Published by

Antique Trader Books

Dubuque, Iowa

Osborne, Jerrry
Rockin' Records Buyers-Sellers Reference Book & Price Guide, 1998 Edition.

Sound Recordings (Phonograph Records), Prices. 2. Sound Recordings, Collectors and Collecting. 3. Music, Popular Songs.

Published by Antique Trader Books, Dubuque, Iowa

Manufactured in the United States of America.

ISBN 0-930625-81-1
ISSN 1052-8768

CONTENTS

ACKNOWLEDGMENTS

The single most important element in the updating and revision of a price and reference guide is reader input. From dealers and collectors, based in every state and in nearly every country, we receive suggestions, additions and corrections for *Rockin' Records*. Every single piece of data we acquire from readers is carefully reviewed, with all the appropriate and usable information utilized in a future printing of this guide—though not necessarily in the very next edition.

As enthusiastically as we encourage your contributions, let us suggest that when you snail mail, e-mail or fax to us, you will either type or print your name clearly on both the envelope and its contents. It is as frustrating for us to receive a packet of useful information, and not be able to credit the sender, as it probably is for the sender to not see his or her name in the Acknowledgments section. If you have a fairly common name, using a middle initial can be helpful.

In compiling this edition, information supplied by the people whose names appear below was of great importance. To these good folks, our deepest gratitude is extended. The amount of data and investment of time, of course, varied, but without each and every one of them this book would have been something less than it is.

Special appreciation is also extended to Village Music and John Goddard for providing the front cover photo of that famous store, in Mill Valley, Calif. Village Music is a shop that you simply must visit.

William O. Adams
Victor Adkins
Cindy Adler
Bob Alaniz
Carol Alaniz
Alice Alexander
Tom Andera
Bill Anderson
James E. Anderson
Mike Anderson
Gary R. Baird
Kim Belculfine
Russ Bell
Andy Benyo
Daniel S. Berkman
Steve Berkos
Jack Berkus
Jean Blankenship
Margaret Blauvelt
Dale Blount
Kenneth Boehm
Jeff Boughton
Thomas L. Boven
Chris G. Bowman
Susan Kim Bowman
Dennis T. Brennan
Art Brink
Bill Brink
Tim Brissette
Michael J. Broussard
Denise M. Brown
John L. Bruno
Chris Buccola
Margie Burns
Robert Byrne
Joe Calato
David A. Campbell
Stephen Carpenito
Angelo Casagrande Jr.
Robert Cassady
Larry L. Christner
Susan Clary
Bob Clere
Julian I. Cohn
Steve Colbert
Steve Cook
John R. Cooper
Perry Cox
Dan Crawford
Christopher Cromley
Kurt Curtis
Robert Dalley
Nicky D'Andrea
Marty Dark
Dave's Record Den
Judy Davis
Charles Dawson
Devon Dawson
Al Dec
Michael De Girolamo
William Deibert
Frank D'Erasmo
Dutch Dillavio
Mark Dillman
John E. Dobroth
J. Taylor Doggett
James M. Doidge
David Dombroski
Fran Donnelly
Doug Dornbos
Dennis Dow
Lee Dresser
Kevin Eaton
Judith M. Ebner
Dan Eddington
Bruce Elrod
Dennis Favreau
Frank Fazio
Ron Feldhaus
Jeff Ferguson
Bill Fingl
Sven Forsberg
Tom Franco
Greg Froelich
John Froidl
Robert Furrer
Emanuel Gambino
Arnie Ganem
Jean-Marc Gargiulo
Kay S. Garvis
Vincent Garvis
Rich Gesner
Jim Gibbons
Gary Giroux
Randy Giroux
James Gladwin
John Goddard
Janice Gordon
Reinhold Gotaskie
David Greenman
James O. Guthrie
Buck Hafeman
Bill Hall Jr.
James Hall
Marshall Hall
Wayne Hall
Terry Hansen
Brewster Harding
Sheldon Harris
Dennis Hartman
Mel Hatton
Alex Havdouglas
Gary M. Hein
"Big" Richie Henchar
Arlo Hennings
Bruce Henningsgaard
James Higgins
Ernie Holland
Tom Holland
Gerard J. Homan
Bill Hoover
Ken Hubert
Lester Hunt
Todd Hutchinson
Jay Hutchison
Terry Mike Jeffrey
F.P. Johns
David R. Johnson Jr.
Colin Johnston
Mark M. Johnston
Kenneth J. Jones
Randy Jones
George H. Kane
Gary Katocs
Norm Katuna
Scott Kelley
Colin Kilts
Kevin King
Don Kirsch
James W. Kolb

Tony Kolodziej
Tracy Kolodziej
David Kopack
Milt Krantz
Wilhelm Kriegl
Nathan Laney
Bruce Laytham
Jim Lear
Al Lee Jr.
Brian Lee
James D. Leggett
Jacqueline D. Le Guyader
Larry Levinson
Craig A. Lewis
Joe Lindsay
Dale Little
David L. Lober
Don Losack
David C. Lovett
Bob Lyon
Ernie Mabrey
Al MacDonald
Jim Macek
Glenn Major
David Mamaux
Cary Mansfield
Franklin Markowitz
Rick Marshall
Dan Martin
Harold D. Mathews
Peter McCullough
Doug McGaghie
Jeffrey McIntyre
Dan McKittrick
James T. Meyer
Wayne Miedema
Mike Mikula
Stephen L. Miller
Vincent P. Miller
Chad Moore
Robert E. Morrison
Don Muller
L. Eddie Muller
Mike Murray
Gary E. Myers
Bill Nadolny
Janis Nagorsen
Tim Nelsen
Charles Neu
Randy L. Nix
Gary Noel
Debbie Oberacker
Bob O'Brien
Robert L. Olive Jr.
Linda Ann Osborne
Roger Osborne
Vic Owens
Steve Pacholl
Sandra A. Pappalardo
George Pardo
Dave Parsons
Jim Patton
Gary Paxton
Victor Pearlin
Alex Peavey
Rick Peirson
Wesley Peterson
Edward F. Pickering
Susan Pineda
Pete Pittman
Emil J. Pohorilla
Jim Powell
Al Price
Toby Proctor
Mike Prosseda
Chester Prudhomme
Fred Preusser
Chuck Proske
John Pumilia
John A. Pyros
Guy Quintino
Leonard J. Ratzman
Tony Renzoni
Andrew R. Richardson
Randy M. Richter
John Riggs
Robert G. Ritter
A.L. Root
Jim Rose
Dick Rosemont
Andy Rosetta
Jim Rossi
Kim Roth
Eileen Rowe
Ron Rowe
Eric Rubin
J. Quentin Russell
Jasper Russell
William R. Sabis
Randall Saksek
Ron Sataloff
Kevin Scanlon
Trish Scarmuzzi
Mark F. Schierbecker
Phil Schwartz
Bill Screws
Melany S. Shapiro
Jerry Sharell
Michael Sharritt
Frank C. Shukstor
Al Silk
Anthony G. Simiele
Bill Sittason
Sherri Six
Russ Skarsten
Andrew P. Smith
Bill Smith
Ed Smith
John Smith
Michael B. Smith
John Sowansky
Phyl Spellman
Jack Stell
Mike Stewart
Dale A. Stirling
Alan Stock
Charlene Storm
Ken Storm
Harvey Street
M. Streeto
Steve Sturdivant
Skip Sullivan
Bill Sweeney
Michael J. Sweeney
Howard A. Sweet
Ed Tataryn
Bill Taylor
Jack L. Thomas
Trevor Thorkildsen
Terry L. Titus
George G. Trabant
Paul Trefzger
Michael Troutman
Tom Tucker
Jim Ulmer
Tom Ulrich
Willem Van Eijk
Nicholas Vasil
Albert J. Wagner
Steve Wallace
Terry Tullos Wayland
Jim Weaver
Joe Wells
Thomas J. Whetstone
Joel Whitburn
Danny A. White
Wild Bill
Al Wilkes
Judy A. Wilkins
Ann Marie Wilson
Morgan Wright
Jerry Zolten
John W. Zurzolo

INTRODUCTION

What's New

Aside from the routine additions and corrections that go into revising every new edition of *Rockin' Records,* we usually choose one or two areas for a more intensive overhaul.

This past year, it has been Soul music that received that special focus – thanks in part to Soul specialist Edward Pickering. Not all of the soulful work planned actually got completed before press time; however, most did. What we didn't get done this time will appear in the 1999 edition.

Speaking of "editions," most folks say it's easier to relate to which edition is which by referring to them by calendar year – rather than by edition number in the series. That's why the cover shows this as the "1998" Edition instead of *Rockin' Records* "19th" Edition.

One change this year came about because of suggestions – or maybe "demands" is more accurate – from readers: the return of reference folios.

Several years ago, when we switched word processing programs, we forfeited the ability to pick up the first artist heading on each page for the folio (top of page) without also picking up the chart information that's on the same line.

We didn't want to move the chart data to a separate line, which would add too many extra pages to an already huge book, so we shelved the folios.

Since many of you asked for the return of the folios, here's the compromise we made:

The reference folios are back; however, we had to give up the luxury of the right page folios being on the right side of the page instead of the left – again because of the chart info.

It's a very slight modification from the traditional right side position that would be our preference, but that tiny inconvenience is more than offset by having the information on each page.

Finally, don't let the page count of this edition fool you. Yes, the *total* count is about the same as the 1997 edition. But that is only because we slightly reduced the size of the type in the Various Artists chapter. This change reduced the total of that section by 51 pages (from 287 to 236) even though many new Various Artists Compilations have been added to the guide.

As for the body of the book – the "A" to "Z" listings – it has grown by 33 full pages – from 583 to 616!

How Prices Are Determined

Record values shown in *Rockin' Records* are averaged using information derived from a number of reliable, proven sources. Most influential in arriving at current values is our long-established "marked copy" review program. Dozens of the world's most active dealers and collectors receive a copy of the most recent edition in which, throughout the year, they track and mark changing prices. When it's time to prepare a revised edition, all marked copies are returned to us for analysis and processing.

Besides the annotated copies, we receive hundreds of letters each year, from folks like yourself, suggesting corrections and/or additions to the guide.

Marketplace publications are another extremely important source of pricing information. Through these, hobbyists buy, sell, and trade music collectibles. We painstakingly review those periodicals, as well as other related publications, carefully comparing prices being asked to those shown in our most recent edition. Keep in mind, however, that while *asking* prices are considered, greater weight is given actual *sales* prices.

If active trading indicates prices in the guide need to be increased or decreased, those changes are made. With our annual publishing schedule, it is never long before the corrected data appear in print.

What makes this step in the pricing process so vital is that nothing more verifiably illustrates the out-of-print record marketplace than everyday sales lists placed by dealers from around the country and around the globe.

Also of great assistance to price tracking are the individual sales catalogs and auction results lists we routinely receive from dealers. Auction results are especially useful – keep 'em coming.

Record prices, as with most collectibles, can vary drastically from one area of the country to another. Having reviewers and annotators in every state — as well as in Europe, Asia, and beyond — enables us to present a realistic average of the highest and lowest current trading prices for an identically graded copy of each record.

Other sources of consequential information include: private set sale and auction lists, record convention trading, personal visits with collectors and to retail locations around the country, and hundreds of hours on the telephone with key advisors.

Although the record marketplace information in this edition was believed accurate at press time, it is ever subject to market changes. At any time, major bulk discoveries, quantity dumps, sudden increases brought about by an artist's death, overnight stardom that creates a greater demand for earlier material, and other such events and trends can easily affect scarcity and demand. Through diurnal research, keeping track of the day-to-day changes and discoveries taking place in the fascinating world of record collecting is a relatively simple and ongoing procedure.

To ensure the greatest possible accuracy, *Rockin' Records* prices are averaged from data culled from all of the aforementioned sources.

When Prices Don't Change

Some prices go unchanged year after year because their values simply do not fluctuate beyond the range given. Others, however, should be shifted and are not. This is because *no one* bothers to advise us of those market changes. With over one million records priced in *Rockin' Records* we cannot keep track of all of them without lots of help.

Don't keep such news a secret. And please don't wait for someone else to do it. Let us know of corrections and updates as soon as possible.

A word of caution here, however. Please *do not* submit any information to us merely because it appears in another record guide. Make certain all information can be verified in some other manner.

How You Can Help

We can never get too much input or have too many reviewers. We wholeheartedly encourage you to submit anything and everything you feel would be useful in building a better record guide. The quantity of data is not a factor — no amount is too little or too much.

The extensive list of names always found in the Acknowledgments chapter indicates the development of our board of advisors. We want *you* to join the team.

When preparing additions for *Rockin' Records* please try to list records in generally the same format as is used in the guide: artist's name, label, selection number, title, year of release (if known), and price range. Since our data base is stored alphabetically by artist, there's no need to note the *Rockin' Records* page number.

Please be very careful to submit information accurately, exactly as it appears on the label. Incomplete copying, especially of artist names, is the reason for embarrassing duplications in the guide. If the credit reads "Winston and the Aardvarks," list it that way. Do not simply tell us it's by the Aardvarks! This oversight can easily create duplicate listings — one under "W" and another under "A." Thank you.

Wax Fax and e-mail

Two frequently used methods of forwarding data to us is by fax and by e-mail. For your convenience, we have a dedicated fax line: (360) 385-6572. Use this service to easily and instantly transmit additions, corrections, price updates, and suggestions. Be sure to include (legibly) your name, address, and phone number so we can acknowledge your contribution and, if necessary, contact you.

Our e-mail address is **jpo@olympus.net.** Again, remember to provide your full name separately since Internet letters normally relay only the sender's e-mail address.

If you help, we want to credit you properly. Just make sure we have — and can read — the information with which to do it.

Send all additions, corrections, and suggestions to:

Jerry Osborne
Box 255
Port Townsend, WA 98368
Fax: (360) 385-6572
e-mail: jpo@olympus.net

Websters Keep Up with Us

For those with on-line capabilities, it's easy to keep up with our busy publishing schedule by regularly visiting our fun and informative web site.

There you'll find a complete listing of every book we have ever done, along with ones currently available as well as what's coming soon from Osborne Enterprieses.

Our home page also provides an instant link to Osborne Fine Art Images, our celebrity, limited edition, fine art publishing company.

Bookmark our cool site and return often:

www.jerryosborne.com

About the Format

Our arrangement of listings is the most logical way to present so much information in a single volume — a format with unlimited potential for expansion.

The structure of *Rockin' Records* allows us to include all of the following in one multi-purpose guidebook: 7-inch 45 rpm singles, both 33 rpm and 45 rpm; 78 rpm singles; 12-inch singles, both 33 and 45 rpm; extended play 33 and 45 rpm EPs; 78 rpm albums, long play 10-inch and 12-inch LPs; picture sleeves; promotional issues, picture discs, and more.

Once you locate an artist's section, their records are listed alphabetically by LABEL. Individual listings for each label appear in numerical order. In many instances, listings that are numerical by selection number are also chronological in sequence of release, but there are times when this is not the case. This format is especially helpful when using the guide along with an artist or label discography. Since the year of release is also provided for each listing, the reader knows immediately the pattern being followed by the label at the time.

Once familiar with the format, you'll find it easy and functional. See the "Sample" page for more information. New users should take time to familiarize themselves with the array. Reading all of the introductory pages should answer most reader questions.

The documenting and pricing of so many recordings is made possible by selectively economizing on space; listing individual titles when necessary but not when it's possible to group a number of equally valuable releases together on one line. Again, *any time* it is necessary to have a separate listing on a record in order to clearly and accurately present the information, we will do it. Also, whenever a specific selection number is noted, whether listed as an exception or not, the title will also be given for easy identification.

One facet of our approach of great concern is the artist who had one or more records of a value indicated for a particular label or series, but who also had one release (or more) that is a notable exception. Every effort has been made to separately document such exceptions, however, due to the sheer bulk of information herein, some may be missed. If you know of any, let us know about them.

You will find that the expansion of an artist's section, moving more toward individual rather than grouped listings, will be as commonplace in subsequent volumes of this series as with this edition. There are hundreds of artists with revised sections in this volume, listing many more individual titles and selection numbers than ever before. With some performers, it is, or perhaps soon will be, necessary to list every single record separately.

The ever-increasing number of pages in the guide are but one indication of how many artists' sections are expanded with individual title listings, over previous editions. Again this year, thousands of records are listed and priced individually that previously were not.

The decision to expand a section is partly based on reader input. Many examples of individual pricing in this edition can be directly attributed to a letter or call suggesting the need to do so.

Non-Rock Guidelines

Since some parameters were necessary to decide which non-rock performers to include in *Rockin' Records,* the following guideline is used.

If a non-rock artist had either a single or an album on the Billboard charts (1950-1987), all recordings known to us by that artist will be found in the guide. This allows for the most popular performers of country, western, jazz, personality, easy listening or other music style to be included, without trying to incorporate every record ever made into one book (although many want us to provide exactly that).

Though these are the parameters, exceptions are not uncommon in *Rockin' Records.* You will find many in this edition who had no charted recordings, but were chosen because of their overall significance in the collectors' marketplace. There are others included simply because we received requests from readers to add them. If there is someone you feel needs to be in this guide, who is not at this time, please write with that suggestion. We are always listening to your suggestions.

Remember, we're only talking non-rock and not particularly in-demand type artists here! If you have a rockin' record — including all forms of black music — not currently listed, we want it in *Rockin' Records.* Whether or not it charted anywhere is of no importance.

Grading and the Price Range

The pricing shown in this edition represents the price *range* for NEAR-MINT condition copies. The value range allows for the countless variables that affect record pricing. Often, the range will widen as the dollar amount increases, making a $500 to $1,000 range as logical as a $5.00 to $10.00 range.

One standardized system of record grading, used and endorsed by Osborne Enterprises as well as buyers and sellers worldwide is as follows:

MINT: A *mint* item must be absolutely perfect. Nothing less can be honestly described as mint. Even brand new purchases can easily be flawed in some manner and not qualify as mint. To allow for tiny blemishes, the highest grade used in our record guide series is *near-mint.* An absolutely pristine mint, or still sealed, item may carry a slight premium above the near-mint range shown in this guide.

VERY GOOD: Records in *very good* condition should have a minimum of visual or audible imperfections, which should not detract much from your enjoyment of owning them. This grade is halfway between good and near-mint.

GOOD: Practically speaking, the grade of *good* means that the item is good enough to fill a gap in your collection until a better copy becomes available. Good condition merchandise will show definite signs of wear and tear, probably evidencing that no protective care was given the item. Even so, records in good condition should play all the way through without skipping.

Most older records are going to be in something less than near-mint, or "excellent" condition. It is very important to use the near-mint price range in this guide only as a starting point in record appraising. Be honest about actual condition. Apply the same standards to the records you trade or sell as you would want one from whom you were buying to observe. Visual grading may be unreliable. Accurate grading may require playing the record (play-grading).

Use the following formula to determine values on lesser condition copies:

For **VERY GOOD** condition, figure about 40% to 60% of the near-mint price range given in this guide.

With many of the older pieces that cannot be found in near-mint, VG or VG+ may be the highest grade available. This significantly narrows the gap between VG and the near-mint range.

For **GOOD** condition, figure about 10% to 20% of the near-mint price range given in this guide.

It will surprise no one to learn that the gulch between GOOD and MINT is gradually becoming a canyon. The drift toward widening the grading gap that began about 10 years ago shows no signs of slowing. To keep pace with this phenomena, changes have been made in the guide to reflect the ever-increasing premiums being paid for mint condition items.

Most industry observers do not foresee a narrowing trend during this millennia.

The 10 Point Grading System

Another recommended grading system is based on the often-used 10 point scale. Many feel that grading with the 10 point system allows for a more precise description of records that are in less than mint condition. Instead of vague terms, such as VG++ (is this the same as M- -?), assigning a specific number provides a more accurate classification of condition.

Most of the records you are likely to buy or sell will no doubt be graded somewhere between 5 and 10.

After using this system ourselves for a few years, we are inclined to agree that it is more precise. Customers who have purchased records from us have, without exception, been pleased with this way of grading.

The table below shows how the 10 point system equates with the more established terms:

10: MINT
9: NEAR-MINT
8: Better than VG but below NM
7: VERY GOOD
6: Better than G but below VG
5: GOOD
4: Better than POOR but below G
3: POOR
2: Really trashed
1: It hurts to think about it

The Bottom Line

All the price guides and reporting of previous sales in the world won't change the fundamental fact that true value is nothing more than what one person is willing to accept and what another is prepared to pay. Actual value is based on scarcity and demand. It's always been that way and always will.

A recording — or anything for that matter — can be 50 or 100 years old, but if no one wants it, the actual value will certainly be minimal. Just because something is old does not necessarily make it valuable. Someone has to want it!

On the other hand, a recent release, perhaps just weeks old, can have exceptionally high value if it has already become scarce and is by an artist whose following has created a demand. A record does not have to be old to be valuable.

Record Types Defined

With the inconsistent language used by the record companies in describing an EP or an LP, we've determined that a language guideline of some kind is needed in order to compile a useful record guide.

Some labels call a 10-inch album an "EP" if it has something less than the prescribed number of tracks found on their LPs. Others call an EP a "Little LP." A few companies have even created special names, associated only with their own label, for the basic record formats.

Having carefully analyzed all of this, we have adopted the following classifications of record configurations, which consistently categorize all types, sizes, and speeds in one section or another:

Singles: 78 rpm are those that play at 78 rpm. Though 78s are almost always 10-inch discs, a few 7-inch 78 rpm singles have been made.

Singles: 7-Inch can be either 45 rpm or 331/3 (always referred to simply as "33") speed singles. If a 7-inch single has more than one track on either side, *Rockin' Records* considers it an EP.

Singles are priced strictly as a disc, with a separate section devoted to picture sleeves (which are often traded separately). If we know that picture sleeves exist for a given artist, a separate grouping will appear for the label, price, and applicable year of release. Should you know of picture sleeves not documented in this edition, please advise us accordingly.

There have been a few 5- and 6-inch discs manufactured, but for the sake of keeping singles with singles (and since we don't want to establish a "Singles: 5-inch" category), such curios will be tossed in with the 7-inch singles, with an explanatory note.

EPs: 7-Inch 33/45 rpm are 7-inch discs that have more than one track on one or both sides. Even if labeled an "EP" by the manufacturer, if it's pressed on a 10-, or 12-inch disc it's an LP in our book. Unless so noted, all EPs are presumed to be accompanied by their original covers, in a condition about equal to the disc. An appropriate adjustment in value should be made to compensate for any differences in this area. Exceptions, such as EPs with paper sleeves or no sleeve at all, are designated as such when known.

LPs: 10/12-Inch 33 rpm is self explanatory. The only possible confusion that might exist here is with 12-inch singles. If it's 10 or 12 inches in diameter, and labeled, priced, and marketed as a 12-inch single (Maxi-Single, etc.), then that's where you'll find it in this guide, regardless of its speed. Often, 12-inch singles will have a 12-inch die-cut cardboard sleeve or jacket; but many have covers that are exactly like LP jackets, with photos of the artist, etc. Unless so noted, all LPs are presumed to be accompanied by their original covers, in a condition about equal to the disc. An appropriate adjustment in value should be made to compensate for any differences in this area.

Other record type headings used such as Picture Sleeves, Promotional Singles, etc., should be clear.

Country Music Records

Recently added and now a permanent part of *Rockin' Records* is the 2,300 or so of America's all-time top-selling country and western artists — from the mid-'20s to present. Among this varied gathering, you'll find all of the Country Music Hall of Fame legends shoulder to shoulder with long-forgotten artists who managed just one insignificant hit.

Qualifying for inclusion in *Rockin' Records* is anyone who managed at one time or another to hit the Billboard C&W chart with a vinyl disc, from 1944 to present. Our chart source here is Joel Whitburn's [Billboard] *Top Country Singles 1944-1993*.

Since Billboard magazine didn't begin publishing separate country music charts until 1944, country music artists who made the pop charts before 1944 are also included.

Knowing this, the reader will understand why the "first charted" reference for some of country music's pioneers (Roy Acuff, Bob Wills, Carter Family, etc.) indicates "P&R" (Pop & Rock, but signifying only "Pop" in this usage) rather than "C&W."

Other two letter abbreviations used include: "LP" (Album chart), "R&B" (Rhythm & Blues/Soul chart), and "D&D" (Dance & Disco chart).

At the other extreme of the time frame — the 1990s — we have encountered a quandary of a different sort. Which recent releases exist on vinyl?

While many collectors have a "who cares" attitude regarding '90s releases, fanciers of certain performers usually are concerned about which singles and albums are manufactured on vinyl, in addition to compact discs. Often they are rarer than ones 20 years old, simply because vinyl production is itself rare in the '90s.

Reliable sources report that a great many country singles are still being made on vinyl, primarily for jukebox use. Though true, knowing with certainty which ones are and which are not on vinyl can be impossible.

We have opted to maintain our usual conservative approach, listing *only* those vinyl discs that we have seen or have been told of by our correspondents. We encourage those of you in the trenches of collecting to submit specifics about other recent vinyl releases.

Price wise, if the most recent year for which we indicate vinyl singles is, say, 1992, it is safe to assume the same price range for singles you might have from 1993 or '94.

Between the first country 78s and digital CDs, *Rockin' Records* now fills a long-standing price guide void. Even though we published a previous guide (1976) for pricing C&W singles and another (1984) for albums and extended plays, this is the first time all C&W formats can be researched and priced with just one volume.

Though we do not anticipate an attempt in the future to include every country or western recording ever made in *Rockin' Records*, we did at least want the complete recorded output of every artist appearing on Billboard's C&W charts — no matter how brief or insignificant their chart success.

In addition to those charted country artists, *Rockin' Records* includes a random assortment of other country music related performers. They may be here because someone submitted the information or because they are somehow significant to the proceedings. Their inclusion should not be viewed as a desire on our part to have every *non-charted* C&W artist in history in the guide.

Cross-Referencing and Multiple Artists' Recordings

The cross-referencing in *Rockin' Records* should provide the easiest possible method of discovering other sections of the book where a particular artist is featured or appears in any capacity.

We've tried to hold to a minimum unexplained cross-references, opting to concentrate more on those cross-references for which the reader can effortlessly understand the rationalization. Minimized is the unnecessary duplication of cross-references. For example, it is not necessary to list every group in which Eric Clapton played, under each and every one of those sections. What we've done is simply indicate "Also see Eric Clapton," where you will find a complete cross-referencing to all other sections where he appears.

Some artists have several sections, one right after the other, because they were involved in different duets and/or compilation releases. In such instances, the primary artist (whose section begins first) is not cross-referenced after each and every subsequent section, but only after the last section wherein that artist is involved. This, in effect, blocks the beginning and the end of releases pertaining to that performer. If you don't find the listing you're searching for right away, remember to check the sections that follow, as the artist may have been joined by someone else on that recording causing it to appear in a separate section.

Cross-references in bold typeface are charted artists; those in normal typeface did not chart.

Artist headings and resultant cross-referencing appear in two different formats in this guide. For example:

LEWIS, Jerry Lee, Carl Perkins & Johnny Cash

Listings under this type heading are those wherein the artists perform *together*. Often these releases will also include solo tracks by one or all of the performers in addition to those on which they collaborate.

LEWIS, Jerry Lee / Carl Perkins / Johnny Cash

This heading, with names separated by a slash, indicates there are selections on *separate* tracks by each of the named artists, but they do not perform together.

ISLEY BROTHERS & DAVE "BABY" CORTEZ

This heading, with all names in upper case letters and no slash, indicates the artists perform *together*.

ISLEY BROTHERS / Brooklyn Bridge

This heading, with names after a slash that are in upper and lower case, indicates artists that perform *separately* – usually each being heard on one side of the disc.

The parameter set for these compilation releases in the body of the book is four different performers or less. Compilations containing five or more individual performers are found in the Various Artists Compilations chapter.

Whenever more than one act is featured on a record, cross-references appear under all of the other artists on the disc, who have a section of their own in this edition, directing the reader to the location of the listing in question. If you're looking up a record with a different artist on each side, and you don't find it under one artist, be sure to try looking for the flip-side artist.

Not all releases containing more than one artist are given separate sections. In some cases it makes more sense to include such records in the primary section for the most important artist. We will rarely create separate sections for multiple artist discs when the other performers on the issue do not have a section of their own in this edition.

To illustrate this point, Hank Williams Jr. had several duet issues with Lois Johnson; Gene Ammons shared an LP with Sonny Stitt. Even though Johnson and Stitt do not have individual sections in this book (they didn't make the Billboard pop singles or LPs charts), such recordings may be important to collectors of Williams and Ammons. For that reason, they are included in their respective artist's section.

On the other hand, a duet by Brenda Lee and Willie Nelson requires a separate section, since either or both may be of interest to the researcher. Also, both are individually pop-charted artists. There are a few isolated exceptions to this policy, simply because every section in this edition was separately prepared and customized in whatever manner necessary to provide the user with the most usable information.

Promotional Issues

Separate documenting and pricing of promotional issues is, in most cases, unnecessary. Because most of the records issued during the primary four decades covered in this guide were simultaneously pressed for promotional purposes, a separate listing of them would theoretically double the size of an already large book.

Rather, we've chosen to list promotional copies separately when we have the knowledge that an alternate price (either higher or lower) consistently is asked for them. For the most part, promos of everyday releases will fall into the same range — usually toward the high end — given for store stock copies. Some may stretch the range slightly, but not enough to warrant separate pricing. Premiums may be paid for promos that have different (longer, shorter, differently mixed, etc.) versions of tunes, even though the artist may not be particularly hot in the collecting marketplace.

When identified as a "Promotional issue," we are usually describing a record with a special promotional ("Not For Sale," "Dee Jay Copy," etc.) label or sleeve, and not a *designate* promo. Designate promos are identical to commercial releases, except they have been rubber or mechanically stamped, stickered, written on by hand, or in some way altered to accommodate their use for promotional purposes. There are very few designate promos listed in this edition, and those that are (such as in the Elvis Presley section) are clearly identified as such.

Colored Vinyl Pressings

Records known to exist on both black vinyl and colored vinyl (vinyl is the term used regardless of whether it's polystyrene or vinyl) are listed separately since there is usually a value difference. However, some colored vinyl releases were never pressed on black vinyl, and since there is no way to have the record other than on colored vinyl, it may or may not be specifically noted as being on colored vinyl.

Because the true color of some colored vinyl pressings may be a judgment call, we once used "colored vinyl" to indicate discs that are not standard black vinyl.

For example, collectors have described the five RCA Victor colored plastic by folks like Arthur "Big Boy" Crudup, the Four Tunes, and others – circa 1940-'50 – as being 1. Red. 2. Pink. 3. Orange. So which is it?

Such dilemmas notwithstanding, because you asked for it, we are gradually replacing "colored" with which color is being used. If you have specific colors for those still shown as "colored," (such as the Four Tunes ones) please send us the information.

Foreign Releases

Originally, *Rockin' Records* listed only U.S. releases. Now, there are many exceptions. A handful of records that were widely distributed in the United States or sold via widespread U.S. advertising, even though manufactured outside the country, are included. Such anomalies would appear only in the more sophisticated sections of the guide.

There are also various Canadian releases in *Rockin' Records*, with more being added to each new edition. The collectors' market for out-of-print Canadian records is mostly a U.S. market. The trading of rare Canadian discs between Canadian collectors is not quite as widespread as those instances that involve a U.S. buyer or seller. Yet it is from Canadian collectors that we receive most of our information on those releases, and we expect to have more listed in future editions.

There are millions of overseas releases that have collector value to fans in those countries as well as to stateside collectors. Unfortunately, the tremendous volume of material and the variances in pricing make it impossible to comprehensively document and price imports.

Bootlegs and Counterfeits

Bootleg and counterfeit records are not priced in this guide, though a few are cited, along with information on how to distinguish them from an original.

For the record, a bootleg recording is one illegally manufactured, usually containing material not previously available in a legitimate form. Often, with the serious collector in mind, a boot will package previously issued tracks that have achieved some degree of value or scarcity. If the material is easily available, legally, then there would be no gain for the bootlegger.

The counterfeit record is one manufactured as close as possible in sound and appearance to the source disc from which it was inspired. Not all counterfeits were created to fool an unsuspecting buyer into thinking he or she was buying an authentic issue, but some were. Many were designated in some way, such as a slight marking or variance, so as not to allow them to be confused with originals. Such a fake record primarily exists to fill a gap in the collector's file until the real thing comes along.

With- both bootleg and with counterfeit records, the appropriate and deserving recipients of royalties are, of course, denied remuneration for their works.

Since most of the world's valuable records have been counterfeited, it is always a good idea to consult with an expert when there is any doubt. The trained eye can usually spot a fake.

This is not to say *unauthorized* releases are excluded from the book. There are many legitimate releases that are unauthorized by one entity or another; records that are neither bootleg or counterfeit. Unauthorized does not necessarily mean illegal.

Group Names and Personnel

One problem that we'll never completely solve involves the many instances where groups using the exact same name are lumped together with other groups who are completely different. Whenever known to be different, these groups are given separate sections; however, there are times when we simply do not know. If you can shed any light in this area, we'd love to hear from you. Thanks to readers, many such groups have been sorted since our last edition.

The listing sequence for artists using the same name is chronological. Thus, the ABC group, Silk, who had a release in 1969, is listed ahead of the Philadelphia International group, Silk, that first recorded in 1979.

As often as not, there will have been group members that have come and gone over the years. Reflecting this turnover in our listing of members' names may cause some confusion, when the reader sees 12 different members shown for a group named the Five Satins. We've tried, whenever possible, to list the original line-up first, followed by later members. Also, the lead singer is usually listed first. We welcome additional information on group members from readers. One of the most reliable sources of this data is the LP covers, which often list members. If you can fill in the members' names on any groups where we don't list that information, we'll see that it gets into our next edition. Hundreds of group members have been added since the ninth edition of this guide.

When group members' names are given, there is a likelihood that not all of the members named appear on *all* of the releases documented. It is also possible that not all of the members named ever recorded with all of the other members shown at the same time.

When names are given for a solo performer, those named are likely noteworthy sidemen.

As more and more group members are named in future editions, there will be added cross-referencing to reflect the constant shuffle of performers from one group to another.

Various Artists Compilations

About the only priority used in determining which compilations are included in this chapter is that special attention is given to include as many as possible from the '50s and '60s, especially ones containing the more collectible rock era artists. Otherwise, we mainly focus on those releases that can easily be documented. We realize there are zillions of various artists LPs from the '70s to present; however, very few of this batch command prices greater than $5.00 to $10.00. While including as many as possible in future editions is planned, you can feel safe for now in assigning that price range to these fairly recent ones.

Crucial to one's appreciation and/or desire of compilation releases is which performers are being featured on them. We are not fond of listing compilation releases without giving you a clue as to whom or what is heard on the disc, though sometimes it could not be helped. We have tried to provide the artist lineup on as many discs as possible. When we lack the complete cast, we provide as many names as possible. Often, just a name or two will offer some insight as to the type of music one might expect on a particular LP.

There are of course many various artists records in *Rockin' Records* that have no artists shown, but by listing them readers will then know which ones we need help with. We encourage you to compare the data here to their actual records, providing missing artists' names as well as other tidbits of information that can be used to make future editions even more complete. Because of the volume of data received, information we receive may not always appear in the very next edition.

Some other notes about the Various Artists Compilations chapter:

- Many records labeled as soundtracks are really various artists compilations in disguise. We have included quite a few soundtracks of this type, but there are plenty of others out there. See *The Official Price Guide to Movie/TV Soundtracks and Original Cast Albums* (also available from Jellyroll Productions) for more listings of this type. Most of the ones we didn't squeeze into this edition are of recent vintage and sell for under $10.00
- Following each label name, one of the following notations will be found:

(M): MONAURAL.

(S): STEREO. Labeled stereo, but may in truth be either true stereo, electronically reprocessed stereo (i.e. fake stereo), or a combination of both.

(SE): Completely electronically reprocessed stereo.

(ST): Completely true stereo.

(SP): Part electronically reprocessed stereo and part true stereo.

(EP): Extended play, 7-inch 45 or 33 rpm.

- Records are listed in alphabetical order by title. Those having titles beginning with numerals are at the beginning of the chapter. To keep things somewhat organized, ones having titles beginning with numbers *spelled out* have been converted to numerals and put in numerical order. We chose this system over listing by label because only by having them in order by title is it possible to always find all of the releases in a specific series grouped together. Also, many find it easier to remember titles than label names.
- Compilation releases that contain tracks by folks like Elvis Presley, the Beatles, and Frank Sinatra — to name just a few — usually command premium prices. Whenever possible we have listed these artists first so that you may quickly see why one particular album is valued higher than others that are similar.
- Regardless of how many tracks appear on an album by an artist, their name is only listed once.
- For the most part, we have made corrections to artists' names that are misspelled on LP covers and labels. You wouldn't believe how many albums show Frankie Lymon as Frankie Lyman, and have countless other similar errors. (Though we have yet to see Arthur Lyman shown as Arthur Lymon.)
- Promotional only samplers that are untitled or part of a continuing series are likely to be listed together in a section under the label name. These releases, set in italics and indented for easy identification, include such well-known issues as the Loss Leader series from Warner Bros., and the Silver Platter Service and Balanced for Broadcast LPs from Capitol.
- At this time, we have chosen not to include vinyl radio shows in this edition. Though there are a few by specific scattered throughout the A-Z body of the book, various artists radio shows are a completely separate pail of worms that we would rather avoid — at least until we have made the rest of the chapter more comprehensive. Same goes for armed forces and public service broadcasting recordings.
- Since we know of no more appropriate section to house sound effects albums, you'll find them listed by title in the Various Artists chapter.
- You will find a few listings that are lacking one piece of information or another, such as a name or selection number. Rather than omit these records entirely, we have included them and used question marks in place of the missing numbers or text. Can you help by providing that portion we're missing?

Parenthetical Notes

Some of the information that may be found in parentheses following the artist heading has already been covered. However, other uses of this space include:

- Complete artist and group or artist and band names. Some artists were shown as being with one group on a few releases, solo on some, and with yet another group on other issues. We've tried to present the information the way, or ways, that it is shown on the actual record label. When encased in quote marks, it means that this particular wording or credit variation is exactly as shown on the label.
- Variations of spelling or names for the same artist. With some artists, it's convenient to have everything in one section; however, when it is illogical to combine listings, perhaps because the performer was popular under more than one name (such as Johnny Cymbal and Derek), you'll find individual sections for each name. Cross-references will be used to help you locate things easily. Having "Kenneth Rogers" in parentheses is not intended to mean that Kenneth is Kenny's real name. Rather, we're letting you know that on at least one of his records he is credited as Kenneth Rogers instead of Kenny Rogers. Same goes for Tony Perkins, who may also be credited as "Anthony Perkins." We may at times provide real names of artists, but only when we feel they need to be given. While we have no desire to give the real names of everyone who has recorded under a pseudonym, there are times when you do need this information. This is especially true when they have also recorded under their real name or when more than one person has recorded under the same pseudonym. To help sort things out, we will, when known,

give you the real name of someone who has recorded under a nom de guerre, such as Guitar Slim (a.k.a. Johnny Winter).

• Names of guest performers who may or may not be credited on the actual label, but who we feel you should know were involved in some of the records listed in that section.

Oldies Labels and Reissues

An effort has been made to include many "oldies" or reissue records in the guide. Though many reissues of this type are of no value beyond their current retail cost, some are. Look at some of the early RCA Victor Gold Standard Series Elvis Presley releases, for example. Once in a blue moon a tune will turn up in true stereo on a reissue label that was previously hard to find in stereo. Otherwise, it's just our desire to report comprehensively on all artists that prompted the listing of reissues.

The main reason we've included these reissues is to eliminate confusion, especially among younger collectors. Often, they'll discover a hit tune on a label like Lana or Lost-Nite, and think it's an original release predating the label that had the hit.

If there are reissues numbered as part of a label's standard release series, and not documented in this edition, please tell us about them.

Using This Guide: Some Additional Points

• A few of the more prolific labels with lengthy names are abbreviated in this guide. They are:

ABC-PAR .... ABC-Paramount
GNP .... GNP/Crescendo
MFSL .... Mobile Fidelity Sound Lab
RCA .... RCA Victor
20TH FOX .... 20th Century-Fox
U.A. .... United Artists
W.B. .... Warner Brothers

To avoid confusion, the short-lived Warner records label, active in 1959, is shown as "Warner," never as "W.B." Also, when an artist has records on the old Memphis Sun label, as well as Shelby Singleton's Nashville-based Sun label, the latter is shown as "SSS/Sun."

• The alphabetization in *Rockin' Records* makes finding any artist or label easy, but a few guidelines may speed the process along for you:

• Names that are simply letters (and are not intended to be pronounced as a word) are found at the beginning of the listings under each letter of the alphabet (i.e., **ABC, AC-DC, GQ, SSQ,** etc.). The same rule applies to acronyms and to initialisms (i.e., **G.T.O, MFSB,** etc.). When known, we'll parenthetically tell you what the abbreviation represents.

• Names are listed in the alphabetical order of the first word. This means you'll find **Rock Squad** before **Rocket.** Hyphenated words are looked upon as whole words (i.e., **Mello-Kings** is treated the same as **Mellokings**). Divided names or names with Spanish articles (i.e., **De Vorzon, Del Satins, El Dorados; Las Vegas, Los Lobos,** etc.) are alphabetically listed as though they were a one-word name.

• Possessive names precede similarly spelled names that are not possessive. For example, **KNIGHT'S** would be found before **KNIGHTS,** regardless of what follows the comma.

• It is flabbergasting to discover how many of the people responsible for crediting bands and groups on record labels have no understanding (or schooling) regarding when to use a possessive apostrophe. This is by far the most frequently found mistake on labels — one which we refuse to blindly copy for our artist headings, lest anyone think that we don't know better. However, for those labels that do credit groups like — to use an actual example — the Capitols (on Gateway) as **CAPITOL'S,** we will indicate that senseless variation under the artist's heading, in parenthesis.

• The articles "A" or "The" have been dropped from group names in this guide even though they may appear on the records as part of the name.

• With record labels in *Rockin' Records* , the listings appear in alphabetical/numerical/chronological order. Selection prefixes are generally not used (they make it more difficult to scan the numbers) unless they are necessary for identification. With some artists (Beatles, Elvis, etc.) it is essential at times because of constant reissues.

• Some sections make use of the label prefixes to sort things out, but most use a number series. If the numbers are duplicated by the label, or if any of a variety of confusing similarities exist, we may resort to the prefixes for clarity.

• Regarding 78 rpms. As to which late '50s and early '60s tunes came out on 78s, we cannot safely assume much of anything. If you know of 78s from end of the 78 rpm era that we do not list, please advise us accordingly. We would be especially happy to learn of charted hits issued after 1957.

• Whenever possible, records priced in the $25.00 to $35.00 range and up are listed individually with label, selection number, and title.

• Anytime we find that the monaural or the stereo issue of a particular record is in need of a separate listing (because there is a price difference for one that is outside the boundaries of the price range of the other), we will gladly provide same. If there is but one listing, this indicates that we have no reason to believe there is much difference in the two forms. A little application of the known variables will help in this area. For example, if the range is $20.00 to $40.00 for a 1960 LP and you know that the stereo issue is in true stereo, it's safe to place the mono at the low end of the range ($20.00 to $30.00) and the stereo at the high end ($30.00 to $40.00). The calculation may be reversed for late '60s and for most electronically reprocessed issues.

• We believe the year or years of release given in the far-right column to be accurate. If we don't know the correct year, the column is left blank. In some cases the record may have been released in one year and debuted on the nation's music charts the following year. This is common for year-end issues and explains why you may remember a hit as being from 1966, although we list it as a 1965 release.

• If you have delta (Δ) numbers for records we do not have release years for, please send them to us. From those numbers we can usually determine year of issue. Delta numbers are found etched in the record's vinyl trail-off area.

• When multiple years are indicated, such as "64-66," it means the records described on that line spanned the years 1964 through

1966. They may have had one issue in 1964 and another in 1966, or may have had eight releases during those years. It does *not* mean that we believe the release came out sometime between 1964 and 1966. If the exact year is not known but the decade of release is, then we will provide that ('50s, '60s, '70s, etc.)

• When a selection number series, such as a "4000 series," is shown, it includes numbers 4000 through 4999. If it were meant to indicate only 4000 through 4099, then separate listings would be found for 4100, 4200, etc.

• Goofy as it seems, a few records have been issued with no artist or label given. You will find this on both singles and albums. These items are filed here by title.

• There are hundreds of double albums (two discs in one package) priced in the guide, but they may not be identified as having two discs. They are, nevertheless, included in the price range.

• Mislabeled records are usually no big deal. We constantly hear from folks who think they have struck gold because one of their records has its labels screwed up in some manner. Either they are reversed, with each side bearing the label intended for the other side, or mislabeled altogether with a label from an entirely different record — perhaps even by a completely different artist. Generally, production errors of this kind do not increase value. They may, in some cases, make the disc even less attractive to a collector. For those very, very few exceptions, the necessary information is already noted in *Rockin' Records*.

• While this guide makes no attempt to fully document gospel recordings per se, the wonderful, soulful harmony of groups like the Swan Silvertones and Soul Stirrers make their records popular among rhythm and blues collectors. For that reason they are included. Others will be added on an as requested basis.

• To conserve space, when the same title is listed as both 45 and 78, we may not list the title in both sections if it requires more than one line. You may therefore find only the label name in the 78 section, whereas the complete number and title will be in the 45 section.

• In most cases, we have no specifics regarding which 78s came on both black and colored plastic. Lacking comments to the contrary, all 78s in *Rockin' Records* are presumed to be black plastic.

• With all recently added listings, when two (or more) releases came out in the same calendar year, a note reading "First issue" will indicate which came first. Most examples of this occurred with independent labels whose records got picked up by one of the major companies, and issued on their own label. Of course, if the years of release differ from one label to the other there is no need for the note. As we run across them, we will make a similar notation to the older listings in the guide.

• When an artist is shown as making their chart debut on the LP charts, but we list no albums and only singles by them – it is because we have yet to confirm any *vinyl* albums. If you find vinyl LPs which we do not list, please let us know of them.

• For those who require an even more comprehensive guide for collectibles by either Elvis Presley or the Beatles, we have separate publications available for each that will take you as far into their records and memorabilia as you want to go.

Presley collectors consider Jerry Osborne's *Presleyana* IV and *Official Price Guide to Elvis Presley Records & Memorabilia* indispensable, whereas Beatles collectors feel the same about Cox & Lindsay's *Official Price Guide to Beatles Records & Memorabilia.*

Also, those who want to know all there is to know about collecting and appraising vinyl soundtracks and original casts will want the latest edition of Jerry Osborne's *The Official Price Guide to Movie/TV Soundtracks & Original Cast Recordings*.

The Elvis and Beatles guides are now available at most bookstores, or by mail from Jellyroll Productions. The movie/TV soundtracks and original casts book is due for publication in early 1997, after which it may also be found at bookstores or ordered from: Jellyroll Productions, Box 255, Port Townsend, WA 98368 (360) 385-1200.

Guidelines for Pricing Records Not in This Edition

Since it is impossible for us to include *every* record ever produced, a few guidelines may assist you in evaluating records not found in this edition:

♦ Pop Singles on 45 rpm: Most pop (i.e. non-rock) vocal and instrumental 45s from the '50s are available for under $15.00. From many rock-oriented dealers, pop singles can often be bought for under $10.00. The few exceptions are likely to be folks with charted hits, and those will be found in the guide.

♦ Pop music singles from the '60s to present are seldom going to sell for over $10.00

♦ Pop Singles on 78 rpm: Most pop 78s are available for under $10.00 Albums of 78s — usually in a gatefold binder with individual paper sleeves — will vary, but most are in the $20.00 to $50.00 range.

♦ Pop Long Play Albums: From the '50s, 12-inch pop LPs generally are found for under $40.00. Ten-inch LPs may go for up to $75.00. Exceptions, such as pop stars who made rock or jazz records, should be found in this book.

♦ Most pop LPs from the '60s to present can be found for $5.00 to $15.00.

♦ Pop Extended Play Albums: Pop EPs are scarce, as are all EPs, but many are still very reasonable. Most can be found for $10.00 to $25.00, often for even less.

♦ Easy Listening Music: The average easy listening record will be worth about half of the price ranges shown for Pop Music. Some exceptions, with higher values, are LPs by certain lounge music performers and virtually any with female models pictured in exotic settings and in alluring poses on their covers.

♦ Country Music on 45 rpm: Most country music vocal and instrumental 45s from the '50s are available for under $15.00; many for less than $10.00. Obvious exceptions are any that border on rockabilly or country rock. Don't take any country record for granted! Play both sides of every disc, as it is always possible you'll discover a great country rocker.

♦ Country music singles from the '60s to present are seldom going to sell for more than $10.00.

♦ Country Music on 78 rpm: Most of the country 78s should fall into the $10.00 to $40.00 range. There are, however, many older 78s with prices well into three figures; some even higher.

♦ Country Music Long Play Albums: From the '50s, 12-inch LPs generally are found for under $30.00 to $60.00. Ten-inch LPs may go for $50 to $100. As always, the range will vary widely depending on the following and collectibility of the artist.

♦ Most country LPs from the '60s to present can be found for $15.00 to $25.00. Again, there are exceptions.

♦ Country Music Extended Play Albums: Very, very few country music EPs were big sellers, which means nearly all are rare. You may find they are in the same price range as the '50s LPs above; some will bring even more than LPs from the same time period.

♦ Jazz Singles on 45 rpm: Most jazz 45s from the '50s are available for under $15.00. The few exceptions are likely to be artists with charted hits, which will be found in the guide.

♦ Jazz singles from the '60s to present are seldom going to sell for more than $10.00.

♦ Jazz Singles on 78 rpm: Most jazz 78s are available for under $20.00. Until the late '40s or early '50s, an *album* was a gatefold binder with a number of 78s, usually in individual paper sleeves. Prices on these jazz albums will vary, but most will fall in the $25.00 to $75.00 range.

♦ Jazz Long Play Albums: From the '50s, 12-inch jazz LPs generally are found for under $50 to $100. Ten-inch LPs may go for $75 to $200.

♦ Most jazz LPs from the '60s to present can still be found for $15.00 to $30.00.

♦ Jazz Extended Play Albums: As with country, very few jazz EPs were big sellers. While all are rare, there is not as much demand for them from jazz collectors as for long-play albums. Of course, outside jazz circles there is virtually no demand for them. You may find they are, in general, worth little more than the prices shown above for jazz singles from the same time period.

♦ Comedy and Personality Long Play Albums: From the '50s and '60s, 12-inch comedy and personality (not soundtrack or original cast) LPs generally are found for under $20.00 to $40.00.

♦ Most comedy and personality LPs from the '70s to present can be had for $10.00 to $15.00.

♦ If we really wanted to add another 100,000 or so listings to *Rockin' Records* (which would make it so thick that the conventional bindery process would be impossible — we'd have to go to two volumes), we could open the door to pre-war blues 78s. For now, the feeling here is "no thanks." You will find quite a number of pre-war blues records already in the guide, but that's usually because those artists either charted or continued to record during the post-war years and are included here for that reason.

♦ In summary, there is no way these few paragraphs can constitute a complete price guide for the millions of non-rock records that exist. If such generic generalizations were possible, while guaranteeing unerring accuracy, the entire price guide would be about ten pages. It is the exceptions that make record pricing so complicated and difficult to document. Our goal here is simply to provide a rough idea of the value of recordings that are outside the parameters of the guide.

What to Expect When Selling Your Records to a Dealer

As most know, there is a noteworthy difference between the prices reported in this guide and the prices that one can expect a dealer to pay when buying records for resale. Unless a dealer is buying for a personal collection and without thoughts of resale, he or she is simply not in a position to pay full price. Dealers work on a percentage basis, largely determined by the total dollar investment, quality, and quantity of material offered as well as the general financial condition and inventory of the dealer at the time.

Another very important consideration is the length of time it will take the dealer to recover at least the amount of the original investment. The greater the demand for the stock and the better the condition, the quicker the return and therefore the greater the percentage that can be paid. Our experience has shown that, day-in and day-out, most dealers will pay from 25% to 50% of *guide* prices. And that's assuming they are planning to resell at guide prices. If they traditionally sell below guide, that will be reflected in what they can pay for stock.

If you have records to sell, it would be wise to check with several shops. In doing so you'll begin to get a good idea of the value of your collection to a dealer.

Also, consult the Directory of Buyers and Sellers in this guide for the names of many dealers who not only might be interested in buying, but from whom many collectible records are available for purchase.

Whether you wish to sell the records you have, or add out-of-print discs to your collection, check out *DISCoveries* magazine. Each issue is packed with ads, features, discographies, collecting tips and more. If getting into the record marketplace is important to you, *DISCoveries* is not just recommended, it is essential. For more information, contact: Trader Publications, PO Box 1050, Dubuque, Iowa 52003. A sample issue is available upon request.

Concluding Thoughts

The purpose of this guide is to report as accurately as possible the most recent prices asked and paid for records within the area of its coverage. There are two key words here that deserve emphasis: **Guide** and **Report**.

We cannot stress enough that this book is only a guide. There always have been and always will be instances of records selling well above and below the prices shown within these pages. These extremes are recognized in the final averaging process; but it's still important to understand that just because we've reported a 30-year-old record as having a $25.00 to $50.00 near-mint value, doesn't mean that a collector of that material should be hesitant to pay $75.00 for it. How badly he or she wants it and how often it's possible to purchase it *at any price* should be the prime factors considered, not the fact that we last reported it at a lower price. Of course, we'd like to know about sales of this sort so that the next edition can reflect the new pricing information.

One extremely difficult area to keep up with is rare R&B releases. We may report a record for $500 to $1,000, which may have been an accurate appraisal at press time. However, before the new edition hits the streets, the price might be $1,000 to $2,000. One or two transactions and six months later it jumps to $2,000 to $4,000. By the time we're close to the following year's guide, this same disc may be considered a bargain at $5,000.

At that point, people may look at the book and wonder how we could show $500 to $1,000 for a $5,000 record. "Our price is a joke," you'll hear. And, at that point, it is.

As in other areas of living, inflation is an undeniable factor in rapidly rising prices of music collectibles

Another component in the inflation equation, however, is the trend for auctioneers to pick the high end of the price range shown in the guide – and make that the *minimum* bid.

Anyone wanting that particular record will likely end up paying more than the posted minimum amount.

Then the results get reported to us.

Some dealers send us only the winning bids, others also submit an average of bids received. A few even send along all of the bid amounts they get.

When we learn *only* of the winning bid, we'll do one of two things:

1. If the item is extremely rare and another sale is unlikely any time soon, we will probably position the winning bid in the middle of our price range. This allows for price movement in either direction.

2. If the item is not so scarce, and other sales are likely, we'll put the winning bid at the high end of the range. This usually provides a realistic price range, since the winning bid is by no means the medium offering – merely the top dollar bid. The average sale price is going to be something less.

Regardless of what the range in our next edition, the cycle begins anew: a new auction is held, using our top price as the new minimum bid.

We mention this truism, not to infer there is anything unethical about the practice, but merely to share one explanation for constantly rising prices.

Meanwhile, please keep in mind that any of the world's more valuable records now have the potential to be worth considerably more in the near future than on that day last spring when work ended on this edition. The key is simply this: is it a money record in the first place? If so, remain open to surprising price increases.

Our objective is to report and reflect record marketplace activity; not to *establish* prices. For that reason, and if given the choice, we'd prefer to be a bit behind the times rather than ahead. With this guide being regularly revised, it will never be long before the necessary changes are reported within these pages.

We encourage record companies, artist management organizations, talent agencies, publicists, and performers to make certain that we are on the active mailing list for new release information, press releases, bios, publicity photos, and anything pertaining to recordings.

There is an avalanche of helpful information in this guide to aid the collector in determining what is valuable and what may not be worth fooling with, but the wise fan will also keep abreast of current trends and news through the pages of the fanzines and publications devoted to his or her favorite forms of music.

Curious?
In case you were wondering:
The number of individual recording artists' sections now found in
Rockin' Records is
OVER 43,900
. . . and Growing.

Osborne Fine Art Images Presents

"Elvis: The Man"

by

Betty Harper

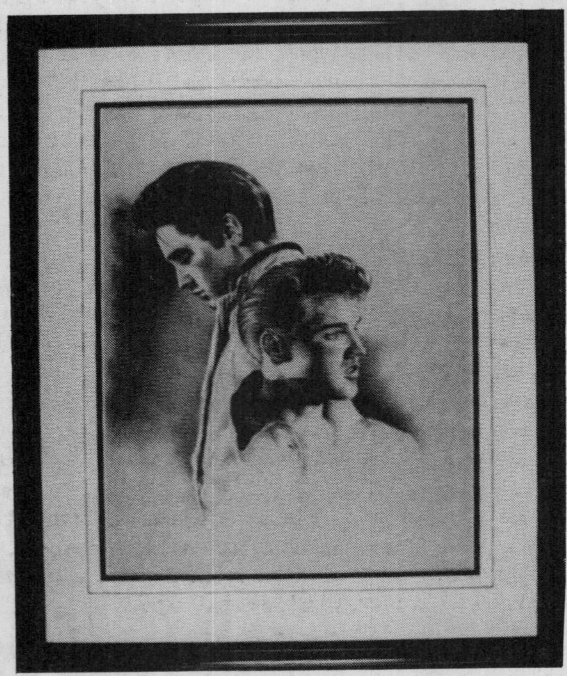

It's the FIRST in our series! Order your copy of this gorgeous, signed, 18" x 24" numbered, limited edition fine art lithograph now! Produced in a tiny edition of only 517 prints, they will likely always be in demand.

As an option for your cherished print, we offer custom, acid-free Museum Quality framing. In frame, size is 26" x 32."

Other signed, limited edition fine art celebrity prints, besides Elvis, available from Osborne Fine Art Images include: DEAN MARTIN, FRANK SINATRA, and MARTY ROBBINS. To view them all in full color, visit our web site: www.jerryosborne.com

Though most folks would no doubt first associate Jerry Osborne's name with his 21 years of Elvis (and other) reference books, his Osborne Fine Art Images has been involved in the limited edition fine art collectibles world even longer — since 1973!

One thing we have learned in two decades of art collecting, is that signed, limited edition lithos are truly a *great* investment. One of the very best available.

Many prints purchased in the '70s and '80s for around $100, are now worth thousands of dollars. And none of those are of Elvis, easily the world's most-collectible celebrity subject. Finally, Elvis hits the fine art scene.

"Elvis: The Man" is a bona fide winner on four counts:

- Any *high-quality*, officially licensed Elvis Presley product is a solid investment. This elegant print and its luxurious packaging (with bonus Harper artwork) are truly first class. Plus, Elvis' many fans worldwide ensure a continual marketplace.
- Most any signed, numbered, limited edition lithograph is highly collectible. With a small Regular Edition run of just 517 prints, the future demand for "Elvis: The Man" is guaranteed. Imagine, all the Elvis fans there are worldwide — and yet so very, very few prints to go around.
- The art of Betty Harper, whether Elvis or her other works, is now more sought-after than ever. "Elvis: The Man" is the FIRST in a series by Osborne/Harper, and the first by any top artist is always more in-demand.
- Having perhaps the most exquisite of all official 20th Anniversary memorabilia is an added bonus for lucky owners of "Elvis: The Man." Don't be left out. Order your print early.

HERE'S OUR AMAZING GUARANTEE: So certain are we of everything we're claiming, that Osborne Fine Art Images will agree to buy back any of our lithographs, for the full purchase price. (Certain restrictions do apply. Inquire for full details of our buy back program.)

"Elvis: The Man" Regular Edition $95
Framed (as pictured) and ready to hang .... Add $150
Shipping & handling (U.S. & Canada) (Framed or unframed) .. $25
Shipping & handling (Overseas by Air pp) (Unframed) $40

(Gallery, dealer and fan club inquiries invited. Buy quantities wholesale and retail through your club as a fund-raiser. Also, some Artist's Proofs are still available. ALL prints include deluxe, signed, numbered outer envelope—with bonus, exclusive Harper art—and certificate of authenticity. Washington residents, add 8% state tax.)

Osborne Fine Art Images
Box 255, Port Townsend WA 98368
(800) 246-3255 – (360) 385-1200 – Fax: (360) 385-6572
Visa/MasterCard accepted
www.jerryosborne.com

FROM SCRATCHY VINYL TO CUSTOMIZED CDs – DO IT YOURSELF

By David Sadler

A major gap in your Beatles collection has been filled with a rare find. The cover is in great shape, the price a steal, but alas the music is damaged. Not to worry! Take the bargain and run. Run right home and use your home computer to restore and create your own "Best Selections" on a music CD from all that music in your collection.

Are we talking about the future? Is this a high priced toy?

No way. The future is today! You can do this right now, at home, and within a budget.

As reported in *Rockin' Records* over the last couple of years, some very sophisticated audio restoration and editing software has been developed for PC computers that lets the PC user do all of the editing and restoration functions that the re-mastering music studios perform when creating re-releases of music selections. The software is powerful and easy to use. Literally anyone with a good PC can utilize the same software as used by the audio pros.

Home remastering is now feasible because the cost of computer CD-R recording devices have come down dramatically. Now we can create our very own music CDs that can be played on any music CD device – in your car, at your friend's place, or even at that theme party next week.

There are even low cost CD label printers available which can be used to create custom labels.

The result for the home music collector is revolutionary. One can go through an entire music collection and affordably produce as many high-quality selections on CD as wanted. Here is an example of how 20 different music titles are restored, and a music CD created from that collection.

The following computer setup is typical:

- At least a 486 DX2 computer equipped with a 1.2 gigabyte disk, a 16 bit sound card, a CD-R reader and recorder, and Windows 95. Of course, Pentiums systems work even better.
- Stereo system with turntable, CD player, cassette, speakers, and so on.
- DART PRO 32 software.

First, install the sound card and connect the stereo system to the PC via one of the "audio out" connectors on the amplifier, to the sound card "audio in" connector. Next install the DART™ PRO 32 software (comes on CD-ROM). DART PRO 32 has a complete multimedia, on-line tutorial and help assistant. It explains with pictures, audio and examples how to do various music editing and restoration functions. And it will show you how to do the music restoration and CD recording.

Next, line up the music selections for recording on a music CD. One music CD can hold about 65 minutes of material – which is approximately 20 to 25 selections. Play a track on the stereo which lets the sound card "hear" the program. DART Wave Manager records the music to a disk file in a "wave" format. Wave Manager is part of DART PRO. The music can come from the phonograph, cassette tape, or even a CD. If in fact the music is from CD, then Wave Manager can read it directly from the CD-R device.

Note the quality of the music and determine if the piece needs restoration. If the music is in good shape, simply add the title (file) to the play list in Wave Manager . If the music has clicks, pops, hiss, or some other damage, use DART PRO 32 to restore the music to near its original condition. When the music is acceptable, add it to the play list. Once there are enough selections to fill the CD, then direct Wave Manager to write the CD from the play list. It shows you how long each selection is, how much total music is in the play list, and lets you position the various titles in the sequence of your choosing. You have complete control over the CD.

It is just that simple. Gather the music from the various sources, restore as necessary, add it to the play list, and record the CD. Your custom music compact disc is now ready for playing on any CD music device.

Now, all those obscure tracks that none of the labels have seen fit to issue on CDs are on *your* CDs.

DART PRO 32 gives you three basic choices for restoring damaged music: DeClick, DeNoise, and DeHiss. It does an exceptional job and you will be amazed at what it can accomplish. In previous editions of *Rockin' Records*, Jeff Klinedinst provided as good a description of these restoration functions as can be written, which we shall repeat.

DeClick

Removing clicks and pops during the restoration process is critical in the restoration of worn vinyl recordings. With DART PRO 32, this is a fairly straightforward and uncomplicated process. An "Outlier Detector" analyzes the material and automatically searches out disturbances which do not fit within the parameters of the source material. It marks these areas and then replaces them with "good" source material, found immediately before or after the disturbance. The program automatically searches out disturbances that are 100 samples or less. It's important to know it won't haphazardly remove cymbal crashes or any other "good," or wanted source material.

For dealing with large scratches or cuts in the source material, DART PRO has a manual reparation mode that allows highlighting an area up to 1500 samples, and replacing it with "good" source material. DeClicking is usually the first stage of the noise restoration process and provides amazing results.

DeNoise

Groove noise, distortion, and any other "constant" noise associated with age and poor quality discs are the next targets. You'll recall that when we recorded the source material, it was mentioned that you should leave a bit at the beginning. Now we make use of that noise. Usually, the noise residing at the beginning of the file is the same as found in the rest of the file. DART PRO can analyze that material then remove it from the entire file. This process is called "Noise Printing."

DeHiss

For the record, DeHiss is an intelligent filtering process which provides maximum hiss removal with minimal source material degradation.

The Noise Audition

One major concern of noise reduction is the fear of damaging the source material in the quest to remove the noise. A key feature of DART PRO allows you to actually subtract your "cleaned" file from your original source and hear only the noise that you've removed. Then, if you hear what you determine to be too much source material amidst the noise, you can always have DART PRO attack the file less aggressively.

If you've been following our updates in previous editions of the guide, you know DART PRO has been available for a few years now. Since its first release, it has been improved a great deal, as you might expect.

The new version, DART PRO 32, still does a great job restoring music, but does it faster – much faster if used with a Pentium system. It is easier than ever to use, and, as outlined above, allows for making customized CDs.

Remember, the multi-media tutorial provides a detailed description on how to do the restoration, along with examples that play the music before and after the process.

Want to try it? A free DART PRO 32 demo – with the tutorial – lets you experiment with your own restorations. Contact ZH Computer (612 844-0915) and they will send you the demo on CD-ROM.

45 RPM SINGLES

A GUIDE TO FIRST PRESSING IDENTIFICATION

By Victor Pearlin and Jerry Osborne

One of the more confusing aspects of record collecting, especially for a newcomer, is identification of 45 rpm pressings—be they first, second or ninth. With some of the better selling releases that seemingly never went out of print, there can be 10 or 20 years worth of releases to try and sort out. Still, it's almost always the first pressing that is of the most interest and the greatest value to collectors.

Except when noted otherwise, all values in this guide are for first pressings. As a general rule, second pressings are valued at about half of first pressings. Third pressings, should there be any, are valued at approximately half of second pressings, etc., etc. The focus of first pressing identification in this guide is on singles only. The subject of long play album label identification has been covered in a separate book.

The catalog numbers shown as points of change in label color and/or design are, in some cases, approximate but, for the most part, accurately researched. The emphasis in this feature is with '50s and early '60s releases though there are exceptions. Largely due to the simultaneous pressing of certain records (usually the better sellers), at different pressing plants, there will always be exceptions to the guidelines presented here. Often, copies pressed in California will carry older labels on East coast releases than we've indicated.

If you should discover records that appear to be an exception to the published information in this edition, please forward the appropriate data to us at Osborne Enterprises. A determination will then be made as to whether our information needs revision or you've simply uncovered a pressing plant variation.

There are tens of thousands of labels in *Rockin' Records* that do not appear in this chapter. Generally, this is because they didn't change their label design or color, thus eliminating any possibility of confusion over what's a first pressing and what's a later pressing. Some labels, Columbia for example, eliminated confusion by not repressing singles with their original catalog numbers. They often utilized a separate series, such as Columbia's "Hall Of Fame" which had both a different number series as well as a somewhat different label design. Overall, most records dealt with in this edition were never reissued or repressed.

Then there's the case of Fortune, a label with many valuable and important releases, but one whose constant change of colors and label art make it absolutely hopeless to trace for you. If there's a way to identify Fortune pressings with certainty, we'd love to know about it. Even the good folks at Fortune can't help us with this problem.

Because some label colors are a tossup as to whether they are maroon or brown (such as Checker and Vee Jay), we'll at least be consistent and call them maroon. Similarities also occur with brown and tan labels. Since we're calling maroon/brown as maroon, we'll call brown/tan as light brown (Argo and Hull are two that come to mind).

You'll find the year or years of releases covered on each line. This will aid you in putting the chronology in proper perspective.

Please address all additions, corrections and suggestions to the publisher or to: Victor Pearlin, P.O. Box 60299, Worcester, MA 01606. Thank you!

ACE

500 through 504 (1955): Black label.
505 through 511 (1955): Yellow label.
512 (1955): Blue label.
513 through 527 (1955-1957): Yellow label.
528 and higher (1957 forward): White label.

This is the Mississippi Ace label, not the New York Ace label that had releases in the 100 series beginning in 1956.

ALADDIN

3000 through 3259 (1947-1954): Blue label.
3260 through 3399 (1954-1957): Maroon label.
3400 and higher (1957 forward): Black label.

Opaque green vinyl exists for 3097, 3104 and 3128 and opaque red vinyl for 3144.

ARGO

5250 through 5281 (1956-1957): Silver and black label with "ship" logo.

5282 through 5360 (1957-1960): Black label, silver lettering, with vertical Argo logo.

5361 and higher (1960 forward): Light brown label with vertical Argo logo. Certain pressing plants used the above black label in the 5300 series.

In late 1965 around number 5515, Argo became Cadet. The name change didn't affect the numbering, as Cadet continued with the 5500 series.

ATCO

6050 through 6090 (1955-1957): Maroon label.

6091 and higher (1957 forward): Yellow and white label.

ATLANTIC

932 through 1083 (1951-1956): Yellow and black label without fan logo.

1084 through 2134 (1956-1962): Red and black label without fan logo.

2135 and higher (1962 forward): Red and black label with fan logo.

Regarding earlier numbers, below 932, Atlantic 919 was issued on 45rpm and there's a possibility that 914 was also on 45. Both labels would be as described for Atlantic 932 through 1083. In the early seventies, Atlantic reissued many of their 932 through 1083 numbers on yellow and black (with fan logo) labels. These used a glossy label stock, whereas the originals were done on a flat paper stock.

BACK BEAT

500 through 530 (1957-1959): White label.

531 and higher (1960 forward): Red "drum" label.

The label name is often shown as one word, "Backbeat."

BRUCE

101 (1953) Script label.

101 through 109 (1953-1954) Has address, "1650 Broadway, N.Y. 19, N.Y." under "Bruce Records." Also has "45 R.P.M." on both sides above the top horizontal line.

110 through 129 (1954-1955) Has "Mfg. by Nu-Way Enterprises, Inc., 1650 Broadway, N.Y. 19, N.Y." under "Bruce Records." Also has "45 R.P.M." on both sides above the top horizontal line.

Exception: Originals of Bruce 111 (*What'll You Do/Tell Me* by the Master-Tones) have "1650 Broadway, N.Y. 19, N.Y." under "Bruce Records" and "45 R.P.M." above the top horizontal line.

Early reissues have "1650 Broadway, N.Y. 19, N.Y." under "Bruce Records" but have "Unbreakable "45 R.P.M." on the left side only, and between the two horizontal lines. Any copies with the sawtooth (wavy) lines are definitely second pressings.

BRUNSWICK

55000 through 55166 (1957-1960): Maroon label.

55167 through 55250 (1960-1963): Orange label.

55251 and higher (1963 forward): Black label with multi-colored arrow.

CAPITOL

791 through 4290 (1949-1959): Purple label with Capitol logo on top.

4291 through 4663 (1959-1961): Purple label with Capitol logo on left side.

4680 through 5999 (1961-1967): Orange and yellow "swirl" label.

Regarding Capitol 4664 through 4679, we've seen enough inconsistencies in this gap to render us unable to make any concrete determinations. Thus far, the highest number we've seen, pressed exclusively on purple, is 4663. The lowest number we know of, pressed exclusively on orange and yellow, is 4680. Many numbers in-between appeared on both Capitol labels. Numbers prior to the beginning of 45 rpm production are reissues of material first issued on 78 rpms.

CHECKER

758 through 800 (1952-1954): Maroon and silver "checkerboard" top label, without "Record Co." under the name Checker.

801 through 876 (1954-1957): Maroon and silver "checkerboard" top label, with "Record Co." under the name Checker.

877 through 1050 (1957-1963): Maroon label, with vertical Checker letters on left side.

1101 and higher (1965 forward): Light blue label, without checkers.

Notes: There is some doubt that 759 and 761 were issued on 45. Some colored plastic exists in the 766-800 series. Several issues after 1101 used the blue label with checkers, but they were inconsistent during that period. A few red vinyl issues appeared in the 766 to 800 series. The first "checkerboard" (maroon) label is often referred to as the "web top" Checker label, however it is a checkerboard and not a spider's web.

Checker 78s as late as 937 exist with the checkerboard design at top, as opposed to 45s which switched designs beginning with 876. Also, 78s as early as 900 have Checker name vertically on left side.

CHESS

1458 through 1670 (1951-1957): Blue and silver label, with three chess pieces at the top.

1671 through 1798 (1957-1961): Blue label, with vertical Chess letters.

1799 through 1840 (1961-1963): Either blue label, with vertical Chess letters, or multi-color label.

1841 through 1950 (1963-1966): Black label, however there are many pressing plant variations. Some 1800 series issues exist on blue and silver, others on multi-color Chess labels.

1951 and higher (1966 forward): Light blue label.

A few red vinyl issues appeared in the 1530-1550 series.

1 through 100 (1951-1956): Glossy red label.

101 and higher (1956 forward): Purple label with Combo name angled across most of the upper left section of the label. No street address shown.

Purple labels with Combo name much smaller (using a reduced portion of the label top) and with street address are reissues. Flat red (almost purple) labels are also reissues.

DECCA

23000 through 29400 (1949-1955): Black label with lines on both sides of the Decca name.

29401 through 31100 (1955-1960): Black label with lines and a star under the Decca name.

31101 and higher (1960 forward): Label is black at the top and bottom, but has a horizontal multi-color band through the center.

An occasional number above 30000 will surface on the label (with lines on both sides of the name Decca) shown for numbers under 29401. Numbers before Decca 45s began (23000 and some as high as 25500—black label with lines on both sides) are 45 rpm reissues of material first issued on 78s

DELUXE

3300 through 3323 (1949-1952): Black label with "AA" following the number. Does not have "Hi-Fidelity" on label. 6000 through 6090 (1953-1955- Black label without "AA" following the number. Does not have "High-Fidelity" on the label.

6091 through 6190 (1955-1959): Black label, with "High-Fidelity" on the label.

6191 through 6200 (1960-1963): Yellow label.

Blue plastic exists between 3318 and 3323. Discs before 45 production began are reissues of material first issued on 78 rpms.

DOOTO

412 through 416 (1957): Maroon and silver label.

417 through 440 (1957-1958): Yellow label with logo in red oval.

441 through 452 (1958-1959): Yellow label with logo in blue oval.

453 through 465 (1959-1961): Black label with multi-color print.

472 and higher (1962 forward): Maroon label with multi-color print.

700 series (1958-1959) Yellow label with logo in blue oval.

Dooto was previously Dootone, and the number series is continued for Dootone's numbering. 466 through 472 were on Dootone instead of Dooto. Some of the changeover numbers are approximate, since many of Dooto's releases were comedy, etc., and we were unable to locate copies of those records.

DOOTONE

300 through 411 (1951-1957) Usually flat maroon labels, but may also be blue, black or glossy red. Yellow, glossy maroon and multi-colored labels are reissues.

466 through 472 (1961-1962) Red label with multi-color print.

1200 series: Red label.

Dootone, in early 1957, changed their name to Dooto, continuing with the same numbering series. 466 through 472 were on Dootone instead of Dooto.

DOT

1000 through 1100 (1950-1952): Glossy maroon label with gold print.

1101 through 1150 (1952-1953): Yellow label with black print.

1151 through 1288 (1953-1957): Maroon label with silver print.

15000 through 15500 (1951-1957): Maroon label with silver print.

15501 and higher (1957 forward): Black label.

A few numbers above 15500 are on the maroon label.

DUKE

101 through 342 (1952-1961): Yellow and purple label.

343 and higher (1961 forward): Orange label.

EMBER

1001 through 1039 (1956-1958): Red or orange labels.

1040 through 1064 (1958-1960): Multi-color label, with name lettered with flaming logs.

1065 and higher (1960 forward): Black label.

An occasional number above 1065 exists on the multi-color label.

END

1000 through 1010 (1957): Black label.

1010 through 1045 (1957-1959): White or gray labels.

1046 and higher (1959 forward): White or multi-color labels.

EXCELLO

2001 through 2057 (1952-1955): Yellow and blue label.

2058 through 2209 (1955-1962): Orange and blue label.

2210 and higher (1962 forward): Red, white and blue label.

FEDERAL

12001 through 12084 (1950-1952): Green label with gold top and "AA" following the number.

12085 through 12129 (1952-1953): Green label with gold top. Does not have the "AA."

12130 through 12196 (1953-1954): Green label with silver top. Some in this series were green with gold top.

12197 through 12244 (1954-1955): Green label, without "Hi-Fidelity."

12245 through 12369 (1955-1959): Green label with "Hi-Fidelity" in small print. Most, if not all, we've seen with this label have an em dash in the selection number between the "45" and 12,000 series number (i.e. 45—12496).

12370 and higher (1959 forward): Green label with "Hi-Fidelity" in larger print. Most, if not all, with this label have a hyphen – not a dash – in the selection number between the "45" and 12,000 series number (i.e. 45-12496).

Blue plastic issues exist between 12050 and approximately 12070.

FEE BEE

201 through 221 (1956-1958): Orange label with "bee" logo. Also, "45 rpm" appears on BOTH sides above the horizontal lines.

222 and higher (1958 forward): Orange label without "bee" on label.

FLASH

101 through 103 (1955): Red label.

104 through 113 (1955-1956): Maroon label.

114 through 127 (1956-1958): Blue label.

128 through 133 (1958-1959): Black label.

FLIP

301 through 305 (1955): Maroon label.

306 and higher (1955 forward): Blue label.

Reissues, through approximately 350, have the matrix number (an "FL" prefix and number) in parentheses.

FURY

1000 through 1019 (1957-1958): Maroon label.

1020 through 1023 (1958-1959): Yellow label without horse head logo.

1024 through 1032 (1959-1960): Yellow label with horse head logo.

1033 through 1039 (1960): Multi-color label.

1040 and higher (1960 forward): Yellow label with horse head logo or multi-color label.

GEE

1 through 12 (1954): Yellow and green label.

1000 through 1021 (1955-1956): Red label, without "Trade Mark" and "Reg. U.S. Pat. Off."

1022 through 1025 (1956): Red label with "Trade Mark" on left and "Reg. U.S. Pat. Off" on the right.

1026 through 1039 (1956-1957): Red label without "Trade Mark" and "Reg. U.S. Pat. Off."

1040 through 1050 (1957-1959): Red label with "Trade Mark" on the left and "Reg. U.S. Pat. Off" on the righ**1051 and higher** (1959 forward): Gray label, although an occasional number will turn up on the red label.

GONE

5001 through 5003 (1957): Black label, with shadow ("drop shadow") of the letters "GONE" shown.

5004 through 5056 (1957-1959): Black label without drop shadow of the letters "GONE."

5057 and higher (1959 forward): Multi-color label.

Some copies of 5012 have the multi-color Gone logo (with the singer's head and open mouth in the letter "O") on black label stock. Others above 5057 occasionally are found on black.

GOTHAM

100 through 288 (1951-1953): Blue label.

289 through 304 (1953-1955): Red label.

305 and higher (1955 forward): Yellow label.

Gotham 304 was also issued on blue and on yellow labels. Red vinyl issues appear for many Gotham discs. Actual selection numbers may be shown with a "7" preceding the above numbers.

GRAND

All Grand first pressings are on thick discs with small lettering on the artist and title lines. Reissues had this print nearly double the size of that used on originals. Pressings with the label's address shown are reissues. First pressings had the catalog number on the bottom whereas later issues had the number on the left side We can't swear to this being true on every Grand 45; however, it applies to all that we have seen.

HERALD

401 through 410 (1953): Black label.

410 through 415 (1953): Yellow label with block print and no flag. (Herald 410 can be found on either black or yellow.)

416 through 528 (1953-1958): Yellow label with script print inside the flag. Some issues in this series appeared with the block style print. Two exceptions in this series are 416 and 432, which can be found on yellow, but without the flag.

529 through 550 (1958-1959): Multi-color label. Some of the higher numbers in this series appeared on a variety of label designs.

551 and higher (1959 forward): Yellow label, with block print inside the flag. A variety of label styles and designs can be found in this series.

Note: Clear red vinyl pressings are found in the 410-421 series.

HOLIDAY

2601 through 2603 (1956-1957): Flat black label.

2604 through 2611 (1957-1958): Glossy red label. (Flat red labels are reissues.)

HULL

711 and 712 (1955-1956): Pink label.

713 through 715 (1956): Black label, without outside ring.

716 through 721 (1956-1957): Black or red label with silver outside ring.

722 through 742 (1957-1961): Red label without outside ring.

743 and higher (1961 forward): Tan label.

IMPERIAL

5000 through 5300 (1952-1954): Blue label with Imperial name in script lettering.

5301 through 5357 (1954-1955): Red label with Imperial name in script lettering.

5358 through 5460 (1955-1957): Maroon label with Imperial name in block lettering.

5461 and higher (1957 forward): Black label.

Opaque red vinyl pressings occur in the 5200-5235 series. Clear red is used on 5262 and "hold to a light" purple can be found in the 5340s. There was a great deal of overlapping, from one style to another, throughout the Imperial catalog. Numbers prior to the beginning of 45 rpm production are issues of material first issued on 78 rpms.

JAMIE

1000 through 1100 (1956-1958): Black label.

1101 through 1124 (1958-1959): Yellow label.

1125 and higher (1959 forward): White and mustard colored label.

JOSIE

760 through 829 (1954-1957): Light brown label with "JOZ" logo and brown print.

830 through 845 (1957-1958): Light brown label with "JOZ" logo and red print.

846 and higher (1958 forward): Light brown label with "JOSIE" logo.

JOYCE

101 through 105 (1957): Blue label, with the "Y" in Joyce larger than the other letters.

JOZ: see JOSIE

JUBILEE

5000 through 5092 (1951-1952): Blue label, with Jubilee in script lettering. No line under "Jubilee."

5093 through 5340 (1952-1958): Black label, with Jubilee in script lettering and underlined.

5341 and higher (1958 forward): Black label.

Clear red vinyl pressings are found in the 5055 to 5120 series. Numbers prior to the beginning of 45 production are reissues of material first issued on 78 rpms.

KING

500 through 1470 (1951-1955): Maroon Label.

1471 through 1502 (1955): Blue label.

4449 through 4544 (1951-1952): Blue label with the letters "AA" following the number and no "High Fidelity" shown.

4545 through 4834 (1952-1955): Blue label without the letters "AA" following the number and no "High Fidelity" shown.

4835 through 5266 (1955-1959): Blue label with "High Fidelity" in small print.

5267 and higher (1959 forward): Blue label with "High Fidelity" in larger print.

Clear colored vinyl (blue, purple, green and red) was pressed in the 1000-1150 and in the 4450-4525 series. Numbers prior to the beginning of 45 production are reissues of material first issued on 78 rpms.

MGM

10000 through 12828 (1949-1959): Yellow label.

12829 and higher (1959 forward): Black label. MGM switched to a blue and yellow label somewhere around 14000 (1969), but we can't pinpoint the exact changeover number.

55000 series (1955-1956): Yellow label.

Numbers prior to the beginning of 45 production are reissues of material first issued on 78 rpms.

MERCURY

5000 through 8999 (1949-1952): Maroon label.

70000 through 71039 (1949-1957): Maroon or black label, though maroon ends around 71100. Also used in this series was a label picturing Mercury (Roman mythological messenger of the gods) in a square, which appeared on maroon, black, pink (R&B):, and green (C&W) stock.

71040 through 72320 (1957-1964) Maroon or black label, with the Mercury ellipse (or oval), or square logo.

72321 and higher (1964 forward): Red label.

METEOR

5000 and 5001 (1953): Yellow label.

5002 through 5030 (1953-1956): Red label.

5031 through 5046 (1956-1958): Black label.

MODERN

779 through 980 (1950-1956): Glossy red or glossy black.

981 through 1028 (1956-1958): Flat black.

MOTOWN

1000 through 1010 (1960-1961): Pink label.

1011 and higher (1961 forward): Blue label.

MUSIC CITY

730 through 795 (1954-1956): Maroon label.

796 through 807 (1956-1957): Flat black label.

808 and higher (1957 forward): Glossy black with multi-colors.

Red, green, and blue plastic exists in the 700 series.

OKEH

6800 through 7092 (1951-1957): Purple label, with small Okeh logo.

7093 through 7140 (1957-1960): Yellow label. A few purple labels overlapped into this series.

7141 and higher (1960 forward): Purple label with large Okeh logo.

OLD TOWN

700 series (1953): Yellow label, with block style (sans-serif) print. Label print is green

1000 through 1012 (1954-1955): Yellow label, with "Old Town" in Old English style lettering. Label print is brown.

1013 through 1028 (1955-1956): Yellow label, with block style (sans-serif) print and horizontal rope-like lines.

1029 through 1051 (1956-1958): Yellow label, with block style (sans-serif) print but with straight, not rope-like, lines.

1052 and higher (1958 forward): Blue label.

Red vinyl pressings occur in the 700 series and in the 1000 series. Beginning with 1094, "There's A Moon Out Tonight," Old Town started using a slightly different blue label, darker and with a yellow moon (probably to tie in with their biggest hit). Later numbers can be found on either of the two blue labels, at least through 1133, which we know was pressed on both of the blue labels.

ONYX

501 through 513 (1956-1957): Glossy black label.

514 through 520 (1957-1958): Flat black and orange or flat black and green label.

PARADISE

101 through 109 (1953-1959): Maroon label with horizontal rope-like lines.

110 and higher (1959 forward): Purple label without horizontal rope-like lines.

PEACOCK

1500 through 1604 (1949-1952): Flat maroon label

1605 through 1675 (1952-1957): Glossy red label.

1676 through 1699 (1957-1961): White label.

1700 through 1899 (1952-1961): Black label.

1900 through 1925 (1961-1962): White label.

1926 and higher (1962 forward): Blue and multi-colored label.

Red plastic exists in the 1700 series. This series was Peacock's gospel series and, as the years indicate, it paralleled their 1600 pop series rather than followed it.

RCA VICTOR

50-0000 through 50-0105 (1950): Gray label, gold print. Red vinyl. (The industry's first 45rpm singles were the early numbers in this series.)

50-0106 through 50-0141 (1950-1951): Gray label, silver print. Black vinyl.

47-2800 through 47-4572 (1948-1952): Turquoise label.

47-4573 through 47-5700 (1952-1954): Flat black label with the dog on right side.

47-5700 through 47-8550 (1954-1965): Glossy black label, with the dog on top.

47-8551 through 47-9650 (1965-1968): Glossy black label, with the dog on the left side.

47-9650 and higher (1968 forward): orange label.

The changeover numbers of 5600, 8550 and 9650 are approximate; our best estimates at this time (especially 5700). If you have releases that can better narrow these down, please let us know. Some numbers in the 6600-6800 series were issued without the dog anywhere on the label.

The "20," "47" and "50" were the most common RCA Victor prefixes, however there were several others in use during this period, including: "21," "22," "23," "25," "28," "40," "46," "48" and "51." None of these specialty series releases were reissued using the same number.

RPM

300 through 362 (1950-1952): "RPM" in script style lettering on either maroon, black or blue labels.

363 through 502 (1952-1956): "RPM" in block (san-serif) style lettering on either red, black or blue labels.

RAINBOW

100 through 250 (1950-1954): Blue label.

251 and higher (1954 forward): Yellow label.

Note: Colored vinyl pressings are found in the 200 series.

RAMA

1 through 196 (1953-1956): Blue label.

197 through 222 (1956-1957): Red label without "Reg. U.S. Pat. Off."

223 through 233 (1957): Red label, with "Reg. U.S. Pat. Off" on left side.

Red plastic exists in some numbers below 50.

RED TOP

100 through 111 (1957): Light blue label.

112 and higher (1957 forward): Red label.

ROULETTE

4001 through 4004 (1957): Orange or red label with roulette wheel circling label.

4005 through 4050 (1957-1958): Orange or red labels with partial roulette wheel or no wheel at all.

4051 through 4420 (1958-1962): White label with six colored "spokes" (lines).

4421 through 4500 (1962-1963): Dark pink label.

4500 and higher (1963 forward): Orange label with broken line and logo circling label.

All changeover numbers are approximate with Roulette. Information helpful in narrowing these down would be appreciated.

SPARK

101 through 108 (1954): Red label, with red letter on a silver top.

109 (1954): Red or blue label, with silver print.

110 through 119 (1955): Red label.

120 through 122 (1955-1956): Yellow and black label.

SPECIALTY

300 through 607 (1951-1957): With saw-tooth (wavy) horizontal lines.

608 and higher (1957 forward): Without saw-tooth (wavy) horizontal lines.

Numbers 500-525 were used in 1946-1948 for 78 rpm issues. Specialty therefore jumped from 499 to 526 in 1954. Colored vinyl pressings are found in the mid-400 series.

TAMLA

100 and 102 (1959): Yellow label with horizontal lines across the top of the label.

5501 (1960): Yellow label with horizontal lines across the top of the label.

54024 through 54043 (1960-1961): Yellow label with horizontal lines across the top of the label.

54044 through 54175 (1961-1968): Yellow label with "globes" logo. Globes may be overlapped or side by side.

54176 and higher (1968 forward): Yellow label, with "box" logo.

VEE JAY

100 through 223 (1953-1956): Maroon label with thin outer silver circle. Does not have "Trademark Reg." or "Made In The U.S.A." on the label.

224 through 286 (1956-1958): Maroon label with thin outer silver circle. Does not have "Trademark Reg." but does have "Made In The U.S.A." on the label.

287 through 353 (1958-1960): Maroon label with thicker outer silver circle. Has "Trademark Reg." but does not have "Made In The U.S.A." on the label.

354 and higher (1960 forward): Black label.

Vee Jay 280 had the thicker outer line, but was an exception to the rule. Red plastic exists in some numbers in the 100 series. When the Beatles became popular in January, 1964, Vee Jay releases poured forth, using a wide assortment of label colors and designs.

WINLEY

212 (1957): Blue label.

213 through 230 (1957-1958): Orange label, "Winley" name is in smaller (3/16-inch) print.

231 and higher (1958 forward): Orange label, "Winley" name is in slightly larger (1/4-inch) print.

ABOUT THE AUTHOR

An avid collector of records for over 35 years, Jerry Osborne has also worked full-time as an author of record price guides and reference books since 1975.

In the 21 years since work began on his first *Record Collector's Price Guide*, the number of Jerry's published works on music now exceeds 200 — including 60 books and 152 periodicals. As busy as ever, he continues to produce several books per year.

Among other music-related ventures, Jerry has, since 1986, written the popular, weekly newspaper feature, *Mr. Music.* This entertaining and informative column answers readers' questions about music and records. (*Mr. Music* is syndicated nationwide by World Features Syndicate. If it does not appear in your area, ask your favorite paper to add it! Sometimes that's all it takes.)

The rest of Osborne's past is also saturated with music. Upon graduation from high school, he began a 14-year career in radio and television (1962–1976) as an announcer, or dee jay.

Over the years, Jerry founded and published three collectors news and marketplace magazines: *Record Digest* and *Music World* and the still-popular *DISCoveries.* In the mid-'80s, he began publication of *The Osborne Report,* a monthly newsletter covering new releases.

Osborne's influence and involvement in record collecting has been chronicled in virtually every major magazine and newspaper in the country: *Reader's Digest, The Wall Street Journal, USA Today, People Magazine, Esquire, Oui, National Enquirer, Money, Changing Times, Photoplay, High Fidelity, Billboard, Cash Box, Music City News, Collectibles, Kiplinger's, Woman's Day* and *Rolling Stone* — to name just a few.

Jerry has been a frequent guest on many major radio and TV talk shows, discussing the record collecting hobby. Among these are: "Good Morning America," The "Today Show" "The Nashville Network," and far too many local and regional shows to enumerate.

He worked in the mid-'80s as a technical advisor and consultant for the critically acclaimed ABC-TV nostalgic news-magazine program, "Our World," and has served as a consultant for HBO, and CBS-TV's "West 57th Street."

Clearly, no one person has been more responsible—directly or indirectly—for the amazing growth in the past 20 years of the music collecting hobby.

A GUIDE TO '50s & '60s CANADIAN PRESSINGS

By Peter S. McCullough

For most record collectors in Canada – and U.S. residents who buy from dealers in Canada – the most perplexing issue is usually accurate identification of original, and later, Canadian issues from the '50s and '60s. This is especially important when trying to use the listings of U.S. releases in *Rockin' Records* to appraise Canadian pressings that do not yet appear in the guide. It should be noted that an effort has been underway in the last few years to include as many important Canadian issues as possible in the guide.

To long-time collectors familiar with the Canadian record companies, the label itself, along with the apparent age of the record, can often identify a Canadian original as well as indicate its U.S. counterpart. Sometimes reference is even made to a U.S. label and number making the task simple.

For U.S. collectors, as well as younger Canadian collectors, unfamiliar with our labels and with searching for clues on those labels, identification of originals may prove a daunting task. Hopefully, the information here will make accurate identification of Canadian originals easier for collectors on both sides of the border.

Aside from the issue of labels and/or pressings, the value of a '50s or '60s Canadian record traded in the U.S. will sometimes depend on a historical context; one with which U.S. collectors may be unfamiliar.

For example, most collectors of The Band know that early releases by the members were with Ronnie Hawkins and the Hawks. But you may not know that some recordings were released in Canada with all the individual band members named.

Similarly, Beatles collectors may be unaware that the first single of *Love Me Do* is a take with session drummer Andy White, rather than with Ringo Starr. Subsequent album releases in both Canada and the U.S. contain the track with Ringo. This special Canadian alternate release was unavailable in the United States until the 1980 release of *Rarities*. Other striking examples will be outlined here as an aid to evaluating certain Canadian releases in their sometimes unfamiliar historical context.

As an aside, it should be noted that in Quebec a virtually separate music industry exists for francophone performers and record companies. Although a few artists and labels are listed here there is no intention to give authoritative information on this area.

Canadian and U.S. Label Differences

The Canadian recording industry was, to be kind, primitive in the early '50s. The majority of records released were from the major U.S. companies (Columbia, Decca, RCA Victor, Mercury, etc.) and marked only as "made in Canada." Canadian labels were few and small. With some exceptions, the established U.S. labels simply reproduced the U.S. "pop" hits for consumption in Canada.

The mid-'50s, however, brought significant changes. With the appearance of many rock and roll recordings by smaller U.S. labels came their need to release their records in Canada. This created a market for a new breed of record company – ones known to collectors as "shadow" labels. The term correctly implies a certain unreality, and these labels had virtually no bands nor artists signed. They existed solely to reproduce for the Canadian market the countless independent U.S. issues. Among our shadow labels were: Quality, Reo, Sparton, Regency, Apex and Delta.

Sometimes the shadows used U.S. selection numbers; sometimes Canadian numbers were shown. Occasionally both were used. Often shadow labels would reflect a licensing agreement with text like: "by arrangement with (fill in blank) Records." Since these records were usually released simultaneously in Canada and the U.S., both must be considered originals. Overall, there were about 10 shadow labels being manufactured by about five plants, with several being produced by Quality Records Limited – the production company, not the record label.

Also, some releases came on a "hybrid" label, where a Canadian shadow company acknowledged the original U.S. label by name, sometimes even showing the U.S. selection number.

For example, Quality releases sometimes denoted "King Series" signifying the disc as a Canadian pressing of a U.S. release from King Records. London records similarly issued some records with "London" at the top and "Liberty" below. These hybrid releases were also simultaneously issued in the U.S. and Canada.

Quite a few Canadian records carried a reproduction of the U.S. label, though some have slightly altered designs and/or different colours. These too are original first pressings. An original '50s and early '60s Warner Bros. release in Canada, for example, was produced by the Compo Company (noted only in fine print) on a deep red label as opposed to the pink label in the U.S. As the pop and rock market grew and production costs dropped, most U.S. labels, majors and independents alike, would "fly their own flag" in Canada, so to speak.

By 1970, virtually all U.S. recordings appeared in Canada simultaneously using a label nearly identical to the U.S. label, but produced by a Canadian manufacturer.

In the early '60s, though, we also saw some discs from truly Canadian independent labels, ones with a stable of Canadian artists. Occasionally one of these releases broke in the U.S. and would be picked up by a U.S. company for distribution. In such cases, the Canadian release usually preceded the U.S. release by a few months, making the Canadian one the true original and potentially more valuable – and probably much rarer – than the U.S. version. More often than not, however, these records failed to realize airplay or sales outside of Canada.

Besides the categories already described, the following minor label variants exist and should be helpful in the area of identification:

British Invasion Oddities

A U.S. subsidiary label, like Capitol Records of Canada, would release a British recording in Canada. The song would only later be released in the U.S., on either an indie or the parent corporation of the Canadian subsidiary, but much later. This particularly applies to the mid-'60s British Invasion years.

Some overseas recordings, primarily British Invasion, came out here exactly as issued in the originating country. Mysteriously, U.S. versions often contained edited or otherwise altered versions of these tracks.

Promotional Issues

Unlike in the States, Canada had very few promotional copies in the '50s and '60s. Dee jays got regular Canadian product, just shipped slightly in advance of commercial release. Certain regular Canadian issues did, however, strongly resemble promos. Atco, for example, used plain white labels with black lettering, but they are clearly store stock and not promos.

Labels from the Past

Canadian issues often used the correct U.S. label and number, but with an older style label design no longer in use in the States.

Identifying Canadian Originals

The detailed description of actual labels falls into basic sections. First, a discussion of the various Canadian labels and Canadian versions of U.S. labels and their identification as true originals and, second, a brief synopsis of certain specific artists and groups, major and minor, whose Canadian original releases pose the greatest problems of identification. This dual approach comes with some risk of duplication, but is necessary in order to avoid even greater confusion overall. When it comes to record identification, too much information is better than too little.

In most cases, appearance on a certain Canadian label usually ties it to a corresponding U.S. company, making it equivalent to either a first pressing or reissue if that's what the U.S. issue is. In other cases, identification must be determined by facts concerning the recording history of the artists themselves.

It should be noted that the bulk of analysis here pertains to singles: 45s and 78 rpms. This format comprises the vast majority of releases. Furthermore, most LPs can be identified using essentially the same information.

Speaking of 78s, those produced in Canada may also need to be reconsidered. Since the attempted inclusion of all 78 releases in *Rockin' Records*, it is becoming increasingly apparent that many late '50s and early '60s singles issued only on 45 in the U.S. came on both formats in Canada. Now, *Rockin' Records* can begin to identify a new Canadian source of certain 78 releases previously thought to be unavailable. Understandably, these previously unknown 78s are quite scarce and in high demand among 78 rpm collectors.

Canadian Shadow Labels

The colour and design characteristics of most original Canadian shadow labels of the '50s and '60s can be summarized as follows: (Unless otherwise indicated, comments apply to 78s, 45s and LPs):

Apex: Singles are reddish brown with silver print where relevant (see below). Most of Cadence's U.S. releases were on Apex in Canada. As a label, Apex predates the '50s with 78s on a dark blue label with silver print. These are all pop music releases and normally would be disregarded by rock and R&B aficionados.

Arc: This budget label has almost no releases of merit. Avoiding them is generally recommended.

Barrell: Singles are black with silver print.

Barry: Singles are white with red print, essentially identical to the later Quality releases.

Birchmont: A Quality-owned budget label used for cheapies and reissues.

Delta: Singles are dark reddish brown with silver print. Produced by Quality Records, most Delta issues tend to be blues or R&B.

London: As of the late '50s and early '60s this label functioned effectively as a UK label with issues in Canada. Labels are mostly blue with silver lettering with a very few labels being reddish brown. As of 1964, the label functions in the U.S. as well (see U.S. variants section below).

Maple Leaf: With early '50s issues only, they are gray with a red maple leaf. Limited pretty much to country and western material.

Pye: Another UK label with product also issued in Canada. Most singles from the '60s are orange/red, though they changed to blue around 1969.

Quality: Singles are a pale yellow, with red printing and a prominent Canadian only selection number on the right side. Early releases may have an identifying reference to a U.S. label (e.g. "King Series").

In the very late '60s, the basic colour changed to white with red lettering. LP labels are dark blue in colour with silver lettering. A few exceptions exist that have the yellow and red label.

Other than changing to gold labels with black lettering, reissues are otherwise virtually identical to originals.

Regency: Singles have mostly green labels with silver printing. Some labels are light brown. Circa 1960, the label changed to medium blue, black print, and some lime green on each side.

Reo: Singles are dark green with silver print. Reissues are gold with black print. Albums may refer to a U.S. label and number on the sleeve, but the disc itself has the green Reo label.

Reo seems to have been consistently used for Canadian releases of product on smaller, independent U.S. labels.

Sparton: Singles are dark reddish brown with silver print. About 1969 the colours changed to purple and black with the same design. If an ABC-Paramount release, as most Sparton discs are, there's a silver half moon (and later black) at the bottom.

Independent Canadian Labels

As already indicated, "independents" are those labels that had their own talent and were not restricted to merely reproducing U.S. releases. Often these labels were strongly associated with one artist (which we'll try to mention) and differ from the "shadow" labels in the sense that the output was limited to a few select recordings.

Aim: Few releases, the most notable being a re-release of the Chateau recordings of Gordon Lightfoot.

Attic: Singles, which have light orange labels, include a wide-ranging catalogue of Canadian artists.

Boo: An offshoot of Rebel Records: silver with black lettering with plant logo similar to marijuana plant. See Grant Smith and the Power.

Chateau: Maritimes-based folk and soft rock releases of the Maritimes. Best known for releasing early Gordon Lightfoot country stylings, most of which Mr. Lightfoot bought back and destroyed. These albums and possibly singles are very rare since Lightfoot demolished most of them. Some labels are white with black printing, others are maroon with silver printing.

Daffodil: Singles have a yellow daffodil with dark green leaves. Canadian bands on Daffodil include Crow Bar and King Biscuit Boy.

Deluxe: Earliest releases were conjoined with Maple Leaf. Subsequent releases are shown as Deluxe only with a black label with silver colouring.

Disques Vogue: (Vogue Records) A francophone version of Vogue. English music released on french translated labels. Black on silver in early sixties later becoming white and green.

Dominion: A budget country and western label. No collectible releases are known.

Fonorama: Quebec-based indie with francophone (i.e. "sung in french") rock releases of mid '60s.

Freedom: Indie of white label and various coloured lettering specializing in releases of David Wilcox.

Melborne: Flat black with silver lettering small indie label with limited folk-type releases from Maritimes.

Nimbus 9: Singles are a pale light brown with black print and a purple logo: This label had the Guess Who in later years although some singles were on RCA and noted simply as a "Nimbus 9" production.

Rebel: Singles are white with blue print with, surprisingly, a Confederate Flag! Primarily associated with Canadian folk singer, Stompin' Tom Connors.

Red Leaf: Mid-'60s, singles are red and white, similar to the present Canadian flag.

Roman: Early singles are black with silver lettering and later medium and light blue with black printing. Includes David Clayton Thomas before his Blood Sweat & Tears years.

Rusticana: Quebec recording company. Green and silver label. Nature of releases consist of pop and light rock.

Skyline: A mid-'70s Quality Records Limited spinoff. Light blue with white lettering. Output is apparently MOR rock.

Snowy River Records: Canadian indie. White label with blue print.

Stone: High quality late '60s rock of a psychedelic nature appears on this shadow label, produced by Sparton.

Tamarac: Light orange on white background with map of Canada on top. Among their few apparent releases are those by Little Caesar and the Consuls.

Tartan: Singles – white and red with a black Scottish kilt design on top – appear restricted to ones by Bobby Curtola. Curtola is a Canadian star who had some Del-Fi U.S. hits in the early '60s, most notably *Fortuneteller*.

Teledisc: Quebec-based indie. Yellow and white with blue and black lettering. Limited to francophone rock.

Tembo: Late '80s indie, white label with red logo.

Vogue: (see Disques Vogue above). Had many Petula Clark releases.

Yorktown: True Canadian indie, whose earliest releases are flat black with silver print. Later releases are yellow with red inset.

Zirkon: Flat black with silver lettering. Releases are primarily ones by Adam Wade.

U.S. Labels Issued in Canada

This list highlights U.S. labels issued in Canada, but *only* ones with significant variations from U.S. labels that most collectors know. If a label is not listed here, one should not necessarily assume the labels to be identical. Rather, it's that no significant label variation has been noted.

Atco: There is no use of yellow. Early '50s labels are primarily white with black print, changing to black with silver print in the late '50s. Atco 78s appear to be only on the black and white labels.

Atlantic: Releases by Atco's parent company pretty much resemble U.S. releases.

Brunswick: Mid-to-late '50s releases that are orange in the States are maroon in Canada.

Columbia: Mid-to-late '60s singles are orange in Canada. Most are red (like album labels) in the U.S.

Deluxe: Sometimes conjoined with "Maple Leaf" logo and colour in early fifties. Later pressings are usually black with grey print.

Era: Canadian releases have a flat black label with silver print.

Imperial: Original Imperial singles and albums are maroon compared to the bright red of U.S. releases. No known Canadian Imperial release has the later black label, common in the U.S. in the '60s.

Liberty: In the late '50s and early '60s (as conjoined with London) singles have labels which are blue in Canada and green in U.S. Album releases may be reddish brown as well.

London: In 1964 – with Rolling Stones releases – U.S. labels (blue and white triangle design) appear. This design is also used in Canada but with an orange and white design.

RCA Victor: (Singles) Very early '50s releases are blue non-photographic dog on side. Post-1954 releases are flat black, the same as pre-'54 U.S. releases. About the time U.S. ceases photographic dog on top, for dog on side, Canadian single releases are dog on top (photographic). With issue of orange label, singles converge in format. Some '69 Canadian singles are red. Also, some Canadian-only Elvis promos have come to light.

RCA Victor: (Albums) Releases of photographic dog on top continue in Canada long after U.S. albums are on the new orange label [around 1970]. See first Youngbloods album.

RCA sometimes functioned as a shadow label, picking up distribution of U.S. releases on indies or subsidiaries, most notably with the Monkees.

Tamla: Original 1961-'62 Canadian pressings of 45s have a dark blue label, followed circa '63 by the U.S. yellow. Canadian *Fingertips,* from 1963, is on the usual yellow label.

Warner Bros.: Labels for 45s are red instead of pink, as in U.S.

Artists and Aberrations

Sometimes it is impossible to correlate Canadian releases to U.S. ones using label information only. Factors relevant to identification to originals often must be tied to specific artists, and this list covers some relevant examples.

Often, a Canadian variant will be identified here that has not yet been noted in *Rockin' Records*. The greatest variations in U.S. and Canadian releases occurred during the British Invasion. In most cases, Britain's hit singles and albums were released (successfully) in Canada, but many of these same releases never saw U.S. release until much later, if ever.

Abbey Tavern Singers: Folksie Canadian release *We're Off to Dublin in the Green* is on Arc 1144.

Ace, Johnny: Early Canadian releases, including *Pledging My Love* are on Quality.

Allen, Barry: Canadian crooner with one big hit, *Lovedrops*. Both his Capitol single and his LP are now very collectible.

Amesbury, Bill: Had one single hit, *Virginia (Touch Me Like You Do),* on Yorktown 45100.

Animals: In the U.S., this group broke in mid-to-late 1964 with *The House of the Rising Sun* 45 and an MGM album, *The Animals*. In Canada, their stuff, including the same LP, came out months earlier on Capitol – though the MGM album was later released in Canada as well. The Capitol release has the full length version of *The House of the Rising Sun*, with a black and white cover. The MGM album has an edited (U.S. single) version, and a colour sleeve. The Canadian Capitol album is much rarer than the MGM issue.

Anka, Paul: All early '50s releases are on Sparton.

Baker, Lavern: Early singles are on Quality with acknowledgment of U.S. Atlantic.

Ballard, Hank: Early releases are on Regency.

Band, The: As mentioned, rocker Ronnie Hawkins developed this group. Early Band singles on Capitol credit their individual names only. Beginning with *Music from Big Pink*, U.S. and Canadian releases were identical and credit The Band.

Barriere, Fernand: Francophone rocker. See *Suspicious* on Fonorama S22.

Beatles: All UK singles were released in Canada on the Capitol yellow swirl label. This includes titles like *She Loves You* and *Twist and Shout*, etc., not issued by Capitol in the U.S. at the time. Those singles eventually released in the U.S. didn't come out there until mid-'64.

The original Capitol single *Help!/I'm Down* in Canada was released with the reference that the song *Help* was from the new motion picture *Eight Arms To Hold You*. The original release in U.S. contains no similar reference, but rather to the ultimate title *Help!* By this time, the original proposed title had been abandoned. Later Canadian pressings refer to the usual movie title *Help!*

Early Canadian albums are significantly different than the U.S. ones. Canada's first album, *Twist and Shout*, is virtually the same as the first UK album, *The Beatles*, but with some songs shuffled to make room for the then-new *She Loves You*. It is also essentially the same as the U.S. issue of *The Early Beatles*.

The second Canadian LP, *Beatlemania*, is identical to the UK's *With the Beatles*, with a similar picture on the front. When finally released in the U.S. as their "first" album, the title became *Meet the Beatles*

Next in Canada came the third album *Long Tall Sally*, released as *The Beatles' Second Album* in the U.S. Obviously, Capitol wouldn't use "Second" when it was their third LP here. (As in the States, Capitol's LP count conveniently ignored Vee Jay's 1963 LP *Introducing the Beatles*.)

From *Beatles '65* forward, U.S. and Canadian albums are mostly identical.

There are no known Canadian releases of the material on the oddball labels (MGM, Atco, Tollie, Vee-Jay, etc.) except as further distributions of U.S. releases. (Already noted is the alternative take of *Love Me Do*.)

Canada's *The Ballad of John and Yoko* came out and received air play in an unexpurgated fashion, with "Christ" intact (not edited) as was common in the U.S.

All Beatles albums through *Rubber Soul* were originally released in mono only. Stereo collectors should seek out the early UK stereo albums. From the UK's *With The Beatles*, they contain limited true stereo, whereas the compact discs are still only in mono. In addition, UK albums appear better-produced. Those recordings offer a more authentic harshness in contrast with both the Canadian and American releases, which, overall, seem to have a sweetened sound. Perhaps this was done to make the releases more palatable to the North American audience.

The 1995 Anthology Series was released in Canada on vinyl (three volumes). So also was the BBC sessions album in 1994.

Beau-Marks: Montreal-based band with singles, *Moonlight Party* (1959), *Clap Your Hands* (1960), *Billy Billy Went A Walkin* (1960-'61) and *Classmate* (1961), on the Quality label. There is also the album, *The Beau-Marks* (Quality 1656).

Bell Notes: Their hits, including the 1959 smash *I've Had It*, came out on Reo.

Bellus, Tony: The single *Robbin' The Cradle* was released in July 1959 as a 78 rpm (only in Canada) on Sparton 739.

Boone, Pat: Reo issued his earliest singles, though later ones are on Dot, as in the U.S.

British Modbeats: Very obscure Canadian band whose album *Mod Is The British Modbeats* is very rare and collectible.

Brown, James: Singles were issued on Regency. King LPs first appear on Regency, then later on King (medium blue label). Regency releases are all originals, though one cannot tell which is which by merely examining the cover. You must look at the disc.

Beau Brummels: All Canadian originals are on Reo.

Cash, Johnny: Early Sun releases came out on Quality. By the late '50s, LPs were being issued in Canada on Sun.

Chanteclairs: Early U.S. R&B music on Dot is on Quality in Canada. *Someday My Love* is Quality 1319.

Chiefs: U.S. releases on Greenich Records released in Canada on Quality. *Apache* is Quality 1726.

Clark, Dave, Five: Canadian releases are on Capitol, whereas Epic handled their U.S. catalog. Albums do have some variations, most notably *Coast to Coast*, a U.S. LP, that appeared here – appropriately – as *Across Canada*. Otherwise the two albums are identical.

Cooke, Sam: Early Specialty releases appear in Canada on Delta. Keen releases were reproduced in Canada with a blue label and a black label.

Cortez, Dave "Baby": Reo issued *The Happy Organ* in Canada.

Crests: Canadian releases are on Quality.

Crowbar: Very collectible, seminal Canadian blues-rock '70s group. All their releases here are on Daffodil.

Danny and the Juniors: Early ABC-Paramount releases are on Sparton (e.g. *At The Hop,* Sparton 516). Their Swan release with Freddie Cannon (*Twistin' All Night Long)* is Quality 1369.

Davis, Spencer, Group: Several Canadian releases appear on Stone – a subsidiary of the shadow label Sparton (*I'm A Man* is Stone 705).

Day, Bobby: Canadian releases of the '50s are on Regency.

Doo, Dicky, and the Don'ts: U.S. Swan releases are on Quality.

Diddley, Bo: Original Checker releases appear on Reo in Canada (*Walkin' and Talkin'* is Reo 8491).

Dixie Cups: U.S. releases on Red Bird appear initially in Canada on Barry (*Chapel of Love* is Barry 3254).

Doggett, Bill: U.S. Regency releases appear on Regency in Canada (green label).

Domino, Fats: Most singles, and all of his albums, were released on Imperial here; however, a few of the early singles did come out on Reo – both 45s and 78s.

Some Reo releases are *So Long* (Reo 8108) and *My Blue Heaven* (Reo 8095). Earliest Canadian pressings are therefore clearly identifiable as on Reo. After those few early issues, all subsequent Fats Domino releases were on Imperial in Canada.

Dove, Ronnie: Diamond releases appear in Canada on Apex.

Downchild Blues Band: Quality blues band in the Chicago style whose releases are primarily on Attic Records.

Drifters: Early Canadian releases of Atlantic releases are on Quality.

Eddy, Duane: Most '50s releases appear on Reo. Post-1960 releases resemble U.S. issues.

Dynatones: One hit wonder (*Steel Guitar Rag,* Bomarc 300) released in Canada on Quality 1918.

Elegants: Canadian *Little Star* is Sparton 620, both 45 and 78.

Esquires: Canadian group had a few good Columbia singles in Canada, which are not scarce. Apparently none other than the 1966 single, *It's a Dirty Shame/Love Hides a Multitude of Sins* (Columbia 43815), came out in the U.S.

Everly Brothers: All Cadence releases came out in Canada on Apex. Warner Bros. records are no different than U.S. issues.

Five Man Electrical Band: An earlier assemblage of this group performed and released records as the Staccatos. As with the better known Five Man Electrical Band, the Staccatos' material was mostly written by Les Emmerson, the spiritual force behind both bands. Records by the Staccatos (on Capitol) are rare and very collectible.

Foundations: Canadian releases are on the blue Pye label.

Freddie and the Dreamers: Original Canadian Capitol album – identical to the UK release – was never released in the U.S. Most of the singles missing, especially *Just For You*, turned up later in the States on a "Greatest Hits" compilation.

Freeman, Bobby: All U.S. Josie singles appeared in Canada on Jubilee – his U.S. LP label and Josie's parent company. We do not yet know of any Canadian LPs by Freeman, but if any exist they are likely on Jubilee. Two of his 1958 hits, *Do You Want to Dance* and *Betty Lou Got a New Pair of Shoes*, came out in Canada on 78s. We have yet to verify U.S. 78s of either.

Birkin, Jane, and Serge Gainsbourg: Had one Canadian hit, *Je T'Aime ... Moi Non Plus,* in 1969.

Grammer, Billy: In Canada, Monument issued a 78 of *Gotta Travel On.* Don't know yet whether this 1959 hit came on 78 in the U.S.

Guess Who: The nucleus of this famous group first recorded as Chad Allen and the Expressions, though the Canadian group got very little air play. Later, in response to disc jockeys who had refused to play their records, the group's singles were sent to radio stations with the credit simply reading "Guess Who?" The lack of a traditional artist credit was meant to be taken literally since their previous identification as a lowly Canadian group resulted in them being virtually ignored by the Canadian media.

The band wanted to tease dee jays, hoping to make them curious enough to play the record – without identifying the band as Canadian. Ironically, the band eventually adopted this jocular name as its own.

Early Canadian singles are on Quality, and a collection of the earliest singles are found on *The Guess Who? Super Golden Oldies* (Birchmount BM 568), a must-have LP for this group's fans.

As in the States, RCA had the band's later hit singles and albums in Canada, followed by releases on Nimbus 9.

Hames Sisters: Obscure female group with *I Promise/Tell Me The Story of Love* on Chateau 102.

Harris, Wynonie: Canadian releases appear on several labels. *Good Rockin' Tonight* is on Maple Leaf 26-104.

Haunted: Montreal-based band whose Canadian releases are on Transworld with up to two album releases. These releases are very rare and quite expensive – especially recordings with *One Two Five.*

Hawkins, Ronnie: Ever-rockin' Ronnie hits after the "Hawks" became The Band (*Down In The Valley/Home From The Forest* on Hawk 302). Roulette albums and singles from the '50s are more common in Canada than in the U.S. and will likely sell for less.

Hayes, Bill: Novelty hit *The Ballad of Davy Crockett* (Cadence) is on Apex 76057.

Herman's Hermits: Early singles in Canada are on Capitol, but their albums turned up on Quality. U.S. releases are on MGM.

Hervey, Pat: Brenda Lee-type rock singer from the Maritimes with one hit on white label Chateau (*Mr. Heartache*).

Honeycombs: All Canadian releases are on orange Pye label.

Hunter, Ivory Joe: MGM releases are virtually identical to U.S. ones. Atlantic discs (e.g. *Since I Met You Baby*) are on Quality with Atlantic acknowledged.

Jackson, Mahalia: It appears Columbia releases were released in Canada with similar selection numbers and sleeves. One Canadian variant is Sparton C33-4906, a Canadian version of the U.S. *Colortone* album, released in both countries, probably in the early '70s.

John, Little Willie: Early Canadian releases are on Delta.

Johnny and the Hurricanes: Canadian releases are on Barry.

Joslin & Fry: Eastern Ontario male/female duo band with one vinyl album release on JM 83133. (Georgette) Fry has later CD releases of high quality.

Kensington Market: Along with the single *I Would Be the One* (Warner Bros. 7221), with its picture sleeve, this band had two albums on Warner Bros. Both are sought after: *Avenue Road* (1754) and *Aardvark* (1780). Releases before Warner Bros. – if any exist – would be extremely rare. Warner Bros. releases are relatively common, although higher grade ones are rare.

King Biscuit Boy: Blues by a very collectible Canadian band. Most of their releases are on Daffodil.

Kingsmen: Original Canadian release of *The Kingsmen in Person* is on Reo. Canadian reissues of that, as well as their later LPs, are on Wand, as in the U.S.

Kinks: Originals of earlier releases are on Pye (orange label).

Knight, Richie and the Mid-Knights: Canadian one-hit rock wonder (*Charlena* Arc 1028).

Knox, Buddy: Canadian *Party Doll* and *Hula Love* (76179) are on Apex.

Kramer, Billy J., and the Dakotas: All discs are on Capitol.

Larks: All Canadian releases are on Reo.

Left Banke: Original LP releases are on Mercury (flat black label with silver lettering) and later pressings are on Smash. Originals can only be distinguished by disc itself, not the sleeve, which indicates Smash.

Les Sultans: Francophone group on Teledisc 24.

Lewis, Jerry Lee: U.S. Sun releases came out on Quality.

Lightfoot, Gordon: Early experimental country releases are on Chateau. Lightfoot bought back and destroyed most copies. These little-known releases are very rare.

Little Caesar and the Consuls: Toronto-based '60s band had one significant hit *(My Girl) Sloopy* (Red Leaf 612) – vaguely similar to subsequent McCoys' version. Also released were *Little Heartbreaker* (Tamarac 202) and *If* (Columbia 629). All these singles are highly collectible.

Little Richard: First few Specialty U.S. singles came out in Canada on Regency, with acknowledgment to Specialty. Early albums have U.S. covers (no reference made to Canada) with the early green/silver Regency label. Later covers were printed in Canada (and identified as such) with the green/silver labels, then again with the ensuing (blue and black) label design. Subsequent U.S. releases on other labels were virtually identical in Canada.

Lords of London: Exemplary band known for live performances and one single, *Cornflakes and Ice Cream* (label and number not yet known).

Lowe, Jim: Earliest Canadian releases, including *Green Door* are on Reo. Later releases are on Dot with corresponding U.S. numbers.

Luke and the Apostles: Worthy late '60s band with two 1967 singles, *Been Burnt* and *You Make Me High* (labels and numbers not yet known).

Lymon, Frankie, and the Teenagers: U.S. Gee releases issued in Canada on Apex (*I Want You to Be My Girl,* Apex 76088).

Mandala: First fronted by George Oliver then later by Roy Kenner, Mandala had two hits, *Opportunity* and *Lovitis*. The album *The Soul Crusade of the Mandala* on Atlantic was also released in the U.S.

Mann, Manfred: First album, on Ascot in the U.S., is on Capitol in Canada. Canadian pressing, like the UK original, includes *Smokestack Lightning* as the lead track. On Ascot issue, the tracks are adjusted to feature *Do Wah Diddy Diddy.*

Marshmallow Soup Group: Obscure eastern Ontario bar band had at least one single on RCA #75-1014, *I Want Candy.*

Mason, Dutch: Canadian blues band leader whose releases appear in Canada on Attic.

McKenna Medelson Mainline: Bluesy rock group with one album on Liberty 583251, *Stink,* relatively common in Ontario. An earlier album, *McKenna Medelson Blues,* on Paragon 15 is extremely rare and very sought after.

Midnighters: Obscure rock and roll instrumental group. Singles released on Barry including *Slow Walk* (Barry 3028).

Monkees: LPs and singles came out here on RCA rather than Colgems.

Moody Blues: Early albums are on London.

Motherlode: Significant '60s Canadian recording group.

Mungo Jerry: Canadian releases are on Pye (blue label).

Music Machine: On Original Sound in the U.S., their label here was Reo.

Nucleus: Experimental psychedelic band with one Mainstream album, *Communication.*

Ocean: Their hit *Put Your Hand in the Hand* is on Yorkville. Later U.S. releases were on Kama Sutra.

Paupers: In 1967, this Canadian group released the *Magic People* LP on Verve, both in the U.S. and Canada. Before that was at least one Canadian-only Verve single, *If I Called You By Some Name.* The exclusively Canadian singles are very scarce.

Pagliaro, Michael: Good Quebec-based rocker (anglophone and francophone vocals) with releases on RCA.

Parsons, Bill: (Bobby Bare) The 1958 U.S. Fraternity hit, *All American Boy* came out on Reo (#8320) in Canada.

Presley, Elvis: Earliest RCA 45s have a blue label and 78s are flat black. Non-photographic dog (on side for 45s - see RCA label comments above). LP sleeves and discs match descriptions of U.S. originals in the Osborne guides.

As long noted in such books as *Rockin' Records* and *Presleyana,* certain Elvis releases are unique to Canada. For example, our 78 of *Blue Suede Shoes* is 20-6492 instead of 20-6636. Interestingly, we know of no U.S. release – by anyone – using the number 20-6492, or 47-6492. Chronologically, that number would have fallen about six months before 20-6636.

Price, Lloyd: Like most ABC-Paramount acts, his Canadian releases are on Sparton.

Quiet Jungle: Late '60s rock band known for *Ship of Dreams* on Yorktown (number and date not yet known).

Rebels/Rockin' Rebels: Canadian band whose hit *Wild Weekend,* on Swan in the U.S., was released here on Reo 8692. There may be an even earlier Canadian release pre-dating both.

Revere, Paul and the Raiders: Rare *In the Beginning* album (U.S. Jerden) issued here on Quality.

Riley, Jeannie C.: U.S. releases on Plantation appeared initially in Canada on Reo, with reissues later on Plantation. Only the Reos are originals.

Rolling Stones: London had all Stones UK singles in Canada: *Time Is on My Side, It's All Over Now* and *Route 66* (not a U.S. single), etc. Original 1963 singles labels are blue with silver lettering replaced with orange/white in 1964 (U.S. singles are on blue and white label).

Sarne, Mike: Minor British Invasion hit *Come Outside,* released only in Canada (Capitol 72043).

Scott, Jack: 78 rpms of *My True Love* (Carlton 462) seem to have been released only in Canada. U.S. and Canadian releases are otherwise fairly identical. Albums are probably less scarce in Canada.

Searchers: All original releases are on Pye (orange label).

Shafto, Bobby: English Invasion obscurity whose U.S. Rust releases appear on Capitol (e.g. *She's My Girl,* yellow swirl 72170).

Smith, Eugene: Blues-oriented vocalist with usually good backup, a.k.a. the "warm-up band" (*Rock By Day* Tembo 8524 released in 1985).

Smith, Grant, and the Power: Excellent band with singles circa 1966, *Keep On Running* and *Her Own Life*. See album release on Boo 6802 (manufactured by Rebel Records). This album and any known singles are very desirable.

Staccatos: Les Emmerson's band had an unknown (to us) number of singles on Capitol before reforming as the Five Man Electrical Band. There's *Half Past Midnight/Weatherman* on Capitol (swirl) 72453, *It's a Long Way Home, Let's Run Away* and probably others, all likely on Capitol.

Stitch N' Tyme: Maritimes (Eastern Canada) band who toured central Canada primarily as a bar band. *Got to Get You Into My Life* (Beatles song) was their big hit in 1967. On Yorkville, all are scarce and in-demand (release numbers not yet known).

Talkabouts: The 1959 single *Sweet Lovin' Baby* was released on 78 in Canada, as well as on 45 (Regency 792).

Thomas, David Clayton: The U.S. Decca album *erroneously* hyphenates his middle and surname: "Clayton-Thomas." Since then, many publications have repeated the blunder. His initial release *Walk That Walk/Hey Hey Hey,* by David Clayton Thomas and his Quartet, appears on Red Leaf 65001. The second 45 was *Take Me Back/Send Her Home,* by David Clayton Thomas and the Shays, on Roman 1101 (black label). Subsequent releases are on Roman (blue label): *Brainwashed/Barbie-Lee* (1105) and *Born With The Blues/Out of the Sunshine* (1102).

Another U.S. album is *Back on the Street Again* (Pickwick 3245) with one side by Thomas and the other by Linda Ronstadt and the Stone Poneys. It includes most of the Red Leaf and Roman A-sides.

Tom, Jim & Garth: Folk releases in the early '60s (*Something to Sing About,* Melborne 3222).

Townsmen: Fine Ottawa-based group with a few releases, the labels and numbers of which we do not yet know.

Ugly Ducklings: Good '60s blues/rock band who issued several discs in Canada. First on Yorktown 45001 (*Nothin'/I Can Tell*) then 45003 (*Just in Case You Wonder*). Another Yorktown issue is *Gaslight* (number not yet known). There's a variant release of *Just in Case You Wonder* with same number but a slightly different title: *Just in Case You're Wondering*. The altered title is obviously an error and may be the original since the song actually mentions "wonder" not "wondering." Their one known album, *Somewhere Outside* (Yorktown 50001) contains above hits, except *Gaslight*.

Veltri, Rudy (and the Tornadoes): Obscure Canadian artist with one Chateau single (105), *Waterfalls of Love/Lost Memories*.

Virtues: Sparton issued their *Guitar Boogie Shuffle* here

Wallis, Ruth: Early singles are on Maple Leaf with acknowledgment of Deluxe, and (subsequently) on the usual flat black Deluxe label.

Wilcox, David: Blues rocker with early releases on Freedom, and later on Capitol.

Williams, Larry: Specialty U.S. releases appear on Regency.

Wray, Link, and the Raymen: *Rumble/The Swag* (Cadence 1347) appears in Canada on Apex 76270. *Rawhide* is on Epic 9300 (same as U.S.). Later Swan releases are on Quality (*Jack the Ripper,* Quality 1536).

Wright, Priscilla: Canadian artist from London, Ontario. U.S. Unique discs are on Sparton in Canada (*The Man in the Raincoat,* Sparton 4-147).

Yemm and the Yemen: Late, obscure British Invasion group with one minor hit *Black is the Night,* released only in Canada (Capitol 72428).

Youngbloods: Their 1969 album, orange in the States, is on RCA's black label here.

Zombies: The early singles are on Parrot.

In Conclusion ...

This essay, put in service with a few selected artists, will be regularly revised and expanded in future editions of *Rockin' Records.*

Every attempt to ensure accuracy has been made, but the intent here – as with the *Rockin' Records* book itself – is merely to provide guidance. As a rule, Canadian releases of U.S. groups will have about the same value as the U.S. pressings of the same discs. But there are many exceptions.

While quantities originally produced of most Canadian and U.S. recordings is not generally known, we do know that some of the unique discs by Canadian acts mentioned here are hard-to-find items, with appropriately higher values.

Now that *Rockin' Records* has undertaken the task of listing and pricing many of the Canadian records, we welcome corrections, additions and price updates from readers.

©1997 Peter S. McCullough
Kingston, Ontario, Canada

SAMPLE LISTING

Artist's primary heading.

FLAMINGOS *R&B '56*
(With Red Holloway's Orchestra)

May also be shown on some releases as ...

Chart or charts and year this artist FIRST appeared on Billboard. For this group, they first hit the R&B chart in 1956.

Singles: 78 rpm

CHANCE (1133 " If I Can't Have You") 100-200 53
CHANCE (1145 "Golden Teardrops") 200-300 53
PARROT (808 "Dream of a Lifetime")................ 100-150 54
PARROT (812 "I'm Yours")................................ 150-200 55

Singles: 7–inch

CHANCE (1133 "If I Can't Have You") 500-750 53
(Black vinyl.)
CHANCE (1133 "If I Can't Have You") 1000-2000 53
(Colored vinyl.)
CHANCE (1145 "Golden Teardrops") 500-750 53
(Black vinyl.)
CHANCE (1145 "Golden Teardrops") 2000-3000 53
(Colored vinyl.)

Near-mint price range.

Helpful explanatory notes.

END (1035 "Please Wait for Me") 30-40 58
(Title later changed to *Lovers Never Say Goodbye*.)
END (1035 "Lovers Never Say Goodbye") 10-20 58
END (1046 "I Only Have Eyes for You"/ "At the Prom")... 10-20 59
END (1046 "I Only Have Eyes for You"/ "Goodnight Sweetheart") 15-25 59
(Note different flip.)
END (1046 "I Only Have Eyes for You")................ 40-50 59
(Stereo.)

Year or years of release.

Label names, selection numbers and titles.

PARROT (808 "Dream of a Lifetime")...............500-1000 54
(Black vinyl.)
PARROT (808 "Dream of a Lifetime")............2000-3000 54
(Colored vinyl.)
PARROT (811 "I Really Don't Want to Know") 1000-2000 55
(Black vinyl.)
PARROT (811 "I Really Don't Want to Know") 3000-5000 55
(Colored vinyl.)

EPs: 7–inch

END (205 "Goodnight Sweetheart") 40-60 59
(Monaural.)
END (205 "Goodnight Sweetheart") 50-85 59
(Stereo.)

Category or type of items listed in each section.

LPs: 10/12–inch

CHECKER (1433 "Flamingos")............................ 75-125 59
(Monaural.)
CHECKER (3005 "Flamingos")............................... 25-50 66
(Stereo.)
END (304 "Flamingo Serenade") 50-100 59
(Monaural.)
END (304 "Flamingo Serenade") 75-125 59
(Stereo.)
END (316 "The Sound of the Flamingos")............. 20-40 62
(Monaural.)
END (316 "The Sound of the Flamingos")............... 25-50 62
(Stereo.)

Members: Sollie McElroy; John Carter; Zeke Carey; Jake Carey; Paul Wilson; Nate Nelson; Tommy Hunt; Terry Johnson.

Also see HUNT, Tommy

References to other, related, sections in the guide.

Names of group members and/or recording session participants.

A

A, B ONE E & C
Singles: 7-inch
MTA 3-5 70

A. DEBBIE
Singles: 7-inch
J-RUDE (1401 "Here Is My Heart") 100-200 65
(Identification number shown since no selection number is used.)

A. JACKS: see JACKS, A., & Cleansers

A OK
Singles: 12-inch
WEST END 4-6 84

A's LP '81
Singles: 7-inch
ARISTA 3-5 79
LPs: 10/12-inch
ARISTA 5-10 79-81
Members: Richard Bush; Rick DiFonzo; Michael Snyder; Terry Bortman; Rocco Nolte.

A.A.B.B.
(Average American Black Band)
Singles: 7-inch
I-DENTIFY 3-5 75

A.B. SKHY P&R '69
Singles: 7-inch
MGM 3-5 69-70
Picture Sleeves
MGM 3-5 69-70
LPs: 10/12-inch
MGM 10-12 69-70
Members: Dennis Geyer; Howard Wales; Jim Liban; Jim Marcotte; Terry Anderson; Gary Karp; Curley Cooke; Rick Jaeger.

ABC P&R/LP '82
Singles: 12-inch
MERCURY 4-6 83-87
Singles: 7-inch
MERCURY 3-4 82-87
Picture Sleeves
MERCURY 3-4 82-87
LPs: 10/12-inch
MERCURY 5-10 82-87
Members: Martin Fry; Steve Singleton; Mark White.

A*B*E: see AMERICAN BLUES EXCHANGE

AC/DC LP '77
Singles: 12-inch
ATLANTIC 8-12 79
(Promotional only.)
Singles: 7-inch
ATCO (7068 "It's a Long Way to the Top") 5-10 77
ATCO (7086 "Problem Child") 5-10 77
ATLANTIC (3499 "Rock & Roll Damnation") 3-5 78
ATLANTIC (3553 "Whole Lotta Rosie") 3-5 79
ATLANTIC (3617 "Highway to Hell") . 3-5 79
ATLANTIC (3644 "Touch Too Much") 3-5 80
ATLANTIC (3761 "You Shook Me All Night Long") 3-5 80
ATLANTIC (3787 "Back in Black") 3-5 80
ATLANTIC (3894 "Let's Get It Up") 3-5 81
ATLANTIC (89614 "Jailbreak") 3-5 82
ATLANTIC (89774 "Guns for Hire") ... 3-5 83
Promotional Singles
ATCO (7068 "It's a Long Way to the Top") 15-25 77
ATCO (7086 "Problem Child") 15-25 77
ATLANTIC (3499 "Rock 'N' Roll Damnation") 10-20 78
ATLANTIC (3553 "Whole Lotta Rosie") 10-20 79
ATLANTIC (3617 "Highway to Hell") 10-20 79
ATLANTIC (3644 "Touch Too Much") 8-12 80
ATLANTIC (3761 "You Shook Me All Night Long") 8-12 80
ATLANTIC (3787 "Back in Black") .. 5-10 80
ATLANTIC (3894 "Let's Get It Up") .. 5-10 81
ATLANTIC (89614 "Jailbreak") 5-10 82
ATLANTIC (89774 "Guns for Hire") 5-10 83
Picture Sleeves
ATLANTIC (3894 "Let's Get It Up") ... 4-8 81
ATLANTIC (89774 "Guns for Hire") ... 4-8 83
LPs: 10/12-inch
ATCO (142 "High Voltage") 15-25 76
ATCO (151 "Let There Be Rock") ... 15-25 77
ATLANTIC (001 "Live from the Atlantic Studios") 20-30 77
(Promotional issue only.)
ATLANTIC (11111 "For Those About to Rock, We Salute You") 5-10 81
ATLANTIC (16018 "Back in Black") .. 5-10 80
ATLANTIC (16033 "Dirty Deeds Done Cheap") 5-10 81
ATLANTIC (19180 "Powerage") 5-10 78
ATLANTIC (19212 "If You Want Blood You've Got It") 5-10 78
ATLANTIC (19244 "Highway to Hell") 5-10 79
EAST/WEST 5-10 90s
Members: Bonn Scott; Angus Young; Mark Evans; Malcomb Young; Phil Rudd; Cliff Williams; Brian Johnson; Chris Slade; Simon Wright.
Also see DIO, Ronnie
Also see FIRM

A-C D-C CURRENTS
Singles: 7-inch
J-GEMS 10-15 63

A.C. DUCEY: see DUCEY, A.C.

ADC BAND R&B/LP '78
Singles: 7-inch
COTILLION 3-5 78-82
LPs: 10/12-inch
COTILLION 5-10 78-82
Members: Michael Judkins; Arwell Mathew Jr; Audrey Mathew; Mark Patterson.

AFO COMBO
Singles: 7-inch
AFO 4-8 61

AFO EXECUTIVES & TAMI LYNN
LPs: 10/12-inch
AFO (0002 "A Compendium") 50-100
Also see LYNN, Tami

AF-TABS
Singles: 7-inch
JET 10-20 65

A-440
Singles: 7-inch
SONA 10-15 67

AKB
Singles: 7-inch
RSO 3-5 79

AM-FM R&B '82
Singles: 7-inch
DAKAR 3-5 82
Also see MASON, Vaughn

A.M.O.S.
Singles: 7-inch
BROWN DAY 3-5 78

APB D&D '83
Singles: 12-inch
IMPORT 4-6 83
SLEEPING BAG 4-6 84
Singles: 7-inch
IMPORT 3-4 83
LPs: 10/12-inch
MCA 5-10 83

A.P.B. HAWAII
Singles
AZRA (18 "Dream Lover") 8-12 89
(Star-shaped picture disc. 500 made.)

ARS NOVA
Singles: 7-inch
ATLANTIC 4-6 69
ELEKTRA 4-8 68
LPs: 10/12-inch
ATLANTIC 10-15 69
ELEKTRA 10-15 68
Members: Mavry Baker; Sam Brown; Wyatt Day; Bill Fowell; Joe Hunt; Art Koenig; Jimmy Owens; Giovanni Papalia; John Pierson; Jonathan Raskin.

AWB: see AVERAGE WHITE BAND

AALON R&B '77
Singles: 7-inch
ARISTA 3-5 77
LPs: 10/12-inch
ARISTA 5-10 77
Members: Aalon Butler; Ronnie Hammond.
Also see WAR

AARDVARK
Singles: 7-inch
ZOOLOGICAL GARDENS (80606 "Wish I Could Tell You") 30-40 67

AARDVARK
Singles: 7-inch
BULLET 3-5 72
Members: Frank Clark; Dave Skillin; Stan Aldous; Daddy Coulter; Steve Milliner.

AARDVARKS
Singles: 7-inch
BELL (1059 "Josephine") 20-30 65
FORTE (2021 "Let's Move Together") 10-15 67
TALPA (68101 "Let's Move Together") 10-15 68

AARDVARKS
Singles: 7-inch
ARCH 15-25 60s
FENTON (2090 "I Don't Believe") .. 20-30 66
VARK (2058 "I'm Higher Than I'm Down") 30-50 66

AARON
LPs: 10/12-inch
JWL 10-12 79

AARON, Lee
LPs: 10/12-inch
VISUAL VINYL (1001 "Lee Aaron Project") 30-40 82
(Picture disc.)

AARON, BRADLEY & LORD
Singles: 7-inch
ATLANTIC 3-6 72

AARONS & ACKLEY
Singles: 7-inch
CAPITOL 3-5 71
LPs: 10/12-inch
CAPITOL 8-10 71

ABACO DREAM P&R/R&B '69
Singles: 7-inch
A&M 4-6 69-70
Members: Paul Douglas; Dave Williams; Dennis Williams; Frank Maid; Mike Sassano.

ABANDONED
Singles: 7-inch
ABANDONED 3-5

ABBA P&R/LP '74
Singles: 12-inch
ATLANTIC 4-8 77-79
Singles: 7-inch
ATLANTIC 3-6 75-82
Picture Sleeves
ATLANTIC 3-6 77-82
LPs: 10/12-inch
ATLANTIC (Except 300) 10-20 74-84
ATLANTIC (300 "Abba") 15-25 78
(Promotional issue only.)
CBS INT'L 8-12 80
EPIC 5-8 79
K-TEL 8-10 80
NAUTILUS (20 "Arrival") 15-25 82
(Half-speed mastered.)
SILVER EAGLE 8-10 84
Members: Anni-frid Lyngstad; Bjorn Ulvaeus; Benny Andersson; Agnetha Faltskog.
Also see BJORN & BENNY
Also see FALTSKOG, Agnetha
Also see FRIDA

ABBA / Spinners / Firefall / England Dan & John Ford Coley
EPs: 7-inch
W.B. SPECIAL PRODUCTS 5-10 78
(Coca-Cola/Burger King promotional issue. Issued with paper sleeve.)
Also see ABBA
Also see ENGLAND DAN & John Ford Coley
Also see FIREFALL
Also see SPINNERS

ABBE
Singles: 7-inch
BUTTERFLY 3-4 80
LPs: 10/12-inch
BUTTERFLY 5-10 80

ABBEY TAVERN SINGERS P&R '66
Singles: 7-inch
HBR 4-8 66
EPs: 7-inch
V.I.P. (60402 "Off to Dublin in the Green") 15-25 66
LPs: 10/12-inch
V.I.P. (402 "Off to Dublin in the Green") 30-60 66

ABBOT, Russ
Singles: 7-inch
EMI/AMERICA 3-4
Picture Sleeves
EMI/AMERICA 3-4

ABBOTT, Billy, & Jewels P&R '63
Singles: 7-inch
PARKWAY 10-15 63-64

ABBOTT, Jay
Singles: 7-inch
SULTAN (1001 "Latanya") 10-20 60
BOMBAY (1313 "Latanya") 10-20 60

ABBOTT, Jerry C&W '78
Singles: 7-inch
CHURCHILL 3-5 78
DALLAS STAR 3-4 82

ABBOTT, Gregory P&R/R&B/LP '86
Singles: 12-inch
COLUMBIA 4-6 86-88
Singles: 7-inch
COLUMBIA 3-4 86-88
Picture Sleeves
COLUMBIA 3-4 86-88
LPs: 10/12-inch
COLUMBIA 5-10 87

ABBOTT, Tony
Singles: 7-inch
WYE 8-15 60s

ABBOTT & COSTELLO
Singles: 78 rpm
ENTERPRISE (501 "Who's on First") 10-20
Members: Bud Abbott; Lou Costello.

ABBOTT SISTERS
Singles: 7-inch
FABOR 5-10 59

ABBY ROAD '78
LPs: 10/12-inch
SPRINGBOARD 5-10 78

ABDNOR, John
(Howard Abdnor)
Singles: 7-inch
ABNAK 3-5 70
LPs: 10/12-inch
ABNAK 10-12 68

ABDO-MEN
Singles: 7-inch
ARCOLA (407 "The Only Bad Thing About Her") 10-15

ABDUL, Paula P&R/R&B/LP '88
(With Wild Pair)
Singles: 7-inch
VIRGIN 3-4 88-91
Picture Sleeves
VIRGIN 3-4 88-89
LPs: 10/12-inch
VIRGIN 5-8 88-89

ABDULLAH
Singles: 7-inch
SOUL 3-5 68

ABEL & STARLINERS
Singles: 7-inch
CHICO (18 "Chicken Hop") 10-20 62

ABEL TWO
Singles: 7-inch
SIDEWALK 4-8 67

ABERNATHY, Lee Roy
Singles: 78 rpm
KING (4223 "Gospel Boogie") 10-15 48
Singles: 7-inch
KING (4223 "Gospel Boogie") 20-40 50s

ABERNATHY, Mack C&W '88
Singles: 7-inch
CMI 3-4 88-89

ABERNATHY, Marion
Singles: 78 rpm
FEDERAL 5-15 51
KING 5-15 47-49
Also see BLUES WOMAN
Also see PAGE, Hot Lips

ABNEY, Bob
Singles: 7-inch
PIK (12 "Ghost Riders in the Sky") .10-15 67

ABNOR, Jon
Singles: 7-inch
ATCO 5-10 65
Also see JON & ROBIN

ABOOTAYS
Singles: 7-inch
VIM (504 "Abootay") 10-15 60

ABOVE THE LAW LP '90
LPs: 10/12-inch
RUTHLESS 5-8 90

ABRAHAM
Singles: 7-inch
HY SIGN 3-5 74
WAND 3-5 70

ABRAHAM & CASANOVAS
Singles: 7-inch
MURCO (1044 "Soul Power") 8-12 60s

ABRAHAM'S CHILDREN
Singles: 7-inch
BUDDAH 3-5 73

ABRAHAMS, Mick, Band
LPs: 10/12-inch
A&M 5-10 71
Also see BLODWYN PIG
Also see JETHRO TULL

ABRAM, J.D.
(With the Handicappers Band)
Singles: 7-inch
REENA (1028 "Doctor of Love") 30-50 68

ABRAMS, Colonel R&B/D&D '84
Singles: 12-inch
MCA 4-6 85-87
STREETWISE 4-6 84
Singles: 7-inch
MCA 3-4 85-87
STREETWISE 3-4 84
Picture Sleeves
MCA 3-4 85-87
LPs: 10/12-inch
MCA 5-8 86

ABRAMS, Miss, & Strawberry Point School Third Grade Class P&R '70
Singles: 7-inch
A&M 3-5 71
REPRISE 3-5 70
Picture Sleeves
REPRISE 3-5 70
LPs: 10/12-inch
REPRISE 8-12 72

ABRAMS, Muhal Richard
LPs: 10/12-inch
BLACK SAINT 5-10 81

ABRAMS, Ray, Band
Singles: 7-inch
JAX (311 "Late Freight") 25-35 53
(Red vinyl.)

ABSHIRE, Nathan, & Pine Grove Boys
Singles: 7-inch
KHOURY'S 10-15 61

ABSOLUTE
Singles: 7-inch
EPIC 3-4 90

ABSOLUTE GREY
LPs: 10/12-inch
MIDNIGHT 5-10

ABSTRAC' P&R '89
Singles: 7-inch
REPRISE 3-4 89
Picture Sleeves
REPRISE 3-4 89
Members: Mary; Marsha; Topaz.

ABSTRACT REALITY
Singles: 7-inch
SPORT (104 "Love Burns") 100-150

ABSTRACT SOUND
Singles: 7-inch
GRAY SOUNDS (006 "Blacked Out Mind") 20-30

ABSTRACTS
Singles: 7-inch
NU CLEAR 5-10 59
CARICATURE 5-10
UP-DOWN 5-10 65
VANTAGE 5-10 63

ABSTRACTS
Singles: 7-inch
POMPEII (66679 "Smell of Incense") 10-15 68
LPs: 10/12-inch
POMPEII (6002 "The Abstracts") ... 20-30 68
Members: Henri Dondini; Tony Francesco Peluso; Michael Thatcher; Pierie Vigeant

ABSTRAK SOUND
Singles: 7-inch
CBM ("You're Gonna Break My Heart") 20-30 66
(No selection number used.)

ACADEMICS
(With the Kingsmen Quintet)
Singles: 7-inch
ANCHO (100 "At My Front Door") 60-80 57
ANCHO (101 "Too Good to Be True") 75-100 57
ANCHOR (101 "Too Good to Be True") 800-1200 57
(First issue.)
ELMONT (1001 "Drive-in Movie") .. 35-45 58
Members: Dave Fisher; Ron Marone; Marty Ganter; Bill Greenberg; Goose Greenberg.
Also see KINGSMEN
Also see PASSENGERS

ACADEMICS / Premiers
LPs: 10/12-inch
PREMAX ("Academics Meet the Premiers") 40-60
Also see ACADEMICS

ACCENT
Singles: 7-inch
PARROT (40022 "Winds of Change") 10-20 67

ACCENTS
(With Jackie Allen)
Singles: 78 rpm
ACCENTS 10-15 56
BLUE MILL 10-15 55
Singles: 7-inch
ACCENTS (1025 "Cool-a-Roo") 15-25 55
ACCENTS (1037 "Name Song") 15-25 56
BLUE MILL (111 "Baby Blue") 15-25 55

ACCENTS P&R '58
(Featuring Robert Draper Jr.)
Singles: 7-inch
BRUNSWICK (55100 "Wiggle Wiggle") 10-20 58
BRUNSWICK (55123 "Ching a Ling") 10-20 59
CORAL (62151 "Autumn Leaves") 10-20 59
JUBILEE (5353 "Red Light") 10-15 59
Members: Robert Draper Jr.; Robert Armstrong; James Jackson; Billy Hood; Arvid Garrett; Israel Goudeau Jr.
Also see THREE SHARPS & FLAT

ACCENTS
Singles: 7-inch
JOKER (200 "Bring Your Love Back") 35-45 62
SULTAN (5500 "Rags to Riches") 50-100 61
Also see ENGLISH, Scott

ACCENTS
Singles: 7-inch
JIVE!! (888 "Our Wonderful Love") 35-50 62
(Pictures well-dressed cat with signboard.)
JIVE!! (888 "Our Wonderful Love") 15-25 62
(Cat not shown on label.)
MATT (0001 "Little Boy Blue") 10-20 62
VEE JAY (484 "Our Wonderful Love") 10-20 62

ACCENTS
Singles: 7-inch
MERCURY 5-8 63

ACCENTS
Singles: 7-inch
M-PAC (7216 "New Girl") 20-30 64
ONE-DERFUL (4833 "You Better Think Again") 10-20 65
Member: Clifford Curry.
Also see CURRY, Clifford

ACCENTS
("Featuring Sandi")
Singles: 7-inch
CHALLENGE 5-10 64
CHARTER 5-10 64
COMMERCE 5-10 64
KARATE 5-10 66
Also see SANDY

ACCENTS
("Featuring Ron Petersen")
Singles: 7-inch
JERDEN 5-10 64
Members: Ron Petersen; Laurie Vitt; Vic Bundy; Pat Jerns; George Palmerton.
Also see BELLINGHAM ACCENTS
Also see FRANTICS

ACCENTS
Singles: 7-inch
BANGAR ("Howlin' for My Baby")....15-25 64
(Selection number not known.)
BANGAR (629 "You Don't Love Me") 15-25 64
BANGAR (648 "Why") 15-25 64
BEAR (1977 "No One Heard You Cry") 25-35 66
GARRETT 15-25 64
TWIN TOWN 15-25 65

ACCENTS
Singles: 7-inch
LIBERTY 5-10 65

ACCENTS
Singles: 7-inch
RCA 3-6 69
LPs: 10/12-inch
RCA 5-10 70

ACCENTS
Singles: 7-inch
BANGAR (0648 "Why") 10-15
GAZARRI (90931 "People Are Funny") 25-35

ACCENTS
Singles: 7-inch
GAZARRI (90931 "People Are Funny") 25-35

ACCENTS (With David Gates): see GATES, David

ACCEPT LP '84
Singles: 7-inch
PORTRAIT 3-4 84-89
Picture Sleeves
PORTRAIT 3-4 84-86
LPs: 10/12-inch
PVC 5-10 83
PASSPORT 5-10 81
PORTRAIT 5-10 84-89

ACCIDENTALS
Singles: 7-inch
BEAU MONDE 5-10 62
FRANKLIN 5-10 62

ACCIDENTALS
Singles: 7-inch
HARBOR (7953 "Loser's Advice") 10-15 67

ACCOLADE
Singles: 7-inch
CAPITOL 3-5 70
LPs: 10/12-inch
CAPITOL 5-10 70

ACCUSED
EPs: 7-inch
MARTHA SPLATTERHEAD 8-12 82
LPs: 10/12-inch
COMBAT 5-10 87
Members: Blaine Cook; Tom Niemeyer; Dana Collins; Alex Sibbald.

ACE P&R/LP '75
Singles: 7-inch
ABC 3-5 76-78
ANCHOR 3-5 75-77
LPs: 10/12-inch
ANCHOR 8-12 74-77
Members: Paul Carrack; Fran Byrne; Tex Comer; Phil Harris; Alan "Bam" King; Jon Woodhead.
Also see CARRACK, Paul
Also see MIGHTY BABY

ACE, Buddy R&B '66
Singles: 78 rpm
DUKE 10-15 56-57
PEACOCK 10-15 55
Singles: 7-inch
DUKE (100 series) 15-25 56-58
DUKE (300 & 400 series) 5-10 60-69
FIDELITY (3011 "Something New") 10-20 59
PAULA 3-5 70-72
PEACOCK (1659 "I Told You So") .20-30 55
SPECIALTY (699 "Oh Why") 10-20 59

ACE, Johnny R&B '52
(With the Beale Streeters; with Johnny Otis Orchestra; with Johnny Board Orchestra)
Singles: 78 rpm
DUKE 15-25 52-55
QUALITY 15-25 54
(Canadian.)
Singles: 7-inch
ABC 3-5 73
DUKE (102 "My Song") 30-40 52
DUKE (107 "Cross My Heart") 20-40 53
DUKE (112 "The Clock") 20-40 53
DUKE (118 "Saving My Love for You") 20-40 53
DUKE (128 "Please Forgive Me") ..20-40 54
DUKE (132 "Never Let Me Go") 20-40 54
DUKE (136 "Pledging My Love"/"No More") 20-40 55
DUKE (136 "Pledging My Love"/"Anymore") 15-25 60
(Different flip. Also has added voices and orchestration.)
DUKE (144 "Anymore") 20-40 55
DUKE (148 "So Lonely") 20-40 55
DUKE (154 "Don't You Know") 20-40 55
DUKE (155 "Back Home") 20-40 55
MCA 3-5 84
QUALITY (1353 "Pledging My Love") 25-50 54
(Canadian.)
EPs: 7-inch
DUKE (71 "Johnny Ace") 15-25 63
(Six-track juke box issue. Includes title strips.)
DUKE (80 "Memorial Album") 150-200 55
DUKE (81 "Tribute Album") 150-200 55
LPs: 10/12-inch
DUKE (70 "Memorial Album") 550-650 55
(10-inch LP.)
DUKE (71 "Memorial Album") 150-250 57
(No playing card shown on cover.)
DUKE (71 "Memorial Album") 60-80 61
(Playing card shown on cover.)
DUKE (X-71 "Memorial Album") 8-10 74
MCA 4-6 83
Also see BLAND, Bobby
Also see OTIS, Johnny

ACE, Johnny / Earl Forrest
Singles: 78 rpm
FLAIR 25-40 53
Singles: 7-inch
FLAIR (1015 "Midnight Hours Journey") 50-100 53
Also see ACE, Johnny
Also see FORREST, Earl

ACE, Sonny
(With the Del Sharps; with Twisters)
Singles: 7-inch
ATLANTIC 5-10 60s
COBRA (1113 "Anymore") 15-25 65
RIVAL (01 "Tamales") 5-10
TNT (153 "If My Teardrops Could Talk") 200-400 58

ACE SPECTRUM P&R '74
Singles: 7-inch
ATLANTIC 3-5 74-76
LPs: 10/12-inch
ATLANTIC 8-10 74-76
Members: Henry Zant; Troy Johnson; Rudy Gay; Elliot Isaac.

ACES
Singles: 7-inch
STELLAR 4-8 64

ACES
Singles: 7-inch
SIRE 3-5 73

ACES, STRAIGHTS & SHUFFLES
Singles: 7-inch
ADA 4-8 75

ACEY, Johnny
Singles: 7-inch
D.J.L. (616 "My Home") 10-20
FALEW (101 "Stay Away Love") 10-20 63
FIRE (1015 "Please Don't Go") 15-25 60
FLING (728 "I Go Into Orbit") 15-25 62

ACHES & PAINS
Singles: 7-inch
PRESS 4-8 66

ACHILLES & FRANK
Singles: 7-inch
NORMAN 4-8 66

ACID CASUALITIES
LPs: 10/12-inch
RHINO 5-10 82

ACKLES, David LP '72
Singles: 7-inch
ELEKTRA 3-6 68-72
LPs: 10/12-inch
COLUMBIA 5-10 73
ELEKTRA 8-12 69-72

ACKLIN, Barbara P&R/R&B/LP '68
Singles: 7-inch
BRUNSWICK 5-10 67-73
CAPITOL 3-5 74-75
ERIC 3-4 83
SPECIAL AGENT (203 "I'm Not Mad Anymore") 25-50
Picture Sleeves
BRUNSWICK 5-10 68
LPs: 10/12-inch
BRUNSWICK 10-20 68-71
CAPITOL 5-10 75
Session: Chi-Lites.
Also see ALLEN, Barbara
Also see CHANDLER, Gene, and Barbara Acklin
Also see CHI-LITES

ACKLIN BROTHERS
Singles: 7-inch
DEVOICE (708 "I Want My Baby")...5-10

ACKROFF, Bob
Singles: 7-inch
ROULETTE 5-8 61

ACOMA
Singles: 7-inch
CERTRON 3-5 71

ACORN, Bobby, & Leaves
(Bobby Mizzell)
Singles: 7-inch
DIAMOND JIM 10-15 62
Also see MIZZELL, Bobby

ACORN SISTERS
Singles: 7-inch
ACORN (593 "Real Gone") 30-40 50s
BOONE (1048 "Wait Until Tomorrow") 10-20 66

ACORNS
Singles: 7-inch
UNART 10-15 58-59

ACOSTA, Bill
Singles: 7-inch
PLATINUM 3-5 71

ACOSTA, Leo
Singles: 7-inch
CAPITOL 3-5 68

ACOUSTICS
Singles: 7-inch
CANALTOWN (254 "My Rights") ... 20-30 66
CHERRY BLOSSOM 4-8

ACQUINETTS
Singles: 7-inch
LILLY (508 "Apple of My Heart") 10-20

ACRE, Seph, & Pets
Singles: 7-inch
ARWIN 5-10 58
Also see PETS

ACROBAT
Singles: 7-inch
TMI 3-5 72-73
LPs: 10/12-inch
TMI 5-10 73
Members: Bob Lehnert; Billy Jones; Mel Senter; Greg Davis; Richie Simpson; Barry Johnson.

ACT
LPs: 10/12-inch
HANNIBAL 5-10 81

ACT I R&B '73
Singles: 7-inch
SPRING 3-5 73-74
LPs: 10/12-inch
SPRING 5-10 74

ACT IV
Singles: 7-inch
CUB (9150 "A Better Man Than I") .10-20 65

ACT OF CREATION
Singles: 7-inch
CAPITOL 4-8 67

ACTION
Singles: 7-inch
STUDIO CITY 8-12 66

ACTION
Singles: 7-inch
CAPITOL 4-8 67

ACTION, Johnny
Singles: 7-inch
ACTION 4-8 67

ACTION UNLIMITED
Singles: 7-inch
PARKWAY 4-8 66

ACTIONEERS
Singles: 7-inch
SHANE (57 "No One Wants Me") .. 15-25 65

ACTIONS
Singles: 7-inch
JEREE (117 "Germ City") 5-10 65

ACTIVE FORCE
Singles: 12-inch
A&M 4-6 83
LPs: 10/12-inch
A&M 5-10 83

ACTOR
Singles: 7-inch
EDIBLE 4-6

ACTORS
Singles: 7-inch
LAURIE 4-8 62

ACTRESS
Singles: 7-inch
PARAMOUNT 3-5 71

ACTUALS: see VOCAL AIRES / Actuals

ACUFF, Roy P&R '38/C&W '44
(With the Smoky Mountain Boys; with Crazy Tennesseeans)
Singles: 78 rpm
BANNER 10-20
CAPITOL 4-8 53-55
COLUMBIA 5-10 45-49
CONQUEROR 10-20
DECCA 4-8 55
MGM 5-10 51
MELOTONE 10-20
OKEH 5-10 40-45
ORIOLE 10-20
PERFECT 10-20
ROMEO 10-20
VOCALION 8-12 38-40
Singles: 7-inch
CAPITOL (2385 thru 3209) 5-10 53-55
COLUMBIA (20000 series) 10-20 52
DECCA 5-10 55
ELEKTRA 3-5 78
HICKORY (314 thru 362) 3-6 73-75
HICKORY (1073 thru 1664) 4-8 58-72
MGM 10-20 51
EPs: 7-inch
CAPITOL (617 "Songs of the Smokey Mountains") 10-15 55
(Price is for any of three volumes.)
COLUMBIA (Except 2895) 10-20 51-57
COLUMBIA (2895 "Roy Acuff EP") 30-50 50s
LPs: 10/12-inch
CAPITOL (617 "Songs of the Smokey Mountains") 20-40 55
CAPITOL (2276 "The Voice of Country Music") 10-20 65
CAPITOL (T-1870 "Country Music Hall of Fame's Roy Acuff") 10-20 63
(Monaural.)
CAPITOL (SM-1870 "Country Music Hall of Fame's Roy Acuff") 5-10 79
(Reprocessed stereo.)
COLUMBIA (9004 "Songs of the Smokey Mountains") 30-50 50
(10-inch LP.)
COLUMBIA (9010 "Old Time Barn Dance") 30-50 50
(10-inch LP.)
COLUMBIA (CS-1034 "Roy Acuff's Greatest Hits") 8-12 70
COLUMBIA (PC-1034 "Roy Acuff's Greatest Hits") 8-12 70
COLUMBIA (39998 "Roy Acuff") 5-8 85
ELEKTRA 5-10 78-82
CAPITOL (2103 "The Great Roy Acuff") 20-30 64
GOLDEN COUNTRY 5-10
HARMONY 8-20 58-70
HICKORY (101 thru 119) 20-35 61-65
HICKORY (125 thru 162) 15-30 65-70
HICKORY/MGM 8-12 74-75
METRO 10-20 65
MGM (3707 "Favorite Hymns") 30-40 58
MGM (4044 "Hymn Time") 15-25 62
PICKWICK 5-10 70s
PICKWICK/HILLTOP 8-15 65-69
ROUNDER 5-8 85
SEARS (123 "Take My Hand, Precious Lord") 15-20
TIME-LIFE 5-10 80s
Session: Jordanaires.
Also see JORDANAIRES
Also see LOUVIN, Charlie, & Roy Acuff
Also see WILLIAMS, Hank / Roy Acuff
Also see NITTY GRITTY DIRT BAND & ROY ACUFF

ACUFF, Roy, & Kitty Wells
Singles: 78 rpm
DECCA 4-6 56
Singles: 7-inch
DECCA 5-10 56
Also see ACUFF, Roy
Also see WELLS, Kitty

AD
LPs: 10/12-inch
CBS ASSOCIATED 5-10 84-85
Members: Kerry Livgren; Dave Hope; Michael Gleason; Warren Ham; Dennis Holt.
Also see LIVGREN, Kerry

AD LIBS P&R/R&B '65
Singles: 7-inch
A.G.P. (100 "New York in the Dark") 100-150 66
BLUE CAT 5-10 65
CAPITOL 3-6 70
ESKEE ("New York in the Dark") 200-300 66
(Selection number not known.)
KAREN (1527 "Think of Me") 15-20 66
PHILIPS 4-8 67
SHARE 3-6 69
Members: Mary Ann Thomas; Danny Austin; Hugh Harris; J.T. Taylor; Norm Donegan; Dave Watts.
Also see CREATORS

AD LIBS
Singles: 7-inch
VE ("Think of Me") 20-30 60s
(Selection number not known.)

AD LIBS / Atlantics / Hudsons / Variations
LPs: 10/12-inch
ACAPPELLA (1001 "New York City to L.A. Acappella All the Way") 100-200
(Dark blue label.)

ADAIR, Robin
Singles: 7-inch
POWERTREE (150 "Alone Alone") 10-15 64

ADAM & ANTS P&R '82
Singles: 12-inch
EPIC 4-8 81
Singles: 7-inch
EPIC 3-5 81
LPs: 10/12-inch
EDITIONS EG 5-10 82
EPIC 8-10 81-82
Members: Adam Ant; Johnny Bivouac; Andy Watson; Dave Barb.
Also see ANT, Adam
Also see BOW WOW WOW

ADAM APPLE
Singles: 7-inch
CAPITOL 4-8 62
Member: Teacho Wiltshire.

ADAM, MIKE & TIM
Singles: 7-inch
LONDON 4-8 65
PRESS 4-8 64

ADAM'S APPLES
Singles: 7-inch
BRUNSWICK (55330 "Don't Take It Out on This World") 50-100 67
BRUNSWICK (55367 "You're the One I Love") 25-45 68

ADAMS, Al
Singles: 7-inch
FRISCO (102 "Two Seconds of Love") 10-15 62

ADAMS, Alberta
Singles: 78 rpm
CHESS 5-10 54
Singles: 7-inch
CHESS 15-25 54
THELMA (2282 "I Got a Feeling") .. 20-40 62

ADAMS, Alicia
Singles: 7-inch
CAPITOL (4545 "Love Bandit") 10-20 60

ADAMS, Andy
Singles: 7-inch
DJM 3-5 80
PYRAMID 4-6 77

ADAMS, Armond
Singles: 7-inch
FORTUNE (572 "The Storm") 10-20 64

ADAMS, Art, & Rhythm Knights
Singles: 7-inch
CHERRY (1005 "Rock Crazy Baby") 75-100 60
CHERRY (1019 "Dancin' Doll") 75-100 60

ADAMS, Arthur
Singles: 7-inch
BLUE THUMB 3-5 73
FANTASY 3-5 76
LPs: 10/12-inch
A&M 5-10 79
BLUE THUMB 8-12 73
FANTASY 8-10 75-77
Also see UPCHURCH, Phil

ADAMS, Arthur K.
(Arthur Adams)
Singles: 7-inch
CHISA (8006 "Let's Make Some Love") 5-10 69
(Black vinyl.)
CHISA (8006 "Let's Make Some Love") 10-20 69
(Colored vinyl. Promotional issue only.)
CHISA (8011 "Can't Wait to See You") 8-12 69
JAMIE (1180 "Willin' to Die") 10-15 61
JETSTAR 5-10 64
MODERN (1034 "Drives Me Out of My Mind") 5-10 67
MODERN (1050 "I'm Lonely for You") 5-10 68

ADAMS, Betty
Singles: 7-inch
NOTES of GOLD 4-6

ADAMS, Billy
(With the Rock-A-Teers; with Georgia & Teens; with Paramounts)
Singles: 7-inch
AMY (893 "You and Me") 8-12 63
APT (25072 "My Happiness") 8-12 63
ARC 5-8 68
CAPITOL (4308 "Count Every Star") 20-30 59
CAPITOL (4373 "Can't Get Enough") 15-25 60
DECCA (30724 "Baby I'm Bugged") 30-50 58
DOT (15689 "You Heard Me Knocking") 10-20 58
FERN (807 "Darling, Take My Hand") 15-25 61
FERN (808 "Tattle Tale") 15-25 61
FERN (812 "Rip Van Winkle") 15-25 61
FERN (813 "Call Me") 10-20 61
HOME OF THE BLUES (239 "Looking for My Baby") 8-12 63
HOME OF THE BLUES (242 "My Happiness") 8-12 63
KO KO 8-12 62
NAU-VOO (802 "You Gotta Have a Duck Tail") 100-200 58
NAU-VOO (805 "Return of the All American Boy") 50-75 59
NAU-VOO (808 "Blue Eyed Ella") .. 25-50 60
QUINCY (932 "Rock Pretty Mama") 1000-1500 59
SUN (389 "Betty & Dupree") 8-10 64
SUN (391 "Trouble in Mind") 8-10 64
SUN (394 "Reconsider Baby") 8-10 64
WAND (133 "Billy Boy") 8-12 63

ADAMS, Billy
Singles: 7-inch
HIT MAN 3-4 83

ADAMS, Bobby R&B '70
Singles: 7-inch
BATTLE (45914 "Better Days Ahead") 5-10 63
BIG B. (778 "The Kind of Man") . 100-200
COLPIX (195 "Here Is One") 10-20 61
COLPIX (604 "I Think You Want My Girl") 20-30 61
HOMETOWN 4-6 70
PET (803 "I Want My Lovin' ") 15-25 58
PURDY (102 "Don't You Feel It") ... 10-20 64
SYMBOL (905 "Don't Leave") 10-20 59
SYMBOL (908 "Little Miss America") 10-20 60

ADAMS, Bobby, & Norma Jean Carpenter
Singles: 7-inch
KINGSTAR 3-5 71

Also see ADAMS, Bobby

ADAMS, Bruce
Singles: 7-inch
BELL 4-8 60s
Also see FRANK, Barry

ADAMS, Bruce / Barry Frank
Singles: 7-inch
BELL (25 "Too Much") 4-8 60s
Also see ADAMS, Bruce
Also see FRANK, Barry

ADAMS, Bryan P&R/LP '82
(B.G. Adams)
Singles: 12-inch
A&M (Black vinyl) 4-6 82-87
A&M (Colored vinyl) 5-10 84
Singles: 7-inch
A&M (Except 474) 3-6 80-87
A&M (474 "Let Me Take You Dancing") 4-6 79
(Black vinyl.)
A&M (474 "Let Me Take You Dancing") 8-12 79
(Colored vinyl.)
Picture Sleeves
A&M (Except 474) 3-5 80-87
A&M (474 "Let Me Take You Dancing") 10-15 79
LPs: 10/12-inch
A&M 5-10 80-87
Also see DION
Also see SWEENY TODD

ADAMS, Bryan, Sting, & Rod Stewart
Singles: 7-inch
A&M 3-4 93
Picture Sleeves
A&M 3-4 93
Also see STEWART, Rod
Also see STING

ADAMS, Bryan, & Tina Turner
Singles: 7-inch
A&M 3-4 85
Picture Sleeves
A&M 3-4 85
Also see ADAMS, Bryan
Also see TURNER, Tina

ADAMS, Candy
Singles: 7-inch
EPIC 4-8 66

ADAMS, Charlie
Singles: 7-inch
COLUMBIA 10-15 57

ADAMS, Christine
Singles: 7-inch
CYCLONE 3-5 69

ADAMS, Cliff
Singles: 7-inch
DOT 4-8 62

ADAMS, Dr. Jo Jo: see ADAMS, Jo Jo

ADAMS, Don C&W '67
(With Greenfield Express)
Singles: 7-inch
ATLANTIC 3-5 73-74
JACK O'DIAMONDS 3-6 67
MUSICOR 4-8 65
Also see YOUNG, Faron

ADAMS, Edie
LPs: 10/12-inch
MGM 10-20 59

ADAMS, Faith
Singles: 7-inch
SAVOY 5-8 61

ADAMS, Faye R&B '53
(With Jimmy Mundy & Orchestra: with Joe Morris Orchestra)
Singles: 78 rpm
ATLANTIC 10-20 53
HERALD 10-20 53-57
IMPERIAL 10-20 57
Singles: 7-inch
ABC 3-4 73
ATLANTIC (1007 "Sweet Talk") 40-60 53
COLLECTABLES 3-4 82
HERALD (416 "Shake a Hand") 20-30 53
HERALD (419 "I'll Be True") 20-30 53
HERALD (429 "Crazy Mixed-Up World") 30-40 54
HERALD (434 "Hurts Me to My Heart") 25-35 54
HERALD (439 "I Owe My Heart") 15-25 54
HERALD (444 "Your Love") 15-25 55
HERALD (450 "You Ain't Been True") 15-25 55
HERALD (457 "Angels Tell Me") 15-25 55
HERALD (462 "No Way Out") 15-25 55
HERALD (470 "Teenage Heart") 15-25 56
HERALD (480 "Takin' You Back") 15-25 56
HERALD (489 "Anytime, Anyplace, Anywhere") 15-25 56
HERALD (512 "Shake a Hand") 10-20 57
IMPERIAL (5443 "Keeper of My Heart") 15-25 57
IMPERIAL (5456 "You're Crazy") 15-25 57
IMPERIAL (5471 "I Have a Twinkle in My Eye") 15-25 57
IMPERIAL (5525 "When We Kiss") 15-25 58
LIDO (603 "It Made Me Cry") 10-15 59
LIDO (606 "I Can't Be Wrong") 10-15 60
WARWICK (550 "Look Around") 10-15 60
WARWICK (590 "Shake a Hand") 10-15 60
WARWICK (620 "Johnny, Don't Believe Her") 10-15 61
LPs: 10/12-inch
COLLECTABLES 6-8 88
SAVOY (14398 "Faye Adams") 8-10 76
WARWICK (2031 "Shake a Hand") 100-200 61
Also see MORRIS, Joe, & His Orchestra

ADAMS, Faye / Little Esther / Maxine Brown
LPs: 10/12-inch
MUSICTONE (7001 "Great Female R&B Package") 20-30 65
Also see BROWN, Maxine

ADAMS, Faye / Little Esther / Shirley & Lee
LPs: 10/12-inch
ALMOR (103 "Golden Souvenirs") 10-20
Also see LITTLE ESTHER
Also see MORRIS, Joe, & His Orchestra
Also see SHIRLEY & LEE

ADAMS, Faye / Jimmy McGriff
Singles: 7-inch
COLLECTABLES 3-5 82
Also see McGRIFF, Jimmy

ADAMS, Faye / Jay McShann
Singles: 7-inch
OLDIES 45 (109 "Shake a Hand") 4-8 60s
Also see ADAMS, Faye
Also see McSHANN, Jay

ADAMS, Gayle R&B '80
Singles: 7-inch
PRELUDE 3-4 80-81
LPs: 10/12-inch
PRELUDE 5-10 82

ADAMS, Greg
Singles: 7-inch
RCA 3-5 79

ADAMS, Jay Boy
Singles: 7-inch
ATLANTIC 3-5 78
LPs: 10/12-inch
ATLANTIC 8-10 77-78

ADAMS, Jeri
Singles: 7-inch
COLUMBIA 10-15 58-59
FRATERNITY 5-10 61
EPs: 7-inch
COLUMBIA 8-12 58

ADAMS, Jerry
Singles: 7-inch
KRASH (5002 "It Doesn't Matter Anymore") 6-12
WHEEL (1003 "Old Black Joe") 100-200 59

ADAMS, Jim
Singles: 7-inch
DANGER 4-8 60s

ADAMS, Jo Jo
(Dr. Jo Jo Adams)
Singles: 78 rpm
ALLADIN 10-15 46
ARISTOCRAT 10-15 47
CHANCE (1127 "Didn't I Tell You") 25-50 52
HY-TONE 10-15 47
MELODY LANE 10-15 46
PARROT (788 "Call My Baby") 20-40 53
Singles: 7-inch
CHANCE (1127 "Didn't I Tell You") 100-150 52
PARROT (788 "Call My Baby") 75-125 53
(Black vinyl.)
PARROT (788 "Call My Baby") 200-300 53
(Colored vinyl.)

ADAMS, Joe
Singles: 7-inch
PENTAGON 5-10

ADAMS, John
LPs: 10/12-inch
ECM 5-10 85

ADAMS, Johnny R&B '62
Singles: 7-inch
ARIOLA AMERICAN 3-5 78
ATLANTIC 3-5 71-72
GAMMA (101 "Best of Luck to You") 3-6 70s
GONE (5147 "Going to the City") 25-50 64
HEP ME 4-8 74-76
J.B. 3-5 76
MODERN (1044 "One Day") 5-10 67
PACEMAKER (249 "When I'll Stop Loving You") 10-15 65
PACEMAKER (255 "Let Them Talk") 10-15 65
PAID 3-4 84
RIC 10-20 59-62
RON 6-12 64-65
SSS INT'L 4-8 68-74
(Black vinyl.)
SSS INT'L (809 "I Won't Cry") 8-12 69
(Colored vinyl.)
TOWNHOUSE 3-5
WATCH (6333 "Part of Me") 20-30 63
LPs: 10/12-inch
ARIOLA AMERICAN 5-10 78
CHELSEA 10-20 77
HEP ME 8-10 74-76
ROUNDER 5-8 80s
SSS INT'L 10-15 70

ADAMS, Johnny, & Gondoliers
Singles: 7-inch
RIC (957 "Knocked Out") 10-20 59
Also see ADAMS, Johnny

ADAMS, Johnny
Singles: 7-inch
MODERN 5-8 67

ADAMS, June
Singles: 7-inch
ROULETTE 4-8 66

ADAMS, Kay C&W '66
(With the Cliffie Stone Group)
Singles: 7-inch
TOWER 4-8 65-68
Picture Sleeves
TOWER (445 "Gonna Have a Good Time") 5-10 68
LPs: 10/12-inch
FRONTLINE 5-10
TOWER 10-15 66-68
Also see STONE, Cliffie

ADAMS, Kaylee C&W '86
Singles: 7-inch
W.B. 3-4 86

ADAMS, Kerry
Singles: 7-inch
CALLA 10-15 65
CHANCELLOR 10-15 60

ADAMS, Lindy
Singles: 7-inch
TRI DISC (108 "A Bird in the Hand") 10-15 62

ADAMS, Link
Singles: 7-inch
A-OKAY (111 "Angel Or Not") 40-50 61

ADAMS, Little Johnnie
Singles: 7-inch
MELATONE (1029 "No In-Between") 10-20

ADAMS, Marie R&B '52
(With Bill Harvey's Band; with Three Tons of Joy)
Singles: 78 rpm
PEACOCK 10-15 51-54
Singles: 7-inch
CAPITOL (4108 "A Fool in Love") 15-25 58
PEACOCK 20-40 51-54
VANTAGE 3-5 73
Also see OTIS, Johnny

ADAMS, Marvin, & Boppers
Singles: 7-inch
ROJAC (8172 "I'm on My Way") 20-30

ADAMS, Little Johnnie
Singles: 7-inch
MELATONE (1029 "No In-Between") 10-20

ADAMS, Mike, & Red Jackets
Singles: 7-inch
KENT 5-10 62
LPs: 10/12-inch
CROWN (312 "Surfers Beat") 20-30 63
(Black vinyl.)
CROWN (312 "Surfers Beat") 50-75 63
(Colored vinyl.)
Members: Mike Adams; Norm Eiserman; Johnny Jones; Kaye Klassy.

ADAMS, Nate
Singles: 7-inch
ATLANTIC 5-8 67

ADAMS, Nick
Singles: 7-inch
MERCURY 10-20 60
RCA 8-12

ADAMS, Oleta LP '90
Singles: 7-inch
FONTANA 3-4 90-91
LPs: 10/12-inch
FONTANA 5-8 90
Also see TEARS for FEARS & Oleta Adams

ADAMS, Pepper
LPs: 10/12-inch
BEHTLEHEM (6056 "Motor City Scene") 50-75 60
INTERLUDE (502 "Pepper Adams") 30-40 59
(Monaural.)
INTERLUDE (1002 "Pepper Adams") 40-50 59
(Stereo.)
METROJAZZ (1004 "Pepper-Knepper Quintet") 50-75 58
MODE (112 "Pepper Adams") 50-100 57
REGENT (6066 "Cool Sound") 50-75 58
RIVERSIDE (265 "10 to 4 at the 5 Spot") 50-75 58
(Monaural.)
RIVERSIDE (1104 "10 to 4 at the 5 Spot") 65-85 58
(Stereo.)
SAVOY 5-10 84-85
WARWICK (2041 "Out of This World") 50-75 61
WORKSHOP JAZZ (219 "Compositions of Charlie Mingus") 30-50 63
WORLD PACIFIC (407 "Critic's Choice") 40-60 58
Also see BYRD, Donald

ADAMS, Ray
Singles: 7-inch
RAINBOW (348 "I'm Gone") 40-50 57

ADAMS, Ray
Singles: 7-inch
LAURIE 4-8 62

ADAMS, Richie
(Ritchie Adams)
Singles: 7-inch
BELTONE (1001 "Right Away") 10-20 61
BELTONE (1011 "Two Initials") 10-20 61
CONGRESS (226 "The King") 10-15 64
CONGRESS (232 "What Am I") 10-15 64
CONGRESS (248 "I Ain't Gonna Make It Without You") 10-15 65
CONGRESS (256 "I Can't Escape from You") 25-50 65
IMPERIAL (5806 "I Got Eyes") 10-15 62
IMPERIAL (5838 "Pakistan") 10-15 62
MCA 3-5 80
MGM (13629 "You Were Mine") 5-10 66
P.I.P. 3-5 76
RIBBON (6910 "Lonely One") 10-20 60
RIBBON (6913 "Back to School") 10-20 60
Also see ARCHIES
Also see FIREFLIES

ADAMS, Rush
Singles: 78 rpm
MGM 4-8 55
Singles: 7-inch
MGM 8-12 55
VIRGO 4-6

ADAMS, Rusty
Singles: 7-inch
BRIAR 5-10
D 3-6 71
HARVARD 5-10 60
Also see McCORMICK, George / Rusty Adams
Also see NULL, Cecil / Rusty Adams

ADAMS, T. Carl
Singles: 7-inch
DORE (541 "Guitar Safari") 15-25 59

ADAMS, Terri
Singles: 7-inch
MUSTANG (101 "You Broke My Heart") 8-12

ADAMS, Terry
LPs: 10/12-inch
PRETZEL 5-10 83
Also see NRBQ

ADAMS, Tony
Singles: 7-inch
CHECKER 4-8 63

ADAMS, Woodrow
(With the Three Bs; with Boogie Blues Blasters)
Singles: 78 rpm
CHECKER (757 "Pretty Baby Blues") 100-150 52
Singles: 7-inch
HOME of the BLUES (109 "Something on My Mind") 15-25 60
METEOR (5018 "Wine Head Woman") 150-200 55

ADANO, Bobby: see ADENO, Bobby

ADANO, Ernie
Singles: 7-inch
ASSAULT 5-10

ADAPTERS
Singles: 7-inch
MONTGOMERY (003 "Why") 15-25 66
MOONGLOW (5015 "Why") 15-25 66
MOONGLOW (5022 "I Want to Know") 15-25 67

ADCOCK, C.A.
Singles: 7-inch
OCEANA 3-4 88
Picture Sleeves
OCEANA 3-4 88

ADDEO, Leo, & His Orchestra LP '61
LPs: 10/12-inch
CAMDEN 5-10 61

ADDEO, Nicky
(With the Darchaes; with Counts; with Plazas; "Uniques Featuring Nickie Addeo")
Singles: 7-inch
EARLS (1533 "Gloria") 20-30 64
MELODY (1417 "Where There Is Love") 15-20 64
REVELATION (101 "Danny Boy") 100-200 64
SAVOY (200 "Gloria") 75-125 63
(Black vinyl)
SAVOY (200 "Gloria") 200-300 63
(Colored vinyl)
SELSOM (104 "Over the Rainbow") 150-250 65
VIK 10-20 50s
EPs: 7-inch
VIK 20-30 50s
Also see BARBAROSO & HISTORIANS
Also see SPRINGSTEEN, Bruce
Also see UNIQUES
Also see WHITE, Ben, & Darchaes

ADDERLEY, Julian "Cannonball" P&R/R&B '61
(Cannonball Adderley Orchestra; Cannonball Adderley Quintet; Cannonball Adderley Sextet)
Singles: 7-inch
BLUE NOTE 5-10 59
CAPITOL 3-8 61-73
RIVERSIDE 5-10 61-64
EPs: 7-inch
EMARCY 10-20 55
LPs: 10/12-inch
BLUE NOTE 20-30 58
(Label reads "Blue Note Records Inc. - New York, U.S.A.")
BLUE NOTE 15-25 66
(Label reads "Blue Note Records - A Division Of Liberty Records Inc.")
CAPITOL (Except 2200 and 2300 series) 8-15 66-80
CAPITOL (2200 and 2300 series) 12-25 64-65
DOBRE 5-8 77
EMARCY (400 series) 8-12 76
EMARCY (36000 series) 30-40 55-58
EVEREST 8-12 71
FANTASY 8-12 73-75
LIMELIGHT 10-20 66
MERCURY (1000 series) 5-10 81
MERCURY (20000 and 60000 series) 15-30 61-62
MILESTONE 6-12 73-82
PACIFIC JAZZ 15-25 62
RIVERSIDE (032 thru 142) 5-8 82-85
RIVERSIDE (200 thru 400 series) 15-30 58-63
RIVERSIDE (1100 series) 20-30 59-60
RIVERSIDE (3000 series) 10-15 68
RIVERSIDE (9000 series) 15-25 60-63
SAVOY (2200 series) 8-12 76
SAVOY (12018 "Presenting Cannonball") 50-75 55
TRIP 5-10 75
VSP 10-20 65
WING 8-12 68
Also see WILSON, Nancy, & Cannonball Adderley

ADDERLEY, Julian "Cannonball," & John Coltrane
LPs: 10/12-inch
LIMELIGHT 10-20 65
MERCURY 20-30 61
Also see COLTRANE, John

ADDERLEY, Julian "Cannonball," & Sergio Mendes
LPs: 10/12-inch
CAPITOL 10-15 68-71
EVEREST 5-10 73
Also see ADDERLEY, Julian "Cannonball"
Also see MENDES, Sergio

ADDERLEY, Tommy
(With the Meteors)
Singles: 7-inch
LEXIAN (10 "I'm Comin' Home") 15-25
MAR-MAR (314 "Whole Lotta Shakin' Goin' On") 15-25 60

ADDICTIONS
Singles: 7-inch
KELLWAY 3-5 72

ADDRISI, Dick
Singles: 7-inch
VALIANT 6-12 66
Also see ADDRISI BROTHERS

ADDRISI BROTHERS P&R '59
Singles: 7-inch
BELL 3-5 74
BRAD 15-20 58
BUDDAH 3-5 77
COLUMBIA 3-5 72-73
DEL-FI 10-15 59
ELEKTRA 3-4 81
IMPERIAL 8-12 60
POM POM 5-10 62
PRIVATE STOCK 3-5 75
SCOTTI BROTHERS 3-5 79
VALIANT 5-10 64-65
W.B. 4-8 62-68
Picture Sleeves
SCOTTI BROTHERS 3-5 79
LPs: 10/12-inch
BUDDAH 5-10 77
COLUMBIA 5-10 72
Members: Dick Addrisi; Don Addrisi.
Also see ADDRISI, Dick

ADDY, Ziggie
Singles: 7-inch
PRIVATE STOCK 3-5 77

ADE, King Sunny LP '83
(With His African Beats)
Singles: 12-inch
MANGO 4-6 83
Singles: 7-inch
MANGO 3-4 83
LPs: 10/12-inch
MANGO 5-10 83

ADELPHIES: see ADELPHIS

ADELPHIS
(With Teacho Wiltshire's Orchestra; Adelphies)
Singles: 7-inch
RIM (2020 "Darlin' It's You") 75-125 58
(Mistakenly credits "Adelphies.")
RIM (2020 "Darlin' It's You") 50-75 58
(Properly credits "Adelphis.")
RIM (2022 "[The Sun Will] Shine Again") 50-75 58
(With parenthetical subtitle.)
RIM (2020 "Shine Again") 20-30 61
(Subtitle omitted.)
20TH FOX (543 "Free Fall") 10-20 64
Also see WILTSHIRE, Teacho

ADELSOHN, Herman
Singles: 7-inch
ROULETTE 3-5 74

ADEN, Terry C&W '81
Singles: 7-inch
AMI 3-4 82
B&B 3-4 81

ADENO, Bobby
(Bobby Adano)
Singles: 7-inch
BACK BEAT (552 "It's a Sad World") 10-15 66
IMPERIAL (5628 "Eager Beaver Heart") 10-15 59
REVUE (552 "Hands of Time") 15-25 60s

ADKINS, Hasil
Singles: 7-inch
AIR (5045 "She's Mine") 50-100 58
ARC 10-15
AVENUE (102 "Get Out My Car") 100-200 57
JODY (1000 "She's Mine") 40-60 58
NORTON 3-5 90
Picture Sleeves
ARC 10-15
NORTON 3-5 90
EPs: 7-inch
NORTON 6-8 83
LPs: 10/12-inch
NORTON 8-10 86-87

ADKINS, Mike
(With Lemon Extract)
Singles: 7-inch
RCA 4-6 67-69
LPs: 10/12-inch
MIKE ADKINS (1061 "Mike Adkins") 15-25

ADKINS, Paul
Singles: 7-inch
OWL 3-5 77

ADKINS, Wendel C&W '77
Singles: 7-inch
HITSVILLE 3-5 77
MC 3-5 77
LPs: 10/12-inch
GILLEY'S (5007 "Live at Gilley's") 10-15 83
(Includes Gilley's club bumper sticker.)
HITSVILLE 5-10 77

ADKINSON, Billy
Singles: 7-inch
GALA (112 "Rock-A-Mo") 10-20 60

ADLIBS
Singles: 7-inch
INTERPHON 5-10 66

ADMIRAL ICE
(Admiral Shohn Ice)
Singles: 7-inch
ADMIRAL ICE ("My Carolina Girl") 20-30
(No selection number used.)
ADMIRAL ICE (3219 "Beach Bum") 20-30

ADMIRAL TONES
Singles: 7-inch
FELSTED (8563 "Rocksville, Pa.") 15-25 59
FUTURE (1006 "Rocksville, Pa.") 25-50 59
HI MAR (1001 "Stompin' U.S.A.") 10-20 62
Member: Paul Gottelshall Jr.
Also see THOMAS, Paul

ADMIRALS
Singles: 78 rpm
KING 20-30 55
Singles: 7-inch
KING (1495 "24 Hours a Day") 75-100 55
KING (4772 "Oh Yes") 100-200 55
KING (4782 "Close Your Eyes") 100-200 55
Members: Richard Beasley; Wesley Devereaux; Willie Barnes; Eugene McDaniels; James Farmer.
Also see MILLINDER, Lucky, & Admirals
Also see RYAN, Cathy
Also see SULTANS

ADMIRALS
Singles: 7-inch
VALMOR (15 "Mr. Blue") 10-20 62

ADMIRALS
Singles: 7-inch
VOLT (125 "King of Love") 15-25 65

ADMIRALS
Singles: 7-inch
PULSE 4-8
SOUL TRAIN 5-10

ADMIRATIONS
Singles: 7-inch
APOLLO (753 "My Baby") 20-30 61

ADMIRATIONS
(With Sammy Lowe Orchestra)
Singles: 7-inch
ATOMIC (12871 "Dear Lady") 75-100
BRUNSWICK 10-20 67
JASON SCOTT 4-8
KELLWAY 3-5 72
MERCURY (71521 "The Bells of Rosa Rita") 20-30 59
MERCURY (71883 "To the Aisle") 75-125 61
Members: Joseph Lorello; John Mallon.
Also see DEDICATIONS

ADMIRATIONS / Bel Mars
Singles: 7-inch
CANDLELITE 3-5 74
Also see HEARTSPINNERS / Admirations
Also see NUTMEGS / Admirations

ADMIRATIONS
Singles: 7-inch
ONE-DERFUL (4849 "Wait 'Til I Get to Know You") 5-10 66
ONE-DERFUL (4851 "Don't Leave Me") 5-10 66
PEACHES (6721 "You Left Me") 100-200
(Also issued as by the Aspirations.)
Also see ASPIRATIONS

ADMIRATIONS
Singles: 7-inch
HULL (1202 "Moonlight") 100-200 64

ADMIRATIONS
Singles: 7-inch
LA CINDY (32769 "Life of Tears") 8-12

ADORABLES
Singles: 7-inch
PEACOCK 5-10 63

ADORABLES
Singles: 7-inch
GOLDEN WORLD (4 "Deep Freeze") 15-20 64
GOLDEN WORLD (5 "Daddy Please") 15-20 64
GOLDEN WORLD (10 "School's All Over") 15-20 64
GOLDEN WORLD (25 "Oh Boy") 20-35 65
Members: Pat Lewis; Diane Lewis; Jackie Winston; Betty Winston.
Also see DEBONAIRES
Also see LEWIS, Diane
Also see LEWIS, Pat

ADRENALIN
Singles: 7-inch
MCA (2833 "Road of the Gypsy") 3-4 86
Picture Sleeves
MCA (2833 "Road of the Gypsy") 3-4 86
LPs: 10/12-inch
MCA (5757 "Road of the Gypsy") 5-8 86
ROCSHIRE 5-10 84

ADRIAN, Lee
(With the Rochester Collegiates)
Singles: 7-inch
RCA 10-20 58
RICHCRAFT (5006 "Barbara, Let's Go Steady") 25-35 60
SMC (1385 "I'm So Lonely") 15-25 59
SMC (1386 "School Is Over") 50-75 59

ADRIAN & SUNSETS
Singles: 7-inch
SUNSET (602 "Breakthrough") 10-20 63
Picture Sleeves
SUNSET (602 "Breakthrough") 30-40 63
LPs: 10/12-inch
SUNSET (601 "Breakthrough") 45-65 63
(Black vinyl.)
SUNSET (601 "Breakthrough") 75-100 63
(Multi-colored vinyl.)
Members: Adrian Lloyd; Ron Eglit; Dick Lambert; Bruce Riddar; Bobby Forest; Clyde Brown.
Also see HOLLYWOOD SUNSETS BAND
Also see RUMBLERS

ADVANCE D&D '83
Singles: 12-inch
POLYDOR 4-6 83
("American Excello") 20-25 81
(Label name and selection number not known. Promotional only picture disc.)
Singles: 7-inch
POLYDOR 3-4 83

ADVANCEMENT
LPs: 10/12-inch
PHILIPS (600328 "Advancement") 30-50 69
Members: Lynne Blessing; Colin Bailey; Hal Gordon.

ADVENTURERS
Singles: 7-inch
CAPITOL 8-12 59
COLUMBIA (3-42227 "Rock & Roll Uprising") 40-60 61
(Compact 33 Single.)
COLUMBIA (4-42227 "Rock & Roll Uprising") 20-30 61
JERDEN 8-12 59
MECCA 10-20 60
MIRACLE 10-15 60
READING (602 "Lover Doll") 10-20 66
LPs: 10/12-inch
COLUMBIA (1747 "Can't Stop Twistin' ") 20-30 61
(Monaural.)
COLUMBIA (8547 "Can't Stop Twistin' ") 30-40 61
(Stereo.)

ADVENTURERS
Singles: 7-inch
BLUE ROCK 3-5 69
COMPASS 4-6 67
RAN-DEE 5-8 62

ADVENTURES P&R/LP '88
Singles: 12-inch
ELEKTRA 4-8 88-90
Singles: 7-inch
ELEKTRA 3-4 88-90
Picture Sleeves
ELEKTRA 3-4 88
LPs: 10/12-inch
ELEKTRA 5-8 88
Member: Terry Sharpe.

ADVENTURES
Singles: 12-inch
CHRYSALIS 4-6 86
Singles: 7-inch
CHRYSALIS 3-4 86
Picture Sleeves
CHRYSALIS 3-4 86
LPs: 10/12-inch
CHRYSALIS 5-10 86

ADVENTURERS
Singles: 7-inch
MUSIC WORLD (110 "Darlin' ") 15-25

ADVENTURES in AGAPELAND: see Picture Discs Chapter

ADVENTURES OF STEVIE V. P&R '90
Singles: 7-inch
MERCURY 3-4 90
Members: Steve Vincent; Melodie Washington; Mick Walsh.

ADVERTS
Singles: 7-inch
ANCHOR 3-4 77
BRIGHT 3-4 77-78
RCA 3-4 79
LPs: 10/12-inch
BRIGHT 5-10 78
RCA 5-10 79

AERIAL
Singles: 7-inch
CAPITOL 3-4 78
LPs: 10/12-inch
CAPITOL 5-10 78

AERIAL LANDSCAPE
Singles: 7-inch
RCA 4-8 68

AEROSMITH P&R/LP '73
Singles: 7-inch
COLUMBIA 3-5 73-80
GEFFEN 3-4 85-91
Picture Sleeves
GEFFEN 3-4 85-89
LPs: 10/12-inch
COLUMBIA (Except KC-32005 and quad issues) 5-15 73-86
COLUMBIA (KC-32005 "Aerosmith") 20-25 73
(Orange cover. Incorrectly shows *Walking the Dog* as "Walking the Dig.")
COLUMBIA (KC-32005 "Aerosmith") 20-25 73
(Blue cover. Incorrectly shows *Walking the Dog* as "Walking the Dig." Promotional issue only.)
COLUMBIA (KC-32005 "Aerosmith") 10-12 73
(Blue cover. Correctly lists *Walking the Dog.*)
COLUMBIA (KCQ-32847 "Get Your Wings") 20-30 74
(Quadraphonic.)
COLUMBIA (PCQ-33479 "Toys in the Attic") 20-30 75
(Quadraphonic.)
COLUMBIA (PCQ-34165 "Rocks") 20-30 76
(Quadraphonic.)
GEFFEN 5-10 85-87
Promotional LPs
COLUMBIA (187 "Pure Gold") 50-55 76
(Boxed set of the group's first three LPs.)
Members: Steve Tyler; Tom Hamilton; Joey Kramer; Joe Perry; Brad Whitford; Rick Dufay; Jimmy Crespo.
Also see CHAIN REACTION
Also see PERRY, Joe, Project
Also see RUN-D.M.C.

AESOP & FABLES
Singles: 7-inch
PANORAMA (29 "Grass") 8-12 60s

AESOPS FABLES
(Sonny Botari)
Singles: 7-inch
ATCO 4-8 67-68
CADET CONCEPT 3-6 68
LPs: 10/12-inch
CADET CONCEPT 10-12 69

AFDEM, Jeff, & Springfield Flute
Singles: 7-inch
BURDETTE 10-15 69
PICCADILLY 10-15 68
LPs: 10/12-inch
BURDETTE (5162 "Something") 30-50 69

AFFECTION COLLECTION
Singles: 7-inch
EVOLUTION 8-12 69
MAUDZ (001 "Time Rests Heavy on My Hands") 20-30 60s
U.A. 5-10 68
LPs: 10/12-inch
EVOLUTION 10-15 69
Members: Mike Doggett; Hal Rowberry; Don Christensen; Tim Comeau; Ray Hassell.

AFFINITY
Singles: 7-inch
PARAMOUNT 3-5 70
LPs: 10/12-inch
PARAMOUNT 15-25 70
Members: Linda Boyle; Lynton Naiff; Mike Jopp; Mo Foster; Grant Serpell.

AFFLUENTS
Singles: 7-inch
CUCA ("I Feel Free") 10-20 67
(Selection number not known.)
USA (901 "Get Ready") 10-20 68

Members: Ted Pfeffer; Jim Morris; Tom Pilizak; Dan Carson; Jeff Schmus; George Shuput; Russ Engelwire.

AFRICA
Singles: 7-inch
EPIC 3-5 72
ODE 4-6 69
LPs: 10/12-inch
JUST SUNSHINE 8-10 74
Also see ALLEY CATS
Also see PIPKINS

AFRICALI
Singles: 12-inch
EASY STREET 4-6 83

AFRICAN BEAVERS
Singles: 7-inch
RCA 4-8 65
Picture Sleeves
RCA 5-10 65

AFRICAN ECHOES
Singles: 7-inch
OVIDE 5-10 60s
PHILA-L.A. of SOUL 4-8 68

AFRICAN MUSIC MACHINE
Singles: 7-inch
JEWEL 3-5
SOUL POWER 3-5 72-74

AFRICAN SUITE
LPs: 10/12-inch
MCA 5-10 80

AFRICANO
Singles: 7-inch
HI 3-5 73

AFRIKA BAMBAATAA: see BAMBAATAA, Afrika

AFRIQUE P&R/R&B/LP '73
Singles: 7-inch
MAINSTREAM 3-5 73
LPs: 10/12-inch
MAINSTREAM 8-12 73
Members: David T. Walker; Chuck Rainey.

AFRO BLUES QUINTET PLUS ONE
Singles: 7-inch
MIRA 5-8 67

AFRO CUBAN BAND R&B '78
Singles: 7-inch
ARISTA 3-4 78
LPs: 10/12-inch
ARISTA 5-10 78

AFRO-SAXONS
Singles: 7-inch
PARAMOUNT 3-5 73

AF-TABS
Singles: 7-inch
FIVE STAR 4-6 69

AFTER ALL
LPs: 10/12-inch
ATHENA ("After All") 15-25 70
(Selection number not known.)
Members: Bill Moon; Charles Short; Alan Gold; Mark Ellerbee.

AFTER HOURS
Singles: 7-inch
CONDOR 5-10

AFTER 7 P&R/LP '89
Singles: 7-inch
VIRGIN 3-4 89-90
Picture Sleeves
VIRGIN 3-4 89-90
LPs: 10/12-inch
VIRGIN 5-8 89
Members: Keith Mitchell; Melvin Edmonds; Kevon Edmonds.

AFTER THE FIRE P&R/D&D/LP '83
Singles: 12-inch
EPIC 4-8 83
Singles: 7-inch
EPIC 3-4 83-84
LPs: 10/12-inch
EPIC 5-10 82
Members: Peter Banks; Andy Piercy; Ivor Twidell; Tim Haywell; Nick Battle.
Also see BANKS, Peter

AFTERBACH R&B '81
Singles: 7-inch
COLUMBIA/ARC 3-4 81
LPs: 10/12-inch
COLUMBIA/ARC 5-10 81
Members: Robert Brooken; Mike Brooken.

AFTERGLOW
LPs: 10/12-inch
MTA (5010 "Afterglow") 75-100 67

AFTERNOON DELIGHTS P&R/R&B '81
Singles: 12-inch
MCA 4-8 81
Singles: 7-inch
MCA 3-4 81
LPs: 10/12-inch
MCA 5-10 81

AGAFON
Singles: 7-inch
GOLDEN NORTH (101 "Walkin' the Dog") 10-15

AGAN, Larry
Singles: 7-inch
SQUIRE (103 "Frankie's New Lover") 30-50 62

AGAPE
LPs: 10/12-inch
MARK (2170 "Gospel Hard Rock") 75-100 71
RENRUT ("Victims of Tradition") 50-80 72

AGARY, Rickey
(With the Mark Anthony Band)
Singles: 7-inch
BEL CANTO 5-10 59
Also see ANTHONY, Mark

AGBAY, Tony, & Continentals
Singles: 7-inch
NEW GLO 20-30

AGE OF BRONZE
Singles: 7-inch
GUAVA (102 "I'm Gonna Love You") 40-60 60s

AGE OF REASON
Singles: 7-inch
ASCOT (2230 "Magnet") 30-50 67
LPs: 10/12-inch
GEORGETOWNE ("Age of Reason") 150-250 69
(No selection number used.)

AGEE, Ray
(With the Four Kings)
Singles: 78 rpm
ALADDIN 10-20 52
CASH 10-20 56
MODERN 10-20 52
QUEEN (101 "Brought It All By Myself") 15-25 52
RECORDED in HOLLYWOOD 10-20 52
RHYTHM & BLUES 10-20 54
SPARK 10-20 55
Singles: 7-inch
ALADDIN (3161 "Deep Trouble") 40-60 52
BORN AGAIN 3-4 84
BRANDIN 5-8
CASH (1032 "Till Death Do Us Part") 25-50 56
CELESTE (612 "I'm the Gambler") 6-12 64
CELESTE (616 "Merry Xmas Time") 6-12 64
CHECK (102 "Pray for Me") 35-50 59
EBB (111 "True Lips") 15-25 57
ELKO (109 "Black Night Is Gone") 10-20 59
FAT BACK (101 "I Can't Work and Watch You") 8-12
HIGHLAND (1192 "Keep Smiling") 5-10 60s
JEWEL 5-8 67
KRAFTON 4-8 67-72
MAR JAN (001 "These Things Are True") 15-25 63
MODERN (883 "Flirtin' Blues") 50-75 52
MODERN (891 "My Lonesome Days Are Gone") 50-75 52
PLAID (105 "Pray for Me") 50-75 59
PROWLIN' 3-5 76
RECORDED in HOLLYWOOD (240 "Troubles Bring Me Down") 50-75 52
RHYTHM & BLUES (111 "Without a Friend") 25-50 54
ROMARK (118 "It's Hard to Explain") 4-8 70s
SHIRLEY (111 "You Hit Me Where It Hurts") 10-15 63
SHIRLEY (123631 "Open Up Your Heart") 10-15 63
SOLID SOUL (802 "Boy and Girl Thing") 10-15
SOUL TOWN 10-15 66
SPARK (119 "Wobble-Lou") 40-60 55
VELTONE 10-20 60
WATTS WAY (642 "My So Called Friend") 5-10
LPs: 10/12-inch
J.W. 8-12
KRAFTON 10-15 68
WHITE 5-10 83
Also see ISOM RAY

AGEE, Ray, & Elly Johnson
Singles: 7-inch
EBB (111 "My Silent Prayer") 20-25 57

AGEE, Ray, & Mary Ann Miles
Singles: 7-inch
CELESTE 6-12 64
Also see AGEE, Ray
Also see MILES, Mary Ann

AGENT ORANGE
Singles: 7-inch
ENIGMA 3-4 86
POSH BOY 3-4 81
LPs: 10/12-inch
ENIGMA 5-10 86-87

AGENTS
Singles: 7-inch
P&L (1001 "You Were Meant for Me") 20-30 60s
RALLY (504 "Gotta Help Me") 20-30 66

AGENTS
LPs: 10/12-inch
SUNSET 15-20 67

AGNES & ORVILLE
Singles: 7-inch
COLUMBIA 4-6 68
Members: Lefty Frizzell; June Stearns.
Also see FRIZZELL, Lefty
Also see STEARNS, June

AGGREGATION
Singles: 7-inch
LHI (1209 "Sunshine Superman")...15-25 68
LPs: 10/12-inch
LHI (12008 "Mind Oydssey") 300-500 68

AGO-GOS
Singles: 7-inch
PEE VEE (2000 "Shake and Fingerpop") 10-15 66

AGRATI, Don
(Don Grady)
Singles: 7-inch
ELEKTRA 3-5 73
LPs: 10/12-inch
ELEKTRA 10-12 73
Also see GRADY, Don
Also see YELLOW BALLOON

AGUA SONICS
Singles: 7-inch
DAKAR 3-5 72

A-HA *P&R/D&D/LP '85*
Singles: 12-inch
W.B. 4-8 85-87
Singles: 7-inch
REPRISE.. 3-6 85-86
W.B. 3-6 85-87
Picture Sleeves
W.B. (Except 29011) 3-6 85-87
W.B. (29011 "Take on Me") 5-8 85
(Promotional issue only with booklet.)
LPs: 10/12-inch
REPRISE.. 5-10 85-86
W.B. 5-10 85-88
Members: Morten Harket; Mags Furuholem; Pal Waaktaar.

AH-MOORS
Singles: 78 rpm
RAINBOW (10060 "Honey, Honey, Honey") 20-40 48

AHRES, Dejah
Singles: 7-inch
VERVE 4-8

AIDA *D&D '84*
Singles: 12-inch
VANGUARD 4-6 84
Singles: 7-inch
VANGUARD 3-4 84
LPs: 10/12-inch
VANGUARD 5-8 84

AIKEN, Ben
Singles: 7-inch
LOMA (2100 "Baby You Move Me") 10-15 67
PHILLY GROOVE.............................. 4-8 71-72
ROULETTE 5-10 65
SQUIRE 4-8

AIKERN, Tony, & Future
Singles: 7-inch
SHYRLDEN 3-5

AIM
Singles: 7-inch
BLUE THUMB 3-5 74
LPs: 10/12-inch
BLUE THUMB 5-10 74
Members: Michael Overly; Patrick O'Connor; Warren Pemberton; Loren Newkirk.

AIMEE, Joyce
Singles: 7-inch
CRYSTALETTE (744 "Playboy Lover") 10-20 61
CRYSTALETTE (746 "Fickle Heart") 10-20 62

AIMES, Steward
Singles: 7-inch
H&W (100 "Angelina") 20-25

AINLEY, Charlie
Singles: 7-inch
NEMPEROR....................................... 3-4 78
LPs: 10/12-inch
NEMPEROR....................................... 5-10 78

AINSFIELD, Freddie
Singles: 7-inch
SCEPTER 5-10 63

AIR
LPs: 10/12-inch
BLACK SAINT 5-10 80-81
EMBRYO 10-15 71
Members: Fred Hopkins; Steve McCall; Henry Threadgill.

AIR FORCE 1
Singles: 12-inch
STREETWISE..................................... 4-6 85

AIR POWER
Singles: 12-inch
A.V.I. 4-8 79

AIR RAID
Singles: 7-inch
20TH FOX 3-4 81
LPs: 10/12-inch
20TH FOX 5-10 81

AIR SUPPLY *P&R/LP '80*
Singles: 7-inch
ARISTA 3-4 80-86
FLASHBACK..................................... 3-4 82
Picture Sleeves
ARISTA 3-4 80-86
LPs: 10/12-inch
ARISTA 5-10 80-86
COLUMBIA...10-15 77
MFSL (113 "The One That You Love") 25-30 84
NAUTILUS (31 "Lost in Love").......15-25 82
Members: Graham Russell; Russell Hitchcock; David Moyse; Criston Barker; Ralph Cooper; David Green; Frank Esler-Smith; Rex Goh.
Also see HITCHCOCK, Russell

AIRBORNE
Singles: 7-inch
COLUMBIA... 3-5 79
SUNRISE 3-6 79
LPs: 10/12-inch
COLUMBIA... 5-10 79
Members: Bearl Hill; David Zychek; Mike Baird; John Pierce; Larry Stewart.

AIRCRAFT
Picture Disc Singles
AZRA (52/53 "Becky") 5-10 82
(Square disc. 60 made with "Rush Records" logo. Promotional only.)
AZRA (52/53 "Becky") 5-10 82
(Square disc. 500 made.)
AZRA (53 "Don't Just Look") 5-10 82
(Square disc. 500 made.)
AZRA (53 "Don't Just Look") 5-10 82
(Square disc. Has "with compliments" print on disc.)

AIRE-DALES
Singles: 7-inch
BRUNSWICK 5-10 65
ROULETTE (4505 "Drumsville") 5-10 63

AIRES, Jimmy / Barry Winston / Billy Logan / Michael Reed
EPs: 7-inch
PROMENADE (14 "Whispering Bells") 15-25 57
(Title shown is of the Aires track. If there is an actual EP title, we're not yet aware of it.)

AIRHEAD
LPs: 10/12-inch
HUMBOLDT'S HIGH 5-10 82

AIRLANE TRIO
Singles: 7-inch
HARMONY 5-10 63

AIRPLAY
Singles: 7-inch
RCA.. 3-4 80
LPs: 10/12-inch
RCA..5-10 80

AIRRACE
Singles: 7-inch
ATCO 3-4 84-85
Picture Sleeves
ATCO 3-4 84
LPs: 10/12-inch
ATCO 5-10 84-85
Member: Jason Bonham.

AIRTO: see MOREIRA, Airto

AIRWAVES *P&R '78*
Singles: 7-inch
A&M 3-4 78-79
LPs: 10/12-inch
A&M 5-10 78-79
Members: John David; Dave Charles; Ray Martinez.

AITKEN, Laurel
Singles: 7-inch
R&B...6-12 60

A-JACKS
Singles: 7-inch
VALIANT (6048 "Knight Ride") 15-20 64

AJACQUES
Singles: 7-inch
CONDOR CLASSICS (38 "Young Love") 8-10 88
(Picture disc.)

AKASHA
LPs: 10/12-inch
DECAMERON 8-10 82
Members: Bill Davis; Willie Waits; Gary Darling; Don Timmons; Marty Fauchier.

AKENS, Jewel *P&R/R&B '65*
Singles: 7-inch
AMERICAN INT'L ARTISTS 3-5 75
CAPEHART (5007 "Wee Bit More of Your Lovin' ") 15-20 61
COLGEMS 5-8 67
CREST ("Wee Bit More of Your Lovin' ") 10-15 62
ERA 6-12 65
ICEPAC (303 "What Would You Do") 10-15
MINASA (6716 "Wee Bit More of Your Lovin' ") 5-10 65
RTV... 3-5 72
WEST-ONE 3-5
LPs: 10/12-inch
ERA (110 "The Birds & Bees") 20-35 65
Also see FOUR DOTS
Also see JEWEL & EDDIE

AKEEM
(Akeem Olajuwan; Hakeem Olajuawan)
Singles: 7-inch
MACOLA 3-4 87
Picture Sleeves
MACOLA 3-4 87

AKI: see ALEONG, Aki

AKIDO
Singles: 7-inch
MERCURY 3-5 72
LPs: 10/12-inch
MERCURY 8-10 72

A'KIES
Singles: 7-inch
PAN WORLD (515 "Haunted Piano") 15-25 59

AKIM & AKTONES
(With the Hank Levine Orchestra; Aki Aleong)
Singles: 7-inch
PAN WORLD (520 "Fall in Love with Me") 50-100 60
Also see ALEONG, Aki
Also see LEVINE, Hank

AKIN, Chuck
Singles: 7-inch
BANDERA 5-10 61

AKIN, Steve
Singles: 7-inch
ASH 10-15

AKINS, Audrey
Singles: 7-inch
PETAL (1030 "Down Came My Tears") 8-12 65

AKINS, J.C., & Dukes
Singles: 7-inch
BOUNTY (5589 "You Upset My Very Soul") 10-20

AKINS, Jim
Singles: 7-inch
MARLO (1517 "Floating on a Cloud") 15-20 61

AKINS, Jerry, & Rockin' Obsidians
Singles: 7-inch
HI MAR..15-20

AKKERMAN, Jan *LP '73*
(With Kaz Lux)
Singles: 7-inch
ATLANTIC...3-4 77-79
LPs: 10/12-inch
ATCO 10-12 73
ATLANTIC...5-10 76-79
SIRE..10-15 73
Also see BRAINBOX
Also see FOCUS

AKLAFF, Pheeroan
LPs: 10/12-inch
GRAMAVISION 5-10 83

AL & BOB
Singles: 7-inch
SUNSET 3-5

AL & DICK
Singles: 7-inch
CARLTON (452 "I'll Wait") 8-12 58
Members: Al Hoffman; Dick Manning.

AL & ECHOES
Singles: 7-inch
ECHO (1003 "Baby, Remember Me") 10-15

AL & EXCLUSIVES
Singles: 7-inch
JOX (015 "Breezy") 10-20 62

AL & JIM
Singles: 7-inch
LOGAN (3117 "Rock-A-Billy Music") 50-75 59

AL & MARGIE
Singles: 7-inch
NRC 5-10 59

AL & NETTIE
(With the Nat Hendrix Band; Al & Nattie)
Singles: 7-inch
ART-TONE (829 "Now You Know") 10-15 62
CHRISTY 20-30 58
GEDINSON'S 10-15 61

AL & RANDY
Singles: 7-inch
MERCURY 4-8 67

AL & TINY
Singles: 7-inch
HURRICANE (6994 "I'm Going Crazy") 15-25

AL B. SURE! *P&R/R&B/LP '88*
Singles: 7-inch
W.B. 3-4 88-90
Picture Sleeves
W.B. 3-4 88-90
LPs: 10/12-inch
W.B. 5-8 88-90
Also see JONES, Quincy, James Ingram, Al B. Sure, El DeBarge & Barry White

AL'S DYNAMICS
Singles: 7-inch
IDEAL...4-8

AL'S UNTOUCHABLES
Singles: 7-inch
HUNT (6007 "Come on Baby") 20-30 66
Member: Al Huntzinger.
Also see UNTOUCHABLES

ALABAMA *C&W '77*
(Alabama Band)
Singles: 7-inch
GRT 8-12 77
LIMBO INT'L ("I Wanna Come Over") 10-20 70s
(Selection number not known.)
MDJ...4-8 79-80
RCA 3-5 80-93
RCA GOLD STANDARD 3-4 82
SSS INT'L (Colored vinyl) 5-10 81
Picture Sleeves
GRT 10-20 77
RCA 3-5 80-90
LPs: 10/12-inch
ACCORD...5-10 81
ALABAMA RECORDS (78 9-01 "The Alabama Band") 200-400 78
PLANTATION (44 "Wild Country") .40-60 81
RCA 5-10 80-90
SONNY 30-50 79
Members: Randy Owen; Jeff Cook; Teddy Gentry; R. Scott; Mark Herndon.
Also see RICHIE, Lionel, & Alabama
Also see WILD COUNTRY

ALABAMA KID
Singles: 7-inch
VARSITY (83 "Rocking Jalopy") 200-300 58

ALABAMA SLIM
(Ralph Willis)
Singles: 78 rpm
SAVOY..10-20 48
Also see WILLIS, Ralph

ALABAMA STATE TROUPERS
LPs: 10/12-inch
ELEKTRA...10-15 72
Members: Furry Lewis; Jeannie Greene; Lonnie Mack; Don Nix.
Also see LEWIS, Furry
Also see MACK, Lonnie
Also see NIX, Don

ALADDIN
Singles: 7-inch
STAR-A-FIRE.....................................4-8

ALADDIN, Johnny
(With the Passions)
Singles: 7-inch
JAMA 4-8
CHIP (1001 "Why Did You Go") 35-50 60
Picture Sleeves
JAMA 5-10
Also see PASSIONS

ALADDIN, Russ
Singles: 7-inch
ALPINE (103 "Me and My Lover") .10-20 60

ALADDIN & GENIES
Singles: 7-inch
DRUMMOND (5001 "Amazon") 20-30 61

ALADDINS
Singles: 7-inch
ALADDIN (3275 "Cry Cry Baby") 100-200 55
ALADDIN (3298 "Get off My Feet") 100-150 55
ALADDIN (3314 "All of My Life") 100-200 56
ALADDIN (3358 "Help Me") 75-150 56
Members: Ed Williams; Alfred Harper; Ted Harper; Gaylord Green.

ALADDINS
Singles: 7-inch
FRANKIE (6 "Dot, My Love") 200-300 58

ALADDINS
Singles: 7-inch
WITCH (109 "Please Love Me") 30-40 62
WITCH (111 "Our Love Will Be") ...20-30 62
Also see BUTLERS / Aladdins

ALADDINS
Singles: 7-inch
DUPLEX..10-20

ALAIMO, Chuck *P&R '57*
(Chuck Alaimo Quartet)
Singles: 78 rpm
KEN..5-10 57
MGM...5-10 57
Singles: 7-inch
KEN (311 "Leap Frog") 15-25 57
MGM...10-20 57-58

ALAIMO, Steve *P&R '62*
(With the Redcoats)
Singles: 7-inch
ABC..5-8 66-67
ABC-PAR 5-10 64-66
ATCO 4-8 67-71
CHECKER...10-15 61-63
DADE (1805 "Love Letters") 15-25 59
DICKSON (6445 "Blue Fire") 10-20 60
ENTRANCE..3-5 71-72
ERIC 3-4 83
IMPERIAL 10-15 60-63
LIFETIME..25-40 58
MARLIN (6064 "I Want You to Love Me") 20-30 59
MARLIN (6067 "She's My Baby") ...15-25 59
EPs: 7-inch
ABC-PAR (531 "Where the Action Is") 10-20 65
(Juke box issue only.)
LPs: 10/12-inch
ABC-PAR (501 "Starring Steve Alaimo") 15-20 65
(Monaural.)
ABC-PAR (S-501 "Starring Steve Alaimo") 20-30 65
(Stereo.)
ABC-PAR (531 "Where the Action Is") 15-20 65
(Monaural.)
ABC-PAR (S-531 "Where the Action Is") 20-30 65
(Stereo.)
ABC-PAR (551 "Steve Alaimo Sings & Swings") 15-20 66
(Monaural.)
ABC-PAR (S-551 "Steve Alaimo Sings & Swings") 20-30 66
(Stereo.)
CHECKER (2981 "Twist") 25-40 63
CHECKER (2983 "Mashed Potatoes") 25-40 62
CHECKER (2986 "Everyday I Have to Cry") 25-50 63
CROWN (5382 "Steve Alaimo") 10-20 63
Also see DELMIRAS
Also see RED COATS
Also see RIVERS, Johnny / Steve Alaimo
Also see UNKNOWNS

ALAIMO, Steve, & Betty Wright
Singles: 7-inch
ATCO 4-8 69
Also see ALAIMO, Steve
Also see WRIGHT, Betty

ALAMO
Singles: 7-inch
ATLANTIC..3-5 71
LPs: 10/12-inch
ATLANTIC...10-12 71
Members: Larry Raspberry; Ken Woodley; Richard Rosebrough; Larry Davis.
Also see RASPBERRY, Larry, & Highsteppers

ALAMO, Tony
Singles: 7-inch
LITTLE MARK 4-8 64

ALAN
LPs: 10/12-inch
ALAN ("A Tribute to Elvis") 30-40 75
(No selection number used.)

ALAN, Buddy *C&W '68*
(With Don Rich & Buckaroos)
Singles: 7-inch
CAPITOL...3-5 68-75
SUN DEVIL (1001 "Ride 'Em Cowboy") 4-8 78
LPs: 10/12-inch
CAPITOL...5-10 70-75
Also see BUCKAROOS
Also see OWENS, Buck, & Buddy Alan

ALAN, Denni
Singles: 7-inch
ACADEMY (434 "Sixth Solid Baby") 20-30 59

ALAN, Edgar, & Po' Boys
Singles: 7-inch
RUST (5053 "Panic Button") 10-15 62

ALAN, Lee
Singles: 7-inch
LEE ALAN PRESENTS ("A Trip to Miami") 400-500 64
(No selection number used. Includes insert sheet. DJ Lee Alan interviews the Beatles.)
LEE ALAN PRESENTS ("A Trip to Miami") 300-400 64
(Without insert sheet.)
Also see BEATLES

ALAN, Lee, & Vandellas
Singles: 7-inch
YMCA/WXYZ (94472 "Set Me Free") 50-75 60s
(Promotional, fund-raising issue.)
Also see ALAN, Lee
Also see MARTHA & VANDELLAS

ALAN, Mark
Singles: 7-inch
PEAK 5-10 60s

ALAN, Phil, & Ardees
(Phil Alan & Ardee's)
Singles: 7-inch
KO CO BO (1010 "Tell Me Why") 200-300

ALAN, Robby
Singles: 7-inch
SAHUARO 8-12

ALAN, Terry
Singles: 7-inch
HART-VAN (0129 "Stompin' Time") 10-20 63

ALAN & ALPINES
Singles: 7-inch
ELKO (16 "Ginger Bread") 100-200

ALARM *LP '83*
Singles: 7-inch
I.R.S. 3-4 83-90
Picture Sleeves
I.R.S. 3-4 83-89
LPs: 10/12-inch
I.R.S. 5-10 83-91
Members: Mike Peters; Nigel Twist; Dave Sharp; Eddie MacDonald.

ALARM CLOCKS
Singles: 7-inch
AWAKE (107 "Yeah") 50-75 66

ALBA, Salix
Singles: 7-inch
JAMIE 3-5 75
STAX...3-5 73

ALBAM, Manny
Singles: 7-inch
COLPIX 4-8

ALBANO, Donny
Singles: 7-inch
ROULETTE 3-5 70

ALBANO, Frankie
Singles: 7-inch
ANOTHER FEATURE 4-8 66
DONDEE (1922 "School Girl") 10-20 60s
TOWER 5-10 65
Session: Davie Allan.
Also see ALLAN, Davie

ALBATROSS
Singles: 7-inch
HARVEST 3-5 71
LION 3-5 73
LPs: 10/12-inch
HARVEST 10-15 71
Members: Jerry Harrison; Ernie Brooks; Jim Mahoney; John Merritt; Geoff Parsons.

ALBEE & CASUALS
Singles: 7-inch
DESTINATION (609 "Your [sic] the Kind of Girl") 15-25 65
Also see CASUALS

ALBEE & FRIENDS
Singles: 7-inch
NIK NIK (74 "Hexorcist – World Premier") 5-8 74

ALBERT
Singles: 7-inch
PERCEPTION 3-5 71
LPs: 10/12-inch
PERCEPTION 10-15 71

ALBERT, Eddie
Singles: 78 rpm
KAPP 5-10 54-56
Singles: 7-inch
BELL 3-5
COLUMBIA 3-5 68
HICKORY 4-8 64-65
KAPP 8-15 54-56
Picture Sleeves
KAPP (134 "Little Child") 10-15 56
LPs: 10/12-inch
COLUMBIA 8-12 68
DOT 8-12
HAMILTON 10-15 59

ALBERT, Eddie, & Sondra Lee *P&R '56*
Singles: 78 rpm
KAPP 4-8 56
Singles: 7-inch
KAPP 5-10 56
Also see ALBERT, Eddie

ALBERT, Fat: see FAT ALBERT

ALBERT, Mel
Singles: 7-inch
APOLLO 8-12 59

ALBERT, Morris *P&R/LP '75*
Singles: 7-inch
RCA 3-5 75-76
LPs: 10/12-inch
RCA 5-10 75-76

ALBERT, Urel *C&W '73*
Singles: 7-inch
TOAST 3-5 73
LPs: 10/12-inch
SPAR (3016 "Saturday Night in Nashville") 20-30
CINNAMON 20-30

ALBERT & CHARLES
Singles: 7-inch
PIONEER (1005 "Weird") 100-150

ALBERTI, Willy *P&R '59*
Singles: 7-inch
EPIC 3-6 59
LONDON 3-6 59
PHILIPS 4-6 65
LPs: 10/12-inch
LONDON 5-15 59

ALBERTINE, Charles
Singles: 7-inch
COLPIX 4-8 64

ALBERTO COMBO
Singles: 7-inch
TAMMY (1025 "Green Monster") 10-20 61

ALBERTS, Al
Singles: 7-inch
COLUMBIA 4-8 63
CORAL 5-10 59
MGM 4-8 60
PRESIDENT 10-20 61
SWAN 5-10 61
LPs: 10/12-inch
CORAL 15-25 59
Also see FOUR ACES

ALBIA ENTERTAINMENT
Singles: 7-inch
FARM OUT (001 "The Last Great Debate") 4-8 80s

ALBIMOOR & LUCKY 13
Singles: 7-inch
PALETTE 4-8 59

ALBIN, Hollis
Singles: 7-inch
HAMMOND (106 "V-8 Ford Boogie") 50-75 59

ALBINO GORILLA
Singles: 7-inch
KAMA SUTRA 3-5 71
LPs: 10/12-inch
KAMA SUTRA 10-15 71

ALBRIGHT, Budd
Singles: 7-inch
RCA 8-12 58

ALBRIGHT, Gerald *R&B '87*
Singles: 7-inch
ATLANTIC 3-4 87-88
LPs: 10/12-inch
ATLANTIC 5-8 88

ALCATRAZZ *LP '84*
Singles: 7-inch
ROCSHIRE 4-8 83
Picture Sleeves
ROCSHIRE 8-15 83
LPs: 10/12-inch
CAPITOL 15-25 85
ROCSHIRE 15-25 83-84
Members: Graham Bonnet; Steve Vai; Yngwie Malmsteen.
Also see RAINBOW
Also see MALMSTEEN, Yngwie J.
Also see SCHENKER, Michael, Group

ALCON SHADES
Singles: 7-inch
BLUE ROCK 5-8 68

ALCONS
Singles: 7-inch
BRUNSWICK 10-15 58
CORAL 10-15 60

ALCORN, Denzil
Singles: 7-inch
CAMARO 5-8 68
GREAT 4-6 69

ALCORN, Sam
Singles: 7-inch
INSTANT 4-8 68

ALCOVES
Singles: 7-inch
CARLTON 10-20 64

ALDA, Alex
(Nick Massi)
Singles: 7-inch
TOPIX (6007 "Little Pony") 40-60 61
(Promotional issue only.)
Also see 4 SEASONS

ALDA RESERVE
LPs: 10/12-inch
W.B./SIRE 5-10 79

ALDEN, Bea
Singles: 7-inch
MINERET (108 "Too Far Above Me") 5-10 63
MINARET (113 "Let's Talk About Love") 5-10 63

ALDEN, Ginger
Singles: 7-inch
MONUMENT 4-6 80

ALDEN & ONE-NIGHTERS
Singles: 7-inch
RCA (7490 "Love-O-Meter") 15-25 59

ALDO NOVA: see NOVA, Aldo

ALDERSON, Johnny
Singles: 7-inch
AVA 5-8 63

ALDO, Buddy
Singles: 7-inch
DIVA 15-25

ALDO, Johnny
Singles: 7-inch
ALDON 8-12

ALDON & EC'S
Singles: 7-inch
GAITY (174 "Endsville") 40-60 59
Members: Al Fremstad; Don Cronkhite; Tex Hanson; Art Hestekin; Kip McFaul; Tom O'Brien.

ALDRICH, Renee *R&B '87*
Singles: 7-inch
JAM PACKED 3-4 87

ALDRICH, Ronnie *LP '61*
LPs: 10/12-inch
LONDON PHASE 4 5-15 61-71

ALDRIDGE, Jim
Singles: 7-inch
RAZORBACK (110 "The Frog") 15-20 61

ALECSTAR
Singles: 7-inch
SMARTALEC 3-5 81

ALEGRETTES
Singles: 7-inch
PACIFIC ("Peter Gunn") 10-20
(Selection number not known.)

ALEEM *R&B/D&D '84*
(Featuring Leroy Burgess; Aleems)
Singles: 12-inch
ATLANTIC 4-6 87
NIA 5-8 85
Singles: 7-inch
ATLANTIC 3-4 86-87
NIA 3-5 84-85
LPs: 10/12-inch
ATLANTIC 5-10 87
Members: Leroy Burgess; Taharqa Aleem; Tunde-Ra Aleem.
Also see BLACK IVORY

ALEEMS: see ALEEM

ALEONG, Aki
(With the Nobels; with Teen Twenty; with His Licorice Twisters; Aki)
Singles: 7-inch
MONA-LEE (130 "How Do I Stand with You") 50-100 59
REPRISE 10-15 61-62
VEE JAY 5-10 63
LPs: 10/12-inch
REPRISE 20-40 62
VEE JAY 20-40 63
Session: Ralph Geddes; Paul Geddes; Marty Smith; Ron Smith; Louis Abella; Rick Gardner.
Also see AKIM & AKTONES
Also see EXPRESSOS

ALEPH
Singles: 7-inch
ROULETTE 3-5 70

ALERT
Singles: 7-inch
ATCO 3-4 90

ALESSI *P&R '82*
Singles: 7-inch
A&M 3-4 77-79
QWEST 3-4 82
Picture Sleeves
A&M 3-4 77-79
LPs: 10/12-inch
A&M 5-10 76-79
QWEST 5-10 82
Members: Bill Alessi; Bob Alessi.
Also see BARNABY BYE

ALEX
Singles: 7-inch
FREE FLIGHT/RCA 3-5 79
KINGSWAY 3-5 72
LPs: 10/12-inch
FREE FLIGHT 5-10 79

ALEXANDER, Alexis
LPs: 10/12-inch
AA (00001 "The Witch in Me") 10-15 84
(Picture disc.)

ALEXANDER, Arthur *P&R/R&B '62*
Singles: 7-inch
AT YOU 3-6
BUDDAH 3-6 75-76
DOT 5-10 62-64
GORDA 4-8
MONUMENT 4-8 68
MUSIC MILL 4-8 77
SOUND STAGE 7 4-8 65-71
W.B. 3-6 72-73
EPs: 7-inch
DOT (434 "You Better Move On") 25-35 62
(Stereo. Juke box issue only.)
LPs: 10/12-inch
DOT (3434 "You Better Move On") 35-45 62
(Monaural.)
DOT (25434 "You Better Move On") 40-55 62
(Stereo.)
W.B. 8-15 72
Also see ALEXANDER, June

ALEXANDER, C., & Natural 3
Singles: 7-inch
GUY JIM (588 "Pay Them No Mind") 15-25 60s

ALEXANDER, Daniele *C&W '89*
Singles: 7-inch
MERCURY 3-4 89-90

ALEXANDER, Daniele, & Butch Baker *C&W '90*
Singles: 7-inch
MERCURY 3-4 90
Also see BAKER, Butch

ALEXANDER, Dave
Singles: 7-inch
ARHOOLIE 5-10 72-73

ALEXANDER, David *R&B '87*
Singles: 7-inch
SOUND TOWN 3-4 87

ALEXANDER, Goldie *R&B '82*
Singles: 7-inch
ARISTA 3-4 82

ALEXANDER, Gordon
Singles: 7-inch
COLUMBIA 4-6 68
LPs: 10/12-inch
COLUMBIA 8-15 68

ALEXANDER, Harold
Singles: 7-inch
ATLANTIC 3-5 74
LPs: 10/12-inch
ATLANTIC 5-10 74

ALEXANDER, J.W.
Singles: 7-inch
ALEXANDER 3-5
THRUSH (105 "Mean Black Snake") 8-12
LPs: 10/12-inch
TRUTH 10-15 70

ALEXANDER, Jeff
(Jeff Alexander Quartet)
Singles: 78 rpm
AARDELL 10-15 55
Singles: 7-inch
AARDELL 20-25 55
LPs: 10/12-inch
FH 10-20

ALEXANDER, Jinx
Singles: 7-inch
PRIVATE STOCK 3-5 75
LPs: 10/12-inch
PRIVATE STOCK 5-10 75

ALEXANDER, Joe
(Joe Alexander's Highlanders)
Singles: 78 rpm
CAPITOL 10-20 46-48
EXCELSIOR 5-15 46
Also see BROOKS, Dusty

ALEXANDER, Joe, & Cubans
Singles: 78 rpm
BALLAD (1008 "Oh Maria") 300-500 55
Singles: 7-inch
BALLAD (1008 "Oh Maria") 1000-1500 55
Members: Joe Alexander; Chuck Berry; Faith Douglas; Freddy Golden.
Also see ALEXANDER, Joe
Also see BERRY, Chuck

ALEXANDER, June
(Arthur Alexander)
Singles: 7-inch
JUDD (1020 "Sally Sue Brown") 25-35 60
Also see ALEXANDER, Arthur

ALEXANDER, La-Jay
Singles: 7-inch
BLACK GOLD 3-5 74

ALEXANDER, Margie *R&B '74*
Singles: 12-inch
CHI-SOUND 4-8 77
Singles: 7-inch
ATLANTIC 3-5 71
CHI-SOUND 3-4 76-77
FUTURE STARS 3-5 74
STAR TOWN 3-5
U.A. 3-5 76

ALEXANDER, Max
Singles: 7-inch
CAPROCK (116 "Little Rome") 75-125 59

ALEXANDER, Mel
Singles: 7-inch
MOVIN' 4-8 62

ALEXANDER, Mike, & Visions
Singles: 7-inch
RICHIE (673 "Pop Goes Love") 20-30 67

ALEXANDER, Nick, & Coquettes
Singles: 7-inch
A-DORA 5-10
EMBEE 10-20 57

ALEXANDER, Norm
Singles: 7-inch
HONEE B (106 "Trusting You") 15-25 59

ALEXANDER, Ray
Singles: 7-inch
LU JUN 4-8

ALEXANDER, Reggie
Singles: 7-inch
LBJ 4-8

ALEXANDER, Texas, & Benton's Busy Bees
Singles: 78 rpm
FREEDOM (1538 "Bottoms Blues") 75-125 50

ALEXANDER, Van
Singles: 7-inch
CAPITOL 10-15

ALEXANDER, Willie
(With the Boom Boom Band)
Singles: 7-inch
MCA 3-5 78
EPs: 7-inch
BOMP 8-10 76
LPs: 10/12-inch
BOMP 5-10 81
MCA 5-10 78

ALEXANDER, Wilmer, Jr.
(With the Dukes)
Singles: 7-inch
APHRODISIAC 3-4 69
LPs: 10/12-inch
APHRODISIAC 5-10 69
Also see WILMER & DUKES

ALEXANDER, Wyvon *C&W '81*
Singles: 7-inch
GERVASI 3-4 81-84

ALEXANDER & GREATS
Singles: 7-inch
ARVEE (5064 "Swanee Stomp") 10-20 63
LIMELIGHT (3040 "Hot Dawg Mustang") 15-25 64

ALEXANDER & HAMILTONS
Singles: 7-inch
W.B. 5-10 66

ALEXANDER RABBIT
Singles: 7-inch
A&M 3-6 69
LPs: 10/12-inch
MERCURY 10-15 70

ALEXANDER'S DISCOTIME BAND
Singles: 7-inch
ARIOLA AMERICA 3-5 76

ALEXANDER'S ROCK TIME BAND
Singles: 7-inch
J&T (2022 "Number One Hippie on the Village Scene") 10-15

ALEXANDER'S TIMELESS BLOOZBAND
Singles: 7-inch
KAPP 5-10 69
MATAMAT 15-20 67
UNI 10-15 68
LPs: 10/12-inch
UNI (73021 "For Sale") 30-50 68
SMACK (1001 "Alexander's Timeless Bloozband") 150-250 67

ALEXANDRA, Sandra
Singles: 7-inch
UNI 4-6 69

ALEXIS
Singles: 7-inch
MCA 3-5 77
LPs: 10/12-inch
MCA 5-10 77
Members: Randy Reeder; Larry Braden; Dave Peters; Robbie Falberg; Eddie Ullibarri; Dave Walker.

ALEXYS
Singles: 7-inch
DOT 4-8 65

ALF
Singles
BURGER KING 3-5 88
(Cardboad, six-inch picture disc. Four different titles.)

ALFI & HARRY *P&R '56*
(David Seville)
Singles: 78 rpm
LIBERTY 4-8 55-57
Singles: 7-inch
LIBERTY 5-10 55-57
Also see SEVILLE, David

ALFIE: see SILAS, Alfie

ALFIE & EXPLOSIONS
Singles: 7-inch
PHIL-L.A. of SOUL 3-5 72

ALFONZO *R&B '82*
(Alfonzo Jones)
Singles: 12-inch
JOE-WES 4-6 83
Singles: 7-inch
JOE-WES 3-4 82
LARC 3-4 82
LPs: 10/12-inch
LARC 5-10 83

ALFORD, Annie
Singles: 78 rpm
GROOVE (0172 "It's Heavenly") 10-20 56
Singles: 7-inch
GROOVE (0172 "It's Heavenly") 35-45 56
VIK (0288 "Easy Baby") 20-30 57
Also see FORD, Ann

ALFORD, Jim
Singles: 7-inch
TAMARA 4-8 64

ALFRED, Chuz
Singles: 78 rpm
SAVOY 5-10 55
Singles: 7-inch
SAVOY (1158 "Buckeye Bounce") 15-25 55
SAVOY (1175 "Rock Along") 15-25 55

ALGEBRA MOTHERS
(A-MOMS)
Singles: 7-inch
AFTERTASTE 3-5 79

ALGERE, Ray
Singles: 7-inch
TOU-SEA (126 "In My Corner") 10-20

ALGERS
Singles: 7-inch
NORTHERN 8-12 60

ALHONA, Richie
Singles: 7-inch
FANTASY 5-10 62

ALI BABA & SULTANS
Singles: 7-inch
FICTION (778 "Open Sesame") 10-15

ALI, Muhammad, & Frank Sinatra
LPs: 10/12-inch
ST. JOHN'S (1 "Ali and His Gang Fight Tooth Decay") 20-40
(Promotional issue only.)
Also see CLAY, Cassius
Also see SINATRA, Frank

ALIAS *LP '90*
Singles: 7-inch
MERCURY 3-5 79-80
LPs: 10/12-inch
EMI 5-8 90
MERCURY 5-10 78

Members: Fred Curci; Steve DeMarchi; Dorman Cogburn; Jimmy Dougherty; Jo Jo Billingsley; Leon Wilkeson; Billy Powell; Barry Harwood; Ricky Powell; Artimus Pyle.
Also see COLLINS, Allen, Band
Also see LYNYRD SKYNYRD
Also see SHERIFF

ALIBI *C&W '87*
Singles: 7-inch
COMSTOCK.................................. 3-4 87-88
POLYDOR.................................. 3-5 80
LPs: 10/12-inch
POLYDOR.................................. 5-10 80

ALICE & Soul Sensations
Singles: 7-inch
PZAZZ.................................. 3-5 70

ALICE COOPER: see COOPER, Alice

ALICE IN CHAINS *LP '91*
LPs: 10/12-inch
COLUMBIA (2192 "Face Lift")........50-75 90
(Promotional issue only.)
COLUMBIA (46075 "Face Lift")....... 5-10 91
COLUMBIA (52475 "Face Lift")....... 5-10 92
COLUMBIA (57804 "Jar of Flies") 12-18 94
(Promotional issue only.)
COLUMBIA (67248 "Jar of Flies"/ "Sap")..............................10-15 94
(Two colored vinyl discs.)

ALICE JEAN & MONDELLOS
Singles: 7-inch
RHYTHM (102 "100 Years from Today")..............................200-400 57
Also see MONDELLOS

ALICE WONDER LAND *P&R '63*
Singles: 7-inch
BARDELL (774 "He's Mine")..........10-20 63
UNITED INTERNATIONAL..........10-15
Also see SWANS

ALICIA & ROCKAWAYS
Singles: 78 rpm
EPIC..................................10-15 56
Singles: 7-inch
EPIC (9191 "Why Can't I Be Loved")..............................20-25 56

ALIEN
LPs: 10/12-inch
ELEKTRA.................................. 5-10 79

ALIENS
Singles: 7-inch
SON of a WITCH (1801 "Season of the Witch")..............................10-20

ALIOTTA - HAYNES
Singles: 7-inch
AMPEX.................................. 3-5 70-71
LPs: 10/12-inch
AMPEX..................................12-15 70
Members: Ted Aliotta; Mitch Aliota; Skip Haynes.

ALIOTTA, HAYNES & JEREMIAH
Singles: 7-inch
ALIOTTA, HAYNES & JEREMIAH ("Lake Shore Drive")........................ 8-10 78
(Yellow label. Shows only title, artist and A/B sides.)
SNOW QUEEN (1000 "Snow Queen"/ "Lake Shore Drive")..................15-20 73
LPs: 10/12-inch
AMPEX..................................10-20 71
BIG FOOT..................................20-25 78
LITTLE FOOT.............................. 8-10 77
Members: Ted Aliotta; Mitch Aliota; Skip Haynes; John Jeremiah.
Also see ALIOTTA-HAYNES
Also see ROTARY CONNECTION

ALISHA *R&B/D&D '84*
Singles: 12-inch
VANGUARD.................................. 4-6 84-86
Singles: 7-inch
MCA.................................. 3-4 90
RCA.................................. 3-4 87
VANGUARD.................................. 3-4 84-86
Picture Sleeves
RCA.................................. 3-4 87
LPs: 10/12-inch
MCA.................................. 5-8 90

ALIVE 'N KICKING *P&R/LP '70*
(Alive 'N Kickin')
Singles: 7-inch
A&M.................................. 3-4
ROULETTE.................................. 4-8 70-71
Picture Sleeves
A&M.................................. 3-4
LPs: 10/12-inch
ROULETTE (42052 "Alive 'N Kickin' ")..............................20-30 70
(Commercial issue.)
ROULETTE (42052 "Alive 'N Kickin' ")..............................40-60 70
(Promotional issue.)

ALKAHOLICS
LPs: 10/12-inch
RCA.................................. 8-10

ALL DYRECTIONS
Singles: 7-inch
BUDDAH.................................. 3-5 73

ALL HEART
Singles: 7-inch
REVOLUTION (6939 "And We Love You")..............................10-20 69

ALL NIGHT WORKERS
Singles: 7-inch
CAMEO..................................5-10 66
MERCURY (72833 "Collector")......15-25 68
ROUND SOUND..............................8-12

ALL NIGHTERS: see ALL-NITERS

ALL OF THE ABOVE
Singles: 7-inch
PARAMOUNT.................................. 3-5 73

ALL POINTS BULLETIN BAND *R&B '76*
Singles: 7-inch
LITTLE CITY.................................. 3-5 75-79

ALL ROOTUS BAND
Singles: 7-inch
RED MARK.................................. 3-5 77

ALL 6
Singles: 7-inch
MTA.................................. 5-8 67

ALL SPORTS BAND *P&R '81*
Singles: 7-inch
RADIO.................................. 3-4 81-82
LPs: 10/12-inch
RADIO..................................5-10 81

ALL STARS
Singles: 7-inch
VON (704 "2-2-5 Special")............40-60 60s

ALL STARS
LPs: 10/12-inch
GRAMOPHONE (20192 "Boogie Woogie")..............................40-50

ALL STARS, Los: see LOS ALL STARS

ALL THE MARBLES
Singles: 7-inch
OLIVER..................................6-12 66

ALL THE PEOPLE
Singles: 7-inch
BLUE CANDLE.................................. 4-6 73

ALLADINS
Singles: 7-inch
PRISM (6001 "Then").............1000-2000 60

ALLAN, Al
Singles: 7-inch
CARLTON..................................5-10 59

ALLAN, Bobby
Singles: 7-inch
ARD (11 "The Only One")............10-20
CHALLENGE (9193 "The Only One")..............................10-15 63

ALLAN, Chad
(With the Expressions)
Singles: 7-inch
MALA.................................. 4-6 70
REPRISE.................................. 3-5 71
LPs: 10/12-inch
SCEPTER..................................20-30 66
Also see ALLEN, Chad
Also see BRAVE BELT
Also see CHADONS
Also see GUESS WHO

ALLAN, Chip
Singles: 7-inch
CORSICAN (651 "Take the Freeway")..............................10-20

ALLAN, Davie *P&R '65*
(With the Arrows)
Singles: 7-inch
A.O.A.................................. 3-6 76
CUDE (101 "War Path")................30-40 63
MARC (3223 "War Path")................20-30 63
MGM.................................. 3-6 71-73
MRC.................................. 3-5 84
PRIVATE STOCK.................................. 3-5 74
SIDEWALK..................................10-15 64
TOWER..................................5-10 65-68
WHAT.................................. 3-5 82
LPs: 10/12-inch
ALKOR..................................5-10 84
ARROW DYNAMICS..................8-12 85
DIONYSUS..................................5-10
TOWER..................................25-40 65-68
WHAT..................................5-10 83
Members: Davie Allan; Steve Pugh; Larry Brown; Paul Johnson; Don Manning; Tony Allwine.
Also see ALBANO, Frankie
Also see ANNETTE
Also see BAND WITHOUT a NAME
Also see BROOKINS, Doug
Also see CURB, Mike
Also see DALE, Dick
Also see DEAN, Tony
Also see FASTEST GROUP ALIVE
Also see FORD, Peter
Also see FROST, Max, & Troopers
Also see GRADS
Also see GREEN BEANS
Also see HANDS of TIME
Also see HATCHER, Harley
Also see HEYBURNERS
Also see HONDELLS
Also see JA DETTS
Also see JOHNSON, Paul
Also see KEN & CAROL
Also see MOORE & MOORE
Also see NAYLOR, Jerry
Also see PARIS SISTERS
Also see PEWTER, Jim
Also see PRISCILLA
Also see RONSTADT, Linda
Also see SHARLETS
Also see SINNERS
Also see SOUNDS of HARLEY
Also see STAFFORD, Terry
Also see STARLETS
Also see STREAMERS
Also see 13TH COMMITTEE
Also see TONY & VIZITORS
Also see VIOT, Russ
Also see VISITORS
Also see ZANIES

ALLAN, Davie / Eternity's Children / Main Attraction / Sunrays
EPs: 7-inch
TOWER (4557 "Selections from April Albums")..............................25-50 68
(Promotional issue only.)
Also see ALLAN, Davie
Also see ETERNITY'S CHILDREN
Also see MAIN ATTRACTION
Also see SUNRAYS

ALLAN, Howie
Singles: 7-inch
LUCK..................................5-8

ALLAN, Johnnie
(Johnnie Allen)
Singles: 7-inch
JIN..................................5-8 63
MGM..................................5-10 59
PIC..................................5-8 64
VIKING..................................5-8 62-63
LPs: 10/12-inch
JIN..................................10-15

ALLAN, Johnny
Singles: 7-inch
MGM..................................8-12 60
MERCURY..................................8-12 60
VIKING (1016 Unfaithful One")......10-15 62

ALLAN, Kent
Singles: 7-inch
ALON (9008 "What Have I Done") 10-20 63

ALLAN, Kirby
Singles: 7-inch
MAZE (140 "Mother Don't Allow Rock & Roll")..............................75-125 50s
(Black vinyl.)
MAZE (140 "Mother Don't Allow Rock & Roll")..............................5-10
(Colored vinyl.)
MAZE (1002 "Don't You Remember")..............................10-20

ALLAN, Scott
Singles: 7-inch
DASH..................................3-5 80

ALLAN & FLAMES
Singles: 7-inch
CAMPBELL (225 "Till the End of Time")..............................25-50 60
COLONIAL (7006 "Till the End of Time")..............................50-75 59

ALLANSON, Susie *C&W '77*
Singles: 7-inch
OAK..................................4-6 77
ELEKTRA/CURB..................................3-5 79
LIBERTY..................................3-4 80-82
TNP..................................3-4 86-87
U.A...................................3-4 80
W.B./CURB..................................3-5 77-78
LPs: 10/12-inch
ABC..................................5-10 79
ELEKTRA/CURB..................................5-8 79
U.A...................................5-8 80
W.B./CURB..................................5-10 78

ALLBERT, Tommy
Singles: 7-inch
JED (0005 "Bless Her Heart")........10-15

ALLEGRO, Joe
Singles: 7-inch
CHAM (001 "Teen-age Clementine")..............................8-12
END (1013 "Web of Dreams")........10-20 58

ALLEN, Adrienne
Singles: 7-inch
RUST (5058 "Dancing with Tears in My Eyes")..............................8-12 63
U.A...................................5-10 64
YALE (240 "When Love Comes Knocking")..............................75-125 60
Also see FIVE DISCS

ALLEN, Al, & Drags
Singles: 7-inch
CARLTON (511 "Egghead")..........15-25 59
RADIANT (1506 "The Drag")..........15-25 62

ALLEN, Annisteen *R&B '53*
(With Her Home Town Boys)
Singles: 78 rpm
CAPITOL..................................10-15 55
DECCA..................................10-15 56-57
FEDERAL..................................10-15 51-52
KING..................................10-15 46-54
Singles: 7-inch
CAPITOL..................................20-30 55
DECCA..................................15-25 56-57
KING..................................20-30 53-54
TODD..................................10-20
TRUE SOUND..................................5-10
WIG..................................5-10 59
Also see ALLEN, Ernestine
Also see GREER, John

ALLEN, Annisteen, & Melvin Moore
Singles: 7-inch
TODD..................................5-10 59
Also see ALLEN, Annisteen

ALLEN, Barbara
Singles: 7-inch
DECCA..................................10-20 58
FELSTED (8583 "Say the Magic Words")..............................10-20 59

ALLEN, Barbara
Singles: 7-inch
SPECIAL AGENT..................................5-8 66
Also see ACKLIN, Barbara

ALLEN, Barbara, & Beverly Taylor
Singles: 7-inch
AMERICAN ARTISTS..................................4-6 68
Also see ALLEN, Barbara

ALLEN, Barry
Singles: 7-inch
DOT..................................4-8 66
Also see DAKUS, Wes

ALLEN, Beau
Singles: 7-inch
HFA (1016 "Give Me Your Love")..15-25 65
EPs: 7-inch
HFA..................................25-35
Also see ALLEN, Bo

ALLEN, Bernie
Singles: 7-inch
CHECKER (862 "You Can Run, But You Can't Hide")..............................15-25 57

ALLEN, Bill
Singles: 7-inch
MAGNOLIA..................................3-5 81

ALLEN, Bill, Trio
Singles: 7-inch
VEE JAY (542 "Money")................10-20 63

ALLEN, Billy
(With the Keynotes; with Back Beats; Bill Allen)
Singles: 7-inch
ELDORADO (505 "Butterfly")..........15-20 57
IMPERIAL (5500 "Please Give Me Something")..............................75-100 58

ALLEN, Billy, & Nomads
Singles: 7-inch
SOMA..................................8-12 60s

ALLEN, Blinky
(Blinky Allen Orchestra)
Singles: 78 rpm
FLAIR..................................10-20 54
SWING TIME..................................15-25 53
Singles: 7-inch
FLAIR..................................20-30 54
PERSONALITY..................................10-15 61
SWING TIME..................................25-35 53

ALLEN, Bo
(Beau Allen)
Singles: 7-inch
ALLEN (1008 "Dreamin' ")..............10-15 68
Also see ALLEN, Beau

ALLEN, Bob
Singles: 7-inch
CLASS (250 "Oh Lonely Night").......5-10 59
DIAMOND (197 "I'm Alone Again")..8-12 66
SOMA..................................5-10 60s

ALLEN, Bobbi
Singles: 7-inch
20TH FOX..................................4-8 65

ALLEN, Bobby
Singles: 7-inch
DOT..................................4-8 68

ALLEN, Bobby, & GPs
Singles: 7-inch
UPPP (101 "Here She Comes Again")..............................10-15

ALLEN, Chad
(With the Reflections)
Singles: 7-inch
CANADIAN AMERICAN (802 "Tribute to Buddy Holly")..............................25-50 64
LAMA (7779 "Little Lonely")............15-20 61
QUALITY..................................15-25 60s
(Canadian.)
RADIANT (1508 "Come on Linda")..8-12 62
SMASH (1720 "Little Lonely").........10-15 61
Also see ALLAN, Chad
Also see ASHLEY, Bob

ALLEN, Charles
Singles: 7-inch
DASH (5017 "God Bless Our Love")..............................10-20 60s

ALLEN, Charlie
Singles: 7-inch
PORTRAIT (107 "Sweetie Pie").......8-12 62

ALLEN, Charlie
Singles: 7-inch
DUNHILL..................................3-5 73
LPs: 10/12-inch
DUNHILL..................................8-12 73
Also see PACIFIC GAS & ELECTRIC

ALLEN, Chip, & Pictures
Singles: 7-inch
ASTRO (117 "Let the Good Times Roll")..............................10-20 67

ALLEN, Chris
Singles: 7-inch
HOLLYWOOD (1098 "Thank You, Mr. Moon")..............................10-15 59

ALLEN, Chris & Peter
Singles: 7-inch
ABC..................................4-8 66
ABC-PAR..................................5-10 66
MERCURY..................................4-8 68
LPs: 10/12-inch
MERCURY..................................10-20 68
Also see ALLEN, Peter

ALLEN, Christy
Singles: 7-inch
DIAMOND (187 "Little Circus Clown")..............................8-12 65
DIAMOND (194 "Heart, Don't Let Him Know")..............................8-12 65
DIAMOND (209 "Any Moment").......8-12 66
POLYDOR..................................3-5 80

ALLEN, Connee
(With Leon Washington's Orchestra)
Singles: 78 rpm
THERON..................................15-25 55
Singles: 7-inch
THERON (114 "I Haven't Got the Heart")..............................50-75 55
THERON (115 "Saving My Love")..50-75 55
Also see RHODES, Todd

ALLEN, Dale, & Rebel Rousers
Singles: 7-inch
VAMPIRE (10762 "Hideaway")......60-80 62
Also see TITANS

ALLEN, Danny
Singles: 7-inch
VALLEY..................................15-25 58

ALLEN, Dave "The Man"
Singles: 7-inch
TIFFANY..................................3-5 71
LPs: 10/12-inch
INT'L ARTISTS (11 "Color Blind")..............................60-75 69
(Green label.)
INT'L ARTISTS (11 "Color Blind")..............................75-100 69
(White label. Promotional issue only.)
INT'L ARTISTS (11 "Color Blind")..............................15-25
(Reissue. Green label. With "RE2" etched in the vinyl trail-off.)

ALLEN, Dayton *LP '60*
LPs: 10/12-inch
GRAND AWARD..................................10-15 60

ALLEN, Dean
Singles: 7-inch
ARGO..................................8-12 57

ALLEN, Deborah *C&W '79*
Singles: 7-inch
CAPITOL..................................3-5 80-82
GIANT..................................3-4 92-93
RCA..................................3-4 80-84
WEA..................................3-4 90s
Picture Sleeves
RCA..................................3-4 83
LPs: 10/12-inch
CAPITOL..................................5-10 80
RCA..................................5-8 84
Also see MANDRELL, Barbara
Also see REEVES, Jim, & Deborah Allen

ALLEN, Dee
Singles: 7-inch
VITA..................................8-12 59

ALLEN, Dick, & Fairlanes
Singles: 7-inch
CUCA (63114 "Dreamin' ")..............15-25 63
Also see NIGHT OWLS

ALLEN, Dickie
Singles: 7-inch
IMPERIAL (5701 "Sally Ann")........25-35 60

ALLEN, Donna *R&B '86*
Singles: 7-inch
OCEANA..................................3-4 88
TWENTY-ONE..................................3-4 86-87
Picture Sleeves
OCEANA..................................3-4 88
LPs: 10/12-inch
OCEANA..................................5-8 88
TWENTY-ONE..................................5-10 86-87

ALLEN, Doris
Singles: 7-inch
MINARET (149 "Shell of a Woman")..............................5-8 70
SSS INT'L..................................4-6 71
Also see HAMILTON, Big John, & Doris Allen

ALLEN, Duane
Singles: 7-inch
KEYNOTE (25 "Surf Around the World")..............................15-25 63

ALLEN, Ernestine
(Annisteen Allen)
Singles: 7-inch
TRU-SOUND (405 "Let It Roll")......10-15 62
LPs: 10/12-inch
TRU-SOUND (15004 "Let It Roll") 25-50 62
Also see ALLEN, Annisteen

ALLEN, Eddy
Singles: 7-inch
AGE (29119 "All About My Baby")..10-15 63

ALLEN, Frankie
Singles: 7-inch
ADONIS (104 "If You Make a Wish")..............................10-20 60

ALLEN, Freddie
Singles: 7-inch
WHITE WHALE ... 3-5 70

ALLEN, George
(George Smith)
Singles: 7-inch
SOTOPLAY (0010 "Tight Dress") ... 10-15 62
SOTOPLAY (0031 "I Must Be Crazy") ... 10-20 62
Also see HARMONICA KING
Also see LITTLE WALTER, JR.
Also see SMITH, George

ALLEN, Harold
Singles: 7-inch
MAR-VEL (1201 "If You Were Mine Again") ... 40-60 57

ALLEN, Jackie
Singles: 7-inch
FELSTED (8678 "I Still Love You") ... 10-15 63

ALLEN, Jason, & Gigolos: see JALOPY FIVE

ALLEN, Jeanie
(With the Beavers)
Singles: 7-inch
ARLISS (1001 "I'm Your Slave") ... 10-20 61
MALA (403 "Nobody to Love Me") .. 10-20 59

ALLEN, Jeffrey
Singles: 7-inch
SOUND STAGE 7 ... 4-8 63

ALLEN, Jesse
Singles: 78 rpm
ALADDIN ... 25-50 52
BAYOU ... 10-20 53
CORAL ... 25-50 51
IMPERIAL ... 25-50 53-55
Singles: 7-inch
ALADDIN (3129 "Rock This Morning") ... 75-150 52
BAYOU (011 "Dragnet") ... 50-75 53
CORAL (65078 "My Suffering") ... 75-150 51
IMPERIAL (5256 "Gotta Call That Number") ... 75-150 53
IMPERIAL (5285 "Sittin' and Wonderin' ") ... 100-200 54
IMPERIAL (5305 "Things I'm Gonna Do") ... 75-150 53
IMPERIAL (5315 "Rockin' & Rollin' ") ... 75-150 55
VIN (1002 "Goodbye Blues") ... 25-50 58

ALLEN, Jim
Singles: 7-inch
TOWER ... 4-8 60s

ALLEN, Jimmy
(With the Two Jays; Jimmie Allen)
Singles: 78 rpm
MGM ... 10-5 52
Singles: 7-inch
AL-BRITE (1200 "My Girl Is a Pearl") ... 75-100 59
CINCH ... 8-10 64
KOOL (1008 "These Lonely Blues") ... 10-15 60
MGM ... 20-30 52

ALLEN, Jimmy, & Tommy Bartella
Singles: 7-inch
AL-BRITE (1300 "When Santa Comes Over the Brooklyn Bridge") ... 15-25 59
Also see ALLEN, Jimmy

ALLEN, Joe C&W '75
Singles: 7-inch
W.B. ... 3-5 75

ALLEN, Joe, & His Alley Cats
Singles: 7-inch
JALO (201 "Baby, Baby Baby") ... 20-40 58
JALO (202 "I Want to Thrill You") .. 20-40 58

ALLEN, Johnnie: see ALLAN, Johnny

ALLEN, Jonelle R&B '78
Singles: 7-inch
ALEXANDER STREET ... 3-4 78

ALLEN, Judy
Singles: 7-inch
LAURIE (3025 "Sentimental Me") .. 15-25 59

ALLEN, Judy C&W '78
Singles: 7-inch
POLYDOR ... 3-5 78
LPs: 10/12-inch
STOP ... 5-10 70s

ALLEN, Kent
Singles: 7-inch
ALON ... 4-8

ALLEN, Lainey
Singles: 7-inch
J.W.J. Ent. (22918 "The Road to Love") ... 10-20 60s

ALLEN, Lee P&R '58
Singles: 78 rpm
ALADDIN ... 10-20 56
EMBER ... 20-40 58
Singles: 7-inch
ALADDIN ... 15-25 56
COLLECTABLES ... 3-4 82
EMBER ... 10-20 58-62
WAND ... 5-10 60s
EPs: 7-inch
EMBER (103 "Walkin' with Mr. Lee") ... 50-75 58
LPs: 10/12-inch
EMBER (200 "Walkin' with Mr. Lee") ... 75-125 58
(Red label.)
EMBER (200 "Walkin' with Mr Lee") ... 60-80 58
("Logs" label. Ember logo is formed with logs.)
EMBER (200 "Walkin' with Mr. Lee") ... 25-40 60
(Black label.)
Also see BIRDSONG, Larry
Also see DOMINO, Fats
Also see BLASTERS
Also see LITTLE RICHARD
Also see NEWSOM, Chubby, & Her Hip Shakers
Also see SMITH, Huey
Also see STRAY CATS

ALLEN, Levinsky
Singles: 7-inch
VITAL (321 "Layed Off") ... 200-300 60

ALLEN, Little Johnny
Singles: 78 rpm
BULLSEYE ... 10-20 56
Singles: 7-inch
BULLSEYE (105 "She's the Girl for Me") ... 20-30 56

ALLEN, Little Marie
Singles: 7-inch
TRIUMPH ... 10-20 59
Also see WARNER, Sonny, & Marie Allen

ALLEN, Lloyd
Singles: 12-inch
EPIC ... 4-6 84
Singles: 7-inch
EPIC ... 3-4 84

ALLEN, Lonnie
Singles: 7-inch
VAL-HILL ... 15-25

ALLEN, Marc
Singles: 7-inch
PRIVATE STOCK ... 3-5 77

ALLEN, Marc, III
Singles: 7-inch
GALLERY ... 3-5 70

ALLEN, Maria
Singles: 7-inch
EXCELLO (2233 "He's Gone") ... 10-15 63

ALLEN, Melody C&W '75
Singles: 7-inch
MERCURY ... 3-5 75

ALLEN, Michael
Singles: 7-inch
ELEKTRA ... 3-5 76
LION ... 3-5 72
LONDON ... 4-6 69
MGM ... 4-8 65-70
MERCURY ... 8-12 62
SLIPPED DISC ... 3-5 77
VERVE ... 3-5 73
LPs: 10/12-inch
CAPITOL ... 10-20 66
LONDON ... 10-15 69
MGM ... 8-12 70

ALLEN, Mike
Singles: 7-inch
MAR-RAY (7001 "Love Is Just a Game") ... 10-20

ALLEN, Mills
Singles: 7-inch
BLACK GOLD (303 "This Is It") ... 15-25 62
BLACK GOLD (304 "This Is It") ... 10-20 62
(Alternate track reissue.)

ALLEN, Milton
(With the Goldens & Paradons)
Singles: 78 rpm
RCA (6994 "Love a, Love a Lover") ... 15-25 57
ROBIN (61824 "My Song") ... 25-50 56
Singles: 7-inch
RCA (6994 "Love a, Love a Lover") ... 15-25 57
RCA (7116 "Don't Bug Me Baby") .. 50-75 58
ROBIN (61824 "My Song") ... 200-300 56

ALLEN, Mimi
(With the Miles Grayson Orchestra)
Singles: 7-inch
THREE SPEED (711 "Do You Miss Me") ... 15-25 61

ALLEN, Na
Singles: 7-inch
ATCO (6753 "Thanks for Nothing") ... 10-15 70
PEDESTAL (120 "Hard to Be Without You") ... 10-15
RONN (47 "Everytime It Rains") ... 10-15

ALLEN, Nancy
Singles: 7-inch
SIANA (715 "Let's Tell Them Tonight") ... 8-12

ALLEN, Pete
Singles: 7-inch
GLORY (300 "Sweet of You") ... 10-20 59

ALLEN, Peter LP '79
Singles: 12-inch
A&M ... 4-8 79
Singles: 7-inch
A&M ... 3-5 74-82
ARISTA ... 3-4 83-84
METROMEDIA ... 3-5 71-73
LPs: 10/12-inch
A&M ... 5-10 74-82
ARISTA ... 5-10 83-84
METROMEDIA ... 10-15 71-72
Also see ALLEN, Chris & Peter

ALLEN, R. Justice R&B '86
Singles: 7-inch
CATAWBA ... 3-4 86

ALLEN, Rance, Group R&B '73
Singles: 7-inch
CAPITOL ... 3-5 77-79
GOSPEL TRUTH ... 3-5 72-73
STAX ... 3-4 78-81
TRUTH ... 3-5 74-75
LPs: 10/12-inch
CAPITOL ... 5-10 77-79
GOSPEL TRUTH ... 8-12 72-74
MYRRH ... 5-10 84
STAX ... 5-10 78-81
TRUTH ... 8-10 75
Members: Rance Allen; Thomas Allen; Steven Allen; Esau Allen; Linda Mendez; Annie Mendez; Judy Mendez.

ALLEN, Ray
(With the Upbeats; with Vinny Catalano & Orchestra)
Singles: 7-inch
BLAST (204 "Peggy Sue") ... 20-30 62
DCP ... 5-10 64
MALA ... 5-10 66
SINCLAIR (1004 "Let Them Talk") ... 25-50 61
LPs: 10/12-inch
BLAST (6804 "A Tribute to Six") ... 50-75 62

ALLEN, Ray
Singles: 7-inch
PARAMOUNT ... 3-5 73
LPs: 10/12-inch
PARAMOUNT ... 8-12 73

ALLEN, Ray, & Carnations
Singles: 7-inch
ACE (130 "A Fool in Love") ... 10-15 59
Also see CARNATIONS

ALLEN, Ray, & Trendells
Singles: 7-inch
CUCA (6544 "Look at Me") ... 15-25 65
CUCA (6562 "Shake a Tail Feather") ... 15-25 65
CUCA (63104 "Who's Gonna Cry") ... 15-25 63
Members: Ray Allen Harbach; Danny Riccio; Larry Rongsvoog; Dick Simon; John Verbraken; Ted Riccio; Duane Gauger; Damon Lee.

ALLEN, Rex C&W '49
(With the Arizona Wranglers & Jerry Byrd)
Singles: 78 rpm
DECCA (Except 30651) ... 5-10 52-57
DECCA (30651 "Knock Knock, Rattle") ... 10-20 56
MERCURY ... 5-10 49-55
Singles: 7-inch
BUENA VISTA ... 4-8 59
DECCA (Except 28000 thru 30000 series) ... 3-8 56-72
DECCA (28000 & 29000 series) ... 5-10 52-56
DECCA (30000 series except 30651) ... 5-10 56
DECCA (30651 "Knock Knock, Rattle") ... 15-20 56
JMI ... 3-5 73
MCA ... 3-5 79
MERCURY ... 5-10 53-62
WILDCAT ... 4-6
Picture Sleeves
MERCURY ... 5-10 63
EPs: 7-inch
DECCA ... 10-20 56
MERCURY ... 10-20 53-56
LPs: 10/12-inch
BUENA VISTA (3307 "Rex Allen Sings 16 Favorites") ... 40-50 61
COLLECTOR'S CLASSICS ... 5-10
CORAL ... 5-10 73
DECCA (5000 series) ... 10-15 68-70
(Decca LP numbers in this series preceded by a "7" or a "DL-7" are stereo issues.)
DECCA (8000 series) ... 20-30 56-58
DESIGN ... 10-15 62
DISNEYLAND ... 6-10 70
HACIENDA (101 "Country Songs I Love") ... 50-60
JMI (4003 "Rex Allen Sings") ... 20-30
MCA ... 5-10
MERCURY (20719 "The Faith of a Man") ... 15-25 62
(Monaural.)
MERCURY (20752 "Rex Allen Sings and Tells Tales") ... 15-25 62
(Monaural.)
MERCURY (60719 "The Faith of a Man") ... 20-30 62
(Stereo.)
MERCURY (60752 "Rex Allen Sings and Tells Tales") ... 20-30 62
(Stereo.)
PICKWICK/HILLTOP ... 10-15 65
VOCALION ... 6-10 70
WING ... 10-15 64-66
Session: Jud Conlon Singers.
Also see CURTIS, Ken / Rex Allen & Arizona Wranglers
Also see PAGE, Patti, & Rex Allen

ALLEN, Rex, Jr. C&W '73
(With Arizona)
Singles: 7-inch
MOON SHINE ... 3-4 83-85
TNP ... 3-4 87
W.B. ... 3-5 73-82
LPs: 10/12-inch
ACCORD ... 5-8 84
OUT OF TOWN ... 5-8 80s
W.B. ... 3-5 74-81
SSS ... 5-10
Session: Rex Allen.

ALLEN, Rex, Jr., & Margo Smith C&W '81
Singles: 7-inch
W.B. ... 3-4 81
Also see SMITH, Margo

ALLEN, Rex, Jr., & Sons of the Pioneers C&W '76
Singles: 7-inch
W.B. ... 3-5 76
Session: Rex Allen.
Also see ALLEN, Rex
Also see SONS of the PIONEERS

ALLEN, Rich, & Ebonistics
Singles: 7-inch
GROOVEY GROOVES (160 "Echo's [sic] of November") ... 20-30 68

ALLEN, Richie P&R '60
(With the Pacific Surfers)
Singles: 7-inch
ERA ... 8-12 61
IMPERIAL ... 10-20 60-63
TOWER ... 5-10 66
LPs: 10/12-inch
IMPERIAL ... 40-60 63
Members: Richie Allen; Ron Lloyd; Jim MacMurdo; Bill Cooper; Ray Pohlman; Sandy Nelson; Les Weiser. Session: Richie Podolor.
Also see NELSON, Sandy
Also see PODOLOR, Dickie

ALLEN, Rick, & Honeytones
Singles: 7-inch
KAY BEE ... 8-12 60s

ALLEN, Ricky R&B '63
Singles: 7-inch
AGE (29104 "For You") ... 15-25 61
AGE (29105 "For You") ... 10-20 62
AGE (29118 "Cut You A-Loose") .. 10-15 63
AGE (29122 "Eighty Hour Week") .. 10-20 63
AGE (29125 "The Big Fight") ... 10-20 64
APOGEE (103 "It's Love Baby") ... 8-10 64
BRIGHT STAR (147 "What Do You Do") ... 5-10 66
BRIGHT STAR (150 "It's a Mess I Tell You") ... 5-10 67
BRIGHT STAR (1038 "I'm Such a Lonely Man") ... 4-8 69
FOUR BROTHERS (401 "I Can't Stand No Signifying") ... 10-15 65
FOUR BROTHERS (402 "Keep It to Yourself") ... 8-12 65
(Retitled reissue of "*I Can't Stand No Signifying.*")
MEL-LON (1004 "Help Me Mama") 10-15 60s
TAM-BOO (6720 "Cut You Loose") ... 5-8 68
U.S.A. (779 "Going or Coming"") ... 8-10 65
U.S.A. (858 "It Ain't Never") ... 8-10 65
Session: Elites.

ALLEN, Robert
Singles: 7-inch
GREGAR ... 3-5 70

ALLEN, Rockin' Dave
(With Thunderbirds)
Singles: 7-inch
JIN (130 "My Broken Heart") ... 6-12 60

ALLEN, Ronnie
Singles: 7-inch
SAN (208 "Juvenille Delinquent") ... 40-60 59
SAN (209 "High School Love") ... 40-60 59
SAN (300 "Gonna Get My Baby') ... 40-60 59

ALLEN, Rosalie C&W '46
(With the Black River Riders; with Sons of the Purple Sage; with Tex Fletcher)
Singles: 78 rpm
BLUEBIRD ... 5-10 49-50
GRAND AWARD ... 12-25 56-57
RCA ... 5-10 46-50
LPs: 10/12-inch
GRAND AWARD (330 "Songsof the Golden West") ... 30-40 56
GRAND AWARD (350 "Rodeo") ... 25-35 57
WALDORF (150 "C&W Hits") ... 25-45 56
Also see BRITT, Elton, Rosalie Allen & Skytoppers
Also see THREE SUNS, Rosalie Allen & Elton Britt

ALLEN, Steve P&R/LP '55
Singles: 78 rpm
BRUNSWICK ... 4-8 53
CORAL ... 4-8 55-56
Singles: 7-inch
BRUNSWICK ... 5-10 53
CORAL ... 5-10 55-56
DOT ... 4-8 59-66
DUNHILL (Except 4097) ... 3-5 67-68
DUNHILL (4097 "Here Comes Sgt. Pepper") ... 4-8 67
SIGNATURE ... 3-6 59-60
Picture Sleeves
DOT ... 5-10 65
EPs: 7-inch
BRUNSWICK ... 10-20 53
COLUMBIA ... 10-15 50s
CORAL ... 10-20 55-56
DECCA ... 15-20 55
WOODBURY'S ... 10-20
LPs: 10/12-inch
COLUMBIA (2554 "Steve Allen") ... 20-30 56
(10-inch LP.)
CORAL (100 "Jazz Story") ... 25-35 59
(Narration by Steve Allen, music by various artists.)
CORAL (57000 series, except 57099) ... 15-20 55-56
CORAL (57099 "The James Dean Story") ... 35-50 56
(With Bill Randle.)
CORAL (57400 series) ... 10-20 63
(Monaural.)
CORAL (7-57400 series) ... 10-20 63
(Stereo.)
DECCA ... 20-25 55
DOT (Except 3472 & 3517) ... 10-20 59-66
DOT (3472 "Steve Allen's Funny Fone Calls") ... 15-20 63
DOT (3517 "More Funny Fone Calls) ... 15-20 63
DUNHILL ... 8-10 67
EMARCY ... 15-20 58
HAMILTON ... 10-15 59-64
MERCURY ... 10-15 61
PETE ... 5-10 69
ROULETTE ... 15-20 59
SIGNATURE (Except 1004) ... 15-20 59
SIGNATURE (1004 "Man on the Street") ... 30-40 59
(With Louis Nye, Tom Poston and Don Knotts.)
Also see FOSTER, Phil
Also see KEROUAC, Jack, & Steve Allen
Also see NYE, Louis
Also see PRESLEY, Elvis

ALLEN, Steve, & Jayne Meadows
Singles: 78 rpm
CORAL ... 4-8 55
Singles: 7-inch
CORAL ... 5-10 55
Also see ALLEN, Steve
Also see MEADOWS, Jayne, & Audrey

ALLEN, Stu
Singles: 7-inch
ROWAX (803 "Jordan Blooper") ... 8-12 63

ALLEN, Sue
Singles: 7-inch
GROOVE (0037 "I Dedicate My Heart") ... 20-40 54
GROOVE (0130 "Think of Tomorrow") ... 20-40 55
WORLD WIDE (8002 "Dance, Dance, Dance") ... 10-15 60
Session: Four Students.
Also see BLACK, Oscar, & Sue Allen
Also see FOUR STUDENTS

ALLEN, Teri
Singles: 7-inch
ABC-PAR (10448 "Poor Little Puppy") ... 10-15 63
CANADIAN AMERICAN (149 "Poor Little Puppy") ... 10-15 63

ALLEN, Tina
Singles: 7-inch
GRANITE ... 3-5 76
TARA ... 5-10 76

ALLEN, Tom, & Saints
Singles: 7-inch
BAND BOX (249 "Lonely One") ... 10-15 62

ALLEN, Tony
(With the Chimes; with Champs; with Twilighters; with Wanderers; with Wonders; with Night Owls; with Arthur Wright Combo; Tony & Barbara)
Singles: 78 rpm
DIG (104 "It Hurts Me So") ... 15-25 56
(Reissue of Ultra 104.)
DIG (109 "I Found an Angel") ... 20-30 56
EBB (115 "Come Back") ... 10-20 57
SPECIALTY (560 "Nite Owl") ... 15-20 55
SPECIALTY (570 "Especially") ... 10-15 56
ULTRA (104 "It Hurts Me So") ... 10-15 56
Singles: 7-inch
BETHLEHEM (3002 "Just Like Before") ... 8-12 61
BETHLEHEM (3004 "It Hurts Me So") ... 8-12 61
BIG TIME (157 "Tell Me") ... 100-200 58
CLASSIC ARTISTS (102 "The Back Door") ... 4-6 89
DIG (104 "It Hurts Me So") ... 20-30 56
DIG (109 "I Found an Angel") ... 50-75 56
DOT ... 10-20 58
EBB (115 "Come Back") ... 15-25 57
IMPERIAL (5523 "Call My Name") 15-25 58
JAMIE (1119 "Looking for My Baby") ... 10-20 59
JAMIE (1143 "Train of Love") ... 10-20 59
KENT (364 "Dreamin' ") ... 10-15 61
ORIGINAL SOUND (13 "Little Lonely Girl") ... 10-15 60
SPECIALTY (560 "Nite Owl") ... 30-50 55
SPECIALTY (570 "Especially") ... 30-40 56
TAMPA (157 "Be My Love") ... 20-30 58
ULTRA (104 "It Hurts Me So") ... 15-25 56
(First issue.)
U.A. (50190 "Now Is Forever") ... 5-10 67
LPs: 10/12-inch
CROWN (5231 "Rock 'n Roll") ... 50-100 60
Also see CHIMES
Also see JAGUARS
Also see OTIS, Johnny
Also see SHIELDS
Also see STARR, Bobby
Also see TWILIGHTERS
Also see WONDERS

ALLEN, Vee R&B '73
Singles: 7-inch
LION ... 3-5 73
MCA ... 3-4 83
LPs: 10/12-inch
MCA ... 5-10 83

ALLEN, Ward
Singles: 7-inch
D ... 8-12 60

ALLEN, Woody LP '64
Singles: 7-inch
U.A. ... 3-5 72
Picture Sleeves
U.A. ... 4-6 72
LPs: 10/12-inch
BELL ... 10-15 67
CAPITOL ... 8-12 68
CASABLANCA ... 8-12 79
COLPIX ... 20-30 64-65
U.A. (800 series) ... 6-10 77
U.A. (9900 series) ... 8-12 72

ALLEN & ALLEN
Singles: 7-inch
MINIT ... 8-12 60

ALLEN & LADS
Singles: 7-inch
BEAVER ... 4-6 60s

ALLEN BROTHERS
Singles: 7-inch
COLPIX ... 5-10 60

ALLEN TRIO / Five Dips
Singles: 7-inch
ORIGINAL (1005 "That's What I Like") ... 250-300 55

ALLENS
Singles: 7-inch
MERCURY ... 3-4 78
MOTOWN ... 3-5 75
LPs: 10/12-inch
MERCURY ... 5-10 77
Members: Larry; Gary; Mitzi; Ronny; Tony.

ALLENS, Arvee
(Ritchie Valens)
Singles: 7-inch
DEL-FI (4111 "Fast Freight") ... 20-30 59
(Reissued as by Ritchie Valens.)
Also see VALENS, Ritchie

ALLER, Michael
Singles: 7-inch
LAURIE ... 5-10 61

ALLER, Michelle
Singles: 7-inch
MOWEST ... 3-5 72

ALLEY, Jim C&W '68
Singles: 7-inch
AVCO (606 "If I Didn't Have a Dime") ... 4-6 75
DOT (17051 "Only Daddy That'll Walk the Line") ... 10-15 68
PEARL (4448 "Dig That Rock & Roll") ... 75-125 50s

ALLEY & SOUL SNEEKERS
Singles: 7-inch
CAPITOL ... 3-5 79
LPs: 10/12-inch
CAPITOL ... 5-10 79

ALLEY BRAT
Singles: 7-inch
BRATMAN ... 3-4
Picture Sleeves
BRATMAN ... 3-5

ALLEY CATS P&R/R&B '63
Singles: 7-inch
EPIC ... 5-10 65
PHILLES (108 "Puddin N' Tain") ... 15-25 62
WHIPPETT (202 "This Thing Called Love") ... 25-50 56
WHIPPETT (209 "Last Night") ... 25-50 57
Members: Chester Pipkin; Gary Pipkin; Bobby Sheen; Sheridan Spencer; Brice Coefield; James Barker. Session: Jack Nitzsche.
Also see NITZSCHE, Jack
Also see PIPKINS
Also see SHEEN, Bobby

ALLEY CATS
LPs: 10/12-inch
MCA ... 5-10 82

ALLEY KATS
Singles: 7-inch
P-C (101 "Alley Kats") ... 15-25 56
Member: Sax Kari.
Also see KARI, Sax

ALLEYNE, Gloria
Singles: 78 rpm
JOSIE ... 10-20 54
Singles: 7-inch
JOSIE (767 "When I Say My Prayer") ... 25-35 54
Also see LYNNE, Gloria

ALLIANCE
Singles: 7-inch
HANDSHAKE ... 3-4 82

ALLIE OOP'S GROUP
Singles: 7-inch
CAPRICE ... 5-10 60

ALLIES
Singles: 7-inch
VALIANT (748 "Sell My Soul") ... 20-30 66

ALLIES
Singles: 7-inch
DEE DAY (120182 "Heartborken Man") ... 4-6 82
Picture Sleeves
DEE DAY (120182 "Heartborken Man") ... 5-8 82
EPs: 7-inch
VICTORIA (100183 "Emma Peel") ... 15-25 83
Members: David Kincaid; Carl Funk; Larry Mason; Andy Pederson; Jerry Battista; Steve Adamek; Gary Shelton.

ALLIGATORS
Singles: 7-inch
SUNWRAY ... 3-5 77

ALLIN, G.G., & Murder Junkies
LPs: 10/12-inch
ALIVE (001 "Brutality and Bloodshed for All") ... 8-12
ALIVE (1000 "Always Was") ... 10-20
AWARENESS (310 "Freaks, Faggots, Drunks & Junkies") ... 8-12

ALLISON
Singles: 7-inch
ANSAP ... 3-5
KING ... 3-5 73
SSS INT'L ... 3-5 75

ALLISON, Dick, & Broughams
Singles: 7-inch
DREEM ... 20-25 60
Also see THOMPSON, Ron, & Broughams

ALLISON, Gene P&R/R&B '57
Singles: 78 rpm
CALVERT ... 10-15 56
DECCA ... 10-15 57
VEE JAY ... 10-20 57
Singles: 7-inch
CALVERT ... 15-25 56
CHAMPION ... 10-15 59
CHEROKEE ... 10-15 59
DECCA ... 10-15 57
MONUMENT ... 5-10 65
REF-O-REE ... 5-10
VALDOT ... 5-10 62
VEE JAY ... 15-25 57-60
LPs: 10/12-inch
VEE JAY (1009 "Gene Allison") ... 100-200 59
(Maroon label.)
VEE JAY (1009 "Gene Allison") ... 50-75 59
(Black label.)
Also see BOB & EARL / Gene Allison

ALLISON, Jerry, & Crickets
Singles: 7-inch
LIBERTY (55742"We Gotta Get Together") ... 10-20 64
LIBERTY (55767 "Now Hear This") ... 10-20 64
Also see CRICKETS
Also see IVAN
Also see PEWTER, Jim

ALLISON, Joe
Singles: 7-inch
DOT ... 8-12 58

ALLISON, Keith
Singles: 7-inch
AMY (024 "Who Do You Love") ... 10-20 68
COLUMBIA ... 10-15 66-70
W.B. (5681 "Sweet Little Rock & Roller") ... 10-20 65
Picture Sleeves
COLUMBIA (44028 "Louise") ... 8-12 67
W.B. (5681 "Sweet Little Rock & Roller") ... 10-20 65
LPs: 10/12-inch
COLUMBIA ... 15-20 67
Also see EZBA, Denny
Also see REVERE, Paul, & Raiders
Also see UNKNOWNS

ALLISON, Leevert
(Levert Allison)
Singles: 7-inch
ELBEJAY (103 "You Made a World") ... 10-15
PONCELLO (7004 "I Want to Give My Heart") ... 15-25 60s

ALLISON, Lori
Singles: 7-inch
ORIGINAL SOUND ... 4-8 64

ALLISON, Luther
Singles: 7-inch
GORDY ... 3-5 73-76
RUMBLE ... 3-4 79
LPs: 10/12-inch
DELMARK ... 5-10 69
GORDY ... 5-8 73-76
RUMBLE (Black vinyl) ... 8-10 79
RUMBLE (Colored vinyl) ... 20-25 79

ALLISON, Mose
Singles: 7-inch
ATLANTIC (5021 "Your Mind Is on Vacation") ... 10-20 62
COLUMBIA ... 8-12 60
PRESTIGE ... 8-15 57-64
LPs: 10/12-inch
ATLANTIC (1389 "I Don't Worry") ... 25-35 62
ATLANTIC (1398 "Swingin' Machine") ... 25-35 63
ATLANTIC (1424 "The Word from Mose") ... 25-35 64
ATLANTIC (1450 "Mose Alive") ... 20-30 66
ATLANTIC (1456 "Wild Man on the Loose") ... 20-30 66
COLUMBIA (1444 "Transfiguration of Hiram Brown") ... 35-50 60
COLUMBIA (1565 "I Love the Life I Live") ... 35-50 60
(Monaural.)
COLUMBIA (8367 "I Love the Life I Live") ... 40-55 60
(Stereo.)
EPIC (16031 "Mose Allison Takes to the Hills") ... 30-40 62
(Monaural.)
EPIC (17031 "Mose Allison Takes to the Hills") ... 35-45 62
(Stereo.)
EPIC (24183 "V-8 Ford Blues") ... 15-25 66
(Monaural.)
EPIC (26183 "V-8 Ford Blues") ... 15-25 66
(Stereo.)
PRESTIGE (7091 "Back Country Suite") ... 40-60 57
PRESTIGE (7121 "Local Color") ... 40-60 58
PRESTIGE (7137 "Young Man Mose") ... 40-60 58
PRESTIGE (7152 "Creek Bank") ... 40-60 58
PRESTIGE (7189 "Autumn Song") ... 40-60 59
PRESTIGE (7215 "Ramblin' ") ... 40-60 59
PRESTIGE (7279 "Sing") ... 35-50 63
PRESTIGE (7423 "Down Home Piano") ... 15-25 65
PRESTIGE (7446 "For Lovers") ... 15-25 66

ALLISONS
Singles: 7-inch
LONDON ... 4-8 61
Picture Sleeves
LONDON ... 5-10 61

ALLISONS P&R '63
Singles: 7-inch
COLUMBIA ... 4-8 61
SMASH ... 4-8 62
TIP (1011 "Surfer Street") ... 15-20 63

ALLMAN, Duane LP '72
LPs: 10/12-inch
CAPRICORN ... 8-12 72-74
Also see DEREK & DOMINOS
Also see JENKINS, Johnny

ALLMAN, Duane & Gregg LP '72
Singles: 7-inch
BOLD ... 5-8 73
LPs: 10/12-inch
BOLD (301 "Duane & Gregg Allman") ... 20-25 72
(Gatefold cover.)
BOLD (301 "Duane & Gregg Allman") ... 8-10 73
(Standard cover.)
SPRINGBOARD ... 8-10 75
Also see ALLMAN, Duane
Also see ALLMAN, Gregg
Also see ALLMAN BROTHERS BAND
Also see ALLMAN JOYS

ALLMAN, Gregg P&R/LP '73
(Gregg Allman Band)
Singles: 7-inch
CAPRICORN ... 3-5 73-77
EPIC ... 3-4 87-89
LPs: 10/12-inch
CAPRICORN ... 8-12 73-77
EPIC ... 5-10 87-89
ROBERT KLEIN ("Interview") ... 40-60 81
(Promotional issue only.)
Also see ALLMAN, Duane & Gregg
Also see ALLMAN & WOMAN
Also see ALLMAN BROTHERS BAND
Also see ALLMAN JOYS
Also see HOUR GLASS

ALLMAN, Sheldon
Singles: 7-inch
HI-FI ... 5-10 60
ORIGINAL SOUND ... 4-8 63
LPs: 10/12-inch
DEL-FI ... 20-25 61
HI-FI ... 15-25 60

ALLMAN & WOMAN
Singles: 7-inch
W.B. ... 3-5 77
LPs: 10/12-inch
W.B. ... 8-10 77
Members: Gregg Allman; Cher.
Also see ALLMAN, Gregg
Also see CHER

ALLMAN BROTHERS BAND LP '70
Singles: 7-inch
ARISTA ... 3-4 80-81
CAPRICORN (Except 036) ... 3-5 71-79
CAPRICORN (036 "Jessica") ... 30-50 73
EPIC ... 3-4 90
Picture Sleeves
ARISTA ... 3-5 81
EPs: 7-inch
ATLANTIC ... 10-20 73
(Juke box issue only.)
CAPRICORN ... 10-20 73
(Juke box issue only.)
LPs: 10/12-inch
ARISTA ... 5-10 80-81
ATCO ... 15-20 69-73
CAPRICORN (Except 802) ... 8-15 72-79
CAPRICORN (802 "The Allman Brothers Band at the Fillmore East") ... 15-20 71
EPIC ... 5-8 90
K-TEL ... 5-10
MFSL (2-157 "Eat a Peach") ... 30-45 85
MFSL (213 "Brothers and Sisters") ... 20-25 94
NAUTILUS (30 "Live at the Fillmore") ... 50-100
(Half-speed mastered.)
POLYDOR (6339 "Best of the Allman Brothers Band") ... 5-10 89
POLYDOR (839-417 "The Allman Brothers Band") ... 25-35 89
(Six-LP boxed set, with booklet.)
Members: Duane Allman; Gregg Allman; Dicky Betts; Berry Oakley; Butch Trucks; Johnny Johanson; Les Dudek; Chuck Leavell; David Goldflies; Paul Hornsby; Dan Toler.
Also see ALLMAN, Duane & Gregg
Also see BETTS, Richard
Also see DUDEK, Les
Also see HOUR GLASS
Also see SEA LEVEL
Also see 31ST of FEBRUARY

ALLMAN JOYS
Singles: 7-inch
DIAL (4046 "Spoonful") ... 25-35 66
LPs: 10/12-inch
DIAL (6005 "Early Allman") ... 10-15 73
Members: Duane Allman; Gregg Allman; Bob Keller; Maynard Portwood; Ralph Balinger; Ronnie Wilkin; Tommy Amato; Jack Jackson; Bobby Dennis; Bill Connell.
Also see ALLMAN, Duane & Gregg
Also see RUBBER BAND

ALL-NITERS
Singles: 7-inch
ERIE (001 "Hey Baby") ... 15-25 65
ERIE (002 "Girl Don't Go") ... 15-25 65
GMA (1 "Summertime Blues") ... 20-30 64
Members: Jay Milhelich; Don Hermanson; Greg Coby; Lloyd Hugo; Tony Defranco; Jimmy Lenten.

ALLRED, Bucky
Singles: 7-inch
BLUEFRONT ... 4-8

ALLRIGHT FAMILY BAND
LPs: 10/12-inch
A.F.B. ... 8-10 80
Also see SAXON, Sky

ALLROY SLAVES
LPs: 10/12-inch
CRUZ ... 8-10
Members: Karl Alvarez; Stephen Egerton; Bill Stevenson; Scott Reynolds.

ALLSPICE
Singles: 7-inch
AT-HOME ... 3-4 77
LPs: 10/12-inch
AT-HOME ... 5-10 77

ALLSTARS
Singles: 7-inch
4 STAR ... 5-10 76

ALLSTARS
LPs: 10/12-inch
ADELPHI ... 8-10 78

ALLSUP, Tommy
(With His Fir Kings)
Singles: 7-inch
GRT ... 4-6 71
POST (1000 "Yas Yas Yas") ... 5-8
LPs: 10/12-inch
REPRISE (6182 "The Buddy Holly Songbook") ... 40-50 65
Also see BOYS from INDIANA
Also see CROW, Alvin
Also see RAIDERS

ALLUMS
Singles: 7-inch
CRYSTAL BALL ... 4-8

ALLURES
Singles: 7-inch
MELRON (5009 "King Love") ... 50-100 64
STARLIGHT (48 "Our Songs of Love") ... 10-12

ALLUSIONS
Singles: 7-inch
BJ (003 "Farewell Darling") ... 10-15
EMBERS ... 8-12

ALLYN, Jack
Singles: 7-inch
NOVART ... 5-10 57

ALLYN, Toby
Singles: 7-inch
HANA HO ... 4-6 68

ALMA-KEYS
(With the Citations Band)
Singles: 7-inch
KISKI (2056 "Please Come Back to Me") ... 300-500 62
(Flexible disc.)
KISKI (2056 "Please Come Back to Me") ... 25-50 62
(Rigid disc.)
Also see CITATIONS

ALMANAC SINGERS
Singles: 78 rpm
GENERAL ... 8-12 41-43
Albums: 78 rpm
COMMODORE ("Deep Sea Chanteys & Whaling Ballads") ... 15-25
(Selection number not known.)
COMMODORE (10 "Sod Buster Ballads") ... 15-25
LPs: 10/12-inch
COMMODORE (002 "Deep Sea Chanteys & Whaling Ballads" & "Sod Buster Ballads") ... 20-30 51
FOLKWAYS (85 "Labor Union Songs") ... 15-25 55
Members: Pete Seeger; Woody Guthrie: Peter Hawes: Millard Lampell
Also see SEEGER, Pete
Also see WEAVERS

ALMARS
Singles: 7-inch
DELTA INT'L ... 4-8 66

ALMEIDA, Laurindo LP '62
(With the Modern Jazz Quartet; with Bossa Nova All Stars)
Singles: 7-inch
ATLANTIC ... 4-6 64
CAPITOL ... 3-8 55-65
PACIFIC JAZZ ... 5-8 55
EPs: 7-inch
CAPITOL ... 5-15 56-59
CORAL ... 5-10 54-56
PACIFIC JAZZ ... 10-15 54
LPs: 10/12-inch
ATLANTIC ... 10-20 64
CAPITOL (Except 8000 series) ... 15-25 59-65
CAPITOL (8000 series) ... 20-35 56-58
CORAL ... 25-45 54-56
CRYSTAL CLEAR ... 5-8 80
DAYBREAK ... 5-10 73
DOBRE ... 5-10 76-77
INNER CITY ... 5-8 79
PACIFIC JAZZ (7 "Laurindo Almeida Quartet") ... 50-75 54
(10-inch LP.)
PACIFIC JAZZ (13 "Laurindo Almeida Quartet, Vol. 2") ... 50-75 54
(10-inch LP.)
SURREY ... 10-20 65
WORLD PACIFIC ... 25-40 56-62
Also see BYRD, Charlie
Also see DAVIS, Sammy, Jr., & Laurindo Almeida
Also see GETZ, Stan, & Laurindo Almeida
Also see SOMMERS, Joanie, & Laurindo Almeida

ALMEIDA, Laurindo / Chico Hamilton
LPs: 10/12-inch
JAZZTONE ... 10-20 64
Also see ALMEIDA, Laurindo
Also see HAMILTON, Chico

ALMER, Tandyn
Singles: 7-inch
W.B. ... 3-5 70

ALMOND, Herschel
Singles: 7-inch
ACE (558 "Let's Get It On") ... 25-50 59
CHALLENGE (59054 "You Are the One") ... 15-25 59
TRUMPET ... 20-30 58

ALMOND, Johnny
Singles: 7-inch
DERAM ... 3-5 69
LPs: 10/12-inch
DERAM ... 10-12 70

ALMOND, Lucky Joe
Singles: 78 rpm
GLOBE ... 25-35 55
TRUMPET ... 10-20 53-54
Singles: 7-inch
GLOBE (240 "Oo Oo Anything Goes") ... 100-200 55
TRUMPET (199 "Rock Me") ... 50-75 53
TRUMPET (221 "Gonna Rock and Roll") ... 50-75 54

ALMOND, Marc P&R/LP '89
Singles: 7-inch
CAPITOL ... 3-4 89
Picture Sleeves
CAPITOL ... 3-4 89
LPs: 10/12-inch
CAPITOL ... 5-8 89
Also see MARK - ALMOND BAND
Also see SOFT CELL

ALMOND LETTUCE
Singles: 7-inch
CAPITOL ... 4-6 69

ALMOST BROTHERS C&W '85
Singles: 7-inch
MTM ... 3-4 85-86
Members: Steve Mosto; Mike Ragogna.

ALONZO & BOPPERS
Singles: 7-inch
ROJAC (8127 "I'm on My Way") ... 25-50 63

ALPACA PHASE III R&B '74
Singles: 7-inch
ATLANTIC ... 3-5 74

ALPACAS
Singles: 7-inch
DOUBLE TAKE (2172 "Sometimes I Love You Girl") ... 20-25
M.M.I. (1237 "Time Marches On") ... 100-200 58

ALPER, Greg, Band
LPs: 10/12-inch
ADELPHI ... 5-10 78

ALPERT, Dore
Singles: 7-inch
A&M ... 5-10 63
AQUARIOUS ... 3-5 76
CARNIVAL ... 8-12 62

DOT ... 5-10 62
RCA (7988 "Little Lost Lover") ... 10-20 62

ALPERT, Herb P&R/LP '62
(With Tijuana Brass; Herbie Alpert)
Singles: 12-inch
A&M ... 4-6 79-84
(Black vinyl.)
A&M ... 5-8 84
(Colored vinyl.)
Singles: 7-inch
A&M (Except 700 series) ... 3-5 66-87
A&M (700 series) ... 3-8 62-66
ANDEX ... 4-6 59
CAROL ... 4-6 59
ROWE/AMI ... 4-8 66
("Play Me" Sales Stimulator promotional issue.)
Picture Sleeves
A&M (Except 700 series) ... 3-5 66-87
A&M (700 series) ... 3-6 65-66
EPs: 7-inch
A&M ... 4-8 65-66
(Juke box issues only.)
LPs: 10/12-inch
A&M (Except 100 series) ... 5-10 66-87
A&M (100 series) ... 8-15 62-66
MFSL (053 "Rise") ... 25-50 81
Members: Lou Pagani; John Pisano; Bob Edmondson; Tonni Kalash; Nick Ceroli; Pat Senatore.
Also see GRAYSON, Milton
Also see HALL, Lani, & Herb Alpert
Also see LOU, Herb B.

ALPERT, Herb, & Hugh Masekela LP '78
Singles: 7-inch
A&M/HORIZON ... 3-4 78
Picture Sleeves
A&M/HORIZON ... 3-5 78
LPs: 10/12-inch
A&M/HORIZON ... 5-10 78
Also see ALPERT, Herb
Also see MASEKELA, Hugh

ALPHA BAND
Singles: 7-inch
ARISTA ... 3-4 76-78
LPs: 10/12-inch
ARISTA ... 5-10 76-78
Members: Matt Betton; T-Bone Burnett; David Jackson; David Mansfield; Steven Soles.
Also see BULLENS, Cindy

ALPHA ZOE
Singles: 7-inch
HIT ... 8-12

ALPHAVILLE P&R/D&D/LP '84
Singles: 12-inch
ATLANTIC ... 4-6 84-86
Singles: 7-inch
ATLANTIC ... 3-4 84-88
Picture Sleeves
ATLANTIC ... 3-4 84-88
LPs: 10/12-inch
ATLANTIC ... 5-10 84-86
Members: Marian Gold; Bernie Lloyd; Frank Mertens.

ALPINES
Singles: 7-inch
CHALLENGE ... 8-12 61

ALQUIN
Singles: 7-inch
RCA ... 3-5 75
LPs: 10/12-inch
RCA ... 8-10 75
Members: Ferdinard Baker; Ronald Ottenhagg; Dick Franssen; Michael Van; Heil Mars; Paul Westrate; Job Tarenskeel.

ALQUIST, Russ
Singles: 7-inch
W.B. ... 4-8 66

ALSTON, Gerald
Singles: 7-inch
MOTOWN ... 3-4 88
LPs: 10/12-inch
MOTOWN ... 5-8 88
Also see MANHATTANS

ALSTON, Henry
Singles: 7-inch
COLPIX (731 "Hey Everybody") ... 10-15 64
SKYLINE (500 "Once in a Beautiful Life"/"I Dare You Baby") ... 20-30 58
SKYLINE (551 "Once in a Beautiful Life"/"What Is There Left for Me") ... 15-25 59

ALSTON, Jo-Ann
(With Gene Redd Jr. & Orchestra)
Singles: 7-inch
VEST (8001 "He Left Me Crying") 25-50 63

ALSTON, Ron
Singles: 7-inch
PHILIPS ... 8-15 66

ALSTON, Shirley
(Shirley Alston-Reeves)
Singles: 7-inch
PRODIGAL ... 4-8 75
LPs: 10/12-inch
STRAWBERRY ... 5-10 77
PRODIGAL (10008 "Shirley Alston with (a Little Help from My Friends") ... 10-15 75
(With the Drifters, Flamingos, Fred Parris & Five Satins, Belmonts, Herman's Hermits, Shep & Limelites, Danny & Juniors, and La La Brooks.)
Also see BELMONTS
Also see CHOLLI MAYE
Also see CRYSTALS
Also see DANNY & JUNIORS
Also see DRIFTERS
Also see FIVE SATINS
Also see FLAMINGOS
Also see HERMAN'S HERMITS
Also see SHEP & LIMELITES
Also see SHIRELLES

ALSTON, Walter
Singles: 7-inch
GAMUT (101 "Hey Baby") ... 10-20 61

ALTAIRS
Singles: 7-inch
AMY (803 "If You Love Me") ... 20-30 60
Member: George Benson.
Also see BENSON, George

ALTAR, Rosalie
Singles: 7-inch
ARCHIE (38 "I Had a Dream") ... 8-12
HARMON (1006 "Be True") ... 8-12 62

ALTAR BOYS
LPs: 10/12-inch
FRONTLINE ... 5-10
Members: Jeff Crandall; Mike Stand.

ALTECS
Singles: 7-inch
CLOISTER ... 10-20 60
DORE ... 8-12 62
FELSTED ... 10-15 61
PAMELA ... 10-15 62

ALTEERS
Singles: 7-inch
G-CLEF (705 "This Lovely Night") ... 50-100 64
LAURIE (3097 "Words Can't Explain") ... 20-30 61

ALTER BOYS
Singles: 7-inch
PRECISIONS ... 3-5 80

ALTERED IMAGES
Singles: 12-inch
PORTRAIT ... 4-6 82
Singles: 7-inch
PORTRAIT ... 3-4 83
Picture Sleeves
PORTRAIT ... 3-4 83
LPs: 10/12-inch
PORTRAIT ... 5-10 82-83
Member: John McElhone.
Also see TEXAS

ALTERNATING BOXES
Singles: 12-inch
POLYDOR ... 4-6 84-85

ALTERNATIVE TV
LPs: 10/12-inch
I.R.S. ... 5-10 81
Members: Chris Bennett; Dennis Burns; Alex Fergusson; Dave George; Mark Lineham; Mark Perry; John Towe; Tyrone Thomas.

ALTHEA & MEMORIES
Singles: 7-inch
RUBBISH ... 3-5

ALTHIA & DONNA
Singles: 7-inch
SIRE ... 3-5 78

ALTON, Johnnie
Singles: 7-inch
ALPHA (8 "Boys Have Feelings Too") ... 10-20
CHESNUT (204 "Please Love Me") ... 10-20 61

ALTON & JIMMY
Singles: 7-inch
SUN (323 "No More Crying the Blues") ... 10-20 59
Members: Alton Lott; Jimmy Harrell.
Also see RILEY, Billy Lee

ALTON & JOHNNY R&B '80
Singles: 7-inch
POLYDOR ... 3-5 80
Members: Johnny Bristol; Alton McClain.
Also see BRISTOL, Johnny
Also see McCLAIN, Alton, & Destiny

ALTON & FLAMES
Singles: 7-inch
DUCHESS ... 10-15

ALTONES
Singles: 7-inch
GARDENA (121 "Eileen") ... 20-30 61

ALUMNI
Singles: 7-inch
STACY ... 5-10 60s

ALVANS
Singles: 7-inch
MAY (102 "Love Is a Game") ... 75-125 61

ALVAREZ
Singles: 7-inch
EPIC ... 4-6 78
POLYDOR ... 4-6

ALVEREZ, Jesus
Singles: 7-inch
VIBRATION ... 3-6

ALVEY, Randy, & Green Fuzz
Singles: 7-inch
BIG TEX (445 "Green Fuzz") ... 50-100 66

ALVIN, Dave LP '87
(With the Red Devils)
Singles: 7-inch
ENIGMA ... 5-8 87
LPs: 10/12-inch
EPIC ... 5-10 87
Also see BLASTERS
Also see X

ALVIN & BILL
Singles: 7-inch
FERNWOOD (124 "Typing Jive") ... 30-50 61

ALVIN & RICKEY
Singles: 7-inch
STANG ... 3-5 71

ALVIN LEE: see LEE, Alvin

ALVON, Tony, & Belairs
Singles: 7-inch
ATLANTIC ... 4-6 68-69

ALWAYS, Billy R&B '82
Singles: 7-inch
EPIC ... 3-4 88
WAYLO ... 3-4 82

ALWYN
Singles: 7-inch
STUDIO (103 "Do You Care") ... 5-10

ALZO
Singles: 7-inch
A&M (1719 "Sunday Kind of Love") 5-10 75
AMPEX (11052 "That's Alright") ... 5-10 71
BELL (45247 "You're Gone") ... 8-12 72
BELL (45288 "Looks Like Rain") ... 8-12 72
LPs: 10/12-inch
AMPEX ... 10-15 71
BELL ... 8-12 72

ALZO & UDDIN
Singles: 7-inch
MERCURY ... 4-8 69
STEED ... 5-10 68
LPs: 10/12-inch
MERCURY ... 10-15 69

AMAKER, Donald
Singles: 7-inch
RAINES (22 "Don't Let Me Shed Anymore Tears") ... 60-80 59

AMANT
Singles: 7-inch
MARLIN ... 3-5 79

AMARILLO C&W '80
(Barry Grant)
Singles: 7-inch
NSD ... 3-4 80-81
Also see GRANT, Barry

AMARO, Tony
(With the Chariots)
Singles: 7-inch
LOMA ... 8-10 67
STACY (920 "Heart and Soul") ... 25-50 60

AMATO, Frankie
Singles: 7-inch
COOL ... 10-15 60

AMATO, Jerry
Singles: 7-inch
TACIT (109 "Dream on Little Fool") ... 25-50 60s

AMATO, Larry
Singles: 7-inch
RCA ... 10-15 58

AMATO, Tony
Singles: 7-inch
PEDDY (1003 "Brenda") ... 10-20 60s

AMAZERS
Singles: 7-inch
BANGAR ... 10-20 68
THOMAS ... 8-12 68

AMAZING BLONDEL
LPs: 10/12-inch
DJM ... 10-12 76
ISLAND ... 10-15 70-73

AMAZING GUITARS
Singles: 7-inch
BLUE SKY ... 3-4 79

AMAZING PICKLES
Singles: 7-inch
PHILIPS ... 4-6 69

AMAZING RHYTHM ACES C&W/P&R/LP '75
Singles: 7-inch
ABC ... 3-5 75-79
COLUMBIA ... 3-4 79
W.B. ... 3-4 80
LPs: 10/12-inch
ABC ... 10-20 75-78
COLUMBIA ... 10-15 79
W.B. ... 8-10 80
Members: Russell Smith; James Brown Jr.; Byrd Burton; Stick Davis; Billy Earhart III; James Hooker; Butch McDade.
Also see BAMA BAND
Also see SMITH, Russell

AMAZULU P&R '87
Singles: 7-inch
MANGO ... 3-4 87
Members: Ann Marie Ruddock; Sharon Bailey; Lesley Beach.

AMBASSADORS
Singles: 78 rpm
TIMELY (1001 "Darling I'm Sorry") ... 200-300 54

AMBASSADORS
(With Johnny L. Chapman Orchestra)
Singles: 7-inch
AIR (5065 "Keep on Trying") .. 1000-1500 56
(Approximately 50 made.)
BON (001 "Power of Love") ... 30-50 62
(First issue.)
PEE VEE (1000 "Too Much of a Good Thing") ... 100-200 61
REEL (117 "Power of Love") ... 20-30 62
Also see GERRY & GEMS / Ambassadors

AMBASSADORS
Singles: 7-inch
FLEET (3500 "Pork Chops") ... 10-20 61

AMBASSADORS
Singles: 7-inch
FEDERAL (12469 "I Have to Cry") 10-15 62

AMBASSADORS
Singles: 7-inch
PLAYBOX (202 "Lorraine") ... 1000-2000 63

AMBASSADORS
Singles: 7-inch
DOT (16528 "Big Breaker") ... 10-15 63

AMBASSADORS
Singles: 7-inch
UPTOWN (734 "I Need Someone") ... 10-20 66

AMBASSADORS R&B '69
Singles: 7-inch
ARCTIC ... 4-8 68-69
ATLANTIC ... 5-10 67-68
SOUND STAGE 7 ... 5-10 67-68
LPs: 10/12-inch
ARCTIC ... 10-20 69
Members: Bobby Todd; Herley Johnson; Orlando Oliphant.
Also see CREME D' COCOA

AMBASSADORS
Singles: 7-inch
DEBROUSSARD (5831 "Do You Ever Think About Me") ... 15-25 60s

AMBASSADORS
Singles: 7-inch
MERCURY ... 3-5 78

AMBASSADORS
Singles: 7-inch
JR (5004 "It's a Lonely Town") ... 8-12

AMBER
Singles: 7-inch
IPM ... 3-5 79
MCA ... 3-4 81
LPs: 10/12-inch
MCA ... 5-10 80

AMBER, Jan
Singles: 7-inch
CLEF-TONE ... 10-15 59

AMBERGRIS
Singles: 7-inch
PARAMOUNT ... 3-6 70
LPs: 10/12-inch
PARAMOUNT ... 10-15 70
Members: Charlie Camiliar; Gil Fields; Lewis Kahl; Larry Harlow; Harry Max; Glen Miller; Billy Shay.

AMBERJACKS
Singles: 7-inch
MIGLIORE ... 4-6

AMBERS
("Featuring Ralph Mathis")
Singles: 7-inch
EBB (142 "Never Let Me Go") ... 50-75 58
TODD (1042 "All of My Darling") .. 75-100 59
Member: Ralph Mathis.

AMBERS
Singles: 7-inch
JEAN ... 3-5 73
NEW ART ... 5-10 65
SMASH ... 10-20 67
VERVE ... 10-20 66
Members: Robert Rhoney; Robert Taylor; Billy Chinn; Ozzie Beek; Jerry White.

AMBERS
Singles: 7-inch
GREEZIE (501 "Listen to Your Heart") ... 20-30 59

AMBERTONES
Singles: 7-inch
DOTTIE (1129 "Chocolate Covered Ants") ... 20-40 65
DOTTIE (1130 "I Need Someone") ... 20-40 65
GNP (329 "Bandido") ... 10-20 64
RAYJACK (1001 "Cruise") ... 20-40 65
RAYJACK (1002 "I Can Only Give You Everything") ... 20-40 65
NEWMAN (601 "Cruise") ... 10-20 65
TREASURE CHEST (1001 "I Can Only Give You Everything") ... 20-30 65

AMBIANCE
LPs: 10/12-inch
DAMON ... 5-10 81-83

AMBITION
Singles: 7-inch
FIREFLY ... 5-10

MERCURY ... 3-4 78

AMBITIONS
Singles: 7-inch
CROSS (1005 "Traveling Stranger") ... 200-300 62

AMBOY DUKES P&R/LP '68
Singles: 7-inch
MAINSTREAM ... 6-12 67-69
LPs: 10/12-inch
AUDIOFIDELITY (1005 "Journey to the Center of the Mind") ... 20-25 83
(Picture disc.)
DISCREET ... 10-20
MAINSTREAM (801 "Journeys and Migrations") ... 15-20 74
MAINSTREAM (6104 "Amboy Dukes") ... 35-55 68
MAINSTREAM (6112 "Journey to the Center of the Mind") ... 35-55 68
MAINSTREAM (6118 "Migration") . 30-40 68
MAINSTREAM (6125 "Best of the Original Amboy Dukes") ... 25-35 69
POLYDOR ... 10-20 70
Members: Ted Nugent; Greg Arama; Rusty Day; John Drake; Steve Farmer; Dave Palmer; Andy Solomon; Rod Grange; K.J. Knight; John Angelos.
Also see DAY, Rusty
Also see KNIGHT, K.J.
Also see NUGENT, Ted
Also see RED RIDER

AMBROSE, Amanda
Singles: 7-inch
B.T. PUPPY (539 "Amanda's Man") ... 10-15 68
RCA (8167 "Crawdad Song") ... 5-8 63
LPs: 10/12-inch
B.T. PUPPY ... 10-20 68
DUNWICH ... 10-20 66
RCA ... 10-20 63

AMBROSE, Johnny
Singles: 7-inch
BETHLEHEM ... 4-8 62
TRIBUTE ... 4-8 62

AMBROSE, Kenny
Singles: 7-inch
HAMILTON (50019 "Come On and Marry Me") ... 15-25 58
WILLET (109 "Your Love Is My Love") ... 10-20 59

AMBROSE, Sammy
Singles: 7-inch
CRAZY HORSE ... 4-8 69
MALA ... 5-10 63
MUSICOR (1061 "This Diamond Ring") ... 10-20 64
MUSICOR (1072 "Welcome to Dreamsville") ... 25-50 64

AMBROSE, Stephen
Singles: 7-inch
BARNABY ... 3-5 72
LPs: 10/12-inch
BARNABY ... 5-10 72

AMBROSE, Tommy
Singles: 7-inch
FONTANA ... 3-5 68
STRAND ... 5-10 60

AMBROSE SLADE
LPs: 10/12-inch
FONTANA (67598 "Ballzy") ... 30-50 69
Also see SLADE

AMBROSIA P&R/LP '75
Singles: 7-inch
20TH FOX ... 3-5 74-78
W.B. ... 3-4 78-82
LPs: 10/12-inch
NAUTILUS ... 10-15 81
(Half-speed mastered.)
20TH FOX ... 8-10 74-78
W.B. ... 5-10 78-82
Members: David Pack; Burleigh Drummond; Joe Puerta; Christopher North.
Also see PACK, David
Also see PARSONS, Alan, Project
Also see TREFETHEN

AMECHE, Don, & Frances Langford LP '62
EPs: 7-inch
COLUMBIA ... 8-15 61
(Promotional only.)
LPs: 10/12-inch
COLUMBIA (1000 & 8000 series) .. 15-20 61-62
COLUMBIA (30000 series) ... 8-12 71

AMELIA
Singles: 7-inch
DIAMOND (107 "Voodoo Doll") ... 10-15 62

AMELIO, Johnny
Singles: 7-inch
BLUE MOON (405 "Jugue") ... 100-125 58
BLUE MOON (408 "Jo-Ann") ... 75-100 58

AMEN CORNER
Singles: 7-inch
DERAM ... 4-8 67
IMMEDIATE ... 3-6 69
LPs: 10/12-inch
DERAM ... 15-20 67
Members: Andy Fairweather-Low; Neil Jones; Blue Weaver; Clive Taylor; Dennis Byron; Alan Jones; Mike Smith.
Also see FAIRWEATHER-LOW, Andy

AMERICA P&R/LP '72

Singles: 7-inch

AMERICAN INT'L 3-5 79
CAPITOL 3-4 79-85
W.B. 3-5 72-77

Picture Sleeves

AMERICAN INT'L 3-6 79
CAPITOL 3-4 82-83
W.B. 3-5 72-74

LPs: 10/12-inch

CAPITOL 5-10 79-85
W.B. (Except 2576) 8-12 72-77
W.B. (2576 "America") 15-25 71
(Does NOT include *A Horse with No Name.*)
W.B. (2576 "America") 8-12 72
(Has *A Horse with No Name.*)
Members: Gerry Beckley; Dan Peek; Dewey Bunnell.
Also see PEEK, Dan

AMERICA'S CHILDREN

Singles: 7-inch

AUDITION 4-8 65

AMERICADE

LPs: 10/12-inch

ADEM 5-10 83

AMERICAN BEATLES

(American Beetles)

Singles: 7-inch

BYP (1001 "She's Mine") 20-30 64
ROULETTE (4550 "Don't Be Unkind") 5-10 64
ROULETTE (4559 "School Days") .. 5-10 64
Members: Bill Ande; Tom Condra; Dave Hieronymous; Jim Tolliver.
Also see RAZOR'S EDGE

AMERICAN BEETLES: see AMERICAN BEATLES

AMERICAN BLUES

Singles: 7-inch

AMY (997 "Your Love Is True") 15-25 67
KARMA (101 "If I Were a Carpenter") 20-30 67

LPs: 10/12-inch

KARMA (1001 "The American Blues Is Here") 250-350 67
UNI (73044 "The American Blues Do Their Thing") 35-55 69
Members: Dusty Hill; Rocky Hill; Doug Davis; Frank Beard.
Also see WARLOCKS
Also see ZZ TOP

AMERICAN BLUES EXCHANGE

(A*B*E)

LPs: 10/12-inch

TAYLUS (1 "Blueprints") 500-750 69
Members: Roy Dudley; Roger Briggs; Pete Hartman; Dan Mixer.

AMERICAN BREED P&R '67

Singles: 7-inch

ABC 3-5 75
ACTA 5-10 67-69
MCA 3-4 84
PARAMOUNT 3-5 70

Picture Sleeves

ACTA (821 "Green Light") 8-12 68

LPs: 10/12-inch

ACTA (38002 "American Breed") ... 15-25 67
ACTA (38003 "Bend Me, Shape Me") 15-25 68
ACTA (38006 "Pumpkin, Powder, Scarlet & Green") 15-25 68
ACTA (38008 "Lonely Side of the City") 15-25 68
Members: Gary Loizzo; Al Ciner; Chuck Colbert; Lee Graziano; Kevin Murphy.
Also see GARY & NITE LITES
Also see RUFUS

AMERICAN CHEESE

Singles: 7-inch

SEAWEST (101 "When the Morning Comes") 20-30 69
Also see GENESIS
Also see KING BISCUIT ENTERTAINERS

AMERICAN COMEDY NETWORK P&R '84

Singles: 7-inch

CRITIQUE 3-4 84

EPs: 7-inch

CRITIQUE (704 "American Comedy Network") 4-6 84

LPs: 10/12-inch

CRITIQUE 5-10 84

AMERICAN DREAM LP '70

Singles: 7-inch

AMPEX 3-5 70
DEMIK 4-8 68

Picture Sleeves

AMPEX 3-5 70

LPs: 10/12-inch

AMPEX 15-20 70
Members: Nick Jameson; Dooley Van Winkle; Nicky Indelicato; Don Ferris; Mickey Brook.

AMERICAN EAGLE

Singles: 7-inch

DECCA 3-5 71

LPs: 10/12-inch

DECCA 10-20 71
Also see VICEROYS

AMERICAN EAGLES

Singles: 7-inch

LIBERTY 4-6 69

AMERICAN EXPRESS

Singles: 7-inch

TEEN TOWN (111 "You & Me") 10-20 69

AMERICAN FLYER P&R/LP '76

Singles: 7-inch

U.A. 3-5 76-77

Picture Sleeves

U.A. 3-5 76-77

LPs: 10/12-inch

U.A. 8-10 76-77
Members: Eric Kaz; Steve Katz; Craig Fuller; Doug Yule.
Also see KAZ, Eric
Also see PURE PRAIRIE LEAGUE
Also see VELVET UNDERGROUND

AMERICAN FOUR

Singles: 7-inch

SELMA (2001 "Luci Baines" 25-50 64
Members: Arthur Lee; John Echols.
Also see LEE, Arthur
Also see LOVE

AMERICAN GIRLS

Singles: 7-inch

I.R.S. 3-4 86

Picture Sleeves

I.R.S. 3-4 86

LPs: 10/12-inch

I.R.S. 5-10 86

AMERICAN GROUP

Singles: 7-inch

AGP 4-6 69

AMERICAN GYPSY

Singles: 7-inch

CHESS 3-5 75

LPs: 10/12-inch

CHESS 8-10 75
Members: Joe Skeefe; Steve Clisby; Michael Hamane; Dale Harrel Jr; Richard James; Lorazo Mills.
Also see GYPSY

AMERICAN LEGEND

Singles: 7-inch

D.J. 8-12 69

AMERICAN MACHINE

Singles: 7-inch

TOWER 4-6 69

AMERICAN NOISE

Singles: 7-inch

PLANET 3-5 80

LPs: 10/12-inch

PLANET 5-10 80

AMERICAN PATROL

LPs: 10/12-inch

VANITY 5-10 83

AMERICAN REBELS

Singles: 7-inch

SUPER (106 "Rebel Song") 10-20 64

AMERICAN REVOLUTION

Singles: 7-inch

FLICK DISC 4-6 68

LPs: 10/12-inch

FLICK DISC (002 "American Revolution") 15-25 68
Members: Richard Barcellona; Daniel Derda; Eddie Haddad; John Keith.
Also see EDGE
Also see Picture Disc Chapter

AMERICAN ROCK REVIVAL

Singles: 7-inch

BELL 4-6 69

AMERICAN SCENE

Singles: 7-inch

DOT 4-6 69

AMERICAN SOUL TRAIN

Singles: 7-inch

A&M 4-6 68

AMERICAN SPRING

Singles: 7-inch

COLUMBIA (45834 "Shyin' Away") 20-30 73

Picture Sleeves

COLUMBIA (45834 "Shyin' Away") 50-80 73
Also see SPRING

AMERICAN STANDARD BAND

Singles: 7-inch

ISLAND 3-5 79
STARIZON 3-5 76

Picture Sleeves

STARIZON 3-5 76

LPs: 10/12-inch

ISLAND 5-10 79

AMERICAN TEA COMPANY

Singles: 7-inch

GOLDEN VOICE (2327 "Don't Leave Your Love") 20-30 69
Members: Gary Testrake; Ken Rogers; Mark Nelson; Tim Haley; Jim Schuh.

AMERICAN TEARS

Singles: 7-inch

COLUMBIA 3-5 74-77

LPs: 10/12-inch

COLUMBIA 8-10 74-77
Members: Craig Evanbrooks; Greg Bale; Tommy Gunn; Glenn Kithcart; Mark Mangold; Kirk Powers.

AMERICAN ZOO

Singles: 7-inch

REENA (1026 "Mr. Brotherhood") .. 20-30 68

AMERSON, Doug

Singles: 7-inch

G&G (105 "Bop Man Bop") 75-100 58
INTRASTATE (25 "Bop Man Bop") 50-75 55

AMES, Durelle C&W '87

Singles: 7-inch

ADVANTAGE 3-4 87-88

AMES, Ed P&R '65

Singles: 7-inch

RCA 3-8 63-73

Picture Sleeves

RCA 3-8 67

LPs: 10/12-inch

CAMDEN 4-8 72-73
RCA 5-15 64-77
Also see AMES BROTHERS

AMES, Marty

Singles: 7-inch

DOT (15876 "Choppin' Cha Cha") 10-15 58

AMES, Nancy P&R '64

Singles: 7-inch

ABC 3-5 68
EPIC (Except 10056) 3-5 66-68
EPIC (10056 "I Don't Want to Talk About It") 8-12 66
LIBERTY 3-6 61-65
SC 3-5 68

Picture Sleeves

EPIC 4-6 66

LPs: 10/12-inch

EPIC 5-12 66-68
LIBERTY 10-20 61-65
SUNSET 5-10 60s
Also see LOPEZ, Trini, with the Ventures & Nancy Ames

AMES, Stacey

Singles: 7-inch

RANDOM (604 "Calendar Boy") 15-25 61

AMES, Stewart

(With Richard Wylie)

Singles: 7-inch

J&W (1000 "King for a Day") 125-175 60s
Also see WYLIE, Richard

AMES BROTHERS P&R '49

Singles: 78 rpm

CORAL 5-15 50-53
RCA (Except E3-VB-291) 5-10 53-57
RCA (E3-VB-291 "The Man with the Banjo") 10-20 54
(Special "National Banjo Week" issue, "Commemorating the Invention of the Banjo. The First Native American Musical Instrument." Promotional issue only.)

Singles: 7-inch

CORAL 10-20 50-53
EPIC 4-8 62-63
MCA 3-5 73
RCA 10-20 53-62

Picture Sleeves

EPIC 4-8 62
RCA 10-20 60

EPs: 7-inch

CORAL 10-25 50-53
RCA 10-25 53-61
RCA SPECIAL PRODUCTS (48 "French's Platter Party") 10-20 50s
(Promotional issue. Made for French's Mustard Co. Paper sleeve.)

LPs: 10/12-inch

CAMDEN 5-10
CORAL 15-30 53-62
EPIC 10-15 63
RCA (1000 series) 5-10 75
MCA 5-8 82
RCA (1200 thru 2200 series) 20-40 55-61
RCA (2800 series) 8-15 64
RCA (6000 series) 5-10 72
RCA SPECIAL PRODUCTS (0207 "The Ames Brothers") 5-10
VOCALION 5-10 68
VOCALION 5-10 68
Members: Ed Ames; Joe Ames; Gene Ames; Vic Ames.
Also see AMES, Ed
Also see COMO, Perry / Ames Brothers / Harry Belafonte / Radio City Music Hall Orch.
Also see LEWIS, Monica, & Ames Brothers
Also see MOONEY, Art, & His Orchestra
Also see ROSS, Lanny, with Stephen Kisley, His Orchestra & Amory Brothers

AMESBURY, Bill P&R '74

Singles: 7-inch

CASABLANCA 3-5 74-75

LPs: 10/12-inch

CAPITOL 5-10 76
CASABLANCA 8-10 74

AMICO, John

Singles: 7-inch

TONER (2306 "Summertime Twist") 8-12 60s

AMIGOS DE MUSICA

Singles: 7-inch

FONTANA 4-8 69-70
Also see MEYERS, Augie
Also see SIR DOUGLAS QUINTET

AMISH

LPs: 10/12-inch

SUSSEX 15-25 72

AMMONS, Albert R&B '47

(With His Rhythm Kings)

Singles: 78 rpm

COMMODORE 10-20 44-47
MERCURY 10-20 45-50

Singles: 7-inch

MERCURY 25-50 51
(We're not yet certain which specific titles are on 45, and which are 78 rpm only.)

EPs: 7-inch

MERCURY (3044 "Boogie Woogie Piano") 50-100 54

LPs: 10/12-inch

BLUES CLASSICS 5-10 83
COMMODORE (20,002 "Boogie Woogie and the Blues") 100-200 52
MERCURY (25012 "Boogie Woogie Piano") 100-200 54
(10-inch LP.)

AMMONS, Albert, & Pete Johnson

(Pete Johnson & Albert Ammons)

Singles: 78 rpm

RCA 5-10 41

EPs: 7-inch

RCA ("EPB" series) 10-20 50s
Also see AMMONS, Albert
Also see JOHNSON, Pete

AMMONS, Gene R&B '47

Singles: 78 rpm

CHESS 10-15 50
DECCA 5-10 54
MERCURY 5-15 47-53
PRESTIGE 5-10 51-57

Singles: 7-inch

ARGO 4-8 62
DECCA 5-10 54
MERCURY 5-10 50-53
PRESTIGE (100 thru 400 series) 3-8 60-68
PRESTIGE (700 series) 3-5 69-73
(This "700" series can easily be distinguished from the early fifties "700" series that follows. The company address is shown as in New Jersey. In the '50s the company was in New York.)
PRESTIGE (713 thru 921) 5-10 51-57
(Black vinyl.)
PRESTIGE (713 thru 921) 10-20 51-57
(Colored vinyl.)
RAY BRA 4-6
SAVOY 4-8 60
UNITED 5-10 53-54

EPs: 7-inch

EMARCY (6052/3 "With Or Without") 25-50 54
(Price for either of two volumes.)
PRESTIGE 25-50 51

LPs: 10/12-inch

ARGO 20-30 62
CHESS 30-40 59
EMARCY (400 series) 8-12 76
EMARCY (26031 "With Or Without") 50-100 54
(10-inch LP.)
ENJA 5-10 81
MERCURY 20-30 60-63
OLYMPIC 5-10 74
PRESTIGE (014 thru 192) 5-10 82-85
PRESTIGE (7010 thru 7132) 25-50 55-58
(Each of the following LPs in this series was reissued using the original selection number but a different title: Prestige 7050, *All Star Jam Session*, was reissued as *Woofin' & Tweetin*; Prestige 7039, *Hi-Fi Jam Session*, was reissued as *Happy Blues*, and Prestige 7060, *Jammin' with Gene*, was reissued as *Not Really the Blues*. These three 1960 reissues are valued in the $20 to $35 range.)
PRESTIGE (7146 thru 7287) 20-35 58-64
PRESTIGE (7300 & 7400 series) ... 10-20 65-68
PRESTIGE (7500 thru 7800 series) . 8-15 68-70
PRESTIGE (10000 series) 5-10 71-74
PRESTIGE (24000 series) 8-12 73-81
ROOTS 5-10 76
SAVOY 15-25 61
TRIP 5-10 73-75
VEE JAY 15-25 60
WING 10-20 60-63
Also see McDUFF, Brother Jack, & Gene Ammons

AMMONS, Gene, & Richard "Groove" Holmes

LPs: 10/12-inch

PACIFIC JAZZ (32 "Groovin' with Jug") 15-25 61
Also see HOLMES, Richard "Groove"

AMMONS, Gene, & Sonny Stitt

Singles: 78 rpm

PRESTIGE 5-10 50-51

Singles: 7-inch

PRESTIGE (700 series) 5-10 50-51
(Black vinyl.)
PRESTIGE (700 series) 10-20 50-51
(Colored vinyl.)

EPs: 7-inch

PRESTIGE 25-50 51

LPs: 10/12-inch

ARGO 25-35 63
CADET 10-20 67
CHESS 30-40 60
PRESTIGE (107 "Gene Ammons") 75-100 51
(10-inch LP.)
PRESTIGE (112 "Gene Ammons with Sonny Stitt") 75-100 51
(10-inch LP.)
PRESTIGE (127 "The Gene Ammons Band") 75-100 52
(10-inch LP.)
PRESTIGE (149 "The Gene Ammons Quartet") 75-100 51
(10-inch LP.)
PRESTIGE (7600 series) 6-10 69
PRESTIGE (10000 series) 5-10 76
VERVE (8400 series) 15-20 61-62
(Reads "MGM Records - a Division of Metro-Goldwyn-Mayer, Inc." at bottom of label.)
VERVE (8800 series) 8-12 72
(Reads "Manufactured By MGM Record Corp.," or mentions either Polydor or Polygram at bottom of label.)
Also see AMMONS, Gene

AMON DUUL

LPs: 10/12-inch

PROPHESY 25-30 70

AMON DUUL II

LIBERTY (56196 "Soap Shop Rock") 10-20 69

LPs: 10/12-inch

ATCO 8-10 75
U.A. (017 "Wolf City") 12-15 73
U.A. (198 "Vive La Trance") 10-12 73
U.A. (5586 "Carnival in Babylon") .. 15-20 72
U.A. (9954 "Dance of the Lemmings") 20-25 71
Members: Renate Knaup Kroetenschwanz; Danny Fischelscher; Dave Anderson; Chris Karrer; Reb Heibl; Kalle Housmann; Lother Meid; Falk Rogner.

AMORY, John

Singles: 7-inch

GULFSTREAM (1065 "Bad") 10-15

AMOS, Betty

Singles: 7-inch

MERCURY 5-10 57

AMOS, Daniel

LPs: 10/12-inch

SOLID ROCK 5-10 81

AMOS, Ira

Singles: 78 rpm

MODERN 10-20 50
OCTIVE 10-20 51
Also see NEW ORLEANS SLIM / Les Mozart

AMOS, Tori

LPs: 10/12-inch

ATLANTIC (81845 "Y Tori Kant Read") 50-75 88
ATLANTIC (82862 "Boys for Pele") 10-15 96
(Two colored vinyl discs.)

AMOS & ANDY P&R '29

Singles: 78 rpm

COLUMBIA 10-15 50s
VICTOR 50-75 29

Singles: 7-inch

COLUMBIA (48002 "The Lord's Prayer") 15-25 50s

AMPAGE

Singles

IRON WORKS (1025 "School of Hard Knox") 10-12 88
(Shaped picture disc. 500 made.)

AMRAM, David

Singles: 7-inch

RCA 3-5 73

AMUZEMENT PARK R&B '82

(Amusement Park Band)

Singles: 7-inch

ATLANTIC 3-4 84-85
OUR GANG 3-4 82-83

LPs: 10/12-inch

ATLANTIC 5-10 84
Members: Paul Richmond; Darryl Ellis; Aaron Jamal; Norval Hodges; Fred Entesari; Reuben Locke Jr.; Rico McFarland.

AMUZULU

Singles: 7-inch

ISLAND 3-4

Picture Sleeves

ISLAND 3-4

AMY C&W '79

Singles: 7-inch

DECADE 3-5 79
SCORPION 3-5 79

AMY, Curtis

(With Hubert Robinson)

Singles: 78 rpm

GOLD STAR 10-15 47
PALOMAR 5-10 65

LPs: 10/12-inch

VERVE 10-15 67
Also see ROBINSON, Hubert

AMY & JARRETTS

Singles: 7-inch

HIT 5-10

ANA P&R '87

Singles: 7-inch

PARC 3-4 87-90

Picture Sleeves

PARC 3-4 87

ANACONDA

Singles: 7-inch

BIG TREE (139 "Rock & Roll") 3-6 72

ANACONDA

LP: 10/12-inch

AZRA (8501 "Anaconda") 5-8 87
(Picture disc.)

ANACOSTIA R&B '72
Singles: 7-inch
COLUMBIA.......3-5 72-75
MCA.......3-4 77
ROULETTE.......3-4 84
TABU.......3-4 78-79
LPs: 10/12-inch
MCA.......5-10 77
TABU.......5-10 78

ANAMARI
LPs: 10/12-inch
ATLANTIC.......10-15 64

ANASTASIA
(With the Nocturnes Orchestra)
Singles: 7-inch
LAURIE (3066 "That's My Kind of Love").......15-25 60
STASI (1000 "Every Road").......300-500 62
STASI (1001 "Seven Days a Week").......100-200 61

ANATHAN
Singles: 7-inch
FONTANA.......5-10 66

ANCIENT GREASE
LPs: 10/12-inch
MERCURY (61305 "Women and Children First").......25-35 70
Members: John Weathers; Phil Ryan; Gary Pickford Hopkins.
Also see EYES of BLUE

ANCRUM, Jimmy
Singles: 7-inch
MUSIC WORLD.......4-8 64

ANDANTES
Singles: 7-inch
DOT (16495 "My Baby's Gone").....15-20 63
V.I.P. (25006 "Nightmare").....1000-2000 64

ANDERKIN, Lonnie
Singles: 7-inch
LADS (700 "Teenage Baby")......300-400 59

ANDERS, Bernie
Singles: 78 rpm
KING.......15-25 55
Singles: 7-inch
KING (4833 "My Heart Believes")..50-75 55

ANDERS, Gliss
Singles: 7-inch
LONDON.......5-10 50s

ANDERS, Lisa, with Victory Five
(Liz Anderson)
Singles: 7-inch
SENATOR (711 "Old Enough")......25-50 60
Also see ANDERSON, Liz

ANDERS, Peter
(Peter Andreoli)
Singles: 7-inch
BUDDAH.......4-8 67
CORVAIR.......5-10
KAMA SUTRA.......4-8 67
LPs: 10/12-inch
FAMILY.......10-15 72
Also see ANDERS & PONCIA
Also see ANDREOLI, Peter

ANDERS, Rick
Singles: 7-inch
TWIN HITS.......4-6

ANDERS, Russ
Singles: 7-inch
ANBEE (3026 "Redheaded, Blue-Eyed Baby Doll").......30-50

ANDERS, Terri
Singles: 7-inch
CHIEF (7027 "All in My Mind").......10-20 60

ANDERS & PONCIA
Singles: 7-inch
KAMA SUTRA.......5-10 67
W.B.......4-8 68-69
LPs: 10/12-inch
W.B.......10-15 69
Members: Peter Anders; Vinnie Poncia.
Also see ANDERS, Peter
Also see INNOCENCE
Also see MULBERRY FRUIT BAND
Also see PENNY ARCADE
Also see PETE & VINNIE
Also see TRADEWINDS
Also see TREASURES
Also see VIDELS

ANDERSEN, Eric LP '72
Singles: 7-inch
ARISTA.......3-4 75-77
COLUMBIA.......3-4 72
W.B.......3-4 68-71
LPs: 10/12-inch
ARISTA.......5-10 75-77
COLUMBIA.......8-10 72
VANGUARD.......15-20 65-70
W.B.......10-15 68-70

ANDERSON, Abby
Singles: 7-inch
KNIGHT.......4-8 64

ANDERSON, Al
Singles: 7-inch
KNIGHTSBRIDGE.......10-20
VANGUARD.......3-5 73
LPs: 10/12-inch
TWIN/TONE.......5-10 88
VANGUARD.......10-15 73
Also see PAYTON, Paul

Also see NRBQ
Also see WILDWEEDS

ANDERSON, Andy
Singles: 7-inch
CARDON (1000 "Double Mirror, Wrap Around Shades").......30-40 58
FELSTEAD (8508 "I-I-I Love You") 10-20 58

ANDERSON, Andy
(With the Dawnbreakers; with Rolling Stones)
Singles: 7-inch
APOLLO (535 "You Shake Me Up").......75-125 59
CENTURY LTD. (601 "Gimmie a Lock of Your Hair").......50-100 60
CENTURY LTD. (602 "Gonna Sit Right Down and Cry").......75-125 60
CENTURY LTD. (603 "Promise Me").......75-125 60
DOT.......15-20 59
FELSTED.......15-25 58
ZYNN (510 I Wanna Boogie").......40-50 59

ANDERSON, Andy
Singles: 7-inch
HERMITAGE (821 "All By Myself").......100-200 60

ANDERSON, Andy
Singles: 7-inch
SCOOT.......8-12

ANDERSON, Anita, & Traits
Singles: 7-inch
CONTACT (502 "Secretly").......15-25 60s

ANDERSON, B.K.
Singles: 7-inch
SWIRL.......10-25

ANDERSON, Bailey
Singles: 7-inch
FANFARE.......3-5 79
RENEGADE.......3-5 72

ANDERSON, Benny, & Teals
Singles: 7-inch
KING.......4-8 64

ANDERSON, Bill C&W '58
(With the Po' Boys; with Po' Folks; with Jordanaires; Whispering Bill Anderson)
Singles: 12-inch
MCA.......4-8 78
Singles: 7-inch
DECCA (30000 series).......10-15 58-59
DECCA (31000 series).......5-10 60-66
DECCA (32000 & 33000 series).......3-8 67-72
MCA.......3-5 73-81
PICKWICK.......5-10 70s
SOUTHERN TRACKS.......3-4 82-87
SWANEE.......3-4 85
TNT (146 "Empty Room").......15-25 57
TNT (165 "Empty Room").......10-20 59
TNT (9015 "City Lights").......15-25 58
Picture Sleeves
DECCA.......5-10 63-69
EPs: 7-inch
DECCA.......5-15 63-65
LPs: 10/12-inch
BILL ANDERSON LABEL (11316 "On the Road").......15-25
(Promotional issue only.)
CORAL.......4-6 73
DECCA (4192 thru 4686).......15-20 62-65
DECCA (4771 thru 5344).......10-15 66-72
(Decca LP numbers in this series preceded by a "7" or a "DL-7" are stereo issues.)
DECCA (7100 series).......15-20 69
DECCA (7200 series).......10-12 72
EPIC.......5-10 82-85
MCA.......5-10 73-80
SOUTHERN TRACKS.......5-10 84
VOCALION.......8-12 68-71
Session: Jordanaires.
Also see COE, David Allan, & Bill Anderson
Also see JORDANAIRES
Also see KERR, Anita
Also see PO' BOYS
Also see WELLS, Kitty / Bill Anderson

ANDERSON, Bill / Jimmie Burton
EPs: 7-inch
TNT (147 "Empty Room"/"Let's Pretend").......30-40 57
(Likely issued without special cover.)
Also see BURTON, James

ANDERSON, Bill, & Jan Howard C&W '66
Singles: 7-inch
DECCA.......3-6 66-71
LPs: 10/12-inch
DECCA.......6-12 68-72
Also see HOWARD, Jan

ANDERSON, Bill, & Mary Lou Turner C&W '78
Singles: 7-inch
MCA.......3-5 78
LPs: 10/12-inch
MCA.......5-10 76-77
Also see ANDERSON, Bill
Also see TURNER, Mary Lou

ANDERSON, Billy
Singles: 7-inch
SOUL HOUSE (13352 "Church").......4-8

ANDERSON, Bob
Singles: 7-inch
ALLAN.......8-12 59
BALLY.......10-15 57
U.A. (372 "Rose, Mose, and Me")..10-20 61

ANDERSON, Brother James
Singles: 7-inch
SUN (406 "I'm Gonna Move in the Room with the Lord").......30-60 68
Also see JANES, Roland

ANDERSON, Bubba
Singles: 7-inch
ACE (662 "Please Don't Leave Me").......20-40 62

ANDERSON, Candy
Singles: 7-inch
GUARANTEED.......5-8 60
W.B.......5-8 59

ANDERSON, Carl R&B '84
Singles: 12-inch
EPIC.......4-6 82-86
Singles: 7-inch
EPIC.......3-4 82-86
LPs: 10/12-inch
EPIC.......5-10 82-86
Also see ELLIMAN, Yvonne / Carl Anderson
Also see LORING, Gloria, & Carl Anderson

ANDERSON, Carol
Singles: 7-inch
BIG TREE (135 "You Boy").......4-6 72
MID-TOWN (271 "You Boy").......5-10 70

ANDERSON, Casey
Singles: 7-inch
ATCO.......3-5 64
REPRISE.......3-4 68-69
LPs: 10/12-inch
ATCO.......12-20 62-65
ELEKTRA.......15-20 60
SUPERSTAR.......5-10
URANIA.......10-15

ANDERSON, Coleman Brooks: see CARRIBIANS

ANDERSON, Curtis
Singles: 7-inch
BROWN BAG.......3-5

ANDERSON, Dale
Singles: 7-inch
RAYNARD (10033 "Tattoo for Rosalie").......10-20 65

ANDERSON, Debra
Singles: 7-inch
COLUMBIA.......3-6
MUSICOR.......5-10 70s

ANDERSON, Elijah
Singles: 7-inch
BOLO.......5-8 62

ANDERSON, Elton P&R/R&B '60
Singles: 7-inch
CAPITOL.......8-12 62
LANOR (514 "I Love You So").......10-15 63
LANOR (516 "The Crawl").......10-15 63
MERCURY (71542 "Cool Down Baby").......10-15 59
MERCURY (71643 "Walking Alone").......10-15 60
MERCURY (71777 "Please Accept My Love").......10-15 61
TREY.......10-15 60
VIN.......10-20 58
Session: Mac Rebennack.
Also see REBENNACK, Mac

ANDERSON, Ernestine LP '58
Singles: 7-inch
MERCURY.......3-4 60-62
SUE.......3-4 63-64
EPs: 7-inch
MERCURY.......5-10 59
LPs: 10/12-inch
CONCORD.......8-12 76-86
MERCURY.......15-25 58-60
OMEGA DISK.......10-15 59
SUE.......10-15 63
WING.......10-15 64

ANDERSON, Flip
Singles: 7-inch
GARPAX.......3-4 79-80

ANDERSON, Gene
(With the Dynamic Psychedelics; with Keynotes; with International Hook-Up)
Singles: 7-inch
HI.......4-6 72-74
ROYAL-TONE (1000 "Baby, I Dig You").......25-35 60s
STAR (246 "Pains in My Heart").......10-20 60s
TOP TEN (252 "Susie").......50-75 60s

ANDERSON, Herb Oscar
Singles: 78 rpm
CAPITOL.......4-8 52
Singles: 7-inch
CAPITOL.......8-12 52

ANDERSON, Ian
LPs: 10/12-inch
CHRYSALIS.......5-10 83
Also see JETHRO TULL
Also see LONDON SYMPHONY ORCHESTRA

ANDERSON, Ivie C&W '44
Singles: 78 rpm
EXCLUSIVE.......5-10 44
Also see ELLINGTON, Duke

ANDERSON, James
Singles: 7-inch
COTILLION.......3-5 70-71
KAT FAMILY.......3-4 82

LPs: 10/12-inch
KAT FAMILY.......5-10 82

ANDERSON, Jesse P&R/R&B '70
Singles: 7-inch
CADET.......4-6 67-68
JEWEL.......3-5 72
OUTTA CYTE (100 "Oh Wow Man").......8-12
THOMAS.......4-8 70

ANDERSON, Jimmy
(With His Joy Jumpers)
Singles: 7-inch
DOT.......10-15 62
EXCELLO.......10-15 64
ZYNN.......10-20 62

ANDERSON, Joe
Singles: 7-inch
HEIDI (110 "How Long Will It Last").8-12

ANDERSON, John C&W '77
Singles: 7-inch
ACE of HEARTS.......4-6 74
MCA.......3-4 87
RCA.......3-4 90s
W.B.......3-5 77-87
LPs: 10/12-inch
W.B.......5-8 77-87
Session: Waylon Jennings.
Also see HAGGARD, Merle
Also see HARRIS, Emmylou
Also see JENNINGS, Waylon

ANDERSON, Jon LP '76
Singles: 12-inch
ATLANTIC.......4-6 82
Singles: 7-inch
ATLANTIC.......3-5 76-82
COLUMBIA.......3-4 88
ELEKTRA (Except 69580).......3-4 84-85
ELEKTRA (69580 "Save All Your Love").......3-4 85
(Black vinyl.)
ELEKTRA (69580 "Save All Your Love").......4-8 85
(Colored vinyl. Special Christmas edition.)
LPs: 10/12-inch
ATLANTIC.......5-10 76-82
COLUMBIA.......5-10 88
ELEKTRA.......5-10 85
Promotional LPs
ATLANTIC ("An Evening with Jon Anderson").......20-30 76
(Jon Anderson interviews, and music from his *Olias of Sunhillow* LP, as well as selections by Yes. Number not known.)
Also see JON & VANGELIS
Also see TANGERINE DREAM / Jon Anderson / Bryan Ferry
Also see YES

ANDERSON, Kip
Singles: 7-inch
ABC-PAR.......8-12 64
ALA.......5-10
CHECKER.......5-10 66-67
DERRICK (1000 "I Want to Be the Only One").......30-50
EVERLAST (5021 "I Feel Good").......10-20 63
EXCELLO.......5-10 67-69
SHARP (102 "Oh My Linda").......15-25 60
TOMORROW.......8-12 65
TRUE SPOT (71001 "Woman, How Do You Make Love").......10-20
VEE JAY.......10-20 60

ANDERSON, Lale P&R '61
Singles: 7-inch
KING.......3-6 61-62
LPs: 10/12-inch
FIESTA.......15-25
UNIVERSE.......10-20 61

ANDERSON, Laurie LP '82
(With John Giorno & William S. Burroughs)
Singles: 12-inch
W.B.......4-6 81
Singles: 7-inch
W.B.......3-4 81-89
EPs: 7-inch
W.B.......3-5 81
LPs: 10/12-inch
GIORNO POETRY (20 "You're the Guy I Want to Share My Money With").......8-12 84
W.B. (Except 25192).......5-10 82-89
W.B. (25192 "United States Live") 35-45 85
(Five-LP set.)
Also see GLASS, Philip
Also see JARRE, Jean-Michael

ANDERSON, Leroy P&R '51
(With His Pops Concert Orchestra)
Singles: 78 rpm
DECCA.......3-5 51-57
Singles: 7-inch
DECCA.......3-8 51-62
MCA.......3-5 73
EPs: 7-inch
DECCA.......5-10 51-58
RCA.......5-10
LPs: 10/12-inch
DECCA.......12-25 51-63
GRAND PRIX.......8-12
MGM.......10-20 62

ANDERSON, Les
(Les "Carrot Top" Anderson)
Singles: 7-inch
ACE-HI.......10-20
CROSBY.......5-8

ANDERSON, Liz C&W '66
Singles: 7-inch
EPIC.......3-5 71-73
RCA (8000 & 9000 series).......3-8 64-70
SCORPION.......3-5 78
LPs: 10/12-inch
CAMDEN.......10-15 66
RCA.......10-20 67-70
TUDOR.......5-8 83
Also see ANDERS, Lisa, & Victory Five
Also see BARE, Bobby, Liz Anderson & Norma Jean

ANDERSON, Liz & Lynn C&W '68
Singles: 7-inch
RCA.......3-6 68
Also see ANDERSON, Liz
Also see ANDERSON, Lynn

ANDERSON, Lynn C&W '66
Singles: 7-inch
CBS (165211 "Isn't It Always Love").......30-50 79
(Picture disc. Promotional issue only. 1200 made.)
CHART.......3-5 66-71
COLUMBIA.......3-4 70-80
MERCURY.......3-4 86-89
PERMIAN.......3-4 83
RCA.......3-5 68
Picture Sleeves
COLUMBIA.......3-6 70-72
EPs: 7-inch
COLUMBIA.......4-8 72
(Promotional only.)
LPs: 10/12-inch
ALBUM GLOBE.......5-10 76
CHART.......10-20 67-72
COLUMBIA.......5-10 70-80
COLUMBIA HOUSE (6033 "Lynn Anderson Treasury").......30-40 73
(Boxed, five-disc set. Mail order offer.)
COLUMBIA HOUSE (6034 "The Ways to Love a Man").......5-10 73
COLUMBIA SPECIAL PRODUCTS.......5-10 83
ERA.......5-8 82
51 WEST.......5-8 82
HARMONY.......5-10 71-73
MOUNTAIN DEW.......5-10
PERMIAN.......5-10 83
PICKWICK.......5-10
TIME-LIFE.......5-10 81
Session: Jordanaires.
Also see ANDERSON, Liz, & Lynn
Also see BRUCE, Ed, & Lynn Anderson
Also see JORDANAIRES
Also see TOMORROW'S WORLD

ANDERSON, Lynn, & Jerry Lane C&W '67
Singles: 7-inch
CHART.......3-5 67
Also see LANE, Jerry

ANDERSON, Lynn, & Gary Morris C&W '83
Singles: 7-inch
PERMIAN.......3-4 83
Also see MORRIS, Gary

ANDERSON, Lynn / Ray Price
LPs: 10/12-inch
COLUMBIA HOUSE (5658 "Heart to Heart").......15-25 72
(Boxed, four-disc set. Mail order offer.)
Also see PRICE, Ray

ANDERSON, Lynn / Charley Pride
LPs: 10/12-inch
TELEHOUSE.......5-8
Also see ANDERSON, Lynn
Also see PRIDE, Charley

ANDERSON, Margie: see LOVE NOTES / Ronald Gill / Nats Walker Orchestra / Margie Anderson

ANDERSON, Michael LP '88
Singles: 7-inch
A&M.......3-4 88
LPs: 10/12-inch
A&M.......5-8 88

ANDERSON, Mildred
Singles: 7-inch
PRESTIGE BLUESVILLE (804 "Person to Person").......8-10 60
LPs: 10/12-inch
PRESTIGE BLUESVILLE (1004 "Person to Person").......25-50 60
PRESTIGE BLUESVILLE (1017 "No More in Life").......25-50 61

ANDERSON, Miller
Singles: 7-inch
DERAM.......3-5 72
LPs: 10/12-inch
DEREM.......8-12 71
Also see SAVOY BROWN

ANDERSON, Paula
Singles: 12-inch
ATLANTIC.......4-6 84-85

ANDERSON, Pink
LPs: 10/12-inch
PRESTIGE BLUESVILLE.......25-30 61-63
RIVERSIDE.......25-30 61

ANDERSON, Ray
LPs: 10/12-inch
SOUL NOTE.......5-10 84

ANDERSON, Rita
Singles: 7-inch
STUDIO ONE ("Hey Senorita")..100-200 50s
(Selection number not known.)

ANDERSON, Roshell R&B '73
Singles: 7-inch
ALBRADELLA (3006 "My Girl")... 5-8
EXCELLO... 4-6 71-73
SUNBURST... 3-5 73-74

ANDERSON, Ross
Singles: 7-inch
CHANNEL... 5-10 61

ANDERSON, Sonny
Singles: 7-inch
IMPERIAL (5634 "Lonely, Lonely Train")... 20-30 59
IMPERIAL (5689 "Fool")... 20-30 60

ANDERSON, Stefan
Singles: 7-inch
CRAZY HORSE... 3-6 69-70

ANDERSON, Vicki
(Vikki Anderson; Vickie Anderson)
Singles: 7-inch
BROWNSTONE... 5-10 71-72
DELUXE... 5-10 66
FONTANA... 5-10 64
KING... 5-10 66-70
SMASH... 5-10 65
TUFF... 5-10 67
Also see BROWN, James, & Vickie Anderson

ANDERSON, BRUFORD, WAKEMAN, HOWE
Singles: 7-inch
ARISTA... 3-4 89
ARISTA... 4-6 89
Picture Sleeves
ARISTA... 4-6 89
LPs: 10/12-inch
ARISTA... 8-10 89
Members: Jon Anderson; Bill Bruford ;Rick Wakeman; Steve Howe.
Also see YES

ANDI & BROWN SISTERS C&W '88
(Andy & the Brown Sisters)
Singles: 7-inch
DOOR KNOB... 3-4 89
KILLER... 3-4 88-89

ANDONI & COUSINS
Singles: 7-inch
BARO... 5-10 60

ANDRE, Billy
Singles: 7-inch
MAGNET... 4-8 65

ANDRE, Dean
Singles: 7-inch
BIG TREE... 3-5 73

ANDRÉ, Jan, & Five Crowns
Singles: 78 rpm
EMERALD... 100-200 55
Singles: 7-inch
EMERALD (2007 "It's Funny to Everyone But Me")... 300-500 55

ANDRE, Tommy
Singles: 7-inch
BROADWAY (503 "One More Try")... 10-15 67

ANDREA, Charles, & Hi Tones
Singles: 7-inch
TORI LTD. (2 "Didn't We Have a Nice Time")... 500-1000 61

ANDREA, John
Singles: 7-inch
MGM... 4-8
REPRISE... 4-8 65

ANDREA, Rod
Singles: 7-inch
COBRA... 4-8 65

ANDREA & HOT MINK
Singles: 12-inch
ROCK 'N' ROLL... 4-6 84

ANDREA TRUE CONNECTION: see TRUE, Andrea

ANDREOLI, Peter
Singles: 7-inch
20TH FOX... 3-4 77
Also see ANDERS, Peter

ANDREW, Ben
Singles: 7-inch
NRC... 8-12 59

ANDREW, Danny
Singles: 7-inch
VERVE (10115 "Bongo Boy")... 20-30 57

ANDREWS, Andy
Singles: 7-inch
SELECT... 8-10 62

ANDREWS, Butch
Singles: 7-inch
JEWEL... 5-10 64

ANDREWS, Chris P&R '66
Singles: 7-inch
ATCO... 5-10 66
RCA... 4-6 69

ANDREWS, Danny
Singles: 7-inch
CHATTAHOOCHEE... 4-8 65

ANDREWS, Ernie
Singles: 78 rpm
ALADDIN... 15-25 47
Singles: 7-inch
CAPITOL... 10-20 65
GNP... 10-20 57
PHILA-L.A. of SOUL... 4-6 70
ROULETTE... 10-15 59
SPARK... 10-15 55
LPs: 10/12-inch
DOT... 10-15 67
GNP... 20-30 57

ANDREWS, Freddy / Fran Cooper
Singles: 7-inch
TWIN HITS (5058 "Stay")... 5-10 64

ANDREWS, Gene
Singles: 7-inch
RUST (5054 "Lonely Room")... 10-15 63

ANDREWS, Hal
Singles: 7-inch
CHOCTAW... 30-40

ANDREWS, Harold
Singles: 7-inch
EARLY BIRD (9663 "You're a Winner")... 10-15
MRM (401 "Party Time")... 10-20 62

ANDREWS, Inez R&B '73
(With the Andrewettes)
Singles: 7-inch
MCA... 3-4 84
SONG BIRD... 3-4 64-73
LPs: 10/12-inch
MCA... 5-10 84
SAVOY... 5-10 80-81

ANDREWS, Jimmy
Singles: 7-inch
BLUE JAY (5003 "Big City Playboy")... 200-300 65
GLORY (288 "Just a Walk with You")... 15-25 59

ANDREWS, Julie P&R '62
Singles: 7-inch
BUENA VISTA... 3-6 65
COLUMBIA... 3-5 67
DECCA... 3-5 67
LONDON... 3-6 60
RCA... 3-4 70
Picture Sleeves
BUENA VISTA... 4-8 65
EPs: 7-inch
RCA... 10-20 56
LPs: 10/12-inch
ANGEL... 15-25 58
COLUMBIA (1700 & 8500 series)... 15-25 62
COLUMBIA (31000 series)... 8-12 72
HARMONY... 8-10 70-72
RCA (1000 series)... 8-12 70
RCA (1400 thru 1600 series)... 20-30 56-58
RCA (3800 series)... 8-15 67
20TH FOX... 8-15 68
Also see VAN DYKE, Dick, & Julie Andrews

ANDREWS, Julie, & Carol Burnett LP '62
LPs: 10/12-inch
COLUMBIA (2200 & 5800 series)... 15-25 62
COLUMBIA (31000 series)... 8-15 72
Also see BURNETT, Carol

ANDREWS, Julie, & Andre Previn
LPs: 10/12-inch
FIRESTONE... 8-12 66
RCA... 8-12 67

ANDREWS, Julie, & Andre Previn / Vic Damone / Jack Jones / Marian Anderson
EPs: 7-inch
RCA (277 "We Wish You a Merry Christmas")... 3-5 69
(Radio Shack "Special Collector's Edition.")
Also see ANDREWS, Julie
Also see DAMONE, Vic
Also see JONES, Jack
Also see PREVIN, Andre

ANDREWS, Lee P&R/R&B '57
(With the Hearts; with Frank Slay Orchestra; Pancho Villa Orchestra)
Singles: 78 rpm
ARGO... 35-50 57
CHESS... 35-50 57
GOTHAM... 50-100 56
MAIN LINE... 50-100 57
RAINBOW... 100-200 54
Singles: 7-inch
ARGO (1000 "Teardrops")... 25-50 57
CASINO (110 "Baby, Come Back")... 25-50 59
CASINO (452 "Try the Impossible")... 500-750 58
(Red and white label, with playing cards at top.)
CASINO (452 "Try the Impossible")... 100-200 58
(Black label.)
CHESS (1665 "Long Lonely Nights")... 20-4 57
(Silver top label with chess pieces.)
CHESS (1665 "Long Lonely Nights")... 10-15
(Blue label.)
CHESS (1675 "Teardrops")... 20-40 57
(Silver top label with chess pieces.)
CHESS (1675 "Teardrops")... 10-15
(Blue label.)
CHESS (9000 series)... 4-6
COLLECTABLES... 3-4 82
CRIMSON... 8-10 67-68
GOTHAM (318 "Bluebird of Happiness")... 200-300 56
GOTHAM (320 "Lonely Room")... 200-300 56
GOTHAM (321 "Just Suppose")... 200-300 56
GOTHAM (323 "Sippin' a Cup of Coffee")... 3-5 81
(Colored vinyl. From a 1956 session.)
GOWEN (1403 "Together Again")... 20-30 61
GRAND (156 "Teardrops")... 10-15 62
GRAND (157 "Long Lonely Nights")... 10-15 62
JORDAN... 15-25 60
LANA... 4-8 64
LOST-NITE... 4-8 65
MAIN LINE (102 "Long Lonely Nights")... 200-300 57
(Green label.)
MAIN LINE (102 "Long Lonely Nights")... 150-250 57
(Black label, with Philadelphia address shown.)
MAIN LINE (102 "Long Lonely Nights")... 25-50 62
(Black label, no address shown.)
MAIN LINE (105 "Teardrops")... 10-15 62
PARKWAY (860 "Gee, But I'm Lonesome")... 15-20 62
PARKWAY (866 "Looking Back")... 15-20 63
RAINBOW (252 "Maybe You'll Be There")... 250-500 54
(Black vinyl.)
RAINBOW (252 "Maybe You'll Be There")... 1000-1500 54
(Red vinyl. Print is small, with the title line being about 1 ½" long.)
RAINBOW (252 "Maybe You'll Be There")... 15-25 62
(Red vinyl. Print is noticeably larger than on 1954 issue.)
RAINBOW (256 "The White Cliffs of Dover")... 500-1000 54
(Yellow label.)
RAINBOW (256 "The White Cliffs of Dover")... 15-25 62
(Blue label.)
RAINBOW (259 "The Bells of St. Mary's")... 500-750 54
(Yellow label.)
RAINBOW (259 "The Bells of St. Mary's")... 15-25 62
(Blue label.)
RCA (8929 "Quiet As It's Kept")... 10-15 66
SWAN (4065 "I Miss You So")... 100-200 60
SWAN (4076 "A Night Like This")... 150-250 61
SWAN (4076 "P.S. I Love You")... 150-250 61
U.A. (123 "Try the Impossible")... 10-20 58
U.A. (136 "Why Do I")... 10-20 58
U.A. (151 "Maybe You'll Be There")... 10-20 58
U.A. (162 "Just Suppose")... 10-20 59
U.A. (592 "Try the Impossible")... 5-10 63
LPs: 10/12-inch
COLLECTABLES... 8-12 81-85
LOST-NITE (1 "Lee Andrews and the Hearts")... 10-15 81
(Red vinyl 10-inch LP.)
LOST-NITE (2 "Lee Andrews and the Hearts")... 10-15 81
(Red vinyl 10-inch LP.)
LOST-NITE (100 series)... 15-25 65
POST... 10-15 70s
Members: Lee Andrews; Arthur Thompson; Roy Calhoun; Wendell Calhoun; Butch Curry; Ted Weems.
Also see FAMOUS HEARTS
Also see HEARTS
Also see SLAY, Frank, & His Orchestra

ANDREWS, Lyn
Singles: 7-inch
TEEN TIME... 10-15 62

ANDREWS, Marg
Singles: 7-inch
CUCA... 5-10 60s

ANDREWS, Mark, & Gents
LPs: 10/12-inch
BIG BOY... 5-10 80

ANDREWS, Patty P&R '49
Singles: 78 rpm
CAPITOL... 3-5 55-56
DECCA... 4-8 50-54
Singles: 7-inch
CAPITOL... 4-8 55-56
DECCA... 5-10 50-54
Also see ANDREWS SISTERS

ANDREWS, Reggie
Singles: 7-inch
MOTOWN... 3-4 83

ANDREWS, Ruby P&R/R&B '67
Singles: 7-inch
ABC... 3-5 76-77
ZODIAC... 6-12 67-71
LPs: 10/12-inch
ABC... 8-10 77
ZODIAC... 10-20 72
Also see STACKHOUSE, Ruby

ANDREWS, Sheila C&W '78
Singles: 7-inch
OVATION... 3-5 78-80
LPs: 10/12-inch
OVATION... 5-8 79

ANDREWS, Sheila, & Joe Sun C&W '80
Singles: 7-inch
OVATION... 3-5 80
Also see ANDREWS, Sheila
Also see SUN, Joe

ANDREWS Suzy
Singles: 7-inch
X (001 "Don't Turn Around")... 3-5 82
X (95034 "Scandal")... 3-5 82
(Colored vinyl.)
LPs: 10/12-inch
X (9510 "Suzy Andrews")... 5-10 82

ANDREWS SISTERS P&R '38
Singles: 78 rpm
CAPITOL... 5-10 56-57
DECCA... 5-10 38-57
Singles: 7-inch
ABC... 3-5 74
CAPITOL... 10-15 56-59
DECCA... 10-20 50-57
DOT... 4-8 63-64
KAPP (309 "I've Got to Pass Your House")... 10-15 59
MCA... 3-5 73-78
PARAMOUNT... 3-5 73-74
Picture Sleeves
DECCA... 10-20 57
KAPP (309 "I've Got to Pass Your House")... 10-15 59
EPs: 7-inch
CAPITOL (973 "Dancing '20s")... 10-20 56
DECCA... 10-20 51-58
LPs: 10/12-inch
ABC... 5-10 74
CAPITOL... 10-20 64
DECCA (4000 series)... 10-15 67
(Decca LP numbers in this series preceded by a "7" or a "DL-7" are stereo issues.)
DECCA (5000 series)... 20-50 49-54
(10-inch LPs.)
DECCA (8000 series)... 15-25 55-58
DOT... 10-20 61-67
HAMILTON... 10-20 64-65
MCA... 8-12 73
PARAMOUNT... 5-10 73-74
VOCALION... 5-10
Members: Patty Andrews; Maxene Andrews; Laverne Andrews.
Also see ANDREWS, Patty
Also see CROSBY, Bing
Also see FOLEY, Red, & Andrews Sisters
Also see MIRANDA, Carmen, & Andrews Sisters
Also see PAUL, Les

ANDREWS SISTERS & ERNEST TUBB C&W '49
(With the Texas Troubadors)
Singles: 78 rpm
DECCA... 5-8 49
Also see TUBB, Ernest

ANDREWS SISTERS & THURL RAVENSCROFT
Singles: 7-inch
DOT (16497 "Mr. Bass Man")... 5-10 63
Also see ANDREWS SISTERS
Also see RAVENSCROFT, Thurl

ANDRIANI, Bobby
Singles: 7-inch
ATCO... 4-8 65

ANDROID SISTERS
LPs: 10/12-inch
VANGUARD... 5-10 85

ANDROMEDA
Singles: 7-inch
AMERICAN INT'L... 3-5 71
Members: John Carr; Ian McClane; Mick Hawksworth.

ANDROZZO, Sandra
Singles: 7-inch
RAINBOW... 3-4

ANDWELLA
Singles: 7-inch
DUNHILL... 3-5 70-71
LPs: 10/12-inch
DUNHILL... 10-15 70-71

ANDY, Randy, & Candymen
LPs: 10/12-inch
DIPLOMAT (114 "Let's Do the Twist")... 15-25 62
(Includes one track by Joey Dee & Starlighters.)
Also see DEE, Joey, & Starlighters

ANDY & BROWN SISTERS: see ANDI & BROWN SISTERS

ANDY & DAVID
Singles: 7-inch
BELL... 3-5 74

ANDY & GINO
Singles: 7-inch
GOLDEN CREST... 3-6 64

ANDY & NANCY
Singles: 7-inch
FIRST... 3-6

ANDY & LIVE WIRES
Singles: 7-inch
APPLAUSE... 15-20 61
LIBERTY... 5-10 61

ANDY & MANHATTANS
Singles: 7-inch
CARDON (1000 "Double Mirror Wrap-Around Shades")... 10-20
MUSICOR (1112 "Skinny Minnie")... 15-25 65

ANDY & MARGLOWS
Singles: 7-inch
LIBERTY... 4-8 63

ANDY & WHEELS
Singles: 7-inch
STATE (700 "Grinding Wheels")... 25-40

ANEKA
Singles: 7-inch
HANDSHAKE... 3-4 81

ANELLO, ANN
Singles: 7-inch
SPI... 3-4 80s
Picture Sleeves
SPI... 3-4 80s

ANELLO, Johnny
Singles: 7-inch
TIARA... 5-10 62

ANEMIC BOYFRIENDS
Singles: 7-inch
RED SWEATER... 3-5 80

ANGEL LP '75
Singles: 7-inch
CASABLANCA... 3-5 75-80
LPs: 10/12-inch
CASABLANCA... 5-10 75-80
Members: Barry Brandt; Frank DiMino; Greg Giuffria; Mickey Jones; Punky Meadows; Felix Robinson.
Also see CHERRY PEOPLE
Also see GIUFFRIA
Also see WILSON, Carl

ANGEL
Singles: 7-inch
TURBO... 3-6

ANGEL, Bobby
(With the Hillsiders; with Nutrockers)
Singles: 7-inch
ASTRA (300 "Submarine Races") 10-15 62
LAP (1003 "Sacannah")... 20-30 62
(Colored vinyl. Also issued as by Bobby Lake.)
RHUM (101 "Baby-O")... 8-12 61
Also see LAKE, Bobby

ANGEL, Eddie
Singles: 7-inch
REBEL RIOT... 6-12 81
Picture Sleeves
REBEL RIOT... 6-12 81
Also see RON & JITTERS
Also see RUBINOWITZ, Tex

ANGEL, Gary
Singles: 7-inch
KAMA (501 "Oh Judy")... 10-20 61

ANGEL, Ginny
Singles: 7-inch
BOW (303 "Tra La La La I'm Yours Tonight")... 15-25 58
MAY (122 "Forever Goodbye Love")... 10-15 62
RCA (7793 "There'll Be Some Changes Made")... 10-15 61

ANGEL, Jimmy
Singles: 7-inch
AVCO... 4-8 69-70
CONDOR CLASSIC (8801 "My Heart's an Open Book")... 8-12 88
(Heart-shaped picture disc. 500 made.)
DE-LITE... 3-6 71
EBB TIDE... 3-4 88
LAURIE... 5-10 77-80
MEGA... 3-5 73
RAMESES... 3-5 76
RIVERBOAT... 4-8
SHANNON... 3-5 77
VALMOR... 4-8
VIGOR... 3-5 75
Picture Sleeves
MEGA... 4-6 73

ANGEL, Johnny
Singles: 78 rpm
EXCELLO (2077 "I Realize")... 10-20 56
Singles: 7-inch
EXCELLO (2077 "I Realize")... 30-40 56
POWER (250 "Starlight")... 100-125 58
VIN... 15-25 58

ANGEL, Johnny
(With the Halos)
Singles: 7-inch
BELL... 3-5 74
FELSTED (8633 "Without Her Heart")... 15-25 61
FELSTED (8646 "One More Tomorrow")... 15-25 62
FELSTED (8659 "Looking for a Fool")... 15-25 62
GARDENA (117 "All Night Party") 15-25 61
IMPERIAL (5673 "Falling Teardrops")... 30-50 60
JAF (2024 "Lonely Nights")... 15-25 61
LIBERTY... 5-10 66
MARKEE (113 "Johnny Angel")... 10-15 63
PARLIMENT... 8-12 63
SWAN (4263 "This Is the Night for Love")... 50-75 66
Also see FRANKIE & JOHNNY

ANGEL, Johnny T: see JOHNNY T. ANGEL

ANGEL, Kenny
Singles: 7-inch
COLISEUM (602 "Teenage Honeymoon")... 10-20 62

ANGEL, Marian
Singles: 7-inch
JUBILEE (5508 "It's Gonna Be All Right")... 10-15 65

ANGEL, Ronnie
Singles: 7-inch
RITA (1011 "Angel Tears")............10-20 60

ANGEL, Tommy
Singles: 7-inch
NASCO....................................10-15 59

ANGEL, Wayne
Singles: 7-inch
WINSTON.................................. 5-10 63

ANGEL & DEVINES
Singles: 7-inch
SIANA 3-4

ANGEL CITY *LP '80*
Singles: 7-inch
EPIC.. 3-4 80-82
LPs: 10/12-inch
EPIC...................................... 5-10 80-82
MCA....................................... 5-10 85
Members: Doc Neeson; Rick Brewster; John Brewster.

ANGEL FACE
Singles: 78 rpm
BIG TOWN..............................10-15
Singles: 7-inch
BIG TOWN..............................10-20 55
DC...8-12 59
GEM......................................15-25 54
OKEH....................................10-20 56
SPECIALTY..............................8-12 60

ANGELA *D&D '85*
Singles: 12-inch
SUTRA 4-6 85

ANGELENOS
Singles: 7-inch
PEEPERS (2824 "As Long As I Have You")..................................30-40 61
PEEPERS (2827 "Come on Baby").....................................15-25 61
Also see BROWN, Camille, & Angelenos

ANGELETTES
Singles: 7-inch
JOSIE (813 "Mine & Mine Alone") 25-50 57

ANGELETTES
Singles: 7-inch
LONDON 3-5 71

ANGELIC GOSPEL SINGERS *R&B '49*
Singles: 78 rpm
GOTHAM................................ 5-10 49

ANGELINE & TEEN TOWNERS
Singles: 7-inch
BERTRAM INT'L (202 "Hula Rock & Roll")..................................15-25 57

ANGELLE
Singles: 7-inch
EPIC...................................... 3-4 77
LPs: 10/12-inch
EPIC..................................... 8-10 77

ANGELLE, Bobby
(Bobby Relf)
Singles: 7-inch
MONEY (123 "I Love")..............15-25 66
MONEY (125 "Living a Lie")........15-25 67
MONEY (128 "Too Much for You").15-25 67
MONEY (137 "You Got Me Dizzy")..................................15-25 67
Also see RELF, Bobby

ANGELLE, Lisa *C&W '85*
Singles: 7-inch
EMI.. 3-4 85

ANGELO
Singles: 7-inch
FANTASY................................ 3-4 76-78
LPs: 10/12-inch
FANTASY................................ 5-10 76-78
Also see RITENOUR, Lee
Also see WILSON, Carl

ANGELO, Bonnie
Singles: 7-inch
BONNY.................................... 3-5 78

ANGELO, Don
Singles: 7-inch
MERCURY (71580 "My Love for You")..................................15-25 60

ANGELO & INITIALS
Singles: 7-inch
CONGRESS................................ 5-8 64

ANGELO'S ANGELS
Singles: 7-inch
BONNY (101 "Macha")..................10-15 63
ERMINE 5-10 64
NEW BREED................................ 5-10 60s
TABB (3230 "Mach 9")................10-15 63

ANGELOS
Singles: 7-inch
CAMEO.................................... 5-10 63
TOLLIE.................................... 5-10 64
TOP RANK................................ 5-10
VEE JAY................................... 8-12 63

ANGELS
(With Jimmy Wright & His Orchestra; with Sonny Gordon)
Singles: 78 rpm
GEE.......................................20-30 56
GRAND...................................50-100 54
Singles: 7-inch
GEE (1024 "Glory of Love").........75-100 56
(Red and black label.)
GEE (1024 "Glory of Love")...........25-50 60
(Gray label.)
GRAND (115 "Wedding Bells Are Ringing in My Ears")..........................500-750 54
(Glossy yellow label. Rigid disc. No company address shown.)
GRAND (115 "Wedding Bells Are Ringing in My Ears")................................50-100 61
(Yellow label. Flexible disc. No company address shown.)
GRAND (115 "Wedding Bells Are Ringing in My Ears")....................................15-25 60s
(Yellow label. Company address is shown.)
GRAND (121 "Lovely Way to Spend an Evening")................................500-750 55
(Glossy yellow label. Rigid disc. No company address shown.)
GRAND (121 "Lovely Way to Spend an Evening")....................................50-100 61
(Yellow label. Flexible disc. No company address shown.)
GRAND (121 "Lovely Way to Spend an Evening").......................................30-50 60s
(Yellow label. Company address is shown.)
Note: Not all of the Grand variations may exist with all of their titles; however, they are listed in case they do exist.
Also see WRIGHT, Jimmy

ANGELS
Singles: 78 rpm
IRMA......................................50-75 56
Singles: 7-inch
AUDIO (203 "A Real Sensation") .75-125 61
IRMA (105 "Leaving You Baby")..75-100 56

ANGELS
Singles: 7-inch
TAWNY (101 "A Lover's Poem")....30-50 59
Also see SAFARIS

ANGELS *P&R '61*
Singles: 7-inch
ASCOT.....................................5-10 63
CAPRICE...................................8-15 61-62
COLLECTABLES........................... 3-4 82
ERIC....................................... 3-4 74
POLYDOR.................................. 3-5 74
RCA..5-10 67-68
SMASH.....................................5-10 63-64
Picture Sleeves
SMASH (1854 "I Adore Him") 10-15 63
EPs: 7-inch
CAPRICE 20-30 62
LPs: 10/12-inch
ASCOT (13009 "The Angels Sing 12 of Their Greatest Hits")..........................20-30 64
(Monaural.)
ASCOT (16009 "The Angels Sing 12 of Their Greatest Hits")..........................30-40 64
(Stereo.)
CAPRICE (LP-1001 "And the Angels Sing")....................................40-50 62
(Monaural.)
CAPRICE (SLP-1001 "And the Angels Sing")....................................50-75 62
(Stereo.)
COLLECTABLES.......................... 5-8 80s
SMASH (27039 "My Boyfriend's Back")....................................30-40 63
(Monaural.)
SMASH (67039 "My Boyfriend's Back")....................................50-75 63
(Stereo.)
SMASH (27048 "A Halo to You") ...30-40 63
(Monaural.)
SMASH (67048 "A Halo to You") ...40-60 63
(Stereo.)
Members: Linda Jansen; Barbara Allbut; Phyllis "Jiggs" Allbut; Peggy Santaglia; Debra Swisher.
Also see DELICATES
Also see DUSK
Also see POWDER PUFFS
Also see SEDAKA, Neil, & Tokens / Angels / Jimmy Gilmer & Fireballs
Also see STARLETS
Also see SWISHER, Debra

ANGELS
Singles: 7-inch
DOVER 8-12

ANGELYNE
Singles: 7-inch
ERIKA (124 "Skin Tight") 40-50 83
(Five-inch picture disc. Includes poster.)
JAEVI 3-5 81
Picture Sleeves
JAEVI 3-5 81
LPs: 10/12-inch
ERIKA (9654 "Angelyne")............40-60 82
(Picture disc.)
PINK KITTEN..............................10-25 85

ANGIE
Singles: 12-inch
WEST END.................................. 4-6 84
Singles: 7-inch
STIFF 3-4 80
Picture Sleeves
STIFF 3-5 80
Also see TOWNSHEND, Peter

ANGIE & CHICKLETTES
Singles: 7-inch
APT (25080 "Treat Him Tender Maureen")..................................15-25 65
Member: Jean Thomas.
Also see RAG DOLLS

ANGIE & CITATIONS
Singles: 7-inch
ANGELA.................................... 5-8

ANGIE & MONOCOS
Singles: 7-inch
WHITETOP..................................10-15 63

ANGLO-AMERICANS
Singles: 7-inch
CHATTAHOOCHEE (705 "The Music Never Stops")..................................15-25 66

ANGLO-EMI & GROUP
Singles: 7-inch
RCA 3-5 73

ANGLOS
Singles: 7-inch
FIRE (512 "A Little Tear") 15-25 62

ANGLOS
Singles: 7-inch
ORBIT.......................................5-10 65

ANGLOS
Singles: 7-inch
SCEPTER..................................10-20 67

ANGLO-SAXON
Singles: 7-inch
TOWER (401 "Ruby")....................15-20 68
TOWER (491 "Ruby")....................15-20 69

ANGLO-SAXONS
Singles: 7-inch
SQUIRE (603 "Brown-Eyed Handsome Man")......................................30-40

ANGORIANS
Singles: 7-inch
TISHMAN.................................10-15

ANGRY MEN
Singles: 7-inch
TORCH (1002 "Come with Me").....20-30 67

ANGUS
Singles: 7-inch
BELL 3-5 71-72

ANILEY, Charlie
Singles: 7-inch
NEMPEROR...................................3-4
Picture Sleeves
NEMPEROR...................................3-5

ANIMAL JACK
Singles: 7-inch
LAURIE (3655 "Gotta Hear the Beat")......................................5-10 77

ANIMAL LOGIC *LP '89*
LPs: 10/12-inch
I.R.S. 5-8 89

ANIMAL NIGHTLIFE
Singles: 12-inch
COLUMBIA..................................4-6 83
Singles: 7-inch
INNERVISIONS..............................3-4
Picture Sleeves
INNERVISIONS..............................3-4

ANIMALS *P&R '64*
(Eric Burdon & the Animals; Original Animals)
Singles: 7-inch
ABKCO.......................................3-5 75
CAPITOL (72171 "The House of the Rising Sun")......................................25-45 64
(Canadian. Mistakenly pressed with full-length [4:28], LP version. Reissued on Quality using edited [2:58] version, as is on original U.S.A. single on MGM.)
COLLECTABLES.............................3-4 82
I.R.S. 3-5 83
JET...3-5 77
MGM 5-15 64-71
QUALITY ("The House of the Rising Sun")..5-10 60s
(Canadian. Edited [2:58] version. Selection number not known.)
STARDUST (1230 "The House of the Rising Sun")..4-6 94
(Full-length [4:28] version. U.S.-made Canadian reissue.)
Promotional Singles
ABKCO.......................................4-6 75
I.R.S. 4-6 83
JET...4-6 77
MGM 10-30 64-71
MGM CELEBRITY SCENE ("The Animals")....................................40-60 66
(Boxed set of five singles with bio insert and title strips.)
Picture Sleeves
MGM (13264 "House of the Rising Sun")......................................10-20 64
MGM (13274 "I'm Crying")............10-15 64
MGM (13298 "Boom Boom") 10-15 64
MGM (13339 "Bring It on Home to Me")......................................8-12 65
MGM (13769 "San Franciscan Nights")......................................5-10 67
MGM (13868 "Monterey")...............5-10 67
LPs: 10/12-inch
ABKCO.......................................8-12 73-76
ACCORD.....................................5-10 82
I.R.S. 5-10 83-85
MGM 15-30 64-69
PICKWICK 5-10 71
SCEPTER/CITATION 5-10 76
SPRINGBOARD 5-10 72
U.A. 5-10 77
WAND...8-12 70
Members: Eric Burdon; Alan Price; Hilton Valentine; Chas Chandler; John Steel; John Weider.
Also see BURDON, Eric
Also see McCULLOCH, Danny
Also see PRICE, Alan
Also see VALENTINE, Hilton
Also see WEIDER, John

ANIMATED EGG
LPs: 10/12-inch
ALSHIRE (5104 "Animated Egg") ..40-60 67

ANIMOTION *D&D '84*
Singles: 12-inch
MERCURY....................................4-6 84-85
Singles: 7-inch
CASABLANCA...............................3-4 86
MERCURY....................................3-4 84-85
POLYDOR....................................3-4 89
Picture Sleeves
CASABLANCA...............................3-4 86
MERCURY....................................3-4 84-85
POLYDOR....................................3-4 89
LPs: 10/12-inch
CASABLANCA...............................5-10 86
MERCURY....................................5-10 84-85
POLYDOR....................................5-8 89
Members: Astrid Plane; Bill Wadhams; Paul Engemann; Cynthia Rhodes; Charles Ottavio.
Also see DEVICE

ANITA & SO-AND-SO'S *P&R '62*
(Anita Kerr Singers)
Singles: 7-inch
RCA (7975 "Joey Baby")................10-15 62
RCA (8050 "To Each His Own").......8-12 62
Also see KERR, Anita

ANKA, Marty
Singles: 7-inch
IMPERIAL (2187 "Tell Me") 10-20 60

ANKA, Paul *P&R/R&B '57*
(With the Don Costa Orchestra)
Singles: 78 rpm
ABC-PAR...................................15-30 57
RPM...15-20 56
SPARTON/ABC (457 "Diana").........10-20 57
(10-inch LP.)
Singles: 12-inch
COLUMBIA 4-6 83
Singles: 7-inch
ABC-PAR (104 "Share Your Love")......................................15-25 58
(Promotional, fan club issue.)
ABC-PAR (296-1 "My Heart Sings")....................................25-35 58
(Stereo Compact 33 Single.)
ABC-PAR (9831 thru 9956)...........10-20 57-58
ABC-PAR (9987 "My Heart Sings")....................................10-15 58
(Monaural.)
ABC-PAR (9987 "My Heart Sings")....................................25-50 58
(Stereo.)
ABC-PAR (10011 "I Miss You So")..10-15 59
(Monaural.)
ABC-PAR (S-10011 "I Miss You So")..25-50 59
(Stereo.)
ABC-PAR (10022 "Lonely Boy").....10-15 59
(Monaural.)
ABC-PAR (S-10022 "Lonely Boy") 25-50 59
(Stereo.)
ABC-PAR (10040 "Put Your Head on My Shoulder")................................10-15 59
(Monaural.)
ABC-PAR (S-10040 "Put Your Head on My Shoulder")................................25-50 59
(Stereo.)
ABC-PAR (10064 "Time to Cry")....10-15 59
(Monaural.)
ABC-PAR (S-10064 "Time to Cry")..25-50 59
(Stereo.)
ABC-PAR (10082 "Puppy Love") ...10-15 60
(Monaural.)
ABC-PAR (S-10082 "Puppy Love")......................................25-50 60
(Stereo.)
ABC-PAR (10106 "My Home Town")....................................10-15 60
(Monaural.)
ABC-PAR (S-10106 "My Home Town")....................................25-50 60
(Stereo.)
ABC-PAR (10132 "Hello Young Lovers")..................................10-15 60
(Monaural.)
ABC-PAR (10132 "Hello Young Lovers")..................................25-50 60
(Stereo.)
ABC-PAR (10147 "Summer's Gone")....................................10-15 60
(Monaural.)
ABC-PAR (S-10147 "Summer's Gone")....................................25-50 60
(Stereo.)
ABC-PAR (10168 "The Story of My Love")......................................10-15 61
(Monaural.)
ABC-PAR (S-10168 "The Story of My Love")......................................25-50 61
(Stereo.)
ABC-PAR (10194 thru 10338).........8-15 61-62
BARNABY 3-6 71
BUDDAH.....................................3-6 72-78
COLUMBIA 3-4 83-85
ERIC..3-5 74
FAME 3-5 73
RCA (Except 2000, 8000, 9000 and 10000 series)......................................3-8 67-79
RCA (2000 series) 10-20 62
(With "VLP" or "VP" prefix. Stereo Compact 33 series.)
RCA (37-7977 "Love Me Warm and Tender")....................................15-25 62
(Compact 33 Single.)
RCA (47-7977 "Love Me Warm and Tender")......................................5-10 62
RCA (8000 series, except 8893) 5-10 62-66
RCA (8893 "I Can't Help Lovin' You")..15-25 66
RCA (9000 series) 5-10 67-69
RCA (10000 series) 3-5 78-81
RPM (472 "I Confess")..................25-50 56
RPM (499 "I Confess")...................20-40 56
SPARTON/ABC (457 "Diana").......10-20 57
(Canadian. Maroon and silver label.)
SPARTON/ABC (457 "Diana").........5-10 60s
(Canadian. Pink and black label.)
U.A. 3-5 75-77
Picture Sleeves
ABC-PAR (Except 9956) 20-30 58-61
ABC-PAR (9956 "Just Young") 50-75 58
COLUMBIA 3-5 83
ERIC 3-5 74
RCA (Except 11000 series) 8-15 62-65
RCA (11000 series) 3-6 78
U.A. 3-6 75
EPs: 7-inch
ABC 15-25 60s
(Juke box issue only.)
ABC-PAR 25-50 59
SIRE 10-12 74
(Juke box issue only.)
LPs: 10/12-inch
ABC-PAR (ABC-240 "Paul Anka") 25-35 58
(Monaural.)
ABC-PAR (ABCS-240 "Paul Anka").......................................35-50 58
(Stereo.)
ABC-PAR (ABC-296 "My Heart Sings")......................................25-35 59
(Monaural.)
ABC-PAR (ABCS-296 "My Heart Sings")......................................35-45 59
(Stereo.)
ABC-PAR (ABC-323 "Big 15")........25-35 60
(Monaural.)
ABC-PAR (ABCS-323 "Big 15")......35-45 60
(Stereo.)
ABC-PAR (ABC-347 "For Young Lovers")......................................25-30 60
(Monaural.)
ABC-PAR (ABCS-347 "For Young Lovers")......................................30-35 60
(Stereo.)
ABC-PAR (ABC-353 "Anka at the Copa")......................................25-30 60
(Monaural.)
ABC-PAR (ABCS-353 "Anka at the Copa")......................................30-35 60
(Stereo.)
ABC-PAR (ABC-360 "It's Christmas Everywhere")............................25-30 60
(Monaural.)
ABC-PAR (ABCS-360 "It's Christmas Everywhere")............................30-35 60
(Stereo.)
ABC-PAR (ABC-371 "Strictly Instrumental")............................20-30 61
(Monaural.)
ABC-PAR (ABCS-371 "Strictly Instrumental")............................25-35 61
(Stereo.)
ABC-PAR (ABC-390 "His Big 15, Vol. 2")....................................20-30 61
(Monaural.)
ABC-PAR (ABCS-390 "His Big 15, Vol. 2")....................................25-35 61
(Stereo.)
ABC-PAR (ABC-409 "His Big 15, Vol. 3")....................................20-30 62
(Monaural.)
ABC-PAR (ABCS-409 "His Big 15, Vol. 3")....................................25-35 62
(Stereo.)
ABC-PAR (ABC-420 "Diana")........20-30 62
(Monaural.)
ABC-PAR (ABCS-420 "Diana").......25-30 62
(Stereo.)
ACCORD......................................5-10 81
BARNABY.....................................8-12
BUDDAH.......................................8-12 71-76
CAMDEN.......................................5-10 74
COLUMBIA 5-10 83-85
LIBERTY.......................................5-10 81-83
PICKWICK 5-10 75
RCA (Except "LPM" & "LSP" series)..5-10 75-81
RCA (2000 thru 4000" series) 10-25 62-70
(With "LPM" prefix. Monaural.)
RCA (2000 thru 4000" series) 15-30 62-70
(With "LSP" prefix. Stereo.)
RANWOOD....................................5-10 81
RIVERA (0047 "Paul Anka and Others")....................................25-40 63
(Has two tracks by Paul Anka.)
RHINO 5-10 86
SIRE 10-12 74-78
U.A. 5-10 74-78
Also see ANN-MARGRET
Also see COSTA, Don, Orchestra
Also see KICKS & COMPANY
Also see MARLO, Micki

ANKA, Paul, & Odia Coates
Singles: 12-inch
EPIC...4-6 77
Singles: 7-inch
EPIC...3-4 76
U.A. 3-4 74-75
Also see COATES, Odia

ANKA, Paul / Sam Cooke / Neil Sedaka
LPs: 10/12-inch
RCA 15-20 64
Also see COOKE, Sam
Also see SEDAKA, Neil

ANKA, Paul, & Karla DeVito
Singles: 12-inch
COLUMBIA.......................................4-6 83
Singles: 7-inch
COLUMBIA....................................... 3-4 83
Also see DE VITO, Karla

ANKA, Paul, George Hamilton IV & Johnny Nash P&R '58
Singles: 7-inch
ABC-PAR (9974 "The Teen Commandments")........................10-15 58
Also see HAMILTON, George
Also see NASH, Johnny

ANKA, Paul / Lloyd Price
EPs: 7-inch
ABC-PAR (14 "Rockin' on 5th Ave.")..35-50 61
(Promotional issue made for Luden's, makers of 5th Avenue candy bars.)
Also see ANKA, Paul
Also see PRICE, Lloyd

ANN, Beverly: see BEVERLY ANN

ANN, Cheryl: see CHERYL ANN

ANN, Chuy
Singles
AMERICAN AUDIOGRAPHICS ("Disco Dynamite")................................. 3-5 79
(Square cardboard picture disc. Made for Scholastic Magazine. No selection number used.)

ANN, Lori: see LORI ANN

ANN, Margaret, & Ja-Das
Singles: 7-inch
W.B. 4-8 59
LPs: 10/12-inch
W.B. 10-20 59
(Not the same singer as Ann-Margret.)

ANN, Maria: see MARIA ANN

ANN, Lorie: see LORIE ANN

ANN MARIE
(Anne Marie)
Singles: 7-inch
EPIC (9465 "Dear Teddy") 5-10 61
JUBILEE (5490 "Runaround") 8-12 64
MGM (13534 "You Won't Be Sorry Baby")...8-12 66
REPRISE (20083 "Nothing Is Forever")...6-10 62
WARWICK (605 "Dream Boy") 10-20 61

ANNE, Patti: see PATTI ANNE & FLAMES

ANNE CHRISTINE
Singles: 7-inch
HBR.. 5-10 66

ANNEBELLE
LPs: 10/12-inch
ALSHIRE 8-10 70

ANNE-MARIE: see ANN MARIE

ANNETTE P&R '59
(Annette Funicello; with the Afterbeats; with Upbeats)
Singles: 78 rpm
DISNEYLAND (102 "How Will I Know")......................................25-50 58
Singles: 7-inch
BUENA VISTA (336, "Jo-Jo the Dog Faced Boy"/"Lonely Guitar")..........10-15 59
BUENA VISTA (336, "Jo-Jo the Dog Faced Boy"/"Love Me Forever")........... 8-15 59
(Note different flip side.)
BUENA VISTA (339 thru 354)......... 8-15 59-60
BUENA VISTA (359 thru 407).......15-25 60-62
BUENA VISTA (414 "Teenage Wedding")...................................20-30 63
BUENA VISTA (427 thru 436).......15-25 63-64
BUENA VISTA (337 "The Wah Watusi")......................................10-15 64
BUENA VISTA (438 "Something Borrowed")...................................15-25 65
BUENA VISTA (440 "The Monkey's Uncle")......................................10-20 65
(With the Beach Boys.)
BUENA VISTA (442 thru 475)........10-15 65-66
DISNEYLAND..................................8-10 57-58
JUGGY..8-10
STARVIEW 5-10 83
TOWER (326 "What's a Girl to Do")..20-25 67
(Name misspelled, shown as "Annettte.")
Picture Sleeves
BUENA VISTA (339 thru 375).......20-30 59-61
BUENA VISTA (384 "Blue Muu Muu")...40-60 62
BUENA VISTA (388 thru 407).......20-30 62
BUENA VISTA (414 "Teenage Wedding")...................................75-100 63
BUENA VISTA (427 "Promise Me Anything")....................................50-75 63
BUENA VISTA (431 thru 436)........20-30 64
BUENA VISTA (437 "The Wah Watusi")......................................15-25 64
BUENA VISTA (438 "Something Borrowed")...................................20-30 65
BUENA VISTA (440 "The Monkey's Uncle")......................................25-35 65
BUENA VISTA (442 thru 475)........10-20 65-66
DISNEYLAND (102 "How Will I Know My Love")..25-45 58
DISNEYLAND (105 "Meetin' at the Malt Shop")..25-45 58
EPs: 7-inch
BUENA VISTA (3301 "Annette") 50-75 59
DISNEYLAND (04 "Tall Paul") 50-75 58
DISNEYLAND (69 "Mickey Mouse Club Featuring Annette")..........................50-75 58
LPs: 10/12-inch
BUENA VISTA (3301 "Annette") 100-200 59
BUENA VISTA (3302 "Annette Sings Anka")..75-125 60
(With bonus color photo.)
BUENA VISTA (3302 "Annette Sings Anka")..50-75 60
(Without bonus photo.)
BUENA VISTA (3303 "Hawaiiannette – Songs of Hawaii")..................................30-60 60
BUENA VISTA (3304 "Italiannette – Songs with Italian Flavor")...........................30-60 60
BUENA VISTA (3305 "Dance Annette")...30-60 61
BUENA VISTA (3312 "Story of My Teens")...30-60 62
BUENA VISTA (3316 "Annette's Beach Party")..30-60 63
BUENA VISTA (3320 "Annette on Campus")..30-60 64
BUENA VISTA (3324 "Annette at Bikini Beach")..30-60 64
BUENA VISTA (3325 "Annette's Pajama Party")..30-60 64
BUENA VISTA (3327 "Annette Sings Golden Surfin' Hits")..............................30-60 65
BUENA VISTA (3328 "Something Borrowed, Something Blue")......................30-60 64
BUENA VISTA (4037 "Annette Funicello")......................................15-25 72
DISNEYLAND (Except 3906)........15-30 62-75
(Various Mouseketeer cast albums that include or feature Annette.)
DISNEYLAND (3906 "Snow White—As Told By Annette")....................................20-50
MICKEY MOUSE (12 thru 24).......35-55 57-58
(Various Mouseketeer cast albums that include or feature Annette.)
RHINO (Except 702)..........................8-10 84
RHINO (702 "Best of Annette") 25-35 84
(Picture disc.)
SILHOUETTE...................................10-15 81
STARVIEW (4001 "Country Album")...8-12 84
(Standard issue.)
STARVIEW (4001 "Country Album")..15-20 84
(Limited Edition series.)
Session: Davie Allan; Phil Baugh; Allan Reuss; Howard Roberts; Tommy Tedesco; Cliff Hils; Ed Hall; Jackie Kelso; Camarata.
Also see ALLAN, Davie
Also see AVALON, Frankie, & Annette
Also see BAUGH, Phil
Also see BEACH BOYS
Also see HONEYS
Also see MacMURRAY, Fred
Also see MOUSEKETEERS
Also see TEDESCO, Tommy
Also see WOOD, Gloria, & Afterbeats

ANNETTE / Jimmy Dodd
Singles: 78 rpm
DISNEYLAND (758 "How Will I Know"/"Annette")..........................25-50 58
(10-inch single.)
DISNEYLAND (758 "How Will I Know"/"Annette")..........................20-30 58
(Five-inch single.)
Picture Sleeves
DISNEYLAND (758 "How Will I Know"/"Annette")..........................25-50 58

ANNETTE / Hayley Mills
LPs: 10/12-inch
BUENA VISTA/DISNEYLAND (3508 "Annette & Hayley Mills") 500-750 64
(Cover reads Buena Vista but label is Disneyland. Issued with paper cover. Mail order only offer. One side by each artist.)
Also see MILLS, Hayley

ANNETTE & TOMMY SANDS
Singles: 7-inch
BUENA VISTA (802 "The Parent Trap")..10-20 61
(45 single.)
BUENA VISTA (802 "The Parent Trap")..25-35 61
(Compact 33 Single.)
Picture Sleeves
BUENA VISTA (802 "The Parent Trap")..15-25 61
Also see ANNETTE
Also see SANDS, Tommy

ANNETTE
Singles: 7-inch
FAM-LEE (1003 "How Can I Carry On")..5-10

ANNIE AMPLE
Singles
AMERICA AUDIOGRAPHICS ("Annie Ample in the Voyeur") 3-5 83
(Square cardboard picture disc. No selection number used.)

ANNIE & ORPHANS
Singles: 7-inch
CAPITOL...10-20 64
Picture Sleeves
CAPITOL...15-25 64

ANNIE G. D&D '84
Singles: 12-inch
MCA 4-6 84
Singles: 7-inch
MCA 3-4 84

ANN-MARGRET P&R '61
Singles: 12-inch
AVCO EMBASSY (4547 "Today") 10-15 70
FIRST AMERICAN (1207 "Everybody Needs Somebody Sometime") 5-10 81
MCA (1867 "Midnight Message") 5-10 80
(Promotional issue only.)
MCA (1867 "What I Do to Men") 5-10 80
OCEAN/ARIOLA AMERICA..............4-8 79-80
RAM (1001 "Everybody Needs Somebody Sometime")..5-10 81
RAM 4-8 81
Singles: 7-inch
FIRST AMERICAN 3-5 81
MCA...3-5 79-80
OCEAN/ARIOLA AMERICA..............3-5 79-80
RCA (VLP-2251 "Vivacious One") 30-50 62
(Five-disc, juke box set. With title strips.)
RCA (37-7857 "Lost Love")............20-40 61
(Compact 33 Single.)
RCA (47-7857 "Lost Love")............10-15 61
RCA (37-7894 "I Just Don't Understand")......................................20-30 61
(Compact 33 Single.)
RCA (47-7894 "I Just Don't Understand")......................................10-15 61
RCA (37-7952 "It Do Me So Good")...20-40 61
(Compact 33 Single.)
RCA (47-7952 "It Do Me So Good")...10-15 61
RCA (7986 thru 9109)..................10-15 61-66
Picture Sleeves
RCA (7894 "I Just Don't Understand")......................................15-25 61
RCA (7952 "It Do Me So Good") 15-25 61
RCA (7986 "What Am I Supposed to Do")..15-25 61
RCA (8061 "Jim Dandy") 15-25 62
RCA (8168 "Bye Bye Birdie") 15-25 63
EPs: 7-inch
RCA (2251 "The Vivacious One") ..15-25 62
RCA (2659 "Mr. Wonderful")...........15-25 63
RCA (4358 "On the Way Up").........15-25 62
RCA (9058 "On the Way Up")..........15-25 62
LPs: 10/12-inch
LHI 10-20 68-69
LAGNIAPPE 1959 ("Be My Guest")..200-300 59
(Cast LP produced by the Boys Tri-Ship Club of New Trier High School. Includes *Tropical Heat Wave* by Ann-Margret Olson.)
MCA...5-10 80
NORTHWESTERN UNIVERSITY/RCA (5760 "Among Friends")......................100-150 60
(Cast LP for the *Waa-Mu Show of 1960* from Northwestern University. Lists Ann-Margret Olson as a dancer.)
RCA (LPM-2399 "And Here She Is")...10-20 61
(Monaural.)
RCA (LSP-2399 "And Here She Is")...15-25 61
(Stereo.)
RCA (LPM-2453 "On the Way Up")...10-20 62
(Monaural.)
RCA (LSP-2453 "On the Way Up")...15-25 62
(Stereo.)
RCA (LPM-2251 "Vivacious One") 10-20 62
(Monaural.)
RCA (LSP-2251 "Vivacious One") 15-25 62
(Stereo.)
RCA (LPM-2659 "Bachelor's Paradise")......................................10-20 63
(Monaural.)
RCA (LSP-2659 "Bachelor's Paradise")......................................15-25 63
(Stereo.)
RCA/NARM ("Tenth Anniversary Convention")....................................40-60 68
(Has *Bye Bye Birdie* by Ann-Margret, plus tracks by the Limeliters, Al Hirt, Paul Anka, Homer & Jethro, Peter Nero, Eddy Arnold, John Gary, Chet Atkins, Floyd Cramer, Anita Kerr Singers, Boots Randolph, Myron Cohen, Barry Sadler, Henry Mancini, Jack Jones, and Harry Belafonte. Promotional, souvenir issue only.)
Also see ANKA, Paul
Also see ARNOLD, Eddy
Also see ATKINS, Chet
Also see BELAFONTE, Harry
Also see COHEN, Myron
Also see CRAMER, Floyd
Also see HOMER & JETHRO
Also see JONES, Jack
Also see KERR, Anita
Also see LIMELITERS
Also see MANCINI, Henry
Also see NERO, Peter
Also see RANDOLPH, Boots
Also see SADLER, Barry
Also see SEDAKA, Neil / Ann-Margret / Browns / Sam Cooke

ANN-MARGRET & JOHN GARY LP '64
LPs: 10/12-inch
RCA (LPM-2947 "Broadway Hits") .10-20 64
(Monaural.)
RCA (LSP-2947 "Broadway Hits")..15-25 64
(Stereo.)
Also see GARY, John

ANN-MARGRET & LEE HAZLEWOOD
Singles: 7-inch
LHI 5-10 68-69
LPs: 10/12-inch
LHI (12007 "The Cowboy and the Lady")..15-20 69
Also see HAZLEWOOD, Lee

ANN-MARGRET & AL HIRT
Singles: 7-inch
RCA (VLP-2690 "Beauty and the Beard")...25-50 64
(Five-disc, juke box set. With title strips.)
RCA (9524 "Slowly")........................5-10 68
EPs: 7-inch
RCA (LSP-2690 "Beauty and the Beard")...15-25 64
LPs: 10/12-inch
RCA (LPM-2690 "Beauty and the Beard")...10-20 64
(Monaural.)
RCA (LSP-2690 "Beauty and the Beard")...15-25 64
(Stereo.)
Also see HIRT, Al

ANN-MARGRET / Kitty Kalen / Della Reese
LPs: 10/12-inch
RCA (2724 "3 Great Girls")............15-20 63
Also see ANN-MARGRET
Also see KALEN, Kitty
Also see REESE, Della

ANN-MICHAEL
Singles: 7-inch
KIP 4-8 63

ANNONYMOUS
Singles: 7-inch
PLANET 10-15 58

ANNUALS
Singles: 7-inch
CONN (2 "Once in a Lifetime") ..200-300 62
MARCONN (1 "Once in a Lifetime")..................................100-150 62

ANONYMOUS
Singles: 7-inch
FLAT 15-20
LPs: 10/12-inch
MAJOR (1002 "Inside the Shadow")...................................200-300 76
Members: Marsha Rollings; Glenn Weaver; Ron Matelic; John Medvescek.

ANONYMOUS FIVE
Singles: 7-inch
HAL & RON (703 "Just a Little")......25-35

ANONYMOUS SOLDIER
Singles: 7-inch
PEACE...3-5 71

ANOTHER BAD CREATION LP '91
LPs: 10/12-inch
MOTOWN 5-8 91

ANQUETTE
LPs: 10/12-inch
LUKE SKYWALKER.............................5-8 88

ANSWER
Singles: 7-inch
WHITE WHALE (225 "I'll Be In")......20-30 65

ANSWER
Singles: 7-inch
COLUMBIA 4-8 67

ANSWERS
Singles: 7-inch
UNITED (212 "Keeps Me Worried All the Time")..50-75 57

ANT, Adam LP '82
Singles: 12-inch
EPIC...4-6 82-85
Singles: 7-inch
EPIC...3-4 82-85
MCA...3-4 90
Picture Sleeves
EPIC...3-4 84
LPs: 10/12-inch
EPIC...5-10 82-85
MCA...5-8 90
Also see ADAM & ANTS
Also see COPELAND, Stewart, & Adam Ant

ANT TRIP CEREMONY
LPs: 10/12-inch
CRC (2129 "24 Hours")..................400-500 67
RESURRECTION ("24 Hours")..........50-75
(Selection number not known.)
Members: Roger Goodman; Gary Rosen; Steve DeTray; George Galt; Mark Stein; Jeff Williams.

ANTEL, Joe
Singles: 7-inch
GONE 8-12 59

ANTELL, Peter P&R '62
(Pete Antell)
Singles: 7-inch
BOUNTY (103 "The Times They Are A-Changin' ")..................................15-25 65
CAMEO (234 "Night Time")............10-20 62
CAMEO (264 "Keep It Up")..............10-20 63
Also see JAYWALKER & PEDESTRIANS
Also see WILD ONES

ANTENNAS
Singles: 7-inch
CLAY (201 "Fujiyama Mama").......15-25 59

ANTHEM
Singles: 7-inch
BUFFALO (003 "It's You") 8-10
REGER (101 "It's You") 5-8 74
LPs: 10/12-inch
BUDDAH (5071 "Anthem") 20-25 71

ANTHONY, Al
(With Gregory Rhodes Orchestra)
Singles: 7-inch
ALA (771 "My Heart Needs You")..50-100 60s

ANTHONY, Al, Quartet
Singles: 7-inch
SHARON...4-8

ANTHONY, Alan R&B '82
Singles: 7-inch
CHALET 3-4 82

ANTHONY, Don
Singles: 7-inch
BEST 3-5 60s

ANTHONY, El
Singles: 7-inch
LA-CINDY 10-15

ANTHONY, Frankie
Singles: 7-inch
DRA (329 "Little Girls Have Big Ears")..8-12 63
JOEY (101 "Goin' to the River").....15-25 62
PARADISE (1003 "Goin' to the River")..10-20 63
REPRISE (20195 "Seven Kisses")...8-12 63

ANTHONY, Jimmy
Singles: 7-inch
ROULETTE 4-8 62

ANTHONY, Joe
Singles: 7-inch
APOLLO..5-8

ANTHONY, Joey
Singles: 7-inch
MYERS 8-12 60

ANTHONY, Johnny
Singles: 7-inch
ACE 8-12 61

ANTHONY, Johnny Ray
Singles: 7-inch
GO 3-5

ANTHONY, Joy, & Dreamers
Singles: 7-inch
SINCLAIR (1001 "Earth Angel").....50-75 61

ANTHONY, Lamont
(La Mont Anthony; Lamont Dozier)
Singles: 7-inch
ANNA (1125 "Popeye")................100-200 60
ANNA (1125-G "Benny the Skinny Man")..25-50 60
(Number at bottom has a "G.")
ANNA (1125 "Benny the Skinny Man")..15-25 60
(Number at bottom has no "G.")
CHECK MATE (1001 "Just to Be Loved")...100-150 61
MEL-O-DY.......................................10-15 64
Also see DOZIER, Lamont

ANTHONY, Marc
Singles: 7-inch
AXTEL (100 "Penny")....................15-25 60
AXTEL (102 "Party Doll")...............15-25 61
DIAMOND (140 "Why Do I Love You")..5-10 63

ANTHONY, Mark
Singles: 7-inch
LA BELLE (779 "I Saw Mama Twistin' with Santa Claus")..................................5-10 62
PORTER (1005 "Wolf Call") 25-35 58
Also see AGARY, Rickey
Also see HOLLYWOOD STARS

ANTHONY, Mark
Singles: 7-inch
TABU 3-4 88

ANTHONY, Markus R&B '86
Singles: 7-inch
ROCK & ROLL 3-4 86

ANTHONY, Mel
Singles: 7-inch
DUEL 5-10 62

ANTHONY, Mike
Singles: 7-inch
IMPERIAL (5813 "Little Linda")......30-40 61

ANTHONY, Nick
Singles: 7-inch
ABC-PAR 15-20 59
CINDY..15-25 58

ANTHONY, Paul
Singles: 7-inch
FIREFLY ("My Promise to You")...50-100 58
(First issue. Selection number not known.)
GAMBIT (1103 "Hello Teardrops, Goodbye Love")..50-75 62
METRO INT'L (1003 "Step Up").......50-75
ROULETTE (4099 "My Promise to You")..20-30 58

ANTHONY, Ray, & His Orchestra P&R '49
Singles: 78 rpm
CAPITOL...3-5 49-57
Singles: 7-inch
CAPITOL...3-6 50-62
RANWOOD..3-5 68
EPs: 7-inch
CAPITOL...5-10 52-59
LPs: 10/12-inch
CAPITOL...5-15 52-62
Also see BEACH BOYS / Ray Anthony

Also see SINATRA, Frank

ANTHONY, Rayburn C&W '76
(Ray B. Anthony)
Singles: 7-inch
MEGA 4-6 71
MERCURY 3-5 79
POLYDOR 3-5 76-78
SUN 15-25 59-62
Member: Brad Suggs.
Also see SUGGS, Brad

ANTHONY, Rayburn, & Kitty Wells C&W '79
Singles: 7-inch
MERCURY 3-5 79
Also see ANTHONY, Rayburn
Also see WELLS, Kitty

ANTHONY, Richard
Singles: 7-inch
CAPITOL 4-8 64
FAYETTE 4-8 64
SWAN (4257 "No Good") 25-45 66
V.I.P. (25022 "I Don't Know What to Do") 10-15 65
VIRTUE (189 "Keep on Livin' ") 100-150 60s

ANTHONY, Sheila
Singles: 7-inch
BUTTERCUP (007 "Livin' in Love") 10-20 60s

ANTHONY, Tony
Singles: 7-inch
HERALD (533 "Lonely One") 15-25 58

ANTHONY, Vince C&W '82
(With the Country Blue Notes)
Singles: 7-inch
HILTON (0007 "Too Hot to Handle") 30-50
MIDNIGHT GOLD 3-4 82
VIKING (1018 "All Over Again") 15-25 60s

ANTHONY, Wayne
(Little Wayne Anthony)
Singles: 7-inch
ROULETTE (4662 "A Thousand Miles Away") 10-15 66
ROULETTE (4672 "Little Miss Lonely") 10-15 66
VEE JAY 8-12 63-64
WALANA (102 "Blow Me a Kiss") 150-250

ANTHONY & AQUA LADS
Singles: 7-inch
GOLD BEE (1650 "I Remember") 40-60 60s

ANTHONY & CAMP R&B '86
Singles: 12-inch
W.B. 4-6 86
Singles: 7-inch
W.B. 3-4 86
Picture Sleeves
W.B. 3-4 86
LPs: 10/12-inch
W.B. 5-10 86
Member: Anthony Malloy.
Also see TEMPER

ANTHONY & DELSONICS
Singles: 7-inch
EMERGE 5-10

ANTHONY & IMPERIALS: see LITTLE ANTHONY & IMPERIALS

ANTHONY & SOPHOMORES
Singles: 7-inch
ABC-PAR (10737 "Gee") 15-25 65
ABC-PAR (10770 "Get Back to You") 10-15 66
ABC-PAR (10844 "Heartbreak") 10-15 66
COLLECTABLES 3-4 82
GRAND (163 "Embraceable You") 50-100 63
JAMIE (1330 "Serenade") 10-15 66
JAMIE (1340 "One Summer Night") 10-15 67
JASON SCOTT 4-8
MERCURY (72103 "Play Those Oldies Mr. D.J.") 50-75 63
(Black label.)
MERCURY (72103 "Play Those Oldies Mr. D.J.") 50-75 63
(White label. Promotional issue only.)
MERCURY (72103 "Play Those Oldies Mr. D.J.") 15-25 65
(Red label.)
MERCURY (72168 "Better Late Than Never") 15-25 63
Member: Anthony "Tony" Maresco.
Also see DYNAMICS, Featuring Tony Maresco
Also see TONY & TWILIGHTS

ANTHRAX LP '85
LPs: 10/12-inch
ISLAND 5-10 85-90
MEGAFORCE 5-10 87-91
Members: Joey Belladonna; Greg D'Angelo; Frank Bello.
Also see WHITE LION

ANTIQUES
Singles: 7-inch
HI (2105 "So Many Ways") 20-30 66
LASALLE (69 "Go for Yourself") 300-400

ANTIX
LPs: 10/12-inch
ENIGMA 5-10 85

ANTOINETTE, Marie
Singles: 7-inch
PROVIDENCE (405 "He's My Dream Boy") 10-20 63

ANTOINETTS
Singles: 7-inch
KAREN 5-10

ANTON, Ray, & Peppermint Men
Singles: 7-inch
ABC-PAR 5-10 65

ANTON, Susan
Singles: 7-inch
COLUMBIA 3-5 78
SCOTTI BROTHERS 3-4 80
Picture Sleeves
COLUMBIA 4-6 78
Also see KNOBLOCK, Fred, & Susan Anton

ANTONES
Singles: 7-inch
BLACKCREST 10-15 57

ANTONS
Singles: 7-inch
TY-TEX (104 "Larry's Tune") 10-20 62

ANTRELL, Dave
Singles: 7-inch
AMARET 3-5 70-72
LPs: 10/12-inch
AMARET 8-12 70
Also see LITTLE FLAYTUS & DREAMAIRES
Also see MAYE, Arthur Lee

ANTWINETTS
Singles: 7-inch
RCA (7398 "Johnny") 25-35 58

ANVIL LP '87
LPs: 10/12-inch
ENIGMA 5-10 87
Members: "Lips;" Dave Allison; Ian Dickson; Robb Reiner.

ANVIL BAND
LPs: 10/12-inch
FREE SPIRIT 5-10 78

ANY TROUBLE
Singles: 7-inch
EMI AMERICA 3-4 83
STIFF 3-4 80
Picture Sleeves
STIFF 3-5 80
LPs: 10/12-inch
EMI AMERICA 5-10 83
STIFF 5-10 80-81

ANYWAY, Ernest, & Mighty Squirrels
Singles: 7-inch
POPLLAMA 3-4 86
LPs: 10/12-inch
POPLLAMA 5-10 86
Members: Rob Morgan; Scott McCaughey; Tad Hutchison; Jimbo Sangster; Chuck Carroll.

AORTA LP '69
Singles: 7-inch
ATLANTIC (2545 "Strange") 10-20 68
COLUMBIA (44870 "Strange") 5-10 69
HAPPY TIGER (567 "Sandcastles") 10-15 70
LPs: 10/12-inch
COLUMBIA (9785 "Aorta") 15-25 69
COLUMBIA (38000 series) 5-10
HAPPY TIGER (1010 "Aorta 2") 35-55 70
Members: Bill Herman; Billy Jones; Jim Donlinger; Jim Nyeholt.

APACHE
LPs: 10/12-inch
AKASHIC (2777 "Maitreya Itali") 1000-1500 71

APACHE
Singles: 7-inch
ROULETTE 3-5 75

APACHE
Singles: 7-inch
EMERALD CITY 3-5 81
LPs: 10/12-inch
EMERALD CITY 5-10 81

APACHEE
Singles: 7-inch
XR-3 4-6 69

APACHES
Singles: 7-inch
HI 5-10 63
MERCURY 4-8 64

APE QUARTET
Singles: 7-inch
PHALANX (1024 "Tarzan") 15-25

APES
Singles: 7-inch
MERCURY 4-8 64

APHRODITES CHILD
Singles: 7-inch
PHILIPS (40536 "Other People") 10-20 68
PHILIPS (40549 "Rain & Tears") 10-20 68
POLYDOR 4-8 69
VERTIGO 3-5 72
LPs: 10/12-inch
VERTIGO (500 "Apocalypse of John") 15-20 72
Members: Demis Roussos; Vangelis Papatharassiou; Lucas Sideras; Silver Koulouris.
Also see ROUSSOS, Demis
Also see VANGELIS

APOCALYPSE
LPs: 10/12-inch
COLOSSUS 8-12 70

APOCRYPHALS
Singles: 7-inch
MAD 4-8 68

APOLLAS
Singles: 7-inch
ABC-PAR 5-10 65
LOMA (2019 "Lock Me in Your Heart") 10-15 65
LOMA (2025 "Nobody's Baby") 8-12 66
LOMA (2039 "Pretty Red Balloons") 8-12 66
LOMA (2053 "Sorry Mama") 8-12 66
W.B. (5893 "Mr. Creator") 40-60 67
W.B. (7060 "Jive Cat") 10-15 67
W.B. (7086 "Who Would Want Me Now") 10-15 67
W.B. (7181 "Seven Days") 10-15 68

APOLLO
Singles: 12-inch
MOTOWN 4-6 79
Singles: 7-inch
GORDY 3-4 79
LPs: 10/12-inch
GORDY 5-10 79

APOLLO, Al
Singles: 7-inch
CUB (9121 "I'm Walkin' Ahead") 10-15 63

APOLLO, Guiseppi
(With the Revels & Mapes Sisters)
Singles: 7-inch
IMPACT (12 "All Because of You") 8-12 61
Also see REVELS

APOLLO, Guy
Singles: 7-inch
ABC-PAR (10732 "Things We Did Last Summer") 8-10 65
HIBACK (106 "Big Man in Town") 8-10 66
LOADSTONE (1603 "Give Me Time") 10-15 64

APOLLO, Johnny
(With the Numbers)
Singles: 7-inch
BONNEVILLE 10-20 62
GNP 5-10 69
LUNA (1001 "Sweet Thing") 15-25
STAR PHONE (11 "Goddess of Love") 10-20 60s
Also see NUMBERS

APOLLO, Tony, & Rhythm Rascals
Singles: 78 rpm
Rockin' Records (101 "For Ages and Ages") 15-25

APOLLO BROTHERS
Singles: 7-inch
CLEVELAND (108 "My Beloved") 35-45 60
LOCKET (108 "My Beloved") 25-35 60
Member: Ruben Guevara.
Also see GUEVARA, Reuben

APOLLO 11 MISSION
Singles: 7-inch
UA (42099 "Man on the Moon – Decade in a Day") 4-8 69
(Promotional issue, "Compliments of the Washington Senators.")
Picture Sleeves
UA (42099 "Man on the Moon – Decade in a Day") 5-10 69
(Promotional issue, "Compliments of the Washington Senators.")

APOLLO 100 P&R/LP '72
Singles: 7-inch
ATCO 3-5 74
EUROGRAM 3-5 77
MEGA 3-5 71-72
LPs: 10/12-inch
MEGA 5-10 72
Member: Tom Parker.

APOLLO'S APACHES
Singles: 7-inch
ANYBODY'S (6088 "Cry Me a Lie") 50-75

APOLLOES
Singles: 7-inch
LOOK 5-8 64

APOLLONIA 6 P&R/R&B/D&D/LP '84
Singles: 12-inch
W.B. 4-6 84-85
Singles: 7-inch
W.B. 3-4 84-85
Picture Sleeves
W.B. 3-4 84-85
LPs: 10/12-inch
W.B. 5-10 84-85
Members: Patty Kotero; Brenda Bennett; Susan Moonsie.
Also see VANITY 6

APOLLOS
Singles: 7-inch
GALAXY (707 "I Can't Believe It") 30-50 61
HARVARD (803 "I Love You Darling") 200-300 59

APOLLOS
Singles: 7-inch
MERCURY (71614 "Just Dreamin' ") 5-10 60
Member: Keith MacKendrick.

APOLLOS
Singles: 7-inch
GLO (5218 "Walk By Myself") 200-400 61
Session: Rocky Hart.
Also see HART, Rocky

APOLLOS
Singles: 7-inch
CITE (5006 "For Pete's Sake") 8-12 64
RAYNARD (602 "Flip Side") 10-20 64
(Also issued as by the Tigers.)
Members: Roland Stone; Denny McCarthy; Pete Miller; Bobby Reindorp.
Also see STEFAN, Paul
Also see STONE, Roland
Also see TIGERS

APOLLOS
LPs: 10/12-inch
CALIFORNIA 20-30 64

APOLLOS
Singles: 7-inch
DELTA (183 "That's the Breaks") 20-30 65
MONTGOMERY (011 "Target Love") 20-30 65
MONTGOMERY (012 "It's a Monster") 20-30 65

APOLLOS
Singles: 7-inch
LOMA (2025 "Nobody's Baby") 5-8 65

APOLLOS
Singles: 7-inch
COLOSSUS 4-6 69

APOLLOS
Singles: 7-inch
BOBBY (5003 "I Know Your Mind") 10-20 60s

APOLLOS
LPs: 10/12-inch
CICADELIC 5-10 86

APOLLOS
Singles: 7-inch
ORLYN (985 "Nora Lee") 25-35

APOSTLE, Johnny, & Willows
Singles: 7-inch
POWER (01 "I Love Ya Honey") 10-15

APOSTLES
Singles: 7-inch
UA 8-12 64

APOSTLES
Singles: 7-inch
A2 10-15 66

APOSTLES
Singles: 7-inch
WGW (18702 "I'm a Lucky Guy") 30-50 66

APOSTLES
Singles: 7-inch
BBS 5-10
KAPP 4-8 69

APOSTLES
Singles: 7-inch
WELHAVEN (125935 "Help Me Find a Way") 40-60 67

APOSTLES
LP: 10/12-inch
SOUND RECORDING 5-10

APPALACHIANS P&R '63
Singles: 7-inch
ABC-PAR 4-8 62-63
GOLDIE 8-10

APPALOOSA LP '69
Singles: 7-inch
CONCORD 3-5 74
LPs: 10/12-inch
COLUMBIA 10-15 69
WHITE GOLD 5-10 82
Members: Robin Batteaux; Al Kooper.
Also see BATTEAUX
Also see KOOPER, Al

APPARITIONS
Singles: 7-inch
CAPED CRUSADER ("She's So Satisfying") 4-8 86
(Colored vinyl.)
Members: Forrest Dieckman; Tom Weir; Doug Retherford; Mike McNerney; Ken Burke.

APPEGGIOS
Singles: 7-inch
ARIES (001 "I'll Be Singing") 30-50 63

APPELL, Dave
(Dave Appell Trio)
Singles: 78 rpm
LONDON 5-8 50
PRESIDENT 8-12 55-56
Singles: 7-inch
CAMEO (184 "The Young Ones") 5-10 60
LONDON 10-15 50
PRESIDENT (1005 "Ring Around My Baby") 15-25 55
PRESIDENT (1006 "Teenage Meeting") 15-25 55
LPs: 10/12-inch
CAMEO (1004 "Alone Together") 35-50 58
Also see APPLEJACKS

APPICE, Carmine
Singles: 7-inch
PASHA 3-4 82
LPs: 10/12-inch
PASHA 8-10 82
Also see BECK, BOGERT & APPICE
Also see HEAR 'N AID
Also see KGB
Also see KING KOBRA
Also see STEWART, Rod

APPLE
Singles: 7-inch
PAGE ONE (21,012 "Buffalo Billycan") 4-8
SMASH 4-8 68

APPLE & APPLEBERRY
Singles: 7-inch
ABC 3-5 74
LPs: 10/12-inch
ABC 8-10 73

APPLE & THREE ORANGES
Singles: 7-inch
STANSON 3-5 71

APPLE GLASS CYNDROM
Singles: 7-inch
COLUMN (691 "Someday") 20-30 69

APPLE PIE MOTHERHOOD BAND
Singles: 7-inch
ATLANTIC 4-6 68-69
LPs: 10/12-inch
ATLANTIC 10-15 68-69

APPLE PIE 'N STOVER
Singles: 7-inch
ERA 3-5 72

APPLEBAUM, Stan
Singles: 7-inch
W.B. 5-10
Also see COVAY, Don

APPLEBEE, Marie
Singles: 7-inch
JUBILEE 4-8 67

APPLEJACKS P&R '58
Singles: 78 rpm
CAMEO 10-20 57-58
DECCA 5-10 54
PRESIDENT 5-10 56
TONE-CRAFT 5-10 55
Singles: 7-inch
CAMEO (100 series) 10-20 57-60
CAMEO (200 & 300 series) 6-12 61-64
DECCA 10-15 54
PRESIDENT 10-20 56
TONE-CRAFT 10-20 55
Member: Dave Appell.
Also see APPELL, Dave

APPLEJACKS
Singles: 7-inch
LONDON 5-10 64
Members: Al Jackson; Gerry Freeman; Don Gould; Phil Cash; Martin Baggott; Megan Davies.

APPLESEED, Johnny
Singles: 7-inch
RAMCO 4-6 68

APPLETON, Charlie
Singles: 7-inch
ROCKET 5-8 61

APPLETON, Jon
LPs: 10/12-inch
FLYING DUTCHMAN 8-10 69-70

APPLETON SYNTONIC MENAGERIE
Singles: 7-inch
FLYING DUTCHMAN 3-6 69
LPs: 10/12-inch
FLYING DUTCHMAN 10-12 69

APPLETREE THEATRE CO.
Singles: 7-inch
VERVE FORECAST 5-10 67-68
LPs: 10/12-inch
VERVE FORECAST (3042 "Playback") 15-25 68
Members: Chuck Rainey; Herb Lovell; Terence Boylan; John Boylan; Larry Coryell; Rick Nelson.
Also see BOYLAN, Terence
Also see ELEVENTH HOUSE
Also see NELSON, Rick

APPOINTMENTS
Singles: 7-inch
DE-LITE (520 "I Saw You There") 200-300 63

APPOLLO BROTHERS
Singles: 7-inch
CLEVELAND (108 "My Beloved One") 50-75 60
LOCKET (108 "My Beloved One") 50-75 60
Member: Ruben Guevara.
Also see GUEVARA, Reuben

APPRECIATIONS
Singles: 7-inch
AWARE (1066 "I Can't Hide It") 400-500 60s
JUBILEE 5-10 66
SPORT (108 "There's a Place in My Heart") 50-100 67
SPORT (111 "It's Better to Cry") 100-200 67

APRIL
(April Stevens)
Singles: 7-inch
A&M 3-5 74
Also see STEVENS, April

APRIL, Johnny
LPs: 10/12-inch
APOLLO....20-30 59

APRIL & NINO: see TEMPO, Nino, & April Stevens

APRIL FOOLS
Singles: 7-inch
MGM....4-8 68
MONUMENT....3-4 70

APRIL MAE & BLUE SKIES
Singles: 7-inch
EMBER....5-10 63

APRIL, MAY & JUNE
Singles: 7-inch
RCA....4-8 65

APRIL WINE P&R '72
Singles: 7-inch
BIG TREE....3-5 72-75
CAPITOL....3-4 78-85
LONDON....3-4 76-78
Picture Sleeves
CAPITOL (Except 4975)....3-4 81-84
CAPITOL (4975 "Just Between You and Me")....3-4 81
(Sleeve opens to a 22"x15" poster.)
CAPITOL (4975 "Just Between You and Me")....3-4 81
(Standard sleeve—no poster.)
LPs: 10/12-inch
AQUARIUS....5-10
ATLANTIC....5-10 81
BIG TREE....10-15 72-75
CAPITOL....5-10 78-85
LONDON....10-12 76-77
Members: Steve Lang; Jerry Mercer; Myles Goodwyn; Brian Greenway; Gary Moffet.
Also see MASHMAKHAN

APTER, Bill
Singles: 7-inch
POLY-T (7968 "Hey Patty")....5-10 74
UNRELEASED GOLD....3-4

AQUA
LPs: 10/12-inch
VIRGIN....5-10

AQUA SONICS
Singles: 7-inch
DAKAR....3-5

AQUAMEN
Singles: 7-inch
HIBACK....5-10 66
SPRING....5-10 66

AQUANAUTS
Singles: 7-inch
SAFARI (1005 "Rumble on the Docks")....20-30 63
SAFARI (1008 "High Divin' ")....20-30 63
SANDE (104 "High Divin' ")....10-15 64
Members: Tom Harding; Steve Harding.

AQUA-NITES
Singles: 7-inch
ASTRA (1000 "Carioca")....8-12 65
ASTRA (2001 "Christy")....50-75 62
ASTRA (2002 "Carioca")....40-60 62

AQUARIAN AGE
Singles: 7-inch
ITCO (102 "Easy to Be Hard")....4-8
MERCURY (72881 "I Can't Grow Flowers in My Yard")....4-8 69
MERCURY (72915 "I Saw the Sky")....4-8 69

AQUARIAN DREAM LP '76
Singles: 7-inch
BUDDAH....3-5 76-77
ELEKTRA....3-4 78
LPs: 10/12-inch
BUDDAH....8-10 76
ELEKTRA....5-10 78-79
Members: Claude Bartee; Pete Bartee; Jacques Burvick; Mike Fowler; Valerie Horn; Gloria Jones; Pat Shannon.
Also see CONNORS, Norman

AQUARIANS LP '69
Singles: 7-inch
UNI....4-6 69
LPs: 10/12-inch
UNI....12-15 69

AQUARIANS
Singles: 7-inch
MGM....4-6 72
Member: Razzy Bailey.
Also see BAILEY, Razzy

AQUATONES P&R/R&B '58
Singles: 78 rpm
FARGO (1001 "You")....25-50 58
Singles: 7-inch
FARGO (1001 "You")....20-25 58
FARGO (1002 "Say You'll Be Mine")....20-25 58
FARGO (1003 "The Drive-In")....20-25 58
FARGO (1005 "My Treasure")....15-25 59
FARGO (1011 "My Darling")....15-25 60
FARGO (1015 "Every Time")....15-25 59
FARGO (1016 "Crazy for You")....15-20 61
FARGO (1022 "My Treasure")....15-20 62
LPs: 10/12-inch
FARGO (3001 "The Aquatones Sing for You")....250-350 64
RELIC/FARGO (5033 "The Aquatones Sing for You")....8-10 80s
Members: Barbara Lee; Larry Vannata; Vic Castro; Russ Nagy; Mike Roma; Tom Vivona.

ARABIAN PRINCE LP '89
Singles: 7-inch
ORPHEUS....3-4 89
LPs: 10/12-inch
ORPHEUS....5-8 89

ARABIANS
(With Earl Williams & His Globes)
Singles: 7-inch
CARRIE (1516 "My One Possession")....200-300 61
CARRIE (1606 "You Upset Me Baby")....50-75 62
JAM (3738 "Heaven Sent You")....150-250 60
LANROD (1606 "You Upset Me Baby")....50-75 60
MAGNIFICANT (102 "Crazy Little Fever")....50-75 60
(Note spelling:"Magnificant" rather than Magnificent.)
MAGNIFICENT (102 "Crazy Little Fever")....500-750 60
(Correct label spelling. Black vinyl. Colored vinyl copies are bootlegs.)
MAGNIFICENT (114 "Teardrops in the Night")....250-350 61
(Colored vinyl.)
TWIN STAR (1018 "Heaven Sent You")....25-50 60
Also see HAMILTON, Edward

ARABIANS
Singles: 7-inch
LEMANS (004 "Take a Chance on Me")....100-150 64
STAFF (1808 "Let Me Try")....20-40 60s

ARABIANS
Singles: 7-inch
JAY-WALKING....8-12 60s

ARAGON, Johnny
Singles: 7-inch
AIRLOK (600 "There Was a Girl")....10-20 60
DONDEE (1044 "I Get So Lonely")....10-20 60
SOUND-O-RAMA (105 "That's All I Want from You")....8-12 62

ARAGON BALLROOM ORCHESTRA
Singles: 12-inch
FANTASY....4-6 78

ARAGONS
Singles: 7-inch
MOSAIC (1009 "Be My Little Girl")....10-15 60s

ARATA, Tony C&W '84
Singles: 7-inch
NOBLE VISION....3-4 84-85

ARBOGAST & ROSS
Singles: 7-inch
LIBERTY (55197 "Chaos")....10-15 59
Picture Sleeves
LIBERTY (55197 "Chaos")....40-50 59
Members: Bob Arbogast; Stan Ross.
Also see ROSS, Stan

ARBORS P&R '66
Singles: 7-inch
CARNEY (1011 "A Symphony for Susan")....10-20 66
COLUMBIA....3-5 73
(Black vinyl.)
COLUMBIA....5-10 73
(Colored vinyl. Promotional only.)
COLUMBIA HALL of FAME....3-4
DATE....4-6 66-70
(Black vinyl.)
DATE....5-10 66-70
(Colored vinyl. Promotional only.)
MERCURY....4-6 65
LPs: 10/12-inch
ARBORS MUSIC....8-10
DATE....12-15 67-68
VANGUARD....15-20 62
Members: Ed Farran; Fred Farran; Scott Herrick; Tom Herrick.

ARBUCKLE
Singles: 7-inch
MUSICAR....3-5 73
LPs: 10/12-inch
MUSICAR....5-10 72

ARC
Singles: 7-inch
LIFESONG....3-5 78
LPs: 10/12-inch
LIFESONG....5-10 78

ARCADE, Gene
Singles: 7-inch
REEL....8-12 59

ARCADES
Singles: 7-inch
COLLECTABLES....3-4 82
GUYDEN (2015 "Blackmail")....10-20 59
JOHNSON (116 "Fine Little Girl")....50-75 62
JOHNSON (320 "Fine Little Girl")....75-125 60
Also see ARKADES

ARCADES
Singles: 7-inch
TRIAD (502 "There's Got to Be a Loser")....75-125 60s

ARCADIA P&R/D&D/LP '85
Singles: 12-inch
CAPITOL....4-6 85-86
Singles: 7-inch
CAPITOL....3-4 85-86
Picture Sleeves
CAPITOL....3-4 85-86
LPs: 10/12-inch
CAPITOL....5-10 85-86
Members: Roger Taylor; Simon LeBon; Nick Rhodes.
Also see DURAN DURAN
Also see TAYLOR, Roger

ARCADOS
Singles: 7-inch
FAM (502 "When You Walked Out")....2000-3000 63

ARCANGEL
Singles: 7-inch
PORTRAIT....3-4 83
LPs: 10/12-inch
PORTRAIT....5-10 83

ARC-ANGELS
Singles: 7-inch
LAN-CET (142 "Goddess")....200-300 61
(Identification number shown since no selection number is used.)

ARCARAZ, Luis
Singles: 7-inch
RCA....5-10 50s

ARCENEAUX, Little Jimmie
Singles: 7-inch
YUCCA (134 "No Nation Ricky")....10-20 61

ARCH OF TRIUMPH
Singles: 7-inch
DATE....4-8 68

ARCHANGEL
Singles: 7-inch
ANDROMEDA TOUR (145 "Barrier")....25-35 60s

ARCHER, Don: see 5 WILLOWS

ARCHER, Frances
LPs: 10/12-inch
DISNEYLAND (1347 "A Child's Garden of Verses")....15-25 55
(10-inch LP.)
DISNEYLAND (3006 "Folk Songs")....20-30 56

ARCHERS
Singles: 7-inch
LAURIE (3207 "Hey Rube")....8-12 63
SUMMER (502 "Motorcycle Michael")....15-25

ARCHIBALD R&B '50
(With Dave Bartholomew's Band)
Singles: 78 rpm
COLONY (105 "Little Miss Muffett")....50-75 51
IMPERIAL (5068 "Stack-A-Lee")....75-125 50
IMPERIAL (5082 "Shake, Baby, Shake")....40-60 50
IMPERIAL (5089 "Frantic Chick")....40-60 50
IMPERIAL (5101 "My Gal")....40-60 50
IMPERIAL (5212 "Early Morning Blues")....40-60 52
IMPERIAL (5358 "Stack-A-Lee")....50-75 55
IMPERIAL (5563 "Stack-A-Lee")....25-50 57
Singles: 7-inch
IMPERIAL (5212 "Early Morning Blues")....150-250 52
IMPERIAL (5358 "Stack-A-Lee")....50-100 55
IMPERIAL (5563 "Stack-A-Lee")....25-50 57
Also see BARTHOLOMEW, Dave

ARCHIBALD PLAYERS
Singles: 7-inch
ARCH (1606 "Mr. Grillon")....10-15 58

ARCHIES P&R/LP '68
Singles: 7-inch
CALENDAR....5-10 68-69
ERIC....3-4 81
KIRSHNER (Except picture discs)....4-8 69-72
KIRSHNER....6-12 70
(5½" picture discs cut-out from cereal boxes. At least seven different songs are on two different picture styles)
RCA....4-8 72
Picture Sleeves
CALENDAR....8-15 68
KIRSHNER....8-10 69-71
LPs: 10/12-inch
ACCORD (7149 "Straight A's")....8-10 81
BACK-TRAC....5-10 85
BRYLEN (4415 "The Archies")....10-20 82
CALENDAR (101 "The Archies")....50-100 68
(With "Everything's Archie" promotional pack, including: red balloon; blue button; *Archie's Laugh-In Joke Book*; blue sticker; "Letter of Introduction" poster; Don "This Man" Kirshner poster; CBS-TV flyer; "Dealer Imprint" flyer; black and white photo of John Goldwater and Don Kirshner; black and white photo of Filmations animated TV production team; Archies record and 8-track flyer; Archies bio sheet; Don Kirshner bio; September 1968 Calendar LP releases flyer.
CALENDAR (101 "The Archies")....15-25 68
(Album only.)
CALENDAR (103 "Everything's Archie")....15-25 69
CALENDAR (103 "Sugar Sugar")....10-15 70
51 WEST (16002 "The Archies")....5-10 79
KIRSHNER (105 "Jingle Jangle")....15-25 69
KIRSHNER (107 "Sunshine")....15-25 70
KIRSHNER (109 "Greatest Hits")....15-25 70
KIRSHNER (110 "This Is Love")....15-25 71
RCA (0221 "The Archies")....15-25 70
(Promotional issue only.)
Members: Ron Dante, Jeff Barry; Toni Wine, plus assorted guests.
Also see ADAMS, Ritchie
Also see BLOOM, Bobby
Also see DANTE, Ron
Also see FASCINATORS
Also see GREENWICH, Ellie
Also see KIM, Andy
Also see STEVENS, Ray
Also see TEMPO, Nino
Also see WINE, Toni

ARCHIES / Johnny Thunder
Singles: 7-inch
COLLECTABLES....3-4 80s
Also see THUNDER, Johnny

ARCTURUS
Singles: 7-inch
TRISTAR....3-4 82

ARDEES: see ALAN, Phil, & Ardees

ARDELLS
Singles: 7-inch
EPIC (9621 "Lonely Valley")....8-12 63
MARCO (102 "Every Day of the Week")....25-35 61
SELMA (4001 "You Can Fall in Love")....20-30 63
Picture Sleeves
EPIC (9621 "Lonely Valley")....15-25 63
Member: Johnny Maestro.
Also see MAESTRO, Johnny

ARDELS
Singles: 7-inch
CAN-CUT (8888 "So Glad You're Mine")....20-30 66
(Canadian.)
CAN-CUT (8963 "Piece of Jewelry")....20-30 66
(Canadian.)

ARDEN, Ray
Singles: 7-inch
ALL STAR....8-10 61

ARDEN, Suzi
Singles: 7-inch
TODD....5-8 62

ARDEN, Toni P&R '49
Singles: 78 rpm
COLUMBIA....3-6 49-54
DECCA....3-6 57-57
RCA....3-6 55-56
Singles: 7-inch
COLUMBIA....8-12 50-54
DECCA....10-20 57-59
MISHAWAKA....3-5
RCA....8-12 55-56
EPs: 7-inch
DECCA....10-20 58
COLUMBIA....10-20 56
LPs: 10/12-inch
DECCA....12-25 57-59
TIARA....10-15

ARDESANA, Rick
Singles: 7-inch
MAGIC TOUCH....3-5 78

ARDIS, Johnny
Singles: 7-inch
ANSO....5-8 62

AREA CODE 212
Singles: 7-inch
FRIENDS & CO....4-8 79

AREA CODE 615 LP '69
Singles: 7-inch
POLYDOR....3-5 69-70
LPs: 10/12-inch
POLYDOR....8-12 69-70
Members: Charlie McCoy; Norbert Putnam.
Also see BAREFOOT JERRY
Also see McCOY, Charlie

AREA CODES
Singles: 7-inch
ARNE (409025 "Pretty Little Angel Eyes")....5-10 70s

ARENA BRASS LP '63
LPs: 10/12-inch
EPIC....10-15 62

ARENA TWINS
Singles: 7-inch
COLUMBIA....4-8 60
KAPP....4-8 60
NOB....4-8 63
Members: Sammy Arena; Andrew Arena.

ARERS, Tinker
Singles: 7-inch
AMBASSADOR....3-4
Picture Sleeves
AMBASSADOR....4-6

ARGENT P&R/LP '72
Singles: 7-inch
DATE....3-6 70
EPIC....4-8 69-74
LPs: 10/12-inch
EPIC....10-20 69-75
U.A.....5-10 76
Members: Rod Argent; Russ Ballard; Robert Henrit; Jim Rodford; John Verity.
Also see BALLARD, Russ
Also see PHOENIX
Also see VERITY, John
Also see WINTER, Johnny / Argent / Chambers Brothers / John Hammond
Also see ZOMBIES

ARGIE & ARKETTS
Singles: 7-inch
RONNIE ("You're the Guy")....25-40 66
(No selection number used.)

ARGIR, Fred
Singles: 7-inch
FLASHLIGHT....4-8 60s

ARGO, Judy C&W '79
Singles: 7-inch
ASI....3-5 79
MDJ....3-4 79

ARGONS
Singles: 7-inch
CASINO....4-8

ARGUS
Singles: 7-inch
BELL....3-5 71

ARGYLES
(With the Prom Orchestra)
Singles: 7-inch
PROM....5-10 55

ARGYLES
Singles: 78 rpm
BALLY (1030 "Moonbeam")....20-30 57
Singles: 7-inch
BALLY (1030 "Moonbeam")....20-40 57

ARGYLES
Singles: 7-inch
BRENT (7004 "Vacation Days Are Over")....15-25 59
Also see HOLLYWOOD ARGYLES

ARGYLES
Singles: 7-inch
JOX....10-15

ARICA
LPs: 10/12-inch
JUST SUNSHINE....10-12 73

ARIEL
Singles: 7-inch
BRENT (7060 "Feels Like I'm Cryin' ")....25-50 66
Also see BANSHEES

ARISTOCATS
LPs: 10/12-inch
HI-FI (610 "Boogie & Blues")....30-40 59

ARISTOCRATS
Singles: 78 rpm
ESSEX (366 "Believe Me")....20-30 54
Singles: 7-inch
ARISTOCRAT....15-25
ESSEX (366 "Believe Me")....30-50 54
Member: Lee Raymond.

ARISTOCRATS
Singles: 7-inch
ARGO....15-20 57

ARISTOCRATS
Singles: 7-inch
W.B.....3-5 73

ARIST-O-KATS
Singles: 7-inch
VITA....20-30 57

ARIZONA
Singles: 7-inch
RCA....3-5 76
LPs: 10/12-inch
RCA....5-10 76
Members: Mary Dobbins; Ken Ashby; Willie Knowles; Doug Holzwarth; Bob Huff; Pat Murphy; Pete Kuch.

ARK
Singles: 7-inch
SENTINEL....4-8

ARK
Singles: 7-inch
MGM....4-8 67

ARK 2
LPs: 10/12-inch
UNI....20-35 70

ARKADE P&R '70
Singles: 7-inch
DUNHILL....4-6 70-71
Picture Sleeves
DUNHILL....4-6 71

ARKADES
Singles: 7-inch
JULIA (1100 "Our Love")....20-40 60
Also see ARCADES

ARKANSAS RIVER BOTTOM
Singles: 7-inch
CAPITOL....3-5 73

ARLEN, Harold, & "Friend"
LPs: 10/12-inch
COLUMBIA (OL-6520 "Harold Sings Arlen")....25-35 66
(Monaural.)
COLUMBIA (OS-2920 "Harold Sings Arlen")....20-40 66
(Stereo.)
COLUMBIA (CSP-2920 "Harold Sings Arlen")....5-10
Members: Harold Arlen; Barbra Streisand.
Also see STREISAND, Barbra

ARLEN, Jan
Singles: 7-inch
BRUNSWICK....4-8 61

ARLIN, Bob
(Bobby Arlin)
Singles: 7-inch
OLYMPIA (500 "East L.A.")............25-30 60
OLYMPIA (823 "East L.A.")............20-25 60
TIKI (3500 "Mushroom Machine") ..10-15 63
Also see LEAVES
Also see HOOK

ARLINGTON, Bruce
Singles: 7-inch
KING (5918 "You Made Me Cry")...15-25 64

ARLINGTON, Roy
Singles: 7-inch
SAFICE (337 "That's Good Enough") 5-10 60s

ARLINGTON, Sue, & Arlisles
Singles: 7-inch
AGAR (776 "The Flip")..............100-150 60s

ARLO, Ray
Singles: 7-inch
CASTLE (501 "She's My Steady Date")..........................25-35 58

ARMADA ORCHESTRA LP '76
LPs: 10/12-inch
SCEPTER 4-8 75

ARMAGEDDON LP '75
Singles: 7-inch
CAPITOL.................................... 3-6 71-72
CREATIVE SOUND........................ 4-6 71
LPs: 10/12-inch
A&M.. 8-12 75
AMOS...15-20 70
Members: Keith Relf; Louis Cennamo; Martin Pugh.
Also see RENAISSANCE
Also see YARDBIRDS

ARMAND, Renee
Singles: 7-inch
A&M.. 3-5 72-73
WINDSONG 3-4 78
LPs: 10/12-inch
WINDSONG (2708 "In Time")......... 8-10 78
(With John Denver.)
Also see COYOTE SISTERS
Also see DENVER, John

ARMANDO
Singles: 7-inch
CUB.. 5-10 60

ARMATRADING, Joan LP '76
Singles: 12-inch
A&M.. 4-6 83
Singles: 7-inch
A&M.. 3-5 74-86
CUBE 4-8 71
Picture Sleeves
A&M.. 3-5 83
EPs: 7-inch
A&M (2391 "Me, Myself + 6 More"). 5-10 83
(Promotional issue only.)
LPs: 10/12-inch
A&M (Except 12) 8-12 73-90
A&M (12 "Talk Under Ladders") 15-25 81
(Promotional issue only.)

ARMEN, Kay P&R '43
Singles: 78 rpm
DECCA... 4-8 42-58
Singles: 7-inch
DECCA... 5-12 55-59
EPs: 7-inch
MGM 10-20 54-55
LPs: 10/12-inch
DECCA (5000 series)....................20-40 54
(10-inch LP)
DECCA (8000 series)....................10-20 59
MGM (200 series) 20-40 54
MGM (3000 series) 15-30 55

ARMEN, Smokey, & Schooners
Singles: 7-inch
PEEK-A-BOO (102 "Say You Love Me")..20-40 65
Also see SCHOONERS
Also see

ARMENIAN JAZZ SEXTET P&R '57
Singles: 78 rpm
KAPP.. 4-6 57
Singles: 7-inch
KAPP.. 5-10 57

ARMENTA D&D '83
Singles: 12-inch
SAVOIR FAIRE 4-6 83

ARMENTO, Micky
Singles: 7-inch
PEEK-A-BOO (1001 "Cheating On Me") 10-15 65

ARMONDA & JAYS
Singles: 7-inch
APOLLO (540 "Present of Love")...25-35 59

ARMORED SAINT LP '84
Singles: 12-inch
CHRYSALIS 4-6 86
Singles: 7-inch
CHRYSALIS 3-4 84-86
LPs: 10/12-inch
CHRYSALIS 5-10 84-87

ARMS, Russell P&R '57
Singles: 78 rpm
EPIC... 3-6 54-56
ERA.. 3-6 56-57
Singles: 7-inch
EPIC... 5-10 54-56
ERA.. 5-10 56-57
LPs: 10/12-inch
ERA.. 10-20 57

ARMSTEAD, Joshie Jo
(Jo Armstead)
Singles: 7-inch
DE LEX.. 8-12 62
GIANT.. 10-15 67-69
GOSPEL TRUTH............................ 4-6 74
INFINITY (28 "Sitting Here Thinking")..................................20-30
Also see IKETTES

ARMSTRONG, Brice, & American Ghouls
Singles: 7-inch
DUCHESS..................................... 5-10 62

ARMSTRONG, Caren
Singles: 12-inch
FANTASY..................................... 4-6 80
Singles: 7-inch
BLACK ROCK 5-10
FANTASY..................................... 3-4 80

ARMSTRONG, Chuck R&B '76
Singles: 7-inch
R&R.. 3-5 76
SOUND STAGE 7 (2640 "How Sweet It Is") 4-6 69

ARMSTRONG, Don
Singles: 7-inch
DON RAY 5-10 60

ARMSTRONG, Frank, & Stingers
Singles: 7-inch
MODERN (1045 "Feel Like I Want to Holler")..10-20 68

ARMSTRONG, Jack
Singles: 7-inch
MARK-X (8012 "Blue Little Angel") 10-15 61

ARMSTRONG, Jimmy
Singles: 7-inch
BROTHERS THREE (1001 "You're Getting Next to Me Baby")........................40-60
ENJOY (1016 "Count the Tears") ...10-15 64
JET SET (768 "I Won't Believe It Till I See It")...20-30
SHRINE (102 "I'm About to Say Goodbye")..................................200-300 65
STOP (105 "Close to You")............15-25
ZELL'S...10-15 63

ARMSTRONG, Joannie
Singles: 7-inch
DIAMOND (262 "I Still Believe in Tomorrow")....................................... 5-10 69

ARMSTRONG, Lil
Singles: 78 rpm
EASTWOOD (101 "East Town Boogie")...10-20

ARMSTRONG, Louis P&R '26
(With His All Stars)
Singles: 78 rpm
CAPITOL...................................... 4-8 56
COLUMBIA (2500 thru 2700 series)......................................15-25 32
COLUMBIA (40000 series)............ 4-8 56-66
DECCA.. 5-15 35-58
OKEH.. 20-30 26-31
RCA.. 4-8 56
VICTOR....................................... 10-20 33
VOCALION................................... 10-20 36
Singles: 7-inch
A&M.. 3-4 88
ABC.. 3-6 67-73
AMSTERDAM................................ 3-5 71
AUDIO FIDELITY 3-5 71
AVCO EMBASSY 3-5 71
BRUNSWICK................................. 4-6 67-68
BUENA VISTA.............................. 4-6 68
CAPITOL...................................... 10-15 56
COLUMBIA................................... 5-15 56-66
CONTINENTAL 3-5 71
DECCA (24752 "That Lucky Old Sun")..20-30 49
DECCA (25000 series).................. 4-8 61-64
DECCA (27000 thru 29000 series) .12-25 50-56
DECCA (30000 thru 31000 series) .10-15 56-59
DOT... 8-12 59
EPIC.. 4-6 69
KAPP... 4-8 64-69
MCA.. 3-5 73
MGM 8-12 59-60
MERCURY.................................... 4-8 64-66
RCA... 10-15 56
U.A.. 4-6 68-69
VERVE... 8-12 59-60
Picture Sleeves
A&M.. 3-4 88
BUENA VISTA.............................. 5-8 68
CONTINENTAL............................. 3-6 71
KAPP... 5-10 64
MGM 10-15 59
MERCURY.................................... 5-10 64
Note: Multi-disc, 1950s boxed sets are in the $15 to $25 range. At this time we do not have specific numbers and titles.
EPs: 7-inch
COLUMBIA................................... 5-15 55-59
DECCA.. 8-15 55-57
RCA... 10-20 53-59
LPs: 10/12-inch
ABC... 5-10 68-76
AMSTERDAM................................ 5-10 70
AUDIO FIDELITY 15-25 60-64
BIOGRAPH................................... 5-10 73
BRUNSWICK (58004 "Jazz Classics").................................50-100 50
(10-inch LP.)
BRUNSWICK (75000 series) 8-15 68-71
BUENA VISTA...............................8-12 68
CHIAROSCURO.............................5-10 77
COLUMBIA (500 thru 900 series)....25-50 54-57
COLUMBIA (2600 series) 8-15 67
COLUMBIA (9400 series) 8-15 67
COLUMBIA (30000 series) 5-12 71-80
CORAL...5-10 73
DECCA (155 "Satchmo")................50-100 65
(Boxed four-disc set. Includes booklet.)
DECCA (195 "Satchmo at Symphony Hall")...30-50 66
(Boxed, two-disc set.)
DECCA (4000 series) 10-20 61-63
DECCA (5000 series) 25-50 51-54
(10-inch LPs.)
DECCA (8000 series) 15-25 55-59
DECCA (9000 series) 8-15 67
(Decca LP numbers in this series preceded by a "7" or a "DL-7" are stereo issues.)
EVEREST......................................5-10 71-76
GNP..8-12 77
GUEST STAR.................................5-10 64
HARMONY.....................................5-10 69
JAZZ HERITAGE 5-10 80
JAZZ PANORAMA (1204 "Fireworks")....................................15-20
JEMI..5-10
KAPP...10-15 64
MCA..6-10 73-82
MERCURY.....................................10-15 66
METRO..10-15 65
MILESTONE...................................5-10 74-75
MOSAIC (146 "Complete Decca Studio Recordings")...................................100-120 90s
(Boxed, eight-disc audiophile set. 7500 made.)
OLYMPIC.......................................5-10 74
PAUSA...5-10 83
RCA (1300 & 1400 series) 25-50 53-56
RCA (2300 thru 2900 series)..........10-20 61-64
(With "LPM" or "LSP" prefix.)
RCA (2600 series) 5-10 77
(With "CPL1" prefix.)
RCA (5500 series) 8-12 77
RCA (6000 series) 8-12 71
SAGA...5-10 72
STORYVILLE..................................5-10 80
TRIP..5-10 72
U.A..8-15 68-69
VANGUARD....................................8-12 76
VERVE...15-20 60-64
VOCALION.....................................5-10 68-69
Also see BARRY, John
Also see BRUBECK, Dave
Also see CROSBY, Bing, Louis Armstrong, Rosemary Clooney & Hi-Los
Also see FITZGERALD, Ella, & Louis Armstrong
Also see KAYE, Danny, & Louis Armstrong
Also see JENKINS, Gordon
Also see MILLS BROTHERS, & Louis Armstrong

ARMSTRONG, Louis, & Duke Ellington
Singles: 7-inch
ROULETTE 4-6 63
LPs: 10/12-inch
MFSL (155 "Recording for the First Time")..25-35 85
ROULETTE (100 series)..................8-12 71
ROULETTE (52000 series) 15-25 63
Also see ELLINGTON, Duke

ARMSTRONG, Louis, & Guy Lombardo
Singles: 7-inch
CAPITOL..3-6 66
Also see LOMBARDO, Guy

ARMSTRONG, Louis, Red Nichols, & Danny Kaye
Singles: 7-inch
DOT...5-10 59
Picture Sleeves
DOT...15-25 59
Also see KAYE, Danny

ARMSTRONG, Louis, & Oscar Peterson
Singles: 7-inch
VERVE...5-10 59
LPs: 10/12-inch
VERVE (6062 "Louis Armstrong Meets Oscar Peterson")..................................15-25 59
(Monaural.)
VERVE (8322 "Louis Armstrong Meets Oscar Peterson")..................................20-30 59
(Stereo.)
Also see PETERSON, Oscar

ARMSTRONG, Louis / Della Reese / Wild Bill Davidson
EPs: 7-inch
AURAVISION/COLUMBIA ("Jazz from Bourbon Street")............................5-8
(Promotional bonus cardboard disc, made for Ancient Age bourbon.)
Also see ARMSTRONG, Louis
Also see REESE, Della

ARMSTRONG, Tal
(Talmadge Armstrong)
Singles: 7-inch
LOVE 4-6 76
SPINDLETOP (15 "Gigi")..................10-20

ARMSTRONG, Vanessa Bell R&B '87
Singles: 7-inch
JIVE...3-4 87
Picture Sleeves
JIVE...3-4 87

ARMSTRONG, Wayne C&W '80
Singles: 7-inch
NSD 3-4 80

ARMSTRONG BROTHERS
Singles: 7-inch
SMACK 3-4
Picture Sleeves
SMACK 3-4

ARNAU, B.J.
Singles: 7-inch
RCA 3-5 73

ARNAZ, Desi
(Desi Arnaz Orchestra)
Singles: 78 rpm
COLUMBIA 5-10 53
RCA 4-8 47
Singles: 7-inch
COLUMBIA (39937 "I Love Lucy")..15-25 53
RCA 8-12 53
EPs: 7-inch
RCA (3096 "Babalu")......................10-20 53
LPs: 10/12-inch
RCA (3096 "Babalu")......................20-40 53
(10-inch LP.)

ARNAZ, Desi, Jr.
Singles: 7-inch
REPRISE 3-5 71
Also see DINO, DESI & BILLY

ARNAZ, Lucie
Singles: 7-inch
CASABLANCA 3-4 79

ARNDT, Bill
Singles: 7-inch
HIT..4-8 60s

ARNE, Skip, & Dukes
Singles: 7-inch
DOT (16627 "Sunshine & Rain") 10-20 60s
LITTLE FORT (8688 "Sunshine & Rain")...15-25 60s
Member: Bob Misky.

ARNELL, Billy
Singles: 7-inch
HOLLY (1001 "Tough Girl") 200-400

ARNELL, Ginny P&R '63
Singles: 7-inch
DECCA...8-12 60
MGM..5-10 63-65
WARWICK (671 "No One Cares") 15-25 61
WARWICK (680 "Married to You").10-20 62
LPs: 10/12-inch
MGM..15-25 64
Also see JAMIE & JANE

ARNELL, Patrici
Singles: 7-inch
ASCOT (2240 "Lost")......................4-8 66

ARNELLS
Singles: 7-inch
ROULETTE (4519 "Take a Look") .10-15 63

ARNETTE, Mae
Singles: 7-inch
BIG TOP (3005 "Fool That I Am") .10-20 58

ARNEZ, Coley
Singles: 7-inch
OLD TOWN (1129 "Fever")..........10-20 62

ARNGRIM, Stefan
Singles: 7-inch
ARTISTS of AMERICA......................3-5 75

ARNIE & SOUL BROTHERS
Singles: 7-inch
EMMES...10-20 61

ARNIE'S LOVE R&B '86
Singles: 12-inch
PROFILE..4-6 85-86

ARNIN - HAMILTON
Singles: 7-inch
INT'L ARTISTS...............................3-5 70

ARNO, Audrey P&R '61
(With the Hazy Osterwald Sextet)
Singles: 7-inch
DECCA...4-8 61

ARNOLD
LPs: 10/12-inch
FIRST AMERICAN...........................5-10 84

ARNOLD, Bee
Singles: 7-inch
GOLDBAND 20-35 54

ARNOLD, Billy "Boy"
(With Bob Carter's Orchestra)
Singles: 78 rpm
COOL...10-20 53
Singles: 7-inch
COOL (103 "I Ain't Got No Money")...25-50 53
LPs: 10/12-inch
PRESTIGE BLUESVILLE (1072 "See What You've Done")..............................25-35 63
PRESTIGE (7389 "Blues on the South")..25-35 65
Also see BILLY BOY
Also see JONES, Johnny, & Billy Boy Arnold

ARNOLD, Calvin P&R/R&B '68
Singles: 7-inch
IX CHAINS 3-5 75
VENTURE 4-8 67-69

ARNOLD, Eddy C&W '45
("The Tennessee Plowboy"; with His Tennessee Plowboys)
Singles: 78 rpm
BLUEBIRD (0520 "Mommie Please Stay Home with Me")..................................50-75 45
BLUEBIRD (0527 "Each Minute Seems Like a Million Years")..............................30-60 45
RCA...10-30 46-57
Singles: 7-inch
DIAMOND P (1009 "If the Whole World Stopped Lovin' ")...............................5-10 73
(Promotional issue only.)
MGM...3-5 73-76
RCA (0001 thru 0476)......................15-30 50-51
(Black vinyl. Black or turquoise labels.)
RCA (0001 thru 0476)......................35-55 50-51
(Colored vinyl. Price for any in this series on colored vinyl, though at this time we lack specific colored vinyl numbers.)
RCA (0120 thru 0747)......................3-6 69-72
(Orange labels.)
RCA (2000 series) 10-15 62
(Stereo Compact 33.)
RCA (3800 thru 6905)......................10-20 50-57
RCA (7040 thru 8296)......................8-15 57-64
RCA (8363 thru 9993)......................3-8 64-71
RCA (10701 thru 13452)...................3-5 76-83
RCA GOLD STANDARD 3-8 59-70s
(With "447" prefix.)
Picture Sleeves
RCA...8-15 56-66
EPs: 7-inch
RCA (100 series) 10-12 61
(With "LPC" prefix. Compact 33 Double.)
RCA (280 "Best Wishes") 10-20
(Promotional issue only.)
RCA (200 thru 900 series) 10-15 52-56
(With "EPA" prefix.)
RCA (1100 & 1200 series) 15-20 55-56
(With "EPB" prefix.)
RCA (1400 & 1500 series) 8-12 57
(With "EPA" prefix.)
RCA (3000 series) 20-40 52-54
(With "EPB" prefix.)
RCA (4000 & 5000 series) 8-15 57-59
(With "EPA" prefix.)
LPs: 10/12-inch
CAMDEN (Except "ACL1" series)..8-18 60-72
CAMDEN ("ACL1" series)..................5-10 72-76
GREEN VALLEY 8-10 76
K-TEL...8-10 74
MGM..8-12 74-76
RCA ("AHL1," "ANL1," "APL1," & "AYL1" series)..5-10 73-81
RCA ("CPL1" series).........................8-12 83
RCA (0051 "Greatest Hits")..............8-12
(Mail order offer.)
RCA (115 "Eddy Arnold Sings Them Again")...15-25 61
RCA (168 "Welcome to My World")..10-20 75
RCA (209 "Eddy Arnold")..................15-20 66
(Promotional issue only.)
RCA (1100 thru 2200 series) 20-30 55-60
(Monaural. with "LPM" prefix.)
RCA (2300 thru 2900 series) 12-20 60-64
(Monaural. with "LPM" prefix.)
RCA (3027 "Country Classics")........50-75 52
(10-inch LP.)
RCA (3031 "All-Time Hits from the Hills")...50-75 52
(10-inch LP.)
RCA (3117 "All-Time Favorites") 50-75 53
(10-inch LP.)
RCA (3219 "Chapel on the Hill") 50-75 54
(10-inch LP.)
RCA (3230 "An American Institution")....................................50-75 54
(10-inch LP.)
RCA (3000 series) 8-12 64-68
(12-inch LPs. with "LPM" prefix.)
RCA (1900 thru 3400 series) 15-25 60-65
(Stereo. with "LSP" prefix. "LSP" numbers below 1900 were reprocessed stereo issues of '50s LPs. They were issued in the '60s and are in the $10-$15 range.)
RCA (3500 thru 4800 series) 10-20 66-73
RCA (6000 series) 8-12 70
RCA SPECIAL PRODUCTS (0051 "Eddy Arnold")...8-12 73
SUNRISE..5-10 79
TIME-LIFE......................................5-10 81
Also see ANN-MARGRET
Also see SOME of CHET'S FRIENDS
Also see PRESLEY, Elvis / Hank Snow / Eddy Arnold / Jim Reeves

ARNOLD, Eddy, & Jaye P. Morgan
Singles: 78 rpm
RCA...5-10
Singles: 7-inch
RCA...5-10

ARNOLD, Eddy, & Jaye P. Morgan / Dorothy Olsen ("The Singing School Teacher")
EPs: 7-inch
RCA (DJ-21 "If 'N'")..........................10-20 56
Also see ARNOLD, Eddy
Also see MORGAN, Jaye P.

ARNOLD, Jack
Singles: 7-inch
WILDCAT..8-12 59

ARNOLD, Jerry
(With the Rhythm Captains)
Singles: 7-inch
SECURITY (106 "Race for Time")...75-125 57
SECURITY (107 "High-Classed Baby")...75-125 58

CAMEO (120 "Race for Time") 50-75 57

ARNOLD, Joe
(With the Davis Combo)
Singles: 7-inch
COTILLION 3-5 70
WAND 4-8 68

ARNOLD, Kokomo
Singles: 78 rpm
DECCA........ 25-50 34-38

ARNOLD, Kokomo / Casey Bill Weldon
LPs: 10/12-inch
YAZOO........ 5-10
Also see WHEATSTRAW, Peetie, & Kokomo Arnold

ARNOLD, Lloyd
Singles: 7-inch
AVET........ 10-15 63
K-ARK 10-15 63
MEMPHIS........ 20-30 64
MYERS (113 "Red Coat, Green Pants and Red Suede Shoes") 75-100 60
RECORD-O-RAMA........ 10-20

ARNOLD, Murray
Singles: 78 rpm
CARDINAL 10-15 54
Singles: 7-inch
CARDINAL (1016 "Boo Boo Boogie") 20-30 54

ARNOLD, P.P.
Singles: 7-inch
ATLANTIC 4-6 69
IMMEDIATE 5-10 67-68
LPs: 10/12-inch
IMMEDIATE 15-20 66

ARNOLD, Paul
LPs:10/12-inch
KAPP........ 10-15

ARNOLD, Rick C&W '89
Singles: 7-inch
LYNN........ 3-4 89

ARNOLD, Sharon
Singles: 7-inch
CUCA (1074 "Cold Cold Heart")..... 15-25 62
CUCA (1110 "I Walk")........ 15-25 62

ARNOLD, Vance, & Avengers
Singles: 7-inch
PHILIPS (40255 "I'll Cry Instead") 15-25 64
Member: Joe Cocker.
Also see COCKER, Joe

ARNOLD & LEE: see VAN BROTHERS

ARNOLD & THOMPSON
Singles: 7-inch
ARISTA 3-4 76

ARNOLD BROTHERS
Singles: 7-inch
IGL 8-12 67
Also see UNIQUES

ARNOLD, MARTIN & MORROW
Singles: 7-inch
BELL 3-5 71-72

ARNOLD SISTERS
Singles: 7-inch
SOUND STAGE 7........ 4-8 64

ARONDIES
Singles: 7-inch
ASTRA (1005 "All My Love") 8-12 65
SHERRY (199 "All My Love")........ 20-30 65

ARP, James, & Tempest
Singles: 7-inch
VELLEZ (1515 "Let It Rock")........ 30-50 64
Also see TEMPESTS

ARONOFF, Benji
LPs:10/12-inch
PRESTIGE 15-25

ARPEGGIO P&R/R&B/LP '79
Singles: 7-inch
POLYDOR........ 3-4 78-80
LPs: 10/12-inch
POLYDOR........ 5-10 78-80

ARPEGGIOS
Singles: 7-inch
ERA........ 5-10 62

ARRANGEMENT
Singles: 7-inch
PULSAR........ 4-6 69
SCEPTER 4-6 69

ARRELL, Gregg
Singles: 7-inch
MCA 3-5 80
LPs: 10/12-inch
MCA 5-10 80

ARRIBIANS
Singles: 7-inch
J.O.B. (1116 "To Look at a Star")........ 550-650 58

ARRINGTON, Steve R&B '82
(Steve Arrington's Hall of Fame)
Singles: 12-inch
ATLANTIC 4-6 83-86
Singles: 7-inch
ATLANTIC 3-4 83-86
KONGLATHER........ 3-4 82
MANHATTAN 3-4 87
LPs: 10/12-inch
ATLANTIC........ 5-10 83-86
Also see SLAVE

ARRIVAL
Singles: 7-inch
EPIC........ 3-5 73
LONDON........ 3-5 70
LPs: 10/12-inch
LONDON........ 10-15 70
Members: Paddy McHugh; Dyan Birch; Frank Collins; Tony O'Malley.
Also see KOKOMO

ARRIVALS
Singles: 7-inch
LUMMTONE........ 5-10

ARROGANCE
Singles: 7-inch
CRESENT CITY 4-6
VANGUARD 4-6 76
W.B. 3-5 79-80
LPs: 10/12-inch
VANGUARD 8-10 76
W.B. 5-10 80
Members: Don Dixon; Robert Kirkland; Scott Davidson; Marty Stout.

ARROGANTS
Singles: 7-inch
BIG A 10-15 60
CANDLELITE 5-10 62
LUTE........ 10-15 62
VANESSA 10-15 62
Member: Ray Morrow.

ARROW
Singles: 12-inch
CHRYSALIS 4-6 84

ARROWS
Singles: 78 rpm
HOLLYWOOD (1065 "Honey Child")........ 50-100 56
HOLLYWOOD (1071 "One Too Many Times") 75-125 56
Singles: 7-inch
HOLLYWOOD (1065 "Honey Child")........ 100-200 56
HOLLYWOOD (1071 "One Too Many Times") 150-250 56
Also see LYONS, Joe, & Arrows

ARROWS
Singles: 7-inch
FLASH (132 "Indian Bop Hop")...... 15-25 58

ARROWS
Singles: 7-inch
CUPID........ 8-12 60

ARROWS
Singles: 7-inch
HUGO (1174 "No Other Arms")..... 15-20 64

ARROWS
Singles: 7-inch
A&M 3-4 83-85
LPs: 10/12-inch
A&M 5-10 83-85

ARROWS (With Davie Allan): see ALLAN, Davie

ARSTA, Marvin
Singles: 7-inch
NSD........ 3-4 81

ARSYNAL
Singles: 7-inch
RAZOR'S EDGE (001 "You Think It's Love")........ 12-18 87
(Square picture disc.)
LP: 10/12-inch
CONDOR CLASSIC ("Mean Line") 10-12 87
(Picture disc. Selection number not known.)

ART, Bobby, & Plainsmen
Singles: 7-inch
CUCA........ 8-12 67
Also see KENNY BEE

ART, Les, & Danceters
Singles: 7-inch
FRATERNITY........ 5-8 83

ART & HONEY
Singles: 7-inch
DUNHILL........ 4-6 69
MOTOWN........ 3-5 73

ART & SCIOTO RHYTHM BOYS
Singles: 7-inch
KARL (8000 "A String Boogie")...... 20-30 56

ART ATTACK D&D '83
Singles: 12-inch
B.M.O........ 4-6 83
Singles: 7-inch
B.M.O........ 3-4 83
LPs: 10/12-inch
B.M.O........ 5-10 83

ART BEARS
LPs: 10/12-inch
RALPH........ 5-10 79

ART FORMS LTD.
Singles: 7-inch
RCA........ 3-6 70-71

ART IN AMERICA LP '83
Singles: 7-inch
PAVILLION........ 3-4 83
LPs: 10/12-inch
PAVILLION........ 5-10 83

ART OF LOVIN'
LPs: 10/12-inch
MAINSTREAM (6113 "Art of Lovin' ")........ 30-50 68
Member: Gail Winnick.

ART OF NOISE D&D '83
Singles: 12-inch
CHINA........ 4-6 86
ISLAND........ 4-6 83-84
Singles: 7-inch
CHINA........ 3-4 86-88
ISLAND........ 3-4 83-84
Picture Sleeves
CHINA........ 3-4 86-88
LPs: 10/12-inch
CHINA........ 5-10 86-88
CHRYSALIS 5-10 86-87
ISLAND 5-10 84-85
Members: Anne Dudley; Gary Langan; J.J. Jeczalik.
Also see ELECTRONIC
Also see HORN, Trevor, Paul Morley, & Art of Noise

ART OF NOISE & DUANE EDDY P&R '86
Singles: 7-inch
CHINA........ 3-4 86
Picture Sleeves
CHINA........ 3-4 86
Also see EDDY, Duane

ART OF NOISE & MAX HEADROOM P&R '86
Singles: 7-inch
CHINA........ 3-4 86
Picture Sleeves
CHINA........ 3-4 86
Also see HEADROOM, Max

ART OF NOISE & TOM JONES P&R '88
Singles: 7-inch
CHINA........ 3-4 88
Picture Sleeves
CHINA........ 3-4 88
Also see ART of NOISE
Also see JONES, Tom

ART NOUVEAUX
Singles: 7-inch
FONTANA........ 5-8 66

ARTFUL DODGER
Singles: 7-inch
ARIOLA AMERICA........ 3-4 80-81
COLUMBIA........ 3-4 76-77
EPs: 7-inch
COLUMBIA........ 8-10 75
LPs: 10/12-inch
ARIOLA AMERICA 5-10 80
COLUMBIA........ 8-10 75-77
Members: Mike Fenech; Gary Herrewig; Gary Cox; Steve Brigida; Steve Cooper; Bill Paliselli.
Also see BADGE
Also see HOMESTEAD

ARTHUR
LPs: 10/12-inch
LHI (12000 "Dreams & Images")..... 20-40 68

ARTHUR, Brooks
Singles: 7-inch
KAPP 4-8 63

ARTHUR, Charline
Singles: 78 rpm
RCA (Except 6297)........ 5-10 54-55
RCA (6297 "Burn That Candle")..... 10-15 55
Singles: 7-inch
COIN 10-20
EL DORADO 4-8 66
RCA (Except 6297)........ 10-15 54-55
RCA (6297 "Burn That Candle")..... 20-30 55

ARTHUR, Gary
Singles: 7-inch
DEBBIE (67 "Little Things") 5-10

ARTHUR, Jay
Singles: 7-inch
SMASH (1805 "Lonely Girl on Sweetheart Mountain")........ 10-15 63

ARTHUR, Maureen
Singles: 7-inch
CARLTON (579 "Don't Make the Angels Cry")........ 5-10 62
LAMA (7787 "Don't Make the Angels Cry") 10-20 62
(First issue.)

ARTHUR & CORVETS
(Arthur Conley & Corvets)
Singles: 7-inch
MRC (232 "Miracles") 15-25 64
NA-R-CO (203 "Poor Girl") 30-50 64
NA-R-CO (232 "Miracles") 30-50 64
NA-R-CO (234 "Aritha")........ 30-50 64
Also see CONLEY, Arthur
Also see CORVETTS

ARTHUR & MARY
Singles: 7-inch
MODERN 4-8 67

ARTHUR, HURLEY & GOTTLIEB
Singles: 7-inch
A&M........ 3-4 75
COLUMBIA........ 3-5 73
LPs: 10/12-inch
A&M........ 5-10 74
COLUMBIA........ 8-10 73

ARTIE & LINDA & PREMERES
(Artie & Lynda)
Singles: 7-inch
CHANCELLOR........ 4-8 63
COLUMBIA........ 3-6 66

ARTIE & PHAROAHS: see LITTLE ARTIE & PHAROAHS

ARTIE & ROSE
Singles: 7-inch
GOLDEN EAGLE 3-4

ARTIE KORNFIELD TREE
Singles: 7-inch
DUNHILL........ 3-5 70

ARTIS, Ray
Singles: 7-inch
A (111 "Art of Love")........ 25-50 61
BUNDY (222 "Dear Liza")........ 15-25 62

ARTISTICS
Singles: 7-inch
S&G (302 "Life Begins at Sixteen")........ 200-300 62

ARTISTICS R&B '65
Singles: 7-inch
BRUNSWICK 4-8 66-73
OKEH........ 5-10 63-66
LPs: 10/12-inch
BRUNSWICK 10-20 67-73
OKEH........ 15-25 67
Members: Marvin Smith; Bernard Reed; Larry Johnson; Tommy Green; Aaron Floyd; Morris Williams.
Also see CHANCE, Nolan
Also see DUKAYS
Also see SMITH, Marvin

ARTISTS UNITED AGAINST APARTHEID P&R/R&B/D&D/LP '85
Singles: 12-inch
MANHATTAN........ 4-6 85
Singles: 7-inch
MANHATTAN........ 3-4 85
Picture Sleeves
MANHATTAN........ 3-4 85
LPs: 10/12-inch
MANHATTAN........ 5-10 85

ARTWOOD, Eddie
Singles: 7-inch
DITTO ("Never Never") 15-25
(Selection number not known.)

ARTY & SUPREMES
Singles: 7-inch
DAYTONE (4311 "Hombre")........ 10-20 64

ARTZ & KRAFTZ
Singles: 7-inch
MOTOWN 3-4 90

ARVAKS
Singles: 7-inch
EVENT........ 4-8

ARVETTES
Singles: 7-inch
HAC........ 5-10 62
IDEAL........ 4-8 66

ARVO PART
LPs: 10/12-inch
ECM........ 5-10 85

ARVON, Bobby P&R '77
Singles: 7-inch
ARIOLA AMERICAN 3-4 76
FIRST ARTISTS........ 3-4 77-78
LPs: 10/12-inch
FIRST ARTISTS........ 5-10 78
MTA 5-10
MERCURY 5-10

ARWIN, Johnny
Singles: 7-inch
ALPINE 8-12 59

ARWOOD, Cerilla, & Barberton 3
Singles: 7-inch
WEL BURN........ 4-8 50s

ARZACHEL
LPs: 10/12-inch
ROULETTE (42036 "Arzachel") 40-50 69
Members: Steve Hillage; Dave Stewart; Mort Campbell; Clive Brooks.
Also see EGG
Also see HILLAGE, Steve

A'SAURUS, Tyrone
(With the Cro-Magnons)
Singles: 7-inch
W.B. (5305 "Monster Twist")........ 10-15 62

ASCENDORS
Singles: 7-inch
LEE (101 "I Won't Be Home")........ 20-30 65

ASCOTS
Singles: 7-inch
ARROW (736 "Is It Really You") 15-25 58

ASCOTS
Singles: 7-inch
J&S (1628 "What Love Can Do") ... 30-50 58

ASCOTS
Singles: 7-inch
DUAL-TONE (1119 "Acapulco Run")........ 15-25 63
Member: Derry Weaver.
Also see GAMBLERS

ASCOTS
Singles: 7-inch
ACE (650 "Perfect Love")........ 20-30 62
BETHLEHEM (3046 "She Did") 10-20 62
KING (5679 "Darling I'll See You Tonight")........ 30-40 62

ASCOTS
Singles: 7-inch
SUPER........ 8-12 65

ASCOTS
Singles: 7-inch
ASCOT (252 "Rail Job") 15-20
M.B.S. 5-10 65

ASCOTS
Singles: 7-inch
MIR-A-DON (1001 "Sometimes I Wonder")........ 35-50 65
MIR-A-DON (1002 "Mother Said")........ 50-75 65

ASCOTS
Singles: 7-inch
NORMANDY (104 "Where I'm Goin' ")........ 8-12 66

ASCOTS
Singles: 7-inch
BLUE FIN (101 "I Won't Cry")........ 25-35 60s
LIVERPOOL........ 15-25 60s
SUPER (102 "Monkey See Monkey Do")........ 15-25 66
SUPER (103 "Midnight Hour") 15-25 66
SUPER (104 "Put Your Arms Around Me")........ 15-25 66
SUPER (105 "I Need You")........ 20-30 67

ASCOTS
Singles: 7-inch
FRAT........ 4-6

ASCOTS
Singles: 7-inch
MIR-A-DON........ 8-12

ASGARD
LPs: 10/12-inch
THRESHOLD........ 10-20 72

ASH
Singles: 7-inch
PROBE........ 4-6 68

ASH, Daniel LP '91
LPs: 10/12-inch
BEGGAR'S BANQUET........ 5-8 91

ASHAYE
Singles: 12-inch
MONTAGE........ 4-6 83

ASHBY, Dorothy
Singles: 7-inch
CADET........ 4-6 68
LPs: 10/12-inch
ATLANTIC........ 8-12
CADET........ 15-20 68-69
PRESTIGE........ 12-15 69

ASHBY, Irving
(Irvin Ashby)
Singles: 7-inch
IMPERIAL 10-15 57
KNIGHT 10-15 58
LPs: 10/12-inch
ACCENT 5-10 77
Also see FREEMAN, Ernie

ASHDOWN, Doug
Singles: 7-inch
FONTANA........ 3-6 69
LPs: 10/12-inch
CORAL........ 10-15 70

ASHE, Clarence P&R/R&B '64
Singles: 7-inch
ABC-PAR........ 8-12 65
CHESS........ 8-12 64
J&S 10-15 64-65
MASTER........ 8-12 65

ASHE, Clarence, & Hartsy Maye
Singles: 7-inch
J&S........ 10-15 65
Also see ASHE, Clarence

ASHELY BROTHERS
Singles: 7-inch
ROULETTE........ 4-6 69

ASHER, Jane
LP: 10/12-inch
LONDON........ 10-20 60s

ASHES
Singles: 7-inch
VAULT (924 "Is There Anything I Can Do")........ 5-10 66
VAULT (936 "Dark on You Now")...... 5-10 67
VAULT (973 "Homeward Bound")..... 5-10 71
LPs: 10/12-inch
VAULT (125 "Ashes") 35-55 68
Members: Pat Taylor; John Merrill; Jim Voight; Alan Brackett.
Also see PEANUT BUTTER CONSPIRACY
Also see PEANUT BUTTER CONSPIRACY / Ashes / Chambers Brothers

ASHFORD, Jack
(With the Charades)
LPs: 10/12-inch
MAGIC DISC........ 5-10 78
Also see CHARADES

ASHFORD, Nick
Singles: 7-inch
ABC 3-6 70
VERVE 4-8 66-68
Also see ASHFORD & SIMPSON

ASHFORD & SIMPSON R&B/LP '73
Singles: 12-inch
CAPITOL 4-6 82-86
W.B. 4-6 79
Singles: 7-inch
CAPITOL 3-4 82-89
EMI AMERICA 3-4 84-85
W.B. 3-5 73-81
Picture Sleeves
CAPITOL 3-4 80-86
W.B. 3-5 70s
LPs: 10/12-inch
CAPITOL 5-10 82-89
W.B. (Except HS series) 5-10 73-81
W.B. ("HS" series) 10-20 79-80
(Half-speed mastered.)
Members: Nick Ashford; Valerie Simpson.
Also see ASHFORD, Nick
Also see JONES, Quincy
Also see SIMPSON, Valerie
Also see VALERIE & NICK

ASHKAN
LPs: 10/12-inch
SIRE 15-20 70
Members: Steve Bailey; Ron Bending; Terry Sims; Bob Weston.

ASHLEY, Bob
(With the Reflections)
REO 15-25 60s
(Canadian.)
Also see ALLEN, Chad

ASHLEY, Del
(David Gates)
Singles: 7-inch
MANCHESTER (101 "There's a Heaven") 30-40 60s
PLANETARY (103 "Little Miss Stuck-Up") 15-25 65
Also see GATES, David

ASHLEY, Hugh, & Four Chords
Singles: 7-inch
ROYALE 5-10 50s

ASHLEY, John
Singles: 7-inch
CAPEHART (5006 "Little Lou") 30-45 61
DOT (15775 "Born to Rock") 50-100 58
DOT (15878 "Let the Good Times Roll") 15-25 58
INTRO (6097 "Let Yourself Go, Go, Go") 25-50
SILVER (1002 "Seriously in Love") 50-75 59
SILVER (1005 "One Love") 20-30 60
Picture Sleeves
INTRO (6097 "Let Yourself Go, Go, Go") 50-75

ASHLEY, Leon C&W '67
Singles: 7-inch
ASHLEY 4-6 67-69
DOT 5-8 64
GOLDBAND 8-12
IMPERIAL 6-10 61
LPs: 10/12-inch
ASHLEY 8-15 69-70
PICKWICK/HILLTOP 10-15 68
RCA 10-20 67

ASHLEY, Leon, & Margie Singleton C&W '67
Singles: 7-inch
ASHLEY 4-6 67-68
LPs: 10/12-inch
ASHLEY 10-15 69
PICKWICK 5-10 70s
Also see ASHLEY, Leon
Also see SINGLETON, Margie

ASHLEY, Robert
Singles: 7-inch
MERCURY (71365 "Comic Strip Rock & Roll") 25-50 58

ASHLEY, Steve
LPs: 10/12-inch
GULL 8-10 76

ASHLEY, Tony
Singles: 7-inch
DECCA (32342 "We Must Have Love") 10-20 69
DECCA (32520 "I'll Go Crazy") 30-60 69

ASHLEY, Tyrone R&B '70
(With the Funky Music Machine)
Singles: 7-inch
PHIL-L.A. of SOUL 3-6 70-71
U.A. 3-5 78
LPs: 10/12-inch
U.A. 5-10 78
Also see DEL LARKS

ASHTON, GARDNER & DYKE P&R/LP '71
Singles: 7-inch
CAPITOL 3-5 70-72
LPs: 10/12-inch
CAPITOL 8-12 70-72
Members: Tony Ashton; Kim Gardner; Roy Dyke.
Also see ASHTON, Tony, & Jon Lord
Also see BADGER

ASHTON, Mark
Singles: 7-inch
20TH FOX 3-4 77
LPs: 10/12-inch
20TH FOX 5-10 76

ASHTON, Tony, & Jon Lord
LPs: 10/12-inch
W.B. 10-15 74
Also see ASHTON, GARDNER & DYKE
Also see LORD, Jon
Also see PAICE, ASHTON & LORD

ASHTON, Zane, & Irrestibles
Singles: 7-inch
EMPALA (117 "Edge of the World") 10-20 60s
LAN-CET (143 "Don't Ever Leave Me") 5-10 61

ASHWORTH, Ernest C&W '60
(Ernie Ashworth)
Singles: 7-inch
DECCA 4-8 60-61
HICKORY 3-6 62-70
O'BRIEN 3-6
LPs: 10/12-inch
HICKORY 10-20 64-68
SEA SHELL 5-8 82
STARDAY 10-20 76

ASIA
Singles: 7-inch
ASIA 8-12 70

ASIA P&R/LP '82
Singles: 12-inch
GEFFEN 4-6 82-85
Singles: 7-inch
GEFFEN 3-4 82-85
Picture Sleeves
GEFFEN 3-4 81-85
LPs: 10/12-inch
GEFFEN 5-10 82-90
Members: Steve Howe; Carl Palmer; John Wetton; Geoff Downes; Mandy Mayer.
Also see BUGGLES
Also see EMERSON, LAKE & PALMER
Also see HOWE, Steve, Band

ASIATICS
Singles: 7-inch
CANTON (1784 "Flu Bug") 15-25 57

ASKEY, Gil
Singles: 7-inch
MOTOWN 3-5 73
LPs: 10/12-inch
RANWOOD 8-12 70

ASLEEP AT THE WHEEL C&W '74
Singles: 7-inch
ARISTA 3-4 90-91
CAPITOL 3-4 75-79
EPIC (06671 thru 08087) 3-4 87-88
EPIC (50000 series) 4-6 74
Picture Sleeves
EPIC 3-5 74
LPs: 10/12-inch
CAPITOL 10-15 75-79
EPIC (BG-33000 series) 15-25 75
EPIC (EG-33000 series) 10-15
EPIC (KE-33000 series) 10-15 74
EPIC (PE-33000 series) 5-10
MCA 5-10 80-84
U.A. 15-25 73
Members: Ray Benson; Chris O'Connell; Danny Levin; Reuben Gosfield. Session: Texas Playboys.
Also see BENSON, Ray
Also see TEXAS PLAYBOYS

ASPHALT JUNGLE R&B '80
Singles: 7-inch
TEC 3-4 80

ASPIRATIONS
Singles: 7-inch
PEACHES (6721 "You Left Me") 100-200
(Also issued as by the Admirations.)
Also see ADMIRATIONS

ASSAGAI
LPs: 10/12-inch
VERTIGO 10-12 71

ASSASSIN OF SILENCE
LPs: 10/12-inch
NEUROLOGICAL 8-10 79

ASSASSINS
LPs: 10/12-inch
SEYMOUR 8-10 87
Members: Jim Thackery; Tom Principato.
Also see MOONEY, John, and Jim Thackery
Also see NIGHTHAWKS
Also see PRINCIPATO, Tom

ASSEMBLEGE
LPs: 10/12-inch
WESTBOUND 8-10 72

ASSEMBLED MULTITUDE P&R '70
Singles: 7-inch
ATLANTIC 3-5 70-72
ERIC 3-4 81
LPs: 10/12-inch
ATLANTIC 8-10 70

ASSEMBLY
Singles: 12-inch
SIRE 4-6 84
Singles: 7-inch
ATLANTIC 3-4 68
SIRE 3-4 84-85
Member: Feargal Sharkey.
Also see SHARKEY, Feargal

ASSOCIATES
LPs: 10/12-inch
SIRE 5-10 82

ASSOCIATION P&R/LP '66
Singles: 7-inch
COLUMBIA 3-5 72
ELEKTRA 3-4 81
JUBILEE 4-8 65
MUMS 3-5 73
RCA 3-5 75
VALIANT 4-8 66
W.B. 3-6 67-71
Picture Sleeves
VALIANT 5-10 66
LPs: 10/12-inch
COLUMBIA 8-10 72
VALIANT 12-20 66
W.B. 8-12 67-71
Members: Gary Alexander; Ted Bluechel Jr; Brian Cole; Russ Giguere; Terry Kirkman; Cliff Nivison; Larry Ramos; Richard Thompson; Jim Yester; Larry Ramos.
Also see GIGUERE, Russ
Also see MAMAS & PAPAS / Association / Fifth Dimension
Also see MIKE & DEAN
Also see NEW CHRISTY MINSTRELS
Also see PEDESTRIANS / Association / Five Americans / Soulblenders

ASSOCIATION / Bobby Vee / Mike Love / Mary MacGregor
LPs: 10/12-inch
HITBOUND (1005 "New Memories") 10-15 83
Also see LOVE, Mike
Also see MacGREGOR, Mary
Also see VEE, Bobby

ASSORTMENT
Singles: 7-inch
SOUNDSPOT (2224 "Bless Our Hippie Home") 30-40 60s

ASTAIRE, Fred P&R '29
Singles: 78 rpm
BRUNSWICK 10-20 35-38
COLUMBIA 15-25 29-34
DECCA 5-10 43
MGM 4-8 51-53
MERCURY 3-6 53
RCA 3-5 55
VERVE 3-5 56
VICTOR 15-20 31-33
Singles: 7-inch
AVA 4-6 63
CHOREO 4-8 62
CLEF 5-10 57
KAPP 4-8 59
MGM 5-10 51-52
MERCURY 5-10 53
RCA 5-10 55
VERVE 5-10 56
EPs: 7-inch
CLEF 10-15 57
EPIC 10-15 57
MGM 10-20 51-53
VERVE 10-15 59
LPs: 10/12-inch
CAMDEN 10-20 59-60
CHOREO 10-20 61
CLEF 15-30 57
EPIC (3000 series) 15-30 57
EPIC (13000 & 15000 series) 8-15 66
KAPP 15-25 59
LION 10-20 59
MGM (100 series) 25-50 52
MGM (3000 series) 15-30 52-55
MONMOUTH EVERGREEN 10-20 71
VERVE 15-30 56-59
VOCALION 8-15 64
"X" 20-25 57
Also see CROSBY, Bing, & Fred Astaire

ASTAIRE, Fred, & Jane Powell P&R '51
Singles: 78 rpm
MGM 4-8 51
Singles: 7-inch
MGM 5-10 51
Also see POWELL, Jane

ASTAIRE, Fred, & Red Skelton / Helen Kane
(With Andre Previn)
EPs: 7-inch
MGM 8-10 50
(Not issued with cover, actually a three-track single.)
Also see ASTAIRE, Fred
Also see PREVIN, Andre
Also see SKELTON, Red

ASTLEY, Jon P&R/LP '87
Singles: 7-inch
ATLANTIC 3-4 87-88
Picture Sleeves
ATLANTIC 3-4 87-88
LPs: 10/12-inch
ATLANTIC 5-10 87

ASTLEY, Rick P&R '87
Singles: 7-inch
RCA 3-4 87-91
Picture Sleeves
RCA 3-4 87-89
LPs: 10/12-inch
RCA 5-8 87-89

ASTIN, John
Singles: 7-inch
U.A. 4-8 65

ASTOR, Rick, & Switchers: see CLARK, Dave, Five / Rick Astor

ASTOR & POTENTIALS
Singles: 7-inch
ARISTO (105 "Give Me What I Want") 5-10

ASTORS P&R/R&B '65
Singles: 7-inch
STAX (139 "What Can It Be") 50-75 63
STAX (170 "Candy") 10-15 65
STAX (179 "Mystery Woman") 10-15 65
STAX (232 "Daddy Didn't Tell You") 8-12 67
Members: Curtis Johnson; Richard Harris; Eddie Stanbeck; Sam Byrnes.
Also see CHIPS

ASTRAKAN, Steve
Singles: 7-inch
MUSICOR 4-6 68

ASTRAL PROJECTION
Singles: 7-inch
MAVERICK (711 "Rosa Lynn") 8-12

ASTRA-LITES
Singles: 7-inch
TRIBUTE (101 "Space Hop") 5-10 62

ASTRA NOVAS
Singles: 7-inch
ALASKA (1020 "Telstar") 10-15

ASTRO JETS
Singles: 7-inch
IMPERIAL 8-12 61

ASTRO TOTS
(With "String Band")
Singles: 7-inch
LINDA (12254 "My Dreams") 10-15 63

ASTRONAUTS
Singles: 7-inch
TRIAL (3521 "Farewell") 100-150 60

ASTRONAUTS
Singles: 7-inch
MERCURY 5-10 60

ASTRONAUTS P&R/LP '63
Singles: 7-inch
PALLADIUM (610 "Come Along Baby") 75-125 61
RCA 10-20 63-65
Picture Sleeves
RCA 20-30 63
EPs: 7-inch
RCA 25-40 63
RCA WURLITZER DISCOTHEQUE (100 "Discotheque Music") 30-40 64
(Promotional issue only.)
LPs: 10/12-inch
RCA 20-30 63-67
Members: Rich Fifield; Jon "Stormy" Patterson; Robert Demmon; Dennis Lindsey; James Gallagher.

ASTRONAUTS / Liverpool Five
LPs: 10/12-inch
RCA (251 "Stereo Festival") 25-45 67
(Promotional issue only.)
Also see ASTRONAUTS
Also see LIVERPOOL FIVE

ASTRONAUTS
Singles: 7-inch
JAN ELL 5-10 62
LUNEY 5-10
VANRUSS 5-10

ASTRONOMERS
Singles: 7-inch
EMBER (1097 "Relay-Son of Telstar") 5-10 63

ASTRO-NOTES
(With Jimmy Lewis & Judi Johns)
Singles: 7-inch
DOT 4-8 64
TROUBADOUR 4-6 67

ASTROS
Singles: 7-inch
GOLDEN STATE 4-8 65

ASTROS
Singles: 7-inch
ANDERSON (125 "Music Maker") 50-75 60s

ASWAD LP '88
LPs: 10/12-inch
ISLAND 5-10 84
MANGO 5-10 84-88
Members: Candy McKenzie; Brinsley Forde; Donald Griffiths; Courtney Hemmings; George Oban; Angus Gaye; Bunny McKenzie; Trevor Bow.

ASYLUM CHOIR
Singles: 7-inch
SHELTER 3-5 71
SMASH 4-6 69
LPs: 10/12-inch
SHELTER (2000 series) 8-10 74
SHELTER (8000 series) 10-15 71
SHELTER (52000 series) 5-10 75
SMASH (67107 "Look Inside") 25-30 68
(With toilet tissue cover.)
SMASH (67107 "Look Inside") 10-15 68
(With photo cover.)
Members: Leon Russell; Marc Benno.
Also see BENNO, Marc
Also see RUSSELL, Leon

ASYLUM KIDS
LPs: 10/12-inch
ENIGMA 5-10 84

AT LAST the 1958 Rock & Roll Show
Singles: 7-inch
EPIC 3-5 68

ATARI, Alexis
Singles: 12-inch
VANGUARD 4-6 83

ATARRAS
Singles: 7-inch
POLARIS 5-10 66

ATCHER, Bob C&W '46
(With the Countrymen; with Bonnie Blue Eyes)
Singles: 78 rpm
COLUMBIA 5-10 46-49
TIFFANY 5-10
VOCALION 8-12
EPs: 7-inch
COLUMBIA 10-20 50s
LPs: 10/12-inch
COLUMBIA (9006 "Early American Folk Songs") 30-50 50s
(10-inch LP.)
COLUMBIA (9013 "Songs of the Saddle") 30-50 50s
(10-inch LP.)
COLUMBIA (2232 "Dean of Cowboy Singers") 20-30 64
(Monaural.)
COLUMBIA (9032 "Dean of Cowboy Singers") 15-25 64
(Stereo.)
HARMONY (7313 "Early American Folk Songs") 15-20 64

ATCHER, Randy
Singles: 7-inch
MGM 15-25 56

ATELLO, Don
(Bernie Schwartz)
Singles: 7-inch
TIDE (1099 "She'll Break Your Heart") 10-20 63
TIDE (2002 "Questions I Can't Answer") 20-30 64
Also see COMFORTABLE CHAIR
Also see PRIDE, Adrian
Also see SCHWARTZ, Bernie
Also see WHEEL

ATENSION
Singles: 7-inch
ATCO/ISLAND 3-4 89

ATHA, Chuck
Singles: 7-inch
C-FLAT 8-12
FOX (006 "Just Me & My Baby") 50-75 57

ATHENS ROGUES
Singles: 7-inch
STOP (185 "She Could Love Me") 8-12

ATHLETIC SUPPORTERS
Singles
K-DISC/ERIKA (00151 "Nolimpix") 5-10 84
(Shaped picture disc.)

ATHLETICO SPIZZ '80
LPs: 10/12-inch
A&M 5-10 80

ATILLA & HUNS
Singles: 7-inch
BEAUX-ART 4-8
Also see ATTILA & HUNS

ATKINS R&B '82
Singles: 7-inch
W.B. 3-4 82
LPs: 10/12-inch
W.B. 5-10 82

ATKINS, Ben
(With the Nomads; Benny Atkins)
Singles: 7-inch
ENTERPRISE 4-6 72
JOSIE (1022 "Mr. Pitiful") 10-20 70
MERCURY (71686 "I'm Following You") 15-25 60
STATUE (7001 "It Would Take a Miracle") 75-125 67
YOUNGSTOWN (609 "Come On Over") 75-125 66

ATKINS, Big Ben C&W '78
Singles: 7-inch
GRT 3-6 78

ATKINS, Bobby
Singles: 7-inch
TORNADO 4-8 67

ATKINS, Chet C&W '55
(With the Anita Kerr Singers)
Singles: 78 rpm
BLUEBIRD (0072 "I Know When I'm Blue") 10-20 50
BULLET (617 "Guitar Blues") 50-100 46
RCA 5-15 47-57
Singles: 7-inch
RCA (0100 thru 0400 series) 12-25 50-51
(Black or turquoise labels.)
RCA (0100 thru 0700 series) 3-5 71-74
(Orange labels.)
RCA (4000 & 5000 series) 10-20 51-55
RCA (6000 & 7000 series) 5-15 55-62
RCA (8000 & 9000 series) 3-8 62-71
RCA (10000 thru 13000 series) 3-5 75-83
Picture Sleeves
RCA 5-10 61-67

EPs: 7-inch
RCA (100 series) ... 8-12 61
(With "LPC" prefix. Compact 33 Double.)
RCA (500 thru 900 series) ... 8-15 55-56
(With "EPA" prefix.)
RCA (1100 & 1200 series) ... 10-20 55-56
(With "EPB" prefix.)
RCA (1300 thru 1500 series) ... 8-15 56-57
(With "EPA" prefix.)
RCA (3000 series) ... 15-25 52-54
(With "EPB" prefix.)
RCA (4000 & 5000 series) ... 5-10 58-60
SESAC (13 "Mr. Atkins, If You Please") ... 20-30 59
LPs: 10/12-inch
CAMDEN ... 8-12 61-72
CANDLELITE ... 10-15
COLUMBIA ... 5-10 83-85
DOLTON ... 15-20 67
PICKWICK/CAMDEN ... 8-10 75
RCA (AHL1, ANL1, APL1, & AYL1 series) ... 5-10 73-83
RCA (CPL1 series) ... 8-12 77
RCA (1000 series) ... 25-35 54
(With "LPM" prefix.)
RCA (1100 thru 2200 series, except 1236) ... 15-25 55-60
(With "LPM" prefix.)
RCA (1236 "Stringin' Along with Chet Atkins") ... 30-40 55
(With "LPM" prefix.)
RCA (2300 thru 2900 series) ... 10-15 60-64
(With "LPM" prefix.)
RCA (3079 "Gallopin' Guitar") ... 150-200 53
(10-inch LP.)
RCA (3163 "Stringing Along") ... 75-125 53
(10-inch LP.)
RCA (3000 series) ... 8-12 64-68
(12-inch LPs. With "LPM" prefix.)
RCA (2000 & 3000 series) ... 10-15 66-69
(With "LSC" prefix.)
RCA (1900 thru 3500 series) ... 10-20 60-66
(Stereo. With "LSP" prefix. LSP numbers below 1900 were reprocessed stereo issues of '50s LPs. They were issued in the '60s are in the $10 to $15 range.)
RCA (3500 thru 4800 series) ... 8-15 68-73
RCA (6000 series) ... 8-12 70-72
SESAC ("Chet Atkins") ... 75-100 59
(Exact title and selection number not known.)
TIME-LIFE ... 5-10 81
Session: Floyd Cramer; Bob Moore; Jack Shook; Murrey Harman; Anita Kerr Singers.
Also see ANN-MARGRET
Also see ATKINS STRING COMPANY
Also see CHARLES, Ray, George Jones, & Chet Atkins
Also see COUNTRY ALL STARS
Also see COUNTRY HAMS
Also see CRAMER, Floyd
Also see EVERLY BROTHERS
Also see GIBSON, Don
Also see KERR, Anita
Also see MOORE, Bob
Also see NASHVILLE ALL-STARS
Also see NELSON, Willie
Also see PRESLEY, Elvis
Also see PURE PRAIRIE LEAGUE
Also see REED, Jerry, & Chet Atkins
Also see RHYTHM ROCKERS
Also see SNOW, Hank, & Chet Atkins

ATKINS, Chet, & Boston Pops
LPs: 10/12-inch
RCA ... 10-20 66-69
Also see BOSTON POPS ORCHESTRA

ATKINS, Chet, Floyd Cramer & Danny Davis
(Chet, Floyd & Danny)
Singles: 7-inch
RCA ... 3-5 77
LPs: 10/12-inch
RCA ... 5-8 77
Also see DAVIS, Danny

ATKINS, Chet, Floyd Cramer & Boots Randolph
LPs: 10/12-inch
PICKWICK ... 5-8 71
Also see CRAMER, Floyd
Also see RANDOLPH, Boots

ATKINS, Chet, & Mark Knopfler
LPs: 10/12-inch
COLUMBIA ... 5-8 90
Also see KNOPFLER, Mark

ATKINS, Chet, & Les Paul
Singles: 7-inch
RCA ... 3-4 78
LPs: 10/12-inch
RCA ... 5-10 76-80
Also see PAUL, Les

ATKINS, Chet, Faron Young, & Anita Kerr Singers
EPs: 7-inch
SESAC (48 "No Greater Love") ... 25-35 59
Also see KERR, Anita
Also see YOUNG, Faron

ATKINS, Chet, & Doc Watson
LPs: 10/12-inch
RCA ... 5-10 80
Also see WATSON, Doc
Also see ATKINS, Chet

ATKINS, Christopher P&R '82
Singles: 7-inch
POLYDOR ... 3-4 82
Picture Sleeves
POLYDOR ... 3-4 82

ATKINS, Dave
(With His Offbeats)
Singles: 7-inch
BACK BEAT (511 "Shake-Kum-Down") ... 40-60 62
HI-Q (5025 "Smokey Mountain Twist") ... 10-15 62
VIV ... 10-15 63

ATKINS, Harold
Singles: 7-inch
APT (25058 "Please Please") ... 10-20 61

ATKINS, J.C., & Dukes
Singles: 7-inch
BOUNTY (5589 "You Upset My Very Soul") ... 10-20 60s

ATKINS, Jim
Singles: 78 rpm
CORAL ... 5-8 53
Singles: 7-inch
CORAL ... 10-20 53

ATKINS, Larry
Singles: 7-inch
HIGHLAND (1193 "Ain't That Love Enough") ... 25-35 60s
ROMARK ... 5-10 68

ATKINS, Walt, & Sabres
Singles: 7-inch
HI-Q (5025 "Big Beat Blues") ... 10-20 60

ATKINS SISTERS
Singles: 7-inch
VANDAN ... 4-8 64

ATKINS STRING COMPANY C&W '75
Singles: 7-inch
RCA ... 3-4 75
LPs: 10/12-inch
RCA ... 5-10 75
Members: Chet Atkins; Johnny Gimble; Paul Yandell; Lisa Silver.
Also see ATKINS, Chet

ATKINSON, Hal
Singles: 7-inch
LOVE DAY ... 4-8 72

ATKINSON, Sweet Pea
Singles: 7-inch
ISLAND ... 3-4 82
LPs: 10/12-inch
ISLAND ... 5-10 82

ATLANTA C&W '83
Singles: 7-inch
MCA ... 3-4 84-85
MDJ ... 3-5 83
SOUTHERN TRACKS ... 3-4 87-88
Picture Sleeves
MDJ ... 3-4 83
LPs: 10/12-inch
MCA ... 5-10 84
Members: Dick Stevens; Brad Griffis; Tony Ingram; Allen David; John Holder; Jeff Baker; Al Collay; Bill Packard.
Also see SPURZZ
Also see VOGUES

ATLANTA DISCO BAND R&B '75
Singles: 7-inch
ARIOLA AMERICA ... 3-4 76
LPs: 10/12-inch
ARIOLA AMERICA ... 5-10 76

ATLANTA JAMES C&W '74
(Mack Vickery)
Singles: 7-inch
MCA ... 3-5 74
Also see VICKERY, Mack

ATLANTA RHYTHM SECTION P&R/LP '74/C&W '79
Singles: 7-inch
COLUMBIA ... 3-4 81
DECCA ... 3-5 72
MCA ... 3-5 73
POLYDOR ... 3-5 74-80
LPs: 10/12-inch
COLUMBIA ... 5-10 81
DECCA ... 12-20 72
MCA ... 5-10 77
MFSL (038 "Champagne Jam") ... 40-60 79
POLYDOR ... 5-10 74-80
Members: Ronnie Hammond; Rodney Justo; Robert Nix; Barry Bailey; James Cobb; Dean Daughtry; Paul Goddard.
Also see BEAVERTEETH
Also see CANDYMEN
Also see CLASSICS IV
Also see MANILOW, Barry / Atlanta Rhythm Section

ATLANTIC
Singles: 7-inch
ATLANTIC ... 3-4 81

ATLANTIC
LPs:10/12-inch
TEKTRA ... 10-20

ATLANTIC, T.C.: see T.C. ATLANTIC

ATLANTIC & PACIFIC
Singles: 7-inch
P.I.P. ... 3-5 75

ATLANTIC OCEAN
Singles: 7-inch
COULEE (137 "I Thought a Lot Today") ... 5-10 71

ATLANTIC FAMILY
Singles: 7-inch
ATLANTIC ... 3-5 78

ATLANTIC SOUNDS
Singles: 7-inch
ATLANTIC ... 4-6 68

ATLANTIC STARR R&B '78
Singles: 12-inch
A&M ... 4-8 79-85
W.B. ... 4-6 89
Singles: 7-inch
A&M ... 3-4 78-86
MANHATTAN ... 3-4 86
W.B. ... 3-4 87-89
Picture Sleeves
A&M ... 3-4 78-86
W.B. ... 3-4 87
LPs: 10/12-inch
A&M ... 5-10 78-85
W.B. ... 5-10 87-89
Members: Sharon Bryant; David Lewis; Wayne Lewis; Jonathan Lewis; William Sudderth; Damon Rentie; Clifford Archer; Joe Phillips; Porter Carroll; Koran Daniels; Barbara Weathers.
Also see BRYANT, Sharon

ATLANTICS
Singles: 7-inch
LINDA (103 "Boo Hoo Hoo") ... 15-25 61
LINDA (107 "Remember the Night") ... 50-100 62

ATLANTICS
Singles: 7-inch
COLUMBIA ... 5-10 63-64
FARO ... 5-10 67
RAMPART ... 5-10 65
Picture Sleeves
FARO ... 10-15 67
RAMPART ... 10-20 65
Also see HODGE, Gaynel
Also see WHITE, Barry, & Atlantics

ATLANTICS
Singles: 7-inch
AMON ... 5-10 64

ATLANTICS
Singles: 7-inch
ABC ... 3-4 78
ALLTIME ... 3-4 80
MCA ... 3-4 79
LPs: 10/12-inch
ABC ... 5-10 79
Members: Bobby Marron; Tom Hauck; Fred Pineau; B. Wilkinson; Ray Fernandes.

ATLANTICS
Singles: 7-inch
CHERRY HILL (2771 "Duke of Earl") ... 15-20

ATLANTIS
Singles: 7-inch
FARO ... 10-20

ATLANTIS
Singles: 7-inch
POLYDOR ... 3-4 75
LPs: 10/12-inch
POLYDOR ... 5-10 75
VERTIGO ... 10-15 73-74
Members: Inga Rumpf; Gaspar Lawal; Jean Kravetz; Karlheinz; Ringo Funk; Dieter Bornschlegel.

ATLANTIS II
Singles: 7-inch
CMS ... 8-12 60s
ZIGGY ... 8-12 60s

ATLEE
Singles: 7-inch
DUNHILL ... 3-5 70
LPs: 10/12-inch
DUNHILL ... 10-12 70

ATMOSPHERES
Singles: 7-inch
LIN (5023 "The Fickle Chicken") ... 10-20 59
RM (1005 "Telegraph") ... 5-10 75
Members: Bill Kramer; Jack Allday; Clarke Brown; Steve Voekel; Ken Waldrop; Ben Hill.

ATOMIC ROOSTER LP '71
Singles: 7-inch
ELEKTRA ... 3-5 71-72
LPs: 10/12-inch
ELEKTRA ... 10-20 71-73
PVC ... 5-10 83
Members: Chris Farlowe; Pete French; Steve Bolton; John Cann; Vincent Crane; Paul Hammond; Carl Palmer; Johnny Mandala; Rick Parnell.
Also see BROWN, Arthur
Also see FARLOWE, Chris

ATTACK
Singles: 7-inch
LONDON ... 4-8 67

ATTACK, Art: see ART ATTACK

ATTALI, Patrick
Singles: 7-inch
AMO ... 3-5
Picture Sleeves
AMO ... 8-12

ATTIC SOUNDS
Singles: 7-inch
MIKE ... 4-8 66

ATTILA
LPs: 10/12-inch
BACK-TRAC ... 5-10 85
D&J ... 5-8 80
EPIC (30030 "Attila") ... 40-50 70
Members: Billy Joel; Jon Small.
Also see JOEL, Billy

ATTILA & HUNS
Singles: 7-inch
MAGIC TOUCH (2009 "Hula Shake") ... 15-25 67
MAGIC TOUCH (2071 "Vineyards of My Mind") ... 15-25 69
SARA (6511 "Cheryl") ... 15-25 65
Members: Mike Pease; Doug Deuel; Barry Berdal; Walter Staniec; Benny Wisniewski; Barb Spence; Dennis Lewan; Rich Legault.
Also see ATILLA & HUNS
Also see FILET of SOUND
Also see HUNS OF TIME

ATTITUDE R&B/D&D '83
Singles: 12-inch
ATLANTIC ... 4-6 83
Singles: 7-inch
ATLANTIC ... 3-4 83
LPs: 10/12-inch
ATLANTIC ... 5-10 83

ATTITUDES
Singles: 7-inch
TIMES SQUARE ... 4-8 67
Members: Randy Silverman; Al Brum; Steve Fineberg; Art Bennanutti; Marty Ziegler.

ATTITUDES P&R/R&B '76
Singles: 7-inch
DARK HORSE ... 3-5 75-76
Picture Sleeves
DARK HORSE ... 3-5 75
LPs: 10/12-inch
DARK HORSE ... 5-10 76-77
Members: Danny Kortchmar; David Foster; Jim Keltner; Paul Stallworth.
Also see BROOKS, Denny
Also see KORTCHMAR, Danny

ATTORNEYS
Singles: 7-inch
VERDICT ... 3-5 81
Member: Vince Megna.
Also see BONNEVILLES
Also see BOYCE, Tommy, & Bobby Hart

ATTRACTIONS
Singles: 7-inch
BELL ... 10-20 67

ATTRACTIONS
Singles: 7-inch
B&B (101 "C.O.D.") ... 5-10
NATIONWIDE ... 10-20
RENFRO ... 3-6

ATTRIBUTES
Singles: 7-inch
U.G.H.A. ... 4-6 79

ATWELL, Winifred
Singles: 78 rpm
COLUMBIA ... 10-15 54
LONDON ... 10-15 53-57
Singles: 7-inch
COLUMBIA (40208 "Five Finger Boogie") ... 10-20 54
COLUMBIA (43472 "Flea Circus") ... 5-10 65
LONDON ... 15-25 53-57

ATWOOD, Eddie, & His Goodies
Singles: 7-inch
SURF (5028 "Hot Saki") ... 15-25 58
Session: Danny Flores.
Also see FLORES, Danny

ATWOOD the ELECTRIC ICEMAN
Singles: 7-inch
UNI ... 4-6 72
Members: Atwood Allen; Sir Douglas Quintet.
Also see SIR DOUGLAS QUINTET

AU GO-GO SINGERS
Singles: 7-inch
ROULETTE (4577 "Pink Polemoniums") ... 10-15 64
LPs: 10/12-inch
ROULETTE (R-25280 "They Call Us Au Go-Go Singers") ... 30-40 64
(Monaural.)
ROULETTE (SR-25280 "They Call Us Au Go-Go Singers") ... 40-50 64
(Stereo.)
Members: Steven (Stephen) Stills; Richie Furay.
Also see FURAY, Richie
Also see STILLS, Stephen

AU GO-GOs
Singles: 7-inch
JEST ... 4-8 65

AU PAIRS
Singles: 7-inch
HUMAN ... 3-4 80-81
21 ... 3-4 79-80
LPs: 10/12-inch
HUMAN ... 5-10 81

AUBREY TWINS
Singles: 7-inch
ABC-PAR ... 4-8 64
EPIC ... 4-8 67
MGM ... 4-8 68
Picture Sleeves
EPIC ... 5-10 67

AUBURN, Jil
Singles: 7-inch
MALA (452 "Push, Sweep") ... 10-15 62

AUBURN, Joan
Singles: 7-inch
ELCLUSIVE (2249 "Cracked Heart") ... 5-10 63

AUDIENCE P&R '71
Singles: 7-inch
ELEKTRA ... 3-5 71-72
LPs: 10/12-inch
AUDIENCE ... 10-15 71-72
ELEKTRA ... 8-12 72
Members: Trevor Williams; Howard Werth; Pat Neubergh; Nick Judd; Tony Connor; Keith Gemmell.
Also see WERTH, Howard, & Moonbeams

AUDIO TWO LP '88
LPs: 10/12-inch
FIRST PRIORITY ... 5-8 88

AUDIOS
Singles: 78 rpm
DIG (105 "Honest I Do") ... 20-25 56
Singles: 7-inch
DIG (105 "Honest I Do") ... 35-45 56
Also see FOSTER, Cell, & Audios

AUDITIONS
Singles: 7-inch
FRECKLES (010 "Get Set, Be Ready") ... 10-20 60s

AUDITONES
Singles: 78 rpm
RAINBOW ... 10-15 47
Also see BROWN, Delores, & Auditones

AUDREY P&R '56
Singles: 78 rpm
PLUS (104 "Dear Elvis") ... 10-20 56
Singles: 7-inch
PLUS (104 "Dear Elvis") ... 20-30 56
(Break-in novelty with excerpts of several Elvis Sun tracks.)
Also see PRESLEY, Elvis

AUGER, Brian P&R/LP '70
(With Trinity; Brian Auger's Oblivion Express)
Singles: 7-inch
ATCO ... 4-6 68-69
RCA ... 3-5 70-74
EPs: 7-inch
ATCO (4536 "Red Beans & Rice") ... 5-8 69
(Labeled an EP by Atco, though only has one track on each side. Not issued with cover.)
LPs: 10/12-inch
ATCO ... 12-15 69
CAPITOL ... 10-12 69
POLYDOR ... 5-10 74
RCA ... 6-10 70-77
W.B. ... 5-10 77
Also see DRISCOLL, Julie, & Brian Auger

AUGIE: see MEYERS, Augie

AUGUST
Singles: 7-inch
BUDDAH ... 3-5 73
Members: G.W. Kenny; Howie Blauvelt; James Santovo.
Also see RAM JAM

AUGUST
Singles: 7-inch
PANTERA ... 3-5

AUGUST, Art
Singles: 7-inch
SOUND-O-RAMA (112 "Hold Out Your Hand") ... 8-12 62
TRANS CONTINENTAL (1014 "Hold Out Your Hand") ... 10-20 60

AUGUST, Jan P&R '46
Singles: 78 rpm
MERCURY ... 3-6 46-57
Singles: 7-inch
MERCURY ... 4-10 50-62
EPs: 7-inch
MERCURY ... 5-15 50-56
LPs: 10/12-inch
MERCURY ... 10-25 50-62
WING ... 6-12 59
Also see HAYMAN, Richard, Orchestra

AUGUST, Joseph
("Mr. Google Eyes")
Singles: 78 rpm
COLEMAN ... 10-15 49
COLUMBIA ... 5-10 50
DOMINO ... 5-10 50
DUKE ... 10-15 54-56
FLIP ... 10-20 54
LEE ... 5-10 51
Singles: 7-inch
DUKE ... 15-20 54-56
FLIP (1001 "Strange Things Happen in the Dark") ... 20-30 54
INSTANT (3239 "Everything Happens At Night") ... 10-20 61
OKEH ... 25-45 51
Also see FORD, Billy
Also see OTIS, Johnny

AUGUST, Jimmy
Singles: 7-inch
SIDEWALK ... 4-8 66

AUGUST, June
Singles: 7-inch
GROOVIE ... 25-40

AUGUST, Kevin
Singles: 7-inch
ANTLER (3003 "Angel")....4-6 81
(Colored vinyl.)

AUGUST, Lord: see LORD AUGUST

AUGUST & DENEEN
Singles: 7-inch
ABC (11082 "We Go Together")....25-50 68

AUGUST & SPUR OF THE MOMENT BAND
Singles: 7-inch
PANTERA (001 "I-95 Asshole Song")....4-6 83

AUGUSTINE TWINS
Singles: 7-inch
DUKE....4-8 67

AUKEMA, Niki
LPs: 10/12-inch
PARAMOUNT....15-20 73
Also see MILKWOOD

AULD, George
Singles: 78 rpm
CORAL....4-8 55
Singles: 7-inch
ABC-PAR....8-12 59
CORAL....8-12 55
U.A.....3-5 77

AUM
Singles: 7-inch
FILLMORE....5-10 69-70
LPs: 10/12-inch
FILLMORE (30002 "Resurrection") 20-30 69
SAN FRANCISCO....10-15 69
SIRE (97007 "Bluesvibes")....30-40 69
Members: Wayne Ceballos; Reese Marin; Larry Martin; Boots Houston; Sean Silverman; Steve Bowman.

AUNE, Steve
Singles: 7-inch
("The Pueblo Incident")....5-8 69
(Neither label name nor selection number used.)

AURA
Singles: 7-inch
MERCURY....3-5 72
TIME....3-4 82
LPs: 10/12-inch
MERCURY....10-12 72
WIZARD....5-10 78

AURACLE
Singles: 7-inch
CHRYSALIS....3-4 78-79
LPs: 10/12-inch
CHRYSALIS....5-10 78-79
Members: Bill Steabell; Ron Wagner; Richard Braun; Stephen Kujala; Steven Rehreil; John Setty Jr.

AURAL EXCITERS
Singles: 12-inch
TOP FLIGHT....4-6 83

AURIE & SIGHS
Singles: 7-inch
ATLANTIC....3-5 81

AURRA R&B '80
Singles: 12-inch
SALSOUL....4-6 82
Singles: 7-inch
DREAM....3-4 80
SALSOUL....3-4 81-83
LPs: 10/12-inch
DREAM....5-10 80
SALSOUL....5-10 81-83
Members: Curt Jones; Starleana Young; Steve Washington; Tom Lockett Jr.; Phillip Fields.
Also see DEJA
Also see SLAVE

AUSSIE BAND
Singles: 7-inch
REAL WORLD....3-4 80

AUSSIES
Singles: 7-inch
TAKE FIVE (6319 "Slippin & Slidin' ")....20-30

AUSTIN, Augie
(With the Chromatics; Little Augie Austin; with Eddie Singleton & Orchestra)
Singles: 7-inch
PONTIAC (101 "My Love for You")....15-20 60
Also see SINGLETON, Eddie, & Chromatics / Augie Austin & Chromatics

AUSTIN, Billy, & Hearts
Singles: 7-inch
APOLLO (444 "Angel Baby")....100-150 53

AUSTIN, Bobby C&W '66
Singles: 7-inch
ATLANTIC....3-5 72-73
CAPITOL....3-6 67-69
CHALLENGE....10-15 59
TALLY....4-8 66
LPs: 10/12-inch
CAPITOL....15-20 67-68
DESIGN....8-12 60s
HURRAH....5-10
SYNDICATE....5-10
Also see STEWART, Wynn

AUSTIN, Chris C&W '88
Singles: 7-inch
W.B.....3-4 88-89
Also see McENTIRE, Reba

AUSTIN, Darlene C&W '82
Singles: 7-inch
CBT....3-4 86
MAGI....3-4 87
MYRTLE....3-4 82-83
LPs: 10/12-inch
MUSIC MASTERS....6-12 80s

AUSTIN, Don
Singles: 7-inch
ALON....3-5

AUSTIN, Donald
Singles: 7-inch
WOODY (105 "Nan Zee")....10-20

AUSTIN, Donald
Singles: 7-inch
EASTBOUND....3-6 73
LPs: 10/12-inch
EASTBOUND....8-12 73

AUSTIN, Donel
Singles: 7-inch
MIDA (113 "Get with It")....15-25 59

AUSTIN, Gene P&R '25
Singles: 78 rpm
COLUMBIA....3-5 54-56
DECCA....3-5 56
VICTOR....4-8 25-35
Singles: 7-inch
COLUMBIA....4-8 54-56
DECCA....4-8 56
RCA....4-8 57
Picture Sleeves
RCA....5-10 57
EPs: 7-inch
RCA....10-15 53
LPs: 10/12-inch
DECCA....15-25 56
DOT....10-15 60s
RCA....20-40 53-57
"X"....15-25 54

AUSTIN, Harold
Singles: 7-inch
ATLAS....8-12

AUSTIN, Jay
Singles: 7-inch
VEE JAY....5-10 63

AUSTIN, Kay C&W '80
Singles: 7-inch
DJ....3-4
E.I.O.....3-4 80
Picture Sleeves
DJ....3-5

AUSTIN, Lee
Singles: 7-inch
I DENTIFY....3-5 75
POLYDOR....3-5 73-78

AUSTIN, Leon
Singles: 7-inch
EXCELLO (2248 "I'm So Glad")....8-12 64
KING....4-6 70

AUSTIN, Patti R&B '69
Singles: 12-inch
QWEST....4-6 84-86
Singles: 7-inch
ABC....5-10 68
CTI....3-6 76-80
COLUMBIA....4-8 71-73
CORAL (62455 "He's Good Enough for Me")....10-20 65
CORAL (62471 "I Wanna Be Loved")....10-20 65
CORAL (62478 "Someone's Gonna Cry")....50-100 66
CORAL (62491 "Take Away the Pain Stain")....10-20 66
CORAL (62500 "Leave a Little Love")....10-20 66
CORAL (62511 "What a Difference a Day Made")....10-20 67
CORAL (62518 "Only All the Time")....10-20 67
CORAL (62541 "You're Too Much a Part of Me")....10-20 67
CORAL (62548 "All My Love")....10-20 68
QWEST....3-4 81-86
U.A.....3-4 69-70
LPs: 10/12-inch
CTI....5-10 77-80
GRP....5-8 90
QWEST....5-10 81-86
Also see JONES, Quincy
Also see WALDEN, Narada Michael, & Patti Austin
Also see YUTAKA

AUSTIN, Patti, & Jerry Butler
Singles: 7-inch
CTI....3-4 83
Also see BUTLER, Jerry

AUSTIN, Patti, & James Ingram P&R '82
Singles: 7-inch
QWEST....3-4 82-84
Also see AUSTIN, Patti
Also see INGRAM, James

AUSTIN, Sil P&R/R&B '56
(With the Allstars)
Singles: 78 rpm
JUBILEE....5-15 54-55
MERCURY....5-15 56-57
WING....5-15 56
Singles: 7-inch
JUBILEE....5-15 54-55
MERCURY....5-15 56-65
SSS INT'L....3-5 70
SEW CITY....4-8 66
WING....5-15 56
EPs: 7-inch
MERCURY....10-15 56-57
LPs: 10/12-inch
MERCURY....10-25 59-67
SSS INT'L....8-10 70-82
WING....10-12 63-68

AUSTIN, Sil, & Red Prysock
Singles: 7-inch
MERCURY....4-6 61
LPs: 10/12-inch
MERCURY (20434 "Battle Royal")..15-25 61
(Monaural.)
MERCURY (60106 "Battle Royal")..20-30 61
(Stereo.)
SSS INT'L....8-10 69
WING....10-12 63-68
Also see AUSTIN, Sil
Also see PRYSOCK, Red

AUSTIN, Tom
Singles: 7-inch
FIRST AMERICAN....3-5 79

AUSTIN, Tom, & Healeys
Singles: 7-inch
OLD TOWN (1147 "Summer's Over")....15-25 62

AUSTIN SISTERS
Singles: 7-inch
EDISON INT'L....5-10 58

AUSTRALIAN CRAWL
Singles: 7-inch
EMI AMERICA....3-4 82
HARVEST....3-5 80
LPs: 10/12-inch
GEFFEN....5-10 84
Members: James Reyne; Simon Binks; Brad Robinson; Paul Williams; Bill McDonough.

AUTIO, Vi, & Pulsations
Singles: 7-inch
BOLO....5-10 62

AUTOGRAPH P&R '84
Singles: 7-inch
RCA....3-4 84-85
Picture Sleeves
RCA....3-4 84-85
LPs: 10/12-inch
RCA....5-10 84-87
Member: Steve Plunkett.

AUTOGRAPHS
Singles: 7-inch
JOKER....5-10
LOMA....5-10 66
OKEH (7293 "I Can Do It")....15-25 67

AUTOMATIC
LPs: 10/12-inch
RMS....5-10 83

AUTOMATIC MAN LP '76
Singles: 7-inch
ISLAND....3-5 76-77
LPs: 10/12-inch
ISLAND....5-10 76-77
Members: Michael Schrieve; Todd Cochran; Doni Harvey; Pat Thrall.

AUTOMATIONS
Singles: 7-inch
CLIFTON....4-8 75

AUTOMATIX
LPs: 10/12-inch
MCA....5-10 83

AUTOSALVAGE
Singles: 7-inch
RCA (9506 "Parahighway")....5-10 68
LPs: 10/12-inch
RCA (3940 "Autosalvage")....25-40 68
Members: Skip Boone; Thomas Danaher; Darius Davenport; Rick Turner.
Also see BEAR
Also see BOYLAN, Terence

AUTRY, Gene P&R '33/C&W '44
(With the Cass County Boys & the Pinafores)
Singles: 78 rpm
BRUNSWICK (12936 "There's An Empty Cot in the Bunkhouse Tonight")....100-200 30s
(Flip side, #12899, is credited to "Gene Autry & Jimmy Long.")
CHAMPION (16096 "Cowboy Yodel")....100-150 30s
CHAMPION (16119 "Texas Blues")....100-150 30s
CHAMPION (16141 "In the Jailhouse Now, No. 2")....100-150 30s
CHAMPION (16210 "Mean Mama Blues")....100-150 30s
CHAMPION (16228 "Pistol Packin' Mama")....100-150 30s
CHAMPION (16245 "Blue Days")....100-150 30s
CHAMPION (16275 "T.B. Blues")....100-150 30s
CLARION (5025 "Hobo Yodel")....75-125 30s
CLARION (5026 "No One to Call Me Darling")....75-125 30s
CLARION (5058 "I'll Be Thinking of You Little Girl")....75-125 30s
CLARION (5075 "Cowboy Yodel")....75-125 30s
CLARION (5154 "Dust Pan Blues")....75-125 30s
CLARION (5155 "Waiting for a Train")....75-125 30s
CLARION (5239 "Left My Gal in the Mountains")....75-125 30s
CLARION (5240 "Daddy and Home")....75-125 30s
CLARION (5243 "Lullaby Yodel")....75-125 30s
CLARION (5272 "True Blue Bill")....75-125 30s
CLARION (5308 "A Gangster's Warning")....75-125 30s
CONQUEROR....30-90 30s
COLUMBIA....5-15 45-56
DECCA (5426 "Blue Days")....50-100 30s
DECCA (5464 "In the Shadow of the Pine")....50-100 30s
DECCA (5488 "Bear Cat Papa Blues")....50-100 30s
DECCA (5501 "My Carolina Sunshine Girl")....50-100 30s
DECCA (5426 "Blue Days")....50-100 30s
DECCA (5517 "T.B. Blues")....50-100 30s
DECCA (5527 "Yodeling Hobo")....50-100 30s
DECCA (5544 "Pistol Packin' Mama")....50-100 30s
DIVA (6030 "Hobo Yodel")....50-100 30s
DIVA (6031 "Waiting for a Train")....50-100 30s
DIVA (6032 "Blue Yodel No. 4")....50-100 30s
DIVA (6033 "Lullaby Yodel")....50-100 30s
DIVA (6035 "No One to Call Me Darling")....50-100 30s
DIVA (6037 "Frankie and Johnny")....50-100 30s
DIVA (6049 "My Rough and Rowdy Ways")....50-100 30s
DIVA (6057 "Cowboy Yodel")....50-100 30s
HARMONY (1046 "Blue Yodel No. 5")....25-50 49
MONTGOMERY WARD (4242 "Bear Cat Papa Blues")....100-200 30s
MONTGOMERY WARD (4243 "My Carolina Sunshine Girl")....100-200 30s
MONTGOMERY WARD (4243 "Don't Do Me That Way")....100-200 30s
MONTGOMERY WARD (4244 "High-Steppin' Mama Blues")....100-200 30s
MONTGOMERY WARD (4245 "Rheumatism Blues")....100-200 30s
MONTGOMERY WARD (4275 "Wildcat Mama")....150-250 30s
MONTGOMERY WARD (4326 "That Ramshackle Shack")....100-200 30s
MONTGOMERY WARD (4333 "I'm Always Dreaming of You")....100-200 30s
MONTGOMERY WARD (4767 "Old Woman and the Cow")....200-300 30s
MONTGOMERY WARD (4767 "There's a Gal in the Mountains")....100-200 30s
MONTGOMERY WARD (4768 "She Wouldn't Do It")....100-200 30s
MONTGOMERY WARD (4768 "She's a Low Down Mama")....150-250 30s
MONTGOMERY WARD (4931 "Pictures of My Mother")....100-200 30s
MONTGOMERY WARD (4932 "Yodeling Hobo")....100-200 30s
MONTGOMERY WARD (4933 "In the Shadow of the Pine")....100-200 30s
MONTGOMERY WARD (4975 "In the Jailhouse Now, No. 2")....100-200 30s
MONTGOMERY WARD (4975 "T.B. Blues")....150-250 30s
MONTGOMERY WARD (4976 "True Blue Bill")....100-200 30s
MONTGOMERY WARD (4977 "Jailhouse Blues")....100-200 30s
MONTGOMERY WARD (4977 "Pistol Packin' Mama")....100-200 30s
MONTGOMERY WARD (4978 "Whisper Your Mother's Name")....150-250 30s
MONTGOMERY WARD (4978 "My Carolina Sunshine Girl")....100-200 30s
MONTGOMERY WARD (8016 "Money Ain't No Use Anyway")....100-200 30s
MONTGOMERY WARD (8017 "Cowboy Yodel")....100-200 30s
MONTGOMERY WARD (8017 "Yodeling Hobo")....100-200 30s
MONTGOMERY WARD (8034 "Train Whistle Blues")....150-250 30s
MONTGOMERY WARD (8034 "Texas Blues")....150-250 30s
Note: Some Montgomery Ward numbers appear to have been used twice, with different titles, and often slightly different pricing. Since this information came from the same source, we are assuming it to be accurate until proven otherwise.)
OKEH....10-20 40-45
PERFECT....30-60
QRS (1044 "I'll Be Thinking of You, Little Gal"/ Living in the Mountains")....3000-5000 29
ROMEO (5109 "Silver Haired Daddy of Mine")....300-500 32
ROMEO (5110 "Jailhouse Blues")....300-500 32
SUPERTONE (9705 "I'll Be Thinking of You, Little Gal"/"Whisper Your Mother's Name")....3000-5000 29
VELVET TONE (2338 "True Bill Bill")....50-100 30s
VELVET TONE (2374 "A Gangster's Warning")....50-100 30s
VELVET TONE (7056 "Hobo Yodel")....50-100 30s
VELVET TONE (7057 "Waiting for a Train")....50-100 30s
VELVET TONE (7058 "Blue Yodel No. 4")....50-100 30s
VELVET TONE (7059 "Lullaby Yodel")....50-100 30s
VELVET TONE (7061 "No One to Call Me Darling")....50-100 30s
VELVET TONE (7063 "Frankie and Johnny")....50-100 30s
VELVET TONE (7075 "My Rough and Rowdy Ways")....50-100 30s
VELVET TONE (7083 "Cowboy Yodel")....50-100 30s
VOCALION....25-50 35-40
Singles: 7-inch
COLUMBIA (06189 "Statue in the Bay")....3-4 86
COLUMBIA (20700 thru 21500 series)....5-10 50-56
COLUMBIA (38700 thru 40500 series)....5-10 50-55
COLUMBIA (44000 series)....3-5 68
MISTLETOE....3-5 74
REPUBLIC....3-8 59-76
Picture Sleeves
COLUMBIA (121 "Three Little Dwarfs")....15-25 51
(May have been a 78 rpm sleeve only.)
COLUMBIA HALL OF FAME (33165 "Rudolph the Red-Nosed Reindeer")....4-6 69
REPUBLIC (2002 "Santa's Comin' in a Whirlybird")....5-10 59
EPs: 7-inch
COLUMBIA....40-50 51-56
LPs: 10/12-inch
BIRCHMOUNT....8-12
BULLDOG....5-10
CHALLENGE....25-30 58
COLUMBIA (55 thru 154)....80-100 51-55
(10-inch LPs.)
COLUMBIA (600 series)....80-100 55
COLUMBIA (1000 series)....8-10 70-82
COLUMBIA (1500 series)....10-20 61
COLUMBIA (2547 "Merry Christmas")....40-60 56
(10-inch LP.)
COLUMBIA (2568 "Easter Favorites")....40-60 57
(10-inch LP.)
COLUMBIA (6020 "Gene Autry Western Classics")....40-60 49
(10-inch LP.)
COLUMBIA (6137 "Merry Christmas")....40-60 50
(10-inch LP.)
COLUMBIA (8000 series)....80-100
COLUMBIA (9001 "Western Classics, Vol. 1")....40-60 51
(10-inch LP.)
COLUMBIA (9002 "Western Classics, Vol. 2")....40-60 51
(10-inch LP.)
COLUMBIA (15000 series)....8-10 81
COLUMBIA (37000 series)....5-10 82
DESIGN....8-10
ENCORE....6-10 80
GRT....10-15 77
GOLDEN AGE....5-10 77
GRAND PRIX....8-10
HALLMARK....8-12
HARMONY (7100 thru 7300 series)....20-30 56-65
HARMONY (9500 series)....15-25 59-64
HARMONY (11000 series)....10-15 64-66
HURRAH....5-10
INTERNATIONAL AWARD....5-10
MELODY RANCH (101 "Melody Ranch")....30-50 65
MISTLETOE....8-12 74
MURRAY HILL (61072 "The Gene Autry Collection")....45-55 83
(Four-LP set.)
MURRAY HILL (897296 "Melody Ranch Radio Show")....45-55 80s
(Four-LP set.)
RCA (2600 series)....25-30 62
RADIOLA....5-10 75
REPUBLIC (1900 series)....5-10
REPUBLIC (6000 series)....5-15 76-78
STARDAY....6-10 78
TIMELESS TREASURES....5-8 83
Also see BOND, Johnny
Also see CLAYTON, Bob
Also see CLAYTON and Breen
Also see DODDS, Johnny
Also see HANDY, John
Also see HATFIELD, Overton
Also see HILL, Sam
Also see JOHNSON, Gene
Also see LONG, Tom
Also see PARKER, Fess, & Buddy Ebsen / Gene Autry
Also see SMITH, Jimmy

AUTRY, Thomas
Singles: 7-inch
TOKEN....8-12

AUTRY, Tom
Singles: 7-inch
BELL....3-5 72

AUTUMN
Singles: 7-inch
COMPLEAT....3-4 84-85
PYE....3-5 73
LPs: 10/12-inch
COMPLEAT....5-10 84-85

AUTUMN PEOPLE
LPs: 10/12-inch
SOUNDTECH (3020 "Autumn People")....75-100 76
Members: Lary Clark; Dan Poff; Steve Barazza; Cliff Spiegel.

AUTUMNS
Singles: 7-inch
AMBER (856 "Never")....................10-15 66
BAB (128 "Dancer").......................10-15
CLIFTON..4-8 80
MEDIEVAL.......................................5-10 62
POWER (871 "Never")..................25-50 66

AVALANCHE '77 R&B '77
Singles: 7-inch
ABC.. 3-5 77
BOBLO... 3-5 77
LPs: 10/12-inch
ABC.. 5-10 77

AVALANCHES
Singles: 7-inch
W.B. 10-15 63-64
LPs: 10/12-inch
W.B. (W-1525 "Ski Surfin' ") 25-35 63
(Monaural.)
W.B. (WS-1525 "Ski Surfin' ")........30-40 63
(Stereo.)
Members: Billy Strange; David Gates; Hal Blaine; Tommy Tedesco; Al DeLory.
Also see BLAINE, Hal
Also see DE LORY, Al
Also see GATES, David
Also see STRANGE, Billy
Also see TEDESCO, Tommy

AVALON
Singles: 7-inch
CAPITOL.. 3-4 82
LPs: 10/12-inch
CAPITOL.. 5-10 82

AVALON, Frankie P&R/R&B '58
("11 Year Old Frankie Avalon")
Singles: 78 rpm
CHANCELLOR..................................25-50 57-58
"X"...10-20 54
Singles: 7-inch
ABC... 3-5 74
AMOS... 4-6 69
BOBCAT... 3-5 83
CHANCELLOR (1 "Shy Guy").........20-40
(Acnecare promotional special products issue.)
CHANCELLOR (1004 "Cupid")........20-30 57
CHANCELLOR (1011 thru 1026)....15-25 57-58
CHANCELLOR (1031 "Venus")......10-20 58
(Monaural)
CHANCELLOR (1031 "Venus")......25-50 58
(Stereo.)
CHANCELLOR (1036 "Bobby Sox to Stockings")..................................10-20 59
(Monaural.)
CHANCELLOR (1036 "Bobby Sox to Stockings")..................................25-50 59
(Stereo.)
CHANCELLOR (1040 "Just Ask Your Heart")...10-20 59
(Monaural.)
CHANCELLOR (1040 "Just Ask Your Heart")...25-50 59
(Stereo.)
CHANCELLOR (1045 "Why").........10-20 59
(Monaural.)
CHANCELLOR (1045 "Why").........25-50 59
(Stereo.)
CHANCELLOR (1048 thru 1131)....10-20 60-63
CHANCELLOR (1134 "Come Fly with Me")...15-25 63
CHANCELLOR (1135 "Cleopatra").10-20 63
CHANCELLOR (1139 "Beach Party")..10-20 64
COLLECTABLES...............................3-4 81
DE LITE...3-6 76-78
ERIC..3-4 73
MCA..3-4 84
METROMEDIA...................................3-5 70
REGALIA..3-5 72
REPRISE... 4-8 68-69
U.A. 5-10 64-65
"X" "(0006 "Trumpet Sorrento").....20-30 54
"X" "(0026 "Trumpet Tarantella")....20-30 54
Picture Sleeves
CHANCELLOR (1026 thru 1045)....20-30 58-59
CHANCELLOR (1048 thru 1125)....10-20 60-63
DE LITE... 4-8 78
U.A. 10-15 64
EPs: 7-inch
CHANCELLOR (300 "Sincerely") ...20-40 59
CHANCELLOR (302 "Guns of Timberland")......................................20-40 60
CHANCELLOR (303 "Ballad of the Alamo")..20-40 60
(Without publicity kit.)
CHANCELLOR (5001 "Frankie Avalon")..20-40 58
CHANCELLOR (5002-A/B "Young Frankie Avalon")...................................20-40 59
(Price is for either of two volumes.)
CHANCELLOR (5004-A/B/C "Swingin on a Rainbow")...................................20-40 59
(Price is for any of three volumes.)
CHANCELLOR (5011-A/B/C "A Summer Scene")..20-40 60
(Price is for any of three volumes.)
CHANCELLOR (5012 "Good Old Summertime")...................................20-40 60
"X" (20 "A Very Young Man with a Horn")...20-40 55
Promotional EPs
CHANCELLOR (303 "Ballad of the Alamo")......................................50-100 60
(With complete publicity kit.)
CHANCELLOR (5004 "Swingin' on a Rainbow")...................................25-50 59
(White label. Includes paper sleeve with note from Frankie, thanking dee jays for their support.)
LPs: 10/12-inch
ABC.. 5-10 73
CHANCELLOR (5001 "Frankie Avalon")...35-50 58
CHANCELLOR (5002 "Young Frankie Avalon")...35-45 59
(Black vinyl.)
CHANCELLOR (5002 "Young Frankie Avalon")...75-100 59
(Colore vinyl.)
CHANCELLOR (5004 "Swingin' on a Rainbow")..................................40-60 59
(With bound-in photo page.)
CHANCELLOR (CHL-5011 "Summer Scene")...30-40 60
(Monaural.)
CHANCELLOR (CHLS-5011 "Summer Scene")...35-45
(Stereo.)
CHANCELLOR (CHL-5018 "A Whole Lot of Frankie")...............................25-35 61
CHANCELLOR (CHL-5022 "About Mr. Avalon")......................................20-30 61
(Monaural.)
CHANCELLOR (CHLS-5022 "About Mr. Avalon")......................................25-35 61
(Stereo.)
CHANCELLOR (CHL-5025 "Frankie Avalon Italiano")..20-25 62
(Monaural.)
CHANCELLOR (CHLS-5025 "Frankie Avalon Italiano")..20-30 62
(Stereo.)
CHANCELLOR (CHL-5027 "You Are Mine")...20-25 62
(Monaural.)
CHANCELLOR (CHLS-5027 "You Are Mine")..20-30 62
(Stereo.)
CHANCELLOR (CHL-5031 "Christmas Album")...20-25 62
(Monaural.)
CHANCELLOR (CHLS-5031 "Christmas Album")...20-30 62
(Stereo.)
CHANCELLOR (CHL-5032 "Cleopatra")......................................20-25 62
(Monaural.)
CHANCELLOR (CHLS-5032 "Cleopatra")......................................20-30 62
(Stereo.)
CHANCELLOR (69801 "Young and in Love")...50-75 60
(LP with felt cover and 3-D portrait, suitable for hanging, in a special box.)
CHANCELLOR (69801 "Young and in Love")...25-40 60
(LP without the box.)
DE-LITE...5-10 76-78
EVEREST...5-10 82
KOALA...8-15
51 WEST..5-10
LIBERTY...5-10 82
MCA...5-10 85
METROMEDIA....................................5-10 70
SUNSET..8-12 69
TRIP...5-10 77
U.A. 15-20 64
(With "UAL" or "UAS" prefix.)
U.A. 5-10 75
(With "UA-LA" prefix.)
Also see FABIAN / Frankie Avalon

AVALON, Frankie, & Annette
Singles: 12-inch
PACIFIC STAR (5698 "Merry Christmas")......................................20-40 81
(Picture disc.)
Singles: 7-inch
PACIFIC STAR (569 "Merry Christmas")... 3-6 81
(Black vinyl.)
PACIFIC STAR (569 "Merry Christmas")......................................15-20 81
(Colored vinyl.)
Picture Sleeves
PACIFIC STAR (569 "Merry Christmas")... 4-8 81
LPs: 10/12-inch
BUENA VISTA (BV-3314 "Muscle Beach Party")..25-50 64
(Monaural. Soundtrack.)
BUENA VISTA (STER-3314 "Muscle Beach Party")..50-100 64
(Stereo. Soundtrack.)
RHINO (205 "Muscle Beach Party")..15-20 86
(Soundtrack.)
Also see ANNETTE
Also see AVALON, Frankie

AVALONS
(With Pancho Villa Orchestra)
Singles: 78 rpm
GROOVE 50-75 56
Singles: 7-inch
BIM BAM BOOM 5-10 72
CASINO (108 "You Do Something to Me")..150-250 59
GROOVE (0141 "Chains Around My Heart")..150-250 56
GROOVE (174 "It's Funny But It's True")..250-350 56
NPC (302 "Begine the Beguine")....15-25 64
OLIMPIC (240 "Begin the Beguine")..50-75 63
UNART (2007 "Hearts Desire") 50-75 58
Members: Ray Ingram; Jim Dozier; Charles Crowley; Bernie Purdie; George Cox.

AVALONS
Singles: 78 rpm
ALADDIN (3336 "I Miss You").........10-20 56
Singles: 7-inch
ALADDIN (3336 "I Miss You").........15-25 56

AVALONS
Singles: 7-inch
DICE (91 "You Broke Our Hearts")..75-125 58

AVALONS
Singles: 7-inch
ROULETTE (4568 "Is It the End")..10-15 64

AVALONS
Singles: 7-inch
PYRAMID..10-20 66

AVALONS
Singles: 7-inch
YOUNG (45104 "Rebel Rouser") ...15-20 60s

AVALONS
Singles: 7-inch
WALLIS...5-10

AVANT-GARDE P&R '68
Singles: 7-inch
COLUMBIA..4-6 67-68

AVANTIES
(Gregory Dee & Avanties)
Singles: 7-inch
APEX (76931 "The Grind")............25-35 64
(First issue.)
BANGAR (602 "Olds Mo William")..15-25 64
BANGAR (620 "The Grind")............15-25 64
BANGAR (646 "I Want to Be with You")...10-20 64
BANGAR (658 "The Slide")............10-20 64
FOX (422 "Watusi Once More").....20-25 66
GARRETT (4007 "Olds Mo William")..15-25 64
GARRETT (4011 "The Grind")........15-25 64
TWIN TOWN (705 "Love Or Magic")..15-25 60s
TWIN TOWN (717 "Because of You")...15-25 60s

AVANTIES
Singles: 7-inch
RANGER (1198 "Next Door to an Angel")..8-12 60s

AVANTIS
Singles: 7-inch
ARGO (5436 "Keep on Dancing") 8-12 63

AVANTIS
Singles: 7-inch
ASTRA (1006 "Wax 'Em Down")......8-12 65
CHANCELLOR (1144 "Wax 'Em Down")...15-20 63
IKON 5-8
REGENCY (108 "Surfin' Granny")..15-25 64
REGENCY (110 "Phantom Surfer")...15-25 64
SPEAR (5 "Swamp Rat") 10-20 60s
Members: Pat Vegas; Lolly Vegas.
Also see VEGAS, Pat & Lolly

AVANTIS
Singles: 7-inch
PEPPER..4-8

AVANTS, Jimmie
Singles: 7-inch
ABS...4-8 61

AVATAR
Singles: 7-inch
TEEN TOWN (120 "Off Your Feet")..10-20 71

AVENGERS
Singles: 7-inch
KAMA (780 "Reflection")...............8-12 65

AVENGERS
Singles: 7-inch
CURRENT (1001 "It's Hard to Hide")..20-30 66
F-G (104 "When It's Over")............10-15 65
STARBURST (125 "Be a Caveman")...30-50 65
STARBURST (128 "I Told You So")...30-50 66
(Selection number not known.)
STARBURST ("Open Your Eyes") 20-30 66
(Selection number not known.)

AVENGERS
Singles: 7-inch
ARDENT (106 "Batarang")............10-20 66

AVENGERS
Singles: 7-inch
AMERICAN 4-8 67
CURRENT...4-8 66
MGM 4-8 66
PYRAMID..8-12 65
Members: Roy Wood; Graeme Edge; Mike Hopkins; Jim Onslow; Gerry Levene.
Also see EDGE, Graeme
Also see WOOD, Roy

AVENGERS
Singles: 12-inch
WHITE NOISE 5-8 70
Singles: 7-inch
WHITE NOISE 3-4 79

AVENGERS
Singles: 7-inch
MR. GENIUS 15-25

AVENGERS VI
Singles: 7-inch
MARK 56 (202 "Time Bomb") 30-40 66
LPs: 10/12-inch
MARK 56 ("Good Humor Presents Real Cool Hits")...................................125-175 66
(Selection number not known. Promotional issue, available only through the Good Humor Ice Cream Company.)

AVENUE BOOGIE BAND
Singles: 7-inch
SALSOUL..3-4 80

AVERAGE, Johnny, Band: see JOHNNY AVERAGE BAND

AVERAGE AMERICAN BLACK BAND: see A.A.B.B.

AVERAGE WHITE BAND P&R/R&B/LP '74
(AWB)
Singles: 7-inch
ARISTA 3-4 80
ATLANTIC..3-4 74-80
MCA..3-5 73-74
LPs: 10/12-inch
ARISTA...5-8 80
ATLANTIC (Except 19000 series)....8-12 74-76
ATLANTIC (19000 series)...............5-10 77-80
MCA (Except 345) 8-10 73-75
MCA (345 "Show Your Hand") 15-20 73
(With "Jack-in-the-box" cover.)
MCA (345 "Show Your Hand") 8-10 73
(With standard cover.)
Members: Roger Ball; Malcolm Duncan; Steve Ferrone; Alan Gorrie; Robbie McIntosh; Onnie McIntyre; Hamish Stuart.
Also see FOREVER MORE
Also see KARP, Charlie
Also see KING, Ben E., & Average White Band
Also see STONE the CROWS

AVERHEART, Booker T.
Singles: 7-inch
KENT 5-10 65
VAULT 4-8 66

AVERNE, Harvey
(Harvey Averne Barrio Band)
Singles: 7-inch
HEAVY DUTY 3-5 72
UP TITE 4-6 69
LPs: 10/12-inch
ATLANTIC..8-10
HEAVY DUTY 8-10 71

AVERSA, Mickey, & Invaders
Singles: 7-inch
LAP (108 "Blast Off")......................20-30 65

AVERY, Jackie
Singles: 7-inch
CAPRICORN...3-5 70

AVERY, Netti Dady, & Florida Gators
Singles: 78 rpm
ASCO (1009 "Reality Blues").........30-40

AVERY & Country Boys
Singles: 7-inch
JAM (903 "Grandpa's Twist") 30-50

AVIARY
LPs: 10/12-inch
EPIC..5-10 79

AVIATOR
LPs: 10/12-inch
EMI-AMERICA 5-10 79-80

AVION
Singles: 7-inch
RCA 3-4 83
LPs: 10/12-inch
RCA 5-10 83

AVIS
Singles: 7-inch
DEB..3-5 60

AVLONS
Singles: 7-inch
PYRAMID..10-15 67

AVO & RAY
Singles: 7-inch
FRATERNITY.......................................4-8 65

AVON, Tony, & Belairs
Singles: 7-inch
ATLANTIC...4-8 68

AVONDIES
Singles: 7-inch
ASTRA (1014 "One Dead Chicken") ..5-8 65

AVONS
Singles: 78 rpm
HULL...20-50 56-57
Singles: 7-inch
ASTRA (1023 "Baby")..................10-20 66
HULL (717 "Our Love Will Never End")...150-200 56
(Black label.)
HULL (717 "Our Love Will Never End")..40-60 56
(Red label.)
HULL (722 "Baby") 100-150 57
HULL (726 "So Close to Me") 100-150 58
HULL (728 "What Will I Do")......100-150 58
HULL (731 "What Love Can Do")..100-150 58
HULL (744 "Whisper") 75-125 61
(White label.)
HULL (744 "Whisper") 75-125 61
(Pink label.)
HULL (744 "Whisper") 50-75
(Brown label.)
HULL (754 "The Grass Is Greener")..100-150 62
(White label.)
HULL (754 "The Grass Is Greener")...50-75 62
(Brown label.)
ROULETTE 3-5 71
LPs: 10/12-inch
HULL (1000 "Hull Records Cordially Invite You to Meet the Avons")...................550-650 60
Members: Robert Lee; Wendell Lee; William Lee; Irv Watson; Curtis Norris; Franklin Cole; George Coleman.

AVONS
Singles: 7-inch
MERCURY...5-10 60

AVONS
Singles: 7-inch
GROOVE 10-15 63-64
Picture Sleeves
GROOVE (0022 :"Oh Gee Baby") 15-25 63

AVONS
Singles: 7-inch
A-BET (9419 "Talk to Me") 10-15 67
EXCELLO (2296 "Since I Met You Baby")...10-15 66
SOUND STAGE 7 ....5-10 66

AVONS
Singles: 7-inch
REF-O-REE (700 "Tell Me Baby") ...8-12

AWALT, Ray
Singles: 7-inch
G.M. 8-12

AXCENTS
Singles: 7-inch
SQUARE 8-12 61

AXE P&R/LP '82
Singles: 7-inch
ATCO...3-4 82-84
MCA..3-4 79-80
LPs: 10/12-inch
ATCO...5-10 82-84
MCA..5-10 79-80
Member: Bobby Barth.
Also see BABYFACE

AXE MASTER
Singles: 7-inch
AZRA (34 "Axe Master") 8-12 89
(Picture disc. 500 made.)

AXEL MARS BLUES BAND
LPs: 10/12-inch
DILL PICKLE 10-15 71

AXIDENTALS
Singles: 7-inch
ABC-PAR (138 "Hello, We're the Axidentals")....................................50-75 55
Member: Maynard Ferguson.
Also see FERGUSON, Maynard

AXIOM
Singles: 7-inch
SIRE 3-5 70
W.B. 3-5 71

AXIS
Singles: 7-inch
PLASTIC EARTH (6993 "I Can't Wait")..10-20 69

AXIS
Singles: 7-inch
RCA 3-4 78
LPs: 10/12-inch
RCA 5-10 78

AXIS, Jon Butcher: see BUTCHER, Jon

AXIS BROTHERHOOD
Singles: 7-inch
WOODY (101 "Signed D.C.") 20-30

AXTON, Hoyt C&W/P&R '74
(With the Sherwood Singers)
Singles: 7-inch
A&M..3-5 73-76
BRIAR..5-10 61
CAPITOL..3-5 71-72
COLGEMS 4-6 67
COLUMBIA..4-6 69
ELEKTRA...3-4 81
HORIZON 5-10 62-63
JEREMIAH 3-5 79-83
MCA..3-5 77-78
20TH FOX..4-8 66
VEE JAY 5-10 64-65
Picture Sleeves
A&M..3-5 73-74
LPs: 10/12-inch
A&M..5-10 73-77
ACCORD..5-10 82
ALLEGIANCE......................................5-10 84
BRYLEN..5-10 82
CAPITOL..8-10 71
COLUMBIA..8-12 69
EXODUS..10-15 66
HORIZON 15-25 62-63
JEREMIAH 8-10 79-82
LAKE SHORE 5-10 81
MCA..5-10 77-78
SURREY 10-20 65
VEE JAY 10-20 64-65
VEE JAY INT'L (Except 1000 series)..5-10 74-77
VEE JAY INT'L (1000 series)..........10-12 74
Session: Linda Ronstadt; Tanya Tucker; Ronee Blakley
Also see RONSTADT, Linda
Also see TUCKER, Tanya

AXTON, Hoyt, & Chambers Brothers
Singles: 7-inch
HORIZON 4-8 62

LPs: 10/12-inch
HORIZON....................15-20 63
Also see AXTON, Hoyt
Also see CHAMBERS BROTHERS

AYALA, Hank
Singles: 7-inch
BACKBEAT 4-8 60

AYERS, Cliff
(With the Dick Quigley Orchestra)
Singles: 7-inch
EMERALD (2004 "Lopsided Love")....................10-15
LINCOLN.................... 4-6
Picture Sleeves
LINCOLN.................... 4-8

AYERS, Cliff, & Continentals
Singles: 7-inch
EMERALD (3000 "I Wonder Why")....................300-400 59

AYERS, Kevin
Singles: 7-inch
ABC.................... 3-4 77
SIRE.................... 3-5 73
LPs: 10/12-inch
ABC.................... 5-10 77
HARVEST 10-15 70
ISLAND 10-12 74
SIRE.................... 8-10 73
Also see CALE, John
Also see NICO

AYERS, Roy LP '74
(Roy Ayers' Ubiquity)
Singles: 12-inch
COLUMBIA.................... 4-6 84-85
POLYDOR.................... 4-6 79
Singles: 7-inch
COLUMBIA.................... 3-4 84-86
POLYDOR.................... 3-4 77
LPs: 10/12-inch
ATLANTIC.................... 8-12 68-76
COLUMBIA.................... 5-10 84-86
ELEKTRA.................... 5-10 78
POLYDOR.................... 6-10 70-82
Also see DUNLAP, Gene
Also see MANN, Herbie
Also see UBIQUITY

AYERS, Roy, and Wayne Henderson
Singles: 7-inch
POLYDOR.................... 3-4 79-80
LPs: 10/12-inch
POLYDOR.................... 5-10 80
Also see AYERS, Roy
Also see HENDERSON, Wayne

AYERS ROCK
Singles: 7-inch
A&M.................... 3-5 75-76
LPs: 10/12-inch
A&M.................... 5-10 75-76
Members: Jimmy Doyle; Duncan McGuire; Col Loughman; Chris Brown; Mark Kennedy.

AYKROYD, Dan, & Pattie Brooks
Singles: 7-inch
BACKSTREET.................... 3-4 83
Also see BLUES BROTHERS
Also see BROOKS, Pattie
Also see U.S.A. for AFRICA

AYO, Zena
Singles: 7-inch
CASE (1004 "Dumb Bell")....................10-15 59

AZALEAS
Singles: 7-inch
ROMULUS (3001 "Hands Off")......20-30 63

AZIMUTH
LPs: 10/12-inch
ECM.................... 5-10 79
Members: John Taylar; Kenny Wheeler; Norma Winstone.

AZITIS
LPs: 10/12-inch
ELCO (5555 "Help")....................1200-1600 71
Members: Steve Nelson; Michael Welch; Dennis Sullivan; Don Lower.

AZTEC CAMERA LP '83
Singles: 12-inch
SIRE.................... 5-10 84
Singles: 7-inch
SIRE.................... 3-6 83-85
Picture Sleeves
SIRE.................... 3-6 84-88
LPs: 10/12-inch
SIRE.................... 8-15 83-87

AZTEC TWO-STEP
Singles: 7-inch
ELEKTRA.................... 3-5 72-73
RCA.................... 3-4 76-78
EPs: 7-inch
RCA (10381 "Meet Aztec Two-Step").................... 5-10 76
(Promotional issue only.)
LPs: 10/12-inch
ELEKTRA....................10-12 72
RCA.................... 5-10 76-80
REFLEX 5-10 86
WATERHOUSE.................... 5-10 80
Members: Rex Fowler; Alan Schwartzberg; Neal Schulman.

AZTECA LP '73
Singles: 7-inch
COLUMBIA.................... 3-5 72-73
LPs: 10/12-inch
COLUMBIA....................10-12 72-73
Members: Coke Escovedo; Tony Smith.
Also see ESCOVEDO, Coke
Also see MALO
Also see SANTANA

AZTECS
Singles: 7-inch
ZIN-A-SPIN (002 "The Answer to My Prayer")....................100-150 62

AZTECS
Singles: 7-inch
CARD (901 "Teenage Hall of Fame")....................25-35 64
SULTAN....................5-10
WORLD ARTISTS.................... 4-8 64
LPs: 10/12-inch
WORLD ARTISTS (2001 "Live at the Ad-Lib Club of London")....................30-60 64

AZTECS
Singles: 7-inch
GNP.................... 4-8 65
SCEPTER.................... 4-6 67
Also see THORPE, Billy, & Aztecs

AZTECS
Singles: 7-inch
RAK.................... 3-5 73

AZTEX
Singles: 7-inch
STAFF (194 "I Said Move")........75-125 67
(150 made.)

AZYMUTH
Singles: 7-inch
MILESTONE.................... 3-4 79-84
LPs: 10/12-inch
MILESTONE....................5-10 79-84

AZZAM, Bob
Singles: 7-inch
MERCURY 5-10 60
LONDON.................... 4-8 62

B

B ANGIE B *LP '91*
LPs: 10/12-inch
CAPITOL ... 5-8 91

B., Jimmy: see JIMMY B.

B., Ty, & Johnny
Singles: 7-inch
RED WING (705 "Meaner Than an Alligator") ... 25-50
Picture Sleeves
RED WING (705 "Meaner Than an Alligator") ... 40-50

B-B
(B.B. Cunningham Jr.)
Singles: 7-inch
COVER (3 "Humbinger") ... 10-20
COVER (1961 "Ivory Marbles") ... 10-20 61
COVER (5931 "Trip to Bandstand") ... 20-30 57
COVER (5981 "Scratchin' ") ... 15-25 58
Also see CUNNINGHAM, B.B., Jr.

B-B / Lyn Vernon
Singles: 7-inch
COVER (4622 "High Pockets Twist") ... 8-12 62
Also see B-B
Also see VERNON, Lynn

B.B.C.S. & A. *R&B '82*
Singles: 7-inch
SAM ... 3-4 82

B.B. & OSCARS
Singles: 7-inch
GUILFORD ... 5-10 68

B.B. & Q. Band *LP '81*
(Brooklyn, Bronx & Queens Band)
Singles: 12-inch
CAPITOL ... 4-6 81-83
Singles: 7-inch
CAPITOL ... 3-5 81-83
IN YOUR FACE ... 3-4 86
LPs: 10/12-inch
CAPITOL ... 5-10 81-83

B.B. BLUNDER
LPs: 10/12-inch
POLYDOR ... 10-12 71

B&B
Singles: 7-inch
MUSICOR ... 3-5 74

B&G RHYTHM
Singles: 7-inch
POLYDOR ... 3-4 78
LPs: 10/12-inch
POLYDOR ... 5-10 78

B. BAKER CHOCOLATE CO.
LPs: 10/12-inch
LRC ... 5-10 79

B. BEAT GIRLS *D&D '83*
Singles: 12-inch
25 WEST ... 4-6 83
Singles: 7-inch
25 WEST ... 3-4 83

B. BUMBLE & STINGERS *P&R '61*
Singles: 7-inch
DYMO ... 5-10
HIGHLAND ... 5-10 60s
MERCURY ... 5-10 66-67
RENDEZVOUS ... 10-15 61-63
TRIAD ... 4-6 74
WAX ... 5-10 64
Members: Billy Brumble; Ron Brady; Fred Richard; Ernie Freeman.
Also see FREEMAN, Ernie

B.C.G.: see CREWE, Bob

B.C. GENERATION
Singles: 7-inch
CASABLANCA ... 3-5 74

B.C.s
Singles: 7-inch
RUFF (1015 "Oh Yeow!") ... 15-25 66

B. FATS *R&B '86*
Singles: 7-inch
POSSE ... 3-4 86

B-52s *LP '79*
Singles: 12-inch
W.B. ... 4-6 86
Singles: 7-inch
B-52s (52 "Rock Lobster") ... 15-20 78
REPRISE ... 3-4 89-91
W.B. (Except 927) ... 3-4 79-86
W.B. (927 "Give Me Back My Man") . 3-5 81
(Promotional issue only.)
Picture Sleeves
B-52s (52 "Rock Lobster") ... 25-50 78
REPRISE ... 3-4 89
W.B. ... 3-5 80-83
LPs: 10/12-inch
REPRISE ... 5-8 89-91
W.B. ... 5-10 79-86
Members: Cindy Wilson; Keith Strickland; Fred Schneider III; Ricky Wilson; Kate Pierson.

B.G. RAMBLERS
Singles: 7-inch
SPARKLE (1297 "Exit Stage Left") ... 10-20 63

B GIRLS
Singles: 7-inch
BOMP ... 3-5 79
Picture Sleeves
BOMP ... 3-5 79
EPs: 7-inch
BOMP ... 5-8 79
Members: Lucasta Rochas; Xenia Holiday; Cynthia Ross.

B-H-Y *R&B '79*
(Baker-Harris-Young)
Singles: 7-inch
SALSOUL ... 3-5 79
LPs: 10/12-inch
SALSOUL ... 5-10 79
Members: Ron Baker; Norman Harris; Earl Young.
Also see MFSB
Also see TRAMMPS

B.I.M.
Singles: 7-inch
ELEKTRA (132 "Thistles") ... 8-12 78

B.J. & BOYS
Singles: 7-inch
BANDERA ... 5-10 61

B.J. & GEMINIS
Singles: 7-inch
ATCO (6364 "Scratch My Back") ... 10-20 65

B.J. & PROFITS
Singles: 7-inch
UPTOWN (705 "Lost Faith") ... 10-15 60s

B. JANE: see JANE, B., & Teenettes

BLT
Singles: 12-inch
GOLD COAST ... 4-6 82

BMI
Singles: 7-inch
PEOPLE ... 3-5 73

BMP
Singles: 12-inch
EPIC ... 4-6 84
Singles: 7-inch
EPIC ... 3-4 84
LPs: 10/12-inch
EPIC ... 5-10 84

B MOVIE
Singles: 12-inch
PVC ... 4-6 82
SIRE ... 4-6 83

B + 3
Singles: 7-inch
CANADIAN AMERICAN (205 "Delia") ... 15-25 67

BQE
(Brooklyn-Queens Expressway)
Singles: 7-inch
STARLIGHT (61 "Tonight") ... 3-5 88

BR5-49
LPs: 10/12-inch
ARISTA (108001 "BR5-49 Live from Roberts") ... 8-12 96

BT & TB
Singles: 7-inch
PHILADELPHIA INT'L ... 3-5 75
Members: Bobby Taylor; Thom Bell.
Also see TAYLOR, Bobby

B.T. EXPRESS *P&R/R&B/LP '74*
Singles: 12-inch
COAST to COAST ... 4-6 81
COLUMBIA ... 4-6 81
Singles: 7-inch
COAST to COAST ... 3-4 82
COLUMBIA ... 3-5 76-80
EARTHTONE ... 3-4 84
ROADSHOW ... 3-5 74-75
SCEPTER ... 3-6 74
LPs: 10/12-inch
COAST to COAST ... 5-10 82
COLUMBIA ... 5-10 76-80
ROADSHOW ... 10-12 74-76
SCEPTER ... 8-10 74
Members: Carlos Ward; Bill Risbrook; Richard Thompson; Michael Jones; Dennis Rowe; Leslie Ming; Barbara Joyce Lomas.

BTO: see BACHMAN - TURNER OVERDRIVE

B.W. & EMERALDS
Singles: 7-inch
RUMBLE (1348 "I Need Your Love") ... 400-600 61

B.W. & NEXT EDITION
Singles: 7-inch
DAKAR ... 3-5 75

B. WILLIE & FEVERS
Singles: 7-inch
TARA (1001 "After Hours") ... 10-20 62

BAAD BOYS
Singles: 7-inch
EPIC ... 10-20 67
Also see BAD BOYS

BAAH, Reebop Kwaku
Singles: 7-inch
ISLAND ... 3-5 72
LPs: 10/12-inch
ISLAND ... 5-10 72

BABALOU
EPs: 7-inch
BABALOU (9851 "Rock Roll Band") ... 5-8 87

BABBIT, Harry / Tony Martin
Singles: 78 rpm
MERCURY/SAV-WAY (3055 "To Me") ... 100-150 47
(Picture disc. Promotional issue only.)
Also see MARTIN, Tony

BABCOCK, Little Lee
Singles: 7-inch
CUCA (6611 "You're the Only One I Know") ... 10-20 66

BABE & LOU
("The Home Run Twins")
Singles: 78 rpm
PERFECT (12382 "Babe & Lou") ... 50-75 20s
Members: Babe Ruth; Lou Gehrig.

BABE RUTH *LP '73*
Singles: 7-inch
CAPITOL ... 3-4 76
HARVEST ... 3-5 73-76
LPs: 10/12-inch
HARVEST ... 5-10 73-76
Members: Ellie Hope; Steve Gurl; Jenny Haan; Dave Hewitt; Ray Knott; Bernie Marsden; Alan Shacklock; Ed Spevock.

BABES
Singles: 7-inch
DEAN (1752 "Buck Fever") ... 8-12

BABES IN TOYLAND
Singles: 7-inch
SUB POP ... 3-5 90

BABIES
Singles: 7-inch
DUNHILL (4085 "You Make Me Feel Like Someone") ... 10-15 67
Picture Sleeves
DUNHILL (4085 "You Make Me Feel Like Someone") ... 20-30 67

BABY
Singles: 7-inch
CHELSEA ... 3-5 76
LPs: 10/12-inch
CHELSEA ... 5-10 76
LONE STARR (3714 "Baby") ... 20-30 74
MERCURY ... 8-12 75
Members: John Camp; Johnny Lee Schell; Stephen Crane; Woody Putman; Tom Scott.

BABY BOY WARREN: see WARREN, Baby Boy

BABY BROTHER
Singles: 7-inch
COTILLION ... 3-4 81
LPs: 10/12-inch
COTILLION ... 5-10 81

BABY BUDDAH
LPs: 10/12-inch
POSH BOY ... 5-10 81

BABY BUGS
Singles: 7-inch
VEE JAY ... 8-10 64
Picture Sleeves
VEE JAY ... 15-25 64
(Promotional sleeve only.)

BABY DOLLS
Singles: 7-inch
BOOM ... 5-10 66
ELGIN (021 "Is This the End") ... 40-50 59
FARGO (1017 "I Should Have Known") ... 20-30 60
GAMBLE ... 5-10 68
HOLLYWOOD (1111 "Why Can't I Love Him Like You") ... 25-35 60
MASKE (103 "I'm Lonely") ... 30-40 61
MASKE (701 "Thanks Mr. Dee-Jay") ... 75-100 61
RCA (7296 "Cause I'm in Love") ... 15-25 58
W.B. (5086 "Hey Baby") ... 10-15 59
Also see BAKER, Bill

BABY EARL & TRINI-DADS
Singles: 7-inch
S.P.Q.R. (3317 "Back Slop") ... 10-20 64

BABY FACE
(Baby Face Leroy; Baby Face Leroy Trio; with the Sunnyland Trio; with Birds; Leroy Foster;)
Singles: 78 rpm
CHESS (1447 "My Head Can't Rest Anymore") ... 75-125 50
J.O.B. (100 "My Head Can't Rest Anymore") ... 100-200 52
J.O.B. (1002 "Pet Rabbit") ... 100-200 52
PARKWAY (104 "Boll Weevil") ... 200-300 50
PARKWAY (501 "Rollin' & Tumblin' ") ... 2000-4000 50
SAVOY (1122 "Red Headed Woman") ... 25-50 54
Singles: 7-inch
SAVOY (1122 "Red Headed Woman") ... 50-100 54
SAVOY (1501 "Red Headed Woman") ... 25-50 58
Session: Muddy Waters; Little Walter.
Also see FOSTER, Leroy, & Muddy Waters
Also see LITTLE WALTER
Also see SUNNYLAND SLIM
Also see SUNNYLAND TRIO

BABY FACE LEROY: see BABY FACE

BABY GRAND
Singles: 7-inch
CUCA ... 4-6 70

BABY GRAND
Singles: 7-inch
HEMISPHERE (1604 "Nature's Way") ... 5-10 72
HEMISPHERE (5009 "Lucy Cain") ... 5-10 72

BABY GRAND
Singles: 7-inch
ARISTA ... 3-5 77-79
LPs: 10/12-inch
ARISTA ... 5-10 77
Members: David Kagan; Rob Hyman; Eric Bazilian; Rick Marotta.

BABY HUEY
(With the Babysitters)
Singles: 7-inch
CURTOM ... 4-6 69
SATELLITE ... 10-20 60s
U.S.A. ... 10-20 60s
LPs: 10/12-inch
CURTOM ... 20-30 71

BABY JANE & ROCK-A-BYES *P&R '63*
(Baby Jane)
Singles: 7-inch
SPOKANE (4001 "Hickory Dickory Dock") ... 10-20 63
(First issue.)
SPOKANE (4004 "Get Me to the Church on Time") ... 10-20 63
(First issue.)
U.A. (505 "Oh Johnny") ... 8-12 62
U.A. (560 "Doggie in the Window") 10-15 63
U.A. (593 "Hickory Dickory Dock") ... 8-12 63

BABY JEAN
Singles: 7-inch
STACY ... 5-10 62

BABY LLOYD
Singles: 7-inch
LOMA ... 5-10 65

BABY RAY *P&R '66*
(Ray Eddlemon)
Singles: 7-inch
CAPACITY (116 "Dance My Tears Away") ... 10-15 60s
IMPERIAL ... 8-15 66-67
LPs: 10/12-inch
IMPERIAL ... 15-20 67

BABY RAY & FERNS
Singles: 7-inch
DONNA (1378 "How's Your Bird") .. 25-35 63
Member: Frank Zappa.
Also see ZAPPA, Frank

BABY ROCKER
LPs: 10/12-inch
A.V.I. ... 8-10 78

BABY STICKS & KINGTONES
Singles: 7-inch
SHELLY ... 8-12 62

BABYFACE *P&R '89*
Singles: 7-inch
ASI ... 3-5 76-77
LPs: 10/12-inch
ASI ... 10-12 77
Also see AXE

BABYFACE *R&B '87*
Singles: 7-inch
SOLAR ... 3-4 87-89
LPs: 10/12-inch
SOLAR ... 5-8 89
EPIC ... 5-8 90s
Members: Kenny "Babyface" Edmonds; Antonio "L.A." Reid.
Also see DEELE

BABYLON A.D. *LP '89*
LPs: 10/12-inch
ARISTA ... 5-8 89

BABYS *P&R/LP '77*
Singles: 7-inch
CHRYSALIS ... 3-5 77-81
Picture Sleeves
CHRYSALIS ... 3-5 80
LPs: 10/12-inch
CHRYSALIS ... 5-10 77-81
Members: Mike Corby; John Waite; Tony Brock; Wally Stocker; Johnthan Cain.
Also see BAD ENGLISH
Also see JOURNEY

BACCARA
Singles: 12-inch
MANHATTAN ... 4-6 78
Singles: 7-inch
MANHATTAN ... 3-5 77
U.A. ... 3-5 78
Picture Sleeves
U.A. ... 3-5 78
LPs: 10/12-inch
MANHATTAN ... 5-10 78

BACCHUS
Singles: 7-inch
MEDALLION ... 5-10

BACCUS, Eddie
Singles: 7-inch
SMASH (1804 "Blues at Dawn") ... 10-20 63

BACH, Don
Singles: 7-inch
WARWICK ... 10-15 61

BACHARACH, Burt *P&R '63*
(Burt Bacharach & Friends)
Singles: 7-inch
A&M ... 3-5 68-74
CABOT ... 3-5
KAPP ... 3-6 63-65
LIBERTY ... 3-5 66
U.A. ... 3-5 67
Picture Sleeves
A&M ... 3-5 71
EPs: 7-inch
A&M ... 4-8 68-73
LPs: 10/12-inch
A&M (Except 1) ... 5-12 67-74
A&M (1 "Radio Interview") ... 8-15 74
(Promotional issue only.)
KAPP ... 8-15 65
MCA ... 5-10 73
Also see CAMPBELL, Glen / Dionne Warwick / Burt Bacharach

BACHELOR THREE
(With Hank Levine & Orchestra)
Singles: 7-inch
VI-WAY (288 "Lover Man") ... 25-50 61
VI-WAY (289 "Whisper") ... 25-50 61
Also see LEVINE, Hank

BACHELORS
Singles: 7-inch
MERCURY (8159 "Yesterday's Roses") ... 150-250 49
Members: Joe Van Loan; Elijah Harvey; Allen Scott; Jim Miller.
Also see VAN LOAN, Joe

BACHELORS
Singles: 7-inch
ALADDIN (3210 "Can't Help Loving You") ... 750-1000 53
POPLAR (101 "After") ... 20-40 57
ROYAL ROOST (620 "You've Lied") ... 200-300 56
Members: Walt Taylor; Jim Walton; Herb Fisher; John Bowie.
Also see JETS
Also see LINKS

BACHELORS
Singles: 78 rpm
EXCEL ... 5-10 55
Singles: 7-inch
EXCEL ... 10-20 55

BACHELORS
Singles: 7-inch
EARL (101 "Delores") ... 100-200 56
EARL (102 "Baby") ... 100-200 57
Members: Dean Barlow; Bill Lindsay; Joe Dias.
Also see BARLOW, Dean

BACHELORS
Singles: 7-inch
MGM (12668 "Teenage Memory") 15-25 58
NATIONAL (104 "A Million Teardrops") ... 15-25 57
NATIONAL (115 "I Want a Girl") ... 15-25 58
TERRY-TONE (201 "Every Night") ... 100-150

BACHELORS
Singles: 7-inch
EPIC ... 5-10 60
INTERNATIONAL (777 "Is This Goodbye") ... 100-150 61
SMASH ... 5-10 61

BACHELORS *P&R/LP '64*
Singles: 7-inch
LONDON ... 5-10 63-72
Picture Sleeves
LONDON ... 10-15 64-65
LPs: 10/12-inch
LONDON ... 10-25 64-72
Members: Con Cluskey; Declan Stokes; John Stokes.

BACHMAN, Randy
Singles: 7-inch
POLYDOR ... 3-4 78
LPs: 10/12-inch
POLYDOR ... 5-10 78
RCA (1100 series) ... 5-10 75
RCA (4300 series) ... 10-15 70
Also see BACHMAN - TURNER - BACHMAN
Also see BACHMAN - TURNER OVERDRIVE
Also see GUESS WHO
Also see IRONHORSE

BACHMAN - TURNER - BACHMAN
LPs: 10/12-inch
REPRISE (2210 "As Brave Belt") ... 8-10 74
Members: Randy Bachman; C.F. Turner; Robin Bachman.
Also see BACHMAN-TURNER OVERDRIVE
Also see BRAVE BELT

BACHMAN - TURNER OVERDRIVE *P&R/LP '73*
Singles: 7-inch
COMPLEAT ... 3-4 84-85
MERCURY ... 3-5 73-79
Picture Sleeves
MERCURY ... 3-5 74-75
LPs: 10/12-inch
COMPLEAT ... 5-10 84-85
CURB ... 5-8 86
MERCURY ... 6-12 73-79
Members: Randy Bachman; C.F. Turner; Robin Bachman; Tim Bachman; Jim Clench; Norman Durkee; Blair Thornton.
Also see BACHMAN, Randy

BACHS
LPs: 10/12-inch
("Out of the Bachs")..............1500-2000 68
(No label name or number used.)
Members: John Peterman; Black Allison; Ben Harrison.

BACHS LUNCH
Singles: 7-inch
TOMORROW..............8-10 67

BACK ALLEY
Singles: 7-inch
DATE..............5-10 68

BACK DOOR
Singles: 7-inch
W.B...............3-5 72-73
LPs: 10/12-inch
W.B...............10-12 72-73
Members: Ron Aspery; Tony Hicks; Colin Hodgkinson; Adrian Tilbrook.

BACK HOME
Singles: 7-inch
ALVA..............3-4
Picture Sleeves
ALVA..............5-8

BACK IN TIME
Singles: 7-inch
ATLANTIC..............3-4 78
LPs: 10/12-inch
ATLANTIC..............5-10 78

BACK POCKET
LPs: 10/12-inch
JOYCE..............8-10 76

BACK PORCH BOYS
Singles: 78 rpm
APOLLO..............15-25 47
Members: Alec Seward; Louis Hayes.
Also see SEWARD, Alec, & Louis Hayes
Also see BLUES BOY

BACK PORCH MAJORITY
Singles: 7-inch
EPIC..............4-8 64-67
LPs: 10/12-inch
EPIC..............10-20 65-67
Member: Michael Johnson.
Also see JOHNSON, Michael

BACK STREET BOYS
Singles: 7-inch
WJG..............4-6

BACK STREET CRAWLER — LP '75
(Crawler)
Singles: 7-inch
EPIC..............3-4 77-78
LPs: 10/12-inch
ATCO..............10-12 75-76
EPIC (Except PAL-349001)..............5-10 77-78
EPIC (PAL-349001 "Crawler")..............35-45 78
(Picture disc. Promotional issue only.)
Members: Tony Braunagel; John Bundrick; Paul Kossoff; Mike Montgomery; Geoff Whitehorn; Terry Wilson Slesser.
Also see CUMMINGS, Burton / Cheap Trick / Crawler
Also see FREE
Also see KOSSOFF, Paul
Also see PIERCE ARROW / Lake / Crawler / Ram Jam

BACK ST. JOURNAL
Singles: 7-inch
FRANKLIN..............12-18 68

BACK WASH RHYTHM BAND
LPs: 10/12-inch
CAPITOL..............15-30 68

BACK WATER BOOGIE BAND
Singles: 7-inch
4 SALE (1003 "Sweet Beach Music")..............5-10

BACKALLEY BANDITS
Singles: 7-inch
LONDON..............3-5 78
LPs: 10/12-inch
LONDON..............5-10 78

BACK-BEAT PHILHARMONIC
Singles: 7-inch
LAURIE..............5-10 61

BACKBONES
LPs: 10/12-inch
MIDNIGHT..............5-10

BACKDOOR SOCIETY
Singles: 7-inch
SHOREMEN..............4-8

BACKGROUNDS
Singles: 7-inch
CENCO (110 "Baby Please Take Me")..............20-30

BACKROADS — C&W '83
Singles: 7-inch
SOUNDWAVES..............3-4 83

BACKSEAT
Singles: 7-inch
LINDA (125 "Where Is Mary")..............8-12 67

BACKSEAT DRIVER
LPs: 10/12-inch
REAR ENTRANCE (001 "Blackout")..............8-10 90

BACKSEAT SALLY
Singles: 7-inch
ATLANTIC..............3-4 83
LPs: 10/12-inch
ATLANTIC..............5-10 83

BACKSTERS
Singles: 7-inch
A&M..............3-4 84
LPs: 10/12-inch
A&M..............5-10 84

BACKTALK
Singles: 12-inch
DEMISUM..............4-6 85

BACKTRACK
(Featuring John Hunt)
Singles: 7-inch
GOLDMINE..............3-4 85

BACKUS, Gus
Singles: 7-inch
CARLTON (471 "You Can't Go It Alone")..............15-20 58
DICO..............4-8
FONO-GRAF..............8-12 61-62
GENERAL AMERICAN..............8-10 63
MGM..............5-10 63
Also see DEL-VIKINGS

BACKUS, Jim — P&R '58
("Jim Backus with Friend"; Mr. McGoo & Dennis Famon Orchestra; Jim Bakus)
Singles: 7-inch
JUBILEE (5330 "Delicious")..............15-25 58
JUBILEE (5351 "Cave Man")..............15-25 58
JUBILEE (5361 "Cave Man")..............15-25 59
(Reissued with different flip side.)
EPs: 7-inch
RCA (1362 "McGoo in Hi-Fi")..............25-35 56
LPs: 10/12-inch
DORE..............8-10 74
RCA (1362 "McGoo in Hi-Fi")..............50-100 56
Also see HOPE, Bob

BACKUS, Jim, & Daws Butler
Singles: 7-inch
DICO (101 "I Was a Teenage Reindeer")..............25-50 59
Also see BACKUS, Jim
Also see BUTLER, Daws

BACKWATER
LPs: 10/12-inch
BONGWATER..............10-12

BACKYARD HEAVIES
Singles: 7-inch
SCEPTER..............3-4 71

BACON, Gar
Singles: 7-inch
BATON (248 "There's Gonna Be Rockin' Tonight")..............30-40 57
DALE (105 "Chains of Love")..............15-25 58
DALE (108 "Dutch Treat")..............15-25 58
OKEH..............8-12 59
RKO UNIQUE..............8-15 57

BACON, Paul, & Poached Eggs
Singles: 7-inch
MALA..............5-8 67

BACON, Woody
Singles: 7-inch
MARBILL (101 "Round House Boogie")..............10-20 61

BACON FAT
LPs: 10/12-inch
BLUE HORIZON (4807 "Grease One for Me")..............25-45 70
Members: George Smith; Buddy Reed; Dick Innes; Greg Schaefer; Jerry Smith; Rod Piazz; J.D. Nicholson.

BAD & GOOD BOYS
Singles: 7-inch
M.O.C. (668 "Fire")..............20-30 68
HI..............5-10 60s

BAD AXE
LPs: 10/12-inch
ALLIGATOR..............5-10 84

BAD BASCOMB: see BASCOMB, Paul

BAD BOY
Singles: 7-inch
BAD BOY..............5-10
(Colored vinyl.)
ELEKTRA..............3-5
U.A...............3-5 77-78
LPs: 10/12-inch
STREETWISE..............5-10 80
U.A...............8-10 77-78
Also see HUNTER, Steve

BAD BOYS
Singles: 7-inch
PAULA (254 "Black Olives")..............10-15 66
W.B...............5-10 65
Also see BAAD BOYS
Also see DANIELS, Charlie, Band

BAD BOYS
Singles: 7-inch
BELL..............8-10 66

BAD BOYS FEATURING K LOVE — R&B/D&D '85
Singles: 12-inch
STARLITE..............4-6 85
Singles: 7-inch
STARLITE..............3-4 85

BAD BRAINS
LPs: 10/12-inch
IMPORTANT..............5-10 83
PVC..............5-10 83

BAD BREATH
Singles: 7-inch
LUV..............5-10

BAD COMPANY — P&R/LP '74
Singles: 12-inch
ATLANTIC..............5-10 88
(Promotional only.)
Singles: 7-inch
ATCO..............3-6 92
ATLANTIC (80000 series)..............3-6 86-89
ATLANTIC (90000 [reissue] series)..............3-5 92
SWAN SONG..............3-6 74-82
Picture Sleeves
ATLANTIC..............3-4 86-89
SWAN SONG..............3-5 79-82
LPs: 10/12-inch
ATCO..............5-8 90-93
ATLANTIC..............5-10 86-88
SWAN SONG..............5-10 74-82
Members: Paul Rodgers; Brian Howe; Boz Burrell; Simon Kirke; Mick Ralphs; Mick Jones.
Also see BOZ
Also see FIRM
Also see FOREIGNER
Also see FREE
Also see KING CRIMSON
Also see NUGENT, Ted
Also see RODGERS, Paul

BAD ENGLISH — P&R/LP '89
Singles: 7-inch
EPIC..............3-4 90
LPs: 10/12-inch
EPIC..............5-8 89
Members: John Waithe; Jonathan Cain; Neal Schon; Ricky Phillips; Dean Castronovo.
Also see BABYS
Also see JOURNEY

BAD GIRLS — R&B '81
Singles: 7-inch
BC..............3-4 81

BAD HABITS
Singles: 7-inch
PAULA..............5-10 70-72
Members: Delaney Bramlett; Bonnie Bramlett.
Also see DELANEY & BONNIE

BAD MANNERS
Singles: 12-inch
PORTRAIT..............4-6 84
Singles: 7-inch
MCA..............3-4 81-84
LPs: 10/12-inch
MCA..............5-10 81-84
PORTRAIT..............5-10 84

BAD NEWS TRAVELS FAST
Singles: 7-inch
CASABLANCA..............3-4 78-79
LPs: 10/12-inch
CASABLANCA..............5-10 78-79

BAD OMENS
Singles: 7-inch
TWIN TOWN..............10-20 67

BAD ROADS
Singles: 7-inch
JIN (21 "Too Bad")..............30-50 67
RAIN TYRE (1000 "Til the End of the Day")..............30-50 66

BAD SEEDS
Singles: 7-inch
J-BECK (1002 "Taste of the Same")..............30-50 65
J-BECK (1003 "Zilch")..............15-25 66
J-BECK (1005 "All Night Long")..............30-50 66

BAD SEEDS
Singles: 7-inch
COLUMBIA..............5-10 66

BAD SMOKE
Singles: 7-inch
CHESS..............3-5 72

BAD WATER
Singles: 7-inch
KYD..............4-6 79

BADALE, Andy, Orchestra — C&W '80
Singles: 7-inch
GP..............3-4 80

BADAROU, Wally — R&B '86
Singles: 7-inch
ISLAND..............3-4 86
LPs: 10/12-inch
ISLAND..............5-10 86

BADAX
Singles: 7-inch
PROGRESSIVE..............3-4 84

BADAXXE
LP: 10/12-inch
AZRA (100 "Feast or Famine")..............10-15 86
(Picture disc. 250 made.)

BADAZZ
Singles: 12-inch
A&M..............5-8 78
Singles: 7-inch
A&M..............3-4 78

BADBEATS
Singles: 7-inch
BEATBAD..............4-8 79
Picture Sleeves
BEATBAD..............5-15 79

BADD BOYS
Singles: 7-inch
EPIC (10119 "Never Goin Back to Georgia")..............30-40 67
EPIC (10165 "I Told You So")..............40-50 67

BADD LADS
Singles: 7-inch
JEREE..............10-15

BADDER THAN EVIL
Singles: 7-inch
BUDDAH..............3-5 73
LPs: 10/12-inch
BUDDAH..............8-12 73

BADFINGER — P&R '69
Singles: 7-inch
AMERICOM (301 "Maybe Tomorrow")..............100-200 69
(Plastic "Pocket Disc" soundsheet.)
APPLE (1815 "Come and Get It")..............5-15 70
APPLE (1822 "No Matter What")..............5-15 70
APPLE (1841 "Day After Day")..............5-15 71
APPLE (1844 "Baby Blue")..............5-15 72
APPLE (1864 "Apple of My Eye")..............10-20 73
ATLANTIC..............3-4 81
ELEKTRA..............3-5 79
RADIO..............3-4 81
W.B...............3-6 74
Promotional Singles
APPLE (1841 "Day After Day")..............100-125 71
(White label.)
APPLE (1844 "Baby Blue")..............100-125 72
(White label.)
APPLE (1864 "Apple of My Eye")..............20-25 73
Picture Sleeves
APPLE (1844 "Baby Blue")..............10-15 72
LPs: 10/12-inch
APPLE (3364 "Magic Christian Music")..............20-30 70
APPLE (3367 "No Dice")..............15-25 70
APPLE (3387 "Straight Up")..............40-60 71
APPLE (3411 "Ass")..............15-25 73
ELEKTRA (175 "Airwaves")..............10-15 79
RADIO (16030 "Say No More")..............5-10 81
RYKODISC (0189 "Day After Day")..............15-25 90
(Clear vinyl.)
W.B. (2762 "Badfinger")..............15-20 74
W.B. (2827 "Wish You Were Here")..............20-30 74
Members: Tom Evans; Mike Gibbons; Pete Ham; Joey Molland; Peter Clarke; Tony Kaye.
Also see IVEYS
Also see MOLLAND, Joey

BADGE
Singles: 7-inch
CMS..............5-10 60s

BADGE
Singles: 7-inch
EXHIBIT..............4-6 71
Member: Bill Paliselli.
Also see ARTFUL DODGER

BADGER — LP '73
LPs: 10/12-inch
ATCO..............10-12 73
EPIC..............8-10 74
Members: Roy Dyke; Kim Gardner; Dave Foster; Tony Kaye; Jackie Lomax; Brian Parrish; Paul Pilnick.
Also see ASHTON, GARDNER & DYKE
Also see LOMAX, Jackie

BADLANDS — LP '89
LPs: 10/12-inch
ATLANTIC..............5-8 89-91

BADMAN, Hickey: see CREEP

BADOWSKI, Henry
Singles: 7-inch
I.R.S...............3-4 80
LPs: 10/12-inch
I.R.S...............5-10 81

BADWATER BLUES REVIVAL
Singles: 7-inch
BLUE ORCHID..............4-8 76
Member: Jim Foley.
Also see FOLEY, Jim

BAER, Carl, & Ascots
Singles: 7-inch
SOMA..............5-10 60s

BAERWALD, David — LP '90
LPs: 10/12-inch
A&M..............5-8 90

BAEZ, Joan — LP '61
Singles: 7-inch
A&M..............3-5 72-77
DECCA..............3-5 72
PORTRAIT..............3-5 77-79
RCA..............3-5 72
VANGUARD (6 "Maria Dolores")..............5-10
(Stereo. Juke box issue.)
VANGUARD (35000 series)..............4-8 63-69
VANGUARD (35100 series)..............3-5 70-71
Picture Sleeves
A&M..............4-6 72
PORTRAIT..............3-5 79
RCA..............4-6 72
VANGUARD (6 "Deportee")..............5-10 60s
(Promotional issue only.)
VANGUARD (35031 "There But for Fortune")..............15-25 65
LPs: 10/12-inch
A&M (Except 8375)..............6-10 72-77
A&M (8375 "Joan Baez - Radio Airplay Album")..............10-15 76
(Promotional issue only.)
EMUS..............5-10 79
FANTASY..............10-15
MFSL (238 "Diamonds & Rust")..............20-25 94
NAUTILUS..............25-35 81
(Half-speed mastered.)
PICKWICK..............5-10 73
PORTRAIT..............5-10 77-79
SQUIRE..............10-20 63
VANGUARD (41/42 "Ballad Book")..............10-15 72
VANGUARD (49/50 "Contemporary Ballad Book")..............10-15 70s
VANGUARD (105/106 "Country Music Album")..............10-20 79
VANGUARD (077 thru 123)..............20-30 60-63
VANGUARD (160 thru 306)..............12-25 64-69
VANGUARD (308 thru 332)..............6-10 69-73
VANGUARD (400 series)..............5-10
(Vanguard numbers 077 through 446 may be preceded by a "2," indicating stereo, or a "9" or "79" for mono issues.)
VANGUARD (6500 series)..............8-12 71
VANGUARD (6500 series)..............10-12 70-71
Also see WILSON, Dennis / Ram Jam / Joan Baez

BAEZ, Joan, Bill Wood & Ted Alevizos
LPs: 10/12-inch
VERITAS (62202 "Folksingers 'Round Harvard Square")..............100-200 60
(Without text in upper right corner reading: "This is the historic album featuring the original first recordings of America's Most Exciting Folk Singer — The Best of Joan Baez." A limited, numbered edition.)
VERITAS (62202 "Folksingers 'Round Harvard Square")..............50-100 61
(Cover has "This is the historic album featuring the original first recordings of America's Most Exciting Folk Singer — The Best of Joan Baez.")
Also see BAEZ, Joan

BAG
Singles: 7-inch
JERDEN..............5-10 66

BAG
Singles: 7-inch
DECCA..............5-8 69
LPs: 10/12-inch
DECCA..............15-20 68
Member: Jimmy Curtiss.
Also see CURTISS, Jimmy

BAGBY, Doc — P&R '57
Singles: 78 rpm
GOTHAM..............10-20 52
KING..............10-20 55
OKEH..............10-20 56-57
Singles: 7-inch
END..............8-12 60
GATOR (Pony Walk")..............5-10 61
GONE (5087 "Pancake Hop")..............8-12 60
GOTHAM "Jumpin' at Smalls")..............25-40 52
HUNT (323 "Muscle Tough")..............15-25 59
KAISER..............10-15 59
KING (4804 "Grinding")..............20-30 55
OKEH..............5-10 56-57
PERRI..............5-10 62
RED TOP..............15-25 59
TALLY HO..............5-10 61
VIM..............5-10 63
EPs: 10/12-inch
EPIC (7190 "Dumplins")..............50-75 57
Also see SELLERS, Johnny
Also see TERRY, Sonny

BAGBY, Doc / Luis Rivera
LPs: 10/12-inch
KING (631 "Battle of the Organs")..............25-35 59
Also see BAGBY, Doc
Also see RIVERA, Luis

BAGBY, Hank
Singles: 7-inch
PROTONE..............25-50

BAGDADS
Singles: 7-inch
DOUBLE SHOT..............4-8 68-70

BAGDASARIAN, Ross
Singles: 78 rpm
MERCURY..............5-8 54
Singles: 7-inch
IMPERIAL..............4-6 69
LIBERTY (55000 thru 55200 series)..............5-15 56-60
LIBERTY (55300 thru 56000 series)..............3-8 61-70
MERCURY..............10-15 54
LPs: 10/12-inch
LIBERTY..............20-30 66
Also see SEVILLE, David

BAGELS
Singles: 7-inch
W.B...............8-10 64

BAGGESE, Charles
Singles: 7-inch
BCS (102 "Tuff")..............10-20 62

BAGGY, Melrose
Singles: 7-inch
BRUNSWICK..............8-12 59

BAGGYS
Singles: 7-inch
PIPELINE (501 "El Surfer")..............25-35 63
Members: Russ Regan; Gene Weed; Joe Saraceno.
Also see REGAN, Russ
Also see WEED, Gene

BAGSHOT ROW
Singles: 7-inch
PIRATE 5-10 73

BAHLER, John
Singles: 7-inch
W.B. 3-5 71

BAILES, Eddy *C&W '76*
(With the Cadillacs with the Accents)
Singles: 7-inch
CIN KAY 3-5 76
RITE (1209 "If This Is Sin") 10-20

BAILEY, Arlene
Singles: 7-inch
AGB (3403 "Closer to You") 4-8
COBRA (0010 "Ain't That Something") 10-20 60s

BAILEY, Arthur
Singles: 12-inch
ATLANTIC 4-6 84
Singles: 7-inch
ATLANTIC 3-4 84

BAILEY, Buddy, & Clovers: see CLOVERS

BAILEY, Dianne
Singles: 7-inch
SWAN 5-10 62

BAILEY, Don
Singles: 7-inch
USA (723 "Be My Own") 25-35 62

BAILEY, Glen *C&W '82*
Singles: 7-inch
YATAHEY 3-4 82

BAILEY, J.R. *R&B '68*
Singles: 7-inch
CALLA 5-15 68
MALA 5-8 60s
MAM 3-5 74
MIDLAND INT'L 3-5 75
RCA 3-5 76
SPRING 3-4 84
TOY 3-5 72-73
U.A. 3-4 78
VIRGO 3-5
LPs: 10/12-inch
MAM 8-10 74
U.A. 5-10 78
Also see CADILLACS
Also see CRICKETS
Also see HAWKINS, Sam
Also see NEW YORKERS 5
Also see VELVETONES

BAILEY, Jack
(With the Naturals)
Singles: 7-inch
FORD (105 "Beneath the Moonlight") 25-50 62
FORD (113 "Your Magic Touch") 50-100 62
FORD (121 "I Cried") 10-20 62
MALA (432 "Memories of You") 10-20 61

BAILEY, Jay Jay
Singles: 7-inch
ATLANTIC 3-5 70

BAILEY, Jimmy
Singles: 7-inch
COLUMBIA 5-10 65
WYNNE (103 "Constantly") 75-125 59
(Also issued as by Jimmy Lane & the Sugartones. We're not sure which came first.)
Also see LANE, Jimmy, & Sugartones

BAILEY, Johnny *C&W '83*
Singles: 7-inch
SOUNDWAVES 3-4 83

BAILEY, Judy *C&W '81*
Singles: 7-inch
COLUMBIA 3-4 81
W.B. 3-4 83
WHITE GOLD 3-4 85
Also see BANDY, Moe, & Judy Bailey

BAILEY, Little Maxie
Singles: 78 rpm
EXCELLO 15-25 53
Singles: 7-inch
EXCELLO (2007 "Brown Skin Woman Blues") 40-60 53

BAILEY, Lynn *C&W '80*
Singles: 7-inch
FRATERNITY 3-5 75
WARTRACE 3-4 80

BAILEY, Mary *C&W '81*
Singles: 7-inch
E&R 3-4 81

BAILEY, Maureen
Singles: 7-inch
BEVERLY HILLS 3-5 73

BAILEY, Max
(Max "Scatman" Bailey; Max "Blues" Bailey)
Singles: 78 rpm
BULLET (306 "Sting-a-Ree") 50-100 49
DOMINO (380 "Leave It Alone") 25-35 51

BAILEY, Mildred, & Charioteers
Singles: 78 rpm
COLUMBIA (80 "Rockin' Chair") 10-15 50
OKEH 5-10 40
VOCALION 8-12 40
Singles: 7-inch
COLUMBIA (80 "Rockin' Chair") 15-25 50
LPs: 10/12-inch
ALLEGRO 10-20 50s
COLUMBIA (6094 "Serenade") 30-50 50
(10-inch LP.)
Also see CHARIOTEERS

BAILEY, Mildred, & Delta Rhythm Boys
Singles: 78 rpm
DECCA 5-10 54
Singles: 7-inch
DECCA (25462 "Ev'rything Depends on You") 15-25 54
Also see BAILEY, Mildred, & Charioteers
Also see DELTA RHYTHM BOYS

BAILEY, Morris, & Thomas Boys
Singles: 7-inch
BAILEY 30-45
Also see INFORMERS

BAILEY, Pearl *R&B '46*
Singles: 78 rpm
COLUMBIA 4-8 46-50
CORAL 3-6 52-55
MERCURY 3-6 56
ROULETTE 3-6 57
SUNSET 3-6 56
VERVE 3-6 56
Singles: 7-inch
COLUMBIA (38000 series) 10-20 50
COLUMBIA (43000 series) 4-6 66
CORAL 10-20 52-55
DECCA 4-6 64
MERCURY 10-15 56
PROJECT 3 3-6 68-70
RCA (500 series) 3-5 71
RCA (9400 series) 4-6 67
ROULETTE 5-10 59-68
SUNSET 10-15 56
VERVE 10-15 56
EPs: 7-inch
COLUMBIA 15-25 52-56
CORAL 15-25 54
ROULETTE 15-25 57
LPs: 10/12-inch
ACCORD 5-10 83
COLUMBIA (900 series) 20-40 57
COLUMBIA (2600 series) 25-50 56
(10-inch LPs.)
COLUMBIA (6000 series) 25-50 50
(10-inch LPs.)
CORAL (56000 series) 25-50 54
(10-inch LPs.)
CORAL (57000 series) 25-50 57
CO-STAR 15-25 58
GUEST STAR 5-10
MERCURY (Except 100 series) 20-40 56-58
MERCURY (100 series) 8-12 69
PROJECT 3 5-10 70
RCA (4500 series) 5-10 71
ROULETTE (100 series) 8-12 71
ROULETTE (25000 & 25100 series) 15-30 57-63
ROULETTE (25200 & 25300 series) 10-20 64-65
ROULETTE (42002 "Back on Broadway") 10-20 60s
VOCALION 15-25 58
WING 15-25 59-63

BAILEY, Pearl, & Margie Anderson
LP: 10/12-inch
CORONET (148 "Singing & Swinging") 10-20 60s

BAILEY, Pearl, & Mike Douglas
Singles: 7-inch
PROJECT 3 4-6 68
Also see DOUGLAS, Mike

BAILEY, Pearl / Rose Murphy / Ivie Anderson
LPs: 10/12-inch
GRAND PRIX 10-15 60s
Also see BAILEY, Pearl
Also see MURPHY, Rose

BAILEY, Philip *R&B/LP '83*
Singles: 12-inch
COLUMBIA 4-6 83-86
Singles: 7-inch
COLUMBIA 3-4 83-86
Picture Sleeves
COLUMBIA 3-4 85-86
LPs: 10/12-inch
COLUMBIA 5-10 83-86
Also see EARTH, WIND & FIRE

BAILEY, Philip, & Phil Collins *P&R/R&B '84*
Singles: 12-inch
COLUMBIA 4-6 84
Singles: 7-inch
COLUMBIA 3-4 84
Picture Sleeves
COLUMBIA 3-4 84
Also see BAILEY, Philip
Also see COLLINS, Phil

BAILEY, Philip, & Little Richard
Singles: 7-inch
WTG (08492 "Twins") 3-4 88
Also see BAILEY, Phil
Also see LITTLE RICHARD

BAILEY, Ramblin' Red
Singles: 7-inch
PEACH 10-20 59

BAILEY, Razzy *P&R '74/C&W '76*
(Razzie Bailey; Razzy)
Singles: 7-inch
ABC-PAR 5-10 67
B&K (103 "Once We Loved") 15-25 59
CAPRICORN 3-5 75
ERASTUS 3-5 76
MCA 3-4 84-86
MGM 3-5 74
1-3-4 4-6 69
PEACH 5-10 66
RCA 3-5 77-84
SOUNDS of AMERICA 3-4 86-89
Picture Sleeves
RCA 3-4 80-81
LPs: 10/12-inch
MCA 5-10 85-86
PLANTATION 5-8 81
RCA 5-10 79-84
Also see AQUARIANS
Also see RAZZY & NEIGHBORHOOD KIDS

BAILEY, Rene
Singles: 7-inch
CARNIVAL (541 "Warm and Tender Love") 10-15 69

BAILEY, Thomas
Singles: 7-inch
FEDERAL (12559 "Fran") 5-10 70
FEDERAL (12567 "Wish I Was Back") 50-100 71

BAILEY, Willie
Singles: 7-inch
LOADSTONE 10-15

BAILLIE & BOYS *C&W '87*
Singles: 7-inch
RCA 3-4 87-91
LPs: 10/12-inch
RCA 5-8 87-90
Members: Kathie Baillie; Mike Bonagura; Alan LeBoeuf.

BAIN, Babette
Singles: 7-inch
RENDEZVOUS 5-10 59

BAIN, Bob
Singles: 7-inch
CAPITOL (3931 "Fender Bender") 15-25 58
RADIANT 10-15 62
RIVIERA 10-15 61
LPs: 10/12-inch
CAPITOL (965 "Rockin' Rollin' Strollin' ") 50-75 58
CAPITOL (1201 "Latin Love") 15-25 58
Also see PILTDOWN MEN

BAINES, Houston
(Houston Boines)
Singles: 78 rpm
BLUES & RHYTHM 25-50 51
Also see BOINES, Houston

BAINES, Vickie
Singles: 7-inch
LOMA 5-10 67
PARKWAY (957 "Losing You") 10-20 65
PARKWAY (966 "Country Girl") 75-125 65

BAIO, Scott *LP '82*
Singles: 7-inch
RCA 3-4 82-83
Picture Sleeves
RCA 3-4 82
LPs: 10/12-inch
RCA 5-10 82-83

BAIRD, Don
Singles: 7-inch
DEF JAM 3-4 90

BAIRD, Randy
Singles: 7-inch
VANGUARD 3-5 75

BAITY, Pamela
Singles: 7-inch
SY-ROC 20-25

BAIZE, Bill
(Bill Baise)
Singles: 7-inch
TRIBUTE (2356 "He Dared to Do His Thing") 5-8
Also see SUMNER, J.D., & Stamps Quartet

BAIZE, Cindy
Singles: 7-inch
MAB 3-4
Picture Sleeves
MAB 4-6

BAJA MARIMBA BAND *P&R '63*
Singles: 7-inch
A&M 3-6 66-67
ALMO 4-8 63-66
BJ 3-5
BELL 3-5 73
SHOUT 3-4 81
Picture Sleeves
A&M 4-8 66-68
EPs: 7-inch
A&M 5-10 68
LPs: 10/12-inch
A&M 5-15 64-70
BELL 5-10 73
Member: Julius Wechter.
Also see DENNY, Martin
Also see MONTEZ, Chris

BAKER, Abie
Singles: 7-inch
LAUREL (1010 "Moccasin Rock") 10-15 59
Also see MAYMIE & ROBERT

BAKER, Adam *C&W '85*
Singles: 7-inch
AVISTA 3-4 86-87
SIGNATURE 3-4 85

BAKER, Adrian
Singles: 7-inch
EPIC 3-5 75

BAKER, Anita *R&B/LP '83*
Singles: 7-inch
BEVERLY GLEN 3-4 83-84
ELEKTRA 3-4 86-90
Picture Sleeves
ELEKTRA 3-4 86-89
LPs: 10/12-inch
BEVERLY GLEN 5-10 83
ELEKTRA 5-10 86-90
Also see CHAPTER 8
Also see WINANS & Anita Baker

BAKER, Arthur *D&D '84*
Singles: 12-inch
ATLANTIC 4-6 84
Singles: 7-inch
ATLANTIC 3-4 84

BAKER, Betty
(With Jaxsis)
Singles: 7-inch
QUICKSAND 3-5
ROULETTE 3-5 70s

BAKER, Bill
(With the Chestnuts; Bill Baker & Del Satins; Bill Baker's Five Satins; Billy Baker & Five Satins)
Singles: 7-inch
AUDICON 10-20 62
CORAL 10-20 60
ETC 10-15 63
ELGIN (007 "Won't You Tell Me, My Heart") 30-45 59
ELGIN (013 "Wonderful Girl") 75-100 59
JANUS GOLD 3-5 77
MUSIC TONE 10-20 61-62
MUSICNOTE (119 "Teenage Triangle") 15-25 63
VIM (515 "Thank Heaven") 50-100 60
LPs: 10/12-inch
DEL CAM (1000 "I'll Be Seeing You") 8-10 87
Also see BABY DOLLS
Also see CHESTNUTS
Also see DAVID & GOLIATH
Also see DEL SATINS
Also see FIVE SATINS
Also see HOOD, Darla

BAKER, Bill, & Twitchers
Singles: 7-inch
DORE (606 "Twitchin' ") 8-12 61
KNICK (172 "Caramba") 15-25 58

BAKER, Butch *C&W '84*
Singles: 7-inch
MERCURY 3-4 84-90
Also see ALEXANDER, Daniele, & Butch Baker
Also see TOMORROW'S WORLD

BAKER, Bob
Singles: 7-inch
VEEDA 4-6 60s

BAKER, C.B.
Singles: 78 rpm
SITTIN' IN WITH (625 "Skin to Skin") 25-35 51

BAKER, Carroll *C&W '81*
Singles: 7-inch
EXCELSIOR 3-4 81
GAIETY 4-6 70
RCA 3-5 77
TEMBO 3-4 85
LPs: 10/12-inch
COLUMBIA 5-10
GAIETY 10-20 70
RCA 5-10 77
TEE VEE 5-10 78

BAKER, Charlie
Singles: 7-inch
LIBERTY (55226 "Star of Wonder") 25-50 60
MUN RAB (106 "Star of Wonder") 100-150 59

BAKER, Dick, Combo
Singles: 7-inch
KIT KAT (711 "Heartless Lover") 200-300
Also see GREENE, Hazel, & Dick Baker

BAKER, Don
Singles: 7-inch
MATTHEW (30103 "Honky Tonk") 10-20 60

BAKER, Donny, & Dimensions
Singles: 78 rpm
RAINBOW 20-30 53
Singles: 7-inch
RAINBOW (219 "Drinkin' Pop Sodee Odee") 30-50 53

BAKER, Francine "Peaches"
Singles: 7-inch
COLUMBIA 4-8 69
Also see PEACHES & HERB

BAKER, George
Singles: 78 rpm
RCA ("How Doth the Little Crocodile") 150-200 38
(Picture disc.)

BAKER, George *P&R/LP '70*
(George Baker Selection)
Singles: 7-inch
COLOSSUS 4-6 70
W.B. 3-5 75-76
Picture Sleeves
COLOSSUS 5-8 70
LPs: 10/12-inch
COLOSSUS 15-20 70
W.B. 10-15 76

BAKER, Ginger *P&R/LP '70*
(Ginger Baker's Air Force)
Singles: 7-inch
ATCO 3-5 70
LPs: 10/12-inch
ATCO 12-15 70-72
AXIOM 8-12 90
SIRE 5-10 77
POLYDOR 8-10 72-79
Also see BAKER - GURVITZ ARMY
Also see BLIND FAITH
Also see CREAM
Also see LAINE, Denny
Also see WINWOOD, Steve

BAKER, Jane
Singles: 7-inch
RCA 6-12

BAKER, Jeanette
Singles: 7-inch
ALADDIN 10-15 58
DUB-TONE (2581 "Johnny") 30-40
Also see DOTS
Also see McLOLLIE, Oscar, & Jeanette Baker

BAKER, Jo-An
(With the Belgianettes)
Singles: 7-inch
DIAMOND (164 "Everybody's Talkin' ") 15-20 64
EMBER (1089 "You're Someone") 15-20 63
Also see BELGIANETTES

BAKER, Joan
Singles: 7-inch
DIAMOND (164 "Everybody's Talking") 25-50 64

BAKER, Johnny
Singles: 7-inch
ASCO (1000 "I Am") 3-5

BAKER, Kenny
Singles: 7-inch
ORBIT 10-15 59

BAKER, LaVern *R&B '55*
(With the Gliders; Lavern Baker; La Verne Baker)
Singles: 78 rpm
ATLANTIC (1004 thru 1136) 20-50 53-57
ATLANTIC (1189 "Whipper Snapper") 20-30 58
ATLANTIC (2001 "It's So Fine") 25-35 58
ATLANTIC (2007 "I Cried a Tear") 40-60 58
Singles: 7-inch
ATLANTIC (1004 "Soul on Fire") 40-60 53
ATLANTIC (1047 "Tweedle Dee") 20-30 55
ATLANTIC (1047 "Bop-Ting-a-Ling") 20-30 55
ATLANTIC (1075 "Play It Fair") 25-50 55
ATLANTIC (1087 "My Happiness Forever") 20-30 56
ATLANTIC (1104 "Still") 20-30 56
ATLANTIC (1116 "Jim Dandy") 20-30 56
ATLANTIC (1136 "Jim Dandy Got Married") 20-30 57
ATLANTIC (1189 "Whipper Snapper") 15-25 58
ATLANTIC (2001 "It's So Fine") 15-25 58
ATLANTIC (2007 "I Cried a Tear") 15-25 58
ATLANTIC (2021 "I Waited Too Long") 15-25 59
ATLANTIC (2033 "So High, So Low") 10-20 59
ATLANTIC (2041 "Tiny Tim") 10-20 59
ATLANTIC (2048 "Shake a Hand") 10-20 60
ATLANTIC (2059 "Wheel of Fortune") 10-20 60
ATLANTIC (2077 "Bumble Bee") 10-20 60
ATLANTIC (2099 "Saved") 10-20 61
ATLANTIC (2109 "Hurtin' Inside") 10-20 61
ATLANTIC (2137 "Must I Cry Again") 10-20 62
ATLANTIC (2162 "See See Rider") 8-15 62
ATLANTIC (2186 "Trouble in Mind") 8-15 63
ATLANTIC (2234 "Go Away") 8-12 64
ATLANTIC (2267 "Fly Me to the Moon") 8-12 65
BRUNSWICK (55291 "Baby") 10-20 66
BRUNSWICK (55297 "Call Me Darling") 10-20 66
BRUNSWICK (55311 "Wrapped, Tied and Tangled") 25-35 67
EPs: 7-inch
ATLANTIC (566 "LaVern Baker - Tweedle Dee") 50-100 56
ATLANTIC (588 "LaVern Baker - Jim Dandy") 50-100 57
ATLANTIC (617 "LaVern Baker - I Cried a Tear") 50-75 58
LPs: 10/12-inch
ATCO (372 "Her Greatest Recordings") 10-15 71
ATLANTIC (1281 "LaVern Baker Sings Bessie Smith") 50-100 58
ATLANTIC (8002 "LaVern") 150-200 57
(Black label.)
ATLANTIC (8002 "LaVern") 25-50 59
(Red label.)
ATLANTIC (8007 "LaVern Baker") 100-150 57
ATLANTIC (8030 "Blues Ballads") 50-75 59
(Black label.)

ATLANTIC (8030 "Blues Ballads") 50-75 59
(White label.)
ATLANTIC (8030 "Blues Ballads") 30-60 59
(Red label.)
ATLANTIC (8036 "Precious Memories") 40-60 59
ATLANTIC (8050 "Saved") 40-60 61
ATLANTIC (8071 "See See Rider") 25-50 63
ATLANTIC (8078 "Best of LaVern Baker") 25-50 63
BRUNSWICK (54160 "Let Me Belong to You") 10-15 70
Session: King Curtis.
Also see KING CURTIS
Also see RHODES, Todd
Also see WILSON, Jackie, & LaVern Baker

BAKER, LaVern, & Ben E. King
Singles: 7-inch
ATLANTIC 10-20 60
Also see KING, Ben E.

BAKER, LaVern, & Jimmy Ricks
Singles: 7-inch
ATLANTIC 10-20 61
Also see BAKER, LaVern
Also see RICKS, Jimmy

BAKER, Little Betty
Singles: 7-inch
ALL PLATINUM 3-5 71

BAKER, Mickey
(Mickey "Guitar" Baker & His House Rockers)
Singles: 78 rpm
RAINBOW 10-20 55
SAVOY 15-25 52-53
Singles: 7-inch
ATLANTIC (2042 "Third Man Theme") 10-15 59
KING 10-15 63-64
MGM 10-20 57
RAINBOW (288 "Shake Walkin' ") 20-30 55
RAINBOW (299 "Bandstand Stomp") 20-30 55
RAINBOW (303 "Old Devil Moon") 20-30 55
RAINBOW (316 "I'm So Glad") 20-30 55
RAINBOW (318 "Forever and for a Day") 20-30 55
SAVOY (867 "Guitar Mambo") 30-40 52
SAVOY (874 "Love You Baby") 30-40 53
LPs: 10/12-inch
ATLANTIC (8035 "Wildest Guitar") 75-125 59
KICKING MULE 5-10 78
KING (839 "But Wild") 50-75 63
Also see BONNIE SISTERS
Also see DARNELL, Larry
Also see DUPREE, Champion Jack, & Mickey Baker
Also see HUMPHRIES, Teddy
Also see McGHEE, Brownie
Also see McHOUSTON, Big Red
Also see MICKEY & KITTY
Also see MICKEY & SYLVIA
Also see MR. BEAR
Also see PAIGE, Hal
Also see RIFF, Eddie
Also see SELLERS, John
Also see TERRY, Sonny
Also see 3 FRIENDS
Also see TURNER, Titus
Also see VALENTINE, Billy
Also see WASHBOARD BILL

BAKER, Penny, & Pillows
Singles: 7-inch
WITCH 20-25 64

BAKER, Robert
LPs: 10/12-inch
GNP 15-20 66

BAKER, Rodney, & Chantiers
Singles: 7-inch
JAN ELL (8 "Teenage Wedding Song") 40-60 61

BAKER, Ron
Singles: 7-inch
OLÉ (9 "This Is It") 8-12

BAKER, Ronnie
(With the Deltones)
Singles: 7-inch
LAURIE (3128 "I Want to Be Loved") 30-40 62
(First issued as by the Beltones.)
LAURIE (3250 "Young at Heart") 10-15 64
Also see BELTONES
Also see BELLTONES

BAKER, Roy Boy
Singles: 7-inch
DESS 15-25 57

BAKER, Sam
Singles: 7-inch
COPA (200-3 "So Long") 200-300 60
ATHENS 10-15 61
EXCELLO 5-10
SAABIA 5-10
SOUND STAGE 7 4-8

BAKER, Teddy
Singles: 7-inch
CASABLANCA 3-4 81

BAKER, Tex
Singles: 7-inch
ABC (1073 "Ontario Valley Rock") 40-50
CROSS WINDS (104 "Ontario Valley Rock") 50-60

BAKER, Willie
Singles: 78 rpm
DELUXE 25-50 53
ROCKIN' 50-75 53
Singles: 7-inch
DELUXE (6023 "Before She Leaves Town") 75-100 53
ROCKIN' (527 "Before She Leaves Town") 100-200 53

BAKER, Yvonne
Singles: 7-inch
JAMIE 5-10 65
JUNIOR (987 "Foolishly Yours") 15-25 63
MODERN 5-10
PARKWAY (140 "You Didn't Say a Word") 50-75 66
Also see SENSATIONS

BAKER - GURVITZ ARMY *LP '75*
Singles: 7-inch
ATCO 3-5 74-76
JANUS 3-5 75
LPs: 10/12-inch
ATCO 8-10 75-76
JANUS 10-12 75
Members: Ginger Baker; Adrian Gurvitz; Paul Gurvitz; Peter Lemer; John Norman; Snips.
Also see BAKER, Ginger
Also see GUN
Also see GURVITZ, Adrian
Also see THREE MAN ARMY

BAKER SISTERS
Singles: 78 rpm
MERCURY 5-10 56
Singles: 7-inch
MERCURY 10-15 56
UNIQUE 4-8

BAKER STREET IRREGULARS: see BEACON STREET IRRELGULARS

BAKER TWINS
Singles: 7-inch
CAMEO 5-10 64

BAKERSFIELD BOOGIE BOYS
LPs: 10/12-inch
RHINO 5-10 81

BAKKER, Tammy Faye
Singles: 12-inch
SUTRA (067 "Ballad of Jim & Tammy") 5-8 87
Singles: 7-inch
SUTRA 3-4 88
Picture Sleeves
SUTRA 3-5 88

BALAAM & ANGEL *LP '88*
LPs: 10/12-inch
VIRGIN 5-10 87-89
Members: Mark Morris; Jim Morris; Des Morris; Ian McKean.

BALANCE *P&R/LP '81*
Singles: 7-inch
PORTRAIT 3-4 81-82
LPs: 10/12-inch
PORTRAIT 5-10 81-82
Also see BLUES MAGOOS

BALBOA
Singles: 7-inch
EVENT 4-8

BALCOM, Bill
("Handsome" Jim Balcom; Jim Balcolm)
Singles: 78 rpm
STARLA (7 "Corrido Rock") 25-50 58
Singles: 7-inch
CADDY (106 "Tribal Dance") 15-25 57
CLASS (249 "Bag Pipe Rock") 10-15 59
CLASS (259 "St. Louis Blues") 10-15 59
DOT (15711 "Corrido Rock") 10-20 58
NORWOOD (102 "Strollin' ") 10-15 59
STARLA (7 "Corrido Rock") 20-30 58
(First issue.)
Also see HERRERA, Little Julian

BALCONES FAULT
Singles: 7-inch
CREAM 3-4 77
LPs: 10/12-inch
CREAM 8-10 77
Members: Steve Blodgett; A. Fletcher Clark; Michael Christian; Don Elam; Jack Jacob; Kerry Kimbrough; Mike McGeary; Riley Osborne; Dean Stimulus.

BALDASSARE, J.F.
Singles: 7-inch
MAGNA-GLIDE 3-5 77

BALDERDASH
LPs: 10/12-inch
MAGNA-GLIDE 5-10 77
UNI 8-10 72

BALDO, Frankie, & Noveltones
Singles: 7-inch
IMPERIAL (5755 "Strange Guitar") 10-20 61

BALDRY, Long John *P&R '68*
(With the Hootchie Cootchie Men)
Singles: 7-inch
A&M 4-6 68
ASCOT 4-8 66-67
EMI AMERICA 3-4 79
W.B. 3-6 68-72
Picture Sleeves
W.B. 4-8 72
LPs: 10/12-inch
ASCOT 15-25 65
CASABLANCA 5-10 75-76
EMI AMERICA 5-10 79-80
JANUS 10-15
MUSICLINE 5-8 86
U.A. 8-10 71
W.B. 8-10 71-72

BALDRY, Long John, & Kathi McDonald
Singles: 7-inch
EMI AMERICA 3-4 79
Picture Sleeves
EMI AMERICA 3-4 79
Also see BALDRY, Long John
Also see McDONALD, Kathi

BALDWIN, Bill
Singles: 7-inch
EPIC 3-4 80

BALDWIN, Clive
Singles: 7-inch
MERCURY 3-6 75

BALDWIN & LEPS
LPs: 10/12-inch
VANGUARD 8-10 71

BALESTRIERI, Brian
Singles: 7-inch
DESMOND 3-5 78
Also see SIDEWALK SKIPPER BAND

BALIN, Marty *P&R/LP '81*
Singles: 7-inch
CHALLENGE 20-25 62
EMI AMERICA 3-4 81-84
Picture Sleeves
EMI AMERICA 3-4 81
LPs: 10/12-inch
EMI AMERICA 8-10 81-83
Also see BODACIOUS, D.F.
Also see JEFFERSON AIRPLANE
Also see JEFFERSON STARSHIP

BALL, Ace
Singles: 7-inch
CAPROCK 10-15 59

BALL, Anita
Singles: 7-inch
RCA 3-5 79

BALL, David *C&W '88*
Singles: 7-inch
RCA 3-4 88-89
WEA 3-4 90s

BALL, Eugene, & Hearts
Singles: 7-inch
MELATONE (1001 "Why Oh Why") 300-500 58

BALL, Kenny
Singles: 7-inch
JERDEN (776 "500 Miles") 10-20 65

BALL, Kenny *P&R/LP '62*
(With His Jazzmen)
Singles: 7-inch
DECCA 3-5 67
GUYDEN 3-5 61
KAPP 3-5 62-64
Picture Sleeves
KAPP 4-8 62
LPs: 10/12-inch
JAZZOLOGY 5-10 79
KAPP 10-25 62-64
Members: Kenny Ball; Johnny Bennett; Dave Jones; Colin Bates; Vic Pitts; Ron Bowden; Diz Disley.

BALL, Marcia *C&W '78*
Singles: 7-inch
CAPITOL 3-5 78
LPs: 10/12-inch
CAPITOL 5-8 78

BALL BROTHERS
Singles: 7-inch
EASY 4-8

BALLACK, Robert John
Singles: 7-inch
ROULETTE 3-5 72

BALLAD, Johnny, & Zodiacs
Singles: 7-inch
WILDCAT 5-10 50s

BALLADEERS
Singles: 78 rpm
RCA (4612 "Goodbye Little Girl") 15-25 52
Singles: 7-inch
RCA (4612 "Goodbye Little Girl") 25-45 52

BALLADEERS
Singles: 78 rpm
JUBILEE (5021 "Red Sails in the Sunset") 200-300 50
JUBILEE (5024 "I Never Knew I Loved You") 200-300 50
Member: Bill Mathews.
Also see MATHEWS, Bill, & Balladeers

BALLADEERS
Singles: 7-inch
DEL-FI 10-15 59-60
LPs: 10/12-inch
DEL-FI (1204 "Alive-O") 20-40 59
(Monaural.)
DEL-FI (1204 "Alive-O") 30-50 59
(Stereo.)
Members: Fred Darian; Al Delory; Joe Van Winkle.
Also see DARIAN, Fred

BALLADEERS
Singles: 7-inch
CORI (31001 "Words I Want to Hear") 5-10 65

BALLADIERS
Singles: 78 rpm
ALADDIN (3008 "Keep Me with You") 75-125 48
ALADDIN (3123 "Forget Me Not") 75-100 52
ANTHRACITE 50-75 55
Singles: 7-inch
ALADDIN (3123 "Forget Me Not") 550-650 52
ANTHRACITE (109 "Starlight Souvenirs") 75-125 55

BALLADIERS
Singles: 7-inch
LOVE LOCK 3-5

BALLADS
(With Jimmy Cris Orchestra)
Singles: 78 rpm
FRANWIL 25-50 56
Singles: 7-inch
FRANWIL (5028 "Before You Fall in Love") 50-100 56
RON-CRIS (1003 "Somehow") 50-100 60
Members: Dick Arnold; Jack McCoy; Sonny Manzo; Phil Babin; Jack Knect.

BALLADS
Singles: 7-inch
TINA (102 "This Is Magic") 25-50 64

BALLADS
Singles: 7-inch
VEE JAY (714 "I Can't See Your Love") 15-25 65

BALLADS *P&R/R&B '68*
Singles: 7-inch
VENTURE (615 "God Bless Our Love") 10-15 68
(Credits "The Ballards.")
VENTURE (615 "God Bless Our Love") 5-10 68
(Credits "The Ballads.")
VENTURE (625 "You're the One") 8-12 68
Members: Nathan Robertson; Jon Foster; Rick Thompson; Lesley LaPalma.

BALLADS
Singles: 7-inch
KLIK 4-8 72
Also see KOLE, Kenny, & Huskies
Also see NUTMEGS

BALLADS
Singles: 7-inch
KIMBERLY (105 "Baby, I'm for Real") 8-12

BALLADS
Singles: 7-inch
BALJA (1002 "Wait") 5-10
HAPPY FOX (503 "Wait") 5-10
(We have yet to determine whether Balja or Happy Fox came first.)
LPs: 10/12-inch
BALJA ("Ballads from the Ground Up") 10-15
(Selection number not known.)

BALLARD, Bud
Singles: 7-inch
SABER (112 "C.C. Rider") 10-20 62

BALLARD, Clint
(Clint Ballard Jr.)
Singles: 7-inch
GUYDEN 5-8 61
IMPERIAL 5-10 61

BALLARD, Florence
Singles: 7-inch
ABC 15-25 68
Picture Sleeves
ABC 20-30 68
Also see SUPREMES

BALLARD, Frank
(With the Philip Reynolds Band)
LPs: 10/12-inch
PHILLIPS INT'L (1985 "Rhythm & Blues Party") 400-600 62

BALLARD, Hank *R&B '68*
(With the Midnight Lighters; with Dapps)
Singles: 7-inch
KING 5-8 68
PEOPLE 4-8 72
POLYDOR 3-5 72
SILVER FOX 4-6 70
STANG 3-5 75
LPs: 10/12-inch
KING (1052 "You Can't Keep a Good Man Down") 15-25 69

BALLARD, Hank, & Midnighters *R&B '59*
Singles: 7-inch
GUSTO 3-4 78
KING (5171 "The Twist") 15-20 59
KING (5195 "Kansas City") 10-15 59
KING (5215 "Sugaree") 10-15 59
(Monaural.)
KING (S-5215 "Sugaree") 20-30 59
(Stereo.)
KING (5245 thru 6131) 5-15 59-67
LE JOINT 3-5 79
Picture Sleeves
KING (5491 "The Continental Walk") 10-15 61
EPs: 7-inch
FEDERAL (333 "Their Greatest Hits") 200-300 54
KING (333 "Their Greatest Hits") 25-50 58
KING (435 "Singin' & Swingin, Vol. 1") 25-35 59
KING (435 "Singin' & Swingin, Vol. 2") 25-35 59
KING (793 "Jumpin' Hank Ballard") 25-35 62
KING (7815 "1963 Sound of Hank Ballard & Midnighters") 15-25 59
LPs: 10/12-inch
FEDERAL (90 "Their Greatest Hits") 5000-10000 54
(10-inch LP.)
FEDERAL (541 "Their Greatest Hits") 500-750 57
(White cover.)
FEDERAL (541 "Their Greatest Hits") 400-500 57
(Tan or red cover.)
KING (541 "Their Greatest Hits") 100-200 58
KING (581 "Midnighters, Volume Two") 100-200 58
KING (618 "Singin' & Swingin' ") 75-125 59
KING (674 "The One & Only") 50-75 60
KING (700 "Mr. Rhythm & Blues") 50-75 60
KING (K-740 "Spotlight on Hank Ballard") 50-75 61
(Monaural.)
KING (KS-740 "Spotlight on Hank Ballard") 75-125 61
(Stereo.)
KING (748 "Let's Go Again") 25-50 61
KING (759 "Sing Along") 25-50 61
KING (781 "Twistin' Fools") 25-50 61
KING (793 "Jumpin' ") 25-50 62
KING (815 "1963 Sound") 25-50 63
KING (867 "Biggest Hits") 25-50 63
KING (896 "A Star in Your Eyes") 20-40 64
KING (913 "Those Lazy Lazy Days") 20-40 65
KING (927 "Glad Songs, Sad Songs") 15-25 66
KING (950 "24 Hit Tunes") 15-25 66
KING (981 "24 Great Songs") 15-25 68
KING (5000 "20 Hits") 8-10 77
POWER PAK (276 "Mr. Rhythm & Blues") 10-15
Also see BALLARD, Hank
Also see MIDNIGHTERS
Also see MOORE, Henry
Also see ROYALS

BALLARD, Hank, & Midnighters / Viceroys
Singles: 7-inch
KING/BETHLEHEM (5719 "That Low Down Move") 10-15 63
(The Viceroys side has a Bethlehem label. Promotional issue only.)
Also see BALLARD, Hank, & Midnighters
Also see VICEROYS

BALLARD, Jerry
Singles: 7-inch
SKIPPY (120-60 "Pinch Me") 15-25 60

BALLARD, Jimmie Lee
Singles: 7-inch
REM 5-10 60

BALLARD, Kenny
(With the Fabulous Soul Brothers)
Singles: 7-inch
GENIE (101 "Lady of Stone") 15-25 60s
KAPP (602 "Mr. Magic") 10-20 64

BALLARD, Lil' Willie
LPs: 10/12-inch
KING (737 "Hit Makers and Record Breakers") 40-50 60

BALLARD, Roger *C&W '93*
Singles: 7-inch
ATLANTIC 3-4 93

BALLARD, Russ *P&R/LP '80*
Singles: 7-inch
EMI AMERICA 3-4 84-85
EPIC 3-5 74-80
LPs: 10/12-inch
EMI AMERICA 5-8 84-85
EPIC 8-10 74-80
Also see ARGENT
Also see UNIT 4+2

BALLARD BROTHERS
Singles: 7-inch
DEBRO 5-10

BALLARDS
Singles: 7-inch
VELTONE (1738 "I Hope I Never Fall in Love") 100-200

BALLARDS (on Venture): see BALLADS

BALLENAIRES
Singles: 7-inch
COLLECTABLES 3-4 81

BALLENGER, Paul, & Flares
Singles: 7-inch
REED (711 "I Still Love You") 100-200 58

BALLEW, Dennis, & Plain Truth
Singles: 7-inch
MARLIN 8-10

BALLEW, Michael *C&W '81*
Singles: 7-inch
LIBERTY 3-4 81-82

BALLIN, Roger
(With the A-Tones)
Singles: 7-inch
NIKE (002 "Why")...25-50 61

BALLIN' JACK P&R/LP '71
Singles: 7-inch
COLUMBIA...3-5 71
MERCURY...3-5 73
LPs: 10/12-inch
COLUMBIA...10-12 70-72
MERCURY...8-10 73-74

BALLISTICS
Singles: 7-inch
JAMIE...3-5 69

BALLOON CORP
Singles: 7-inch
BELL...4-8 69
DUNHILL...4-8 69

BALLOON FARM P&R '68
Singles: 7-inch
LAURIE (3405 "A Question of Temperature")...8-12 68
LAURIE (3445 "Hurry Up Sundown")...10-15 68

BALLOONS
Singles: 7-inch
BLUE RIBBON...5-10 70s

BALLOU, Classie, & His Tempo Kings
Singles: 7-inch
EXCELLO...10-20 58
GOLDBAND...15-20
LANOR...4-6
NASCO...10-20 57

BALTIMORA P&R '85
Singles: 12-inch
MANHATTAN...4-6 86
Singles: 7-inch
MANHATTAN...3-4 85-86
Picture Sleeves
MANHATTAN...3-4 85
LPs: 10/12-inch
MANHATTAN (53026 "Living in the Background")...5-10 85
Also see TECHNOTRONIC Featuring Ya Kid K / Baltimora

BALTIMORE & OHIO MARCHING BAND P&R '67
Singles: 7-inch
JUBILEE...3-6 67
LPs: 10/12-inch
JUBILEE...10-15 67

BALTINEERS
Singles: 78 rpm
TEENAGE...50-75 56
Singles: 7-inch
LOST NITE...4-8
TEENAGE (1000 "Moments Like This")...150-200 56
TEENAGE (1002 "Tears in My Eyes")...200-250 56

BALUM & ANGELS
LPs: 10/12-inch
VIRGIN...5-8 87

BAMA P&R '79
Singles: 7-inch
FREE FLIGHT (Black vinyl)...3-5 79
FREE FLIGHT (Colored vinyl)...4-6 79
(Promotional issues only.)
LPs: 10/12-inch
FREE FLIGHT...5-10 79

BAMA BAND C&W '82
Singles: 7-inch
COMPLEAT...3-4 85-87
MERCURY...3-4 88-89
OASIS...3-5 82-83
SOUNDWAVES...3-4 83
LPs: 10/12-inch
COMPLEAT...5-10 86
Members: Lamar Morris; Billy Earhart III.
Also see AMAZING RHYTHM ACES
Also see MORRIS, Lamar
Also see WILLIAMS, Hank, Jr.

BAMBAATAA, Afrika P&R/R&B '82
(With James Brown; with Soul Sonic Force; with Family)
Singles: 12-inch
TOMMY BOY...4-6 83-86
Singles: 7-inch
EMI...3-4 88
TOMMY BOY...3-5 82-86
Picture Sleeves
EMI...3-4 88
LPs: 10/12-inch
TOMMY BOY...5-10 83-86
Also see BROWN, James
Also see SHANGO

BAMBINOS
Singles: 7-inch
DOT (16238 "Algiers")...10-15 61

BAMBOO
LPs: 10/12-inch
ELEKTRA...10-15 69
Members: Mike Rickfors; Will Donicht; Daniel Lee Hall; Brenden Harkin; Sanford Konikoff; Dave Ray; Red Rhodes; Peter Hodgson; Ken Jenkins.
Also see HOLLIES

BAN
Singles: 7-inch
BRENT (7049 "Bye Bye")...15-25 65

BAN LONS
Singles: 7-inch
FIDELITY (4051 "Hey Baby")...15-25 59
FIDELITY (4056 "I Like It")...15-20 59

BANANA & BUNCH
Singles: 7-inch
W.B. ...3-5 72
LPs: 10/12-inch
W.B. ...10-12 72
Members: Ed "Banana" Denson; Michael Kane; Joe Bauer; Eddie Ottenstein.
Also see YOUNGBLOODS

BANANA BOYS
Singles: 7-inch
UNI...3-5 70

BANANA BROTHERS
Singles: 7-inch
BGO...3-5 75

BANANA SPLITS P&R '69
Singles: 7-inch
DECCA...4-8 68-69
Picture Sleeves
DECCA...8-10 69-70
EPs: 7-inch
KELLOGG...8-12 69
LPs: 10/12-inch
DECCA...10-15 69

BANANA'S BUNCH
Singles: 7-inch
FUN-E-BONE (320 "King Kong Goes Ape")...4-8 76

BANANARAMA P&R/D&D/LP '83
Singles: 12-inch
LONDON...4-6 83-88
Singles: 7-inch
LONDON...3-4 82-88
Picture Sleeves
LONDON...3-4 82-88
LPs: 10/12-inch
LONDON...5-10 83-88
Members: Sarah Dallin; Keren Woodward; Siobhan Fahey.
Also see BAND AID

BANBARRA
Singles: 7-inch
U.A. ...3-5 75

BANCHEE
Singles: 7-inch
ATLANTIC (2708 "Train of Life")...5-8 70
LPs: 10/12-inch
ATLANTIC (8240 "Banchee")...15-25 69
POLYDOR (4066 "Thinkin' ")...30-50 71
Members: Victor Digilio; Michael Marino; Jose Dejesus; Peter Alongi.

BANCO
LPs: 10/12-inch
MANTICORE...8-10 75
Members: Franceso DiGiacomo; Pier Luigi Calderoni; Renato D'Angelo; Rodolfo Maltese; Gianni Nocenzi; Vittorio Nocenzi.

BAND, The P&R/LP '68
Singles: 7-inch
CAPITOL (Except 2000 series)...3-5 71-77
CAPITOL (2000 series)...4-8 67-70
W.B. ...3-4 78
Picture Sleeves
CAPITOL (2705 "Rag Mama Rag")...4-8 70
LPs: 10/12-inch
CAPITOL (Except 2955)...10-15 69-85
CAPITOL (2955 "Music from Big Pink")...15-20 68
MFSL (039 "Music from Big Pink")...75-100 80
W.B. (737 "The Last Waltz")...20-30 78
(Promotional issue only.)
W.B. (3146 "The Last Waltz")...15-20 78
(Three-LP set.)
Members: Levon Helm; Rick Danko; Garth Hudson; Richard Manuel; Robbie Robertson.
Also see CANADIAN SQUIRES
Also see DANKO, Rick
Also see DYLAN, Bob
Also see HAWKINS, Ronnie
Also see HELM, Levon
Also see LEVON & HAWKS
Also see MILLER, Steve / Band / Quicksilver Messinger Service
Also see ROBERTSON, Robbie

BAND, The
Singles: 7-inch
TENER (1006 "Mr. Guitar Man")...15-25 60s

BAND AID P&R '84
Singles: 7-inch
COLUMBIA (04749 "Do They Know It's Christmas")...3-4 84
Picture Sleeves
COLUMBIA (04749 "Do They Know It's Christmas")...3-5 84
Members: Bananarama; Paul McCartney; Boomtown Rats; Boy George; Phil Collins; Duran Duran; Bob Geldof; Heaven 17; Kool & Gang; George Michael; John Moss; Spandau Ballet; Status Quo; Sting; U2; Ultravox; Paul Weller; Paul Young.
Also see BANANARAMA
Also see BOOMTOWN RATS
Also see COLLINS, Phil
Also see CULTURE CLUB
Also see DURAN DURAN
Also see GELDOF, Bob
Also see HEAVEN 17
Also see KOOL & GANG
Also see SPANDAU BALLET
Also see STATUS QUO
Also see STING
Also see STYLE COUNCIL
Also see U2
Also see ULTRAVOX
Also see WHAM
Also see YOUNG, Paul

BAND AKA
Singles: 12-inch
BOUVIER...4-6 83
Singles: 7-inch
PPL...3-4 81-82
LPs: 10/12-inch
PPL...5-10 81-82

BAND OF ANGELS
Singles: 7-inch
MIDLAND INT'L...3-5 75
MUMS...3-5 75

BAND OF GOLD P&R/R&B '84
Singles: 7-inch
RCA...3-4 85

BAND OF JOY
Singles: 7-inch
POLYDOR...3-4 78
LPs: 10/12-inch
POLYDOR...5-10 78
Members: Robert Plant; John Bonham; Paul Lockey; Kevin Hammend; John Pasternak; Michael Chetwood; Francisco Nizza.
Also see LED ZEPPELIN

BAND OF OZ
Singles: 7-inch
MEGA...3-5
SURFSIDE...3-5 82

BAND OF BLACK WATCH P&R/LP '76
Singles: 7-inch
PRIVATE STOCK...3-5 75-76
LPs: 10/12-inch
PRIVATE STOCK...5-10 76

BAND OF IRISH GUARDS
LPs: 10/12-inch
TOWER...5-15 65

BAND OF THIEVES
LPs: 10/12-inch
OVATION...5-10 77

BAND WITHOUT A NAME
Singles: 7-inch
SIDEWALK (913 "Thunder Alley")...10-20 67
TOWER...10-15 66
Session: Davie Allan
Also see ALLAN, Davie

BAND X
Singles: 7-inch
S.M.F. (95096 "How Good the Rain")...5-10 60s

BANDANA C&W '82
(BANDANNA)
Singles: 7-inch
HAVEN...3-5 76
PARAMOUNT...3-5 73
W.B. ...3-4 81-86
LPs: 10/12-inch
W.B. ...5-10 86
Also see PLAYER

BANDERA
Singles: 7-inch
MCA...3-4 81
LPs: 10/12-inch
MCA...5-10 81

BANDES, Cindy
Singles: 7-inch
PLATINUM SOUND...3-4 85

BANDIDOS
Singles: 7-inch
SHELLEY (129 "Ape Walk")...10-20 60

BANDIT
Singles: 7-inch
ABC...3-5 75
ARISTA...3-5 77
LPs: 10/12-inch
ABC...8-10 75
ARISTA...6-10 77
Members: Jim Diamond; Danny McIntosh; James Litherland; Cliff Williams; Graham Broad.

BANDIT
Singles: 7-inch
ARIOLA AMERICA...3-5 79
POLYDOR...3-5 79
LPs: 10/12-inch
ARIOLA AMERICA...5-10 78-79
Members: Joey Newman; Kevin Barnhill; Tommy Eaton; Danny Gorman; David Rossa.

BANDIT BAND C&W '87
Singles: 7-inch
PEGASUS...3-4 87

BANDIT BROTHERS C&W '91
Singles: 7-inch
CURB...3-4 91

BANDITOS
Singles: 7-inch
ELKAY (2001 "Mark of Zorro")...10-20 64
IGL (189 "Peggy Sue")...10-15 60s

BANDITS
Singles: 7-inch
GOAL...10-15
TWIN TOWN...10-20 65

BANDITS
Singles: 7-inch
JERDEN...5-10 66
PANORAMA (34 "Queen Jane")...10-15 60s
LP: 10/12-inch
WORLD PACIFIC (1833 "Electric")...10-15 60s
Also see CALLIOPE

BANDITS
Singles: 7-inch
RCI...3-4 83

BANDITS / Dynamics
Singles: 7-inch
EMJAY (1928 "Nothing Can Change My Love for You"/"That's Bad")...30-50 63
EMJAY (1935 "Nothing Can Change My Love for You"/"This Love of Ours")...15-25 63

BANDLONS
Singles: 7-inch
SONIC (82661 "Miserlou")...20-30 61

BANDOLERO D&D '84
Singles: 12-inch
SIRE...4-6 84
Singles: 7-inch
SIRE...3-4 84
LPs: 10/12-inch
ECLIPSE...8-10 75

BANDS OF GOLD
Singles: 7-inch
SMASH...10-20 66

BANDWAGON R&B '68
Singles: 7-inch
EPIC...4-6 68

BANDY, Moe C&W '74
(With Janie Fricke)
Singles: 7-inch
COLUMBIA...3-5 75-85
CURB...3-4 88-89
FOOTPRINT...5-10 74
GRC...3-5 74-75
MCA/CURB...3-4 86-87
LPs: 10/12-inch
COLUMBIA...5-10 76-85
FANFARE...5-10
GRC...10-15 74-75
MCA/CURB...5-8 86
Session: Janie Fricke; Jordanaires; Merle Haggard; Bobby Wood; Johnny Gimble; Laverna Moore; Pig Robbins; Terry McMillan.
Also see FRICKE, Janie
Also see HAGGARD, Merle
Also see JORDANAIRES
Also see ROBBINS, Hargus "Pig"

BANDY, Moe, & Becky Hobbs C&W '83
Singles: 7-inch
COLUMBIA...3-4 83
Also see HOBBS, Becky

BANDY, Moe, & Joe Stampley C&W '79
(Moe & Joe)
Singles: 7-inch
COLUMBIA...3-5 79-85
LPs: 10/12-inch
COLUMBIA...5-10 81-84
Also see BANDY, Moe
Also see STAMPLEY, Joe

BANG P&R//LP '72
Singles: 7-inch
CAPITOL...3-5 72-74
LPs: 10/12-inch
CAPITOL...8-12 72-73

BANG TANGO LP '89
LPs: 10/12-inch
MECHANIC...5-8 89-91

BANG - BANG
Singles: 7-inch
EPIC...3-4 85
Picture Sleeves
EPIC...3-4 85
LPs: 10/12-inch
EPIC...5-10 85

BANGERS
Singles: 7-inch
R&B (101 "Baby, Let Me Bang Your Box")...15-25 65

BANGLES LP '84
Singles: 12-inch
COLUMBIA...4-6 85-88
FAULTY (1000 "The Real World")...6-12 83
Singles: 7-inch
COLUMBIA...3-4 84-88
DEF JAM...3-4 87
DOWNKIDDIE (001 "Getting Out of Hand")...5-10 81
Picture Sleeves
COLUMBIA...3-4 84-88
DEF JAM...3-4 87
DOWNKIDDIE (001 "Getting Out of Hand")...10-20 81
(Back of sleeve shows Downkiddie Records as being in Los Angeles, California.)
DOWNKIDDIE (001 "Getting Out of Hand")...8-15 81
(Back of sleeve shows Downkiddie Records as being in Torrance, California.)
LPs: 10/12-inch
COLUMBIA (Except 2270)...5-10 84-90
COLUMBIA (2270 "Interchords")...10-20 86
(Promotional issue only.)
I.R.S. ...6-10 83
Members: Vicki Peterson; Debbi Peterson; Susanna Hoffs; Annette Zilinskas; Micki Steele.
Also see BANGS
Also see HOFFS, Susanna
Also see RAIN PARADE
Also see RUNAWAYS

BANGLES / Joan Jett
Singles: 7-inch
DEF JAM...3-4 87
Picture Sleeves
DEF JAM...3-4 87
Also see BANGLES
Also see JETT, Joan

BANGOR FLYING CIRCUS LP '69
Singles: 7-inch
DUNHILL...3-5 70
LPs: 10/12-inch
DUNHILL...12-15 69
Members: Michael Tegza; David Wolinski; Alan DeCarlo.

BANGS
Singles: 7-inch
DOWNKIDDIE (001 "Getting Out of Hand")...20-30 81
Picture Sleeves
DOWNKIDDIE (001 "Getting Out of Hand")...30-50 81
Members: Vicki Peterson; Debbi Peterson; Susanna Hoffs.
Also see BANGLES

BANISTER, James, & His Combo
Singles: 78 rpm
STATES (141 "Gold Digger")...50-75 54
Singles: 7-inch
STATES (141 "Gold Digger")...150-200 5

BANKS, Artie, & Tellers
Singles: 7-inch
IMPERIAL (5788 "Oriental Baby")...10-20 61

BANKS, Barbara
Singles: 7-inch
MGM...5-10 67
VEEP (1247 "Living in the Past")...10-15 66

BANKS, Bessie
Singles: 7-inch
QUALITY...3-5 76
SPOKANE...8-10 63
TIGER (102 "Go Now")...10-15 64
VERVE...4-6 67
VOLT...3-5 74
WAND...8-12 64
Also see JONES, Linda / Bessie Banks

BANKS, Bunny, Trio R&B '43
Singles: 78 rpm
SAVOY...5-10 43
Members: Ernie Ransom; Henry Padgett; Clem Moorman.

BANKS, Darrell P&R/R&B '66
Singles: 7-inch
ATCO (6471 "Here Comes the Tears")...10-20 67
ATCO (6484 "Angel Baby")...15-25 67
COTILLION...5-10 68
REVILOT...10-20 66
SOULTOWN...5-10 66
VOLT...4-8 69
LPs: 10/12-inch
ATCO (216 "Darrell Banks Is Here")...15-25 67
(Monaural.)
ATCO (216 "Darrell Banks Is Here")...25-30 67
(Stereo.)
VOLT...10-15 69

BANKS, Dick
Singles: 7-inch
LIBERTY (55145 "You Dirty Dog")...20-30 58

BANKS, Douglas
(Doug Bnaks)
Singles: 7-inch
ARGO (5483 "I Just Kept on Dancing")...25-50 64
GUYDEN (2082 "Ain't That Just Like a Woman")...25-50 63

BANKS, Eddie
(With the Five Dreamers)
Singles: 78 rpm
GALE...10-15 56
JOSIE (804 "Rock a Bye Blues")...15-20 56
Singles: 7-inch
GALE...15-25 56
JOSIE (804 "Rock a Bye Blues")...40-60 56

BANKS, Homer
Singles: 7-inch
GENIE (1000 "Hooked by Love")...25-50
MINIT (32000 "A Lot of Love")...15-25 66
MINIT (32008 "Sixty Minutes of Your Love")...15-25 66
MINIT (32020 "Hooked by Love")...15-25 67

BANKS, Johnny, & Everglades
Singles: 7-inch
BPV ("While Sitting in the Corner")...200-300 63
(No selection number used.)

BANKS, Larry
Singles: 7-inch
KAPP (865 "I'm Not the One")...15-25 67

SELECT (722 "Will You Wait") 10-20 63
SPRING (105 "We Got a Problem") 10-15 70

BANKS, Mack
Singles: 7-inch
FAME (580 "Be-Boppin' Daddy") 500-750 59
(500 made.)

BANKS, Otis, & Majors
Singles: 7-inch
GALE (1002 "Don't Take My Word") 25-35 58

BANKS, Patryce "Choc'let"
Singles: 7-inch
T-ELECTRIC 3-4 80
LPs: 10/12-inch
T-ELECTRIC 5-10 80

BANKS, Peter LP '73
Singles: 7-inch
CAPITOL 3-5 73
LPs: 10/12-inch
CAPITOL 10-12 73
Also see AFTER the FIRE
Also see BLODWYN PIG
Also see FLASH
Also see YES

BANKS, Ron R&B '83
Singles: 12-inch
CBS ASSOCIATED 4-6 83
Singles: 7-inch
ABC 3-5 75
CBS ASSOCIATED 3-4 83
LPs: 10/12-inch
CBS ASSOCIATED 5-10 83
Also see DRAMATICS

BANKS, Rose R&B '76
Singles: 7-inch
MOTOWN 3-5 76
SOURCE 3-4 80
LPs: 10/12-inch
MOTOWN 8-10 76
Also see SLY & Family Stone

BANKS, Tony LP '79
Singles: 7-inch
ATLANTIC 3-4 83
CHARISMA 3-4 79
LPs: 10/12-inch
ATLANTIC 5-10 83
CHARISMA 5-10 79
Also see GENESIS

BANKS & HAMPTON R&B '77
Singles: 7-inch
W.B. 3-5 76-77
LPs: 10/12-inch
W.B. 5-10 77
Members: Homer Banks; Carl Hampton.

BAN-LONS
Singles: 7-inch
FIDELITY (4051 "Hey Baby") 100-150 62
FIDELITY (4056 "I Like It") 100-150 62

BANNED
Singles: 7-inch
FONTANA 4-8 68
Picture Sleeves
FONTANA 5-10 68

BANNERS
Singles: 7-inch
MGM 5-10 60

BANNON, Eddie
Singles: 7-inch
VERVE (10608 "Baby Hold On") 10-20 67

BANNON, R.C. C&W '77
Singles: 7-inch
COLUMBIA 3-5 77-80
RCA 3-4 82
Also see MANDRELL, Louise, & R.C. Bannon

BANSHEES
Singles: 7-inch
DUNWICH (129 "Project Blue") 15-25 66
Also see ARIEL

BANSHEES
Singles: 7-inch
SOLO (1 "They Prefer Blondes") 20-30 66

BANTA, Benny
Singles: 7-inch
VIV (101 "Cry Little Girlie") 30-50

BANTAMS
Singles: 7-inch
W.B. 4-8 66
Picture Sleeves
W.B. 5-10 66
LPs: 10/12-inch
W.B. 15-20 66

BANZAII P&R/R&B '75
Singles: 7-inch
SCEPTER 3-5 75

BARA, Tony
Singles: 7-inch
ATCO 5-10 60

BARAKAT, Johnny, & Vestells
Singles: 7-inch
DELL STAR (103 "Happy Time") 25-35 64
Session: Johnny Barakat; Dave Tunno; Dan Bilbery; Danny Poore; Mark Piscatelli; Terry Gibbon.

BARB, Gerry
Singles: 7-inch
ATB 25-35 60s

BARBARA, Jo
Singles: 7-inch
MARKIE 5-10

BARBARA & BELIEVERS
Singles: 7-inch
CAPITOL 10-15 67

BARBARA & BOYS
Singles: 7-inch
DOT 8-12 58

BARBARA & BRENDA
Singles: 7-inch
AVANTI (1600 "Let's Get Together") 10-15 63
DYNAMO (103 "Too Young to Be Fooled") 4-8 67
DYNAMO (108 "Sally's Party") 4-8 67
HEIDI (104 "That's When You've Got Soul") 8-12 64
HEIDI (106 "You Don't Love Me Anymore") 8-12 66
HEIDI (109 "One More Chance") 8-12 66
Member: Brenda Holloway.
Also see HOLLOWAY, Brenda

BARBARA & BROWNS P&R/R&B '64
Singles: 7-inch
CADET 4-8 66
SOUND of MEMPHIS 3-5 72
STAX 5-10 64
Member: Barbara Brown.
Also see BROWN, Barbara

BARBARA & DELIGHTS
Singles: 7-inch
U.A. 3-5 75

BARBARA & ERNIE
LPs: 10/12-inch
COTILLION 8-10 71

BARBARA & GWEN
Singles: 7-inch
NEW CHICAGO SOUND 3-6 69-70
Members: Barbara Livsey; Gwen Livsey.
Also see BARBARA & UNIQUES

BARBARA & UNIQUES R&B '70
Singles: 7-inch
ABBOTT 3-6 72
ARDEN 4-8 70
NEW CHICAGO SOUND 3-6 70
20TH FOX 3-5 74
Members: Barbara Livsey; Gwen Livsey; Doris Lindsey.
Also see BARBARA & GWEN
Also see BLAKE, Barbara, & Uniques
Also see DU-ETTES

BARBARA JEAN
(With the Lyrics)
Singles: 7-inch
BIG HIT (107Any Two Can Play") ..25-50
COMET (2162 "Don't Remind Me of Tommy") 5-10

BARBARA JO: see BARBARA, Jo

BARBARA LYNN: see LYNN, Barbara

BARBARIANS P&R '65
Singles: 7-inch
JOY (290 "Hey Little Bird") 20-30 65
LAURIE (3308 "Are You a Boy or Are You a Girl") 10-15 65
LAURIE (3321 "What the New Breed Say") 10-20 65
LAURIE (3326 "Moulty") 10-20 66
LPs: 10/12-inch
LAURIE (2033 "The Barbarians") ...50-70 66
RHINO 5-10 79
Also see ELEGANTS

BARBAROSO & HISTORIANS
Singles: 7-inch
JADE (120 "Zoom") 50-75 64
Also see ADDEO, Nicky

BARBARY, Richard
Singles: 7-inch
A&M 3-5 69
SPRING 4-6 67
LPs: 10/12-inch
A&M 10-20 68

BARBATA, Johnny
LPs: 10/12-inch
DEL-FI 25-35 63
Also see FULLER, Bobby
Also see SENTINELS

BARBED WIRE DOLLS
EPs: 7-inch
GET HIP 3-5 90
(Issued with paper sleeve and photo inserts.)

BARBEE, Lucille
Singles: 7-inch
REPUBLIC 5-10 50s

BARBEES
Singles: 7-inch
STEPP (236 "The Wind") 100-200 62
Members: Carolyn Gill, Sandra Tilley; Betty Kelly.
Also see VELVELETTES

BARBER, Ava C&W '77
Singles: 7-inch
OAK 3-5 81
RANWOOD 3-5 77-78
LPs: 10/12-inch
RANWOOD 5-10 77-78

BARBER, Cecil
Singles: 7-inch
SOUTHTOWN (214 "I'm Not a Know It All") 10-15 62

BARBER, Chris P&R/R&B '59
(Chris Barber's Jazz Band)
Singles: 7-inch
ATLANTIC 5-10 59
LAURIE 5-10 58-63
LONDON 4-8 62
Picture Sleeves
LAURIE 10-20 59
LPs: 10/12-inch
ARCHIVE of FOLK MUSIC 8-12 68
ATLANTIC 15-25 59
COLPIX 15-25 59
LAURIE 20-30 59-62
Also see DR. JOHN & Chris Barber

BARBER, Debra C&W '75
Singles: 7-inch
RCA 3-5 73-75
SOUNDS of MEMPHIS 3-5 73

BARBER, Don, & Dukes
Singles: 7-inch
PERSONALITY (3505 "I'll Be Blue") 150-250 62
THUNDERBIRD (105 "What's Your Name") 20-30 60

BARBER, Frank, Orchestra P&R/LP '82
Singles: 7-inch
VICTORY 3-4 82
LPs: 10/12-inch
VICTORY 5-10 82

BARBER, Glenn C&W '64
Singles: 78 rpm
STARDAY (Except 166 & 249) 5-10 54-56
STARDAY (166 "Ice Water") 10-20 54
STARDAY (249 "Shadow My Baby") 15-25 56
Singles: 7-inch
CENTURY 21 ......3-5 78-79
GROOVY 3-5 77
HICKORY 3-8 68-74
MMI 3-5 79
PIC (137 "We'll Take Our Last Walk Tonight") 10-20 62
SIMS 4-8 64
SKILL (002 "April Fool") 8-12 62
STARDAY (Except 166, 249 & 600 series) 8-12 54-56
STARDAY (166 "Ice Water") 25-50 54
STARDAY (249 "Shadow My Baby") 50-75 56
STARDAY (600 series") 4-8 64
SUNBIRD 3-4 80
LPs: 10/12-inch
BRYLEN 5-10 83-84
HICKORY 8-12 70-72
HICKORY/MGM 5-10 74
TUDOR 5-10 83

BARBIERI, Gato LP '73
Singles: 7-inch
A&M 3-5 76-79
U.A. 3-5 73
LPs: 10/12-inch
A&M 5-10 76-79
ARISTA 8-10 75
FLYING DUTCHMAN 5-10 70-80
IMPULSE 8-10 73-75
U.A. 5-10 73

BARBOUR, Dave P&R '50
Singles: 78 rpm
CAPITOL 5-10 50-51
Singles: 7-inch
ARWIN 4-8 59
CAPITOL 5-10 50-51
EPs: 7-inch
CAPITOL 5-15 54
DECCA 5-15 53
LPs: 10/12-inch
DECCA 15-25 53

BARBOUR, Gene
(With the Cavaliers)
Singles: 7-inch
HIT 10-15 60s
JCP (1020 "Nobody") 10-20 64

BARBOUR, Keith P&R/LP '69
Singles: 7-inch
BARNABY 3-5 71
EPIC 3-6 69-70
LPs: 10/12-inch
EPIC 15-20 69

BARBOZA, Daniel
Singles: 7-inch
BARCLIFF 3-6

BARBUSTERS P&R '87
Singles: 7-inch
CBS ASSOCIATED 3-4 87
Also see JETT, Joan

BARCARI, Angela
Singles: 7-inch
RCA 3-5 76

BARCLAY, Eddie P&R '55
(Eddie Barclay & His Orchestra)
Singles: 78 rpm
MERCURY 10-20 57
RAMA 5-10 55
TICO 5-10 55
U.A. 5-10 59
Singles: 7-inch
MERCURY (71098 "Ten Little Tears") 10-20 57
RAMA 5-10 55
TICO 5-10 55
LPs: 10/12-inch
MONUMENT 10-20 66
U.A. (3023 "Americans in Paris") ...15-25 59

BARCLAY, Nickey
Singles: 7-inch
ARIOLA AMERICA 3-5 75-76
LPs: 10/12-inch
ARIOLA AMERICA 5-10 76
Also see FANNY

BARCLAY, Phil
Singles: 7-inch
DOKE 20-30 59

BARCLAY JAMES HARVEST LP '77
Singles: 7-inch
HARVEST 3-5 73
MCA 3-5 76-77
POLYDOR 3-5 75-79
SIRE 5-10 68
LPs: 10/12-inch
HARVEST 8-12 73
MCA 8-10 77
POLYDOR 8-10 74-80
SIRE 10-15 70-71
Members: Les Holroyd; John Lees; John Pritchard; Stewart "Wolly" Wolstenholme.

BARCLAY STARS
LPs: 10/12-inch
ATCO (194 "Guitars Unlimited") 20-30

BARD, Annette
Singles: 7-inch
IMPERIAL 20-25 60
Also see CONNORS, Carol

BARDENS, Peter LP '87
(Pete Bardens)
Singles: 7-inch
CAPITOL 3-4 87
Picture Sleeves
CAPITOL 3-4 87
LPs: 10/12-inch
CAPITOL 5-10 87
VERVE/FORECAST 10-12 71
Also see CAMEL
Also see KEATS
Also see SHOTGUN EXPRESS
Also see THEM

BARDEUX P&R/LP '88
Singles: 7-inch
ENIGMA 3-4 89
SYNTHICIDE 3-4 88
Picture Sleeves
SYNTHICIDE 3-4 88
LPs: 10/12-inch
ENIGMA 5-8 89
SYNTHICIDE 5-8 88
Members: Stacy Smith; Jazz; Melanie Taylor.

BARDI, Dick, & Orchids
Singles: 7-inch
MAESTRO (409 "Stormy Weather") 15-25

BARDOT, Brigitte
Singles: 7-inch
MGM (13099 "Sidonie") 5-10 62
LPs: 10/12-inch
BURLINGTON CAMEO (1000 "Special Bardot") 75-125 68
(TV soundtrack. Promotional issue made for Burlington Cameo.)
DECCA (8685 "And God Created Woman") 60-75 58
(Soundtrack.)
PHILIPS 15-25 63
POPLAR (1002 "The Girl in the Bikini") 175-225 59
(Soundtrack.)
U.A. (4135 "Viva Maria") 12-15 66
(Soundtrack. Monaural.)
U.A. (5135 "Viva Maria") 15-25 66
(Soundtrack. Stereo.)
W.B. 10-20
Also see DISTEL, Sacha, & Brigitte Bardot
Also see RUGOLO, Pete, & His Orchestra

BARDS
Singles: 78 rpm
DAWN 50-100 54
Singles: 7-inch
DAWN (208 "I'm a Wine Drinker") 150-200 54
DAWN (209 "Avalon") 150-200 54

BARDS
Singles: 7-inch
CUCA (1038 "Unicorn Song") 10-15 61

BARDS
Singles: 7-inch
BURDETTE 10-15 67
CAPITOL 10-15 67-68
JERDEN 5-10 68
NO LABEL NAME (2148 "The Owl & the Pussycat"/"Light of Love") 15-25 67
(No label name shown.
PARROT 8-12 69-70
PICCADILLY 10-20 66-67
Picture Sleeves
CAPITOL (2148 "The Owl & the Pussycat") 10-20 67
LPs: 10/12-inch
PICCADILLY/FIRST AMERICAN (3419 "The Bards") 30-50 80

BARDS
Singles: 7-inch
EMCEE (13 "Alibis") 20-30 66

BARE, Bobby C&W/P&R '62
(With the All American Boys; with Hillsiders; with Bobby Bare Jr; Bobby Bare & Family; with Jeannie Bare)
Singles: 78 rpm
CAPITOL 5-10 57
Singles: 7-inch
CAPITOL 10-15 57
COLUMBIA 3-5 78-85
EMI AMERICA 3-4 85-86
FRATERNITY 10-20 58-61
MERCURY 3-5 70-72
RCA (Except 8000 & 9000 series) 3-6 69-77
RCA (8000 & 9000 series) 4-8 62-68
RICE 3-5 73-75
Picture Sleeves
RCA 5-15 62-65
LPs: 10/12-inch
CAMDEN 8-12 68-73
COLUMBIA 5-10 78-85
MERCURY 10-15 70-72
OVATION 5-10 80
PHONORAMA 5-8 82
PICKWICK 5-10 75-80
PICKWICK/HILLTOP 10-15 65
RCA (ANL1 & APL1 series) 8-12 73-77
RCA (AYL1 series) 5-10 81
RCA (0079 "Singin' in the Kitchen") 15-25 74
(Promotional issue only.)
RCA (LPM-2776 thru LPM-3994) ...10-20 63-68
(Monaural.)
RCA (LSP-2776 thru LSP-3994) 15-25 63-68
(Stereo.)
RCA (4000 series) 10-15 69-71
RCA (6000 series) 8-15 73
SEARS 10-15
SUN (136 "Bobby Bare's Greatest Hits") 15-25 74
U.A. 8-12 75-76
Session: Anita Kerr Singers; Floyd Cramer; Lacy J. Dalton; Charlie Daniels; Waylon Jennings.
Also see BOWMAN, Don
Also see CASH, Rosanne, & Bobby Bare
Also see CRAMER, Floyd
Also see DALTON, Lacy
Also see DANIELS, Charlie
Also see JENNINGS, Waylon
Also see KERR, Anita
Also see ORBISON, Roy / Bobby Bare / Joey Powers
Also see PARSONS, Bill
Also see SOME of CHET'S FRIENDS
Also see TENNESSEE PULLYBONE

BARE, Bobby, Liz Anderson & Norma Jean C&W '66
Singles: 7-inch
RCA 4-6 66
LPs: 10/12-inch
BARE TRACKS 8-12
RCA 15-20 67
Also see ANDERSON, Liz
Also see NORMA JEAN

BARE, Bobby, & Skeeter Davis C&W '65
(Skeeter Davis & Bobby Bare)
Singles: 7-inch
RCA (8000 & 9000 series) 3-6 65-70
LPs: 10/12-inch
RCA 15-20 65-70
Also see DAVIS, Skeeter

BARE, Bobby, / Donna Fargo / Jerry Wallace
LPs: 10/12-inch
OUT of TOWN DIST 5-10 82
Also see BARE, Bobby
Also see FARGO, Donna
Also see WALLACE, Jerry

BARE, Spence
Singles: 78 rpm
MCI (1001 "Boogie Billy") 15-25 56
Singles: 7-inch
MCI (1001 "Boogie Billy") 25-35 56

BARE, Steve
Singles: 7-inch
CHEROKEE (785 "Smooth") 8-12

BARE BLUE WATER
Singles: 7-inch
TARGET (1012 "In the Midnight Hour") 8-12 70

BARE FACTS
Singles: 7-inch
JOSIE ("To Think") 10-15
(Selection number not known.)
JUBILEE (5544 "Bad Part of Town") 15-25 66

BARE FAT
Singles: 7-inch
BANG 3-5 70
Members: Jim White; Kurt Kuzulka; Steve Beau; Gene Diest; Randy Lindert.

BAREFOOT JERRY
Singles: 7-inch
CAPITOL 13-5 71
MONUMENT 3-5 74-77
W.B. 3-5 73
LPs: 10/12-inch
CAPITOL 10-15 71
MONUMENT 5-10 74-77
W.B. 8-12 73
Also see AREA CODE 615

Also see McCOY, Charlie

BARENAKED LADIES LP '94
Singles: 7-inch
REPRISE (17499 "The Old Apartment") ... 3-5 97
Members: Tyler Stewart; Jim Creeggan; Andrew Creeggan; Ed Robertson.

BARES
Singles: 7-inch
DEAN ("Buck Fever") ... 15-25 60
(Selection number not known.)

BARFIELD, Johnny, & Men of S.O.U.L.
LPs: 10/12-inch
SSS INT'L ... 4-8 67

BARGE, Gene
Singles: 78 rpm
CHECKER ... 10-20 54
LEGION ... 5-10
Singles: 7-inch
CHECKER (839 "Way Down Home") ... 20-30 54
CHECKER (1110 "Fine Twine") ... 5-10 65
LEGION ... 8-10
LEGRAND (1006 "Thinking of You") ... 15-25 60
PARAMOUNT ... 3-5 72
LPs: 10/12-inch
CHECKER (2994 "Dance with Daddy G") ... 20-30 65
Also see BONDS, Gary "U.S."
Also see CHURCH STREET FIVE
Also see DADDY G
Also see WILLIS, Chuck

BARIAN, Bullet Bob
Singles: 7-inch
MAGIC TOUCH (2004 "Bat-Mo") ... 10-20 67
Also see COMIC BOOKS

BARIN, Pete
(With the Pete Bennett Orchestra)
Singles: 7-inch
SABRINA (504 "So Wrong") ... 35-50 62
SABRINA (512 "Look Out for Cindy") ... 20-40 63
Session: Belmonts.
Also see BELMONTS

BARINNO BROTHERS
Singles: 7-inch
INVICTUS ... 3-5 73

BARISH, Jesse
Singles: 7-inch
RCA ... 3-4 78
LPs: 10/12-inch
RCA ... 5-10 78-80

BARITONES
Singles: 7-inch
DORE (501 "After School Rock") ... 30-50 58

BARKAN, Mark
Singles: 7-inch
MGM ... 3-5 70

BAR-KAYS P&R/R&B '67
Singles: 12-inch
MERCURY ... 4-6 79-85
Singles: 7-inch
MERCURY ... 3-5 76-89
STAX ... 3-5 78-81
VOLT ... 4-8 67-74
Picture Sleeves
MERCURY ... 3-4 88-89
LPs: 10/12-inch
MERCURY ... 5-10 76-87
STAX ... 5-10 78-81
VOLT ... 10-15 67-74
Members: Jimmy King; Phalon Jones; Carl Cunningham; Ron Caldwell; Larry Dodson; James Alexander; Charles Allen; Vernon Burch; Ben Cauley; Donnelle Hagan; Harvey Henderson; Winston Stewart.
Also see NEWCOMERS
Also see REDDING, Otis

BARKDULL, Wiley
Singles: 7-inch
ALL STAR ... 8-12 62
HICKORY (1074 "Hey Honey") ... 25-50 58

BARKER, Blue Lu R&B '48
Singles: 78 rpm
APOLLO ... 5-10 46-48
CAPITOL ... 10-15 48-50
DECCA ... 10-20 39-40
Singles: 7-inch
CAPITOL ... 20-30 50

BARKER, Delbert
Singles: 78 rpm
KING ... 10-15 56
TOP TUNES ... 5-10 54
Singles: 7-inch
KING ... 20-30 56
TOP TUNES ... 8-12 54

BARKER, Francine
Singles: 7-inch
COLUMBIA ... 4-6 68

BARKER, Freddie
Singles: 7-inch
DOUBLE SHOT ... 3-5 70

BARKER BROTHERS
Singles: 78 rpm
DECCA ... 10-15 57
Singles: 7-inch
DECCA ... 15-20 57-58

BARKING SPYDERS
Singles: 7-inch
AUDIO PRECISION (45001 "I Want Your Love") ... 20-30 66

BARKLE, Al
Singles: 7-inch
FRANTIC (Frantic 108 "Muscle Beach") ... 25-50
M&M (4041 "Jumpin from Six to Six") ... 75-125

BARKLEY, Sparkley
Singles: 7-inch
KEEN ... 5-10 58

BARKLEY, Tyrone R&B '79
Singles: 7-inch
MIDSONG INT'L ... 3-4 79

BARKSDALE, Everett
Singles: 7-inch
COLPIX (660 "Firewater") ... 10-20 62

BARLOW, Dean
(With the Crickets; with Charles Shirley & Orchestra)
Singles: 78 rpm
JAY-DEE ... 50-75 54
Singles: 7-inch
BEACON (463 "True Love") ... 10-20 59
JAY-DEE (785 "Your Love") ... 100-200 54
JAY-DEE (786 "Just You") ... 100-200 54
JAY-DEE (789 "Are You Looking for a Sweetheart") ... 100-200 54
JAY-DEE (795 "I'm Going to Live My Life Alone") ... 100-200 54
LESCAY (3004 "Baby Doll") ... 10-20 61
LESCAY (3010 "The Night Before Last") ... 10-20 61
RUST (5068 "Don't Let Him Take My Baby") ... 8-10 63
7 ARTS (704 "Little Sister") ... 10-15 61
TCF (12 "Glory of Love") ... 10-15 64
UT (4001 "You're Mine") ... 100-200 59
WARWICK (618 "It's All in Your Mind") ... 15-25 61
Also see BACHELORS
Also see CRICKETS

BARLOW, Dean, & Crickets / Deep River Boys
Singles: 78 rpm
BEACON ... 40-60 54
Singles: 7-inch
BEACON (104 "Be Faithful"/"Sleepy Little Cowboy") ... 50-100 54
Also see BARLOW, Dean
Also see CRICKETS
Also see DEEP RIVER BOYS

BARLOW, Dean, & Montereys
Singles: 78 rpm
ONYX ... 20-40 57
Singles: 7-inch
ONYX (513 "Dearest One") ... 50-75 57
ONYX (517 "Angel") ... 50-75 57
Also see BARLOW, Dean
Also see MONTEREYS

BARLOW, Jack C&W '68
Singles: 7-inch
ANTIQUE ... 3-5 75
APEX ... 5-10 60s
DIAL ... 5-10 65
DOT ... 3-8 68-73
EPIC ... 4-6 67
GOLDEN RING ... 5-10 64
SOMA ... 5-12 62-64
LPs: 10/12-inch
ANTIQUE ... 5-10 75
DOT ... 8-12 69-70
Also see FENSTER, Zoot

BARLOW, Randy C&W '74
Singles: 7-inch
CAPITOL ... 3-4 74
GAZELLE ... 3-5 76-83
JAMEX ... 3-5
PAID ... 3-4 80-81
REPUBLIC ... 3-5 78-84
SOUL, COUNTRY & BLUES ... 3-6 75
LPs: 10/12-inch
GAZELLE ... 6-12 77
PAID ... 5-10 81
REPUBLIC ... 5-10 78-79

BARMBY, Shane C&W '89
Singles: 7-inch
MERCURY ... 3-4 89
Also see TOMORROW'S WORLD

BARNABY BYE
Singles: 7-inch
ATLANTIC ... 3-5 73-75
LPs: 10/12-inch
ATLANTIC ... 10-12 73-74
Members: Billy Alessi; Bobby Alessi; Peppy Castro; Mike Ricciardella.
Also see ALESSI
Also see PRINE, John / Daryl Hall & John Oates / Barnaby Bye / Delbert & Glen

BARNER, Juke Boy, & Group
(Juke Boy Bonner)
Singles: 7-inch
IRMA (111 "Rock with Me Baby") ... 200-300 58
Also see BONNER, Juke Boy

BARNES, Benny C&W '56
Singles: 78 rpm
STARDAY ... 10-20 56-57
Singles: 7-inch
D (1052 "Gold Records in the Snow") ... 25-50 59
GUYDEN ... 4-6 74
HALL-WAY ... 4-8 64
MEGA ... 8-12 72
MERCURY ... 10-20 58-61
MUSICOR ... 4-6 65-66
PLAYBOY ... 4-8 77
STARDAY (200 series) ... 15-30 56-57
STARDAY (400 series) ... 15-20 58
LPs: 10/12-inch
CRAZY CAJUN ... 5-10
Also see JONES, George / Benny Barnes

BARNES, Betty
Singles: 7-inch
BODWAY ... 10-12

BARNES, Big Syl
Singles: 7-inch
ASTRA (1007 "Cherry") ... 5-10 65
CORVAIR (900 "Cherry") ... 25-35 60

BARNES, Billy
(Willie Barnes)
Singles: 7-inch
LIBERTY (55421 "Until") ... 15-20 62
U.A. (157 "I'm Coming to See You") ... 10-15 59
Also see SULTANS

BARNES, Bobby
Singles: 78 rpm
MARVEL ... 5-10

BARNES, Cheryl P&R '79
Singles: 7-inch
MILLENNIUM ... 3-4 77
POLYDOR ... 3-4 80
RCA ... 3-4 79

BARNES, David
Singles: 7-inch
SAN (302 "Lovin' on My Mind") ... 40-60

BARNES, Dena
Singles: 7-inch
INFERNO (2002 "Who Am I") ... 150-200 60s

BARNES, Diane
Singles: 7-inch
AJAY (902 "I Suffer for You") ... 5-10

BARNES, Don
Singles: 7-inch
BEJAY ... 3-4 78

BARNES, Dorothy
Singles: 7-inch
MILKY WAY ... 20-30 64
Members: Arlie Neaville; Dave Marten.
Also see NEAVILLE, Arlie

BARNES, Eddie
Singles: 7-inch
CLOCK ... 10-20 58
FIESTA ... 25-35 58

BARNES, George
Singles: 78 rpm
DECCA ... 10-15 52
Singles: 7-inch
DECCA (27939 "State Street Boogie") ... 15-25 52
MERCURY (71968 "Spooky") ... 15-25 62
PLEASURE (1002 "Hot Shortnin' Bread") ... 15-25 59
LPs: 10/12-inch
MERCURY (2020 "Guitars Galore") ... 15-25 62
(Monaural.)
MERCURY (6020 "Guitars Galore") ... 20-30 62
(Stereo.)

BARNES, George, & Carl Kress
LPs: 10/12-inch
U.A. ... 10-20 64

BARNES, George, Carl Kress, & Flo Handy
LPs: 10/12-inch
CARNEY ... 10-20 62
Also see BARNES, George

BARNES, J.J. P&R/R&B '66
(With the Dell Fi's)
Singles: 7-inch
BUDDAH (120 "I'll Keep Coming Back") ... 10-15 69
GROOVESVILLE (1006 "Chains of Love") ... 10-15 67
GROOVESVILLE (1008 "Forgive Me") ... 10-15 67
INVASION (1001 "My Baby") ... 8-10 70
KABLE (913 "Won't You Let Me Know") ... 75-125 60
MAGIC TOUCH (1000 "Cloudy Days") ... 5-10 70
MICKAY'S (351 "Teenage Queen") ... 50-75 62
MICKAY'S (353 "So Far Away") ... 50-75 62
MICKAY'S (3004 "Just One More Time") ... 50-75 63
MICKAY'S (3014 "These Chains of Love") ... 50-75 63
MICKAY'S (4471 "Lonely No More") ... 50-75 63
PERCEPTION (546 "You Are Just a Living Doll") ... 5-10 73
REVILOT (216 "Hold On to It") ... 10-20 68
REVILOT (218 "Sad Day a Coming") ... 10-20 68
REVILOT (222 "Out Love Is in the Pocket") ... 50-75 68
REVILOT (225 "So-Called Friends") ... 10-20 69
RICH (1005 "Won't You Let Me Know") ... 50-100 60
RIC-TIC (106 "Please Let Me In") ... 10-20 65
RIC-TIC (110 "A Real Humdinger") ... 10-20 66
RIC-TIC (115 "Day Tripper") ... 10-20 66
RIC-TIC (117 "Say It") ... 10-20 66
RING (101 "She Ain't Ready") ... 20-30 64
SCEPTER (1266 "Just One More Time") ... 20-30 64
VOLT (4027 "Snowflakes") ... 10-15 69
LPs: 10/12-inch
PERCEPTION ... 10-20 74

BARNES, J.J., & Steve Mancha
LPs: 10/12-inch
VOLT (6001 "Rare Stamps") ... 10-20 69
Also see BARNES, J.J.
Also see HOLIDAYS
Also see MANCHA, Steve

BARNES, James, & Agents
Singles: 7-inch
GOLDEN HIT ... 3-5

BARNES, Jimmy
(With the Gibralters)
Singles: 7-inch
GIBRALTAR (101 "No Regrets") ... 10-20 59
GIBRALTAR (102 "I Need You So Much") ... 10-20 59
SAVOY (1581 "Our Wedding Day") ... 10-15 59
SAVOY (1590 "You Thrill Me So Much") ... 10-15 60

BARNES, Jimmy P&R/LP '86
Singles: 7-inch
GEFFEN ... 3-4 86-88
Picture Sleeves
GEFFEN ... 3-4 88
LPs: 10/12-inch
GEFFEN ... 5-10 86
Also see COLD CHISEL
Also see INXS & Jimmy Barnes

BARNES, Johnny
Singles: 7-inch
CAP CITY (122 "Real Nice") ... 15-25 60s
JABA (801 "Nothing Without Your Love") ... 150-250

BARNES, Kathy C&W '75
(With Larry Barnes)
Singles: 7-inch
MGM ... 3-5 75
REPUBLIC ... 3-4 76-78
Picture Sleeves
REPUBLIC ... 3-4 76
LPs: 10/12-inch
REPUBLIC (Except 5002) ... 6-12 76-78
REPUBLIC (5002 "Kathy Barnes Sings Gene Autry") ... 10-20 78

BARNES, Larry
Singles: 7-inch
CALLIOPE (6502 "Patiently") ... 5-10 61

BARNES, Mae
EPs: 7-inch
ATLANTIC (502 "Mae Barnes Sings") ... 25-50
LPs: 10/12-inch
ATLANTIC (404 "Fun with Mae Barnes") ... 150-200 53
(With the Three Flames. 10-inch LP.)
VANGUARD ... 20-30 58
Also see THREE FLAMES

BARNES, Max D. C&W '77
Singles: 7-inch
OVATION ... 3-4 80-81
POLYDOR ... 3-5 77-78
LPs: 10/12-inch
OVATION ... 6-10 77-80

BARNES, Myra
Singles: 7-inch
KING ... 3-5 70

BARNES, Ortheia
Singles: 7-inch
CORAL ... 8-12
MICKAY'S ... 10-20 60s

BARNES, Roosevelt "Booba," & Playboys
LPs: 10/12-inch
ROOSTER BLUES ... 5-8 90

BARNES, Sidney
Singles: 12-inch
PARACHUTE ... 4-6 78
Singles: 7-inch
BLUE CAT (125 "I Hurt on the Other Side") ... 75-125 66
BLUE STONE (402 "Shindig") ... 10-15 60s
CHESS (2094 "Baloney") ... 6-10 65
PARACHUTE ... 3-4 79
RED BIRD (10039 "You'll Always Be in Style") ... 25-35 65
LPs: 10/12-inch
PARACHUTE ... 5-10 78
Also see ROTARY CONNECTION
Also see SERENADERS

BARNES, Syl: see BARNES, Big Syl

BARNES, Tawanda
Singles: 7-inch
A&M ... 10-20 70
GROOVY ... 5-10

BARNES & BARNES
Singles: 7-inch
LUMANIA ... 4-8 79
RHINO ... 3-4 82
Picture Sleeves
LUMANIA ... 3-5 79
LPs: 10/12-inch
BRYLEN ... 5-10 84
RHINO ... 5-10 80-84
Members: Bill Mumy; Robert Haimer.

BARNESS, Johnny
Singles: 7-inch
FLIPPIN' ... 10-20

BARNET, Charlie, & Orchestra
R&B '42
Singles: 78 rpm
APOLLO ... 4-8 48
BANNER ... 4-8 34
BLUEBIRD ... 5-10 35-41
CONQUEROR ... 4-8 34
DECCA ... 4-8 42-43
MELOTONE ... 4-8 34
ORIOLE ... 4-8 34
PERFECT ... 4-8 33
ROMEO ... 4-8 33
LPs: 10/12-inch
FM VERI SONICS ... 5-10

BARNETT, Billy
Singles: 7-inch
DOUBLE B (1113 "Romp and Stomp") ... 150-200
PARKWAY (826 "Marlene") ... 10-20 61
TEX (105 "Tired of Your Honky Tonk Love") ... 10-15
Also see BURNETTE, Billy Joe
Also see FIENDS

BARNETT, Bobby C&W '60
Singles: 7-inch
BANNISTER ... 3-5 73
CIN KAY ... 3-5 78
COLUMBIA ... 4-6 68-69
HERITAGE ... 3-5 74
K-ARK ... 4-6 67
PRESTA ... 4-6 60s
RAZORBACK ... 5-10 60
SIMS ... 4-8 64
LPs: 10/12-inch
COLUMBIA ... 8-15 68
HERITAGE ... 5-10 74
SIMS (118 "At the Crystal Palace") ... 15-25 64

BARNETT, Don
Singles: 7-inch
CHAPARRAL ... 3-4 80
MEDALLION ... 3-4 80

BARNETT, James
Singles: 7-inch
FAME (1001 "Take a Good Look") ... 10-20 66

BARNETT, Julian, & Talents
Singles: 7-inch
HERALD (519 "Come Back to Me") ... 25-35 58

BARNETT, Spot
(Spot Barnett Combo)
Singles: 7-inch
MASTER (101 "Pony Race") ... 10-20 61
WILDCAT (0040 "Sweet Meats") ... 15-25 59

BARNETTE, Billy
(With the Searchers; with Divots and Ron Sunshine Orchestra)
Singles: 7-inch
MT. VERNON (500 "Don't Let Our Love Go Wrong") ... 500-1000
MT. VERNON (501 "Billy the Kid") ... ??
(We're listing this because we have seen it; however, we have no opinions yet as to value. We cannot automatically assume it to be in the range of Mt. Vernon 500. Readers?)

BARNETTE, Johnny
Singles: 7-inch
VANCE (481 "Shadow My Baby") ... 50-75

BARNEY & GOOGLES
Singles: 7-inch
SHIMMY (1055 "Doin' the Shimmy") ... 50-75 60

BARNHILL, Joe C&W '89
(Joe Bob Barnhill)
Singles: 7-inch
UNIVERSAL ... 3-4 89
LPs: 10/12-inch
RPA ... 5-10

BARNHILL, Leslie C&W '78
Singles: 7-inch
REPUBLIC ... 3-4 78-79

BARNICOAT, Alan
Singles: 7-inch
ROCKET ... 10-15 59

BARNSTORM
LPs: 10/12-inch
DUNHILL ... 8-12 72-73
Members: Joe Walsh; Brian Garafalo; Rock Grace; Joe Lala; Kenny Passarelli; Joe Vital; Tom Stevenson.
Also see WALSH, Joe

BARNSTORMERS
Singles: 7-inch
CAPITOL ... 5-10 62

BARNUM, H.B. P&R '61
Singles: 7-inch
CAPITOL (Except 5932) ... 5-10 65-68
CAPITOL (5932 "Heartbreaker") ... 20-40 67
DECCA ... 3-5 71
ELDO ... 5-10 60-61
FIDELITY ... 5-10
IMPERIAL ... 8-12 58-64

MUN RAB 8-12 59
RCA (Except 8112) 8-12 61-63
RCA (8112 "It Hurts Too Much to Cry") 40-60 62
ULTRA SONIC 8-12 60
U.A. 3-5 73
Picture Sleeves
RCA (8112 "It Hurts Too Much to Cry") 50-75 62
LPs: 10/12-inch
CAPITOL 12-20 65
RCA 15-20 62
TROPIC ISLE 15-25 59
Also see NORMAN, Jimmy
Also see MAD LADS
Also see MARTY & Mellow Yellow Bunch
Also see ROBINS

BARON, Bill
Singles: 7-inch
YES (18 "Love Came to Me") 100-150 63

BARON, Billy
Singles: 7-inch
APT 10-20 58

BARON, Elliott
Singles: 7-inch
GOLDEN WORLD (11 "The Spare Rib") 15-25 64

BARON, Nancy
Singles: 7-inch
DIAMOND 4-8 63

BARON, Sandy
Singles: 7-inch
DUEL 5-10 62
LPs: 10/12-inch
A&M 8-10 72
ROULETTE 10-15 64
20TH FOX 8-10 77

BARON, Steve
Singles: 7-inch
BELL 3-5 70
LPs: 10/12-inch
PARAMOUNT 8-10 74

BARONAIRS
Singles: 7-inch
CARRIE 10-15 60

BARONE
Singles: 12-inch
SILVER BLUE 4-6 84

BARONE, Joe, & His Rockets
Singles: 78 rpm
POINT 5-10 56
Singles: 7-inch
POINT 10-15 56

BARONETS
Singles: 7-inch
VEE JAY 10-15 65

BARONS
Singles: 78 rpm
MODERN (818 "Forever") 25-50 51

BARONS
Singles: 78 rpm
DECCA 35-50 54
Singles: 7-inch
DECCA (29293 "Exactly Like You") 75-100 54
DECCA (48323 "Year and a Day") 75-100 54
Members: Leon Harrison; Roger Wainwright; Maurice Hicks; Luther Dixon.
Also see BUDDIES
Also see FOUR BUDDIES

BARONS / Mel Williams & Montclairs
EPs: 7-inch
DECCA 75-100 56
LPs: 10/12-inch
DECCA (8315 "He's a Rug Cutter") 100-150 56
Also see WILLIAMS, Mel

BARONS
Singles: 7-inch
DEMON (1520 "Fight") 10-15 59
KEY (1001 "If You Want a Little Lovin' ") 75-125 59

BARONS R&B '56
Singles: 78 rpm
IMPERIAL 25-75 55-56
Singles: 7-inch
IMPERIAL (5343 "Eternally Yours") 150-250 55
(Black vinyl.)
IMPERIAL (5343 "Eternally Yours") 400-600 55
(Purple vinyl. Promotional issue only.)
IMPERIAL (5359 "My Dream My Love") 200-300 55
(Red label.)
IMPERIAL (5359 "My Dream My Love") 50-100 55
(Black label.)
IMPERIAL (5370 "Cold Kisses") 100-200 55
IMPERIAL (5383 "So Long My Darling") 100-150 56
IMPERIAL (5397 "Don't Walk Out") 100-150 56
IMPERIAL (66057 "Silence") 10-15 64

BARONS
Singles: 7-inch
DART (126 "Lonely Loretta") 20-30 60
DART (134 "Perfect Love") 15-25 60

BARONS
("Formerly the Peppermints")
Singles: 7-inch
SOUL (837 "Money Don't Grow on Trees") 15-25 61
SPARTAN (400 "I've Been Hurt") ...15-25 61
SPARTAN (402 "Money Don't Grow on Trees") 15-25 61
(We're not yet certain whether Soul or Spartan is the first issue.)
Also see PEPPERMINTS

BARONS
Singles: 7-inch
BELLAIRE (103 "Bandit") 5-10 63

BARONS
Singles: 7-inch
EPIC (9586 "Pledge of a Fool") 25-35 63
EPIC (9747 "Remember Rita") ...200-300 63
EPIC (10093 "Pledge of a Fool") 10-15 66

BARONS
Singles: 7-inch
JAFES (985 "Try a Little Love with Me") 200-300 65
TENDER 5-10
Also see CHANCE, Larry
Also see LONNIE & CAROLLONS / Barons

BARONS
Singles: 7-inch
BROWNFIELD (1035 "Don't Burn It") 30-50 66
TORCH (101 "You're Gonna Cry") .15-20 65
TORCH (102 "I'll Never Be Happy") 10-15 65
TORCH (103 "Live and Die") 20-30 66

BARONS
Singles: 7-inch
MOHAWK (902 "Wild Weekend") ..10-20 65
MONOCLE (001 "Come to Me") 20-30 67

BARONS
Singles: 7-inch
BASF 3-5 73
RCA 10-20 67

BARONS
Singles: 7-inch
E&M (2901 "Dianna") 15-25
SUN-Y 10-15

BARONS
Singles: 7-inch
ESPIRIT (2210 "On This Earth") 10-15 60s
ETAH (102 "Clap Your Little Hands") 15-20 60s

BARONS LTD.
Singles: 7-inch
CHIMNEYVILLE (436 "Sympathy of Gratitude") 15-20 70
CHIMNEYVILLE (440 "Gypsy Read Your Cards for Me") 15-20 72

BAROOGA
(Barooga Bandit)
Singles: 7-inch
CAPITOL 3-4 79
LPs: 10/12-inch
CAPITOL 5-10 80

BAROQUE BROTHERS
Singles: 7-inch
BACK BEAT 10-20 66

BAROQUE ENSEMBLE OF MERSEYSIDE
LPs: 10/12-inch
ELEKTRA 12-20 64

BAROQUE INEVITABLE
Singles: 7-inch
COLUMBIA 3-6 66
LPs: 10/12-inch
COLUMBIA 12-15 66

BAROQUES
Singles: 7-inch
BAROQUE (4554 "I Will Not Touch You") 15-25 68
CHESS 10-15 67
LPs: 10/12-inch
BAROQUE (9005 "The Baroques") ..8-12 80s
CHESS (1516 "The Baroques") 40-60 67
Members: Rick Bieniewski; Jay Borkenhagen; Jacques Hutchinson; Dean Nimmer.
Also see MAJOR ARCANA

BAROQUES
Singles: 7-inch
VAN GOGH (2020 "Bad Girl") 20-30 67

BA-ROZ
Singles: 7-inch
PISCES 5-10 60s

BARR, Chuck
(With the Playboys)
Singles: 7-inch
ELSAN (1001 "Susie or Mary Lou") 30-50
RPC 10-15

BARR, Kathy
LPs: 10/12-inch
AVA 10-15 64

BARR, Phil
Singles: 7-inch
LAURIE 4-8 68

BARR, Rico, & Boston Barristers
Singles: 7-inch
BOSSTOWN (1113 "I Need You Babe") 15-25

BARR, Walt
LPs: 10/12-inch
MUSE 8-10 78-81

BARRA, Rocky
LPs: 10/12-inch
BARRATONE 10-15

BARRABAS LP '75
Singles: 7-inch
ATCO 3-5 75-76
LPs: 10/12-inch
ATCO 5-10 75-76
RCA 8-10 72-73
Members: Jo Tejada; Ricky Morales; Miquel Morales; Juan Videl; Daniel Louis; Ernest Duarte.

BARRACLOUGH, Elizabeth
Singles: 7-inch
BEARSVILLE 3-4 79
LPs: 10/12-inch
BEARSVILLE 5-10 79

BARRACUDA
Singles: 7-inch
RCA (9660 "The Dance at St. Francis") 10-20 68
RCA (9743 "Julie") 5-10 69
Picture Sleeves
RCA (9660 "The Dance at St. Francis") 20-35 68

BARRACUDA
Singles: 7-inch
20TH FOX 3-5 73

BARRACUDA D&D '83
Singles: 12-inch
EPIC 4-6 83
Singles: 7-inch
EPIC 3-4 83

BARRACUDAS
Singles: 7-inch
VOLT (123 "Yank Me Doodle") 10-20 64

BARRACUDAS
Singles: 7-inch
CANJO (104 "Boss Barracuda") 15-20 64
MFI 5-10
SMASH 10-20 68

BARRACUDAS
Singles: 7-inch
CUDA ("I Can't Believe") 10-20 66
(No selection number used.)
CUDA ("Days of a Quiet Sun") 8-12 69
(No selection number used.)
LPs: 10/12-inch
JUSTICE (143 "Plane View") 250-350 68

BARRACUDAS
Singles: 7-inch
ZUNDAK (101 "Baby Get Lost") 15-25 66

BARRACUDAS
Singles: 7-inch
THUNDERBIRD (877 "Saturn") 20-30 60s

BARRACUDAS
Singles: 7-inch
SATORI 10-20

BARRACUDAS
EPs: 7-inch
VOXX 3-5
LPs: 10/12-inch
VOXX 5-10

BARRAGE, Harold: see BURRAGE, Harold

BARRAN, Rob
Singles: 7-inch
SILVER STREAK (311 "Mother Goose Hop") 100-150 60

BARRELHOUSE SAMMY
(Willie Samuel)
Singles: 78 rpm
ATLANTIC (891 "Broke Down Engine Blues") 75-125 49
Also see McTELL, Blind Willie

BARRELL HOUSE BLOTT & LEE
(With the St. Louisians)
Singles: 7-inch
CHANCE (1136 "Brand New Man") 50-75 53
(Black vinyl.)
CHANCE (1136 "Brand New Man") 150-200 53
(Colored vinyl.)

BARRERE, Paul
Singles: 7-inch
MIRAGE 3-4 83
LPs: 10/12-inch
MIRAGE 5-10 83
Also see LITTLE FEAT

BARRETT, David
Singles: 7-inch
BROTHER 3-4 82
LP: 10/12-inch
BROTHER 5-8 83

BARRETT, Hugh
(With the Victors)
Singles: 7-inch
DYNAMIC SOUND (2003 "Moonlight Down by the River") 15-25 66
LUCKY FOUR (1015 "Devil's Love") 50-75 61
MADISON (164 "Got the Bull By the Horns") 30-50 61

BARRETT, Ray, & Expressions
Singles: 7-inch
EXPRESS 10-15

BARRETT, Richard P&R '58
(With the Chantels; with Sevilles)
Singles: 7-inch
ATLANTIC 5-10 62
CRACKERJACK 10-15 63
GONE 15-25 59
MGM 15-25 58
METRO 10-15 58
ORCHID (5004 "Come Softly to Me") 20-30
SEVILLE 10-15 60
20TH FOX 8-12 59
Also see CHANTELS
Also see IMPERIALS
Also see VALENTINES

BARRETT, Ron
(With the Duals; with Buckskins)
Singles: 7-inch
INFINITY (32 "Big Race") 10-15 62
JUGGY (321 "Big Race") 15-25 62
MAGNUM (715 "Louie Louie") 10-20 64

BARRETT, Rona
LPs: 10/12-inch
MR 15-20 74

BARRETT, Ruth, & Cynthia Smith
Singles: 7-inch
KICKING MULE 3-4 83
LPs: 10/12-inch
KICKING MULE 5-10 83

BARRETT, Susan
Singles: 7-inch
RCA (8888 "Grain of Sand") 10-20 66
RCA (9017 "Walking Happy") 10-20 66
RCA (9296 "What's It Gonna Be") 25-35 67
RCA (9384 "Sunny") 10-20 67
LPs: 10/12-inch
RCA (3738 "Susan Barrett") 20-40 67

BARRETT, Syd LP '74
Singles: 12-inch
CAPITOL 8-12 88
(Promotional only. With special cover.)
LPs: 10/12-inch
CAPITOL 5-10 74-88
HARVEST (Except 11314) 10-20 70-74
HARVEST (11314 "Madcap Laughs") 20-30 70
Members: Syd Barrett; Dave Gilmour; Roger Waters; Vic Seywell; Mike Ratledge.
Also see PINK FLOYD

BARRETT, Vance, & Col-Lee-Jets
Singles: 7-inch
NORTHWESTERN 15-20 58

BARRETTO, Ray P&R/R&B '63
Singles: 78 rpm
TICO (419 "El Watusi") 150-250 63
Singles: 7-inch
ASCOT 5-10 66
ATLANTIC 3-6 77-78
FANIA 5-15 68-72
RIVERSIDE 5-10 61
ROULETTE 3-4
TICO 5-10 63
U.A. 5-10 65-67
LPs: 10/12-inch
ATLANTIC 5-10 76-78
CTI 5-10 81
FANIA 5-10 68-73
FANTASY 8-10 73
RIVERSIDE 10-15 61-66
TICO 10-15 62-63
U.A. 8-15 65-67
Also see LYTLE, Johnny, & Ray Barretto

BARRI, Steve
(Steve Barrie)
Singles: 7-inch
RONA (1003 "Please Let It Be You") 30-50 61
RONA (1004 "Story of the Ring") ...20-40 61
RONA (1005 "Two Different Worlds") 20-40 62
RONA (1006 "Never Before") 20-40 62
TABB (103 "Flowers Mean Forgiveness") 20-30 60s
Also see FANTASTIC BAGGYS
Also see LIFEGUARDS
Also see RHYTHM HERITAGE
Also see STORYTELLERS

BARRIE, J.J.
Singles: 7-inch
JANUS 3-5 77

BARRIES
Singles: 7-inch
DI-NAN (101 "Loneliest Man in Town") 30-50 65
EMBER (1101 "Tonight-Tonight") ..40-60 64
VERNON (102 "Why Don't You Write Me") 50-75 63
Members: Joe Marturiello; Al Battista; Guy Villano; Jimmy O'Connor; Nick Delano; Andy Smith.
Also see CHOSEN FEW
Also see DELTONS

BARRINO BROTHERS
Singles: 7-inch
INVICTUS 3-5 70-72
LPs: 10/12-inch
INVICTUS 8-10 73

BARRIS, Chuck
(With the Gong Show)
Singles: 7-inch
CAPITOL 4-6 69
GONG SHOW (100 "Theme Theme") 5-10 78
Picture Sleeves
GONG SHOW (100 "Theme Theme") 8-10 78

BARRIS, Marti
Singles: 7-inch
CALENDAR (1 "Crazy Shoes") 10-15 60
KEEN (4016 "Sweet Talk") 10-20 59
KEEN (4018 "Ahbe Casabe") 15-25 58
WILCO (7 "Who's Gonna Walk Me Down the Aisle") 10-15

BARRIX, Billy
Singles: 78 rpm
CHESS (1662 "Cool off Baby") 500-1000 57
Singles: 7-inch
CHESS (1662 "Cool Off Baby") 2500-5000 57
SHREVEPORT ("Cool Off Baby") 7500-10000 57
(Selection number not known.)

BARRIX, Curley
Singles: 7-inch
DUNWICH 5-10 67

BARRON, Lonnie
Singles: 7-inch
SAGE 15-20 57

BARRON, Ronnie
Singles: 7-inch
SOUNDEX 10-20
WHEELER DEALERS (505 "The Grass Looks Greener") 5-8
Also see PRIME MINISTERS

BARRON KNIGHTS P&R '79
Singles: 7-inch
DECCA 5-10 67
EPIC (Except 9835) 3-5 79
EPIC (9835 "Pop Go the Workers") .5-10 65
MERCURY 3-5 72
Members: Barron Anthony; Peanut Langford; Butch Baker; Dave Ballinger; Duke D'mond.

BARRONS
Singles: 7-inch
ALITHIA 3-5 73
SUPERDOME 5-10

BARROW, Barbara: see SMITH, Mike, & Barbara Barrow

BARROW, Keith R&B '78
Singles: 12-inch
COLUMBIA 4-6 79
Singles: 7-inch
CAPITOL 3-4 80
COLUMBIA 3-4 76-79
JEWEL 3-5 73
LPs: 10/12-inch
CAPITOL 5-10 80
UMBIA 5-10 77
JEWEL 8-10 73

BARRY, Bolean
Singles: 7-inch
FABOR (137 "Long Sideburns") 50-75 56

BARRY, Claudja P&R/LP '78
Singles: 12-inch
CHRYSALIS 4-6 79
EPIC 4-6 86-87
PERSONAL 4-6 83
TSR 4-6 85
Singles: 7-inch
CHRYSALIS 3-4 79-84
EPIC 3-4 86-87
MIRAGE 3-4 82
PERSONAL 3-4 83
SALSOUL 3-4 77-78
LPs: 10/12-inch
CHRYSALIS 5-10 79-84
HANDSHAKE 5-10 82
SALSOUL 5-10 77-78

BARRY, Claudja, & Ronnie Jones
LPs: 10/12-inch
HANDSHAKE 5-10 82
Also see BARRY, Claudja

BARRY, Dave, & Daws Butler
Singles: 7-inch
CAPITOL 3-5 65
Also see BUTLER, Daws

BARRY, Dave, & Sara Berner
Singles: 78 rpm
RPM 8-12 56
Singles: 7-inch
RPM (469 "Out of This World with Flying Saucers") 15-20 56

BARRY, Gene
Singles: 7-inch
FELSTED 4-6 62
RCA 3-4 83
LPs: 10/12-inch
RCA 15-20 64

BARRY, Jack
(With Ray Charles Singers)
Singles: 78 rpm
DECCA 4-8
Singles: 7-inch
DECCA 4-8
Picture Sleeves
DECCA ("Huckleberry Finn") 8-15
Also see CHARLES, Ray, Singers

BARRY, Jan: see BERRY, Jan

BARRY, Jay
Singles: 7-inch
ABC-PAR 5-10 61

BARRY, Jeff
Singles: 7-inch
A&M 3-5 73
BELL 3-5 71
DECCA 15-20 60
RCA (7477 "It's Called Rock & Roll") 20-30 60
RCA (7797 "Lonely Lips") 15-25 60
RCA (7821 "Teen Quartet") 10-20 60
RED BIRD 5-10 65
LPs: 10/12-inch
A&M 10-12 73
Session: King Curtis.
Also see KING CURTIS
Also see RAINDROPS
Also see REDWOODS

BARRY, Joe P&R/R&B '61
Singles: 7-inch
ABC/DOT 3-4 77
JIN 10-15 60-62
NUGGET 4-8
SHOW-BIZ (2001 "I Can't Do Without You") 15-25 59
SMASH 4-8 61-62
Picture Sleeves
SMASH 10-15 61
LPs: 10/12-inch
ABC/DOT 5-10 77

BARRY, John, Orchestra P&R '65
Singles: 12-inch
CASABLANCA (20146 "The Chase") 10-12 78
Singles: 7-inch
A&M 3-4 83
CAPITOL (4200 series) 4-6 59
CAPITOL (5400 series) 3-4 86
COLUMBIA 3-5 65-70
EPIC 3-4 72
KING 3-6 61
MCA 3-4 85
MGM 3-5 66
MERCURY 3-6 64
20TH FOX 3-5 64
U.A. 3-6 63-65
W.B. 3-5 68
Picture Sleeves
U.A. 5-10 65
LPs: 10/12-inch
CAPITOL (2500 series) 10-15 66
COLUMBIA (1003 "Ready When You Are Mr. J.B.") 8-12 70
COLUMBIA (2493 "Great Movie Themes") 10-15 66
COLUMBIA (2708 "You Only Live Twice") 8-12 67
(Stereo.)
COLUMBIA (9293 "Great Movie Themes") 10-15 66
COLUMBIA (9508 "You Only Live Twice") 8-12 67
(Monaural.)
U.A. (91 "James Bond Tenth Anniversary") 8-12 72
U.A. (3424 "Goldfinger and Other Favorites") 8-12 65
U.A. (6424 "Goldfinger and Other Favorites") 10-12 65
For a complete listing of soundtracks by this artist, consult *The Official Price Guide to Movie/TV Soundtracks and Original Cast Albums.*
Also see ARMSTRONG, Louis
Also see BASIE, Count
Also see BASSEY, Shirley
Also see JONES, Tom
Also see MONRO, Matt
Also see SINATRA, Nancy

BARRY, Len P&R/R&B/LP '65
Singles: 7-inch
AMY 4-6 68-69
BUDDAH 3-5 72
CAMEO 5-10 64
DECCA 5-10 65-66
MCA 3-4 73-83
MERCURY 5-10 64
PARAMOUNT 3-5 73
PARKWAY 5-10 65
RCA 5-10 67-68
SCEPTER 4-6 69-70
EPs: 7-inch
DECCA (74720 "1-2-3") 8-15 65
(Juke box issue only.)
LPs: 10/12-inch
BUDDAH 10-15 72
CAMEO 20-25 64
DECCA 20-25 65
RCA 15-20 67
Also see DOVELLS

BARRY, Sandra
Singles: 7-inch
PARKWAY 4-8 66-67

BARRY, Tony
Singles: 7-inch
PARROT 4-8 67

BARRY & DEANS
Singles: 7-inch
ZIRKON 8-10 60

BARRY & HIGHLIGHTS
Singles: 7-inch
AIRMASTER (700 "Xmas Bell Rock") 25-45 60
BAYE (511 "Xmas Bell Rock") 40-60 60
(First issue.)
PLANET (1048 "The Wonderful Years") 500-750 61

BARRY & IN GROUP
Singles: 7-inch
MUSIC WORLD (105 "The Rooster") 10-20 65

BARRY & TAMERLANES P&R/R&B '63
Singles: 7-inch
VALIANT 8-12 63-65
LPs: 10/12-inch
A&M 10-15
VALIANT (406 "I Wonder What She's Doing Tonight") 50-75 63
Members: Barry DeVorzon; Terry Smith; Bodie Chandler.
Also see DE VORZON, Barry

BARRY & VI-COUNTS
Singles: 7-inch
FINE (102 "Love Forever") 500-750

BARRY SISTERS
Singles: 7-inch
CADENCE 4-8 55
Singles: 7-inch
ABC-PAR 4-8 65
CADENCE 5-10 55
ROULETTE 5-10 59
LP: 10/12-inch
ABC-PAR 10-15 65
ROULETTE 10-15 59
Members: Claire Barry; Merna Barry.

BARRY'S TRUCKERS
Singles: 7-inch
LULU 5-10 70s

BARRYS
Singles: 7-inch
SURPRISE 3-5 71

BARSANTI, Tom, & Invaders
Singles: 7-inch
DELTA (2134 "You Can't Sit Down") 20-30 65

BARTEL
LPs: 10/12-inch
PERCEPTION 8-12 71

BARTEL, Bob: see WINSTONS Featuring Bob Bartel

BARTEL, Eddie
Singles: 7-inch
MODERN SOUND (6900 "Steady Eddie") 8-12

BARTEL, Johnny, & Soul Masters
Singles: 7-inch
SOLID STATE (2514 "I Waited Too Long") 50-100 60s

BARTEL, Lou
(With Don Costa & Orchestra)
Singles: 78 rpm
APOLLO (473 "I Pray") 50-75 55
Singles: 7-inch
ABC-PAR (9877 "I'm Gonna Kiss My Baby Goodnight") 15-25 57
APOLLO (473 "I Pray") 75-125 55

BARTHOLOMEW, Dave R&B '50
Singles: 78 rpm
BAYOU 20-30 53
DECCA 20-40 51
DELUXE 10-20 47-50
IMPERIAL 20-50 50-57
JAX 10-20 50
KING 40-80 51-52
Singles: 7-inch
DECCA (48216 "Tra-La-La") 75-100 51
IMPERIAL (5210 "Who Drank the Beer While I Was in the Rear") 75-100 52
IMPERIAL (5249 "No More Black Nights") 75-100 51
IMPERIAL (5273 "Texas Hop") 75-125 53
IMPERIAL (5322 "Another Mule") 20-40 54
IMPERIAL (5350 "Every Night Every Day") 20-40 55
IMPERIAL (5373 "Shrimp and Gumbo") 20-30 56
IMPERIAL (5390 "Would You") 20-30 56
IMPERIAL (5408 "Lovin' You") 15-25 56
IMPERIAL (5500 thru 5800 series) 10-20 56-61
KING (4482 "Sweet Home Blues") 100-150 51
KING (4508 "In the Alley") 100-200 52
KING (4523 "Lawdy, Lawdy Lard") 100-150 52
(Black vinyl.)
KING (4523 "Lawdy, Lawdy Lard") 200-300 52
(Red vinyl.)
KING (4544 "My Ding-A-Ling") 100-200 52
KING (4559 "The Golden Rule") 50-100 52
KING (4585 "High Flying Woman") 50-100 53
LPs: 10/12-inch
IMPERIAL (9162/12076 "Fats Domino Presents Dave Bartholomew & His Great Big Band") 40-50 61
IMPERIAL (9217/12217 "New Orleans House Party") 40-50 63
Imperial 9000 numbers are mono, 12000 are stereo.
Also see ARCHIBALD
Also see DOMINO, Fats
Also see KING, Jewel
Also see RHODES, Todd
Also see LEWIS, Smiley

BARTLEY, Charlene
(With Al Donahue & His Orchestra)
Singles: 78 rpm
PRESIDENT 5-10 55
Singles: 7-inch
PRESIDENT 10-15 55

BARTLEY, Chris P&R/R&B '67
Singles: 7-inch
BUDDAH 3-5 71
MUSICOR 3-5 72
VANDO 4-8 67-68
LPs: 10/12-inch
VANDO 15-20 67

BARTLEY, Jack
Singles: 7-inch
KENCO 5-10 62

BARTOCK & LANSKY
Singles: 7-inch
MCA 3-4 82
LPs: 10/12-inch
MCA 5-10 82

BARTON, Bart
Singles: 7-inch
E&M 25-40

BARTON, Billy
(Billy Boy Barton)
Singles: 7-inch
BARTON (1007 "A Day Late and a Dollar Short") 25-50
BILLY BARTON ("Crazy Lover") 50-75
(No label name other than "Billy Barton" used.)
GULF REEF 10-15
KING 10-15
RADIO 10-20 58
SIMS 10-15 64
VIDOR (1007 "Crazy Lover") 30-50

BARTON, Eileen P&R '50
Singles: 78 rpm
CORAL 4-8 51-56
MERCURY 4-8 53
NATIONAL 5-10 50
Singles: 7-inch
CORAL 10-20 51-56
CREST 4-8 62
MGM 5-8 59
MERCURY 5-10 53
NATIONAL (9109 "Honey, Won't You Honeymoon with Me") 15-25 50
(Can someone confirm a 45 of National 9103, *If I Knew You Were Comin'*?)
NATIONAL (9112 "May I Take Two Giant Steps") 15-25 50
20TH FOX 3-6 63
U.A. (Except 206) 4-8 59
U.A. (206 "The Joke") 15-25 60
EPs: 7-inch
CORAL 5-10 54
LPs: 10/12-inch
CORAL 15-25 54
Also see BREWER, Teresa / Eileen Barton
Also see DESMOND, Johnny, Eileen Barton & McGuire Sisters

BARTON, Ernie
Singles: 7-inch
PHILLIPS INT'L (3528 "Stairway to Nowhere") 10-15 58
PHILLIPS INT'L (3541 "Open the Door Richard") 100-125 59
Also see JANES, Roland

BARTON, Fifi
Singles: 7-inch
ACE 5-10 60

BARTON, Lou Ann LP '82
Singles: 7-inch
ASYLUM 3-4 82
LPs: 10/12-inch
ANTONE'S 5-10 89
ASYLUM 8-12 82

BARTON, Rod
EPs: 7-inch
AIR (508 "Rock & Roll Blues") 200-300 50s

BARTON, Willene
Singles: 7-inch
SKY-MAC (1001 "Rice Pudding") 10-20 62

BARTZ, Gary R&B '77
(Gary Bartz Nu Troop)
Singles: 7-inch
ARISTA 3-4 80
CAPITOL 3-4 77-78
LPs: 10/12-inch
ARISTA 5-10 80
CAPITOL 5-10 77-78
CATALYST 5-10 76
MILESTONE 10-15 68-69
PRESTIGE 6-10 73-75
VEE JAY 5-10 78

BASCOM, Bernadette
Singles: 12-inch
PENGUIN 4-6 88
Singles: 7-inch
SOLIDARITY 3-4 83-85

BASCOMB, Dud
Singles: 7-inch
SAVOY (1580 "Geechie Blues") 15-25 59
SHARP (111 "Grumpy") 10-20 60

BASCOMB, Paul
(Bad Bascomb)
Singles: 78 rpm
ALERT 8-12 46
LONDON 5-10 51
MANOR 8-12 46-47
MERCURY 5-10 52
PARROT 10-20 54-55
STATES 5-10 52-53
Singles: 7-inch
MERCURY (8299 "Nona") 25-50 52
PARAMOUNT 3-5 73-74
PARROT (792 "Jan") 30-50 54
PARROT (817 "Alley B on Fifth Avenue") 30-50 55
STATES (102 "Blackout") 20-30 52
STATES (110 "Coquette") 20-30 52
STATES (121 "Body & Soul") 20-30 53
LPs: 10/12-inch
DELMARK 5-10 77
PARAMOUNT 8-10 73

BASCOMB, Paul, & Five Arrows / Gloria Valdez
Singles: 78 rpm
PARROT 50-100 55
Singles: 7-inch
PARROT (816 "Pretty Little Thing") 200-250 55
Also see BASCOMB, Paul

BASEBALL ("HOW TO" SERIES)
Singles: 7-inch
MARS CANDY (1 "How to Hit") 10-20 62
(Promotional issue, made for Mars Candy.)
MARS CANDY (2 "How to Pitch") 10-20 62
(Promotional issue, made for Mars Candy.)
MARS CANDY (3 "How to Field") 10-20 62
(Promotional issue, made for Mars Candy.)
Picture Sleeves
MARS CANDY (1 "How to Hit") 25-50 62
(Pictures MLB players, such as Stan Musial, Ernie Banks, Duke Snider and Ken Boyer. Promotional issues, made for Mars Candy.)
MARS CANDY (2 "How to Pitch") 25-50 62
(Pictures MLB players, such as Don Drysdale, Warren Spahn, Joey Jay and Johnny Padres. Promotional issues, made for Mars Candy.)
MARS CANDY (3 "How to Field") 25-50 62
(Pictures MLB players, such as Johnny Roseboro, Willie Mays, Gil Hodges and Don Hoak. Promotional issues, made for Mars Candy.)
Also see DRYSDALE, Don
Also see MAYS, Willie

BASEMAN, M.R., & Symbols / Marty & Symbols
Singles: 7-inch
GRAPHIC ARTS (1000 "Rip Van Winkle") 75-125 63
Session: Richie Cordell.
Also see CORDELL, Richie

BASEMENT WALL
Singles: 7-inch
SENATE (2109 "Never Existed") 25-35 68

BASH, Otto
Singles: 78 rpm
HIDS 5-10 56
RCA 10-15 56
Singles: 7-inch
HIDS ((2008 "My Babe") 10-15 56
RCA (6426 "Later Alligator") 15-25 56
RCA (6585 "The Elvis Blues") 15-25 56
Also see MARTIN, Janis / Otto Bash

BASIA P&R/LP '88
(Basia Trzetrzelewska)
Singles: 7-inch
EPIC 3-4 88-90
LPs: 10/12-inch
EPIC 5-8 88-90

BASIC BLACK LP '90
Singles: 7-inch
MOTOWN 3-4 90
LPs: 10/12-inch
MOTOWN 5-8 90

BASIC BLACK & PEARL
Singles: 7-inch
POLYDOR 3-5 75

BASIE, Count P&R '37
Singles: 78 rpm
COLUMBIA 5-10 43-51
CLEF 4-8 52-56
DECCA (Except 1300 thru 3000 series) 5-10 41-53
DECCA (1300 thru 3000 series) 8-15 37-40
MERCURY 4-8 52-53
OKEH 4-8 52
Singles: 7-inch
ABC-PAR 3-5 66
BRUNSWICK 3-5 67
CLEF 5-10 52-56
COLUMBIA (33000 series) 3-4 76
COLUMBIA (38000 & 39000 series) 5-10 50-51
COMMAND 3-5 67
DECCA 5-10 53
HAPPY TIGER 3-5 70
MERCURY 5-10 52-53
OKEH 5-10 52
REPRISE 3-6 63
ROULETTE (Except "SSR" series) 4-8 58-63
ROULETTE ("SSR" series) 8-15 59
(Stereo.)
U.A. 3-5 66
VERVE 3-5 60-67
EPs: 7-inch
BRUNSWICK 10-15 54
CAMDEN 8-15 58
CLEF 10-20 52-55
COLUMBIA 10-20 50
CORAL 10-20
DECCA 10-20 53
EPIC 10-20 55
RCA (Except 5000 series) 10-20 54
RCA (5000 series) 8-12 59
ROULETTE 8-12 58-60
VERVE 10-15 56
LPs: 10/12-inch
ABC 5-10 76
ABC-PAR 10-15 66
ACCORD 5-10 82-83
AMERICAN 15-25 57
BRIGHT ORANGE 5-10 73
BRUNSWICK (54000 series) 10-20 63-67
BRUNSWICK (58000 series) 25-35 54
(10-inch LPs.)
CAMDEN 10-20 58-60
CIRCLE 40-50 54
CLEF (120 "Count Basie & His Orchestra") 100-200 52
(10-inch LP.)
CLEF (148 "The Count Basie Big Band") 100-200 52
(10-inch LP.)
CLEF (164 "The Count Basie Sextet") 100-200 52
(10-inch LP.)
CLEF (626 "Dance Session") 50-100 53
CLEF (647 "Dance Session, Volume 2") 50-100 53
CLEF (633 "Basieana") 50-100 53
CLEF (666 "Basie") 50-100 54
CLEF (678 "Basie Swings - Joe Williams Sings") 50-100 55
CLEF (685 "Count Basie") 50-80 56
CLEF (700 series) 20-30 56
COLISEUM 8-12 67
COLUMBIA (700 & 900 series) 20-30 56-57
COLUMBIA (6079 "Dance Parade") 25-35 49
(10-inch LPs)
COLUMBIA (31000 series) 10-12 72
COMMAND 10-15 66-71
CORAL 10-20
CROWN ("Music Composed By Count Basie") 10-15 60s
(Selection number not known. Credits: "Members of the Count Basie Orchestra—B.B. King Guest Vocalist.")
DAYBREAK 6-10 71
DECCA (100 series) 15-25 64
DECCA (5000 series) 25-35 50-53
(10-inch LPs.)
DECCA (8000 series) 10-15 65
DOCTOR JAZZ 5-10 85-86
DOT 8-12 68
EMARCY (26000 series) 30-45 54
(10-inch LPs.)
EMUS 5-10 79
EPIC (1000 & 1100 series) 25-35 54
(10-inch LPs.)
EPIC 25-35 55
FLYING DUTCHMAN 6-10 71
HAPPY TIGER 8-12 70
HARMONY (7000 series) 10-20 60
HARMONY (11000 series) 5-10 67-69
IMPULSE 10-20 62
JAZZ PANORAMA 50-75 52
MCA 8-12 77-82
MGM 6-10 70
MFSL (129 "Basie Plays Hefti") 25-30 85
MFSL (237 "April in Paris") 20-25 94
MPS 10-12 72
MERCURY (25000 series) 25-35 50-51
(10-inch LPs.)
METRO 6-10 65-66
MOSAIC (135 "Complete Roulette Live Recordings of Count Basie") 100-125 90s
(12 LP boxed set. 7500 made.)
MOSAIC (149 "Complete Roulette Studio Recordings of Count Basie") 200-225 90s
(15 audiophile LP boxed set. 3500 made.)
OLYMPIC 5-10 74
PABLO 5-10 74-83
PAUSA 5-10 83
PRESTIGE 5-10 82
RCA (500 series) 10-15 65
RCA (1100 series) 25-35 54
REPRISE 10-15 63-65
ROULETTE (100 series) 12-18 71
ROULETTE (52003 thru 52106) 15-20 58-64
ROULETTE (52111/12/13 "The World of Count Basie") 30-40 64
(Three-disc set.)
SCEPTER 5-10 74
SOLID STATE 8-12 68
TRIP 5-10 75
U.A. 10-15 66
VSP 10-15 66
VANGUARD 15-25 57
VERVE 5-10 73-84
(Reads "Manufactured By MGM Record Corp.," or mentions either Polydor or Polygram at bottom of label.)
VERVE (2000 series) 20-30 56
(Reads "Verve Records, Inc." at bottom of label.)
VERVE (2500 series) 8-12 77-82
VERVE (2600 series) 5-10 82
VERVE (6000 series) 20-30 56
(Reads "Verve Records, Inc." at bottom of label.)
VERVE (8000 & 8100 series) 15-25 56-57
(Reads "Verve Records, Inc." at bottom of label.)
VERVE (8200 thru 8400) 15-20 58-61
(Reads "Verve Records, Inc." at bottom of label.)
VERVE (8500 thru 8600 series) 10-15 62-67
(Reads "MGM Records - a Division of Metro-Goldwyn-Mayer, Inc." at bottom of label.)
VERVE (8700 series) 6-10 69
(Reads "MGM Records - a Division of Metro-Goldwyn-Mayer, Inc." at bottom of label.)
VERVE (68000 series) 10-20 63-65
(Reads "MGM Records - a Division of Metro-Goldwyn-Mayer, Inc." at bottom of label.)
Also see BARRY, John
Also see BENNETT, Tony, & Count Basie

Also see BREWER, Teresa, & Count Basie
Also see CROSBY, Bing, & Count Basie
Also see DAVIS, Sammy, Jr., & Count Basie
Also see FITZGERALD, Ella, & Count Basie
Also see JACQUET, Illinois, & Count Basie
Also see KING, B.B.
Also see MILLS BROTHERS, & COUNT BASIE
Also see PRYSOCK, Arthur, & Count Basie
Also see SINATRA, Frank, & Count Basie
Also see STARR, Kay, & Count Basie
Also see WILLIAMS, Joe
Also see WILSON, Jackie, & Count Basie
Also see YOUNG, Lester

BASIE, Count, & Tony Bennett
EPs: 7-inch
ROULETTE 6-10 59
LPs: 10/12-inch
ROULETTE 10-20 59-63
Also see BENNETT, Tony

BASIE, Count, & Billy Eckstine
Singles: 7-inch
ROULETTE (Except "SSR" series) ... 4-8 59
ROULETTE ("SSR" series) 8-15 59
LPs: 10/12-inch
ROULETTE 15-20 59
Also see ECKSTINE, Billy

BASIE, Count, & Duke Ellington
Singles: 7-inch
COLUMBIA 4-6 62
LPs: 10/12-inch
ACCORD 5-10 82
COLUMBIA 15-20 62
Also see ELINGTON, Duke

BASIE, Count, & Maynard Ferguson
LPs: 10/12-inch
ROULETTE 10-20 65
Also see FERGUSON, Maynard

BASIE, Count, & Benny Goodman
LPs: 10/12-inch
ABC 8-12 73
VANGUARD 15-25 59
Also see GOODMAN, Benny

BASIE, Count, & Oscar Peterson
LPs: 10/12-inch
PABLO 5-10 75-83
VERVE 15-20 59
Also see PETERSON, Oscar

BASIE, Count, & Sarah Vaughan
LPs: 10/12-inch
ROULETTE 15-20 61

BASIE, Count, Sarah Vaughan & Joe Williams
Singles: 7-inch
ROULETTE 4-8 60
LPs: 10/12-inch
ROULETTE 15-20 60
Joe Williams is also a featured vocalist on many of the recordings included in the section of listings for Count Basie.
Also see BASIE, Count
Also see VAUGHAN, Sarah

BASIL
Singles: 7-inch
GRT 8-12

BASIL, Toni *P&R/LP '82*
Singles: 12-inch
CHRYSALIS 4-6 82-85
Singles: 7-inch
A&M (791 "Breakaway") 100-200 66
CHRYSALIS 3-4 82-85
CHRYSALIS/VIRGIN (2638 "Mickey") 4-6 81
(With Radialchoice logo.)
Picture Sleeves
CHRYSALIS 3-4 82-84
LPs: 10/12-inch
CHRYSALIS 5-10 82-84

BASILE, Vinnie
Singles: 7-inch
DAVY JONES 8-10 67

BASIN STREET BOYS
Singles: 78 rpm
EXCLUSIVE 20-40 46-49
FLAME (1002 "I Sold My Heart to the Junkman") 20-30 53
Also see BROWN, Charles / Basin Street Boys
Also see WILSON, Ormond, & Basin Street Boys

BASIN ST. SIX
Singles: 7-inch
MERCURY 5-10 50s

BASKERVILLE, Hayes, & Five Chestnuts / Norveen Baskerville & Five Chestnuts
Singles: 7-inch
DRUM (003 "Billy") 300-500 58
Also see FIVE CHESTNUTS

BASKERVILLE, Marvin, & Five Chestnuts
Singles: 7-inch
DRUM (001 "Chapel in the Moonlight") 300-500 58

BASKERVILLE, Marvin, & Five Chestnuts / Hayes Baskerville & Five Chestnuts
Singles: 7-inch
DRUM (002 "Chi Chi") 200-400 58
Also see BASKERVILLE, Marvin, & Five Chestnuts

BASKERVILLE, Norveen, & Admirations
Singles: 7-inch
X-TRA (100 "Gonna Find My Pretty Baby") 40-60 50s
Also see BASKERVILLE, Hayes, & Five Chestnuts / Norveen Baskerville & Five Chestnuts

BASKERVILLE HOUNDS *P&R '69*
Singles: 7-inch
AVCO EMBASSY (4504 "Hold Me") .. 4-6 69
BUDDAH 5-10 67
DOT 5-10 67
TEMA (135 "Hold Me") 8-12 68
TEMA (125 "Debbie") 8-12 66
TEMA (128 "Space Rock") 8-12 67
TEMA (131 "Christmas Is Here") 8-12 67
LPs: 10/12-inch
DOT 15-20 67
Also see TULU BABIES

BASKIN & COPPERFIELD
Singles: 7-inch
AVALANCHE 3-5 71

BASS, Fontella *P&R/R&B '65*
Singles: 7-inch
ABC 3-4 74
BOBBIN (134 "Brand New Love") .. 10-15 62
CHECKER 5-10 65-66
CHESS 3-8 75-85
ERIC 3-5 73
GUSTO 3-4
MCA 3-4 83
PAULA 3-5 74
PRANN (5005 "My Good Lovin' ") ... 8-12 63
SONJA (2006 "Poor Little Fool") 5-8 70
(First issue credits Fontella Bass & Tina Turner.)
LPs: 10/12-inch
CHECKER (2997 "New Look") 15-25 66
CHESS 5-10 70s
PAULA (2203 "Free") 8-12 71

BASS, Fontella, & Bobby McClure *P&R/R&B '65*
Singles: 7-inch
CHECKER 5-10 65-66
Also see McCLURE, Bobby

BASS, Fontella, & Tina Turner
Singles: 7-inch
VESUVIUS (1002 "Poor Little Fool") 15-20 63
(Reissue on Sonja credits only Fontella Bass.)
Also see BASS, Fontella
Also see TURNER, Tina

BASS, Hulan
Singles: 7-inch
BRILL (100 "Little Bitty Man") 20-30

BASS, Leon
Singles: 7-inch
TUNE (209 "Come on Baby") 30-50 60
WHIRL-AWAY (1058 "Country Hicks") 40-60

BASS, Sam D. *C&W '80*
Singles: 7-inch
3J 3-5 80
Also see McAULIFFE, Leon

BASSETT, Tony
Singles: 7-inch
ORCHID (873 "Rockin' Little Mama") 25-50 61

BASSETT HAND
Singles: 7-inch
JOSIE 4-8 65

BASSETTE, John
EPs: 7-inch
TINKERTOO ("Weed & Wine") 8-10
(No number shown.)
Members: John Bassette; Willis Lyman; Dan Mahoney; Norman Tischler; David Krauss.

BASSEY, Shirley *P&R/LP '65*
Singles: 78 rpm
COLUMBIA 5-10 57
Singles: 12-inch
U.A. 4-6 79
Singles: 7-inch
COLUMBIA 5-10 57
EPIC 4-8 59
MGM 3-6 60
U.A. 3-5 61-79
LPs: 10/12-inch
EPIC 10-20 62
LIBERTY 4-6 81-82
MGM 12-20 60
PHILIPS 10-15 65
SPRINGBORAD 5-10 75
U.A. 4-6 80
(With "LM" prefix.)
U.A. 10-15 62-72
(With "UAL" or "UAS" prefix.)
U.A. 5-10 73-79
(With "UA-LA" prefix.)
Also see BARRY, John
Also see NELSON, Willie / Nat "King" Cole / Johnny Mathis / Shirley Bassey

BASSMEN
Singles: 7-inch
GALLANTRY (745 "Last Laugh") ... 15-25
VAUGHN LTD (101 "I Need You") .20-30

BASTILE, Jimmy
Singles: 7-inch
CAPITOL 10-15

BASTILLES
Singles: 7-inch
PHILIPS (40453 "Vengeance") 10-20 67

BASTOS, J.
Singles: 7-inch
GUYDEN 3-5 71
SIRE 3-5 73

BATAAN
Singles: 7-inch
EPIC 3-6 75
UPTITE 5-10 70
LPs: 10/12-inch
EPIC 8-10 75

BATAAN, Joe *R&B '69*
(With the Mestizo Band)
Singles: 7-inch
FANIA 5-15
SALSOUL 3-4 80
UPTITE 3-5 69
LPs: 10/12-inch
SALSOUL 5-10 80-81

BATCH
Singles: 7-inch
GROOVE SOUP 8-12 60s

BATCHLER, Willie: see BATCHELOR, Willie

BATCHELOR, Harry
Singles: 7-inch
ROULETTE 5-8 69

BATCHELOR, Willie
(Willie Batchler)
Singles: 7-inch
FORMULA (101 "I Need a Hit") 15-25 60s
GIBBS (101 "Baby if You Do Right") 10-15

BATDORF, John
LPs: 10/12-inch
20TH FOX 5-10 81
Also see SILVER

BATDORF & RODNEY *LP '72*
Singles: 7-inch
ARISTA 3-5 75
ASYLUM 3-5 72
ATLANTIC 3-5 71-72
LPs: 10/12-inch
ATLANTIC 8-12 71
ARISTA 6-10 75
ASYLUM 8-10 72
Members: John Batdorf: Mark Rodney.
Also see BATDORF, John

BATEMAN, Carroll
Singles: 7-inch
TWIN TOWN 20-25 67
Also see CARROL, Evans, & Tempos

BATEMAN, Gil
Singles: 7-inch
JERDEN 10-20 65
PANORAMA 10-20 65
PICCADILLY 10-20 66

BATEMON, June
(June Bateman)
Singles: 78 rpm
HOLIDAY (2606 "Yes I Will") 20-30 57
Singles: 7-inch
ARRAWAK 10-15
CLAMIKE 4-8
FURY (1030 "Believe Me Darling") 20-25 60
HOLIDAY (2606 "Yes I Will") 25-45 57
ODESSA 10-15 61
Also see MARQUIS

BATES, Deacon L.J.
(Blind Lemon Jefferson)
Singles: 78 rpm
PARAMOUNT (12386 "I Want to Be Like Jesus in My Heart") 150-200 26
(Also issued as by Deacon Jackson.)
Also see JACKSON, Deacon
Also see JEFFERSON, Blind Lemon

BATES, Lee
Singles: 7-inch
INSTANT 10-20 70
SANSU (1002 "Shake, Baby, Shake") 10-20

BATES, Lefty Guitar
(With "His Recording Band")
Singles: 7-inch
APEX (951 "Rock Alley") 15-25 59
APEX (952 "Ena") 15-25 59
BOXER (203 "Say Whoa") 10-20
MAD (1011 "Back Ground") 25-35 58
Also see PALM, Horace M., with Lefty Bates Orchestra
Also see FOSTER BROTHERS
Also see MOROCCOS

BATH-HOUSE BRASS
Singles: 7-inch
CAPITOL 3-5 68
Member: Ken Handler.

BATMAN
Singles: 7-inch
SALSOUL 3-5 75
LPs: 10/12-inch
SALSOUL 5-10 75

BATMAN, Elmo
Singles: 7-inch
GRANITE (519 "I'm a Spy for the F.B.I.") 5-10 75

BATON ROUGE *LP '90*
LPs: 10/12-inch
ATLANTIC 5-8 90

BATORS, Stiv
(With the Dead Boys)
Singles: 12-inch
BOMP 5-10 87
Singles: 7-inch
BOMP 3-4 79
EPs: 7-inch
BOMP 5-10 79
LPs: 10/12-inch
BOMP 8-10 80
Also see DEAD BOYS
Also see LORDS of the NEW CHURCH

BATS
Singles: 7-inch
FLAME (5155 "Batmobile") 20-25 64
HBR 5-10 65
Member: Gene Moles.
Also see MOLES, Gene

BATT, Mike
Singles: 7-inch
EPIC 3-4 83
LPs: 10/12-inch
EPIC 5-10 83

BATTALION TWEED
Singles: 7-inch
MR. G. 4-8 68

BATTAN
Singles: 7-inch
SALSOUL 3-4 75

BATTAN, Joe
Singles: 7-inch
UPTITE 3-6 69

BATTEAUX
Singles: 7-inch
A&M 3-4 76
COLUMBIA 3-5 73
LPs: 10/12-inch
A&M 5-10 76
COLUMBIA 8-10 73
Members: David Batteaux; Robin Batteaux.
Also see APPALOOSA
Also see PIERCE ARROW

BATTEN, Cecelia
Singles: 7-inch
COLONIAL 5-10 57

BATTERED ORNAMENTS
LPs: 10/12-inch
HARVEST 15-25 70
Members: Chris Spedding; Pete Brown.

BATTERY PARK
Singles: 7-inch
VINTAGE 4-6 72-73

BATTIN, Skip
(Skip Battyn & Groop; Clyde Battin; Skip Batten Combo)
Singles: 7-inch
AURORA (159 "Dating Game") 10-15 66
GROOVE (0055 "Searchin") 25-35 64
GROOVE (0065 "What's Mine Is Mine") 25-35 65
INDIGO (143 "Can't Stop Twistin' ") 10-20 62
MAY (108 "Twister") 10-20 62
SIGNPOST 4-6 73
LPs: 10/12-inch
SIGNPOST 8-10 72
Also see BYRDS
Also see FLYING BURRITO BROTHERS
Also see NEW RIDERS of the Purple Sage
Also see SKIP & FLIP
Also see VINCENT, Gene

BATTISTE, Rose
Singles: 7-inch
GOLDEN WORLD (33 "Sweetheart Darling") 15-25 66
REVILOT (204 "Hit & Run") 40-60 66
REVILOT (206 "Come Back in a Hurry") 15-25 66
RIC-TIC 10-15 65
THELMA (102 "Someday") 75-125 64

BATTLE, Jean
Singles: 7-inch
CLINTONE 5-8
RED LITE 3-5 72

BATTLE, P.R.
Singles: 7-inch
A&M 3-4 77

BATTS, Ray
Singles: 78 rpm
EXCELLO (2028 "Stealin' Sugar") .. 15-25 54
Singles: 7-inch
EXCELLO (2028 "Stealin' Sugar") 40-60 54

BATTYN, Skip: see BATTIN, Skip

BAUER, Kathy *C&W '83*
Singles: 7-inch
NSD 3-4 83

BAUGH, Phil *C&W '65*
Singles: 7-inch
CREST 5-10 62
ERA 4-6 69
LONGHORN 4-6 65
LPs: 10/12-inch
ERA (801 "California Guitar") 10-15 69
LONGHORN (002 "Country Guitar") 30-50 65
TORO (502 "Country Guitar II") 15-25 74
Also see ANNETTE
Also see NASHVILLE SUPERPICKERS

BAUHAUS *LP '89*
Singles: 7-inch
A&M 3-4 83
LPs: 10/12-inch
A&M 5-10 83
BEGGARS BANQUET 8-12 89
Members: Daniel Ash; David Jor; Kevin Haskins.
Also see LOVE & ROCKETS

BAUM, Allen
(Alden Bunn)
Singles: 78 rpm
RED ROBIN 50-100 53
Singles: 7-inch
RED ROBIN (124 "My Kinda Woman") 200-300 53
Also see BUNN, Allen

BAUM, Bruce "Baby Man"
Singles: 7-inch
HORN 3-4 81
LPs: 10/12-inch
HORN 5-10 81

BAUMANN, Ace, & Crossfires
Singles: 7-inch
LEAF (6238 "All American Twister") 8-12 62
Members: Ace Baumann; Phil Alagna; Denny Geyer; Harry Jay.
Also see CROSSFIRES

BAUMANN, Peter *D&D '83*
Singles: 12-inch
PORTRAIT 4-6 82-83
Singles: 7-inch
PORTRAIT 3-4 83
LPs: 10/12-inch
PORTRAIT 5-10 82-83
VIRGIN 8-10 77
Also see TANGERINE DREAM

BAUTISTA
(Roland Bautista)
Singles: 7-inch
ABC 3-4 77
LPs: 10/12-inch
ABC 5-10 77-79

BAXTER
Singles: 7-inch
PARAMOUNT 3-5 73
LPs: 10/12-inch
PARAMOUNT 8-10 73

BAXTER, Betty: see BAXTER, Harmon

BAXTER, Betty Jo
Singles: 7-inch
VIK (0337 "I Cross My Heart") 10-20 57

BAXTER, Duke *P&R '69*
Singles: 7-inch
MERCURY 3-5 70
VMC 5-10 69
LPs: 10/12-inch
VMC 15-20 69

BAXTER, Harmon / Betty Baxter
(With the Baxters)
Singles: 7-inch
HI FI (103 "Wild Bill") 25-50 64

BAXTER, Les *P&R '51*
(With His Orchestra & Chorus; Les Baxter Balladeers)
Singles: 78 rpm
CAPITOL 3-6 50-57
Singles: 7-inch
A/S 3-4 70
CAPITOL 4-8 50-61
GNP 3-5 64-69
LINK 3-5 64
REPRISE 3-5 62-63
Picture Sleeves
REPRISE (20120 "Theme from *The Manchurian Candidate*" 40-60 62
(A Frank Sinatra collectible, as his name is shown on this cover.)
EPs: 7-inch
CAPITOL 5-10 51-56
GNP 5-10 67-69
RCA 5-10 52
REPRISE 4-8 64
LPs: 10/12-inch
ALSHIRE 5-10 70-85
AMERICAN INT'L (1028 "Dunwich Horror") 20-25 70
(Soundtrack.)
CAPITOL (200 thru 900 series) 10-20 51-58
CAPITOL (1000 thru 1800 series) 5-15 58-63
CAPITOL (11000 series) 4-6 77-79
GNP 5-10 69
RCA 15-25 52
REPRISE 10-15 62-63
VARESE SARABANDE (81103 "Dunwich Horror") 8-10 79
Also see CHEERS
Also see CROSBY, Bing, & Bob Hope
Also see WAKELY, Jimmy

BAXTER, Ronnie
Singles: 7-inch
GONE (5036 "Gates of Heaven") .. 20-30 58
MARK-X (8001 "It's Magic") 5-10 59

BAXTER, Terry
LPs: 10/12-inch
COLUMBIA.. 8-10

BAXTER, BAXTER & BAXTER *C&W '81*
Singles: 7-inch
A.M.I.. 3-4 83
SUN.. 3-5 81
Members: Duncan Baxter; Mark Baxter; Rick Baxter.

BAXTER'S CHAT
Singles: 7-inch
PEARCE (5812 "Don't Come Around Today")..15-25

BAY BOPS
Singles: 7-inch
CORAL (61975 "Follow the Rock")..30-40 58

BAY BROTHERS
Singles: 7-inch
MILLENNIUM 3-4 80-82

BAY CITY FIVE
Singles: 78 rpm
JAGUAR..50-75 54
Singles: 7-inch
JAGUAR (3001 "Basin Street Blues")..150-250 54
JAGUAR (3002 "Oh Marie").......150-250 54

BAY CITY ROLLERS *P&R/LP '75*
Singles: 7-inch
ARISTA 3-4 75-78
BELL 3-5 72-76
FLASHBACK 3-4 80
Picture Sleeves
ARISTA 3-4 75-77
LPs: 10/12-inch
ARISTA 5-10 75-79
BELL 6-12 74
Members: Les McKeowen; Eric Faulkner; Stuart Wood; Alan Longmuir; Derek Longmuir; Billy Lyall; Pat McGlynn; Ian Mitchell.
Also see ROLLERS
Also see STONE, Rosetta

BAY RIDGE
Singles: 7-inch
ATLANTIC 4-6 67

BAY RIDGE BAND
LPs: 10/12-inch
MUSICOR 5-10 78

BAYER, Carole: see SAGER, Carole Bayer

BAYETE
(Todd Cochran)
Singles: 7-inch
PRESTIGE 3-5 72-73
LPs: 10/12-inch
PRESTIGE 8-10 72-73

BAYLANDERS
(Journeymen)
Singles: 7-inch
IONA (1115 "Surfers Rule") 15-25 63
(Also issued as by the Journeymen.)
Also see JOURNEYMEN

BAYMEN
Singles: 7-inch
MERRI (6000 "Bonzai").................10-20 63
Members: Bob Knight; Robert Edwards; Fred Buxton.
Also see EDDIE & SHOWMEN

BAYNOTES
Singles: 7-inch
PHOENIX (1 "The Swingin' A's")....... 4-8 70s
Picture Sleeves
PHOENIX (1 "The Swingin' A's")..... 5-10 70s

BAYOU, Billy
Singles: 7-inch
E&M (1632 "Rattlesanke")..............10-15 62

BAYOU BOYS
Singles: 78 rpm
CHECKER (765 "Dinah") 50-75 52
Singles: 7-inch
CHECKER (765 "Dinah") 75-100 52

BAYSIDERS
Singles: 7-inch
EVEREST... 5-10 60
LPs: 10/12-inch
EVEREST (5124 "Over the Rainbow")..50-70 61

BAYTOVENS
Singles: 7-inch
BELFAST 10-15

BAZIL BLAVIS CHIOTA: see CHIOTA, Bazil Blavis

BAZOOKA
Singles: 7-inch
BANG.. 4-8 68
WHITE WHALE 3-6 70

BAZUKA *P&R/R&B '75*
(Tony Camillo's Bazuka)
Singles: 7-inch
A&M 3-5 75
VENTURE 3-4 79
LPs: 10/12-inch
A&M 5-10 75

BAZZELL, Jimmy
Singles: 7-inch
ACE.. 4-8 62

BEACH, Bill
Singles: 7-inch
KING (4940 "Peg Pants")..........100-150 56

BEACH, Freddie
Singles: 7-inch
SUMMIT (222 "Little Red Sports Car")..10-20 50s

BEACH, Scott
Singles: 7-inch
CAPTAIN.. 4-8

BEACH BOYS
Singles: 7-inch
KAPP.. 3-5 59

BEACH BOYS *P&R/LP '62*
Singles: 12-inch
CAPITOL (9711 "Rock & Roll to the Rescue")..10-15 86
(Promotional issue only.)
CAPITOL (9796 "California Dreamin' ")..10-15 86
(Promotional issue only.)
CAPITOL (15234 "Rock & Roll to the Rescue")..5-10 86
CARIBOU (2080 "Getcha Back") ...10-15 86
(Promotional issue only.)
CARIBOU (9028 "Here Comes the Night")..5-10 79
CARIBOU (9028 "Here Comes the Night")..20-25 79
(Promotional issue only.)
Singles: 7-inch
BROTHER..5-10 67
CANDIX (301 "Surfin' ") 200-250 61
(No mention of Era distribution.)
CANDIX (301 "Surfin' ") 150-250 61
(Label reads "Distributed by Era Record Sales Inc.")
CANDIX (331 "Surfin' ")...............125-175 62
CAPITOL (2000 series except 2765)..5-10 67-69
CAPITOL (2765 "Cottonfields")........15-20 70
CAPITOL (3924 "Surfin' USA")......... 3-5 74
(Some copies indicate "Stereo" but play mono; others indicate "Mono" but play stereo.)
CAPITOL (4000 series except 4880)..8-12 62-63
CAPITOL (4880 "Ten Little Indians")..15-20 62
CAPITOL (5000 series, except 5096 & 5312)..5-10 63-66
(Orange/yellow labels.)
CAPITOL (5096 "Little Saint Nick") 12-18 63
CAPITOL (5312 "The Man with All the Toys")..12-18 63
CAPITOL (5000 series)................ 3-4 81-86
(Black labels.)
CAPITOL (6000 series)................5-10 67-68
CAPITOL (44000 series)................ 3-4 89
CARIBOU 3-5 79-86
ODE '70...12-15 71
REPRISE (0101 thru 0107")............. 4-6 73
("Back to Back" reissue series.)
REPRISE (0894 "Add Some Music to Your Day")..5-10 70
REPRISE (0929 "Slip On Through")..5-10 70
REPRISE (0957 "Tears in the Morning")..12-15 70
REPRISE (0998 "Cool, Cool Water")..60-75 71
REPRISE (1015 "Long Promised Road")..20-25 71
REPRISE (1047 "Long Promised Road")..20-25 71
REPRISE (1058 "Surf's Up")..........45-50 71
REPRISE (1091 "Cuddle Up").........25-30 72
REPRISE (1101 "Marcella")............25-30 72
REPRISE (1138 "Sail on Sailor")..... 8-12 73
REPRISE (1156 "California Saga")..10-15 73
REPRISE (1310 "I Can Hear Music")..3-5 74
REPRISE (1321 "Child of Winter").20-30 74
REPRISE (1325 "Sail on Sailor")......5-10 75
REPRISE (1336 "Wouldn't It Be Nice")..5-10 75
REPRISE (1354 thru 1394)............. 3-5 76-78
X (301 "Surfin'")...........................300-500 61
Promotional Singles
CAPITOL (2360 "Bluebirds over the Mountain")..15-20 69
CAPITOL (2936/7 "Salt Lake City")..175-200 65
CAPITOL (4093 "Little Honda")......15-20 75
CAPITOL CUSTOM ("Spirit of America")..125-150 63
CARIBOU (557 "Here Comes the Night")..10-12 79
(Blue vinyl.)
CARIBOU (557 "Here Comes the Night")..50-60 79
(Special Edition autographed copies. Blue vinyl.)
CARIBOU (9026 "Here Comes the Night")..10-15 79
EVA-TONE (0300 "Living Doll") 3-4 87
(Barbie Doll promotional issue.)
ODE '70 (66016 "Wouldn't It Be Nice-Live Version")..35-40 71
REPRISE (557-2 "Sail on Sailor")..75-100 73
REPRISE (0998 "Cool, Cool Water")..45-50 71
REPRISE (1310 "I Can Hear Music")..30-50 74
WHAT'S IT ALL ABOUT (449/450 & 507/508)..20-25
(Public service radio station issues. Program disc 449/450 has the Beach Boys on one side and Dr. Hook on the flip. 507/508 features the Beach Boys on one side and the Rolling Stones on the other.)
Note: Promo singles not listed separately are presumed to fall into the same price range as commercial issues.
Picture Sleeves
BROTHER (1001 "Heroes and Villains")..40-80 67
CAPITOL (1001 "Heroes and Villains")..250-500 66
(Canadian edition. Made in the US before it was known that the single would not be on Capitol, then exported to Canada. When issued there, the Capitol number, 5826, was blocked out and the Canadian number added.)
CAPITOL (2068 "Darlin' ")..............10-20 67
CAPITOL (4777 "Surfin' Safari") 20-30 62
CAPITOL (4880 "Ten Little Indians")..75-100 62
CAPITOL (5118 "Fun, Fun, Fun") ..10-20 63
CAPITOL (5174 "I Get Around") 10-20 64
CAPITOL (5245 "When I Grow Up")..10-20 64
CAPITOL (5306 "Dance, Dance, Dance")..10-20 64
CAPITOL (5372 "Do You Wanna Dance")..10-20 65
CAPITOL (5395 "Help Me Rhonda")..10-20 65
CAPITOL (5464 "California Girls") 10-20 65
CAPITOL (5540 "The Little Girl I Once Knew")..10-20 65
CAPITOL (5561 "Barbara Ann").100-125 65
CAPITOL (5595 "Rock 'N' Roll to the Rescue")..3-5 86
CAPITOL (5602 "Sloop John B.")...10-20 66
CAPITOL (5676 "Good Vibrations")..10-20 66
CAPITOL (5826 "Heroes and Villains")..400-800 66
(Not issued with the Brother disc, which has its own sleeve. Made before it was known that the single would not be on Capitol, then exported to Canada and elsewhere – some of which worked their way back to the US.)
CARIBOU..3-6 79-86
EPs: 7-inch
BROTHER (1 "Radio Spot Backing Tracks")..225-250 73
(Promotional issue only.)
CAPITOL (189 "Best of the Beach Boys")..15-20 66
(With "LLP" prefix. Juke box issue only.)
CAPITOL (1981 "Surfer Girl") 45-55 63
CAPITOL (2027 "Shut Down, Vol. 2")..45-55 64
CAPITOL (2269 "The Beach Boys Today")..50-75 65
(Juke box issue only.)
CAPITOL (2293/94 "Beach Boys' Party")..125-150 65
(Juke box issue only.)
CAPITOL (2545 "Best of the Beach Boys")..50-75 66
(With "DU" prefix. Juke box issue only.)
CAPITOL (2545 "Best of the Beach Boys")..15-20 66
CAPITOL (2754/55 "Brian Wilson Introduces Selections")..350-375 64
(Promotional issue only. Includes selections from *Beach Boys Concert* and *Beach Boys Songbook.*)
CAPITOL (5267 "4 by the Beach Boys")..35-45 66
REPRISE (2118 "Mount Vernon and Fairway")..8-10 73
(Originally packaged with Reprise LP 2118, "Holland.")
ROCK SHOPPE ("The Beach Years")..75-100 75
(Demo disc for "A Six Hour Radio Special." Also contains excerpts by Jan & Dean, Dick Dale, and the Surfaris. Narrated by Roger Christian. Promotional issue, pressed in a quantity of 200 copies.)
SUB-POP ("I Just Wasn't Made for These Times")..5-8 96
(Three track disc.)
W.B. (422 "Sunflower Promotional Spots")..100-125 70
W.B. (534 "Vote '72")....................35-45 72
(Promotional issue only.)
WHAT'S IT ALL ABOUT 20-25 70s
(Promotional issue only.)
LPs: 10/12-inch
ACCORD..5-10 83
AUDIO FIDELITY (335 "Beach Boys")..8-12 84
(Picture disc.)
AXIS/CAPITOL (8 "Their 22 Greatest Hits")..6-12 73
BROTHER (9001 "Smiley Smile")..15-20 67
BROTHER/SUNKIST (9431 "25 Years of Good Vibrations")..10-20 86
(Includes tour booklet. Sold at Beach Boys concerts.)
CAPITOL (133 "20/20")..................10-20 69
CAPITOL (133 "20/20")..................30-35 69
(With "SKAO-8" prefix. Capitol Record Club issue.)
CAPITOL (253 "Close Up")............35-40 69
CAPITOL (442 "Good Vibrations") .20-25 70
CAPITOL (500 "All Summer Long"/"California Girls")..8-12 70
CAPITOL (701 "Dance, Dance, Dance"/"Fun, Fun, Fun")..8-12 71
CAPITOL (702 "Fun, Fun, Fun") 5-8 71
CAPITOL (1808 thru 1998) 15-25 63-67
(With "DT" prefix.)
CAPITOL (1808 thru 1998) 5-10 75-78
(With "SM" prefix.)
CAPITOL (1808 thru 1998) 20-35 62-63
(With "T" or "ST" prefix.)
CAPITOL (2027 "Shut Down, Vol. 2")..8-15 63
(With "DT" prefix.)
CAPITOL (2027 "Shut Down, Vol. 2")..5-10 75
(With "SM" prefix.)
CAPITOL (2027 "Shut Down, Vol. 2")..15-20 63
(With "T" or "ST" prefix.)
CAPITOL (2110 "All Summer Long")..25-30 64
(With "Don't Break Down." On this pressing, *Don't Back Down* is incorrectly shown as "Don't Break Down.")
CAPITOL (2110 "All Summer Long")..15-20 64
(With "Don't Back Down" shown correctly.)
CAPITOL (2164 "Beach Boys' Christmas Album")..5-10 75
(With "SM" prefix.)
CAPITOL (2164 "Beach Boys' Christmas Album")..20-35 64
(With "T" or "ST" prefix.)
CAPITOL (2198 "Beach Boys Concert")..10-15 64
(With "T" or "ST" prefix.)
CAPITOL (2198 "Beach Boys Concert")..5-10
(With "SM" prefix.)
CAPITOL (2269 "The Beach Boys Today")..15-20 65
(With "T" or "DT" prefix.)
CAPITOL (2354 "Summer Days and Summer Nights")..20-35 65
(With "T" or DT" prefix.)
CAPITOL (2398 "Beach Boys Party")..50-75 65
(With "MAS" or "SMAS" prefix. Price includes 15 bonus photos. Deduct $20 to $40 if these photos are missing.)
CAPITOL (2458 "Pet Sounds") 15-20 66
(With "T" or DT" prefix.)
CAPITOL (2545 "Best of the Beach Boys")..10-15 66
(With "T" or DT" prefix.)
CAPITOL (2706 "Best of the Beach Boys, Vol. 2")..10-15 67
(With "T" or "DT" prefix.)
CAPITOL (2813 "Beach Boys Deluxe Set")..100-125 67
(With "TCL" prefix.)
CAPITOL (2813 "Beach Boys Deluxe Set")..35-40 67
(With "DTCL" prefix.)
CAPITOL (2859 "Wild Honey") 10-15 67
(With "T" or "ST" prefix.)
CAPITOL (ST-8-2891 "Smiley Smile")..60-75 69
(With "ST-8" prefix. Capitol Record Club issue.)
CAPITOL (2893 "Stack-o-Tracks")..100-150 68
(With music-lyrics booklet.)
CAPITOL (2893 "Stack-o-Tracks")..50-75 68
(Without music-lyrics booklet.)
CAPITOL (2893 "Stack-o-Tracks")..100-125 69
(With "ST-8" prefix. Capitol Record Club issue.)
CAPITOL (2895 "Friends")............10-15 68
CAPITOL (2945 "Best of the Beach Boys, Vol. 3")..35-40 68
CAPITOL (3352 "Sunflower")..........30-35 70
(With "SKAO-9" prefix. Capitol Record Club issue.)
CAPITOL (8300 series)...................5-8 83
CAPITOL (6994 "Golden Years of the Beach Boys")..25-30 75
(TV mail-order offer.)
CAPITOL (48421 "Pet Sounds") 5-8 90
CAPITOL (11000 thru 16000, except 11384)..5-15 74-86
CAPITOL (11384 Spirit of America")..15-20 75
CAPITOL (29600 series)................10-15 96
(Digitally remastered.)
CAPITOL (90427 "Beach Boys Concert")..10-15 96
CAPITOL (92639 "Still Cruisin' ") 5-10 89
CAPITOL (123946 "Best of the Beach Boys, Vol. 1")..20-25 74
(RCA Record Club issue.)
CAPITOL (153477 "Rarities").........20-25 75
(RCA Record Club issue.)
CAPITOL (233559 "Endless Summer")..20-25 74
(RCA Record Club issue.)
CAPITOL (233593 "American Summer")..20-25 75
(RCA Record Club issue.)
CAPITOL STARLINE........................10-15 60s
CARIBOU..5-10 78-85
ERA..12-18 69
EVEREST 5-10 81
HIGHLIGHT (9926 "Beach Boys")......5-8 80s
MFSL (116 "Surfer Girl")................20-35 84
PAIR...10-12 84
PICKWICK 8-12 72-75
REPRISE (2118 "Holland")............15-20 73
(With *Mount Vernon & Fairway* EP.)
REPRISE (2118 "Holland")..............8-12 73
(Without *Mount Vernon & Fairway* EP.)
REPRISE (2166 "Wild Honey"/"20-20")..8-10 74
REPRISE (2166 "Friends/Smiley Smile")..8-10 74
REPRISE (2223 "Good Vibrations"/"Best of the Beach Boys") 8-10 75
REPRISE (2251 "15 Big Ones")........8-10 76
REPRISE (2258 "Love You")............8-10 77
REPRISE (2268 "M.I.U. Album") 8-10 78
REPRISE (6382 "Sunflower") 8-12 70
REPRISE (6453 "Surf's Up")..........20-25 71
(Capitol Record Club issue.)
REPRISE (6484 "The Beach Boys in Concert")..8-10 73
RONCO..8-10 78
SCEPTER 8-12
SEARS (608 "Summertime Blues")..100-125 70
(Sold only at Sears retail stores.)
SESSIONS..15-20 80
SPRINGBOARD (4021 "Greatest Hits: 1961-1963")..8-12 72
SUNDAZED (5005 "Lost & Found")..10-15
(Colored vinyl.)
WAND (688 "Greatest Hits")..........10-15 72
Promotional LPs
BROTHER (9431 "Good Vibrations from the Beach Boys")..10-15 86
(Sunkist promotional issue.)
CAPITOL (1 "Open House") 175-200 78
CAPITOL (2754/5 "Beach Boys' Concert")..300-350 64
CAPITOL (3123 "Silver Platter Service")..75-100 64
(With selections by the Hollyridge Strings.)
CAPITOL (3133 "Silver Platter Service")..125-150 64
("Beach Boys Christmas Special.")
CAPITOL (3266 "Silver Platter Service")..75-100 67
CARIBOU (1024 "Keepin' the Summer Alive")..45-50 80
CRAWDADDY ("Brian Wilson Interview")..90-100 77
(Issued to radio stations only.)
MORE MUSIC (03-179-72 "Good Vibrations from London")..50-60
MUTUAL RADIO ("Dick Clark Presents the Beach Boys")..150-175 81
(Three-LP boxed set.)
REPRISE ("Radio Spot Backing Tracks for Beach Boys in Concert") 225-250 73
TIME-LIFE..10-15 86
Members: Brian Wilson; Carl Wilson; Dennis Wilson; Mike Love; Al Jardine; David Marks; Bruce Johnston; Ricky Fataar; Blondie Chaplin.
Note: Promos NOT listed separately are priced in the same range as commercial issues.
Also see ANNETTE
Also see BEATLES / Beach Boys / Buddy Holly
Also see CAMPBELL, Glen
Also see CAPTAIN & TENNILLE
Also see CHICAGO
Also see CHRISTIAN, Roger
Also see CLAYTON, Merry
Also see DALE, Dick / Surfaris / Surf Kings
Also see DR. HOOK
Also see EVERLY BROTHERS & Beach Boys
Also see FAT BOYS & Beach Boys
Also see HONEYS
Also see JAN & DEAN / Beach Boys
Also see JETT, Joan
Also see JOHNSTON, Bruce
Also see KENNY & CADETS
Also see LOVE, Mike
Also see MARKS, David
Also see PETERSEN, Paul
Also see ROLLING STONES
Also see ROTH, David Lee
Also see SURVIVORS
Also see WILSON, Brian
Also see WILSON, Brian, and Mike Love
Also see WILSON, Carl
Also see WILSON, Dennis

BEACH BOYS / Ray Anthony
EPs: 7-inch
CAPITOL (2186/2185 "Complete Selections from *Surfin' Safari* by the Beach Boys")..500-750 64
(Promotional issue only.)
Also see ANTHONY, Ray

BEACH BOYS / Jan & Dean
LPs: 10/12-inch
CAPITOL (8149 "The Beach Boys/Jan & Dean")..10-20 81
(Sold only at Radio Shack stores. Realistic #S1-7010.)
EXACT..5-8 81
Also see JAN & DEAN

BEACH BOYS / Little Richard
(Beach Boys & Little Richard / Beach Boys) *P&R '88*
Singles: 7-inch
CRITIQUE (99392 "Happy Endings").3-5 87
ELEKTRA (69385 "Kokomo") 3-4 88
Picture Sleeves
CRITIQUE (99392 "Happy Endings").3-5 87
Also see LITTLE RICHARD

BEACH BOYS / Tony & Joe
Singles: 7-inch
ERA 3-5 70
Also see TONY & JOE

BEACH BOYS with FRANKIE VALLI & 4 SEASONS
Singles: 7-inch
FBI..3-5 84
Also see 4 SEASONS

BEACH BOYS / Carl Wilson
LPs: 10/12-inch
BROTHER (2083 "Pet Sounds"/"So Tough")..10-20 72
Also see BEACH BOYS

BEACH BUMS
Singles: 7-inch
ARE YOU KIDDING ME? (1010 "The Ballad of the Yellow Baret")....25-35 66
Members: Bob Seger; Doug Brown.
Also see BROWN, Doug
Also see SEGER, Bob

BEACH CONTINENTALS
Singles: 7-inch
VERSATILE (114 "Something Else")....10-20 62

BEACH GIRLS
Singles: 7-inch
DYNA VOX....10-20 65
VAULT....10-20 63

BEACH NUTS
Singles: 7-inch
BANG (504 "Out in the Sun")....25-35 65
Member: Lou Reed.
Also see REED, Lou

BEACH NUTS
Singles: 7-inch
CORONADO (131 "Surf Beat '65")....10-20 65
Picture Sleeves
CORONADO (131 "Surf Beat '65")....25-35 65

BEACHAM, Rufus
(With His Tampa Tappers)
Singles: 78 rpm
CHART....10-15 56
KING....10-15 55
Singles: 7-inch
CHART (627 "I Can't Believe")....20-40 56
JAX (300 "Since I Fell for You")...50-100 52
(Red vinyl.)
KING (4807 "Love Have Mercy")...25-50 55
KING (4820 "Let Me Be")....25-50 55
SCEPTER (1214 "No Man Is King")....15-25 60

BEACHCOMBERS
Singles: 7-inch
BIG AL ("Memories")....50-75 62
(No selection number used.)
Also see KRAFTONES

BEACHCOMBERS
Singles: 7-inch
DOT (16354 "Lone Survivor")....10-15 62

BEACHCOMBERS
Singles: 7-inch
DIAMOND (168 "This Is My Love")....15-25 64
SPAR....10-15 65

BEACHCOMBERS
Singles: 7-inch
JERDEN (719 "Purple Peanuts")..... 8-12 63
PANORAMA (11 "The Wheeley")...15-25 63

BEACHMAN, Rufus "Mr. Soul"
Singles: 7-inch
SCEPTER.... 5-10

BEACH-NIKS
Singles: 7-inch
MMC.... 5-10 65
SEA MIST.... 5-10

BEACON STREET IRREGULARS
(Baker Street Irregulars)
Singles: 7-inch
LARGO.... 4-8
SIMPER-FI.... 4-8

BEACON STREET UNION LP '68
Singles: 7-inch
MGM.... 5-10 67-69
RTP.... 5-10 69
LPs: 10/12-inch
MGM (4517 "The Eyes of the Beacon Street Union")....15-25 68
MGM (4568 "The Clown Died in Marvin Gardens")....15-25 68
Members: John Lincoln Wright; Robert Rhodes; Paul Tartachny; Wayne Ulaky; Richard Weisberg.
Also see EAGLE

BEAD GAME
Singles: 7-inch
AVCO EMBASSY (4539 "Sweet Medusa").... 5-10 70
LPs: 10/12-inch
AVCO EMBASSY (33009 "Welcome")....30-50 70
Members: Jim Hodder; John Sheldon.
Also see STEELY DAN

BEAGLE & FOUR LIVERPOOL WHIGS
LPs: 10/12-inch
SUTTON.... 8-12 64

BEAGLES
Singles: 7-inch
ERA.... 5-10 64
Picture Sleeves
ERA....10-20 64

BEAGLES
Singles: 7-inch
COLUMBIA....10-20 66
LPs: 10/12-inch
HARMONY....10-12 67

BEAGLES / Fred York
Singles: 7-inch
HIT.... 5-15 64

BEAL, Billy
Singles: 7-inch
RAYNARD (10027 "Foolish Me")...15-25 65

BEAGLES
LPs: 10/12-inch
HARMONY....10-12 67

BEALE STREET BOYS
Singles: 78 rpm
MGM (10141 "Teach Me Baby")....20-30 48
MGM (10197 "Wedding Bells")....20-30 48
MGM (10273 "Home")....20-30 48
MGM (10505 "I Wish I Had a Dime")....20-30 49
PARADISE....25-35 55
Singles: 7-inch
PARADISE (100 "There Is Nothing Greater")....50-75 55

BEALE STREET BOYS
Singles: 7-inch
OBA (102 "There's Nothing Greater Than a Prayer")....75-125 60

BEAM, Tommy "Jim"
(With the Four Fifths)
Singles: 7-inch
100 PROOF (101 "My Little Jewel")....200-300 58
SPARKETTE (1004 "Golden Boy")....50-100 59

BEAN, Arnold
LPs: 10/12-inch
SSS INT'L (21 "Cosmic Bean")....20-30

BEAN, Carl
Singles: 12-inch
MOTOWN.... 4-6 78
Singles: 7-inch
AIRWAVE.... 3-4 83
MOTOWN.... 3-4 78

BEAN, Jim C&W '88
Singles: 7-inch
HUB.... 3-4 88

BEANO
Singles: 7-inch
DERAM....5-10

BEANS
Singles: 7-inch
AVALANCHE.... 3-5 72
LPs: 10/12-inch
AVALANCHE....12-15 71

BEAR
Singles: 7-inch
VERVE/FORECAST....5-10 69
LPs: 10/12-inch
VERVE (3059 "Greetings")....15-25 70
Members: Eric Kaz; Steve Soles; Artie Traum; Skip Boone; Darius Davenport.
Also see AUTOSALVAGE
Also see KAZ, Eric

BEAR
Singles: 7-inch
RCA.... 3-5 78

BEAR, Edward: see EDWARD BEAR

BEAR, Richard T.
Singles: 7-inch
RCA.... 3-4 78-79
LPs: 10/12-inch
RCA....5-10 78-79

BEAR CREEK Featuring Leonda C&W '88
Singles: 7-inch
BEAR CREEK.... 3-4 88

BEAR ESSENCE STARRING MARIANNA D&D '84
Singles: 12-inch
MOBY DICK.... 4-6 84

BEAR FAX
Singles: 7-inch
FUZZ (0901 "Love Is a Beautiful Thing")....15-25 66
FUZZ (4141 "Out of Our Tree")....20-30 66

BEARCATS
Singles: 7-inch
CAMEO....5-10 63

BEARCUTS
LPs: 10/12-inch
SOMERSET....15-20 64

BEARD, Dean
(With the Rhythm Rebels)
Singles: 78 rpm
ATLANTIC....40-60 57
FOX....25-50 55
Singles: 7-inch
ATLANTIC (1137 "Rakin' and Scrapin' ")....50-75 57
ATLANTIC (1162 "Party Party")....50-75 57
ATLANTIC (1182 "Hold Me Close")....10-20 58
BOOTS & SADDLE ("Judy Judy") 25-35 66
(No selection number used.)
CANDIX (341 "The Day That I Lost You")....5-10 62
CHALLENGE (59048 "Little Lover")....15-25 59
EDMORAL (1011 "Rakin' and Scrapin' ")....300-500 57
FOX (405 "Red Rover")....75-125 55
GAYLO (112 "The Day That I Lost You")....10-20 62
GINA (1116 "Strawberry Shake").... 5-8 64
INTERNATIONAL (107 "Big D")....5-8 63
JOED (715 "Tropical Nights")....10-15 62
SANGELO (55 "Party Party")....75-100 58
SIMS....5-8 66
WINSTON....10-15 62-63
Also see CHAMPS

BEARD, Herbert
Singles: 78 rpm
COOL (101 "Gal! You Need a Whippin' ")....35-50 53

BEARDS C&W '88
Singles: 7-inch
BEARDO....3-4 88
Members: Randy Beard; Ron Beard.

BEARFOOT
Singles: 7-inch
EPIC....3-5 74-75
LPs: 10/12-inch
EPIC....10-12 73
Member: Dwayen Ford.

BEARINGS
Singles: 7-inch
PYRAMID (6953 "Anything You Want")....20-40 66
Members: Dave Britt; George Pittman; Lance Walters.

BEARS LP '88
LPs: 10/12-inch
I.R.S. 8-10 87-88

BEA'S
Singles: 7-inch
CHATTAHOOCHEE....4-8 65

BEAS
Singles: 7-inch
DEE GEE (3010 "Doctor Goldfoot and the Bikini Machine")....5-10 67
Also see HONEY CONE

BEASLEY, Billy
Singles: 7-inch
DEE CAL (500 "Too Long")....15-25 59

BEASLEY, Good Rockin' Sam
(Good Rockin' Beasley)
Singles: 78 rpm
EXCELLO....12-25 53-55
Singles: 7-inch
EXCELLO (Except 2011)....15-30 54-55
EXCELLO (2011 "Lord Goody")....25-50 53

BEASLEY, Good Rockin' Sam / Kid King's Combo
Singles: 78 rpm
EXCELLO....10-20 55
Singles: 7-inch
EXCELLO....20-40 55
Also see BEASLEY, Good Rockin' Sam
Also see KING, Kid

BEASLEY, Jimmy
(With the Rockets)
Singles: 78 rpm
MODERN....5-10 56-57
SILHOUETTE....5-10 56
Singles: 7-inch
MODERN....10-20 56-57
SILHOUETTE....10-20 56
LPs: 10/12-inch
CROWN (5014 "The Fabulous Jimmy Beasley")....50-75 57
CROWN (5247 "Twist with Jimmy Beasley")....20-30 61
MODERN (1214 "The Fabulous Jimmy Beasley")....75-125 56
Also see ROCKETS

BEASLEY, Walter R&B '87
Singles: 12-inch
POLYDOR....4-6 88
Singles: 7-inch
POLYDOR....3-4 87-88
LPs: 10/12-inch
POLYDOR....5-10 87-88

BEASLEY, Watson
Singles: 7-inch
W.B. 3-4 80

BEAST
Singles: 7-inch
TEE PEE (106 "Love Your Life")....15-25 69

BEAST LP '69
Singles: 7-inch
EVOLUTION....4-8 70
LPs: 10/12-inch
COTILLION....10-12 69
EVOLUTION....8-10 70
Also see BEDLAM

BEASTIE BOYS P&R/R&B/LP '86
Singles: 12-inch
DEF JAM....4-6 86-87
Singles: 7-inch
DEF JAM....3-4 86-87
LPs: 10/12-inch
CAPITOL (Except 79461)....5-8 89
CAPITOL (79461 "Hip Hop Sampler")....35-45 89
(Promotional issue only.)
DEF JAM....5-10 86-87
Members: Adam Horovitz; Adam Yaunch; Michael Diamond.

BEASTMASTER R&B '84
Singles: 12-inch
TOMMY BOY....4-6 84

BEASTS
Singles: 7-inch
HIT (159 "Sha La La")....10-20 60s

BEAT, The
Singles: 7-inch
COLUMBIA....3-4 79-80
LPs: 10/12-inch
COLUMBIA....5-10 79
PASSPORT....5-10 83
Members: Paul Collins; Steve Huff; Larry Whitman; Michael Ruiz.
Also see COLLINS, Paul
Also see SINCEROS / Hounds / The Beat / Jules & Polar Bears

BEAT, B: see B. BEAT GIRLS

BEAT BROTHERS
Singles: 7-inch
MGM....5-10 61

BEAT FARMERS LP '85
Singles: 7-inch
RHINO....3-4 85
LPs: 10/12-inch
MCA/CURB....5-10 86-87
RHINO....5-10 85

BEAT HAPPENING
Singles: 7-inch
SUB POP....3-4 91

BEAT HOVEN
Singles: 7-inch
WIZDOM....3-5 70

BEAT MERCHANTS: see FREDDIE & DREAMERS

BEAT OF EARTH
LPs: 10/12-inch
RADISH (0001 "The Beat of the Earth")....250-350 68
Members: Morgan Chapman; Karen Darby; J.R. Nichols; Ron Collins; Bill Phillips; Sherry Phillips.

BEAT RODEO
Singles: 7-inch
I.R.S. 3-4 86
Picture Sleeves
I.R.S. 3-4 86

BEAT-A-MANIA
LPs: 10/12-inch
STEREO-SPECTRUM....10-20 64
("Beat-A-Mania" is the title of the LP. No artist is credited.)

BEATIN' PATH
Singles: 7-inch
FONTANA (1583 "The Original Nothing People")....20-30 67
JUBILEE (5556 "Doctor Stone")....10-15 66
Also see STARLITES

BEATLE BUDDIES
LPs: 10/12-inch
DIPLOMAT....15-20 64

BEATLE BUGS
Singles: 7-inch
CASTLE....10-15 64

BEATLE MANIACS
Singles: 7-inch
LIN....35-50 64

BEATLE-ETTES
Singles: 7-inch
ASSAULT....10-20 64
JUBILEE....5-10 65

BEATLEMANIA
EPs: 7-inch
EVA-TONE (324771 "Beatlemania") 5-10 78
(Promotional issue only.)
LPs: 10/12-inch
ARISTA....10-15 78
Members: Joseph Pecorino; Mitch Weissman; Les Fradkin; Justin McNeil.

BEATLERAMA: see MANCHESTERS

BEATLES P&R '64
Singles: 12-inch
CAPITOL (SPRO-9758 "Movie Medley")....40-50 81
(Promotional issue only.)
ULTIMIX (120 "Twist and Shout")....100-125 88
(Promotional issue only.)
Singles: 7-inch
APPLE....8-15 69-75
APPLE....25-35 71
(With black star on label.)
ATCO (6302 "Sweet Georgia Brown")....175-200 64
(Shown as by "The Beatles with Tony Sheridan.")
ATCO (6308 "Ain't She Sweet")....50-60 64
(Yellow and white label. Without cut-out hole.)
ATCO (6308 "Ain't She Sweet")....20-30 64
(Yellow and white label. With cut-out hole.)
ATCO (6308 "Ain't She Sweet")....30-40 69
(Yellow and white label with "Mfg by Atlantic.." print.)
ATLANTIC....10-20 83-85
APPLE (2056 "Hello Goodbye")....25-35 71
(With black star on label.)
APPLE (2056 "Hello Goodbye")....10-20 71
(No black star on label.)
APPLE (2138 "Lady Madonna")....25-35 71
(With black star on label.)
APPLE (2138 "Lady Madonna")....10-20 71
(No black star on label.)
APPLE (2276 "Hey Jude")....10-15 68
(Apple label with Capitol logo.)
APPLE (2276 "Hey Jude")....5-10 71
(Apple label with "Mfd by Apple, etc." perimeter print.)
APPLE (2276 "Hey Jude")....15-20 75
(Apple label with "All Rights Reserved, etc." perimeter print.)
APPLE (2654 "Something")....75-100 69
(Apple label with Capitol logo.)
APPLE (2654 "Something")....8-12 71
(Apple label with "Mfd by Apple, etc." perimeter print.)
APPLE (2654 "Something")....15-20 75
(Apple label with "All Rights Reserved, etc." perimeter print.)
APPLE (2764 "Let It Be")....8-12 69
(Apple label with Capitol logo, or with "Mfd by Apple, etc." perimeter print.)
APPLE (2764 "Let It Be")....15-20 75
(Apple label with "All Rights Reserved, etc." perimeter print.)
APPLE (2832 "Long and Winding Road")....15-20 69
(Apple label with Capitol logo.)
APPLE (2832 "Long and Winding Road")....6-10 71
(Apple label with "Mfd by Apple, etc." perimeter print.)
APPLE (2832 "Long and Winding Road")....15-20 75
(Apple label with "All Rights Reserved, etc." perimeter print.)
APPLE (2490 "Get Back")....6-10 69
(Apple label with Capitol logo, or with "Mfd by Apple, etc." perimeter print.)
APPLE (2490 "Get Back")....15-20 75
(Apple label with "All Rights Reserved, etc." perimeter print.)
APPLE (2531 "Ballad of John and Yoko")....10-15 69
APPLE (5112 "I Want to Hold Your Hand")....30-40 71
(Has black star on label.)
APPLE (5112 "I Want to Hold Your Hand")....10-15 71
(No black star on label.)
APPLE (5150 "Can't Buy Me Love")....25-35 71
(Has black star on label.)
APPLE (5150 "Can't Buy Me Love")....10-15 71
(No black star on label.)
APPLE (5222 "A Hard Day's Night")....25-35 71
(With black star on label.)
APPLE (5222 "A Hard Day's Night")....10-15 71
(No black star on label.)
APPLE (5327 "I Feel Fine")....25-35 71
(With black star on label.)
APPLE (5327 "I Feel Fine")....10-15 71
(No black star on label.)
APPLE (5234 "I'll Cry Instead")....25-35 71
(With black star on label.)
APPLE (5234 "I'll Cry Instead")....10-15 71
(No black star on label.)
APPLE (5235 "And I Love Her")....25-35 71
(With black star on label.)
APPLE (5235 "And I Love Her")....10-15 71
(No black star on label.)
APPLE (5255 "Matchbox")....25-35 71
(With black star on label.)
APPLE (5255 "Matchbox")....10-15 71
(No black star on label.)
APPLE (5371 "Eight Days a Week")....25-35 71
(Has black star on label.)
APPLE (5371 "Eight Days a Week")....10-15 71
(No black star on label.)
APPLE (5407 "Ticket to Ride")....25-35 71
(With black star on label.)
APPLE (5407 "Ticket to Ride")....10-15 71
(No black star on label.)
APPLE (5476 "Help!")....25-35 71
(With black star on label.)
APPLE (5476 "Help!")....10-15 71
(No black star on label.)
APPLE (5498 "Yesterday")....25-35 71
(With black star on label.)
APPLE (5498 "Yesterday")....10-15 71
(No black star on label.)
APPLE (5555 "We Can Work It Out")....25-35 71
(With black star on label.)
APPLE (5555 "We Can Work It Out")....10-15 71
(No black star on label.)
APPLE (5587 "Nowhere Man")....25-35 71
(With black star on label.)
APPLE (5587 "Nowhere Man")....10-15 71
(No black star on label.)
APPLE (5651 "Paperback Writer")....25-35 71
(With black star on label.)
APPLE (5651 "Paperback Writer")....10-15 71
(No black star on label.)
APPLE (5715 "Yellow Submarine")....25-35 71
(With black star on label.)
APPLE (5715 "Yellow Submarine")....10-15 71
(No black star on label.)
APPLE (5810 "Penny Lane")....25-35 71
(With black star on label.)
APPLE (5810 "Penny Lane")....10-15 71
(No black star on label.)
APPLE (5964 "All You Need Is Love")....25-35 71
(With black star on label.)
APPLE (5964 "All You Need Is Love")....10-15 71
(No black star on label.)

BRS (1/2 "Murray the 'K' and the Beatles As It Happened")..........30-40 64
CAPITOL (2056 "Hello Goodbye")..........20-30 67
(Yellow/orange swirl label without "Subsidiary of Capitol, etc." perimeter print.)
CAPITOL (2056 "Hello Goodbye")..........40-50 68
(Yellow/orange swirl label with "Subsidiary of Capitol, etc." perimeter print.)
CAPITOL (2056 "Hello Goodbye")..........55-65 69
(Red/orange label with dome logo.)
CAPITOL (2056 "Hello Goodbye")..........15-20 69
(Red/orange label with round logo.)
CAPITOL (2056 "Hello Goodbye") 5-8 76
(Orange label.)
CAPITOL (2056 "Hello Goodbye") .10-15 78
(Purple or black label.)
CAPITOL (2138 "Lady Madonna")..........20-30 68
(Yellow/orange swirl label without "Subsidiary of Capitol, etc." perimeter print.)
CAPITOL (2138 "Lady Madonna")..........40-50 68
(Yellow/orange swirl label with "Subsidiary of Capitol, etc." perimeter print.)
CAPITOL (2138 "Lady Madonna")..........55-65 69
(Red/orange label with dome logo.)
CAPITOL (2138 "Lady Madonna")..........15-20 69
(Red/orange label with round logo.)
CAPITOL (2138 "Lady Madonna")..... 5-8 76
(Orange or purple or black label.)
CAPITOL (2276 "Hey Jude")............ 5-8 76
(Orange or purple or black label.)
CAPITOL (2490 "Get Back")............ 5-8 76
(Orange or purple or black label.)
CAPITOL (2531 "Ballad of John and Yoko")..........5-8 78
(Purple or black label.)
CAPITOL (2654 "Something")........... 5-8 76
(Orange or purple or black label.)
CAPITOL (2764 "Let It Be")............. 5-8 76
(Orange or purple or black label.)
CAPITOL (2832 "Long and Winding Road")..........5-8 76
(Orange or purple or black label.)
CAPITOL (4274 "Got to Get You into My Life")..........5-10 76
(Orange or purple or black label.)
CAPITOL (4347 "Ob-La-Di, Ob-La-Da")..........5-10 76
(Orange or purple or black label.)
CAPITOL (4612 "Sgt. Pepper's Lonely Hearts Club Band" & "With A Little Help From My Friends")..........5-8 78
(Purple or black label.)
CAPITOL (B-5100 "Movie Medley"/"Fab Four on Film")..........40-50 82
(First issued with *Movie Medley* backed with *Fab Four on Film*, the Beatles talking about the film *A Hard Day's Night*.)
CAPITOL (B-5107 "Movie Medley"/"I'm Happy Just to Dance with You")..........3-4 82
CAPITOL (5112 "I Want to Hold Your Hand")..........35-45 64
(Yellow/orange swirl label without "Subsidiary of Capitol, etc." perimeter print. Perimeter has *white* print. Reissue in 1984 has *black* perimeter print.)
CAPITOL (5112 "I Want to Hold Your Hand")..........60-70 68
(Yellow/orange swirl label with "Subsidiary of Capitol, etc." perimeter print.)
CAPITOL (5112 "I Want to Hold Your Hand")..........65-75 69
(Red/orange label with dome logo.)
CAPITOL (5112 "I Want to Hold Your Hand")..........15-25 69
(Red/orange label with round logo.)
CAPITOL (5112 "I Want to Hold Your Hand")..........5-10 76
(Orange label.)
CAPITOL (5112 "I Want to Hold Your Hand")..........10-15 78
(Purple label "Mfd. by Capitol, etc." perimeter print.)
CAPITOL (5112 "I Want to Hold Your Hand")..........3-5 84
(Yellow/orange swirl label with *black* perimeter print. Original 1964 issue has *white* perimeter print.)
CAPITOL (5112 "I Want to Hold Your Hand")..........5-8 86
(Black label.)
CAPITOL (5112 "I Want to Hold Your Hand")..........4-6 88
(Purple label with "Manufactured by Capitol, etc." perimeter print.)
CAPITOL (5112 "I Want to Hold Your Hand")..........3-5 94
(Yellow/orange swirl label. Has "NR-58123" in trail-off area.)
CAPITOL (5150 "Can't Buy Me Love")..........25-35 64
(Yellow/orange swirl label without "Subsidiary of Capitol, etc." perimeter print.)
CAPITOL (5150 "Can't Buy Me Love")..........40-50 68
(Yellow/orange swirl label with "Subsidiary of Capitol, etc." perimeter print.)
CAPITOL (5150 "Can't Buy Me Love")..........60-70 69
(Red/orange label with dome logo.)
CAPITOL (5150 "Can't Buy Me Love")..........15-20 69
(Red/orange label with round logo.)
CAPITOL (5150 "Can't Buy Me Love")..........5-8 76
(Orange label.)
CAPITOL (5150 "Can't Buy Me Love")..........10-15 78
(Purple label.)
CAPITOL (B-5189 "Love Me Do")..... 4-6 82
(Yellow/orange or black or purple label.)
CAPITOL (5222 "A Hard Day's Night")..........25-35 64
(Yellow/orange swirl label without "Subsidiary of Capitol, etc." perimeter print.)
CAPITOL (5222 "A Hard Day's Night")..........40-50 64
(Yellow/orange swirl label with "Subsidiary of Capitol, etc." in *white* perimeter print.)
CAPITOL (5222 "A Hard Day's Night")..........75-100 64
(Yellow/orange swirl label with "Subsidiary of Capitol, etc." in *black* perimeter print.)
CAPITOL (5222 "A Hard Day's Night")..........60-70 69
(Red/orange label with dome logo.)
CAPITOL (5222 "A Hard Day's Night")..........15-20 69
(Red/orange label with round logo.)
CAPITOL (5222 "A Hard Day's Night")..........5-8 76
(Orange label.)
CAPITOL (5222 "A Hard Day's Night")..........10-15 78
(Purple label.)
CAPITOL (5234 "I'll Cry Instead") ..25-35 64
(Yellow/orange swirl label without "Subsidiary of Capitol, etc." perimeter print.)
CAPITOL (5234 "I'll Cry Instead") ..50-70 64
(Yellow/orange swirl label with "Subsidiary of Capitol, etc." perimeter print.)
CAPITOL (5234 "I'll Cry Instead") ..60-75 69
(Red/orange label with dome logo.)
CAPITOL (5234 "I'll Cry Instead") ..15-20 69
(Red/orange label with round logo.)
CAPITOL (5234 "I'll Cry Instead") 5-8 76
(Orange label.)
CAPITOL (5234 "I'll Cry Instead") ..10-15 78
(Purple label.)
CAPITOL (5235 "And I Love Her")..........25-35 64
(Yellow/orange swirl label without "Subsidiary of Capitol, etc." perimeter print.)
CAPITOL (5235 "And I Love Her")..........40-50 64
(Yellow/orange swirl label with "Subsidiary of Capitol, etc." in *white* perimeter print.)
CAPITOL (5235 "And I Love Her")..........60-70 64
(Yellow/orange swirl label with "Subsidiary of Capitol, etc." in *black* perimeter print.)
CAPITOL (5235 "And I Love Her")..........60-70 69
(Red/orange label with dome logo.)
CAPITOL (5235 "And I Love Her").15-20 69
(Red/orange label with round logo.)
CAPITOL (5235 "And I Love Her").... 5-8 76
(Orange label.)
CAPITOL (5235 "And I Love Her").10-15 78
(Purple label.)
CAPITOL (5255 "Matchbox")..........25-35 64
(Yellow/orange swirl label without "Subsidiary of Capitol, etc." perimeter print.)
CAPITOL (5255 "Matchbox")..........40-50 64
(Yellow/orange swirl label with "Subsidiary of Capitol, etc." perimeter print.)
CAPITOL (5255 "Matchbox")..........60-70 69
(Red/orange label with dome logo.)
CAPITOL (5255 "Matchbox")..........15-20 69
(Red/orange label with round logo.)
CAPITOL (5255 "Matchbox")........... 5-8 76
(Orange label.)
CAPITOL (5255 "Matchbox")..........10-15 78
(Purple label.)
CAPITOL (5327 "I Feel Fine")........25-35 64
(Yellow/orange swirl label without "Subsidiary of Capitol, etc." perimeter print.)
CAPITOL (5327 "I Feel Fine")........40-50 64
(Yellow/orange swirl label with "Subsidiary of Capitol, etc." perimeter print.)
CAPITOL (5327 "I Feel Fine")........60-70 69
(Red/orange label with dome logo.)
CAPITOL (5327 "I Feel Fine")........15-20 69
(Red/orange label with round logo.)
CAPITOL (5327 "I Feel Fine")........... 5-8 76
(Orange label.)
CAPITOL (5327 "I Feel Fine")........10-15 78
(Purple label.)
CAPITOL (5371 "Eight Days a Week")..........25-35 65
(Yellow/orange swirl label without "Subsidiary of Capitol, etc." perimeter print.)
CAPITOL (5371 "Eight Days a Week")..........40-50 68
(Yellow/orange swirl label with "Subsidiary of Capitol, etc." perimeter print.)
CAPITOL (5371 "Eight Days a Week")..........60-70 69
(Red/orange label with dome logo.)
CAPITOL (5371 "Eight Days a Week")..........15-20 69
(Red/orange label with round logo.)
CAPITOL (5371 "Eight Days a Week")..........5-8 76
(Orange label.)
CAPITOL (5371 "Eight Days a Week")..........10-15 78
(Purple label.)
CAPITOL (5407 "Ticket to Ride")...25-35 64
(Yellow/orange swirl label without "Subsidiary of Capitol, etc." perimeter print.)
CAPITOL (5407 "Ticket to Ride")...40-50 64
(Yellow/orange swirl label with "Subsidiary of Capitol, etc." in *white* perimeter print.)
CAPITOL (5407 "Ticket to Ride").75-100 64
(Yellow/orange swirl label with "Subsidiary of Capitol, etc." in *black* perimeter print.)
CAPITOL (5407 "Ticket to Ride")...60-70 69
(Red/orange label with dome logo.)
CAPITOL (5407 "Ticket to Ride")...15-20 69
(Red/orange label with round logo.)
CAPITOL (5407 "Ticket to Ride").......5-8 76
(Orange label.)
CAPITOL (5407 "Ticket to Ride")...10-15 78
(Purple label.)
CAPITOL (5476 "Help!")..........25-35 65
(Yellow/orange swirl label without "Subsidiary of Capitol, etc." perimeter print.)
CAPITOL (5476 "Help!")..........40-50 68
(Yellow/orange swirl label with "Subsidiary of Capitol, etc." in *white* perimeter print.)
CAPITOL (5476 "Help!")..........75-100 68
(Yellow/orange swirl label with "Subsidiary of Capitol, etc." in *black* perimeter print.)
CAPITOL (5476 "Help!")..........60-70 69
(Red/orange label with dome logo.)
CAPITOL (5476 "Help!")..........15-20 69
(Red/orange label with round logo.)
CAPITOL (5476 "Help!")..........5-8 76
(Orange label.)
CAPITOL (5476 "Help!")..........10-15 78
(Purple label.)
CAPITOL (5498 "Yesterday")..........20-30 64
(Yellow/orange swirl label without "Subsidiary of Capitol, etc." perimeter print.)
CAPITOL (5498 "Yesterday")..........40-50 68
(Yellow/orange swirl label with "Subsidiary of Capitol, etc." in *white* perimeter print.)
CAPITOL (5498 "Yesterday").......75-100 68
(Yellow/orange swirl label with "Subsidiary of Capitol, etc." in *black* perimeter print.)
CAPITOL (5498 "Yesterday")..........60-70 69
(Red/orange label with dome logo.)
CAPITOL (5498 "Yesterday")..........15-20 69
(Red/orange label with round logo.)
CAPITOL (5498 "Yesterday")..........5-8 76
(Orange label.)
CAPITOL (5498 "Yesterday")..........10-15 78
(Purple label.)
CAPITOL (5555 "We Can Work It Out")..........20-30 66
(Yellow/orange swirl label without "Subsidiary of Capitol, etc." perimeter print.)
CAPITOL (5555 "We Can Work It Out")..........40-50 68
(Yellow/orange swirl label with "Subsidiary of Capitol, etc." perimeter print.)
CAPITOL (5555 "We Can Work It Out")..........1200-1500 69
(Red and white label. "Starline" series.)
CAPITOL (5555 "We Can Work It Out")..........60-75 69
(Red/orange label with dome logo.)
CAPITOL (5555 "We Can Work It Out")..........15-20 69
(Red/orange label with round logo.)
CAPITOL (5555 "We Can Work It Out")..........5-8 76
(Orange label.)
CAPITOL (5555 "We Can Work It Out")..........10-15 78
(Purple label.)
CAPITOL (5587 "Nowhere Man")...25-50 66
(Yellow/orange swirl label without "Subsidiary of Capitol, etc." perimeter print.)
CAPITOL (5587 "Nowhere Man")...40-50 68
(Yellow/orange swirl label with "Subsidiary of Capitol, etc." perimeter print.)
CAPITOL (5587 "Nowhere Man")...60-75 69
(Red/orange label with dome logo.)
CAPITOL (5587 "Nowhere Man")...15-20 69
(Red/orange label with round logo.)
CAPITOL (5587 "Nowhere Man").......5-8 76
(Orange label.)
CAPITOL (5587 "Nowhere Man")...10-15 78
(Purple label.)
CAPITOL (B-5624 "Twist and Shout")..........4-6 86
(Black or purple label.)
CAPITOL (5651 "Paperback Writer")..........25-50 66
(Yellow/orange swirl label without "Subsidiary of Capitol, etc." perimeter print.)
CAPITOL (5651 "Paperback Writer")..........40-50 68
(Yellow/orange swirl label with "Subsidiary of Capitol, etc." in *white* perimeter print.)
CAPITOL (5651 "Paperback Writer")..........75-100 68
(Yellow/orange swirl label with "Subsidiary of Capitol, etc." in *black* perimeter print.)
CAPITOL (5651 "Paperback Writer")..........60-75 69
(Red/orange label with dome logo.)
CAPITOL (5651 "Paperback Writer")..........15-20 69
(Red/orange label with round logo.)
CAPITOL (5651 "Paperback Writer")..........5-8 76
(Orange label.)
CAPITOL (5651 "Paperback Writer")..........10-15 78
(Purple label.)
CAPITOL (5715 "Yellow Submarine")..........20-30 66
(Yellow/orange swirl label without "Subsidiary of Capitol, etc." perimeter print.)
CAPITOL (5715 "Yellow Submarine")..........40-50 68
(Yellow/orange swirl label with "Subsidiary of Capitol, etc." perimeter print.)
CAPITOL (5715 "Yellow Submarine")..........60-70 69
(Red/orange label with dome logo.)
CAPITOL (5715 "Yellow Submarine")..........15-20 69
(Red/orange label with round logo.)
CAPITOL (5715 "Yellow Submarine")..........5-8 76
(Orange label.)
CAPITOL (5715 "Yellow Submarine")..........10-15 78
(Purple label.)
CAPITOL (5810 "Penny Lane")......25-35 66
(Yellow/orange swirl label without "Subsidiary of Capitol, etc." perimeter print.)
CAPITOL (5810 "Penny Lane")......40-50 68
(Yellow/orange swirl label with "Subsidiary of Capitol, etc." perimeter print.)
CAPITOL (5810 "Penny Lane")......60-70 69
(Red/orange label with dome logo.)
CAPITOL (5810 "Penny Lane")......15-20 69
(Red/orange label with round logo.)
CAPITOL (5810 "Penny Lane")..........5-8 76
(Orange label.)
CAPITOL (5810 "Penny Lane")......10-15 78
(Purple label.)
CAPITOL (5964 "All You Need Is Love")..........20-30 67
(Yellow/orange swirl label without "Subsidiary of Capitol, etc." perimeter print.)
CAPITOL (5964 "All You Need Is Love")..........40-50 68
(Yellow/orange swirl label with "Subsidiary of Capitol, etc." perimeter print.)
CAPITOL (5964 "All You Need Is Love")..........60-75 69
(Red/orange label with dome logo.)
CAPITOL (5964 "All You Need Is Love")..........15-20 69
(Red/orange label with round logo.)
CAPITOL (5964 "All You Need Is Love")..........5-8 76
(Orange label.)
CAPITOL (5964 "All You Need Is Love")..........10-15 78
(Purple label.)
CAPITOL (6061 "Twist and Shout")..........100-125 65
(Green label. "Starline" series.)
CAPITOL (6062 "Love Me Do") . 100-125 65
(Green label. "Starline" series.)
CAPITOL (6063 "Please Please Me")..........100-125 65
(Green label. "Starline" series.)
CAPITOL (6064 "Do You Want to Know a Secret")..........100-125 65
(Green label. "Starline" series.)
CAPITOL (6065 "Misery")..........100-125 65
(Green label. "Starline" series.)
CAPITOL (6065 "Misery")..........20-30 71
(Red/orange label. "Starline" series.)
CAPITOL (6066 "Kansas City")......70-90 65
(Green label. "Starline" series.)
CAPITOL (6066 "Kansas City")......20-30 71
(Red/orange label. "Starline" series.)
CAPITOL (A-6278 "I Want to Hold Your Hand")..........15-25 81
(Blue label reads "stereo" but plays mono. "Starline" series.)
CAPITOL (A-6278 "I Want to Hold Your Hand")..........20-30 81
(Blue label reads "mono." "Starline" series.)
CAPITOL (X-6278 "I Want to Hold Your Hand")..........10-15 81
(Blue label reads "mono." "Starline" series.)
CAPITOL (A-6279 "Can't Buy Me Love")..........5-8 81
(Blue label reads "stereo" but plays mono. "Starline" series.)
CAPITOL (A-6279 "Can't Buy Me Love")..........15-25 81
(Blue label reads "mono." "Starline" series.)
CAPITOL (X-6279 "Can't Buy Me Love")..........4-6 81
(Blue label reads "mono." "Starline" series.)
CAPITOL (6279 "Can't Buy Me Love")..........4-6 86
(Black or purple label. "Starline" series.)
CAPITOL (A-6281 "A Hard Day's Night")..........5-8 81
(Blue label reads "stereo" but plays mono. "Starline" series.)
CAPITOL (A-6281 "A Hard Day's Night")..........15-25 81
(Blue label reads "mono." "Starline" series.)
CAPITOL (X-6281 "A Hard Day's Night")..........4-6 81
(Blue label reads "mono." "Starline" series.)
CAPITOL (6281 "A Hard Day's Night")..........4-6 86
(Black or purple label "Starline" series.)
CAPITOL (A-6282 "I'll Cry Instead")...5-8 81
(Blue label reads "stereo" but plays mono. "Starline" series.)
CAPITOL (A-6282 "I'll Cry Instead")..........15-25 81
(Blue label reads "mono." "Starline" series.)
CAPITOL (X-6282 "I'll Cry Instead")...4-6 81
(Blue label reads "mono." "Starline" series.)
CAPITOL (6282 "I'll Cry Instead")......4-6 86
(Black or purple label "Starline" series.)
CAPITOL (A-6283 "And I Love Her") .5-8 81
(Blue label reads "stereo" but plays mono. "Starline" series.)
CAPITOL (A-6283 "And I Love Her")..........15-25 81
(Blue label reads "mono." "Starline" series.)
CAPITOL (X-6283 "And I Love Her")..........4-6 81
(Blue label reads "mono." "Starline" series.)
CAPITOL (6283 "And I Love Her").....4-6 86
(Black or purple label. "Starline" series.)
CAPITOL (A-6284 "Matchbox")..........5-8 81
(Blue label reads "stereo" but plays mono. "Starline" series.)
CAPITOL (A-6284 "Matchbox")......15-25 81
(Blue label reads "mono." "Starline" series.)
CAPITOL (X-6284 "Matchbox")..........4-6 81
(Blue label reads "mono." "Starline" series.)
CAPITOL (6284 "Matchbox")..........4-6 86
(Black or purple label. "Starline" series.)
CAPITOL (A-6286 "I Feel Fine")..........5-8 81
(Blue label reads "stereo" but plays mono. "Starline" series.)
CAPITOL (A-6286 "I Feel Fine") 15-25 81
(Blue label reads "mono." "Starline" series.)
CAPITOL (X-6286 "I Feel Fine")........4-6 81
(Blue label reads "mono." "Starline" series.)
CAPITOL (6286 "I Feel Fine")..........4-6 86
(Black or purple label. "Starline" series.)
CAPITOL (A-6287 "Eight Days a Week")..........5-8 81
(Blue label reads "stereo" but plays mono. "Starline" series.)
CAPITOL (A-6287 "Eight Days a Week")..........15-25 81
(Blue label reads "mono." "Starline" series.)
CAPITOL (X-6287 "Eight Days a Week")..........4-6 81
(Blue label reads "mono." "Starline" series.)
CAPITOL (6287 "Eight Days a Week")..........4-6 86
(Black or purple label. "Starline" series.)
CAPITOL (A-6288 "Ticket to Ride")...5-8 81
(Blue label reads "stereo" but plays mono. "Starline" series.)
CAPITOL (A-6288 "Ticket to Ride")..........15-25 81
(Blue label reads "mono." "Starline" series.)
CAPITOL (X-6288 "Ticket to Ride") ...4-6 81
(Blue label reads "mono." "Starline" series.)
CAPITOL (6288 "Ticket to Ride").......4-6 86
(Black or purple label. "Starline" series.)
CAPITOL (A-6290 "Help!")..........5-8 81
(Blue label reads "stereo" but plays mono. "Starline" series.)
CAPITOL (A-6290 "Help!")..........15-25 81
(Blue label reads "mono." "Starline" series.)
CAPITOL (X-6290 "Help!")..........4-6 81
(Blue label reads "mono." "Starline" series.)
CAPITOL (6290 "Help!")..........4-6 86
(Black or purple label "Starline" series.)
CAPITOL (A-6291 "Yesterday")..........5-8 81
(Blue label reads "stereo" but plays mono. "Starline" series.)
CAPITOL (A-6291 "Yesterday").....15-25 81
(Blue label reads "mono." "Starline" series.)
CAPITOL (X-6291 "Yesterday")........4-6 81
(Blue label reads "mono." "Starline" series.)
CAPITOL (6291 "Yesterday")..........4-6 86
(Black or purple label "Starline" series.)
CAPITOL (A-6293 "We Can Work It Out")..........5-8 81
(Blue label reads "stereo" but plays mono. "Starline" series.)
CAPITOL (A-6293 "We Can Work It Out")..........15-25 81
(Blue label reads "mono." "Starline" series.)
CAPITOL (X-6293 "We Can Work It Out")..........4-6 81
(Blue label reads "mono." "Starline" series.)
CAPITOL (6293 "We Can Work It Out")..........4-6 86
(Black or purple label "Starline" series.)
CAPITOL (A-6294 "Nowhere Man")...5-8 81
(Blue label reads "stereo" but plays mono. "Starline" series.)
CAPITOL (A-6294 "Nowhere Man")..........15-25 81
(Blue label reads "mono." "Starline" series.)
CAPITOL (X-6294 "Nowhere Man") ...4-6 81
(Blue label reads "mono." "Starline" series.)
CAPITOL (6294 "Nowhere Man").......4-6 86
(Black or purple label "Starline" series.)
CAPITOL (A-6296 "Paperback Writer")..........5-8 81
(Blue label reads "stereo" but plays mono. "Starline" series.)
CAPITOL (A-6296 "Paperback Writer")..........15-25 81
(Blue label reads "mono." "Starline" series.)
CAPITOL (X-6296 "Paperback Writer")..........4-6 81
(Blue label reads "mono." "Starline" series.)
CAPITOL (6296 "Paperback Writer")..........4-6 86
(Black or purple label "Starline" series.)
CAPITOL (A-6297 "Yellow Submarine")..........5-8 81
(Blue label reads "stereo" but plays mono. "Starline" series.)
CAPITOL (A-6297 "Yellow Submarine")..........15-25 81
(Blue label reads "mono." "Starline" series.)
CAPITOL (X-6297 "Yellow Submarine")..........4-6 81
(Blue label reads "mono." "Starline" series.)
CAPITOL (6297 "Yellow Submarine")..........4-6 86
(Black or purple label "Starline" series.)
CAPITOL (A-6299 "Penny Lane")......5-8 81
(Blue label reads "stereo" but plays mono. "Starline" series.)
CAPITOL (A-6299 "Penny Lane") ..15-25 81
(Blue label reads "mono." "Starline" series.)
CAPITOL (X-6299 "Penny Lane")......4-6 81
(Blue label reads "mono." "Starline" series.)
CAPITOL (6299 "Penny Lane")..........4-6 86
(Black or purple label "Starline" series.)
CAPITOL (A-6300 "All You Need Is Love")..........5-8 81
(Blue label reads "stereo" but plays mono. "Starline" series.)
CAPITOL (A-6300 "All You Need Is Love")..........15-25 81
(Blue label reads "mono." "Starline" series.)
CAPITOL (X-6300 "All You Need Is Love")..........4-6 81
(Blue label reads "mono." "Starline" series.)
CAPITOL (6300 "All You Need Is Love")..........15-20 86
(Black label. "Starline" series.)
CAPITOL (17488 "Birthday")..........40-50 94
(Black vinyl, 30th Anniversary juke box issue.)
CAPITOL (17488 "Birthday")..........3-5 94
(Colored vinyl, 30th Anniversary juke box issue.)
CAPITOL (17488 "Birthday")..........3-5 94
(Colored vinyl, 30th Anniversary juke box issue.)

CAPITOL (17688 "She Loves You").. 3-5 94
(Colored vinyl, 30th Anniversary juke box issue.)
CAPITOL (17689 "I Want to Hold Your Hand") 3-5 94
(Colored vinyl, 30th Anniversary juke box issue.)
CAPITOL (17690 "Can't Buy Me Love") 3-5 94
(Colored vinyl, 30th Anniversary juke box issue.)
CAPITOL (17691 "Help!") 3-5 94
(Colored vinyl, 30th Anniversary juke box issue.)
CAPITOL (17692 "A Hard Day's Night") 3-5 94
(Colored vinyl, 30th Anniversary juke box issue.)
CAPITOL (17693 "All You Need Is Love") 3-5 94
(Colored vinyl, 30th Anniversary juke box issue.)
CAPITOL (17694 "Hey Jude") 3-5 94
(Colored vinyl, 30th Anniversary juke box issue.)
CAPITOL (17695 "Let It Be") 3-5 94
(Colored vinyl, 30th Anniversary juke box issue.)
CAPITOL (17696 "Eleanor Rigby").... 3-5 94
(Colored vinyl, 30th Anniversary juke box issue.)
CAPITOL (17697 "Penny Lane") 3-5 94
(Colored vinyl, 30th Anniversary juke box issue.)
CAPITOL (17698 "Something") 3-5 94
(Colored vinyl, 30th Anniversary juke box issue.)
CAPITOL (17699 "Twist and Shout") 3-5 94
(Colored vinyl, 30th Anniversary juke box issue.)
CAPITOL (17700 "Here Comes the Sun") 3-5 94
(Colored vinyl, 30th Anniversary juke box issue.)
CAPITOL (17701 "Sgt. Pepper's Lonely Hearts Club Band") 3-5 94
(Colored vinyl, 30th Anniversary juke box issue.)
CAPITOL (18889 "You've Got to Hide Your Love Away") 3-5 96
(Colored vinyl.)
CAPITOL (18890 "Magical Mystery Tour") 3-5 96
(Colored vinyl.)
CAPITOL (18891 "Across the Universe") 3-5 96
(Colored vinyl.)
CAPITOL (18892 "While My Guitar Gently Sleeps") 3-5 96
(Colored vinyl.)
CAPITOL (18893 "It's All Too Much") 3-5 96
(Colored vinyl.)
CAPITOL (18894 "Nowhere Man").... 3-5 96
(Colored vinyl.)
CAPITOL (18895 "Can't Buy Me Love") 3-5 96
(Colored vinyl.)
CAPITOL (18896 "Lucy in the Sky with Diamonds") 3-5 96
(Colored vinyl.)
CAPITOL (18897 "Here, There and Everywhere") 3-5 96
(Colored vinyl.)
CAPITOL (18898 "Long and Winding Road") 3-5 96
(Colored vinyl.)
CAPITOL (18899 "Got to Get You into My Life") 3-5 96
(Colored vinyl.)
CAPITOL (18900 "Ob-La-Di, Ob-La-Da") 3-5 96
(Colored vinyl.)
CAPITOL (18901 "Yesterday") 3-5 96
(Colored vinyl.)
CAPITOL (18902 "Paperback Writer") 3-5 96
(Colored vinyl.)
CAPITOL (56785 "Love Me Do") 25-30 92
(Intended to be black vinyl but issued on red vinyl by mistake. Reportedly 1,500 made. 30th Anniversary juke box issue.)
CAPITOL (56785 "Love Me Do") 3-5 92
(Black vinyl. 30th Anniversary juke box issue.)
CAPITOL (58123 "I Want to Hold Your Hand") 3-5 96
CAPITOL (58497 "Free As a Bird") .. 3-5 96
CAPITOL (58544 "Real Love") 3-5 96
CAPITOL (72133 "Roll Over Beethoven") 20-30 64
(Canadian [Capitol of Canada].)
CAPITOL (72144 "All My Loving") .20-30 64
(Canadian. [Capitol of Canada].)
CAPITOL (72144 "All My Loving") 80-100 71
(An error in production created a U.S. pressing of the Canadian release, *All My Loving/This Boy*.)
CAPITOL (79551 "Love Me Do")....20-25 92
(Mail-order only.)
CARROLL JAMES (3301 "The Carroll James Interview with the Beatles") 4-8 84
CICADELIC/BIODISC (001 "A Hard Day's Night") 15-20 90
(Open-end interview picture disc. With script.)
CICADELIC/BIODISC (001 "A Hard Day's Night") 25-35 90
(Open-end interview picture disc. With script. Promotional only issue made for "Records, Etc. of Payson, Az." 55 made.)
CICADELIC/BIODISC (002 "Help!: Open-end Interview") 5-8 90
(With script.)
COLLECTABLES 3-4 82
CREATIVE RADIO (B-1 "The Beatle Invasion") 10-20 80s
(Radio show demo. Flip side is "Inside Paul McCartney.")
DECCA (31382 "My Bonnie") 8000-12000 62
(Shown as by Tony Sheridan & Beat Brothers. Note: Price is for a *COMMERCIAL*, not promotional, issue. Commercial copies are on Decca's black label with silver print and a multi-color stripe across the center of the label. Black and silver Decca labels without the other colors are bootlegs.)
IBC (0082 "Murray the 'K' and the Beatles As It Happened") 8-10 76
MGM (13213 "My Bonnie") 40-50 64
(Shown as by the Beatles with Tony Sheridan.)
MGM (13227 "Why") 100-125 64
(Shown as by the Beatles with Tony Sheridan.)
MURRAY the "K" & BEATLES 20-25 64
(33 Single. Reissued in 1976 as IBC 0082.)
OLDIES 45 .... 8-15 65
SILHOUETTE (1451 "Timeless 2 ½") 10-15 83
(Picture disc.)
SWAN (4152 "She Loves You") .600-650 63
(White label, with red or blue print.)
SWAN (4152 "She Loves You") 25-50 64
(Black label.)
SWAN (4182 "Sie Liebt Dich") 125-150 64
(White label with red print.)
SWAN (4182 "Sie Liebt Dich") 150-175 64
(White label with orange print.)
TOLLIE (9001 "Twist and Shout") 60-70 64
(Black label.)
TOLLIE (9001 "Twist and Shout") ..60-80 64
(Yellow label with purple print.)
TOLLIE (9001 "Twist and Shout") ..50-60 64
(Yellow label with blue print.)
TOLLIE (9001 "Twist and Shout") ..50-75 64
(Yellow label with black print.)
TOLLIE (9001 "Twist and Shout") ..60-80 64
(Yellow label with green print has logo in box.)
TOLLIE (9001 "Twist and Shout") ..40-50 64
(Yellow label with green print has logo without box.)
TOLLIE (9008 "Love Me Do") 50-60 64
(Black label.)
TOLLIE (9008 "Love Me Do") 40-50 64
(Yellow label.)
TOPAZ (1353 "Seattle Press Conference") 4-6 89
VEE JAY (498 "Please Please Me") 1400-1600 63
(Credits "BEATTLES." Black label with rainbow circle. Has thin lettering and oval logo.)
VEE JAY (498 "Please Please Me") 800-1000 63
(Credits "BEATTLES." Black label with rainbow circle. Has bold lettering and oval logo.)
VEE JAY (498 "Please Please Me") 1500-1800 63
(Credits "BEATLES." Black label with rainbow circle. Has thin lettering and oval label logo.)
VEE JAY (498 "Please Please Me") 700-900 63
(Credits "BEATLES." Black label with rainbow circle. Has bold lettering and oval label logo.)
VEE JAY (498 "Please Please Me") 1800-2000 63
(Credits "BEATLES." Black label with rainbow circle. Has brackets label logo.)
VEE JAY (522 "From Me to You") 700-800 63
(Black label with horizontal silver lines.)
VEE JAY (522 "From Me to You") 800-900 63
(Black label with rainbow circle and brackets logo.)
VEE JAY (522 "From Me to You") 500-700 63
(Black label with rainbow circle and oval logo.)
VEE JAY (581 "Please Please Me") 200-250 64
(Purple label.)
VEE JAY (581 "Please Please Me") 140-160 64
(White label. Not a promotional issue.)
VEE JAY (581 "Please Please Me") 60-75 64
(Yellow label.)
VEE JAY (581 "Please Please Me") 35-45 64
(Black label with horizontal silver lines.)
VEE JAY (581 "Please Please Me") 50-75 64
(Black label. No rainbow circle.)
VEE JAY (581 "Please Please Me") 50-60 64
(Black label with rainbow circle.)
VEE JAY (587 "Do You Want to Know a Secret") 35-45 64
(Solid black label with horizontal silver lines.)
VEE JAY (587 "Do You Want to Know a Secret") 50-65 64
(Solid black label or yellow label.)
VEE JAY (587 "Do You Want to Know a Secret") 40-50 64
(Black label with rainbow circle.)

Picture Sleeves

APPLE (2531 "Ballad of John & Yoko") 60-80 69
APPLE (2764 "Let It Be") 60-80 70
APPLE (2832 "Long and Winding Road") 60-80 70
ATCO (6308 "Ain't She Sweet") .350-500 64
BRS (1/2 "Murray the 'K' and the Beatles As It Happened") 150-200 64
CAPITOL/HOLIDAY INN 800-1000 64
(Promotional sleeve, pictures the four Beatles on front and their first three Capitol LPs on the back. Not known to have been issued containing any particular single.)
CAPITOL (2056 "Hello Goodbye") 60-80 67
CAPITOL (2138 "Lady Madonna") 70-90 68
CAPITOL (2138 "Lady Madonna") 15-20 68
(Fan Club flyer insert.)
CAPITOL (4274 "Got to Get You into My Life") 3-6 88
CAPITOL (4347 "Ob-La-Di, Ob-La-Da") 5-8 76
CAPITOL (4506 "Girl") 10-15 78
CAPITOL (4612 "Sgt. Pepper's Lonely Hearts Club Band" & "With A Little Help From My Friends") 15-20 78
CAPITOL (B-5100 "Movie Medley"/"Fab Four on Film") 15-20 82
CAPITOL (B-5107 "Movie Medley"/"I'm Happy Just to Dance with You") 3-4 82
CAPITOL (B-5189 "Love Me Do")......3-4 82
CAPITOL (5112 "I Want to Hold Your Hand") 50-75 64
(This original sleeve has no periods placed at end of the small print in "Reg. U.S. Pat. Off." in Capitol logo. Reissue in 1994 has periods.)
CAPITOL (5112 WMCA Radio Promotional Sleeve) 2000-2200 64
(Back side of this sleeve pictures WMCA dee jays. Front side is identical to standard commercial issue.)
CAPITOL (5112 "I Want to Hold Your Hand") 4-6 84
(This reissue sleeve is clearly dated "1984" in lower left corner.)
CAPITOL (5112 "I Want to Hold Your Hand") 4-6 94
(This reissue sleeve has periods placed at end of the small print in "Reg. U.S. Pat. Off." in Capitol logo. Original in 1964 has no periods.)
CAPITOL (5150 "Can't Buy Me Love") 550-650 64
CAPITOL CUSTOM (2637 "Music City KFWBeatles") 800-1000 64
(Promotional sleeve for the "Souvenir Record" from KFWB and Wallichs Music City.)
CAPITOL (5222 "A Hard Day's Night") 50-75 64
CAPITOL (5234 "I'll Cry Instead") 140-160 64
CAPITOL (5235 "And I Love Her") 125-150 64
CAPITOL (5255 "Slow Down") 50-75 64
CAPITOL (5327 "I Feel Fine") 50-70 64
CAPITOL (5371 "Eight Days a Week") 25-50 65
CAPITOL (5407 "Ticket to Ride") 75-100 65
CAPITOL (5439 "Leave My Kitten Alone") 35-45 85
CAPITOL (5476 "Help!") 50-75 65
CAPITOL (5498 "Yesterday") 50-75 65
CAPITOL (5555 "We Can Work It Out") 50-75 65
CAPITOL (5587 "Nowhere Man")...40-50 66
CAPITOL (5651 "Paperback Writer") 50-75 66
CAPITOL (5715 "Yellow Submarine") 75-100 66
CAPITOL (5810 "Penny Lane")...75-100 67
CAPITOL (5964 "All You Need Is Love") 40-50 67
CAPITOL (58123 "I Want to Hold Your Hand") 3-4 96
CAPITOL (58497 "Free As a Bird")....3-4 96
CAPITOL (58544 "Real Love") 3-4 96
CAPITOL (79551 "Love Me Do") ...15-20 92
CARROLL JAMES (3301 "The Carroll James Interview with the Beatles") 4-8 84
CICADELIC/BIODISC (002 "Help!: Open-end Interview") 5-8 90
COLLECTABLES 3-4 82
IBC (0082 "Murray the 'K' and the Beatles As It Happened") 6-10 76
MGM (13213 "My Bonnie") 75-100 64
MGM (13227 "Why") 300-400 64
SWAN (4152 "She Loves You") 100-125 63
TOLLIE (9008 "Love Me Do") 100-125 64
TOPAZ 4-6 89
U.A. (42370 "Let It Be") 100-150 70
(Custom mailer envelope for promo radio spots single.)
VEE JAY SPECIAL CHRISTMAS SLEEVE 70-90 64
(Standard center-cut paper sleeve printed with the Beatles' faces and "We Wish You a Merry Christmas and a Happy New Year." Issued with assorted Vee Jay singles during the holiday season.)
VEE JAY (581 "Please Please Me") 400-500 64
(Pictures the four Beatles.)
VEE JAY (581 "Please Please Me") 2000-3000 64
(Promotional only sleeve. Reads "The Record That Started Beatlemania" across the top. Does not picture the group.)
VEE JAY (587 "Do You Want to Know a Secret") 100-125 64

Promotional Singles

APPLE ("Let It Be") 50-60 70
(Identified as "Beatles Promo 1970." Single-sided promo issue.)
ATCO (6302 "Sweet Georgia Brown") 175-200 64
ATCO (6308 "Ain't She Sweet") .250-300 64
BACKSTAGE (1112 "Oui Presents the Silver Beatles") 20-25 82
(*Oui* magazine promotional giveaway. Features a *Like Dreamers Do/Love of the Loved* montage. Mailing also included *Oui* News Release and subscription form. This is not a picture disc single, as the other Backstage 1100 series singles are.)
BACKSTAGE (1122 "Love of the Loved") 20-25 83
(Promotional only picture disc.)
BACKSTAGE (1133 "Like Dreamers Do") 20-25 83
(Promotional only picture disc.)
BACKSTAGE (1133 "Like Dreamers Do") 40-50 83
(Picture disc, with photo of *Penthouse* "Pet.")
CAPITOL (2056 "Hello Goodbye") 200-250 67
CAPITOL (2138 "Lady Madonna") 150-200 68
CAPITOL (4274 "Got to Get You Into My Life") 30-40 76
CAPITOL (4274 "Helter Skelter") ... 30-40 76
CAPITOL (4347 "Ob-La-Di, Ob-La-Da") 30-40 76
CAPITOL (4506 "Girl") 175-200 78
CAPITOL (4612 "Sgt. Pepper's Lonely Hearts Club Band" & "With a Little Help From My Friends") 30-40 78
CAPITOL (PB-5100 "Movie Medley"/"Fab Four on Film") 20-25 82
CAPITOL (P-5112/PRO-9076 "I Want to Hold Your Hand") 10-15 84
CAPITOL (PB-5150 "Can't Buy Me Love") 5000-10000
(Yellow vinyl. Experimental pressing only.)
CAPITOL (PB-5150 "Can't Buy Me Love") 4000-6000
(Black and yellow vinyl. Experimental pressing only.)
CAPITOL (PB-5189 "Love Me Do") 10-15 82
CAPITOL (PB-5624 "Twist and Shout") 10-15 86
CAPITOL (5810 "Penny Lane")..250-300 67
(With trumpet solo at end of song.)
CAPITOL (5810 "Penny Lane")..550-650 67
(No trumpet solo at end of song.)
CAPITOL (5964 "All You Need Is Love") 200-250 67
(This promo, as well as many Capitol issues by other artists, was shipped in a "Rush" paper sleeve. It's possible a slight premium may be placed on these sleeves, although they were NOT identified in any way as a Beatles item.)
CAPITOL CUSTOM (2637 "Music City KFWBeatles") 800-1000 64
(Radio KFWB and Wallichs Music City promo disc, "The Beatles Talking"/"You Can't Do That.")
CARROLL JAMES (3301 "The Carroll James Interview with the Beatles") 6-8 84
DECCA (31382 "My Bonnie"). 1500-2000 62
(Shown as by Tony Sheridan & Beat Brothers. Pink label with black lettering.)
MBRF (55551 "Decade") 150-250 74
(Contains radio spots for the "Beatles 1962-1966" and "Beatles 1967-1970." May be bootleg, and not an authorized record.)
MGM (13213 "My Bonnie") 200-250 64
(Shown as by the Beatles with Tony Sheridan.)
MGM (13227 "Why") 200-250 64
(Shown as by the Beatles with Tony Sheridan.)
SWAN (4152 "She Loves You") 450-500 63
SWAN (4152 "I'll Get You") 550-650 64
(Single-sided pressing. Flip side has blank grooves.)
SWAN (4182 "Sie Liebt Dich")...400-450 64
TOLLIE (9001 "Twist and Shout") 100-125 64
TOLLIE (9008 "Love Me Do") 400-450 64
TOPAZ (1353 "Seattle Press Conference") 4-8 89
U.A. (2357 "A Hard Day's Night") 2000-3000 64
(Theater lobby advertisements. Orange label.)
U.A. (10029 "A Hard Day's Night") 1200-1500 64
(Open-end interview. Has small play hole.)
U.A. (42370 "Let It Be") 1000-1200 70
(Has three radio advertisements for the film.)
VEE JAY (8 "Anna"/"Ask Me Why") 10000-12000 64
VEE JAY (498 "Please Please Me") 500-1000 63
VEE JAY (522 "From Me to You") 400-500 63
VEE JAY (581 "Please Please Me") 500-600 64
(Blue and white label.)
VEE JAY (587 "Do You Want to Know a Secret") 550-650 64
WHAT'S IT ALL ABOUT 15-20

Plastic Soundsheets/Flexi-Discs

AMERICOM ("Yellow Submarine") 1500-1800 69
(Plastic "Pocket Disc" soundsheet. Number not known.)
AMERICOM (221 "Hey Jude") ... 250-300 69
(Plastic "Pocket Disc" soundsheet.)
AMERICOM (335 "Get Back") .800-1000 69
(Plastic "Pocket Disc" soundsheet.)
AMERICOM (382 "Ballad of John & Yoko") 600-800 69
(Plastic "Pocket Disc" soundsheet.)
EVA-TONE (830771 "Till There Was You") 4-6 83
EVA-TONE (420826 "All My Loving") 5-10 82
(Back side reads either "Compliments of Musicland.")
EVA-TONE (420826 "All My Loving") 15-25 82
(Back side reads "Compliments of Sam Goody" or "Compliments of Discount.")
EVA-TONE (420827 "Magical Mystery Tour") 5-10 82
(Back side reads either "Compliments of Musicland")
EVA-TONE (420827 "Magical Mystery Tour") 15-25 82
(Back side reads "Compliments of Sam Goody" or "Compliments of Discount.")
EVA-TONE (420828 "Rocky Raccoon") 5-10 82
(Back side reads either "Compliments of Musicland".)
EVA-TONE (420828 "Rocky Raccoon") 15-25 82
(Back side reads "Compliments of Sam Goody" or "Compliments of Discount.")
EVA-TONE (1214825 "The Beatles German Medley") 50-60 83
OFFICIAL BEATLES FAN CLUB ("1964 Season's Greetings from the Beatles") 250-300 64
OFFICIAL BEATLES FAN CLUB ("1965 Beatles Christmas Record") 150-175 65
(Includes picture sleeve.)
OFFICIAL BEATLES FAN CLUB ("1966 Season's Greetings from the Beatles") 125-150 66
OFFICIAL BEATLES FAN CLUB ("1967 Christmas Time Is Here Again") 125-150 67
OFFICIAL BEATLES FAN CLUB ("1968 Beatles Christmas Record") 100-125 68
(Includes picture sleeve.)
OFFICIAL BEATLES FAN CLUB ("1969 Happy Christmas") 75-100 69
(Includes picture sleeve.)

EPs: 7-inch

CAPITOL (EAP 1-2121 "Four by the Beatles") 30-400 64
CAPITOL (R-5365 "4-by the Beatles") 200-250 65
CAPITOL (58348 "Baby It's You")......4-6 95
CAPITOL COMPACT 33 (2047 "Meet the Beatles") 500-700 64
(Juke box issue only. Add $15 to 25 for each insert.)
CAPITOL COMPACT 33 (2080 "The Beatles' Second Album") 500-700 64
(Juke box issue only. Add $15 to 25 for each insert.)
CAPITOL COMPACT 33 (2108 "Something New") 700-900 64
(Juke box issue only. Add $10 to 30 for each insert.)
VEE JAY (VJEP 1-903 "Souvenir of Their Visit to America") 200-225 64
(Solid black label with either oval or brackets or block style Vee Jay logo.)
VEE JAY (VJEP 1-903 "Souvenir of Their Visit to America") 80-100 64
(Black label with rainbow color-band with oval logo.)
VEE JAY (VJEP 1-903 "Souvenir of Their Visit to America") 200-225 64
(Black label with rainbow color-band with brackets logo.)

Promotional EPs

CAPITOL COMPACT 33 (2548/49 "Open-End Interview") 1200-1500 64
(Issued with a paper sleeve/script, which represents about $700-$800 of the value.)
CAPITOL COMPACT 33 (2598/99 "Second Open-End Interview") 1200-1400 64
(Issued with a paper sleeve/script, which represents about $600-$700 of the value.)
CAPITOL (2720/21 "The Beatles Introduce New Songs") 1500-2000 64
(45 rpm EP with John Lennon about Cilla Black's *It's for You*, and Paul talking about Peter & Gordon's *I Don't Want to See You Again*.)
CAPITOL 33 COMPACT (2905/06 "The Capitol Souvenir Record") 400-500 64
(Issued with a paper sleeve and script, which represents about $200-$250 of the value. Contains excerpts of 15 different songs by 15 artists, including the Beatles.)
POLYGRAM (PRO-1113 "Backbeat") 40-50 94
(Soundtrack.)
VEE JAY (903 "Souvenir of Their Visit to America") 300-350 64
(White label with blue print. Price is for disc only.)
VEE JAY (VJEP 1-903 "Ask Me Why") 7500-8500 64
(The high price is for the paper, EP sleeve promoting *Ask Me Why* but still with the same Vee Jay EP number as *Souvenir of Their Visit to America*.)

LPs: 10/12-inch

ADIRONDACK (8146 "Happy Michaelmas") 15-20 81
APPLE ("Beatles Special Limited Edition") 1000-1200 74
(10 LP boxed set.)
APPLE (101 "The Beatles") 100-150 68
(With Capitol logo at bottom of label. Limited numbered edition. Includes photos and poster.)
APPLE (101 "The Beatles") 40-50 71
(Without Capitol logo at bottom of label. Includes photos and poster.)
APPLE (101 "The Beatles") 15-25 76-83
(Orange labels, or purple labels, or black labels. Includes photos and poster.)
APPLE (153 "Yellow Submarine") .20-30 69
(With Capitol logo at bottom of label.)
APPLE (153 "Yellow Submarine") 15-25 71
(Without Capitol logo at bottom of label.)
APPLE (383 "Abbey Road") 50-75 69
(With Capitol logo at bottom of label.)
APPLE (383 "Abbey Road") 15-25 71
(Without Capitol logo at bottom of label.)
APPLE (385 "Hey Jude") 30-35 70
(Has title, *The Beatles Again* on label.)
APPLE (385 "Hey Jude") 60-80 70
(With Capitol logo at bottom of label.)
APPLE (385 "Hey Jude") 15-25 71
(Without Capitol logo at bottom of label.)
APPLE (ST-2047 "Meet the Beatles") 25-35 68
(With Capitol logo at bottom of label.)

APPLE (ST-2047 "Meet the Beatles")..15-25 71
(Without Capitol logo at bottom of label.)
APPLE (ST-2080 "The Beatles' Second Album")..25-35 68
(With Capitol logo at bottom of label.)
APPLE (ST-2080 "The Beatles' Second Album")..15-25 71
(Without Capitol logo at bottom of label.)
APPLE (ST-2108 "Something New")..25-35 68
(With Capitol logo at bottom of label.)
APPLE (ST-2108 "Something New")..15-25 71
(Without Capitol logo at bottom of label.)
APPLE (ST-2222 "The Beatles' Story")..40-50 68
(With Capitol logo at bottom of label.)
APPLE (ST-2222 "The Beatles' Story")..30-40 71
(Without Capitol logo at bottom of label.)
APPLE (ST-2228 "Beatles '65") 25-35 68
(With Capitol logo at bottom of label.)
APPLE (ST-2228 "Beatles '65") 15-25 71
(Without Capitol logo at bottom of label.)
APPLE (ST-2309 "Early Beatles") 25-35 68
(With Capitol logo at bottom of label.)
APPLE (ST-2309 "Early Beatles") 15-25 71
(Without Capitol logo at bottom of label.)
APPLE (ST-2358 "Beatles VI").......25-35 68
(With Capitol logo at bottom of label.)
APPLE (ST-2358 "Beatles VI").......15-25 71
(Without Capitol logo at bottom of label.)
APPLE (ST-2386 "Help!") 25-35 68
(With Capitol logo at bottom of label.)
APPLE (ST-2386 "Help!") 15-25 71
(Without Capitol logo at bottom of label.)
APPLE (ST-2442 "Rubber Soul") ...25-35 68
(With Capitol logo at bottom of label.)
APPLE (ST-2442 "Rubber Soul") ...15-25 71
(Without Capitol logo at bottom of label.)
APPLE (2553 "Yesterday and Today")..25-35 68
(With Capitol logo at bottom of label.)
APPLE (2553 "Yesterday and Today")..15-25 71
(Without Capitol logo at bottom of label.)
APPLE (ST-2576 "Revolver") 25-35 68
(With Capitol logo at bottom of label.)
APPLE (ST-2576 "Revolver") 15-25 71
(Without Capitol logo at bottom of label.)
APPLE (SMAS-2653 "Sgt. Pepper's Lonely Hearts Club Band")........................30-40 68
(With Capitol logo at bottom of label.)
APPLE (SMAS-2653 "Sgt. Pepper's Lonely Hearts Club Band")........................15-25 71
(Without Capitol logo at bottom of label.)
APPLE (SMAL-2835 "Magical Mystery Tour")..30-40 68
(With Capitol logo at bottom of label.)
APPLE (SMAL-2835 "Magical Mystery Tour")..15-25 71
(Without Capitol logo at bottom of label.)
APPLE (3403 "1962-1966")............30-40 73
APPLE (3404 "1967-1970")............30-40 73
APPLE (34001 "Let It Be").............20-30 70
ATCO (169 "Ain't She Sweet") ...250-300 64
(Monaural. Also contains selections by the Swallows.)
ATCO (169 "Ain't She Sweet") ...300-400 64-69
(Stereo. Also contains selections by the Swallows.)
AUDIO FIDELITY (339 "First Movement").. 8-12 82
AUDIO FIDELITY (339 "First Movement")..15-20 82
(Picture disc.)
AUDIO RARITIES (2452 "The Complete Silver Beatles)..10-15 82
AUDIO RARITIES (30003 "The Silver Beatles)..20-25 82
(Picture disc.)
BACKSTAGE (201 "Like Dreamers Do")..40-60 82
(Two-LP set. One picture disc and one colored vinyl.)
BACKSTAGE (1111 "Like Dreamers Do")..30-40 82
(Three-LP set. Contains two picture discs and a white vinyl LP.)
BACKSTAGE (1111 "Like Dreamers Do")..70-90 82
(Three-LP set. Contains two picture discs and a GRAY vinyl LP.)
BACKSTAGE (1111 "Like Dreamers Do")..50-60 82
(Three-LP set. Includes any of the custom issues, which had various logos printed on the reverse side of the picture discs.)
BACKSTAGE (1111 "Like Dreamers Do")..30-40 82
(Three-LP set. No custom artwork on picture disc. With gatefold cover.)
BACKSTAGE (1165 "Beatles Talk with Jerry G. Volume 1")..15-20 82
(Picture disc.)
BACKSTAGE (1175 "Beatles Talk with Jerry G. Volume 2")..15-20 82
(Picture disc.)
CAPITOL (101 "The Beatles")........20-25 76
(Orange label.)
CAPITOL (101 "The Beatles")........15-20 78
(Purple label.)
CAPITOL (101 "The Beatles")........25-30 83
(Black label.)
CAPITOL (153 "Yellow Submarine").. 8-12 76
(Orange label.)
CAPITOL (153 "Yellow Submarine").. 6-10 78
(Purple label.)
CAPITOL (153 "Yellow Submarine")..10-15 84
(Black label.)
CAPITOL (383 "Abbey Road") 8-12 76
(Orange label.)
CAPITOL (383 "Abbey Road") 6-10 78
(Purple label.)
CAPITOL (383 "Abbey Road") 20-30 83
(Black label.)
CAPITOL (385 "Hey Jude")............8-12 76
(Orange label.)
CAPITOL (385 "Hey Jude")............6-10 78
(Purple label.)
CAPITOL (385 "Hey Jude")...........30-50 83
(Black label.)
CAPITOL (T-2047 "Meet the Beatles")..50-100 64
(Monaural.)
CAPITOL (ST-2047 "Meet the Beatles")..80-100 64
(Stereo. Black label with white print around border. Does not have "Subsidiary of Capitol, etc." perimeter print.)
CAPITOL (ST-2047 "Meet the Beatles")..40-50 64
(Stereo. Black label with white print around border. Has "Subsidiary of Capitol, etc." print.)
CAPITOL (ST-2047 "Meet the Beatles")..30-40 69
(Green label.)
CAPITOL (ST-2047 "Meet the Beatles")..8-12 76
(Orange label.)
CAPITOL (ST-2047 "Meet the Beatles")..6-10 78
(Purple label.)
CAPITOL (ST-2047 "Meet the Beatles")..10-15 83
(Black label with black print around border.)
CAPITOL (ST-8-2047 "Meet the Beatles")..200-250 64
(Capitol Record Club issue, black label.)
CAPITOL (ST-8-2047 "Meet the Beatles")..80-100 69
(Capitol Record Club issue, green label.)
CAPITOL (T-2080 "The Beatles' Second Album")..50-100 64
(Monaural.)
CAPITOL (ST-2080 "The Beatles' Second Album")..90-100 64
(Stereo. Black label with white print around border. Does not have "Subsidiary of Capitol, etc." perimeter print.)
CAPITOL (ST-2080 "The Beatles' Second Album")..40-50 64
(Stereo. Black label with white print around border. Has "Subsidiary of Capitol, etc." print.)
CAPITOL (ST-2080 "The Beatles' Second Album")..40-50 69
(Green label.)
CAPITOL (ST-2080 "The Beatles' Second Album")..8-12 76
(Orange label.)
CAPITOL (ST-2080 "The Beatles' Second Album")..6-10 78
(Purple label.)
CAPITOL (ST-2080 "The Beatles' Second Album")..10-15 83
(Black label with black print around border.)
CAPITOL (ST-8-2080 "The Beatles' Second Album")..400-450 64
(Capitol Record Club issue, black label.)
CAPITOL (ST-8-2080 "The Beatles' Second Album")..300-350 69
(Capitol Record Club issue, green label.)
CAPITOL (T-2108 "Something New")..50-100 64
(Monaural.)
CAPITOL (ST-2108 "Something New")..80-90 64
(Stereo. Black label with white print around border. Does not have "Subsidiary of Capitol, etc." perimeter print.)
CAPITOL (ST-2108 "Something New")..40-50 64
(Stereo. Black label with white print around border. Has "Subsidiary of Capitol, etc." print.)
CAPITOL (ST-2108 "Something New")..30-40 69
(Green label.)
CAPITOL (ST-2108 "Something New")..8-12 76
(Orange label.)
CAPITOL (ST-2108 "Something New")..6-10 78
(Purple label.)
CAPITOL (ST-2108 "Something New")..10-15 83
(Black label with black print around border.)
CAPITOL (ST-8-2108 "Something New")..200-250 64
(Record Club issue, black label.)
CAPITOL (ST-8-2108 "Something New")..80-120 69
(Record Club issue, green label.)
CAPITOL (TBO-2222 "The Beatles' Story")..200-250 64
(Monaural.)
CAPITOL (STBO-2222 "The Beatles' Story")..125-175 64
(Stereo. Black label with white print around border. Does not have "Subsidiary of Capitol, etc." perimeter print.)
CAPITOL (STBO-2222 "The Beatles' Story")..50-60 69
(Stereo. Black label with white print around border. Has "Subsidiary of Capitol, etc." print.)
CAPITOL (STBO-2222 "The Beatles' Story")..40-50 69
(Green label.)
CAPITOL (STBO-2222 "The Beatles' Story")..15-20 76
(Orange labels, or purple labels.)
CAPITOL (STBO-2222 "The Beatles' Story")..40-50 83
(Black label with black print around border.)
CAPITOL (T-2228 "Beatles '65")..50-100 65
(Monaural.)
CAPITOL (ST-2228 "Beatles '65") 70-90 65
(Stereo. Black label with white print around border.)
CAPITOL (ST-2228 "Beatles '65") 30-40 69
(Green label.)
CAPITOL (ST-2228 "Beatles '65")....8-12 76
(Orange label.)
CAPITOL (ST-2228 "Beatles '65")....6-10 78
(Purple label.)
CAPITOL (ST-2228 "Beatles '65") 10-15 83
(Black label with black print around border.)
CAPITOL (T-2309 "The Early Beatles")..50-100 65
(Monaural.)
CAPITOL (ST-2309 "The Early Beatles")..80-120 65
(Stereo. Black label with white print around border. Does not have "Subsidiary of Capitol, etc." perimeter print.)
CAPITOL (ST-2309 "The Early Beatles")..40-50 69
(Stereo. Black label with white print around border. Has "Subsidiary of Capitol, etc." print.)
CAPITOL (ST-2309 "The Early Beatles")..30-40 69
(Green label.)
CAPITOL (ST-2309 "The Early Beatles")..8-12 76
(Orange label.)
CAPITOL (ST-2309 "The Early Beatles")..6-10 78
(Purple label.)
CAPITOL (ST-2309 "The Early Beatles")..15-25 83
(Black label with black print around border.)
CAPITOL (T-2358 "Beatles VI") ...50-100 65
(Monaural.)
CAPITOL (ST-2358 "Beatles VI")...70-90 65
(Stereo. Black label with white print around border.)
CAPITOL (ST-2358 "Beatles VI")...30-40 69
(Green label.)
CAPITOL (ST-2358 "Beatles VI").....8-12 76
(Orange label.)
CAPITOL (ST-2358 "Beatles VI").....6-10 78
(Purple label with "Mfd.." perimeter print.)
CAPITOL (ST-2358 "Beatles VI")...10-15 83
(Black label with black print around border.)
CAPITOL (ST-2358 "Beatles VI")...60-80 88
(Purple label with "Manufactured by Capitol, etc." perimeter print.)
CAPITOL (ST-8-2358 "Beatles VI")..250-300 69
(Green label. Capitol Record Club issue.)
CAPITOL (MAS-2386 "Help!") 50-100 65
(Monaural.)
CAPITOL (SMAS-2386 "Help!").....60-80 65
(Stereo. Black label with white print around border. Does not have "Subsidiary of Capitol, etc." perimeter print.)
CAPITOL (SMAS-2386 "Help!").....40-50 69
(Stereo. Black label with white print around border. Has "Subsidiary of Capitol, etc." print.)
CAPITOL (SMAS-2386 "Help!").....30-40 69
(Green label.)
CAPITOL (SMAS-2386 "Help!").......8-12 76
(Orange label.)
CAPITOL (SMAS-2386 "Help!").......6-10 78
(Purple label.)
CAPITOL (SMAS-2386 "Help!").....10-15 83
(Black label with black print around border.)
CAPITOL (SMAS-8-2386 "Help!")..300-500 65
(Capitol Record Club, or Longines Symphonette Record Club issue, black label.)
CAPITOL (SMAS-8-2386 "Help!")..200-300 69
(Capitol Record Club issue, green label.)
CAPITOL (T-2442 "Rubber Soul")..50-100 65
(Monaural.)
CAPITOL (ST-2442 "Rubber Soul")..70-90 65
(Stereo. Black label with white print around border. Does not have "Subsidiary of Capitol, etc." perimeter print.)
CAPITOL (ST-2442 "Rubber Soul")..40-50 65
(Stereo. Black label with white print around border. Has "Subsidiary of Capitol, etc." print.)
CAPITOL (ST-2442 "Rubber Soul")..30-40 69
(Green label.)
CAPITOL (ST-2442 "Rubber Soul")..8-12 76
(Orange label.)
CAPITOL (SW-2442 "Rubber Soul")..6-10 78
(Purple label.)
CAPITOL (SW-2442 "Rubber Soul")..10-15 83
(Black label with black print around border.)
CAPITOL (ST-8-2442 "Rubber Soul")..200-250 65
(Capitol Record Club issue, black label.)
CAPITOL (ST-8-2442 "Rubber Soul")..80-100 69
(Capitol Record Club issue, green label.)
CAPITOL (T-2553 "Yesterday and Today")..2000-3000 66
(Monaural. FIRST STATE "Butcher cover" issues.)
CAPITOL (ST-2553 "Yesterday and Today")..5000-7000 66
(Stereo. FIRST STATE "Butcher Cover" issues.)
CAPITOL (T-2553 "Yesterday and Today")..500-700 66
(Monaural. PASTE OVER or PEELED "Butcher cover" copies.)
CAPITOL (ST-2553 "Yesterday and Today")..1000-1200 66
(Stereo. PASTE OVER or PEELED "Butcher cover" copies.)
Note: the wide range of values exists here due to varied opinions on the practice of peeling the "Trunk cover" from the "Butcher cover." The expertise used in the peeling is also a major factor affecting the value of these LPs.
CAPITOL (T-2553 "Yesterday and Today")..50-100 66
(Monaural. "Trunk cover.")
CAPITOL (ST-2553 "Yesterday and Today")..80-100 66
(Stereo. Black label with white print around border. Does not have "Subsidiary of Capitol, etc." perimeter print.)
CAPITOL (ST-2553 "Yesterday and Today")..40-50 69
(Stereo. Black label with white print around border. Has "Subsidiary of Capitol, etc." print. "Trunk cover.")
CAPITOL (ST-2553 "Yesterday and Today")..30-40 69
(Green label.)
CAPITOL (ST-2553 "Yesterday and Today")..8-12 76
(Orange label.)
CAPITOL (ST-2553 "Yesterday and Today")..6-10 78
(Purple label.)
CAPITOL (ST-2553 "Yesterday and Today")..10-15 83
(Black label with black print around border.)
CAPITOL (ST-8-2553 "Yesterday and Today")..200-250 66
(Capitol Record Club issue, black label.)
CAPITOL (ST-8-2553 "Yesterday and Today")..80-100 69
(Capitol Record Club issue, green label.)
CAPITOL (T-2576 "Revolver").....50-100 66
(Monaural.)
CAPITOL (ST-2576 "Revolver") 70-90 66
(Stereo. Black label with white print around border. Does not have "Subsidiary of Capitol, etc." perimeter print.)
CAPITOL (ST-2576 "Revolver") 40-50 66
(Stereo. Black label with white print around border. Has "Subsidiary of Capitol, etc." print.)
CAPITOL (ST-2576 "Revolver") 30-40 69
(Green label.)
CAPITOL (ST-2576 "Revolver") 250-300 71
(Red label.)
CAPITOL (ST-2576 "Revolver") 8-12 76
(Orange label.)
CAPITOL (ST-2576 "Revolver") 6-10 78
(Purple label.)
CAPITOL (ST-2576 "Revolver") 10-15 83
(Black label with black print around border.)
CAPITOL (ST-8-2576 "Revolver")..175-200 66
(Capitol Record Club issue, black label.)
CAPITOL (ST-8-2576 "Revolver")..70-90 69
(Capitol Record Club issue, green label.)
CAPITOL (ST-8-2576 "Revolver")..175-200 76
(Capitol Record Club issue, orange label.)
CAPITOL (MAS-2653 "Sgt. Pepper's Lonely Hearts Club Band")........................200-250 67
(Monaural.)
CAPITOL (SMAS-2653 "Sgt. Pepper's Lonely Hearts Club Band")........................125-150 67
(Stereo. Black label with white print around border. Does not have "Subsidiary of Capitol, etc." perimeter print.)
CAPITOL (SMAS-2653 "Sgt. Pepper's Lonely Hearts Club Band")........................50-60 69
(Stereo. Black label with white print around border. Has "Subsidiary of Capitol, etc." print.)
CAPITOL (SMAS-2653 "Sgt. Pepper's Lonely Hearts Club Band")........................40-50 69
(Green label.)
CAPITOL (SMAS-2653 "Sgt. Pepper's Lonely Hearts Club Band")........................8-12 76
(Orange label.)
CAPITOL (SMAS-2653 "Sgt. Pepper's Lonely Hearts Club Band")........................6-10 78
(Purple label.)
CAPITOL (SMAS-2653 "Sgt. Pepper's Lonely Hearts Club Band")........................10-15 83
(Black label with black print around border.)
CAPITOL (MAL-2835 "Magical Mystery Tour")..200-250 67
(Monaural.)
CAPITOL (SMAL-2835 "Magical Mystery Tour")..70-90 67
(Stereo. Black label with white print around border. Does not have "Subsidiary of Capitol, etc." perimeter print.)
CAPITOL (SMAL-2835 "Magical Mystery Tour")..40-50 68
(Stereo. Black label with white print around border. Has "Subsidiary of Capitol, etc." print.)
CAPITOL (SMAL-2835 "Magical Mystery Tour")..40-50 69
(Green label.)
CAPITOL (SMAL-2835 "Magical Mystery Tour")..8-12 76
(Orange label.)
CAPITOL (SMAL-2835 "Magical Mystery Tour")..6-10 78
(Purple label.)
CAPITOL (SMAL-2835 "Magical Mystery Tour")..10-15 83
(Black label with black print around border.)
CAPITOL (3403 "The Beatles/ 1962-1966")..15-20 78
CAPITOL (3404 "The Beatles/ 1967-1970")..15-20 78
CAPITOL (SPRO-8969 "Rarities") .40-50 78
(Bonus LP in *Beatles Collection* boxed set.)
CAPITOL (11537 "Rock 'n' Roll Music")..30-40 76
CAPITOL (11638 "Beatles at the Hollywood Bowl")..8-10 77
CAPITOL (11711 "Love Songs")....30-40 77
CAPITOL (11840 "Sgt. Pepper's Lonely Hearts Club Band")........................20-30 78
(Picture disc.)
CAPITOL (11840 "Sgt. Pepper")....30-45 78
(Picture disc. Has drum photo on both sides.)
CAPITOL (11841 "The Beatles") 100-200 78
(Gray splash-colored vinyl. Experimental item only.)
CAPITOL (11841 "The Beatles")....30-40 78
(White vinyl.)
CAPITOL (11842 "The Beatles/ 1962-1966")..30-40 78
(Colored vinyl.)
CAPITOL (11843 "The Beatles/ 1967-1970")..30-40 78
(Colored vinyl.)
CAPITOL (11900 "Abbey Road") ...50-60 78
(Picture disc.)
CAPITOL (11921 "A Hard Day's Night")..8-10 80
(Purple label with "Mfd..." perimeter print.)
CAPITOL (11921 "A Hard Day's Night")..10-15 84
(Black label with black print around border.)
CAPITOL (11921 "A Hard Day's Night")..15-25 88
(Purple label with "Manufactured..." perimeter print.)
CAPITOL (11922 "Let It Be")...........8-12 79
(Purple label.)
CAPITOL (11922 "Let It Be")........10-15 83
(Black label with black print around border.)
CAPITOL (12009 "Rarities") 200-250 78
CAPITOL (12080 "Rarities") 15-20 80
CAPITOL (12199 "Reel Music").......8-12 82
CAPITOL (12245 "The Beatles 20 Greatest Hits")..15-25 82-88
(Purple or black label.)
CAPITOL (16020 "Rock 'N' Roll Music, Volume I")..5-10 80
CAPITOL (16021 "Rock 'N' Roll Music, Volume II")..5-10 80
CAPITOL (31796 "Live at the BBC")..40-60 94
CAPITOL (34445 "Anthology I")...75-100 96
CAPITOL (34448 "Anthology II")....50-75 96
CAPITOL (34451 "Anthology III")...50-75 96
CAPITOL (46435 thru 46447, except 46443)..15-25 87-94
CAPITOL (46443 "The Beatles")....30-40 88
CAPITOL (48062 "Magical Mystery Tour")..15-25 87
CAPITOL (90043 "Past Masters, Vol. 1")..6-10 88
CAPITOL (90044 "Past Masters, Vol. 2")..6-10 88
CAPITOL (90435 thru 90454) 20-30 88
CAPITOL (91302 "Beatles Deluxe Box Set")..200-250 88
(14 LP boxed set.)
CICADELIC..6-12 85-87
CLARION (601 "The Amazing Beatles & Other Great English Sounds")............150-200 66
(Stereo. Back cover lists song titles. Also contains selections by the Swallows.)
CLARION (601 "The Amazing Beatles & Other Great English Sounds")............175-200 66
(Stereo. Back cover does NOT list song titles. Also contains selections by the Swallows.)
CLARION (601 "The Amazing Beatles & Other Great English Sounds")............100-125 66
(Monaural. Also contains selections by the Swallows.)
CREATIVE RADIO ("The Beatle Invasion")..35-45 80s
(Three-LP set, includes 12x19 poster.)
DESERT VIBRATIONS 20-25 82
GREAT NORTHWEST MUSIC CO. (4007 "Beatle Talk")..5-10 78
GREAT NORTHWEST MUSIC CO. (4007 "Beatle Talk")..25-50 78
(Columbia Record Club issue.)
HALL of MUSIC..30-40 81
HERITAGE SOUND 30-40 82
I-N-S RADIO NEWS ("American Tour with Ed Rudy #2")..15-25 80
LINGASONG (7001 "Live at the Starclub in Hamburg Germany-1962")..............15-20 77
(Black vinyl.)
LLOYDS (AG-8146 "The Great American Tour 1965 Live Beatlemania Concert")..500-700 65
(With selections by the Liverpool Lads.)
METRO (M-563 "This Is Where It Started")..80-100 66
(Also contains selections by Tony Sheridan and by the Titans.)
METRO (MS-563 "This Is Where It Started")..175-225 66
(Also contains selections by Tony Sheridan and by the Titans.)
MFSL (1 "The Beatles, the Collection")..400-500 82
(Boxed, 14-disc set. Includes booklet and alignment tool.)
MFSL (023 "Abbey Road")............40-50 79
MFSL (047 "Magical Mystery Tour")..55-65 81
MFSL (2-072 "The Beatles")..........40-50 82
MFSL (UHQR 100 "Sgt. Pepper's Lonely Hearts Club Band")..250-300 82
(Boxed set. Silver label.)
MFSL (100 "Sgt. Pepper's Lonely Hearts Club Band")..30-40 85
(White label.)
MFSL (101 "Please Please Me")....25-35 86
MFSL (102 "With the Beatles") ..150-200 86
MFSL (103 "A Hard Day's Night") ..30-40 87
MFSL (104 "Beatles for Sale").......30-40 87
MFSL (105 "Help!")......................30-40 85
MFSL (106 "Rubber Soul")...........30-40 84
MFSL (107 "Revolver")..................30-40 86
MFSL (108 "Yellow Submarine")....50-60 87
MFSL (109 "Let It Be")..................30-40 87
(Gatefold cover.)

MFSL (109 "Let It Be")..............150-200 87
(Single pocket cover.)
MGM (E-4215 "The Beatles with Tony Sheridan and Guests")..........................200-225 64
(Monaural. With selections by Tony Sheridan and by the Titans.)
MGM (SE-4215 "The Beatles with Tony Sheridan and Guests")..............600-800 64
(Stereo. With selections by Tony Sheridan and by the Titans.)
MUSIC INTERNATIONAL.............40-50 85
PAC.......................................30-50 81
PBR INT'L................................70-90 78
(Colored vinyl.)
PBR INT'L................................50-60 78
(Black vinyl.)
PHOENIX 10................................8-12 82
PHOENIX 20..............................15-20 82-83
PICKWICK (Except 90071)..........20-30 78-79
PICKWICK (90071 "Recorded Live in Hamburg, 1962, Volume 3")..........30-40 78
POLYDOR (4504 "In the Beginning, Circa 1960")......................................20-30 70
(With gatefold cover.)
POLYDOR (4504 "In the Beginning, Circa 1960")..6-12 81-84
(With standard cover.)
POLYDOR (93199 "In the Beginning, Circa 1960")......................................20-30 70
(Capitol Record Club issue.)
POLYDOR (422-825-073 "In the Beginning, Circa 1960")............................15-20 88
RAVEN (8911 "Talk Down Under")..5-10 81
RPN (RADIO PULSEBEAT NEWS) ("American Tour with Ed Rudy #2")..............40-50 64
(This LP was occasionally issued with a "Teen Talk" booklet. The value of the booklet is approximately the same as for the LP. This edition has NO pictures of the Beatles on the LP cover.)
RPN (RADIO PULSEBEAT NEWS) ("1965 Talk Album, Ed Rudy/New US Tour")......................................100-150 65
SAVAGE (69 "The Savage Young Beatles")..............................1200-1500 68
(Label is yellow. Cover is glossy orange.)
SAVAGE (69 "The Savage Young Beatles")................................100-125 68
(Label is orange. Cover is orange.)
SILHOUETTE (10004 "Timeless").20-30 81
(Picture disc.)
SILHOUETTE (10010 "Timeless II")...20-30 82
(Picture disc.)
SILHOUETTE (10013 "The British Are Coming")..................................10-15 84
(Black vinyl.)
SILHOUETTE (10013 "The British Are Coming")..................................40-80 84
(Colored vinyl.)
SILHOUETTE (10015 "The Golden Beatles")....................................10-15 85
(Black vinyl.)
SILHOUETTE (10015 "The Golden Beatles")....................................40-80 85
(Colored vinyl.)
STERLING PRODUCTIONS (6481 "I Apologize")...........................300-350 66
(Price includes bonus 8" x 10" photo, which represents $15 to $25 of the value.)
U.A. (UAL-3366 "A Hard Day's Night")..................................150-225 64
(Monaural.)
U.A. (UAS-6366 "A Hard Day's Night")..................................200-250 64
(Stereo. Black label. Black vinyl.)
U.A. (UAS-6366 "A Hard Day's Night")......................................50-60 69
(Stereo. Pink and orange or black and orange label.)
U.A. (UAS-6366 "A Hard Day's Night")......................................15-25 71
(Stereo. Tan label.)
U.A. (UAS-6366 "A Hard Day's Night")......................................15-20 77
(Stereo. Orange and yellow label.)
U.A. (T-90828 "A Hard Day's Night")..................................800-900 65
(Monaural. Capitol Record Club issue.)
U.A. (ST-90828 "A Hard Day's Night")..................................400-500 65
(Stereo. Capitol Record Club issue.)
VEE JAY (202 "Hear the Beatles Tell All")..................................250-350 64
(Monaural. Black label with rainbow color-band.)
VEE JAY (202 "Hear the Beatles Tell All")..5-10 79
(Stereo.)
VEE JAY (202 "Hear the Beatles Tell All")...20-30 87
(Shaped picture disc.)
VEE JAY (1062 "Introducing the Beatles")..............................1800-2000 63
(Monaural. With *Love Me Do* and *P.S. I Love You.* Back cover pictures 25 other Vee Jay albums.)
VEE JAY (1062 "Introducing the Beatles")..............................6000-7000 63
(Stereo. With *Love Me Do* and *P.S. I Love You.* Back cover pictures 25 other Vee Jay albums.)
VEE JAY (1062 "Introducing the Beatles")..................................900-1100 63
(Monaural. With *Love Me Do* and *P.S. I Love You.* Back cover is blank.)
VEE JAY (1062 "Introducing the Beatles")..............................3000-4000 63
(Stereo. With *Love Me Do* and *P.S. I Love You.* Back cover is blank.)
VEE JAY (1062 "Introducing the Beatles")..................................800-900 64
(Monaural. With *Love Me Do* and *P.S. I Love You.* Back cover lists contents. Has brackets style label logo.)
VEE JAY (1062 "Introducing the Beatles")..............................2500-5000 64
(Stereo. With *Love Me Do* and *P.S. I Love You.* Back cover lists contents. Has brackets style label logo. As with all Vee Jay STEREO discs, the title, *Introducing the Beatles*, and artist credit, "The Beatles," is printed above the hole. Counterfeits have that text divided by the hole.)
VEE JAY (1062 "Introducing the Beatles")..................................700-800 64
(Monaural. With *Love Me Do* and *P.S. I Love You.* Back cover lists contents. Oval style label logo.)
VEE JAY (1062 "Introducing the Beatles")...........................20,000-25,000 64
(Stereo. With *Love Me Do* and *P.S. I Love You.* Back cover lists contents. Oval style label logo.)
VEE JAY (1062 "Introducing the Beatles")..............................2000-3000 64
(Stereo. With *Love Me Do* and *P.S. I Love You* listed on cover and disc, but actually plays *Ask Me Why* and *Please Please Me.*)
VEE JAY (1062 "Introducing the Beatles")..............................1800-2200 64
(Stereo. With *Ask Me Why* and *Please Please Me.* For any of the label styles or logo designs.)
VEE JAY (1062 "Introducing the Beatles")..................................250-350 64
(Monaural, rainbow color-band label. With *Ask Me Why* and *Please Please Me.* Add $50 to $75 if accompanied by "Featuring Twist and Shout" and "Please Please Me" sticker.)
VEE JAY (1062 "Introducing the Beatles")..................................250-350 64
(Monaural, black label, no color-band. With *Ask Me Why* and *Please Please Me.* With "Vee Jay Records" printed under "VJ" logo, or oval style logo. Add $50 to $75 if accompanied by "Featuring Twist and Shout" and "Please Please Me" sticker.)
VEE JAY (1062 "Introducing the Beatles")..............................1000-1200 64
(Monaural, black label, no color-band. With *Ask Me Why* and *Please Please Me.* With brackets logo. Add $50 to $75 if accompanied by "Featuring Twist and Shout" and "Please Please Me" sticker.)
VEE JAY (1092 "Songs, Pictures and Stories")..................................300-400 64
(Monaural.)
VEE JAY (1092 "Songs and Pictures")..8-10
(Reissue.)

Promotional LPs

APPLE (SBC-100 "The Beatles' Christmas Album")..................................200-250 70
(Special issue for Beatles fan club members.)
APPLE (SPRO 11206/207 "College Radio Sampler")..................................125-175 96
APPLE FILMS (KAL 1004 "The Yellow Submarine")..............................900-1200 69
(Contains the advertisements used on radio stations to promote the film.)
ATCO (169 "Ain't She Sweet")...700-900 64
(Also contains selections by the Swallows.)
BACKSTAGE (1111 "Like Dreamers Do")..30-40 82
(Colored vinyl)
CAPITOL ("The Platinum Beatles Collection")..................................500-600 84
(Boxed, 18-disc set.)
CAPITOL (SMAS-11638 "Beatles at the Hollywood Bowl")......................300-400 77
(Promotional issue.)
CAPITOL (SMAS-11638 "Beatles at the Hollywood Bowl")..........................15-25 77
(Without bar code [UPC] symbol.)
CAPITOL (SMAS-11638 "Beatles at the Hollywood Bowl")..........................30-40 89
(With bar code [UPC] symbol.)
CAPITOL (12199 "Reel Music").....30-40 82
(Promotional issue. Colored vinyl. White cover.)
CAPITOL (12199 "Reel Music").....15-20 82
(Promotional issue. Colored vinyl. Regular cover.)
CAPITOL/EMI (BC-13 "The Beatles Collection")..................................400-450 78
(Boxed, 14-disc set.)
I-N-S RADIO NEWS (DOC-1 "Beatlemania Tour Coverage")..........................900-1200 64
(Promotional only issue. An open-end interview. Includes a script.)
LINGASONG (7001 "Live at the Starclub in Hamburg Germany-1962")............30-40 77
(Promotional issue. Black vinyl.)
LINGASONG (7001 "Live at the Starclub in Hamburg Germany-1962")........250-350 77
(Promotional issue. Colored vinyl.)
ORANGE (12880 "Silver Beatles")..250-350 85
RAVEN (8911 "Talk Down Under")..60-80 81
SILHOUETTE..................................30-40 84
U.A. (UA-HELP "United Artists Presents *Help!*")..800-900 65
(Contains the advertisements used on radio stations to promote the film.)
U.A. (UA-HELP INT "Special Open-End Interview")..............................1000-1200 65
(Price includes script and programming information, which represents about $75-100 of the value.)
U.A. (UA-HELP-SHOW "United Artists Presents *Help!*")..............................2000-2200 65
(Single-sided open-end interview. Price includes script which represents about $75 to $100 of the value.)
U.A. (2359/60 "Special Beatles Half Hour Open End Interview")..........................1000-1200 64
(Price includes 12-pages of script and programming information, which represents about $75 to $100 of the value.)
U.A. (2362/63 "United Artists Presents *A Hard Day's Night*")..............................700-800 64
(Contains the advertisements used on radio stations to promote the film.)
U.A. (UAL-3366 "A Hard Day's Night")..............................2000-2500 64
(Monaural. White label.)
U.A. (UAL-6366 "A Hard Day's Night")..............................10000-12000 64
(Pink vinyl. Likely an experimental pressing.)
VEE JAY (202 "Hear the Beatles Tell All")..............................8000-10000 64
(Label reads "Promotional" on left and "Not For Sale" on right.)
VEE JAY (1092 "Songs, Pictures and Stories")..............................2000-2200 64
(Stereo.)
Members: John Lennon; Paul McCartney; George Harrison; Pete Best; Ringo Starr.
Note: Nearly every valuable Beatles record has been counterfeited. If in doubt, have potential purchases authenticated by an expert.
Also see ALAN, Lee
Also see BEST, Pete
Also see CLAY, Tom
Also see HARRISON, George
Also see LENNON, John
Also see MARTIN, George
Also see McCARTNEY, Paul
Also see MOORE, Harv
Also see NICOL, Jimmy, & Shubdubs
Also see PRESLEY, Elvis / Beatles
Also see PRESTON, Billy
Also see RESIDENTS
Also see SHANKAR, Ravi
Also see SILKIE
Also see STARR, Ringo

BEATLES / Beach Boys / Buddy Holly

LPs: 10/12-inch

CREATIVE RADIO SHOWS (Demo of "Specials")..................................75-100 79
(Promotional issue only.)
Also see HOLLY, Buddy

BEATLES / Beach Boys / Kingston Trio

Plastic Soundsheets/Flexi-Discs:

EVA-TONE (8464 "Surprise Gift from the Beatles, Beach Boys & Kingston Trio")..................................450-550 64
(Seven-inch tri-fold card.)
EVA-TONE (8464 "Surprise Gift from the Beatles, Beach Boys & Kingston Trio")..................................300-350 64
(Five-inch round plastic soundsheet.)
EVA-TONE (8464 "Surprise Gift from the Beatles, Beach Boys & Kingston Trio")..............................2000-2550 64
(Mailer envelope for five-inch round plastic soundsheet.)
Also see BEACH BOYS
Also see KINGSTON TRIO

BEATLES / Jerry Blabber

Singles: 7-inch

QUEST..5-10 65

BEATLES / 4 Seasons — LP '64

LPs: 10/12-inch

VEE JAY (DX-30 "Beatles Vs. the Four Seasons")..................................600-800 64
(Monaural.)
VEE JAY (DXS-30 "Beatles Vs. the Four Seasons")..............................1800-2000 64
(Stereo.)
Price includes a bonus Beatles poster, which represents $150 to $200 of the value.
Also see 4 SEASONS

BEATLES / Frank Ifield — LP '64

LPs: 10/12-inch

VEE JAY (1085 "The Beatles & Frank Ifield")..............................2500-3000 64
(Monaural. Pictures the Beatles on cover.)
VEE JAY (1085 "The Beatles & Frank Ifield")..............................8000-9000 64
(Stereo. Pictures the Beatles on cover.)
VEE JAY (1085 "Jolly What! the Beatles & Frank Ifield")..................................200-250 64
(Monaural. Pictures an Englishman on cover.)
VEE JAY (1085 "Jolly What! the Beatles & Frank Ifield")..................................500-600 64
(Stereo. Pictures an Englishman on cover.)
Also see IFIELD, Frank

BEATLES / Loretta Lynn

Singles: 7-inch

VEE JAY (581 "Please Please Me"/"Before I'm Over You")..................................50-100 64
(This pairing is the result of a production error.)
Also see BEATLES
Also see LYNN, Loretta

BEATLES BLAST AT STADIUM (Described by Erupting Fans)

LPs: 10/12-inch

AUDIO JOURNAL..............................10-20 66
(*Beatles Blast at Stadium* is the title of the LP. Featuring only noise, made by fans at a Shea Stadium concert. No artists are credited.

BEATLES COSTELLO

EPs: 7-inch

PIOUS..5-10 78
Members: Andy Paley; Jim Freeman; Jim Skinner; Joe Pope; Eric Rosenfield.
Also see PALEY BROTHERS

BEATLETTES

Singles: 7-inch

ASSULT..10-20 64
JAMIE..5-10 64

BEATMASTER

Singles: 7-inch

TOMMY BOY..3-4 84

BEATNICKS

Singles: 7-inch

KEY-LOCK (913 "Blue Angel")..................................500-1000 60

BEATNIKS

(Beat-Niks)

Singles: 7-inch

PERFORMANCE (500 "Get Yourself a Ready")..10-20 60s
ROULETTE ("Beatnik Blues")........15-25 59
TAMPA..10-15 58
Also see RAYE, Patsy, & Beatniks

BEATS

Singles: 7-inch

COLUMBIA (41781 "Beatnik Bounce")..8-12 60

BEATS

Singles: 7-inch

DESIGN (827 "Bagdad Daddy")........6-12 64

LPs: 10/12-inch

DESIGN..10-20 64
RONDO (2026 "New Merseyside Sound")..25-35 64
(Also issued as by the Liverpool Beats.)
Also see LIVERPOOL BEATS

BEATS INTERNATIONAL — P&R/LP '90

LPs: 10/12-inch

ELEKTRA..5-8 90
Members: Norman Cook; Lester Noel; Lindy Layton; Andy Boucher; Luke Cresswell.
Also see HOUSEMARTINS

BEATSTALKERS

Singles: 7-inch

PRESS..10-15 66

BEATTY, E.C. — P&R '59

Singles: 7-inch

CAMPBELL..5-10 64
COLONIAL..8-15 59-61

BEATTY, Pamela

Singles: 7-inch

TIP (1018 "Talking Eyes")..............20-30 60s

BEATTY, Susi — C&W '89

Singles: 7-inch

STARWAY..3-4 89

BEAU, Bill

(Bill Beau Trio)

Singles: 7-inch

DUNHILL..4-8 65

BEAU, Kenny

(With the Whirlwinds; Kenny Bolognese)

Singles: 7-inch

PL (1015 "You're the Right One")..250-350
Member: Kenny Chandler.
Also see CHANDLER, Kenny

BEAU, Toby: see TOBY BEAU

BEAU BRUMMELS — P&R/LP '65

Singles: 7-inch

AUTUMN (8 "Laugh Laugh")............8-12 64
(White label.)
AUTUMN (8 "Laugh Laugh")............5-10 64
(Orange label. Different edit than on white label.)
AUTUMN (10 thru 24)..............................5-10 65
PEP..3-4
RHINO..3-4 82
VAULT..4-6 67
W.B...4-8 66-75

Picture Sleeves

PEP..3-4
RHINO..3-4 82

LPs: 10/12-inch

ACCORD..5-10 82
AUTUMN (103 "Introducing the Beau Brummels")..40-50 65
AUTUMN (104 "Beau Brummels, Vol. 2")..40-50 65
JAS..8-10
POST..8-10
RHINO..5-10 81-82
VAULT (114 "Best of the Beau Brummels")..25-30 67
VAULT (121 "Beau Brummels, Vol. 44")..15-20 68
W.B. (Except 1644)..............................20-25 67-75
W.B. (1644 "Beau Brummels '66")..30-35 66
Members: Sal Valentino; Ron Elliott; Ron Meagher; Declan Mulligan; John Petersen.
Session: Van Dyke Parks.
Also see ELLIOTT, Ron
Also see VALENTINO, Sal
Also see PARKS, Van Dyke

BEAU COUP — P&R '87

Singles: 7-inch

AGORA (82734 "Still in My Heart")..5-10
AMHERST..3-4 87
ROCK & ROLL..............................3-4 84-85

BEAU DENTURIES

Singles: 7-inch

ENCORE (1001 "Straight Home")..10-20 66
Also see ZOO

BEAU DOLLAR & COINS

Singles: 7-inch

FRATERNITY..4-8 66
PRIME..4-8 66

BEAU GENTS

Singles: 7-inch

PO CHA MO (794 "Three Letter Word")..20-30

BEAU JENS

Singles: 7-inch

SOUND of the SCREEM (2162 "She Was Mine")..30-40 67

BEAU JIVES

(Beau-Jives)

Singles: 7-inch

LORD BINGO (102 "Brightest Star in the Sky")..50-75 62
LORD BINGO (103 "Dip Dip")........50-100 62
LORD BINGO (107 "Brightest Star in the Sky")..25-50 63
LORD BINGO (108 "Here We Go")..15-25 63
SHEPHERD (2202 "I'll Never Be the Same")..50-75 61
VISION (111 "Dip Dip")..............50-100 62

BEAU PHENOM

Singles: 7-inch

CO-OP..4-6 69

BEAU-BELLS

Singles: 7-inch

ARROW..10-20 58
COLPIX..5-10 59

BEAUBIENS

Singles: 7-inch

MALIBU (67001 "Time's Passed")..............................100-200

BEAUCHEMINS

Singles: 7-inch

MUSTANG..4-8 66

BEAU-HANNON

Singles: 7-inch

UNITED SOUTH..............................10-20

BEAU-JIVES: see BEAU JIVES

BEAU-Ks

Singles: 7-inch

MERCURY..4-8 63-64

BEAU-MARKS — P&R '60

Singles: 7-inch

MAINSTREAM (688 "Clap Your Hands")..5-10 68
PORT (70029 "Lovely Little Lady") 15-25 62
QUALITY ("Clap Your Hands")......20-40 60
(Canadian. Selection number not known.)
QUALITY ("Cause We're in Love")..20-40 60
(Canadian. Selection number not known.)
QUALITY (1404 "Tender Years")...20-30 61
(Canadian.)
QUALITY (1423 "Tender Years")...15-25 62
(Canadian.)
RUST (5035 "School Is Out")........20-30 61
RUST (5050 "Tender Years") 15-25 61
SHAD (5017 "Clap Your Hands")...10-15 60
SHAD (5021 "Cause We're in Love")..10-15 60
TIME (1032 "Rockin' Blues")........20-30 61
(Previously issued in Canada only, credited to the Del Tones.)
Also see DEL TONES

BEAUMONT, Ashley

(Ashley Beaumont the 18th)

Singles: 7-inch

WORTHY (1003 "Shimmy Doll")...35-45 58

BEAUMONT, Donnie

Singles: 7-inch

MERCURY..3-5 75

BEAUMONT, Jimmy — P&R '61

(With the Skyliners; Jimmie Beaumont)

Singles: 7-inch

BANG (525 "You Got Too Much Going for You")..15-20 66
CAPITOL..3-5 74
COLPIX..5-10 61
DOC..5-10
DRIVE..3-5 76
GALLANT (3012 "Love Is a Dangerous Game")..5-10 60s
MAY..8-10 61-63
Also see SKYLINERS

BEAUREGARD

Singles: 7-inch

INT'L ARTISTS (123 "Popcorn Popper")..15-20 68

LPs: 10/12-inch

EMPIRE ("Beauregarde")............75-100 69
(No selection number used.)
SOUND (7104 "Beauregarde").......50-75 69
Members: Greg Sage; Dave Kopel.

BEAUREGARD & TUFFS

Singles: 7-inch

DECCA..4-8 65

BEAUTIFUL APOLLO

Singles: 7-inch

BARRA-DONNA ("Why I")............30-50

BEAUTIFUL BEND

Singles: 7-inch

MARLIN..3-5 78

BEAUTIFUL DAZE
Singles: 7-inch
RPR (101 "City Jungle")....................20-30 67
SPREAD CITY (101 "City Jungle")..10-15 68

BEAUTIFUL MORNING
Singles: 7-inch
CAPITOL.. 3-5 73

BEAUTIFUL PEOPLE
Singles: 7-inch
ROULETTE...................................... 4-8 67

BEAUVOIR, Jean P&R/LP '86
Singles: 12-inch
COLUMBIA..................................... 4-6 86
Singles: 7-inch
COLUMBIA..................................... 3-4 86
Picture Sleeves
COLUMBIA..................................... 3-4 86
LPs: 10/12-inch
COLUMBIA..................................... 5-10 86
Also see LITTLE STEVEN & Disciples of Soul
Also see PLASMATICS

BEAUX JENS
Singles: 7-inch
SOUND OF THE SCEEN (2162 "She Was Mine")....................................10-20 67

BEAVER, D.
Singles: 7-inch
TMI.. 3-5 73
LPs: 10/12-inch
TMI.. 8-10 73

BEAVER, Paul
LPs: 10/12-inch
RAPTURE......................................20-30

BEAVER, Stan
Singles: 7-inch
PETAL (1012 "Got a Rocket in My Pocket")....................................25-30 60

BEAVER & KRAUSE
Singles: 7-inch
W.B. 3-5 70-72
LPs: 10/12-inch
LIMELIGHT....................................20-30 69
NONESUCH...................................15-25 68
W.B. 10-12 70-72
Members: Paul Beaver; Bernard Krause.

BEAVER & TRAPPERS
Singles: 7-inch
WHITE CLIFFS (236 "Happiness").40-60 66

BEAVER BROWN
Singles: 7-inch
COASTLINE.................................... 3-4 80
Picture Sleeves
COASTLINE.................................... 3-4 80

BEAVER PATROL
Singles: 7-inch
COLUMBIA.....................................10-20 65-67
Members: Jim Biesoe; Floyd Humphrys; Jimmy Becker.

BEAVERS
Singles: 78 rpm
CORAL...50-100 49-50
Singles: 7-inch
CORAL (65018 "If You See Tears in My Eyes")....................................200-250 49
CORAL (65026 "Big Mouth Mama")......................................200-250 50
Members: Fred Hamilton; Richard Palmer; Ray Johnson; John Wilson.
Also see LANCE, Herb

BEAVERS
Singles: 7-inch
CAPITOL.......................................10-20 58

BEAVERS, Clyde C&W '60
(Clyde Beavers / Jim Martin)
Singles: 7-inch
DECCA... 5-10 60
HICKORY.. 4-6 66
KA$H.. 4-6 65
TEMPWOOD..................................... 4-8 63
LPs: 10/12-inch
KASH COUNTRY............................. 5-10
SOMERSET...................................... 8-12

BEAVERS, Clyde, & Red Sovine
LPs: 10/12-inch
ALSHIRE... 5-10
Also see BEAVERS, Clyde
Also see SOVINE, Red

BEAVERS, Jackey
(With the Fam Gang; Jackey Beavers Show)
Singles: 7-inch
CHECKER (1119 "I Need Sombody")....................................10-20 65
GRAND LAND (9000 "Bring Me All Your Heartaches")....................................15-25 60s
MAINSTREAM................................... 4-8 69
NATION ("Come Back My Love") ..20-40 60s
(No selection number used.)
REVILOT (208 "I Need My Baby")..150-250 66
SEVENTY-SEVEN............................. 4-6 72-73
SOUND PLUS.................................... 4-6 72
SOUND STAGE 7.............................. 5-8 69-72
W.B. 3-6 72
Also see JOHNNY & JACKEY

BEAVERTEETH
Singles: 7-inch
RCA.. 3-5 77
LPs: 10/12-inch
RCA.. 8-10 77-78

Members: Rodney Justo; John Adkins.
Also see ATLANTA RHYTHM SECTION
Also see CANDYMEN

BE-BOP DELUXE LP '76
Singles: 7-inch
HARVEST... 3-5 75-78
LPs: 10/12-inch
HARVEST (Black vinyl)...................5-10 76-78
HARVEST (Colored vinyl)..............15-20 77-78
Promotional LPs
HARVEST (8531 "Be Bop's Biggest")..25-35 75
Members: Richard Brown; Robert Bryan; Nicholas Chatterton-Dew; Andrew Clarke; Simon Fox; Paul Jeffreys; Milton R. James; Bill Nelson; Ian Parkin; Charles Tumahai.

BECHER, Curt, & California
(Curt Boetcher)
Singles: 7-inch
W.B. 3-4 77
Also see BOETCHER, Curt
Also see CALIFORNIA

BECK, Becky Lee
Singles: 7-inch
CHALLENGE....................................5-10 64

BECK, Bobby
Singles: 7-inch
ABC-PAR..10-20 60

BECK, Carlton
Singles: 7-inch
TROY (100 "The Girl I Left Behind")..400-600 63
(First issued as by Carlton.)
Also see CARLTON

BECK, Floyd
Singles: 12-inch
PRECISION..................................... 4-6 81
Singles: 7-inch
PRECISION..................................... 3-4 80

BECK, Jeff P&R/LP '68
(Jeff Beck Group; with Terry Bozzio & Tony Hymas; with Jan Hammer)
Singles: 7-inch
EPIC (10000 series)........................5-10 67-69
EPIC (50000 series)........................ 3-6 75-76
LPs: 10/12-inch
ACCORD (7141 "Early Anthology")..5-10 81
EPIC (151 "Everything You Always Wanted to Hear")..20-30 76
(Promotional issue only.)
EPIC (796 "Musical Montage").......20-30 79
(Promotional issue only.)
EPIC (850 "Then and Now").............25-35 80
(Two discs. Promotional issue only.)
EPIC (26413 "Truth")......................10-15 68
EPIC (26478 "Bec-Ola")...................10-15 69
EPIC (KE-30973 "Rough and Ready")..10-15 71
EPIC (EQ-30973 "Rough and Ready")..20-30 74
(Quadraphonic.)
EPIC (KE-31331 "Jeff Beck Group")..10-15 72
EPIC (EQ-31331 "Jeff Beck Group")..20-30 72
(Quadraphonic.)
EPIC (PE-33409 "Blow By Blow") ..10-15 75
EPIC (PEQ-33409 "Blow By Blow")..10-15 75
(Quadraphonic.)
EPIC (PE-33849 "Wired")................10-15 75
EPIC (33779 "Truth"/"Beck-Ola")...10-15 75
(Two discs.)
EPIC (PEQ-33849 "Wired") 10-15 75
(Quadraphonic.)
EPIC (34433 "Live")..........................8-12 77
EPIC (35684 "There and Back").......8-12 80
EPIC (39483 "Flash")........................8-12 85
EPIC (44313 "Guitar Shop")..............8-12 89
EPIC (43409 "Blow By Blow")........15-25 75
(Half-speed mastered.)
EPIC (43849 "Wired")......................10-15 75
(Half-speed mastered.)
MFP (5219 "Most of Jeff Beck").......8-10
SPRINGBOARD (4039 "Shapes of Things")..5-10 75
Members: Rod Stewart; Ronnie Wood; Nicky Hopkins; Tony Newman; Bob Tench; Max Middleton; Cozy Powell. Session: Jan Hammer; Jimmy Hall; Terry Bozzio; Tony Hymas.
Also see BECK, BOGERT & APPICE
Also see CLAPTON, Eric, Jeff Beck & Jimmy Page
Also see DONOVAN & Jeff Beck Group
Also see G.T.O.
Also see HALL, Jimmy
Also see HAMMER, Jan
Also see HARRISON, George / Jeff Beck / Dave Edmunds
Also see HONEYDRIPPERS
Also see HOPKINS, Nicky
Also see LORD SUTCH
Also see MISSING PERSONS
Also see POWELL, Cozy
Also see STEWART, Rod
Also see WOOD, Ron
Also see YARDBIRDS

BECK, Jeff, & Rod Stewart P&R '85
Singles: 7-inch
EPIC (05416 "People Get Ready").... 3-4 85
Picture Sleeves
EPIC (05416 "People Get Ready").... 3-5 85
Also see BECK, Jeff
Also see STEWART, Rod

BECK, Jimmy P&R '59
(With His Orchestra)
Singles: 7-inch
ASTRA (1015 "Pipe Dreams") 5-10 65
CHAMPION (1002 "Pipe Dreams") 10-20 59
ZIL (9004 "Carnival")......................15-25 58

BECK, Joe LP '75
(With the Highlites)
Singles: 7-inch
CHARLES (478 "I've Got to Win Your Love")..15-25
CHARLES (577 "Daddy Cool").......10-20
POLYDOR...3-5 77
RADAR (1010 "Cool Moose").........10-20 62
LPs: 10/12-inch
KUDU..8-10 75
POLYDOR...5-10 77
VERVE/FORECAST..........................10-15 69
Also see PHILLIPS, Esther, & Joe Beck

BECK, Johnny
Singles: 78 rpm
SITTIN' IN WITH (531 "Locked in Jail Blues")..75-125 50

BECK, Lee
Singles: 7-inch
KING...3-6 69

BECK, Robin
Singles: 12-inch
MERCURY..4-6 79
Singles: 7-inch
MERCURY..3-4 79-80
LPs: 10/12-inch
MERCURY..5-10 79

BECK, BOGERT & APPICE
Singles: 7-inch
EPIC..3-5 73
LPs: 10/12-inch
EPIC..10-12 73
Members: Jeff Beck; Tim Bogert; Carmine Appice.
Also see BECK, Jeff
Also see CACTUS
Also see SCOTT, Neal
Also see VANILLA FUDGE

BECK BROTHERS
Singles: 7-inch
MID WEST ("Big Rocker") 15-25 59
(Selection number not known.)

BECK FAMILY R&B '79
Singles: 7-inch
LE JOINT 3-5 79
Members: Tony Beck; Tyrone Beck; Mendy Beck; Joanna Beck; Donnie Wilson; Nick Mundy.

BECKER, Francis
Singles: 7-inch
CUCA (1505 "Musicians Play All Night")..4-8 70

BECKER, Gloria
(With the Don Ralke Quintet)
Singles: 78 rpm
REAL (1304 "Sixteen Pounds")........5-10 55
Singles: 7-inch
REAL (1304 "Sixteen Pounds")......10-15 55
Also see RALKE, Don

BECKETT
Singles: 7-inch
CASABLANCA.................................3-4 77
LPs: 10/12-inch
CASABLANCA.................................5-10 77
Members: Robert Barton; Kenny Mountain; Keith Fisher; Ian Murray; Terry Wilson Slesser; Tim Hinkley.

BECKETTE QUINTET
Singles: 7-inch
A&M...4-6 65
GEMCOR..4-6 65

BECKHAM, Bob P&R '59
Singles: 7-inch
DECCA...4-8 59-63
MONUMENT......................................3-5 67
SMASH...3-6 65
Picture Sleeves
DECCA...5-10 59
LPs: 10/12-inch
DECCA...15-20 59

BECKHAM, C.
Singles: 7-inch
TRAVEL..3-4 78

BECKHAM, Charlie C&W '88
Singles: 7-inch
OAK...3-4 88

BECKIES
Singles: 7-inch
SIRE..3-5 76
LPs: 10/12-inch
SIRE..8-12 76
Members: Michael Brown; Gary Hodgden; Scotty Trusty.
Also see LEFT BANKE

BECKMEIER, Freddie
Singles: 7-inch
CASABLANCA.................................3-4 80
LPs: 10/12-inch
CASABLANCA.................................5-10 80

BECKMEIER BROTHERS P&R '79
Singles: 7-inch
CASABLANCA.................................3-4 79
LPs: 10/12-inch
CASABLANCA.................................5-10 79

Members: Fred Beckmeier; Steve Beckmeier.

BECKY & Red Pony
Singles: 7-inch
BARNABY..3-5 70

BECKY & LOLLIPOPS
Singles: 7-inch
EPIC...5-10 64
TROY..10-15 64

BECKY & MONTCLAIRS
Singles: 7-inch
ACCENT 8-12 64

BECTION, James
(L'il Jimmy Bection)
Singles: 7-inch
SEA BIRD 10-20
TMI..3-5 73

BED OF ROSES
Singles: 7-inch
DELTRON..5-10 66
TEA (2577 "Quiet")..........................50-100

BEDBUGS
Singles: 7-inch
LIBERTY 6-10 64
Also see CHIPMUNKS

BEDFORD, Scott
(Scott Bedford Four)
Singles: 7-inch
CONGRESS.......................................4-8 65
JOY...4-8 65

BEDFORD INCIDENT
Singles: 7-inch
KAPP 3-6 69

BEDFORDE SET
Singles: 7-inch
RCA (9068 "The World Through a Tear").............................10-15 67

BEDIENT, Jack
(With the Chessmen)
Singles: 7-inch
COLUMBIA.......................................5-10 67-68
ERA (3050 "The Mystic One")..........5-10 61
EXECUTIVE PRODUCTIONS............8-12 60s
FANTASY (595 "Double Whammy")...15-25 65
R-E-V (104 "Glimmer Sunshine")...15-25 66
TROPHY (1001 "Pretty One").........10-15 65
LPs: 10/12-inch
EXECUTIVE PRODUCTIONS ("Jack Bedient")......................................50-75 60s
FANTASY (3365 "Live at Harvey's")..40-50 65
SATORI (1001 "Where Did She Go")...40-60 66
TROPHY (101 "Two Sides")..............40-60 64
Also see CHESSMEN

BEDLAM
Singles: 7-inch
CHRYSALIS.......................................3-5 73
LPs: 10/12-inch
CHRYSALIS.......................................10-12 73
Members: Frank Aiello; Dave Ball; Dennis Ball; Andy Fraser; Cozy Powell; Chris Speeding.
Also see BEAST
Also see POWELL, Cozy

BEDLAM FOUR
Singles: 7-inch
ARMADA (001 "Hydrogen Atom")..200-300 67
LE JAC (3006 "Watch It Baby") 40-60 66
Also see ECHOMEN

BEDPOST ORACLE
Singles: 7-inch
CORBY (230 "Break of Dawn")......20-30 68
ORACLE (29002 "Somebody to Love")...20-30 68

BEDROCK
Singles: 7-inch
EPIC...3-5 71
LPs: 10/12-inch
EPIC...8-10 71

BEDROCKS
Singles: 7-inch
SIRE...3-6 69

BEDS
LPs: 10/12-inch
ELEKTRA...5-10 81

BEDWELL, Tommy
Singles: 7-inch
ACE (626 "Maybe I'm Wrong") 10-15 61
DEBUT (7674 "I Met an Angel").....30-40 60
Also see BEDWELLS

BEDWELLS
Singles: 7-inch
DEL-FI..5-10 63
Also see BEDWELL, Tommy

BEE, Betty
Singles: 7-inch
VOKES...4-8 66-67

BEE, Celi: see CELI BEE

BEE, Charlie
(Charlie Bee Combo)
Singles: 7-inch
ATCO...8-10 61

BEE, Davey, & Sonics
Singles: 7-inch
PEARL (408 "Linda Lee") 50-75 58
(Colored vinyl.)

BEE, Eddie
Singles: 7-inch
GOLDISC (3025 "Eddie's Train") ... 10-20 61

BEE, Jackie
Singles: 7-inch
SALEM (190 "Moments of Infatuation")....................................20-25 60s

BEE, Jay, & Kats
Singles: 7-inch
BANGAR (606 "Tension")..............15-25 62

BEE, Jimmy R&B '76
(With Ernie Fields Jr.'s Orchestra)
Singles: 7-inch
ALA...3-5 73
CALLA...3-5 76
KENT..3-5 70
KIMBERLY..5-10
HAMILTON..5-10 59
20TH FOX...5-8 66-67
U.A...3-5 71
LPs: 10/12-inch
ALA (1975 "Live")..........................10-15 73

BEE, Joe
Singles: 7-inch
STOP (402 "Trip to Moscow")............4-8 71

BEE, Kathy C&W '88
Singles: 7-inch
LILAC...3-4 88

BEE, Kenny: see KENNY BEE

BEE, Molly P&R '53
Singles: 78 rpm
CAPITOL...3-8 53-58
CORAL..3-6 55
DOT..3-6 56
Singles: 7-inch
CAPITOL...5-10 53-58
CORAL..5-10 55
DOT..5-10 56
GRANITE...3-5 74-75
LIBERTY..4-8 63-64
MGM...3-6 65-67
Picture Sleeves
MGM...5-10 65
EPs: 7-inch
CAPITOL...5-10 58
LPs: 10/12-inch
ACCORD..5-10 82
ALBUM GLOBE.....................................5-10
CAPITOL...15-25 58
GRANITE...5-10 74
MGM...10-15 65-67

BEE, Tee C.
Singles: 7-inch
LODESTONE (1850 "By the River")..10-20 66

BEE, Tom
Singles: 7-inch
MOTHER EARTH..................................4-8
Also see XIT

BEE, Tommy
Singles: 7-inch
SEPTEMBER...5-10 64

BEE BOPS
Singles: 7-inch
DOT..10-20 64

BEE GEES P&R/LP '67
Singles: 12-inch
W.B...5-10 80s
Singles: 7-inch
ATCO..4-10 67-72
ATLANTIC..3-5
RSO..3-5 73-84
W.B...3-4 87-89
Picture Sleeves
RSO..3-5 83
W.B...3-4 87-89
EPs: 7-inch
ATCO (4523 Horizontal")..................15-25 68
(Promotional issue only. Tracks are from *Horizontal*, though shown only as "Atco LP 33-233" on this label.)
ATCO (4535 Odessa")......................10-20 69
(Promotional issue only.)
ATCO (37264 "Rare, Precious and Beautiful")..8-15 69
(Promotional issue only.)
RSO (200 "Greatest Hits")................5-10 79
(Promotional issue only.)
LPs: 10/12-inch
ATCO (Except TL-ST-142) 12-25 67-72
ATCO (TL-ST-142 "Odessa")..............30-50 69
(Promotional issue only.)
NAUTILUS..15-25
(Half-speed mastered.)
RSO (Except 1 & 3042).....................5-10 73-84
RSO (1 "Words and Music")..............40-60
(Promotional issue only.)
RSO (3042 "Spirits Having Flown")..10-15 79
(Picture disc.)
W.B...5-10 87-89
Members: Barry Gibb; Maurice Gibb; Robin Gibb; Vince Melouney; Colin Petersen. Session: Alan Kendall; Blue Weaver; Dennis Bryon.
Also see GIBB, Andy
Also see GIBB, Barry
Also see GIBB, Maurice
Also see GIBB, Robin
Also see SANG, Samantha

BEE HIVES
Singles: 7-inch
FLEETWOOD (215 "Beatnik Baby") 15-25 61
KING 8-12 64

BEE JAY
Singles: 7-inch
CLOCK (1743 "I'll Go On") 15-20 61

BEE JAYS
(With Bob Swanson)
Singles: 78 rpm
MERCURY 5-10 57
Singles: 7-inch
MERCURY 10-15 57
PRIME (1001 "I'll Find You") 100-200 65
RSP 4-8 66

BEE KAYS
Singles: 7-inch
GAMBLE 5-8 67

BEEBEE TWINS
Singles: 7-inch
DOT 5-10 58

BEECH RESORTS
Singles: 7-inch
KEY (1830 "Springtime") 40-60

BEECHER, Johnny, & His Buckingham Road Quintet P&R '63
Singles: 7-inch
ASTRA (1019 "Sax 5th Avenue") 4-8 65
CHARTER (6 "Summit Ridge Drive") 5-10 63
CHARTER (10 "She's Gone Away") 5-10 63
CHARTER (1019 "Sax 5th Avenue") 10-20 63
OMEGA (116 "Sax 5th Avenue") ...15-25 58
W.B. (5341 "Sax 5th Avenue") 5-10 63
LPs: 10/12-inch
CHARTER (102 "Sax 5th Avenue") 20-40 63
CHARTER (104 "On the Scene") ...20-30 63

BEECHER, Melody
Singles: 7-inch
PAUL-MEL 3-4 83

BEECHMAN, Laurie
Singles: 7-inch
EPIC 3-4 84

BEECHMONTS
LPs: 10/12-inch
FORTUNA 5-10 60s

BEECHNUTS
Singles: 7-inch
SHOWCASE (9902 "My Iconoclastic Life") 10-20

BEECHWOODS
Singles: 7-inch
SMASH 5-8 63

BEEDS
Singles: 7-inch
BUDDADH 10-15 70-71
TEAM 15-20 68

BEEFCAKE
Singles: 7-inch
DERAM 3-5 70

BEEFEATERS
Singles: 7-inch
ELEKTRA (45013 "Please Let Me Love You") 50-75 64
Members: David Crosby; Gene Clark; Jim McGuinn.
Also see BYRDS

BEEFHEART, Captain: see CAPTAIN BEEFHEART

BEEFUS, Barry "Barefoot"
Singles: 7-inch
LOMA 4-8 66

BEEHIVES
Singles: 7-inch
KING 8-10 64

BEELINE, Danny, & Rich Kids
Singles: 7-inch
RCA (8883 "Summer Girl") 5-10 66

BEEMAN, Johnny
Singles: 7-inch
AMY (809 "Rockin' Beatnik") 10-20 61

BEEP BEEP & ROADRUNNERS
Singles: 7-inch
AUDIO DYNAMICS (162 "Don't Run") 10-15 67
VINCENT (222 "Shiftin' Gears") 40-60 65

BEEPERS
Singles: 12-inch
MCA 4-6 83
Singles: 7-inch
MCA 3-4 83

BEER GARDEN
Singles: 7-inch
SMASH (1778 "New Generation") 10-20 62

BEES
Singles: 78 rpm
IMPERIAL (5314 "Toy Bell") 100-150 54
IMPERIAL (5320 "Get Away Baby") 300-400 54
Singles: 7-inch
IMPERIAL (5314 "Toy Bell") 300-500 54
(Glossy red label.)
IMPERIAL (5314 "Toy Bell") 100-150 54
(Flat red label.)
IMPERIAL (5320 "Get Away Baby") 1000-2000 54

BEES
Singles: 7-inch
FINCH (7321 "Oh Yes") 200-300 59

BEES
Singles: 7-inch
MIRA 8-12 65
MIRWOOD 8-12 65

BEES
Singles: 7-inch
LIVERPOOL (62225 "Voices Green and Purple") 50-75 66
Picture Sleeves
LIVERPOOL (62225 "Voices Green and Purple") 75-100 66

BEETHOVEN 4
Singles: 7-inch
DON LEE (0003 "Oh Pretty Baby") 15-25 66

BEETHOVEN 4
(Beethoven Four; Beethovens)
Singles: 7-inch
TAG (4000 "Don't Call on Me") 40-60 66
TALOS (1313 "She Sets My Soul on Fire") 40-60 67
Members: Joey Hall; Hayward Fowler; Larry McBrayer; Larry Butler. Session: Bill Johnson.
Also see JOHNSON, Bill

BEETHOVEN SOUL
Singles: 7-inch
DOT 4-6 67
LPs: 10/12-inch
DOT 10-15 67

BEETHOVEN'S FIFTH
Singles: 7-inch
MGM 10-20 67

BEETHOVENS: see BEETHOVEN 4

BEETLES
Singles: 7-inch
BLUE CAT 8-10 65

BEGGARS
Singles: 7-inch
JEREE 8-10

BEGGARS OPERA
Singles: 7-inch
VERVE 3-5 71
LPs: 10/12-inch
VERVE 10-12 71
Members: Martin Griffiths; Alan Park; Raymond Wilson; Ricky Gardiner; Marshall Erskine; Gordon Sellar; Virginia Scott.

BEGINNERS
Singles: 7-inch
DOT 4-8 64

BEGINNING OF THE END P&R/R&B '71
Singles: 7-inch
ALSTON 3-5 71-72
LPs: 10/12-inch
ALSTON 10-12 71-76

BEHAN, Dominic
Singles: 7-inch
HICKORY 4-8 64

BEHRKE, Richard, Trio
LPs: 10/12-inch
ATCO (141 "Bobby Darin Presents the Richard Behrke Trio: West Side Story") 15-25 62
Also see DARIN, Bobby

BEHUNIN, Ronnie, & Rockeys Raiders
Singles: 7-inch
COTTONWOOD (112 "Mary Jane") .8-12 61

BEISBIER, Julie Ann
Singles: 7-inch
FLASH 3-5 72

BEK BROTHERS
(With the Collarmen)
Singles: 7-inch
CUCA (1216 "Ebony") 10-20 64
CUCA (1284 "My Rhonda") 10-15 66
CUCA (1294 "Today") 10-15 66

BEL CANTOS
Singles: 7-inch
DOWNEY 8-10 65
Also see RUMBLERS

BEL MARS: see ADMIRATIONS / Bel Mars

BEL TONES
Singles: 7-inch
DEL AMO (4647 "Break Time") 15-25 64

BELAFONTE, Harry P&R '52
Singles: 78 rpm
JUBILEE 8-12 54
RCA 5-10 57
ROOST (501 "Lean on Me") 10-15 49
Singles: 7-inch
COLUMBIA 3-4 81
JUBILEE 10-20 54
RCA (0300 series) 5-10 57
RCA (0400 thru 0600 series) 3-5 71-72
RCA (4000 & 5000 series) 10-20 52-55
RCA (6000 & 7000 series) 5-10 55-62
RCA (8000 & 9000 series) 4-6 62-67
Picture Sleeves
RCA (Except 9200 series) 10-15 55-59
RCA (9200 series) 4-8 69
EPs: 7-inch
CAPITOL (619 "Close You Eyes") .15-20 55
JUBILEE 20-30 54
RCA (Except 24) 10-20 54-61
RCA (SPD-24 "Best of Belafonte") .40-60 56
(Ten-EP boxed set, with inserts.)
LPs: 10/12-inch
BOOK of the MONTH RECORDS ..15-20 83
CAMDEN 5-10 73-74
COLUMBIA 5-10 81
CORONET 8-15
RCA (0000 thru 0900 series) 5-10 73
RCA (1000 thru 1900 series) 15-25 54-59
(With "LOP," "LPM" or "LSP" prefix.)
RCA (2400 series) 5-10 78-81
(With "AYL1 or "CPL1" prefix.)
RCA (2000 & 3000 series, except 2449) 10-20 60-67
(With "LPM" or "LSP" prefix.)
RCA (2449 "The Midnight Special") 20-40 62
(Has Bob Dylan playing harmonica on the title track—his first appearance on record.)
RCA (1000 series) 5-10
RCA (3800 series) 5-10 75
RCA (4000 series) 10-15 68-71
RCA (6000 series) 15-25 59-72
Also see ANN-MARGRET
Also see COMO, Perry / Ames Brothers / Harry Belafonte / Radio City Music Hall Orch.
Also see DYLAN, Bob
Also see ROBINSON, Sugar "Chile" / Harry Belafonte

BELAFONTE, Harry, & Lena Horne LP '59
LPs: 10/12-inch
RCA 15-25 59
Also see HORNE, Lena

BELAFONTE, Harry / Islanders
LPs: 10/12-inch
CELEBRITY 10-20
Also see ISLANDERS

BELAFONTE, Harry, & Miriam Makeba LP '65
LPs: 10/12-inch
RCA 10-15 65
Also see MAKEBA, Miriam

BELAFONTE, Harry, & Nana Mouskouri LP '66
LPs: 10/12-inch
RCA 10-15 66
Also see BELAFONTE, Harry
Also see MOUSKOURI, Nana

BEL-AIR FIVE
Singles: 7-inch
USA 15-25 64

BEL-AIRE GIRLS
Singles: 7-inch
EVEREST 8-10 59
LPs: 10/12-inch
EVEREST 20-30 60

BEL-AIRE POPS ORCHESTRA
LPs: 10/12-inch
LIBERTY 10-12 65

BEL-AIRES
Singles: 78 rpm
FLIP 25-50 54-55
Singles: 7-inch
FLIP (303 "This Paradise") 75-125 54
(Maroon label.)
FLIP (303 "This Paradise") 40-60 55
(Blue label.)
FLIP (304 "White Port and Lemon Juice") 75-125 55
Members: Donald Woods; Randy Bryant; Ira Foley.
Also see GREEN, Vernon, & Medallions
Also see VEL-AIRES
Also see WOODS, Donald

BEL-AIRES
Singles: 78 rpm
CROWN (126 "Cherry Pie") 15-25 54
Singles: 7-inch
CROWN (126 "Cherry Pie") 40-60 54

BEL-AIRES
Singles: 7-inch
DECCA (30631 "My Yearbook") 25-30 58

BEL-AIRES
Singles: 7-inch
ARC 8-12 59
M.Z. 125-175 59
Member: Larry Lee.

BEL-AIRES
Singles: 7-inch
LUCKY TOKEN (107 "Baggies") ...10-20 62
NU SOUND 5-10 62
PIV 5-10
SPARTAN 5-10

BEL-AIRES
Singles: 7-inch
DISCOTHEQUE (1004 "Ya Ha Be Be") 25-35 67
PLANET (58 "Ya Ha Be Be") 15-25 67

BEL-AIRES
Singles: 7-inch
BRUT 3-5 74

BELAIRS
Singles: 7-inch
ARVEE (5034 "Mr. Moto") 15-25 61
ARVEE (5054 "Volcanic Action") ...15-25 61
TRIUMPH (54 "Kami-Kaze") 10-20 63
Members: Richard Delvy; Eddie Bertrand; Jim Roberts; Paul Johnson; Chaz Stewart.
Also see CHALLENGERS
Also see DELVY, Richard
Also see EDDIE & SHOWMEN
Also see EVERPRESENT FULLNESS
Also see GOOD GUYS

BELAIRS
Singles: 7-inch
RAFT (604 "Are You My Girl") ...100-200 62

BEL-AIRS
Singles: 7-inch
SARA (6431 "Forever Loving You") 500-750 63
Members: Wayne Demmer; Dennis Gehrke; Bob Wickert; Pete Miller.

BELAIRS
Singles: 7-inch
ACTION (110 "I Tried") 25-35
LEWIS (107 "As You Go") 8-12

BELAIRS / Decoys
Singles: 7-inch
TIMES SQUARE 6-10 63
Also see DECOYS

BELAND, John
Singles: 7-inch
BIG TREE 3-4 78
LPs: 10/12-inch
BIG TREE 5-10 78
WHAT 5-10 82

BELANGER, Rick
Singles: 7-inch
LION 3-5 73

BELDON, Billy
Singles: 7-inch
VULCAN 3-5 72

BELEW, Adrian LP '82
Singles: 7-inch
ATLANTIC 3-4 89-90
Picture Sleeves
ATLANTIC 3-4 89
LPs: 10/12-inch
ATLANTIC 5-8 89-90
ISLAND 5-10 82-83
Also see KING CRIMSON

BELEW, Carl C&W '59
(With His Riff Riders)
Singles: 7-inch
BRUNSWICK 5-10 58
DECCA (Except 30947) 3-8 59-72
DECCA (30947 "Cool Gator Shoes") 25-35 59
4 STAR (1700 series) 10-20 58-59
MCA 3-5 74
RCA 4-8 62-68
SOWDER (248 "I'm Long Gone") 500-1000 57
EPs: 7-inch
DECCA 8-12 60
LPs: 10/12-inch
BUCKBOARD 5-10
DECCA (4074 "Carl Belew") 20-25 60
(Monaural.)
DECCA (7-4074 "Carl Belew") 25-35 60
(Stereo.)
FORUM 5-10
PICKWICK/HILLTOP 10-20 65
PLANTATION 5-10 81
RCA 10-20 64-68
VOCALION 10-15 66-67
WRANGLER 15-25 62

BELEW, Carl, & Betty Jean Robinson C&W '71
Singles: 7-inch
DECCA 3-5 71
LPs: 10/12-inch
DECCA 8-12 71
Also see BELEW, Carl
Also see ROBINSON, Betty Jean

BELFAST GYPSYS
Singles: 7-inch
LOMA 8-12 66
Members: Kim Fowley; Pat McAuley; Jackie McAuley.
Also see FOWLEY, Kim
Also see THEM

BELFEGORE
LPs: 10/12-inch
ELEKTRA 5-10 84

BELGIANETTES
Singles: 7-inch
OKEH 5-10 63
Also see BAKER, Jo-An

BELGIANS
(With Benny & the Sportsman)
Singles: 7-inch
TEEK (4824 "Pray Tell Me") 100-125 64

BELIEVERS
Singles: 7-inch
APT 5-8 65
CAPITOL 4-8 68

BELISLE, Girard
Singles: 7-inch
ROMAR 3-5 72

BELL, Archie P&R/R&B/LP '68
(With the Drells)
Singles: 12-inch
PHILADELPHIA INT'L 4-6 79
PLAYHOUSE 4-6 84
Singles: 7-inch
ATLANTIC 4-8 68-72
BECKETT 3-4 81-84
EAST-WEST 3-4
GLADES 3-5 73
OVIDE (228 "Tighten Up") 15-25 67
PHILADELPHIA INT'L 3-6 76-79
TSOP 3-6 75-76
LPs: 10/12-inch
ATLANTIC 10-15 68-69
BECKETT 5-10 81-84
PHILADELPHIA INT'L 8-10 75-79
TSOP 5-8 75
Members: Archie Bell; Huey Butler; James Wise; Joe Cross; Lee Bell; Willie Parnell.
Also see PHILADELPHIA INTERNATIONAL ALL STARS
Also see T.S.U. TORONADOS

BELL, Benny P&R '75
(Featuring Paul Wynn)
Singles: 78 rpm
COCKTAIL PARTY SONGS (202 "Shaving Cream") 15-25 46
Singles: 7-inch
ENTERPRISE 4-8 62
VANGUARD 3-5 75
LPs: 10/12-inch
BELL ENTERPRISES 10-20
VANGUARD 10-15 75
ZION 10-20

BELL, Bill
Singles: 7-inch
MIDA (112 "Little Bitty Girl") 50-75 59

BELL, Billy
Singles: 7-inch
WEB 3-5 70

BELL, Brother
Singles: 78 rpm
BLUES & RHYTHM (7002 "If You Feel Froggish") 25-50 51

BELL, Carey
LPs: 10/12-inch
BLUESWAY 8-12 73
DELMARK 10-20 69
Also see COTTON, James, Carey Bell, Junior Wells, & Billy Branch
Also see HORTON, Big Walter

BELL, Carl, & Novars
Singles: 7-inch
LAURIE (3014 "Open House in Your Heart") 10-15 58

BELL, Danny
Singles: 7-inch
DOWN to EARTH 3-5 73
FRATERNITY 5-10 58

BELL, Delia C&W '83
Singles: 7-inch
W.B. 3-4 83
LPs: 10/12-inch
W.B. 5-8 83

BELL, Dennis
Singles: 7-inch
IMPERIAL 8-10 61-62
LEP-RE-CHAUN 5-10 61
RCA 5-10 62
TOP RANK 5-10 60

BELL, Donnie
Singles: 7-inch
REECE RAWSON 5-10

BELL, Dwain
Singles: 7-inch
SUMMIT (110 "Rock & Roll on Saturday Night") 200-300 59

BELL, Eddie
(With the Rock-A-Fellas; with Bel-Aires)
Singles: 7-inch
COED 10-20 59
LUCKY FOUR (1005 "Johnny B. Goode Is in Hollywood") 75-100 61
LUCKY FOUR (1012 "The Great Pumpkin") 15-25 61
MERCURY (71677 "Masked Man") 10-20 60
MERCURY (71763 "Knock, Knock, Knock") 30-50 61
Also see ROCK-A-FELLAS

BELL, Freddie, & Bell Boys
Singles: 78 rpm
TEEN 10-20 55
MERCURY 8-12 56
WING 8-12 56
Singles: 7-inch
TEEN 20-30 55
MERCURY 10-20 56
WING 10-20 56
LPs: 10/12-inch
MERCURY (20289 "Rock & Roll...All Flavors") 50-100 57
20TH FOX (4146 "Bells Are Swinging") 20-30 64
(With Roberta Linn.)

BELL, Freddy
Singles: 7-inch
AUDICON 8-12 59
WYNNE 5-10 60

BELL, Gwenn, & Brown Dots
Singles: 78 rpm
MANOR....15-20 49
Also see WATSON, Deek, & Brown Dots

BELL, Hugh, & Twiggs
Singles: 78 rpm
BLAZE (109 "Redcap")....10-20 55
Singles: 7-inch
BLAZE (109 "Redcap")....20-40 55
Also see MOORE, Johnny

BELL, James C&W '68
(James Mullins)
Singles: 7-inch
BELL....4-8 67-68
Also see VELVIT, Jimmy

BELL, Jerry
Singles: 7-inch
YUCCA (119 "Jungle Bunny")....10-20 60

BELL, Jerry R&B '81
Singles: 7-inch
MCA....3-4 80-81

BELL, Jessica
Singles: 7-inch
FIRE-SIGN....5-10 77

BELL, Joey, & Chick Foster
Singles: 7-inch
ROCK (1000 "Don't Be Late")....10-20 59
Also see FOSTER, Chick

BELL, Johnny
(Johnny Bell Tones; Johnny Bell Quartet)
Singles: 7-inch
BRUNSWICK (55142 "Flip, Flop and Fly")....100-150 59
CECIL (5050 "Ev'ry Day")....100-150 57
FLEETWOOD (1001 "Ev'ry Day") 25-50 59
UNIVERSAL (104 "Cricket Rock") 15-25 59

BELL, Johnny
Singles: 7-inch
REALLY SINCERE....4-6

BELL, Kay
(Kay Bell & Spacemen)
Singles: 7-inch
BUENA VISTA (428 "Surfer's Blues")....10-20 63
Also see TUFFS

BELL, Larry
(With the Soul Pack)
Singles: 7-inch
CLARIDGE....3-5 77-78
PHILIPS....4-6 69

BELL, Leigh
Singles: 7-inch
RUST....5-10 61

BELL, Madeline P&R/R&B '68
Singles: 7-inch
ASCOT....5-8 64-65
BRUT....3-5 73
MOD....4-6 67
PHILIPS....4-6 67-68
PYE....3-5 76
LPs: 10/12-inch
PHILIPS....15-20 68
PYE....8-10 76
Also see BLUE MINK
Also see HUMMINGBIRD
Also see MANN, Manfred
Also see SPACE
Also see WATERS, Roger

BELL, Maggie P&R/LP '74
Singles: 7-inch
ATLANTIC....3-5 73-74
SWAN SONG....3-5 76
LPs: 10/12-inch
ATLANTIC....10-12 74
SWAN SONG....8-10 75
Also see STONE the CROWS

BELL, Maggie, & B.A. Robertson
Singles: 7-inch
SWAN SONG....3-4
Picture Sleeves
SWAN SONG....3-4

BELL, Maggie, & Bobby Whitlock
Singles: 7-inch
SWAN SONG....3-4 83-84
Also see BELL, Maggie
Also see WHITLOCK, Bobby

BELL, Randy P&R '84
Singles: 7-inch
EPIC....3-4 84
Picture Sleeves
EPIC....3-4 84

BELL, Reuben R&B '72
Singles: 7-inch
ALARM....3-5 75-77
DELUXE....3-6 72-73
HOUSE OF ORANGE (2403 "I Can't Feel This Way at Home")....5-10
MURCO (1035 "It's Not That Easy")....15-25 68
MURCO (1046 "You're Gonna Miss Me")....25-50 68
SILVER FOX....5-10 69

BELL, Tommy C&W '82
Singles: 7-inch
GOLD SOUND....3-4 82-83
ZIL (9001 "Swamp Gal")....50-75 60

BELL, Trudy
Singles: 7-inch
PHILIPS....5-10 62-63

BELL, Vincent P&R/LP '70
(With the Bell Men; Vinnie Bell)
Singles: 7-inch
DECCA....4-8 67-70
INDEPENDENT (102 "Quicksand")....20-30 60
INDEPENDENT (1214 "Caravan")....20-30 60
MUSICOR....5-10 64
VERVE (10308 "Shindig")....8-12 63
LPs: 10/12-inch
DECCA....10-15 67-70
INDEPENDENT....20-30 60
MUSICOR....10-20 64
VERVE....10-20 64
Also see FERRENTE & TEICHER
Also see RAMRODS

BELL, Vivian C&W '77
Singles: 7-inch
GRT....3-5 77

BELL, William P&R '62
Singles: 7-inch
ANDEE....5-8
KAT FAMILY....3-4 83-84
MERCURY....3-5 76-77
STAX (Except 100 series)....3-8 67-74
STAX (100 series)....10-15 61-67
WILBE....3-4 86
LPs: 10/12-inch
KAT FAMILY....5-10 83-84
MERCURY....8-10 77
STAX....10-15 67-74
Also see CLAY, Judy, & William Bell
Also see DEL RIOS

BELL, William, & Janice Bullock R&B '86
Singles: 7-inch
WILBE....3-4 86
Also see BULLOCK, Janice

BELL, William, & Mavis Staples
Singles: 7-inch
STAX....4-6 69
Also see STAPLES, Mavis

BELL, William, & Carla Thomas
Singles: 7-inch
STAX....4-6 69-70
Also see BELL, William
Also see THOMAS, Carla

BELL AIRES: see BELLAIRES

BELL & ARC
Singles: 7-inch
COLUMBIA....3-5 72
LPs: 10/12-inch
COLUMBIA....8-10 71

BELL & JAMES R&B '78
Singles: 12-inch
A&M....4-6 79
LORIMAR....4-6 80
Singles: 7-inch
A&M....3-4 78-84
LORIMAR....3-4 80
Picture Sleeves
A&M....3-5 78-81
LPs: 10/12-inch
A&M....5-10 79-84
Members: Leroy Bell; Casey James.

BELL BIV DeVOE P&R/LP '90
Singles: 7-inch
MCA....3-4 90
LPs: 10/12-inch
MCA....5-8 90
Members: Ricky Bell; Michael Bivins; Ronnie DeVoe.
Also see NEW EDITION

BELL BOYS
Singles: 7-inch
JAMAR (728 "I Don't Want to Lose You")....50-100
(At least one source shows this number as 101. We don't know yet who's right.)

BELL BROTHERS
Singles: 7-inch
SURE SHOT....4-8 65-68

BELL HOPS
Singles: 78 rpm
DECCA....25-50 51
Singles: 7-inch
DECCA (48208 "For the Rest of My Life")....50-100 51
DECCA (48239 "I'm All Yours")....50-100 51

BELL HOPS
Singles: 78 rpm
TIN PAN ALLEY....40-60 56
Singles: 7-inch
TIN PAN ALLEY (153 "Please Don't Say No to Me")....100-150 56

BELL HOPS
Singles: 7-inch
BARB (100 "Angelita")....15-25 58
BARB (101 "Teenage Years")....15-25 58

BELL NOTES P&R/R&B '59
Singles: 7-inch
AUTOGRAPH....10-20 60
ERIC....3-5 73
MADISON....5-10 60
TIME (Blue label)....15-20 59
TIME (Red label)....5-10 59-60
EPs: 7-inch
TIME (100 "I've Had It")....60-100 59
Members: Carl Bonura; Ray Ceroni; Lenny Giambalvo; Pete Kane; John Casey.

BELL SISTERS P&R '52
(With Phil Harris; with Rex)
Singles: 78 rpm
BERMUDA....4-8 53
RCA....4-8 50-53
Singles: 7-inch
BERMUDA....5-10 53
BRAD (2210 "Honey Baby")....8-12
RCA....5-10 50-53
Members: Kay Bell; Cynthia Bell.
Also see HARRIS, Phil
Also see RENE, Henri, & His Orchestra

BELL TONES
Singles: 78 rpm
RAMA (170 "Heart to Heart")....50-75 55
Singles: 7-inch
RAMA (170 "Heart to Heart")....100-200 55

BELL TONES
Singles: 7-inch
CLOCK....10-15 61

BELLAIRES
Singles: 78 rpm
RUBY....40-60 55
Singles: 7-inch
RUBY (103 "I'd Never Forgive Myself")....100-150 55

BELLAIRES
Singles: 7-inch
BELLAIRE....3-4 79

BELLAMY, David P&R '75
Singles: 7-inch
W.B.....3-5 75
Also see BELLAMY BROTHERS

BELLAMY BROTHERS C&W/P&R/LP '76
Singles: 7-inch
CURB....3-4 84-87
CURB/MCA....3-4 88-89
ELEKTRA/CURB....3-4 82
MCA....3-4 87
W.B./CURB....3-4 76-83
LPs: 10/12-inch
ELEKTRA....5-10 83
MCA/CURB....5-10 84-90
W.B.....8-10 76-83
Members: David Bellamy; Howard Bellamy.
Also see BELLAMY, David

BELLAMY BROTHERS & Forester Sisters C&W '86
Singles: 7-inch
CURB....3-4 86
W.B.....3-4 90
Also see BELLAMY BROTHERS
Also see FORESTER SISTERS

BELLAND & SOMERVILLE
Singles: 7-inch
BARNABY....4-6 69
Members: Bruce Belland; David Somerville.
Also see DIAMONDS
Also see FOUR PREPS

BELLANTE, John & Carl
Singles: 7-inch
NAMI....3-5 75

BEL-LARKS
(With the Eternals; with Eternals Orchestra)
Singles: 7-inch
HAMMER (6313 " A Million and One Dreams ")....1000-2000 63
RANSOM (5001 "A Million and One Dreams")....250-500 63
(Opinions vary as to which is the first issue, though the Hammer is the rarer disc.)

BELLATONES
Singles: 7-inch
BELLA (20 "Carol Lee")....20-30 59
BELLA (21 "Forgotten Spring")....20-30 59

BELLCO RHYTHM BOYS
Singles: 7-inch
BELLCO (210 "Ruby Ann")....5-15 63

BELLE, Bobby
Singles: 12-inch
AIRWAVE....4-6 83

BELLE, Regina P&R/R&B/LP '87
Singles: 7-inch
COLUMBIA....3-4 87-89
ELEKTRA....3-4 87-88
LPs: 10/12-inch
COLUMBIA....5-10 87-88
Also see BRYSON, Peabo, & Regina Belle

BELLE, Vada
Singles: 78 rpm
MERCURY....5-10 57
Singles: 7-inch
MERCURY....8-12 57

BELLE EPOQUE P&R/R&B '78
Singles: 7-inch
BIG TREE....3-4 78

BELLE STARS P&R/D&D/LP '83
Singles: 12-inch
W.B.....4-6 83-84
Singles: 7-inch
CAPITOL....3-4 89
W.B.....3-4 83-84
Picture Sleeves
W.B.....3-4 83
LPs: 10/12-inch
W.B.....5-10 83-84

BELLES
Singles: 7-inch
CHOICE....10-15 61-63
MIRWOOD....5-10 66
TIARA (100 "Melvin")....15-25 66
TIARA (703 "La Bamba")....10-20 60s
Members: Debbie Teaver; Pan Kent; Marina Perez; May Perez.

BELLETTO, Al
Singles: 7-inch
KING....5-10 60

BELLINE, Denny
(With the Dwellers; with Rich Kids)
Singles: 7-inch
COLUMBIA (45123 "Living Without You")....5-10 70
RCA (8665 "Little Lonely Girl")....8-12 65
RCA (10171 "Rosemary Blue")....4-8 75
LPs: 10/12-inch
RCA (3655 "Denny Belline and the Rich Kids")....25-45 66
Members: Denny Belline; Richard Supa.
Also see SUPA, Richard

BELLINGHAM ACCENTS
Singles: 7-inch
JERDEN (746 "Sampan")....5-10 65
Members: Kathi McDonald; Pat Jerns; Laurie Vitt; Bill Capp; Gary Carb; Vic Bundy; Doug Ling; Harvey Redman.
Also see ACCENTS
Also see McDONALD, Kathi
Also see UNUSUALS

BELLINO
(Bill Bamal)
Singles: 7-inch
DUEL (520 "Bossa Rock")....5-10 62
Also see RAMAL, Bill

BELLINO, Johnny
Singles: 7-inch
DECCA....4-8 65

BELLOWS, Bob
Singles: 7-inch
IRIS....5-10 61

BELLS
Singles: 78 rpm
RAMA....200-300 55
Singles: 7-inch
RAMA (166 "What Can I Tell Her Now")....1000-1500 55
Members: Joe Van Loan; Willie Ray; Willis Sanders; Bob Kornegay.
Also see DIXIEAIRES
Also see DU DROPPERS
Also see RAVENS
Also see VALIANTS

BELLS P&R/LP '71
Singles: 7-inch
MGM....3-5 73
POLYDOR....3-5 70-73
LPs: 10/12-inch
POLYDOR....10-15 71-72
Members: Jacki Ralph; Cliff Edwards; Frank Mills.
Also see MILLS, Frank

BELLS OF JOY
Singles: 7-inch
ABC....3-5 73
WILDCAT....5-10

BELLS OF RHYMNY
Singles: 7-inch
DICTO (1001 "She'll Be Back")....15-25

BELLTONES
Singles: 78 rpm
GRAND (102 "Estelle")....250-500 54
Singles: 7-inch
GRAND (102 "Estelle")....2000-3000 54
(Black vinyl. Blue label.)
GRAND (102 "Estelle")....4000-6000 54
(Red vinyl.)

BELL-TONES
(With the Shytone 5 Orchestra; Belltones)
Singles: 78 rpm
SCATT (1609 "The Merengue")....50-100 56
Singles: 7-inch
J&S (1609 "The Merengue")....200-300 58
SCATT (1609 "The Merengue")....300-500 56
Members: Ronnie Baker; Al Brandon; Billy Lee; Joe Raguso; Paul Fernandez.
Also see BAKER, Ronnie
Also see CAPRIS

BELL-TONES
Singles: 7-inch
CLOCK (71889 "There She Goes")....75-125 61
(Clock disc has the Mercury selection number.)
MERCURY (71889 "There She Goes")....25-50 61

BELLTONES
Singles: 7-inch
ITZY (1 "To Understand Me")....15-25 63
OLIMPIC (241 "Swingin' Little Chickie")....30-50 63
OLIMPIC (1068 "Please Try to Understand Me")....30-50 62

BELLUS, Tony P&R '59
Singles: 7-inch
ABC....3-4 73
COLLECTABLES....3-4 81
KING....4-8 65
NRC....10-20 59-60
Picture Sleeves
NRC (035 "Hey Little Darlin' ")....25-40 59
NRC (051 "The Echo of an Old Song")....20-30 60
LPs: 10/12-inch
NRC (8 "Robbin' the Cradle with Tony Bellus")....50-100 60
SHI-FI (11 "Gems of Tony Bellus") 20-40

BELLY, P.J.
(Rob Gamble)
Singles: 7-inch
NOR VA JAK....3-4 87

BELMONT, Bobby
Singles: 7-inch
LAURIE....4-8 65

BELMONTS P&R '61
("The Belmonts with Dion")
Singles: 12-inch
STRAWBERRY (1107 "I'll Never Fall in Love Again")....5-10 76
Singles: 7-inch
COLLECTABLES....3-4 81
CRYSTAL BALL....5-8 79
DOT (17173 "Reminiscences")....10-15 68
DOT (17257 "Answer Me My Love")....10-15 68
LAURIE (3080 "We Belong Together")....10-20 61
LAURIE (3631 "Brand New Song")....4-8 75
MOHAWK (106 "Teenage Clementine")....25-50 57
ROULETTE....3-5
SABINA (502 "I Need Someone")..15-25 61
SABINA (503 "Hombre")....15-25 62
SABINA (505 "Come on Little Angel")....15-25 62
SABINA (507 "Diddle-Dee-Dum")..15-25 62
SABINA (509 "Ann Marie")....15-25 63
SABINA (513 "Let's Call It a Day").15-25 64
SABINA (519 "Why")....15-25 64
SABINA (521 "Nothing in Return")....75-125 64
SABRINA (500 "Tell Me Why")....20-30 61
SABRINA (501 "Don't Get Around Much Anymore")....20-30 61
(In 1961, after #502, Sabrina changed its name, slightly, to Sabina.)
STRAWBERRY (106 "Cheek to Cheek")....4-6 76
SURPRISE (1000 "Tell Me Why")....75-125 61
U.A. (809 "I Don't Know Why")....10-15 64
U.A. (904 "Then I Walked Away")...10-15 65
U.A. (966 "I Got a Feeling")....10-15 66
U.A. (50007 "Come with Me")....15-20 66
LPs: 10/12-inch
BUDDAH (5123 "Cigars, Acappella, Candy")....25-50 72
CRYSTAL BALL....8-12 81
DOT (25949 "Summer Love")....25-30 69
SABINA (5001 "Carnival of Hits")....100-150 62
STRAWBERRY....10-15 76
UPTOWN....5-10 88
Members: Carlo Mastrangelo; Fred Milano; Angelo D'Aleo; Frank Lyndon.
Also see ALSTON, Shirley
Also see BARIN, Pete
Also see CARLO
Also see DION & BELMONTS
Also see LYNDON, Frank
Also see SHEPPARD, Buddy, & Holidays
Also see SOUL, Jimmy / Belmonts
Also see STRANGE BROTHERS SHOW

BELMONTS, Freddy Cannon & Bo Diddley
Singles: 12-inch
ROCK & ROLL TRAVELLING SHOW....4-6
LPs: 10/12-inch
DOWNTOWN....5-10
Also see BELMONTS
Also see CANNON, Freddy
Also see DIDDLEY, Bo

BELOUIS SOME P&R/D&D '85
Singles: 12-inch
CAPITOL....4-6 85
Singles: 7-inch
CAPITOL....3-4 85
LPs: 10/12-inch
CAPITOL....5-8 85

BELOVED, The LP '90
LPs: 10/12-inch
ATLANTIC....5-8 90

BELOVED ONES
Singles: 7-inch
BOYD ("Peep Peep Pop Pop")....20-30 66
Also see DEARLY BELOVEDS
Also see INTRUDERS
Also see QUINSTRELS

BELOYD R&B '77
Singles: 7-inch
20TH FOX....3-4 77

BELTONES
Singles: 78 rpm
HULL (721 "I Talk to My Echo")....25-50 57
Singles: 7-inch
COLLECTABLES....3-4 81
HULL (721 "I Talk to My Echo")...75-100 57
(Black label)
HULL (721 "I Talk to My Echo")....25-50 58
(Red label)
ROULETTE....3-5 77

BELTONES
Singles: 7-inch
JELL (188 "I Want to Be Loved") 100-150 62
(Reissued as by Ronnie Baker & the Deltones.)
Also see BAKER, Ronnie

BEL-TONES
Singles: 7-inch
DEL AMO 5-10

BELUSHI, John P&R '78
Singles: 7-inch
MCA 3-4 78
Also see BLUES BROTHERS
Also see NATIONAL LAMPOON

BELVA & Randolph Brothers
Singles: 7-inch
RANDOLPH BROTHERS 5-8

BELVADERES
Singles: 78 rpm
HUDSON 25-50 56
Singles: 7-inch
HUDSON (4 "Don't Leave Me to Cry") 75-150 55

BELVEDERES Featuring Dick Dawson
Singles: 7-inch
JOPZ (1771 "Buona Sera") 250-300 58

BELVEDERES
Singles: 7-inch
COUNT ("From Out of Nowhere") 10-20 61
(No selection number used.)
LUCKY FOUR (1003 "He's a Square") 30-40 61

BELVEDERS
Singles: 78 rpm
BATON 10-20 55
Singles: 7-inch
BATON (217 "We Too") 20-30 55
DOT 10-15 58
POPLAR 10-15 62

BELVEDERS
Singles: 7-inch
RHAPSODY (5163 "The McCoy") ..15-25
TREND (9 "Let's Get Married") 20-30 58

BELVIN, Andy
Singles: 7-inch
ATCO 8-12 64
GEE KAY 8-12 60s
VAULT 8-12 63
Also see VOWELS

BELVIN, Jesse R&B '56
(With the Sharptones)
Singles: 78 rpm
CASH 25-50 56
HOLLYWOOD 50-75 53-56
MODERN 20-30 56-57
SPECIALTY (435 "Confusin' Blues") 40-60 52
SPECIALTY (550 "Gone") 25-50 55
Singles: 7-inch
ALADDIN (3431 "Let Me Dream") ..25-40 58
CASH (1056 "Beware") 150-200 56
(Reissued in 1959 as by the Capris.)
CLASS (267 "Deep in My Heart") ...10-20 60
COLLECTABLES 3-4 81
CUSTOM 4-8
ERIC 3-5 73
HOLLYWOOD (412 "Love Comes Tumbling Down" 150-250 53
HOLLYWOOD (1059 "Betty My Darling" 100-200 56
IMPACT (23 "Tonight My Love") 10-15 62
JAMIE (1145 "Goodnight My Love") 10-20 59
KENT (236 "Sentimental Reasons") 10-20 59
KNIGHT (2012 "Little Darling") 10-20 59
MODERN (1005 "Goodnight My Love") 25-50 56
MODERN (1025 "You Send Me") ...20-30 57
MODERN (1027 "Just to Say Hello") 20-40 57
RCA (7310 "Volare") 15-25 58
RCA (7387 "Funny") 15-25 58
RCA (47-7469 "Guess Who") 15-25 59
(Monaural.)
RCA (61-7469 "Guess Who") 25-45 59
(Stereo.)
RCA (7543 "Here's a Heart") 15-25 59
RCA (7596 "Give Me Love") 15-25 59
RCA (7675 "Something Happens to Me") 10-20 60
RCA (8040 "Guess Who") 5-10 62
SPECIALTY (435 "Confusin' Blues") 75-100 52
SPECIALTY (550 "Gone") 25-50 55
TENDER (518 "Beware") 25-50 59
EPs: 7-inch
RCA (2089 "Just Jesse Belvin") 25-50 59
RCA (2105 "Mr. Easy") 25-50 60
LPs: 10/12-inch
CAMDEN (960 "Jesse Belvin's Best") 15-20 66
CORONET 8-12 60s
CROWN (5145 "Jesse Belvin Sings") 25-35 60
CROWN (5187 "Unforgettable") 25-35 60
RCA (0966 "Yesterdays") 8-12 75
RCA (LPM-2089 "Just Jesse Belvin") 30-50 59
(Monaural.)
RCA (LSP-2089 "Just Jesse Belvin") 30-60 59
(Stereo.)
RCA (LPM-2105 "Mr. Easy") 30-50 60
(Monaural.)
RCA (LSP-2105 "Mr. Easy") 30-60 60
(Stereo.)
UNITED (7220 "Jesse Belvin...But Not Forgotten") 10-15 60s
Also see BENTON, Brook / Jesse Belvin
Also see CAPRIS
Also see CHARGERS
Also see CLIQUES
Also see GASSERS
Also see JESSE & MARVIN
Also see SHIELDS
Also see T-BIRDS

BELVIN, Jesse, & Five Keys / Feathers
Singles: 7-inch
CANDLELITE (427 "Love Song") ...10-20 63
Also see FEATHERS
Also see FIVE KEYS

BELVIN, Jesse, & Three Dots and a Dash
Singles: 78 rpm
IMPERIAL (5115 "All That Wine Is Gone") 75-125 51
IMPERIAL (5164 "I'll Never Love Again") 75-125 51
Singles: 7-inch
IMPERIAL (5115 "All That Wine Is Gone.) 400-500 51
IMPERIAL (5164 "I'll Never Love Again") 400-500 51
Also see BELVIN, Jesse
Also see THREE DOTS and a Dash

BEN, LaBrenda
(With the Vandellas; with Beljeans; with Andantes)
Singles: 7-inch
GORDY (7009 "Camel Walk") 30-50 63
GORDY (7021 "Just Be Yourself") 30-50 63
MOTOWN (1033 "Camel Walk") 200-400 63
(First issued as by Saundra Mallett & the Vandellas.)
Also see MARTHA & VANDELLAS
Also see MALLETT, Saundra, & Vandellas

BEN, Toby
(Toby Ben Blues Band)
Singles: 7-inch
COLUMBIA 3-5

BEN & BEA
Singles: 7-inch
PHILIPS 4-8 62

BEN & CHEERS
Singles: 7-inch
MOCHA 3-5

BEN & SPENCE
Singles: 7-inch
ATLANTIC 4-8 67-68

BEN GAY: see GAY, Ben

BENARD, Chuck: see BERNARD, Chuck

BENATAR, Pat P&R/LP '79
Singles: 12-inch
CHRYSALIS 4-8 79-86
COLUMBIA ("Le Bel Age") 10-15
(No selection number used. Promotional issue only.)
Singles: 7-inch
CHRYSALIS 4-8 79-89
SUNSHINE 8-12 78
TRACE (5293 "Day Gig") 20-30 74
Picture Sleeves
CHRYSALIS 4-8 79-89
LPs: 10/12-inch
CHRYSALIS 5-10 79-91
MFSL (057 "In the Heat of the Night") 30-40 81
Also see COXON'S ARMY

BENAY, Ben
Singles: 7-inch
GARPAX 5-8 64
EPs: 7-inch
CAPITOL (4047 "Big Blues Harmonica of Ben Benay") 15-25 66
(Promotional issue only.)
LPs: 10/12-inch
CAPITOL ("Big Blues Harmonica of Ben Benay") 15-25 66
Members: Jerry Scheff; James Burton; Jim Troxel; Mike Henderson; Mike Deasy.
Also see BURTON, James
Also see FRIAR TUCK
Also see GOLDENROD

BENAY, Vince
Singles: 7-inch
U.T. 4-6

BENDER, D.C.
(D.C. Bendy)
Singles: 7-inch
IVORY 15-25 58
Also see TILLIS, Big Son
Also see WASHINGTON, D.C.

BENDER, Freddy
Singles: 7-inch
PARKWAY 8-10 63

BENDER, Riley
Singles: 7-inch
SKOKIE 4-8 63

BENDER SISTERS
Singles: 7-inch
LOWE 5-10 59

BENDERS
Singles: 7-inch
JAMAKA (1927 "Sharpest Little Girl") 100-150 59

BENDERS
Singles: 7-inch
BIG SOUND (3006 "Can't Tame Me") 40-60 66
Picture Sleeves
BIG SOUND (3006 "Can't Tame Me") 50-75 66
Members: Gerry Cain; Tom Noffke; Geno Jansen; Paul Barry.

BENDETH BAND
Singles: 7-inch
ENSIGN 3-4 81
LPs: 10/12-inch
ENSIGN 5-10 81

BENDIX, Ralf
Singles: 7-inch
ABC-PAR (10340 "Baby Sittin' Boogie") 15-20 62

BENDS
Singles: 7-inch
REBEL 5-10

BENEDICT
Singles: 7-inch
EARTH 5-10 72

BENEDICT, Ernie, & His Polkateers C&W '49
(With the Kendall Sisters)
Singles: 78 rpm
RCA 4-6 49
LPs: 10/12-inch
CONTINENTAL 8-10

BENEFIELD, Marvin
(Vince Everett)
Singles: 7-inch
ROYALTY (505 "I'm Snowed") 30-60 58
Also see EVERETT, Vince

BENEFIELD, Red, & Blades
Singles: 7-inch
47M (6400 "Blade Rock") 8-12

BENGMIN, Marcellas Lord
Singles: 78 rpm
JVB 10-15 56
Singles: 7-inch
JVB (51 "Jorae's Shuffle") 15-25 56

BENITEZ, Marga, & Mello-Tones
Singles: 78 rpm
DECCA 50-100 54
Singles: 7-inch
DECCA (48318 "Man Love Woman") 200-300 54
Also see MELLO-TONES

BENJAMIN, Tom
Singles: 7-inch
RCA 3-5 79

BENJAMIN & POT
Singles: 7-inch
CC 4-6 69

BENNET, Connie, Bill Smyth, & Harlem-Aires
LPs: 10/12-inch
HOLLYWOOD (30 "Rhythm & Blues in the Night") 50-100 55
Also see HARLEMAIRES

BENNET, Ron
Singles: 7-inch
TA-RAH ("Dingle Dangle Doll") 20-40 61
(Previously issued as by Mike & the Jays.)
Also see MIKE & JAYS

BENNETT, Barbara
Singles: 7-inch
SWADE (101 "You Can Make It if You Try") 20-30 59

BENNETT, Biff, Band
Singles: 7-inch
JUBILEE (5397 "Riverside Band") ...5-10 61

BENNETT, Bob
Singles: 7-inch
PRIORITY 5-10 82

BENNETT, Bobby
(With the Dynamics)
Singles: 7-inch
LEN 10-15 60
LOMA 5-10 65
MALIBU 5-10 63
PHIL-L.A. of SOUL 10-20 69
SUNSET 4-8
V-TONE 5-10 63

BENNETT, Bobby "Guitar"
Singles: 7-inch
JUNIOR (1009 "You Did It Again") 25-50
WORLD ARTISTS 8-12 65

BENNETT, Boyd P&R/R&B '55
(With the Rockets; with Southlanders)
Singles: 78 rpm
KING 15-25 54-57
Singles: 7-inch
KING (1400 series) 25-50 54-55
(Maroon labels.)
KING (1400 series) 20-30 56
(Blue labels.)
KING (4000 series) 20-40 56-58
KING (5000 series) 10-15 58-63
MERCURY 10-20 59-61
EPs: 7-inch
KING (377 "Boyd Bennett") 100-200 56
KING (383 "Rock & Roll with Boyd Bennett & His Rockets") 100-200 56
LPs: 10/12-inch
KING (594 "Boyd Bennett") 1500-2000 58
(Counterfeits exist.)

BENNETT, Buddy
Singles: 7-inch
BLUE MOON 10-15 59

BENNETT, Buster, Trio
Singles: 78 rpm
COLUMBIA (36873 "Reefer Head Woman") 10-20 45

BENNETT, Carole
(With the Satisfiers)
Singles: 7-inch
SHAD 10-15 58
VERVE 10-15

BENNETT, Chuck
Singles: 7-inch
BONNIE (101 "Seven Days") 25-35 62

BENNETT, Cliff, & Rebel Rousers
Singles: 7-inch
ABC 5-10 66
AMY 8-12 65
ASCOT 8-12 64
CAPITOL (4621 "I'm in Love with You") 40-60 61
Also see TOE FAT

BENNETT, Duster
LPs: 10/12-inch
BLUE HORIZON 8-12 70-71

BENNETT, Eddie
(Eddie Bennett's Three Loose Nuts and a Bolt; with Teacho Wiltshire & Orchestra)
Singles: 78 rpm
AVALON 10-15 53
Singles: 7-inch
AVALON (63696 "Caught My Sister Doin' It") 20-30 53
Also see WILTSHIRE, Teacho

BENNETT, Harold, & Soul Brothers
Singles: 7-inch
COPA 20-40

BENNETT, Jerry
Singles: 7-inch
ARCH 20-30 59

BENNETT, Joe, & Sparkletones P&R/R&B '57
Singles: 78 rpm
ABC-PAR 25-50 57-58
Singles: 7-inch
ABC 3-4 73
ABC-PAR 15-25 57-58
PARIS 10-15 59-60
LPs: 10/12-inch
MCA 5-10 83

BENNETT, Linda
Singles: 7-inch
COMMAND 3-6 70
MERCURY 3-5 75
RCA 3-5 75
Picture Sleeves
COMMAND 4-6 70

BENNETT, Lorna
Singles: 7-inch
CAPITOL 3-5 73

BENNETT, Pete, & Embers
Singles: 7-inch
CANADIAN AMERICAN (112 "Dark Eyes") 5-10 60
CUPID 10-15 59
SILVER BIRD (1019 "Rocket Twist") 5-10 62
SUNSET 5-10 61

BENNETT, Ron
Singles: 7-inch
TA-RAH 10-15 61

BENNETT, Sheldon
LPs: 10/12-inch
NRC 20-35 58

BENNETT, Tony P&R '51
Singles: 78 rpm
COLUMBIA 4-8 50-57
Singles: 7-inch
BRUT 3-5 74
COLUMBIA (1600 series) 5-10
(Colored vinyl. Promotional issue only.)
COLUMBIA (06000 series) 3-4 86
COLUMBIA (38000 thru 41000 series) 8-15 50-61
COLUMBIA (42000 thru 45000 series) 4-10 61-70
COLUMBIA/AUROVISION ("Ca C'est L'Amour") 5-10 60s
(Square cardboard picture disc. Promotional issue made for Waterman Pens.)
IMPROV 3-4 75-77
MGM 3-5 73
VERVE 3-5 72-73
Picture Sleeves
COLUMBIA (1600 series) 5-10
(Promotional issue only.)
COLUMBIA (40000 & 41000 series) 5-10 53-61
COLUMBIA (42000 thru 44000 series) 3-6 61-67
IMPROV 3-4 75
EPs: 7-inch
COLUMBIA 5-15 55-59
LPs: 10/12-inch
COLUMBIA (Except 600 thru 1200 series) 6-12 59-86
COLUMBIA (600 thru 1200 series) 10-25 55-59
FANTASY 8-12
GUEST STAR 5-10
HARMONY 5-10 69-73
IMPROV 5-10 75-78
MGM 6-10 73
MGM/VERVE 6-10 72
MFSL 20-30 84
Also see GETZ, Stan
Also see MATHIS, Johnny / Tony Bennett / North Carolina Ramblers / Ray Conniff & Jerry Vale with Eugene Ormandy
Also see SHARON, Ralph

BENNETT, Tony, & Count Basie
EPs: 7-inch
COLUMBIA 6-10 59
LPs: 10/12-inch
COLUMBIA 10-20 59
Also see BASIE, Count

BENNETT, Tony, & Bill Evans
LP: 10/12-inch
MFSL (117 "Tony Bennett & Bill Evans") 25-35 84

BENNETT, Tony / Al Tornello
LPs: 10/12-inch
GUEST STAR 5-10 64
Also see BENNETT, Tony

BENNETT, Wayne
Singles: 7-inch
GIANT 4-8 67

BENNETTE, Cora
Singles: 7-inch
SWINGIN' (635 "Little Cupid") 5-10 61

BENNETTS
Singles: 7-inch
AMCAN 4-8 64

BENNINGHOFF'S BAD ROCK BLUES BAND
LPs: 10/12-inch
PLANTATION 5-10
SSS INT'L 5-10 71

BENNINGS, John
Singles: 7-inch
CLOCK 5-10 59
VIM 5-10 60

BENNIS, Barbara
Singles: 7-inch
MALA 5-10 63

BENNO, Marc LP '72
Singles: 7-inch
A&M 3-5 71-79
LPs: 10/12-inch
A&M 8-12 70-79
MCA 5-10
Also see ASYLUM CHOIR

BENNY, "Scat": see SMITH, Hank

BENNY & BEDBUGS
Singles: 7-inch
DCP 8-10 64
Picture Sleeves
DCP 15-25 64

BENNY & JETS
LPs: 10/12-inch
RCA 8-10 75

BENNY & TINA
Singles: 7-inch
BLUE ROCK 4-6 69

BENOIT, Dave LP '88
Singles: 7-inch
A.V.I. 3-4 78-82
LPs: 10/12-inch
A.V.I. 5-10 78-80
GRP 5-8 88-90

BENONI, Arne C&W '89
Singles: 7-inch
ROUND ROBIN 3-4 89

BENSKIN, Sammy
(With the Spacemen; with Clouds)
Singles: 7-inch
CLOCK 8-10 60
SPARKLE 8-10 61

BENSON, Barbara
Singles: 7-inch
PAGE 5-10 72

BENSON, Gary
Singles: 7-inch
ARISTA 3-4 78
PRIVATE STOCK 3-4 76

BENSON, George LP '69
(George "Bad" Benson)
Singles: 78 rpm
GROOVE 10-15 54
Singles: 12-inch
W.B. 4-6 80-83
Singles: 7-inch
A&M 3-6 68-70
ARISTA 3-5 77
CTI 3-5 75-78
COLUMBIA 4-8 66-67
GROOVE (0024 "It Should Have Been Me #2") 20-40 54
PRESTIGE 4-8 64
W.B. 3-4 76-89
Picture Sleeves
ARISTA 3-5 77

W.B. 3-4 78-86
LPs: 10/12-inch
A&M 8-12 68-76
CTI 8-10 71-78
COLUMBIA 8-10 66-67
(With "CL" or "CS" prefix.)
COLUMBIA 5-10 76
(With "CG" or "PC" prefix.)
MFSL (011 "Breezin'") 25-50 78
POLYDOR 5-10 76
VERVE 10-12 69
W.B. 5-10 75-89
Also see ALTAIRS
Also see FRANKLIN, Aretha, & George Benson
Also see McDUFF, Brother Jack

BENSON, George, & Earl Klugh *LP '87*
LPs: 10/12-inch
W.B. 5-8 87
Also see BENSON, George
Also see KLUGH, Earl

BENSON, Jane
Singles: 7-inch
ATCO 5-10 59

BENSON, Jo Jo
Singles: 7-inch
SSS INT'L (768 "Eternally") 4-8 69
Also see SCOTT, Peggy, & Jo Jo Benson

BENSON, Joe
Singles: 7-inch
DELUXE 10-15 59

BENSON, Matt *C&W '89*
Singles: 7-inch
STEP ONE 3-4 89

BENSON, Ray *C&W '91*
Singles: 7-inch
ARISTA 3-4 91
Also see ASLEEP at the WHEEL

BENSON, Robby
Singles: 7-inch
BELL 3-5 74-75
MCA 3-4 79
W.B. 3-4 80

BENSON, Sharon
Singles: 12-inch
MALACO 4-6 84
Singles: 7-inch
MALACO 3-5 84

BENSON - OGLETREE
Singles: 78 rpm
PARROT (822 "Uptown Stomp") 10-15 55
Singles: 7-inch
PARROT (822 "Uptown Stomp") 20-25 55

BENT FABRIC: see FABRIC, Bent

BENT FORCEP: see FORCEP, Bent, & Patients

BENT MYGGEN
Singles: 7-inch
W.B. 3-5 78

BENTLEY, Erlene *D&D '83*
Singles: 12-inch
MEGATONE 4-6 83
TVI 4-6 84
Singles: 7-inch
MEGATONE 3-4 83

BENTLEY, Jay, & Jet Set
Singles: 7-inch
GNP 5-8 64-65

BENTLEYS
Singles: 7-inch
SMASH (1967 "She's My Hot Rod Queen") 10-20 65
SMASH (1988 "Why Didn't I Listen to Mother") 25-50 65
(Previously issued as by the Vampires.)
Also see VAMPIRES

BENTLEYS
Singles: 7-inch
DEVLET (444 "Now It's Gone") 35-55

BENTON, Barbi *C&W '75*
Singles: 7-inch
PLAYBOY 3-5 74-77
Picture Sleeves
PLAYBOY 4-8 74-76
LPs: 10/12-inch
PLAYBOY 8-12 74-77
Also see GILLEY, Mickey, & Barbi Benton

BENTON, Brook *P&R '58*
(With the Dixie Flyers)
Singles: 78 rpm
EPIC 8-15 56
OKEH 8-15 55
Singles: 7-inch
ALL PLATINUM 3-5 76
BRUT 3-5 73
COTILLION 5-10 68-72
EPIC 10-20 56
MGM 3-5 72
MERCURY (10000 series) 8-15 59-65
(Monaural.)
MERCURY (70000 series) 10-15 60
(Monaural.)
MERCURY (70000 series) 15-25 60-61
(Stereo.)
MUSICOR 3-5 77
OKEH 15-25 55
OLDE WORLD 3-5 77-78
POLYDOR 3-5 79
RCA 6-12 65-67
REPRISE 4-8 67-68
STAX 3-5 74
VIK 10-20 57-58
Picture Sleeves
MERCURY 10-20 60-64
RCA 10-15 65
EPs: 7-inch
MERCURY (3394 "Brook Benton") 15-25 59
MERCURY (4033 "It's Just a Matter of Time") 15-25 61
MERCURY (4046 "The Boll Weevil Song") 15-25 61
LPs: 10/12-inch
ALL PLATINUM 8-10 76
CAMDEN (Except 564) 8-10 70
CAMDEN (564 "Brook Benton") 15-20 60
COTILLION 8-10 69-72
EPIC (3573 "Brook Benton at His Best") 15-25 59
HARMONY 8-12 65
MGM 8-10 73
MERCURY (20000 series) 15-30 59-65
(Monaural.)
MERCURY (60000 series) 20-35 59-65
(Stereo.)
MERCURY (822321 "Greatest Hits") 5-8 84
MUSICOR 8-10 77
OLDE WORLD 5-10 77
RCA (APL1 series) 8-10 75
(With "APL1" prefix.)
RCA (LPM/LSP series) 10-12 66
(With "LPM" or "LSP" prefix.)
REPRISE 8-12 67-68
TEE VEE 5-10
WING 8-10 66
Session: King Curtis.
Also see KING CURTIS
Also see SANDMEN
Also see TROGGS / Brook Benton

BENTON, Brook / Jesse Belvin
LPs: 10/12-inch
CROWN 12-15 63
Also see BELVIN, Jesse

BENTON, Brook, & Damita Jo
Singles: 7-inch
MERCURY 5-10 63
Also see DAMITA JO

BENTON, Brook / Chuck Jackson / Jimmy Soul
LPs: 10/12-inch
ALMOR (106 "Stargazing") 10-20 60s
Also see JACKSON, Chuck
Also see SOUL, Jimmy

BENTON, Brook / Jackie Jocko
LPs: 10/12-inch
STRAND (1121 "The Dynamic Brook Benton Sings") 15-25 63

BENTON, Brook, & Dinah Washington *P&R '60*
Singles: 7-inch
MERCURY (10032 "A Rockin' Good Way") 15-25 60
(Stereo.)
MERCURY (71565 "Baby") 8-12 60
MERCURY (71629 "A Rockin' Good Way") 8-12 60
(Monaural.)
Picture Sleeves
MERCURY (71629 "A Rockin' Good Way") 10-20 60
EPs: 7-inch
MERCURY (4028 "Two of Us") 15-25 60
LPs: 10/12-inch
MERCURY (20588 "Two of Us") 25-35 60
(Monaural.)
MERCURY (60244 "Two of Us") 30-40 60
(Stereo.)
Also see BENTON, Brook
Also see WASHINGTON, Dinah

BENTON, Buster
Singles: 7-inch
JEWEL 4-8 74
MELLOWAY 10-15
RONN 3-6 78-79
SUPREME 5-10
LPs: 10/12-inch
RONN 5-10 78-81

BENTON, Merv
Singles: 7-inch
MARVEL 10-20 66

BENTON, Walt
Singles: 7-inch
SCOTTIE (1321 "Summer School Blues") 40-60 60
STARO (2 "Do It Again") 50-100
20TH FOX (143 "Stuck Up") 50-75 59

BENTWOOD ROCKER
LPs: 10/12-inch
QUALITY/RFC 5-10 83

BEOWULF
LPs: 10/12-inch
MORRHYTHM 5-10 80

BERBERIAN, John
(With the Rock East Ensemble)
LPs: 10/12-inch
MAINSTREAM (6123 "Impressions East") 75-100 69
VERVE/FORECAST (3073 "Middle Eastern Rock") 30-40 69

BERG, Gertrude *LP '65*
LPs: 10/12-inch
AMY 10-15 65

BERG, Matraca *C&W '90*
Singles: 7-inch
RCA 3-4 90-91

BERGEN, Polly *LP '57*
Singles: 78 rpm
COLUMBIA 3-6 57
JUBILEE 4-6 56
RCA 4-8 50-51
RKO UNIQUE 4-6 57
Singles: 7-inch
COLUMBIA 5-10 57-61
JUBILEE 5-10 56
RCA 5-10 50-51
RKO UNIQUE 5-10 57
EPs: 7-inch
COLUMBIA 5-15 57
JUBILEE 5-15 56
LPs: 10/12-inch
CAMDEN 15-20 56
COLUMBIA 15-25 57-61
HARMONY 10-20 60
JUBILEE 15-25 56
PHILIPS 10-20 63

BERGEN, Polly / Fran Warren / Lynn Roberts
LPs: 10/12-inch
RKO 10-20 59
Also see BERGEN, Polly

BERGER, Michael
Singles: 7-inch
ATLANTIC 3-4 82
LPs: 10/12-inch
ATLANTIC 5-10 82

BERGMAN, Ingrid, & Orphans' Chorus / Malcolm Arnold & London Philharmonic
Singles: 7-inch
20TH FOX (126 "This Old Man") 5-10 58
Picture Sleeves
20TH FOX (126 "This Old Man") 15-25 58

BERK, Sammy
(Sammy Berk "At the Piano")
Singles: 7-inch
TRIPLE A (98 "Cool Cat Crawl") 15-25 58

BERKELEY FIVE
Singles: 7-inch
BOSS (004 "You're Gonna Cry") 15-25 66

BERKELEY KITES
Singles: 7-inch
MINARET (132 "Hang-Up City") 20-35 66
MINARET (140 "Alice in Wonderland") 10-20 67
MINARET (145 "Willow Run") 10-20 67

BERLIN *P&R/D&D/LP '83*
Singles: 12-inch
GEFFEN 4-6 83-84
Singles: 7-inch
COLUMBIA 3-4 86
GEFFEN 3-4 82-86
I.R.S. 3-4 80
Picture Sleeves
COLUMBIA 3-4 86
GEFFEN 3-4 83-86
LPs: 10/12-inch
ENIGMA ("Pleasure Victim") 50-100 82
GEFFEN 5-10 82-86
Members: Terri Nunn; John Crawford; Rob Brill.

BERLIN / Madonna
Singles: 7-inch
GEFFEN 3-5 85
Picture Sleeves
GEFFEN 3-5 85
Also see BERLIN
Also see MADONNA

BERLIN EXPRESS
Singles: 12-inch
PORTRAIT 4-6 82

BERLIN PHILHARMONIC *P&R '70*
(Conducted by Karl Böhm)
Singles: 7-inch
POLYDOR 4-6 69
Member: Karl Boehm.

BERLINGER, Jay
LPs: 10/12-inch
MAINSTREAM 8-10 73

BERMAN, Shelley *LP '59*
LPs: 10/12-inch
METRO 8-12 65
VERVE (15000 series) 10-20 59-64

BERMUDA JAM
LPs: 10/12-inch
DYNAVOICE 10-15 69

BERMUDAS *P&R '64*
Singles: 7-inch
ERA 5-10 64
Member: Rickie Page.

BERNA-DEAN
Singles: 7-inch
GNP 5-10 64
IMPERIAL 10-20 61-63
POST (10002 "I Don't Know") 5-10 63

BERNADETTE
(With the Swingin' Bears)
Singles: 7-inch
BEACH 5-10 61
GOLD COAST 5-10
JULIA 5-10 62

BERNADETTE, Sunny, & Her Fabulous Guys
Singles: 7-inch
U.A. (50970 "That's Happy") 10-20 69
Also see SHY GUYS

BERNAL, Gil
Singles: 78 rpm
AMERICAN 5-10 56
SPARK 10-20 54
Singles: 7-inch
AMERICAN 8-15 56
SPARK 15-25 54
VERVE 5-10

BERNARD, Chris
Singles: 7-inch
McVOUTIE 3-5
REVUE 4-8

BERNARD, Chuck *R&B '66*
(Chuck Benard)
Singles: 7-inch
MAVERICK (1009 "Indian Giver") 5-10 67
(Different recording than issued on Satellite.)
MI BOUTE 8-12 60s
ST. LAWRENCE 5-10 67
SATELLITE 5-10 65-66
ZODIAC 3-6 70-71

BERNARD, Rod *P&R/R&B '59*
(With the Twisters)
Singles: 7-inch
ABC 3-4 74
ARBEE 4-8 65-66
ARGO 8-10 59
CARL 10-20 57
COLLECTABLES 3-4 81
COPYRIGHT 4-6 68
CRAZY CAJUN 3-4 78
HALL 5-10 61-64
HALLWAY 5-10 61-64
JIN (105 "This Should Go On Forever") 25-40 59
JIN (200 series) 3-5 74-76
MERCURY 5-10 59-61
TEARDROP 5-10 64-65
LPs: 10/12-inch
JIN (4007 "Rod Bernard") 50-75 60s
Also see MIZZELL, Bobby
Also see SHONDELLS / Rod Bernard / Warren Storm / Skip Stewart

BERNARD, Rod / Clifton Chenier
Singles: 7-inch
JIN (9014 "Boogie in Black") 10-15
Also see BERNARD, Rod
Also see CHENIER, Clifton

BERNDT, Robert
Singles: 7-inch
CUCA (1041 "False Dreams") 15-25 61

BERNELL, Bobby
Singles: 7-inch
FORTUNE 4-8 62

BERNELL, G.L.
Singles: 7-inch
AMARET 3-5 72

BERNIE & LEE
Singles: 7-inch
MATT 5-10 61
TODD 8-12 59

BERNIER, Carolyne
Singles: 7-inch
PRIVATE STOCK 3-4 78
LPs: 10/12-inch
DERAM 5-10 77
PRIVATE STOCK 5-10 78

BERNS, Mike
Singles: 7-inch
ABC 5-10 63

BERNSTEIN, Elmer, & Orchestra *P&R '56*
Singles: 78 rpm
DECCA 3-6 56
Singles: 7-inch
AVA 3-8 62-65
CAPITOL 4-8 59-60
CHOREO 3-5 62
COLUMBIA 3-5 65
DECCA 4-8 56
DOT 3-5 66
U.A. 3-5 65-68
EPs: 7-inch
CAPITOL 3-8 59
LPs: 10/12-inch
CAPITOL 4-8 59-60
COLUMBIA 5-15 60
DOT 10-15 59
HAMILTON 4-8 59
Also see CARR, Vikki
For a complete listing of soundtracks by this artist, consult *The Official Price Guide to Movie/TV Soundtracks and Original Cast Albums.*

BERNSTEIN, Leonard, & His Orchestra *LP '60*
LPs: 10/12-inch
CAMDEN 8-15 55-56
COLUMBIA (919 "What Is Jazz") 20-40 56
COLUMBIA (31000 series) 5-10 71
COLUMBIA MASTERWORKS 10-20
For a complete listing of soundtracks by this artist, consult *The Official Price Guide to Movie/TV Soundtracks and Original Cast Albums.*

BERNSTEIN, Leonard, & Dave Brubeck
LPs: 10/12-inch
COLUMBIA 12-25 60
Also see BERNSTEIN, Leonard, & His Orchestra
Also see BRUBECK, Dave

BERRIES
Singles: 7-inch
IGL (133 "I've Been Looking") 15-25

BERRINGTON, Lou
Singles: 7-inch
PARKWAY 5-8 66

BERRY, Al, & Furness Bros.
(With Max Dickman & Orchestra)
Singles: 7-inch
MELMAR (115 "Please Don't Call Me Fool") 15-25 50s
Also see FURNESS BROTHERS

BERRY, Bill
(Bill Berry Quartet)
Singles: 7-inch
GMA (7 "Heavenly Angel") 50-75 64
LPs: 10/12-inch
DIRECTIONAL SOUND 15-20 67

BERRY, Brooks
Singles: 7-inch
PRESTIGE BLUESVILLE 3-5 63
LPs: 10/12-inch
PRESTIGE BLUESVILLE 15-20 63

BERRY, Brooks, & Scrapper Blackwell
LPs: 10/12-inch
PRESTIGE BLUESVILLE (1074 "My Heart Struck Sorrow") 20-30 64
Also see BERRY, Brooks
Also see BLACKWELL, Francis "Scrapper"

BERRY, Charles
Singles: 7-inch
JET STREAM (722 "Don't Call on Me") 10-20 60s

BERRY, Chuck *P&R/R&B '55*
Singles: 78 rpm
CHESS (1600 series) 30-60 55-58
CHESS (1700 "Carol") 50-100 58
CHESS (1709 "Sweet Little Rock & Roller") 50-100 58
CHESS (1722 "Almost Grown") 50-100 59
CHESS (1729 "Memphis, Tennessee") 75-125 59
CHESS (1737 "My Childhood Sweetheart") 100-150 59
CHESS (1747 "Too Pooped to Pop") 100-200 60
QUALITY 20-40 55
(Canadian.)
Singles: 7-inch
ATCO 3-5 79
CHESS (1604 "Maybellene") 30-40 55
CHESS (1610 "Thirty Days") 30-40 55
CHESS (1615 "No Money Down") 30-40 56
CHESS (1626 "Roll Over Beethoven") 30-40 56
CHESS (1635 "Too Much Moneky Business") 30-40 56
CHESS (1645 "You Can't Catch Me") 30-40 57
CHESS (1653 "School Day") 30-40 57
CHESS (1664 "Oh Baby Doll") 30-40 57
CHESS (1671 "Rock & Roll Music") 30-40 57
CHESS (1683 "Sweet Little Sixteen") 30-40 58
CHESS (1691 "Johnny B. Goode") 30-40 58
CHESS (1697 "Beautiful Delilah") 30-40 58
CHESS (1700 "Carol") 30-40 58
CHESS (1709 "Sweet Little Rock & Roller") 30-40 58
CHESS (1716 "Anthony Boy") 30-40 59
CHESS (1722 "Almost Grown") 30-40 59
CHESS (1729 "Back in the USA") 30-40 59
CHESS (1737 "My Childhood Sweetheart") 15-25 59
CHESS (1747 "Too Pooped to Pop") 15-25 60
CHESS (1754 thru 1926) 10-15 60-65
CHESS (1943 thru 1926) 6-12 65-69
CHESS (2000 & 9000 series) 4-6 70-73
ERIC 3-4 73
MERCURY 4-8 66-72
PHILO 8-15 66
("Hip Pocket" Record.)
QUALITY (1413 "Maybelline") 50-100 55
(Canadian. Note slightly different spelling.)
QUALITY (1467 "No Money Down") 50-100 56
(Canadian.)
Picture Sleeves
CHESS (1898 "No Particular Place to Go") 10-20 64
CHESS (1906 "You Never Can Tell") 10-20 64
CHESS (1912 "Little Marie") 10-20 64
CHESS (1916 "Promised Land") 10-20 64
EPs: 7-inch
CHESS (5118 "After School Session") 50-100 57
CHESS (5118 "Head Over Heels") 75-125 57
CHESS (5119 "Rock & Roll Music") 50-100 58
CHESS (5121 "Sweet Little 16") 50-100 58
CHESS (5124 "Pickin' Berries") 50-100 58
CHESS (5126 "Sweet Little Rock & Roller") 50-100 58

LPs: 10/12-inch
ACCORD 5-10 82
ATCO 5-10 79
AUDIO FIDELITY 8-10 84
(Picture disc.)
BROOKVILLE 12-15 73
CHESS (Except 1400 & 9000 series) 10-20 66-76
CHESS (1426 "After School Session") 50-75 57
CHESS (1432 "One Dozen Berrys") 50-75 58
CHESS (1435 "Chuck Berry's on Top") 50-75 59
CHESS (1448 "Rockin' at the Hops") 50-75 59
CHESS (1456 "Chuck Berry's New Juke box Hits") 25-40 61
CHESS (1465 "More Chuck Berry") 30-40 62
CHESS (1465 "Chuck Berry Twist") 20-25 62
(Reissue with title change.)
CHESS (1480 "Chuck Berry on Stage") 20-25 63
CHESS (1485 "Chuck Berry's Greatest Hits") 25-30 64
CHESS (1488 "St. Louis to Liverpool") 20-25 64
CHESS (1495 "Chuck Berry in London") 25-30 65
CHESS (1498 "Fresh Berrys") 20-25 65
CHESS (9000 series) 5-10 85
CHESS/MCA 5-8 89
EVEREST 8-10 76
GUSTO 5-10 78
MCA 8-12 86-87
MAGNUM 10-12 69
MERCURY 15-25 67-72
PICKWICK 8-10 72
TRIP 8-10 78
UPFRONT 5-10 79
Also see ALEXANDER, Joe, & Cubans
Also see DIDDLEY, Bo, & Chuck Berry
Also see MILLER, Steve

BERRY, Chuck, & Howlin' Wolf
LPs: 10/12-inch
CHESS 15-20 69
Also see BERRY, Chuck
Also see HOWLIN' WOLF

BERRY, Dave
Singles: 7-inch
LONDON 4-8 64-68
PARROT 4-8 67

BERRY, Debbie
Singles: 7-inch
BIG K (1001 "Music City Schemer") 5-8 76
MERCURY 3-5 73

BERRY, Delorise
Singles: 7-inch
COTILLION 4-6 68

BERRY, Dorothy
(With the Swans)
Singles: 7-inch
BIG THREE (401 "Don't Give Me Love") 15-25 60s
CHALLENGE 8-10 63
DOT 4-8 64
LITTLE STAR (111 "The Girl Who Stoped the Duke of Earl") 10-15 62
LITTLE STAR (117 "I'll Come Back to You") 10-15 62
PLANETARY 10-15 65
TANGERINE 3-5 71
VANCE 4-8
Also see NORMAN, Jimmy, & Dorothy Berry

BERRY, Dorothy, & Jimmy Norman
Singles: 7-inch
LITTLE STAR (122 "Your Love") 10-15 62
Also see BERRY, Dorothy
Also see NORMAN, Jimmy

BERRY, Gordon
Singles: 7-inch
SPORT (103 "How Lonely") 15-25 60s

BERRY, Huckle
Singles: 78 rpm
MGM 4-8 52
Singles: 7-inch
MGM 8-12 52

BERRY, Jan
(Jan; Jan Barry)
Singles: 7-inch
A&M 5-10 77-78
LIBERTY (55845 "The Universal Coward") 10-15 66
ODE '70 (Except 66023 & 66034) 15-20 72-77
ODE '70 (66023 "Mother Earth") 20-40 72
(With insert note from Jan. Promotional issue only.)
ODE '70 (66023 "Mother Earth") 20-30 72
(Without insert note from Jan.)
ODE '70 (66034 "Don't You Just Know It") 30-40 73
(With Brian Wilson.)
RIPPLE (6101 "Tomorrow's Teardrops") 30-45 61
Picture Sleeves
LIBERTY (55845 "The Universal Coward") 100-125 66
Also see JAN & ARNIE
Also see JAN & DEAN
Also see WILSON, Brian

BERRY, Jody
Singles: 7-inch
STACK 5-10 59

BERRY, John
Singles: 7-inch
DOT 5-10 60

BERRY, Lou, & Bel Raves
Singles: 7-inch
DREEM (1001 "Hot Rod") 300-400 59
(Reissued as by Red & Lou Berry.)
Also see BERRY, Red & Lou

BERRY, Mike
(With the Outlaws)
Singles: 7-inch
CORAL 10-20 62-66
EPIC 3-4 79-80
MCA 3-4 75
SOO 5-10
LPs: 10/12-inch
EPIC 5-10 79
SIRE 10-15 76

BERRY, Panda
Singles: 7-inch
CHALLENGE 4-8 63
EVEREST 4-8 63

BERRY, Red & Lou
Singles: 7-inch
20TH FOX (169 "Hot Rod") 150-200 59
Also see BERRY, Lou, & Bel Raves

BERRY, Richard
(With the Dreamers; with Pharaohs; with Lockettes; with Soul Searchers; with Soul Serchers; with Silks)
Singles: 78 rpm
FLAIR 15-25 55
FLIP 15-25 56-57
RPM 15-25 56
Singles: 7-inch
AMC (616 "Go Go Girl") 10-15
ARC (7463 "Soulin' in C-Minor") 5-10
BOLD SOUL 3-5 71
CIRAY 4-6
FLAIR (1016 "One Little Prayer") 40-60 53
FLAIR (1052 "At Last") 40-60 55
FLAIR (1055 "The Big Break") 40-60 54
FLAIR (1058 "Daddy, Daddy") 40-60 55
FLAIR (1064 "Get Out of the Car") 40-60 55
FLAIR (1068 "God Gave Me You") 40-60 55
FLAIR (1075 "Jelly Roll") 40-60 55
FLIP (318 "Take the Key") 25-35 57
FLIP (321 "Louie Louie"/"You Are My Sunshine") 35-50 57
FLIP (321 "Louie Louie"/"Rock Rock Rock") 20-40 57
FLIP (327 thru 349) 20-30 57-60
JONCO (51 "Doin' It") 5-10
K&G (9001 "I'm Your Fool") 50-75 61
PAXLEY (751 "Give It Up") 10-15 61
(Both Paxley – PAXton and FowLEY – and K&G – Kim & Gary – were owned by Kim Fowley and Gary Paxton.)
RPM (465 "Yama Yama Pretty Mama") 25-50 56
RPM (477 "Wait for Me") 25-50 56
SMASH 8-12 62-63
UNITY 3-6
W.B. (5164 "Walk Right In") 25-50 60
LPs: 10/12-inch
CROWN (5371 "Richard Berry and the Dreamers") 20-25 63
KENT 5-10 86
PAM (1001 "Live from H.D. Hover Century Restaurant") 20-25 68
PAM (1002 "Wild Berry Live") 20-25
Also see BLOSSOMS
Also see DREAMERS
Also see FLAIRS
Also see FOWLEY, Kim
Also see JAMES, Etta
Also see LOCKETTES
Also see MAYE, Arthur Lee
Also see PAXTON, Gary
Also see PHARAOHS
Also see RICKIE & JENNELL
Also see RICKY
Also see ROBINS
Also see SIX TEENS / Donald Woods / Richard Berry

BERRY, Ron, & Dreamers
Singles: 7-inch
KEN-H (11290 "I'll Give You All My Love") 200-300 63
(Identification number used since no label number is shown.)
PIXIE (4864 "I'm Crazy 'Bout That Woman") 30-40 65

BERRY, Sleepy Jim
Singles: 7-inch
BERRY 5-10

BERRY, Wayne
Singles: 7-inch
RCA 3-5 74

BERRY BOYS
Singles: 7-inch
SOMA 8-12 60s

BERRY BROTHERS
Singles: 7-inch
DREEM 25-50 60s
(Title and selection number not known.)

BERRY KIDS
Singles: 78 rpm
MGM 25-50 56-57
Singles: 7-inch
MGM (12379 "Go, Go, Go Right Into Town") 40-80 56
MGM (12496 "Rootie Tootie") 40-80 57

BERRY STREET STATION
Singles: 7-inch
KARAT 5-8 67
LE CAM 5-8
Members: Sonny Threatt; Phyllis Brown-Threatt.
Also see SONNY & PHYLLIS

BERRYMAN, Lou & Peter
LPs: 10/12-inch
CORNBELT 5-10
MOUNTAIN RAILROAD 5-10

BERRYS
Singles: 7-inch
CHALLENGE (59358 "Midnight Hour") 8-12 67

BERSIN, Johnny
Singles: 7-inch
HALL WAY 4-8 62

BERT & RAY
Singles: 7-inch
ALPINE (51 "Slow Drag") 10-20 59
Member: Link Wray
Also see WRAY, Link

BERTEI, Adele *D&D '83*
Singles: 12-inch
GEFFEN 4-6 83
Singles: 7-inch
GEFFEN 3-4 83

BERTOLET, Tony
Singles: 7-inch
DORE 5-10 62
STRAND 5-10 61

BERTRAM, Bob
Singles: 7-inch
BERTRAM INT'L (205 "I'll Roam No More") 15-20 57
Also see DADDY BOB

BERTRAND, Plastic *P&R '78*
Singles: 7-inch
SIRE 4-6 78
Picture Sleeves
SIRE 5-10 78

BERWICK, Brad
Singles: 7-inch
CLINTON 10-15 64
DEEM 4-8 65
Picture Sleeves
CLINTON 15-25 64

BESAW, Ron, & Mojo Men
Singles: 7-inch
TARGET (2002 "I'm Sorry") 10-20 71
Members: Ronnie (Besaw) Fuller; Jesse Vasquez; Bobby Borlee.
Also see FULLER, Ronnie
Also see NEW RAGING STORMS

BESIG, Paul
Singles: 7-inch
RHYTHMAIRE 5-10 59

BEST, Billy, & Ditalians
Singles: 7-inch
MERCURY 4-6 69

BEST, James
Singles: 7-inch
SCOTTI BROTHERS 3-4 82

BEST, Peter
("Pete Best Formerly of the Beatles"; "Best of the Beatles, Peter Best")
Singles: 7-inch
BEATLES BEST (800 "I'll Try Anyway") 150-175 64
CAMEO (391 "Boys") 50-75 66
CAMEO (391 "Boys") 60-70 66
(Promotional issue.)
CAPITOL (2092 "Carousel of Love") 25-35 67
CAPITOL (2092 "Carousel of Love") 15-25 67
(Promotional issue.)
COLLECTABLES 4-8 87
HAPPENING (1117 "If You Can't Get Her") 125-150 66
HAPPENING (405 "Don't Play with Me Little Girl") 150-175 66
MR. MAESTRO (711 "I Can't Do Without You Now") 200-250 65
(Colored vinyl.With photo insert flyer.)
MR. MAESTRO (711 "I Can't Do Without You Now") 100-150 65
(Colored vinyl.Without photo insert flyer.)
MR. MAESTRO (711 "I Can't Do Without You Now") 150-200 65
(Black vinyl.)
MR. MAESTRO (712 "Casting My Spell") 125-150 65
(Black vinyl.)
MR. MAESTRO (712 "Casting My Spell") 150-200 65
(Colored vinyl.)
ORIGINAL BEATLES DRUMMER (800 "I'll Try Anyway") 40-50 64
Picture Sleeves
CAMEO (391 "Boys") 75-100 66
LPs: 10/12-inch
BEST FAN CLUB 25-30 66
PB 15-25 81
PHOENIX 10 10-15 82
SAVAGE (71 "Best of the Beatles") 150-200 65
Also see BEATLES

BEST EVER
Singles: 7-inch
STARWAY 4-8 75
Member: Muhammad Ali.
Also see CLAY, Cassius

BEST OF BOTH WORLDS
Singles: 7-inch
CALLA 5-8 60s

BEST PEOPLE
Singles: 7-inch
CUCA (6894 "Rainbow") 10-20 68

BEST THINGS
Singles: 7-inch
U.A. 10-20 66

BETH, Karen *LP '69*
Singles: 7-inch
BUDDAH 3-5 75
LPs: 10/12-inch
BUDDAH 8-10 75
DECCA 8-12 69

BETHANY
Singles: 7-inch
RCI 3-4 83-84

BETHEA, Harmon *R&B '73*
(Bethea; with Maskman & the Agents)
Singles: 7-inch
BBC 3-5
CAP CITY 3-5
DYNAMO 5-10 69-71
INTERSTATE 3-5 74
JAN JAN 3-5 74
LEBBY 3-5 72
MUSICOR 10-20 70-74
ROADHOUSE 3-5
RUJAC 3-5
SMITHS 3-5 76
Also see BETHEA & CAP-TANS
Also see MASKMAN & AGENTS
Also see PROGRESSIVE FOUR

BETHEA & CAP-TANS
Singles: 7-inch
ANNA 5-10 60
DC 3-5
LOOP 3-5 72
SABU 5-10 63-64
Also see BETHEA, Harmon
Also see CAP-TANS
Also see WAILING BETHEA & CAP-TANS

BETHLEHEM ASYLUM
Singles: 7-inch
AMPEX 3-5 70-71
LPs: 10/12-inch
AMPEX 12-15 70-71

BETHLEHEM EXIT
Singles: 7-inch
JABBERWOCK 10-20

BETTER DAYS
LPs: 10/12-inch
EXIT 10-20 69
Members: Lynn Weyts; Joe Mendyk; Phil Salvaggio; Jerry Warner.
Also see FRONTIERS

BETTER HALF
Singles: 7-inch
CHATIM 3-5

BETTER HALF DOZEN
Singles: 7-inch
U-DOE (105 "I'm Gonna Leave You") 20-30

BETTER SWEET
Singles: 7-inch
M.O.C. (667 "Like the Flowers") 20-30 67

BETTERS, Harold *P&R/R&B '64*
Singles: 7-inch
GATEWAY 4-6 63-65
REPRISE 4-6 66-67
LPs: 10/12-inch
GATEWAY 10-20 64-66
REPRISE 10-20 65-67

BETTS, Dickey: see BETTS, Richard

BETTS, Harry
Singles: 7-inch
RCA 3-6 69
LPs: 10/12-inch
RCA 10-15 69

BETTS, Richard *LP '74*
(Dickey Betts & Great Southern; Dickey Betts Band)
Singles: 7-inch
ARISTA 3-5 77-78
CAPRICORN 3-5 74-76
LPs: 10/12-inch
ARISTA 5-10 77-78
CAPRICORN 8-10 74
EPIC 5-8 88
Also see ALLMAN BROTHERS BAND

BETTY & CHARLES
Singles: 7-inch
CAPITOL (2143 "Someone for Everyone") 5-10 68
CRAZY HORSE 3-6 70

BETTY & DUPREE
Singles: 7-inch
KENT 5-10 59

BETTY & KAREN
Singles: 7-inch
MGM 4-8 66

BETTY & RAY
Singles: 7-inch
RENDEZVOUS 5-10 62

BETTY & ROSE
Singles: 7-inch
PRESS 5-10 62

BETTY & ROY
Singles: 7-inch
SAFICE (335 "I'll Be There") 5-10

BETTY & SUE
Singles: 7-inch
RCA 5-10 60

BETTY JANE & TEENETTES
Singles: 7-inch
CARELLEN (101 "Show Your Love") 15-25 61
CARELLEN (107 "I'm No Longer Jimmy's Girl") 15-25 61
Also see JONES, Billy, & Teenettes

BEV & SAL
Singles: 7-inch
DON-MAR 5-10 59

BEVAN, Alex
Singles: 7-inch
BIG TREE 3-5 71
LPs: 10/12-inch
BIG TREE 10-15 71

BEVEL, Charles *R&B '74*
(Charles "Mississippi" Bevel)
Singles: 7-inch
A&M 3-5 73-74
LPs: 10/12-inch
A&M 8-10 73-74

BEVERLEE & SIDRO
(With the Sneakers)
Singles: 7-inch
W.B. 4-6 69

BEVERLEY
Singles: 7-inch
DERAM 4-8 67

BEVERLEY SISTERS: see BEVERLY SISTERS

BEVERLY, Frankie
(With the Butlers; with Raw Soul; Frankie Beverley)
Singles: 7-inch
FAIRMOUNT (1017 "Because of My Heart") 150-250
GAMBLE 3-5
GREGAR (220 "If That's What You Wanted") 50-75 71
ROUSER (1017 "Because of My Heart") 200-300
SASSY (1002 "If That's What You Wanted") 20-30
Also see BUTLERS
Also see MAZE

BEVERLY, Stan, & Hollywood Saxons
(With the "Hollywood Saxon's")
Singles: 7-inch
ENTRA (1214 "Diamonds") 150-250 60s
(Red label.)
ENTRA (1214 "Diamonds") 50-75 60s
(Black label.)
Also see HOLLYWOOD SAXONS

BEVERLY & DUANE *R&B '78*
Singles: 7-inch
ARIOLA AMERICA 3-5 78-79
Members: Beverly Wheeler; Duane Williams.

BEVERLY & MIKE
Singles: 7-inch
LONDON 4-8 64

BEVERLY & DEL-CAPRIS
Singles: 7-inch
COLUMBIA 5-10 64

BEVERLY & DONUTS
Singles: 7-inch
BOBBI 10-15

BEVERLY & MOTOR SCOOTERS
Singles: 7-inch
EPIC 4-8 64

BEVERLY ANN
Singles: 7-inch
RCA 8-10 68

BEVERLY HILLS BLUES BAND
Singles: 7-inch
W.B. 3-5 76
Members: Dino Martin; Desi Arnaz Jr; Tony Martin; Terry Melcher.
Also see DINO, DESI & BILLY
Also see MARTIN & FINLEY
Also see MELCHER, Terry

BEVERLY HILLS PAINTERS
Singles: 7-inch
GATEWAY (700 "Believe Me") 20-40 64

BEVERLY HOT SPOTS
Singles: 7-inch
M.O.C. (652 "Carroll County Blues") 10-15 63

BEVERLY O. & BONNEVILLES
Singles: 7-inch
KA HI 5-10 59

BEVERLY SISTERS P&R '56
(Beverley Sisters)
Singles: 78 rpm
LONDON 4-6 56
Singles: 7-inch
LONDON 5-10 56
MERCURY 5-10 60
LPs: 10/12-inch
CAPITOL 10-20 61

BEY, Salome, & Brotherhood
Singles: 7-inch
BUDDAH 3-5 76

BEY SISTERS
Singles: 78 rpm
JAGUAR 8-12 55-56
Singles: 7-inch
JAGUAR 15-25 55-56

BHANG
Singles: 7-inch
MONSTER 4-8

BIANCO, Cappy
Singles: 7-inch
ABC-PAR 5-10 59
CASA BLANCA 5-10 59

BIANCO, Frank
Singles: 78 rpm
ATCO 4-8 57
Singles: 7-inch
ATCO 5-10 57

BIANCO, Gene
Singles: 7-inch
VISCOUNT (530 "Harp Rock Boogie") 15-25 58

BIANCO, Lory
Singles: 7-inch
RCA 3-5 80

BIBB, Leon
LPs:10/12-inch
LIBERTY 10-15
VANGUARD 15-25
WASHINGTON 12-15

BIBBS, Betty
Singles: 7-inch
GENEVA 8-12
KENT 5-8 66

BIBLE
LPs: 10/12-inch
CHRYSALIS 5-8 88

BICENTENNIAL NEWS TEAM
Singles: 7-inch
ST. JOHNS 4-6 76

BICKERSONS: see AMECHE, Don, & Frances Langford

BICKHARDT, Craig C&W '84
Singles: 7-inch
LIBERTY 3-4 84
Also see SCHUYLER, KNOBLOCH & BICKHARDT

BIDDU P&R/R&B '75
(Biddu Orchestra)
Singles: 7-inch
COLOSSUS 3-5 70
EPIC 3-5 75-77
LPs: 10/12-inch
EPIC 5-10 76-77

BIENER, Tommy
Singles: 7-inch
GOLDEN CREST (501 "Top 40") ... 10-15 58

BIG "A" RAN
Singles: 7-inch
BEAU MONDE 4-8 62

BIG AL & HI-FIs
Singles: 7-inch
PIZZA (1 "Flip, Flop & Fly") 25-30

BIG AL T.
Singles: 7-inch
VIRTUE 4-6 69

BIG AMOS
(Amos Patton)
Singles: 7-inch
HI 4-8 66-67

BIG AMOS / Big Lucky / Don Hines
LPs: 10/12-inch
HI 8-12 71
Also see BIG AMOS
Also see HINES, Don

BIG APPLE
Singles: 7-inch
PRO-GRESS 4-8 75
Members: Pete Source; John Beilfuss; John Dombeck.
Also see SOURCE, Pete

BIG AUDIO DYNAMITE LP '85
Singles: 12-inch
COLUMBIA (1739 "James Brown") . 6-10 89
(Promotional issue only.)
COLUMBIA (1899 "Contact") 5-8 89
(Promotional issue only.)
COLUMBIA (2302 "Medicine Show") 5-8 86
(Promotional issue only.)
COLUMBIA (2520 "C'mon Every Beatbox") 5-8 86
(Promotional issue only.)
COLUMBIA (2697 "Hollywood Boulevard") 5-8 86
(Promotional issue only.)
COLUMBIA (07955 "Just Play Music") 4-6
COLUMBIA (8133 "Other 99") 5-8 88
(Promotional issue only.)
COLUMBIA (5000 thru 8000 series) .. 4-6 85-90
Singles: 7-inch
COLUMBIA (5000 series except 5841) 3-5 85
COLUMBIA (5841 "Medicine Show") 4-6 85
(White label. Promotional issue only.)
COLUMBIA (6000 series, except 6053) 3-5 86
COLUMBIA (6053 "E = MC²") 4-6 85
(White label. Promotional issue only.)
COLUMBIA (6364 "C'mon Every Beatbox") 4-6 86
(White label. Promotional issue only.)
COLUMBIA (6708 "Badrock City") 4-6 86
(White label. Promotional issue only.)
COLUMBIA (8000 series) 3-5 88
Picture Sleeves
COLUMBIA (5841 "Medicine Show"). 5-8 85
(Promotional issue only.)
COLUMBIA (6053 "E = MC²") 5-8 85
(Promotional issue only.)
COLUMBIA (8094 "Other 99") 4-6 88
LPs: 10/12-inch
COLUMBIA 5-10 85-89
MCA 5-10
Members: Mick Jones; Don Letts; Leo Williams; Greg Roberts; Dan Donovan; Flea.
Also see BIG AUDIO DYNAMITE II
Also see CLASH

BIG AUDIO DYNAMITE II
Singles: 12-inch
COLUMBIA (4044 "Rush Dance") 5-8 91
COLUMBIA (657640 "Rush") 5-10 91
(Promotional issue only.)
LPs: 10/12-inch
COLUMBIA 8-10 91
Members: Mick Jones; Gary Stonadge; Chris Kavanagh; Nick Hawkins.
Also see BIG AUDIO DYNAMITE

BIG BEATS
Singles: 7-inch
COLUMBIA (41072 "Clark's Expedition") 10-20 58
COLUMBIA (41199 "Rush Me") 10-20 58s
PLAY 10-20 59
Member: Trini Lopez.
Also see LOPEZ, Trini

BIG BEATS
Singles: 7-inch
TEL 8-12 59

BIG BEATS
Singles: 7-inch
STE SO (714 "Big Beat Blues") 10-20 64

BIG BEATS
Singles: 7-inch
LIBERTY 5-10 65
LPs: 10/12-inch
LIBERTY 15-25 65
Member: Arlin Harmon.

BIG BEATS
Singles: 7-inch
TONKA 4-8

BIG BEN
(Scatman Crothers)
Singles: 7-inch
ENTERPRISE 3-5 72
RIC 4-8 65
Also see CROTHERS, Scatman

BIG BEN BANJO BAND
LPs: 10/12-inch
CAPITOL 5-10 67
Member: Norrie Paramor.

BIG BERTHA: see HENDERSON, Big Bertha, with Al Smith Orchestra

BIG BILL: see BROONZY, Bill

BIG BILL TWISTER: see TWISTER, Big Bill

BIG BIRD & HIS BLOWERS
Singles: 7-inch
MAGIC CARPET 6-12

BIG BITE & MAC
Singles: 7-inch
FUN-E-BONE (4322 "Deep Tooth") .. 4-8 76

BIG BLACK
(Big Black & Blues)
Singles: 7-inch
UNI 4-8 67
LPs: 10/12-inch
UNI 8-15 67-72

BIG BLUE WRECKING CREW
Singles: 7-inch
ELEKTRA 3-4 81
Picture Sleeves
ELEKTRA 3-4 81
Members: Steve Yeager; Rick Monday; Jay Johnstone; Jerry Reuss.

BIG BO
(With the Arrows featuring Fred Lowery)
Singles: 7-inch
CHECKER 5-10 64
DUCHESS 5-10 59-62
GAY SHELL 5-10 64
Member: Fred Lowery.

BIG BOB
Singles: 7-inch
JARO (77003 "Your Line Was Busy") 25-35 59
STACY 5-10 62
CHECKER 4-8 64
DUCHESS 5-10 59-62
GAY SHELL 5-10 64
Member: Fred Lowery.

BIG BOB & DOLLARS
Singles: 7-inch
GLOBE (400 "Gordie Howe") 10-15 63
(Canadian.)
Also see DAVIS, Bob

BIG BOPPER P&R/R&B '58
(Jape Richardson; Jiles Perry Richardson Jr.)
Singles: 7-inch
D (1008 "Chantilly Lace") 150-250 58
MERCURY (71343 "Chantilly Lace") 10-15 58
MERCURY (71375 "Big Bopper's Wedding") 10-15 58
MERCURY (71416 "Walking Through My Dreams") 10-15 59
(Black label.)
MERCURY (71416 "Walking Through My Dreams") 20-30 59
(White label. Has alternate take of A-side. Promotional issue only.)
MERCURY (71451 "It's the Truth Ruth") 10-15 59
MERCURY (71482 "Pink Petticoats") 10-15 59
MERCURY CELEBRITY SERIES (30072 "Chantilly Lace") 5-10 60
WING (17000 "Chantilly Lace") 5-10 60s
LPs: 10/12-inch
MERCURY (20402 "Chantilly Lace") 250-300 59
(Black label.)
MERCURY (20402 "Chantilly Lace") 250-300 59
(White or pink label. Promotional issue only.)
MERCURY (20402 "Chantilly Lace") 75-100 64
(Red label.)
MERCURY (20402 "Chantilly Lace") 10-15 81
(Chicago "skyline" label.)
PICKWICK 20-30 73
RHINO 5-8 89
Also see DAMERON, Donna
Also see DEL-VIKINGS / Diamonds / Big Bopper / Gaylords
Also see RICHARDSON, Jape

BIG BOSS BAND
Singles: 7-inch
RENEGADE 3-5 86
Picture Sleeves
RENEGADE 4-6 86

BIG BOSSMAN
(Bob Barian)
Singles: 7-inch
MAGIC TOUCH (2004 "Do the Bat-Mo") 5-10 66
Also see COMIC BOOKS

BIG BROTHER
(Featuring Ernie Joseph)
Singles: 7-inch
ALL AMERICAN (5718 "E.S.P.") 20-30 69
LPs: 10/12-inch
ALL AMERICAN (5770 "Big Brother") 75-125 70

BIG BROTHER & HOLDING CO.
(Big Brother) LP '67
Singles: 7-inch
COLUMBIA 5-10 68-71
MAINSTREAM 5-10 67-68
Picture Sleeves
COLUMBIA (44626 "Piece of My Heart") 10-20 68
LPs: 10/12-inch
COLUMBIA 15-25 68-71
MADE to LAST 5-10 84
MAINSTREAM (6099 "Big Brother and the Holding Company") 20-35 67
Members: Janis Joplin; David Getz; Sam Andrew; Peter Albin; Jim Gurley; David Schallock; Nick Gravenites; Kathi McDonald.
Also see GRAVENITES, Nick
Also see JOPLIN, Janis
Also see McDONALD, Kathi

BIG BROWN
LPs: 10/12-inch
KENT 8-10 73

BIG BUDDY K.
Singles: 7-inch
VEE JAY 4-8 63

BIG CHENIER
(Morris Chenier; Big Chenier & His Night Owls)
Singles: 7-inch
GOLDBAND 6-12 58-61

BIG CHIEF
Singles: 7-inch
GET HIP 3-5 90

BIG CHIEF TRIO
(Big Chief & His Trio; Wilbert Ellis)
Singles: 78 rpm
SITTIN' IN WITH (523 "She's Gone") 25-35 49
SITTIN' IN WITH (530 "Poor Man's Blues") 25-35 49
Also see ELLIS, Big Boy

BIG CITY
Singles: 7-inch
20TH FOX 3-5 74

BIG CITY DOWN RIVER
Singles: 7-inch
LIONEL 3-5 70

BIG COUNTRY P&R/D&D/LP '83
Singles: 12-inch
MERCURY 4-6 83-86
Singles: 7-inch
MERCURY 3-4 83-86
REPRISE 3-4 88-89
Picture Sleeves
MERCURY (Except 811450) 3-4 83-84
MERCURY (811450 "Fields of Fire") 4-8 84
(Poster sleeve.)
REPRISE 3-4 89
LPs: 10/12-inch
MERCURY 5-10 83-86
REPRISE 5-8 88
Members: Stuart Adamson; Bruce Watson; Mark Brzezicki; Tony Butler.

BIG DADDY
(Frankie Brunson)
Singles: 7-inch
CRAKERJACK 8-12 61
GEE 10-20 57-60
PMB (7220 "Hard Top") 15-25 59
WYNNE 8-12 59
LPs: 10/12-inch
GEE (704 "Big Daddy's Blues") 35-55 60
(Red label)
GEE (704 "Big Daddy's Blues") 25-35 61
(Gray label)
REGENT (6106 "Twist Party") 20-25 62
Also see BRUNSON, Frankie

BIG DADDY
Singles: 7-inch
RHINO 3-4 83
LPs: 10/12-inch
RHINO 5-10 83-91
Members: Marty Kaniger; David Stams; Bob Wayne; Tom Lee; Gary Hoffman; John Hatton; Vince Ciavarella; Jim Reeves; Don Raymond; Norman A. Norman; Bob Sandman; Damon DeGrignon.

BIG DADDY & HIS BOYS
Singles: 78 rpm
KING 8-12 56
Singles: 7-inch
KING 10-20 56

BIG DADDY TRIO
Singles: 7-inch
PMB 5-10
SPOT 5-10 59

BIG DADDY & LITTLE SISTERS
Singles: 7-inch
ROYAL 10-15 59

BIG DAVE
Singles: 78 rpm
CAPITOL 10-15 54
Singles: 7-inch
CAPITOL (2742 "One Stop") 15-25 54
CAPITOL (2794 "Cat from Coos Bay") 15-25 54

BIG DOG
Singles: 7-inch
JOEY (501 "Doris") 50-100 62

BIG DON
Singles: 7-inch
MERRI 5-10 62

BIG DON'S REBELLION
Singles: 7-inch
ETHON (101 "It Was True") 15-25

BIG DUKE
Singles: 78 rpm
FLAIR 10-20 53
Singles: 7-inch
FLAIR (1018 "Hey, Dr. Kinsey") 25-50 53
FLAIR (1029 "Beggin' and Pleadin' ") 25-50 53

BIG ED & HIS COMBO
(Eddie Burns)
Singles: 78 rpm
CHECKER 50-75 54
Singles: 7-inch
CHECKER (790 "Biscuit Baking Mama") 150-250 54
Also see BURNS, Eddie

BIG EL
Singles: 7-inch
QUADRA (7774 "I Love You Because") 4-8 78

BIG ELLA
Singles: 7-inch
LO LO 5-10 69
RUSH 5-10
SALEM (1009 "Too Hot to Hold") ... 10-20 60s

BIG EXCHANGE
Singles: 7-inch
FANIA 3-5 75

BIG FIVE
Singles: 7-inch
JUNIOR (5000 "Wob-Ding-A-Ling") 15-25
SHAD (5019 "Stardust in Her Eyes") 50-100 60

BIG FIVE + THREE
Singles: 7-inch
MANHATTAN (4000 "Draggin' ") 15-25

BIG FOOT
Singles: 7-inch
SUE INT'L 3-6
WINRO 5-10 69
LPs: 10/12-inch
WINRO (1004 "Big Foot") 20-25 69
Members: Art Munson; David Garland; Virgil Beckham; Spence Earnshaw.
Also see BOBBY & MIDNITES
Also see WACKERS

BIG FOUR
Singles: 7-inch
MOON (306 "Outa Tune") 10-15 59

BIG FRANK & ESSENCE
Singles: 7-inch
BLUE ROCK (4012 "Secret") 150-250 65
PHILIPS (40283 "Secret") 50-100 65

BIG FROG
Singles: 7-inch
PHILIPS 4-6 69

BIG GAME HUNTERS
Singles: 7-inch
UNI 4-8 67

BIG GUITAR
Singles: 7-inch
HANOVER (4518 "Tony's Folly") ... 15-25 59

BIG GUITAR SUNNY & EL PAST RAMBLERS
Singles: 7-inch
REPRISE 4-6 69

BIG GUITARS FROM TEXAS
LPs: 10/12-inch
JUNGLE 10-12 85

BIG GUYS
Singles: 7-inch
PALETTE 10-20 64

BIG GUYS
Singles: 7-inch
W.B. (7047 "Hang My Head") 25-45 67

BIG HUGH BABY
Singles: 7-inch
LIBERTY 4-8 66-67

BIG INNERS
Singles: 7-inch
PANORAMA (16 "Do You Wonder") 5-10

BIG J.J.
(Jimmy Wisner)
Singles: 7-inch
DAY DELL (1005 "Harpsichord Blues") 5-10 59
Also see WISNER, Jimmy

BIG JACK
Singles: 7-inch
JC 5-8

BIG JEFF & PLAYBOYS
Singles: 78 rpm
DOT (1088 "Move on Baby") 20-40 52
Singles: 7-inch
DOT (1088 "Move on Baby") 40-60 52

BIG JIM & SUNDOWNERS
Singles: 7-inch
CHIP (1008 "Poor Little Sad-Eyed Sue") 40-60 61

BIG JIM'S BORDER CROSSING
Singles: 7-inch
ZANZEE (103 "You're Good for Me Girl") 10-20 60s

BIG JIMMY G
Singles: 78 rpm
TAMPA (114 "Big Boy") 10-15 56
Singles: 7-inch
TAMPA (114 "Big Boy") 15-25 56

BIG JOE
(Joseph McCoy)
Singles: 78 rpm
BLUEBIRD 5-10 42
Singles: 7-inch
WOW (902 "My Ding-A-Ling") 5-10

BIG JOHN & BUZZARDS
Singles: 78 rpm
COLUMBIA 10-20 54
OKEH 10-20 54
Singles: 7-inch
COLUMBIA 25-40 54
OKEH 25-40 54

BIG JOHN & FABULOUS BLENDS
Singles: 7-inch
CASA GRANDE (Black vinyl) 8-12 64
CASA GRANDE (Colored vinyl) 15-25 64

BIG JOHN & PHILADELPHIANS / Vince Montana
Singles: 7-inch
GUYDEN 6-10 63

BIG JOHN'S SWING CARAVAN
Singles: 7-inch
J.F.J (600 "Lila Cha-Cha") 50-100 60s

BIG LOSER
Singles: 7-inch
GROOVE (012 "This Is Monte") 10-15 50s

BIG LOST RAINBOW
LPs: 10/12-inch
("Big Lost Rainbow") 1000-1200 73
(Approximately 200 made. No label or number used.)

BIG MAC
Singles: 7-inch
DAWN 5-10 65
JEWEL 4-8 67
RONN 4-8 67

BIG MACEO R&B '45
(Major Merriweather)
Singles: 78 rpm
BLUEBIRD 15-30 42-45
FORTUNE (137 "Leavin' Blues") 25-50 52
FORTUNE (805 "Worried Life Blues, No. 2") 20-40 52
GROOVE 10-20 54
RCA 15-25 47-48
SPECIALTY (320 "Do You Remember") 10-20 49
SPECIALTY (346 "One Sunday Morning") 10-20 49
Singles: 7-inch
GROOVE (5001 "Chicago Breakdown") 30-50 54
RCA (50-0002 "Chicago Breakdown") 75-125 49
(Red vinyl.)
LPs: 10/12-inch
BLUEBIRD 10-12 75
Also see BRIM, John
Also see TAMPA RED

BIG MACK & SHUFFLERS
Singles: 7-inch
TRI-MAC (501 "Out of My Mind") 15-25 58

BIG MAYBELLE R&B '53
(Mable Smith)
Singles: 78 rpm
KING 10-20 48-49
OKEH 10-20 53-56
SAVOY 10-20 56-58
Singles: 7-inch
BRUNSWICK 5-10 63
CHESS 4-8 66
OKEH 20-40 53-56
PARAMOUNT 3-5 73
PORT 5-10 65
ROJAC 10-15 64-69
SAVOY 10-20 56-61
SCEPTER 10-15 64
EPs: 7-inch
EPIC (7071 "Big Maybelle Sings the Blues") 40-60 57
LPs: 10/12-inch
BRUNSWICK 15-25 62-68
ENCORE 10-15 67
EPIC 8-10 83
PARAMOUNT 8-10 73
ROJAC 10-12 67-69
SAVOY (14005 "Big Maybelle Sings") 50-100 57
SAVOY (14011 "Blues, Candy and Big Maybelle") 50-100 57
SCEPTER 15-20 64
UPFRONT 8-10 73
Also see CHATMAN, Christine

BIG MIKE
Singles: 78 rpm
SAVOY 5-10 55
Singles: 7-inch
SAVOY 10-15 55

BIG MILLER
(With the Five Pennies)
Singles: 78 rpm
SAVOY 10-15 56
Singles: 7-inch
SAVOY 15-20 56
LPs: 10/12-inch
U.A. (3047 "Did You Ever Hear the Blues") 20-40 59
(Monaural.)
U.A. (6047 "Did You Ever Hear the Blues") 40-60 59
(Stereo.)
Also see FIVE PENNIES

BIG MOOSE
Singles: 7-inch
THE BLUES 3-6

BIG MOOSE & JAMS
Singles: 7-inch
AGE 5-10 62
Also see WALKER, Moose John

BIG MOUTH
Singles: 7-inch
SPINDIZZY 3-5 72
LPs: 10/12-inch
SPINDIZZY 10-12 71

BIG MOUTH & LITTLE EVE
Singles: 7-inch
MERCURY 3-5 75

BIG NOISE P&R '89
Singles: 7-inch
ATCO 3-4 89
Member: Anthony Fenelle.

BIG PETE & MINUTE MEN
Singles: 7-inch
BRENT 10-20 61

BIG PIG P&R/LP '88
Singles: 7-inch
A&M 3-4 88
Picture Sleeves
A&M 3-4 88

BIG REGGIE
Singles: 7-inch
STUDIO CITY 10-20 63

BIG RIC P&R '83
Singles: 7-inch
ROCK & ROLL 3-4 83
SCOTTI BROTHERS 3-4 83
LPs: 10/12-inch
SCOTTI BROTHERS 5-10 83-84
Member: Joel Porter.

BIG RIVERS
Singles: 7-inch
POP-LINE (0209 "Land of Make Believe") 8-12

BIG ROCK & TADPOLE
Singles: 7-inch
OUTHOUSE (711 "Ain't Hit a Shame") 5-10
OUTHOUSE (713 "She's Got the Biggest Box in Town") 10-20

BIG ROCKER
(With His 1950s Rock & Roll Band)
Singles: 7-inch
CRALEN (3001 "Rock & Roll Romance") 5-10
LUCKY FOUR (1002 "No Privacy") 10-15 61
LUCKY FOUR (1009 "Rock & Roll Romance") 40-60 62
Member: Lenny LaCour.
Also see LACOUR, Lenny

BIG RON
Singles: 7-inch
COIN (1510 "Shufflin' Guitar") 10-20

BIG ROSS & MEMPHIS SOUND
LPs: 10/12-inch
PICKWICK 10-15

BIG SAM
Singles: 7-inch
BIG SAM 5-8
LPs: 10/12-inch
ROULETTE (25099 "Sounds in the Night") 15-20

BIG SAMBO P&R '62
(With the House Wreckers)
Singles: 7-inch
ERIC 4-8 62

BIG SANDY & FLY-RITE TRIO
Singles: 7-inch
DIONYSUS 3-4 91
Picture Sleeves
DIONYSUS 3-4 91
Members: Big Sandy; T.K. Smith; Wally Hersom; Bobby Tremble.

BIG SHORTY
Singles: 7-inch
GINCHEE 5-10 59

BIG SIR
Singles: 7-inch
GRT 3-6 69

BIG SLIM
Singles: 7-inch
SAVOY 5-10 61
STARLITE 3-5 70

BIG SONNY & FURYS
Singles: 7-inch
BEST (112 "U-2") 10-20 63

BIG STAR
Singles: 7-inch
ARDENT 12-25 72-74
PRIVILEGE 4-6
LPs: 10/12-inch
ARDENT 20-25 72-74
BIG STAR FAN CLUB 15-20
(Promotional fan club issues only.)
PVC 8-10 78
PEACEABLE (1 "Peacable") 30-45 74
Members: Alex Chilton; Chris Bell; Andy Hummell; Jody Stepenson.
Also see BOX TOPS
Also see CHILTON, Alex

BIG T. & PEACE MAKERS
Singles: 7-inch
NASCO 3-5 73

BIG TEDDY & RAMBLERS
Singles: 7-inch
COLUMBIA 10-15 60

BIG THREE
Singles: 7-inch
STERE-O-CRAFT 3-5
EPs: 7-inch
STERE-O-CRAFT 10-15
Members: Marty; Chubby, Mickey.

BIG THREE
Singles: 7-inch
FM 5-10 63
ROULETTE 4-8 66
TOLLIE 4-8 64
LPs: 10/12-inch
ACCORD 5-10 82
FM 15-25 63-64
ROULETTE 15-20 68
Members: Cass Elliott; Tim Rose; Denny Dougherty.
Also see ELLIOTT, Cass
Also see MAMAS & PAPAS
Also see ROSE, Tim

BIG THREE TRIO R&B '48
Singles: 78 rpm
BULLET (275 "Signifying Monkey") 25-35 47
COLUMBIA 20-30 47-51
DELTA 20-30 49
DOT 15-25 52
OKEH 20-30 51-53
Singles: 7-inch
COLUMBIA (30239 "Blip Blip") 50-75 51
OKEH (6807 "Lonesome") 50-75 51
OKEH (6842 "It's All Over Now") ... 50-75 51
OKEH (6863 "Blue Because of You") 50-75 52
OKEH (6901 "My Love Will Never Die") 50-75 52
OKEH (6944 "Come Here Baby") 50-75 53
Members: Willie Dixon; Leonard "Baby Doo" Caston; Bernard Dennis.
Also see DIXON, Willie
Also see HOWARD, Rosetta

BIG TIME SARAH
Singles: 7-inch
AIRWAY 3-6

BIG TIMERS
Singles: 7-inch
MASON (2123 "Surfin' Love") 10-20 60s

BIG TOPS
Singles: 7-inch
WARNER (1017 "I'm in Love") 100-125 58

BIG TOWN BOYS
Singles: 7-inch
BELL 4-8 65

BIG TOWN SENDERS
Singles: 7-inch
SOUND of the BIG TOWN 5-8 69

BIG TROUBLE P&R '87
Singles: 7-inch
EPIC 3-4 87
Picture Sleeves
EPIC 3-4 87
Member: Bobbi Eakes.

BIG TWIST & MELLO FELLOWS
LPs: 10/12-inch
ALLIGATOR 5-10 83
FLYING FISH 6-12 80-82

BIG TWO
Singles: 7-inch
WREN (150 "Puppet Bop") 15-25 59

BIG VERNON
(Joe Turner)
Singles: 78 rpm
STAG 20-30 47
Also see TURNER, Joe

BIG WALTER
(Walter Horton)
Singles: 78 rpm
STATES 50-100 54
Singles: 7-inch
STATES (145 "Hard Hearted Woman") 150-200 54
Also see HORTON, Big Walter, & His Combo

BIG WALTER
(With the Thunderbirds; Walter Price)
Singles: 78 rpm
PEACOCK 10-20 56-57
TNT 25-50 55
Singles: 7-inch
GLOBAL (409 "Watusi Freeze") 8-10 62
GOLDBAND (1080 "San Antonio") .. 10-20 59
GOLDBAND (1098 "Oh Ramona") 10-20 59
MYRL (406 "It's How You Treat Me") 10-15 61
MYRL (409 "Watusi Freeze") 8-10 62
(First issue.)
PEACOCK (1661 "Shirley Jean") ... 25-35 56
PEACOCK (1666 "Pack Fair and Square") 25-35 56
PEACOCK (1669 "Just Lookin' for a Home") 25-35 56
PEACOCK (1674 "I Gotta Go") 25-35 57
PEACOCK (1680 "Ramona") 25-35 57
TNT (8005 "Junior Jumped In") 75-125 55
TNT (8006 "Six Weeks of Misery") 75-125 55
TNT (8009 "This Is All") 75-125 55
Also see PRICE, Big Walter
Also see YOUNG, Johnny, & Big Walter

BIG WHA-KOO
Singles: 7-inch
ABC 3-5 77
LPs: 10/12-inch
ABC 8-10 77
Members: David Palmer; Danny Douma; Don Francisco; Rick Van Maarth; Richard Kosinski; Andrew Silvester; Claude Pepper; Peter Frieberger.
Also see WHA-KOO

BIG WHEELIE
(Big Wheelie & the Hubcaps)
Singles: 7-inch
MCA 4-8 78
SCEPTER 5-10 73
LPs: 10/12-inch
AMHERST 5-10 75
BANDSTAND 8-10 73

BIG WILLIE
(Willie Mabon)
Singles: 78 rpm
APOLLO (450 "Bogy Man") 50-100 53
Singles: 7-inch
APOLLO (450 "Bogy Man") 150-250 53
Also see MABON, Willie

BIG WOLFE
Singles: 7-inch
INSTANT 4-8 66

BIG YOUTH
Singles: 7-inch
SUN SPLASH 3-4 84

BIGBEATS
Singles: 7-inch
TONKA (488 "Beware") 10-20 60s

BIG-BITE & MAC
Singles: 7-inch
FUN-E-BONE 4-6 75

BIGFOOT
Singles: 7-inch
SUE INT'L 3-5

BIGGER SAM & COPY CATS
Singles: 7-inch
20TH FOX 4-8 67

BIGGIE RATT
(Vernon Garrett)
Singles: 7-inch
WATTS U.S.A. (2003 "We Don't Need No Music") 30-40
Also see GARRETT, Vernon

BIGGS, Kenny
Singles: 7-inch
B-W 5-10 61
CHART 4-8 66
TIARA 4-8 67

BIGGS, Travis
LPs: 10/12-inch
SOURCE 5-10 79

BIGHAM, Rex
Singles: 7-inch
TOPPA 5-10 60

BIGHORN
Singles: 7-inch
COLUMBIA 3-4 79
LPs: 10/12-inch
COLUMBIA 5-10 79

BIJOU
Singles: 7-inch
A&M 3-5 75

BIKINIS
Singles: 7-inch
DOT (15808 "Kitchy Koo") 20-30 58
DOT (15872 "Chop Stick Rock") 20-30 58
ROULETTE (4073 "Boogie Rock and Roll") 10-15 58
TOP RANK (2032 "Spunky") 8-12 60

BILK, Mr. Acker P&R/R&B/LP '62
(With His Paramount Jazz Band; with Leon Young String Chorale)
Singles: 7-inch
ATCO 4-6 61-66
REPRISE 4-6 62
LPs: 10/12-inch
ASCOT 10-20 62
ATCO 10-20 62-66

BILK, Mr. Acker, & Bent Fabric
(Mr. Acker Bilk / Bent Fabric)
Singles: 7-inch
ATCO (6378 "Stranger on the Shore"/"Alley Cat") 4-6 65
LPs: 10/12-inch
ATCO (175 "Together") 10-20 65
Also see BILK, Mr. Acker
Also see FABRIC, Bent

BILL & CLIFF
Singles: 7-inch
BEECEE 50-75

BILL & HOWDY
Singles: 7-inch
VERVE/FORECAST 4-6 67
LPs: 10/12-inch
VERVE/FORECAST 10-15 67

BILL & SHERRY
Singles: 7-inch
TANGERINE 4-6 66

BILL & TAFFY
Singles: 7-inch
RCA 3-6 74
LPs: 10/12-inch
RCA 10-12 73-74
Members: Bill Danoff; Taffy Danoff.
Also see FAT CITY
Also see STARLAND VOCAL BAND

BILL & WILL
(With the Souls)
Singles: 7-inch
CHECKER 5-10 64
SHURFINE 5-10

BILL BLACK'S COMBO: see BLACK, Bill

BILLARD, Doug, & Soul Patrol
Singles: 7-inch
PARKWAY (126 "Emily") 20-30 67

BILLAY, Rich
Singles: 7-inch
ATCO 3-5 76

BILLBOARDS
(With the Red Julian Orchestra)
Singles: 7-inch
VISTONE (2023 "With All My Heart") 200-400 61
(Black vinyl.)
VISTONE (2023 "With All My Heart") 500-1000 61
(Yellow vinyl.)

BILLIE & MARK
Singles: 7-inch
DEMON 10-15 59

BILLIE & RICKY
Singles: 7-inch
SUE 10-15 59

BILLIE JEAN
Singles: 7-inch
DORE 5-8 63

BILLION DOLLAR BABIES LP '77
Singles: 7-inch
POLYDOR (Except 14406) 4-6 77
POLYDOR (14406 "Too Young") 8-12 77
(Promotional issue only.)
LPs: 10/12-inch
POLYDOR (Except 022) 12-15 77
POLYDOR (022 "Battle Axe") 20-25 77
(Promotional issue only.)
Also see COOPER, Alice

BILLION DOLLAR BAND
LPs: 10/12-inch
GOOD SOUNDS 5-10 77

BILLS, Dick
Singles: 7-inch
CREST (1089 "Rockin' & Rollin' ") 50-75 61
Session: Glen Campbell.
Also see CAMPBELL, Glen

BILLUPS, Eddie
(Eddie Billips & the C.C.C.'s)
Singles: 7-inch
GAR•PAX (123 "Shake Off That Dream") 4-6 77
JOSIE 5-10 66-67
PEACHTREE (104 "Soldier's Prayer") 50-100

BILLUPS, Shorty
Singles: 7-inch
HELPP 5-10
TRI BORO 5-10

BILLY
Singles: 7-inch
SELECT 3-4 82

BILLY ALWAYS: see ALWAYS, Billy

BILLY & AR-KETS
Singles: 7-inch
RALLY 5-10

BILLY & BABY GAP R&B '85
Singles: 7-inch
TOTAL EXPERIENCE 3-4 85
Members: Billy Young; Anthony Walker
Also see GAP BAND

BILLY & BEATERS LP '81
Singles: 7-inch
ALFA 3-4 81
Picture Sleeves
ALFA 3-4 81
LPs: 10/12-inch
ALFA 5-10 81
Member: Billy Vera.
Also see VERA, Bill

BILLY & BETTY
Singles: 7-inch
SAG PORT 5-10

BILLY & BLOODKNOTS
Singles: 7-inch
JOSIE 4-8 68

BILLY & BOINGERS
Singles: 7-inch
EVA-TONE 3-4 87
(Flexi-disc. Included with the book "Bloom County Bootleg.")

BILLY & BOSSTONES
Singles: 7-inch
GUYDEN 5-10 63

BILLY & CAROL
Singles: 7-inch
CALIFORNIA 4-8 63

BILLY & CLIFF
Singles: 7-inch
CHALLENGE (59089 "The Gun, the Gold and the Girl") 10-15 60
DORE (534 "Summer's End") 10-15 59
Member: Billy Mize.
Also see MIZE, Billy

BILLY & DAWN
Singles: 7-inch
MERCURY 5-8 64

BILLY & ECHOES
Singles: 7-inch
GALA 5-10 62

BILLY & EDDIE
Singles: 7-inch
TOP RANK 15-25 59

BILLY & ESSENTIALS
(Little Billy & Essentials)
Singles: 7-inch
CAMEO (334 "The Actor") 10-15 65
CHELTENHAM ("The Actor") 250-500 65
(Selection number not known.)
CRYSTAL BALL 4-8
JAMIE (1229 "Steady Girl") 10-15 62
JAMIE (1239 "Maybe You'll Be There") 20-30 62
LANDA (691 "Steady Girl") 20-30 62
(First issue.)
MERCURY (72127 "Lonely Weekend") 15-25 63
MERCURY (72210 "Last Dance") ..15-25 63
SSS INT'L (706 "I Wrote the Song") 5-10 67
SMASH (2045 "Babalu's Wedding Day") 10-15 66
SMASH (2071 "Don't Cry") 50-75 66
Picture Sleeves
CRYSTAL BALL 4-8
LPs: 10/12-inch
CRYSTAL BALL (127 "Billy and the Essentials") 8-10 81
Members: Billy Carlucci; Phil D'Antonio; Pete Torres; Mike Lenihan; Jim Sofia; Johnny Caulfield; Richie Grasso.
Also see HEATWAVES
Also see KAY, Gary
Also see LITTLE BILLY
Also see MARSHMALLOW WAY

BILLY & FLEET
Singles: 7-inch
ARLEN (514 "Power Shift") 15-20 63

BILLY & GLENS
Singles: 7-inch
JARO (77006 "I Believe in You") 20-30 59

BILLY & KID
Singles: 7-inch
DECCA 5-8 66

BILLY & KIDS
Singles: 7-inch
LINIPHONE ("Only You") 15-25 60s
(No selection number used.)
LUTE (6016 "Take a Chance on Love") 75-125 61

BILLY & KIDS
(Chapelles)
Singles: 7-inch
HARMIKE (1300 "Nightrider") 20-30 62
TRIANGLE (2 "Nightrider") 20-30 62
(First issued as by the Chapelles.)
Also see CHAPELLES

BILLY & KIDS
Singles: 7-inch
JULIAN (104 "Say You Love Me") ..20-30 65
JULIAN (109 "When I See You") 20-30 66

BILLY & KING BEES
Singles: 7-inch
VOLT 5-10 63

BILLY & LILLIE P&R/R&B '58
(Billy Ford & the Thunderbirds with "Vocal by Freddie Pinkard")
Singles: 78 rpm
SWAN (4002 "La Dee Dah") 25-50 57
Singles: 7-inch
ABC 3-5 73
ABC-PAR (10421 "Love Me Sincerely") 15-25 63
ABC-PAR (10489 "Carry Me 'Cross the Threshold") 10-15 63
CAMEO 4-8 66
CASINO (105 "Lucky Ladybug") 10-15 59
COLLECTABLES 3-4 81
CROSS ROADS (101 "Baby, You Just Don't Know") 8-10
SWAN (4002 "La Dee Dah") 15-25 57
SWAN (4005 "Happiness") 15-20 58
SWAN (4011 "Greasy Spoon") 15-20 58
SWAN (4017 "Draggin' ") 15-20 58
SWAN (4020 "Lucky Ladybug") 15-20 58
SWAN (4030 "The Cat Alloysius Horatio Thomas") 10-20 59
SWAN (4036 "Bells Bells Bells") 10-20 59
SWAN (4042 "Swampy") 10-20 59
SWAN (4058 "Over the Mountain, Across the Sea") 10-20 60
SWAN (4069 "Bananas") 10-20 61
Members: Billy Ford; Lillie Bryant.
Also see BRYANT, Lillie
Also see FORD, Billy

BILLY & LISA
Singles: 7-inch
MCA 3-4 88
Picture Sleeves
MCA 3-4 88

BILLY & LOVERS
Singles: 7-inch
DRAGON (4403 "Hold Me Close") 25-35 65

BILLY & MICKEY
Singles: 7-inch
IMPALA (203 "I Desire") 10-15 59

BILLY & MOONLIGHTERS
Singles: 7-inch
CRYSTAL BALL (Black vinyl) 5-10
CRYSTAL BALL (Colored vinyl) 10-15

BILLY & MYLA
Singles: 12-inch
COLUMBIA 4-6 83
Singles: 7-inch
COLUMBIA 3-4 84
LPs: 10/12-inch
COLUMBIA 5-10 84

BILLY & PATIOS
Singles: 7-inch
LITE (9002 "Love Is a Story") 100-150 61
Member: Billy Galante.

BILLY & RICKEY
Singles: 7-inch
SUE (711 "Baby Doll") 10-15 59
SUE (716 "Buttercup") 10-15 59

BILLY & RUGBEATERS
LPs: 10/12-inch
BARNSTORMER 15-20

BILLY & STENOTONES
Singles: 7-inch
RUST (5038 "Phyllis") 30-50 61

BILLY & SUE
Singles: 7-inch
CREW 3-5 70
Members: William Oliver Swofford; Lesley Gore.
Also see GORE, Lesley
Also see OLIVER

BILLY & WOLFE
Singles: 7-inch
CORAL 4-8 67

BILLY BEAU: see BEAU, Billy

BILLY BOY
Singles: 78 rpm
VEE JAY 15-25 55-57
Singles: 7-inch
VEE JAY (146 "I Was Fooled") 20-40 55
VEE JAY (171 "I Ain't Got You") 20-40 56
VEE JAY (192 "Here's My Picture") 20-40 56
VEE JAY (238 "My Heart Is Crying") 20-40 57
VEE JAY (260 "Prisoner's Plea") 20-40 57
VIVID (109 "Prisoner's Plea") 10-20
Also see ARNOLD, Billy "Boy"

BILLY HILL C&W '89
Singles: 7-inch
REPRISE 3-4 89
Member: Dennis Robbins.
Also see ROBBINS, Dennis
Also see TOMORROW'S WORLD

BILLY JOE & CHECKMATES P&R '62
(Billy Joe Hunter)
Singles: 7-inch
DORE 5-15 61-66
Also see RICKY & HITCH-HIKERS

BILLY JOE & CHESSMEN
Singles: 7-inch
WOLFIE 5-10 63

BILLY JOE & CONFIDENTIALS
Singles: 7-inch
B-J 10-15

BILLY JOE & TOKES
Singles: 7-inch
DORE 3-5 73

BILLY JOHN & CONTINENTALS
Singles: 7-inch
JIN 4-8 66
N-JOY 4-8 65

BILLY "K"
Singles: 7-inch
BALD EAGLE 5-10 59

BILLY LEE & RUGBEATERS
Singles: 7-inch
BARNSTORMER 3-4 85

BILLY SATELLITE P&R/LP '84
Singles: 7-inch
CAPITOL 3-4 84
Picture Sleeves
CAPITOL 3-4 84
LPs: 10/12-inch
CAPITOL 5-10 84
Member: Monty Bryom.

BILLY "T"
(Billy Tabbert)
Singles: 7-inch
SRO 3-4 85

BILLY THE BARON
(With Smokin' Chali)
Singles: 7-inch
GRILL 3-5 75

BILLY THE KID
Singles: 7-inch
KAPP 5-10 59

BILLY THE KID C&W '79
Singles: 7-inch
CYCLONE 3-4 79

BIMBO JET P&R '75
Singles: 7-inch
SCEPTER 3-5 75

BINDER, Dennis
(Long Man Binder & His Thin Men)
Singles: 7-inch
MODERN 25-50 54
UNITED 20-40 55

BINDER, Long Man: see BINDER, Dennis

BINDERS
Singles: 7-inch
ANKH 5-10
SARA 8-12

BINDIGER, Emily
Singles: 7-inch
HANDSHAKE 3-4 81

BING, Jimmy
Singles: 7-inch
COLPIX 4-8 65

BINGENHEIMER, Rodney
EPs: 7-inch
BOMP 5-10

BINGHAM, J.B.
Singles: 7-inch
U.A. 10-20 76
W.B. 5-10 74

BINGHAMPTON BLUES BOYS
Singles: 7-inch
EASTSIDE ("Cross Cut Saw") 75-100 64
FORD ("Cross Cut Saw") 75-100 64
XL (901 "Cross Cut Saw") 65-90 64

BINGO
Singles: 7-inch
SILVER BLUE 3-5 73

BINKLEY, Jimmy
(With the Teasers)
Singles: 78 rpm
ALADDIN 25-50 53
CHANCE 50-75 53
CHECKER (789 "Wine Wine Wine") 75-100 55
CHECKER (835 "Messin' Around") 50-75 56
DOT (1183 "Blue, Blue Night") 10-15 53
Singles: 7-inch
ALADDIN (3193 "Night Life") 75-100 53
CHANCE (1134 "Hey, Hey Sugar Ray") 100-150 53
CHECKER (789 "Wine Wine Wine") 100-150 55
CHECKER (835 "Messin' Around") 50-100 56
DOT (1183 "Blue, Blue Night") 20-30 53
NOTE (10002 "Why Oh Why") ...100-200 57
Also see TEASERS

BINTANGS
Singles: 7-inch
PHILIPS 3-5 70

BIOHAZARD
LPs: 10/12-inch
W.B. (45595 "State of the World Address") 10-15 94
(Colored vinyl. Issued in clear plastic bag with title sticker. Limited edition, promotional issue only.)

BIONDI, Dick
Singles: 7-inch
IRC (6904 "The Pizza Song") 10-20 62
(Promotional issue, made for WLS Radio and Pepsi Cola.)
Picture Sleeves
IRC (6904 "The Pizza Song") 20-30 62
(Promotional issue, made for WLS Radio and Pepsi Cola.)

BIONIC BOOGIE R&B/LP '78
Singles: 12-inch
RP 4-8
Singles: 7-inch
POLYDOR 3-4 77-78
LPs: 10/12-inch
POLYDOR 5-10 78
Member: Gregg Diamond.

BIRCH, Peter
Singles: 7-inch
RHAPSODY 8-12 60

BIRCH, Sadie
(With Kelly Owens & Band)
Singles: 78 rpm
RED ROBIN 10-15 53
Singles: 7-inch
RED ROBIN (121 "The Man I Crave") 15-25 53

BIRCHETT, Tony
Singles: 7-inch
L.B.J. (293 "You're Good People") 20-30 60s

BIRD, Bobby
Singles: 7-inch
TOPIC (8042 "Proud to Be with You") 5-10 60s

BIRD, J. D&D '84
Singles: 12-inch
WARRIOR 4-6 84

BIRD, Vicki C&W '87
Singles: 7-inch
AVCO 3-5 74
16TH AVE. 3-4 87-89

BIRD DOGS
Singles: 7-inch
IGL 10-12 64

BIRDIES
Singles: 7-inch
CHARTER 4-8 65

BIRDLEGS & PAULINE & THEIR VERSATILITY BIRDS P&R/R&B '63
Singles: 7-inch
CUCA (1125 "Spring") 20-35 63
(Credits "Birdlegs & His Versatility Birds.")
VEE JAY (510 "Spring") 5-10 63
LPs: 10/12-inch
CUCA (4000 "Birdlegs & Pauline") 50-100 64
Members: Sidney Banks; Pauline Shivers Banks.
Also see LITTLE BEAVER
Also see PAULINE & BOBBY
Also see SHIVERS, Pauline

BIRDMEN
Singles: 7-inch
ROCK-IT (1003 "Dance the Jaybird") 10-20 61

BIRDS
Singles: 7-inch
BINGO (1000 "Foggy River") 15-25 59

BIRDS
Singles: 7-inch
SUE 4-8 65

BIRDS
Singles: 7-inch
PRIDE 4-8

BIRDS OF A Feather
Singles: 7-inch
ARMOUR 3-5 77
DJM 4-8 71
PAGE ONE 3-5 70
Member: Caleb Quaye.
Also see JOHN, Elton

BIRDSONG, Edwin R&B '81
Singles: 12-inch
PHILADELPHIA INT'L 4-6 78-79
SALSOUL 4-6 81-84
Singles: 7-inch
BAMBOO 3-6 75
PHILADELPHIA INT'L 3-5 78
POLYDOR 3-5 71-72
SALSOUL 3-4 81-84
LPs: 10/12-inch
PHILADELPHIA INT'L 5-10 78
POLYDOR 8-10 71-73

BIRDSONG, Jimmy
Singles: 7-inch
EXCELLO (2183 "It's All Over Now") 8-12 60

BIRDSONG, Larry R&B '56
(With Louis Brooks & His Hi-Toppers)
Singles: 78 rpm
CALVERT 10-20 56
DECCA 10-15 56
EXCELLO 10-15 55-56
Singles: 7-inch
ACE (589 "Who Do You Love") 10-20 60
CALVERT (102 "Now That We're Together") 15-25 56
CALVERT (104 "Three Times Seven") 15-25 56
CHAMPION (1003 "Live the Life I Sing About") 15-25 59
CHAMPION (1015 "Somewhere, Somewhere") 15-25 59
CHAMPION (1018 "Young and Fancy Free") 15-25 59
DECCA (30186 "Let's Try It Again") 20-30 56
EXCELLO (2064 "You Won't Be Needin' Me No More") 20-30 56
EXCELLO (2076 "Pleadin' for Love") 20-30 56
HOME of the BLUES (116 "Stay with Me") 10-15 61
HOME of the BLUES (121 "Sooner Or Later") 10-15 61
HOME of the BLUES (231 "Continental Time") 10-15 61
HOME of the BLUES (240 "Aunt Mattie") 10-15 62
REF-O-REE 5-10
VEE JAY (254 "If You Don't Want Me No More") 15-25 57
VEE JAY (262 "My Darling") 15-25 57
VEE JAY (277 "Fannie's Place") 15-25 58
Session: Lee Allen.
Also see ALLEN, Lee

BIRDWATCHERS
Singles: 7-inch
GEMINX 10-15 66-67
LAURIE 5-10 67
MALA (536 "I'm Gonna Love You Anyway") 15-25 66
MALA (548 "I'm Gonna Do It to You") 15-25 66
MALA (555 "Mary Mary") 10-15 66
SCOTT (27 "Girl I Got News for You") 25-45 66
Member: Jerry Schils; Bobby Puccetti; Eddie Martinez; Jim Tolliver; Dave Chiodo; Sammy Hall; Joey Murcia; Craig Caraglior.
Also see LEGENDS

BIRKIN, Jane, & Serge Gainsbourg P&R '69
Singles: 7-inch
FONTANA 3-6 69
LPs: 10/12-inch
FONTANA 6-12 70

BIRMINGHAM RHYTHM SECTION
Singles: 7-inch
SOUND STAGE 7 ....3-5 77

BIRMINGHAM SAM & HIS MAGIC GUITAR
(John Lee Hooker)
Singles: 78 rpm
SAVOY (5558 "Low Down Midnight Boogie") 20-40 49
Also see HOOKER, John Lee

BIRTH CONTROL
LPs: 10/12-inch
PROPHESY 25-35 70

BIRTH OF SPRING
Singles: 7-inch
MERCURY 4-8 67

BIRTHA
Singles: 7-inch
DUNHILL 3-5 73
LPs: 10/12-inch
DUNHILL 8-10 72-73

BIRTLES & GOBLE
LPs: 10/12-inch
CAPITOL 5-10 80

BISCAINES
Singles: 7-inch
FELSTED (8615 "Menagerie") 8-10 61
YUKON (101 "Menagerie") 10-20 61

BISCAYNE BAY SURFERS
(With Professor Marcell & Collegians)
Singles: 7-inch
MAYHAMS (214 "Surfing Is a Sight to See") 15-25 64

BISCAYNES
Singles: 7-inch
RIDGE (6601 "Mis-Beat") 50-100 60s
VPM 10-15 61

BISCAYNES & CO-ENCIDENTALS
Singles: 7-inch
CO-EN (1 "Midnight in Montevideo") 20-30 62

BISCAYNES / Surfaris: see SURFARIS / Biscaynes

BISCUIT DAVIS
LPs: 10/12-inch
FLYING DUTCHMAN 10-12 73

BISHOP
LPs: 10/12-inch
LOU-NEITA 10-12 70

BISHOP, Bob C&W '68
(Bobby Bishop; Bobby Sykes)
Singles: 7-inch
ABC 3-5 68
GOLDISC 5-10 61
MALA 5-10 60
WAYSIDE 4-8 67
LPs: 10/12-inch
ABC 8-10 68
Also see ROBBINS, Marty
Also see SYKES, Bobby

BISHOP, Eddie
Singles: 7-inch
ABC (10799 "Call Me") 25-50 65
ABC (10858 "Hanky Panky") 10-20 66

BISHOP, Elvin P&R/LP '74
(Elvin Bishop Group; with Crabshaw Rising)
Singles: 7-inch
CAPRICORN 3-5 74-79
EPIC 3-5 72-75
FILLMORE 3-5 70-71
W.B. 3-5 72
LPs: 10/12-inch
ALLIGATOR 5-8 91
CAPRICORN 8-12 74-78
EPIC 8-12 72-75
FILLMORE 10-15 69-72
Also see BUTTERFIELD, Paul
Also see GRATEFUL DEAD / Elvin Bishop Group

BISHOP, Jimmy
Singles: 7-inch
ARTIC 5-10

BISHOP, Joni C&W '87
Singles: 7-inch
COLUMBIA 3-4 87

BISHOP, Oscar
Singles: 7-inch
RIP CORD 5-10

BISHOP, Randy
(With the Underdogs)
Singles: 7-inch
A&M 3-5 77
LPs: 10/12-inch
PASHA 5-10 82

BISHOP, Stephen P&R '76
Singles: 7-inch
ABC 3-5 76-78
W.B. 3-4 80-83
Picture Sleeves
ABC (12435 "Animal House") 4-8 78
LPs: 10/12-inch
ABC 6-12 76-78
MCA 5-10 80
W.B. 5-10 80
Also see GRUSIN, Dave
Also see NEWMAN, Randy

BISHOP, Stephen, & Yvonne Elliman
Singles: 7-inch
W.B. 3-4 80
Also see BISHOP, Stephen
Also see ELLIMAN, Yvonne

BISHOP, Terri C&W '78
Singles: 7-inch
U.A. 3-5 78

BISHOP, Thom
LPs: 10/12-inch
STUFF 5-10 82

BISHOPS
Singles: 7-inch
CAPITOL....5-10 65
LUTE (6010 "Open Your Heart")....40-50 61
RALSTON....10-15
Also see LINDSEY, Bobby

BISHOPS & MELLOWTONES
Singles: 7-inch
BRIDGES (1105 "The Wedding")....100-200 61

BISKITTS
Singles: 7-inch
PARACHUTE....3-4 84

BIT
Singles: 7-inch
ALLIED ARTISTS....3-4 83
LPs: 10/12-inch
ALLIED ARTISTS....5-10 83

BIT'A SWEET
Singles: 7-inch
ABC (11125 "2086")....10-15 68
MGM (13695 "Out of Sight, Out of Mind")....10-20 67
LPs: 10/12-inch
ABC (640 "Hypnotic 1")....25-40 68
Members: Mitch London; Russ Leslie.

BITETTI, Calie
Singles: 7-inch
SUSAN....4-8 63

BI-TONES
Singles: 7-inch
BLUEJAY (1000 "Oh How I Love You So")....10-15 60
Also see CHIMES

BITS & PIECES *R&B '81*
(Bits 'N' Pieces)
Singles: 7-inch
MANGO....3-4 81
NASCO....3-5 73-74
PARAMOUNT....3-5 74

BITS 'N' PIECES
Singles: 7-inch
BITS 'N' PIECES....10-15
DEE GEE (2005 "Look Out Linda")....20-30

BITTER END SINGERS
Singles: 7-inch
ATCO....4-8 66
MERCURY....4-8 65
MUSICOR....4-8 66
LPs: 10/12-inch
MERCURY....10-20 65

BITTER SWEETS
Singles: 7-inch
HYPE....10-15 60s
CAMEO....5-10 65
ORIGINAL SOUND....10-15 67
TEMA....6-12 60s

BITTERSWEET
Singles: 7-inch
BIG TREE....3-5 76
WHITE WHALE....3-6 69

BITTERSWEET, Richard, Blues Band
Singles: 7-inch
PAGE (1086 "Call Out")....4-8

BITTLE, Arkie
Singles: 7-inch
CLAUDRA (110 "Teenage Blues")....40-60 59

BIVINS, Steve
Singles: 7-inch
BULLDOG....3-5 76

BIZ MARKIE *R&B '86*
(Marcel Hall)
Singles: 7-inch
COLD CHILL....3-4 88-90
PRISM....3-4 86
Picture Sleeves
COLD CHILL....3-4 90
LPs: 10/12-inch
COLD CHILL....5-8 88-90

BIZARROS
LPs: 10/12-inch
MERCURY....5-10 79

BJORN & BENNY
Singles: 7-inch
PLAYBOY....8-10 72-74
(With Anna and Freida.)
Members: Bjorn Ulvaeus; Benny Anderson.
Also see ABBA
Also see HEP STARS

BLACK, Alan
Singles: 7-inch
ABC-PAR (9784 "Harmonica Rock")....15-25 57
RADAR....10-15 59

BLACK, Alan, & Karen Stewart
Singles: 7-inch
EPIC....8-12 60
Also see BLACK, Alan

BLACK, Alder Ray, & Fame Gang
Singles: 7-inch
SOUND PLUS....3-5 72

BLACK, Anna
Singles: 7-inch
EPIC....3-6 69
LPs: 10/12-inch
EPIC....10-15 68

BLACK, Bill *P&R/R&B '59*
(Bill Black's Combo)
Singles: 7-inch
COLUMBIA....3-5 70
ECHO....3-5 72
GUSTO....3-4 83
HI (Except 2000 series)....3-6 67-78
HI (2000 series)....5-15 59-66
LONDON....3-4 84
MEGA....3-5 71-74
MOTOWN....3-4 83
Picture Sleeves
HI....5-10 60-62
EPs: 7-inch
HI (52 "King of the Road")....8-12 64
HI (22001 "Dee J. Special")....10-20 60s
(Promotional only issue.)
MEGA (192 "Juke box Favorites")....5-10 72
(Juke box issue.)
LPs: 10/12-inch
COLUMBIA....8-10 69-70
51 WEST....5-10 84
HI (6000 & 8000 series)....5-10 77-78
HI (12001 "Smokie")....30-60 60
HI (12002 thru 12005)....20-40 60-62
HI (12006 thru 12041)....10-20 62-68
(Monaural.)
HI (32000 thru 32010)....15-30 61-63
(Stereo.)
HI (32011 thru 32110)....10-20 63-77
(Stereo.)
MEGA....5-10 71-74
ZODIAC....8-12 77
Also see CANNON, Ace
Also see LOYD, Jay B.
Also see POINDEXTER, Doug, & Starlite Wranglers
Also see PRESLEY, Elvis

BLACK, Cane
Singles: 7-inch
OKEH....4-8 68

BLACK, Cilla *P&R '64*
Singles: 7-inch
BELL....3-4 68
CAPITOL....5-10 64-66
DJM....3-6 68-70
EMI AMERICA....3-5 74
PRIVATE STOCK....3-5 75-76
LPs: 10/12-inch
CAPITOL (T-2308 "Is It Love")....20-30 65
(Monaural.)
CAPITOL (ST-2308 "Is It Love")....25-35 65
(Stereo.)

BLACK, Clint *C&W/LP '89*
Singles: 7-inch
RCA....3-4 89-92
LPs: 10/12-inch
RCA....5-8 89-90
Also see ROGERS, Roy, & Clint Black

BLACK, Cody
Singles: 7-inch
D-TOWN (1057 "You Must Be in Love")....25-50 60s
D-TOWN (1066 "Too Many Irons")....25-50 60s
GIG (201 "It's Our Time to Fall in Love")....200-300
RAM BROCK (2002 "Going, Going, Gone")....15-25 60s
STON-ROC....5-10 70

BLACK, Donna
Singles: 7-inch
BASIC SOUNDS LTD.....3-5 72

BLACK, Flip
Singles: 7-inch
ACE....5-10 60
BERGEN....5-10 59
CAPITOL....5-10 59
JUBILEE....4-8 65-66
WHITE CLIFFS....4-6 67

BLACK, Geronimo: see GERONIMO BLACK

BLACK, Jay *P&R '80*
Singles: 12-inch
MILLENIUM (20614 "Love Is in the Air")....15-20 78
(Single-sided disc. Promotional issue only.)
MILLENIUM (20614 "Love Is in the Air"/"Please Stay")....8-12 78
Singles: 7-inch
ATLANTIC/MIGRATION....3-5 75
K-TEL (562 "This Magic Moment")....30-40 82
(Canadian. Credited to "Jay Black of Jay and the Americans.")
MIDSONG....3-4 80
MILLENNIUM....3-5 78
PRIVATE STOCK....3-5 76
ROULETTE (7198 "One Night Affair")....10-15 76
(Same track on both sides. Promotional issue only.)
U.A.....4-8 67
Picture Sleeves
U.A.....5-10 67
Also see EMPIRES
Also see JAY & AMERICANS
Also see TWO CHAPS

BLACK, Jay / Caress
Singles: 12-inch
ROULETTE (2005 "One Night Affair")....10-15 76
(For the promotional issue, with Jay Black on both sides, see his section above.)
Also see BLACK, Jay
Also see CARESS

BLACK, Jeanne *C&W/P&R/R&B '60*
Singles: 7-inch
CAPITOL....4-8 60-62
LPs: 10/12-inch
CAPITOL....15-20 60

BLACK, Jim, & Stardusters Combo
Singles: 7-inch
FLO (100 "Flashy")....10-20 62

BLACK, Jimmy Carl
Singles: 7-inch
MCA (1914 "Jimmy Carl Black Raps About Geronimo Black")....10-15 71
(Promotional issue only.)
Also see G.T.O.
Also see GERONIMO BLACK
Also see MOTHERS of INVENTION

BLACK, Joe, & His Boogie Woogie Boys
Singles: 78 rpm
CORAL....15-25 51
DERBY....5-10 49
Singles: 7-inch
CORAL (65067 "Flag Wavin' Boogie")....25-35 51

BLACK, June
Singles: 7-inch
TOPIC....5-10 59

BLACK, Lincoln
Singles: 7-inch
MONUMENT....3-5 70

BLACK, Marjorie
Singles: 7-inch
SUE (132 "One More Hurt")....15-25

BLACK, Marc
(Marc Black Band)
LPs: 10/12-inch
SUMA....5-10 83

BLACK, Marion *R&B '71*
Singles: 7-inch
AVCO EMBASSY....3-5 71
SHAKAT....3-5 74

BLACK, Memphis
Singles: 7-inch
ASCOT....4-8 68

BLACK, Oscar *P&R '61*
Singles: 78 rpm
ATLANTIC....25-50 51
GROOVE....15-25 54-55
Singles: 7-inch
ATLANTIC (956 "Troubled Mind Blues")....50-100 51
GROOVE....25-50 54-55
SAVOY....5-10 61

BLACK, Oscar, & Sue Allen
Singles: 78 rpm
GROOVE....10-20 54-56
Singles: 7-inch
GROOVE (0012 "I'll Get By")....20-40 54
GROOVE (0102 "Don't Leave Me Here to Cry")....20-40 55
GROOVE (0115 "Baby, Please Don't Go")....20-40 55
GROOVE (0168 "Into Each Heart")....20-40 56
Also see ALLEN, Sue
Also see BLACK, Oscar

BLACK, Pauline
LPs: 10/12-inch
A&M....5-10 84

BLACK, Sharon
Singles: 7-inch
PHILIPS....8-12 65

BLACK, Shelly *R&B '76*
Singles: 7-inch
VIGOR....3-5 76-77

BLACK, Stanley, & His Orchestra *LP '62*
LPs: 10/12-inch
LONDON PHASE 4....5-15 62-65

BLACK, T.J.
Singles: 7-inch
JUBILEE....4-8 65

BLACK, Terry *P&R '64*
Singles: 7-inch
DUNHILL....4-8 65-66
TOLLIE....5-10 64-65
Picture Sleeves
TOLLIE....5-10 65

BLACK, Terry, & Laurel Ward *P&R '72*
Singles: 7-inch
KAMA SUTRA....3-5 72
Also see BLACK, Terry

BLACK, Wally
Singles: 7-inch
FABLE....15-25 58
FEDORA....5-10 61
TOPPA....5-10 59-63

BLACK, Zell
Singles: 7-inch
MOTOWN....3-5 74
W.B.....3-5 75-76

BLACK ABBOTS
Singles: 7-inch
ROULETTE....3-5 72

BLACK ACE
LPs: 10/12-inch
ARHOOLIE....12-15

BLACK AMERICANS
Singles: 7-inch
JEWEL....3-5 74

BLACK & BLUE
Singles: 7-inch
GAME (395 "Of All the Hearts to Break")....10-15
MERCURY....3-5 70

BLACK & BLUES
Singles: 7-inch
TALUN STEREO....3-5 70
U.A.....4-8 67

BLACK BLOOD *R&B '75*
Singles: 7-inch
CHRYSALIS....3-5 77
MAINSTREAM....3-5 75
LPs: 10/12-inch
CHRYSALIS....5-10 77
MAINSTREAM....8-10 75

BLACK BOX *P&R/LP '90*
Singles: 7-inch
RCA....3-4 90
LPs: 10/12-inch
RCA....5-8 90
Member: Martha Wash.
Also see WEATHER GIRLS

BLACK BRITON
Singles: 7-inch
VIRGIN....3-4 87
Picture Sleeves
VIRGIN....3-4 87

BLACK CATS & KITTEN
Singles: 78 rpm
OKEH....20-40 40-41

BLACK CROWES *P&R/LP '90*
Singles: 7-inch
DEF AMERICAN....3-4 91
LPs: 10/12-inch
DEF AMERICAN....5-8 90
W.B.....5-8 90s
Members: Chris Robinson; Rich Robinson; Steve Cease; Johnny Colt; Steve Gorman.

BLACK DEATH
Singles: 7-inch
CATHEDRAL (417 "Rock & Roll with Ork")....40-60 60s

BLACK DIAMOND
(James Butler)
Singles: 78 rpm
JAXYSON (6 "Lonesome Blues")....75-125 49

BLACK DIAMOND / Goldrush
Singles: 78 rpm
JAXYSON (50 "T.P. Railer")....75-125 48
Also see BLACK DIAMOND

BLACK DIAMOND
Singles: 7-inch
ATLANTIC....3-5 77

BLACK DIAMONDS
LPs: 10/12-inch
ALSHIRE....10-12 71

BLACK DYKE MILLS BAND: see FOSTER, John, & Sons Ltd.

BLACK EYED PEAS
(Black Eyes Peas)
Singles: 7-inch
DETO....5-8 68
ULTRA CITY....4-6 70
Member: Kripp Johnson.
Also see JOHNSON, Kripp

BLACK FLAG
Singles: 7-inch
SST....3-4
LPs: 10/12-inch
SST....5-10 85-89
Members: Greg Ginn; Chuck Dukowski; Brian Migdol; Keith Morris; Chavo; Dez Cadena; Henry Rollins; Bill Stevenson; Emil.

BLACK FLAMES *R&B '87*
Singles: 7-inch
DEF JAM....3-4 87

BLACK FOX
Singles: 7-inch
TRANSPLANT....15-20

BLACK GRASS
(Phyllis Lindsey)
Singles: 7-inch
SHELTER....3-5 73
LPs: 10/12-inch
SHELTER....8-10 73
Also see RUSSELL, Leon

BLACK HEAT *R&B '73*
Singles: 7-inch
ATLANTIC....3-5 72-74
LPs: 10/12-inch
ATLANTIC....8-10 72-75

BLACK ICE *R&B '77*
Singles: 7-inch
AMHERST....3-5 76
HDM....3-5 77
MONTAGE....3-4 81-84
LPs: 10/12-inch
AMHERST....8-10 76
MONTAGE....5-10 82

BLACK IVORY *R&B '71*
Singles: 7-inch
BUDDAH....3-5 75-84
KWANZA....3-5 74
PANORAMIC....3-4 85
PERCEPTION....3-5 72
TODAY....4-6 71-73
LPs: 10/12-inch
BUDDAH....5-10 75-84
TODAY....10-12 72-73
Member: Leroy Burgess.
Also see ALEEM

BLACK LIGHTNING
Singles: 7-inch
MCA....3-5 74
LPs: 10/12-inch
TOWER....12-20 68

BLACK MAGIC
Singles: 7-inch
ATCO....3-5 75
LPs: 10/12-inch
ATCO....10-15 70
Also see BREAKWATER

BLACK MAGIC & HOWARD STRUTT
Singles
ERIKA (8663 "Good Ole Boys")....15-20 84
(Shaped picture disc. Includes poster.)
LP: 10/12-inch
VISUAL VINYL (1002 "Spellbound")....30-40 83
(Picture disc.)

BLACK MAMBA *D&D '84*
Singles: 12-inch
GARAGE....4-6 84

BLACK MERDA
Singles: 7-inch
CHESS (2095 "Reality")....5-10 70
LPs: 10/12-inch
CHESS (1551 "Black Merda")....30-50 70

BLACK 'N BLUE *LP '84*
Singles: 7-inch
GEFFEN....3-4 84-88
LPs: 10/12-inch
GEFFEN....5-10 84-88

BLACK NASTY
Singles: 7-inch
ENTERPRISE....3-5 71-74

BLACK OAK ARKANSAS *LP '71*
(Black Oak)
Singles: 7-inch
ATCO....3-5 71-75
CAPRICORN....3-5 77-78
ENTERPRISE....3-5 70
MCA....3-5 75-77
LPs: 10/12-inch
ATCO....8-15 71-84
CAPRICORN....8-10 77-78
MCA....8-12 75-77
STAX....10-15 74
Members: Jim Mangrum; Ruby Starr; Rickie Reynolds; Stanley Knight; Harvey Jett; Jimmy Henderson; Pat Daugherty; Tom Aldridge.
Also see KNOWBODY ELSE
Also see STARR, Ruby

BLACK OAK ARKANSAS / Cooper Brothers
LPs: 10/12-inch
CAPRICORN (0005 "I'd Rather Be Sailing")....10-15 78
(Promotional issue only.)
Also see BLACK OAK ARKANSAS
Also see COOPER BROTHERS

BLACK PEARL *LP '69*
Singles: 7-inch
ATLANTIC....3-6 69
PROPHESY....3-6 70
LPs: 10/12-inch
ATLANTIC....12-15 69
PROPHESY....15-20 70

BLACK RABBIT
Singles: 7-inch
IMPERIAL....4-6 70
Also see CLASSICS IV

BLACK RIVER CIRCUS
Singles: 7-inch
MAJOR....10-15
MONUMENT....4-8 70

BLACK ROSE
Singles: 7-inch
MICHIGAN NICKEL (001 "Love Handles")....10-20 67

BLACK ROSE
Singles: 7-inch
RCA....3-5 75

BLACK ROSE
Singles: 7-inch
CASABLANCA....3-4 80-84
LPs: 10/12-inch
CASABLANCA....5-10 80
Members: Cher; Les Dudek; Ron Ritchotle; Michael Finnigan; Trey Thompson; Gary Ferguson; Warren Ham.
Also see CHER
Also see DUDEK, Les

BLACK RUSSIAN
Singles: 7-inch
MOTOWN....3-4 80
LPs: 10/12-inch
MOTOWN....5-10 80

Members: Serge Kapustin; Natasha Kapustin; Vladimir Shneider.

BLACK SABBATH *P&R/LP '70*
Singles: 7-inch
I.R.S. ... 3-4 89
W.B. ... 3-5 70-76
EPs: 7-inch
W.B. (241 "Sabbath Bloody Sabbath") ... 15-25 74
(Juke box EP.)
LPs: 10/12-inch
I.R.S. ... 5-8 89
W.B. (PRO-417 "Radio Spots") 150-200 69
W.B. (Except 1000 & 2000 series) .. 5-10 76-84
W.B. (1000 & 2000 series) ... 8-15 70-76
W.B. ... 5-10 87
Members: Ozzy Osbourne; Tony Iommi; Kip Treavor; Bill Ward; Ronnie Dio; Terry "Geezer" Butler.
Also see DIO, Ronnie
Also see OSBOURNE, Ozzy

BLACK SATIN *R&B '75*
(Featuring Fred Parris)
Singles: 7-inch
BUDDAH ... 3-5 75
LPs: 10/12-inch
BUDDAH (5654 "Black Satin") ... 8-10 76
BUDDAH (5654 "Black Satin") ... 25-35 76
(Promotional issue.)
Members: Fred Parris; Rich Freeman; Jimmy Curtis; Nate Marshall.
Also see FIVE SATINS

BLACK SHEEP
Singles: 7-inch
COLUMBIA ... 10-20 66-67

BLACK SHEEP
Singles: 7-inch
CAPITOL ... 3-5 75
CHRYSALIS ... 3-5 74
LPs: 10/12-inch
CAPITOL ... 10-12 75
Members: Lou Gramm; Donald Mancuso; Mike Bonafede; Larry Cruzier; Bruce Turson.
Also see GRAMM, Lou

BLACK SLATE
LPs: 10/12-inch
ALLIGATOR ... 5-10 80-81

BLACK SOCIETY
Singles: 7-inch
MCA ... 3-5 73
STAX ... 3-5 72

BLACK TIE *C&W '90*
Singles: 7-inch
BENCH ... 3-4 90
LPs: 10/12-inch
BENCH ("When the Night Falls") ... 20-30 85
(Selection number not known.)
Members: James Griffin; Billy Swan; Randy Meisner; T-Bone Burnett; Robb Royer.
Also see BURNETT, T-Bone
Also see GRIFFIN, James
Also see MEISNER, Randy
Also see SWAN, Billy

BLACK UHURU *LP '82*
Singles: 7-inch
ISLAND ... 3-4 84
LPs: 10/12-inch
ISLAND ... 5-10 84
MANGO ... 5-10 80-85
MESA ... 5-8 90

BLACK VELVET
Singles: 7-inch
BRT ... 8-12
EMBER ... 4-8 70
OKEH (7330 "Come On Heart") ... 10-15 69
LPs: 10/12-inch
OKEH (14130 "Love City") ... 15-25 69
Members: Pete Morris; Clinton Creasey; Lynton Steel; Brian Clark.

BLACK WATCH
Singles: 7-inch
FENTON (2508 "Left Behind") ... 25-50 67

BLACK WHIP THRILL BAND
LPs: 10/12-inch
SPINDIZZY ... 8-10 73

BLACK WIDOW
LPs: 10/12-inch
U.A. ... 15-20 70

BLACKBEARD & PIRATES
Singles: 7-inch
AD PRESENTS (101 "Lovers Never Say Goodbye") ... 75-125 58
MAIN MAN (50 "Lovers Never Say Goodbye") ... 50-100 61

BLACKBERRIES
Singles: 7-inch
A&M ... 3-5 73-74
Members: Billy Barnum; Vanetta Fields; Clydie King.
Also see KING, Clydie

BLACKBERRY WINTER
Singles: 7-inch
CHAMUS ... 3-5 75

BLACKBONE
Singles: 7-inch
ACE ... 3-5 74

BLACKBURN, Lou
Singles: 7-inch
IMPERIAL (5943 "Grand Prix") ... 10-20 63

BLACKBURN & SNOW
Singles: 7-inch
VERVE ... 5-10 67
Member: Jeff Blackburn.
Also see MOBY GRAPE

BLACKBURN TWINS & Jerry Collins
Singles: 7-inch
CROSLEY (211 "That Tickles") ... 8-10

BLACKBYRDS *P&R/R&B/LP '74*
Singles: 7-inch
FANTASY ... 3-5 74-84
LPs: 10/12-inch
FPM ... 10-12 75
FANTASY ... 10-15 74-84
Members: Gary Hart; Joe Hall III; Stephe Johnson; Keith Killgo; Orville Saunders; Kevin Toney.
Also see BYRD, Donald

BLACKELL, Eugene
Singles: 7-inch
SEASIDE ... 10-20

BLACKFOOT *P&R/LP '79*
Singles: 7-inch
ATCO ... 3-4 79-84
LPs: 10/12-inch
ANTILLES ... 5-10 78
ATCO ... 5-10 79-84
EPIC ... 8-10 76
ISLAND ... 10-12 75
Members: Rick Medlocke; Jackson Spires; Charlie Hargrett; Greg Walker.
Also see LYNYRD SKYNYRD
Also see MEDLOCKE, Rick, & Blackfoot

BLACKFOOT, J.D. *R&B '83*
(With Ann Hines; J. Blackfoot)
Singles: 7-inch
EDGE ... 3-4 86-87
FANTASY ... 4-8 74
PHILIPS ... 8-12 69-70
SOUND TOWN ... 3-5 83-86
LPs: 10/12-inch
FANTASY (9468 "Song of Crazy Horse") ... 15-25 74
FANTASY (9487 "Southbound & Gone") ... 15-25 75
MERCURY (61288 "The Ultimate Prophecy") ... 40-60 70
SOUND TOWN ... 5-10 84-85
Also see SOUL CHILDREN

BLACKFOOT SUE
Singles: 7-inch
A&M ... 3-6 72
LPs: 10/12-inch
IMPORT ... 8-10 77-78

BLACKHAWK
Singles: 7-inch
PLAYBOY ... 3-5

BLACKHAWK COUNTRY
Singles: 7-inch
SEAGULL ... 4-8 74

BLACKHOLES
Singles: 7-inch
BLACKHOLE ... 3-5 79

BLACKHORSE
LPs: 10/12-inch
DSDA ... 8-10 79

BLACKJACK *P&R/LP '79*
Singles: 7-inch
POLYDOR ... 3-5 79-84
20TH FOX ... 4-8 76
LPs: 10/12-inch
POLYDOR ... 5-10 79-80
Members: Michael Bolotin; Tony Battaglia; Bruce Kulick; Chuck Kirkpatrick; Jan Mullaney.
Also see BOLTON, Michael
Also see KISS

BLACKLIGHT CHAMELEONS
Singles: 12-inch
VOXX ... 4-8

BLACKMAN, Hank, & Killers
Singles: 7-inch
BRENT ... 10-15 62

BLACKMAN, Hank / Tip Tops
Singles: 7-inch
HALO (1003 "Everyone Has Someone") ... 20-30
Also see BLACKMAN, Hank, & Killers
Also see TIP TOPS

BLACKMAN, Honor
LPs: 10/12-inch
LONDON ... 10-20 64

BLACKMAN, Robert
Singles: 12-inch
RIVERWINDS ... 4-6 84

BLACKMORE, Ritchie
(Ritchie Blackmore's Rainbow)
Singles: 7-inch
POLYDOR ... 3-5 75
LPs: 10/12-inch
POLYDOR (6049 "Ritchie Blackmore's Rainbow") ... 8-10 75
Also see BLACKMORE'S RAINBOW
Also see LORD SUTCH

BLACKMORE'S RAINBOW *LP '75*
Singles: 7-inch
OYSTER ... 3-5 76
POLYDOR ... 3-5 75-79
LPs: 10/12-inch
OYSTER ... 8-12 75-76
Members: Ritchie Blackmore; Roger Glover; Ronnie Dio.
Also see BLACKMORE, Ritchie
Also see DEEP PURPLE
Also see DIO, Ronnie
Also see ELF
Also see RAINBOW

BLACKOUT
LPs: 10/12-inch
BOOT ... 5-10 81

BLACKROCK
Singles: 7-inch
BLACKROCK ... 3-5 75
SELECTOHITS ... 3-6 70

BLACKSHEEP
Singles: 7-inch
BELLCOR ... 3-5

BLACKSMOKE *R&B '76*
Singles: 7-inch
CHOCOLATE CITY ... 3-5 76

BLACKSTONE
Singles: 7-inch
EPIC ... 3-5 71
LPs: 10/12-inch
EPIC ... 10-12 71

BLACKSTONE, Bob, & Co. Walkers
Singles: 7-inch
ARCOLA ... 8-12 60s

BLACKTEARS
(Kevin & the Blacktears)
EPs: 7-inch
KEVIN KAT (118 "Juanita and a Texas Tornado") ... 3-4 93
(Issued in plain paper sleeve, with insert.)
Also see KEVIN & BLACKTEARS

BLACKWELL *P&R '69*
Singles: 7-inch
ASTRO ... 3-6 69-70
BUTTERFLY ... 3-4 78
LPs: 10/12-inch
ASTRO ... 8-10 69
BUTTERFLY ... 5-10 78

BLACKWELL, Angie
Singles: 7-inch
CONCORDE ... 3-5 76

BLACKWELL, Charlie *P&R '59*
Singles: 7-inch
W.B. ... 5-10 59

BLACKWELL, Eugene
Singles: 7-inch
CELESTE (111 "Jump Back") ... 8-12

BLACKWELL, Francis "Scrapper"
LPs: 10/12-inch
PRESTIGE BLUESVILLE (1047 "Mr. Scrapper's Blues") ... 50-100 62
Also see BERRY, Brooks, & Scrapper Blackwell

BLACKWELL, George
Singles: 7-inch
SMOKE (100 "Mister Loser") ... 25-50 65
SMOKE (200 "Can't Lose My Head") ... 100-200 66

BLACKWELL, Karon *C&W '77*
(Kay-Ron Blackwell)
Singles: 7-inch
BLACKLAND ... 3-5 76-77

BLACKWELL, Lou
Singles: 78 rpm
CHANCE ... 50-75 53
Singles: 7-inch
CHANCE (1130 "How Blue the Night") ... 100-200 53

BLACKWELL, Manner
Singles: 7-inch
W.B. ... 4-6 67

BLACKWELL, Otis
Singles: 78 rpm
ATLANTIC ... 15-25 57-58
GALE ... 20-30 57
GROOVE ... 20-30 55
JAY-DEE ... 15-25 55-57
RCA ... 20-30 52-53
Singles: 7-inch
ATLANTIC (1165 "Make Ready for Love") ... 20-30 57
ATLANTIC (1178 "Turtle Dove") ... 20-30 58
CUB (9092 "I'd Rather Kiss You Than Eat") ... 10-15 61
CUB (9107 "Sister Twister") ... 10-15 62
DATE (1006 "Don't Run Away") ... 15-25 58
EPIC (10654 "It's All Over") ... 20-30 70
FEVER ... 3-5 80
GALE (102 "It's Love and It's Real") ... 15-25 57
GROOVE (34 "Oh What a Babe") 30-50 55
JAY-DEE (784 "Daddy Rolling Stone") ... 30-50 54
JAY-DEE (787 "You're My Love") .. 30-50 54
JAY-DEE (791 "On That Power Line") ... 30-50 54
JAY-DEE (792 "Nobody Met the Train") ... 30-50 54
JAY-DEE (794 "My Josephine") ... 30-50 54
JAY-DEE (798 "Go Away Mr. Blues") ... 30-50 55
JAY-DEE (802 "My Poor Broken Heart") ... 30-50 55
JAY-DEE (808 "Oh What a Wonderful Time") ... 30-40 55
MGM (13090 "Kiss Away") ... 10-15 62
RCA (5069 "Wake Up Fool") ... 45-65 52-53
RCA (5225 "Number 000") ... 45-65 52-53
LPs: 10/12-inch
DAVIS (109 "Singin' the Blues") 200-300 56
INNER CITY (1032 "These Are My Songs") ... 8-12 77
Also see WATKINS, Viola

BLACKWELLS
Singles: 7-inch
G&G ... 10-15 59
GUYDEN ... 10-20 59
HICKORY ... 4-8 64-65
JAMIE ... 10-15 59-61
LIBERTY ... 4-8 64
Picture Sleeves
JAMIE (1150 "Honey Honey") ... 15-25 60
Members: Dewayne Blackwell; Ronald Blackwell.

BLACKWOOD
Singles: 7-inch
BLACKWOOD ... 4-6 73

BLACKWOOD, R.W. *C&W '76*
(With the Blackwood Singers)
Singles: 7-inch
CAPITOL ... 3-5 76
SCORPION ... 3-5 78
LPs: 10/12-inch
CAPITOL ... 5-10 76

BLACKWOOD APOLOGY
LPs: 10/12-inch
FONTANA ... 12-18 69
Also see CASTAWAYS

BLADE FAMILY
Singles: 7-inch
KING JAMES ... 3-5

BLADES, Carol
(With the Harptones)
Singles: 78 rpm
GEE ... 50-75 57
Singles: 7-inch
GEE (1029 "When Will I Know") ... 100-200 57
Also see HARPTONES

BLADES, Emery
Singles: 7-inch
ARVIS (110 "I Feel Like a Million") 40-60 60
RUBY (120 "Rock & Roll Carpenter") ... 40-60 57
RUBY (230 "Look What You Done to Me") ... 25-50 57
RUBY (340 "Try, Try Again") ... 20-35 57

BLADES, Ruben *LP '88*
Singles: 7-inch
ATLANTIC ... 3-5
ELEKTRA ... 3-4 88

BLADES OF GRASS *P&R '67*
Singles: 7-inch
FINE (57027 "It Isn't Easy") ... 20-30 67
JUBILEE ... 4-8 67-68
LPs: 10/12-inch
JUBILEE ... 12-20 67
Members: Bruce Ames; Marc Black; Frank DiChiara; Dave Gordon.

BLAINE, Gerry
Singles: 7-inch
ARVEE ... 8-12 60

BLAINE, Hal
(With the Young Cougars; Col. with Hollywood Raiders)
Singles: 7-inch
DUNHILL ... 5-10 65-69
MELODY HOUSE ... 10-20 62
RCA ... 10-15 62-63
ROCK-IT (1000 "Alamo Rock") ... 20-30 59
LPs: 10/12-inch
DUNHILL ... 15-25 65-67
RCA (2834 "Deuces, T's Roadsters and Drums") ... 30-50 63
Also see AVALANCHES
Also see CATALINAS
Also see DENVER, John
Also see FABARES, Shelley
Also see GOOD GUYS
Also see KNIGHTS
Also see JAN & DEAN
Also see MONTEZ, Chris
Also see RIP CHORDS
Also see SANDS, Tommy
Also see PRESLEY, Elvis

BLAIR, Kenny *C&W '88*
Singles: 7-inch
AWESOME ... 3-4 88

BLAIR, Ronnie
Singles: 7-inch
CREST (1084 "Twenty-One") ... 5-8 61

BLAIR, Sallie
Singles: 7-inch
BETHLEHEM ... 4-8 62
SCEPTER ... 5-8 61
TOP RANK ... 5-8 60
LP: 10/12-inch
MGM ... 10-15

BLAIR, Sandy
Singles: 7-inch
BOBBY (111 "When the Bells Stop Ringing") ... 30-50 60s

BLAIR, Sunny
Singles: 78 rpm
RPM (354 "Five Foot Three Blues") ... 100-200 52
Singles: 7-inch
METEOR (5006 "Please Send My Baby Back") ... 250-350 52
(Though credited to Blair, the flip, *Gonna Let You Go*, is reportedly by Baby Face Turner.)
Also see TURNER, Baby Face

BLAIR, Tom
(With the West Coasters)
Singles: 7-inch
DECCA (31223 "West Coast") ... 15-25 61
DOT (16095 "Rock It") ... 25-40 60
TEEN-TUNES (767 "Rock It") ... 50-100 60

BLAIZE, Rupert
Singles: 7-inch
ALITHIA ... 3-5 74

BLAKE, Barbara, & Uniques
LPs: 10/12-inch
20TH FOX ... 8-10 75
Also see BARBARA & UNIQUES

BLAKE, Buddy
Singles: 78 rpm
DECCA ... 4-8 55
Singles: 7-inch
COVER ... 5-10 59
DECCA ... 5-10 55
PHILLIPS INT'L ... 15-25 58
RIVER ... 5-10

BLAKE, Cicero
Singles: 7-inch
BRAINSTORM (123 "Shing-a-ling") ... 10-20 60s
MAR-V-LUS ... 5-10 65
PAULA ... 3-5
RAINBOWS END ... 5-10
RENEE ... 5-10 64
SOUND PLUS ... 4-8
SUCCESS (108 "See What Tomorrow Brings") ... 25-35 63
SUE ... 3-5 85
TOWER ... 4-8 68

BLAKE, Dick
Singles: 7-inch
BLAKE (001 "The Robbie") ... 10-15

BLAKE, Harriette
Singles: 7-inch
LTD ... 4-8 66
MONUMENT ... 4-6 68-69
PARKWAY ... 4-8 65
VINCENT (114 "Teenager's Prayer") ... 4-8 60s

BLAKE, Johnny, & Clippers
Singles: 78 rpm
GEE (1027 "I'm Yours") ... 20-40 57
Singles: 7-inch
GEE (1027 "I'm Yours") ... 30-50 57

BLAKE, Melvin
Singles: 7-inch
RODNEY ("Judy") ... 15-25
(Selection number not known.)

BLAKE, Paul, & Blood Fire Posse
Singles: 12-inch
REAL AUTHENTIC SOUND ... 4-6 84

BLAKE, Ran
LPs: 10/12-inch
OWL ... 5-10 84

BLAKE, Sonny "Harmonica"
EPs: 7-inch
ROOSTER BLUES ... 3-5 81

BLAKE, Theresa
Singles: 7-inch
EXCELLO ... 4-8 64

BLAKE, Tommy
(With the Rhythm Rebels)
Singles: 7-inch
BUDDY ... 15-25 58
CHANCELLOR ... 5-10 62
RCA (6925 "Mister Hoody") ... 15-25 57
RECCO (1006 "Folding Money") ... 15-20 60
SUN (278 "Flat Foot Sam") ... 50-100 57
SUN (300 "I Dig You Baby") ... 75-100 58

BLAKE & HINES *R&B '87*
Singles: 7-inch
MOTOWN ... 3-4 87
Members: Cory Blake; Andra Hines.

BLAKELY, Cliff
Singles: 7-inch
STARDAY (352 "High Steppin' ") ... 50-80 58
STARDAY (369 "Get off My Toes") ... 50-80 58

BLAKELY, Cornell
(Bouncing Cornell Blakely)
Singles: 7-inch
CARRIE (1503 "Tell Me More") ... 50-100 60s
FULTON (2453 "Don't Touch the Moon") ... 50-75 57
RICH (1007 "You Ain't Gonna Find") ... 50-75 61
(No mention of distribution by Mercury.)
RICH (71853 "You Ain't Gonna Find") ... 15-25 61
("With "Distributed by Mercury.")
RICH (1747 "You Broke My Heart") ... 40-60 61
RICH (1801 "I've Got That Feeling") ... 40-60 62

BLAKELY, Ronee
Singles: 7-inch
ELEKTRA ... 3-5 72
LPs: 10/12-inch
ELEKTRA ... 8-10 72

Also see COHEN, Leonard

BLAKELY, Virginia

Singles: 7-inch

MAJO (101 "Let Nobody Love You") ... 150-250

BLAKELY, Wellington

Singles: 78 rpm

VEE JAY (104 "Sailor Joe") ... 50-100 53

Singles: 7-inch

VEE JAY (104 "Sailor Joe") ... 200-400 53

BLAKER, Clay, & Texas Honky-Tonk Band C&W '87

(With the Texas Honkey-Tonk Band)

Singles: 7-inch

RAIN FOREST ... 3-4 88
TEXAS ... 3-4 87

BLAKEY, Don

Singles: 7-inch

PHARAOH (107 "Only Love") ... 15-20

BLAKNEY, Bobby, & Pastels

Singles: 7-inch

CHANG'N TIMES (300 "Beautiful Day") ... 10-15

BLAM BLAM BLAM

LPs: 10/12-inch

ENIGMA ... 5-10 84

BLANC, Mel P&R '48

(With the Sportsmen & Billy May; with Alan Reed)

Singles: 78 rpm

CAPITOL (5221 "Seasons Greetings from Capitol") ... 10-20 49
(Promotional issue only. Also contains greetings from other Capitol artists.)
CAPITOL ... 10-20 48-54

Singles: 7-inch

CAPITOL (Except PRO-15) ... 20-30 50-54
CAPITOL (PRO-15 "I Taut I Taw a Record Dealer") ... 30-50 51
(Mel Blanc provides the voice of assorted cartoon characters, though he is not credited on label. Promotional issue only.)
PETER PAN ... 3-5 72
W.B. ... 5-10 60

EPs: 7-inch

CAPITOL (436 "Party Panic") ... 40-60 53

LPs: 10/12-inch

CAPITOL (436 "Party Panic") ... 50-100 53
(10-inch LP.)
CAPITOL (3251 "Woody Woodpecker & His Talent Show") ... 15-25 61
CAPITOL (3257 "Bugs Bunny & His Friends") ... 25-35 61
CAPITOL (3261 "Tweety Pie") ... 15-25 63
CAPITOL (3266 "Bugs Bunny in Storyland") ... 15-25 63
CAPITOL (6686 "Bozo & His Pals") ... 15-25
COLPIX (302 "The Flintstones") ... 75-150 61
(TV Soundtrack.)
GOLDEN (66 "Songs of the Flintstones") ... 125-175 61
Also see HUNT, Pee Wee
Also see LE BLANC

BLANCH, Arthur C&W '78

Singles: 7-inch

MC ... 3-5 78
RIDGETOP ... 3-5 79

BLANCH, Jewel C&W '78

Singles: 7-inch

RCA ... 3-5 78-79

BLANCHARD, Bonnie, & Aaron

Singles: 7-inch

CRS (2 "You're the Only One") ... 10-20 60s

BLANCHARD, Edgar

Singles: 78 rpm

SPECIALTY ... 10-15 56

Singles: 7-inch

RIC ... 10-20 59
SPECIALTY ... 15-25 56

BLANCHARD, Jack, & Misty Morgan C&W '69

Singles: 7-inch

EPIC ... 3-4 73-75
MEGA ... 3-5 71-73
WAYSIDE ... 3-5 69-70

LPs: 10/12-inch

MEGA ... 8-12 72
WAYSIDE ... 10-15 70

BLANCHARD, Jackie

Singles: 7-inch

MIDA (111 "King of Hearts") ... 30-60 58

BLANCHARD, Red

Singles: 7-inch

COLUMBIA ... 10-20 57
Also see NERVOUS NORVUS

BLANCMANGE D&D '83

Singles: 12-inch

ISLAND ... 4-6 83-84
LONDON ... 5-8 83
SIRE ... 4-6 84-85

Singles: 7-inch

ISLAND ... 3-4 83-84
SIRE ... 3-4 84-85

LPs: 10/12-inch

ISLAND ... 5-10 82-84
SIRE ... 5-10 84-85

BLAND, Billy P&R/R&B '60

Singles: 78 rpm

OLD TOWN ... 10-20 55-57

Singles: 7-inch

ATLANTIC ... 3-5 84
COLLECTABLES ... 3-4 81
TIP TOP ... 10-20 58
OLD TOWN (1016 thru 1035) ... 15-25 55-57
OLD TOWN (1076 thru 1143) ... 10-15 60-63

BLAND, Billy

(McKinley Mitchell)

Singles: 7-inch

ST. LAWRENCE (1018 "I'm Sorry About That") ... 5-10 66
Also see MITCHELL, McKinley

BLAND, Bobby R&B '57

(Bobby "Blue" Bland)

Singles: 78 rpm

CHESS (1489 "Crying") ... 20-40 54
DUKE (105 "I.O.U. Blues") ... 40-60 54
DUKE (115 "No Blow No Show") ... 25-50 54
DUKE (141 "It's My Life, Baby") ... 20-40 56
DUKE (146 thru 196) ... 15-30 57-58
MODERN (848 "Crying All Night Long") ... 15-25 52
MODERN (868 "Good Lovin' ") ... 15-25 52

Singles: 7-inch

ABC ... 3-5 73-78
DUKE (105 "I.O.U. Blues") ... 75-100 54
DUKE (115 "No Blow No Show") ... 50-100 54
DUKE (141 "It's My Life, Baby") ... 30-60 56
DUKE (146 thru 196) ... 15-30 57-58
DUKE (300 series) ... 5-10 60-66
DUKE (400 series) ... 4-8 66-72
DUNHILL ... 3-5 74
FAIRWAY ... 8-10 79
KENT ... 5-10
MCA ... 3-5 79-84
MALACO ... 3-5
ST. LAWRENCE ... 4-8

EPs: 7-inch

DUKE (75 "Here's the Man") ... 20-30 62
(Juke box issue only. Includes title strips.)
DUKE (78 "Ain't Nothing You Can Do") ... 20-30 64
(Juke box issue only. Includes title strips.)

LPs: 10/12-inch

ABC ... 5-10 75-78
ABC/DUKE ... 5-10 73
BLUESWAY ... 5-10 73
DUKE (74 "Two Steps from the Blues") ... 50-75 61
DUKE (75 "Here's the Man") ... 45-55 62
DUKE (77 "Call On Me") ... 35-50 63
DUKE (78 "Ain't Nothing You Can Do") ... 35-50 64
DUKE (79 "Soul of the Man") ... 25-45 66
DUKE (84 "Best of Bobby Bland") ... 25-40 67
DUKE (86 "Best of Bobby Bland, Vol. 2") ... 25-40 68
DUKE (88 "Touch of the Blues") ... 25-40 68
DUKE (89 "Spotlighting the Man") ... 20-40 69
DUKE (90 "If Loving You Is Wrong") ... 15-25 70
DUKE (92 "Introspective") ... 20-25 74
DUNHILL ... 8-15 73-74
MCA ... 5-10 79-84
Also see ACE, Johnny

BLAND, Bobby, & B.B. King R&B '76

Singles: 7-inch

ABC ... 3-4 78
IMPULSE ... 3-5 76

LPs: 10/12-inch

DUNHILL ... 10-12 74
IMPULSE ... 8-10 76
MCA ... 5-10 82
Also see KING, B.B.

BLAND, Bobby / Little Junior Parker

LPs: 10/12-inch

DUKE (DLP-72 "The Barefoot Rock") ... 100-150 58
DUKE (X-72 "The Barefoot Rock") ... 10-12 74
Also see PARKER, Little Junior

BLAND, Bobby, & Ike Turner

Singles: 7-inch

KENT ... 5-10 62
Also see TURNER, Ike

BLAND, Bobby / Johnny Guitar Watson

LPs: 10/12-inch

CROWN (5358 "2 in Blues") ... 20-30 63
Also see BLAND, Bobby
Also see WATSON, Johnny

BLAND, Glenn

Singles: 7-inch

SARG (159 "Mean Jean") ... 40-75 58
SARG (164 "When My Baby Passes By") ... 40-75 58

BLAND, Len, & Hi Notes

Singles: 78 rpm

HI-Q ... 15-25 56

Singles: 7-inch

HI-Q (5048 "Operator") ... 30-40 56

BLAND, Sammy

Singles: 7-inch

PROGRESS (206 "Lovies Love Groove") ... 10-20 64

BLANDERS

Singles: 7-inch

SMASH (2005 "Jitterbug") ... 30-40 65

BLANDING, Gil

Singles: 7-inch

READY ... 4-8

BLANDING, Virgil

Singles: 7-inch

VERVE ... 10-20 66

BLANDON, Curtis

Singles: 7-inch

PORT ... 5-10 63
TOWER ... 4-8 67
WAND ... 3-5 71

BLANDON, Richard, & Dubs: see DUBS

BLANE, Marcie P&R/R&B '62

Singles: 7-inch

LONDON ... 3-4 84
SEVILLE ... 5-10 62-65

BLANKENSHIP BROTHERS

Singles: 78 rpm

SKYLINE ... 20-30 56

Singles: 7-inch

SKYLINE (105 "Don't Tell Me You're Sorry") ... 50-100 56
SKYLINE (106 "That's Why I'm Blue") ... 100-150 56
SKYLINE (107 "Waitin' for a Train") ... 100-200 56

BLANKET OF SECRECY

Singles: 7-inch

W.B. ... 3-4 82

LPs: 10/12-inch

W.B. ... 5-10 82

BLANN, Sammy

Singles: 7-inch

PROGRESS ... 4-8 64

BLANTON, Harry

Singles: 7-inch

GRT ... 3-5 76

BLANTON, Loy C&W '85

Singles: 7-inch

SOUNDWAVES ... 3-4 85

BLARNEYS

Singles: 7-inch

ROMULUS ... 20-30 63

BLASERS

(Featuring Tommy "Mary Jo" Braden)

Singles: 78 rpm

UNITED ... 10-20 55

Singles: 7-inch

UNITED (191 "She Needs to Be Loved") ... 15-25 55
(Previously issued as by the Four Blazes.)
Member: Tommy Braden.
Also see BRADEN, Tommy
Also see FOUR BLAZES

BLASKEY, Lindy

(With the Lavells)

Singles: 7-inch

CHALLENGE (59354 "You Ain't Tuff") ... 10-15 67
LAVETTE (5005 "What's Her Name") ... 10-15 67
SPACE (0003 "My Baby Done Left Me") ... 15-25 65
SPACE (0005 "Papa-Oom-Mow-Mow") ... 15-25 65
SPACE (0007 "You Ain't Tuff") ... 15-25 66
SPACE (0009 "Sweets for My Sweet") ... 15-25 66
Also see LINDY & LAVELLS

BLASSIE, Freddie

(With the Geekettes)

Singles: 7-inch

GEEKBEAT (002 "Pencil-Neck Geek") ... 10-15 77
RAUNCHY TONK ... 5-8 76

Picture Sleeves

GEEKBEAT (002 "Pencil-Neck Geek") ... 15-25 77

LPs: 10/12-inch

RHINO (Colored vinyl) ... 5-10 83
RHINO (Picture disc) ... 10-15 83

BLAST

Singles: 7-inch

CAPE (1999 "Canaveral Rock") ... 10-20 60s

BLAST

Singles: 7-inch

COLUMBIA ... 3-4 79

LPs: 10/12-inch

COLUMBIA ... 5-10 79

BLAST, C.L. R&B '80

Singles: 7-inch

ATLANTIC ... 4-8 69
CLIMTONE (009 "Leftover Love") 10-20
COTILLION ... 3-5 80
PARK PLACE ... 3-4 85
STAX ... 5-10 67
UNITED ... 5-10 70-71

LPs: 10/12-inch

COTILLION ... 5-10 80

BLASTERS

LPs: 10/12-inch

CROWN ... 15-20 63

BLASTERS LP '82

Singles: 7-inch

MCA ... 3-4 84
SLASH ... 3-5 81-85

Picture Sleeves

SLASH ... 3-4 81-85

LPs: 10/12-inch

ROLLIN' ROCK (021 "American Music") ... 50-75 80
SLASH ... 8-12 81-85
Members: David Alvin; Phil Alvin; John Bazz; Gene Taylor; Bill Bateman; Steve Berlin; Lee Allen.
Also see ALLEN, Lee
Also see ALVIN, Dave
Also see HARTMAN, Dan / Blasters
Also see X

BLATTNER, Jules

(With His Teen Tones; with Warren Groovy Band; Warren Groovy All Stars)

Singles: 7-inch

BLUE RIBBON ... 5-10 76
BOBBIN (105 "Rock & Roll Blues") ... 75-100 59
BOBBIN (113 "Green Stuff") ... 20-30 59
BUDDAH ... 5-10 71
CINE VISTA ... 10-20 69
CORAL ... 5-10 64
DMA ... 5-10 69
GASLIGHT ... 10-20 62
K-ARK (609 "Till I'm with You") ... 20-30 60
K-ARK (612 "One More Time") ... 20-30 60
METROMEDIA ... 5-10 73
MGM ... 10-20 72
NORMAN (Except 1020) ... 15-20 61-65
NORMAN (1020 "New Orleans") ... 3-4 89
TARGET ... 8-12 71
TEE PEE ... 10-20 67

LPs: 10/12-inch

BUDDAH ... 10-20 71
DESMOND ... 5-10 79
MOUNTAIN ... 10-20 74
Also see J.B.G. & JULES
Also see LUNARTICS
Also see RENTTALB, Seluj

BLAVAT, Jerry

(With the Geatorettes; with Yon-Teens; Geator with the Heater)

Singles: 7-inch

BOND ... 4-8 70
CAMEO ... 4-8 66
EPIC ... 5-10 67
FAVOR ... 10-15 65
ROULETTE ... 3-5 70

LPs: 10/12-inch

CRIMSON ... 6-10
LOST-NITE ... 8-12
Also see DUPREES / RIVIERAS

BLAZE P&R '76

Singles: 7-inch

EPIC ... 3-5 76-77
FRATERNITY ... 3-5 76

BLAZE, Johnny

(With Eddie Konecnik Orchestra)

Singles: 7-inch

APON (2142 "Oh Lovin' Baby") ... 25-35 59

BLAZER, Jimmy "Boo Boo"

Singles: 7-inch

EBONY ... 5-10

BLAZER & Little Archie Taylor

Singles: 7-inch

TREND ... 5-10 59

BLAZER BOY

(James Locks)

Singles: 78 rpm

IMPERIAL ... 25-50 52-53

Singles: 7-inch

IMPERIAL (5199 "Morning Train") ... 50-100 52
IMPERIAL (5244 "Surprise Blues") ... 50-100 53
IMPERIAL (5800 series) ... 10-15 62
Also see LOCKS, James

BLAZERS

(Featuring Frankie Tucker)

LPs: 10/12-inch

HARMONY (7103 "Rock & Roll by the Blazers") ... 25-35 59
Also see HARMONY BLAZERS

BLAZERS

(Featuring Dave "Baby" Cortez on Organ)

Singles: 7-inch

WINLEY ... 5-10 61
Also see CORTEZ, Dave

BLAZERS

(Blasers)

Singles: 7-inch

LYONS (108 "You Are the Only One") ... 10-15 61
Also see HOLLIDAYS

BLAZERS

(With Li'l Ray Armstrong)

Singles: 7-inch

EMPIRE (2001 "Boom Boom") ... 10-20 62

BLAZERS

Singles: 7-inch

SINGULAR (1003 "Sit Down") ... 10-20 62

BLAZERS

Singles: 7-inch

ACREE (101 "Beaver Patrol") ... 25-35 63
ACREE (102 "Sound of Mecca") ... 25-35 63
BRASS (306 "I Don't Need You") ... 15-25 63
Members: Vernon Acree; Larry Robbins; Chris Holguin; John Morris.

BLAZERS

Singles: 7-inch

DOT (16623 "Masked Grandma") ... 10-15 64
GOLDEN CREST ... 8-10
MUNDO ... 8-10 63

BLAZERS

LP: 10/12-inch

ABC-PAR ... 10-20

BLAZONS

Singles: 7-inch

BRAVURA (5001 "Magic Lamp") ... 100-125 58
FANFARE (5001 "Magic Lamp") ... 250-500 58
(First issue.)

BLEACH BOYS

Singles: 7-inch

STUDIO CITY (1030 "Must Be Love") ... 40-60 64

BLEAK, Charles

Singles: 7-inch

P.I.P. ... 3-5 76

LPs: 10/12-inch

P.I.P. ... 8-10 76

BLEATERS

Singles: 7-inch

GUYDEN ... 5-10 62-64

BLEDSOE, Gerry, & Fatback

Singles: 12-inch

SPRING ... 4-6 84

Singles: 7-inch

SPRING ... 3-4 84

BLEDSOE, Steve

Singles: 7-inch

SCOPE ... 10-15
SUPERSTAR ... 3-5 73
VEM ... 5-10 60
WITCH ... 10-15 61

BLEND P&R '78

Singles: 7-inch

MCA ... 3-4 78-79

LPs: 10/12-inch

MCA ... 5-10 78-79
Member: Jim Drown.

BLEND TONES: see BLENDTONES

BLEND-AIRES

Singles: 7-inch

STORY UNTOLD ... 4-8

BLENDAIRS

Singles: 7-inch

TIN PAN ALLEY (252 "My Love Is Just for You") ... 100-150 58

BLENDED SPICE

Singles: 7-inch

QUEEN BEE ... 3-5

BLENDELLES

Singles: 7-inch

JOTEE ... 4-6

BLEN-DELLS

Singles: 7-inch

BELLA (608 "Forever") ... 50-75 62

BLENDELLS P&R '64

Singles: 7-inch

COLLECTABLES ... 3-4 81
COTILLION ... 4-8 68
ERA ... 3-5 73
RAMPART ... 8-10 64
REPRISE ... 4-8 64-65
Also see SONNY & CHER / Bill Medley / Lettermen / Blendells

BLENDELLS

Singles: 7-inch

CAPTOWN (4029 "Night After Night") ... 250-350
DON-TEE ("You Need Love") ... 20-30 60s
(Selection number not known.)

BLENDERS

Singles: 78 rpm

DECCA (27403 "I'm Afraid the Masquerade Is Over") ... 75-125 51
DECCA (27587 "Busiest Corner in My Home Town") ... 75-125 51
DECCA (28092 "I'd Be a Fool Again") ... 75-125 52
DECCA (28241 "Never in a Million Years") ... 75-125 52
DECCA (48156 "Gone") ... 50-100 50
DECCA (48158 "Count Every Star") ... 50-100 50
DECCA (48183 "I'm So Crazy for Love") ... 50-100 50
DECCA (48244 "My Heart Will Never Forget") ... 50-100 51
JAY DEE (780 "Don't Play Around with Love") ... 50-100 53
MGM (11488 "If That's the Way You Want It Baby") ... 50-100 53
MGM (11531 "Please Take Me Back") ... 50-100 53
NATIONAL (9092 "I Can Dream, Can't I") ... 50-75 49

Singles: 7-inch

DECCA (27403 "I'm Afraid the Masquerade Is Over") ... 300-400 51
DECCA (27587 "Busiest Corner in My Home Town") ... 300-400 51
DECCA (28092 "I'd Be a Fool Again") ... 300-400 52
DECCA (28241 "Never in a Million Years") ... 300-400 52
DECCA (48156 "Gone") ... 300-400 50
DECCA (48158 "Count Every Star") ... 300-400 50
DECCA (48183 "I'm So Crazy for Love") ... 300-400 50
DECCA (48244 "My Heart Will Never Forget") ... 300-400 51
JAY DEE (780 "Don't Play Around with Love") ... 200-300 53
MGM (11488 "If That's the Way You Want It Baby") ... 200-300 53
MGM (11531 "Please Take Me Back") ... 200-300 53

Members: Ollie Jones; Tommy Adams; Abe DeCosta; James DeLoach; Ernie Brown; Dick Palmer; Ray Johnson; Nappy Allen.
Also see BLENDERS / Sparrows
Also see MILLIONAIRES

BLENDERS / Sparrows
Singles: 78 rpm
("Don't F#*K Around with Love") 15-25
(Label is blank.)
Singles: 7-inch
KELWAY (101 "Don't F#*K Around with Love")..........10-15 71
Also see BLENDERS
Also see SPARROWS

BLENDERS
Singles: 78 rpm
RCA..........10-20 56
Singles: 7-inch
RCA (6591 "I've Told Every Little Star")..........25-50 56
RCA (6712 "Wake Up to the Music")..........15-25 56

BLENDERS
Singles: 7-inch
ALADDIN (3449 "Two Loves")..500-1000 59
CLASS (236 "Little Rose") 50-75 58
WANGER (189 "Angel")..........30-50 59

BLENDERS
Singles: 7-inch
PARADISE (111 "I Won't Tell the World")..........30-50 59
Member: Herman Dunham.
Also see VOCALEERS

BLENDERS
Singles: 7-inch
COBRA.......... 5-10
WONDER..........10-15 59

BLENDERS
Singles: 7-inch
AFO (305 "It Takes Time")..........250-300 62

BLENDERS P&R '63
Singles: 7-inch
CORTLAND.......... 5-10 62
MAR-V-LUS ("Your Love Has Got Me Down")..........100-200 66
(No selection number used.)
VISION (1000 "I Asked for Your Hand")..........40-50 57
WITCH (114 "Daughter")..........10-20 62
WITCH (117 "Boys Think")..........10-20 63
WITCH (122 "One Time")..........10-20 63
Also see CANDLES

BLENDERS
LPs: 10/12-inch
DOT..........15-20 65

BLENDERS LTD.
Singles: 7-inch
GRAYSLAK..........10-15

BLENDORS
Singles: 7-inch
DECCA..........15-25 61

BLENDS
(With the Eden Rockers; with Frank Paul's Orchestra)
Singles: 7-inch
CASA GRANDE (3037 "Now It's Your Turn")..........30-50 60
CASA GRANDE (5000 "A Thousand Miles Away")..........30-50 61
CASA GRANDE (5001 "Baby You're Wrong")..........25-50 61
(Colored vinyl.)
SKYLARK (108 "Tell Me")..........25-35 61
TALENT (110 "Tell Me")..........100-125 60
(Credits: "Music by the Eden Rockers.")
TALENT (110 "Tell Me")..........75-100 60
(No mention of the Eden Rockers.")

BLENDS
Singles: 7-inch
MCA.......... 3-4 78
LPs: 10/12-inch
MCA.......... 5-10 78

BLENDTONES
Singles: 7-inch
MGM (12782 "Lilly")..........15-25 59

BLENDTONES
(Blend-Tones; Blend Tones)
Singles: 7-inch
CHIC-CAR (100 "She's Gone")..........25-50 61
DON-EL (106 "She's Gone")..........50-75 61
(First issue.)
IMPERIAL (5758 "She's Gone")..........15-25 61
SUCCESS (101 "Lovers")..........25-35 63
SUCCESS (105 "Come on Home")..........25-35 63

BLESSED END
LPs: 10/12-inch
TNS (248 "Movin' On")..........200-300 71
Members: Doug Teti; Jim Shugarts; Ken Carson.

BLESSED ONES
Singles: 7-inch
SMOGVILLE..........4-8 67

BLESSING, Lynn
LPs: 10/12-inch
EPIC..........10-15 69

BLESSING, Michael
(Michael Nesmith)
Singles: 7-inch
COLPIX (792 "Until It's Time for You to Go")..........15-25 65
Also see NESMITH, Michael

BLESSITT, Arthur
LPs: 10/12-inch
CREATIVE SOUND..........8-10

BLEU, Frankie
LPs: 10/12-inch
UNICORN..........5-10 82

BLEU LIGHTS
Singles: 7-inch
BAY SOUND (67003 "Forever")..........30-40 68
BAY SOUND (67007 "Lonely Man's Prayer")..........15-25 68
BAY SOUND (67010 "Yes I Do")..........10-15 69

BLEUS
(Bleues)
Singles: 7-inch
AMY.......... 4-8 68
DIAMOND.......... 4-6 69
SWING LTD (2 "A Fella")..........8-12

BLEVINS, Bill
Singles: 7-inch
N.H.F. (101 "Crazy Blues")..........20-30 58

BLEVINS, Chuck
Singles: 7-inch
FOXIE..........10-20 59

BLEY, Paul
LPs: 10/12-inch
OWL..........5-10 84
SOUL NOTE..........5-10 85

BLEYER, Archie P&R '54
(With Maria Alba)
Singles: 78 rpm
ARC..........8-15 35
CADENCE..........5-10 54-57
VOCALION..........8-15 34
Singles: 7-inch
CADENCE..........8-15 54-57
SCHOLASTIC (2701 "Bedtime for Francis").......... 3-5 74
(Compact 33 single.)
LPs: 10/12-inch
CADENCE (3044 "Moonlight Serenade")..........15-25 62
(Monaural.)
CADENCE (25044 "Moonlight Serenade")..........20-30 62
(Stereo.)
Also see CHORDETTES
Also see GODFREY, Arthur, with Archie Bleyer
Also see HAYES, Bill

BLIFFERT
(Fred Bliffert; Freddy Bliffert)
LPs: 10/12-inch
O NO..........10-12
ZERO..........10-12 77
Also see FREELOADERS
Also see HENRY, Freddy

BLIGE, Mary J.
LPs: 10/12-inch
MCA..........8-10 90s

BLIHOVDE, Marv
Singles: 7-inch
KAY BEE (6001 "Been Away Too Long")..........25-35 60
LINDY (1113 "Cigarette & Coffee Blues")..........40-60 59
LINDY (1551 "Sweet Little Wife")..25-35 59
Also see DENNIS, Marv
Also see MINNESOTA MARV

BLIND BLAKE
LPs: 10/12-inch
BYG..........5-10
BIOGRAPH..........10-15 70

BLIND DATE
Singles: 7-inch
WINDSONG.......... 3-5 79
LPs: 10/12-inch
WINDSONG..........5-10 79

BLIND FAITH LP '69
Singles: 7-inch
RSO.......... 3-6 77
LPs: 10/12-inch
ATCO (304A "Blind Faith")..........20-30 69
(Front cover pictures a nude girl.)
ATCO (304B "Blind Faith")..........10-12 69
(Front cover pictures the group.)
MFSL (186 "Blind Faith")..........25-35 69
(Half-speed mastered.)
RSO..........5-10 76
(Reissue. Pictures nude girl.)
Members: Eric Clapton; Ginger Baker; Steve Winwood; Rick Grech.
Also see BAKER, Ginger
Also see CLAPTON, Eric
Also see FAMILY
Also see WINWOOD, Steve

BLIND HOG
Singles: 7-inch
VULCAN (106 "Rockin' Pneumonia & Boogie Woogie Flu")..........10-15 58
VULCAN (112 "Memphis")..........5-10 72

BLIND MELON
LPs: 10/12-inch
CAPITOL..........5-10 90s

BLIND WILLIE: see McTELL, Willie

BLINDERS
Singles: 7-inch
ANKH..........3-5 77
SARA..........3-5 77

BLINKY
(Sandra Williams)
Singles: 7-inch
MOTOWN (Except 1168)..........3-6 68-73
MOTOWN (1168 "How You Gonna Keep It")..........50-100 68
MOWEST..........3-5 72-73
SOUL..........3-5 71
Also see STARR, Edwin, & Blinky

BLISS, Melvin
Singles: 7-inch
SUNBURST..........3-5

BLISS, Peter: see BLISS BAND

BLISS
Singles: 7-inch
CANYON (34 "Gangster of Love") .10-20 68
LPs: 10/12-inch
CANYON (7707 "Bliss")..........75-100 68

BLISS BAND
Singles: 7-inch
COLUMBIA..........3-5 78-79
U.A...........3-5 77
LPs: 10/12-inch
COLUMBIA..........5-10 78-79
U.A...........8-12 77
Member: Peter Bliss.

BLISTERS
Singles: 7-inch
LIBERTY..........4-8 63
TITANIC..........5-10 63

BLIXSETH, Tim, & Kathy Walker C&W '85
Singles: 7-inch
COMPLEAT..........3-4 85

BLIZZARD
Singles: 7-inch
METROMEDIA..........3-5 70-72

BLOBS
Singles: 7-inch
VERVE..........3-5 72

BLOCH, Ray, & Orchestra P&R '46
Singles: 78 rpm
CORAL..........4-8 52-57
SIGNATURE..........4-8 47
Singles: 7-inch
CORAL..........6-12 53
SIGNATURE..........4-6 60-61
Picture Sleeves
CORAL (9-1327 "From Here to Eternity")..........300-500 53
(Pictures Frank Sinatra, Burt Lancaster, Montgomery Clift, Donna Reed, and Deborah Kerr.)
LPs: 10/12-inch
AMBASSADOR..........8-12
CORAL..........10-25 52-57
Also see SINATRA, Frank

BLOCH, Rene, Orchestra & Chorus
Singles: 7-inch
ANDEX..........3-6 59
ATCO..........3-5 63
CAPITOL..........10-15 60-61
HI FI..........3-6 59
LPs: 10/12-inch
ANDEX..........10-20 59
ATCO..........10-15 63
HI FI..........15-25 59

BLOCH, Sonny, & Coralairs
(With Sy Hoffman & His Orchestra)
Singles: 7-inch
REGAL (7503 "Ask Me No Questions")..........10-15 58

BLOCK, Doug C&W '84
Singles: 7-inch
REVOLVER..........3-4 84
Also see DOUGLAS

BLOCK, Hal
Singles: 78 rpm
JUBILEE..........5-10 54
Singles: 7-inch
JUBILEE..........10-15 54

BLOCK, Rory
Singles: 7-inch
CHRYSALIS..........3-5 77-79
LPs: 10/12-inch
BLUE GOOSE..........8-10 76
CHRYSALIS..........5-10 77-79
RCA..........10-12 75
ROUNDER..........5-10 82

BLOCKBUSTERS
Singles: 78 rpm
ALADDIN..........10-15 56
INTRO..........10-15 56
Singles: 7-inch
ALADDIN (3319 "Why Baby Why")..........20-30 56
INTRO (6093 "All the Way")..........20-30 56

BLOCKBUSTERS
Singles: 78 rpm
ANTLER..........10-20 56-57
Singles: 7-inch
ANTLER (4006 "Full Time Baby")..20-40 56
ANTLER (4008 "Nobody to Love").20-40 57
Also see NEW BLOCKBUSTERS

Also see OLENN, Johnny

BLOCKBUSTERS
Singles: 7-inch
CRYSTALETTE (725 "Boogie Bop")..........10-20 59

BLOCKBUSTERS
Singles: 7-inch
ENTREE..........5-10 64
ROCKIN (500/1 "Muddy")..........5-10 64

BLOCKER, Dan
(With John Mitchum)
LPs: 10/12-inch
RCA..........10-20 64
TREY..........15-20 61

BLODWYN PIG LP '69
Singles: 7-inch
A&M..........3-6 69-70
LPs: 10/12-inch
A&M (3000 series)..........5-10 82
A&M (4000 series)..........10-15 69-70
Members: Blodwyn; Mick Abrahams; Peter Banks; Ron Berg; Clive Bunker; Jack Lancaster; Andy Pyle.
Also see ABRAHAMS, Mick, Band
Also see BANKS, Peter
Also see NETWORK

BLOIS, Larry
(With the Lincolns)
Singles: 7-inch
SEVENTEEN..........10-15 59

BLOKES
Singles: 7-inch
DANTE (2545 "All American Girl") 20-40 66

BLOND
Singles: 7-inch
FONTANA..........5-10 68
Picture Sleeves
FONTANA..........8-12 68
LPs: 10/12-inch
FONTANA..........15-20 69

BLONDE BOMBER
Singles: 7-inch
HULL (763 "Strollie Bun")..........30-45 60

BLONDE ON BLONDE
LPs: 10/12-inch
JANUS..........12-15 69

BLONDELL BREED & IMPORTS
Singles: 7-inch
ACTA..........4-8 68

BLONDIE LP '78
Singles: 12-inch
CHRYSALIS..........5-10 78-84
Singles: 7-inch
CHRYSALIS..........3-5 77-84
PRIVATE STOCK..........6-10 76-77
Picture Sleeves
CHRYSALIS..........3-8 79-82
LPs: 10/12-inch
CAPITOL (32748 "Remix Project") 10-15 90s
CHRYSALIS (Except 5001)..........5-10 76-84
CHRYSALIS (5001 "Parallel Lines")..........15-25 78
(Picture disc.)
MFSL (050 "Parallel Lines")..........20-40 81
PRIVATE STOCK..........15-20 75
Members: Deborah Harry; Clem Burke; Jimmy Destri; Chris Stein; Gary Valentine; Fred Smith; Nigel Harrison.
Also see HARRY, Debbie
Also see LITTLE GIRLS
Also see SILVERHEAD

BLOOD, SWEAT & TEARS LP '68
Singles: 7-inch
ABC..........3-4 78
COLUMBIA..........3-5 69-77
Picture Sleeves
COLUMBIA..........3-5 70-72
LPs: 10/12-inch
ABC..........5-10 77
COLUMBIA (Except 9619 & 49619)..........10-15 69-76
COLUMBIA (9619 "Child Is Father to the Man")..........20-30 68
COLUMBIA (49619 "Child Is Father to the Man")..........25-35 68
(Half-speed mastered.)
LAX (1865 "Nuclear Blues")..........5-10 80
(Black vinyl.)
LAX (1865 "Nuclear Blues")..........10-12 80
(Colored vinyl. Promotional issue only.)
MFSL (251 "Blood, Sweat & Tears")..........15-25
Members: David Clayton-Thomas; Al Kooper; Jerry Hyman; Fred Lipsius; Dick Halligan; Bobby Colomby; Lew Soloff; Chuck Winfield; Steve Katz; James Thomas Fielder; Dave Bargeron; Georg Wadenius; Lou Matini Jr.; Bobby Doyle; Jerry Fisher.
Also see CLAYTON-THOMAS, David
Also see DOYLE, Bobby
Also see FISHER, Jerry
Also see FRANKLIN, Aretha / Union Gap / Blood, Sweat & Tears / Moby Grape
Also see KOOPER, Al
Also see STREISAND, Barbra

BLOOD BROTHERS
Singles: 7-inch
W.B...........4-8 66

BLOOD BROTHERS
LPs: 10/12-inch
SUGARHILL..........5-10 81

BLOOD FEAST
LP: 10/12-inch
NEW RENAISSANCE (35 "Face Fate")..........10-15 88
(Picture disc.)

BLOODGOOD
LPs: 10/12-inch
FRONTLINE..........5-10

BLOODROCK P&R '71
Singles: 7-inch
CAPITOL..........3-6 69-75
Promotional Singles
CAPITOL (3451 "Bloodrock Interview by Sol Smaizys")..........4-8 72
LPs: 10/12-inch
CAPITOL..........15-35 69-75
Members: James Rutledge; Eddie Grundy; Steve Hill; Lee Pickens; Nick Taylor; Warren Ham.
Also see RUTLEDGE, James

BLOODSTONE P&R/R&B/LP '73
Singles: 12-inch
MOTOWN..........4-6 79
T-NECK..........4-6 82-85
Singles: 7-inch
EPIC..........3-4 82
LONDON..........3-5 73-76
MOTOWN..........3-4 79
T-NECK..........3-4 82-85
Picture Sleeves
LONDON..........3-5 74-76
LPs: 10/12-inch
LONDON..........8-10 73-74
MOTOWN..........5-10 78
T-NECK..........5-10 82
Members: Harry Williams; Charles McCormick; Charles Love; Steve Ferrone; Roger Lee Durham; Willis Draffen.

BLOODWORTH, Ray
Singles: 7-inch
DYNOVOICE..........4-8 68

BLOODY MARY
LPs: 10/12-inch
FAMILY..........10-15 72

BLOOM, Bobby. P&R/LP '70
Singles: 7-inch
EARTH..........4-8 69
KAMA SUTRA..........5-10 67
L&R..........4-8 70
MGM..........5-10 70-73
ROULETTE..........3-5 70
WHITE WHALE..........4-8 69
LPs: 10/12-inch
BUDDAH..........8-12 71
L&R..........10-15 70
Also see ARCHIES
Also see CAPT. GROOVEY & His Bubblegum Army
Also see IMAGINATIONS
Also see MANN, Bobby
Also see MUSIC EXPLOSION

BLOOM, James
Singles: 7-inch
20TH FOX..........3-5 73

BLOOMFIELD, Mike LP '69
LPs: 10/12-inch
CLOUDS..........5-10 78
COLUMBIA (9000 series)..........12-15 69
COLUMBIA (37000 series)..........6-10 81-83
GUITAR PLAYER..........8-10 77
HARMONY..........8-10 71
TAKOMA..........5-10 77-81
W.B. (7674 "Steelyard Blues")..........4-8 73
WATERHOUSE..........5-10 81
Also see DYLAN, Bob
Also see KGB

BLOOMFIELD, Mike, Dr. John & John Paul Hammond LP '73
LPs: 10/12-inch
COLUMBIA..........8-10 73
Also see DR. JOHN
Also see HAMMOND, John

BLOOMFIELD, Mike, & Nick Gravenites
LPs: 10/12-inch
COLUMBIA..........10-12 69
Also see ELECTRIC FLAG

BLOOMFIELD, Mike, & Al Kooper LP '69
LPs: 10/12-inch
COLUMBIA..........12-20 68
MFSL (178 "Super Session")..........15-25 85
Also see KOOPER, Al
Also see MOBY GRAPE

BLOOMFIELD, Mike, Al Kooper & Steve Stills LP '68
Singles: 7-inch
COLUMBIA..........3-6 68
LPs: 10/12-inch
COLUMBIA..........10-15 68
MFSL (178 "Super Session")..........20-30 85
Also see BLOOMFIELD, Mike
Also see STILLS, Stephen

BLOOMSBURY PEOPLE
Singles: 7-inch
MGM (14158 "Witch Helen")..........10-15 70
PAGE (1119 "Have You Seen Them Cry")..........10-15 69
LPs: 10/12-inch
MGM (2184 "Bloomsbury People")..........15-25 70

Members: Sigmund Snopek III; Jon Wyderka; Dennis Lanting; Greg Janick; Michael DuJardin; Rick Harris; Michael Lorenz.
Also see MAJOR ARCANA

BLOONTZ
Singles: 7-inch
EVOLUTION... 3-5 73
LPs: 10/12-inch
EVOLUTION... 10-15 73

BLOOP GROUP
Singles: 7-inch
LIBERTY... 4-6 68

BLOOPERS
Singles: 7-inch
ROWAX (803 "Bloopers Morse Code")... 10-20 63

BLOOS PHASE
Singles: 7-inch
TEE PEE (37/38 "Will You Love Me")... 15-25 67

BLOSSOMS *P&R '61*
Singles: 7-inch
BELL... 4-8 69-70
CAPITOL (3822 "Move On")... 15-25 57
CAPITOL (3878 "Little Louie")... 15-25 58
CAPITOL (4072 "Have Faith in Me")... 15-25 58
CHALLENGE (9138 "Big Talking Jim")... 10-15 62
CHALLENGE (59122 "Write Me a Letter")... 20-30 62
CLASSIC ARTISTS... 4-6 89
EEOC (8172 "Things Are Changing")... 75-100 65
(Equal Employment Opportunity Center promotional issue.)
EPIC... 3-5 77
LION... 3-5 72
MGM... 8-12 68
ODE... 5-10 67-69
OKEH... 8-12 62-63
REPRISE... 4-8 65-67
Picture Sleeves
EEOC (8172 "Things Are Changing")... 75-100 65
(Promotional issue only.)
LPs: 10/12-inch
LION... 8-12 72
Members: Darlene "Love" Wright; Gloria Jones; Fanita James-Barrett; Annette Williams; Nanette Williams-Jackson; Grazia Nitzsche; Jean King.
Also see BERRY, Richard
Also see BOB B. SOXX & Blue Jeans
Also see DON & DEWEY
Also see EDDY, Duane
Also see EVERETT, Betty
Also see HALE & HUSHABYES
Also see LOVE, Darlene
Also see PLAYGIRLS
Also see PRESLEY, Elvis
Also see WILDCATS
Also see WILSON, Brian

BLOSSOMS / Coeds
Singles: 7-inch
CHALLENGE (9109 "Son-in-Law") 10-15 61
Also see BLOSSOMS

BLOTT, Barrel House: see BARREL HOUSE BLOTT

BLOTTO
Singles: 12-inch
BLOTTO... 5-10 79
Singles: 7-inch
BLOTTO... 3-4 81
LPs: 10/12-inch
BLOTTO... 5-10 83

BLOUNT, Tina, & Bobby Newton
Singles: 7-inch
INTREPID... 3-6 69
Also see NEWTON, Bobby

BLOW, Kurtis *P&R/R&B/LP '80*
Singles: 12-inch
MERCURY... 4-6 80-86
Singles: 7-inch
MERCURY... 3-4 80-86
POLYDOR... 3-4 85
LPs: 10/12-inch
MERCURY... 5-10 80-86
Also see KING DREAM CHORUS & Holiday Crew
Also see KRUSH GROVE ALL STARS

BLOW MONKEYS *P&R/LP '86*
Singles: 12-inch
RCA... 4-6 85-87
Singles: 7-inch
RCA... 3-4 85-87
LPs: 10/12-inch
RCA... 5-10 85-87
Members: Robert Howard; Tony Kiley; Neville Henry; Mick Anker.

BLOW PUPS
Singles: 7-inch
GET HIP... 3-5 90
Picture Sleeves
GET HIP... 3-5 90
LPs: 10/12-inch
GET HIP... 5-10 92
Members: Nick Randazzo; Tim Buckley; Mike Jarvis; John Daniels.

BLOW TOP LYNN: see LYNN, Blow Top

BLOWFISH
EPs: 7-inch
VARULVEN... 5-10 77
Member: Paul Lovell.

BLOWFLY *LP '80*
Singles: 7-inch
WEIRD WORLD... 3-4 80
LPs: 10/12-inch
WEIRD WORLD... 8-10 80

BLOWTORCH
Singles: 7-inch
PARAMOUNT... 4-6 71
Member: Buddy Randell.
Also see RANDELL, Buddy

BLOW-UP
Singles: 7-inch
CAPITOL... 3-4 80

BLOX
Singles: 7-inch
SOLAR (235 "Say Those Magic Words")... 5-10 67
SOLAR (237 "Hangin' Out")... 20-30 67

BLU, Nikki
Singles: 7-inch
PARKWAY... 4-8 64

BLU, Peggi *R&B '87*
Singles: 7-inch
CAPITOL... 3-4 87

BLU, Peggi, & Bert Robinson *R&B '87*
Singles: 7-inch
CAPITOL... 3-4 87
Also see BLU, Peggi
Also see ROBINSON, Bert

BLUE *P&R '77*
Singles: 7-inch
IRIS... 3-4
MCA/PIG (Colored vinyl)... 4-6 77
(Promotional issue only.)
RSO... 3-5 73-75
ROCKET... 3-5 77
LPs: 10/12-inch
RSO... 8-10 73
ROCKET... 5-10 77
Members: Tim Donald; Ian MacMillan; Jimmy McCullough; Hugh Nicholson.
Also see MARMALADE

BLUE, Annie
Singles: 7-inch
20TH FOX... 3-5 75-76

BLUE, Babbity
Singles: 7-inch
LONDON... 4-8 65

BLUE, Barry
Singles: 7-inch
ARISTA... 3-5 75
BELL... 3-5 73-74

BLUE, Bill
LPs: 10/12-inch
ADELPHI... 8-10 79-80
FEATHER... 10-12 75

BLUE, Bobby *C&W '86*
(Bobby & Blue Jays)
Singles: 7-inch
CANADIAN AMERICAN... 5-10 63
HEARTBREAK... 5-10 64
HERALD... 5-10 64
IMPERIAL... 4-8 69-70
LOVE... 8-12 59
MUSIC VOICE... 5-10 64
NITE... 3-4 86

BLUE, David *P&R '73*
(David Cohen)
Singles: 7-inch
ASYLUM... 3-5 73
REPRISE... 3-6 69
LPs: 10/12-inch
ASYLUM... 8-10 73-76
ELEKTRA... 12-15 66
REPRISE... 12-15 68
Also see COUNTRY JOE & FISH

BLUE, Jay
Singles: 7-inch
IMPERIAL (5587 "Get off My Back")... 50-75 59

BLUE, Johnny
Singles: 7-inch
TAMMY (1008 "Runaway Guitar")... 8-12 60

BLUE, Little Joe: see LITTLE JOE BLUE

BLUE, Kattie, & Peppermints
Singles: 7-inch
HOB (114 "Doing All Right")... 30-50 60
Also see PEPPERMINTS

BLUE, Lucy
Singles: 7-inch
BIG TREE... 3-5 71

BLUE, Peggy
Singles: 7-inch
MCA... 3-4 80
LPs: 10/12-inch
MCA... 5-10 80

BLUE, Roger
Singles: 7-inch
CALL (102 "Crazy Mixed-Up World") 4-8 61
Picture Sleeves
CALL (102 "Crazy Mixed-Up World")... 5-10 61
(Has die-cut hole.)

BLUE ANGEL
Singles: 7-inch
POLYDOR... 3-5 81
LPs: 10/12-inch
POLYDOR (6300 "Blue Angel")... 15-25 80
POLYDOR (6300 "Blue Angel")... 50-100 80
(White label. Promotional issue only.)
Members: Cyndi Lauper; John Turi; Art Neilson; Ron Halee; John Morelli; Lee Brovitz.
Also see LAUPER, Cyndi

BLUE ANGELS
Singles: 7-inch
CRAZY (100 "To-Geth-Er")... 50-75 50s

BLUE ANGELS
Singles: 7-inch
EDSEL (781 "Deserie")... 25-50 60
PALETTE... 10-20 60-61

BLUE ANGELS
Singles: 7-inch
SSS INT'L... 10-15 70

BLUE ANGELS
Singles: 7-inch
CAP (076 "Quicksand")... 10-15
CAP (077 "Shake a Tail Feather") 10-15

BLUE ASH
Singles: 7-inch
MERCURY... 3-5 73-74
PLAYBOY... 3-5 77
LPs: 10/12-inch
MERCURY... 10-12 73
PLAYBOY... 8-10 77
Members: Bill Bartolin; David Evans; Jimmy Kendzor; Frank Secich.

BLUE BANANA
Singles: 7-inch
KANWIC (152 "My Luv")... 20-30 67
Picture Sleeves
KANWIC (152 "My Luv")... 30-50 67

BLUE BARRON & His Orchestra *P&R '38*
Singles: 78 rpm
BLUEBIRD... 4-6 38-41
MGM... 3-6 47-55
Singles: 7-inch
MGM... 4-6 50-55
EPs: 7-inch
MGM... 4-8 54-55
LPs: 10/12-inch
MGM... 10-20 54

BLUE BARRONS
LPs: 10/12-inch
PHILIPS... 20-25 62

BLUE BEARDS
(With the Jacks)
Singles: 7-inch
GUIDE (1002 "Romance")... 50-75 58

BLUE BEATS
Singles: 7-inch
BEOWOLF ("Superman")... 20-30 66
(No selection number used.)
COLUMBIA (43790 "Extra Girl")... 15-25 66
COLUMBIA (44098 "Born in Chicago")... 20-30 67
Picture Sleeves
COLUMBIA (43790 "Extra Girl")... 60-80 66
(Promotional issue only.)
LPs: 10/12-inch
A.A. (133 "Beatle Beat")... 20-30 64
Members: Lance Drake; Jack Lee; Peter Robbins; Louie Mazza.
Also see ONE

BLUE BELLES
Singles: 78 rpm
ATLANTIC... 25-50 53
Singles: 7-inch
ATLANTIC (987 "Cancel the Call")... 100-150 53

BLUE BELLES
(Blue-Belles; Starlets)
Singles: 7-inch
PEAK... 10-20 62
RAINBOW (1903 "Youre Just Fooling Yourself")... 10-20
(Selection number may be something other than "1903," which we suspect is just an identification number.)
Picture Sleeves
PEAK... 15-25 62
Also see PATTON, Robert G.
Also see STARLETS

BLUE BELLS
Singles: 7-inch
LAST CHANCE (1 "Atlantis")... 8-12 61

BLUE BELLS (With Patti LaBelle): see LABELLE, Patti

BLUE BOYS
Singles: 7-inch
INDIGO... 5-10 60
U.A.... 5-10 61

BLUE BOYS *C&W '67*
Singles: 7-inch
RCA... 5-10 65-68
LPs: 10/12-inch
RCA... 15-25 65-68
Members: Bud Logan; Leo Jackson; Bunky Keels; Mel Rogers.
Also see LOGAN, Bud, & Wilma Burgess
Also see REEVES, Jim

BLUE BULL
Singles: 7-inch
UNI... 3-6 69

BLUE CHARLIE
Singles: 7-inch
NASCO (6002 "I'm Gonna Kill That Hen")... 50-75 57

BLUE CHEER *P&R/LP '68*
Singles: 7-inch
MERCURY... 3-5 76
PHILIPS... 8-12 68-70
Picture Sleeves
PHILIPS (40516 "Summertime Blues")... 10-15 68
LPs: 10/12-inch
MEGAFORCE... 5-10 85
PHILIPS (9001 "Vincebus Eruption")... 5-10 80
PHILIPS (200264 "Vincebus Eruption")... 40-60 68
(Monaural.)
PHILIPS (600264 "Vincebus Eruption")... 30-50 68
(Stereo.)
PHILIPS (600278 "Outside Inside")... 40-60 68
PHILIPS (600305 "New! Improved!")... 30-50 69
PHILIPS (600333 "Blue Cheer")... 30-50 70
PHILIPS (600347 "Original Human Being")... 30-50 70
PHILIPS (600350 "Oh Pleasant Hope")... 40-60 71
Members: Leigh Stephens; Paul Whaley; Dick Peterson; Randy Holden; Tony Rainer; Bruce Stephens; Ralph Kellogg; Gary Yoder.
Also see GROUP B
Also see HOLDEN, Randy
Also see KAK
Also see MINT TATTOO
Also see OXFORD CIRCLE
Also see PILOT
Also see STEPHENS, Leigh

BLUE CHIEFTAINS
Singles: 7-inch
DIESEL ONLY (8421 "I Think Hank Woulda Dont It This Way")... 3-5 92
(Blue vinyl.)

BLUE CHIPS
Singles: 78 rpm
DELUXE (6100 "Come Back")... 50-100 56
Singles: 7-inch
DELUXE (6100 "Come Back")... 150-200 56
(Black label.)
DELUXE (6100 "Come Back")... 200-225 56
(White label with bio. Promotional issue only.)
Member: Carlton Lankford.

BLUE CHIPS
Singles: 7-inch
GROOVE (0006 "Promise")... 10-20 62
LAUREL (1026 "Double Dutch Twist")... 15-25 61
RCA (7923 "Puddle of Tears")... 10-20 61
RCA (7935 "Let It Ride")... 10-20 61
ROARING... 5-10 67
SHASTAIN (001 "Dynamo")... 20-30 58
WREN (302 "I'm So in Love with You")... 10-20 59
WREN (304 "Little Street")... 10-20 59
WREN (305 "A Song and a Prayer")... 10-20 60

BLUE CHIPS
Singles: 7-inch
SPARTA (001 "Wishing Well")... 500-750 62
(Similar selection number [Sparta 001-BB] used for an Ivorys release.)
Also see IVORYS

BLUE CHRISTIE
Singles: 7-inch
SUN... 3-5 79

BLUE COMETS
Singles: 7-inch
EPIC... 5-8 66
Picture Sleeves
EPIC... 8-12 66

BLUE CRYSTALS
Singles: 7-inch
MERCURY... 5-10 59

BLUE CRYSTALS
Singles: 7-inch
COURIER (116 "Be Bop a Lula")... 10-15

BLUE DIAMONDS
Singles: 78 rpm
SAVOY (1134 "Honey Baby")... 15-25 54
Singles: 7-inch
SAVOY (1134 "Honey Baby")... 35-50 54
Member: Ernie Kador.
Also see K-DOE, Ernie

BLUE DIAMONDS *P&R '60*
Singles: 7-inch
LONDON... 5-10 62-63
LP: 10/12-inch
LONDON... 10-20 63
Members: Riem de Wolf; Rudy de Wolf.

BLUE DOTS
Singles: 78 rpm
DELUXE... 20-40 54
Singles: 7-inch
ACE (526 "Please Don't Tell 'Em")... 40-60 57
DELUXE (6052 "Don't Do That Baby")... 50-75 54
DELUXE (6055 "Don't Hold It")... 75-100 54
DELUXE (6061 "God Loves You") 50-75 54
DELUXE (6067 "Hold Me Tight")... 50-75 54

BLUE ECHOES
Singles: 7-inch
ADERAY (4156 "Rebel Train")... 10-15
ADERAY (5178 "Maharajah of Magador")... 10-15
BON ("It's Witchcraft")... 75-100 58
(No selection number used.)
BRISTOL (101 "Blue Bell Bounce")... 10-15 63
GILSTEN (3134 "Cool Guitar")... 10-20 63
ITZY... 8-12
LAWN (225 "Blue Bell Bounce")... 8-15 63
RAYNARD (10019 "Moonride")... 15-20 65
RAYNARD (4005 "Moonride")... 10-15 68

BLUE EMOTIONS
Singles: 7-inch
AMBIENT SOUND ("Doo Wop All Night Long")... 5-10 82
(Selection number not known.)
LPs: 10/12-inch
AMBIENT SOUND... 10-15 82
Also see EMOTIONS

BLUE EYED SOUL
Singles: 7-inch
CAMEO... 5-10 66
SAND CITY... 5-10
Member: Billy Vera.
Also see VERA, Billy

BLUE FALCONS
Singles: 7-inch
BELMONT (4005 "Run Like the Wind")... 10-20 62

BLUE FEELING
Singles: 7-inch
NIGHT OWL (6861 "Tell Her No") 15-25 68
Members: Ross Baldock; Steve Fuedner; Jack Westfall; Tommy Raml.

BLUE FLAMERS
Singles: 78 rpm
EXCELLO... 25-50 54
Singles: 7-inch
EXCELLO (2026 "Driving Down the Highway")... 50-75 54

BLUE FLAMES
Singles: 7-inch
SPRY (113 "That Crazy Little House")... 75-100 61
SPRY (115 "Close to Me")... 75-125 62
STRAND... 8-12 59

BLUE GIN
Singles: 7-inch
NWI (2767 "Light Blue")... 5-10
Picture Sleeves
NWI (2767 "Light Blue")... 5-10

BLUE GOOSE
LPs: 10/12-inch
ANCHOR... 8-10 75
Members: Nick Hograth; Mike Dodman; Alan Callan; Sean Locke; Chris Perkey; Nick South.

BLUE GRASS ERVIN
Singles: 7-inch
QUEEN... 5-10

BLUE HAZE *P&R '72*
Singles: 7-inch
A&M... 3-5 72-74

BLUE HEAVEN
Singles: 7-inch
EPIC... 3-5 74
LPs: 10/12-inch
EPIC... 8-10 74

BLUE HILLS
Singles: 7-inch
VALIANT... 4-8 64

BLUE HORIZON
Singles: 7-inch
VANGUARD... 3-5 70

BLUE HOUR
Singles: 7-inch
I.R.S. (9932 "Raise the Dragon")... 3-5 84
(Blue vinyl.)
I.R.S. (9932 "Raise the Dragon")... 3-5 84
(Brown vinyl. Promotional issue only.)

BLUE JAYS
Singles: 78 rpm
CHECKER... 250-450 53
Singles: 7-inch
CHECKER (782 "White Cliffs of Dover")... 2000-3000 53

BLUE JAYS
EPs: 7-inch
DIG THIS RECORD (777 "Earth Angel")... 75-100 56
DIG THIS RECORD (778 "Tweedlee Dee")... 75-100 56
(With vocals by Bernie Bridges. Includes one Diggers instrumental.)
Members: Chester Pipkin; Lee Godeau; Don Harris; Dewey Terry.
Also see DON & DEWEY
Also see SQUIRES

BLUE JAYS
Singles: 7-inch
LAURIE... 5-10 59
ROULETTE... 5-10 59-60

BLUE JAYS
(With "Music By Nat Sledge")
Singles: 7-inch
BLUEJAY (1002 "Write Me a Letter") 150-250 61

BLUE JAYS P&R '61
("Lead Vocal - Leon Peels"; Leon Peels & the Bluejays)
Singles: 7-inch
CLASSIC ARTISTS (111 "Once Upon a Love") 4-6 89
COLLECTABLES 3-4 81
ERA 3-5 72
MILESTONE (2008 "Lover's Island") 15-30 61
(Blue label. Opinions differ as to which came first—the dark blue, or light blue and white label.)
MILESTONE (2008 "Lover's Island") 10-15 61
(Green label.)
MILESTONE (2009 "Tears Are Falling") 25-35 61
MILESTONE (2010 "Let's Make Love") 15-25 61
MILESTONE (2012 "The Right to Love") 15-25 62
MILESTONE (2014 "Venus My Love") 50-75 62
Member: Leon Peels.
Also see PEELS, Leon

BLUE JAYS / Little Caesar & Romans
LPs: 10/12-inch
MILESTONE (1001 "Blue Jays Meet Little Caesar & Romans") 50-100 62
(Black vinyl.)
MILESTONE (1001 "Blue Jays Meet Little Caesar & Romans") 150-200 62
(Colored vinyl.)
Also see BLUE JAYS
Also see LITTLE CAESAR & ROMANS

BLUE JAYS
Singles: 7-inch
MAP CITY 3-6 69-71
W.B. 3-6 69
LPs: 10/12-inch
MAP CITY 10-15 70
Also see BLUEJAYS as one word.

BLUE JEANS
Singles: 7-inch
SOUVENIR (1006 "Cool Martini") .. 10-20 61
SOUVENIR (1007 "Moon Mist") 10-20 61

BLUE JUG
Singles: 7-inch
ARIOLA AMERICA 3-4 78
CAPRICORN 3-5 75
LPs: 10/12-inch
ARIOLA AMERICA 5-10 78
CAPRICORN 8-10 75
Members: Bill Burnett; Clint DeLong; Bill Little; Ed Ratzeloff; Paul Walkley.

BLUE KATS
Singles: 7-inch
GAITY (674 "Oh Yeah") 100-200 60s
(Colored vinyl.)

BLUE KNIGHTS
Singles: 7-inch
KITTEN (6970 "Madness") 15-25 59
STRATFORD (6502 "Take the Last Train Home") 10-20

BLUE LIGHTS
Singles: 7-inch
BLACKSBACK 3-4 81

BLUE LITES
Singles: 7-inch
BAY SOUND 20-25

BLUE MAGIC R&B '73
Singles: 12-inch
MIRAGE 4-6 83
Singles: 7-inch
ATCO 3-5 73-76
CAPITOL 3-4 81
LIBERTY 3-6 69
MIRAGE 3-4 83
WMOT 3-5 76
LPs: 10/12-inch
ATCO 8-10 74-77
ATLANTIC 5-10 83
CAPITOL 5-10 81
COLLECTABLES 6-8 86
MIRAGE 5-10 83
Members: Ted Mills; Margie Joseph; Vernon Sawyer; Wendell Sawyer; Richard Pratt; Keath Beaton.
Also see JOSEPH, Margie

BLUE MARBLE
Singles: 7-inch
A&M 3-5 74
LPs: 10/12-inch
A&M 8-10 74

BLUE MARBLE FAUN
Singles: 7-inch
LOOK 4-8 68-69

BLUE MERCEDES P&R/LP '88
Singles: 7-inch
MCA 3-4 88
Picture Sleeves
MCA 3-4 88
LPs: 10/12-inch
MCA 5-8 88
Members: David Titlow; Duncan Millar.

BLUE MINK P&R '70
Singles: 7-inch
BELL 3-5 71-72
MCA 3-5 73-74
PHILIPS 3-6 69-70
Picture Sleeves
PHILIPS 4-8 70
LPs: 10/12-inch
MCA 8-10 73
PHILIPS 12-15 69-70
Members: Madeline Bell; Roger Cook; Barry Morgan; Herbie Flowers; Alan Parker; Ann Odell; Roger Coulan; Ray Cooper.
Also see BELL, Madeline
Also see COOK, Roger

BLUE MITCHELL: see MITCHELL, Blue

BLUE MOONS
Singles: 7-inch
JAGUAR 8-10

BLUE MOUNTAIN EAGLE
Singles: 7-inch
ATCO 3-5 70
LPs: 10/12-inch
ATCO 15-20 70

BLUE MURDER LP '89
Singles: 7-inch
GEFFEN 3-4 89
LPs: 10/12-inch
GEFFEN 5-8 89
Member: Tony Franklin.
Also see FIRM

BLUE NILE LP '90
LPs: 10/12-inch
A&M 5-8 90

BLUE NOTES
(With Melino & His Orchestra)
Singles: 78 rpm
RAMA (25 "If You'll Be Mine") 50-75 53
TICO (1083 "Charlotte Amalie") 40-60 54
Singles: 7-inch
PORT (70021 "If You Love Me") 25-50 58
RAMA (25 "If You'll Be Mine") 200-300 53
TICO (1083 "Charlotte Amalie") 100-200 54

BLUE NOTES P&R '60
Singles: 78 rpm
JOSIE 35-75 56-57
Singles: 7-inch
COLLECTABLES 3-4 81
GAMUT (1000 "My Heart Cries for You") 15-25 61
JALYNNE 20-40 60
(Title and number not known.)
JOSIE (800 "If You Love Me") ... 100-200 56
JOSIE (814 "Letters") 75-125 57
JOSIE (823 "Retribution Blues") ... 75-125 57
LOST NITE 4-8
RED TOP (135 "My Hero") 20-40 63
3 SONS (103 "W-P-L-J") 50-100 62
UNI 5-10 69
VAL-UE (213 "My Hero") 50-100 60
VAL-UE (215 "O Holy Night") 50-100 60
LPs: 10/12-inch
COLLECTABLES 5-10 82
Members: Harold Melvin; Jesse Gillis Jr.; Roosevelt Brodie; Frank Peaker; Bernard Williams; John Atkins; Lawrence Brown.
Also see BLUENOTES
Also see MELVIN, Harold, & Blue Notes
Also see RANDALL, Todd

BLUE NOTES
Singles: 7-inch
COLONIAL (434 "Page One") 10-15 58
COLONIAL (9999 "Never Never Land") 10-15 58
TNT (150 "Darling of Mine") 15-25 58

BLUE NOTES
Singles: 7-inch
INSTANT ACTION (101 "She Is Mine") 50-75 60s
LOST (104 "She Is Mine") 150-250 60
(First issue.)

BLUE NOTES
Singles: 7-inch
ACCENT (1069 "Your Tender Lips") 10-20 61
TWENTIETH CENTURY (1213 "Blue Star") 10-15 61

BLUE NOTES
Singles: 7-inch
BLUCO ("Rigor Mortis") 10-20 60
(No selection number used.)

BLUE NOTES
Singles: 7-inch
U.A. 5-10 62

BLUE NOTES
Singles: 7-inch
HARTHON (136 "Needless to Say") 8-12 64
LANDA (703 "You May Not Love Me") 10-15 64

BLUE NOTES
Singles: 12-inch
FANTASY 4-6 78
Singles: 7-inch
ABC 3-5
CHECKER 4-8 68
FANTASY 3-4 78
UNI 3-6 69
LPs: 10/12-inch
GLADES 5-10 77

BLUE ORCHIDS
Singles: 7-inch
LONDON 5-8

BLUE OYSTER CULT LP '72
Singles: 12-inch
COLUMBIA 4-6 80
Singles: 7-inch
COLUMBIA 3-4 72-84
WHAT'S IT ALL ABOUT 8-12
(Promotional issue only.)
Picture Sleeves
COLUMBIA (02000 & 04000 series) ... 3-4 81-84
COLUMBIA (45000 series) 4-8 72
EPs: 7-inch
COLUMBIA (40 "Bootleg EP") 20-25 72
LPs: 10/12-inch
ABC RADIO ("A Night on the Road") 35-50 81
(Promotional issue only.)
COLUMBIA (Except 31000 thru 33000 series) 5-10 76-84
COLUMBIA (31000 thru 33000 series) 6-12 72-75
Members: Al Bouchard; Joe Bouchard; Eric Bloom; Alan Lanier; Donald "Buck Dharma" Roeser.
Also see SOFT WHITE UNDERBELLY

BLUE PRINT D&D '83
Singles: 12-inch
FANTASY 4-6 83

BLUE RAYS
Singles: 7-inch
PHILIPS 8-10 64

BLUE REALM
Singles: 7-inch
OASIS 4-8 67

BLUE RIDGE RANGERS C&W/P&R '73
(John Fogerty)
Singles: 7-inch
FANTASY 3-5 72-73
Picture Sleeves
FANTASY 4-8 72
LPs: 10/12-inch
FANTASY 10-12 73
Also see FOGERTY, John

BLUE RODEO
Singles: 7-inch
ATLANTIC 3-4 88
Picture Sleeves
ATLANTIC 3-4 88

BLUE RONDOS
Singles: 7-inch
PARKWAY 5-10 64

BLUE ROSE
Singles: 7-inch
EPIC 3-5 72
ESTATE 3-4 83
LPs: 10/12-inch
EPIC 12-15 72
ESTATE 5-10 83

BLUE SANDLEWOOD SOAP
Singles: 7-inch
AESOP'S LABLE (103 "Friends I Haven't Met Yet") 10-15 68

BLUE SATINS
Singles: 7-inch
SCARLET 8-12

BLUE SCEPTER
Singles: 7-inch
RARE EARTH 10-15 72
Also see SRC

BLUE SHOES
Singles: 7-inch
LIVING ROOM 3-4 81
Picture Sleeves
LIVING ROOM 3-4 81

BLUE SMITTY & HIS STRING MEN
(Clarence Smith)
Singles: 78 rpm
CHESS (1522 "Crying") 25-50 52
Singles: 7-inch
CHESS (1522 "Crying") 75-100 52

BLUE SMOKE
(With Blue Smoke)
LPs: 10/12-inch
MANSION 8-10 88
Members: Bill Turner; Eric Knutsen; John Triolo; Tony Benson; Laura Marie Tate; Kathy Forgetta; Keith Sammut; John Widgren; Ira Zadikow; Tim Sullivan; Jay Richards.

BLUE SONNETS
Singles: 7-inch
COLUMBIA (42793 "Thank You Mr Moon") 30-40 63
Member: Eric Nathanson.
Also see VOCALAIRES

BLUE SOUNDS
Singles: 7-inch
FONTANA 4-8 65

BLUE STARS P&R '55
Singles: 78 rpm
MERCURY 3-6 55-56
Singles: 7-inch
MERCURY 5-10 55-56
Member: Blossom Dearie.

BLUE STARS
Singles: 7-inch
ARCADE (Black vinyl) 3-5 76
ARCADE (Colored vinyl) 4-8 76

BLUE STEEL
Singles: 7-inch
ASYLUM 3-4 81
INFINITY 3-4 79
LPs: 10/12-inch
ELEKTRA 5-10 80
INFINITY 5-10 79

BLUE STONE
Singles: 7-inch
DIMENSIONS 3-4 80

BLUE STREAM
Singles: 7-inch
CATAMOUNT (133 "I Want a Girl") 15-25 66

BLUE SUBWAY
Singles: 7-inch
DECCA 4-8 68

BLUE SWEDE P&R/LP '74
Singles: 7-inch
EMI AMERICA 3-5 73-75
Picture Sleeves
EMI AMERICA 3-5 73-74
LPs: 10/12-inch
EMI AMERICA 8-10 74-75
Members: Bjorn Skifs; Jan Guldback; Bosse Liljedahl; Michael Areklew; Ladislau Balaz; Tommy Berglund; Hinke Ekestubble.
Also see SKIFS, Bjorn

BLUE TALE FLY
Singles: 7-inch
CHIEF OSHKOSH 4-8 70s
Member: Pat Nugent.
Also see COBBLERS

BLUE TATTOO
Singles: 7-inch
PARAMOUNT 3-5 72

BLUE THINGS: see BLUETHINGS

BLUE TONES
Singles: 7-inch
BLUE JAY 5-10
GUSTO 3-5 84
KING (5088 "Shake Shake") 20-30 57
REGENCY (670 "Shake Shake") ... 40-60 57
Member: Billy Gayles.

BLUE VELVET BAND
Singles: 7-inch
W.B. 3-6 69
LPs: 10/12-inch
W.B. 15-20 69

BLUE VELVETS: see FOGERTY, Tom

BLUE WOOD
Singles: 7-inch
JET SET 4-8

BLUE YONDER
Singles: 7-inch
ATLANTIC 3-4 87
Picture Sleeves
ATLANTIC 3-4 87

BLUE ZONE U.K. P&R '88
Singles: 7-inch
ARISTA 3-4 88
Picture Sleeves
ARISTA 3-4 88
Members: Lisa Stansfield; Andy Morris; Ian Devaney.

BLUE ZOO
Singles: 12-inch
RCA 4-6 83
LPs: 10/12-inch
RCA 5-10 83

BLUEBEARDS
Singles: 7-inch
DATE 5-10 67
GUIDE 20-40 60s

BLUEBELLS
Singles: 7-inch
TREND (30002 "Squeegie") 15-25 59

BLUEBELLS
Singles: 7-inch
SIRE 3-4 84
LPs: 10/12-inch
SIRE 5-10 83-85

BLUEBERRY HILL BAND
Singles: 7-inch
TOWER 4-8 66

BLUEBIRD
Singles: 7-inch
BUDDAH 3-5 70
BURDETTE 4-8
JERDEN 5-10 60s
PICADILLY 10-15 60s
LPs: 10/12-inch
PICADILLY ("Country Boy Blues") 40-60 60s
(Selection number not known.)

BLUEBIRDS
Singles: 78 rpm
RAINBOW 200-300 53

BLUEDOTS
Singles: 7-inch
HURRICANE (104 "My Very Own") 100-200 59

BLUEFIELD
Singles: 7-inch
MERCURY 3-5 76

LPs: 10/12-inch
MERCURY 8-10 75

BLUEJAYS: see BLUE JAYS

BLUEJEANS
Singles: 7-inch
SOUVENIR 5-10 61

BLUENOTES P&R '59
Singles: 7-inch
BROOKE (111 "I Don't Know What It Is") 10-20 59
BROOKE (116 "Forever on My Mind") 10-20 60
BROOKE (119 "Summer Love") 10-20 60
Picture Sleeves
BROOKE 25-45 60
Members: Tom Underwood; Joe Tanner; Pat Patterson; Ralph Harrington.
Also see BLUE NOTES
Also see FRANKLIN, Doug
Also see HAMILTON, George, IV

BLUENOTES / Five Echoes / Five Chances
LPs: 10/12-inch
CONSTELLATION (5 "Collectors Showcase, Groups Three") 20-25 64
Also see BLUENOTES
Also see FIVE CHANCES
Also see FIVE ECHOES

BLUE-NOTES
Singles: 7-inch
BEECH WOOD (1000 "Shake It Up") 10-20 65

BLUEPRINT
Singles: 12-inch
FANTASY 4-6 83
Singles: 7-inch
FANTASY 3-4 83

BLUEPRINTS
Singles: 7-inch
EXCALIBUR (101 "I've Been Duped") 8-12

BLUERAYS
Singles: 7-inch
PHILIPS 4-8 64

BLU-EREBUS
Singles: 7-inch
KING JAMES (9255 "Plastic Year") 10-20 60s

BLUES, Los: see LOS BLUES

BLUES BLASTERS
LPs: 10/12-inch
RIGHT ON RED 8-10

BLUES BOY
(Guitar Slim & Jelly Belly)
Singles: 78 rpm
SUPER DISC (1053 "In Love Blues") 20-40 48
TRU-BLUE (101 "Smilin' Blues") 25-50 47
TRUE BLUES (102 "Ungrateful Woman Blues") 25-50 47
LPs: 10/12-inch
ARHOOLIE 10-15
Also see BACK PORCH BOYS
Also see BLUES KING
Also see SEWARD, Slim, & Fat Boy Hayes

BLUES BOY WILLIE
LPs: 10/12-inch
ICHIBAN 5-10

BLUES BOY BILL: see BLUESBOY BILL

BLUES BREAKERS: see MAYALL, John

BLUES BROTHERS P&R/LP '78
Singles: 7-inch
ATLANTIC 3-5 78-81
(Black vinyl.)
ATLANTIC 5-10
(Colored vinyl. Promotional issue only.)
Picture Sleeves
ATLANTIC 3-6 78-80
LPs: 10/12-inch
ATLANTIC 10-15 78-81
Members: Dan Aykroyd; John Belushi.
Also see AYKROYD, Dan, & Pattie Brooks
Also see BELUSHI, John

BLUES BUSTERS
Singles: 7-inch
BRA 5-10
CAPITOL 5-10 62
NEW ORLEANS 5-10 62
SHOUT 4-8 68

BLUES CLIMAX
LPs: 10/12-inch
HORNE (333 "Blues Climax") 50-75 69
HORNE (888 "The Alan Franklin Explosion") 50-75 70
Members: Alan Franklin; Chris Russel; Dave Dix; Buzzy Meekins; Bill Vermillion.

BLUES COMPANY
Singles: 7-inch
GREAT LAKES (3002 "Experiment in Color") 10-20
PEAR ("Love Machine") 25-35
(No selection number used.)
PEAR ("You're Dead My Friend") 25-35
(No selection number used.)

BLUES CRUSADER
Singles: 7-inch
SHOW TOWN 3-6 69

BLUES DIMENSION
Singles: 7-inch
HAVOC (141 "Chains") ... 3-6 60s
Picture Sleeves
HAVOC (141 "Chains") ... 4-8 60s

BLUES EXPRESS ORCH.
Singles: 78 rpm
GEM (206 "Honkin' Away") ... 15-20 53
Singles: 7-inch
GEM (206 "Honkin' Away") ... 30-40 53

BLUES GROOVE
Singles: 7-inch
VERVE ... 4-8 66

BLUES IMAGE LP '69
Singles: 7-inch
ATCO ... 4-8 69-71
LPs: 10/12-inch
ATCO ... 10-20 69-70
Members: Mike Pinera; Joe Lala; Frank Konte; Malcolm Jones; Manuel Bertematti.
Also see PINERA, Mike

BLUES INC.
Singles: 7-inch
POWER (19362 "Out of the Darkness") ... 15-25 60s
UNITED AUDIO ("7 and 7 Is") ... 25-35 60s
(Selection number not known.)

BLUES KING
Singles: 78 rpm
SOLO ... 25-50 46
Members: Alec Seward; Louis Hayes.
Also see BLUES BOY
Also see SEWARD, Alec, & Louis Hayes

BLUES KINGS
Singles: 7-inch
D (1061 "Lover Come Back") ... 30-40 59

BLUES MAGOOS P&R/LP '66
Singles: 7-inch
ABC ... 4-8 68-70
GANIM (1000 "Who Do You Love") ... 20-40 69
MERCURY (30000 series) ... 3-5 76
MERCURY (70000 series) ... 8-12 66-68
VERVE/FOLKWAYS (5006 "So I'm Wrong") ... 20-30 66
VERVE/FOLKWAYS (5044 "So I'm Wrong") ... 15-25 67
Picture Sleeves
MERCURY (72660 "Pipe Dream") .10-20 67
MERCURY (72692 "One by One") .10-20 67
LPs: 10/12-inch
ABC ... 8-10 69-70
MERCURY (21096 "Psychedelic Lollipop") ... 40-50 66
(Monaural.)
MERCURY (21104 "Electric Comic Book") ... 30-40 67
(Monaural. Add $5 to $10 if accompanied by comic book insert.)
MERCURY (61096 "Psychedelic Lollipop") ... 25-40 66
(Red label. Stereo.)
MERCURY (61096 "Psychedelic Lollipop") ... 8-10
(Chicago "skyline" label.)
MERCURY (61104 "Electric Comic Book") ... 30-45 67
(Stereo. Add $5 to $10 if accompanied by comic book insert.)
MERCURY (61167 "Basic Blues Magoos") ... 20-30 68
Members: Geoff Daking; Mike Esposito; Ron Gilbert; Ralph Scala; Emil Thielhelm.
Also see BALANCE
Also see FELIX & ESCORTS

BLUES PROJECT LP '66
Singles: 7-inch
CAPITOL ... 5-8 72
MCA ... 3-5 73
VERVE/FOLKWAYS ... 10-15 66-67
LPs: 10/12-inch
CAPITOL ... 10-15 72
ELEKTRA ... 5-10 80
MCA ... 8-10 73
MGM ... 8-12 70-74
VERVE/FOLKWAYS ... 15-25 66
VERVE/FORECAST ... 12-20 66-70
Members: Al Kooper; Roy Blumenfeld; David Cohen; Tommy Flanders; Richard Green; John Gregory; Don Gretmar; Danny Kalb; Steve Katz; Andy Kulbert; Bill Lussenden; Chicken Hirsch.
Also see KOOPER, Al
Also see SEATRAIN

BLUES ROCKERS
Singles: 78 rpm
ARISTOCRAT (407 "Trouble in My Home") ... 25-50 50
ARISTOCRAT (413 "When Times Are Getting Better") ... 25-50 50
CHESS (1483 "Little Boy, Little Boy") ... 25-50 50
EXCELLO (2062 "Calling All Cows") ... 15-25 55
Singles: 7-inch
EXCELLO (2062 "Calling All Cows") ... 30-50 55

BLUES SCENE
Singles: 7-inch
UNI ... 4-8 67

BLUES SLIM
Singles: 7-inch
PIONEER INT'L ... 5-10 61

BLUES TRAVELER LP '91
LPs: 10/12-inch
A&M ... 5-8 91

BLUES WOMAN R&B '46
(Marion Abernathy)
Singles: 78 rpm
JUKE BOX ... 10-15 46
Also see ABERNATHY, Marion

BLUESBAG
Singles: 7-inch
PSYCHEDELIC (101 "I Wanna Be Your Lovin' Man") ... 4-6

BLUESBOY BILL
Singles: 78 rpm
BLUESMAN (101 "Come On Baby") ... 50-100 48

BLUESBUSTERS
Singles: 7-inch
CAPITOL ... 4-8 67
U.A. ... 4-8 67
LPs: 10/12-inch
U.A. INT'L ... 15-20 67

BLUESBUSTERS
LPs: 10/12-inch
LANDSLIDE ... 8-10 86
Member: Catfish Hodge.
Also see CATFISH

BLUESMEN REVUE
Singles: 7-inch
COLUMBIA ... 4-8 68

BLUESTONE C&W '80
Singles: 7-inch
DIMENSION ... 3-5 80
SCOTTI BROTHERS ... 3-4 82
Members: Ray Pennington; Jerry McBee.
Also see PENNINGTON, Ray

BLUESTYLE
Singles: 7-inch
YORKSHIRE (153 "Night Time Woman") ... 15-25

BLUESVILLE
Singles: 7-inch
JERDEN (788 "As Tears Go By") ... 8-12 66

BLUESY MAE MAE
Singles: 7-inch
CAMARO (3446 "He's an Ugly Man") ... 10-20 60s

BLUETHINGS
(Blue Things)
Singles: 7-inch
RCA (8692 "La Do Da Da") ... 15-25 65
RCA (8860 "Doll House") ... 15-25 66
RCA (8998 "The Orange Rooftop of Your Mind") ... 15-25 66
RCA (9203 "Twist & Shout") ... 15-25 67
RCA (9308 "Somebody Help Me") .15-25 67
RUFF (1000 "Mary Lou") ... 25-35 65
RUFF (1002 "Pretty Thing") ... 25-35 65
Picture Sleeves
RCA (8692 "La Do Da Da") ... 25-40 66
LPs: 10/12-inch
CICADELIC ... 8-10 87
RCA (LPM-3603 "Blue Things") ... 60-80 66
(Monaural.)
RCA (LSP-3603 "Blue Things") ... 75-100 66
(Stereo.)
Members: Van Stoecklein; Richard Scott; Robert Day; Larry Burton; Mike Chapman.
Also see STOECKLEIN, Val

BLUETONES
(With "Lead Vocal By Joe Villa")
Singles: 7-inch
BLUEJAY (101 "I'll Love You") ... 200-300 65
(Reissued on Swan as by the Royal Teens.)
Also see ROYAL TEENS
Also see VILLA, Joey

BLUEWATER
Singles: 7-inch
H&L ... 3-5 77
LPs: 10/12-inch
H&L ... 5-10 77

BLUJAYS
Singles: 7-inch
BLUJAY (1002 "Write Me a Letter") ... 300-400 61

BLUNSTONE, Colin
Singles: 7-inch
EPIC ... 3-5 72-73
ROCKET ... 3-5 78
LPs: 10/12-inch
EPIC ... 10-12 72-74
ROCKET ... 5-10 78
Also see KEATS
Also see PARSONS, Alan
Also see ZOMBIES

BLUR, Ben
Singles: 7-inch
MARK X (8007 "Chariot Race") ... 10-20 60
Also see PARSONS, Alan, Project

BLUSHING BRIDES
LPs: 10/12-inch
RCA ... 5-10 83

BO, Billy, & Arrows
Singles: 7-inch
POLARIS (400 "Voodoo Rhythm") 10-20 66

BO, Eddie P&R/R&B '69
Singles: 78 rpm
ACE (515 "I'm So Tired") ... 10-20 56
APOLLO (486 thru 504) ... 10-20 55-56
APOLLO (509 "Dearest One") ... 30-60 57
Singles: 7-inch
ACE (515 "I'm So Tired") ... 25-35 56
ACE (555 "I'll Keep on Trying") ... 15-25 59
APOLLO (486 "I'm Wise") ... 30-50 56
APOLLO (496 "Please Forget Me") ... 30-50 56
APOLLO (499 "I Cry Oh") ... 30-50 56
APOLLO (504 "Tell Me Why") ... 40-60 56
APOLLO (509 "Dearest One") ... 40-60 57
AT LAST ... 8-12 63
BLUE JAY (154 "Come to Me") ... 4-8 64
BO-SOUND ... 3-5 71
CAPITOL (4617 "Dinky Doo") ... 8-10 61
CHECKER (877 "Indeed I Do") ... 10-15 58
CHESS (1692 "My Dearest Darling") ... 10-15 58
CHESS (1833 "You Are the Only One") ... 8-10 62
CINDERELLA (1203 "Shake, Rock & Soul") ... 8-12 63
RIC (156 "You Are the Only One") ... 10-15 62
RIC (962 "Hey There Baby") ... 10-15 59
RIC (964 "You Got Your Mojo Working") ... 10-15 59
RIC (969 "Tell It Like It Is") ... 10-15 60
RIC (981 "Dinky Doo") ... 10-15 61
RIC (987 "Check Mr. Popeye") ... 10-15 62
RIC (985 "I Got to Know") ... 8-12 59
RIP ... 10-20
SEVEN B ... 4-8 66-68
SCRAM ... 4-8 69
SWAN (4099 "Check Mr. Popeye") .. 8-10 62
ZIP (803 "You Are the Only One") .10-15 62
LPs: 10/12-inch
ROUNDER ... 5-8
Also see LITTLE BO
Also see PARKER, Robert

BO, Eddie, & Inez Cheatham
Singles: 7-inch
SEVEN B ... 4-8 68
Also see BO, Eddie

BO, Little
(Eddie Bo)
Singles: 78 rpm
ACE (501 "Baby") ... 25-50 55
Singles: 7-inch
ACE (501 "Baby") ... 50-75 55
Also see BO, Eddie

BO, Phil
Singles: 7-inch
JIN (123 "Tough") ... 10-20 60
SMASH ... 5-10 62

BO & RUTH: see KIRKLAND, Bo, & Ruth Davis

BO & BELIEVERS
Singles: 7-inch
ELF ... 4-8 68

BO & WEEVILS
Singles: 7-inch
ALLEN (1001 "My Time") ... 20-30 69
ALLEN (1004 "Love Hurts") ... 20-30 69
SAHARA (513 "Rosalee") ... 20-30

BO DIDDLEY: see DIDDLEY, Bo

BO GRUMPUS
LPs: 10/12-inch
ATCO (246 "Before the War") ... 15-20 68
Members: Ronnie Blake; Jim Colegrove; Joe Hutchinson; Ed Mottau.
Also see JOLLIVER ARKANSAS

BO PETE
(Harry Nilsson)
Singles: 7-inch
CRUSADER (103 "Baa Baa Black Sheep") ... 20-30 64
TRY (501 "Groovy Little Suzy") ... 20-40 64
Also see NILSSON

BO STREET RUNNERS
Singles: 7-inch
KR (104 "Aladdin") ... 25-35
(Single-sided promotional issue.)

BO WEEVELS
(Carl Lertzman & Bo-Weevels)
Singles: 7-inch
UNITED STATES (1934 "The Beetles Will Getcha") ... 8-12 64
Picture Sleeves
UNITED STATES (1934 "The Beetles Will Getcha") ... 10-20 64

BOA
LPs: 10/12-inch
SNAKEFIELD (001 "Wrong Road") ... 200-300 69
Members: Bob Maledon; Brian Walton.

BOA
Singles: 7-inch
WOODEN NICKEL ... 3-5 75
LPs: 10/12-inch
WOODEN NICKEL ... 10-15 75

BOARDMAN HIGH SCHOOL CHOIR
Singles: 7-inch
CAPRICE ... 4-8 60

BOARDO, Liz C&W '87
Singles: 7-inch
MASTER ... 3-4 87

BOATMAN, Tooter
Singles: 7-inch
GAYLO ... 5-10 62
REBEL (108 "Poor Gal") ... 150-200 58
TWINKLE (501 "Thunder and Lightning") ... 150-200 58
Also see CHAPARRALS

BOATWRIGHT, Henry
Singles: 7-inch
CAPITOL ... 3-6 68

BOATZ
Singles: 7-inch
CAPRICORN ... 3-4 79

BOB & AVERONES
Singles: 7-inch
BRENT ... 8-12 66

BOB & BARRY
Singles: 7-inch
ACCENT ... 4-8 62

BOB & BOB
Singles: 7-inch
POLYDOR ... 3-4 83
LPs: 10/12-inch
POLYDOR ... 5-10 83

BOB & BOBBY
Singles: 7-inch
TOWER (154 "12:04") ... 15-25 65

BOB & CAROL
Singles: 7-inch
W.B. ... 5-10 60-61
Members: Bob Montgomery; Carol Montgomery.
Also see MONTGOMERY, Bob

BOB & DELCADES
Singles: 7-inch
FOX (107 "A New Day") ... 50-75 59

BOB & DENNY
Singles: 7-inch
HEP (2145 "Hush, Hush Little Baby") ... 25-35 59

BOB & EARL
Singles: 7-inch
CLASS (213 "That's My Desire") ... 20-30 57
CLASS (231 "Gee Whiz") ... 15-25 58
CLASS (232 "Chains of Love") ... 15-25 58
CLASS (247 "That's My Desire") ... 10-20 59
HI OLDIES ... 3-5
MALYNN (232 "Chains of Love") ... 10-20 59
Members: Bobby Byrd; Earl Nelson.
Also see BYRD, Bobby
Also see HOLLYWOOD FLAMES
Also see LEE, Jackie

BOB & EARL P&R '62
(With René Hall Orchestra)
Singles: 7-inch
ABC ... 3-5 73
CHENE (103 "Sissy Baby") ... 5-10 64
COLLECTABLES ... 3-4 81
CRESTVIEW (9011 "Dancing Everywhere") ... 4-8 69
ISLAND ... 3-5
LOMA (2004 "Everybody Jerk") ... 5-10 64
MARC (104 "Harlem Shuffle") ... 8-12 63
MARC (105 "Puppet on a String") .. 10-15 64
MARC (106 "Baby, Your Time Is My Time") ... 10-15 64
MIRWOOD (5507 "It's Over") ... 8-12 66
MIRWOOD (5517 "Baby, It's Over") .. 5-8 66
(Reissue. Note slight title change.)
MIRWOOD (5526 "Baby, Your Time Is My Time") ... 5-8 66
TEMPE (102 "Don't Ever Leave Me") ... 15-25 62
TEMPE (104 "Oh Baby Doll") ... 15-25 62
TIP (1013 "As We Dance") ... 8-12 64
UNI (55196 "Love's Vibration") ... 4-8 70
UNI (55248 "Honey, Sugar, My Sweet Thing") ... 4-8 70
WHITE WHALE (310 "Harlem Shuffle") ... 10-15 69
LPs: 10/12-inch
CRESTVIEW (3055 "Bob & Earl") .15-20 69
TIP (9011 "Harlem Shuffle") ... 20-30 64
UPFRONT (118 "Bob & Earl") ... 10-15
Members: Bobby Relf; Earl Nelson; Earl Wilson.
Also see HALL, René
Also see NELSON, Earl
Also see WHITE, Barry

BOB & EARL / Gene Allison
Singles: 7-inch
TRIP (75 "Harlem Shuffle"/"You Can Make It if You Try") ... 3-5 75
Also see ALLISON, Gene
Also see BOB & EARL

BOB & EARL
Singles: 7-inch
BIG MACK (6101 "I'll Be on My Way") ... 100-200

BOB & GENE
(With Mama Spiegleman)
Singles: 7-inch
ACCENT ... 5-10 66

BOB & JERRY
Singles: 7-inch
COLUMBIA ... 4-8 61
MUSICOR ... 4-8 62
RENDEZVOUS ... 5-10 59
Members: Bob Feldman; Jerry Goldstein.

BOB & JIM
Singles: 7-inch
COLUMBIA (41487 "Stood Up") ... 10-15 59
COLUMBIA (41559 "I Love Only You") ... 10-15 60
SUNBEAM (129 "Dumbell") ... 10-15 59

BOB & JOE
Singles: 7-inch
A (112 "Little Girl of My Dreams") .. 10-20 61
A (318 "Suzie Q") ... 10-20 61

BOB & JUDY
Singles: 7-inch
IMPRESSION ... 4-8 65

BOB & JUSTINE
Singles: 7-inch
FRANSIL ... 10-20

BOB & KEN
Singles: 7-inch
W.B. ... 4-8 63

BOB & KIM
Singles: 7-inch
DOT ... 4-8 66

BOB & KIT
Singles: 7-inch
HBR ... 4-8 66
Picture Sleeves
HBR ... 5-10 66

BOB & LARRY
Singles: 7-inch
KING ... 5-8 60-61

BOB & LUCILLE
Singles: 7-inch
DITTO (121 "Eeny Meeny Miney Moe") ... 50-75 62
DITTO (126 "What's the Password") ... 50-75 62
KING (5631 "Eeny Meeny Miney Moe") ... 20-30 62
Member: Lucille Starr.
Also see CANADIAN SWEETHEARTS
Also see REGAN, Bob, & Lucille Starr
Also see STARR, Lucille

BOB & MARCIA
Singles: 7-inch
A&M ... 3-5 71
EPIC ... 3-5 73
TAMLA ... 3-5 70

BOB & MESSENGERS
Singles: 7-inch
RUST (5069 "Splash Down") ... 10-20 63

BOB & MICHÉLE
Singles: 7-inch
BOSH ... 5-8

BOB & NEPTUNES
Singles: 7-inch
CARRIE ... 8-12

BOB & PEGGY
Singles: 7-inch
PEACOCK (1927 "Everybody's Talking") ... 5-10 63

BOB & PHIL
Singles: 7-inch
PROJECT 3 (1302 "Pussyfoot") ... 10-20 61

BOB & RAY
Singles: 78 rpm
ACE ("Mule Train") ... 10-20 49
(With Mary McGoon.)
CORAL ... 5-10 56
Singles: 7-inch
CORAL (61338 "This Is Your Bed") ... 10-15 56
LPs: 10/12-inch
B&R CLASSICS ... 10-20
COLUMBIA (30412 "The Two and Only") ... 10-15 71
(Original cast.)
GEG ... 8-12 76
GENESIS ... 8-12 73-76
GOULDING-ELLIOT-GREYBAR (112301 "Mary Backstage, Nobel Wife") ... 30-40
RCA (1773 "Stereo Spectacular") .30-40 58
RCA (2131 "Bob & Ray on a Platter") ... 20-30 59
U.S. ENVIRONMENTAL PROTECTION SOCIETY (72435 "Bob & Ray") ... 25-35
(Promotional issue only.)
UNICORN (1001 "Write If You Get Work") ... 20-40 54
(10-inch LP.)
Members: Bob Elliott; Ray Goulding.
Also see ELLIOTT, Bob

BOB & RAY
Singles: 7-inch
MODERN SOUND ... 10-20
NASCO ... 10-15 59

BOB & ROBYN
(Bob 'N Robyn)
Singles: 7-inch
LINDA ... 4-8 65

BOB & ROCKBILLIES
Singles: 7-inch
BLUE CHIP (11 "Your Kind of Love") ... 30-50 57

BOB & SHERI
Singles: 7-inch
SAFARI (101 "Surfer Moon") ... 600-800 61
(Brian Wilson's first record production. Original commercial copies had a light blue label; promotional copies had a white label. Beware! Near-perfect counterfeits exist.)
Members: Bob Norberg; Sheri Pomeroy.
Also see SURVIVORS
Also see WILSON, Brian

BOB & SHIRLEY
Singles: 7-inch
BAND BOX..................5-10 60

BOB & TRAVIS
Singles: 7-inch
MERCURY..................5-8 61

BOB B. SOXX & BLUE JEANS P&R/R&B '62
Singles: 7-inch
PHILLES (107 "Zip-a-Dee Doo-Dah")..................10-15 62
PHILLES (110 "Why Do Lovers Break Each Other's Heart")..................10-15 63
PHILLES (113 "Not Too Young to Get Married")..................10-15 63
LPs: 10/12-inch
PHILLES (4002 "Zip-a-Dee Doo-Dah")..................75-125 63
Members: Bobby Sheen; Darlene Love; Carolyn Willis; Fanita James-Barrett.
Also see BLOSSOMS
Also see HONEY CONE
Also see LOVE, Darlene
Also see RONETTES / Crystals / Darlene Love / Bob B. Soxx & Blue Jeans
Also see SHEEN, Bobby

BOB'S BOYS
Singles: 78 rpm
CONTINENTAL..................3-6

BOBBEJAAN
Singles: 7-inch
PALETTE..................4-8 62

BOBBETTES P&R/R&B '57
Singles: 78 rpm
ATLANTIC..................20-40 57
Singles: 7-inch
ATLANTIC..................15-25 57-60
DIAMOND..................8-12 62-65
END..................10-20 61
GALLIANT..................10-20 60
GONE..................10-20 61
JUBILEE..................8-12 62
KING..................8-12 61-62
MAYHEW..................3-5 72-74
RCA..................10-20 66
TRIPLE-X..................10-20 60
Members: Emma Pought; Jannie Pought; Heather Dixon; Laura Webb; Helen Gathers.
Session: King Curtis.
Also see KING, Ben E.
Also see KING CURTIS

BOBBI & MICHI
Singles: 7-inch
JOSIE..................5-10 66

BOBBIDAZZLER
Singles: 7-inch
A&M..................3-5 75
LPs: 10/12-inch
RCA..................5-10 77

BOBBIE & BEAUS
Singles: 7-inch
UNART..................10-15 59

BOBBIE & BOOBIE
Singles: 7-inch
DICE (480 "Teenage Party")......100-150

BOBBIE & BOYS
Singles: 7-inch
PHILLIPS INT'L..................10-15 59

BOBBIE & PLEASERS
Singles: 7-inch
JAMIE..................10-15 59

BOBBIE & RONALD
Singles: 78 rpm
KING (4961 "When Oh When")..........5-10 56
Singles: 7-inch
KING (4961 "When Oh When")..........10-15 56

BOBBIE & VALIANTS
Singles: 7-inch
ARCO (100 "Rambunkshus")..........10-15 63

BOBBIE JEAN
Singles: 7-inch
BLUE RIBBON..................5-10 59
SUN..................5-10 60

BOBBIES
Singles: 7-inch
CRUSADER..................5-10 65
SONNY..................4-8 66

BOBBI-PINS: see BOBBY PINS

BOBBS, Billy, & Chips
Singles: 7-inch
EDISON INT'L..................15-25 58

BOBBSEY TWINS
Singles: 7-inch
CADENCE..................10-15 57

BOBBY & BENGALS
Singles: 7-inch
B-W (1 "No Parking!")..................20-40 60

BOBBY & BILLY
Singles: 7-inch
STARFIRE..................8-12 62
U.A...................5-10 59-60

BOBBY & Blue Jays: see BLUE, Bobby

BOBBY & BUDDY
Singles: 78 rpm
FURY..................20-40 58
Singles: 7-inch
FURY (1008 "What's the Word, Thunderbird")..................15-25 58
HIT (180 "Bless You Little Girl").......8-12

BOBBY & BUZZ
Singles: 7-inch
MONUMENT..................4-8 66

BOBBY & CASTELEERS
Singles: 7-inch
DIAMOND JIM..................8-12

BOBBY & CONSOLES
(Bobby Pedrick Jr.)
Singles: 7-inch
DIAMOND (141 "My Jelly Bean")...40-60 63
VERVE (10402 "Karine")..........15-25 66
Also see PEDRICK, Bobby, Jr.

BOBBY & COUNTS
("Vocal by Fred Ciaschi"; Bobby Comstock)
Singles: 7-inch
COUNT (6985 "Three Signs of Love")..................35-50 58
MARLEE (104 "Tra-La-La")......100-200 58
Also see COMSTOCK, Bobby

BOBBY & DEAMONS
Singles: 7-inch
MCI (1028 "The Woo")..................35-50 56

BOBBY & DUKES
Singles: 7-inch
PHILIPS..................10-20 65

BOBBY & EXPRESSIONS
Singles: 7-inch
KING..................8-12 66

BOBBY & FERRARIS
Singles: 7-inch
TUFF-NUFF ("Pretty")..................15-20 65
(No selection number used.)
Member: Bobby Hughes.

BOBBY & GALAXIES
Singles: 7-inch
TUFF-NUFF..................10-20
Member: Bobby Hughes.

BOBBY & HEAVYWEIGHTS
Singles: 7-inch
ATLANTIC..................4-8 68

BOBBY & I
Singles: 7-inch
IMPERIAL..................3-6 69
LPs: 10/12-inch
IMPERIAL..................10-15 69

BOBBY & JIM
Singles: 7-inch
CAPITOL..................5-10 58

BOBBY & LAURIE
Singles: 7-inch
LTD..................4-8 66

BOBBY & MIDNITES LP '81
Singles: 7-inch
ARISTA..................3-4 81
COLUMBIA..................3-4 84
LPs: 10/12-inch
ARISTA..................5-10 81
COLUMBIA..................5-10 84
Members: Bob Weir; David Garland.
Also see BIG FOOT
Also see WEIR, Bob

BOBBY & ORBITS
Singles: 7-inch
GONE..................5-10 62
SEECO (6005 "Felicia")..........15-25 59
SEECO (6030 "Teenage Love").....10-20 60

BOBBY & PREMIERS
Singles: 7-inch
SOULED OUT of TEXAS (36202 "Gotta Have a Reason")..................10-15 60s
Member: Bobby Rosales.

BOBBY & ROSEMARY
Singles: 7-inch
FEDERAL..................5-10 62

BOBBY & SYLVIA
Singles: 7-inch
BATTLE..................5-10 62
Member: Bobby Hebb.
Also see HEBB, Bobby

BOBBY & TEASERS
Singles: 7-inch
FLEETWOOD (1012 "She's a Tease")..................20-30 60

BOBBY & TEMPS
Singles: 7-inch
ABC-PAR..................8-10 63

BOBBY & VALIANTS
Singles: 7-inch
ARCO..................5-10

BOBBY & VELVETS
Singles: 7-inch
RASON (501 "I Promised")........100-200 59
Member: Bobby Sanders.
Also see EXTREMES
Also see SANDERS, Bobby

BOBBY & WALTER
Singles: 7-inch
SANNS (8805 "One, Two, Three").10-20 60s

BOBBY GENE SIX PAC
Singles: 7-inch
MERCURY..................3-5 70

BOBBY JIMMY: see JIMMY, Bobby

BOBBY JOHN: see JOHN, Bobby

BOBBY LEE: see LEE, Bobby

BOBBY O
Singles: 12-inch
O RECORDS..................4-6 82

BOBBY PINS
(Bobbi-Pins)
Singles: 7-inch
MERCURY..................5-10 64-65
OKEH (7110 "I Want You")..........10-20 60s

BOBBY SUE & FREELOADERS
Singles: 78 rpm
HARLEM..................50-75 55
Singles: 7-inch
HARLEM (2335 "It Takes a Lot of Love")..................75-100 55

BOB-CHORDS
Singles: 7-inch
SIOUX (8260 "Hi-Voltage")..........10-20 60

BOBO
Singles: 7-inch
COLUMBIA..................3-4 78-79
LPs: 10/12-inch
COLUMBIA..................5-10 78-79

BOBO, Bobby
Singles: 7-inch
DECCA..................5-10 61
SAGE..................10-15 56

BOBO, Jim
Singles: 7-inch
EKO (506 "Jungle Rock")..........200-300 58
(Labels crediting Bobo may or may not have a sticker indicating singer is Hank Mizell.)
Also see MIZELL, Hank, & Jim Bobo

BOBO, Mr. Soul
Singles: 7-inch
HI..................4-6 72
OVIDE (252 "Answer to the Want Ads")..................10-15 68
OVIDE (258 "Hitchhike to Heartbreak Rd.")..................8-12 68

BOBO, Willie LP '66
(With the Bo-Gents)
Singles: 7-inch
BLUE NOTE..................3-5 77
CAPITOL..................3-5 76
JUPITER JAZZ..................3-5 75
TICO..................8-12 59
VERVE..................4-8 65-69
LPs: 10/12-inch
BLUE NOTE..................5-10 77
COLUMBIA..................8-10 78-79
MGM..................5-10
ROULETTE..................15-25 63-64
SUSSEX..................8-10
TICO..................10-20
TRIP..................5-10
VERVE..................10-20 65-69
Also see DIXIE HUMMINGBIRDS
Also see HANCOCK, Herbie, & Willie Bobo

BOBO MR. SOUL: see BOBO, Mr. Soul

BOBOLINKS
Singles: 7-inch
KEY (Except 573)..................10-20 59
KEY (573 "Elvis Presley's Sergeant")..................25-40 59
TUNE (226 "Lonesome Wind")......10-15 61

BOB-o-LINKS
Singles: 7-inch
HI-HO (101 "I Promise")..................30-50 62
(Is this the same recording as on Way-Lin 101, credited to the Memories?)
Also see MEMORIES

BOBSLED & TOBOGGANS
Singles: 7-inch
CAMEO..................8-12 66
Also see JOHNSTON, Bruce

BOBSMITHS
Singles: 7-inch
CLICK (57 "Hello Baby")..................5-10 64
LP: 10/12-inch
NATIONAL..................10-20 71
RUSTICANA..................15-25 64
Also see DAVIS, Bob

BOCEPHUS
(Hank Williams Jr.)
Singles: 7-inch
VERVE (10540 "Meter Reader Maid")..................20-30 67
VERVE (10572 "Splish Splash")....20-30 67
(May have been issued only as a promo.)
Also see WILLIAMS, Hank, Jr.

BOCKY & VISIONS
(Bocky)
Singles: 7-inch
PHILIPS..................10-20 64
REDDA..................10-20 64-66
Member: Bocky Dipasquate.

BODACIOUS, D.F.
LPs: 10/12-inch
RCA (AFL1 series)..................10-12 77
RCA (APL1 series)..................12-15 73
RCA (AYL1 series)..................5-10 82
Members: Marty Balin; Vic Smith; Mark Ryan; Charlie Hickox; Greg Dewey.
Also see BALIN, Marty

BODAFORD, Bill
Singles: 7-inch
BACK BEAT (507 "Little Girl")......20-30 58

BoDEANS LP '86
Singles: 7-inch
SLASH..................3-4 86-89
LPs: 10/12-inch
SLASH..................5-10 86-89
SLASH/REPRISE..................5-8 91
Members: Sammy Llanas; Kurt Neumann; Guy Hoffman; Bob Griffin.

BODINE
Singles: 7-inch
JEWEL..................3-4 81
LPs: 10/12-inch
MGM..................10-12 69
WEA INT'L..................5-10 83

BODINE, Rita Jean
Singles: 7-inch
20TH FOX..................3-5 74
LPs: 10/12-inch
20TH FOX..................8-10 74

BODNER, Phil, Sextet
Singles: 7-inch
RCA..................3-6 63
Also see BRASS RING

BODROCKERS
Singles: 7-inch
BOLO..................10-15 66

BODY & SOUL
Singles: 7-inch
NATIONAL GENERAL..................3-5 70
LPs: 10/12-inch
NATIONAL GENERAL..................10-12 71

BOENZEE CRYQUE
Singles: 7-inch
CHICORY (406 "Sky Gone Gray") 15-25 67
UNI (55012 "Sky Gone Gray").......10-15 67
Members: Sam Bush; Rusty Young; George Grantham; Mort Mitchell; Jed Neddo.
Also see POCO

BOERSMA, Amy
Singles: 7-inch
BELL..................3-5 73

BOETCHER, Curt
Singles: 7-inch
ELEKTRA..................3-5 73
TOGETHER..................4-8 69
LPs: 10/12-inch
ELEKTRA..................12-15 72
Also see BECHER, Curt, & California
Also see FRIAR TUCK
Also see GOLDEBRIARS
Also see MILLENIUM
Also see SAGITTARIIUS
Also see SONG

BOFFALONGO
Singles: 7-inch
U.A...................3-5 70
LPs: 10/12-inch
U.A...................10-20 69-70

BOFILL, Angela R&B/LP '79
Singles: 12-inch
ARISTA..................4-6 81-85
Singles: 7-inch
ARISTA..................3-4 81-85
GRP..................3-5 79
LPs: 10/12-inch
ARISTA..................5-10 81-85
GRP..................8-10 78-79

BO'FLYERS
Singles: 7-inch
PYE..................3-4 76

BOGAN, Ted / Carl Martin
Singles: 7-inch
ROCKY ROAD (4501 "Seaboard Stomp")..................10-20 68

BOGART, Humphrey
MARK 56 ("The Enforcer")..........60-80
(Picture disc.)

BOGGS, Lucky / Howard Perkins
Singles: 7-inch
BISHOP (1012 "Drillin' Rig Boogie")..4-8

BOGGS, Prof. Harold
Singles: 78 rpm
KING..................15-25 53
Singles: 7-inch
KING (4643 "Inside the Beautiful Gate")..................25-50 53
KING (4660 "I Want to Live Right")..................25-50 53

BOGGUSS, Suzy C&W '87
Singles: 7-inch
CAPITOL..................3-4 87-91
LPs: 10/12-inch
CAPITOL..................5-8 87-90
Also see TOMORROW'S WORLD

BOGIE, Col. Doug
Singles: 7-inch
ABC..................3-5 75

BOGIN, Laurie
LPs: 10/12-inch
BUDDAH..................5-10 75
CHAMP (3403 "I Think You'll Find")..................10-15 66
Members: Jimmy Dentici; Glen Frank; Rick Skow; Dave Frasheski; Mike Kowaleski.
Also see MANIFEST DESTINY

Also see ROAD RUNNERS

BOGLE, Jim, & Beaumen
Singles: 7-inch
TEXAS RECORD CO. (2629 "Letter to My Love")..................100-200 62

BOGUSH, Paul
(Paul Bogush Band)
Singles: 7-inch
PRIVATE STOCK..................3-5 76
RCA..................3-5 74

BOHANNA
Singles: 7-inch
SCEPTER..................3-6 69

BOHANNON R&B '74
(Hamilton Bohannon)
Singles: 12-inch
COMPLEAT..................4-6 84-85
MERCURY..................5-8 77-80
MCA..................4-6 84
PHASE II..................4-6 80-83
Singles: 7-inch
DAKAR..................3-5 73-75
MERCURY..................3-4 77-80
PHASE 2..................3-4 80-83
LPs: 10/12-inch
DAKAR..................10-12 73-75
MERCURY..................8-10 77-80
PHASE 2..................5-10 80-83
Session: Carolyn Crawford.
Also see CRAWFORD, Carolyn

BOHANNON, Bill
Singles: 7-inch
PAULA..................4-8 67-68

BOHANNON, Hamilton, & Dr. Perri Johnson R&B '81
Singles: 12-inch
PHASE 2..................4-6 81
Singles: 7-inch
PHASE 2..................3-4 81
Also see BOHANNON

BOHANON, George, Quartet
Singles: 7-inch
WORKSHOP JAZZ (2006 "Bobbie")..................15-25 63
LPs: 10/12-inch
WORKSHOP JAZZ (207 "Boss Bossa Nova")..................40-60 63
WORKSHOP JAZZ (214 "Bold")....40-60 64

BOHEMIA
LPs: 10/12-inch
VU..................15-20 80

BOHEMIAN VENDETTA
Singles: 7-inch
MAINSTREAM (681 "Riddles and Fairytales")..................10-15 68
U.A. (50174 "Enough")..................10-20 67
LPs: 10/12-inch
MAINSTREAM (6106 "Bohemian Vendetta")..................75-100 68
Members: Brian Cooke; Nick Manzi.

BOHEMIANS
Singles: 7-inch
CHEX (1007 "Say Sweet Things") 10-20 62
EPs: 7-inch
BOHEMIAN..................5-10

BOHET, Nal
Singles: 7-inch
KARATE..................4-8 66
LPs: 10/12-inch
KARATE..................15-20 67

BOHLER, Herb
Singles: 7-inch
TORE..................5-10 59

BOHN, Rudi, & His Band LP '61
LPs: 10/12-inch
LONDON PHASE 4..................5-12 61

BOHORN, Jimmy
Singles: 7-inch
ALSTON..................3-5 75

BOILING POINT R&B '78
Singles: 7-inch
BULLET..................3-5 78

BOINES, Houston
("With Rhythm Acc.")
Singles: 78 rpm
RPM (364 "Monkey Motion")......150-200 51
(7-inch 78rpm single.)
RPM (364 "Monkey Motion")..........50-75 51
(10-inch single.)
Also see BAINES, Houston
Also see GILMORE, Boyd /Houston Boines / Charlie Booker

BO-JAC
Singles: 7-inch
SMASH..................3-5 70

BOLAN, Marc
LPs: 10/12-inch
REPRISE (511 "Interview with Marc Bolan of T-Rex")..................50-75 71
(Promotional issue only.)
RHINO (Picture disc)..................8-10
WHAT..................5-10 82
Also see T. REX

BOLD
LPs: 10/12-inch
ABC (705 "Bold")..................12-20 70
Member: Rick LaFrenier.
Also see BUSTERS

Also see EAGLES

BOLD
Singles: 7-inch
CAMEO (430 "Gotta Get Some") ... 15-20 66
Also see CLEAN LIVING
Also see WALKER, Steve, & Bold

BOLDEN, James
Singles: 7-inch
FANTASY ... 3-5 80
IVY (1001 "Caught Up in the Middle") ... 10-15

BOLDEN, Lonnie
Singles: 7-inch
DORE (810 "Live It Up") ... 10-20 68

BOLES, Calvin
Singles: 7-inch
YUCCA (Except 141 & 161) ... 10-20 59-64
YUCCA (141 "If You've Got a Lot of Dough") ... 20-25 62
YUCCA (161 "Stompin' on a Hardwood Floor") ... 50-75 63

BOLGER, Ray P&R '49
Singles: 78 rpm
DECCA ... 4-8 49-51
Singles: 7-inch
ARMOUR ... 3-6 63
DECCA ... 5-10 50-51
LPs: 10/12-inch
DISNEYLAND ... 6-10 65

BOLIN, Tommy LP '75
Singles: 7-inch
NEMPEROR ... 3-5 76
LPs: 10/12-inch
COLUMBIA ... 8-10 76
NEMPEROR (400 series) ... 10-12 75
NEMPEROR (37000 series) ... 5-10 81
Also see CHATEAUX
Also see DEEP PURPLE
Also see JAMES GANG
Also see ZEPHYR

BOLING, Wayne
Singles: 7-inch
SPOT (1111 "Please Cry") ... 15-25

BOLINS, Chet
LPs: 10/12-inch
STRAIGHT FACED ... 8-10 82

BOLL WEEVIL
Singles: 7-inch
FUNN (1001 "Free-Dumb Riders") 15-20 62

BOLL WEEVILS
Singles: 7-inch
HIT ... 5-15 64

BOLLAND
Singles: 7-inch
A&M ... 3-4 81
LPs: 10/12-inch
A&M ... 5-10 81

BOLLIN, Zu Zu
Singles: 78 rpm
TORCH (6910 "Why Don't You Eat Where You Slept Last Night") ... 40-60 52
TORCH (6912 "Cry Cry Cry") ... 40-60 52

BOLLINGER, William
Singles: 7-inch
CHESS ... 4-8 67

BOLOTON, Michael: see BOLTON, Michael

BOLT, Al C&W '76
Singles: 7-inch
CIN KAY ... 3-5 76

BOLT, Ben
Singles: 7-inch
MGM ... 3-6
Picture Sleeves
MGM ... 5-10

BOLT, Shirley, & Baroque-Adelics
Singles: 7-inch
CONTRAST ... 4-8 67

BOLTON, Amy
Singles: 12-inch
ATLANTIC ... 4-6 83
Singles: 7-inch
ATLANTIC ... 3-4 83

BOLTON, Michael P&R/LP '83
(Michael Boloton)
Singles: 12-inch
COLUMBIA ... 4-8 85
(Promotional issue only.)
Singles: 7-inch
COLUMBIA ... 3-4 83-91
RCA ... 3-5 75-76
Picture Sleeves
COLUMBIA ... 3-4 88
LPs: 10/12-inch
COLUMBIA ... 5-10 83-91
RCA ... 8-10 75-76
Also see BLACKJACK
Also see JOY

BOMARCS
Singles: 7-inch
DOT (15934 "Undecided") ... 8-12 59

BOMBERS
Singles: 78 rpm
ORPHEUS ... 15-25 55-56
Singles: 7-inch
ORPHEUS (1101 "I'll Never Tire of You") ... 50-75 55
(Black vinyl.)
ORPHEUS (1101 "I'll Never Tire of You") ... 100-150 55
(Colored vinyl.)
ORPHEUS (1105 "Two-Time Heart") ... 50-75 56
(Black vinyl.)
ORPHEUS (1105 "Two-Time Heart") ... 100-150 56
(Colored vinyl.)

BOMBERS R&B '79
Singles: 7-inch
WEST END ... 3-5 79
LPs: 10/12-inch
WEST END ... 8-12 79

BOMIS PRENDIN
LPs: 10/12-inch
ARTIFACTS ... 5-10 79

BOMPERS
Singles: 7-inch
HBR ... 5-10 65
Also see CONNORS, Carol

BON, Joann, & Coquettes
Singles: 7-inch
MTA ... 5-10 67-69
LPs: 10/12-inch
MTA ... 10-20 68

BON BON & BUDDIES
Singles: 78 rpm
DECCA ... 10-20 41-42

BON BONS
Singles: 78 rpm
APOLLO ... 10-20 48

BON BONS
(With Ray Conniff)
Singles: 78 rpm
COLUMBIA ... 8-12 57
LONDON ... 5-10 55
Singles: 7-inch
COLUMBIA (40800 "Three Teens") ... 10-15 57
COLUMBIA (40887 "The Kiss in Your Eyes") ... 10-15 57
LONDON ... 8-12 55
Also see CONNIFF, Ray

BON BONS
Singles: 7-inch
CORAL ... 10-20 64

BON JOVI, Jon P&R/LP '84
(Bon Jovi)
Singles: 7-inch
MERCURY ... 3-4 84-90
Picture Sleeves
MERCURY ... 3-4 84-89
LPs: 10/12-inch
MERCURY ... 5-10 84-90
POLYGRAM (830 822 "Slippery When Wet") ... 15-20 87
(Picture disc.)
POLYGRAM (422-863 499 "New Jersey") ... 15-20 88
(Picture disc.)
Members: Jon Bon Jovi; Richie Sambora; David Bryan; Alec John Such; Tico Torres.

BON ROCK D&D '84
Singles: 12-inch
EARTHTONE ... 4-6 84
LPs: 10/12-inch
EARTHTONE ... 5-10 84
Member: Keith Rogers.

BONADUCE, Danny
Singles: 7-inch
LION ... 3-5 73
LPs: 10/12-inch
LION ... 10-12 73
Also see PARTRIDGE FAMILY

BONAFEDE, Carl
Singles: 7-inch
IMPALA (2123 "Baby Sittin' Blues") ... 75-125
Also see SCREAMING WILDMAN

BON-AIRES
Singles: 78 rpm
KING (4975 "Bermuda") ... 10-15 56
Singles: 7-inch
KING (4975 "Bermuda") ... 15-25 56

BON-AIRES
Singles: 7-inch
PRO-GRESS (2468 "La Versatile") ... 10-20 69

BON-AIRES
Singles: 7-inch
CATAMOUNT ... 3-5 71
FLAMINGO ... 3-5 76
RUST (3 "Blue Beat") ... 20-30 62
RUST (5000 series) ... 10-20 64

BONAIRS / Ernie Tavares Trio
Singles: 78 rpm
DOOTONE (325 "It's Christmas") ... 25-50 53
Singles: 7-inch
DOOTONE (325 "It's Christmas") . 75-100 53

BONAPARTE, Gonzalez
Singles: 7-inch
INSTANT ... 5-10 61
MADISON ... 5-10 61
Also see O'SEA, Shad

BONAROO
Singles: 7-inch
W.B. ... 3-5 75
LPs: 10/12-inch
W.B. ... 5-10 75
Members: Bill Cuomo; Michael Hossack; Robert Lichtig; Jerry Weems; Bobby Winkelman.

BOND
Singles: 7-inch
COLUMBIA ... 3-4 75

BOND, Angelo R&B/LP '75
Singles: 7-inch
ABC ... 3-5 75-76
LPs: 10/12-inch
ABC ... 8-10 75-77

BOND, Bobby C&W '72
Singles: 7-inch
DANCELAND ... 5-10 61
HICKORY ... 3-5 72
MGM ... 3-5 68
PARROT ... 4-8 66
WAND ... 4-8 65
W.B. ... 3-5 69
LPs: 10/12-inch
ALSHIRE ... 8-10 69
SOMERSET/STEREO FIDELITY .. 10-20 60s
TIME ... 15-25 64

BOND, Chris, Band
Singles: 12-inch
CEEVEEBEE ... 15-20 83
Members: Rob Stoner; Freddy Frogs.

BOND, Christopher
Singles: 7-inch
DISC REET ... 3-5 74

BOND, Eddie
(With the Stompers; with Legend Makers)
Singles: 78 rpm
EKKO ... 50-75 55
MERCURY ... 25-50 56-57
Singles: 7-inch
ADVANCE ... 3-5 76
AMERICAN IMAGE ... 3-6 89-91
CORAL (62200 "Little Black Book") ... 10-20 60
D (1016 "Standing in Your Window") ... 15-25 58
DECCER ... 4-8 75-78
DIPLOMAT (8566 "The Monkey and the Baboon") ... 50-75 63
EKKO (1015 "Talkin' off the Wall") ... 100-200 55
EKKO (1016 "Love Makes a Fool") ... 75-125 55
ENTERPRISE ... 4-8 72
ERWIN (2001 "Here Comes that Train") ... 10-15 75
(Opinions vary about the year of release. Though reported to us as accurate, some question it, saying this version predates the Memphis one from 1965. We do know that year is right. IF the Erwin came first, then its price would likely be in the $30 to $50 range.)
GOLDWAX ... 5-10 65
HIGH COURT ... 3-5 80
K-ARK ... 5-10 65
MEMPHIS (114 "Raunchy") ... 15-25 65
MEMPHIS (115 "Here Comes That Train") ... 15-25 65
MERCURY (70826 "Rockin' Daddy") ... 50-75 56
MERCURY (70882 "Slip, Slip, Slipin' In") ... 50-75 56
MERCURY (70941 "Boppin' Bonnie") ... 50-75 56
MERCURY (71000 series) ... 10-20 57
MEMPHIS (105 "Make the Parting Sweet") ... 10-15 64
MEMPHIS (114 "Cold Dark Waters") ... 10-15 65
MEMPHIS (115 "Here Comes the Train") ... 20-30 65
MILLIONAIRE ... 5-10 65-67
PEN ... 8-10 62
ROCK-IT ... 3-5 79
SPA (1001 "I Walk Alone") ... 10-15 61
STARGEM ... 3-6 91
STOMPER TIME ... 15-20 59
TAB (677 "Rocking Daddy") ... 10-20 68
TAB (669 "Juke Joint Johnnie") ... 10-20 68
TAGG ... 5-10 67
THREE STARS ... 3-5 78
UNITED SOUTHERN ARTISTS (506 "Second Chance") ... 10-15 61
WILDCAT (58 "Can't Win for Losing") ... 15-25 61
XL ... 5-10 68
LPs: 10/12-inch
COUNTRY CIRCLE (6605 "My Choice Is Eddie Bond") ... 15-25 73
ENTERPRISE (1038 "The Legend of Buford Pusser") ... 10-20 73
(Includes bonus single, booklet and music sheet.)
M.C.C.R. ... 25-35 69
MILLIONAIRE ... 25-35 67
PHILLIPS INT'L (1980 "Greatest Country Gospel Hits") ... 200-300 62
Also see BURLISON, Paul

BOND, Graham
(Graham Bond Organization)
Singles: 7-inch
ASCOT ... 5-10 66
PULSAR ... 3-6 69
LPs: 10/12-inch
MERCURY ... 10-12 70-71
PULSAR ... 12-15 69
W.B. ... 10-12 70

BOND, Graham, & Rory O'Donoghue
Singles: 7-inch
POLYDOR ... 3-5 75
Also see BOND, Graham

BOND, Johnny C&W '47
(With the Red River Valley Boys)
Singles: 78 rpm
COLUMBIA (Except 21521) ... 5-15 45-56
(Columbia 20545 through 20787 were also issued on 7-inch 33 singles, any of which may be in the $15 to $25 range.)
COLUMBIA (21521 "The Little Rock Roll") ... 8-12 56
Singles: 7-inch
COLUMBIA (Except 21521) ... 10-20 51-56
COLUMBIA (21521 "The Little Rock Roll") ... 30-45 56
CONQUEROR ... 10-25
DITTO ... 5-10 59
GILLETTE ... 3-4
KING ... 3-4
LAMB & LION ... 3-5 74
LONDON ... 3-5
MGM ... 3-5 73
OKEH ... 8-15 41-45
REPUBLIC (2000 series) ... 5-10 60
SMASH ... 4-6 62
STARDAY (618 thru 951) ... 4-8 63-72
STARDAY (7021 thru 9292) ... 3-4 72-74
20TH FOX ... 4-8 60
EPs: 7-inch
COLUMBIA ... 10-20 58
REPUBLIC ... 10-20 60
STARDAY ... 10-15 63
LPs: 10/12-inch
CMH ... 5-10 77
CAPITOL ... 8-12 69
CATTLE ... 15-20
DANNY ... 15-20
HARMONY ... 10-20 64-65
LAMB & LION ... 5-10 74
NASHVILLE ... 5-10 71
SHASTA ... 10-15
STARDAY (147 thru 298) ... 20-30 61-64
STARDAY (333 "Ten Little Bottles") ... 15-20 65-66
STARDAY (354 "Famous Hot Rodders I Have Known") ... 25-30 65
STARDAY (368 thru 472) ... 20-30 66-71
STARDAY (900 series) ... 6-10 74
Also see AUTRY, Gene
Also see HANK & FRANK
Also see TRAVIS, Merle, & Johnny Bond

BOND, Johnny, & Lefty Frizzell
Singles: 78 rpm
COLUMBIA ... 5-10 56-57
Singles: 7-inch
COLUMBIA ... 10-15 56-57
Also see BOND, Johnny
Also see FRIZZELL, Lefty

BOND, Lou
Singles: 7-inch
BRAINSTORM ... 5-10
FONTANA ... 4-8 66

BOND, Luther
(With the Emeralds)
Singles: 78 rpm
SAVOY ... 20-30 55
Singles: 7-inch
FEDERAL (12368 "Old Mother Nature") ... 30-50 59
SAVOY (1124 "What If") ... 50-75 55
SAVOY (1131 "Starlight Starbright") ... 50-75 55
SAVOY (1159 "Written in the Stars") ... 50-75 55
SHOWBOAT (1501 "Gold Will Never Do") ... 15-25 59
SHOWBOAT (1505 "Someone to Love Me") ... 75-100 60
Also see EMERALDS

BONDS, Dave
Singles: 7-inch
AVI ... 3-4 84

BONDS, Gary "U.S." P&R/R&B '60
(U.S. Bonds; Gary Bonds)
Singles: 12-inch
EMI (9666 "Gary U.S. Bonds") ... 25-30 81
(Promotional issue only.)
Singles: 7-inch
ABC ... 3-4 73
ATCO ... 3-6 69
BLUFF CITY ... 3-5 74
BOTANIC ... 4-6 68
COLLECTABLES ... 3-4 81
EMI AMERICA ... 3-4 81-82
LEGRAND (1003 thru 1012) ... 10-20 60-61
(Purple label.)
LEGRAND (1003 thru 1012) ... 6-12 62-63
(Multi-color label.)
LEGRAND (1015 thru 1020) ... 8-15 62
LEGRAND (1022 thru 1041) ... 10-20 62-66
LEGRAND (1043 thru 1046) ... 10-15 66-67
MCA ... 3-4 84
PRODIGAL ... 3-5 75
SKY DISC (641 "Joy to the World") ... 3-6 70s
SUE ... 3-6 70
Picture Sleeves
EMI AMERICA ... 4-8 81-82
LEGRAND (1008 "Quarter to Three") ... 10-15 61
LEGRAND (1009 "School Is Out") 10-15 61
LPs: 10/12-inch
EMI AMERICA ... 5-10 81-82
LEGRAND (1000 series) ... 5-10 79-86
LEGRAND (3001 "Dance 'Till Quarter to Three") ... 40-60 61
LEGRAND (3002 "Twist Up Calypso") ... 40-60 62
LEGRAND (3003 "Greatest Hits") .. 40-60 62
MCA ... 5-10 84
PHOENIX ... 5-10 84
RHINO ... 5-10 84
Session: Bruce Springsteen.
Also see BARGE, Gene
Also see BONDSMEN
Also see CHECKER, Chubby / Gary U.S. Bonds
Also see CHURCH STREET FIVE
Also see GREENWICH, Ellie
Also see JACKSON, Chuck
Also see KING, Ben E.
Also see SPRINGSTEEN, Bruce

BONDS, Lee
Singles: 78 rpm
CAPITOL ... 10-20 54
DECCA ... 10-15 54
REPUBLIC ... 10-20 52
TENNESSEE ... 20-30 52
Singles: 7-inch
CAPITOL (2692 "Done Gone Crazy") ... 20-30 54
DECCA (29338 "I'm Looking for Some Lovin' ") ... 15-25 54
REPUBLIC (7007 "How About a Date") ... 25-40 52
TENNESSEE (804 "Uh-Huh Honey") ... 50-75 52
TENNESSEE (826 "Wild Cattin' Woman") ... 50-75 52
TODD (1055 "Walking with the Blues") ... 10-20 60

BONDS, U.S: see BONDS, Gary "U.S."

BONDSMEN
Singles: 7-inch
AMH (6704 "I See the Light") ... 20-30 67
GUILLOTINE ... 10-15 66

BONDSMEN / Derbys
Singles: 7-inch
DAWN (303 "Wipe Out '66") ... 15-25 66
USA (887 "Shotgun") ... 10-20 68

BONE
Singles: 7-inch
POISON RING (712 "Easy Thing") 10-15 70
Members: Danny Gomes; Rick Simpson; Fred O'Brien; Bob Sheehan; Brooks Barnett; Vic Mattson; Charles Hickox.

BONE, Jimmy, & Jokers
Singles: 7-inch
GRACE (510 "Little Mama") ... 75-125

BONE SYMPHONY D&D '83
Singles: 12-inch
CAPITOL ... 4-6 83
Singles: 7-inch
CAPITOL ... 3-4 83
LPs: 10/12-inch
CAPITOL ... 5-10 83

BONES P&R '72
Singles: 7-inch
MCA ... 3-5 73
SIGNPOST ... 4-6 72
LPs: 10/12-inch
MCA ... 8-10 73
SIGNPOST ... 10-12 72
Members: Dan Faragher; Jimmy Faragher.
Also see FARAGHER BROTHERS

BONES, Elbow: see ELBOW BONES

BONES, Mr. Goon, & Mr. Ford: see MR. GOON BONES & MR. FORD

BONETREES, Ches
Singles: 7-inch
FONTANA ... 3-6 70

BONEY M P&R '77
Singles: 12-inch
CARRERE ... 4-6 85
SIRE ... 4-6 79
Singles: 7-inch
ATCO ... 3-5 76-77
ATLANTIC ... 3-5 77
SIRE ... 3-4 78-79
Picture Sleeves
SIRE ... 3-4 79
LPs: 10/12-inch
ATCO ... 10-12 76
ATLANTIC ... 8-10 77
SIRE ... 5-10 77-79
Members: Marcia Barrett; Bobby Farrell; Liz Mitchell; Maizie Williams.

BONFIRE, Mars
(Dennis Edmonton)
Singles: 7-inch
COLUMBIA ... 4-6 68-69
LPs: 10/12-inch
COLUMBIA ... 12-15 69
UNI ... 12-15 68
Also see NELSON, Sandy
Also see IMITATION LIFE
Also see SPARROWS

BONGALIS
Singles: 7-inch
M-S ... 4-8 67

BONGI & JUDI
Singles: 7-inch
BUDDAH ... 4-8 67
EPIC ... 4-8 67

BONGO
(Georgie Bongo)
Singles: 7-inch
DORE (573 "Outer Space") ... 10-20 60

BONGOS
Singles: 7-inch
SPLASH 10-20 59

BONGOS
LPs: 10/12-inch
PVC 5-10 82
RCA 5-10 83-85

BONHAM P&R/LP '89
Singles: 7-inch
WTG 3-4 89
LPs: 10/12-inch
WTG 5-8 89
Members: Daniel MacMaster; Jason Bonham; Ian Hatton; John Smithson.

BONI, Johnny
Singles: 7-inch
BLACK 5-10

BONN, Bob
Singles: 7-inch
FABLE 15-20 57

BONNAVILLES
Singles: 7-inch
QUESTION MARK (101 "High Noon Stomp") 15-25 62
QUESTION MARK (103 "Bonnavilles Stomp") 15-25 62
Picture Sleeves
QUESTION MARK (101 "High Noon Stomp") 20-35 62

BONNER, Garry
Singles: 7-inch
ATLANTIC 3-5 74-75
COLUMBIA 5-10 67-68
VERVE 4-6 72
Also see MAGICIANS

BONNER, James
Singles: 7-inch
B.P.L. 3-5 71

BONNER, Juke Boy
Singles: 7-inch
GOLDBAND 15-25 61
LPs: 10/12-inch
ARHOOLIE 5-10
Also see BARNER, Juke Boy, & Group

BONNER, Lil' Joe, & Idols
(With the Fabulous Playboys)
Singles: 78 rpm
B&S B-DISC-S 100-200 55
Singles: 7-inch
B&S B-DISC-S (1570 "Tell Me Baby") 500-750 55

BONNER, Louis
LPs: 10/12-inch
FOLKWAYS 10-12

BONNER, Wheldon: see BONNER, Juke Boy

BONNERS C&W '88
Singles: 7-inch
OL 3-4 88
Members: James Bonner; Edith Bonner.

BONNETS
Singles: 7-inch
UNICAL (3010 "You Gotta Take a Chance") 10-20 63

BONNETT, Neil
Singles: 7-inch
SPEEDWAY (1 "The Men Who Race for the Checkered Flag") 5-10

BONNEVILLES
Singles: 7-inch
DRUM BOY (45101 "Bacardi") 10-20 62
DRUM BOY (45102 "Don't You Dare") 10-20 62
FENWAY (7000 "Sky Dive") 10-20 60
CORAL (62273 "Johnny") 10-20 61
Picture Sleeves
DRUM BOY 10-20 62
LPs: 10/12-inch
DRUM BOY (1001 "Meet the Bonnevilles") 40-60 62
Members: John Cerniglia; Larry Lynne; Teddy Peplinski; Dennis Madigan; Pete Funck; Vince Megna; Tony Kolp; Howard Wales; Bob Merkt; Rick Allen; Johnny Edwards; Paul Frederick; Tom Hahn..
Also see ATTORNEYS
Also see COLBY, Wendy, & Bonnevilles
Also see CONTINENTALS
Also see ELLIS, Herb, & Vince Megna.
Also see LYNNE, Larry, Group
Also see SKUNKS

BONNEVILLES
Singles: 7-inch
BARRY (104 "Zu Zu") 25-50 62
CAPRI (102 "Give Me Your Love") 50-100 59
COLLECTABLES 3-4 81
MUNICH (103 "Zu Zu") 150-250 60
(Red label.)
MUNICH (103 "Zu Zu") 75-125 60
(Black label.)
WHITEHALL (30,002 "I Do") 100-200 59

BONNEVILLES
Singles: 7-inch
SCOTTY (643 "Let's Go") 10-20 60s
SPOTLIGHT (102 "I'm Walking the Dog") 10-20 60s

BONNEVILLES
Singles: 7-inch
PLEASON (1002 "Caravan") 8-12 63
QUESTION MARK 5-10

BONNEVILLES
Singles: 7-inch
NOW 3-6 70

BONNEVILLES
Singles: 7-inch
PRIVATE STOCK (101 "Don't Break the Spell of Love") 10-15

BONNEY, Graham
Singles: 7-inch
CAPITOL 4-8 66-68
MIKE 4-8 66

BONNIE
Singles: 7-inch
W.B. 4-8 66

BONNIE & BUDDY C&W '69
Singles: 7-inch
PARAMOUNT 3-5 69
Members: Bonnie Guitar; Buddy Killen.
Also see GUITAR, Bonnie

BONNIE & BUTTERFLYS
Singles: 7-inch
SMASH 10-15 64

BONNIE & CLYDE
Singles: 7-inch
IN SOUND (405 "I Want a Boyfriend [Girlfriend]") 4-8 68

BONNIE & DENIMS
Singles: 7-inch
LLP 5-10 65

BONNIE & LEE
Singles: 7-inch
FAIRMOUNT 4-8 67

BONNIE & LITTLE BOYS BLUE
Singles: 7-inch
NIKKO (611 "Bells") 5000-7000 58

BONNIE & RUSTY
Singles: 7-inch
KING (5110 "La Dee Dah") 10-20 58

BONNIE & SHEILA
Singles: 7-inch
KING 3-5 71

BONNIE & TREASURES P&R '65
(Featuring Charlott O'Hara)
Singles: 7-inch
PHI DAN (5505 "Home of the Brave") 20-30 65
Also see MID AMERICANS / Bonnie & Treasures

BONNIE LOU C&W '53
(Bonnie Lou Kath)
Singles: 78 rpm
KING 4-8 53-55
Singles: 7-inch
FRATERNITY 5-10 58
KING 5-10 53-55
TODD (1073 "Twenty-four Hours of Loneliness") 5-10 62
EPs: 7-inch
KING 10-15 58
LPs: 10/12-inch
KING (595 "Bonnie Lou Sings") 25-50 58
WRAYCO 5-10

BONNIE SISTERS P&R '56
(With Mickey "Guitar" Baker Orch; with Randy Carlos Cha Cha Rhythms)
Singles: 78 rpm
RAINBOW 10-15 56
Singles: 7-inch
RAINBOW 15-20 56
Members: Jean Bonnie; Pat Bonnie; Sylvia Bonnie. Session: Mickey Baker.
Also see BAKER, Mickey

BONNIWELL, T.S.
Singles: 7-inch
CAPITOL 5-8 69
LPs: 10/12-inch
CAPITOL 15-20 69
Member: Sean Bonniwell.
Also see BONNIWELL'S MUSIC MACHINE

BONNIWELL'S MUSIC MACHINE
Singles: 7-inch
BELL 5-10 69
W.B. 8-12 67-68
Picture Sleeves
W.B (7093 "Bottom of the Soul") 15-25 67
LPs: 10/12-inch
W.B. 12-15 67
Member: Sean Bonniwell.
Also see BONNIWELL, T.S.
Also see FRIENDLY TORPEDOS
Also see MUSIC MACHINE

BONNY, Billy
Singles: 7-inch
MARK 56 (830 "Bootleg Rock") 15-25 59

BONNY, William
Singles: 7-inch
MERCURY 4-8 66
(Is he the same person as Billy Bonny?)

BONNY LEE
Singles: 7-inch
EBONY 5-10

BONO, Sonny: see SONNY

BONOFF, Karla LP '77
Singles: 7-inch
COLUMBIA 3-4 77-84
Picture Sleeves
COLUMBIA 3-4 77-84
LPs: 10/12-inch
COLUMBIA 5-10 77-82
Also see BRYNDLE

BONQUETS, Tootie
Singles: 7-inch
PARKWAY 15-25 63

BONSALL, Joe
Singles: 7-inch
GOLDBAND 4-6
Also see OAK RIDGE BOYS
Also see SAWYER BROWN & "Cat" Joe Bonsall

BONTY, Jay
Singles: 7-inch
M&R (5 "The Shape") 10-20 67

BONUS, Jack
Singles: 7-inch
GRUNT 3-5 72
LPs: 10/12-inch
GRUNT 8-10 72

BONZO DOG BAND LP '72
(Bonzo Dog Doo-Dah Band)
Singles: 7-inch
IMPERIAL 3-6 69
LIBERTY 4-8 68
U.A. 3-5 71-72
LPs: 10/12-inch
IMPERIAL 15-20 68-70
LIBERTY 5-10 83
U.A. 10-15 71-74
Members: Vivian Stanshall; Neil Innes; Roger Ruskin Spear; Hughie Flint; Tony Kaye; Dave Richards; Andy Roberts.
Also see PLAINSONG
Also see RUTLES
Also see SPEAR, Rodger Ruskin

BONZO GOES TO WASHINGTON D&D '84
Singles: 12-inch
SLEEPING BAG 4-6 84

BOO BOO & BUNKIE
Singles: 7-inch
BRENT 4-8 65

BOOGALOO R&B '56
(With the Gallant Crew; Kent Harris)
Singles: 78 rpm
CREST 10-20 56
Singles: 7-inch
CREST (1030 "Cops & Robbers") ..15-25 56
(Black vinyl.)
CREST (1030 "Cops & Robbers") ..35-55 56
(Colored vinyl.)

BOOGIE BOYS R&B/D&D/LP '85
Singles: 12-inch
CAPITOL 4-6 84-88
Singles: 7-inch
CAPITOL 3-4 84-88
Picture Sleeves
CAPITOL 3-4 86
LPs: 10/12-inch
CAPITOL 5-10 85-88
Member: William Stroman.

BOOGIE DOWN PRODUCTIONS LP '88
LPs: 10/12-inch
JIVE 5-8 88-91

BOOGIE JAKE
(Matthew Jacobs)
Singles: 7-inch
CHESS (1746 "Bad Luck & Trouble") 20-30 59
INSTANT 10-15 61
MINIT (602 "Bad Luck & Trouble") 15-20 60

BOOGIE KINGS
Singles: 7-inch
MONTEL 4-8 65-67
PAULA 4-6 67
PIC 1 (129 "This Is Blue-Eyed Soul") 10-15 60s
LPs: 10/12-inch
MONTEL (104 "Boogie Kings") 30-50 66
MONTEL (109 "Blue-Eyed Soul") 30-50 66
Members: Gee Gee Shin; Jerry Lacroix.

BOOGIE MAN
(John Lee Hooker)
Singles: 78 rpm
ACORN (308 "Morning Blues") 30-50 50
Also see HOOKER, John Lee

BOOGIE MAN ORCHESTRA R&B '75
Singles: 7-inch
BOOGIE MAN 3-5 75

BOOGIE RAMBLERS
Singles: 78 rpm
GOLDBAND (1130 "Cindy Lou") 50-75 57
Singles: 7-inch
GOLDBAND (1130 "Cindy Lou") 30-50 57
Member: Huey Thierry.
Also see COOKIE & CUPCAKES

BOOGIE WOOGIE RED
LPs: 10/12-inch
BLIND PIG 5-10 74-78

BOOK OF CHANGES
Singles: 7-inch
TOWER (337 "I Stole the Goodyear Blimp") 15-25 67

Members: Bob Bailey; Frank Smith; Joseph Bracket; Arthur Penthollow; Roland Stone.

BOOK OF LOVE D&D '85
Singles: 12-inch
SIRE 4-6 84-85
Singles: 7-inch
SIRE 3-4 84-90
Picture Sleeves
SIRE 3-4 88
LPs: 10/12-inch
SIRE 5-10 86-91

BOOK OF MATCHES
Singles: 7-inch
BELL 3-6 69
20TH FOX 3-5 70

BOOKE, Sorrell
Singles: 7-inch
SCOTTI BROTHERS 3-4 82

BOOKENDS
Singles: 7-inch
CAPITOL 5-10 61

BOOKER, Bea
Singles: 7-inch
PEACOCK 5-8 58

BOOKER, Charley
(Charlie Booker)
Singles: 78 rpm
BLUES & RHYTHM (7003 "Rabbit Blues") 150-200 51
(Seven-inch 78rpm single.)
BLUES & RHYTHM 50-75 51
(10-inch single.)
MODERN (878 "Moonrise Blues") 50-75 51
Singles: 7-inch
MODERN (878 "Moonrise Blues") 100-200 51
Also see GILMORE, Boyd /Houston Boines / Charlie Booker

BOOKER, Chuckii P&R/LP '89
Singles: 7-inch
ATLANTIC 3-4 89
LPs: 10/12-inch
ATLANTIC 5-8 89

BOOKER, Connie Mack: see McBOOKER, Connie

BOOKER, Harry T.
Singles: 7-inch
W.B. 3-5 76

BOOKER, James P&R/R&B '60
Singles: 7-inch
PEACOCK 6-12 60-64
LPs: 10/12-inch
ROUNDER 5-10 84
Also see DEL-TONES
Also see LITTLE BOOKER

BOOKER, Jay C&W '87
Singles: 7-inch
EMI 3-4 87

BOOKER, John Lee
(John L. Booker; John Lee Hooker)
Singles: 78 rpm
CHANCE 100-200 51
CHESS (1462 "Mad Man Blues") 25-50 51
DELUXE 25-50 53
GONE (60 "Mad Man Blues") 150-250 51
MODERN 20-30 51
ROCKIN' 25-50 53
Singles: 7-inch
CHANCE (1108 "Miss Lorraine") 300-500 51
CHANCE (1110 "Graveyard Blues") 300-500 51
CHANCE (1122 "609 Boogie") 300-500 51
DELUXE (6004 "Blue Monday") 75-100 53
DELUXE (6032 "Pouring Down Rain") 50-100 53
DELUXE (6004 "Blue Monday") 50-100 53
DELUXE (6046 "My Baby Don't Love Me") 50-100 53
MODERN (852 "Ground Hog Blues") 50-75 51
ROCKIN' (525 "Stuttering Blues") 75-100 53
Also see HOOKER, John Lee

BOOKER, Ronnie, & Boardwalkers
Singles: 7-inch
REX (103 "She Won't Go Steady") 800-1200 61

BOOKER T. & MGs P&R/R&B/LP '62
Singles: 12-inch
A&M 4-8 82-84
Singles: 7-inch
A&M 3-4 81-82
ASYLUM 3-5 77
EPIC 3-5 75
STAX (Except 100 series) 4-8 67-71
STAX (100 series) 5-10 62-66
VOLT (102 "Green Onions") 20-30 62
LPs: 10/12-inch
A&M 8-10 72-81
ASYLUM 5-10 77
ATLANTIC 10-12 68
ATLANTIC/ATCO (113 "Excerpts from *In the Christmas Spirit*) 15-20 66
(Promotional issue only. One side is excerpts from *Soul Christmas*, a various artists LP.)
EPIC 8-10 74
PICKWICK 5-10
STAX (700 series, except 701 & 713) 20-30 65-68
STAX (701 "Green Onions") 25-40 62
STAX (713 "In the Spirit of Christmas") 25-35 66
(Hands and keyboard drawing on front cover. Back has 1966 copyright date.)
STAX (713 "In the Spirit of Christmas") 15-25 67
(Christmas ornament cover. Back has 1967 copyright date.)
STAX (2000 series) 10-20 68-71
STAX (8000 series) 5-10 81-84
Members: Booker T. Jones; Steve Cropper; Al Jackson Jr.; Louis Steinberg; Willie Hall.
Also see BOOKER T. & PRISCILLA
Also see CROPPER, Steve
Also see MGs
Also see MAR-KEYS / Booker T. & MGs
Also see RANDLE, Del
Also see REDDING, Otis
Also see SANTANA
Also see SIMON, PAUL
Also see TRIUMPHS

BOOKER T. & PRISCILLA LP '71
Singles: 7-inch
A&M 3-5 71-73
LPs: 10/12-inch
A&M 8-10 71-73
Members: Booker T. Jones; Priscilla Coolidge-Jones.
Also see COOLIDGE-JONES, Priscilla

BOOKWORMS
Singles: 7-inch
TITAN (1714 "Ditchin' ") 10-20 61
Member: Ray Stanley.

BOOM, Taka P&R/R&B/LP '79
Singles: 7-inch
ARIOLA 3-4 79
MIRAGE 3-4 85
LPs: 10/12-inch
ARIOLA 5-10 79
Also see UNDISPUTED TRUTH

BOOMERANG
Singles: 7-inch
RCA 3-5 71
LPs: 10/12-inch
RCA 15-20 71

BOOMERANGS
Singles: 7-inch
BANDERA 4-8 64
CHECKER 4-8 64

BOOMTOWN RATS LP '79
Singles: 7-inch
COLUMBIA 3-4 79-80
LPs: 10/12-inch
COLUMBIA 5-10 79-85
MERCURY 8-12 77
Members: Bob Geldof; Pete Briquette; Gerry Cott; Simon Crowe; Johnny Fingers; Garry Roberts.
Also see BAND AID
Also see GELDOF, Bob

BOONA
Singles: 7-inch
MGM 4-8 67

BOONE, Daniel P&R/LP '72
Singles: 7-inch
EPIC 3-5 72
MERCURY 3-5 72-74
PYE 3-4 75
LPs: 10/12-inch
MERCURY 10-12 72

BOONE, Debby P&R/C&W/LP '77
Singles: 7-inch
LAMB & LION 3-4 80-84
W.B./CURB 3-4 77-81
Picture Sleeves
W.B./CURB 3-4 78
LPs: 10/12-inch
LAMB & LION 5-10 80-84
W.B./CURB 5-10 77-80
Also see BOONE, Pat, & Boone Girls
Also see BOONE GIRLS

BOONE, Jesse, & Astros
Singles: 7-inch
ATLANTIC 3-5 68
SOUL-PO-TION 3-4 70-71

BOONE, Larry C&W '86
Singles: 7-inch
MERCURY 3-4 86-91

BOONE, Len
Singles: 12-inch
CHRYSALIS 4-6 79
Singles: 7-inch
CHRYSALIS 3-4 78

BOONE, Len, & Holly Sherwood
Singles: 12-inch
CHRYSALIS 4-6 79
Singles: 7-inch
CHRYSALIS 3-4 78
Also see BOONE, Len

BOONE, Pat P&R/R&B '55
Singles: 78 rpm
DOT 10-25 55-58
REPUBLIC 5-10 54
Singles: 7-inch
ABC 3-4 74-75
BUENA VISTA 3-5 73
CAPITOL 3-5 70
CHEVROLET/RCA (4988 "June Is Bustin' Out All Over") 10-15 58
(Promotional issue for Chevrolet dealers. Narration by Bob Lund.)
DOT (200 series) 10-20 59-60
(Stereo.)

DOT (15000 series) 10-20 55-57
(Maroon label.)
DOT (15000 & 16000 series, except 16658).......................................6-12 57-66
(Black label.)
DOT (16658 "Beach Girl")..............8-12 64
(With Bruce Johnston and Terry Melcher.)
DOT (17000 series) 3-6 66-75
HITSVILLE 3-5 76-77
LION...3-4 72
MC...3-4 77
MCA..3-4 84
MGM 3-5 71-73
MELODYLAND.....................................3-5 74-76
ORCHID 3-4 89
REPUBLIC...10-15 54
SRG 3-4 88
TETRAGRAMMATON 3-5 69
W.B. 3-4 80-81

Picture Sleeves

DOT...8-15 57-62

EPs: 7-inch

DOT...8-12 57-60

LPs: 10/12-inch

ABC...5-10 74
BIBLE VOICE 5-10 70
CANDLELITE 6-10
(Mail-order offer.)
DOT (3000 series) 20-35 55-56
(Maroon label.)
DOT (3000 series, except 3501) 10-20 57-67
(Black label. Monaural series.)
DOT (3501 "Pat Boone Sings Guess Who")...25-35 63
DOT (9000 "April Love") 30-40 57
(Soundtrack.)
DOT (25000 series, except 25270 & 25501)..10-20 58-68
(Stereo series.)
DOT (25270 "Moonglow") 10-20 60
(Black vinyl.)
DOT (25270 "Moonglow") 30-50 60
(Colored vinyl.)
DOT (25501 "Pat Boone Sings Guess Who")...25-40 63
FAMOUS TWINSET 5-8 74
HAMILTON...10-12 65
HITSVILLE 8-10 76
LAMB & LION 5-10 73-81
MC...5-10 77
MCA..5-10 82
MGM 5-10 73
PARAMOUNT..5-10 74
PICKWICK 5-10 79
SUPREME...6-10 70
TETRAGRAMMATON 10-12 69
WORD..5-10 75-84
Also see BRUCE & TERRY
Also see FONTANE SISTERS
Also see HUSKY, Ferlin / Pat Boone
Also see JENKINS, Gordon, & His Orchestra
Also see WARD, Robin

BOONE, Pat & Shirley
(Pat Boone Family)

Singles: 7-inch

DOT...4-6 62-64
MGM 3-5 72
MELODYLAND.....................................3-5 75
MOTOWN 3-5 74
W.B. 3-4 79

EPs: 7-inch

DOT...5-10 59

LPs: 10/12-inch

DOT...10-20 62
LION...5-10 72
WORD..5-10 71

BOONE, Pat, & Boone Girls

Singles: 7-inch

LION...3-4 72
Also see BOONE, Pat & Shirley
Also see BOONE GIRLS

BOONE, Richard

Singles: 7-inch

NOCTURNE 3-5 70

BOONE BROTHERS

Singles: 12-inch

ATLANTIC 4-6 83

Singles: 7-inch

ATLANTIC 3-4 83

BOONE CREEK

LPs: 10/12-inch

ROUNDER 5-10 77
SUGAR HILL 5-8 79
Members: Ricky Skaggs; Jerry Douglas; Terry Baucom; Wes Golding.
Also see SKAGGS, Ricky

BOONE FAMILY: see BOONE, Pat & Shirley

BOONE GIRLS
(Boones)

Singles: 7-inch

LAMB & LION 3-4 77
LION...3-4 72
MGM 3-5 71-73
MOTOWN 3-5 75
W.B. 3-4 77

LPs: 10/12-inch

LAMB & LION 5-10 77-83
Also see BOONE, Debbie
Also see BOONE, Pat, & Boone Girls

BOONE'S JUMPIN' JACKS — R&B '43

Singles: 78 rpm

DECCA (8644 "Please Be Careful")...25-50 43
Members: Chester Boone; George Johnson; Chauncey Graham; Vernon King; Lloyd Phillips; Buster Smith.

BOONES FARM

Singles: 7-inch

COLUMBIA 3-5 72

LPs: 10/12-inch

COLUMBIA...10-12 72

BOOT

Singles: 7-inch

AGAPE..3-5 72

LPs: 10/12-inch

AGAPE (2601 "Boot").....................15-25 72
Also see SPLIT ENDS

BOOT

Singles: 7-inch

GUINNESS..8-12 77

BOOT, Joe, & Fabulous Winds
(With the Floyd Standifer Orchestra)

Singles: 7-inch

CELESTIAL (111 "Rock and Roll Radio")..40-60 58

BOOTEE, Duke — R&B '82

Singles: 7-inch

MERCURY 3-4 84
Also see MELLE MEL & Duke Bootee

BOOTH, Ann

Singles: 7-inch

EPIC..3-5 71

BOOTH, Charlie

Singles: 7-inch

LORI (9537 "Lord Made Man").......20-30 62
LORI (9534 "Fishin' Fits")..............25-50 62

BOOTH, Chico
(With Upsetters; Quintet)

Singles: 7-inch

LEN (1012 "Skippin") 10-20 61
PALM (200 "Hot Peppers")..............10-15 60
TRIEST ("Hot Pepper").....................15-25 60
(First issue. Selection number not known.)

BOOTH, Henry

Singles: 7-inch

DELUXE..15-20 61
Also see MIDNIGHTERS
Also see ROYALS

BOOTH, Larry — C&W '78

Singles: 7-inch

CREAM 3-5 78

BOOTH, Lori

Singles: 7-inch

LORI (9537 "Lord Made Man").........5-10
LORI (9538 "Give Me a Chance") 5-10

BOOTH, Sonny

Singles: 7-inch

REVOLVO 4-8 64

BOOTH, Tony — C&W '70

Singles: 7-inch

CAPITOL..3-5 71-75
MGM 3-5 70
U.A. 3-5 77

LPs: 10/12-inch

CAPITOL..10-20 72-74
MGM 10-20 70
Also see WATSON, Gene

BOOTHE, Betty

Singles: 7-inch

FALEW...4-8 65

BOOTHE, Ken

LPs: 10/12-inch

GENERATION..5-10 79

BOOTHE, Ken / Beverley's All Stars

Singles: 7-inch

BEVERELY'S 3-5
Also see BOOTHE, Ken

BOOTHE, Patrick

Singles: 12-inch

COLUMBIA..4-6 82

Singles: 7-inch

COLUMBIA..3-4 82

BOOTHMAN, Michael

LPs: 10/12-inch

TABU..8-10 77

BOOTIQUES

Singles: 7-inch

DATE 4-8 66

BOOTLES

Singles: 7-inch

GNP...8-10 64

BOOTMEN

Singles: 7-inch

ETIQUETTE (10 "Black Widow") 10-20 64
RIVERTON (104 "Wherever You Hide")..25-50 66
Members: F. Dickerson; M. Moore; D. McCaslin.

BOOTS

Singles: 7-inch

DATE (1635 "Even the Bad Times Are Good") 10-15 69

BOOTS, Joe

Singles: 7-inch

CONTINENTAL 30-50

BOOTSY'S RUBBER BAND — R&B/LP '76
(William "Bootsy" Collins; Bootsy)

Singles: 12-inch

W.B. 5-10 79-82

Singles: 7-inch

W.B. 3-4 75-82

Picture Sleeves

W.B. 3-4 75-82

LPs: 10/12-inch

W.B. 5-15 76-82
Members: William "Bootsy" Collins; Phelp Collins; Frankie Waddy; Gary Cooper; Fred Wesley; Rick Gardner; Robert Johnson; Maceo Parker; Gary Shider; Mike Hampton; Bennie Worrell.
Also see PARLIAMENT
Also see SWEAT BAND
Also see ZAPP

BOOTY PEOPLE — R&B '76

Singles: 7-inch

CALLA..3-5 76

LPs: 10/12-inch

ABC...5-10 77

BOO-YAA T.R.I.B.E. — LP '90

LPs: 10/12-inch

4TH & BROADWAY 5-8 90

BOOZE, Bea — R&B '42
(Muriel Nichols)

Singles: 78 rpm

APOLLO...15-25 50
DECCA...20-35 42-44

BOP, Charlie, Trio

Singles: 7-inch

CAPITOL..10-20 58

BOP INCORPORATED

Singles: 7-inch

CRUNCH...3-5 74

BOP SHOP

Singles: 7-inch

HORIZON..3-5
JOKE (101 "The Stars")........................4-6 88
KELWAY..3-5 72
LARRIC...3-5

LPs: 10/12-inch

RETRO-METRO......................................8-10 89

BOP-A-LOOS

Singles: 78 rpm

MERCURY 5-10 55

Singles: 7-inch

MERCURY 10-15 55

BOP - CHORDS
("Featuring Ernest Harriston")

Singles: 78 rpm

HOLIDAY 50-100 57

Singles: 7-inch

HOLIDAY (2601 "Castle in the Sky")..100-200 57
(Black label.)
HOLIDAY (2601 "Castle in the Sky")..25-50 60s
(Glossy red label. Has double horizontal lines.)
HOLIDAY (2601 "Castle in the Sky")..15-25 60s
(Flat red label. Has single horizontal line.)
HOLIDAY (2603 "When I Woke Up This Morning")......................................100-200 57
(Black label.)
HOLIDAY (2603 "When I Woke Up This Morning") 25-50
(Glossy red label.)
HOLIDAY (2608 "Baby") 200-300 57
(Glossy red label.)
LOST NITE..3-5 80s
SIOUX (8260 "Hi-Voltage")...........10-20 60

LPs: 10/12-inch

LOST-NITE 8-12 81
Members: Ernest Harriston; Kenny "Butch" Hamilton; Morris "Mickey" Smarr; Leon Ivey; William Dailey; Peggy Jones; Skip Boyd.
Also see CHARTS / Bop - Chords / Ladders / Harmonaires
Also see 5 WINGS

BOPPERS — R&B '79

Singles: 7-inch

FANTASY..3-4 78

BOPPIN' BILLIES

Singles: 7-inch

MOPIC (9682 "Greens Rock")........15-25 59
(Identification number used since no selection number is shown. Has group photo on label.)
Member: Bill Green.

BOPTONES

Singles: 7-inch

EMBER (1043 "I Had a Love").......25-35 58

BORCHERS, Bobby — C&W '76

Singles: 7-inch

EPIC...3-5 78-79
LONGHORN...3-4 87
PLAYBOY 3-5 76-78

LPs: 10/12-inch

PLAYBOY 8-12 77

BORDEN, Sandy

Singles: 7-inch

DIPLOMACY 4-8 65

BORDERLINE

Singles: 7-inch

AVALANCHE..3-5 73

LPs: 10/12-inch

AVALANCHE..8-10 73
Members: Vassar Clements; Jim Colegrove; Dave Gershen; Jon Gershen; Ben Keith; Dick Handle; Ken Koselk; Camp Malaqua; Billy Mundi; Jim Rooney; Dave Sanborn.
Also see MOTHER EARTH

BORDERS, Tony

Singles: 7-inch

DELTA 5-10 61
HALL 4-8 64
QUINVY (001 "For My Woman's Love") 10-15
REVUE..4-8 68-69
SOUTH CAMP (7009 "You Better Believe It") 10-15
TCF 4-8 66

BORDERSONG

Singles: 7-inch

GREAT NORTHWEST (704 "She's a Good Woman") 10-20 76

LPs: 10/12-inch

REAL GOOD (1001 "Morning")....75-100 75
Members: Ann Wilson; Nancy Wilson.
Also see HEART

BOREN, Bill

Singles: 7-inch

HOME of the BLUES 5-10 61

BORIS, Chuck

Singles: 7-inch

ENTERPRISE 3-5 70

BORROWED THYME

Singles: 7-inch

U.A. 3-5 71-72

BORUM, Memphis Willie
(Memphis Willie B.)

LPs: 10/12-inch

BLUESVILLE......................................20-30 61-63

BOSEMAN, Bobby

Singles: 7-inch

EVEJIM (1941 "Another Man's Woman")..10-15

BOSMAN, Millie

Singles: 7-inch

CAT...3-5

BOSS

LPs: 10/12-inch

RCA 5-10 85

BOSS, Billy, & Boss Tones

Singles: 7-inch

GUYDEN..5-10 63

BOSS, Jerry, & Boss Guitars

Singles: 7-inch

HOUND 5-10 64

BOSS, Jim & Sundowners

Singles: 7-inch

MIRACLE (1301 "G-Stringer")..........5-10 65

BOSS BLUES

Singles: 7-inch

COBBLESTONE (702 "Takin' Life Easy")..4-8 68
DIRECTION (101 "So, Go")............10-15 67

BOSS CAMP

Singles: 7-inch

HI FI 4-8 67

BOSS COMBO

Singles: 7-inch

CORAL..5-10 62

LPs: 10/12-inch

CORAL..15-20 62

BOSS FIVE

Singles: 7-inch

IMPACT (1003 "You Cheat Too Much")..15-25 66

BOSS FOUR

Singles: 7-inch

RIM (2025 "Walkin' By") 15-25 60s

BOSS GUITARS

Singles: 7-inch

KAPP 4-8 65

LPs: 10/12-inch

KAPP 12-20 65

BOSS MAN

Singles: 7-inch

GAMBLE 4-8 68

BOSS MEN

Singles: 7-inch

BUSY BEE (1001 "Fear of Love")..10-15

BOSS TWEADS

Singles: 7-inch

STUDIO CITY (1056 "Goin' Away") 100-150 66

BOSS TWEEDS

Singles: 7-inch

CHATTAHOOCHEE (689 "Little Bad News")..15-20 65
CHATTAHOOCHEE (701 "She Belongs to Me")..15-20 67
COLUMBIA (44961 "Love Is a Happening")..5-10 69

BOSSA RIO

Singles: 7-inch

BLUE THUMB 3-5 70

LPs: 10/12-inch

BLUE THUMB 8-12 70

BOSSMAN, Billy / Bossmen

Singles: 7-inch

HBR 4-8

BOSSMEN

Singles: 7-inch

SCORE (1001 "Mashed Potatoes") 15-25 64
Members: Jesse Perales; Pete Perez; Vince Nares.
Also see MANDO & CHILI PEPPERS

BOSSMEN

Singles: 7-inch

VIM (72 "Take It Easy" 5-10 64

BOSSMEN

Singles: 7-inch

BURDLAND ("Soul Fine")...............15-20 66
Members: Jackie Lee Blount; Chris Sappington; Barry Amos; Ronnie Saucier.

BOSSMEN
(Boss-Men)

Singles: 7-inch

BECK (112 "Take a Look") 10-20 60s
DICTO (1001 "Here"s Congratulations")...............................10-20 65
DICTO (1002 "Wait and See").......10-20 65
LUCKY ELEVEN (001 "Tina Marie") 8-12 60s
LUCKY ELEVEN (227 "Wait and See")..8-12 66
LUCKY ELEVEN (231 "Baby Boy") .8-12 66
M&L (1809 "Help Me Baby")..............8-12
SOFT (121 "Take a Look") 10-20 60s

BOSSTONES
(Boss-Tones)

Singles: 7-inch

BOSS (401 "Mope-Itty Mope") 50-100 59
(Credits "Boss-Tones.")
BOSS (501 "Moptity Mope") 100-150 59
(Despite higher selection number, this seems to be the first pressing. Certainly copies of 401 with "Dist. Nationally - Ember" are later issues. Each has a differently spelled title and artist.)
LOST-NITE 4-6 70s
V-TONE (208 "Mope-Itty Mope")....40-60 60

BOSTELS

Singles: 7-inch

FUN (1092 "Oriental Goddess"). 100-125 66
(Identification number shown since no selection number is used.)

BOSTIC, Earl — R&B '48

Singles: 78 rpm

GOTHAM 5-15 46-51
KING 5-15 47-58
MAJESTIC 5-10 46
QUALITY/KING 8-12 54
(Canadian.)

Singles: 7-inch

GOTHAM (7154 "845 Stomp")......25-35 51
KING (500 series)...................................3-5 77
KING (4000 series, except 4491)...10-20 50-57
(Black vinyl.)
KING (4491 "I Got Loaded") 25-40 52
KING (4000 series).........................25-50 52-56
(Colored vinyl.)
KING (5000 series)...........................5-15 57-65
KING (6000 series)............................4-8 65-69
KING (15000 series) 3-5 72
QUALITY/KING (4289 "These Foolish Things") 15-25 54
(Canadian.)
20TH FOX (5017 "Hot Sauce! Boss")..10-20

EPs: 7-inch

KING 10-25 52-62

LPs: 10/12-inch

GRAND PRIX (416 "Earl Bostic")....15-20 60s
KING (64 "Earl Bostic & His Alto Sax")..50-100 51
(Black vinyl. 10-inch LP.)
KING (64 "Earl Bostic & His Alto Sax")..100-200 51
(Colored vinyl. 10-inch LP.)
KING (72 "Earl Bostic & His Alto Sax")..50-100 52
(10-inch LP.)
KING (76 "Earl Bostic & His Alto Sax")..50-100 52
(10-inch LP.)
KING (77 "Earl Bostic & His Alto Sax")..50-100 52
(10-inch LP.)
KING (78 "Earl Bostic & His Alto Sax")..50-100 52
(10-inch LP.)
KING (79 "Earl Bostic & His Alto Sax")..50-100 52
(10-inch LP.)
KING (95 "Earl Bostic Plays Old Standards")...................................50-100 54
(10-inch LP.)
KING (103 "Earl Bostic & His Alto Sax")..50-100 54
(10-inch LP.)
KING (119 "Earl Bostic & His Alto Sax")..50-100 54
(10-inch LP.)
KING (500 series)............................20-50 55-58
KING (600 thru 1000 series) 8-18 59-70
KING (5000 series).........................10-15 77
Also see HAMPTON, Lionel
Also see PAGE, Hot Lips

BOSTIC, Earl, & Bill Doggett

Singles: 78 rpm

KING 6-12 56

Singles: 7-inch

KING 10-15 56
Also see BOSTIC, Earl

BOSTIC, Earl / Jimmie Lunceford

LP: 10/12-inch

ALLEGRO 8-12
Also see DOGGETT, Bill

Also see LUNCEFORD, Jimmie

BOSTIC, Sam R&B '85
Singles: 7-inch
ATLANTIC 3-4 85

BOSTICK, Calvin
Singles: 78 rpm
CHESS (1530 "Christmas Won't Be Christmas") 25-50 52
CHESS (1571 "Four Eleven Boogie") 15-25 53
Singles: 7-inch
CHESS (1530 "Christmas Won't Be Christmas") 50-100 52
CHESS (1571 "Four Eleven Boogie") 25-50 53

BOSTON P&R/LP '76
Singles: 12-inch
EPIC (491 "Don't Look Back") 5-8 78
(Promotional issue only.)
Singles: 7-inch
EPIC 3-5 76-79
MCA 3-4 85-87
Picture Sleeves
MCA 3-4 85-87
LPs: 10/12-inch
EPIC (E99-34188 "Boston") 15-25 78
(Picture disc. Without cover.)
EPIC (E99-34188 "Boston") 30-40 78
(Picture disc. With cover.)
EPIC (HE-34188 "Boston") 12-15 80
(Half-speed mastered.)
EPIC (34188 "Boston") 15-25 76
(With "JE" or "PE" prefix.)
EPIC (35000 series, except 35050) 10-12 78
EPIC (35050 "Don't Look Back") 10-20 78
(Promotional black vinyl issue.)
EPIC (35050 "Don't Look Back") 50-60 80
(Picture disc.)
EPIC (35050 "Don't Look Back") 65-75 80
(Promotional picture disc.)
EPIC (HE-45000 series) 12-15 81
(Half-speed mastered.)
MCA 5-10 85-87
MFSL (249 "Boston") 15-25
Members: Brad Delp; Tom Scholz; Barry Goudreau; Sib Hashian; Fran Sheehan.
Also see GOUDREAU, Barry
Also see ORION the HUNTER

BOSTON CRABS
Singles: 7-inch
CAPITOL 4-8 65
TOWER 4-8 66-67

BOSTON HITSMEN
Singles: 7-inch
MTA 4-8 66

BOSTON POPS ORCHESTRA P&R '38
(Conducted by Arthur Fiedler)
Singles: 78 rpm
RCA 3-5 49-57
VICTOR 3-6 38
Singles: 7-inch
POLYDOR 3-4 70
RCA 3-8 50-65
RCA RED SEAL (Colored vinyl) 5-10 50s
Picture Sleeves
RCA (8378 "I Want to Hold Your Hand") 10-15 64
EPs: 7-inch
RCA 4-8 50-61
RCA RED SEAL (Colored vinyl) 8-12 50s
LPs: 10/12-inch
CAMDEN 4-8
DEUTSCHE GRAMMOPHON 4-8 78
FLEETWOOD 4-8 72
MIDSONG INT'L 4-8 79
PICKWICK/CAMDEN 4-8
POLYDOR 5-10 71-72
QUINTESSENCE 4-8
RCA 5-20 50-69
RCA/READER'S DIGEST (48 "Boston Pops Orchestra") 25-50 67
(Boxed, 10-disc set.)
Also see ATKINS, Chet, & Boston Pops
Also see ELLINGTON, Duke, & Boston Pops
Also see GETZ, Stan, & Boston Pops Orchestra
Also see HIRT, Al, & Boston Pops
Also see NERO, Peter
Also see SHERMAN, Allan

BOSTON POPS ORCHESTRA LP '80
(Conducted by John Williams)
LPs: 10/12-inch
PHILIPS 5-10 80-86
Also see WILLIAMS, John

BOSTON ROCKABILLY MUSIC CONSPIRACY
(B.R.M.C.)
Singles: 7-inch
BLACK ROSE 3-5 82
EPs: 7-inch
BLACK ROSE 5-10 81-83
LPs: 10/12-inch
BLACK ROSE 8-10 88
Members: Vic Layne; John Tate; Rick Gallant; Jim Scoppa; Chuck Myra; Ray Gillette.

BOSTON TEA PARTY
Singles: 7-inch
BIG BOSS (1002 "Words") 30-40 67
CHALLENGE (59368 "Words") 20-30 67
FLICK-DISC (900 "Free Service") 15-25 68
FONA (311 "Is It Love") 20-30 67
VOGUE INT'L (101 "My Daze") 20-30 67
LPs: 10/12-inch
FLICK DISC (45,000 "The Boston Tea Party") 50-75 68
Members: Travis Fields; Mike Stevens; Richard De Perna; Robert De Perna; Dave Novogroski.

BOSTONIANS
Singles: 7-inch
PLATINUM BLUE ROSE 3-4 81

BOSTWEEDS
Singles: 7-inch
CHATTAHOOCHEE 5-10 65
EVE ("Faster Pussycat!") 10-20 65

BOSWELL, Bolliver
Singles: 7-inch
PYRO 5-10

BOSWELL, Connee P&R '32
Singles: 78 rpm
BRUNSWICK 5-10 32-44
DECCA 5-10 35-56
Singles: 7-inch
CHARLES 4-8 62
DECCA 5-10 50-56
EPs: 7-inch
DECCA 5-15 56
RCA 5-10 57
LPs: 10/12-inch
DECCA 15-25 56
DESIGN 5-10 60s
RCA 10-20 57
Also see BOSWELL SISTERS
Also see CROSBY, Bing, & Connee Boswell

BOSWELL, Paul
Singles: 7-inch
TOP-PIC 4-8 63

BOSWELL SISTERS P&R '31
Singles: 78 rpm
BRUNSWICK 5-15 31-35
DECCA 5-10 35-37
Members: Connie Boswell; Martha Boswell; Vet Boswell.
Also see BOSWELL, Connie

BOTIQUES
Singles: 7-inch
DATE 4-8 67

BOTTLE COMPANY
Singles: 7-inch
HIDEOUT (1230 "Lives for No One") 100-150 60s

BOTTLE UPS
EPs: 7-inch
RAINBOW 8-10 84

BOTTLES
Singles: 7-inch
MCA 3-4 79-82
LPs: 10/12-inch
MCA 5-10 79

BOTTOM & COMPANY R&B '74
Singles: 7-inch
MOTOWN 3-5 74-75
LPs: 10/12-inch
GORDY 8-10 76

BOTTOM LINE R&B '76
Singles: 7-inch
GREEDY 3-5 76
LPs: 10/12-inch
GREEDY 8-10 76

BOTTOMS, Dennis C&W '85
Singles: 7-inch
W.B. 3-4 85

BOTTS, Harley
Singles: 7-inch
FELSTED 5-10 58

BOTUMLESS PIT
Singles: 7-inch
PSYCHEDELIC (113 "13 Stories High") 10-15

BOUBARERE, Marie
Singles: 7-inch
NOLA (731 "I Know") 8-10 67

BOUCHER, Pegi
Singles: 7-inch
HIBACK 4-8 66
Picture Sleeves
HIBACK 5-10 66

BOUGALIEU
Singles: 7-inch
ROULETTE (4767 "Let's Do Wrong") 15-20 67
ROULETTE (4776 "Let's Do Wrong") 10-15 67
(A different take than on #4767.)

BOUGHN, Christy, & Dale Kahr
Singles: 7-inch
FOGGY LOVE 3-6 69

BOULANGER, Leon
Singles: 7-inch
HEP 4-8 67

BOULDER
Singles: 7-inch
ELEKTRA 3-4 80
LPs: 10/12-inch
ELEKTRA 5-10 79

BOULEVARD
Singles: 7-inch
PYE 3-5 72

BOULEVARDS
Singles: 7-inch
EVEREST (19316 "Delores") 20-30 59

BOUNCIN' BEATS
Singles: 7-inch
BEAT (4839 "The Bounce") 8-12
EPIC (9788 "Need Your Love") 10-20 65

BOUND BROOK SOUND
Singles: 7-inch
SCEPTER 4-8 66

BOUNEE
LPs: 10/12-inch
REBOUND 5-10 81

BOUNTY, Rick, & Rockits
Singles: 7-inch
BOW (6144 "It'll Be Me") 100-150 58
MASSABESIC 3-5 86
Picture Sleeves
MASSABESIC 3-5 86

BOUNTY HUNTERS
Singles: 7-inch
HURON 5-10 61
ROMAIN 5-10

BOUQUETS
Singles: 7-inch
BLUE CAT (115 "Welcome to My Heart") 15-25 65
MALA 4-8 64
VEST 4-8 63

BOURBONS
Singles: 7-inch
ROYAL FAMILY (267 "A Dark Corner") 20-30 67

BOURGEOIS, Gene
Singles: 7-inch
CAPITOL 4-8 68
Also see JIVIN' GENE

BOURGEOIS, Marye
Singles: 7-inch
DJO 3-5

BOURGEOIS - TAGG P&R/LP '86
Singles: 7-inch
ISLAND 3-4 86-87
LPs: 10/12-inch
ISLAND 5-10 86-87
Members: Brent Bourgeois; Larry Tagg.

BOURLAND, Jan
Singles: 7-inch
DYNASTY 5-10 59

BOURQUE, Butch
Singles: 7-inch
BELMONT 4-6 84

BOW RIBBONS
Singles: 7-inch
MOTIF 5-10 59
TRANS-CONTINENTAL 3-5 59

BOW STREET RUNNERS
LPs: 10/12-inch
B.T. PUPPY (1026 "Bow Street Runners") 800-1200 70
Member: Mick Fleetwood.
Also see FLEETWOOD, Mick

BOW WOW WOW LP '81
Singles: 12-inch
RCA 4-6 83
Singles: 7-inch
RCA 3-4 81-84
Picture Sleeves
RCA 3-4 82
LPs: 10/12-inch
HARVEST 5-10 82
RCA 5-10 81-84
Promotional LPs
RCA ("Special Radio Series") 10-15 81
Members: Annabella Lu Win; Matt Ashman; Dave Barbarossa; Leroy Gorman.
Also see ADAM & ANTS

BOWE, Linda
Singles: 7-inch
20TH FOX 3-5 60

BO-WEEVILS
Singles: 7-inch
UNITED STATES 10-15 64

BOWEN, Bill
Singles: 78 rpm
METEOR 50-100 56
Singles: 7-inch
METEOR (5033 "Have Myself a Ball") 150-250 56

BOWEN, Billy, & Butterball Four
Singles: 78 rpm
MGM 15-25 52
Singles: 7-inch
MGM (11271 "You Broke My Heart") 25-45 52

BOWEN, Danny
Singles: 7-inch
TOPPA 4-8 63

BOWEN, Jeff
Singles: 7-inch
MERCURY 4-8 64

BOWEN, Jimmy P&R/R&B '57
Singles: 78 rpm
ROULETTE 25-50 57
Singles: 7-inch
CAPEHART 5-10 61-62
CREST 5-10 61
REPRISE 5-10 64-66
ROULETTE (Except 4002) 10-20 57-60
ROULETTE (4002 "Party Doll") 30-40 57
(Credited to "Jimmy Bowen with the Rhythm Orchids" though actually by Buddy Knox.)
Picture Sleeves
CAPEHART (5005 "Teenage Dreamworld") 30-40 61
EPs: 7-inch
ROULETTE (302 "Jimmy Bowen") 50-75 57
LPs: 10/12-inch
REPRISE (6210 "Sunday Morning with the Comics") 20-25 66
ROULETTE (25004 "Jimmy Bowen") 75-100 57
(Black label.)
ROULETTE (25004 "Jimmy Bowen") 100-150 57
(White label. Promotional issue only.)
ROULETTE (25004 "Jimmy Bowen") 5-10
(Reissue for the Outlet Book Co. and Publishers Central Bureau, and labeled as such.)
Members (Rhythm Orchids): Buddy Knox; Jimmy Bowen; Dave Alldred; Don Lanier.
Also see KNOX, Buddy / Jimmy Bowen

BOWEN, Rick
Singles: 7-inch
GEMINI 3-5

BOWEN & RICHARDS
Singles: 7-inch
RANWOOD 3-5 76

BOWENS, Pvt. Charles
Singles: 7-inch
ROJAC 15-20

BOWER, Chuck, & Stardusters
Singles: 78 rpm
BLUE RIBBON 10-15 55
Singles: 7-inch
BLUE RIBBON (101 "Cy Boogie") 15-25 55

BOWER, Maurice
Singles: 7-inch
HI 4-8 65

BOWERS, Bob
Singles: 7-inch
DART 5-10 60

BOWERS, Chuck
Singles: 78 rpm
CHOICE 10-20 56
Singles: 7-inch
CHOICE 15-25 56

BOWERS, Kenny
Singles: 7-inch
COLUMBIA 5-10 58

BOWERS, Richard
Singles: 7-inch
COLUMBIA 5-10 50s

BOWERY BOYS
Singles: 7-inch
HEMISPHERE 3-6 69-72

BOWES, Margie C&W '59
Singles: 7-inch
DECCA 4-6 63-64
HICKORY 5-10 59-60
MERCURY 4-8 61-63
LPs: 10/12-inch
DECCA 15-25 67-69

BOWIE, David P&R/LP '72
Singles: 12-inch
EMI AMERICA 5-10 82-87
RCA 10-15 79-80
Promotional 12-inch Singles
EMI AMERICA 8-15 82-87
RCA 15-25 79-80
Singles: 7-inch
BACKSTREET 3-5 82
DERAM (85009 "Rubber Band") 20-40 67
EMI AMERICA 3-5 83-87
(Black vinyl.)
EMI AMERICA (8231 "Blue Jean") 5-8 84
(Colored vinyl.)
LONDON (20079 "The Laughing Gnome") 15-25 73
MCA/BACKSTREET ("Cat People") 50-65 82
(Promotional only picture disc. No selection number used.)
MCA/BACKSTREET ("Cat People") 75-90 82
(Promotional only picture disc. No selection number used. B-side says: "Filmex" promo.)
MERCURY (72949 "Space Oddity") 30-50 69
MERCURY (73075 "Memory of a Free Festival") 35-50 70
MERCURY (73173 "All the Madmen") 40-60 71
RCA 3-6 71-84
W.B. (5815 "Can't Help Thinking About Me") 50-75 66
Picture Sleeves
BACKSTREET (1767 "Cat People") 4-8 82
EMI AMERICA 3-5 83-87
RCA (0001 "Time") 200-400 73
RCA (0719 "Starman") 15-20 72
RCA (0876 "Space Oddity") 10-15 73
RCA (12078 "Ashes to Ashes") 10-15 80
RCA (12134 "Fashion") 5-10 80
RCA (13660 "White Light White Heat") 3-5 83
RCA (13769 "1984") 3-5 80
Promotional Singles
BACKSTREET 5-10 82
DERAM (85009 "Rubber Band") 30-40 67
EMI AMERICA (8158 thru 8190) 4-8 83-84
EMI AMERICA (8231 "Blue Jean") 4-8 84
EMI AMERICA (8246 thru 8308) 4-8 83-86
EMI AMERICA (8380 "Day in Day Out") 4-8 87
EMI AMERICA (8380 "Day in Day Out") 15-20 87
(Colored vinyl. Boxed edition.)
EMI AMERICA (43000 series) 4-8 87
LONDON (20079 "The Laughing Gnome") 15-25 73
MERCURY (311 "All the Madmen") 40-60 70
MERCURY (72949 "Space Oddity") 30-50 69
MERCURY (73075 "Memory of a Free Festival") 40-60 70
RCA 5-12 71-84
W.B. (5815 "Can't Help Thinking About Me") 50-75 66
WHAT'S IT ALL ABOUT 10-20 70s
EPs: 7-inch
RCA 20-25 70s
(Promotional issues only.)
LPs: 10/12-inch
DERAM (16003 "David Bowie") 100-125 67
(Monaural.)
DERAM (18003 "David Bowie") 100-150 67
(Stereo.)
EMI AMERICA 5-10 83-87
LONDON 10-20 73-85
MFSL (064 "Rise and Fall of Ziggy Stardust") 40-60 82
MFSL (083 "Let's Dance") 25-35 82
MERCURY (61246 "Man of Words/Man of Music") 75-100 69
MERCURY (61246 "Space Oddity") 10-15 72
MERCURY (61325 "The Man Who Sold the World") 25-40 71
PRECISION (1 "Don't Be Fooled By the Name") 20-25 81
(10-inch LP.)
RCA (0291 "Bowie Pin Ups") 10-15 73
RCA (0576 "Diamond Dogs") 1500-2000 74
(With "Dog Genitals" cover.)
RCA (0576 "Diamond Dogs") 10-15 74
(With dog's genitals covered.)
RCA (0700 thru 1300 series) 10-15 74-76
RCA (1732 "Changesone Bowie") 100-150 76
(With alternate take of *John, I'm Only Dancing*.)
RCA (1732 "Changesone Bowie") 10-20 76
(With the commonly issued take of *John, I'm Only Dancing*.)
RCA (2000 thru 2500) 10-15 77
RCA (2743 "Peter and the Wolf") 10-15 78
(Black vinyl. With Eugene Ormandy & Philadelphia Orchestra.)
RCA (2743 "Peter and the Wolf") 35-55 78
(Colored vinyl. With Eugene Ormandy & Philadelphia Orchestra.)
RCA (2900 thru 4200 series) 5-10 79-82
RCA (4600 thru 4800 series) 10-15 71-73
(With "LSP" prefix.)
RCA (4700 thru 4900 series, except 4862) 5-10 83-84
(With "AFL," "AYL" or "CPL" prefix.)
RCA 4862 "Ziggy Stardust") 5-10 83
(Black vinyl.)
RCA 4862 "Ziggy Stardust") 40-80 83
(Clear vinyl.)
RYKODISC (Except 0120/2) 8-12 87-90
RYKODISC (0120/2 "Sound and Vision") 50-75 89
(Boxed, six-disc set.)
Promotional LPs
DERAM (18003 "David Bowie") 200-300 67
EMI AMERICA (9960 "Let's Talk") 40-70 83
MERCURY (61246 "Man of Words/Man of Music") 75-125 69
MERCURY (61325 "The Man Who Sold the World") 75-125 71
RCA (0200 thru 4800 series) 20-40 71-73
(With programmer's strip on front cover.)
RCA (2697 "Bowie Now") 30-50 78
RCA (3016 "An Evening with David Bowie") 100-200 78
RCA (3545 "Bowie 1980") 50-75 80
RCA (3829 "RCA Special Radio Series") 30-50 80
RCA (3840 "Interview") 35-50 80
RCA (11306 "Peter and the Wolf") 30-40 78
Also see HOUSTON, Cissy
Also see KHAN, Chaka
Also see QUEEN & David Bowie
Also see SPIDERS from MARS
Also see TURNER, Tina
Also see VANDROSS, Luther

BOWIE, David / Joe Cocker / Youngbloods
LPs: 10/12-inch
MERCURY (SRD-2-29 "Zig Zag Festival") 40-60 70
(Promotional issue only.)
Also see COCKER, Joe
Also see YOUNGBLOODS

BOWIE, David, & Bing Crosby
Singles: 7-inch
RCA (13400 "Peace on Earth") 8-12 77
(Promotional issue only.)
RCA 3-6 83
Picture Sleeves
RCA (13400 "Peace on Earth") 8-12 77
(Promotional issue only.)

RCA ... 4-8 83
Also see CROSBY, Bing

BOWIE, David, & Mick Jagger *P&R/D&D '85*
Singles: 12-inch
EMI AMERICA (19200 "Dancing in the Streets") ... 8-12 85
Singles: 7-inch
EMI AMERICA (8288 "Dancing in the Streets") ... 3-4 85
Picture Sleeves
EMI AMERICA (8288 "Dancing in the Streets") ... 3-5 85
Also see JAGGER, Mick

BOWIE, David, & Pat Metheny Group *P&R/D&D '85*
Singles: 12-inch
EMI AMERICA ... 4-8 85
Singles: 7-inch
EMI AMERICA ... 3-4 85
Picture Sleeves
EMI AMERICA ... 3-4 85
LPs: 10/12-inch
EMI AMERICA ... 5-10 85
Also see METHENY, Pat

BOWIE, David / Iggy Pop
Singles: 12-inch
RCA (10956 "Sound and Vision") ... 30-50 77
(Promotional issue only.)
Also see BOWIE, David
Also see POP, Iggy

BOWIE, Larry
Singles: 7-inch
CHICKEN SCRATCH ... 3-4 84

BOWIE, Pat
Singles: 7-inch
PRESTIGE ... 4-8 65
LPs: 10/12-inch
PRESTIGE ... 10-15

BOWIE, Roz
Singles: 7-inch
BLUESTEM (17834 "The Boz") ... 3-5 87
(Red vinyl.)
Picture Sleeves
BLUESTEM ... 3-5 87
LPs: 10/12-inch
BLUESTEM ... 5-10 87

BOWIE, Sam, & Blue Feelings
Singles: 7-inch
WINGATE (002 "Times We Had Together") ... 15-20 65

BOWLEGS
Singles: 7-inch
VEE JAY ... 8-12 61
ZAB ... 10-15 61-62

BOWLES, Doug, & Rubarbs
Singles: 7-inch
TUNE (206 "Cadillac Cutie") ... 25-50 59

BOWLES, Rick *P&R '82*
Singles: 7-inch
POLYDOR ... 3-4 82
LPs: 10/12-inch
POLYDOR ... 5-10 82

BOWLING, Roger *C&W '78*
Singles: 7-inch
LOUISIANA HAYRIDE ... 3-5 78
MERCURY ... 3-4 81
NSD ... 3-4 80

BOWMAN, Billy Bob, with Bearmont Bag & Burlap Company *C&W '72*
(Biff Collie)
Singles: 7-inch
U.A. ... 3-5 72

BOWMAN, Bob
Singles: 7-inch
REVELLO (1001 "Betty Lou") ... 25-50 59

BOWMAN, Don *C&W '64*
(With "Friends")
Singles: 7-inch
LAGREE ... 3-5 70s
RCA ... 4-8 64-69
LPs: 10/12-inch
LONE STAR ... 5-10 79
MEGA ... 6-12 72
RCA ... 10-20 64-70
Session: Waylon Jennings; Bobby Bare; Willie Nelson.
Also see BARE, Bobby
Also see DAVIS, Skeeter, & Don Bowman
Also see JENNINGS, Waylon
Also see NELSON, Willie
Also see SOME of CHET'S FRIENDS

BOWMAN, Jane
Singles: 7-inch
SAPIEN (1002 "Dearest Little Angel") ... 150-250 61

BOWMAN, Jimmy
Singles: 7-inch
JAYBO ... 5-10 60s
KAY BEE ... 8-12 60s
PENNY ... 8-12 60s
SOMA ... 8-12 60s

BOWMAN, Leon
EPs: 7-inch
REED (903 "Rockin' the Blues") 250-350

BOWMAN, Mickey
Singles: 7-inch
JACK BEE ... 5-10 59

BOWMAN, Priscilla
Singles: 78 rpm
VEE JAY ... 10-15 56
Singles: 7-inch
ABNER ... 5-10 59
FALCON (1008 "Sugar Daddy") ... 10-20 58
VEE JAY ... 10-20 56
Also see MC SHANN, Jay, & Priscilla Bowman

BOWMAN BROTHERS & Norman Petty Trio
Singles: 7-inch
COLUMBIA (41176 "Hey Pumpkin") ... 10-15 58

BOWMEN
Singles: 7-inch
DOT ... 8-12 63-64

BOWN, Alan
(Alan Bown Set)
Singles: 7-inch
DERAM ... 3-6 69
MGM ... 4-8 68
MUSIC FACTORY ... 4-8 67-68
LPs: 10/12-inch
DERAM ... 12-15 69
ISLAND ... 10-12 71
MUSIC FACTORY ... 15-20 68
VERVE/FORECAST ... 10-12 70
Also see PALMER, Robert

BOWN, Andy
Singles: 7-inch
MERCURY ... 3-5 72-73
LPs: 10/12-inch
EMI AMERICA ... 5-10 76
MERCURY ... 8-10 73

BOWS & ARROWS
Singles: 7-inch
GNP ... 4-8 65

BOWSER, Donnie *C&W '89*
(Little Donnie Bowshier & Radio Ranch Boys; Donnie Bowshier)
Singles: 7-inch
BAMBOO ... 5-10 61
CHOICE ... 4-8
DESS (7002 "Rock & Roll Joys") ... 150-200 57
DESS (7004 "I Love You Baby") ... 10-20 57
ERA ... 5-10 60
FRATERNITY (801 "I Love You Baby") ... 20-40 58
J.D. ... 5-10
RIDGEWOOD ... 3-4 89
ROBBINS (1001 "I Love You Baby") ... 50-75 58
ROME ... 4-8
SAGE ... 10-20 58
Also see BOWSHIER, Little Donnie, & Radio Ranch Boys

BOWSHIER, Little Donnie: see BOWSER, Donnie

BOWTIES
Singles: 78 rpm
ROYAL ROOST ... 10-15 55-56
Singles: 7-inch
ROYAL ROOST ... 15-25 55-56
Members: Cirino & Bowties; Cirino Colocrai; Jimmy Piro; John Granada; Vince Sepaldo.

BOWYER, Brendan
Singles: 7-inch
TOWER ... 4-8 65

BOX
Singles: 7-inch
BOARDWALK ... 3-4 81

BOX, David
(With Bob Moore's Orchestra & Chorus)
Singles: 7-inch
CANDIX (339 "I've Had My Moments") ... 8-12 62
JOED (116 "Little Lonesome Summer Girl") ... 10-20 64
Also see CRICKETS
Also see MOORE, Bob

BOX, Euel
Singles: 7-inch
PAMS ... 4-8 62
(Special advertising release from the manufacturer of Fritos.)

BOX & BLEACHER SOCIETY
Singles: 7-inch
MAMMOTH ... 4-8 65

BOX OF FROGS *LP '84*
Singles: 7-inch
EPIC ... 3-4 84-86
LPs: 10/12-inch
EPIC ... 5-10 84-86
Members: Chris Dreja; Jim McCarty; Jeff Beck.
Also see YARDBIRDS

BOX TOPS *P&R/R&B/LP '67*
Singles: 7-inch
BELL ... 3-5 70-71
GUSTO ... 3-4 84
HI ... 3-5 72-73
MALA ... 4-8 67-69
SPHERE SOUND ... 4-8 67
STAX ... 3-5 74
LPs: 10/12-inch
BELL ... 10-20 67-69
COTILLION ... 10-15 71
KORY ... 5-10 76
RHINO ... 5-10 82
Members: Alex Chilton; Rick Allen; Tom Boggs; Harold Cloud; Bill Cunningham; John Evans; Swain Scharfar; Gary Talley; Danny Smythe; Rick Stevens.
Also see BIG STAR
Also see CHILTON, Alex

BOXCAR WILLIE *C&W '80*
(Lecil T. Martin)
Singles: 7-inch
ARISTA ... 3-4 89
COLUMN ONE ... 3-5 80
MAIN STREET ... 3-4 81-84
LPs: 10/12-inch
AMERICAN HERITAGE ... 8-12 70
COLUMN ONE ... 6-12 76-80
MAIN STREET ... 5-10 82-84
STAR FLEET ... 10-15 81
SUFFOLK MARKETING ... 5-10 80-83

BOXER
Singles: 7-inch
VIRGIN ... 3-5 76-77
Picture Sleeves
VIRGIN ... 3-5 76
LPs: 10/12-inch
EPIC ... 5-10 77
VIRGIN ... 8-10 76
Members: Mike Patto; Keith Ellis; Ollie Halsall; Tony Newman.
Also see PATTO
Also see SPOOKY TOOTH

BOXER, Karl
Singles: 7-inch
DOT ... 10-15 66

BOXKITE, Bristol
Singles: 7-inch
WORLD PACIFIC ... 3-6 68

BOXX, Freda, & Rockin' Aces
Singles: 7-inch
MARLO (1513 "Havin' a Ball") ... 15-25 50s

BOY
Singles: 7-inch
CAMEO ... 4-8 65

BOY BLUES
Singles: 7-inch
FRANTIC (2131 "Coming Down to You") ... 20-30 67

BOY GEORGE *P&R/R&B/LP '87*
(George O'Dowd)
Singles: 7-inch
VIRGIN ... 3-4 87-89
Picture Sleeves
VIRGIN ... 3-4 87
LPs: 10/12-inch
VIRGIN ... 5-10 87-89
Also see CULTURE CLUB
Also see SUN FERRY AID

BOY FRIENDS
Singles: 7-inch
GLASER ... 5-10 61

BOY HOWDY *C&W '92*
Singles: 7-inch
CURB ... 3-4 92

BOY MEETS GIRL *P&R/LP '85*
Singles: 7-inch
A&M ... 3-4 85
RCA ... 3-4 88-89
Picture Sleeves
A&M ... 3-4 85
RCA ... 3-4 88-89
LPs: 10/12-inch
A&M ... 5-10 85
RCA ... 5-8 88
Members: George Merrill; Shannon Rubicam.

BOYCE, Jesse
Singles: 7-inch
COMPLEAT ... 3-4 83-84

BOYCE, Tommy *P&R '62*
Singles: 7-inch
A&M (Except 826) ... 4-8 66
A&M (826 "In Case the Wind Should Blow") ... 10-12 66
CAPITOL ... 3-5 71
COLPIX ... 8-10 66
DOT ... 10-15 60
MGM ... 8-10 65
RCA (7000 series) ... 15-25 61
RCA (8000 series) ... 8-12 62-63
R-DELL ... 15-25 58
WOW ... 8-12 61
LPs: 10/12-inch
CAMDEN ... 15-20 68
Also see CLOUD, Christopher

BOYCE, Tommy, & Bobby Hart *P&R/LP '67*
(Boyce & Hart)
Singles: 7-inch
A&M ... 4-8 67-69
AQUARIAN ... 3-6 68
Picture Sleeves
A&M ... 5-10 67-69
AQUARIAN ... 5-8 68
LPs: 10/12-inch
A&M ... 10-20 67-69
Also see ATTORNEYS
Also see BOYCE, Tommy
Also see DOLENZ, JONES, BOYCE & HART
Also see HART, Bobby

BOYD, Bill, & Cowboy Ramblers *C&W '45*
(With Jim Boyd)
Singles: 78 rpm
BLUEBIRD ... 10-15 34-45
RCA ... 5-10 46
Singles: 7-inch
RCA GOLD STANDARD ... 5-10 50s
LPs: 10/12-inch
BLUEBIRD ... 20-30
TEXAS ROSE ... 10-20

BOYD, Billy
LPs: 10/12-inch
CROWN (196 "Twangy Guitars") ... 15-20 63
(Stereo. Black vinyl.)
CROWN (196 "Twangy Guitars") ... 50-75 63
(Stereo. Colored vinyl.)
CROWN (5170 "Twangy Guitars") 15-20 63
(Monaural.)
Also see DAILEY, Don

BOYD, Bobby
(With the Playboys)
Singles: 7-inch
CHATTANOOGA ... 4-8 67
VEEP ... 4-8 65

BOYD, Danny
Singles: 7-inch
L'AMI ... 4-8 67
UPTOWN ... 3-6 69

BOYD, Donnie
(With the 4 D's)
Singles: 7-inch
DART ... 25-50 58-60
LAUREL (1022 "Brahm's Express 9") ... 15-25 59
TWIN STAR ... 20-30 60

BOYD, Eddie *R&B '52*
(With His Chess Men; Eddie Boyd Blues Combo; Little Eddie Boyd & His Boogie Band)
Singles: 78 rpm
CHESS ... 15-25 52-56
HERALD ... 50-75 52
J.O.B. ... 25-75 52-57
RCA ... 15-25 47-50
Singles: 7-inch
ART TONE (832 "I'm Comin' Home") ... 10-15 62
BEA & BABY (101 "I'm Comin' Home") ... 20-30 59
BEA & BABY (107 "Blue Monday Blues") ... 20-30 59
BEA & BABY (108 "Come Home") ... 20-30 59
CHESS (1523 "Cool Kind Treatment") ... 40-60 52
CHESS (1533 "24 Hours") ... 40-60 53
CHESS (1541 "Third Degree") ... 40-60 53
CHESS (1552 "That's When I Miss You") ... 40-60 53
CHESS (1561 "Picture in the Frame") ... 40-60 54
CHESS (1573 "Hush Baby, Don't You Cry") ... 40-60 54
CHESS (1576 "Driftin' ") ... 20-40 54
CHESS (1582 "The Story of Bill") ... 20-40 55
CHESS (1595 "Real Good Feeling") ... 20-40 55
CHESS (1606 "I'm a Prisoner") ... 20-40 55
CHESS (1634 "Just a Fool") ... 20-40 56
CHESS (1660 "I Got a Woman") ... 20-40 56
CHESS (1674 "I Got the Blues") ... 20-40 57
CHESS (Colored vinyl) ... 150-200 54
(We are unable at this time to specify exactly which Chess numbers were pressed on colored vinyl.)
HERALD (406 "I'm Goin' Downtown") ... 75-125 52
J.O.B. (1007 "Five Long Years") ... 75-125 52
(Black vinyl.)
J.O.B. (1007 "Five Long Years") ... 200-300 52
(Red vinyl.)
J.O.B. (1009 "It's Miserable to Be Alone") ... 40-60 53
J.O.B. (1114 "I Love You") ... 30-50 57
LA SALLE (503 "I Cry") ... 10-20 61
MOJO (2167 "It's Too Bad") ... 8-12 60s
ORIOLE (1316 "Five Long Years") 20-30 58
PALOS (1206 "Empty Arms") ... 8-12 63
PUSH (1050 "Ten to One") ... 8-12 62
RCA (50-0006 "What Makes These Things Happen to Me") ... 35-50 50
(Colored vinyl.)
EPs: 7-inch
ESQUIRE (247 "Eddie Boyd Blues Combo") ... 25-50 60
LPs: 10/12-inch
EPIC (26409 "7936 South Rhodes") ... 15-25 69
LONDON (554 "I'll Dust My Broom") ... 15-20 69
Session: Willie Dixon; Howard Dixon; J.T. Brown; James Clark; Lonnie Graham; Sax Mallard; Bill Casimir; Willie Lacey.
Also see BOYD, Ernie
Also see DIXON, Willie
Also see GREEN, Peter

BOYD, Ernie
(Eddie Boyd)
Singles: 78 rpm
REGAL (3305 "Why Don't You Be Wise, Baby") ... 35-50 50
Also see BOYD, Eddie

BOYD, Idalia
Singles: 7-inch
DIMENSION ... 10-20 63

BOYD, Jim
Singles: 7-inch
SIMS ... 4-8 64
TAKE TEN ... 4-8 63

BOYD, Jimmy *P&R/C&W '52*
(Little Jimmy Boyd)
Singles: 78 rpm
COLUMBIA (Except 21571) ... 4-8 52-56
COLUMBIA (21571 "Rockin' Down the Mississippi") ... 10-15 56
Singles: 7-inch
CAPITOL ... 4-8 63
COLUMBIA (152 "I Saw Mommy Kissing Santa Claus") ... 10-20 52
COLUMBIA (21571 "Rockin' Down the Mississippi") ... 30-40 56
COLUMBIA (39000 & 40000 series) ... 10-20 52-56
IMPERIAL ... 3-6 66-67
MGM (12788 "Cream Puff") ... 40-50 59
TAKE TEN ... 4-8 63
VEE JAY ... 4-8 65
Picture Sleeves
COLUMBIA (152 "I Saw Mommy Kissing Santa Claus") ... 15-25 52
(With die-cut center hole.)
EPs: 7-inch
COLUMBIA (1913 "Jimmy Boyd") ... 10-15 50s
Also see LAINE, Frankie, & Jimmy Boyd

BOYD, Jimmy, & Rosemary Clooney *P&R '53*
Singles: 78 rpm
COLUMBIA ... 4-8 53
Singles: 7-inch
COLUMBIA (39000 series) ... 8-12 53
COLUMBIA (41000 series) ... 4-8 60
Also see BOYD, Jimmy
Also see CLOONEY, Rosemary

BOYD, Little Eddie: see BOYD, Eddie

BOYD, Melvin
Singles: 7-inch
ERA (3167 "Exit Loneliness, Enter Love") ... 12-25 66

BOYD, Mickey, & Plain Viewers
(Keith McCormick)
Singles: 7-inch
7 ARTS (700 "Tell the World") ... 20-30 61
Also see STRING-A-LONGS

BOYD, Mike *C&W '76*
Singles: 7-inch
BLAST-OFF ... 3-6 69
CLARIDGE ... 3-5 76
INERGI ... 3-5 78
MBI ... 3-5 77

BOYD, Oscar
Singles: 7-inch
HERMES ... 5-10
SUCCESS ... 5-10 63

BOYD, Reggie
Singles: 7-inch
AGE (29110 "Nothing But Good") ... 10-20 62
LIBERTY (55621 "Cotton Picker") 10-20 63

BOYD, Robert
Singles: 78 rpm
WASCO (201 "East St. Louis Baby") ... 75-125 50
Also see PROFESSOR LONGHAIR

BOYD, Sylvester
Singles: 7-inch
KING ... 3-5 73

BOYD, Terry
Singles: 7-inch
COED ... 4-8 64

BOYD, Tim, & Esquires
(With the Bill Gibbs Combo)
Singles: 7-inch
ODESSA (101 "My Dearest, My Darling") ... 500-1000 60s
Also see ESQUIRES
Also see GIBBS, Bill

BOYD SISTERS
Singles: 7-inch
ROULETTE ... 4-8 65

BOYE, Franny
Singles: 7-inch
COLPIX ... 4-8 60
GONE ... 4-8 61

BOYELL, Dick
Singles: 7-inch
DUNHILL ... 4-8 67

BOYER, Bonnie *P&R '79*
Singles: 12-inch
COLUMBIA ... 4-6 79
Singles: 7-inch
COLUMBIA ... 3-4 79
LPs: 10/12-inch
COLUMBIA ... 5-10 79

BOYER, Charles *LP '66*
Singles: 7-inch
VALIANT ... 3-6 65
LPs: 10/12-inch
VALIANT ... 10-20 65

BOYER, Gina
Singles: 7-inch
LIBERTY ... 5-8 61-62

BOYER, Jim
(With the Chocolate Pickles; with Newports)
Singles: 7-inch
A.D.A.V. 10-15 64
DARN (10 "Hey You") 50-100

BOYER TWINS C&W '80
Singles: 7-inch
GUSTO 3-4 78
SABRE 3-4 80-81
Members: Gene Boyer; Dean Boyer.

BOYFRIENDS
(With Mort Garson Orchestra)
Singles: 7-inch
KAPP (569 "Let's Fall in Love") 150-200 64
(Black label.)
KAPP (569 "Let's Fall in Love") 150-200 64
(White label. Title at top, artist credits at bottom. Promotional issue only.)
KAPP (569 "Let's Fall in Love") 100-150 64
(White label. Top is blank. Title and artist credits at bottom. Promotional issue only.)
Members: Steve Bray; Pat Collier; Mark Henry; Chris Skornia; Chris Smith.
Also see FIVE DISCS

BOYFRIENDS
EPs: 7-inch
BOMP 5-10

BOYKIN, Jerald
Singles: 7-inch
OZARK ("Walkin' Talkin' Baby Doll") 50-100
(Selection number not known.)

BOYKIN, Wayne
Singles: 7-inch
ATLANTIC 3-6 69

BOYLAN, Terence LP '77
Singles: 7-inch
ASYLUM 3-4 77-80
LPs: 10/12-inch
ASYLUM 5-10 77-80
VERVE/FORECAST 12-15 69
Session: Darius Davenport.
Also see APPLETREE THEATRE CO.
Also see AUTOSALVAGE

BOYLE, Bobby
Singles: 7-inch
JANIE 4-8 65
BRITE STAR 4-8 67
BRYTE 4-8 62-65
ROY 4-8 65
TIARA 5-10 59

BOYNTON, Hugh
(Huriah Boynton)
Singles: 7-inch
LANOR 4-8

BOYS
Singles: 7-inch
DOT (15794 "Cobra") 10-20 58
LIL-TEE (1003 "Shake It Up") 10-20
#1 (0001 "Cobra") 20-30 58
(First issue.)

BOYS
Singles: 7-inch
CAMEO 10-15 65
KAMA SUTRA (203 "Every Morning") 15-25 65
SVR (1001 "Angel of Mine") 20-30 64
SVR (1002 "It's Hopeless") 25-50 64

BOYS
Singles: 7-inch
EMCEE (15 "You Deceived Me") 25-35 66

BOYS P&R/LP '88
Singles: 7-inch
MOTOWN 3-4 88-90
Picture Sleeves
MOTOWN 3-4 88-90
LPs: 10/12-inch
MOTOWN 5-8 88-90

BOY & GIRL: see JOHNSON, Budd

BOYS & GIRLS
Singles: 7-inch
SMASH 4-6 68

BOYS BAND P&R '82
Singles: 7-inch
ELEKTRA 3-4 82
Picture Sleeves
ELEKTRA 3-4 82
LPs: 10/12-inch
ASYLUM 5-10 82
Members: Rusty Golden; Chris Golden; Greg Gordon; B.J. Lowry.
Also see GOLDENS

BOYS BLUE
Singles: 7-inch
ABC-PAR 4-8 65

BOYS CLUB P&R/LP '88
Singles: 7-inch
MCA 3-4 88
Picture Sleeves
MCA 3-4 88
LPs: 10/12-inch
MCA 5-8 88
Members: Joe Pasquale; Gene Hunt.
Also see JETS

BOYS DON'T CRY P&R/LP '86
Singles: 12-inch
PROFILE 4-6 86
Singles: 7-inch
ATLANTIC 3-4 88
PROFILE 3-4 86
Picture Sleeves
ATLANTIC 3-4 88
PROFILE 3-4 86
LPs: 10/12-inch
PROFILE 5-10 86
Member: Nick Richards.

BOYS FROM CALIFORNIA
Singles: 7-inch
DATOM 3-4 82

BOYS FROM INDIANA
Singles: 7-inch
OLD HERITAGE 3-4 88
Picture Sleeves
OLD HERITAGE 3-4 88
Members: Aubrey Holt; Jerry Holt; Tom Holt; Harley Gabbard; Tommy Allsup; Bob Hoban; Ken Buttrey; Charlie McCoy; Roy Huskey; J.W. Murray.
Also see ALLSUP, Tommy
Also see McCOY, Charlie

BOYS FROM NEW YORK CITY
Singles: 7-inch
LAURIE 4-6 67-68

BOYS FROM NOWHERE
LPs: 10/12-inch
SKYCLAD 5-10 90
Members: Mick Divvens; Johnny Bernardo.

BOYS IN THE BAND P&R/R&B '70
Singles: 7-inch
SPRING 3-5 70

BOYS NEXT DOOR
Singles: 78 rpm
RAINBOW 10-15 55
VIK 5-10 56
Singles: 7-inch
RAINBOW (349 "We Belong Together") 30-50 55
VIK 10-20 56

BOYS NEXT DOOR
Singles: 7-inch
ATCO 8-12 66-67
BAD 12-18 67
CAMEO 12-18 66
SOMA (Except 1428) 12-18 65
SOMA (1428 "Central High Playmate") 20-25 65
Also see FOUR WHEELS

BOYS ON THE BLOCK R&B '87
Singles: 7-inch
FANTASY 3-4 87

BOYS TOWN GANG
LPs: 10/12-inch
FANTASY 5-10 84
MOBY DICK 5-10 81

BOYZ
Singles: 7-inch
DESTINATION 5-8 66
KIDERIAN 8-12

BOYZ II MEN P&R/R&B/LP '91
Singles: 7-inch
MOTOWN 3-4 91
LPs: 10/12-inch
MOTOWN 5-8 91

BOYZZ
Singles: 7-inch
EPIC 3-4 78-79
LPs: 10/12-inch
EPIC 5-10 78

BOZ
(Boz Burrell)
Singles: 7-inch
EPIC 4-8 66
Picture Sleeves
EPIC 8-12 66
Also see BAD COMPANY
Also see KING CRIMSON

BOZE, Calvin R&B '50
(With His All-Stars)
Singles: 78 rpm
ALADDIN 20-50 50-52
G&G (1029 "Safronia B.") 30-60 46
SCORE (4003 "Satisfied") 15-25 48
Singles: 7-inch
ALADDIN (3045 "Waitin' and Drinkin'") 100-150 50
ALADDIN (3055 "Safronia B.") 100-150 50
ALADDIN (3065 "Lizzie Lou") 50-100 50
ALADDIN (3072 "Stinkin' from Drinkin'") 50-100 50
ALADDIN (3079 "Beale Street on Saturday Night") 50-100 51
ALADDIN (3086 "Slippin' and Slidin'") 50-100 51
ALADDIN (3100 "I've Got News for You") 50-100 51
ALADDIN (3110 "I'm Gonna Steam Off the Stamp") 50-100 52
ALADDIN (3160 "Shamrock") 50-100 52
ALADDIN (3122 "My Friend Told Me") 50-100 52
ALADDIN (3132 "Good Time Sue") 50-100 52
ALADDIN (3147 "Looped") 50-100 52
ASTRA 5-10
IMPERIAL 10-15 62
Also see JOHNSON, Marvin, & His Orchestra

BOZE, Ed
Singles: 7-inch
AVCO 3-5 73

BOZEMAN, John
Singles: 7-inch
PILOT 3-4 80

BOZEMAN, Johnny
Singles: 7-inch
SANDY (1001 "Blues and I") 50-75 57

BOZEMAN, Ken
Singles: 7-inch
SANDY 5-10 61

BRACELETS
Singles: 7-inch
CONGRESS 10-15 62
20TH FOX 4-8 64

BRACKENS, Ray
Singles: 7-inch
SCRAM (101 "Come On, It's Cranival") 10-15

BRACKETT, Lee
(Alan Lee Brackett)
Singles: 7-inch
BELL 3-6 72
DUNHILL 3-6 71
EXCELLO 4-8 72
VAULT 5-10 64-65

BRADBURY, Ray
LP: 10/12-inch
TOWER 10-20 60s

BRADDOCK, Bobby C&W '67
Singles: 7-inch
ELEKTRA 3-5 79-80
MGM 4-6 67-69
LPs: 10/12-inch
ELEKTRA 6-12 79-80
RCA 5-10 83-84
Also see ROBBINS, Marty

BRADEN, John
LPs: 10/12-inch
A&M 10-15 69

BRADEN, Tommy
(Tommy "Mary Jo" Braden; with His Flames)
Singles: 78 rpm
UNITED 10-15 54
Singles: 7-inch
UNITED 15-25 54
Also see BLASERS
Also see FOUR BLAZES

BRADFORD, Chuck
Singles: 7-inch
ATLANTIC 5-10 64
FIRE (511 "You Can't Hurt Me Anymore") 15-25 62

BRADFORD, Clea
Singles: 7-inch
CADET 4-6 68
HI-Q 8-12 60s
LPs: 10/12-inch
CADET 10-15

BRADFORD, Don
Singles: 7-inch
SPOT 5-10 59

BRADFORD, Eddie
Singles: 7-inch
CHESS (2133 "Pride Aside") 4-8 72

BRADFORD, Floyd
Singles: 7-inch
LOGAN 5-10 59

BRADFORD, Keith C&W '78
Singles: 7-inch
MU-SOUND 3-5 78
SCORPION 3-5 79

BRADFORD, Scott
LPs: 10/12-inch
PROBE 10-15 69

BRADFORD, Sylvester
Singles: 7-inch
ATCO 8-12 58

BRADFORD, Willie
Singles: 7-inch
FIRE (500 "Wanna Be Loved") 15-25 61

BRADFORD & BELL
Singles: 7-inch
SPIRIT 3-4 80
Members: B. Bradford; S. Bell.

BRADFORD BOYS
Singles: 78 rpm
RAINBOW (307 "That Feeling") 50-75 55
Singles: 7-inch
RAINBOW (307 "That Feeling") 100-125 55

BRADING, Susie C&W '84
Singles: 7-inch
RIDDLE 3-4 84

BRADIX, Big Charley
Singles: 78 rpm
ARISTOCRAT (418 "Numbered Days") 75-100 48
BLUE BONNET (153 "Boogie Like You Wanna") 75-100 48
COLONIAL (108 "Boogie Like You Wanna") 40-60 48

BRADLEY, Allen, Quintet
Singles: 7-inch
OKEH (7100 "Space Race") 15-25 57

BRADLEY, James R&B '79
(With the Bill Smith Combo)
Singles: 7-inch
CHESS 5-10 60
MALACO 3-4 79-84
MANCO 5-10 61
LPs: 10/12-inch
MALACO 5-10 84

BRADLEY, Jan P&R/R&B '63
Singles: 7-inch
ADANTI (1050 "Back in Circulation") 5-10 65
CHESS 5-10 62-68
DOYLEN 4-8 70
ERIC 3-4 73
FORMAL (1014 "Crufew Blues") 8-10 62
FORMAL (1044 "Mama Didn't Lie") 15-25 62
HOOTENANNY 5-8 62
NIGHT OWL (1055 "Behind the Curtains") 10-20 63
SOUND SPECTRUM (36002 "Back in Circulation") 8-12 65
Session: Impressions.
Also see IMPRESSIONS
Also see JAN & CHUCK

BRADLEY, Mamie
Singles: 7-inch
SUE (702 "The Patty Cake") 10-20 58

BRADLEY, Mike
Singles: 7-inch
SOFT 4-8 67

BRADLEY, Owen C&W/P&R '49
(Owen Bradley Quintet)
Singles: 78 rpm
CORAL 4-8 49-50
DECCA 5-10 54-57
Singles: 7-inch
CORAL 5-10 50
DECCA 5-15 54-61
EPs: 7-inch
CORAL 10-20 54
DECCA 10-20 58
LPs: 10/12-inch
CORAL 20-30 53-55
DECCA 15-25 58-60
VOCALION 5-15 60s
Also see PLEIS, Jack, & Owen Bradley
Also see SHANNON, Pat

BRADLEY, Patrick
Singles: 7-inch
DECCA (32148 "Just One More Chance") 100-150 67
(Multi-color label.)
DECCA (32148 "Just One More Chance") 50-75 67
(Pink label. Promotional issue only.)

BRADLEY, Rockin': see ROCKIN' BRADLEY

BRADLEY, Sid
Singles: 7-inch
CONTEST 5-10 60
SAB 15-20

BRADLEY, Will
(With Ray McKinley; with His Boogie-Woogie Boys; with Will Bradley Jr.)
Singles: 78 rpm
ATLANTIC 10-20 50
BEACON 5-15 44
COLUMBIA 5-15 42
EPIC 8-12 56
SIGNATURE 5-15 47
Singles: 7-inch
EPIC 10-20 56
EPs: 7-inch
EPIC 15-30 54-56
LPs: 10/12-inch
EPIC (1005 "Boogie Woogie") 75-100 54
(10-inch LP.)
EPIC (1127 "Will Bradley") 50-75 56
EPIC (3115 "Boogie Woogie") 40-50 56
EPIC (3199 "The House of Bradley") 40-50 56
Also see BROWN, Ruth

BRADLEY, Will, & Johnny Guarnieri Band
LPs: 10/12-inch
RCA 15-25 60
Also see BRADLEY, Will

BRADSHAW, Bobby
Singles: 7-inch
WAND 3-5 70s

BRADSHAW, Carolyn C&W '53
Singles: 78 rpm
ABBOTT 4-8 53
Singles: 7-inch
ABBOTT 5-10 53

BRADSHAW, Jack
Singles: 78 rpm
MAR-VEL 15-25 54-55
Singles: 7-inch
GLENN 10-20 59
MAR-VEL (750 "Don't Tease Me") 25-40 54
MAR-VEL (751 "Searchin'") 20-30 55
MAR-VEL (752 "It Just Ain't Right") 20-30 58
MAR-VEL (753 "Jo Jo") 25-50 58
MAR-VEL (756 "Saturday Night Special") 15-25 59

BRADSHAW, Terry C&W/P&R '76
Singles: 7-inch
BENSON 3-4 80
MERCURY 3-5 76
Picture Sleeves
BENSON 3-4 80
LPs: 10/12-inch
BENSON 5-10 80
HEARTWARMING 5-10 82
MERCURY 6-12 76

BRADSHAW, Tiny R&B '50
Singles: 78 rpm
KING (4357 "I Hate You") 15-25 50
KING (4397 "Butterfly") 15-25 50
KING (4457 "Bradshaw Boogie") 15-25 50
KING (4487 "T-99") 25-50 52
KING (4497 "The Train Kept A-Rollin'") 25-50 52
KING (4547 "Rippin' & Runnin'") 25-50 52
KING (4577 thru 4787) 10-20 52-55
MANOR (1147 "I Found Out Too Late") 10-20 48
MANOR (1181 "Six Shooter") 10-20 49
REGIS (1010 "Bradshaw Bounce") 10-20 44
REGIS (1011 "After You've Gone") 10-20 44
SAVOY (650 "These Things Are Love") 10-20 47
SAVOY (655 "If I Had a Million Dollars") 10-20 47
Singles: 7-inch
GUSTO 3-4 80-83
KING (4357 "I Hate You") 25-50 50
KING (4397 "Butterfly") 25-50 50
KING (4457 "Bradshaw Boogie") 25-50 50
KING (4487 "T-99") 75-150 52
KING (4497 "The Train Kept A-Rollin'") 75-150 52
KING (4547 "Rippin' & Runnin'") 75-150 52
KING (4577 thru 4787) 20-40 52-55
(For King 4000 series colored vinyl singles, the price range will double or triple.)
EPs: 7-inch
KING (208 thru 360) 25-50 52-56
LPs: 10/12-inch
KING (74 "Off and On") 100-200 52
(10-inch LP.)
KING (501 "Tiny Bradshaw") 75-125 55
KING (653 "Great Composer") 30-50 59
KING (953 "24 Great Songs") 20-30 66

BRADY, Bob
(With the Con Chords)
Singles: 7-inch
A&M 3-5 72
CHARIOT 4-8 66-69

BRADY, Dave, & Stars
Singles: 7-inch
DARBY (8189 "Ridin' High") 20-25 67

BRADY, George, & Kingsmen
Singles: 7-inch
HAPPY HEARTS 5-8 61

BRADY, Jim, & Sonics
Singles: 7-inch
JERDEN 4-8 69
PULSAR 4-8 69

BRADY, June & George
Singles: 78 rpm
ABC-PAR 5-10 57
Singles: 7-inch
ABC-PAR 10-15 57

BRADY, Liz
Singles: 7-inch
CAPITOL 4-8 65

BRADY, Pal
Singles: 7-inch
KING 5-8 63

BRADY, Paul
Singles: 7-inch
21 3-4 81

BRADY, Pete, & Blazers
LPs: 10/12-inch
ABC-PAR (310 "Murder Ballads") 15-25 59

BRADY & CORVETTES
Singles: 7-inch
ARCO (104 "Shasta") 10-20 60s

BRADY & GRADY: see SNEED, Brady & Grady

BRADY BUNCH
Singles: 7-inch
PARAMOUNT 5-10 72-73
Picture Sleeves
PARAMOUNT 10-20 72-73
LPs: 10/12-inch
PARAMOUNT (5026 "Merry Christmas from the Brady Bunch") 30-60 70
PARAMOUNT (6032 "Meet the Brady Bunch") 20-50 72
PARAMOUNT (6037 "Kids from the Brady Bunch") 20-50 72
PARAMOUNT (6058 "Brady Bunch Phonographic Album") 20-50 73
Members: Barry Williams; Maureen McCormick, Mike Lookinland, Eve Plumb; Chris Knight; Susan Olsen.
Also see KNIGHT, Chris, & Maureen McCormick

BRADY BUNCH KIDS
Singles: 7-inch
PARAMOUNT 3-5 73
Also see BRADY BUNCH

BRAGA SISTERS
Singles: 7-inch
FELSTED 5-10 59
MANCO 5-10 61

BRAGG, Billy *LP '88*
Singles: 7-inch
ELEKTRA 3-4 88
LPs: 10/12-inch
ELEKTRA 5-8 88

BRAGG, Doug
Singles: 7-inch
D (1018 "Daydreaming Again") 75-125 58
D (1045 "Calling Me Back") 10-20 59
D (1087 When the Blues Came Walking In") 10-20 59
DIXIE (2002 "Red Rover") 50-75 58
DIXIE (2004 "Jerry") 20-40 58

BRAGG, Doug, & Cheri Robbins
Singles: 7-inch
SKIPPY 10-20 59
Also see BRAGG, Doug
Also see ROBBINS, Cheri

BRAGG, Joe
Singles: 7-inch
ARLISS 10-15 62
ATLAS 10-15 60
BOCART (101 "I've Got to Make It") 50-75 63

BRAGG, Johnny
(With the Marigolds)
Singles: 78 rpm
EXCELLO 15-25 56
Singles: 7-inch
DECCA 10-15 59
ELBEJAY 5-10 60
EXCELLO (2057 "Rollin' Stone") 25-50 56
EXCELLO (2091 "It's You Darling, It's You") 25-50 56
Also see MARIGOLDS
Also see PRISONAIRES

BRAGGS, Al "TNT"
Singles: 7-inch
PEACOCK 8-15 60-64
Also see FIVE NOTES

BRAHMAN
Singles: 7-inch
MERCURY 3-5 71
LPs: 10/12-inch
MERCURY 12-15 71

BRAIN POLICE
Singles: 7-inch
HEAD 10-15 65

BRAIN TRAIN
Singles: 7-inch
TITAN 4-8 67

BRAINBOX
Singles: 7-inch
CAPITOL 3-5 70
ELEKTRA 3-5 69
LPs: 10/12-inch
CAPITOL 10-12 70
Also see AKKERMAN, Jan

BRAINS
Singles: 7-inch
GRAY MATTER (1 "Money Changes Everything") 3-5 78
MERCURY 3-4 80
Picture Sleeves
GRAY MATTER (1 "Money Changes Everything") 4-8 78
LPs: 10/12-inch
LANDSLIDE 5-10 82
MERCURY 5-10 80-81
Members: Tom Gray; Rick Price; Bryan Smithwick.

BRAINSTORM
Singles: 7-inch
CALLA (164 "Movin' ") 5-10 70

BRAINSTORM *P&R/R&B/LP '77*
Singles: 12-inch
TABU 4-6 77-79
Singles: 7-inch
RCA 3-4 82
TABU 3-4 76-79
LPs: 10/12-inch
RCA 5-10 82
TABU 5-10 77-79
Members: Belita Woods; Charles Overton; Jeryl Bright; Larry Sims; Jerry Kent; Renell Gousalves; Willie Wooten; Lamont Johnson; Trenita Womack.

BRAITHWAITE, Mitchell
Singles: 7-inch
PROBE 3-5 69

BRAKEMEN
Singles: 7-inch
LSK (2391 "Movin' ") 25-35

BRAM RIGG SET
Singles: 7-inch
KAYDEN (400 "I Can Only Give You Everything") 15-20 66
Members: Pete Neri; Jerry Poulton; Benet Segal; Rich Bednarzyck; Bobby Schlosser.
Also see PULSE

BRAM TCHAIKOVSKY: see TCHAIKOVSKY, Bram

BRAMBLETT, Randall
Singles: 7-inch
POLYDOR 3-5 75
LPs: 10/12-inch
POLYDOR 8-10 75-76

BRAMLETT, Bonnie *LP '75*
Singles: 7-inch
CAPRICORN 3-5 75-78
COLUMBIA 3-5 72-73
REFUGE 3-4 81
LPs: 10/12-inch
CAPRICORN 8-10 75-78
COLUMBIA 10-12 72-73
Also see DELANEY & BONNIE
Also see LITTLE FEAT

BRAMLETT, Delaney
(With Bekka Bramlett; with Blue Diamond)
Singles: 7-inch
COLUMBIA (45950 "Are You a Beatle Or a Rolling Stone") 5-10 73
CREAM 3-4 81
GNP 4-8 64-66
INDEPENDENCE 4-8 67
LPs: 10/12-inch
COLUMBIA 8-10 72-73
MGM 8-10 75
PRODIGAL 8-10 77
Also see DELANEY & BONNIE
Also see RIO, Chuck, & Delaney

BRAN, Greg
Singles: 7-inch
CROSS COUNTRY 3-6 89

BRANCH, Ben
(With the Downhomers; with Operation Breadbasket)
Singles: 7-inch
CADET 4-8 66-68
DOT 5-8 61
HI 3-5 73

BRANCH, Judy
Singles: 7-inch
REPRISE 4-8 66-67

BRANCH, Tom
Singles: 7-inch
ROCKY BLUF 5-10 77

BRANCH ESTATE
Singles: 7-inch
CAROUSEL 3-4

BRAND, Jack
Singles: 7-inch
SHANE 3-5 77

BRAND, Oscar
LPs:10/12-inch
ELEKTRA 15-25
FOLKWAYS 10-15
KAPP 10-15
RIVERSIDE 20-25
TRADITION 10-20

BRAND, Saddhu
LPs: 10/12-inch
UNI 8-10 71

BRAND NEW FUNK
Singles: 7-inch
VIBRATION 3-5

BRAND NUBIAN *LP '91*
LPs: 10/12-inch
ATLANTIC 4-8 91

BRAND X *LP '76*
Singles: 7-inch
PASSPORT 3-4 78
LPs: 10/12-inch
PASSPORT 5-10 76-84
Members: Phil Collins; John Goodsall; Percy Jones; Robin Lumley; Morris Pert.
Also see COLLINS, Phil

BRAND X
Singles: 7-inch
SEQUOIA (501 "She Lied") 5-10
STEEL BREEZE (3786 "Come on Home") 10-20

BRANDEN, Don
Singles: 7-inch
CESSNA (973 "The Girl with the Golden Hair") 10-20 60s

BRANDMEIER, Jonathan
(Johnny & His Leisure Suits)
Singles: 7-inch
LOON 3-5 81-83
Picture Sleeves
LOON 3-6 81
LPs: 10/12-inch
LOON 10-15 82
Members: Jonathan Brandmeier; Steve Goddard; Willie Carmichael; Dave Cook; Brian Page; Brad Patrick; Garry Stafford.
Also see GODDARD, Steve

BRANDING IRON
Singles: 7-inch
STAG 3-6
VOLT 3-5 71
LPs: 10/12-inch
VOLT 10-12 70

BRANDON, Bill *R&B '72*
Singles: 7-inch
BELL (733 "Rainbow Road") 5-10 68
MOONSONG 10-20 72-73
PIEDMONT 3-6 76
PRELUDE 3-5 77-78
QUINVY (7007 "Strange Feeling") 50-75
SOUTH CAMP 5-10 67
TOWER (430 "Rainbow Road") 20-30 68

BRANDON, Bob
Singles: 7-inch
EMCEE 4-8 62

BRANDON, Cal
Singles: 7-inch
HIT MAN 3-5 76

BRANDON, Don
Singles: 7-inch
CHALLENGE 10-15 64
DOT 10-15 64
Also see COMPETITORS

BRANDON, Johnny
Singles: 78 rpm
KING 5-10 56
LONDON 5-10 56
Singles: 7-inch
KING 8-12 56
LAURIE 5-10 59
LONDON 8-12 56

BRANDON, Kathy
Singles: 7-inch
CRYSTALETTE 5-15 61-64

BRANDON, Little Eddie
Singles: 7-inch
DORE 5-8 64

BRANDON, Luther
Singles: 7-inch
FRATERNITY (852 "Tuff-E-Nuff") 15-25 59

BRANDON, Patty
Singles: 78 rpm
ABC-PAR 5-10 57
CHANCELLOR 5-10 57
Singles: 7-inch
ABC-PAR 10-15 57
CHANCELLOR 10-15 57

BRANDON, T.C. *C&W '89*
Singles: 7-inch
BEAR 3-4 89

BRANDOS *LP '87*
LPs: 10/12-inch
RELATIVITY 5-10 87

BRANDT TRIO
Singles: 7-inch
WYN 5-10 59

BRANDY, Charles
Singles: 7-inch
BLUE CAT (126 "I Can't Get Enough of You") 150-250 65

BRANDYE
LPs: 10/12-inch
KAYVETTE 5-10 79
Also see JACKSON, Millie

BRANDYWINE
LP: 10/12-inch
BRUNSWICK 10-15

BRANDYWINE SINGERS
Singles: 7-inch
JOY 4-8 63

BRANÉ, Sherry *C&W '78*
Singles: 7-inch
E.I.O. 3-4 80
MMI 3-4 79
OAK 3-5 78
TEJAS 3-5 80

BRANIGAN, Laura *P&R/LP '82*
Singles: 12-inch
ATLANTIC 4-8 82-87
Singles: 7-inch
ATLANTIC 3-4 80-90
EMI AMERICA 3-4 84
Picture Sleeves
ATLANTIC 3-4 80-87
LPs: 10/12-inch
ATLANTIC 5-10 82-90
EMI AMERICA 5-10 84
Also see COHEN, Leonard
Also see MEADOW

BRANIGAN, Laura, & Joe Esposito
Singles: 7-inch
ATCO 3-5
Picture Sleeves
ATCO 5-8
Also see BRANIGAN, Laura
Also see ESPOSITO, Joe "Bean"

BRANNEN, John *LP '88*
LPs: 10/12-inch
APACHE 5-8 88

BRANNON, Janie
Singles: 7-inch
ZODIAC 3-5 76-77

BRANNON, Kippi *C&W '81*
Singles: 7-inch
MCA 3-4 81-82

BRANNON, Linda
Singles: 7-inch
CHESS 5-10 59
EPIC 4-8 63-64
PHILLIPS 5-8 62
RAM 10-20 59

BRANT, Bobby
Singles: 7-inch
EAST WEST (124 "Piano Nellie") .. 50-75 59
WHITE ROCK (1114 "Piano Nellie") 75-100 59

BRANTLEY, Bill
Singles: 7-inch
SOUND STAGE 7 .... 3-5 76
STAX 3-4 84

BRANTLEY, Charles
(Charlie Brantley)
Singles: 78 rpm
KING 10-20 53
Singles: 7-inch
JAX (301 "Beggin' Blues") 75-125 53
(Red vinyl.)
KING (4616 "Movin' on Now") 25-50 53
KING (4619 "Fog Horn") 25-50 53
KING (4640 "Look at Me") 25-50 53

BRANTLEY, Dan
Singles: 7-inch
DELUXE 5-10 69
FEDERAL 4-8 70
HOLLYWOOD 5-10 68
SIMS (101 "Can't Take No More") 20-30 55

BRANTLEY, Johnny
(Johnny Brantley's All Stars)
Singles: 7-inch
CARLTON (453 "The Place") 15-20 58

BRASHER, Cathy
(Miss Cathy Brasher; Cathy Fischer)
Singles: 7-inch
CHATTAHOOCHEE 8-12 65
ERA 8-12 64
LAP 8-12 64
Also see MURMAIDS

BRASS BREED
LPs: 10/12-inch
WYNCOTE 5-10 65

BRASS CONSTRUCTION *P&R/R&B/LP '76*
Singles: 12-inch
CAPITOL 4-6 83
LIBERTY 4-6 82
Singles: 7-inch
CAPITOL 3-4 83
DOCC 3-5
LIBERTY 3-4 82
U.A. 3-5 75-80
Picture Sleeves
U.A. 3-5
LPs: 10/12-inch
CAPITOL 5-10 83
U.A. 5-10 75-80
LIBERTY 5-10 82
Members: Randy Muller; Wade Williamston; Joe Wong; Wayne Parris; Mickey Grudge; Morris Price; Jesse Ward; Sandy Billups; Larry Payton.

BRASS FEVER *R&B '77*
Singles: 7-inch
IMPULSE 3-5 76-77
LPs: 10/12-inch
IMPULSE 8-10 76

BRASS MONKEY
Singles: 7-inch
RARE EARTH 3-5 71
LPs: 10/12-inch
RARE EARTH 8-10 71

BRASS RAIL
Singles: 7-inch
BUDDAH 3-5 71

BRASS RING *P&R/LP '66*
Singles: 7-inch
ABC 3-5 70
DUNHILL (Except 4090) 4-6 66-69
DUNHILL (4090 "Love in the Open Air") 10-20 67
ITCO 3-5 69
Picture Sleeves
DUNHILL (4090 "Love in the Open Air") 15-25 67
(Billed on sleeve as "Paul McCartney's First NON Beatle Song.")
LPs: 10/12-inch
DUNHILL 8-12 66-73
ITCO 6-10 70
PROJECT 3 .... 6-10 72
Members: Phil Bodner.
Also see BODNER, Phil, Sextet
Also see McCARTNEY, Paul

BRASS TOAD
Singles: 7-inch
TWO WORLDS (1071 "In the Back of My Mind") 20-30

BRASSETTES
Singles: 7-inch
EBB (107 "Brassette Rock") 15-25 57

BRASSEUR, Andre
(With the Burners)
Singles: 7-inch
CONGRESS (271 "The Kid") 10-20 65
4 CORNERS 8-15 65-66

BRASSO, Larry
Singles: 7-inch
JIN 3-5 73
KING 4-6 69
MONTEL 4-8 66

BRASWELL, Jimmy
Singles: 7-inch
KING (6374 "I Can't Give You My Heart") 30-50 71
QUINVY (7004 "Home for the Summer") 20-30

BRAT
LPs: 10/12-inch
FATIMA 8-10 81

BRAT PACK *P&R '90*
Singles: 7-inch
VENDETTA 3-4 90

BRATTS
Singles: 7-inch
TOLLIE 5-10 64

BRAUN, Bob *P&R/LP '62*
(With the Fun Bunch)
Singles: 7-inch
AUDIO FIDELITY 3-6 65
APPLEGATE 4-6
CANDEE 4-8
DECCA 4-8 62
FRATERNITY 3-6 64-66
KING 4-8 59
QCA 3-5 73
U.A. 3-5 67
WRAYCO 3-5 71
Picture Sleeves
DECCA 5-8 62
QCA 3-5 73
EPs: 7-inch
DECCA 5-10 63
LPs: 10/12-inch
AUDIO FIDELITY 8-12 65
DECCA 10-20 62
U.A. 8-12 67
WRAYCO 5-10 71

BRAVE BELT
Singles: 7-inch
REPRISE 3-5 71-72
LPs: 10/12-inch
REPRISE (2057 "Brave Belt II") 15-20 72
REPRISE (6447 "Brave Belt") 15-20 71
Members: Chad Allan; Randy Bachman; Robert Bachman; C.F. Turner.
Also see ALLAN, Chad
Also see BACHMAN - TURNER - BACHMAN

BRAVE BUTTER
Singles: 7-inch
HAPPY TIGER 3-5 70

BRAVE COMBO
Singles: 12-inch
FOUR DOT 4-6
LPs: 10/12-inch
FOUR DOT 5-10
Member: Carl Finch.

BRAVE NEW WORLD
Singles: 7-inch
EPIC (10123 "It's Tomorrow") 10-15 66
PICCADILLY (225 "It's Tomorrow") 20-30 66
LP: 10/12-inch
PANORAMA 15-25 60s

BRAVERMAN, Cory: see CORY

BRAVES
Singles: 7-inch
VANTAGE (701 "Mo-Combo") 10-15 62

BRAVO, Sonny
Singles: 7-inch
COLUMBIA 4-6 68
LPs: 10/12-inch
COLUMBIA 8-12 68

BRAVOS, Los: see LOS BRAVOS

BRAVURA
Singles: 7-inch
BRAVURA/DECCA ("The Man Who Hears a Different Drummer") 4-8 69
(No artist credited or number used. Promotional issue made for Bravaura.)
Picture Sleeves
BRAVURA/DECCA ("The Man Who Hears a Different Drummer") 4-8 69
(No artist credited or number used. Promotional issue made for Bravaura.)

BRAWLEY, Jewel
(Jewel Brawley Trio)
Singles: 7-inch
SHASTA 5-10 59

BRAXTON, Dhar *R&B '86*
(With Chocolette)
Singles: 12-inch
SLEEPING BAG 4-6 86
Singles: 7-inch
SLEEPING BAG 3-4 86

BRAZELL, Nicky, & Satellites
Singles: 7-inch
SPARR (2259 "Betty Jo") 25-45

BREAD *LP '69*
(David Gates & Bread)
Singles: 7-inch
ASYLUM (45054 "Make It with You") . 4-6 70s
(Label misprint; Asylum should be Elektra.)
ELEKTRA (Except 45666 & 45668) ... 3-5 70-77
ELEKTRA (45666 "Dismal Day") 5-8 69
ELEKTRA (45668 "Could I") 4-6 69
Picture Sleeves
ELEKTRA 4-8 70-72
LPs: 10/12-inch
ELEKTRA (100 & 1000 series) 8-12 73-77
ELEKTRA (5000 series) 15-25 72-73
(Quadrophonic series.)
ELEKTRA (74000 & 75000 series, except 75015 & 75056) 10-15 69-73
ELEKTRA (75015 "Baby I'm a Want You") 15-25 72
(With die-cut cover.)
ELEKTRA (75015 "Baby I'm a Want You") 10-15 72
(Standard cover.)
ELEKTRA (75056 "Best of Bread") 25-35 73
K-TEL 5-10 82
Members: David Gates; James Griffin; Mike Botts; Larry Knechtel; Robb Royer.
Also see CEYLEIB PEOPLE

Also see GATES, David
Also see GRIFFIN, James
Also see JOSHUA FOX
Also see PLEASURE FAIR

BREAD & BUTTER
Singles: 7-inch
TARA 3-5 74

BREAD, LOVE & DREAMS
LPs: 10/12-inch
LONDON 10-12 67-69

BREAK
Singles: 7-inch
ELEKTRA 3-5 72

BREAK MACHINE R&B/D&D '84
Singles: 12-inch
SIRE 4-6 84
Singles: 7-inch
BLACK SCORPIO 3-5
SIRE 3-4 84
Members: Lindell Blake; Lindsay Blake; Cortez Jordan.

BREAKAWAYS
Singles: 7-inch
CAMEO 8-10 64
LONDON 5-10 64
MELBOURNE 5-10 64
Also see CAREFREES
Also see VERNON'S GIRLS

BREAKERS
Singles: 7-inch
MOXIE 5-10 63

BREAKERS
Singles: 7-inch
BRANA (1001 "Kami-Kaze") 20-30 63
DJB (116 "Jet Stream") 15-25 64
DJB (116 "Super Jet Rumble") 15-25 64
(Same number is used twice.)
IMPACT (14 "Surfin' Tragedy") 15-25 63
(Black vinyl.)
IMPACT (14 "Surfin' Tragedy") 30-50 63
(Colored vinyl.)
MARSH (206 "Balboa Memories") 50-75 63
Also see WALLER, Jim, & Deltas

BREAKERS
Singles: 7-inch
AMY 5-10 65

BREAKERS
(Wailers)
Singles: 7-inch
JERDEN (789 "All My Nights") 15-20 66
RIVERTON (102 "All My Nights") 25-35 66
Also see WAILERS

BREAKFAST BARRY C&W '79
(Barry Grant)
Singles: 7-inch
COUNTRYSTOCK 3-5 79
Also see GRANT, Barry

BREAKFAST CLUB P&R/R&B/LP '87
Singles: 7-inch
MCA 3-4 87
Picture Sleeves
MCA 3-4 87
LPs: 10/12-inch
MCA 5-10 87

BREAKOUTS
Singles: 7-inch
SOLITARY (9762 "The Chase") 10-20 62
SPIDER 5-8 64

BREAKS
Singles: 7-inch
RCA 3-4 84
LPs: 10/12-inch
RCA 5-10 83

BREAKWATER R&B/LP '79
Singles: 7-inch
ARISTA 3-5 79-80
LPs: 10/12-inch
ARISTA 5-10 79-80
Members: Kae Williams; Lincoln Gilmore; James Jones; Gene Robinson Jr.; Vince Garnell; Greg Scott; John Braddock; Steve Green.
Also see BLACK MAGIC

BREATHE P&R/LP '88
Singles: 12-inch
A&M 4-8 87
Singles: 7-inch
A&M 3-4 87-90
Picture Sleeves
A&M 3-8 88-89
LPs: 10/12-inch
A&M 5-10 87-90
Members: David Glasper; Ian Spice; Michael Delahunty; Marcus Lillington.

BREATHLESS P&R '80
Singles: 7-inch
EMI AMERICA 3-4 79
LPs: 10/12-inch
EMI AMERICA 5-10 79-80

BRECKER BROTHERS P&R/R&B/LP '75
Singles: 7-inch
ARISTA 3-5 75-80
LPs: 10/12-inch
ARISTA 5-10 75-81
Members: Mike Brecker; Randy Brecker; Dave Sanborn.
Also see DREAMS

BREED, Allen
Singles: 7-inch
ABC-PAR 4-8 63

BREEDLOVE, Jimmy
Singles: 78 rpm
ATCO 10-20 57
Singles: 7-inch
ATCO (6094 "Over Somebody Else's Shoulder") 15-25 57
DIAMOND (144 "Jealous Fool") 15-25 63
EPIC (9270 "Could This Be Love") 10-20 58
EPIC (9283 "Whirlpool") 10-20 58
EPIC (9289 "Ooh-Wee Good Gosh A-Mighty") 15-25 58
EPIC (9319 "All Is Forgiven") 10-15 59
EPIC (9360 "To Belong") 10-15 60
JUBILEE 4-8 66
OKEH (7145 "Anytime You Want Me") 8-12 62
OKEH (7152 "Queen Bee") 8-12 62
ROULETTE 4-6 68
EPs: 7-inch
CAMDEN (447 "Rock 'N' Roll Music") 25-40 58
LPs: 10/12-inch
CAMDEN (430 "Rock 'N' Roll Hits") 40-60 58
Also see CUES

BREEN, Bobby
Singles: 7-inch
CHIC (1003 "If the Night Could Tell You") 5-8
LYRIC (106 "It's a Sin") 10-15
MOTOWN (1053 "How Can We Tell Him") 10-20 64
MOTOWN (1059 "Here Comes the Heartache") 10-20 64
Picture Sleeves
MOTOWN (1059 "Here Comes the Heartache") 40-50 64

BREESE, Lou
Singles: 78 rpm
BALLY 4-8 56
Singles: 7-inch
BALLY 5-10 56

BREEZE
Singles: 7-inch
A&M 3-5 69
WMOT 3-4 78
LPs: 10/12-inch
JUST SUNSHINE 8-10 74
Also see WELLS, Brandi

BREEZE, Cool: see COOL BREEZE

BREGMAN, Buddy
Singles: 78 rpm
RCA 5-10 56
Singles: 7-inch
RCA 10-20 56

BRELYN, Bobby
Singles: 7-inch
JOREL (5396 "Hanna") 25-35 60s

BREMERS, Beverly P&R '71
Singles: 7-inch
COLUMBIA 3-5 75-77
ERIC 3-4 83
SCEPTER 3-5 71-75
Picture Sleeves
SCEPTER 4-6 72
LPs: 10/12-inch
SCEPTER 8-10 72

BRENDA & CAROLYN
(Stephenson Sisters)
Singles: 7-inch
CR 5-8
Members: Brenda Stephenson; Carolyn Stephenson.

BRENDA & HERB R&B '78
Singles: 7-inch
H&L 3-5 78
Members: Brenda Reid; Herb Rooney.
Also see EXCITERS
Also see MASTERS

BRENDA & PETE: see LEE, Brenda, & Pete Fountain

BRENDA & BIG DUDES R&B '86
Singles: 12-inch
CAPITOL 4-6 86
Singles: 7-inch
CAPITOL 3-4 86
LPs: 10/12-inch
CAPITOL 5-10 86

BRENDA & TABULATIONS
P&R/R&B/LP '67
Singles: 12-inch
CHOCOLATE CITY 4-6 77
Singles: 7-inch
CHOCOLATE CITY 3-5 76-77
DIONN 5-10 67-69
EPIC 3-5 72-75
TOP & BOTTOM 4-8 69-71
LPs: 10/12-inch
CHOCOLATE CITY 5-10 77
DIONN (2000 "Dry Your Eyes") 20-30 67
TOP & BOTTOM 15-20 70
Members: Brenda Payton; Jerry Joures; Eddie Jackson; Maurice Coates; Dennis Dozier; Donald Ford; Deborah Martin; Lee Smith; Kenneth Wright; Pat Mercer. Also see SIX TEENS / Brenda & Tabulations

BRENDA LEE: see LEE, Brenda

BRENDON
Singles: 7-inch
ARIOLA AMERICA 3-5 77
U.K. 3-5 74

BRENNAN, Buddy
(Buddy Brennan Quartet)
Singles: 7-inch
THUNDER (103 "Big River") 10-20 59
WARWICK (517 "Big River") 10-15 59
WARWICK (532 "Blue River") 8-12 60

BRENNAN, Cody
Singles: 7-inch
SWAN 5-8 61

BRENNAN, J.D., & Gold Fever
LPs: 10/12-inch
SCYNE (5283 "Guitar Slinger") 8-10 90
Members: J.D. Brennan; Scotty Esty; Tom Flynn; Bruce Esty; Carl Illyes; Monica Lauderdale; Sandra Lauderdale.

BRENNAN, Michael
Singles: 7-inch
CAPITOL 3-5 70

BRENNAN, Walter P&R '60
(With Billy Vaughn's Orchestra & Chorus; with Patriots)
Singles: 7-inch
DOT 5-10 60
KAPP 3-5 71
LIBERTY 4-8 62-64
RPC 8-10 61
Picture Sleeves
DOT 10-15 60
LIBERTY 8-12 62-63
LPs: 10/12-inch
DOT 20-30 60
EVEREST 20-30 60
HAMILTON 15-25 65
LIBERTY 20-30 62
LONDON 15-20 70
RPC 20-30 62
SUNSET 8-10 66
U.A. 5-10 75
Also see GOLDWATER, Barry
Also see PATRIOTS
Also see VAUGHN, Billy

BRENSTON, Jackie R&B '51
(With His Delta Cats)
Singles: 78 rpm
CHESS (Except 1458) 15-30 51-53
CHESS (1458 "Rocket 88") 50-100 51
(See note below regarding 45 rpms.)
FEDERAL 15-40 56-57
Singles: 7-inch
CHESS (1458 "Rocket 88") 300-500 51
(With Ike Turner on guitar. Original 45s from 1951 are not known to exist. There are legit reissue 45s, made circa 1954. These have a delta symbol [Δ] and the number stamped in the trail-off. Fakes, without the delta mark, also exist.)
CHESS (1469 "In My Real Gone Rocket") 150-250 51
CHESS (1472 "Juiced") 150-250 52
CHESS (1496 "Leo the Louse") 100-150 52
CHESS (1532 "The Blues Got Me Again") 50-100 53
FEDERAL 20-40 56-57
SUE 5-10 61
Also see TURNER, Ike

BRENSTON, Jackie / Muddy Waters
Singles: 7-inch
CHESS (113 "Rocket 88") 3-5
Also see BRENSTON, Jackie
Also see WATERS, Muddy

BRENT, Bryan, & Cut Outs
Singles: 7-inch
PENNY (2201 "Vacation Time") 200-400 62

BRENT, Carolyn
Singles: 7-inch
CONGRESS 5-8 64

BRENT, Frankie
(With the Counts; Frankie Brent Revue Featuring Little Linda Lou)
Singles: 7-inch
CALVERT (201 "No Rock & Rollin' Here") 50-75 57
CAMEO (181 "More of Everything") 8-12 60
CAMEO (187 "Hi Ho Silver") 8-12 61
CAMEO (196 "Rang Dang Do") 8-12 61
CUTTY ("All I Have to Do Is Dream") 5-10
(Selection number not known.)
EPIC 5-10 64
PALETTE (5016 "Time After Time") 8-12 59
PALETTE (5018 "Should We Tell") 8-12 59
STRAND (25014 "No Rock & Rollin' Here") 15-25 60
VIK 10-20 58
Picture Sleeves
EPIC 8-12 64

BRENT, Randy
Singles: 7-inch
CUPID 5-10 59

BRENT, Ronnie
Singles: 7-inch
COLT-45 10-20 59
U.A. 20-30 58

BRENT, Tony
Singles: 7-inch
ROULETTE 5-10 58

BRENT & SPECTRAS
Singles: 7-inch
SPECTRA ("Oh Darling") 30-40
(Selection number not known.)

BRENTWOOD C&W '83
Singles: 7-inch
HOT SCHATZ 3-4 83-84

BRENTWOODS
Singles: 7-inch
DORE (559 "Midnight Star") 25-35 60
TALENT 10-15 63

BRENTWOODS
Singles: 7-inch
OUR (101 "Yeah Yeah, No, No") 20-30 67

BRESH, Tom C&W '76
Singles: 7-inch
ABC 3-5 78
ABC/DOT 3-5 77-78
FARR 3-5 76-77
LPs: 10/12-inch
ABC 5-10 78
ABC/DOT 5-10 77-78
FARR 6-12 76-77

BRESH, Tom, & Lane Brody C&W '82
Singles: 7-inch
LIBERTY 3-4 82
Also see BRESH, Tom
Also see BRODY, Lane

BRESSLAW, Bernard
Singles: 7-inch
CAPITOL 10-15 58

BRET & TERRY
Singles: 7-inch
PRESTIGE (313 "Beatle Hop") 10-15 64

BRETHREN
Singles: 7-inch
TEEN TOWN (124 "Can This Be Real") 10-20 60s

BRETHREN
LPs: 10/12-inch
TIFFANY 10-15 70-71

BRETT, Paul
LPs: 10/12-inch
ABC 10-20 69
JANUS 10-15 71
RCA 5-10 78

BREW
Singles: 7-inch
ABC 10-12 69

BREWED
Singles: 7-inch
ATLANTIC 4-8 70

BREWER, Deanna
Singles: 7-inch
LEMCO (885 "I've Gotta Know") 10-20 60s

BREWER, Gordon
Singles: 7-inch
TOPPA 4-8 62

BREWER, Michael
Singles: 7-inch
FULL MOON 3-4 83
LPs: 10/12-inch
FULL MOON 5-10 83

BREWER, Spencer
Singles: 7-inch
WILLOW ROSE 3-4 84

BREWER, Teresa P&R '50
(With the Lancers; with Dixieland Band; with Mickey Mantle; with Bobby Wayne)
Singles: 78 rpm
CORAL 5-15 52-57
LONDON 5-15 50-52
Singles: 7-inch
ABC 3-5 67
AMSTERDAM 3-5 72-73
CORAL (60000 & 61000 series) 10-20 52-58
CORAL (62000 & 65000 series) 5-15 58-64
DOCTOR JAZZ 3-4 83
FLYING DUTCHMAN 3-5 72
LONDON 10-20 50-52
PHILIPS 4-8 63-67
PROJECT 3 3-4 82
RCA (11882 "Merry Christmas") 4-6 79
(With picture label. Special products issue.)
SSS INT'L 4-6 68
SIGNATURE 3-4 74-83
Picture Sleeves
CORAL 10-15 58-60
SIGNATURE 3-5 80
EPs: 7-inch
CORAL 10-20 55-60
LONDON (6039 "Teresa Brewer") 20-30 51
LONDON (6041 "Teresa Brewer") 20-30 51
LPs: 10/12-inch
AMSTERDAM 6-10 73-74
COLUMBIA 5-10 81
CORAL (7 "Best of Teresa Brewer") 15-25 65
CORAL (56072 "A Bouquet of Hits from Teresa Brewer") 50-75 52
(10-inch LP.)
CORAL (56093 "Till I Waltz Again with You") 50-75 53
(10-inch LP.)
CORAL (57027 thru 57297) 25-50 55-59
(Monaural. Stereo numbers in the 57000 series are preceded by a "7.")
CORAL (57315 thru 57414) 15-30 60-65
(Monaural. Stereo numbers in the 57000 series are preceded by a "7.")
DOCTOR JAZZ 5-10 79-83
FLYING DUTCHMAN 6-10 73-74
IMAGE 5-10 78
LONDON (1006 "Teresa Brewer") 50-100 51
(10-inch LP.)
MCA 5-10 83
PHILIPS 10-20 63-67
PROJECT 3 5-10 82
RCA 5-10 75
SIGNATURE 5-10 74-75
VOCALION 8-15 69
WING 8-10 66
Also see CORNELL, Don, & Teresa Brewer
Also see McGUIRE SISTERS / Lancers / Dorothy Collins / Teresa Brewer

BREWER, Teresa / Eileen Barton
Singles: 78 rpm
CORAL 5-10 50s
Also see BARTON, Eileen

BREWER, Teresa, & Count Basie
LPs: 10/12-inch
DOCTOR JAZZ 5-10 84
Also see BASIE, Count

BREWER, Teresa, & Duke Ellington
LPs: 10/12-inch
COLUMBIA 5-10 81
FLYING DUTCHMAN 6-10 74
Also see BREWER, Teresa
Also see ELLINGTON, Duke

BREWER, Tommy
Singles: 7-inch
CRYSTALETTE (701 "Drag, Brother, Drag") 15-20 56
(Colored vinyl.)

BREWER & SHIPLEY P&R/LP '71
Singles: 7-inch
A&M 4-8 68-69
BUDDAH 3-5 70
CAPITOL 3-5 74-75
KAMA SUTRA 3-5 70-73
Picture Sleeves
KAMA SUTRA 3-6 72
LPs: 10/12-inch
A&M 12-15 68
ACCORD 5-10 83
CAPITOL 8-10 74-75
KAMA SUTRA 10-12 70-76
Members: Mike Brewer; Tom Shipley.

BREWSTER, Ray
Singles: 7-inch
ALTO 5-10 61
Also see HOLLYWOOD FLAMES

BREWSTER, Ray, & Cadillacs
Singles: 7-inch
ARCTIC 5-10 64
Also see BREWSTER, Ray
Also see CADILLACS

BRIAN, Neil
Singles: 7-inch
PARKWAY 4-8 64
20TH FOX 4-8 67

BRIAN, Russ
Singles: 7-inch
HORIZON (1001 "Hillbill's Rock") 300-500

BRIAN, Steve
Singles: 7-inch
CLEFF-TONE 5-10 59

BRIAN & BRENDA R&B '78
Singles: 7-inch
ROCKET 3-5 76-78
Members: Brian Russell; Brenda Russell.

BRIANS, Robin Hood
Singles: 7-inch
FRATERNITY (803 "Dis Itty Bitty Girl") 50-100 58
UNI 10-15 66

BRIARWOODS
Singles: 7-inch
RISING SONS 4-8 69
Members: Stan Beach; Bob Hoffman; Harry Scholes; Barry Bobst; Dorinda Duncan.

BRICK P&R/R&B/LP '76
Singles: 12-inch
BANG 4-6 79-82
Singles: 7-inch
BANG 3-5 76-82
MAINSTREET 4-8 76
STREET 3-5 76
LPs: 10/12-inch
BANG 5-10 76-82
Members: Jimmy Brown; Regi Hargis; Eddie Irons; Ray Ransom; Don Nevins.

BRICK WALL
Singles: 7-inch
CAPITOL 3-6 69

BRICKELL, Edie P&R/LP '88
(With the New Bohemians)
Singles: 7-inch
GEFFEN 3-4 88-90
Picture Sleeves
GEFFEN 3-4 88-89
LPs: 10/12-inch
GEFFEN 5-8 88-90

BRICKLIN
LPs: 10/12-inch
A&M (5124 "Bricklin'") 5-10 86

BRIDES OF FUNKENSTEIN R&B/LP '78
Singles: 7-inch
ATLANTIC 3-4 78-80
LPs: 10/12-inch
ATLANTIC 5-10 78-80
Members: Lynn Mabry; Dawn Silva.
Also see PARLIAMENT
Also see YOUNG, Val

BRIDESHEAD
Singles: 7-inch
CHRYSALIS 3-4 82
LPs: 10/12-inch
CHRYSALIS 5-10 82

BRIDGE
Singles: 7-inch
CO-OP (519 "A Beautiful Day") 8-12 69
KIRZO (1 "Love Is There") 10-20 70
ROULETTE (7081 "Love Is There") 8-12 70
Members: Leon D'Amato; Dennis D'Amato; Paul Tortora; Charlie Claude; John Mariano.

BRIDGE
(Brooklyn Bridge)
Singles: 7-inch
BUDDAH 3-5 72
LPs: 10/12-inch
BUDDAH 8-12 72
Also see BROOKLYN BRIDGE

BRIDGE
LPs: 10/12-inch
BRENTWOOD.................................. 5-10 82

BRIDGER, Bobby
Singles: 7-inch
NUGGET.................................. 5-10

BRIDGES, Alicia P&R/R&B/LP '78
Singles: 12-inch
SECOND WAVE.................................. 4-6 84
POLYDOR.................................. 4-6 78-79
Singles: 7-inch
A.V.I. 3-4 82
MEGA.................................. 3-5 72
POLYDOR.................................. 3-4 78-79
SECOND WAVE.................................. 3-4 84
ZODIAC.................................. 3-5 73
LPs: 10/12-inch
POLYDOR.................................. 5-10 78-79

BRIDGES, Chuck
(With L.A. Happening)
Singles: 7-inch
SCOOP (03 "Don't You Make Me Cry")..........................10-20 60s
VAULT.................................. 4-8 69
LPs: 10/12-inch
VAULT.................................. 10-15 69
Members: Adrian Tappia; Pete Marchica; Kenny Sawhill; Jim Sawyer; Bob O'Donnel; Stu Blomberg; Gary Green; John Hobbs; Pete Woodford.

BRIDGES, Curly, & Frank Motley
Singles: 7-inch
DC.................................. 5-8 62

BRIDGES, Willy
Singles: 7-inch
BUDDAH.................................. 3-4 77
LPs: 10/12-inch
BUDDAH.................................. 5-10 77

BRIDGEWATER, Dee Dee R&B/LP '78
Singles: 12-inch
ELEKTRA.................................. 4-6 79-80
Singles: 7-inch
ELEKTRA.................................. 3-5 78-79
LPs: 10/12-inch
ATLANTIC.................................. 8-10 76
ELEKTRA.................................. 5-10 78-80

BRIEF ENCOUNTER R&B '76
Singles: 7-inch
CAPITOL.................................. 3-5 76-77
SEVENTY SEVEN.................................. 3-5 72-73
Members: Maurice Whittington; Gary Bailey; Larry Bailey; Belmont Bailey; Monte Bailey.

BRIGADE
LPs: 10/12-inch
BAND 'N' VOCAL (1066 "Last Laugh")..........................1000-2000 70
Members: Peter Belknap; Ed Wallo; Mark Hartman; Bob Anderson; Eric Anderson; Tim Vetter; Dennis Steindal.

BRIGADIERS
Singles: 7-inch
MALA 10-15 61

BRIGANDS
Singles: 7-inch
EPIC.................................. 10-15 66

BRIGATI
Singles: 7-inch
ELEKTRA.................................. 3-5 76
LPs: 10/12-inch
ELEKTRA.................................. 8-10 76
Members: Eddie Brigati; David Brigati; Ed Kobylarz.
Also see RASCALS

BRIGGS, Brian
Singles: 7-inch
BEARSVILLE.................................. 3-4 80-81
Picture Sleeves
BEARSVILLE.................................. 3-4 80-81
LPs: 10/12-inch
BEARSVILLE.................................. 5-10 80-82

BRIGGS, David
Singles: 7-inch
DECCA.................................. 4-8 63
DOT 4-6 66
LPs: 10/12-inch
HARMONY.................................. 8-12 72
MONUMENT.................................. 10-12 69
Also see KENYON, Joe
Also see McDOWELL, Ronnie
Also see NELSON, Willie
Also see ROBBINS, Marty
Also see PRESLEY, Elvis

BRIGGS, Freddie
(Fred Briggs)
Singles: 7-inch
CONGRESS.................................. 5-10 64
GROOVE CITY ("I'm So Sorry") 50-75
(Selection number not known.)

BRIGGS, Jimmy
Singles: 7-inch
CAPITOL.................................. 4-8 63

BRIGGS, Katie
Singles: 7-inch
COLUMBIA.................................. 5-10 68
MOS-RAY.................................. 10-20

BRIGGS, Lillian P&R '55
Singles: 78 rpm
EPIC.................................. 5-10 56
Singles: 7-inch
ABC-PAR 4-8 61
CORAL.................................. 5-10 59-60
EPIC.................................. 10-20 56
SUNBEAM.................................. 5-10 58
EPs: 7-inch
EPIC (7163 "High Priestess of Rock 'N Roll")..........................20-30 56
Also see HAWKINS, Screamin' Jay / Lillian Briggs

BRIGGS, Rick
Singles: 7-inch
ROCKIN'.................................. 5-10

BRIGHT, Bobby, & Laurie Allen
Singles: 7-inch
LTD 4-8 66

BRIGHT, Cal
Singles: 7-inch
AZETTA 3-5

BRIGHT, Jerry, & Embers
Singles: 7-inch
YUCCA (139 "Jim's Jive")..............20-30 61
YUCCA (143 "Be Mine")..............20-30 62

BRIGHT, Judy
LPs:10/12-inch
DOT 15-25

BRIGHT, Larry P&R '60
(Pete Roberts)
Singles: 7-inch
BRIGHT.................................. 4-8 65
DEL-FI (Except 4204)..................5-10 63-64
DEL-FI (4204 "Surfin' Queen") 10-20 63
DIPLOMAT.................................. 4-8
DONNA.................................. 4-8 64
DOT 4-8 66
EDIT.................................. 8-12 62
HIGHLAND.................................. 8-12 61
JOJO.................................. 3-5 76
ORIGINAL SOUND.................................. 3-5 71
RENDEZVOUS (124 "Hold Me") 8-10 60
(Reissued as by Pete Roberts.)
TIDE (006 thru 1083)..................10-20 60-62
Also see GREASERS
Also see HUMDINGERS
Also see ROBERTS, Pete

BRIGHT, Larry / Humdingers
Singles: 7-inch
JAYE JOSEPH.................................. 4-8 64
Also see BRIGHT, Larry

BRIGHTER SIDE OF DARKNESS P&R/R&B '72
Singles: 7-inch
STAR VUE.................................. 5-10
20TH FOX.................................. 3-5 72-75
LPs: 10/12-inch
20TH FOX.................................. 8-10 73
Members: Darryl Lamont; Ralph Eskridge; Larry Washington; Randolph Murph.

BRIGHTLIGHTS
Singles: 7-inch
SILVER FOX 3-5 69

BRIGHTMAN, Sarah, & Hot Gossip
Singles: 7-inch
ARIOLA.................................. 3-5 78
Also see RICHARD, Cliff, & Sarah Brightman

BRIGHTON, Connie
Singles: 12-inch
HANDSHAKE.................................. 4-6 82

BRIGHTONES
Singles: 7-inch
W.B. (5472 "Rumors")..................10-15 64

BRIGIDI SISTERS
Singles: 7-inch
CHANCELLOR (1032 "That Tickles")..........................10-20 59

BRIGMAN, George
(With Split)
EPs: 7-inch
BONA FIDE.................................. 5-10 85
LPs: 10/12-inch
SOLID (001 "Jungle Rot")............75-125 75
Also see SPLIT

BRIKS
Singles: 7-inch
BISMARK (1013 "Can You See Me")..........................25-35 66
DOT (16878 "Can You See Me") ...15-20 66

BRIKTA, Danny
Singles: 7-inch
NITRO (998 "Sweet Little Angel")..........................50-100 63

BRILEY, Jebry Lee C&W '79
Singles: 7-inch
IBC.................................. 3-5 79
PAID.................................. 3-4 82
Also see HILKA & JEBRY

BRILEY, Martin P&R '83
Singles: 7-inch
EMI AMERICA.................................. 3-4 84
MERCURY.................................. 3-4 81-84
LPs: 10/12-inch
MERCURY.................................. 5-10 81-85
Also see GREENSLADE

BRILEY, Pat
Singles: 7-inch
WHIZ MASTERS.................................. 4-8 67

BRILL, Marty
Singles: 78 rpm
MERCURY.................................. 5-10 56
Singles: 7-inch
MERCURY.................................. 8-12 56
LPs: 10/12-inch
MERCURY.................................. 20-25 56

BRILL, Marty, & Larry Foster
LPs: 10/12-inch
COLPIX.................................. 10-20 65
LAURIE.................................. 15-20 62
Also see BRILL, Marty

BRILLIANT, Ashleigh
LPs: 10/12-inch
DORASH (1001 "Ashleigh Brilliant in the Haight Ashbury")..........................30-60 67

BRILLIANT KORNERS
Singles: 7-inch
MODERN (1059 "Three Lonely Guys")..........................10-20 68

BRIM
Singles: 7-inch
ATLANTIC.................................. 3-6 69

BRIM, Grace
Singles: 78 rpm
J.O.B. (117 "Man Around My Door")..........................75-100 52
Also see BRIM, John
Also see BRIM, Mrs. John

BRIM, John
(With His Combo; Trio; with His Gary Kings; with His Stompers.)
Singles: 78 rpm
FORTUNE (801 "Strange Man") ..75-125 50
J.O.B. (110 "Trouble in the Morning")..........................50-75 52
J.O.B. (1011 "Drinking Woman") ...50-75 53
(Though not credited, the flip of J.O.B. 1011, *Woman Trouble*, is by Sunnyland Slim & His Boys.)
RANDOM (201 "Dark Clouds").....75-125 51
Singles: 7-inch
CHESS (1588 "Go Away")............75-125 55
CHESS (1624 "I Would Hate to See You Go")..........................75-125 56
PARROT (799 "Tough Times") ..100-150 53
(Black vinyl.)
PARROT (799 "Tough Times") ..150-250 53
(Colored vinyl.)
Members: Little Walter; Robert Lockwood Jr. Big Maceo; James Watkins.
Also see BIG MACEO
Also see BRIM, Grace
Also see JAMES, Elmore, & John Brim
Also see LITTLE WALTER
Also see SUNNYLAND SLIM

BRIM, Mrs. John
(Grace Brim)
Singles: 78 rpm
RANDOM (202 "Going Down the Line")..........................75-125 51
Also see BRIM, Grace

BRIMMER, Charles R&B '75
Singles: 7-inch
CHELSEA.................................. 4-8 75-76
LPs: 10/12-inch
CHELSEA.................................. 8-10 76-77

BRIMSTONE
Singles: 7-inch
FIREBIRD ("Blowin' in the Wind") 8-12 69
(Selection number not known.)
LANGCO (3122 "Home Cooking") .10-15
LPs: 10/12-inch
BRIMSTONE ("Paper Winged Dreams")..........................150-250 60s
(No selection number used.)
Members: Gregg Andrews; Chris Wintrip; Ken Miller; Bernie Nau; Jim Papatoukakis.

BRIMSTONE
Singles: 7-inch
BIG TREE 3-5 71

BRIMSTONES
Singles: 7-inch
MGM (13653 "It's All Over But the Crying")..........................10-20 66

BRIMSTONES
Singles: 7-inch
WORLD PACIFIC (77834 "Cold Hearted Woman")..........................15-25 66

BRINK, Fred
Singles: 7-inch
RINGO 4-8 65

BRINK, James
Singles: 7-inch
ROTARY (101 "It's Rough")...........50-75

BRINKLEY, Bobby
Singles: 7-inch
MONUMENT.................................. 4-8 62

BRINKLEY, Charles
Singles: 7-inch
MUSIC MACHINE 3-5 75

BRINKLEY, Jay
Singles: 78 rpm
DOT 5-10 55
Singles: 7-inch
DOT 10-15 55
KLIFF (100 "Guitar Smoke")..........10-20 58
ROULETTE (4117 "The Creep")....15-25 58

BRINKLEY, Jimmy
Singles: 78 rpm
ALADDIN (3100 series)..................15-25 53

BRINKLEY, Larry
Singles: 7-inch
WESTWOOD (202 "Jackson Dog")..........................30-50 59

BRINKLEY & PARKER R&B '74
Singles: 7-inch
DARNEL.................................. 3-5 74

BRINSLEY SCHWARZ: see SCHWARZ, Brinsley

BRINSON, Lee
Singles: 7-inch
BRUNSWICK.................................. 4-8 66
DAL MOR.................................. 4-8 66

BRIODY, Billy
Singles: 7-inch
ARCO.................................. 4-8 67

BRISBOIS, Buddy
Singles: 7-inch
A.N.B. 4-8 66

BRISCO, Dotti
Singles: 7-inch
TOPPA.................................. 4-8 62-63

BRISCOE, Bill
Singles: 7-inch
HANOVER 5-8 60

BRISCOE, Jimmy, & Little Beavers R&B '73
Singles: 7-inch
ATLANTIC.................................. 3-5 71
J-CITY.................................. 3-5 72
PHI-KAPPA.................................. 3-5 73-75
SALSOUL.................................. 3-4 79
WANDERICK.................................. 3-5 77
LPs: 10/12-inch
PHI-KAPPA.................................. 10-12 74
WANDERICK.................................. 8-10 77
Members: Jimmy Briscoel; Stanford Stansbury; Robert Makins; Kevin Brown; Maurice Pully.

BRISCOE, Joey
Singles: 78 rpm
DECCA (30414 "Eternal Love") 15-25 57
Singles: 7-inch
DECCA (30414 "Eternal Love") 15-25 57
GREENWICH (413 "Pretty Kisses")..........................10-20 59
Also see DEL-VIKINGS

BRISTOL, Johnny P&R/R&B/LP '74
Singles: 7-inch
ATLANTIC.................................. 3-5 76-78
HANDSHAKE.................................. 3-4 80-81
MGM.................................. 3-5 74-75
LPs: 10/12-inch
ATLANTIC.................................. 5-10 76-78
HANDSHAKE.................................. 5-10 81
MGM.................................. 8-12 74-75
Also see ALTON & JOHNNY
Also see JOHNNY & JACKEY
Also see STEWART, Amii, & Johnny Bristol

BRISTOL, Johnny, & Spyder Turner
Singles: 7-inch
POLYDOR.................................. 3-4 83
Also see BRISTOL, Johnny
Also see TURNER, Spyder

BRISTOL, Marc
LPs: 10/12-inch
KING NOODLE 5-10 87
Also see OKIE DOKE BAND

BRISTOLS
Singles: 7-inch
AUDIO DYNAMICS 4-8 67

BRITAIN BROTHERS
Singles: 7-inch
TCF.................................. 4-8 65

BRITANNIA
Singles: 7-inch
MIDLAND INT'L.................................. 3-5 76

BRITINS
Singles: 7-inch
BANANAS.................................. 3-5 77
NOVA.................................. 3-4 79

BRITISH CASUALS
Singles: 7-inch
LONDON.................................. 3-6
MAINSTREAM.................................. 5-8 69
LPs: 10/12-inch
MAINSTREAM.................................. 15-20 69
Also see CASUALS

BRITISH LIONS P&R/LP '78
Singles: 7-inch
RSO.................................. 3-5 78
LPs: 10/12-inch
RSO.................................. 5-10 78
Members: John Fiddler; Dale Griffin; Overend Watts; Ray Major; Morgan Fisher.
Also see MOTT the HOOPLE

BRITISH ROAD RUNNERS
Singles: 7-inch
LAURIE.................................. 4-8 68

BRITISH WALKERS
Singles: 7-inch
CAMEO.................................. 5-10 67
CHARGER (108 "The Girl Can't Help It")..........................10-20 65
MANCHESTER (651120 "Watch Yourself")..........................15-25 65
TRY (502 "I Found You")...............10-20 64

BRITNY FOX P&R/LP '88
Singles: 7-inch
COLUMBIA.................................. 3-4 88-89
LPs: 10/12-inch
COLUMBIA.................................. 5-8 88-89
Member: Dean Davidson.

BRITO, Phil
Singles: 7-inch
BRUNSWICK.................................. 10-15 59

BRITT, Darryl
Singles: 7-inch
BLUE (1199 "Lover, Lover") 50-100

BRITT, Elton C&W '45
(With the Skytoppers with Zeke Manners Band)
Singles: 78 rpm
BLUEBIRD.................................. 10-15 40-45
RCA.................................. 5-10 49-56
VICTOR.................................. 8-12 46-48
Singles: 7-inch
ABC-PAR.................................. 5-8 60
RCA (0006 thru 6429)..................10-20 49-56
RCA (9000 series)..................4-6 68-69
EPs: 7-inch
RCA.................................. 10-20 55-56
LPs: 10/12-inch
ABC-PAR (293 thru 521)..............20-30 59
ABC-PAR (322 thru 521)..............15-25 60-66
ABC-PAR (744 "16 Great Country Performances")..........................10-15 71
CAMDEN.................................. 10-20 69
CERTRON.................................. 8-12 70
KOALA.................................. 8-10 79
PREMIER.................................. 5-10 60s
RCA (1288" Yodel Songs") 30-50 56
RCA (2669 "Best of Elton Britt").....20-30 63
RCA (3222" Yodel Songs") 50-100 54
(10-inch LP.)
RCA (4822 "Best of Elton Britt, Vol. 2")..........................5-10 73
SPIN-O-RAMA.................................. 8-15 60s
Also see MANNERS, Zeke, & His Band
Also see THREE SUNS, Rosalie Allen & Elton Britt

BRITT, Elton, Rosalie Allen & Skytoppers C&W '50
(Elton Britt / Rosalie Allen)
Singles: 78 rpm
RCA.................................. 5-10 50
EPs: 7-inch
RCA.................................. 15-25 55
LPs: 10/12-inch
GRAND AWARD (262 "Starring Elton Britt & Rosalie Allen")..........................15-25 66
WALDORF (1206 "Rosalie Allen & Elton Britt")..........................20-30 57
Also see ALLEN, Rosalie
Also see BRITT, Elton

BRITT, Lynn
Singles: 7-inch
DOT.................................. 5-10 61
MIKI.................................. 10-15 61

BRITT, Mel
Singles: 7-inch
FESTIVAL INT'L (650 "She'll Come Running Back")..........................150-250 60s

BRITT, Steve
Singles: 7-inch
U.A..................................... 4-6 68

BRITT, Tina R&B '65
Singles: 7-inch
EASTERN (604 "The Real Thing")..........................8-12 65
MINIT.................................. 5-10 69
VEEP.................................. 5-10 68-69
LPs: 10/12-inch
MINIT.................................. 15-25 69

BRITT, Tommy
Singles: 7-inch
ADMIRAL.................................. 4-8 62
UNISON.................................. 5-10 59-60

BRITTAN, Bob
Singles: 7-inch
RIDER.................................. 5-10 60

BRITTEN, Benjamin *LP '63*
LPs: 10/12-inch
LONDON ... 10-20 63

BRITTON, Aldora
Singles: 7-inch
COLUMBIA ... 4-8 67
DECCA ... 4-6 69-70

BRITTON, Marilyn
Singles: 7-inch
VEE JAY ... 4-8 62

BRITTON, Nikki
Singles: 7-inch
DOT ... 4-6 68-69

BROAD STREET GANG
Singles: 7-inch
COUGAR ... 3-5

BROADCASTERS
LPs: 10/12-inch
ENIGMA ... 5-10 87
Also see FINN & SHARKS

BROADUS, Batiste
Singles: 7-inch
CAPA (124 "I Need Time") ... 15-25

BROADWAY *P&R/R&B '76*
Singles: 7-inch
GRANITE ... 3-5 76
HILLTAK ... 3-4 78
LPs: 10/12-inch
HILLTAK ... 8-10 79

BROADWAY EXPRESS
Singles: 7-inch
ABBOTT ... 5-10
I&D (1006 "What Love Can Do") ... 15-25 60s
PHILLY GROOVE ... 5-10 60s

BROADWAY MAINTENANCE TICKLE CO.
Singles: 7-inch
HARBOUR ... 3-6 69

BROADWAYS
Singles: 7-inch
MGM ... 4-8 66

BROCHURES
Singles: 7-inch
APOLLO (757 "They Lied") ... 15-25 61
Members: Ed McLwain; Lucius Hood; Robert Hood; Butch Hogan.

BROCK
Singles: 7-inch
20TH FOX ... 3-5 74

BROCK, B.
(With the Sultans; with Vibratos)
Singles: 7-inch
CROWN ... 10-15 64
LA BROC (101 "Hang Five") ... 15-25 63
LPs: 10/12-inch
CROWN ... 15-20 64

BROCK, Bill
(With the Clansmen)
Singles: 7-inch
BILBRO ... 4-6 60s
GENE NORMAN PRESENTS ... 5-10 62
LIBERTY ... 4-8 63-64
SAMPSON ... 4-8 64
TOPIC ... 4-8 65

BROCK, Joe *C&W '76*
Singles: 7-inch
RONNIE ... 3-5 76

BROCK, Mike
Singles
EVATONE/SPORTS NETWORK ("Mike Brock") ... 10-15 76
(Square cardboard picture disc.)

BROCK, Norma, & Keynoters
(With the Jack Hale Orchestra)
Singles: 7-inch
PEPPER (896 "Evergood") ... 25-50 59

BROCK, Tom
Singles: 7-inch
20TH FOX ... 3-5 74
LPs: 10/12-inch
20TH FOX ... 8-10 74

BROCKETT, Jamie
LPs: 10/12-inch
ADELPHI ... 5-10 77
CAPITOL ... 10-12 69-71
ORACLE ... 10-15 69

BROCKINGTON, Alfreda
Singles: 7-inch
PHIL L.A. of SOUL ... 8-15 69-70

BROCKINGTON, Julius
Singles: 7-inch
BURMAN ... 3-5
TODAY ... 3-5
LPs: 10/12-inch
TODAY ... 8-10 72-73
Also see BROCKINGTONS

BROCKINGTONS
LPs: 10/12-inch
TODAY ... 8-10 72
Member: Julius Brockington.
Also see BROCKINGTON, Julius

BRODIAN, Stewart
LPs: 10/12-inch
MOUNTAIN ... 5-10 84

BRODIE, Henry, & Red Toppers
Singles: 7-inch
DAN (3214 "All Night Jump") ... 10-20 61

BRODY, Lane *C&W '82*
Singles: 7-inch
EMI ... 3-4 84-85
LIBERTY ... 3-4 82-84
Picture Sleeves
EMI ... 3-4 84
Also see BRESH, Tom, & Lane Brody
Also see LEE, Johnny, & Lane Brody

BRODY, Marsha
Singles: 7-inch
HEART & SOUL ... 4-8 67
HOT SHOT ... 4-8 66

BRODY, Michael J.
Singles: 7-inch
RCA ... 4-6 70

BROG & WEINER
Singles: 7-inch
GREEN MENU ... 3-5 77

BROGAN, Michael
Singles: 7-inch
ARISTA ... 3-4 80

BROGUES
Singles: 7-inch
CHALLENGE (59311 "But Now I Find") ... 20-25 65
CHALLENGE (59316 "Don't Shoot Me Down") ... 20-25 65
TWILIGHT (408 "But Now I Find") ... 40-50 65
Members: Eddie Rodrigues; Rick Campbell; Gary Duncan; Greg Elmore.
Also see QUICKSILVER

BROKEN ARROW
Singles: 7-inch
VAULT ... 3-5 70

BROKEN EDGE
Singles: 7-inch
POLYDOR ... 3-4 83
LPs: 10/12-inch
POLYDOR ... 5-10 83

BROKEN GLASS
Singles: 7-inch
CAPITOL ... 3-5 76
LPs: 10/12-inch
CAPITOL ... 8-10 76
Members: Stan Webb; Robbie Blunt: Bob Daisley; Rob Rowlinson; Mac Poole.

BROKEN HEARTS
Singles: 7-inch
DIAMOND ... 8-10 62

BROKEN HOME
Singles: 7-inch
ATLANTIC ... 3-4 80
LPs: 10/12-inch
ATLANTIC ... 5-10 80

BROKENJO
Singles: 7-inch
SANFRIS ... 3-5 70

BROMBERG, David *LP '72*
Singles: 7-inch
COLUMBIA ... 3-5 72-73
FANTASY ... 3-4 77-79
LPs: 10/12-inch
ATLANTIC ... 5-10 80
COLUMBIA ... 8-12 72-77
FANTASY ... 8-12 76-80
Also see CLEMENTS, Vassar
Also see GRATEFUL DEAD
Also see FREAK SCENE
Also see HARRISON, George
Also see KEITH & DONNA
Also see LOGGINS & MESSINA / David Bromberg
Also see SAHM, Doug

BRONCO
Singles: 7-inch
ISLAND ... 3-5 71
LPs: 10/12-inch
ISLAND ... 10-12 71
Members: Jess Roden; Robbie Blunt; Kevyn Gammend; John Pasternak; Pete Robinson.

BRONNER BROTHERS *R&B '84*
Singles: 7-inch
JEWEL ... 4-6 75
NEIGHBOR ... 3-4 84
Picture Sleeves
NEIGHBOR ... 3-4 84
Members: Bernard Bronner; Nate Bronner.

BRONSKI BEAT *P&R/D&D '84*
Singles: 12-inch
MCA ... 4-6 84-86
Singles: 7-inch
MCA ... 3-4 84-86
Picture Sleeves
MCA ... 3-4 84-86
LPs: 10/12-inch
MCA ... 5-10 85-86
Members: Jimmy Somerville; Steve Bronski; Larry Steinbachek.
Also see COMMUNARDS
Also see SOMERVILLE, Jimmy

BRONSON, Marty
Singles: 7-inch
NORMAN ... 4-8 62-63
LPs: 10/12-inch
NORMAN ... 12-15 63

BRONSON, Sonny
Singles: 7-inch
MALA ... 5-10 59

BRONSTEIN, Stan
LPs: 10/12-inch
MUSE ... 5-10 76

BRONX CHEER
Singles: 7-inch
PYE ... 3-5 72

BRONZ
LPs: 10/12-inch
BRONZE ... 5-10 84

BRONZETTES
Singles: 7-inch
PARKWAY ... 5-10 64

BRONZVILLE, Lewis
(Lewis Bronzville Five)
Singles: 78 rpm
BLUEBIRD ... 40-60 40
MONTGOMERY WARD ... 20-40

BROOD
Singles: 7-inch
DOT ... 3-5 71

BROOD
Singles: 7-inch
GET HIP ... 3-4 90
Picture Sleeves
GET HIP ... 3-4 90
LPs: 10/12-inch
GET HIP ... 5-10 90
ESTRUS ... 5-10 92
Members: Chris Horne; Betsy Mitchell; Crystal Light; Asch Gregory.

BROOD, Herman *P&R/LP '79*
(With Wild Romance)
Singles: 7-inch
ARIOLA AMERICA ... 3-4 79
LPs: 10/12-inch
ARIOLA AMERICA ... 8-10 79-80
TOWNHOUSE ... 5-10 82

BROOK, Shannon
Singles: 7-inch
ACCENT ... 3-5 71

BROOK, Skippy
Singles: 7-inch
EXCELLO ... 8-12 60

BROOK BROTHERS
(Brooks)
Singles: 7-inch
LONDON ... 5-10 61-64

BROOKE, Stormy, & Escapades
Singles: 7-inch
ASTRONAUT ... 5-10 61

BROOKFIELDS
Singles: 7-inch
EMBER ... 5-8 63

BROOKER, Gary
Singles: 7-inch
CHRYSALIS ... 3-4 79
POLYGRAM ... 3-4 82
LPs: 10/12-inch
CHRYSALIS ... 5-10 79
MERCURY ... 5-10 82
RCA ... 5-8 85
Also see CLAPTON, Eric
Also see PARSONS, Alan, Project
Also see PROCOL HARUM
Also see RENWICK, Tim

BROOKES, Bobby
Singles: 7-inch
CAPITOL ... 4-8 62
CARLTON ... 8-12 59
RCA ... 5-10 58

BROOKFIELDS
Singles: 7-inch
EMBER ... 5-10 63

BROOKINS, Doug
Singles: 7-inch
IMPERIAL ... 4-8 68
Session: Davie Allan.
Also see ALLAN, Davie

BROOKINS, Robert *R&B '86*
Singles: 12-inch
MCA ... 4-6 86
Singles: 7-inch
MCA ... 3-4 86
Picture Sleeves
MCA ... 3-4 87

BROOKLYN BOYS
Singles: 78 rpm
DYNAMIC ... 40-60 56
FERRIS ... 10-15 56
Singles: 7-inch
DYNAMIC (107 "If She Should Call") ... 100-200 56
(First issue.)
FERRIS (902 "If She Should Call") ... 15-25 56

BROOKLYN BRATS
LP: 10/12-inch
IRON WORKS (1002 "Brooklyn Brats") ... 5-10 86
(Picture disc.)

BROOKLYN BRIDGE *P&R '68*
(Johnny Maestro & Brooklyn Bridge)
Singles: 7-inch
BROOKLYN BRIDGE (881 "Christmas Is") ... 10-15 88
BUDDAH ... 4-8 68-72
COLLECTABLES ... 3-4 84
ERIC ... 3-5 78
FLASHBACK ... 3-5 70s
HARVEY (500 "Worst That Could Happen") ... 5-10 81
(Colored vinyl.)
RADIO ACTIVE GOLD ... 3-5
LPs: 10/12-inch
BUDDAH (5000 series) ... 20-25 69-72
BUDDAH (69000 series) ... 5-10 84
COLLECTABLES ... 5-10 82
Members: Johnny Maestro; Fred Ferrara; Les Cauchi; Mike Gregorio; Tom Sullivan; Carolyn Wood; Jimmy Rosica; Richie Macioce; Artie Cantanzarita; Shelly Davis; Joe Ruvio.
Also see BRIDGE
Also see DEL SATINS
Also see FANN BAND
Also see ISLEY BROTHERS / Brooklyn Bridge
Also see MAESTRO, Johnny

BROOKLYN DREAMS *P&R '77*
Singles: 12-inch
CASABLANCA ... 4-6 79
MILLENNIUM ... 4-6 78
Singles: 7-inch
CASABLANCA ... 3-4 79-80
MILLENNIUM ... 3-5 77-78
LPs: 10/12-inch
CASABLANCA ... 5-10 79-80
MILLENNIUM ... 8-10 77
Members: Joe Esposito; Eddie Hokenson; Bruce Sudano.
Also see ESPOSITO, Joe "Bean"
Also see SUMMER, Donna

BROOKLYN PEOPLE
Singles: 7-inch
CHERI ... 3-5 76

BROOKS: see BROOK BROTHERS

BROOKS, Albert
Singles: 7-inch
ASYLUM (45259 "Party from Outer Space") ... 4-8 75

BROOKS, Arthur
Singles: 7-inch
JEFF ... 5-10 59

BROOKS, Billy
(With the Red Saunders Band)
Singles: 78 rpm
DUKE ... 10-20 55-56
PEACOCK ... 15-25 53
Singles: 7-inch
DUKE (142 "Song of the Dreamer") ... 20-30 55
DUKE (149 "I Want Your Love Tonight") ... 20-30 56
PEACOCK (1629 "I Called My Baby") ... 25-50 53

BROOKS, Billy
LPs: 10/12-inch
CROSSOVER ... 8-10 75

BROOKS, Blondie
Singles: 7-inch
GULF REEF ... 5-10 62

BROOKS, Bobby
Singles: 78 rpm
RAINBOW ... 5-10 56
Singles: 7-inch
RAINBOW ... 10-15 56
EPs: 7-inch
RCA (1/2-1598 "This Is the Night") ... 20-40 58
(Price is for either of two volumes.)
RCA (4273 "Teenagers Dance to Bobby Brooks") ... 20-40 58
LPs: 10/12-inch
RCA (1598 "This Is the Night") ... 50-75 58
Also see JALOPY FIVE

BROOKS, Bonnie
Singles: 7-inch
U.A. ... 5-10 64

BROOKS, Chuck
Singles: 7-inch
AGP ... 3-5 69
CHIMNEYVILLE ... 3-5
VOLT ... 3-5 70

BROOKS, Chuck, & Sharpies
Singles: 7-inch
DUB (2844 "Spinning My Wheels") ... 150-200 58

BROOKS, Clinton, & Bs
Singles: 7-inch
APACHE (1828 "Tom Dooley Rock") ... 30-50 59

BROOKS, Dale
Singles: 7-inch
BISHOP ... 4-8
DOLPHIN ... 5-10 65
TWIRL ... 4-8 66

BROOKS, David
Singles: 78 rpm
CHART (618 "Bus Ride") ... 10-15 56
Singles: 7-inch
CHART (618 "Bus Ride") ... 15-25 56

BROOKS, Denny
Singles: 7-inch
BELL ... 3-5 73
BUDDAH ... 3-5 77
MCA ... 3-5 76
LPs: 10/12-inch
W.B. (1822 "Denny Brooks") ... 10-20 69
Members: Denny Brooks; Bernie Leadon; Jim Keltner; Carl Radle; David Marks.
Also see ATTITUDES
Also see DAVE & MARKSMEN
Also see DEREK & DOMINOES
Also see LEADON, Bernie

BROOKS, Dianne
Singles: 12-inch
TOWNHOUSE ... 4-6 81
Singles: 7-inch
REPRISE ... 3-5 76
TOWNHOUSE ... 3-4 81
LPs: 10/12-inch
REPRISE ... 8-10 76

BROOKS, Donnie *P&R '60*
Singles: 7-inch
CHALLENGE ... 4-8 66
COLLECTABLES ... 3-4 81
DJ ... 4-8 65
ERA (3000 series) ... 8-15 59-62
ERA (3100 series) ... 4-6 68
HAPPY TIGER ... 3-5 70-71
MIDSONG ... 3-5 79
OAK ... 3-5 71
REPRISE ... 3-5 64-65
USA ... 10-15 60s
YARDBIRD ... 4-6 68-69
Picture Sleeves
ERA ... 10-20 60-61
Promotional Singles
ERA ("Mission Bell"/"Doll House") . 50-75 60
(Distributed during a personal appearance.)
LPs: 10/12-inch
ERA (105 "The Happiest") ... 30-40 61
OAK ... 8-10 71
WISHBONE ... 5-10 75
Also see BUSH, Dick
Also see FAIRE, Johnny
Also see JORDAN, Johnny

BROOKS, Dusty
(With the Four Tones; with Tones)
Singles: 78 rpm
COLUMBIA ... 15-25 50-51
DOOTONE ... 10-20 52
LAMARR STAR (101 "I'll Follow You") ... 15-25 46
LAMARR STAR (102 "Seclusion") 15-25 46
LAMARR STAR (103 "Little Chum") ... 15-25 46
MAJESTIC (123 "Ole' Man River") 15-25 50
MAJESTIC (127 "Shuffle Board Boogie") ... 15-25 50
MEMO (1001 "Play Jackpot") ... 15-25 46-48
MEMO (1002 "Little Chum") ... 15-25 46-48
MEMO (1003 "Please Don't Rush Me") ... 15-25 46-48
MEMO (1005 "Put Your Cards on the Table") ... 15-25 46-48
MEMO (7001 "Please Don't Rush Me") ... 15-25 48
PREVIEW (666 "Someone Over Here Loves Someone Over There") ... 20-30 45
PREVIEW (668 "Two Tears Met") 20-30 45
SUN (182 "Heaven Or Fire") ... 100-200 53
SUPREME ... 10-20 49
Singles: 7-inch
SUN (182 "Heaven Or Fire") .. 1000-1500 53
Members: Dusty Brooks; Juanita Brown; Joe Alexander.
Also see ALEXANDER, Joe
Also see BROWN, Juanita

BROOKS, Elkie
Singles: 7-inch
A&M ... 3-4 77-80
PARROT ... 4-8 64
LPs: 10/12-inch
A&M ... 5-10 75-80

BROOKS, Ella *R&B '87*
Singles: 7-inch
QMI ... 3-4 87
Picture Sleeves
QMI ... 3-4 87

BROOKS, Eloise, & Dreamers
Singles: 78 rpm
ALADDIN (3303 "My Plea") ... 50-100 55
Singles: 7-inch
ALADDIN (3303 "My Plea") ... 100-200 55

BROOKS, Garth *C&W '89*
Singles: 7-inch
CAPITOL ... 3-4 89-92
LPs: 10/12-inch
CAPITOL ... 5-8 90-92

BROOKS, Genie
Singles: 7-inch
MINARET (130 "Fine Time") ... 5-8 66
MINARET (142 "Helping Hand") ... 5-8 66

BROOKS, George E., & Ink Spots
Singles: 7-inch
PAULA ... 3-5 72
Also see INK SPOTS

BROOKS, Hadda *R&B '47*
(Hadda Brooks Trio)
Singles: 78 rpm
LONDON ... 15-25 50
MODERN ... 15-30 45-56
MODERN MUSIC ... 15-25 47
OKEH ... 10-20 54
Singles: 7-inch
WIN ... 4-6 69

ARWIN (1001 "Careless Years")........8-12 59
KENT (321 "The Thrill Is Gone")......8-12 59
LONDON (684 "I Hadn't Anyone Till You")..........25-50 50
MODERN (100 series)..................15-25 52
MODERN (804 "Let's Be Sweethearts Again")..........50-100 51
MODERN (825 "When a Woman Cries")..........50-100 51
MODERN (841 "I Feel So Good")..........50-100 51
MODERN (861 "Romance in the Dark")..........50-100 52
MODERN (1008 "Close Your Eyes")..........25-50 56
MODERN MUSIC (Colored vinyl).....4-6 86
OKEH..........20-40 54
EPs: 7-inch
LONDON (6149 "Presenting Hadda Brooks")..........50-75 54
MODERN (114 "Boogie")..........50-100 52
LPs: 10/12-inch
CROWN (5010 "Femme Fatale")....40-60 57
CROWN (5374 "Hadda Brooks Sings and Swings")..........15-25 63
MODERN (1210 "Femme Fatale")..........100-200 56
Members: Hadda Brooks; Basie Day; Al Wichard; Jim Black.

BROOKS, Hadda / Pete Johnson
LPs: 10/12-inch
CROWN (5058 "Boogie")..........35-45 58
Also see BROOKS, Hadda
Also see JOHNSON, Pete

BROOKS, Jean
Singles: 7-inch
G-NOTE..........10-20

BROOKS Jeff
Singles: 7-inch
MOONGLOW (216 "Fat Louise")....5-10 63
MOONGLOW (216 "Fat Louise")....10-20 63
(Colored vinyl. Promotional issue only.)

BROOKS, Joe
(Joe Brooks Group)
Singles: 7-inch
ATLANTIC..........3-4 78
METROMEDIA..........3-5 70
LPs: 10/12-inch
METROMEDIA..........10-15 70

BROOKS, Joey
Singles: 7-inch
AURORA..........5-10 65
CANADIAN AMERICAN (105 "I Have Waited")..........20-30 59
COLUMBIA..........5-10 61
MUSICOR..........5-10 64

BROOKS, John Benson
LPs: 10/12-inch
DECCA..........10-15 68

BROOKS, Junior
Singles: 78 rpm
RPM (343 "Lone Town Blues")........40-60 51

BROOKS, Karen *C&W '82*
Singles: 7-inch
W.B. 3-4 82-85
LPs: 10/12-inch
W.B. 5-8 82-84
Also see CROWELL, Rodney
Also see SHEPPARD, T.G., & Karen Brooks

BROOKS, Karen, & Johnny Cash *C&W '85*
Singles: 7-inch
W.B. 3-4 85
Also see BROOKS, Karen
Also see CASH, Johnny

BROOKS, Kix *C&W '83*
Singles: 7-inch
AVION..........3-5 83
CAPITOL..........3-4 89
Also see BROOKS & DUNN
Also see TOMORROW'S WORLD

BROOKS, Lillian
(With the Moroccos)
Singles: 78 rpm
KING..........8-15 56
MGM..........5-10 57
Singles: 7-inch
B&F..........5-10 59-60
KING..........10-20 56
MGM..........8-12 57-58
NEWPORT..........5-10 61-63
ORIOLE..........5-10 59
Also see MOROCCOS

BROOKS, Little Genie
Singles: 7-inch
CAROL..........4-8 66

BROOKS, Lonnie
(Lee Baker)
Singles: 7-inch
ALLIGATOR..........3-4 81
CHESS..........5-10
CHIRRUP..........10-20
MIDAS..........5-10
PALOS (005 "The Train")..........8-12
SECOND CITY..........4-8
U.S.A. 5-10 64
LPs: 10/12-inch
ALLIGATOR..........6-12 79-83
BLACK & BLUE..........8-10 75
Also see GUITAR JR.

BROOKS, Louis *R&B '55*
(With His Hi-Toppers)
Singles: 78 rpm
EXCELLO..........15-25 52-57
Singles: 7-inch
EXCELLO (2000 series)..........25-50 52-53
EXCELLO (2100 series)..........15-25 57-59

BROOKS, Mel *R&B '82*
Singles: 7-inch
WMOT..........3-4 82
Also see REINER, Carl, & Mel Brooks

BROOKS, Nancy *P&R '79*
Singles: 7-inch
ARISTA..........3-4 79

BROOKS, Nancy / Bud Roman
Singles: 7-inch
TOPS..........20-35

BROOKS, Pattie
Singles: 12-inch
CASABLANCA..........4-6 78-79
Singles: 7-inch
BACKSTREET..........3-4 83-84
CASABLANCA..........3-4 77-80
MIRAGE..........3-4 83
LPs: 10/12-inch
CASABLANCA..........5-10 77-80
MIRAGE..........5-10 83
Also see AYKROYD, Dan, & Pattie Brooks

BROOKS, Pattie, & Joe Esposito
Singles: 7-inch
CASABLANCA..........3-4 79
Also see ESPOSITO, Joe "Bean"

BROOKS, Pattie, & Paul Jabara
Singles: 7-inch
CASABLANCA..........3-4 78
Also see BROOKS, Patti

BROOKS, Ramona *R&B '77*
Singles: 7-inch
MANHATTAN..........3-5 77
U.A. 3-5 77
LPs: 10/12-inch
MANHATTAN..........8-10 78

BROOKS, Rosa Lee
Singles: 7-inch
REVIS (1013 "My Diary")..........20-40 63
Also see HENDRIX, Jimi

BROOKS, Rose
Singles: 7-inch
SOUL CITY..........4-8 66

BROOKS, Senator
Singles: 7-inch
LEE..........10-20

BROOKS, Skippy, Combo
Singles: 7-inch
EXCELLO (2188 "Doin' the Horse")..........10-20 60

BROOKS, Smokey
Singles: 7-inch
VEEP..........4-8 68

BROOKS, Sonny, & Savoys
Singles: 78 rpm
TIP TOP..........50-75 56
Singles: 7-inch
TIP TOP (1007 "Here I Am")......100-150 56
TIP TOP (1008 "Sweetheart Darling")..........100-150 56

BROOKS, Terry, & Strange
Singles: 12-inch
STAR PEOPLE..........8-10 81
Singles: 7-inch
HIGH FREQUENCY (4178 "Disco Queen")..........5-10 80s
STAR PEOPLE (001 "Bottom Line")..........10-15 81
STAR PEOPLE (002 "Bottom Line") 8-12 81
STAR PEOPLE (003 "Disco Queen")..........5-10 80s
Picture Sleeves
HIGH FREQUENCY (4178 "Disco Queen")..........5-10 80s
STAR PEOPLE (003 "Disco Queen")..........5-10 80s
LPs: 10/12-inch
STAR PEOPLE (005 "To Earth with Love")..........10-20 81
Also see STRANGE

BROOKS, Tommy
Singles: 7-inch
CAPITOL..........3-5 70
IN ARTS..........4-8 68

BROOKS, Wayne, & Cyclones
Singles: 7-inch
TOP RANK (2099 "Runaway")........10-20 61
(First issue; by about four or five months.)
WARWICK (629 "Runaway")........10-15 61

BROOKS: see BROOK BROTHERS

BROOKS & BROWN
Singles: 78 rpm
DUKE..........8-15 57
Singles: 7-inch
DUKE..........10-20 57

BROOKS & DUNN *C&W '91*
Singles: 7-inch
ARISTA..........3-4 91
Members: Kix Brooks; Ronnie Dunn.
Also see BROOKS, Kix
Also see DUNN, Ronnie

BROOKS & JERRY
Singles: 7-inch
DYNAMO..........4-8 67
Member: Jerry Williams.
Also see WILLIAMS, Jerry

BROOKS & KORNFELD
Singles: 7-inch
EPIC..........4-8 67
Member: Joe Brooks.

BROOKS BOND FOOD
Singles: 7-inch
GINK (9612 "Red Rose Tea")........35-45

BROOKS BROTHER FIDELIS
Singles: 7-inch
BANGAR..........4-8 60s

BROOKS BROTHERS
Singles: 78 rpm
DECCA..........15-25 47-48
DIAMOND..........15-25 46

BROOKS BROTHERS *C&W '85*
(Brooks Brothers Band)
Singles: 7-inch
BUCKBOARD..........3-4 85
YATAHEY..........3-4 80
Members: Randy Brooks; Bill Brooks.

BROOKS FOUR
Singles: 7-inch
SINCLAIR..........5-8 62

BROOKTONES
Singles: 7-inch
COED..........8-12 58

BROOM, Bobby *R&B '81*
Singles: 7-inch
ARISTA..........3-4 81-84
GRP..........3-4 81
LPs: 10/12-inch
GRP..........5-10 81

BROOME, Charlie
Singles: 7-inch
O.E.K. 5-10 61

BROONZY, Big Bill
(With His Fat Four; Little Sam; Big Bill & His Rhythm Band; Chicago Bill)
Singles: 78 rpm
CHESS (1546 "Little City Woman")..........50-75 53
COLUMBIA..........15-25 45-47
HUB..........15-25 45
MELODISC..........15-25 51
MERCURY..........15-25 49-51
OKEH..........15-25 40s
VOCALION..........20-50 40s
VOGUE..........10-20 49-51
Singles: 7-inch
CHESS (1546 "Little City Woman")..........250-350 53
MERCURY (8122 "I Love My Whiskey")..........25-50 51
MERCURY (8126 "I Wonder")........25-50 51
MERCURY (8160 "You've Been Mistreatin' Me")..........25-50 51
EPs: 7-inch
MERCURY..........15-20 63
LPs: 10/12-inch
ARCHIVE of FOLK MUSIC..........10-12 67
BIOGRAPH..........8-10 73
COLUMBIA (111 "Big Bill's Blues")..........50-100 57
DISC..........12-20 65
EMARCY (26034 "Folk Blues")......50-75 54
EMARCY (26137 "Blues by Broonzy")..........50-75 55
EPIC..........10-12 69
FOLKWAYS..........15-30 57-58
GNP..........8-10 74-75
MERCURY..........20-30 63-64
PERIOD (1114 "Big Bill Broonzy Sings")..........50-100 55
ROOTS N' BLUES..........5-8 90
TRIP..........8-10 75
VERVE (3000-5 "The Big Bill Broonzy Story")..........50-100 61
(Boxed, five-disc set.)
VERVE (3001 "Last Session, Vol. 1")..........15-25 61
VERVE (3001 "Last Session, Vol. 2")..........15-25 61
VERVE (3001 "Last Session, Vol. 3")..........15-25 61
YAZOO..........8-12 69-70
Also see CHICAGO BILL
Also see GILLUM, Jazz
Also see LITTLE SAM
Also see McGHEE, Brownie, & Sonny Terry
Also see WHITE, Josh & Big Bill Broonzy
Also see WHITE, Josh / Leadbelly / Bill Broonzy

BROONZY, Big Bill, & Pete Seeger
LPs: 10/12-inch
FOLKWAYS..........10-15 65
Also see SEEGER, Pete

BROONZY, Big Bill, & Washboard Sam
LPs: 10/12-inch
CHESS (1468 "Big Bill Broonzy & Washboard Sam")..........35-45 62
Also see BROONZY, Big Bill
Also see WASHBOARD SAM

BROS *P&R/LP '88*
Singles: 7-inch
EPIC..........3-4 88
Picture Sleeves
EPIC..........3-4 88

LPs: 10/12-inch
EPIC..........5-8 88

BROTH
LPs: 10/12-inch
MERCURY..........10-12 70

BROTHER
Singles: 7-inch
EPIC..........3-5 71

BROTHER BLUES & BACK ROOM BOYS
(Champion Jack Dupree)
Singles: 78 rpm
ABBEY (3015 "Featherweight Mama")..........20-40 50
Also see DUPREE, Champion Jack

BROTHER BONES *R&B '49*
(With His Shadows)
Singles: 78 rpm
TEMPO (652 "Sweet Georgia Brown")..........15-25 48
TEMPO (4566 "Bubber's Boogie") 10-15 54
Singles: 7-inch
HARLEM GLOBETROTTER (300 "Sweet Georgia Brown")..........5-15
(Reissue of Tempo 652.)
TEMPO (4566 "Bubber's Boogie") 15-25 54
Member: Joe Darensbourg.
Also see DARENSBOURG, Joe

BROTHER BULLDOG
Singles: 7-inch
CITATION..........3-5 70

BROTHER FOX & TAR BABY
Singles: 7-inch
CAPITOL..........3-6 70
LPs: 10/12-inch
CAPITOL..........20-30 70
ORACLE..........15-25 70

BROTHER FROG
Singles: 7-inch
MGM..........3-5 73

BROTHER JOHN
Singles: 7-inch
A&M..........3-5 70

BROTHER L. CONGREGATION
Singles: 7-inch
KUMQUAT (1 "Bringing Me Down")..........20-30 68

BROTHER MAKES TWO
Singles: 7-inch
CAPITOL..........4-8 68

BROTHER NIGEL'S PROXY PARTY
Singles: 7-inch
FANTASY..........3-6 69

BROTHER SISTERS
Singles: 78 rpm
MERCURY..........5-10 57
Singles: 7-inch
MERCURY..........10-20 57

BROTHER TO BROTHER *P&R/R&B '74*
Singles: 7-inch
SUGAR HILL..........3-4 81
TURBO..........3-5 74-77
WIN OR LOSE..........3-5
LPs: 10/12-inch
SUGAR HILL..........5-10 81
TURBO..........10-12 74-77
Members: Michael Burton; Bill Jones; Frankie Prescott; Yogi Horton.

BROTHERHOOD *R&B '76*
Singles: 7-inch
COLUMBIA..........3-5 70
DIAL..........3-6 69
MCA..........3-4 78
RCA..........3-6 69
Picture Sleeves
RCA..........4-8 69
LPs: 10/12-inch
MCA..........5-10 78
RCA..........12-15 69
Members: Drake Levin; Michael Smith; Phil Volk; Ron Collins.
Also see REVERE, Paul, & Raiders
Also see WOMACK, Bobby

BROTHERHOOD BLUES BAND
MOVIN' OUT (701 "More & More")....3-5

BROTHERHOOD OF MAN *P&R/LP '70*
Singles: 7-inch
BELL..........3-5 74
DERAM..........3-6 70-72
LONDON..........5-8
PRELUDE..........3-5 78
PRIVATE STOCK..........3-5 77
PYE..........3-5 75-76
LPs: 10/12-inch
DERAM..........10-12 70
PYE..........8-10 76
Members: Tony Burrows; Sunny; Johnny Goddison; Hal Atkinson; Nicky Stevens; Sandra Stevens; Martin Lee; Lee Sheridan.
Also see BURROWS, Tony

BROTHERLY LOVE *R&B '72*
Singles: 7-inch
MUSIC MERCHANT..........5-10 72
LPs: 10/12-inch
MUSIC MERCHANT (104 "Brotherly Love")..........25-50 72

BROTHERLY LOVES
Singles: 7-inch
ESKEE..........4-8 66

BROTHERS
Singles: 7-inch
ARGO..........10-20 58-59
CHECKER..........8-15 61
Members: Dean Mathis; Marc Mathis.
Also see DEAN & MARC

BROTHERS
Singles: 7-inch
RCA..........4-8 66
WHITE WHALE..........4-8 67-70
ZANZEE (112 "Secret Place")......10-15
LPs: 10/12-inch
COLUMBIA..........10-12 73

BROTHERS
Singles: 7-inch
RCA..........3-5 75-76
LPs: 10/12-inch
RCA..........10-12 75-76

BROTHERS & OTHERS
Singles: 7-inch
RCA..........3-5 71

BROTHERS & SISTERS
Singles: 7-inch
SOFT (979 "And I Know")..........20-30 66
TOWER (262 "And I Know")........15-25 66

BROTHERS & SISTERS
(Featuring Merry Clayton)
Singles: 7-inch
CAPITOL..........5-10 67
ODE..........4-8 68
TODDLIN' TOWN..........5-10 69
Also see CLAYTON. Merry

BROTHERS & SISTERS OF L.A.
LPs: 10/12-inch
ODE '70..........10-15 69

BROTHERS & SISTERS OF SOUL
Singles: 7-inch
DUKE..........4-8 64

BROTHERS "B"
LPs: 10/12-inch
RAINBOW..........5-10 73

BROTHERS BY CHOICE *R&B '78*
Singles: 7-inch
ALA..........3-4 78-80
FRETONE..........3-5 75

BROTHERS CAIN
Singles: 7-inch
ACTA..........10-20 67-68
MERCURY..........10-20 65

BROTHERS FOUR *P&R/LP '60*
Singles: 7-inch
AURAVISION (6725 "San Francisco Bay Blues")..........10-15 64
(Cardboard flexi-disc, one of six by six different artists. Columbia Record Club "Enrollment Premium." Set came in a special paper sleeve.)
COLUMBIA (Except 43547)..........5-10 59-69
COLUMBIA (43547 "Ratman & Bobbin in the Clipper Caper")..........8-12 69
FANTASY..........3-5 70
Picture Sleeves
COLUMBIA..........10-15 60-63
LPs: 10/12-inch
COLUMBIA..........10-20 59-69
FANTASY..........8-12 70
FIRST AMERICAN..........5-10 81
GRT..........10-12 77
HARMONY..........6-10 69-72
Members: Bob Flick; Dick Foley; John Paine; Mike Kirkland.

BROTHERS GRIMM
Singles: 7-inch
MERCURY..........4-8 65
TRIPLE TIGRRR (7 "You'll Never Be Mine")..........15-25 65

BROTHERS GUIDING LIGHT *R&B '73*
(Featuring David)
Singles: 7-inch
MERCURY..........3-5 73

BROTHERS IN CO-OP
Singles: 7-inch
BUNKY..........5-10 70s

BROTHERS JOHNSON *P&R '75*
Singles: 12-inch
A&M (Black vinyl)..........4-6 78-85
A&M (Colored vinyl)..........5-10 78-85
Singles: 7-inch
A&M..........3-4 76-88
Picture Sleeves
A&M..........3-5 76-85
LPs: 10/12-inch
A&M (Except PR-4714)..........5-10 76-85
A&M (PR-4714 "Blam")..........6-12 79
(Picture disc. No tour info on B-side.)
A&M (PR-4714 "Blam")..........20-30 79
(Picture disc. Has tour information on B-side. 250 made.)
Members: Louis Johnson; George Johnson.
Also see JONES, Quincy, & Brothers Johnson

BROTHERS JONES
Singles: 7-inch
OVATION..........3-4 80
LPs: 10/12-inch
OVATION..........5-10 80

BROTHERS LEGARD
Singles: 7-inch
ERA 3-6

BROTHERS OF GHETTO
Singles: 7-inch
GHETTO 3-5

BROTHERS OF HOPE
Singles: 7-inch
GAMBLE 3-5 70

BROTHERS OF LOVE
Singles: 7-inch
BLUE ROCK 4-8 68-69
INTREPID 3-5 70
MERCURY 3-5 70-71

BROTHERS OF SOUL R&B '68
Singles: 7-inch
BOO (111 "You Better Believe It") 15-25 70
BOO (112 "Love Is Fever") 15-25 70
BOO (1004 "Hurry Don't Linger") 15-25 68
BOO (1005 "Come On Back") 15-25 68
BOO (1006 "I'd Be Grateful") 50-100 69
CRISS-CROSS (1001 "Can't Get You Out of My Mind") 25-50 60s
SHOCK (1314 "Candy") 15-25 60s
Members: Richard Knight; Robert Eaton; Fred Bridges.

BROTHERS PRIDE
Singles: 7-inch
GNP 3-4 71

BROTHERS RE-BORN
LPs: 10/12-inch
KENT 10-20 68
Members: Raphael & Ramon Velez.

BROTHERS THREE
Singles: 7-inch
T-NECK 3-6 69

BROTHERS TWO
Singles: 7-inch
CAPITOL 3-5 73
CRIMSON 4-8 67
INSTANT 3-5 73
JONAH 10-20

BROTHERS UNLIMITED
Singles: 7-inch
CAPITOL 3-5 70
LPs: 10/12-inch
CAPITOL 10-15 70

BROUGHAM CLOSET
Singles: 7-inch
MOTHER BEAR 4-8

BROUGHTON, Edgar
(Edgar Broughton Band)
LPs: 10/12-inch
CAPITOL 10-15 74
HARVEST 15-20 69

BROUGHTON, Edna
Singles: 78 rpm
MODERN (773) 40-60 50
(Exact title not known.)

BROUGHTON, John, & Muffins / Shawkey Seau & Muffins
Singles: 7-inch
PLANET (59 "Walk Alone") 10-20 66

BROUSSARD, Van
Singles: 7-inch
MALA 4-6 68
REX 4-8 61

BROWN, Abigail
Singles: 7-inch
PRIVATE STOCK 3-5 77

BROWN, Al
(Al Brown Rhythm Band)
Singles: 7-inch
BM 4-8
SOUND GEMS 3-5 75

BROWN, Al, & His Tunetoppers P&R/R&B '60
(Featuring Cookie Brown)
Singles: 7-inch
AMY 5-10 60-61
EPs: 7-inch
AMY (1 "Madison Dance Party") 35-45 60
LPs: 10/12-inch
AMY (1 "Madison Dance Party") 45-50 60

BROWN, Alex P&R/D&D '85
Singles: 12-inch
MERCURY 4-6 85
Singles: 7-inch
MERCURY 3-4 85
ROXBURY 3-5 76

BROWN, Andrew
Singles: 7-inch
4 BROTHERS (444 "Let's Get Together") 10-15 65
4 BROTHERS (446 "If We Try") 8-12 65
4 BROTHERS (449 "Can't Let You Go") 8-12 65

BROWN, Anglo-Saxon
Singles: 7-inch
ATLANTIC 3-5 76
LPs: 10/12-inch
ATLANTIC 8-10 76

BROWN, Arlene
(Arelean Brown)
Singles: 7-inch
DUD SOUND (4730 "I Am a Streaker") 4-6 74
DYNAMITE (8664 "You're Gonna Miss Me") 4-6 74
SIMMONS (432 "Eagle Stirs His Nest") 4-6

BROWN, Arthur P&R/LP '68
(Crazy World of Arthur Brown; Arthur Brown's Kingdom Come)
Singles: 7-inch
ATLANTIC 4-8 68
TRACK 4-6 68-69
LPs: 10/12-inch
ATLANTIC 15-20 68
GULL 8-10 75
PASSPORT 10-12 74
RECKLESS 5-10 88
REPUBLIC (001 "Speak No Tech") 10-20 82
(Picture disc.)
TRACK 10-15 68
Also see ATOMIC ROOSTER
Also see PARSONS, Alan, Project

BROWN, Arthur Lee
Singles: 7-inch
LAVA 10-20 72

BROWN, B., & His McVouts
Singles: 78 rpm
FLASH (102 "Good Woman Blues") 200-250 55
Singles: 7-inch
FLASH (102 "Good Woman Blues") 750-1000 55

BROWN, B., & Rockin' McVouts
(Buster Brown)
Singles: 7-inch
EVERLAST (5014 "Rockin' with B") 20-30 60
VEST (827 "My Baby Left Me") 20-30 60
VEST (830 "Fannie Mae Is Back") 20-30 60
Despite incredible name similarities, there seems to be no connection between this artist and the previous one, who recorded for Flash.
Also see BROWN, Buster

BROWN, Barbara
Singles: 7-inch
ATCO 5-10 68
CARNIVAL (508 "So in Love") 10-20 65
SOUNDS of MEMPHIS 4-6 72
TOWER 5-10 68
Also see BARBARA & BROWNS

BROWN, Beaver: see BEAVER BROWN

BROWN, Beckett
Singles: 7-inch
RCA 3-5 75

BROWN, Benny
Singles: 78 rpm
GOTHAM 15-25 53
Singles: 7-inch
GOTHAM (293 "Slick Baby") 30-40 53
(Black vinyl.)
GOTHAM (293 "Slick Baby") 75-100 53
(Colored vinyl.)

BROWN, Benson
Singles: 7-inch
POLYDOR 3-5 72
SOUND SYNDICATE 3-5 72

BROWN, Bep
(J.T. Brown)
Singles: 78 rpm
METEOR 40-60 53
Singles: 7-inch
METEOR (5001 "Kickin' the Blues Around") 75-100 53
Also see BROWN, J.T.

BROWN, Betty
Singles: 7-inch
BETHLEHEM 5-10 61-62

BROWN, Bill
Singles: 7-inch
CUSTOM SOUND (164 "Tight Levis and Boots") 35-50 57

BROWN, Billie, & Ballards
Singles: 7-inch
ELTONE (439 "Why Baby Why") 250-500

BROWN, Billie Bea
Singles: 7-inch
TOPIC 5-10 66

BROWN, Billy
Singles: 7-inch
CHALLENGE 4-6 69
COLUMBIA 10-20 57-59
REPUBLIC 8-12 60

BROWN, Billy C&W '79
Singles: 7-inch
ACCENT 3-5 75
BERNES 3-4 79

BROWN, Billy, & Ballads
Singles: 7-inch
EL TONE 4-8 63

BROWN, Bobby
(With the Curios)
Singles: 7-inch
CURIO (100 "Falling from Paradise") 30-40 63
KING (5214 "I'm Beggin' You Baby") 10-15 59
KING (S-5214 "I'm Beggin' You Baby") 20-40 59
KING (5246 "Pleading") 10-15 59
PAK (1313 "Falling from Paradise") 50-100 62
VADEN (100 "Down at Mary's House") 75-100 59
VADEN (109 "Please, Please Baby") 75-100 59
(With Larry Donn.)
VERVE 4-8 68
Also see DONN, Larry

BROWN, Bobby
LPs: 10/12-inch
DESTINY (4001 "Live") 75-100 72
DESTINY (4002 "The Enlightening Beam of Axonda") 100-150 72

BROWN, Bobby P&R/R&B/LP '86
Singles: 12-inch
MCA 4-6 86
Singles: 7-inch
MCA 3-4 86-89
Picture Sleeves
MCA 3-4 86-89
LPs: 10/12-inch
MCA 5-10 86-89
Also see BROWN, B., Posse
Also see MEDEIROS, Glenn, & Bobby Brown
Also see NEW EDITION

BROWN, Boots P&R '58
(With Blockbusters; with Pelugelpipers; with Dan Drew; Shorty Rogers)
Singles: 78 rpm
RCA 5-15 53-57
Singles: 7-inch
DOT 4-6 67-68
RCA 8-15 53-60
EPs: 7-inch
GROOVE (1000 "Rock That Beat") 25-50 55
LPs: 10/12-inch
GROOVE (1000 "Rock That Beat") 50-100 55
Also see COOL, Calvin
Also see ROGERS, Shorty

BROWN, Brian
(Brian Brown Trio)
Singles: 7-inch
ACADEMY 5-10 60

BROWN, Bucky, & Curios
Singles: 7-inch
XYZ (610 "Dream Date") 20-30 60

BROWN, Buster P&R/R&B '60
(With Chas. Lucas & Thrillers)
Singles: 78 rpm
FIRE (1008 "Fannie Mae") 300-400 59
Singles: 7-inch
ABC 3-4 73
CHECKER 10-15 63
FIRE 15-25 59-62
GWENN 10-15 62
NOCTURN (1000 "I Love You for Sentimental Reasons") 25-50 64
OLDIES 45 4-6
RCA 4-6 74
ROULETTE 3-5 72
SEROCK 10-15 63
LPs: 10/12-inch
COLLECTABLES 6-8 88
FIRE (101/102 "The New King of the Blues") 300-400 60
(Blue cover. Track listing includes *Blueberry Hill* and *When Things Go Wrong*. Disc number is 101 though cover indicates 102.)
FIRE (101/102 "The New King of the Blues") 150-300 60
(White cover. With *Blueberry Hill* and *When Things Go Wrong* replaced by *Going on a Picnic* and *Corena*. Disc number is 101 though cover indicates 102.)
KOALA 8-12
SOUFFLE 10-20 73
Also see BROWN, B., & Rockin' McVouts

BROWN, Camille, & Angelenos
Singles: 7-inch
PEEPERS (2825 "Angels in Heaven") 50-100 61
Also see ANGELENOS

BROWN, Capability
Singles: 7-inch
CHARISMA 3-5 72
PASSPORT 3-5 74
LPs: 10/12-inch
PASSPORT 8-10 74

BROWN, Charity
Singles: 7-inch
A&M 3-5 75-76

BROWN, Charles R&B '49
(With Johnny Moore's Three Blazers; "Charles Brown singing and accompanying himself on piano")
Singles: 78 rpm
ALADDIN 15-25 49-57
CASH 15-25 57
HOLLYWOOD 15-25 54
SWING TIME 25-50 52
Singles: 7-inch
ACE (561 "Educated Fool") 8-12 59
ACE (599 "Boys Will Be Boys") 8-12 60
ALADDIN (3076 "Black Night") 50-100 51
ALADDIN (3091 "I'll Always Be in Love with You") 50-75 51
ALADDIN (3092 "Seven Long Days") 50-75 52
ALADDIN (3116 "Hard Times") 50-75 52
ALADDIN (3120 "My Last Affair") 50-75 52
ALADDIN (3138 "Without Your Love") 50-75 52
ALADDIN (3157 "Rollin' Like a Pebble in the Sand") 50-100 52
ALADDIN (3163 "Evening Shadows") 25-50 53
ALADDIN (3176 "Take Me") 25-50 53
ALADDIN (3191 "Lonesome Feeling") 25-50 53
ALADDIN (3200 "All My Life") 20-40 53
ALADDIN (3235 "Cryin' Mercy") 20-40 54
ALADDIN (3254 "Foolish") 20-40 54
ALADDIN (3272 "Honey Sipper") 20-40 55
ALADDIN (3284 "Walk with Me") 20-40 55
ALADDIN (3290 "Fool's Paradise") 20-40 55
ALADDIN (3296 "My Heart Is Mended") 20-40 55
ALADDIN (3316 "One Heart to One") 20-40 56
ALADDIN (3339 "Soothe Me") 20-40 56
ALADDIN (3342 "Confidential") 20-40 56
ALADDIN (3348 "Merry Christmas Baby") 20-40 56
ALADDIN (3366 "It's a Sin to Tell a Lie") 20-40 57
CENCO (123 "I Want to Go Home") 5-10
EAST-WEST 15-25 58
GALAXY 5-8 66
HOLLYWOOD (1006 "Pleading for Your Love") 20-40 54
IMPERIAL (018 "Black Night") 5-8 62
IMPERIAL (5830 "Fool's Paradise") 5-10 62
IMPERIAL (5902 "Merry Christmas Baby") 5-10 62
IMPERIAL (5905 "Black Night") 5-8 63
IMPERIAL (5961 "I'm Savin' My Love for You") 5-8 63
JEWEL 3-5 71-74
KING (5439 "Angel Baby") 8-10 61
KING (5523 "Butterfly") 8-10 61
KING (5530 "Christmas in Heaven") 8-10 61
KING (5570 "Without a Friend") 8-10 61
KING (5722 "I'm Just a Drifter") 8-10 62
KING (5726 "It's Christmas Time") 8-10 62
KING (5731 "Wrap Yourself in a Christmas Package") 8-10 62
KING (5802 "I Wanna Be Close") 5-8 63
KING (5825 "Lucky Dreamer") 5-8 63
KING (5852 "Come Home") 5-8 64
KING (5946 "Christmas Blues") 5-8 64
KING (5947 "Christmas") 5-8 64
LIBERTY 3-4 84
LILLY (506 "Bon Voyage") 8-10 62
MAINSTREAM (607 "Pledging My Love") 5-8 65
NOLA (702 "I'll Love You") 5-10 63
STARDAY 4-6 69
SWING TIME (253 "I'll Miss You") 50-100 52
SWING TIME (259 "Be Fair with Me") 50-100 52
LPs: 10/12-inch
ALADDIN (702 "Mood Music") 400-600 52
(10-inch LP. Black vinyl.)
ALADDIN (702 "Mood Music") 2000-3000 52
(10-inch LP. Red vinyl.)
ALADDIN (809 "Mood Music") 100-200 57
BIG TOWN 8-10 77-78
BLUES SPECTRUM 4-6
BLUESWAY 8-10 70
IMPERIAL (9178 "Million Sellers") 50-75 62
JEWEL 8-15 72
KING (775 "Christmas Songs") 30-50 61
KING (878 "The Great Charles Brown") 30-50 63
KING (5000 series) 5-10
MAINSTREAM (300 series) 8-12 72
MAINSTREAM (6035 "Ballads My Way") 10-20 65
(Monaural.)
MAINSTREAM (56035 "Ballads My Way") 10-20 65
(Stereo.)
SCORE (4011 "Driftin' Blues") 100-150 57
Also see BROWN, Floyd
Also see CHARLES, Ray / Charles Brown
Also see 5 EMBERS
Also see McCRACKLIN, Jimmy / T-Bone Walker / Charles Brown
Also see MOORE, Johnny
Also see SCOTT, Mabel

BROWN, Charles / Basin Street Boys
Singles: 78 rpm
CASH 15-25 57
Singles: 7-inch
CASH (1052 "Lost in the Night") 30-40 57
Also see BASIN STREET BOYS

BROWN, Charles / Lloyd Glenn
(With Johnny Moore's 3 Blazers)
Singles: 78 rpm
HOLLYWOOD 10-20 54
Singles: 7-inch
HOLLYWOOD (1021 "Merry Christmas Baby") 20-30 54
Also see GLENN, Lloyd

BROWN, Charles, & Jimmy McCracklin
LPs: 10/12-inch
IMPERIAL (9257 "Best of the Blues") 25-50 64
Also see McCRACKLIN, Jimmy

BROWN, Charles, & Amos Milburn
(Charles Brown / Amos Milburn)
Singles: 7-inch
ACE 5-10 59
KING (5464 "My Little Baby") 8-10 61
KING (6000 series) 3-5 75
LPs: 10/12-inch
GRAND PRIX (421 "Original Blues Sound") 10-15 64
(With Jackie Shane and Bob Marshall & Crystals.)
Also see BROWN, Charles
Also see MILBURN, Amos

BROWN, Charlie
Singles: 78 rpm
ROSE 25-50 55
Singles: 7-inch
ROSE (101 "Mean Mama") 100-150 55
ROSE (102 "Have You Heard the Gossip") 50-75 55

BROWN, Charlie
(Charlie Brown's Generation)
Singles: 7-inch
ATCO 4-8 66

BROWN, Charlie
LPs: 10/12-inch
CONTACT 10-15 73
POLYDOR 10-15 70-71

BROWN, Charlie "Cole Black"
Singles: 7-inch
JEWEL 3-5 73

BROWN, Chuck
Singles: 7-inch
EXCELLO 4-8 62

BROWN, Chuck, & Soul Searchers R&B '78
Singles: 12-inch
SOURCE 4-8 78-79
Singles: 7-inch
MCA 3-5 79
SOUL SEARCHERS 3-4 84
SOURCE 3-5 78-80
T.T.E.D. 3-4 84
LPs: 10/12-inch
SOURCE 5-10 79
Also see SOUL SEARCHERS

BROWN, Clarence "Gatemouth" R&B '49
Singles: 78 rpm
ALADDIN 15-25 47
PEACOCK 10-20 49-54
Singles: 7-inch
CINDERELLA (1021 "Okie Dokie") 10-20 65
CINDERELLA (1022 "Chicken Shake") 10-20 65
CINDERELLA (1024 "It's Alright") 10-20 65
CUE (1050 "Leftover Blues") 8-10 64
PEACOCK (1600 "Baby Take It Easy") 50-100 52
PEACOCK (1607 "You Got Money") 20-40 52
PEACOCK (1617 "Boogie Uproar") 20-40 53
PEACOCK (1619 "Please Tell Me Baby") 20-40 53
PEACOCK (1633 "Midnight Hour") 20-40 54
PEACOCK (1637 "Okie Dokie Stomp") 20-40 54
PEACOCK (1692 "Just Before Dawn") 10-25 60
PEACOCK (1696 "Slop Time") 10-25 60
LPs: 10/12-inch
BLUE STAR 30-40
MUSIC IS MEDICINE 8-12 78
ROUNDER 5-10 82
Also see McVEA, Jack

BROWN, Clarence "Gatemouth"/ Camille Howard / Bill Johnson Quartet / Van "Piano Man' Walls
EPs: 7-inch
BIG TOWN (150 "Without Me Baby") 25-50 50s
(Probably not issued with cover. For reference, title shown is of Brown track, not EP overall.)
Also see BROWN, Clarence "Gatemouth"
Also see HOWARD, Camille
Also see WALLS, Van

BROWN, Cleo R&B '49
Singles: 78 rpm
BLUE 10-20 51
CAPITOL 10-20 49

BROWN, Clyde R&B '73
Singles: 7-inch
ATLANTIC 3-5 73-74

BROWN, Craig
Singles: 7-inch
SELECT 5-10 62
20TH FOX 10-20 59
U.A. 10-20 60

BROWN, Danny
Singles: 7-inch
EARTH 4-8 62

BROWN, Danny
Singles: 7-inch
I.M.I.................3-5 76

BROWN, Danny Joe, & Danny Joe Brown Band LP '81
Singles: 7-inch
EPIC.................3-4 81
LPs: 10/12-inch
EPIC.................5-10 81
Also see MOLLY HATCHET

BROWN, Dave
Singles: 7-inch
JARVEY.................5-10 61

BROWN, David & Jeremiah
LPs: 10/12-inch
UNI.................8-10 72

BROWN, Dee
Singles: 7-inch
DEE.................3-5 72
JEWEL.................3-5 71

BROWN, Dee, & Lola Grant R&B '66
Singles: 7-inch
SHURFINE.................4-8 66

BROWN, Dennis R&B '82
Singles: 12-inch
A&M.................4-6 82
Singles: 7-inch
A&M.................3-4 81-82
STUDIO ONE.................3-5 72
LPs: 10/12-inch
A&M.................5-10 81-82

BROWN, Dennis, & Atomics
Singles: 7-inch
ATOMIC (101 "Show Me the Rose").................250-350 57

BROWN, Dizzy, & Dancing Tamborines
Singles: 7-inch
TEEN.................5-10 60
EPs: 7-inch
ABC.................5-10

BROWN, Dolores, & Auditones
Singles: 78 rpm
STERLING.................15-25 47
Also see AUDITONES

BROWN, Don P&R '78
Singles: 7-inch
FIRST AMERICAN.................3-5 77-78
LPs: 10/12-inch
FIRST AMERICAN.................5-10 78

BROWN, Doug
(With the Omens)
Singles: 7-inch
CHECKER (1001 "Swingin' Sue")..10-20 61
PUNCH (1008 "T.G.I.F.").................25-50 65
(Reportedly 500 made.)
Session: Bob Seger; Lenny Drake.
Also see BEACH BUMS
Also see LENNY & THUNDERTONES
Also see SEGER, Bob
Also see THUNDERTONES

BROWN, Doug, & Ones
Singles: 7-inch
STREET.................4-8 81
LPs: 10/12-inch
STREET.................8-12 81

BROWN, Dusty
Singles: 78 rpm
PARROT.................40-60 55
Singles: 7-inch
BANDARA (2503 "Please Don't Go").................15-25 59
PARROT (820 "Yes, She's Gone").................75-125 55

BROWN, Earl
Singles: 78 rpm
CHECKER.................15-25 54
SWING TIME.................20-40 52
Singles: 7-inch
CHECKER (802 "The Cat's Wiggle").................40-60 54
KAPPA (207 "Tambourine").................15-25 58
SWING TIME (307 "Dust My Broom").................50-100 52
Also see FULSON, Lowell

BROWN, Elaine
Singles: 7-inch
BLACK FORUM.................3-5 73
RAY STAR (782 "If There's a Chance").................15-25 61
LPs: 10/12-inch
BLACK FORUM.................8-10 73
VAULT.................10-15 69

BROWN, Edith
Singles: 7-inch
FOUR BROTHERS (403 "You Did It").................8-10 67
Also see SAM & KITTY

BROWN, Ella
Singles: 7-inch
LANOR.................4-8 72

BROWN, Estelle
Singles: 7-inch
U.A. (727 "Stick Close").................5-10 64
Also see SWEET INSPIRATIONS

BROWN, Faith
Singles: 7-inch
BELL.................3-5 73

BROWN, Family: see FAMILY BROWN

BROWN, Finley
Singles: 7-inch
ENTERPRISE.................3-5 71
M.O.C.................4-8 67

BROWN, Floyd
(With Charles Brown)
Singles: 7-inch
ACE.................5-10 62
ENTERPRISE.................3-6 69
HERITAGE.................3-4 80
MAGNUM.................3-4 83
Also see BROWN, Charles

BROWN, Floyd C&W '77
Singles: 7-inch
ABC/DOT.................3-5 77
MAGNUM.................3-4 83

BROWN, Gabriel
Singles: 78 rpm
BEACON.................15-25 45-46
CORAL.................10-20 49
GENNETT.................15-25 45-46
JOE DAVIS.................15-25 45-46
MGM.................10-15 53

BROWN, Gary
(With the Chants)
Singles: 7-inch
BROWNIE (103 "Would You Laugh at Me").................35-45 60s
DYNAMIC SOUND (2005 "Would You Laugh at Me").................8-12 67
USA (821 "Cold Day in June").................6-10 66
VENUS (101 "Cold Day in June")...10-15 66

BROWN, Gatemouth: see BROWN, Clarence "Gatemouth"

BROWN, Gene
Singles: 7-inch
DOT (15709 "Big Door").................40-60 58
4 STAR (28 "Big Door").................50-75 58

BROWN, Genie
Singles: 7-inch
DUNHILL.................3-5 73

BROWN, George Washington
(Van Dyke Parks)
Singles: 7-inch
W.B.................5-10 67
Also see PARKS, Van Dyke

BROWN, Gloria
Singles: 7-inch
CHECKER.................4-8 63

BROWN, Gloria D. R&B '86
Singles: 7-inch
KRYSTAL.................3-4 86

BROWN, Hank
Singles: 7-inch
ROYALTY (123 "Operation Stomp").................10-20

BROWN, Harry C.
Singles: 78 rpm
COLUMBIA (1999 "Nigger Love a Watermelon Ha Ha Ha").................50-100 09

BROWN, Hash
(With His Ignunt Strings)
Singles: 7-inch
PHILIPS.................5-10 62
LPs: 10/12-inch
PHILIPS (200018 "Hash Brown Sounds").................20-30 62
(Monaural.)
PHILIPS (600018 "Hash Brown Sounds").................30-40 62
(Stereo.)

BROWN, Honey
(With Lefty Bates' Combo)
Singles: 78 rpm
CLUB "51" (107 "No Good Daddy").................25-50 55
Singles: 7-inch
CLUB "51" (107 "No Good Daddy").................75-100 55

BROWN, Hubert
Singles: 7-inch
PEACH.................5-10 59

BROWN, J.T.
(Sax Man Brown; with the Broomdusters)
Singles: 78 rpm
HARLEM.................20-30 49-50
JOB (1103 "Boogie Baby").................75-100 54
METEOR.................25-50 54
Singles: 7-inch
JOB (1103 "Boogie Baby").................75-100 54
METEOR (5016 "Dumb Woman Blues").................50-100 54
METEOR (5024 "Flaming Blues").................50-100 54
LPs: 10/12-inch
PEARL.................5-10 78
Session: Elmore James.
Also see BROWN, Bep
Also see BROWN, Nature Boy
Also see JAMES, Elmore

BROWN, James
Singles: 78 rpm
MGM.................3-6 55
Singles: 7-inch
MGM.................5-10 55
Picture Sleeves
MGM.................8-12 55

BROWN, James R&B '56
(With His Famous Flames; with the J.B.s)
Singles: 12-inch
CHURCHILL.................4-6 83
POLYDOR.................4-6 78
Singles: 78 rpm
FEDERAL (Except 12348).................20-40 56-58
FEDERAL (12348 "I Want You So Bad").................50-100 59
Singles: 7-inch
AUGUSTA.................3-4 83
BACKSTREET.................3-4 83
BETHLEHEM.................8-15 69
CHURCHILL.................3-4 83
FEDERAL (12258 "Please Please Please").................50-100 56
FEDERAL (12258 "Please Please Please").................15-25 60s
(Has audience noises added to give a live concert effect.)
FEDERAL (12277 "No No No No").................50-75 57
FEDERAL (12289 "Just Won't Do Right").................50-75 57
FEDERAL (12290 "I Won't Plead No More").................50-75 57
FEDERAL (12300 "I Walked Alone").................50-75 57
FEDERAL (12311 "Baby Cries Over the Ocean").................50-75 57
FEDERAL (12337 "Try Me").................40-60 58
FEDERAL (12337 "Try Me").................15-25 60s
(Has added strings and instrumentation.)
FEDERAL (12348 "I Want You So Bad").................30-50 59
FEDERAL (S-12352 "I've Got to Change").................25-35 59
(Monaural.)
FEDERAL (S-12352 "I've Got to Change").................50-75 59
(Stereo.)
FEDERAL (S-12361 "Good, Good Lovin' ").................25-35 59
(Monaural.)
FEDERAL (S-12361 "Good, Good Lovin' ").................50-75 59
(Stereo.)
FEDERAL (12370 "Think").................20-30 60
FEDERAL (12378 "This Old Heart").................20-30 60
Note: For more details on Federal first pressings and reissues, see the chapter on *45 RPM Singles – A Guide to First Pressing Identification*, in the introductory pages.
KING (5000 series).................15-25 60-65
KING (6000 series).................5-15 65-71
PEOPLE.................3-6 71-76
POLYDOR (Except 14304).................3-6 71-84
POLYDOR (14304 "For Sentimental Reasons").................5-10 70s
RIPETE.................3-4 80s
SCOTTI BROTHERS.................3-4 85-88
SMASH.................8-15 64-66
T.K.................3-5 80-81
Picture Sleeves
KING (5842 "Oh Baby Don't You Weep").................10-20 64
POLYDOR.................3-5 72-84
SCOTTI BROTHERS.................3-4 85-86
SMASH (1898 "Caledonia").................10-15 64
SMASH (1908 "The Things That I Used to Do").................10-15 64
SMASH (1919 "Out of Sight").................10-15 64
EPs: 7-inch
KING ("Month of Soul").................25-50
(Promotional issue only. No selection number used.)
KING (430 "Please Please Please").................30-50 59
KING (826 "Live at the Apollo").................20-40 63
SMASH (703 "Grits & Soul").................15-25 65
(Juke box issue only. Includes title strips.)
SMASH (707 "James Brown Plays the New Breed").................15-25 66
(Juke box issue only. Includes title strips.)
LPs: 10/12-inch
AGUSTA SOUND.................5-8
AUDIO FIDELITY (326 "James Brown").................10-15 83
(Picture disc.)
CHURCHILL.................5-10 83
HRB.................8-10 73
KING (610 "Please, Please, Please").................100-200 59
(Cover pictures a woman's legs.)
KING (635 "Try Me").................100-200 59
(Cover pictures a woman with a smoking gun.)
KING (683 "James Brown & His Famous Flames *Think*").................200-300 60
(Cover pictures a baby.)
KING (683 "James Brown & His Famous Flames *Think*").................25-40 61
(Cover has pictures of James Brown.)
KING (743 "The Always Amazing James Brown and the Famous Flames").................50-75 61
(Cover is pink and blue.)
KING (771 "Jump Around").................50-75 62
KING (780 "The Exciting James Brown").................50-75 62
KING (804 "James Brown and the Famous Flames Tour the U.S.A.").................50-75 62
KING (826 "Apollo Theatre Presents, in Person, the James Brown Show").................40-60 63
KING (851 "Prisoner of Love").................30-50 63
KING (883 "Pure Dynamite").................25-50 64
KING (900 series).................15-25 65-66
KING (1000 & 1100 series, except 1024 and 1038).................10-15 67-71
KING (1024 "Show of Tomorrow").................100-150 67
KING (1038 "Thinking About Little Willie John").................30-35 68
POLYDOR.................5-10 71-84
SCOTTI BROTHERS.................5-8 86-88
SMASH.................10-20 64-68
SOLID SMOKE.................5-10 80-81
T.K.................5-10 80
Also see BAMBAATAA, Afrika, James Brown
Also see BYRD, Bobby, & James Brown
Also see J.B.s
Also see KENDRICK, Nat, & Swans
Also see POETS

BROWN, James, & Vicki Anderson P&R '67
Singles: 7-inch
KING.................4-6 67-70
Also see ANDERSON, Vicki

BROWN, James, Band
Singles: 7-inch
KING.................4-8 61
Also see WESLEY, Fred, & Horny Horns

BROWN, James, & Lyn Collins P&R/R&B '72
Singles: 7-inch
POLYDOR.................3-5 72
Also see COLLINS, Lyn

BROWN, James / Martha & Vandellas
Singles: 7-inch
A&M (3022 "I Got You").................3-4 88
Picture Sleeves
A&M (3022 "I Got You").................3-4 88
Also see MARTHA & VANDELLAS

BROWN, James, & Marva Whitney
Singles: 7-inch
KING.................3-6 69
Also see BROWN, James
Also see WHITNEY, Marva

BROWN, James
Singles: 7-inch
STATLER (829 "Papa's Got a Brand New Bag").................4-6
(This is not the same James Brown who had the 1965 hit of this song.)

BROWN, James "Widemouth"
(With Henry Hayes)
Singles: 7-inch
JAX (306 "A Weary Silent Night").................100-200 51
(Red vinyl.)
Also see HAYES, Henry

BROWN, Jay
(Jay Brown & the Jets)
Singles: 7-inch
ATCO.................5-10 66
PEACH (736 "Rockin' the Guitar") 10-20 60

BROWN, Jericho
Singles: 7-inch
DEL-FI (4103 "I Need You").................10-20 58
RKO UNIQUE (412 "Little Neava") 15-25 57
W.B. (5161 "Look for a Star").................8-10 60
W.B. (5408 "He's Taken My Baby") 8-10 60

BROWN, Jewel
Singles: 7-inch
LIBERTY.................4-8 62

BROWN, Jim, & Four Bells
Singles: 78 rpm
BELL.................6-12 54
Singles: 7-inch
BELL.................15-25 54

BROWN, Jim Ed C&W '65
(Jim Edward Brown)
Singles: 7-inch
RCA (Except 8000 & 9000 series).....3-5 69-81
RCA (8000 & 9000 series).................3-8 65-68
LPs: 10/12-inch
PICKWICK.................5-8 80
RCA (Except 3000 & 4000 series)....5-10 73-81
RCA (3000 & 4000 series).................8-15 66-72
(With "LPM" or "LSP" prefix.)
Session: Mary Cates; Margie Cates.
Also see BROWNS
Also see CATES SISTERS
Also see SOME OF CHET'S FRIENDS

BROWN, Jim Ed, & Helen Cornelius C&W '76
Singles: 7-inch
RCA.................3-5 76-81
LPs: 10/12-inch
RCA.................5-10 76-82
Also see BROWN, Jim Ed
Also see CORNELIUS, Helen

BROWN, Jim Edward & Maxine: see BROWNS

BROWN, Jim Edward, Maxine & Bonnie: see BROWNS

BROWN, Jimmy
Singles: 7-inch
A-BET.................5-10 67-68
KENO (1001 "Hootchi Koo").................10-20 61

BROWN, Jocelyn P&R/R&B/D&D '84
Singles: 12-inch
JELLYBEAN.................4-6 86
VINYL DREAMS.................4-6 84
Singles: 7-inch
JELLYBEAN.................3-4 86
VINYL DREAMS.................3-4 84
W.B.................3-4 86-87
LPs: 10/12-inch
JELLYBEAN.................5-10 86
VINYL DREAMS.................5-10 84
Also see INNER LIFE
Also see SALSOUL ORCHESTRA

BROWN, Joe
(With Bruvvers)
Singles: 7-inch
BELL.................3-5 73
CAMEO.................4-8 63
DOT.................4-8 63
HICKORY.................4-8 65
JAMIE.................4-8 66
KAPP.................3-6 70
LONDON (Except 10507).................4-8 62-66
LONDON (10507 "Popcorn").................5-10 66
STELLAR.................4-8 63
W.B.................4-8 67

BROWN, Joe, & Dell Shirley
Singles: 7-inch
LOGAN.................5-10 59

BROWN, John, L.
Singles: 7-inch
LIKE IT IS (690 "I'm Losing You")..15-25 60s

BROWN, John, Trio
Singles: 7-inch
FENTON.................15-25 68

BROWN, Johnny
(With His Joy Boys)
Singles: 7-inch
ATLANTIC.................5-10 68
COLUMBIA.................4-8 61
DUKE.................5-10 60
DYNASTY.................5-10 59
EPs: 7-inch
COLUMBIA.................5-10 61

BROWN, Josie C&W '73
Singles: 7-inch
RCA.................3-5 73-74

BROWN, Juanita
Singles: 78 rpm
ALADDIN.................10-20 49
Also see BROOKS, Dusty

BROWN, Judy
Singles: 7-inch
FIFO.................5-10 61
SKYLA.................5-10 61

BROWN, Julie LP '85
Singles: 7-inch
BULLETZ.................3-5 83
RHINO.................3-4 84
SIRE.................3-4 87
Picture Sleeves
BULLETZ.................3-5 83
LPs: 10/12-inch
RHINO.................5-10 85

BROWN, Julius D&D '83
Singles: 12-inch
WEST END.................4-6 83-84

BROWN, Kay
Singles: 78 rpm
CROWN (127 "Oop-Shoop").................5-10 54
MGM (12694 "If I Had You").................5-10 58
Singles: 7-inch
CROWN (127 "Oop-Shoop").................10-20 54
MGM (12694 "If I Had You").................8-12 58

BROWN, Kenny
Singles: 78 rpm
PEP.................5-10 55-56
Singles: 7-inch
PEP.................15-25 55-56
SUNDOWN.................5-10 60
TOPPA.................5-10 61

BROWN, Lattimore
(Sir Lattimore Brown)
Singles: 7-inch
DUCHESS (1002 "Night Time Is the Right Time").................15-20 61
DUCHESS (1015 "Say What").................10-15 62
EXCELLO (2196 "Somebody's Gonna Miss Me").................8-12 61
RENEGADE (101 "I Wish I Felt This Way at Home").................10-15 60s
RENEGADE (1201 "I Will").................10-15 69
SEVENTY 7.................5-10 60s
SOUND STAGE 7.................5-10 65-68
ZIL (9005 "It Hurts Me So").................10-20 60
ZIL (9006 "Always My Love").................10-20 60

BROWN, Leadell
Singles: 7-inch
MASON (1101 "Seven Years of Torture").................5-10 66

BROWN, Lee, & His Barbeton Boogie Woogie Cats
(Lee Brown "The Heartbreaker")
Singles: 78 rpm
CHICAGO.................20-30 46
QUEEN.................20-30 46

BROWN, Les, & His Orch. P&R '39
(With His Band of Renown; with His Duke University Blue Devils)
Singles: 78 rpm
BLUEBIRD.................5-10 38-40
CAPITOL.................3-5 56-57
COLUMBIA.................5-10 42-57
CONQUEROR.................5-10 41
CORAL.................3-6 53-57
DECCA.................5-10 36-40
OKEH.................5-10 41-42
Singles: 7-inch
CAPITOL.................3-8 56-59
COLUMBIA.................5-10 50-60
CORAL.................3-6 53-59
SIGNATURE.................3-6 60
EPs: 7-inch
CAPITOL.................5-10 56-58
COLUMBIA.................5-10 54-56

CORAL 5-10 53-56
LPs: 10/12-inch
CAPITOL 10-20 56-59
COLUMBIA 10-25 50-61
CORAL 15-30 55-60
HARMONY 8-15 59
KAPP 8-15 59
MEDALLION 8-15 61
Also see DAY, Doris

BROWN, Les, Jr.
Singles: 7-inch
GNP 8-12 62
LPs: 10/12-inch
GNP 10-20 62

BROWN, Lewis
LPs: 10/12-inch
ALLEGIANCE 5-10 84

BROWN, Little Brother
Singles: 78 rpm
OKEH 10-15 51
Singles: 7-inch
OKEH 15-25 51

BROWN, Little Jimmy
Singles: 7-inch
BRENT (7022 "Tell It Like It Is") 10-20 61

BROWN, Little Tommy: see BROWN, Tommy

BROWN, Little Willie
Singles: 78 rpm
SUNTAN 15-25 56
Singles: 7-inch
DO-RA-ME (1404 "Cut It Out") 20-30 61
SUNTAN (1112 "Going Back to the Country") 50-75 56
TOPIC 25-35

BROWN, Louise P&R '61
Singles: 7-inch
WITCH (101 "Son-in-Law") 25-45 61

BROWN, Lover Boy
Singles: 78 rpm
REGENT (1007 "Just the Blues") 10-15 49

BROWN, Lynn
Singles: 7-inch
PZAZZ 3-6 70

BROWN, Magica
Singles: 7-inch
20TH FOX (553 "I Won't Be Back") 8-12 65

BROWN, Mara Lynn
Singles: 7-inch
LAURIE 3-5 73
PHONOGRAPH (1 "Super Duper Pooper Scooper") 4-6
Picture Sleeves
PHONOGRAPH (1 "Super Duper Pooper Scooper") 5-10
ROULETTE 3-5 70
SPIRAL 4-6 68-69

BROWN, Marti C&W '73
Singles: 7-inch
ATLANTIC 3-5 73
LPs: 10/12-inch
ATLANTIC 8-10 73

BROWN, Mathew
Singles: 7-inch
SEW CITY 4-8 68

BROWN, Matt
Singles: 7-inch
SOFT 5-10

BROWN, Max C&W '79
Singles: 7-inch
DOOR KNOB 3-5 79

BROWN, Maxine P&R '60
(With the Leroy Glover Orchestra)
Singles: 7-inch
ABC 3-4 75
ABC-PAR (10235 "Think of Me") 8-12 61
ABC-PAR (10255 "My Life") 8-12 61
ABC-PAR (10290 "I Got a Funny Kind of Feeling") 8-12 62
ABC-PAR (10315 "Forget Him") 8-12 62
ABC-PAR (10327 "Wanting You") 8-12 62
ABC-PAR (10343 "If I Knew Then") 8-12 62
ABC-PAR (10370 "Promise Me Anything") 8-12 62
ABC-PAR (10388 "Life Goes On Just the Same") 8-12 62
AVCO EMBASSY 3-5 71
COLLECTABLES 3-4 81
COMMONWEALTH UNITED 4-6 69-70
EPIC 5-10 69
ERIC 3-4 83
NOMAR (103 "All in My Mind") 10-20 60
NOMAR (106 "Funny") 10-20 61
NOMAR (107 "Heaven in Your Arms") 20-30 61
WAND 5-15 63-67
WHAM 4-8
Picture Sleeves
WAND (135 "Ask Me") 10-15 63
WHAM (7036 "All in My Mind") 10-15
EPs: 7-inch
COMMONWEALTH UNITED (1001 "Maxine Brown") 5-10 69
(Promotional issue only.)
LPs: 10/12-inch
COLLECTABLES 6-8 88
COMMONWEALTH UNITED 10-12 69
GUEST STAR 10-12 64
WAND 15-25 63-67
Also see ADAMS, Faye / Little Esther / Maxine Brown
Also see JACKSON, Chuck, & Maxine Brown

BROWN, Maxine / Irma Thomas
LPs: 10/12-inch
GRAND PRIX 12-15 64
Also see BROWN, Maxine
Also see THOMAS, Irma

BROWN, Maxine C&W '68
Singles: 7-inch
CHART 4-6 68
LPs: 10/12-inch
CHART 10-20 69
Also see BROWNS

BROWN, Mel
LPs: 10/12-inch
BLUESWAY 5-10 73
IMPULSE 10-15 68

BROWN, Michael
Singles: 7-inch
KAMA SUTRA 3-5 73
Also see LEFT BANKE
Also see STORIES

BROWN, Michael
Singles: 12-inch
ESTATE 4-6 83
Singles: 7-inch
ESTATE 3-4 83
Also see BROWN, Michael, & Janice Dempsey

BROWN, Michael, & Janice Dempsey
Singles: 7-inch
PORTRAIT 3-4 81
Also see BROWN, Michael

BROWN, Millie
Singles: 7-inch
GAYLORD 4-8 63

BROWN, Milt
Singles: 7-inch
SANDY 4-8 62

BROWN, Miquel D&D '83
Singles: 12-inch
TSR 4-6 83
Singles: 7-inch
POLYDOR 3-4 79
TSR 3-4 83
Picture Sleeves
TSR 3-4 83
LPs: 10/12-inch
POLYDOR 5-10 78
TSR 5-10 85

BROWN, Nappy P&R/R&B '55
(With the Gibralters; with Southern Sisters)
Singles: 78 rpm
REO (8033 "Pitter Patter") 15-25 55
(Canadian.)
SAVOY 10-20 55-57
Singles: 7-inch
REO (8033 "Pitter Patter") 30-40 55
(Canadian.)
SAVOY (1129 "That Man") 25-35 54
SAVOY (1135 "Is It True") 25-35 54
SAVOY (1135 "Don't Be Angry") 25-35 55
SAVOY (1162 "Pitter Patter") 25-35 55
SAVOY (1167 "Just a Little Love") 25-35 55
SAVOY (1176 "Sittin' in the Dark") 25-35 55
SAVOY (1187 "Open Up That Door") 25-35 56
SAVOY (1196 "Am I") 25-35 56
SAVOY (1511 "Pretty Girl") 15-25 57
SAVOY (1514 "Goody Goody Gum Drop") 15-25 57
SAVOY (1525 "The Right Time") 25-50 57
(Dionne Warwick's first appearance on record, as a backup vocalist.)
SAVOY (1530 "I'm in the Mood") 15-25 58
SAVOY (1547 "I Cried Like a Baby") 15-25 58
SAVOY (1555 "Skiddy Woe") 15-25 58
SAVOY (1562 "A Long Time") 15-25 59
SAVOY (1566 "Little By Little") 15-25 59
SAVOY (1569 "This Is My Confession") 15-25 59
SAVOY (1575 "So Deep") 15-25 59
SAVOY (1579 "Too Shy") 15-25 59
SAVOY (1582 "Down in the Alley") 15-25 59
SAVOY (1587 "Baby Cry, Cry Baby") 15-25 60
SAVOY (1588 "Apple of My Eye") 15-25 60
SAVOY (1592 "Nobody Can Say") 15-25 60
SAVOY (1594 "Coal Miner") 15-25 61
SAVOY (1598 "Don't Be Angry") 10-20 61
SAVOY (1616 "Don't You Know") 10-20 62
SAVOY (1621 "Lock on the Door") 10-20 61
LPs: 10/12-inch
ICHIBAN 5-10
LANDSLIDE 5-10
SAVOY (14002 "Nappy Brown Sings") 150-200 57
SAVOY (14025 "The Right Time") 50-100 60
SAVOY (14427 "Nappy Brown") 8-15 77
Session: Gospelaires (featuring Dionne Warwick).
Also see WARWICK, Dionne

BROWN, Nat
Singles: 7-inch
BRENT (7019 "Three Pictures") 5-10 61
SELMA (1002 "If This Is Goodbye") 10-20 60s

BROWN, Nature Boy, & His Blues Ramblers
(J.T. Brown)
Singles: 78 rpm
UNITED 10-20 51-52
Singles: 7-inch
B&F 5-10 60
UNITED (103 "Windy City Boogie") 50-75 51
UNITED (106 "Rock 'Em") 50-75 51
UNITED (121 "Strictly Gone") 50-75 52
(Black vinyl.)
UNITED (121 "Strictly Gone") 75-125 52
(Colored vinyl.)
Also see BROWN, J.T.

BROWN, Neal
Singles: 7-inch
CHART SOUND (129 "If By Chance") 15-20 60s

BROWN, O.W.
LPs: 10/12-inch
CHECKER 10-15 68

BROWN, O'chi R&B '86
Singles: 12-inch
MERCURY 4-6 86
Singles: 7-inch
MERCURY 3-4 86
LPs: 10/12-inch
MERCURY 5-10 86

BROWN, Odell LP '67
(With the Organ-izers)
Singles: 7-inch
CADET 3-6 67-68
LPs: 10/12-inch
CADET 10-15 67-69
PAULA 8-10 74

BROWN, Oscar, Jr. P&R/R&B '74
Singles: 7-inch
ATLANTIC 3-5 74
COLUMBIA 5-10 60-62
FONTANA 4-8 65-66
MAD 8-12 59
LPs: 10/12-inch
ATLANTIC 5-10
COLUMBIA 15-25 61-63
FONTANA 10-15 66

BROWN, Otis
(With the Haywood Singers)
Singles: 7-inch
EX SPECT MORE (10655 "You Girl") 10-20 60s
EX SPECT MORE (66551 "I Don't Wanna Cry") 10-20 60s
EXPECT MORE (106551 "I Don't Wonn'a Cry") 5-10 60s
(Note slight label name variation.)
LUJUNA (10655 "Will You Wait") 10-20 60s
OLÉ (100 "South Side Chicago") 15-25 60s
OLÉ (102 "What Would You Do") 15-25 60s

BROWN, Pat
Singles: 7-inch
SEVEN B 4-8 67

BROWN, Pep
Singles: 7-inch
LAVA 4-8 72
POLYDOR 3-5 73-74

BROWN, Peter P&R/R&B '77
Singles: 12-inch
COLUMBIA 4-6 84
RCA 4-6 83
Singles: 7-inch
COLUMBIA 3-4 84
DRIVE 3-5 77-80
RCA 3-4 83
Picture Sleeves
COLUMBIA 3-4 84
LPs: 10/12-inch
COLUMBIA 5-10 84
DRIVE 5-10 78
RCA 5-10 82-83

BROWN, Peter, & Betty Wright P&R/R&B '78
Singles: 7-inch
DRIVE 3-5 78
Also see BROWN, Peter
Also see WRIGHT, Betty

BROWN, Phyllis
(With the Neighbors)
Singles: 7-inch
AUSTIN 5-10
FOLK MUSIC 5-10
RAINBO 10-20
Also see SONNY & PHYLLIS

BROWN, Piney
Singles: 78 rpm
JUBILEE 10-15 54
KING 10-15 53
Singles: 7-inch
CIMARRON 4-8 63
DEEP GROOVE 3-5
JUBILEE 15-25 54
KING 15-25 53
MAD 8-12 59
SOUND STAGE 3-6 69

BROWN, Polly P&R/R&B '75
Singles: 7-inch
ARIOLA AMERICA 3-5 75-76
BEL 3-5 73
GTO 3-5 74
Also see PICKETTYWITCH
Also see SWEET DREAMS

BROWN, Preston
Singles: 7-inch
OLD TOWN 5-10 58

BROWN, Randy R&B '78
(Randy Brown & Company)
Singles: 12-inch
MILLENNIUM 4-6 78
Singles: 7-inch
CHOCOLATE CITY 3-4 80-81
IX CHAINS 3-5 75
PARACHUTE 3-5 78-79
STAX 3-4 80
TRUTH 3-5 74-75
LPs: 10/12-inch
CHOCOLATE CITY 5-10 80-81
PARACHUTE 5-10 78-79
STAX 5-10 80-81

BROWN, Ray, & Whispers
Singles: 7-inch
GNP 8-12 65
PARKWAY 8-12 66

BROWN, Rayfield
Singles: 7-inch
DUMAS 15-20 64

BROWN, Richard
Singles: 7-inch
STEELTOWN 8-12

BROWN, Richie: see JALOPY FIVE

BROWN, Robert Lynn
(With the Elephant City Band)
Singles: 7-inch
MBM 3-5 71

BROWN, Rocky
Singles: 7-inch
MELRON (5001 "Den of Love") 50-75 64
Also see STUDENTS

BROWN, Romaine, & Romaines
Singles: 78 rpm
DECCA 10-20 56-57
Singles: 7-inch
DECCA (30122 "Hold 'Em Joe") 15-25 56
DECCA (30399 "Satin Doll") 15-25 57

BROWN, Ronnie
Singles: 7-inch
ABC (10904 "Robin Hood") 5-10 67
CELESTE (618 "Soul") 5-10 60s

BROWN, Rose, & Jimmie Harris
Singles: 78 rpm
G.S.T. 25-35

BROWN, Roy R&B/C&W '48
(With His Mighty-Mighty Men)
Singles: 78 rpm
DELUXE 25-50 47-51
GOLD STAR (636 "Deep Sea Diver") 50-75 48
IMPERIAL 15-25 57
KING 15-25 52-57
Singles: 7-inch
BLUESWAY 4-8 67
DELUXE (3319 "Bar Room Blues") 150-200 51
(Black vinyl.)
DELUXE (3319 "Bar Room Blues") 200-400 51
(Colored vinyl.)
DELUXE (3323 "I've Got the Last Laugh Now") 75-100 51
(Black vinyl.)
DELUXE (3323 "I've Got the Last Laugh Now") 150-250 51
(Colored vinyl.)
FRIENDSHIP 5-10
GUSTO 3-4 83
HOME of the BLUES (107 "Man with the Blues") 15-25 60
HOME of the BLUES (110 "Rockin' All the Time") 15-25 60
HOME of the BLUES (115 "Sugar Baby") 15-25 60
HOME of the BLUES (122 "Rock & Roll Jamboree") 15-25 61
IMPERIAL (5422 "Saturday Night") 20-30 57
IMPERIAL (5427 "Party Doll") 20-30 57
IMPERIAL (5439 "Let the Four Winds Blow") 20-30 57
IMPERIAL (5510 "Hip Shakin' Baby") 20-30 57
KING (4602 "Travelin' Man") 25-50 53
(Black vinyl.)
KING (4602 "Travelin' Man") 100-150 53
(Colored vinyl.)
KING (4609 "Money Can't Buy Love") 25-50 53
KING (4627 "Gamblin' Man") 25-50 53
KING (4637 "Old Age Boogie") 25-50 53
KING (4654 "Laughing But Crying") 25-50 53
KING (4669 "A Fool in Love") 25-50 53
KING (4684 "Midnight Lover Man") 25-50 53
KING (4704 "Bootleggin' Baby") 25-50 54
KING (4715 "This Is My Last Goodbye") 25-50 54
KING (4722 "Don't Let It Rain") 25-50 54
KING (4731 "Ain't It a Shame") 25-50 54
KING (4743 "Worried Life Blues") 25-50 54
KING (4761 "Fanny Brown Got Married") 25-50 54
KING (4816 "Letter to Baby") 25-50 55
KING (4834 "She's Gone Too Long") 25-50 55
KING (5000 series) 10-20 56-60
MERCURY 3-5 71
MOBILE FIDELITY 3-5 72
TRU-LOVE 4-6
EPs: 7-inch
KING (254 "Roy Brown") 50-100 53
LPs: 10/12-inch
BLUESWAY 10-20 68-73
EPIC 10-15 71
GUSTO 8-12
INTERMEDIA 5-10 84
KING (956 "24 Hits") 35-45 66
KING (1100 series) 10-15 71
KING (5000 series) 8-10 79
Also see HARRIS, Wynonie / Roy Brown
Also see VINSON, Eddie / Roy Brown / Wynonie Harris

BROWN, Russell L.
Singles: 7-inch
POLYDOR 3-5 78

BROWN, Ruth R&B '49
(With the Rhythmakers)
Singles: 78 rpm
ATLANTIC 15-30 49-57
Singles: 7-inch
ATLANTIC (919 "Teardrops from My Eyes") 200-250 50
ATLANTIC (948 "Shine On") 40-60 51
ATLANTIC (962 thru 993) 30-40 52-53
ATLANTIC (1005 thru 1091) 20-30 53-56
ATLANTIC (1100 series) 15-25 57-58
ATLANTIC (2000 series) 10-15 59-60
DECCA 4-8 64
LG (102 "Time After Time") 5-10
MAINSTREAM 5-8
NOSLEN 4-8 64
PHILIPS 5-10 62
SKYE 4-8 69
EPs: 7-inch
ATLANTIC (505 "Ruth Brown Sings") 50-75 53
ATLANTIC (535 "Ruth Brown Sings") 50-75 53
ATLANTIC (585 "Ruth Brown") 35-60 57
PHILIPS 10-15 62
LPs: 10/12-inch
ATLANTIC (1308 "Last Date with Ruth Brown") 100-200 59
ATLANTIC (SD-1308 "Last Date with Ruth Brown") 150-250 59
(Stereo.)
ATLANTIC (8004 "Ruth Brown") 50-75 57
(Black label.)
ATLANTIC (8004 "Ruth Brown") 30-40 60
(Red label.)
ATLANTIC (8026 "Miss Rhythm") 35-50 59
(Black label.)
ATLANTIC (8026 "Miss Rhythm") 75-100 59
(Multi-color label.)
ATLANTIC (8026 "Miss Rhythm") 35-50 59
(White label.)
ATLANTIC (8026 "Miss Rhythm") 15-25 60
(Red label.)
ATLANTIC (8080 "Best of Ruth Brown") 15-25 63
COBBLESTONE 8-10 72
DOBRE 5-10 78
MAINSTREAM (300 series) 8-10 72
MAINSTREAM (6000 series) 12-15 65
PHILIPS 12-15 62
SKYE 10-12 70
Also see BRADLEY, Will, & Ray McKinley
Also see JACKSON, Willis
Also see JOHNSON, Buddy

BROWN, Ruth, & Clyde McPhatter R&B '55
Singles: 78 rpm
ATLANTIC 10-20 55
Singles: 7-inch
ATLANTIC 10-20 55
Also see BROWN, Ruth
Also see McPHATTER, Clyde

BROWN, Sam P&R '89
Singles: 7-inch
A&M 3-4 89
Picture Sleeves
A&M 3-4 89

BROWN, Sammy
Singles: 7-inch
BEE BEE (701 "I'm in Love") 15-25 64

BROWN, Savoy: see SAVOY BROWN

BROWN, Sawyer: see SAWYER BROWN

BROWN, Sax Man: see BROWN, J.T.

BROWN, Sedatrius
Singles: 7-inch
MGM 4-8 67
ROULETTE 4-8 65

BROWN, Sharon R&B '82
Singles: 12-inch
PROFILE 4-6 83
Singles: 7-inch
PROFILE 3-4 82-83

BROWN, Shawn R&B/D&D '85
Singles: 12-inch
JWP 4-6 85
Singles: 7-inch
JWP 3-4 85

BROWN, Shenny "Goofy"
Singles: 7-inch
B.T. PUPPY 4-8 67

BROWN, Sheree R&B '81
Singles: 12-inch
CAPITOL 4-6 81
Singles: 7-inch
CAPITOL 3-4 81-82

LPs: 10/12-inch
CAPITOL 5-10 81-82

BROWN, Shirley P&R/R&B '74
Singles: 12-inch
MERCURY 4-6 83
Singles: 7-inch
ABET 4-6 71
ARISTA 3-5 77-78
CHELSEA AVE 4-6
SOUND TOWN 3-4 84-85
STAX 3-5 79
TRUTH 3-5 74-76
20TH FOX 3-4 80
LPs: 10/12-inch
ARISTA 5-10 77
COLUMBIA 10-15 68-72
SOUND TRACK 5-10 85
STAX 5-10 77-79
TRUTH 8-10 75

BROWN, Sir Lattimore: see BROWN, Lattimore

BROWN, Skip, & Shantons
Singles: 7-inch
PAM (112 "Why Don't You Believe Me") 20-30 61
Also see JACKSON, Skip
Also see SHANTONS

BROWN, Skippy
Singles: 78 rpm
CHANCE 50-75 52
Singles: 7-inch
CHANCE (1129 "So Many Days") 100-200 52

BROWN, Stanky: see STANKY BROWN GROUP

BROWN, T. Graham C&W '85
Singles: 7-inch
CAPITOL 3-4 85-90
Also see TOMORROW'S WORLD
Also see TUCKER, Tanya, & T. Graham Brown

BROWN, Terry, & Marquees
Singles: 7-inch
JO ANN 8-12 61
Also see MARQUEES

BROWN, Texas Johnny
Singles: 78 rpm
ATLANTIC (876 "The Blues Rock") 50-75 49

BROWN, Timmy
Singles: 7-inch
EMBER 5-8 64
IMPERIAL 5-8 62
MERCURY 5-8 62-64

BROWN, Tom, & Tom Toms
Singles: 7-inch
JARO INT'L (77023 "Tomahawk") 40-60 60

BROWN, Tommy
(Little Tommy Brown)
Singles: 78 rpm
ACORN 30-40 51
GROOVE 10-20 55
IMPERIAL 15-25 57
KING 15-25 53
SAVOY 10-20 52
UNITED (183 "Remember Me") 20-40 54
Singles: 7-inch
ABC-PAR 5-10 65
GROOVE (0132 "Don't Leave Me") 15-25 55
GROOVE (0143 "The Thrill Is Gone") 15-25 55
IMPERIAL (5476 "Rock My Blues Away") 20-40 57
KING (4658 "How Much Do You Think I Can Stand") 75-125 53
KING (4679 "Goodbye I'm Gone") 25-50 53
SAVOY (838 "Never Trust a Woman") 25-50 52
UNITED (183 "Remember Me") 75-125 54

BROWN, Toni, & Terry Garthwaite
Singles: 7-inch
CAPITOL 3-5 73
Also see JOY of COOKING
Also see GARTHWAITE, Terry

BROWN, Veda R&B '73
Singles: 7-inch
RAKEN 3-5 75
STAX 3-5 73-74

BROWN, Walter
(With Ben Webster)
Singles: 78 rpm
CAPITOL (806 "Nasty Attitude") 15-25 50
ZIP (4686 "Alley Cat") 25-50 56
Singles: 7-inch
CAPITOL (806 "Nasty Attitude") 40-50 50
LUNNAR #2 (006 "Alley Cat") 3-5 78
ZIP (4686 "Alley Cat") 50-75 56
Also see McSHANN, Jay

BROWN, Watson T.
Singles: 7-inch
OKEH 4-6 69

BROWN, Waymon
Singles: 78 rpm
DECCA (48264 "Barefoot Susie") 15-25 51
Singles: 7-inch
DECCA (48264 "Barefoot Susie") 30-40 51

BROWN, Wini R&B '52
(With the Boyfriends)
Singles: 78 rpm
COLUMBIA 10-20 51
MERCURY 25-50 52
Singles: 7-inch
COLUMBIA (872 "A Good Man Is Hard to Find") 15-25 51
JARO (77018 "Gone Again") 10-15 60
MERCURY (5870 "Here in My Heart") 75-125 52
MERCURY (8270 "Be Anything") 75-125 52
Members: Wini Brown; Joe Van Loan; Percy Green; Fred Francis; Warren Suttles.
Also see DOGGETT, Bill
Also see DREAMERS
Also see HAMPTON, Lionel
Also see VAN LOAN, Joe
Also see WILLIAMS, Cootie, & Wini Brown

BROWN, Yvonne
Singles: 12-inch
MONTAGE 4-6 82-83
Singles: 7-inch
MONTAGE 3-4 82

BROWN & HARPER
Singles: 7-inch
CRYSTAL 10-15

BROWN BEAVER
Singles: 7-inch
COASTLINE 3-4 80

BROWN BROTHERS
Singles: 7-inch
ALADDIN 10-15 58

BROWN BROTHERS
Singles: 7-inch
COLUMBIA 3-5 73

BROWN BROTHERS OF SOUL
Singles: 7-inch
SPECIALTY 3-5 70

BROWN DOTS
(Deek Watson & Brown Dots)
Singles: 78 rpm
CASTLE 15-25 48
MAJESTIC 10-20 48
MANOR 10-20 45-49
VARSITY 15-25 42
Members: Deek Watson; Pat Best; Jimmy Gordon; Jimmie Nabbie.
Also see BELL, Gwenn, & Brown Dots
Also see INK SPOTS
Also see FOUR DOTS
Also see FOUR TUNES
Also see NABBIE, Jimmie

BROWN PAPER BAG
Singles: 7-inch
JOX (065 "Something Tells Me") 15-25 67

BROWN RICE
Singles: 7-inch
LION 3-5 72
MGM 3-5 73

BROWN SISTERS
Singles: 7-inch
GOLDEN CREST 4-6 64

BROWN SUGAR P&R '76
Singles: 7-inch
ABKCO 3-5 72
CAPITOL 3-5 76
CHELSEA 3-5 73-74
Member: Clydie King.
Also see KING, Clydie

BROWN SUGAR INC.
Singles: 7-inch
IMPEL 4-6

BROWNE, Al
(Al Browne & His Band; Al Brown)
Singles: 7-inch
BM (2835 "The Whip") 10-20 60s
GENEVA 5-10 65
LAKE 5-10
RIC (409 "Buggy Boo") 10-20 60s
XAVIER ("Hot Dog Twist") 10-20 60
(No selection number used.)
Also see CRESTS
Also see CONCEPTS
Also see DEL COUNTS
Also see EDDIE & STARLITES
Also see JIMMY & CRESTONES
Also see ROULETTES
Also see STARLITES
Also see STYLISTS
Also see TWINKLES
Also see VELTONES
Also see VERDICTS
Also see VIOLINS

BROWNE, Bertha Belle
Singles: 7-inch
MAINSTREAM 3-4 74
LPs: 10/12-inch
MAINSTREAM 8-12 73

BROWNE, Brian
(Brian Browne Trio)
Singles: 7-inch
ACADEMY 4-8 66

BROWNE, Doris
(With the Capris)
Singles: 78 rpm
GOTHAM 20-40 53
Singles: 7-inch
COLLECTABLES 3-4 81
GOTHAM (290 "Please Believe Me") 50-75 53
GOTHAM (296 "Until the End of Time") 50-75 53
GOTHAM (298 "The Game of Love") 50-75 53
GOTHAM (303 "Am I Asking Too Much") 50-75 53
Also see CAPRIS

BROWNE, Duncan LP '79
Singles: 7-inch
IMMEDIATE 3-6 69
RAK 3-5 72
SIRE 3-4 79
Picture Sleeves
IMMEDIATE 5-10 68
LPs: 10/12-inch
IMMEDIATE 10-15 68
SIRE 5-10 79

BROWNE, Jackson P&R/LP '72
Singles: 12-inch
ASYLUM 4-6 81-82
ELEKTRA 4-8 89
(Promotional only.)
Singles: 7-inch
ASYLUM 3-4 72-86
COLUMBIA 3-4 86
ELEKTRA 3-4 80-89
Picture Sleeves
ASYLUM 3-5 80-86
ELEKTRA 4-8 80
LPs: 10/12-inch
ASYLUM (Except 5051) 8-10 72-86
ASYLUM (5051 "Jackson Browne") 10-15 72
(With burlap cover.)
ASYLUM (5051 "Jackson Browne") 8-10 72
(Without burlap.)
ELEKTRA ("Jackson Browne's First Album") 25-35 67
(Promotional issue only.)
ELEKTRA (60830 "World in Motion") 5-8 89
MFSL (055 "Pretender") 25-50 81
Also see CLEMONS, Clarence, & Jackson Browne
Also see LINDLEY, David
Also see SPRINGSTEEN, Bruce / Jackson Browne

BROWNE, Jann C&W '89
Singles: 7-inch
CURB 3-4 89

BROWNE, Jericho
Singles: 7-inch
CHANCELLOR 4-8 62
MERCURY 4-8 65
W.B. 5-10 60-64

BROWNE, Reno, & Her Buckaroos: see HALEY, Bill

BROWNE, Severin
Singles: 7-inch
MOTOWN 3-5 74-75
Picture Sleeves
MOTOWN 3-5 74
LPs: 10/12-inch
MOTOWN 8-10 73-74
MOWEST 10-12 70

BROWNE, Tedd
LPs:10/12-inch
CAPO 15-20
CLEVELAND CURSILLO 10-20

BROWNE, Thomas F.
LP: 10/12-inch
VERTIGO (1011 "Wednesday's Child") 8-12

BROWNE, Tom LP '79
Singles: 12-inch
ARISTA 4-6 83
Singles: 7-inch
ARISTA 3-4 83-84
GRP 3-4 79-82
LPs: 10/12-inch
ARISTA 5-10 83-84
GRP 5-10 79-82

BROWNER, Duke, & Kaddo Strings
Singles: 7-inch
IMPACT (1008 "Crying Over You") 50-75 66
Also see KADDO STRINGS

BROWNETTES
Singles: 7-inch
KING (6153 "Never Find a Love Like Mine") 10-15 68

BROWNHILL STAMP DUTY
Singles: 7-inch
GRIT 3-5 71

BROWNING
Singles: 7-inch
AMARET 3-5 70-71

BROWNING, Bill
Singles: 7-inch
ISLAND (4 "Hula Rock") 25-50 59
ISLAND (7 "Born with the Blues") 50-75 59
ISLAND (10 "Breaking Hearts") 20-40 60
ISLAND (11 "Sinful Woman") 50-75 60

BROWNING, Bill
Singles: 7-inch
LUCKY (1 "I'll Pay You Back") 100-150 59
STARDAY (432 "Don't Push, Don't Shove") 50-75 59
Also see BROWNING, Zeke

BROWNING, Zeke
(With the Dynamics)
Singles: 7-inch
LUCKY (5 "Bad Case of the Blues") 20-40 59
LUCKY (11 "Spinning Wheel Rock") 60-90 61
Also see BROWNING, Bill

BROWNMARK R&B '88
Singles: 7-inch
MOTOWN 3-4 88
Also see MAZARATI
Also see PRINCE

BROWN'S HOME BREW
Singles: 7-inch
VERTIGO 3-5 74
LPs: 10/12-inch
VERTIGO 8-10 74

BROWNS C&W '54
(Jim Edward & Maxine Brown; Jim Edward, Maxine & Bonnie Brown; with the Louisiana Hayride Band; Browns featuring Jim Edward Brown)
Singles: 78 rpm
FABOR 5-15 54-55
RCA 5-15 56-57
Singles: 7-inch
COLUMBIA 4-8 62
FABOR 10-20 54-55
RCA (6480 thru 7427) 10-15 56-58
RCA (47-7555 "The Three Bells") 5-10 59
(Monaural.)
RCA (61-7555 "The Three Bells") 10-15 59
(Stereo.)
RCA (47-7614 "Scarlet Ribbons") 5-10 59
(Monaural.)
RCA (61-7614 "Scarlet Ribbons") 10-15 59
(Stereo.)
RCA (47-7700 "Old Lamplighter") 5-10 60
(Monaural.)
RCA (61-7700 "Old Lamplighter") 10-15 60
(Stereo.)
RCA (47-7755 "Lonely Little Robin") 5-10 60
(Monaural.)
RCA (61-7755 "Lonely Little Robin") 10-15 60
(Stereo.)
RCA (47-7780 "Wiffenpoof Song") 5-10 60
(Monaural.)
RCA (61-7780 "Wiffenpoof Song") 10-15 60
(Stereo.)
RCA (47-7820 "Send Me the Pillow You Dream On") 5-10 60
(Monaural.)
RCA (61-7820 "Send Me the Pillow You Dream On") 10-15 60
(Monaural.)
RCA (7820 "Blue Christmas") 5-10 60
RCA (37-7866 "Angel's Dolly") 10-15 61
(Compact 33 single.)
RCA (47-7866 "Angel's Dolly") 4-8 61
RCA (37-7917 "My Baby's Gone") 10-15 61
(Compact 33 single.)
RCA (47-7917 "My Baby's Gone") 4-8 61
RCA (37-7969 "Foolish Pride") 10-15 61
(Compact 33 single.)
RCA (47-7969 "Foolish Pride") 4-8 61
RCA (37-7997 "Remember Me") 10-15 62
(Compact 33 single.)
RCA (47-7997 "Remember Me") 4-8 62
RCA (8066 thru 9364) 4-8 62-67
Picture Sleeves
RCA (7700 "The Old Lamplighter") 10-15 60
RCA (7755 "Lonely Little Robin") 10-15 60
RCA (7780 "Wiffenpoof Song") 10-15 60
EPs: 7-inch
RCA 10-20 57-60
LPs: 10/12-inch
CAMDEN 8-12 65-68
CANDLELITE (0422 "Beautiful Country Music of the Browns") 5-10 80
(Mail order offer.)
MCA/DOT 5-8 86
RCA (524 "20 of the Best") 5-8 85
RCA (1000 thru 3000 series) 5-10 75-81
(With "ANL1" or "AYL1" prefix.)
RCA (1438 Jim Edward, Maxine & Bonnie Brown") 35-55 57
(With "LPM" prefix.)
RCA (2000 series) 15-30 59-65
(With "LPM" or "LSP" prefix.)
RCA (3000 series) 12-20 65-67
(With "LPM" or "LSP" prefix.)
Members: Jim Edward Brown; Maxine Brown; Bonnie Brown.
Also see BROWN, Jim Ed
Also see BROWN, Maxine
Also see COOKE, Sam / Rod Lauren / Neil Sedaka / Browns
Also see SEDAKA, Neil / Ann-Margret / Browns / Sam Cooke

BROWNSMITH
Singles: 7-inch
CAPITOL 3-5 76
LPs: 10/12-inch
CAPITOL 8-10 76

BROWNSTONE
Singles: 7-inch
PLAYBOY 3-5 73
LPs: 10/12-inch
PLAYBOY 8-10 73

BROWNSVILLE
Singles: 7-inch
EPIC 3-4 79
LPs: 10/12-inch
EPIC (Black vinyl) 8-10 79
EPIC (Colored vinyl) 12-18 79
Also see BROWNSVILLE STATION

BROWNSVILLE STATION P&R/LP '72
Singles: 7-inch
BIG TREE 3-5 72-74
EPIC 3-5 79
HIDEOUT (1957 "Rock & Roll Holiday") 8-12 69
PALLADIUM (1075 "Be-Bop Confidential") 5-10 70
POLYDOR 3-5 70
PRIVATE STOCK 3-5 77
W.B. (7501 "That's Fine") 4-8 71
LPs: 10/12-inch
BIG TREE 10-12 72-75
EPIC (Black vinyl) 8-10 78
EPIC (Colored vinyl) 10-20 78
(Promotional issue only.)
PALLADIUM (1004 "Brownsville Station") 20-25 70
PRIVATE STOCK 8-10 77
W.B. 12-15 70
Members: Tony Driggins; Cub Koda; Michael Lutz; Henry Weck; Bruce Nazarian.
Also see BROWNSVILLE
Also see GOON, Peter
Also see KODA, Cub
Also see SEGER, Bob

BROXTON, Parrish
Singles: 7-inch
SMASH 4-8 66

BRUBECK, Dave, Quartet LP '55
(Dave Brubeck Trio; Octet; with Paul Desmond)
Singles: 78 rpm
COLUMBIA 4-8 55-57
FANTASY 4-8 52-55
Singles: 7-inch
COLUMBIA (Except 40000 & 41000 series) 3-6 62-65
COLUMBIA (40000 & 41000 series) 5-10 55-61
FANTASY (500 series) 5-10 52-55
Picture Sleeves
COLUMBIA 5-10 61-63
EPs: 7-inch
COLUMBIA 10-25 55-59
FANTASY 15-30 51-57
LPs: 10/12-inch
ATLANTIC (79 "Fantasy Years") 8-12 74
COLUMBIA (566 "Jazz Goes to College") 50-75 54
COLUMBIA (590 "Dave Brubeck at Storyville") 50-75 54
COLUMBIA (622 "Brubeck Time") 40-60 55
COLUMBIA (699 "Jazz: Red Hot and Cool") 40-60 55
COLUMBIA (826 "Dave Brubeck Quintet at Carnegie Hall") 20-30 63
COLUMBIA (878 "Brubeck Plays Brubeck") 30-50 56
COLUMBIA (932 "Brubeck, Jay & Kai at Newport") 30-50 57
COLUMBIA (984 "Jazz Impressions of the U.S.A.") 30-50 57
COLUMBIA (1000 thru 1200 series) 20-35 57-59
(Monaural.)
COLUMBIA (1300 thru 2300 series) 12-25 59-65
(Monaural.)
COLUMBIA (6321 "Jazz Goes to College") 50-100 54
(10-inch LP.)
COLUMBIA (6322 "Jazz Goes to College") 50-75 54
(10-inch LP.)
COLUMBIA (6330 "Dave Brubeck at Storyville") 50-75 54
(10-inch LP.)
COLUMBIA (6331 "Dave Brubeck at Storyville") 50-75 54
(10-inch LP.)
COLUMBIA (8000 series) 20-45 57-59
(Stereo.)
COLUMBIA (8100 thru 9300 series) 15-30 59-66
(Stereo.)
CROWN 10-15 62-64
FANTASY (1 "Dave Brubeck Trio") 100-150 51
(10-inch LP. Colored vinyl.)
FANTASY (2 "Dave Brubeck Trio") 100-150 51
(10-inch LP. Colored vinyl.)
FANTASY (3 "Dave Brubeck Octet") 100-150 52
(10-inch LP. Colored vinyl.)
FANTASY (5 "Dave Brubeck Quartet with Paul Desmond") 100-150 52
(10-inch LP. Colored vinyl.)
FANTASY (7 "Dave Brubeck Quartet with Paul Desmond") 100-150 53
(10-inch LP. Colored vinyl.)
FANTASY (8 "At Storyville") 100-150 53
(10-inch LP. Colored vinyl.)
FANTASY (10 "Jazz at the Black Hawk") 100-150 53
(10-inch LP. Colored vinyl.)
FANTASY (11 "Jazz at Oberlin") 100-150 53
(10-inch LP. Colored vinyl.)
FANTASY (13 "Jazz at the College of the Pacific") 100-150 54
(10-inch LP. Colored vinyl.)
FANTASY (16 "Old Sounds from San Francisco") 100-150 55
(10-inch LP. Colored vinyl.)
FANTASY (204 "Dave Brubeck Trio") 75-125 56
(Colored vinyl.)
FANTASY (205 "Dave Brubeck Trio") 50-100 56

FANTASY (210 "Jazz at the Black Hawk")...50-100 56
FANTASY (223 "Jazz at the College of the Pacific")...50-100 56
FANTASY (229 "Dave Brubeck Quartet with Paul Desmond")...50-100 56
FANTASY (230 "Dave Brubeck Quartet with Paul Desmond")...50-100 56
FANTASY (239 "Dave Brubeck Octet")...50-100 56
FANTASY (240 "At Storyville")...50-100 57
FANTASY (245 "Jazz at Oberlin")...50-100 57
FANTASY (3300 series)...15-25 62
HORIZON...5-10 76
JAZZTONE (1272 "Dave Brubeck")...25-50 57
Members: Dave Brubeck; Paul Desmond; Cal Tjader; Dick Collins; David Van Kriedt; Joe Morello; Eugene Wright.
Also see ARMSTRONG, Louis
Also see BERNSTEIN, Leonard, & Dave Brubeck
Also see RUSHING, Jimmy
Also see TJADER, Cal

BRUBECK, Dave, & Paul Desmond
LP '76

Singles: 7-inch
A&M...3-5 76
HORIZON...3-5 75
LPs: 10/12-inch
HORIZON...6-10 74-75
As a member of Dave Brubeck's group, Paul Desmond was often credited prominently on releases which, for consistency, appear in the Brubeck section.
Also see DESMOND, Paul

BRUBECK, Dave, & Gerry Mulligan
Singles: 7-inch
COLUMBIA...4-6 68
LPs: 10/12-inch
COLUMBIA...8-15 68-73
VERVE...8-12 73

BRUBECK, Dave, Gerry Mulligan, & Paul Desmond
LP: 10/12-inch
MFSL (216 "We're All Together Again for the First Time")...20-25 90s
Also see BRUBECK, Dave
Also see DESMOND, Paul
Also see MULLIGAN, Gerry

BRUCE, Donn, & Little Beats
Singles: 78 rpm
TUXEDO...15-25 56
Singles: 7-inch
TUXEDO (914 "Love Leads a Fool")...40-60 56

BRUCE, Ed
C&W '67
(Edwin Bruce)
Singles: 78 rpm
SUN (276 "Rock Boppin' Baby")...50-100 57
Singles: 7-inch
EPIC...3-5 77-78
GOOD BUDDY...3-5 76
MCA...3-4 80-85
MONUMENT...4-6 68-69
RCA (5000 series)...3-4 86
RCA (47-7842 "Flight 303")...5-10 61
(Monaural.)
RCA (61-7842 "Flight 303")...10-20 61
(Stereo Compact 33.)
RCA (9000 series)...4-8 66-68
RCA (13000 & 14000 series)...3-4 84-86
SUN (276 "Rock Boppin' Baby")...25-50 57
SUN (292 "Sweet Woman")...20-40 58
TRANS-SONIC...10-20 60s
U.A....3-5 73-76
WAND...10-20 63
Promotional Singles
MCA (52109 "Ever Never Lovin' You")...3-5 82
(5 1/4-inch disc with LP size hole and label. Packaged in a special sleeve that unfolds to make a 1983 calendar.)
LPs: 10/12-inch
EPIC...6-10 77-78
MCA...5-10 80-83
MONUMENT...10-15 69
RCA (3948 "If I Could Just Go Home")...20-30 68
RCA (5000 series)...5-10 84-85
U.A....8-10 76
Session: Willie Nelson.
Also see NELSON, Willie

BRUCE, Ed, & Lynn Anderson
Singles: 7-inch
RCA...3-4 86
Also see ANDERSON, Lynn
Also see BRUCE, Ed

BRUCE, Jack
LP '69
(Jack Bruce Band; with Friends)
Singles: 7-inch
RSO...3-5 74-75
LPs: 10/12-inch
ATCO...10-15 69-71
EPIC...5-10 80
POLYDOR...8-12 72
RSO...5-10 74-77
Also see CREAM
Also see MAYALL, John
Also see ROCKET 88
Also see WEST, BRUCE & LAING

BRUCE, Jack, & Robin Trower
LP '82
LPs: 10/12-inch
CHRYSALIS (1352 "Truce")...5-10 82

BRUCE, Jack, Bill Lordan & Robin Trower
LP '81
LPs: 10/12-inch
CHRYSALIS (1324 "B.L.T.")...5-10 81
Also see BRUCE, Jack
Also see TROWER, Robin

BRUCE, James, & Del Catos
Singles: 7-inch
PALOS (1203 "Brand New Baby")...75-125

BRUCE, Joe, & Steppers
Singles: 7-inch
ROBIN...4-8

BRUCE, Lenny
LP '75
Singles: 7-inch
FANTASY (Black vinyl)...5-10
FANTASY (Colored vinyl)...10-15
Picture Sleeves
W.B. (598 "The Law, Language and Lenny Bruce")...20-30 74
EPs: 7-inch
FANTASY (2 "Curran Theater Concert")...10-20
(Promotional issue only.)
LPs: 10/12-inch
CAPITOL (2630 "Why Did Lenny Bruce Die")...15-20 66
DOUGLAS...15-25 68-71
FANTASY (1 "Lenny Bruce")...50-75
(Promotional issue only.)
FANTASY (7001 "Lenny Bruce's Interviews of Our Times")...30-40 58
(THICK red vinyl.)
FANTASY (7001 "Lenny Bruce's Interviews of Our Times")...15-25
(Black vinyl.)
FANTASY (7001 "Lenny Bruce's Interviews of Our Times")...8-12
(THIN red vinyl.)
FANTASY (7003 "The Sick Humor of Lenny Bruce")...30-40 58
(THICK red vinyl.)
FANTASY (7003 "The Sick Humor of Lenny Bruce")...15-20
(Black vinyl.)
FANTASY (7003 "The Sick Humor of Lenny Bruce")...8-12
(THIN red vinyl.)
FANTASY (7007 "I Am Not a Nut, Elect Me")...30-40 59
(THICK red vinyl.)
FANTASY (7007 "I Am Not a Nut, Elect Me")...15-20
(Black vinyl.)
FANTASY (7007 "I Am Not a Nut, Elect Me")...8-12
(THIN red vinyl.)
FANTASY (7011 "Lenny Bruce, American")...30-40 62
(THICK red vinyl.)
FANTASY (7011 "Lenny Bruce, American")...15-20
(Black vinyl.)
FANTASY (7011 "Lenny Bruce, American")...8-12
(THIN red vinyl.)
FANTASY (7012 "The Best of Lenny Bruce")...25-30 63
(THICK red vinyl.)
FANTASY (7012 "The Best of Lenny Bruce")...15-20
(Black vinyl.)
FANTASY (7012 "The Best of Lenny Bruce")...8-12
(THIN red vinyl.)
FANTASY (7017 "Thank You Masked Man")...10-15 72
FANTASY (34201 "Lenny Bruce Live at the Curran Theatre")...10-15 72
FANTASY (79003 "The Real Lenny Bruce")...8-12 75
LENNY BRUCE RECORDS ("Recordings Submitted As Evidence in the San Francisco Obscenity Trial in March, 1962")..75-100 62
PHILLES (4010 "Lenny Bruce Is Out Again")...50-75 66
REPRISE (6329 "The Berkeley Concert")...15-20 69
U.A. (3580 "Midnight Concert")...15-20 67
U.A. (9800 "At Carnegie Hall")...15-25 71
(3 LPs.)
W.B. (9101 "The Law, Language and Lenny Bruce")...10-20 74
(Promotional issue only.)

BRUCE, Michael
Singles: 12-inch
ETR...4-6 83
Also see COOPER, Alice

BRUCE, Richie
Singles: 7-inch
ROULETTE...4-8 66

BRUCE, Tommy
Singles: 7-inch
CAPITOL...5-10 60-65

BRUCE & CHERYL
Singles: 7-inch
TOWNE HOUSE...5-10

BRUCE & DUTCH
Singles: 7-inch
LIBERTY...4-8 68

BRUCE & JERRY
Singles: 7-inch
ARWIN...5-10 59

BRUCE & SHERL
Singles: 7-inch
PACEMAKER (230 "Cold Lonely Nights")...4-8 60s
VALERIE (104 "Runaway")...5-10 60s

BRUCE & TERRY
P&R '64
Singles: 7-inch
COLUMBIA (Except 11)...5-10 64-66
COLUMBIA (11 "Spinning Wheel Rock")...10-20 64
Members: Bruce Johnston; Terry Melcher.
Also see BOONE, Pat
Also see CALIFORNIA MUSIC
Also see HONDELLS
Also see JOHNSTON, Bruce
Also see MELCHER, Terry, & Bruce Johnston
Also see NEWTON, Wayne
Also see RIP CHORDS
Also see ROGUES
Also see SAGITTARIUS

BRUDICK, Doni
Singles: 7-inch
SOUND IMPRESSION (6808 "I Have Faith in You")...50-100 60s

BRUFORD
LPs: 10/12-inch
EDITIONS EG...5-10 81

BRUFORD, Bill
LP '79
Singles: 7-inch
POLYDOR...3-5 78-80
LPs: 10/12-inch
POLYDOR...5-10 79-80
Also see KING CRIMSON
Also see YES

BRUINS
Singles: 7-inch
COMET...15-20 64
GENERAL AMERICAN (721 "Go on and Cry")...25-30 65
ROULETTE (4566 "Believe Me")...10-15 64

BRUMBLE, Don
Singles: 7-inch
MANCO...4-8 63

BRUNEL, Bunny
LPs: 10/12-inch
INNER CITY...5-10

BRUNER, June
(With Dick Taylor & His Taylor Made Music)
Singles: 78 rpm
MASTER...4-8 55
Singles: 7-inch
MASTER...5-10 55

BRUNO, Bruce
Singles: 7-inch
ROULETTE (4386 "Hey Little One")...15-25 61
ROULETTE (4427 "Dear Joanne")...50-75 62
Session: Del Satins.
Also see DEL SATINS

BRUNO, Don
Singles: 7-inch
BARRY (3056 "Highland Rock")...10-20 61
(Canadian.)

BRUNO, Ric
Singles: 7-inch
TWILIGHT...4-8 62

BRUNO & GLADIATORS
Singles: 7-inch
VAULT...10-20 62

BRUNO SISTERS
Singles: 78 rpm
IMPERIAL (5364 "Dreaming")...5-10 55
Singles: 7-inch
IMPERIAL (5364 "Dreaming")...10-15 55

BRUNSON, Frankie
("Little" Frankie Brunson; "Big Daddy")
Singles: 78 rpm
GROOVE...5-10 56
RCA...5-10 57
Singles: 7-inch
FAIRMOUNT...5-10 63
GEE (1063 "Give Me Something to Live For")...10-20 60
GROOVE (0173 "Charmaine")...10-20 56
RCA...10-20 57
Also see BIG DADDY
Also see FASHIONS
Also see PEOPLE'S CHOICE

BRUNSON, Tyrone "Tystick"
R&B '82
Singles: 12-inch
BELIEVE in a DREAM...4-6 82-84
Singles: 7-inch
BELIEVE in a DREAM...3-4 82-84
MCA...3-4 86-87
Picture Sleeves
MCA...3-4 86
LPs: 10/12-inch
BELIEVE in a DREAM...5-10 82-84
Also see SPECIAL DELIVERY

BRUNZELL, Jim
LPs: 10/12-inch
MATLAND (14622 "Matlands")...25-30
(Picture disc.)

BRUSH ARBOR
C&W '72
Singles: 7-inch
CAPITOL...3-5 72-73
MONUMENT...3-5 75-77
LPs: 10/12-inch
CAPITOL...8-12 72-73
MONUMENT...5-10 75-77
MYRRH...5-10

BRUSSEL SPROUT
Singles: 7-inch
MCA...3-5 75-76

BRUTAL FORCE
Singles: 7-inch
PHIL-LA of SOUL...4-6

BRUTE FORCE
Singles: 7-inch
COLUMBIA...4-8 67
W.B....4-8 68
LPs: 10/12-inch
B.T. PUPPY...10-15 71
COLUMBIA...15-20 67
EMBRYO...10-15 70

BRUTES
Singles: 7-inch
NOVA (7401 "Make Me Happy, Girl")...20-30 66

BRUTHERS
Singles: 7-inch
RCA (8920 "Bad Way to Go")...10-20 66

BRUTUS
Singles: 12-inch
PHILLY WORLD...4-6 83

BRUZER
Singles: 7-inch
HANDSHAKE...3-4 82
LPs: 10/12-inch
HANDSHAKE...5-10 82

BRYAN
Singles: 7-inch
ABC...4-6 68

BRYAN, Bill, & Gold Tones
Singles: 7-inch
PIKE (5913 "Rocking Chair")...15-25 62

BRYAN, Billy
(Gene Pitney)
Singles: 7-inch
BLAZE (351 "Going Back to My Love")...20-30 59
Also see PITNEY, Gene

BRYAN, Billy
Singles: 7-inch
EVEREST...4-8 61

BRYAN, Danny
Singles: 7-inch
ENTERPRISE...3-5 73

BRYAN, Dave, & Choraltones
Singles: 78 rpm
SPECK (103 "Please Forgive Me")...100-200 56
Singles: 7-inch
SPECK (103 "Please Forgive Me")...550-650 56

BRYAN, Dora
Singles: 7-inch
FONTANA...10-15 64

BRYAN, Eddie
Singles: 7-inch
ARLEN (733 "Your Lips")...10-20 60s

BRYAN, Larry
Singles: 7-inch
VISCOUNT...4-8 62

BRYAN, Lenny
Singles: 7-inch
DOLTON...4-8 63

BRYAN, Steve
Singles: 7-inch
NORELL...4-8 62

BRYAN, Wes
Singles: 7-inch
CLOCK...15-20 59
ROULETTE...5-10 60
U.A....15-25 57-58
Picture Sleeves
U.A....15-30 57-58

BRYANT, Anita
P&R '59
Singles: 7-inch
CARLTON...4-8 58-61
COLUMBIA...4-8 61-67
DISNEYLAND...3-4
TRIP...3-5
Picture Sleeves
COLUMBIA...4-8 61-67
DISNEYLAND...3-5
EPs: 7-inch
ACSP (1779 "See America with AC")...5-10
(Promotional issue for AC Spark Plugs.)
LPs: 10/12-inch
CARLTON...10-20 59-61
COLUMBIA...8-15 62-67
HARMONY...6-12

BRYANT, Anita / Jo Stafford & Gordon MacRae
Singles: 7-inch
COLUMBIA...5-10 60
Also see MacRAE, Gordon, & Jo Stafford

BRYANT, Ardie
Singles: 7-inch
AD&A (101 "What's It All About")...15-25 60s

BRYANT, Audrey
Singles: 7-inch
DO-RA-ME (1405 "Someone Like You")...25-35 59

BRYANT, Ben
Singles: 78 rpm
SABRE...10-15 53
Singles: 7-inch
SABRE (101 "Blue Midnight")...15-25 53

BRYANT, Beulah
(Big Beulah Bryant)
Singles: 78 rpm
EXCELLO...50-75 54
Singles: 7-inch
DO-KAY-LO...5-10 63
EXCELLO (2049 "Prize Fighting Papa")...100-150 54

BRYANT, Bobby
LPs: 10/12-inch
CADET...8-10 75
WORLD PACIFIC...8-10

BRYANT, Boudleaux
(With the Sparks)
Singles: 7-inch
HICKORY...8-12 59
MONUMENT (007)...5-10 63
(Title not known. Promotional issue only.)
MONUMENT...3-5 72
Picture Sleeves
MONUMENT (007)...8-12 63
(Title not known. Promotional only issue.)
EPs: 7-inch
MONUMENT...5-10 63
(Compact 33 single.)
LPs: 10/12-inch
MONUMENT...15-20 63

BRYANT, Browning
Singles: 7-inch
DOT...4-6 69
RCA...3-5 70
REPRISE...3-5 74-75
LPs: 10/12-inch
DOT...15-20 69
RCA...12-15 70
REPRISE...8-10 74

BRYANT, Charles
Singles: 7-inch
PEACH...5-10 60

BRYANT, Dee Dee
Singles: 7-inch
ALFA...10-20

BRYANT, Denis
Singles: 7-inch
DISC REET...3-5 75

BRYANT, Donald
(Don Bryant)
Singles: 7-inch
HI...5-10 65-69
LPs: 10/12-inch
HI...15-20 69
Also see MITCHELL, Willie
Also see 1 PLUS 1

BRYANT, Gary
Singles: 7-inch
DECCA...10-15 58
FOUR CORNERS...4-8 64

BRYANT, Helen
Singles: 7-inch
FURY...5-10 61

BRYANT, Jay Dee
(With the Kiddie-O's; J.D. Bryant & USA)
Singles: 7-inch
ALFA (501 "Don't Stop Now")...25-35
CEE=JAY (577 "Searching for Tomorrow")...50-75 60
ENJOY...10-15 63
GRASSROOTS...3-6 73
HERALD (570 "Come Summer")...10-15 63
JOSIE...5-10 68
SHRINE (108 "I Won't Be Coming Back")...3000-5000 66
STOP (103 "Come Summer")...8-12 64

BRYANT, James
Singles: 7-inch
PARROT...5-10 65
RENEE...5-10 60s

BRYANT, Jeannie
Singles: 7-inch
NCP...3-5 75-76

BRYANT, Jesse
Singles: 7-inch
DAY...5-10 61

BRYANT, Jimmy, & Pacesetters
Singles: 7-inch
ADKORP...4-6 71

BRYANT, Ken
Singles
NSFD (NFSD "Destination Love") 10-15 88
(Bus-shaped picture disc. 500 made.)
NSFD (NFSD "Destination Love") 15-20 88
(Rectangle picture disc. 100 made.)

BRYANT, Larry
Singles: 7-inch
SANTA FE...10-15 59

BRYANT, Laura
Singles: 7-inch
CAMEO...6-12 57-58

BRYANT, Leon R&B '81
Singles: 7-inch
DE-LITE 3-4 81-84
LPs: 10/12-inch
DE-LITE 5-10 84

BRYANT, Lillie
Singles: 7-inch
CAMEO (122 "Good Good Morning, Baby") 15-25 58
SWAN (4029 "I'll Never Be Free") .. 10-20 59
TAYSTER (6016 "Meet Me Half Way") 200-300
Also see BILLY & LILLIE

BRYANT, Paul
Singles: 7-inch
FANTASY (576 "Sister Lovie") 10-20 64

BRYANT, Ray P&R/R&B '60
(Ray Bryant Combo; Ray Bryant Quintet)
Singles: 7-inch
ATLANTIC 5-10
CADET 4-8 66-67
COLUMBIA 5-10 60-64
SIGNATURE 5-10 60
SUE 5-10 61
Picture Sleeves
CADET 5-10 67
COLUMBIA 10-15 60
LPs: 10/12-inch
CADET 10-20 66-67
COLUMBIA 15-30 60-62
EPIC (3279 "Ray Bryant Trio") 40-60 56
PRESTIGE/NEW JAZZ 15-25 62
SIGNATURE 15-25 60
SUE 15-30 60-64
Also see CARTER, Betty, & Ray Bryant

BRYANT, Ronnie C&W '89
Singles: 7-inch
EVERGREEN 3-4 89

BRYANT, Rusty
(With the Carolyn Club Band)
Singles: 78 rpm
CAROLYN 10-15 53
DOT 5-10 54-59
Singles: 7-inch
CAROLYN (333 "Castle Rock") 20-30 53
DOT 10-20 54-59
PRESTIGE 3-5 71
EPs: 7-inch
DOT (1023 "All Night Long") 25-35 55
DOT (1047 "Rusty Bryant and the Carolyn Club Band") 20-30 56
LPs: 10/12-inch
DOT (3006 "All Night Long") 50-100 55
PRESTIGE 10-12 70-74

BRYANT, Sharon P&R/LP '89
Singles: 7-inch
WING 3-4 89
Picture Sleeves
WING 3-4 89
LPs: 10/12-inch
WING 5-8 89
Also see ATLANTIC STARR

BRYANT, Soda, & Jordanaires
Singles: 7-inch
COVER 5-10 63
Also see JORDANAIRES

BRYANT, Terri
Singles: 7-inch
VERVE (10508 "When I'm in Your Arms") 10-20 67
VERVE (10553 "Straighten Up and Fly Right") 10-20 67

BRYCE, Sherry C&W '73
Singles: 7-inch
MGM 3-5 73-77
LPs: 10/12-inch
MGM 5-10 74-75
Also see TILLIS, Mel, & Sherry Bryce

BRYDS
Singles: 7-inch
RAYNARD ("Your Lies") 20-40

BRYE, Betsy
(Betty Brye)
Singles: 7-inch
CANADIAN AMERICAN 5-10 60
MALA 5-10 61
PEACOCK 4-8 62
SANTE FE 5-10 59

BRYER & AMUNSON
Singles: 7-inch
NOLTA 5-10 61

BRYLLIG & Nymbol Swabes
Singles: 7-inch
TRX 4-8 68

BRYM-MARS
Singles: 7-inch
eEe (2772 "Keep on Goin' ") 5-10

BRYM-STONZ LTD.
Singles: 7-inch
CUSTOM (143 "Times Gone By") ... 5-10

BRYNDA & BELLAIRES
Singles: 7-inch
BELLAIRE 3-4 79

BRYNDLE
Singles: 7-inch
A&M 3-5 71
Members: Andrew Gold; Karla Bonoff; Wendy Waldman; Kenny Edwards.
Also see BONOFF, Karla
Also see GOLD, Andrew
Also see WALDMAN, Wendy

BRYSON, Eldon
Singles: 78 rpm
STELLA 20-30 55
Singles: 7-inch
STELLA (1043 "Rock & Roll Daddy") 35-50 55

BRYSON, Peabo R&B '76
Singles: 7-inch
BULLET 3-5 76-77
CAPITOL 3-4 77-83
COLUMBIA 3-4 91
ELEKTRA 3-4 84-88
MCA 3-4 84
SHOUT 3-5 75
Picture Sleeves
CAPITOL 3-4 81-83
ELEKTRA 3-4 85-88
LPs: 10/12-inch
BULLET 8-10 76
CAPITOL 5-10 78-84
COLUMBIA 5-8 91
ELEKTRA 5-10 84-86
Also see COLE, Natalie, & Peabo Bryson
Also see MANCHESTER, Melissa, & Peabo Bryson
Also see ZAGER, Michael, Moon Band, & Peabo Bryson

BRYSON, Peabo, & Regina Belle R&B '87
Singles: 7-inch
ELEKTRA 3-4 88
Picture Sleeves
ELEKTRA 3-4 88
Also see BELLE, Regina
Also see COLE, Natalie, & Peabo Bryson
Also see FLACK, Roberta, & Peabo Bryson

BUA, Gene
Singles: 7-inch
ABC-PAR (9928 "Golly Gee") 10-15 58
HERITAGE 4-6 69
RUST 4-8 67
SAFARI 15-25 58
W.B. 5-10 59
WARWICK 5-10 60
Picture Sleeves
HERITAGE 3-6 69

BUBBA
LPs: 10/12-inch
COLUMBIA 10-15 70
HERITAGE 10-15 69

BUBBLE
Singles: 7-inch
DOT 4-6 68

BUBBLE BUSTERS
Singles: 7-inch
DOT 4-8 64

BUBBLE GUM MACHINE
Singles: 7-inch
SENATE 4-8 68
LPs: 10/12-inch
SENATE 12-20 68

BUBBLE PUPPY P&R/LP '69
Singles: 7-inch
INT'L ARTISTS (128 "Hot Smoke and Sasafrass") 15-20 69
INT'L ARTISTS (133 "Beginning") .. 15-25 69
INT'L ARTISTS (136 "Days of Our Time") 15-25 70
INT'L ARTISTS (138 "Hurry Sundown") 15-25 69
Promotional Singles
INT'L ARTISTS (Black vinyl) 20-30 69-70
INT'L ARTISTS (Colored vinyl) 25-50 70
LPs: 10/12-inch
INT'L ARTISTS (10 "A Gathering of Promises") 100-125 69
(Green label)
INT'L ARTISTS (10 "A Gathering of Promises") 150-200 69
(White label. Promotional issue only.)
Members: Rod Prince; Todd Potter; Roy Cox; M. Taylor; Dave Fore.
Also see DEMIAN
Also see MUSIC MACHINE / Bubble Puppy

BUBBLEROCK
Singles: 7-inch
U.K. 3-5 74

BUBBLES, John W.
Singles: 7-inch
VEE JAY 4-8 64
LPs: 10/12-inch
VEE JAY 12-20 64

BUBBLES & CO.
Singles: 7-inch
BLUE CAT 5-10 65

BUBBLES, BANGLES & BEADS
Singles: 7-inch
CLARIDGE 5-10 66

BUBBLING GARFUNKELS
Singles: 12-inch
BUZZ 4-8 90

BUBI & BOB
Singles: 7-inch
SPHINX (1201 "The Mummy") 10-15 59

BUCCANEERS
(With the Matthew Child & His Drifters)
Singles: 78 rpm
RAINBOW (211 "Fine Brown Frame") 100-200 53
RAMA (21 "The Stars Will Remember") 100-200 53
RAMA (24 "In the Mission of St. Augustine") 100-200 53
SOUTHERN (101 "Fine Brown Frame") 200-400 53
Singles: 7-inch
RAINBOW (211 "Fine Brown Frame") 500-750 53
RAMA (21 "The Stars Will Remember") 1000-2000 53
RAMA (24 "In the Mission of St. Augustine") 1000-2000 53
SOUTHERN (101 "Dear Ruth") 1500-2500 53
(Red vinyl.)
Members: Ernest Smith; Julius Robinson; Richard Gregory; Sam Johnson; Don Marshall.

BUCCANEERS
Singles: 78 rpm
TIFFANY 10-20 54
Singles: 7-inch
TIFFANY 20-30 54

BUCCANEERS
Singles: 7-inch
CRYSTALETTE (718 "Blonde Hair, Blue Eyes & Ruby Lips" 10-20 58

BUCCANEERS
Singles: 7-inch
CUPID (5006 "Bye Bye Baby") ... 100-150 58
Members: Robert Mansfield; Robert Wentworth; Donald Emilian; Lee de Felice.
Also see DUSTERS

BUCHANAN, Al
Singles: 7-inch
LOST GOLD (41193 "Easter Parade") 3-5 95
(Colored vinyl.)

BUCHANAN, Big Jim
Singles: 78 rpm
CENTURY 10-15 54
Singles: 7-inch
CENTURY 15-25 54

BUCHANAN, Bill
Singles: 7-inch
GONE (5032 "The Thing") 15-25 58
U.A. 8-12 62
Also see BUCHANAN & ANCELL
Also see BUCHANAN & CELLA
Also see BUCHANAN & GOODMAN
Also see BUCHANAN & GREENFIELD
Also see LAWRENCE, Syd, & Friends / Billy Mure

BUCHANAN, Roy LP '72
Singles: 7-inch
ALLIGATOR 3-4 85-86
ATLANTIC 3-4 76-78
BOMARC 10-15 61
POLYDOR 3-5 72-75
SWAN 4-8 61
LPs: 10/12-inch
ALLIGATOR 5-10 85
ATLANTIC 5-10 76-77
BIOYA 30-40 71
POLYDOR 8-15 72-75
WATERHOUSE 10-15 81
Also see CANNON, Freddy
Also see GREGG, Bobby
Also see HAWKINS, Dale
Also see MOORE, Bob, & Temps

BUCHANAN, Wes C&W '68
Singles: 7-inch
COLUMBIA 4-6 68
PEP (114 "Give Some Love My Way") 15-25 58

BUCHANAN & ANCELL P&R '57
Singles: 78 rpm
FLYING SAUCER 20-30 57
Singles: 7-inch
FLYING SAUCER (501 "The Creature") 20-30 57
Members: Bill Buchanan; Bob Ancell.
Also see BUCHANAN, Bill

BUCHANAN & CELLA
Singles: 7-inch
ABC-PAR (10033 "String Along with Pal-O-Mine") 10-20 59
Member: Bill Buchanan.
Also see BUCHANAN, Bill

BUCHANAN & GOODMAN P&R/R&B '56
Singles: 78 rpm
LUNIVERSE (101 "The Flying Saucer") 25-35 56
(Label is printed "Universe," with a handwritten "L," making "Luniverse.")
LUNIVERSE (101 "The Flying Saucer") 15-25 56
(Label is "Luniverse.")
LUNIVERSE (101X "Back to Earth") 25-50 56
LUNIVERSE (102 thru 108) 15-25 56-58
RADIO-ACTIVE 20-30 56
Singles: 7-inch
COMIC (500 "Flying Saucer the 3rd") 10-20 59
LUNIVERSE (101 "The Flying Saucer") 30-40 56
(Label is printed "Universe," with a handwritten "L," making "Luniverse.")
LUNIVERSE (101 "The Flying Saucer") 15-25 56
(Label is "Luniverse.")
LUNIVERSE (101X "Back to Earth") 100-125 56
LUNIVERSE (102 "Buchanan & Goodman on Trial") 20-30 56
LUNIVERSE (103 "The Banana Boat Story") 20-30 56
LUNIVERSE (105 "Flying Saucer the 2nd") 20-30 57
LUNIVERSE (107 "Santa & the Satellite") 20-30 57
LUNIVERSE (108 "Flying Saucer Goes West") 20-30 57
NOVELTY (301 "Frankenstein '59") 10-20 59
RADIO-ACTIVE (101 "The Flying Saucer") 50-75 56
(No artist credit shown. Unauthorized issue.)
Members: Bill Buchanan; Dickie Goodman.
Session: Paul Sharman.
Also see BUCHANAN, Bill
Also see GOODMAN, Dickie
Also see INVADERS

BUCHANAN & GREENFIELD
Singles: 7-inch
NOVEL (711 "The Invasion") 15-20 64
(Red label.)
NOVEL (711 "The Invasion") 3-5 72
(Red and white label.)
Members: Bill Buchanan; Howard Greenfield.
Also see BUCHANAN, Bill

BUCHANAN BROTHERS C&W '46
Singles: 78 rpm
VICTOR 5-10 46

BUCHANAN BROTHERS P&R '69
Singles: 7-inch
EVENT 3-6 69-71
LPs: 10/12-inch
EVENT (101 "Medicine Man") 20-25 69
Members: Terry Cashman; Gene Pistilli; Tommy West.
Also see CASHMAN, PISTILLI & WEST

BUCHANANS: see JALOPY FIVE

BUCHWALD, Art
Singles: 7-inch
CAPITOL 4-6 65
LPs: 10/12-inch
CAPITOL 10-20 65

BUCK
Singles: 7-inch
SPRINGFELLOWS 10-15 67

BUCK R&B '75
Singles: 7-inch
PLAYBOY 3-5 75

BUCK, Charlie
Singles: 7-inch
TAD 5-8 62

BUCK, Gary C&W '63
Singles: 7-inch
CHATEAU 5-10 62
DIMENSION 3-4 82
PETAL 4-6 63-64
TOWER 4-6 66-67
LPs: 10/12-inch
PETAL 15-20 64
TOWER 10-15 67

BUCK, John, & His Blazers
Singles: 7-inch
CADENCE 10-15 58
W.B. 10-15 59-62

BUCK ROGERS MOVEMENT
Singles: 7-inch
21ST CENTURY (601 "Baby Come On") 25-50 67
21ST CENTURY (603 "Take It from Me Girl") 10-20 67

BUCKACRE
Singles: 7-inch
MCA 3-5 76-78
Members: Alan Thacker; Dick Halley; Dick Verruchi; Darrel Data; Les Lockridge.

BUCKAROOS C&W '67
(Featuring Don Rich)
Singles: 7-inch
CAPITOL 4-8 67-69
LPs: 10/12-inch
CAPITOL (322 "Roll Your Own") 15-25 69
CAPITOL (440 "Rompin & Stompin' ") 15-25 70
CAPITOL (550 "Boot Hill") 15-25 70
CAPITOL (767 "The Buckaroos Play the Hits") 15-25 70
CAPITOL (2436 "The Buck Owens Songbook") 20-30 66
CAPITOL (2828 "Again") 20-30 67
CAPITOL (2973 "Meanwhile, Back at the Ranch") 15-25 68
Members: Don Rich; Doyle Holly; Tom Brumley; Willie Cantu.
Also see ALAN, Buddy
Also see HOLLY, Doyle
Also see OWENS, Buck
Also see RICH, Don

BUCKEYE P&R '79
Singles: 7-inch
POLYDOR 3-4 79
LPs: 10/12-inch
POLYDOR 5-10 79
Member: Ronn Price.

BUCKEYE POLITICIANS
Singles: 7-inch
SCEPTER 3-5 71
UTOPIA 3-5 76
LPs: 10/12-inch
UTOPIA 8-10 76

BUCKEYES
("Vocal by the Buckeyes with Orchestra")
Singles: 78 rpm
DELUXE (6110 "Since I Fell for You") 50-100 57
DELUXE (6126 "Dottie Baby") ... 100-125 57
Singles: 7-inch
DELUXE (6110 "Since I Fell for You") 200-300 57
DELUXE (6126 "Dottie Baby") ... 250-350 57
Also see STEREOS

BUCKINGHAM, Lindsey P&R/LP '81
Singles: 7-inch
ASYLUM 3-4 81
ELEKTRA 3-4 84
W.B. 3-4 83
Picture Sleeves
ASYLUM 3-4 81
ELEKTRA 3-4 84
LPs: 10/12-inch
ASYLUM 5-10 81
ELEKTRA 5-10 84
Also see BUCKINGHAM NICKS
Also see EGAN, Walter
Also see FLEETWOOD MAC
Also see STEWART, John

BUCKINGHAM IV
Singles: 7-inch
IMPERIAL 4-8 65

BUCKINGHAM NICKS
Singles: 7-inch
POLYDOR (14335 "Down Let Me Down Again") 20-30 76
POLYDOR (14428 "Crying in the Night") 20-30 77
Picture Sleeves
POLYDOR (14428 "Crying in the Night") 40-60 77
LPs: 10/12-inch
POLYDOR (5058 "Buckingham Nicks") 30-40 73
Members: Lindsey Buckingham; Stevie Nicks.
Also see BUCKINGHAM, Lindsey
Also see NICKS, Stevie

BUCKINGHAMS
Singles: 7-inch
LAURIE 4-8 64
SEG-WAY 5-8 61

BUCKINGHAMS P&R '66
Singles: 7-inch
COLUMBIA 4-8 67-70
RED LABEL 3-4 85
ROWE/AMI 10-20 66
("Play Me" Sales Stimulator promotional issue.)
SPECTRA-SOUND 10-20 67
U.S.A. 10-15 66-67
Picture Sleeves
COLUMBIA 8-15 67-68
RED LABEL 3-4 85
LPs: 10/12-inch
COLUMBIA 15-25 67-75
RED LABEL 5-10 85
U.S.A. (107 "Kind of a Drag") 50-75 67
(With 13 tracks.)
U.S.A. (107 "Kind of a Drag") 30-40 67
(With 12 tracks.)
Members: Dennis Tufano; Carl Giammarese; Nick Fortune; Marty Grebb; Dennis Miccoli; Jon-Jon Poulos.
Also see CENTURIES
Also see EXCEPTIONS
Also see FALLING PEBBLES
Also see TUFANO & GIAMMARESE

BUCKINS, Mickey, & New Breed
Singles: 7-inch
SOUTH CAMP 4-8 67

BUCKLE
Singles: 7-inch
LPI (1001 "Woman") 15-25 67

BUCKLEY, Betty
Singles: 7-inch
GEFFEN 3-4 83

BUCKLEY, Lord
(With Lyle Griffin's All Star Jazz Band; Lord Richard Buckley, Professor of Hipology)
Singles: 7-inch
HIP (270 "Flight of the Saucer") ... 75-100 56
(With "Space Correspondent" Lyle Griffin.)
EPs: 7-inch
HIP (301 "The Gettysburg Address [Narration and Hip Translation]") 20-40 56
(Colored vinyl. Autographed copies—which were available in 1956 for $1.50 via mail order—may be valued at double this price range. Issued in a brown paper sleeve.)
HIP (302 "James Dean's [Message to Teenagers]") 75-100 56
(Issued in a brown paper sleeve.)
RCA (3246 "Hipsters, Flipsters, and Finger-Poppin' Daddies, Knock Me Your Lobes") 75-125 54
(Two Eps in double-pocket cover.)
LPs: 10/12-inch
BIZARRE/REPRISE (6389 "A Most Immaculately Hip Aristocrat") 10-20 70
CRESTVIEW (CRV-801 "The Best of Lord Buckley") 25-40 63
(Monaural.)
CRESTVIEW (CRV-801 "The Best of Lord Buckley") 25-40 63
(Promotional issue only. Monaural.)
CRESTVIEW (CRV7-801 "The Best of Lord Buckley") 40-60 63
(Stereo.)

ELEKTRA (74047 "The Best of Lord Buckley")..........15-25 69
(Repackage of the 1963 Crestview LP.)
RCA (3246 "Hipsters, Flipsters, & Finger Poppin' Daddies")..........150-175 54
(10-inch LP. With the Royal Court Orchestra.)
REPRISE (6389 "A Most Immaculately Hip Aristocrat")..........12-25 70
STRAIGHT (1054 "A Most Immaculately Hip Aristocrat")..........15-30 70
STRAIGHT (1054 "A Most Immaculately Hip Aristocrat")..........25-35 70
(White label. Promotional issue only.)
VAYA (1715 "Euphoria")..........150-200 51
(10-inch LP. Colored vinyl.)
VAYA (101 "Euphoria, Vol. 1")..........75-125 55
VAYA (107 "Euphoria, Vol. 2")..........125-175 56
WORLD PACIFIC (1279 "Way Out Humor")..........50-75 59
(Back cover may read "Far Out Humor" instead of "Way Out Humor.")
WORLD PACIFIC (1815 "Lord Buckley in Concert")..........20-40 64
(Repackage of *Way Out Humor*.)
WORLD PACIFIC (1849 "Blowing His Mind [And Your's Too]")..........30-50 66
WORLD PACIFIC (21879 "Buckley's Best")..........25-40 68
WORLD PACIFIC (21889 "Bad Rapping of the Marquis De Sade")..........20-30 69
Session: Dodo Marmarosa; Lucky Thompson.

BUCKLEY, Tim — LP '67
Singles: 7-inch
DISC REET..........3-5 73-74
ELEKTRA..........4-8 66-67
LPs: 10/12-inch
DISC REET..........8-10 73-74
ELEKTRA (Except 74004)..........15-20 67-70
ELEKTRA (74004 "Tim Buckley")..........25-35 66
RHINO..........5-10 83
STRAIGHT (Except 1060)..........15-25 70
STRAIGHT (1060 "Blue Afternoon")..........25-35 69
W.B...........10-15 70-72

BUCKLEY, William, Jr.
LPs: 10/12-inch
JUBILEE..........15-25 68

BUCKNASTY, Thomas
LPs: 10/12-inch
RCA..........8-10 80

BUCKNER, Joe
Singles: 78 rpm
VEE JAY..........10-15 56
Singles: 7-inch
VEE JAY..........10-20 56

BUCKNER, Milt
Singles: 7-inch
ARGO..........10-15 60
BETHLEHEM..........5-10 63
CAPITOL..........15-25 57-59
SAVOY..........10-20 52

BUCKNER & GARCIA — P&R '80
Singles: 12-inch
COLUMBIA..........4-6 82
Singles: 7-inch
BGO (1001 "Pac-Man Fever")..........5-8 81
(First issue.)
COLUMBIA (Except 02945)..........3-4 81
COLUMBIA (02945 "Pac-Man Fever")..........8-12 82
(Square picture disc.)
Picture Sleeves
COLUMBIA..........3-4 81
LPs: 10/12-inch
COLUMBIA..........5-10 82
Members: Jerry Buckner; Gary Garcia.
Also see WILLIS "The Guard" & Vigorish

BUCKS FIZZ
Singles: 7-inch
RCA..........3-4 81
LPs: 10/12-inch
RCA..........5-10 82

BUCKSHOTS
Singles: 7-inch
MONOGRAM..........4-8 63

BUCKWEET
Singles: 7-inch
ACT II..........4-6 71
Member: Joey Miranda.
Also see STRAWBED

BUCKWHEAT
Singles: 7-inch
RATHSKELLER..........10-20 70
Also see GESTURES

BUCKWHEAT — P&R/LP '72
Singles: 7-inch
LONDON..........3-5 71-73
LPs: 10/12-inch
LONDON..........10-12 71-73

BUCKWHEAT
LPs: 10/12-inch
SUPER K..........10-12

BUCKWHEAT ZYDECO — LP '87
LPs: 10/12-inch
ISLAND..........5-10 87-90

BUCKY & STRINGS
Singles: 7-inch
STRAND..........5-10 61

BUD, Billy
Singles: 7-inch
JUBILEE..........4-8 67

BUD & BUD
Singles: 7-inch
TONKA..........3-5 71

BUD & KATHY
Singles: 7-inch
DOWNEY (136 "Hang It Out to Dry")..........15-25 65

BUD & TRAVIS — P&R '60
Singles: 7-inch
LIBERTY..........5-10 59-65
WORLD PACIFIC..........5-10 59
LPs: 10/12-inch
LIBERTY..........10-20 59-65
SUNSET..........8-15 67
Members: Bud Dashiel; Travis Edmonson.
Also see DASHIEL, Bud, & Kinsmen
Also see EDMONSON, Travis

BUDD, Billy
Singles: 7-inch
JUBILEE..........4-6
20TH FOX..........3-5

BUDD, Julie
(Julie)
Singles: 7-inch
A&M..........3-4 81
ALSTON..........3-4 77
BELL..........3-5 70
MGM..........4-6 68
RCA..........3-5 72-73
TOM CAT..........3-5 76-77
LPs: 10/12-inch
MGM..........12-20 68
RCA..........10-15 71
Also see JULIE

BUDD, Landon, & "Grunion"
Singles: 7-inch
ALERT (1002 "Killer Reef")..........20-35 62

BUDDE, Rusty — C&W '86
Singles: 7-inch
BPC..........3-4 86

BUDDIES
Singles: 78 rpm
GLORY..........25-50 55
Singles: 7-inch
GLORY (230 "I Stole Your Heart")..........75-100 55
Members: Leon Harrison; Luther Dixon; Roger Wainwright; Danny Ferguson.
Also see BARONS

BUDDIES
Singles: 78 rpm
DECCA..........5-10 56-57
Singles: 7-inch
DECCA..........10-15 56-57

BUDDIES
Singles: 7-inch
OKEH..........5-10 59
TIARA..........10-20 59

BUDDIES
Singles: 7-inch
COMET..........10-20 61

BUDDIES
Singles: 7-inch
SWAN (4170 "The Beatle")..........10-20 64
Members: John Mahoney; Dave Zelinski; Dave Marsciak; Bob Horbette.

BUDDIES
Singles: 7-inch
SWING (102 "On the Go")..........10-20 64
Members: Jay Siegel; Henry Medress; Mitch Margo; Phil Margo.
Also see TOKENS

BUDDIES
Singles: 7-inch
CRC..........8-12 65

BUDDIES
LPs: 10/12-inch
WING (12306 "Go Go with the Buddies")..........20-30 65
(Monaural.)
WING (16306 "Go Go with the Buddies")..........25-35 65
(Stereo.)

BUDDIES / Compacts
LPs: 10/12-inch
WING (12293 "The Buddies and the Compacts")..........25-35 65
(Monaural.)
WING (16293 "The Buddies and the Compacts")..........30-40 65
(Stereo.)
Also see BUDDIES

BUDDIES
Singles: 7-inch
DECCA (31000 series)..........4-8 66

BUDDY ALAN: see ALAN, Buddy

BUDDY & BON BONS
Singles: 7-inch
CORSICAN..........8-12 61

BUDDY & CITATIONS
Singles: 7-inch
IRC (6918 "Don't Let Her Have Her Way")..........100-150 64
Member: Bob Penney.
Also see SECOND COMING

BUDDY & CLAUDIA — R&B '55
Singles: 78 rpm
CHESS..........8-10 55
Singles: 7-inch
CHESS..........10-15 55
Members: Buddy Griffin; Claudia Swann.

BUDDY & DIMES
Singles: 7-inch
EMI..........4-6

BUDDY & EDNA
Singles: 7-inch
SAVOY (1543 "No Change")..........15-25 58
Members: Buddy Lucas; Edna McGriff.
Also see LUCAS, Buddy
Also see McGRIFF, Edna

BUDDY & FADS
Singles: 7-inch
MOROCCO..........10-20 58

BUDDY & GERRIE
Singles: 7-inch
SKYLARK..........5-10 61

BUDDY & HEARTS
Singles: 7-inch
LANDA (701 "Let It Rock")..........8-12 64
Member: Kirby St. Romain.
Also see ST. ROMAIN, Kirby

BUDDY & STACEY
(Buddy & Stacy)
Singles: 7-inch
RAID..........4-8
TWIRL..........4-8 65

BUDDY & WILDCATS
Singles: 7-inch
RUST..........4-8 63

BUDDY WAYNE: see WAYNE, Buddy

BUDGIE
Singles: 7-inch
KAPP..........3-5 72
MCA..........3-5 75
LPs: 10/12-inch
A&M..........8-15 76-78
ACTIVE..........12-15 80
KAPP (3656 "Budgie")..........30-40 71
KAPP (3669 "Squawk")..........30-40 71
MCA..........10-12 74
Members: Pete Boot; Tony Bourge; Ray Phillips; Burke Shelley; Steve Williams.

BUELL, Bebe
(With the B-Sides)
EPs: 7-inch
RHINO..........4-6 81
LPs: 10/12-inch
RHINO..........5-10 81
VISUAL VINYL (1006 "Windy Words")..........15-20 84
(Picture disc.)

BUELOW, Bob
Singles: 7-inch
20TH FOX..........3-5 74-75

BUENA VISTAS — P&R '66
Singles: 7-inch
BB (4001 "Sunset")..........10-20 60s
MARQUEE..........5-10 68
SWAN..........10-15 66

BUFF, Beverly — C&W '62
Singles: 7-inch
BETHLEHEM..........4-8 62-63
SUR-SPEED..........4-8 67

BUFF, Paul
(Buff Organization)
Singles: 7-inch
DONNA..........4-8 63
ORIGINAL SOUND..........4-6 68

BUFF ORGANIZATION
Singles: 7-inch
ORIGINAL SOUND..........10-15 60s

BUFFALO, Cecil, & Prophets
Singles: 7-inch
SHO BOAT (102 "Big Red")..........10-20 60s
Also see FIVE SOUNDS / Cecil Buffalo

BUFFALO, Norton
Singles: 7-inch
CAPITOL..........3-5 77
LPs: 10/12-inch
CAPITOL..........5-10 77
Member: Norton Buffalo; Byron Alred; Gary Creller; John McFee; Dave Shipiro; Bill Champlin; Mickey Hart.
Also see HART, Mickey

BUFFALO & BRANDY
Singles: 7-inch
KM..........3-4 82

BUFFALO BILL
Singles: 7-inch
COMMONWEALTH..........5-8

BUFFALO HIGHLITES
Singles: 7-inch
COLLEGIATE (1001 "Spyder")..........15-25 63

BUFFALO NICKEL
Singles: 7-inch
DOME..........3-4

BUFFALO NICKEL JUGBAND
LPs: 10/12-inch
HAPPY TIGER..........15-25 71

BUFFALO REBELS
Singles: 7-inch
MAR-LEE..........15-20 60-61
Also see REBELS
Also see ROCKIN' REBELS

BUFFALO SMOKE
Singles: 12-inch
RCA..........4-8 76
Singles: 7-inch
RCA..........3-5 76

BUFFALO SOLDIER
Singles: 7-inch
SMC..........3-5 70-71

BUFFALO SPRINGFIELD — P&R/LP '67
Singles: 7-inch
ATCO..........5-10 67-68
LPs: 10/12-inch
ATCO (105 "Retrospective")..........8-10 75
ATCO (200 "Buffalo Springfield")..........30-50 66
(Contains *Baby Don't Scold Me*.)
ATCO (200 "Buffalo Springfield")..........15-25 67
(*Baby Don't Scold Me* replaced by *For What It's Worth*.)
ATCO (226 thru 283)..........20-30 67-69
ATCO (806 "Buffalo Springfield")..........15-20 73
Members: Stephen Stills; Neil Young; Jim Messina; Richie Furay; Jim Fielder; Doug Hastings; Dewey Martin; Bruce Palmer.
Also see FURAY, Richie
Also see MARTIN, Dewey, & Medicine Ball
Also see MESSINA, Jim
Also see PALMER, Bruce
Also see POCO
Also see STILLS, Stephen
Also see YOUNG, Neil

BUFFALOS
Singles: 7-inch
GMC (10000 "She Wants Me")..........10-20 60s

BUFFETT, Jimmy — C&W '73
Singles: 7-inch
ABC..........3-5 75-78
ASYLUM..........3-4 80
BARNABY..........3-5 70-72
DUNHILL..........3-5 73-75
FULL MOON..........3-4 80
MCA (Black vinyl)..........3-4 79-86
MCA (Colored vinyl)..........3-6 85
Picture Sleeves
ABC..........3-5
MCA..........3-4
LPs: 10/12-inch
ABC..........8-10 76-78
BARNABY (6014 "High Cumberland Jubilee")..........50-100 76
BARNABY (30093 "Down to Earth")..........150-250 70
DUNHILL..........10-15 73-74
MCA..........5-10 79-90
U.A...........8-10 75

BUFFETT, Mary — D&D '84
Singles: 12-inch
MOBY DICK..........4-6 84
Singles: 7-inch
MOBY DICK..........3-4 84

BUFFOONS
Singles: 7-inch
BRIGHT ORANGE..........4-8

BUFORD, Mojo
(George Buford)
Singles: 7-inch
ADELL (103 "Mojo Woman")..........20-25 60s
BANGAR (622 "Whole Lot a Woman")..........20-25 64
GARRETT (4020 "Craw-Dad Hole")..........20-25 65
GARRETT (4021 "Rag Pickers")..........20-25 65
INDIGO (139 "Something on My Mind")..........25-35 62
TWIN TOWN (736 "Bird Nest on the Ground")..........20-25 60s
TWIN TOWN (739 "Love Nest")..........20-25 60s
Picture Sleeves
ADELL (103 "Mojo Woman")..........25-35 60s
Also see LITTLE MOJO
Also see MOJO

BUG, Professor: see PROFESSOR BUG

BUG ALLEY
LPs: 10/12-inch
P.M...........5-10 80

BUG COLLECTORS
Singles: 7-inch
CATCH..........15-20 64

BUG MEN
Singles: 7-inch
DOT (16592 "Beatles, You Bug Me")..........15-25 64

BUGALOOS
Singles: 7-inch
CAPITOL..........3-5 70
LPs: 10/12-inch
CAPITOL..........10-15 70

BUGATTI & MUSKER
Singles: 7-inch
EPIC..........3-5 74

BUGGERBEE, L.J.
Singles: 7-inch
DORE..........5-10 60

BUGGLES — P&R/LP 79
Singles: 7-inch
CARRERE..........3-4 82
ISLAND..........3-4 79-83
Promotional Singles
CARRERE ("Fade Away")..........3-4 82
(Soundsheet. Originally included in a magazine.)
LPs: 10/12-inch
CARRERE..........5-10 82
ISLAND..........5-10 80
Members: Trevor Horn; Geoff Downes.
Also see ASIA
Also see YES

BUGGS
Singles: 7-inch
SOMA (1413 "She Loves You")..........20-25 64
Picture Sleeves
SOMA (1413 "She Loves You")..........40-60 64

BUGGS
LPs: 10/12-inch
CORONET (212 "Beetle Beat")..........25-30 64
Also see 4 SEASONS / Connie Francis / Barbara Brown & Buggs
Also see RASCALS / Buggs / Four Seasons / Johnny Rivers

BUGGS
Singles: 7-inch
BITTNER'S (16024 "It's All Right") 30-50

BUGNON, Alex — LP '89
LPs: 10/12-inch
ORPHEUS..........5-8 89-90

BUGS / Chellows
Singles: 7-inch
HIT..........5-15 64
Also see JALOPY FIVE

BUGS
Singles: 7-inch
ASTOR (001 "Stranger in the Night")..........15-25 66
ASTOR (002 "Pretty Girl")..........20-30 66
POLARIS (001 "Pretty Girl")..........10-20 66

BUGS TOMORROW
Singles: 7-inch
CASABLANCA..........3-4 80
LPs: 10/12-inch
CASABLANCA..........5-10 80

BUGSY
(Bugsy Maugh)
Singles: 7-inch
DOT..........3-6 69
LPs: 10/12-inch
DOT..........10-12 69

BUHL, Davey
Singles: 7-inch
MEGA..........3-4 70
Picture Sleeves
MEGA..........3-4 70

BUIE & COBB
Singles: 7-inch
CAPITOL..........3-6 69
Member: James Cobb.
Also see CLASSICS IV

BULAWAYO SWEET RHYTHM BOYS
Singles: 78 rpm
LONDON..........4-8 54
Singles: 7-inch
LONDON..........5-10 54

BULL
Singles: 7-inch
BELL..........3-5 72
PARAMOUNT..........3-5 71-72
LPs: 10/12-inch
PARAMOUNT..........10-12 71

BULL, Sandy
LPs: 10/12-inch
VANGUARD..........10-12 72-74

BULL, Smokey John
Singles: 7-inch
AVCO EMBASSY..........3-5 71

BULL & EL CAPALARS
("Bull & El Capalar's")
Singles: 7-inch
BELL..........4-8

BULL & MATADORS — P&R/R&B '68
Singles: 7-inch
TODDLIN' TOWN..........5-10 68-69

BULL ANGUS
Singles: 7-inch
MERCURY..........3-5 72
LPs: 10/12-inch
MERCURY..........10-15 71-72

BULL DOG BREED
Singles: 7-inch
CORAL..........4-8 68

BULLARD, John
(John Bullard Quartet; with Bobby Sands)
Singles: 78 rpm
DELUXE..........25-50 52
INDEX (300 "Don't Talk Dem Trash")..........50-75 50
Singles: 7-inch
DELUXE (6019 "Western Union Blues")..........75-100 52
DELUXE (6035 "Mary Lou")..........75-100 52

BULLDOG — P&R/LP '72
Singles: 7-inch
BUDDAH..........3-5 72-74
DECCA..........3-5 72
GUYDEN..........3-5 71
MCA..........3-5 73
LPs: 10/12-inch
BUDDAH..........8-12 74
DECCA..........12-20 72
Members: Gene Cornish; Dino Danelli; Billy Hocher; Eric Thorngren; John Turi.
Also see RASCALS

BULLDOGS
Singles: 7-inch
MERCURY 10-15 64

BULLENS, Cindy P&R '79
Singles: 7-inch
CASABLANCA 3-4 79-80
U.A. 3-4 78-79
LPs: 10/12-inch
CASABLANCA 5-10 79
U.A. 5-10 78
Also see ALPHA BAND

BULLET P&R '71
Singles: 7-inch
BIG TREE 3-5 71-72

BULLET
Singles: 7-inch
ARISTA 3-4 84
LPs: 10/12-inch
ARISTA 5-10 84

BULLETBOYS LP '88
Singles: 7-inch
W.B. 3-4 89
Picture Sleeves
W.B. 3-4 89
LPs: 10/12-inch
W.B. 5-8 89

BULLOCK, Janice R&B '87
Singles: 7-inch
WRC 3-4 87
Also see BELL, William, & Janice Bullock

BULLS
Singles: 7-inch
KLONDIKE 3-5 70

BULLSEYE
Singles: 7-inch
COLUMBIA 3-4 79
LPs: 10/12-inch
COLUMBIA 5-10 79

BULLY BOYS BAND
LPs: 10/12-inch
DUNHILL 10-15 70

BUMBLE, B: see B. BUMBLE & STINGERS

BUMBLE BEE SLIM
(Amos Easton)
Singles: 78 rpm
FIDELITY (3004 "Lonesome Old Feeling") 25-50 51
LPs: 10/12-inch
PACIFIC JAZZ (54 "Back in Town") 75-125 62
Also see EASTON, Amos, & His Orchestra

BUMBLE BEE UNLIMITED P&R/R&B '76
Singles: 12-inch
RED GREG 4-8 70s
Singles: 7-inch
MERCURY 3-5 76-77
RCA 3-4 79
LPs: 10/12-inch
RCA 5-10 79

BUMBLE BEES
Singles: 7-inch
JOEY (6220 "A Girl Called Love") 25-50 63

BUMP
Singles: 7-inch
PIONEER (2147 "Winston Built That Bridge") 20-40 70
LPs: 10/12-inch
PIONEER (2150 "Bump") 350-550 70

BUMPERS
Singles: 7-inch
ROULETTE 3-5 76
LPs: 10/12-inch
ROULETTE 8-10 76

BUMPS
Singles: 7-inch
PICCADILLY (245 "Hey Girl") 10-20 67
PICCADILLY (251 "Hard Woman") 10-20 67
SINAWAY 10-15
WALRUS 10-15

BUMPUS, Cornelius
LPs: 10/12-inch
BROADBEACH 5-10 82
Also see DOOBIE BROTHERS

BUMPY & JAGUARS
Singles: 7-inch
DEPRI (226 "Here I Go Again") 25-35

BUNCH
LPs: 10/12-inch
A&M 10-15 72

BUNDY, Jim, Combo
Singles: 7-inch
MAR-J ("Goofin' ") 10-15 62
(No selection number used.)
MAR-J ("Rebel Twist") 10-15 62
(No selection number used.)
Members: Jim Bundy; Charlie Boykin; Jesse Ennis; Jeff Duke; Wayne DeLisse.

BUNGI
Singles: 7-inch
TARGET (2005 "Six Days on the Road") 4-6 71
Picture Sleeves
TARGET (2005 "Six Days on the Road") 5-10 71

BUNGLE, Barney, & Klarence Kleen
Singles: 7-inch
PARTEE (1302 "UFO Landing") 5-8 73

BUNKER HILL
Singles: 7-inch
MALA 4-8 65

BUNKY & JAKE
LPs: 10/12-inch
MERCURY 10-15 69
Member: Jake Jacobs.
Also see JAKE & Family Jewels

BUNN, Allen
(Alden Bunn)
Singles: 78 rpm
APOLLO 35-50 52
RED ROBIN 50-75 54
Singles: 7-inch
APOLLO (436 "She'll Be Sorry") ..75-100 52
APOLLO (439 "Discouraged") 75-100 52
RED ROBIN (124 "My Kinda Woman") 175-225 54
Also see BAUM, Allen
Also see LARKS
Also see TARHEEL SLIM & LITTLE ANN
Also see WHEELS

BUNN, Bennie
(With the Cadets)
Singles: 7-inch
EASTMAN (790 "If I Were King") ...20-40 59
SHERWOOD (211 "You Must Be an Angel") 100-150 60
Also see DALTON, Martine, & Bennie Bunn
Also see CADETS

BUNN, Bennie, & Martine Dalton
Singles: 7-inch
TCF 8-12 60s
Also see BUNN, Bennie

BUNN, Billy, & His Buddies
Singles: 78 rpm
RCA 50-100 51-52
Singles: 7-inch
RCA (4483 "I Need a Shoulder to Cry On") 200-300 51
RCA (4657 "That's When Your Heartaches Begin") 250-400 52

BUNNIES
Singles: 7-inch
ROOMATE 4-8 65

BUNNY, Bobby, & Jackrabbits
Singles: 7-inch
ARROW (714 "Scatty Cat") 15-25 57

BUNNY & CINDY
Singles: 7-inch
NEPTUNE 4-6 69

BUNNY & ROYALETTES
Singles: 7-inch
CAVALCADE 5-10 64

BUNNY BOPPERS
Singles: 7-inch
BLUE JEANS 5-8

BUNNY PAUL: see PAUL, Bunny

BUNYAN, John
(John Bunyan's Progressive Pilgrims)
LPs: 10/12-inch
ALSHIRE 8-10 69

BUONO, Victor LP '71
Singles: 7-inch
DORE 3-5 71
FAMILY 3-5 71
LPs: 10/12-inch
DORE 5-10 71

BUOY, Danny
Singles: 7-inch
DATE LINE 5-10 60

BUOYS P&R '71
Singles: 7-inch
POLYDOR 3-5 73
RANSOM 5-10
SCEPTER 4-6 69-71
Picture Sleeves
SCEPTER 4-6 70
LPs: 10/12-inch
SCEPTER 10-15 71
Members: Jerry Hludzik; Bill Kelly; Chris Hanlon; Fran Brozena; Carl Siracuse.
Also see DAKOTA
Also see JERRY KELLY

BURBANK, Gary, & Band McNally / Tennessee Valley Authority
C&W/P&R '80
Singles: 7-inch
OVATION 3-5 80

BURBANK STATION C&W '88
Singles: 7-inch
PRAIRIE 3-4 88-89

BURCH, Bobby
Singles: 7-inch
REPRISE 3-5 72

BURCH, Doc
Singles: 7-inch
CHALLENGE (59038 "Catch a Little Moonbeam") 8-12 59

BURCH, Doug
Singles: 7-inch
KAY-BAR DANE 5-10

BURCH, Ray
LPs: 10/12-inch
YELLOWSTONE 8-10 72

BURCH, Vernon R&B '75
Singles: 12-inch
CHOCOLATE CITY 4-6 79-80
SPECTOR 4-6 81
Singles: 7-inch
CHOCOLATE CITY 3-4 78-80
COLUMBIA 3-4 77-78
SPECTOR 3-4 81-84
U.A. 3-5 75
LPs: 10/12-inch
CHOCOLATE CITY 5-10 79-80
COLUMBIA 8-10 77-78
SPECTOR 5-10 81-84
U.A. 8-10 74-76

BURCH SISTERS C&W '88
Singles: 7-inch
MERCURY 3-4 88-89
Members: Cindy Burch; Cathy Burch; Charlene Burch.
Also see TOMORROW'S WORLD

BURCHETT, Dave, & Mark Smith
Singles: 7-inch
BIRDIE 5-10

BURCHETTE, Wilburn
LPs: 10/12-inch
AMOS (7014 "Occult Concert") 75-100 71
BURCHETTE BROS (1 "Guitar Grimore") 40-60 73
BURCHETTE BROS (2 "Psychic Meditation") 40-60 74
BURCHETTE BROS (3 "The Godhead") 40-60 74
BURCHETTE BROS (4 "Trancendental Music for Meditation") 40-60 76
BURCHETTE BROS (7 "Mind Storm") 40-60 77
EBOS (0001 "Seven Gates of Transcendental Consciousness") 50-100 72

BURDEN, Billy
Singles: 7-inch
NSD 3-5 80

BURDEN, Ray
Singles: 7-inch
ADONIS (112 "Hot Rodder's Dream") 15-25 60
CULLMAN (6403 "That Kind of Carryin' On") 40-60 58

BURDEN LIFTERS
Singles: 7-inch
BIG CHANCE (202 "Farewell, Goodbye") 10-20

BURDETTE, Lew
Singles: 7-inch
DOT (15672 "Three Strikes and You're Out") 10-20 58

BURDON, Eric LP '74
(Eric Burdon Band)
Singles: 7-inch
CAPITOL 3-5 74
LPs: 10/12-inch
CAPITOL 8-10 74-75
LAX 5-10 81-84
VERVE 10-12 72
Also see ANIMALS

BURDON, Eric, & War P&R/LP '70
(With Sharon Scott)
Singles: 7-inch
ABC 3-5 76
CAPITOL 5-10 74-75
LIBERTY 3-5
MGM 5-10 70
Picture Sleeves
MGM 4-6 70
LPs: 10/12-inch
ABC 8-10 77
MGM (Except 4710) 10-15 70
MGM (4710 "Black Man's Burdon") 20-30 70
(Promotional issue only.)
Also see WAR

BURDON, Eric, & Jimmy Witherspoon
Singles: 7-inch
MGM 3-5 71
LPs: 10/12-inch
MGM 10-15 71
Also see BURDON, Eric
Also see WITHERSPOON, Jimmy

BURGAN, Debbie
Singles: 7-inch
A&M 3-5 75
Also see BURGANS

BURGAN, Ken
LPs: 10/12-inch
BLUE THUMB 8-10 74

BURGANDY RUNN
Singles: 7-inch
LAVETTE (5014 "Stop") 15-25 66

BURGANDYS
Singles: 7-inch
EXCLUSIVE (2281 "Ridin' Shotgun") 10-20 64

BURGANS
Singles: 7-inch
A&M 3-5 75
Member: Debbie Burgan
Also see BURGAN, Debbie

BURGESS, Dave
(With Chimes; with Buddy Cole Quartet; with Toppers)
Singles: 78 rpm
CHALLENGE 10-20 57
GILMAR 10-15 56
OKEH 10-15 53-55
TAMPA 10-15 55
Singles: 7-inch
CHALLENGE 10-20 57-59
GILMAR 10-20 56
OKEH 15-20 53-55
TAMPA 15-20 55
EPs: 7-inch
TOPS 10-20 56
(Not issued with cover. May have tracks by Neil Hunt, Norma Zimmer, Jerry Case, and the Lew Raymond Orchestra.)
LPs: 10/12-inch
TOPS 20-30 57
Also see CHAMPS
Also see DUPRE, Dave
Also see FLEAS
Also see TROPHIES

BURGESS, Dewayne, with Rhythm Group
Singles: 7-inch
BRAMLEY (103 "Moments to Recall") 100-200 50s

BURGESS, Frank C&W '88
Singles: 7-inch
TRUE 3-4 88-89

BURGESS, Leroy
Singles: 12-inch
SALSOUL 4-6 83

BURGESS, Richard James D&D '84
Singles: 12-inch
CAPITOL 4-6 84
Singles: 7-inch
CAPITOL 3-4 84
LPs: 10/12-inch
CAPITOL 5-10 84

BURGESS, Sonny
(With the Pacers; with King IV)
Singles: 78 rpm
SUN 50-100 56-57
Singles: 7-inch
ARA 4-8 67
PHILLIPS INT'L (3551 "Sadie's Back in Town") 20-30 59
RAZORBACK (120 "Mary Lou") 5-10 64
RAZORBACK (126 "School Days") 5-10 65
RAZORBACK (130 "Bamboo") 5-10 65
RAZORBACK (132 "Restless") 5-10 66
RAZORBACK (136 "Odessa") 5-10 66
ROLANDO 10-15 68
SUN (247 "We Wanna Boogie") 40-60 56
SUN (263 "Ain't Got a Thing") 15-25 57
SUN (285 "My Bucket's Got a Hole in It") 15-25 58
SUN (304 "Thunderbird") 15-25 58
TSBS 4-8 70
Members: Sonny Burgess; Bobby Crafford; Johnny Hubbard; Kern Kennedy.
Also see PACERS
Also see PERKINS, Carl / Sonny Burgess

BURGESS, Sonny, & Larry Donn
Singles: 7-inch
AD-BUR (100 "The Girl Next Door") 100-150 61
LPs: 10/12-inch
WHITE 8-12 80
Also see BURGESS, Sonny
Also see DONN, Larry

BURGESS, Wilma C&W '65
Singles: 7-inch
DECCA 3-6 64-70
SHANNON 3-5 73-75
U.A. 5-8 62
LPs: 10/12-inch
CORAL 5-10 73
DECCA 10-20 66-69
Also see LOGAN, Bud, & Wilma Burgess

BURGETT, Jim
(With the Make Believers)
Singles: 7-inch
COLUMBIA (41962 "Living Dead") 10-20 61
COLUMBIA (41962 "Living Dead") 20-30 61
(Compact 33.)
GO (6565 "Pick Up a Coupl'a of Records") 50-75
LAMA (7784 "Sugaree") 10-15
MGM 3-6 69
ORO (1502 "Live It Up") 25-50 60
ORO (1505 "Scene of the Crime") .25-50 60
LPs: 10/12-inch
WOLFGANG ("For the Swim Set") 30-40

BURGUNDY, Willie, Five
Singles: 7-inch
MGM 3-5 74
LPs: 10/12-inch
MGM 10-12 74

BURHAM, Buzz: see BURNAM, Buzz

BURK, Tommy
(With the Counts; Counts with "Vocal By Tommy Burk")
Singles: 7-inch
ATCO (6340 "You Better Move On") 10-20 65
H.I.P. (101 "Rainy Day Lovin' ") 20-30 64
NAT (100 "You'll Feel It Too") 25-50 62
NAT (101 "Stormy Weather") 25-50 63
(First issue.)

RICH-ROSE (1001 "Cute") 40-60 64
RICH-ROSE (1002 "You Took My Heart") 40-60 64
SMASH (1821 "Stormy Weather") 10-20 63
SOUTHERN ARTISTS (2026 "Without Me") 20-30 60s
Also see COUNTS

BURKE, Alan
LPs: 10/12-inch
AUDIO FIDELITY 10-12 67

BURKE, Aloha
Singles: 7-inch
COBBLESTONE 4-6

BURKE, Buddy
Singles: 7-inch
BULLSEYE (1002 "That Big Old Moon") 100-200 59

BURKE, Ceele R&B '43
Singles: 78 rpm
CAPITOL 10-15 43

BURKE, Cubie
Singles: 12-inch
RISSA CHRISSA 4-6 83
Also see FIVE STAIRSTEPS

BURKE, Dave
Singles: 7-inch
TRUMP 5-10 61

BURKE, Fiddlin' Frenchie C&W '74
(Fiddlin' Frenchie Bourque & Outlaws; Frenchie Bruke)
Singles: 7-inch
CHERRY 3-5 78
DELTA 3-4 81
20TH CENTURY 3-5 74-75
LPs: 10/12-inch
DELTA 5-10 80-82
20TH CENTURY 6-12 75
Also see BUSH, Johnny

BURKE, Keni R&B '81
Singles: 7-inch
DARK HORSE 3-5 77-78
RCA 3-4 81-82
LPs: 10/12-inch
DARK HORSE 8-10 77
RCA 5-10 81-82
Also see FIVE STAIRSTEPS

BURKE, Linda
Singles: 7-inch
SOFT 4-8 65

BURKE, Phyllis
Singles: 7-inch
ARCHER (1003 "Baby Sitter") 10-20

BURKE, Ron
Singles: 7-inch
POWER HOUSE 3-5 73

BURKE, Solomon P&R/R&B '61
Singles: 12-inch
SAVOY 4-6 84
Singles: 78 rpm
APOLLO 15-25 56-57
Singles: 7-inch
ABC/DUNHILL 3-5 74
AMHERST 3-5 78
APOLLO (500 "No Man Walks Alone") 15-25 56
APOLLO (505 "A Picture of You") ..15-25 56
APOLLO (511 "This Is It") 15-25 57
APOLLO (511 "My Heart Is a Chapel") 15-25 58
ATLANTIC 5-12 61-68
BELL 4-8 69-70
CHESS 3-5 75-77
DUNHILL 3-5 74
INFINITY 3-5 79
MGM 4-6 70-73
ODEON 4-6
PRIDE 3-5 72-73
SINGULAR 5-10 60
SOULTOWN (3001 "Bettin' on America") 3-5 81
EPs: 7-inch
ATLANTIC (SD-8109 "The Best of Solomon Burke") 10-20 65
(Stereo. Juke box issue only. Includes title strips.)
LPs: 10/12-inch
ABC/DUNHILL 10-12 74
APOLLO (498 "Solomon Burke") .60-100 62
ATLANTIC (8000 series) 25-45 62-64
ATLANTIC (8100 series) 15-30 65-68
(No W.B. logo on label.)
ATLANTIC (8100 series) 5-10 80s
(Has Warner Bros. logo on label.)
BELL 15-20 69
CHESS 8-10 75-76
CLARION 12-20 64
INFINITY 5-10 79
KENWOOD 12-20 64
MGM 10-15 71-72
PRIDE 8-12 73
ROUNDER 5-10 84
SAVOY 5-10 81-83
Session: Ray Charles Singers.
Also see CHARLES, Ray / Somomon Burke
Also see SOUL CLAN

BURKE, Solomon, & Lady Lee
Singles: 7-inch
PRIDE 3-5 73
Also see BURKE, Solomon

BURKE, Tommy: see BURK, Tommy

BURKE, Vinnie
Singles: 7-inch
ASTRO....5-10 60

BURKEY, Eddie
Singles: 7-inch
GEMCOR....4-8 65

BURKS, Donny
Singles: 7-inch
BRUNSWICK....3-5 77

BURKS, Gene
Singles: 7-inch
AROCK (1001 "Monkey Man")....10-20 63
AROCK (1006 "Shirley Jean")....10-20 64
CALLA (138 "You Got It")....8-12 67

BURLAND, Sascha, & Skip Jack Choir
Singles: 7-inch
COLUMBIA (42009 "Gorilla Walk")..8-10 61
RCA....4-8 63
Picture Sleeves
RCA....5-10 63
Also see NUTTY SQUIRRELS

BURLEY, Dan
(With His Skiffle Boys)
Singles: 78 rpm
ARKAY....10-20 47
CIRCLE....10-20 46
EXCLUSIVE....10-20 49

BURLINGTON EXPRESS
Singles: 7-inch
CAVERN (2207 "Memories")....20-30 60s

BURLISON, Paul
(Johnny Burnette's Rock & Roll Trio and Their Rockin' Friends from Memphis)
LPs: 10/12-inch
ROCK-A-BILLY (1001 "A Tribute to Johnny & Dorsey Burnette")....10-15 85
Members: Charlie Feathers, Eddie Bond, Malcolm Yelvington, Glenn Honeycutt, Jim Dickinson, Johnny Foster, Robert Geisley, Al Hobson, Tony Austin, Johnny Black, Marcus Van Story, J.M. Van Eaton and J.L. Smith.
Also see BOND, Eddie
Also see BURNETTE, Johnny, & Rock'n Roll Trio
Also see DICKINSON, Jim
Also see FEATHERS, Charlie
Also see HONEYCUTT, Glenn
Also see YELVINGTON, Malcolm

BURN, Alan
(With the Ushers)
Singles: 7-inch
ISLAND....4-8 64
MALA....4-8 65
TUESDAY (11 "Whirlpool")....15-25 67

BURNADETTES
Singles: 7-inch
DIVINITY (99007 "I'm Going Home")....15-25 60s

BURNAM, Buzz
(Buzz Burham)
Singles: 78 rpm
VIV (4000 "Mama Lou")....50-75 56
Singles: 7-inch
VIV (4000 "Mama Lou")....100-150 56

BURNETT, Carl, & Hustlers
Singles: 7-inch
CARMAX (102 "Sweet Memories")....25-50 65
Session: Barry White.
Also see LITTLE CAESAR & ROMANS
Also see WHITE, Barry

BURNETT, Carol LP '72
Singles: 7-inch
RCA....4-6 67
LPs: 10/12-inch
DECCA....15-25 61-64
COLUMBIA....8-12 71
RCA....10-15 67
TETRAGRAMMATON....8-12 69
VOCALION....8-12 68
Also see ANDREWS, Julie, & Carol Burnett

BURNETT, Frances
Singles: 7-inch
CORAL (62092 "Come to Me")....50-75 60
CORAL (62164 "Too Proud")....50-75 60
CORAL (62214 "She Was Taking My Baby")....50-75 60

BURNETT, Geraldine
Singles: 7-inch
RENO (171 "Poor Girl's Dream")....5-10 62

BURNETT, J. Henry
Singles: 7-inch
UNI....4-6 72
LPs: 10/12-inch
UNI....10-15 72
Also see BURNETT, T-Bone

BURNETT, T-Bone LP '83
(J. Henry Burnett)
Singles: 7-inch
W.B.....3-4 83
LPs: 10/12-inch
TAKOMA....5-10 80
W.B.....5-10 82-83
Also see BLACK TIE
Also see BURNETT, J. Henry
Also see LEGENDARY STARDUST COWBOY

BURNETTE, Billy C&W '79
(With Jawbone)
Singles: 7-inch
A&M....3-5 76
COLUMBIA....3-4 80-81
CURB....3-4 86
POLYDOR....3-5 79
W.B. (7300 series)....4-6 69
LPs: 10/12-inch
COLUMBIA....5-10 80-81
ENTRANCE....10-12 72
MCA/CURB....5-10 86
POLYDOR....5-10 79
Also see FLEETWOOD MAC

BURNETTE, Billy, & Christine McVie
Singles: 12-inch
MCA/CURB (17040 "It Ain't Over")....5-8 85
(Promotional issue only.)
Also see BURNETTE, Billy
Also see McVIE, Christine

BURNETTE, Billy Joe C&W '90
(Billy Burnette)
Singles: 7-inch
BADGER....3-4 90
DEVILLE (134 "Blue Misery")....8-12 65
GOLD STANDARD....3-5
GUSTO-STARDAY (167 "Welcome Home Elvis")....4-8 77
GUSTO-STARDAY (9009 "The Colonel and the King")....8-12 78
(Promotional issue only.)
K-ARK....3-5 70
MAGIC LAMP (613 "Miss Ping Pong")....10-15 65
PD....3-5
PALOMINO....3-5
TEDDY BEAR....4-6 77
TELEMEDIA....3-4 81
W.B.....4-8 69
LPs: 10/12-inch
GUSTO....10-20 77
Also see BARNETT, Billy
Also see LEGENDS

BURNETTE, Dorsey P&R '60
Singles: 78 rpm
ABBOTT....15-25 56
Singles: 7-inch
ABBOTT (188 "Devil's Queen")....25-50 56
ABBOTT (190 "At a Distance")....25-50 56
CALLIOPE....3-5 77
CAPITOL....3-5 71-74
CEE-JAM (16 "Bertha-Lou")....50-100 57
COLLECTABLES....3-4 81
CONDOR....4-6 70
DOT (16230 "Raining in My Heart")....10-15 61
DOT (16265 "Sad Boy")....10-15 61
ELEKTRA....3-5 79-80
ERA....8-15 60-69
HAPPY TIGER....4-6 70
HICKORY....4-8 67
IMPERIAL (5561 "Try")....15-25 59
IMPERIAL (5597 "Misery")....15-25 59
IMPERIAL (5668 "Your Love")....15-25 60
IMPERIAL (5987 "Circle Rock")....10-15 63
LIBERTY (56087 "The Greatest Love")....5-10 69
MC....3-5 77
MEL-O-DY (113 "Little Acorn")....10-15 64
MEL-O-DY (116 "Jimmy Brown")....10-15 64
MEL-O-DY (118 "Ever Since the World Began")....10-15 64
MELODYLAND....3-5 75-76
MERRI (206 "Lucy Darling")....8-12 60
MOVIE STAR....4-8
MUSIC FACTORY....4-8 68
REPRISE....10-20 62-63
SMASH....5-10 66
SURF (5019 "Bertha Lou")....150-200 57
U.S. NAVY ("Be a Navy Man")....10-20 60s
(U.S. Navy recruiting promotional issue.)
Picture Sleeves
ERA (3033 "The River and the Mountain")....15-25 61
REPRISE (246 "4 for Texas")....20-40 63
U.S. NAVY ("Be a Navy Man")....15-25 60s
(U.S. Navy recruiting promotional issue.)
LPs: 10/12-inch
BUCKBOARD (1024 "Dorsey")....8-10
CALLIOPE....8-10 77
CAPITOL....10-12 72-73
DOT (3456 "Dorsey Burnette Sings")....20-40 63
(Monaural.)
DOT (25456 "Dorsey Burnette Sings")....25-50 63
(Stereo.)
ERA (EL-102 "Tall Oak Tree")....40-80 60
(Monaural.)
ERA (ES-102 "Tall Oak Tree")....100-150 60
(Stereo.)
ERA (800 series)....15-20 69
GUSTO....5-10 79
TRIP....8-12 74
Also see BURNETTE, Johnny & Dorsey

BURNETTE, Hank C.
Singles: 7-inch
SEA GULL....3-6 72
LPs: 10/12-inch
SUN....5-10 80

BURNETTE, J. Henry
Singles: 7-inch
UNI....3-5 72

BURNETTE, Jan
Singles: 7-inch
KAPP....4-8 63

BURNETTE, Johnny P&R '60
(With the Rock'n Roll Trio)
Singles: 78 rpm
CORAL....40-60 56-57
VON (106 "Go Mule Go")....100-150 54
Singles: 7-inch
CAPITOL (5023 "All Week Long")..10-15 63
CAPITOL (5114 "The Opposite")...10-15 64
CAPITOL (5176 "Sweet Suzie")....10-15 64
CHANCELLOR (1116 "I Wanna Thank You Folks")....10-20 62
CHANCELLOR (1129 "Remember Me")....10-20 62
CORAL (61651 "Tear It Up")....100-200 56
CORAL (61675 "Midnight Train")....100-200 56
CORAL (61719 "Honey Hush")..100-200 56
CORAL (61758 "Lonesome Train")....100-200 56
CORAL (61829 "Eager Beaver Baby")....100-200 57
CORAL (61869 "Drinkin' Wine Spo-Dee-O-Dee")....100-200 57
CORAL (61918 "Rock Billy Boogie")....100-200 57
FREEDOM (44001 "I'm Restless") 30-50 58
FREEDOM (44011 "Gumbo")....30-50 59
FREEDOM (44017 "Sweet Baby Doll")....30-50 59
LIBERTY....15-25 60
(Green and silver label.)
LIBERTY....10-15 60-62
(Multi-color label.)
LIBERTY ALL-TIME HITS....3-5
MAGIC LAMP (515 "Bigger Man") 20-30 64
SAHARA (512 "Fountain of Love")...8-12 64
U.A.....3-5 84
VON (106 "Go Mule Go")....300-600 54
Picture Sleeves
LIBERTY (55285 "You're Sixteen") 15-20 60
LIBERTY (55298 "Little Boy Sad") 15-20 61
LIBERTY (55318 "Big, Big World") 15-20 61
MAGIC LAMP (515 "Bigger Man")....75-100 64
EPs: 7-inch
LIBERTY (1004 "Dreamin'")....40-60 60
LIBERTY (1011 "Johnny Burnette's Hits")....50-75 61
LPs: 10/12-inch
CORAL (57080 "Johnny Burnette and the Rock'n Roll Trio")....3000-4000 56
(Counterfeits can be identified by their lack of printing on the spine and hand-etched identification numbers in the trail-off. Originals have the numbers mechanically stamped. Canadian issues are worth at least as much as U.S. issues.)
LIBERTY (3179 "Dreamin'")....30-40 60
(Monaural.)
LIBERTY (3183 "Johnny Burnette")....30-40 61
(Monaural.)
LIBERTY (3190 "Johnny Burnette Sings")....30-40 61
(Monaural.)
LIBERTY (3206 "Johnny Burnette's Hits and Other Favorites")....30-40 62
(Monaural.)
LIBERTY (3255 "Roses Are Red") 30-40 62
(Monaural.)
LIBERTY (3389 "The Johnny Burnette Story")....40-50 64
(Monaural.)
LIBERTY (7179 "Dreamin'")....40-60 60
(Stereo.)
LIBERTY (7183 "Johnny Burnette")....40-50 61
(Stereo.)
LIBERTY (7190 "Johnny Burnette Sings")....40-50 61
(Stereo.)
LIBERTY (7206 "Johnny Burnette's Hits and Other Favorites")....40-50 62
(Stereo. Black & rainbow colored label with gold & white logo.)
LIBERTY (7206 "Johnny Burnette's Hits and Other Favorites")....15-25 66
(Stereo. Black & rainbow label with box style logo.)
LIBERTY (7206 "Johnny Burnette's Hits and Other Favorites")....5-10 91
(Stereo. Peach and coral colored label.)
LIBERTY (7255 "Roses Are Red") 40-50 62
(Stereo.)
LIBERTY (7389 "The Johnny Burnette Story")....50-60 64
(Stereo.)
LIBERTY (7300 series)....25-30 63
LIBERTY (10000 series)....5-10 81
MCA....5-10 82
SOLID SMOKE (Black vinyl)....5-10 78-80
SOLID SMOKE (Colored vinyl)....10-15 78
SUNSET....15-25 67
U.A.....10-15 75
Members (Trio): Johnny Burnette; Dorsey Burnette; Paul Burlison.
Also see BURLISON, Paul
Also see BURNETTE, Dorsey
Also see BURNETTE, Johnny
Also see VEE, Bobby / Johnny Burnette / Ventures / Fleetwoods

BURNETTE, Johnny & Dorsey
(Burnette Brothers)
Singles: 7-inch
CORAL (62190 "Blues Stay Away from Me")....25-35 60
IMPERIAL (5509 "Warm Love")....40-60 58
REPRISE (20153 "Hey Sue")....10-15 63
Also see BURNETTE, Dorsey
Also see BURNETTE, Johnny
Also see SHAMROCKS
Also see TEXANS

BURNETTE, Linda
Singles: 7-inch
PERRY (5 "Rattle Bones Rock")....100-150 58

BURNETTE, Randy, & Rocky Burnette
Singles: 7-inch
BURNETTE....3-4 90
Picture Sleeves
BURNETTE....3-4 90

BURNETTE, Rocky P&R/LP '80
(With the Rock 'N Roll Trio)
Singles: 7-inch
EMI AMERICA....3-5 80
LPs: 10/12-inch
EMI AMERICA....5-10 80-82
GOODS....5-10 82
KYD....5-10 83
Also see BURNETTE, Randy, & Rocky Burnette

BURNEY, Mac, & Four Jacks
Singles: 78 rpm
ALADDIN....100-150 54
HOLLYWOOD....50-100 56
Singles: 7-inch
ALADDIN (3274 "Tired of Your Sexy Ways")....300-500 55
HOLLYWOOD (1058 "Let Me Get Next to You")....200-300 56
Also see FOUR JACKS

BURNING BUSH
Singles: 7-inch
MERCURY (72657 "Keep on Burning")....10-15 67

BURNING EMOTIONS
(Burning Emotion)
Singles: 7-inch
ABC....4-8 69
BANG (553 "New World")....4-8 68

BURNING ROME
Singles: 7-inch
A&M....3-4 82
LPs: 10/12-inch
A&M....5-10 82

BURNING SENSATIONS LP '83
Singles: 7-inch
CAPITOL....3-4 83
LPs: 10/12-inch
CAPITOL....5-10 83

BURNING SLICKS
Singles: 7-inch
BATTLE (45926 "Midnight Drag")..10-15 63
RIVERSIDE (4571 "Midnight Drag")....15-25 63

BURNING SPEARS
LPs: 10/12-inch
ISLAND....5-10 76-83
MANGO....5-10 76-77
Members: Delroy Hines; Winston Rodney; Rupert Willington.

BURNS, Becky
Singles: 7-inch
VANDAN....4-8 64

BURNS, Brenda
Singles: 7-inch
CAVALCADE INT'L....3-6 70

BURNS, Brent C&W '78
Singles: 7-inch
PANTHEON DESERT....3-5 78

BURNS, Eddie
Singles: 78 rpm
CHESS....15-25 57
DELUXE....40-60 52
JVB....25-50 57
Singles: 7-inch
CHESS (1672 "Treat Me Like I Treat You")....20-30 57
DELUXE (6024 "Hello Miss Jessie Lee")....100-150 52
HARVEY (111 "Orange Driver")....50-75 62
HARVEY (115 "The Thing to Do") 20-30 62
HARVEY (118 "Orange Driver")....20-30 62
JVB (82 "Treat Me Like I Treat You")....50-75 57
RED BIRD....3-4 83
VON....4-8 65
Also see BIG ED & His Combo
Also see GAYE, Marvin
Also see HOOKER, John Lee / Eddie Kirkland / Eddie Burns / Sylvester Cotton
Also see PICKENS, Slim
Also see SWING BROTHERS

BURNS, George P&R/C&W/LP '80
Singles: 7-inch
MERCURY....3-4 80-81
Picture Sleeves
MERCURY....3-4 80
EPs: 7-inch
COLPIX....5-10 60s
LPs: 10/12-inch
BUDDAH....6-10 72
MERCURY....5-10 80
PRIDE....5-10
Also see MARTIN, Dean

BURNS, George, & Gracie Allen P&R '33
Singles: 78 rpm
COLUMBIA....10-20 33
LPs: 10/12-inch
MARK 56....8-15
Also see BURNS, George

BURNS, Hughie C&W '80
Singles: 7-inch
C-S-I....3-4 80

BURNS, Jackie
(With the Bo-Bells)
Singles: 7-inch
CROSBY....5-10 62
DEL-FI (4102 "You Are My Dream")....10-15 58
MGM....5-10 63

BURNS, Jackie C&W '69
Singles: 7-inch
HONOR BRIGADE....3-6 69
JMI....3-5 72

BURNS, Jimmy
Singles: 78 rpm
COMBO....15-25 53
Singles: 7-inch
COMBO (28 "Nervous")....35-50 53

BURNS, Jimmy
(Jimmy & the Epics)
Singles: 7-inch
ERICA (02 "I Really Love You").200-300
MINIT....3-5 70
TIP TOP (14 "You're Gonna Miss Me")....15-25
(At least one source shows this number as 2013. We don't know yet who's right.)

BURNS, Linda
Singles: 7-inch
TY-TEX (121 "The Reason Why")..10-20 60s

BURNS, Lisa
Singles: 7-inch
HUMAN....3-4 80

BURNS, Mary
Singles: 7-inch
MCA....3-4 80
LPs: 10/12-inch
MCA....5-10 80

BURNS, Randy
(With the Sky Dog Band)
Singles: 7-inch
MERCURY....3-5 71
POLYDOR....3-5 72
LPs: 10/12-inch
ESP....10-20 66-70
MERCURY....10-15 71
POLYDOR....10-12 72-73

BURNS, Roy
(With the Dick Grove Band)
LPs: 10/12-inch
FPM....10-15 73

BURNS, Sonny
Singles: 78 rpm
STARDAY....8-12 54
Singles: 7-inch
STARDAY....15-25 54

BURNSIDE, R.L.
Singles: 7-inch
HIGH WATER....3-4 84

BURNT SUITE
LPs: 10/12-inch
BJW (9 "Burnt Suite")....100-150 68

BURNT TOAST & COFFEE
Singles: 7-inch
MCWT (1 "I Love You Girl")....10-15

BURR, Francis
Singles: 7-inch
SALEM....8-12

BURRAGE, Harold R&B '65
(Harold Barrage)
Singles: 78 rpm
ALADDIN....15-25 52
COBRA....15-25 56-57
DECCA....15-25 50
STATES....25-50 54
Singles: 7-inch
ALADDIN (3194 "Sweet Brown Gal")....25-50 52
COBRA....20-40 56-58
DECCA (48175 "Hi-Yo")....30-60 50
FOXY....8-12 62
M-PAC....5-10 62-65
PASO....8-12 61
STATES (144 "Feel So Fine")....50-100 54
(Black vinyl.)
STATES (144 "Feel So Fine")...100-200 50
(Red vinyl.)
VEE JAY....10-20 60
VIVID....4-8 64

BURRELL R&B '88
Singles: 7-inch
VIRGIN....3-4 88

BURRELL, Boz: see BOZ

BURRELL, Carl
Singles: 7-inch
ARRAWAK....4-8 64

BURRELL, Joe
Singles: 7-inch
JUNIOR....4-8 64

BURRELL, Kenny LP '63
Singles: 7-inch
CADET....4-8 66
LPs: 10/12-inch
CADET....10-20 66
VERVE....10-15 68

BURRELL, Kenny, & Jimmy Smith LP '63
LPs: 10/12-inch
VERVE...10-20 66-68
Also see BURRELL, Kenny
Also see SMITH, Jimmy

BURRIS, Daisy
Singles: 7-inch
PORT (3007 "Take the Same Thing")...15-25 65

BURRIS, Warren
Singles: 7-inch
ECLIPSE...10-20

BURRIS, Warren G. & Michelle
Singles: 12-inch
BECKET...4-6 84
Also see BURRIS, Warren

BURRITO BROTHERS C&W '81
Singles: 7-inch
CURB...3-4 81-84
EPIC...3-4 81
LPs: 10/12-inch
A&M...8-10 80
CURB...5-10 81-82
Members: Pete Battin; Pete Kleinow; Greg Harris; Ed Ponder; Gib Guilbeau; John Beland.
Also see BATTIN, Pete
Also see FLYING BURRITO BROTHERS
Also see SWAMPWATER

BURROUGHS, William
LPs: 10/12-inch
ESP (1050 "Call Me Burroughs")...20-40

BURROWS, Tony P&R '70
Singles: 7-inch
BELL...4-6 70-71
Also see BROTHERHOOD of MAN
Also see DOMINO
Also see EDISON LIGHTHOUSE
Also see FIRST CLASS
Also see FLOWERPOT MEN
Also see PIPKINS
Also see WHITE PLAINS

BURTON, John: see JONES, John "Boris"

BURRUS, Terry & Transe
Singles: 7-inch
ARISTA...3-4 83

BURT, Tom
Singles: 7-inch
CAMEO...4-8 65

BURT, Wanda
(With the Creschendos)
Singles: 7-inch
MUSIC CITY (840 "Scheming")...50-75 61
(Black vinyl.)
MUSIC CITY (840 "Scheming")..100-150 61
(Colored vinyl.)
Also see CRESCHENDOS

BURT & CHARLIE
Singles: 7-inch
KOOL...5-10 59

BURTNICK, Glen P&R/LP '87
Singles: 7-inch
A&M...3-4 87
Picture Sleeves
A&M...3-4 87
LPs: 10/12-inch
A&M...5-10 87

BURTON, Allen
Singles: 7-inch
ABC...3-5 74

BURTON, Ben
Singles: 78 rpm
MODERN...10-20 54
Singles: 7-inch
MODERN...20-30 54

BURTON, Bob
Singles: 78 rpm
MAR-VEL...20-50 53
Singles: 7-inch
MAR-VEL (951 "Boogie Woogie Baby of Mine")...75-125 53
MAR-VEL (952 "Don't Cry Little Girl")...40-60 55
MAR-VEL (953 "Tired of Rocking")...75-125 56

BURTON, Bob, & Ginny Carter
Singles: 78 rpm
MAR-VEL...20-40 53
Singles: 7-inch
MAR-VEL (950 "40 Acres of My Heart")...35-50 53
(Black vinyl.)
MAR-VEL (950 "40 Acres of My Heart")...75-100 53
(Colored vinyl.)
Also see BURTON, Bob

BURTON, Debbie
Singles: 7-inch
CAPITOL...4-8 66

BURTON, James
(Jimmy Burton)
Singles: 7-inch
GUYDEN...3-6 72
MIRAMAR (108 "Jimmy's Blues")...20-30 65
ROMAN (101 "Christmas Party")...20-30 65
(Colored vinyl. Music is *Jimmy's Blues* [Miramar 108] reworked.)
TNT (187 "Wild River")...30-40 61
LPs: 10/12-inch
A&M (4293 "James Burton")...15-20 71
Also see ANDERSON, Bill / Jimmie Burton
Also see BENAY, Ben
Also see BURTON, James, & Ralph Mooney
Also see DENVER, John
Also see DOBRO, Jimmie
Also see EDDY, Duane
Also see HAGGARD, Merle
Also see HARRIS, Emmylou
Also see HAWKINS, Dale
Also see HILLMAN, Chris
Also see JENNINGS, Waylon
Also see JIM & JOE
Also see LONGBRANCH PENNYWHISTLE
Also see NELSON, Ricky
Also see PRESLEY, Elvis

BURTON, James, & Ralph Mooney
Singles: 7-inch
CAPITOL (2140 "Corn Pickin' ")...10-15 68
LPs: 10/12-inch
CAPITOL (2822 "Corn Pickin' and Slick Slidin' ")...50-100 68
Also see BURTON, James
Also see MOONEY, Ralph

BURTON, Jenny R&B/D&D '83
Singles: 12-inch
ATLANTIC...4-6 83-85
Singles: 7-inch
ATLANTIC...3-4 83-86
LPs: 10/12-inch
ATLANTIC...5-10 83-85
Also see C-BANK

BURTON, Jenny, & Patrick Jude P&R '84
Singles: 7-inch
ATLANTIC...3-4 84
Picture Sleeves
ATLANTIC...3-4 84
Also see BURTON, Jenny

BURTON, Johnny
Singles: 7-inch
BROADWAY...8-12

BURTON, Lori
Singles: 7-inch
COLUMBIA...3-5 71
MERCURY...4-8 67
ROULETTE...4-8 65
LPs: 10/12-inch
MERCURY...10-20 67

BURTON, Michael
Singles: 7-inch
TURBO...4-8

BURTON, Richard P&R '65
Singles: 7-inch
MGM...4-6 65

BURTON, Ronnie
Singles: 7-inch
M&M...3-6 68

BURTON, Scott
Singles: 7-inch
BIGTOP (3084 "Nashville Express")...10-20 61

BURTON, Ward, & Music Men Inc.
Singles: 7-inch
PANTHER (1 "Salty Dog")...15-25 60s
Also see BURTON, Willard

BURTON, Wendy
Singles: 7-inch
COLUMBIA...4-8 62

BURTON, Willard
(Willard Burton & Funky Four; Ward Burton)
Singles: 7-inch
CAPITOL...3-5 71
PANTHER (5 "Sweet Temptation")...10-20 60s
PARADISE (1018 "The Freeze")...10-20 60s
PEACOCK...10-20 60-62
MONEY...3-5 76
Also see BURTON, Ward, & Music Men Inc.
Also see PIANO SLIM

BURTON & CUNICO
Singles: 7-inch
FAMILY...3-5 72
LPs: 10/12-inch
PARAMOUNT...10-15 71

BUS BOYS LP '80
Singles: 7-inch
ARISTA...3-4 80-84
LPs: 10/12-inch
ARISTA...5-10 80-82
Members: Gus Loundermon; Brian O'Neal; Kevin O'Neal; Michael Jones; Victor Johnson; Steve Felix.

BUSBEE, Buford
(With the Epitomes)
Singles: 7-inch
DEE DEE...8-12 59
DORE...5-10 60-61

BUSBY, Buzz
Singles: 7-inch
EMPIRE (507 "Pretty Polly")...10-20 58

BUSBY, Jay
Singles: 7-inch
BETHLEHEM...10-20 64

BUSBY, Johnny
Singles: 7-inch
TALENT...5-10 60

BUSBY, Wayne
Singles: 7-inch
EMPIRE (506 "Goin' Back to Dixie")...50-100 58
OTT (201 "Goin' Back to Dixie")...50-100 58

BUSCH, Lou, Orchestra P&R '55
Singles: 78 rpm
CAPITOL...3-5 55-56
Singles: 7-inch
CAPITOL...4-8 55-56
Also see CARR, Joe "Fingers"

BUSCHER, Dick, & Cliches
(Dick Busher)
Singles: 7-inch
CUCA (1040 "Outlaw")...10-20 61
CUCA (1054 "Two Hearts in Love")...10-20 61
CUCA (1077 "I Wonder Why")...10-20 62
CUCA (1105 "Sixteen Tons")...10-20 62
CUCA (1168 "Baby Come on Home")...10-20 64
CUCA (1235 "Don't Say You're Sorry")...10-15 65
Members: Nick White; Ton Weig; Harry Bluett; Benny Bryson; Denny Tranel; Terry William; Joe Huseman.
Also see CLICHES

BUSEY, Gary
Singles: 7-inch
EPIC/AMERICAN INT'L (50607 "Clear Lake Medley")...4-8 78
Also see CARP

BUSH
Singles: 7-inch
HIBACK (102 "Got Love if You Want It")...10-20 65
HIBACK (104 "To Die Alone")...10-20 66
HIBACK (108 "Sad & Lonely")...10-20 66
HIBACK (110 "Who Killed the Ice Cream Man")...10-20 66
Picture Sleeves
HIBACK (102 "Got Love if You Want It")...20-30 65

BUSH
Singles: 7-inch
DUNHILL...4-6 70
LPs: 10/12-inch
DUNHILL...10-15 70

BUSH, Dick
(Donnie Brooks)
Singles: 7-inch
ERA (1067 "Hollywood Party")...30-40 58
Also see BROOKS, Donnie

BUSH, Eddie
Singles: 7-inch
JAXON (503 "Little Darling")...50-75 57
PHILLIPS INT'L (3558 "Baby, I Don't Care")...15-20 60

BUSH, Johnny C&W '67
(With Bill Freeman & His Texas Plainsmen)
Singles: 7-inch
ALLSTAR (7166 "In My World All Alone")...100-125 57
ALLSTAR (7172 "Your Kind of Love")...75-100 57
DELTA...3-4 81-82
GUSTO...3-5 78
MILLION...3-6 72
NEW STAR...4-6 60s
RCA...3-5 72-74
STOP...4-8 67-71
WHISKEY RIVER...3-5 79
LPs: 10/12-inch
BUCKBOARD...5-10
DELTA...10-15 80-83
MILLION...15-25 72
PICKWICK...5-10 70s
PICKWICK/HILLTOP...10-15
POWER PAK...5-10 74
RCA...10-15 73
STOP...10-20 68-72
WHISKEY RIVER...15-20
Session: Fiddlin' Frenchie Burke.
Also see BURKE, Fiddlin' Frenchie
Also see NELSON, Willie
Also see PRICE, Ray
Also see SOME of CHET'S FRIENDS

BUSH, Kate P&R '79
Singles: 12-inch
EMI AMERICA...4-6 85-86
Singles: 7-inch
COLUMBIA...3-4 89
EMI AMERICA (8000 series)...3-8 78-86
EMI AMERICA (9605 "Hounds of Love")...8-10 85
(Long version/Short version. Promotional issue only.)
EMI AMERICA (EMR-20490 "Them Heavy People")...25-50
(Promotional issue only.)
GEFFEN...3-4 87
HARVEST...5-8 78-79
Picture Sleeves
EMI AMERICA (8285 "Running Up That Hill")...4-6 85
EMI AMERICA (8302 "Hounds of Love")...4-6 85
EMI AMERICA (EMR-20490 "Them Heavy People")...25-50
(Promotional issue only.)
GEFFEN...3-4 87
HARVEST...10-15 78
LPs: 10/12-inch
COLUMBIA...5-10 89
EMI AMERICA...6-12 78-86
HARVEST...10-15 78
Also see GABRIEL, Peter, & Kate Bush
Also see SUN FERRY AID

BUSH, Little David
(David Ruffin)
Singles: 7-inch
VEGA (1002 "You and I")...150-200 59
Also see RUFFIN, David

BUSH, Oliver
Singles: 7-inch
GAMBLE...4-6
JUBILEE...5-8 67

BUSH, Stan
Singles: 7-inch
COLUMBIA...3-4 84
LPs: 10/12-inch
COLUMBIA...5-10 83

BUSH, Tommy
Singles: 7-inch
RIKA (108 "I Like It")...50-75
SPECIALTY...3-5 71-72

BUSH BOYS
Singles: 7-inch
CAPITOL...5-10 59

BUSHER, Dick: see BUSCHER, Dick

BUSHKIN, Joe LP '56
LPs: 10/12-inch
CAPITOL...20-30 56
REPRISE...10-20 63

BUSHMEN
Singles: 7-inch
DIMENSION (1049 "Baby")...20-30 65
SMASH (2054 "Friends and Lovers Forever")...5-10 66

BUSKIN, David
Singles: 7-inch
CAPITOL...3-5 70
EPIC...3-5 71-72
Picture Sleeves
EPIC...3-5 71
LPs: 10/12-inch
EPIC...10-15 72

BUSKIRK, Kenny
Singles: 7-inch
COWTOWN...4-8

BUSKIRK, Paul, & His Little Men (Featuring Hugh Nelson)
Singles: 7-inch
R (502 "Nite Life")...50-100 64
(Selection number not known. Last edition we showed 1959 as release year. We've been told to change it to '64. Hopefully that is correct.)
Members: Willie Hugh Nelson; Paul Buskirk; Dick Shannon.
Also see NELSON, Willie

BUSKIRK, Ronny
Singles: 7-inch
COLUMBIA...3-6 69

BUSS
Singles: 78 rpm
ONYX...10-15 57
Singles: 7-inch
ONYX...10-15 57

BUSSCHER, Pam
Singles: 7-inch
FENTON...15-25 68

BUSSEY, George
(George Bussey Experience)
Singles: 7-inch
ATLANTIC...3-4 79
LPs: 10/12-inch
ATLANTIC...5-10 79

BUSSY, Terry
Singles: 7-inch
JAZZMAR (103 "How Could You")...250-500 57

BUSTER & EDDIE
Singles: 7-inch
CLASS (1518 "Can't Be Still")...50-75 66

BUSTER & JAMES
Singles: 7-inch
CEE JAM...4-8

BUSTERS P&R '63
Singles: 7-inch
ARLEN (735 "Bust Out")...10-20 63
ARLEN (740 "All American Surfer")...10-20 63
ARLEN (745 "Heartaches")...10-20 64
Members: Jack Baker; Fran Parda; Rick LaFrenier; Richard Eriksen; Tink Hermanson.
Also see BOLD
Also see COLE, Fred E.
Also see TROPHIES

BUSY BODY
LPs: 10/12-inch
LIZ-DE...8-10 74

BUSYBODIES
Singles: 7-inch
DIAL...4-8 65

BUTALA, Tony
Singles: 7-inch
CAPITOL...3-5 73
LUTE...8-12
TOPIC...10-15 59
Also see LETTERMEN

BUTANES P&R '61
Singles: 7-inch
ENRICA...10-20 61

BUTCH, Peggy, & Little John
Singles: 7-inch
OLD TOWN...4-8 64

BUTCH, Sam, & Station Band
Singles: 12-inch
PRIVATE I...4-6 85
Singles: 7-inch
PRIVATE I...3-4 85

BUTCH GREASER & HOODS
Singles: 7-inch
TOILET (7135 "Teenager with V.D.")...20-25 60s

BUTCHER, Jon P&R '83
(John Butcher Axis)
Singles: 7-inch
CAPITOL...3-4 85-89
POLYDOR...3-4 83-84
Picture Sleeves
CAPITOL...3-4 85-87
LPs: 10/12-inch
CAPITOL...5-10 85-89
POLYDOR...5-10 83-84
Members: Jon Butcher; Thom Gimbell; Derek Blevins; Bob Jefferies.

BUTCHERS
Singles: 7-inch
NOTOWN ("A Hardship")...3-5 85
(No selection number used. Colored vinyl.)

BUTERA, Sam
(With the Witnesses)
Singles: 78 rpm
CADENCE...5-10 56
GROOVE...5-10 54-55
PREP (105 "10 Little Women")...10-15 57
RCA...5-10 53
Singles: 7-inch
CADENCE...10-20 56
CAPITOL (Except 4862)...5-10 58-62
CAPITOL (4862 "Later Baby, Later")...15-20 62
DOT...8-12 59-62
GROOVE...10-15 54-55
PREP (105 "10 Little Women")...20-40 57
PRIMA...3-5 63
RCA...10-20 53
EPs: 7-inch
CAPITOL...10-20 58
"X"...15-25 54
LPs: 10/12-inch
CAPITOL...20-30 58-62
DOT...15-25 60-62
PREP...5-10 84
PRIMA...15-20 64
Also see PRIMA, Louis
Also see DAVIS, Sammy, Jr., & Sam Butera

BUTLER, Andy
Singles: 7-inch
TANGERINE (988 "Coming Apart at the Seams")...10-20 68

BUTLER, Angeline
Singles: 7-inch
COBURT...3-5 70
LPs: 10/12-inch
COBURT...10-12 70

BUTLER, Anthony, & Invaders
Singles: 7-inch
BIG DEAL...3-6 69

BUTLER, Art
Singles: 7-inch
EPIC...4-8 67
Also see JAYNETTS

BUTLER, B.B.
(Bee Bee Butler)
Singles: 7-inch
BARRY...4-8 64
SMC...3-6 71

BUTLER, Billy P&R/R&B '65
(With the Chanters; with Infinity; with Enchanters)
Singles: 7-inch
BRUNSWICK...6-12 66-68
CURTOM...3-5 76
OKEH...4-8 63-66
MEMPHIS...3-5 71
OKEH (Except 7207)...6-12 63-66
OKEH (7207 "My Sweet Woman")...10-20
PRIDE...3-5 72-73
LPs: 10/12-inch
EDSEL...5-10 86
OKEH...15-20 66
PRESTIGE...10-15 69-70
PRIDE...10-12 73
Members: Billy Butler; Earl Batts; Jess Tillman; Larry Wade; Phyllis Know.
Also see CHANTERS
Also see INFINITY

BUTLER, Bobby "Sofine" C&W '76
Singles: 7-inch
IBC...3-5 79
PANTHEON DESERT...3-5 76

BUTLER, Buddy
(Buddy Butler Band)
Singles: 7-inch
VERRO...5-10 60

BUTLER, Buz
Singles: 78 rpm
MERCURY...5-8

BUTLER, Carl C&W '61
Singles: 78 rpm
CAPITOL 5-10 51-52
OKEH 4-8 54-55
Singles: 7-inch
CAPITOL 8-12 51-52
COLUMBIA 4-8 59-63
OKEH 6-10 54-55
LPs: 10/12-inch
COLUMBIA 10-20 63
HARMONY 8-15 66-71

BUTLER, Carl & Pearl C&W '62
Singles: 7-inch
COLUMBIA 4-8 62-69
LPs: 10/12-inch
CMH 5-10 80
CHART 3-5 71
COLUMBIA 10-20 64-70
HARMONY 8-12 72
PEDACA 5-10
Also see BUTLER, Carl
Also see BUTLER, Pearl

BUTLER, Champ P&R '51
Singles: 78 rpm
COLUMBIA 3-8 50-54
CORAL 3-8 55-56
Singles: 7-inch
COLUMBIA 5-10 50-54
CORAL 5-10 55-56
GILLETTE 4-6 62
VISCOUNT 5-10 59
EPs: 7-inch
COLUMBIA 8-15 53
LPs: 10/12-inch
GILLETTE 10-20 62

BUTLER, Champ, & George Cates
Singles: 78 rpm
CORAL 3-5 55
Singles: 7-inch
CORAL 4-8 55
Also see BUTLER, Champ
Also see CATES, George

BUTLER, Cliff
(With the Doves; with Lovers; with His Band)
Singles: 78 rpm
KIT (885 "Rent's Too High") 10-20 55
STATES (123 "When You Love") 50-75 53
Singles: 7-inch
EXCELLO (2126 "Lover's Plea") 20-30 58
FAVORITE (600) 50-100
(Title not known.)
FRANTIC (801 "I Can't Believe") 100-200 50s
KIT (885 "Rent's Too High") 25-50 55
NASCO (6003 "My Mood") 20-30 57
STATES (123 "When You Love") 300-400 53
(Red vinyl.)

BUTLER, Davy
Singles: 7-inch
JCP (1032 "If I Had a Girl") 10-20 64
JCP (1044 "She's a Baby") 10-20 65

BUTLER, Daws
(As Huckleberry Hound)
Singles: 7-inch
MERRI 5-10 64
Picture Sleeves
MERRI 10-20 64
Also see BACKUS, Jim, & Daws Butler
Also see BARRY, Dave, & Daws Butler

BUTLER, Daws, & Don Messick
LPs: 10/12-inch
COLPIX (208 "Mr. Jinks, Pixie & Dixie") 25-45 61
Also see BUTLER, Daws

BUTLER, Freddy
LPs: 10/12-inch
KAPP 10-20 67

BUTLER, Gene
Singles: 7-inch
ZODIAC (333 "L.C.") 10-20 63

BUTLER, George "Wild Child"
Singles: 7-inch
JEWEL 4-8 67-68
LPs: 10/12-inch
MERCURY 10-15 70
ROOTS 8-10 77

BUTLER, Howie, & Reflections
Singles: 7-inch
GAITY (6017 "Treasure of Love") 25-50 60

BUTLER, Jerry P&R/R&B '58
(With the Impressions; with Riley Hampton's Orchestra)
Singles: 78 rpm
ABNER (1013 "For Your Precious Love") 50-100 58
ABNER (1024 "Lost") 75-125 59
FALCON (1013 "For Your Precious Love") 50-100 58
Singles: 7-inch
ABNER (1013 "For Your Precious Love") 25-50 58
ABNER (1024 "Lost") 15-25 59
ABNER (1028 "Hold Me Darling") 15-25 59
ABNER (1030 "I Was Wrong") 15-25 59
ABNER (1035 "I Found a Love") 15-25 60
COLLECTABLES 3-4 81
ERIC 3-4 73
FALCON (1013 "For Your Precious Love") 50-75 58
FOUNTAIN 3-4 82
ICHIBAN 3-4 92-93
MCA 3-4 83
MERCURY 3-8 67-74
MISTLETOE 3-5 75
MOTOWN 3-5 76-77
OLDIES 45 3-5
PHILADELPHIA INT'L 3-4 78-81
TRIP 3-5
VEE JAY (280 "For Your Precious Love") 3000-4000 58
VEE JAY (354 thru 715) 5-10 60-66
VEE JAY (1971 "Aware of Love") 15-25 63
(Stereo compact 33 single.)
Picture Sleeves
VEE JAY 8-12 61-64
LPs: 10/12-inch
ABNER (2001 "Jerry Butler Esquire") 200-300 59
BUDDAH 12-20 69
EXODUS 5-10
FOUNTAIN 5-10 82
DYNASTY 12-18
KENT 10-15 68
LOST-NITE 8-12 81
MERCURY 8-15 67-84
MOTOWN 5-10 76-77
PHILADELPHIA INT'L 5-10 78-81
POST 5-10
PRIDE 8-10 72
UPFRONT 8-10
SCEPTER 8-10
SIRE 8-12 77
SUNSET 10-12 68
TRIP 10-12 71-78
U.A. 8-10 75
VEE JAY (1000 series, except 1038) 25-45 60-64
VEE JAY (1038 "Aware of Love") 40-60
VEE JAY (1100 series) 20-30 64-65
Members (Impressions): Jerry Butler; Sam Gooden; Richard Brooks; Arthur Brooks; Curtis Mayfield.
Also see AUSTIN, Patti, & Jerry Butler
Also see CHANDLER, Gene, & Jerry Butler
Also see ICE MAN'S BAND
Also see IMPRESSIONS
Also see McPHATTER, Clyde / Little Richard / Jerry Butler
Also see RIVERS, Johnny / 4 Seasons / Jerry Butler / Jimmy Soul

BUTLER, Jerry, & Brenda Lee Eager P&R/R&B '72
Singles: 7-inch
MERCURY 3-4 71-73
LPs: 10/12-inch
MERCURY 8-10 73
Also see EAGER, Brenda Lee

BUTLER, Jerry, & Betty Everett LP '64
Singles: 7-inch
ABC 3-4 73
VEE JAY 3-5 64
LPs: 10/12-inch
BUDDAH 10-15 69
TRADITION 5-10 82
VEE JAY 20-30 64
Also see DELLS
Also see EVERETT, Betty

BUTLER, Jerry, & Debra Henry R&B '82
Singles: 7-inch
PHILADELPHIA INT'L 3-4 80
Also see SILK

BUTLER, Jerry, & Stix Hooper
Singles: 7-inch
MCA 3-4 83
Also see HOOPER, Stix

BUTLER, Jerry, & Thelma Houston LP '77
Singles: 7-inch
MOTOWN 3-5 77
LPs: 10/12-inch
MOTOWN 5-10 77
Also see BUTLER, Jerry
Also see HOUSTON, Thelma

BUTLER, Jesse
Singles: 7-inch
PHILIPS 4-8 67
LPs: 10/12-inch
PHILIPS 12-15 67

BUTLER, Joan Carol
Singles: 7-inch
CAPITOL 3-5 76
LPs: 10/12-inch
CAPITOL 8-10 76

BUTLER, Joe
Singles: 7-inch
KAMA SUTRA 3-6 69
Also see LOVIN' SPOONFUL

BUTLER, Jonathan LP '86
Singles: 7-inch
JIVE 3-4 86-89
Picture Sleeves
JIVE 3-4 87-89
LPs: 10/12-inch
JIVE 5-10 86-88
Also see TURNER, Ruby

BUTLER, Larry, & Friends
LPs: 10/12-inch
PICKWICK (3726 "Larry Butler & Friends, Featuring Crystal Gayle & Billy Jo Spears") 5-10 77
Also see GAYLE, Crystal
Also see SPEARS, Billy Jo

BUTLER, Marty
Singles: 7-inch
EPIC 3-5 73

BUTLER, Pearl
Singles: 7-inch
COLUMBIA 3-5 69
Also see BUTLER, Carl & Pearl

BUTLER, Phil
Singles: 7-inch
EPIC 10-15 62

BUTLER, Rod
Singles: 7-inch
ARTEEN (1005 "Yellow Moon") 10-20 60

BUTLER, Ron, & Ramblers
Singles: 7-inch
PLAYBOY 3-5 75

BUTLER, Tommy
Singles: 7-inch
CHATTAHOOCHEE 10-20 65-66
ROULETTE 5-10 61

BUTLER, Wild Child: see BUTLER, George "Wild Child"

BUTLERS
Singles: 7-inch
GAMBLE 5-10
GUYDEN (2081 "Lovable Girl") 75-125 63
(White label. Promotional issue only.)
GUYDEN (2081 "Lovable Girl") 50-75 63
(Purple and silver label.)
GUYDEN (2081 "Lovable Girl") 35-50 63
(Purple and blue label.)
LIBERTY BELL (1024 "She Tried to Kiss Me") 15-25 64
PARKWAY 10-15 67
PHILA 5-10 64
Also see BEVERLY, Frankie

BUTLERS / Aladdins
Singles: 7-inch
WITCH (109 "Lovable Girl"/"Please Love Me") 5-8
Also see ALADDINS
Also see BUTLERS

BUTTER BALL PAIGE
Singles: 7-inch
ROSE 4-8 68

BUTTER REBELLION
Singles: 7-inch
MAUDZ (002 "Aftermath") 15-20 60s

BUTTERCUPS
Singles: 7-inch
SILVER STAR 5-8

BUTTERFIELD, Billy
Singles: 78 rpm
CAPITOL 4-8 49
ESSEX 4-8 55
Singles: 7-inch
CAPITOL 5-10 49
ESSEX 5-10 55

BUTTERFIELD, Erskine
(With His Blue Boys)
Singles: 78 rpm
CORAL 6-10 49
Singles: 7-inch
CORAL 15-25 49

BUTTERFIELD, Paul LP '65
(Butterfield Blues Band; Paul Butterfield's Better Days)
Singles: 7-inch
BEARSVILLE 3-5 73-81
ELEKTRA 4-8 67-69
Picture Sleeves
ELEKTRA 4-8 67
LPs: 10/12-inch
AMHERST 5-8 86
BEARSVILLE 8-10 73-81
ELEKTRA 10-20 65-76
RED LIGHTNIN' ("An Offer You Can't Refuse") 30-40 72
(Single-sided promotional LP.)
Also see BISHOP, Elvin

BUTTERFLYS P&R '64
(Ellie Greenwich)
Singles: 7-inch
RED BIRD 10-20 64
Also see GREENWICH, Ellie

BUTTERMILK BOTTOM
Singles: 7-inch
POLYDOR 3-5 70

BUTTERSCOTCH
Singles: 7-inch
RCA 3-6 70
RENEE 4-6 72

BUTTERSCOTCH CABOOSE
Singles: 7-inch
AGP 3-6 69
AMY 4-8 68
GAP 4-8

BUTTERWORTH, Donna
Singles: 7-inch
REPRISE 4-8 66

BUTTERWORTH, Mary: see MARY BUTTERWORTH

BUTTONDOWNS
Singles: 7-inch
DOT 5-8 63

BUTTONS
Singles: 7-inch
ARLEN (719 "You Set My Soul on Fire") 8-12 63
CAPITOL (4223 "Jerry") 8-12 59
COLUMBIA (42618 "Shimmy Shimmy Watusi") 5-10 62
COLUMBIA (42700 "Popeye Does the Mashed Potatoes") 5-10 63
COLUMBIA (42834 "Foot Stompin' U.S.A.") 5-10 63
DOT (15988 "Calendar of Love") 15-25 59
EMBER (1100 "Absence Makes the Heart Grow Fonder") 8-12 64

BUTTONS, Red P&R '53
Singles: 78 rpm
COLUMBIA 3-6 53
Singles: 7-inch
COLUMBIA 5-10 53

BUTTONS & BEAUS
Singles: 7-inch
ZEN (104 "Never Leave Your Sugar") 10-20 63

BUTTS, Hindal
Singles: 7-inch
MS 3-5

BUTTS, Nancy
Singles: 7-inch
KING 3-5 72
FLAMING ARROW 4-6 69

BUTTS BAND
Singles: 7-inch
BLUE THUMB 3-5 74-75
LPs: 10/12-inch
BLUE THUMB 8-10 73-75

BUX
Singles: 7-inch
CAPITOL 3-5 76
LPs: 10/12-inch
CAPITOL 10-15 76
Members: Punky Meadows; James Newton; Ralph Mormon; Mickey Jones; Rocky Isaac.

BUXTON, Sonny
Singles: 7-inch
BOLO 4-8 67

BUZON, John, Trio
Singles: 7-inch
LIBERTY (55189 "Lizette") 15-25 59
LPs: 10/12-inch
LIBERTY (3108 "Inferno") 20-40 59
LIBERTY (3124 "Cha Cha on the Rocks") 20-40 59

BUZZ
Singles: 7-inch
CORAL 4-8 66

BUZZ & AL
Singles: 7-inch
ABC-PAR 5-10 60
COLUMBIA 4-8 62
JIMSKIP 5-10 59
MGM 5-10 61

BUZZ & BUCKY
Singles: 7-inch
AMY (924 "Tiger a Go-Go") 15-20 65
Members: Buzz Cason; Bucky Wilkin.
Also see CASON, Buzz
Also see RONNY & DAYTONAS

BUZZ & JOEY
Singles: 7-inch
SARA 4-8 66

BUZZ & TRACI
Singles: 7-inch
ELF 4-8 67

BUZZARD, Dr: see DR. BUZZARD

BUZZARDS
Singles: 7-inch
ALBERTA 3-5 70

BUZZCOCKS LP '80
Singles: 7-inch
I.R.S. 3-5 79-80
Picture Sleeves
I.R.S. 3-5 79
LPs: 10/12-inch
I.R.S. 5-10 79
Members: Pete Shelley; Steve Diggle; Howard Devoto; Steve Garvey; John Maher.
Also see SHELLEY, Pete

BUZZI, Ruth C&W '77
Singles: 7-inch
U.A. 3-5 77

BUZZIE
Singles: 7-inch
GORDY 3-5 70

BUZZO'S BANDITS & FRIENDS
LPs: 10/12-inch
UNITED SOUND 8-10

BUZZSAW
Singles: 7-inch
RCA 5-10 62

BUZZY
Singles: 7-inch
THRESHOLD (001 "Tinted Class") 3-5 82

BY ALL MEANS R&B '88
Singles: 7-inch
ATCO/VIRGIN 3-4 89-90
ISLAND 3-4 88-89
LPs: 10/12-inch
ISLAND 5-8 89
Members: James Vomer; Lynn Roderick; Billy Sheppard.
Also see SKOOL BOYZ

BY THE MORRISON
Singles: 7-inch
VIKING (376 "Gonna Have That Girl") 15-20

BYARS, Bernard
Singles: 7-inch
END 5-10 60-61

BYAS, Don R&B '48
Singles: 78 rpm
SAVOY 10-20 48

BYE, Tammy, & Friend
Singles: 7-inch
SWAMI 5-10

BYE BYES
Singles: 7-inch
MERCURY 8-12 59

BYERS, Ann
Singles: 7-inch
ACADEMY (109 "Dead End") 25-50 64
ACADEMY (111 "Here I Am") 25-50 65
ACADEMY (124 "Happy Without You") 50-100 66

BYERS, Billy
Singles: 7-inch
SCEPTER 5-8 64

BYERS, Brenda C&W '68
Singles: 7-inch
MTA 3-6 66-71
LPs: 10/12-inch
MTA 8-12 70

BYGONES
Singles: 7-inch
BLUES (401 "Cycle") 15-25

BYKE, Silver
Singles: 7-inch
BANG 4-8 68

BYLINERSZ
Singles: 7-inch
FELSTED 5-10 61-62

BYNUM, Chuck
Singles: 7-inch
W.B. 3-4 80

BYNUM, James
Singles: 7-inch
INTEGRA 5-10 68

BYRAM, Judy C&W '87
Singles: 7-inch
F&L 3-4 87
REGAL 3-4 88

BYRD, Bernie
(Bernie Byrd Show)
Singles: 7-inch
ERA 3-5 74

BYRD, Bobby
(Robert Byrd & His Birdies; Bobby Day)
Singles: 78 rpm
CASH 20-30 56
JAMIE 15-25 57
SAGE & SAND 10-20 55
SPARK 15-25
Singles: 7-inch
BROWNSTONE 8-10
CASH (1031 "The Truth Hurts") 50-80 56
JAMIE (1039 "Bippin' and Boppin' Over You") 10-15 57
SAGE & SAND (203 "Please Don't Hurt Me") 20-30 55
SPARK (501 "Bippin' and Boppin' Over You") 20-35 57
STRAWBERRY 3-5
Also see BOB & EARL
Also see DAY, Bobby
Also see HOLLYWOOD FLAMES
Also see IMPALAS
Also see LAURELS
Also see NUNN, Bobby
Also see SOUNDS
Also see VOICES

BYRD, Bobby R&B '65
(With the Byrds; with James Brown Band)
Singles: 7-inch
BROWNSTONE 3-5 71-72
FEDERAL 5-10 63
INTERNATIONAL BROTHERS 3-5 75
KING 3-6 67-71
KWANZA 3-5 73
SMASH 8-15 64-65
ZEPHYR 15-20 57
LPs: 10/12-inch
KING 10-15 70
Also see KING, Anna, & Bobby Byrd

BYRD, Bobby, & James Brown R&B '68
Singles: 7-inch
KING 4-6 68
Also see BROWN, James
Also see BYRD, Bobby

BYRD, Carolyn
Singles: 7-inch
LIONEL 3-5 71

BYRD, Charlie P&R '62
(Charlie Byrd Trio)
Singles: 7-inch
COLUMBIA 3-6 69
RIVERSIDE 3-6 62-63
LPs: 10/12-inch
COLUMBIA 15-25 65-69

FANTASY (9429 "Chrystal Silence")....10-15 73
MFSL (515 "At the Village Gate")...25-30 80s
OFFBEAT....25-35 59-60
RIVERSIDE....15-25 62-82
SAVOY....30-50 58
Also see ALMEIDA, Laurindo
Also see GETZ, Stan, & Charlie Byrd

BYRD, Charlie, & Woody Herman
LPs: 10/12-inch
EVEREST....10-20 63
PICKWICK....6-12 66
Also see BYRD, Charlie
Also see HERMAN, Woody

BYRD, Curtis
Singles: 7-inch
CANDIX....15-20 62

BYRD, Danny
Singles: 7-inch
SAVAGE....3-5 76

BYRD, Donald *LP '64*
Singles: 7-inch
BLUE NOTE....3-5 75-77
ELEKTRA....3-4 78-82
LPs: 10/12-inch
BETHLEHEM....15-25 60
BLUE NOTE....15-25 59-65
(Label reads "Blue Note Records Inc. - New York, U.S.A.")
BLUE NOTE....10-20 66-77
(Label reads "Blue Note Records - a Division of Liberty Records Inc.")
COLUMBIA (998 "Jazz Lab")....40-60 57
(With Gigi Gryce.)
COLUMBIA (1058 "Jazz Lab, Vol. 2, Modern Jazz Perspective")....40-60 57
(With Gigi Gryce.)
ELEKTRA....5-10 78-82
JAZZLAND (6 "Hard Bop")....30-40
JUBILEE (1059 "Jazz Lab")....40-60 57
(With Gigi Gryce.)
PRESTIGE (7062 "Two Trumpets")....75-100 56
(Yellow label. With Art Farmer.)
PRESTIGE (7080 "Youngbloods")..60-80 57
(Yellow label. With Phil Woods.)
PRESTIGE (7092 "Three Trumpets")....60-80 57
(Yellow label. With Art Farmer & Idrees Sulieman.)
REGENT (6056 "Jazz Eyes")....40-60 57
SAVOY (12032 "Byrd's Word")....40-60 56
(With Frank Foster.)
TRANSITION (4 "Byrd's Eye View")....50-80 55
(With Hank Mobley.)
TRANSITION (5 "Byrd Jazz")....50-80 55
(With Yusef Lateef.)
TRANSITION (17 "Byrd Blows on Beacon Hill")....50-80 56
VERVE....20-30 58
Also see BLACKBYRDS

BYRD, Gary *R&B '83*
(With G.B. Experience)
Singles: 12-inch
WONDIRECTION....4-6 83
Singles: 7-inch
RCA....3-5 73
REAL THING....3-5

BYRD, George
Singles: 7-inch
TANGERINE (1002 "You Better Tell Her So")....8-15 69

BYRD, Jerry *P&R '50*
Singles: 78 rpm
MERCURY....4-6 53-55
Singles: 7-inch
MERCURY....4-8 53-55
MONUMENT....4-6 60-67
EPs: 7-inch
DECCA....8-12 58
MERCURY....10-20 53-55
RCA....8-12 58
LPs: 10/12-inch
DECCA....20-35 58
LEHUA....8-10
MERCURY (Except 25000 series)..10-20 58-64
MERCURY (25000 series)....20-40 53-54
(10-inch LPs.)
MONUMENT....12-25 61-63
RCA (1687 "Hawaiian Beach Party")....30-40 59
SESAC....40-60 59
WING....10-15 60-66
Also see ALLEN, Rex
Also see KIRK, Red

BYRD, Joe, & Field Hippies
Singles: 7-inch
COLUMBIA....10-20 70
LPs: 10/12-inch
COLUMBIA (7317 "American Metaphysical Circus")....35-55 69
Members: Joe Byrd; Ted Greene; John Clauder; Gregg Kovner; Dana Chalberg; Fred Selden; Tom Scott; Meyer Hirsch.
Also see UNITED STATES of AMERICA

BYRD, John
Singles: 7-inch
20TH FOX....3-5 74-75

BYRD, Robert: see BYRD, Bobby

BYRD, Roy *R&B '50*
(With His Blues Jumpers; Roy "Bald Head" Byrd; with His New Orleans Rhythm; Roland Byrd)
Singles: 78 rpm
ATLANTIC (947 "Hey Little Girl")....150-250 50
FEDERAL (12061 "K.C. Blues") 150-250 52
(All Federal 45s known to exist are bootlegs.)
FEDERAL (12073 "Rockin' with Fess")....75-125 52
MERCURY (8175 "Bald Head")....50-100 50
MERCURY (8184 "Her Mind Is Gone")....50-100 50
Also see PROFESSOR LONGHAIR

BYRD, Russell *P&R '61*
Singles: 7-inch
SYMBOL....5-10 62
WAND....5-10 61

BYRD, Tanya
(With Jimmy & Rene)
Singles: 7-inch
VISTONE....3-6 68

BYRDS
Singles: 7-inch
RAYNARD (10038 "Your Lies")....50-100 65

BYRDS *P&R/LP '65*
Singles: 7-inch
ASYLUM....4-6 73
COLUMBIA (1600 series)....4-6 73
COLUMBIA (43271 "Mr. Tambourine Man")....8-10 65
(Black vinyl.)
COLUMBIA (43271 "Mr. Tambourine Man")....50-75 65
(Colored vinyl. Promotional issue only.)
COLUMBIA (43332 "I'll Feel a Whole Lot Better")....8-10 65
(Black vinyl.)
COLUMBIA (43332 "I'll Feel a Whole Lot Better")....50-75 65
(Colored vinyl. Promotional issue only.)
COLUMBIA (43332 "All I Really Want to Do")....8-10 65
(Black vinyl.)
COLUMBIA (43332 "All I Really Want to Do")....50-75 65
(Colored vinyl. Promotional issue only.)
COLUMBIA (43424 "Turn, Turn, Turn")....8-10 65
(Black vinyl.)
COLUMBIA (43424 "Turn, Turn, Turn")....50-75 65
(Colored vinyl. Promotional issue only.)
COLUMBIA (43501 thru 45761)....6-12 66-72
Picture Sleeves
COLUMBIA (43271 "Mr. Tambourine Man")....100-200 65
(Promotional issue only.)
COLUMBIA (43578 "Eight Miles High")....25-35 65
COLUMBIA (44157 "Have You Seen Her Face")....25-35 65
EPs: 7-inch
COLUMBIA (10287 "The Byrds")...50-75 66
(Columbia Special Products issue for the Scholastic Book Services. Issued with paper cover.)
COLUMBIA (116003/4 "Fifth Dimension Open-End Interview")....50-100 66
(Promotional issue only.)
LPs: 10/12-inch
ASYLUM (5058 "Byrds")....8-12 73
COLUMBIA (2372 "Mr. Tambourine Man")....25-50 65
(Monaural.)
COLUMBIA (2454 "Turn, Turn, Turn")....20-40 65
(Monaural.)
COLUMBIA (2549 "Fifth Dimension")....20-40 66
(Monaural.)
COLUMBIA (2642 "Younger Than Yesterday")....20-40 67
(Monaural.)
COLUMBIA (2716 "Greatest Hits")..20-40 67
(Monaural.)
COLUMBIA (2775 "Notorious Byrd Brothers")....20-40 68
(Monaural.)
COLUMBIA (9172 "Mr. Tambourine Man")....20-30 65
(Stereo.)
COLUMBIA (9254 "Turn, Turn, Turn")....20-30 65
(Stereo.)
COLUMBIA (9349 "Fifth Dimension")....20-30 66
(Stereo.)
COLUMBIA (9442 "Younger Than Yesterday")....20-30 67
(Stereo.)
COLUMBIA (9516 "Greatest Hits") 20-30 67
(Stereo.)
COLUMBIA (9575 "Notorious Byrd Brothers")....20-30 68
(Stereo.)
COLUMBIA (9670 "Sweetheart of the Rodeo")....20-30 68
(Stereo.)
COLUMBIA (9755 "Dr. Byrds & My Hyde")....20-30 69
(Stereo.)
COLUMBIA (9942 "The Ballad of Easy Rider")....20-30 69
(Stereo.)
COLUMBIA (30127 "The Byrds")...10-20 70
COLUMBIA (30640 "Byrdmaniax")...8-15 71
COLUMBIA (31050 "Farther Along")....8-15 71
COLUMBIA (31795 "The Best of the Byrds")....8-15 72
COLUMBIA (32183 "Preflyte")....8-15 73
COLUMBIA (34000 thru 37000 series)....6-12 75-81
COLUMBIA (46773 "The Byrds")...30-50 90
(Four-disc set. Includes 55-page booklet.)
MURRAY HILL....5-10 87
PAIR....10-12 83
REALM....8-12 76
RHINO....5-10 88
TOGETHER (1001 "Preflyte")....15-25 69
Promotional LPs
BROADCAST ("Byrds Live")....35-50 81
COLUMBIA (2000 series)....50-100 65-67
(White label.)
COLUMBIA (9000 series)....35-55 65-69
(White label.)
COLUMBIA (116003/4 "*Fifth Dimension* Interview Album")....100-200 66
Members: Jim (Roger) McGuinn; Gene Clark; David Crosby; Chris Hillman; Michael Clarke; Gram Parsons; Clarence White; Gene Parsons; John York; Skip Battin. Session: Jay Dee Maness; Bayard Jones; Jim Wessely; Frank Laurie; John Jamnick; Frank Inman; Robert Stanley. Session: Van Dyke Parks.
Also see BATTIN, Skip
Also see BEEFEATERS
Also see CLARK, Gene
Also see CROSBY, David
Also see HILLMAN, Chris
Also see McGUINN, Roger
Also see PACIFIC STEEL CO.
Also see PARKS, Van Dyke
Also see PARSONS, Gram
Also see REVERE, Paul, & Raiders / Simon & Garfunkel / Byrds / Aretha Franklin
Also see WEST COAST POP ART EXPERIMENTAL BAND

BYRNE, David *LP '81*
Singles: 12-inch
SIRE....4-6 82
LPs: 10/12-inch
ECM....5-8 85
LUAKA BOP....5-8 89
SIRE....5-10 81
Also see ENO, Brian
Also see GLASS, Philip
Also see TALKING HEADS

BYRNE, Jerry
Singles: 7-inch
SPECIALTY (635 "Lights Out")....20-40 58
SPECIALTY (662 "Carry On")....20-40 59

BYRNE, Robert
Singles: 7-inch
MERCURY....3-5 78-79
LPs: 10/12-inch
MERCURY....5-10 79

BYRNE, Tony
Singles: 7-inch
CAPITOL....3-6 70

BYRNES, Edd "Kookie," with Joanie Sommers & Mary Kaye Trio
Singles: 7-inch
W.B....5-10 59
Picture Sleeves
W.B....8-12 59
Also see KAYE, Mary
Also see SOMMERS, Joanie

BYRNES, Edward *P&R '59*
(Edd "Kookie" Byrnes; with Connie Stevens & Don Ralke's Orchestra; with Friend; with Mary Kaye Trio.)
Singles: 7-inch
W.B. (5047 "Kookie Kookie")....5-10 59
W.B. (S-5047 "Kookie Kookie")....10-20 59
(Stereo.)
W.B. (5087 thru 5121)....5-10 59
Picture Sleeves
W.B....15-20 59
EPs: 7-inch
W.B. (1309 "Edd "Kookie" Byrnes")....15-25 59
LPs: 10/12-inch
W.B. (1309 "Kookie")....25-35 59
Also see BYRNES, Edd "Kookie," with Joanie Sommers & Mary Kaye Trio
Also see RALKE, Don
Also see STEVENS, Connie

BYRON, Andy
Singles: 7-inch
SPIN-IT....3-4 81
Picture Sleeves
SPIN-IT....3-4 81

BYRON, April
Singles: 7-inch
INTERPHON....4-8 64

BYRON, D.L. *LP '80*
Singles: 7-inch
ARISTA....3-4 80
Picture Sleeves
ARISTA....3-5 80
LPs: 10/12-inch
ARISTA....5-10 80

BYRON, David
Singles: 7-inch
MERCURY....3-5 76
LPs: 10/12-inch
MERCURY....8-10 76

BYRON, Jimmy
Singles: 7-inch
EVEREST....5-10 60
TEEN....20-30 57

BYRON, Junior *D&D '83*
Singles: 12-inch
VANGUARD....4-6 83

BYRON, Lord Douglas
Singles: 7-inch
DOT....10-20 65

BYRON, Lord Douglas / Continentals
Singles: 7-inch
UNION (505 "Big Bad Ho-Dad")....20-30 62
Also see BYRON, Lord Douglas
Also see CONTINENTALS

BYRON & MORTALS
Singles: 7-inch
X-PRESHUN (2 "Do You Believe Me")....25-35 66

BYSTANDERS
Singles: 7-inch
ON TAP....15-25 64

BYZANTIUM
LPs: 10/12-inch
W.B....10-12 73
Members: Charles Jankel; Robin Lamble; Steve Corduner; Nick Ramsden.

B'ZZ
Singles: 7-inch
EPIC....3-4 83-84
LPs: 10/12-inch
EPIC....5-10 83-84

KING
E.P.
SPECIAL D.J
NOT FOR RESALE
SIDE 1
JAMES BROWN
MONTH OF SOUL
PLEASE, PLEASE, PLEASE 2:04
TRY ME 2:28
Formal
FORMAL RECORDS — Chicago, Illinois
Curtom
Publishing Co
B.M.I. 2:10
Produced By
D. Talty
FR 1044
"MAMA DIDN'T LIE"
"Mayfield"
JAN BRADLEY

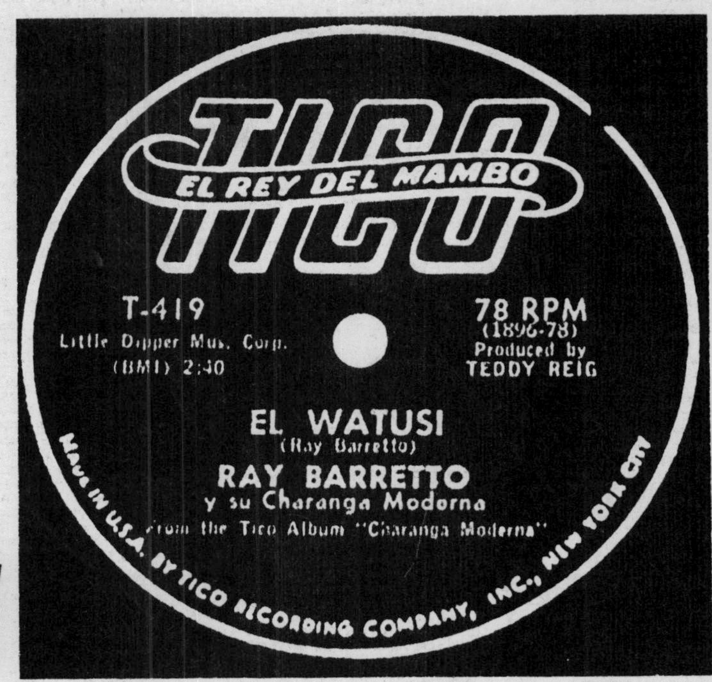
TICO
EL REY DEL MAMBO
T-419
Little Dipper Mus. Corp.
(BMI) 2:40
78 RPM
(1896-78)
Produced by
TEDDY REIG
EL WATUSI
(Ray Barretto)
RAY BARRETTO
y su Charanga Moderna
From the Tico Album "Charanga Moderna"
MADE IN U.S.A. BY TICO RECORDING COMPANY, INC., NEW YORK CITY

Kit RECORDS INC.
AL BUBIS PRODUCTIONS
45-885
Al Bubis Assoc.
BMI
Time 2:59
RENT'S TOO HIGH
(Butler-Broadwater)
CLIFF BUTLER
And His Band
804 CHURCH STREET
NASHVILLE, TENNESSEE

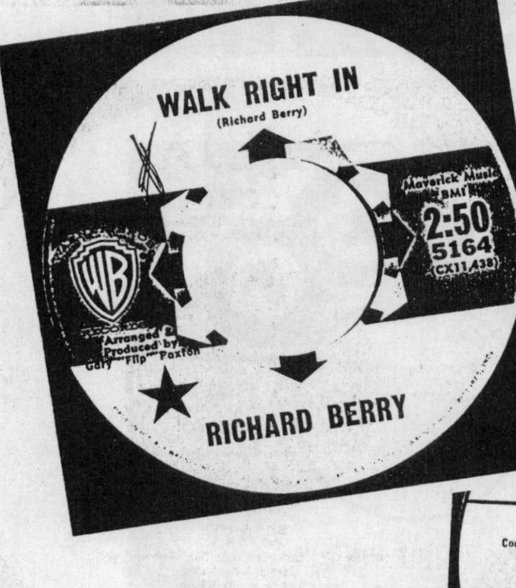
WALK RIGHT IN
(Richard Berry)
Maverick Music
BMI
2:50
5164
(CX11,438)
WB
Arranged &
Produced by
Gary "Flip" Paxton
RICHARD BERRY

CAMEO
Conley Music
BMI
C-122 A
Time: 2:22
GOOD GOOD MORNING, BABY
(Frank C. Slay, Jr. - Bob Crewe)
LILLIE BRYANT
BILLY FORD
Orch. and Chorus

Josie
Record No.
45-804
Time: 2:37
45 R.P.M.
(45-JOZ-140)
Vocal with
Orch. Acc.
Choppell (ASCAP)
ROCK A BYE BLUES
(Benjomin-Marcus)
EDDIE BANKS
(with The Five Dreamers)

DEB
RECORDS
1650 BROADWAY, NEW YORK 19, N. Y.
UNBREAKABLE
45 R.P.M.
RECORD NO.
D500-B
Draxon-Freida
Music Corp.
BMI
Time 2:51
"THE REASON"
(J. Dixon)
* THE CHANELS *

BAND
BOX
RECORDS
REG. U.S. PAT. OFF.
#329
Val-Jean
Music Pub.
BMI
Time 2:59
45 RPM
SIDE ONE
P4KB-1011
CRISIS AT OLE MISS
(J. L. Parker)
CHILLY CHARLIE
5136 W. 41ST AVE. • DENVER 12, COLORADO

6425 HOLLYWOOD BOULEVARD • HOLLYWOOD 28, CALIFORNIA U.S.A.
IMPERIAL
X3002
BMI 2:23
KAVELIN
MUSIC CORP.
Vocal
Not For Sale
SITTIN' AND ROCKIN'
(Schelbach, Scott and Duncan)
EDDIE CLETRO
IF-705

Vee-Jay
RECORDS
S-161
Vocal-BMI
Time 2:40
Norgelde-Tollie
MY LOVE
(Charles Murray)
THE CO-HEARTS
Produced by
H. Norton & B. Goldstein
VJ 289

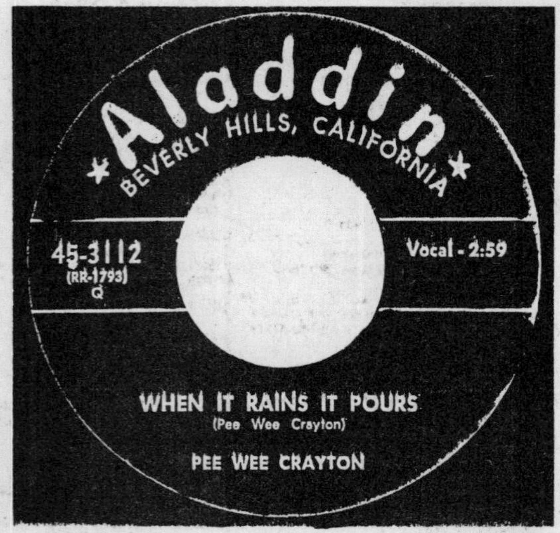
Aladdin
BEVERLY HILLS, CALIFORNIA
45-3112
(RR-1793)
Q
Vocal - 2:59
WHEN IT RAINS IT POURS
(Pee Wee Crayton)
PEE WEE CRAYTON

TOLT
Pub: Sunflower Mus.,
Inc.-Garnet Pub. Co.
ASCAP Time: 2:44
TR 6032
45-787-V
I'M A LITTLE MIXED UP
(James; Johnson)
COSMO
Music by The Carnations
Made in U.S.A.
DISTRIBUTED BY LONDON RECORDS, INC.

C

C & C BOYS
Singles: 7-inch
DUKE 10-20 62-64

C & C MUSIC FACTORY LP '91
(Clivilles & Cole)
Singles: 7-inch
COLUMBIA 3-4 90-91
LPs: 10/12-inch
COLUMBIA 5-8 91

C & SHELLS R&B '69
Singles: 7-inch
COTILLION 4-6 69
ZANZEE 3-6 72
Members: Calvin White; Andrea Bolden; Lonzine Wright.
Also see SANDPEBBLES

C.A. QUINTET
Singles: 7-inch
CANDY FLOSS (102 "Smooth As Silk") 40-60 68
FALCON (70 "Mickey's Monkey") 25-50 67
FALCON (71 "Blow to My Soul") 25-50 67
LPs: 10/12-inch
CANDY FLOSS (7764 "A Trip Through Hell") 1000-1500 68
Members: Jim Erwin; Ken Erwin; Doug Reynolds; Tom Pohling; Paul Samuels; Rick Johnson; Rick Patron; Donnie Chapin; Tony Wright.

C.A.T.
Singles: 7-inch
AZRA ("I Essener Schalldlatten") 8-12
(Picture disc. No Selection number used.)
MAGNA-GILDE 3-5 77
Also see CRISPINO, John, & C.A.T.

C COMPANY Featuring Terry Nelson C&W '71
Singles: 7-inch
PLANTATION 3-5 71
LPs: 10/12-inch
PLANTATION 5-10 71

C-BANK R&B/D&D '83
(Featuring Jenny Burton)
Singles: 7-inch
NEXT PLATEAU 3-4 83
Also see BURTON, Jenny

C-BRAND
Singles: 12-inch
SPRING 4-6 83
Singles: 7-inch
SPRING 3-4 83

C.B.'S BANDSTAND
(With D.J. Hollywood)
Singles: 7-inch
MERCURY 3-4 83

C.C. & COMPANY P&R '76
Singles: 7-inch
SUSSEX 3-5 75
20TH CENTURY/WESTBOUND 3-5 75
Also see C.J. & CO.

C.C.S. P&R/LP '71
(Collective Consciousness Society)
Singles: 7-inch
BELL 3-5 73
RAK 4-8 71
LPs: 10/12-inch
RAK 15-20 71-72
Member: Alexis Korner.

C.D. BAND
Singles: 7-inch
CASABLANCA 3-4 79
LPs: 10/12-inch
CASABLANCA 5-10 79

C.J.
LPs: 10/12-inch
OVATION 5-10 77

C.J. & CO. P&R '77
(C.C. & COMPANY)
Singles: 7-inch
WESTBOUND 3-5 77-78
LPs: 10/12-inch
WESTBOUND 5-10 77-78
Members: Dennis Coffey; Cornelius Brown; Joni Tolbert; Charles Clark; Connie Durden; Curtis Durden.
Also see C.C. & COMPANY
Also see COFFEY, Dennis

C.K. STRONG
LPs: 10/12-inch
EPIC 10-20 69

C.L. & PICTURES
Singles: 7-inch
CADETTE (8005 "Love Will Find a Way") 15-25 60s
DUNES (2010 "I'm Asking Forgiveness") 10-15 62
DUNES (2017 "Afraid") 10-15 62
DUNES (2023 "I'm Sorry") 15-25 63
JAMIE (1398 "You Really Slipped One") 10-15 70
MONUMENT (854 "He'll Only Hurt You") 5-10 64
MONUMENT (888 "Could This Be") 5-10 65
MONUMENT (958 "Baby, Not Now") 5-10 66
SABRA 3-6 79
SILVER BULLET 3-5 84-86
Member: Charlie Broyles.

C.L. BLAST: see BLAST, C.L.

C-MINORS
Singles: 7-inch
IMPRESSION (106 "Don't Go") 20-30 66

C-NOTES
Singles: 78 rpm
EVERLAST 30-50 57
Singles: 7-inch
ARC (4447 Last Saturday Night") 20-30 59
EVERLAST (5005 "From Now On") 30-50 57

C.O.D.
Singles: 7-inch
CASABLANCA 3-4 79
LPs: 10/12-inch
CASABLANCA 5-10 79

C.O.D.s P&R '65
Singles: 7-inch
KELLMAC (1003 "Michael") 5-10 65
KELLMAC (1005 "Pretty Baby") 8-12 66
KELLMAC (1012 "Coming Back Girl") 50-100 66
Members: Larry Brownlee; Robert Lewis; Carl Washington.
Also see LOST GENERATION
Also see MYSTIQUE

C.P.W.
Singles: 7-inch
CAPITOL 3-5 71

C.Q.D. D&D '83
Singles: 12-inch
EMERGENCY 4-6 83

C - QUENTS
Singles: 7-inch
CAPTOWN (4027 "Merry Christmas Baby") 150-250 68
ESSICA (004 "Dearest One") 15-25 60s

C-QUINS
Singles: 7-inch
CHESS (1815 "My Only Love") 10-20 62
DITTO (501 "My Only Love") 20-40 62

C.S. ANGELS
LPs: 10/12-inch
JIVE 5-10 83

CTs
Singles: 7-inch
SUNBURST 4-8 67

C.U.B.
Singles: 7-inch
CAPITOL 3-5 72
EMI 3-5 73

C.Y. WALKIN'
Singles: 7-inch
PARACHUTE 3-5 79
LPs: 10/12-inch
PARACHUTE 5-10 79

CABARETS
Singles: 7-inch
SAXONY (1002 "There Must Be a Way") 30-50 62
SAXONY (2006 "There Must Be a Way") 4-6 97

CABBOT, Johnny
Singles: 7-inch
COLUMBIA (3-42283 "Night and Day") 50-75 62
(Compact 33 Single.)
COLUMBIA (4-42283 "Night and Day") 30-40 62
Also see 4 SEASONS

CABELL, Sly
Singles: 12-inch
SALSOUL 4-6 82
Singles: 7-inch
SALSOUL 3-4 82

CABIN CREW
Singles: 7-inch
DIMENSION 5-10 64

CABINEERS
Singles: 78 rpm
ABBEY (72 "Whirlpool") 75-150 49
ABBEY (3001 "Tell Me Now") 75-150 49
ABBEY (3003 "Whirlpool") 75-150 49
PRESTIGE (902 "My My My") 50-100 51
PRESTIGE (904 "Each Time") 50-100 52
PRESTIGE (917 "Baby Mine") 50-100 55
Singles: 7-inch
PRESTIGE (904 "Each Time") 200-300 52
PRESTIGE (917 "Baby Mine") 300-400 55

CABLES
Singles: 7-inch
RCA 4-8 61
Also see LIMELITERS

CABOOSE P&R '70
Singles: 7-inch
ENTERPRISE 3-5 70
LPs: 10/12-inch
ENTERPRISE 10-15 71

CACLA, Paula
LPs: 10/12-inch
ALEXANDER STREET 5-10 81

CACTUS LP '70
Singles: 7-inch
ATCO 5-8 70-72
LPs: 10/12-inch
ATCO 20-25 70-72
Members: Carmine Appice; Tim Bogert; Pete French; Werner Fritzschings; Duane Hitchings; Jerry Norris; Mike Pinera; Roland Robinson; Rusty Day; Jim McCarty.
Also see BECK, BOGERT & APPICE
Also see DAY, Rusty
Also see NEW CACTUS BAND
Also see PINERA, Mike
Also see THEE IMAGE

CACTUS WORLD NEWS LP '86
Singles: 7-inch
MCA 3-4 86
LPs: 10/12-inch
MCA 5-10 86

CADALINAS
Singles: 7-inch
MINUTEMAN 5-10 65
SHER-A-TUNE 10-15

CADAVER
Singles: 7-inch
KALEIDOSCOPE 4-8 68
Picture Sleeves
KALEIDOSCOPE 8-12 68

CADD, Brian
Singles: 7-inch
CAPITOL 3-4 77-78
CHELSEA 3-5 73-75
LPs: 10/12-inch
CAPITOL 5-10 76-78
CHELSEA 8-10 73-74

CADDELL, Freddie
Singles: 7-inch
ARDENT (12 "At the Rockhouse") 100-125

CADDELL, Shirley
Singles: 78 rpm
COLUMBIA (40939 "Part Time Gal") 8-12 57
Singles: 7-inch
COLUMBIA (40939 "Part Time Gal") 5-10 57
LESLEY 4-8 63

CADETS P&R/R&B '56
Singles: 78 rpm
MODERN (Except 971) 20-50 55-57
MODERN (971 "If It Is Wrong") 50-75 55
Singles: 7-inch
COLLECTABLES 3-4 81
MODERN (Except 971) 25-50 55-57
MODERN (971 "If It Is Wrong") 75-125 55
LPs: 10/12-inch
CROWN (370 "The Cadets") 50-75 63
(Stereo.)
CROWN (5015 "Rockin' 'N' Reelin'") 100-200 57
(Monaural.)
CROWN (5370 "The Cadets") 50-75 63
(Monaural.)
RELIC 10-15
Members: Ted Taylor; Aaron Collins; Will "Dub" Jones; Willie Davis; Lloyd McCraw; Prentice Moreland; Tom Fox; Randolph Jones.
Also see CLASS-NOTES
Also see FLARES
Also see JACKS
Also see JONES, Will, & Cadets
Also see PEPPERS
Also see ROCKETEERS
Also see THOR-ABLES
Also see TAYLOR, Ted

CADETS
Singles: 7-inch
JAN-LAR (102 "Don't") 30-50 60
Members: Willie Davis; Aaron Collins; George Hollis; Tom Miller; Robbie Robinson; Beverley Harris.
Also see BUNN, Bennie
Also see PEPPERS

CADILLAC, Flash: see FLASH CADILLAC

CADILLAC SALLY
(Barbara Raney)
LPs: 10/12-inch
MINNESOTA PRODUCTIONS 10-15 81
Also see DEEPWATER REUNION
Also see RANEY, Barbara

CADILLACS P&R '55
(With the Jesse Powell Orchestra)
Singles: 78 rpm
JOSIE (765 "Gloria") 75-125 54
JOSIE (769 "Wishing Well") 50-75 54
JOSIE (773 thru 820) 25-50 55-57
JUBILEE (846 "Peek-a-Boo") 30-50 58
(Canadian.)
REO 25-75 55-57
(Canadian.)
Singles: 7-inch
ABC 3-5 73
ARCTIC (101 "Fool") 50-100 64
CAPITOL (4825 "White Gardenia") 10-20 62
JOSIE (765 "Gloria") 300-500 54
JOSIE (769 "Wishing Well") 350-550 54
JOSIE (773 "No Chance") 50-75 55
JOSIE (778 "Down the Road") 75-100 55
JOSIE (785 "Speedoo") 50-75 55
JOSIE (792 "Zoom") 40-60 56
JOSIE (798 "Betty My Love") 40-60 56
JOSIE (805 "The Girl I Love) 20-40 56
JOSIE (807 "Shock-a-Doo) 20-40 56
JOSIE (812 "Sugar Sugar) 20-40 57
JOSIE (820 "My Girl Friend") 40-60 57
JOSIE (836 "Speedoo Is Back") 20-30 58
JOSIE (842 "I Want to Know") 20-30 58
JOSIE (846 "Peek-a-Boo") 20-30 58
JOSIE (857 "Copy Cat") 20-30 59
JOSIE (861 "Please Mr Johnson") 20-30 59
JOSIE (866 "Romeo") 20-30 59
JOSIE (870 "Big Dan McGoon") 20-30 59
JOSIE (883 "That's Why") 15-25 60
JOSIE (915 "I'll Never Let You Go") 10-15 63
JUBILEE (846 "Peek-a-Boo") 20-30 58
(Canadian.)
JUBILEE (9010 "Romeo") 40-60 59
(Stereo.)
LANA 4-6 64
MERCURY (71738 "I'm Willing") 30-40 61
REO (8002 "No Chance") 75-125 55
(Canadian.)
REO (8071 "Speedoo") 50-100 55
(Canadian.)
REO (8100 "Zoom") 50-100 55
(Canadian.)
REO (8139 "Shock-a-Doo") 50-100 56
(Canadian.)
REO (8150 "Sugar Sugar") 50-100 57
(Canadian.)
REO (8163 "My Girl Friend") 50-100 57
(Canadian.)
SMASH (1712 "You Are to Blame") 15-20 61
VIRGO 3-5 72-73
LPs: 10/12-inch
CADAVER 5-10
HARLEM HITPARADE 10-15 70s
JUBILEE (1045 "The Fabulous Cadillacs") 300-400 57
(Blue label.)
JUBILEE (1045 "The Fabulous Cadillacs") 200-250 59
(Flat black label.)
JUBILEE (1045 "The Fabulous Cadillacs") 100-150 60
(Glossy black label.)
JUBILEE (1089 "The Crazy Cadillacs") 150-250 58
(Flat black label.)
JUBILEE (1089 "The Crazy Cadillacs") 100-150 60
(Glossy black label.)
JUBILEE (5009 "Twistin' with the Cadillacs") 50-100 62
(Monaural.)
JUBILEE (5009 "Twistin' with the Cadillacs") 100-150 62
(Stereo.)
MURRAY HILL (1195 "The Very Best of the Cadillacs") 5-10 88
MURRAY HILL (1285 "The Cadillacs") 30-40
(Boxed, five-disc set.)
Members: Earl "Speedoo" Carroll; Jim "Papa" Clark; Gus Willingham; Bobby Phillips; Laverne Drake; Charles Brooks; James Bailey; Earl Wade.
Also see BAILEY, J.R.
Also see BREWSTER, Ray, & Cadillacs
Also see CARROL, Earl, & Original Cadillacs
Also see CRICKETS
Also see CRYSTALS
Also see FIVE CROWNS
Also see HOWARD, Gregory
Also see MISSLES
Also see NEW YORK CITY
Also see OPALS
Also see ORIGINAL CADILLACS
Also see PEARLS
Also see POWELL, Jesse
Also see RAY, Bobby, & Cadillacs
Also see SCHOOLBOYS
Also see SOLITAIRES
Also see SPEEDO & CADILLACS

CADILLACS / Orioles
LPs: 10/12-inch
JUBILEE (1117 "The Cadillacs Meet the Orioles") 75-100 61
Also see CADILLACS
Also see ORIOLES

CADO BELLE
Singles: 7-inch
ANCHOR 3-5 77
LPs: 10/12-inch
ANCHOR (1 "The Cado Belle EP") 10-15 77
(10-inch disc.)
ANCHOR (2015 "Cado Belle") 8-12 77
Members: Maggie Reilly; Alan Darby; Gavin Hodgson; Stuart Mackillop; Davy Roy; Colin Tully.

CADWELL, Don, & Revolvers
Singles
CONDOR CLASSIX (8804 "Santa Stole My Sock") 8-12 88
(Santa shaped picture disc. 500 made.)

CAESAR, Pearline
Singles: 7-inch
AMY 4-8 63

CAESAR, Shirley P&R/R&B '75
(With the Caesar Singers)
Singles: 7-inch
HOB/SCEPTER 3-5 73-75
ROADSHOW 3-5 77-78
LPs: 10/12-inch
HOB 8-12 70-75
ROADSHOW 5-10 77
TRIP 5-10 77

CAESAR & CLEO P&R '65
Singles: 7-inch
REPRISE 10-15 64-65
VAULT 15-25 63
Picture Sleeves
REPRISE (0419 "Let the Good Times Roll") 25-50 65
Members: Salvatore "Sonny" Bono; Cher LaPiere.
Also see SONNY & CHER

CAESAR & ROMANS: see LITTLE CAESAR & ROMANS

CAESARS R&B '67
Singles: 7-inch
LANIE (2001 "Lala I Love You") 75-125 67
LANIE (2002 "Girl I Miss You") 25-35 67

CAFE
(With the Hearns Sisters)
Singles: 12-inch
MONTAGE 4-6 84

CAFE CREME
Singles: 12-inch
RSO 5-10 78
Singles: 7-inch
RSO 3-5 78
LPs: 10/12-inch
RSO 5-10 78

CAFFEE & REAPERS
Singles: 7-inch
DOVE (101 "Hawg Jawls") 10-20 61

CAFFERTY, John LP '83
(With the Beaver Brown Band)
Singles: 7-inch
SCOTTI BROTHERS 3-4 84-86
Picture Sleeves
SCOTTI BROTHERS 3-4 84-86
LPs: 10/12-inch
SCOTTI BROTHERS 5-10 84-89
Also see EDDIE & CRUISERS

CAFFERY, Robert
Singles: 78 rpm
CHESS (1470 "Ida Bee") 50-75 51

CAGER, Willie
Singles: 7-inch
CONTACT (504 "He's a Player") 10-20

CAGLE, Aubrey
Singles: 7-inch
GLEE (1000 "Be-Bop") 100-150 60
GLEE (1001 "Come Along Little Girl") 75-100 60
HOUSE of SOUNDS (504 "Real Cool") 150-250 59

CAGLE, Buddy C&W '63
Singles: 7-inch
CAPITOL 4-8 63
IMPERIAL 4-6 66-68
MERCURY 4-6 65
U.A. 3-5 70
LPs: 10/12-inch
IMPERIAL 8-5 66-68
Also see THOMPSON, Hank

CAGLE, Wade, & Escorts
Singles: 7-inch
SUN 5-10 61

CAHAN, Andy
Singles: 7-inch
PHANANA (7247 "Trick or Treat") 5-10 82
PANDA (83 "Trick or Treat") 5-10 83
Picture Sleeves
PANDA (83 "Trick or Treat") 5-10 83
EPs: 7-inch
ERIKA/PANDA (883 "Mooch") 5-10 83
(Uncut panda bear picture disc.)
ERIKA/PANDA (883 "Mooch") 10-20 83
(Panda bear shaped picture disc.)
LP: 10/12-inch
PANDA ("Andy Cahan Band") 10-15 83
(Selection number not known.)

CAHILL, Graig, & Off-Beats
Singles: 7-inch
MERRITT (0001 "Landslide") 15-25 63
MERRITT (0002 "Grind") 15-25 63
MERRITT (0003 "Surfin' Elephant") 15-25 64
Also see OFF-BEATS

CAHILL, Mike
Singles: 7-inch
FORD 4-8 62
FOXIE 4-8 61

CAHMERE
Singles: 7-inch
BABYLON 3-5 74

CAHPERONES
(Chaperones)
Singles: 7-inch
JOSIE (880 "Cruise to the Moon") 50-75 60
(Repressed to show group as the Chaperones.)
Also see CHAPERONES

CAIN
Singles: 7-inch
ASI 8-12 60s
LPs: 10/12-inch
ASI 15-20 75-77
Also see GRASSHOPPERS

CAIN, Bobby
(Bob Cain)
Singles: 7-inch
BIG TOP (3109 "I Don't See Me in Your Eyes Anymore") 8-10 62

MINARET (117 "Everything") 5-8 64
VULCAN (1011 "Chance of a Lifetime") 10-15
20TH FOX (118 "Spider") 15-25 58

CAIN, Hunter C&W '88
Singles: 7-inch
DISCOVERY 3-4 88-89

CAIN, Jeff
Singles: 7-inch
ALTERA 8-12

CAIN, Jeffrey
Singles: 7-inch
W.B. 3-5 70-72
LPs: 10/12-inch
W.B. 8-12 70-72

CAIN, Joe, & Red Parrot Orchestra R&B '83
Singles: 7-inch
ZOO YORK 3-4 83

CAIN, Jonathan P&R '76
(Jonathan Cain Band)
Singles: 7-inch
BEARSVILLE 3-5 76
OCTOBER 3-5 75-76
LPs: 10/12-inch
BEARSVILLE 5-10 77
Also see BABYS
Also see CAIN, Tane
Also see JOURNEY

CAIN, Kenny
Singles: 7-inch
HI 4-8 62

CAIN, Marie
Singles: 7-inch
COLUMBIA 3-5 76
LPs: 10/12-inch
COLUMBIA 8-10 76

CAIN, Pat
Singles: 7-inch
GREAT 3-5 71
PEACH 10-15 60

CAIN, Perry
Singles: 78 rpm
GOLD STAR 25-50 48

CAIN, Tane P&R/LP '82
Singles: 7-inch
RCA 3-4 82-83
LPs: 10/12-inch
RCA 5-10 82
Also see CAIN, Jonathan

CAIN, Tasso: see TASSO-CAIN

CAIN, Thomas
Singles: 7-inch
RCA 3-5 75

CAIN & ABEL
Singles: 7-inch
ABELL 5-10 59

CAIN & New Generation
Singles: 7-inch
PHILIPS 4-8 66

CAINE, General R&B '82
Singles: 12-inch
CAPITOL 4-6 84
TABU 4-6 82-84
Singles: 7-inch
CAPITOL 3-4 84
TABU 3-4 82-84
LPs: 10/12-inch
TABU 5-10 82-84

CAINE, Gladys
Singles: 7-inch
TO GO (602 "Please Mr. DJ") 25-35 63

CAINE, Simon
LPs: 10/12-inch
RCA 10-15 70

CAINES, Joe
Singles: 7-inch
ARCADIA 8-12 59

CAIOLA, Al P&R '60
Singles: 78 rpm
CORAL 5-10 57
RCA 4-8 53-55
REGENCY 4-8 56
Singles: 7-inch
AVLANCHE 3-4 73
CORAL (61855 "Honky Tonk Parade") 5-10 57
CORAL (61890 "Blue Angel Blues") 5-10 58
PREFERRED 5-10 59-60
RCA 5-10 53-55
REGENCY 5-10 56
U.A. 4-8 60-68
EPs: 7-inch
RCA (551 "Latin Beat") 10-15 53
RCA (555 "Guitar Sketches") 10-15 53
SESAC (85 "Boffola Caiola") 10-15 60
LPs: 10/12-inch
ATCO 10-15 60
BAINBRIDGE 5-8 80
CAMDEN 8-12 62
CHANCELLOR 10-15 60
RCA 10-15 59
ROULETTE 10-15 60
SAVOY 15-25 58
TIME 10-20 60-61
TWO WORLDS 8-10 72
UNART 8-12 67
U.A. 10-15 60-69
Also see JUVENILES
Also see TONES

CAIROS
Singles: 7-inch
SHRINE (111 "Don't Fight It") 150-250 66
Members: Keni Lewis; Famon Johnson; Tommy Montier; Gerald Richardson; Wilford Ruffin.

CAITON, Richard
Singles: 7-inch
GNP (327 "You Look Like a Flower") 30-40 64
(Blue label.)
GNP (327 "You Look Like a Flower") 10-15
(Yellow label.)

CAJUN HART
Singles: 7-inch
W.B. (7258 "Got to Find a Way") 8-12 69

CAJUNS
Singles: 7-inch
FRATERNITY (836 "Cajun Blues") 15-25 58
SAGE (321 "One, One, One") 10-20 60s
Member: Rusty York.
Also see YORK, Rusty

CAKE
Singles: 7-inch
DECCA 5-10 67-68
Picture Sleeves
DECCA 5-10 68
LPs: 10/12-inch
DECCA (74927 "The Cake") 40-50 67
DECCA (75039 "A Slice of the Cake") 40-50 68
Members: Jeanette Jacobs; Barbara Morillo.

CAKEKITCHEN
LPs: 10/12-inch
HOMESTEAD 5-10 91
Members: Graeme Jefferies; Rachael King; Robert Key; Russell Hoffman; David Mitchell.

CAL & CHUCK
Singles: 7-inch
DORE 4-8 64

CAL & IVAN
Singles: 7-inch
SKOOP (1052 "Lazy") 10-15 59
STARDAY (475 "Lazy") 5-10 60

CALAMITY JANE C&W '81
Singles: 7-inch
COLUMBIA 3-4 81-82
LPs: 10/12-inch
COLUMBIA 5-10 82
LYLE (9183 "Calamity Jane") 30-40 82
(Picture disc. Promotional issue only.)
Members: Pam Rose; Mary Fiedler; Linda Moore; Mary Ann Kennedy.
Also see ROSE, Pam

CAL-CONS
Singles: 7-inch
ALLRITE 15-25 62

CALDERA R&B/LP '77
Singles: 7-inch
CAPITOL 3-5 76
LPs: 10/12-inch
CAPITOL 8-10 76-79

CALDWELL, Andy
Singles: 7-inch
LIBERTY 10-20 58

CALDWELL, Bobby P&R/R&B/LP '78
Singles: 12-inch
MCA 4-6 84-85
Singles: 7-inch
CLOUDS 3-4 78-80
PBR INT'L 3-4 76
POLYDOR 3-4 82-83
MCA 3-4 84-85
LPs: 10/12-inch
CLOUDS 5-10 78-80
MCA 5-10 84
POLYDOR 5-10 82
Also see CAPTAIN BEYOND

CALDWELL, Clinton
Singles: 7-inch
OMNI 3-5 74

CALDWELL, Everett, & Rock-A-Billies
Singles: 7-inch
HAPPY HEARTS 5-10 61

CALDWELL, Harry
Singles: 7-inch
CARNIVAL 4-8

CALDWELL, Joe
(With the Majestics)
Singles: 7-inch
BIM (1 "How Long Will It Last") 100-200
ESTA (100 "Rollin' Tears") 200-250 59
(Esta 100 is also used for an Escos release.)
M.C. (1 "Guess I'm the Lonely One") 1000-2000 50s
Also see ESCOS
Also see FOUR PHARAOHS

CALDWELL, Louise Harrison
LPs: 10/12-inch
RECAR (2012 "All About the Beatles") 50-75 64

CALDWELL, Rue R&B/D&D '83
Singles: 12-inch
CRITIQUE 4-6 83
Singles: 7-inch
CRITIQUE 3-4 83

CALE, J.J. P&R/LP '72
Singles: 7-inch
LIBERTY (55840 "Dick Tracy") 5-10 66
MERCURY 3-4 83-84
SHELTER 3-5 71-81
LPs: 10/12-inch
MCA 5-10 81
MERCURY 5-10 82-85
SHELTER 10-15 71-79
SILVERTONE 5-8 80
Also see LEATHERCOATED MINDS

CALE, John LP '81
Singles: 7-inch
A&M 3-4 81
COLUMBIA 3-5 70
I.R.S. 3-4 79-80
REPRISE 3-5 72
Picture Sleeves
I.R.S. 3-4 79-80
LPs: 10/12-inch
A&M 5-10 81
COLUMBIA 12-15 70-71
I.R.S. 5-10 79
ISLAND 8-10 75-77
PASSPORT 5-10 84
REPRISE 10-12 72-73
ZE 5-10 83
Also see AYERS, Kevin
Also see EARTH OPERA
Also see PRIMITIVES
Also see REED, Lou, & John Cale
Also see VELVET UNDERGROUND

CALE, Johnny
Singles: 7-inch
CHAN (101 "Ain't That Lovin' You Baby") 20-30 61
MERCURY 8-12

CALEB & PLAYBOYS
(With the Emporers [sic]; with Gary K. Pepper & Orchestra)
Singles: 7-inch
OLIMPIC (4575 "I'm Yours") 250-500 63
Member: Caleb Talbert.

CALEDONIA
Singles: 7-inch
BIG TREE 3-5 77

CALELLO, Charlie
Singles: 7-inch
ARIOLA AMERICA 3-5 76
MIDSONG INT'L 3-4 80
LPs: 10/12-inch
MIDSONG INT'L 5-10 80

CALELLO, Pat
Singles: 7-inch
OLIVER 4-8 66

CALEN, Frankie P&R '61
Singles: 7-inch
BEAR 4-8 62
EPIC 4-8 63-64
KIP (1517 "Pretty Dimple") 8-12
NRC (029 "Angel Face") 5-10 59
NRC (5008 "Angel Face") 5-10 59
SPARK 15-20 61
U.A. 4-8 62

CALENDAR
Picture Sleeves
NRC (5008 "Angel Face") 10-20 59
LPs: 10/12-inch
PI KAPPA 8-12 76

CALENDAR GIRLS
Singles: 7-inch
4 CORNERS of the WORLD 4-8 65

CALENDARS
Singles: 7-inch
CYCLONE (5012 "If I Could Hold Your Hand") 1000-2000 59

CALENDARS
Singles: 7-inch
CHATTAHOOCHEE (722 "You Don't Fall in Love") 150-200 62
COED (564 "I'm Gonna Laugh at You") 150-200 61
PALACE (104 "Weekend") 10-20 61

CALHOON R&B '75
Singles: 12-inch
W.B./SPECTOR 4-8 75
Singles: 7-inch
W.B./SPECTOR 3-5 75-76

CALHOUN, Charles, & Four Students
Singles: 78 rpm
GROOVE (149 "Jamboree") 10-20 56
Singles: 7-inch
GROOVE (149 "Jamboree") 25-35 56
Also see CALHOUN, Charlie
Also see FOUR STUDENTS

CALHOUN, Charlie
(With His Orchestra & Chorus)
Singles: 78 rpm
MGM 5-10 55
Singles: 7-inch
MGM (11989 "Smack Dab in the Middle") 15-25 55
Also see CALHOUN, Charles, & Four Students

CALHOUN, Lena
(With the Emotions)
Singles: 7-inch
FLIP 15-20 61
Also see EMOTIONS

CALHOUN, Linda C&W '79
Singles: 7-inch
GRAPE 3-5 79

CALHOUN, Rory
Singles: 78 rpm
MGM 5-10 56
Singles: 7-inch
MGM (12359 "Flight to Hong Kong") 5-10 56
Picture Sleeves
MGM (12359 "Flight to Hong Kong") 15-25 56

CALIA, Billy
Singles: 7-inch
HULL 5-10 60

CALICO
Singles: 7-inch
BIG TREE 3-5 73
U.A. 3-5 74-76
LPs: 10/12-inch
U.A. 8-12 75-76

CALICO WALL
Singles: 7-inch
DOVE ("Flight Reaction") 5-10
(Colored vinyl. Number not known.)
TURTLE (1107 "Flight Reaction") 150-250 67
(Reissued in '87, but we do not yet have the details as to how to identify originals.)

CALIFORNIA
Singles: 7-inch
COLUMBIA 3-6 69

CALIFORNIA
Singles: 7-inch
RCA 3-4 79
RSO 3-5 78
Member: Curt Becher.
Also see BECHER, Curt, and California

CALIFORNIA
Singles: 7-inch
LAURIE 3-4 81

CALIFORNIA
Singles: 7-inch
VIVA 3-4 84

CALIFORNIA, Randy
Singles: 7-inch
EPIC 4-8 72
LPs: 10/12-inch
EPIC (31755 "Kapt. Kopter") 20-30 76
Also see KAPT. KOPTER & Fabulous Twirly Birds
Also see SPIRIT

CALIFORNIA EARTHQUAKE
Singles: 7-inch
U.A. 3-5 71
WORLD PACIFIC 4-6 69
LPs: 10/12-inch
U.A. 8-12 71
WORLD PACIFIC 10-15 69

CALIFORNIA GIRLS
Singles: 7-inch
DOORWAY 3-5 72

CALIFORNIA GOLD
Singles: 7-inch
LARUPIN 3-5 77
Members: David Vega; Tom Miller; Doug Clifford; Bobby Whitlock.

CALIFORNIA GOLD RUSH
Singles: 7-inch
SCEPTER 3-5 71

CALIFORNIA LICENSE
Singles: 7-inch
PHILIPS 3-6 70

CALIFORNIA MALIBUS
Singles: 7-inch
M&M (633 "I Stand Alone") 8-12

CALIFORNIA MUSIC
Singles: 7-inch
RCA/EQUINOX 10-15 74-76
Members: Dean Torrence; Bruce Johnston; Terry Melcher; Kenny Hinkle.
Also see BRUCE & TERRY
Also see HINKLE, Kenny
Also see JAN & DEAN

CALIFORNIA POPPY PICKERS
Singles: 7-inch
A/S 4-8 70
LPs: 10/12-inch
ALSHIRE 15-20 69

CALIFORNIA RAISINS LP '87
Singles: 7-inch
ATLANTIC 3-4 88
PRIORITY (Black vinyl) 3-4 87-88
PRIORITY (7915 "What Does It Take to Win Your Love") 4-6 88
(Colored vinyl.)
Picture Sleeves
ATLANTIC 3-5 88
PRIORITY 3-5 87-88
LPs: 10/12-inch
PRIORITY 5-10 87-88
Member: Buddy Miles.
Also see MILES, Buddy

CALIFORNIA ROCK CHOIR
Singles: 7-inch
CYCLONE 3-5 69

CALIFORNIA SMOG
Singles: 7-inch
IMPERIAL 5-10 69

CALIFORNIA SONS
Singles: 7-inch
COASTLINE 4-8 66

CALIFORNIA SUNS
Singles: 7-inch
IMPERIAL 4-8 66

CALIFORNIANS
Singles: 78 rpm
FEDERAL (12231 "My Angel") 50-100 55
Singles: 7-inch
FEDERAL (12231 "My Angel") 200-300 55

CALIFORNIANS
Singles: 7-inch
CRAFT (1001 "Please Don't Tell Me") 15-25 50s
(Colored vinyl.)
CRAZY HORSE 4-6 69

CALIMAN, Hadley
LPs: 10/12-inch
CATALYST 8-10 76-78
MAINSTREAM 10-12 71-72

CALIPHS
Singles: 7-inch
SARA (6772 "Today, Tomorrow") 15-25 67
SCATT (111 "Mother Dear") 500-750 58
VINTAGE 4-6 73

CALL, The P&R/LP '83
Singles: 12-inch
ELEKTRA 4-6 86
Singles: 7-inch
ELEKTRA 3-4 86
MCA 3-4 89
MERCURY 3-4 83
Picture Sleeves
ELEKTRA 3-4 86
MCA 3-4 89
MERCURY 3-4 83
LPs: 10/12-inch
ELEKTRA 5-10 86-87
MCA 5-8 89
MERCURY 5-10 82-83

CALL, Alex
Singles: 7-inch
ARISTA 3-4 83
LPs: 10/12-inch
ARISTA 5-10 83

CALL, Bob
Singles: 78 rpm
CORAL 20-40 49

CALLAHAN, Ginger
Singles: 78 rpm
JOYCE 8-12 50s
Singles: 7-inch
JOYCE 10-15 50s

CALLAHAN, Mike
Singles: 7-inch
PRO-TONE 10-15

CALLAHAN, Mike & Judy
Singles: 7-inch
DECCA 3-6 66

CALLAN, Mickey
(Michael Callan)
Singles: 7-inch
COLPIX (134 "Marina") 5-10 59
Picture Sleeves
COLPIX (134 "Marina") 10-20 59

CALLAWAY, Bob
(With the Spiro Hep Cats; with Chicks)
Singles: 7-inch
BIG RED 25-40 58
RCA 10-15 59

CALLAWAY, Virgil
(Virgil Callaway Combo)
Singles: 7-inch
PLANET EARTH 4-8 67

CALLENDER, Bobby P&R '63
(Bob Callender)
Singles: 7-inch
CORAL 10-15 67
GOLD (102 "Baby, I'm Ready") 50-100 61
ROULETTE (4471 "Little Star") 15-25 63
LPs: 10/12-inch
MGM (4557 "Rainbow") 75-125 68
(Includes lyrics insert.)

CALLENDER, Red
(Red Callender Sextet; with Buddy Collette)
Singles: 78 rpm
FEDERAL 5-10 51
RECORDED IN HOLLYWOOD 5-10 50-51
Singles: 7-inch
FEDERAL (12045 "Dolphin Street Boogie") 15-25 51
(Reissue of Recorded in Hollywood tracks.)
LPs: 10/12-inch
CROWN (5012 "Speaks Low") 40-60 57
CROWN (5025 "Swingin' Suite") 40-60 57
METROJAZZ (1007 "The Lowest") 20-30 59
MODERN (1201 "Swingin' Suite") 60-80 56
Also see COLLETTE, Buddy
Also see CRAYTON, Pee Wee
Also see LEE, Julia
Also see YOUNG, Lester

CALLICOAT, Mississippi Joe
LPs: 10/12-inch
BLUE HORIZON 10-15 72
SIRE 12-20 69

CALLICUTT, Dudley
(With the Go Boys)
Singles: 7-inch
DC (412 "Get Ready Baby")........50-100 59

CALLIER, J.J.
Singles: 7-inch
MAISON ("Just You and Me") 15-25
(Selection number not known.)

CALLIER, Terry R&B '79
Singles: 12-inch
ERECT 4-6 82
Singles: 7-inch
CADET (Except 5623) 50-75 68
CADET (5623 "Look at Me Now").... 5-10 69-73
ELEKTRA....................................... 3-5 78-79
LPs: 10/12-inch
CADET 10-12 72-73
CHESS..10-15 71
ELEKTRA...................................... 8-10 78-79

CALLIOPE
Singles: 7-inch
BUDDAH 4-6 69
EPIC... 5-8 68
JET SET.. 5-8 68
SHAMLEY 4-6 69
LPs: 10/12-inch
BUDDAH 15-20 68
Also see BANDITS
Also see O'KEEFE, Danny

CALLIOPE
Singles: 7-inch
AUDIO SEVEN (151 "Everybody's High")......................................30-40 67
AUDIO SEVEN (152 "Streets of Boston")...............................25-35 67

CALLOWAY P&R/LP '90
Singles: 7-inch
SOLAR 3-4 89-90
Picture Sleeves
SOLAR 3-4 90
LPs: 10/12-inch
SOLAR 5-8 90
Members: Cino-Vincent Calloway; Reggie Calloway.
Also see MIDNIGHT STAR

CALLOWAY, Al
Singles: 7-inch
CASH (1048 "Uncle John") 25-50 57

CALLOWAY, Baby
Singles: 7-inch
BAYTONE 12-25 59

CALLOWAY, Cab P&R '30
(With Cab Jivers; with Caballiers)
Singles: 78 rpm
ABC-PAR 5-10 56
BANNER 8-12 31-32
BELL 4-8 53-55
BLUEBIRD..................................... 5-10 49
BRUNSWICK 5-15 30-36
CAMEO 6-12
COLUMBIA.................................... 5-10 42-49
CONQUEROR................................. 6-12 38-41
DOMINO.......................................10-15 30
FILMOPHONE................................ 8-12
HI-TONE.. 5-10 49
JEWEL... 8-12 31
MEL-O-DEE.................................10-15 31
MELOTONE 8-12 32-33
OKEH 5-10 40-42
ORIOLE... 8-12 32-33
PERFECT...................................... 8-12 32
RCA... 4-8 49
REGAL 6-12 31-51
ROMEO.. 8-12 32-33
SIGNATURE................................... 5-8 49
VARIETY....................................... 8-12 33-37
VICTOR... 5-15 33-34
VOCALION..................................... 5-10 38-40
Singles: 7-inch
ABC-PAR 5-10 56
BOOM 4-6 65
CORAL 4-8 61-62
GONE... 8-15 58
OKEH (6896 "Willow Weep for Me")..20-30 52
RCA (007 "Rooming House Boogie")....................................50-75 49
RCA (8000 series) 4-6 62
RCA (11000 series)........................ 3-5 78
EPs: 7-inch
EPIC (7016 "Cab Calloway & His Orchestra")................................15-25 53
LPs: 10/12-inch
BRUNSWICK (58010 "Cab Calloway")..................................40-60 52
COLUMBIA....................................10-20 73
CORAL (57408 "Blues Make Me Happy")..15-20 62
(Monaural.)
CORAL (757408 "Blues Make Me Happy")..20-30 62
(Stereo.)
EPIC (3265 "Cab Calloway")..........30-50 57
GONE (101 "Cotton Club Revue") .30-50 58
GUEST STAR.................................10-15 60s
MARK 56..15-25 60s
RCA (LPM-2021 "Hi De Hi De Ho")...15-25 60
(Monaural.)
RCA (LSP-2021 "Hi De Hi De Ho")...25-35 60
(Stereo.)

CALLOWAY, Chris
Singles: 7-inch
CUB.. 4-8 67

CALLOWAY, Janet
Singles: 7-inch
ENJOY 10-15 62

CALS
Singles: 7-inch
LOADSTONE (1600 "Amazon Bossa Nova")..25-35

CALVAES
Singles: 78 rpm
COBRA 50-100 56
Singles: 7-inch
CHECKER (928 "So Bad")..............20-30 59
COBRA (5003 "Fine Girl")..........300-400 56
COBRA (5014 "Born with Rhythm")......................................300-400 57
Member: Oscar Boyd.

CALVANES
(With the Val Anthony Combo)
Singles: 78 rpm
DOOTONE 50-75 55
Singles: 7-inch
CLASSIC ARTISTS 4-6 90
DECK (579 "Dreamworld").........100-150 58
DECK (580 "My Love Song") 100-150 58
DOOTONE (371 "Crazy Over You")......................................150-250 55
DOOTONE (380 "Florabelle") 100-150 56
EPs: 7-inch
DOOTO (205 "Voices for Lovers")......................................50-100 60
DOOTONE (205 "Voices for Lovers")....................................400-500 56
Members: Stewart Crunk; Joe Hampton; Jack Harris; Lorenzo Adams.
Also see NUGGETS
Also see PENGUINS / Meadowlarks / Medallions / Calvanes

CALVERT, Duane
(With the Kittens)
Singles: 7-inch
DMD (102 "Somewhere Shoehow")..................................50-100 64

CALVERT, Eddie P&R '53
Singles: 78 rpm
CAPITOL... 3-5 56
ESSEX.. 3-5 53-54
Singles: 7-inch
ABC-PAR 4-6 60-61
CAPITOL... 4-8 56
ESSEX.. 4-8 53-54
LPs: 10/12-inch
ABC-PAR 10-15 60-62

CALVERTS
Singles: 7-inch
SALEM (1302 "Listen for the Raindrops") 15-25 60s

CALVEYS Featuring Gino Romano
Singles: 7-inch
COMMA (445 "The Wind")............30-50 61

CALVIN, Lee
Singles: 7-inch
ENRICA... 4-8 67

CALVIN, Tony
Singles: 7-inch
RADAR... 4-8 62

CALVIN & CLARENCE
Singles: 7-inch
FAIRLANE....................................... 5-8 61-62

CALVIN & VAN DYKES: see VAN DYKES

CAMACHO, Thelma
Singles: 7-inch
AIM.. 3-5 71
CASABLANCA 3-4 80-84
REPRISE... 3-6 69
LPs: 10/12-inch
CASABLANCA 5-10 80-84
Also see FIRST EDITION

CAMACHO, Ray, & Teardrops
Singles: 7-inch
COPPER STATE ("I Told You So")...10-20
(Selection number not known.)

CAMBRIDGE, Dottie
Singles: 7-inch
MGM 10-20 67-68

CAMBRIDGE, Godfrey LP '64
LPs: 10/12-inch
EPIC...10-20 64-68

CAMBRIDGE FIVE
Singles: 7-inch
USA (850 "Floatin")......................10-15 66

CAMBRIDGE STRINGS & SINGERS P&R '61
Singles: 7-inch
LONDON... 3-5 61
Also see KNIGHTSBRIDGE STRINGS

CAMEL LP '74
Singles: 7-inch
JANUS 3-5 74-77
LPs: 10/12-inch
ARISTA 5-10 79
JANUS 8-10 74-77
PASSPORT.....................................5-10 81
Members: Peter Bardens; Doug Ferguson; Andy Latimer; Andy Ward.
Also see BARDENS, Peter
Also see STRANGE BREW

CAMEL DRIVERS
Singles: 7-inch
BUDDAH (61 "Sunday Morning") 5-10 68
BUDDAH (85 "Don't Throw Stones at My Window")..5-10 68
TOP DOG (100 "The Grass Looks Greener")......................................10-15 68
TOP DOG (103 "Sunday Morning") 10-15 68
(First issue.)
TOP DOG (200 "You Made a Believer Out of Me")..10-15 68

CAMELOTS
(With Al Browne & the Cordials)
Singles: 7-inch
AANKO (1001 "Your Way")...........30-50 63
AANKO (1004 "Sunday Kind of Love")...30-50 63
COMET (2150 "Chase")..................8-12 62
COMET (2158 "Scratch")................8-12 63
CRIMSON 8-12 61
DREAM (1001 "I Wonder")..............5-10 67
EMBER (1108 "Pocahontas")........15-25 64
INVICTA (9005 "Bad Girl")............10-15 63
NIX (101 "Lulu")............................10-20 61
PORTRAIT (108 "Thirsty")............10-15 62
Also see EBONAIRES / Camelots

CAMELOTS / Suns
Singles: 7-inch
TIMES SQUARE (32 "Dance Girl") 10-15 64
(Colored vinyl.)

CAMEO R&B/LP '77
Singles: 12-inch
ATLANTA ARTISTS 4-6 83-86
CHOCOLATE CITY 4-6 78-80
Singles: 7-inch
ATLANTA ARTISTS 3-4 83-88
CHOCOLATE CITY 3-5 75-82
Picture Sleeves
ATLANTA ARTISTS 3-4 86-88
LPs: 10/12-inch
ATLANTA ARTISTS 5-10 83-90
CHOCOLATE CITY 5-10 77-82
Members: Tomi Jenkins; Larry Blackmon; Nathan Leftenant.
Also see EAST COAST
Also see SINGLETON, Charlie

CAMEOS
Singles: 78 rpm
DOOTONE (365 "Craving") 50-75 55
Singles: 7-inch
DOOTONE (365 "Craving") 75-125 55

CAMEOS
(With the Emeralds; with Shipmates)
Singles: 78 rpm
CAMEO..25-50 57
Singles: 7-inch
CAMEO (123 "Merry Christmas") 50-100 57
CAMEO (176 "Best of the Can Can")...15-25 58
COLLECTABLES 3-4 81
DEAN (504 "Wait Up")..............100-150 60
FLAGSHIP (115 "Please Love Me")..50-75 59
GIGI (100 "Can You Remember") 15-25 63
JOHNSON (108 "Wait Up")...........50-75 61
MATADOR (1808 "I Remember When")......................................75-125 63
(Orange label.)
MATADOR (1808 "I Remember When")..50-75 60
(Maroon label.)
MATADOR (1808 "I Remember When")..25-50 60
(Blue label.)
MATADOR (18138 "Never Before")..15-25 63
SOUNDCRAFT ("Can You Remember")...................................15-25
(Selection number not known.)
Picture Sleeves
CAMEO (176 "Best of the Can Can")...10-20 58

CAMEOS Featuring Billy Rome
Singles: 7-inch
ALL (501 "Penny Penny")..............30-40 60
Also see ROME, Billy

CAMERON R&B/LP '80
(Rafael Cameron)
Singles: 7-inch
SALSOUL...3-4 80-82
LPs: 10/12-inch
SALSOUL.......................................5-10 80-82

CAMERON, Bart C&W '86
Singles: 7-inch
REVOLVER.......................................3-4 86

CAMERON, Etta
Singles: 7-inch
ANNUIT COEPTIS 3-5 76

CAMERON, G.C. R&B '71
Singles: 7-inch
MALACO 3-4 83
MOTOWN 3-5 73-77
MOWEST...3-5 71-73
LPs: 10/12-inch
MOTOWN 5-10 74-77
Also see SPINNERS

CAMERON, George
Singles: 7-inch
PORTRAIT 8-12

CAMERON, Jimmy & Vella
Singles: 7-inch
REPRISE 15-25 66

UNLIMITED GOLD 3-4 80-81
LPs: 10/12-inch
UNLIMITED GOLD 5-10 81

CAMERON, Joanne
Singles: 7-inch
NORMAN 4-8 62

CAMERON, Johnny
(With the Camerons)
Singles: 7-inch
ATLANTIC..3-5 70
RCA 5-10 62
20TH FOX (179 "Fantastic") 10-15 60
Picture Sleeves
20TH FOX (179 "Fantastic") 15-25 60

CAMERON, Rafael: see CAMERON

CAMERONS
Singles: 7-inch
COUSINS (1-2 "Cheryl")...........150-200 61
CRYSTAL BALL 4-8
Also see TAYLOR, Mike

CAMERONS
Singles: 7-inch
COUSINS (1003 "Guardian Angel") 200-250 61
(This is a different group than the one above who recorded *Cheryl*, though both recorded for Cousins.)
FELSTED (8638 "Guardian Angel")..25-50 62
Also see DEMILLES

CAMILLE, Bob
(With the Lollipops; "Lil" Bob Camille)
Singles: 7-inch
LA LOUISIANNE (8122 "Soul Woman")..10-15
WHIT (6906 "Got to Get Away") 10-15 70
Also see LITTLE BOB

CAMILLI, Jim
Singles: 7-inch
("A Tribute to the King of Rock & Roll")..10-20 77
(Yellow vinyl. No label name or selection number used.)
Picture Sleeves
("A Tribute to the King of Rock & Roll")..10-20 77

CAMILLO, Tony: see BAZUKA

CAMINOS
Singles: 7-inch
LAVENDER (1925 "Camino Flip") 10-20 67

CAMMAROTA, H.
Singles: 7-inch
UNIVERSAL ARTISTS (1762 "Comanche Getaway")...8-12

CAMON, David
Singles: 7-inch
MOONSONG 3-5 72

CAMOTIONS
Singles: 7-inch
LA RO KE (751 "Sonny")...............12-18

CAMOUFLAGE P&R '88
Singles: 12-inch
ROULETTE 4-6 79
Singles: 7-inch
ATLANTIC..3-4 88
ROULETTE 3-5 76
Picture Sleeves
ATLANTIC..3-4 88
LPs: 10/12-inch
ATLANTIC..5-8 88

CAMP
Singles: 7-inch
SCEPTER (12159 "Marching") 50-75 66

CAMP, Bob
(With the Nighthawks; with His Buddies)
Singles: 78 rpm
DECCA...10-15 49
EBONY 10-15
ESSEX..10-15 52
SOUTHERN 10-15 45

CAMP, Colleen C&W '82
Singles: 7-inch
MOON PICTURES 3-4 82

CAMP, Hamilton P&R '68
(Hamid Hamilton Camp & Skymonters; Bob Camp)
Singles: 7-inch
AMERICAN INT'L.................................3-5 71
W.B. 4-8 68
LPs: 10/12-inch
ELEKTRA (200 series)....................12-15 64
ELEKTRA (75000 series)...................8-10 73
MOUNTAIN RAILROAD 5-10
W.B. 10-15 67-69
Also see GIBSON, Bob, & Bob Camp

CAMP GALORE
LPs: 10/12-inch
D&M...8-10 76

CAMP HILLTOP
Singles: 7-inch
A&M 3-6 69

CAMPANELLA, David, & Dellchords
Singles: 7-inch
KANE (25593 "Somewhere Over the Rainbow")......................................50-60 59

CAMPANIONS
Singles: 7-inch
DEE-DEE (1047 "I Want a Yul Brynner Haircut")..20-30 61
Also see DEL SATINS

CAMPBELL, Archie C&W '60
Singles: 7-inch
ELEKTRA..3-5 76-77
RCA (0147 thru 0766)........................3-5 72-73
RCA (7660 thru 9987).........................4-8 60-71
STARDAY 4-8 61-64
LPs: 10/12-inch
ELEKTRA...5-10 76
NASHVILLE 10-15 68
RCA 10-15 66-71
STARDAY (167 "Bedtime Stories for Adults")..20-25 62
STARDAY (223 "The Joker Is Wild")...15-20 63
STARDAY (377 "Grand Ole Opry's Good Humor Man") 10-20 66
Also see SOME of CHET'S FRIENDS

CAMPBELL, Archie, & Lorene Mann C&W '68
Singles: 7-inch
RCA 4-6 68
LPs: 10/12-inch
RCA 8-12 68
Also see MANN, Lorene

CAMPBELL, Archie, & Junior Samples
LPs: 10/12-inch
CHART...10-15 68
MOUNTAIN DEW..................................5-8
Also see CAMPBELL, Archie

CAMPBELL, Bernie
(With the Four Ekkos)
Singles: 7-inch
FINE (26571 "When I Find My Baby")...15-25
Also see FOUR EKKOS

CAMPBELL, Blind James
LPs: 10/12-inch
ARHOOLIE...8-10 63

CAMPBELL, Carl
(With Henry Hayes' 4 Kings.)
Singles: 78 rpm
FREEDOM 15-25 49
PEACOCK...15-25 50
Also see HAYES, Henry

CAMPBELL, Cecil C&W '49
(With the Tennessee Ramblers)
Singles: 78 rpm
MGM (12118 "Steel Guitar Waltz") ..5-10 55
MGM (12245 "Dixieland Rock") 10-20 56
MGM (12482 "Rock & Roll Fever")..25-50
MGM (12605 "On the Prado").........10-15 57
RCA 5-8 49
Singles: 7-inch
MGM (12118 "Steel Guitar Waltz")..10-15 55
MGM (12245 "Dixieland Rock") 25-50 56
MGM (12482 "Rock & Roll Fever")..75-100 57
MGM (12605 "On the Prado") 15-25 57
LPs: 10/12-inch
STARDAY (254 "Steel Guitar Jamboree")..30-40 63

CAMPBELL, Choker
(With Horace Williams; Walter Campbell)
Singles: 78 rpm
ATLANTIC...15-25 53-54
FORTUNE..25-35 53
Singles: 7-inch
APT (25011 "Walk a While") 40-60 58
ATLANTIC (1014 "Last Call for Whiskey")..20-30 53
ATLANTIC (1038 "Have You Seen My Baby")..20-30 54
CANDY APPLE (740 "Carioca").........5-8
FORTUNE (808 "Rocking and Jumping") 40-60 53
MAGIC CITY (2 "Going Christmas Shopping")..20-30 60s
MOTOWN (1072 "Come See About Me")..10-20 65
EPs: 7-inch
MOTOWN (60620 "Hits of the '60s")...25-35 64
LPs: 10/12-inch
MOTOWN (620 "Hits of the '60s")...50-75 64
Also see FULSON, Lowell

CAMPBELL, Chris
Singles: 7-inch
U.S.A. (885 "You Gotta Pay Dues") ...4-8 67

CAMPBELL, Cookie
Singles: 7-inch
KAPP 4-8 63

CAMPBELL, Debbie P&R '75
Singles: 7-inch
PLAYBOY 3-5 75

CAMPBELL, Dick
Singles: 7-inch
CUCA (6962 "Train to Hollywood")..10-20 69
GREAT (4703 "She's My Girl") 30-60 63
MERCURY (72511 "Blues Peddlers")..15-25 65
LP: 10/12-inch
MERCURY 15-25 65
Also see STOKER, Billy

CAMPBELL, Don
Singles: 7-inch
STANSON (509 "Campbell Lock") ... 10-20 65

CAMPBELL, Eddie C.
Singles: 7-inch
ROOSTER BLUES ... 3-4 81
Also see ERNIE & EDDIE

CAMPBELL, George, & Kool 5
Singles: 7-inch
WITCH'S BREW (121 "Sugar") ... 15-25

CAMPBELL, Glen P&R '61/C&W '62
(With the Glen-Aires; with Green River Boys; with Bandits)
Singles: 7-inch
ATLANTIC AMERICA ... 3-4 82-86
CAPEHART ... 10-20 61
CAPITOL (2000 & 3000 series) ... 3-6 68-74
CAPITOL (4000 series) ... 3-5 75-81
(Orange or purple labels.)
CAPITOL (4783 thru 5360) ... 5-10 61-65
(Orange/yellow swirl labels.)
CAPITOL (5441 "Guess I'm Dumb") ... 30-40 65
(With Brian Wilson.)
CAPITOL (5504 thru 5939, except 5927) ... 4-8 65-67
CAPITOL (5927 "My Baby's Gone/Kelli Hoedown") ... 6-12 67
(Has alternate takes. Promotional issue only.)
CAPITOL STARLINE ... 3-5
CENECO (1324 "Dreams for Sale") ... 10-25 59
CENECO (1356 "You, You, You") 10-15 60s
CREST (1087 "Turn Around Look at Me") ... 10-20 61
(Mistakenly credits "Glen Cambpbell" on some Crest labels.)
CREST (1096 "Miracle of Love") ... 15-25 61
EVEREST ... 3-6 69
STARDAY ... 3-6 68
MCA ... 3-4 84-89
MIRAGE ... 3-4 81
UNIVERSAL ... 3-4 89
W.B. ... 3-4 80
Picture Sleeves
ATLANTIC AMERICA ... 3-4 85-86
CAPITOL (Except 4856 & 5279) ... 3-6 68-74
CAPITOL (4856 "Long Black Limousine") ... 10-15 62
CAPITOL (5279 "Summer, Winter, Spring and Fall") ... 8-12 64
EPs: 7-inch
CAPITOL ... 5-10 68-69
(Juke box issues.)
CAPITOL/CHEVROLET (55 "The Glen Campbell Good Time Hour") ... 5-10 60s
CAPITOL CREATIVE PRODUCTS ... 5-10 60s
LPs: 10/12-inch
ATLANTIC AMERICA ... 5-10 82-86
BUCKBOARD ... 8-10
CAPITOL (103 thru 752) ... 8-15 68-71
CAPITOL (1810 "Big Bluegrass Special") ... 25-75 62
(Credits the "Green River Boys Featuring Glen Campbell.")
CAPITOL (1881 thru 2392) ... 10-20 63-65
(With "T" or "ST" prefix.)
CAPITOL (2809 thru 2978) ... 8-15 67-69
(With "T" or "ST" prefix.)
CAPITOL (SM-300 series) ... 5-10 82
CAPITOL (SM-2000 series) ... 5-10 78
CAPITOL (4000 series) ... 5-10 73
CAPITOL (11000 thru 16000 series) ... 5-10 72-85
CAPITOL (11722 "Basic") ... 50-100 78
(Picture disc. Promotional issue only. One of a four-artist, four-LP set. 250 made.)
CAPITOL (80000 series) ... 5-10
CAPITOL (94000 series) ... 8-15 72
(Capitol Record Club issues.)
CAPITOL (120000 series) ... 5-10
(Capitol Record Club issues.)
CAPITOL CREATIVE PRODUCTS 8-12
CAPITOL SPECIAL PRODUCTS ... 5-8 84
CUSTOM TONE ... 15-20
LONGINES (5408 "Gentle on My Mind") ... 5-10 69
LONGINES ("Glen Campbell's Golden Favorites") ... 20-30 72
(Boxed, six-disc set.)
PAIR ... 5-8 84
PICKWICK ... 8-10 64-79
SEARS ... 8-12
STARDAY ... 15-20 68-69
Session: Jerry Puckett.
Also see BACHARACH, Burt / Glen Campbell / Dionne Warwick
Also see BEACH BOYS
Also see BILLS, Dick
Also see CAPEHART, Jerry
Also see CHAMPS
Also see FABARES, Shelley
Also see FANN BAND
Also see FLEAS
Also see FOLKSWINGERS
Also see FORD, Tennessee Ernie, & Glen Campbell
Also see GEE CEES
Also see HONDELLS
Also see IN-GROUP
Also see JAN & DEAN
Also see KNIGHTS
Also see LEGENDARY MASKED SURFERS
Also see MARTIN, Dean / Glen Campbell
Also see MR. TWELVE STRING
Also see NELSON, Willie
Also see PUCKETT, Jerry
Also see RIP CHORDS
Also see ROGERS, Weldon
Also see SAGITTARIUS
Also see SWEET SOULS
Also see TILLIS, Mel, & Glen Campbell
Also see TUCKER, Tanya, & Glen Campbell
Also see WILSON, Brian
Also see YORK, Dave, & Beachcombers

CAMPBELL, Glen, & Rita Coolidge C&W/P&R '80
Singles: 7-inch
CAPITOL ... 3-4 80
Also see COOLIDGE, Rita

CAMPBELL, Glen, & Bobbie Gentry C&W/LP '68
Singles: 7-inch
CAPITOL ... 3-5 68-70
EPs: 7-inch
CAPITOL ... 8-10 68
(Juke box issue only.)
LPs: 10/12-inch
CAPITOL ... 8-10 68
Also see GENTRY, Bobbie

CAMPBELL, Glen / Lettermen / Ella Fitzgerald / Sandler & Young
LPs: 10/12-inch
CAPITOL (56 "B.F. Goodrich Presents Christmas 1969") ... 10-15 69
(Promotional, special products issue.)
Also see FITZGERALD, Ella
Also see LETTERMEN
Also see SANDLER & YOUNG

CAMPBELL, Glen, & Anne Murray C&W/P&R/LP '71
Singles: 7-inch
CAPITOL ... 3-5 71-72
LPs: 10/12-inch
CAPITOL ... 5-10 71-80

CAMPBELL, Glen / Anne Murray / Kenny Rogers / Crystal Gayle
LPs: 10/12-inch
CAPITOL/U.A. (11743-F-19 "Glen/Anne/Kenny/Crystal") ... 300-500 78
(Four framed picture disc set. Promotional issue only. 250 made)
Also see GAYLE, Crystal
Also see MURRAY, Anne
Also see ROGERS, Kenny
CAMPBELL, Glen, & Billy Strange
LPs: 10/12-inch
SURREY ... 12-20 65
Also see STRANGE, Billy

CAMPBELL, Glen / Texas Opera Company
Singles: 7-inch
W.B./VIVA ... 3-5 80

CAMPBELL, Glen, & Steve Wariner C&W '87
Singles: 7-inch
MCA ... 3-4 87
Also see WARINER, Steve

CAMPBELL, Glen / Dionne Warwick / Burt Bacharach
LPs: 10/12-inch
CHEVROLET (6658 "On the Move") ... 5-10 70
(Chevrolet promotional issue.)
Also see CAMPBELL, Glen

CAMPBELL, Jim P&R '70
Singles: 7-inch
LAURIE ... 3-6 69-70

CAMPBELL, Jimmy
LPs: 10/12-inch
VERTIGO ... 8-10 71

CAMPBELL, Jo Ann P&R '60
Singles: 78 rpm
ELDORADO ... 25-50 57
POINT ... 10-20 56
Singles: 7-inch
ABC-PAR ... 10-20 60-62
(Monaural.)
ABC-PAR (10134 "Kookie Little Paradise") ... 20-40 60
(Stereo.)
CAMEO ... 5-10 62-63
ELDORADO (504 "Forever Young") ... 15-25 57
GONE ... 10-20 59
POINT ... 15-25 56
RORI ... 5-10 62
LPs: 10/12-inch
ABC-PAR (393 "Twistin' and Listenin' ") ... 40-50 62
(Monaural.)
ABC-PAR (393 "Twistin' and Listenin' ") ... 50-60 62
(Stereo.)
CAMEO (1026 "All the Hits of Jo Ann Campbell") ... 25-30 62
CORONET (199 "Starring Jo Ann Campbell") ... 10-20 62
END (306 "I'm Nobody's Baby") ... 40-60 59
Also see JO ANN & TROY

CAMPBELL, Junior
Singles: 7-inch
DERAM ... 3-5 72
Also see MARMALADE

CAMPBELL, King
Singles: 7-inch
LEWIS ... 3-5 72

CAMPBELL, Little Milton
Singles: 7-inch
CHECKER ... 3-6 70
Also see LITTLE MILTON

CAMPBELL, Louis
Singles: 78 rpm
EXCELLO ... 25-50 54
Singles: 7-inch
EXCELLO (2035 "Gotta Have You Baby") ... 75-100 54
Also see LEAP FROGS

CAMPBELL, Michael Edward
(Michael Campbell)
Singles: 7-inch
MOTOWN ... 3-5 74
MOWEST ... 3-5 73
LPs: 10/12-inch
MOTOWN ... 8-12 74

CAMPBELL, Mike C&W '81
Singles: 7-inch
COLUMBIA ... 3-4 81-84
RSVP ... 4-6

CAMPBELL, Mike, & Tom Garvin
LPs: 10/12-inch
ITI ... 5-10 84
Also see CAMPBELL, Mike

CAMPBELL, Rev. Anthony, Hank Davis, & Calvin Morris
EPs: 7-inch
FOLKART (5002 "How Long Have You Been a Negro") ... 15-25 64
LPs: 10/12-inch
FOLKART (5002 "God Made the Blues") ... 25-50 64
FOLKART ... 10-15 64
Also see DAVIS, Hank

CAMPBELL, Stacy Dean C&W '92
Singles: 7-inch
COLUMBIA ... 3-4 92

CAMPBELL, Tevin
Singles: 7-inch
QWEST ... 3-4 89
LPs: 10/12-inch
QWEST ... 5-8 89
Also see JONES, Quincy, & Tevin Campbell

CAMPBELL, Sam
(Sammy Campbell)
Singles: 7-inch
GALAXY ... 5-8 70
QUEEN CITY ... 10-20

CAMPBELL, Sonny
Singles: 7-inch
APT ... 8-12 59
CARLTON ... 5-8 63

CAMPBELL, Vi
Singles: 7-inch
PEACOCK ... 4-8 65

CAMPBELL BROTHERS
Singles: 7-inch
AMHERST ... 3-5 75

CAMPELS
Singles: 7-inch
JOY ... 5-10 63

CAMPER VAN BEETHOVEN LP '88
LPs: 10/12-inch
VIRGIN ... 5-8 88-89

CAMPERS
Singles: 7-inch
PARKWAY (974 "The Ballad of Batman") ... 20-25 66
(Previously issued as by the Camps.)
Members: Sonny Curtis & Crickets.
Also see CAMPS
Also see CRICKETS
Also see CURTIS, Sonny

CAMPERS
Singles: 7-inch
COLUMBIA ... 4-8 66

CAMPI, Ray
Singles: 78 rpm
DOT ... 25-50 57
Singles: 7-inch
COLPIX ... 5-10 60
D (1047 "Ballad of Donna and Peggy Sue" ... 20-35 59
DOMINO (700 "My Screamin' Mimi") ... 20-30 59
DOT (15617 "Give That Love to Me") ... 25-50 57
ROLLIN' ROCK ... 3-5 78-83
TNT (145 "Play It Cool") ... 50-75 58
WINSOR (001 "Billie Jean") ... 15-25 64
Picture Sleeves
DOMINO (700 "My Screamin' Mimi") ... 50-100 59
EPs: 7-inch
TNT ("Ray Campi") ... 50-75 58
(Selection number not known. Title is uncertain.)
LPs: 10/12-inch
ROLLIN' ROCK ... 8-10 77-83
ROUNDER ... 5-10
Also see MACK, Ronnie
Also see McCOY BOYS

CAMPLIN, Bill
Singles: 7-inch
TOOL ROOM ... 3-5 76
LP: 10/12-inch
TOOL BOX ... 10-15 76

CAMPO, Lucy
Singles: 7-inch
RCA ... 8-12 62

CAMPO, Phil
Singles: 7-inch
IMPACT ... 5-10 60

CAMPS
Singles: 7-inch
PARKWAY (974 "The Ballad of Batman") ... 25-30 65
(Later issued as by the Campers.)
Members: Sonny Curtis & Crickets.
Also see CAMPERS
Also see CRICKETS
Also see CURTIS, Sonny

CAMPUS KIDS
Singles: 7-inch
ABC-PAR ... 4-8 62

CAMPUS QUEENS
Singles: 7-inch
GONE ... 5-8 62

CAMPUS SINGERS
LPs: 10/12-inch
ARGO ... 15-25 63

CAMS
Singles: 7-inch
INDIE (1303 "Smashin' ") ... 15-25 58

CAN
Singles: 7-inch
U.A. ... 3-5 74
Picture Sleeves
U.A. ... 3-5 74
LPs: 10/12-inch
U.A. ... 8-12 73-75
Members: Malcolm Mooney; Holger Czukay; Rosko Gee; Michael Karoli; Reebob Baah; Jacki Liebezeit; Irmin Schmidt; Kenji Suzuki.
Also see TRAFFIC

CANADA
Singles: 7-inch
CREAM ... 3-5 71

CANADA GOOSE
Singles: 7-inch
TONSIL ... 3-6 70

CANADIAN BEADLES
Singles: 7-inch
TIDE ... 10-15 64
LPs: 10/12-inch
TIDE (2005 "Three Faces North") ... 35-50 65
Members: Vic Blunt; Paul Case; Bruce Pollard.
Also see MOJO MEN

CANADIAN CLASSICS
Singles: 7-inch
VALIANT (723 "Gone Away") ... 25-35 65
Also see CLASSICS
Also see COLLECTORS

CANADIAN METEORS
Singles: 78 rpm
BULLSEYE ... 50-75 57
Singles: 7-inch
BULLSEYE (1002 "Street of Sorrow") ... 50-75 57

CANADIAN ROCK THEATRE
LPs: 10/12-inch
LION ... 10-15 72

CANADIAN ROGUES
Singles: 7-inch
CHARAY (19 "Keep in Touch") ... 20-30 66
FULLER ("You Better Stop") ... 15-25 66
PALMER (5017 "Keep in Touch") ... 20-30 67
PARIS TOWER (112 "Run and Hide") ... 15-25 67
ROGUE (1967 "Do You Love Me") 15-20 67

CANADIAN SQUIRES
Singles: 7-inch
APEX ... 10-20
WARE ... 15-20
Also see BAND

CANADIAN SWEETHEARTS C&W '64
Singles: 7-inch
A&M ... 5-10 63
EPIC ... 4-8 68
SOMA (1156 "No Help Wanted") ... 30-50 61
LPs: 10/12-inch
A&M (106 "Introducing the Canadian Sweethearts") ... 20-30 64
EPIC ... 15-25 72
Member: Lucille Starr.
Also see BOB & LUCILLE
Also see STARR, Lucille

CANADIAN V.I.P's
Singles: 7-inch
ARAGON (401 "Lucille") ... 25-35

CANALE, Vinnie
Singles: 7-inch
INTREPID ... 4-6 69

CANARIES
Singles: 7-inch
DIMENSION ... 10-15 63

CANARIES
LPs: 10/12-inch
B.T. PUPPY (1007 "Flying High with the Canaries") ... 20-30 70

CANARIOS, Los: see LOS CANARIOS

CANDANCE LOVE: see LOVE, Candance

CAN-DEE
Singles: 12-inch
KEE WEE ... 4-6 84

CANDEE, Bobby
(Bob Candee)
Singles: 7-inch
DORE ... 10-15 63
PENTAGRAM ... 3-5 71

CANDELA R&B '82
Singles: 12-inch
ARISTA ... 4-6 83
Singles: 7-inch
ARISTA ... 3-4 82-83

CANDI P&R '88
Singles: 7-inch
I.R.S. ... 3-4 88
Picture Sleeves
I.R.S. ... 3-5 88

CANDIDO
Singles: 7-inch
POLYDOR ... 3-5 73
SALSOUL ... 3-4 79-80
LPs: 10/12-inch
BLUE NOTE ... 8-10 71
POLYDOR ... 8-10 73
SALSOUL ... 5-10 79-80
SOLID STATE ... 10-12 70

CANDIES
Singles: 7-inch
EMBER ... 4-8 63
FLEETWOOD ... 10-20 63

CANDLE
Singles: 7-inch
GREEN BOTTLE ... 3-5 72
LPs: 10/12-inch
GREEN BOTTLE ... 10-12 72

CANDLELIGHTERS
Singles: 7-inch
DELTA (203 "Would You Do the Same for Me") ... 1000-2000 58

CANDLEMASS LP '89
LPs: 10/12-inch
METAL BLADE ... 5-8 89

CANDLES
(Blenders)
Singles: 7-inch
NIKE (1016 "Down on My Knees") 25-50 63
Session: Johnny Pate.
Also see BLENDERS
Also see PATE, Johnny

CANDLETTES
Singles: 7-inch
RONDA (1001 "Moments to Remember") ... 50-100 61

CANDLETTS
Singles: 7-inch
VITA (179 "Angel Love") ... 30-40 58
VITA (182 "My Only Love") ... 30-40 59
Members: Ruth Christie; Cathy Saunders.
Also see CHRISTIE, Ruth
Also see SAUNDERS, Kathy

CANDLEWICK GREEN
Singles: 7-inch
BASF ... 3-5 74
MPS ... 3-5 72
LPs: 10/12-inch
BASF ... 8-12 75
Members: Terry Webb; Jimmy Nunnen; Andy Leland; Derek Cleary; Andy Ball.

CANDOLI, Pete
Singles: 7-inch
NAN ... 8-12 64

CANDOLI BROTHERS
Singles: 7-inch
DOT (15614 "Rockin' Boogie") ... 15-25 57

CANDY
Singles: 7-inch
TAO ... 3-5 77

CANDY, Penny
Singles: 7-inch
DWAIN (816 "Come on Over") ... 10-15 60
FLIPPIN' (201 "Rockin' Lady") ... 25-35 59

CANDY & KISSES P&R/R&B '64
Singles: 7-inch
CAMEO ... 10-15 64
COLLECTABLES ... 3-4 81
DECCA ... 4-8 68
R&L ... 10-15 63
SCEPTER ... 8-12 65-66
Members: Candy Nelson; Suzanne Nelson; Jeanette Johnson.

CANDY & SUGARTONES
Singles: 7-inch
JACKPOT (46008 "Hurtin' All Over") ... 10-15 58

CANDY & SWEETS
Singles: 7-inch
20TH FOX ... 3-5 73

CANDY APPLE
Singles: 7-inch
A/S ... 3-5 70
BEVERLY HILLS ... 3-5 73

CANDY COMPANY
Singles: 7-inch
ABC ... 4-8 66

CANDY GIRLS
Singles: 7-inch
ROTATE (5001 "Tomorrow My Love") ... 10-20 63
Also see LORIN, Tempi, & Candy Girls

CANDY MAKERS
Singles: 7-inch
URBAN 4-8

CANDY STORE
LPs: 10/12-inch
DECCA 20-25 69

CANDY STRIPES
Singles: 7-inch
VIM 15-20 61

CANDY YAMS
Singles: 7-inch
CAT 3-5 80
Member: Sax Kari.

CANDYMAN P&R/LP '90
Singles: 7-inch
EPIC 3-4 90
LPs: 10/12-inch
EPIC 5-8 90

CANDYMEN
Singles: 7-inch
PROMENADE (24 "Spearmint Twist") 5-8 62
LPs: 10/12-inch
DIPLOMAT 10-15 62

CANDYMEN P&R/LP '67
Singles: 7-inch
ABC 4-8 67-69
LIBERTY 3-6 70
LPs: 10/12-inch
ABC 15-25 67-68
Members: Rodney Justo; Barry Bailey; Dean Daughtry; Billy Gilmore; Paul Goddard; John Adkins; Bob Nix.
Also see ATLANTA RHYTHM SECTION
Also see BEAVERTEETH
Also see CLASSICS IV
Also see ORBISON, Roy

CANE, Gary P&R '60
(With His Friends)
Singles: 7-inch
SHELL 8-12 60-61

CANE, Stacey
Singles: 7-inch
JUBILEE 4-8 65

CANECUTTERS
Singles: 78 rpm
CHECKER 75-125 54
Singles: 7-inch
CHECKER (795 "No More Heartaches") 300-400 54

CANES
Singles: 7-inch
STAX 8-12 62

CANFIL, Chase
Singles: 7-inch
DART 5-10 59-60

CANNA, Little Junior
Singles: 7-inch
BIG STAR 10-15

CANNATA, Jeff
Singles: 7-inch
MIRAGE 3-4 81

CANNED HEAT LP '67
(Heat Brothers)
Singles: 7-inch
ALA 3-4 84
ATLANTIC 3-5 74
LIBERTY 4-8 68-71
U.A. 3-5 71-73
Picture Sleeves
LIBERTY 5-10 67-69
LPs: 10/12-inch
ACCORD 5-10 81
ALA 8-10 84
ATLANTIC 10-12 73-74
HAPPY BIRD (90135 "Dog House Blues") 10-20 83
(Picture disc.)
JANUS (3009 "Vintage") 10-15 69
LIBERTY (1000 series) 5-10 80
LIBERTY (3526 "Canned Heat") 25-40 67
(Monaural.)
LIBERTY (7526 "Canned Heat") 15-25 67
(Stereo.)
LIBERTY (7541 "Boogie") 15-25 68
LIBERTY (7618 "Hallelujah") 15-20 69
LIBERTY (10000 series) 5-10 81
LIBERTY (11000 "Cook Book") 10-15 69
LIBERTY (11002 "Future Blues") 10-15 70
LIBERTY (27200 "Living the Blues") 10-20 68
PICKWICK 5-10 70s
SCEPTER 10-15
SPRINGBOARD 5-10
SUNSET 10-15 71
U.A. 10-15 71-75
WAND 15-20 70
Members: Bob Hite; Joel Scott Hill; Harvey Mandel; Mark Andes; Ed Bayer; Frank Cook; Richard Hite; Chris Morgan; James Shane; Gene Taylor; Larry Taylor; Henry Vestine; Alan Wilson; Adolfo "Fito" de la Parra.
Also see GAMBLERS
Also see HILL, Joel
Also see HOOKER, John Lee, & Canned Heat
Also see LITTLE RICHARD
Also see MANDEL, Harvey
Also see SMOKE

CANNED HEAT & CHIPMUNKS
Singles: 7-inch
LIBERTY 15-25 68-70
Also see CANNED HEAT
Also see CHIPMUNKS

CANNERY ROW
Singles: 7-inch
WORLD PACIFIC 4-6 69

CANNIBAL & HEADHUNTERS P&R/LP '65
Singles: 7-inch
AIRES 5-10 68
CAPITOL 4-8 69
COLLECTABLES 3-4 81
DATE 5-10 66
ERA 3-5 73
RAMPART 10-15 65-66
LPs: 10/12-inch
DATE (3001 "Land of 1000 Dances") 20-30 66
RAMPART (3302 "Land of 1000 Dances") 40-60 65
Members: Frankie "Cannibal" Garcia; Robert Jaramillo; Joe Jaramillo; Richard Lopez.

CANNON, Ace P&R '61
(Johnny "Ace" Cannon)
Singles: 7-inch
FERNWOOD (135 "Hoe Down Rock") 5-10 63
FERNWOOD (137 "Big Shot") 5-10 64
(First issued as by Johnny Cannon.)
HI (2000 series) 5-10 61-66
HI (2100 thru 2300 series) 3-8 66-76
LOUIS (2001 "Tuff") 20-30 61
MOTOWN 3-4 82
SANTO 5-10 62
Picture Sleeves
HI 5-10 62-63
EPs: 7-inch
HI (1133 "In the Spotlight") 5-10 68
(Juke box issue.)
LPs: 10/12-inch
ALLEGIANCE 5-10 84
GUSTO 5-10 80
HI (007 thru 040) 10-20 62-67
(Numbers in this series are preceeded by a "12" for mono or a "32" for stereo issues.)
HI (043 thru 090) 8-15 68-75
(Numbers in this series are preceded by a "32," indicating stereo.)
HI (6000 & 8000 series) 8-10 77-79
MOTOWN 5-10 83
Also see BLACK, Bill
Also see CANNON, Johnny

CANNON, Dean
Singles: 7-inch
VALIANT 4-8 63

CANNON, Dyan
LP: 10/12-inch
HMF (001 "Having It All") 60-80 83
(Picture disc. Promotional issue only.)

CANNON, Freddy P&R/R&B '59
(Freddie Cannon; Freddie Cannon / Cannon's Express)
Singles: 78 rpm
QUALITY (1897 "Tallahassee Lassie") 50-100 59
(Canadian.)
Singles: 7-inch
AMHERST 3-5 88
ANDEE 3-5 75
BUDDAH 3-5 71
CLARIDGE 3-5 74-76
ERIC 3-4 78
HQ ("Kennywood Park") 4-6 87
(KDKA promotional issue only. No selection number used.)
MCA 3-5 74
METROMEDIA 3-5 72
QUALITY (1897 "Tallahassee Lassie") 20-30 59
(Canadian.)
ROYAL AMERICAN 3-6 69-70
SIRE 4-6 69
SWAN (4031 "Tallahassee Lassie") 10-20 59
SWAN (4038 "Okefenokee") 10-20 59
SWAN (4043 "Way Down Yonder in New Orleans") 10-20 59
SWAN (4050 "Chattanooga Shoe Shine Boy") 10-20 60
SWAN (4053 "Jump Over") 10-20 60
SWAN (4057 "Happy Shades of Blue") 10-20 60
SWAN (4061 "Humdinger") 10-20 60
SWAN (4066 "Muskrat Ramble") 10-20 60
SWAN (4071 "Buzz Buzz A-Diddle-It") 10-20 61
SWAN (4078 "Transistor Sister") 10-20 61
SWAN (4083 thru 4178) 8-15 61-64
W.B. 6-12 64-67
WE MAKE ROCK & ROLL RECORDS 4-8 68
Picture Sleeves
HQ ("Kennywood Park") 5-8 87
(KDKA promotional issue only. No selection number used.)
SWAN (4043 "Way Down Yonder in New Orleans") 15-25 59
SWAN (4050 "Chattanooga Shoe Shine Boy") 15-25 60
SWAN (4053 "Jump Over") 15-25 60
SWAN (4057 "Happy Shades of Blue") 15-25 60
SWAN (4061 "Humdinger") 15-25 60
SWAN (4066 "Muskrat Ramble") 15-25 60
SWAN (4071 "Buzz Buzz A-Diddle-It") 15-25 61
SWAN (4078 "Transistor Sister") 15-25 61
W.B. (5616 "In the Night") 10-20 64
LPs: 10/12-inch
RHINO 5-10 82
SWAN (502 "The Explosive Freddy Cannon") 50-100 60
(Monaural.)
SWAN (502 "The Explosive Freddy Cannon") 75-125 60
(Stereo.)
SWAN (504 "Happy Shades of Blue") 50-75 62
SWAN (505 "Solid Gold Hits") 100-200 61
SWAN (507 "Palisades Park") 50-75 62
SWAN (511 "Freddy Cannon Steps Out") 50-75 62
W.B. (1544 "Freddie Cannon") 30-40 64
W.B. (1612 "Action") 30-40 64
W.B. (1628 "Greatest Hits") 30-40 64
Also see BUCHANAN, Roy
Also see CANNON'S EXPRESS
Also see DANNY & JUNIORS
Also see G-CLEFS
Also see SLAY, Frank, & His Orchestra
Also see SPINDRIFTS

CANNON, Freddy, & Belmonts
Singles: 7-inch
MIA SOUND 4-6 81
Also see BELMONTS, Freddy Cannon & Bo Diddley
Also see CANNON, Freddy

CANNON, Gus
Singles: 7-inch
STAX 4-8 63
LPs: 10/12-inch
STAX (702 "Walk Right In") 50-75 62
(Stax appears to have recalled this LP shortly after release, as the number 702 was also used for a various artists collection, *Hit Sounds of the South.*)

CANNON, Jack, & Continental Allegros
LPs: 10/12-inch
POMPEII 10-15 71

CANNON, Jackie
Singles: 7-inch
CHAN (103 "Proof of Your Love") 30-40 61
CHESS (1807 "Proof of Your Love") 8-12 61

CANNON, Jim
Singles: 7-inch
FRETONE 3-5 73

CANNON, Jimmi C&W '81
Singles: 7-inch
W.B. 3-4 81-82
Also see GOLDDIGGERS

CANNON, Johnny
(Ace Cannon)
Singles: 7-inch
FERNWOOD (117 "Big Shot") 15-25 60
Also see CANNON, Ace

CANNON, Lonzine
Singles: 7-inch
PHILIPS (40128 "One at a Time") 10-15 63
PHILIPS (40190 "You Still Love Her") 10-15 64
PHILIPS (40240 "Quit While You're Ahead") 50-100 64
CADET (5623 "Look at Me Now") 25-50 68-73

CANNON BROTHERS
Singles: 7-inch
RIC (107 "Surfin' in Bermuda") 15-25 63

CANNON SISTERS
Singles: 7-inch
VALIANT 5-10 62

CANNON'S EXPRESS
Singles: 7-inch
ANDEE (4001 "Chomp Chomp, Sooey Sooey") 5-10 75
Also see CANNON, Freddie

CANNONBALL
Singles: 7-inch
BLAST 4-8 73
KNIGHTSBRIDGE (050 "No Good to Cry") 10-20 60

CANNONBALLS
Singles: 7-inch
BOBBY (222 "Johnny B. Goode") 15-25
BRUNSWICK 5-10 61-62

CANNONS
Singles: 7-inch
LONDON 5-10 60

CANNONS C&W '83
Singles: 7-inch
COMPLEAT 3-4 83
MERCURY 3-4 86-87
Members: Carla Cannon; Darla Cannon; Larry Cannon.

CANO, Eddie LP '62
Singles: 7-inch
DUNHILL 3-6 66-67
GNP 4-6 62
REPRISE 4-8 62-65
LPs: 10/12-inch
DUNHILL 10-15 67
GNP 10-20 61-62
RCA 10-20 62
REPRISE 10-20 62-65

CANO, Eddie, & Nino Tempo
LP: 10/12-inch
ATCO 10-15
Also see CANO, Eddie
Also see TEMPO, Nino

CANOISE
Singles: 7-inch
IGL 12-18 67
SONIC 12-18 67
TRIM 8-12 66

CANOVA, Diana
Singles: 7-inch
20TH FOX 3-4 81
Picture Sleeves
20TH FOX 3-6 81

CANS
Singles: 7-inch
PHILIPS 3-5 70

CANTELON, Willard
LPs: 10/12-inch
SUPREME (113 "LSD Battle for the Mind") 25-30 66

CANTERBURY, Chip
Singles: 7-inch
RIVERSIDE 3-5 77

CANTERBURY FAIR
Singles: 7-inch
KOALA 4-8

CANTERBURY MUSIC FESTIVAL
Singles: 7-inch
B.T. PUPPY 4-8 68

CANTINA, Sarah, Band
Singles: 7-inch
SAMAR 10-20

CANTINA BAND P&R '81
Singles: 7-inch
MILLENNIUM 5-8 81
Member: Lou Christie.
Also see CHRISTIE, Lou

CANTRELL, Lana LP '68
Singles: 7-inch
EAST COAST 3-4 74
POLYDOR 3-4 74-75
RCA 3-6 66-69
LPs: 10/12-inch
RCA 8-15 67-69

CANTRELLS
Singles: 7-inch
KASH 4-8 65

CANTU, Vince, & Rockin' Dominoes
Singles: 7-inch
FOX 8-12

CANTY, Capt. John, U.S.A.F.
Singles: 7-inch
MGM (14192 "M.I.A.-P.O.W.") 3-6 70

CANUCKS
Singles: 7-inch
DIADON 5-10 60

CANYON
Singles: 7-inch
COLUMBIA 3-6 70
LPs: 10/12-inch
COLUMBIA 10-12 70

CANYON
Singles: 7-inch
MERCURY 3-6 70
Member: Eddie Haddad.

CANYON P&R '75
Singles: 7-inch
MAGNA-GLIDE 3-5 75

CANYON C&W '88
Singles: 7-inch
16TH AVENUE 3-4 88-90

CANYON, Rusty
(With the Banana Boys)
Singles: 7-inch
TEENERAMA 5-10 58

CANYON BROTHERS
Singles: 7-inch
TOPPA 5-10 61

CAPABILITY BROWN
Singles: 7-inch
CHARISMA 3-5 72
LPs: 10/12-inch
CHARISMA 10-12 72
PASSPORT 8-10 74
Members: Tony Ferguson; Dave Nevin; Roger Willis; Grahame White Kenny Rowe; Joe Williams.

CAPALDI, Jim P&R/LP '72
Singles: 12-inch
ISLAND 4-8 88
(Promotional only.)
RSO 4-6 79
Singles: 7-inch
ATLANTIC 3-4 83
ISLAND 3-5 72-88
RSO 3-4 78
Picture Sleeves
ATLANTIC 3-4 83
LPs: 10/12-inch
ATLANTIC 5-10 83
CAPITOL 8-10 72
ISLAND 6-12 73-88
RSO 5-10 78-79
Also see TRAFFIC

CAPEHART, Jerry
(Jerry Neal)
Singles: 7-inch
CASH (1021 "Rollin' ") 25-40 56
(With the Cochran Brothers.)
CREST (1101 "Song of New Orleans") 20-30 62
(With Eddie Cochran and Glen Campbell.)
Also see CAMPBELL, Glen
Also see COCHRAN, Eddie
Also see COCHRAN BROTHERS
Also see NEAL, Jerry

CAPELLO, Lenny
(With the Dots)
Singles: 7-inch
RIC 15-25 60-62

CAPER BROTHERS
Singles: 7-inch
ROULETTE 4-8 65

CAPERS
Singles: 7-inch
VEE JAY 10-20 58-59

CAPERS
Singles: 7-inch
DORE 4-8 61

CAPERS, Valerie
LPs: 10/12-inch
ATLANTIC 12-20 66

CAPERS & CARSON
Singles: 7-inch
JANUS 3-5 73
LPs: 10/12-inch
JANUS 10-15 73

CAPES
Singles: 78 rpm
CHAT (5005 "The Vow") 250-450 50s
Singles: 7-inch
CHAT (5005 "The Vow") 1500-2000 50s

CAPES & MASKS
LPs: 10/12-inch
MAINSTREAM 15-20 66

CAPES OF GOOD HOPE
Singles: 7-inch
ROUND (1001 "Shades") 10-20 66
ROUND (1002 "Winter's Children") 10-20 66

CAPISTRANOS: see LITTLETON, John

CAPITAL CITY ROCKETS
Singles: 7-inch
ELEKTRA 3-5 73
LPs: 10/12-inch
ELEKTRA 15-20 73
Members: Jamie Lyons; Jerry Hertig; Bob Hill; Eric Moore; Michael Warner.
Also see GODZ
Also see LYONS, Jamie

CAPITAL PUNISHMENT
Singles: 7-inch
THUMB (9840 "Berkowitz Hop") 5-10

CAPITALS
Singles: 7-inch
TRIUMPH 10-15 59

CAPITALS C&W '80
Singles: 7-inch
RIDGETOP 3-4 80-81

CAPITOL CITY BOYS
Singles: 7-inch
COMPASS 3-4 83
NSD 3-4 83

CAPITOL CITY SINGERS
Singles: 7-inch
SONG BIRD 4-6

CAPITOL'S MYSTERY ARTIST
(Nancy Wilson)
Singles: 7-inch
CAPITOL (1667 "Something Wonderful Happens") 5-10 60
(Promotional issue only. Nancy's name is not shown on label.)
Also see WILSON, Nancy

CAPITOLS
Singles: 7-inch
CARLTON (461 "I Let Her Go") 300-400 58

CAPITOLS P&R/R&B/LP '66
Singles: 7-inch
COLLECTABLES 3-4 81
KAREN 4-8 66-68
LPs: 10/12-inch
ATCO 15-20 66
COLLECTABLES 6-8 88
SOLID SMOKE 5-10 85
Members: Sam George; Don Storball; Richard McDougall.

CAPITOLS
Singles: 7-inch
PET (807 "Angel of Love") 150-250 58

CAPITOLS
Singles: 7-inch
PORTRAIT (109 "I'll Drink a Toast") 50-75 62

CAPITOLS
EPs: 7-inch
MTR 5-10 62

CAPITOLS
Singles: 7-inch
KORAN (1526 "In the Groove") 20-30

CAPITOLS
(Capitol's)
Singles: 7-inch
GATEWAY (721 "Little Things") 250-350 64
(Beige label.)
GATEWAY (721 "Little Things")...75-125 64
(White label. Promotional issue only.)
Also see TOLIVER, Mickey, & Capitols

CAPONE, Susan
(With the Four Esquires)
Singles: 78 rpm
PILGRIM...10-20 56
Singles: 7-inch
EVENT (4288 "I Understand")...8-12 58
PILGRIM (704 "I'll be Dancing")...10-20 56
PILGRIM (718 "Chick-a-Dee")...10-20 56
Also see FOUR ESQUIRES

CAPOTE, Truman
LPs: 10/12-inch
U.A....10-20 68

CAPP, Joe,
(With the Count Downs; with Starfires)
Singles: 7-inch
ROULETTE...8-12 62
Member: Bill Ramal.
Also see RAMAL, Bill

CAPPEL, Larry
Singles: 7-inch
RCA...4-8 67

CAPPS, Al
(Al Capps Band)
Singles: 7-inch
BELL...3-5 73
COLUMBIA...3-5 70

CAPPS, Hank C&W '72
Singles: 7-inch
CAPITOL...3-5 72

CAPPS, Jimmy
Singles: 7-inch
PAPA JOE...3-5 71-72

CAPPS, Judy
Singles: 7-inch
CHERRY (1009 "You Can Have My Love")...40-60 60

CAPREE, Jonathan
Singles: 7-inch
MINI (101 "Mindy")...5-10

CAPREES
Singles: 7-inch
BUCCANEER (502 "If I Should Lose You")...75-125 62

CAPREES / Dawns
Singles: 7-inch
STOOP SOUNDS (503 "If I Should Lose You")...100-150 96
(Limited edition. Estimates range from less than 10 to a few dozen made.)
Also see CAPREES

CAPREEZ
Singles: 7-inch
SOUND (126 "Rosanna")...10-15 66
SOUND (126 "Roseanna")...15-25 66
(Note spelling error.)
SOUND (149 "It's Good to Be Home Again")...25-50 67
SOUND (171 "Time")...10-20 67
TOWER (370 "Time")...5-10 67

CAPRELLS R&B '77
Singles: 7-inch
ARIOLA AMERICA...3-5 76
BANO (100 "Walk On By")...8-10
CRS (008 "Which One Will It Be")...5-8

CAPRI, Bobby
(With the Velvet Satins)
Singles: 7-inch
ARISTE (101 "One Sided Love")...100-200 61
JOHNSON (124 "You and I")...50-100 63
JOHNSON (126 "The Night")...100-200 63
Also see VELVET SATINS

CAPRI, John
(With the Fabulous Fours)
Singles: 7-inch
BOMARC (306 "When I'm Lonely")...30-50 59

CAPRI SISTERS
Singles: 78 rpm
JUBILEE...4-8 56
Singles: 7-inch
ABC-PAR...5-10 60
DOT...5-10 58
HANOVER...5-10 59
JUBILEE...8-12 56
NEWTOWN...5-10 62
WARWICK...5-10 61

CAPRICORN
Singles: 7-inch
RUST...4-8 67

CAPRICORNS
Singles: 7-inch
RCA...4-8 66

CAPRIES
Singles: 7-inch
RAINBOW ("Hey Girl")...10-20
(No selection number used.)

CAPRIS
("With Rhythm Accompaniment")
Singles: 78 rpm
GOTHAM...50-75 54-56
RAGE...50-75 54
Singles: 7-inch
CANDLELITE (422 "Oh, My Darling")...10-20 63
GOTHAM (304 "God Only Knows")...100-200 54
(Blue label.)
GOTHAM (304 "God Only Knows")...75-125 54
(Red label.)
GOTHAM (304 "God Only Knows")...50-75 56
(Yellow label.)
GOTHAM (306 "It Was Moonglow")...100-150 55
GOTHAM (308 "It's a Miracle")...75-125 56
LIFETIME (1001 "Oh, My Darling")...50-100 61
RAGE (101 "Fools Fall in Love")...100-150 54
TWENTIETH CENTURY (1201 "My Weakness")...25-50 57
TWENTIETH CENTURY (7304 "That's What You're Doing to Me")...10-15
LPs: 10/12-inch
COLLECTABLES...8-10 80
Members: Bobby Smart; Herb Johnson; Larry Scott; Rubin Wright.
Also see BELLTONES
Also see BROWNE, Doris

CAPRIS
(Capri's)
Singles: 7-inch
FABLE (665 "This Is Goodbye")...400-600 59
SABRE (201 "My Promise to You")...300-500 59

CAPRIS
Singles: 7-inch
TENDER (518 "Endless Love"/"Beware")...75-125 59
(*Beware* is by Jesse Belvin, and was issued in 1956 on Cash by him.)
Member: Jesse Belvin.
Also see BELVIN, Jesse

CAPRIS P&R '60
Singles: 7-inch
AMBIENT SOUND...5-10 82
JANUS (714 "Why Did I Cry")...4-6 77
COLLECTABLES...3-4 81
DELTA (3118 "There's a Moon Out Tonight")...10-20 61
(Canadian.)
LOST-NITE (101 "There's a Moon Out Tonight")...40-60 60
(Pink label. Black vinyl.)
LOST-NITE (101 "There's a Moon Out Tonight")...75-125 60
(Pink label. Red vinyl.)
LOST NITE (101 "There's a Moon Out Tonight")...5-10 60s
(Yellow label.)
MR. PEEKE (118 "Limbo")...10-20 63
OLD TOWN (1094 "There's a Moon Out Tonight")...10-20 60
OLD TOWN (1099 "Where I Fell in Love")...25-35 60
OLD TOWN (1103 "Why Do I Cry")...20-30 60
OLD TOWN (1107 "Girl in My Dreams")...30-50 61
PLANET (1010 "There's a Moon Out Tonight")...250-350 60
TROMMERS (101 "There's a Moon Out Tonight")...30-40 60
LPs: 10/12-inch
AMBIENT SOUND...8-12 82
COLLECTABLES...5-10 84
Members: Nick "Santos" Santamaria; Mike Mitchell; Vince Narcardo; John Apostol; Frank Reina.
Also see COLE, Clay

CAPRISIANS
Singles: 7-inch
INDIGO (109 "Lovely Way to Spend an Evening")...20-35 60
LAVENDER (4 "Oh What a Nite")..20-40 61

CAPS
Singles: 7-inch
LEO...20-40 57
WHITE STAR (102 "Red Headed Flea")...10-20 59
WHITE STAR (103 "Daddy Dean Part Two")...10-20 59

CAPTAIN & TENNILLE P&R/LP '75
Singles: 7-inch
A&M...3-5 75-78
BUTTERSCOTCH CASTLE (001 "The Way I Want to Touch You")...50-75 73
JOYCE (101 "The Way I Want to Touch You")...20-40 74
CASABLANCA...3-5 79-80
Picture Sleeves
A&M...4-6 75-78
LPs: 10/12-inch
A&M...8-10 75-79
CASABLANCA...5-10 79
Members: Daryl Dragon; Toni Tennille.
Also see BEACH BOYS
Also see DRAGONS
Also see TENNILLE, Toni
Also see YELLOW BALLOON

CAPTAIN BEEFHEART LP '72
(With His Magic Band)
Singles: 7-inch
A&M (794 "Diddy Wah Diddy")...50-75 66
A&M (818 "Moonchild")...40-60 66
BUDDAH...4-8 67-69
EPIC...3-5 82
MCA (40897 "Hard Workin' Man")...4-8 70s
MERCURY...3-5 74
REPRISE...3-6 72
VIRGIN...3-5 82
Promotional Singles
REPRISE (434 "Lick My Decals Off, Baby")...40-50 70
REPRISE (447 "Talking About")...40-50 71
REPRISE (514 "Click Clack")...50-75 71
REPRISE (547 "Low Yo Yo Stuff").40-50 72
(Issued with gatefold, EP-like, cover.)
LPs: 10/12-inch
A&M...5-10 84
ACCORD...5-10 83
BIZARRE...10-12 72
BLUE THUMB (1 "Strictly Personal")...20-30 68
(Black label.)
BLUE THUMB (1 "Strictly Personal")...10-15 69
(Tan label.)
BUDDAH (1001 "Safe As Milk")...25-35 67
(Monaural. Add $10 to $15 if accompanied by 4" x 15" *Safe As Milk* bumper sticker.)
BUDDAH (5001 "Safe As Milk")...25-30 67
(Stereo. Add $10 to $15 if accompanied by 4" x 15" *Safe As Milk* bumper sticker.)
BUDDAH (5077 "Mirror Man")...10-15 71
BUDDAH (5063 "Safe As Milk")...8-12 70
D.I.R. (57 "Direct News, Week of 12-18-78")...35-45 78
(Five, 5-minute radio programs, one of which has an interview with Don Van Vliet. Promotional issue only.)
EPIC...5-10 82
MERCURY (709 "Unconditionally Guaranteed")...8-12 74
MERCURY (1018 "Bluejeans and Moonbeams")...8-12 74
REPRISE (2027 "Trout Mask Replica")...8-12 77
REPRISE (2050 "Spotlight Kid")...10-15 72
REPRISE (2115 "Clear Spot")...10-20 72
(With embossed "Clear Spot" plastic bag.)
REPRISE (2115 "Clear Spot")...15-20 72
(White label. Has printed inserts instead of standard cover. Promotional issue only.)
STRAIGHT (1053 "Trout Mask Replica")...30-40 68
(With lyrics sleeve.)
STRAIGHT (1053 "Trout Mask Replica")...20-25 68
(Without lyrics sleeve.)
STRAIGHT (6420 "Lick My Decals Off, Baby")...10-15 70
VIRGIN...5-10 80-82
W.B....5-15 78
Members: Don "Captain Beefheart" Van Vliet; Doug Moon; Paul Blakely; Alex St. Claire; Jerry Handley; Ry Cooder; Jeff Cotton; John French; Bill "Zoot Horn Rollo" Harkleroad; Rockette Morton; Jimmy Semens; Jerry Handsley; Ty Grimes.
Also see COODER, Ry
Also see MALLARD
Also see MOTHERS of INVENTION
Also see MU
Also see TRIANGLE

CAPTAIN BEYOND LP '72
Singles: 7-inch
CAPRICORN...3-5 73
LPs: 10/12-inch
CAPRICORN (Except 0105)...8-12 72-73
CAPRICORN (0105 "Captain Beyond")...45-55 72
(With 3-D cover.)
CAPRICORN (0105 "Captain Beyond")...15-25 72
(With standard cover.)
W.B....8-10 77
Members: Bobby Caldwell; Rod Evans; Willie Daffern; Lee Dorman; Larry Reinhardt.
Also see CALDWELL, Bobby
Also see DEEP PURPLE
Also see IRON BUTTERFLY

CAPTAIN CHAMELEON
Singles: 7-inch
MILLENNIUM...3-4 81

CAPTAIN COOKIE
LPs: 10/12-inch
PARACHUTE...5-10 83

CAPTAIN FREAK
(With the Lunacycle Band)
Singles: 7-inch
JAMIE...3-5 71
PHIL L.A. of SOUL...3-5 74

CAPT. GROOVEY & HIS BUBBLEGUM ARMY
Singles: 7-inch
SUPER K...4-6 69
Member: Bobby Bloom.
Also see BLOOM, Bobby

CAPTAIN KANGAROO
Singles: 7-inch
CHELSEA...3-5 74
Picture Sleeves
CHELSEA...3-5 74

CAPTAIN LOCKHEED & STARFIGHTERS
Singles: 7-inch
U.A....3-5 73

CAPTAIN MATCHBOX WHOOPEE BAND
LPs: 10/12-inch
ESP...10-15 73

CAPTAIN MILK
Singles: 7-inch
TETRAGRAMMATON...4-6 69

CAPTAIN RAPP D&D '83
Singles: 12-inch
BECKET...4-6 83
Singles: 7-inch
BECKET...3-4 83

CAPTAIN REDFEATHER
Singles: 7-inch
CONTE...3-4

CAPTAIN SENSIBLE
Singles: 7-inch
A&M...3-5 82
LPs: 10/12-inch
A&M...5-10 83
Also see DAMNED

CAPTAIN SKY R&B '78
(Daryl Cameron)
Singles: 12-inch
WMOT...4-6 81
Singles: 7-inch
A.V.I....3-5 79-82
TEC...3-4 80
TRIPLE...3-4 86
WMOT...3-4 81
LPs: 10/12-inch
A.V.I....5-10 78-82
TEC...5-10 80

CAPTAIN STUBBY & BUCCANEERS: see STUBBY & BUCCANEERS

CAPTAIN VIDEO
Singles: 78 rpm
RCA (2008 "And the Captives of Saturn")...5-10 82
RCA (2000 "And His Video Rangers")...5-10 82
Singles: 7-inch
RCA...3-5 82
Picture Sleeves
RCA (2008 "And the Captives of Saturn")...5-10 82
(Sleeve for 78 rpm.)
RCA (2000 "And His Video Rangers")...5-10 82
(Sleeve for 78 rpm.)

CAPTAIN WILLIE
Singles: 7-inch
POLYDOR...3-5 74

CAPTAIN ZAP & MOTORTOWN CUT-UPS
Singles: 7-inch
MOTOWN (1151 "Luney Landing")...10-20 69

CAPTAIN ZERO
Singles: 7-inch
GULL (23 "Space Walk")...8-12

CAPTAIN ZOOM
(With the Androids)
Singles: 7-inch
A&M...4-8 65

CAPTANS
Singles: 7-inch
DC...5-10 59
SAVOY...4-8 59

CAP-TANS
Singles: 78 rpm
CORAL...50-75 51
DOT...25-50 50-53
Singles: 7-inch
ANNA (1122 "I'm Afraid")...15-25 60
CORAL (65071 "Asking")...100-200 51
DOT (15114 "I'm So Crazy for Love")...50-75 53
(First issued in 1950 on 78 rpm as Dot 1009.)
GOTHAM (233 "My, My, Ain't She Pretty")...100-200 50
GOTHAM (268 "Yes, I Thought I Could Forget")...100-200 51
LOOP...10-20
Members: Harmon Bethea; Les Fountain; Buddy Slaughter; Floyd Bennett.
Also see BETHEA & CAP-TANS
Also see L'CAP-TANS

CAPTIONS
Singles: 7-inch
KAYHAM (8 "Turn Out the Lights") 10-20

CAPTIVATIONS
Singles: 7-inch
GARPAX (44179 "Red Hot Scrambler–Go")...10-20 64
(Reissue: note slightly different title.)
PENTACLE (1635 "Red Hot Scramblers–Go")...20-35 64

CAR, Billy
Singles: 7-inch
C&P...5-10 59

CARA, Irene P&R '80
(Irene Cara / Helen St. John; Irene Cara / Contemporary Gospel Chorus)
Singles: 12-inch
CASABLANCA...4-6 83
GEFFEN...4-6 83
Singles: 7-inch
CASABLANCA...3-4 83
ELEKTRA...3-4 87
GEFFEN...3-4 83-85
RSO...3-5 80
NETWORK...3-4 81
Picture Sleeves
ELEKTRA...3-4 87
GEFFEN...3-4 83
LPs: 10/12-inch
GEFFEN...5-10 83-85
NETWORK...5-10 82
RSO...5-10 80

CARAMEN, Art "Turk"
Singles: 7-inch
DASA (101 "Eternity of Love")...25-50 62

CARAVAN LP '75
Singles: 7-inch
BTM...3-5 75
DK...3-4 83
LONDON...3-5 71
LPs: 10/12-inch
ARISTA...5-10 76
BTM...5-10 75
LONDON...12-15 71-75
VERVE/FORECAST...15-20 69
Members: Steve Miller; Richard Coughlan; Pye Hastings; John Perry; Geoff Richards; Jan Schelhaas; Dave Sinclair; Richard Sinclair; Mike Wedgewood.
Also see HATFIELD & NORTH

CARAVAN, Jimmy
LPs: 10/12-inch
TOWER...15-20 68
VAULT...15-20 69

CARAVANS
Singles: 7-inch
T.J....4-8 65

CARAVANS
Singles: 7-inch
VEE JAY...4-8 62

CARAVELLES
Singles: 7-inch
STAR MAKER (1925 "Angry Angel")...15-25 61

CARAVELLES
Singles: 7-inch
JOEY (301 "Fallin' for You")...75-125 63
JOEY (6208 "One Little Kiss")...75-125 62

CARAVELLES
Singles: 7-inch
ONACREST (502 "Lovin' Just My Style")...15-25 66

CARAVELLES P&R '63
Singles: 7-inch
SMASH...4-8 63-65
LPs: 10/12-inch
SMASH (27044 "You Don't Have to Be a Baby to Cry")...20-40 63
(Monaural.)
SMASH (67044 "You Don't Have to Be a Baby to Cry")...20-40 63
(Stereo.)
Members: Lois Wilkinson; Andrea Simpson.

CARAWAY, Bobby
Singles: 7-inch
JUDD (1230 "Dr. Jones")...5-8
Also see JANES, Roland

CARAWAY, Bobby & Terry
Singles: 7-inch
CREST (1065 "Ballin' Keen")...65-85 59
Also see CARAWAY, Bobby

CARBO, Chic
(Chick Carbo)
Singles: 7-inch
INSTANT (3245 In the Night")...8-12 63
REVUE...4-6 68

CARBO, Chuck
Singles: 78 rpm
IMPERIAL...20-40 57
Singles: 7-inch
ACE...10-20 61-63
"504"...5-10
IMPERIAL...20-30 57
INSTANT...5-10 62
REX...10-20 58-60
Also see SPIDERS

CARBO, Claude & Hank
Singles: 7-inch
CASTLE...4-6 68
Also see CARBO, Hank

CARBO, Hank
Singles: 7-inch
HCP...3-5 73
JANUARY...3-4 78
Also see CARBO, Calude & Hank

CARBONE, Jackie
(With the Concords; with Eddie Bartel & Orchestra)
Singles: 7-inch
CIRO'S...5-10 60
FOX (103 "Sugar Eyes")...10-15 59
STAR-X (503 "Just Foolin' ")...10-20 57

CARDBOARD ZEPPELIN
Singles: 7-inch
LAURIE (3433 "City Lights")...15-25 68
Also see REGENTS

CARDEL, Tony
Singles: 7-inch
SPACE...5-10 60

CARDELL, Johnny, & Three Pals
Singles: 78 rpm
RAMA....25-50 57
Singles: 7-inch
RAMA (227 "Rock-A-Billy Yodeler")....50-75 57
Also see LA RUE, Roc, & Three Pals

CARDELL, Nick
Singles: 7-inch
AMCAN (405 "Everybody Jump")...15-25 64
(Flip is not *I Stand Alone.*)
AMCAN (405 "I Stand Alone")....50-100 64
(Flip is *Everybody Jump.*)
LIBERTY (55556 "Arlene")....30-50 63

CARDELL, Vince
LPs: 10/12-inch
A.V.I.... 5-10 82

CARDELL & WHITE
Singles: 7-inch
WHITE CARD.... 3-5 76

CARDELLS
("Featuring Wm. Gardner")
Singles: 78 rpm
MIDDLE-TONE (011 "Helen")....50-100 56
Singles: 7-inch
MIDDLE-TONE (011 "Helen")....250-350 56
Members: William Gardner; Sonny Mayberry; Robert Carey; Charles Bearden.

CARDENAS, Luis P&R '86
Singles: 7-inch
ALLIED ARTISTS.... 3-4 86
Picture Sleeves
ALLIED ARTISTS.... 3-4 86
LPs: 10/12-inch
ALLIED ARTISTS.... 5-10 86
Also see RENEGADE

CARDIGAN BROTHERS
Singles: 7-inch
CHAIRMAN.... 5-10 63
MOTION.... 5-10 62

CARDIGANS
Singles: 78 rpm
MERCURY....25-50 57
Singles: 7-inch
MERCURY (71251 "Your Graduation Means Goodbye")....15-25 57
MERCURY (71349 "It's Better That You Love")....10-20 58
MERCURY (71367 "Poor Boy")....10-20 58
SPANN (431 "Make Up Your Mind")....25-40 59

CARDILLE, Bill
Singles: 7-inch
VAMPIRE (104 "Chilly Billy's Vamp").... 5-10 66

CARDINAL, Vin
Singles: 7-inch
A&M.... 3-5 70-71
MOTOWN.... 3-5 73

CARDINALS R&B '51
Singles: 78 rpm
ATLANTIC (938 "Shouldn't I Know")....50-100 51
ATLANTIC (958 thru 1126)....25-75 51-57
Singles: 7-inch
ATLANTIC (952 "I'll Always Love You")....150-250 51
ATLANTIC (958 "Wheel of Fortune")....150-250 52
ATLANTIC (972 "The Bump")....50-100 52
ATLANTIC (995 "You Are My Only Love")....100-200 53
ATLANTIC (1025 "Under a Blanket of Blue")....100-200 54
ATLANTIC (1054 "The Door Is Still Open")....50-75 55
ATLANTIC (1067 "Two Things I Love")....50-75 55
ATLANTIC (1079 "There Goes My Heart to You")....50-75 55
ATLANTIC (1090 "Off Shore")....25-50 56
ATLANTIC (1103 "The End of the Story")....15-25 56
ATLANTIC (1126 "Near You")....15-25 57
EPs: 7-inch
BIM BAM BOOM (1000 "The Cardinals").... 6-12 70s
Members: Ernie Warren; Meredith Brothers; Leon Hardy; Donald Johnson; Jack "Sam" Aydelotte; Luther MacArthur; James Brown; Lee Tarver.

CARDINALS
Singles: 7-inch
ROSE (835 "Why Don't You Write Me")....1000-1500 63

CARDINALS
Singles: 7-inch
CHA CHA (740 "I Want You")....20-30 66
CHA CHA (748 "I'm Gonna Tell on You")....20-30 66
CHA CHA (1441 "Hatchet Face")....20-30 60s

CARDWELL, Jack C&W '53
Singles: 78 rpm
KING.... 5-15 53-55
Singles: 7-inch
KING....10-15 53-55
SANDY.... 8-10 59

CARE
Singles: 7-inch
HEARTLAND.... 3-5 74

CARE PACKAGE
Singles: 7-inch
JUBILEE.... 4-8 67
LIBERTY....8-12 70

CAREFREES P&R '64
Singles: 7-inch
LONDON INT'L (10614 "We Love You Beatles")....8-12 64
LONDON INT'L (10615 "Paddy Wack").... 5-8 64
Picture Sleeves
LONDON INT'L (10614 "We Love You Beatles")....10-20 64
LPs: 10/12-inch
LONDON (379 "We Love You All")....35-45 64
Members: Lyn Cornell; Betty Prescott; Barbara Kay.
Also see BREAKAWAYS
Also see VERNON'S GIRLS

CARELESS FIVE
Singles: 7-inch
CAREFUL (1010 "I'm Lonely")....35-50 62

CARESS
Singles: 7-inch
W.B.... 3-4 79
LPs: 10/12-inch
W.B....5-10 79
Also see BLACK, Jay / Caress

CARESSORS
Singles: 7-inch
RU-JAC (0020 "Who Can It Be")....25-50

CARETAKERS
Singles: 7-inch
RIP OFF....8-10 68

CARETAKERS OF DECEPTION
Singles: 7-inch
SANCTUS (11 "Cuttin' Grass")....20-30 67

CAREW, Bennie
Singles: 7-inch
FENTON....10-20 66

CAREY, Bill
Singles: 78 rpm
CORAL....5-10 56
DOT (15618 "Single")....5-10 57
Singles: 7-inch
CORAL....10-15 56
DOT (15618 "Single")....10-15 57
DOT (16755 "I Am").... 4-8 65

CAREY, Charlie
Singles: 7-inch
LE CAM....5-10 61

CAREY, Mariah P&R/LP '90
Singles: 7-inch
COLUMBIA.... 3-4 90-93
LPs: 10/12-inch
COLUMBIA.... 5-8 90

CAREY, Tony P&R/LP '83
Singles: 7-inch
MCA.... 3-4 84
ROCSHIRE.... 3-4 83
Picture Sleeves
MCA.... 3-4 84
ROCSHIRE.... 3-4 83
LPs: 10/12-inch
MCA....5-10 84
ROCSHIRE....5-10 83
Also see PLANET P PROJECT
Also see RAINBOW

CAREY, Vince
Singles: 7-inch
TURNTABLE (712 "Don't Worry")..10-15 65
TURNTABLE (717 "Love Letters") ..10-15 65

CARGILL, Henson P&R/C&W '67
Singles: 7-inch
ARCO.... 4-6 67
ATLANTIC.... 3-5 73-74
COPPER MOUNTAIN.... 3-4 79-80
ELEKTRA.... 3-5 75
MEGA.... 3-5 71-73
MONUMENT.... 4-6 67-70
RUFF.... 4-6
TOWER.... 3-6 68
LPs: 10/12-inch
ATLANTIC....6-10 73
BUCKBOARD....5-10
HARMONY....6-10 72
MEGA....6-10 72
MONUMENT....8-12 68-70

CARGO
Singles: 7-inch
ATLANTIC.... 3-4 83
RELATIVITY.... 3-4 83

CARGOE
Singles: 7-inch
ARDENT.... 3-5 72-73
LPs: 10/12-inch
ARDENT (2802 "Cargoe")....15-20 72

CARI, Eddie
Singles: 7-inch
MERMAID (104 "This Love of Mine")....20-30 63

CARIANS
Singles: 7-inch
INDIGO (136 "She's Gone")....75-125 62
MAGENTA (04 "Only a Dream") ..50-100 61
Also see CORDIALS

CARIBBEANS
Singles: 7-inch
20TH FOX (112 "Keep Her By My Side")....20-35 58

CARILLO
(Frank Carillo)
Singles: 7-inch
ATLANTIC....3-5 78-79
Picture Sleeves
ATLANTIC....3-5 78
LPs: 10/12-inch
ATLANTIC....5-10 78-79

CARL, Bobby
Singles: 7-inch
SILVER BELL....10-15

CARL, Carolyn
Singles: 7-inch
AMPEX....3-5 71

CARL, Donnie
Singles: 7-inch
TY TEX....5-10 65

CARL, Eddie, & Emblems
Singles: 7-inch
OH MY (1000 "Every Little Dream Comes True")....100-200 62

CARL, Joe
Singles: 7-inch
ROCKO....4-8
TOP RANK....5-10 60

CARL, Johnny
Singles: 7-inch
GONE....5-10 62
NELBER....5-10 63

CARL, Max
Singles: 12-inch
MCA....4-8 85
(Promotional issue only.)

CARL, Steve, & Jags
Singles: 7-inch
METEOR (5046 "Curfew")....150-200 58

CARL & COMMANDERS
("Vocal Marco King")
Singles: 7-inch
CAMEO (197 "Farmer John")....10-20 61
JADCO (161 "I Need Your Love")....50-100 64

CARL & HAIRCUTS
Singles: 7-inch
DAY DELL....10-15 64

CARL & SPINDLE TOPPERS
Singles: 7-inch
ABC-PAR....5-10 62

CARL JUNIOR
Singles: 7-inch
MILLS (0489 "Look Who's Lonely")....15-25

CARLA & JO
Singles: 7-inch
MARKIE....4-8 63

CARLA & RUFUS: see RUFUS & CARLA

CARLE, Bobby, & Blendaires
(With Jack Pleis & His Orchestra)
Singles: 7-inch
DECCA (30655 "Walk with Me")....15-25 58
DECCA (30699 "I Couldn't Stand It")....15-25 58
DECCA (30938 "I Got It Bad and That Ain't Good")....15-25 59
Also see PLEIS, Jack, & His Orchestra

CARLETTE C&W '85
(Carlette Ruff)
Singles: 7-inch
LUV....3-4 85-87
OAK....3-4 85

CARLETTS
Singles: 7-inch
CAPITOL....3-6 70

CARLILE, Tom C&W '81
Singles: 7-inch
DOOR KNOB....3-4 81-83
Picture Sleeves
DOOR KNOB....3-4 81

CARLIN, George LP '72
Singles: 7-inch
LITTLE DAVID....3-5 72-75
RCA....4-8 67
Picture Sleeves
LITTLE DAVID....5-10 72
LPs: 10/12-inch
ATLANTIC....5-10 81
CAMDEN....8-10 72
EARDRUM....5-10 84
ERA....8-12 72
LITTLE DAVID....5-10 72-85
RCA....10-15 67

CARLISLE, Belinda P&R/LP '86
Singles: 12-inch
I.R.S....4-6 86
Singles: 7-inch
I.R.S....3-4 86-87
MCA....3-4 87-90
Picture Sleeves
I.R.S....3-4 86-87
MCA....3-4 87-88
LPs: 10/12-inch
I.R.S....5-10 86-87
MCA....5-10 87-90
Also see GO-GOs

CARLISLE, Bill C&W '48
(With the Carlisles; Bill Carlisle's Kentucky Boys)
Singles: 78 rpm
BLUEBIRD (Except 6478)....10-15
BLUEBIRD (6478 "Rattlin' Daddy")....25-40
DECCA....10-20 30s
FEDERAL....5-10
KING....5-10 48
MERCURY....4-8 53
VOCALION (02520 "Rattle Snake Daddy")....20-40
VOCALION (02946 "I'm Gonna Kill Myself")....20-40
Singles: 7-inch
COLUMBIA....4-8 62
HICKORY....4-8 65
MERCURY....10-15 53
EPs: 7-inch
MERCURY....10-20 56
LPs: 10/12-inch
BRYLEN....5-10 83
HICKORY....10-20 66
Also see CARLISLES

CARLISLE, Jim
Singles: 7-inch
MONEY (103 "Sweet Baby")....10-15 64

CARLISLE, Ken
Singles: 7-inch
JUNGLE....5-10 60

CARLISLE, Steve P&R '81
Singles: 7-inch
MCA....3-4 81-82
LPs: 10/12-inch
MCA....5-10 82

CARLISLE, Una Mae
Singles: 78 rpm
BEACON....10-15 45

CARLISLES C&W '46
(Carlisle Brothers; Carlisle Family)
Singles: 78 rpm
DECCA....10-15 40-41
KING....8-12 46
MERCURY....5-10 53-56
Singles: 7-inch
MERCURY....10-20 51-54
EPs: 7-inch
MERCURY....10-20 55
LPs: 10/12-inch
GUEST STAR....10-15 60s
KING (643 "Fresh from the Country")....15-25 59
MERCURY (20359 "On Stage")....30-40 58
OLD HOMESTEAD....5-8 80s
Members: Bill Carlisle; Cliff Carlisle.
Also see CARLISLE, Bill

CARLLILE, Kathy C&W '80
Singles: 7-inch
FRONTLINE....3-5 80

CARLO
(With the Glen Stuart Orchestra; Carlo Mastrangelo)
Singles: 7-inch
LAURIE (3151 "Baby Doll")....20-30 63
LAURIE (3157 "Little Orphan Girl") 15-25 63
LAURIE (3175 "Five Minutes More")....20-30 63
LAURIE (3227 "Ring-A-Ling")....35-45 64
RAFTIS....8-12 70
Also see BELMONTS
Also see CARLO & JIMMY
Also see CARLO'S CROWN JEWEL
Also see DEMILLES
Also see ENDLESS PULSE
Also see PULSE
Also see STUART, Glen

CARLO, Johnny
Singles: 7-inch
CONCORD....5-10 60

CARLO & JIMMY
Singles: 7-inch
LAURIE (3063 "Happy Tune")....10-20 60
Also see CARLO

CARLO & SECRETS
Singles: 7-inch
THRONE....5-10 62

CARLO'S CROWN JEWEL
Singles: 7-inch
TOWER....10-20 69
Also see CARLO

CARLOS
Singles: 7-inch
DORE....3-6 69

CARLOS, Barry, & Night-Caps
Singles: 7-inch
AMBER....4-8 65

CARLOS, Randy
Singles: 7-inch
FIESTA (Monaural)....5-10 59
FIESTA (Stereo)....15-20 59

CARLOS, Walter LP '69
LPs: 10/12-inch
COLUMBIA....8-12 69-72

CARLOS BROTHERS
Singles: 7-inch
DEL-FI....10-15 59-61
ZEN....5-10

CARLSON, Cathy
Singles: 7-inch
ABC....4-8
DCP....3-5 71
GRIFFIN....3-4 73
MGM....3-5 70-71
PHILIPS....4-8 68

CARLSON, Dave
Singles: 7-inch
HIFI (590 "Dave's Blues")....10-20 60

CARLSON, Harry, & Bandeleros
Singles: 7-inch
FRATERNITY....4-8 68

CARLSON, Lenny
Singles: 7-inch
ITI....5-10

CARLSON, Paulette C&W '83
Singles: 7-inch
RCA....3-4 83-84
Also see HIGHWAY 101

CARLSON & DURIO
Singles: 7-inch
A&M....3-5 74

CARLTON
(Carlton Beck)
Singles: 7-inch
PENNEY (1306 "The Girl I Left Behind")....800-1200 62
(Reissued as by Carlton Beck.)
Also see BECK, Carlton

CARLTON, Carl P&R/R&B '68
(Little Carl Carlton)
Singles: 12-inch
20TH FOX....4-6 80
Singles: 7-inch
ABC....3-5 73-76
BACK BEAT....3-6 68-75
CASABLANCA....3-4 86
GOLDEN WORLD (23 "Nothin' No Sweeter Than Love")....10-20 65
LANDO (8527 "So What")....30-40 65
MCA....3-4 84
MERCURY....3-5 77
RCA....3-4 82
20TH FOX....3-4 81-82
LPs: 10/12-inch
ABC....10-12 74
BACK BEAT....10-15 73
CASABLANCA....5-10 86
RCA....5-10 82
20TH FOX....5-10 81

CARLTON, Chick
(With the Majestics)
Singles: 7-inch
ATCO....4-6 70
FARO (592 "So You Want to Rock")....10-20 59
FARO (611 "Turkey Time")....5-10 61
IMPERIAL (5873 "Tomorrow Never Comes")....15-25 62

CARLTON, Eddie
Singles: 7-inch
CRACKERJACK (4009 "Wait")....15-20 64
SWAN (4218 "Misery")....20-30 64

CARLTON, John
LPs: 10/12-inch
STERLING....8-10 70

CARLTON, Johnny, & Escorts
Singles: 7-inch
BEAUMONT....4-8 65

CARLTON, Kenny
Singles: 7-inch
BLUE ROCK (4054 Lost and Found")....50-100 68
VALLI (305 "You're 16")....10-15 64

CARLTON, Larry LP '78
Singles: 7-inch
GRP....3-4 90
MCA....3-4 85-86
UNI....4-6 68-69
W.B....3-5 78-83
LPs: 10/12-inch
ATLANTIC....5-10 84
BLUE THUMB....10-12 73
GRP....5-8 90
MCA....5-10 85-87
UNI....12-18 68
W.B....5-10 78-83
Also see CRUSADERS
Also see POST, Mike

CARLTON, Richard
Singles: 7-inch
UPTIGHT ("I Like to Get Near You")....10-20 60s
(No selection number used.)

CARLTONS
Singles: 7-inch
ARGO....4-8 64-65
CADET....4-8 65

CARLYLE
Singles: 7-inch
STEVENSON'S (680068 "Is It")....10-20 60s

CARLYLE, Russ, Orchestra
Singles: 78 rpm
ABC-PAR....4-8 57
CAPITOL....4-8 50
Singles: 7-inch
ABC-PAR....5-10 57-63
CAPITOL....5-10 50
MERCURY....4-8 59

RE-CAR ... 4-8
TEMPUS ... 5-10 59
LPs: 10/12-inch
ABC-PAR ... 10-20 58-63
STEPHENY ... 10-15 60

CARMACKS
Singles: 7-inch
AUTOGRAPH (205 "With All My Heart") ... 10-20 60

CARMAN, Billy
Singles: 7-inch
METROMEDIA ... 3-6 69

CARMAN, Pauli R&B '86
Singles: 12-inch
COLUMBIA ... 4-6 86
Singles: 7-inch
COLUMBIA ... 3-4 86-87
LPs: 10/12-inch
COLUMBIA ... 5-10 86

CARMEL
Singles: 7-inch
MGM ... 4-8 67-68
Also see GRAPEVINE

CARMEL
Singles: 7-inch
W.B. ... 3-4 84
LPs: 10/12-inch
W.B. ... 5-10 84

CARMEL, Eddie
Singles: 7-inch
RADAR ... 4-8 62

CARMEL COVERED POPCORN
Singles: 7-inch
VISTONE (2055 "Suzie Q") ... 10-15 68

CARMEL SISTERS
Singles: 7-inch
COLPIX (767 "Go Go GTO") ... 50-75 65
JUBILEE (5464 "Joey's Comin' Home") ... 15-25 63
Members: Carol Carmel (a.k.a. Carol Connors); Cheryl Carmel.
Also see CAROL & CHERYL

CARMELETTES
Singles: 7-inch
ALPINE ... 10-20 59-60

CARMEN
LPs: 10/12-inch
DUNHILL ... 10-15 74
EPIC ... 12-20 69
MERCURY ... 8-12 75
PRIORITY ... 5-10 82-83

CARMEN
Singles: 7-inch
JODAY (1003 "False Hearted Love") ... 200-300 63

CARMEN, Eric P&R/LP '75
Singles: 12-inch
GEFFEN ... 4-6 85
Singles: 7-inch
ARISTA (Except 9000 series) ... 3-5 75-80
ARISTA (9000 series) ... 3-4 88
COOL ... 3-4 86
EPIC ... 3-6 70
GEFFEN ... 3-4 84-85
RCA ... 3-4 87
Picture Sleeves
ARISTA (0266 "She Did It") ... 3-5 77
ARISTA (0295 "Boats Against the Current") ... 4-6 77
(Promotional issue only.)
ARISTA (9000 series) ... 3-4 88
COOL (101 "The Rock Stops Here") ... 3-4 86
GEFFEN ... 3-4 85
LPs: 10/12-inch
ARISTA (Except 4057) ... 5-10 77-88
ARISTA (AL-4057 "Eric Carmen") ... 8-10 75
ARISTA (AQ-4057 "Eric Carmen") 15-20 75
(Quadraphonic.)
GEFFEN ... 5-10 85
Also see CYRUS ERIE
Also see MANDRELL, Louise, & Eric Carmen
Also see QUICK
Also see RASPBERRIES

CARMEN, Eric / Tom Johnston
Singles: 7-inch
RCA ... 3-4 87
Also see CARMEN, Eric
Also see JOHNSTON, Tom

CARMEN, Jay
Singles: 7-inch
MINK ... 5-10 59

CARMEN, Jerry
Singles: 7-inch
BARRISH (500 "Cherry Pie") ... 50-100 62

CARMEN, Tony, & Spitfires
Singles: 7-inch
ABEL ... 5-10 59
Also see TONY & Day Dreams

CARMICHAEL, Bill
Singles: 7-inch
HIT ... 4-8 62

CARMICHAEL, Carol
Singles: 7-inch
BELL ... 3-5 72

CARMICHAEL, Danny
Singles: 7-inch
LINCO ... 5-10 60

CARMICHAEL, Lucky
Singles: 7-inch
LOMA ... 4-8 64
SHAR ... 5-10 60

CARMINE & CO.
Singles: 7-inch
MERCURY ... 3-5 75

CARMON, Joey
Singles: 7-inch
TRC ... 3-4 79

CARN, Jean: see CARNE, Jean

CARNABY STREET RUNNERS
Singles: 7-inch
BUDDAH ... 4-8 68
SUPER K ... 4-8 69

CARNABY STREET SET
Singles: 7-inch
COLUMBIA ... 10-15 67

CARNATIONS
Singles: 78 rpm
DERBY ... 50-100 52
SAVOY ... 15-25 55
Singles: 7-inch
DERBY (789 "Tree in the Meadow") ... 250-350 52
SAVOY (1172 "The Angels Sent You to Me") ... 25-50 55
Members: Bill Reid; Horace Holmes.

CARNATIONS
Singles: 7-inch
ACE (130 "A Fool in Love") ... 60-80 60
TERRY-TONE (199 "Barbary Coast") ... 15-25 60

CARNATIONS
(With the Eddie Wilcox Orchestra)
Singles: 7-inch
ENRICA (1001 "Love open Up My Heart") ... 10-20 59

CARNATIONS
Singles: 7-inch
FRATERNITY ... 8-12 60
UNIVERSITY ... 8-12 60

CARNATIONS
(With the Joe René Orchestra)
Singles: 7-inch
LESCAY (3002 "Long Tall Girl") ... 50-100 61
LOST-NITE ... 10-20 60s
Members: Matt Morales; Harvey Arrington; Carl Hatton; Ed Kennedy; Tommy Blackwell.
Also see STARTONES

CARNATIONS
Singles: 7-inch
LAURIE ... 10-15 63
TILT ... 5-10 61
Also see COSMO

CARNE, Jean R&B/LP '77
(Jean Carn)
Singles: 7-inch
ATLANTIC ... 3-4 88
MOTOWN ... 3-4 82
OMNI ... 3-4 86
PHILADELPHIA INT'L ... 3-4 77-80
TSOP ... 3-4 81
LPs: 10/12-inch
OMNI ... 5-10 86
PHILADELPHIA INT'L ... 5-10 76-80
MOTOWN ... 5-10 82
TSOP ... 5-10 81
Also see JOHNSON, Al, & Jean Carn
Also see MILITELLO, Bobby, & Jean Carn

CARNE, Judy
Singles: 7-inch
REPRISE ... 3-6 68

CARNEGIE, Ross
Singles: 7-inch
EL CON ... 5-8 68

CARNES, Kim P&R '79
Singles: 12-inch
EMI AMERICA ... 4-6 80-85
Singles: 7-inch
A&M ... 3-5 75-82
AMOS ... 3-6 71-72
EMI AMERICA ... 3-4 79-86
ELEKTRA ... 3-4 84
Picture Sleeves
EMI AMERICA ... 3-4 80-86
LPs: 10/12-inch
A&M (3000 series) ... 5-10 82
A&M (4000 series) ... 8-10 75-77
AMOS ... 12-18 71
EMI AMERICA ... 5-10 79-86
MCA ... 5-10 84
MFSL (073 "Mistaken Identity") ... 25-35 82
Session: Lyle Lovett.
Also see COTTON, Gene, & Kim Carnes
Also see LOVETT, Lyle
Also see ROGERS, Kenny, & Kim Carnes
Also see STREISAND, Barbra, & Kim Carnes
Also see SUGAR BEARS
Also see U.S.A. for AFRICA

CARNES, Kim, & Dave Ellington
Singles: 7-inch
AMOS ... 3-5 72
Also see CARNES, Kim

CARNES, Preston
Singles: 7-inch
STACY ... 4-8 63

CARNES, Rick & Janis C&W '82
Singles: 7-inch
ELEKTRA ... 3-4 82
MCA ... 3-4 84
W.B. ... 3-4 83

CARNEY, Art
Singles: 78 rpm
COLUMBIA ... 5-10 54-56
Singles: 7-inch
COLUMBIA ... 10-20 54-56
Picture Sleeves
COLUMBIA ... 20-30 54-56
EPs: 7-inch
COLUMBIA (2034 "Art Carney") ... 25-45 55

CARNEY, Paul
LPs: 10/12-inch
THRESHOLD ... 8-10 71

CARNEY, Sandy
Singles: 7-inch
HEADLINE ... 5-10 59

CARNEY, Tom
Singles: 7-inch
GONE ... 8-10 61

CARNIVAL LP '69
Singles: 7-inch
U.A. ... 3-5 71
WORLD PACIFIC ... 3-6 69
LPs: 10/12-inch
WORLD PACIFIC ... 10-15 69
Member: Terry Fisher.
Also see FISHER, Terry

CARNIVAL CONNECTION
Singles: 7-inch
CAPITOL ... 4-8 68

CARNIVAL KINGS
Singles: 7-inch
CARNIVAL ... 3-5 70

CARNIVAL OF SOUND
Singles: 7-inch
U.S.A. (892 "I Can't Remember") ... 15-20 67
Also see TROLLS

CARO
Singles: 7-inch
ROCSHIRE ... 3-4 83
LPs: 10/12-inch
ROCSHIRE ... 5-10 83

CARO, Nydia
Singles: 7-inch
ROULETTE ... 4-8 64

CARO, Tony
Singles: 7-inch
CRYSTALETTE ... 5-10 59-60

CAROL, Angie
Singles: 7-inch
INSOUNDS ... 3-5 70

CAROL, Benae
Singles: 7-inch
FRESH ... 5-10 61

CAROL, Cammy
(Cammy Carol & Halos)
Singles: 7-inch
ELMOR (302 "Until the Day I Die") 20-30 61
WARWICK ... 10-15 60

CAROL, Ce Cee
Singles: 7-inch
TRANS WORLD ... 5-10 60

CAROL, Faye
Singles: 7-inch
HIT ... 4-8 67

CAROL, Fran
Singles: 7-inch
PORT ... 4-8 65

CAROL, Jacqueline, & Louis St. Louis
Singles: 7-inch
STEED ... 4-8 67

CAROL, Lily Ann, & Jimmy Saunders
(With Chris Griffin's Cornball Serenaders)
Singles: 78 rpm
SIGNATURE (15289 "Walkin' with the Blues") ... 15-25 51
Also see SAUNDERS, Jimmy

CAROL & CHERYL
Singles: 7-inch
COLPIX (767 "Go Go GTO") ... 50-75 65
Members: Carol Carmel (Carol Connors); Cheryl Carmel (Cheryl Connors).
Also see CONNORS, Carol
Also see CARMEL SISTERS

CAROL & GERRI
Singles: 7-inch
MGM (13568 "How Can I Ever Find the Way") ... 20-30 66

CAROL & SHERRY
Singles: 7-inch
MGM ... 4-8 65
POP SIDE ... 4-8 62

CAROL ANN
Singles: 7-inch
PJ ... 4-8 63

CAROL, LINDA & CATHY
Singles: 7-inch
UNITED ... 10-15 57

CAROLE, Nancy
Singles: 7-inch
LUXOR (1029 "The Memories We Share") ... 50-100 63
UNITED INT'L (500 "Polar Bear") ... 10-15 63

CAROLFRAN
Singles: 7-inch
ROULETTE ... 4-8 67

CAROLINA SLIM
(Ed Harris)
Singles: 78 rpm
ACORN (319 "Come Back, Baby") ... 25-50 51
ACORN (323 "Blues Knocking at My Door") ... 25-50 52
ACORN (324 "Rag Mama") ... 25-50 52
ACORN (3015 "Mama's Boogie") ... 25-50 51
LPs: 10/12-inch
SHARP (2002 "Blues from the Cottonfields") ... 50-100 59
Also see COUNTRY PAUL
Also see JAMMIN' JIM
Also see LAZY SLIM JIM

CAROLINA TIKIS
Singles: 7-inch
CHARAY (1010 "Four Season Girl") ... 10-20 60s

CAROLINES
Singles: 7-inch
ROULETTE ... 4-8 66

CAROLONS
Singles: 7-inch
MELLOMOOD ... 10-15 64

CAROLS
Singles: 78 rpm
COLUMBIA ... 15-25 50
SAVOY ... 25-50 53
Singles: 7-inch
SAVOY (896 "Fifty Million Women") ... 75-125 53
Members: Tommy Evans; Richard Coleman; Wilbert Tindle; William Davis; James Worthy; Ken Duncan.

CAROLS
Singles: 78 rpm
LAMP ... 15-25 56
Singles: 7-inch
LAMP (2001 "My Search Is Over") ... 20-40 56

CARON, Don, Orchestra
Singles: 7-inch
IRC ... 8-15
VEEP ... 4-8 65

CARON, Jack
Singles: 7-inch
CAPITOL ... 3-6 69

CARONATORS
Singles: 7-inch
CLOCK (1045 "Long Hot Summer") ... 15-25 60
CLOCK (1047 "Lonely Street") ... 15-25 61
CLOCK (1049 "This Is the Time") ... 15-25 61

CAROSONE, Renato P&R '58
Singles: 7-inch
CAPITOL ... 4-8 58

CAROTHERS, Scat Man: see CROTHERS, Scatman

CAROUSEL
Singles: 7-inch
ABC ... 5-8 67
TEEN TOWN ... 10-15 69

CAROUSELS
Singles: 7-inch
G.C. (601 "Fading Away") ... 250-350 60
JAGUAR (3029 "Rendezvous") ... 50-75 59
SPRY (116 "I've Cried Enough") ... 100-150 62
SPRY (121 "Rendezvous") ... 75-125 62

CAROUSELS
Singles: 7-inch
GONE (Except 5118) ... 10-20 61-62
GONE (5118 "You Can Come If You Want To") ... 25-40 61
GONE (5118 "If You Want to") ... 10-20 61
GONE (5131 "Never Let Him Go") ... 10-15 61
ROULETTE ... 3-5 71

CAROUSELS
Singles: 7-inch
AUTUMN ... 5-10 65
GUYDEN ... 4-8 64

CAROUSELS
Singles: 7-inch
VINTAGE ... 3-6 73

CARP
Singles: 7-inch
EPIC ... 3-5 70
LPs: 10/12-inch
EPIC ... 15-20 70
Member: Gary Busey.
Also see BUSEY, Gary

CARPENTER, Carleton, & Debbie Reynolds P&R '51
Singles: 78 rpm
MGM ... 5-10 51
Singles: 7-inch
MGM ... 8-12 51
EPs: 7-inch
MGM (1008 "Debbie Reynolds & Carleton Carpenter Sing") ... 10-15 51
Also see REYNOLDS, Debbie

CARPENTER, Chris
(Preston Carnes)
Singles: 7-inch
OCEAN-SIDE ... 6-10 68
U.A. ... 4-8 68
Also see LENNY & THUNDERTONES
Also see PRESTON

CARPENTER, Everett
Singles: 7-inch
SQUARE DEAL (501 "Let Your Hair Down Baby") ... 75-100

CARPENTER, Ike
(With the Merry Macs)
Singles: 78 rpm
ALADDIN ... 10-20 53
DECCA ... 10-15 53
INTRO ... 10-15 52
DISCOVERY ... 5-10 50
MODERN ... 15-25 47-48
RCA ... 5-10 49
Singles: 7-inch
ALADDIN ... 15-25 53
DECCA ... 15-25 53
INTRO ... 15-25 52
MODERN (116 "Yesterdays") ... 30-50 51
MODERN (117 "Day Dream") ... 30-50 51
LPs: 10/12-inch
ALADDIN (811 "Light's Out") ... 75-125 57
INTRO (950 "Lights Out") ... 100-200 52
(10-inch LP.)
SCORE (4010 "Light's Out") ... 50-75 57
Members: Ike Carpenter; Nick Fatool; Stan Black; John Kitzmiller.
Also see FERGUSON, Maynard
Also see SMITH, Effie
Also see ZENTNER, Si

CARPENTER, Karen
Singles: 7-inch
MAGIC LAMP (704 "Looking for Love") ... 100-200 66
Members: Karen Carpenter; Richard Carpenter; Wes Jacobs.
Also see CARPENTERS

CARPENTER, Kris C&W '81
Singles: 7-inch
DOOR KNOB ... 3-4 81

CARPENTER, Marion: see MARION

CARPENTER, Marlyn
Singles: 7-inch
HEP ... 4-8 67

CARPENTER, Mary Chapin C&W/LP '89
Singles: 7-inch
COLUMBIA ... 3-4 89-92
LPs: 10/12-inch
COLUMBIA ... 5-8 89-90

CARPENTER, Richard
LPs: 10/12-inch
A&M ... 5-8 87
Also see CARPENTERS

CARPENTER, Ronnie
Singles: 7-inch
NEW STAR ... 4-6 69

CARPENTER, Steve
Singles: 7-inch
BRUNSWICK (55322 "You're Putting Me On") ... 20-30 63

CARPENTER, Thelma P&R '60
Singles: 78 rpm
COLUMBIA ... 5-10 50
MAJESTIC ... 5-10 45-46
Singles: 7-inch
COLUMBIA ... 10-15 50
CORAL (Except 62272) ... 5-10 60-62
CORAL (62272 "Heartaches") ... 20-30 61
LPs: 10/12-inch
CORAL (57433 "Thinking of You Tonight") ... 15-25 63
(Monaural.)
CORAL (7-57433 "Thinking of You Tonight") ... 25-35 63
(Stereo.)

CARPENTER BROTHERS
Singles: 7-inch
KASH ... 4-8 65

CARPENTERS P&R/LP '70
Singles: 7-inch
A&M (Except 2735) ... 3-6 69-85
A&M (2735 "Yesterday Once More") ... 10-15 85
(Promotional issue only.)
Picture Sleeves
A&M (Except 2735) ... 5-12 70-81
A&M (2735 "Yesterday Once More") ... 10-15 85
(Promotional issue only. With paper sleeve.)
EPs: 7-inch
A&M ... 10-15 72-85
LPs: 10/12-inch
A&M (3000 series) ... 8-15 71-85
A&M (4000 series, except 4205) ... 8-15 70-83
A&M (4205 "Offering") ... 20-35 69
A&M (4205 "Ticket to Ride") ... 10-15 71
A&M (5100 series") ... 5-8 90
A&M (50000 series) ... 15-25 74-75
(Quadraphonic series.)
A&M (6000 series) ... 8-12 85
MFP (50431 "Ticket to Ride") ... 10-15 70
Members: Karen Carpenter; Richard Carpenter; Tony Peluso.
Also see CARPENTER, Karen
Also see CARPENTER, Richard

CARPETBAGGERS
Singles: 7-inch
LTD (407 "Let Yourself Go") 20-30

CARPETBAGGERS
Singles: 7-inch
MUSIC of AMERICA 8-10

CARPETS
Singles: 78 rpm
FEDERAL 50-100 56
Singles: 7-inch
FEDERAL (12257 "Why Do I") 250-350 56
FEDERAL (1226 "Lonely One") 250-350 56
Also see CHANDELIERS

CARR, Barbra
(Barbara Carr)
Singles: 7-inch
CHESS 4-8 66
PAULA 3-5

CARR, Billy
Singles: 7-inch
CAPITOL 4-8 68
COLPIX 4-8 65
EPIC 4-8 65
WHEELER DEALER 4-8

CARR, Bob, & Bill Kahl
LPs: 10/12-inch
GROTESQUE 10-15 70

CARR, Cathy *P&R '56*
Singles: 78 rpm
CORAL 5-10 53-56
FRATERNITY 5-15 55-56
Singles: 7-inch
ABC 3-4 73
COLLECTABLES 3-4 81
CORAL 8-10 53-56
FRATERNITY 10-20 55-56
LAURIE 5-10 62-63
ROULETTE (Except 4152) 5-10 59-61
ROULETTE (4152 "I'm Gonna Change Him") 5-10 59
(Monaural.)
ROULETTE (SSR-4152 "I'm Gonna Change Him") 15-25 59
(Stereo.)
SMASH 4-8 61
EPs: 7-inch
BRUNSWICK 10-20 57
LPs: 10/12-inch
DOT 15-25 66
FRATERNITY (1005 "Ivory Tower") 50-100 57
RCA 15-25 64
ROULETTE (R-25077 "Shy") 30-40 59
(Monaural.)
ROULETTE (SR-25077 "Shy") 40-60 59
(Stereo.)

CARR, Craig
Singles: 7-inch
DOT (16926 "What's Your Game") 15-20 66

CARR, Danny
Singles: 7-inch
A 5-10 59-60
ARC 5-10 59

CARR, Eddie
Singles: 7-inch
PEOPLE (1004 "Your Love Is Indescribably Delicious") 4-8 60s

CARR, Eddie, & Navajos
Singles: 7-inch
A&M 4-8 68

CARR, Eddie Lee *C&W '89*
Singles: 7-inch
EVERGREEN 3-4 89

CARR, Georgia
Singles: 7-inch
VEE JAY 5-10 65
LPs: 10/12-inch
ROULETTE 10-15
TOPS 8-12
VEE JAY 15-25 64

CARR, Gunter Lee
(Cecil Gant)
Singles: 78 rpm
DECCA 10-20 50
Singles: 7-inch
DECCA (48167 "Goodnight Irene") 20-30 50
DECCA (48170 "We're Gonna Rock") 20-30 50
Also see GANT, Cecil

CARR, Ian
(Ian Carr's Nucleus)
Singles: 7-inch
CAPITOL 3-4 79
LPs: 10/12-inch
CAPITOL 5-10 79

CARR, James *P&R/R&B '66*
Singles: 7-inch
ATLANTIC 3-5 71
GOLDWAX 4-8 65-69
LPs: 10/12-inch
GOLDWAX 12-20 67-68
Also see SOUL STIRRERS

CARR, Jamie
Singles: 7-inch
KIRSHNER 3-5 72

CARR, Jerry *R&B '81*
Singles: 7-inch
CHERIE 3-4 81

CARR, Joe "Fingers" *P&R '50*
(Lou Busch)
Singles: 78 rpm
CAPITOL 3-6 50-57
Singles: 7-inch
CAPITOL 5-10 50-59
CORAL 4-6 63
DOT 3-6 66
W.B. 4-8 60-62
EPs: 7-inch
CAPITOL 5-15 51-57
LPs: 10/12-inch
CAPITOL (Except 2000 series) 15-30 51-61
CAPITOL (2000 series) 10-15 64
CORAL 10-15 63
DOT 10-15 66
W.B. 10-20 60-62
Also see BUSCH, Lou
Also see FORD, Tennessee Ernie, & Joe "Fingers" Carr
Also see FRAZIER, Dallas, & Joe "Fingers" Carr
Also see PROVINE, Dorothy, & Joe "Fingers" Carr
Also see YOUNG, Vicki, & Joe Carr

CARR, Johnnie
(Featuring Jerry Parker)
Singles: 7-inch
SELMA (1003 "Rockin' Shock") 5-10

CARR, Kenny *C&W '88*
Singles: 7-inch
KOTTAGE 3-4 88-89

CARR, Leroy
LPs: 10/12-inch
BIOGRAPH 8-12 73
COLUMBIA (1911 "Blues Before Sunrise") 20-30 62
(Monaural.)
COLUMBIA (8511 "Blues Before Sunrise") 25-35 62
(Stereo.)
COLUMBIA (30000 series) 8-10 71

CARR, Linda
(With the Impossibles; with Love Squad)
Singles: 7-inch
BELL 4-8 67
DCP 5-10 65
RAY STARR (779 "Shy One") 150-200 61
ROMAR 3-5 72
ROXBURY 3-5 75
SKYLA (1052 "Happy Teenager") 15-25 61
LPs: 10/12-inch
ROXBURY 8-12 74

CARR, Pete
Singles: 7-inch
BIG TREE 3-5 78
LPs: 10/12-inch
BIG TREE 8-12 78
Also see LE BLANC & CARR

CARR, Scott
Singles: 7-inch
DC 4-8 64

CARR, Timmy, & Persianettes
Singles: 7-inch
GUYDEN 5-10 63
Also see PERSIANETTES
Also see TIMMY & PERSIANETTES

CARR, Timothy
Singles: 7-inch
HOT BISCUIT 4-8 68

CARR, Valerie *P&R '58*
Singles: 7-inch
ATLAS 4-8 64
ROULETTE 5-10 58-61
LPs: 10/12-inch
ROULETTE (25094 "Ev'ry Hour, Ev'ry Day") 25-35 59

CARR, Vikki *LP '64*
Singles: 7-inch
COLUMBIA 3-5 71-75
LIBERTY 4-8 62-69
Picture Sleeves
COLUMBIA 3-5 74
LIBERTY 4-8 67
LPs: 10/12-inch
COLUMBIA 8-10 71-75
LIBERTY (Except 10000 series) 10-20 63-70
LIBERTY (10000 series) 5-10 81
SPRINGBOARD 5-10
SUNSET 8-12
U.A. 5-10 71-80
Also see BERNSTEIN, Elmer

CARR, Wynona *R&B '57*
(Sister Wynona Carr)
Singles: 78 rpm
SPECIALTY 5-15 56-58
Singles: 7-inch
REPRISE 5-10 61-63
SPECIALTY 10-20 56-60
LPs: 10/12-inch
REPRISE 15-25 62
SPECIALTY 8-10 88

CARR & COMPANY
Singles: 7-inch
KIRSHNER 3-5 72

CARRACK, Paul *P&R/LP '82*
Singles: 12-inch
CHRYSALIS 4-8 87
(Promotional only.)
Singles: 7-inch
CHRYSALIS 3-4 87
EPIC 3-4 82
Picture Sleeves
CHRYSALIS 3-4 87-88
LPs: 10/12-inch
CHRYSALIS 5-10 87-89
EPIC 5-10 82
Also see ACE
Also see MIKE + the MECHANICS
Also see ROXY MUSIC
Also see SQUEEZE

CARRADINE, Keith *P&R/LP '76*
Singles: 7-inch
ABC 3-5 75
ASYLUM 3-5 78
VALA 3-4 83
LPs: 10/12-inch
ASYLUM 8-10 76

CARRASCO, Joe
(Joe "King" Carrasco & Crowns)
Singles: 78 rpm
STIFF/CROWN ("Bueno") 5-8 80
(10-inch 78. Promotional issue only.)
Singles: 7-inch
GEE BEE 3-4 80
HANNIBAL 3-4 82-83
Picture Sleeves
GEE BEE 3-5 80
LPs: 10/12-inch
HANNIBAL 5-10 82

CARRERA
Singles: 7-inch
W.B. 3-4 83
LPs: 10/12-inch
W.B. 5-10 83

CARRETTES
Singles: 7-inch
ANTLER 4-8 64

CARRIAGE TRADE
Singles: 7-inch
FILMWAYS 4-8 66

CARRIBEANS
Singles: 7-inch
AMY (871 "Wonderful Girl") 30-50 62
CARRIE 10-15 60

CARRIBIANS
(Coleman Brooks Anderson)
Singles: 7-inch
BROOKS (2000 "Baby") 250-350 59
CLIFTON ("Baby") 4-8

CARRIE: see LUCAS, Carrie

CARRIE, Len, & Krakerjacks
Singles: 78 rpm
DECCA 5-10 56
Singles: 7-inch
DECCA 10-15 56

CARRINGTON, Curtis
Singles: 7-inch
GEE 5-10 60

CARRINGTON, Sunny
Singles: 7-inch
DEEP (004 "The Girl That Every Guy Should Know") 10-15

CARRINGTON, Terri Lyne *LP '89*
LPs: 10/12-inch
FORECAST 5-8 89

CARROLL, Andrea *P&R '63*
Singles: 7-inch
BIG TOP (515 "The Doolang") 30-40 64
BIG TOP (3156 "It Hurts to Be Sixteen") 8-12 63
EPIC (9438 "Young and Lonely") 50-100 61
(Yellow label.)
EPIC (9438 "Young and Lonely") 50-75 61
(White label. Promotional issue.)
EPIC (9450 "Please Don't Talk to the Lifeguard") 10-15 61
EPIC (9471 "Gee Dad") 15-20 61
EPIC (9523 "Fifteen Shades of Pink") 15-20 62
RCA (8618 "Sally Fool") 10-20 65
Picture Sleeves
EPIC (9471 "Gee Dad") 25-35 61
RCA (8618 "Sally Fool") 15-25 65
U.A. (982 "The World Isn't Big Enough") 8-15 66
U.A. (50039 "Hey Beach Boy") 8-15 66

CARROLL, Andrea / Beverly Warren
LPs: 10/12-inch
B.T. PUPPY (1017 "Andrea Carroll and Beverly Warren – Side by Side") 50-75 63
Also see CARROLL, Andrea
Also see WARREN, Beverly

CARROLL, Barbara
Singles: 7-inch
KAPP (297 "North by Northwest") 5-10 59
Picture Sleeves
KAPP (297 "North by Northwest") 15-30 59

CARROLL, Bat
Singles: 7-inch
ACE 8-10 59-61

CARROLL, Bernadette *P&R '64*
Singles: 7-inch
COLLECTABLES 3-4 81
JULIA 4-8 62
LAURIE 5-10 63-64

CARROLL, Bert
Singles: 7-inch
WARWICK 8-12 59

CARROLL, Billy
Singles: 7-inch
FASCINATION (2000 "Big Green Car") 50-75

CARROLL, Bob *P&R '53*
Singles: 78 rpm
BALLY 5-10 56-57
DERBY 4-8 53
MGM 4-8 55
Singles: 7-inch
BALLY 5-10 56-57
DERBY 5-10 53
DOT 3-6 66
MGM 5-10 55
MURBO 3-6 67
UNART 4-8 59
U.A. 4-8 59-59
Picture Sleeves
U.A. 5-10 58
Also see JENKINS, Gordon, & His Orchestra

CARROLL, Candy
Singles: 7-inch
DOUBLE L 4-8 63-64

CARROLL, Carmen
Singles: 7-inch
MIRA 4-8 67

CARROLL, Cathy *P&R '62*
Singles: 7-inch
CHEER 10-15 63-64
DOT 4-8 66
MUSICOR 4-8 65
PHILIPS 4-8 63
TRIODEX 10-15 61
W.B. 5-10 62-63

CARROLL, Chelsey
Singles: 7-inch
MINARET (155 "Hippie from Mississippi") 5-8 69

CARROLL, Corkey, & His Fabulous Corketts
Singles: 7-inch
JET 3-5 77
PACIFIC ARTS 3-5 78

CARROLL, Dave
Singles: 7-inch
GROOVY 4-8 65

CARROLL, David, Orchestra *P&R '54*
Singles: 78 rpm
MERCURY 3-5 53-57
Singles: 7-inch
MERCURY 4-8 53-62
EPs: 7-inch
MERCURY 5-10 54-59
LPs: 10/12-inch
MERCURY 8-18 53-62
WING 5-10 59
Also see CONTINO, Dick

CARROLL, Delores, & Four Tops
(With Maurice King & His Wolverines)
Singles: 78 rpm
CHATEAU (2002 "Everybody Knows") 50-100 56
Singles: 7-inch
CHATEAU (2002 "Everybody Knows") 150-250 56
Also see FOUR TOPS
Also see HAYES, Carolyn, & Four Tops

CARROLL, Diahann
Singles: 78 rpm
RCA 4-8 56
Singles: 7-inch
COLUMBIA 4-6 66-68
DISQUE D-OR 4-6 65
RCA 5-10 56
U.A. 4-8 59-60
EPs: 7-inch
RCA (1-1467 "Sings Harold Arlen") 10-20 57
LPs: 10/12-inch
ATLANTIC 15-25 61
CAMDEN 10-15 62
COLUMBIA 10-15 67
DISQUE D-OR 10-15 65
MOTOWN 5-8 74
RCA (1467 "Dianne Carroll Sings Harold Arlen") 30-40 57
SUNSET 10-15 69
U.A. 10-20 62
VIK (1131 "Best Beat Forward") 20-30 58

CARROLL, Diahann, & Duke Ellington Orchestra
(Conducted by Mercer Ellington)
LPs: 10/12-inch
ORINDA (133 "Tribute to Ethel Waters") 10-20 78
Also see ELLINGTON, Duke

CARROLL, Diahann, & Andre Previn
Singles: 7-inch
U.A. 4-8 60
LPs: 10/12-inch
U.A. 15-25 59-60
Also see CARROLL, Diahann
Also see PREVIN, Andre

CARROLL, Dottie
Singles: 7-inch
LAURIE 5-10 61

CARROLL, Earl, & Original Cadillacs
Singles: 7-inch
JOSIE (829 "Buzz-Buzz-Buzz") 20-30 57
REO (8195 "Buzz-Buzz-Buzz") 20-30 57
(Canadian. One source gives this number as 8199. We're not sure yet which is correct.)
Also see CADILLACS
Also see COASTERS
Also see ORIGINAL CADILLACS
Also see SPEEDO & CADILLACS

CARROLL, Eddie
Singles: 7-inch
FERNWOOD (138 "Golden Door Night Club") 8-12 64
GUYDEN (2046 "Rules of Love") 20-30 61
SANTO (504 "I'm Sorry") 10-20 62

CARROLL, Gregory
Singles: 7-inch
EPIC (9416 "Stand By Me") 10-15 60
OKEH (7129 "Twinkle") 15-25 60

CARROLL, Jack
(With the Joe Leahy Orchestra & Chorus; Jack Carroll & Eliot Glen's Orchestra)
Singles: 78 rpm
UNIQUE 4-8 56
Singles: 7-inch
LAURIE 4-8 59
TALENT 4-8 62
UNIQUE (354 "Story of James Dean") 5-10 56

CARROLL, Jim *LP '80*
(Jim Carroll Band)
Singles: 12-inch
ATLANTIC 4-8 83
(Promotional only.)
Singles: 7-inch
A&M 3-5 72
ATCO 3-4 80-81
ATLANTIC 3-4 83
LPs: 10/12-inch
A&M 10-15 71
ATCO 5-10 80-82
ATLANTIC 5-10 83

CARROLL, Jimmy
Singles: 7-inch
CAROUSEL (44 "Angelina") 10-15 59
(Monaural.)
CAROUSEL (44 "Angelina") 25-35 59
(Stereo.)
FASCINATION (2000 "Big Green Car") 50-75 58
(Whether this disc is by Billy Carroll or Jimmy Carroll *or both* has not yet been resolved.)
Picture Sleeves
CAROUSEL (44 "Angelina") 15-25 59

CARROLL, Johnny
Singles: 78 rpm
DECCA 25-50 56
PHILLIPS INT'L 50-75 57
SARG 25-50 56
Singles: 7-inch
DECCA (29940 "Rock and Roll Ruby") 50-75 56
DECCA (29941 "Wild, Wild Women") 50-75 56
DECCA (30013 "Hot Rock") 50-75 56
PHILLIPS INT'L (3520 "That's the Way I Love") 50-75 57
SARG (144 "I'll Think of You") 40-60 56
W.B. 10-20 59-60
LPs: 10/12-inch
ROLLIN' ROCK 8-12 78

CARROLL, Linda
Singles: 7-inch
CAMELOT (113 "I Wanna Go Home") 8-12 60s

CARROLL, Lisa
Singles: 7-inch
KEYMAN (701 "Diamonds & Pearls") 8-12 63

CARROLL, Lois
Singles: 7-inch
LOVE-U-MAC 4-8 63

CARROLL, Marsha
Singles: 7-inch
ROULETTE 4-8 63

CARROLL, Mickey
LPs: 10/12-inch
RCA 8-12

CARROLL, Milton Chesley
Singles: 7-inch
MINARET 3-5 70
LP: 10/12-inch
RCA 8-12 72

CARROLL, Pat
Singles: 7-inch
BRENT 4-8 66

CARROLL, Pete
Singles: 7-inch
CAMEO (279 "You're a Dog") 5-10 63
Also see CARROLL BROTHERS

CARROLL, Ronnie *P&R '63*
Singles: 7-inch
PHILIPS 4-8 63-66

CARROLL, Scotty
(With the Metropolitans)
Singles: 78 rpm
RKO UNIQUE 5-10 57
Singles: 7-inch
RKO UNIQUE 8-15 57
VIM 5-10 60

CARROLL, Toni
Singles: 7-inch
MGM 4-8 59-65
CARROLL, Vickie
Singles: 7-inch
DECCA 4-8 64
ROULETTE 4-8 62
CARROLL, Wayne
Singles: 78 rpm
KING 20-40 57
Singles: 7-inch
KING (5123 "Chicken Out") 25-50 57
KING (5134 "Rocking Chair Mama") 25-50 57
KING (5146 "He Created") 25-50 57
CARROLL, Yvonne
(Yvonne Caroll)
Singles: 7-inch
CHALLENGE (59275 "A Little Bit of Soap") 8-12 65
CHALLENGE (59297 "Mister Loveman") 15-20 65
DOMAIN (1018 "Gee What a Guy") 10-15 63
VEE JAY (592 "There He Goes") 5-10 64
CARROLL & CHARLOTTE
Singles: 7-inch
COLPIX 8-10 61
CARROLL BROTHERS P&R '62
Singles: 7-inch
CAMEO (140 "Red Hot") 50-75 58
CAMEO (213 "Bo Diddley") 8-10 62
CAMEO (221 "Sweet Grorgia Brown") 8-10 62
FELSTED (8550 "I Found You") 10-15 59
LPs: 10/12-inch
CAMEO (C-1015 "College Twist Party") 30-40 62
(Monaural.)
CAMEO (SC-1015 "College Twist Party") 40-50 62
(Stereo.)
Members: Pete Carroll; Dick Noble; Bill McGraw; Jimmy Chick; Kenneth Dorn.
Also see CARROLL, Pete
CARROLL COUNTY BOYS
Singles: 78 rpm
FLAIR 5-10 53-55
Singles: 7-inch
FLAIR (1001 "Carroll County Blues") 15-25 53
FLAIR (1023 "Carroll County Boogie") 15-25 54
FLAIR (1046 "Eyes of Texas") 15-25 54
FLAIR (1061 "Dizzy") 15-25 55
Also see CRAYTON, Pee Wee
CARROLL SISTERS
Singles: 7-inch
DELTA 3-5 76
LUCKY ELEVEN 3-5 75
CARRON, Billy
Singles: 7-inch
MIRASONIC 5-10 59
CARROT TREE
Singles: 7-inch
RCA 3-5 70
CARROW, George
Singles: 7-inch
COLUMBIA 4-8 67
CARRUTH, Paul
Singles: 7-inch
FLAG 5-10 61
SPECTATOR 4-8 66
CARRY, Benjamin, Ltd.
Singles: 7-inch
VIVA 4-8 60s
CARS P&R/LP '78
Singles: 12-inch
ELEKTRA 5-10 86
(Promotional issues only.)
Singles: 7-inch
ELEKTRA 3-5 78-88
Picture Sleeves
ELEKTRA 3-5 78-88
LPs: 10/12-inch
ELEKTRA (Except 5E-567) 5-10 78-87
ELEKTRA (5E-567 "Shake It Up") 120-140 81
(Picture disc with blank B-side. Promotional issue only. 500 made.)
ELEKTRA (5E-567 "Shake It Up") 150-175 81
(Picture disc with KMET radio logo on B-side. Promotional issue only. 50 made.)
NAUTILUS (14 "The Cars") 20-40 82
(Half-speed mastered.)
NAUTILUS (49 "Candy-O") 20-40 82
(Half-speed mastered.)
Members: Ric Ocasek; Elliot Easton; Benjamin Orr; Greg Hawkes; Dave Robinson.
Also see EASTON, Elliot
Also see MILKWOOD
Also see MODERN LOVERS
Also see OCASEK, Ric
Also see ORR, Benjamin
CARSON, Cindy
(With Cliffie Stone Group)
Singles: 7-inch
BIG J 4-8 60s
CAPITOL 4-6 67
Also see STONE, Cliffie

Singles: 7-inch
CARSON, Cobey
Singles: 7-inch
COED 5-8 63
CARSON, Deedee
Singles: 7-inch
CRYSTALETTE 5-10 60
CARSON, Don
(With the Whirlaways; with Casuals)
Singles: 7-inch
CREST 10-20 58
BERTRAM INT'L (209 "Jungle Bungalow") 20-30 59
CARSON, Eddie
(With Buddy Lucas Orchestra; Big Blues Carson)
Singles: 78 rpm
JOSIE (776 "Jailbird Blues") 10-15 55
Singles: 7-inch
FORTUNE 5-10 63
JOSIE (776 "Jailbird Blues") 20-30 55
M.R.C. (1203 "The Devastating Bombs") 40-60 60s
CARSON, Joe C&W '63
Singles: 7-inch
LIBERTY 4-8 63-64
LPs: 10/12-inch
LIBERTY 20-30 64
CARSON, Johnny
LPs: 10/12-inch
COLUMBIA (2199 "Introduction to New York and the World's Fair") 20-30 62
CARSON, Kay
Singles: 78 rpm
CAPITOL 5-8 56
Singles: 7-inch
CAPITOL (3595 "There's a Shadow Between Us") 8-12 56
CARSON, Ken
Singles: 78 rpm
MEDIA 4-8 55
Singles: 7-inch
MEDIA 5-10 55
Also see HALEY, Bill
CARSON, Kit P&R '55
Singles: 78 rpm
CAPITOL 4-8 55
Singles: 7-inch
CAPITOL 8-10 55
CARSON, Martha
Singles: 78 rpm
RCA 5-10 55-57
Singles: 7-inch
RCA 10-20 55-57
LPs: 10/12-inch
CAMDEN 5-10 65
Also see PRESLEY, Elvis / Martha Carson / Lou Monte / Herb Jeffries
CARSON, Mindy P&R '46
Singles: 78 rpm
COLUMBIA 5-10 52-58
Singles: 7-inch
COLUMBIA 8-12 52-58
JOY 5-10 60
RCA 8-12 50-52
Also see MITCHELL, Guy, & Mindy Carson
CARSON, Mr. Blues
Singles: 78 rpm
ALLEN 10-20 53
Singles: 7-inch
ALLEN 20-30 53
CARSON, Vince
Singles: 7-inch
BLUE BELL (105 "Boulevard of Broken Dreams") 30-40
CHANCELLOR 5-10 62
CARSON, Wayne C&W '73
Singles: 7-inch
EMH 3-4 83
ELEKTRA 3-5 76-77
MONUMENT 3-5 70-73
LPs: 10/12-inch
MONUMENT 6-10 72
CARSON, Whitey
Singles: 78 rpm
REGIS 4-6
CARSTAIRS
Singles: 7-inch
OKEH 5-10 69
RED COACH 5-10
CARTEE, Alan C&W '77
Singles: 7-inch
GROOVY 3-5 77
Also see CARTEE BROTHERS
CARTEE, Wayne
Singles: 7-inch
GROOVY 3-4 77
CARTEE BROTHERS
(Cartees)
Singles: 7-inch
QUALLA 4-8 65
REPRISE 4-8 66
Members: Alan Cartee; Wayne Cartee.
Also see CARTEE, Alan
Also see CARTEE, Wayne
CARTELL, Larry
Singles: 7-inch
COLOSSAL 3-6 68

GLENOLDEN 4-8
CARTELLA, Helen
Singles: 7-inch
BLAST 4-8 65
CARTER, Anita C&W '51
Singles: 78 rpm
COLUMBIA 4-8 53-54
RCA 4-8 51-56
Singles: 7-inch
CAPITOL 3-5 71
COLUMBIA 5-10 53-54
JAMIE 4-8 60
MERCURY 4-8 63-64
RCA (0426 thru 0493) 10-20 51-53
RCA (6000 series) 8-15 55-56
RCA (8000 & 9000 series) 4-8 66-67
U.A. 4-6 68-69
LPs: 10/12-inch
CAPITOL 8-10 72
MERCURY 15-25 63-64
Also see CARTER FAMILY
Also see CARTER SISTERS
Also see DARRELL, Johnny, & Anita Carter
Also see JENNINGS, Waylon, & Anita Carter
Also see SNOW, Hank, & Anita Carter
CARTER, Ann
Singles: 78 rpm
BLUE LAKE 50-100 53
Singles: 7-inch
BLUE LAKE (103 "Lovin' Daddy Blues") 150-300 53
CARTER, B.B.
Singles: 7-inch
EMANUEL 5-10 64
CARTER, Ben
Singles: 78 rpm
4 STAR 5-10 46
CARTER, Benny, & His Orchestra R&B/C&W '44
(Featuring Savannah Churchill)
Singles: 78 rpm
BLUEBIRD 4-8 41
BRUNSWICK 4-8 46
CAPITOL 4-8 42-44
COLUMBIA (2898 "Devil's Holiday") 10-20 33
(Colored plastic.)
DECCA 4-8 40
OKEH 4-8 40
VOCALION 4-8 35-40
Also see CHURCHILL, Savannah
CARTER, Betty
Singles: 7-inch
ATCO 4-8 63
LPs: 10/12-inch
ATCO 15-20 63
BET-CAR 10-12 80
COLUMBIA 5-10 80
IMPULSE 8-10 76
ROULETTE 8-10 76
Also see CHARLES, Ray, & Betty Carter
Also see HAMPTON, Lionel
CARTER, Betty, & Ray Bryant
LPs: 10/12-inch
EPIC (3202 "Meet Betty Carter and Ray Bryant") 50-75 56
Also see CARTER, Betty
Also see BRYANT, Ray
CARTER, Billy
(Bill Carter)
Singles: 7-inch
CHALLENGE 5-10 60
OZARK 15-25 57
TALLY 15-25 57
CARTER, Bo
LPs: 10/12-inch
YAZOO 10-15 71-73
CARTER, Bob
Singles: 7-inch
DEN (11229 "Downtown Twist") 50-75 62
DEN (25731 "Every Night") 50-100 61
Picture Sleeves
DEN (11229 "Downtown Twist") 100-150 62
(Fold-out, promotional only sleeve.)
CARTER, Bob
Singles: 7-inch
ASTERIA (Colored vinyl) 5-10 81
CARTER, Calvin
(Cal Carter)
Singles: 7-inch
VEE JAY 5-10 62
LPs: 10/12-inch
VEE JAY 20-30 62
Also see CHANDLER, Gene
CARTER, Carl
Singles: 7-inch
DOT 5-10 58
CARTER, Carlene C&W '79
(With Rockpile)
Singles: 7-inch
EPIC 3-4 83
REPRISE 3-4 90-91
W.B. 3-4 78-82
Picture Sleeves
W.B. (8576 "Who Needs Words") 3-5 78
LPs: 10/12-inch
EPIC 5-10 83
W.B. 5-10 78-82
Also see CARTER FAMILY
Also see EDMUNDS, Dave, & Carlene Carter
Also see ORRALL, Robert Ellis
Also see ROCKPILE
Also see SOUTHERN PACIFIC & Carlene Carter
CARTER, Carlene, & Dave Edmunds C&W '80
Singles: 7-inch
W.B. 3-4 80
Also see CARTER, Carlene
Also see EDMUNDS, Dave
CARTER, Carol
Singles: 7-inch
MERCURY 4-8 61
CARTER, Carolyn
Singles: 7-inch
JAMIE 4-8 65
CARTER, Cecil "Count"
Singles: 78 rpm
FEDERAL 10-20 53
Singles: 7-inch
FEDERAL (12130 "What's Wrong with Me") 20-30 53
FEDERAL (12135 "I Know, I Know") 20-30 53
CARTER, Chuck
Singles: 7-inch
BRUNSWICK 4-8 66
CARTER, Clarence P&R/R&B '67
Singles: 12-inch
ICHIBAN 4-6 88
Singles: 7-inch
ABC 3-5 75-76
ATLANTIC (2000 series) 4-8 68-72
ATLANTIC (13000 series) 3-4
FAME (Except 1000 series) 3-5 72-73
FAME (1000 series) 4-8 67
FUTURE STARS 3-5
ICHIBAN 3-4 88-92
RONN 3-5 77
VENTURE 3-4 80-81
LPs: 10/12-inch
ABC 8-10 74-76
ATLANTIC 10-20 68-71
BIG C 5-10 83
BRYLEN 5-10 84
FAME 10-12 73
ICHIBAN 5-10 86-88
VENTURE 5-10 80-81
CARTER, Clarence & Candi
Singles: 7-inch
ATLANTIC 3-5 72
Also see CARTER, Clarence
CARTER, Darryl
Singles: 7-inch
HI 3-5 73
PERCEPTION 3-5 71
TTC 3-5 72
CARTER, Dean
(Dean Carter Sound; Arlie Neaville)
Singles: 7-inch
LIMELIGHT (3019 "Sixteen Tons") 10-15 64
(With Arlie Miller.)
MILKY WAY (003 "Number-One Girl") 250-350 65
(With Arlie Miller, Dave Marten & Kookie.)
MILKY WAY (004 "The Rockin' Bandit") 5-10 65
MILKYWAY (010 "Run Rabbit Run") 40-60 66
(Has Milky Way as "Milkyway" [one word].)
MILKY WAY (011 "Rebel Woman") 40-50 67
TELL INT'L (369 "Mary Sue") 20-40 68
(With Jerry Merritt.)
TELL INT'L (373 "Good Side of My Mind") 75-100 69
Picture Sleeves
TELL (373 "Good Side of My Mind") 100-125 69
Also see KOOKIE
Also see MARTEN, Dave
Also see MERRITT, Jerry
Also see MILLER, Arlie, & Bullets
Also see NEAVILLE, Arlie
CARTER, Ed
(With the Carterays; Eddie Carter Quartet)
Singles: 78 rpm
GRAND (107 "Take Everything But You") 200-300 54
MGM (11405 "Don't Turn Your Back on Me") 20-30 53
SOUND (105 "Oh Baby") 50-75 54
Singles: 7-inch
GRAND (107 "Take Everything But You") 1500-2500 54
(Reissued as by the Carter Rays.)
MGM (11405 "Don't Turn Your Back on Me") 75-100 53
SOUND (105 "Oh Baby") 200-300 54
Also see CARTER RAYS
CARTER, Eloise
Singles: 7-inch
SUE 5-10 61
CARTER, Fred
Singles: 7-inch
MAY 3-6
CARTER, Fred, Jr. C&W '67
Singles: 7-inch
MONUMENT 4-6 67
LPs: 10/12-inch
U.A. 8-12 67
Also see TWITTY, Conway

CARTER, Goree
(With His Hep Cats; Gory Carter)
Singles: 78 rpm
CORAL 20-40 50
FREEDOM 20-40 49-50
MODERN 15-25 51
SITTIN' IN WITH 15-25 50
Also see LITTLEFIELD, Little Willie / Goree Carter
Also see THOMPSON, Rocky
CARTER, Goree / Clarence Samuels
Singles: 78 rpm
BAYOU (010 "Drunk Or Sober") 10-20 54
Singles: 7-inch
BAYOU (010 "Drunk Or Sober") 50-75 54
Also see CARTER, Goree
Also see SAMUELS, Clarence
CARTER, Henry
Singles: 7-inch
DON-EL 5-10 60
CARTER, J.T., & Co.
(Jay Carter)
Singles: 7-inch
DECCA (31785 "Closer to Your Heart") 8-12 65
Also see CRESTS
CARTER, James
(With the Sentimentals; with Twilights)
Singles: 7-inch
TUXEDO (922 "Wild Hog Baby") 50-100 57
Also see NICHOLS, Ann, & Sentimentals
Also see SENTIMENTALS
CARTER, Jean
Singles: 7-inch
DECCA (31965 "Like One") 35-55 66
SUNFLOWER (101 "I Bet You") 25-50
CARTER, Jimmy
Singles: 7-inch
HANOVER 10-15 59
CARTER, Jimmy, & Broken Pieces
Singles: 7-inch
RADNOR 4-6 69
CARTER, Jimmy, & Dolettes
Singles: 7-inch
CAYCE (2002 "I'll Never Let You Go") 25-50
CARTER, Joanne
Singles: 7-inch
SQUARE 5-10 60
CARTER, Joe
Singles: 7-inch
B&J 4-8 64
CARTER, Joe L.
(With Johnnie M. Matthews)
Singles: 7-inch
AUDREY (112 "My Life Story") 10-20
CARTER, Joey
(With Friends)
Singles: 7-inch
EPIC 5-10 60
CARTER, June C&W '71
(June Carter Cash)
Singles: 78 rpm
COLUMBIA 5-10 55-56
RCA 5-10 50-51
Singles: 7-inch
COLUMBIA (21000 series) 5-10 55-56
COLUMBIA (40700 series) 5-10 56
COLUMBIA (42000 thru 45000 series) 3-5 63-71
LIBERTY 4-8 61-62
RCA (0355 thru 0439) 8-12 50-51
LPs: 10/12-inch
COLUMBIA 6-10 75
Also see CARTER FAMILY
Also see CARTER SISTERS
Also see CASH, Johnny, & June Carter
Also see HOMER & JETHRO with June Carter
CARTER, Kenny
(With Barbara Webb Singers)
Singles: 7-inch
JOLA 8-10
RCA (8791 "I've Gotta Find Her") 15-25 66
RCA (8841 "I've Got to Get Myself Together") 15-25 66
RCA (8970 "Don't Go") 10-20 66
RENEE (3001 "Why Do You Have to Go") 4-6
U.A. (308 "Hey Lover") 15-25 61
CARTER, King
Singles: 7-inch
SPECIALTY 3-5 72
CARTER, Lynda
Singles: 7-inch
EPIC 3-5 78
LPs: 10/12-inch
EPIC (KE-35308 "Portrait") 8-12 78
EPIC (JE-35308 "Portrait") 75-100 78
(Picture disc. 1000 made.)
CARTER, Martha
Singles: 7-inch
RON 5-10 61
CARTER, Mel P&R/R&B '63
Singles: 7-inch
ABKCO 3-4 84
AMOS 3-6 69-70
ARWIN (23 "I'm Coming Home") 10-15 60
BELL 3-6 68-69

CREAM 3-5 81
DERBY (1003 "When a Boy Falls in Love") 10-15 63
DERBY (1005 "Time of Young Love") 10-15 63
DERBY (1008 "Why I Call Her Mine") 10-15 64
IMPERIAL 5-8 64-66
LIBERTY (1 "The Star Spangled Banner") 8-10 67
(Promotional issue only.)
LIBERTY (55000 & 56000 series) 4-6 67-68
MERCURY 5-10 62
PHILIPS 5-10 62
ROMAR 3-5 73-74
TRI-STATE 10-20 59

LPs: 10/12-inch

AMOS 10-12 70
DERBY (702 "When a Boy Falls in Love") 50-100 63
IMPERIAL 15-20 65-66
LIBERTY 12-20 67
SUNSET 10-12 68-70

CARTER, Mel / Vic Dana

EPs: 7-inch

ROWE/AMI 5-10 60s
(Colored vinyl. Juke box issue.)
Also see DANA, Vic

CARTER, Mel, & Clydie King

Singles: 7-inch

PHILIPS 4-8 62
Also see CARTER, Mel
Also see KING, Clydie, & Sweet Things

CARTER, Melvin

Singles: 7-inch

PEACOCK 10-20 65-67

CARTER, Nell

Singles: 7-inch

RCA 3-5

CARTER, Nelson

(With His Guitar)

Singles: 78 rpm

SITTIN' IN WITH (557 "My Baby Left Me") 20-30 50

CARTER, Penny

Singles: 7-inch

VERVE 4-8 66

CARTER, Prince

Singles: 7-inch

GO 5-10 61

CARTER, Ralph *P&R/R&B '75*

Singles: 7-inch

MERCURY 3-5 75-76

CARTER, Roman

Singles: 7-inch

JEWEL 4-8 68

CARTER, Ron *LP '77*

LPs: 10/12-inch

MILESTONE 5-10 77-78
MOTOWN 5-8 84

CARTER, Sonny

Singles: 78 rpm

KING 15-25 54

Singles: 7-inch

CARLTON (481; Crying, Crying Over You") 40-60 58
DOT (15921 "Crying, Crying Over You") 20-30 59
KING (4739 "There Is No Greater Love") 25-50 54
KING (4756 "It's Strange But True") 20-40 54

CARTER, Tal

Singles: 78 rpm

COMBO 10-15 54

Singles: 7-inch

COMBO (29 "Echo Blues") 15-25 54

CARTER, Tom, & Ramrods

Singles: 7-inch

CARRAM (106 "El Cumbanchero") 10-20 60s
NORTHWAY SOUND (1005 "Flyin' Saucer Twist") 10-20 62

CARTER, Valerie *LP '77*

Singles: 7-inch

COLUMBIA 3-4 77-79

LPs: 10/12-inch

COLUMBIA 8-10 77-78
Also see LITTLE FEAT
Also see MONEY, Eddie, & Valerie Carter

CARTER, Valerie, & Henry Paul

Singles: 7-inch

ATLANTIC 3-4 82
Also see CARTER, Valerie

CARTER, Woody, & Hoedown Boys *C&W '49*

Singles: 78 rpm

LUCKY 10-15 52
MACY'S 10-15 49

CARTER BROTHERS *R&B '65*

Singles: 7-inch

COLEMAN 10-15 64
JEWEL 5-10 65-67
MISTY 4-8
TALENT SCOUT 4-6
Members: Jerry Carter; Al Carter; Roman Carter.
Also see CARTER, Roman

CARTER FAMILY *P&R '28/C&W '72*

Singles: 78 rpm

BANNER 15-25 35
BLUEBIRD 15-25 30s
DECCA 10-20 30s
ELEKTRADISK 25-50 32-33
(Made for sale through Woolworth Stores.)
MONTEGOMERY WARD 15-25 30s
VICTOR (20000 series) 50-150 28
VICTOR (40000 series) 25-75 28
VOCALION 25-35

EPs: 7-inch

ACME 25-50 50s
DECCA 10-20 65

LPs: 10/12-inch

ACME (1 "All Time Favorites") 100-200 50s
ACME (2 "In Memory of A.P. Carter: Keep on the Sunny Side") 100-200 50s
ANTHOLOGY of COUNTRY MUSIC 10-15
COLUMBIA ("CL" & "CS" series) 10-20 64-67
DECCA (4404 "Carter Family") 20-30 63
DECCA (4557 "More Favorites") 20-30 65
LIBERTY 15-25 62
CAMDEN (Except 586) 71-74
CAMDEN (586 "Original and Great Carter Family") 15-20 62
COLUMBIA ("KC" & "PC" series) 5-10 72-80s
HARMONY (7280 "Famous Carter Family") 15-25 61
HARMONY (7300 "Carter Family") 15-25 63
HARMONY (7344 "Home Among the Hills") 15-25 65
HARMONY (7396 "Sacred Songs") 10-15 66
HARMONY (7422 "Country Sounds") 10-20 67
HARMONY (11000 series) 10-15 69-70
J.E.M.F. 10-15
OLD HOMESTEAD 5-8
OLD TIME CLASSICS 5-10
PICKWICK 5-10 75
PINE MOUNTAIN 8-10
RCA (Except 2772) 5-15 75-78
RCA (2772 "Mid the Green Fields of Virginia") 15-25 63
STARDAY (248 "Echoes") 15-25 63
SUNSET 10-15 67
Members: A.P. Carter; Sara Carter; Maybelle Carter; Anita Carter; June Carter; Helen Carter; Joe Carter; Janette Carter; Carlene Carter.
Session: Johnny Cash.
Also see CARTER, Anita
Also see CARTER, June
Also see CARTER SISTERS
Also see CASH, Johnny, & Carter Family
Also see HAGGARD, Merle

CARTER RAYS

Singles: 78 rpm

GONE 100-200 57
GRAND 50-100 54
LYRIC 200-300 57

Singles: 7-inch

COLLECTABLES 3-4 81
GONE (5006 "My Secret Love") 250-500 57
(First issue.)
GRAND (107 "Take Everything But You") 200-300 54
(Previously issued as by the Ed Carter Quartet.)
LYRIC (2001 "My Secret Love") 500-750 57
MALA (433 "Keep Listening to Your Heart") 50-75 61
Also see CARTER, Ed
Also see MANN, Gloria, & Carter Rays

CARTER SISTERS

(With Mother Maybelle)

Singles: 78 rpm

COLUMBIA 5-10 52-53
RCA 5-10 50-51

Singles: 7-inch

COLUMBIA 10-15 52-53
RCA 10-15 50-51
Members: Anita Carter; June Carter; Helen Carter.
Also see CARTER, Anita
Also see CARTER, June
Also see CARTER FAMILY

CARTEY, Ric

Singles: 78 rpm

RCA 50-100 56-57
STARS (539 "Oooh-Eee") 50-75 56

Singles: 7-inch

ABC-PAR 4-8 63
NRC (503 "Scratching on My Screen") 30-50 59
RCA (6751 "Oooh-Eee") 50-75 56
RCA (6828 "Heart Throb") 50-75 57
RCA (6920 "Born to Love One Woman") 75-100 57
RCA (7011 "My Babe") 75-100 57
STARS (539 "Oooh-Eee") 75-100 56

CARTEY, Ric / Paul Evans

EPs: 7-inch

RCA (DJ-73 "Heart Throb") 100-150 57
(Promotional issue only. Not issued with cover.)
Also see CARTEY, Ric
Also see EVANS, Paul

CARTHAYS

Singles: 7-inch

TAG 5-10 61

CARTOON CANDY CARNIVAL

Singles: 7-inch

METROMEDIA 3-6 69

CARTOONE

Singles: 7-inch

ATLANTIC (Except 2598) 3-6 69-70
ALTANTIC (2598 "Mr. Poor Man") 4-8 69

LPs: 10/12-inch

ATLANTIC 10-15 69
Member: Jimmy Page.
Also see PAGE, Jimmy

CARTOONS

Singles: 7-inch

TUBA 4-8 66

CARTRIDGE, Flip *P&R '66*

Singles: 7-inch

PARROT 4-8 66-67

CARTUNES

Singles: 7-inch

ROULETTE 4-8 68

CARTWRIGHT, Jonathan

Singles: 7-inch

VEEP 4-8 67

CARTWRIGHT, Lionel *C&W '88*

Singles: 7-inch

MCA 3-4 90-92

CARTWRIGHT FAMILY

(With Grandpappy Smith & Western Valley Boys)

Singles: 78 rpm

ORBIT 5-10 56

Singles: 7-inch

ORBIT 10-20 56

CARUSO, Dick

Singles: 7-inch

MGM 15-25 59-61

CARUSO, Johnny

Singles: 7-inch

CAPITOL 5-10 60

CARUSO, Marian

Singles: 78 rpm

DECCA 3-6 54-55
DEVON 3-6 52

Singles: 7-inch

DECCA 5-10 54-55
DEVON 5-10 52

CARVELS

Singles: 7-inch

TWIRL 4-8 66

CARVELS

Singles: 7-inch

LIFESONG 3-4 78

CARVER, Coney

Singles: 7-inch

BRYTE 4-8 62

CARVER, Johnny *C&W '67*

Singles: 7-inch

ABC 3-5 73-75
ABC/DOT 3-5 75-77
DOT 4-6 66
EQUITY 3-5 80
EPIC 3-5 71-72
IMPERIAL 4-6 67-70
REL 4-8
TANGLEWOOD 3-4 80
U.A. 3-5 70

LPs: 10/12-inch

ABC 8-15 74-75
ABC/DOT 8-12 76-77
HARMONY 8-12 73
IMPERIAL 10-15 67-69
Session: Anita Kerr Singers.
Also see KERR, Anita

CARVER, Keith

Singles: 7-inch

SPIN 5-10 62

CARVETTES

Singles: 7-inch

COPA (200-1 "Lover's Prayer") 550-650 59

CARYL, Naomi

Singles: 78 rpm

EMBER 10-20 56

Singles: 7-inch

EMBER (1006 "Before You Say Goodbye") 15-25 56
Also see FIVE SATINS

CARZLE, Lee

Singles: 7-inch

ERWIN 5-10 60

CASA, Kathleen

Singles: 7-inch

NSD 3-4 78

CASAL, Carlos, Jr.

Singles: 7-inch

EMGE (1005 "Don't Meet Mr. Frankenstein") 10-15 58

CASALS

Singles: 7-inch

SEVILLE 5-10 60

CASANOVA

Singles: 12-inch

SALSOUL 4-6 84

CASANOVA, Jimmy

Singles: 7-inch

FELSTED 5-10 59

CASANOVA, Tony

Singles: 7-inch

AMERICAN INT'L (533 "Diary of a Highschool Bride") 25-35 59
CHARIOT (1001 "My Little Nancy") 10-20
CREST (1053 "Yea! Yea! Come Another Day") 30-50 58
DORE (535 "Boogie Woogie Feeling") 50-75 59

CASANOVA & CHANTS

Singles: 7-inch

SAPHIRE 15-25

CASANOVA JR.

Singles: 78 rpm

PORT (7001 "Sally Mae") 25-50 57

Singles: 7-inch

PORT (7001 "Sally Mae") 25-50 57

CASANOVA II

Singles: 7-inch

EARLY BIRD (49658 "We've Got to Keep On") 10-20 60s

CASANOVAS

Singles: 78 rpm

APOLLO 25-75 55-57

Singles: 7-inch

APOLLO (471 "That's All") 50-75 55
APOLLO (474 "It's Been a Long Time") 75-100 55
APOLLO (477 "I Don't Want You to Go") 75-100 55
APOLLO (483 "My Baby's Love") 75-100 55
APOLLO (519 "Please Be Mine") 50-75 57
APOLLO (523 "Good Lookin' Baby") 50-75 57

CASANOVAS

Singles: 7-inch

PLANET (1027 "In the Land of Dreams") 150-250 62

CASASSA, Tommy

Singles: 7-inch

VALLI (103 "Three Rows Over") 10-20 60s

CASCADES *P&R/R&B/LP '63*

Singles: 7-inch

ABC 3-4 73
ARWIN 5-8 66
CANBASE 3-5 72
CHARTER 10-15 64
COLLECTABLES 3-4 81
GOLDIES 3-5 73
LIBERTY 5-8 65
PROBE 4-6 68
RCA 5-10 63-64
RENEE 10-20
SMASH 4-8 67
UNI 4-8 69-70
VALIANT 8-15 62-63
W.B. 3-4

Picture Sleeves

PROBE 4-8 68
RCA 8-12 63

LPs: 10/12-inch

BLOSSOM 10-15
CASCADES (6820 "What Goes on Inside the Cascades") 20-35
UNI 15-20 69
VALIANT (W-405 "Rhythm of the Rain") 40-60 63
(Monaural.)
VALIANT (WS-405 "Rhythm of the Rain") 50-100 63
(Stereo.)
Members: John Gummoe; David Stevens; David Zabo; Eddie Snyder; David Wilson.
Also see YOUNG, Neil

CASCADES / Sir Douglas Quintet

Singles: 7-inch

TRIP 3-5 70s
Also see CASCADES
Also see SIR DOUGLAS QUINTET

CASCADES

Singles: 7-inch

McCORMICK (105 "Pains in My Heart") 25-30 64
Also see VON GAYELS

CASDEN, Jack

Singles: 7-inch

MERCURY 5-10 59-60

CASE, Allen

Singles: 78 rpm

COLUMBIA (40585 "Watch Out") 15-25 57

Singles: 7-inch

COLUMBIA (40585 "Watch Out") 15-25 57
GOTHIC 5-10 61

CASE, Jimmy

Singles: 7-inch

WILCO 20-30

CASE, Scot Richard: see SRC

CASEY, Al *P&R/R&B '62*

(Al Casey Combo; with the K-C Ettes)

Singles: 78 rpm

DOT 20-30 56-57
MCI 10-20 55

Singles: 7-inch

BLUE HORIZON (925 "Cookin' ") 15-25 62
CHALLENGE 5-10 60
DOT (15524 "A Fool's Blues") 10-20 56
DOT (15563 "Guitar Man") 15-25 57
GREGMARK (5 "Caravan") 5-10 61
(Shown as by Duane Eddy, but actually by Al Casey.)
HIGHLAND (1002 "Got the Teenage Blues") 25-40 59
HIGHLAND (1004 "Night Beat") 15-25 60
LIBERTY 10-20 58
MCI 15-25 55
RAMCO 8-10 61
STACY (Except 962) 10-20 62-64
STACY (962 "Surfin' Hootenany") 10-20 63
(Black vinyl.)
STACY (962 "Surfin' Hootenany") 25-50 63
(Colored vinyl.)
U.A. (158 "Stinger") 10-20 59

LPs: 10/12-inch

STACY (100 "Surfin' Hootenany") 30-50 63
(Black vinyl.)
STACY (100 "Surfin' Hootenany") 100-125 63
(Colored vinyl.)
Also see CLARK, Sanford
Also see EDDY, Duane
Also see EXOTIC GUITARS
Also see HONEYS
Also see JONES, Art
Also see RAINTREE COUNTY SINGERS
Also see REYNOLDS, Jody
Also see ROGERS, Frantic Johnny
Also see SHARPE, Ray
Also see STORMS

CASEY, Gene

Singles: 7-inch

TRU-SOUND 5-10 61

CASEY, Jo

Singles: 7-inch

HONEE B 5-10 60

CASEY, Joe, & Fresh Heir

Singles: 7-inch

GMI 3-4 79

CASEY, June

Singles: 7-inch

DE-LITE 3-5 75

CASEY, Karen *C&W '80*

Singles: 7-inch

WESTERN PRIDE 3-5 80

CASEY, Patti

Singles: 7-inch

HOLLYWOOD 5-10 60

CASEY, Ruth

Singles: 78 rpm

CADILLAC 3-5

CASEY & Pressure Group

Singles: 7-inch

WIZDOM 3-5 70

CASH, Alvin *P&R '65*

(With Crawlers; with Registers)

Singles: 7-inch

CHESS 3-5 70
COLLECTABLES 3-4 81
DAKAR 3-5 76
ERIC 3-4 73
MAR-V-LUS 5-10 65-67
SEVENTY SEVEN 3-5 72
SOUND STAGE 7 8-12
TODDLIN' TOWN 5-10 68-69
TRIP 4-6
WESTBOUND 3-6
XL ("Twine Time") 20-30 65
(Selection number not known.)

LPs: 10/12-inch

MAR-V-LUS 15-20 65
SOUND STAGE "7" 10-15 73

CASH, Bobby

Singles: 7-inch

KING (5844 "Teen Love") 15-25 64
KING (5864 "It's Only Make Believe") 15-25 64
KING (5894 "Answer to My Dreams") 15-20 64

EPs: 7-inch

KING (25327 "Bobby Cash") 10-15 80
(Bonus EP, packaged with the various artists, Elvis sound-alikes LP, *The Other Kings*, [Revival 002]. Not issued with special cover.)

CASH, Eddie

(With the Cashiers)

Singles: 7-inch

PEAK (1001 "Doing All Right") 100-125 58
PEAK (1010 "Come on Home") 8-12 60
ROULETTE 5-10 61
TODD 10-15 60

CASH, Gordon

Singles: 7-inch

TAMBORINE 4-6 68

CASH, J.D.

Singles: 7-inch

GRT 5-10 77
SOUTH STAR 4-8 83
Also see LEADERS

CASH, J.D., & Bob Kuban Brass

LPs: 10/12-inch

NORMAN 8-12 87
RIPETE 5-10 88
Also see CASH, J.D.
Also see KUBAN, Bob

CASH, Johnny *C&W '55*

(With the Tennessee Two; with Tennessee Three)

Singles: 78 rpm

SUN 20-40 55-57

Singles: 7-inch

CACHET (4506 "Wings in the Morning") 3-5 80
COLUMBIA (02189 thru 05896) 3-5 81-86
COLUMBIA (10066 thru 11424) 3-5 74-81

COLUMBIA (30427 "Five Feet High and Rising") 10-20 59
(Stereo Seven single.)
COLUMBIA (30843 "Loading Coal") 10-20 60
(Stereo Seven single.)
COLUMBIA (30844 "Lumberjack") .10-20 60
(Stereo Seven single.)
COLUMBIA (30846 "Boss Jack")....10-20 60
(Stereo Seven single.)
COLUMBIA (30847 "Run Softly, Blue River") 10-20 60
(Stereo Seven single.)
COLUMBIA (3-41804 "Loading Coal") 10-20 60
(Compact 33 single.)
COLUMBIA (4-41804 "Loading Coal") 8-12 60
COLUMBIA (3-41995 "The Rebel – Johnny Yuma") 10-20 61
(Compact 33 single.)
COLUMBIA (4-41995 "The Rebel – Johnny Yuma") 8-12 61
COLUMBIA (3-42147 "Tennessee Flat-Top Box") 10-20 61
(Compact 33 single.)
COLUMBIA (4-42147 "Tennessee Flat-Top Box") 8-12 61
COLUMBIA (3-42301 "The Big Battle") 10-20 62
(Compact 33 single.)
COLUMBIA (4-42301 "The Big Battle") 8-12 62
COLUMBIA (3-42425 "In the Jailhouse Now") 10-20 62
(Compact 33 single.)
COLUMBIA (4-42425 "In the Jailhouse Now") 8-12 62
COLUMBIA (3-42512 "Bonanza")...10-20 62
(Compact 33 single.)
COLUMBIA (4-42512 "Bonanza")... 8-12 62
COLUMBIA (3-42615 "Were You There") 10-20 62
(Compact 33 single.)
COLUMBIA (4-42615 "Were You There") 8-12 62
COLUMBIA (42665 thru 46028) 3-8 63-74
COLUMBIA (60516 "The Baron") 3-5 81
COLUMBIA BOOK/RECORD LIBRARY ("The Bug That Tried to Crawl Around the World") 4-8 60s
COLUMBIA HALL OF FAME 3-8 59-64
SSS/SUN (Black vinyl) 3-5 69-70
SSS/SUN (Colored vinyl) 5-10 69-70
(Promotional issues only.)
SCOTTI BROS 3-5 82
SUN (200 series) 20-30 55-58
SUN (300 series) 10-25 58-62

Picture Sleeves

CACHET (4506 "Wings in the Morning") 3-5 80
COLUMBIA (10000 series)............ 3-6 79
COLUMBIA (41000 series)........... 10-20 58-61
COLUMBIA (42000 series)............ 5-15 61-64
COLUMBIA (44000 series)............ 5-10 68
SUN (295 "Guess Things Happen That Way") 15-25 58

EPs: 7-inch

COLUMBIA (2155 "Johnny Cash Sings The Rebel – Johnny Yuma")...............20-30 59
COLUMBIA (12531/2/3 "Fabulous Johnny Cash") 20-30 58
(Price is for any of three volumes.)
COLUMBIA (12841 /2/3 "Hymns By Johnny Cash") 15-25 59
(Price is for any of three volumes.)
COLUMBIA (13391/2/3 "Songs of Our Soul") 20-30 59
(Price is for any of three volumes.)
COLUMBIA (14631/2/3 "Now There Was a Song") 20-30 60
(Price is for any of three volumes.)
COLUMBIA (12531 "Fabulous") 20-30 58
SUN (111 "Johnny Cash Sings Hank Williams") 25-35 58
SUN (112 "Johnny Cash")..............25-35 58
SUN (113 "Johnny Cash")..............25-35 58
SUN (114 "Johnny Cash with the Tennessee Two") 25-35 58
SUN (116 "Johnny Cash")..............25-35 58
SUN (117 "Johnny Cash")..............25-35 58

LPs: 10/12-inch

AMERICAN.................................. 8-10 90s
BLAINE HOUSE 6-12
(Mail order offer.)
BUCKBOARD 5-10
CBS.. 5-10 82
CACHET.. 5-10
COLUMBIA (29 "The World of Johnny Cash") 8-12 70
COLUMBIA (363 "Legends and Love Songs") 10-15 68
(Columbia Record Club issue.)
COLUMBIA (1200 thru 1799) 15-30 58-61
(With "CL" prefix. Monaural.)
COLUMBIA (8100 thru 8599) 20-40 58-61
(With "CS" prefix. Stereo.)
COLUMBIA (1800 thru 2650) 10-20 62-68
(With "CL" prefix. Monaural.)
COLUMBIA (2004 "The Heart of Johnny Cash") 15-25 60s
(Columbia Star Series.)
COLUMBIA (8600 thru 9478) 10-20 62-68
(With "CS" prefix. Stereo.)
COLUMBIA (9726 "Holy Land")......12-18 69
(With 3-D cover.)
COLUMBIA (9726 "Holy Land")...... 8-12 69
(Standard cover.)
COLUMBIA (9827 thru 9943).......... 8-12 69-70
COLUMBIA (10000 series)............. 5-10 73
COLUMBIA (30000 thru 38000 series) 5-15 70-82
COLUMBIA SPECIAL PRODUCTS.................................. 5-10 75
COLUMBIA/SUFFOLK 8-10 79
DESIGN 5-8
DORAL..20-40
(Promotional mail-order LP from Doral cigarettes.)
HARMONY 8-12 69
IMPERIAL HOUSE 5-10
(Mail order offer.)
LONGINES.......................................5-8
(Mail order offer.)
MERCURY 5-10 87
OUT of TOWN DIST.........................5-10 82
PICKWICK 5-10 70s
POWER PAK 5-10
PRIORITY 5-10 81-82
SSS/SUN...5-15 69-84
(Some may be colored vinyl.)
SHARE 5-10
STACK-O-HITS 5-8
SUN (1220 "Johnny Cash and His Hot and Blue Guitar") 20-40 56
SUN (1235 "Songs That Made Him Famous") 20-40 58
SUN (1240 "Greatest")..................20-30 59
SUN (1245 "Johnny Cash Sings Hank Williams and Other Favorties") 15-25 60
SUN (1255 "Now Here's Johnny Cash") 15-25 61
SUN (1270 "All Aboard the Blue Train") 15-25 63
SUN (1275 "Original Sun Sound of Johnny Cash") 15-25 64
SUN/CAPITOL (90000 series) 15-20 60s
(Record club issues.)
SUNRISE MEDIA 5-10 81
SUNNYVALE 5-8
TIME-LIFE ("Johnny Cash")...........10-15 82
(Three-disc set.)
TRIP 8-10 74
U.A. 10-12 68
Session: George Jones; Marty Robbins; Waylon Jennings.
Also see BROOKS, Karen, & Johnny Cash
Also see DEL RAY, Martin
Also see HARRIS, Emmylou
Also see JONES, George
Also see KILGORE, Merle
Also see RICH, Charlie
Also see ROBBINS, Marty / Johnny Cash / Ray Price
Also see STATLER BROTHERS
Also see STUART, Marty
Also see TUBB, Ernest

CASH, Johnny, & June Carter

(Johnny Cash & June Carter Cash) C&W '64

Singles: 7-inch

COLUMBIA (10000 series).............. 3-5 76
COLUMBIA (43145 thru 45929)........ 3-8 64-73

LPs: 10/12-inch

COLUMBIA (9500 series) 10-20 64-67
COLUMBIA (32000 series)..............5-10 73
HARMONY 6-10 72
Also see CARTER, June
Also see JENNINGS, Waylon, Willie Nelson, Johnny Cash, & Kris Kristofferson

CASH, Johnny, & Carter Family C&W '63

(Carter Family with Johnny Cash)

Singles: 7-inch

COLUMBIA 3-8 63-72

CASH, Johnny, Carter Family & Oak Ridge Boys C&W '73

Singles: 7-inch

COLUMBIA... 3-5 73
Also see CARTER FAMILY
Also see OAK RIDGE BOYS

CASH, Johnny, & Mother Maybelle Carter C&W '73

Singles: 7-inch

COLUMBIA... 3-5 73
Also see CARTER FAMILY

CASH, Johnny, Rosanne Cash & Everly Brothers C&W '89

Singles: 7-inch

MERCURY (872 420-7 "Ballad of a Teenage Queen") 3-5 89
Also see CASH, Rosanne
Also see EVERLY BROTHERS

CASH, Johnny / Roy Clark / Linda Ronstadt

LPs: 10/12-inch

POINTED STAR (10178 "Concert Behind Prison Walls") 10-15 78
(NAPA special products TV soundtrack.)
Also see CASH, Rosanne
Also see CLARK, Roy
Also see RONSTADT, Linda

CASH, Johnny / Billy Grammer / Wilburn Brothers

LPs: 10/12-inch

PICKWICK/HILLTOP...................10-15 65
Also see GRAMMER, Billy

CASH, Johnny, & Levon Helm

Singles: 7-inch

A&M 3-4 80
Also see HELM, Levon

CASH, Johnny, & Waylon Jennings C&W '86

Singles: 7-inch

COLUMBIA.. 3-4 78-86
EPIC.. 3-4 80
Also see JENNINGS, Waylon

CASH, Johnny / Jerry Lee Lewis / Jeanie C. Riley

LPs: 10/12-inch

PICKWICK 5-10 70s
Also see RILEY, Jeanie C.

CASH, Johnny, Carl Perkins & Jerry Lee Lewis

LPs: 10/12-inch

COLUMBIA..5-10 82
Also see PERKINS, Carl, Jerry Lee Lewis, Roy Orbison & Johnny Cash

CASH, Johnny / Jeanie C. Riley

LPs: 10/12-inch

LONGINES (5288 "Rock Island Line") 5-8
(Mail order offer.)
Also see RILEY, Jeanie C.

CASH, Johnny, & Hank Williams Jr. C&W '88

Singles: 7-inch

MERCURY 3-4 88
Also see WILLIAMS, Hank, Jr.

CASH, Johnny / Tammy Wynette

LPs: 10/12-inch

COLUMBIA (5418 "King & Queen") 10-15
(Columbia Musical Treasury issue.)
Also see CASH, Johnny
Also see WYNETTE, Tammy

CASH, Rosanne C&W '80

Singles: 7-inch

COLUMBIA...3-4 80-90

Picture Sleeves

COLUMBIA..3-4 81

EPs: 7-inch

COLUMBIA..4-8 85

LPs: 10/12-inch

COLUMBIA..5-10 79-90
Session: Bobby Bare; Rodney Crowell; Emmylou Harris; Ricky Skaggs.
Also see CASH, Johnny, Rosanne Cash & Everly Brothers
Also see CROWELL, Rodney, & Rosanne Cash
Also see HARRIS, Emmylou
Also see NITTY GRITTY DIRT BAND, Rosanne Cash & John Hiatt
Also see SKAGGS, Ricky

CASH, Rosanne, & Bobby Bare C&W '79

Singles: 7-inch

COLUMBIA..3-4 79
Also see BARE, Bobby
Also see CASH, Rosanne

CASH, Sharon

Singles: 7-inch

A&M 3-5 71
PLAYBOY 3-4 73

LPs: 10/12-inch

PLAYBOY 8-10 73
Also see HONEY CONE

CASH, Tommy C&W '68

Singles: 7-inch

AUDIOGRAPH 3-4 83
ELEKTRA...3-5 75
EPIC...3-6 68-73
MONUMENT 3-4 77-79
MUSICOR 4-8 65
20TH FOX 3-4 76
U.A. 4-6 66-68

LPs: 10/12-inch

ELEKTRA...5-10 75
EPIC...8-12 69-72
MONUMENT 5-10 78
U.A. 10-12 68

CASH & CARRY

Singles: 7-inch

TARA 3-5 74
UNI...3-5 70

CASHBOARD, BILLBOX & YOUNG

Singles: 7-inch

HERITAGE...3-5 70

CASHELLES

Singles: 7-inch

DECCA..4-8 64

CASHER, Billy

Singles: 7-inch

EPIC...20-30 61

CASHEWS

Singles: 7-inch

FILM TOWN 5-10 61

CA$HFLOW R&B/LP '86

Singles: 12-inch

ATLANTA ARTISTS 4-6 86

Singles: 7-inch

ATLANTA ARTISTS 3-4 86
MERCURY 3-4 86

LPs: 10/12-inch

ATLANTA ARTISTS 5-10 86

CASHMAN, Terry P&R '76

(With The Men)

Singles: 7-inch

BOOM (005 "Try Me")......................8-10 66
LIFESONG (Except 45096 thru 45115) 3-5 76-82
LIFESONG (45096 thru 45115 "Talkin' Baseball") 3-5 76
(Price is for any individual disc. Complete set of 20 versions may be valued at $50 to $125.)

Picture Sleeves

LIFESONG (45096 thru 45115 "Talkin' Baseball") 3-8 76
(Price is for any individual sleeve. Complete set of 20 may be valued at $50 to $125.)

LPs: 10/12-inch

LIFESONG 5-10 76-77

CASHMAN & WEST P&R/LP '72

Singles: 7-inch

ABC...3-4 74
DUNHILL..3-5 72-74
LIFESONG 3-5 75

Picture Sleeves

DUNHILL...3-5 72

LPs: 10/12-inch

ABC...8-10 74
DUNHILL...8-12 72-74
Members: Terry Cashman; Tommy West.
Also see CROCE, Jim
Also see GENE & TOMMY
Also see MORNING MIST

CASHMAN & WEST / Gordon Jenkins & His Orchestra

LPs: 10/12-inch

DUNHILL (SPDJ-17 "Manhattan Tower") 10-15 72
(10-inch LP.)
Also see CASHMAN & WEST
Also see JENKINS, Gordon, & His Orchestra

CASHMAN, PISTILLI & WEST

Singles: 7-inch

ABC...4-6 68
CAPITOL...3-5 69-71

LPs: 10/12-inch

ABC...12-15 68
CAPITOL...10-15 69-71
Members: Terry Cashman; Gene Pistilli; Tommy West.
Also see BUCHANAN BROTHERS
Also see CASHMAN, Terry
Also see PISTILLI, Gene
Also see WEST, Tommy

CASHMAN, PISTILLI & WEST / Steve Karmen

Singles: 7-inch

PONTIAC ("GTO Rock")..................10-15 70
(Promotional issue of "1970 Pontiac Theme Music.")
Also see CASHMAN, PISTILLI & WEST

CASHMERE R&B/D&D '83

Singles: 12-inch

PHILLY WORLD...................................4-6 83
TNT 4-6 84

Singles: 7-inch

PHILLY WORLD...................................3-4 83-85

LPs: 10/12-inch

PHILLY WORLD.................................5-10 83-85

CASHMERE, Charlie

Singles: 7-inch

GOOMBIE 5-10 66

CASHMERES

Singles: 78 rpm

HERALD...25-50 56
MERCURY 25-50 54-55

Singles: 7-inch

ACA (1216 "Stairsteps to Heaven") 50-100 59
HERALD (474 "Little Dream Girl") 50-100 56
MERCURY (70501 "My Sentimental Heart") 50-100 54
MERCURY (70617 "Don't Let It Happen Again") 50-100 55
MERCURY (70679 "There's a Rumor") 50-100 55

CASHMERES

Singles: 7-inch

JOSIE (894 "Where Have You Been") 10-15 61
LAKE (703 "Four Lonely Nights")...15-25 60
LAKE (705 "Satisfied")..................15-25 60
LAURIE (3078 "A Very Special Birthday") 10-15 60
LAURIE (3088 "I Gotta Go") 5-10 61
LAURIE (3105 "Poppa Said")...........5-10 61
RELIC 4-8 72
Members: Windsor King; Bill Jordan; Jean Reeves; Robert Bowers; Neta Arnold.
Also see ROYAL SONS QUINTET
Also see KING & SHARPETTES

CASHMERES

Singles: 7-inch

HEM (1000 "Show Stopper").......200-400 65

CASHMIR, Kid, & Winnie LeCoux

Singles: 7-inch

PHANTOM 3-5 76

CASINO

Singles: 7-inch

MCA...3-5 76

LPs: 10/12-inch

MCA...8-10 76

CASINO ROYALES

Singles: 7-inch

COLISEUM 4-8 67

CASINOS

Singles: 7-inch

CASINO (111 "My Love for You") ...25-50 60
MASKE (803 "I'm Falling")...........50-100 59

CASINOS

Singles: 7-inch

ALTO (2002 "I Like It Like That") ...15-25 61
S&G (301 "Please Let Her").........75-125 62

CASINOS P&R/LP '67

(Gene Hughes & Casinos; with Saturns; Casino's)

Singles: 7-inch

ABC 3-5 73
AIRTOWN (002 "That's the Way") 10-15 67
CAROL (201 "Wisdom of a Fool") 4-6 80
CAROL (1001 "You Belong to Me") ...4-6 80
CERTRON 5-8 70
COLLECTABLES 3-4 81
FRATERNITY.....................................6-12 65-71
ITZY (2 "Do You Recall").................40-60 63
MILLION..5-8 72
NAME (001 "Do You Recall").....200-300 62
OLIMPIC (251 "Do You Recall") 100-150 63
(Re-recording of Name release.)
TERRY (115 "Gee Whiz")..............50-75 64
TERRY (116 "Too Good to Be True") 35-55 64
TRIP 3-5
U.A. 4-6 68

LPs: 10/12-inch

FRATERNITY (1019 "Then You Can Tell Me Goodbye") 20-30 67
Members: J.T. Sears; Pete Bolton; Gene Hughes; Pete Bolton; Joe Patterson; Ray White; Denny Frecke; Mickey Denton; Bob Armstrong; Bill Hawkins; Tommy Matthews.
Also see DENTON, Mickey

CASINOS / Fireflies

Singles: 7-inch

ERA 3-5 70s
Also see CASINOS
Also see FIREFLIES

CASINOS

Singles: 7-inch

SIMS...4-8 66

CASINOS

Singles: 7-inch

DEL VAL (1002 "Everybody Can't Be Pretty") 12-18

CASIOPEA

LPs: 10/12-inch

ALFA...5-10 81-82
MILESTONE 5-10 85

CASLONS P&R '61

Singles: 7-inch

AMY...10-20 61-62
SEECO 10-20 61

CASON, Buzz

Singles: 7-inch

CAPRICE 3-5 72
CAPRICORN...3-5 72
ELF 3-6 69
Also see BUZZ & BUCKY
Also see LEE, Brenda
Also see MILES, Garry
Also see RONNY & DAYTONAS
Also see STATUES

CASON, Rich, & Galactic Orchestra R&B '83

Singles: 12-inch

PRIVATE I..4-6 84

Singles: 7-inch

LARC 3-4 83
PRIVATE I..3-4 84

CASPAR

Singles: 7-inch

SUNFLOWER 4-6 71

CASPER R&B '80

Singles: 7-inch

A.V.I. 3-4 84
ATLANTIC...3-4 83-84

LPs: 10/12-inch

A.V.I. 5-10 84
ATLANTIC...5-10 83

CASRAN

Singles: 7-inch

SOUTH 3-5 73

CASS, Mama: see ELLIOTT, Cass

CASSADY, Gene

Singles: 7-inch

PURE GOLD 4-8 64

CASSADY, Linda C&W '76

(With Bobby Spears)

Singles: 7-inch

CIN KAY...3-5 76-78

LPs: 10/12-inch

AMIGO...5-10 70s
CIN KAY...5-10 77
Also see SPEARS, Bobby

CASSARO, Al

(Alan Cassaro)

Singles: 7-inch

INTEGRITY...5-10 64
OLD TOWN...4-8 66
Also see CASSARO, Lane
Also see LEATHERWOOD, Alan

CASSARO, Lane

(Alan Cassaro)

Singles: 7-inch

MAHALO 8-12 63
Also see CASSARO, Al

CASSETTA, John

Singles: 7-inch

TRU LITE 4-8 62

CASSIDY
Singles: 7-inch
EPIC... 3-5 71

CASSIDY, Dan
LPs: 10/12-inch
LITTLE DAVID... 8-10 72

CASSIDY, David P&R '71
Singles: 7-inch
BELL... 3-5 71-73
FLASHBACK... 3-5 73
MCA (41101 "Hurt So Bad")... 3-5 79
RCA... 3-5 75-77
Picture Sleeves
BELL (45150 "Cherish")... 3-5 71
BELL (45187 "Could It Be Forever")... 3-5 72
MCA (41101 "Hurt So Bad")... 3-5 79
LPs: 10/12-inch
BELL... 10-15 72-74
RCA... 8-12 74-76
Also see PARTRIDGE FAMILY
Also see WILSON, Carl

CASSIDY, Pam
Singles: 7-inch
MOON... 3-4 77

CASSIDY, Shaun P&R/LP '77
Singles: 7-inch
W.B.... 3-4 77-80
Picture Sleeves
W.B.... 3-4 77-78
LPs: 10/12-inch
W.B.... 8-10 77-80

CASSIDY, Shaun, and Todd Rundgren's Utopia
Singles: 7-inch
W.B.... 3-4 80
Also see CASSIDY, Shaun
Also see UTOPIA

CASSIDY, Ted
("Ted Cassidy as Lurch [of TV's Addams Family] with the Music of Gary Paxton")
Singles: 7-inch
CAPITOL (5503 "The Lurch")... 10-15 65
Picture Sleeves
CAPITOL (5503 "The Lurch")... 15-25 65
Also see PAXTON, Gary

CASSIDY SISTERS
(With the Titanics)
Singles: 7-inch
HOP (505 "Stardust Waltz")... 25-50 58

CASSIETTA, George
Singles: 7-inch
AUDIO ARTS... 5-8

CASSINOS
Singles: 7-inch
ALPHA... 4-8 66

CAST, Ernie
Singles: 7-inch
EMBER (1033 "Betty Morretti")... 15-25 58

CAST OF THOUSANDS
Singles: 7-inch
AMY (11040 "Long Way to Go")... 8-12 68
AMY (11056 "Country Gardens")... 8-12 68
SOFT (1002 "Have It Your Way")... 15-20 67
TOWER (276 "Girl")... 15-20 66

CASTALEERS
("With Rhythm Accompaniment"; "Solo - Richard A. Jones")
Singles: 7-inch
DONNA (1349 "That's Why I Cry")... 20-30 61
FELSTED (8504 "Come Back")... 50-75 58
FELSTED (8512 "Lonely Boy")... 50-75 58
FELSTED (8585 "You're My Dream")... 75-125 59
PLANET (44 "That's Why I Cry")... 30-50 60
Member: Richard A. Jones.

CASTANETS
Singles: 7-inch
TCF... 4-8 64

CASTAWAYS
Singles: 78 rpm
EXCELLO (2038 "I Wish")... 10-20 54
Singles: 7-inch
EXCELLO (2038 "I Wish")... 20-30 54

CASTAWAYS
Singles: 7-inch
CAPITOL... 5-10 60
VIV... 5-10 61

CASTAWAYS
Singles: 7-inch
GNP... 5-10 63-64

CASTAWAYS
Singles: 7-inch
WITCH (124 "Don't You Just Know It")... 20-25 63

CASTAWAYS P&R '65
Singles: 7-inch
APEX... 12-18 65
BEAR (2000 "Feel So Fine")... 25-35 67
COLLECTABLES... 3-4 81
ERA... 3-5 72
ERIC... 3-4 78
FONTANA... 12-18 68
LANA... 4-6 64
SOMA (Except 1461)... 8-12 65
SOMA (1461 "Girl in Love")... 15-25 67
TAUNAH (7745 "I Feel So Fine")... 15-25 67
TERRIFIC... 4-8
EPs: 7-inch
SOMA (03 "Liar Liar")... 10-20
(Reportedly 500 made.)
Members: Merlin Dean; Richard Robey; Robert Folschon; Ron Hensley; James Donna; Dennis Craswell.
Also see BLACKWOOD APOLOGY
Also see CROW
Also see DEAN, Merlin
Also see ROBY, Dick

CASTAWAYS / Gestures
Singles: 7-inch
TERRIFIC... 4-6 60s
Also see CASTAWAYS
Also see GESTURES

CASTAWAYS
Singles: 7-inch
STAR DELTA... 4-8 63

CASTAWAYS
Singles: 7-inch
ASTRA (1002 "I Found You")... 5-10 65

CASTAWAYS
Singles: 7-inch
EEE... 3-5 80

CASTAWAYS
Singles: 7-inch
ASSAULT... 8-12

CASTAWAYS
Singles: 7-inch
HEARTBEAT (0010 "The Girl Next Door")... 10-20
PIT (100,001 "If Our Love Is Strong")... 15-25
SMOKE (215 "Love Me Baby")... 25-35
TORNADO... 15-20

CASTAWAYS FIVE
Singles: 7-inch
RAOL (001 "Revenge")... 15-20

CASTELLANOS, Al
Singles: 7-inch
MARDI-GRAS... 5-10

CASTELLES
(George Grant & Castelles)
Singles: 78 rpm
ATCO... 25-50 56
GRAND (Blue label)... 200-400 54
GRAND (Yellow label)... 100-200 54
Singles: 7-inch
ATCO (6069 "Happy and Gay")... 75-100 56
CLASSIC ARTISTS... 4-6 89-90
COLLECTABLES... 3-4 81
GRAND (101 "My Girl Awaits Me")... 2000-4000 53
(Glossy blue label. Reportedly 600 made.)
GRAND (101 "My Girl Awaits Me")... 1000-2000 53
(Flat blue label.)
GRAND (101 "My Girl Awaits Me")... 250-500 50s
(Yellow label. Rigid disc. No company address shown.)
GRAND (101 "My Girl Awaits Me")... 50-100 61
(Yellow label. Flexible disc. No company address shown.)
GRAND (101 "My Girl Awaits Me")... 15-25 60s
(Yellow label. Company address is shown.)
GRAND (103 "This Silver Ring")... 1000-2000 54
(Glossy yellow label. Rigid disc. No company address shown.)
GRAND (103 "This Silver Ring")... 50-100 61
(Yellow label. Flexible disc. No company address shown.)
GRAND (103 "This Silver Ring")... 15-25 60s
(Yellow label. Company address is shown.)
GRAND (105 "Do You Remember")... 1000-2000 54
(Glossy yellow label. Rigid disc. No company address shown.)
GRAND (105 "Do You Remember")... 50-100 61
(Yellow label. Flexible disc. No company address shown.)
GRAND (105 "Do You Remember")... 15-25 60s
(Yellow label. Company address is shown.)
GRAND (109 "Over a Cup of Coffee")... 2000-2500 54
(Blue label.)
GRAND (109 "Over a Cup of Coffee")... 250-500 50s
(Glossy yellow label. Rigid disc. No company address shown.)
GRAND (109 "Over a Cup of Coffee")... 50-100 61
(Yellow label. Flexible disc. No company address shown.)
GRAND (109 "Over a Cup of Coffee")... 15-25 60s
(Yellow label. Company address is shown.)
GRAND (114 "Marcella")... 2000-2500 54
(Cream color label. Rigid disc. No company address shown.)
GRAND (114 "Marcella")... 50-100 61
(Yellow label. Flexible disc. No company address shown.)
GRAND (114 "Marcella")... 15-25 60s
(Yellow label. Company address is shown.)
GRAND (122 "Heavenly Father")... 1000-2000 55
(Cream color label. Rigid disc. No company address shown.)
GRAND (122 "Heavenly Father")... 50-100 61
(Yellow label. Flexible disc. No company address shown.)
GRAND (122 "Heavenly Father")... 15-25 60s
(Yellow label. Company address is shown.)
LOST-NITE... 4-6 70s
COLLECTABLES ("Castells")... 5-10 81
(Selection number not known.)
COLLECTABLES ("Castells")... 10-15 82
(Picture disc.)
Note: Not all of the Grand variations may exist with all of their titles; however, they are listed in case they do exist.
Members: George Grant; Frank Vance; William Taylor; Ron Everett; Octavius Anthony; Walt Miller; Clarence Scott.

CASTELLS P&R '61
Singles: 7-inch
COLLECTABLES... 3-4 80
DECCA (31834 "The Angel Cried")... 5-10 65
DECCA (31967 "Life Goes On")... 5-10 66
ERA... 10-20 61-63
LAURIE (3444 "Rocky Ridges")... 15-20 68
U.A. (50324 "Two Lovers")... 5-10 68
W.B. (5421 "I Do")... 40-60 64
W.B. (5445 "Could This Be Magic")... 8-12 64
W.B. (5486 "Love Finds a Way")... 8-12 64
LPs: 10/12-inch
ERA (EL-109 "So This Is Love")... 50-100 62
(Monaural.)
ERA (ES-109 "So This Is Love")... 100-150 62
(Stereo.)
Members: Chuck Girard; Bob Ussery; Tom Hicks; Joe Kelly.
Also see GIRARD, Chuck
Also see WILSON, Brian

CASTELS
Singles: 7-inch
BLACK GOLD (306 "Save a Chance")... 20-40
SOLOMON... 10-20 67
WILDFIRE ("Save a Chance")... 20-40
(Selection number not known. Different version than on Black Gold.)

CASTER, Jimmy: see CASTOR, Jimmy

CASTILES
Singles: 7-inch
MAGENTA... 8-12 61

CASTINOS
(Castino's)
Singles: 7-inch
C&M (440 "Loapin")... 10-20 58

CASTLE, Angee
Singles: 7-inch
CUB... 5-10 59

CASTLE, Ann
Singles: 7-inch
X-POWER... 15-25 59

CASTLE, Birdie
(With Stardusters)
Singles: 7-inch
PORT (70005 "Crazy Beat")... 15-25 58

CASTLE, Chuck
Singles: 7-inch
DORIAN... 5-10 59

CASTLE, David P&R '77
Singles: 7-inch
PARACHUTE... 3-5 77-79
LPs: 10/12-inch
PARACHUTE... 8-10 77-79

CASTLE, Diane
Singles: 7-inch
DECCA... 4-8 64
MGM... 4-8 64

CASTLE, Joey
(With the Daddy-O's)
Singles: 7-inch
HEADLINE (1008 "Rock & Roll Daddy-O")... 50-75 59
RCA (7283 "That Ain't Nothin' But Right")... 30-50 58

CASTLE, Nan
Singles: 7-inch
RCA... 8-12 57

CASTLE, Ric
Singles: 7-inch
AARDVARK... 5-10 65
RAYNE... 5-10 62
W.B.... 4-8 63

CASTLE, Tony
(With the Raiders)
Singles: 7-inch
EAST WEST... 10-20 57
GONE... 5-10 61
TREY... 5-10 60

CASTLE KINGS
Singles: 7-inch
ATLANTIC... 5-10 61-62

CASTLE SISTERS P&R '62
Singles: 7-inch
ROULETTE... 5-10 59-60
TERRACE... 5-10 62-63
TRIODEX... 5-10 61
Picture Sleeves
TERRACE... 10-15 62

CASTLEBERRY, Leo
Singles: 7-inch
UNITED SOUTHERN ARTISTS (101 "Teenage Blues")... 20-40 61

CASTLEMAN, Boomer P&R '75
(Boomer Clarke)
Singles: 7-inch
CREME... 3-4 86
MUMS... 3-5 75
SRO (218 "Summertime Blues")... 4-6 86
(Promotional issue only.)
Also see LEWIS & CLARKE

CASTLES
Singles: 7-inch
TRIBUTE (100 "I Was a Fool")... 75-125 61

CASTLE-TONES
(With Jimmy Johnson's Band; Castlestones)
Singles: 7-inch
FIRE FLY... 10-20 60
RIFT (502 "Goodnight")... 75-125 59
(Has company address under name: "Rift.")
RIFT (502 "Goodnight")... 40-60 61
(Has no address under name: "Rift Records.")
RIFT (504 "We Met at a Dance")... 75-125 59

CASTON, Bobbe
Singles: 7-inch
ATLAS (1103 "Call Me Darling")... 75-100 58

CASTON & MAJORS
LPs: 10/12-inch
MOTOWN... 8-10 74
Also see RADIANTS

CASTOR, Jimmy P&R/R&B '66
(Jimmy Castor Bunch; Jimmy Caster Quintet)
Singles: 12-inch
SALSOUL... 4-6 83
Singles: 7-inch
ATLANTIC... 3-5 74-77
CAPITOL... 4-6 68-69
CLOWN... 5-10 62
COMPASS... 4-6 68
COTILLION... 3-4 79
DECCA... 4-8 66
DREAM... 3-4 84-85
DRIVE... 3-4 78
HULL (758 "Poor Loser")... 10-20 63
JET SET... 4-8 65
KINETIC... 3-6 70
LM... 5-8
LONG DISTANCE... 3-4 81
RCA... 3-5 71-73
SALSOUL... 3-4 82
SLEEPING BAG... 3-4 88
SMASH... 4-8 66-67
LPs: 10/12-inch
ATLANTIC... 8-10 74-77
COTILLION... 5-10 79
CRYSTAL BALL... 8-10 81
DREAM... 5-10 83
DRIVE... 5-10 78
LONG DISTANCE... 5-10 80
PAUL WINLEY... 5-15
RCA... 10-15 72-75
SMASH... 15-20 67
Members: Jimmy Castor; Gerry Thomas; Doug Gibson; Lenny Fridie Jr.; Harry Jensen; Bobby Manigault.
Also see CLINTONIAN CUBS
Also see JOEY & TEENAGERS
Also see LYMON, Lewis, & Teenchords

CASTOR, Jimmy, & Juniors
Singles: 78 rpm
ATOMIC... 75-150 57
WING... 50-75 56
Singles: 7-inch
ATOMIC (100 "This Girl of Mine")... 100-200 57
WING (90078 "I Promise")... 75-125 56
Also see CASTOR, Jimmy

CASTRO, Bernadette
Singles: 7-inch
COLPIX (747 "Sports Car Sally")... 25-30 64
COLPIX (759 "Get Rid of Him")... 25-30 64

CASTRO, Frankie
Singles: 78 rpm
WING... 4-8 56
Singles: 7-inch
WING... 5-10 56

CASTRO, Phil
Singles: 7-inch
COLPIX... 5-10 59

CASTRO, Skip, Band
LPs: 10/12-inch
MIDNIGHT... 5-10

CASTRO, Vince
Singles: 7-inch
APT... 8-12 58-60
DOE (102 "Bong Bong")... 25-40 58
ORCHID... 5-10 60

CASTROES
Singles: 7-inch
COLLECTABLES... 3-4 81
GRAND (2002 "Dearest Darling")... 75-125 59

CASTROS
Singles: 7-inch
LASSO (501 "Lucky Me")... 1000-2000 59
(Reportedly 100 made.)
LASSO (502 "In My Dreams")... 1000-2000 59
(Reportedly 100 made.)

CASUAL CRESCENDOS
Singles: 7-inch
MRC (12001 "Wish That You Were Here")... 250-350 63

CASUAL TEENS
Singles: 7-inch
FELSTED... 10-20 58

CASUAL THREE
Singles: 7-inch
LUNIVERSE (109 "Invisible Thing")... 25-35 58
MARK-X (7009 "Candy Store Blues")... 20-30 57
Also see GOODMAN, Dickie

CASUALAIRS
Singles: 7-inch
AUTUMN (21 "Just for You")... 15-25 65
CRAIG (5001 "Cruising")... 15-25 61
MONA-LEE (136 "At the Dance")... 15-25 59

CASUAL-AIRES
Singles: 7-inch
BRUNSWICK... 10-15 58
C.B.... 10-15 63
CRAIG (5001 "Cruising")... 25-50 62
ENTERPRISE (1000 "The Millionaire")... 50-100 63

CASUALEERS
Singles: 7-inch
LAURIE... 4-8 67-68
ROULETTE... 4-8 67

CASUALS
Singles: 78 rpm
DOT... 5-10 57
Singles: 7-inch
BLACK HAWK... 3-5
DOT (15557 "My Love Song for You")... 10-15 57
DOT (15671 "Hello Love")... 10-15 57

CASUALS
("Featuring Gary Mears")
Singles: 78 rpm
BACK BEAT... 15-25 57
Singles: 7-inch
ABC... 3-5 73
BACK BEAT (503 "So Tough")... 20-30 57
BACK BEAT (510 "Ju-Judy")... 15-25 58
Picture Sleeves
BACK BEAT (503 "So Tough")... 20-30 57
Also see ORIGINAL CASUALS

CASUALS
Singles: 7-inch
SCOTTY (628 "Darling, Do You Love Me")... 150-250 59

CASUALS
("Vocal Joe Hoffman")
Singles: 7-inch
MOONBEAM (71613 "Some Day")... 50-100 63

CASUALS
Singles: 7-inch
MINARET (109 "Money")... 10-15 63
MONUMENT... 5-10 65-66
SOUND STAGE 7... 10-15 64

CASUALS
Singles: 7-inch
FEATURE... 8-12 65
Picture Sleeves
FEATURE... 10-20 65
Members: Albee Clausen; Keith Bener; Steve Acklam; Mike Morales.
Also see ALBEE & CASUALS

CASUALS
(British Casuals)
Singles: 7-inch
MAINSTREAM... 5-10 68
Also see BRITISH CASUALS

CASUALS
Singles: 7-inch
TOLTEC (12 "Johnny B. Goode")... 8-12

CASUALTONES
Singles: 7-inch
SUCCESS... 5-10 63

CASUALTONES
Singles: 7-inch
LIBRARY... 8-12 63

CASWELL, Johnny P&R '63
Singles: 7-inch
DECCA (32017 "I.O.U.")... 50-75 66
LUV (250 "Faces")... 8-12 67
SMASH... 5-10 63-64
Also see CRYSTAL MANSION

CAT
Singles: 7-inch
RCA... 3-6 69-70
LPs: 10/12-inch
RCA... 10-12 70

CAT MOTHER P&R/LP '69
(With the All Night News Boys)
Singles: 7-inch
POLYDOR... 3-6 69-72
LPs: 10/12-inch
POLYDOR... 20-30 69-73

CAT'S CRADLE
Singles: 7-inch
BIG TREE... 3-5 73

CAT'S PAJAMAS
Singles: 7-inch
AMERICAN WORLD... 10-15

CATALANO, Vinny
Singles: 7-inch
HAMMER 4-8

CATALINA SIX
Singles: 7-inch
FLAGSHIP (126 "Moon 2000") 15-25 62

CATALINA SIX
Singles: 7-inch
CANDLELITE (413 "It Had to Rain") . 4-6 74

CATALINAS
Singles: 7-inch
LITTLE (811 "Give Me Your Love") 75-125 57
Members: Jimmy Colwell; Johnny Luth; Artie DeNicholas; Johnny Kunz; Tom Juliano.
Also see VAN DYKES

CATALINAS
Singles: 7-inch
GLORY (285 "Marlene") 25-35 58

CATALINAS
Singles: 7-inch
BACK BEAT (513 "Speechless") 20-25 58
CRYSTAL BALL 4-8

CATALINAS
Singles: 7-inch
FORTUNE (535 "Long Walk") 10-15 60

CATALINAS
("Featuring Bob Meyer")
Singles: 7-inch
CATALINAS 3-4 82
DOMINANT 8-15
RITA (107 "Ring of Stars") 20-30 60
RITA (108 "Wooly Wooly Willy") 15-20 60
S.E.I. 3-4 82
SCEPTER 8-15 67
SUGARBUSH 4-6 75
SUMMERTIME SOUNDS (15 "Tick Tock") 15-25 60s
ZEBRA (101 "Hey Little Girl") 50-100 61
LPs: 10/12-inch
CATALINAS 5-10 82
Members: Bob Meyer; Tommy Black; Buddy Emmerke; Johnny Wyatt; O.C. Gravitte; Reggie Smith; Jack Stallings; Johnny Edwards; Tom Plyler; Sidney Smith; Rob Thorne; Bobby Pace; Gary Barker; Ken Carriker; Mike Hewat; Rex Cole; Mark Goins; Mike Suddreth; Bobby Nantz; Earl Dawkins.

CATALINAS
Singles: 7-inch
20TH FOX (299 "Safari") 10-20 61

CATALINAS
Singles: 7-inch
CUCA (1094 "War Party") 10-20 62
KNIGHT (101 "Come to Me") 15-25 65
MEAN MT. (1422 "Dee Dee") 3-5 82
MUNDO (1000 "Hey Little Girl") 4-8 63
SARA (6392 "By My Window") 15-20 63
TARGET (101 "Varsity Club Song") 15-25 66
TEE PEE (117 "Dee Dee") 15-25 67
Picture Sleeves
MUNDO (1000 "Hey Little Girl") 8-12 63
Members: Al Posniak; Harry Wheelock; Bob Dix; Jim Kelly; Roger Loos; Pete Sorce; Judy Lee Reeths; Denny Noie.
Also see NOIE, Denny
Also see SOURCE, Pete

CATALINAS
Singles: 7-inch
DEE JAY (1010 "Bail Out") 20-30 63
RIC (113 "Banzai Washout") 15-25 64
RIC (164 "Surfer Boy") 15-25 65
SIMS (134 "Bail Out") 10-20 63
LPs: 10/12-inch
RIC (1006 "Fun, Fun, Fun") 30-45 64
Members: Tommy Tedesco; Steve Douglas; Hal Blaine; Leon Russell; Bruce Johnston; Billy Strange; Jerry Cole.

CATALINAS
Singles: 7-inch
DIAL 5-10 63
MILLION (77 "Stormy Weather") .. 50-100 63
ORIGINAL SOUND (48 "Your Tender Lips") 10-15 64
PAGODA 5-10 68

CATALON, Nathan
Singles: 7-inch
MERCURY 5-10 59

CATAMORANDS
Singles: 7-inch
DGMR (101 "Over You") 20-30

CATAPILLA
LPs: 10/12-inch
VERTIGO 10-20 71

CATAPULT
Singles: 7-inch
SCEPTER 4-6 72

CATCH
Singles: 7-inch
DOT 3-6 69
LPs: 10/12-inch
DOT 10-15 69

CATCH R&B '84
Singles: 12-inch
COLUMBIA 4-6 84-85
Singles: 7-inch
COLUMBIA 3-4 84-85

CATCH III
Singles: 7-inch
CRIKET 4-8

CATE, Billy
Singles: 7-inch
JUDY 4-8 62

CATE BROTHERS P&R/R&B/LP '76
(Cates Gang)
Singles: 7-inch
ASYLUM 3-5 76-78
ELEKTRA 3-4 77
METROMEDIA 3-5 70
LPs: 10/12-inch
ASYLUM 5-10 75-77
ATLANTIC 5-10 79
METROMEDIA 10-12 70-73
Members: Earl Cate; Ernie Cate.

CATERPILLARS
Singles: 7-inch
COLUMBIA 4-8 61

CATERPILLARS
Singles: 7-inch
PORT 5-10 64

CATES: see CATES SISTERS

CATES, George P&R '55
Singles: 78 rpm
CORAL 3-6 51-57
Singles: 7-inch
CORAL 5-10 51-57
DOT 3-6 62
SIGNATURE 3-6 59-60
EPs: 7-inch
CORAL 5-10 54-57
LPs: 10/12-inch
CORAL 10-20 54-57
Also see BUTLER, Champ, & George Cates

CATES, Phoebe
Singles: 7-inch
COLUMBIA 3-4 82
Picture Sleeves
COLUMBIA 3-4 82

CATES, Phoebe, & Bill Wray
Singles: 7-inch
MCA 3-4 83
Also see CATES, Phoebe

CATES, Ronnie
Singles: 7-inch
TERRACE (7501 "Long Time") 50-100 62
TERRACE (7508 "Long Time") 50-100 62
(Reissue with different flip side.)
Session: Travellers.

CATES GANG: see CATE BROTHERS

CATES SISTERS C&W '76
(The Cates)
Singles: 7-inch
CAPRICE 3-5 76-78
OVATION 3-5 79-80
LPs: 10/12-inch
CAPRICE 5-10 77
OVATION 5-10 79
Members: Mary Cates; Margie Cates.
Also see BROWN, Jim Ed

CATFISH
(Bob Hodge)
Singles: 7-inch
EASTBOUND 3-5 73
EPIC 3-6 69-70
LPs: 10/12-inch
ADELPHI 5-10 79-81
EASTBOUND 8-10 73-74
EPIC 10-12 70-71
Also see BLUESBUSTERS

CATHERINE WHEEL
LPs: 10/12-inch
POLYDOR (526850 "Happy Days") 10-15 90s

CATHOLIC GIRLS
Singles: 7-inch
MCA 3-4 82-83
Picture Sleeves
MCA 3-4 82
LPs: 10/12-inch
MCA 5-10 82

CATHY & JOE P&R '64
Singles: 7-inch
SMASH 4-8 64-65
Members: Cathy Bunn; Joe Wegman.

CATHY & RICHETTES
Singles: 7-inch
GROOVE MERCHANT 4-6 75

CATHY JEAN P&R '61
(With the Roomates)
Singles: 7-inch
ERIC 3-4 73
PHILIPS (Except 40014) 8-12 63
PHILIPS (40014 "Believe Me") 10-20 62
QUALITY (1251 "Please Love Me Forever") 10-15 61
(Canadian.)
VALMOR 10-15 61-62
LPs: 10/12-inch
VALMOR (78 "At the Hop") 400-500 62
(Reissue. Has titles printed on cover. Does not picture the group.)
VALMOR (789 "At the Hop") 350-450 61
(Pictures Cathy Jean & Roomates. Note different number.)
Also see ROOMATES

CAT-KEYS
Singles: 7-inch
BLUE ROCK 3-6 69

CATMAN & TOENAIL
Singles: 7-inch
FUN-E-BONE (4612 "Election '76") 5-8 76
Also see HARRIS, Dave / Catman & Toenail

CATO, Connie C&W '74
Singles: 7-inch
CAPITOL 3-5 74-77
MCA 3-4 80
LPs: 10/12-inch
CAPITOL 5-10 74-77

CATO, Joe
Singles: 7-inch
CHESS 4-8 67

CATS
Singles: 78 rpm
FEDERAL 20-40 55
Singles: 7-inch
FEDERAL (12238 "I Don't Care No More") 100-150 55
FEDERAL (12248 "You're So Nice") 75-125 55
Members: Gene Ford; Bill Boyd.

CATS
Singles: 7-inch
ELEKTRA 3-4 80
FANTASY 3-5 72-74
MCA 3-5 76
RARE EARTH 3-5 70
SIRE 3-6 69
LPs: 10/12-inch
ELEKTRA 5-10 80
FANTASY 8-12 74
RARE EARTH 10-12 70

CATS & FIDDLE
Singles: 78 rpm
BLUEBIRD 20-30 39-42
DECCA 10-20 50
GOTHAM 15-25 49-50
MANOR 15-25 45-48
MONTGOMERY WARD 15-25
RCA 10-20 46-50
REGIS 15-25 45
Singles: 7-inch
DECCA (48151 "Wine Drinker") . 100-200 50
LPs: 10/12-inch
RCA 10-12 76
Members: Austin Powell; Jim Henderson; Ernie Price; Chuck Barksdale; Tiny Grimes; Herb Miles; Shirley Moore; Johnny Davis.
Also see DAVIS, June, with Cats & Fiddle
Also see POWELL, Austin

CATS & FIDDLE / Four Clefs
Singles: 78 rpm
RCA 50-100 50
Singles: 7-inch
RCA (0077 "I Miss You So") 150-250 50
(Colored vinyl.)
RCA (4393 "I Miss You So") 100-150 50
(Black vinyl.)
Also see CATS & FIDDLE
Also see FOUR CLEFS

CATS 'N' JAMMER THREE: see SAMUELS, Bill

CATS MEOW
Singles: 7-inch
DECCA 4-8 66

CATTIVA, Savina
Singles: 7-inch
LOVE 5-10 59
RANDOM 5-10 61

CAUDELL, Ann
Singles: 7-inch
QUICK 10-20

CAUDELL, Lane C&W '87
Singles: 7-inch
MCA 3-4 78
METROMEDIA 3-5 73
PRIVATE STOCK 3-5 76
16TH AVE. 3-4 87-88
LPs: 10/12-inch
MCA 8-10 78-79

CAULSTON, Jerry
Singles: 7-inch
CHRISTY 5-10 60

CAUSEY, Buddy
Singles: 7-inch
ATLANTIC 3-5 70
U.A. 3-5 70

CAUSEY, Sam
Singles: 7-inch
DEB 5-10 59
SCOTTIE 5-10 59

CAUTIONS
Singles: 7-inch
IKON (113 "Groovin' ") 15-25 63
SHRINE (104 "Watch Your Step") 150-200 65
SHRINE (115 "No Other Way") .. 300-400 66
TORÈ (1010 "On Our Way to School") 75-125 59
Member: Joe Clyburn.

CAVALIER, Johnny
Singles: 7-inch
HI CLASS (105 "Rockin' Chair Roll") 30-45 59
Picture Sleeves
HI CLASS (105 "Rockin' Chair Roll") 40-50 59

CAVALIERE, Felix P&R '80
Singles: 7-inch
BEARSVILLE 3-5 74-75
EPIC 3-4 80
LPs: 10/12-inch
BEARSVILLE 10-12 74-75
EPIC (705 "Castles in the Air") 15-20 79
(Interview and music. Promotional issue only.)
EPIC (35990 "Castles in the Air") 5-10 79
Also see KARP, Charlie
Also see RASCALS
Also see 3 GIRLS
Also see TREASURE

CAVALIERS
Singles: 78 rpm
DECCA 5-10 55
Singles: 7-inch
DECCA (29556 "Somewhere, Sometime, Someday") 15-20 55

CAVALIERS
Singles: 7-inch
APT (25004 "Dance, Dance, Dance") 25-40 58

CAVALIERS
Singles: 7-inch
MUSIC WORLD (101 "Magic Age of Sixteen") 20-30 63
NRC (028 "Charm Bracelet") 20-30 59

CAVALIERS
Singles: 7-inch
CORAL (62245 "Teen Fever") 5-10 61
GALENA 10-20 60
Also see NASH, Lloyd, & Cavaliers

CAVALIERS
Singles: 7-inch
ASKEL (12 "Crazy Guitar") 10-20 60s
GUM (1002 "I Wanna Know") 15-25 62
GUM (1004 "The Right Time") 15-25 62

CAVALIERS
Singles: 7-inch
JOSIE (924 "Tears of Happiness") ... 8-12 64
Also see WILSON, J. Frank

CAVALIERS
Singles: 7-inch
RCA (9054 "Hold on to My Baby") 20-30 66
RCA (9321 "I Really Love You") 10-20 67

CAVALIERS
Singles: 7-inch
CUCA (1437 "Cavalier's Twist") 10-20 68

CAVALIERS
Singles: 7-inch
FLARE 10-20 60s
Member: Kink Middleliest.
Also see CROW

CAVALIERS
Singles: 7-inch
CAVALIER 3-5 76

CAVALIERS QUARTET
Singles: 78 rpm
ATLAS (1031 "You Thrill Me") 75-125 53
Singles: 7-inch
ATLAS (1031 "You Thrill Me") ... 300-500 53
Members: Lester Gardner; Ron Anderson; Cecil Holmes; Lowe Murray.
Also see CHANCES
Also see FI-TONES

CAVALLARO, Carmen P&R '45
Singles: 78 rpm
DECCA 3-6 45-57
Singles: 7-inch
DECCA 4-8 50-61
EPs: 7-inch
DECCA (Except 844) 5-10 50-59
DECCA (844 "The Eddy Duchin Story") 20-30 56
(Boxed three-EP set.)
LPs: 10/12-inch
DECCA (Except "The Eddy Duchin Story") 10-20 50-61
DECCA (DL-8289 "Eddy Duchin Story") 25-35 56
(Soundtrack. Monaural.)
DECCA (DL7-8289 "The Eddy Duchin Story") 25-30 59
(Soundtrack. Stereo.)
DECCA (8396 "The Eddy Duchin Story") 60-75 56
(Soundtrack. Also has music from three other shows.)
DECCA (DL-9121 "The Eddy Duchin Story") 10-15 65
(Soundtrack. Monaural.)
DECCA (DL7-9121 "The Eddy Duchin Story") 10-15 65
(Soundtrack. Stereo.)
VOCALION 10-15 59

CAVALLARO, Carmen, Featuring Al Cernick
Singles: 78 rpm
DECCA (24330 "Dream Girl") 15-25 48
DECCA (24410 "Evelyn") 15-25 48
DECCA (24488 "Ah, But It Happens") 15-25 48
Also see CAVALLARO, Carmen
Also see MITCHELL, Guy

CAVALLI, Pierre
Singles: 7-inch
JAMIE 5-10 59

CAVALLO, Jimmy: see CAVELLO, Jimmy

CAVALRY MEN
Singles: 7-inch
U.A. 4-8 61

CAVALRY TWILL
Singles: 7-inch
MGM 4-8 67

CAVANAUGH, Page
Singles: 78 rpm
HUB 25-35

CAVE DWELLERS
Singles: 7-inch
ABC-PAR 10-20 65
BAYTOWN 10-20 68

CAVE MEN
Singles: 7-inch
CHELLE (148 "It's Trash") 25-35 66

CAVELL, Marc
(With the Classmates)
Singles: 7-inch
CANDIX (322 "That's All I Want") 8-12 61
CANDIX (329 "I Didn't Lie") 20-30 61
WESBURN 5-10 60

CAVELLO, Jimmy, & His House Rockers
(With His Quintet; Jimmy Cavallo)
Singles: 78 rpm
BSD 50-100 52
CORAL 10-20 56-57
Singles: 7-inch
BSD (1005 "Leave Married Women Alone") 150-250 52
CORAL (61689 "Soda Shop Rock") 20-30 56
CORAL (61728 "Rock Rock Rock") 20-30 56
CORAL (61787 "Ooh-Wee") 20-30 57
CORAL (61868 "Yo Yo Baby") 20-30 57
CORAL (61919 "Dream Toy") 20-30 57
DARCY (5001 "Fanny Brown") 50-75 61
SUNNYSIDE (3105 "Don't Move Me No More") 10-20 59
Also see FREED, Alan

CAVEMEN
Singles: 7-inch
CAPITOL STAR ARTIST (18285 "All About Love") 15-25 66
(Identification number shown since no selection number is used.)
Members: Al Cretacci Jr.; Jim Crouse; Ron Gorski; Skip Maciezewski; Joey Calato.

CAVEMEN
Singles: 7-inch
20TH FOX (6643 "Small World") ... 10-20 66
Members: Bob Friedman; Vic Rose; Hector Sorano; Eddie Rayez; Willy Rayez.

CAVEMEN
LPs: 10/12-inch
MIDNIGHT 5-10

CAVER, Bobby
Singles: 7-inch
CORAL 4-8 62

CAVES, Johnny
Singles: 7-inch
NA-R-CO 4-8 64

CAVIN, Mel, & Kokonuts
Singles: 7-inch
BERTRAM INT'L (215 "I Love You") 20-25 60

CAY, Phil, & Blue Notes
Singles: 7-inch
HART (1001 "Meet Me in the Barnyard") 75-125 59

CAYENNE
LPs: 10/12-inch
BUCKSNORT 8-10 75

CAZZ P&R '78
(Robert Lewis)
Singles: 7-inch
NUMBER 3-4 78

CAZZ, Lue
Singles: 7-inch
ART TONE 4-8 62
CLOCK 5-10 60
VEE JAY 4-8 63

CECIL & EMMITT
(Cecil - Emmitt)
Singles: 7-inch
REVOLVO (27 "Don't Let My Dream Come True") 10-15 59
Members: Cecil Null; Emmitt Luttrell.
Also see NULL, Cecil

CECILIO & KAPONO
Singles: 7-inch
COLUMBIA 3-5 75-77
LPs: 10/12-inch
COLUMBIA 8-10 75-77

CEDAR CREEK C&W '81
Singles: 7-inch
MOON SHINE 3-4 81-83
Members: Dave Holcraft; Garland Craft; Chris Golden.
Also see GOLDENS

CEE, Billy
Singles: 7-inch
CHIMNEYVILLE 3-5 76

GSF 3-5 74
ONNED 4-8 62

CEE, David, & Prince Eddie
Singles: 7-inch
SKYTONE 4-8 63

CEE, Jimmy, & Earls
Singles: 7-inch
BO-P-C 3-5 78
BODY SHOP 3-5
Also see EARLS

CEE, Richie
Singles: 7-inch
CONCEPT 5-8

CEE JAYS
Singles: 7-inch
MOSAIC 5-10 63

CEE VEE
Singles: 7-inch
CARROLLTON 5-10 59

CEEDS
Singles: 7-inch
EMLAR (1001 "You Won't Do That") 10-20 66

CELEBRATION
Singles: 7-inch
CHALLENGE 4-8 67
U.A. 4-8 68

CELEBRATION
Singles: 7-inch
MOWEST 5-10 72
LPs: 10/12-inch
MOWEST 10-20 72

CELEBRATION P&R '78
(Featuring Mike Love)
Singles: 7-inch
MCA 3-4 78
PACIFIC ARTS 5-10 79
Promotional Singles
MCA (1982 "Almost Summer, KRTH 101 Version") 10-12 78
(Made for radio station KRTH.)
LPs: 10/12-inch
MCA (3037 "Almost Summer") 8-10 78
(Soundtrack.)
PACIFIC ARTS 8-12 79
Members: Mike Love; Charles Lloyd; Steve Leach; Ron Altbach; Linda Mallah; Suzanne Wallach; Irene Cathaway; Al Perkins; Tim Weston.
Also see LOVE, Mike

CELEBRATED RENAISSANCE BAND
Singles: 7-inch
LION (1001) 10-20 68
(Exact title not known.)
Picture Sleeves
LION (1001) 25-35 68

CELEBRITIES
Singles: 7-inch
MUSIC MAKERS 10-15 61
ROUND 15-20 59

CELEBRITIES
Singles: 7-inch
BOSS ("You Didn't Tell the Truth") 10-20 60s

CELEBRITYS
Singles: 78 rpm
CAROLINE 150-250 56
Singles: 7-inch
CAROLINE (2301 "Juanita") 500-750 56
Also see HAMMOND, Clay, with Johnnie Young & Celebritys

CELENTANO, Adriano
Singles: 7-inch
COLUMBIA 3-5 74
REPRISE (0266 "Sabato Triste") 4-6 64
Picture Sleeves
REPRISE (0266 "Sabato Triste") 5-8 64

CELESTE, C.R.
Singles: 7-inch
SAPIEN 4-8 61

CELESTIALS
Singles: 7-inch
SATIN (007 "Hoochie Koochie Koo") 8-12

CELESTINE
Singles: 7-inch
ADORE (900 "One More Chance") .25-35 64

CELESTRALS
Singles: 7-inch
DON-EL (125 "Alone") 20-30 63
DON-EL (126 "Checkerboard Lover") 40-50 63
RCA (9016 "Chain Reaction") 15-25 66

CELI BEE & BUZZY BUNCH
P&R/R&B/LP '77
Singles: 7-inch
APA 3-5 77-78
LPs: 10/12-inch
APA 5-10 77-79

CELIA & MUTATIONS
Singles: 7-inch
U.A. 3-5 77

CELIA MARIE
Singles: 7-inch
ERA 4-8 62

CELLAR CIRCLE
Singles: 7-inch
EDMARK 5-10 65

CELLAR DWELLERS
Singles: 7-inch
CENTURY (24501 "Child of the Devil") 10-20 60s
LANCE (111 "Love Is a Beautiful Thing") 15-20 67

CELLAR DWELLERS
Singles: 7-inch
GET HIP 3-5 90

CELLARFUL OF NOISE P&R '88
Singles: 7-inch
CBS 3-4 88

CELLOPHANE
Singles: 12-inch
SALSOUL 4-8 78

CELLOS P&R '57
Singles: 78 rpm
APOLLO (Except 510) 25-50 57
APOLLO (510 "Rang Tang Ding Dong") 50-75 57
(No subtitle used.)
APOLLO (510 "Rang Tang Ding Dong [I Am the Japanese Sandman]") 15-25 57
(With subtitle.)
Singles: 7-inch
APOLLO (510 "Rang Tang Ding Dong") 50-100 57
(No subtitle used.)
APOLLO (510 "Rang Tang Ding Dong [I Am the Japanese Sandman]") 15-25 57
(With subtitle.)
APOLLO (515 "Under Your Spell") .25-50 57
APOLLO (516 "The Be-Bop Mouse") 25-50 57
APOLLO (524 "I Beg for Your Love") 40-60 58
Members: Cliff Williams; Ken Levinson; Alvin Campbell; Bill Montgomery; Alton Thomas.

CELLS, Ronnie, & His Continentals
Singles: 7-inch
VALMON (67 "Chicken") 15-20

CELLUTRON & INVISIBLE
LPs: 10/12-inch
GREEN MOUNTAIN 5-10 78

CELTICS
Singles: 7-inch
AL-JACK'S (0002 "Can You Remember") 2000-3000 62
(Approximately 200 made.)
WAR CONN (2216 "Darline, Darling") 200-300 62

CELTICS
Singles: 7-inch
CORONADO (133 "Wondering Why") 20-30
LINJO (106 "And She'll Cry") 15-25 66

CELTICS
Singles: 7-inch
BRIDGES 3-5 73

CELTS, Bonnie, & Continentals
Singles: 7-inch
VALMON (067 "Chicken") 25-35 65

CENCI, Ettore
Singles: 7-inch
DIAMOND 4-8 67

CENICOLA, P.G.
Singles: 7-inch
PEPSI 3-5

CENTAURS
Singles: 7-inch
ROCKET (65219 "Weird Turtle") 10-20 65

CENTAURUS
LP: 10/12-inch
AZRA (002 "Centaurus") 15-20 78
(Numbered edition picture disc. 1000 made. Promotional issue only.)

CENTENNIALS
Singles: 7-inch
DOT 5-10 61

CENTER, Sandy, & Rainbow Rhythmaires
Singles: 7-inch
RUBY (260 "Come On Baby, It's Christmas") 15-25 57

CENTER STAGE
Singles: 7-inch
MARC 5-10
RCA (0480 "Someday Someway") . 10-15 71

CENTERFOLD R&B '88
Singles: 7-inch
COLUMBIA 3-4 88

CENTRAL CITY BAND
Singles: 7-inch
HOOK CITY 3-4 81

CENTRAL LINE P&R/R&B '81
Singles: 12-inch
MERCURY 4-6 84-85
Singles: 7-inch
MERCURY 3-4 81-85
LPs: 10/12-inch
MERCURY 5-10 82-85
Members: Linton Beckles; Lipson Francis; Henry Defoe; Camelle Hinds.

CENTRAL NERVOUS SYSTEM
Singles: 7-inch
LAURIE 4-8 68
LPs: 10/12-inch
MUSIC FACTORY 15-20 68
Members: Doug Billard; Bruce Cassidy; Keith Jollimore; Jack Lilly; Richard Oakley; Jim White.

CENTRAL PARK
Singles: 7-inch
AMY 3-5 68

CENTRAL PARK WEST
Singles: 7-inch
EVENT 3-6 68-69

CENTURIANS
Singles: 7-inch
TIGER (1001 "We Mean More to Each Other") 30-50 60

CENTURIANS (on Del-Fi): see JOHNSTON, Bruce

CENTURIES
Singles: 7-inch
DOOTO (469 "Geraldine") 15-25 62
LIFE (501 "In This Whole World") 50-75 61

CENTURIES
Singles: 7-inch
CARLTON (588 "Anniversary Hop") 5-10 63

CENTURIES
Singles: 7-inch
CLEOPATRA (2 "Outer Limits") 15-25 63
(Black vinyl.)
CLEOPATRA (2 "Outer Limits") 30-50 63
(Colored vinyl. Promotional issue only.)
CLEOPATRA (3 "Jack 23") 15-25 64
Member: Tom Falcone

CENTURIES
Singles: 7-inch
RICH (102 "I'd Cry for You") 20-30

CENTURIES
Singles: 7-inch
SPECTRA-SOUND 15-20
Also see BUCKINGHAMS

CENTURIES / Jaytone
Singles: 7-inch
TIMES SQUARE (5 "Crying for You") 15-25 63
(Colored vinyl.)
Also see CENTURIES / Revlons

CENTURIES / Revlons
Singles: 7-inch
TIMES SQUARE (15 "Betty") 15-25 63
Also see CENTURIES / Jaytones

CENTURY FIVE
Singles: 7-inch
BELMONT (4003 "La Moomba Kasa Boo Boo Cha Cha") 25-50 61

CENTURYS
Singles: 7-inch
FORTUNE (553 "Take My Hand") 15-20 59

CENTURYS
Singles: 7-inch
VELTONE (104 "Strollin' Time") 10-20 60

CENTURYS
Singles: 7-inch
MICRO (6344 "Her Love") 15-25 63
LP: 10/12-inch
MARKUS 10-15 72
Members: Phil Cornelisen; Jim Morrison; Paul Willems; Donne Cornell; David K. Pilz; Eddie Farah; Dave Parpovich; Mark Helniak; James Copeland Scovell.
Also see 2ND CENTURY

CENTURYS
Singles: 7-inch
MARK C (101 "Whole Lot of Shakin' Going On") 10-20 64
Members: Wink; Bill Bellamy Jr.; Jim "Tex" Taylor Jr.

CENTURYS
(With Carson Sisters)
Singles: 7-inch
BANGAR 10-15 64
STUDIO CITY 8-12 60s

CENTURYS
Singles: 7-inch
B-B (4002) 25-35 67
(Title not yet known.)
RENCO (115 "The 83") 20-30 65
RENCO (116 "Don't Bother") 20-30 65
SWAN (4265 "Hard Times") 15-25 66
EPs: 7-inch
BONA FIDE (7001 "The Centurys") 8-10 84
(Repackage of the four Renco tracks.)
Members: Bob Koch; Billy Beard; Bernie Orner; Larry McKinney; John Iacovone.

CEPHAS SYSTEM
Singles: 78 rpm
ABBOTT 4-8 54
Singles: 7-inch
ABBOTT 5-10 54

CEPTORS
Singles: 7-inch
PANORAMA (1001 "I Can't Make It") 20-30

CERF, Christopher
(Chris Cerf)
Singles: 7-inch
AMY (954 "Sweet Music") 20-40 66
AMY (977 "Watch Your Step") 15-25 66
CUB (9116 "Cheerleader") 15-25 62
MGM (13103 "Cheerleader") 10-15 62

CERRITO C&W '89
Singles: 7-inch
SOUNDWAVES 3-4 89

CERRONE P&R/R&B/LP '77
(Jean-Marc Cerrone)
Singles: 12-inch
PAVILLION 4-6 82
PERSONAL 4-6 84
Singles: 7-inch
ATLANTIC 3-4 79
COTILLION 3-5 77-78
PAVILLION 3-4 82
PERSONAL 3-4 84
LPs: 10/12-inch
ATLANTIC 5-10 79
COTILLION 5-10 77-79
PAVILLION 5-10 82

CERRONE & LA TOYA JACKSON R&B '86
Singles: 12-inch
PALASS 4-6 86
Also see CERRONE
Also see JACKSON, La Toya

CERTAIN AMOUNT
Singles: 7-inch
PRESS to HIT (620671 "Is This the Dream") 5-10

CERTAIN SCENE
Singles: 7-inch
ERA 4-8 68

CERVENKA, Exene, & Wanda Coleman
LPs: 10/12-inch
FREEWAY 5-8 85
Also see X

CESANA
LPs: 10/12-inch
MODERN 15-20 64

CESAR
LPs: 10/12-inch
FLYING DUTCHMAN 8-10 75

CETERA, Peter LP '82
Singles: 7-inch
FULL MOON 3-4 82-88
Picture Sleeves
FULL MOON 3-4 82-88
LPs: 10/12-inch
FULL MOON 5-10 81-88
W.B. 5-8 86
Also see CHER & Peter Cetera
Also see CHICAGO
Also see EXCEPTIONS
Also see FALTSKOG, Agnetha, & Peter Cetera

CETERA, Peter, & Amy Grant P&R '87
Singles: 7-inch
FULL MOON 3-4 86
Picture Sleeves
FULL MOON 3-4 86
Also see CETERA, Peter
Also see GRANT, Amy

CEYLEIB PEOPLE
Singles: 7-inch
VAULT (940 "Changes") 10-15 68
LPs: 10/12-inch
VAULT (117 "Tanyet") 60-100 68
Members: Larry Knechtel; Ry Cooder; Joe Osborn; Mike Deasy; Sean Deasy.
Also see BREAD
Also see COODER, Ry
Also see DILLARDS

CEZANNES Featuring Cerressa
Singles: 7-inch
MARKAY (108 "Pardon Me") ... 500-1000 63

CHABUKOS R&B '73
Singles: 7-inch
MAINSTREAM 3-5 73

CHACHERE, Louis
Singles: 7-inch
PAULA 3-5

CHACKSFIELD, Frank, Orchestra P&R '53
Singles: 78 rpm
LONDON 3-6 53-57
Singles: 7-inch
LONDON 4-8 53-61
EPs: 7-inch
LONDON 5-10 53-61
LPs: 10/12-inch
LONDON 5-15 53-61
RICHMOND 5-12 59-62

CHAD R&B '87
Singles: 7-inch
RCA 3-4 87-88

CHAD & JEREMY P&R/LP '64
Singles: 7-inch
COLLECTABLES 3-4 81
COLUMBIA (Except 43277) 4-8 65-68
COLUMBIA (43277 "Before & After") . 4-8 65
(Black vinyl.)
COLUMBIA (43277 "Before & After") 10-15 65
(Colored vinyl. Promotional issues only.)
ERIC 3-4 73
LANA 3-6 60s
ROCSHIRE 3-4 84
TEEN SCOOP ("Interview") 20-30 60s
(Square cardboard picture disc still bound in *Teen Scoop* magazine.)
TEEN SCOOP ("Interview") 15-20 60s
(Square cardboard picture disc by itself)
TRIP 3-5 70s
WORLD ARTISTS 5-10 64-65
Picture Sleeves
COLUMBIA 5-10 65-66
WORLD ARTISTS 8-12 64-65
LPs: 10/12-inch
CAPITOL (2000 series) 15-20 66
CAPITOL (12000 & 16000 series) 5-10 80
COLUMBIA 20-25 65-68
FIDU 10-12
HARMONY 12-15 69
MDA (6000 "Olde English Gold") ... 10-20
ROCSHIRE 5-10 84
SIDEWALK 12-20 69
TRADITION REST 10-12
WORLD ARTISTS (2002 "Yesterday's Gone") 20-40 64
(Monaural.)
WORLD ARTISTS (2005 "Chad & Jeremy Sing for You") 20-40 65
(Monaural.)
WORLD ARTISTS (3002 "Yesterday's Gone") 30-50 64
(Stereo.)
WORLD ARTISTS (3005 "Chad & Jeremy Sing for You") 30-50 65
(Stereo.)
Members: Chad Stuart; Jeremy Clyde.
Also see STUART, Chad

CHADONS
Singles: 7-inch
CHATTAHOOCHEE 5-10 64-65
Member: Chad Allen.
Also see ALLEN, Chad

CHADWICK, Bill
Singles: 7-inch
DOT 4-6 69

CHAFFIN, Dickie
Singles: 7-inch
KARL 5-10 59

CHAFFIN, Ernie
Singles: 78 rpm
FINE 20-30 56
SUN 25-50 57
Singles: 7-inch
FINE (1010 "Stop Look & Listen") .. 35-50 56
RKP 10-15
SUN (262 "Feelin' Low") 15-25 57
SUN (275 "I'm Lonesome") 15-25 57
SUN (307 "My Love for You") 10-20 58
SUN (320 "Don't Ever Leave Me") 10-20 59
VILLAGE 10-20

CHAFIN, Ray
Singles: 7-inch
CHANCELLOR 4-8 68
IMPERIAL 4-8 67
LHI 4-6 69
TOWER 4-8 66

CHAFNER, Linda
Singles: 7-inch
ROSE C 4-8 62

CHAIN
Singles: 7-inch
AVALANCHE 3-5 71

CHAIN, Michael A.
Singles: 7-inch
20TH FOX 3-5 73

CHAIN REACTION
Singles: 7-inch
DATE (1538 "When I Needed You") 15-25 66
Member: Steve Tallarico (a.k.a. Steve Tyler).
Also see AEROSMITH

CHAIN REACTION R&B '77
Singles: 7-inch
ARIOLA AMERICA 3-5 76
DELICKS 5-10 69
DIAL 5-10 68
GRT 4-6 70
OSHOWLEO (1 "Lady in Red") 10-15
VERVE 10-20 68
Member: Norris Harris.
Also see CHOCOLATE SYRUP
Also see MOMENT of TRUTH

CHAIN REACTION
Singles: 7-inch
EARL (1003 "Chain Reaction") 35-45

CHAINO
Singles: 7-inch
ORB 8-12
TAMPA (142 "The Slide") 15-25 58
TAMPA (144 "Ubangi Rock") 15-25 58

CHAINS
Singles: 7-inch
PEACOCK 4-8 63

CHAINS
Singles: 7-inch
HBR (460 "Carol's Got a Cobra") ... 15-20 66
PINPOINT (6902 "You're in Love") 20-30 67
PINPOINT (6903 "It's a Shame") ... 20-30 68

CHAIR
Singles: 7-inch
W.B. 3-5 70

CHAIRMEN OF BOARD *P&R/R&B/LP '70*
(Chairmen; Chairman of the Board)
Singles: 7-inch
INVICTUS.... 3-6 70-76
SURFSIDE.... 4-8 82
Picture Sleeves
INVICTUS.... 3-5 70-72
LPs: 10/12-inch
INVICTUS.... 12-20 70-74
Members: General Norman Johnson; Eddie Curtis; Harrison Kennedy; Danny Woods.
Also see JOHNSON, General

CHAISSON, Billy Don
Singles: 7-inch
TAB (1011 "Soul Walk").... 15-25 66

CHAKA
Singles: 7-inch
COLUMBIA.... 4-6 69

CHAKA KHAN: see KHAN, Chaka

CHAKACHAS *P&R/R&B/LP '72*
Singles: 7-inch
AVCO EMBASSY.... 3-5 72
JANUS.... 3-5 74
POLYDOR.... 3-5 71-75
LPs: 10/12-inch
AVCO EMBASSY.... 8-10 72
POLYDOR.... 8-12 72

CHAKIRIS, George *LP '62*
Singles: 7-inch
CAPITOL.... 3-6 62-65
HORIZON.... 4-6 62
Picture Sleeves
CAPITOL.... 5-10 63
LPs: 10/12-inch
CAPITOL.... 10-20 62-65
HORIZON.... 15-20 62

CHAKRA
Singles: 7-inch
MEDIARTS.... 3-6 70

CHAKRAS
Singles: 7-inch
REPRISE.... 8-12 69

CHALAWA
Singles: 12-inch
GENERATION.... 4-8 79

CHALETS
Singles: 7-inch
COLLECTABLES.... 3-4 81
DART.... 10-15 61
MUSIC NOTE.... 10-15 61
TRU-LITE.... 10-20 61
TRU-LITE (1001 "Who's Laughing").... 25-35 61

CHALFONTES
Singles: 7-inch
MERCURY.... 4-8 65

CHALICE
LPs: 10/12-inch
SUNSPLASH.... 5-10 83

CHALKIT MILK REVUE
Singles: 7-inch
MR. G.... 4-8 68

CHALLENGERS
Singles: 7-inch
DEBONAIR (105 "Troubles at an End").... 100-200 50s

CHALLENGERS
Singles: 7-inch
TRIODEX.... 10-20 60-61

CHALLENGERS
Singles: 7-inch
TRI-PHI (1012 "Stay with Me").... 15-25 62
Also see CHALLENGERS III

CHALLENGERS
Singles: 7-inch
EXPLOSIVE (3621 "Why").... 100-150 63
(First issued as by the Executives.)
Also see EXECUTIVES

CHALLENGERS
Singles: 7-inch
CHALLENGE.... 8-10 62
GNP.... 4-8 65-68
PRINCESS.... 10-20 65
TRIUMPH.... 10-20
VAULT.... 8-15 63-65
LPs: 10/12-inch
FANTASY.... 8-12 73
GNP (600 series).... 10-20 67
GNP (2010 thru 2045).... 10-20 65-68
GNP (2056 thru 2093).... 8-12 70-77
RHINO.... 5-10 82
TRIUMPH (100 "The Challengers Go Sidewalk Surfing").... 25-30 65
VAULT (100 "Surfbeat").... 30-45 63
(Black vinyl.)
VAULT (100 "Surfbeat").... 50-75 63
(Colored vinyl.)
VAULT (101 Lloyd Thaxton Goes Surfin' with the Challengers).... 40-50 63
(Black vinyl.)
VAULT (101 Lloyd Thaxton Goes Surfin' with the Challengers).... 60-80 63
(Colored vinyl.)
VAULT (101 Surfing with the Challengers).... 30-40 63
(Black vinyl.)
VAULT (101 Surfing with the Challengers).... 50-75 63
(Colored vinyl.)
VAULT (102 "The Challengers on the Move Surfing Around the World").... 25-45 63
VAULT (107 "K-39").... 25-45 64
VAULT (109 "Surf's Up-the Challengers on TV").... 25-45 65
VAULT (110 "Challengers a Go Go").... 25-40 66
VAULT (111 "Greatest Hits").... 25-40 67
Members: Richard Delvy; Jim Roberts; Glen Grey; Randy Nauert; Nick Hefner; Ed Fornier; Art Fisher; Phil Pruden; Phil Miles.
Also see BELAIRS
Also see DELVY, Richard
Also see EDDIE & SHOWMEN
Also see JOURNEYMEN
Also see SURFARIS / Challengers
Also see SURFRIDERS
Also see THAXTON, Lloyd

CHALLENGERS & BILLY STRANGE
LPs: 10/12-inch
GNP.... 15-20 66
Also see CHALLENGERS
Also see STRANGE, Billy

CHALLENGERS
Singles: 7-inch
CHESS.... 4-8 66

CHALLENGERS
Singles: 7-inch
KIX INT'L (2263 "Moon, Send My Baby").... 25-35 66

CHALLENGERS
(Challengers of Who)
Singles: 7-inch
AGE OF AQUARIUS (1500 "Hear My Message").... 10-15 70
NIGHT OWL (1457 "Leave Me Be").... 15-25 69
NIGHT OWL (6794 "Challengers Take a Ride on the Jefferson Airplane").... 15-25 67
Members: John McCurdy; Mike Hoolihan; Keith Pentler; Pat Clark; John Beaster; David Wayne; Chris Connors.

CHALLENGERS III
(Featuring Ann Bogan; Challengers)
Singles: 7-inch
TRI-PHI (1012 "Stay").... 25-35 62
TRI-PHI (1020 "Every Day").... 25-35 62
Also see CHALLENGERS

CHALMERS, Charles
Singles: 7-inch
CHESS.... 4-8 67-68
LPs: 10/12-inch
CHESS.... 12-20 67

CHALONS
Singles: 7-inch
DICE (89 "Oh You").... 250-350 58
(Pictures a hand throwing dice, with "Dice Records, New York, N.Y." below.)

CHAMAELEON CHURCH
Singles: 7-inch
MGM.... 5-10 68
LPs: 10/12-inch
MGM (4574 "Chamaeleon Church").... 15-20 68
Members: Chevy Chase; Ted Myers; Tony Scheuren; Kyle Garrahan.
Also see CHASE, Chevy
Also see ULTIMATE SPINACH

CHAMBER OF COMMERCE
Singles: 7-inch
DCA.... 3-5

CHAMBERLAIN, Cathy
Singles: 7-inch
KAMA SUTRA.... 3-5 72
LPs: 10/12-inch
BUDDAH.... 8-10 77
KAMA SUTRA.... 10-15 72
W.B.... 5-10 77

CHAMBERLAIN, David *C&W '88*
Singles: 7-inch
COUNTRY INT'L.... 3-4 88

CHAMBERLAIN, Richard *P&R '62*
Singles: 7-inch
MCA.... 3-4 77
MGM.... 4-6 62-65
Picture Sleeves
MGM.... 5-10 62-65
LPs: 10/12-inch
MGM.... 15-20 63-65
METRO.... 8-12 66

CHAMBERLAIN, Wilt "The Stilt"
Singles: 7-inch
END.... 10-15 60

CHAMBERLIN BROTHERS
Singles: 7-inch
COLUMBIA (41227 "Debbie Jean").... 10-15 58
PORTER.... 3-5

CHAMBERS, Billy
Singles: 7-inch
DJ.... 4-8 62

CHAMBERS, Buddy
Singles: 7-inch
EMPALA.... 4-8 65

CHAMBERS, Carl *C&W '81*
Singles: 7-inch
PRAIRIE DUST.... 3-5 81

CHAMBERS, Cliff
Singles: 7-inch
GARDENA (104 "Time Has Made Her Change").... 10-20 60
KENT (4523 "Just for You").... 4-8 69
TOWER.... 5-10 68
Also see VERNON & CLIFF

CHAMBERS, Don
Singles: 7-inch
SWASTIKA (1000 "I Overlooked an Orchid").... 15-25 59

CHAMBERS, George
Singles: 7-inch
HBR.... 4-8 66

CHAMBERS, Homer
Singles: 7-inch
GOLDEN.... 3-5

CHAMBERS, Marilyn
Singles: 7-inch
ROULETTE.... 3-5 77

CHAMBERS, Tony
Singles: 7-inch
MOPRES.... 4-8

CHAMBERS BROTHERS *P&R/LP '68*
(Chambers Brothers Quartet)
Singles: 7-inch
AVCO.... 3-6 74-75
COLUMBIA.... 6-15 66-73
PROVERB (1021 "I Trust in God") 10-20 60s
ROXBURY.... 3-6 76
S B W (101 "I Trust in God").... 20-30 60s
(First issue.)
TEAR DROP.... 3-6 74
VAULT.... 8-15 65-69
Picture Sleeves
COLUMBIA.... 6-12 68-69
LPs: 10/12-inch
AVCO.... 8-12 74-75
CHELSEA.... 8-10 77
COLUMBIA (20 "Love, Peace and Happiness").... 20-30 69
(Two LPs, the second being *The Chambers Brothers Live at Bill Graham's Fillmore East.*)
COLUMBIA (2000 & 9000 series).. 15-20 67-68
COLUMBIA (30000 series, except 31158).... 10-20 71-75
COLUMBIA (31158 "Oh My God").... 40-60 72
FANTASY.... 10-15 74
RIVERSIDE.... 10-15 68
ROXBURY.... 8-10 76
VAULT (100 series).... 15-20 67-70
VAULT (9003 "People Get Ready").... 20-30 65
Members: Joe Chambers; Willie Chambers; Lester Chambers; George Chambers; Brian Keenan.
Also see AXTON, Hoyt, & Chambers Brothers
Also see DANE, Barbara, & Chambers Brothers
Also see PEANUT BUTTER CONSPIRACY / Ashes / Chambers Brothers
Also see WINTER, Johnny / Argent / Chambers Brothers / John Hammond

CHAMBLEE, Eddie *R&B '49*
(With His Orchestra)
Singles: 78 rpm
CORAL.... 10-20 52
FEDERAL.... 15-25 52
MERCURY.... 15-25 57
UNITED.... 15-25 54
MIRACLE.... 10-20 47-51
UNITED.... 10-15 53
Singles: 7-inch
CORAL (65080 "Southern Comfort").... 20-40 52
FEDERAL.... 20-40 52
MERCURY.... 10-20 57
UNITED (160 "Walkin' Home").... 15-25 54
UNITED (181 "Come on In").... 15-25 54
LPs: 10/12-inch
EMARCY (36124 "Chamblee Music").... 30-60 58
EMARCY (36131 "Doodin' ").... 30-60 58
(Monaural.)
EMARCY (80007 "Doodin' ").... 50-100 59
(Stereo.)
MERCURY (60127 "Chamblee Music").... 30-40 59
PRESTIGE (7321 "Eddie Chamblee").... 25-35 64
(Yellow label.)
PRESTIGE (7321 "Eddie Chamblee").... 20-30 64
(Blue label.)
Also see WASHINGTON, Dinah

CHAMELEON
Singles: 7-inch
ELEKTRA.... 3-5 79
LPs: 10/12-inch
ELEKTRA.... 5-10 79
PLATINUM (744 "Chameleon").... 5-10 82
(Includes poster/lyrics insert.)
PLATINUM (927 "Techno-Color").... 5-10 82
(Includes poster/lyrics insert.)
U.S.A. PLATINUM.... 5-10 82
Members: Yanni; Charlie Adams; Dugan McNeill; Mark Anthony; Johnny Donaldson.
Also see YANNI

CHAMELEONS U.K.
LPs: 10/12-inch
MCA.... 5-10 84

CHAMP, Billy
Singles: 7-inch
ABC-PAR (10518 "Believe Me").... 20-25 64

CHAMP BUTLER: see BUTLER, Champ

CHAMPAGNE *P&R '77*
Singles: 7-inch
ARIOLA AMERICA.... 3-5 77-78
Picture Sleeves
ARIOLA AMERICA.... 3-5 77

CHAMPAGNE BROTHERS
Singles: 7-inch
TYPHOON (2002 "Chickawawa").... 8-12

CHAMPAGNES
Singles: 7-inch
LAURIE.... 5-10 63
SKYMAC.... 5-10 63

CHAMPAIGN *P&R/R&B/LP '81*
Singles: 12-inch
COLUMBIA.... 4-6 83
Singles: 7-inch
COLUMBIA.... 3-4 81-85
LPs: 10/12-inch
COLUMBIA.... 5-10 81-85
Members: Rena Jones; Pauli Carman; Michael Day; Dana Walden; Michael Reed; Howard Reeder; Rocky Maffit.

CHAMPELLS
Singles: 7-inch
PACIFIC.... 5-10

CHAMPION
Singles: 7-inch
EPIC.... 3-4 78
LPs: 10/12-inch
EPIC.... 5-10 78

CHAMPION, Hollis
Singles: 7-inch
STRIP (501 "Long Gone Lonesome Blues").... 100-150 64

CHAMPION, Micky
(Mickie Champion)
Singles: 7-inch
LILLY (505 "Bam-a-Lam").... 10-20 62
LILLY (509 "Wait for Me").... 10-20 62
MUSETTE (9115 "What Good Am I").... 20-40 60s
Also see MILTON, Roy, & Mickey Champion

CHAMPIONS
Singles: 78 rpm
CHART.... 15-25 55-56
SCOTT.... 25-45 55
Singles: 7-inch
ACE (541 "I'm So Blue").... 25-35 58
CHART (602 "Annie Met Henry").... 30-50 55
CHART (611 "It's Love It's Love").... 30-50 56
CHART (620 "Same Old Story").... 30-50 56
CHART (631 "Come On").... 30-50 56
SCOTT ("Annie Met Henry").... 50-100 55
(Selection number not known.)

CHAMPIONS
Singles: 7-inch
TOWER.... 4-8 64

CHAMPLAINS
Singles: 7-inch
U.A. (346 "Ding Dong").... 40-50 61
Also see FIVE SATINS

CHAMPLIN, Bill *P&R '81*
Singles: 7-inch
ELEKTRA.... 3-4 81-82
EPIC.... 3-5 78
LPs: 10/12-inch
ELEKTRA.... 5-10 82
EPIC.... 5-10 78
Also see CHICAGO
Also see LABELLE, Patti, & Bill Champlin
Also see SONS of CHAMPLIN

CHAMPS
Singles: 7-inch
CHATAM (350 "Teenage Sweetheart").... 150-250 50s
(Previously issued as by the Mystics.)
Also see MYSTICS

CHAMPS *P&R/R&B '58*
Singles: 78 rpm
CHALLENGE (1016 "Tequila").... 35-55 58
Singles: 7-inch
CHALLENGE.... 10-20 58-65
ERIC.... 3-4 78
HI OLDIES.... 3-5 77
LANA.... 3-6 64
REPUBLIC (246 "Tequila '76").... 3-5 76
Picture Sleeves
CHALLENGE (59143 "I've Just Seen Her").... 20-30 61
REPUBLIC (246 "Tequila '76").... 4-6 76
EPs: 7-inch
CHALLENGE (7100 "Tequila").... 40-60 58
CHALLENGE (7101 "Caramba").... 40-60 58
LPs: 10/12-inch
CHALLENGE (601 "Go Champs Go!").... 50-100 58
(Black vinyl.)
CHALLENGE (601 "Go Champs Go!").... 250-350 58
(Colored vinyl.)
CHALLENGE (605 "Everybody's Rockin' with the Champs").... 50-75 58
CHALLENGE (613 "Go Champs Go!").... 40-60 62
CHALLENGE (614 "The Champs Play *All American*").... 40-60 62
(Monaural.)
CHALLENGE (2514 "The Champs Play *All American*").... 50-75 62
(Stereo.)
DESIGN SPOTLIGHT SERIES.... 10-20 60s
INTERNATIONAL AWARD.... 10-20 60s
POINT.... 10-20 60s
SPECTRUM.... 10-20 60s
Members: Dave Burgess; Danny "Chuck Rio" Flores; Gene Alden; Dale Norris; Joe Burness; Van Norman; Jim Seals; Dash Crofts; Dean Beard; Bob Morris; Glen Campbell; Jerry Cole; Keith MacKendrick; Chuch Downs; Rich Grissom; Keith MacKendrick; Mo Marshall; Dean McDaniel; Johnny Meeks; Gary Nieland; Curtis Paul; Jerry Puckett; Leon Sanders; Dave Smith; John Trombatore.
Also see APOLLOS
Also see BEARD, Dean
Also see BURGESS, Dave
Also see CAMPBELL, Glen
Also see COLE, Jerry
Also see DEMONS
Also see MORRIS, Bob
Also see PUCKETT, Jerry
Also see RIO, Chuck
Also see ROXSTERS
Also see SEALS & CROFTS
Also see SHADOWS FIVE
Also see THINGS to COME
Also see VINCENT, Gene

CHAMPS / Cyclones
LPs: 10/12-inch
DESIGN SPOTLIGHT SERIES.... 10-20 60s
Also see CHAMPS

CHAMPS' BOYS ORCHESTRA *P&R/R&B '76*
Singles: 7-inch
JANUS.... 3-5 76

CHAN, Joie
Singles: 7-inch
CHATTAHOOCHEE.... 4-8 64

CHANACLAIRS
Singles: 78 rpm
COLEMAN (1056 "Yuletide Love").... 30-50 49

CHANCE *C&W '85*
Singles: 7-inch
MERCURY.... 3-4 85-86
Member: Jeff Chance
Also see CHANCE, Jeff

CHANCE, Bob
Singles: 7-inch
ALWIN.... 4-8 66
OUTSTANDING.... 3-5 74
LPs: 10/12-inch
MORRHYTHM.... 5-10 80

CHANCE, Jeff *C&W '88*
Singles: 7-inch
CURB.... 3-4 88
Also see CHANCE

CHANCE, Larry
(With the Earls Today)
Singles: 7-inch
BARRY (110 "Let Them Talk").... 30-40 64
CHANCE.... 10-15 83
Also see BARONS
Also see EARLS

CHANCE, Nolan
(Charles Davis)
Singles: 7-inch
BUNKY (161 "Just Like the Weather").... 150-250 65
CONSTELLATION (144 "She's Gone").... 10-20 65
CONSTELLATION (161 "Just Like the Weather").... 50-100 65
THOMAS (802 "I'll Never Forget You").... 10-20 60s
Also see ARTISTICS
Also see DUKAYS

CHANCE, Tony
Singles: 7-inch
SWEETHEART (301 "Only Time Will Tell").... 100-150 50s

CHANCE, Wayne
Singles: 7-inch
WHIRLYBIRD.... 10-15 64

CHANCELLORS
Singles: 78 rpm
UNIQUE.... 15-25 56
XYZ.... 25-50 57
Singles: 7-inch
PORT (5000 "Tell Me You Love Me").... 30-45 58
(Also issued as by the Five Chancellors.)
STORM (503 "My Thoughts of You").... 50-75 59
UNIQUE (341 "Too Many Memories").... 10-20 56
XYZ (104 "I'm Coming Home").... 15-25 57
XYZ (105 "Seaport at Sunrise").... 10-15 58
XYZ (601 "I'm Coming Home").... 10-15 59

CHANCELLORS
Singles: 7-inch
BRENT (7031 "Straightaway").... 10-20 62
CAP CITY (107 "All the Way from Heaven").... 10-20 69
CAP CITY (112 "Girls Do Wonderful Things for Boys").... 10-20 69
CORBY (200 "Jam").... 10-20 62
EL CID.... 5-10 60s
U.S.A.... 8-12 65

CHANCELLORS
Singles: 7-inch
APEX.... 10-20 60s
SOMA (1421 "Little Latin Lupe Lu").... 10-15 65

Picture Sleeves
SOMA (1421 "Little Latin Lupe Lu")...100-125 65

CHANCELLORS
Singles: 7-inch
FENTON (2066 "Once in a Million")...25-40 66
FENTON (2072 "Dear John")...25-40 66

CHANCELLORS LTD.
Singles: 7-inch
DENE (101 "You Be the Judge")...20-30

CHANCERS
Singles: 7-inch
DOT (15870 "Shirley Ann")...30-40 58

CHANCES
Singles: 7-inch
BEA & BABY (130 "One More Chance")...15-25 61
(Monaural, though label reads: "Stereo Hi-Fi.")
Members: Darla; Moria; Sharonne.

CHANCES
(With Cecil Holmes Jr. & Orchestra)
Singles: 7-inch
ROULETTE (4549 "Through a Long and Sleepless Night")...50-75 64
Members: Milton Love; Bob Baylor; Reggie Barnes; Fred Barksdale; Cecil Holmes; Monte Owens.
Also see CAVERLIERS QUARTET

CHANCES
Singles: 7-inch
DOT (16634 "Blackgrass")...10-15 64

CHANCES R
Singles: 7-inch
QUILL (105 "I'll Have You Cryin' ") 10-20 65

CHANCETEERS
Singles: 78 rpm
CHANCE (1107 "The Flame")...10-20 52
Singles: 7-inch
CHANCE (1107 "The Flame")...20-30 52
Also see PORTER, Johnny

CHANDELIERS
(Chandeliers Quintet)
Singles: 7-inch
ANGLE TONE (521 "Blueberry Sweet")...200-250 58
(Credits "Chandeliers Quintet." Black vinyl.)
ANGLE TONE (521 "Blueberry Sweet")...100-200 58
(Credits "Chandeliers." Black vinyl.)
ANGLE TONE (521 "Blueberry Sweet")...250-350 58
(Colored vinyl.)
ANGLE TONE (529 "Dolly")...100-150 58
Also see CARPETS

CHANDELIERS
Singles: 7-inch
SUE...5-10 62

CHANDELIERS
Singles: 7-inch
LOADSTONE...4-8 64-65

CHANDELLES
Singles: 7-inch
DOT (16553 "El Gato")...10-20 63

CHAN-DELLS
Singles: 7-inch
ARC (8101 "Sand Surfer")...15-25 63

CHANDLER, Barbara
Singles: 7-inch
ABC-PAR...5-10 62-63
KAPP...4-8 63-64
MUSICOR...3-6 68

CHANDLER, Bobbie
Singles: 7-inch
ATLAS (1090 "Just You & Me")...10-20 58

CHANDLER, Bobby
(With His Stardusters)
Singles: 7-inch
HI...8-12 59
OJ (1005 "Shadows of Love")...25-35 57

CHANDLER, Chuckie
Singles: 7-inch
DEL-FI...5-10 61

CHANDLER, Deniece
Singles: 7-inch
TODDLIN TOWN...8-10 60s

CHANDLER, Deniece, & Lee Sain
Singles: 7-inch
TODDLIN TOWN...8-10 60s

CHANDLER, Denise
Singles: 7-inch
LOCK...5-8

CHANDLER, Dub
Singles: 7-inch
SUNDOWN...5-10 59

CHANDLER, Gary
LPs: 10/12-inch
EASTBOUND...8-10 73

CHANDLER, Gene P&R/R&B/LP '62
(Eugene Dixon)
Singles: 12-inch
20TH FOX...4-8 79
Singles: 7-inch
BRUNSWICK...4-8 67-68
CHECKER...5-10 66-69
CHI-SOUND...3-5 79-82
COLLECTABLES...3-4 81
CONSTELLATION...6-12 63-66
CURTOM...3-6 72-73
ERIC...3-4 73
FASTFIRE...3-4 86
MCA...3-4 84
MARSEL...3-5 76
MERCURY...4-6 70
SOLID SMOKE...3-4 84
20TH FOX...3-4 78-79
VEE JAY (Black label)...5-10 61-63
VEE JAY (White labes)...10-20 61
(Promotional issues only.)
U.A....3-5 78
LPs: 10/12-inch
BRUNSWICK...12-15 67-69
CHECKER...15-20 67
CHI-SOUND/20TH-FOX...5-10 78-79
CONSTELLATION...15-25 64-66
KENT...5-10 86
MERCURY...10-15 70
SOLID SMOKE...5-10 84
20TH FOX...5-10 78-81
UPFRONT...8-10
VEE JAY (1040 "The Duke of Earl")...50-100 62
(Monaural.)
VEE JAY (1040 "The Duke of Earl")...100-150 62
(Stereo.)
At least six early Vee Jay tracks, including *Duke of Earl*, are actually by the Dukays, not just Gene Chandler.
Also see CARTER, Calvin
Also see DUKAYS
Also see DUKE of EARL

CHANDLER, Gene, & Barbara Acklin P&R/R&B '68
Singles: 7-inch
BRUNSWICK...4-8 68-69
Also see ACKLIN, Barbara

CHANDLER, Gene, & Jerry Butler P&R/R&B/LP '71
(Gene & Jerry)
Singles: 7-inch
MERCURY...3-6 70
Also see BUTLER, Jerry

CHANDLER, Gene, & Jamie Lynn R&B '83
Singles: 7-inch
SALSOUL...3-4 83
Also see CHANDLER, Gene

CHANDLER, Guy
Singles: 7-inch
PIED PIPER...3-5 74

CHANDLER, Howard
Singles: 78 rpm
WAMPUS (100 "Wampus Cat")...20-30 56
Singles: 7-inch
WAMPUS (100 "Wampus Cat") 100-200 56

CHANDLER, Jeff P&R '54
Singles: 78 rpm
DECCA...4-8 54
Singles: 7-inch
DECCA...8-10 54
LIBERTY (3067 "Sings to You")...15-25 57
LIBERTY (3074 "Warm & Easy")...15-25 57

CHANDLER, Karen P&R '52
(With the Jacks; Eve Young)
Singles: 78 rpm
CORAL...4-8 52-55
DECCA...4-8 56
Singles: 7-inch
CARLTON...5-10 60
CORAL...5-10 52-58
DECCA...8-15 56
DOT...3-5 67-68
MOHAWK...4-8 62
STRAND...5-10 61
SUNBEAM...5-10 59
TIVOLI...4-6 65
EPs: 7-inch
CORAL...8-15 52
LPs: 10/12-inch
STRAND...10-20 61
Also see FONTAINE, Eddie, & Karen Chandler

CHANDLER, Karen, & Jimmy Wakely
Singles: 78 rpm
DECCA...4-8 56
Singles: 7-inch
DECCA...5-10 56
Also see CHANDLER, Karen
Also see WAKELY, Jimmy

CHANDLER, Kenny P&R '63
(Kenny Bolognese)
Singles: 7-inch
AMY (890 "Happy to Be Unhappy") .5-10 63
COLLECTABLES...3-4 81
CORAL (62309 "It Might Have Been")...5-10 62
EPIC...4-8 65-66
LAURIE (3140 "Leave Me if You Want To")...8-10 62
LAURIE (3158 "Heart")...8-10 63
LAURIE (3181 "I Tell Myself")...8-10 63
TOWER...5-10 67-68
U.A. (342 "Drums")...10-12 61
U.A. (384 "What Kind of Love Is Yours")...8-10 61
Also see BEAU, Kenny
Also see KENNY, FRANK & RAY
Also see TREE SWINGERS

CHANDLER, Lee, & Blue Rhythms
Singles: 7-inch
BAND BOX (224 "Consideration")..15-25 58

CHANDLER, Len
Singles: 7-inch
COLUMBIA...4-8 67
LPs: 10/12-inch
COLUMBIA...10-20 67

CHANDLER, Lorraine
Singles: 7-inch
GIANT (703 "What Can I Do")...25-50 66
RCA (8810 "What Can I Do")...15-25 66
RCA (8980 "I Can't Hold On")...15-25 66
RCA (9349 "I Can't Change")...35-45 67

CHANDLER, Paul
Singles: 7-inch
GARDENA...5-10 61
RENDEZVOUS...4-8 62

CHANDLER, Ronnie
Singles: 7-inch
VEEDA...10-15 59

CHANDLER, Shirley
Singles: 7-inch
U PLAY...4-8 62

CHANDLERS
Singles: 7-inch
BLEU ROSE (100 "Your Love Keeps Drawing Me Closer")...15-25 68

CHANEL, Jean
Singles: 7-inch
CREST...5-10 62

CHANELS
Singles: 78 rpm
DEB (500 "The Reason")...20-40 58
Singles: 7-inch
DEB (500 "The Reason")...35-50 58
(Reissued as by the 5 Chanels.)
Also see 5 CHANELS
Also see VIRGIL & 4 Chanels

CHANEY, Al
Singles: 7-inch
SOUND STAGE 7...4-8 64

CHANEY, Hank C&W '86
Singles: 7-inch
CMI...3-4 86

CHANEY, Lon
Singles: 7-inch
TOWER...4-8 64

CHANEY, Ray
Singles: 7-inch
SHAH...4-8 64

CHANFER, Linda
Singles: 7-inch
ROSE (3342 "My Own Angel Love")...10-15

CHANGE
Singles: 7-inch
KAPP...3-5 72

CHANGE P&R/R&B/LP '80
Singles: 12-inch
ATLANTIC...4-6 84
RFC...4-6 83
Singles: 7-inch
ATLANTIC...3-4 81-85
RFC...3-4 80
W.B....3-4 80
LPs: 10/12-inch
ATLANTIC...5-10 81-85
RFC...5-10 80
W.B....5-10 80
Members: Paolo Granolio; David Romani; James Robinson; Deborah Cooper.
Also see VANDROSS, Luther

CHANGE OF PACE
Singles: 7-inch
STONE LADY (006 Bring My Buddies Back")...10-15 60s
TABOO (100 "You Can Depend on Me")...8-12 60s

CHANGES
Singles: 7-inch
MARTI...3-6

CHANGIN' TIMES P&R '65
Singles: 7-inch
PHILIPS...10-20 65-66

CHANGIN' TIMES
Singles: 7-inch
BELL...10-20 67

CHANGING COLORS
Singles: 7-inch
TOWER...4-8 68-69
Member: Jerry Vance.

CHANGING SCENE
Singles: 7-inch
FONTANA...5-10 69

CHANGING TIMES
Singles: 7-inch
MARK VII (1013 "I'm Alone")...20-30 67
Members: Dale Hastings; Rick Laymon; Sandy Charles; Rick Davidson; Garry Ford; Joe Reynolds.

CHANGING TIMES
Singles: 7-inch
VIBRA ("Free As the Wind")...30-40 60s
(Selection number not known.)

CHANGING TYDES REVUE
Singles: 7-inch
NIGHT OWL (6837 "Love Is a Beautiful Thing")...8-12 68

CHANGING TYMES
Singles: 7-inch
R.D. (1 "You Make It Hard")...15-25 66

CHANGING TYMES
Singles: 7-inch
HARD TYMES (5811 "You Had It Made")...10-15 60s

CHANGO
LPs: 10/12-inch
ABC...8-10 75
MERCURY...5-10 76

CHANIER, Cliston
("King of the South"; Clifton Chenier)
Singles: 78 rpm
ELKO (920 "Louisiana Stomp")...50-75 54
IMPERIAL (5352 "Louisiana Stomp")...20-30 54
Singles: 7-inch
ELKO (920 "Louisiana Stomp")..100-200 54
IMPERIAL (5352 "Louisiana Stomp")...50-75 54
Also see CHENIER, Clifton

CHANNEL
LPs: 10/12-inch
EPIC...5-10 84

CHANNEL 3
Singles: 7-inch
DAKAR (4520 "The Sweetest Thing")...10-15

CHANNEL, Bruce P&R/R&B/LP '62
(With the Straitjackets)
Singles: 7-inch
BROWNFIELD (29 "Don't Let Go") 8-12 65
CHARAY...4-6 68
COLLECTABLES...3-4 81
ELEKTRA...3-5 80
KING...10-20 59-60
JADE...5-10 60s
LE CAM (122 "Going Back to Louisiana")...4-8
LE CAM (125 "Blue Monday")...8-12 64
LE CAM (953 "Hey Baby")...15-25 61
LE CAM (963 "Number One Man") 10-20 62
LE CAM (1100 series)...3-5 77
LE CAM (7277 "The King Is Free")...5-8 77
MALA...5-10 67-68
MANCO (1035 "Run Romance, Run")...10-20 62
MEL-O-DY (112 "Satisfied Mind")..10-15 64
MEL-O-DY (114 "You Never Looked Better")...10-15 64
NAP...3-5
SHAH (304 "Court of Love")...8-12 64
SMASH...5-10 62-63
SOFT...5-10 60s
TEEN AGER (601 "Run Romance, Run")...20-30 59
SHALIMAR...5-10
ZUMA...3-5 77
Picture Sleeves
SMASH...10-15 62-63
LPs: 10/12-inch
SMASH (27008 "Hey! Baby")...30-50 62
(Monaural.)
SMASH (67008 "Hey! Baby")...25-40 62
(Stereo.)
Session: Delbert McClinton.
Also see McCLINTON, Delbert
Also see STRAITJACKETS

CHANNEL, Bruce / Paul & Paula
Singles: 7-inch
ERA...3-4
Also see CHANNEL, Bruce
Also see LUKE, Jimmy, & Bruce Channel
Also see PAUL & PAULA

CHANNELLS
Singles: 7-inch
HIT RECORD (700 "In My Arms to Stay")...25-50 63
Members: Tony Williams; Gene Williams; Larry Hampden; Revo Hodge.
Also see CHANNELS

CHANNELS
(Earl Lewis & Channels)
Singles: 78 rpm
FURY...50-100 58
GONE...50-75 57
WHIRLIN' DISC...50-75 56
Singles: 7-inch
ABC...3-4 73
CHANNEL (Black vinyl)...8-12 71-74
CHANNEL (Colored vinyl)...10-20 70s
CLASSIC ARTISTS...4-6 90
COLLECTABLES...3-4
FIRE (1001 "My Heart Is Sad")...30-50 59
FLASHBACK...4-8 65
FURY (1021 "Bye Bye Baby")...40-60 58
FURY (1071 "Bye Bye Baby")...25-50 63
GONE (5012 "That's My Desire")...50-100 57
(Black label.)
GONE (5012 "That's My Desire")...20-40 60
(Multi-color label.)
GONE (5019 "Altar of Love")...50-75 58
(Black label.)
GONE (5019 "Altar of Love")...20-30 58
(Multi-color label.)
KING TUT...4-8
PORT (70014 "The Closer You Are")...15-25 59
PORT (70017 "The Gleam in You Eyes")...15-25 60
PORT (70022 "Flames in My Heart")...15-25 61
PORT (70023 "I Really Love You") 15-25 61
RARE BIRD...5-10 71
ROULETTE...3-5 71
VIRGO...3-5 72-73
WHIRLIN' DISC (100 "The Closer You Are")...150-250 56
(Label name is in a sans serif—or block—typestyle. Label stock is glossy. Publisher credited is "Bob-Dan Music.")
WHIRLIN' DISC (100 "The Closer You Are")...100-200 56
(Label name is in a sans serif—or block—typestyle. Publisher credited is "Spinning Wheel Music.")
WHIRLIN' DISC (100 "The Closer You Are")...100-200 56
(Label name is in a serif style type.)
WHIRLIN' DISC (102 "The Gleam in Your Eyes")...100-200 56
WHIRLIN' DISC (107 "I Really Love You")...100-200 56
WHIRLIN' DISC (109 "Flames in My Heart")...100-200 57
LPs: 10/12-inch
CHANNEL...10-20 73-80
COLLECTABLES (5012 "Earl Lewis & the Channels")...10-15 82
(Picture disc.)
LOST-NITE...10-15 81
RELIC...5-10 90
Members: Earl Lewis; Larry Hampden; Bill Morris; Ed Dolphin; Cliff Wright; John Felix; Alton Thomas.

CHANNELS
Singles: 7-inch
MERCURY...5-10 59
Members: Charlie Reynolds; Gene DiGienerio; James Liott; Charles Toole.

CHANNELS
Singles: 7-inch
ENJOY (2001 "My Love")...10-20 63
GROOVE (0046 "Anything You Do")...10-20 64
GROOVE (0061 "You Can Count on Me")...10-20 65
Members: Tony Williams; Gene Williams; Larry Hampden.
Also see CHANNELLS

CHANSON P&R/LP '78
Singles: 7-inch
ARIOLA AMERICA...3-4 78-79
LPs: 10/12-inch
ARIOLA AMERICA...5-10 78
Also see EVANS, Linda

CHANSONETTES, Les: see LES CHANSONETTES

CHANT, The
LPs: 10/12-inch
SAFETY NET (5 "Three Sheets to the Wind")...10-15 85
Walter Czachowski; James B. Johnson; Todd Barry; Rich DeFinis.

CHANT PAUL
Singles: 7-inch
FELSTED...4-8 64

CHANTAYS P&R/R&B/LP '63
Singles: 7-inch
ABC...3-4 74
COLLECTABLES...3-4 81
DOT...4-8 63
DOWNEY (104 "Pipeline")...20-30 63
DOWNEY (108 "Monsoon")...15-25 63
DOWNEY (116 thru 130)...10-20 63-65
MCA...3-4 84
LPs: 10/12-inch
DOT (3516 "Pipeline")...25-30 63
(Monaural.)
DOT (25516 "Pipeline")...30-40 63
(Stereo.)
DOT (3771 "Two Sides of the Chantays")...25-30 63
(Monaural.)
DOT (25771 "Two Sides of the Chantays")...30-40 63
(Stereo.)
DOWNEY (1002 "Pipeline")...150-200 63
Members: Bob Marshall; Bob Welch; Bob Spickard; Brian Carman; Steve Cahn; Warren Waters
Also see ILL WINDS
Also see LEAPING FERNS

CHANTECLAIRS
Singles: 78 rpm
DOT...15-30 54-55
Singles: 7-inch
DOT (1227 "Someday My Love Will Come My Way")...30-60 54
DOT (15404 "Believe Me, Beloved")...25-50 55
Member: Prentice Moore.
Also see MORELAND, Prentice

CHANTEERS
Singles: 7-inch
MERCURY (72037 "Just a Little Boy")...25-35 62

CHANTEL, Dale
Singles: 7-inch
JIN...8-15 60

CHANTELLES
Singles: 7-inch
GNP...4-8 68

CHANTELS P&R '57
Singles: 78 rpm
END........25-50 57-58
Singles: 7-inch
ABC........3-5 73
CARLTON (555 "Look in My Eyes")........10-20 61
CARLTON (564 "Well I Told You").10-20 61
CARLTON (569 "Here It Comes Again")........10-20 61
END (1001 "He's Gone")........40-60 57
(Black label.)
END (1005 "Maybe")........30-50 57
(Black label.)
END (1005 "Maybe")........15-25 50s
(White label.)
END (1005 "Maybe")........10-15 60s
(Multi-color label.)
END (1015 "Every Night")........25-50 59
(White label.)
END (1015 "Every Night")........10-15 60s
(Multi-color label.)
END (1020 "I Love You So")........20-40 58
END (1026 "Sure of Love")........20-40 58
END (1030 "Congratulations")........20-40 58
END (1037 "I Can't Take It")........20-40 58
END (1048 "I'm Confessin' ")........20-30 59
END (1069 "Whoever You Are")....15-25 60
END (1103 "Believe Me")........15-25 61
END (1105 "There's Our Song").....15-25 61
END (1120 "To Live My Life Again")........15-25 63
ERIC........3-4 73
LANA........4-8 64
LUDIX (101 "Eternally")........25-50 63
LUDIX (106 "That's Why You're Happy")........15-25 63
RCA........3-6 70
ROULETTE........3-6 69-71
TCF........5-10 65
VERVE........5-10 66
EPs: 7-inch
END (201 "I Love You So")........100-150 58
END (202 "I Love You So")........100-150 58
LPs: 10/12-inch
CARLTON (LP-144 "The Chantels on Tour – Look in My Eyes")........50-100 62
(Monaural.)
CARLTON (STLP-144 "The Chantels on Tour – Look in My Eyes")........75-150 62
(Stereo.)
END (301 "We're the Chantels")........1000-2000 58
(Pictures the group on front cover.)
END (301 "The Chantels")........150-300 59
(Pictures a juke box on front cover.)
END (312 "There's Our Song Again")........50-100 62
FORUM (9104 "The Chantels Sing Their Favorites")........25-50 64
MURRAY HILL (000385 "Arlene Smith & the Chantels")........20-30 87
(Three discs. Includes booklet.)
ROULETTE........5-10
Members: Arlene Smith; Lois Harris; Rene Minus; Sonia Gorring; Jackie Landry; Annette Smith; Sandra Dawn. Session: Richard Barrett; Buddy Lucas Orchestra.
Also see BARRETT, Richard
Also see SMITH, Arlene
Also see VENEERS

CHANTELS
Singles: 7-inch
FANTASTIC (3662 "Tu N'Avais Pas Besoin de Moi")........10-20
MW (1001 "Shaggy Baggy Joe")...20-30

CHANTELS & AQUA LADS
Singles: 7-inch
AQUA (8755 "I'll Never Know")......15-20

CHANTER SISTERS
Singles: 7-inch
POLYDOR........3-5 76-77
LPs: 10/12-inch
POLYDOR........5-10 76
Members: Doreen Chanter; Irene Chanter.

CHANTERS
(Featuring Ethel Brown & Brother Woodman's Combo)
Singles: 78 rpm
COMBO (78 "Why")........100-150 55
COMBO (92 "I Love You")........75-125 55
KEM (2740 "Lonesome Me")........50-75 55
RPM (415 "Tell Me, Thrill Me")......50-75 54
Singles: 7-inch
COMBO (78 "Why")........300-400 55
COMBO (92 "I Love You")........250-350 55
KEM (2740 "Lonesome Me")........150-200 55
RPM (415 "Tell Me, Thrill Me")..150-200 54
Members: Ethel Brown; Gene Ford; Billy Boyd; Alan Boyd.

CHANTERS P&R/R&B '61
Singles: 7-inch
DE LUXE (6162 "My My Darling")..30-50 58
DE LUXE (6166 "Row Your Boat") 25-40 58
(Black label.)
DE LUXE (6166 "Row Your Boat").15-25
(Yellow label.)
DE LUXE (6172 "Five Little Kisses")........30-50 58
DE LUXE (6191 "No, No, No")........30-50 61
DE LUXE (6194 "My My Darling")..20-40 61
DE LUXE (6200 "Row Your Boat") 10-20 63
GUSTO........3-4 77
SSP (1001 "Heavenly You")........15-20
Members: Bud Johnson Jr; Larry Pendegrass; Fred Paige; Bobby Thompson; Elliot Green.

CHANTERS
Singles: 7-inch
MGM........3-5 67
Also see BUTLER, Billy

CHANTEURS
(With King Kolax & His Band)
Singles: 7-inch
LA SALLE (501 "Wishin' Well")...100-200 61
VEE JAY (519 "You've Got a Great Love")........10-20 63
Members: Eugene Record; Sollie McElroy; Robert Lester; Clarence Johnson.
Also see CHI-LITES
Also see McELROY, Sollie
Also see MOROCCOS
Also see RECORD, Eugene

CHANTEURS
Singles: 7-inch
BOLO........8-12 64
Also see DYNAMICS
Also see HANNA, Jimmy

CHANTICLEERS
Singles: 7-inch
ARC........15-25 59
LYRIC (103 "To Keep Your Love").20-30 58
OLD TOWN........10-15 63

CHANTIERS
Singles: 7-inch
DJB........10-15 64

CHANTILLY C&W '82
(Featuring Kim Williams)
Singles: 7-inch
F&L........3-4 82-84
JAROCO........3-5 82
Members: Kim Williams; Debbie Pierce; P.J. Allman; Joci Stevens.

CHANTONES
Singles: 7-inch
CAPITOL........10-15 61
CARLTON........10-20 58
TOP RANK........10-15 60
Also see SCOTT, Jack

CHANTS
Singles: 7-inch
CAPITOL........8-12 58
CHECKER........4-8 68
EKO........10-15 61
MGM........5-10 61
TRU EKO........5-10 61
U.W.R........5-10 62
VERVE........5-10 61
Picture Sleeves
CAPITOL........15-30 58

CHANTS
Singles: 7-inch
CAMEO........8-12 63-64
INTERPHON........8-12 64

CHANTS
Singles: 7-inch
NITE-OWL (40 "Heaven and Paradise")........200-300 60
(Maroon label.)
NITE-OWL (40 "Heaven and Paradise")........50-100 60
(Black label. Colored vinyl.)
NITE-OWL (40 "Heaven and Paradise")........25-50 60
(Black label. Black vinyl.)

CHANTS
Singles: 7-inch
B. WARE (869 "Hypnotized")........15-25

CHAPARALS
(Featuring Tooter Boatman)
Singles: 7-inch
REBEL (108 "Poor Gal")........150-250 58
Also see BOATMAN, Tooter

CHAPARRAL BROTHERS C&W '68
Singles: 7-inch
CAPITOL........3-6 68-70
LPs: 10/12-inch
CAPITOL........8-12 68-70
Members: John Chaparral; Paul Chaparral.

CHAPARRALS
Singles: 7-inch
MONEY TOWN (102 "Burning Up in Love")........10-15
ROULETTE........5-10 60

CHAPARRO, Tommy C&W '83
Singles: 7-inch
COMPASS........3-4 83

CHAPEL, Jean
Singles: 78 rpm
SUN........15-25 56
RCA........10-20 56
Singles: 7-inch
CHALLENGE........4-8 66-68
KAPP........4-6 69
SMASH........4-8 63
SUN........15-25 56
RCA........10-20 56
Also see PRESLEY, Elvis / Jean Chapel

CHAPELAIRES
(With Lenny Martin Orchestra)
Singles: 7-inch
GATEWAY (744 "Lonely Star")......20-30 64
GATEWAY (746 "Vacation Time") 30-40 64
HAC (101 "Not Good Enough")...200-300 61
HAC (102 "Gloria")........20-30 61

CHAPELLES
(Billy & the Kids)
Singles: 7-inch
ADARA (101 "Nightrider")........25-35 61
(Reissued as by Billy & Kids.)
Also see BILLY & KIDS

CHAPELLS
Singles: 7-inch
DOUBLE CHECK (4001 "Are You Ready")........20-30 60s

CHAPERONES
Singles: 7-inch
JOSIE (880 "Cruise to the Moon") 15-20 60
(First issued crediting the Cahperones.)
JOSIE (885 "Shining Star")........15-20 60
JOSIE (891 "Blueberry Sweet")........25-35 61
Also see CAHPERONES
Also see JORDAN, Lou

CHAPIN, Harry P&R/LP '72
Singles: 7-inch
BOARDWALK........3-4 80-81
DUNHILL........3-4 88
ELEKTRA........3-5 72-79
LPs: 10/12-inch
BOARDWALK........5-10 80
DUNHILL........5-10 88
ELEKTRA........8-12 72-79

CHAPIN, Sandy
Singles: 7-inch
EMPIRE........5-8

CHAPIN, Tom
Singles: 7-inch
FANTASY........3-5 77
SPECTOR........3-4 81
LPs: 10/12-inch
FANTASY........5-10 76
SPECTOR........5-10 81

CHAPINS
(With Will Jordan & Friends)
Singles: 7-inch
EPIC........3-5 71
ROCK-LAND........4-8 67
Picture Sleeves
ROCK-LAND........10-15 67
LPs: 10/12-inch
ROCK LAND (66 "Chapin Music")..20-30 67
Members: Tom Chapin; Steve Chapin; Phil Forbes; Doug Walkers.

CHAPLAIN, Paul P&R '60
(With His Emeralds; Paul Chaplin)
Singles: 7-inch
ELGIN........5-10
HARPER........10-20 60-61
PAT (101 "Caledonia")........60-80

CHAPLIN, Angelica R&B '87
Singles: 7-inch
MERCURY........3-4 87

CHAPLIN, Blondie
Singles: 7-inch
ASYLUM........3-5 77
LPs: 10/12-inch
ASYLUM........5-10 77
Also see FLAME

CHAPLIN, Paul: see CHAPLAIN, Paul

CHAPMAN, Andy
Singles: 7-inch
ATCO........3-5 68

CHAPMAN, Cee Cee C&W '88
(With Santa Fe)
Singles: 7-inch
CURB........3-4 88-89

CHAPMAN, Gary C&W '88
Singles: 7-inch
RCA........3-4 88

CHAPMAN, Grady
(With the Suedes; with Don Ralke's Orchestra)
Singles: 78 rpm
MONEY........50-100 55
Singles: 7-inch
IMPERIAL (5591 "Garden of Memories")........10-15 59
IMPERIAL (5611 "Come Away")....10-15 59
KNIGHT (1754 "Say You'll Be Mine")........20-25 58
MERCURY (71771 "I'll Never Question Your Love")........8-12 61
MERCURY (71698 "Ambush")........30-50 60
MONEY (204 "I Need You So")..250-350 55
ZEPHYR (016 "My Love Will Never Change")........10-15 60s
Also see RALKE, Don
Also see ROBINS

CHAPMAN, Marshall C&W '77
Singles: 7-inch
EPIC........3-5 76-80
LPs: 10/12-inch
EPIC........8-12 77-79
ROUNDER........5-10 82

CHAPMAN, Michael
LPs: 10/12-inch
HARVEST........10-15 71
PACIFIC ARTS........5-10 80

CHAPMAN, Ronnie
Singles: 7-inch
COLUMBIA (41469 "Annie B. Is Gone")........20-30 59

CHAPMAN, Tracy P&R/LP '88
Singles: 7-inch
ELEKTRA........3-4 88-89
Picture Sleeves
ELEKTRA........3-4 88-89
LPs: 10/12-inch
ELEKTRA........5-8 88-89

CHAPPELL, Walter
Singles: 7-inch
FERNWOOD........8-12

CHAPPELLS
Singles: 7-inch
BEDFORD........5-10

CHAPPIES
Singles: 7-inch
CHELTON (750 "Suddenly There Were Tears")........75-125

CHAPS
Singles: 7-inch
BRENT........5-10 60
MATADOR (1814 "There'll Never Be")........25-35 61

CHAPS
Singles: 7-inch
PAULA........4-8 66

CHAPTER ONE
Singles: 7-inch
TOXSAN........8-10
20TH FOX........3-5 76

CHAPTER II
Singles: 7-inch
MORRHYTHM........3-5 77

CHAPTER III
Singles: 7-inch
DIAL........3-5 70

CHAPTER FOUR
Singles: 7-inch
DOT........4-8 65

CHAPTER FOUR
Singles: 7-inch
P.I.P........3-5 75

CHAPTER V
Singles: 7-inch
VERVE FORECAST........10-20 67

CHAPTER SIX
Singles: 7-inch
MERCURY........4-8 66

CHAPTER VI
Singles: 7-inch
ORIGINAL SOUND........4-8 68

CHAPTER 8 R&B '79
Singles: 12-inch
ARIOLA AMERICA........4-8 79
BEVERLY GLEN........4-6 85
Singles: 7-inch
ARIOLA AMERICA........3-5 79-80
BEVERLY GLEN........3-4 85
Members: Anita Baker; Michael Powell; David Washington; Carolyn Crawford; Valerie Pinkston.
LPs: 10/12-inch
ARIOLA AMERICA........5-10 79
Also see BAKER, Anita
Also see CRAWFORD, Carolyn
Also see DETROIT EMERALDS

CHAPTER THIRTEEN
Singles: 7-inch
PLAYBOY........3-5 74

CHAPTERS
("With Band")
Singles: 78 rpm
REPUBLIC........100-150 53
Singles: 7-inch
REPUBLIC (7038 "Goodbye, My Love")........250-350 53
Also see FOSTER, Helen

CHARACTERS
Singles: 7-inch
PIP........8-12 59
VIRTRON........5-10
LPs: 10/12-inch
PIP (1900 "Smash Flops")........30-50 59

CHARADE
Singles: 7-inch
EPIC........3-5 70

CHARADE D&D '83
(Featuring Jessica)
Singles: 12-inch
PROFILE........4-6 83

CHARADES
Singles: 7-inch
LANCER........10-20 58

CHARADES
Singles: 7-inch
U.A. (132 "Make Me Happy")........20-30 58
U.A. (183 "Let Me Love You")....100-200 59
Member: Billy Storm.
Also see STORM, Billy

CHARADES
(Charades Band; "Featuring Syl Grigsby")
Singles: 7-inch
AVA (154 "Please Be My Love Tonight")........20-30 63
CHARADE........3-5 75-82
IMPACT (2 "Christina")........15-25 63
NORTHRIDGE (1002 "For You") .75-125 62
ORIGINAL SOUND........10-20 64
LPs: 10/12-inch
CHARADE........10-15 82
Members: Syl Grisby; Raymond A. Baradat; Tom Johnston; Ed Cuellar.
Also see ASHFORD, Jack
Also see EL TRIO DEL PUEBLO
Also see JOHNSTON, Tom
Also see GAYE, Marvin
Also see MASERANG
Also see RHYTHM KINGS

CHARADES
Singles: 7-inch
MGM (13540 "Key to My Happiness")........25-35 66
MERCURY........5-10 65
MONUMENT........5-10 66
OKEH........5-10 64
SKYLARK........5-10 64
W.B........5-10 64

CHARADES
Singles: 12-inch
BLUE PARROT........4-6 84
Singles: 7-inch
CHARADE........3-5 75-82

CHARAYS
Singles: 7-inch
VIVA (101 "Afraid")........8-12

CHARGERS P&R '58
Singles: 7-inch
RCA (7301 "Old MacDonald")........15-25 58
RCA (7417 "Here in My Heart")....15-25 58
Members: Jesse Belvin; James Scott; Ben Easley; Dunbar White; Johnny White; Mitchell Alexander; Jimmy Norman.
Also see BELVIN, Jesse
Also see FEATHERS
Also see NORMAN, Jimmy

CHARGERS
Singles: 7-inch
B.E.A.T........10-15 58

CHARGERS
Singles: 7-inch
HOLLYWOOD........15-20 64

CHARGERS
Singles: 7-inch
VANGUARD........3-5 72

CHARIOT
LPs: 10/12-inch
NAT'L GENERAL (2003 "Chariot").50-75 71
Members: Mike Koplan; Larry Gould; Pug Baker.

CHARIOTEERS P&R '40
Singles: 78 rpm
BRUNSWICK........25-50 38-39
COLUMBIA........25-50 39-49
DECCA........20-30 35
JOSIE........15-25 55
KEYSTONE........10-20 52
LANG-WORTH........10-20 40s
(16-inch transcriptions.)
MGM........20-30 57
OKEH........15-25 40-42
TUXEDO........15-25 55
VOCALION........15-25 38-39
Singles: 7-inch
COLUMBIA (168 "A Kiss and a Rose")........400-600 50
(Microgroove 33 single.)
COLUMBIA (363 "This Side of Heaven")........400-600 50
(Microgroove 33 single.)
JOSIE (787 "I've Got My Heart on My Sleeve")........50-75 55
MGM (12569 "The Candles")........50-75 57
TUXEDO (891 "Thanks for Yesterday")........50-75 55
LPs: 10/12-inch
COLUMBIA (6014 "Sweet and Low")........150-200 49
(10-inch LP.)
HARMONY (7089 "The Charioteers & Billy Williams")........50-100 57
Members: Billy Williams; Eddie Jackson; Ira Williams; Howard Daniel; James Sherman.
Also see BAILEY, Mildred, & Charioteers
Also see PARTICK, Gladys
Also see SINATRA, Frank, & Charioteers
Also see WILLIAMS, Billy

CHARIOTS
Singles: 7-inch
RSVP (1105 "Tiger in the Tank")....15-25 64
TIME (1006 "Gloria")........25-35 59

CHARISMA
Singles: 7-inch
ROULETTE........3-5 71
LPs: 10/12-inch
ROULETTE........10-15 69

CHARISMA BAND
Singles: 7-inch
BUDDAH (483 "Ain't Nothing Like Your Love")........4-6 75
COLUMBIA........3-5 77

CHARITY
Singles: 7-inch
PHILIPS........4-8 69
UNI........4-8 69
LPs: 10/12-inch
UNI........10-20 69
Member: Kent Henry.
Also see GENESIS

CHARITY SHAYNE
Singles: 7-inch
AUTUMN........5-10 65

CHARLATANS
Singles: 7-inch
KAPP (779 "The Shadow Knows") 40-50 66
PHILIPS (40610 "High Coin")........30-40 69

PHILIPS (44824 "Date: May 19, 1969") ... 40-60 69
(Promotional issue only.)
KAPP (779 "The Shadow Knows") ... 50-75 66
PHILIPS (40610 "High Coin") ... 50-75 69
LPs: 10/12-inch
PHILLIPS (600309 "The Charlatans") ... 75-125 69
Members: Dan Hicks; George Hunter; Michael Ferguson; Richard Olson; Mike Wilhelm; Patrick Bogert; Terry Wilson; Sam Linde.
Also see HICKS, Dan, & His Hot Licks
Also see HUGHES, Lynne
Also see WILHELM

CHARLATANS UK LP '90
LPs: 10/12-inch
BEGGARS BANQUET ... 5-8 90

CHARLEE
LPs: 10/12-inch
MIND DUST MUSIC ... 5-10 84

CHARLENA & ROCKETTES
Singles: 7-inch
MORGAN (9018 "Ramrod") ... 10-20 65

CHARLENE P&R '77
(Charlene Duncan)
Singles: 7-inch
MOTOWN ... 3-5 76-85
PRODIGAL ... 3-5 76-77
Picture Sleeves
PRODIGAL ... 3-5 77
LPs: 10/12-inch
MOTOWN ... 5-10 82-85
PRODIGAL ... 8-10 76

CHARLENE & Stevie Wonder P&R '82
Singles: 7-inch
MOTOWN ... 3-4 82
Picture Sleeves
MOTOWN ... 3-4 82
Also see CHARLENE
Also see WONDER, Stevie

CHARLENE & Soul Serenaders
Singles: 7-inch
VOLT ... 3-6 70

CHARLES
Singles: 7-inch
CALLIOPE ... 4-6

CHARLES, Adam
Singles: 7-inch
DOT ... 4-8 63

CHARLES, Andy, & Blues Kings
Singles: 7-inch
D (1061 "Baby Don't Go") ... 40-60 59
(Yellow label.)
D (1061 "Baby Don't Go") ... 10-20 59
(Tan label.)

CHARLES, Bobby R&B '56
Singles: 78 rpm
CHESS (1609 thru 1638) ... 15-30 55-56
CHESS (1647 thru 1670) ... 25-50 57
Singles: 7-inch
BEARSVILLE ... 3-5 73
CHESS (1609 "On Bended Knee") ... 20-40 55
CHESS (1617 "Why Did You Leave") ... 20-40 56
CHESS (1628 "Time Will Tell") ... 20-40 56
CHESS (1638 "Laura Lee") ... 20-40 56
CHESS (1647 "Put Your Arms Around Me Honey") ... 20-40 57
CHESS (1658 "No More") ... 20-30 57
CHESS (1670 "One-Eyed Jack") ... 20-30 57
HUB CITY ... 5-10 63
IMPERIAL ... 8-15 58-60
JEWEL ... 5-10 64
PAULA ... 4-8 65
RICE & GRAVY ... 3-4 86-90
LPs: 10/12-inch
BEARSVILLE ... 10-15 72
CHESS ... 8-12 76

CHARLES, Bobby
(With the Apollos)
Singles: 7-inch
HIGHLAND ... 5-10
TIDE ... 5-10 62

CHARLES, Bobby, Quartet
Singles: 7-inch
FENTON ... 10-15 66

CHARLES, Buddy
(With Richard Phillips & Orchestra)
Singles: 7-inch
CHARMAN (0001 "Be a Man") ... 15-25

CHARLES, Claire
(With the Terrytones)
Singles: 7-inch
WYE ... 5-10 60
Also see TERRYTONES

CHARLES, Donnie
Singles: 7-inch
SMASH ... 5-10 62
WORLD ARTISTS ... 4-8 64

CHARLES, Doug
(With the Boogie Kings; featuring Skip Morris)
Singles: 7-inch
TODD ... 5-10 59

CHARLES, Elaine
Singles: 7-inch
ACAMA ... 4-8 62

CHARLES, Harry
Singles: 7-inch
BOYD ... 3-6 68

ROWAX ... 4-8 63

CHARLES, Jimmy P&R/R&B '60
(With the Revelletts)
Singles: 7-inch
ABC ... 3-5 73
COLLECTABLES ... 3-4 81
ERIC ... 3-5 79
MCA ... 3-4 84
PROMO (1002 "A Million to One") ... 10-20 60
PROMO (1003 "The Age for Love") ... 10-15 60
PROMO (1004 "I Saw Mommy Kissing Santa Claus") ... 10-15 60
PROMO (1005 "Christmasville U.S.A.") ... 10-15 61
ROULETTE ... 3-5 71
Picture Sleeves
PROMO (1003 "The Age for Love") ... 15-25 60
PROMO (1004 "I Saw Mommy Kissing Santa Claus") ... 15-25 60
PROMO (1005 "Christmasville U.S.A.") ... 15-25 61
Also see JOHNNIE & JOE / Jimmy Charles

CHARLES, Kim C&W '79
Singles: 7-inch
MCA ... 3-5 79

CHARLES, Lee R&B '68
Singles: 7-inch
BAMBOO ... 4-6 70-71
BRUNSWICK ... 5-10 69
HOT WAX ... 3-5 73
INVICTUS ... 3-5 74
REVUE ... 10-15 68

CHARLES, Nick
Singles: 7-inch
GUYDEN ... 15-25 61
SATELLITE ... 5-10 61
STAX ... 5-10 62

CHARLES, Norman
Singles: 7-inch
COLUMBIA ... 4-8 67
TRY ME ... 5-10 63
VEE JAY ... 5-10 62

CHARLES, Owen
Singles: 7-inch
GUYDEN ... 5-10 59

CHARLES, Ray R&B '51
(With the Raelettes)
Singles: 78 rpm
ATLANTIC (900 & 1000 series) ... 15-25 52-57
ATLANTIC (2000 series) ... 25-50 58
JAX (641 "Baby Let Me Hear You Call My Name") ... 100-200 52
ROCKIN' ... 15-25 53
SWING BEAT ... 20-40 49
SWING TIME ... 20-40 50-53
Singles: 7-inch
ABC ... 3-8 66-73
ABC-PAR (Monaural) ... 5-10 60-66
ABC-PAR (Stereo) ... 10-20 61-62
ABC/TRC ... 3-6
ATLANTIC (976 "Roll with Me Baby") ... 50-75 52
ATLANTIC (984 "The Sun's Gonna Shine Again") ... 30-60 53
ATLANTIC (999 "Mess Around") ... 30-60 53
ATLANTIC (1000 series) ... 20-40 53-57
ATLANTIC (2000 series) ... 5-15 58-68
ATLANTIC (3000 series) ... 3-5 77-79
BARONET (7111 "See See Rider") ... 8-10 62
COLUMBIA ... 3-4 82-87
CROSSOVER ... 3-5 73-78
DUNHILL GOLDIES ... 3-4 73
HURRAH ... 8-12
IMPULSE ... 8-10 61
JAX (641 "Baby Let Me Hear You Call My Name") ... 300-500 52
MAYFAIR (121 "Pony Boy") ... 4-8
(With "Uncle Stu.")
RCA ... 3-5 76
ROCKIN' (504 "Walkin' and Talkin' ") ... 100-200 53
SITTIN' IN WITH (641 "Baby Let Me Hear You Call My Name") ... 75-150 52
SWING TIME (250 "Baby Let Me Hold Your Hand") ... 75-100 51
SWING TIME (274 "Kiss Me Baby") ... 75-100 52
SWING TIME (300 "Baby Let Me Hear You Call My Name") ... 75-100 52
SWING TIME (326 "The Snow Is Falling") ... 50-100 53
TANGERINE ... 3-5 71
TIME ... 5-10 62
Picture Sleeves
ABC (11045 "That's a Lie") ... 4-8 68
BARONET (7111 "See See Rider") ... 10-15 62
EPs: 7-inch
ABC-PAR (335 "Basin St. Blues") ... 15-25 60
(Stereo. Juke box issue only.)
ABC-PAR (415 "Greatest Hits") ... 15-25 62
(Stereo. Juke box issue only.)
ABC-PAR (465 "Ingredients in a Recipe for Soul") ... 15-25 63
(Stereo. Juke box issue only.)
ATLANTIC (567 "Ray Charles") ... 25-45 56
ATLANTIC (587 "Ray Charles") ... 25-45 57
ATLANTIC (597 "The Great Ray Charles") ... 25-45 57
ATLANTIC (607 "Rock with Ray Charles") ... 25-45 58
ATLANTIC (614 "Soul Brothers") ... 25-45 58
(With Milt Jackson.)
ATLANTIC (619 "The Genius of Ray Charles") ... 25-45 59
ATLANTIC (8029 "What'd I Say") ... 25-45 59
U.A. (1004 "In the Heat of the Night") ... 10-20 67
(Promotional issue only.)
LPs: 10/12-inch
ABC (Except 590) ... 10-12 66-73
ABC (590 "A Man and His Soul") ... 20-25 67
ABC-PAR (300 series) ... 15-25 60-61
ABC-PAR (400 & 500 series) ... 10-20 62-66
AHED ... 8-12
(TV mail-order offer.)
ARCHIVES ... 8-12
ATLANTIC (500 series) ... 10-15 73
ATLANTIC (900 "The Ray Charles Story, Vols. 1 & 2") ... 30-40 62
(Combines Atlantic 8063 and 8064.)
ATLANTIC (1259 "The Great Ray Charles") ... 50-75 57
ATLANTIC (1279 "Soul Brothers") ... 40-60 58
(With Milt Jackson.)
ATLANTIC (1289 "Ray Charles at Newport") ... 40-60 58
ATLANTIC (1312 "The Genius of Ray Charles") ... 30-50 59
ATLANTIC (1360 "Soul Meeting") ... 25-35 62
(With Milt Jackson. Number indicates a '61 release, but not actually issued until 1962.)
ATLANTIC (1369 "Genius After Hours") ... 25-35 61
ATLANTIC (1500 series) ... 10-20 70
ATLANTIC (3700 series) ... 20-25 82
ATLANTIC (7000 series) ... 15-20 64
ATLANTIC (8006 "Ray Charles") ... 50-100 57
(Black label.)
ATLANTIC (8006 "Ray Charles") ... 25-45 59
(Red label.)
ATLANTIC (8025 "Yes Indeed") ... 40-60 59
(Black label.)
ATLANTIC (8025 "Yes Indeed") ... 25-45 60
(Red label.)
ATLANTIC (8029 "What'd I Say") ... 40-50 59
(Black label.)
ATLANTIC (8029 "What'd I Say") ... 25-45 60
(Red label.)
ATLANTIC (8039 "Ray Charles in Person") ... 30-50 60
(Black label.)
ATLANTIC (8039 "Ray Charles in Person") ... 25-35 60
(Red label.)
ATLANTIC (8052 "The Genius Sings the Blues") ... 20-30 61
ATLANTIC (8054 "Dot the Twist") ... 20-30 61
ATLANTIC (8063 "The Ray Charles Story, Vol. 1") ... 20-25 62
ATLANTIC (8064 "The Ray Charles Story, Vol. 2") ... 20-25 62
ATLANTIC (8083 "The Ray Charles Story, Vol. 3") ... 20-25 63
ATLANTIC (8094 "The Ray Charles Story, Vol. 4") ... 20-25 64
ATLANTIC (19000 series) ... 5-12 77-80
BARONET ... 15-20 62
BLUESWAY ... 8-10 73
BULLDOG ... 5-10 84
COLUMBIA ... 5-10 83-86
CORONET ... 8-12 60s
CROSSOVER ... 8-15 73-76
DESIGN ... 10-20 62
EVEREST ... 8-10 70-82
GRAND PRIX ... 10-20 60s
GUEST STAR ... 10-20 64
HOLLYWOOD (504 "The Original Ray Charles") ... 100-150 59
HOLLYWOOD 505: see CHARLES, Ray / Charles Brown)
HURRAH ... 8-15
IMPULSE ... 20-30 61
INTERMEDIA ... 5-10 84
JAZZ INT'L ... 15-25
KING ... 8-10 77
PALACE ... 5-10
PREMIER ... 8-10
SCEPTER ... 8-12
SPIN-O-RAMA ... 10-15 60s
STRAND ... 10-15 60s
TANGERINE ... 10-12 70-73
UPFRONT ... 8-10 70s
Also see COOKIES
Also see GUITAR SLIM
Also see FULSON, Lowell
Also see HENDRIX, Margie
Also see JOEL, Billy, & Ray Charles
Also see JONES, Quincy, Ray Charles & Chaka Khan
Also see MAXIM TRIO
Also see RAELETTES
Also see U.S.A. for AFRICA

CHARLES, Ray / Charles Brown
LPs: 10/12-inch
HOLLYWOOD (505 "The Fabulous Artistry of Ray Charles") ... 100-150 59
(Brown, barely credited, provides four tracks.)

CHARLES, Ray / Solomon Burke
LPs: 10/12-inch
GRAND PRIX ... 10-20 64
Also see BURKE, Solomon

CHARLES, Ray, & Betty Carter LP '61
Singles: 7-inch
ABC-PAR ... 5-10 61-62
LPs: 10/12-inch
ABC-PAR (ABC-385 "Ray Charles & Betty Carter") ... 50-75 61
(Monaural.)
ABC-PAR (ABCS-385 "Ray Charles & Betty Carter") ... 75-100 61
(Stereo.)
DCC (2005 "Ray Charles & Betty Carter") ... 10-15 95
(Audiophile issue.)
Also see CARTER, Betty

CHARLES, Ray, & Clint Eastwood C&W '80
Singles: 7-inch
W.B. ... 3-4 80
Also see EASTWOOD, Clint

CHARLES, Ray, & Mickey Gilley C&W '85
Singles: 7-inch
COLUMBIA ... 3-4 85
Also see GILLEY, Mickey

CHARLES, Ray / Ivory Joe Hunter / Jimmy Rushing
LPs: 10/12-inch
DESIGN (909 "Three of a Kind") ... 15-20 60s
(Black label, silver print.)
DESIGN (909 "Three of a Kind") ... 10-15 60s
(Black, red, blue and yellow label.)
Also see HUNTER, Ivory Joe
Also see RUSHING, Jimmy

CHARLES, Ray, George Jones & Chet Atkins C&W '83
Singles: 7-inch
COLUMBIA ... 3-4 83
Also see ATKINS, Chet
Also see JONES, George

CHARLES, Ray, & Cleo Laine LP '76
LPs: 10/12-inch
RCA ... 10-12 76
Also see LAINE, Cleo

CHARLES, Ray & Jimmy Lewis P&R/R&B '69
Singles: 7-inch
ABC ... 3-4 69
TANGERINE ... 3-6 68
Also see LEWIS, Jimmy

CHARLES, Ray / Little Richard / Sam Cooke
LPs: 10/12-inch
ALMOR (102 "Soul Blues") ... 10-20
Also see COOKE, Sam
Also see LITTLE RICHARD

CHARLES, Ray, & Willie Nelson C&W '84
Singles: 7-inch
COLUMBIA ... 3-4 84
Also see NELSON, Willie

CHARLES, Ray / Arbee Stidham / Li'l Son Jackson / James Wayne
LPs: 10/12-inch
MAINSTREAM ... 8-12 71
Also see JACKSON, Li'l Son
Also see STIDHAM, Arbee
Also see WAYNE, James

CHARLES, Ray, & B.J. Thomas C&W '84
Singles: 7-inch
COLUMBIA ... 3-4 85
Also see THOMAS, B.J.

CHARLES, Ray, & Hank Williams Jr. C&W '85
Singles: 7-inch
COLUMBIA ... 3-4 85
Also see WILLIAMS, Hank, Jr.

CHARLES, Ray, & Jimmy Witherspoon
LPs: 10/12-inch
CROWN ... 15-25 60s
Also see CHARLES, Ray
Also see WITHERSPOON, Jimmy

CHARLES, Ray, Singers P&R '55
Singles: 78 rpm
JUBILEE ... 3-5 54
MGM ... 3-6 51-56
Singles: 7-inch
COMMAND ... 3-5 64-70
DECCA ... 3-6 58-59
JUBILEE ... 4-8 54
MGM ... 4-8 51-56
EPs: 7-inch
CADENCE ... 5-10 50s
DECCA ... 5-10 59
ESSEX ... 5-10 50s
JAMESTOWN ... 8-15 57
MGM ... 5-15 55-57
LPs: 10/12-inch
ABC ... 5-10 73
ALSHIRE ... 5-10 70
ATCO ... 8-12 68
CAMDEN ... 6-10 67
COMMAND ... 8-12 62-71
DECCA ... 10-15 58-60
MCA ... 4-6 82
MGM (100 series) ... 5-10 71
MGM (3000 series) ... 10-20 55-60
MGM (4000 series) ... 8-15 63-66
METRO ... 6-10 65
SOMERSET ... 5-10 64
VOCALION ... 8-10 66
Also see BARRY, Jack
Also see COMO, Perry
Also see KNIGHT, Evelyn

CHARLES, Ronnie
LPs: 10/12-inch
20TH FOX ... 8-12 75

CHARLES, Roosevelt
LPs: 10/12-inch
VANGUARD ... 10-20 64

CHARLES, Sonny P&R/R&B '69
(With Checkmates Ltd.)
Singles: 7-inch
A&M ... 4-8 68-73
CAPITOL ... 4-8 66-67
FRATERNITY (935 "Speechless") ... 5-10 64
HIGHRISE ... 3-4 82
PENQUIN (1000 "It's Only Make Believe") ... 10-15 58
RCA ... 3-5 72
Note: Confirmation sought as to whether the Fraternity and Penquin releases are by the same Sonny Charles as the other 45s.
LPs: 10/12-inch
HIGHRISE ... 5-10 82
A&M ... 15-25 69
Also see CHECKMATES LTD.

CHARLES, Tina
Singles: 12-inch
COLUMBIA ... 4-6 77-78
Singles: 7-inch
COLUMBIA ... 3-5 75-78
MAM ... 3-5 71
LPs: 10/12-inch
COLUMBIA ... 5-10 75-77

CHARLES, Tommy P&R '56
Singles: 78 rpm
DECCA ... 10-20 56
WILLETT (111 "Hey There Baby") ... 50-100 57
Singles: 7-inch
DECCA ... 10-20 56
WILLETT (111 "Hey There Baby") ... 40-60 57
Session: Anita Kerr Singers.
Also see KERR, Anita

CHARLES & CARL
Singles: 7-inch
RED ROBIN ("One More Chance") ... 50-75 55
Members: Charles Sampson; Carl Hazan.

CHARLES & ESQUIRES
Singles: 7-inch
SALEM (22064 "Sometime Beats No Time") ... 10-20 60s

CHARLES & IVORY
Singles: 7-inch
GENEVA (106 "My Little Baby") ... 5-10

CHARLES & KAYE
LPs: 10/12-inch
CHARKAYA ... 10-15 73
Members: Jack Charles Wagner; Andy Kaye.
Also see SOLID GOLD

CHARLES & WALTER
Singles: 7-inch
CHENE ... 4-8 64

CHARLES RIVER BOYS
LPs: 10/12-inch
ELEKTRA ... 10-15 67

CHARLESTON CITY ALL STARS LP '57
EPs: 7-inch
WALDORF MUSIC HALL ... 5-10
LPs: 10/12-inch
GRAND AWARD ... 5-15 57-59

CHARLESTON EXPRESS & JESSE WALES C&W '84
Singles: 7-inch
SOUNDWAVES ... 3-4 84-85

CHARLETTES
Singles: 7-inch
ANGIE (1002 "The Fight's Not Over") ... 15-20 60s

CHARLETTS
Singles: 7-inch
PALA ... 5-10 61

CHARLEY D. & MILO
LPs: 10/12-inch
EPIC ... 8-12 70
Members: Charlie D. Harris; Lon Milo Duquette; Joe Wilson; Dave Dunn; Dave Ledbetter.

CHARLIE P&R/LP '77
Singles: 7-inch
ARISTA ... 3-5 79
JANUS ... 3-4 77-78
MIRAGE ... 3-4 83
RCA ... 3-4 81
Picture Sleeves
ARISTA ... 3-5 79
MIRAGE ... 3-4 83
LPs: 10/12-inch
ARISTA ... 5-10 79
COLUMBIA ... 8-10 76
JANUS ... 8-10 77-78
MIRAGE ... 5-10 83
RCA ... 5-10 81
Member: Terry Thomas.

CHARLIE
(Charles Reinhart)
Singles: 7-inch
C&E (101 "Beatles") ... 4-8 79

CHARLIE & BILLY
Singles: 7-inch
DWAIN (806 "Steel Guitar Polka") ... 8-12 59
("Ramblin' Boogie") ... 8-12 59
(No label name or number shown.)
Member: Billy Mure.
Also see MURE, Billy

CHARLIE & CHAN
Singles: 7-inch
KAPP (582 "Rickshaw Drag Race")....10-15 64

CHARLIE & DON
Singles: 7-inch
DUEL (513 "Hush Little Baby")....15-25 62

CHARLIE & RAY
Singles: 78 rpm
HERALD....15-30 54-57
Singles: 7-inch
FLASHBACK (006 "I Love You Madly")....4-8 65
HERALD (438 "I Love You Madly")....30-50 54
HERALD (447 "My Lovin' Baby")....30-50 55
HERALD (454 "Certainly Baby")....20-40 55
HERALD (461 "Oh Gee-Oo-Wee")....20-40 55
HERALD (472 "Little Fool")....20-40 56
HERALD (487 "Mad with You Baby")....20-40 56
HERALD (503 "I Love You Madly")....15-25 57
HERALD (515 "Dearest One")....15-25 58
HI (436 "I Love You Madly")....4-6
JANUS (727 "I Love You Madly")....4-6
JOSIE (789 "Alright, Okay, You Win")....8-10 68
TEL (1005 "This Is Love")....15-20 59

CHARLIE & JIVES
Singles: 7-inch
HOUR (104 "The Coffee Grind")....8-12 62
Also see JIVES
Also see ROYAL JESTERS

CHARLIE & PEP BOYS
Singles: 7-inch
A&M....3-5 76
LPs: 10/12-inch
A&M....8-10 76

CHARLIE & ROSIE
Singles: 78 rpm
RCA....8-12 56
Singles: 7-inch
RCA (6634 "Don't Call the Wagon")....10-20 56
Members: Charlie Singleton; Rose Marie McCoy.
Also see SINGLETON, Charlie

CHARLIE'S ANGELS
Singles: 7-inch
P&P....3-6

CHARLIE'S CHILDREN
Singles: 7-inch
HOLIDAY INN....4-6 68

CHARLINE & DOTTIE
Singles: 7-inch
EL DORADO....4-8 63

CHARLOTTE RUSSE
Singles: 7-inch
PHILIPS....4-8 68

CHARM
Singles: 7-inch
CLIFTON....4-8 83
LPs: 10/12-inch
CLIFTON....8-12 83

CHARM KINGS
Singles: 7-inch
MARK (146 "Tell Me a Tale")....800-1200 60

CHARMAINE
Singles: 7-inch
SEROCK....4-8 62
20TH FOX....4-8 64

CHARMAINES
Singles: 7-inch
FRATERNITY (873 "If You Were Mine")....5-10 61
FRATERNITY (880 "All You Gotta Do")....5-10 61

CHARMAINES
Singles: 7-inch
DOT (16351 "Where Is the Boy Tonight")....8-12 62
Also see SEARS, J.T., & Roebux / Charmaines

CHARMAINES
Singles: 7-inch
DATE....4-8 66
Also see GIGI & CHARMAINES

CHARME R&B '84
Singles: 7-inch
ATLANTIC....3-4 84
RCA....3-4 79-85
LPs: 10/12-inch
RCA....5-10 79-85

CHARMELS
Singles: 7-inch
VOLT....4-8 67-68

CHARMERS
("With Rhythm Acc.")
Singles: 78 rpm
CENTRAL....100-200 54
TIMELY (1009 "I Was Wrong")....200-300 54
TIMELY (1011 "Church on the Hill")....200-300 54
Singles: 7-inch
CENTRAL (1002 "The Beating of My Heart")....500-750 54
CENTRAL (1006 "Tony, My Darling")....500-1000 54
TIMELY (1009 "I Was Wrong")....500-1000 54
Member: Vicki Burgess.
Also see JOYTONES

CHARMERS
Singles: 78 rpm
ALADDIN....15-25 56
Singles: 7-inch
ALADDIN (3337 "All Alone")....30-50 56
ALADDIN (3341 "He's Gone")....30-50 56

CHARMERS
Singles: 7-inch
SILHOUETTE (521 "Rock Rhythm & Blues")....40-50 57
(This same number was used for *Sent Up*, by the Falcons.)
Also see FALCONS

CHARMERS
Singles: 7-inch
JAF (2021 "Little Fool")....15-25 61

CHARMERS
Singles: 7-inch
CO-REC (101 "Watch What You Do")....15-25 63
SURE PLAY (104 "Lesson from the Stars")....200-300 62

CHARMERS
Singles: 7-inch
ALLISON (921 "Magic Rose")....35-45 62
TERRACE (7512 "Visiting Day")....10-20 62

CHARMERS
Singles: 7-inch
TAHOE....5-10 63

CHARMERS
Singles: 7-inch
LAURIE....10-15 62-63
LOUIS....5-10 65
PIP....5-10 64
STUYVESANT....8-10

CHARMETTES P&R/R&B '63
(Charmetts)
Singles: 7-inch
FEDERAL (12345 "Johnny Johnny")....25-35 59
HI....10-15 59
KAPP (547 "Please Don't Kiss Me Again")....15-25 63
KAPP (570 "He's a Wise Guy")....10-20 64
MALA....5-10 64
MARKAY (101 "Donnie")....25-35 62
MARLIN (16001 "One More Time")....20-30 62
MELOMEGA....5-10 62
MONA (553 "The Deeds to My Heart")....25-35 60
TRI DISC (103 "Why Oh Why")....10-20 62
WORLD ARTISTS (1053 "Sugar Boy")....10-20 65
Also see MARGARET & CHARMETTES

CHARMETTS
Singles: 7-inch
PHILOMEGA....4-6 73-74

CHARMS P&R/R&B '54
(Otis Williams & the Charms; Otis Williams & His New Group; Otis Williams)
Singles: 78 rpm
CHART....20-35 55-56
DELUXE....25-75 54-57
QUALITY/KING....40-60 54
(Canadian.)
ROCKIN'....50-75 53
Singles: 7-inch
CHART (608 "Love's Our Inspiration")....30-50 55
(Has "Vocal Group The Charms" between the horizontal line patterns.)
CHART (608 "Love's Our Inspiration")....25-35 55
(Has "Vocal Group The Charms" below horizontal rope-like lines.)
CHART (613 "Heart of a Rose")....30-50 56
CHART (623 "I'll Be True")....50-100 56
DELUXE (6000 "Heaven Only Knows")....100-200 53
DELUXE (6014 "Happy Are We")....100-200 53
DELUXE (6034 "Bye-Bye Baby")....100-200 54
DELUXE (6050 "Quiet Please")....100-200 54
DELUXE (6056 "My Baby Dearest Darling")....100-200 54
DELUXE (6062 "Who Knows")....50-100 54
DELUXE (6065 "Two Hearts")....25-50 54
DELUXE (6072 "Crazy Crazy Crazy")....25-50 54
DELUXE (6076 "Ling Ting Tong")....25-50 54
DELUXE (6080 "Ko Ko Mo")....25-50 55
DELUXE (6082 "Whadya Want")....15-25 55
DELUXE (6087 "When We Get Together")....20-40 55
DELUXE (6088 "Tell Me Now")....20-40 55
DELUXE (6089 "One Fine Day")....20-40 55
DELUXE (6090 "Save Me, Save Me")....20-40 55
DELUXE (6091 "That's Your Mistake")....15-25 55
DELUXE (6092 "Rolling Home")....15-25 55
DELUXE (6093 "Ivory Tower")....15-25 56
DELUXE (6095 "It's All Over")....15-25 56
DELUXE (6097 "I'd Like to Thank You Mr. Dee Jay")....20-40 56
DELUXE (6098 "I'll Remember You")....15-25 56
DELUXE (6105 "Blues Stay Away from Me")....15-25 56
DELUXE (6115 "Walking After Midnight")....15-25 57
DELUXE (6130 "Nowhere on Earth")....20-40 57
DELUXE (6137 "Talking to Myself")....25-35 57
DELUXE (6138 "United")....25-35 57
DELUXE (6149 "Dynamite Darling")....15-25 57
DELUXE (6158 "Could This Be Magic")....15-25 57
DELUXE (6160 "Baby-O")....20-40 57
DELUXE (6165 "Burning Lips")....15-25 58
DELUXE (6174 "Don't Wake Up the Kids")....15-25 58
DELUXE (6178 "My Friends")....15-25 58
DELUXE (6181 "Welcome Home")....15-25 59
DELUXE (6183 "My Prayer Tonight")....15-25 59
DELUXE (6185 "Tears of Happiness")....15-25 59
(Monaural.)
DELUXE (6185 "Tears of Happiness")....50-75 59
(Stereo.)
DELUXE (6186 "Who Knows")....15-25 59
DELUXE (6187 "Blues Stay Away from Me")....15-25 59
GUSTO....3-5 77
KING (5323 "It's a Treat")....15-25 60
KING (5332 "Rickety Rickshaw Man")....15-25 60
KING (5372 "Image of a Girl")....25-50 60
KING (5389 "So Be It")....10-20 60
KING (5421 "Wait")....10-20 60
KING (5455 "Little Turtle Dove")....10-20 61
KING (5497 "Just Forget About Me")....10-20 61
KING (5527 "Pardon Me")....10-20 61
KING (5558 "Two Hearts")....10-20 61
KING (5682 "When We Get Together")....10-20 62
KING (5816 "It Just Ain't Right")....10-20 63
KING (5880 "Unchain My Heart")....10-20 63
OKEH (7225 "Baby, You Turn Me On")....8-12 65
OKEH (7235 "I Fall to Pieces")....8-12 65
OKEH (7248 "Welcome Home")....8-12 66
OKEH (7261 "Your Sweet Love")....8-12 66
QUALITY/KING (4302 "Hearts of Stone")....50-100 54
(Canadian.)
QUALITY/KING (4323 "Two Hearts")....50-100 54
(Canadian.)
ROCKIN' (516 "Heaven Only Knows")....200-350 53
STOP....5-8
EPs: 7-inch
DELUXE (357 "Hits By the Charms")....200-300 55
DELUXE (364 "Hits By the Charms")....200-300 55
DELUXE (385 "Otis Williams and the Charms")....200-300 56
KING (357 "Hits By the Charms")....50-100 58
KING (364 "Hits By the Charms, Vol. 2")....50-100 58
KING (385 "Otis Williams and His Charms")....50-100 58
LPs: 10/12-inch
DELUXE (570 "All Their Hits")....300-500 58
(With color photo of the group on cover.)
KING (614 "This Is Otis Williams and the Charms")....100-200 59
KING/GUSTO....8-10 78
POWER PAK....8-10 74
Members: Otis Williams; Ron Bradley; Don Peak; Joe Penn; Richard Parker; Rollie Willis.
Also see ESCOS
Also see TINY TOPSY
Also see WILLIAMS, Otis
WILLIS, Rollie, & Contenders

CHARMS
Singles: 7-inch
CANADIAN-AMERICAN (193 "Ram-Bunk-Shush")....10-15 64
EMERSON (101 "Ram-Bunk-Shush")....12-18 64
JAY DEE....25-35 62
MAURY....25-35 63
STUDIO CITY (1009 "Night Train to Memphis")....25-35 64
Member: Gary Ray Emerson.
Also see FINNEY, Maury

CHARMS
(Charms Ltd.)
Singles: 7-inch
EMBLEM (104 "If You Got the Notion")....20-25
EMBLEM (109 "What Goes Up")....20-25

CHARMS
Singles: 7-inch
ESTILL....4-8 69
Member: Linda Evans.
Also see EVANS, Linda

CHARNE, Billy
Singles: 7-inch
RCA....3-5 70
SUSSEX....3-5 72-73
LPs: 10/12-inch
SUSSEX....8-10 72

CHARNEY, Kim
Singles: 7-inch
DOT....10-20 59-60
LAGREE....5-10 59

CHARO LP '77
(With the Salsoul Orchestra)
Singles: 7-inch
CAPITOL....3-5 76
SALSOUL....3-5 77-78
Picture Sleeves
SALSOUL....3-5 78
LPs: 10/12-inch
SALSOUL....5-10 77-78
Also see SALSOUL ORCHESTRA

CHARO, Bert
Singles: 7-inch
AMP....5-10 59

CHARPEES
Singles: 7-inch
ONE-DERFUL....5-10 66

CHARTBUSTERS P&R '64
Singles: 7-inch
BELL....4-8 67
CRUSADER....8-12 65
MUTUAL....5-10 64-65

CHARTERS
(With the Wanderers)
Singles: 7-inch
ALVA (1001 "I Lost You")....200-300 63
MEL-O-DY (104 "Trouble Lover")....1000-1500 62
MERRY GO ROUND (103 "Lost in a Dream")....40-60 64
TARX (1003 "My Rose")....100-200 62

CHARTS P&R '57
Singles: 78 rpm
EVERLAST (5001 "Deserie")....100-150 57
Singles: 7-inch
ABC....3-4 73
COLLECTABLES....3-4 80s
ENJOY (1002 "Deserie")....20-30 62
EVERLAST (5001 "Deserie")....50-100 57
EVERLAST (5002 "Dance Girl")....50-100 57
EVERLAST (5006 "You're the Reason")....50-75 58
EVERLAST (5008 "All Because of Love")....50-75 58
EVERLAST (5010 "My Diane")....60-80 58
EVERLAST (5026 "Deserie")....10-20 63
GUYDEN (2021 "For the Birds")....10-15 59
LOST-NITE....4-8
VEL-V-TONE (102 "Keep Dancing with Me")....50-100
WAND (1112 "Deserie")....15-25 66
WAND (1124 "Livin' the Nightlife")....25-50 66
LPs: 10/12-inch
COLLECTABLES....8-10 86
LOST-NITE....8-12 81
Members: Joe Grier; Steve Brown; Ross Buford; Glen Jackson; Leroy Binns.
Also see COOPER, Les

CHARTS / Bop-Chords / Ladders / Harmonaires
LPs: 10/12-inch
EVERLAST (201 "Our Best to You")....100-200
Also see BOP - CHORDS
Also see CHARTS
Also see LADDERS
Also see HARMONAIRES

CHASE P&R/LP '71
Singles: 7-inch
EPIC....3-5 71-76
LPs: 10/12-inch
EPIC....10-12 71-76
Members: Bill Chase; Jerry Van Blair; Jay Burrid; Dennis Johnson; Ted Piercefield; Phil Porter; Terry Richards; Angel South; Alan Ware.

CHASE, Allan
Singles: 7-inch
CINEMA....5-10 61-62
COLUMBIA....8-12 59-60
JIN....5-10 60

CHASE, Becky C&W '85
Singles: 7-inch
SPRIT HORSE....3-4 85

CHASE, Bobby
Singles: 7-inch
ASCOT (2195 "Missing Someone")....15-25 65

CHASE, Buddy
Singles: 7-inch
20TH FOX....5-10 60

CHASE, Carol C&W '79
Singles: 7-inch
CASABLANCA....3-4 79-80
JANUS....3-5 75
MCA....3-4 80
LPs: 10/12-inch
CASABLANCA....5-10 80
Also see WEST, Jim

CHASE, Chevy
Singles: 7-inch
ARISTA....3-4 80
LPs: 10/12-inch
ARISTA....5-10 80
Also see CHAMAELEON CHURCH
Also see NATIONAL LAMPOON

CHASE, Eddie
Singles: 7-inch
VISCOUNT....15-25 59

CHASE, Ellison P&R '76
Singles: 7-inch
BIG TREE....3-5 76-77
COLUMBIA....3-4 82
MAGNA-GLIDE....3-5 75
LPs: 10/12-inch
COLUMBIA/ARC....5-10 82

CHASE, Jason
Singles: 7-inch
ATCO....4-8 68

CHASE, Lincoln
Singles: 78 rpm
DAWN....8-12 56
DECCA....8-12 53
RCA....8-12 53
Singles: 7-inch
COLUMBIA....5-10 61
DAWN....10-15 56
DECCA....10-15 53
RCA....10-15 53
SPLASH....8-12 59
SWAN....4-8 62
LPs: 10/12-inch
LIBERTY (3076 "The Explosive Lincoln Chase")....30-50 57
PARAMOUNT....8-12 74

CHASER
Singles: 7-inch
CAPITOL....3-4 78

CHASTAIN, Dawn C&W '78
Singles: 7-inch
OAK....3-5 79
PRAIRIE DUST....3-5 78
SRC....3-5 79

CHASTAIN, Jody
Singles: 7-inch
KAY (1002 "My My")....100-150 58

CHASTAIN, Tilfer
Singles: 7-inch
REFLECTOR....3-5 71

CHATEAUS
Singles: 78 rpm
EPIC (9163 "Let Me Tell")....50-75 56
Singles: 7-inch
EPIC (9163 "Let Me Tell")....75-100 56

CHATEAUS
(With Leroy Kirkland & Orchestra)
Singles: 7-inch
W.B. (5023 "Satisfied")....25-50 58
W.B. (5043 "If I Didn't Care")....25-50 59
W.B. (5071 "Ladder of Love")....25-50 59

CHATEAUS
Singles: 7-inch
CORAL (62364 "Honest I Will")....25-40 63

CHATEAUS
Singles: 7-inch
BOSS....10-15 65
JAM....10-15 65
SMASH....5-10 66
SOUND STAGE 7....10-15 65

CHATEAUX
Singles: 7-inch
EYE (100 "Reference Man")....40-60 68
Member: Tommy Bolin
Also see BOLIN, Tommy
Also see SHATTOES

CHATEAUX, Nicky C.
Singles: 7-inch
BAY-SOUND (67012 "Those Good Times")....10-20

CHATER, Kerry P&R '77
Singles: 7-inch
W.B.....3-5 76-78
LPs: 10/12-inch
W.B.....5-10 77-78
Also see PUCKETT, Gary

CHATMAN, Christine
(With Mabel Smith)
Singles: 78 rpm
DECCA (8660 "Hurry Hurry")....10-15 44
Also see BIG MAYBELLE

CHATMAN, Earl
Singles: 7-inch
FORTUNE....10-20 58

CHATMAN, Sam, & Sparks
Singles: 7-inch
BOSS....15-25

CHATTERS
Singles: 7-inch
VIKING (1001 "Teenage Love Affair")....15-25 59

CHAUMONTS
Singles: 7-inch
BAY SOUND (2740 "I Need Your Love")....25-50 67
BAY SOUND (2750 "All of My Life")....20-30 69
CARAVELLE (2470 "I Need Your Love")....50-100 67

CHAUVIGNY, Robert
Singles: 7-inch
TOP RANK....5-10 59

CHAVELLES
Singles: 78 rpm
VITA (127 "Valley of Love")....50-100 56
Singles: 7-inch
VITA (127 "Valley of Love")....150-200 56
Members: Billy Storm; Sheridan Spencer; Gary Pipkins; Bruce Corfield.
Also see STORM, Billy
Also see UNTOUCHABLES
Also see VALIANTS

CHAVELLES
Singles: 7-inch
I-SAY....4-6

CHAVERS, Elliott, & His Blazers
Singles: 7-inch
KING 5-10 61

CHAVEZ, Freddie
Singles: 7-inch
LOOK (5010 "They'll Never Know Why") 50-100 68

CHAVIN
LPs: 10/12-inch
CP 8-10 78

CHAVIS, Boozoo
(Wilson Chavis)
Singles: 78 rpm
FOLK STAR 25-50 55
IMPERIAL 15-25 56
Singles: 7-inch
FOLK STAR (1197 "Boozoo Stomp") 50-75 55
FOLK STAR (1201 "Forty-One Days") 50-75 55
GOLDBAND 5-10 63
IMPERIAL (5374 "Boozoo Stomp") 25-35 56

CHAVIS, Danny
(With the Chavis Brothers)
Singles: 7-inch
GRAPE 4-8
LPs: 10/12-inch
ROC-CO 12-15 78
Also see CHAVIS BROTHERS

CHAVIS BROTHERS
Singles: 7-inch
ASCOT 8-12 65
CLOCK (1025 "So Tired") 25-35 60
CORAL (62270 "Baby, Don't Leave Me") 25-35 61
LPs: 10/12-inch
HOW (410 "Dedicated to You") 50-75 63
Member: Danny Chavis.
Also see CHAVIS, Danny

CHAYNS
(Chaynes)
Singles: 7-inch
CHAYN REACTION ("Night Time") 25-35 67
(No selection number used.)
CHAYN REACTION (002 "Run and Hide") 20-30 68
INTERNATIONAL ARTISTS (114 "Night Time") 15-25 67
INTERNATIONAL ARTISTS (119 "There's Something Wrong") 15-25 67

CHAZ R&B '82
Singles: 7-inch
PROMISE 3-4 82

CHAZ PLUS 2
Singles: 7-inch
MAB JAB 4-8 62

CHEAP SKATES
Singles: 7-inch
BANG 4-8 66

CHEAP TRICK LP '77
Singles: 12-inch
EPIC 5-15 83
Singles: 7-inch
ASYLUM 3-4 81
COLUMBIA 3-4 86
EPIC 3-5 77-91
PASHA 3-4 84
W.B. 3-4 83
Picture Sleeves
EPIC (Except 50814) 3-5 79-88
EPIC (50814 "Voices") 5-10 79
(Promotional issue only.)
EPs: 7-inch
CSP 5-10 81
(Promotional issue only. Made for Nestle's.)
LPs: 10/12-inch
EPIC (Except 35773) 5-10 76-90
EPIC (35773 "Dream Police") 35-40 80
(Picture disc. Promotional issue only.)
EPIC/NU-DISC 10-15 80
(Includes bonus single.)
PASHA 5-10 84
Members: Robin Zander; Tom Petersson; Rick Nielson; Bun E. Carlos; Jon Brant.
Also see CUMMINGS, Burton / Cheap Trick / Crawler
Also see FUSE
Also see GRIM REAPERS
Also see NAZZ
Also see PAEGENS

CHEAP TRICK / Aldo Nova / Saxon
Singles
CBS ("Southwest Tour") 8-12 82
(Square cardboard picture disc. Selection number not known.)
Also see CHEAP TRICK
Also see NOVA, Aldo
Also see SAXON

CHEATER
LPs: 10/12-inch
MALLARD 5-10 80

CHEATERS
(Vic Pitts & Cheaters)
Singles: 7-inch
BREWTOWN 3-5 72
JEWEL 3-5 74
RAYNARD (1056 "You're Mine") 10-15 66
Members: Beverly Pitts; Vic Pitts; Sharon Pitts; Omar Dupree; Lee Brown; Van Patterson; E.C. Reynolds; Ray Maxwell; Bertha Downs; Al Vance; Rollo Armstead; Greg Browder.
Also see PITTS, Beverly, & Cheaters

CHEATERS
Singles: 7-inch
WAX (213 "Suzanne") 25-50 65

CHEATHAM, Inez: see BO, Eddie, & Inez Cheatham

CHEATHAM, Oliver R&B '83
Singles: 7-inch
CRITIQUE 3-4 86-87
MCA 3-4 83
LPs: 10/12-inch
MCA 5-10 83

CHECKER, Chubby P&R '59
(With Dee Dee Sharp)
Singles: 7-inch
ABKCO 3-4 72
AMHERST 3-5 76
BUDDAH 4-6 69
MCA 3-4 82
PARKWAY (006 "The Jet") 10-15 62
PARKWAY (100 series) 5-10 66
PARKWAY (706 "Twist to Blueberry Hill") 10-20 60s
(Promotional issue only.)
PARKWAY (804 thru 810) 10-20 59-60
PARKWAY (811 "The Twist"/ "Toot") 15-25 60
(White label.)
PARKWAY (811 "The Twist"/ "Toot") 10-15 60
(Orange label.)
PARKWAY (811 "The Twist"/ "Twistin' U.S.A.") 5-10 61
(Yellow/orange or orange label.)
PARKWAY (811 "The Twist") 20-30 61
(Colored vinyl.)
PARKWAY (813 thru 959, except 824) 5-10 60-66
PARKWAY (824 "Let's Twist Again") 5-10 61
(Black vinyl.)
PARKWAY (824 "Let's Twist Again") 20-30 61
(Colored vinyl.)
PARKWAY (965 "You Just Don't Know") 100-200 66
PARKWAY (989 "Hey You! Little Boo-Ga-Loo") 5-10 66
20TH FOX 4-6 73-74
Picture Sleeves
PARKWAY 8-15 61-65
EPs: 7-inch
PARKWAY 15-20 61
(Includes Compact 33 Doubles.)
LPs: 10/12-inch
ABKCO 8-12 72
D.C.M. 5-10
EVEREST 5-10 81
51 WEST 5-10 84
MCA 8-10 82
PARKWAY (5001 "Chubby Checker") 20-30 62
PARKWAY (7001 "Twist with Chubby Checker") 20-30 60
PARKWAY (7002 "For Twisters Only") 20-30 60
PARKWAY (7002 "For Teen Twisters Only") 20-30 61
(Monaural.)
PARKWAY (SP-7002 "For Teen Twisters Only") 30-40 61
(Stereo.)
PARKWAY (7003 "It's Pony Time") 20-30 61
PARKWAY (7004 "Let's Twist Again") 20-30 61
PARKWAY (7007 "Your Twist Party with the King of the Twist") 20-30 61
PARKWAY (7008 "Twistin' 'Round the World") 20-30 62
(Monaural.)
PARKWAY (SP-7008 "Twistin' 'Round the World") 30-40 62
(Stereo.)
PARKWAY (7009 "For Teen Twisters Only") 25-35 62
PARKWAY (SP-7009 "For Teen Twisters Only") 30-40 62
PARKWAY (7014 "All the Hits") 20-30 62
(Monaural.)
PARKWAY (SP-7014 "All the Hits") 25-35 62
(Stereo.)
PARKWAY (7020 "Limbo Party") ... 20-30 62
(Monaural.)
PARKWAY (SP-7020 "Limbo Party") 25-35 62
(Stereo.)
PARKWAY (7022 "Biggest Hits") ... 20-30 62
(Monaural.)
PARKWAY (SP-7022 "Biggest Hits") 25-35 62
(Stereo.)
PARKWAY (7026 "In Person") 20-30 63
(Monaural.)
PARKWAY (SP-7026 "In Person") 25-35 63
(Stereo.)
PARKWAY (7027 "Let's Limbo Some More") 20-30 63
(Monaural.)
PARKWAY (SP-7027 "Let's Limbo Some More") 25-35 63
(Stereo.)
PARKWAY (7030 "Beach Party") ... 20-30 63
(Monaural.)
PARKWAY (SP-7030 "Beach Party") 25-35 63
(Stereo.)
PARKWAY (7036 "Chubby Checker") 20-30 63
(Monaural.)
PARKWAY (SP-7036 "Chubby Checker") 25-35 63
(Stereo.)
PARKWAY (7040 "Folk Album") 20-30 63
(Monaural.)
PARKWAY (SP-7040 "Folk Album") 25-35 63
(Stereo.)
PARKWAY (7045 "Discoteque") 15-25 65
(Monaural.)
PARKWAY (SP-7045 "Discoteque") 20-30 65
(Stereo.)
PARKWAY (7048 "18 Golden Hits") 15-25 66
(Monaural.)
PARKWAY (SP-7048 "18 Golden Hits") 20-30 66
(Stereo.)
Also see DREAMLOVERS
Also see FAT BOYS & Chubby Checker
Also see LITTLE SISTERS

CHECKER, Chubby / Gary U.S. Bonds
LPs: 10/12-inch
EXACT 5-10 80
Also see BONDS, Gary "U.S."

CHECKER, Chubby, & Bobby Rydell LP '61
Singles: 7-inch
CAMEO (12 "Your Hits & Mine") 10-20 61
(Promotional issue only.)
CAMEO (200 series) 8-15 61-62
Picture Sleeves
CAMEO 5-10 61
LPs: 10/12-inch
CAMEO (1013 "Chubby Checker & Bobby Rydell") 20-30 61
CAMEO (1063 "Chubby Checker & Bobby Rydell") 20-30 63
Also see RYDELL, Bobby

CHECKER, Chubby, & Dee Dee Sharp LP '62
Singles: 7-inch
PARKWAY (835 "Slow Twistin' ") 5-10 62
PARKWAY (7041 "The Twist") 10-15 63
(Promotional issue only. Bonus single, packaged with *Oldies By the Dozen, Vol. 2*)
LPs: 10/12-inch
CAMEO (1029 "Down to Earth") 20-30 62
Also see CHECKER, Chubby
Also see SHARP, Dee Dee

CHECKER BOARD SQUARE
Singles: 7-inch
VILLA (705 "Double Cooking") ... 100-200

CHECKER DOTS
Singles: 7-inch
PEACOCK (1688 "Alpha Omega") . 20-30 59

CHECKERBOARD SQUARES
Singles: 7-inch
SIM 10-15

CHECKERLADS
Singles: 7-inch
RCA (8986 "Shake Yourself Down") 10-20 66

CHECKERS
Singles: 78 rpm
KING (4558 "Flame in My Heart") 100-200 52
KING (4581 "Night's Curtains") .. 100-200 52
KING (4596 "My Prayer Tonight") 100-200 53
KING (4626 "I Wanna Know") 100-200 53
KING (4673 "I Promise You") 50-100 53
KING (4675 "White Cliffs of Dover") 50-100 53
KING (4710 "House with No Windows") 50-100 54
KING (4719 "Over the Rainbow") 50-100 54
KING (4751 "I Wasn't Thinkin', I Was Drinkin' ") 50-100 54
KING (4764 "Trying to Hold My Girl") 50-100 54
Singles: 7-inch
FEDERAL (12355 "Sentimental Heart") 25-50 59
FEDERAL (12375 "White Cliffs of Dover") 25-50 60
GUSTO 3-5 80
KING (4558 "Flame in My Heart") 500-1000 52
KING (4581 "Night's Curtains") 500-1000 52
KING (4596 "My Prayer Tonight") 500-1000 53
KING (4626 "I Wanna Know") .. 500-1000 53
KING (4673 "I Promise You") 300-500 53
KING (4675 "White Cliffs of Dover") 300-500 53
KING (4710 "House with No Windows") 300-500 54
KING (4719 "Over the Rainbow") 300-500 54
KING (4751 "I Wasn't Thinkin', I Was Drinkin' ") 300-500 54
KING (4764 "Trying to Hold My Girl") 300-500 54
KING (5156 "Heaven Only Knows") 300-500 58
Members: Charlie White; Bill Brown.
Also see DOMINOES
Also see ORIGINAL CHECKERS

CHECKERS
Singles: 7-inch
KING (5199 "Teardrops Are Falling") 30-50 59
(Previously issued as by the Five Wings.)
Also see FIVE WINGS

CHECKERS
Singles: 7-inch
ARVEE (5035 "Skooby Doo") 10-20 61
JERDEN (710 "Black Cat") 10-20 63
PATRICE (8720 "Double Jump") ... 10-20 60

CHECKERS
Singles: 7-inch
SKYLA (1120 "Cascade") 10-20 61

CHECKERS
Singles: 7-inch
MERCURY 5-8 64

CHECKERS
Singles: 7-inch
MICKAY'S (3008 "Applesauce") 10-20 65

CHECKERS
Singles: 7-inch
DOTTIE (1001 "Big Car") 5-10

CHECKERS
Singles: 7-inch
SUR-SPEED 10-20

CHECK-MATES
Singles: 7-inch
BLACK DOG (1001 "Scrappy") 15-25 59
(Reissued as by the Shamrocks.)
Member: Jim Ford.
Also see FORD, Jim
Also see SHAMROCKS

CHECKMATES
Singles: 7-inch
CHAMP 15-20
LONDON INT'L 5-10 63
RUFF 8-12 65

CHECK-MATES
Singles: 7-inch
REGENCY 5-10 64

CHECKMATES
LPs: 10/12-inch
JUSTICE (149 "Checkmate") 350-500 68
Members: Billy Carden; Baron Conklin; Dave Mack; John McCurdy; Jon Mueller; George Outlaw; Roddy Porter; Sammy Winston.

CHECKMATES LTD. P&R/LP '69
(Featuring Sonny Charles)
Singles: 7-inch
A&M 4-6 69
CAPITOL (5603 "Do the Walk") 10-20 66
CAPITOL (5753 "Kissin' Her and Cryin' for You") 20-30 66
CAPITOL (5814 "Please Don't Take My World Away") 10-20 67
CAPITOL (5922 "A&I") 10-20 67
FANTASY 3-5 77-78
GREEDY 3-5 77
RUSTIC 3-5 74
LPs: 10/12-inch
A&M (4183 "Love Is All We Have to Give") 15-25 69
CAPITOL (2840 "Live") 25-35 67
FANTASY 8-10 77
IKON 5-10
POLYDOR 8-10 76
RUSTIC 8-10 74
Members: Sonny Charles; Bill Van Buskirk; Marvin Smith; Bobby Stevens; Harvey Trees.
Also see CHARLES, Sonny
Also see STEVENS, Bobby, & Checkmates Ltd.

CHECKPOINT CHARLIE
LPs: 10/12-inch
RHINO 5-10 82

CHEECH & CHONG LP '71
Singles: 7-inch
A&M 3-4
EPIC/ODE 3-5 77
MCA 3-4 85
ODE 3-5 71-77
W.B. 3-4 78
Picture Sleeves
A&M 3-4
MCA 3-4 85
ODE 8-12 73-77
W.B. 3-4 78
EPs: 7-inch
ODE (8 "Cheech & Chong") 5-8 71
LPs: 10/12-inch
("Cheech & Chong") 40-50 83
(No label name or selection number used. Promotional only, unplayable picture disc.)
EPIC/ODE 8-10 77
MCA 5-8 85
ODE 8-12 71-76
W.B. 8-10 78-80
Members: Richard Marin; Thomas Chong.
Also see TAYLOR, Bobby

CHEE-CHEE & PEPPY P&R/R&B '71
Singles: 7-inch
BUDDAH 3-5 71
LPs: 10/12-inch
BUDDAH 10-15 72
Members: Dorothy Moore; Keith Bolling.
Also see MOORE, Dorothy

CHEEK
EPs: 7-inch
VOXX 5-10

CHEEK & TONG PLAYERS
Singles: 7-inch
GESUNDHEIT (0000 "The Light Before Christmas") 5-10 77
Members: Steve Baron; Brian Mason; Rick Northcutt.

CHEEK-O-VASS & SOLA-TEARS
Singles: 7-inch
TWY-LITE (752 "Bo-Peep Rock") 100-150
Also see VANCE, Chico

CHEEKS
Singles: 7-inch
CAPITOL 3-4 80

CHEEKS, Judy P&R/R&B '78
Singles: 7-inch
DREAM 3-4 80
SALSOUL 3-4 78
U.A. 3-5 73
LPs: 10/12-inch
SALSOUL 5-10 78
U.A. 8-10 73

CHEEKS, Maurice
Singles: 12-inch
SUTRA 4-6 84
Singles: 7-inch
SUTRA 3-4 84

CHEEPSKATES
Singles: 7-inch
MIDNIGHT 3-4
LPs: 10/12-inch
MIDNIGHT 5-10

CHEER LEADERS
Singles: 7-inch
ENCORE 4-8 62

CHEERFUL EARFULLS
Singles: 7-inch
STEPHENY 5-10 58
ZALE 5-10

CHEERIOS
Singles: 7-inch
INFINITY (011 "Ding Dong Honeymoon") 150-250 61
GOLDEN OLDIES (1 "Ding Dong Honeymoon") 10-20

CHEERS P&R '54
(With Les Baxter's Orchestra & Chorus)
Singles: 78 rpm
CAPITOL 10-20 54-56
MERCURY 10-15 57
Singles: 7-inch
CAPITOL 20-30 54-56
MERCURY 15-25 57
EPs: 7-inch
CAPITOL (584 "Bazoom") 50-100 55
Members: Bert Convy; Gil Garfield; Susan Allen.
Also see BAXTER, Les
Also see CONVY, Bert

CHEERS
Singles: 7-inch
NRC 8-12 58

CHEERS
Singles: 7-inch
OKEH 3-6 69-70
PENNY 4-8 66-67

CHEERLEADERS
Singles: 7-inch
RSVP 5-8 66

CHEERTONES
Singles: 7-inch
ABC-PAR 5-10 61

CHEESE CAKES
Singles: 7-inch
LAURIE 4-8 66

CHEESEDOOS
EPs: 7-inch
CHEDDAR PUP ("Cheesedoos") ... 10-15 81
(No selection number used.)

CHEESMAN, Judy
Singles: 7-inch
REDD HEDD 3-5 76
Members: Arlie Miller; Arlie Neaville.
Also see MILLER, Arlie, & Bullets
Also see NEAVILLE, Arlie

CHEETAH
Singles: 7-inch
ATLANTIC 3-4 82
LPs: 10/12-inch
ATLANTIC 5-10 82

CHEETAHS
Singles: 7-inch
COLUMBIA 4-8 67
PHILIPS 4-8 64

CHEEZ-IT-RITZ
Singles: 7-inch
PIGFACE (003 "Disco Diarrhea") ... 10-15
Picture Sleeves
PIGFACE (003 "Disco Diarrhea") ... 10-20

CHEEZMO
EPs: 7-inch
KATZ PAJAMAZ 4-8 82
(With paper sleeve.)

CHEKKERS
Singles: 7-inch
LOOK 4-8 67

CHELETTE, Mary Jo
Singles: 78 rpm
STARDAY 10-20 53-54
Singles: 7-inch
STARDAY (101 "Cat Fishing") 15-25 53
STARDAY (112 "Son of Mexican Joe") 15-25 53
STARDAY (121 "He Likes Me") 15-25 54

CHELL-MARS
Singles: 7-inch
HI-MAR (505 "Roamin' Heart") 15-25 60s
JAMIE 10-15 63
Also see CHELMARS

CHELLO, Peter
Singles: 7-inch
TIARA 5-10 59

CHELLOS
Singles: 7-inch
WGW 8-12 62

CHELLOWS
Singles: 7-inch
PONCELLO (713 "Be My Baby") 25-50 60s

CHELMARS
Singles: 7-inch
SELECT 10-15 63
Also see CHELL-MARS

CHELSEA
LPs: 10/12-inch
DECCA 10-15 71
I.R.S. 5-10 80-82
Also see GENERATION X
Also see IDOL, Billy
Also see IF

CHELSEA BEIGE
Singles: 7-inch
EPIC 3-5 71
LPs: 10/12-inch
EPIC 10-12 71

CHELSEA BOYS
Singles: 7-inch
KEF 3-6 69

CHEMAY, Joe P&R '81
(Joe Chemay Band)
Singles: 7-inch
UNICORN 3-4 81
LPs: 10/12-inch
UNICORN 5-10 81

CHENAULT, Eva Lena
Singles: 7-inch
VOKES 4-8 67

CHENAULT, Teenie
Singles: 7-inch
ALEAR 5-10 64-67

CHENIER, Big: see BIG CHENIER

CHENIER, Clifton
(With the Red Hot Louisiana Band)
Singles: 78 rpm
ARGO 15-25 56-57
POST 20-30 54
SPECIALTY 10-20 55
Singles: 7-inch
ARGO 20-30 56-58
ARHOOLIE 4-8 64-76
BAYOU 5-10 65-66
BELL 4-6 69
CHECKER 10-15 60
CRAZY CAJUN 4-8
POST (2010 "Rockin' the Bop") 30-50 54
POST (2016 "Rockin' Hop") 30-50 54
SPECIALTY 15-25 55
ZYNN 5-10 61
LPs: 10/12-inch
ALLIGATOR 5-10 82
ARHOOLIE 8-10 69-83
BLUE THUMB (8815 "Very Best") 15-25 70
GNP 8-10 78
PROPHESY 10-15 70
SPECIALTY 8-10 70
UTOPIA 10-12 76
Also see BERNARD, Rod / Clifton Chenier
Also see CHANIER, Cliston
Also see PERSIANS / Clifton Chenier

CHENIER, Rosco
Singles: 7-inch
REYNAUD (1018 "I Broke the Yo Yo") 15-25 63

CHENTELLES
Singles: 7-inch
FENTON (2032 "Be My Queen") 50-75 67

CHEPITO, Jose
Singles: 7-inch
COLUMBIA 3-5 74
LPs: 10/12-inch
COLUMBIA 8-10 74

CHEQUERED PAST LP '84
Singles: 7-inch
EMI AMERICA 3-4 84
LPs: 10/12-inch
EMI AMERICA 5-10 84
Members: Clem Burke; Nigel Harrison.
Also see LITTLE GIRLS
Also see SILVERHEAD

CHEQUERS
Singles: 7-inch
SCEPTER 3-5 75

CHEQUES
Singles: 7-inch
HIP 5-10 69
SUR-SPEED 10-20

CHER P&R/LP '65
(Cher Bono; Cher Allman)
Singles: 12-inch
CASABLANCA 8-10 79-82
Singles: 7-inch
ATCO 3-6 69-72
ATLANTIC 4-6 69
CASABLANCA 3-5 79
COLUMBIA 3-5 82
GEFFEN 3-4 87-91
IMPERIAL 5-10 64-68
KAPP 3-5 71-72
LIBERTY 3-4 82
MCA 3-5 73-75
U.A. 3-5 71-72
W.B. 3-5 75-77
W.B./SPECTOR 3-5 74
Picture Sleeves
COLUMBIA 3-5 82
GEFFEN 3-4 87-89
LPs: 10/12-inch
ATCO 15-20 69
CASABLANCA (Except NBPIX-7133) 8-12 79
CASABLANCA (NBPIX-7133 "Take Me Home") 50-75 79
(Picture disc.)
COLUMBIA 5-10 82
GEFFEN 5-12 87-91
IMPERIAL 15-25 65-68
KAPP 12-15 71-72
LIBERTY 5-10 81
MCA 10-15 73-74
SPRINGBOARD 8-10 72
SUNSET 8-10 70
U.A. 8-10 71-75
W.B. 8-15 75-77
Also see ALLMAN & WOMAN
Also see BLACK ROSE
Also see CHERILYN / Cherilyn's Group
Also see MASON, Bonnie Jo
Also see SONNY & CHER

CHER & Peter Cetera P&R '89
Singles: 7-inch
GEFFEN 3-4 89
Picture Sleeves
GEFFEN 3-4 89
Also see CETERA, Peter

CHER & NILSSON
Singles: 7-inch
SPECTOR 3-5 75
Members: Cher; Harry Nilsson.
Also see CHER
Also see NILSSON, Harry

CHERI P&R/R&B '82
Singles: 12-inch
21 4-6 83
Singles: 7-inch
21 3-4 83
VENTURE 3-4 82
Members: Rosalind Hunt; Amy Roslyn.

CHERILYN / Cherilyn's Group
(Cher Bono)
Singles: 7-inch
IMPERIAL (66081 "Dream Baby") 20-30 64
Also see CHER

CHERLOS
Singles: 78 rpm
ULTRA D'OR 50-75 56
Singles: 7-inch
ULTRA D'OR (8 "99 ½ Won't Do") 100-150 56

CHERMAY, Joe
Singles: 7-inch
UNICORN 3-5 80

CHEROKEE
Singles: 7-inch
ABC 3-6 71
LPs: 10/12-inch
ABC 12-15 70
Member: Dee Donaldson.
Also see ROBBS

CHEROKEE, Chris
Singles: 7-inch
TURRET 4-8 67

CHEROKEES
Singles: 78 rpm
GRAND 200-300 54
PEACOCK 50-75 55
Singles: 7-inch
COLLECTABLES 3-4 84
GRAND (106 "Rainbow of Love") 500-1000 54
(Yellow label. Rigid disc.)
GRAND (110 "Please Tell Me So") 500-1000 54
(Yellow label. Rigid disc.)
PEACOCK (1656 "Is She Real") 100-200 55
Member: Russell Carter.

CHEROKEES
Singles: 7-inch
GUYDEN 5-10 60
Picture Sleeves
GUYDEN 10-20 60

CHEROKEES
Singles: 7-inch
U.A. (367 "My Heavenly Angel") 50-75 61
Member: Fred Parris.
Also see PARRIS, Fred

CHEROKEES
Singles: 7-inch
CHALLENGE 5-10 62

CHEROKEES
Singles: 7-inch
MGM 4-8 65

CHERRELLE P&R/R&B/D&D/LP '84
Singles: 12-inch
TABU 4-6 84-86
Singles: 7-inch
TABU 3-4 84-88
Picture Sleeves
TABU 3-4 88
LPs: 10/12-inch
TABU 5-10 84-88
Also see O'NEAL, Alexander, & Cherrelle

CHERRIES & Rhythm King
Singles: 7-inch
DELLA 5-10

CHERRY, Ava R&B '80
Singles: 12-inch
CAPITOL 4-6 82
Singles: 7-inch
CAPITOL 3-4 82
CURTOM 3-4 80
RSO 3-4 80
LPs: 10/12-inch
RSO 5-10 80

CHERRY, Carl
Singles: 7-inch
TENE (1023 "The Itch") 150-250 59

CHERRY, Chuckle: see CHERRY, Miss Chuckle

CHERRY, Don P&R '54
Singles: 78 rpm
COLUMBIA 5-10 55-57
DECCA 5-10 50-56
Singles: 7-inch
COLUMBIA 5-10 55-59
DECCA 8-12 50-56
MONUMENT 3-5 65-78
STRAND 4-8 59
VERVE 4-8 62
WARWICK 4-8 60
EPs: 7-inch
COLUMBIA 8-15 56
LPs: 10/12-inch
COLUMBIA 15-25 56
HARMONY 10-15 59
MONUMENT 8-12 66-73
Also see DAY, Doris, & Don Cherry
Also see TUNESMITHS with Rosemary Clooney & Don Cherry

CHERRY, Jo Ann
Singles: 7-inch
LOCKET 4-8

CHERRY, Miss Chuckle
Singles: 7-inch
GRASSROOTS 4-8 72

CHERRY, Neneh P&R/LP '89
Singles: 7-inch
VIRGIN 3-4 89
Picture Sleeves
VIRGIN 3-4 89
LPs: 10/12-inch
VIRGIN 5-8 89

CHERRY, Tommy, & Niteriders
Singles: 7-inch
SMOKE 5-10 60

CHERRY BLEND
Singles: 7-inch
KING 3-5 72

CHERRY PEOPLE P&R '68
Singles: 7-inch
HERITAGE 4-8 68-69
Picture Sleeves
HERITAGE 6-10 68
LPs: 10/12-inch
HERITAGE 15-20 68
Members: Punky Meadows; Doug Grimes; Chris Grimes; Rocky Isaac.
Also see ANGEL

CHERRY SLUSH
Singles: 7-inch
COCONUT GROVE (2032 "I Cannot Stop You") 20-30 67
U.S.A. (895 "I Cannot Stop You") 10-20 68
U.S.A. (904 "Gotta Take It Easy") 10-20 68

CHERRYHILL TRIO
Singles: 7-inch
CAPITOL 4-8 63

CHERUBS
Singles: 7-inch
DORE 5-10 60

CHERVAL, Frank
(With Cinnamon Calliope)
Singles: 7-inch
ACE 4-8 62
BIG B 20-25
CONGRESS 4-8 65
LAURIE 4-8 63
MERCURY 4-8 64
MGM 5-10 62
NOLA 4-8 66
WIZDOM 4-6 70

CHERYL
Singles: 7-inch
TAHOE 3-4 82

CHERYL & PAM
Singles: 7-inch
STAX 4-8 63

CHERYL ANN
Singles: 7-inch
PATTY (52 "I Can't Let Him") 50-100

CHERYL LYNN: see LYNN, Cheryl

CHESAPEAKE JUKE BOX BAND
Singles: 7-inch
GREENE BOTTLE 3-5 72
LPs: 10/12-inch
GREENE BOTTLE 8-12 72

CHESNUT, Jim C&W '77
Singles: 7-inch
ABC/HICKORY 3-5 77-78
LIBERTY 3-4 81
MCA 3-5 79
U.A. 3-4 80
LPs: 10/12-inch
ABC/HICKORY 6-12 77-78

CHESNUTT, Mark C&W/LP '90
Singles: 7-inch
MCA 3-4 90-91
LPs: 10/12-inch
MCA 5-8 90-91

CHESS & CHECKER
Singles: 7-inch
CHICORY 4-8 64

CHESS, Tubby, & His Candy Stripe Twisters
LPs: 10/12-inch
GRAND PRIX 10-15 62

CHESSMAN SQUARE
Singles: 7-inch
LION (1002 "Circles") 15-25 69
Picture Sleeves
LION (1002 "Circles") 25-50 69

CHESSMEN
Singles: 7-inch
SAFARI (1011 "Keeper of My Love") 150-250 58

CHESSMEN
(With the Karol-Thorn Orchestra)
Singles: 7-inch
MIRASONIC (1002 "I Live for You") 100-200 58

CHESSMEN
Singles: 7-inch
GOLDEN CREST (2661 "Bells Bells") 1000-2000 59

CHESSMEN
Singles: 7-inch
PAC (100 "Lola") 100-200 61
(Blue label.)
PAC (100 "Lola") 400-500 61
(White label. Promotional issue.)

CHESSMEN
Singles: 7-inch
AMC (101 "Mr. Cupid") 20-30 62
AMY (841 "Stormy Dreams") 20-30 62
DON-DEE (101 "Mr. Cupid") 10-20 63

CHESSMEN
Singles: 7-inch
GMA (12 "Touchdown") 20-30 60s
(Canadian.)
JERDEN (743 "Mustang") 10-15 64
LONDON (17334 "Mustang") 15-25 64
(First issue. Canadian.)
Also see BEDIENT, Jack, & Chessmen

CHESSMEN
("Featuring Tom Salem")
Singles: 7-inch
G-CLEF (707 "Sorry") 50-100 64
Member: Tom Salem.

CHESSMEN
Singles: 7-inch
SALEM (001 "It'll Be Me") 150-200 65

CHESSMEN
Singles: 7-inch
RELIC (1015 "I Apologize") 5-10 65
RELIC (1016 "Ways of Romance") 5-10 65
RELIC (1017 "That's My Desire") 5-10 65

CHESSMEN
Singles: 7-inch
CHESS (1950 "Why Can't I Be Your Man") 15-25 66
MERCURY (72498 "Love Didn't Die") 5-10 65
MERCURY (72498 "Love Didn't Die") 5-10 65
MERCURY (72559 "Running Wild") 5-10 66
RAZORBACK (119 "She's the One for Me") 5-10 65

CHESSMEN
Singles: 7-inch
PHALANX (1018 "You Can't Catch Me") 40-50 66

CHESSMEN
Singles: 7-inch
BISMARK (1010 "Dreams and Wishes") 10-20 66
BISMARK (1012 "I Need You There") 15-25 66
BISMARK (1014 "No More") 15-25 66

CHESSMEN
Singles: 7-inch
COULEE 10-15

CHESTER
Singles: 7-inch
BELL 3-5 73-74

CHESTER, Gary
Singles: 7-inch
CORAL 4-8 63
LPs: 10/12-inch
DCP (6803 "Yeah, Yeah, Yeah") 15-25 64

CHESTER, John, & Chessmen
Singles: 7-inch
INTERPHON 4-8 64

CHESTER, Johnny, & Thunderbirds
Singles: 7-inch
MELBOURNE 5-10

CHESTERFIELD KINGS
Singles: 7-inch
LIVING EYE (1 "Exit 9") 8-12 80
LIVING EYE (2 "You Can't Catch Me") 8-12 82
LIVING EYE (3 "Exit 9") 8-12 82
MIRROR ("A Dark Corner") 3-5 83
(No selection number used.)
MIRROR ("She Told Me Lies") 3-5 84
(No selection number used.)
MIRROR (2061 "I'm Going Home") 3-5 82
Picture Sleeves
LIVING EYE (1 "Exit 9") 8-12 80
LIVING EYE (3 "Exit 9") 8-12 82
MIRROR ("A Dark Corner") 3-5 83
(No selection number used.)
MIRROR ("She Told Me Lies") 3-5 84
(No selection number used.)
MIRROR (2061 "I'm Going Home") 3-5 82
LPs: 10/12-inch
MIRROR 8-12 82-90

CHESTERFIELDS
Singles: 78 rpm
CHESS (1559 "I'm in Heaven") 50-100 54
Singles: 7-inch
CHESS (1559 "I'm in Heaven") 200-300 54

CHESTERFIELDS
Singles: 7-inch
CUB 10-20 58
Member: Al Reno.
Also see RENO, Al

CHESTERFIELDS
Singles: 7-inch
PHILIPS (40060 "A Dream Is But a Dream") 100-200 62

CHESTERFIELDS
Singles: 7-inch
A&M 4-6 78

CHESTERS
Singles: 78 rpm
APOLLO 20-30 57
Singles: 7-inch
APOLLO (521 "The Fires Burn No More") 25-50 57
Members: "Little Anthony" Guardine; Tracy Lord; Ernest Wright; Nat Rogers; Keith Williams; Clarence Collins.
Also see LITTLE ANTHONY & IMPERIALS

CHESTNUT, Morris
Singles: 7-inch
AMY (981 "Too Darn Soulful") 100-200 66

CHESTNUT TREE
Singles: 7-inch
PARAMOUNT 4-8

CHESTNUTS
Singles: 78 rpm
MERCURY (70489 "Don't Go") 25-50 54
Singles: 7-inch
MERCURY (70489 "Don't Go") 75-100 54
Member: Louis Heyward.

CHESTNUTS
(Lyman Hopkins & Chestnuts; Ruby Whitaker & Chestnuts; "Featuring Ruby Whitaker")
Singles: 78 rpm
DAVIS 35-50 56
ELDORADO 25-50 57
STANDORD 100-200 57
Singles: 7-inch
DAVIS (447 "Love Is True") 100-150 56
(Copies on Crescent [45-201] are boots.)
DAVIS (452 "Forever I Vow") 150-250 56
ELDORADO (511 "Who Knows Better Than I") 50-100 57
STANDORD (100 "Who Knows Better Than I") 150-250 57
Members: Ruby Whitaker; Lyman Hopkins; Franklin Hopkins; Reuben White; Jimmy Curtis; Sylvester Hopkins; Bill Baker.
Also see BAKER, Bill, & Chestnuts

CHESTNUTS
Singles: 7-inch
ALADDIN (3444 "This Is My Love") 25-35 58

CHESTNUTS
Singles: 7-inch
CORAL (62176 "Endless Love") 8-12 60

CHESTNUTS
Singles: 7-inch
NIGHT TRAIN (906 "Rock & Roll Tragedy") 20-30 50s

CHET & CHARLIE
Singles: 7-inch
SMART (1002 "The Apartment") 5-10

CHET, FLOYD & DANNY: see ATKINS, Chet, Floyd Cramer & Danny Davis

CHEVALIER, Jay
Singles: 7-inch
GOLDBAND (1105 "Castro Rock") 15-25 60

MINARET (120 "Big Wheels")......... 8-12 64
PEL (201 "High School Days")...100-200 58
RECCO (1002 "Ballad of Earl K. Long") 10-15 60

CHEVALIER, Jay, & Shelley Ford C&W '79
Singles: 7-inch
CREOLE GOLD............................ 3-5 78
Also see CHEVALIER, Jay

CHEVELLE V
Singles: 7-inch
ASKEL (7 "Come Back Bird").........20-30 66
TITAN (1737 "Dangling Little Friends")...............................10-20 67
UMI (100 "Come Back Bird")..........10-20 66
Picture Sleeves
TITAN (1737 "Dangling Little Friends")...............................20-25 67

CHEVELLES
Singles: 7-inch
CHEVELLE (101 "Riptide") 25-35 63
FLAMING ARROW......................... 5-10 68
SD 15-25

CHEVELLES
Singles: 7-inch
BANGAR (603 "Blue Chevelle").....25-35 64
BANGAR (603 "Chevelle Stomp") 20-30 64
Picture Sleeves
BANGAR (603 "Blue Chevelle").....60-80 64
Also see DEE JAY & RUNAWAYS
Also see STOREY, Denny

CHEVELLES
Singles: 7-inch
INFINITY (029 "I'm Sorry")..............15-25 64
Also see TURNER, Betty

CHEVELLS
Singles: 7-inch
JUSTICE (1004 "Pretty Little Girl") 75-100

CHEVELS
Singles: 7-inch
GASS (1001 "Hendersonville").......10-15 63
MUSICLAND 10-15

CHEVELS
Singles: 7-inch
BUTANE...15-25

CHEVIES
Singles: 7-inch
DOVE (1033 "Love That Girl") 250-350 59

CHEVIES & PREMIERS
Singles: 7-inch
INTERN... 4-8 63

CHEVRONS
Singles: 7-inch
BRENT (7000 "That Comes with Love")..25-50 59
BRENT (7007 "Lullabye")..............25-50 59
BRENT (7015 "Little Star")............25-50 60
TIME (1 "Come Go with Me").........20-30 60
LPs: 10/12-inch
TIME (10008 "Sing-A-Long Rock & Roll")..................................100-200 61

CHEVRONS
Singles: 7-inch
SARA 10-15 63-64
Member: Dave Zadra; Fred Herrmann; Tom Olivas; Jim Woelfel; Ken Vanslett; Tom Louchbaum.

CHEVRONS
Singles: 7-inch
KISKI (2065 "The Jones Girl")........25-35 64

CHEVRONS
Singles: 7-inch
FENTON (2092 "Hey Little Teaser") 15-25 66

CHEVRONS
Singles: 7-inch
INDEPENDENCE 10-15 68
MMC...10-20 68

CHEV-RONS
Singles: 7-inch
GAIT (100 "The Defense Rest")...75-125 62
(Also issued on the same label, by Lee Ward.)
Also see WARD, Lee

CHEW
Singles: 7-inch
CAPITOL.. 3-4 83
LPs: 10/12-inch
CAPITOL.. 5-10 83

CHEYENNE
Singles: 7-inch
BELL 3-5 74
CENTURY VII 3-4 80
CURRENT ATTRACTIONS 3-5 71
LPs: 10/12-inch
SHADYBROOK 8-10 76

CHEYNE R&B/D&D '85
Singles: 12-inch
MCA 4-6 85

CHI CHI
(With the Bill Beau Trio)
Singles: 7-inch
DUNHILL... 4-8 65
KAPP.. 4-6 66

CHIC P&R/R&B/LP '77
Singles: 12-inch 33/45
ATLANTIC (Except 131) 4-8 78-83
ATLANTIC (131 "Le Freak")...........20-25 78
(Picture disc. Promotional issue only.)
Singles: 7-inch
ATLANTIC.. 3-5 77-83
MIRAGE 3-4 82
Picture Sleeves
ATLANTIC 3-5 78-80
LPs: 10/12-inch
ATLANTIC.......................................5-10 77-82
Also see HONEYDRIPPERS
Also see NORMA JEAN
Also see RODGERS, Nile
Also see ROUNDTREE

CHIC / Leif Garrett / Roberta Flack / Genesis
EPs: 7-inch
W.B. SPECIAL PRODUCTS...........8-12 78
(Coca-Cola/Burger King promotional issue. Issued with paper sleeve.)
Also see CHIC
Also see FLACK, Roberta
Also see GARRETT, Leif
Also see GENESIS

CHIC & DIPLOMATS
Singles: 7-inch
IVANHOE 4-8

CHICAGO P&R/LP '69
Singles: 12-inch
COLUMBIA.. 4-8 80
Singles: 7-inch
COLUMBIA.. 3-6 69-80
FULL MOON 3-4 82-86
REPRISE... 3-4 88-91
W.B... 3-4 87
Picture Sleeves
COLUMBIA.. 3-6 69-77
FULL MOON 3-4 84-86
REPRISE... 3-4 88-89
W.B... 3-4 87
EPs: 7-inch
COLUMBIA.....................................10-15 70-73
(Juke box issues only.)
LPs: 10/12-inch
ACCORD.. 5-10 81
COLUMBIA ("Chicago")...............200-250 76
(No selection number used. Boxed set of first 10 LPs [17 discs]. Promotional issue only.)
COLUMBIA (8 "Chicago Transit Authority")......................................25-35 69
COLUMBIA (24 "Chicago II") 20-30 70
COLUMBIA (C2-30110 "Chicago III")...................................10-20 70
COLUMBIA (C2Q-30110 "Chicago III")...................................20-25 74
(Quadrophonic.)
COLUMBIA (30863 "Chicago IV") ..15-20 71
COLUMBIA (CAX-30865 "Chicago IV")....................................20-30 71
(Boxed, four-disc set. Includes three posters, booklet and card.)
COLUMBIA (CQ-30865 "Chicago IV")....................................20-30 74
(Quadrophonic.)
COLUMBIA (31102 thru 38590) 8-15 72-82
(With "C2," "FC," "HC," "KC," "JC," or "PC" prefix.)
COLUMBIA (31102 thru 34200)...15-25 74-76
(Quadrophonic. With "CQ," "C2Q," "GQ," or "PCQ" prefix.)
COLUMBIA (43000 & 44000 series)...15-25 82
(Half-speed mastered.)
FULL MOON 5-10 82-86
MFSL (2-128 "Chicago Transit Authority")......................................30-40 85
REPRISE... 5-8 88-89
SHOWCASE (121 "Chicago Live") ..8-10 85
MAGNUM 10-12 78
W.B. 5-8 86
Members: Peter Cetera; Terry Kath; Robert Lamm; James Pankow; Lee Loughnane; Daniel Seraphine; Walter Parazaider; Bill Champlin; Donnie Dacus; Jason Scheff.
Also see BEACH BOYS
Also see CETERA, Peter
Also see CHAMPLIN, Bill
Also see GUERCIO, James William
Also see LAMM, Robert

CHICAGO, Artie
(Artie Chicago from the Bronx)
Singles: 7-inch
LAURIE 5-10 68
Also see MARESCA, Ernie
Also see TREMONTS

CHICAGO BEARS SHUFFLIN' CREW P&R/R&B '86
Singles: 12-inch
RED LABEL.. 4-8 85
Singles: 7-inch
RED LABEL... 3-4 85
Picture Sleeves
RED LABEL... 3-4 85
Members: Walter Payton; Willie Gault; Mike Singletary; Jim McMahon; Otis Wilson; Steve Fuller; Mike Richardson; Richard Dent; Gary Fencik; William Perry.

CHICAGO BILL
(Bill Broonzy)
Singles: 78 rpm
MELODISC.......................................10-20 51
Also see BROONZY, Big Bill

CHICAGO BLUES ALLSTARS
LPs: 10/12-inch
BASF...8-10

CHICAGO FIRE
Singles: 7-inch
U.S.A. 4-8 68

CHICAGO GANGSTERS R&B '75
Singles: 7-inch
GOLD PLATE.....................................3-5 75-76
RCA 3-5 78
RED COACH.......................................3-5 74-75
LPs: 10/12-inch
GOLD PLATE.................................10-12 75-76
Members: Sam McCant; James McCant; Larry McCant; Chris McCant.

CHICAGO LOOP P&R '66
Singles: 7-inch
DYNO VOICE.......................................4-8 66-67
MERCURY...4-8 67-68

CHICAGO PROHIBITION - 1931
Singles: 7-inch
BUDDAH 4-8 68

CHICAGO SLIM & STU RAMSAY
LPs: 10/12-inch
CAPITOL..10-15 69
Also see RAMSAY, Stu

CHICAGO STRUGGLERS
Singles: 7-inch
MAESTRO 4-8 65

CHICAGO SUNNY BOY
(Joe Hill Louis)
Singles: 78 rpm
METEOR (5004 "Western Union Man")....................................200-300 53
METEOR (5008 "Love You Baby")....................................200-300 53
Singles: 7-inch
METEOR (5004 "Western Union Man")....................................500-750 53
(Though a higher number than *Western Union Man* original 45s of 5008 are not known to exist.)
Also see LOUIS, Joe Hill

CHICAGO TRANSIT AUTHORITY: see CHICAGO

CHICAGO WOMEN'S LIBERATION ROCK BAND
LPs: 10/12-inch
ROUNDER 5-10 72

CHICANO, El: see EL CHICANO

CHICK, Tony
Singles: 7-inch
HY-JOY (1001 "A Car")...................15-25

CHICK & HOT RODS C&W '61
Singles: 7-inch
KING 5-10 61
Members: Don Reno; Red Smiley.
Also see RENO & SMILEY

CHICK & NOBLES
Singles: 7-inch
U.S.A. (772 "I Cry")............................8-12 65
Also see NOBLES

CHICK & RICK
Singles: 7-inch
KENCO 8-10 61

CHICKEN SHACK
Singles: 7-inch
BLUE HORIZON...................................3-5 70-72
DERAM 3-5 73
EPIC...4-8 68
LPs: 10/12-inch
BLUE HORIZON...............................10-15 69-70
DERAM 10-12 72-73
EPIC..10-20 68
LONDON 10-15 73
Members: Stan Webb; Christine McVie; Tony Ashton; Dave Bidwell; Bob Daisley; Paul Hancock; John Glascock; Chris Mercer; Alan Powell; Paul Raymonde; Andy Silvester; Mac Poole.
Also see McVIE, Christine
Also see SAVOY BROWN

CHIC-LETS
Singles: 7-inch
JOSIE...8-12 64

CHIC-LETS
LPs: 10/12-inch
BOLD 5-10 80

CHICO: see HOLIDAY, Chico

CHICO & CHA CHA
Singles: 7-inch
SCORPI 4-8 67

CHICORY P&R '72
(Chicory Tip)
Singles: 7-inch
EPIC...3-5 72-73
LPs: 10/12-inch
EPIC..10-12 72

CHIEF WING NUT
Singles: 7-inch
WHITE WHALE.....................................3-5 70

CHIEFS
Singles: 7-inch
GREENWICH (408 "Apache")........10-20 58
GREENWICH (410 "Enchiladas") ..10-20 58
VALIANT 10-15 63

CHIEFTAINS LP '76
Singles: 7-inch
ISLAND 3-5 76
LPs: 10/12-inch
COLUMBIA 5-10 78-80
ISLAND 5-10 75-78
Also see MORRISON, Van, & Chieftains

CHIEFTONES
Singles: 7-inch
CUCA (1287 "Do Lord") 10-15 66
Also see THUNDERKLOUD, Billy, & Chieftones

CHIFFONS P&R '60
Singles: 7-inch
B.T. PUPPY (558 "My Secret Love") 4-8 70
BIG DEAL (6003 "Tonight's the Night")......................................50-100 60
BUDDAH (171 "So Much in Love") 4-8 71
LAURIE 5-10 63-76
REPRISE (20103 "Doctor of Hearts")..20-30 62
WILDCAT (601 "Never Never") 20-30 61
LPs: 10/12-inch
B.T. PUPPY (1011 "My Secret Love")..35-45 70
COLLECTABLES 5-10 87
LAURIE (2018 "He's So Fine").......35-50 63
LAURIE (2020 "One Fine Day") 40-60 63
LAURIE (LLP-2036 "Sweet Talkin' Guy")...35-45 66
(Monaural.)
LAURIE (SLP-2036 "Sweet Talkin' Guy")...40-50 66
(Stereo.)
LAURIE (4001 "Everything You Always Wanted to Hear") 10-20 74
Members: Judy Craig; Barbara Lee; Patricia Bennett; Sylvia Peterson.
Also see CHRISTIE, Lou, & Classics / Isley Brothers / Chiffons
Also see COASTERS / Crew-Cuts / Chiffons
Also see FOUR PENNIES

CHILD
Singles: 7-inch
JUBILEE (5673 "You'll Never Walk Alone")..5-10 69
LPs: 10/12-inch
JUBILEE (8029 "Child") 25-35 68

CHILD
LPs: 10/12-inch
ARIEL..5-10 80

CHILD, Desmond, & Rouge P&R/R&B/LP '79
Singles: 12-inch
CAPITOL...4-8 79
Singles: 7-inch
CAPITOL (Black vinyl)........................3-4 79-82
CAPITOL (Colored vinyl).....................4-6 79
LPs: 10/12-inch
CAPITOL (Black vinyl).......................5-10 79
CAPITOL (Colored vinyl)..................15-20 79
Also see VIDAL, Maria

CHILD, Harold
(Harold Child Group)
Singles: 7-inch
LIMELIGHT 3-6 68

CHILD, Jane P&R/LP '90
Singles: 7-inch
W.B. 3-4 90
LPs: 10/12-inch
W.B. 3-4 90

CHILD'S GARDEN OF GRASS
LPs: 10/12-inch
ELEKTRA (75012 "A Pre-Legalization Comedy")......................................20-30 70
Members: Anton Greene; Carl Esser; Michael Gwynne; Ron Jacobs; Jack S. Margolis; Cyrus Faryar; Anna-Lee Austin; Dorina May; Oz Knox; Dr. Franklin D. Wacco; George Savage; Mary Howard; Tom Rounds; Marty Stone; Renais Faryar; John Horton; Peter Gallway; Alex Hassilev; Murray Roman.
Also see GALLWAY, Peter
Also see RON & JON

CHILDE, Sonny
Singles: 7-inch
MUSIC FACTORY.................................4-6 68

CHILDREN
Singles: 7-inch
ATCO (6633 "Maypole") 10-15 68
CINEMA (025 "Pills") 15-25 68
DRAGONET...5-10
LARAMIE (666 "Picture Me") 20-30 67
MAP CITY 4-8 70
ODE '70 (66005 "From the Very Start")..10-15 70
ODE '70 (66013 "Fire Ring")..........10-15 71
SWEET SMOKE (2 "Jumping Jack Flash")..10-15 68
LPs: 10/12-inch
ATCO (271 "Rebirth")....................15-25 68
CINEMA (0001 "Rebirth") 100-200 67
Members: Stephen Perron; Cassell Webb; Ken Corday; William Ash; Andrew Szuch Jr.; Louis Cabaza.
Also see MIND'S EYE
Also see STOICS

CHILDREN OF DARKNESS
Singles: 7-inch
ROYCE (5140 "She's Mine")..........15-25 66

CHILDREN OF GOD
Singles: 7-inch
A&M...3-6 69
LPs: 10/12-inch
A&M...10-15 69

CHILDREN OF NIGHT
Singles: 7-inch
MOON ROCK (100 "Dinner with Drac") 5-10

CHILDREN OF ONE
LPs: 10/12-inch
REAL (101 "Children of One") ...100-200 70

CHILDREN OF PARADISE
Singles: 7-inch
COLUMBIA 4-8 67

CHILDREN OF PRAGUE
LPs: 10/12-inch
MERCURY 10-15 70

CHILDREN OF THE MUSHROOM
Singles: 7-inch
SOHO (101 "You Can't Erase a Mirror")..10-20 68

CHILDREN OF NIGHT
Singles: 7-inch
BELLA (101 "World of Tears").......25-35 67
LPs: 10/12-inch
P.I.P. 15-20 76
Member: John DiBella

CHILDREN OF THE WORLD
(With Herve Villechaize)
Singles: 7-inch
EPIC/CLEVELAND INT'L.....................3-4 80
Picture Sleeves
EPIC/CLEVELAND INT'L.....................3-4 80

CHILDRESS, Buddy
Singles: 7-inch
DUB (2838 "My Lovin' Arms").......15-25

CHILDRESS, Howard, & Clefts
Singles: 7-inch
KNOX (101 "Whoa!").......................10-20

CHILDRESS, Lisa C&W '86
Singles: 7-inch
AMI 3-4 86-87
TRUE 3-4 88-89

CHILDRESS, Norma
Singles: 7-inch
WEBER..3-6

CHILDS, Billy
Singles: 7-inch
REKA (100 series)..........................10-15 60
REKA (200 series)............................8-12 62

CHILDS, Leon
Singles: 7-inch
VIN...5-10 60

CHILDS, Matthew
Singles: 7-inch
RAE COX (1002 "Funky Onions") ..10-20 63

CHILDS, Toni P&R/LP '88
Singles: 7-inch
A&M...3-4 88-90
Picture Sleeves
A&M...3-4 88
LPs: 10/12-inch
A&M...5-8 88-91

CHILES, Buddy
Singles: 78 rpm
GOLD STAR (660 "Mistreated Blues")..25-50 49

CHI-LITES P&R/R&B/LP '69
Singles: 12-inch
LARC 4-8 83
PRIVATE 1..4-6 84
Singles: 7-inch
BLUE ROCK (4007 "I'm So Jealous")..15-25 65
BLUE ROCK (4020 "The Monkey")..15-25 65
BLUE ROCK (4037 "She's Mine")..25-50 65
BRUNSWICK 3-8 69-78
CHI-SOUND...3-4 80-82
EPIC 3-4 83
INPHASION 3-5 79
LARC 3-4 83
MERCURY...3-5 76-77
O'RETTA..4-8 70
PRIVATE I..3-4 84
REVUE...5-10 67-68
20TH FOX...3-4 81
LPs: 10/12-inch
BRUNSWICK 10-15 69-74
CHI-SOUND...5-8 80-82
EPIC 5-10 83-84
LARC 5-10 83
MERCURY...5-10 77
PICKWICK...5-10 70s
20TH FOX..5-10 80-81
Members: Eugene Record; Creadel Jones; Robert Lester; Marshall Thompson; Danny Johnson.
Also see ACKLIN, Barbara
Also see CHANTEURS
Also see HI-LITES
Also see JOHNSON, Danny
Also see MARSHALL & CHI-LITES
Also see PITMAN, Donnell
Also see RECORD, Eugene
Also see WILSON, Jackie, & Chi-Lites

CHILL FACTOR R&B '87
Singles: 7-inch
W.B. 3-4 87

CHILL FAC-TORR
Singles: 7-inch
PHILLY WORLD 3-4 83

CHILL TOWN *D&D '83*
Singles: 12-inch
A&M 4-6 83

CHILLIWACK *P&R '72*
Singles: 12-inch
MUSHROOM (0611 "Dreams, Dreams, Dreams") 10-15 78
(Clear vinyl. Promotional issue only.)
Singles: 7-inch
A&M 3-5 72
MILLENNIUM 3-4 81-83
MUSHROOM 3-5 76-80
PARROT 3-5 71
SIRE 3-5 74-76
LPs: 10/12-inch
A&M 10-15 71-73
MILLENNIUM 5-10 81-82
MUSHROOM 8-12 77-80
PARROT 15-20 70
SIRE 10-15 75
Members: Bill Henderson; Howard Froese; Claire Lawrence; Glen Miller; Ross Turney.
Also see COLLECTORS

CHILLY
Singles: 7-inch
POLYDOR 3-4 78
LPs: 10/12-inch
POLYDOR 5-10 79-80

CHILLY CHARLIE
Singles: 7-inch
BAND BOX (329 "Cirsis at Ole Miss") 10-20 63
Picture Sleeves
BAND BOX (329 "Cirsis at Ole Miss") 30-40 63

CHILTON, Alex
EPs: 7-inch
BIGTIME 4-8 85-86
LPs: 10/12-inch
BIGTIME 5-10 87
Also see BOX TOPS

CHILTON, Bob
Singles: 7-inch
CREST 5-8 61

CHIMERA
LPs: 10/12-inch
PETERS INT'L 8-10 74

CHIMES
Singles: 78 rpm
FLAIR 200-300 54
Singles: 7-inch
FLAIR (1051 "My Heart's Crying for You") 500-750 54
Members: Cornell Gunter; Young Jessie; Richard Berry; Beverly Thompson; Tom Fox.
Also see FLAIRS

CHIMES
Singles: 78 rpm
ROYAL ROOST (577 "Dearest Darling") 75-125 55

CHIMES
(With the Bumps Blackwell Band)
Singles: 78 rpm
SPECIALTY 20-30 55-56
Singles: 7-inch
JAY TEE (1000 "Losing You Baby") 100-200 50s
SPECIALTY (555 "Tears on My Pillow") 50-75 55
(Rigid disc.)
SPECIALTY (555 "Tears on My Pillow") 40-60 55
(Fleixble disc.)
SPECIALTY (574 "Pretty Little Girl") 35-50 56
Also see ALLEN, Tony

CHIMES
Singles: 7-inch
ARROW (724 "Please Call") 20-40 58
ARROW (726 "Lovin' Baby") 20-40 58
Member: Freddy Scott.
Also see SCOTT, Freddie

CHIMES *P&R '60*
Singles: 7-inch
ABC 3-4 75
COLLECTABLES 3-4 81
ERIC 3-4 70s
LAURIE (3211 "Who's Heart Are You Breaking Now") 10-15 63
LOST-NITE 4-8 70s
METRO (1 "Who's Heart Are You Breaking Now") 25-35 63
MUSIC NOTE (1101 "Once in Awhile") 15-25 61
RESERVE (120 "When School Starts Again") 30-50 57
TAG (444 "Once in Awhile"/"Summer Night") 50-75 60
(Maroon label. "Tag" in normal letters.)
TAG (444 "Once in Awhile"/"Summer Night") 100-150 60
(Blue label. "Tag" in normal letters.)
TAG (444 "Once in Awhile"/"Summer Night") 15-25 60
(Green label. Has "Tag" in a triangle.)
TAG (444 "Once in Awhile"/"Oh How I Love You So") 15-25 60
(Though shown as by the Chimes, *Oh How I Love You So* is by the BiTones.)
TAG (445 "I'm in the Mood for Love") 15-25 61
TAG (447 "Let's Fall in Love") 15-25 61
TAG (450 "My Love") 15-25 62
TRIP 3-5 70s
LPs: 10/12-inch
CHIMES 10-15 83
Member: Lenny Cocco.
Also see BI-TONES
Also see CHYMES
Also see LENNY & CHIMES
Also see RIFFS
Also see THREE CHIMES

CHIMES / Huey "Piano" Smith
Singles: 7-inch
OLDIES 45 3-5
Also see CHIMES
Also see SMITH, Huey

CHIMES
Singles: 7-inch
HOB (3 "Tears from an Angel's Eyes") 50-75 60

CHIMES
Singles: 7-inch
LIMELIGHT (3000 "Cry Baby, Cry") 15-25 63
LIMELIGHT (3002 "Du Wap") 15-25 63

CHIMES *P&R/LP '90*
LPs: 10/12-inch
COLUMBIA 5-8 90
Member: Pauline Henry.

CHIMES
Singles: 7-inch
MATRIX (777 "Foolish Pride") 10-20

CHIMES, Les
Singles: 7-inch
GAY 5-10 60

CHINA
Singles: 7-inch
EPIC 3-4 81-82
ROCKET 3-4 77
LPs: 10/12-inch
EPIC 5-10 81
ROCKET 8-10 77
Members: Davey Johnstone; Dennis Conway; James Howard; Roger Pope; Jo Partridge; Cooker LoPresti.
Also see JOHN, Elton

CHINA CRISIS *D&D '84*
Singles: 12-inch
VIRGIN 4-6 82
W.B. 4-6 83-84
Singles: 7-inch
VIRGIN 3-4 82
W.B. 3-4 84
LPs: 10/12-inch
A&M 5-10 87
W.B. 5-10 84-85

CHINGAS, Johnny
Singles: 12-inch
COLUMBIA 4-6 83

CHINNOCK, Bill *C&W '85*
Singles: 7-inch
ATLANTIC 3-5 78
NORTH COUNTRY 3-5 80
PARADISE 3-4 85
PARAMOUNT 3-5 74
LPs: 10/12-inch
ATLANTIC 5-10 78
NORTH COUNTRY 5-10 80
PARAMOUNT 8-10 74

CHINOOK
Singles: 7-inch
CHINOOK 4-6
CLARIDGE 3-5 74-75

CHIOTA, Bazil Blavis
Singles: 7-inch
UA 10-15 66

CHIP & DAVE TRIO
Singles: 7-inch
DECCA 4-8 67

CHIP & QUARTERTONES
Singles: 7-inch
CARLTON (604 "Simple Simon") 75-125 64
Members: Chip Kopaczewski; Tony Galantino; Jim Murkens; Dick Curry.
Also see INTENTIONS

CHIP E. INC. Featuring K. Joy *D&D '85*
Singles: 12-inch
D.J. INT'L 4-6 85

CHIP HAND
Singles: 7-inch
MOTOWN 3-5 75
RCA 3-5 71-72

CHIPMUNKS *P&R/R&B '58*
("Starring Alvin, Theodore, & Simon;" "Featuring David Seville;" David Seville & Chipmunks)
Singles: 7-inch
AMERICAN TELECARD 10-15 64
DOT (16997 "Sorry About That Herb") 4-8 67
LIBERTY (Except 77000 series) 5-10 58-74
LIBERTY (77000 series) 10-20 59
(Stereo.)
MISTLETOE 3-5 75
SUNSET 3-6 68
U.A. 3-5 74
Picture Sleeves
LIBERTY 5-10 59-65
EPs: 7-inch
LIBERTY 10-20 59-64
LPs: 10/12-inch
LIBERTY (3132 "Let's All Sing with the Chipmunks") 20-30 59
(Monaural. Black vinyl. Cover shows Chipmunks as animals. If Chipmunks are drawn as cartoon characters, deduct 50%.)
LIBERTY (3132 "Let's All Sing with the Chipmunks") 25-40 59
(Monaural. Colored vinyl. Cover shows Chipmunks as animals. If Chipmunks are drawn as cartoon characters, deduct 50%.)
LIBERTY (3159 "Sing Again with the Chipmunks") 20-30 60
(Monaural. Cover shows Chipmunks as animals. If Chipmunks are drawn as cartoon characters, deduct 50%.)
LIBERTY (3170 "Around the World with the Chipmunks") 20-30 60
(Monaural. Cover shows Chipmunks as animals. If Chipmunks are drawn as cartoon characters, deduct 50%.)
LIBERTY (3200 thru 3400 series) 10-20 61-65
(Monaural.)
LIBERTY (7132 "Let's All Sing with the Chipmunks") 20-35 59
(Stereo. Black vinyl. Cover shows Chipmunks as animals. If Chipmunks are drawn as cartoon characters, deduct 50%.)
LIBERTY (7132 "Let's All Sing with the Chipmunks") 25-45 59
(Stereo. Colored vinyl. Cover shows Chipmunks as animals. If Chipmunks are drawn as cartoon characters, deduct 50%.)
LIBERTY (7159 "Sing Again with the Chipmunks") 20-35 60
(Stereo. Cover shows Chipmunks as animals. If Chipmunks are drawn as cartoon characters, deduct 50%.)
LIBERTY (7170 "Around the World with the Chipmunks") 20-35 60
(Stereo. Cover shows Chipmunks as animals. If Chipmunks are drawn as cartoon characters, deduct 50%.)
LIBERTY (7200 thru 7400 series) 10-20 61-65
(Stereo.)
LIBERTY (10000 series) 5-10 82
PICKWICK 5-10 80
SUNSET 8-15 68-69
U.A. 5-10 74-76
Also see BEDBUGS
Also see CANNED HEAT & CHIPMUNKS
Also see SEVILLE, David

CHIPMUNKS *LP '80*
(Starring Alvin, Theodore, & Simon; Featuring David Seville Jr.)
Singles: 7-inch
EPIC 3-4 92
EXCELSIOR 3-4 80
RCA 3-4 81-82
Picture Sleeves
EXCELSIOR 3-4 80
RCA 3-4 81
LPs: 10/12-inch
EXCELSIOR 5-10 80
PICKWICK INT'L 5-10 80
RCA 5-10 81-82

CHIPPENDALES
Singles: 7-inch
ANDIE 10-15 59
RUST 4-8 61

CHIPPER & His Playmates
LPs: 10/12-inch
U.A. 10-15 64

CHIPPS, Jimmy, & Christmas Belles
Singles: 7-inch
OVO 4-8 64

CHIPS
Singles: 78 rpm
JOSIE (803 "Rubber Biscuit") 25-50 56
Singles: 7-inch
JOSIE (803 "Rubber Biscuit") 50-100 56
(With "Joz" logo.)
JOSIE (803 "Rubber Biscuit") 25-50 58
(With "Josie" logo.)
VIRGO 4-8 73
Members: Kinrod Johnson;Nathaniel "Lil John" Epps; Bubbie Lincoln; Paul Fulton; Charles Johnson; Sam Strain.
Also see LITTLE ANTHONY & IMPERIALS
Also see O'JAYS

CHIPS
Singles: 7-inch
SATELLITE (105 "As You Can See") 75-125 61
Members: Curtis Johnson; Richard Harris; Eddie Stanbeck; Sam Byrnes.
Also see ASTORS

CHIPS
Singles: 7-inch
STRAND (25027 "Darling") 20-40 61
VENICE (101 "Darling") 75-125 60

CHIPS
Singles: 7-inch
EMBER (1077 "Bye Bye My Love") 15-25 61
TOLLIE (9042 "Party People") 8-10 65
TRACK 5-10 64
Also see SOUTH, Joe

CHIPS
Singles: 7-inch
PHILIPS (40520 "Break It Gently") 4-8 68
Picture Sleeves
PHILIPS (40520 "Break It Gently") 8-10 68

CHIPS & CO.
(Chips)
Singles: 7-inch
ABC (11157 "When You Hold Me Baby") 5-10 68
ABC-PAR (10749 "Every Night") 8-12 65
ABC-PAR (10769 "Walk Tall") 8-12 66
M5 (191 "Let the Winds Blow") 20-30 66

CHIRCO
Singles: 7-inch
CRESTED BUTTE 4-8 72
LPs: 10/12-inch
CRESTED BUTTE ("Visitation") 30-45 72
(Selection number not known.)
Members: Alvin Roth; John Naylor.

CHIYO & CRESCENTS: see CRESCENTS

CHOATES, Harry *C&W '47*
(Harry Coates)
Singles: 78 rpm
ALLIED 10-15
GOLD STAR 10-15 46-50
MACY'S 10-15
MODERN MOUNTAIN 10-15 46
LPs: 10/12-inch
ARHOOLIE 5-10
D (7000 "Jole Blon") 25-35
D (7000 "Original Cajun Fiddle") 10-15
(Repackage of *Jole Blon.*)

CHOB
(Choäb)
Singles: 7-inch
LAVETTE (5016 "Ain't Gonna Eat Out My Heart Anymore") 20-30 66
Q.Q. (224 "Why Am I Alone") 20-30 66

CHOCO
LPs: 10/12-inch
AUDIO FIDELITY 12-15 63

CHOCOLATE CHIPS
Singles: 7-inch
DORE (822 "Come Softly to Me") 10-15

CHOCOLATE COMPANY
Singles: 7-inch
EUREKA 3-6 69

CHOCOLATE JAM CO.
Singles: 7-inch
EPIC 3-4 79
LPs: 10/12-inch
EPIC 5-10 79

CHOCOLATE MILK *R&B/LP '75*
Singles: 12-inch
RCA 4-6 83
Singles: 7-inch
RCA 3-5 75-83
LPs: 10/12-inch
RCA 5-10 77-82
Members: Frank Richard; Amadee Castanell; Robert Doban; Joe Foxx; Mario Tio; Dwight Richards.

CHOCOLATE MOOSE
Singles: 7-inch
SPOTLIGHT (1012 "Take a Ride") 20-30 66
SPOTLIGHT (1015 "Rosie") 20-30 66

CHOCOLATE SYRUP *R&B '71*
Singles: 7-inch
AVCO EMBASSY 3-5 71
BROWN DOG 3-5 74
LAW TON 3-5
Members: L.J. Reynolds; Lenny Wolfe; Jimmy Holiday; Norris Harris.
Also see CHAIN REACTION
Also see MOMENT of TRUTH
Also see REYNOLDS, L.J.

CHOCOLATE TELEPHONE POLE
Singles: 7-inch
JACK O' DIAMONDS 5-10 67

CHOCOLATE TUNNEL
Singles: 7-inch
ERA 4-8 67

CHOCOLATE WATCH BAND
Singles: 7-inch
TOWER (373 "No Way Out") 30-40 67
UPTOWN (740 "Baby Blue") 30-40 67
UPTOWN (749 "Misty Lane") 30-40 67
LPs: 10/12-inch
RHINO 5-10 83
TOWER (5096 "No Way Out") 150-200 67
TOWER (5106 "Inner Mystique") 150-200 68
TOWER (5153 "One Step Beyond") 125-150 69
Also see HOGS

CHOCOLATEERS
Singles: 78 rpm
PARROT 25-50 54
Singles: 7-inch
OWL 3-5 73
PARROT (781 "Bartender Blues") 60-100 54

CHOCOLATS
LPs: 10/12-inch
TOM 'N' JERRY 8-10 77

CHOCOLETE *D&D '85*
Singles: 12-inch
SUPERTRONICS 4-6 85

CHOICE
Singles: 7-inch
POLYDOR 3-4 80

CHOICE FOUR *R&B '74*
Singles: 7-inch
RCA 3-5 74-76
LPs: 10/12-inch
RCA 8-10 74-75
Members: Bobby Hamilton; Pete Marshall; Ted Maduro; Charles Blagmore.

CHOICE MCs FEATURING FRESH GORDON *R&B/D&D '85*
Singles: 12-inch
TOMMY BOY 4-6 85
Singles: 7-inch
TOMMY BOY 3-4 85

CHOICE OF COLOUR
Singles: 7-inch
APT 10-15 72

CHOIR *P&R '67*
Singles: 7-inch
CANADIAN AMERICAN (203 "It's Cold Outside") 25-35 67
INTREPID 4-6 70
ROULETTE 10-15 67-68
EPs: 7-inch
BOMP 8-10 76
Members: Wally Bryson; David Smalley; Jim Bonfanti.
Also see RASPBERRIES

CHOIRBOYS *P&R '89*
Singles: 7-inch
WTG 3-4 89
Member: Mark Gable.

CHOLLI MAYE
(Shirley Alston)
Singles: 7-inch
GOLD (212 "You Will Never Get Away") 5-10
Also see ALSTON, Shirley

CHOPPER
Singles: 12-inch
POSSE 4-6 83
Singles: 7-inch
ARIOLA AMERICA 3-4 79
LPs: 10/12-inch
ARIOLA AMERICA 5-10 79

CHOPPERS
Singles: 7-inch
DORE 5-10 60

CHOPS *R&B '84*
Singles: 12-inch
ATLANTIC 4-6 84
Singles: 7-inch
ATLANTIC 3-4 84
LPs: 10/12-inch
ATLANTIC 5-10 84

CHORALETTES
Singles: 7-inch
FARGO (1063 "Won't You Call on Me") 10-20 64

CHORALS
Singles: 78 rpm
DECCA (29914 "In My Dream") 25-50 56
Singles: 7-inch
DECCA (29914 "In My Dream") 50-75 56

CHORDCATS
Singles: 78 rpm
CAT (109 "Zippety Zum") 15-20 54
CAT (112 "Hold Me, Baby") 20-25 54
Singles: 7-inch
CAT (109 "Zippety Zum") 20-30 54
CAT (112 "Hold Me, Baby") 30-50 54
Members: Carl Feaster; Claude Feaster; Jimmy Keys; Floyd McRae; William Edwards.
Also see CHORDS

CHORDELLS
Singles: 78 rpm
ONYX 100-200 56
Singles: 7-inch
ONYX (504 "Here's a Heart for You") 250-350 56

CHORDELLS
Singles: 7-inch
JARO INT'L (77005 "At Last") 25-50 59

CHORDELLS
Singles: 7-inch
TIGRE (601 "Quit While You're Ahead") 20-30 63

CHORDETTES *P&R '54*
(With Archie Bleyer; with Jeff Kron & Jackie Ertel)
Singles: 78 rpm
CADENCE 5-10 54-57
COLUMBIA 5-10 50-54
Singles: 7-inch
BARNABY 3-5 70-76
CADENCE 8-15 54-63
COLUMBIA 10-15 50-54
ERIC 3-4 78
Picture Sleeves
CADENCE (Except 1366) 10-20 58-61
CADENCE (1366 "No Wheels") 15-25 59
(Promotional issue only. Pictures Jeff and Jackie. Sleeve and disc has *No Wheels* on both sides.)
CADENCE (1366 "A Girl's Work Is Never Done") 10-15 59
(Pictures only Jackie.)
EPs: 7-inch
CADENCE 10-20 57-61
COLUMBIA (Except 201 thru 401) 10-25 54-57
COLUMBIA (201 "Harmony Time") 30-40 50
(Boxed, four-disc set.)
COLUMBIA (241 "Harmony Time, Vol. 2") 30-40 51
(Boxed, four-disc set.)

COLUMBIA (309 "Harmony Encores") 30-40 52
(Boxed, four-disc set.)
COLUMBIA (401 "Your Requests") 30-40 53
(Boxed, four-disc set.)
LPs: 10/12-inch
BACK-TRAC.... 5-10
BARNABY 8-10 76
CADENCE (1002 "Close Harmony") 20-30 55
CADENCE (3001 "Chordettes")....20-35 57
CADENCE (3020 "Barbershop Harmonies") 20-30 58
CADENCE (3062 "Never on Sunday") 20-30 62
CADENCE (25062 "Never on Sunday") 25-35 62
COLUMBIA (956 "Listen") 20-35 57
COLUMBIA (2519 "Chordettes") 25-35 56
(10-inch LP.)
COLUMBIA (6111 "Harmony Time") 30-40 50
(10-inch LP.)
COLUMBIA (6170 "Harmony Time, Vol. 2") 30-40 51
(10-inch LP.)
COLUMBIA (6218 "Harmony Encores") 30-40 52
(10-inch LP.)
COLUMBIA (6285 "Your Requests") 30-40 53
(10-inch LP.)
EVEREST.... 5-10 82
HARMONY 12-15 59
Members: Margie Needham; Janet Ertel; Carol Bushman; Lynn Evans.
Also see BLEYER, Archie

CHORDIALS
Singles: 7-inch
BIG TOP.... 5-8 64

CHORD'R NOTES
Singles: 7-inch
FARGO (1061 "How Still the Night") 20-30 64

CHORDS
Singles: 78 rpm
GEM (211 "In the Woods") 25-50 53

CHORDS *P&R/R&B '54*
Singles: 78 rpm
CAT (104 "Sh-Boom"/"Cross Over the Bridge") 20-40 54
CAT (104 "Sh-Boom"/"Little Maiden") 15-25 54
CAT (109 "Zippety Zum") 10-20 54
QUALITY (1268 "Sh-Boom") 35-50 54
(Canadian.)
QUALITY (1293 "Zippety Zum") 10-20 54
(Canadian.)
Singles: 7-inch
CAT (104 "Sh-Boom"/"Cross Over the Bridge") 50-100 54
CAT (104 "Sh-Boom"/"Little Maiden") 25-50 54
CAT (109 "Zippety Zum") 25-50 54
LOST-NITE.... 4-8
QUALITY (1268 "Sh-Boom") 150-200 54
(Canadian.)
QUALITY (1293 "Zippety Zum") 15-25 54
(Canadian.)
Members: Carl Feaster; Claude Feaster; Jimmy Keys; Floyd McRae; William Edwards.
Also see CHORDCATS
Also see SH-BOOMS
Also see THORPE, Lionel

CHORDS
Singles: 7-inch
METRO 8-12 59

CHORDS
Singles: 7-inch
CASINO....15-25 58

CHORDS / Jalopy Five: see JALOPY FIVE

CHOSEN FEW
Singles: 7-inch
MARSH (201 "Jump Down") 20-30 62
Members: Scott Engel; John Stewart.
Also see ENGEL, Scott, & John Stewart

CHOSEN FEW
Singles: 7-inch
AUTUMN.... 5-10 65
NORTH BEACH.... 8-12 66

CHOSEN FEW
Singles: 7-inch
CANYON.... 8-12 60s
CRYSTAL.... 8-12 60s
DART 8-12 67
LIBERTY 10-20 66-67
MAPLE 3-5 71
PLAYBOY.... 8-12 65
POWER INT'L (872 "Forget About the Past") 25-35 66
ROULETTE 5-10 68
LPs: 10/12-inch
MAPLE 10-20

CHOSEN FEW
Singles: 7-inch
DENIM.... 5-10 66
Members: Warren Mittlestadt; Gary Huboldt; Des Smith; Dave Huegel; John Baker.

CHOSEN FEW
Singles: 7-inch
B.F.D. 10-20 66

CHOSEN FEW
Singles: 7-inch
CANUSA 5-10 68
CO-OP 8-12 66-67
Members: Bobby White; Billy Paul; Harry Jeroleman; Jimmie O'Connor; Mike Helske; Richard Zwick; Mike Helske.
Also see BARRIES
Also see SONICS

CHOSEN FEW
Singles: 7-inch
RCA.... 4-6 69
TALUN STEREO 4-8 69
LPs: 10/12-inch
RCA....10-20 69
Also see FAITH BAND

CHOSEN FEW
Singles: 7-inch
BANDIT (2521 "Lift This Hurt") 5-10

CHOSEN LOT
Singles: 7-inch
SIDRA 4-8 66

CHOSEN THREE
Singles: 7-inch
CLARIDGE.... 4-8 65

CHOWDER HEAD & BOSTON BEANS
Singles: 7-inch
DELITE (1020 "Boston Stroll") ....5-10 -

CHOWNING, Randle
(Randle Chowning Band)
Singles: 7-inch
A&M 3-5 78
LPs: 10/12-inch
A&M 5-10 78

CHOZEN ONES
Singles: 7-inch
FROG.... 4-8 67

CHRIS, Tommy
Singles: 7-inch
OUR GANG.... 3-4 81

CHRIS & CYTATIONS
Singles: 7-inch
CATAMOUNT (100 "Glory of Love") 15-25 63
(Colored vinyl.)

CHRIS & CRAIG
Singles: 7-inch
CAPITOL.... 4-8 66

CHRIS & KATHY
(Chris Montez & Kathy Young)
Singles: 7-inch
MONOGRAM (517 "All You Had to Do") 10-15 64
MONOGRAM (520 "Shoot That Curl") 10-15 64
Members: Chris Montez; Kathy Young.
Also see MONTEZ, Chris
Also see YOUNG, Kathy

CHRIS & LENNY *C&W '89*
Singles: 7-inch
HAPPY MAN 3-4 89

CHRIS & SHACK
Singles: 7-inch
VOLT (4036 "Goodies") 4-8 70

CHRIS D.
LPs: 10/12-inch
ENIGMA 5-10 85

CHRIST CHILD
LPs: 10/12-inch
BUDDAH....5-10 78

CHRISTENSEN, John
LPs: 10/12-inch
ROBBINS (5001 "The Spirit: Every Little Thing") 30-40 87
(Picture disc.)

CHRISTENSEN, Nedra
Singles: 7-inch
HUMMINGBIRD 4-8 65

CHRISTI, Al, & Coastiers / Gateway Trio
Singles: 7-inch
COAST to COAST....8-12 59

CHRISTI, Christine
Singles: 7-inch
DOUBLETALK.... 3-6 69

CHRISTIAN, Bobby
Singles: 78 rpm
BALLY....5-10 57
Singles: 7-inch
BALLY....5-10 57
FORMAL (1002 "Grasshopper Jump") 10-20 60s
MERCURY 4-8 63
SALEM....5-10
STEPHENY 15-25 58
TOP RANK (2004 "Bobby's Tune") 15-25 59

CHRISTIAN, Chris
Singles: 7-inch
BOARDWALK 3-4
TESTA....5-10 59
Picture Sleeves
BOARDWALK 3-4

CHRISTIAN, Chris *P&R '81*
(With Amy Holland)
Singles: 7-inch
BOARDWALK 3-4 81-82
Picture Sleeves
BOARDWALK....3-4 81
LPs: 10/12-inch
BORADWALK 5-10 81
HOME SWEET HOME 5-10 81
MYRRH 5-10 83-84
Also see COTTON, LLOYD & CHRISTIAN
Also see HOLLAND, Amy

CHRISTIAN, Diane
Singles: 7-inch
BELL 4-8 65
SMASH 4-8 64

CHRISTIAN, Hans
Singles: 7-inch
TOWER....4-8 68

CHRISTIAN, Janice
Singles: 7-inch
SWAN 4-8 64

CHRISTIAN, Joel
Singles: 7-inch
ABC-PAR 4-8 65
IMPERIAL 4-8 66

CHRISTIAN, Little Johnny
LPs: 10/12-inch
BIG BOY 10-12 90

CHRISTIAN, Michael
Singles: 7-inch
U.A. 3-4 79
LPs: 10/12-inch
U.A. 5-10 79

CHRISTIAN, Neil
Singles: 7-inch
MORNINGSTAR....3-5 76
RCA 4-8 66
Also see DALLON, Miki

CHRISTIAN, Oliver
Singles: 7-inch
LEGRAND....5-15 84
NORFOLK INT'L....3-5 77

CHRISTIAN, Rick
Singles: 7-inch
MERCURY 3-4 78
LPs: 10/12-inch
COLUMBIA....5-10 83

CHRISTIAN, Roger
Singles: 7-inch
NBI (100 "Big Bad Ho-Dad") 25-35 63
RENDEZVOUS....10-15 62
Also see BEACH BOYS
Also see SUPER STOCKS / Hot Rod Rog / Shutdown Douglas

CHRISTIAN, T.V.
Singles: 7-inch
NSD 3-4 83

CHRISTIAN DEATH
LPs: 10/12-inch
FRONTIER....5-10 82

CHRISTIANS *LP '88*
LPs: 10/12-inch
ISLAND 5-8 88

CHRISTIAN'S CRUSADERS
Singles: 7-inch
RCA 4-8 65

CHRISTIANSEN, Chris
(Jim Christiansen)
Singles: 7-inch
IMPERIAL 4-8 64
UNITY 4-8 64

CHRISTIE *P&R/LP '70*
Singles: 7-inch
EPIC....3-5 70-71
LPs: 10/12-inch
EPIC....10-15 70
Members: Jeff Christie; Mike Blakely; Vic Elmes.

CHRISTIE, Charles: see CHRISTY, Charles

CHRISTIE, Christine
Singles: 7-inch
DOUBLETALK....3-5 76

CHRISTIE, Dave
Singles: 7-inch
ASSOCIATED ARTISTS 4-8 66
MERCURY 4-6 68

CHRISTIE, Dean *P&R '62*
(Dean Christy)
Singles: 7-inch
MERCURY 4-8 63-64
SWL....5-10 62
SELECT (715 "Heart Breaker") 10-15 62
SELECT (718 "Teenage Jezebel") .15-25 62
TOP FLIGHT (113 "So Much") 20-30 60s

CHRISTIE, Gaylon
(Gaylon Christy & Downbeats Featuring Roy Robinson)
Singles: 7-inch
BID....4-8 63
CAPRI....4-8 60s
FAME....10-20 60s

CHRISTIE, Janice *D&D '85*
Singles: 12-inch
SUPERTRONICS 4-6 85-86
Singles: 7-inch
SUPERTRONICS....3-4 85-86
Also see FATBACK

CHRISTIE, Joel
Singles: 7-inch
IMPERIAL 4-8 65-66

CHRISTIE, John
Singles: 7-inch
CAPITOL....3-5 74
Picture Sleeves
CAPITOL....3-5 74

CHRISTIE, Ken, & Sunday People
Singles: 7-inch
RARE EARTH 3-5 71

CHRISTIE, Lou *P&R/R&B/LP '63*
(With the Classics; Lou Christy)
Singles: 12-inch
PLATEAU (101 "Guardian Angels") 40-50 81
(Promotional issue only.)
PLATEAU (4551 "Guardian Angels") 40-50 81
Singles: 7-inch
ABC....3-5 73
ALCAR (207 "Close Your Eyes") 25-35 63
ALCAR (208 "You're with It") 30-50 63
AMERICAN MUSIC MAKERS (006 "The Jury") 25-30
BUDDAH....5-15 68-72
C&C (102 "The Gypsy Cried") 75-100 62
CO & CE (235 "Outside the Gates of Heaven") 5-10 66
COLPIX....10-15 64-66
COLUMBIA....10-15 67
EPIC....10-15 76
MGM (Except 13473) 5-10 65-66
MGM (13473 "Rhapsody in the Rain") 10-15 66
(With "making out in the rain" lyrics.)
MGM (13473 "Rhapsody in the Rain") 5-10 66
(With "fell in love in the rain" lyrics.)
MIDLAND INT'L....10-15 76-77
MIDSONG....10-12 77
PLATEAU (4551 "Guardian Angels") 40-50 81
POLYDOR (519 "Rhapsody in the Rain") 3-5
RHINO 3-5 90s
ROULETTE (4457 "The Gypsy Cried") 15-20 62
(White label with color spokes.)
ROULETTE (4457 "The Gypsy Cried") 5-10 63
(Pink label.)
ROULETTE (4481 "Two Faces Have I") 15-25 63
(White label with color spokes.)
ROULETTE (4481 "Two Faces Have I") 5-10 63
(Pink label.)
ROULETTE (4457 thru 4527) 5-10 62-63
ROULETTE (4545 "Stay") 10-15 64
ROULETTE (4554 "When You Dance") 20-25 64
SLIPPED DISC....10-15 75
THREE BROTHERS 5-15 73-75
WORLD (1002 "The Jury") 25-30
Picture Sleeves
COLPIX (799 "Big Time") 10-20 66
MGM (13473 "Rhapsody in the Rain") 8-12 66
MGM (13533 "Painter") 8-12 66
MGM (13576 "If My Car Could Only Talk") 20-25 66
LPs: 10/12-inch
BUDDAH (5052 "I'm Gonna Make You Mine") 10-15 69
BUDDAH (5073 "Paint America Love") 15-20 71
CO & CE (1231 "Lou Christie Strikes Back") 30-50 66
(Label may read: "Lou Christie Strkes Again.")
COLPIX (4001 "Lou Christie Strikes Again") 20-25 66
(Gold label.)
COLPIX (4001 "Lou Christie Strikes Again") 10-20 66
(Blue label.)
CSP (18260 "Lou Christie Does Detroit") 5-8
51 WEST ("Lou Christie Does Detroit") 10-15 83
MGM (4360 "Lightnin' Strikes") 12-18 66
MGM (4394 "Painter of Hits") 15-20 66
RHINO 5-8 88
ROULETTE (25208 "Lou Christie") 50-60 63
(Cover has a blue background.)
ROULETTE (25208 "Lou Christie") 30-40 63
(Cover has white wall background.)
ROULETTE (25332 "Lou Christie Strikes Again") 20-30 63
(Repackage of Co & Ce 1231, *Lou Christie Strikes Back.*)
UNDERGROUND (50002 "Self Expression") 8-10 83
(Canadian.)
THREE BROTHERS (2000 "Lou Christie") 15-20 74
Also see CANTINA BAND
Also see CHRISTY, Chic
Also see CLASSICS
Also see CRITTERS / Young Rascals / Lou Christie
Also see DEE, Dave
Also see GORE, Leslie, & Lou Christie
Also see JACK, Johnny
Also see LA RUE, D.C.
Also see LUGEE & LIONS
Also see MARCY JOE
Also see RENEE & Rhinestone Rambles
Also see RICHIE & RUNAROUNDS
Also see SACCO
Also see ZADORA, Pia, & Lou Christie

CHRISTIE, Lou / Len Barry & Dovells / Bobby Rydell / Tokens
LPs: 10/12-inch
WYNCOTE....10-20 60s
Also see DOVELLS
Also see RYDELL, Bobby
Also see TOKENS

CHRISTIE, Lou, & Classics / Isley Brothers / Chiffons
LPs: 10/12-inch
SPIN-O-RAMA (173 "Lou Christie and the Classics") 20-30 66
Also see CHIFFONS
Also see ISLEY BROTHERS

CHRISTIE, Lynn, & Deckers
Singles: 7-inch
NAR 8-12 57

CHRISTIE, Ruth
(Ruth Christy)
Singles: 7-inch
TIDE....5-15 61-67
UPTOWN 4-8 66
Also see CANDLETTS
Also see CHRISTY SEXTET

CHRISTIE, Susan *P&R '66*
Singles: 7-inch
COLUMBIA 4-8 66-67

CHRISTIE, Tony
Singles: 7-inch
KAPP 3-5 71-72
MCA....3-5 74-77
MGM 3-6 68

CHRISTINE, Anne *C&W '71*
Singles: 7-inch
CME....3-8 71

CHRISTLAND SINGERS
Singles: 7-inch
CHECKER (1000 "God Has Done So Much") 10-20 61

CHRISTMAN, Chris
Singles: 7-inch
CAPRICORN....3-5 74
LPs: 10/12-inch
CAPRICORN....8-10 75

CHRISTMAS, Connie
Singles: 7-inch
CHECKER....4-8 62

CHRISTMAS, Johnny, & Dynamics
Singles: 7-inch
P.D.Q. (5002 ""Soft Lips") 100-150 59

CHRISTMAS, Keith
Singles: 7-inch
MANTICORE....3-5 75
LPs: 10/12-inch
MANTICORE....5-10 75
POLYDOR....8-10 71

CHRISTMAS SPIRIT
Singles: 7-inch
WHITE WHALE (290 "Christmas Is My Time of Year") 50-75 69
Members: Mark Volman; Howard Kaylan; Linda Ronstadt.
Also see RONSTADT, Linda
Also see TURTLES

CHRISTMON, John
Singles: 78 rpm
EXCELLO (2031 "My Baby's Gone") 15-25 54
Singles: 7-inch
EXCELLO (2031 "My Baby's Gone") 25-35 54

CHRISTOPHER
Singles: 7-inch
BELL....8-12 67
DATE 4-8 69
20TH FOX....3-5 76
WOODEN NICKEL....3-5 74
LPs: 10/12-inch
BELL 10-15 70

CHRISTOPHER
LPs: 10/12-inch
METROMEDIA (1024 "Christopher") 50-100 70
Members: Ron Cramer; Terry Hand; Richard Avitts; Doug Tull; John Simpson; Doug Walden.

CHRISTOPHER
LPs: 10/12-inch
CHRIS-TEE (12411 "What'cha Gonna Do") 2500-3000 70
(Reportedly 100 made.)
Members: Frank Smoak; Gary Lucas; Steve Nagle; Bill McKee.

CHRISTOPHER, Artie
Singles: 7-inch
ATLANTIC....3-6 68

CHRISTOPHER, Gavin *R&B '79*
Singles: 7-inch
E.M.I. 3-4 88
ISLAND 3-5 76
MANHATTAN....3-4 86
RSO....3-4 79

Picture Sleeves
MANHATTAN 3-4 86
LPs: 10/12-inch
ISLAND 8-10 76
MANHATTAN 5-10 86
RSO 5-10 79

CHRISTOPHER, Johnny
Singles: 7-inch
ABC 4-8 67
LIBERTY 4-8 66

CHRISTOPHER, Jordan
Singles: 7-inch
JUBILEE 4-6 63
Picture Sleeves
JUBILEE 4-8 63

CHRISTOPHER, Lyn
Singles: 7-inch
AVCO EMBASSY 3-5 70
GRANITE (527 "Harmony") 3-5 75
LPs: 10/12-inch
PARAMOUNT 10-15 73
Also see SIMMONS, Gene

CHRISTOPHER, Paul & Shawn — P&R '75
Singles: 7-inch
CASABLANCA 3-5 75
Also see CHRISTOPHER, Shawn

CHRISTOPHER, Rod
Singles: 7-inch
TRU LITE 10-20 62

CHRISTOPHER, Ron
Singles: 7-inch
PYRO (54 "Debra") 10-15 66

CHRISTOPHER, Shawn — R&B '82
Singles: 7-inch
LARC 3-4 83
Also see CHRISTOPHER, Paul & Shawn

CHRISTOPHER & CHAPS
Singles: 7-inch
FONTANA 4-8 65

CHRISTOPHER & SOULS
Singles: 7-inch
PHARAOH (151 "Diamonds, Rats and Gum") 20-30 66

CHRISTOPHER MILK
(John Mendelsohn)
LPs: 10/12-inch
U.A. 8-12 71
EPs: 7-inch
U.A. 10-15 71
(Promotional mail order offer.)

CHRISTOPHER SUNDAY
Singles: 7-inch
DOT 4-6 68

CHRISTY, Alvin
(Al Christy)
Singles: 7-inch
ACTION 5-10
BB (4003 "My Girl") 15-25 66
KEY JO 4-8
PIN POINT (101 "I'm So Proud") 8-12 70
VIVA (732 "Devil Darling") 8-12 64

CHRISTY, Charles
(With the Crystals; Charles Christie)
Singles: 7-inch
HBR (455 "Cherry Pie") 10-15 65
HBR (473 "In the Arms of a Girl") 10-15 66
Picture Sleeves
HBR (473 "In the Arms of a Girl") 15-25 66

CHRISTY, Chic
Singles: 7-inch
HAC (103 "With This Kiss") 20-30 62
Members: Lou Christie; Kay Chick; Susan Christie.
Also see CHRISTIE, Lou

CHRISTY, Dean: see CHRISTIE, Dean

CHRISTY, Don
(Sonny Bono)
Singles: 7-inch
FIDELITY 10-15 60
GO 10-15 60
NAME 10-15 60
SPECIALTY 10-15 59
Also see SONNY

CHRISTY, Gaylon: see CHRISTIE, Gaylon

CHRISTY, Jack
Singles: 7-inch
S.W.R. 5-8

CHRISTY, June — P&R '53
Singles: 78 rpm
CAPITOL 3-8 51-57
Singles: 7-inch
CAPITOL (1800 thru 3900 series) 5-10 51-58
CAPITOL (4000 thru 4800 series) 3-8 59-62
EPs: 7-inch 33/4rpm
CAPITOL 5-15 53-55
LPs: 10/12-inch
CAPITOL (516 "Something Cool") 25-40 54
(With "H" prefix. 10-inch LP.)
CAPITOL (516 "Something Cool") 15-25 55
(Green label. With "T" prefix.)
CAPITOL (516 "Something Cool") 10-20 60
(Black label. With "T" or "ST" prefix.)
CAPITOL (516 "Something Cool") 5-10 75
(With "SM" prefix.)
CAPITOL (600 thru 900 series) 15-25 55-57
(Green label.)
CAPITOL (600 thru 900 series) 10-15 60
(Black label.)
CAPITOL (1000 thru 2400 series) 10-20 60-65
CAPITOL (11000 series) 5-10 79
DISCOVERY 5-10 82
SEABREEZE 5-10 80

CHRISTY, June, with Stan Kenton
EPs: 7-inch
CAPITOL 5-10 56
LPs: 10/12-inch
CAPITOL (656 "Duet") 20-35 56
(10-inch LP.)
Also see JONES, Jonah
Also see KENTON, Stan, & His Orchestra

CHRISTY, June / Fran Warren
LP: 10/12-inch
CAMAY 8-12
Also see CHRISTY, June
Also see WARREN, Fran

CHRISTY, Lou: see CHRISTIE, Lou

CHRISTY SEXTET
Singles: 7-inch
VITA 5-10 59
Member: Ruth Christie.
Also see CHRISTIE, Ruth

CHROMATICS
Singles: 7-inch
GALAXY 5-10 66

CHROMATICS
Singles: 78 rpm
BLEND 25-50 55
CREST 25-50 56
MILLION 25-50 55-56
Singles: 7-inch
BLEND (1005 "Believe Me") 50-75 55
BLEND (1006 "I'll Never Change") 50-75 55
CREST (1011 "Wild Man, Wild") 50-75 56
DUCKY 5-10 60
MILLION (2010 "Here in the Darkness") 50-75 55
MILLION (2014 "Here in the Darkness") 50-75 56
Also see SINGLETON, Eddie
Also see WASHINGTON, Sherry, & Chromatics
Also see WYNN, Lee, & Chromatics

CHROME
Singles: 7-inch
INFINITY 3-5 79

CHROMIUM
Singles: 7-inch
INFINITY 3-5 79
LPs: 10/12-inch
INFINITY 5-10 79

CHRONICLE
LPs: 10/12-inch
ALL EARS 8-10 77

CHRYSALIS
LPs: 10/12-inch
MGM 10-15 68

CHRYSLERS: see LITTLE NATE & CHRYSLERS

CHUBB ROCK — LP '91
LPs: 10/12-inch
SELECT 5-8 91

CHUBBY & DOMINOES
LPs: 10/12-inch
DYNA DISC 15-20

CHUBBY & TURNPIKES
Singles: 7-inch
CAPITOL (5840 "I Didn't Try") 15-25 67
Also see TAVARES

CHUBUKOS
Singles: 7-inch
MAINSTREAM 3-5 74
PARAMOUNT 3-5 73

CHUCK, Charlie
Singles: 7-inch
CHANSON 4-6 69

CHUCK & BETTY
Singles: 7-inch
DECCA 8-12 58-59

CHUCK & BILL
Singles: 78 rpm
BRUNSWICK 10-20 57
Singles: 7-inch
BRUNSWICK 15-25 57

CHUCK & CHUCKLES
Singles: 7-inch
SHAD (5015 "One Hundred Baby") 10-20 59

CHUCK & CLEO
Singles: 7-inch
BLUE ROCK 4-8 65

CHUCK & DAYLIGHTERS: see DAYLIGHTERS

CHUCK & EDDIE
Singles: 7-inch
S.I.G.N. (127 "Good Thing Going") 15-25

CHUCK & GENE: see DAVIS, Gene / Chuck & Gene

CHUCK & JOE
Singles: 7-inch
DECCA 4-8 65

CHUCK & RAY
Singles: 7-inch
TOWER 4-8 66

CHUCK & RITA
Singles: 7-inch
CHESS 3-6 69

CHUCK & SANDY
Singles: 7-inch
REVOLVO 5-10 61

CHUCK & SENTRIES
Singles: 7-inch
RENDEZVOUS (207 "Sentinal Walk") 10-20 63

CHUCK-A-LUCKS
Singles: 7-inch
BOW (305 "Heaven Knows") 50-100 57
JUBILEE 10-20 61
LIN (5010 "Who Am I") 25-35 58
LIN (5014 "Disc Jockey Fever") 50-75 58
MEL-O-DY (106 "Sugar Cane Curtain") 25-35 63
W.B. (5198 "Long John") 10-20 61
W.B. (5234 "Cotton Pickin' Love") 10-20 61
Members: Charles Dickerson; Adrian McLish; Ruben Noel.

CHUCKLES
(Featuring Teddy Randazzo)
Singles: 7-inch
ABC-PAR (10276 "Runaround") 8-12 61
Also see RANDAZZO, Teddy
Also see THREE CHUCKLES

CHUCKLES
Singles: 7-inch
WEST SIDE (1019 "On the Street Where You Live") 20-30 63
Also see CONSORTS

CHUG & DOUG
Singles: 7-inch
CHARGER 10-20 64

CHUNG, Wang: see WANG CHUNG

CHUNKY A — P&R/LP '89
(Arsenio Hall)
Singles: 7-inch
MCA 3-4 89
Picture Sleeves
MCA 3-4 89
LPs: 10/12-inch
MCA 5-8 89

CHUNKY, NOVI & ERNIE
Singles: 7-inch
W.B. 3-5 77
LPs: 10/12-inch
REPRISE 8-12 74
W.B. 8-10 77

CHURCH — LP '86
Singles: 7-inch
ARISTA 3-4 88-90
CAPITOL 3-4 82
W.B. 3-4 84-86
Picture Sleeves
ARISTA 3-4 88
W.B. 3-4 86
LPs: 10/12-inch
ARISTA 5-8 88-90
CAPITOL 5-10 82
W.B. 5-10 84-86
Member: Steve Kilbey.

CHURCH, Eugene — P&R/R&B '58
(With the Fellows)
Singles: 7-inch
CLASS 10-20 58-60
COLLECTABLES 3-4 81
KING 8-12 61-63
RENDEZVOUS 10-15 60
SPECIALTY 15-25 57
WORLD PACIFIC (77866 "Dollar Bill") 10-15 67
Also see CLIQUES

CHURCH, Jimmy
(Jimmy Church Orchestra)
Singles: 7-inch
OKEH (7186 "The Hurt") 15-25 64
PEACHTREE (101 "Thinkin' About the Good Times") 50-100 60s
SOUND STAGE 7 5-10 66-67
VERVE (10126 "Corrido Rock") 15-25 58

CHURCH, Loreen
Singles: 7-inch
CHATTAHOOCHEE 4-8 64

CHURCH MICE
Singles: 7-inch
HOUSE of GUITARS (43 "Baby, We're Not Part of Society") 20-30 60s
Picture Sleeves
HOUSE of GUITARS (43 "Baby, We're Not Part of Society") 40-60 60s

CHURCH STREET FIVE
("Featuring Gene 'Daddy G' Barge")
Singles: 7-inch
LEGRAND (1004 "A Night with Daddy G") 10-20 61
LEGRAND (1010 "Fallen Arches") 10-20 61
LEGRAND (1014 "Church Street Walk") 10-20 61
LEGRAND (1021 "Daddy G Rides Again") 10-20 62
LEGRAND (1026 "Moonlight in Vermont") 10-20 63
Also see BARGE, Gene
Also see BONDS, Gary "U.S."
Also see DADDY G

CHURCHILL
Singles: 7-inch
ATTARACK 3-5 70
LPs: 10/12-inch
ATTARACK 10-15 70

CHURCHILL, Chick
LPs: 10/12-inch
CHRYSALIS 8-10 73

CHURCHILL, Kenneth
Singles: 7-inch
JOYCE (304 "Fate of Rock & Roll") 30-40

CHURCHILL, Savannah — R&B '45
(With the Five Kings; with Striders; with Four Tunes)
Singles: 78 rpm
ARGO 5-10 56
DECCA 5-10 53-55
KAY-RON 5-10 56
MANOR 5-10 45-48
RCA 5-10 51-52
REGAL (3309 "Once There Lived a Fool") 25-50 50
REGAL (3313 "Wedding Bells") 5-10 50
Singles: 7-inch
ARGO 10-20 56
DECCA 10-25 53-55
(Black label with sliver print.)
DECCA 5-10
(Multi-color label.)
JAMIE 10-15 60
KAY-RON 10-15 56
RCA 15-25 51-52
REGAL (468 "Once There Lived a Fool") 100-200 50
(Differs from 78 rpm number series.)
EPs: 7-inch
CAMDEN (270 "Love and Sin") 35-50 55
CAMDEN (282 "Savannah Churchill Sings") 35-50 55
Also see CARTER, Benny, & Orchestra
Also see FIVE KINGS
Also see FOUR TUNES
Also see STRIDERS

CHURCHILL DOWNS
Singles: 7-inch
AMAZING 3 (101 "Amazing Three") 5-10 68
INCANDESCENT (101 "It's Only a Matter of Time") 5-10 68

CHURCHWELL, Jimmy
Singles: 7-inch
WARE 4-8 65

CHURLS
Singles: 7-inch
A&M 3-6 69
LPs: 10/12-inch
A&M 10-15 69
Members: Bob O'Neill; John Barr; Brad Fowles; Sam Hurrie; Harry Ames.

CHY GUYS
Singles: 7-inch
MOBIE 4-8 66

CHYLDS
Singles: 7-inch
GIANT (101 "Hay Girl") 15-25 67
W.B. (7058 "Hay Girl") 10-15 67
W.B. (7095 "Psychedelic Soul") 10-15 67

CHYMES
(Four Chymes)
Singles: 7-inch
CHATTAHOOCHEE 5-10 62
DOWN to EARTH 5-10
MUSICTONE 10-15 64
Also see CHIMES

CHYMES
Singles: 7-inch
OKEH 4-8 66

CI CI — R&B '85
Singles: 7-inch
CREATIVE FUNK 3-4 85

CIARI, Claude
Singles: 7-inch
MURBO 4-8 67

CICADAS
Singles: 7-inch
RCA 4-8 64

CICCARELLI, Mike
Singles: 7-inch
HI 3-5 71

CICCONE, Don
Singles: 7-inch
KAMA SUTRA 4-6 70
Also see CRITTERS
Also see DON & CHEVELLS
Also see 4 SEASONS

CIGARETZ
LPs: 10/12-inch
CANCER 15-25 79
Members: Throb; Bindee; Johnny Guitar; Jimmy Jones; Ed McMuffin.

CIMMARON
(Cimmaron Show Review)
Singles: 7-inch
BEAT TREE 3-4 83
GREENTREE 3-5 76
HAMMERHEAD 3-5 79
Picture Sleeves
GREENTREE 3-5 76
LPs: 10/12-inch
BEAT TREE 5-10 85
Members: John Guelig; Larry Wolfe.

CINCINNATI MUSIC CO.
Singles: 7-inch
KAPP 4-6 68

CINCINNATIANS
Singles: 7-inch
EMERALD (16116 "Magic Genie") 20-30 63
ROSEVELT LEE (16116 "Magic Genie") 50-75 63
(First issue.)

CINCO'S
Singles: 7-inch
TALENT (104 "So Cold") 8-12

CINDERELLA — P&R/LP '86
Singles: 12-inch
MERCURY 4-8 88
(Promotional only.)
Singles: 7-inch
MERCURY 3-4 86-90
Picture Sleeves
MERCURY 3-4 86-89
LPs: 10/12-inch
MERCURY 5-10 86-90
Members: Tom Keifer; Fred Coury; Eric Brittingham; Jeff LaBar.

CINDERELLAS
Singles: 7-inch
COLUMBIA 10-15 60
DECCA 10-20 59
ESCAPADE 5-10 63
MERCURY 5-10 65
TAMARA 5-10 64

CINDERELLAS
Singles: 7-inch
DIMENSION (1026 "Baby Baby") 30-40 64
Member: Margaret Ross.
Also see COOKIES

CINDERMEN
Singles: 7-inch
MOONGLOW 15-25 66-68

CINDERS
Singles: 7-inch
ORIGINAL SOUND 4-8 64
W.B. 4-8 62

CINDERS
Singles: 7-inch
RIK (156 "Poison Ivy") 10-20 65
Member: John David Souther
Also see JOHN DAVID & CINDERS
Also see SOUTHER, J. D.

CINDY & LINDY
Singles: 7-inch
ABC-PAR 8-12 57
CORAL 5-10 59-61
PILGRIM 5-10 60
Members: Cindy Lord; Linda Doherty.

CINDY & PLAYMATES
Singles: 7-inch
JAY PEE (127 "Now That School Is Through") 8-12

CINDY & ROY — R&B '79
Singles: 12-inch
CASABLANCA 4-8 79
Singles: 7-inch
CASABLANCA 3-4 79
LPs: 10/12-inch
CASABLANCA 5-10 79
Member: Cynthia Biggs.

CINDY & SANDY
Singles: 7-inch
TAILSPIN 5-10 60

CINDY & SUE
Singles: 7-inch
ERA 5-10 61-62

CINDY LYNN & IN-SOUNDS
Singles: 7-inch
IN-SOUND (402 "Meet Me at Midnight") 40-60 67

CINDY RELLA: see RELLA, Cindy

CINEEMAS
Singles: 7-inch
DAVE (911 "Never Gonna Cry") 15-25 64

CINEMA — D&D '84
Singles: 12-inch
PROFILE 4-6 84

CINERAMAS
Singles: 7-inch
CHAMP (103 "It Must Be Love") 20-30 59
CLIFTON 4-8 74
RHAPSODY (71964 "Crying Over You") 50-75 60
Members: Frankie Palmer; Joey Bennett.
Also see ROWLAND, Roc

CINNAMON
Singles: 7-inch
MORNING THUNDER 81 4-8
LPs: 10/12-inch
BRADFORD (2824 "Cinnamon") 10-15 76(Recorded at Bradford's Studio, but no actual label name used.)
Members: Doug Morgan; Bruce Rowell; Jim Bannister; Dean Anderson.

CINNAMON
Singles: 7-inch
PAID 3-4 84

CINNAMON ANGELS
Singles: 7-inch
B.T. PUPPY 4-8 69
Also see SATANS FOUR / Cinnamon Angels

CINNAMON EMPIRE
Singles: 7-inch
ABC 3-6 69

CINNAMON SHIP
Singles: 7-inch
RCA 3-6 69

CINNAMONS
Singles: 7-inch
B.T. PUPPY 4-8 64-65

CIOLINO, Pete
Singles: 7-inch
RECORTE (401 "Daddy Joe") 75-100 58

CIRCA 58 / Peanut Gallery
Singles: 7-inch
BUDDAH 3-6 71

CIRCLE CITY BAND
Singles: 12-inch
BECKET 4-6 84

CIRCLE JERKS
Singles: 7-inch
LAX 3-4 83
LPs: 10/12-inch
LAX 5-10 83
POLYDOR (526948 Oddities, Abnormalities & Curiosities") 8-10 90s
(Colored vinyl.)
Member: Chuck Biscuits.
Also see DANZIG

CIRCLE O' FIRE
Singles: 7-inch
STAX 3-5 78
LPs: 10/12-inch
STAX 5-10 78

CIRCLE OF FIVE
Singles: 7-inch
A/S 3-4 84

CIRCULATIONS
Singles: 7-inch
HESS (3498 "Tell Me") 10-15

CIRCUS
Singles: 7-inch
REMBRANDT 10-20 66
U.S.A. 8-12 68

CIRCUS
Singles: 7-inch
OFFE (101 "Bad Seed") 15-25 67

CIRCUS *P&R '73*
Singles: 7-inch
METROMEDIA 3-6 72-73
LPs: 10/12-inch
HEMISPHERE 10-15 74
METROMEDIA 15-25 73
Members: Tom Dobeck; Frank Salle; Craig Balzer; Phil Alexander; Mick Sabol; Bruce Balzer.
Also see STANLEY, Michael, Band

CIRCUS
Singles: 7-inch
MAGIC CARPET 5-10
Picture Sleeves
MAGIC CARPET 5-10

CIRCUS MAXIMUS
LPs: 10/12-inch
VANGUARD 15-25 67-68
Members: Jerry Jeff Walker; Bob Bruno; David Scherstrom; Peter Troutner; Gary White.
Also see WALKER, Jerry Jeff

CIRCUS OF POWER *LP '88*
LPs: 10/12-inch
RCA 5-8 88

CIRCUT *D&D '84*
Singles: 12-inch
4TH & BROADWAY 4-6 84-85

CIRELL, Terry
(With the Backbeats)
Singles: 7-inch
VEKO 10-15 61

CIRINO & BOWTIES: see BOWTIES

CIRDO, Vic
Singles: 7-inch
DRAGON 4-8 61-64

CIRKYT
Singles: 7-inch
JODY (6701 "That's the Way Life Is") 20-30 67
Picture Sleeves
JODY (6701 "That's the Way Life Is") 20-30 67

CISSEL, Chuck *R&B '79*
Singles: 7-inch
ARISTA 3-5 79-80
LPs: 10/12-inch
ARISTA 5-10 80

CISSEL, Chuck, & Marva King *R&B '82*
Singles: 7-inch
ARISTA 3-4 82
Also see CISSEL, Chuck
Also see KING, Marva

CISUM
Singles: 7-inch
EPIC 4-6 68

CISYK, Kacey *P&R '77*
("Original Cast of You Light Up My Life")
Singles: 7-inch
ABC 3-5 78
ARISTA 3-5 78

CITADELS
Singles: 7-inch
MONOGRAM (501 "Let's Fall in Love") 150-200 62

CITATIONS
Singles: 7-inch
SWAN (4062 "Fire Ritual") 10-15 60

CITATIONS
Singles: 7-inch
CANADIAN AMERICAN 10-15 61
Member: Nicki North.

CITATIONS
Singles: 7-inch
DON-EL (113 "It Hurts Me") 40-60 62

CITATIONS
Singles: 7-inch
JUST (101 "That Is You") 10-15 62

CITATIONS
Singles: 7-inch
EPIC (9603 "Moon Race") 10-20 63
SARA (3301 "Moon Race") 20-30 63
Members: Brad Meyers; Ted Kasper; David Gustin; Bob Sanderson; Joe Halser; Tom Lamanchek; Kenny Stupek; Bob Sanderson; Plamen Sisters.
Also see MEYERS, Brad, & Citations

CITATIONS
Singles: 7-inch
FRATERNITY (910 "The Girl Next Door") 15-25 63
FRATERNITY (992 "The Girl Next Door") 10-15 67
VANGEE (301 "The Girl Next Door") 25-50 63

CITATIONS
Singles: 7-inch
MAJESTIC (1001 "Panda Bear") 10-20 60
MGM (13373 "That Girl of Mine") 10-20 65
MERCURY 5-10 64
PRINCESS 5-10 66
ROME (196 "Chartreuse") 8-12
ROULETTE 4-8 65
SWAN 5-10 60
UNIVERSITY ("Phantom Freighter") 8-12
(Selection number not known.)
Also see ALMA-KEYS

CITATIONS
Singles: 7-inch
BALLAD (101 "I Will Stand by You") 75-125 67

CITI
LPs: 10/12-inch
DELITE 5-10 79

CITIES SERVICE BAND
(Cities Service Green & White Quartet)
Singles: 78 rpm
RCA 3-5 50s
Singles: 7-inch
RCA 4-8 50s
EPs: 7-inch
RCA 5-10 50s
Member: Paul Lavalle.

CITISPEAK *R&B /D&D'84*
Singles: 7-inch
STREETWISE 3-4 84

CITIZEN
LPs: 10/12-inch
OVATION 5-10 80

CITIZEN KAINE
Singles: 7-inch
DUNHILL 4-8 68-69

CITIZENS BAND
Singles: 7-inch
CLARIDGE 3-5 75
COLUMBIA 3-4 83

CITY
Singles: 7-inch
ODE 8-12 68-69
LPs: 10/12-inch
ODE (44012 "Now That Everything's Been Said") 75-100 69
(Color photo on front cover.)
ODE (44012 "Now That Everything's Been Said") 8-12 71
(Black and white photo on front cover.)
Members: Carole King; Danny Kortchmar; Charles Larkey; Jim Gordon.
Also see KING, Carole
Also see KORTCHMAR, Danny

CITY
LPs: 10/12-inch
CHRYSALIS 5-10 86

CITY BOY *LP '76*
Singles: 7-inch
AIRBOY 3-5 77
ATLANTIC 3-4 79-81
MERCURY 3-5 76-78
Picture Sleeves
MERCURY 3-5 78
LPs: 10/12-inch
ATLANTIC 5-10 80
MERCURY 8-10 76-78
Members: Steve Broughton; Lol Mason; Mike Slamer; Max Thomas; Roy Ward; Chris Dunn; Roger Kent.

CITY BOYS
Singles: 7-inch
OVATION 3-5 76

CITY LIGHTS
Singles: 7-inch
SIRE 3-5 75
LPs: 10/12-inch
SIRE 8-10 75
Members: Mark Abel; John Berenzy; Leland Bobbe; Don Wilkins.

CITY LIMITS
Singles: 7-inch
CAMELIA (100 "There She Goes") 20-30 60s
UPTOWN 5-10 66
Member: Rocky Rhoades.
Also see IMPERIALS

CITY LIMITS
Singles: 7-inch
TSOP 3-5 75
LPs: 10/12-inch
TSOP 5-10 76

CITY LIMITZ
Singles: 7-inch
VIRTUE 3-5 70

CITY SQUIRES
Singles: 7-inch
TEMA (141 "Is It Time") 8-12 68

CITY STREETS
LPs: 10/12-inch
RCA 5-10 79

CITY SURFERS
Singles: 7-inch
CAPITOL 15-20 63-64

CITY THRILLS
LPs: 10/12-inch
STAR RHYTHM 8-10 81

CITY ZU
Singles: 7-inch
COLUMBIA (44342 "Give a Little Bit") 10-15 67
DOT 5-10 68-69

CIULO, Jerry
Singles: 7-inch
JEREE (114 "Fools Fall in Love") 10-15 65

CIVIL ATTACK
Singles: 7-inch
SALSOUL 3-4 83

CIX BITS
Singles: 7-inch
ENTERPRISE 3-5 73

CLAIRE, Nancy
Singles: 7-inch
RONA 5-10 61

CLANCY BROTHERS
(With Lou Killen; with Robbie O'Connell)
LPs: 10/12-inch
AUDIO FIDELITY 8-12 71-73
COLUMBIA 8-15 70
VANGUARD 5-12 74-83

CLANCY BROTHERS & TOMMY MAKEM *LP '63*
Singles: 7-inch
COLUMBIA 4-6 62-69
LPs: 10/12-inch
COLUMBIA 10-20 62-69
GWP 10-15
HARMONY 6-10 71-72
SHANACHIE 5-10
TRADITION 10-15 67-69
Also see CLANCY BROTHERS

CLANDESTINE *D&D '84*
Singles: 12-inch
SLEEPING BAG 4-6 84

CLANFORD, Kris
Singles: 7-inch
ABC-PAR 10-15 68

CLANN
Singles: 7-inch
G.A.R. (103 "Stubborn Kind of Fellow") 20-30 66
G.A.R. (109 "Tall Towers") 15-25 67
Members: Ross Dickerson; Dave Dister; Bill Stone; Jeff Gorman; Terry Kolkmann.

CLANNAD *LP '86*
LPs: 10/12-inch
RCA 5-10 84-88

CLANTON, Bobby, & Cyclones
Singles: 7-inch
CYCLONE (500 "Angel") 50-100

CLANTON, Darrell *C&W '83*
Singles: 7-inch
AUDIOGRAPH 3-4 83-84
W.B. 3-4 84-85
LPs: 10/12-inch
AUDIOGRAPH 5-8 83

CLANTON, Ike *P&R '60*
Singles: 7-inch
ACE 5-10 59-60
MERCURY 5-10 62-63
Also see DEL-VIKINGS / Ike Clanton
Also see EDDY, Duane

CLANTON, Jimmy *P&R/R&B '58*
(With His Rockets; Jimmie Clanton)
Singles: 78 rpm
ACE 25-50 57
Singles: 7-inch
ABC 3-4 73
ACE (Except 567) 8-15 57-63
ACE (567 "My Own True Love") 10-15 59
(Monaural.)
ACE (567 "My Own True Love") 25-50 59
(Stereo.)
COLLECTABLES 3-4 81
ERIC 3-4 73
IMPERIAL 4-8 67-68
LAURIE 4-8 69
MALA 4-8 65
OLDIES 45 3-5
PHILIPS 4-8 63-64
SPIRAL 3-5 71
STARCREST 3-5 76
STARFIRE (Except picture discs) 3-5 78
STARFIRE ("I Wanna Go Home") 10-15 81
(Picture disc. Selection number not known.)
VIN 4-8 62
Promotional Singles
ACE (664 "Venus in Blue Jeans") 15-25 62
ACE (51860 "The Slave") 10-20 60
(Promotional, bonus disc with the *Jimmy's Happy/Jimmy's Blue* LP.)
U.A. ("Teenage Millionaire") 10-20 62
(Cardboard 6-inch flexi-disc.)
Picture Sleeves
ACE (Except 51860) 8-15 59-63
ACE (51860 "The Slave") 15-25 60
(Promotional only, mail-order bonus offer to buyers of the *Jimmy's Happy/Jimmy's Blue* LP. All copies of this sleeve were autographed by Clanton.)
PHILIPS 5-10 64
STARCREST 4-6 76
EPs: 7-inch
ACE ("Jimmy's Happy/Jimmy's Blue") 25-50 60
(Colored vinyl. Exact title and selection number not known.)
ACE (101 "Just a Dream") 20-40 59
ACE (102 "Thinking of You") 20-40 59
ACE (103 "I'm Always Chasing Rainbows") 20-30 59
ACE (642 "Teenage Millionaire") 15-25 61
LPs: 10/12-inch
ACE (100 "Jimmy's Happy/Jimmy's Blue") 50-75 60
(Black vinyl.)
ACE (100 "Jimmy's Happy/Jimmy's Blue") 75-125 60
(Colored vinyl.)
ACE (1001 "Just a Dream") 50-75 59
ACE (1007 "Jimmy's Happy") 40-50 60
ACE (1008 "Jimmy's Blue") 40-50 60
ACE (1011 "My Best to You") 50-75 61
ACE (1014 "Teenage Millionaire") 50-75 61
ACE (1026 "Venus in Blue Jeans") 40-60 61
MONTAGNE 10-15 81
PHILIPS 15-25 64
Also see DALE, Jimmy

CLANTON, Jimmy / Frankie Ford / Jerry Lee Lewis / Patsy Cline
EPs: 7-inch
MEMORY LANE 3-5 92
(Promotional issue only. Not issued with cover.)
Also see CLINE, Patsy
Also see FORD, Frankie
Also see LEWIS, Jerry Lee

CLANTON, Jimmy / Bristow Hopper
LPs: 10/12-inch
DESIGN 15-20
Also see HOPPER, Bristow

CLANTON, Jimmy, & Mary Ann Mobley
Singles: 7-inch
ACE 5-10 61
Picture Sleeves
ACE 10-15 61
Also see CLANTON, Jimmy

CLAN-TONES
Singles: 7-inch
EMONY (1021 "May I Never Love Again") 25-50 59

CLAP
LP: 10/12-inch
NOVA SOL 8-12

CLAPTON, Eric *P&R/LP '70*
Singles: 12-inch
W.B. (2248 "Forever Man") 5-10 85
(Promotional issue only.)
W.B. (2683 "Miss You") 5-10 85
(Promotional issue only.)
Singles: 7-inch
ATCO 4-6 70-71
DUCK 3-4 83-86
POLYDOR 3-5 72-73
RSO 3-5 74-82
W.B. 3-4 86
Picture Sleeves
DUCK 3-4 85-89
POLYDOR 3-6
RSO 3-5 80-81
W.B. 3-4 86
LPs: 10/12-inch
ATCO (329 "Eric Clapton") 20-30 70
ATCO (803 "History of Eric Clapton") 20-30 72
DUCK 5-10 83-89
MFSL (030 "Slowhand") 75-100 79
MFSL (183 "Bluesbreakers") 25-35 87
MFSL (220 "Eric Clapton") 20-25 94
NAUTILUS (32 "Just One Night") 75-100 80
(Half-speed mastered.)
POLYDOR (Except 835261) 8-15 72-73
POLYDOR (835261 "Crossroads") 30-40 88
(Boxed, six-disc set.)
RSO (Except 035, 1009 & 4801) 8-20 73-82
RSO (035 "Slowhand") 20-25 77
(Colored vinyl. Promotional issue only.)
RSO (1009 "Limited Backless") 40-50 78
(Colored vinyl. Promotional issue only.)
RSO (4801 "461 Ocean Blvd.") 8-12 74
(With *Give Me Strength*.)
RSO (4801 "461 Ocean Blvd.") 5-10 74
(*Give Me Strength* is replaced with *Better Make It Through the Day*.)
Also see BLIND FAITH
Also see BROOKER, Gary
Also see COOLIDGE, Rita
Also see CREAM
Also see CURTIS, Sonny
Also see DELANEY & BONNIE
Also see DEREK & DOMINOES
Also see GUY, Buddy, with Dr. John & Eric Clapton / Buddy Guy & J. Geils Band
Also see HARRISON, George
Also see LEVY, Marcy
Also see LOMAX, Jackie
Also see MAYALL, John
Also see RUSSELL, Leon
Also see SPANN, Otis
Also see STARR, Ringo
Also see TOWNSHEND, Pete, & Ronnie Lane
Also see WATERS, Roger
Also see YARDBIRDS

CLAPTON, Eric, Jeff Beck & Jimmy Page
LPs: 10/12-inch
RCA (4624 "Guitar Boogie") 10-15 71
Also see BECK, Jeff
Also see PAGE, Jimmy

CLAPTON, Eric, & Tina Turner
Singles: 7-inch
DUCK 3-4 87
Picture Sleeves
DUCK 3-4 87
Also see CLAPTON, Eric
Also see TURNER, Tina

CLARE
Singles: 7-inch
A&M 3-5 71

CLARE SISTERS
Singles: 7-inch
VAN (1922 "Cool, Cool, Cool") 15-25

CLAREMONTS
Singles: 78 rpm
APOLLO 25-50 57
Singles: 7-inch
APOLLO (517 "Why Keep Me Dreaming") 25-50 57
APOLLO (751 "Why Keep Me Dreaming") 10-20 63

CLARENCE & CALVIN
Singles: 7-inch
DUKE 5-10 63

CLARK, Al Brisco
Singles: 7-inch
FONTANA 4-8 64

CLARK, Alan
Singles: 7-inch
CLARK 3-5 75

CLARK, Alice
Singles: 7-inch
MAINSTREAM (5520 "I Keep It Hid") 4-6 72
RAINY DAY (8004 "You Got a Deal") 5-10 68
W.B. (7270 "You Hit Me") 20-40 69
LPs: 10/12-inch
MAINSTREAM 10-12 72

CLARK, Ann
Singles: 78 rpm
ACE (512 "I Had a Dream") 10-15 56
Singles: 7-inch
ACE (512 "I Had a Dream") 10-20 56

CLARK, Becky
Singles: 7-inch
JC 4-8 62

CLARK, Billy
Singles: 7-inch
ORANGE 5-10 59
PEACH 5-10 59

CLARK, Billy, & Lucille Brown
Singles: 7-inch
DYNAMO 4-6 69

CLARK, Billy, & Maskman
Singles: 7-inch
DYNAMO 4-8 68
Also see CLARK, Billy, & Lucille Brown

CLARK, Bobby
Singles: 7-inch
CMH 3-4 83
Also see OUTLAW BAND
Also see RIPPLES
Also see VELVIT, Jimmy

CLARK, Bobby, & Rhythm Knights
Singles: 7-inch
SOMA....12-18 60

CLARK, Bruce, & Qs
Singles: 7-inch
HULL (762 "Penny for Your Thoughts")....25-35 63

CLARK, Charles
Singles: 7-inch
ARTISTIC....15-25 58

CLARK, Chris R&B '66
Singles: 7-inch
MOTOWN....10-15 67-68
V.I.P. (25031 "Do Right Baby Do Right")....10-15 66
V.I.P. (25038 "Love's Gone Mad")..50-60 66
(Title incorrect on label.)
V.I.P. (25038 "Love's Gone Bad")..10-20 66
(Title corrected.)
V.I.P. (25041 "I Love You")....10-15 67
LPs: 10/12-inch
MOTOWN (664 "Soul Sounds")....40-60 67
WEED (801 "CC Rides Again")....50-75

CLARK, Chuck
Singles: 7-inch
RELIABLE....4-8 62
SHERATON....4-8 62
U.A.....4-8 62

CLARK, Claudine P&R/R&B '62
(With the Spinners)
Singles: 7-inch
CHANCELLOR....5-10 62-63
COLLECTABLES....3-4 81
ERIC....3-4 73
HERALD (521 "Teenage Blues")....20-30 58
JAMIE....4-8 64
TCF....4-8 64
LPs: 10/12-inch
CHANCELLOR (5029 "Party Lights")....40-60 62
Also see DAWN, Joy

CLARK, Connie
Singles: 7-inch
JOKER (716 "My Sugar Baby")....75-125 60s

CLARK, Cortelia
LPs: 10/12-inch
RCA....10-15 66

CLARK, Dave, Five P&R/LP '64
(With Friends)
Singles: 7-inch
CONGRESS (212 "I Knew It All the Time")....10-15 64
EPIC (2000 series)....4-6 72
EPIC (9656 thru 10894)....5-15 64-72
EPIC MEMORY LANE....3-5
HOLLYWOOD....3-4 93
JUBILEE (5476 "Chaquita")....10-20 64
LAURIE (3188 "I Walk the Line")....25-35 63
RUST (5078 "I Walk the Line")....20-30 64
Promotional Singles
EPIC (9656 thru 9833)....10-20 64-65
EPIC (9863 "Over & Over")....10-20 65
(Black vinyl.)
EPIC (9863 "Over & Over")....25-35 65
(Colored vinyl.)
EPIC (9882 thru 10894)....10-20 65-72
Picture Sleeves
CONGRESS (212 "I Knew It All the Time")....15-25 64
EPIC (2000 series)....5-8 72
EPIC (9656 thru 10265)....10-20 64-67
EPIC (10375 thru 10684)....15-25 68-72
HOLLYWOOD (65909 "Over and Over")....4-6 93
HOLLYWOOD (65912 "Do You Love Me")....4-6 93
EPs: 7-inch
COLUMBIA/AURAVISION ("Catch Us If You Can")....30-50 65
(Promotional issue made for Ponds. Single-sided, square, cardboard picture disc.)
EPIC....15-25 66
(Juke box issues only. Include title strips.)
LPs: 10/12-inch
EPIC (24093 "Glad All Over")....75-125 64
(Instruments are not pictured on cover.)
EPIC (24093 "Glad All Over")....20-30 64
(Instruments are pictured on cover.)
EPIC (24104 "The Dave Clark Five Return")....20-30 64
EPIC (24117 "American Tour")....20-30 64
EPIC (24128 "Coast to Coast")....20-30 64
EPIC (24139 "A Weekend in London")....20-30 65
EPIC (24162 "Having a Wild Weekend")....20-30 65
EPIC (24178 "I Like It Like That")...20-30 65
EPIC (24185 "Greatest Hits")....20-30 66
EPIC (24198 "Try Too Hard")....20-30 66
EPIC (24212 "Satisfied with You") 20-30 66
EPIC (24221 "More Greatest Hits")....20-30 66
EPIC (24236 "5 by 5")....20-30 67
EPIC (24312 "You Got What It Takes")....20-30 67
EPIC (24354 "Everybody Knows") 20-30 68
EPIC (26000 series)....15-25 64-68
(Reprocessed stereo issues.)
EPIC (30434 "Dave Clark Five")....35-50 71
EPIC (33459 "Glad All Over Again")....20-25 75
Promotional LPs
EPIC (77238 "The Dave Clark Interviews")....40-45 65
I-N-S RADIO NEWS (1006 "It's Here Luv")....75-100 64
Members: Dave Clark; Mike Smith; Lenny Davidson; Denny Payton; Rick Huxley.

CLARK, Dave, Five / Rick Astor & Switchers
LPs: 10/12-inch
CORTLEIGH (1073 "Dave Clark Five")....15-25 66
(Has only two Dave Clark Five tracks.)

CLARK, Dave, Five / Lulu
Singles: 7-inch
EPIC (10260/65 "Everybody Knows"/"Best of Both Worlds")....10-20 67
(Promotional issue only.)
Also see LULU

CLARK, Dave, Five / New Christy Minstrels / Bobby Vinton / Jerry Vale
EPs: 7-inch
COLUMBIA SPECIAL PRODUCTS (223 "Limited Edition")....10-15 65
Also see NEW CHRISTY MINSTRELS
Also see VALE, Jerry
Also see VINTON, Bobby

CLARK, Dave, Five / Playbacks
LPs: 10/12-inch
CROWN (400 "Playbacks")....20-25 64
(Stereo.)
CROWN (5400 "Playbacks")....20-25 64
(Monaural.)
CROWN (473 "Chaquita - In Your Heart")....20-25 65
(Stereo.)
CROWN (5473 "Chaquita - In Your Heart")....20-25 65
(Monaural.)
CUSTOM (1098 "It's Happening")..15-20 65
(Each Crown and Custom LP has only two Dave Clark Five tracks.)

CLARK, Dave, Five / Simon & Garfunkel / Yardbirds / New Christy Minstrels
EPs: 7-inch
COLUMBIA SPECIAL PRODUCTS (468 "Great Shakes Shake-Out")....20-30 65
(Mail-order promotional offer from General Foods.)
Also see CLARK, Dave, Five
Also see NEW CHRISTY MINSTRELS
Also see SIMON & GARFUNKEL
Also see YARDBIRDS

CLARK, Dee P&R/R&B '58
(With the Riley Hampton Orchestra)
Singles: 78 rpm
ABNER (1019 "Nobody But You")..50-75 59
ABNER (1029 "Hey Little Girl")....50-100 59
FALCON (1002 "Gloria")....15-25 57
Singles: 7-inch
ABC....3-4 73
ABNER (Monaural)....10-20 58-60
ABNER (Stereo)....40-50 59-60
CHELSEA....3-5 75
COLLECTABLES....3-4 83
ERIC....3-4 73
COLUMBIA....5-10 67
CONSTELLATION....8-15 63-65
FALCON (1002 "Gloria")....15-25 57
LIBERTY....8-15 70
MCA....3-4 84
ROCKY....3-5 73
VEE JAY (Monaural)....5-10 60-63
VEE JAY (Stereo)....25-40 60-63
U.A.....3-5 71
WAND....4-8 68
W.B.....3-5 73
Picture Sleeves
ABNER (1029 "Hey Little Girl")....15-25 59
EPs: 7-inch
ABNER (900 "Dee Clark")....40-60 61
VEE JAY (900 "Dee Clark")....25-50 61
LPs: 10/12-inch
ABNER (LP-2000 "Dee Clark")....40-60 59
(Monaural.)
ABNER (SR-2000 "Dee Clark")....50-75 59
(Stereo.)
ABNER (LP-2002 "How About That")....40-60 59
(Monaural.)
ABNER (SR-2002 "How About That")....50-75 59
(Stereo.)
SOLID SMOKE....5-10 84
SUNSET (5217 "Wondering")....10-15 68
VEE JAY (1019 "You're Looking Good")....20-30 60
VEE JAY (1028 "Dee Clark")....20-30 61
VEE JAY (1037 "Hold On, It's Dee Clark")....20-30 61
VEE JAY (1047 "The Best of Dee Clark")....20-30 64
Also see DELEGATES
Also see DELLS
Also see KOOL GENTS
Also see SAUNDERS, Red
Also see UPCHURCH, Phil

CLARK, Dee Dee
Singles: 7-inch
TWIN HITS....3-5

CLARK, Delores
Singles: 7-inch
ANTARAS....4-8 66

CLARK, Dick
Singles: 7-inch
BUDDAH ("Inside Stories")....8-12 70s
(Square cardboard picture disc. Issued with "20 Years of Rock N Roll" compilation album.)
DICK CLARK....10-15
DUNHILL....4-8 67
LIBERTY....4-6 69

CLARK, Dorisetta
Singles: 7-inch
LIBRA (217 "My Baby's Gone")....50-100
MERCURY (71253 "You Love Me")....75-125 58

CLARK, Dottie
(Dotty Clark)
Singles: 7-inch
BIG TOP....5-10 61
HOLLYWOOD....4-8 68
LPs: 10/12-inch
TIME....10-20 64

CLARK, Doug
(With the Nuts; with the Hot Nuts)
Singles: 7-inch
JUBILEE (5536 "Baby Let Me Bang Your Box")....10-15 66
JUBILEE (5546 "Go Doug, Go")....10-15 66
PORT (70043 "Peanuts")....8-12 65
EPs: 7-inch
GROSS (1000 "Excerpts")....15-20
(Excerpts from Gross LPs, 102, 103 & 105.)
GROSS (2065 "Burlesque")....15-20
LPs: 10/12-inch
GROSS (101 "Nuts to You")....20-30
GROSS (102 "On Campus")....20-30
GROSS (103 "Homecoming")....20-30
GROSS (104 "Rush Week")....20-30
GROSS (105 "Panty Raid")....20-30
GROSS (106 "Summer Session")..20-30
GROSS (107 "Hell Night")....20-30
GROSS (108 "Freak Out")....20-30
GROSS (109 "With a Hat On")....20-30

CLARK, Fred
Singles: 78 rpm
FEDERAL....10-20 53
Singles: 7-inch
FEDERAL (12136 "Walkin' and Wonderin'")....20-30 53
Also see JACKSON, Jump / Fred Clark

CLARK, Freddie
Singles: 78 rpm
X-TRA (105 "Ward 13")....15-25 57
Singles: 7-inch
X-TRA (105 "Ward 13")....15-25 57

CLARK, Gene LP '74
(With the Gosdin Brothers)
Singles: 7-inch
ASYLUM....3-5 74
COLUMBIA (43000 series)....5-8 66
RSO....3-4 77
LPs: 10/12-inch
A&M....10-15 71
ASYLUM....8-10 74
COLUMBIA (2618 "Gene Clark")....20-30 67
(Monaural.)
COLUMBIA (9418 "Gene Clark")....25-35 67
(Stereo.)
COLUMBIA (31123 "Early L.A. Sessions")....10-15 72
RSO....5-10 77
TAKOMA....5-10 84
Also see BYRDS
Also see DILLARD & CLARK
Also see NEW CHRISTY MINSTRELS

CLARK, Gene, & Carla Olson
LPs: 10/12-inch
RHINO....5-8 87
Also see CLARK, Gene
Also see TEXTONES

CLARK, Guy C&W '79
Singles: 7-inch
RCA....3-5 76
W.B.....3-5 78-83
LPs: 10/12-inch
RCA....5-10 75-83
W.B.....5-8 78-83
Session: Waylon Jennings.
Also see COE, David Allan
Also see JENNINGS, Waylon

CLARK, Harvey, & Dawn Monet Singers
Singles: 7-inch
KAPP....4-6 69

CLARK, Jackie
Singles: 7-inch
XYZ (2005 "Walkie Talkie")....15-25 59

CLARK, James "Beale Street"
Singles: 78 rpm
COLUMBIA....10-20 46
Also see MEMPHIS JIMMY

CLARK, Jay C&W '85
Singles: 7-inch
CONCORDE....3-4 85-86

CLARK, Jimmy
(Jimmy "Soul" Clark; with Benny & Sportsmen)
Singles: 7-inch
KAREN (101 "I Blew a Good Thing")....10-15 60s
KAREN (1539 "Do It Right Now")....10-15 68
MOIRA (104 "Tell Her")....8-12 69
SOULHAWK (001 "Come on and Be My Sweet Darlin'")....10-20 67
SOULHAWK (003 "I'll Be Your Winner")....25-50 67
TEEK (4824 "Shook Up Over You")....20-30
TEEK (4829 "Nothing Like a Mother")....20-30

CLARK, Jimmy, Trio
Singles: 7-inch
ROUND (1001 "The Cat")....15-25 59

CLARK, Jo Jo
LPs: 10/12-inch
ALLEGIANCE....5-10 84

CLARK, Kitty
Singles: 7-inch
HOUSE of ORANGE (2400 "Big Wheel")....10-15 70

CLARK, Lee
Singles: 7-inch
ATCO....4-8 63

CLARK, Lewis
Singles: 7-inch
BRENT....4-8
FULLER....5-10 68
RED RAM (13672 "I Got My Eyes on You")....10-20 60s
TIGERTOWN (004 "If You Ever, Ever Leave Me")....15-25 60s

CLARK, Lori
Singles: 7-inch
CELESTIAL....4-8 67

CLARK, Lucky
Singles: 7-inch
CHESS (1782 "So Sick")....10-20 61
CHESS (1806 "Feeling of Love")....8-12 61

CLARK, Lucky C&W '77
Singles: 7-inch
POLYDOR....3-5 76-77
PUMA....3-5 76

CLARK, Lynda
Singles: 7-inch
ABC....4-8 66

CLARK, Michael
Singles: 7-inch
IMPERIAL....10-15 62-63

CLARK, Michael
Singles: 7-inch
CAPITOL....3-5 76-79
LPs: 10/12-inch
CAPITOL....8-10 77

CLARK, Mickey C&W '83
Singles: 7-inch
EVERGREEN....3-4 87
MONUMENT....3-4 83

CLARK, Mike
Singles: 7-inch
SMASH....4-6 68

CLARK, Paul
LPs: 10/12-inch
CREATIVE SOUND....10-12 72
SEED....8-10
SUNRISE....10-12 74

CLARK, Petula P&R '64
(Pet Clark)
Singles: 78 rpm
CORAL....5-15 53-54
KING....5-15 54
MGM....5-15 55
Singles: 7-inch
CORAL....10-20 53-54
DUNHILL....3-5 74
ERIC....3-4 83
IMPERIAL....5-10 59-60
JANUS....3-5 76
KING....10-20 54
LAURIE....4-8 62-63
LONDON....4-8 62
MGM (12000 series)....10-20 55
MGM (14000 series, except 14392)...3-6 72-74
MGM (14392 "Little Bit of Lovin'")..15-25
ROWE/AMI....5-10 66
("Play Me" Sales Stimulator promotional issue.)
SCOTTI BROTHERS....3-4 82
W.B.....3-8 64-69
WARWICK....5-10 61
EPs: 7-inch
W.B.....5-10 65-66
(Juke box issues only.)
LPs: 10/12-inch
GNP....5-8 73
IMPERIAL (9079 "Pet Clark")....20-40 59
(Monaural.)
IMPERIAL (9281 "Uptown")....15-25 65
IMPERIAL (12027 "Pet Clark")....20-30 65
(Stereo.)
LAURIE (2032 "In Love")....20-25 65
(Monaural.)
LAURIE (S-2032 "In Love")....25-35 65
(Stereo.)
LAURIE (2043 "Petula Clark Sings for Everybody")....15-20 65
(Monaural.)
LAURIE (2043 "Petula Clark Sings for Everybody")....20-25 65
(Stereo.)
MGM....8-12 72
PREMIER....15-25 64
SUNSET....10-20 66
W.B.....10-20 65-71
Also see ELLIOTT, Ron
Also see FELICIANO, Jose / Petula Clark

CLARK, Rickie
(Rickie Clark Company)
Singles: 12-inch
BECKET....4-6 84

CLARK, Robin
Singles: 7-inch
CAPITOL....5-10 61-62

CLARK, Rosalind
Singles: 7-inch
W.B.....3-5 74

CLARK, Roy C&W/P&R '63
(With Buck Trent)
Singles: 78 rpm
4 STAR....15-25 54
Singles: 7-inch
ABC....3-5 74-79
ABC/DOT....3-5 75-77
CAPITOL....4-8 61-66
CHURCHILL....3-4 82-84
DOT....3-6 68-74
4 STAR (1659 "Mysteries of Life")....25-50 54
HALLMARK....3-4 89
MCA....3-4 79-84
SILVER DOLLAR....3-4 86
SONGBIRD....3-4 81
TOWER....3-6 67
LPs: 10/12-inch
ABC....5-10 77-79
ABC/DOT....6-10 74-77
ABC SPECIAL PRODUCTS (1002 "Roy Clark")....10-15 78
(Promotional issue, made for Pringles.)
CAPITOL (300 series)....10-12 69
CAPITOL (1700 thru 2500 series)....10-25 62-66
(With "T" or "ST" prefix.)
CAPITOL (2400 series)....5-10 81
(With "SM" prefix.)
CAPITOL (11000 series)....8-12 74-75
CAPITOL (12000 thru 16000 series)....5-10 80-81
CHURCHILL....5-10 82
DOT....8-12 68-74
GUEST STAR....8-12 60s
MCA....5-8 79-84
PICKWICK....5-10 70s
PICKWICK/HILLTOP....8-15 66
SONGBIRD....5-10 81
TOWER....10-15 67-68
WORD....5-10 75
Also see CASH, Johnny / Roy Clark / Linda Ronstadt

CLARK, Royce
Singles: 7-inch
AIRWAYS (1001 "Losing Side of Town")....4-6 81
MINARET (204 "Oh Boy")....25-50
VEEDA ("They'll Never Know")..100-150 60s
(Selection number not known.)
VEEDA (4011 "Like a Man")....100-150 60s

CLARK, Sally & Marvin
Singles: 7-inch
PATMAK....4-8 65

CLARK, Sanford P&R/R&B/C&W '56
Singles: 78 rpm
DOT....15-25 56
MCI (1003 "The Fool")....25-50 55
REO....35-55 57
(Canadian.)
Singles: 7-inch
ABC....3-5 74
DOT (15481 "The Fool")....20-40 56
(Maroon label.)
DOT (15481 "The Fool")....15-25 57
(Black label.)
DOT (15481 "The Fool")....15-25 57
(Black label.)
DOT (15516 "A Cheat")....20-40 56
(Maroon label.)
DOT (15534 "9 Lb Hammer")....20-30 57
DOT (15556 "The Glory of Love")..20-30 57
DOT (15585 "Loo Be Doo")....20-30 57
DOT (15646 "Swanee River Rock")....20-30 57
DOT (15738 "Modern Romance")....75-100 58
JAMIE (1120 "Bad Luck")....10-20 59
JAMIE (1129 "Run Boy Run")....10-20 59
JAMIE (1153 "Pledging My Love")..10-20 60
LHI (9 "Footprints in Her Yard")....4-8 68
LHI (9 "Farm Labor Camp #9")....4-8 69
LHI (1203 "Son of Hickory Holler's Tramp")....4-8 68
LHI (12003 "Return of the Fool")....8-15 68
MCI (1003 "The Fool")....50-100 55
RAMCO (1972 "The Fool")....5-10 66
REO (8143 "9 Lb. Hammer")....20-30 57
(Canadian.)
TREY (3016 "It Hurts Me Too")....10-15 61
W.B.....6-12 64-65
Also see CASEY, Al
Also see REYNOLDS, Jody

CLARK, Sanford, & Duane Eddy
Singles: 7-inch
JAMIE (1107 "Sing 'Em Some Blues")....15-25 58
Also see CLARK, Sanford
Also see EDDY, Duane

CLARK, Sharen, & Product of Time
Singles: 7-inch
APT....3-5 72

CLARK, Steve C&W '84
Singles: 7-inch
MERCURY....3-4 84

CLARK, Suzanne
Singles: 7-inch
JAF....5-10 61

CLARK, Suzie
Singles: 7-inch
RENDEZVOUS....4-8 63

CLARK, Suzy
Singles: 7-inch
CRUSADER....4-8 65

CLARK, Toni
Singles: 7-inch
TUCSON 3-5 70-71

CLARK, Wilbur
Singles: 7-inch
JOB (1124 "I'll Give My Whole Life") 200-300 58

CLARK & MARILYN
Singles: 7-inch
CREAM 3-5 71

CLARK & McMULLEN
Singles: 78 rpm
ABBEY 4-8
Singles: 7-inch
ABBEY 5-10

CLARK - HUTCHINSON
LPs: 10/12-inch
DERAM 10-12 71
SIRE 10-15 70

CLARK SISTERS
Singles: 7-inch
DOT 4-8 59
LPs: 10/12-inch
CORAL 10-20 60-62
DOT 10-20 59

CLARK SISTERS R&B/D&D '83
Singles: 12-inch
ELEKTRA 4-6 83
Singles: 7-inch
ELEKTRA 3-4 83

CLARKE, Allan P&R '78
Singles: 7-inch
ASYLUM 3-5 76
ATLANTIC 3-5 78
ELEKTRA 3-4 80
EPIC 3-5 72
LPs: 10/12-inch
ASYLUM 8-10 76
ATLANTIC 5-10 78
ELEKTRA 5-10 80
EPIC 10-15 72
Also see HOLLIES
Also see PARSONS, Alan, Project

CLARKE, Billy
Singles: 7-inch
DYNAMO 3-5

CLARKE, Bruce
Singles: 7-inch
WYNNE 5-10 60

CLARKE, Gary
Singles: 7-inch
DECCA (31511 "The Virginian") 5-10 63
RCA 5-10 61
Picture Sleeves
DECCA (31511 "The Virginian") 15-25 63

CLARKE, Jimmy
Singles: 7-inch
DIAMOND 4-8 64

CLARKE, Stanley LP '75
(Stan Clarke)
Singles: 12-inch
EPIC 4-6 83-85
NEMPEROR 4-8 79
Singles: 7-inch
EPIC 3-4 80-85
NEMPEROR 3-5 75-79
LPs: 10/12-inch
EPIC 5-10 80-85
NEMPEROR 8-12 74-79
POLYDOR 10-12 73
Also see RETURN to FOREVER

CLARKE, Stanley, & George Duke P&R/R&B '81
Singles: 12-inch
EPIC 4-6 83
Singles: 7-inch
EPIC 3-4 81-84
LPs: 10/12-inch
EPIC 5-10 81-83
Also see CLARKE, Stanley
Also see DUKE, George

CLARKE, Tony P&R/R&B '64
Singles: 7-inch
CHESS 6-12 64-65
CHICKORY 4-6 70
ERIC 3-5 78
M-S (206 "A Wrong Man") 50-100 68

CLARKE, William
LPs: 10/12-inch
ALLIGATOR 5-8 90

CLASH LP '79
Singles: 12-inch
EPIC (617 "Gates of the West") 15-20 79
(Promotional issue only.)
EPIC (723 "Clampdown") 15-20 79
(Promotional issue only.)
EPIC (905 "Magnificent Seven") 15-20 80
(Promotional issue only.)
EPIC (2036 "Call Up") 8-12 81
(Blue label. Promotional issue only.)
EPIC (2036 "Call Up") 8-12 81
(Roulette wheel label. Promotional issue only.)
EPIC (2230 "This Is England") 8-12 85
(Promotional issue only.)
EPIC (2277 "Fingerpoppin' ") 8-12 85
(Blue label. Promotional issue only.)
EPIC (2662 "This Is Radio Clash") .15-20 81
(Promotional issue only.)
EPIC (3144 "Rock the Casbah") 8-12 82
EPIC (6899 "Radio Clash") 5-10 87
EPIC (7829 "Rock the Casbah") 5-10 89
(Mixed masters issue.)
Singles: 7-inch
EPIC (1178 "Gates of the West") 4-6 79
(Promotional issue only. Issued with promo edition of *The Clash.*)
EPIC (3006 "Should I Stay") 8-10 82
(Promotional issue only.)
EPIC (3088 "London Calling") 5-8 80
(Hall of Fame series.)
EPIC (3245 "Rock the Casbah") 8-10 82
(Promotional issue only.)
EPIC (3547 "Should I Stay") 3-5 82
EPIC (3571 "Should I Stay") 15-20 82
(Single-sided disc. Promotional issue only.)
EPIC (5749 "Train in Vain") 15-20 79
(10-inch single. Promotional issue only.)
EPIC (5788 "Clampdown") 15-20 79
(10-inch single. Promotional issue only.)
EPIC (8470 "Should I Stay") 5-8 82
(Hall of Fame series.)
EPIC (20000 series) 3-5 82
EPIC (30000 series) 3-5 82
EPIC (50000 series, except 50738, 50851 & 51013) 3-5 79-81
EPIC (50738 "White Man in Hammersmith Palais") 5-10 79
EPIC (50851 "Train in Vain") 10-15 79
(Promotional issue only.)
EPIC (51013 "Hitsville UK") 10-15 80
(Promotional issue only.)
Picture Sleeves
EPIC (3061 "Should I Stay") 10-15 82
(Shown as "Special Limited Edition.")
EPIC (3547 "Should I Stay") 5-10 82
(Lists B-side, *Cool Confusion.*)
EPIC (3547 "Should I Stay") 10-15 82
(No B-side shown. Promotional issue only.)
LPs: 10/12-inch
EPIC (913 "Sandinista Now") 15-20 80
(Promotional issue only.)
EPIC (952 "If Music Could Talk") ...15-20 81
(Promotional issue only.)
EPIC (1574 "World According to Clash") 30-35 82
(Black cover, with printing.)
EPIC (1574 "World According to Clash") 25-30 82
(Black cover, with no printing.)
EPIC (1592 "Combat Rock") 40-50 82
(Logo picture disc, with "Face the Future" sticker. Promotional issue only.)
EPIC (35543 "Give 'Em Enough Rope") 8-12 78
(Orange label.)
EPIC (35543 "Give 'Em Enough Rope") 5-10 78
(Blue label.)
EPIC (35543 "Give 'Em Enough Rope") 10-15 78
(White label. Promotional issue only. With insert.)
EPIC (36060 "The Clash") 5-10 79
EPIC (36060 "The Clash") 15-20 79
(White label. Promotional issue only. With lyric insert and bonus single, #1178 *Gates of the West*)
EPIC (36328 "London Calling") 10-15 79
EPIC (36328 "London Calling") 15-20 79
(White label. Promotional issue only. With lyric sleeve.)
EPIC (37037 "Sandinista") 15-20 80
(Promotional issue only. With *Armagideon Times #3*)
EPIC (37037 "Sandinista") 10-15 80
(With *Armagideon Times #3.*)
EPIC (37689 "Combat Rock") 8-10 82
(Black label.)
EPIC (37689 "Combat Rock") 5-8 82
(Blue label.)
EPIC (37689 "Combat Rock") 10-15 82
(Promotional issue only. With lyric sleeve.)
EPIC (37689 "Combat Rock") 40-50 82
(Limited edition, camouflage vinyl. Promotional issue only. With "Face the Future" sticker.)
EPIC (38540 "Black Market Clash") .5-10 80
EPIC (40017 "Cut the Crap") 5-10 85
EPIC (40017 "Cut the Crap") 10-15 85
(Promotional issue only.)
EPIC (44035 "Story of the Clash") .10-15 88
EPIC (53191 "Super Black Market Clash") 30-40 93
(Limited edition, three 10-inch LPs.)
EPIC/NU-DISC (36846 "Black Market Clash") 10-15 80
(10-inch LP.)
Members: Joe Strummer; Mick Jones; Nick Sheppard; Pete Howard; Paul Simonon; Topper Headon; Terry Chimes; Vince White.
Also see BIG AUDIO DYNAMITE
Also see STRUMMER, Joe

CLASS ACTION D&D '83
Singles: 12-inch
SLEEPING BAG 4-6 83

CLASS MATES
Singles: 7-inch
MARQUEE (101 "Don't Make Me Cry") 15-25 60
SEG-WAY (104 "Homework") 15-25 61

CLASS MATES
Singles: 7-inch
BRIGHT STAR (157 "You Can Do Me Some Good") 8-10 67

CLASS NOTES: see CLASS-NOTES

CLASS REUNION
Singles: 7-inch
PARADE 4-8 67

CLASS SET
Singles: 7-inch
MOD ART 3-5

CLASS-AIRS
Singles: 7-inch
HONEY BEE (81631 "Too Old to Cry") 1000-2000
(Identification number shown since no selection number is used.)
JASON SCOTT 5-10

CLASSETTS
Singles: 7-inch
ULTRA CLASS 3-5

CLASSIC EXAMPLE
Singles: 7-inch
GSF 3-6

CLASSIC FOUR
(Classic IV)
Singles: 7-inch
ALGONQUIN (1650 "Early Christmas") 35-50 61
ALGONQUIN (1651 "What Will I Do") 75-125 61
TWIST (1001 "What Will I Do") ...50-100 62
(Twist credits "Classics IV," and shows title with subtitle: *What Will I Do (Without You)*, whereas on Algonquin they're the "Classics Four" and there is no subtitle.)
TWIST (1004 "Heavenly Bliss") 1000-2000 62

CLASSIC IV: see CLASSIC FOUR or CLASSICS IV

CLASSIC SULLIVANS R&B '73
Singles: 7-inch
KWANZA 4-6 73
MASTER KEY (03 "Shame, Shame, Shame") 15-25
Members: Eddie Sullivan; Lorraine; Barbara Sullivan.

CLASSICAL GUYS
Singles: 7-inch
BLUE 4-6

CLASSICAL HEADS
LPs: 10/12-inch
PROBE 10-12 70

CLASSICAL SMOKE
LPs: 10/12-inch
PISCES 10-12 77

CLASSICALS
Singles: 7-inch
KENT (379 "One More River") 50-75 62
PRUDENTIAL (1002 "Help Me") 10-20 61

CLASSICS
Singles: 7-inch
CLASS (219 "If Only the Sky Was a Mirror") 50-75 57

CLASSICS
Singles: 7-inch
RO-ANN (1002 "Je Vous Aime") 200-300 59

CLASSICS
Singles: 7-inch
CREST (1063 "Let Me Dream") ...50-100 59

CLASSICS
Singles: 7-inch
STARR (508 "Close Your Eyes") 100-200 60
(Reissued on Alcar 207, credited to Lou Christie & Classics.)
Members: Lou Christie; Kay Chick; Shirley Herbert; Ken Krease.
Also see CHRISTIE, Lou
Also see LUGEE & LIONS

CLASSICS
Singles: 7-inch
TOP RANK (2061 "Burning Love") .15-25 60

CLASSICS R&B '61
Singles: 7-inch
BED-STUY (222 "Again") 15-25
COLLECTABLES (1275 "P.S. I Love You") 3-4 83
(Colored vinyl.)
DART (1015 "Cinderella") 20-30 60
DART (1024 "Life Is But a Dream") 100-200 61
DART (1032 "Angel Angela") 30-50 61
ERIC 3-4 82
MERCURY (71829 "Life Is But a Dream Sweetheart") 20-30 61
MUSICNOTE (118 "P.S. I Love You") 20-30 63
(White label.)
MUSICNOTE (118 "P.S. I Love You") 10-20 63
(Blue label.)
MUSICNOTE (1116 "Till Then") 10-20 63
(Black vinyl.)
MUSICNOTE (1116 "Till Then") 100-200 63
(Colored vinyl.)
PICCOLO (500 "I Apologize") 15-25 65
STORK (2 "You'll Never Know") 15-25 64
STREAMLINE (1028 "Life's But a Dream") 15-25 61
TRIP 3-5
LPs: 10/12-inch
CRYSTAL BALL 8-10 84
Members: Emil Stuccio; Tony Victor; John Gamble; Jamie Troy.

CLASSICS
Singles: 7-inch
JERDEN (742 "Till I Met You") 20-30 64
Also see CANADIAN CLASSICS

CLASSICS
Singles: 7-inch
WIDE WORLD (62767 "Looking for a Love") 50-100 60s

CLASSICS
Singles: 7-inch
SHELTER 3-5 72

CLASSICS IV
Singles: 7-inch
TWIST (1001 "Island of Paradise") 50-75 62
TWIST (1003 "Heavenly Bliss") . 150-250 62

CLASSICS IV
Singles: 7-inch
ARLEN (746 "It's Too Late") 15-25 64

CLASSICS IV P&R '67
(Dennis Yost & Classics IV; Classics)
Singles: 7-inch
AMERICAN PIE 3-4 90s
CAPITOL 10-15 66-67
GUSTO 3-4
IMPERIAL (Except 66328) 4-8 67-70
IMPERIAL (66328 "Stormy"/"Ladies Man") 10-20 68
IMPERIAL (66328 "Stormy"/"24 Hours of Loneliness") 4-8 68
(Note different flip.)
LIBERTY (Except SP-36) 3-5 70
LIBERTY (SP-36 "Song") 15-25 70
(Radio spots. Promotional issue only.)
MGM 3-5 75
MGM/SOUTH 3-5 72-73
PLAYBACK 3-4 90
SILVER SPOTLIGHT SERIES 3-5
U.A. 3-5 71
LPs: 10/12-inch
IMPERIAL 12-20 68-69
KOALA (14258 "Greatest Hits of the Classic IV") 8-10 79
(Mistakenly credits group as the "Classic IV.")
LIBERTY (10000 series) 5-10 81-85
LIBERTY (11000 series) 10-12 70
MGM/SOUNDS of the SOUTH 8-10 73
SUNSET 10-12 70
U.A. 8-10 75
Members: Dennis Yost; James Cobb; Dean Daughtry; Wally Eaton; Auburn Burrell; Kim Venable; Joe Wilson; Mike Sharpe.
Also see ATLANTA RHYTHM SECTION
Also see BLACK RABBIT
Also see BUIE & COBB
Also see CANDYMEN
Also see YOST, Dennis

CLASSICS IV / Mac Davis
LPs: 10/12-inch
VINTAGE 10-15
Also see CLASSICS IV
Also see DAVIS, Mac
Also see SHARPE, Mike

CLASSINETTES
Singles: 7-inch
MARKAY (107 "Little Boy") 25-75 62

CLASSIX NOUVEAUX
Singles: 7-inch
LIBERTY 3-4 81
LPs: 10/12-inch
EMI AMERICA 5-10 84
LIBERTY 5-10 81

CLASSMATES
Singles: 78 rpm
SILHOUETTE 5-10 56
Singles: 7-inch
SILHOUETTE 10-15 56

CLASSMATES
Singles: 78 rpm
DOT 10-15 56-57
KING 10-15 55
Singles: 7-inch
DOT (15460 "Return My Heart") 15-25 56
DOT (15464 "Break Down and Love Me") 15-25 56
DOT (15504 "Friends") 15-25 56
DOT (15589 "You Do Something to Me") 15-25 57
FELSTED (8673 "Cotton Pickin,' Pickle Packin,' Fish Strippin,' Claw Hoppin,' Hands") 5-10 63
KING (1487 "A Kiss Is Not a Kiss") 15-25 55
STACY (935 "Did You Ever") 5-10 62

CLASSMATES
("Vocal: David London - Music: Al Greiner")
Singles: 7-inch
RADAR (2624 "Graduation") 15-25 62
RADAR (3962 "All I Want Is to Love You") 15-25 62
Member: David London.

CLASSMATES / Johnny Mastrio & Classmates
Singles: 7-inch
FRANKIE 15-25 57
Members: John DeLisa; Pete DeLisa.
Also see DE LISA, Pete
Also see MASTRIO, Johnny

CLASSMATES
(With Henry J. Beau Orchestra; with Heini Beau Orchestra)
Singles: 7-inch
MARQUEE (101 "High School") 50-75 60
MARQUEE (102 "Pretty Little Pet") 40-60 60
(Letters in "Marquee" are almost touching each other at the bottom.)
MARQUEE (102 "Pretty Little Pet") 30-50 60
(Letters in "Marquee" have extra space between each character.)

CLASSMATES
Singles: 7-inch
HIT (338 "Classical Gas") 5-10 68

CLASSMEN
Singles: 7-inch
C-M (8464 "I Wont Cry") 50-100 63
IMPACT (1012 "Susie Jones") 20-30 66
J&R (5006 "Why Did You Put Me On") 25-50 60s
J&R (5008 "Look Out World") 25-50 65
J&R (5009 "Ping Pong") 15-25 65
LIMELIGHT 5-10 63-64
PEARCE (5806 "Julie") 10-20 67
PEARCE (5913 "Yang Yang") 10-20 67
VOLKANO (5002 "Susie Jones") .75-100 66

CLASS-NOTES
Singles: 7-inch
DOT (15786 "You Inspire Me") 50-75 58
HAMILTON (50011 "Take It Back") 50-75 58
Also see CADETS
Also see ROCKETEERS

CLAUD, Vernon
Singles: 78 rpm
DECCA 15-25 56
Singles: 7-inch
DECCA (30174 "Jungle of Cement and Stone") 20-40 56

CLAUDE & HIGHTONES
Singles: 7-inch
BAY-TONE (113 "Bucket Head") ...15-25 59
PAM-MAR 8-12 64

CLAUDIA & BUDDY
Singles: 78 rpm
CHESS 15-25 55
Singles: 7-inch
CHESS (1586 "Please Come Back to Me") 25-35 55

CLAUDIA & CRYSTALS
Singles: 7-inch
DORE 10-15 61

CLAUSER, Al, & Oklahomans: see PAGE, Patti

CLAY, Andrew Dice LP '89
LPs: 10/12-inch
DEF AMERICAN 5-8 89-91

CLAY, Cassius LP '63
(Cassius Marcellus Clay Jr; Muhammed Ali)
Singles: 7-inch
COLUMBIA (43007 "Stand By Me") 10-20 64
COLUMBIA (75717 "Will the Real Sonny Liston Please Fall Down") 25-40 64
(Promotional issue only.)
Picture Sleeves
COLUMBIA (43007 "Stand By Me") 25-35 64
LPs: 10/12-inch
COLUMBIA (2093 "I Am the Greatest") 30-40 63
(Monaural.)
COLUMBIA (8893 "I Am the Greatest") 35-45 63
(Stereo.)
Also see ALI, Muhammad, & Frank Sinatra
Also see BEST EVER

CLAY, Chris
Singles: 7-inch
VELTONE (111 "Santa Under Analysis") 10-20 60

CLAY, Clarence, & William Scott
LPs: 10/12-inch
PRESTIGE BLUESVILLE 15-20 63

CLAY, Clifford
Singles: 7-inch
MCM 5-8

CLAY, Georgia
Singles: 7-inch
SIRE 4-6 69

CLAY, Jeffrey
(With the Diggers)
Singles: 78 rpm
CORAL 5-10 55
Singles: 7-inch
CORAL 10-15 55
MGM 4-8 65

CLAY, Jenny
Singles: 7-inch
COLUMBIA 4-8 66

CLAY, Joe
Singles: 78 rpm
VIK 40-60 56
Singles: 7-inch
VIK (0211 "Duck Tail") 50-100 56
VIK (0218 "Get on the Right Track") 50-100 56

CLAY, Judy R&B '70
Singles: 7-inch
ATLANTIC 3-5 69-70
EMBER 5-10 61-62
LA VETTE (1004 "Let It Be Me") 5-10
SCEPTER 4-8 64-66
STAX 4-6 68-69
Also see VERA, Billy, & Judy Clay

CLAY, Judy, & William Bell P&R/R&B '68

Singles: 7-inch

STAX...4-6 68

Also see BELL, William

Also see CLAY, Judy

CLAY, Otis R&B '67

Singles: 12-inch

PAULA...4-8 85

Singles: 7-inch

COTILLION...3-6 68-71

DAKAR...3-6 69

ECHO (2002 "Check It Out")...8-12

ELKA...4-6 75

GLADES (1736 "All I Need Is You")...5-10

HI...3-6 72-73

KAYVETTE...3-5 77

ONE-DERFUL...4-8 65-67

LPs: 10/12-inch

HI...8-12 73-77

CLAY, Rayna

Singles: 7-inch

ATHENA...5-10 60

CLAY, Sonji

Singles: 7-inch

SONGEE...3-6 69

CLAY, Tiggi: see TIGGI CLAY

CLAY, Tom P&R/R&B/LP '71

(With the Blackberries; with Raybor Voices)

Singles: 7-inch

BIG TOP (3055 "That's All")...10-15 60

CHANT (103 "Marry Me")...50-100 59

MOTOWN...3-4 81

MOWEST...3-5 71

OFFICIAL IBBB INTERVIEW (97436 "Remember, We Don't Like Them, We Love Them")...50-75 64

(Tom Clay interviews the Beatles. Promotional issue only.)

OFFICIAL IBBB INTERVIEW (45629 "We Don't Like Them, We Love Them")...125-150 65

(Tom Clay interviews the Beatles. Promotional issue only.)

Picture Sleeves

OFFICIAL IBBB INTERVIEW (97436 "Remember, We Don't Like Them, We Love Them")...100-150 64

LPs: 10/12-inch

MOWEST...10-15 71

Also see BEATLES

CLAY, Verna Rae

Singles: 7-inch

SURE SHOT...8-10 64

CLAY COUNTY PLAYBOYS

Singles: 7-inch

LIFETIME...4-8 67

CLAYBURN, Larry

Singles: 7-inch

MERCURY...4-8 65

CLAYBURNS

PYRO (51 "What Did He Mean")...10-20 66

Singles: 7-inch

CLAYDERMAN, Richard LP '84

LPs: 10/12-inch

COLUMBIA...5-8 84

CLAYTON, BOB

(Gene Autry)

Singles: 78 rpm

BROADWAY (4004 "Dallas County Jail Blues")...25-75

BROADWAY (4062 "In the Jailhouse Now, No. 2")...25-75

BROADWAY (4067 "Jailhouse Blues")...25-75

BROADWAY (4073 "Silver Haired Daddy of Mine")...25-75

BROADWAY (4093 "Crimes I Didn't Do")...25-75

BROADWAY (4094 "Back to Old Smokey Mountain")...25-75

BROADWAY (4095 "My Carolina Mountain Home")...25-75

Also see AUTRY, Gene

Also see CLAYTON & BREEN

CLAYTON, Doctor

(Peter Clayton)

Singles: 78 rpm

BLUEBIRD...10-20 41-42

GROOVE (5006 "Hold That Train Conductor")...15-25 56

OKEH...15-25 39

RCA...10-20 46

Singles: 7-inch

GROOVE (5006 "Hold That Trai , Conductor")...30-50 54

CLAYTON, Lee

Singles: 7-inch

CAPITOL...3-4 79-81

LPs: 10/12-inch

CAPITOL...5-10 79-81

CLAYTON, Merry P&R '70

Singles: 7-inch

CAPITOL...5-8 63-65

MCA...3-4 80-88

ODE '70...3-5 70-76

TELDISC (501 "The Doorbell Rings")...10-15 62

LPs: 10/12-inch

MCA...5-10 80

ODE (34000 series)...5-10 77

ODE (77000 series)...10-12 71-75

Also see BEACH BOYS

Also see BROTHERS & SISTERS

Also see FIVE SATINS / Merry Clayton

Also see HASKELL, JIMMY

Also see RAELETTES

Also see SCOTT, Tom

Also see SISTERS LOVE

Also see SMITH, Leslie, & Merry Clayton

Also see WYCOFF, Michael

CLAYTON, Pat

Singles: 7-inch

SILVER TIP...10-20

CLAYTON, Paul

Singles: 7-inch

MONUMENT...4-6 64

LPs: 10/12-inch

ELEKTRA...20-25

MONUMENT...10-20 65

TRADITION...10-20

WASHINGTON...10-20

CLAYTON, Rich, & Rumbles

Singles: 7-inch

DAWN CORY (1003 "Flip Side")...20-30 63

Also see FABULOUS RUMBLES

Also see RUMBLES LTD.

CLAYTON, Steve

Singles: 7-inch

DECCA...4-8 63

EPIC...4-8 64

JAMIE...4-8 67

MEDALLION...5-10 59

SPIRAL...4-8 65-71

T-BIRD...4-8 63

CLAYTON, Steve & Suzanne

Singles: 7-inch

RX...4-8 68

Also see CLAYTON, Steve

CLAYTON, Von

Singles: 7-inch

SURE PLAY (1003 "Bandstand")...8-12

CLAYTON, Willie R&B '84

Singles: 7-inch

COMPLEAT...3-4 85

CLAYTON & BREEN

Singles: 78 rpm

BROADWAY (4095 "Alone with My Sorrows")...25-75

Member: Gene Autry.

Also see AUTRY, Gene

Also see CLAYTON, Bob

CLAYTON SQUARES

Singles: 7-inch

MGM...5-10 65

CLAYTON-THOMAS, David: see THOMAS, David Clayton

CLAYTONS

Singles: 7-inch

COLUMBIA...3-6 69

CLEAN, ATHLETIC & TALENTED

Singles: 7-inch

DESTINY...3-4 82

LPs: 10/12-inch

DESTINY...5-10 82

CLEAN, Don, & Clean Cut Clan

Singles: 7-inch

ACCENT...15-25 62

CLEAN LIVING P&R '72

Singles: 7-inch

VANGUARD...3-5 72

LPs: 10/12-inch

VANGUARD...8-12 72-73

Also see BOLD

CLEAN SWEEPS

Singles: 7-inch

PHILIPS...4-6 68

CLEANLINESS & Godliness Skiffle Band

LPs: 10/12-inch

VANGUARD (79285 "Greatest Hits")...10-20 68

Also see MASKED MARAUDERS

CLEAR BLUE SKY

Singles: 7-inch

ROMAT (1005 "Morning of Creation")...20-30 60s

CLEAR LIGHT LP '67

Singles: 7-inch

ELEKTRA...5-10 67

LPs: 10/12-inch

ELEKTRA (4011 "Clear Light")...15-25 67

Members: Cliff DeYoung; Douglas Lubahn; Michael Ney; Ralph Schuckett; Bob Seal; Dallas Taylor.

CLEARWATER, Eddie

Singles: 7-inch

ATOMIC...10-15

CLEARTONE...3-5

FEDERAL (12446 "I Was Gone")...20-30 62

LPs: 10/12-inch

ROOSTER BLUES...5-10 81

CLEARY, Eddie

Singles: 7-inch

KAWANA (102 "Think It Over Baby")...50-100 59

CLEARY, Mark, with Bill German & His Bob Cats

Singles: 7-inch

BOP CAT (101 "Two Drops of Water")...10-15

CLEE-SHAYS

Singles: 7-inch

TRIUMPH (65 "Dynamite")...10-15 66

LPs: 10/12-inch

TRIUMPH (101 "Super Spy Themes")...15-25 66

CLEE-SHAYS

Singles: 7-inch

ZOOM (101 "My Dream")...200-400

CLEF DWELLERS

Singles: 7-inch

SINGULAR...10-15 58

CLEFFTONES

Singles: 78 rpm

OLD TOWN...200-400 55

Singles: 7-inch

OLD TOWN (1011 "My Dearest Darling")...1000-2000 55

Member: Cas Bridges.

Also see FOUR FELLOWS

Also see VICTORIANS

CLEFMEN

Singles: 7-inch

CHERRY (7889 "Shimmer")...10-20 64

CLEFS

Singles: 78 rpm

CHESS (1521 "We Three")...50-100 52

PEACOCK...25-50 54

Singles: 7-inch

CHESS (1521 "We Three")...200-300 52

PEACOCK (1643 "I'll Be Waiting")...50-75 54

Members: Scotty Mann; Frank Newman; Pav Bess; Leroy Flack; Fred Council; Leo Carter.

Also see MANN, Scotty, & Masters

CLEFS

("Vocal: Lonnie Hathaway Jr.")

Singles: 7-inch

RED BIRD (1210 "Don't Cry")...150-200 50s

CLEFS

Singles: 7-inch

TRI EM...3-5

CLEFS OF LAVENDER HILL P&R '66

Singles: 7-inch

DATE (1510 "Stop! Get a Ticket")...10-20 66

DATE (1530 "One More Time")...10-20 66

DATE (1533 "Play with Fire")...10-20 66

DATE (1567 "Gimme One Good Reason")...10-20 67

THAMES (100 "Stop! Get a Ticket")...25-35 66

Members: Travis Fairchild; Coventry; Bill Moss; Fred Moss.

CLEFTONES P&R/R&B '56

(Herb Cox & Cleftones)

Singles: 78 rpm

GEE...20-30 56-57

ROULETTE...30-40 58

Singles: 7-inch

ABC...3-5 73

CLASSIC ARTISTS...4-6 90

GEE (1000 "You Baby You")...50-75 56

GEE (1011 "Little Girl of Mine")...40-60 56

GEE (1016 "Can't We Be Sweethearts")...25-50 56

(Red and black label.)

GEE (1016 "Can't We Be Sweethearts")...15-25 60

(Gary label.)

GEE (1025 "String Around My Heart")...25-50 56

GEE (1031 "Why Do You Do Me Like You Do")...20-40 56

GEE (1038 "See You Next Year")...20-40 57

GEE (1041 "Hey Babe")...20-40 57

GEE (1048 "Lover Boy")...20-40 57

(Red and black label.)

GEE (1048 "Lover Boy")...15-25 60

(Gray label.)

GEE (1064 "Heart & Soul")...20-30 61

GEE (1067 "For Sentimental Reasons")...20-30 61

GEE (1074 "Earth Angel")...20-30 62

GEE (1077 "Again")...20-30 62

GEE (1079 "There She Goes")...20-30 62

GEE (1080 "How Deep Is the Ocean")...20-30 62

ROULETTE (4094 "She's So Fine")...15-25 58

ROULETTE (4161 "Mish-Mash Baby")...15-25 59

ROULETTE (4302 "She's Gone")...15-25 59

ROULETTE GOLDEN GOODIES...3-5 70s

WARE (6001 "He's Forgotten You")...10-20 64

LPs: 10/12-inch

EMUS...5-10 79

GEE (GLP-705 "Heart & Soul")...100-200 61

(Monaural.)

GEE (SGLP-705 "Heart & Soul")...200-300 61

(Stereo.)

GEE (GLP-707 "For Sentimental Reasons")...150-250 62

(Monaural.)

GEE (SGLP-707 "For Sentimental Reasons")...250-350 62

(Stereo.)

Members: Herbie Cox; Berman Patterson; Bill McClain; Charles James; Warren Corbin; Pat Span; Eugene Pearson.

Also see COX, Herbie

Also see DRIFTERS

Also see HARPTONES / Cleftones

CLEFTS

Singles: 7-inch

V-TONE...10-20 60

CLEGG, Johnny, & Savuka LP '88

Singles: 7-inch

CAPITOL...3-4 88-89

LPs: 10/12-inch

CAPITOL...5-8 88-90

CLEMENS, T.L.

Singles: 7-inch

COMBO (168 "I Love You So")...25-35 59

CLEMENT, Henry

(With the Trojans; with Dewdrops)

Singles: 7-inch

SPOT...10-15 62

ZYNN (503 "I'm So in Love with You")...40-60 58

ZYNN (1006 "I'll Be Waiting")...20-30 61

CLEMENT, Jack C&W '78

Singles: 78 rpm

SUN...15-25 57

Singles: 7-inch

ELEKTRA...3-5 78

HALL-WAY (1796 "Time After Time, After Time")...4-8 63

HALL-WAY (1912 "Banks of the Ohio")...4-8 64

RCA (7602 "Whole Lotta Lookin' ") 10-20 59

SUN (291 "Ten Years")...20-30 57

SUN (311 "Wrong")...15-25 57

LPs: 10/12-inch

ELEKTRA...5-10 78

Also see CLEMENT TRAVELERS

CLEMENT TRAVELERS

Singles: 7-inch

PHILLIPS INT'L...5-10 59

Also see CLEMENT, Jack

CLEMENTINO, Clairette

Singles: 7-inch

CAPITOL...4-8 63-64

ENCORE...5-10 61-62

CLEMENTS, Boots C&W '86

Singles: 7-inch

WEST...3-4 86

CLEMENTS, Don

Singles: 7-inch

PUSH...3-5 70

CLEMENTS, Sonny

Singles: 7-inch

DRAGON (411 "Sleepy Guitar")...10-20 61

CLEMENTS, T.

Singles: 7-inch

HOT (107 "Kick That Tiger")...10-20 64

CLEMENTS, Vassar C&W '80

Singles: 7-inch

FLYING FISH...3-5 80

SHIKATA...3-4 88

LPs: 10/12-inch

FLYING FISH...5-10 77-81

MCA...5-10 77-84

MERCURY...6-12 75

MIND BEST...5-8 84

ROUNDER...5-10 80s

RURAL RHYTHM...8-12

Session: Doug Jernigan; David Bromberg.

Also see BROMBERG, David

Also see GRATEFUL DEAD

Also see HOT TUNA

Also see JIM & JESSE

Also see MARSHALL TUCKER BAND

Also see MONROE, Bill

Also see NITTY GRITTY DIRT BAND

Also see YOUNG, Faron

CLEMMONS, Angela R&B '80

Singles: 12-inch

PORTRAIT...4-6 82

Singles: 7-inch

EPIC...3-4 80

PORTRAIT...3-4 82-87

LPs: 10/12-inch

PORTRAIT...5-10 82

CLEMMONS, Jerome

Singles: 7-inch

ABC-PAR...4-8 64

CLEMONS, Clarence LP '83

(With the Red Bank Rockers)

Singles: 7-inch

COLUMBIA...3-4 83-85

LPs: 10/12-inch

COLUMBIA...5-10 83-85

Also see FRANKLIN, Aretha

Also see SPRINGSTEEN, Bruce

CLEMONS, Clarence, & Jackson Browne P&R '85

Singles: 7-inch

COLUMBIA...3-4 85

Also see BROWNE, Jackson

CLEMONS, Gregg

Singles: 7-inch

NEMPEROR...3-4 80

LPs: 10/12-inch

NEMPEROR...5-10 80

CLEMONS, T.L.

(T. Clemons)

Singles: 7-inch

COMBO...10-20 60-62

CLEO & CRYSTALIERS: see CRYSTALIERS

CLEOPATRA

Singles: 7-inch

SHERYL (335 "Heaven Only Knows")...400-600 61

CLERVERS

(Clerver's)

Singles: 7-inch

REEL (114 "Tears")...100-200

CLE-SHAYS

Singles: 7-inch

MONEX (5232 "Spend All My Money")...15-25 68

CLESS, Rod

Singles: 78 rpm

BLACK & WHITE...10-15

CLETRO, Eddie

Singles: 78 rpm

IMPERIAL (3002 "Sittin' and Rockin' ")...20-40 56

Singles: 7-inch

IMPERIAL (3002 "Sittin' and Rockin' ")...50-100 56

LARIAT ("Flyin' Saucer Boogie")...300-400 50s

(Selection number not known.)

CLEVELAND, Holly

Singles: 7-inch

ATCO...4-8 65

CLEVELAND, Sara

LPs:10/12-inch

PHILO...10-15

CLEVES SCHOOL CHOIR

Singles: 7-inch

BELL...3-5 72

CLIATT, Chuck

Singles: 7-inch

BOSS...3-5 72

CLIC CLAX

Singles: 7-inch

STARFIRE...4-8 64

CLICHES

Singles: 7-inch

CUCA (1040 "Outlaw")...10-20 61

Also see BUSCHER, Dick, & Cliches

CLICHES

(Cliché's)

Singles: 7-inch

MAARC (1530 "What's Your Name")...25-50 62

WES MAR (1020 "Save it for Me")...20-30

CLICK

Singles: 7-inch

LAURIE...5-10 67

CLICK-CLACKS

Singles: 7-inch

ALGONQUIN (715 "A Kiss Goodbye")...20-30 58

APT (25010 "Pretty Little Pearly")...15-25 58

APT (25032 "Rocket Roll")...15-25 59

CLICKER

Singles: 7-inch

CLICKER...3-5 73-75

HEMISPHERE...3-5 73

LPs: 10/12-inch

CLICKER...10-15 75

HEMISPHERE...10-15 73

CLICKETTES

(Click-Ettes)

Singles: 7-inch

CHECKER (1060 "I Just Can't Help It")...10-15 63

COLLECTABLES...3-4 82

DICE (83 "A Teenager's First Love")...50-100 58

DICE (92 "To Be a Part of You")...50-100 59

(Pictures a hand throwing dice, with "Dice Records, New York, N.Y." below.)

DICE (94 "Warm, Soft and Lovely")...50-100 59

(Pictures a hand throwing dice, with "Dice Records, New York, N.Y." below.)

DICE (96 "Lover's Prayer")...75-125 59

(Pictures a hand throwing dice, with "Distributed Exclusively by Memo Record Corp." below.)

DICE (96 "Lover's Prayer")...40-60 59

(Reads: "Nationally Distributed by Jubilee Recors" at bottom.)

DICE (100 "But Not for Me")...50-100 60

GUYDEN (2043 "Where Is He")...15-25 60

LOST NITE...3-5

TUFF (373 "I Understand Him")...10-15 63

CLICKS

Singles: 78 rpm

JOSIE...50-75 55

Singles: 7-inch

JOSIE (780 "Come Back to Me")...150-250 55

CLIENTELLS

Singles: 7-inch

M.B.S. (07 "Church Bells May Ring")...100-200 61

CLIF & MARTY

Singles: 7-inch

MOSAIC...3-5 72

CLIFF, Benny
(With the Benny Cliff Trio)
Singles: 7-inch
DRIFT (1441 "Shake Um Up Rock")....1000-2000 59

CLIFF, Jimmy P&R '69
Singles: 12-inch
COLUMBIA....4-6 83-84
Singles: 7-inch
A&M....3-6 69-70
COLUMBIA....3-4 82-84
MANGO....3-5 73-75
MCA....3-5 81
REPRISE....3-5 73-77
VEEP....4-8 67-68
Picture Sleeves
A&M....3-6 69
LPs: 10/12-inch
A&M....10-20 70
COLUMBIA....5-10 82
ISLAND....8-10 74
MCA....5-10 80-81
MANGO....8-10 75
REPRISE....8-10 73-76
VEEP....15-20 69
W.B....5-10 78

CLIFF, Jimmy, Elvis Costello & Attractions
Singles: 12-inch
COLUMBIA....5-10 86
(Promotional issue only.)
Singles: 7-inch
COLUMBIA....3-4 86
Picture Sleeves
COLUMBIA....3-4 86
Also see CLIFF, Jimmy
Also see COSTELLO, Elvis

CLIFF, Zelma
Singles: 7-inch
BATTLE....4-8 63
SPINO (1011 "I Don't Believe")....12-18

CLIFF & SUN-RAYS
Singles: 7-inch
ZIL (9002 "No Treason In My Heart")....10-20

CLIFF DWELLERS
Singles: 7-inch
LIZA....8-12

CLIFF OF RHYTHM BAND
Singles: 7-inch
DIT DOT....5-10 67

CLIFFORD, Buzz P&R/C&W/R&B '61
Singles: 7-inch
BOW ("14 Karet")....20-30 59
(Selection number not known.)
CAPITOL....4-8 67
COLUMBIA (41774 "Hello Mr. Moonlight")....10-15 60
COLUMBIA (41876 "Baby Sittin' Boogie")....30-50 60
(With "3" prefix. Compact 33 Single.)
COLUMBIA (41979 "Simply Because")....30-50 61
(With "3" prefix. Compact 33 Single.)
COLUMBIA (42019 "I'll Never Forget")....30-50 61
(With "3" prefix. Compact 33 Single.)
COLUMBIA (42290 "Forever")....30-50 62
(With "3" prefix. Compact 33 Single.)
COLUMBIA (41876 "Baby Sitter Boogie")....20-30 60
(Note slightly different title. With "4" prefix.)
COLUMBIA (41876 "Baby Sittin' Boogie")....5-10 61
(With "4" prefix.)
COLUMBIA (41979 "Simply Because")....15-25 61
(With "4" prefix.)
COLUMBIA (42019 "I'll Never Forget")....15-25 61
(With "4" prefix.)
COLUMBIA (42177 "Moving Day")..5-10 61
(With "4" prefix.)
COLUMBIA (42290 "Forever")....15-25 62
(With "4" prefix.)
DOT....4-6 69-70
ERIC....3-4 83
RCA....4-8 66
ROULETTE....5-10 62-63
Picture Sleeves
COLUMBIA (41774 "Hello Mr. Moonlight")....15-25 60
COLUMBIA (41876 "Baby Sittin' Boogie")....15-25 60
COLUMBIA (41979 "Simply Because")....15-25 61
COLUMBIA (42019 "I'll Never Forget")....15-25 61
COLUMBIA (42177 "Moving Day")....15-25 61
COLUMBIA (42290 "Forever")....15-25 62
LPs: 10/12-inch
COLUMBIA (1616 "Baby Sittin' Boogie")....50-75 61
(Monaural.)
COLUMBIA (8416 "Baby Sittin' Boogie")....50-100 61
(Monaural.)
DOT....15-20 69
Also see DAVE & MARKSMEN

CLIFFORD, Doug
(Doug "Cosmo" Clifford)
Singles: 7-inch
FANTASY....3-5 72
LPs: 10/12-inch
FANTASY....10-15 72
Also see CREEDENCE CLEARWATER REVIVAL

CLIFFORD, Linda R&B '74
Singles: 12-inch
CAPITOL....4-6 82
RSO....4-8 79
RED LABEL....4-6 85
Singles: 7-inch
CAPITOL....3-4 80-82
CURTOM....3-4 77-78
GEMIGO....3-5 75
PARAMOUNT....3-5 74
POLYDOR....3-5 73
RSO....3-4 79-80
RED LABEL....3-4 84-85
LPs: 10/12-inch
CAPITOL....5-10 80-82
CURTOM....8-10 77-80
RSO....5-10 79-80
Also see MAYFIELD, Curtis, & Linda Clifford

CLIFFORD, Mike P&R '62
Singles: 7-inch
AIR....3-5 71
AMERICAN INT'L....3-5 70
CAMEO....4-8 65-66
COLUMBIA....4-8 61-62
LIBERTY....5-10 59
SIDEWALK....4-8 67-68
U.A....4-8 62-65
Picture Sleeves
COLUMBIA....5-10 61
LPs: 10/12-inch
U.A....15-25 65

CLIFFORD, Mike, with Patience & Prudence
Singles: 7-inch
LIBERTY....8-12 59
Also see CLIFFORD, Mike
Also see PATIENCE & PRUDENCE

CLIFFTERS
Singles: 7-inch
PHILIPS....5-10 62

CLIFTON, Bill
Singles: 7-inch
LONDON....8-12 64

CLIFTON, Johnny, & His String Band
(Bill Haley)
Singles: 78 rpm
CENTER (102 "Stand Up and Be Counted")....1000-1500 50
Also see HALEY, Bill

CLIFTON, Paul
Singles: 7-inch
FLASH (127 "Are You Alright")....15-25 58
Also see TAYLOR, Little Johnny

CLIMATES
Singles: 7-inch
HOLIDAY INN....8-12 67
SUN....15-20 67

CLIMATICS
(With Clark Darie & His Combo)
Singles: 7-inch
RE-NO (1000 "My Gift from Heaven")....100-200 62
REQUEST (3008 "All Alone")....250-500 59

CLIMAX P&R/LP '72
(Sonny Geraci & Climax)
Singles: 7-inch
ARISTA....3-4 81
BELL....3-5 71
CAROUSEL....3-5 70-71
FLASHBACK....3-4 73
PARAMOUNT....3-5 70
PATTI PLATTERS....4-8 67
ROCKY ROAD....3-5 72-73
LPs: 10/12-inch
ROCKY ROAD....12-15 72
Members: Sonny Geraci; John Bahler; Tom Bahler; Jon Jon Gultman; Walt Nims.
Also see GERACI, Sonny
Also see LOVE GENERATION
Also see OUTSIDERS

CLIMAX BLUES BAND LP '70
Singles: 7-inch
SIRE....3-5 71-79
W.B....3-4 79-82
LPs: 10/12-inch
SIRE (Except 6000 series)....10-15 69-76
SIRE (6000 series)....8-10 77-79
VIRGIN....5-10 83
W.B....5-10 79-81
Members: Climax Chicago Blues Band; Colin Cooper; John Cuffley; Peter Haycock; Derek Holt; Richard Jones; Arthur Wood.

CLIMBERS
("With Orchestra")
Singles: 7-inch
J&S (1652 "My Darlin' Dear")....500-1000 57
(With straight horizontal lines.)
J&S (1652 "My Darlin' Dear")....25-50 60s
(With wavy horizontal lines.)
J&S (1658 "I Love You")....1000-1500 57

CLIMIE FISHER P&R/LP '88
Singles: 7-inch
CAPITOL....3-4 88
Picture Sleeves
CAPITOL....3-4 88
LPs: 10/12-inch
CAPITOL....5-8 88
Members: Simon Clime; Rob Fisher.
Also see NAKED EYES

CLINE, Cecil
Singles: 7-inch
BLUE HEN....15-25 59

CLINE, Patsy C&W/P&R '57
Singles: 78 rpm
CORAL....20-30 55-56
DECCA (30221 "Walking After Midnight")....50-80 57
Singles: 7-inch
CORAL (61464 "Honky Tonk Merry Go Round")....25-50 55
CORAL (61523 "Turn the Cards Slowly")....25-50 55
CORAL (61583 "I Love You Honey")....25-50 56
(First issue.)
DECCA (25000 series)....4-8 65-69
DECCA (29963 thru 30846)....10-25 57-59
DECCA (30929 "Gotta Lot of Rhythm in My Soul")....10-20 59
DECCA (31000 series)....5-10 59-64
DECCA (74282 "Decca Artist of the Week: Patsy Cline")....125-175 62
(Envelope/sleeve with five singles from LP *Sentimentally Yours*. A "7" Stereo 33 1/3 rpm Pop Pre-Pak." Includes five juke box title strips and color photo of LP. Promotional issue only.)
EVEREST (2000 series)....5-10 62-64
EVEREST (20005 "I Can't Forget")....10-15 62
4 STAR (11 "I Love You Honey")....20-30 56
4 STAR (1033 "Life's Railway to Heaven")....3-5 78
KAPP....4-8 65
MCA....3-5 73-80
STARDAY (7000 series)....4-8 65
STARDAY (8000 series)....3-5 71
Picture Sleeves
DECCA (Except 30221)....10-20 62-63
DECCA (30221 "Walkin After Midnight")....20-30 57
EPs: 7-inch
CORAL (81159 "Songs By Patsy Cline")....50-75 58
DECCA (Except 2542)....15-25 61-65
DECCA (2542 "Patsy Cline")....35-50 57
4 STAR ("Patsy Cline")....25-35 57
(Reissue of *Patsy Cline* [Decca 2542]. Issued with paper sleeve. Number not known. Promotional issue only.)
PATSY CLINE....25-35 57
LPs: 10/12-inch
ACCORD....5-10 81
ALBUM GLOBE....5-10
ALLEGIANCE....5-10 84
AUDIO FIDELITY (204 "Patsy Cline")....10-15 84
(Picture disc.)
AUDIO FIDELITY (205 "Crazy Dreams")....25-50 84
(Picture disc.)
BREAKAWAY....5-10
BULLDOG....5-10
COLUMBIA....12-15 69
(Columbia Musical Treasury issue.)
COUNTRY FIDELITY....5-10 82
DECCA (176 "Patsy Cline Story")..25-40 63
(Monaural. Includes booklet.)
DECCA (7-176 "Patsy Cline Story")....30-50 63
(Stereo. Includes booklet.)
DECCA (4202 "Showcase")....20-30 61
(Monaural.)
DECCA (7-4202 "Showcase")....25-35 61
(Stereo.)
DECCA (4282 "Sentimentally Yours")....15-25 62
(Monaural.)
DECCA (4282 "Sentimentally Yours")....20-30 61
(Stereo.)
DECCA (4508 "Portrait")....15-25 64
(Monaural.)
DECCA (7-4508 "Portrait")....20-30 64
(Stereo.)
DECCA (4586 "That's How a Heartache Begins")....30-50 64
(Monaural.)
DECCA (7-4586 "That's How a Heartache Begins")....40-60 64
(Stereo.)
DECCA (4854 "Greatest Hits")....10-15 67
(Monaural.)
DECCA (7-4854 "Greatest Hits")....10-15 67
(Stereo.)
DECCA (8611 "Patsy Cline")....30-50 57
EVEREST (300 series)....5-10 75
EVEREST (1200 series)....15-20 62-64
EVEREST (90000 series)....8-12
51 WEST....5-10 82
H.S.R.D....8-10 84
LONGINES....8-12
MCA....5-10 80-89
METRO....10-20 65
MUSIC MASTERS....5-10
PICCADILLY....5-10 80
PICKWICK....5-12 70s
PICKWICK/HILLTOP....10-12 65-68
ROLLER SKATE....5-10 82
SEARS....10-15
VOCALION....10-15 65-69
Session: Jordanaires; Anita Kerr Singers.
Also see HAGGARD, Merle / Patsy Cline
Also see JORDANAIRES
Also see KERR, Anita
Also see PIERCE, Webb / Patsy Cline / T. Texas Tyler
Also see REEVES, Jim, & Patsy Cline
Also see TUBB, Ernest

CLINE, Patsy / Cowboy Copas / Hawkshaw Hawkins
LPs: 10/12-inch
STARDAY....15-20 65
Also see HAWKINS, Hawkshaw

CLINE, Patsy / Cowboy Copas / Johnny Horton
LPs: 10/12-inch
HILLTOP....10-15 60s
Also see COPAS, Cowboy
Also see HORTON, Johnny

CLINE, Patsy / Hank Locklin / Miller Brothers / Eddie Marvin
EPs: 7-inch
4 STAR (136 "Hidin' Out")....25-50 56
(Promotional 10-inch, 45 rpm. Not issued with cover.)
Also see LOCKLIN, Hank

CLINE, Patsy / Pete Pike / Jack Bradshaw / Miller Brothers
EPs: 7-inch
4 STAR (137 "Come On In")....25-50 56
(Promotional 10-inch, 45 rpm. Not issued with cover.)

CLINE, Patsy / T. Texas Tyler / Bill Taylor / Eddie Marvin
EPs: 7-inch
4 STAR (139 "Dear God")....25-50 56
(Promotional 10-inch, 45 rpm. Not issued with cover.)
Also see CLINE, Patsy
Also see TYLER, T. Texas

CLINGER, Peggy
Singles: 7-inch
CHELSEA....3-5 72-73
Also see CYMBAL & CLINGER

CLINGER SISTERS
Singles: 7-inch
TOLLIE....8-12 64

CLINGERS
Singles: 7-inch
MGM....3-5 70
U.A....3-6 69
Also see KAPTAIN KOOL & KONGS

CLINGMAN, Loy
(L.C.)
Singles: 7-inch
CAPITOL....4-8 68
ELKO (15 "Blue Black Hair")....5-10 63
LIBERTY BELL (9012 "It's Nothing to Me")....15-25
RIMROCK....5-10
VIV (2000 "Uranium Blues")....10-15
VIV (3401 "Rockin' Down Mexico Way")....15-25
EPs: 7-inch
VIV (2002 "Loy Clingman")....15-20
Also see HAWKS

CLINGMAN CLAN
Singles: 7-inch
4 CORNERS....5-10 64
VIV....5-10 82
LPs:10/12-inch
TREY (900 "At the Baboquivari")...25-35 60s
Member: Loy Clingman.
Also see CLINGMAN, Loy

CLINIC
LPs: 10/12-inch
ROULETTE....10-15 73

CLINKING BEARD
Singles: 7-inch
JERDEN (922 "Pay Yourself Loretta")....4-8 70

CLINT & TOMMY
Singles: 7-inch
FONTANA....4-8 65

CLINTON, Buddy
Singles: 7-inch
MADISON....5-10 60
TIME....5-10 59

CLINTON, Debby
Singles: 7-inch
PLATINUM SOUND....3-4 80

CLINTON, George R&B/LP '82
(George Clinton Band)
Singles: 12-inch
CAPITOL....4-8 82-86
Singles: 7-inch
ABC....3-5 74
CAPITOL....3-4 83-86
PAISLEY PARK....3-4 89
Picture Sleeves
CAPITOL....3-4 83
LPs: 10/12-inch
ABC....8-10 74
CAPITOL....5-10 82-86
INVICTUS....10-12 73
PAISLEY PARK....5-8 89
Also see PARLIAMENTS

CLINTON, Larry
Singles: 78 rpm
JUBILEE....10-15 57
RCA....5-10 49
Singles: 7-inch
DYNAMO (300 "She's Wanted in Three States")....100-200
JUBILEE....10-15 57
LAWN....4-8 64
RCA....5-10 49
EPs: 7-inch
TOPS....5-10

CLINTON, Mac, & Straitjackets
Singles: 7-inch
LE CAM (714 "Wake Up Baby")....35-50 60
Members: Delbert McClinton; Robert Harwell; Ralph Dixon; Billy Cox; Ray Clark.
Also see McCLINTON, Delbert
Also see STRAITJACKETS

CLINTON, Terry, & Berry Cups
Singles: 7-inch
KHOURY'S (710 "Hurt by a Letter")....30-40 59
Also see COOKIE & CUPCAKES

CLINTONIAN CUBS
Singles: 7-inch
MY BROTHER'S (508 "She's Just My Size")....1000-2000 60
Member: Jimmy Castor.
Also see CASTOR, Jimmy

CLINTONS
Singles: 7-inch
COYOTE....3-6 84
Picture Sleeves
COYOTE....4-8 84

CLINTS
LPs: 10/12-inch
SKYCLAD....5-8 89
Members: Clint Ambuter; Clint Wade; Clint Harrison; Clint Villalobos.

CLIP, Sod
Singles: 7-inch
CONTOUR....4-8 67

CLIPPERS
Singles: 78 rpm
BATON (233 "The Clipper")....10-15 56
Singles: 7-inch
BATON (233 "The Clipper")....15-25 56
BEACON....5-10 60
TRI....5-10 61

CLIPS
(With Jimmy Beck & His Band)
Singles: 78 rpm
CALVERT....50-100 56
REPUBLIC....100-150 54
Singles: 7-inch
CALVERT (105 "Kiss Away")....150-200 56
REPUBLIC (7102 "Wish I Didn't Love You So")....200-300 54

CLIQUE
Singles: 7-inch
ABC-PAR....4-8 65

CLIQUE P&R '69
Singles: 7-inch
ABC....3-5 73
CINEMA (001 "Splash")....25-35 67
SCEPTER....10-20 67
WHITE WHALE....8-15 69-71
LPs: 10/12-inch
WHITE WHALE (7126 "The Clique")....10-20 69
Also see LAVENDER HOUR

CLIQUE
Singles: 7-inch
MERCURY....3-5 69
SASSY....4-8 67

CLIQUE
Singles: 7-inch
FRETONE....3-5 74

CLIQUE
LPs: 10/12-inch
GRAPHIC....5-10 83

CLIQUES P&R '56
Singles: 78 rpm
MODERN....10-20 56
Singles: 7-inch
MODERN (987 "The Girl in My Dreams")....20-30 56
Members: Jesse Belvin; Eugene Church.
Also see BELVIN, Jesse
Also see CHURCH, Eugene

CLOCK, Thomas
Singles: 7-inch
COOKING (109 "Where You Go") 10-20 62

CLOCKS P&R '82
Singles: 7-inch
BOULEVARD....3-4 82
LPs: 10/12-inch
BOULEVARD....5-10 82

CLOCKS & CLASSMEN
Singles: 7-inch
MAIL CALL (1011 "It's Written")...75-125 62

CLOCKWATCHERS
Singles: 7-inch
DOT....10-15 67

CLOCKWORK
LPs: 10/12-inch
GREENE BOTTLE....10-12 73

CLOCKWORK R&B/D&D '84
Singles: 12-inch
PRIVATE I....4-6 84
Singles: 7-inch
PRIVATE I....3-4 84

CLOCK-WORK ORANGE
Singles: 7-inch
CREOLE (1002 "Your Golden Touch")....10-20 67

RUST (5119 "Help Me")................10-20 67
RUST (5126 "What Am I Without You")................10-20 68

CLOCKWORK ORANGES
Singles: 7-inch
LIBERTY 4-8 66

CLOD, El: see EL CLOD

CLOONEY, Rosemary P&R '51
(Clooney Sisters)
Singles: 78 rpm
COLUMBIA................4-8 50-57
Singles: 7-inch
APCO................3-5 75
COLUMBIA................10-20 50-57
CORAL................5-10 59
DOT................4-6 68
GIBSON/COLUMBIA................10-20 55
("Musicards," with fold-out covers.)
MGM................5-15 59-65
RCA................5-10 60-61
REPRISE................5-10 63-64
SATURDAY EVENING POST (1055 "Hollywood's Favorite Songbird")...15-25 54
(Promotional issue only. Includes interview script.)
Picture Sleeves
RCA................10-15 60
EPs: 7-inch
COLUMBIA................15-25 51-56
EPIC (7139/7140/7141 "Clooney Sisters")................10-20 56
(Price is for any of three volumes.)
MGM................8-15 58-60
LPs: 10/12-inch
COLUMBIA (500 thru 1200 series, except 6297)................15-25 54-58
COLUMBIA (2500 series)................20-30 50s
(10-inch LPs.)
COLUMBIA (6297 "While We're Young")................25-35 51
(10-inch LP.)
CONCORD JAZZ................5-10 78-83
CORAL................15-25 59
EPIC (3160 "Clooney Sisters")................20-30 56
HARMONY................8-15 59-68
MGM (Except 1000 series)................10-15 59-62
MGM (1000 series)................8-12 67
RCA................15-25 60-63
REPRISE................10-25 63-64
Also see BOYD, Jimmy, & Rosemary Clooney
Also see CROSBY, Bing, Louis Armstrong, Rosemary Clooney & Hi-Los
Also see GOODMAN, Benny, Trio, & Rosemary Clooney
Also see HERMAN, Woody
Also see HOPE, Bob, & Rosemary Clooney
Also see TUNESMITHS with Rosemary Clooney & Don Cherry

CLOONEY, Rosemary, & Bing Crosby
Singles: 7-inch
RCA................4-8 59
LPs: 10/12-inch
CAMDEN................6-10 69
CAPITOL (2300 series)................8-12 65
CAPITOL (11000 series)................5-10 77
Also see CROSBY, Bing

CLOONEY, Rosemary, & Marlene Dietrich
Singles: 78 rpm
COLUMBIA................4-8 52
Singles: 7-inch
COLUMBIA................5-10 52
EPs: 7-inch
COLUMBIA (1699 "Rosie & Marlene")................15-20 52
Also see DIETRICH, Marlene

CLOONEY, Rosemary, & Duke Ellington
LPs: 10/12-inch
COLUMBIA (872 "Blue Rose")................15-25 56
Also see ELLINGTON, Duke

CLOONEY, Rosemary, & Jose Ferrer
Singles: 78 rpm
COLUMBIA................4-8 54
EPs: 7-inch
MGM................10-20 58
Also see FERRER Jose

CLOONEY, Rosemary, & Hi-Los LP '57
EPs: 7-inch
COLUMBIA................5-10 57
LPs: 10/12-inch
COLUMBIA (1006 "Ring Around Rosie")................20-25 57
Also see HI-LOs

CLOONEY, Rosemary, & Dick Haymes
LPs: 10/12-inch
EXACT................5-10 80
Also see HAYMES, Dick

CLOONEY, Rosemary, & Guy Mitchell P&R '51
(With Joanne Gilbert)
EPs: 7-inch
COLUMBIA (377 "Red Garters")................15-20 54
(Soundtrack.)
LPs: 10/12-inch
COLUMBIA (6282 "Red Garters")..40-50 54
(10-inch LP. Soundtrack.)
Also see MITCHELL, Guy

CLOONEY, Rosemary, & Perez Prado
Singles: 7-inch
RCA................4-8 60
LPs: 10/12-inch
RCA................10-12 60
Also see CLOONEY, Rosemary
Also see PRADO, Perez

CLOSE
LPs: 10/12-inch
ISLAND................5-10 84

CLOUD
Singles: 7-inch
AUDIO FIDELITY................3-5 69

CLOUD, Bruce
Singles: 7-inch
ERA (3087 "Lucky Is My Name")...20-40 63
ERA (3101 "Little Spark of Fire")......5-10 63
MOTIF (015 "Let Me Come Back Home"................50-75 63
LPs: 10/12-inch
CAPITOL................10-20 69

CLOUD, Christopher
(Tommy Boyce)
Singles: 7-inch
CHELSEA................3-5 72-73
LPs: 10/12-inch
CHELSEA................10-15 73
Also see BOYCE, Tommy

CLOUD, Claude, & His Thunderclaps
Singles: 78 rpm
MGM................5-10 54-57
Singles: 7-inch
MGM (12386 "Close Out")................8-12 57
MGM (55003 "One Bone")................8-12 54

CLOUD WALKERS
Singles: 7-inch
CAPCO................4-8 65

CLOUDS
Singles: 78 rpm
COBRA (5001 "I Do")................150-250 56
Singles: 7-inch
COBRA (5001 "I Do")................550-650 56
Member: Albert Hunter.
Also see MAPLES

CLOUDS
Singles: 7-inch
SKYLARK (116 "Baby It's Me")..100-200 61

CLOUDS
Singles: 7-inch
ROUND (1008 "Darling I Love You")................100-200 59

CLOUDS
Singles: 7-inch
MEDLEY (1001 "Night Owl")................15-25 64
Member: Bill Medley.
Also see MEDLEY, Bill

CLOUDS
Singles: 7-inch
INDEPENDENCE................10-20 67
Also see LOOKING GLASSES

CLOUDS
Singles: 7-inch
NORTHLAND................3-6 69-71
LPs: 10/12-inch
DERAM................10-15 70-71

CLOUDS
Singles: 7-inch
VOUS (1000 "A Lovely Way to Spend an Evening")................100-150 60s

CLOUR, Deral, & Charley Drake
Singles: 7-inch
HU-SE-CO (1056 "Sundown")................25-50

CLOUT P&R '78
Singles: 7-inch
EPIC................3-4 78-79
LPs: 10/12-inch
EPIC................5-10 79-80

CLOVER
Singles: 7-inch
CHS................5-10 60s

CLOVER
Singles: 7-inch
FANTASY................3-6 70
MCA................3-5 77
MERCURY................3-5 77-78
LPs: 10/12-inch
FANTASY................10-15 70-71
MERCURY................8-10 77
Also see LEWIS, Huey, & News

CLOVER, Timothy
Singles: 7-inch
TOWER................4-8 68

CLOVER LEAF
Singles: 7-inch
BANG................3-5 72

CLOVERS R&B '51
("Featuring Buddy Bailey")
Singles: 78 rpm
ATLANTIC................20-50 51-57
RAINBOW (122 "Yes Sir, That's My Baby")................200-400 51
Singles: 7-inch
ATLANTIC (934 "Don't You Know I Love You")................150-250 51
ATLANTIC (944 "Fool, Fool, Fool")................100-200 51
ATLANTIC (963 "One Mint Julep")................75-125 52
ATLANTIC (969 "Ting-A-Ling")....75-125 52
ATLANTIC (977 "I Played the Fool")................75-125 52
ATLANTIC (989 "Yes It's You")....75-125 53
ATLANTIC (1000 "Good Lovin' ")................75-125 53
ATLANTIC (1010 "Comin' On")....75-125 53
ATLANTIC (1022 "Lovey Dovey")................75-125 54
ATLANTIC (1035 "Your Cash Ain't Nothin' But Trash")................75-125 54
ATLANTIC (1046 "I Confess")......75-125 54
ATLANTIC (1052 "Blue Velvet")...75-125 54
ATLANTIC (1060 "Love Bug")......75-125 55
ATLANTIC (1073 "Nip Sip")........75-125 55
ATLANTIC (1083 "Devil Or Angel")................75-125 56
ATLANTIC (1094 "Your Tender Lips")................50-100 56
ATLANTIC (1107 "From the Bottom of My Heart")................25-50 56
ATLANTIC (1118 "A Lonely Fool") 25-50 56
ATLANTIC (1129 "You Good Looking Woman")................25-50 57
ATLANTIC (1139 "So Young")......25-50 57
ATLANTIC (1152 "Down in the Alley")................25-50 57
ATLANTIC (1175 "Wishing for Your Love")................25-50 58
ATLANTIC (2129 "Drive It Home").10-20 61
BRUNSWICK (55249 "Love Love Love")................10-20 63
JOSIE................5-10 68
POPLAR (110 "The Gossip Wheel")................15-25 58
POPLAR (111 "The Good Old Summertime")................15-25 58
PORT (3004 "Poor Baby")................10-20 65
PORWIN (1001 "Stop Pretending")................15-25 63
(Has sans-serif logo and straight horizontal lines.)
PORWIN (1002 "Stop Pretending")................10-20 63
(Has serif logo and wavy horizontal lines.)
RIPETE................3-5 88
U.A.................10-15 59-61
WINLEY (255 "Wrapped Up in a Dream")................20-30 61
WINLEY (655 "I Need You Now")..20-30 62
EPs: 7-inch
ATLANTIC (504 "The Clovers Sing")................100-200 56
ATLANTIC (537 "The Clovers Sing")................100-200 56
ATLANTIC (590 "The Clovers") . 100-150 57
LPs: 10/12-inch
ATCO................10-15 71
ATLANTIC (1248 "The Clovers")................300-400 56
ATLANTIC (8009 "The Clovers")................200-300 57
(Black label.)
ATLANTIC (8009 "The Clovers") .50-100 59
(Red label.)
ATLANTIC (8034 "The Clovers' Dance Party")................50-100 59
GRAND PRIX................10-20 64
POPLAR (1001 "The Clovers in Clover")................100-150 58
TRIP................8-10 72
U.A. (3033 "Clovers in Clover")....50-100 59
(Monaural.)
U.A. (6033 "Clovers in Clover")..100-125 59
(Stereo.)
U.A. (3099 "Love Potion Number Nine")................50-100 60
(Monaural.)
U.A. (6099 "Love Potion Number Nine")................100-125 60
(Stereo.)
Members: John "Buddy" Bailey; Harold Winley; Hal Lucas; Bill Harris; Matthew McQuater; Charlie White; Billy Mitchell. Session: King Curtis.
Also see FABULOUS CLOVERS
Also see HARPTONES / Paragons / Jesters / Clovers
Also see JACKSON, Willis
Also see KING CURTIS
Also see MITCHELL, Billy

CLOWER, Jerry
Singles: 7-inch
MCA................3-5 70s
LPs: 10/12-inch
DECCA (75286 "Mississippi Talkin' ")................10-20 71
DECCA (75342 "Mouth of the Mississippi")................10-15 72
MCA................5-10 73-83

CLOWNEY, David, Band
(David Cortez Clowney)
Singles: 78 rpm
EMBER (1010 "Soft Lights")..........15-25 56
Singles: 7-inch
EMBER (1010 "Soft Lights")..........20-40 56
PARIS (513 "Shakin' ")................15-25 58
Also see CORTEZ, Dave, "Baby"
Also see JESTERS

CLUB HOUSE P&R/R&B '83
Singles: 12-inch
ATLANTIC................4-6 83
Singles: 7-inch
ATLANTIC................3-4 83

CLUB NOUVEAU R&B/LP '86
Singles: 12-inch
W.B.................4-6 86
Singles: 7-inch
TOMMY BOY................3-4 88
W.B.................3-4 86-88
LPs: 10/12-inch
W.B.................5-10 86-88

CLUE
Singles: 7-inch
BYRON (101 "Bad Times")................20-25 67

CLUE J. & BLUES BLASTERS: see MELLOW LARKS

CLUSTERS
Singles: 7-inch
END (1115 "Darling Can't You Tell")................15-25 62
EPIC (9330 "Forecast of Our Love")................100-150 59
TEE GEE (102 " Darling Can't You Tell")................100-150 58
(Publisher shown as "Emkay Music." No mention of distribution by Gone.)
TEE GEE (102 " Darling Can't You Tell")................75-100 58
(Publisher shown as "Emkay Music." Reads: "Nat Dist. Gone Records.")
TEE GEE (102 " Darling Can't You Tell")................50-75 58
(Publisher shown as "RealGone Music." No mention of distribution by Gone.)

CLUSTERS
Singles: 7-inch
LOOK................3-5 70

CLYDE
(Dick Hyman)
Singles: 7-inch
COLUMBIA (413332 "Clyde's Blast")................10-20 59
Also see HYMAN, Dick

CLYDE & BIRD WATCHERS
Singles: 7-inch
REALM................4-8 62

CLYDE & BLUE JAYS
Singles: 7-inch
LOMA................4-8 64

COACHMEN
Singles: 78 rpm
"X" (0044 "Fame & Fortune")................5-10 54
Singles: 7-inch
"X" (0044 "Fame & Fortune")........10-20 54

COACHMEN
Singles: 7-inch
HI-FI................10-15 59
ORBIT................10-15 59

COACHMEN
("Vocal by Ricky Mann")
Singles: 7-inch
IONA (1004 "Teen Bride")................20-30 60

COACHMEN
Singles: 7-inch
PICO ("Gonna Take a Chance") 100-200 60
(Selection number not known.)

COACHMEN
Singles: 7-inch
AUSTIN (65120 "El Dorado")........10-20 65
SPOTLITE (5025/6 "Splash Day") .10-20 60s
TYPE (3580 "Movin' ")................10-20 63

COACHMEN
Singles: 7-inch
BEAR (819 "Mr. Moon")................10-15 65
BEAR (1976 "Linda Lou")................10-15 66
MMC (010 "Mr. Moon")................10-20 65
(Black vinyl)
MMC (010 "Mr. Moon")................35-50 65
(Colored vinyl)
MMC (013 "My Generation")........10-15 66
MMC (014 "Tyme Won't Change") 10-15 66

COACHMEN
Singles: 7-inch
CAPITOL................4-8 67
ROULETTE................4-6 68
SSS INT'L................4-6 69

COACHMEN
Singles: 7-inch
TARGET................5-8 69
Members: Ray Johnson; Rick Preis; James Kaminski; Jeff Greenthal; Leon Klekowski; Paul Strand; Jim Paolo; Byron Weiman.

COACHMEN FIVE Featuring Ray Davis
Singles: 7-inch
JANSON (100 "Oh Joan")................75-125
Member: Ray Davis.

COALITIONS
Singles: 7-inch
PHIL L.A. of SOUL................3-5 74-75
RE-DUN (5 "How Are You")................8-12

COALKITCHEN
Singles: 7-inch
EPIC................3-5 77
LPs: 10/12-inch
EPIC................8-10 77

COANJOS
Singles: 7-inch
DAPT................5-10 61

COASTERS P&R/R&B '56
Singles: 78 rpm
ATCO (6064 thru 6126)................10-30 57-58
ATCO (6132 "Charlie Brown")................25-50 59
ATCO (6141 "Along Came Jones")................50-75 59
ATCO (6146 "Poison Ivy")................50-100 59
ATCO (6153 "What About Us").....75-125 59
Singles: 7-inch
ATCO (6064 "Down in Mexico")...50-100 56
(Maroon label.)
ATCO (6073 "One Kiss Led to Another")................40-60 56
(Maroon label.)
ATCO (6087 "Searchin' ")................30-50 57
(Maroon label.)
ATCO (6087 "Searchin' ")................15-25 57
(Yellow and white label.)
ATCO (6098 "Idol with the Golden Head")................20-30 57
ATCO (6104 "Sweet Georgia Brown")................20-30 57
ATCO (6111 "Dance")................15-25 58
ATCO (6116 "Yakety Yak")................15-25 58
ATCO (6126 "The Shadow Knows")................15-25 58
ATCO (6132 "Charlie Brown")........15-25 59
ATCO (6141 "Along Came Jones") 15-25 59
ATCO (6146 "Poison Ivy")................15-25 59
ATCO (6153 "What About Us")........10-20 59
ATCO (6163 "Besame Mucho")........10-20 60
ATCO (6168 "Wake Me, Shake Me")................10-20 60
ATCO (6178 "Shoppin for Clothes")................10-20 60
ATCO (6186 thru 6356)................8-15 61-65
ATCO (6379 "Crazy Baby")................20-30 65
ATCO (6407 "She's a Yum Yum")...8-10 66
DATE................5-10 67-68
KING................3-6 71-73
KING/GUSTO................3-5 79
TURNTABLE................4-8 69
EPs: 7-inch
ATCO (4501 "Rock & Roll with the Coasters")................50-70 58
ATCO (4503 "Keep Rockin' ")........50-70 58
ATCO (4506 "The Coasters")........30-50 59
ATCO (4507 "Top Hits")................30-50 59
LPs: 10/12-inch
ARCHIVES................8-12
ATCO (101 "The Coasters")........75-100 58
(Yellow label.)
ATCO (101 "The Coasters")................25-50 59
(Yellow and white label.)
ATCO (111 "Greatest Hits")................50-75 59
ATCO (123 "One by One")................40-50 60
(Monaural.)
ATCO (SD-123 "One By One")......50-60 60
(Stereo.)
ATCO (135 "Coast Along")................30-40 59
(Monaural.)
ATCO (SD-135 "Coast Along")......40-50 59
(Stereo.)
ATCO (371 "Their Greatest Recordings")................10-20 71
ATLANTIC................10-12 82
CLARION................10-15 64
GUSTO................5-8
KING................10-15 71
PHOENIX 20................5-8
POWER PAK................5-10 83
TRIP................8-10 72-76
WEST-ONE................8-15
Members: Bobby Nunn; Leon Hughes; Carl Gardner; Billy Guy; Adolph Jacobs; Cornel Gunter; Will Jones; Earl Carroll; Ronnie Bright; Jimmy Norman. Session: King Curtis.
Also see CARROLL, Earl, & Original Cadillacs
Also see COASTERS TWO PLUS TWO
Also see GUY, Billy
Also see HENDRICKS, Bobby
Also see KING, Ben E.
Also see KING CURTIS
Also see NORMAN, Jimmy
Also see NUNN, Bobby
Also see ROBINS

COASTERS / Crew-Cuts / Chiffons
LPs: 10/12-inch
EXACT................5-10 80
Also see CHIFFONS
Also see CREW-CUTS

COASTERS / Drifters
LPs: 10/12-inch
TVP................10-15
(TV mail-order offer.)
Also see DRIFTERS

COASTERS
Singles: 7-inch
COAST (187 "The Angels Listened In")................15-25

COASTERS TWO PLUS TWO
Singles: 7-inch
CHELAN................3-5 75
Also see COASTERS

COASTIERS
(With the Coastiers Orchestra)
Singles: 7-inch
COAST to COAST (1265 "16 Candles")................10-15 58
COAST to COAST (1287 "The Angels Listened In")................10-15 59

COASTLINERS
Singles: 7-inch
ASTRO (109 "Lonely Sea")............15-25 65
BACK BEAT (554 "Alright")..........10-15 66
BACK BEAT (566 "She's My Girl").15-20 66
DEAR................8-12 67
INT'L ARTISTS (101 "Alright")........15-25 65

COATES, Dorothy Love
LPs: 10/12-inch
NASHBORO................10-20
OKEH................8-18
SAVOY................10-20
SPECIALTY................8-18
TRIP................5-15

COATES, Harry: see CHOATES, Harry

COATES, Jesse

Singles: 78 rpm

HEADLINE 50-75 55

Singles: 7-inch

HEADLINE (101 "Nobody Can Take My Baby") 100-200 55

COATES, Odia P&R '75

Singles: 12-inch

EPIC 4-6 77

Singles: 7-inch

BUDDAH 3-5 73
EPIC 3-4 78
U.A. 3-4 74-75

LPs: 10/12-inch

U.A. 8-10 75
Also see ANKA, Paul, & Odia Coates
Also see RAELETTES
Also see SISTERS LOVE

COBB, Arnett

(With His Orchestra & Suttle's Dreamers)

Singles: 78 rpm

APOLLO 5-15 47-49
ATLANTIC 15-25 54-55
COLUMBIA 5-10 50-51
HAMP-TONE 5-15 46
MERCURY 5-10 53
OKEH (Except 6912 and 6928) 5-10 51-52
OKEH (6912 "Someone to Watch Over Me") 25-50 52
(With the Ravens.)
OKEH (6928 "Linger Awhile") 25-50 52
(With the Ravens.)
VEE JAY 5-15 56

Singles: 7-inch

ATLANTIC (1031 "Night") 25-50 54
ATLANTIC (1042 "Horse Laff") 25-50 54
ATLANTIC (1056 "Flying Home Mambo") 25-50 55
COLUMBIA 10-15 50-51
MERCURY 10-15 53
OKEH (Except 6912 and 6928) 10-15 51-52
OKEH (6912 "Someone to Watch Over Me") 50-100 52
(With the Ravens.)
OKEH (6928 "Linger Awhile") 50-100 52
(With the Ravens.)
PRESTIGE 4-8 59-61
VEE JAY 10-20 56

LPs: 10/12-inch

APOLLO (105 "Swingin' with Arnett Cobb") 75-100 52
(10-inch LP.)
PRESTIGE (7151 "Blow, Arnett, Blow") 25-50 59
(Yellow label.)
PRESTIGE (7151 "Blow, Arnett, Blow") 15-20 64
(Blue label.)
PRESTIGE (7165 "Party Time") 25-50 59
(Yellow label.)
PRESTIGE (7165 "Party Time") 15-20 64
(Blue label.)
PRESTIGE (7175 "More Party Time") 25-50 60
(Yellow label.)
PRESTIGE (7175 "More Party Time") 15-20 64
(Blue label.)
PRESTIGE (7184 "Smooth Sailing") 25-50 61
(Yellow label.)
PRESTIGE (7184 "Smooth Sailing") 15-20 64
(Blue label.)
PRESTIGE (7216 "Movin' Right Along") 25-40 61
(Yellow label.)
PRESTIGE (7216 "Movin' Right Along") 15-20 64
(Blue label.)
PRESTIGE/MOODSVILLE (14 "Ballads by Cobb") 15-25 61
Also see DREAMERS
Also see RAVENS
Also see VAN LOAN, Joe

COBB, Danny

Singles: 78 rpm

SAVOY 15-25 52

COBB, Johnny

(With the Attractions; with Mellow Souls)

Singles: 7-inch

CRISS COBB (100 "Yes I Do") 10-20 60s
JAGUAR (468 "Love Doesn't Pay") 10-20 60s

COBB, Joyce P&R '79

Singles: 7-inch

CREAM 3-4 79-80
TRUTH 3-5 75

COBB, Julius

Singles: 7-inch

BETHLEHEM (3024 "Oh Baby, I Want You Back Home") 15-20 62

COBB, June

Singles: 7-inch

GOLDEN RULE 5-10 60

COBB, Terry

Singles: 7-inch

BOOT HILL (101 "I'll Try") 8-12

COBBLERS

Singles: 7-inch

STUDIO CITY (1060 Smokin' at the Half Note") 50-75 66
Members: Ron Spanbauer; Pat Nugent; Mike Meidl; Bob Weisapple; Bob Misky; Nick Christas.
Also see BLUE TALE FLY
Also see SYNDICATE

COBBLESTONE

Singles: 7-inch

MERCURY (73051 "She Loves Me") 8-10 70

COBBLESTONES

Singles: 7-inch

MOBIE (3425 "Flower People") 20-30 67

COBBS, Danny Boy

Singles: 78 rpm

ACORN 20-30

COBBS, Willie

Singles: 7-inch

ASCOT (2113 "Don't Say Goodbye") 8-12 62
BRACOB ("C.C. Rider") 10-20 60s
C&F 10-20 62
CHIMNEYVILLE 4-6 77
HOME of the BLUES (230 "You Don't Love Me") 15-25 61
(First issue.)
JOB 15-20 63
MINARET (147 "Don't Worry About Me") 8-10 69
MOJO 15-25 61
PHILWOOD (254 "Why Did You Change Your Mind") 4-6 76
PURE GOLD (313 "Come on Home") 5-10 65
RICE BELT 8-12 63
RICELAND (111 "I'll Love Only You") 10-20 60s
RULER 5-10
SHIELD 5-10
SOUL BEAT (113 "Worst Feeling") 10-20 60s
VEE JAY (411 "You Don't Love Me") 10-15 61
WHIRL-A-WAY 5-10
Also see WILLIE C.

COBHAM, Billy LP '73

(Billy Cobham's Glass Menagerie; with George Duke Band)

Singles: 12-inch

COLUMBIA 4-6 80

Singles: 7-inch

ATLANTIC 3-5 75-77
COLUMBIA 3-4 78-80

Picture Sleeves

ATLANTIC 3-5 70s

LPs: 10/12-inch

ATLANTIC 5-10 73-79
COLUMBIA 5-10 77-80
ELEKTRA 5-10 82-83
Also see DUKE, George
Also see SINGLETON, Charlie

COBRA

LPs: 10/12-inch

EPIC 5-10 83
Member: Jim Jameson.
Also see SURVIVOR

COBRA BROTHERS

Singles: 7-inch

MAGNET 5-10 60

COBRA KINGS

Singles: 7-inch

BLACK GOLD (200 "Night Walk") 15-25
BLACK GOLD (300 "Tragedy") 15-25

COBRAS

Singles: 78 rpm

MODERN (964 "Sindy") 50-100 55
MODERN (964 "Cindy") 25-50 55

Singles: 7-inch

MODERN (964 "Sindy") 150-250 55
MODERN (964 "Cindy") 75-125 55
(Note different spellings.)

COBRAS

Singles: 7-inch

CASINO (1309 "La La") 50-75 63
COLLECTABLES 3-4 81
MONOGRAM 4-8 64
STAX 5-10 64
SWAN (4176 "La La") 15-25 64

COBRAS

Singles: 7-inch

PEACH (150 "Hammerhead") 8-12 65

COBRAS

Singles: 7-inch

BIG BEAT (1002 "Instant Heartache") 20-25 66

COBRAS

Singles: 7-inch

MILKY WAY 15-20 66

COBRAS

Singles: 7-inch

SCOOP 5-10

COBRAS Featuring Stevie Ray Vaughan

Singles: 7-inch

ARMADILLO (79-1 "Blow Joe, Blow") 50-100 80
Also see VAUGHAN, Stevie Ray

COBURN, Kimball

(With the Six O'Clock Boys; with Sy Rose Orchestra)

Singles: 7-inch

CHALLENGE (59009 "My Little Girl") 15-25 58
CHAN (106 "No Reason Why") 20-40 62
COVER (6061 "What a Day") 30-50 60
HI (2010 "Teenage Love") 50-100 58
HI (2016 "If I Were King") 50-100 59
PHILLIPS 8-12 64-65
RCA (7592 "I'm My Own Grandpaw") 15-20 59
RIVERMONT (1159 "Cute") 75-125 58

COBY, Carole

Singles: 7-inch

EPIC 4-8 64
ROULETTE 4-8 65

COCA-NUTS

Singles: 7-inch

("Bring It Back!") 3-5 86
(No label name or selection number used.)

COCCIANTE, Richard P&R '76

Singles: 7-inch

20TH FOX 3-5 76

LPs: 10/12-inch

20TH FOX 5-10 76

COCCO, Lenny, & Chimes: see LENNY & CHIMES

COCCOMO, Carl

Singles: 7-inch

TREND 4-8 62

COCHISE P&R '71

Singles: 7-inch

U.A. 3-5 71

EPs: 7-inch

U.A. 10-12 71

LPs: 10/12-inch

U.A. 10-12 71
Member: Mick Grabham.

COCHRAN, Cliff C&W '74

Singles: 7-inch

ENTERPRISE 3-5 74-75
RCA 3-4 79

COCHRAN, Don

Singles: 7-inch

BIG-K (40064 "Pig Pen Boogie") 10-20 64

COCHRAN, Eddie P&R/R&B '57

Singles: 78 rpm

CREST (1026 "Skinny Jim") 75-125 56
LIBERTY 75-125 57-58

Singles: 7-inch

CAPEHART (5003 "Rough Stuff") 10-20 60
CREST (1026 "Skinny Jim") 200-300 56
LIBERTY (54000 series) 5-10 62
LIBERTY (55056 "Sittin' in the Balcony") 15-25 57
LIBERTY (55070 "Mean When I'm Mad") 15-25 58
LIBERTY (55087 "Drive in Show") 15-25 57
LIBERTY (55112 "Twenty Flight Rock") 20-30 58
LIBERTY (55123 "Jeannie Jeannie Jeannie") 20-30 58
LIBERTY (55138 "Pretty Girl") 15-25 58
LIBERTY (55144 "Summertime Blues") 15-25 58
LIBERTY (55166 "C'mon Everybody") 15-25 58
(Green label.)
LIBERTY (55166 "C'mon Everybody") 10-20 58
(Black label.)
LIBERTY (55177 "Teenage Heaven") 15-25 59
LIBERTY (55203 "Somethin' Else") 15-25 59
(With horizontal silver lines.)
LIBERTY (55203 "Somethin' Else") 10-20 59
(Without horizontal silver lines.)
LIBERTY (55217 "Hallelujah, I Love Her So") 10-20 59
LIBERTY (55242 "Cut Across Shorty") 15-25 60
(Green label.)
LIBERTY (55242 "Cut Across Shorty") 10-20 61
(Black label.)
LIBERTY (55278 "Sweetie Pie") 10-20 60
LIBERTY (55389 "Weekend") 20-30 61

Picture Sleeves

CAPEHART (5003 "Rough Stuff") 35-50 60
LIBERTY (55070 "Mean When I'm Mad") 750-1000 58

EPs: 7-inch

LIBERTY (3061-1/2/3 "Singin' to My Baby") 100-150 58
(Price is for any of three volumes.)

LPs: 10/12-inch

LIBERTY (3061 "Singin' to My Baby") 200-300 58
(Green label.)
LIBERTY (3061 "Singin' to My Baby") 40-60 60
(Black label.)
LIBERTY (3172 "Memorial Album") 50-100 60
LIBERTY (3220 "Never to Be Forgotten") 50-100 62
(Black label.)
LIBERTY (3220 "Never to Be Forgotten") 75-90 62
(Yellow label. Promotional issue only.)
LIBERTY (10000 series) 5-10 81-83
SUNSET (1123 "Summertime Blues") 30-40 66
U.A. (428 "Very Best of Eddie Cochran") 10-15 75
U.A. (9959 "Legendary Masters") ... 15-20 71
Also see CAPEHART, Jerry
Also see COCHRAN BROTHERS
Also see DAVIS, Bo
Also see DENSON, Lee
Also see GEE CEES
Also see HOLLY TWINS
Also see KELLY FOUR
Also see KEY, Troyce
Also see NEAL, Jerry
Also see STANLEY, Ray

COCHRAN, Hank C&W '62

Singles: 7-inch

CAPITOL 3-4 78
DOT 3-5 70
ELEKTRA 3-4 80
GAYLORD 4-8 62-63
LIBERTY 4-8 62-63
MONUMENT 3-6 67-68
RCA 4-8 64-66

LPs: 10/12-inch

CAPITOL 10-20 78
ELEKTRA 5-10 80
MONUMENT 10-15 68
RCA 10-20 65
Session: Jack Greene; Merle Haggard; Willie Nelson; Jeannie Seely; Rafe Van Hoy
Also see COCHRAN BROTHERS
Also see GREENE, Jack
Also see HAGGARD, Merle
Also see SEELY, Jeannie

COCHRAN, Hank, & Willie Nelson

Singles: 7-inch

CAPITOL 3-5 78
Also see COCHRAN, Hank
Also see NELSON, Willie

COCHRAN, Jackie Lee

(Jack Cochran)

Singles: 78 rpm

DECCA (30206 "Mama Don't You Think I Know") 100-150 57
SIMS (107 "Riverside Jump") 50-100 56

Singles: 7-inch

ABC-PAR (9930 "Buy a Car") 50-80 58
DECCA (30206 "Mama Don't You Think I Know") 100-150 57
JAGUAR (3031 "I Want to See You") 75-125 59
SIMS (107 "Riverside Jump") ... 100-200 56
SPRY (120 "Endless Love") 200-250 59
VIV (988 "Buy a Car") 100-150 58

LPs: 10/12-inch

ROLLIN' ROCK 10-15 70s

COCHRAN, Wayne LP '68

(With the C.C. Riders; with Fabulous C.C. Riders; with Rockin' Capris)

Singles: 7-inch

BETHLEHEM (3097 "Hey Jude") 4-8 69
BOBLO (101 "Hey Baby") 5-10 68
CHESS 5-10 67-68
CONFEDERATE (155 "Linda Lu") 10-20 63
DECK (151 "Monkey Monkey") 10-20 63
DRIVE (6249 "Sea Cruise") 4-6 76
EPIC 3-5 72
ERA (18 "Last Kiss") 3-5 78
(Credits Cochran but track is by J. Frank Wilson.)
GALA (117 "Last Kiss") 10-20 62
GALICO (105 "Last Kiss") 15-25 61
KING (5000 series) 5-15 63-65
KING (6000 series) 4-8 69-71
KING GOLD 3-5 72
MERCURY 4-8 65-67
SCOTTIE (1303 "The Coo") 25-50 59
SOFT (779 "Harlem Shuffle") 8-12 65
SOFT (1009 "Hang on Sloopy") 5-10 68
SOFT (1010 "Hey Baby") 5-10 68

Picture Sleeves

CHESS (2020 "Some-A Your Sweet Love") 5-10 67
MERCURY (72507 "Harlem Shuffle") 8-12 65

EPs: 7-inch

PLAYBACK (32 "Long Long Day") ... 8-12 72
(Also has tracks by other artists.)

LPs: 10/12-inch

BETHLEHEM (10002 "High & Ridin' ") 10-20 70
CHESS (1519 "Wayne Cochran") .. 20-30 68
EPIC (30989 "Cochran") 8-12 72
KING (1116 "Alive & Well") 15-25 70
KING (16001 "Old King Gold") 5-10 75
Also see GREAT SEBASTIAN
Also see REDDING, Otis
Also see ROCKIN' CAPRIS
Also see WILSON, J. Frank

COCHRAN BROTHERS

Singles: 78 rpm

EKKO (1003 "Two Blue Singing Stars") 50-100 56
EKKO (1005 "Guilty Conscience") 50-100 56
EKKO (3001 "Tired & Sleepy") 75-125 56

Singles: 7-inch

EKKO (1003 "Two Blue Singing Stars") 350-500 56
EKKO (1005 "Guilty Conscience") 350-500 56
EKKO (3001 "Tired & Sleepy") 450-650 56
Members: Eddie Cochran; Hank Cochran.
(Eddie and Hank were not really brothers).
Also see CAPEHART, Jerry
Also see COCHRAN, Eddie
Also see COCHRAN, Hank

COCHRANE, Ron, & Entertainers

Singles: 7-inch

JUBILEE 4-8 67

COCHRANE, Tom LP '86

(With Red Rider)

Singles: 7-inch

CAPITOL 3-4 86
RCA 3-4 88

Picture Sleeves

RCA 3-5 88

LPs: 10/12-inch

CAPITOL 5-10 86
RCA 5-8 88
Also see RED RIDER

COCHRANE TWINS

Singles: 7-inch

GARPAX (4084 "Hey, Mr. Weatherman") 20-30 64
Members: Lani Cochrane; Boni Cochrane.

COCK ROBIN P&R/D&D '85

Singles: 12-inch

COLUMBIA 4-6 85

Singles: 7-inch

COLUMBIA 3-4 85

Picture Sleeves

COLUMBIA 3-5 85

LPs: 10/12-inch

COLUMBIA 5-10 85-87
Members: Peter Kingsbery; Anna LaCazio.

COCKBURN, Bruce P&R/LP '80

Singles: 7-inch

GOLD MOUNTAIN 3-4 84
MCA 3-4 86
MILLENNIUM 3-4 80

LPs: 10/12-inch

EPIC 10-15 71-72
GOLD CASTLE 5-8 89
GOLD MOUNTAIN 5-10 84
ISLAND 8-10 77-78
MCA 5-10 86
MILLENNIUM 5-10 80-81
TRUE NORTH 8-10 77-78

COCKER, Joe P&R '68

(With the Chris Stainton Band)

Singles: 7-inch

A&M 3-6 68-78
ASYLUM 3-4 78-79
CAPITOL 3-4 84-88
ISLAND 3-4 82-83
PHILIPS 10-15 65

Picture Sleeves

A&M 3-5 69-74
CAPITOL 3-4 84
ISLAND 3-4

LPs: 10/12-inch

A&M (Except 3100 series) 8-15 69-77
A&M (3100 series) 5-10 82
ASYLUM (Except 145) 5-10 78-79
ASYLUM (145 "Luxury You Can Afford") 5-10 79
ASYLUM (145 "Luxury You Can Afford") 15-25 79
(Picture disc. Promotional issue only.)
CAPITOL 5-10 84-90
ISLAND 5-8 82
MFSL (223 "Sheffield Steel") 20-25 94
Also see ARNOLD, Vance, & Avengers
Also see BOWIE, David / Joe Cocker / Youngbloods
Also see CRUSADERS
Also see GREASE BAND
Also see RUSSELL, Leon

COCKER, Joe, & Jennifer Warnes P&R '82

Singles: 7-inch

ISLAND 3-4 82

Picture Sleeves

ISLAND 3-4 82
Also see COCKER, Joe
Also see WARNES, Jennifer

COCKERHAM, Chuck

Singles: 7-inch

MALA ("Have I the Right") 10-20 60s
(No selection number used.)

COCKNEY REBEL

Singles: 7-inch

EMI AMERICA 3-5 74

LPs: 10/12-inch

EMI AMERICA 8-10 74
Also see PARSONS, Alan, Project

COCKRELL, Charles

Singles: 7-inch

HI 5-10 59

COCKRELL, Mat

Singles: 78 rpm

FLAIR (1037 "Baby Please") 15-25 54

Singles: 7-inch

FLAIR (1037 "Baby Please") 25-50 54

COCKRELL & SANTOS

Singles: 7-inch

A&M 3-4 78

LPs: 10/12-inch

A&M 5-10 78

COCO, El: see EL COCO

COCOAS

Singles: 78 rpm

CHESTERFIELD 50-75 55

Singles: 7-inch

CHESTERFIELD (364 "Flip Your Daddy") 150-250 55
(Label name in script typeface. Has clef and staff above name.)
CHESTERFIELD (364 "Flip Your Daddy") 75-125 55
(Label name in normal—not script—typeface. No clef and staff shown.)

COCONUTS

Singles: 12-inch

EMI AMERICA 4-6 83

Singles: 7-inch

EMI AMERICA 3-4 83

LPs: 10/12-inch

EMI AMERICA 5-10 83

COCTEAU TWINS LP '88
LPs: 10/12-inch
CAPITOL 5-8 88
4AD 5-8 90

CODA
Singles: 7-inch
CAPITOL 3-5 74

CODAS
Singles: 7-inch
BELL (122 "Sleepwalk") 15-25 59

CODAY, Bill R&B '71
Singles: 7-inch
CRAJON (48202 "Sixty Minute Teaser") 10-15 69
CRAJON (48203 "Right On Baby") 50-75 70
CRAJON (48204 "Get Your Lie Straight") 4-8 71
(At least one source shows this label as "Crayon." We're not yet sure who's right.)
EPIC 4-8 73-75
GALAXY (777 "Get Your Lie Straight") 4-6 71
GALAXY (779 "When You Find a Fool, Bump His Head") 4-8 71
GALAXY (781 "I Got a Thing") 4-8 71

CODD, Pat
Singles: 7-inch
UK 3-5 74

CODE BLUE
Singles: 7-inch
W.B. 3-4 80
LPs: 10/12-inch
INDEX 5-10 84
W.B. (Black vinyl) 5-10 80
W.B. (Colored vinyl) 10-15 80

CODY
Singles: 7-inch
ATCO 3-5 72

CODY, Betty C&W '53
Singles: 78 rpm
RCA 4-8 53-55
Singles: 7-inch
RCA 5-10 53-55

CODY, Carl
Singles: 7-inch
VISTONE 4-8 68

CODY, Commander: see COMMANDER CODY

CODY, Michele
Singles: 7-inch
SAFARI 3-4 78

CODY, Philip
(Phil Cody)
Singles: 7-inch
KIRSHNER 3-5 72
LPs: 10/12-inch
REPRISE 8-10 76

CODY SISTERS
Singles: 7-inch
ARCH 4-8 59

COE, David Allan C&W '74
Singles: 7-inch
COLUMBIA 3-5 74-87
PLANTATION 3-5 73
SSS INT'L (Black vinyl) 3-5 71-72
SSS INT'L (Colored vinyl) 5-10 71-72
(Promotional issues only.)
Picture Sleeves
COLUMBIA 3-5
LPs: 10/12-inch
COLUMBIA 5-10 72-86
SSS INT'L (9 "Penitentiary Blues") 25-40 70
Session: Lacy J. Dalton; Dianne Sherrill; Eve Shaprio; Bill Anderson; George Jones; Dickey Betts; Kris Kristofferson; Guy Clark; Larry Jon Wilson; Waylon Jennings.
Also see CLARK, Guy
Also see DALTON, Lacy J.
Also see JENNINGS, Waylon
Also see JONES, George
Also see JONES, George, & David Allan Coe
Also see KRISTOFFERSON, Kris
Also see WILSON, Larry Jon

COE, David Allan, & Bill Anderson
Singles: 7-inch
COLUMBIA 3-5 80
Also see ANDERSON, Bill

COE, David Allan, & Willie Nelson C&W '86
Singles: 7-inch
COLUMBIA 3-4 86
Also see COE, David Allan
Also see NELSON, Willie
Also see NELSON, Willie / Jerry Lee Lewis / Carl Perkins / David Allan Coe

COE, Frankie
(Franky Coe)
Singles: 7-inch
BRUNSWICK 3-6 69
OKEH 4-8 67

COE, Jamie
(Jamie Coe & Gigolos)
Singles: 7-inch
ABC-PAR 10-15 60-61
ADDISON 10-15 59
BIG TOP 10-20 62-63
CAMEO 10-15 66
ENTERPRISE 5-10 64-65
REPRISE 5-10 64
Also see GIGOLOS

COE, Jimmy, & His Gay Cats of Rhythm
(Jimmy Coe & His Cohorts)
Singles: 78 rpm
STATES 15-25 52
Singles: 7-inch
INTRO (002 "Cold Jam for Breakfast") 10-20 66
NOTE (10013 "Wazoo") 15-25 58
STATES (118 "After Hours Joint") 20-40 52
(Black vinyl.)
STATES (118 "After Hours Joint") 50-100 52
(Red vinyl.)
STATES (129 "Raid on the After Hour Joint") 20-40 52
(Black vinyl.)
STATES (129 "Raid on the After Hour Joint") 50-100 52
(Red vinyl.)
STATES (155 "Run Jody, Run") 20-40 52
Also see COHORTS

COE, Tommy
Singles: 78 rpm
PEP (110 "Teenage Heart") 4-8 56
Singles: 7-inch
PEP (110 "Teenage Heart") 8-12 56

CO-EDS
(Featuring Gwen Edwards)
Singles: 78 rpm
OLD TOWN 25-35 56
Singles: 7-inch
OLD TOWN (1027 "Love You Baby All the Time") 40-60 56
OLD TOWN (1033 " I Love an Angel") 40-60 57

CO-EDS
Singles: 78 rpm
CAMEO 25-50 57-58
Singles: 7-inch
CAMEO 15-25 57-58
CHA CHA 8-12 61
CHECKER (996 "Annabelle Lee") 15-25 61
DWAIN 8-12 59
SHERYL 8-12 61

COEDS
(With the Tokens)
Singles: 7-inch
SWING 10-20 64
Also see TOKENS

COEDS / Blossoms: see BLOSSOMS / Coeds

COEFIELD, Brice
Singles: 7-inch
MADISON 15-25 60
OMEN 4-8 66

COETTES
Singles: 7-inch
POP-SIDE 5-10 61
COFF, Dennis
(Dennis Coffey)
Singles: 7-inch
MAVERICK (107 "It's Your Thing") 4-8 69
Also see COFFEY, Dennis

COFFEE R&B '82
Singles: 7-inch
DELITE 3-4 80-82

COFFEE HOUSE
LPs: 10/12-inch
DORIAN (1001 "Coffee House") 20-30 59
Members: Judy Henske; Paul Sykes.
Also see HENSKE, Judy

COFFEY, Dennis P&R/LP '71
(With the Detroit Guitar Band; with Lyman Woodward Trio)
Singles: 7-inch
SUSSEX 3-5 70-74
W.B. 3-5 74
20TH CENTURY/WESTBOUND 3-5 75-76
WESTBOUND 3-4 77-78
LPs: 10/12-inch
SUSSEX 10-12 70-75
20TH CENTURY/WESTBOUND 8-10 75-76
WESTBOUND 5-10 77
Also see C.C. & COMPANY
Also see C.J. & CO.
Also see COFF, Dennis
Also see FRONTERA, Tommy

COFFMAN, Howard, & Johnny Dabbs
Singles: 7-inch
TOPPA 5-10 61

COFIELD, Peter
Singles: 7-inch
CORAL 3-6 69
LPs: 10/12-inch
CORAL 10-12 69

COGAN, Alma
Singles: 78 rpm
RCA 10-15 55-56
Singles: 7-inch
AMERICAN ARTS (4 "I Love You Much Too Much") 5-10 64
CAPITOL (4547 "Just Couldn't Resist Her with Her Pocket Transistor") 15-25 61
RCA (6063 "Blue Again") 15-25 55
RCA (6236 "Got'n Idea") 20-30 55
RCA (6573 "Pickin' a Chicken") 15-25 56

COGAN, Don
Singles: 7-inch
MGM 8-12 58

COGAN, Shaye
Singles: 7-inch
MGM 5-10 59
ROULETTE 5-10 57

COGGSWELL, Alice
Singles: 7-inch
MIDLAND INT'L 3-5 74

COGICS
Singles: 7-inch
SIMPSON 3-5

COGNACS
Singles: 7-inch
ROULETTE (4340 "Charlena") 15-25 61

CO-HEARTS
Singles: 7-inch
VEE JAY (289 "My Love") 50-100 58

COHEN, Joe
LPs: 10/12-inch
FRIENDSHIP STORE MUSIC 5-10 82

COHEN, Laurie Kaye
Singles: 7-inch
PLAYBOY 3-5 73
LPs: 10/12-inch
PLAYBOY 10-12 73

COHEN, Leonard LP '68
Singles: 7-inch
COLUMBIA 3-6 68-73
LPs: 10/12-inch
COLUMBIA 10-12 68-85
W.B. 8-12 77
Also see BLAKELY, Ronee
Also see BRANIGAN, Laura

COHEN, Mike
LPs: 10/12-inch
PACIFIC ARTS 5-10 80

COHEN, Myron LP '66
LPs: 10/12-inch
RCA 10-15 66
Also see ANN-MARGRET

COHEN, Sidney: see SCHILLER, Lawrence

CO-HIERS
Singles: 7-inch
JCP (1009 "She Cried") 10-20 64

COHN, Marc C&W/LP '91
Singles: 7-inch
ATLANTIC 3-4 91
LPs: 10/12-inch
ATLANTIC 5-8 91

COHN, Stephen
Singles: 7-inch
MOTOWN 3-5 75
LPs: 10/12-inch
MOTOWN 10-12 73

COHORTS
Singles: 7-inch
NOTE (20001 "Country Blues") 20-30 57
Also see COE, Jimmy, and His Gay Cats of Rhythm

COHRON, Phil C&W '90
Singles: 7-inch
AIR 3-4 89-90

COIN, R.C. C&W '87
Singles: 7-inch
BGM 3-4 87

COINS
("Vocal Don Trotter & Al Perry")
Singles: 78 rpm
GEE 200-400 54
MODEL (2001 "Loretta") 200-400 56
Singles: 7-inch
GEE (10 "Cheatin' Baby") 1000-2000 54
(Black vinyl.)
GEE (10 "Cheatin' Baby") 2000-3000 54
(Red vinyl.)
GEE (11 "Look at Me Girl"/"S.R. Blues") 1000-2000 54
MODEL (2001 "Loretta") 1000-2000 55
Members: Don Trotter; Al Perry.

COINS / Colonials
Singles: 78 rpm
GEE 100-150 54
Singles: 7-inch
GEE (1007 "Look at Me Girl"/"Two Loves Have I") 400-600 56
Also see COINS
Also see GORDON, Bill "Bass," & Colonials

COIT, James
Singles: 7-inch
PHOOF 4-8 68

COKEFIELD, Brice
Singles: 7-inch
OMEN 5-8

COKER, Al
(Alvadean Coker)
ABBOTT 15-25 54-55
DECCA 20-30 57
Singles: 7-inch
ABBOTT (163 "Sugar Doll") 20-30 54
ABBOTT (167 "Funny Little Things") 20-30 54
ABBOTT (176 "We're Gonna Bop") 50-75 55
DECCA (30053 "Don't Go Baby") 20-30 57
DECCA (30490 "One More Chance") 20-30 57
Also see REEVES, Jim / Alvadean Coker

COKER, Sandy
Singles: 78 rpm
ABBOTT 10-15 54
DECCA 10-15 50s
Singles: 7-inch
ABBOTT 15-25 54
DECCA (30051 "Rock Island Ride") 15-25 56
DECCA (30534 "Under Cover") 15-25 58

COKIE & TY RONES
Singles: 7-inch
AL-FANG (16790 "Let's Start Anew") 400-600 66

COLANTINIO, Cris
Singles
ERIKA (12335 "Last Mile") 4-8 84
(Picture disc.)

COLAVITA, Don
Singles: 7-inch
PLAID 15-25 60

COLBERT, Andre
Singles: 7-inch
PALETTE 5-10 59

COLBERT, Bertha
Singles: 7-inch
COLUMBIA 4-8 63

COLBERT, Chuck
Singles: 7-inch
BEE 10-15 67

COLBERT, Godoy
Singles: 7-inch
REVUE 3-6 69

COLBERT, John
Singles: 7-inch
SUR-SPEED (222 "Congratulations") 8-10

COLBERT, Melrose
Singles: 78 rpm
ATLANTIC 10-20 48
PLAZA 10-15 49

COLBERT, Phil
Singles: 7-inch
PHILIPS 10-20 65-66

COLBURN, Lou
Singles: 7-inch
MAYAN 15-25 62

COLBY, Mark
Singles: 7-inch
TAPPAN ZEE/COLUMBIA 3-4 78-79
LPs: 10/12-inch
TAPPAN ZEE/COLUMBIA 5-10 79

COLBY, Wendy, & Bonnevilles
Singles: 7-inch
DRUM BOY 5-10 63
Also see BONNEVILLES

COLD BLOOD LP '69
(Lydia Pense & Cold Blood)
Singles: 7-inch
ABC 3-5 75
REPRISE 3-5 72-73
SAN FRANCISCO 3-6 70
EPs: 7-inch
SAN FRANCISCO (3309 "Cold Blood") 5-10 70
(Promotional issue only.)
LPs: 10/12-inch
ABC 8-10 76
REPRISE 10-12 72-73
SAN FRANCISCO 12-15 69-70
W.B. 8-10 74
Members: Lydia Pense; Michael Andreas; Rod Ellicott; Frank Davis; Jerry Jonutz; Danny Hull; Larry Field; Raul Matute; Larry Jonutz; David Padron.
Also see PENSE, Lydia, & New Invaders

COLD CHISEL LP '81
Singles: 7-inch
ELEKTRA 3-4 81
LPs: 10/12-inch
ELEKTRA 5-10 80-82
Members: Jimmy Barnes; Don Walker; Steve Prestwich; Phil Small; Ian Moss.
Also see BARNES, Jimmy

COLD CRUSH BROTHERS
Singles: 12-inch
TUFF CITY 4-6 83
Singles: 7-inch
TUFF CITY 3-4 83

COLD FIRE
Singles: 7-inch
CAPITOL 3-4 81
LPs: 10/12-inch
CAPITOL 5-10 81

COLD GRITS
Singles: 7-inch
ATCO 3-5 69

COLD WATER FLAT
Singles: 7-inch
OUTBURST 3-5 71

COLDER, Ben C&W/P&R '62
(Sheb Wooley)
Singles: 7-inch
MGM 4-8 62-73
PORTLAND 3-6 78
SCORPION 3-5 79-80
SUNBIRD 3-4 80
TPL 3-5 87
LPs: 10/12-inch
LAKESHORE (621 "Ben Colder & Sheb Wooley") 10-20
(Mail order offer.)
LAKESHORE/GUSTO (110 "Greatest Hits of Sheb Wooley & Ben Colder") 8-12 79
(Mail order offer.)
MGM (139 "Ben Colder") 8-12 70
MGM (4421 thru 4876) 10-20 66-73
MGM (4173 "Spoofing the Big Ones") 15-25 63
Also see WOOLEY, Sheb

COLDIRON, Curley: see SUNDOWNERS

COLDWATER ARMY
LPs: 10/12-inch
AGAPE 10-15 71

COLE, Ann R&B '56
(With the Suburbans; with Cole-Miners)
Singles: 78 rpm
BATON 15-25 55-57
TIMELY 10-20 54
Singles: 7-inch
BATON (218 "Are You Satisfied") 20-40 55
BATON (224 "New Love") 20-30 56
BATON (229 "My Tearful Heart") 20-30 56
BATON (232 "In the Chapel") 20-40 56
BATON (237 "Got My Mojo Working") 15-25 57
BATON (243 "No Star Is Lost") 15-25 57
BATON (247 "Give Me Love Or Nothing") 15-25 57
BATON (258 "The Love in My Heart") 15-25 58
MGM (12954 "In the Chapel") 10-20 60
ROULETTE (4452 "Have Fun") 10-20 62
SIR (272 "That's Enough") 10-20 59
SIR (275 "A Love of My Own") 10-20 60
TIMELY (1006 "Danny Boy") 20-30 54
TIMELY (1007 "I'll Find a Way") 20-30 54
TIMELY (1010 "So Proud of You") 20-30 54
Also see SUBURBANS

COLE, Bobby P&R '68
Singles: 7-inch
DATE 4-8 68-69

COLE, Brenda C&W '87
Singles: 7-inch
MELODY DAWN 3-4 87-88

COLE, Candy
Singles: 7-inch
MUSICOR 4-8 62

COLE, Carmen
Singles: 7-inch
GROOVE 4-8 64-65

COLE, Carson, & RU4
LPs: 10/12-inch
FRONTLINE 5-10

COLE, Cindy
Singles: 7-inch
TOWER 4-8 65-67

COLE, Clay
Singles: 7-inch
IMPERIAL (5771 "Happy Times") 10-15 61
IMPERIAL (5804 "Twist Around the Clock") 15-25 61
ROULETTE (4280 "Skip Skip") 10-15 60
Session: Capris.
Also see CAPRIS

COLE, Cozy R&B '44
(With His All Stars; with Gary Chester; with Pete Johnson; with Red Norvo; Cozy Cole Septet)
Singles: 78 rpm
KEYNOTE 10-15 44
MGM 5-10 54
Singles: 7-inch
ARTISTIQUE 4-8 61
BETHLEHEM 4-8 63
CHARLIE PARKER 4-8 62
COLUMBIA 4-8 66
CORAL 4-8 62-67
FELSTED 5-10 58
GRAND AWARD 5-8 58
KING 4-8 59-60
LOVE 10-15 58-59
MGM 5-10 54
MERCURY 5-8 58
RANDOM 4-8 60
Picture Sleeves
RANDOM 5-10 60
EPs: 7-inch
AFTER HOURS 15-20 55
MGM 15-20 54
WALDORF 5-8
LPs: 10/12-inch
AFTER HOURS 25-30 55
CHARLIE PARKER 15-20 62
COLUMBIA 10-15 66
CORAL 15-20 62-64
EVEREST 8-10 74
FELSTED 15-20 59
KING 20-25 59-60
LOVE 20-25 59
PARIS 20-25 58
SAVOY 8-12 72-77
TRIP 8-10 74
Also see HAMPTON, Lionel
Also see PAGE, Hot Lips, & Cozy Cole
Also see SHEARING, George, Quintet

COLE, Cozy, & Illnois Jacquet
LPs: 10/12-inch
AUDITION 25-35 55
Also see COLE, Cozy
Also see JACQUET, Illinois

COLE, Diana
Singles: 78 rpm
JOSIE 10-20 57
Singles: 7-inch
ALLISON 4-8 62
JOSIE (808 "So Much Rockin' to Do") 10-15 57
STRAND 5-10 59

COLE, Don
Singles: 78 rpm
RPM (502 "Snake Eyed Mama") 40-60 57
Singles: 7-inch
COED 10-15 61
GUYDEN 10-15 61
KENT (305 "Sweet Lovin' Honey") 40-60 58
RPM (502 "Snake Eyed Mama") 40-60 57
Also see GIGOLOS
Also see HAWKS
Also see RIO ROCKERS
Also see TIARAS

COLE, Don & Alleyne
Singles: 7-inch
SON-RAY 5-10 65
TOLLIE (9015 "Something's Got a Hold on Me") 10-15 64
LPs: 10/12-inch
TOLLIE (56001 "Live at the Whiskey A-Go-Go") 20-30 64

COLE, Eddie
(Eddie Cole's Solid Swingers)
Singles: 78 rpm
DECCA (7210 "Honey Hush") 25-50 36
DECCA (7215 "Stompin' at the Panama") 25-50 36
Members: Eddie Cole; Nat "King" Cole; Bill Wright; Tom Thompson; Ken Roane.
Also see COLE, Nat "King"

COLE, Eddie & Betty
Singles: 7-inch
LARK 8-12 59

COLE, Fred E.
(Northern Lights; with Northern Lights; with Northsiders; Freddie Cole)
Singles: 7-inch
BAND BOX (284 "Don't Be Mad") 75-125 61
DELITE 3-5
DOT 5-10 60
LOIS 5-10 61
PATT (058 "All Alone") 15-25 59
PATT (059 "Please Love Me Now") 15-25 60
WINLEY (222 "One More Night") 15-25 57
TRU GLO TOWN 5-10
LPs: 10/12-inch
NATURAL RESOURCES 5-10 73
PATT (101 "College Hop") 75-100 60
Members: Jack Baker; John Kowecki; John Kosic; John Chappel; Fran Parda; Alan Orkins; Freddie Cole; Don Gates Jr.
Also see BUSTERS

COLE, Gardner P&R '88
Singles: 7-inch
W.B. 3-4 88
Picture Sleeves
W.B. 3-4 88

COLE, Ike
Singles: 7-inch
DEE GEE 4-8 66
PERSONALITY 10-15
LPs: 10/12-inch
DEE GEE 8-12 66

COLE, J.C.
Singles: 7-inch
VALIANT 3-5 66

COLE, Jerry
(With the Spacemen; with Trinity; with Stingers: Jerry Kole)
Singles: 7-inch
CAPITOL 5-10 63-65
HAPPY TIGER 4-6 70
MIDGET 3-5 75
W.B. 3-5 75
Promotional Singles
CAPITOL ("Movin' Surf"/"Racing Waves") 5-10 64
(Bonus single, packaged with the *Summer Surf* LP by Dick Dale & His Del-Tones.)
LPs: 10/12-inch
CAPITOL (T-2044 "Outer Limits") 20-30 63
(Monaural.)
CAPITOL (ST-2044 "Outer Limits") 25-35 63
(Stereo.)
CAPITOL (T-2061 "Hot Rod Dance Party") 20-30 63
(Monaural.)
CAPITOL (ST-2061 "Hot Rod Dance Party") 25-35 63
(Stereo.)
CAPITOL (T-2112 "Surf Age") 25-35 63
(Monaural. With *Thunder Wave*, a bonus single by Dick Dale & His Del-Tones.)
CAPITOL (T-2112 "Surf Age") 20-30 63
(Monaural. Without bonus single.)
CAPITOL (ST-2112 "Surf Age") 35-45 63
(Stereo. With *Thunder Wave*, a bonus single by Dick Dale & His Del-Tones.)
CAPITOL (ST-2112 "Surf Age") 30-40 63
(Stereo. Without bonus single.)
CROWN 15-20 65
CUSTOM 15-20
VOGUE 15-25 63
Also see CATALINAS
Also see CHAMPS
Also see DALE, Dick
Also see ID
Also see KICKSTANDS
Also see KNIGHTS
Also see RIVERS, Johnny / Jerry Cole
Also see SUPER STOCKS
Also see VALENS, Ritchie / Jerry Kole

COLE, Johnny
(With the Reptiles)
Singles: 7-inch
DORE (605 "How the Time Flies") 10-20 61
ORIGINAL SOUND (24 "Love of Diane") 10-20 62
PARADE (202 "Stop the Rain") 5-10 64
RADIANT (1503 "Wrap My Heart in Velvet") 75-125 61
(Orange label.)
RADIANT (1503 "Wrap My Heart in Velvet") 40-60 61
(Black label.)

COLE, Jude P&R/LP '90
Singles: 7-inch
REPRISE 3-4 90
LPs: 10/12-inch
REPRISE 5-8 90
Also see MARTIN, Moon

COLE, Junior
(Jr. Cole & Crescents; with Johnny Winter's Band)
Singles: 7-inch
FROLIC 5-10 64
JIN (163 "I Won't Cry") 30-50 62
Also see WINTER, Johnny

COLE, King, Trio: see COLE, Nat King

COLE, Lee
Singles: 7-inch
MIST (1010 "Cool Baby") 70-80 59

COLE, Les
Singles: 7-inch
D (1010 "Bee Boppin' Daddy") 200-250 58

COLE, Leslie
Singles: 7-inch
JODY 5-8

COLE, Lloyd, & Commotions
LPs: 10/12-inch
GEFFEN 5-10 84

COLE, Mandee
Singles: 7-inch
MERCURY 5-10 62

COLE, Maria
(Mrs. Nat Cole)
LPs: 10/12-inch
CAPITOL 10-15 66

COLE, Nat "King" R&B '42
(King Cole Trio; Quintet; Quartet)
Singles: 78 rpm
AMMOR 15-25 42
ATLAS 10-20 43-45
CAPITOL (100 thru 700 series) 5-10 43-49
CAPITOL (800 thru 4600 series) 4-8 50-58
CAPITOL (15000 series) 3-8 47-49
DAVIS & SCHWEGLER 20-40 39-40
DECCA 10-20 42-47
DISC 15-25 42
EXCELSIOR 10-20 42-45
PREMIER 10-20 44
SAVOY 10-15 46
VARSITY 15-25 40
Singles: 7-inch
CAPITOL (Except 889 thru 5683) 3-6
(Orange labels.)
CAPITOL (889 thru 3619) 10-15 50-57
(Purple labels.)
CAPITOL (3702 "When Rock & Roll Came to Trinidad") 15-25 57
CAPITOL (3737 thru 4623) 6-12 57-61
(Purple labels.)
CAPITOL (4804 thru 5683) 4-8 62-66
(Orange/yellow labels.)
CAPITOL STARLINE 4-6 60s
TAMPA (134 "Vom-Vim-Veedle") 8-12 57
Picture Sleeves
CAPITOL 10-20 59-66
TAMPA (134 "Vom-Vim-Veedle") 15-25 57
EPs: 7-inch
CAPITOL 10-20 50-60
DECCA 10-20 56
LPs: 10/12-inch
CAMAY 8-12
CAPITOL (Except 100 thru 2900 series) 5-15 61-82
CAPITOL (H-156 "Nat 'King' Cole at the Piano") 50-100 49
(10-inch LP.)
CAPITOL (H-177 "Nat 'King' Cole Trio") 50-75 49
(10-inch LP.)
CAPITOL (H-220 "Nat 'King' Cole Trio") 50-75 50
(10-inch LP.)
CAPITOL (H-332 "Penthouse Serenade") 50-75 52
(10-inch LP.)
CAPITOL (H-357 "Unforgettable") 50-75 52
(10-inch LP.)
CAPITOL (100 thru 900 series) 20-35 55-58
(With "T" or "W" prefix.)
CAPITOL (1000 thru 2900 series) 10-20 58-68
(With "T," "ST" or "W" prefix.)
CAPITOL 5-10
(With "SM" prefix.)
CAPITOL (4903 "Nat 'King' Cole") 10-20 65
(Commemorative, promotional issue only. Signed by Cole's widow.)
CROWN 8-12 64
DECCA (8260 "In the Beginning") 35-50 56
DYNAMIC HOUSE 5-10 72
MCA 5-10 73
MARK 56 5-10 76
MONARCH ("Nat 'King' Cole") 75-100 53
(Colored vinyl.)
PICKWICK 5-10 70s
SCORE (4019 "King Cole Trio") 20-40 58
SPINORAMA 10-15 60s
VSP 10-15 66
WYNCOTE 10-15 63
Members (King Cole Trio): Harry Edison; Willie Smith; Juan Tizol.
Also see COLE, Eddie
Also see COLE, Maria
Also see FOUR KNIGHTS
Also see KENTON, Stan
Also see LUTCHER, Nellie, & Nat "King" Cole
Also see MARTIN, Dean, & Nat "King" Cole
Also see NELSON, Willie / Nat "King" Cole / Johnny Mathis / Shirley Bassey
Also see PRESLEY, Elvis
Also see PRESLEY, Elvis / Frank Sinatra / Nat "King" Cole
Also see SINATRA, Frank / Nat "King" Cole
Also see YOUNG, Lester, & Nat "King" Cole

COLE, Nat "King" / Phil Flowers
LPs: 10/12-inch
EXCELSIOR 5-10
Also see FLOWERS, Phil

COLE, Nat "King," & Stubby Kaye
Singles: 7-inch
CAPITOL 3-6 65
Picture Sleeves
CAPITOL 4-8 65

COLE, Nat "King," & His Trio / George Kingston
LPs: 10/12-inch
WYNCOTE 10-15 60s

COLE, Nat "King," & George Shearing
LPs: 10/12-inch
CAPITOL 20-30 61
Also see COLE, Nat "King"
Also see SHEARING, George, Quintet

COLE, Nat, Jr.
Singles: 7-inch
STAFF 4-6 80

COLE, Natalie P&R/R&B/LP '75
(With George Shearing)
Singles: 12-inch
EMI 4-6 88
EPIC 4-6 83
MODERN 4-6 85
Singles: 7-inch
CAPITOL 3-4 75-80
EMI 3-4 88-89
EPIC 3-4 83
MANHATTAN 3-4 87
MODERN 3-4 85
Picture Sleeves
EMI 3-4 88-89
MANHATTAN 3-4 87
MODERN 3-4 85
LPs: 10/12-inch
CAPITOL (Except 11928) 8-12 75-82
CAPITOL (11928 "I Love You So") 20-25 79
(Promotional only picture disc.)
EMI 5-8 89
ELEKTRA 5-8 91
EPIC 5-10 83
MANHATTAN 5-10 87
MFSL (032 "Thankful") 30-50 79
MFSL (081 "Natalie Cole Sings George Shearing Plays") 25-40 82
MODERN 5-10 85
Also see PARKER, Ray, Jr., & Natalie Cole
Also see SHEARING, George, Quintet

COLE, Natalie, & Peabo Bryson R&B/LP '79
Singles: 7-inch
CAPITOL 3-4 79
LPs: 10/12-inch
CAPITOL 5-10 79
Also see BRYSON, Peabo
Also see COLE, Natalie

COLE, Patsy C&W '89
Singles: 7-inch
TRA-STAR 3-4 89

COLE, Sami Jo C&W/P&R '74
(Sami Jo & Friends; Sami Jo Cole)
Singles: 7-inch
ELEKTRA 3-4 81
FAME 3-5 71-72
MGM 3-5 74-75
POLYDOR 3-5 76
LPs: 10/12-inch
MGM 5-10 74-75

COLE, Skip
Singles: 7-inch
BAND BOX 5-10 62

COLE, Sonny, & Rhythm Roamers
EXCELL 20-30 56
Singles: 7-inch
EXCELL (123 "I Dreampt I Was Elvis") 75-100 56
EXCELL (124 "Robinson Crusoe Bop") 50-75 56
ROLLIN' ROCK 5-10 69

COLE, Tony P&R '72
Singles: 7-inch
20TH FOX 3-4 73-74
LPs: 10/12-inch
20TH FOX 8-10 73

COLE BROTHERS
Singles: 7-inch
JAMIE 4-6 68-69
MILLMONT 10-20 60s

COLE & EMBERS
Singles: 7-inch
STAR-TREK (1220 "Hey Girl") 15-25 68

COLEMAN, Albert C&W '82
(Albert Coleman's Atlanta Pops)
Singles: 7-inch
EPIC 3-4 82
LPs: 10/12-inch
EPIC 5-8 83

COLEMAN, Carlton: see COLEMAN, King

COLEMAN, David
Singles: 7-inch
BARRY 10-15 67

COLEMAN, Diane
Singles: 7-inch
COED 4-8 62

COLEMAN, Durell R&B/LP '85
Singles: 7-inch
ISLAND 3-4 85
LPs: 10/12-inch
ISLAND 5-10 85

COLEMAN, Gary B.B.
LPs: 10/12-inch
ICHIBAN 5-10

COLEMAN, George
Singles: 7-inch
77 5-10 59

COLEMAN, Herb
Singles: 7-inch
KAPP 5-10 59

COLEMAN, Honey
Singles: 78 rpm
COMBO 20-40 52
Singles: 7-inch
COMBO (3 "Talk About a Girl Child Being Down") 50-75 52

COLEMAN, Hooks
Singles: 7-inch
EXCELLO 5-10 60

COLEMAN, Jimmy
Singles: 7-inch
REVUE 4-8 67

COLEMAN, Joe
Singles: 7-inch
REM 5-10 60

COLEMAN, King
(Carlton "King" Coleman)
Singles: 7-inch
ATLANTIC 5-10 61
COLUMBIA 5-10 61
KAREN 5-10 59
KENCO 5-10 61
KING 3-6 67-71
PORT 4-8 66
SYLVIA 5-10 65
SYMBOL 5-10 60
TOGO 4-8 63
Picture Sleeves
KING 4-6 71

COLEMAN, Lenny
(With Nino & the Ebb Tides)
Singles: 7-inch
LAURIE (3290 "Four Seasons") 20-30 65
Also see NINO & Ebb Tides

COLEMAN, Ray
Singles: 7-inch
ARCADE (147 "Juke box Rock & Roll") 100-150 58
SALIANO (111 "My Rock & Roll Baby") 50-75
SKYROCKET (1002 "Toodle Oo-Bamboo") 50-75 59

COLEMAN, Richard
Singles: 7-inch
PRIMA 5-10 59

COLEMAN, Trudy
Singles: 7-inch
MANCO 4-8 63

COLEMANS
(Coleman Brothers)
Singles: 78 rpm
ARCO 5-10 49
CORAL 5-10 49
DECCA 10-15 44-47
MANOR 8-12 45-47
REGAL 10-15 50

COLES, Johnny
LPs: 10/12-inch
MAINSTREAM 10-12 72

COLESCENTS
Singles: 7-inch
DOUBLE PLAY 4-8 67

COLEY, John Ford
(With Leslie & Kelly Coley)
Singles: 7-inch
A&M 3-5 81
LPs: 10/12-inch
A&M 5-10 81
Also see ENGLAND DAN & John Ford Coley

COLICCHIO, Victor
Singles: 12-inch
3C (839 "His Music Will Never Die") 10-15 88
(With cover.)

COLIN, Jesse: see YOUNG, Jesse Colin

COLL, Brian, & Plattermen
Singles: 7-inch
PARROT 4-8 66

COLLAGE R&B '83
Singles: 12-inch
CONSTELLATION 4-6 86
MCA 4-6 85
SOLAR 4-6 83
Singles: 7-inch
CONSTELLATION 3-4 86
MCA 3-4 85
SOLAR 3-4 82-83
LPs: 10/12-inch
CONSTELLATION 5-10 86
SOLAR 5-10 81-83

COLLAGE
Singles: 7-inch
BELL 3-6 70
SMASH 4-8 68
LPs: 10/12-inch
CREAM 8-10 71
SMASH 10-12 68

COLLARMEN
Singles: 7-inch
CUCA 4-8 67

COLLAY, Allan
Singles: 7-inch
ACE 4-8 61
INSTANT 5-10 62

COLLAY & SATELLITES P&R '60
Singles: 7-inch
SHO-BIZ (1002 "Last Chance") 15-25 60

COLLECTION
Singles: 7-inch
HOT BISCUIT COMPANY 4-8 68
RCA 4-6 68

COLLECTORS
Singles: 7-inch
LONDON 8-12 70
VALIANT (760 "Old Man") 20-30 67
W.B. (7059 "Listen to the Words") 10-20 67
W.B. (7159 "Fat Bird") 10-20 68
W.B. (7194 "Lydia Purple") 8-15 68
W.B. (7300 "Easy Morning") 6-12 69
LPs: 10/12-inch
W.B. (1746 "The Collectors") 20-35 68
W.B. (1774 "Grass and Wild Strawberries") 20-30 69
Also see CANADIAN CLASSICS
Also see CHILLIWACK

COLLEGIANS
Singles: 78 rpm
CAT 8-15 54
GROOVE 10-20 56
Singles: 7-inch
CAT (110 "Rickety Tickety Melody") 10-20 54
GROOVE (0163 "Blue Solitude") 20-30 56

COLLEGIANS
Singles: 78 rpm
WINLEY 25-50 57
Singles: 7-inch
LOST-NITE 4-8
TIMES SQUARE 5-10 63
WINLEY (224 "Zoom Zoom Zoom") 50-75 57
(Rigid disc.)
WINLEY (224 "Zoom Zoom Zoom") 15-25 57
(Flexible disc.)
WINLEY (261 "Oh, I Need Your Love") 15-25 62
WINLEY (263 "Right Around the Corner") 15-25 62
X-TRA (108 "Heavenly Night") 100-250 58
(Titles and artists shown on label in print approximately 1/8-inch letters. Label also has double horizontal lines.)
X-TRA (108 "Heavenly Night") 25-50
(Titles and artists shown in print approximately 1/4-inch letters.)
LPs: 10/12-inch
LOST-NITE 8-12 81
WINLEY (6004 "Sing Along with the Collegians") 200-300 62
Members: Roger Hayes; Vernon Riley; Henry Brown; William Tarkenton; Holland Jackson.

COLLEGIANS
Singles: 7-inch
HILLTOP 10-15 60-61
POST 8-12 62

COLLEGIATES
Singles: 7-inch
CAPO (001 "Brief Romance") 5-10 59

COLLEGIATES
(With the Classmates)
Singles: 7-inch
CAMPUS (10 "Say Hello to My Angel") 40-60 60

COLLEGIATES
Singles: 7-inch
HERITAGE (105 "I Had a Dream")..15-25 61

COLLEGIATES
Singles: 7-inch
CABELL..........5-10 66-67
SMASH..........5-10 66

COL-LE-JETS
Singles: 7-inch
NORTHWESTERN (2477 "Jam and Jelly")..........10-20 60

COLLETT, Jimmy
Singles: 78 rpm
ARCADE..........20-30 52-53
Singles: 7-inch
ARCADE..........20-40 52-53

COLLETTE, Buddy
LPs: 10/12-inch
CROWN (5019 "Bongo Madness")..........25-35 57
Also see CALLENDER, Red

COLLETTI, Gus, & Clusters
Singles: 7-inch
TIN PAN ALLEY (206 "Hold My Hand")..........150-250 58
TIN PAN ALLEY (207 "My Darling, Wait for Me")..........150-250 58

COLLEY, Keith P&R '63
Singles: 7-inch
CHALLENGE..........4-6 66-70
COLUMBIA..........4-6 68
ERA..........5-10 61-62
JAF..........5-10 60s
UNICAL..........5-10 63-64
VEE JAY..........4-8 65

COLLEY, Steve
Singles: 7-inch
EXCELLO..........5-10 59

COLLIE, Mark C&W '90
Singles: 7-inch
MCA..........3-4 90-92

COLLIE, Shirley C&W '61
Singles: 7-inch
LIBERTY..........5-10 61
Also see NELSON, Willie, & Shirley Collie
Also see SMITH, Warren, & Shirley Collie

COLLIER, George, & Columbians
Singles: 7-inch
KLUB (4148 "Forever Mine")..........12-18

COLLIER, Mitty R&B '63
Singles: 7-inch
CHESS..........5-10 61-68
ENTRANCE..........3-5 72
ERIC..........3-4 78
PEACHTREE..........3-6 69-70
LPs: 10/12-inch
CHESS..........15-25 65-66
GOSPEL ROOTS..........5-10 79

COLLIER, Ralph
Singles: 7-inch
SIMS..........4-8 64

COLLINS, Aaron
Singles: 7-inch
CRAZY HORSE..........4-8 68-69
DYNASTY..........5-10 60
MAJOR..........5-8
Also see CADETS
Also see FLARES
Also see THOR-ABLES / Aaron Collins

COLLINS, Al
Singles: 78 rpm
ACE (500 "I Got the Blues for You")..........15-25 55
Singles: 7-inch
ACE (500 "I Got the Blues for You")..........75-100 55

COLLINS, Al
Singles: 7-inch
DOT (15944 "Beat Love")..........8-12 59

COLLINS, Al P&R '53
(Al "Jazzbo" Collins)
Singles: 78 rpm
BRUNSWICK..........10-15 53
Singles: 7-inch
BRUNSWICK (86001 "Little Red Riding Hood")..........10-20 53
IDONGOTOSHOWYOUNOSTINKINBADGES (1225 "Hip Nite B-4 Xmas")..........10-15
(Label name is correct—as in "I Don't Got to Show You No Stinkin' Badges" and is not the result of a typist gone berserk.)
SINCERELY YOURS (3491 "Lullaby")..........5-10
Picture Sleeves
BRUNSWICK (86001 "Little Red Riding Hood")..........20-30 53
LPs: 10/12-inch
CORAL (57035 "East Coast Jazz Scene")..........50-100 56
Also see FREED, Alan, Steve Allen, Al "Jazzbo" Collins & Modernaires

COLLINS, Al "Jazzbo," & Lou Stein
Singles: 78 rpm
BRUNSWICK (80226 "Three Little Pigs")..........5-10 53
CAPITOL..........5-10 53
Singles: 7-inch
BRUNSWICK (80226 "Three Little Pigs")..........10-15 53
CAPITOL (2580 "Snow White and the Seven Dwarfs")..........10-20 53
Also see COLLINS, Al
Also see STEIN, Lou

COLLINS, Albert R&B/LP '72
(With the Ice Breakers; with His Rhythm Rockers)
Singles: 12-inch
ALLIGATOR (5 "Cold Snap")..........5-10 86
(Promotional issue only.)
Singles: 7-inch
GREAT SCOTT (007 "Albert's Alley")..........15-25 59
HALL..........8-12 64
HALL WAY..........8-12 63
IMPERIAL..........4-6 69
KANGAROO (103 "Freeze")..........25-50 58
LIBERTY..........3-5 70
TCF HALL..........4-8 65-66
TRACIE (2003 "I Don't Know")..........10-20 62
TUMBLEWEED..........3-5 72-73
20TH FOX..........5-10 68
LPs: 10/12-inch
ALLIGATOR..........6-10 79-87
BLUE THUMB..........10-15 69
BRYLEN..........5-10 84
IMPERIAL..........12-25 69-70
MFSL (226 "Cold Snap")..........15-25
TCF HALL (8002 "Cool Sound of Albert Collins")..........30-35 65
TUMBLEWEED..........10-15 71

COLLINS, Albert, Robert Cray & Johnny Copeland LP '86
Singles: 12-inch
ALLIGATOR (5 "T-Bone Shuffle")....5-10 86
(Promotional issue only.)
LPs: 10/12-inch
ALLIGATOR..........5-10 86
MFSL (217 "Showdown")..........20-25 90s
Also see COLLINS, Albert
Also see COPELAND, Johnny
Also see CRAY, Robert

COLLINS, Allen, Band
LPs: 10/12-inch
MCA..........5-8 83
Members: Allen Collins; Leon Wilkeson; Barry Harwood; Jimmy Dougherty; Billy Powell; Derek Hess; Randall Hall.
Also see ALIAS
Also see LYNYRD SKYNYRD

COLLINS, Big Tom
(Brownie McGhee)
Singles: 78 rpm
KING..........50-75 51-52
Singles: 7-inch
KING (4483 "Heartache Blues")...75-100 51
KING (4568 "Heart Breaking Woman")..........75-100 52
Also see McGHEE, Brownie

COLLINS, Bill
Singles: 7-inch
BRENT..........5-10 59

COLLINS, Bob
Singles: 7-inch
MARK IV..........4-8

COLLINS, Bob, & Fabulous Five
Singles: 7-inch
JOKERS THREE..........5-10
MAINLINE..........15-20

COLLINS, Bonnie
Singles: 7-inch
RINGO..........4-8 65

COLLINS, Boots
Singles: 7-inch
UPLAND..........4-8 64

COLLINS, Brian C&W '71
Singles: 7-inch
ABC/DOT..........3-5 74-77
DOT..........3-5 73-74
MEGA..........3-5 71-72
PRIMERO..........3-4 82-83
RCA..........3-5 78-79
LPs: 10/12-inch
ABC..........5-10 77
ABC/DOT..........6-12 74
DOT..........8-12 73

COLLINS, Carol
Singles: 7-inch
DUNES (2005 "Dear One")..........15-25 61
Also see CONNORS, Carol

COLLINS, Cecil
Singles: 7-inch
BLUE MOON (414 "Rockin' Baby")..........50-75 59

COLLINS, Choo Choo
Singles: 7-inch
TORNADO (1007 "My Competition")..........10-20

COLLINS, Dave
Singles: 7-inch
CAPITOL..........3-5 73

COLLINS, Dave & Ansell P&R '71
Singles: 7-inch
BIG TREE..........3-5 71-72
LPs: 10/12-inch
BIG TREE..........10-12 71
Also see COLLINS, Dave

COLLINS, Dave, & Scrubs
Singles: 78 rpm
IMPERIAL (5294 "Don't Break-a-My Heart")..........50-75 54
Singles: 7-inch
IMPERIAL (5294 "Don't Break-a-My Heart")..........200-400 54

COLLINS, Della Sue
Singles: 7-inch
THUNDERHEAD..........3-4
Picture Sleeves
THUNDERHEAD..........8-10

COLLINS, Dorothy P&R '55
Singles: 78 rpm
AUDIOVOX..........4-8 54-55
CORAL..........4-8 55-56
DECCA..........4-8 52
MGM..........4-8 50-51
Singles: 7-inch
AUDIOVOX..........5-10 54-55
CORAL..........5-10 55-56
DECCA..........5-10 52
GOLD EAGLE..........4-8 61
MGM..........5-10 50-51
ROULETTE..........4-6 63
TOP RANK..........5-10 59-60
EPs: 7-inch
CORAL..........5-10 55-56
MGM..........5-10 55
LPs: 10/12-inch
CORAL..........15-25 55-57
MOTIVATION..........10-15 62
TOP RANK..........10-15 60
VOCALION..........5-10 65
Also see McGUIRE SISTERS / Lancers / Dorothy Collins / Teresa Brewer

COLLINS, Dugg C&W '77
Singles: 7-inch
SCR..........3-5 77

COLLINS, Eddie
Singles: 7-inch
FERNWOOD (104 "Patience Baby")..........50-75 58

COLLINS, Ernie
Singles: 7-inch
FIRST ARTISTS..........3-4 78

COLLINS, Glenda
Singles: 7-inch
LAWN..........4-8 64

COLLINS, Gwen
Singles: 7-inch
BRAGG..........4-8 65
NEW WORLD..........4-8 66

COLLINS, Gwen & Jerry C&W '70
Singles: 7-inch
BRAGG..........4-8 65
CAPITOL..........3-6 69-70
NEW WORLD..........4-6 67
Also see COLLINS, Gwen

COLLINS, Jim C&W '85
Singles: 7-inch
TKM..........3-4 86
WHITE GOLD..........3-4 85

COLLINS, Jimmy
Singles: 7-inch
J&S..........5-10 60
ORBIT..........10-20

COLLINS, Judy LP '64
Singles: 7-inch
ELEKTRA (Except 45253 & 45008 thru 45680)..........3-5 70-84
ELEKTRA (45253 "Send in the Clowns")..........3-5 75
ELEKTRA (45008 thru 45680)..........4-8 64-69
Picture Sleeves
ELEKTRA (Except "The Hostage")....3-5 69-84
ELEKTRA ("The Hostage")..........4-8 73
(Promotional issue only.)
LPs: 10/12-inch
ELEKTRA (Except 200 & 300 series)..........10-15 67-84
ELEKTRA (209 "Maid of Constant Sorrow")..........30-40 61
ELEKTRA (222 "Golden Apples of the Sun")..........25-35 62
ELEKTRA (243 "Judy Collins No. 3")..........20-30 63
(Monaural.)
ELEKTRA (7-243 "Judy Collins No. 3")..........25-35 63
(Stereo.)
ELEKTRA (253 "Running for My Life")..........5-8 80
ELEKTRA (300 series)..........15-20 65-68
(Monaural.)
ELEKTRA (7-300 series)..........15-20 65-72
(Stereo.)
ELEKTRA (60001 "Times of Our Lives")..........5-8 82
Session: Van Dyke Parks.
Also see PARKS, Van Dyke

COLLINS, Judy, & T.G. Sheppard C&W '84
Singles: 7-inch
ELEKTRA..........3-4 84
Also see COLLINS, Judy
Also see SHEPPARD, T.G.

COLLINS, Keanya R&B '69
(Kenya Collins)
Singles: 7-inch
BLUE ROCK..........3-6 69
ITCO..........3-6 69
KEANYA (1 "Love Bandit")..........15-25

PM..........3-5

COLLINS, L.
(With the Counts)
Singles: 7-inch
BALKAN..........5-10 59

COLLINS, Larry
Singles: 7-inch
COLUMBIA..........8-12 61-62
MONUMENT..........3-5 70
Also see COLLINS KIDS

COLLINS, Linda
Singles: 7-inch
TIME..........10-20 61

COLLINS, Lorrie
Singles: 7-inch
COLUMBIA (41541 "That Lonesome Road")..........10-15 59
COLUMBIA (41673 "That's Your Affair")..........5-10 60
Also see COLLINS KIDS

COLLINS, Lyn P&R/R&B '72
(With the Famous Flames)
Singles: 7-inch
PEOPLE..........3-5 72-76
LPs: 10/12-inch
PEOPLE..........10-12 72-75
Also see BROWN, James & Lyn Collins

COLLINS, Marty
Singles: 7-inch
RENNER..........4-8 62

COLLINS, Paul
(Paul Collins Beat)
Singles: 7-inch
COLUMBIA..........3-4 82
LPs: 10/12-inch
COLUMBIA..........5-10 82
Also see BEAT

COLLINS, Phil P&R/LP '81
Singles: 12-inch
ATLANTIC..........4-6 84-86
Singles: 7-inch
ATLANTIC..........3-4 81-90
Picture Sleeves
ATLANTIC..........3-4 81-90
LPs: 10/12-inch
ATLANTIC..........5-10 81-90
Also see BAILEY, Philip, & Phil Collins
Also see BAND AID
Also see BRAND X
Also see FLAMING YOUTH
Also see GENESIS

COLLINS, Phil, & Marilyn Martin P&R '85
Singles: 7-inch
ATLANTIC..........3-4 85
Picture Sleeves
ATLANTIC..........3-4 85
Also see COLLINS, Phil
Also see MARTIN, Marilyn

COLLINS, Ramona
Singles: 7-inch
CLARK'S (346 "You've Been Cheating")..........300-400

COLLINS, Rodger R&B '67
(Roger Collins)
Singles: 7-inch
FANTASY..........3-5 73
GALAXY..........3-8 66-73
POMPEII..........3-6 69

COLLINS, Sue
(Sue Collins & D.H.S. Swingers)
Singles: 7-inch
VANDAN..........4-8 66
Also see DAVIS, Paul

COLLINS, Terry
Singles: 7-inch
KWANZA..........3-5
SILVER BLUE..........3-5

COLLINS, Tom, & Mixers
Singles: 7-inch
("Mixer's Rock")..........250-500 59
(Label name and selection number not known.)
Members: Laurie Collins; Pete Glystein; Bob Merkt; Gene Stoiber; Tony Kolp.

COLLINS, Tommy C&W '54
(With Wanda Collins)
Singles: 78 rpm
CAPITOL..........10-20 54-56
Singles: 7-inch
CAPITOL (2000 & 3000 series)..........15-25 54-58
CAPITOL (4000 & 5000 series except 4495)..........5-15 58-64
CAPITOL (4495 "Black Cat")..........20-30 61
COLUMBIA..........5-8 66-68
EPs: 7-inch
CAPITOL (607 "Tommy Collins")...30-50 54
CAPITOL (776 "Words and Music Country Style")..........25-40 56
(Price is for any of three volumes in this series.)
CAPITOL (1100 series)..........10-20 59
LPs: 10/12-inch
CAPITOL (776 "Words and Music Country Style")..........30-50 56
CAPITOL (1125 "Light of the Lord")..........50-60 59
CAPITOL (1196 "This Is Tommy Collins")..........30-40 59
CAPITOL (1436 "Songs I Love to Sing")..........30-40 61
COLUMBIA..........20-35 66-68
GOLDEN COUNTRY..........5-8 83
STARDAY..........10-15 72
TOWER..........15-25 66-68
VERVE (10565 "I Wanna Thank You")..........10-15 67
Session: Buck Owens.
Also see OWENS, Buck
Also see SIPES, Leonard, & Rhythm Oakies

COLLINS, Tommy, & Paragons
Singles: 7-inch
WINLEY..........10-20 59
Also see PARAGONS

COLLINS, Tyler P&R/LP '90
Singles: 7-inch
RCA..........3-4 90
LPs: 10/12-inch
RCA..........5-8 90

COLLINS, Vivian
Singles: 7-inch
SEROCK..........4-8 62

COLLINS, Wil, & Willpower
Singles: 7-inch
MERCURY..........3-5 75

COLLINS, William: see BOOTSY'S RUBBER BAND

COLLINS, Willie R&B '86
Singles: 7-inch
CAPITOL..........3-4 86

COLLINS & COLLINS R&B '80
Singles: 7-inch
A&M..........3-4 80
LPs: 10/12-inch
A&M..........5-10 80
Members: Bill Collins; Tonee Collins.

COLLINS KIDS
Singles: 78 rpm
COLUMBIA..........20-50 55-57
Singles: 7-inch
COLUMBIA (21470 "Hush Money")..........15-25 55
COLUMBIA (21514 "Rockaway Rock")..........15-25 56
COLUMBIA (21543 "I'm in My Teens")..........15-25 56
COLUMBIA (21560 "Rock & Roll Polka")..........15-25 56
COLUMBIA (40824 "Move a Little Closer")..........20-30 57
COLUMBIA (40921 "Hop, Skip and Jump")..........20-30 57
COLUMBIA (41012 "Party")..........50-75 57
(Black vinyl.)
COLUMBIA (41012 "Party")..........100-200 57
(Purple vinyl. Promotional issue only.)
COLUMBIA (41087 "Hoy Hoy")..........30-45 58
COLUMBIA (41149 "Mercy")..........30-45 58
COLUMBIA (41225 "Whistle Bait") 35-55 58
COLUMBIA (41329 "Sugar Plum")..10-20 59
LPs: 10/12-inch
COLUMBIA..........8-12 83
Members: Larry Collins; Lawrencine "Lorrie" Collins.
Also see COLLINS, Larry
Also see COLLINS, Lorrie

COLLOM, Tookie, & Roller Coasters
Singles: 7-inch
HOLIDAY INN..........4-8

COLMAN, Ken
Singles: 7-inch
EPIC..........4-8 65

COLOGNES
Singles: 7-inch
LUMMTONE (102 "A River Flows")..........75-125 59

COLOMBIER, Michel
LPs: 10/12-inch
CHRYSALIS..........5-10 79
COLUMBIA..........8-10 83

COLOMBO, Chris: see COLUMBO, Chris

COLOMBO, Joe
Singles: 7-inch
AMP 3..........5-10
DOMINO (1000 "Cha-Rock")..........8-12 61
STYLE..........8-10
TAURUS (359 "I Need You")..........25-35 63

COLONAIRS
Singles: 78 rpm
EMBER (1017 "Can't Stand to Lose You")..........40-60 57
Singles: 7-inch
EMBER (1017 "Can't Stand to Lose You")..........35-55 57
TRU-LITE (127 "Do-Pop-Si")..........30-45 63

COLONEL ABRAMS: see ABRAMS, Colonel

COLONEL BAGSHOT
LPs: 10/12-inch
CADET CONCEPT..........10-12 71

COLONEL JOYE
(With the Joy Boys; Col Joye)
Singles: 7-inch
DECCA (30933 "Rockin' Rollin' Clementine")..........75-125 59
FONO GRAF (1241 "Please Give It a Chance")..........200-300 62

COLONEL SPLENDID
Singles: 7-inch
LUCKY TOKEN..........4-8 65

COLONIALS
Singles: 7-inch
SENATE (1003 "Where Is My Love") ... 25-35
TRU-LITE (127 "Little Miss Muffet") ... 50-75 64

COLONNA, Johnny Jay
Singles: 7-inch
MAGNET ... 4-8 63

COLONY
Singles: 7-inch
SUNDERLAND (2293 "Psuedo-Pscyho Intuition") ... 30-50

COLONY
Singles: 7-inch
PLATTER (105 "All I Want") ... 5-10

COLOR ME BAD
Singles: 7-inch
GIANT ... 3-4 91

COLOR ME GONE
Singles: 7-inch
A&M ... 3-4 84
LPs: 10/12-inch
A&M ... 5-10 84

COLORADO
Singles: 7-inch
UNI ... 3-5 71

COLORBLIND
Singles: 7-inch
CAPITOL ... 3-4 84
LPs: 10/12-inch
CAPITOL ... 5-10 84

COLORING BOOK
Singles: 7-inch
PACIFIC CHALLENGE (117 "Smokestack Lightning") ... 15-25

COLORS *D&D '83*
Singles: 12-inch
FIRST TAKE ... 4-6 83
Singles: 7-inch
BECKET ... 3-4 82
INFINITE ... 3-4 80s
Picture Sleeves
INFINITE ... 3-5 80s

COLORS OF LOVE
Singles: 7-inch
PAGE ONE ... 4-8 68

COLOSSEUM *LP '71*
Singles: 7-inch
DUNHILL ... 3-6 69-71
LPs: 10/12-inch
DUNHILL ... 10-15 69-70
W.B. ... 10-15 71
Members: Jon Heisman; Dick Heckstall-Smith; David Greenslade; Dave Clempson; Mark Clarke; Chris Farlowe; Barbara Thompson; Louis Gennamo.
Also see FARLOWE, Chris

COLOSSEUM II
LPs: 10/12-inch
MCA ... 8-10 77-78

COLOUR BOX
Singles: 12-inch
A&M ... 4-6 83

COLOUR FIELD
Singles: 7-inch
CHRYSALIS ... 3-4 85
LPs: 10/12-inch
CHRYSALIS ... 5-10 85

COLOUR RADIO
Singles: 7-inch
GOLD MOUNTAIN ... 3-4 83
LPs: 10/12-inch
GOLD MOUNTAIN ... 5-10 83

COLOURS
Singles: 7-inch
DOT ... 4-8 68-69
LPs: 10/12-inch
DOT ... 15-20 68-69

COLQUITT, Bobby, & Renaults
Singles: 7-inch
COLTON (101 "I'm Not a Know It All") ... 25-50

COLT, Alisa
Singles: 7-inch
CHELSEA ... 3-5 75

COLT, Steve
(With the Mustangs; with Blue Knights; with 45s; with Fabulous Counts; Steve Colt's Paradox)
Singles: 7-inch
AMOS ... 4-8 69
BIG BEAT ... 5-10
FLEETWOOD (4550 "Gloria") ... 200-400 62
(Credits "Steve Colt and The Mustangs.")
FLEETWOOD (4550 "Gloria") ... 50-100 62
(Credits "Steve Colt and The Blue Knights.")
MIRANDA (265 "In the Still of the Night") ... 100-200 60s
RCA ... 4-8 66
VANGUARD ... 3-5 71
LPs: 10/12-inch
VANGUARD ... 10-12 71

COLTER, Jessi *C&W/P&R '75*
(Mirriam Johnson; Mirriam Eddy)
Singles: 7-inch
CAPITOL ... 3-5 75-82
RCA ... 3-6 69-72
LPs: 10/12-inch
CAPITOL ... 5-10 75-81
RCA (4333 "A Country Star Is Born") ... 10-20 70
Session: Waylon Jennings; Gary Scruggs.
Also see EDDY, Duane & Mirriam
Also see JENNINGS, Waylon, & Jessi Colter
Also see JOHNSON, Mirriam
Also see SOME of CHET'S FRIENDS

COLTIN, R.J.
Singles: 7-inch
VISTA INT'L ... 3-5
EPs: 12-inch
COLT (101 "'87 Reunion in Nashville") ... 10-15 87
Members: R.J. Coltin; D.J. Fontana; Charlie Hodge; Jordanaires.
Also see FONTANA, D.J., Band
Also see JORDANAIRES
Also see PRESLEY, Elvis

COLTON, Tony
(With the Concords)
Singles: 7-inch
ABC-PAR ... 10-15 65
ROULETTE ... 10-20 63

COLTRANE, Alice *LP '71*
LPs: 10/12-inch
IMPULSE ... 8-10 71-74
W.B. ... 5-10 77-78

COLTRANE, Alice, & Carlos Santana *LP '74*
LPs: 10/12-inch
COLUMBIA ... 6-10 74
Also see SANTANA

COLTRANE, Alice, & Pharoah Sanders
LP: 10/12-inch
ARISTA ... 6-10 70s
Also see COLTRANE, Alice
Also see SANDERS, Pharoah

COLTRANE, Chi *P&R/LP '72*
Singles: 7-inch
CLOUDS ... 3-5 78
COLUMBIA ... 3-5 72-73
LPs: 10/12-inch
CLOUDS ... 5-10 77
COLUMBIA ... 8-12 72-73

COLTRANE, John *LP '67*
Singles: 78 rpm
PRESTIGE ... 10-20 57
Singles: 7-inch
ATLANTIC ... 4-8 60-61
PRESTIGE ... 5-10 57-64
LPs: 10/12-inch
ATLANTIC (1300 & 1400 series) ... 20-40 59-66
BLUE NOTE (1577 "Blue Train") ... 100-150 51
(Label gives New York street address for Blue Note Records.)
BLUE NOTE (1577 "Blue Train") ... 35-55 59
(Label reads "Blue Note Records Inc. - New York, U.S.A.")
COLTRANE (4950 "Cosmic Music") ... 150-200 66
COLTRANE (5000 "Cosmic Music") ... 150-200 66
IMPULSE (Except 6 thru 77) ... 10-25 66-71
IMPULSE (6 thru 77) ... 25-45 61-65
JAZZLAND ... 20-40 61
PRESTIGE (7043 "Two Tenors") ... 50-100 56
(Yellow label.)
PRESTIGE (7043 "Two Tenors") ... 25-35 64
(Blue label.)
PRESTIGE (7105 "Coltrane") ... 50-100 57
(Yellow label.)
PRESTIGE (7105 "Coltrane") ... 25-35 57
(Blue label.)
PRESTIGE (7123 "John Coltrane & Red Garland Trio") ... 50-75 57
(Yellow label.)
PRESTIGE (7123 "Traneing In") ... 25-35 64
(Blue label, logo on right. Reissue of *John Coltrane & Red Garland Trio.*)
PRESTIGE (7123 "Traneing In") ... 15-25 69
(Blue label, logo at top.)
PRESTIGE (7142 "Soultrane") ... 40-70 58
(Yellow label.)
PRESTIGE (7158 "Cattin' ") ... 40-70 59
(Yellow label.)
PRESTIGE (7158 "Cattin' ") ... 25-35 64
(Blue label.)
PRESTIGE (7131 "Wheelin' and Dealin' ") ... 40-70 59
(Yellow label.)
PRESTIGE (7188 "Lush Life") ... 40-70 60
(Yellow label.)
PRESTIGE (7188 "Lush Life") ... 25-35 64
(Blue label.)
PRESTIGE (7200 series) ... 20-40 61-64
(Yellow label.)
PRESTIGE (7200 series) ... 15-25 64
(Blue label.)
PRESTIGE (7300 series) ... 15-25 65
U.A. ... 25-35 62
Also see ADDERLEY, Julian "Cannonball," & John Coltrane
Also see ELLINGTON, Duke, & John Coltrane

COLTRANE, John, & Miles Davis
LPs: 10/12-inch
PRESTIGE ... 10-20 64
Also see DAVIS, Miles

COLTRANE, John, & Thelonious Monk
LPs: 10/12-inch
JAZZLAND ... 20-30 61
MILESTONE ... 8-12 73
RIVERSIDE (Except 039) ... 10-20 65-68
RIVERSIDE (039 "Thelonious Monk & John Coltrane") ... 5-10 82
Also see COLTRANE, John
Also see MONK, Thelonious

COLTS *R&B '55*
Singles: 78 rpm
ANTLER (4003 "Never No More") ... 50-75 57
ANTLER (4007 "Guiding Angel") ... 50-75 57
MAMBO (112 "Adorable") ... 100-150 55
VITA (112 "Adorable") ... 35-55 55
VITA (121 "Sweet Sixteen") ... 25-50 56
VITA (130 "Never No More") ... 25-50 56
Singles: 7-inch
ANTLER (4003 "Never No More") ... 75-100 57
ANTLER (4007 "Guiding Angel") ... 75-100 57
MAMBO (112 "Adorable") ... 200-500 55
PLAZA (505 "Sweet Sixteen") ... 15-25 62
VITA (112 "Adorable") ... 100-200 55
VITA (121 "Sweet Sixteen") ... 75-100 56
VITA (130 "Never No More") ... 75-100 56
Members: Eddie Williams; Joe Crunby; Rubin Grunby; Leroy Smith; Carl Moland; Don Wyatt.
Also see CREATIVE SOURCE
Also see FORTUNES

COLTS
("Featuring Joe Grundy")
Singles: 7-inch
DELCO (4002 "I Never Knew") ... 15-25 59
(First issued as by the Red Coats.)
Member: Joe Grundy.
Also see RED COATS

COLUCCI, Jill
Singles: 7-inch
CASABLANCA ... 3-4 82

COLUMBIANS
(Featuring George Collier)
Singles: 7-inch
KLUB (4148 "Forever More") ... 8-12

COLUMBO, Chris *P&R '63*
(Chris Colombo Quintet)
Singles: 7-inch
BATTLE ... 4-8 62
MAXX ... 3-6 64
STRAND ... 4-8 63
LPs: 10/12-inch
MERCURY ... 5-10 75
STRAND ... 10-15 63

COLUMBUS, Ray
(With the Invaders; with Art Collection)
Singles: 7-inch
COLSTAR (1001 "Kick Me") ... 15-25 67
MEMORY ... 8-10 67
PHILIPS ... 4-8 64-65

COLUMBUS PHARAOHS
(With the Tommy Wills Orchestra; 4 Pharaohs)
Singles: 7-inch
ESTA (290 "Give Me Your Love") ... 500-1000 58
Members: Morris Wade; Bobby Taylor; Ron Wilson; Bernard Wilson.
Also see EGYPTIAN KINGS
Also see 4 PHARAOHS
Also see TAYLOR, Bobby

COLVIN, Shawn *LP '89*
LPs: 10/12-inch
COLUMBIA ... 5-8 89

COLWELL, Gerald Red
Singles: 7-inch
GLOBE STAR ... 5-10 59

COLWELL BROTHERS
Singles: 7-inch
PACE ... 4-8 67

COLWELL-WINFIELD BLUES BAND
Singles: 7-inch
VERVE/FORECAST ... 4-6 69
LPs: 10/12-inch
VERVE/FORECAST (3056 "Cold Wind Blues") ... 10-20 68
ZA-ZOO (1 "Live Bust") ... 20-30 71

COMANCHEROS
Singles: 7-inch
TEEN ... 10-15 64

COMANOR, Jeffrey
Singles: 7-inch
EPIC ... 3-5 74-76
LPs: 10/12-inch
EPIC ... 10-15 74-76

COMATEENS *D&D '83*
Singles: 12-inch
MERCURY ... 4-6 83-84
Singles: 7-inch
MERCURY ... 3-4 83-84
LPs: 10/12-inch
CACHALOT ... 5-10 81
MERCURY ... 5-10 83

COMBENASHUNS
Singles: 7-inch
LEO (3801 "What'cha Gonna Do") ... 5-10 66
Picture Sleeves
LEO (3801 "What'cha Gonna Do") ... 10-20 66
(Plain white sleeve with "Introducing the Combinashuns" printed at the bottom.)

COMBINATION, INC.
Singles: 7-inch
STACEY (2616 "Adam & Eve") ... 10-15

COMBINATIONS
Singles: 7-inch
COMBO (167 "Back Home Again") ... 25-35 59

COMBINATIONS
Singles: 7-inch
RCA ... 4-8 68

COMBINATIONS
Singles: 7-inch
CARRIE (614 "Just One More Chance") ... 100-150 62
KIM-TONE (1001 "Goddess of Love") ... 15-25 60s

COMBO AUDIO
Singles: 7-inch
EMI AMERICA ... 3-4 83
LPs: 10/12-inch
EMI AMERICA ... 5-10 83

COMBO KINGS
Singles: 7-inch
CHASE ... 5-10 64
FLO-JO ... 8-12 62
IMPERIAL ... 5-10 63
JAMIE ... 4-8 66
Member: Pervis Herder.
Also see HERDER, Pervis

COMBOAIRES
Singles: 7-inch
DART (1010 "Wicked") ... 15-25 59
RESCUE (31044 "Topaz") ... 10-20 60s

COMBONATION
Singles: 7-inch
W.B. ... 3-4 84
Picture Sleeves
W.B. ... 3-4 84
LPs: 10/12-inch
W.B. ... 5-10 84

COMBONETTES
Singles: 78 rpm
COMBO (74 "If I Had My Wish") ... 10-20 55
Singles: 7-inch
COMBO (74 "If I Had My Wish") ... 25-35 55

COMBS, Jerry
(With Mannix)
Singles: 7-inch
CAPITOL ... 3-6 68
W.B. ... 3-6 68

COMER, Chuck
Singles: 7-inch
VADEN (302 "A Little More Lovin' ") ... 35-50 60

COMER, Judy
Singles: 7-inch
UPLAND ... 4-6 68

COMER, Tony & Crosswinds *R&B '84*
Singles: 7-inch
VIDCOM ... 3-4 84

COMFORTABLE CHAIR
Singles: 7-inch
ODE '70 ... 5-10 68
LPs: 10/12-inch
ODE '70 (44005 "Comfortable Chair") ... 15-25 68
Members: Barbara Wallace; Bernie Schwartz; Greg Leroy; Taz Baczec; Gary Davis.
Also see ATELLO, Don

COMIC BOOKS
("""Comic Books""")
Singles: 7-inch
CITATION (5001 "Manuel") ... 50-75 62
DYNAMIC SOUND (2005 "The First Time in My Life") ... 15-25 67
MAGIC TOUCH ... 10-20 62
NEW PHOENIX (6199 "Manuel") 50-100 61
Members: Bob Barian; Bob Casper; Ronnie Premier; Floyd Dorsey; Bill Dorsey; Lloyd Johnson; James Pike; Greg Browder.
Also see BARIAN, Bullet Bob
Also see BIG BOSSMAN
Also see FUN & GAMES
Also see PREMIERE, Ronnie

COMICS
Singles: 7-inch
MINARET (152 "Red Rider") ... 4-8 69

COMING TIMES
Singles: 7-inch
JOSIE ... 4-8 66

COMMANCHES
Singles: 7-inch
HICKORY ... 4-8 64

COMMAND PERFORMANCE
Singles: 7-inch
VIKING ... 3-5 70
LPs: 10/12-inch
VIKING ... 10-15 70

COMMANDER
LPs: 10/12-inch
IRON WORKS (1028 "High 'N' Mighty") ... 10-20 89
(Picture disc. 100 made. Promotional issue only.)

COMMANDER CODY *LP '71*
(With His Lost Planet Airmen)
Singles: 7-inch
ABC ... 3-5 75
ARISTA ... 3-5 77
DOT ... 3-5 73-74
MCA ... 3-4 83
PARAMOUNT ... 3-5 71-74
W.B. ... 3-5 75
Picture Sleeves
PARAMOUNT ... 3-5 72-73
LPs: 10/12-inch
ARISTA ... 5-10 77
PARAMOUNT ... 10-12 71-74
W.B. ... 8-10 75-76

COMMANDERS
Singles: 78 rpm
MODERN (567 "Lonesome Road") 10-20 48
DECCA ... 5-10 53
Singles: 7-inch
DECCA ... 8-12 53
MODERN (567 "Lonesome Road") 10-20 48
(Flexidisc.)

COMMANDOS
Singles: 7-inch
SYMBOL ... 8-12 59
Members: King Curtis; Jimmy Spruill.
Also see KING CURTIS

COMMANDS
(With the Dell Tones)
Singles: 7-inch
DYNAMIC (104 "No Time for You") ... 25-35 64

COMMANDS
Singles: 7-inch
BACK BEAT ... 10-20 66

COMMERCIALS
Singles: 7-inch
DAYHILL (2012 "Power in Your Love") ... 20-30

COMMISSION
Singles: 7-inch
ATLANTIC ... 3-5 70

COMMITTEE
Singles: 7-inch
WHITE WHALE ... 4-8 67
LPs: 10/12-inch
LITTLE DAVID ... 10-12 73

COMMODORES
Singles: 78 rpm
DOT ... 10-20 55-56
Singles: 7-inch
DOT ... 15-25 55-56

COMMODORES
Singles: 78 rpm
CHALLENGE ... 10-20 57
Singles: 7-inch
CHALLENGE (1004 "Sweet Angel") ... 10-15 57
CHALLENGE (1007 "Faith") ... 10-15 57

COMMODORES *P&R/R&B/LP '74*
Singles: 12-inch
MOTOWN ... 4-8 79-85
POLYDOR ... 4-6 86
Singles: 7-inch
ATLANTIC ... 5-10 69
MOTOWN ... 3-5 74-85
(Black vinyl.)
MOTOWN (1307 "Machine Gun") ... 4-8 74
(Colored vinyl. Promotional issue only.)
MOTOWN (1381 "Sweet Love") ... 4-8 75
(Colored vinyl. Promotional issue only.)
MOWEST ... 3-5 72
POLYDOR ... 3-4 86
Picture Sleeves
MOTOWN ... 3-5 85
POLYDOR ... 3-4 86
LPs: 10/12-inch
MOTOWN (Except 39) ... 8-10 74-87
MOTOWN (39 "1978 Platinum Tour") ... 15-20 78
(Promotional issue only.)
POLYDOR ... 5-10 86
Members: Lionel Ritchie; William King; Ronald LaPread; Tommy McClary; Walter Orange; Milan Williams.
Also see McCLARY, Thomas
Also see RICHIE, Lionel

COMMON BOND
LPs: 10/12-inch
FRONTLINE ... 5-10 86-87

COMMON COLD
Singles: 7-inch
ATCO ... 4-8 67

COMMON PEOPLE
Singles: 7-inch
CAPITOL ... 4-8 69
LPs: 10/12-inch
CAPITOL (266 "Of the People/By the People/for the People") ... 50-75 69

COMMON SENSE *R&B '81*
Singles: 7-inch
BC ... 3-4 81

COMMONS LTD.
Singles: 7-inch
MOD (1005 "Change the World") ... 25-35

COMMOTIONS
Singles: 7-inch
BLUE ROCK ... 4-8 68
CAPITOL ... 4-6 69

COMMUNARDS *P&R/LP '86*
Singles: 12-inch
MCA ... 4-6 86

Singles: 7-inch
MCA 3-4 86-88
LPs: 10/12-inch
MCA 5-10 86-88
Members: Jimmy Sommerville; Sara Jane Morris; Richard Coles.
Also see BRONSKI BEAT
Also see SOMERVILLE, Jimmy

COMMUNE
Singles: 7-inch
FLIPPIN' 3-6 70

COMMUNICATION AGGREGATION
Singles: 7-inch
RCA 4-8 66

COMMUNION
Singles: 7-inch
MERCURY 3-5 71

COMO, Amos, & His Tune Toppers
Singles: 78 rpm
STARDAY (257 "Hole in the Wall") 20-40 56
Singles: 7-inch
STARDAY (257 "Hole in the Wall") 50-100 56

COMO, Chuck
Singles: 7-inch
FOXY 5-10

COMO, Nicky
(With the Glen Stuart Orchestra)
Singles: 7-inch
LAURIE (3061 "Look for a Star") 8-12 60
TANG (1231 "Your Guardian Angel") 25-50 60s
Session: Del Satins.
Also see DEL SATINS
Also see STUART, Glen

COMO, Perry P&R '43
(With Hugo Winterhalter's Orchestra; with Ramblers; with Ray Charles Singers)
Singles: 78 rpm
BLUEBIRD 5-10 50
RCA 5-10 43-58
Singles: 7-inch
BLUEBIRD 10-20 50
(May also be shown as RCA Victor "Bluebird Children's Records.")
RCA (237 "Supper Club Favorites") 15-25 49
(Three disc set.)
RCA (0071 "Ave Maria") 10-15 49
(Black vinyl.)
RCA (0071 "Ave Maria") 15-25 49
(Colored vinyl.)
RCA (0100 thru 0900 series) 3-6 69-73
RCA (VP-2000 series) 8-12 59
(Stereo.)
RCA (2700 thru 7400 series) 8-20 48-59
RCA (61-7000 series) 8-12 58-60
(Stereo.)
RCA (7500 thru 9700 series) 4-10 59-69
RCA (10000 thru 13000 series) 3-5 74-83
Picture Sleeves
RCA (3800 thru 7100 series) 10-20 53-58
RCA (7200 thru 9700 series) 5-15 58-69
EPs: 7-inch
CAMDEN 5-10 50s
RCA (Except SPD series) 10-25 52-70
RCA (SPD-27 "Perry Como") 40-60 56
(Boxed 10-EP set. Includes inserts and biography booklet.)
RCA (SPD-28 "Perry Como Highlighter") 20-30 56
(Sampler from Kleenex Tissue. Includes picture cover.)
LPs: 10/12-inch
CAMDEN 5-15 57-74
RCA (0100 thru 4000 series) 5-15 73-83
(With "AFL1," "ANL1," "APL1," "AQL1," "AYL1," "CPL1," or "DVL2" prefix.)
RCA (1004 "Saturday Night with Mr. C") 20-30 58
RCA (1007 "Golden Records") 20-30 58
RCA (LPM-1085 "So Smooth") 20-40 55
RCA (LPM-1172 "I Believe") 20-40 56
RCA (LPM-1176 "Relaxing with Perry Como") 20-40 56
RCA (LPM-1177 "Sentimental Date with Perry Como") 20-40 56
RCA (LPM-1191 "Perry Como Sings Hits from Broadway Shows") 20-40 56
RCA (LPM-1243 Perry Sings Christmas Music") 20-40 56
RCA (LPM-1463 We Get Letters") 20-30 57
RCA (LPM-1800 thru LPM-2900 series) 15-25 58-63
RCA (LSP-1085 thru LSP-1463) 10-20 62-68
(Electronic stereo reissues.)
RCA (LSP-1800 thru LSP-2900 series) 15-30 58-63
(Stereo.)
RCA (3013 "TV Favorites") 25-50 52
(10-inch LP.)
RCA (3044 "Supper Club Favorites") 25-50 52
(10-inch LP.)
RCA (3124 "Broadway") 25-50 53
(10-inch LP.)
RCA (3133 "Christmas") 25-50 53
(10-inch LP.)
RCA (3188 "I Believe") 25-50 53
(10-inch LP.)
RCA (3224 "Golden Records") 25-50 54
(10-inch LP.)
RCA (3300 thru 4500 series) 8-15 64-71
(With "LPM" or "LSP" prefix.)
READER'S DIGEST 8-15 75
Also see CHARLES, Ray, Singers

COMO, Perry / Ames Brothers / Harry Belafonte / Radio City Music Hall Orchestra
EPs: 7-inch
RCA (SP-35 "Merry Christmas") 10-20 56
(Record dealer giveaway. Issued with paper sleeve.)
Also see AMES BROTHERS
Also see BELAFONTE, Harry
Also see WINTERHALTER, Hugo, & His Orchestra

COMO, Perry, & Eddie Fisher P&R '52
Singles: 78 rpm
RCA 4-8 52
Singles: 7-inch
RCA 5-10 52
Also see FISHER, Eddie

COMO, Perry, & Fontane Sisters P&R '50
Singles: 78 rpm
RCA 4-8 50-51
Singles: 7-inch
RCA 8-15 50-51
Also see FONTANE SISTERS

COMO, Perry, & Betty Hutton P&R '50
Singles: 78 rpm
RCA 4-8 50
Singles: 7-inch
RCA 8-15 50
Also see HUTTON, Betty

COMO, Perry, & Jaye P. Morgan
Singles: 78 rpm
RCA 4-8 55
Singles: 7-inch
RCA 5-10 55
Also see COMO, Perry
Also see MORGAN, Jaye P.

COMO, Sue
Singles: 7-inch
SMART 5-10 60

COMPACTS
Singles: 7-inch
CARLA 10-20

COMPAGNONS DE LA CHANSON: see LES COMPAGNONS DE LA CHANSON

COMPANION
LPs: 10/12-inch
RAV 8-10 78

COMPANIONS
(With Bob Mersey Orchestra)
Singles: 7-inch
DOVE (240 "Falling") 75-100 58

COMPANIONS
(With Abie Baker & Orchestra)
Singles: 7-inch
AMY (852 "No Fool Am I") 30-50 63
ARLEN (722 "It's Too Late") 20-40 63
BROOK'S (100 "I Didn't Know") 75-125 59
COLLECTABLES 3-4 81
FEDERAL (12397 "I Didn't Know") 35-55 61
GINA (722 "It's Too Late") 20-30 63

COMPANIONS
Singles: 7-inch
DEE DEE (1047 "I Want a Yul Brynner Haircut") 15-25 50s

COMPANIONS
Singles: 7-inch
COLUMBIA (42279 "I'll Always Love You") 25-35 62

COMPANIONS
Singles: 7-inch
GENERAL AMERICAN 5-10 64

COMPANY
Singles: 7-inch
PLAYBOY 3-5 72
LPs: 10/12-inch
PLAYBOY 8-10 72

COMPANY B P&R/LP '87
Singles: 7-inch
ATLANTIC 3-4 87-89
LPs: 10/12-inch
ATLANTIC 5-10 87-89
Members: Donna Huntley; Julie Marie; Susan Johnson; Lori L.

COMPANY FRONT
Singles: 7-inch
RISING SONS 4-8 68-69

COMPANY OF WOLVES LP '90
LPs: 10/12-inch
MERCURY 5-8 90

COMPASS
Singles: 7-inch
AJP 3-6 70

COMPETITORS
Singles: 7-inch
DOT 10-20 63
LPs: 10/12-inch
DOT (3542 "Hits of the Street and Strip") 30-40 63
(Monaural.)
DOT (25542 "Hits of the Street and Strip") 40-50 63
(Stereo.)
Members: Don Brandon; Larry Brown.
Also see BRANDON, Don

COMPLAMENTS
Singles: 7-inch
DAKAR 3-5 77

COMPLIMENTS
Singles: 7-inch
CONGRESS (252 "The Time of Her Life") 25-50 65
MIDAS (304 "Beware, Beware") 20-30 60s

COMPOSERS
Singles: 7-inch
ERA 15-20 63

COMPOSERS
Singles: 7-inch
AMPEN (221 "Woe Is Me") 200-300 63
Session: Johnny Moore
Also see MOORE, Johnny

COMPOSERS
Singles: 7-inch
COMPLEX 3 .... 3-6 70

COMPOST
LPs: 10/12-inch
COLUMBIA 10-12 72

COMPTON, Burt, & Steve Mele
LPs: 10/12-inch
WIZARD 8-10 78

COMPTON BROTHERS C&W '66
Singles: 7-inch
ABC/DOT 3-5 75
DOT 3-6 66-73
Picture Sleeves
DOT 5-10
LPs: 10/12-inch
DOT 10-15 68-72
Members: Bill Compton; Harry Compton.

COMPTON'S MOST WANTED LP '90
LPs: 10/12-inch
ORPHEUS 5-8 90-91

COMPUTER & LITTLE FOOLER
Singles: 7-inch
MAURCI (106 "S-w-w-w-l-s-s-s-h") 4-8 67
Also see SIMMONS, Simtec

COMRADE X
Singles: 7-inch
ERA 8-12 61

COMSATS
Singles: 7-inch
FELSTED (8705 "Astronaut") 10-20 64

COMSTOCK, Bill
Singles: 7-inch
MC2 10-15

COMSTOCK, Bobby P&R '59
(With the Counts)
Singles: 7-inch
ASCOT 8-15 64-66
ATLANTIC 10-15 60
BLAZE (349 "Tennessee Waltz") 10-20 59
ERIC 3-4 73
FESTIVAL 10-15 61
JUBILEE 5-10 60-63
LAWN 8-12 62-64
MOHAWK 10-15 61
TRIUMPH 10-15 59
LPs: 10/12-inch
ASCOT (16026 "Out of Sight") 30-45 66
BLAZE ("Tennessee Waltz") 100-150
Session: King Curtis.
Also see BOBBY & COUNTS
Also see KING CURTIS

COMSTOCK LTD
Singles: 7-inch
BELL 3-6 69-72

CON CHORDS
Singles: 7-inch
CHARIOT 5-10

CON FUNK SHUN P&R/R&B/LP '77
Singles: 12-inch
MERCURY 4-6 83-86
Singles: 7-inch
FRETONE 3-5 74
MERCURY 3-4 77-86
LPs: 10/12-inch
51 WEST 5-10 83
MERCURY (Except 3754) 5-10 76-86
MERCURY (3754 "Candy") 10-20 79
(Picture disc. Has die-cut cover.)
MERCURY (3754 "Candy") 15-25 79
(Picture disc. Has plastic cover. Promotional issue only.)
Members: Michael Cooper; Louis McCall; Karl Fuller; Paul Harrell; Danny Thomas; Felton Pilate II.
Also see COOPER, Michael

CONANT, Susan
Singles: 7-inch
CAPITOL 4-8 64

CONAWAY, Jeff
Singles: 7-inch
COLUMBIA 3-4 80
LPs: 10/12-inch
COLUMBIA 5-10 80

CONCEPT R&B '85
Singles: 7-inch
TUCKWOOD 3-4 85

CONCEPTION
Singles: 7-inch
PERFECTION (1001 "Babylon") 15-25 68

CONCEPTION CORPORATION
Singles: 7-inch
COTILLION 3-6 72
LPs: 10/12-inch
COTILLION 10-15 70-72
Members: Ira Miller; Howard Cohen.
Also see MOGAN DAVID & WINOS

CONCEPTS
Singles: 7-inch
TOPS ("Heaven Help Me") 150-200 50s
(Selection number not known.)

CONCEPTS
(With Al Browne's Orchestra)
Singles: 7-inch
APACHE (1515 "Whisper") 250-350 61
MUSICTONE (1109 "Whisper") 15-25 61
Member: Johnnie James.
Also see BROWNE, Al

CONCEPTS
Singles: 7-inch
ABC-PAR (10526 "Sad Little Boy") 10-15 64
CATAMOUNT (112 "The Vow") 8-12 66
(Black vinyl.)
CATAMOUNT (112 "The Vow") 15-20 66
(Colored vinyl.)

CONCEPTS & EMANONS
Singles: 7-inch
J&J (3000 "Cry") 50-100
Also see EMANONS

CONCHORDS
Singles: 7-inch
AGA 5-8

CONCORDS
Singles: 78 rpm
EMBER 25-50 56
HARLEM 100-200 54
Singles: 7-inch
EMBER (1007 "I'm Satisfied with Rock & Roll") 50-75 56
HARLEM (2328 "Candlelight") ... 250-350 54
Members: Milton Love; Joe Willis; Bob Thompson; Jimmy Hunter.
Also see REAVES, Pearl, & Concords

CONCORDS
Singles: 7-inch
BOOM (60,021 "Down the Aisle of Love") 30-40 66
EPIC (9697 "Should I Cry") 50-75 64
GRAMERCY (304 "Cross My Heart") 150-200 61
(Special Christmas issue, with two candy canes on each side of label.)
GRAMERCY (304 "Cross My Heart") 40-60 62
(No candy canes on label.)
GRAMERCY (305 "My Dreams") ... 30-40 62
HERALD (576 "Marlene") 20-30 62
HERALD (578 "Cold and Frosty Morning") 25-35 62
POLYDOR (14036 "Down the Aisle of Love") 5-10 70
RCA (7911 "Again") 20-30 61
RUST (5048 "One Step from Heaven") 25-35 62
Also see KENNY, Sue
Also see LISA & LULLABIES
Also see LISI, Ricky
Also see ROBERTS, Wayne
Also see SCOTT, Neal
Also see SHERWOODS
Also see SNOWMEN

CONCRETE BLONDE LP '87
Singles: 7-inch
I.R.S. 3-4 87-90
LPs: 10/12-inch
I.R.S. 5-10 87-90
Members: Johnette Napolitano; James Mankey.

CONCRETE COWBOY BAND C&W '81
Singles: 7-inch
EXCELSIOR 3-4 81
LPs: 10/12-inch
EXCELSIOR 5-10 81

CONDELLO
(Michael Condello; Commodore Condello's Salt River Navy Band)
Singles: 7-inch
SCEPTER 4-6 68
EPs: 7-inch 33/45
BLOSSOM KIDS REVUE 8-12
LPs: 10/12-inch
SCEPTER 15-25 66
Also see HUB KAPP & WHEELS

CONDOLI, Conti
Singles: 78 rpm
CHANCE (1153 "Flamingo") 15-25 54
Singles: 7-inch
CHANCE (1153 "Flamingo") 35-50 54
Members: Chubby Jackson; Ira Sullivan; R. Winn; T. Papa; G. Esposito.

CON-DONS
Singles: 7-inch
CARLTON 4-8 63

CONDORS
Singles: 7-inch
HUNTER (2504 "Sweetest Angel") 1000-2000 60

CONDUCTOR P&R '82
Singles: 7-inch
JAMIE 5-10 61
MONTAGE 3-4 82
LPs: 10/12-inch
MONTAGE 5-10 82

CONE, Jimmy
Singles: 7-inch
BELL 5-10

CONERLY, Bobby
Singles: 7-inch
DUKE 8-12 70

CONES
Singles: 7-inch
LECTRON 4-8 64

CONEY, King, & Hot Dogs
Singles: 7-inch
LEGRAND (1038 "Ba-Pa-Da") 10-20 63

CONEY HATCH LP '83
LPs: 10/12-inch
MERCURY 5-10 83-85

CONEY ISLAND KIDS
Singles: 78 rpm
JOSIE 15-25 56
JUBILEE 15-25 55
Singles: 7-inch
JOSIE (791 "I Love It") 25-35 56
JOSIE (802 "We Want a Rock & Roll President") 15-25 56
JOSIE (809 "Popcorn & Candy") 15-25 56
JUBILEE (5215 "Moonlight Beach") 25-35 55
Also see TUCKER, George / Coney Island Kids

CONFEDERACY
Singles: 7-inch
UA 10-15 64

CONFEDERATE RAILROAD C&W '92
Singles: 7-inch
ATLANTIC 3-4 92-93
Members: Danny Shirley; Chris McDaniel.
Also see SHIRLEY, Danny

CONFEDERATES
Singles: 7-inch
BBB 4-8
DOT 5-10 60s

CONFESSIONS
Singles: 7-inch
EPIC (9474 "Be Bop Baby") 15-25 61

CONFIDENTIALS
Singles: 7-inch
BJ 8-12

CONFINERS
Singles: 7-inch
ELECTRO (261 "Harmonica Boogie") 150-200 61

CONFORTI, Donna
Singles: 7-inch
GLENCO 4-8 62
Also see CONFORTI SISTERS

CONFORTI SISTERS
Singles: 7-inch
GLENCO 4-8 62
Also see CONFORTI, Donna

CONGO KID
Singles: 7-inch
BULL DOG 8-12 59

CONGO RHYTHM BOYS
Singles: 78 rpm
INTERNATIONAL (607 "Week End Blues") 25-50 50
INTERNATIONAL (611 "Please Don't Cry") 25-50 50

CONGREGATION
Singles: 7-inch
JUBILEE 3-6 68-69
REPRISE 4-8 67

CONGRESS ALLEY
LPs: 10/12-inch
AVCO 8-10 74

CONGRESS OF WONDERS
LPs: 10/12-inch
FANTASY 10-12 71-72

CONIGLIARO, Tony
Singles: 7-inch
MAGNA-GLIDE 3-5 75
PENN-TONE 5-10
RCA 4-8 65-66
Picture Sleeves
RCA (8577 "I Can't Get Over You") 15-20 65

CONJUR
Singles: 7-inch
SUNFLOWER 3-5 71

CONLEE, John C&W '78
Singles: 7-inch
ABC 3-4 78
ABC/DOT 3-4 76-77
COLUMBIA 3-4 86-87
MCA 3-4 79-85
16TH AVE. 3-4 89-90
LPs: 10/12-inch
ABC 8-10 78
COLUMBIA 5-10 86-87
MCA 5-10 79-86

CONLEY, Arthur P&R/R&B/LP '67
Singles: 7-inch
ATCO 4-8 67-70
CAPRICORN 4-6 71-74
FAME (1007 "In The Same Old Way") 8-12 66
FAME (1009 "Take Me") 8-12 66

JOTIS (472 "Who's Fooling Who").. 5-10 66
LPs: 10/12-inch
ATCO 15-25 67-69
Also see ARTHUR & CORVETS
Also see CORVETTS
Also see SOUL CLAN

CONLEY, Earl Thomas C&W '75
(Earl Conley; ETC Band)
Singles: 7-inch
ALTO 5-8
GRT 4-6 75-76
RCA 3-4 81-92
SUNBIRD 3-4 80-81
W.B. 3-5 78-79
Picture Sleeves
RCA 3-4
LPs: 10/12-inch
RCA 5-10 81-84
SUNBIRD 8-15 80
Also see HARDIN, Gus, & Earl Thomas Conley
Also see WHITLEY, Keith, & Earl Thomas Conley

CONLEY, Earl Thomas, & Emmylou Harris C&W '88
Singles: 7-inch
RCA 3-4 88
Also see HARRIS, Emmylou

CONLEY, Earl Thomas, & Anita Pointer C&W '86
Singles: 7-inch
RCA 3-4 87
Also see CONLEY, Earl Thomas
Also see POINTER, Anita

CONLEY, Patricia, & Royal Robins
Singles: 7-inch
ALDO 10-15 62

CONLEY, Prince
Singles: 7-inch
SATELLITE 5-10 61

CONLON, Chuck
Singles: 7-inch
MARLIN (16007 "Won't You Say Yes") 10-15 67
W.B. 3-5 75
Also see CONLON & CRAWLERS

CONLON, Jud
Singles: 7-inch
ZEPHYR 10-20 57

CONLON & CRAWLERS
Singles: 7-inch
MARLIN (16006 "I Won't Tell") 15-20 67
Member: Chuck Conlon.
Also see CONLON, Chuck
Also see NIGHTCRAWLERS

CONN, Bennie
Singles: 7-inch
MAGNUM (741 "I'm So Glad to Be Back Home") 5-10
SOULTOWN (107 "Have You Had a Love") 5-10
LPs: 10/12-inch
GROOVE TIME 5-10 81

CONN, Billy
Singles: 7-inch
FEDERAL (12500 "I Promise Myself") 5-10 63

CONN, Dean
Singles: 7-inch
A&M 3-4 80-81
LPs: 10/12-inch
A&M 5-10 80

CONN, Tony
Singles: 7-inch
DECCA (30813 "Like Wow") 20-35 59
DECCA (30865 "Run Rabbit Run") 10-20 59

CONNELL, Doug, & Hot Rods
Singles: 7-inch
ALTON 10-15 59

CONNELL, Harvey, & Efics
Singles: 7-inch
FRATERNITY 10-15 61

CONNELLS LP '89
LPs: 10/12-inch
TVT 5-10 87-90
Members: Michael Connell; David Connell; Doug Macmillan; Peele Wilberley; George Huntley.

CONNELLY, Chris
Singles: 7-inch
PHILLIPS 4-6 65
Picture Sleeves
PHILLIPS 4-8 65
LPs: 10/12-inch
PHILLIPS 10-15 65

CONNELLY, Earl
Singles: 7-inch
ALTO (2003 "Just to Hold My Hand") 20-30
MASTER (120 "Tell Me Why") 20-30
MAYCON (Except 100) 15-25
MAYCON (100 "I Don't Know Why") 40-60

CONNER, Buddy
Singles: 7-inch
BREAKTHROUGH ("When You're Alone") 100-200
(Selection number not known.)

CONNER, Lynn
Singles: 7-inch
MONUMENT 8-15 63

CONNER, Ted
Singles: 7-inch
CAPRICE 4-8 63

CONNEXION
Singles: 7-inch
ERA 3-5 76

CONNEY'S COMBO: see Connie's Combo

CONNICK, Harry, Jr. LP '89
(Harry Connick Jr. Trio)
LPs: 10/12-inch
COLUMBIA 5-8 90-91

CONNIE R&B/D&D '85
Singles: 12-inch
SUNNYVIEW 4-6 85-86
Singles: 7-inch
SUNNYVIEW 3-4 85-86

CONNIE & BELLHOPS
Singles: 7-inch
DAMON ("Shot Rod") 20-30 64
(Selection number not known.)
R (505 "Shot Rod") 30-50 64

CONNIE & CONES
Singles: 7-inch
NRC 10-20 59
ROULETTE 8-15 60-61

CONNIE & LEE
Singles: 7-inch
GONE 10-15 58
LOOK 10-20 58

CONNIE'S COMBO
(Connie's Combo)
Singles: 78 rpm
EDDIE'S (1203 "Why Don't You Come Back") 15-25 48
FREEDOM (1508 "Ugly Mae") 15-25 48
Members: Conrad Johnson; L.C. Williams.
Also see JOHNSON, Conrad
Also see WILLIAMS, L.C.

CONNIFF, Ray P&R/LP '57
(With the Rockin' Rhythm Boys; Ray Conniff Orchestra & Chorus)
Singles: 78 rpm
BRUNSWICK 4-8 57
COLUMBIA 3-5 56-57
CORAL 4-8 55
Singles: 7-inch
BRUNSWICK 5-10 57
COLUMBIA 3-8 56-82
CORAL 5-10 55
Picture Sleeves
COLUMBIA 3-8 60-64
EPs: 7-inch
COLUMBIA (Except 10041/2/3) 5-10 56-59
COLUMBIA (10041/2/3 "Dance the Bop") 8-12 57
(Price is for either volume.)
LPs: 10/12-inch
COLUMBIA (Except 925 & 1004) 5-15 58-82
COLUMBIA (925 "S'Wonderful") 10-20 56
COLUMBIA (1004 "Dance the Bop") 15-25 57
HARMONY 4-8 69
Also see MATHIS, Johnny
Also see MATHIS, Johnny / Tony Bennett / North Carolina Ramblers / Ray Conniff & Jerry Vale with Eugene Ormandy
Also see ROBBINS, Marty

CONNOR, Chris P&R '56
Singles: 78 rpm
ATLANTIC 5-15 56-57
BETHLEHEM 5-10 54-55
Singles: 7-inch
ATLANTIC 8-15 56-62
BETHLEHEM (1200 & 1300 series) 10-20 54-55
BETHLEHEM (3000 series) 4-8 64
FM 4-8 63
EPs: 7-inch
ATLANTIC (593/4/5/6 "Chris Connor Sings the George Gershwin Almanac") 30-40 57
(Price is for any of four volumes.)
ATLANTIC (580 "I Miss You So") ...30-40 57
ATLANTIC (615 "Jazz Date") 30-40 58
BETHLEHEM 20-40 54-56
LPs: 10/12-inch
ABC-PAR 10-20 65-66
ATLANTIC (601 "Chris Connor Sings the George Gershwin Almanac") 50-100 57
ATLANTIC (1240 "He Loves Me He Loves Me Not") 50-100 57
ATLANTIC (1228 "Chris Connor") 50-100 57
ATLANTIC (1286 "Jazz Date") 50-75 58
ATLANTIC (1290 "Chris Craft") 50-75 58
ATLANTIC (1307 "Sad Cafe") 50-75 59
(Monaural.)
ATLANTIC (SD-1307 "Sad Cafe") ..60-80 59
(Stereo.)
ATLANTIC (8014 "I Miss You So") 50-75 58
ATLANTIC (8032 "Witchcraft") 50-75 59
(Monaural.)
ATLANTIC (SD-8032 "Witchcraft") 60-80 59
(Stereo.)
ATLANTIC (8040 "In Person") 40-60 59
(Monaural.)
ATLANTIC (SD-8040 "In Person") 50-75 59
(Stereo.)
ATLANTIC (8046 "A Portrait") 30-50 60
(Monaural.)
ATLANTIC (SD-8046 "A Portrait") ..40-60 60
(Stereo.)
ATLANTIC (8061 "Free Spirits") 25-50 62
(Monaural.)
ATLANTIC (SD-8061 "Free Spirits") 30-60 62
(Stereo.)
BETHLEHEM (20 "This Is Chris") 50-100 55
(Maroon label.)
BETHLEHEM (56 "Chris") 50-100 56
(Maroon label.)
BETHLEHEM (1001 Lullabys of Birdland") 100-200 54
(10-inch LP.)
BETHLEHEM (1002 Lullabys for Lovers") 100-200 54
(10-inch LP.)
BETHLEHEM (6000 series) 10-12 78
(Gray label.)
BETHLEHEM (6004 "Lullabys of Birdland") 50-100 56
(Maroon label.)
BETHLEHEM (6005 "Lullabys for Lovers") 50-100 56
(Maroon label.)
FM 10-15 63
Also see BON BONS
Also see FERGUSON, Maynard, & Chris Connor
Also see SIMONE, Nina, Chris Connor & Carmen McRae

CONNOR, Chris / Julie London / Carmen McRae
LPs: 10/12-inch
BETHLEHEM (6006 "Bethlehem Girlfriends") 50-100 56
(Maroon label.)
Also see CONNOR, Chris
Also see LONDON, Julie
Also see McRAE, Carmen

CONNORS, Bob
Singles: 7-inch
WTVN RADIO (102657 "1977 Buckeye Preview") 4-6 77

CONNORS, Carol
(With Hank Levine & His Orchestra; Annette Klienbard)
Singles: 7-inch
CAPITOL (5152 "Never") 10-20 64
COLUMBIA (41976 "You Are My Answer") 25-40 61
(With "3" prefix. Compact 33 Single.)
COLUMBIA (41976 "You Are My Answer") 10-20 61
COLUMBIA (42155 "Listen to the Beat") 30-40 61
(With "3" prefix. Compact 33 Single.)
COLUMBIA (42155 "Listen to the Beat") 10-20 61
COLUMBIA (42337 "What Do You See in Him") 30-40 62
(With "3" prefix. Compact 33 Single.)
COLUMBIA (42337 "What Do You See in Him") 10-20 62
ERA (3084 "Two Rivers") 10-20 62
ERA (3096 "I Wanna Know") 10-20 62
MIRA (219 "My Baby Looks, But He Don't Touch") 10-20 66
N.T.C. (3131 "Yum-Yum Yamaha") 20-25 64
(Single-sided pressing.)
Picture Sleeves
MIRA (219 "My Baby Looks, But He Don't Touch") 15-25 66
N.T.C. (3131 "Yum-Yum Yamaha") 25-50 64
Also see BARD, Annette
Also see BOMPERS
Also see CAROL & CHERYL
Also see COLLINS, Carol
Also see LEVINE, Hank
Also see STORYTELLERS
Also see SURFETTES
Also see TEDDY BEARS

CONNORS, Chuck
(With the Salvation Army Chorus)
Singles: 7-inch
DECCA 5-10 60

CONNORS, Greg
Singles: 7-inch
GUYDEN (2017 "Till the End") 10-15 59
TREY (3003 "Your Love Tears Me Up") 15-20 60

CONNORS, Norman R&B/LP '75
Singles: 7-inch
ARISTA 3-4 78-81
BUDDAH 3-5 74-77
CAPITOL 3-4 88
LPs: 10/12-inch
ARISTA 5-10 78-81
BUDDAH 10-12 75-78
NOVUS 5-10 81
Session: Michael Henderson; Pharoah Sanders; Jean Cain; Phyllis Hyman; Prince Phillip Mitchell.
Also see AQUARIAN DREAM
Also see HENDERSON, Michael
Also see HYMAN, Phyllis

CONNOTATIONS
Singles: 7-inch
CLIFTON 4-8
GRECO 5-10
TECHNICHORD (1000 "Two Hearts Fall in Love") 75-125 62
(Black vinyl.)
TECHNICHORD (1000 "Two Hearts Fall in Love") 200-300 62
(Colored vinyl.)

CONNY
Singles: 7-inch
CAPITOL 8-12 61
LPs: 10/12-inch
CAPITOL 20-25 60

CONNY & BELLHOPS
Singles: 7-inch
DAMON (12315 "Shot Rod") 20-30 60
R (OUR) (505 "Shot Rod") 15-25 61
(Rerecorded version.)

CONQUEROO
Singles: 7-inch
SONOBEAT (103 "I've Got Time"). 10-20 68
Picture Sleeves
SONOBEAT (103 "I've Got Time"). 20-30 68
LPs: 10/12-inch
FIVE HOURS (8 "From the Vulcan Gas Co.") 10-15 87

CONQUERORS
Singles: 7-inch
LU PINE (108 "Bill Is My Boyfriend") 25-50 62

CONQUEST
Singles: 7-inch
GAIL (114 "Is It Right") 15-25 67

CONQUEST, June
Singles: 7-inch
CURTOM 4-6
FAME 4-8 65
WINDY C 4-8 66
Also see HATHAWAY, Donny, & June Conquest

CONQUISTADORS
Singles: 7-inch
ACT (4 "Just Can't Stop Lovin' You") 50-100
CATCH 5-10 64

CONRAD, Bob
Singles: 7-inch
W.B. 4-8 61
Picture Sleeves
W.B. 5-10 61

CONRAD, John
Singles: 7-inch
ALLEY 4-8 62

CONRAD, Jerry
Singles: 7-inch
JUKE 3-5

CONRAD & HURRICANE STRINGS
Singles: 7-inch
DAYTONE (6401 "Hurricane") 15-25 64
ERA (3130 "Hurricane") 8-12 64
Members: Conrad Couwenberg; Pat Couwenberg; Ed Sigarlaki; Don Sigarlaki.

CONRAD & VAN-DELLS
Singles: 7-inch
BMC (1001 "Dead End") 15-25 60s

CONROY, Bert, & Misfits
Singles: 7-inch
DEB-CO 10-15 63

CONSENTING ADULTS
Singles: 7-inch
DREAMLAND 3-4 81
LPs: 10/12-inch
DREAMLAND 5-10 81

CONSERVATIVES
Singles: 7-inch
EBONIC (6569 "That's All") 15-25 60s
ON TIME (100 "Happiness") 10-20 60s
TRIBE 5-10 68

CONSIDINE, Tim
Singles: 78 rpm
DISNEYLAND 10-20 57
Singles: 7-inch
DEL-FI 5-10 63
DISNEYLAND 8-12 57
Picture Sleeves
DISNEYLAND 15-25 57

CONSORTIUM
Singles: 7-inch
UNI 3-6 69

CONSORTS
Singles: 7-inch
APT (25066 "Please Be Mine") 75-125 62
COUSINS (1004 "Please Be Mine") 200-400 61
CRYSTAL BALL 4-8
Members: Bruce Laurent; Sal Donnarumma; William Abbatte.
Also see CHUCKLES
Also see 4 CLEFS

CONSPIRACY
Singles: 7-inch
CAPITOL 3-5 76-77
EXCALIBUR 3-5

CONSPIRATORS
Singles: 7-inch
SUNDAY (306326 "Waterloo '73") 4-8 73
Member: Bob Shannon.

CONSTELLATION ORCHESTRA
LPs: 10/12-inch
PRELUDE 5-10 78

CONSTELLATIONS
(With Jonah Jones)
Singles: 78 rpm
GROOVE 10-20 56
Singles: 7-inch
GROOVE (0140 "Come Sit By Me") 50-75 56

CONSTELLATIONS
Singles: 7-inch
GEMINI STAR 5-10 68
PROCESS (127 "Quoidas") 15-25 65
SMASH (1923 "Tear It Up Baby") ..15-20 64
VIOLET (1053 "My Dear") 25-35 63

CONSTELLATIONS
Singles: 7-inch
SONDAY 3-5 70

CONSTRUCTION
Singles: 7-inch
SYNC (6 "Hey Little Way Out Girl") 50-75

CONSULS
Singles: 7-inch
ABEL (222 "Runaway") 35-45 59

CONSUMER RAPPORT P&R/R&B '75
Singles: 7-inch
WING and a PRAYER 3-5 75-76
Member: Frank Floyd.

CONTACTS
Singles: 7-inch
QUADRAN 3-5 71

CONTARDO, Johnny
Singles: 7-inch
BECKET 3-4 80
Picture Sleeves
BECKET 3-4 80
LPs: 10/12-inch
BECKET 5-10 80
Also see SHA NA NA

CONTELLA, Sandy
Singles: 7-inch
SUE 5-8 65

CONTELS
Singles: 7-inch
WARWICK (104 "Lovers Dream") 50-100 59

CONTEMPORARIES
Singles: 7-inch
RICHIE (672 "Fool for Temptation") 15-25 66

CONTENDERS
Singles: 7-inch
JACKPOT (48002 "Tequila") 10-20 59
Member: Chuck "Tequila" Rio.
Also see RIO, Chuck

CONTENDERS
Singles: 7-inch
CHATTAHOOCHEE (644 "Dune Buggy") 10-20 64
CHATTAHOOCHEE (656 "Johnny B Goode") 10-20 64

CONTENDERS
Singles: 7-inch
EDGE (506 "Do What You Gotta Do") 15-25 65

CONTENDERS
(With the Rogues)
Singles: 7-inch
JAVA (101 "The Clock") 50-100 66
(Gold label.)
JAVA (101 "The Clock") 15-25 66
(Red label.)
JAVA (102 "Surprise") 25-50 66
JAVA (103 "I Like It Like That") 25-50 66
JAVA (104 "Hetta Hetta") 50-100 66

CONTENTS ARE:
Singles: 7-inch
ROK (6707 "Future Days") 25-35 67
ROK (6709 "I Don't Know") 25-35 67

CONTESSAS
Singles: 7-inch
E 10-15
WITCH 10-15 63

CONTI, Bill P&R '77
Singles: 7-inch
ARISTA 3-4 82
U.A. 3-5 77-78
LPs: 10/12-inch
MCA 5-10 79
U.A. 8-12 78-79

CONTINDERS
(Featuring Clifford Curry)
Singles: 7-inch
BLUE SKY (105 "Mr. Dee Jay") 500-750 59
Also see CURRY, Clifford

CONTINENTAL CO-ETS
Singles: 7-inch
IGL (105 "I Don't Love You No More") 40-60 66

CONTINENTAL COMPLEX
Singles: 7-inch
MONUMENT 3-6 69

CONTINENTAL COUSINS
Singles: 7-inch
PALETTE 4-8 61-63

CONTINENTAL FOUR
Singles: 7-inch
FORTUNE (863 "Jack the Ripper") . 8-10 64

CONTINENTAL 4 *P&R/R&B '71*
(Continental Four)
Singles: 7-inch
JAY WALKING 4-8 71-72
LPs: 10/12-inch
JAY WALKING 10-15 71
Members: Fred Kelly; Anthony Burke; Ronnie McGregor; Larry McGregor.

CONTINENTAL FIVE
(With the Lil Walters Band)
Singles: 7-inch
NU KAT ("Perdelia") 50-75 59
(No selection number used.)
NU KAT (105 "My Lonely Friend") 100-150 59
Also see VELVATONES / Continentals

CONTINENTAL V
Singles: 7-inch
CONTINENTAL (101 "Wake Me Up Girl") 30-50 67
RADEL (107 "Wake Me Up Girl") ...15-25 67

CONTINENTAL 5
Singles: 7-inch
LIFETIME (1038 "Yours")..............10-20 68

CONTINENTAL GEMS / Anthony Montalbono
Singles: 7-inch
GUYDEN (2091 "My Love Will Follow You").................................1000-2000 63

CONTINENTAL MINIATURES *P&R '78*
Singles: 7-inch
LONDON 3-5 78
Picture Sleeves
LONDON 3-5 78

CONTINENTAL ROCKERS
Singles: 7-inch
NIMBO 5-10 64

CONTINENTAL UPTIGHT BAND
Singles: 7-inch
CAPITOL... 3-5 70

CONTINENTALS
Singles: 78 rpm
WHIRLIN' DISC 50-75 56
Singles: 7-inch
DAVIS (466 "Sweet As a Flower")..20-30 59
PORT 15-25 60-61
VIRGO... 3-4 72
WHIRLIN' DISC (101 "Dear Lord") 75-125 56
WHIRLIN' DISC (105 "Picture of Love") 75-125 56
Member: Daniel Hicks.

CONTINENTALS
Singles: 78 rpm
KEY (517 "Take a Gamble on Me")..20-40 56
RAMA (190 "You're an Angel")...................................300-400 56
(Blue label.)
RAMA (190 "You're an Angel").......25-50 56
(Red label.)
Singles: 7-inch
HUNTER (3503 "It Doesn't Matter")............................1000-2000 60
KEY (517 "Take a Gamble on Me")...50-75 56
RAMA (190 "You're an Angel")..........................1000-2000 56
(Blue label.)
RAMA (190 "You're an Angel")...100-200 56
(Red label.)
ROULETTE 3-5 70
Members: James Gooden; Sidney Gray; Bill Davis; Demetrius Cleare.

CONTINENTALS
Singles: 7-inch
RIVIERA (101 "Music Shop Hop") 15-25 58

CONTINENTALS
Singles: 7-inch
ERA (3003 "Cool Penguin") 10-15 59
PENGUIN (1002 "Cool Penguin")...15-25 59

CONTINENTALS
Singles: 7-inch
BOLO (720 "I'm Coming Home")....15-25 60
Member: Don Stevenson.

CONTINENTALS
Singles: 7-inch
CUCA (1063 "Tic-Toc")...................15-25 61
Member: Vince Megna; Rusty Harding; Roger Roessler; Ron Evans; Dennis Madigan; Lee Breest.
Also see BONNEVILLES
Also see LINDEMAN, Bob, & Continentals

CONTINENTALS
Singles: 7-inch
UNION (505 "Big Bad Ho-Dad") 10-20 62
Also see BYRON, Lord Douglas / Continentals

CONTINENTALS
Singles: 7-inch
M (500 "Saxy Twist")......................10-20 62

CONTINENTALS
Singles: 7-inch
CANDI (1029 "Give Us Your Blessing")......................................10-20 63

CONTINENTALS
Singles: 7-inch
LIFETIME..5-10 66

CONTINENTALS
Singles: 7-inch
A-OK (1025 "Take Me") 10-20 66
GAYLO (124 "I'm Gone") 20-30 60s

CONTINENTALS
Singles: 7-inch
MITCH 5-8 60s

CONTINENTALS
LPs: 10/12-inch
EPIC..5-10 80

CONTINENTALS
Singles: 7-inch
BLUE FOX (101 "Funky Fox").......... 3-5 70

CONTINENTALS
Singles: 7-inch
VANDAN (8065 "Suave") 10-15
VANDAN (8453 "Pink Champagne") 10-15

CONTINENTALS & COUNTS OF RHYTHM
Singles: 7-inch
(10476 "Don't Leave Me")......2000-3000 60s
(No label name used. Also, identification number shown since no selection number is used.)

CONTINETTES
Singles: 7-inch
RITCHIE.. 4-8 63

CONTINGENT
Singles: 7-inch
FREEFORM 3-5 71

CONTINO, Dick *P&R '54*
Singles: 78 rpm
MERCURY 3-5 54-57
Singles: 7-inch
DOT 3-6 66-67
MERCURY 4-8 54-64
EPs: 7-inch
MERCURY 5-10 55-59
LPs: 10/12-inch
DOT 5-15 64-66
HAMILTON.....................................5-10 64-66
MERCURY 8-15 56-63
WING 5-10 63
Also see CARROLL, David

CONTORTIONS / Teenage Jesus & Jerks / Mars / D.N.A.
LPs: 10/12-inch
ANTILLES (2067 "No New York") 8-12

CONTOURS
Singles: 7-inch
BULLSEYE.....................................15-20 58

CONTOURS *P&R/R&B '62*
(With Jack Surrell)
Singles: 12-inch
MOTOWN 4-8 88
Singles: 7-inch
GORDY 8-15 62-67
HOB (116 "I'm So Glad") 75-100 61
MOTOWN (400 series) 3-4 82-88
MOTOWN (1008 "Whole Lotta Woman")......................................350-450 61
MOTOWN (1012 "Funny") 450-650 61
TAMLA (7012 "Shake Sherry").....75-125 62
(Tamla label with Gordy selection number.)
ROCKET 3-4 80
Picture Sleeves
MOTOWN 3-4 88
EPs: 7-inch
MOTOWN (2002 "The Contours") .15-25 60s
LPs: 10/12-inch
GORDY (901 "Do You Love Me")...200-300 62
MOTOWN 5-10 82
Members: Dennis Edwards; Bill Gordon; Sylvester Potts; Billy Hoggs; Joe Billingslea; Joe Stubbs; Hubert Johnson; Huey Davis.
Also see EDWARDS, Dennis
Also see HANKS, Mike
Also see HI-FIDELITIES
Also see ORIGINALS
Also see STUBBS, Joe

CONTRABAND
LPs: 10/12-inch
EPIC...10-15 71

CONTRABAND
Singles: 7-inch
RCA 3-5 72-73

CONTRABAND
Singles: 7-inch
PORTRAIT 3-4 78
LPs: 10/12-inch
PORTRAIT 5-10 78

CONTRABAND *LP '91*
LPs: 10/12-inch
IMPACT... 5-8 91

CONTRAILS
("Vocal By Dick and Jack")
Singles: 7-inch
DIAMOND (213 "Someone")..........20-25 66
REUBEN (711 "Someone")..........50-100 64

CONTRAILS
Singles: 7-inch
LOVE MUSIC 5-10 60s
MILLAGE..5-10 60s

CONTRASTS
("Vocalist: Colin Hopkins")
Singles: 7-inch
RHAPSODY (71965 "Steady")...100-150 60
Member: Colin Hopkins.

CONTRASTS
Singles: 7-inch
MONUMENT 4-6 68
LPs: 10/12-inch
JANUS 10-12 69
Member: Bob Morrison.

CONTRIBUTORS OF SOUL
Singles: 7-inch
EMASE (1053 "Yum Yum Man")......5-10
NEW MISS (123 "I Don't Know")....10-20 60s
TAD...5-10 68

CONTROLLERS *R&B '76*
(With Valerie DeMece)
Singles: 12-inch
MCA 4-6 85-86
Singles: 7-inch
JUANA 3-4 76-82
MCA 3-4 85-88
LPs: 10/12-inch
JUANA 8-10 77-79
MCA 5-10 86
WINDHAM HILL 5-10 85
Members: Larry McArthur; Regie McArthur; Ricky Lewis; Leonard Brown.

CONVENTION
Singles: 7-inch
BUDDAH 4-8 68

CONVENTIONALS
Singles: 7-inch
SWAN 8-12 64

CONVERTERS
Singles: 7-inch
STAR HI (10560 "Dave's Place")...10-15 60

CONVERTION *R&B '81*
Singles: 7-inch
SAM 3-4 81
VANGUARD 3-4 83
LPs: 10/12-inch
VANGUARD 5-10 83

CONVERTS
Singles: 7-inch
RAMPRO (117 "Don't Leave Me") 15-25 66

CONVINCERS
(With Al Clark's Band)
Singles: 7-inch
MOVIN (100 "Rejected Love") ...250-500 62

CONVY, Bert
(With the Cheers)
Singles: 78 rpm
CAPITOL...5-10 56
MERCURY 10-20 57
Singles: 7-inch
CAPITOL...8-12 56
CONTENDER..................................5-10 58
ERA 3-5 74
MERCURY 8-12 57
MOONGLOW 5-8 62
STORM 5-10
Also see CHEERS

CONWAY, Dave *C&W '77*
Singles: 7-inch
TEDDY BEAR (17505 "Jingle Bears")..20-30 85
(Picture disc.)
TRUE 3-5 77

CONWAY, Inez
Singles: 7-inch
EMERSON (2106 "You Fool").......12-18

CONWAY, Russ
Singles: 7-inch
POLARIS (200 "I'm Still Missing You")...10-20

CONWAY BROTHERS *R&B '85*
Singles: 7-inch
ICHIBAN...3-4 87
PBT 3-4 86
PAULA 3-4 85
Members: Huston Conway; Jim Conway; Fredrick Conway; Hiawatha Conway.

CONWELL, James
Singles: 7-inch
FOUR J (511 "Trouble with Girls") .30-50 64

CONWELL, Tommy, & Young Rumblers *P&R/LP '88*
Singles: 12-inch
COLUMBIA.....................................4-8 88
(Promotional only.)
Singles: 7-inch
COLUMBIA.....................................3-4 88
Picture Sleeves
COLUMBIA.....................................3-4 88
LPs: 10/12-inch
ANTENNA 10-15 86
COLUMBIA.....................................5-8 88
Members: Tommy Conwell; Rob Miller; Paul Slivka; Jim Hannum; Chris Day.
Also see HOOTERS

COO-COO RACHAS
Singles: 7-inch
CAPITOL...5-10 59

COO-COOS
Singles: 7-inch
WYNNFIELD 10-15

COODER, Ry *LP '72*
Singles: 7-inch
MUSICOR 4-8 66
REPRISE 3-6 69-72
W.B. 3-5 77-82
LPs: 10/12-inch
MFSL (085 "Jazz")..........................25-50 82
REPRISE 8-12 72-76
W.B. 5-10 77-87
Session: Van Dyke Parks.
Also see CAPTAIN BEEFHEART
Also see CEYLEIB PEOPLE
Also see ELLIOTT, Ron
Also see LENNEAR, Claudia
Also see LITTLE FEAT
Also see LONGBRANCH PENNYWHISTLE
Also see PARKS, Van Dyke
Also see RISING SONS

COOK, Bennie
Singles: 7-inch
TELA STAR 4-8 63

COOK, Bill, & Marshalls
Singles: 78 rpm
SAVOY (828 "Just Because") 50-100 51
Singles: 7-inch
SAVOY (828 "Just Because") 100-200 51
Also see MARSHALL BROTHERS

COOK, Billy
Singles: 7-inch
LAWN 4-8 63

COOK, Ira
Singles: 7-inch
IMPERIAL 5-10 59

COOK, J. Lawrence
LPs: 10/12-inch
MERCURY 15-25 59

COOK, Jack
Singles: 7-inch
RAMCO...5-10 62
RUBY 4-8 63

COOK, Jerry
Singles: 7-inch
CAPITOL (5981 "Take What I've Got")...20-30 67

COOK, Joe
Singles: 7-inch
JOYETTE..10-15 59

COOK, Johnnie
Singles: 7-inch
FIDELITY 3-5 62

COOK, Ken
(With Roy Orbison)
Singles: 7-inch
PHILLIPS INT'L (3534 "I Was a Fool")..20-30 59
Also see ORBISON, Roy

COOK, Little Becky, & Mad Lads
Singles: 7-inch
CBM (504 "Let's Dance") 30-50 61

COOK, Little Joe
Singles: 7-inch
FURY 10-20 62
HOT (1003 "I'm Falling in Love") 50-100
J.J. 10-20
LOMA 8-12 66
LOVE TOWN 10-20
OKEH 8-12 64
20TH FOX 8-12 63
Also see DE-LOS
Also see IVY TONES
Also see LITTLE JOE & THRILLERS

COOK, Red
Singles: 78 rpm
RICHTONE 5-10

COOK, Roger
Singles: 7-inch
CAPRICORN 3-5 77
KAMA SUTRA 3-5 72-73
MCA 3-5 74
Picture Sleeves
KAMA SUTRA 4-6 72
LPs: 10/12-inch
KAMA SUTRA 8-10 72-73
W.B. 8-10 76
Also see BLUE MINK
Also see DAVID & JONATHAN

COOK, Roland
Singles: 78 rpm
ACE 15-25 57
Singles: 7-inch
ACE 10-20 57
Also see COOKIE

COOK, Ronnie
(With the Gaylords; with Gaylads; Ronnie Cooke)
Singles: 7-inch
ASTRA (1013 "Scotch") 5-10 65
DORE (565 "My Angel") 5-10 60
DORE (600 "If I May") 5-10 61
DORE (721 "Only the Lonely") 5-10 64
TRI DISC (105 "Such a Night") 8-12 62
(Same selection number also used for an Olympics release.)

COOK, Steven Lee *C&W '79*
Singles: 7-inch
GRINDER'S SWITCH 3-5 79

COOK, Tony *D&D '84*
Singles: 12-inch
HALFMOON 4-6 84

COOK, Vic, & Esquires
Singles: 7-inch
TYME (106 "Teenage Heartbreak")..........................75-125

COOK BROTHERS
Singles: 7-inch
ARCADE 5-10 60
EMPEROR 5-10 59

COOK COUNTY
Singles: 7-inch
MOTOWN 3-4 79-80

COOK E. JARR
Singles: 7-inch
EPIC 3-5 71
RCA 4-6 69
LPs: 10/12-inch
RCA 10-15 69

COOKE, Curley
LPs: 10/12-inch
FIRST AMERICAN (7767 "Curley Cooke")...20-30 80

COOKE, Dale
(Sam Cooke)
Singles: 78 rpm
SPECIALTY (596 "Forever")..........15-25 57
Singles: 7-inch
SPECIALTY (596 "Forever")..........15-25 57
Also see COOKE, Sam

COOKE, James Curley
LPs: 10/12-inch
FIRST AMERICAN............................5-10 80

COOKE, L.C.
(L.C. Cook)
Singles: 7-inch
CHECKER 10-15 59
DESTINATION 5-10 65
SAR 5-10 60-62
WAND 10-20 68
LPs: 10/12-inch
BLUE ROCK 15-20 65
Also see L.C.

COOKE, Pete
(With the Baby Dolls)
Singles: 7-inch
DIMENSION (1037 "I Won't Cry")....5-10 64
LOGO (503 "Take It and Git").........8-12 60s

COOKE, Ronnie: see COOK, Ronnie

COOKE, SAM *P&R/R&B '57*
(With the Soul Stirrers; with Bumps Blackwell Orchestra; with René Hall Orchestra; with Don Ralke Orchestra)
Singles: 78 rpm
KEEN (2005 "Stealing Kisses").......50-75 58
KEEN (2006 "Win Your Love for Me")..50-75 58
KEEN (2008 "Love You Most of All")..50-75 58
KEEN (2018 "Everybody Likes to Cha Cha Cha")...50-100 59
KEEN (2022 "Only Sixteen")...........75-125 59
KEEN (4002 "For Sentimental Reasons")..50-75 58
KEEN (4009 "Lonely Island") 50-75 58
KEEN (4013 "You Send Me")..........25-50 57
SPECIALTY (619 "I'll Come Running Back to You")..25-50 57
Singles: 7-inch
CHERIE 4-6 71
COLLECTABLES 3-4 81
KEEN (2005 "Stealing Kisses").......20-30 58
KEEN (2006 "Win Your Love for Me")..15-25 58
KEEN (2008 "Love You Most of All")..20-30 58
KEEN (2018 "Everybody Likes to Cha Cha Cha") 15-25 59
(Monaural.)
KEEN (S-2018 "Everybody Likes to Cha Cha Cha")..35-50 59
(Stereo.)
KEEN (2022 "Only Sixteen")...........15-25 59
(Monaural.)
KEEN (S-2022 "Only Sixteen") 35-50 59
(Stereo.)
KEEN (2101 "Summertime")............15-25 59
KEEN (2105 "There I've Said It Again")...15-25 59
KEEN (2111 "No One")....................15-25 60
KEEN (2112 "Wonderful World") 15-25 60
KEEN (2117 "With You") 15-25 60
KEEN (2118 "So Glamorous") 15-25 60
KEEN (2122 "Mary, Mary Lou") 15-25 61
KEEN (4002 "For Sentimental Reasons")..20-30 58
KEEN (4009 "Lonely Island") 20-30 58
KEEN (4013 "You Send Me")..........25-35 57
Note: Some Keen numbers in the 2000 and 4000 series have either a "3" or and "8" preceding the 2000 or 4000 series number.
RCA (47-7701 "Teenage Sonata") 10-20 60
(Monaural.)
RCA (61-7701 "Teenage Sonata") 35-50 60
(Stereo.)
RCA (47-7730 "I Belong to Your Heart")...15-25 60
(Monaural.)
RCA (61-7730 "I Belong to Your Heart")...40-60 60
(Stereo.)
RCA (47-7783 "Chain Gang") 10-20 60
(Monaural.)
RCA (61-7783 "Chain Gang") 35-50 60
(Stereo.)
RCA (47-7816 "Sad Mood") 10-20 60
(Monaural.)

RCA (61-7816 "Sad Mood") 35-50 60
(Stereo.)
RCA (37-7853 "That's It – I Quit, I'm Movin' On") 35-50 61
(Compact 33 Single.)
RCA (47-7853 "That's It – I Quit, I'm Movin' On") 10-20 61
RCA (37-7883 "Cupid") 30-40 61
(Compact 33 Single.)
RCA (47-7883 "Cupid") 10-15 61
RCA (37-7927 "Feel It") 30-40 61
(Compact 33 Single.)
RCA (47-7927 "Feel It") 10-15 61
RCA (37-7927 "Twistin' the Night Away") 30-40 62
(Compact 33 Single.)
RCA (47-7927 "Twistin' the Night Away") 6-12 62
RCA (8036 thru 8934) 5-15 62-66
RCA GOLD STANDARD 3-8
(With "447" prefix.)
SAR (122 "Just for You") 10-20 61
SPECIALTY (SPBX series) 15-20 87
(Boxed set of six colored vinyl singles.)
SPECIALTY (619 "I'll Come Running Back to You") 15-25 57
SPECIALTY (627 "I Don't Want to Cry") 15-25 58
SPECIALTY (667 "Happy in Love") 15-25 59
SPECIALTY (900 series) 3-5 70-72

Picture Sleeves

RCA (7730 "I Belong to Your Heart") 20-30 60
RCA (7783 "Chain Gang") 10-20 60
RCA (7883 "Cupid") 10-20 60
RCA (7927 "Feel It") 10-20 61
RCA (8088 "Nothing Can Change This Love") 10-20 62
RCA (8129 "Send Me Some Lovin' ") 10-20 63
RCA (8164 "Another Saturday Night") 10-20 63
RCA (8215 "Frankie & Johnny") 10-20 63
RCA (8247 "Little Red Rooster") 10-20 63
RCA (8631 "Sugar Dumpling") 10-20 65

EPs: 7-inch

KEEN (2001/2002/2003 "Songs by Sam Cooke") 30-40 57
(Price is for any of three volumes.)
KEEN (2012/2013/2014 "Tribute to the Lady") 20-30 59
(Price is for any of three volumes.)
KEEN (2006 "Encore") 20-40 58
KEEN (2008 "Encore, Vol. 2") 20-40 58
RCA (126 "Sam Cooke Sings") 25-50 61
(Compact 33.)
RCA (3373 "Sam Cooke") 25-30 64
(Juke box issue only. Includes title strips.)
RCA (4375 "Another Saturday Night") 15-25 63

LPs: 10/12-inch

CAMDEN (0445 "You Send Me") 5-10 74
CAMDEN (2264 "One & Only") 8-12 68
CAMDEN (2433 "Sam Cooke") 8-12 70
CAMDEN (2610 "Unforgettable") 8-12 73
CANDLELITE 15-20 74
(Mail-order offer.)
CHERIE (1001 "Right On") 8-10 71
FAMOUS (502 "Sam's Songs") 10-20 69
FAMOUS (505 "Only Sixteen") 10-20 69
FAMOUS (508 "So Wonderful") 10-20 69
FAMOUS (509 "You Send Me") 10-20 69
FAMOUS (512 "Cha-Cha-Cha") 10-20 69
KEEN (2001 "Sam Cooke") 60-100 58
KEEN (2003 "Encore") 50-75 58
KEEN (2004 "Tribute to the Lady") 30-50 59
KEEN (86101 "Hit Kit") 100-200 59
KEEN (86103 "I Thank God") 100-200 60
KEEN (86106 "The Wonderful World of Sam Cooke") 50-100 60
PHOENIX 10 .... 5-10 81
PICKWICK 5-10 76
RCA (2221 "Cooke's Tour") 20-30 60
RCA (2236 "Hits of the '50s") 20-30 60
RCA (2293 "Sam Cooke") 15-25 61
RCA (2392 "My Kind of Blues") 15-25 61
RCA (2555 "Twistin' the Night Away") 15-25 62
RCA (2625 "Best of Sam Cooke") 15-25 62
RCA (2658 "At the Copa") 5-10 78
RCA (2673 "Mr. Soul") 15-25 63
RCA (2709 "Night Beat") 15-25 63
RCA (2899 "Ain't That Good News") 15-25 64
RCA (2970 "At the Copa") 15-25 64
RCA (3367 "Shake") 15-25 65
RCA (3373 "Best of Sam Cooke, Vol. 2") 15-25 65
RCA (3435 "Try a Little Love") 15-20 65
RCA (3466 "Best of Sam Cooke") 8-10 79
RCA (3517 "Unforgettable") 15-20 66
RCA (3863 "Best of Sam Cooke") 5-8 81
RCA (3991 "The Man Who Invented Soul") 10-20 68
RCA (5000 series) 5-10 78-85
(With "AFL1," "ANL1" or "AYL1" prefix.)
RCA (7000 series) 8-12 86
SAR 3-5 61
SOUFFLE 5-10
SPECIALTY (2119 "Two Sides of Sam Cooke") 6-12 69
TRIP (8030 "Golden Sounds") 8-10 72
UPFRONT (160 "The Billie Holiday Story") 8-10 73
Also see ANKA, Paul / Sam Cooke / Neil Sedaka
Also see CHARLES, Ray / Little Richard / Sam Cooke
Also see COOKE, Dale
Also see HALL, René
Also see RALKE, Don
Also see RAWLS, Lou
Also see SEDAKA, Neil / Ann-Margret / Browns / Sam Cooke
Also see SOUL STIRRERS

COOKE, Sam / Rod Lauren / Neil Sedaka / Browns

EPs: 7-inch

RCA (33-99 "Compact 33 Double") 15-20 60
(Has the same four songs on each side, mono on one side, stereo on the reverse.)
Also see BROWNS
Also see LAUREN, Rod
Also see SEDAKA, Neil

COOKE, Sam / Johnny Morisette

Singles: 7-inch

CAPITOL STAR LINE 4-8 65
Also see MORISETTE, Johnnie

COOKE, Sam / Lloyd Price / Larry Williams / Little Richard

LPs: 10/12-inch

SPECIALTY (2112 "Our Significant Hits") 25-35 60
(Black and gold label.)
Also see COOKE, Sam
Also see LITTLE RICHARD
Also see PRICE, Lloyd
Also see WILLIAMS, Larry

COOKE, Samona

Singles: 7-inch

EPIC 3-5 76-77
MERCURY 3-5 78

COOKE, Sarah

Singles: 7-inch

BIG TOP (519 "Please Don't Go") 25-50 64

COOKER — P&R '74

(Norman Des Rosiers)

Singles: 7-inch

SCEPTER 3-5 73-74

LPs: 10/12-inch

SCEPTER 8-10 74

COOKER, John Lee

(John Lee Hooker)

Singles: 7-inch

KING (4504 "Stomp Boogie") 50-100 52
Also see HOOKER, John Lee

COOKIE

(Roland Cook)

Singles: 7-inch

PRESIDENT 8-12 61
RCA (7305 "That's What You Do to Me") 15-25 58
Also see COOK, Roland

COOKIE & CHARLIE

Singles: 7-inch

CAL (1002 "Bye Bye Baby, Don't Cry") 40-60
JEFF (1212 "Let's Go Rock & Roll") 15-20

COOKIE & CUPCAKES — P&R '59

(Cookie & His Berry Cups)

Singles: 7-inch

CHESS 5-10 63
JUDD 10-20 59
KHOURY'S (703 "Matilda") 20-30 59
LYRIC 10-15 63-64
MERCURY 8-10 61
PAULA 4-8 65-68
Members: Terry "Cookie" Clinton; Shelton Dunaway; Lil' Alfred.
Also see BOOGIE RAMBLERS
Also see CLINTON, Terry, & Berry Cups

COOKIE & HIS CUPCAKES / Little Alfred

Singles: 7-inch

LYRIC 8-12 64
Also see COOKIE & His Cupcakes
Also see LITTLE ALFRED

COOKIE CREW

Singles: 7-inch

TVT 3-4 88

COOKIE & CRUMBS

Singles: 7-inch

VEST 5-10 66

COOKIEFOOT

Singles: 7-inch

MSP 4-8 72
Also see JOKERS WILD

COOKIES — R&B '56

Singles: 78 rpm

ATLANTIC 10-25 55-57
JOSIE (822 "King of Hearts") 15-25 57
LAMP (8008 "Don't Let Go") 10-20 54

Singles: 7-inch

ATLANTIC (1061 "Precious Love") 15-25 55
ATLANTIC (1084 "Passing Time") 15-25 56
ATLANTIC (1110 "My Lover") 10-20 56
ATLANTIC (2079 "Passing Time") 10-15 60
JOSIE (822 "King of Hearts") 15-25 57
LAMP (8008 "Don't Let Go") 20-30 54
Members: Earl-Jean McCree; Margie Hendrix; Pat Lyles.
Also see CHARLES, Ray
Also see COOKIES (Group that follows)
Also see DILLARD, Varetta
Also see WILLIS, Chuck

COOKIES — P&R/R&B '62

Singles: 7-inch

ABC 3-5 74
DIMENSION (1002 "Chains") 10-20 62
DIMENSION (1008 "Don't Say Nothin' Bad About My Baby") 10-20 63
DIMENSION (1012 "Will Power") 10-20 63
DIMENSION (1020 "Girls Grow Up Faster Than Boys") 10-20 63
DIMENSION (1032 "The Old Crowd") 15-25 63
ERIC 3-5 73
MCA 3-5 83
Members: Earl-Jean McCree; Margaret Ross; Dorothy Jones.
Also see CINDERELLAS
Also see EARL-JEAN

COOKIES / Little Eva / Carole King

LPs: 10/12-inch

DIMENSION (6001 "The Dimension Dolls, Vol. 1") 50-75 63
Also see COOKIES
Also see KING, Carole
Also see LITTLE EVA

COOKIES

Singles: 7-inch

W.B. 4-8 67

COOKS, Donald

Singles: 78 rpm

JADE (202 "Trouble-Making Woman") 15-25 51
Also see COOKS, Silver, & Gondoliers

COOKS, Silver, & Gondoliers

(Donald Cooks)

Singles: 78 rpm

PEACOCK (1510 "Mr. Ticket Man") 50-75 49
Also see COOKS, Donald

COOL, Calvin

(With the Surf Knobs; Shorty Rogers)

Singles: 7-inch

CHARTER (7 "Beach Bash") 10-20 63

LPs: 10/12-inch

CHARTER (103 "Surfer's Beat") 30-40 63
Also see BROWN, Boots
Also see KINGSMEN / Calvin Cool
Also see ROGERS, Shorty

COOL, Harry / Frances Langford

Singles: 78 rpm

MERCURY/SAV-WAY (3066 "Ragtime Cowboy Joe") 100-150 47
(Picture disc. Promotional issue only.)

COOL, Harry, & Helen Mayfair

Singles: 7-inch

CRYSTAL 5-10 60

COOL, Joe, & Rumblers

Singles: 7-inch

ARROW DYNAMIC 3-4 88

Picture Sleeves

ARROW DYNAMIC 3-4 88

COOL, Larry

Singles: 7-inch

SONIC 4-8 67

COOL, Oliver

Singles: 7-inch

BRAND (6789 "Nobody Can Like Joanne") 40-50 62
ROULETTE 5-10 60-61

COOL BREEZE & HIS BAND

(With the Little Cool Breezes; with Jimmy Petty, Rupert Jones & the Senders)

Singles: 7-inch

EBONY (1015 "Won't You Come In") 1000-2000 59

COOL GENTS

Singles: 7-inch

CEE JAY 15-25 61

COOL HEAT — P&R '70

Singles: 7-inch

FORWARD (152 "Are You Nuts") 5-10 70
Also see WIND

COOL PAPA

(Haskell Sadler)

Singles: 7-inch

BLACK GOLD 8-10
Also see SADLER, Haskell, & His Orchestra

COOL SOUNDS

Singles: 7-inch

PULSAR (2421 "Comin' Home") 35-45 69
W.B. (7538 "I'll Take You Back") 10-20 71
W.B. (7575 "Love Like Ours Could Last a Million Years Or More") 15-25 71
W.B. (7615 "Free") 15-25 71

COOL TONES

Singles: 7-inch

RADIANT 5-10 62
WARWICK 10-15 59
Also see COOLTONES (one word).

COOLBREEZERS

(With the Don Costa Orchestra; with Al White & Band)

Singles: 78 rpm

ABC-PAR 50-75 57

Singles: 7-inch

ABC-PAR (9865 "My Brother") 50-75 57
BALE (100 "Eda Weda Bug") 40-60 58
BALE (102 "Hello Mr. New Year") 150-250 58
Also see COSTA, Don, Orchestra

COOLEY, Eddie — P&R '56

(With the Dimples)

Singles: 78 rpm

ROYAL ROOST 20-40 56-57

Singles: 7-inch

ABC 3-4 73
ROULETTE 5-10 60
ROYAL ROOST 10-20 56-57
TRIUMPH 8-12 59

COOLEY, Jack

Singles: 7-inch

STATES (125 "Could, But I Ain't") 50-75 53
(Colored vinyl.)

COOLEY, Spade, & His Orchestra — C&W '45

(With the Buckle Busters; with Tex Williams)

Singles: 78 rpm

BLUEBIRD 5-10
COLUMBIA 5-10 46-47
DECCA 4-8 51-55
OKEH 5-10 45-46
RCA 5-10 47-48

Singles: 7-inch

DECCA 8-10 51-52

EPs: 7-inch

DECCA (2225/2226 "Dance-O Rama") 10-20 55
(Price is for either volume.)

LPs: 10/12-inch

CLUB of SPADE 8-15
COLUMBIA (9007 "Sagebrush Swing") 40-80 50s
(10-inch LP.)
COLUMBIA (37000 series) 5-10
DECCA (5563 "Dance-O-Rama") 30-50 55
RAYNOTE (RN-5007 "Fidoodlin' ") 20-30 59
(Monaural.)
RAYNOTE (RS-5007 "Fidoodlin' ") 30-40 59
(Stereo.)
ROULETTE (R-25145 Fidoodlin' ") 15-20 61
(Monaural.)
ROULETTE (S-25145 Fidoodlin' ") 20-25 61
(Stereo.)
Also see ROGERS, Roy, with Spade Cooley's Buckle Busters

COOLIDGE, Rita — P&R '69

Singles: 7-inch

A&M 3-5 71-83
PEPPER 4-8 68-69

Picture Sleeves

A&M 3-6 72-83

LPs: 10/12-inch

A&M 5-10 71-83

Promotional LPs

A&M ("In-Store Sampler - Rita Coolidge") 10-15
Also see CAMPBELL, Glen, & Rita Coolidge
Also see CLAPTON, Eric
Also see KRISTOFFERSON, Kris, & Rita Coolidge

COOLIDGE-JONES, Priscilla

(Priscilla)

Singles: 7-inch

CAPRICORN 3-4 79
YORK 4-8 67-68

LPs: 10/12-inch

A&M 8-12 71
CAPRICORN 5-10 79
SUSSEX 8-12 70
Also see BOOKER T. & Priscilla

COOLTONES

Singles: 7-inch

DICE (750 "Cry All Night") 40-60
Also see COOL TONES, as two words.

COON ELDER BAND

LPs: 10/12-inch

MERCURY 8-10 77
Member: Brenda Patterson.
Also see PATTERSON, Brenda

COOPER, Al, & Savoy Sultans

LPs: 10/12-inch

DECCA 15-25 64

COOPER, Alan

Singles: 7-inch

20TH FOX 4-8 62

COOPER, Alice — LP '69

(Alice Cooper Group)

Promotional Singles: 12-inch

EPIC (1347 "I Got a Line on You") 5-8
EPIC (1663 "Poison") 5-8 89
EPIC (1686 "Trash") 5-8 89
EPIC (1890 "I'm Your Gun") 5-8 89
MCA (17177 "He's Back") 5-8 86
MCA (17205 "Give It Up") 5-8 86
W.B. (864 "Clones") 10-15 80
W.B. (1059 "I Like Girls") 5-8

Singles: 7-inch

ATLANTIC 3-5 75
EPIC 3-4 89-90
MCA 3-4 86-87
STRAIGHT (101 "Reflected") 15-25 69
STRAIGHT (7398 "Shoe Salesman") 15-20 70
W.B. 3-5 70-82

Promotional Singles

ATLANTIC 5-10 75
MCA 3-6 86-87
W.B. 8-12 70-80

Picture Sleeves

MCA 3-4 87
W.B. 4-8 72-80

EPs: 7-inch

W.B. 15-25 73
(Juke box issues only.)

LPs: 10/12-inch

ATLANTIC 5-10 75-78
EPIC 5-8 89
MFSL (063 "Welcome to My Nightmare") 40-60 82
MCA 5-10 86-87
STRAIGHT (1051 "Pretties for You") 30-40 69
(Cover has a drawing of a woman raising her dress, with a yellow sticker covering her crotch area. Price is for cover with sticker still intact.)
STRAIGHT (1051 "Pretties for You") 20-30 69
(Cover shows the woman with the sticker removed and panties showing.)
W.B. (Except 1883, 2567 & 2623) 8-12 73-84
W.B. (1883 "Love It to Death") 25-30 71
(Black cover has Cooper's right thumb showing through his wrap. Does NOT have white block reading "Including Their Hit *I'm Eighteen.*")
W.B. (1883 "Love It to Death") 15-20 71
(Black cover has Cooper's right thumb showing through his wrap. Has white block reading "Including Their Hit *I'm Eighteen.*" Also includes issue with huge white stripes at top and bottom of cover.)
W.B. (1883 "Love It to Death") 5-10 71
(Black cover does NOT have Cooper's right thumb showing through his wrap. Has the white block reading "Including Their Hit *I'm Eighteen.*")
W.B. (2567 "Killer") 15-18 71
(With poster and 1972 calendar.)
W.B. (2567 "Killer") 5-10 72
(Without poster and calendar.)
W.B. (2623 "School's Out") 30-40 72
(With panties attached. Panties came in four different colors: pink, white, yellow, and blue. Back cover does not list titles.)
W.B. (2623 "School's Out") 15-20 72
(With panties attached. Back cover lists titles.)
W.B. (2623 "School's Out") 5-10 72
(With no paper panties. Back cover lists titles.)
W.B. (2685 "Billion Dollar Babies") 5-10 73
W.B. (BS4-2685 "Billion Dollar Babies") 20-25 73
(Quad issue.)
W.B. (2748 "Muscle of Love") 5-10 73
W.B. (BBS4-2748 "Muscle of Love") 20-25 73
(Quad issue.)
W.B. (2803 thru 3581) 5-10 74-81
W.B./STRAIGHT (1051 "Pretties for You") 15-18 69
W.B./STRAIGHT (1845 "Easy Action") 30-35 70
(With the name "Alice Cooper" in black letters on front cover.)
W.B./STRAIGHT (1845 "Easy Action") 5-10 70
(With "Alice Cooper" in white letters on front.)

Promotional LPs

CHELSEA PROD ("Allison's Tea House") 25-30 74
STRAIGHT (1051 "Pretties for You") 45-55 69
(Cover has drawing of a woman raising her dress, with a yellow sticker covering her crotch area. Price is for cover with sticker still intact.)
STRAIGHT (1051 "Pretties for You") 30-40 69
(Cover shows the woman with the sticker removed and panties showing.)
STRAIGHT (1845 "Easy Action") 25-30 70
STRAIGHT (1883 "Love It to Death") 20-25 71
W.B. 20-40 71-78
(Includes all white label promo labels.)
W.B./STRAIGHT ("Pretties for You") 25-30 69
Members: Alice Cooper; Dennis Dunaway; Glen Buxton; Michael Bruce; Neal Smith; Kane Roberts; Ken K. Mary.
Also see BILLION DOLLAR BABIES
Also see BRUCE, Michael
Also see FROST
Also see NAZZ
Also see SPIDERS

COOPER, Angel

Singles: 7-inch

NOLA ("You Beat Me to the Punch") 10-15 60s

COOPER, Babs

Singles: 7-inch

INDIGO 4-8 62

COOPER, Becky

Singles: 7-inch

ACCENT 4-8 63

COOPER, Bo

(Ron Dante)

Singles: 7-inch

BELL 4-8 74
Also see DANTE, Ron

COOPER, Christine

Singles: 7-inch

PARKWAY (971 "S.O.S." 15-25 66
PARKWAY (983 "Bad Boy") 30-50 66

COOPER, D.B.

Singles: 7-inch

W.B. 3-4 81

LPs: 10/12-inch

W.B. 5-10 81

COOPER, Dana

Singles: 7-inch

ELEKTRA 3-4 73

LPs: 10/12-inch

ELEKTRA 10-12 73

COOPER, Dave, & Continentals

Singles: 7-inch

WESTCO (7 "Church Key") 15-20 60s

COOPER, Dolly
(With the Four Buddies)
Singles: 78 rpm
DOT 5-10 56
EBB 5-10 57
MODERN 10-15 55
SAVOY 10-15 53-54
Singles: 7-inch
DOT 4-8 56
EBB 4-8 57
MODERN (965 "My Man") 20-40 55
MODERN (977 "Teenage Prayer") 30-50 55
MODERN (986 "Teenage Wedding Bells") 30-50 55
SAVOY (891 "I'd Climb the Highest Mountain") 10-20 53
SAVOY (1121 "Love Can't Be Blind") 15-25 54
Also see FOUR BUDDIES
Also see WANDERERS

COOPER, Don
Singles: 7-inch
ROULETTE 3-6 69
LPs: 10/12-inch
ROULETTE 10-12 69

COOPER, Ed
Singles: 7-inch
NIMROD ("Just Like a Hero") 10-20
(Selection number not known.)

COOPER, Eula
Singles: 7-inch
ATLANTIC 4-6 69
NOTE 4-8

COOPER, Garnell, & Kinfolks
Singles: 7-inch
JUBILEE 4-8 63

COOPER, Herb
Singles: 78 rpm
OKEH (7037 "Ready, Miss Betty") 10-15 54
Singles: 7-inch
OKEH (7037 "Ready, Miss Betty") 20-30 54

COOPER, Horace
Singles: 7-inch
VEST (831 "The Squeeze") 8-10 60
Members: Horace Cooper; Jimmy Spruill. Session: King Curtis.
Also see KING CURTIS

COOPER, Jackie
Singles: 78 rpm
DOT 15-25 57
Singles: 7-inch
DOT 15-25 57

COOPER, James
Singles: 7-inch
SPECIALTY (728 "Highway 280") 5-8 72

COOPER, Jerry
Singles: 7-inch
CLIMAX 5-10 60

COOPER, Jerry C&W '87
Singles: 7-inch
BEAR 3-4 87-88

COOPER, Joey
(With the Conspiracy)
Singles: 7-inch
A&M 3-5 71
CHALLENGE 5-10 61
CHANCELLOR 5-10 62
INDEPENDENCE 4-8 67
RCA 8-12 65
REPRISE 4-8 64

COOPER, John Lee
Singles: 78 rpm
KING (4504 "Stomp Boogie") 10-15 52
Singles: 7-inch
KING (4504 "Stomp Boogie") 20-30 52

COOPER, Johnny
Singles: 7-inch
BARRINGTON 5-10
CHALLENGE 5-10 67
ERMINE (Except 38) 10-15 62-63
ERMINE (38 "Little Bride") 15-25 62
PLANTATION 4-6 69
TODDLIN' TOWN 5-10 65

COOPER, Les, & Soul Rockers P&R/R&B '62
Singles: 7-inch
ABC 3-4 73
ARRAWAK 4-8 65
ATCO 3-6 69
DIMENSION (1023 "Motor City") 10-15 64
ENJOY 4-8 65
EVERLAST 5-10 62
SAMAR 4-8 66
LPs: 10/12-inch
EVERLAST (202 "Wiggle Wobble") 40-60 63
Members: Les Cooper; Joe Grier.
Also see CHARTS
Also see EMPIRES
Also see WHIRLERS

COOPER, Little: see LITTLE COOPER

COOPER, Marty
(Marty Cooper Clan)
Singles: 7-inch
CAPITOL 4-8 67
CREST (1043 "You Bet Your Little Life") 15-25 58
DOPPLER (7501 "American Farming Man") 4-8 60s
(Asgrow Seed Special products issue.)
HOLIDAY 4-8 64
RCA 5-10 63
UNLIMITED GOLD 3-4 80-81
Picture Sleeves
DOPPLER (7501 "American Farming Man") 4-8 60s
(Asgrow Seed Special products issue.)
LPs: 10/12-inch
RCA 15-25 63

COOPER, Michael R&B '87
Singles: 7-inch
W.B. 3-4 87-88
LPs: 10/12-inch
W.B. 5-8 88
Also see CON FUNK SHUN

COOPER, Micky
Singles: 78 rpm
SWING BEAT 10-15 49
Singles: 7-inch
RUBY 8-12

COOPER, Mike
LPs: 10/12-inch
JANUS 10-12 69

COOPER, Pat LP '66
LPs: 10/12-inch
U.A. 10-15 66-69

COOPER, Prince
Singles: 78 rpm
CLUB 51 (101 "The Wiggler") 15-25 55
Singles: 7-inch
CLUB 51 (101 "The Wiggler") 25-35 55
Members: Prince Cooper; H. Wynne; J. Cosby; J. Slaughter; H. Ashby.

COOPER, Rattlesnake
Singles: 78 rpm
TALENT (804 "Rattlesnake Blues") 150-250 49

COOPER, Shirley
Singles: 7-inch
COVER 5-10 60

COOPER, Tommy
Singles: 7-inch
HIGHLAND 4-8 66
PHIL TONE 5-10 60
W.B. 4-8 62

COOPER, Wade
Singles: 7-inch
EMBER 5-10 60
HERALD 5-10 60

COOPER, Willie, & Webs
Singles: 7-inch
DYNAMIC (105 "You Don't Love Nobody") 15-25 60s

COOPER, Wilma Lee & Stoney C&W '56
(With the Clinch Mountain Clan; with Carolee & Clinch Mountain Clan)
Singles: 78 rpm
COLUMBIA 4-8 54-55
HICKORY 4-8 56-57
Singles: 7-inch
COLUMBIA 5-10 54-55
HICKORY 5-10 56-64
EPs: 7-inch
COLUMBIA 10-15 59
LPs: 10/12-inch
COUNTY 5-10
DECCA 15-20 66
HARMONY 15-25 60-66
HICKORY 10-20 60-62
POWER PAK 6-10
ROUNDER 5-10
SKYLIGHT COUNTRY 8-12
STARDAY 8-12 77
Also see WILMA LEE

COOPER & ROSS
Singles: 7-inch
MCA 3-4 82
LPs: 10/12-inch
MCA 5-10 82

COOPER BROTHERS P&R '78
Singles: 7-inch
CAPRICORN 3-4 78-79
LPs: 10/12-inch
CAPRICORN 5-10 78-79
Members: Richard Cooper; Brian Cooper.
Also see BLACK OAK ARKANSAS / Cooper Brothers

COOPER DODGE BAND
Singles: 7-inch
ATCO 3-4 80

COOPERETTES
Singles: 7-inch
ABC 3-5 69
BRUNSWICK (55296 "Goodbye School") 8-15 66
BRUNSWICK (55307 "Don't Trust Him") 8-15 66
BRUNSWICK (55329 "Shing-a-ling") 15-25 67

CO-OPS
Singles: 7-inch
VERSAILLES 5-10 59

COOTER, Daniel
Singles: 7-inch
CONNECTION 3-4 80
RIVA 3-4 80

COPA COMBO
(Ben Denton Singers)
Singles: 7-inch
SOLA 5-10 64
Also see DENTON, Ben, Singers

COPAS, Cowboy C&W '46
(Cowboy "Poppy" Copas; Lloyd Copas; with Kathy Copas)
Singles: 78 rpm
KING 5-15 44-57
Singles: 7-inch
DOT 10-20 57-58
KING (951 thru 1507) 10-20 50-55
KING (4865 thru 5270) 8-12 55-59
KING (5392 thru 5734) 5-10 60-63
STARDAY (476 thru 750) 5-10 60-66
STARDAY (7000 series) 4-6 64
STARDAY (8000 series) 3-5 71
EPs: 7-inch
KING 15-25 52-53
STARDAY 10-20 60
LPs: 10/12-inch
BUCKBOARD 5-10
GUEST STAR 10-15
KING (553 "All-Time Hits") 45-55 57
KING (556 "Favorite Sacred Songs") 40-50 57
KING (619 thru 835) 25-35 59-64
KING (894 thru 1049) 8-15 64-69
MONTGOMERY WARD 10-15 60s
NASHVILLE 8-12 68-70
PICKWICK/HILLTOP 10-20 66
STARDAY (113 "All Time Country Music Great") 20-30 60
STARDAY (133 "Inspirational Songs") 20-30 61
STARDAY (144 "Songs That Made Him Famous") 20-30 62
STARDAY (157 "Opry Star Spotlight") 20-30 63
STARDAY (175 "Mr. Country Music") 20-30 64
STARDAY (200 series) 12-25 64-67
STARDAY (300 series) 10-20 65-67
STARDAY (400 series) 8-12 68-70
TRIO CLUB 5-10 82
Also see COPAS, Lloyd
Also see MULLICAN, Moon / Cowboy Copas / Red Sovine
Also see ROCKING MARTIN

COPAS, Cowboy / Hawkshaw Hawkins
LPs: 10/12-inch
KING 12-25 63-66
Also see CLINE, Patsy / Cowboy Copas / Hawkshaw Hawkins
Also see COPAS, Cowboy
Also see HAWKINS, Hawkshaw

COPAS, Lloyd
Singles: 7-inch
DOT (15735 "Circle Rock") 60-80 58
Also see COPAS, Cowboy

COPE, Julian P&R/LP '87
Singles: 7-inch
ISLAND 3-4 87-88
Picture Sleeves
ISLAND 3-4 87
LPs: 10/12-inch
ISLAND 5-10 87-88
Also see TEARDROP EXPLODES

COPELAND, Jimmy
Singles: 7-inch
ALLSTAR 5-8 60-62

COPELAND, Johnny
(With the Soul Agents)
Singles: 7-inch
ALL BOY 5-10 62
ATLANTIC 4-8 68-69
BRAGG 5-10 64
CRAZY CAJUN 3-5 77
EVENT 5-10
GHETT CHILD 5-10
GOLDEN EAGLE 5-10 63-64
JET STREAM (802 "Sufferin' City") 10-15
KENT 4-6 70-71
MERCURY (71280 "Rock and Roll Lilly") 20-30 58
MR. R&B 3-5 83
RESCO 3-5 75
WAND 5-8 66
WET SOUL 4-6
LPs: 10/12-inch
ROUNDER 5-10 81-83
Also see COLLINS, Albert, Robert Cray & Johnny Copeland
Also see MEYERS, Augie

COPELAND, Ken
Singles: 78 rpm
IMPERIAL 10-20 57
Singles: 7-inch
DOT (15686 "Where the Rio De Rosa Flows") 15-25 58
IMPERIAL (5453 "Teenage") 10-20 57
KAI (5352 "Hey! Little Girl") 8-12 60s
LIN (5017 "Fanny Brown") 30-50 58

COPELAND, Ken / Mints P&R '57
Singles: 78 rpm
IMPERIAL 10-20 57
LIN 10-20 57
Singles: 7-inch
IMPERIAL (5432 "Pledge of Love") 10-20 57
LIN (5007 "Pledge of Love") 25-30 57
Also see COPELAND, Ken
Also see FOUR MINTS

COPELAND, Rudy
Singles: 7-inch
FANTASY 3-5

COPELAND, Ruth
Singles: 7-inch
INVICTUS 3-5 71
RCA 3-5 77
LPs: 10/12-inch
INVICTUS 10-15 70-71
RCA 8-10 76
Also see HALL, Daryl, & Ruth Copeland
Also see NEW PLAY
Also see PARLIAMENT

COPELAND, Stewart LP '83
(Stuart Copeland)
LPs: 10/12-inch
A&M 5-10 83-85
Also see CURVED AIR
Also see FROLK HEAVEN
Also see POLICE

COPELAND, Stewart, & Adam Ant
Singles: 7-inch
MCA/I.R.S. 3-4 86
Also see ANT, Adam

COPELAND, Stewart, & Stan Ridgway
Singles: 7-inch
A&M 3-4 83
Also see COPELAND, Stewart
Also see WALL of VOODOO

COPELAND, Tony
Singles: 7-inch
ARCO 3-5 77

COPELAND, Vivian R&B '69
Singles: 7-inch
D'ORO 3-6 69
MALA 4-8 67

COPELIN, Roger
Singles: 7-inch
R.C. 3-5 89

COPESETICS
Singles: 78 rpm
PREMIUM 50-75 56
Singles: 7-inch
PREMIUM (409 "Believein Me") 100-125 56

COPNEY, Bobby
Singles: 7-inch
TUFF (414 "Ain't No Good") 10-15 66

COPPER 'N BRASS
Singles: 7-inch
AMAZON 3-5 70

COPPER PLATED INTEGRATED CIRCUIT
LPs: 10/12-inch
COMMAND 10-15 69

COPPERHEAD
Singles: 7-inch
COLUMBIA 3-5 73
LPs: 10/12-inch
COLUMBIA 12-15 73
Also see QUICKSILVER MESSENGER SERVICE
Also see SAN FRANCISCO ALL STARS

COPPERPENNY
Singles: 7-inch
BIG TREE 3-5 73
CAPITOL 3-5 75
RCA 3-6 69
LPs: 10/12-inch
RCA 10-15 70

COPS 'N ROBBERS
Singles: 7-inch
CORAL 8-12 65
PARROT 10-15 64

COPYCATS
Singles: 7-inch
PRINCE 8-12 60
RUST 8-12 60

COQUETTES
Singles: 78 rpm
COLUMBIA 5-10 57
RCA 5-10 55
Singles: 7-inch
COLUMBIA 5-10 57
JAC-LYN 5-10
MGM 5-10 59
RCA 8-12 55

CORALAIRS
Singles: 7-inch
BEE (1543 "Baby Blue Eyes") 40-50
NRC 5-10 59

CORALITES
Singles: 7-inch
CARIB 15-25

CORALS
Singles: 7-inch
CHEER 5-10 62
RAYNA 5-10 62

CORALS
Singles: 7-inch
BIG SOUND (308 "Blue Moon") 10-20 66
BIG SOUND (311 "Baby My Heart") 10-20 67
Member: Ray Kannon; James Curley Cooke.
Also see KANNON, Ray, & Corals

CORALS
Singles: 7-inch
KRAM 15-25

CORBETT, Louise
Singles: 7-inch
MOSRITE 4-8 66

CORBETTA, Jerry
(With Bob Webber)
Singles: 7-inch
CLARIDGE 3-5 75-78
W.B. 3-4 78
Picture Sleeves
CLARIDGE 4-6 70s
LPs: 10/12-inch
W.B. 5-10 78
Also see 4 SEASONS
Also see SUGARLOAF

CORBIN, Harold
LPs: 10/12-inch
ROULETTE 15-25 61

CORBIN, Ray C&W '69
Singles: 7-inch
COLUMBIA 4-6 69-70
MONUMENT 4-6 67-68
TREND 5-10 60s

CORBIN & HANNER C&W '79
(Corbin-Hanner Band)
Singles: 7-inch
ALFA 3-5 81-82
LIFESONG 3-5 78-82
MERCURY 3-4 90-92
LPs: 10/12-inch
ALFA 5-10 81-82
Members: Bob Corbin; Dave Hanner.

CORBITT, Jerry
Singles: 7-inch
POLYDOR 3-5 71

CORBY, Chuck
(With the Chances; with Entrees)
Singles: 7-inch
CHESS 5-10 69
FEE BEE (219 "Honey Let Me Stay") 50-75 58
SONIC (118 "City of Strangers") 15-25
SOUND (717 "Man Loves Two") 15-25
VEEP (1235 "Happy Go Lucky") 10-20 66

CORBY, Doug
Singles: 7-inch
JC (121 "Heartbreak Train") 50-75 61

CORBY, Ron
Singles: 78 rpm
VIK (0262 "Destiny Is a Woman") 10-15 57
Singles: 7-inch
VIK (0262 "Destiny Is a Woman") 10-20 57
Also see FORD, Billy, & Thunderbirds / Ron Corby

CORBY & CHAMPAGNE
Singles: 7-inch
COMPASS 4-8 67

CORCORAN, Noreen
(With Nino Tempo)
Singles: 7-inch
VEE JAY (555 "Love Kitten") 5-10 63
Also see TEMPO, Nino

CORDEL, Pat
(With the Crescents "Later Known As the Elegants"; with Cherokee & Band; with Elegants)
Singles: 7-inch
CLUB (1011 "Darling Come Back") 250-500 56
MICHELE (503 "Darling Come Back") 100-200 59
VICTORY (1001 "Darling Come Back") 50-75 63
Also see ELEGANTS
Also see PICONE, Vito

CORDELL, Lucky
Singles: 7-inch
COTILLION 3-6 69
HAPPINESS 5-10
NICKEL 3-5

CORDELL, Phil
Singles: 7-inch
JANUS 3-6 70

CORDELL, Richie
Singles: 7-inch
AMY 10-15 64
RORI (707 "Tick Tock") 50-75 62
STREETCAR 5-10 65
Also see BASEMAN, M.R., & Symbols / Marty & Symbols
Also see GENTRY, Bo, & Ritchie Cordell
Also see INNER LITE

CORDELL, Sandy
Singles: 7-inch
SUNBIRD 5-10 60

CORDELLS
Singles: 7-inch
ADOR (6402 "Happy Time") 15-25 64
BARGAIN (5004 "The Beat of My Heart") 35-55 62
BULLSEYE (1017 "Please Don't Go") 50-75 58
CASKET 5-10

CORDELLS / Tabulations
Singles: 7-inch
SMITHVILLE (5766 "The Beat of My Heart") 5-8

Also see CORDELLS

CORDENES
Singles: 7-inch
CALWEST 15-25

CORDER FAMILY
Singles: 7-inch
KENT 3-5 73

CORDIALS
Singles: 7-inch
BETHLEHEM (3019 "I'm Not Crying Anymore") 20-30 62
PANIC (1000 "Blue Moon") 10-20 62

CORDIALS
Singles: 7-inch
FELSTED (8653 "Once in a Lifetime") 20-30 62
7 ARTS (707 "Dawn Is Almost Here") 50-75 61
Members: Bobby Pickett; Leonard Capizzi; Bill Capizzi; Ron Deltorto; Lou Toscano.
Also see PICKETT, Bobby
Also see STOMPERS

CORDIALS
(With the Cutups)
Singles: 7-inch
CORDIAL (1001 "I'm Ashamed") 75-125 60
REVEILLE (106 "Eternal Love") 100-200 62
Also see CARIANS

CORDIALS
("Vocal by Lee Dorian")
Singles: 7-inch
STAN (111 "A Fool in Love") 75-125 61

CORDIALS
Singles: 7-inch
WHIP (276 "Listen My Heart") 150-250 61

CORDIALS
Singles: 7-inch
LIBERTY (55784 "Oh How I Love Her") 15-25 65
LPs: 10/12-inch
CATAMOUNT (902 "Blue Eyed Soul") 10-20 67

CORDIALS
Singles: 7-inch
BUNDY 5-10 66

CORDIC, Rege
Singles: 7-inch
GATEWAY 4-8 64

CORDING, Henry
(With Big Mike & His Parisian Rockets)
Singles: 78 rpm
COLUMBIA 20-30 56
Singles: 7-inch
COLUMBIA (40762 "Hiccough Rock") 40-60 56

COR-DONS
(Cor-Don's; with Ron Butko & Orchestra)
Singles: 7-inch
ROWE (100 "Some Kinda Wonderful") 500-750 62

CORDOUROYS
Singles: 7-inch
HALE (100 "Forever Yours") 40-50 61

CORDOVANS
Singles: 7-inch
COLLECTABLES 3-4 81
JOHNSON (731 "My Heart") 10-20 60

CORDS
Singles: 7-inch
ATCO (6687 "I'll Do Just What I Want to Do") 10-20 69
RAKKI (101 "Termites") 10-20 63
Member: Billy Stull.

CORDS
Singles: 7-inch
CUCA (1512 "Cords Inc.") 20-30 66
CUCA (1513 "Ghost Power") 15-25 70
Member: Jim Bertler.

CORDUROYS
Singles: 7-inch
PLANET 4-8 67

COREA, Chick LP '76
Singles: 7-inch
POLYDOR 3-4 79
LPs: 10/12-inch
BLUE NOTE 8-12 75-78
ECM 5-10 75-80
ELEKTRA 5-8 83
PACIFIC JAZZ 5-8 81
POLYDOR 6-12 76-78
VERVE 8-10 76
W.B. 5-8 80-81
Also see HANCOCK, Herbie, & Chick Corea
Also see RETURN to FOREVER

COREY, Don, & Montereys
Singles: 7-inch
MONTEREY (106 "I Wish You Love") 200-300

COREY, Ed
Singles: 7-inch
MALA 4-8 62

COREY, Herb
Singles: 7-inch
TOP RANK 10-15 59

COREY, Jill P&R '54
Singles: 78 rpm
COLUMBIA 3-6 54-57
Singles: 7-inch
COLUMBIA 5-10 54-60
MERCURY 4-8 62
20TH FOX 5-10 64
EPs: 7-inch
COLUMBIA 8-12 55-57
LPs: 10/12-inch
COLUMBIA 15-25 56-57

COREY, Joey
Singles: 7-inch
MAGIC CARPET 5-10

COREY, John
Singles: 7-inch
VEE JAY (466 "Pollyanna") 20-30 62
(With the 4 Seasons.)
VEE JAY (514 "Hey Little Runaround")) 8-12 63
Also see 4 SEASONS

CORI, Troy
Singles: 7-inch
BINGO (1002 "Torture") 10-15 59
Also see CORY, Troy

CORIN, Terry
(With Her Boy Friends)
Singles: 7-inch
COLONY (110 "Dream Date") 20-30 60
MOHAWK (127 "My Ding Dong Heart") 15-25 60
Also see TERRY & MELLOS

CORKEY
Singles: 7-inch
1-2-3 4-6 69

CORLETTES
Singles: 7-inch
KANSOMA (02 "I Love You") 50-75 62
NITA (711 "Tears on My Pillow") 75-125 60s

CORLEY, Al P&R '85
Singles: 7-inch
MERCURY 3-4 85
Picture Sleeves
MERCURY 3-4 85

CORLEY, Bob P&R '55
Singles: 78 rpm
RCA 3-5 56
STARS 10-20 55
Singles: 7-inch
RCA 5-10 56
STARS 20-25 55

CORLINA, Ray
Singles: 7-inch
RICCIO 4-8 63

CORLISS, Mike
Singles: 7-inch
BOSS 3-5 72
LPs: 10/12-inch
NATURAL RESOURCES 8-10 72

CORMAN, Gene
LPs: 10/12-inch
THIMBLE 8-10 75

CORNBREAD & BISCUITS
(With Lea Lendon & Orchestra) P&R/R&B '60
Singles: 7-inch
ANNA (102 "The Big Time Spender") 25-50 59
(This is the Maske disc with an Anna label sticker applied to each side, covering "Maske.")
MASKE (102 "The Big Time Spender") 15-25 60

CORNBREAD & JERRY
Singles: 7-inch
LIBERTY (55322 "Lil' Ole Me") 10-15 61
Member: Jerry Smith.
Also see SMITH, Jerry

CORNELIUS, Don
Singles: 7-inch
SOUL TRAIN 3-5 75

CORNELIUS, Helen C&W '76
Singles: 7-inch
AMERI-CAN 3-4 83
CAPITOL 3-5 71
COLUMBIA 3-5 73
ELEKTRA 3-4 81
RCA 3-5 76-79
Also see BROWN, Jim Ed, & Helen Cornelius

CORNELIUS, Ron
LPs: 10/12-inch
POLYDOR 8-10 71

CORNELIUS & CAROL: see ENTERTAINMENT UNLIMITED

CORNELIUS BROTHERS & SISTER ROSE P&R/R&B '71
Singles: 7-inch
PLATINUM 8-12 70
U.A. 3-5 70-74
LPs: 10/12-inch
PICKWICK 5-10 76
U.A. 10-15 72-76
Members: Ed Cornelius; Carter Cornelius; Rose Cornelius.

CORNELL
Singles: 7-inch
BOSSSOUND 3-4 80

CORNELL, Don P&R '50
Singles: 78 rpm
CORAL 5-10 52-57
RCA 5-10
Singles: 7-inch
ABC-PAR 3-6 65
CORAL 5-15 52-57
DOT 4-8 59-60
JAYBEE 3-5 69
JUBILEE 3-6 62
SIGNATURE 4-8 59-60
20TH FOX 3-6 64
EPs: 7-inch
CORAL 5-10 54-56
LPs: 10/12-inch
ABC-PAR 8-12 66
CORAL 15-25 54-57
DOT 10-15 59
MOVIETONE 5-10 66
SIGNATURE 10-15 59
VOCALION 8-15 59
Also see KAYE, Sammy

CORNELL, Don, & Teresa Brewer
(With Jack Pleis Orchestra)
Singles: 78 rpm
CORAL 4-6 52
Singles: 7-inch
CORAL (60829 "You'll Never Get Away") 8-12 52
Also see BREWER, Teresa
Also see PLEIS, Jack, & His Orchestra

CORNELL, Don, Johnny Desmond & Alan Dale P&R '53
Singles: 78 rpm
CORAL 3-6 53
Singles: 7-inch
CORAL 5-10 53
EPs: 7-inch
CORAL 5-10 54
Also see CORNELL, Don
Also see DALE, Alan
Also see DESMOND, Johnny

CORNELL, Doug
(With the Hot Rods; Douglas Cornell)
Singles: 7-inch
BRUNSWICK 10-15 58
DEB (1000 "Hong Kong Rock") 15-25 59

CORNELL, Jackie
Singles: 7-inch
LIONEL 3-5 70

CORNELL SISTERS
Singles: 7-inch
LABEL 5-10 59

CORNELLS
Singles: 7-inch
GAREX 15-25 62-63
LPs: 10/12-inch
GAREX (100 "Beach Bound") 40-60 63
Members: Bob Linkletter; Peter Young; James O'Keefe; Charles Cornell; Tom Crumpler.

CORNER, Eddie, & Discords
Singles: 7-inch
SMOKE (101 "World of Make Believe") 20-30 59

CORNER BOYS R&B '69
Singles: 7-inch
NEPTUNE 4-6 69
Members: Victor Drayton; Jerry Akines; Reginald Turner; Ernie Brooks; Johnny Bellman.
Also see FORMATIONS

CORNERS FOUR
Singles: 7-inch
PHILIPS 10-20 67

CORNERSTONES
Singles: 7-inch
METROBEAT (4447 "You Rule Me") 30-40 67

CORNERSTONES
Singles: 7-inch
LIBERTY 4-6 69-70

CORNICHE
Singles: 7-inch
WINDSONG 3-4 79
Picture Sleeves
WINDSONG 3-6 79

CORNISH, Chuck
Singles: 7-inch
WHITE CLIFFS 4-8 67

CORNISH, Gene
(With the Unbeatables)
Singles: 7-inch
DAWN (550 "Do the Capri") 20-30 64
DAWN (557 "I Want to Be a Beetle") 25-35 64
VASSAR 15-20 62
Also see FOTOMAKER
Also see RASCALS
Also see UNBEATABLES

CORNOR, Randy C&W '75
Singles: 7-inch
ABC/DOT 3-5 75-77
CHERRY 3-5 78
LPs: 10/12-inch
ABC/DOT 6-12 76

CORONA
Singles: 7-inch
REGINA 8-12

CORONADOS
Singles: 7-inch
COLUMBIA 5-10 59-60

CORONADOS
Singles: 7-inch
PEERLESS 4-8 61
RIC 5-10 61

CORONADOS
Singles: 7-inch
PURDY 4-8 64
TODD 4-8 64

CORONADOS
Singles: 7-inch
BRIGHT STAR (157 "You Can Do Me Some Good") 8-12 67
Members: John Dandsby; Ann Dandsby; Glenn; Charles.

CORONADOS
Singles: 7-inch
PARLIAMENT 5-10 67

CORONADOS
Singles: 7-inch
JUBILEE 4-6 68-70
LPs: 10/12-inch
JUBILEE 10-15 69

CORONADOS
Singles: 7-inch
ARLINGWOOD (6467 "Florida Sun") 20-30

CORONAS
Singles: 7-inch
CORONA 5-8 65

CORONETS R&B '53
(With Sax Mallard & Combo)
Singles: 78 rpm
CHESS 25-50 53
GROOVE 25-50 55
Singles: 7-inch
CHESS (1549 "Nadine") 150-250 53
(Silver top label with chess pieces.)
CHESS (1549 "Nadine") 10-20
(Blue label.)
CHESS (1553 "It Would Be Heavenly") 250-350 53
(Black vinyl. Silver top label with chess pieces.)
CHESS (1553 "It Would Be Heavenly") 10-20 53
(Black vinyl. Blue label.)
CHESS (1553 "It Would Be Heavenly") 750-1000 53
(Red vinyl.)
GROOVE (0114 "I Love You More") 200-300 55
GROOVE (0116 "Hush") 200-300 55
Members: Charles Carothers; Lester Russaw; George Lewis; William Griggs; Sam Griggs; Babby Ward.
Also see MALLARD, Sax

CORONETS
(With the Bill Reese Quintet)
Singles: 78 rpm
STERLING 50-100 55
Singles: 7-inch
STERLING (903 "Don't Deprive Me") 150-250 55

CORPORATE BODY
Singles: 7-inch
MGM 3-4 69
MUSIC FACTORY 3-5 68
LPs: 10/12-inch
MGM 10-12 69

CORPORATE IMAGE
Singles: 7-inch
MGM 4-8 66

CORPORATION
Singles: 7-inch
MUSICOR (1418 "Candida") 5-10 68

CORPORATION LP '69
Singles: 7-inch
AGE OF AQUARIUS (1496 "You Make Me Feel So Good") 10-20 69
CAPITOL (2467 "Highway") 10-15 69
CUCA (1496 "You Make Me Feel Good") 10-15 68
LPs: 10/12-inch
AGE of AQUARIUS (4150 "The Corporation") 30-50 70
AGE of AQUARIUS (4250 "Hassels in My Mind") 20-30 69
CAPITOL (175 "The Corporation") 20-30 69
Members: Danny Peil; Ken Berdoll; John Kondos; Nicholas Kondos; Pat McCarthy; Gerald Smith.
Also see PEIL, Danny

CORPS
Singles: 7-inch
REDD HEDD 15-20 71

CORPUS
LPs: 10/12-inch
ACORN (1001 "Creation of a Child") 100-150 71
Members: William Grate; James Castilla; Richard Deleon; Gilbert Pena.

CORRADO, Arnie
Singles: 7-inch
COLUMBIA 4-8 67
DATE 4-8 66-67

CORREIA, Djalma
Singles: 7-inch
RCA 3-5 77

CORRELL, Dennis
Singles: 7-inch
A&M 3-5 74

CORRELL, Denny
LPs: 10/12-inch
MARANTHA 5-10 79
MYRRH 5-10 80-82

CORRENTE, Sal
Singles: 7-inch
ROULETTE (4673 "Run Run Run") 8-12 66
Also see DIALS
Also see LAW, Johnny, Four
Also see LITTLE DAVID
Also see 1929 DEPRESSION
Also see TRACES

CORRESPONDENTS
Singles: 7-inch
SUNSHINE (803 "Not So Great Debate") 4-6 80

CORRIDORS
(Corridor's)
Singles: 7-inch
WILDCAT (57 "Dear One") 15-25 63
ZONE (2160 "Dear One") 50-75 59

CORSAIRS
Singles: 78 rpm
COLUMBIA (38700 "Four Letters") 5-10 50
COLUMBIA (38715 "Jonathan") 5-10 50

CORSAIRS
Singles: 7-inch
HY-TONE (110 "Goodbye Darling") 1000-2000 58

CORSAIRS P&R '61
(Featuring Jay "Bird" Uzzell)
Singles: 7-inch
CHESS (1808 "Smokey Places") 8-12 61
CHESS (1818 "I'll Take You Home") 8-12 62
ERIC 3-4 78
SMASH (1715 "Time Waits") 10-15 61
TUFF (1 "The Ring") 15-25 61
TUFF (375 "Save a Little Monkey") 5-10 64
TUFF (1808 "Smokey Places") 10-15 61
TUFF (1818 "I'll Take You Home") 10-15 62
(First issue.)
TUFF (1830 "While") 15-25 62
TUFF (1840 "At the Stroke of Midnight") 10-15 62
TUFF (1847 "Stormy") 10-15 63
TUFF (3027 "Time Waits") 10-15 60s
Members: Jay "Bird" Uzzell; "King" Moe Uzzell; James Uzzell; George Wooten.
Also see McNEIL, Landy

CORSELLS
Singles: 7-inch
HUDSON 4-8 64

CORSO, Bob
Singles: 7-inch
PHILIPS 4-8 61-62

CORT, Bob, Skiffle Group
Singles: 78 rpm
LONDON 5-10 56
Singles: 7-inch
LONDON 10-15 56

CORTEZ, Alberto
LPs: 10/12-inch
TOLLIE 15-20 64

CORTEZ, Dave, & Moon People
Singles: 7-inch
SPEED 3-6 69
TETRAGRAMMATON 3-6 69

CORTEZ, Dave "Baby" P&R/R&B '59
(With the Moon People; Baby Cortez)
Singles: 78 rpm
CLOCK (1006 "You're the Girl") 15-25 58
CLOCK (1009 "The Happy Organ") 50-75 59
Singles: 7-inch
ABC 3-4 74
ALL PLATINUM 3-5 72
ARGO 4-8 64
CHESS 4-8 63
CLOCK 10-20 58-62
COLLECTABLES 3-4 81
EMIT 5-10 62
ERIC 3-4 73
FIRE 5-10 60
HI OLDIES 4-6 77
JULIA (1829 "Rinky Dink") 15-25 62
OKEH (7100 series) 15-25 58
OKEH (7200 series) 10-15 64
ROULETTE 4-8 65-68
SOUND 3-5 71
SPEED 3-5
T-NECK 3-6 69
WINLEY 4-8 62
EPs: 7-inch
CLOCK (4039 " Dave 'Baby' Cortez & His Happy Organ") 20-30 61
RCA (EPA-4342 "Dave 'Baby' Cortez & His Happy Organ") 20-30 59
(Monaural.)
RCA (ESP-4342 "Dave 'Baby' Cortez & His Happy Organ") 35-50 59
(Stereo.)
LPs: 10/12-inch
CHESS 25-30 62
CLOCK 25-35 60-63
CORONET 10-15 60s
CROWN 15-20 63
DESIGN 10-15 60s
METRO 10-20 65

RCA (LPM-2099 "Dave 'Baby' Cortez & His Happy Organ") ... 25-35 59
(Monaural.)
RCA (LSP-2099 "Dave `Baby' Cortez & His Happy Organ") ... 35-50 59
(Stereo.)
ROULETTE ... 15-20 65-66
Also see BLAZERS
Also see CLOWNEY, David, Band
Also see ISLEY BROTHERS & Dave "Baby" Cortez
Also see JESTERS
Also see PARAGONS
Also see PEARLS
Also see VALENTINES

CORTEZ, Dave "Baby" / Jerry's House Rockers
LPs: 10/12-inch
CROWN ... 10-20 63
Also see CORTEZ, Dave "Baby"

CORTEZ & ENTERTAINERS
Singles: 7-inch
YOUR TOWN (711 "Life") ... 15-25 60s

CORVAIRS
(With Little Joe Williams; with Ross Aldrich & Orchestra)
Singles: 7-inch
CLOCK (1037 "Love Her So") ... 25-35 61
COLLECTABLES ... 3-4 81
CROWN (004 "Darlin'") ... 15-25 61
CUB (9065 "Yeah Yeah") ... 10-20 60
You") ... 20-30 63
TWIN (1001 "Gee Whiz") ... 150-250 62
(Red label. Reads "Twin Records" at top.)
TWIN (1001 "Gee Whiz") ... 50-75 62
(Blue label. Reads only "TWIN" at top.)
TWIN (19671 "I Need You So") ... 50-75 62
Also see JIVE FIVE
Also see SMITH, Bill, & & Corvairs

CORVAIRS
Singles: 7-inch
COLUMBIA (43603 "Swinging Little Government") ... 10-15 66
COLUMBIA (43861 "Ain't No Soul") ... 10-20 66
COMET (2145 "True True Love") ... 20-25 62
(Black label.)
COMET (2145 "True True Love") ... 10-15 62
(Yellow label.)
LEOPARD (5005 "Don't Wanna Be Without You") ... 20-30 63
SYLVIA (5003 "A Victim of Her Charms") ... 8-12 60s
Members: Edward Alston; Nelson Shields; Joe Shepard; Ronald Judge; Prince McKnight; Bill Fiason; Edgar Brown
Also see LEADERS

CORVAIRS / Valroys
EPs: 7-inch
MAGIC CARPET ... 5-10

CORVAIRS
Singles: 7-inch
HICKORY ... 4-8 67

CORVANS
("Vocal By Bobby Arsena")
Singles: 7-inch
CABOT (131 "Sleepless Nights") ... 35-50 59

CORVELLS
(With the Royalteens)
Singles: 7-inch
ABC-PAR (10324 "Take My Love") ... 100-150 62
BLAST (203 "The Bells") ... 100-150 61
CUB (9122 "The Joke's on Me") ... 15-25 63
LIDO (509 "We Made a Vow") ... 250-350 57
(First issue.)
LU PINE (104 "He's So Fine") ... 10-20 62
TIP TOP (509 "We Made a Vow") ... 100-200 57

CORVELLS
Singles: 7-inch
CENTURY (19805 "Dune Buggy Ride") ... 15-20
Picture Sleeves
CENTURY (19805 "Dune Buggy Ride") ... 20-30

CORVETS
Singles: 7-inch
ABC-PAR (9891 "String Band Hop") ... 15-25 58

CORVETS
(With Vince Catalano & Orchestra)
Singles: 7-inch
LAUREL (1012 "So Long") ... 25-40 60
20TH FOX (223 "Only Last Night") ... 15-25 60
WAY-OUT (101 "Lenora") ... 75-100 58
Members: Vince Zeccola; George DeAlfonso; Jules Hahn; Joe Lento; Vance Hallup Hank Shuh.
Also see LYNN, Sandy

CORVETS
Singles: 7-inch
SURE (1003 "I'm Pleadin'") ... 100-200 60

CORVETS
Singles: 7-inch
RE-CAR ... 8-12 64
SOMA (1164 "Wallin' Wallin'") ... 75-125 61
SOMA (1425 "You Don't Want Me") ... 10-20 65

CORVETTES
Singles: 7-inch
CORVETTE (1000 "Corvette") ... 40-60 60

CORVETTES & TODDETTES
Singles: 7-inch
DUTCH (1061 "Today") ... 15-25 61
FAN JR. (1000 "Jeri") ... 15-25 61
Members: Shane Todd; Tom Van Maren; Bob Gugel; Gene Clifford; George Moll; Bruce Benson; Jim Bisbee.
Also see TODD, Shane

CORVETTES
Singles: 7-inch
DOT ... 5-10 69
Members: John Ware; John London; Linda Ronstadt.
Also see NESMITH, Mike
Also see RONSTADT, Linda

CORVETTES
Singles: 7-inch
BEE DEE (102 "Tears Are Free") ... 25-35 60s
BITCHEN (100 "Surf Don't Walk") ... 10-20 60s

CORVETTES
(With Bill Duzan)
Singles: 7-inch
DUNCAN (401 "Janice") ... 20-30 60s

CORVETTS
Singles: 7-inch
SHERATON (201 "In the Chapel") ... 75-125 61

CORVETTS
Singles: 7-inch
MOON (100 "I'm Going to Cry") ... 500-750 59
Member: Arthur Conley.
Also see ARTHUR & CORVETS
Also see CONLEY, Arthur

CORVETTS
Singles: 7-inch
TONE CRAFT (1009 "Voodoo Baby") ... 250-500 60s

CORWIN, Roy
Singles: 7-inch
HOB (111 "The World Is a Better Place") ... 25-35 61

CORWINS
Singles: 7-inch
GILMAR (222 "Little Star") ... 10-20 57
Also see MARKS, Steve / Jack Richards / Corwins

CORY
(Cory Braverman)
Singles: 7-inch
PHANTOM ... 3-5 76-77
LPs: 10/12-inch
PHANTOM ... 6-10 76

CORY, Troy
Singles: 78 rpm
SPECIALTY (620 "Yearning") ... 20-30 58
Singles: 7-inch
HIGHLAND (1030 "Teeny Weeny Wiggle") ... 8-12 62
MERCURY (71548 "Little Pink Toe") ... 10-15 60
SPECIALTY (620 "Yearning") ... 15-25 58
SQUARE BLOCK ... 3-5 72
Picture Sleeves
SQUARE BLOCK ... 3-5 72
Also see CORI, Troy

CORYELL, Larry *LP '69*
LPs: 10/12-inch
ARISTA ... 5-10 76
VANGUARD ... 10-15 69
Also see ELEVENTH HOUR / ELVENTH HOUSE
Also see MOUZON, Alphonse, & Larry Croyell

COSBY, Bill *LP '64*
Singles: 12-inch
MOTOWN (110 "Super Special for Radio") ... 5-10 82
(Promotional issue only.)
Singles: 7-inch
CAPITOL ... 3-5 76-78
UNI ... 3-6 69-70
W.B. ... 3-5 65-67
EPs: 7-inch
W.B. (274 "A Taste of Cosby") ... 5-10
(Promotional issue only.)
LPs: 10/12-inch
CAPITOL ... 5-10 76-78
COLUMBIA (40270 "Music from the Bill Cosby Show") ... 5-10 86
(Featuring Grover Washington Jr.)
GEFFEN ... 5-10 86
MCA ... 5-10 73
MOTOWN ... 5-10 82
PARTEE ... 5-10
TETRAGRAMMATON ... 6-10 69
UNI ... 5-10 69-72
W.B. (Except 249) ... 10-15 64-70
W.B. (249 "Best of Bill Cosby") ... 15-20 69
(Promotional issue only.)
Also see ROSS, Diana, & Bill Cosby / Diana Ross & Jackson Five
Also see WASHINGTON, Grover, Jr.

COSBY, Bill, & Ozzie Davis
LPs: 10/12-inch
BLACK FORUM ... 8-12 72
Also see COSBY, Bill

COSGREN, Wally
Singles: 7-inch
WABR (21784 "Blues, Stay Away") ... 50-100

COSHART, Terry
(Tiny Coshart)
Singles: 7-inch
COULEE (105 "Why") ... 15-25 64
COULEE (125 "Double Life") ... 10-20 68

COSMETIC
Singles: 12-inch
GRAMAVISION ... 4-6 83
Member: Jamaaladeen Tacuma.

COSMETICS
Singles: 7-inch
I.R.S. ... 3-4 84
LPs: 10/12-inch
I.R.S. ... 5-10 84

COSMIC BROTHERHOOD
Singles: 7-inch
A&M ... 4-6 69

COSMIC RAYS
(With Le Sun Ra & Arkestra; with Sun Ra & Arkestra)
Singles: 7-inch
SATURN (222 "Bye Bye") ... 1000-2000 60
SATURN (401 "Dreaming") ... 1000-2000 60

COSMIC ROCK SHOW
Singles: 7-inch
BLITZ (464 "Rising Sun") ... 50-75 68

COSMO
(With the Carnations)
Singles: 7-inch
JAN ... 15-25 58
SOUND STAGE 7 (2504 "Small Town Gossip") ... 8-10 63
SOUND STAGE 7 (2520 "You Gotta Dance") ... 8-10 64
TILT (787 "I'm a Little Mixed Up") ... 30-50 62
TILT (789 "Just Words") ... 15-25 62
Also see CARNATIONS

COSMO, Tony
Singles: 7-inch
FLING ... 5-10 60
ROULETTE ... 5-10 60
VANN ... 5-10 61
Picture Sleeves
FLING ... 10-20 60

COSMO WAVE & CADETS
Singles: 7-inch
EPIC (50811 "Star Trekking") ... 3-5 79
EPIC (50812 "Star Trekking") ... 3-5 79

COSMOLOGY
LPs: 10/12-inch
VANGUARD ... 8-10 77

COSMOS
Singles: 7-inch
BIG "L" (502 "Angel, Angel") ... 75-100

COSSEN, Ray, Jr.
Singles: 7-inch
MUSICOR (1246 "Try Some Soul") ... 10-20 67

COSTA, Buddy
Singles: 7-inch
PYRAMID ... 20-30

COSTA, Don, Orchestra *P&R '59*
(With the Mello-Larks)
Singles: 78 rpm
ABC-PAR ... 4-8 56-57
EPIC ... 4-8 55
ESSEX ... 4-8 55
Singles: 7-inch
ABC-PAR ... 5-10 56-57
COLUMBIA ... 4-6 62-63
DCP ... 4-6 64-65
EPIC ... 5-10 55
ESSEX ... 5-10 55
JAMIE ... 5-10 59
MGM ... 4-6 66-72
MERCURY ... 3-5 68
U.A. ... 5-10 59-62
VERVE ... 3-5 67
Picture Sleeves
U.A. (234 "Never on Sunday") ... 10-15 60
VERVE ... 4-8 67
LPs: 10/12-inch
ABC-PAR ... 15-30 56-61
COLUMBIA ... 10-20 62-63
DCP ... 5-10 64-65
HARMONY ... 5-10 65
MERCURY ... 5-10 68-69
U.A. ... 10-20 59-62
VERVE ... 5-10 67
Also see ANKA, Paul
Also see BARTEL, Lou
Also see COOLBREEZERS
Also see DE CASTRO SISTERS
Also see GALLOP, Frank
Also see HAWKINS, Dolores
Also see MANN, Gloria
Also see READ, Bernadine

COSTA, Joey
(Joe Costa)
Singles: 78 rpm
RCA ... 4-8 53
Singles: 7-inch
DOT ... 4-8 62
LOCKET ... 8-12
MURBO ... 4-8 65
RCA ... 5-10 53-64
W.B. ... 4-8 62-63

COSTANDINOS, Alec R. *LP '78*
(With the Syncophonic Orchestra)
Singles: 7-inch
CASABLANCA ... 3-4 79
LPs: 10/12-inch
CASABLANCA ... 5-10 78-79

COSTANZO, Greg
Singles: 7-inch
TAXI ... 3-4 81

COSTANZO, Jack
Singles: 7-inch
GNP (100 series) ... 8-12 57
GNP (400 series) ... 4-8 72
LPs: 10/12-inch
LIBERTY ... 8-15

COSTELLO, Danny
Singles: 7-inch
CORAL ... 5-10 59-60
ESCAPADE ... 4-8 63

COSTELLO, Elvis *LP '77*
(With the Attractions; Costello Show)
Singles: 12-inch
COLUMBIA ... 5-15 83-85
Singles: 7-inch
CBS (Black vinyl) ... 3-6 79
CBS (Red vinyl) ... 15-25 79
COLUMBIA ... 3-6 77-86
W.B. ... 3-5 89
Promotional Singles
COLUMBIA ... 5-15 77-86
Picture Sleeves
COLUMBIA (04502 "Everyday I Write the Book") ... 3-6 83
COLUMBIA (10919 "Accidents Will Happen") ... 15-20 78
(Promotional issue only.)
COLUMBIA (60519 "Watching Your Step") ... 4-6 81
W.B. (22981 "Veronica") ... 3-5 89
EPs: 7-inch
COLUMBIA (529 "Live at Hollywood High") ... 10-20 78
(Bonus EP. Included with the LP *Armed Forces*.)
COLUMBIA (1171 "Elvis Costello & the Attractions") ... 25-35 78
(Promotional issue only.)
COLUMBIA (11251 "I Can't Stand Up for Falling Down") ... 10-20 80
COLUMBIA (11251 "I Can't Stand Up for Falling Down") ... 20-30 80
(White label. Promotional issue only.)
LPs: 10/12-inch
COLUMBIA (30000 series, except 35709) ... 8-12 77-86
COLUMBIA (35709 "Armed Forces") ... 15-25 79
(Includes the bonus EP *Live at Hollywood High*.)
COLUMBIA (35709 "Armed Forces") ... 8-12 79
(Without *Live at Hollywood High* EP.)
COLUMBIA (35709 "Armed Forces") ... 30-40 79
(Colored vinyl.)
COLUMBIA/COSTELLO (35331 "This Year's Model") ... 20-30 78
COLUMBIA (40000 series, except 48157) ... 5-8 85-86
COLUMBIA (48157 "Imperial Bedroom") ... 30-40 82
(Half-speed mastered.)
W.B. ... 5-10 89-91
Promotional LPs
COLUMBIA ("My Aim Is True"/"This Year's Model") ... 125-150 79
(Picture disc. No number given.)
COLUMBIA (529 "Live at Hollywood High") ... 30-45 79
COLUMBIA (958 "Tom Snyder Interview") ... 25-35 81
COLUMBIA (1318 "Almost Blue") ... 25-35 81
COLUMBIA (35709 "Armed Forces") ... 20-25 79
(With programming sticker on cover.)
COLUMBIA/COSTELLO (847 "Taking Liberties") ... 30-35 80
KING BISCUIT FLOWER HOUR (For July 13, 1980) ... 75-125
WESTWOOD ONE ("Off the Record") ... 40-60
Session: Daryl Hall; Paul McCartney.
Also see CLIFF, Jimmy, Elvis Costello & Attractions
Also see HALL, Daryl
Also see HIATT, John
Also see McCARTNEY, Paul
Also see NICK & ELVIS
Also see WHEELER, Caron

COSTELLO, Jack
Singles: 78 rpm
SILHOUETTE ... 4-6 56
Singles: 7-inch
SILHOUETTE ... 8-12 56

COSTELLO, Lois
Singles: 7-inch
TEMPUS ... 5-10 59
VARIETY ... 5-10 60

COSTELLO SISTERS
Singles: 7-inch
SOUND ... 3-5

COSTER, Tom
LPs: 10/12-inch
FANTASY ... 5-10 81-82

COSYTONES
Singles: 78 rpm
MELBA ... 25-35 56
Singles: 7-inch
MELBA ("Speak to Me of Love") ... 25-50 56
WILLOW (1001 "I'm Alone") ... 20-40 58
Members: Windsor King; Kathy King; Ralph King; Eloise King; Mitch McPhee.
Also see ROYAL SONS QUINTET

COTA, Joe
Singles: 7-inch
LOCKET ... 4-8

COTILLIONS
Singles: 7-inch
ALLEY ... 10-15 62
Member: Larry Donn.
Also see DONN, Larry

COTILLIONS
Singles: 7-inch
ASCOT (2105 "What Kind of Day Has It Been") ... 15-25 62

COTILLIONS
Singles: 7-inch
ABC-PAR ... 4-8 63
ALLEY ... 10-15 62

COTNER, Carl
Singles: 7-inch
CHALLENGE ... 5-10 60

COTT, Gerry
Singles: 12-inch
EPIC ... 4-6 83

COTTON
Singles: 7-inch
DAKAR ... 3-5 72

COTTON, Gene *P&R '74*
Singles: 7-inch
ABC ... 3-5 75-77
ARIOLA AMERICA ... 3-5 77-79
GENE COTTON ("Child of Peace") ... 4-6 81
(No actual label name or number. A gift to radio stations. With explanatory insert.)
KNOLL ... 3-4 81-82
MYRRH ... 3-5 74
LPs: 10/12-inch
ABC ... 8-10 76-77
ACCORD ... 5-10 83
ARIOLA AMERICA ... 5-10 78-79
BUDDAH ... 8-10 74-75
CAPITOL ... 8-10 71
IMPACT ... 15-20
KNOLL ... 5-10 81-82
MYRRH ... 8-10 73

COTTON, Gene, & Kim Carnes *P&R '78*
Singles: 7-inch
ARIOLA AMERICA ... 3-4 78
Also see CARNES, Kim
Also see COTTON, Gene

COTTON, James *LP '67*
(James Cotton Blues Band; with Matt "Guitar" Murphy & Luther Tucker)
Singles: 12-inch
ERECT ... 4-6 82
Singles: 78 rpm
SUN (199 "My Baby") ... 200-300 54
SUN (206 "Cotton Crop Blues") ... 200-300 54
Singles: 7-inch
BACKROOM ... 4-6
BUDDAH ... 3-5 75
LOMA ... 10-15 66
SUN (199 "My Baby") ... 400-600 54
SUN (206 "Cotton Crop Blues") ... 550-650 54
VERVE/FOLKWAYS ... 4-8 67
VERVE/FORECAST ... 4-8 67-69
LPs: 10/12-inch
ACCORD ... 5-10 83
ALLIGATOR ... 5-10 84
ANTONE'S ... 5-10 88
BUDDAH (Except 5661) ... 10-15 74-76
BUDDAH (5661 "Live and on the Move") ... 20-25 76
CAPITOL ... 10-12 71
ERECT ... 5-10 82
INTERMEDIA ... 5-10 84
VANGUARD ... 10-15 68
VERVE/FOLKWAYS ... 10-20 67
VERVE/FORECAST ... 10-15 66-69
Also see HOWLIN' WOLF
Also see WATERS, Muddy

COTTON, James, Carey Bell, Junior Wells, & Billy Branch
LPs: 10/12-inch
ALLIGATOR (4790 "Harp Attack") ... 5-10 90
Also see BELL, Carey
Also see WELLS, Junior

COTTON, Josie *P&R/LP '82*
Singles: 12-inch
BOMP ... 5-10 80
ELEKTRA (11538 "Johnny Are You Queer") ... 5-10 82
Singles: 7-inch
ELEKTRA (Black vinyl) ... 3-4 82-84
ELEKTRA (Colored vinyl) ... 5-10 82
WEA (79292 "Johnny Are You Queer") ... 3-5 82
Picture Sleeves
ELEKTRA ... 3-4 82-84
WEA (79292 "Johnny Are You Queer") ... 3-5 82
LPs: 10/12-inch
ELEKTRA ... 5-10 82

COTTON, Little Willie
Singles: 78 rpm
SWING TIME (319 "Gonna Shake It Up and Go") ... 20-30 52

COTTON, Loyce
Singles: 7-inch
AQUARIUS ... 3-5

COTTON, Paul
LPs: 10/12-inch
SISPA (414 "Changing Horses") ... 5-8 90
Also see POCO

COTTON, Sammy
Singles: 7-inch
SAVOY ... 5-10 61

COTTON, Sylvester
Singles: 78 rpm
MODERN (655 "Ugly Woman Blues") ... 20-40 49
SENSATION (7000 "Ugly Woman Blues") ... 75-100 49
Also see HOOKER, John Lee

COTTON CANDY
(Leah Kunkel)
Singles: 7-inch
DUNHILL ... 4-8 69
Also see KUNKEL, Leah

COTTON, LLOYD & CHRISTIAN P&R '75
Singles: 7-inch
20TH FOX ... 3-5 75-76
LPs: 10/12-inch
20TH FOX ... 8-12 75-76
Members: Darryl Cotton; Michael Lloyd; Chris Christian.
Also see CHRISTIAN, Chris
Also see LLOYD, Michael

COTTONMOUTH
Singles: 7-inch
MUSICOR ... 3-6 71
RCA ... 3-5 77

COTTONWOOD
Singles: 7-inch
ABC ... 3-5 71
LPs: 10/12-inch
ABC ... 8-10 71
Member: Doug Phillips.
Also see PHILLIPS, Doug, & New Concepts

COUCH, C.C.
Singles: 7-inch
EPIC ... 3-4 81

COUCH, Orville C&W '62
Singles: 7-inch
CUSTOM ... 6-10 62
DERBY
MERCURY ... 5-10 60
MONUMENT ... 4-8 66
VEE JAY ... 4-8 62-64
LPs: 10/12-inch
VEE JAY ... 15-25 64

COUCH, Stanley
LPs: 10/12-inch
FLYING DUTCHMAN ... 10-12 69

COUCHOIS LP '79
Singles: 7-inch
W.B. ... 3-4 79-80
LPs: 10/12-inch
W.B. ... 5-10 79-80

COUGAR, John: see MELLENCAMP, John Cougar

COUGAR, Johnny
Singles: 7-inch
MCA ... 3-5 76
LPs: 10/12-inch
MCA ... 8-10 76

COUGHLIN, Jack Lincoln
EPs: 7-inch
BARON (503 "It'll Be Me") ... 5-10
(Colored vinyl.)

COULSON, Dean
LPs: 10/12-inch
SIRE ... 8-10 73

COULSON, Dennis
LPs: 10/12-inch
ELECTRA ... 8-10 73

COULSON, Dick, & Letter O
LPs: 10/12-inch
POLYDOR ... 5-10 83

COULSTON, Jerry
Singles: 7-inch
CHRISTY (112 "Cave Man Hop") .50-100 59
CHRISTY (119 "Go Ask Your Mama") ... 100-150 59
CHRISTY (131 "Bon-Bon Baby") .50-100 60

COULTAS, Michael, & Quick Change
Singles: 7-inch
STARGEM ... 3-4 82

COULTER, Clifford R&B '80
Singles: 7-inch
COLUMBIA ... 3-4 80
LPs: 10/12-inch
COLUMBIA ... 5-10 80

COULTERS C&W '83
Singles: 7-inch
DOLPHIN ... 3-4 83
EPIC ... 3-5 80

COUNT & COLONY
Singles: 7-inch
PA-GO-GO (121 "Can't You See") 15-25 66
SSS INT'L ... 8-12 67

COUNT BASIE: see BASIE, Count

COUNT FERRELL
Singles: 7-inch
ASTRA (1017 "Wizard of Ahs") ... 4-8 65

COUNT FIVE P&R/LP '66
Singles: 7-inch
APEX (77019 "Psychotic Reaction") ... 10-20 66
(Canadian.)
DOUBLE-SHOT (104 "Psychotic Reaction") ... 10-15 66
(Label name at top.)
DOUBLE-SHOT (104 "Psychotic Reaction") ... 5-10 66
(Label name on left side.)
DOUBLE-SHOT (106 thru 141) ... 5-15 66-69
LPs: 10/12-inch
DOUBLE-SHOT (1001 "Psychotic Reaction") ... 25-35 66
(Monaural.)
DOUBLE-SHOT (5001 "Psychotic Reaction") ... 30-40 66
(Stereo.)
PERFORMANCE (398 "Psychotic Reaction") ... 8-10

COUNT 5
Singles: 7-inch
LES COUNTS (3447 "Count 5") ... 20-30 60s

COUNT V
Singles: 7-inch
LEMCO ... 10-20

COUNT FLOYD
LPs: 10/12-inch
RCA ... 5-10 82-83

COUNT HASTINGS: see HASTINGS, Count

COUNT LORRY & BITERS
Singles: 7-inch
DRAGON (4406 "Frankenstein Stomp") ... 5-10 65

COUNT POPEYE
Singles: 7-inch
KENT ... 4-8 65

COUNT ROCKIN' SYDNEY
(With His Dukes)
Singles: 7-inch
BOLD ... 5-10
GOLDBAND ... 8-10 65-66
Also see ROCKIN' SYDNEY

COUNT VICTORS
Singles: 7-inch
CORAL ... 4-8 62
RUST ... 5-10 61
Also see HARRISON, Danny

COUNT YATES
Singles: 7-inch
REGIS ... 3-5

COUNTDOWN 5
(Countdown Five)
Singles: 7-inch
CINEMA (1310 "Uncle Kirby") ... 10-20 67
CINEMA (1326 "Maybe I'll Love You") ... 10-20 67
COBBLESTONE (745 "Money Man") ... 10-20 69
PIC 1 (123 "Shout") ... 15-25 65
PIC 1 (131 "My Own Style") ... 15-25 66
TOUCAN (1 "Uncle Kirby") ... 15-25 67
Picture Sleeves
TOUCAN (1 "Uncle Kirby") ... 25-35 67

COUNTDOWNS
Singles: 7-inch
IMAGE ... 8-12 61
RORI ... 8-12 62
SUMIT (0004 "Lost Horizon") ... 20-30 63

COUNTDOWNS
Singles: 7-inch
BEAR (1968 "You Know I Do") ... 50-75 66
FIJI (691 "You Know I Do") ... 50-75 66

COUNTDOWNS
Singles: 7-inch
LINK (101 "I Can't Explain") ... 20-30 66
LINK (102 "Don't Take My Dreams") ... 10-15 66
Picture Sleeves
LINK (101 "I Can't Explain") ... 35-50 66

COUNTDOWNS
Singles: 7-inch
ANDERSON (110 "Do It") ... 10-20 66

COUNTDOWNS
Singles: 7-inch
APOLLO (71669 "Creative Soul") .. 10-15 60s
WG (1 "She Works All Night") ... 10-15 67

COUNTDOWNS
(Ron Gray & Countdowns)
Singles: 7-inch
N-JOY (1013 "No More") ... 20-30 60s
N-JOY (1015 "Cover of Night") ... 15-25 60s
Member: Ron Gray.

COUNTER POINTS
Singles: 7-inch
JA-WES ... 3-5 70-71

COUNTRY
LPs: 10/12-inch
CLEAN ... 10-15 71

COUNTRY ALL STARS
Singles: 78 rpm
RCA ... 5-10 52-56
Singles: 7-inch
RCA ... 10-20 52-56
Members: Chet Atkins; Homer & Jethro.
Also see ATKINS, Chet
Also see HOMER & JETHRO

COUNTRY BOYS
Singles: 7-inch
DEL-FI (4248 "Oakie Surfer") ... 25-35 64
Member: David Gates.
Also see GATES, David

COUNTRY BOYS & City Girls R&B '76
Singles: 7-inch
HAPPY FOX ... 3-5 76
Member: Lee Maye.
Also see MAYE, Arthur Lee

COUNTRY CAVALEERS C&W '73
Singles: 7-inch
COUNTRY SHOWCASE AMERICA .3-6 72-76
MGM ... 3-5 73
Members: James Marvell; Buddy Good.
Also see MARVELL, James
Also see MERCY

COUNTRY COALITION P&R '70
Singles: 7-inch
ABC ... 3-5 70-73
ABC/BLUESWAY ... 3-5 70
LPs: 10/12-inch
ABC/BLUESWAY ... 10-12 70

COUNTRY FEVER
Singles: 7-inch
BELL ... 3-6 69

COUNTRY FUNK
Singles: 7-inch
POLYDOR ... 3-5 70
LPs: 10/12-inch
POLYDOR ... 8-10 70

COUNTRY GJs
Singles: 7-inch
VALLEY (250 "Go Girl, Go") ... 150-250

COUNTRY GENTLEMEN C&W '65
Singles: 78 rpm
RCA ... 5-8 56
Singles: 7-inch
BRENT (7058 "For You") ... 15-25 67
RCA (6000 series) ... 8-12 56
REBEL ... 4-8 65
EPs: 7-inch
STARDAY ... 5-10
LPs: 10/12-inch
CIMMARON (2001 "Songs of the Pioneers") ... 25-35 62
CROWN ... 10-15 60s
DESIGN ... 5-10 63
FOLKWAYS (2409 "Country Gentlemen, Vol. 1") ... 15-25 60
(Includes booklet.)
FOLKWAYS (2410 "Country Gentlemen, Vol. 2") ... 15-25 60
(Includes booklet.)
FOLKWAYS (2411 "Country Gentlemen, Vol. 3") ... 15-25 60
(Includes booklet.)
FOLKWAYS (31031 "Going Back to the Blue Ridge Mountains") ... 10-15
GUSTO ... 5-10
MERCURY ... 10-20 63
PICKWICK/HILLTOP ... 10-15 60s
REBEL ... 5-10 70s
SUGAR HILL ... 5-10 83
STARDAY (109 "Traveling Dobro Blues") ... 25-50 59
STARDAY (174 "Bluegrass at Carnegie Hall") ... 15-25 62
STARDAY (311 "Songs of the Pioneers") ... 15-20 65
VANGUARD (40021 "The Country Gentlemen") ... 15-25 73
(Quardaphonic.)
VANGUARD (79331 "The Country Gentlemen") ... 10-15 73
(Stereo.)
ZAP ... 10-15
Members: Charlie Waller; Ricky Skaggs.
Also see SKAGGS, Ricky

COUNTRY HAMS
Singles: 7-inch
EMI (3977 "Walking in the Park with Eloise") ... 10-20 74
Picture Sleeves
EMI (3977 "Walking in the Park with Eloise") ... 50-60 74
Promotional Singles
EMI (3977 "Walking in the Park with Eloise") ... 25-35 74
Members: Paul McCartney & Wings; Chet Atkins; Floyd Cramer.
Also see ATKINS, Chet
Also see CRAMER, Floyd
Also see McCARTNEY, Paul

COUNTRY JIM
(James Bledsoe)
Singles: 78 rpm
IMPERIAL ... 35-50 49-50
LPs: 10/12-inch
IMPERIAL ... 15-20 70
Also see HOT ROD HAPPY

COUNTRY JOE & FISH P&R/LP '67
Singles: 7-inch
VANGUARD ... 5-10 67-69
Picture Sleeves
VANGUARD ... 8-15 68
EPs: 7-inch
RAG BABY (1001 "Rag Baby") ... 30-40 66
RAG BABY (1002 "Rag Baby") ... 30-40 66
RAG BABY (1003 "Rag Baby") ... 30-40 66
LPs: 10/12-inch
FANTASY ... 8-10 75-77
VANGUARD (Except 9266) ... 10-20 67-71
VANGUARD (9266 "I Feel Like I'm Fixin' to Die") ... 20-30 67
(With cut-out pictures and poster game.)
VANGUARD (9266 "I Feel Like I'm Fixin' to Die") ... 10-20 67
(Without pictures and poster.)
Members: Country Joe McDonald; David Cohen; Mark Kapner; Barry Melton; Bob Steele; Richard Saunders; Mark Ryan.
Also see BLUE, David
Also see McDONALD, Country Joe
Also see MELTON, Barry
Also see REBECCA & SUNNY BROOK FARMERS

COUNTRY MILE
Singles: 7-inch
WORLD PACIFIC ... 4-6 69

COUNTRY PAUL
("Country Paul on His Guitar"; Edward Harris)
Singles: 78 rpm
KING ... 50-100 51-52
Singles: 7-inch
KING (4517 "Your Picture Done Faded") ... 300-500 51
KING (4532 "One More Time") .. 200-400 52
KING (4560 "I'll Never Walk in Your Door") ... 200-400 52
KING (4573 "Sidewalk Boogie") 200-400 52
Also see CAROLINA SLIM
Also see JAMMIN' JIM
Also see LAZY SLIM JIM

COUNTRY SLIM / Miss Country Slim
(Ernest Lewis)
Singles: 78 rpm
HOLLYWOOD (1005 "What Wrong Have I Done") ... 50-100 53
Also see LEWIS, Ernest

COUNTRY STORE
Singles: 7-inch
T.A. ... 4-8 68-70

COUNTRYMAN, Freddy
Singles: 7-inch
VALTONE ... 5-10 63
W.E.D. (23 "Raven") ... 30-40 62
Also see FREDDY & LONNIE
Also see FREDDY & RAVENS

COUNTS R&B '54
Singles: 78 rpm
DOT ... 15-25 53-56
NOTE (20000 "Sweet Names") ... 50-75 56
Singles: 7-inch
DOT (1199 "Hot Tamales") ... 25-50 54
DOT (1188 "Darling Dear") ... 25-50 53
DOT (1210 "My Dear My Darling") 40-60 54
DOT (1226 "Baby, I Want You") ... 40-60 54
DOT (1235 "Let Me Go Lover") ... 25-50 54
DOT (1243 "From This Day On") ... 25-50 55
DOT (1265 "Sally Walker") ... 20-30 55
DOT (1275 "Heartbreaker") ... 20-30 56
DOT (16105 "Darling Dear") ... 15-25 60
NOTE (20000 "Sweet Names") 100-200 56

COUNTS
Singles: 7-inch
MERCURY ... 10-15 58
VIK ... 15-25 58

COUNTS
Singles: 7-inch
MANCO (1060 "Surfer's Paradise") ... 15-25 64
COUNT (5 "The Beat") ... 10-20

COUNTS
Singles: 7-inch
PANORAMA (9 "Chitlins, Etc.") ... 6-12 65
PANORAMA (33 "Since I Fell for You") ... 6-12 66
SEA CREST (6003 "Turn On Song") ... 10-20 64
SEA CREST (6004 "Doggin' ") ... 10-15 64

COUNTS
Singles: 7-inch
SHRINE (117 "My Only Love") .. 200-300 60s

COUNTS
Singles: 7-inch
TWIN TOWN ... 5-10 60s

COUNTS
Singles: 7-inch
KEY (15131 "All Night") ... 10-20 60s

COUNTS
Singles: 7-inch
RICH ROSE (102 "Georgi's Theme") ... 8-12 60s
RICH ROSE (711 "Just a Little Bit") ... 8-12 60s

COUNTS LP '72
Singles: 7-inch
AWARE ... 3-5 74
WESTBOUND ... 3-5 72
YES (103 "Ask the Lonely") ... 8-10
LPs: 10/12-inch
AWARE ... 8-10 75
AWARE/GRC ... 8-10 73
GRC ... 8-10 73
TCB ... 4-8
WESTBOUND ... 8-10 72

COUNTS
Singles: 7-inch
DYNAMO (50 "Someday I'm Gonna Get You") ... 15-25

COUNTS
Singles: 7-inch
SPIRAL (1002 "My Babe") ... 15-20

COUNTS (With Tommy Burk): see BURK, Tommy

COUNTS IV
Singles: 7-inch
DATE ... 10-15 66
JCP (1006 "Listen to Me") ... 15-25 67

COUNTS of RHYTHM: see CONTINENTALS & COUNTS OF RHYTHM

COUP
Singles: 7-inch
A&M ... 3-4 84
LPs: 10/12-inch
A&M ... 5-10 84

COUPE DE VILLES
Singles: 7-inch
PHILLY GROOVE ... 4-6 69

COUPLINGS
Singles: 7-inch
JOSIE ... 10-15 58
PRISM ... 4-8 64-65

COUQUETTES
Singles: 7-inch
SIMS ... 4-8 63

COURCY, Joanne
(Jo Ann Courcy)
Singles: 7-inch
TWIRL (2020 "Silly Girl") ... 15-25 66
TWIRL (2026 "I Got the Power") 100-200 66

COURIERS
("Vocal: Steve Kurtz")
Singles: 7-inch
C.V. (500 "Stomping Time Again") ... 50-75 67
TEE PEE (114 "You Honey Baby") 10-15 67
Member: Steve Kurtz.

COURT JESTERS
Singles: 7-inch
BLAST (201 "Roaches") ... 35-50 61
BLAST (208 "Roaches") ... 15-25 63
COLLECTABLES ... 3-4 81
ROULETTE ... 4-8 67

COURT JESTERS
Singles: 7-inch
JESTER (2034 "Drive Me Crazy") 15-25

COURTIAL
Singles: 7-inch
PIPELINE ... 3-5

COURTIERS
Singles: 7-inch
CASE (107 "I've Been Mistreated") ... 200-300 59

COURTNEY, Bill
Singles: 7-inch
RCA ... 5-10 59
ROULETTE ... 5-10 60
VERSATILE ... 4-8 62

COURTNEY, Claire
Singles: 7-inch
BEVERLY HILLS ... 3-5 73
EDGE ... 3-5 74-76

COURTNEY, David LP '75
LPs: 10/12-inch
U.A. ... 8-10 75

COURTNEY, Dean
Singles: 7-inch
MGM (13776 "You Just Can't Walk Away") ... 75-125 67
PARAMOUNT (0214 "It Makes Me Nervous") ... 10-15 73
RCA (8919 "We Have a Good Thing") ... 10-15 66
RCA (9049 "I'll Always Need You") 15-25 66

COURTNEY, Del
Singles: 78 rpm
MERCURY/SAV-WAY (5054 "Hawaiian War Chant") ... 100-150 47
(Picture disc. Promotional issue only.)

COURTNEY, Lou P&R/R&B '67
(Lew Courtney)
Singles: 7-inch
BUDDAH ... 10-15 69
EPIC ... 3-5 73-75
HURDY GURDY ... 3-5
IMPERIAL ... 5-10 63-64
PHILIPS (40287 "I Watched You Slowly Slip Away") ... 50-100 65
POP SIDE ... 5-10 67
RAGS ... 4-8 73
RIVERSIDE ... 5-10 66-67
VERVE ... 5-10 68
LPs: 10/12-inch
EPIC ... 8-10 74
RCA ... 8-10 76
RIVERSIDE ... 15-20 67

COURTNEY, Peter
Singles: 7-inch
VIVA ... 4-8 67

COURTNEY & WESTERN
Singles: 7-inch
DIESEL ONLY (8423 "Hands Off") 3-5 92
(Blue vinyl.)

COURTSHIP P&R '72
Singles: 7-inch
CAPITOL 3-5 70
GLADES 3-5 72
TAMLA 3-5 72

COURVALE, Keith
Singles: 7-inch
DOT (15844 "Trapped Love") 30-50 58

COUSIN ICE D&D '85
Singles: 12-inch
URBAN ROCK 4-6 85

COUSIN JOE
LPs: 10/12-inch
BLUESWAY 8-10 73

COUSIN LEROY
(Leroy Rozier)
Singles: 78 rpm
EMBER 25-50 57
GROOVE 20-40 55
Singles: 7-inch
EMBER (1016 "Will a Matchbox Hold My Clothes") 25-40 57
EMBER (1023 "I'm Lonesome") 25-35 57
GROOVE (0123 "Goin' Back Home") 40-60 55
HERALD (546 "Waiting at the Station") 20-30 60

COUSINS
Singles: 7-inch
FIDELITY (3010 "Love Is Blind") 15-25 59
DECCA (30609 "Be Nice to Me") 10-20 58

COUSINS
(With Teacho Wiltshire & Orchestra)
Singles: 7-inch
VERSATILE (105 "Lonely Road") 50-75 60
Also see WILTSHIRE, Teacho

COUSINS
Singles: 7-inch
PARKWAY 10-15 61-63
LPs: 10/12-inch
PARKWAY (7005 "Music of the Strip") 20-25 61

COUSINS
Singles: 7-inch
WYNNE (132 "Guilty") 250-500 62

COUSINS
Singles: 7-inch
SHOVE LOVE 3-5
Also see KANE'S COUSINS

COUSINS, Dave
LPs: 10/12-inch
PASSPORT 8-10 80

COUTO & MULLIGAN
Singles: 7-inch
MULLCO 3-4 80
LPs: 10/12-inch
MULLCO 8-10 80

COUTY, Doc
Singles: 7-inch
AQUARIUS 5-10 64
Also see YOUNG SAVAGES

COVAY, Dave
Singles: 7-inch
MERCURY 3-5 73
LPs: 10/12-inch
MERCURY 8-10 73

COVAY, Don P&R '62
(With the Goodtimers; with Jefferson Lemon Blues Band; with Stan Applebaum Orchestra; Don "Pretty Boy" Covay)
Singles: 7-inch
ARNOLD (1002 "Pony Time") 10-15 61
ATLANTIC 5-10 65-70
BIG TOP (3033 "Beauty and the Beast") 10-20 60
BLAZE (350 "Standing in the Doorway") 20-30 58
CAMEO 8-15 62-63
COLUMBIA (42197 "Now That I Need You") 75-100 61
LANDA 5-10 64
MERCURY 3-6 72-75
NEWMAN 3-4 80
PARKWAY 10-20 63-64
PHILADELPHIA INT'L 3-6 76
ROSEMART 5-10 64
SUE (709 "Believe It Or Not") 20-30 58
U-VON 5-10 77
LPs: 10/12-inch
ATLANTIC 15-25 65-69
JANUS 8-12 72
MERCURY 8-10 74
PHILADELPHIA INT'L 8-10 76
VERSATILE 8-10 78
Also see APPLEBAUM, Stan
Also see GOODTIMERS
Also see PRETTY BOY
Also see RAINBOWS
Also see SOLDIER BOYS
Also see SOUL CLAN

COVELLE, Buddy
Singles: 7-inch
CORAL (62181 "Lorraine") 250-350 60
Also see HACKERT, Veline

COVEN P&R '71
Singles: 7-inch
BUDDAH 3-5 74
LION 3-5 71
MGM 3-5 71-73
MERCURY 3-6 69
SGC 5-8 68
W.B. 3-5 71-73
LPs: 10/12-inch
BUDDAH 8-10 74
MGM 10-12 71-72
MERCURY 12-15 69
Members: Jinx Dawson; Teresa Kelly.

COVER GIRLS P&R/R&B/LP '87
Singles: 7-inch
FEVER 3-4 87-88
Picture Sleeves
FEVER 3-4 87-88
LPs: 10/12-inch
CAPITOL 5-8 89-90
FEVER 5-10 87

COVERDALE, David
(David Coverdale's Whitesnake)
Singles: 7-inch
U.A. 3-5 78
LPs: 10/12-inch
U.A. 5-10 78
Also see DEEP PURPLE
Also see WHITESNAKE

COVERDALE & PAGE
Singles: 7-inch
GEFFEN 3-4 91
Members: David Coverdale; Jimmy Page.
Also see COVERDALE, David
Also see PAGE, Jimmy

COVERDALE, Larry, & Four Horsemen
Singles: 7-inch
ROULETTE 10-20 66

COVEY, Julian, & Time Machine
Singles: 7-inch
PHILIPS 4-8 68

COVINAS
(With the Dayna Tones)
Singles: 7-inch
HILTON (3752 "Five Minutes More") 20-25 65
Session: Tommy Dee.
Also see DEE, Tommy

COVINGTON, Gloria
Singles: 7-inch
CASABLANCA 3-4 80

COVINGTON, Joe E.
(With Fat Fandango)
Singles: 7-inch
GRUNT 3-5 73
LPs: 10/12-inch
GRUNT 8-10 73

COVINGTON, Joey
Singles: 7-inch
ORIGINAL SOUND 4-8 67

COVINGTON, Sonny
Singles: 7-inch
BAND BOX (228 "Hey-Hey Hey-Hey") 35-50 61

COW, Henry: see HENRY COW

COWARD, Noel LP '56
(With Leo Reisman Orchestra)
EPs: 7-inch
COLUMBIA 5-10 55
LPs: 12-inch 78 rpm
COLUMBIA (5063 "Noel Coward at Las Vegas") 20-30 55
RCA VICTOR (39002 "RCA Presents Noel Coward") 300-400 30s
(Picture disc.)

COWBOY
Singles: 7-inch
CAPRICORN 3-5 74-78
LPs: 10/12-inch
CAPRICORN 8-12 70-77
Member: Scott Boyer.
Also see 31ST of FEBRUARY

COWBOY COPAS: see COPAS, Cowboy

COWBOY CHURCH SUNDAY SCHOOL P&R '55
Singles: 78 rpm
DECCA 3-5 54-55
VOSS 3-5 54
Singles: 7-inch
DECCA 5-10 54-55
VOSS 5-10 54
Picture Sleeves
DECCA 10-20 54
EPs: 7-inch
DECCA 8-12 55

COWBOY JUNKIES LP '89
Singles: 7-inch
RCA 3-4 89
Picture Sleeves
RCA 3-4 89
LPs: 10/12-inch
RCA 5-8 89-90

COWBOYS INTERNATIONAL
LPs: 10/12-inch
VIRGIN 5-10 80

COWELL, Stanley
LPs: 10/12-inch
ARISTA 8-10 75-77
GALAXY 8-10 77-81
STRAT-EAST 8-10 76

COWSILL, Bill
Singles: 7-inch
MGM 3-5 70
LPs: 10/12-inch
MGM 8-10 70
Also see COWSILLS

COWSILL, John
Singles: 7-inch
MGM 4-6 68
Also see COWSILLS

COWSILL, Susan
Singles: 7-inch
W.B. 3-5 76
LPs: 10/12-inch
W.B. 8-10 76-77
Also see COWSILLS

COWSILLS P&R/LP '67
Singles: 7-inch
JODA (103 "All I Really Want to Be Is Me") 10-20 65
LONDON 3-4 71-72
MGM 3-5 67-71
PHILIPS 4-8 66-67
Picture Sleeves
MGM 4-8 67-69
PHILIPS 5-10 66
EPs: 7-inch
MGM (1 "The Cowsills") 15-25 68
(Promotional issue from the American Dairy Assocaition.)
LPs: 10/12-inch
LONDON 8-10 71
MGM 10-12 67-71
WING 10-12 68
Members: Bill Cowsill; Barry Cowsill; John Cowsill; Susan Cowsill; Bob Cowsill; Paul Cowsill; Barbara Cowsill.
Also see COWSILL, Bill
Also see COWSILL, John
Also see COWSILL, Susan

COX, Danny
Singles: 7-inch
CASABLANCA 3-5 74
LPs: 10/12-inch
CASABLANCA 8-10 74
DUNHILL 8-10 71
SUNFLOWER 8-10 70
TOGETHER 8-10 70

COX, Dave
Singles: 7-inch
GOLDEN LEAF (105 "Skateland Bounce") 5-10 62

COX, Don C&W '79
Singles: 7-inch
ARC 3-5 79

COX, Herbie
Singles: 7-inch
RAMA (233 "Leave My Woman Alone") 25-40 61
Also see CLEFTONES

COX, Ida
LPs: 10/12-inch
ROSETTA 5-10 85

COX, Jerry
(With the Cavaliers)
Singles: 7-inch
BUZ (100 "Lover Man") 50-75 58
FRANTIC (751 "Sherry") 175-225 59

COX, Mick
(Mick Cox Band)
Singles: 7-inch
CAPITOL 3-5 73
LPs: 10/12-inch
CAPITOL 8-10 73

COX, Wally P&R '53
Singles: 78 rpm
RCA 3-5 53
Singles: 7-inch
ARVEE 4-8 60
GEORGE 4-8 61
RCA (5278 "What a Crazy Guy") 5-10 53
WAND 3-5 70
Picture Sleeves
RCA (5278 "What a Crazy Guy") 10-20 53

COXHILL, Lol
Singles: 7-inch
AMPEX 3-5 71
LPs: 10/12-inch
AMPEX 15-20 71

COXON'S ARMY
LPs: 10/12-inch
TRACE ("Coxson's Army") 300-500 75
(No selection number used.)
Members: Phil Coxson; Pat Benatar.
Also see BENATAR, Pat

COYNE, Kevin
LPs: 10/12-inch
VIRGIN 8-10 74-77

COYNE, Ricky, & His Guitar Rockers
(Rick Coyne)
Singles: 7-inch
EVENT (4289 "Rollin' Pin Mim") 50-75 58
EVENT (4290 "Little Darleen") 30-40 59
EVENT (4294 "I Want You to Know") 30-40 59
FENWICK (1011 "Rollin' Pin Mim") 200-300 58
MGM 4-8 67
Also see RICKOCHETS

COYOTE
Singles: 7-inch
CAPITOL 3-5 76-77

COYOTE SISTERS P&R '84
Singles: 7-inch
MOROCCO 3-4 84
Picture Sleeves
MOROCCO 3-4 84
LPs: 10/12-inch
MOROCCO 5-10 84
Members: Leah Kunkel; Marty Gwinn; Renee Armand.
Also see ARMAND, Renee

COZYTONES: see COSYTONES

C-QUENTS
Singles: 7-inch
CAPTOWN (4027 "Merry Christmas Baby") 150-250
CAPTOWN (4028 "Dearest One") 250-350
ESSICA (004 "Dearest One") 15-25

C-QUINS
Singles: 7-inch
CHESS 5-8 62
DITTO 10-20 62

CRAB & CREECH: see MALLARD, Earl, & His Web Feet of Rhythm

CRABBY APPLETON P&R/LP '70
Singles: 7-inch
ELEKTRA 3-5 70-72
LPs: 10/12-inch
ELEKTRA 8-10 70-71
Member: Michael Fennelly.
Also see FENNELLY, Michael

CRABEAU, Bobby, & Teenettes
Singles: 7-inch
CREST 15-25 59

CRACK OF DAWN
Singles: 7-inch
EPIC 3-5 76

CRACK THE SKY LP '76
Singles: 12-inch
GRUDGE 4-8 88
(Promotional only.)
Singles: 7-inch
GRUDGE 3-4 88-90
LIFESONG 3-5 76-79
LPs: 10/12-inch
GRUDGE 5-8 88-90
LIFESONG (Except 8000 series) 10-15 75-78
LIFESONG (8000 series) 5-10 81
Members: Rick Withowski; Joe Macre; Joe D'Amico.
Also see TAYLOR, B.E., Group

CRACKERJACK SOCIETY
Singles: 7-inch
COLUMBIA 4-8 67
Picture Sleeves
COLUMBIA 5-10 67

CRACKERS
Singles: 7-inch
W.B. 3-5 75-76
LPs: 10/12-inch
EDISON 5-10 83

CRACKIN'
Singles: 7-inch
POLYDOR 3-5 75
W.B. 3-5 77-78
LPs: 10/12-inch
POLYDOR 8-10 75
W.B. 8-10 77-78

CRADDOCK, Billy "Crash"
(Billy Craddock "Crash" Craddock; Billy Graddock) P&R '59/C&W '71
Singles: 7-inch
ABC 3-5 72-78
ABC/DOT 3-5 75-77
ATLANTIC 3-4 89
CAPITOL 3-5 78-82
CARTWHEEL 3-5 71-72
CEE CEE 3-4 83
CHART 3-6 67-73
COLONIAL 10-15 58
COLUMBIA 5-10 59-60
DATE 8-12 58
KING (Except 5912) 5-10 64-65
KING (5912 "Betty Betty") 15-25 64
MERCURY 5-10 61-62
SKY CASTLE ("Smacky Mouth") 20-30
(No selection number used. Shows Columbia identification numbers, 26671/26672.)
Picture Sleeves
COLUMBIA (41470 "Don't Destroy Me") 15-25 59
COLUMBIA (41619 "All I Want Is You") 15-25 60
EPs: 7-inch
ABC 5-10 74
(Juke box issue only.)
LPs: 10/12-inch
ABC 6-10 72-78
ABC/AT EASE 10-12 78
(Special issue for the Armed Forces.)
ABC/DOT 8-10 76-77
CAPITOL 5-10 78-83
CARTWHEEL 10-12 71-72
CHART 8-12 73
HARMONY 10-12 73
KING (912 "I'm Tore Up") 45-55 64
PICKWICK 5-10 79
POWER PAK 5-10 75
STARDAY 8-10
MCA 5-10 82

CRADLE
Singles: 7-inch
JUBILEE 4-8 66

CRAFFORD, Bobby
(With the Pacers)
Singles: 7-inch
RAZORBACK (114 "Red Headed Woman") 40-50 63
RAZORBACK (122 "Short Squashed Texan") 10-15 65
RAZORBACK (128 thru 135) 5-15
Also see PACERS

CRAFT, Morty
Singles: 7-inch
MGM 5-10 58
SMASH 4-8 66
TOD (122 "All Mixed Up") 15-25 57
WARWICK 5-10 59
Also see CRAFTSMEN

CRAFT, Paul C&W '74
Singles: 7-inch
RCA 3-5 77-78
TRUTH 3-5 74

CRAFTSMEN
Singles: 7-inch
SCOUT 5-10 61
WARWICK 10-20 60-62
Also see CRAFT, Morty
Also see JOHNNY & HURRICANES

CRAFTYS
Singles: 7-inch
ELMOR 15-25 62
SEVEN ARTS 5-10 61

CRAIG, The
Singles: 7-inch
FONTANA (1579 "I Must Be Mad") 20-25 67

CRAIG, Anna
Singles: 7-inch
DECCA 5-10 65
20TH FOX 10-20 64

CRAIG, Charlie
Singles: 7-inch
GUSTO 3-4 78

CRAIG, Deran
Singles: 7-inch
CURB 3-4 83

CRAIG, Earl, & Downbeats
Singles: 7-inch
DOMINION ("Craig's Crazy Boogie") 15-25 58
(No selection number used.)
DOMINION (1003 "Saki") 10-20 60

CRAIG, Gloria
Singles: 7-inch
SHERITON 5-10 60

CRAIG, Greer
(With the Shufflers)
Singles: 7-inch
JCP 10-20 60s
TRAIL (1862 "Love Me") 3-5 77
(Includes photo/bio insert.)

CRAIG, Jimmy
(Jimmie Craig)
Singles: 7-inch
BRILL (1 "Gonna Love My Baby") 50-75 59
IMPERIAL (5592 "Oh Little Girl") 30-40 59
WARWICK (542 "Drifter") 15-20 60

CRAIG, Jonathan
Singles: 7-inch
FLIP (1001 "Rock a Billy Gal") 20-30 57

CRAIG, Ken
Singles: 7-inch
BERTRAM INT'L 5-10 59

CRAIG, Ken & Karol
Singles: 7-inch
BERTRAM INT'L 10-15 61
Also see CRAIG, Ken

CRAIG, Lee
Singles: 7-inch
JOSIE 5-10 59

CRAIG, Vilas
(With the Viscounts)
Singles: 7-inch
CUCA (1011 "Don't You Just Know It") 8-12 60
FAN JR. (1706 "Poor Loser") 5-10 62
FAN JR. (4792 "Walkin' Down the Avenue") 5-10 62
INT'L ARTISTS (2120 "Little Miss Mary") 20-25 60
INT'L ARTISTS (2122 "The Spin") 20-25 60
INT'L ARTISTS (6334 "Gotta Find My Baby") 20-25 63
INT'L ARTISTS (6335 "Chumba") 20-25 63
INT'L ARTISTS (6336 "Black Out") 20-25 63
INT'L ARTISTS (6337 "Poor Loser") 20-25 63
RIFF (1148 "Spring Fever") 8-12 59
RIFF (2119 "If I May") 8-12 60
SIMS (259 "Unlucky Am I") 10-20 65
Members: Ronnie McDonald; Dick Faith; Gary Kirschner; Bob Smitke; Jack Goodwiler; Gene Moller; Hal Block; George Cash; Roger Hessling; Steve Prestigard; Pete Steele; Carl Gillingham; Jim Chitwood; Bobby Greenwood; Bill McCorkle; Al Sugden; Tom Levarda.

CRAIG, Vilas & Royal Lancers / Badgers
Singles: 7-inch
CUCA (1072 "Skinny Minnie Twist")....10-15 62
Also see CRAIG, Vilas

CRAIG, Wick, & Autochords
Singles: 7-inch
COOL (6354 "Auto Hop")....10-20 60

CRAIG, Windy
Singles: 7-inch
CEVETONE....4-8 63

CRAIG & His Daddy
Singles: 7-inch
AMY....4-8 62

CRAIG & ETHICS
Singles: 7-inch
SPYDER....15-25

CRAIN, Billy
Singles: 7-inch
DEMO....3-5 77
FLORIDA SOUNDS....3-5 87

CRAIN, Jimmy: see CRANE, Jimmy

CRAMER, Floyd *P&R '54/C&W '60*
(With the Louisiana Hayride Band; with Keyboard Kick Band)
Singles: 78 rpm
ABBOTT....3-5 53-54
MGM....3-5 55-57
Singles: 7-inch
ABBOTT....5-10 53-54
MGM....5-8 55-57
RCA (Except 7000 & 8000 series)....3-5 67-81
RCA (7000 & 8000 series)....4-8 61-66
Picture Sleeves
RCA....6-12 61-63
EPs: 7-inch
MGM....8-12 57
RCA....5-10 61-63
LPs: 10/12-inch
ALSHIRE....8-12 68
CAMDEN....6-12 65-74
MGM (3500 series)....15-20 57
MGM (4200 series)....10-15 64
MGM (4600 series)....8-12 70
RCA (0100 thru 4000 series)....5-10 73-81
(With "AHL1," ANL1," "APD1," "APL1," or "AYL1" prefix.)
RCA (2000 thru 4000 series)....10-20 60-73
(With "LPM" or "LSP" prefix.)
Also see ANN-MARGRET
Also see ATKINS, Chet, Floyd Cramer & Danny Davis
Also see ATKINS, Chet, Floyd Cramer & Boots Randolph
Also see BARE, Bobby
Also see COUNTRY HAMS
Also see FRANCIS, Connie
Also see NASHVILLE ALL-STARS
Also see PRESLEY, Elvis
Also see REEVES, Jim
Also see SOME of CHET'S FRIENDS
Also see STARR, Frank, & His Rock-Away Boys

CRAMER, Floyd / Peter Nero / Frankie Carle
LPs: 10/12-inch
RCA....10-15 63
Also see CRAMER, Floyd
Also see NERO, Peter

CRAMPS
("Cramps with Bryan & Miriam")
Singles: 12-inch
BIG BEAT (6 "Smell of Female")....15-25 83
(Black vinyl. With paper sleeve.)
BIG BEAT (6 "Smell of Female")....15-25 83
(Colored vinyl. With paper sleeve.)
BIG BEAT (110 "Can Your Pussy Do the Dog")....15-20 85
(10-inch 45 rpm.)
BIG BEAT (110 "Can Your Pussy Do the Dog")....15-20 85
(12-inch 45 rpm.)
BIG BEAT (135 "Eyeball in My Martini")....8-12 91
(With paper sleeve.)
BIG BEAT (115 "What's Inside a Girl")....15-20 86
(With paper sleeve.)
ENIGMA (19 "All Women Are Bad")....15-20 90
(With paper sleeve.)
I.R.S. (1008 "The Crusher")....30-40 81
(With paper sleeve.)
POW WOW (02 "What's Inside a Goul")....200-300 82
(Colored vinyl. Interview with Cramps' Poison Ivy and Lux Interior. No music on disc.)
Singles: 7-inch
CRAMPS/NEW ROSE (1 "Smell of Female – Special Limited Edition")....80-100 84
(Seven colored vinyl discs. Includes one track, *Psychotic Reaction*, not on LP. Numbered edition of approximately 10,000.)
CREATION (196 "Naked Girl Falling Down the Stairs")....5-8 95
("Limited Colored Vinyl Editon.")
ENIGMA (17 "Bikini Girls with Machine Guns"/"Jackyard Backoff")....50-75 90
(Die-cut picture disc. Has 12-inch sleeve.)
I.R.S. (9021 "Goo Goo Muck")....4-8 81
I.R.S. (9021 "Goo Goo Muck")....35-50 81
(Colored vinyl.)
ILLEGAL/I.R.S. (9014 "Garbageman")....5-10 80
LUX (102 "Hurricane Fighter Plane")....15-25 77
VENGEANCE ("Human Fly")....50-75 78
(Demo version. Colored vinyl. No number used.)
VENGEANCE (666 "Surfin' Bird")....25-35 77
(Counterfeits exist but are easily identified. Their labels are all orange, whereas originals are orange and black.)
VENGEANCE (668 "Human Fly")....25-35 78
(Counterfeits exist but are easily identified. Their labels are all orange, whereas originals are orange and black.)
Picture Sleeves
CREATION (196 "Naked Girl Falling Down the Stairs")....5-8 95
("Limited Editon.")
I.R.S. (9014 "Garbage Man")....10-20 80
I.R.S. (9021 "Goo Goo Muck")....10-20 81
ILLEGAL/I.R.S. (9014 "Garbageman")....10-15 80
LUX (102 "Hurricane Fighter Plane")....15-25 77
(Sleeve is also titled *The Cramps in Dance of the Cannibals of Sex*)
VENGEANCE (666 "Surfin' Bird")....25-35 78
(Counterfeits exist but are easily identified. They lack color and their photos are enlarged. Originals have color and smaller photos.)
VENGEANCE (668 "Human Fly")....50-75 78
(Fold-out, comic book cover.)
VENGEANCE (668 "Human Fly")....25-35 78
(Counterfeits exist but are easily identified. They lack color and their photos are enlarged. Originals have color and smaller photos.)
LPs: 10/12-inch
BIG BEAT (46 "A Date with Elvis")....15-25 86
BIG BEAT (101 "Look Mom, No Head")....15-25 91
CAVE (001 "Tales from the Cramps")....300-400 77
ENIGMA (1001 "Stay Sick")....30-50 90
(Limited edition vinyl pressing.)
GIANT (24592 "Flame Job")....12-18 94
I.R.S. (70042 "Bad Music for Bad People")....20-30 84
ILLEGAL/I.R.S. (007 "Songs the Lord Taught Us")....10-15 79
(Tracks on disc are different than those shown on the cover, and in a different sequence than shown on label.)
ILLEGAL/I.R.S. (012 "Off the Bone")....15-20 83
(With 3-D cover and glasses.)
ILLEGAL/I.R.S. (012 "Off the Bone")....5-10 83
(With standard cover.)
ILLEGAL/I.R.S. (012 "Off the Bone")....50-80 85
(Picture disc. Includes one extra track.)
ILLEGAL (501 "Gravest Hits")....10-20 79
ILLEGAL/I.R.S. (70016 "Psychedelic Jungle")....8-10 81
LAST RECORD (2022 "Transylvania Tapes")....100-150 78
MIDNIGHT....15-20 78
NST....5-10 85
PRAIRIE DOG ("Totally Destroy Seattle")....300-500
(Colored vinyl. Reportedly 100 made.)
W.B. (86449 "Flame Job")....8-10 90s
(Colored vinyl.)
Members: Lux Interior; Congo Powers; Bryan Gregory; Nick Knox; Ivy "Poison Ivy" Rorschach.

CRAMPTON SISTERS *P&R '64*
Singles: 7-inch
ABC....4-8 66
DCP....5-10 64

CRANDALL, Eddie
Singles: 7-inch
SCARLET....5-10 59

CRANE
Singles: 7-inch
CAPITOL....3-5 77
LPs: 10/12-inch
CAPITOL....5-10 78

CRANE, Carol
("Mrs. Brown's Lovely Daughter")
Singles: 7-inch
CHALLENGE....4-8 65

CRANE, Jimmy
(Jimmy Crain)
Singles: 7-inch
MERLENE (95611 "Break a Heart Each Night")....10-15 60s
PRISM....15-25
SPANGLE (2009 "Shing a Shag")....50-75 59
VINCENT (5048 "Why Worry")....50-75 59
Picture Sleeves
SPANGLE (2009 "Shing a Shag")....75-100 59
LPs: 10/12-inch
RAY-O (2005 "Miles to Go")....40-60 60

CRANE, Joe, & Hoodoo Rhythm Devils
Singles: 7-inch
CAPITOL....3-5 71

CRANE, Les *P&R/LP '71*
Singles: 7-inch
W.B.....3-5 71
Picture Sleeves
W.B.....4-8 71
LPs: 10/12-inch
W.B.....5-10 71

CRANE, Lor
Singles: 7-inch
BOARDWALK....4-8 60-65
RADIANT....4-8 62

CRANE, Sherry
Singles: 7-inch
SUN....8-12 59

CRANK
Singles: 7-inch
BLUE ROSE....8-10
UA....8-12 64

CRANSTON, Lamont
(Lamont Cranston Band)
Singles: 7-inch
RCA....3-4 82
LPs: 10/12-inch
SHADOW....10-15 78
WATERHOUSE....5-10 80-84

CRASH STREET KIDS
LPs: 10/12-inch
FAT CITY....5-10 82

CRASH TEST DUMMIES
LPs: 10/12-inch
ARISTA....5-8 91

CRAVEN HOUSE
Singles: 7-inch
VEE JAY....4-8 63

CRAVENS
Singles: 7-inch
SABRE....5-8

CRAVER, Sonny
Singles: 7-inch
CELESTIAL....3-5 78
MUSETTE....8-12 66
TERI DE (007 "I'm No Fool")....15-25 71

CRAVERS
Singles: 7-inch
CHOCK (109 "Flavor Craver")....15-25 60s
Also see GARVIN, Rex, & Mighty Cravers
Also see MIGHTY CRAVERS

CRAWDADDY
Singles: 7-inch
COLOSSUS....3-6 69-71

CRAWDADDYS
Singles: 7-inch
VOXX....3-4 80s
EPs: 7-inch
VOXX....5-10 80s
LPs: 10/12-inch
VOXX....5-10 86

CRAWFORD, Bixie
Singles: 78 rpm
KING....15-25 49
Singles: 7-inch
EMPIRE....10-15
INDIGO....5-10 60

CRAWFORD, Blackie
(With the Western Cherokees)
Singles: 78 rpm
CORAL....5-10 52
STARDAY (Except 116)....5-10 53-54
STARDAY (116 "Stop Boogie")....20-30 54
Singles: 7-inch
STARDAY (Except 116)....10-20 53-54
STARDAY (116 "Stop Boogie")....35-50 54

CRAWFORD, Bobby
Singles: 7-inch
DEL-FI....4-8 63
Also see CRAWFORD BROTHERS

CRAWFORD, Caroline: see CRAWFORD, Carolyn

CRAWFORD, Carolyn *R&B '65*
(Caroline Crawford)
Singles: 7-inch
MERCURY....3-4 78-79
MOTOWN (1050 "Forget About Me")....20-40 63
MOTOWN (1064 "My Smile Is Just a Frown Turned Upside Down")....25-50 64
MOTOWN (1064 "My Smile Is Just a Frown [Turned Upside Down]")....15-25 64
(Repressing—note title variation.)
MOTOWN (1070 "My Heart")....30-40 64
PHILADELPHIA INT'L....3-5 74-75
LPs: 10/12-inch
MERCURY....6-12 78-79
Also see BOHANNON
Also see CHAPTER 8

CRAWFORD, D.J.
Singles: 7-inch
JUCA....3-5

CRAWFORD, Dave
Singles: 7-inch
L-A....3-5

CRAWFORD, Don
Singles: 7-inch
BLUE RIVER....4-8 67
CAPITOL....3-5 70
CHALLENGE....4-6 68-69
CONDOR....5-10 61
LOMA....4-8 66
MIKE....4-8 62
ROULETTE....3-5 71
VALIANT....4-8 65
VERVE/FOLKWAYS....4-8 66
W.B.....4-8 67
LPs: 10/12-inch
VERVE/FOLKWAYS....10-12 66

CRAWFORD, Faye
Singles: 7-inch
RCA ((8555 "So Many Lies")....10-20 65

CRAWFORD, Fred
Singles: 78 rpm
STARDAY (Except 243)....10-15 54-55
STARDAY (243 "Rock Candy Rock")....20-30 56
Singles: 7-inch
STARDAY (Except 243)....10-20 54-55
STARDAY (243 "Rock Candy Rock")....35-40 56

CRAWFORD, Gene
Singles: 7-inch
BOW & ARROW....4-8 63
HALA....4-8 67
MTA....4-8 67-68
METROMEDIA....4-6 69

CRAWFORD, Hank *LP '64*
Singles: 7-inch
ATLANTIC....3-8 61-70
KUDU....3-5 72
LPs: 10/12-inchs
ATLANTIC....10-20 61-73
KUDU....10-12 72-76
MFSL (224 "Soul of the Ballad")....20-25 94
Also see KING, B.B.

CRAWFORD, Ian
Singles: 7-inch
INTERPHON....4-8 65

CRAWFORD, James
(James "Sugar Boy" Crawford)
Singles: 78 rpm
IMPERIAL....10-20 57
Singles: 7-inch
ACE (625 "Have a Little Mercy")....15-25 61
BLUE ROCK....5-10 65
IMPERIAL (5424 "She's Gotta Wobble")....20-30 57
IMPERIAL (5513 "I Need Your Love")....20-30 58
KING....5-8 67
MERCURY....10-20 64-65
MONTELL....10-20 59
OMEN....5-10 64-66
LPs: 10/12-inch
CHESS....8-12 76
Also see SMITH, Huey
Also see SUGAR BOY & His Cane Cutters

CRAWFORD, Jimmy, Frank Motley & His Crew
Singles: 78 rpm
GEM (215 "That Ain't Right")....25-45 54
Singles: 7-inch
GEM (215 "That Ain't Right")....60-75 54
(Also issued as by Frank Motley.)
Also see MOTLEY, Frank

CRAWFORD, Johnny *P&R '61*
Singles: 7-inch
ABC....3-4 73
CINDY....4-6
COLLECTABLES....3-4 81
DEL-FI....5-10 61-64
SIDEWALK....4-8 67-68
WYNNE (124 "Ask")....10-15 60
Picture Sleeves
DEL-FI....10-15 61-63
SIDEWALK....5-8 68
EPs: 7-inch
GRASON (6515 "The Restless Ones")....10-15 66
LPs: 10/12-inch
DEL-FI (1220 "The Captivating Johnny Crawford")....20-30 62
DEL-FI (1223 "A Young Man's Fancy")....20-30 62
DEL-FI (1224 "Rumors")....20-30 63
DEL-FI (1229 "His Greatest Hits")....20-30 63
DEL-FI (1248 "Greatest Hits Vol. 2")....20-30 63
GUEST STAR....15-20 63
RHINO....5-10 82
SUPREME (110 "Songs from *The Restless Ones*)....15-20 66
(Soundtrack. Monaural.)
SUPREME (210 "Songs from *The Restless Ones*)....20-30 66
(Soundtrack. Stereo.)
Also see CRAWFORD BROTHERS
Also see MOUSEKETEERS

CRAWFORD, Kris
Singles: 7-inch
ABC....4-8 66

CRAWFORD, Michael *LP '88*
LPs: 10/12-inch
COLUMBIA....5-8 88

CRAWFORD, Peter
Singles: 7-inch
SANDY (1039 Dancing with My Lover")....500-1000 63

CRAWFORD, Randy *R&B '79*
Singles: 12-inch
W.B.....4-6 83
Singles: 7-inch
COLUMBIA....3-5 72-73
MCA....3-4 81
W.B.....3-5 77-86
Picture Sleeves
COLUMBIA....3-5 72
LPs: 10/12-inch
RCA....5-10 84
W.B.....8-10 76-89
Also see CRUSADERS
Also see JARREAU, Al, & Randy Crawford
Also see SPRINGFIELD, Rick, & Randy Crawford

CRAWFORD BROTHERS
Singles: 7-inch
ALADDIN (3375 "Midnight Mover Groover")....15-25 57

CRAWFORD BROTHERS
Singles: 7-inch
DEL-FI....5-10 62
Picture Sleeves
DEL-FI....10-15 62
Members: Johnny Crawford; Bobby Crawford.
Also see CRAWFORD, Bobby
Also see CRAWFORD, Johnny

CRAWLER: see BACK STREET CRAWLER

CRAWLING WALLS
LPs: 10/12-inch
VOXX....5-10

CRAY, Jackie
Singles: 7-inch
LIMELIGHT (3001 "Maybelle")....50-75 58

CRAY, Robert *LP '86*
(Robert Cray Band)
Singles: 12-inch
MERCURY....4-8 88
(Promotional only.)
Singles: 7-inch
MERCURY....3-4 87-88
Picture Sleeves
MERCURY....3-4 87-88
LPs: 10/12-inch
HIGHTONE....5-10 83-87
MERCURY....5-10 86
TOMATO....10-20 80
Also see COLLINS, Albert, Robert Cray & Johnny Copeland

CRAY, Robert, Band, & Memphis Horns *LP '90*
LPs: 10/12-inch
MERCURY....5-8 90
Also see CRAY, Robert
Also see MEMPHIS HORNS

CRAYONS
(Cray-Ons)
Singles: 7-inch
COUNSEL (121 "Teach Me Mama")....15-25 63
COUNSEL (122 "Love at First Sight")....15-25 63
Also see RONNIE & CRAYONS

CRAYSELL, Rudy, & T-Birds
Singles: 7-inch
AWARD (130 "You'll Be Mine")....25-35 59

CRAYTON, Maxine
Singles: 7-inch
STEELTOWN....10-15 69

CRAYTON, Pee Wee *R&B '48*
(With Red Callender Sextette)
Singles: 78 rpm
ALADDIN....40-60 51
FLAIR....15-25 55
4 STAR (1304 "After Hours Boogie")....25-50 47
IMPERIAL....25-50 54-55
MODERN....25-50 49-51
POST....25-50 55
RECORDED in HOLLYWOOD....40-60 54
VEE JAY....20-30 56-57
Singles: 7-inch
ALADDIN (3112 "When It Rains It Pours")....100-200 51
BLACK DIAMOND....15-25
BLUES SPECTRUM (15 "Texas Bop")....10-20
EDCO (1009 "Ev'ry Night 'Bout This Time")....20-30
EDCO (1010 "Money Tree")....25-50
FLAIR (1061 "Central Avenue Blues")....25-50 55
(Actually by Pee Wee Crayton though shown as by the Carroll County Boys. The flip, *Dizzy*, is by the Carroll County Boys.)
FOX (10069 "Give Me One More Chance")....15-25
GUYDEN (2048 "I'm Still in Love with You")....10-20 61
IMPERIAL (5288 "Do Unto Others")....50-75 54
IMPERIAL (5297 "Win-o")....50-75 54
IMPERIAL (5321 "I Need Your Love")....50-75 54
IMPERIAL (5338 "My Idea About You")....50-75 55
IMPERIAL (5345 "Eyes Full of Tears")....50-75 55
IMPERIAL (5353 "Yours Truly")....50-75 55
JAMIE (1190 "Little Bitty Things")....10-15 61
MODERN (892 "Cool Evening")....50-75 51
MODERN (892 "Cool Evening")....50-75 51
POST (2007 "I Must Go On")....50-75 55
RECORDED in HOLLYWOOD (408 "Crying & Walking")....75-125 54
RECORDED in HOLLYWOOD (426 "Baby Pat the Floor")....75-125 54
SMASH (1774 "Hillbilly Blues")....10-15 62
VEE JAY (214 "Frosty Night")....40-60 56
VEE JAY (252 "I Found Peace of Mind")....40-60 57
VEE JAY (266 "Fiddle De Dee")....40-60 57
LPs: 10/12-inch
CROWN (5175 "Pee Wee Crayton")....50-100 60
(Back cover has text about Crayton and lists other Crown LPs. No photos used. Company address shown is in Culver City, Calif. Black label.)

CROWN (5175 "Pee Wee Crayton") ... 10-20 69
(Generic back cover makes no mention of Crayton and pictures other Crown LPs. Company address shown is in Los Angeles, Calif. Gray label.)
MURRAY BROTHERS ... 5-10 83
VANGUARD ... 8-12 71
Also see CALLENDER, Red
Also see CARROLL COUNTY BOYS
Also see HOMER the GREAT

CRAYTON TRIO
Singles: 78 rpm
GRUVTONE ... 25-35

CRAZY CRICKETS
Singles: 7-inch
BAND BOX (290 "Honey Walk") ... 10-20 61

CRAZY D
Singles: 7-inch
SUNDAY NIGHT (100 "81 Luncheon") ... 4-6 81

CRAZY ELEPHANT — P&R '69
Singles: 7-inch
BELL ... 4-8 69-70
SPHERE SOUND ... 4-6 69
LPs: 10/12-inch
BELL ... 15-20 69
Member: Robert Spencer.

CRAZY EMMA
Singles: 7-inch
SCEPTER ... 3-5 72

CRAZY GIRLS
(With the Javelins)
Singles: 7-inch
CAPITOL ... 4-8 63

CRAZY HORSE — LP '71
Singles: 7-inch
EPIC ... 3-5 72
M.O.C. ... 4-8
REPRISE ... 3-5 71-72
LPs: 10/12-inch
EPIC ... 8-12 72-76
RCA ... 5-10 78
REPRISE ... 10-15 71-72
Members: Ralph Molina; Billy Talbot; Leon Whitsell; George Whitsell; Ry Cooder; Mike Curtis; Greg Leroy; Bob Notkoff; Neil Young.
Also see ROCKETS
Also see YOUNG, Neil

CRAZY JACKS
Singles: 7-inch
LONDON ... 4-8 63

CRAZY JOE & Variable Speed Band
Singles: 7-inch
CASABLANCA ... 3-4 80-81
LPs: 10/12-inch
CASABLANCA ... 5-10 81

CRAZY KATS
Singles: 7-inch
DEAUVILLE ... 4-8 62

CRAZY LUKE
Singles: 7-inch
DO BROOKS ... 4-8 63

CRAZY MORLEY
Singles: 7-inch
CAMEO ... 5-10 58

CRAZY OTTO — P&R/LP '55
Singles: 78 rpm
DECCA ... 3-5 55-57
Singles: 7-inch
DECCA ... 4-8 55-61
MGM ... 3-5 62
EPs: 7-inch
DECCA ... 5-10 55-58
LPs: 10/12-inch
DECCA ... 8-18 55-61
MGM ... 6-12 63
VOCALION ... 8-10 59

CRAZY PAVING
Singles: 7-inch
KAPP ... 3-5 71

CRAZY TEENS
Singles: 7-inch
SCOTT ... 10-15

CRAZY WORLD of ARTHUR BROWN: see BROWN, Arthur

CREACH, Johnny
Singles: 7-inch
ERA ... 4-8 67

CREACH, Papa John — LP '72
Singles: 7-inch
BUDDAH ... 3-5 76
DJM ... 3-4 79
GRUNT ... 3-5 71-72
LPs: 10/12-inch
BUDDAH ... 8-12 75-77
DJM ... 6-10 77-78
GRUNT ... 10-15 71-74
Also see HOT TUNA
Also see JEFFERSON STARSHIP
Also see SUNRISE

CREAM — LP '67
Singles: 7-inch
ATCO ... 4-8 67-70
EPs: 7-inch
ATCO ("Goodbye Cream") ... 10-15 69
(Promotional issue only.)
LPs: 10/12-inch
ATCO (206 "Fresh Cream") ... 25-35 67
(With *I Feel Free*. On RSO reissues, this track is replaced with *Spoonful*.)
ATCO (206 "Fresh Cream") ... 10-20 67
(Without *I Feel Free*.)
ATCO (232 "Disraeli Gears") ... 20-30 67
ATCO (291 "The Best of Cream") ... 20-30 69
ATCO (328 "Live Cream") ... 20-30 70
ATCO (700 "Wheels of Fire") ... 20-30 68
ATCO (7001 "Goodbye Cream") ... 20-30 69
ATCO (7005 "Live Cream, Vol. 2") ... 20-30 72
MFSL (066 "Wheels of Fire") ... 40-60 82
POLYDOR ... 10-12 72-73
RSO (Except 015) ... 5-10 72-83
RSO (015 "Classic Cuts") ... 35-45 75
(Promotional issue only.)
SPRINGBOARD ... 10-12
Members: Eric Clapton; Jack Bruce; Ginger Baker.
Also see BAKER, Ginger
Also see BRUCE, Jack
Also see CLAPTON, Eric

CREAM / Vanilla Fudge
LPs: 10/12-inch
ATCO (7001/278 "Promotional LP for Record Department-in-Store Play") ... 25-35 68
(Promotional issue only.)
Also see CREAM
Also see VANILLA FUDGE

CREAM SODA: see CREME SODA

CREAMCHEEZE GOOD-TIME BAND
Singles: 7-inch
MCA ... 3-5 73

CREATION
Singles: 7-inch
PLANET (116 "Making Time") ... 10-15 66
PLANET (119 "Painter Man") ... 10-15 66

CREATION
Singles: 7-inch
ATCO ... 3-5 74
DECCA ... 4-8 67
LPs: 10/12-inch
ATCO ... 10-15 73

CREATION
Singles: 7-inch
HITBOUND ... 10-15
PROLIFIC (704 "I'm So Lonely") ... 10-15
Member: Billy Scott.
Also see GEORGIA PROPHETS

CREATION
Singles: 7-inch
GLOBE (103 "Times Are Changing") ... 8-12

CREATION OF SUNLIGHT
LPs: 10/12-inch
WINDI (1001 "Creation of Sunlight") ... 400-600 68
Members: G.C. Prophet; J. Griffin.
Also see SUNLIGHT
Also see SUNLIGHT'S SEVEN

CREATION'S DISCIPLE
Singles: 7-inch
DAWN (309 "Psychedelic Retraction") ... 50-75 66

CREATIONS
Singles: 78 rpm
LIDO (501 "There Goes the Girl I Love") ... 50-100 56
TIP TOP (400 "Every Night I Pray") ... 50-100 56
TIP TOP (501 "You Are My Darling") ... 100-200 57
Singles: 7-inch
LIDO (501 "There Goes the Girl I Love") ... 100-150 56
TIP TOP (400 "Every Night I Pray") ... 100-200 56
TIP TOP (501 "You Are My Darling") ... 100-200 57

CREATIONS
Singles: 7-inch
JAMIE (1134 "Where's My Love") ... 15-20 59
JAMIE (1197 "The Bells") ... 10-15 61

CREATIONS
Singles: 7-inch
EMBER (1076 "This Is My Love") ... 15-25 61

CREATIONS
Singles: 7-inch
PATTI-JO (1703 "Seventeen") ... 300-500 62

CREATIONS
Singles: 7-inch
MEL-O-DY (101 "This Is Our Night") ... 75-100 62
MERIDIAN (7550 "The Wedding") ... 50-75 62
(Identification number shown since no selection number is used.)
PINE CREST (101 "Woke Up in the Morning") ... 300-400 61
RADIANT (103 "Don't Listen to What Others Say") ... 15-25 64

CREATIONS
Singles: 7-inch
GLOBE (102 "Just Remember Me") ... 15-25 62
GLOBE (103 "I've Got to Find Her") ... 10-20 62
GLOBE (1000 "Oh Baby!") ... 10-20 61
HULL ... 10-15 60s
LIBERTY BELL (013 "Peek-A-Boo") ... 15-20 60s
VIRTUE ... 3-5 71-73
ZODIAC ... 5-10 67

CREATIONS
Singles: 7-inch
PENNY (9022 "Let the We're in Love") ... 50-100 62
TAKE TEN (1501 "We're in Love") ... 25-50 63
(Note title change to something that makes sense.)

CREATIONS
Singles: 7-inch
RADIANT ... 10-15 64

CREATIONS
Singles: 7-inch
TOP HAT (1003 "Crash") ... 15-25 64
TOP HAT (1004 "Don't Be Mean") ... 25-35 65
Picture Sleeves
TOP HAT (1003 "Crash") ... 25-35 64
TOP HAT (1004 "Don't Be Mean") ... 50-75 65
Members: Chuck Delaney; Howard Plant; James Burnham; Danny Gomes.

CREATIONS
Singles: 7-inch
AFCO ... 5-10

CREATIONS IV
Singles: 7-inch
HBR ... 10-20 65

CREATIVE FUNK
Singles: 7-inch
CREATIVE FUNK ... 3-5 72

CREATIVE SOURCE — R&B '73
Singles: 7-inch
POLYDOR ... 3-5 75
SUSSEX ... 3-5 73-74
LPs: 10/12-inch
POLYDOR ... 8-10 75-76
SUSSEX ... 10-12 74
Members: Don Wyatt; Celeste Rhodes; Steve Flanagan; Barbara Berryman; Barbara Lewis.
Also see COLTS
Also see FORTUNES

CREATORS
Singles: 7-inch
DOOTO (463 "I've Had You") ... 15-25 61
DORE (635 "Too Far to Turn Around") ... 40-60 62
Members: Gentry Bradley; Charles Perry; Gerald Middleton; Donald Neal; Thomas Harris; Hillary Connody.
Also see HAMILTON, Little Johnny, & Creators

CREATORS
Singles: 7-inch
EPIC (9605 "Crazy Love") ... 10-15 63
HI-Q (5021 "Wear My Ring") ... 30-40 61
(Label print is a normal.)
HI-Q (5021 "Wear My Ring") ... 10-20 60s
(Label print is bold, or thick.)
TIME (1038 "Do You Remember") ... 15-20 61

CREATORS / Jaynells
Singles: 7-inch
JASON SCOTT ... 4-8
Also see CREATORS
Also see JAYNELLS

CREATORS
Singles: 7-inch
PHILIPS (40058 "Boy, He's Got It") ... 15-25 62
PHILIPS (40083 "I'll Stay Home") ... 200-300 62
T-KAY (110 "I'll Never Never Do It Again") ... 50-100 62
Members: Johnny Allen; Chris Coles; Danny Austin; Hugh Harris; Jimmy Wright; J.T. Taylor.
Also see AD LIBS

CREATORS
Singles: 7-inch
RCA ... 3-5 80

CREATURES
LPs: 10/12-inch
RCA (LPM-1923 "Monster Rally" ... 25-35 58
(Monaural.)
RCA (LSP-1923 "Monster Rally" ... 35-45 58
(Stereo.)

CREATURES
Singles: 7-inch
COLUMBIA ... 5-8 66-67

CREATURES — LP '90
LPs: 10/12-inch
GEFFEN ... 5-8 90

CREDIBILITY GAP
Singles: 7-inch
CAPITOL ... 4-6 68
EPs: 7-inch
W.B. (517 "Credibility Gap") ... 5-10 73
(Promotional issue only.)
LPs: 10/12-inch
CAPITOL ... 20-25 71
REPRISE ... 10-12 73
Members: David L. Lander; Michael McKean.
Also see LENNY & SQUIGTONES
Also see SPINAL TAP

CREDIT, Joni
Singles: 7-inch
HAPPY TIGER (102 "A Girl Named Harry") ... 5-8 70s

CREECH, Alice — C&W '71
Singles: 7-inch
TARGET ... 3-5 71-72

CREED
Singles: 7-inch
ASYLUM ... 3-4 78
LPs: 10/12-inch
ASYLUM ... 8-10 78

CREEDENCE CLEARWATER REVIVAL — P&R/LP '68
Singles: 12-inch
FANTASY (238 "Creedence Medley") ... 10-15 85
FANTASY (759 "I Heard It Through the Grapevine") ... 15-20 76
(Promotional issue only.)
Singles: 7-inch
FANTASY (Except 2832) ... 3-6 69-85
FANTASY (2832 "45 Revolutions Per Minute") ... 40-60 70
LIBERTY ... 3-5
SCORPIO (412 "Porterville") ... 15-25 68
Picture Sleeves
FANTASY (Except 2832) ... 5-10 69-76
FANTASY (2832 "45 Revolutions Per Minute") ... 20-25 70
LPs: 10/12-inch
BEVERLY ("Willie and the Poor Boys") ... 75-100
(Half-speed mastered. Number not known.)
FANTASY (1 thru 70) ... 8-15 73-78
FANTASY (4500 series) ... 5-10 80-85
(Includes reissues of 8382 through 9404.)
FANTASY (8382 thru 9404) ... 8-15 68-72
FANTASY (9418 thru 9621) ... 5-10 72-82
K-TEL ... 8-12 78
MFSL (037 "Cosmo's Factory") ... 75-125 79
SWEET THUNDER (13 "Green River") ... 75-100 75
(Half-speed mastered.)
W.B. SPECIAL PRODUCTS (3514 "Greatest Hits") ... 10-15 85
(TV mail-order offer.)
Members: John Fogerty; Tom Fogerty; Doug Clifford; Stuart Cook.
Also see CLIFFORD, Doug "Cosmo"
Also see DA SHIELL, Russell
Also see FOGERTY, John
Also see FOGERTY, Tom
Also see GOLLIWOGS
Also see HARRISON, Don, Band
Also see SOUTHERN PACIFIC

CREEL SISTERS
Singles: 78 rpm
ABBOTT ... 5-10 56
Singles: 7-inch
ABBOTT ... 10-15 56

CREELS
Singles: 7-inch
JUDD ... 10-20 59

CREEP
(Committee to Rip-off Each and Every Politician; Creep / Hickey Badman)
Singles: 7-inch
MR. G (826 "Halderman, Erlichman, Mitchell & Dean") ... 5-10 73
NIXXXON (1976 "Convention '76") ... 4-8 76

CREEPER
Singles: 7-inch
ABC ... 3-5 75

CREEPS
Singles: 7-inch
GINCHEE (1002 "The Whip") ... 15-25 59

CREME, Lol, & Kevin Godley: see GODLEY, Kevin, & Lol Creme

CREME CARAMEL
Singles: 7-inch
JANUS ... 3-6 69

CREME D'COCOA — R&B '78
Singles: 7-inch
VENTURE ... 3-5 78-80
LPs: 10/12-inch
VENTURE ... 8-10 79
Also see AMBASSADORS
Also see EBONYS

CREME SODA
Singles: 7-inch
KIDERIAN (45121 "Keep It Heavy") ... 10-20 74
KIDERIAN (45122 "I'm Chewing Gum") ... 10-20 74
TRINITY (112 "Keep It Heavy") ... 25-35 75
TRINITY (45121 "Keep It Heavy") ... 15-25 75
TRINITY (45122 "Chewin' Gum") ... 15-25 75
LPs: 10/12-inch
TRINITY (11 "Tricky Fingers") ... 300-500 75

CRENSHAW, Marshall — P&R/LP '82
Singles: 12-inch
SHAKE (104 "Marshall Crenshaw") ... 20-25 81
W.B. ... 5-10 82
Singles: 7-inch
W.B. ... 3-4 82-85
LPs: 10/12-inch
W.B. ... 5-10 82-85

CRENSHAWS
Singles: 7-inch
W.B. (5254 "Moonlight in Vermont") ... 10-20 61
W.B. (5505 "Wishing Star") ... 10-20 62
EPs: 7-inch
W.B. (5505 "Crenshaws") ... 25-50 61
(Promotional only. Issued without cover.)
Members: Al Frazier; Carl White; Sonny Harris; Turner Wilson; Matthew Nelson.
Also see RIVINGTONS

CREOLE, Kid: see KID CREOLE

CRESCENDOS
Singles: 78 rpm
ATLANTIC (1109 "Sweet Dreams") ... 10-20 56
Singles: 7-inch
ATLANTIC (1109 "Sweet Dreams") ... 15-25 56
ATLANTIC (2014 "Sweet Dreams") ... 8-12 59

CRESCENDOS — P&R/R&B '58
Singles: 78 rpm
NASCO (6005 "Oh Julie") ... 50-75 57
SPARTON (525 "Oh Julie") ... 25-35 57
(Canadian.)
Singles: 7-inch
ABC ... 3-5 73
MCA ... 3-4 84
NASCO (6005 "Oh Julie") ... 10-20 57
NASCO (6009 "School Girl") ... 10-20 58
NASCO (6021 "Young and in Love") ... 10-20 58
SCARLET (4007 "Let's Take a Walk") ... 10-20 60
SCARLET (4009 "Angel Face") ... 10-20 61
SPARTON (525 "Oh Julie") ... 25-35 57
(Canadian.)
TAP (7027 "Oh Julie") ... 10-15 57
Picture Sleeves
NASCO (6009 "School Girl") ... 20-30 58
NASCO (6021 "Young and in Love") ... 20-30 58
TAP (7027 "Oh Julie") ... 15-25 57
LPs: 10/12-inch
GUEST STAR (1453 "Oh Julie") ... 20-30 62
Members: George Lanuis; Ken Brigham; James Hall; Tommy Fortner.
Also see 4 SEASONS
Also see GREEN, Janice

CRESCENDOS
("Lead Voice Wanda Burt")
Singles: 7-inch
GONE (5100 "My Heart's Desire") ... 20-30 61
MUSIC CITY (831 "My Heart's Desire") ... 300-500 60
(Green label. "Music City" on two lines.)
MUSIC CITY (831 "My Heart's Desire") ... 200-250 60
(Maroon label. "Music City" on one line.)
MUSIC CITY (831 "My Heart's Desire") ... 15-25 60s
(Black label with multi-color print.)
Member: Wanda Burt.
Also see BURT, Wanda
Also see CRESCHENDOS

CRESCENDOS
Singles: 7-inch
DOMAIN (1025 "A Fellow Needs a Girl") ... 75-125 63
IMPRO (5006 "Tidal Wave") ... 20-30 62
NU-SOUND (1007 "Count Down") ... 15-25 61
NU-SOUND (1014 "Movin' Wild") ... 15-25 61

CRESCENT SIX
Singles: 7-inch
RUST ... 10-20 65

CRESCENT STREET STOMPERS
Singles: 7-inch
20TH FOX ... 3-5 75

CRESCENTS
Singles: 78 rpm
RESERVE (105 "Julie") ... 100-200 56
Singles: 7-inch
RESERVE (105 "Julie") ... 300-500 56

CRESCENTS
Singles: 7-inch
ARLEN (743 "Smoke Gets in Your Eyes") ... 10-20 63
DOT (16447 "Hey There") ... 15-25 63
HAMILTON (50003 "Hey There") ... 40-60 63

CRESCENTS — P&R '63
(Chiyo & Crescents)
Singles: 7-inch
BREAK OUT (4 "Pink Dominos") ... 15-25 63
(With straight horizontal lines.)
BREAK OUT (4 "Pink Dominos") ... 15-20 63
(With jagged horizontal lines.)
ERA (3116 "Pink Dominos") ... 5-10 63

CRESCENTS
Singles: 7-inch
BLUE RIVER ... 5-10 66
SEVEN B (2159 "I'll Make a Vow") ... 50-75 65

CRESCHENDOES
Singles: 7-inch
SATURN (404 "Surfin' Strip") ... 15-25 63
Member: Chuck Rio.
Also see CRUCHENDOES
Also see RIO, Chuck

CRESCHENDOS
(Crescendos)
Singles: 7-inch
MUSIC CITY (839 "Teenage Prayer") ... 200-250 61
Also see CRESCENDOS

CRESENTS
Singles: 7-inch
JOYCE (102 "Everybody Knew But Me") ... 150-250 57
(Every copy we have seen credits "Cresents." We're not yet aware of copies crediting the

"Crescents." Was the group's name really "Cresents," or is there an error on the labels?)
JOYCE (108 "Dolores") 4-6 90s

CRESHENDALS
Singles: 7-inch
FORTUNE (566 "Oh My Love") 10-20 64

CRESHENDOS
Singles: 7-inch
AQUARIUS (822 "You're Still on My Mind") 8-12

CRESTERS
Singles: 7-inch
CAPITOL 5-10 64

CRESTMEN
Singles: 7-inch
SYLVIA 4-8 65

CRESTONES
Singles: 7-inch
MARKIE 10-15 64-65
U.S.A. 5-10 65

CRESTRIDERS
Singles: 7-inch
CRYSTALETTE (756 "Surf Stomp") 10-15 63
(Previously issued as *Boomerang*, by the Spinners and as *The Lion*, by Duke Mitchell.)
Also see MITCHELL, Duke
Also see SPINNERS

CRESTS — P&R '57
(With Johnny Maestro; with "Johnny Mastro;" Original Crests; with Al Browne & His Orchestra; "Crest's")
Singles: 78 rpm
JOYCE 103 ("Sweetest One") 75-125 57
JOYCE 105 ("No One to Love") ...75-125 57
Singles: 7-inch
ABC 3-4 73
APT (25075 "She's All Mine Alone") 10-20 65
CAMEO (256 "I'll Be True") 25-35 64
CAMEO (305 "Lean on Me") 10-20 64
COED (501 "Pretty Little Angel") 100-200 58
COED (506 "16 Candles") 25-50 58
(Red label.)
COED (506 "16 Candles") 15-25 61
(Black label.)
COED (509 "Six Nights a Week") ..25-50 59
COED (511 "Molly Mae") 25-50 59
COED (515 "The Angels Listened In") 25-50 59
COED (521 "A Year Ago Tonight") 20-40 59
COED (525 "Step By Step") 20-40 60
COED (531 "Trouble in Paradise") .20-40 60
COED (535 "Journey of Love") 20-40 60
COED (537 "Isn't It Amazing") 20-40 60
COED (543 "In the Still of the Night") 20-40 60
COED (561 "Little Miracles") 15-25 61
COLLECTABLES 3-4 81-83
CORAL (62403 "You Blew Out the Candles") 15-25 64
ERIC 3-5 73
GOLDIES 45 3-4
HARVEY (501 "16 Candles") 5-10 81
(Colored vinyl.)
JOYCE 103 ("Sweetest One") 100-200 57
(With the oversize letter "Y" in the Joyce logo.)
JOYCE 103"(Sweetest One") 15-25
(With all of the letters the same size in the Joyce logo.)
JOYCE 105"(No One to Love") 100-200 57
KING TUT 4-8
LANA 4-8 64
LOST-NITE 4-8
MCA 3-5 73
MUSICTONE (1106 "Sweetest One") 20-30 62
ORIGINAL SOUND 3-5 87
QUALITY 15-30
(Canadian.)
SELMA (311 "Guilty") 20-40 62
SELMA (4000 "Did I Remember") 30-50 63
TIMES SQUARE (2 "No One to Love") 30-40 62
(Colored vinyl.)
TIMES SQUARE (6 "Baby") 15-25 64
(Black vinyl. Selection number on both sides is 6.)
TIMES SQUARE (6 "Baby") 30-40 64
(Colored vinyl.)
TIMES SQUARE (97 "Baby") 20-30 64
(Selection number on B-side is 6.)
TRANS ATLAS (696 "The Actor") 25-50 62
TRIP 3-5 70s
EPs: 7-inch
COED (101 "The Angels Listened In") 300-400 59
LPs: 10/12-inch
COED (901 "The Crests Sing All Biggies") 250-500 60
COED (904 "Best of the Crests") 200-350 60
COLLECTABLES (5009 "Greatest Hits") 8-10 82
COLLECTABLES (P-5009 "Greatest Hits") 10-15 82
(Picture disc.)
POST 8-12 70s
RHINO 5-10 90
Members: Johnny Maestro; Tom Gough; Harold Torres; Jay Carter; James Ancrum.
Also see BROWNE, Al
Also see CARTER, J.T.
Also see MAESTRO, Johnny

CRESTS / Skyliners
Singles: 7-inch
ORIGINAL SOUND 3-4 84
Also see SKYLINERS

CRESTS / Cal York & Roamers
Singles: 7-inch
HIT 5-15 60s
Also see CRESTS

CRESTWOODS
Singles: 7-inch
IMPACT (6 "Angel of Love") 25-50 61
(Colored vinyl.)

CRESTWOODS
Singles: 7-inch
SOMAR 5-10 66

CRETONES — P&R/LP '80
Singles: 7-inch
PLANET 3-4 80-81
Picture Sleeves
PLANET 3-4 80
LPs: 10/12-inch
PLANET 5-10 80-81

CREW
Singles: 7-inch
BRASS (194 "Big Junk") 15-25 63
(No London distribution noted.)
BRASS (2900 "Big Junk") 10-20 63
(Reads: "Dist. by London Records, Inc.")
YUCCA (713 "Flight 889") 15-25 59

CREW, Tom
Singles: 7-inch
BELL 4-8 64

CREW-CUTS — P&R '54
Singles: 78 rpm
MERCURY 8-15 54-57
Singles: 7-inch
ABC-PAR 4-8 63
CHESS 4-6 64
FIREBIRD 3-5 70
MERCURY 10-20 54-57
RCA 6-12 58-60
VEE JAY 4-8 63
WARWICK 5-10 60-61
WHALE 4-8 62
EPs: 7-inch
MERCURY 10-20 54-57
LPs: 10/12-inch
CAMAY (3002 "Folk") 10-15
MERCURY (20067 "Crew-Cuts Go Long Hair") 30-40 55
MERCURY (20140 "On the Campus") 30-40 56
MERCURY (20143 "Crew-Cut Capers") 30-40 56
MERCURY (20144 "Rock & Roll Bash") 35-50 56
MERCURY (20199 "Music A La Carte") 30-40 57
MERCURY (25200 "On the Campus") 40-60 55
(10-inch LP.)
PICCADILLY 8-10 80
RCA (1933 "Surprise Package") 20-30 58
RCA (2037 "Crew-Cuts Sing") 20-30 59
RCA (2067 "You Must Have Been a Beautiful Baby") 20-30 60
WING (12180 "High School Favorites") 15-25 60
WING (12195 "Swing the Masters") 15-25 60
Members: Ray Perkins; John Perkins; Rudi Maugeri; Pat Barrett.
Also see COASTERS / Crew-Cuts / Chiffons

CREW-CUTS / Junior Powell & Charlotte Grubic
LPs: 10/12-inch
RCA CUSTOM ("The Crew-Cuts Have a Ball") 20-30 59
(Special products issue for Ebonite Co. One side has "Bowling Tips By Top Stars")
Also see CREW-CUTS

CREWE, Bob — P&R '60
(Bob Crewe Generation; B.C.G.; with Rays)
Singles: 78 rpm
CORAL 5-10 56
Singles: 7-inch
ABC-PAR 10-15 61
DYNO VOICE 5-10 66-68
CORAL 10-20 56
CREWE 3-5 71
ELEKTRA 3-5 76-77
ERIC 3-4 73
GAMBLE 3-5 69
JUBILEE 10-20 54
MELBA 10-20 57
METROMEDIA 3-5 72
SPOTLIGHT 15-25 56
20TH FOX 3-5 76
U.T. 10-15 59
VIK (0337 "Charm Bracelet") 20-30 57
WARWICK 10-15 59-61
Picture Sleeves
DYNO VOICE 4-8 67
LPs: 10/12-inch
CGC 10-12 70
CREWE 10-15
DYNO VOICE 10-12 67-68
ELEKTRA 8-10 76-77
GAMBLE 3-4 69
PHILIPS (200150 "All the Song Hits of the 4 Seasons") 15-20 64
(Monaural. Includes lyrics sheet.)
PHILIPS (200238 "The 4 Seasons Hits") 10-15 67
(Monaural.)
PHILIPS (600150 "All the Song Hits of the 4 Seasons") 15-20 64
(Stereo. Includes lyrics sheet.)
PHILIPS (600238 "The 4 Seasons Hits") 10-15 67
(Stereo.)
WARWICK (2009 "Kicks") 25-35 60
WARWICK (2034 "Crazy in the Heart") 25-35 61
Also see LA ROSA, Julius, & Bob Crew Generation

CREWNECKS
(With Khakis)
Singles: 7-inch
RHAPSODY (71959 "I'll Never Forget You") 50-75 59
RHAPSODY (71961 "Rockin' Zombie") 50-75 60
Members: Bob Martin; Boyd "Porky" Hoats; Larry Choper; Jerry Pauley; Bruce Miles.

CREWS, Dwayne — C&W '90
Singles: 7-inch
KILLER 3-4 90

CRIB & BEN
Singles: 7-inch
DECCA 3-6 69

CRIBBINS, Bernard
Singles: 7-inch
CAPITOL 4-8 67

CRICKET
LPs: 10/12-inch
Z-BRAH 5-10 80

CRICKET, Obie
Singles: 7-inch
RUST 4-8 63

CRICKETONES
Singles: 7-inch
CRICKET 4-6
Picture Sleeves
CRICKET 4-8

CRICKETS — R&B '53
(Crickets Featuring Dean Barlow)
Singles: 78 rpm
BEACON 40-60 54
JAY-DEE 50-75 53
MGM 50-75 53
Singles: 7-inch
BEACON (104 "Be Faithful"/"I'm Not the One You Love") 75-100 54
BEACON (555 "Be Faithful"/"I'm Not the One You Love") 20-30 63
DAVIS (459 "I'm Going to Live My Life Alone") 50-100 58
JAY-DEE (777 "Dreams and Wishes") 150-250 53
JAY-DEE (781 "I'm Not the One You Love") 150-250 53
MGM (11428 "You're Mine") 150-250 53
MGM (11507 "For You I Have Eyes") 150-250 53
LPs: 10/12-inch
RELIC 8-12
Members: Harold Johnson; Leon Carter; Eugene Stapleton; Rodney Jackson; Grover "Dean" Barlow; J.R. Bailey; Robert Spencer; Freddy Barksdale; Robert Bynum; William Lindsay; Joe Dias.
Also see BAILEY, J.R.
Also see BARLOW, Dean
Also see BARLOW, Dean, & Crickets / Deep River Boys
Also see CADILLACS

CRICKETS
Singles: 7-inch
BARNABY 15-25 72
BRUNSWICK (55124 "Love's Made a Fool of You") 15-25 59
BRUNSWICK (55153 "When You Ask About Love") 15-25 59
CORAL (62198 "More Than I Can Say") 15-25 60
EPIC (08028 "T-Shirt") 3-4 88
LIBERTY 10-20 61-65
(Black labels.)
LIBERTY 15-25 61-65
(Promotional issues. With cream color or white labels.)
MGM 10-15 73
MUSIC FACTORY 15-20 68
Note: Records by Buddy Holly & Crickets, even if credited only to the Crickets, are listed in the BUDDY HOLLY section.
Promotional Singles
BRUNSWICK (55124 "Love's Made a Fool of You") 20-30 59
BRUNSWICK (55153 "When You Ask About Love") 20-30 59
CORAL (62198 "More Than I Can Say") 20-30 60
EPIC (08028 "T-Shirt") 3-4 88
EPs: 7-inch
B.H.M.S. 3-6 78
CORAL (81192 "The Crickets") 75-100 63
(With Buddy Holly on one track, *It's Too Late*.)
LPs: 10/12-inch
BARNABY (30268 "Rockin' '50s Rock & Roll") 15-25 70
CORAL (57320 "In Style") 40-60 60
KOALA 8-10
LIBERTY (3272 "Something Old, Something New, Something Blue, Somethin' Else") 30-40 64
(Monaural.)
LIBERTY (3351 "California Sun") ...30-40 64
(Monaural.)
LIBERTY (7272 "Something Old, Something New, Something Blue, Somethin' Else") 40-50 64
(Stereo.)
LIBERTY (7351 "California Sun") ...40-50 64
(Stereo.)
VERTIGO 10-20 73
Note: Records by Buddy Holly & Crickets, even if credited only to the Crickets, are listed in the BUDDY HOLLY section.
Members: Sonny Curtis; Jerry Naylor; Glen D. Hardin; Jerry Allison; Joe Mauldin; Earl Sinks; David Box.
Also see ALLISON, Jerry, & Crickets
Also see BOX, David
Also see CAMPERS
Also see CURTIS, Sonny
Also see HOLLY, Buddy
Also see IVAN
Also see JENNINGS, Waylon
Also see NAYLOR, Jerry
Also see PRESLEY, Elvis
Also see SULLIVAN, Niki
Also see VEE, Bobby, & Crickets

CRIDER, Tommy
Singles: 7-inch
TOKEN 4-8 63

CRIKITT, Jiminy
Singles: 7-inch
UNI 3-5 70

CRIME
Singles: 7-inch
CRIME MUSIC 3-5 78

CRIMINAL NATION
Singles: 12-inch
NASTYMIX 4-8 90

CRIMPTON, Roy Gene
Singles: 7-inch
REVUE 3-6 69

CRIMSON, King: see KING CRIMSON

CRIMSON & CLOVER
Singles: 7-inch
BELL 3-5 72

CRIMSON BRIDGE
LPs: 10/12-inch
MYRRH 5-10 72

CRIMSON SHADES
Singles: 7-inch
CINEMASOUND (8134 "I Wrote My Love a Letter") 100-150 64

CRIMSON TIDE
Singles: 7-inch
CAPITOL 3-4 78-79
LPs: 10/12-inch
CAPITOL (Except 11806) 5-10 78-79
CAPITOL (11806 "Crimson Tide") ...5-10 78
(Black vinyl.)
CAPITOL (11806 "Crimson Tide") .10-15 78
(Colored vinyl. Promotional issue only.)
Members: Wayne Perkins; J.J. Jackson; Greg Straub; Bobby Delander; Dale Perkins.
Also see RUSSELL, Leon

CRISPINO, John, & C.A.T.
Singles
ERIKA (58 "Madman Jack") 8-12 81
(Football-shaped picture disc. 1000 made. Tribute to Jack Lambert.)
Singles: 7-inch
AZRA (102 "Bad Night") 4-6 81
ERIKA 4-6 81
(Picture disc. Promotional issue only.)
Also see C.A.T.

CRISS, Gary
Singles: 7-inch
DIAMOND (except 228) 5-10 62-67
DIAMOND (228 "Welcome Home to My Heart") 10-20 67
SALSOUL 3-5 79
STRAND 10-15 61

CRISS, Peter — LP '78
Singles: 7-inch
CASABLANCA 3-5 79-80
LPs: 10/12-inch
CASABLANCA (7122 "Peter Criss") 25-50 78
CASABLANCA (PIX-7122 "Peter Criss") 50-60 79
(Picture disc.)
CASABLANCA (7240 "Out of Control") 25-50 80
Note: We have yet to learn of a U.S. release of the European-issued *Let Me Rock You*.
Also see KISS

CRISS, Sonny
Singles: 7-inch
IMPERIAL 5-10 60
PEACOCK 4-8 61
LPs: 10/12-inch
IMPERIAL 20-25 63

CRISTALE, Danny, & Tornadoes
Singles: 7-inch
HOME of the BLUES 5-10 60

CRISTINA
Singles: 7-inch
ZE 3-4 80
LPs: 10/12-inch
MERCURY 5-10 83
ZE 8-10 80

CRISTO, Bobby
Singles: 7-inch
U.A. 4-8 67

CRITERIONS
Singles: 7-inch
CECILIA (1010 "Don't Say Goodbye") 25-50 59
(Blue label.)
CECILIA (1010 "Don't Say Goodbye") 15-25 60s
(Orange label.)
CECILIA (1208 "I Remain Truly Yours") 50-75 59
LAURIE (3305 "I Remain Truly Yours") 10-15 65
PRINCE (1210 "Island Fever") 5-10 61
ROULETTE (4076 "Choo Choo Rock") 15-25 58
Members: Tommy West; Tim Hauser.
Also see MANHATTAN TRANSFER
Also see WEST, Tommy

CRITICAL MASS
LPs: 10/12-inch
MCA 5-10 80

CRITICS
Singles: 7-inch
PANOMA 3-4 80

CRITTERS — P&R/LP '66
Singles: 7-inch
KAPP 5-10 65-69
MCA 3-5 73-84
MUSICOR (1044 "Georgianna") 10-20 65
PRANCER 4-8 68
PROJECT 3 .... 4-8 67-69
Picture Sleeves
KAPP (769 "Mr. Dieingly Sad") 8-12 66
PROJECT 3 .... 4-8 67-69
LPs: 10/12-inch
BACK-TRAC 5-10 85
KAPP (1485 "Younger Girl") 20-30 66
(Monaural.)
KAPP (3485 "Younger Girl") 25-35 66
(Stereo.)
PROJECT 3 .... 15-20 68
Members: Don Ciccone; Chris Darway.
Also see CICCONE, Don

CRITTERS / Young Rascals / Lou Christie
LPs: 10/12-inch
BOTIQUE 10-20 66
(Tracks shown as by the Young Rascals are actually by Felix & Escorts.)
Also see CHRISTIE, Lou
Also see CRITTERS
Also see FELIX & ESCORTS

CRITTERS
Singles: 7-inch
KOUNTRY KARAVAN (115 "The Lady Took Me In") 8-12 73

CROCE, Jim — P&R/LP '72
Singles: 7-inch
ABC 3-5 72-74
LIFESONG 3-5 75-76
Picture Sleeves
ABC (11413 "Time in a Bottle") 4-8 73
EPs: 7-inch
ABC (769 "Life and Times") 10-12 73
(Juke box issue only.)
LPs: 10/12-inch
ABC (100 "A Jim Croce Christmas Programming Sampler") 15-20 73
(Promotional issue only.)
ABC (769 thru 835) 8-12 72-74
ABC/COMMAND (40006 "You Don't Mess Around with Jim") 15-25 74
(Quadraphonic.)
ABC/COMMAND (40007 "Life and Times") 15-25 74
(Quadraphonic.)
ABC/COMMAND (40008 "I Got a Name") 15-25 74
(Quadraphonic.)
ABC/COMMAND (40020 "Photographs and Memories") 15-25 74
(Quadraphonic.)
BURNS MEDIA (1-2 "The Faces I've Been") 40-60 75
(Two discs. Promotional issue only.)
CASHWEST (77024 "The Jim Croce Collection") 8-10 77
LIFESONG 10-15 75-78
MFSL (079 "You Don't Mess Around with Jim") 25-50 82
Session: Maury Muehleisen; Tommy West; Gary Chester; Marty Nelson; Joe Macho; Terry Cashman; Ellie Greenwich; David Spinozza.
Also see CASHMAN & WEST
Also see GREENWICH, Ellie

CROCE, Jim & Ingrid
(Jim & Ingrid)
Singles: 7-inch
CAPITOL 10-15 69
LPs: 10/12-inch
CAPITOL (315 "Croce") 30-35 69
PICKWICK (3332 "Another Day, Another Town") 8-12 70s
Also see CROCE, Jim

CROCHET, Cleveland — P&R '60
(With the Sugar Bees; with His Hillbilly Ramblers)
Singles: 7-inch
GOLDBAND 5-10 60-61
LYRIC 5-10
LPs: 10/12-inch
GOLDBAND (7749 "Cleveland Crochet and All the Sugar Bees") 50-75 61

CROCKER, Frankie "Loveman"
Singles: 7-inch
TURBO (1 "Ton of Dynamite") 25-50

CROCKER, Jack
Singles: 7-inch
FRETONE 3-5 74

CROCKETT, Franky
Singles: 7-inch
ABC-PAR 5-10 60

CROCKETT, G.L. P&R/R&B '65
(G. Davy Crockett)
Singles: 78 rpm
CHIEF (7010 "Look Out Mabel") 50-75 57
Singles: 7-inch
CHECKER (1121 "Look Out Mabel") 20-30 65
CHIEF (7010 "Look Out Mabel") 50-75 57
4 BROTHERS (445 "It's a Man Down There") 8-10 65
4 BROTHERS (448 "Every Good-bye Ain't Gone") 8-10 65
4 BROTHERS (451 "Think Twice Before You Go") 8-10 66

CROCKETT, Howard C&W '73
Singles: 78 rpm
DOT (15593 "If You'll Let Me") 35-50 57
Singles: 7-inch
DOT (15593 "If You'll Let Me") 35-50 57
DOT (17000 series) 3-5 73
MANCO 5-10 60
MEL-O-DY 10-20 64-65

CROCKETT, P.C.
Singles: 7-inch
VERVE 3-6 68

CROCKETT BROTHERS
Singles: 7-inch
DEL-FI (4213 "Mother, Mother, Can I Go Surfin' ") 10-20 63
DONNA (1389 "Fastest Car in Town") 10-20 63
Members: Joel Crockett; Jeremy Crockett; Chris Crockett.

CROFFORD, Cliff
Singles: 78 rpm
TALLY 15-30 56-57
Singles: 7-inch
TALLY (104 "Ain't Nothin' Happenin' to Me") 20-30 56
TALLY (109 "A Night for Love") 20-30 57

CROFT, Hal
Singles: 7-inch
JAB 4-8 67

CROFT, Sandy C&W '83
Singles: 7-inch
ANGELSONG 3-4 83
CAPITOL 3-4 84-85

CROFTERS
LPs: 10/12-inch
LONDON 10-15 71

CROISETTE
LPs: 10/12-inch
A.V.I. 5-10 79

CROMAGNON
LPs: 10/12-inch
ESP (2001 "Cromagnon") 20-30 69

CROME SYRCUS
Singles: 7-inch
COMMAND 5-10 68
JERDEN 4-8 69
MERRILYN 8-12 60s
PICCADILLY 5-10 68
LPs: 10/12-inch
COMMAND (925 "Love Cycle") 15-25 68

CROMER, Allen
Singles: 7-inch
EDGE 4-8 63

CROMWELL, George
(With Larry Love Orchestra)
Singles: 7-inch
BRUNSWICK 5-10 59
GLORY 10-20 58

CROMWELL, Link
Singles: 7-inch
HOLLYWOOD 4-8 66

CRONIN, Jerry, & Flashes
Singles: 7-inch
FLAME (113 "Rock-A-Me Baby") ... 30-45 59

CROOK, Ed
Singles: 7-inch
TRI SOUND (601 "That's Alright") .. 15-25

CROOK, General R&B '70
Singles: 7-inch
CAPITOL 3-6 69
DOWN to EARTH 3-6 70-71
WAND 3-5 74
LPs: 10/12-inch
CAPITOL 10-15 70
WAND 10-12 74

CROOK, Howard
Singles: 7-inch
PHILIPS 4-8 62

CROOK, Reni
Singles: 7-inch
TMI 3-5 72

CROOM BROTHERS
Singles: 7-inch
VEE JAY (283 "It's You I Love") 40-50 58
Member: Dillard Croom Jr.

CROPPER, Steve
Singles: 7-inch
MCA 3-5 81-82
LPs: 10/12-inch
MCA 5-10 81-82
VOLT 12-15 69
Also see BOOKER T. & MGs
Also see MGs
Also see MAR-KEYS
Also see NERVOUS EATERS
Also see REDDING, Otis

CROSBY, Beverly R&B '77
Singles: 7-inch
BAREBACK 3-5 77

CROSBY, Bing P&R '31
(With the Andrews Sisters; with Gary Crosby; with Victor Young Orchestra; with Grady Martin & His Slew Foot Five)
Singles: 78 rpm
BRUNSWICK 10-20 32-34
DECCA 5-15 34-57
KAPP 3-5 57
VICTOR 10-20 31
Singles: 7-inch
AMOS 3-5 69
CAPITOL 4-6 63
COLUMBIA 4-6 59
CROWLEY'S/CROSBY ("How Lovely Is Christmas") 10-20
(Promotional issue made for Crowley's Milk Co.)
DAYBREAK 3-5 71
DECCA (23281 thru 30828) 5-10 51-59
DECCA (31000 series) 4-8 61-65
KAPP 4-6 57
LONDON 3-4 77
MGM 4-6 60
POLYDOR 3-4 78
RCA 4-6 60
REPRISE 4-6 64-67
U.A. 3-5 75
VERVE 4-6
Picture Sleeves
DECCA 5-10 53-63
DAYBREAK 3-5 71
KAPP 4-8 57
EPs: 7-inch
BRUNSWICK 5-15 50-55
COLUMBIA 8-12 50-57
DECCA ("Old Masters") 20-30
(Boxed EP set. No number shown.)
DECCA (Except 1700) 8-15 50-59
DECCA (1700 "Deluxe Box Set") 75-100 54
(Boxed, 17-disc set.)
RCA 5-10 57
THREE on ONE (407 "Bing Crosby Sings 2 New Christmas Songs") 5-10 50s
(Though labeled "45 Extended Play," actually has only one song on each side. May not have been issued with cover.)
VERVE (5022 "Bing Sings While Bregman Swings") 10-15 59
(With envelope/sleeve.)
LPs: 10/12-inch
AMOS 8-10 69
ARGO 10-15 76
BIOGRAPH 5-10 73
BRUNSWICK (54000 series) 15-25 55
BRUNSWICK (58000 series) 25-40 52
(10-inch LPs.)
CAPITOL (2300 series) 8-12 65
CAPITOL (11000 series) 5-10 77-78
CITADEL 5-10 78
COLUMBIA (43 "Bing in Hollywood") 10-15 67
COLUMBIA (2502 "Der Bingle") 20-30 56
(10-inch LP.)
COLUMBIA (6027 "Classics") 20-40 49
(10-inch LP.)
COLUMBIA (6105 "Classics, Vol. 2") 20-40 50
(10-inch LP.)
COLUMBIA (35000 series) 5-10 78-79
COLUMBIA SPECIAL PRODUCTS .. 5-8 77
DECCA (154 "Bing") 50-100 54
(Boxed, five-disc set. Includes booklet.)
DECCA (184 "Best of Bing Crosby") 10-15 65
DECCA (4000 series) 20-50 61-64
DECCA (5000 series) 15-25 49-55
(10-inch LPs.)
DECCA (6000 series) 25-50 55-56
(10-inch LPs.)
DECCA (8000 series) 15-25 54-59
(Black label with silver print.)
DECCA (8000 series) 8-15 60-72
(Black label with horizontal rainbow stripe.)
DECCA (8700 series) 8-12 64
DECCA (9000 series) 10-20 61-62
(Decca LP numbers in this series preceded by a "7" or a "DL-7" are stereo issues.)
DECCA CUSTOM (34461 "Bing Crosby") 10-20
(Promotional issue, made for La-Z-Boy.)
ENCORE 8-10 68
GOLDEN 10-15 57-59
HARMONY (7000 series) 10-15 57
HARMONY (11000 series) 5-10 69
LONDON 5-10 77
MCA 5-10 73-82
MGM 10-15 61-64
METRO 5-10 65
P.I.P. 5-10 71
POLYDOR 5-10 77
RCA (500 series) 6-10 72
RCA (1400 thru 2000 series) 10-20 57-59
(With "LPM" or "LSP" prefix.)
RCA (2000 series) 5-10 77
(With "CPL1" prefix.)
REPRISE 8-12 64
20TH FOX 5-10 79
U.A. 5-10 76
VERVE/MGM (2030 "Bing Sings While Bregman Swings") 25-50 56
VOCALION (3600 series) 10-15 57
VOCALION (3700 series) 5-10 66
W.B. 10-15 60-62
"X" 15-25 54
Also see ANDREWS SISTERS
Also see BOWIE, David, & Bing Crosby
Also see CROSBY, Gary, & Friend
Also see CROSBY, Gary, Phillip, Dennis, Lindsay & Bing
Also see DORSEY, Jimmy
Also see MARTIN, Grady, & His Slew Foot Five
Also see SINATRA, Frank, Bing Crosby & Dean Martin
Also see YOUNG, Victor

CROSBY, Bing & Gary P&R '50
Singles: 78 rpm
DECCA 3-5 50-51
Singles: 7-inch
DECCA 4-8 50-51

CROSBY, Bing, & Louis Armstrong P&R '51
Singles: 78 rpm
CAPITOL 3-5 56
DECCA 3-5 51
Singles: 7-inch
CAPITOL 4-8 56
DECCA 4-8 51
MGM 3-5 60
LPs: 10/12-inch
MGM (100 series) 5-10 70
MGM (3800 series) 10-20 60
SOUNDS RARE 5-10 83

CROSBY, Bing, Louis Armstrong, Rosemary Clooney & Hi-Los
Singles: 7-inch
COLUMBIA (6277 "Music to Shave By") 5-10 50s
(Special products flexi-disc from Remington.)
Also see ARMSTRONG, Louis
Also see CLOONEY, Rosemary
Also see CROSBY, Bing, & Louis Armstrong

CROSBY, Bing, & Fred Astaire
LPs: 10/12-inch
U.A. 5-8 77
Also see ASTAIRE, Fred

CROSBY, Bing, & Count Basie
LPs: 10/12-inch
DAYBREAK 8-12 72
Also see BASIE, Count

CROSBY, Bing, & Connee Boswell P&R '37
Singles: 78 rpm
DECCA 4-8 37-40
LPs: 10/12-inch
DECCA 15-25 52
Also see BOSWELL, Connee

CROSBY, Bing, & Judy Garland P&R '45
Singles: 78 rpm
DECCA 5-10 45
Also see GARLAND, Judy

CROSBY, Bing, Dick Haymes & Andrews Sisters P&R '47
Singles: 78 rpm
DECCA 5-10 47
Also see HAYMES, Dick

CROSBY, Bing, & Bob Hope P&R '45
Singles: 78 rpm
DECCA 5-10 45
EPs: 7-inch
CAPITOL CUSTOM (2263 "Vacation Road to Minnesota") 5-10
(Issued to promote Minnesota tourism.)
Also see BAXTER, Les
Also see HOPE, Bob

CROSBY, Bing, & Louis Jordan P&R '45
Singles: 78 rpm
DECCA 5-10 45
Also see JORDAN, Louis

CROSBY, Bing, & Grace Kelly / Bing Crosby & Frank Sinatra P&R '56
(With Johnny Green's Orchestra)
Singles: 78 rpm
CAPITOL 3-5 56
Singles: 7-inch
CAPITOL 5-10 56

CROSBY, Bing / Grace Kelly / Frank Sinatra / Celeste Holm
CAPITOL (281 "Interviews for use with Capitol Soundtrack LP, *High Society*") 50-100 56
(Promotional issue only.)
Also see SINATRA, Frank

CROSBY, Bing, & Peggy Lee
Singles: 78 rpm
DECCA 3-5 52
Singles: 7-inch
DECCA 5-10 52
Also see LEE, Peggy

CROSBY, Bing, & Johnny Mercer P&R '38
Singles: 78 rpm
DECCA 5-8 38-40
Also see MERCER, Johnny

CROSBY, Bing, & Mills Brothers P&R '31
(With Connee Boswell)
Singles: 78 rpm
BRUNSWICK 5-10 31-32
Also see MILLS BROTHERS

CROSBY, Bing, & Frank Sinatra
Singles: 78 rpm
CAPITOL 3-5 56
Singles: 7-inch
CAPITOL 5-10 56
Also see SINATRA, Frank

CROSBY, Bing, & Mel Torme P&R '46
(With the Mel-Tones)
Singles: 78 rpm
DECCA 4-8 46
Also see TORME, Mel

CROSBY, Bing, & Orson Welles
LPs: 10/12-inch
DECCA (6000 "The Small One, the Happy Prince") 10-25 50
(10-inch LP.)
Also see CROSBY, Bing
Also see WELLES, Orson

CROSBY, Chris P&R '64
Singles: 7-inch
ATLANTIC 4-8 67
CHALLENGE 4-8 64-65
COLUMBIA 3-6 69
DORE 4-8 61
MGM 4-8 64
W.B. 3-5 63
Picture Sleeves
MGM 5-10 64
LPs: 10/12-inch
MGM 15-20 64

CROSBY, David LP '71
Singles: 7-inch
ATLANTIC 3-5 71
LPs: 10/12-inch
A&M 5-8 89
ATLANTIC 10-15 71
Also see BYRDS
Also see GRATEFUL DEAD
Also see JEFFERSON AIRPLANE
Also see SLICK, Grace

CROSBY, David, & Graham Nash P&R '71
Singles: 7-inch
ABC 3-5 75-77
ATLANTIC 3-5 72
LPs: 10/12-inch
ABC 8-10 75-78
ATLANTIC 10-15 72
MCA 5-10 75
Also see CROSBY, David
Also see NASH, Graham

CROSBY, Eddie C&W '49
Singles: 78 rpm
DECCA 4-8 49

CROSBY, Gary
Singles: 7-inch
DECCA 5-10 55
GREGMARK (11 "That's Alright Baby") 20-25 62
HICKORY (1448 "Town Girl") 5-10 66

CROSBY, Gary, & Friend (Bing Crosby)
EPs: 7-inch
DECCA (2001 "Gary Crosby & Friend") 10-15 54

CROSBY, Gary, Phillip, Dennis, Lindsay & Bing P&R '50
Singles: 78 rpm
DECCA 5-8 50
Singles: 7-inch
DECCA (40181 "A Crosby Christmas") 10-15 50
Picture Sleeves
DECCA (1-134 "A Crosby Christmas") 20-40 50
(Sleeve for 45)
DECCA (796 "A Crosby Christmas") 10-20 50
(Sleeve for 78.)
Also see CROSBY, Bing
Also see CROSBY, Gary

CROSBY, Harold
Singles: 7-inch
TOP 50 8-12

CROSBY, Lindsay
Singles: 7-inch
RCA 4-8 58

CROSBY, Rob C&W '90
Singles: 7-inch
ARISTA 3-4 90-92

CROSBY, STILLS & NASH P&R/LP '69
Singles: 7-inch
ATLANTIC 3-6 69-89
Picture Sleeves
ATLANTIC 3-8 70-89
LPs: 10/12-inch
ATLANTIC (Except 8229) 8-10 77-83
ATLANTIC (8229 "Crosby, Stills & Nash") 15-20 69
Members: David Crosby; Stephen Stills; Graham Nash.

CROSBY, STILLS, NASH & YOUNG P&R/LP '70
Singles: 7-inch
ATLANTIC 3-5 70
Picture Sleeves
ATLANTIC 3-6 70
EPs: 7-inch
ATLANTIC 10-15 70
(Juke box issue only.)
LPs: 10/12-inch
ATLANTIC (165 "Celebration Copy") 25-35 70s
(Promotional issue only.)
ATLANTIC (902 "4-Way Street") ... 12-20 71
(With photo applied to cover.)
ATLANTIC (7200 "Deja Vu") 15-20 70
(With photo applied to cover.)
ATLANTIC (7200 "Deja Vu") 8-12
(With photo *printed* on cover.)
ATLANTIC (16000 thru 19000 series) 5-10 74-82
ATLANTIC (8000 series) 5-10 83
MFSL (088 "Deja Vu") 40-60 82
Promotional LPs
Members: David Crosby; Stephen Stills; Graham Nash; Neil Young.
Also see CROSBY, David
Also see CROSBY, STILLS & NASH
Also see NASH, Graham
Also see STILLS, Stephen
Also see YOUNG, Neil

CROSBY BROTHERS
Singles: 7-inch
DOT 4-6 61-62

CROSS, Christopher P&R/LP '80
Singles: 7-inch
COLUMBIA 3-4 85
REPRISE 3-4 88
W.B. 3-4 79-85
Picture Sleeves
REPRISE 3-4 88
W.B. 3-4 80-85
LPs: 10/12-inch
COLUMBIA 5-10 85
REPRISE 5-8 88
W.B. (Except 1172) 3-4 79-85
W.B. (1172 "Theme from *Arthur*") 20-25 81
(Picture disc. Promotional issue only.)
Also see McDONALD, Michael

CROSS, Don
Singles: 7-inch
MEDIAN 3-4 78-79

CROSS, Gay, & Good Humor Six
Singles: 78 rpm
REPUBLIC (7027 "G.C. Rock") 10-15 53
Singles: 7-inch
REPUBLIC (7027 "G.C. Rock") 20-30 53

CROSS, Jimmy P&R '65
Singles: 7-inch
CHICKEN 4-8 65
RECORDO 5-10 61
RED BIRD 5-10 65
REO 8-12 64
(Canadian.)
TOLLIE 5-10 64

CROSS, Judy
Singles: 7-inch
CLARION 4-8
MGM 5-10 60

CROSS COUNTRY P&R/LP '73
(Tokens)
Singles: 7-inch
ATCO 3-6 73-74
LPs: 10/12-inch
ATCO 10-15 73
Members: Jay Siegel; Phil Margo; Mitch Margo.
Also see TOKENS

CROSS KEYS
Singles: 7-inch
DOT 4-8 61

CROSS TOWN TRAFFIQUE
Singles: 7-inch
NECTAR 3-5 70

CROSSE, Gay
(Gay Crosse & His Good Humor Six)
Singles: 78 rpm
GOTHAM 10-15 51
MERCURY 10-20 47
QUEEN 10-20 46
RCA 10-20 49-50
Singles: 7-inch
RCA (0033 "Saturday Night Fish Fry") 25-50 49
(Colored vinyl.)
RCA (0050 "It Ain't Gonna Be That Way") 25-50 50
(Colored vinyl.)

CROSSEN, Ray, Jr.
Singles: 7-inch
MUSICOR 10-20 67

CROSSFIRE
Singles: 7-inch
SMASH 3-5 70

CROSSFIRE
LPs: 10/12-inch
HEADFIRST 5-10 81

CROSSFIRES
Singles: 7-inch
CUCA 8-12 61
Members: Ace Baumann.
Also see BAUMANN, Ace, & Crossfires

CROSSFIRES
Singles: 7-inch
TOWER...10-20 66
Also see FOUNTAIN of YOUTH

CROSSFIRES
LPs: 10/12-inch
STRAND (1083 "Limbo Rock")...15-25 63
Members: Les Philbrick; Dennis Day; David Kent.

CROSSFIRES
Singles: 7-inch
CAPCO (104 "Dr. Jekyll & Mr. Hyde")...20-30 63
LUCKY TOKEN (112 "One Potato, Two Potato")...5-10 65
LPs: 10/12-inch
RHINO...5-10 81
Members: Howard Kaylan; Mark Volman; Don Murray; Chuck Portz; Al Nichol; Dale Walton.
Also see TURTLES

CROSSLEY, Charlotte, Sharon Redd & Ula Hedwig
Singles: 7-inch
COLUMBIA...3-4 78
LPs: 10/12-inch
COLUMBIA...8-10 78

CROSSROADS
Singles: 7-inch
ATCO...3-5 70

CROSSTONES
Singles: 78 rpm
JAGUAR (3014 "Lies")...50-75 55
Singles: 7-inch
JAGUAR (3014 "Lies")...100-150 55

CROSSTOWN BUS
Singles: 7-inch
MCA...4-8 70
WILDCAT (99999 "I Crave Your Love")...20-30

CROSSTOWNERS
Singles: 7-inch
AMY...4-8 62

CROTHERS, Scatman
(Scat Man; Scat Man Carothers; Scatman Crothers Mellow Men)
Singles: 78 rpm
CAPITOL...10-20 48-49
CN...10-15 55
CENTURY...10-15 55
DECCA...10-15 54
INTRO...10-20 51
LONDON...10-20 50
MGM...10-15 56
RECORDED in HOLLYWOOD...10-20 51
Singles: 7-inch
CN...10-20 55
CENTURY (712 "Where Or When")...15-25 55
CHALLENGE...4-8 60
DECCA...10-20 54
DOOTO...5-10 61
HBR...3-6 66
LONDON (30081 "Television Blues")...40-60 50
MGM...10-15 56
EPs: 7-inch
DOOTO...5-15 61
LPs: 10/12-inch
CRAFTSMAN...15-25 60
DOOTO...10-15 61
MOTOWN...10-12 73
TOPS (1511 "Rock & Roll with Scat Man")...30-50 56
Also see BIG BEN

CROTHERS, Scatman / Gene Merlino / Bud Roman
(With the Toppers)
EPs: 7-inch
TOPS (286 "Transfusion")...15-25 56
Also see CROTHERS, Scatman

CROUCH, Andrae R&B '80
(With His Disciples)
Singles: 7-inch
LIGHT...3-4 76-80
W.B....3-4 81
LPs: 10/12-inch
ACCORD...82 5-8
LIGHT...5-8 68-82
W.B....5-8 81
Also see JACKSON, Michael

CROUCH, Dub
Singles: 7-inch
PROFESSIONAL ARTISTS...3-5 77

CROW P&R/LP '69
(David Wagner)
Singles: 7-inch
AMARET...3-6 69-72
INNER EAR (427 "Autumn of Tomorrow")...25-50
PEAK...8-12 83
(Colored vinyl)
LPs: 10/12-inch
AMARET...10-15 69-73
PEAK...4-8 83
Members: David Waggoner; Dennis Craswell; Kink Middlellest.
Also see CASTAWAYS
Also see CAVALIERS
Also see SOUTH 40
Also see WAGGONER, David

CROW, Alvin C&W '77
(With the Pleasant Valley Boys; with Tommy Allsup; with Jesse Ashlock)
Singles: 7-inch
POLYDOR...3-5 77-78
LPs: 10/12-inch
LONGNECK...6-12 76
POLYDOR...5-10 76-77
Also see ALLSUP, Tommy

CROW, Sheryl P&R/LP '94
Singles: 7-inch
A&M...3-4 94-96

CROWBAR
Singles: 7-inch
EPIC...3-5 74
PARAMOUNT...4-6 70-71
LPs: 10/12-inch
EPIC...8-10 74
PARAMOUNT...10-15 70-71

CROWD PLEASERS R&B '79
Singles: 7-inch
WESTBOUND...3-4 79
LPs: 10/12-inch
WESTBOUND...5-10 79

CROWD PLUS 1
Singles: 7-inch
CAPITOL...4-6 68-69

CROWDED HOUSE LP '86
Singles: 12-inch
CAPITOL...4-6 86
Singles: 7-inch
CAPITOL...3-4 86-88
Picture Sleeves
CAPITOL...3-4 87-88
LPs: 10/12-inch
CAPITOL...5-10 86-88
Members: Neil Finn; Paul Hester; Nick Seymour; Tim Finn.
Also see SPLIT ENZ

CROWDER, Bud
Singles: 7-inch
TOPPA...4-8 62

CROWELL, Rodney C&W '78
Singles: 7-inch
COLUMBIA...3-4 86-90
W.B....3-4 78-82
LPs: 10/12-inch
COLUMBIA...5-8 86-90
W.B....5-10 78-81
Session: Karen Brooks.
Also see BROOKS, Karen
Also see HARRIS, Emmylou
Also see SHAVER, Billy Joe
Also see STEWART, Gary

CROWELL, Rodney, & Rosanne Cash C&W '88
Singles: 7-inch
COLUMBIA...3-4 88
Also see CASH, Rosanne
Also see CROWELL, Rodney

CROWFOOT
Singles: 7-inch
ABC...3-5 71
PARAMOUNT...3-5 70-71
LPs: 10/12-inch
ABC...10-12 71
Members: Sam McCue; Rick Jaeger; Russell Dashiel.
Also see DASHIEL, Russell
Also see LEGENDS
Also see McCUE, Sam

CROWLEY, J.C. C&W '88
Singles: 7-inch
RCA...3-4 88
Also see PLAYER

CROWLEY, Sheryl
Singles: 78 rpm
FLASH...15-25 56
Singles: 7-inch
FLASH (112 "It Ain't to Play With")...25-35 56
Also see CURRY, James / Sheryl Crowley

CROWN, Bobby, & Kapers
Singles: 7-inch
FELCO (102 "One Way Ticket")...300-500 59

CROWN HEIGHTS AFFAIR R&B '74
Singles: 12-inch
SBK...4-6 89
Singles: 7-inch
DELITE...3-5 75-82
RCA...3-5 73-74
LPs: 10/12-inch
DELITE...5-10 75-82
RCA...10-12 74-78
Members: Phil Thomas; Ray Rock; Bert Reid; James Baynard; Ray Reid; William Anderson; Howard Young; Muki Wilson.

CROWNS (With Arthur Lee Maye) see MAYE, Arthur Lee

CROWNS
Singles: 7-inch
R n B (6901 "Kiss and Make Up")...50-75 58
Members: Ben E. King; James Clark; Charlie Thomas; Dock Green; Elsbeary Hobbs.
Also see DRIFTERS
Also see DUVALS
Also see FIVE CROWNS
Also see KING, Ben E.
Also see MOONGLOWS

CROWNS
Singles: 7-inch
WHEEL (1001 "Heart Breaking Train")...100-200 59

CROWNS
Singles: 7-inch
CHORDETTE (1001 "Party Time")...8-12 62

CROWNS
Singles: 7-inch
BALL (1015 "Why Did You Go Away")...25-35 63
VEE JAY (546 "I Wonder Why")...10-15 63
Member: Philip Harris.

CROWNS
Singles: 7-inch
OLD TOWN (1171 "Watch Out")...30-40 64

CROWNS
Singles: 7-inch
LIMELIGHT (3031 "It's Still Love")...15-25 64

CROWS P&R/R&B '54
(With Melino & His Orchestra)
Singles: 78 rpm
QUALITY (1236 "Gee")...50-75 53
(Canadian.)
RAMA (3 "Seven Lonely Days")...100-200 53
RAMA (5 "Gee")...50-100 53
RAMA (10 "Heartbreaker")...50-100 53
RAMA (29 "Baby")...75-125 54
RAMA (30 "Miss You")...100-200 54
RAMA (50 "Baby Doll")...50-100 54
TICO (1082 "Mambo Shevitz")...50-100 51
Singles: 7-inch
QUALITY (1236 "Gee")...100-150 53
(Canadian.)
RAMA (3 "Seven Lonely Days")...500-750 53
RAMA (5 "Gee")...50-100 53
(Black vinyl. Blue label. No clouds or lines around "Rama" logo.)
RAMA (5 "Gee")...40-60 53
(Black vinyl. Blue label. With clouds and lines around "Rama" logo.)
RAMA (5 "Gee")...300-500 53
(Red vinyl.)
RAMA (5 "Gee")...20-40 56
(Red label.)
RAMA (10 "Heartbreaker")...300-500 53
(Black vinyl.)
RAMA (10 "Heartbreaker")...1000-2000 53
(Red vinyl.)
RAMA (29 "Baby")...200-300 54
RAMA (30 "Miss You")...250-350 54
(Black vinyl.)
RAMA (30 "Miss You")...1000-2000 54
(Red vinyl.)
RAMA (50 "Baby Doll")...250-350 54
TICO (1082 "Mambo Shevitz")...200-300 51
(Black vinyl.)
TICO (1082 "Mambo Shevitz")...500-750 51
(Red vinyl.)
LPs: 10/12-inch
MURRAY HILL...5-8 88
Members: Daniel "Sonny" Norton; Harold Major; Jerry Hamilton; Mark Jackson; Bill Davis.
Also see ELLIS, Lorraine
Also see HARPTONES / Crows
Also see HUMPHRIES, Fat Man, & Four Notes
Also see JEWELS
Also see WATKINS, Viola

CRUCHENDOES
Singles: 7-inch
TOPPA...5-10
Member: Chuck Rio.
Also see RIO, Chuck

CRUCIBLES
Singles: 7-inch
MAD TOWN (401 "You Know I Do")...40-60 66
Members: Ed Erickson; Greg Kimmerly; Treble Lysenko; Bruce Hull; Tom Fisher; John Edland; Dave Brownley; Rod Butler; Fred Elwakil.
Also see KIRIAE CRUCIBLE

CRUDUP, Big Boy R&B '45
(Arthur "Big Boy" Crudup)
Singles: 78 rpm
ACE (503 "I Wonder")...200-300 53
BLUEBIRD...20-50 41-46
CHAMPION (108 "I Wonder")...200-300 52
GROOVE...20-30 53-54
RCA...20-50 47-53
Singles: 7-inch
FIRE (1501 "Mean Ol' Frisco")...10-20 62
FIRE (1502 "Katie Mae")...10-20 62
GROOVE (0011 "I Love My Baby")...30-50 53
GROOVE (0026 "She's Got No Hair")...30-50 54
GROOVE (5005 "Mean Ol' Frisco")...30-50 54
RCA (0000 "That's All Right")...200-225 49
(Colored vinyl.)
RCA (0001 "Boy Friend Blues")...50-100 49
(Colored vinyl.)
RCA (0013 "Shout Sister Shout") 50-100 49
(Colored vinyl.)
RCA (0032 "Hoodoo Lady Blues")...50-100 50
(Colored vinyl.)
RCA (0046 "Come Back Baby")...50-100 49
(Colored vinyl.)
RCA (0074 "Dust My Broom")...50-100 50
(Colored vinyl.)
RCA (0092 "Mean Old Santa Fe")...50-100 50
(Colored vinyl.)
RCA (0100 "Lonesome World to Me")...50-100 50
(Colored vinyl.)
RCA (0105 "She's Just Like Caldonia")...50-100 50
(Colored vinyl.)
RCA (0117 "Nobody Wants Me")...50-100 50
(Colored vinyl.)
RCA (0126 "Roberta Blues")...50-100 50
(Colored vinyl.)
RCA (0141 "Too Much Competition")...50-100 50
(Colored vinyl.)
RCA (4367 "Love Me Mama")...50-100 51
RCA (4572 "Goin' Back to Georgia")...50-75 52
RCA (4753 "Worried About You Baby")...50-75 52
RCA (4933 "Second Man Blues")...50-75 52
RCA (5070 "Pearly Lee")...50-75 52
RCA (5167 "Keep on Drinkin' ")...50-75 53
RCA (5563 "My Wife & Women")...50-75 53
EPs: 7-inch
CAMDEN (415 "Arthur 'Big Boy' Crudup")...100-125 57
LPs: 10/12-inch
COLLECTABLES...6-8 88
DELMARK...15-25 69
FIRE (103 "Mean Ol' Frisco")...150-200 62
RCA...10-20 71
TRIP (7501 "Mean Ol' Frisco")...8-12 75
Also see CRUDUP, Percy Lee
Also see CRUMP, Arthur
Also see JAMES, Elmore
Also see LITTLE RICHARD / Arthur Crudup / Red Callendar Sextet

CRUDUP, Percy Lee
(Arthur Crudup)
Singles: 78 rpm
CHECKER (754 "Open Your Book")...25-50 52
Also see CRUDUP, Big Boy

CRUISE, Johnny
Singles: 7-inch
JARO...5-10 59

CRUISE, Julee LP '90
LPs: 10/12-inch
W.B....5-8 90

CRUISE, Pablo: see PABLO CRUISE

CRUISER
LPs: 10/12-inch
NETWORK...5-10 81

CRUISERS
("Featuring Leroy Jones")
Singles: 7-inch
FINCH (353 "The Moon Is Yours") 25-35 57

CRUISERS
Singles: 7-inch
ARCH (1611 "I Said Hear")...25-50 59
CODA (3005 "Betty Ann")...25-50 59
COLLECTABLES...3-4 83
DORE (500 "Bouys & Gulls")...10-20 58
ERA (1052 "Bouys & Gulls")...20-30 57
JASON SCOTT...4-8
WINSTON (1033 "My Mary Lou")...30-50 59
ZEBRA (119 "There's a Girl")...150-250 58

CRUISERS
Singles: 7-inch
GAMBLE...5-8 67-70
GUYDEN (2069 "Cryin' Over You")...10-15 62
V-TONE (207 "Miss Fine")...25-50 60
(Blue label.)
V-TONE (207 "Miss Fine")...15-25 60
(Orange label.)
V-TONE (213 "Cryin' Over You")...15-25 60
(Blue label.)

CRUISERS
Singles: 7-inch
PHARAOH (125 "An Angel Like You")...25-35 61
PHARAOH (128 "Another Lonely Night")...15-25 61

CRUISERS
LPs: 10/12-inch
SPRINGBOARD...8-10 78

CRUM, Simon C&W '55
(Ferlin Husky)
Singles: 78 rpm
CAPITOL...5-15 55-57
Singles: 7-inch
ABC...3-5 74
CAPITOL...5-15 55-63
LPs: 10/12-inch
CAPITOL (1880 "The Unpredictable Simon Crum")...75-100 63
Also see HUSKY, Ferlin

CRUM, Tom
Singles: 7-inch
UNIVERSAL SOUND...3-5 71

CRUMB, Robert, & His Cheapsuit Serenaders
LPs: 10/12-inch
BLUE GOOSE...10-15 74

CRUMBACHER
LPs: 10/12-inch
FRONTLINE...5-10

CRUME, Dillard, Soul Rockers
Singles: 7-inch
GRIT...3-5 71
LPs: 10/12-inch
ALSHIRE...8-12 70

CRUME BROTHERS
Singles: 7-inch
ATCO...4-8 63
CHESS...4-6 68
PEACOCK...4-8 62

CRUMP, Arthur
(Arthur Crudup)
Singles: 78 rpm
CHAMPION ("I Wonder")...75-100
Also see CRUDUP, Big Boy

CRUMPETS
Singles: 7-inch
TECHNIQUE (101 "Mama Baby")...20-30 65

CRUNCH BAND
Singles: 7-inch
DG...3-5 79

CRUSADE
Singles: 7-inch
GOLDEN NORTH (103 "Psychedelic Woman")...20-35 60s

CRUSADERS
Singles: 7-inch
D.K.R. (12565 "Seminole")...20-30 62
(No selection number shown. "12565" is the identification number.)
CAMEO...5-10 63
DOOTO...10-15 63

CRUSADERS LP '71
Singles: 7-inch
ABC...3-4 78
BLUE THUMB...3-5 72-77
CHISA...3-5 71
MCA (8783 "Street Life")...20-30 79
(Picture disc. Promotional issue only. Reportedly 125 made.)
MOWEST...3-5
LPs: 10/12-inch
BLUE THUMB...10-12 73-77
GRP...5-8 91
MCA...8-10 79-86
MFSL (010 "Chain Reaction")...25-50 78
(Half-speed mastered.)
MOTOWN...10-12 73
MOWEST...10-12 72
Members: Larry Carlton; Pops Popwell.
Also see CARLTON, Larry
Also see COCKER, Joe
Also see CRAWFORD, Randy
Also see HOOPER, Stix
Also see JAZZ CRUSADERS
Also see SAMPLE, Joe

CRUSADERS & B.B. KING
Singles: 7-inch
MCA...3-4 82
LPs: 10/12-inch
MCA...8-10 82
Also see CRUSADERS
Also see KING, B.B.

CRUTCHFIELD, Jerry
Singles: 7-inch
CORAL...4-8 64
DOT...5-10 60-63
EUPHONIC...4-8
FELSTED...4-8 62

CRUZ, Ernie
Singles: 7-inch
BIG ISLAND...3-4
LPs: 10/12-inch
BIG ISLAND...5-8
Member: Chip Douglas.
Also see MODERN FOLK QUARTET

CRUZADOS LP '85
Singles: 7-inch
ARISTA...3-4 85
LPs: 10/12-inch
ARISTA...5-10 85-87
Members: Tito Larriva; Chalo Quintana; Steve Hufsteter; Tony Marsico; Marshall Rohner.
Also see PLUGZ

CRY
Singles: 7-inch
VIRGIN...3-5 78
Picture Sleeves
VIRGIN...3-5 78

CRY BEFORE DAWN
LPs: 10/12-inch
EPIC...5-10 87

CRY 3
LPs: 10/12-inch
CLEAR LIGHT...10-12 75

CRYAN' SHAMES P&R '66
Singles: 7-inch
COLUMBIA...4-8 66-70
DESTINATION...5-10 66
Picture Sleeves
COLUMBIA...8-12 67
LPs: 10/12-inch
BACK-TRAC...5-10 85
COLUMBIA (2589 "Sugar and Spice")...20-25 66
(Monaural.)
COLUMBIA (2786 "A Scratch in the Sky")...20-25 67
(Monaural.)
COLUMBIA (9389 "Sugar and Spice")...15-20 66
(Stereo.)
COLUMBIA (9586 "A Scratch in the Sky")...15-20 67
(Stereo.)
COLUMBIA (9719 "Synthesis")...15-20 69
Also see GUILLORY, Isaac

CRYERS
Singles: 7-inch
MERCURY ... 3-5 78
20TH FOX ... 3-4 79
LPs: 10/12-inch
MERCURY (Except 3734) ... 5-10 78
MERCURY (3734 "The Cryers") ... 10-15 79
(Picture disc. Promotional issue only.)

CRYIN' SHAMES
Singles: 7-inch
LONDON ... 4-8 66

CRYSTAL, Billy P&R/D&D/LP '85
Singles: 12-inch
A&M ... 4-6 85
Singles: 7-inch
A&M ... 3-4 85
Picture Sleeves
A&M ... 3-5 85
LPs: 10/12-inch
A&M ... 5-10 85

CRYSTAL, Cathy
Singles: 7-inch
DAY DELL ... 3-5

CRYSTAL, Lou
Singles: 7-inch
SFAZ (1001 "Dreaming of an Angel") ... 25-35 62

CRYSTAL BALL
Singles: 7-inch
SMASH ... 10-15 67

CRYSTAL CHANDELIER
Singles: 7-inch
COBBLESTONE (730 "Suicidal Flowers") ... 30-40 69
U.A. (50284 "Setting of Despair") ... 10-20 68

CRYSTAL CLEAR
Singles: 7-inch
POLYDOR ... 3-4 80-81

CRYSTAL GAYLE: see GAYLE, Crystal

CRYSTAL GRASS R&B '75
Singles: 7-inch
POLYDOR ... 3-5 75
PRIVATE STOCK ... 3-5 76
LPs: 10/12-inch
MERCURY ... 5-10 78
POLYDOR ... 8-10 75

CRYSTAL IMAGE
Singles: 7-inch
IX CHAINS ... 3-5 76

CRYSTAL JUNKYARD
Singles: 7-inch
TRX ... 3-5 71

CRYSTAL MANSION P&R '68
Singles: 7-inch
CAPITOL ... 3-6 68-70
COLOSSUS ... 3-5 70-71
RARE EARTH ... 3-5 72
20TH FOX ... 3-4 79
LPs: 10/12-inch
CAPITOL ... 12-15 69
RARE EARTH ... 10-12 72
20TH FOX ... 5-10 79
Also see CASWELL, Johnny

CRYSTAL MOTION
Singles: 7-inch
SOUND GEMS ... 3-5 75

CRYSTAL PALACE & CHANDELIERS
Singles: 7-inch
JEANNIE HITMAKER ... 3-4 80

CRYSTAL REVELATION
Singles: 7-inch
FINE (2709 "Life") ... 10-15 70

CRYSTAL TONES
Singles: 7-inch
M.Z. (008 "A Girl I Love") ... 250-500 59
Also see JAMES, Billy, & Crystaltones

CRYSTAL WATERS BAND
EPs: 7-inch
MR (001 "Crystal Waters Band") ... 8-10

CRYSTALAIRES OF LANCASTER, PA.
Singles: 7-inch
SOUND SOUVENIR (1 "Nobody Nowhere") ... 300-500 63
(Record store [Stan's Record Bar] promotional issue only.)

CRYSTALETTES
Singles: 7-inch
CRYSTALETTE ... 6-12 62-63

CRYSTALIERS
(Cleo & Crystaliers)
Singles: 7-inch
CINDY (3003 "Please Be My Guy") ... 150-250 57
JOHNSON (103 "Please Be My Guy") ... 500-750 57
(First issue.)

CRYSTALS
("Vocal by the Crystals with Orchestra")
Singles: 78 rpm
DE LUXE ... 50-100 54
LUNA ... 50-75 54
ROCKIN' ... 50-100 53
Singles: 7-inch
DE LUXE (6013 "My Dear") 200-300 53
DE LUXE (6037 "Have Faith in Me") ... 200-300 54
DE LUXE (6077 "My Girl") ... 150-250 54
LUNA (101 "Come to Me Darling") ... 350-500 54
(Reads "Recorded at Mastertone Studios, New York, N.Y." at bottom.)
LUNA (101 "Come to Me Darling") ... 250-350 54
(No mention of Mastertone Studios.)
LUNA (5001 "Come to Me Darling") ... 150-250 50s
ROCKIN' (518 "My Girl") ... 250-350 53
Members: Earl Wade; Johnny Hopson; Martin Brown; Ted Williams.
Also see CADILLACS
Also see OPALS

CRYSTALS
Singles: 78 rpm
ALADDIN ... 35-50 57
Singles: 7-inch
ALADDIN (3355 "I Love My Baby") ... 35-50 57

CRYSTALS
Singles: 7-inch
SPECIALTY ... 10-15 58

CRYSTALS
Singles: 7-inch
FELSTED ... 10-20 59

CRYSTALS
(With Ray Ellis & Orchestra)
Singles: 7-inch
METRO (20026 "Better Come Back to Me") ... 20-30 59
Also see ELLIS, Ray, Orchestra

CRYSTALS
Singles: 7-inch
BRENT (7011 "Gypsy Ribbon") ... 10-20 60
CUB (9064 "Watchin' You") ... 15-25 60
INDIGO (114 "Dreams & Wishes") ... 15-25 60
REGALIA (17 "Pony in Dixie") ... 8-10 61

CRYSTALS P&R/R&B '61
Singles: 7-inch
GUSTO ... 3-5 80s
MICHELLE (4113 "Ring-a-Ting-a-Ling") ... 5-10 67
PAVILLION ... 4-6 82
PHILLES (100 "There's No Other") ... 10-20 61
PHILLES (102 "Uptown") ... 10-20 62
PHILLES (105 "He Hit Me") ... 20-30 62
PHILLES (106 "He's a Rebel") ... 10-20 62
PHILLES (109 "He's Sure the Boy I Love") ... 10-20 62
PHILLES (111 "Let's Dance the Screw") ... 1000-2000 63
(White label. Promotional issue Only.)
PHILLES (111 "Let's Dance the Screw") ... 2000-4000 63
(Blue label. Has "Let's Dance" in smaller print and in parenthesis. Also has identification numbers *stamped* in vinyl. Blue label copies with "Let's Dance" in the same size print as "The Screw - Part 1" and with identification numbers hand etched are counterfeits.)
PHILLES (112 "Da Do Ron Ron") ... 10-20 63
PHILLES (115 "Then He Kissed Me") ... 10-20 63
PHILLES (119 "Little Boy") ... 15-25 63
PHILLES (119X "Little Boy") ... 200-300 63
(Single-sided disc.)
PHILLES (122 "All Grown Up") ... 10-20 64
U.A. (927 "My Place") ... 5-10 65
U.A. (994 "I Got a Man") ... 5-10 66
LPs: 10/12-inch
PHILLES (4000 "The Crystals Twist Uptown") ... 200-300 62
(Monaural. Blue label.)
PHILLES (4000 "The Crystals Twist Uptown") ... 550-750 62
(Monaural. White label. Promotional issue only.)
PHILLES (4000 "The Crystals Twist Uptown") ... 500-650 62
(Stereo.)
PHILLES (4001 "He's a Rebel") ... 200-300 63
(Monaural. Blue label.)
PHILLES (4001 "He's a Rebel") ... 500-750 63
(White label. Promotional issue only.)
PHILLES (4003 "Crystals") ... 150-250 63
(Monaural. Blue label.)
PHILLES (4003 "Crystals") ... 500-750 63
(White label. Promotional issue only.)
PHILLES (90722 "The Crystals Twist Uptown") ... 750-1000 62
(Capitol Record Club issue.)
Members: Barbara Alston; Lala Brooks; Dee Dee Kennibrew; Patricia Wright; Mary Thomas.
Also see ALSTON, Shirley
Also see LOVE, Darlene
Also see RONETTES / Crystals / Darlene Love / Bob B. Soxx & Blue Jeans

CRYSTALTONES: see CRYSTAL TONES

CRYSYS
LPs: 10/12-inch
METALWORKS ... 5-10 83

CUA, Rick
Singles: 7-inch
REFUGE ... 3-5 82
SPARROW ... 3-5 82
LPs: 10/12-inch
REFUGE ... 8-10 83
REUNION ... 5-8 88-90
SPARROW ... 5-8 85-87
Also see OUTLAWS

CUBA, Joe P&R/R&B/LP '66
(Joe Cuba Sextet)
Singles: 7-inch
ROULETTE ... 3-5 71
TICO ... 4-6 66
LPs: 10/12-inch
SEECO ... 10-15
TICO ... 10-15 66-67
Session: Jose Feliciano.
Also see FELICIANO, Jose

CUBANS
Singles: 7-inch
FLASH (133 "Tell Me") ... 50-60 58

CUBS
Singles: 78 rpm
SAVOY ... 15-25 56
Singles: 7-inch
SAVOY (1502 "I Hear Wedding Bells") ... 20-30 56

CUBY & BLIZZARDS
Singles: 7-inch
PHILLIPS ... 3-5 70
LPs: 10/12-inch
PHILLIPS ... 10-12 69-70

CUCA R&B '88
Singles: 7-inch
ALPHA INT. ... 3-4 88

CUCUMBER
Singles: 7-inch
COBBLESTONE (715 "Under") ... 15-25 68

CUES P&R '55
Singles: 78 rpm
CAPITOL ... 10-15 55-56
JUBILEE ... 10-15 55
LAMP ... 10-15 54
PREP ... 10-20 57
Singles: 7-inch
CAPITOL ... 15-25 55-56
JUBILEE ... 15-20 55
LAMP ... 10-20 54
PREP ... 10-15 57
Members: Ollie Jones; Jimmy Breedlove; Abe DeCosta; Robey Kirk; Eddie Barnes.
Also see BREEDLOVE, Jimmy
Also see NUGGETS
Also see RAVENS

CUFF LINKS
Singles: 78 rpm
DOOTO ... 25-50 56-57
DOOTONE ... 30-50 56
Singles: 7-inch
DOOTO (409 "Guided Missles") ... 25-50 56
DOOTO (413 "How You Lied") ... 25-50 57
DOOTO (414 "Twinkle") ... 25-50 57
DOOTO (422 "It's too Late Now") ... 25-50 57
DOOTO (474 "Chancing My Love") ... 15-25 63
DOOTONE (409 "Guided Missles") ... 50-100 56
Members: Robert Truesdale; Everett Tyson; John Anderson; Al Gaitwood; Marshall Lamb; Henry Huston.
Also see CUFFLINKS
Also see CUFFLINX
Also see HANK & Sugar Pie

CUFF LINKS P&R/LP '69
Singles: 7-inch
ATCO ... 3-5 72
DECCA ... 3-6 69-71
MCA ... 3-4 84
Picture Sleeves
DECCA (32533 "Tracy") ... 5-10 69
(Gatefold sleeve. Promotional issue only.)
LPs: 10/12-inch
DECCA ... 15-25 69-70
Members: Ron Dante; Rupert Holmes.
Also see DANTE, Ron
Also see HOLMES, Rupert

CUFFLINKS
Singles: 7-inch
GAIT (1445 "Only One Love") ... 200-300 65
Member: Al Gaitwood.
Also see CUFF LINKS

CUFFLINX
Singles: 78 rpm
DOOTO ... 25-50 57
Singles: 7-inch
DOOTO (433 "So tough") ... 20-30 57
DOOTO (434 "A Fool's Fortune") ... 20-30 57
DOOTO (438 "Lawful Wedding") ... 20-30 57
Members: Robert Truesdale; Moses Walker; Johnny Simmons; Henry Houston; Ray Dierdan.
Also see CUFF LINKS

CUGAT, Xavier P&R '35
Singles: 78 rpm
COLUMBIA ... 4-8 41-55
RCA ... 3-6 50-57
VICTOR ... 4-8 35-41
Singles: 7-inch
COLUMBIA ... 5-10 50-55
DECCA ... 3-5 65
MERCURY ... 4-6 62-64
RCA ... 5-10 50-62
EPs: 7-inch
COLUMBIA ... 5-15 55-59
MERCURY ... 5-15 53-54
LPs: 10/12-inch
CAMDEN ... 10-15 59
COLUMBIA ... 10-20 62
DECCA ... 10-20 65-69
HARMONY ... 10-15 60
MERCURY ... 10-30 53-67
RCA (Except 3021) ... 15-25 58-60
RCA (3021 "Siboney") ... 25-40 53
(10-inch LP.)

CUGAT, Xavier, & Dinah Shore
LPs: 10/12-inch
RCA (3022 "Tangos") ... 25-40 53

CUGINI P&R '79
(Donald Cugini)
Singles: 7-inch
SCOTTI BROTHERS ... 3-5 79

CULLEN, Dave
Singles: 7-inch
B 'N KC ... 4-6 63

CULLEY, Frank R&B '49
(Frank "Floorshow" Culley; with the Buddy Tate Orchestra)
Singles: 78 rpm
ATLANTIC ... 20-40 49-51
BATON ... 10-20 56
LENOX ... 15-25 49
Singles: 7-inch
BATON ... 15-25 56
EPs: 7-inch
BATON (7001/2 "Rock & Roll") ... 50-100 56
(Price is for either volume.)
LPs: 10/12-inch
BATON (1201 "Rock & Roll") ... 150-250 56
Also see RUSHING, Jimmy

CULLENS, Tommy
Singles: 7-inch
CORINA (2002 "Need Your Love") ... 300-500 60
(Credits Cullens, bu may be by the Five Chances. We have yet to learn if copies credited to the Five Chances exist.)

CULMER, Little Iris
(With the Majestics)
Singles: 7-inch
MARLIN (803 "Frankie, My Eyes Are On You") ... 2000-3000 57
Also see MAJESTICS

CULT
Singles: 7-inch
20TH FOX ... 4-8 66

CULT LP '85
(Southern Death Cult; Southern Cult; Death Cult)
Singles: 12-inch
BEGGARS BANQUET (260T "Heart of Soul") ... 5-10 86
(Limited numbered edition.)
BEGGARS BANQUET (2691 "Love Removal Machine") ... 5-10 87
(Promotional issue only.)
SIRE ... 4-6 85-86
Singles: 7-inch
SIRE ... 3-4 85-89
Picture Sleeves
SIRE ... 3-4 85-89
LPs: 10/12-inch
BEGGARS BANQUET (98 "Sonic Temple") ... 10-15 89
(Colored vinyl.)
SIRE ... 5-10 85-89
Members: Ian Astbury; Billy Duffy; Jamie Stewart; Les Warner; Matt Sorum.
Also see GUNS 'N' ROSES

CULT
LPs: 10/12-inch
STARBURST ... 10-12

CULTURE
LPs: 10/12-inch
VIRGIN INT'L ... 5-10 80

CULTURE CLUB P&R '82
(Featuring Boy George)
Singles: 12-inch
EPIC/VIRGIN ... 4-6 82-86
Singles: 7-inch
EPIC/VIRGIN ... 3-4 82-86
Picture Sleeves
EPIC/VIRGIN ... 3-4 83-86
LPs: 10/12-inch
EPIC/VIRGIN (Except 39237) ... 5-10 82-86
EPIC/VIRGIN (39237 "Colour by Numbers") ... 8-10 84
(Picture disc.)
VIRGIN (2330 "Waking Up with the House on Fire") ... 8-10 84
(Picture disc.)
Members: Boy George; Jon Moss; Roy Hay; Michael Craig.
Also see BAND AID
Also see BOY GEORGE
Also see STEWART, Jermaine

CULVER, Bruce
Singles: 7-inch
M.M.I. (1235 "Square Record") ... 20-30 58

CULVER STREET PLAYGROUND
Singles: 7-inch
SEVILLE ... 4-8 67

CUMBO, Linda
Singles: 7-inch
SELECT ... 4-8 65

CUMMINGS, Barbara C&W '66
Singles: 7-inch
LONDON ... 4-8 66-67

CUMMINGS, Burton P&R/LP '76
Singles: 7-inch
ALFA ... 3-4 81
PORTRAIT ... 3-6 76-78
Picture Sleeves
ALFA ... 3-4 81
PORTRAIT ... 3-6 78
EPs: 7-inch
PORTRAIT ... 4-8 77
(Issued with a paper sleeve.)
LPs: 10/12-inch
ALFA ... 5-10 81
PORTRAIT ... 8-10 76-78
Also see DEVERONS
Also see GUESS WHO
Also see ROGERS, Dann

CUMMINGS, Burton / Cheap Trick / Crawler
EPs: 7-inch
COLUMBIA (1129 "Music for Every Ear") ... 15-25 77
(Promotional issue only.)
Also see CHEAP TRICK
Also see CUMMINGS, Burton
Also see BACK STREET CRAWLER
Also see WILSON, Dennis / Ram Jam / Joan Baez

CUMMINGS, Carol
Singles: 7-inch
CHECKER ... 10-15 61

CUMMINGS, Larry
Singles: 7-inch
CHESS ... 5-10 60
MOCKINGBIRD ... 4-6

CUMMINGS, William
Singles: 7-inch
BANG BANG ("Make My Love a Hurtin' Thing") ... 20-30 60s
(No selection number used.)

CUMMINS, Christy
Singles: 7-inch
ELECT ... 5-10 64
PRO ... 10-15 61
ROULETTE (4319 "Till Then") ... 15-25 61
VENETT ... 10-15 63

CUNHA, Rick P&R/C&W '74
Singles: 7-inch
COLUMBIA ... 3-5 75
GRC ... 3-5 74
LPs: 10/12-inch
COLUMBIA ... 8-10 75
GRC ... 10-12 74
SIERRA BRIAR ... 5-10
Also see HEARTS & FLOWERS
Also see JENNINGS, Waylon

CUNHA & DAWSON
Singles: 7-inch
PETE ... 3-6 69

CUNNINGHAM
Singles: 7-inch
HAVEN ... 3-5 74
Picture Sleeves
HAVEN ... 3-5 74

CUNNINGHAM, B.B., Jr.
Singles: 7-inch
JANUS ... 3-5 74
Also see B-B

CUNNINGHAM, Buddy
Singles: 78 rpm
SUN (208 "Right Or Wrong") ... 200-300 54
Singles: 7-inch
SUN (208 "Right Or Wrong") ... 400-600 54

CUNNINGHAM, Dale
Singles: 7-inch
CASH (1067 "Trust Me") ... 20-30 58

CUNNINGHAM, Diane
Singles: 7-inch
FONTANA ... 4-8 67

CUNNINGHAM, J.C. C&W '80
Singles: 7-inch
SCOTTI BROS ... 3-5 80
VIVA ... 3-4 84

CUNNINGHAM, Johnny
Singles: 7-inch
CAPITOL ... 3-5 72

CUNNINGHAM, Larry, & Mighty Avons
Singles: 7-inch
CAROL ... 4-8 67
DECCA ... 4-8 66

CUNNINGHAM, Skip
Singles: 7-inch
CORAL ... 4-8 64
KAPP ... 10-15 62
20TH FOX ... 4-8 65

CUPCAKES
Singles: 7-inch
DIAMOND ... 4-8 65
TIME ... 8-12 59

CUPID
Singles: 7-inch
BROWN BAG ... 3-5 72

CUPID'S INSPIRATION
Singles: 7-inch
BELL ... 3-6 69
COLUMBIA ... 3-6 69
DATE ... 3-6 70
EPIC ... 4-6 68
LPs: 10/12-inch
DATE ... 10-12 70
Member: Terry Rice-Milton.
Also see RICE-MILTON, Terry

CUPIDS
Singles: 78 rpm
DECCA 20-30 57
Singles: 7-inch
DECCA (30279 "Answer to Your Prayer") 20-30 57

CUPIDS
Singles: 7-inch
ALADDIN (3404 "Now You Tell Me") 25-50 58
(Brown label.)
ALADDIN (3404 "Now You Tell Me") 10-20 58
(Black label.)

CUPIDS
Singles: 7-inch
CHAN (107 "Troubles Not at End") 50-100 62
UWR (4241 "True Love True Love") 25-50 62

CUPIDS *P&R '63*
Singles: 7-inch
AANKO (1002 "Brenda") 50-100 63
(First issue.)
KC (115 "Brenda") 25-50 63

CUPIDS
Singles: 7-inch
MUSICNOTE 10-15 63

CUPIDS
Singles: 7-inch
TIMES SQUARE 8-10 64

CUPIDS
Singles: 7-inch
GALAXY (734 "For You") 10-20 66

CUPIT, Earl
Singles: 7-inch
MYRL 4-8 61

CUPIT
Singles: 7-inch
NEPTUNE 3-5 70

CUPP, Pat
(With the Flying Saucers)
Singles: 78 rpm
RPM 20-30 56
Singles: 7-inch
RPM (461 "Do Me No Wrong") 40-60 56
RPM (473 "Long Gone Daddy") 40-60 56
Also see SMITH, Ray / Pat Cupp

CUPS
Singles: 7-inch
TETRAGRAMMATON 3-5 69

CURB, Mike *P&R/LP '70*
(Mike Curb Congregation; with Sidewalk Sounds; with Curbstones; with Rebalairs; with Waterfall)
Singles: 7-inch
BUENA VISTA 3-5 75
FORWARD 3-6 69
MGM 3-4 70
REPRISE (0287 "Hot Dawg") 10-20 64
SMASH (1938 "The Rebel") 10-15 64
TOWER 10-15 66
W.B. 3-5 77
Picture Sleeves
BUENA VISTA 5-10 75
FORWARD 4-8 69
LPs: 10/12-inch
BUENA VISTA 8-12
COBURT 8-12 70
FORWARD 5-10
MGM 5-10 71
Also see ALLAN, Davie
Also see DAVIS, Sammy, Jr.
Also see HANDS of TIME
Also see HEYBURNERS
Also see OSMONDS
Also see OWENS, Gary
Also see SIDEWALK SOUNDS
Also see WILLIAMS, Hank, Jr.

CURBSTONES
Singles: 7-inch
MGM 3-5 73
Picture Sleeves
MGM 3-5 73

CURE *D&D/LP '83*
Singles: 12-inch
ELEKTRA 4-6 85-86
SIRE 4-6 83-85
Singles: 7-inch
ELEKTRA 3-4 85-89
SIRE 3-4 83-85
Picture Sleeves
ELEKTRA 3-4 86-89
LPs: 10/12-inch
A&M 8-10 81
ELEKTRA 5-10 85-89
PVC 8-10 80
SIRE 5-10 83-85
Members: Robert Smith; Laurence Tolhurst.

CURFEW
Singles: 7-inch
U.A. 3-5 70
LPs: 10/12-inch
U.A. 10-15 70
Also see FANN BAND

CURFEWS
Singles: 7-inch
MONTGOMERY (008 "Look at Me") 10-20 60s

CURINGTON, Harold
Singles: 7-inch
TAD (100 "One Day Girl") 10-15 60s

CURIOS
Singles: 7-inch
CURIO 4-8 63
FARGO 4-8 62

CURIOSITIES
Singles: 7-inch
SEEBURG (3011 "Walkin' the Dog") 20-35 65
SEEBURG (3013 "Money") 20-35 65
SEEBURG (3014 "Twist and Shout") 20-35 65
SEEBURG (3015 "Johnny B. Goode") 20-35 65

CURIOSITY KILLED THE CAT *P&R/LP '87*
Singles: 7-inch
MERCURY 3-4 87
Picture Sleeves
MERCURY 3-4 87
LPs: 10/12-inch
MERCURY 5-8 87

CURIOUS GEORGE
LPs: 10/12-inch
B.F.S. 8-12 90-91

CURLESS, Dick *C&W '65*
Singles: 7-inch
ALLAGASH (101 "A Tombstone Every Mile") 10-15 65
CAPITOL 3-6 70-73
TOWER 4-8 65-68
LPs: 10/12-inch
BELMONT 6-10 78-80
CAPITOL 10-20 70-73
INTERSTATE 8-12 76
PICKWICK/HILLTOP 8-15 70s
TIFFANY (1016 "Songs of the Open Country") 50-75 58
TIFFANY (1028 "Singin' Just for Fun") 50-75 59
TIFFANY (1033 "I Love to Tell a Story") 75-100 60
TOWER 15-25 65-68

CURLEY, Jim
Singles: 7-inch
METRO (100 "Rock & Roll Itch") 150-200 58
MIDA (100 "Rock & Roll Itch") 75-125 58
MIDA (108 "Sloppy, Sloopy Susie") 75-125 58

CURLEY & JADES
Singles: 7-inch
MUSIC MAKERS (109 "Boom Stix") 20-30 61
REPRISE (20046 "Boom Stix") 10-15 62

CURLS
Singles: 7-inch
EVEREST 5-10 59-60

CURNUTTE, Jim
LPs: 10/12-inch
NEUROLOGICAL 5-10 80

CURRENT *P&R '77*
Singles: 7-inch
PLAYBOY 3-4 77

CURRENTS
Singles: 7-inch
LAURIE 10-20 63

CURREY, Diana Sicily *C&W '89*
Singles: 7-inch
CONDOR 3-4 90

CURRIE, Bob
Singles: 7-inch
STRAND 4-8 60s

CURRIE, Cherie & Marie *P&R '79*
Singles: 7-inch
CAPITOL 3-5 79-80
Picture Sleeves
CAPITOL 3-5 79
LPs: 10/12-inch
CAPITOL 5-10 79-81
Also see RUNAWAYS

CURRY, Clifford *P&R/R&B '67*
(Cliff Curry)
Singles: 7-inch
ABBOTT 3-6 72
C.C. 4-8
CAPRICE 3-6 72
ELF 10-20 67-69
RIDGECREST (1202 "Kiss Kiss Kiss") 20-25 59
SSS INT'L (812 "Soul Ranger") 10-15 70
LP: 10/12-inch
WOODSHED 8-12
Session: Bergen White.
Also see ACCENTS
Also see CONTINDERS
Also see FIVE PENNIES
Also see NOTATIONS
Also see WHITE, Bergen

CURRY, Dalyce, & Roulettes
Singles: 7-inch
ANGLE 8-12 63
Also see ROULETTES

CURRY, Dan
Singles: 7-inch
CRIMSON (1 "She's My Girl") 20-30

CURRY, Earl
(With the Blenders)
Singles: 78 rpm
R&B 75-125 55
RPM 50-75 54
Singles: 7-inch
R&B (1304 "I Want to Be with You") 125-175 54
R&B (1313 "Dream") 150-200 55
RPM (402 "One Whole Year Baby") 50-100 54

CURRY, Ed
Singles: 7-inch
BRUNSWICK 5-10 58
DOL (101 "Don't Be Long") 10-15 57

CURRY, Irma
Singles: 7-inch
VEE JAY 4-8 65

CURRY, James "King"
Singles: 78 rpm
FLASH (110 "My Promise") 10-20 56
Singles: 7-inch
FLASH (110 "My Promise") 15-25 56
MOVIN' (100-19 "Saturday Night Shakin") 15-25 57
Also see JAYHAWKS

CURRY, James / Sheryl Crowley
Singles: 78 rpm
FLASH 10-15 56
Singles: 7-inch
FLASH (107 "Still Longing for You") 15-25 56
Also see CROWLEY, Sheryl

CURRY, Louis *R&B '68*
Singles: 7-inch
M-S 5-10 68
REEL 10-20

CURRY, Mini *R&B '87*
Singles: 7-inch
TOTAL EMP. 3-4 87

CURRY, Tim *P&R/LP '79*
(With Original Roxy Cast)
Singles: 7-inch
A&M 3-4 78-81
ODE 3-5 76
ODE '70 3-4 74
Picture Sleeves
A&M 3-4 79
LPs: 10/12-inch
A&M 5-10 78-89
Also see WILSON, Brian

CURTAIN CALLS
Singles: 7-inch
DOT 4-6 68

CURTICE, Robbi
Singles: 7-inch
SIDEWALK 4-8 68

CURTIE & BOOMBOX *P&R/D&D '85*
Singles: 12-inch
RCA 4-6 85
Singles: 7-inch
RCA 3-4 85
Member: Curtie Fortune.

CURTIN, Jim E.
Singles: 7-inch
STARFIRE (101 "Love Me Tender") 3-5 78
(Red vinyl.)
Picture Sleeves
STARFIRE (101 "Love Me Tender") 4-6 78

CURTIN, Lee
Singles: 7-inch
END (1118 "Hot Dog") 15-25 62
GIZMO (003 "Hot Dog") 35-50 61

CURTIS, Benny
(With the Millionaires)
Singles: 7-inch
BRIDGES (1102 "I Wonder") 250-500 61
DYNAMITE 5-10 63
RESIST (502 "Dirty Hearts") 25-35 60s

CURTIS, Betty
Singles: 7-inch
CGD 4-8 63

CURTIS, Bill
Singles: 7-inch
ARC (4443 "Panic Stricken") 35-50 58

CURTIS, C.C.: see CURTISS, C.C.

CURTIS, Chantal *R&B '79*
Singles: 7-inch
KEYLOCK 3-5 79

CURTIS, Clem
Singles: 7-inch
IMPERIAL 4-8 69

CURTIS, Cry Baby
Singles: 7-inch
CASH (1062 "I Wanna") 100-150 58
JULET (1005 "There Will Be Some Changes Made") 5-10
ROMARK (110 "There Will Be Some Changes Made") 25-35
TREVOR (103 "Don't Just Stand There 25-35

CURTIS, Danny S.
Singles: 7-inch
JAMCO 4-8 62

CURTIS, Dave
Singles: 7-inch
DON RAY 3-5 60

CURTIS, Dean
Singles: 7-inch
PAULA 3-5 71

CURTIS, Don
(Butch McClary)
Singles: 7-inch
KLIFF (104 "Rough Tough Man") 50-75 58
Also see McCLARY, Butch

CURTIS, Don Day
Singles: 7-inch
ABC-PAR 10-15 63

CURTIS, Eddie
(Eddie "Tex"Curtis)
Singles: 78 rpm
DOT 10-20 56
GEE 15-25 54
OKEH 10-20 55
Singles: 7-inch
ABC-PAR 5-8 62-63
BEAR CAT 5-10 60
DECCA 4-8 61-62
DOT (15505 "You're Much Too Pretty") 15-25 56
GEE 20-30 54
JELL 5-8 65
JOSIE 5-8 66
OKEH 15-25 55

CURTIS, Frank
Singles: 7-inch
PALETTE 5-8 59

CURTIS, James
Singles: 7-inch
COMSTOCK 3-4 83

CURTIS, Jimmy
Singles: 7-inch
U.A. 15-25 60

CURTIS, Ken
LPs: 10/12-inch
CAPITOL 30-40 66
DOT 25-35 67
PICKWICK 10-20

CURTIS, Ken / Rex Allen & Arizona Wranglers
Singles: 78 rpm
MERCURY/SAV-WAY (6045 "Lemme Outa Here") 100-150 47
(Picture disc. Promotional issue only.)
Also see ALLEN, Rex
Also see CURTIS, Ken
Also see SONS of PIONEERS

CURTIS, King: see KING CURTIS

CURTIS, Lance
(With the Uniques)
Singles: 7-inch
'TEEN (507 "Bye Bye Baby") 50-75 59
'TEEN (509 "Sympathy") 100-150 60

CURTIS, Larry *C&W '78*
Singles: 7-inch
SCRIMSHAW 3-5 78

CURTIS, Lee
Singles: 7-inch
GIZMO 8-12 61

CURTIS, Lennie
Singles: 7-inch
END (1127 "Nothing Can Help You Now") 50-100 63

CURTIS, Lindy
Singles: 7-inch
MALA 4-8 61

CURTIS, Little Joe: see REDDING, Otis / Little Joe Curtis

CURTIS, Mac *C&W '68*
Singles: 78 rpm
KING 25-75 56-57
Singles: 7-inch
DOT 4-8 62
EPIC 4-6 68-70
FELSTED (8592 "Come Back Baby") 10-15 60
GRT 3-6 70
KING (4927 "If I Had Me a Woman") 50-100 56
(Blue label.)
KING (4927 "If I Had Me a Woman") 100-150 56
(White bio label. Promotional issue only.)
KING (4949 "Grandaddy's Rockin'") 100-200 56
KING (4965 "You Ain't Treatin' Me Right") 100-200 56
KING (4995 "That Ain't Nothin' But Right") 100-200 56
KING (5059 "Say So") 25-50 57
KING (5107 "What You Want") 40-60 57
KING (5121 "Little Miss Linda") 40-60 58
SHAH (982 "Singing the Blues") 10-15 61
SHALIMAR 5-10 63
TOWER 4-8 67
LPs: 10/12-inch
EPIC 12-20 68
GRT 10-15 71
ROLLIN' ROCK 8-10
Session: Ron-dells.

CURTIS, Mac / Ron-Dels
Singles: 7-inch
MARIDENE (111 "100 Pounds of Honey") 10-15 63
Also see CURTIS, Mac
Also see RON-DELS

CURTIS, Mary Anne
(Mary Ann Curtis)
Singles: 7-inch
PONTIAC 5-10 60
RAYDIN 4-8 66

CURTIS, Mickey
Singles: 7-inch
JOSAN 5-10 60

CURTIS, Rhoda
Singles: 7-inch
U.A. 3-5 77
LPs: 10/12-inch
U.A. 8-10 77

CURTIS, Rick
Singles: 7-inch
AVCO EMBASSY 3-5 70
LPs: 10/12-inch
AVCO EMBASSY 8-10 70

CURTIS, Rita
Singles: 7-inch
WOLFF (102 "This Little Girl") 50-100
(Canadian.)

CURTIS, Sal
Singles: 7-inch
TRIBUTE 4-8 62

CURTIS, Sonny
Singles: 78 rpm
CORAL 5-10 53
Singles: 7-inch
CORAL (61023 "The Best Way to Hold a Girl") 10-15 53
CORAL (62207 "Red Headed Stranger") 10-15 60

CURTIS, Sonny *C&W '66*
Singles: 7-inch
A&M (1359 "The Lights of L.A.") 20-30 72
CAPITOL 8-12 75-76
DIMENSION 8-12 63-64
DOT 10-20 58
ELEKTRA 3-4 79-81
LIBERTY 10-15 64
MERCURY 8-12 73
OVATION 10-15 70
'STEEM 3-4 85
VIVA 8-10 66-69
LPs: 10/12-inch
ELEKTRA 8-15 79-81
IMPERIAL (9276 "Beatle Hits") 25-35 64
(Monaural.)
IMPERIAL (12276 "Beatle Hits") 30-40 64
(Stereo.)
VIVA (36012 "1st of Sonny Curtis") 20-30 68
VIVA (36021 "The Sonny Curtis Style") 20-30 69
Also see CAMPERS
Also see CAMPS
Also see CLAPTON, Eric
Also see CRICKETS
Also see HOLLY, Buddy
Also see PEWTER, Jim

CURTIS, T.C. *D&D '85*
Singles: 12-inch
SIRE 4-6 85

CURTIS, Tommy
Singles: 7-inch
BRAGG 4-8 65

CURTIS & DEL
Singles: 7-inch
MONUMENT 4-8 61-63

CURTIS & GALAXIES
Singles: 7-inch
GAITY (6014 "Laura Lee") 25-35 60

CURTIS BROTHERS
Singles: 7-inch
CAPITOL 4-8 68
POLYDOR 3-5 76

CURTISS, C.C.
Singles: 7-inch
AUDICON (109 "Aunt Minnie") 10-15 60
WINK (1001 "Please Let Me Know") 10-15 60

CURTISS, Dave, & Clive Maldoon
(Curtiss-Maldoon)
LPs: 10/12-inch
PURPLE 10-12 72
Also see MALDOON

CURTISS, Dave, & Tremors
Singles: 7-inch
KARATE 4-8 66

CURTISS, Jackie
(Sgt. Jackie Curtiss & Rex Dennis Singers)
Singles: 7-inch
DYNASTY 5-10 59
RADIANT 4-8 62
U.A. 4-8 62

CURTISS, Jimmy
Singles: 7-inch
LAURIE (3312 "You're What's Happening Baby") 8-12 65
LAURIE (3315 "Let's Dance Close") 20-30 65
LAURIE (3383 "Psychedelic Situation") 15-20 67
U.A. 5-10 60
W.B. 5-10 62
Also see BAG
Also see HOBBITS
Also see TREMONTS

CURTOLA, Bobby *P&R '62*
(With the Martells)
Singles: 7-inch
DEL-FI........ 8-12 61-63
KING........ 4-8 67
TARTAN........ 5-10 63-66
Picture Sleeves
DEL-FI........ 10-15 61-62

CURVED AIR
Singles: 7-inch
W.B. 3-5 71
LPs: 10/12-inch
BTM........ 8-10 75
W.B. 10-12 71-72
Members: Florian Pilkington; Darryl Way; Sonja Kristina; Ian Eyre; Francis Monkman; Stewart Copeland.
Also see COPELAND, Stewart

CURVES
Singles: 7-inch
ALLEGIANCE........ 3-4 83
LIBERTY........ 3-4 81
LPs: 10/12-inch
ALLEGIANCE........ 5-10 84
LIBERTY........ 5-10 81

CUSSICK, Ian
Singles: 7-inch
A&M........ 3-4 84
LPs: 10/12-inch
A&M........ 5-10 84

CUSSON, Lorraine
Singles: 7-inch
PENI........ 5-10 59

CUSTER & SURVIVERS
Singles: 7-inch
GOLDEN STATE........ 5-10 65

CUSTER'S LAST BAND
Singles: 7-inch
GOLDEN CHARIOT (70001 "I Couldn't Last a Day Without Your Love")........ 10-20

CUSTOMS
Singles: 7-inch
REGANO (1062 "Steppin' Out")........ 25-35 62
(Reissued as *Surfin' '63*, as by the Original Sufaris.)
Also see QUADS / Grand Prix / Customs
Also see SURFARIS (Original Surfaris)

CUSTOMS
Singles: 7-inch
ARLEN........ 5-10 63

CUSTOMS
Singles: 7-inch
SHAKE IT........ 8-12
Picture Sleeves
SHAKE IT........ 10-15

CUSTOMS FIVE
Singles: 7-inch
TASK (108 "Let's Go")........ 15-25 68

CUT *R&B '86*
Singles: 7-inch
SUPERTRONICS........ 3-4 86

CUT GLASS
Singles: 7-inch
CUT GLASS........ 4-8
20TH FOX........ 3-4 80

CUT OUTS
Singles: 7-inch
V.A.C. (2006 "Keep Talking")........ 10-15

CUTCHINS, Bobby
Singles: 7-inch
LASSO (503 "I Did It Again")........ 10-20 60s

CUTE TEENS
Singles: 7-inch
ALADDIN (3458 "When My Teenage Days Are Over")........ 100-200 59
Member: Raynoma Gordy.

CUTTING CREW *P&R/LP '87*
Singles: 12-inch
VIRGIN (1003 "I Just Died in Your Arms")........ 10-15 87
(Saw blade-shaped disc. Promotional issue only.)
Singles: 7-inch
VIRGIN........ 3-4 87-89
Picture Sleeves
VIRGIN........ 3-4 87-89
LPs: 10/12-inch
VIRGIN........ 5-10 87-89

CUTTING EDGE
Singles: 12-inch
MCA........ 4-6 83

CUTUPS
Singles: 7-inch
JIM........ 4-8
MUSIC MAKERS........ 5-10 62

CUT-UPS
Singles: 7-inch
MECCA........ 5-10 59

CUT-UPS
Singles: 7-inch
HICKORY........ 4-8 67

CWAZY WABBITS – ROCK STONE & AL MOORE
Singles: 7-inch
CHECKER (950 "The Bunny's Easter Song")........ 8-12 60
Picture Sleeves
CHECKER (950 "The Bunny's Easter Song")........ 10-20 60

CY & CYCLONES
Singles: 7-inch
SHELLEY........ 5-10 62

CYAN
Singles: 7-inch
RCA........ 3-5 71

CYBERMEN
Singles: 7-inch
WHAAAM (002 "She's Raining")........ 3-5 86
Picture Sleeves
WHAAAM (002 "She's Raining")........ 3-5 86
EPs: 7-inch
GET HIP (117 "Every Night & Day")........ 3-5 90
(Issued with paper sleeve.)
Members: Bill Boeddeker; Michael Grimm; Steve Ostrov; Mike Huegen; James Grapes.

CYBOTRON *R&B '83*
Singles: 12-inch
FANTASY........ 4-6 82-84
Singles: 7-inch
FANTASY........ 3-4 83-84
LPs: 10/12-inch
FANTASY........ 5-10 83-84

CYCLE V
Singles: 7-inch
CASABLANCA........ 3-4 84

CYCLONE III
Singles: 7-inch
PHILIPS (40258 "You've Got a Bomb")........ 15-25 65

CYCLONES
Singles: 78 rpm
FLIP (324 "My Dear")........ 100-200 57
Singles: 7-inch
FLIP (324 "My Dear")........ 150-250 57

CYCLONES *P&R '58*
Singles: 7-inch
QUALITY (1796 "Bullwhip Rock")........ 20-30 58
TROPHY (500 "Bullwhip Rock")........ 20-30 58
TROPHY (503 "Aftermath")........ 20-30 58
Member: Bill Taylor.

CYCLONES
Singles: 7-inch
FORWARD (313 "Good Goodnight")........ 300-400 59

CYCLONES
Singles: 7-inch
BAND BOX (211 "Cyclone")........ 8-12 60

CYCLONES
Singles: 7-inch
FESTIVAL (25003 "Give Me Love")........ 20-30 61

CYCLONES
Singles: 7-inch
LEE (5467 "She's No Good")........ 10-20 60s

CYCLONES
Singles: 7-inch
LITTLE RICKY........ 3-5 81
LPs: 10/12-inch
PLEXUS TRADING........ 5-10 83

CYD & CHERI
Singles: 7-inch
LUTE........ 5-10 61

CYMANDE *P&R/R&B/LP '73*
Singles: 7-inch
JANUS........ 3-5 72-73
LPs: 10/12-inch
JANUS........ 10-12 72-74

CYMARRON *P&R/LP '71*
Singles: 7-inch
ENTRANCE........ 3-5 71-72
LPs: 10/12-inch
ENTRANCE........ 10-12 71
Members: Rick Yancey; Richard Mainegra; Sherrill Parks.
Also see REMINGTONS

CYMBAL, Johnny *P&R '63*
Singles: 7-inch
AMARET........ 3-6 69
COLUMBIA........ 4-8 66
DCP (1135 "Go VW, Go")........ 10-15 65
KAPP........ 8-15 63-64
KEDLEN........ 10-15 63
MCA........ 3-5 73-84
MGM........ 8-15 60-61
MUSICOR........ 4-8 67
VEE JAY........ 4-8 63
Picture Sleeves
DCP (1135 "Go VW, Go")........ 15-25 65
LPs: 10/12-inch
KAPP (1324 "Mr. Bass Man")........ 25-40 63
(Monaural.)
KAPP (3324 "Mr. Bass Man")........ 35-50 63
(Stereo.)
Also see DEREK
Also see MILK
Also see TAURUS

CYMBAL & CLINGER
Singles: 7-inch
CHELSEA........ 3-5 73
MGM........ 3-5 71
MARINA........ 3-5 71
LPs: 10/12-inch
CHELSEA........ 10-12 72
Members: Johnny Cymbal; Peggy Clinger.
Also see CLINGER, Peggy
Also see CYMBAL, Johnny

CYMBALS
Singles: 7-inch
AMAZON (709 "One Step Too Far")........ 20-40 62
DOT (16472 "Voice of a Fool")........ 5-10 63

CYMBOLS & REVELERS
Singles: 7-inch
AVR........ 5-10 60

CYKLE
Singles: 7-inch
LABEL (101 "If You Can")........ 15-25 69
Picture Sleeves
LABEL (101 "If You Can")........ 25-50 69
LPs: 10/12-inch
LABEL (101 "Cykle")........ 400-600 69
Also see YOUNG ONES

CYMONE, Andre *R&B '82*
Singles: 12-inch
COLUMBIA........ 4-6 82-86
Singles: 7-inch
COLUMBIA........ 3-4 82-86
Picture Sleeves
COLUMBIA........ 3-4 83
LPs: 10/12-inch
CBS (99869 "Love")........ 15-20 83
(Promotional only picture disc.)
COLUMBIA........ 5-10 82-86
Also see PRINCE
Also see WATLEY, Jody

CYNARA
LPs: 10/12-inch
CAPITOL (547 "Cynara")........ 20-30 70

CYNEMAN VYNE
Singles: 7-inch
COCONUT GROVE (2042 "Changes")........ 50-100

CYNICS
(With Pete Buck & Mike Mills)
Singles: 12-inch
GET HIP........ 4-8 90
Singles: 7-inch
GET HIP........ 3-5 90-92
Picture Sleeves
GET HIP........ 3-5 90-92
EPs: 7-inch
GET HIP........ 3-5 90
LPs: 10/12-inch
GET HIP/SKYCLAD........ 5-10 90-93
Members: Michael Kastelic; Gregg Kostelich; Mike Michalski; Tom Hohn.
Also see R.E.M.

CYNICS / Frampton Brothers
Singles: 7-inch
GET HIP (150 "I Got You Babe")........ 3-4 92
Picture Sleeves
GET HIP (150 "I Got You Babe")........ 3-4 92
Also see CYNICS
Also see FRAMPTON BROTHERS

CYNARA
LPs: 10/12-inch
CAPITOL........ 10-12 70

CYNTHIA
Singles: 7-inch
BARRY........ 4-8 66

CYNTHIA & JOHNNY O *P&R '90*
LPs: 10/12-inch
MICMAC........ 5-8 90

CYNTHIA & IMAGINATIONS
Singles: 7-inch
BLUE ROCK........ 3-5 69
MAGIC CITY........ 4-8 68

CYR, Joe
Singles: 7-inch
ALLEY........ 15-20

CYR, Ray
Singles: 7-inch
MAGNET........ 4-6 68

CYRÉ *R&B '87*
Singles: 7-inch
FRESH........ 3-4 87

CYRESS, Buddy
Singles: 78 rpm
FLASH........ 25-35 57
Singles: 7-inch
FLASH (118 "I'm in Love with You")........ 25-35 57

CYRKLE *P&R/LP '66*
Singles: 7-inch
COLUMBIA (Except picture discs and 43589)........ 5-10 65-68
COLUMBIA ("Interview")........ 15-20 66
(Square-shaped cardboard picture disc.)
COLUMBIA ("Interview")........ 20-30 66
(Square-shaped cardboard picture disc. Still bound in *Teen Scoop* magazine.)
COLUMBIA (43589 "Red Rubber Ball")........ 5-10 65
(Black vinyl.)
COLUMBIA (43589 "Red Rubber Ball")........ 10-15 65
(Colored vinyl. Promotional issue only.)
Picture Sleeves
COLUMBIA........ 20-30 66-68
LPs: 10/12-inch
COLUMBIA (2544 "Red Rubber Ball")........ 20-25 66
COLUMBIA (9344 "Red Rubber Ball")........ 25-30 66
COLUMBIA (2632 "Neon")........ 20-25 67
(Monaural.)
COLUMBIA (9432 "Neon")........ 20-30 67
(Stereo.)
FLYING DUTCHMAN/AMSTERDAM (12007 "The Minx")........ 20-25 70
(Soundtrack.)

CYRKLE / Paul Revere & Raiders
Singles: 7-inch
COLUMBIA (466 "Camaro"/ "SS 396")........ 10-15 66
(Special Products Chevrolet promotional issue only.)
Picture Sleeves
COLUMBIA (466 "Camaro"/ "SS 396")........ 15-25 66
(Special Products Chevrolet promotional issue only.)
COLUMBIA (43000 series)........ 5-10 66-67
Members: Don Danneman; Marty Fried; Tom Dawes; John Simon; Michael Losekamp.
Also see CYRKLE
Also see REVERE, Paul, & Raiders
Also see SIMON, Paul

CYRUS
Singles: 7-inch
ELEKTRA........ 3-5 71
LPs: 10/12-inch
ELEKTRA........ 10-12 71

CYRUS ERIE
Singles: 7-inch
EPIC........ 8-10 69
Member: Eric Carmen.
Also see CARMEN, Eric

CZARNEK, Harry
Singles: 7-inch
GUIDE........ 3-4

CZARS OF RHYTHM
Singles: 7-inch
DE'VOICES (782 "You Show Me the Way")........ 100-200 65

D

D., Ronnie, & Valiants
Singles: 7–inch
SEA LOCK (27 "Hound Dog Guitar") 10-20

D MEN
Singles: 7–inch
KAPP (691 "So Little Time") 8-12 65
VEEP (1206 "Don't You Know") 10-15 64
VEEP (1209 "I Just Don't Care") 10-15 65
Members: Wayne Wadhams; Rick Engler; Doug Ferrara; Bill Shute; Ken Evans.
Also see FIFTH ESTATE

D MOB *P&R '89*
(Featuring Cathy Dennis)
Singles: 7–inch
FFRR.......................... 3-4 89-90
LPs: 10/12–inch
FFRR.......................... 3-4 89

D - NICE *LP '90*
LPs: 10/12–inch
JIVE.......................... 5-8 90

"D" TRAIN *LP '82*
Singles: 12–inch
PRELUDE.......................... 4-6 81-85
Singles: 7–inch
PRELUDE.......................... 3-4 81-85
LPs: 10/12–inch
PRELUDE.......................... 5-10 82-85
Members: James "D Train" Williams; Hubert Eaves III.
Also see WILLIAMS, James "D Train"

D., Eddie: see EDDIE D.

D., Jimmy: see JIMMY "D"

D.A.
Singles: 7–inch
RASCAL (102 "Ready 'N Steady") .25-35 79
LPs: 10/12–inch
FRONTLINE.......................... 5-10 85-86

D.A.D. *LP '89*
LPs: 10/12–inch
W.B. 5-8 89

D&M
Singles: 12–inch
POLYDOR (054 "On the Shelf")........ 5-8 79
Members: Donnie Osmond; Marie Osmond.
Also see OSMOND, Donny & Marie

DB's *LP '87*
LPs: 10/12–inch
I.R.S. 5-10 87

DBM
(Disco BeatleMania)
Singles: 12–inch
A.V.I. 8-10 78
Singles: 7–inch
A.V.I. 3-5 78

DBMT: see DOZY, BEAKY, MICK & TICH

D.C. BLOSSOMS
Singles: 7–inch
SHRINE (107 "I Know About Her") 200-300 66

D.C. DRIFTERS
Singles: 7–inch
REACTION (1008 "I Know")..........40-60 60s

D.C. EXPRESS
Singles: 12–inch
SOUND of NEW YORK 4-6
Singles: 7–inch
SOUND of NEW YORK 3-4

D.C. MAGNATONES
Singles: 7–inch
D.C. MAGNATONES (216 "Does She Love Me")..........................500-750 63

D.C. PLAYBOYS
Singles: 7–inch
AROCK.......................... 3-5

D.D.T. & REPELLENTS
Singles: 7–inch
RCA (8064 "Fly Swatter")..............10-15 62

DFX2 *LP '83*
Singles: 7–inch
MCA 3-4 83
LPs: 10/12–inch
MCA 5-10 83

D.J. & CATS
Singles: 7–inch
HEP (2100 "Jeanie 16") 35-50 59
HEP (2101 "Lightning Strikes") 35-50 59

D.J. DAN
Singles: 7–inch
STAR STAGE (7710 "Star Warn") 4-6 77
STAR STAGE (8083 "Jawed") 4-6 77

D.J. DOC & SPYDER D.
Singles: 7–inch
PROFILE.......................... 4-6 86

D.J. JAZZY JEFF & FRESH PRINCE *R&B '86*
Singles: 7–inch
JIVE 3-4 87-89
WORD-UP.......................... 3-4 86
Picture Sleeves
JIVE 3-4 88-89
LPs: 10/12–inch
JIVE 5-10 87-89
Also see SIMPSONS

D.J. MAGIC MIKE *LP '90*
LPs: 10/12–inch
CHEETAH 5-8 90
Also see VICIOUS BASE Featuring D.J. Magic Mike

DJ QUIK *LP '91*
LPs: 10/12–inch
PROFILE.......................... 5-8 91

D.J. PAUL
Singles: 7–inch
DOR 4-8

DMX, Davy: see DAVY DMX

DMZ
EPs: 7–inch
BOMP.......................... 5-10
LPs: 10/12–inch
SIRE.......................... 8-10 78
VOXX.......................... 5-10

DNA Featuring Suzanne Vega *P&R '90*
Singles: 7–inch
A&M 3-4 90
Also see VEGA, Suzanne

D.O.A. *LP '90*
LPs: 10/12–inch
RESTLESS.......................... 5-8 90

D.O.C. *LP '89*
LPs: 10/12–inch
RUTHLESS 5-8 89

D.O.X.
(Defenders of the Cross)
LPs: 10/12–inch
FRONTLINE.......................... 5-10 86

DRs
Singles: 12–inch
EPIC.......................... 4-6 83
Singles: 7–inch
EPIC.......................... 3-4 83
LPs: 10/12–inch
EPIC.......................... 5-10 83

D.R.I. *LP '88*
LPs: 10/12–inch
METAL BLADE.......................... 5-8 88-89

DVC
Singles: 7–inch
ALFA 3-4 82
LPs: 10/12–inch
ALFA 5-10 81

D-Y & MOTIVATORS
Singles: 7–inch
LINJO.......................... 10-20 65-66

DA BUSH BABEES
Singles: 12–inch
REPRISE (41150 "Swing It")............ 4-6 94

DA YOOPERS
Singles: 7–inch
YOU GUYS 3-5 87

DAARTS
Singles: 7–inch
DYNA.......................... 5-10 61

DABETTES
Singles: 7–inch
ADVANCE.......................... 4-8 62

D'ABO, Michael
Singles: 7–inch
A&M 3-5 73-74
BELL 3-5 71
LPs: 10/12–inch
A&M 8-10 72-74
Also see MANFRED MANN

D'ACCORDS
Singles: 7–inch
DON-EL.......................... 15-25 61

DACHE, Bertell
Singles: 7–inch
U.A. (290 "Not Just Tomorrow, But Always")..........................25-30 60-61
Members: Tony Orlando; Carole King.
Also see KING, Carole
Also see ORLANDO, Tony

DA CORSI, Gail
Singles: 7–inch
DOLTON (314 "Touch of Yesterday")..........................8-12 66

DA COSTA, Rita
Singles: 7–inch
MOHAWK (703 "Don't Bring Me Down")..........................15-25
PANDORA (7049 "Don't Bring Me Down")..........................100-200
TOWER.......................... 8-12 65

DADA
LPs: 10/12–inch
ATCO.......................... 10-12 70

DADDARIO, Joe
Singles: 7–inch
D-TOWN.......................... 3-4 85

DADDY BOB
(Bob Bertram)
Singles: 7–inch
BERTRAM INT'L (1835 "Welcome Home Elvis")..........................8-12 77
(With insert of 1959 drawing of Elvis Presley, by Bob Bertram.)
BERTRAM INT'L (1835 "Welcome Home Elvis")..........................5-8 77
(Without insert.)
Also see BERTRAM, Bob

DADDY CLEANHEAD
(Fred Higgins)
Singles: 78 rpm
SPECIALTY.......................... 8-12 55
Singles: 7–inch
SPECIALTY (541 "Let Me Come Back Home")..........................15-25 55

DADDY COOL
Singles: 78 rpm
REPRISE (522 "Teenage Heaven")..........................15-25 72
(Promotional issue only.)
Singles: 7–inch
BLUE SKY.......................... 8-10
REPRISE.......................... 3-8 71-72
LPs: 10/12–inch
REPRISE (2088 "Teenage Heaven")..........................15-25 72
REPRISE (6471 "Daddy Who? Daddy Cool")..........................20-25 71

DADDY COOL
Singles: 7–inch
BLUE SKY (107 "Story of Daddy Cool")..........................4-6 70s

DADDY DEWDROP *P&R '71*
Singles: 7–inch
CAPITOL.......................... 3-5 75
INPHASION.......................... 3-4 78-79
SUNFLOWER.......................... 3-6 70-72
SUNFLOWER/MGM.......................... 3-5 73
LPs: 10/12–inch
SUNFLOWER 12-15 71

DADDY G
("Daddy;" Gene Barge)
Singles: 7–inch
LEGRAND (1028 "Look Alive")......20-30 63
Also see BARGE, Gene
Also see CHURCH STREET FIVE

DADDY GOODLOWE
(Daddy Goodloe)
Singles: 7–inch
RUFUS (502 "Just One More Drink")..........................5-10 62
VEE JAY (421 "Jamil")..........................4-8 62

DADDY LICKS BAND
LPs: 10/12–inch
EMOTIONAL.......................... 10-12

DADDY MERRITT: see MERRITT, Daddy

DADDY O's *P&R '58*
Singles: 7–inch
CABOT.......................... 8-10 58

DADISTICS
Singles: 7–inch
QUARK 3-5

DADURIA, Dan
Singles: 7–inch
BERTRAM INT'L (222 "Ukelele in Orbit")..........................8-12 62

DAE, Danny, & Defiants
Singles: 7–inch
ARLEN (521 "Beatle Mania") 15-20 64

DAE, Tommy
(With the High Tensions; with Tensionettes; Tom Dae)
Singles: 7–inch
DIAMOND 4-8 67
GLO (5245 "Candy Heart") 5-10 60s
HITT ("Tampico Rage") 4-8
(No selection number used.)
HITT (01 "Vibrations")..........................4-6 78
HITT (03 "So Dedicated") 4-6 78
HITT (6401 "Watch Out")..........................4-8

DAE, Toni
Singles: 7–inch
TEIA.......................... 5-10 64

DAFFAN, Ted *C&W '44*
(With His Texans)
Singles: 78 rpm
COLUMBIA.......................... 4-8 46-55
OKEH.......................... 4-8 44-45
Singles: 7–inch
COLUMBIA (21400 "Born to Lose") 8-12 55
Members: George Strange; Chuck Keeshan; Leon Seago.

DAFFODILS & Carl Jones
(With Ike Perkins Band)
Singles: 7–inch
C.J. (100 "Wine")..........................75-100 57

DAGENITES
Singles: 7–inch
HEIGH-HO 4-8 65-66

D'AGOSTIN, Dick
(With the Swingers)
Singles: 7–inch
ACCENT (1046 "I'm Your Daddy-O")..........................15-25
ACCENT (1049 "Mean Mean Woman")..........................10-15
DOT (15773 "Nancy Lynne")...........35-50 58
DOT (15867 "Night Walk")............15-25 58
LIBERTY.......................... 5-10 59

DAHCOTAH
Singles: 7–inch
COGNITO 4-8

DAHILLS
Singles: 7–inch
CLIFTON.......................... 4-8 76
CRYSTAL BALL.......................... 4-8
MUSICOR (1041 "Why Do We Have to Say Goodbye")..........................10-20 64

DAHL, Dick
Singles: 7–inch
ORIGINAL SOUND 8-12 65

DAHL, Jeff
Singles: 7–inch
BOMP 3-4 87

DAHL, Steve, & Teenage Radiation *P&R '79*
Singles: 7–inch
COHO 3-5 79
OVATION.......................... 3-5 79
Picture Sleeves
OVATION.......................... 3-5 79

DAHL, Tiny, & Robyns
Singles: 7–inch
U.A. 5-10 62

DAHLIAS
Singles: 7–inch
BIG H (612 "Go Away")..........................50-100 57

DAHLQUIST, Patricia
Singles: 7–inch
EPIC.......................... 3-5 75

DAHLSTROM, Patti
Singles: 7–inch
20TH FOX.......................... 3-5 74-76
UNI 3-5 72
LPs: 10/12–inch
20TH FOX.......................... 8-10 73-76
UNI.......................... 10-15 72

DAHROUGE, Ray
Singles: 7–inch
BELL.......................... 4-8 73-74

DAIDEMS
Singles: 7–inch
GOLDIE 10-15 61
LAVERE.......................... 8-10 61
STAR 10-15

DAILEY, Don
LPs: 10/12–inch
CROWN (314 "Surf Stompin' ") 15-25 63
Also see BOYD, Billy

DAILEY, Jack
Singles: 7–inch
GUYDEN.......................... 5-10 60
JAMIE 5-10 60

DAILEY, Wayne
Singles: 7–inch
MOONGLOW.......................... 4-8 66

DAILY, E.G. *P&R/R&B '86*
(Elizabeth G. Daily)
Singles: 12–inch
A&M 4-6 86
Singles: 7–inch
A&M 3-4 86
Picture Sleeves
A&M 3-4 86
LPs: 10/12–inch
A&M 5-10 86

DAILY FLASH
Singles: 7–inch
PARROT 8-10 66
UNI.......................... 5-10 67
EPs: 7–inch
MOXIE 5-10 83

DAILY NEWS
Singles: 7–inch
PARROT 4-8 68

DAISIES
Singles: 7–inch
CAPITOL (5667 "Cold Wave").......15-25 66
ROULETTE.......................... 5-10 64

DAISY, Pat *C&W '72*
Singles: 7–inch
RCA 3-5 72-73

DAISY CHAIN
Singles: 7–inch
FONTANA.......................... 4-6 68
LPs: 10/12–inch
UNITED INT'L 10-15

DAISY DILLMAN BAND: see DILLMAN BAND

DAISY MAE & HER HEPCATS
Singles: 78 rpm
GOTHAM 10-20 56
RICHLOY 15-25 56
20TH CENTURY 15-25 57
Singles: 7–inch
GOTHAM (7-317 "Lonesome Playgirl")..........................15-25 56
RICHLOY (102 "Want Me a Man").25-35 56
20TH CENTURY (1204 "Hop Scotch!")..........................25-35 57

DA-KARS
Singles: 7–inch
JOSIE 5-8 68

DAKIL, Floyd, Combo
Singles: 7–inch
EARTH (402 "Bad Boy") 30-40 65
EARTH (403 "Kitty Kitty") 25-35 65
EARTH (404 "Stronger Than Dirt")..........................25-35 65
GUYDEN (2111 "Dance Franny Dance")..........................10-15 65
JETSTAR (103 "Dance Franny Dance")..........................30-50 64
POMPEII (66687 "One Girl") 10-20 68

DAKILA
Singles: 7–inch
EPIC.......................... 3-5 72-73
LPs: 10/12–inch
EPIC 10-12 72

DAKOTA
Singles: 7–inch
COLUMBIA 3-4 80
MGM.......................... 3-5 70
LPs: 10/12–inch
COLUMBIA 5-10 80
GROOVE MERCHANT 8-10 75
Members: Bill Kelly; Jerry Huldzik.
Also see BUOYS

DAKOTAS
Singles: 7–inch
LIBERTY.......................... 5-10 63
Also see KRAMER, Billy J., & Dakotas

DA'KRASH *R&B/LP '88*
Singles: 7–inch
CAPITOL.......................... 3-4 88
LPs: 10/12–inch
CAPITOL.......................... 5-8 88

DAKUS, Wes
(With the Rebels; with Barry Allen; with Dennis Paul; with Club 93 Rebels)
Singles: 7–inch
CAPITOL.......................... 8-12 64-67
GALLIO (102 "Dog Food")..........15-25 63
KAPP 4-8 67
QUALITY.......................... 10-20 60
(Canadian.)
SWAN.......................... 8-12 65
U.A. (Except 722).......................... 5-10 64
U.A. (722 "Sidewinder")..........15-25 64
LPs: 10/12–inch
CAPITOL (6120 "The Wes Dakus Album")..........................25-35 60s
(Canadian.)
KAPP (3536 "Wes Dakus' Rebels")..........................25-35 67
Also see ALLEN, Barry
Also see PAUL, Dennis

DALBELLO *D&D '84*
Singles: 12–inch
CAPITOL.......................... 4-6 84
Singles: 7–inch
CAPITOL.......................... 3-4 84

DAL BELLO, Lisa
(With Michael McDonald)
Singles: 7–inch
TALISMAN (Black vinyl) 3-4 78
TALISMAN (Colored vinyl) 3-5 78
(Promotional issues only.)
Picture Sleeves
TALISMAN.......................... 3-5 78
Also see McDONALD, Michael

DALE, Alan *P&R '48*
(With Connie Haines)
Singles: 78 rpm
COLUMBIA 4-6 50-51
CORAL.......................... 3-6 52-56
DECCA 3-5 52
Singles: 7–inch
ABC-PAR.......................... 4-8 64
ADVANCE.......................... 3-6
COLUMBIA 5-15 50-51
CORAL (60000 & 61000 series).......5-15 52-56
CORAL (62000 series).......................... 5-8 63
DECCA.......................... 8-12 52
EMKAY 4-8 62
FTP.......................... 4-8 61
JUBILEE 4-6 67
MGM.......................... 5-8 59
SINCLAIR (1003 "A Teenage Girl")..........................15-25 61
EPs: 7–inch
CORAL.......................... 5-15 52-56
LPs: 10/12–inch
CORAL.......................... 15-25 55-56
FORD.......................... 10-15 63
U.A. 10-15 60
Also see CORNELL, Don, Johnny Desmond & Alan Dale

DALE, Bill
Singles: 7–inch
JCP (1053 "Speaker Ban Ballad")....5-10 65

DALE, Billy, Quartet
Singles: 78 rpm
KING.......................... 5-10 54-55
Singles: 7–inch
KING.......................... 10-15 54-55

DALE, Bobby
Singles: 7-inch
DE ROSE (8469 "You, You Love Me Only in Your Dreams")....................25-50

DALE, Denny, & Honeymoons
(Denny Dale Gudin)
Singles: 7-inch
BRANDY 3-4 85
DOOR KNOB................................ 3-4 93
HOMELY 3-5 80
LEJAC 10-15 65
SOMA (1447 "Mr. Moon") 10-15 65
Also see FENDERMEN

DALE, Dick P&R '61
(With His Del-tones)
Singles: 7-inch
CAPITOL (4939 "Miserlou") 8-12 62
CAPITOL (4940 "Peppermint Man") 8-12 63
CAPITOL (4963 "King of the Surf Guitar")................................ 8-12 63
CAPITOL (5010 "Secret Surgin' Spot")..................................... 8-12 63
CAPITOL (5048 "The Scavenger").. 8-12 63
CAPITOL (5098 "The Wedge") 8-12 63
CAPITOL (5140 "Mr. Eliminator").... 8-12 64
CAPITOL (5187 "Wild Wild Mustang")................................ 8-12 64
CAPITOL (5225 "Eyes of a Child").. 8-12 64
CAPITOL (5290 "Who Can He Be") 8-12 64
CAPITOL (5389 "Let's Go Trippin' ")................................ 8-12 64
COLUMBIA.................................... 3-5 87
CONCERT ROOM (371 "We'll Never Hear the End of It")........................... 4-8 63
COUGAR (712 "Taco Wagon") 4-8 67
CUPID (105 "We'll Never Hear the End of It")......................................15-25 60
DELTONE (4939 "Misirlou")...........40-60 58
DELTONE (4940 "Peppermint Man")......................................40-60 58
DELTONE (5012 "Oh Wee Marie") 35-50 58
DELTONE (5013 "Stop Teasing") ..35-50 59
DELTONE (5014 "Jessie Pearl")....35-50 60
DELTONE (5017 "Let's Go Trippin' ")...................................15-25 61
(No mention of Rendezvous Records.)
DELTONE (5017 "Let's Go Trippin' ")...................................10-20 61
(Reads: "Distributed by Rendezvous Records.")
DELTONE (5018 "Shake and Stomp")...................................20-30 62
DELTONE (5019 "Miserlou")..........15-25 62
(Reissue of 4939. Note slight spelling change.)
DELTONE (5020 "Peppermint Man")......................................15-25 62
DELTONE (5028 "Run for Life")......15-25 63
GNP (804 "Let's Go Trippin' ")........... 4-8 75
RENDEZVOUS (204 "Reincarnation Parts 1 & 2")..10-20 62
SATURN (401 "We'll Never Hear the End of It")..10-20 63
YES (7014 "We'll Never Hear the End of It")..10-20
Promotional Singles
CAPITOL ("Thunder Wave"/"Spanish Kiss")......................................10-20 64
(Bonus single, packaged with the *Surf Age* LP by Jerry Cole and His Spacemen.)
CAPITOL (2320 "Peppermint Man")......................................35-50 63
(Compact 33 Single)
Picture Sleeves
CAPITOL (2320 "Peppermint Man")......................................35-55 63
(Promotional Compact 33 Single sleeve.)
CAPITOL (4963 "King of the Surf Guitar")...................................20-30 63
COLUMBIA.................................... 4-6 87
LPs: 10/12-inch
BALBOA.. 5-10 83
CAPITOL (T-1930 "King of the Surf Guitar")...................................30-40 63
(Monaural.)
CAPITOL (ST-1930 "King of the Surf Guitar")...................................40-50 63
(Stereo.)
CAPITOL (T-2002 "Checkered Flag")......................................25-35 63
(Monaural.)
CAPITOL (ST-2002 "Checkered Flag")......................................30-40 63
(Stereo.)
CAPITOL (T-2053 "Mr. Eliminator")...................................30-35 64
(Monaural.)
CAPITOL (ST-2053 "Mr. Eliminator")...................................35-40 64
(Stereo.)
CAPITOL (T-2111 "Summer Surf")......................................50-75 64
(Monaural. With *Movin' Surf*, a bonus single by Jerry Cole & His Spacemen.)
CAPITOL (T-2111 "Summer Surf")......................................35-45 64
(Monaural. Without bonus single.)
CAPITOL (ST-2111 "Summer Surf")......................................45-55 64
(Stereo. With *Movin' Surf*, a bonus single by Jerry Cole & His Spacemen.)
CAPITOL (ST-2111 "Summer Surf")......................................40-50 64
(Stereo. Without bonus single.)
CAPITOL (T-2293 "Rock Out with Dick Dale Live at Ciro's")...........................30-35 65
(Monaural.)
CAPITOL (2293 "Rock Out with Dick Dale Live at Ciro's")..................................35-40 65
(Stereo.)
DELTONE (1001 "Surfer's Choice")...................................30-40 61
DELTONE (1886 "Surfer's Choice")...................................40-60 63
(Distributed by Capitol.)
DUBTONE......................................15-20 63
GNP 8-12 75
Also see ALLAN, Davie
Also see BEACH BOYS / Dick Dale / Surfaris / Surf Kings
Also see HOLLYWOOD SURFERS / Dick Dale
Also see STOMPERS / Dick Dale
Also see TROY, Bo, & His Hot Rods / Dick Dale
Also see VAUGHAN, Stevie Ray, & Dick Dale

DALE, Dick / Jerry Cole / Super Stocks / Mr. Gasser & Weirdos
EPs: 7-inch
CAPITOL (2663 "The Big Surfing Sounds")...................................35-50 64
(Promotional issue only.)
Also see COLE, Jerry
Also see MR. GASSER & WEIRDOS
Also see SUPER STOCKS

DALE, Dick / Surfaris / Fireballs
LPs: 10/12-inch
ALMOR (108 "World of Surfin' ")....10-20 60s
ALMOR (109 "Hot Rod Drag Races")......................................10-20 60s
Also see FIREBALLS

DALE, Dick / Surfaris / Surf Kings (Beach Boys)
LPs: 10/12-inch
GUEST STAR (1433 "Surf Kings")......................................20-30 63
(Credits the Beach Boys, though there are no tracks by the Beach Boys. Also, tracks credited to the Surfaris are by the Original Surfaris.)
GUEST STAR (1433 "Surf Kings")......................................15-20 63
(Does not credit the Beach Boys.)
Also see SURFARIS (Original Surfaris)

DALE, Dick, His Del-Tones, & Francine York / Craig Adams & His Country Cousins
(With the Overland Swingin' Top Brass)
Singles: 7-inch
UNITED STATES ARMY (1301 "Enlistment Twist")......................................10-20 62
(Colored vinyl. Promotional issue only.)
Picture Sleeves
UNITED STATES ARMY (1301 "Enlistment Twist")......................................10-20 62
Also see DALE, Dick

DALE, Dick
Singles: 7-inch
ACCENT.. 3-5 68
LPs: 10/12-inch
ACCENT..8-12 67

DALE, Gary
Singles: 7-inch
GONE (5007 "Pretty Baby")...........15-25 57

DALE, Glen
Singles: 7-inch
MALA (001 "I've Got You on My Mind")..8-12 68
Also see FORTUNES

DALE, Ginny
Singles: 7-inch
LAWN... 4-8 64

DALE, Jeff
Singles: 7-inch
ATCO (6352 " Where Did I Go") 10-15 65
ATCO (6405 "Our Love Will Grow Stronger")....................................10-15 66

DALE, Jim
Singles: 7-inch
CAPITOL......................................15-25 58

DALE, Jim, & Comancheroes
Singles: 7-inch
TEEN..5-10

DALE, Jimmie
Singles: 7-inch
PALAMINO.....................................5-10
SABRE (708 "Baby Doll")..............25-35

DALE, Jimmy
(Jimmy Clanton)
Singles: 7-inch
DREW-BLAN (1003 "My Pride and Joy")..15-25 61
Also see CLANTON, Jimmy

DALE, Kenny C&W '77
Singles: 7-inch
BGM.. 3-4 86
CAPITOL...................................... 3-5 77-80
FUNDERBURG 3-4 82
REPUBLIC 3-4 84
SABA.. 3-4 85
LPs: 10/12-inch
CAPITOL.......................................6-12 77-81

DALE, Kenny
Singles: 7-inch
PICTURE (310 "Cindy Lee") 10-20

DALE, Larry
Singles: 78 rpm
GROOVE 15-25 54
HERALD..15-25 55
Singles: 7-inch
ATLANTIC (2133 "Drinkin' Wine Spo-Dee-O-Dee")..8-12 62
ELBRIDGE (12762 "Crying Over You")..20-30
FIRE... 4-8 68
GLOVER (203 "Big Muddy") 10-20 60
GLOVER (208 "Let the Doorbell Ring")..10-20 60
GROOVE (0029 " You Better Heed My Warning")....................................30-40 54
HERALD (463 "Feelin' All Right")...30-40 55
RAM 4-6 68
Also see DUPREE, Jack, & Mr. Bear
Also see McHOUSTON, Big Red
Also see WILLIAMS, Paul

DALE, Robin
Singles: 7-inch
LIBERTY (55297 "Cry, Cry, Cry").....5-10 61

DALE, Terry C&W '82
Singles: 7-inch
LANEDALE......................................3-4 82

DALE & GRACE P&R/R&B '63
Singles: 7-inch
COLLECTABLES 3-4 70s
ERIC 3-4 70s
GUYDEN 3-5 72
HBR 4-8 66
MICHELLE 5-10 63-64
MONTEL..4-8 63-67
MONTEL MICHELLE (942 "What Am I Living For")...4-8 64
(Shows both label names.)
TRIP...3-4 70s
LPs: 10/12-inch
MONTEL (100 "I'm Leaving It Up to You")...35-50 64
Members: Dale Houston; Grace Broussard.
Also see HOUSTON, Dale

DALE & DEL-HEARTS
Singles: 7-inch
HERALD...10-15 61

DALE & UNIQUES
Singles: 7-inch
UNIQUE 20-30

DALES
Singles: 78 rpm
ONYX...25-50 57
Singles: 7-inch
ONYX (509 "If You Are Meant to Be")..25-50 57

DALES
(Dale's Boys)
Singles: 7-inch
CREST (1045 "The Big Jump")......15-20 58
CREST (1069 "Rockin' Nellie") 10-15 60

DALEY, Jimmy, & Ding-A-Lings
Singles: 78 rpm
DECCA..20-30 56-57
Singles: 7-inch
DECCA (30163 "Rock Pretty Baby")..20-30 56
DECCA (30532 "Hole in the Wall")..20-30 57
EPs: 7-inch
DECCA (2480 "Rock Pretty Baby")..50-75 56
(Soundtrack.)
LPs: 10/12-inch
DECCA (8429 "Rock Pretty Baby")......................................100-150 56
(Soundtrack. With Rod McKuen, Alan Copeland, & Hal Dickinson.)

DALHART, Vernon P&R '17
(With Gladys Rice; with Al Bernard)
Singles: 78 rpm
BANNER 15-25 20s
BLACK PATTI 75-125
BRUNSWICK 10-20 20s
BUDDY..50-100
CAMEO...15-25 20s
CHAMPION 15-25 20s
CLARION 10-20
COLUMBIA......................................5-15 22-30s
DOMINO 15-25 20s
EDISON 20-50 17-20s
EDISON AMBEROL 15-25 20s
GENNETT 15-25 20s
HARMONY.......................................15-25 20s
HERSCHEL.......................................25-50
HERWIN..25-50
OKEH..10-20 24
PATH 15-25 20s
PERFECT 15-25 20s
RCA 5-10 49
REGAL..15-25 20s
SILVERTONE....................................15-25
VICTOR...10-20 21-30s
VOCALION.......................................15-25 20s
Singles: 7-inch
RCA (0016 "Prisoner's Song")........15-25 49
LPs: 10/12-inch
DAVIS UNLIMITED 10-20
GOLDEN OLDEN COUNTRY.................8-10
MARK 56..8-10
OLD HOMESTEAD 8-10

DALHART, Vernon, & Carson Robison P&R '28
Singles: 78 rpm
VICTOR...10-20 27-28
Also see DALHART, Vernon
Also see ROBISON, Carson

DALICE C&W '90
Singles: 7-inch
COUNTRY PRIDE................................3-4 90

DALIDA
Singles: 7-inch
FELSTED 10-15 59

DALLAIRE, Art, & Watchmen
Singles: 7-inch
FLIP (202 "A Cryin' Shame") 20-30

DALLARA, Tony P&R '58
Singles: 7-inch
MERCURY 5-10 58-60
VESUVIUS 4-8 61-62
LPs: 10/12-inch
VESUVIUS..8-10 62

DALLAS, Jackie
(With the Tiaras)
Singles: 7-inch
ALLIANCE (1690 "All I Want").......10-20 60s
FAWN (6002 "Lorraine")................25-35
Also see TIARAS

DALLAS, Johnny C&W '66
Singles: 7-inch
LITTLE DARLIN'...............................4-6 66

DALLAS, Leroy
Singles: 78 rpm
JADE (707 "Your Sweet Man's Blues")..15-25 49
SITTIN' IN WITH (522 "I'm Down Now, But I Won't Be Always")..........................20-30 49
SITTIN' IN WITH (526 "Good Morning Blues")...20-30 49
SITTIN' IN WITH (537 "Your Sweet Man's Blues")...20-30 49

DALLAS, Suzie
Singles: 7-inch
TODD..5-10 59

DALLAS COUNTY
Singles: 7-inch
ENTERPRISE 3-6 70
LPs: 10/12-inch
ENTERPRISE 8-12 70

DALLIS, Chuck
Singles: 7-inch
GLENN (2201 "Come on Let's Go")...40-60 61
GLENN (2202 "Moon Twist") 20-40 62
GLENN (2203 "Good Show, But No Go")...20-40 62
K.C. (102 "Come on Let's Go") 30-50 62

DALLMAN, Jerry, & Knightcaps
Singles: 7-inch
PUNCH (6000 "The Bug")...............15-20 63

DALLON, Lee
Singles: 7-inch
TARA 3-5 74

DALLON, Miki
Singles: 7-inch
RCA 8-12 65
Also see CHRISTIAN, Neil
Also see MIKI
Also see SORROWS

DALLTIN, Dusty
Singles: 7-inch
UNIQUE (100 "Shotgun")...............15-25 62

DALMATIANS
Singles: 7-inch
ABC-PAR 4-8 62

DALTON, Bob C&W '70
Singles: 7-inch
MEGA 3-5 70

DALTON, Danny
Singles: 7-inch
TEEN 5-10 59

DALTON, James & Sutton
Singles: 7-inch
NATIONAL GENERAL.........................10-20
RCA 4-6 72-73

DALTON, Kathy P&R/LP '74
Singles: 7-inch
DISC REET..3-5 74
LPs: 10/12-inch
DISC REET..8-12 73-74
Session: Van Dyke Parks.
Also see PARKS, Van Dyke

DALTON, Lacy J. C&W '79
Singles: 7-inch
CAPITOL..3-4 90
COLUMBIA..3-5 79-86
UNIVERSAL..3-4 89
LPs: 10/12-inch
CBS...5-10
COLUMBIA..6-12 78-83
Also see BARE, Bobby
Also see COE, David Allan
Also see JONES, George, & Lacy J. Dalton

DALTON, Larry, & Dolton Gang C&W '81
Singles: 7-inch
SOUNDWAVES 3-4 81

DALTON, Martine, & Bennie Bunn
Singles: 7-inch
TCF (10 "No Matter What the People Say")...10-20 64
Also see BUNN, Bennie

DALTON & DUBARRI R&B '79
Singles: 7-inch
ABC...3-5 76
COLUMBIA..3-5 73-74
HILLTAK..3-4 79
LPs: 10/12-inch
ABC...8-10 76
COLUMBIA..10-12 73-74
HILLTAK..5-10 79
Members: Gary Dalton; Kent Dubarri.

DALTON BOYS
(With Henry Jerome & His Orchestra)
Singles: 7-inch
CORAL (62387 "Silver Dollar") 10-20 63
PORT CITY (355 "Anyone Who Had a Heart")..10-20 63
SKYLA (1124 "Much Stronger").......20-30 62
TEEN (505 "Who's Gonna Hold Your Hand")..30-50 60s
V.I.P. (25025 "Take My Hand")....75-125 65
V.I.P. (25025 "Something's Bothering You")..30-50 65
Member: Danny Dalton.
Also see JEROME, Henry, & His Orchestra

DALTON BOYS
Singles: 7-inch
CAROL...5-10 65

DALTON BROTHERS
Singles: 7-inch
MARTAY (2001 "I Only Came to Dance with You")..20-30 63
Members: Scott Engel; John Stewart.
Also see ENGEL, Scott, & John Stewart

DAL-TONES: see PARKER, Wayne / Dal-Tones

DALTREY, David
LPs: 10/12-inch
SCEPTER 10-12 71

DALTREY, Roger P&R/LP '73
Singles: 7-inch
A&M...3-5 75-76
ATLANTIC...3-4 84-87
MCA...3-5 73-82
MCA/GOLDHAWKE 3-5 75-77
ODE...3-5 72-73
POLYDOR...3-4 80-81
TRACK..3-5 73
Picture Sleeves
ATLANTIC...3-4 84-85
POLYDOR...3-5 80
LPs: 10/12-inch
ATLANTIC...5-10 84-87
MCA...10-15 71-82
POLYDOR...5-8 80
TRACK..10-12 73
Also see WHO

DALTREY, Roger, & Steve Gibbons
Singles: 12-inch
MCA...5-10
(Promotional issue only.)
Also see GIBBONS, Steve, Band

DALTREY, Roger, & Rick Wakeman
Singles: 7-inch
A&M...3-5 75
LPs: 10/12-inch
A&M...8-10 75
Also see DALTREY, Roger
Also see WAKEMAN, Rick

DALY, Durwood
Singles: 7-inch
CAPROCK (108 "That's the Way It Goes")..25-40 59

DALY, Sandra
Singles: 7-inch
T.J. (101 "My Only Cure Is You") 50-100 61

DALY, Terry
Singles: 7-inch
MARK (122 "You Don't Bug Me")..200-300 58

DALYS
Singles: 7-inch
FONTANA (1647 "Early Momin' Rain")..8-12 69

DAMAL & RASHEED
Singles: 7-inch
GREAT...4-8 62

DAMARIS R&B '84
Singles: 7-inch
COLUMBIA...3-4 84

DAMASCANS
Singles: 7-inch
PYRAMID (6372 "Go 'Way Girl") 10-15 66

DAMASKAS, BARNES & BARNES
Singles: 7-inch
ASININE...4-8 79
Picture Sleeves
ASININE...5-10 79

D'AMBRA, Joe, & Embers
Singles: 7-inch
MERCURY...5-10 60

DAME, Freddy
(With Bobby's Trailers; with Fables)
Singles: 7-inch
HERITAGE (813 "Sometimes I Don't Like Me")...5-10 71
NIC NAC (331 "Love Is a Game")...35-45
Also see FREDDY & CLAIRE

DAMERON, Donna
(With the Big Bopper)
Singles: 7-inch
DART (113 "Bopper 486609")......75-125 59
(With "The Story Behind the Record" photo-insert.)
DART (113 "Bopper 486609").........25-50 59
(Without insert.)
Also see BIG BOPPER

DAMIAN, Michael P&R '81
Singles: 7-inch
CYPRESS ... 3-4 89
LEG ... 3-4 81
Picture Sleeves
CYPRESS ... 3-4 89
LEG ... 3-4 81
LPs: 10/12-inch
CYPRESS ... 5-8 89

DAMIANO, Joe P&R '59
(Josef Damiano)
Singles: 7-inch
CHANCELLOR ... 5-10 59-60

D'AMICO, Ted
Singles: 7-inch
CAVLALIER (902 "Mr. Switchman") ... 25-50 61

DAMIN EIH: see EIH, Damin

DAMION & DENITA
LPs: 10/12-inch
ROCKET ... 5-10 80
Members: Damion Micheals; Denita James.
Also see HODGES, JAMES & SMITH

DAMITA JO P&R '53
(Damita Joe)
Singles: 78 rpm
HOLLYWOOD ... 5-10 52
RCA ... 4-8 53
Singles: 7-inch
BANG BANG ... 4-8
EPIC (Black vinyl) ... 3-5 65-67
EPIC (Colored vinyl) ... 4-8 66
HOLLYWOOD (182 "Way Up High") ... 10-15 52
MELIC ... 4-6 64
MERCURY ... 4-8 60-64
RCA ... 8-12 53
RANWOOD ... 3-5 68-71
VEE JAY ... 4-6 65
Picture Sleeves
EPIC ... 4-8 65
MERCURY ... 5-10 61-63
EPs: 7-inch
MERCURY ... 5-10 60-61
LPs: 10/12-inch
CAMDEN ... 6-10 65
EPIC ... 8-15 65-67
MERCURY ... 12-25 61-63
RANWOOD ... 5-10 68
VEE JAY ... 10-15 65
Also see BENTON, Brook, & Damita Jo

DAMITA JO & BILLY ECKSTINE
Singles: 7-inch
MERCURY ... 3-6 63
Also see ECKSTINE, Billy

DAMITA JO with STEVE GIBSON & RED CAPS
Singles: 78 rpm
RCA (6281 "Always") ... 8-15 55
Singles: 7-inch
ABC-PAR ... 5-10 61
RCA (6281 "Always") ... 10-20 55
LPs: 10/12-inch
ABC-PAR (378 "Big 15") ... 40-60 61
Also see DAMITA JO
Also see GIBSON, Steve

DAMN YANKEES P&R/LP '90
Singles: 7-inch
W.B. ... 3-4 90
LPs: 10/12-inch
W.B. ... 5-8 90
Members: Ted Nugent; Jack Blades; Tommy Shaw; Michael Cartellone.
Also see NIGHT RANGER
Also see NUGENT, Ted
Also see STYX

DAMNATION LP '70
(Featuring Adam Blessing)
Singles: 7-inch
U.A. ... 3-5 71-72
LPs: 10/12-inch
U.A. ... 10-15 69-71

DAMNED
Singles: 7-inch
MCA ... 3-4 87
Picture Sleeves
MCA ... 3-4 87
LPs: 10/12-inch
I.R.S. ... 5-10 80
STIFF COU-B/SEEZ ... 8-10 77
Members: Dave Vanian; Captain Sensible; Brian James; Rat Scabies; Algy Ward; Roman Jugg; Bryn Marek.
Also see CAPTAIN SENSIBLE

DAMON
LPs: 10/12-inch
ANKH ("Song of a Gypsy") ... 2500-3000 70
(No selection number used.)

DAMON, Dennis
Singles: 7-inch
CAMPO (953 "Satisfy You") ... 15-20
U.A. ... 4-8 66

DAMON, Jimmy
Singles: 7-inch
JIST ... 4-8 64

DAMON, Liz P&R '70
(Liz Damon's Orient Express)
Singles: 7-inch
ABC ... 3-5 73
ANTHEM ... 5-10 71-72
DONCY ... 5-8 78
MAKAHA ... 5-10 70
WHITE WHALE ... 3-5 70
LPs: 10/12-inch
ANTHEM ("Liz Damon and the Orient Express") ... 15-25 71
DELILAH ... 8-12
MAKAHA ... 10-20 70
WHITE WHALE ... 8-12 71
Also see ORIENT EXPRESS

DAMON, Mark, & Jordanaires
Singles: 7-inch
WYNNE ... 8-10 59
Picture Sleeves
WYNNE ... 10-20 59
Also see JORDANAIRES

DAMON, Russ
Singles: 7-inch
ABC-PAR ... 4-8 65
LAURIE ... 4-8 63
MUSICOR ... 4-8 65

DAMON, Sterling
Singles: 7-inch
1A (108 "Rejected") ... 10-20 66

DAMONE, Vic P&R '47
Singles: 78 rpm
COLUMBIA ... 3-6 56-57
MERCURY ... 3-6 48-55
MERCURY/SAV-WAY (5053 "Ivy") ... 100-150 47
(Picture disc. Promotional issue only.)
Singles: 7-inch
CAPITOL ... 4-6 61-64
COLUMBIA ... 5-10 56-61
DOLTON ... 4-6 62
MGM ... 3-5 72-73
MERCURY ... 5-10 50-55
RCA ... 3-6 66-69
REBECCA ... 3-5 77
UNITED TALENT ... 3-5 70
W.B. ... 4-6 65-66
EPs: 7-inch
CAPITOL CUSTOM ("Vic Damone Swings with A&W") ... 10-15 62
(Special products issue for A&W Root Beer.)
COLUMBIA ... 5-10 56-58
MERCURY ... 8-12 50-56
LPs: 10/12-inch
CAPITOL ... 10-20 61-64
COLUMBIA (900 thru 1500 series) ... 15-25 56-61
COLUMBIA (1900 series) ... 10-20 62
COLUMBIA (8000 thru 8300 series) ... 20-30 58-61
COLUMBIA (8700 series) ... 10-15 62
DOLTON ... 10-15 64
HARMONY ... 5-10 66-67
HOLLYWOOD ... 5-10
MERCURY (Except 25000 series) ... 8-12 69
MERCURY (25000 series) ... 15-30 50-56
RCA ... 8-12 66-68
UNITED TALENT ... 5-10
W.B. ... 10-15 65
WING ... 10-15 59-63
Also see ANDREWS, Julie & Andre Previn / Vic Damone / Jack Jones / Marian Anderson
Also see FISHER, Eddie / Vic Damone / Dick Haymes
Also see PAGE, Patti, & Vic Damone

DAMONE, Vic / Dick "Two Ton" Baker
Singles: 78 rpm
MERCURY/SAV-WAY (5056/5055 "You Do") ... 100-150 47
(Picture disc. Promotional issue only.)

DAMPHIER, Tom
Singles: 7-inch
KIRSHNER ... 4-8
Also see TOKENS

DAMRON, Alan
Singles: 7-inch
FRANC ... 4-8 64

DAMRON, Dick
Singles: 7-inch
QUALITY (1213 "Julie") ... 30-45

DAN & CLEAN-CUTS
(Dan & the Clean Cut-Guys)
Singles: 7-inch
ACCENT ... 10-20 64
SCEPTER ... 10-20 65-66

DAN & DALE
Singles: 7-inch
NEWARK (229 "Love Is Blue") ... 4-8 68
TIFTON (125 "Batman Theme") ... 5-10 66
Picture Sleeves
TIFTON (125 "Batman Theme") ... 10-20 66
LPs: 10/12-inch
DIPLOMAT ... 10-20 60s
TIFTON (78002 "Batman and Robin") ... 20-30 66
(Includes color Batman & Robin inner sleeve.)

DAN & LOU
Singles: 7-inch
SIGMA (1002 "Girl in My Dreams") ... 8-12 60

DAN the MAN
Singles: 7-inch
DAN the MAN (13836 "Reagon-Omics") ... 4-6 82
DAN the MAN (18467 "High-Priced Gasoline") ... 3-5 90

DANA
Singles: 7-inch
ARIOLA AMERICA ... 3-5 76-77
EPIC ... 3-5 79
LONDON ... 3-5 72

DANA, Bill LP '60
(Jose Jimenez; Bill Dana & Friends)
Singles: 7-inch
A&M ... 4-8 65-66
KAPP ... 5-15 61-63
SIGNATURE ... 5-10 60
Picture Sleeves
KAPP ... 10-20 61-62
EPs: 7-inch
KAPP ... 10-20 61
LPs: 10/12-inch
A&M ... 8-12 68
CAPITOL ... 6-10 70
HBR ... 8-10 66
KAPP ... 12-25 60-64
ROULETTE ... 12-25 61
SIGNATURE ... 20-25 60

DANA, Jeff
Singles: 7-inch
FLEETWOOD ... 10-15

DANA, Kenny
Singles: 7-inch
SHELL ... 5-10 61

DANA, Vic P&R '61
Singles: 7-inch
CASINO ... 3-5 76
COLUMBIA ... 3-5 71
DOLTON ... 4-8 61-65
LIBERTY ... 3-6 68-70
MGM ... 3-5 75
Picture Sleeves
DOLTON ... 5-10 62-66
LPs: 10/12-inch
DOLTON (Except 2013/8013) ... 15-25 62-65
DOLTON (2013 "This Is Vic Dana") ... 15-25 61
(Monaural.)
DOLTON (8013 "This Is Vic Dana") ... 20-30 61
(Stereo.)
LIBERTY ... 8-15 67-70
SUNSET ... 8-10 67
Also see CARTER, Mel / Vic Dana

DANA & DEXTER
Singles: 7-inch
IMPERIAL ... 5-10 61

DANA DANE: see DANE, Dana

DANCER
Singles: 7-inch
A&M ... 3-5 76
HITTIE ... 3-4 80
LPs: 10/12-inch
A&M ... 8-10 76

DANCER, Terri R&B '86
Singles: 7-inch
REFLECTION ... 3-4 86

DANCER, PRANCER & NERVOUS P&R '59
Singles: 7-inch
CAPITOL ... 5-10 59
Picture Sleeves
CAPITOL ... 8-10 59
Member: Russ Regan.
Also see REGAN, Russ
Also see SUMMERS, Little Davey

DANCING PANTHER
(Dancing Panther Orchestra; Dancing Panther Band)
Singles: 7-inch
W.B. ... 4-8 61

DANCO, Carl
Singles: 7-inch
DANCO ... 8-12 64

DANCY, Mel
Singles: 7-inch
DUCKY ... 5-10 59

DAN-DEES
Singles: 7-inch
VEST ... 5-10 63

DANDELION WINE
Singles: 7-inch
SUSSEX ... 4-8

DANDERLIERS R&B '55
("James Campbell & Dallas Taylor Vocalists")
Singles: 78 rpm
STATES (147 "Chop Chop Boom") ... 75-125 55
STATES (150 "Shu-Wop") ... 50-75 55
STATES (152 "May God Be with You") ... 50-75 56
STATES (160 "My Love") ... 75-125 56
Singles: 7-inch
B&F (150 "Shu-Wop") ... 12-20 60
B&F (160 "My Love") ... 12-20 60
B&F (1344 "Shu-Wop") ... 10-15 61
MIDAS (9004 "All the Way") ... 10-20 67
STATES (147 "Chop Chop Boom") ... 150-250 55
(Black vinyl.)
STATES (147 "Chop Chop Boom") ... 600-800 55
(Red vinyl.)
STATES (150 "Shu-Wop") ... 75-100 55
STATES (152 "May God Be with You") ... 100-150 56
STATES (160 "My Love") ... 100-150 56
Members: Dallas Taylor; James Campbell; Richard Thomas; Walter Stephenson; Bernard Dixon; Louis Johnson.

DANDEVILLES
Singles: 7-inch
FORTÉ (314 "Heavenly Angel") ... 200-300 59

DANDEVILLES
Singles: 7-inch
GUYDEN (2014 "There's a Reason") ... 10-20 59
Also see GUIDES
Also see UPTONES

DANDIE, Professor Jim, & Kampus Kids
Singles: 7-inch
BULLSEYE (1006 "Teacher's Comin' ") ... 10-20 58

DANDIES
Singles: 7-inch
PEACH (726 "Have I Lost You Love") ... 25-50 58

DANDLEERS: see DANLEERS

DANDO SHAFT
LPs: 10/12-inch
NEON ... 10-12 71

D'ANDREA, Ann
Singles: 7-inch
JAMIE (1352 "Don't Stop Lookin' ") ... 10-15 69
PHILIPS ... 4-8 64

D'ANDREA, Bob
Singles: 7-inch
TRIBUTE ... 4-8

D'ANDREA, Dick, & Melody Kings with 5 Teens
Singles: 7-inch
BALD EAGLE (1002 "Git Outta the House") ... 15-20

D'ANDREA, John, & Young Gyants
Singles: 7-inch
PARKWAY ... 4-6 67
LPs: 10/12-inch
PARKWAY ... 10-15 67

DANDRIDGE, Ruby, & Her Rhythmanians
Singles: 7-inch
SAND (245 "Hot Tamale Blues") ... 10-20 57

DANDY C&W '79
(With the Doolittle Band)
Singles: 7-inch
COLUMBIA ... 3-4 80
W.B. ... 3-5 79

DANE, Barbara
(With the Earl Hines Orchestra)
Singles: 7-inch
TREY ... 10-15 60
LPs: 10/12-inch
CAPITOL (1758 "On My Way") ... 15-25 62
DOT (3177 "Livin' with the Blues") ... 15-25 59
(Monaural.)
DOT (25177 "Livin' with the Blues") ... 20-30 59
(Stereo.)
FOLKWAYS (2471 "The Blues") ... 10-20 64
HORIZON (1602 "When I Was a Young Girl") ... 15-25 62
(Black vinyl.)
HORIZON (1602 "When I Was a Young Girl") ... 30-40 62
(Colored vinyl.)

DANE, Barbara, & Chambers Brothers
LPs: 10/12-inch
FOLKWAYS (2468 "Barbara Dane and the Chambers Brothers") ... 20-30 64
Also see CHAMBERS BROTHERS
Also see DANE, Barbara

DANE, Bill, & Hot Dogs
Singles: 78 rpm
CREST ... 10-20 56
Singles: 7-inch
CREST (1008 "Boogie Woogie Cha Cha") ... 15-25 56
CREST (1021 "Tears of Joy") ... 15-25 56

DANE, Dana R&B '85
Singles: 12-inch
PROFILE ... 4-6 85
Singles: 7-inch
PROFILE ... 3-4 85-90
LPs: 10/12-inch
PROFILE ... 5-10 86-90

DANE, Johnny
Singles: 7-inch
VEE JAY ... 5-10 59

DANES
(With the Marvino Four)
Singles: 7-inch
CHARAY (303 "Just a Dream") ... 15-25 60s
LE CAM (718 "Most of All") ... 500-750 61
(Reissued as by the Team Mates.)
SMASH ... 5-10 65
TOWER ... 5-10 66
Also see TEAM MATES

DANETTA & STARLETS
(With Carl H. Davis & Orchestra)
Singles: 7-inch
OKEH (7155 "You Belong to Me") ... 50-100 62

D'ANGELO, Nick, & Farmers
Singles: 7-inch
CHIME (109 "Mr. Zeppelin Man") ... 5-10

DANGER, Nick
Singles: 7-inch
BARSTOW ... 3-5 90
(With insert flyer.)

DANGER DANGER LP '89
LPs: 10/12-inch
EPIC ... 5-8 89

DANGERFIELD, Rodney LP '80
Singles: 12-inch
RCA ... 4-6 83
Singles: 7-inch
RCA ... 3-4 83
Picture Sleeves
RCA ... 3-4 83
LPs: 10/12-inch
DECCA ... 15-20 66
CASABLANCA ... 5-10 80
RCA ... 5-10 83
RHINO ... 5-10 80

DANGEROUS FRIENDS
LPs: 10/12-inch
MASQUE (8701 "Dangerous Friends") ... 5-10 88
(Picture disc. 500 made.)

DANGEROUS TOYS LP '89
Singles: 7-inch
COLUMBIA ... 5-8 89-90
LPs: 10/12-inch
COLUMBIA ... 5-8 89-91

DANIEL C&W '77
(Daniel Willis)
Singles: 7-inch
LS ... 3-5 77-78

DANIEL, Cooter C&W '80
Singles: 7-inch
CONNECTION ... 3-4 80

DANIEL, Davis C&W '91
Singles: 7-inch
MERCURY ... 3-4 91

DANIEL, Godfrey
Singles: 7-inch
NOSTALGIA ... 3-5
LPs: 10/12-inch
ATLANTIC ... 10-20 72

DANIEL, Jay
Singles: 7-inch
DART ... 4-8 62
MERCURY ... 4-8 61

DANIEL, Jody
Singles: 7-inch
N-JOY ... 4-8 65

DANIEL, Johnny, & Soul Malibus
Singles: 7-inch
SM (08 "I'm Gonna Make You Mine") ... 8-12

DANIEL, Pebble C&W '80
Singles: 7-inch
ELEKTRA ... 3-4 80

DANIEL, Stan
Singles: 7-inch
HOLIDAY INN ... 4-8 62

DANIEL, Yvann
Singles: 7-inch
TRIBUTE ... 4-8 62

DANIEL AMOS
LPs: 10/12-inch
MARANATHA MUSIC ... 5-10 75-77

DANIELLE
LPs: 10/12-inch
CASABLANCA ... 5-10 80

DANIELLE, Tina C&W '86
(With the Laverna Moore Singers; with Carol Lee Singers)
Singles: 7-inch
CHARTA ... 3-4 86-87

DANIELS, The
Singles: 7-inch
LANTAM (01 "Finally") ... 15-25 60s

DANIELS, Bill
Singles: 78 rpm
MERCURY ... 5-10 52
Singles: 7-inch
MERCURY (5822 "That's How It Goes") ... 10-20 52

DANIELS, Charlie C&W/P&R/LP '73
(Charlie Daniels Band; with the Jaguars)
Singles: 7-inch
CAPITOL ... 3-4 90s
EPIC ... 3-5 76-86
HANOVER (4541 "Robot Romp") ... 10-20 59
KAMA SUTRA ... 3-6 73-76
PAULA (200 series) ... 5-10 66
PAULA (400 series) ... 3-5 76
Picture Sleeves
EPIC ... 3-4
EPs: 7-inch
KAMA SUTRA (10 "Volunteer Jam") ... 5-8 74
(Bonus EP packaged with *Fire on the Mountain* LP.)
LPs: 10/12-inch
CAPITOL (11000 series) ... 8-10 75
CAPITOL (16000 series) ... 5-10 80
EPIC (Except 273) ... 5-10 76-91
EPIC (273 "Everything You Always Wanted to Hear") ... 10-15 77
(Promotional issue only.)
EPIC/CBS (35751 "Million Mile Reflection") ... 35-45 79

(Picture disc. Six variations, each with a different logo on back side. 250 made of each of the six. Promotional issue only.)
KAMA SUTRA 10-15 73-76
MFSL (176 "Million Mile Reflections") 20-30 85
Members: Tom Crain; Taz DiGregorio; Fred Edwards; Charles Hayward.
Also see BAD BOYS
Also see BARE, Bobby
Also see HELM, Levon, Johnny Cash, Emmylou Harris & Charlie Daniels
Also see LEE, Johnny, Michael Martin Murphey, & Charlie Daniels
Also see TUBB, Ernest

DANIELS, Danny
Singles: 7-inch
VITA 5-10 59

DANIELS, Dotty
Singles: 7-inch
AMY (885 "I Wrote You a Letter") ..10-15 63
AMY (891 "A Casual Look") 10-15 63

DANIELS, Duke
Singles: 7-inch
EASTERN (002 "Backfire") 15-25 60s

DANIELS, Eddie
(With His Daniels Nine)
Singles: 7-inch
EBB (108 "Playin' Hide and Seek") 25-40 57
EBB (113 "I Wanna Know") 20-30 58
EDDIE MAE'S (501 "Little Ishana Man") 8-12
STARLA 10-20 60

DANIELS, J.J.
Singles: 7-inch
SURE SHOT 4-8 67

DANIELS, Jack
Singles: 7-inch
GATEWAY 4-8
JERDEN 4-8 66

DANIELS, Jeff
(Luke McDaniels)
Singles: 7-inch
ASTRO (108 "Foxy Dan") 50-75 61
BIG HOWDY (777 "Switch Blade Sam") 75-100 59
BIG HOWDY (8120 "Uh-Huh") 40-60 59
BIG HOWDY (8121 "Foxy Dan") 50-75 59
DUELL 3-5 79
MELADEE (117 "Daddy-O Rock") 100-150 58
Also see McDANIELS, Luke

DANIELS, Larry
Singles: 7-inch
COUNTRY CAPERS (104 Buckshot") 5-10

DANIELS, Maxine
Singles: 7-inch
TREND (014 "A Foggy Day") 5-10 58

DANIELS, Mike
Singles: 7-inch
GROOVE 4-8 64

DANIELS, Tex
Singles: 78 rpm
DIXIE 10-20

DANIELS, Yvonne
Singles: 7-inch
STERLING 8-10

DANIELS, Zak
LPs: 10/12-inch
AZRA (063 "Ground Zero") 5-10 83
(Picture disc. Promotional issue only. 500 made.)

DANISH LOST & FOUND
Singles: 7-inch
LAURIE 4-6 69

DANKO, Rick *LP '77*
Singles: 7-inch
ARISTA 3-4 78
LPs: 10/12-inch
ARISTA 8-10 77
Also see BAND

DANKS
LPs: 10/12-inch
COLOSSUS 10-12 70

DANKWORTH, Johnny *P&R '56*
(Johnnie Dankworth)
Singles: 78 rpm
CAPITOL 3-8 55-56
Singles: 7-inch
CAPITOL 4-8 55-56
FONTANA 3-5 63-66
20TH FOX 3-5 66
LPs: 10/12-inch
FONTANA (Except 7559) 6-12 64-69
FONTANA (27559 "The Idol") 15-20 66
(Soundtrack. Monaural.)
FONTANA (67559 "The Idol") 20-25 66
(Soundtrack. Stereo.)
ROULETTE 10-15 60-61
TOP RANK 10-15 60

DANLEERS *P&R/R&B '58*
(Dandleers)
Singles: 7-inch
ABC 3-4 75
AMP 3 (1005 " One Summer Night") 20-30
(Credits Danleers.)
AMP 3 (2115 " One Summer Night") 50-100 58
(Credits "Dandleers.")
COLLECTABLES 3-4 80s
EPIC (9367 "Half a Block from an Angel") 25-50 60
EPIC (9421 "Little Lover") 50-75 60
EVEREST (19412 "Foolish") 20-30 61
LE MANS (005 "The Truth Hurts") 15-25 64
LE MANS (008 "I'm Sorry") 15-25 64
MERCURY (71322 "One Summer Night") 15-25 58
MERCURY (71356 "I Really Love You") 15-25 58
(Blue label.)
MERCURY (71356 "I Really Love You") 25-50 58
(Black label.)
MERCURY (71401 "Picture of You") 25-35 58
MERCURY (71441 "Your Love") 40-60 59
SMASH (1872 "If") 15-25 64
SMASH (1895 "Where Is My Love") 15-25 64
Members: Jimmy Weston; Johnny Lee; Nat McCune; Willie Ephriam; Roosevelt Mays; Doug Ebron; Louis Williams; Terry Wilson; Frank Clemens; Bill Carey.
Also see FOUR FELLOWS
Also see WEBTONES

D'ANNA, Darin
Singles: 7-inch
WORLD ARTISTS 4-8 65

DANNON, Mark
Singles: 7-inch
WYNNE 5-10 59

DANNY & ACCENTS
Singles: 7-inch
VALLI 4-8 65

DANNY & COUNTS
Singles: 7-inch
CORONADO (136 "You Need Love") 20-30

DANNY & CROWNS
Singles: 7-inch
MERCURY 5-10 62-63

DANNY & DEBONAIRS
Singles: 7-inch
DEBONAIR (2250 "I Guess I'm Through with Love") 100-200 61
(Identification number shown since no selection number is used.)

DANNY & DIEGO
Singles: 7-inch
MUSICOR 4-8 65

DANNY & DREAMERS
Singles: 7-inch
DREAM (7 "Forgive Me") 25-30 62

DANNY & FAT BOYS
LPs: 10/12-inch
ALADDIN (102 "American Music") 75-100 76
Member: Danny Gatton.
Also see GATTON, Danny

DANNY & GADABOUTS
Singles: 7-inch
SUBTOWN 5-10

DANNY & GWEN
Singles: 7-inch
LIBERTY 5-8 62

DANNY & HITMAKERS
Singles: 7-inch
CAVALCADE 4-8 64

DANNY & JERRY
Singles: 7-inch
RONN (12 "I've Got Pride") 5-10 67
RONN (24 "I Can't See Nobody") 5-10 67
Member: Danny Rapp.
Also see DANNY & JUNIORS

DANNY & JUNIORS *P&R/R&B '57*
(With Joe Terry)
Singles: 78 rpm
ABC-PAR 25-75 57-58
SPARTON 50-75 58
(Canadian.)
Singles: 7-inch
ABC 3-5 73
ABC-PAR (9871 "At the Hop") 20-30 57
ABC-PAR (9888 "Rock & Roll Is Here to Stay") 20-30 58
ABC-PAR (9926 "Dottie") 20-30 58
ABC-PAR (9953 "Crazy Cave") 15-25 58
ABC-PAR (9978 "I Feel So Lonely") 15-25 58
ABC-PAR (10004 "Do You Love Me") 15-25 59
ABC-PAR (10052 "Playing Hard to Get") 15-25 59
CRUNCH 4-6 73
DOWNTOWN 3-4 93
GOLDIES 45 .... 3-5 73
GUSTO 3-5 79
GUYDEN (2076 "Now & Then") 15-25 62
LUV 5-10 68
MCA 3-4 70s
MERCURY (72240 "Sad Girl") 10-20 64
ROULETTE 3-5 70s
SINGULAR (711 "At the Hop") ...200-400 57
(Blue label.)
SINGULAR (711 "At the Hop") 10-15
(Black label.)
SPARTON (582 "Dottie") 40-60 58
(Canadian.)
SWAN (4060 "Twistin' USA") 10-20 60
(With Freddy Cannon.)
SWAN (4064 "Candy Cane Sugar Plum") 15-25 60
SWAN (4068 "Pony Express") 10-20 61
SWAN (4072 "Cha Cha Go Go") 10-20 61
SWAN (4082 "Back to the Hop") 15-20 61
SWAN (4084 "Just Because") 10-20 61
SWAN (4100 "Mashed Potatoes") 10-20 62
SWAN (4113 "Funny") 10-20 62
TOPAZ 3-6 87
Picture Sleeves
SWAN (4064 "Candy Cane Sugar Plum") 50-75 60
EPs: 7-inch
ABC-PAR (11 "At the Hop") 250-350 58
SWAN (4084 "Just Because") 75-125 62
(Not issued with cover. Promotional issue only.)
LPs: 10/12-inch
MCA (1555 "Rockin' with Danny and the Juniors") 5-10 83
Members: Danny Rapp; Frank Maffei; Joe Terry; Dave White.
Also see ALSTON, Shirley
Also see CANNON, Freddy
Also see DANNY & JERRY
Also see JUNIORS
Also see WHITE, Dave

DANNY & MEMORIES
Singles: 7-inch
VALIANT (6049 "Can't Help Lovin' That Girl of Mine") 25-50 64
Member: Neil Young.
Also see YOUNG, Neil

DANNY & ROC-KETTS
Singles: 7-inch
NU SOUND 5-10 61

DANNY & SAINTS
Singles: 7-inch
FANELLE (101 "Long, Long Ago") 100-150
W.B. (5134 No One Has Eyes for Me") 25-35 59

DANNY & SENIORS
Singles: 7-inch
PANORAMA (26 "Oh Devil") 10-15 66

DANNY & SESSIONS
Singles: 7-inch
COBRA 8-12 65
SALIGO 10-15 60s

DANNY & VELAIRES
Singles: 7-inch
BRENT (7072 "What Am I Livin' For") 20-30 67
RAMCO (1983 "I Found a Love") 30-40 67

DANNY & ZELTONES
Singles: 7-inch
BIGTOP (3074 "Steel Guitar Rag") 10-20 61
Member: Danny Zella.
Also see ZELLA, Danny

DANNY BOY
Singles: 7-inch
DOT (16140 "Send Me Some Lovin' ") 40-60 60
KENT (300 "Don't Go, Pretty Baby") 40-60 58

DANNY BOY & HIS BLUE GUITAR
(Danny Thomas)
Singles: 7-inch
TIFCO 8-12 61

DANNY THE DREAMER
Singles: 7-inch
LUTE 5-10 61

DANNY WILSON *P&R/LP '87*
Singles: 7-inch
VIRGIN 3-4 87
Picture Sleeves
VIRGIN 3-4 87
LPs: 10/12-inch
VIRGIN 5-10 87
Members: Gary Clark; Kit Clark; Ged Grimes.

DANNY'S REASONS
Singles: 7-inch
CARNABY (101 "Under My Thumb") 60-80 67
GREAT HALL 5-10
HAND 10-15 69
IRC (6935 "Little Diane") 40-60 66
UNCLE SAM 5-10 72

DANO, Tony, & Robbie Reed
Singles: 7-inch
BLAST 5-10 63

DAN-RAYS
Singles: 7-inch
REGENCY (105 "Surfin' Granny") ..20-30 63

DANSE SOCIETY *D&D '84*
Singles: 12-inch
ARISTA 4-6 84
Singles: 7-inch
ARISTA 3-4 84

DANSER'S INFERNO
(John Danser)
LPs: 10/12-inch
THIMBLE 8-10 75

DANTE
Singles: 7-inch
DARROW (515 "How Much I Care") 20-30 60
DECCA 10-15 60-61
MERCURY (71621 "How Much I Care") 10-15 60
TIDE 10-15 60

DANTE *P&R '60*
(With the Evergreens; with His Friends)
Singles: 7-inch
A&M 5-10 66
IMPERIAL 15-25 61-62
MADISON 8-12 60-61
LPs: 10/12-inch
MADISON (1002 "Dante and the Evergreens") 150-200 61
Members: Don "Dante" Drowty; Bill Young; Frank Rosenthal; Tony Moon.
Also see EMERALD CITY BANDITS

DANTE, David
Singles: 7-inch
RCA 8-12 61-62

DANTE, Rob
Singles: 7-inch
HARLAN 4-8 62
MARCO 4-8 62

DANTE, Ron
(Ronnie Dante)
Singles: 7-inch
ALMONT 4-8 64
BELL 3-5 74
COLUMBIA 4-8 66
DOT 4-8 67
HANDSHAKE 3-5 80
KIRSHNER 3-5 70
MERCURY 4-8 68
MUSIC VOICE 5-10 64
MUSICOR 4-8 65
RCA 3-5 75-77
SCEPTER 3-5 71
Picture Sleeves
KIRSHNER 4-8 70
LPs: 10/12-inch
HANDSHAKE 5-10 81-82
KIRSHNER 10-12 70
Also see ARCHIES
Also see COOPER, Bo
Also see CUFF LINKS
Also see DANTE'S INFERNO
Also see DETERGENTS
Also see NOAH'S ARK
Also see PEARLY GATE
Also see ROSE, C.G.
Also see RONNIE & Dirt Riders
Also see TWO DOLLAR QUESTION
Also see WEBSPINNERS

DANTE, Troy
Singles: 7-inch
KAPP 4-8 69

DANTE & EVERGREENS: see DANTE

DANTE & His Friends: see DANTE

DANTE'S INFERNO
Singles: 78 rpm
LIDO (507 "My First True Love") 10-20 57
Singles: 7-inch
LIDO (507 "My First True Love") 10-20 57

DANTE'S INFERNO
Singles: 12-inch
INFINITY 4-8 79
Singles: 7-inch
INFINITY 3-5 79
LPs: 10/12-inch
INFINITY 5-10 79
Members: Ron Dante; Monica Burruss; Toni Lund.
Also see DANTE, Ron
Also see LADY FLASH

DANTÉS
Singles: 7-inch
COURTNEY (713 "Zebra Shoot") ..15-25 64
ROTATE (5008 "Top Down Time") 50-75 64

DANTES
Singles: 7-inch
CAMEO 10-20 66
JAMIE 10-20 66

DANTES
Singles: 7-inch
MAIN LINE 5-10 67

DANTON, Tommy
(With the Echoes)
Singles: 7-inch
DOT (15650 "Oh Yeah") 30-40 57
KAREN (60549 "Kerry Pipers' Rock") 8-12 59
PAR (235 "Oh Yeah") 50-75 57

DANZIG *LP '88*
Singles: 7-inch
DEF AMERICAN 3-4 88-90
LPs: 10/12-inch
DEF AMERICAN 5-8 88-90
Members: Glenn Danzig; John Christ; Chuck Biscuits; Eerie Von.
Also see CIRCLE JERKS

DAPPER DANS
Singles: 7-inch
EMBER 5-10 60

DAPPERS
Singles: 78 rpm
PEACOCK 25-50 55
RAINBOW 15-25 56
Singles: 7-inch
EPIC (9432 "My Love Is Real") 20-30 60
PEACOCK (1651 "Come Back to Me") 250-350 55
RAINBOW (373 "Bop Bop Bu") 50-75 56

DAPPERS
Singles: 78 rpm
GROOVE 50-75 56
Singles: 7-inch
GROOVE (0156 "Unwanted Love") 75-125 56

DAPPERS
Singles: 7-inch
STAR-X (505 "We're in Love") ...100-150 58

DAPPERS
Singles: 7-inch
FOXIE (7005 "Lonely Street") 25-35 61

DAPPS
Singles: 7-inch
KING (6147 "Bringing Up the Guitar") 8-15 68

DA-PREES
Singles: 7-inch
TWIST (70913 "Payday") 100-200 63

DAPS
Singles: 78 rpm
MARTERRY 20-40 56
Singles: 7-inch
MARTERRY (5249 "When You're Alone") 50-75 56

DARBY, Huey
Singles: 7-inch
N-JOY 4-8 65

DARBY, Nobles C.
Singles: 7-inch
FELSTED 4-6 60

D'ARBY, Terence Trent *P&R/R&B/LP '87*
Singles: 7-inch
COLUMBIA 3-4 87-89
Picture Sleeves
COLUMBIA 3-4 87-89
LPs: 10/12-inch
COLUMBIA 5-10 87-89

DARBY, Ward, & Ravens
Singles: 7-inch
DOT (15952 "Wham-O") 5-10 59
PETITE (501 "Wham-O") 15-25 59
(First issue.)
STAR (511 "Kentucky Blue Grass") 10-20 62

DARBY SISTERS
Singles: 7-inch
COLUMBIA 5-10 60
CUB 5-10 59
METRO 8-10 59
MUSICOR 4-8 61

DARCELLS
Singles: 7-inch
TOP TEN 5-10 62

DARCEY, Frankie
Singles: 7-inch
RORI 5-10 62

DARCUS
Singles: 7-inch
RCA 3-4 77-78
LPs: 10/12-inch
RCA 8-10 77

DARCY, Johnny
Singles: 7-inch
SYCAMORE (103 "Rockin' the Arc") 15-25 58

DARDENELLES
Singles: 7-inch
CAMEO (271 "Alright") 8-12 63

DARDENELLES
Singles: 7-inch
ENTRE (102 "Now You're Gone") ..25-50
PLAYGIRL (501 "Soft Is the Breeze") 50-75 60s

DARE, Timothy
Singles
NFSD (005 "Russian Roulette") 15-20 89
(Picture disc, shaped like cigarette pack. 100 made with small picture.)
NFSD (005 "Russian Roulette") 8-12 89
(Picture disc, shaped like cigarette pack. 500 made with large picture.)

DARELYCKS
Singles: 7-inch
FINE (111 "Bad Trip") 25-35 66
FINE (57027 "Bad Trip") 10-15

DARENSBOURG, Joe, & His Dixie Flyers *P&R '58*
Singles: 7-inch
LARK 4-8 58-59
LPs: 10/12-inch
DIXIELAND JUBILEE 5-10 75
GHB 5-10 77
Also see BROTHER BONES

DARIAN, Fred *P&R '61*
(Freddy Darian)
Singles: 7-inch
DEL-FI 5-10 60
GARDENA 5-10 61
JAF 4-8 61-63
MAHALO 4-8 63
OKEH 5-10 59
RCA 5-10 59

U.A. 4-8 63
Also see BALLADEERS

DARIANS
Singles: 7-inch
CARLSON INT'L (3670027 "Tell Me Love") 50-75

DARIL, Johnny
Singles: 7-inch
VITA 5-10 59

DARIN, Bobby *P&R/R&B/C&W '58*
(With the Jaybirds; with Rinky Dinks; Bob Darin)
Singles: 78 rpm
ATCO (6092 "So Mean") 25-35 57
ATCO (6103 "Pretty Betty") 25-35 57
ATCO (6109 "Just in Case You Change Your Mind") 25-35 58
ATCO (6117 "Splish Splash") 25-50 58
ATCO (6121 "Early in the Morning") 40-60 58
ATCO (6127 "Queen of the Hop") .. 40-60 58
ATCO (6128 "Mighty Mighty Man") 50-75 58
DECCA 50-75 56-57
Singles: 7-inch
ATCO ("She's Tanfastic") 25-35
(Promotional issue only. No selection number used.)
ATCO (6092 "So Mean") 15-25 57
ATCO (6103 "Pretty Betty") 25-35 57
ATCO (6109 "Just in Case You Change Your Mind") 25-35 58
ATCO (6117 "Splish Splash") 15-25 58
ATCO (6121 "Early in the Morning") 20-30 58
(This same track was previously issued as by "The Rinky Dinks on Atco and by the Ding Dongs on Brunswick.")
ATCO (6127 "Queen of the Hop") .. 15-25 58
ATCO (6128 "Mighty Mighty Man") 25-35 58
ATCO (6133 "Plain Jane") 15-25 59
(Monaural.)
ATCO (SD-45-6133 "Plain Jane") .. 35-50 59
(Stereo.)
ATCO (6140 "Dream Lover") 10-15 59
ATCO (6147 "Mack the Knife") 10-15 59
ATCO (6158 "Beyond the Sea") 10-15 60
ATCO (6161 "Clementine") 10-15 60
ATCO (6167 "Won't You Come Home Bill Bailey") 10-15 60
ATCO (6173 "Beachcomber") 10-15 60
ATCO (6179 "Artificial Flowers") 10-15 60
ATCO (6183 "Christmas Auld Lang Syne") 10-20 60
ATCO (6188 "Lazy River") 8-15 61
ATCO (6196 "Nature Boy") 8-15 61
ATCO (6206 "You Must Have Been a Beautiful Baby") 8-15 61
ATCO (6211 "Ave Maria") 10-20 61
ATCO (6214 "Multiplication") 8-12 61
ATCO (6221 "What'd I Say") 8-12 61
ATLANTIC 5-8 65-67
CAPITOL (2263 "18 Yellow Roses") 20-30 63
(Promotional issue only.)
CAPITOL 5-8 62-65
DECCA (29883 "Rock Island Line") 20-30 56
DECCA (29922 "Blue Eyed Mermaid") 30-50 56
DECCA (30031 "The Greatest Builder") 20-30 56
DECCA (30225 "Dealer in Dreams") 25-40 57
DECCA (30737 "Dealer in Dreams") 10-20 59
DIMENSION 3-6 70
DIRECTION 3-6 68-70
MOTOWN 3-5 71-73
Picture Sleeves
ATCO (6133 "Plain Jane") 25-40 59
ATCO (6140 "Dream Lover") 20-40 59
ATCO (6147 "Mack the Knife") 20-30 59
ATCO (6158 "Beyond the Sea") 20-30 60
ATCO (6161 "Clementine") 20-30 60
ATCO (6167 "Won't You Come Home Bill Bailey") 15-25 60
ATCO (6173 "Beachcomber") 15-25 60
ATCO (6179 "Artificial Flowers") 15-25 60
ATCO (6183 "Christmas Auld Lang Syne") 15-25 60
ATCO (6188 "Lazy River") 15-25 61
ATCO (6196 "Nature Boy") 15-25 61
ATCO (6206 "You Must Have Been a Beautiful Baby") 15-25 61
ATCO (6211 "Ave Maria") 75-100 61
ATCO (6214 "Multiplication") 10-20 61
ATCO (6221 "What'd I Say") 10-20 61
CAPITOL (2263 "18 Yellow Roses") 25-50 63
(Promotional issue only.)
CAPITOL (4837 thru 5443) 10-20 62-65
EPs: 7-inch
ATCO (115 "This Is Darin") 50-100 59
(Promotional issue only. Issued with paper sleeve.)
ATCO (1001 "Bobby Darin for Teenagers Only") 50-100 60
(Promotional issue only. Issued with paper sleeve.)
ATCO (4502 "Bobby Darin") 35-50 58
ATCO (4504 "That's All") 25-40 59
ATCO (4505 "Queen of the Hop") .. 30-50 59
ATCO (4508 "This Is Darin") 20-40 59
ATCO (4512 "Darin at the Copa") .. 20-40 60
ATCO (4513 "For Teenagers Only") 30-50 60
CAPITOL (1791 "Look at Me Now") 25-50 62
(Juke box issue only.)
CAPITOL CUSTOM ("Scripto Presents Bobby Darin") 25-50 63
(Promotional issue only. Made with two different color paper sleeves, each offered in conjunction with a different pen: One with light blue sleeve came with Scripto Wordmaster ball point pen; one with yellow sleeve came with ink cartridge fountain pen. Picture of Bobby Darin is the same on both sleeves.)
CAPITOL CUSTOM/ARTISTIC ("Bobby Darin") 25-50 63
(Promotional issue only. Issued with paper sleeve.)
DECCA (2676 "Here Them Bells") 50-75 60
LPs: 10/12-inch
ATCO (102 "Bobby Darin") 50-75 58
ATCO (104 "That's All") 25-45 58
(Monaural.)
ATCO (SD-104 "That's All") 35-55 58
(Stereo.)
ATCO (115 "This Is Darin") 15-25 60
(Monaural.)
ATCO (SD-115 "This Is Darin") 20-30 60
(Stereo.)
ATCO (122 "Darin at the Copa") 15-25 60
(Monaural.)
ATCO (SD-122 "Darin at the Copa") 20-30 60
(Stereo.)
ATCO (124 "It's You Or No One") .. 15-25 63
(Monaural.)
ATCO (SD-124 "It's You Or No One") 20-30 63
(Stereo.)
ATCO (125 "The 25th Day of December") 25-35 60
(Monaural.)
ATCO (SD-125 "The 25th Day of December") 35-50 60
(Stereo.)
ATCO (131 "The Bobby Darin Story") 35-45 61
(Monaural. White cover.)
ATCO (SD-131 "The Bobby Darin Story") 45-55 61
(Stereo. White cover.)
ATCO (131 "The Bobby Darin Story") 10-15 72
(Black cover.)
ATCO (134 "Love Swings") 15-25 61
(Monaural.)
ATCO (SD-134 "Love Swings") 20-30 61
(Stereo.)
ATCO (138 "Twist") 15-25 61
(Monaural.)
ATCO (SD-138 "Twist") 20-30 61
(Stereo.)
ATCO (140 "Bobby Darin Sings Ray Charles") 15-25 62
(Monaural.)
ATCO (SD-140 "Bobby Darin Sings Ray Charles") 20-30 62
(Stereo.)
ATCO (146 "Things") 15-25 61
(Monaural.)
ATCO (SD-146 "Things") 20-30 61
(Stereo.)
ATCO (167 "Winners") 15-25 64
(Monaural)
ATCO (SD-167 "Winners") 20-30 64
(Stereo.)
ATCO (1001 "Bobby Darin for Teenagers Only") 100-150 60
(With color foldout photo.)
ATLANTIC 15-25 66-67
BAINBRIDGE 5-10 81
CANDLELITE 15-20 76
CAPITOL 20-25 62-66
CLARION 15-20 64
DIRECTION 12-20 68-70
IMPERIAL HOUSE 12-15 76
MOTOWN (100 series) 5-10 82
MOTOWN (738 "Finally") 150-250 72
(Promotional issue only.)
MOTOWN (753 "Bobby Darin") 10-20 72
MOTOWN (813 "Darin: 1936-1973") 10-20 74
W.B. (3501 "Original Bobby Darin") 20-30 76
(Three-LP mail-order offer.)
Session: King Curtis.
Also see BEHRKE, Richard, Trio
Also see DING DONGS
Also see KING CURTIS
Also see MOGAMBOS
Also see RINKY DINKS

DARIN, Bobby, & Johnny Mercer
LPs: 10/12-inch
ATCO (126 "Two of a Kind") 15-25 61
(Monaural.)
ATCO (SD-126 "Two of a Kind") 25-40 61
(Stereo.)
Also see DARIN, Bobby
Also see MERCER, Johnny

DARIN, Curt
Singles: 7-inch
BUDDAH 3-5

DARING, Peter: see PETER DARING

DARIUS
LPs: 10/12-inch
CHARTMAKER (1102 "Darius") 100-150 68
Session: Jerry Scheff; Toxie French; Ben Benay.
Also see GOLDENROD

DARK, Danny
Singles: 7-inch
REPRISE 4-8 65

DARK, Johnny
Singles: 7-inch
BIG BEN (1004 "Land of a Thousand Dances") 10-20 65

DARK AGE
LPs: 10/12-inch
GARNLY/GREENWOOD (1001 "Dark Age") 20-25 85
(Picture disc.)

DARK ANGEL *LP '89*
Singles: 7-inch
COMBAT 3-4 89
METAL STORM (8602 "Merciless Death") 15-25 87
(Saw blade-shaped picture disc. 25 made.)
METAL STORM (8602 "Merciless Death") 10-20 87
(Rectangular picture disc. 50 made.)
METAL STORM (8602 "Merciless Death") 5-8 87
(Skull or torture wheel shape picture disc. 500 made of each.)
METAL STORM (8817 "We Have Arrived") 10-20 88
(Cross shaped picture disc. 25 made. Promotional issue only.)
METAL STORM (8817 "We Have Arrived") 5-8 88
(Square picture disc. 500 made.)
LPs: 10/12-inch
COMBAT 5-8 89
METALSTORM (8501 "We Have Arrived") 10-15 87
(Picture disc. 500 made for USA. 500 made for Europe.)

DARK HORSEMEN
Singles: 7-inch
DARK HORSE ("You Lied") 20-45

DARKE, Ronny
Singles: 7-inch
LOND 5-10 59

DARLENE & DARLA
Singles: 7-inch
NEPTUNE 5-10 61

DARLENE & JOKERS
Singles: 7-inch
DANCO (115 "Frankie") 25-50 60
Also see JOKERS

DARLENES
Singles: 7-inch
STACY 10-20 63

DARLETTES
Singles: 7-inch
MIRA 5-10 65
TAFFI 5-10
Also see DIANE & DARLETTES

DAR-LETTS
Singles: 7-inch
SHELL 5-10 64

DARLIN, Brenda
Singles: 7-inch
BIG J 8-10

DARLIN, Chris
Singles: 7-inch
DORE 4-8 61

DARLIN, Florraine *P&R '62*
Singles: 7-inch
EPIC 8-10 62-63
RIC 4-8 64

DARLIN, Molly
Picture Sleeves
WORLD 4-6 70s

DARLING
Singles: 7-inch
CHARISMA 3-5 79
LPs: 10/12-inch
CHARISMA 5-10 79

DARLING, Fay
Singles: 7-inch
KOOL 4-8 63

DARLING, Johnny
Singles: 7-inch
DELUXE (6167 "Don't Want to Wind Up in Love") 75-100 58

DARLING CRUEL *LP '89*
LPs: 10/12-inch
MIKA 5-8 89

DARLINGS
(With the Snub Mosley Quintet)
Singles: 7-inch
PENGUIN (06-98 "In the Evening") 40-60 59

DARLINGS
Singles: 7-inch
DORE (663 "To Know Him Is to Love Him") 10-15 63
DORE (677 "My Pillow") 10-15 63
MERCURY (72185 "Two Time Loser") 10-15 63

DARNEL, Bill
(With the Heathertones)
Singles: 78 rpm
CORAL 3-5 50-51
DECCA 3-5 52-53
Singles: 7-inch
CORAL 5-10 50-51
DECCA 5-10 52-53
JUBILEE 4-8 59
LONDON (Except 1665) 5-10 56
LONDON (1665 "Rock-a-Boogie Baby") 10-15 56
PARIS 10-15 59
"X" 5-10 54-55
EPs: 7-inch
"X" 10-20 55
LPs: 10/12-inch
"X" 20-30 55

DARNELL, Angie
Singles: 7-inch
LOST GOLD (2 "Sweet Love") 3-4 89
(Red vinyl.)
LOST GOLD (1004 "Mommy") 3-4 90
(Red vinyl.)
LOST GOLD (1005 "This Might Be the Day") 3-4 90
(Gold vinyl.)
Picture Sleeves
LOST GOLD (2 "Sweet Love") 3-4 90
LOST GOLD (1004 "Mommy") 3-4 90
LOST GOLD (1005 "This Might Be the Day") 3-4 90
Session: Al Pearson; Frank Wilkie; Charlie Miller; Ricky Godfrey; Christine Schwarz; Stephen Hill.

DARNELL, Gracie
Singles: 7-inch
RUTH (101 "So Long Lover") 20-30

DARNELL, Kissy
Singles: 7-inch
G.T.O. 4-8 66

DARNELL, Larry *R&B '49*
(With the Fortunes)
Singles: 78 rpm
DELUXE 15-25 57
OKEH 10-20 51-53
REGAL 10-20 49-51
SAVOY 10-20 55
Singles: 7-inch
ANNA (1109 (With Tears in My Eyes") 200-300 60
ARGO (5364 "Look at Me") 20-30 60
ARGO (5372 "With Tears in My Eyes") 15-25 60
DELUXE 15-25 57
MISTY 4-6
OKEH 10-20 51-53
REGAL 10-20 51
SAVOY (1151 "That's All I Want from You") 15-25 55
WARWICK 8-12 59
EPs: 7-inch
EPIC (7072 "For You My Love") 30-40 61
Session: Mickey Baker.
Also see BAKER, Mickey

DARNELL, Paul
Singles: 7-inch
CREST 4-8 62
DELTONE 4-8 64

DARNELL, Ravon
(With the Earl Hyde & His Orchestra)
Singles: 78 rpm
TAMPA (119 "Chicken Little") 10-20 56
Singles: 7-inch
TAMPA (119 "Chicken Little") 40-60 56

DARNELL & DREAMS
Singles: 7-inch
WEST SIDE (1020 "I Had a Love") 20-30 64

DARNELLS
(Marvelettes)
Singles: 7-inch
GORDY (7024 "Too Hurt to Cry, Too Much in Love to Say Goodbye") 50-75 63
Also see MARVELETTES

DARNELLS
Singles: 7-inch
SARA (1055 "She, She, Little Shelia") 15-20 61
TIDE (1090 "Spooner") 5-10 63
SARA (5016 "Fate of a Fool") 15-20 62
Members: Tom Fabares; Bruce Welch; Jerry Saworski; Tommy Hahn; Denny King; Gary Myers.
Also see HAHN, Tommy, & Mojo Men
Also see KING, Denny
Also see MAD LADS
Also see MOJO MEN
Also see MYERS, Gary
Also see PORTRAITS

DARNELS
Singles: 7-inch
BANA (525 "My Little Homin' Pigeon") 25-50 57

DARRELL, Guy "Daddy Cool"
Singles: 7-inch
WARWICK 8-12 61

DARRELL, Johnny *C&W '65*
Singles: 7-inch
CAPRICORN 3-5 74-75
CARTWHEEL 3-5 71-72
GUSTO 3-4 78
MONUMENT 3-5 73
U.A. 4-6 65-70
Picture Sleeves
U.A. 3-6 67
LPs: 10/12-inch
CAPRICORN 6-10 75
GUSTO 5-10
SUNSET 6-10 68-70
U.A. 8-12 66-70

DARRELL, Johnny / George Jones / Willie Nelson
LPs: 10/12-inch
SUNSET 8-12 69
Also see DARRELL, Johnny
Also see JONES, George
Also see NELSON, Willie

DARRELL & OXFORDS
(Tokens)
Singles: 7-inch
ROULETTE (4174 "Picture in My Wallet") 20-30 59
ROULETTE (4230 "Can't You Tell") 20-30 60
Also see TOKENS

DARRELLS
Singles: 7-inch
LYCO (1003 "So Tenderly") 25-50 61

DARREN, Danny
Singles: 7-inch
ALAN DALE (3063 "Lonliness") .... ?? 67
COULEE (141 "Medals for Mother") 5-10 72
DRAERER (360 "Road Side Rag") 25-50 66
DRAEGER (4561 "Fool About You") 200-250 66
KL (KS10 "Love Make the World Go Round") 5-10 72
PYRAMID (15 "No Reason to Quit") 5-10 73
PYRAMID (18 "Take These Charms") 5-10 73
RAINBOW (201 "Go Menasi") 5-10 72
SILVER STAR (1039 "Nothing to Write Home About") 5-10 70

DARREN, James *P&R '59*
(Jimmy Darren)
Singles: 7-inch
ABC 3-4 74
BUDDAH 3-5 70
COLPIX (102 "There's No Such Thing") 5-10 58
COLPIX (113 "Gidget") 5-10 59
COLPIX (119 "Angel Face") 5-10 59
(Monaural.)
COLPIX (SCP-119 "Angel Face") .. 10-20 59
(Stereo.)
COLPIX (128 thru 708) 5-10 59-63
COLPIX (758 "Punch and Judy") .. 10-20 64
COLPIX (765 "Married Man") 5-10 64
ERIC 3-4
KIRSHNER 3-5 71-72
MCA 3-4
MGM 3-5 73
PRIVATE STOCK 3-5 75-77
RCA 3-5 78
W.B. 4-8 65-68
Picture Sleeves
COLPIX 8-15 58-61
EPs: 7-inch
RMR JUNIORS ("James Darren") 10-15
(Promotional issue, with fashion spots.)
LPs: 10/12-inch
COLPIX (406 "Album No. 1") 20-30 60
COLPIX (418 "Gidget Goes Hawaiian") 20-30 61
COLPIX (424 "For All Sizes") 20-30 62
COLPIX (428 "Love Among the Young") 20-30 62
(Monaural.)
COLPIX (SCP-428 "Love Among the Young") 30-40 62
(Stereo.)
KIRSHNER 10-20 71-72
W.B. 15-20 67

DARREN, James / Shelley Fabares / Paul Petersen *LP '63*
LPs: 10/12-inch
COLPIX (444 "Teenage Triangle") 25-35 63
COLPIX (468 "More Teenage Triangle") 25-35 63
Also see DARREN, James
Also see FABARES, Shelley
Also see PETERSEN, Paul

DARRIN, Diana
Singles: 7-inch
VIRGO 4-8 61-62

DARRIS, Ann
Singles: 7-inch
SKYWAY 4-8 62

DARRIS, Frank
Singles: 7-inch
THUNDER 8-12 59

DARRO, George
Singles: 7-inch
NATIONWIDE (100 "Eye'n You Up") 30-45 59

DARRO, Tony
Singles: 7-inch
CROSLEY 5-10 59-60

DARROW, Danny
Singles: 12-inch
MIGHTY 4-6 83
Singles: 7-inch
ALMONT 4-8 63
MIGHTY (Except 101) 3-4 83
MIGHTY (101 "Handsome Man") 5-10 60
STRAND (25031 "Impulse") 20-40 61
LPs: 10/12-inch
MIGHTY 5-10

DARROW, Jay
Singles: 7-inch
KEEN (82124 "Girl in My Dreams")....................25-50 61
ORIGINAL SOUND....................5-10 62

DARROW, Johnny
(Johnny Moore)
Singles: 7-inch
MELIC....................8-12
SUE....................8-12 60-61
Also see DRIFTERS

DARROW, Ken
Singles: 7-inch
GARY (1007 "Everytime")....................8-10 57

DARROW, Neil
(With the Quarter Notes)
Singles: 7-inch
ADMIRAL (751 "Action Central")....................5-10 64
CAMEO....................5-10 61
SWAN....................5-10 65
WHIZZ....................10-15 59

D'ARROW, Phillip
Singles: 7-inch
POLYDOR....................3-4 79
LPs: 10/12-inch
POLYDOR....................5-10 79-80

DARRYL WAY'S WOLF
LPs: 10/12-inch
DERAM....................8-10
LONDON....................8-10 73

DART
Singles: 7-inch
GARLAND....................10-15 68
LPs: 10/12-inch
GARLAND (4567 "Presenting Dart")....................30-40 68
GARLAND (4578 "Dart")....................25-35 70
HOOT (4568 "Sound of Dart")....................25-35 70

DART, Jimmy
Singles: 7-inch
HITT (185 "You Won't Care")....................40-50 59

DARTELLS *P&R/R&B/LP '63*
Singles: 7-inch
ARLEN (509 "Hot Pastrami")....................8-12 63
(Black vinyl.)
ARLEN (509 "Hot Pastrami")....................20-30 63
(Colored vinyl.)
ARLEN (513 "Dance Everybody, Dance")....................10-15 63
DOT....................4-8 63-64
HBR....................4-8 66
LPs: 10/12-inch
DOT (3522 "Hot Pastrami")....................25-30 63
(Monaural.)
DOT (25522 "Hot Pastrami")....................25-30 63
(Stereo.)
Member: Doug Phillips.
Also see PHILLIPS, Doug, & New Concepts
Also see RAIN

DARTS
Singles: 7-inch
APT....................10-20 58

DARTS
Singles: 7-inch
DOT....................10-15 58

DARTS
LPs: 10/12-inch
DEL-FI (1244 "Hollywood Drag")....................25-35 63

DARTS
Singles: 7-inch
KAT FAMILY....................3-4 81
POLYDOR....................3-4 78-80
U.A.....................3-5 77
LPs: 10/12-inch
KAT FAMILY....................5-10 81
MAGNET....................5-10 78
POLYDOR....................5-10 79-80
U.A.....................8-10 78

DARTY, Chuck
Singles: 7-inch
CHART (649 "My Steady Girl")....................15-25 57
RAMA (229 "My Steady Girl")....................8-12 57
ROULETTE....................5-10 59

DARVELL, Barry
(With Hash Brown & His Orchestra)
Singles: 7-inch
ATLANTIC....................10-20 61-62
COLT 45 (Except 107)....................8-10 59-63
COLT 45 (107 "Geronimo Stomp")....................40-60 59
COLUMBIA....................5-10 67
CUB (9088 "Fountain of Love")....................10-15 61
PROVIDENCE (404 "When You're Alone")....................8-12 64
WORLD ARTISTS....................5-10 65
Also see DEMOLYRS

DARVELS
Singles: 7-inch
EDDIES (69 "I Lost My Baby")....................20-30 63
(Black vinyl.)
EDDIES (69 "I Lost My Baby")....................50-75 63
(Colored vinyl.)
Member: Warren Gradis.

DARWIN
(Darwin Lamm)
Singles: 7-inch
DORE....................5-8 63-65
Also see DARWIN & CUPIDS

DARWIN, Ricky
(With the Bobby Smith Orchestra & Chorus)
Singles: 7-inch
BUZZ (103 "The Great Great Thinker")....................30-40 59

DARWIN & CUPIDS
Singles: 7-inch
JERDEN (1 "How Long")....................10-20 60
JERDEN (9 "Goodnight My Love")....................10-20 60
Member: Darwin Lamm.
Also see DARWIN

DARWINS
Singles: 7-inch
VEE JAY....................4-8 63

DARWYN, Jane
Singles: 7-inch
RONKO....................4-8 62
VEE JAY....................4-8 63

DARYLL, Teddy
Singles: 7-inch
UTOPIA....................4-8 61

DASH, Frankie
Singles: 7-inch
COOL (106 "Rock to the Moon")....................75-100 58

DASH, Julian
(With His Sextet; Julian Dash Orchestra)
Singles: 78 rpm
SITTIN' IN WITH (600 "Hot Rod")....................15-25 51
VEE JAY (144 "Zero")....................15-25 54
Singles: 7-inch
VEE JAY (144 "Zero")....................30-40 54
Also see HAWKINS, Erskine

DASH, Sarah *P&R/R&B/LP '79*
Singles: 12-inch
MEGATONE....................4-6 83
Singles: 7-inch
KIRSHNER....................3-4 79-81
LPs: 10/12-inch
KIRSHNER....................5-10 78-81
Also see LABELLE, Patti

DASH & DOT
Singles: 7-inch
SKYLA....................5-10 61

DASH RIP ROCK
LPs: 10/12-inch
MAMMOTH....................5-8 90
Members: Bill Davis; Ned Hickel; Chris Luckette.

DASHIEL, Bud, & Kinsmen
Singles: 7-inch
W.B.....................4-8 61
LPs: 10/12-inch
W.B.....................10-20 61
Also see BUD & TRAVIS

DASHIELL, Russell
LPs: 10/12-inch
EPIC....................8-12 78
Session: Doug Clifford; Stu Cook.
Also see CREEDENCE CLEARWATER REVIVAL
Also see CROWFOOT

DATE, Ronnie
Singles: 7-inch
MUSICOR....................4-8 65

DATE with SOUL
Singles: 7-inch
YORK (408 "Yes Sir That's My Baby")....................15-25 67
(Previously issued as by Hale & Hushabyes. See that listing for members)
Also see HALE & HUSHABYES

DATONS
Singles: 7-inch
KICK OFF (501 "The Whip")....................8-12

DAUGHTERS OF ALBION
Singles: 7-inch
FONTANA....................5-10 68
LPs: 10/12-inch
FONTANA....................10-20 68

DAUGHTERS OF EVE
Singles: 7-inch
CADET....................4-8 68
U.S.A.....................4-8 67

DAUN, Bobby
Singles: 7-inch
TWIN STAR....................5-10 60

DAVANI, Dave
(Dave Davani Four)
Singles: 7-inch
CAPITOL....................4-8 66

DAVE & BOB
Singles: 7-inch
M&F (169 "Two Old Sparrows")....................25-30

DAVE & CARDIGANS
Singles: 7-inch
BAY (216 "My Falling Star")....................100-150

DAVE & CUSTOMS
Singles: 7-inch
DAC (500 "Shortnin' Bread")....................25-35 65
DAC (501 "You Should Be Glad")....................25-35 65
DAC (502 "Bony Maronie")....................25-35 66
Members: Dave Zdunich; Mark Zdunich; Ken Cook.

DAVE & MARKSMEN
(David Marks)
Singles: 7-inch
A&M (730 "Cruisin' ")....................15-25 64
Also see BEACH BOYS
Also see BROOKS, Denny
Also see CLIFFORD, Buzz
Also see HONEYS
Also see MOON

DAVE & ORBITS
Singles: 7-inch
AMERICAN ARTS (14 "Chili Beans")....................20-40 65

DAVE & PONCHO
Singles: 7-inch
CUCA (6661 "Riders in the Sky")....................10-15 66

DAVE & SAINTS
Singles: 7-inch
BAND BOX (341 "Leavin' Surf City")....................10-20 63

DAVE & SANDY
Singles: 7-inch
GAYE....................4-8 66

DAVE & SHADOWS
Singles: 7-inch
CHECK MATE (1011 "Hereafter")....................25-50 62
CHECK MATE (1016 "Cheek to Cheek")....................35-55 62
FENTON (942 "Playboy")....................40-60 64

DAVE & STEREOS
Singles: 7-inch
PENNANT (1001 "Roamin' Romeo")....................20-30 61

DAVE & SUGAR *C&W '75*
(Dave Rowland & Sugar)
Singles: 7-inch
ELEKTRA....................3-4 81
RCA....................3-5 75-82
LPs: 10/12-inch
ELEKTRA....................5-10 81
RCA....................5-10 76-82
Members: Dave Rowland; Vicki Hackeman-Baker; Jackie Frantz; Sue Powell; Melissa Dean; Jamie Kaye.
Also see POWELL, Sue
Also see PRIDE, Charley
Also see ROWLAND, Dave

DAVE & VEE
Singles: 7-inch
DELUXE....................4-6 69

DAVE C & HIS SHARPTONES
Singles: 7-inch
DOLLEE (2615 "Dolly Waddle")....................5-10 60s
WHIRL (13157 "Hi Spy")....................10-15 60s
Member: Dave Cox.

DAVE, STAN & ROBIN
Singles: 7-inch
STARTIME....................4-8 66

DAVE T & DEL-RAYS
("Dave T [Del-Rays]")
Singles: 7-inch
CAROUSEL (213 "Girl in My Heart")....................50-100 64

DAVENPORT, Cow Cow
(Charles "Cow Cow" Davenport)
Singles: 78 rpm
BRUNSWICK (80022 "Cow Cow Blues")....................10-20 49
COMET....................10-20 45

DAVENPORT SISTERS
Singles: 7-inch
TRI-PHI (1008 "You've Got Me Crying Again")....................25-50 62

DAVEY, Lee
Singles: 7-inch
DCP....................4-8 65

DAVEY & BADMEN
LPs: 10/12-inch
KRW (054 "Wanted")....................60-75

DAVEY & DOLPHINS
Singles: 7-inch
20TH FOX (529 "She Likes Older Boys")....................20-30 64
Member: David Liska.
Also see DAVY & DOLPHINS

DAVEY & DOO RAYS
Singles: 7-inch
GUYDEN....................10-15 58

DAVI
Singles: 7-inch
STARK (110 "Reason for Love")....................150-250 62

DAVID
(The David)
Singles: 12-inch
AZRA (100 "Mother's Warning")....................10-15 85
(Picture disc. 500 made.)
Singles: 7-inch
20TH FOX (6663 "40 Miles")....................15-25 66
VMC (716 "I'm Not Alone")....................10-20 68
LPs: 10/12-inch
VMC (124 "Another Day, Another Lifetime")....................50-100 68
Members: Tim Harrison; Warren Hansen; Mark Bird; Charles Spieth.

DAVID, Clifford
Singles: 7-inch
OKEH....................4-8 63

DAVID, F.R. *P&R '83*
Singles: 7-inch
CARRERE AMERICA....................3-4 83
LPs: 10/12-inch
CARRERE AMERICA....................5-10 83

DAVID, Geater
Singles: 7-inch
HOUSE of ORANGE....................3-5 70

DAVID, John, & Cinders
Singles: 7-inch
W.B.....................5-8 66

DAVID, Johnny
Singles: 7-inch
DOT (16078 "Race with the Devil")....................15-25 60
GIL (104 "Race with the Devil")....................40-60 60

DAVID, Kal, & Exceptions
Singles: 7-inch
TOLLIE (9007 "Searchin' ")....................8-12 64
Also see EXCEPTIONS

DAVID, Lee
Singles: 7-inch
BELL....................4-8 60s

DAVID, Mogan: see MOGAN DAVID

DAVID, Mogen: see MOGEN DAVID

DAVID & BOYS NEXT DOOR
Singles: 7-inch
SKIPPER (1240 "Land O' Love")....................15-25

DAVID & DAVID *P&R/LP '86*
Singles: 7-inch
A&M....................3-4 86-87
Picture Sleeves
A&M....................3-4 86-87
LPs: 10/12-inch
A&M....................5-10 86
Members: David Baerwald; David Rickets.

DAVID & DIVERSIFIED SOUND
Singles: 7-inch
FENTON....................10-15 67

DAVID & FREDDIE
Singles: 7-inch
BULLSEYE....................10-20 58
Member: David Ellin.

DAVID & GIANTS
Singles: 7-inch
CAPITOL (2893 "Don't Say No")....................5-10 70

DAVID & GOLIATH
Singles: 7-inch
TOMARO (101 "Like Strangers")....................15-20 65
Members: Bill Baker; Roger Koob.
Also see BAKER, Bill
Also see KOOB, Roger

DAVID & JONATHAN *P&R '66*
Singles: 7-inch
AMY....................4-8 68
CAPITOL....................4-8 66-67
20TH FOX....................4-6 66
Picture Sleeves
CAPITOL....................5-10 66
LPs: 10/12-inch
CAPITOL (2473 "Michelle")....................20-30 66
Members: Roger Greenaway; Roger Cook.
Also see COOK, Roger
Also see PHILWIT & PEGASUS

DAVID & LEE
Singles: 7-inch
G.S.P. (1 "Sad September")....................20-30 62
Members: David Gates; Leon Russell.
Also see GATES, David
Also see RUSSELL, Leon

DAVID & GIANTS
Singles: 7-inch
CRAZY HORSE....................10-20 68-69
FAME (1467 "Letter to Josephine")....................15-25 67
LPs: 10/12-inch
PRIORITY....................5-10 82
Members: David Huff; Raybum Huff; Claybum Huff; Keith Thibodeaux.

DAVID & RUBEN
Singles: 7-inch
RAMPART (662 "Girl in My Dreams")....................50-100 69
W.B. (7316 "Girl in My Dreams")....................25-50 69

DAVIDSON, Frankie
Singles: 7-inch
MELBOURNE....................3-5 62
WYNNE....................8-12 61

DAVIDSON, John *LP '66*
Singles: 7-inch
COLUMBIA....................3-6 66-71
MERCURY....................3-5 73
20TH FOX....................3-5 73-77
Picture Sleeves
COLUMBIA....................4-6 66-69
LPs: 10/12-inch
COLPIX....................10-15 65
COLUMBIA....................5-10 66-80
HARMONY....................4-6 72
MERCURY....................5-10 73
20TH FOX....................5-10 74-76

DAVIE, Hutch *P&R '58*
(With His Honky-Tonkers)
Singles: 7-inch
ATCO....................10-15 58-59
CANADIAN AMERICAN....................5-10 61
CLARIDGE....................4-8 66
CONGRESS....................5-10 62
DYNO VOICE....................4-6 68
NEW VOICE....................4-8 67
LPs: 10/12-inch
ATCO (105 "Much Hutch")....................30-40 59
CONGRESS (3004 "Piano Memories")....................25-35 62
Also see RAY, James

DAVIE, Robert
Singles: 7-inch
CONGRESS....................4-8 64

DAVIE & KARTOON
Singles: 7-inch
OLIVER....................4-8 66

DAVIES, Bob: see DAVIS, Bob

DAVIES, Brian
Singles: 7-inch
DOT....................8-10 59

DAVIES, Cyril, All Stars
Singles: 7-inch
DOT....................4-8 64

DAVIES, Dave *LP '80*
Singles: 7-inch
RCA....................3-5 80
REPRISE....................15-20 67-68
W.B.....................3-4 83
Picture Sleeves
RCA (12089 "Wild Man")....................10-15 80
LPs: 10/12-inch
RCA....................8-12 80-81
W.B.....................5-10 83
Also see KINKS

DAVIES, Gail *C&W '78*
Singles: 7-inch
LIFESONG....................3-5 78-79
MCA....................3-4 89
RCA....................3-4 84-85
W.B.....................3-5 79-84
LPs: 10/12-inch
LIFESONG....................6-12 78
MCA....................5-8 89
RCA....................5-8 85
W.B.....................5-10 80-83
Also see WILD CHOIR

DAVIES, Ron
Singles: 7-inch
A&M....................3-5 71

DA VINCI, Paul
Singles: 7-inch
MERCURY....................3-5 72-74

DAVIS, Al
Singles: 7-inch
MANCO....................4-8 61-62

DAVIS, Andrea
(Minnie Riperton)
Singles: 7-inch
CHESS....................5-10 66
Also see RIPERTON, Minnie

DAVIS, Artie
Singles: 7-inch
COOL (123 "Book of Love")....................30-50 60

DAVIS, Bette
Singles: 7-inch
BELL....................4-8 65
MERCURY....................4-8 65

DAVIS, Bette, & Debbie Burton
Singles: 7-inch
MGM....................4-8 62
Picture Sleeves
MGM....................15-25 62
Also see DAVIS, Bette

DAVIS, Betty *R&B '73*
Singles: 7-inch
ISLAND....................3-5 75-76
JUST SUNSHINE....................3-5 73-74
LPs: 10/12-inch
ISLAND....................5-10 75
JUST SUNSHINE....................6-10 73-74

DAVIS, Bill
Singles: 7-inch
SARA (1449 "Tell Me")....................15-25 60s
SARA (1450 "I'll Say Yes")....................15-25 60s

DAVIS, Billie
Singles: 7-inch
JERDEN....................4-8 65
LONDON....................5-10 68

DAVIS, Billy, & Legends
Singles: 7-inch
PEACOCK....................5-10 60

DAVIS, Billy Guitar
Singles: 78 rpm
GOTHAM....................10-15 56
Singles: 7-inch
GOTHAM (322 "Warm and Cooler")....................15-25 56

DAVIS, Billy, Jr. *R&B '75*
(Billy Davis)
Singles: 7-inch
ABC....................3-5 75
COBBLESTONE....................4-6 69
EPSOM....................4-8 61
HI....................4-8 68
LPs: 10/12-inch
SAVOY....................5-10 82
Also see EMERALDS
Also see FIFTH DIMENSION

DAVIS, Blind Gary
LPs: 10/12-inch
PRESTIGE BLUESVILLE (1015 "Harlem Street Singer") 40-80 61

DAVIS, Blind John
(Blind Johnny Davis & Blind Johnny Davis Trio)
Singles: 78 rpm
MGM 15-30 49-51
Singles: 7-inch
MGM (10919 "Telegram to My Baby") 50-75 51
MGM (10976 "The Day Will Come") 25-50 51
LPs: 10/12-inch
ALLIGATOR 8-10 77

DAVIS, Bo
Singles: 78 rpm
CREST 20-40 56
Singles: 7-inch
CREST (1027 "Let's Coast Awhile") 50-75 56
Also see COCHRAN, Eddie

DAVIS, Bob
(With the Rhythm Jesters; Bob Davies)
Singles: 78 rpm
RAMA (224 "Never Anymore") 20-30 57
Singles: 7-inch
APEX (76135 "Never Anymore") 10-20 57
(Canadian.)
BROADLAND 4-8 71
(Canadian.)
CLICK 4-8 63-64
(Canadian.)
RAMA (224 "Never Anymore") 20-30 57
ZIRCON (1003 "That's How Young Love Should Be") 10-20 59
(Canadian.)
LP: 10/12-inch
CELINA 5-10 78
(Canadian.)
RUSTICANA 25-25 63
(Canadian.)
Session: Joyce Germain.
Also see BIG BOB & DOLLARS
Also see BOBSMITHS
Also see MASON, Little Billie
Also see RHYTHM JESTERS

DAVIS, Bob, Quartet
Singles: 7-inch
DOOTO (414 "Off Day Blues") 15-25 57

DAVIS, Bobby
(With the Rhythm Rockers)
Singles: 7-inch
BANDARA (2508 "She's a Problem") 10-15 61
M-PAC (7200 "A Human's Prayer") 8-12 63
VEST (8003 "Get with It") 8-12 64

DAVIS, Bonnie, & Piccadilly Pipers
Singles: 78 rpm
"X" 10-20 54
Singles: 7-inch
MELMAR (101 "If You Only Knew") 25-50 50s
"X" (0086 "I Wanna") 25-50 54

DAVIS, Carl, & Chi-Sound Orchestra R&B '77
Singles: 7-inch
CHI-SOUND 3-5 77

DAVIS, Carrie C&W '89
Singles: 7-inch
FOUNTAIN HILLS 3-4 89

DAVIS, Charlie
Singles: 78 rpm
IMPERIAL (5011 "Rainin' Blues") 25-35 47

DAVIS, Chuck
Singles: 7-inch
TILT (1101 "Teaser") 15-25 58

DAVIS, Cliff
(Cliff Davis Sextet; Clifford Davis)
Singles: 7-inch
BANANA (501 "Hard Hearted Girl") 75-100 57
CATHAY 5-10 66
FEDERAL 8-12 59-60
JAY JAY (161 "Rocky Road Blues") 25-50 56
OKEH 10-15 63
LPs: 10/12-inch
EPIC 15-20 65

DAVIS, Curtis
Singles: 7-inch
BEV MAR (1001 "Somebody") 5-10

DAVIS, Dale, & His Tomcats
Singles: 78 rpm
STARDALE 40-80 56
Singles: 7-inch
STARDALE (100 "Gotta Rock") 75-125 56
STARDALE (104 "Crazy, Batty and Gone") 40-60 56
STARDALE (333 "Gotta Rock") 75-125 56

DAVIS, Danny LP '69/C&W '70
(With the Nashville Brass; with Arlene Baird; with Titans; with Nashville Strings; Danny Davis Orchestra;)
Singles: 78 rpm
BLUE JAY 3-5 54
HICKORY 3-5 54
MGM 3-6 51-53
Singles: 7-inch
BLUE JAY 4-8 54
CABOT 3-6 59
HICKORY 4-8 54
LIBERTY (55213 "Glory Bugle") 10-15 59
MGM (11000 series) 5-10 51-53
MGM (13000 series) 3-5 62-65
RCA 3-4 69-84
THUNDER (102 "Glory Bugle") 15-25 59
VERVE 3-5 61
LPs: 10/12-inch
MGM 8-18 61-65
RCA SPECIAL PRODUCTS (0176 "America 200 Years Young") 10-15 76
(Special Products issue for the Amana Corp.)
RCA 5-10 69-84
Also see ATKINS, Chet, Floyd Cramer & Danny Davis
Also see LOCKLIN, Hank, with Danny Davis & Nashville Brass
Also see SOME of CHET'S FRIENDS
Also see TITANS

DAVIS, Danny, & Byron Lee
Singles: 7-inch
MGM 4-6 64

DAVIS, Danny, Nashville Brass & Dona Mason C&W '87
Singles: 7-inch
JAROCO 3-4 87

DAVIS, Danny, Willie Nelson, & Nashville Brass LP '80
Singles: 7-inch
RCA 3-4 80
LPs: 10/12-inch
RCA 5-10 80
Also see DAVIS, Danny
Also see LOCKLIN, Hank
Also see NEWMAN, Jimmy C., Danny Davis & Nashville Brass

DAVIS, Denny
Singles: 7-inch
AGE (29121 "I Love You") 20-30

DAVIS, Dianne C&W '89
Singles: 7-inch
16TH AVE. 3-4 89

DAVIS, Don, & His Groovers
Singles: 7-inch
NORTHERN (3735 "Let's Do It") 75-100 61
Also see MAGNIFICENT SEVEN

DAVIS, Doug
Singles: 7-inch
NITE STAR 5-10 61

DAVIS, Earl, & Arabian Knights
Singles: 7-inch
LARO (1301 "Night in Arabia") 40-60

DAVIS, Eddie
Singles: 78 rpm
MODERN 10-20 48
VITA 25-35 57
Singles: 7-inch
VITA (170 "To Be Or Not to Be") 25-35 57

DAVIS, Eddie "Lockjaw"
(Featuring Henry Glover)
Singles: 78 rpm
APOLLO 10-15 47
BIRDLAND 5-10 50
HAVEN 10-15 46
KING (Except 4321) 5-10 55-59
KING (4321 "Mountain Oysters") 50-100 49
LENNOX 8-10 48
REGENT 5-10 50
ROOST 4-8 52-53
SAVOY 6-12 47-48
SIGNATURE 8-12 47
SITTIN' IN WITH 5-10 49
Singles: 7-inch
JAZZLAND 4-8 60-61
KING 5-10 55-59
PRESTIGE 5-10 58
RCA 3-5 66
EPs: 7-inch
KING 10-20 56-59
LPs: 10/12-inch
BETHLEHEM 20-30 60
CONTINENTAL (5140 "Kickin' and Wailin'") 25-35
JAZZLAND 20-30 60-62
KING (500 & 600 series) 25-50 56-59
MOODSVILLE 20-30 63
PRESTIGE 20-40 58-65
RCA 10-20 66-68
RIVERSIDE 20-30 61-62
ROULETTE 20-30 58-60
Also see DOGGETT, Bill
Also see GLOVER, Henry

DAVIS, Emmett
Singles: 7-inch
BELTONE 5-10 61
CRAIG 4-8 63
M&B (101 "How About It") 50-75 59
Also see PARKER, Jack "The Bear"

DAVIS, Eunice
(With Freddie Mitchell Orchestra)
Singles: 78 rpm
ATLANTIC 15-25 53
CORAL 5-15 52
DELUXE 10-15 54
DERBY 5-15 51
GRAND 5-15 55
Singles: 7-inch
ATLANTIC (992 "Go to Work Pretty Daddy") 25-50 53
CORAL 8-12 52
DELUXE 15-25 54
DERBY (752 "Rock Little Daddy") 15-25 51
GRAND 8-10 55

DAVIS, Freddy, & Counts
Singles: 7-inch
COUNT 15-25 58

DAVIS, Gary
(Reverend Gary Davis)
LPs: 10/12-inch
CONTINENTAL 20-40
VANGUARD 15-20

DAVIS, Geater R&B '70
(Geater "Jeater" Davis; Jeater Davis; Geater "Blues" Davis)
Singles: 12-inch
MT (005 "Better Days") 5-10 83
Singles: 7-inch
ACE (3006 "Nice and Easy") 5-10 74
ACE (3019 "Tired of Busting My Brain") 4-8 76
HOUSE OF ORANGE (2401 "Don't Marry a Fool") 6-12 70
HOUSE OF ORANGE (2402 "My Love Is Strong for You") 5-10 71
HOUSE OF ORANGE (2405 "For Your Precious Love") 5-10 71
HOUSE OF ORANGE (2407 "I Know") 5-10 72
HOUSE OF ORANGE (2410 "Cold Love") 4-6 77
HOUSE OF ORANGE (2615 "Breath Taking Girl") 4-6 76
HOUSE OF ORANGE (79100 "I'll Play the Blues for You")") 3-6 79
LUNA (801 "I've Got to Pay the Price") 5-10 72
LUNA (804 "I Don't Worry") 5-10 72
MT (001 "Right Back for More") 3-6 81
MT (002 "I'll Take Care of You") 3-6 81
MT (005 "Better Days") 3-6 83
MT (007 "Go Your Way") 3-6 83
ODDS & ENDS (7600 "I'll Play the Blues for You") 4-8 75
SEVENTY-SEVEN (124 "Why Does It Hurt So Bad") 4-8 72
SEVENTY-SEVEN (130 "Your Heart Is So Cold") 4-8 73
SEVENTY-SEVEN (136 "I've Got to Pay the Price") 4-8 73
SUN BELT (7179 "Where Ever You Are") 3-6 79
LPs: 10/12-inch
HOUSE OF ORANGE (6000 "Geater Davis") 8-12 72
MT (0001 "Geater Davis") 8-10 83

DAVIS, Gene
Singles: 7-inch
CHALLLENGE 5-10 60
LIBERTY 4-8 63-64
SUPER-SONIC 4-8 61
EPs: 7-inch
BOOGIE BOY 8-12

DAVIS, Gene / Chuck & Gene
Singles: 7-inch
R-DELL (107 "Curfew") 5-10
Also see DAVIS, Gene
Also see MILLS, Chuck

DAVIS, Gene C&W '76
Singles: 7-inch
MAVERICK 3-5 76

DAVIS, George
Singles: 7-inch
PHILIPS (40082 "Out of a Million Girls") 100-125 62

DAVIS, Ginger
(With the Snaps)
Singles: 7-inch
MGM 8-12 65
SWAN 10-15 61

DAVIS, Glee
Singles: 7-inch
SOUND STAGE 7 4-8 65

DAVIS, Hal
(With Brenda Holloway; Hal "Sonny" Davis)
Singles: 7-inch
ALDEN (1301 "Sweet & Lovely") 25-50 59
ALDEN (1303 "King of Lovers"") 25-50 59
DEL-FI (4146 "You're Playing with Me") 15-25 60
DYNAMITE (1010 "Why Did You Go Away") 100-150 62
FEDERAL (12429 "My Only Flower") 10-20 61
G.S.P. (2 "I Don't Know") 15-25 63
GARDENA (125 "One More Chance") 25-50 62
KELLEY (105 "Way to My Heart") 50-100
(Colored vinyl.)
M.J.C. (104 "You'll Find Love") 50-100 63
(Colored vinyl.)
MARIE (1010 "Why Did You Go Away") 25-50 60s
MINASA (6714 "It's You") 15-25 60s
WIZARD (101 "What Do You Mean to Me") 50-75 61
(Black label.)
WIZARD (101 "What Do You Mean to Me") 25-50 61
(Yellow label.)
WIZARD (102 "I Need Someone") 25-50 61
VEE JAY (387 " What Do You Mean to Me") 15-25 61
Also see HOLLOWAY, Brenda

DAVIS, Hal, & Ercelle Tisby
Singles: 7-inch
EDSEL 10-20 60
Also see DAVIS, Hal

DAVIS, Hank
(Hank & the Elektras)
Singles: 7-inch
STACY (911 "Real Soon") 35-50 59
WIZZ (716 "I Want You to Be My Baby") 20-30 59
LPs: 10/12-inch
DUCKTAIL 10-12
RR 10-15
REDITA 10-12
Also see CAMPBELL, Rev. Anthony, Hank Davis, & Calvin Morris
Also see HANK & CAROLEE
Also see HANK & ELECTRAS
Also see RADLEY, Raunch

DAVIS, Happy Jack
Singles: 7-inch
LLUVIA 4-8 61

DAVIS, Harley, & Teenaires
Singles: 7-inch
WILDCAT 5-10 61

DAVIS, Hayward
Singles: 7-inch
CHRISTY (103 "Bubble Gum Rock") 10-20 60
CHRISTY (103 "Showdown") 10-20 60
(Retitled reissue of *Bubble Gum Rock*.)

DAVIS, J.C.
Singles: 7-inch
ARGO 4-8 61
CHESS 4-8 62-63

DAVIS, James
Singles: 7-inch
DUKE 4-8 62-66
FEDERAL 5-10 59

DAVIS, Jan
(With the Routers; "The Jan Davis Guitar")
Singles: 7-inch
A&M 8-12 64
ALJO (104 "Surfing Matador") 15-25 64
BEAR 4-6 69
BIG BIRD 4-8 67
COLUMBIA 4-8 65
DIRECT HIT 4-8
1ST PRESIDENT 5-10 60
GUILD (1900 "Destination Love") 100-200 58
HOLIDAY 4-8 64
QUAD-ETT (10039 "Hot Sauce") 4-8 74
RCA 4-8 66
RANWOOD 3-5 75
RCA 4-8 66
RENDEZVOUS (Except 214) 5-10 61-63
RENDEZVOUS (214 "You're Not Welcome") 15-25 63
SHAMLEY 4-6 69
SMASH (1863 "Surfing Matador") 10-15 64
SOAP 3-4 82
UNI 4-8 67
Also see HOLLYWOOD PRODUCERS

DAVIS, Jerry
Singles: 7-inch
IMPERIAL 4-8 62
RAMCO 5-10 61

DAVIS, Jess
(With Freddie Flynn & Flashes)
Singles: 7-inch
BOB-O-LINK (100 "With All My Heart and Soul") 20-30 59
BOB-O-LINK (102 "Do You Love Me") 10-20 60

DAVIS, Jesse
Singles: 7-inch
ERA (3189 "Gonna Hang in There Girl") 50-100 66
ERA (3192 "Something to Think About") 40-60 66

DAVIS, Jesse Ed
Singles: 7-inch
ATCO 3-6 71-72
COLUMBIA 4-8 70
EPs: 7-inch
EPIC (1067 "Interview with Jesse Ed Davis") 8-10 73
(Promotional issue only.)
LPs: 10/12-inch
ATCO 10-15 70-72
EPIC 10-12 73
Member: Johnny "Angel" Angelos.
Also see RED RIDER

DAVIS, Jimmie C&W '44
(With the Jimmie Davis Singers; with Anita Kerr Singers)
Singles: 78 rpm
BLUEBIRD 25-75 30s
DECCA (1500 thru 6100 series) 20-40 35-45
DECCA (20000 & 30000 series) 8-15 43-57
Electradisk 100-200 30s
(Made for sale through Woolworth Stores.)
SUNRISE (3128 "Bear Cat Mama from Homer Corners") 100-200 33
SUNRISE (3237 "It's All Coming Home to You") 100-200 33
SUNRISE (3267 "I Wonder If She's Blue") 100-200 33
SUNRISE (3400 "There's Evil in Ye Children Gather 'Round") 100-200 33
SUNRISE (3440 "I Want Her Tailor Made") 100-200 33
VICTOR (23000 series) 75-150 30s
EPs: 7-inch
DECCA 5-15 55-65
LPs: 10/12-inch
CANAAN 4-8 74-81
CORAL 4-8 73
DECCA 8-20 55-72
MCA 4-10 75
PAULA 6-10 74-75
PLANTATION 6-12 78-81
RIVERSONG 5-8
VOCALION 5-15 60-69
Also see FOLEY, Red / Jimmie Davis
Also see KERR, Anita

DAVIS, Jimmy & Junction P&R/LP '87
Singles: 7-inch
QMI MUSIC 3-4 87
Picture Sleeves
QMI MUSIC 3-4 87
LPs: 10/12-inch
MCA 5-10 87

DAVIS, Joe Arnold, Combo
Singles: 7-inch
2 SPOT 10-12

DAVIS, Joey C&W '78
Singles: 7-inch
MRC 3-5 78

DAVIS, John, & Monster Orchestra R&B '76
Singles: 12-inch
COLUMBIA 4-8 79
Singles: 7-inch
COLUMBIA 3-5 78-79
SAM 3-5 76-78
LPs: 10/12-inch
COLUMBIA 5-10 79

DAVIS, Johnny
Singles: 7-inch
SMASH 4-8 63

DAVIS, Joyce
Singles: 7-inch
COLUMBIA 4-8 63
OKEH 3-6 66
U.A. 4-8 60-62

DAVIS, Joyce, & Nelson Dupree
Singles: 7-inch
U.A. 4-8 61
Also see DAVIS, Joyce

DAVIS, Judge
Singles: 78 rpm
FLASH 10-15 57
Singles: 7-inch
FLASH 10-15 57

DAVIS, June, with Cats & Fiddle
Singles: 78 rpm
MANOR 10-20 46
Also see CATS & FIDDLE

DAVIS, Keith
Singles: 7-inch
BROADWAY 4-8 61

DAVIS, Ken
(With Honey Bees)
Singles: 7-inch
BADGER (250 "Shook Shake") 25-50 59
BADGER (251 "Oh So Blue") 15-25 59
KAY DEE (031 "Play Ginger Play") 5-10 67
MEAN MT. (1419 "Shook Shake") 3-4 82
PFAU (3057 "Sittin' Pretty") 40-60 58
SINGING BLUE ("Next Little Town") 15-25 62
(No selection number used.)
STARLIGHT (1002 "Uh Huh, That's Right") 50-75 58
STARLIGHT (1006 "Shook Shake") 100-150 58
Picture Sleeves
MEAN MT. (1419 "Shook Shake") 3-5 82

DAVIS, Ken
Singles: 7-inch
DOT (16654 "Drop Out") 25-35 64

DAVIS, King
Singles: 78 rpm
HOLLYWOOD 20-30 54
Singles: 7-inch
HOLLYWOOD (422 "Someday You'll Understand") 40-50 54

DAVIS, Krystal D&D '85
Singles: 12-inch
URBAN ROCK 4-6 85

DAVIS, Larry
Singles: 7-inch
DUKE (192 "I Tried") 15-25 58
DUKE (313 "My Little Girl") 15-25 59
HUB CITY (629-73 "Same Thing They Did to Me") 5-10
KENT 10-15 69
ROOSTER BLUES (47 "Since I Been Loving You") 4-6 82
VIRGO 5-10
Session: Oliver Sain.
Also see SAIN, Oliver

DAVIS, Larry & Dixie
Singles: 7-inch
KANGAROO (13 "Gonna Live It Up") 30-40 58

DAVIS, Laurie
Singles: 7-inch
GUARANTEED 5-10 61

DAVIS, Lem
Singles: 7-inch
PATTERN (103 "Hot Chocolate") 15-25 58

DAVIS, Lenny
Singles: 7-inch
DO-RA-ME 15-25 61
SHEEN 5-10 59

EPs: 7-inch
DE VAY (8900 "Lenny Davis") ... 5-10

DAVIS, Linda C&W '88
Singles: 7-inch
CAPITOL ... 3-4 90-91
EPIC ... 3-4 88-89
Also see ROGERS, Kenny

DAVIS, Link
Singles: 78 rpm
NU-CRAFT ... 25-35 55
SARG ... 25-40 56
STARDAY ... 15-25 56
Singles: 7-inch
ALLSTAR ... 5-10 60
COLUMBIA ... 10-15 55
KOOL ... 5-10 64
NU-CRAFT (2026 "Grasshopper Rock") ... 35-50 55
PRINCESS (4057 "Face in the Glass") ... 10-20
SARG (136 "Cockroach") ... 50-75 56
STARDAY (235 (16 Chicks") ... 50-75 56
STARDAY (242 (Grasshopper Rock") ... 50-75 56
STARDAY (255 (Trucker from Tennessee") ... 50-75 56
STARDAY (275 (Bayou Buffalo") ... 20-30 56
STARDAY (293 (Slippin and Slidin' ") ... 50-75 57
STARDAY (331 (Big Connie") ... 20-30 57
TANKER (715 "Airliner") ... 50-75 59

DAVIS, Little Sam
Singles: 78 rpm
DELUXE ... 25-50 53
ROCKIN' ... 40-60 53
Singles: 7-inch
DELUXE (6025 "She's So Good to Me") ... 50-75 53
ROCKIN' (512 "Goin' Home to Mother") ... 60-80 53
ROCKIN' (519 "She's So Good to Me") ... 75-100 53

DAVIS, Lynda
Singles: 7-inch
STARR MOUNT ... 5-10

DAVIS, Mac C&W/P&R '70
Singles: 7-inch
CAPITOL ... 4-8 65
COLUMBIA ... 3-5 70-78
CASABLANCA ... 3-4 80-84
JAMIE (1227 "I'm a Poor Loser") ... 10-20 62
MCA ... 3-4 85-86
VEE JAY (492 "Lookin' at Linda") ... 8-12 63
VEE JAY (565 "Honey Love") ... 8-12 63
Picture Sleeves
COLUMBIA ... 3-5 70-75
LPs: 10/12-inch
ACCORD ... 5-10 82
BUCKBOARD ... 5-10
CASABLANCA ... 5-10 81-85
COLUMBIA ... 8-10 70-83
MCA ... 5-10 86
SPRINGBOARD ... 6-10
TRIP ... 8-10 73
Also see CLASSICS IV / Mac Davis

DAVIS, Martha R&B '48
Singles: 78 rpm
CORAL ... 5-10 51-52
DECCA ... 5-10 48
JEWEL ... 5-15 48
URBAN ... 5-15 46
Singles: 7-inch
CORAL ... 10-20 51-52
LPs: 10/12-inch
ABC-PAR (213 "Tribute to Fats Waller") ... 40-50 57
Also see JORDAN, Louis

DAVIS, Martha P&R/LP '87
Singles: 7-inch
CAPITOL ... 3-4 87
Picture Sleeves
CAPITOL ... 3-4 87
LPs: 10/12-inch
CAPITOL ... 5-10 87
Also see MOTELS

DAVIS, Martha, & Sly Stone
Singles: 7-inch
A&M ... 3-4 86
Also see STONE, Sly

DAVIS, Mary R&B '87
Singles: 7-inch
FAT BACK ... 5-8
TABU ... 3-4 87
Also see S.O.S. Band

DAVIS, Maxine
Singles: 7-inch
GUYDEN ... 10-15 63
TRINITY ... 8-10

DAVIS, Maxwell
(With His Blenders; with Harlem Brass)
Singles: 78 rpm
GOTHAM ... 10-15 51
RPM ... 10-15 56
MILTONE ... 10-20 47
RPM ... 10-20 53-56
SWING BEAT ... 10-20 49
Singles: 7-inch
KENT (454 "Green Hornet") ... 5-10 67
RPM (449 "Thunderbird") ... 15-25 55
RPM (482 "Tempo Rock") ... 15-25 56
EPs: 7-inch
ALADDIN ... 20-30 56
LPs: 10/12-inch
ALADDIN (709 "Maxwell Davis") ... 30-50 56
(10-inch LP. Black vinyl.)
ALADDIN (709 "Maxwell Davis") ... 50-100 56
(10-inch LP. Colored vinyl.)
ALADDIN (804 "Maxwell Davis") ... 25-40 56
SCORE (4016 "Blue Tango") ... 20-35 57
Also see FABULOUS FOUR
Also see LITTLE CAESAR
Also see MARY ELLEN

DAVIS, Melvin
(With the Nite Sounds)
Singles: 7-inch
FORTUNE (551 "Playboy") ... 20-30 63
GROOVESVILLE (1003 "I Must Love You") ... 100-150 60s
KE-KE (1815 "It's No News") ... 200-300
MALA (590 "Save It") ... 20-30 67
MALA (12009 "Faith") ... 10-15 68
WHEEL CITY (1003 "Find a Quiet Place") ... 300-400 60s
Also see NITE SOUNDS

DAVIS, Meyer
Singles: 7-inch
WARWICK ... 4-8 61
LPs: 10/12-inch
CAMEO (C-1014 "The Twist") ... 10-20 61
(Monaural.)
CAMEO (SC-1014 "The Twist") ... 15-25 61
(Stereo.)

DAVIS, Mighty Mike
Singles: 7-inch
DEAN (1395 "All American Boy") ... 10-20

DAVIS, Miles LP '61
(Miles Davis Sextet)
Singles: 78 rpm
BLUE NOTE ... 10-20 54-56
PRESTIGE ... 10-20 52-57
Singles: 7-inch
BLUE NOTE (1600 series) ... 5-10 54-56
COLUMBIA (02000 thru 03000 series) ... 3-4 81-83
COLUMBIA (10000 series) ... 3-6 75
COLUMBIA (41000 thru 46000 series) ... 3-8 61-74
PRESTIGE (100 thru 400 series) ... 5-10 57-66
PRESTIGE (700 thru 900 series) ... 15-25 52-55
EPs: 7-inch
BLUE NOTE ... 15-25 52
CAPITOL (459 "Jeru") ... 50-100 53
COLUMBIA ... 6-10 59
PRESTIGE ... 12-20 52-53
LPs: 10/12-inch
BLUE NOTE (100 series) ... 8-12 73
BLUE NOTE (1500 series) ... 25-50 56-58
(Label gives New York street address for Blue Note Records.)
BLUE NOTE (1500 series) ... 15-25 58
(Label reads "Blue Note Records Inc. - New York, U.S.A.")
BLUE NOTE (1500 series) ... 10-20 66
(Label shows Blue Note Records as a division of either Liberty or United Artists.)
BLUE NOTE (5013 "Miles Davis") ... 100-150 52
(10-inch LP.)
BLUE NOTE (5022 "Tempus Fugit") ... 100-150 53
(10-inch LP.)
BLUE NOTE (5044 "Miles Davis") ... 100-150 54
(10-inch LP.)
CAPITOL (H-459 "Jeru") ... 100-150 53
(10-inch LP.)
CAPITOL (T-459 "Jeru") ... 35-50 53
CAPITOL (762 "Birth of Cool") ... 50-75 56
CAPITOL (1900 series) ... 10-20 63
CAPITOL (11000 series) ... 8-12 72
CAPITOL (16000 series) ... 5-10 81
COLUMBIA (20 "Friday and Saturday Nights in Person") ... 25-30 61
(Monaural.)
COLUMBIA (26 "Bitches Brew") ... 8-12 70
COLUMBIA (820 "Friday and Saturday Nights in Person") ... 30-40 61
(Stereo.)
COLUMBIA (900 thru 1600 series) ... 20-35 57-61
(With six black Columbia "eye" logos on red label.)
COLUMBIA (1800 thru 2300 series) ... 15-25 61-65
COLUMBIA (8000 thru 8400 series) ... 20-35 58-62
(With six black Columbia "eye" logos on red label.)
COLUMBIA (8600 thru 9800 series) ... 10-20 61-69
COLUMBIA (10000 series) ... 6-10 73
COLUMBIA (30000 series, except 36976) ... 6-12 70-85
COLUMBIA (36976 "The Miles Davis Collection") ... 30-40 80
(Boxed, six-disc set.)
COLUMBIA (40000 series) ... 8-12 81-85
DEBUT (043 "Blue Moods") ... 5-8 83
DEBUT (120 "Blue Moods") ... 50-100 55
FANTASY ... 15-20 62
FONTANA ... 10-15 65
MFSL (177 "Someday My Prince Will Come") ... 20-30 85
MOODSVILLE ... 15-20 63
MOSAIC (158 "Complete Plugged Nickel Sessions") ... 125-150 90s
(10 audiophile LP boxed set. 5000 made.)
MOSAIC (164 "Complete Columbia Studio Recordings") ... 135-160 90s
(11 audiophile LP boxed set. 5000 made. With Gil Evans.)
NEW JAZZ ... 10-15 64
PRESTIGE (004 thru 093) ... 5-8 80-85
PRESTIGE (100 series) ... 50-100 52-54
(10-inch LPs.)
PRESTIGE (7007 thru 7166) ... 40-60 55-59
(Yellow label.)
PRESTIGE (7168 thru 7281) ... 20-30 60-64
(Yellow label.)
PRESTIGE (7000 thru 7600 series) ... 6-12 64-69
(Blue label.)
PRESTIGE (7700 thru 7800 series) ... 6-12 70-71
PRESTIGE (24000 series) ... 8-12 72-78
SAVOY ... 12-20 61
TRIP ... 5-10 73
U.A. ... 8-10 71
W.B. ... 5-10 86-90
Also see COLTRANE, John, & Miles Davis
Also see FORREST, Jimmy

DAVIS, Miles, & Thelonious Monk
LPs: 10/12-inch
COLUMBIA ... 10-20 64
Also see DAVIS, Miles
Also see JACQUET, Illinois, & Miles Davis
Also see MONK, Thelonious

DAVIS, Miz R&B '76
Singles: 7-inch
NEW ... 3-5 76

DAVIS, Myler
Singles: 7-inch
CAMEO ... 4-8 62

DAVIS, Pat
Singles: 7-inch
ACTS ... 5-10 60

DAVIS, Paul C&W '60
Singles: 7-inch
DOKE ... 5-10 60

DAVIS, Paul P&R '70
(With Susan Collins)
Singles: 7-inch
ARISTA ... 3-4 81-82
BANG (Except 500 series) ... 3-5 73-80
BANG (500 series) ... 4-6 68-72
CAPITOL/CURB ... 3-4 86
FLASHBACK ... 3-4 82
SOLID GOLD ... 3-5 73
LPs: 10/12-inch
ARISTA ... 5-10 81
BANG ... 10-12 72-82
Also see COLLINS, Sue
Also see OSMOND, Marie, & Paul Davis
Also see TUCKER, Tanya, Paul Davis & Paul Overstreet

DAVIS, Phil
Singles: 7-inch
JOHNSON ... 4-8 62

DAVIS, Rainy R&B '86
Singles: 12-inch
SUPERTRONICS ... 4-6 86
Singles: 7-inch
COLUMBIA ... 3-4 87-88
SUPERTRONICS ... 3-4 86

DAVIS, Ramp
Singles: 78 rpm
MODERN ... 10-20 51

DAVIS, Ray: see COACHMEN FIVE

DAVIS, Rebel
Singles: 7-inch
DIXIE-AIRE (1962 "Free Ride") ... 8-12

DAVIS, Reverend Gary
Singles: 78 rpm
LENOX ... 10-20 48
LPs: 10/12-inch
BIOGRAPH ... 8-10 71
FANTASY ... 10-15 72
FOLK LYRIC ... 10-15
KICKING MULE ... 8-10 74
PRESTIGE BLUESVILLE ... 20-25 62

DAVIS, Ray, & Starlighters
Singles: 7-inch
LADY J ... 3-5 81

DAVIS, Rocky
Singles: 7-inch
BLUE SKY (102 "Hot Rod Baby") ... 400-600 59

DAVIS, Ronny
Singles: 7-inch
SHERIDAN ... 5-10 64

DAVIS, Rufe
Singles: 7-inch
DOT ... 5-10 61

DAVIS, Ruth R&B '78
Singles: 7-inch
CLARIDGE ... 3-4 78
Also see KIRKLAND, Bo, & Ruth Davis

DAVIS, Sammy, Jr. P&R '54
(With Morton Stevens Orchestra; Sammy Davis)
Singles: 78 rpm
DECCA ... 5-10 54-57
Singles: 7-inch
A.L.B.B. (38032 "The House I Live In") ... 3-5
(Promotional issue only.)
APPLAUSE ... 3-4 82
D.D.R. (101 "Who Needs Spring") ... 5-10
(Red vinyl.)
DECCA (25500 series) ... 4-6 62
DECCA (29000 thru 31000 series) ... 8-15 54-60
DECCA (32000 series) ... 3-5 69
ECOLOGY ... 3-4 71
MGM ... 3-5 71-79
VERVE ... 5-8 60
REPRISE ... 4-8 61-71
20TH FOX ... 3-5 75-76
W.B. ... 3-4 77
Picture Sleeves
A.L.B.B. (38032 "The House I Live In") ... 5-10
(Promotional issue only.)
EPs: 7-inch
CAPITOL (555 "Sammy Davis Jr.") ... 10-20 54
DECCA ... 10-20 54-55
LPs: 10/12-inch
DECCA (100 series) ... 10-20 66
DECCA (4000 series) ... 10-20 61-65
DECCA (8100 thru 8700 series) ... 20-30 54-58
DECCA (8900 series) ... 10-20 59
DECCA (9032 "Mr. Wonderful") ... 60-70 56
(Soundtrack.)
HARMONY ... 5-10 69-71
MCA ... 5-10 77
MGM ... 5-10 72-73
MOTOWN ... 6-10 70
RCA (1086 "Three Penny Opera") ... 15-25 64
REPRISE ... 10-20 61-69
20TH FOX (Except 5014) ... 5-10 76
20TH FOX (FXG-5014 "Of Love and Desire") ... 25-30 64
(Soundtrack. Monaural.)
20TH FOX (SXG-5014 "Of Love and Desire") ... 35-40 64
(Soundtrack. Stereo.)
W.B. ... 5-10 77
U.A. (5187 "Salt and Pepper") ... 15-20 68
(Soundtrack.)
VOCALION ... 5-10 68
Also see CURB, Mike
Also see SINATRA, Frank, Sammy Davis Jr. & Dean Martin

DAVIS, Sammy, Jr., & Sam Butera
LP: 10/12-inch
REPRISE ... 10-15 64
Also see BUTERA, Sam

DAVIS, Sammy, Jr., & Laurindo Almeida
LPs: 10/12-inch
REPRISE ... 10-15 67
Also see ALMEIDA, Laurindo

DAVIS, Sammy, Jr., & Count Basie LP '65
Singles: 7-inch
VERVE ... 3-5 65
LPs: 10/12-inch
MGM ... 6-10 73
VERVE ... 10-15 65
Also see BASIE, Count

DAVIS, Sammy, Jr., & Carmen McRae
Singles: 7-inch
DECCA ... 5-10 55
EPs: 7-inch
DECCA ... 5-10 59
LPs: 10/12-inch
DECCA ... 10-20 59
Also see McRAE, Carmen

DAVIS, Sammy, Jr., & Buddy Rich
LPs: 10/12-inch
REPRISE ... 10-20 66
Also see RICH, Buddy

DAVIS, Sammy, Jr. / Joya Sherril
LPs: 10/12-inch
DESIGN ... 5-10 60s
Also see DAVIS, Sammy, Jr.

DAVIS, Sherry
(With Buddy Holly)
Singles: 7-inch
FASHION (1001 "Humble Heart") ... 50-75 57
Also see HOLLY, Buddy

DAVIS, Skeeter C&W '58
Singles: 7-inch
MERCURY ... 3-5 76-77
PART TWO ... 3-5 80
RCA (Except 7000 thru 9600 series) ... 3-6 69-74
RCA (7000 thru 8300 series) ... 6-15 58-64
RCA (8400 thru 9600 series) ... 5-10 64-68
Picture Sleeves
RCA ... 5-10 63
EPs: 7-inch
RCA ... 5-10 63
LPs: 10/12-inch
CAMDEN ... 5-10 65-74
GUSTO ... 5-10 78
RCA (2179 thru 4818, except 3790) ... 10-20 60-73
RCA (3790 "Skeeter Davis Sings Buddy Holly") ... 20-30 67
TUDOR ... 5-10 84
Also see BARE, Bobby, & Skeeter Davis
Also see DAVIS SISTERS
Also see HAMILTON, George, IV, & Skeeter Davis
Also see JENNINGS, Waylon
Also see POSEY, Sandy / Skeeter Davis
Also see SOME of CHET'S FRIENDS
Also see WAGONER, Porter, & Skeeter Davis

DAVIS, Skeeter, & Don Bowman C&W '68
Singles: 7-inch
RCA ... 4-8 68
LPs: 10/12-inch
RCA ... 10-15 68
Also see BOWMAN, Don

DAVIS, Skeeter, & George Hamilton IV C&W '70
Singles: 7-inch
RCA ... 3-5 70
LPs: 10/12-inch
RCA ... 10-12 70
Also see HAMILTON, George, IV

DAVIS, Skeeter, & NRBQ
Singles: 7-inch
ROUNDER ... 3-5 85
Also see DAVIS, Skeeter
Also see NRBQ

DAVIS, Sonny Boy
Singles: 78 rpm
TALENT (802 "Rhythm Blues") ... 50-100 49

DAVIS, Spencer P&R '66
(Spencer Davis Group; with Peter Jameson)
Singles: 7-inch
ALLEGIANCE ... 3-4 84
ATCO ... 5-10 66
FONTANA ... 8-12 64
U.A. ... 4-8 66-72
VERTIGO ... 3-4 73-74
Picture Sleeves
U.A. ... 8-12 66-67
LPs: 10/12-inch
ALLEGIANCE ... 5-10 84
DATE ... 10-12 70
FONTANA ... 20-30 66
ISLAND ... 5-10 83
MEDIARTS ... 10-12 71
RHINO ... 5-10 84
U.A. ... 15-30 67-75
VERTIGO ... 10-12 73-74
WING ... 10-15
Members: Spencer Davis; Steve Winwood; Pete York; Brian Dexter; Ray Fenwick; Ken Salmon; Muff Winwood.
Also see WINWOOD, Steve

DAVIS, Tim P&R '72
(With the Chordairs)
Singles: 7-inch
LEAF (6467 "Wine Wine Wine") ... 10-20 64
METROMEDIA ... 3-5 72-73
LPs: 10/12-inch
METROMEDIA ... 8-10 72-73
Members: Jim Marcotte; David Chaffee; Curley Cooke; Jim Peterman; Dick Personett; Denny Geyer.
Also see MILLER, Steve

DAVIS, Tyrone P&R/R&B '68
(Tyrone "Wonder Boy" Davis)
Singles: 7-inch
ABC ... 4-6 68
COLUMBIA ... 3-5 76-81
DAKAR ... 4-8 68-77
EPIC ... 3-4 83
FUTURE ... 3-4 87-88
HIGHRISE ... 3-5 82-83
HIT SOUND (888 "I'm Confessin' ") ... 5-10 70
ICHIBAN ... 3-4 91-94
OCEAN FRONT ... 3-4 83-84
SACK ... 10-20
LPs: 10/12-inch
COLUMBIA ... 8-10 76-81
DAKAR ... 10-15 69-76
EPIC ... 5-10 83
HIGHRISE ... 5-10 82
ICHIBAN ... 5-10
Also see TYRONE (The Wonder Boy)

DAVIS, Walter
Singles: 78 rpm
BLUEBIRD ... 25-50 33-42
BULLET ... 15-25 49-50
RCA ... 15-25 46-52
Singles: 7-inch
RCA (5012 "You Made My World So Bright") ... 75-100 52
RCA (5168 "So Long Baby") ... 75-100 52

DAVIS & JONES & DEFENDERS
Singles: 7-inch
DERRY ... 4-8 64

DAVIS SISTERS C&W '53
Singles: 78 rpm
FORTUNE (174 "Kaw-Liga") ... 10-20 52
RCA ... 10-15 53-56
Singles: 7-inch
FORTUNE (174 "Kaw-Liga") ... 15-25 52
FORTUNE (3000 series) ... 4-8
RCA (5000 & 6000 series) ... 10-15 53-56
Members: Skeeter Davis; Betty J. "Bee Jay" Davis.
Also see DAVIS, Skeeter

DAVIS SISTERS / Chuck Hatfield & the Treble-Aires
Singles: 7-inch
FORTUNE ... 10-15 52
Singles: 7-inch
FORTUNE (175 "Heartbreak Ahead") ... 15-25 52

DAVIS SISTERS / Roy Hall & His Cahutta Mountain Boys
Singles: 78 rpm
FORTUNE (170 "Jealous Love") ... 10-20 53
Singles: 7-inch
FORTUNE (170 "Jealous Love") ... 20-40 53
Also see DAVIS SISTERS
Also see HALL, Roy

DAVISON, Brian
LPs: 10/12-inch
MERCURY ... 10-12 71

DAVISON, Leo
Singles: 7-inch
GREAT SCOTT 10-15

DAVY, Dick
LPs: 10/12-inch
COLUMBIA 10-15 67

DAVY D: see DAVY DMX

DAVY & DOLPHINS
Singles: 7-inch
SUBTOWN 10-20 60s
Member: David Liska.
Also see DAVEY & DOLPHINS

DAVY DMX R&B/D&D '84
(Davy D; David Reeves)
Singles: 12-inch
CBS ASSOCIATED 4-6 84
Singles: 7-inch
CBS ASSOCIATED 3-4 84
DEF JAM 3-4 87

DAWE, Tim
LPs: 10/12-inch
STRAIGHT 12-15 69
W.B. 10-15 70

DAWGS
Singles: 7-inch
GREENLINE 3-4 80

DAWKINS, Earl
(With the Aqua Lads)
Singles: 7-inch
AQUA (8903 "Ain't Gonna Ride") 8-10

DAWKINS, Jimmy
LPs: 10/12-inch
DELMARK 10-12 69-76
EXCELLO 8-12 72

DAWN
Singles: 7-inch
APT 4-8 65
CADET 4-6 69
U.A. 4-8 66

DAWN
(Five Discs)
Singles: 7-inch
LAURIE 5-10 67
RUST 5-10 66
Also see FIVE DISCS

DAWN P&R/LP '70
(With Tony Orlando)
Singles: 7-inch
BELL 3-5 70-72
FLASHBACK 3-5 70s
LPs: 10/12-inch
BELL 10-12 70-71
Members: Tony Orlando; Joyce Wilson; Telma Hopkins.
Also see ORLANDO, Tony, & Dawn

DAWN
Singles: 7-inch
ARISTA 3-5 75
ELEKTRA 3-5 76-77
Members: Joyce Wilson; Telma Hopkins.
Also see ADORABLES
Also see DAWN (With Tony Orlando)
Also see DEBONAIRES

DAWN, Billy
Singles: 7-inch
ABC-PAR 4-8 61
COED 5-10 59

DAWN, Billy, Quartet
(Billy Dawn Smith; with Connie Frederick & Orchestra)
Singles: 78 rpm
DECATUR 75-125 52
Singles: 7-inch
DECATUR (3001 "This Is the Real Thing Now") 150-250 52
VINTAGE 3-5 73
Also see HERALDS
Also see MIGHTY DUKES

DAWN, Debbie
Singles: 7-inch
W.B. (7721 "Hands") 4-6 73

DAWN, Diana
Singles: 7-inch
ED-NEL (66-3 "Wonder Boy") 15-25 66
Picture Sleeves
ED-NEL (66-3 "Wonder Boy") 30-40 66

DAWN, Dolly
Singles: 7-inch
VANTONE 4-8 65

DAWN, Ginger
Singles: 7-inch
LEE 5-10 59

DAWN, Janice
Singles: 7-inch
BROOKE 5-10 59

DAWN, Joy
(Claudine Clark)
Singles: 7-inch
SWAN 5-10 63
Also see CLARK, Claudine

DAWN, Tommy, & Sunsets
Singles: 7-inch
WHITE CLIFFS (246 "Wanted: $10,000 Reward") 15-25

DAWN & JOE
Singles: 7-inch
UNICORN 4-8 65

DAWN & TWILIGHTS
Singles: 7-inch
FINER ARTS 4-8 67

DAWN BEATS
Singles: 7-inch
CENTURY (17380 "Road Block") 5-10

DAWN SISTERS
Singles: 7-inch
SOUTHTOWN 4-8 64

DAWNBEATS
Singles: 7-inch
AMP (792 "Midnight Express") 10-20 59

DAWNE, Billie
Singles: 7-inch
FELSTED 5-10 60

DAWNELLS
Singles: 7-inch
BOGAN ("Scorpion") 20-30 65
(No selection number used.)

DAWNS
(With Sid Feller Orchestra)
Singles: 7-inch
CLIMAX (104 "Why Did You Let Me Love You") 30-50 59

DAWNS
Singles: 7-inch
ATCO (6296 "It Seems Like Yesterday") 10-15 64

DAWNS
Singles: 7-inch
CATALINA (1000 "Trav'lin' ") 350-450 59
(One source gives a 1958 release date for this disc. Another says '64. We don't know yet who's right.)

DAWNS / Caprees: see CAPREES / Dawns

DAWSON, Cliff R&B '82
Singles: 7-inch
BOARDWALK 3-4 82

DAWSON, Cliff, & Renee Diggs R&B '83
Singles: 7-inch
BOARDWALK 3-4 83
Also see DAWSON, Cliff
Also see STARPOINT

DAWSON, Dandee, & Ginger Snaps
Singles: 7-inch
DUNHILL 4-8 65

DAWSON, Jim
Singles: 7-inch
APPLE RIDGE 3-4 80
KAMA SUTRA 3-5 72-73
RCA 3-5 74-75
LPs: 10/12-inch
KAMA SUTRA 10-12 72-76
RCA 8-10 74-75

DAWSON, Jimmy
Singles: 7-inch
COUNTRY FAIR (711 "Big Black Bug Boogie") 10-15 60s
(Includes photo insert.)
FAN JR. (1992 "Playboy") 10-15 60s
K-ARK (775 "Big Black Bug Boogie") 10-15 60s
RUSTIC (808 "It Took An Older Woman") 75-125
Also see DIXIE DRIFTER

DAWSON, Leah
Singles: 7-inch
MAGIC CITY (001 "My Mechanical Man") 10-20 60s
OKEH 5-10 68

DAWSON, Les
Singles: 7-inch
FORD 20-30 58

DAWSON, Ronnie
(Commonwealth Jones)
Singles: 7-inch
BACKBEAT 15-25 58
BANNER 5-10
LEVEE 4-6 70
MAVERICK 15-25 61
ROCKIN' (1 "Rockin' Bones") 75-100 59
SWAN 10-15 60
Session: Ron-Dels
Also see DEE, Ronnie
Also see JONES, Commonwealth
Also see RON-DELS

DAWSON, Tommy
Singles: 7-inch
CHANCELLOR 4-8 63

DAX
Singles: 7-inch
DORE 3-5 72

DAY, Arlan P&R '81
Singles: 7-inch
PASHA 3-4 81

DAY, Bing
Singles: 7-inch
FEDERAL (12320 "Pony Tail Partner") 30-50 58
MERCURY (71446 "I Can't Help It") 15-25 59
MERCURY (71494 "How Do I Do It") 5-10 59

DAY, Bobby P&R '57
(With the Satellites; with Blossoms; Bobby Byrd)
Singles: 78 rpm
CLASS 20-40 57-58
Singles: 7-inch
CLASS (207 "So Long Baby") 20-30 57
CLASS (211 "Little Bitty Pretty One") 15-25 57
CLASS (215 "Beep Beep Beep") 15-25 57
CLASS (225 "Little Turtle Dove") 15-25 58
CLASS (229 "Rockin' Robin") 15-25 58
CLASS (241 "The Bluebird, the Buzzard and the Oriole") 15-25 58
CLASS (245 "That's All I Want") 15-25 59
CLASS (252 "Mr. & Mrs. Rock & Roll") 15-25 59
CLASS (255 "Ain't Gonna Cry No More") 15-25 59
CLASS (257 "Unchained Melody") 15-25 59
CLASS (263 "I Don't Want To") 15-25 60
HIGHLAND (1100 "Little Turtle Dove") 8-10 64
RCA (8133 "Another Country, Another World") 15-25 63
RCA (8196 "Buzz Buzz Buzz") 8-12 63
RCA (8230 "Down on My Knees") 8-12 63
RCA (8316 "When I See My Baby Smile") 8-12 64
RENDEZVOUS (130 "Teenage Philosopher") 10-15 60
RENDEZVOUS (136 "Over and Over") 10-15 60
RENDEZVOUS (146 "Life Can Be Beautiful") 10-15 61
RENDEZVOUS (158 "The King's Highway") 8-12 61
RENDEZVOUS (167 "Don't Worry 'Bout Me") 8-12 62
RENDEZVOUS (175 "Undecided") 8-12 62
SURE SHOT 4-8 67
LPs: 10/12-inch
CLASS (5002 "Rockin' with Robin") 100-150 59
RHINO 5-10 84
Also see BYRD, Bobby
Also see SATELLITES

DAY, Caroline
Singles: 7-inch
DIMENSION 8-12 64

DAY, Chuck, & Young Gyants
Singles: 7-inch
PARKWAY 4-8 67
Also see D'ANDREA, John, & Young Gyants

DAY, Cora Lee
LPs: 10/12-inch
ROULETTE 15-20 60

DAY, Danny
Singles: 7-inch
FRONT (122 "Look at Me Now") 25-35 60s
V.I.P. (25019 "This Time Last Summer") 10-20 65

DAY, Darlene
Singles: 7-inch
MUSIC MAKERS (106 "I Love You So") 50-100 61
Session: Imaginations.
Also see IMAGINATIONS

DAY, Dave Diddle
Singles: 78 rpm
FEE BEE 8-12 57
MERCURY 5-10 57
Singles: 7-inch
FEE BEE 8-12 57
MERCURY 5-10 57

DAY, DAWN & DUSK
("Featuring Charlie Laverne & His Guitars"; with "Chas. Laverne Orch."; Day Dawn, Dusk Trio)
Singles: 78 rpm
APOLLO 10-20 55
DENT 8-12 55
HERALD 8-12 54
JOSIE 10-20 56
Singles: 7-inch
APOLLO (476 "Miss Petunia") 15-25 55
DENT (519 "Let the Tears Fall") 20-30 55
HERALD (5000 "All Through the Years") 15-20 54
JOSIE (794 "Anytime, Anyplace, Anywhere") 15-25 56

DAY, Debbie
Singles: 7-inch
DOWNBEAT 4-8 65

DAY, Dennis P&R '47
(With Jack Benny)
Singles: 78 rpm
CAPITOL 3-5 56
RCA 3-5 47-54
Singles: 7-inch
CAPITOL 4-8 56
RCA 4-8 50-54
REPRISE 3-6 62
SHAMROCK 3-6 59
EPs: 7-inch
CAPITOL 5-10 56
RCA 5-10 50-59
LPs: 10/12-inch
BLUEBIRD 5-10 60
CAMDEN 5-10 64-66
CAPITOL 10-20 56
DESIGN 5-10
MASTERSEAL 10-20
RCA (3036 "My Wild Irish Rose") 15-25 52
REPRISE 5-10 63
ROULETTE 10-15 63

DAY, Doris P&R '47
(With the Mellomen; with Norman Luboff Choir; with Buddy Clark)
Singles: 78 rpm
COLUMBIA 5-15 47-57
Singles: 7-inch
ARWIN (250 "Everlasting Arms") 5-15 50s
COLUMBIA (38000 & 39000 series) 5-15 50-53
COLUMBIA (40000 thru 44000 series) 4-8 54-67
Picture Sleeves
COLUMBIA 10-20 57-61
EPs: 7-inch
COLUMBIA 10-30 50-59
LPs: 10/12-inch
COLUMBIA (1 "Listen to Day") 20-30 60
COLUMBIA (600 thru 1300 series) 15-30 55-59
COLUMBIA (1400 thru 2100 series) 10-20 60-64
COLUMBIA (2500 series) 20-35 56
(10-inch LPs.)
COLUMBIA (6000 series) 25-50 49-55
(10-inch LPs.)
COLUMBIA (8000 thru 8900 series) 15-30 58-64
COLUMBIA (2200 thru 2300 series) 10-25 64-65
(Monaural.)
COLUMBIA (9000 thru 9100 series) 15-35 64-65
(Stereo.)
HARMONY 8-12 66-72
Also see BROWN, Les, & His Orchestra
Also see STREISAND, Barbra / Doris Day / Jim Nabors / Andre Kostelanetz

DAY, Doris, & Don Cherry
EPs: 7-inch
COLUMBIA 10-20 56
Also see CHERRY, Don

DAY, Doris, & Frankie Laine P&R '52
Singles: 78 rpm
COLUMBIA 5-10 52
Singles: 7-inch
COLUMBIA 5-15 52
Also see LAINE, Frankie

DAY, Doris, & Andre Previn
LPs: 10/12-inch
COLUMBIA 10-20 62
Also see PREVIN, Andre

DAY, Doris, & Johnnie Ray P&R '53
Singles: 78 rpm
COLUMBIA 5-10 52-53
Singles: 7-inch
COLUMBIA 5-15 52-53
Also see RAY, Johnnie

DAY, Doris, & Frank Sinatra P&R '49
Singles: 78 rpm
COLUMBIA 5-10 49
Singles: 7-inch
COLUMBIA 5-15 49

DAY, Doris / Frank Sinatra LP '55
EPs: 7-inch
COLUMBIA (571 "Young at Heart") 10-20 55
COLUMBIA (34178 "Young at Heart") 30-50 54
(Promotional issue only.)
LPs: 10/12-inch
COLUMBIA (6339 "Young at Heart") 40-60 55
(Soundtrack. 10-inch LP.)
Also see DAY, Doris, & Frank Sinatra
Also see SINATRA, Frank

DAY, Doris, & Danny Thomas
EPs: 7-inch
COLUMBIA (289 "I'll See You in My Dreams") 10-15
Also see DAY, Doris
Also see THOMAS, Danny

DAY, Eddie, & Night Timers
Singles: 7-inch
BB (4005 "How to Be a Musician") 15-25 66

DAY, Jack
Singles: 7-inch
ARCADE (115 "Rattle Bone Boogie") 20-30 59

DAY, Jackie
Singles: 7-inch
MODERN (1028 "Before It's Too Late") 10-20 67
PHELECTRON (382 "Naughty Boy") 200-300
SUGAR HILL 4-6 69
SPECIALTY 4-6 69

DAY, Joey, & Nite Tymes
Singles: 7-inch
BEAVER (8662 "Good Times") 20-30

DAY, Johnny
Singles: 7-inch
DORE 15-25 60

DAY, Little Sunny, & Clouds
Singles: 7-inch
TANDEM (7001 "Lou Ann") 200-300 61

DAY, Margie R&B '50
Singles: 78 rpm
CAT (118 "Ho-Ho") 10-20 55
DECCA 5-10 54
DOT 5-10 54
Singles: 7-inch
CAT (118 "Ho-Ho") 20-30 55
COED 4-8 61
DECCA 15-25 54
DOT 15-20 54
LEGRAND 10-20 62
MARTHAY 10-20 60s
Also see GRIFFIN BROTHERS

DAY, Morris P&R/R&B/D&D/LP '85
Singles: 12-inch
W.B. 4-6 85-86
Singles: 7-inch
W.B. 3-4 85-88
Picture Sleeves
W.B. 3-4 85-88
LPs: 10/12-inch
W.B. 5-10 85-88
Also see TIME

DAY, Reginald
Singles: 7-inch
MIDAS (9005 "Lost Love") 10-20 60s

DAY, Roberta
Singles: 7-inch
ABNER 10-15

DAY, Rusty
Singles: 7-inch
MALTESE (104 "I Gotta Move") 15-25 66
MALTESE (110 "I Gotta Move") 15-25 66
Also see AMBOY DUKES
Also see CACTUS

DAY, Sonny
(With the Versatiles; with Rare Breed; Little Sunny Day & the Clouds)
Singles: 78 rpm
STAR 15-25 56
Singles: 7-inch
ABC-PAR 15-20 58
CHECKER (886 "Speedillac") 40-60 58
JUBILEE 5-10 66
MALA (481 "37 Men") 15-25 63
STAR (226 "Creature from Outer Space") 35-50 56
POWER 5-8
TANDEM (7001 "Lou Ann") 200-300 61

DAY, Terry
(Terry Melcher)
Singles: 7-inch
COLUMBIA (3-42427 "I Waited Too Long") 30-40 62
(Compact 33 Single.)
COLUMBIA (3-42678 "Be a Soldier") 40-50 63
(Compact 33 Single.)
COLUMBIA (4-42427 "I Waited Too Long) 8-12 62
COLUMBIA (4-42678 "Be a Soldier") 10-15 63
Picture Sleeves
COLUMBIA (42678 "Be a Soldier") 30-40 63
Also see MELCHER, Terry

DAY & KNIGHT
Singles: 7-inch
JOSIE 8-12 60

DAY BIRDS
Singles: 7-inch
JAMA (502) 5-10 62
(Answer to *Please Mr. Postman*, but exact title not yet known.)
Member: Bobby Day.

DAY BLINDNESS
Singles: 7-inch
STUDIO 10 (2494 "Horse and Dog") 10-15 70
LPs: 10/12-inch
STUDIO 10 (101 "Day Blindness") 40-60 69

DAY BROTHERS
Singles: 7-inch
CHANCELLOR 5-10 60
COLUMBIA 4-8 64
FIREBIRD 15-25 63

DAYBREAK P&R '70
Singles: 7-inch
PRELUDE 3-4 80
UNI 3-4 70

DAYBREAK
Singles: 7-inch
PAP (003 "I Need Love") 10-20

DAYBREAKERS
Singles: 7-inch
ALADDIN (3434 "I Wonder Why") 25-35 58
LAMP (2016 "I Wonder Why") 30-50 58

DAYBREAKERS
Singles: 7-inch
DIAL (4066 "Psychedelic Siren") 10-20 67

DAYCHORDS
Singles: 7-inch
DON-EL (120 "One More Time") 15-25 62
Also see ROXY & DAYCHORDS

DAYDREAMS
Singles: 7-inch
DIAL 4-8 66

DAYE, Billie
Singles: 7-inch
BLISS.......10-20 61

DAYE, Carolyn
Singles: 7-inch
CHALLENGE (9150 "Fragile").......10-20 62
LIBERTY.......5-10 66

DAYE, Cory P&R/LP '79
Singles: 7-inch
N.Y.I.......3-5 79
Picture Sleeves
N.Y.I.......3-5 79
LPs: 10/12-inch
N.Y.I.......5-10 79
Also see DR. BUZZARD'S ORIGINAL SAVANNAH BAND

DAYE, Eddie
(With the Four Bars; Eddie Daye's 4 Bars with Soul Bandits)
Singles: 7-inch
DAYCO (2500 "Stay on the Job").......50-100 62
SHRINE (112 "Guess Who Loves You").......300-400 66
Also see FOUR BARS

DAYE, Frankie, & His Knights
Singles: 7-inch
DA-MAR (2001 "Dance Party Rock").......10-15
STUDIO (9904 "Drag It").......10-20 59

DAYE, Johnny R&B '65
Singles: 7-inch
JOMADA.......4-8 65-66
PARKWAY.......4-8 66
STAX.......4-6 68

DAYE, Roberta
Singles: 7-inch
ABNER (7002 "Every Day").......20-30 62

DAYE, Sonny
Singles: 7-inch
C-FLAT.......10-20
POWER (203 "Come Back Sandy").......15-25 60s
POWER (208 "Long Long Road")..15-25 60s
ST. CLARK.......5-10 65

DAYE, Stu
LPs: 10/12-inch
COLUMBIA.......8-10 76

DAYJOBBERS
Singles: 7-inch
TMP-TING (116 "Hootchie Koochie Man").......20-30

DAYLIGHTERS
(Chuck & Daylighters; with Al Perkins Band; "Strings by Johnny Pate)
Singles: 7-inch
ASTRA (1001 "This Heart of Mine").......8-12 65
BEA & BABY (103 "Mad House Jump").......25-35 59
C&J (614 "Tough Love").......25-35 60
CHECKER (1051 "War Hoss Mash").......10-15 63
DOMINO (904 "I'll Never Let You Go").......15-25 61
DOT (16326 "Oh What a Way to Be Loved").......15-25 62
NIKE (1011 "This Heart of Mine").......50-100 61
NIKE (10011 "Why Do You Do Me Wrong").......100-150 61
SMASH (2040 "Tell Me").......8-10 66
TIP TOP (2001 "Oh What a Way to Be Loved").......15-25 62
TIP TOP (2002 "Cool Breeze").......15-25 62
TIP TOP (2006 "I Can't Stop Crying").......10-20 63
TIP TOP (2007 "Whisper of the Wind").......10-20 63
TIP TOP (2008 "Oh Mom").......10-20 64
TIP TOP (2009 "Magic Touch").......10-20 64
TIP TOP (2010 "For My Baby").......10-20 65
TOLLIE (9028 "Whisper of the Wind").......8-12 64
Members: Tony Gideon; Levi Moreland; Eddie Thomas; George Wood; Dorsey Wood; Gerald Sims; Curtis Burrell; Ulysses McDonald; Gary & Knight Lites.
Also see DONALD & DELIGHTERS
Also see EVERETT, Betty
Also see GARY & NITE LITES
Also see PATE, Johnny
Also see SIMS, Gerald
Also see PERKINS, Al

DAYLIGHTS
Singles: 7-inch
PROPULSION (601 "A Tear Fell from My Eyes").......15-25 63

DAYNE, Taylor P&R '87
Singles: 7-inch
ARISTA.......3-4 87-90
Picture Sleeves
ARISTA.......3-4 87-90
LPs: 10/12-inch
ARISTA.......5-8 87-90

DAY'S END
Singles: 7-inch
EPIC (10751 "Runnin' Home").......3-6 71

DAYS, Paul
Singles: 7-inch
LOMA.......4-8 66

DAYTON R&B '81
Singles: 7-inch
CAPITOL.......3-4 82-85
LIBERTY.......3-4 81-82
U.A.......3-4 80
LPs: 10/12-inch
CAPITOL.......5-10 83
LIBERTY.......5-10 81-82
U.A.......5-10 80

DAYTON, Dan
Singles: 7-inch
JENKL (3290 "Skylab").......4-6 74

DAYTON, David, & Colos
Singles: 7-inch
LOMAR (704 "I Gotta Have Love") 10-15 64

DAYTON, Jerry
Singles: 7-inch
EPIC.......4-8 64

DAYTONAS
Singles: 7-inch
AMY.......10-20 65

DAYTONES
Singles: 7-inch
JUBILEE.......5-10 63

DAYTONS
Singles: 7-inch
NORGOLDE (101 "King of Broken Hearts").......200-300 59

DAYTONS
Singles: 7-inch
DAYTON.......8-10

DAYTRIPPERS
Singles: 7-inch
AMM (005 "You Cheated").......20-30 66
KARATE (524 "That's Part of the Game").......10-15 66

DAYWINS
Singles: 7-inch
ARWIN (22 "Heartbeat").......10-20 60
D-F (1000 "Thump Thump").......10-20 60s

DAZE OF THE WEEK
Singles: 7-inch
PIECE (1003 "One Night Stand").......6-12

DAZZ BAND R&B '80
Singles: 12-inch
GEFFEN.......4-6 86
MOTOWN.......4-8 80-85
Singles: 7-inch
GEFFEN.......3-4 86
MOTOWN.......3-4 80-85
RCA.......3-4 88
LPs: 10/12-inch
GEFFEN.......5-10 86
MOTOWN.......5-10 80-85
Members: Rob Harris; Michael Calhoun; Kenny Pettus; Ike Wiley; Mike Wiley; Ed Meyers; Skip Martin; Pierre De Mudd; Eric Fearman; Kevin Kendrick; Marlon McClain.
Also see KINSMAN DAZZ

DAZZLE
LPs: 10/12-inch
DELITE.......5-10 79

DAZZLERS
Singles: 7-inch
KNICK.......8-12
LEE (100 "Something Baby").......40-60 58
LEE (102 "Gee Whiz").......40-60 58

D'COCOA, Creme: see CREME D'COCOA

DE LA SOUL LP '89
Singles: 12-inch
TOMMY B.......4-6 89
Singles: 7-inch
TOMMY B.......3-4 89

DEACON & Rock & Rollers
Singles: 7-inch
NAU-VOO (804 "Rockin' on the Moon").......50-100 59
Member: Deacon Gilliland.

DEACONS
Singles: 7-inch
RE-CAR (9004 "Baldie Stomp").......25-35 64
SOMA (1452 "Empty Room").......40-60 65

DEACONS R&B '68
Singles: 7-inch
CAMELOT.......8-10
SHAMA.......10-20 68

DEAD BEATS
Singles: 7-inch
CUE WEST (002 "Can't Go On This Way").......15-25 67

DEAD BOLTS
Singles: 7-inch
COFFIN (9009 "Torture Chamber").......15-25 84
(500 made.)
Picture Sleeves
COFFIN (9009 "Torture Chamber").......15-25 84
(500 made.)
Members: Russ Bell; Dave Wall; Rob Hislop; Stefanie Cassandra Bell.

DEAD BOYS LP '77
Singles: 7-inch
SIRE.......3-5 77-78
SIRE.......5-10 77-78
(Promotional issues only.)
LPs: 10/12-inch
BOMP.......8-10 80
SIRE.......15-25 77-78
Members: Stiv Bators; Jimmy Zero, John Blitz; Cheetah Chrome; Jeff Jizz.
Also see BATORS, Stiv

DEAD KENNEDYS
Singles: 7-inch
ALTERNATIVE TENTACLES.......4-8 83-86
LPs: 10/12-inch
ALTERNATIVE TENTACLES.......10-20 83-86
I.R.S.......10-12 81
VIRUS (45 "Frankenchrist").......30-40
(With Geiger poster.)
Members: Jello Biafra; East Bay Ray; Deron Peligro; Klaus Fluoride.

DEAD MILKMEN LP '87
Singles: 7-inch
ENIGMA.......3-4 87-90
LPs: 10/12-inch
ENIGMA.......5-10 87-90

DEAD ON LP '90
LPs: 10/12-inch
SBK.......5-8 90

DEAD OR ALIVE D&D '84
Singles: 12-inch
EPIC.......4-6 84-86
Singles: 7-inch
EPIC.......3-4 84-89
Picture Sleeves
EPIC.......3-4 84-89
LPs: 10/12-inch
EPIC.......5-10 84-89
Members: Pete Burns; Wayne Hussey.
Also see MISSION
Also see SISTERS of MERCY

DEAD SEA FRUIT
Singles: 7-inch
ATCO.......10-15 67

DEAD WUNZ
Singles: 7-inch
ORLYN (5123 "Drums").......10-20 66

DEADBEATS
Singles: 7-inch
CROQUETTE (201066 "Hungry Monday").......10-15 66

DEADEYE DICK
Singles: 7-inch
ICHIBAN (232 "Prefect Family").......4-6 94
(Colored vinyl.)

DEADLY NIGHTSHADE P&R '76
Singles: 7-inch
PHANTOM.......3-5 76
LPs: 10/12-inch
PHANTOM.......8-10 76

DEADLY ONES
LPs: 10/12-inch
VEE JAY (1090 "It's Monster Surfing Time").......20-35 64

DEAF SCHOOL
LPs: 10/12-inch
W.B.......8-12 77-78

DEAL, Bill P&R '69
(With the Rhondels; with Pleasers; with Big Deals)
Singles: 7-inch
BEACH (1601 "May I").......25-35 60s
BUDDAH.......4-6 71-72
CHESLICK.......4-8
COLLECTABLES.......3-4 80s
ERIC.......3-5 70s
HERITAGE.......4-8 68-70
MALA (502 "Don't Put Me Down").15-25 64
POLYDOR.......4-6 70-73
RED LION.......3-5 79
ROLL CALL ("Lucious").......15-20
(No selection number used.)
Picture Sleeves
HERITAGE (812 "I've Been Hurt") 10-15 69
HERITAGE (812 "Swingin' Tight") .10-15 69
LPs: 10/12-inch
HERITAGE (35003 "Vintage Rock").......15-20 69
HERITAGE (35006 "Best of Bill Deal & the Rondells").......15-20 69
RHINO.......5-10 86
Members: Bill Deal; Jeff Pollard; Mike Kerwin; Ken Dawson; Ronny Rosenbaum; Bob Fisher; Don Quisenburry; Ammon Tharp.
Also see SOUL, Jimmy

DEAL, Don C&W '79
Singles: 7-inch
CAPITOL.......4-8 63
CHALLENGE.......4-8 68
DONJIM.......3-5 79
ERA.......10-15 57-58
MGM.......4-8 64
SAND.......4-6 69

DEAL, Harry, & Galaxies
Singles: 7-inch
ATLANTIC.......3-6 70
COMPANION.......5-10
ECLIPSE.......3-5 70-82
ETIQUETTE.......10-20 65-66
JUBILEE.......8-12 66
LAURIE.......5-10 63
PETAL.......5-10 64
SSS INT'L.......4-6
LPs: 10/12-inch
ECLIPSE.......5-10 82
Also see SONICS / Wailers / Galaxies

DEAL, Kenneth
Singles: 7-inch
PEACOCK.......10-20 62

DEALERS
Singles: 7-inch
BIG BUNNY.......4-8 66
DEAL (999 "This Rock Is Rollin' ") 40-60

DEAN, Al
(Al Dean & All Stars)
Singles: 7-inch
BOP-TEX.......5-8
KIK-R.......10-15 67
WARRIOR.......15-25 59

DEAN, Alan P&R '52
Singles: 78 rpm
LONDON.......3-5 51
MGM.......3-5 51-56
RAMA.......4-6 56-57
Singles: 7-inch
LONDON.......5-10 51
MGM.......4-8 51-56
RAMA.......5-10 56-57

DEAN, Berna: see BERNA-DEAN

DEAN, Bill
Singles: 7-inch
CORAL.......5-10 62

DEAN, Billy C&W '90
Singles: 7-inch
CAPITOL/SBK.......3-4 90-91
LPs: 10/12-inch
CAPITOL/SBK.......5-8 91
Also see NELSON, Willie, & Billy Dean

DEAN, Bob
Singles: 7-inch
ARCADE.......10-15 68
SUMMIT.......8-12 64

DEAN, Bobby
Singles: 7-inch
CHESS (1673 "Wild Over Rock & Roll").......25-40 57
CHESS (1710 "Go Mr. Dillon").......20-30 58
PROFILE (4006 "It's a Fad").......20-30 59

DEAN, Charles
Singles: 7-inch
BENTON (103 "Itchy").......150-200 58

DEAN, Danny
Singles: 7-inch
DOLLY.......10-15

DEAN, David
Singles: 78 rpm
PEACOCK.......10-15 54
Singles: 7-inch
PEACOCK.......15-25 54
Also see ROBINSON, Fention / David Dean's Combo

DEAN, Debbie P&R '61
(With the Petites; with Paulette Singers)
Singles: 7-inch
MOTOWN (1007 "Don't Let Him Shop Around").......25-35 61
MOTOWN (1014 "Itsy Bity Pity Love").......15-25 62
MOTOWN (1025 "Everybody's Talking About My Baby").......20-30 62
TREVA (223 "Take My Hand").......10-15 66
V.I.P. (25044 "Why Am I Lovin' You").......100-200 68
Picture Sleeves
MOTOWN (1025 "Everybody's Talking About My Baby").......50-100 62

DEAN, Donnie
Singles: 7-inch
APT.......4-8 65

DEAN, Eddie C&W '48
(With the Frontiersmen; with Cort Johnson)
Singles: 78 rpm
CAPITOL.......4-8 51-52
CORAL.......4-8 52
CRYSTAL.......5-10 48
SAGE & SAND.......4-8 54-55
Singles: 7-inch
CAPITOL.......5-10 51-52
CORAL.......5-10 52
SAGE & SAND.......5-10 54-55
LPs: 10/12-inch
CRICKET.......5-10
CROWN.......10-20 60s
DESIGN.......10-20 60s
KING (686 "Favorites of Eddie Dean").......30-40 60
SAGE (1 "Greatest Westerns").......25-50 56
SAGE (5 "Hi-Country").......25-50 57
SAGE (16 "Hillbilly Heaven").......20-30 61
SHASTA.......8-12 74
SOUND (603 "Greatest Westerns").......25-50 56
SUTTON.......10-20
TIARA.......5-10
WFC.......5-10 76
Also see WILLING, Foy, Eddie Dean & His Riders of the Purple Sage

DEAN, Elvis
Singles: 7-inch
LARK.......3-5 77

DEAN, Frank
Singles: 7-inch
TREND.......5-10 58

DEAN, Hannah
Singles: 7-inch
COLUMBIA.......5-8 60

DEAN, Hazell D&D '83
(Hazel Dean)
Singles: 12-inch
QUALITY.......4-6 84
TSR.......4-6 83
Singles: 7-inch
LONDON.......3-5 76

DEAN, James
(With Bob Romeo)
Singles: 7-inch
ROMEO (129 "Ad-Lib Jam Session").......15-25 57
Picture Sleeves
ROMEO (129 "Ad-Lib Jam Session").......50-75 57
LPs: 10/12-inch
SANDY HOOK (2103 "Rare Broadcast Recordings").......15-20 84
(Picture disc.)
Also see MANTOVANI
Also see MOONEY, Art
Also see PERKINS, Tony / James Dean

DEAN, Jerry
Singles: 7-inch
CREOLE (1002 "Walking in My Sleep").......40-60

DEAN, Jimmy C&W '53
(Jimmie Dean)
Singles: 78 rpm
COLUMBIA.......5-10 57
4 STAR.......5-10 54
MERCURY.......4-8 56
Singles: 7-inch
CASINO.......3-5 76
CHURCHILL.......3-4 83
COLUMBIA (40000 thru 43000 series, except 42175).......5-10 57-66
COLUMBIA (42175 "Big John").......10-12 61
(Dean says: "At the bottom of this mine lies one hell of a man.")
COLUMBIA (42175 "Big Bad John").......4-8 61
(Dean says: "At the bottom of this mine lies a big, big man." Note slight title change.)
COLUMBIA (45000 & 46000 series)..3-5 74
4 STAR (1600 series).......10-15 54
4 STAR (1700 series).......5-8 59
KING.......4-6 64
MERCURY.......5-10 56
RCA.......3-6 66-71
Picture Sleeves
COLUMBIA (Except 41025).......5-10 59-66
COLUMBIA (41025 "Little Sandy Sleighfoot").......10-20 57
EPs: 7-inch
COLUMBIA.......8-12 57
LPs: 10/12-inch
ACCORD.......5-10 82
BRYLEN.......5-10
CASINO.......5-10 76
COLUMBIA (1025 thru 2500 series).......10-25 57-66
(Monaural.)
COLUMBIA (8000 & 9000 series).......10-25 61-68
(Stereo. With "CS" prefix.)
COLUMBIA (9200 series).......5-10
(With "PC" prefix.)
COLUMBIA (10000 series).......6-10 73
COLUMBIA SPECIAL PRODUCTS.......5-10
CROWN.......10-15 60s
CUSTOM.......5-10
GRT.......5-10 77
GUEST STAR.......8-10 60s
HARMONY.......8-12 60-69
KING (686 "Favorites of Jimmy Dean").......25-35 60
LA BREA (8014 "Bummin' Around with Jimmy Dean").......20-30
MERCURY (20319 "Jimmy Dean Sings His Television Favorites").......15-25 57
PICKWICK.......5-10 70s
PICKWICK/HILLTOP.......10-12 65
PREMIER.......5-10
RCA.......8-12 67-71
SPIN-O-RAMA.......8-10 60s
WING.......8-12 64
Also see SOME OF CHET'S FRIENDS

DEAN, Jimmy / Luke Gordon
LPs: 10/12-inch
PREMIER.......10-15 60s
SPIN-O-RAMA.......10-15 60s

DEAN, Jimmy / Johnny Horton
LPs: 10/12-inch
STARDAY.......15-20 65
Also see HORTON, Johnny

DEAN, Jimmy / David Houston / Warner Mack / Autry Inman
LPs: 10/12-inch
DIPLOMAT.......10-15 60s
Also see HOUSTON, David
Also see INMAN, Autry
Also see MACK, Warner

DEAN, Jimmy / Marvin Rainwater
LPs: 10/12-inch
MOUNT VERNON.......5-10
PREMIER (9054 "Nashville Showtime").......5-10

DEAN, Jimmy / Marvin Rainwater / Rusty Evans
LPs: 10/12-inch
ALMOR.......5-10 60s
Also see EVANS, Rusty
Also see RAINWATER, Marvin

DEAN, Jimmy / Stoneman Family
LPs: 10/12-inch
WYNCOTE 5-10 62

DEAN, Jimmy, & Dottie West
Singles: 7-inch
RCA 3-5 71
LPs: 10/12-inch
RCA 10-20 70
Also see DEAN, Jimmy
Also see WEST, Dottie

DEAN, Joanna
Singles: 7-inch
KENT 5-10 59

DEAN, Junior
Singles: 7-inch
MIKE (7328 "Chick Chick") 100-200 58

DEAN, Larry
Singles: 7-inch
BALBOA 5-10
BRUNSWICK 5-10 58
JUNIOR 5-10 60

DEAN, Larry *C&W '89*
Singles: 7-inch
USA 3-4 89

DEAN, Lee
Singles: 7-inch
MANCO 4-8 62

DEAN, Lenny, & Rockin' Chairs
Singles: 7-inch
RECORTE (512 "Girl of Mine") 30-35 59
Also see ROCKIN' CHAIRS

DEAN, Lonnie
Singles: 7-inch
KING (6234 "Navajo") 10-20 68

DEAN, Merlin
Singles: 7-inch
BANGAR 5-10 60s
Also see CASTAWAYS

DEAN, Paul *LP '89*
LPs: 10/12-inch
COLUMBIA 5-8 89

DEAN, Ricky
Singles: 7-inch
DEL-FI 4-8 62

DEAN, Ritchie
Singles: 7-inch
IMPERIAL 5-10 63
SWIRL 5-10 61
TOWER 5-10 65-66

DEAN, Russell
LPs: 10/12-inch
METROMEDIA 8-10 71

DEAN, Terri
Singles: 7-inch
LAUREL 10-15 59
LAURIE 5-10 59
MADISON 5-10 61

DEAN, Tommy
Singles: 7-inch
VEE JAY 5-10 60

DEAN, Tony
Singles: 7-inch
JUBILEE 4-6 69
MANHATTAN 4-8 66
Session: Davie Allan.
Also see ALLAN, Davie

DEAN, Wally
Singles: 7-inch
ARTIC (102 "Rockin' with Rosie") 30-45 59
ARTIC (103 "Saddle Up a Satellite") 35-50 59
ARTIC (65221 "Drinkin' Wine Spo-Dee-O-Dee") 10-15 60
GLOBE (238 "Cool, Cool Daddy") 35-50 59

DEAN, William
Singles: 7-inch
D-TOWN 3-4 85

DEAN & DEL-TONES
Singles: 7-inch
PYRAMID 12-18 66

DEAN & JEAN *P&R '63*
Singles: 78 rpm
EMBER (1048 "We're Gonna Get Married") 25-50 58
Singles: 7-inch
EMBER 5-10 58-62
RUST 5-8 63-65
Members: Welton Young; Brenda Lee Jones.
Also see JONES, Brenda

DEAN & MARC *P&R '59*
Singles: 7-inch
BULLSEYE (1025 "Tell Him No") 10-20 59
BULLSEYE (1026 "Beginning of Love") 10-20 59
CHECK MATE (1008 "Boogie-Woogie Twist") 15-25 61
HICKORY 5-10 63-65
MAY 5-10 63
Members: Dean Mathis; Marc Mathis.
Also see BROTHERS
Also see NEWBEATS

DEAN BROTHERS
Singles: 7-inch
PILGRIM 3-5 76-79
LPs: 10/12-inch
PILGRIM 8-10 76
Members: John Dean; Robert Dean; Jeff Steele; Jimmy Johns.

DEANE, Christopher
Singles: 7-inch
SIDEWALK 10-15 66

DEANE, Debbie: see DEAN, Debbie

DEANE, Eddie V.
Singles: 7-inch
CHARGER 5-8 66
SELECT 5-8 63

DEANE, Janet
(With the Skyliners)
Singles: 7-inch
GATEWAY (719 "Another Night Alone") 20-30
MASTODON (101 "Another Night Alone") 4-8
(Colored vinyl.)
Also see SKYLINERS

DEANE, Shelbra *R&B '76*
Singles: 7-inch
CASINO 3-5 76-77

DEANNA
(Deanna McClary)
EPs: 7-inch
JEREMIAH (1007 "Deanna") 5-10 80

DEANS
Singles: 7-inch
LAURIE (3114 "Little White Gardenia") 15-20 61
MOHAWK (114 "My Heart Is Low") 20-30 60
MOHAWK (119 "Humpty Dumpty") 10-20 60
MOHAWK (126 "It's You") 30-50 61
STAR MAKER (1928 "Oh Little Star") 100-200 63
STAR MAKER (1931 "Chills, Chills, Chills") 40-60 63
TIN PAN ALLEY (316 "I'm Gonna Love You") 100-200
TIN PAN ALLEY (319 "Pretty Nola") 50-75
Also see LONNIE & CAROLLONS / Deans

DEANS, Rich
Singles: 7-inch
NEW EUROPE 5-10 81
Picture Sleeves
NEW EUROPE 5-10 81

DEARBORN, Billie
Singles: 7-inch
DYNO VOICE (223 "Down") 5-8 66
LHI (1210 "Firday's Child") 5-8 68

DEARDORFF, Danny
Singles: 7-inch
MAIDEN VOYAGE 3-5 81

DEARLY BELOVEDS
Singles: 7-inch
COLUMBIA 5-10 66-67
SPLITSOUND (5 "Flight 13") 10-20 67
Also see BELOVED ONES
Also see INTRUDERS
Also see QUINSTRELLS

DEASY, Mike
LPs: 10/12-inch
CAPITOL 8-10 73
SPARROW 8-10 76

DEATH ANGEL *LP '88*
LPs: 10/12-inch
ENIGMA 5-8 88

DEATH CULT: see CULT

DEATON, Billy
Singles: 7-inch
SHANNON 4-8 63
SMASH 4-8 61-62
TNT 5-10 60-61

DEATON, Frank
(Franklin Deaton; with the Mad Lads)
Singles: 7-inch
ALTA (2000 "I Was Framed") 15-25
BALLY (1042 "Just a Little Bit More") 40-60 57
BANNER 10-20 60
TARGET 8-12 60

DEAUVILLE, Ronnie *LP '57*
Singles: 7-inch
ERA (1056 "Laura") 10-15 58
IMPERIAL (5559 "King of Fools") 8-12 59
Picture Sleeves
ERA (1056 "Laura") 20-40 58
LPs: 10/12-inch
ERA (20002 "Smoke Dreams") 20-40 57

DEB, Debbie: see DEBBIE DEB

DEBANAIRS
Singles: 7-inch
B.S. 4-8 67-68

DE BARGE *R&B/LP '82*
(DeBarges)
Singles: 12-inch
GORDY 4-6 85-86
Singles: 7-inch
GORDY 3-4 85-86
STRIPED HORSE 3-4 87
Picture Sleeves
GORDY 3-4 85-86
STRIPED HORSE 3-4 87
LPs: 10/12-inch
GORDY 5-10 81-86
MOTOWN 5-8 80s
Members: Eldra BeBarge; Marty DeBarge; James DeBarge; Bunny De Barge.
Also see DE BARGE, Bunny
Also see DE BARGE, EL
Also see JONES, Quincy, James Ingram, Al B. Sure, El DeBarge & Barry White
Also see KING DREAM CHORUS & Holiday Crew
Also see SWITCH

DE BARGE, Bunny *R&B/LP '87*
Singles: 12-inch
GORDY 4-6 87
Singles: 7-inch
GORDY 3-4 87
LPs: 10/12-inch
MOTOWN 5-8 87
Also see DE BARGE

DE BARGE, Chico *P&R/R&B/LP '86*
Singles: 12-inch
MOTOWN 4-6 86-87
Singles: 7-inch
MOTOWN 3-4 86-88
Picture Sleeves
MOTOWN 3-4 86
LPs: 10/12-inch
MOTOWN 5-10 86-87

DE BARGE, El *R&B/D&D '85*
(With DeBarge)
Singles: 12-inch
GORDY 4-6 86-87
Singles: 7-inch
GORDY 3-4 81-87
LPs: 10/12-inch
GORDY 5-10 81-87
Also see DE BARGE

DEBELAIRES
Singles: 7-inch
LECTRA 4-8 62

DE BERRY, Jimmy
Singles: 78 rpm
SUN 100-200 53
Singles: 7-inch
SUN (185 "Take a Little Chance") 250-350 53
Also see JIMMY & WALTER

DEBBIE, A.: see A. DEBBIE

DEBBIE & DARNELS
Singles: 7-inch
COLUMBIA 10-15 62
Members: Dorothy Yutenkas; Joan Yutenkas; Marie Broncotti.
Also see TEEN DREAMS

DEBBIE & Teen Dreams: see TEEN DREAMS

DEBBIE DEB *R&B/D&D '84*
Singles: 12-inch
JAMPACKED 4-6 85
SUNNYVIEW 4-6 84
Singles: 7-inch
JAMPACKED 3-4 84-87
Also see TRINERE / Freestyle / Debbie Deb

DEBLANC *R&B '76*
Singles: 7-inch
ARISTA 3-5 75-76
Members: Ralph DeBlanc; Linda Carriere.
Also see DYNASTY
Also see STARFIRE

DE 'BONAIRS
Singles: 78 rpm
PING 75-125 56
Singles: 7-inch
PING (1000 "Lanky Linda") 200-250 56
PING (1001 "Say a Prayer for Me") 200-300 56

DEBONAIRES
Singles: 7-inch
MASKE (804 "Every Other Day") 20-30 59

DEBONAIRES
Singles: 78 rpm
GEE (1008 "Won't You Tell Me") 20-30 56
HERALD (509 "Darlin' ") 40-50 57
Singles: 7-inch
DORE (526 "Every Once in a While") 40-60 59
DORE (592 "Every Once in a While") 15-25 61
DORE (702 "Every Once in a While") 10-20 64
DORE (712 "Everybody's Movin' ") 8-10 61
GEE (1008 "Won't You Tell Me") 40-60 56
GEE (1054 "We'll Wait") 10-20 59
HERALD (509 "Darlin' ") 40-50 57
(Previously issued as by the Five Debonaires.)
Also see FIVE DEBONAIRES

DEBONAIRES
Singles: 7-inch
ELMONT (1004 "This Must Be Paradise") 200-300 58

DEBONAIRES
Singles: 7-inch
B&F (1353 "Fools in Love") 50-75 61

DEBONAIRES
(Debonairs)
Singles: 7-inch
GOLDEN WORLD 10-20 64-66
SOLID HIT (101 "I'm in Love Again") 20-40 67
SOLID HIT (102 "Loving You Takes All My Time") 250-350 67
Members: Joyce Vincent; Telma Hopkins.
Also see ADORABLES
Also see DAWN

DEBONAIRES *C&W '85*
Singles: 7-inch
MTM 3-4 85

DEBONAIRES
Singles: 7-inch
GALAXY 5-8
RITE (785 "Never Mistaken") 5-10

DEBONAIRS
Singles: 78 rpm
COMBO (129 "Bill Collector") 50-75 57
Singles: 7-inch
COMBO (129 "Bill Collector") 75-100 57
COMBO (149 "Cause of a Bad Romance") 50-75 58

DEBONAIRS
Singles: 7-inch
CAROL ANN 15-20 62
SOUTHSIDE 4-8 62

DEBONAIRS
Singles: 7-inch
FENWAY (1712 "The Holly Lynn") 4-8 60s

DEBONAIRS
Singles: 7-inch
TOBIN 8-12
WINTER 10-15

DE BORD, Sharon
Singles: 7-inch
SHAMLEY 4-6

DE BREE, Peter, & Wanderers
Singles: 7-inch
FORTUNE (193 "My Bucket's Got a Hole in It") 10-20 58
FORTUNE (200 "Hey, Mr. Presley") 25-30 58

DEBRIS
LPs: 10/12-inch
STATIC DISPOSAL (0000 "Debris") 50-100 76
Members: John Gregg; Richard Davis; Charles Ivy.

DEBS
Singles: 78 rpm
BRUCE 30-40 55
CROWN 10-20 55
Singles: 7-inch
BRUCE (129 "Shoo Doo-Be Doo") 40-50 55
CROWN (153 "If You Were Here Tonight") 20-30 55

DEBS
Singles: 78 rpm
KEEN (34003 "Johnny Darling") 10-20 57
Singles: 7-inch
KEEN (34003 "Johnny Darling") 10-20 57

DEBS
Singles: 7-inch
JOSIE 10-15 58

DEBS
Singles: 7-inch
DOUBLE L 5-10 63
ECHO 8-12 61

DEBS
Singles: 7-inch
SQUALOR (1314 "Stars in the Sky") 40-60 62

DEBS
Singles: 7-inch
MERCURY 10-15 65-66

DEB-TONES
Singles: 7-inch
RCA 8-12 58-59

DE BURGH, Chris *P&R '83*
Singles: 7-inch
A&M 3-5 75-87
Picture Sleeves
A&M 3-4 86-87
LPs: 10/12-inch
A&M 8-10 76-86

DEBUTANTES
Singles: 78 rpm
SAVOY 10-20 56
Singles: 7-inch
SAVOY (1191 "Just Leave It to Me") 15-25 56

DEBUTANTES
Singles: 7-inch
KAYO (928 "Going Steady") 100-200 58

DEBUTANTES
Singles: 7-inch
GAIL & RICE (101 "Little Latin Lupe Lou") 10-15
LUCKY ELEVEN (237 "Love Is Strange") 8-12
STANDOUT (601 "Shake a Tail Feather") 10-15

DEBUTS
Singles: 7-inch
ATCO (6591 "If I Cry") 10-15 68
SCUDDER (101 "Gettin' Mellow") 20-30 68

DECADES
Singles: 7-inch
DAYTONE (1306 "Dance Forever") 15-25 63
DAYTONE (6403 "Lonely Drummer") 15-20 64
ERA (3174 "I'm Gonna Dance") 10-15 67
LADY LUCK ("On Sunset") 50-75 66
(Selection number not known.)
LADY LUCK (101 "I'm Gonna Dance") 50-75 66

DECADES
Singles: 7-inch
JANIE (10646 "Strange World") 15-25 64

DECADES
Singles: 7-inch
AVENUE D (0001 "Please Say It Isn't So") 30-50 80
(Clear vinyl. Reportedly 10 made.)
AVENUE D (0001 "Please Say It Isn't So") 20-30 80
(Orange vinyl. Reportedly 20 made.)
AVENUE D (0002 "Teenage Roses") 8-10 81
AVENUE D (0003 "To Make a Long Story Short") 10-20 82
(Yellow/orange vinyl. Reportedly 60 made.)
DAYTONE 5-10
GREAT SCOTT (1002 "Pledging My Love") 15-25
Members: Tom Jones; Dennis Nagel; Jeff Beckman; Bobby Cannizzaro; Chris Mahoney; Marc Scott.
Also see SUBWAY SERENADERS

DE CAMPO, Vinnie
Singles: 7-inch
REV 8-10 59

DE CARLO, Don
Singles: 7-inch
LITTLE TOWN (290 "Sweet Cora Lee") 8-12 62
Also see DINO

DE CARO, Nick *P&R/LP '69*
Singles: 7-inch
A&M 3-5 67-69
LPs: 10/12-inch
A&M 5-10 69
BLUE THUMB 5-10 77

DE CASTRO, Gregory
Singles: 12-inch
AZRA (210 "Island's Embrace") 10-15 83
(Picture disc. 500 made.)
Singles
ERIKA (109 "Love Letter to Malvinas") 8-12 83
(8-inch picture disc.)
ERIKA (109 "Love Letter to Malvinas") 15-25 83
(Heart-shaped picture disc. 150 made.)
ERIKA (109 "Love Letter to Malvinas") 10-15 83
(Square picture disc. 500 made.)

DE CASTRO, Peggy
Singles: 7-inch
SPOTLITE 5-15 62
Also see DE CASTRO SISTERS

DE CASTRO SISTERS *P&R '54*
(With Don Costa's Orchestra; with Joe Reisman's Orchestra & Chorus)
Singles: 78 rpm
ABBOTT 4-8 54-56
RCA 4-8 56
TICO 4-8 52
Singles: 7-inch
ABC-PAR 5-10 58
ABBOTT 10-20 54-56
CAPITOL 5-10 60-61
RCA 8-12 56
TICO 10-15 52
ZODIAC 3-5 77
LPs: 10/12-inch
ABBOTT (5002 "DeCastro Sisters") 40-60 56
CAPITOL 15-25 60-61
20TH FOX 8-15 65
Members: Peggy DeCastro; Babette DeCastro; Cherie DeCastro.
Also see COSTA, Don, Orchestra
Also see DE CASTRO, Peggy
Also see RAVENSCROFT, Thurl
Also see REISMAN, Joe, & His Orchestra

DE CASTRO SISTERS / Hugo Winterhalter & His Orchestra
EPs: 7-inch
RCA (DJ-51 "I Never Meant to Hurt You") 10-20 56
(Promotional issue only. Not issued with cover.)
Also see DE CASTRO SISTERS
Also see WINTERHALTER, Hugo, & His Orchestra

DECEMBER, Bobby
Singles: 7-inch
ORCHESTRA (100 "Bye Bye Baby") 20-30 60s
ORCHESTRA (209 "Invasion") 10-20 60s

DECEMBER'S CHILDREN
Singles: 7-inch
CAPITOL 5-10 67
COLUMBIA 5-10 66
LIBERTY 5-10 70
TWIN 5-10
WORLD PACIFIC 4-8 68-69

DECEMBER'S CHILDREN
Singles: 7-inch
MAINSTREAM (728 "Sweet Talking Woman") 8-12 70

LPs: 10/12-inch
MAINSTREAM (6128 "December's Children")..........20-30 70
Members: Bill Petti; Craig Balzer; Bruce Balzer.

DECEMBER'S CHILDREN LTD.
Singles: 7-inch
DOMESTIC SOUND (123 "Signed D.C.")..........40-50 67

DE CESARE, Dom
(With the Impalas; De Cesare)
Singles: 7-inch
FRATERNITY..........4-6 75
EPs: 7-inch
METRO-MEDIA (5203 "Don DeCesare")..........10-15 65

DECISIONS
Singles: 7-inch
TOPPER (1013 "Tears, Tears")..........15-25 66

DECISIONS
Singles: 7-inch
SUSSEX..........3-5 71

DECKERS
Singles: 7-inch
YEADON (101 "Sincerely with All My Heart")..........50-75 58
YEADON (1041 "Sincerely with All My Heart")..........10-20

DECO R&B '83
Singles: 12-inch
QWEST..........4-6 84-85
Singles: 7-inch
QWEST..........3-4 84-85
LPs: 10/12-inch
QWEST..........5-10 84
Members: Philip Ingram; Zane Giles.
Also see PAYNE, Scherrie
Also see SWITCH

DE COSTA, Barbara
Singles: 7-inch
RIC-TIC (103 "The One in Your Arms")..........15-25 62

DECOU, Art
(Art Decoy)
Singles: 7-inch
FORM..........5-10 59
STARLA..........15-25
SUTTER..........8-12

DECOYS
Singles: 7-inch
AANKO (1005 "I Want Only You")..........300-400 64
TIMES SQUARE (9 "I Want Only You")..........15-25 64
VELVET (1001 "Listen to Me")..........100-200 64
Also see BELAIRS / Decoys

DECOYS / Four Fellows
Singles: 7-inch
ALJON (1261 "Memories")..........20-30 72
Also see DECOYS

DEDICATED FOLLOWERS: see GEARS / Emeralds / Dedicated Followers / Internal Canitery Sin

DEDICATIONS
Singles: 7-inch
AVENUE D (0008 "Why Don't You Write Me")..........5-10 83
(Black vinyl.)
AVENUE D (0008 "Why Don't You Write Me")..........10-20 83
(Red vinyl. Reportedly 150 made.)
AVENUE D (0009 "Crazy for You")..........10-20 83
(Blue vinyl. Reportedly 200 made.)
BELL (611 "Toy Boy")..........5-10 65
C&A (506 "Shining Star")..........150-200 63
CARD (2001 "Why Don't You Write Me")..........25-35 62
CLIFTON (86 "Flower of Love")..........4-8 90
CLIFTON (92 "For Your Love")..........4-8 91
(Colored vinyl.)
JASON SCOTT..........5-10
RAMARCA (602 "Someone to Love")..........10-20 63
WHITE WHALE (340 "Teardrops")..........20-30 70
Members: Freddie; Charlie; Tony; Marty; Lou; Mike Paquette; Joe Burke; John Mallon; Ronni Petri; Steve Petri.
Also see ADMIRATIONS

DEE, Billy
(With the Superchargers)
Singles: 7-inch
LE CAM (127 "Moon Maid")..........10-20 64
WESTFORD (101 "Curb Service")..........10-20 63

DEE, C. / F. York
Singles: 7-inch
HIT (43 "My Coloring Book")..........4-6

DEE, Charlie
Singles: 7-inch
USA (101 "World on the Moon")..........40-50

DEE, Dave
Singles: 7-inch
BELL..........4-6 70
Also see CHRISTIE, Lou
Also see DEE, Dave, Dozy, Beaky, Mick & Tich

DEE, Dave, Dozy, Beaky, Mick & Tich LP '67
Singles: 7-inch
ATLANTIC..........3-4 83
FONTANA..........5-10 66-67
IMPERIAL..........4-8 67-68
LPs: 10/12-inch
FONTANA (27567 "Greatest Hits")..........20-30 67
(Monaural.)
FONTANA (67567 "Greatest Hits")..........25-30 67
(Stereo.)
IMPERIAL (12402 "Time to Take Off")..........20-25 68
Also see DEE, Dave
Also see DOZY, BEAKY, MICK & TICH

DEE, Davey, & Mudcats
Singles: 7-inch
EMBER (1055 "Puddle Jumper")..........10-20 59

DEE, Davey, & Redcoats
Singles: 78 rpm
KAPP (163 "Calypso")..........10-15 56
Singles: 7-inch
KAPP (163 "Calypso")..........15-25 56

DEE, David
Singles: 7-inch
DOT (16085 "Mr. D")..........10-20 60
VANESSA..........4-6

DEE, Donna
(With the Clouds; with Penetrators)
Singles: 7-inch
ABC-PAR (10296 "Television")..........10-15 62
RAMADA (501 "The More I See Him")..........25-50 61

DEE, Duane C&W '67
Singles: 7-inch
ABC..........3-5 74
CAPITOL..........4-6 67-68
CARTWHEEL..........3-5 71-72
LPs: 10/12-inch
CAPITOL..........8-12 68

DEE, Fern
Singles: 7-inch
EMBER..........15-20 58

DEE, Frankie
(With the Mastertones; Frank Detrano)
Singles: 7-inch
ABCO (1002 "Walking in the Rain")..........10-20
FUTURE (1001 "I Made a Boo Boo")..........8-12 58
FUTURE (1003 "Let's Go Steady")..........30-50 57
RCA (7276 "Shake It Up Baby")..........30-50 58
TEE JAY (333 "Darling Arlene")..........500-750 61
20TH FOX (146 "Swinging in a Hammock")..........15-25 59

DEE, Georgie, & Ladds
Singles: 7-inch
KON-TI-KI ("I Can Go on Like This")..........150-250
(No selection number used.)

DEE, Gina
Singles: 7-inch
HOME of the BLUES..........5-10 62

DEE, Gordon C&W '84
Singles: 7-inch
SOUTHERN TRACKS..........3-4 84

DEE, Gregory, & Avanties: see AVANTIES

DEE, Jackie
(Jackie DeShannon)
Singles: 78 rpm
GONE (5008 "I'll Be True")..........50-100 57
Singles: 7-inch
GONE (5008 "I'll Be True")..........30-50 57
LIBERTY (55148 "Buddy")..........25-45 58
Also see DE SHANNON, Jackie

DEE, James, & A Piece of the Action
(With the Primettes)
Singles: 7-inch
ENRICA (1020 "Jealous Over Love")..........15-25 62

DEE, Jay R&B '74
(Earl Nelson)
Singles: 7-inch
W.B...........3-5 74
Also see NELSON, Earl

DEE, Jean
Singles: 7-inch
COLUMBIA..........5-10 60
DECCA..........5-10 59
KING..........4-8 63
PHILLIPS INT'L..........5-10 61

DEE, Jerry & Gino
Singles: 7-inch
DAREM..........4-8 64

DEE, Jimmy P&R '58
(With the Offbeats; with Universals)
Singles: 78 rpm
DOT (15664 "Henrietta")..........50-75 57
TNT (148 "Henrietta")..........75-125 57
Singles: 7-inch
CUTIE..........4-8 63
DOT (15664 "Henrietta")..........15-25 57
DOT (15721 "You're Late Miss Kate")..........20-30 58
HEAR ME..........5-10
INNER-GLO (105 "Guitar Pickin' Man")..........75-100 57
SCOPE (103 "I Ain't Givin' Up Nothin' ")..........15-25 59
TNT (148 "Henrietta")..........25-50 57
TNT (152 "You're Late Miss Kate")..........50-75 58
TNT (161 "I Feel Like Rockin' ")..........40-60 59
TAPER (101 "I Ain't Givin' Up Nothin' ")..........30-50 59
V-TONE..........15-25 62

DEE, Joe, & Top Hands
Singles: 7-inch
PAT RICCIO..........5-10 62
Also see TREMONTS

DEE, Joey P&R/R&B/LP '61
(With the Starliters; with Starlites; with New Starliters; with the Hawk)
Singles: 7-inch
ABC..........3-4 73
BONUS (7009 "Lorraine")..........25-50 63
CANEIL..........4-6
JANUS..........4-8 70s
JUBILEE..........5-10 66-67
LITTLE (813 "Lorraine")..........1000-2000 60
ROULETTE..........10-20 61-65
ROULETTE GOLDEN GOODIES..........3-4
SCEPTER (1210 "Face of an Angel")..........15-25 60
SUNBURST..........3-5 73
TONSIL RECORDS..........4-8 70
VASELINE HAIR TONIC (12 "Learn to Dance the Peppermint Twist")..........15-25 62
(Special products issue from Chesebrough-Ponds.)
Picture Sleeves
BONUS (7009 "Lorraine")..........50-75 63
ROULETTE..........15-25 62
LPs: 10/12-inch
ACCORD..........5-10 82
JUBILEE (8000 "Hitsville")..........15-25 66
ROULETTE..........15-25 61-63
SCEPTER (503 "The Peppermint Twisters")..........15-25 62
Members: Joey Dee; Tony Scuito; John Yanic; Vinnie Correo; Ralph Fazio; Roger Freeman; David Brigati; Joe Pesci; Willie Davis; Carlton Latimore.
Session: Ronettes.
Also see HAWK
Also see HI-FIVES
Also see RASCALS
Also see RONETTES

DEE, Joey, & Starliters / Dion
Singles: 7-inch
MONUMENT ("YaYa Twist")..........8-12 61
(No selection number used. Promotional issue only.)
Also see DION

DEE, Joey, & Starliters / Randy Andy & Candymen
EPs: 7-inch
DIPLOMAT (66-2 "The Girl I Walk to School")..........10-20 62
LPs: 10/12-inch
DIPLOMAT (66-2 "Come Twist with Me")..........15-25 62
Also see ANDY, Randy, & Candymen
Also see DEE, Joey

DEE, Joey, & Lois Lee
Singles: 7-inch
STEADY (37004 "Storybook Children")..........3-6 70s
Also see DEE, Joey
Also see LEE, Lois

DEE, Joey, & Top Hands
Singles: 7-inch
PAT RICCIO (1105 "Honky Tonk Guitar")..........10-20 62

DEE, Johni
Singles: 7-inch
GUSTO..........3-4 82

DEE, Johnny P&R '57
(John D. Loudermilk; "Featuring Joe Tanner on Guitar")
Singles: 78 rpm
COLONIAL (430 "Sittin' in the Balcony")..........25-50 57
Singles: 7-inch
COLONIAL (430 "Sittin' in the Balcony")..........15-20 57
(Has "45 RPM" on left side of label.)
COLONIAL (430 "Sittin' in the Balcony")..........10-15 57
(Has "45 RPM" on right side of label.)
COLONIAL (430 "Sittin' in the Balcony")..........8-12 57
(No "45 RPM" on label. Reads "Dist. by AM-PAR Record Corp.")
COLONIAL (435 "1000 Concrete Blocks")..........15-20 57
DOT..........5-10 58
Picture Sleeves
COLONIAL (430 "Sittin in the Balcony")..........30-40 57
Also see LOUDERMILK, John D.
Also see TANNER, Joe

DEE, Johnny
Singles: 7-inch
ALLSTAR..........4-8 62

DEE, Johnny, Trio
Singles: 78 rpm
JUBILEE..........5-10 52
Singles: 7-inch
JUBILEE..........8-15 52

DEE, Kathy C&W '63
Singles: 7-inch
B-W (619 "If I Never Get to Heaven")..........4-8 63
U.A...........4-8 63-64
Picture Sleeves
B-W (619 "If I Never Get to Heaven")..........10-20 63
LPs: 10/12-inch
B-W..........10-20 63
GUEST STAR..........10-20 64

DEE, Kiki P&R '71
(Kiki Dee Band)
Singles: 7-inch
LIBERTY..........4-6 68
MCA..........3-5 73-77
POSSE..........3-4 81
RCA..........3-4 81
RARE EARTH..........3-5 71
ROCKET..........3-5 73-79
TAMLA..........3-6 70
WORLD PACIFIC..........4-8 66
Picture Sleeves
TAMLA..........3-6 70
LPs: 10/12-inch
LIBERTY (7600 series)..........15-20 69
LIBERTY (10000 series)..........5-10 81
MCA/ROCKET..........8-12 73-74
RCA..........5-10 81
ROCKET..........8-10 77-78
TAMLA..........15-20 70
Also see JOHN, Elton, & Kiki Dee

DEE, Larry
Singles: 7-inch
LAGREE..........5-10 61

DEE, Lenny P&R/LP '55
Singles: 78 rpm
DECCA..........3-4 56-61
Singles: 7-inch
DECCA..........3-5 56-61
EPs: 7-inch
DECCA..........4-8 59
LPs: 10/12-inch
DECCA..........5-15 55-70
Also see HALEY, Bill / Lionel Hampton / Sal Salvador Quartet / Lenny Dee

DEE, Little Jimmy
Singles: 7-inch
INFINITY..........5-10 61

DEE, Lola P&R '54
(With Stubby & the Buccaneers)
Singles: 78 rpm
BALLY..........4-8 57
MERCURY..........3-5 54-56
WING..........5-10 55-56
Singles: 7-inch
BALLY..........5-10 57
MERCURY..........5-10 54-56
WING..........10-20 55-56

DEE, Lola, & Rusty Draper
Singles: 78 rpm
MERCURY..........3-6 56
Singles: 7-inch
MERCURY..........5-10 56
Also see DEE, Lola
Also see DRAPER,Rusty

DEE, Lynn, & Statics
Singles: 7-inch
MANTIS (101 "Little Girl's Dream")..........100-200
Also see STATICS

DEE, Marcy: see MARCY DEE

DEE, Mary
Singles: 7-inch
CHALLENGE..........4-8 61
LILLY..........4-8 62

DEE, Mercy: see MERCY DEE

DEE, Neecy D&D '85
Singles: 12-inch
TNT..........4-6 85

DEE, Nicky
Singles: 7-inch
EBBTIDE..........4-8 63

DEE, Ricky
(With the Embers)
Singles: 7-inch
NEWTOWN..........4-8 62
PALETTE..........5-10 60

DEE, Ronnie
Singles: 7-inch
BACK BEAT (522 "Action Packed")..........75-100 62
WYE..........10-15 61
Also see DAWSON, Ronnie

DEE, Sandra
Singles: 7-inch
DECCA..........5-10 60-61
Picture Sleeves
DECCA..........15-25 60

DEE, Sonny
Singles: 7-inch
ARCADE..........15-20 54
KAPP (421 "Here I Stand")..........25-35 61
Session: Regents.
Also see REGENTS

DEE, Tommy P&R '59
(With the Mellotones)
Singles: 7-inch
A&M..........3-4 80
CHALLENGE..........8-10 60
CREST (1067 "Angel of Love")..........8-12 59
K-ARK..........3-5 70
PIKE..........5-10 61
SIMS..........10-15 66
Also see COVINAS
Also see SANFORD, Sandy

DEE, Tommy, with Teen Tones & Orchestra / Teen Tones P&R '59
Singles: 7-inch
CREST (1057 "Three Stars")..........15-25 59
(Flip, *I'll Never Change*, is also credited to Teen Tones here and to Carol Kay and the Teen-Aires on copies below. The track is exactly the same on both discs.)

DEE, Tommy, with Carol Kay & Teen-Aires / Carol Kay & Teen-Aires P&R '59
Singles: 7-inch
CREST (1057 "Three Stars")..........15-25 59
(Monaural.)
CREST (1057 "Three Stars")..........35-50 59
(Stereo.)
Also see DEE, Tommy
Also see KAYE, Carol

DEE, Toni
Singles: 7-inch
BRUNSWICK..........8-10 64
RINGO..........4-8 65

DEE, Tony
(With the Pageants; Tony I. Dee)
Singles: 7-inch
ARLEN (731 "Saturday Romance")..........25-50 63
KAYSAL (103 "Good Lovin' ")..........10-20 60s
DU-WELL (101 "Saturday Romance")..........100-200 61
Also see PAGEANTS

DEE & DI
Singles: 7-inch
KEEN..........10-15 60-61

DEE & DON
Singles: 7-inch
A-BET (9429 "I Can't Stand It")..........10-15 68

DEE & JOE
Singles: 7-inch
JUBILEE (5670 "I Found a Love")..........10-15 69

DEE & LOLA
Singles: 7-inch
JOSIE..........5-8 66

DEE & PATTY
Singles: 78 rpm
MERCURY..........20-30 57
Singles: 7-inch
D (1020 "Sweet Lovin' Baby")..........25-35 58
MERCURY (71252 "First Date")..........25-35 57

DEE & TEE
Singles: 7-inch
CORAL (62507 "Something's Comin' ")..........10-15 66

DEE & YEOMEN
Singles: 7-inch
BELL (633 "Why Why Why")..........10-15 65
WOLFF (101 "Say Baby")..........20-30

DEE CALS
Singles: 7-inch
CO ED (1960 "Stars in the Blue What Should I Do")..........60-100 59
MAYHAMS (1960 "Stars in the Blue What Should I Do")..........75-125 61

DEE JAN & ELGINS: see DE JAN & ELGINS

DEE JAY & MICKIE
Singles: 7-inch
ALTO..........5-10 60

DEE JAY & RUNAWAYS P&R '66
Singles: 7-inch
COULEE (109 "Love Bug Crawl")..........25-35 64
DEE JAY..........3-6 82
IGL (100 "Jenny Jenny")..........100-150 65
IGL (103 "Peter Rabbit")..........20-40 66
SMASH..........5-10 66
SONIC (132 "Don't You Ever")..........25-50 66
STONE (45 "Don't You Ever")..........25-50 66
Picture Sleeves
DEE JAY..........4-8 82
(With insert)
Members: Denny Storey; John Senn; Gary Lind; Terry Klein; Bob; Tom.
Also see CHEVELLES
Also see KLEIN, Terry, with Dee Jay & Runaways
Also see STOREY, Denny
Also see TEMPTORS

DEE JAYES
Singles: 7-inch
HIGHLAND (1031 "Bongo Beach Party")..........15-20 62

DEE-JAYS
(Dee-Jay's)
Singles: 7-inch
SONATA (1100 "You Took Your Love from Me")..........200-300 62

DEEE-LITE P&R/LP '90
LPs: 10/12-inch
ELEKTRA..........5-8 90

DEELE R&B '83
Singles: 7-inch
SOLAR..........3-4 83-88

LPs: 10/12-inch
SOLAR ... 5-10 84-88
Members: Kenny "Babyface" Edmonds; Antonio "L.A." Reid; Darnell Bristol; Kevin Roberson; Carlos Green.
Also see BABYFACE
Also see MANCHILD

DEE-LITES
Singles: 7-inch
BRITTON (Colored vinyl) ... 8-12

DEEP, The
LPs: 10/12-inch
PARKWAY (7051 "Psychedelic Moods") ... 200-400 66
Members: Members: David Bromberg; Rusty Evans; Mark Barkan.
Also see FREAK SCENE

DEEP PURPLE *P&R/LP '68*
Singles: 12-inch
MERCURY ... 4-8 87
Singles: 7-inch
GRP ... 3-5 73
MERCURY ... 3-4 84-87
TETRAGRAMMATON ... 5-10 68-69
W.B. ... 3-6 70-73
W.B./PURPLE ... 3-4 74-75
Picture Sleeves
MERCURY ... 3-5 85
TETRAGRAMMATON ... 8-15 68
W.B./PURPLE ... 3-5 74-75
EPs: 7-inch
W.B./PURPLE ... 10-20 74
(Juke box issue.)
LPs: 10/12-inch
MERCURY ... 6-12 84-88
PASSPORT ... 5-10 88
PORTRAIT ... 5-10 82
RCA ... 5-8 90
SCEPTER/CITATION ... 8-10 72
TETRAGRAMMATON (102 "Shades of Deep Purple") ... 20-30 68
TETRAGRAMMATON (107 "Book of Taliesyn") ... 20-30 69
TETRAGRAMMATON (119 "Deep Purple") ... 20-30 69
W.B. (Except 3000 series) ... 15-25 70-74
W.B. (3000 series) ... 5-10 77
W.B./PURPLE ... 10-15 74-80
Members: Ritchie Blackmore; Jon Lord; Ian Paice; Rod Evans; Nick Simper; Roger Glover; Ian Gillan; David Coverdale; Tommy Bolin.
Also see BLACKMORE'S RAINBOW
Also see BOLIN, Tommy
Also see CAPTAIN BEYOND
Also see COVERDALE, David
Also see GILLAN, Ian
Also see GLOVER, Roger
Also see LORD, Jon
Also see PAICE, ASHTON & LORD
Also see TRAPEZE
Also see WHITESNAKE

DEEP RIVER BAND
LPs: 10/12-inch
ERECT ... 5-10 82

DEEP RIVER BOYS *P&R '48*
Singles: 78 rpm
BEACON ... 20-30 52-54
BLUEBIRD (10676 "I Was a Fool to Let You Go") ... 20-40 40
BLUEBIRD (10847 "Bird in the Hand") ... 20-40 40
BLUEBIRD (11178 "My Heart at Thy Sweet Voice") ... 20-40 41
BLUEBIRD (11217 "I Wish I Had Died in My Cradle") ... 20-40 41
JAY-DEE ... 15-25 54
LANG-WORTH ... 10-25
(16-inch transcriptions, made in the '40s.)
PILOTONE ... 10-25 46
RCA ... 10-25 40-53
VICTOR ... 15-25 40
VIK ... 10-15 56
Singles: 7-inch
BEACON (104 "Sleepy Little Cowboy") ... 40-60 54
BEACON (9143 "Truthfully") ... 40-60 52
BEACON (9146 "All I Need Is You") ... 40-60 52
GALLANT ... 10-15 59
JAY-DEE (788 "No One Else Will Do") ... 25-35 54
MICHELLE ... 4-8 65
RCA (0078 "Free Grace") ... 30-50 50
(Colored vinyl.)
RCA (5268 "Biggest Fool") ... 20-30 53
SEECO ... 10-15 60
VIK (0205 "All My Love Belongs to You") ... 15-20 56
VIK (0224 "You're Not to Old") ... 15-20 56
WAND ... 5-10 61
Picture Sleeves
GALLANT (2001 "I Don't Know Why") ... 15-25 59
EPs: 7-inch
CAMDEN (341 "Presenting the Deep River Boys") ... 30-50 56
WALDORF MUSIC HALL (113 "Songs of Jubilee") ... 50-75 56
(May also be shown as *Spirituals and Jubilees.*)
WALDORF MUSIC HALL (114 "Songs of Jubilee") ... 50-75 56
(Black vinyl. Has picture of group on cover.
WALDORF MUSIC HALL (114 "Spirituals and Jubilees") ... 75-100 56
(Colored vinyl. No picture of group on cover.)
LPs: 10/12-inch
CAMDEN (303 "Presenting the Deep River Boys") ... 40-60 56
CAPITOL (6050 "Presenting Harry Douglas and the Deep River Boys") ... 20-40
(Canadian.)
QUE (104 "Midnight Magic") ... 50-75 57
WALDORF MUSIC HALL (108" Songs of Jubilee") ... 75-125 56
(10-inch LP. Label gives title as *Spirituals and Jubilees.*)
"X" (1019 "Deep River Boys") ... 60-80 56
Members: Harry Douglas; Vernon Gardner; George Lawson; Ed Ware; Carter Wilson.
Also see BARLOW, Dean, & Crickets / Deep River Boys

DEEP SIX
Singles: 7-inch
LIBERTY ... 4-8 65-66
SAW-MAN ... 5-10 65
SOFT ... 4-8 65
LPs: 10/12-inch
LIBERTY ... 15-20 66

DEEP TONES
Singles: 78 rpm
CORAL (65062 "The Night You Said Goodbye") ... 50-100 51

DEEP VELVET *R&B '73*
Singles: 7-inch
AWARE ... 3-5 73

DEEPEST BLUE
Singles: 7-inch
BLUE-FIN (102 "Somebody's Girl") ... 10-20 66

DEEPWATER REUNION
(Deepwater)
Singles: 7-inch
JERRAL ... 4-8 69
RCA ... 4-8 68
LPs: 10/12-inch
DEEPWATER ... 8-10
JERRAL (1009 "Deepwater Water Reunion") ... 20-25 69
Also see CADILLAC SALLY
Also see RANEY, Barbara

DEER
LPs: 10/12-inch
STREET SWEEPER ... 8-10 80-81

DEER, John *C&W '70*
(John Deer Company)
Singles: 7-inch
ROYAL AMERICAN ... 3-5 70

DEERFIELD
LPs: 10/12-inch
FLAT ROCK ("Nil Desperandum") ... 75-125 71
(Selection number not known.)

DEERFIELD, Johnny
(With the Del-ites)
Singles: 7-inch
CAPITOL ... 5-10 60
DELL ... 4-8 63
TOWER ... 4-8 66

DEES, Ashley
(Melodies from Ashley Dees)
Singles: 7-inch
FRANKIE STARR ... 5-10

DEES, Rick *P&R/R&B '76*
(With His Cast of Idiots; Rick & Cast of Idiots)
Singles: 12-inch
RSO ... 4-8 78
STAX ... 4-8 78
Singles: 7-inch
ATLANTIC (89481 "I Wanna Be Elvis") ... 4-8 85
FRETONE (040 "Disco Duck") ... 5-10 76
RSO (Except 860) ... 3-5 76-77
RSO (860 "He Ate Too Many Jelly Donuts") ... 8-10 77
RSO/POLYDOR ... 3-5 76-77
STAX ... 3-5 78
Picture Sleeves
ATLANTIC ... 3-4 86
STAX ... 3-5 78
LPs: 10/12-inch
ATLANTIC ... 5-10 85
RSO ... 8-10 77

DEES, Sam *R&B '73*
Singles: 7-inch
ATLANTIC ... 3-5 73-75
CHESS ... 3-5 71
LOLO ... 4-6 69
POLYDOR ... 3-4 78
SSS INT'L (732 "I Need You Girl") ... 15-25 68
LPs: 10/12-inch
ATLANTIC ... 5-10 75

DEES, Sam, & Bettye Swann
Singles: 7-inch
BIG TREE ... 3-5 76
Also see DEES, Sam
Also see SWANN, Bettye

DEES, Stephen
Singles: 7-inch
RCA ... 3-5 77
LPs: 10/12-inch
RCA ... 8-10 77

DEE-VINES
(With Quentin Solano Orchestra)
Singles: 7-inch
LANO (2001 "I Believe") ... 35-50 60
(White label.)
LANO (2001 "I Believe") ... 25-40 60
(Red label.)
RELIC (514 "I Believe") ... 5-10 64

DEF LEPPARD *LP '80*
Singles: 12-inch
MERCURY ... 4-8 80-87
(Promotional only.)
Singles: 7-inch
MERCURY ... 3-4 80-89
EPs: 7-inch
BLUDGEON RIFFOLA ... 10-15 78
Picture Sleeves
MERCURY (Except 811-215-7) ... 3-4 80-89
MERCURY (811-215-7 "Photograph") ... 4-6 83
LPs: 10/12-inch
MERCURY (Except 832-962) ... 5-10 80-88
MERCURY (832-962 "Hysteria") ... 25-35 87
(Picture disc.)
Members: Joe Elliott; Pete Willis; Rick Allen; Steve Clark; Phil Collen; Rick Savage; Vivian Campbell
Also see DIO, Ronnie

DE-FENDERS
Singles: 7-inch
WORLD PACIFIC (382 "Wild One") ... 10-20 63
LPs: 10/12-inch
DEL-FI (1242 "Drag Beat") ... 20-30 63
WORLD PACIFIC (1810 "The De-Fenders Play the Big Ones") ... 20-30 63
(Black vinyl.)
WORLD PACIFIC (1810 "The De-Fenders Play the Big Ones") ... 45-60 63
(Colored vinyl.)

DE-FENDERS / Deuce Coupes
Singles: 7-inch
DEL-FI (4226 "Little Deuce Coupe") ... 10-20 63
Also see DE-FENDERS
Also see DEUCE COUPES

DEFENDERS
Singles: 7-inch
PARKWAY ... 8-10 64
REALM ... 8-10 64

DEFIANT 4
Singles: 7-inch
DELTA (2195 "Away from Home") ... 25-30

DEFIANT ONES
Singles: 7-inch
ESSAR (1000 "Deep Six") ... 20-30 61
ESSAR (1002 "Defiant Drums") ... 20-30 61
REAL FINE (834 "Defiant Drums No. 2") ... 15-25 62

DEFIANTS
Singles: 7-inch
BARONET (5 "Surfer's Twist") ... 15-25 62

DEFIANTS
Singles: 7-inch
STUDIO CITY (10442 "Bye Bye Johnny") ... 20-25 66

DEFINITIVE ROCK CHORALE
Singles: 7-inch
PHILIPS ... 4-8 67-68

DE FRANCIS, Nick
Singles: 7-inch
DWAIN (815 "Don't Ask") ... 5-10 60

DE FRANCO FAMILY *P&R/LP '73*
(Featuring Tony DeFranco)
Singles: 7-inch
20TH FOX (Except 2214) ... 3-5 73-74
20TH FOX (2214 "We Belong Together") ... 4-8 75
Picture Sleeves
20TH FOX ... 3-5 73-74
LPs: 10/12-inch
20TH FOX ... 8-12 73-74
Members: Tony DeFranco; Benny DeFranco; Merlina DeFranco; Marisa DeFranco; Nino DeFranco.

DEGARMO & KEY BAND
LPs: 10/12-inch
LAMB & LION ... 5-10 78-80

DE GRANT, Tony
Singles: 7-inch
EXCELLO ... 5-10 60

DE GRINDA, Joe
Singles: 7-inch
BOFUZ (19694 "Smokestack Lightning") ... 25-35 69

DeHAVEN, Penny *C&W '69*
Singles: 7-inch
IMPERIAL ... 3-6 69-70
MAIN STREET ... 3-4 82-84
MERCURY ... 3-5 73-74
STARCREST ... 3-5 76
U.A. ... 3-5 70-72
LPs: 10/12-inch
MAIN STREET ... 5-8 84
U.A. ... 8-12 72
Also see BOXCAR WILLIE & Penny DeHaven
Also see REEVES, Del, & Penny DeHaven
Also see STARR, Penny

DEHONEY, Jimmy
Singles: 7-inch
NABOR ... 10-20

DE-ICERS
Singles: 7-inch
DE-ICER (100 "After Five") ... 15-25 57

DEJA *P&R/R&B/LP '87*
Singles: 7-inch
VIRGIN ... 3-4 87-88
Picture Sleeves
VIRGIN ... 3-4 87-88
LPs: 10/12-inch
VIRGIN ... 5-10 87-88
Members: Curt Jones; Starleana Young.
Also see AURRA
Also see SLAVE

DEJA VOODOO
Singles: 12-inch
MIDNIGHT (112 "Too Cool to Live, Too Smart to Die") ... 5-10 85
Singles: 7-inch
DV (01 "Monsters in My Garage") ... 4-6 82
Picture Sleeves
DV (01 "Monsters in My Garage") ... 10-20 82
DV (01 "The Original Mosters in My Garage") ... 4-6 82
(Note title variation, which is only on sleeve.)
LPs: 10/12-inch
OG (4 "Cemetary") ... 10-15 84
(With black and white cover.)
OG (4 "Cemetary") ... 8-10 84
(With color cover.)
OG (11 "Swamp of Love") ... 8-10 86
OG (14 "Worst of Deja Voodoo") ... 8-10 87
OG (18 "Big Pile of Mud") ... 8-10 88

DEJA VU
Singles: 7-inch
CAPITOL ... 3-5 76-77
LPs: 10/12-inch
CAPITOL ... 8-10 76-77

DE JAN & ELGINS
Singles: 7-inch
LESSIE (0099 "That's My Girl") ... 3000-5000 60

DE JOHN SISTERS *P&R '54*
Singles: 78 rpm
COLUMBIA ... 8-12 57
EPIC ... 4-8 54-56
OKEH ... 4-8 53
Singles: 7-inch
COLUMBIA ... 10-15 57
EPIC ... 8-12 54-56
OKEH ... 10-15 53
SUNBEAM ... 8-12 59
U.A. ... 4-8 60
LPs: 10/12-inch
U.A. ... 15-25 60
Members: Julie DeGiovanni; Dux DeGiovanni.

DEJONAY, Zena *D&D '84*
Singles: 12-inch
TVI ... 4-6 84

DEK, Tony
Singles: 7-inch
DE ROSE ... 4-8 61

DEKKER, Desmond, & Aces *P&R/LP '69*
Singles: 7-inch
UNI ... 3-6 69-70
LPs: 10/12-inch
UNI ... 20-25 69

DEKLE, Mike *C&W '84*
Singles: 7-inch
NSD ... 3-4 84

DE KNIGHT, Jimmy
(With the Knights of Rhythm)
Singles: 7-inch
APT (25034 "Rock Around the Clock") ... 5-10 59
BANDBOX ... 8-12 61
PEAK (105 "Rock Around the Clock") ... 8-12 59

DEL AMITRI *LP '90*
LPs: 10/12-inch
A&M ... 5-8 90

DEL & ESCORTS
Singles: 7-inch
ROME (103 "Baby Doll") ... 20-30 61
Also see EARLS
Also see ESCORTS

DEL & RIC
Singles: 7-inch
LOOK (5001 "I'm Looking for Someone") ... 20-30 64
Members: Del Trolinder; Ric Matlock.

DELACARDOS *P&R '61*
Singles: 7-inch
ELGEY (1001 "Letter to a School Girl") ... 50-75 59
IMPERIAL (5992 "On the Beach") ... 10-15 63
SHELL (308 "Dream Girl") ... 15-25 61
SHELL (311 "Love Is the Greatest Thing") ... 15-25 62
U.A. (276 "I Got It") ... 10-15 60
U.A. (310 "Hold Back the Tears") ... 10-15 61

DELACARDOS
Singles: 7-inch
ATLANTIC ... 5-10 66-67
DIMENSION ... 10-15 64

DELAFOSE, John
LPs: 10/12-inch
MAISON de SOUL ... 8-10 90

DEL-AIRES
Singles: 7-inch
CORAL (62370 "Elaine") ... 20-25 63
CORAL (62404 "My Funny Valentine") ... 20-25 63
CORAL (62419 "Arlene") ... 30-40 64
DELSEY (302 "It Took a Long Time") ... 30-40 65
Also see RONNIE & DELAIRES

DEL-AIRS
Singles: 7-inch
M.B.S. (001 "While Walking") ... 15-25 60

DEL-AIRS
Singles: 7-inch
ARRAWAK (1003 "I'm Lonely") ... 15-20 62

DEL AMOS
Singles: 7-inch
NIKKO (703 "She's So Wonderful") ... 30-50 59

DELANCEYS
Singles: 7-inch
ABC-PAR (10353 "High Voltage") ... 10-20 62

DELANEY & BONNIE *LP '69*
(Delaney & Bonnie and Friends)
Singles: 7-inch
ATCO ... 3-6 70-72
COLUMBIA ... 3-5 72-73
ELEKTRA ... 4-6 69
INDEPENDENCE ... 5-10 67
STAX ... 4-8 68-69
LPs: 10/12-inch
ATCO ... 15-25 70-72
COLUMBIA ... 15-25 72
ELEKTRA ... 15-25 69
GNP ... 15-25 70
STAX ... 15-25 69
Members: Delaney Bramlett; Bonnie Bramlett.
Also see BAD HABITS
Also see BRAMLETT, Bonnie
Also see BRAMLETT, Delaney
Also see CLAPTON, Eric
Also see ROGERS, Dann
Also see SHINDOGS
Also see WHITLOCK, Bobby

DE LA SOUL
LPs: 10/12-inch
TOMMY BOY ... 5-8 89-91

DELATONES
Singles: 7-inch
TNT (9028 "Teenagers Love") ... 250-500 60

DELBERT & GLEN *P&R '72*
Singles: 7-inch
CLEAN ... 3-5 72-73
LPs: 10/12-inch
CLEAN (601 "Subject to Change") ... 15-20 72
Members: Delbert McClinton; Glen Clark.
Also see McCLINTON, Delbert
Also see PRINE, John / Daryl Hall & John Oates / Barnaby Bye / Delbert & Glen

DEL-BROOKS
Singles: 7-inch
KID (101 "Darling Barbara") ... 100-150 58

DELCADES
Singles: 7-inch
J.W. FOX ... 4-8 62

DEL CADES
Singles: 7-inch
UNITED SOUND ASSOCIATES (175 "Two to Fall in Love") ... 15-25 64
Picture Sleeves
UNITED SOUND ASSOCIATES (175 "Two to Fall in Love") ... 25-50 64

DEL CAPRIS
(Del-Capris)
Singles: 7-inch
AMBER (854 "Up on the Roof") ... 10-15 66
CATAMOUNT (115 "Teardrops Follow Me") ... 8-12 66
(Black vinyl.)
CATAMOUNT (115 "Teardrops Follow Me") ... 10-20 66
(Colored vinyl.)

DEL CAPRIS
Singles: 7-inch
KAMA SUTRA ... 5-10 67
RONJERDON (39 "Hey Little Girl") ... 10-15 67

DEL CAPRIS
Singles: 7-inch
ALMONT (304 "Teresa") ... 30-50 63

DEL CHONTAYS
Singles: 7-inch
STEELTOWN (2467 "Baby I Need You") ... 20-30
Session: Emmett Smith.
Also see EXCITING INVICTAS

DEL-CHORDS
Singles: 7-inch
COOL (5816 "Marsha-Mellow") ... 200-300 58

DEL-CHORDS
Singles: 7-inch
JIN (126 "Help Me") ... 30-50 60
(Has tiny bubbles in the vinyl.)
JIN (126 "Help Me") ... 10-20 60
(No bubbles in vinyl.)
KANE (5593 "Over the Rainbow") ... 75-125 59

DEL-CHORDS
Singles: 7-inch
IMPALA (215 "Everybody's Gotta Lose Someday") ... 25-50 63
MR. GENIUS (401 "Everybody's Gotta Lose Someday") ... 50-100 62
MR. GENIUS (1028 "Your Mommy Lied to Your Daddy") ... 40-60 60s
Members: Dave Bupp; Buddy King.
Also see MAGNIFICENT MEN

DEL CONTE, Dave
Singles: 7-inch
MERRI (6003 "Lonely Surfer") 15-25 63

DELCOS
(With Buddy Kay's Band; Delco's)
Singles: 7-inch
EBONY (01 "Arabia") 100-150 63
SHOWCASE (2501 "Arabia") 40-60 64
(White label. Promotional issue only.)
SHOWCASE (2501 "Arabia") 40-50 64
(Blue label.)
SHOWCASE (2501 "Arabia") 30-40 64
(Green label.)
SHOWCASE (2501 "Arabia") 15-25 64
(Red label.)
SHOWCASE (2515 "Still Miss You So") 20-30 64
SOUND STAGE 7 (2501 "Arabia") .15-25 65
SOUND STAGE 7 (2515 "Still Miss You So") 20-40 65
Members: Glenn Madison; Ralph Woods; Otis Smith; Richard Greene; Pete Woodard.
Also see MADISON, Glenn

DEL COUNTS
(With Al Browne's Orchestra)
Singles: 7-inch
ROSE (22 "Lone Stranger") 75-125 60
Also see BROWNE, Al

DEL COUNTS
Singles: 7-inch
APA 8-12 73
APEX (77058 "What Is the Reason") 20-30 67
(First issue.)
HAND 8-12 72
MAPLE LEAF 8-12 74
MAR-BIL (109 "Ain't Got the Time") 10-20 68
MOON SOUND 8-12 74
SOMA (1430 "Bird Dog") 15-25 66
SOMA (1465 "What Is the Reason") 15-25 67
Picture Sleeves
MOON SOUND 8-12 74

DELEGATES
(Kool Gents)
Singles: 78 rpm
VEE JAY (243 "Mother's Son") 25-50 57
Singles: 7-inch
VEE JAY (243 "Mother's Son") 25-50 57
Members: Dee Clark; Johnny Carter; John McCall; Ted Long; Doug Brown.
Also see CLARK, Dee
Also see EL DORADOS
Also see KOOL GENTS

DELEGATES / Big Jay McNeely
Singles: 78 rpm
VEE JAY (212 "The Convention") ..20-30 57
Singles: 7-inch
VEE JAY (212 "The Convention") ..20-30 57
Also see DELEGATES
Also see McNEELY, Big Jay

DELEGATES
Singles: 7-inch
AURA 4-8 65
WORLD PACIFIC 4-8 65-66
LPs: 10/12-inch
AURA (3002 "The Delegates") 15-20 65
WORLD PACIFIC 15-20 65-66
Member: Billy Larkin.

DELEGATES *P&R '72*
Singles: 7-inch
MAINSTREAM (5525 "Convention '72") 5-10 72
MAINSTREAM (5530 "Richard Nixon Faces the Issues") 5-10 72
LPs: 10/12-inch
MAINSTREAM (100 "The Delegates") 10-15 73

DELEGATES OF SOUL
Singles: 7-inch
UPLOOK (51470 "I'll Come Running Back") 15-25 60s

DELEGATION *P&R/R&B/LP '79*
Singles: 12-inch
SHADYBROOK 4-8 77
Singles: 7-inch
MCA 3-5 76
MERCURY 3-4 80-81
SHADYBROOK 3-4 77-79
LPs: 10/12-inch
MERCURY 5-10 80-81
SHADYBROOK 5-10 79
Members: Ray Patterson; Ricky Bailey; Bruce Dunbar.

DE LEON, Sir Lon
Singles: 7-inch
DU WELL 4-8 61

DEL-FIS
("Del-Fi's Combo - Vocal By Pete Bosquez")
Singles: 7-inch
CADETTE (8010 "The Magic of Your Love") 50-75 60s
1001 (101 "Let's Start All Over") 200-300 63
Also see DEL-PHIS
Also see HANKS, Mike

DELFONICS
Singles: 7-inch
FLING (727 "There They Go") 25-35 62
Member: Carlton Lee.

DELFONICS *P&R/R&B '68*
Singles: 7-inch
CAMEO 4-8 67
COLLECTABLES 3-4 80s
FLASHBACK 3-5 70s
MOON SHOT 4-8 68
PHILLY GROOVE 3-6 68-73
ROULETTE 3-5 73
LPs: 10/12-inch
KORY 8-10 76
PHILLY GROOVE 10-20 68-74
POOGIE 5-10 81
COLLECTABLES 6-8 88
Members: Major Harris; William Hart; Wilbert Hart; Randy Cain; Richie Daniels.
Also see HARRIS, Major

DEL 4s
Singles: 7-inch
ZENITH 8-12 64

DEL FUEGOS *LP '85*
Singles: 7-inch
CZECH 4-8 82
SLASH 3-4 85-87
Picture Sleeves
CZECH 5-10 82
SLASH 3-4 86
LPs: 10/12-inch
RCA 5-8 89
SLASH 5-10 85-87

DELI-CADOS
Singles: 7-inch
PMP (4979 "Now I've Confessed") 500-1000 60
(Identification number shown since no selection number is used.)

DELICATES
Singles: 7-inch
CELESTE 15-25 59
CHALLENGE 5-10 64-65
DEE DEE (677 "My Pillow") 15-25 61
ROULETTE 10-15 61
UNART (2024 "Ringa Ding") 15-20 59
SOUL TOWN 10-20
U.A. 10-15 60-61
UNART (2017 "Black & White Thunderbird") 15-20 59
Also see ANGELS
Also see SOUL SURFERS / Delicates

DELICATESSEN
Singles: 7-inch
GNP 4-8 67

DELICATO, Paul *C&W '75*
Singles: 7-inch
ARTISTS of AMERICA 3-5 75-76
LPs: 10/12-inch
A.V.I. 6-10 77-78
ARTISTS of AMERICA 8-10 76

DELIGHTS
Singles: 7-inch
NITE (1034 "My One Desire") 30-35 61

DELIGHTS
Singles: 7-inch
ARLEN 10-15 64
DELAWARE 10-20 65

DE-LIGHTS
Singles: 7-inch
AD-LIB (346 "I'm Comin' Home") 25-50 62
(Previously issued as by the Del Knights.)
Also see DEL KNIGHTS

DELIGHTS / Planotones: see PLANOTONES with Prof. LaPlano / Delghts

DELILAH
Singles: 7-inch
SHIRLEY 4-8 64

DELILAH
LPs: 10/12-inch
ABC 5-10 79

DE LISA, Pete
(With the Johnny Mastrio Quintet)
Singles: 7-inch
FRANKIE 5-10 62
Also see CLASSMATES
Also see MASTRIO, Johnny

DELIVERANCE *P&R '80*
Singles: 7-inch
COLUMBIA 3-4 80

DELKATES
Singles: 7-inch
ROULETTE 4-8

DEL KNIGHTS
Singles: 7-inch
UNART (2008 "Everything") 10-15 59

DEL KNIGHTS
Singles: 7-inch
SHERYL (339 "I'm Comin' Home") 50-100 61
(Reissued as by the De-Lights.)
Also see DE-LIGHTS

DEL KNIGHTS
Singles: 7-inch
BRONKO (502 "Speedy Gonzales") 10-15 62
CHANCELLOR (1075 "Whoever You Are") 15-25 61

DELL, Danny
(With the Trends)
Singles: 7-inch
GUARANTEED (220 "I'll Wait") 10-15 61
ROCKIN' (160 "Froggy Went a Courting") 150-200 60
WORLD PACIFIC (824 "Froggy Went a Courting") 100-150 60

DELL, Dicky, & Bing Bongs
(With Sonny Dale Orchestra)
Singles: 7-inch
DRAGON (10205 "Ding-A-Ling-A-Ling-Ding Dong") 75-100 58
Also see TROYS

DELL, Don
(With the Up Starts; with Montereys; with Dominants)
Singles: 7-inch
EAST COAST (102 "Time") 50-75 61
EAST COAST (105 "A Special Love") 75-125 61
ROMAN (2963 "Make Believe Love") 35-55 64

DELL, Evelyn, & Vibrations
Singles: 7-inch
ABC-PAR 10-20 61

DELL, Frank
Singles: 7-inch
VALISE (6900 "He Broke Your Game Wide Open") 10-20
VALISE (6901 "Baby, You've Got It") 10-20

DELL, Jeanie
Singles: 7-inch
JOSIE 15-20 60
RITZ 15-20

DELL, Jimmy
(Jimmy Delbridge)
Singles: 7-inch
PHILIPS 4-8 63
RCA 10-15 58
Also see JIMMY & DUANE

DELL, Joey
Singles: 7-inch
ROULETTE 4-8 62

DELL, Jovan
Singles: 7-inch
BALLY 8-12 58

DELL, Lenny, & Demensions: see DEMENSIONS

DELL, Richie
Singles: 7-inch
KING (5888 "King Lover") 10-15 64

DELL, Roy
Singles: 7-inch
ESCO 8-12 59

DELL, Tony
Singles: 7-inch
KING (5766 "My Girl") 25-35 63

DELL, Wailin' Bill
Singles: 7-inch
OJ (1003 "You Gotta Be Loose") 150-250 56

DELL & ESCORTS
Singles: 7-inch
SYMBOL (913 "You Don't Love Me") 300-500 60

DELL BOYS / Shallows
Singles: 7-inch
FORLIN 5-10 63

DELLA SISTERS
Singles: 7-inch
URANIA 8-12 59

DEL-LARDS
Singles: 7-inch
STOP 8-12

DEL-LARKS
Singles: 7-inch
EAST WEST (116 "Remember the Night") 50-75 58
Also see ASHLEY, Tyrone

DEL-LARKS
Singles: 7-inch
QUEEN CITY (2004 "Job Opening") 500-750

DELL-COEDS
Singles: 7-inch
DOT 5-10 62
ENITH 15-20 62

DELL-ITES
Singles: 7-inch
DELL 5-10 63

DELL KINGS
Singles: 7-inch
RENCO 5-10 62

DELL MATES
Singles: 7-inch
FONTANA 4-8 64

DELLORDS
Singles: 7-inch
MIDAS (9 "In Togetherness") 50-75 62

DEL-LOURDS & THE SHADES
Singles: 7-inch
SOLAR (1001 "Alone") 20-30 63
SOLAR (1003 "Gloria") 20-30 63

DELL-RAYS
Singles: 7-inch
BOPTOWN (102 "Pauline") 50-75 58

DELL RAYS
Singles: 7-inch
DICE (479 "DiDi") 20-30

DELLS *R&B '56*
Singles: 78 rpm
VEE JAY (166 "Dreams of Contentment") 50-75 55
VEE JAY (200 series) 20-50 56-57
Singles: 12-inch
ABC 4-6 79
Singles: 7-inch
ABC 3-5 73-78
ARGO (5415 "God Bless the Child") 8-12 62
ARGO (5428 "Eternally") 8-12 62
ARGO (5442 "If It Ain't One Thing It's Another") 5-10 63
CADET 4-8 67-75
CHESS 3-5 73
COLLECTABLES 3-4 80s
MCA 3-4 79
MERCURY 3-5 75-77
OLDIES 45 .... 4-8 60s
PRIVATE I 3-4 84
20TH FOX 3-5 80-82
VEE JAY (166 "Dreams of Contentment") 100-150 55
Note: Vee Jay 134, *Tell the World*, is listed in the following section for DELLS / Count Morris.
VEE JAY (204 "Oh, What a Night") 50-75 56
VEE JAY (230 "Movin' On") 20-40 56
VEE JAY (236 "Why Do You Have to Go") 20-40 57
VEE JAY (251 "Distant Love") 20-40 57
VEE JAY (258 "Pain in My Heart") 20-40 57
VEE JAY (274 "The Springer") 15-25 58
VEE JAY (292 "I'm Calling") 15-25 58
VEE JAY (300 "Wedding Day") 50-75 58
VEE JAY (324 "Dry Your Eyes") 20-40 58
VEE JAY (338 thru 712) 5-15 59-65
LPs: 10/12-inch
ABC 8-10 78
BUDDAH 10-15 69
CADET 10-20 68-75
LOST-NITE 8-12 81
MERCURY 10-15 75-77
PRIVATE I 5-10 84
TRIP 10-12 73
20TH FOX 5-10 80-81
UPFRONT 10-15 68
VEE JAY (1010 "Oh What a Night") 400-500 59
(Maroon label, with thin circular ring.)
VEE JAY (1010 "Oh What a Night") 300-400 59
(Maroon label, with thick circular ring.)
VEE JAY (1010 "Oh What a Night") 100-200 61
(Black label. Monaural.)
VEE JAY (1010 "Oh What a Night") 100-200 61
(Black label. Stereo.)
VEE JAY (1141 "It's Not Unusual") 100-200 65
Members: Johnny Funches; Mike McGill; Marvin Junior; Vern Allison; Johnny Carter.
Also see BUTLER, Jerry, & Betty Everett
Also see CLARK, Dee
Also see EL RAYS
Also see GREENE, Barbara
Also see LEWIS, Barbara
Also see SOUTH, Joe / Dells

DELLS / Count Morris
Singles: 78 rpm
VEE JAY (134 "Tell the World") 100-200 55
Singles: 7-inch
VEE JAY (134 "Tell the World") 400-500 55
(Black vinyl.)
VEE JAY (134 "Tell the World") 700-900 55
(Red vinyl.)
Also see DELLS

DELLS & DRAMATICS *R&B '75*
Singles: 7-inch
CADET 3-5 75
Also see DELLS
Also see DRAMATICS

DELL SATINS: see DEL SATINS

DELLTONES
(Dell-Tones; with Kelly Owens Orchestra)
Singles: 78 rpm
BATON 20-30 55-56
BRUNSWICK 50-75 53
RAINBOW 50-75 54
Singles: 7-inch
BATON (212 "Don't Be Long") 15-25 55
BATON (223 "My Special Love") 15-25 56
BRUNSWICK (84015 "My Heart's on Fire") 100-150 53
RAINBOW (244 "I'm Not in Love with You") 75-100 54

DELLWOODS
Singles: 7-inch
BIG TOP (3127 "Don't Put Onions on Your Hamburger") 10-15 63
EPs: 7-inch
MAD ("She Got a Nose Job") 10-15 62
(Cardboard cutout picture disc, attached to *The Worst of Mad* magazine. Pictures Alfred E. Neuman. No selection number used.)

DELLWOODS / Mike Russo / Jeanne Hayes
LPs: 10/12-inch
BIG TOP (1305 "Mad Twists Rock 'N' Roll") 50-75 63
Also see DELLWOODS
Also see RUSSO, Mike

DELMAR, Eddie
Singles: 7-inch
MADISON (168 "Love Bells") 25-35 61
VEGAS (628 "Garden in the Rain") 10-20 65
Session: Bob Knight Four.
Also see KNIGHT, Bob, Four

DEL-MARS
Singles: 7-inch
ABC-PAR (10426 "That's My Desire") 10-15 63
MERCURY (72244 "Snacky Poo") ...8-12 64

DEL-MINGOS
Singles: 7-inch
LOMAR (702 "Goodnite My Love") 20-30 63

DELMIRAS
Singles: 7-inch
DADE (1821 "Dry Your Eyes") 750-1000 61
Session: Steve Alaimo.
Also see ALAIMO, Steve

DELMIRAS / Sof-Tones
Singles: 7-inch
STOOP SOUNDS (500 "Dry Your Eyes") 100-150 96
(Limited edition. Estimates range from less than 10 to a few dozen made.)
Also see DELMIRAS

DELMONICOS
Singles: 7-inch
AKU (6139 "Teenage Idol") 30-50 63
AKU (6318 "There They Go") 50-75 63
MUSICTONE (6122 "Until You") 15-25 64
Also see GERMAINE, Denise

DELMONICS
Singles: 7-inch
BENGAL (1002 "Come Go with Me") 5-10

DELMORE BROTHERS *C&W '46*
(Delmores)
Singles: 78 rpm
BLUEBIRD 20-40 30s-41
COLUMBIA (15724 "Alabama Lullaby") 25-50 30s
DECCA 10-20 40-48
KING 5-15 43-57
Singles: 7-inch
KING (769 thru 5407) 10-25 51-60
(Black vinyl.)
KING (1023 "I'll Be There") 30-50 51
(Colored vinyl.)
EPs: 7-inch
KING 10-20
LPs: 10/12-inch
COUNTY 5-10
KING (589 thru 785) 30-60 58-62
KING (910 thru 1090) 10-30 64-70
OLD HOMESTEAD 5-8
STARDAY 5-10
Members: Alton Delmore; Rabon Delmore.

DELONGS
Singles: 7-inch
ARTFLOW 8-12

DE LORY, Al *P&R '70*
Singles: 7-inch
CAPITOL 3-6 68-71
CHAAT (1001 "Hot Saki") 5-10
EUREKA 4-8 61
PHI DAN 4-8 65
LPs: 10/12-inch
CAPITOL 5-15 69-70
Also see AVALANCHES

DE-LOS
Singles: 7-inch
CEDAR (302 "Lullabye Serenade") 50-75
Session: Joe Cook.
Also see COOK, Little Joe

DEL-PHIS
Singles: 7-inch
CHECK MATE (1005 "It Takes Two") 100-200 61
Members: Gloria Williamson; Martha Reeves; Annette Beard; Rosalind Ashford.
Also see DEL-FIS
Also see HANKS, Mike
Also see MARTHA & VANDELLAS
Also see VELLS

DELPHS, Jimmy *P&R/R&B '68*
Singles: 7-inch
CARLA (1904 "Dancing a Hold in the World") 100-200 68
CARLA (2535 "Almost") 10-20 67
KAREN 5-10 68

DEL-PRADOS
Singles: 7-inch
LUCKY FOUR (1021 "Oh, Baby") ...30-35 62

DEL PRIS
("By Baby Washington")
Singles: 7-inch
VARBEE (2003 "The Time") 100-150 61
Members: Harold Shields; Bill Cyrus; Jack Derbish; Wilson Rue; Dan Carr.
Also see WASHINGTON, Baby

DEL RAY, Martin *C&W '85*
(With Johnny Cash)
Singles: 7-inch
ATLANTIC 3-4 91
Also see CASH, Johnny
Also see MARTIN, Mike

DELRAYS
Singles: 7-inch
BOPTOWN (102 "Darling I Pray") 30-50 58
JASON SCOTT 4-8

DEL RAYS
Singles: 7-inch
FUTURE (7210 "When We're Alone") 75-125 58
(Identification number shown since no selection number is used.)

DELRAYS
(Del Rays)
Singles: 7-inch
CORD (1001 "Our Love Is True") 3000-4000 58
MOON (110 "Have a Heart") 200-300 59
W.B. (5022 "My Darling") 50-75 58

DEL-RAYS
(Del-Ray's)
Singles: 7-inch
PLANET (52 "Lorraine") 250-350 61

DEL-RAYS
Singles: 7-inch
TAMMY (1020 "Run-Around-Lou") 75-125 61

DEL-RAYS
Singles: 7-inch
SWINGLINE (1800 "Freeze") 10-20 62

DEL RAYS
Singles: 7-inch
TEISLO/DEL RAY (6142 "Wipe Out") 20-30 63

DEL RAYS
Singles: 7-inch
WIDE 5-10 64-66

DEL-RAYS
Singles: 7-inch
ATCO 5-10 65
STAX 5-10 64

DEL RAYS
Singles: 7-inch
R&H (1002 "Night Prowl") 10-20 65

DEL RAYS
Singles: 7-inch
CUCA (68121 "I Feel a Whole Lot Better") 10-20 68

DELRAYS INC.
Singles: 7-inch
SALEM 8-12 65

DEL REYS
Singles: 7-inch
COLUMBIA (41784 "Let's Stay Together") 10-15 60

DEL-REYS
Singles: 7-inch
DELRECO (500 Should I Ever Love Again") 20-30 60

DEL-RHYTHMETTES
Singles: 7-inch
JVB (5000 "I Need Your Love") 40-60 59

DEL-RICOS
Singles: 7-inch
620 .... 10-20 64
GAITY ("Buggin' The Boogie") 40-60 60s
(Selection number not known.)

DEL RIOS
(With the Bearcats)
Singles: 78 rpm
METEOR (5038 "Lizzie") 50-100 56
Singles: 7-inch
METEOR (5038 "Lizzie") 150-250 56

DEL RIOS
(Del Rio's)
Singles: 7-inch
BET..T (7001 "Heavenly Angel") 300-400 62
BIG H (613 "The Vines of Love") 200-300 57
RUST (5066 "Valerie") 20-40 63

DEL-RIOS
Singles: 7-inch
NEPTUNE (108 "I'm Crying") 40-50 59
STAX (125 "There's a Love") 30-40 62
Members: William Bell; David Brown; Melvin Jones; Harrison Austin.
Also see BELL, William
Also see OVATIONS

DEL-RONS
Singles: 7-inch
LAURIE (3252 "Leave Us Alone") .. 10-20 64
Members: Mary Aiese; Sheila Reillie; Carol Drobnicki.
Also see REPARATA

DELRONS
Singles: 7-inch
FORUM (700 "This Love of Ours") 500-750 61

DEL ROYALS
Singles: 7-inch
MINIT (610 "She's Gone") 10-20 61
MINIT (620 "Close to You") 10-20 61
MINIT (637 "I Fell in Love with You") 10-20 61

DEL ROYALS
(Featuring Willie Johnson)
Singles: 7-inch
MERCURY 4-8 69

DEL ROYS
Singles: 7-inch
CAROL (4113 "Love Me Tenderly") 20-30 61
(Rigid disc.)
CAROL (4113 "Love Me Tenderly") 8-12 61
(Flexible disc.)
Members: Ronald Coleman; Ray Pain; Norman Baquie; Cliff Davis.
Also see DELROYS

DELROYS
(Milton Sparks with the Delroys; with Larry Greenwich & Orchestra; Delroy's)
Singles: 78 rpm
APOLLO (514 "Bermuda Shorts") .. 20-40 57
Singles: 7-inch
APOLLO (514 "Bermuda Shorts") .. 15-25 57
SPARKELL (102 "Wise Old Owl") 300-500 59
Members: Reggie Walker; John Blunt; Ronald Coleman; Robert Coleman; Bobby Taylor; Junior Talbot.
Also see DEL ROYS
Also see SPARKS, Milton

DEL SATINS
(Del-Satins; Dell Satins)
Singles: 7-inch
B.T. PUPPY (506 "My Candy Apple Vette") 10-20 65
B.T. PUPPY (509 "A Girl Named Arlene") 25-45 65
B.T. PUPPY (509 "A Girl Named Arlene") 50-75 65
(White label. Promotional issue only.)
B.T. PUPPY (513 "The Bells of St. Mary's") 15-25 65
COLLECTABLES 3-4 80s
COLUMBIA (42802 "Feelin' No Pain") 15-25 63
DIAMOND (216 "Love, Hate, Revenge") 10-15 67
(Black vinyl.)
DIAMOND (216 "Love, Hate, Revenge") 15-25 67
(Colored vinyl—brown when held to light.)
END (1096 "I'll Pray for You") 100-200 61
LAURIE (3132 "Teardrops Follow Me") 15-25 62
LAURIE (3149 "Does My Love Stand a Chance") 15-25 62
MALA (475 "Two Broken Hearts") 15-25 64
WIN (702 "Counting Tear Drops") 100-200 61
(Black label.)
WIN (702 "Remember") 50-100 61
(Orange label.)
Picture Sleeves
COLUMBIA (42802 "Who Cares") 20-30 63
LPs: 10/12-inch
B.T. PUPPY (1019 "Out to Lunch") 100-150 72
Members: Stan Sommers; Rich Green; Fred Ferrara; Tom Ferrara; Les Cauchi.
Also see BAKER, Bill
Also see BROOKLYN BRIDGE
Also see BRUNO, Bruce
Also see CAMPANIONS
Also see COMO, Nicky
Also see DION
Also see FOREIGN INTRIGUE
Also see LAURIE, Linda
Also see MAESTRO, Johnny
Also see MARESCA, Ernie
Also see SATANS FOUR
Also see SUNDOWNERS
Also see ZISKA, Stosh

DEL SHAYS
Singles: 7-inch
CHARGER (102 "I'll Love You Forever") 75-125 64
CHARGER (102 "[Love You] Forever") 75-100 64
Note slight variation of title.)

DEL-STARS
Singles: 7-inch
MELLOMOOD (1001 "For Your Love") 15-25 64
MELLOMOOD (1004 "Why Do You Have to Go") 15-25 64
RELIC 4-8

DELSU & SMARTS
Singles: 7-inch
DORE 4-6 69

DELTA JOE
(Albert Luandrew)
Singles: 78 rpm
CHANCE (1115 "4 O'Clock Blues") 40-50 53
OPERA (5 "Roll, Tumble & Slip") ... 50-60 53
Also see SUNNYLAND SLIM

DELTA JOHN
(John Lee Hooker)
Singles: 78 rpm
REGENT (1001 "Helpless Blues") .. 40-60 49
Also see HOOKER, John Lee

DELTA MERCHANTS
LPs: 10/12-inch
EXCELLO 8-10 70

DELTA RHYTHM BOYS *P&R/R&B '46*
Singles: 78 rpm
ATLANTIC (889 "The Laugh's on Me") 50-75 49
ATLANTIC (900 "Nobody Knows") 40-60 50
DECCA 20-30 42-55
MUSICRAFT 15-25 49
RCA 15-25 47-48
Singles: 7-inch
DECCA (29000 series) 20-35 54-55
DECCA (48140 "You Are Closer to My Heart") 50-75 50
DECCA (48148 "It's All in Your Mind") 50-75 50
LONDON (1145 "Blow Out the Candle") 15-25 52
MERCURY (1407 "I've Got You Under My Skin") 20-30 52
MERCURY (1408 "They Didn't Believe Me") 20-30 52
MERCURY (1409 "All the Things You Are") 10-20 52
PHILIPS 5-10 62
RCA (5094 "I'll Never Get Out of This World Alive") 25-35 53
RCA (5217 "Long Gone Baby") 20-25 53
EPs: 7-inch
RCA (3085 "Dry Bones") 75-100 50
(Double EP.)
LPs: 10/12-inch
CAMDEN (313 "The Delta Rhythm Boys") 40-50 56
CORAL (57358 "Swingin' Spirituals") 20-30 60
(Monaural.)
CORAL (757358 "Swingin' Spirituals") 25-40 60
(Stereo.)
ELEKTRA (138 "The Delta Rhythm Boys") 25-35 57
JUBILEE (1022 "Delta Rhythm Boys in Sweden") 25-50 57
(Black vinyl.)
JUBILEE (1022 "Delta Rhythm Boys in Sweden") 75-100 57
(Colored vinyl.)
MERCURY (25153 "The Delta Rhythm Boys") 75-100 53
(10-inch LP.)
RCA (3085 "Dry Bones") 100-150 50
(10-inch LP.)
Members: Traverse Crawford; Karl Jones; Kell Pharr; Lee Gaines.
Also see BAILEY, Mildred, & Delta Rhythm Boys
Also see FOUR SHARPS
Also see LUNCEFORD, Jimmie, & Orchestra

DELTA SOUTHERNAIRES
Singles: 7-inch
IMPERIAL 5-10 63

DELTAIRS
Singles: 7-inch
IVY (101 "Lullaby of the Bells") 75-150 57
(Yellow label.)
IVY (101 "Lullaby of the Bells") 15-25 58
IVY (105 "Standing at the Altar") 15-25 58
VINTAGE 3-5 73
Also see MALDONEERS

DELTAIRS
Singles: 7-inch
FELSTED 15-25 58

DELTAS
Singles: 7-inch
GONE (5010 "Let Me Share Your Dream") 300-500 57
(Black label.)
GONE (5010 "Let Me Share Your Dream") 50-75 61
(Multi-color label.)
Also see PREMIERS

DELTAS
Singles: 7-inch
CAMBRIDGE (124 "Goodnight My Love") 50-75 62
PHILIPS 8-12 62

DELTAS
Singles: 7-inch
CENTURY (1028 "In the Shade") 8-12 60s
EMP (10001 "She's My Girl") 15-25

DELTEENS
(With the Orbits and Devora Brown Orchestra)
Singles: 7-inch
FORTUNE (541 "Listen to the Rain") 30-50 61

DELTEENS
Singles: 7-inch
FEDERAL (12487 "Hokey Pokey") . 10-20 63

DEL-TINOS
Singles: 7-inch
DEL-TINO 15-20 63-66
SONIC 15-20 64
LPs: 10/12-inch
SOUNDS INTERESTING 5-10 84
Members: Cub Koda Doug Hankes; Rusty Creech.
Also see KODA, Cub

DEL TONES
(The Beau-Marks)
Singles: 7-inch
QUALITY (1881 "Moonlight Party"/"Rockin' Blues") 75-125 58
(Canadian. Both sides later issued as by the Beau-Marks.)
Also see BEAU-MARKS

DELTONES
Singles: 7-inch
VEE JAY (288 "Early Morning Rock") 10-15 58
VEE JAY (303 "A Lovers Prayer") 20-30 58

DEL-TONES
Singles: 7-inch
RO-ANN (1001 "Best Wishes") .. 150-250 59

DEL-TONES
Singles: 7-inch
JUBILEE (5374 "Bow-Legged Annie") 10-15 59
PEACH (714 "Could I") 5-10 59

DEL TONES
Singles: 7-inch
BRUNSWICK (85015 "Your's Alone") 15-25 50s

DELTONES
(With Tony Bruno Orchestra)
Singles: 7-inch
DAYHILL (1002 "Since I Met You") 50-75 61

DEL-TONES
(With Sal & Side Man)
Singles: 7-inch
USA (711 "Please Talk to Me") .. 200-300 61

DEL-TONES
Singles: 7-inch
STORM (982 "Taboo") 10-15 61

DELTONES
Singles: 7-inch
TCF (175 "Framed") 8-12 60s

DEL-TONES
("Featuring James 'Mr. Piano' Booker")
Singles: 7-inch
ACE (3009 "Everybody's Doin Somthin [sic]") 5-10 74
Also see BOOKER, James

DELTONS
Singles: 7-inch
DRUM 10-15 64
Member: Andy Smith.
Also see BARRIES
Also see SHAGS

DELVERTS
(With the Migraters)
Singles: 7-inch
SALEM (1302 "Listen for the Raindrops") 10-15

DELVETTS
Singles: 7-inch
END 15-25 61-62

DEL-VETTS
Singles: 7-inch
DUNWICH (125 "Last Time Around") 10-20 66
DUNWICH (142 "I Call My Baby STP") 10-20 66
SEEBURG (3018 "Ram Charger") . 20-35 65
(Monaural.)
SEEBURG (3018 "Ram Charger") . 25-40 65
(Stereo.)
Picture Sleeves
DUNWICH (142 "I Call My Baby STP") 20-30 66
(Includes bonus decal.)
Members: Jim Lauer; Bob Good; Paul Wade; Les Goldboss.

DEL-VIKINGS *P&R/R&B '57*
(Featuring Krips Johnson; with Joey Biscoe; Original Dell Vikings; Del Vikings; Dell-Vikings)
Singles: 78 rpm
DOT 25-50 57
FEE BEE 20-40 56-57
MERCURY 20-40 57
Singles: 7-inch
ABC 3-5 75
ABC-PAR (10208 "I'll Never Stop Crying") 20-30 61
ABC-PAR (10248 "I Hear Bells") 50-75 61
ABC-PAR (10278 "Kiss Me") 15-25 62
ABC-PAR (10304 "One More River to Cross") 25-50 62
ABC-PAR (10341 "Confession of Love") 15-25 62
ABC-PAR (10385 "An Angel Up in Heaven") 75-100 63
(Vinyl pressing.)
ABC-PAR (10385 "An Angel Up in Heaven") 50-75 63
(Polystyrene pressing.)
ABC-PAR (10425 "Too Many Miles") 15-25 63
ALPINE (66 "The Sun") 100-200 60
BVM 3-5 90
BIM BAM BOOM 4-8 72
BLUE SKY 3-5
BROADCAST 3-5
COLLECTABLES 3-4 80
CRUISIN' 3-5
DRC (101 "Can't You See") 30-50 57
DOT (15538 "Come Go with Me") .. 15-25 57
DOT (15571 "What Made Maggie Run") 15-25 57
DOT (15592 "Whispering Bells") 15-25 57
DOT (16092 "Come Go with Me") .. 10-15 60
DOT (16236 "Come Go with Me") .. 10-15 61
FEE BEE (173 "Welfare Blues") 5-8 77
FEE BEE (205 "Come Go with Me") 100-150 56
(Has "45 RPM" on each side at top of label. With two sets of thin, horizontal, double parallel lines.)
FEE BEE (205 "Come Go with Me") 20-30 61
(Does not have "45 RPM." With one set of lines, one thick, one thin.)
FEE BEE (206 "Down in Bermuda") 50-100 57
FEE BEE (210 "What Made Maggie Run"/"Down by the Stream") 50-100 57
FEE BEE (210 "What Made Maggie Run"/"Uh Uh Baby") 50-100 57
FEE BEE (210 "What Made Maggie Run"/"When I Come Home") 75-125 57
FEE BEE (214 "Whispering Bells") 100-150 57
FEE BEE (218 "I'm Spinning") 50-75 58
(First issued, on 218-A, as by the "Del Viking Kripp Johnson." See his section for that listing.)
FEE BEE (221 "Willette") 50-75 58
(First issued as by the "Dell Viking Kripp Johnson and Charles Jackson." See their section for that listing.)
FEE BEE (227 "Tell Me") 20-30 59
FEE BEE (902 "True Love") 20-30 61
GATEWAY (743 "We Three") 15-25 64
GOLDIES 3-4
JOJO 3-6 76
LIGHTNING 3-4
LUNIVERSE (106 "Somewhere Over the Rainbow") 50-100 57
LUNIVERSE (110 "Heaven in Paradise") 50-100 58
LUNIVERSE (113 "White Cliffs of Dover") 50-100 58
LUNIVERSE (114 "There I Go") ... 50-100 58
MCA 3-4 70s
MERCURY (30112 "Come Along with Me") 10-15 61
MERCURY (71132 "Cool Shake") 15-25 57
MERCURY (71180 "Come Along with Me") 15-25 57
MERCURY (71198 "I'm Spinning") 15-25 59
MERCURY (71241 "Your Book of Life") 15-25 57
MERCURY (71266 "Voodoo Man") 15-25 58
MERCURY (71345 "You Cheated") 25-35 58
(Blue label.)
MERCURY (71345 "You Cheated") 15-25 58
(Black label.)
MERCURY (71390 "How Could You") 20-30 58
SCEPTER (12367 "Come Go with Me") 4-6 72
SHIP 3-4
SPARTON/ABC-PAR (1104 "Confession of Love") 15-25 62
(Canadian.)
Picture Sleeves
ALPINE (66 "The Sun") 150-250 60
EPs: 7-inch
DOT (1058 "Come Go with Us") 200-300 57
MERCURY (3359 "They Sing, They Swing") 50-100 57
MERCURY (3362 "They Sing, They Swing") 75-100 57
MERCURY (3363 "They Sing, They Swing") 75-100 57
LPs: 10/12-inch
BVM 5-10 91
COLLECTABLES (Except picture discs) 5-10 80-83
COLLECTABLES 10-15 82
(Picture disc.)
DOT (3695 "Come Go with Me") 200-400 66
JANGO (778 "Greatest Hits") 15-20
LUNIVERSE (1000 "Come Go with the Del Vikings") 500-750 57
MERCURY (20314 "They Sing, They Swing") 100-200 57
MERCURY (20353 "Del Vikings' Record Session") 100-200 58
Members: Kripp Johnson; Norman Wright; Clarence Quick; Don Jackson; Gus Backus; Joey Briscoe; David Lerchey; Bill Blakely; Ritzi Lee; Billy Woodruff.
Also see BACKUS, Gus
Also see BRISCOE, Joey
Also see JOHNSON, Kripp
Also see JOHNSON, Kripp, and Chuck Jackson
Also see KING, Ben E.

DEL-VIKINGS / Ike Clanton
Singles: 7-inch
ERA 3-5
Also see CLANTON, Ike

DEL-VIKINGS / Diamonds / Big Bopper / Gaylords
Singles: 7-inch
MERCURY (53 "60 Second Spots") 20-40 58
(Promotional issue only.)
Also see BIG BOPPER
Also see DIAMONDS
Also see GAYLORDS

DEL-VIKINGS / Sonnets
LPs: 10/12-inch
CROWN (5368 "The Del-Vikings and the Sonnets") 20-30 63
(Tracks shown by the Sonnets are actually by either the Meadowlarks or the Sounds.)
Also see DEL-VIKINGS
Also see JULIAN, Don, & Meadowlarks
Also see SONNETS
Also see SOUNDS

DELVONS
Singles: 7-inch
J.D.F. (760 "Stay Clear of Love") 5-10 67
(Black vinyl.)
J.D.F. (760 "Stay Clear of Love") 15-20 67
(Colored vinyl.)

DEL VUES
("Featuring W. Voss")
Singles: 7-inch
U TOWN (8008 "My Confession") 500-750

DELVY, Richard
Singles: 7-inch
TRIUMPH (55 "Atlantis") 10-20 63
Also see BELAIRS
Also see CHALLENGERS

DE LYON, Leo
(With the Musclemen)
Singles: 7-inch
MUSICOR 5-10 60
LPs: 10/12-inch
LONDON 15-25 60

DEMANDS
Singles: 7-inch
CLIM ("Say It Again") 15-25
(Selection number not known.)

DEMAR, Jerry
Singles: 7-inch
FORD (1003 "Cross-eyed Alley Cat") 175-225

DE MARCO, Billy
Singles: 7-inch
KEEFO 15-20

DE MARCO, Gloria
Singles: 7-inch
ARROW 8-12 58

DEMARCO, Lou
("With Vocal Quartet & Orchestra [Rock & Roll]")
Singles: 78 rpm
FERRIS 10-15 56
Singles: 7-inch
FERRIS (903 "Careless Love") 15-25 56

DE MARCO, Phil, & Valiants
Singles: 7-inch
DEBBY (065 "Lonely Guy") 200-250 64

DE MARCO, Ralph *P&R '59*
(With Billy Mure & Orchestra)
Singles: 7-inch
GUARANTEED (202 "Old Shep") 10-15 59
SHELLEY (1011 "Donna") 50-100 60
20TH FOX (309 "Lonely for a Girl") 5-10 62
Picture Sleeves
GUARANTEED (202 "Old Shep") 20-30 59
Also see MURE, Billy
Also see PARAMOUNTS

DE MARCO SISTERS
(Five DeMarco Sisters)
Singles: 78 rpm
DECCA 3-6 54-56
MGM 3-6 54
Singles: 7-inch
DECCA 5-10 54-56
MGM 5-10 54
Members: Gloria DeMarco; Jean DeMarco; Arlene DeMarco; Terri DeMarco; Ann DeMarco.

DE MARINO, Ronnie, & Rockin' Kings
Singles: 7-inch
JUBILEE (5377 "Ding Dong Daddy Wants to Rock") 40-55 59

DE MATTEO, Nicky *P&R '60*
(With the Sorrows)
Singles: 7-inch
ABC-PAR 5-10 61
ACE (110 "Please Don't Go Away") 20-30 57
CAMEO 5-10 65-66
DIAMOND 5-15 63
END (1021 "School House Rock") 15-25 58
GUYDEN 5-10 60
PARIS 8-12 59
TORE 8-12 59

DEMENS
Singles: 7-inch
TEENAGE (1006 "Take Me As I Am") 150-250 58
TEENAGE (1007 "I'm Not in Love with You") 150-250 58
TEENAGE (1008 "The Greatest of Them All") 150-250 58
(Company address shown as on Eighth Avenue.)
TEENAGE (1008 "The Greatest of Them All") 50-100 58
(Company address shown as on 125th Street.)
Members: Eddie Jones; Tom Cook; Frank Cook; Joe Caines.
Also see EMERSONS

DEMENSIONS *P&R '60*
(Dimensions: Lenny Dell & Demensions)
Singles: 7-inch
COLLECTABLES 3-4 80s
CORAL (62277 "Again") 20-30 61
CORAL (62293 "As Time Goes By") 20-30 61
CORAL (62323 "Young at Heart") 20-30 62
CORAL (62344 "My Foolish Heart") 20-30 63
CORAL (62359 "Fly Me to the Moon") 20-30 63
CORAL (62382 "Just a Shoulder to Cry On") 20-30 63
CORAL (62392 "A Little White Gardenia") 20-30 64
CORAL (62432 "My Old Girl Friend") 20-30 64
CORAL (62444 "Once a Day") 20-30 65
CORAL (65559 "Over the Rainbow") 20-30 62
CORAL (65611 "As Time Goes By") 5-10 67
MOHAWK (116 "Over the Rainbow") 30-40 60
(Maroon label.)
MOHAWK (116 "Over the Rainbow") 15-25 60
(Brown label.)
MOHAWK (116 "Over the Rainbow") 10-20 61
(Red label.)
MOHAWK (120 "Zing Went the Strings of My Heart") 15-25 60
MOHAWK (121 "God's Christmas") 30-40 60
MOHAWK (123 "A Tear Fell") 40-60 60
OLD HIT 3-5
Picture Sleeves
CORAL (62344 "My Foolish Heart") 30-50 63
LPs: 10/12-inch
CORAL (57430 "My Foolish Heart") 100-150 63
(Monaural.)
CORAL (7-57430 "My Foolish Heart") 150-250 63
(Stereo.)
CRYSTAL BALL 8-10 82
MCA 5-10
Members: Lenny Dell; Phil Del Giudice; Howard Margolin; Marisa Martelli.

DEMENTIA 13
LPs: 10/12-inch
MIDNIGHT 5-10

DEMERITTE, Kenny, & Swinging Vibrations
Singles: 7-inch
GRAND BAHAMA (3305 "Sitting and Thinking Alone") 200-400

DE MERLE, Les
Singles: 7-inch
TOURNAMENT (404 "Bulldozer") 8-12

DEMETRIUS
Singles: 7-inch
LENOX 5-10 63

DEMETRONS
Singles: 7-inch
SELECT 5-10 65

DEMIAN
Singles: 7-inch
ABC (11297 "Face the World") 5-10 70
LPs: 10/12-inch
ABC (718 "Demian") 25-30 70
Members: Rod Prince; Todd Potter; Roy Cox; Dave Fore.
Also see BUBBLE PUPPY

DEMIAN, Max *LP '79*
(Max Demian Band)
Singles: 7-inch
RCA 3-4 79
LPs: 10/12-inch
RCA 8-10 79-80

DEMILLES
Singles: 7-inch
LAURIE (3230 "Donna Lee") 15-25 64
LAURIE (3247 "Cry and Be On Your Way") 25-40 64
Also see CAMERONS
Also see CARLO

DE MILO, Cordella
Singles: 78 rpm
MODERN (954 "Lonely Girl") 15-25 55
Singles: 7-inch
MODERN (954 "Lonely Girl") 50-75 55

DEMIRES
Singles: 7-inch
LUNAR (519 "Wheels of Love") 25-35 59

DEMOLYRS
(With Hash Brown & His Orchestra)
Singles: 7-inch
JASON SCOTT 4-8
UWR (900 "Rain") 500-1000 64
Also see DARVELL, Barry

DEMONS
Singles: 7-inch
UNART (2002 "Doo Doo Dah") 15-25 58

DEMONS
Singles: 7-inch
GEMCO (1001 "El Lobo") 10-20 60s
KEET (1000 "Big D Blues") 10-20 63
KEET (1001 "Night Train") 10-20 63

DEMONS
Singles: 7-inch
CLOVER (338 "Island of Romance") 20-30 66
Members: Johnny Manasia; Dave Smith.
Also see CHAMPS

DEMONS
LPs: 10/12-inch
MERCURY 8-10 77

DEMONSTRATORS
Singles: 7-inch
W.B. 4-8 64

DEMOPOULOS, Jimmy
Singles: 7-inch
PHILLIPS INT'L 5-10 59

DEMOTRONS
Singles: 7-inch
DORSET 5-10 61
ENRICA 10-20 61
RADAR 5-10 62
RUST (5025 "Home on the Pad") 10-15 60
SCEPTER 5-10 66

DEMOTRONS
Singles: 7-inch
CAMEO 4-8 67

DEMPSEY, Little Jimmy
Singles: 7-inch
ABC 3-5 70
FOX (5 "Bop Hop") 100-150 58
TREND (662 "Be-Bop-a-Lulu") 10-20 66

DEMURES
Singles: 7-inch
BRUNSWICK (55284 "Raining Teardrops") 50-75 65

DENATO, Johnny
Singles: 7-inch
BEAR 4-8 62

DENBY, Junior
Singles: 78 rpm
KING 20-30 54
Singles: 7-inch
KING (4717 "With This Ring") 40-60 54
KING (4725 "This Fool Has Learned") 40-60 54
Also see SWALLOWS

DENE, Glenna
Singles: 7-inch
EUNICE 5-10 61

DENELS
Singles: 7-inch
BAMBOO (517 "Here Come the Ho-Dads") 20-30 62
UNION (502 "Here Come the Ho-Dads") 15-25 62

DENET, Mike
(Mike De Net)
Singles: 7-inch
RAYNARD (1015 "Ghost of Your Love") 10-15 62
STACY (995 "Ghost of Your Love") 5-10 63

DENHAMS
Singles: 7-inch
NOTE (10009 "I'm So Lonely") 35-45 57

DENIM
Singles: 7-inch
EPIC 3-5 77
LPs: 10/12-inch
EPIC 8-10 77

DENIMS
Singles: 7-inch
CAVORT ("Salty Dog") 10-20 63
(No selection number used. Promotional issue, made for Salty Dog Scrub Denim/Canton Textile Mills.)
COLUMBIA (43312 "I'm Your Man") 8-12 65
COLUMBIA (43367 "Everybody, Let's Dance") 8-12 65
COLUMBIA SPECIAL PRODUCTS (1 "The Adler Sock") 15-25 65
(Special product for the Adler Sock Co.)
Picture Sleeves
CAVORT ("Salty Dog") 15-25 63
(No selection number used. Promotional issue, made for Salty Dog Scrub Denim/Canton Textile Mills.)

DENIMS
Singles: 7-inch
MERCURY 4-8 66

DENISON, Homer
(Homer Denison Jr.)
Singles: 7-inch
BRUNSWICK (55150 "Chickie Run") 15-20 59
TIME 5-10 61

DENMAN, Chuck
Singles: 7-inch
GARPAX (44173 "The Fool") 5-10 63

DENNIS, Allen, & Disco Turkeys
Singles: 7-inch
BROWN DOG 3-5

DENNIS, Bill
Singles: 7-inch
SHRINE (113 "I'll Never Let You Get Away") 300-400 66

DENNIS, Bradford
Singles: 7-inch
CANADIAN ("The Wings of an Angel") 20-30
(No selection number used.)

DENNIS, Cathy *LP '90*
LPs: 10/12-inch
POLYDOR 5-8 90

DENNIS, Chuck
Singles: 7-inch
VERNA 5-10 61

DENNIS, Gloria
Singles: 7-inch
RUST 4-8 62-63

DENNIS, Keith
Singles: 7-inch
REPRISE 4-8 65

DENNIS, Marv
(Marv Dennis IV)
Singles: 7-inch
BAGDAD 15-25 62
BEAR 10-15 65
COULEE 5-10 72
FILM 10-15 65
KAY BEE 10-15 60s
SPARTON 10-15 65
LPs: 10/12-inch
COULEE 10-15 72
GARPAX 20-30 65
Members: Marv Dennis Blihovde; Ed Cree; Leo Breidel; Terry Meale.
Also see BLIHOVDE, Marv
Also see MINNESOTA MARV

DENNIS, Marv, & Ed Cree
LPs: 10/12-inch
D&C 15-25 62
Also see DENNIS, Marv

DENNIS, Quitmann
Singles: 7-inch
EPIC 8-12 64
Also see SLIDERS

DENNIS, Richie
Singles: 7-inch
CAMEO 4-8 66
JULIA 10-15 60

DENNIS & EXPLORERS
Singles: 7-inch
CORAL (62295 "Remember") 20-25 61
Also see EXPLORERS

DENNIS & MENACES
Singles: 7-inch
DOT 5-10 60

DENNIS & SUPERTONES
Singles: 7-inch
SMASH 4-8 63

DENNY, Burch *C&W '89*
Singles: 7-inch
OAK 3-4 89

DENNY, D.
Singles: 7-inch
ACCENT 4-8 65

DENNY, Dotty
Singles: 7-inch
A440 (415 "Rainbow Train") 5-10
Members: Dotty Denny; Charlie Scardino; Buddy Saltzman.

DENNY, Galen
Singles: 7-inch
LIBERTY 10-15 58

DENNY, Martin *P&R/R&B/LP '59*
(Exotic Sounds of Martin Denny)
Singles: 7-inch
LIBERTY (55000 series) 3-8 59-67
LIBERTY (56000 series) 3-5 69
LIBERTY (77000 series) 5-15 59-60
(Stereo.)
Picture Sleeves
LIBERTY 5-15 59-63
EPs: 7-inch
LIBERTY 5-15 59
LPs: 10/12-inch
FIRST AMERICAN 5-10 81
LIBERTY 20-30 59-60s
(With bird calls and animal sounds and covers picturing model Sandy Warner. Perhaps a Martin Denny fan will provide us with a list of which specific LPs are included in this group.)
LIBERTY 5-10 60s
(Without bird calls and covers picturing model Sandy Warner.)
SUNSET 5-10 66-68
U.A. 5-10 74-80
Also see BAJA MARIMBA BAND
Also see ZENTER, Si

DENNY, Sandy *LP '74*
Singles: 7-inch
A&M 3-5 72-73
LPs: 10/12-inch
A&M 8-12 71-72
ISLAND 8-10 74-76
Also see FAIRPORT CONVENTION
Also see FOTHERINGAY
Also see LED ZEPPELIN

DENNY, Sandy, & Strawbs
LPs: 10/12-inch
PICKWICK 10-15 73
Also see DENNY, Sandy
Also see STRAWBS

DENNY & DEDICATIONS
Singles: 7-inch
SUSAN 15-25 65

DENNY & JAY
Singles: 7-inch
CAPITOL 4-8 64

DENNY & JENNY
Singles: 7-inch
CORONET 5-10 59
INVICTA 5-10 62

DENNY & LP's
(B.B. Butler & Band)
Singles: 7-inch
ROCK-IT (001 "Why Not Give Me Your Heart") 30-50

DENNY & LENNY
Singles: 7-inch
CHANCE 4-8 63
RADAR 4-8 62

DENNY-O
Singles: 7-inch
BLIND JUSTICE (101 "Trial of the President") 5-8 74

DE NOBLE, Tommy
Singles: 7-inch
SHERYL 5-10
STAR SATELLITE 8-12 59

DE NOIA, Paul
Singles: 7-inch
KENCO 4-8 62

DENOTATIONS
Singles: 7-inch
LAWN (253 "Lone Stranger") 75-125 65

DENSMORE, John, & Robby Kreiger
LPs: 10/12-inch
RHINO 5-10
Also see DOORS

DENSON, Lee
Singles: 78 rpm
VIK 15-25 56
Singles: 7-inch
ENTERPRISE 3-5 73
KENT (306 "High School Hop") 30-50 58
VIK (0251 "Heart of a Fool") 20-40 56
VIK (0281 "New Shoes") 35-60 56
Also see COCHRAN, Eddie

DENSON, Wee Willie
Singles: 7-inch
MAY 4-8 62-63

DENTON, Ben, Singers
Singles: 7-inch
GONE 5-10 58
Also see COPA COMBO
Also see LANGFORD, Jerry, & Ben Denton Singers

DENTON, Bobby
(Bob Denton)
Singles: 7-inch
CHANCELLOR 4-8 62
DOT 10-20 58
JUDD 10-15 58-59

DENTON, Jack *C&W '89*
Singles: 7-inch
M.V.P. 3-4 89

DENTON, Johnny
Singles: 7-inch
MEL-O-TONE (1147 "Hey Babe") 15-25 57

DENTON, Mickey
(With the New York Express)
Singles: 7-inch
AMY (902 "Top 10") 8-12 64
BIG TOP (3078 "Steady Kind") 15-25 61
BIG TOP (3094 "Ain't Nobody") 10-20 62
BIG TOP (3114 "Tell Her") 10-20 62
BIG TOP (3142 "Dance with Me Mary") 10-20 63
IMPACT (1002 "Ain't Love Grand") 15-20 65
IMPACT (1011 "Heartache Is My Name") 15-20 65
WORLD ARTISTS (1043 "One More Time") 8-12 65
LPs: 10/12-inch
CHERIE 5-10 82
Also see CASINOS
Also see PATTI & MICKEY

DENVER, Danny
Singles: 7-inch
CHANCELLOR 5-10 62
DEVILLE (104 "Long Hairy Arms") 10-15 67
GO-GO 10-15
LPs: 10/12-inch
WRAYCO 8-10

DENVER, John *LP '69*
Singles: 12-inch
RCA (11189 "Bet on the Blues") 5-10 77
(Promotional issue only.)
Singles: 7-inch
ALLEGIANCE 3-4
CBS 3-4 90s
CHERRY MOUNTAIN (02 "Flying Or Me") 3-5 86
RCA (Except 0067 thru 0955) 3-5 74-86
RCA (0067 thru 0955) 4-8 70-74
Promotional Singles
EVA-TONE (106026 "Trees for America") 3-5 86
RCA (2008 "Rocky Mountain High") 5-10 72
Picture Sleeves
ALLEGIANCE 3-4
CBS 3-4 90s
CHERRY MOUNTAIN (02 "Flying Or Me") 3-5 86
RCA (Except 2008) 3-5 74-86
RCA (2008 "Rocky Mountain High") 5-10 72
(Promotional issue only.)
LPs: 10/12-inch
HJD (66 "John Denver Sings") 200-300 66
(Promotional issue only. Less than 300 copies made as Christmas gifts for friends.)

MOS ("Something to Sing About") 50-100 66
(Promotional issue only. No actual label name is used. Various artists LP with three Denver tracks not available elsewhere.)
MERCURY (704 "Beginnings") 10-15 72
(Pictures John Denver on cover.)
MERCURY (704 "Beginnings") 8-10 74
(With mountain scene photo on cover.)
RCA (0101 thru 3449) 5-10 73-80
RCA (0075 "The John Denver Radio Show") 20-30 74
(Single-sided LP. Promotional issue only.)
RCA (0683 "The Second John Denver Radio Show") 20-30 74
RCA (4000 series) 10-15 69-72
(Orange labels.)
RCA (4000 & 5000 series) 5-10 81-85
(Black labels.)
RCA (5398 "The John Denver Holiday Radio Show") 10-20 84
(Promotional issue only.)
WINDSTAR 5-8 90
Session: Hal Blaine; John Sommers; Steve Weisberg; Dick Kniss; Lee Holdridge; James Burton.
Also see ARMAND, Renee
Also see BLAINE, Hal
Also see BURTON, James
Also see DENVER, BOISE & JOHNSON
Also see FAT CITY
Also see MITCHELL, Chad, Trio
Also see MURPHEY, Michael
Also see TRAVERS, Mary
Also see WONDER, Stevie / John Denver

DENVER, John, & Placido Domingo
P&R '82
Singles: 7-inch
COLUMBIA 3-4 82
Also see DOMINGO, Placido

DENVER, John, & Emmylou Harris
C&W '83
Singles: 7-inch
RCA 3-4 83
Also see HARRIS, Emmylou

DENVER, John, & Muppets
LP '79
Singles: 7-inch
RCA 3-4 79
LPs: 10/12-inch
RCA 5-10 79-83
Also see MUPPETS

DENVER, John, & Olivia Newton-John
P&R '75
Singles: 7-inch
RCA 3-5 75
Also see NEWTON-JOHN, Olivia

DENVER, John, & Nitty Gritty Dirt Band
C&W '89
Singles: 7-inch
UNIVERSAL 3-4 89
Also see NITTY GRITTY DIRT BAND

DENVER, John / Diana Ross
Singles: 7-inch
WHAT'S IT ALL ABOUT 4-8 81
(Public service, radio station issue.)
Also see ROSS, Diana

DENVER, John, & Sylvie Vartan
Singles: 7-inch
RCA 3-4 84

DENVER, BOISE & JOHNSON
Singles: 7-inch
REPRISE (0695 "Take Me to Tomorrow") 5-10 68
Member: John Denver; Michael Johnson.
Also see DENVER, John
Also see JOHNSON, Michael

DENVER MINT LTD.
Singles: 7-inch
SMALL TOWN (106 "I've Got to Find Myself") 25-35

DEODATO
P&R/R&B/LP '73
(Eumir Deodato)
Singles: 12-inch
W.B. 4-6 84
Singles: 7-inch
CTI 3-4 73-77
MCA 3-4 74-76
W.B. 3-4 78-84
Picture Sleeves
CTI 3-4 73
LPs: 10/12-inch
CTI 8-10 73-74
MCA 6-10 76
MUSE 8-10 73-76
W.B. 5-10 78-82
Also see MOREIRA, Airto
Also see TROPEA

DE ORIAN, Pam
Singles: 7-inch
LIBERTY 5-10 59

DE PAUL, Lynsey
Singles: 7-inch
MAM 3-5 73
MERCURY 3-5 75

DE PAUL, Ray
Singles: 7-inch
ABC-PAR 5-10 58

DEPECHE MODE
LP '81
Singles: 12-inch
SIRE (Except 2271 & 2952) 4-6 81-87
SIRE (2271 "Blasphemous Rumors") 40-50 80s
(Promotional issue only.)
SIRE (2952 "Behind the Wheel") ... 20-30 87
(Promotional issue only.)
Singles: 7-inch
REPRISE 3-5 97
SIRE 3-5 81-90
Picture Sleeves
SIRE 3-5 85-88
LPs: 10/12-inch
SIRE 5-10 81-90
Members: Vince Clarke; David Gahan; Martin Gore; Andy Fletcher; Alan Wilder.
Also see ERASURE

DEPENDABLES
Singles: 7-inch
U.A. 3-6 71
LPs: 10/12-inch
U.A. 10-20 71

DE PERALTA, Diana Grave
Singles: 7-inch
BAKSHEESH 4-6 78

DEPOLIS, Chris
Singles: 7-inch
CAMEO 4-8 64

DEPRESSIONS
Singles: 7-inch
MADD (123167 "Can't Tell You") ... 50-75 67

DEPUTIES
LPs: 10/12-inch
WYNCOTE 8-12 66

DER PLAN
LPs: 10/12-inch
OPTIONAL MUSIC 5-10

DE RAE, Eddie
Singles: 7-inch
DECCA 4-8 64

DERBY-HATVILLE
Singles: 7-inch
SEA ELL (102 "You'll Forget Me") 30-40 67

DERBYS
Singles: 7-inch
KC (111 "The Huckster") 10-15 63
MERCURY (71437 "Night After Night") 40-60 59
SAVOY (1609 "Travelin' Man") 15-25 62

DERBYS / Bondsmen: see BONDSMEN / Derbys

DEREK
P&R '68
(Johnny Cymbal)
Singles: 7-inch
BANG 4-8 68-69
SOLID GOLD 3-5 73
Also see CYMBAL, Johnny

DEREK B
R&B '88
Singles: 7-inch
PROFILE 3-4 88

DEREK, Lance
Singles: 7-inch
BLACK BIRD 4-8 62

DEREK, Tommy
Singles: 7-inch
FLAG 8-12 62

DEREK & CYNDI
R&B '74
Singles: 7-inch
THUNDER 3-5 74
Picture Sleeves
THUNDER 3-5 74

DEREK & DOMINOS
LP '70
Singles: 7-inch
ATCO 3-5 70-72
RSO 3-4 73
LPs: 10/12-inch
ATCO (704 "Layla") 20-30 70
MFSL (2-239 "In Concert") 25-35 90s
POLYDOR 8-10 74
RSO 5-10 77
Members: Eric Clapton; Jim Gordon; Carl Radle; Bobby Whitlock; Duane Allman.
Also see ALLMAN, Duane
Also see BROOKS, Denny
Also see CLAPTON, Eric
Also see WHITLOCK, Bobby

DEREK & HOWARD
Singles: 7-inch
FESTIVAL 4-8 62

DEREK & RAY
Singles: 7-inch
MERCURY (72744 "To Sir with Love") 5-10 67
RCA (9111 "Interplay") 10-20 67

DE RIEUX, Larry
Singles: 7-inch
ARCO (102 "Chicken Session") ... 75-100

DERKSEN, Arnie
Singles: 7-inch
DECCA 15-25 59

DERMONTTE, Jo-Jo & Starlings
Singles: 7-inch
FRANTIC (114 "The Big Egg") 4-6
Picture Sleeves
FRANTIC (114 "The Big Egg") 5-8

DERONS
Singles: 7-inch
JEWL (1001 "It's Okay") 10-20

DE ROSA, Frank
Singles: 7-inch
BIGTOP (3019 "Hubcaps") 15-25 59
DOT (15696 "Big Guitar") 10-15 58
KEN (25 "Big Guitar") 25-35 57

DE ROSE, Marty
Singles: 7-inch
LANE 15-25 58

DERRINGER, Rick
LP '73
(With the McCoys; Derringer)
Singles: 7-inch
BLUE SKY 3-5 74-80
EPIC 3-4 83
LPs: 10/12-inch
BLUE SKY 8-18 73-81
MERCURY 10-20 74
PASSPORT 5-10 83
Also see DUST
Also see GLASS, Dick, & Rick Derringer & McCoys
Also see LA CROIX, Jerry
Also see McCOYS
Also see TIN HOUSE
Also see WINTER, Edgar, & Rick Derringer

DERRINGERS
Singles: 7-inch
CAPITOL 5-10 61

DESALVO, Albert, & Bugs
Singles: 7-inch
ASTOR (001 "Albert Albert") 20-30

DESANTO, Sugar Pie
R&B '60
("Sugar Pie" De Santo; Umpeylia Balinton)
Singles: 7-inch
BRUNSWICK 5-10 67-68
CADET 5-10 66
CHECK 10-20 60
CHECKER 5-10 63-66
GEDINSON 5-10 62
JASMAN 4-6 74
SOUL CLOCK 4-6 69
VELTONE 10-20 60
WAX 8-12 64
EPs: 7-inch
CHECKER (2979 "Sugar Pie") 30-50 61
(Stereo. Juke box issue only.)
LPs: 10/12-inch
CHECKER (2979 "Sugar Pie") 50-100 61
Also see HANK & Sugar Pie
Also see JAMES, Etta, & Sugar Pie DeSanto
Also see KINGSLEY, Pee Wee
Also see SUGAR & Pee Wee

DE SARIO, Teri
P&R '78
Singles: 7-inch
CASABLANCA 3-5 78
LPs: 10/12-inch
CASABLANCA 5-10 80
DAYSPRING 5-8 85

DE SARIO, Teri, & K.C.
R&B '80
Singles: 7-inch
CASABLANCA 3-5 79-80
Also see DE SARIO, Teri
Also see K.C. & Sunshine Band

DES BARRES, Michael
Singles: 7-inch
A&M 3-4 80
LPs: 10/12-inch
DREAMLAND 5-10 80
Also see DETECTIVE

DES BARRES, Michael, & Holly Knight
Singles: 7-inch
A&M 3-4 84
Also see DES BARRES, Michael
Also see KNIGHT, Holly

DESCENDANTS
Singles: 7-inch
MTA (112 "Lela") 20-30 66

DESDA
Singles: 7-inch
DEL-FI 4-8 62

DESERT RATS
Singles: 7-inch
MINK (5001 "High Noon") 10-15

DESERT ROSE BAND
C&W '87
Singles: 7-inch
CURB/MCA 3-4 87-92
LPs: 10/12-inch
CURB/MCA 5-8 87-92
Members: Chris Hillman; Herb Pedersen; John Jorgenson.
Also see HILLMAN, Chris
Also see PEDERSEN, Herb

DESERTERS
LPs: 10/12-inch
CAPITOL 5-10 81-83

DE SHANNON, Jackie
P&R '63
Singles: 7-inch
AMHERST 6-12 78
ATLANTIC 5-10 72-74
CAPITOL 5-10 71
COLUMBIA (Except 10221) 5-10 75
COLUMBIA (10221 "Boat to Sail") . 10-15 76
(With Brian Wilson.)
EDISON INT'L (416 "I Wanna Go Home") 50-100 60
EDISON INT'L (418 "Put My Baby Down") 50-100 60
IMPERIAL 5-10 65-70
LIBERTY (55000 series, except 55602) 15-25 60-64
LIBERTY (55602 "Little Yellow Roses") 8-10 63
(Black vinyl.)
LIBERTY (55602 "Little Yellow Roses") 15-25 63
(Colored vinyl. Promotional issue only.)
LIBERTY (56000 series) 5-10 70
MGM 4-8 65
RCA 3-4 80
Picture Sleeves
LIBERTY (55526 "Faded Love") .. 75-100 63
LPs: 10/12-inch
AMHERST (1010 "You're the Only Dancer") 15-25 77
ATLANTIC 10-15 72-74
CAPITOL 15-20 71
COLUMBIA 10-15 75
IMPERIAL (9286 "This Is Jackie De Shannon") 25-50 65
(Monaural.)
IMPERIAL (9294 "You Won't Forget Me") 25-50 65
(Monaural.)
IMPERIAL (9296 "In the Wind") 25-50 65
(Monaural.)
IMPERIAL (9328 "Are You Ready for This") 25-50 66
(Monaural.)
IMPERIAL (9344 "New Image") 25-50 67
(Monaural.)
IMPERIAL (9352 "For You") 25-50 67
(Monaural.)
IMPERIAL (12286 "This Is Jackie De Shannon") 25-50 65
(Stereo.)
IMPERIAL (12294 "You Won't Forget Me") 25-50 65
(Stereo.)
IMPERIAL (12296 "In the Wind") ... 25-50 65
(Stereo.)
IMPERIAL (12328 "Are You Ready for This") 25-50 66
(Stereo.)
IMPERIAL (12344 "New Image") ... 25-50 67
(Stereo.)
IMPERIAL (12352 "For You") 25-50 67
(Stereo.)
IMPERIAL (12386 "Me About You") 25-50 68
IMPERIAL (12404 "What the World Needs Now Is Love") 25-50 68
IMPERIAL (12415 "Laurel Canyon") 25-50 68
IMPERIAL (12442 "Put a Little Love in Your Heart") 25-50 69
IMPERIAL (12453 "To Be Free") ... 25-50 70
LIBERTY (3320 "Jackie De Shannon") 50-100 63
(Monaural.)
LIBERTY (3390 "Breakin' It Up On the Beatles Tour") 50-100 64
(Monaural.)
LIBERTY (7320 "Jackie De Shannon") 75-100 63
(Stereo.)
LIBERTY (7390 "Breakin' It Up on the Beatles Tour") 75-100 64
(Stereo.)
LIBERTY (10000 series) 5-10 82
SUNSET 10-15 68-71
U.A. 8-10 75
Also see DEE, Jackie
Also see HALE & HUSHABYES
Also see SHANNON, Jackie
Also see WILSON, Brian

DE SHANNON, Jackie / Bobby Vee / Eddie Hodges
LPs: 10/12-inch
LIBERTY (3430 "C'mon Let's Live a Little") 15-20 66
(Monaural. Soundtrack)
LIBERTY (7430 "C'mon Let's Live a Little") 20-25 66
(Stereo. Soundtrack)
Also see DE SHANNON, Jackie
Also see HODGES, Eddie
Also see VEE, Bobby

DESHAWN, Tony
R&B '87
Singles: 7-inch
AMAZON 3-4 87

DESIGN
LPs: 10/12-inch
EPIC 10-15 71

DESIRES
Singles: 7-inch
HERALD (532 "Bobby You") 15-25 58

DESIRES
Singles: 7-inch
HULL (730 "Let It Please Be You") 50-75 59
HULL (733 "Rendezvous with You") 50-75 60
ROULETTE 3-5 73
Members: Robert White; Charles Hurston; George Smith; Charles Powell; James Whittier.
Also see JIVE TONES

DESIRES
Singles: 7-inch
DEE ("Need Someone") 250-500 62
(Selection number not known.)
SMASH (1763 "I Never Loved Like This Before") 10-20 62
MONEYTOWN (602 "Need Someone") 150-250 62
20TH FOX (195 "I Don't Know Why") 15-25 60
Picture Sleeves
20TH FOX (195 "I Don't Know Why") 20-35 60

DESIRES
Singles: 7-inch
DASA (102 "The Girl for Me") 20-40 62

DESIRES
(With Billy Mure & Orchestra)
Singles: 7-inch
SEVILLE (118 "Story of Love") 25-50 62
Also see REGENTS
Also see MARESCA, Ernie
Also see MURE, Billy

DESIRES
Singles: 7-inch
STARVILLE (1206 "Oh What a Lonely Night") 20-30

DESMOND, Johnny
P&R '46
Singles: 78 rpm
CORAL 3-5 52-56
MGM 3-6 50-51
Singles: 7-inch
COLUMBIA 4-8 59-60
CORAL 5-10 52-56
DIAMOND 3-6 62
EDGEWOOD 3-6 62
MGM 5-10 50-51
MUSICANZA 3-4
RCA 3-6 63
RED LITE 5-8
20TH FOX 3-6 64
VIGOR 3-4 73
Picture Sleeves
CORAL 5-10 55
EPs: 7-inch
CORAL 8-15 54-56
MGM 10-20 52
P.R.I. (11 "So Nice") 5-10
LPs: 10/12-inch
CAMDEN 10-20 53-54
COLUMBIA 5-10 59-60
CORAL 15-25 55-56
EVON 10-15 50s
LION 10-15 56
MGM 10-20 55
MAYFAIR 10-15 58
MOVIETONE 5-10 66
P.R.I. (98 "90th Anniversary Album") 10-20
(Colored vinyl. Promotional issue for Montgomery Ward stores.)
VOCALION 5-10 66
Also see CORNELL, Don, Johnny Desmond & Alan Dale

DESMOND, Johnny, Eileen Barton & McGuire Sisters
P&R '54
Singles: 78 rpm
CORAL 4-8 54
Also see BARTON, Eileen
Also see McGUIRE SISTERS

DESMOND, Johnny / John Gary / Gordon MacRae
LPs: 10/12-inch
INT'L AWARD 8-15 60s
Also see DESMOND, Johnny
Also see GARY, John
Also see MacRAE, Gordon

DESMOND, Paul
LP '63
(Paul Desmond Quartet)
Singles: 7-inch
A&M 3-5 69-70
RCA VICTOR 3-8 62-63
LPs: 10/12-inch
A&M 5-15 69-76
CTI 8-12 75
CAMDEN 8-12 73
DISCOVERY 5-8 81
FANTASY (21 "Paul Desmond") .. 50-100 54
(10-inch LP.)
FANTASY (220 "Paul Desmond") .. 40-60 56
RCA (2400 & 2500 series) 15-25 62-63
RCA (2800 series) 10-20 78
RCA (3300 & 3400 series) 10-20 65-66
W.B. 20-30 60
Also see BRUBECK, Dave, & Paul Desmond
Also see MULLIGAN, Gerry, & Paul Desmond

DE SOTO, Bobby
Singles: 7-inch
CLARO (5914 "The Cheater") 35-50 59

DESTINAIRES
Singles: 7-inch
OLD TIMER (609 "Teardrops") 10-15 65
OLD TIMER (610 "Chapel Bells") .. 20-30 65
(Colored vinyl.)
Also see ZIRCONS / Destinaires

DESTINAIRES / Lancers
Singles: 7-inch
OLD TIMER (614 "You're Cheating on Me") 10-15 65
Also see DESTINAIRES
Also see LANCERS

DESTINATION
R&B '77
Singles: 12-inch
BUTTERFLY 4-6 79
Singles: 7-inch
A.V.I. 3-5 77
BUTTERFLY 3-4 79
LPs: 10/12-inch
A.V.I. 8-10 77
BUTTERFLY 5-10 79

DESTINATION SOUL
Singles: 7-inch
UPTOWN (753 "Ease My Mind") 8-15 67

DESTINATIONS
Singles: 7-inch
FORTUNE (864 "Valley of Tears") ... 75-125 64

DESTINATIONS
Singles: 7-inch
CAMEO (422 "I'd Rather Be Hurt") . 10-20 66

DESTINATIONS
Singles: 7-inch
DESTINATION ... 5-10 67
Member: Reid Kailing; Sid Rice; Bruce Robertson; Fred Hadler; Bill Wilson; Rick Sorgel.
Also see GRASS ROOTS

DESTINATIONS
Singles: 7-inch
AND (114 "I Can't Leave You") .. 100-200 60s

DESTINEERS
Singles: 7-inch
RCA ... 5-10 62

DESTINY
Singles: 7-inch
TAMPA ... 5-10 58

DESTINY'S CHILDREN
Singles: 7-inch
PYRO (52 "For Me") ... 15-25 66
VENTURAL (730 "Your First Time") ... 35-45 60s

DESTINYS
Singles: 7-inch
ALTA (102 "What's Up") ... 10-20 61
(First issue.)
DIAMOND (105 "What's Up") ... 5-10 61

DESTRO, Bill, & Destinys
Singles: 7-inch
STARLA ... 5-10

DESTROY ALL MONSTERS
Singles: 7-inch
IDBI (1 "Bored") ... 5-8 78
Picture Sleeves
IDBI (1 "Bored") ... 8-12 78
EPs: 7-inch
BLACK HOLE (18551 "Live") ... 5-10 79
Member: Michael Davis.
Also see MC 5

DESTRY, Johnny, & Destiny
Singles: 7-inch
MILLENNIUM ... 3-5 80
LPs: 10/12-inch
MILLENNIUM ... 5-10 80

DET REIRRUC & CLUB RAPPERS *D&D '85*
Singles: 12-inch
CLUB ... 4-6 85

DETECTIVE *LP '77*
Singles: 7-inch
SWAN SONG ... 3-5 77-78
LPs: 10/12-inch
SWAN SONG ... 10-12 77-78
Member: Michael Des Barres.
Also see DES BARRES, Michael

DETERGENTS *P&R '64*
Singles: 7-inch
KAPP ... 5-10 66
ROULETTE ... 5-10 64-65
Picture Sleeves
ROULETTE (4590 "Leader of the Laundromat") ... 15-25 64
LPs: 10/12-inch
ROULETTE (25308 "The Many Faces of the Detergents") ... 25-35 65
Members: Ron Dante; Tommy Wynn; Danny Jordan.
Also see DANTE, Ron

DETERMINATIONS
Singles: 7-inch
SPACE (304 "O My Love, Sweet Love") ... 15-25 59

DETERMINATIONS
Singles: 7-inch
KING (6297 "Girl, Girl, Girl") ... 10-15 70
IMPORTANT (1010 "You Can't Hold on to Love") ... 35-50 67

DETOURS
Singles: 7-inch
ATCO ... 10-20 66
McSHERRY ... 10-20 64

DETROIT *LP '72*
Singles: 7-inch
PARAMOUNT ... 3-5 70-71
LPs: 10/12-inch
PARAMOUNT ... 10-15 71-72
Also see DETROIT WHEELS
Also see ROCKETS
Also see RYDER, Mitch, & Detroit Wheels

DETROIT & INTRUDERS
(Detroit & Invaders)
Singles: 7-inch
DELLWOOD (778 "Let Me Love You") ... 30-50 60s
DELLWOOD (10677 "There She Goes") ... 30-50 60s

DETROIT CITY LIMITS
Singles: 7-inch
OKEH ... 4-8 68
LPs: 10/12-inch
OKEH ... 12-15 68

DETROIT COUNT
(The Detroit Count)
Singles: 78 rpm
JVB (75830 "Hastings Street Opera, Part 1") ... 40-80 48
JVB (75831 "Crazy About You") ... 40-80 48
KING (4264 "Hastings Street Opera, Part 1") ... 20-40 48
KING (4265 "Crazy About You") ... 20-40 48
KING (4279 "Little Tille Willie") ... 20-40 48

DETROIT EMERALDS *P&R/R&B '68*
Singles: 7-inch
RIC TIC (135 "Showtime") ... 10-15 68
WESTBOUND ... 3-6 70-78
LPs: 10/12-inch
WESTBOUND ... 10-15 71-78
Members: Abrim Tilmon; Ivory Tilmon; Cleophus Tilmon; Raymond Tilmon; James Mitchell; Paul Riser; Maurice King; Johnny Allen.
Also see CHAPTER 8

DETROIT JR.
(With the Delrays)
Singles: 7-inch
BEA & BABY ... 10-15 60
C.J. ... 5-10 64
CHECKER ... 5-10
FOXY ... 10-15 61
TIP TOP ... 5-8 67
U.S.A. (807 "Talk Fast") ... 10-15 65

DETROIT LAND APPLES
Singles: 7-inch
SHOTGUN ... 5-8

DETROIT RIOTS
Singles: 7-inch
DEARBORN (582 "Fast Way to Die") ... 6-12 68

DETROIT ROAD RUNNERS
Singles: 7-inch
ABC ... 4-6 68-69

DETROIT SOUL
Singles: 7-inch
MUSIC TOWN (208 "Love Without Meaning") ... 10-20 60s
MUSIC TOWN (502 "Mr. Hip") ... 10-20 67

DETROIT WHEELS
Singles: 7-inch
INFERNO (5002 "Tally Ho") ... 10-20 68
Also see DETROIT
Also see RYDER, Mitch, & Detroit Wheels

DETROIT'S MOST WANTED
Singles: 12-inch
BRYANT ... 4-6 91
LPs: 10/12-inch
BRYANT ... 5-8 91

DETROYT *R&B '84*
Singles: 7-inch
TABU ... 3-4 84

DEUCE COUPES
LPs: 10/12-inch
CROWN ... 15-20 63
DEL-FI (1243 "Hotrodder's Choice") ... 25-35 63
Also see DE-FENDERS / Deuce Coupes

DEUCES of RHYTHM: see DUCES of RHYTHM

DEUCES WILD
(With Don Ralke's Orchestra)
Singles: 7-inch
FARO ... 4-8 64
SHEEN ... 5-10 60
SPECIALTY ... 5-10 59
VAULT ... 4-8 64
Also see RALKE, Don

DEUCES WILD
Singles: 7-inch
SALMAR (100 "Come Easy Go") ... 5-10
SALMAR (102 "Hey Little One") ... 5-10

DEUCES WILD
Singles: 7-inch
CORBY (211 "Keep On") ... 3-5

DEUTSCH, Patti
Singles: 7-inch
RSVP ... 4-8 66

DEVASTATING AFFAIR
Singles: 7-inch
MOWEST ... 3-5 72
Members: Andrew Porter; Harold Johnson; Greg Wright; Karin Patterson; Olivia Foster.
Also see FINISHED TOUCH

DE VAUGHN, William *P&R/R&B/LP '74*
Singles: 7-inch
ROXBURY ... 3-5 74
TEC ... 3-4 80
LPs: 10/12-inch
ROXBURY ... 8-10 74
TEC ... 5-10 80
Also see MFSB

DE-VAURS
(With Cliff Driver & His Orchestra; De Vaurs)
Singles: 7-inch
D-TONE (3 "Baby Doll") ... 150-250 58
MOON (105 "Where Are You") .. 100-125 59
RED FOX (104 "Where Are You") ... 20-30 65

DE VELLS
Singles: 7-inch
EMANUEL ... 20-25

DEVENS, Sammy
Singles: 7-inch
DUAL ... 5-10 61

DEVERONS
Singles: 7-inch
REO (8892 "Blue Is the Night") .. 150-250 65
(Canadian. Title and selection number not known.)
Members: Burton Cummings; Edd Smith; Ronn Savoie; Derek Blake.
Also see CUMMINGS, Burton

DEVERONS
Singles: 7-inch
RAYNARD (1046 "On the Road Again") ... 5-8 66

DEVIANTS
LPs: 10/12-inch
SIRE (97001 "Ptooff") ... 30-40 68
SIRE (97005 "Disposable") ... 30-40 69
SIRE (97016 "Deviants, No. 3") ... 30-40 69
Members: Mick Farren; Russ Hunter; Steve Sparks; Duncan Sanderson; Jon Weber.

DEVICE *P&R/LP '86*
Singles: 12-inch
CHRYSALIS ... 4-8 86
(Promotional issue only.)
Singles: 7-inch
CHRYSALIS ... 3-4 86
Picture Sleeves
CHRYSALIS ... 3-4 86
LPs: 10/12-inch
CHRYSALIS ... 5-8 86
Members: Paul Engemann; Holly Knight; Gene Black.
Also see ANIMOTION
Also see KNIGHT, Holly

DEVIL'S ANVIL
LPs: 10/12-inch
COLUMBIA (2664 "Hard Rock from the Middle East") ... 15-20 67
(Monaural.)
COLUMBIA (9464 "Hard Rock from the Middle East") ... 15-20 67
(Stereo.)

DEVIL'S BRIGADE
Singles: 7-inch
U.A. ... 4-8 68

DEVIL'S OWN
Singles: 7-inch
EXIT (1907 "I Just Wanna Make Love") ... 20-30 66

DEVILE, Cecile
Singles: 7-inch
EVEREST ... 10-15 59

DEVILED HAM
LPs: 10/12-inch
SUPER K (6003 "I Had too Much to Dream Last Night") ... 15-25 68

DEVILLE SISTERS
Singles: 7-inch
IMPERIAL ... 8-12 58

DE VILLES
Singles: 7-inch
ALADDIN (3423 "Kiss Me Again") .. 20-30 58

DE VILLES
Singles: 7-inch
NAUVOO (806 "I Didn't Do It") ... 50-75 59

DEVILLES
Singles: 7-inch
DIXIE (1108 "Without Warning") ... 25-50 60
Also see JOHNS, Sammy, & DeVilles

DEVILLES
Singles: 7-inch
ACCLAIM (1002 "Give Your Love to Me") ... 25-50 61
ARRAWAK (201 "I Do Believe") ... 50-75 62
(Green label.)
ARRAWAK (201 "I Do Believe") ... 25-50 63
(Yellow label.)
ORBIT (540 "Tell Me So") ... 20-30 59
SPARTON ("Tell Me So") ... 10-15 61
(Selection number not known.)
TALENT (103 "Goddess of Angels") ... 50-75 60

DEVILLES
Singles: 7-inch
KERRY (1109 "Baby Blue") ... 60-80 66
KERRY (1110 "Denise") ... 150-175 66
STUDIO CITY (1045 "Cry Baby") ... 40-60 66
Also see SECOND THOUGHT

DEVILLES
Singles: 7-inch
JERDEN (107 "Searchin' for Love") ... 5-10 60s

DEVILS
Singles: 7-inch
SARA (1449 "Tell Me") ... 15-25 67
SARA (1450 "I'll Be There When You Come") ... 15-25 67

DEVINE, Skippy
Singles: 7-inch
D-S-D (105 "Am I Wasting My Time") ... 10-20

DE VITO, Karla
Singles: 7-inch
A&M ... 3-4 86
EPIC (Except 0304) ... 3-4 81-82
EPIC (0304 "Santa Claus Is Coming to My House") ... 3-5 82
(Includes 9" x 14" poster. Promotional issue only.)
LPs: 10/12-inch
A&M ... 5-10 86
EPIC ... 5-10 81
Also see ANKA, Paul, & Karla DeVito

DEVLIN, Johnny
Singles: 7-inch
CORAL ... 4-8 62

DEVO *LP '78*
Singles: 12-inch
ENIGMA ... 4-6 88
W.B (Except 2006) ... 4-8 80-85
W.B. (2006 "That's Good") ... 15-20 83
(Picture disc. Promotional issue only.)
Singles: 7-inch
ASYLUM ... 3-4 81
BOOJI BOY ... 4-8 78
ENIGMA ... 3-4 88
FULL MOON ... 3-4 81
W.B. (Except 49826) ... 3-6 78-85
W.B. (49826 "Beautiful World") ... 10-15 81
(Space helmet shaped picture disc.)
W.B. (49826 Beautiful World") ... 40-80 81
(Space helmet shaped colored vinyl. Experimental pressing only. 20 made.)
Picture Sleeves
FULL MOON ... 3-4 81
W.B. ... 3-5 79-85
LPs: 10/12-inch
ENIGMA ... 5-10 88
W.B. ... 5-10 78-88
Members: Mark Mothersbaugh; Bob Mothersbaugh; David Kendrick; Bob Casale; Gerald Casale.
Also see JACKSON, Jermaine

DE VOL, Frank, Orchestra *P&R '50*
(With the Rainbow Strings)
Singles: 78 rpm
CAPITOL ... 3-5 50-56
KEM ... 3-5 55
Singles: 7-inch
ABC-PAR ... 3-5 64-65
CAPITOL ... 3-6 50-56
COLGEMS ... 3-5 68
COLUMBIA ... 3-5 59-62
KEM ... 3-6 55
Picture Sleeves
COLGEMS ... 3-5 68
LPs: 10/12-inch
ABC-PAR ... 5-10 65-66
COLGEMS (COM-108 "Guess Who's Coming to Dinner") ... 20-25 68
(Soundtrack. Monaural.)
COLGEMS (COS-108 "Guess Who's Coming to Dinner") ... 25-30 68
(Soundtrack. Stereo.)
COLGEMS (COMO-5006 "The Happening") ... 15-20 67
(Soundtrack. Monaural.)
COLGEMS (COSO-5006 "The Happening") ... 20-25 67
(Soundtrack. Stereo.)
COLUMBIA ... 8-10 59-63
HARMONY ... 5-10 65

DEVONAIRES
Singles: 7-inch
DEVON ... 8-12 60
GOLDEN WORLD ... 5-10 64

DEVONNES
Singles: 7-inch
COLOSSUS (142 "I'm Gonna Pick Up My Toys") ... 10-20 71

DEVONS
Singles: 7-inch
DECCA (31777 "Free Fall") ... 25-35 65
DECCA (31899 "Come On") ... 25-35 66
Members: Chuck Girard; Gary Usher.
Also see GIRARD, Chuck
Also see USHER, Gary

DEVONS
(Sir Douglas Quintet)
Singles: 7-inch
PIC ONE ... 10-15 66
Also see SIR DOUGLAS QUINTET

DEVONS *R&B '69*
Singles: 7-inch
KING ... 3-6 69

DEVONSQUARE
Singles: 7-inch
ATLANTIC ... 3-4
BLIND DATE ... 3-4 84

DEVORE, Florence
Singles: 7-inch
PHIL-DAN (5000 "Kiss Me Now") ... 10-20 65

DEVORINE, Shura
Singles: 7-inch
ASCOT ... 4-8 64

DE VORZON, Barry *LP '76*
Singles: 7-inch
COLUMBIA ... 8-12 59-61
RCA ... 10-20 57-59
W.B. ... 3-4 81
LPs: 10/12-inch
A&M ... 5-10 76
ARISTA ... 5-10 76
Also see BARRY & TAMERLANES

DE VORZON, Barry, & Perry Botkin Jr. *P&R '76*
Singles: 7-inch
A&M ... 3-5 76-77
Picture Sleeves
A&M ... 3-5 76
LPs: 10/12-inch
A&M ... 5-10 76
Also see DE VORZON, Barry
Also see McCOY BOYS

DEVOTIONS *P&R '64*
Singles: 7-inch
DELTA (1001 "Rip Van Winkle") .. 50-100 61
KAPE ... 5-10
ROULETTE (4406 "Rip Van Winkle") ... 25-50 61
(White label.)
ROULETTE (4541 "Rip Van Winkle") ... 10-15 64
(Orange label.)
ROULETTE (4556 "Sunday Kind of Love") ... 25-35 64
ROULETTE (4580 "Snow White") 10-20 64
Members: Joe Pardo; Frank Pardo; Bob Weisbrod; Ray Sanchez; Bob Havorka; Louis DeCarlo; Larry Frank
Also see FIVE DISCS / Devotions

DEVOTIONS
Singles: 7-inch
TRI-SOUND ... 4-8 66

DEVOTIONS *R&B '70*
Singles: 7-inch
COLOSSUS ... 3-6 70

DEVOTIONS
Singles: 7-inch
AVENUE D (0022 "Erlene") ... 4-6 94
(Black vinyl.)
AVENUE D (0022 "Erlene") ... 8-12 94
(Yellow vinyl.)

DEVOTIONS
Singles: 7-inch
NATION ("It's Alright") ... 100-200
(Selection number not known.)

DEVOTO, Howard
Singles: 12-inch
I.R.S. ... 4-6 86
Singles: 7-inch
I.R.S. ... 3-4 86
LPs: 10/12-inch
I.R.S. ... 5-10 86
Also see MAGAZINE

DEVROE, Billy & Devilaires
(Billy Dev-roe; Devroe's Devilaires)
Singles: 78 rpm
TAMPA ... 10-25 55-57
Singles: 7-inch
TAMPA (107 "Ice and Fire") ... 10-15 55
TAMPA (109 "Will You Love Me") . 10-15 56
TAMPA (127 "Buttercup") ... 10-15 57
TAMPA (133 "I'm Packin'") ... 20-40 58
Picture Sleeves
TAMPA (127 "Buttercup") ... 50-75 57
LPs: 10/12-inch
TAMPA (31 "Billy Devroe and the Devilaires, Vol. 1") ... 25-35 58
TAMPA (39 "Billy Devroe and the Devilaires, Vol. 2") ... 25-35 58

DEVRONS
Singles: 7-inch
LOTUS ... 3-5 62

DEW DROPS
Singles: 7-inch
JEFF (1963 "No Other Guy") ... 20-30 63

DE WAYNE & BELDETTAS
Singles: 7-inch
HBR (506 "Big Time") ... 5-10 66

DEWEY, George & Jack
Singles: 7-inch
RAVEN (700 "Flying Saucers Have Landed") ... 20-25

DeWITT, Lew *C&W '85*
Singles: 7-inch
COMPLEAT ... 3-4 85
Also see STATLER BROTHERS

DE WOLF, Dean
LPs: 10/12-inch
ARGO ... 15-20 65

DEXTER, Al, & Troopers *P&R/R&B '43*
Singles: 7-inch
COLUMBIA ... 4-8 46
EKKO ... 4-6 55
OKEH ... 5-10 43-44
VOCALION ... 10-20
Singles: 7-inch
EKKO ... 5-10 55
LPs: 10/12-inch
AUDIO LAB ... 8-12
CAPITOL (1701 "Greatest Hits") ... 20-30 62
COLUMBIA (9005 "Songs of the Southwest") ... 30-40
(10-inch LP.)
HARMONY ... 8-10
HILLTOP ... 8-10

DEXTER, Levi
LPs: 10/12-inch
PVC ... 8-15 81
Also see LEVI & ROCKATS

DEXY'S MIDNIGHT RUNNERS *P&R/LP '83*
Singles: 7-inch
EMI AMERICA ... 3-4 81
MERCURY ... 3-4 82-83
Picture Sleeves
MERCURY ... 5-10 82-83
LPs: 10/12-inch
EMI AMERICA ... 5-10 81
MERCURY ... 5-10 82-83

DEY, Tracey P&R '63
Singles: 7-inch
AMY 8-12 63-65
COLUMBIA 5-10 66
LIBERTY 10-20 63
VEE JAY 10-20 62
Also see DEY & KNIGHT

DEY & KNIGHT
Singles: 7-inch
COLUMBIA (43466 "Young Love").. 5-10 65
COLUMBIA (43693 "Ooh Da La") ... 5-10 66
Members: Tracey Dey; Gary Knight.
Also see DEY, Tracey

DE YOUNG, Cliff P&R '74
Singles: 7-inch
MCA 3-5 73-75
Picture Sleeves
MCA 3-5 74
LPs: 10/12-inch
MCA 10-12 73-75

DE YOUNG, Dennis P&R/LP '84
Singles: 12-inch
MCA 4-8 88
(Promotional only.)
Singles: 7-inch
A&M 3-4 83-86
Picture Sleeves
A&M 3-4 84-86
LPs: 10/12-inch
A&M 5-10 84-86
MCA 5-8 88
Also see STYX

DE ZASTA, Gen.
Singles: 7-inch
ROULETTE 5-10 59

DEZEL, Neice
Singles: 7-inch
J&S 10-15

D'FANO, Bobby
Singles: 7-inch
PALETTE 4-8 61-63
STAR SATELLITE 4-8 59

DIABLOS R&B '56
(Featuring Nolan Strong; with Maurice King Orchestra)
Singles: 78 rpm
FORTUNE 10-25 54-57
Singles: 7-inch
FORTUNE (509 thru 522) 15-25 54-56
FORTUNE (525 thru 563) 10-20 57-64
FORTUNE (574 "The Way You Dog Me Around") 10-15 80
(Colored vinyl.)
Picture Sleeves
FORTUNE 15-25 64
LPs: 10/12-inch
FORTUNE (8010 "Fortune of Hits") 50-75 61
FORTUNE (8012 "Fortune of Hits, Vol. 2") 40-60 62
FORTUNE (8015 "Mind Over Matter") 40-60 63
FORTUNE (80810 "Fortune of Hits") 10-15
Members: Nolan Strong; Bob "Chico" Edwards; Juan Guiterriez; Willie Hunter, Quentin Eubanks; Jim Strong; George Scott; J.W. Johnson.
Also see STRONG, Nolan

DIABLOS
Singles: 7-inch
JUBILEE 10-20 67

DIABOLIQUES
Singles: 7-inch
MERRI (6005 "Bubbles") 10-20 63
Picture Sleeves
MERRI (6005 "Bubbles") 10-20 63

DIACO, Al
Singles: 7-inch
FOUR SEASONS ("Lover's Hideaway") 75-100 65
(No selection number used.)

DIADEMS
(With Buddy Sharpe & the Shakers)
Singles: 7-inch
GOLDIE (715 "I'll Do Anything") 25-35 61
LAVERE 5-8
STAR (514 "Why Don't You Believe Me") 30-40 63
Also see HILTON, Jerry, & Diadems

DIAL, Buddy
Singles: 7-inch
MARK LTD. (1007 "Baby") 10-15

DIAL, Harry
Singles: 7-inch
YORKSHIRE 4-8 64

DIAL TONES
(Dynamic Dial Tones)
Singles: 7-inch
HORIZON (1596 "Boss") 10-15 61

DIALOGUE
LPs: 10/12-inch
COLD ("Dialogue") 300-400 68
(Selection number not known.)

DIALS
Singles: 7-inch
HILL TOP (219 "No Hard Feelings") 75-125 61
HILL TOP (2009 "School Bells Are Ringing") 350-500 60
HILL TOP (2010 "Wondering About Your Love") 150-250 60
NORGOLDE (105 "Ring Ting-a-Ding") 50-75 59

DIALS
Singles: 7-inch
PHILIPS (40040 "These Foolish Things") 75-125 62
Member: Sal Corrente.
Also see CORRENTE, Sal

DIALS
Singles: 7-inch
TIME 4-8 63
LPs: 10/12-inch
TIME (2100 "It's Monkey Time") 15-25 64

DIALTONES
Singles: 7-inch
DANDY DAN 15-25 59
LAWN 10-20 63

DIALTONES
Singles: 7-inch
GOLDISC 10-15 60-61
Also see RANDY & RAINBOWS

DIALTONES
Singles: 7-inch
DIAL 10-20 67

DIAMOND
Singles: 7-inch
PARAMOUNT 3-5 73
LPs: 10/12-inch
PARAMOUNT 8-10 74

DIAMOND, Bobby
Singles: 7-inch
MGM 4-8 62

DIAMOND, Brian
(Brian Diamond & Cutters)
Singles: 7-inch
HICKORY 4-8 65

DIAMOND, Dave
Singles: 7-inch
VISION 5-8 62

DIAMOND, Dave
(With the Higher Elevation)
Singles: 7-inch
CHICORY (408 "Diamond Mine") ... 15-25 66
CLARIDGE 5-10 75-76
Also see HIGHER ELEVATION
Also see SOOTHSAYERS

DIAMOND, Dyan
Singles: 7-inch
MCA 3-4 78
LPs: 10/12-inch
MCA 5-10 78

DIAMOND, Gerri
Singles: 7-inch
HBR 4-8 66

DIAMOND, Gerry
Singles: 7-inch
DWAIN (811 "Nancy") 5-10 60

DIAMOND, Gregg R&B '78
(Gregg Diamond's Starcruiser; Gregg Diamond's Bionic Boogie)
Singles: 12-inch
POLYDOR 4-6 79
Singles: 7-inch
MARLIN 3-5 78
POLYDOR 3-4 79-80
LPs: 10/12-inch
MARLIN 5-10 78
MERCURY 5-10 79
POLYDOR 5-10 77-78

DIAMOND, Hank & Carol
Singles: 7-inch
WORKSHOP JAZZ (2001 "I Remember You") 15-25 60s

DIAMOND, Joel P&R '81
(Joel Diamond Experience)
Singles: 12-inch
CASABLANCA 4-6 79
Singles: 7-inch
ATLANTIC 3-4 82
CASABLANCA 3-4 79-84
MOTOWN 3-4 81
LPs: 10/12-inch
CASABLANCA 8-10 79

DIAMOND, Larry
Singles: 7-inch
ARGO 5-10 59
DIMAX 8-12 60
GARDENA (112 "Betty Booper") 30-45 61

DIAMOND, Lee
Singles: 7-inch
LIKE YOUNG 4-8 65
MINIT 5-10 60
VEE JAY 10-15 58

DIAMOND, Leo P&R '53
Singles: 78 rpm
AMBASSADOR 3-5 51-53
RCA 3-5 55
ROULETTE 4-8 57
Singles: 7-inch
AMBASSADOR 4-8 53
RCA 3-6 55
ROULETTE 5-10 57

DIAMOND, Neil P&R/LP '66
Singles: 12-inch
COLUMBIA (99-1586 "Heartlight") . 30-40 83
(Picture disc. Promotional issue only.)
CONTINUUM II (001 "We Wrote a Song Together") 1500-2000 76
(Made exclusively for Neil's son Jesse's grade school class. Has Neil and a band composing and recording, with children, in a studio. Includes an alternative version of *Beautiful Noise*. Neil made and autographed a copy for each child in attendence – estimated to be 30 to 40 copies.)
Singles: 7-inch
BANG (100 series) 3-4
("Best Hits" reissue series.)
BANG (500 & 700 series) 5-10 66-73
CAPITOL 3-5 80-81
COLUMBIA (02600 thru 06100 series) 3-4 81-86
COLUMBIA (10000 & 11000 series) ... 3-6 74-80
COLUMBIA (33000 series) 3-4
("Hall of Fame" series.)
COLUMBIA (42809 "Clown Town") 550-650 63
COLUMBIA (45000 series) 3-6 73-74
MCA (40000 series) 3-6 73
MCA (60000 series) 3-6 73
PHILCO 25-30 66-67
("Hip-Pocket" flexi-discs.)
SOLID ROCK 5-8
UNI 4-8 68-72
Promotional Singles
BANG (Except 55075) 10-15 66-73
UNI (55075 "Two-Bit Manchild") 40-50 68
(Colored vinyl.)
CAPITOL 3-5 80-81
COLUMBIA (1115 "Song Sung Blue") 4-8 77
COLUMBIA (1193 "September Morn") 4-8 79
(Alternative version.)
COLUMBIA (02600 thru 11000) 3-8 74-86
COLUMBIA (42809 "Clown Town") 300-400 63
COLUMBIA (45000 series) 4-8 73-74
MCA 3-6 73
UNI 8-12 68-72
WHAT'S IT ALL ABOUT 20-30 70s
(Public service disc, made for radio stations.)
Picture Sleeves
CAPITOL 3-6 80-81
COLUMBIA 3-6 73-86
UNI 5-10 68-70
EPs: 7-inch
COLUMBIA (32919 "Serenade") 35-40 74
(Juke box issue only. Includes title strips.)
MCA (34989 "12 Greatest Hits") 25-30 74
(Juke box issue only. Includes title strips.)
UNI (34818 "Neil Diamond Gold") .. 25-30 71
(Juke box issue only. Includes title strips.)
UNI (34871 "Stones") 45-50 71
(Juke box issue only. Includes title strips.)
LPs: 10/12-inch
BANG (214 "The Feel of Neil Diamond") 125-150 66
BANG (217 "Just For You") 25-50 67
BANG (219 "Greatest Hits") 25-50 68
BANG (221 "Shilo") 40-50 70
BANG (224 "Do It") 40-50 71
BANG (227 "Double Gold") 25-30 73
CAPITOL 5-10 80
COLUMBIA (30000 series, except 39915) 8-12 73-86
COLUMBIA (39915 "Primitive") 35-40 84
(Picture disc.)
COLUMBIA (40000 series) 8-10 86-89
COLUMBIA (42550 "Jonathan Livingston Seagull") 25-30 81
(Half-speed mastered.)
COLUMBIA (45025 "Best Years of Our Lives") 5-8 89
COLUMBIA (46525 "You Don't Bring Me Flowers") 30-35 80
(Half-speed mastered.)
COLUMBIA (47628 "On the Way to the Sky") 45-50 82
(Half-speed mastered.)
DIRECT-TO-DISK 25-30
FROG KING (1 "Early Classics") ... 65-75 78
(Includes music and lyrics songbook. Columbia Record Club issue.)
HARMONY (30023 "Chartbusters") 75-100 70
(Various artists LP, containing the 1963 Columbia tracks, and the otherwise unavailable *I've Never Been the Same.*)
MCA 6-15 72-81
MFSL (2-024 "Hot August Night") .. 40-50 79
MFSL (071 "Jazz Singer") 30-40 82
UNI (11 Neil Diamond Sampler") 150-200 71
(With paper envelope cover. Has sticker promoting a special event. Promotional souvenir "Hits" pakage for those attending.)
UNI (11 Neil Diamond D.J. Sampler") 100-125 71
(With paper envelope cover. Does not have sticker promoting the event. Promotional issue for dee jays only.)
UNI (1913 "Open-End Interview with Neil Diamond") 75-100 72
(Promotional issue only.)
UNI (73030 "Velvet Gloves and Spit") 50-60 68
(Gatefold cover pictures Neil and some female mannequins. Does not contain *Shilo.*)
UNI (73030 "Velvet Gloves and Spit") 40-50 68
(Gatefold cover pictures Neil and some female mannequins. Contains *Shilo.*)
UNI (73030 "Velvet Gloves and Spit") 15-25 70
(Standard cover – no mannequins. Contains *Shilo.*)
UNI (73047 "Brother Love's Traveling Salvation Show") 40-50 69
(Gatefold cover pictures Neil on a wagon on front side and a game board on the back. Known as "Purple Wagon" cover.)
UNI (73047 "Sweet Caroline – Brother Love's Traveling Salvation Show") 15-25 69
(Standard cover – reworked, including revised title. No game board.)
UNI (73071 "Touching You, Touching Me") 15-25 69
UNI (73084 "Gold") 15-25 70
UNI (73092 "Tap Root Manuscript") 15-25 70
(Some 70000 series LPs were reissued in the 90000 series, with the only change being the first digit.)
UNI (93106 "Stones") 15-25 71
UNI (93136 "Moods") 15-25 72
UNI (93501 "Tap Root Manuscript") 15-25 70
(Capitol Record Club issue.)
Also see JUDAS PRIEST
Also see NEIL & JACK
Also see STREISAND, Barbra, & Neil Diamond
Also see TEN BROKEN HEARTS

DIAMOND, Neil / Diana Ross & Supremes
LPs: 10/12-inch
MCA (734727 "It's Happening") 30-40 72
(One side of LP devoted to each artist.)
Also see DIAMOND, Neil
Also see SUPREMES

DIAMOND, Nelson
Singles: 7-inch
HI 3-6 69

DIAMOND, Ronnie
Singles: 7-inch
IMPERIAL (Except 5588) 5-10 58-59
IMPERIAL (5588 "Life Begins at 4 O'Clock") 30-45 59

DIAMOND HEAD
Singles: 7-inch
DUNHILL 3-5 73
HAVEN 3-5 75
MCA 3-4 83
LPs: 10/12-inch
MCA 5-10 83

DIAMOND JIM
Singles: 7-inch
PANJO 4-8 69

DIAMOND JOE
Singles: 7-inch
INSTANT 5-8 65
MINIT 5-10 62
SANSU 4-8 66-67

DIAMOND REO P&R '75
Singles: 7-inch
BIG TREE 3-5 75
BUDDAH 3-5 77
LPs: 10/12-inch
BIG TREE 8-10 75
KAMA SUTRA 8-10 76
PICCADILLY 5-10 79
Members: Frank Czuri; Bob McKeag.
Also see SILENCERS

DIAMOND RIO C&W/LP '91
Singles: 7-inch
ARISTA 3-4 91
LPs: 10/12-inch
ARISTA 5-8 91
Members: Marty Roe; Dan Truman; Brian Prout; Jim Olander; Dana Williams; Gene Johnson.

DIAMONDS
Singles: 78 rpm
ATLANTIC (981 "A Beggar for Your Kisses") 150-250 52
ATLANTIC (1003 "Two Loves Have I") 100-200 53
ATLANTIC (1017 "Cherry") 100-200 53
Singles: 7-inch
ATLANTIC (981 "A Beggar for Your Kisses") 400-600 52
ATLANTIC (1003 "Two Loves Have I") 300-500 53
ATLANTIC (1017 "Cherry") 300-500 53
Members: Harold Wright; Ernest Ward; Myles Hardy; Dan Stevens.
Also see METRONOMES

DIAMONDS P&R/R&B '56
(With Dick Jacobs & Orchestra)
Singles: 78 rpm
CORAL 5-10 55-56
MERCURY (Except 71060) 5-15 56-57
MERCURY (71060 "Little Darlin' ") 25-50 57
Singles: 7-inch
CHURCHILL 3-4 87
CORAL 10-20 55-56
MERCURY (Maroon label) 15-25 56
MERCURY (Black label) 10-20 56-62
Picture Sleeves
MERCURY (71291 "High Sign") 15-25 58
EPs: 7-inch
BRUNSWICK 15-20 57
MERCURY 10-20 56-61
LPs: 10/12-inch
MERCURY 20-45 57-60
WING 20-25 59
Members: David Somerville; Phil Leavitt; Bill Reed; Ted Kowalski; Bob Duncan.
Also see DEL-VIKINGS / Diamonds / Big Bopper / Gaylords
Also see JACOBS, Dick, & Orchestra
Also see SOMERVILLE, David
Also see VEE, Bobby / Diamonds / Drifters

DIAMONDS / Georgia Gibbs / Sarah Vaughan / Florian Zabach
EPs: 7-inch
MERCURY (4026 "Tops in Pops") 15-20 50s
Also see GIBBS, Georgia
Also see VAUGHAN, Sarah
Also see ZABACH, Florian

DIAMONDS & PETE RUGOLO
LPs: 10/12-inch
MERCURY (60076 "The Diamonds Meet Pete Rugolo") 45-55 59
Also see BELLAND & SOMERVILLE
Also see DIAMONDS
Also see RUGOLO, Pete, & His Orchestra

DIAMONDS C&W '87
Singles: 7-inch
CHURCHILL 3-5
Member: Bob Duncan.

DIAMONDS IV
Singles: 7-inch
JAMAKA (8346 "Panic Beat") 10-15 59

DIAMONDS, Jerry, & Sparkles
Singles: 7-inch
RCA 15-20 58

DIAMONETTES
Singles: 7-inch
ALSTON 3-5 71

DIAN, Humevist
Singles: 7-inch
VOLTONE 10-15 62

DIAN & Greenbriar Boys
Singles: 7-inch
ELEKTRA 4-8 63
Member: James Dian.

DIANA C&W '79
(Diana Murrell)
Singles: 7-inch
ADAMAS 3-4 82
ELEKTRA 3-5 79
SUNBIRD 3-4 81

DIANE & ANNITA
Singles: 7-inch
WAND 4-8 66

DIANE & DARLETTES
Singles: 7-inch
DUNES 15-20 62

DIANE RAY: see RAY, Diane

DIANTE, Denny
Singles: 7-inch
HOLIDAY (1210 "Little Lover") 50-75 64

DIAPER RASH
Singles: 7-inch
LAURIE 3-5 70

DIATONES
Singles: 7-inch
BANDERA (2509 "Oh, Baby Come Dance with Me") 50-75 61

DIAZ, Carlos, & Royal Tones
Singles: 7-inch
TRIANGLE (001 "Only One Love") 75-125

DIAZ, Louis
Singles: 7-inch
SECTON 10-15

DIAZ, Vic
(Vickie Diaz)
Singles: 7-inch
DEL-FI (4149 "For Eternity") 20-30 60
DONNA (1351 "Mr. Moon") 5-10 61

DIBANGO, Manu P&R/R&B/LP '73
Singles: 7-inch
ATLANTIC 3-5 73
LPs: 10/12-inch
ATLANTIC 8-10 73

DI BLANDA, Kareen
Singles: 7-inch
ROULETTE 5-8 60

DICE, Roland
Singles: 7-inch
JAMIE (1257 "Velma") 5-10 63

DICK, Deadeye: see DEADEYE DICK

DICK, Moby: see MOBY DICK

DICK & DEEDEE P&R '61
(With the Don Ralke Orchestra)
Singles: 7-inch
DOT 4-8 68-69
LAMA (7778 "The Mountain's High") 15-25 61
LAMA (7780 "Goodbye to Love") ... 15-25 61
LAMA (7783 "Tell Me") 15-25 61
LIBERTY 5-10 61-62
U.A. 3-4
W.B. 4-8 62-69
Picture Sleeves
W.B. 12-25 63-64
LPs: 10/12-inch
LIBERTY (3236 "Tell Me"/"The Mountain's High") 40-50 62
(Monaural.)
LIBERTY (7236 "Tell Me"/"The Mountain's High") 40-50 62
W.B. (1500 "Young and in Love") .. 20-30 63

W.B. (1538 "Turn Around")...20-30 64
W.B. (1586 "Thou Shalt Not Steal")...25-35 65
W.B. (1623 "Songs We've Sung on Shindig")...20-30 65
Members: Dick St. John; Dee Dee Sperling.
Also see RALKE, Don
Also see ST. JOHN, Dick

DICK & DON: see ADDRISI BROTHERS

DICK & JACK
Singles: 7-inch
PROFILE...5-10 60

DICK & RICHARD
Singles: 7-inch
CAPITOL...4-8 63

DICK & TEENBEATS
Singles: 7-inch
BIGTOP (3144 "Strawberries")...10-20 63
Also see FIVE TEENBEATS

DICK LEE: see LEE, Dick

DICKENS, Doles, Quintet
Singles: 78 rpm
CONTINENTAL...15-25 47
DECCA...15-25 49-55
GOTHAM...15-25 49
SUPERDISC...15-25 47
Singles: 7-inch
DECCA (29490 "Gonna Rock This Morning")...20-30 55
DECCA (48199 "Blues in the Back Room")...40-50 51
DECCA (48229 "Gonna Rock This Morning")...40-50 51
DECCA (48242 "Blues in the Evening")...40-50 51

DICKENS, Jimmy *C&W '49*
(Little Jimmy Dickens; Jimmie Dickens)
Singles: 78 rpm
COLUMBIA...5-10 49-57
Singles: 7-inch
COLUMBIA (10000 series)...3-5 76
COLUMBIA (20000 & 21000 series)...10-20 50-56
COLUMBIA (40000 series)...8-12 56
COLUMBIA (41000 series, except 41173)...8-12 57-60
COLUMBIA (41173 "I Got a Hole in My Pocket")...30-45 57
COLUMBIA (42000 thru 44000 series)...4-8 60-67
DECCA...3-6 67-69
LITTLE GEM...3-5 75
PARTRIDGE...3-4 80
STARDAY...3-5 73
U.A....3-5 70-72
EPs: 7-inch
COLUMBIA (Except 2800 series)...15-20 52-57
COLUMBIA (2800 series)...10-15 57-58
LPs: 10/12-inch
COLUMBIA (1047 "Raisin' the Dickens")...40-50 57
COLUMBIA (1500 thru 2500 series)...10-20 60-66
(Monaural.)
COLUMBIA (8300 thru 9600 series, except 9025)...15-25 60-68
(Stereo.)
COLUMBIA (9025 "The Old Country Church")...50-100 54
(10-inch LP.)
COLUMBIA (10000 & 11000 series)...6-10 70-73
COLUMBIA (38000 series)...5-10 84
DECCA...10-15 68-69
GUSTO...5-10
HARMONY (7000 series)...15-25 64-65
HARMONY (11000 series)...8-12 67
QCA...5-10 75

DICKERSON, John: see SENATORS

DICKERSON, Suzy
Singles: 7-inch
TREY...5-10 60

DICKEY, Dan *C&W '79*
Singles: 7-inch
CHARTWHEEL...3-5 79

DICKEY, Milt
Singles: 78 rpm
SHOME...10-15

DICKIE & CUTOUTS
Singles: 7-inch
("A Pimple on the Ass of Progress")...6-12 91
(Picture disc. Promotional issue only. No label name or number used.)

DICKIE & DEBONAIRES
Singles: 7-inch
ASTA (101 "Stomp")...10-20 61
JASON SCOTT...4-8
VALLI (302 "Yo Yo Girl")...100-150

DICKIE & EBBTIDES
Singles: 7-inch
GOLDEN WORLD (45 "One Boy, One Girl")...15-25 66

DICKIE & POSEIDONS
Singles: 7-inch
MOTOWN...3-5 75

DICKLESS
Singles: 7-inch
SUB POP...3-5 91

DICKY DOO & DONT'S *P&R/R&B '58*
Singles: 7-inch
ASCOT...4-8 65
CASINO...3-5
COLLECTABLES...3-4 80s
DANNA...4-8 67
ITZY...4-8
SWAN...8-12 58-59
U.A....8-10 60-61
LPs: 10/12-inch
DANNA (1566 "Live at Eagle Rock")...40-60 60s
U.A. (3094 "Madison and Other Dances")...25-30 60
(Monaural.)
U.A. (3097 "Teen Scene")...25-30 60
U.A. (6094 "Madison and Other Dances")...30-40 60
(Stereo.)
U.A. (6097 "Teen Scene")...30-40 60
(Stereo.)
Members: Gerry Granahan; Harvey Davis; Jerry Grant; Ray Gangi; Joey Paige.
Also see GRANAHAN, Gerry

DICKIE LEE: see LEE, Dickie

DICKIE, Tom, & Desires
Singles: 7-inch
MERCURY...3-4 81
LPs: 10/12-inch
MERCURY...5-10 81

DICKIE G & DON'TS
Singles: 7-inch
ASI (1013 "Rocky & the Angel")...4-8 70s

DICKIES
Singles: 7-inch
A&M...3-4 79
LPs: 10/12-inch
A&M (4742 "Incredible Shrinking Dickies")...5-10 79
A&M (12008 "The Dickies")...20-30 79
(Colored vinyl. Promotional issue only.)

DICKINSON, Bruce *LP '90*
LPs: 10/12-inch
COLUMBIA...5-8 90

DICKINSON, Hal *C&W '66*
Singles: 7-inch
GRASS...4-8 66

DICKINSON, James Luther
LPs: 10/12-inch
ATLANTIC...8-10 72
Also see DR. JOHN
Also see MANNING, Terry
Also see PATTERSON, Brenda

DICKINSON, Jim
Singles: 7-inch
SOUTHTOWN...4-8 65
Also see BURLISON, Paul

DICKINSON, Pam
Singles: 7-inch
GAMBIT...4-8 63
MONUMENT...4-8 65-66

DICKSON, Barbara
Singles: 7-inch
COLUMBIA...3-4 80
MCA...3-4 77
RSO...3-4 77
LPs: 10/12-inch
COLUMBIA...8-10 80

DICKSON, Don
Singles: 7-inch
PHILIPS...4-8 64

DICKSON, Duke
Singles: 7-inch
GLOBAL (716 "My Baby Doll")...30-50 58
GLOBAL (720 "Is You Is Or Is You Ain't")...20-30 59

DICKSON, Richie
Singles: 7-inch
CLASS...4-8 63

DICKY & Watergate Bugs
Singles: 7-inch
STEADY...5-8 73

DICTATORS *LP '77*
Singles: 7-inch
ASYLUM...3-4 77
LPs: 10/12-inch
ASYLUM...8-12 77-78
EPIC...10-12 75

DIDDLEY, Bo *R&B '55*
Singles: 78 rpm
CHECKER (814 thru 907)...25-50 55-58
CHECKER (914 "I'm Sorry")...40-60 59
CHECKER (924 "Crackin' Up")...50-75 59
REO (8022 "Bo Diddley")...50-75 55
(Canadian.)
Singles: 7-inch
ABC...3-5 74
CHECKER (814 "Bo Diddley")...25-50 55
CHECKER (819 "Diddley Daddy")...25-50 55
CHECKER (827 "Pretty Thing")...25-50 55
CHECKER (832 "Diddy Wah Diddy")...25-50 56
CHECKER (842 "Who Do You Love")...25-50 56
CHECKER (850 "Cops & Robbers")...25-50 56
CHECKER (860 "Hey, Bo Diddley")...20-40 57
CHECKER (878 "Say, Boss Man")...20-40 57
CHECKER (896 "Hush Your Mouth")...20-40 58
CHECKER (907 "Bo Meets the Monster")...20-40 58
CHECKER (914 "I'm Sorry")...15-25 59
CHECKER (924 "Crackin' Up")...15-25 59
CHECKER (931 "Say Man")...15-25 59
CHECKER (936 "Say Man, Back Again")...15-25 59
CHECKER (942 "Road Runner")...15-25 60
CHECKER (951 "Crawdad")...15-25 60
CHECKER (965 "Gunslinger")...15-25 61
CHECKER (976 "Not Guilty")...15-25 61
CHECKER (985 "Call Me")...15-25 61
CHECKER (997 "Bo Diddley")...10-20 61
CHECKER (1019 thru 1200)...5-15 62-69
CHESS...3-5 71-72
GOLDEN GOODIES...4-6
RCA...3-5 76
REO (8022 "Bo Diddley")...50-100 55
(Canadian.)
EPs: 7-inch
CHESS (5125 "Bo Diddley")...50-75 58
(With cardboard cover.)
CHESS (5125 "Bo Diddley")...40-50 58
(With paper cover.)
LPs: 10/12-inch
ACCORD...5-10 82
CHECKER (1436 "Go Bo Diddley")...75-100 57
CHECKER (2974 "Have Guitar Will Travel")...50-75 59
CHECKER (2976 "Bo Diddley in the Spotlight")...50-75 60
CHECKER (2977 "Bo Diddley Is a Gunslinger")...65-75 61
CHECKER (2980 "Bo Diddley in a Lover")...40-60 61
CHECKER (2982 "Bo Diddley's a Twister")...40-50 62
CHECKER (2984 "Bo Diddley")...35-45 62
CHECKER (2985 "Bo Diddley and Company")...40-60 63
CHECKER (2987 "Surfin' with Bo Diddley")...35-45 63
(Most of the tracks on this LP are by the Megatons.)
CHECKER (2988 "Bo Diddley's Beach Party")...35-45 63
CHECKER (2989 "Bo Diddley's 16 All-Time Greatest Hits")...25-35 63
CHECKER (2992 "Hey Good Lookin' ")...25-35 64
CHECKER (2996 "500% More Man")...25-35 64
CHECKER (3001 "The Originator")...25-35 66
CHECKER (3006 "Go Bo Diddley")...25-35 67
CHECKER (3007 "Boss Man")...40-60 67
CHECKER (3013 "The Black Gladiator")...25-35 69
CHESS (1431 "Bo Diddley")...75-100 58
CHESS (8000 series)...5-10 83
CHESS (60000 series)...15-25 74
MCA/CHESS...5-8 88
RCA (1229 "20th Anniversary of Rock 'N Roll")...10-20 76
(With numerous guest stars.)
Session: Jody Williams; Cliff James; Frank Kirkland; Jerome Green. Session: Willie Dixon; Otis Spann; Moonglows.
Also see BELMONTS, Freddy Cannon & Bo Diddley
Also see DIXON, Willie
Also see McCAIN, Jerry
Also see MOONGLOWS
Also see SPANN, Otis

DIDDLEY, Bo, & Chuck Berry
Singles: 7-inch
CHECKER (13370 "Bo's Beat")...4-8 64
LPs: 10/12-inch
CHECKER (2991 "Two Great Guitars")...20-25 64
Also see BERRY, Chuck

DIDDLEY, Bo, Howlin' Wolf & Muddy Waters
LPs: 10/12-inch
CHECKER (3010 "Super Super Blues Band")...15-20 68
Also see DIDDLEY, Bo
Also see HOWLIN' WOLF
Also see WATERS, Muddy

DIDDLEY OOHS
Singles: 7-inch
DORE...4-8 62

DIDDLY, Squiddly: see SQUIDDLY DIDDLY

DIEHL, Aleta
Singles: 7-inch
MINUTEMAN...4-8 65

DIESEL *P&R/LP '81*
Singles: 7-inch
REGENCY...3-4 81
LPs: 10/12-inch
REGENCY...8-10 81

DIETRICH, Marlene
Singles: 78 rpm
COLUMBIA...4-8 55
Singles: 7-inch
COLUMBIA...5-10 55
LPs: 10/12-inch
COLUMBIA (105 "Marlena Dietrich Overseas")...40-60 52
(10-inch LP.)
COLUMBIA (316 "Dietrich in Rio")...25-35 59
COLUMBIA (2615 "Marlena Dietrich Overseas")...30-50 56
(10-inch LP.)
COLUMBIA (4975 "At the Cafe de Paris")...30-50 55
DECCA (5100 "Souvenir Album")...40-60 49
(10-inch LP.)
DECCA (7021 "Curtain Call")...30-40 51
DECCA (8465 "Marlene Dietrich")...25-35 57
MCA (1501 "Her Complete Recordings")...5-10 70s
VOX (3040 "Dietrich Sings")...50-75
Also see CLOONEY, Rosemary, & Marlene Dietrich

DIETZEL, Elroy, & Rhythm Bandits
Singles: 7-inch
BO-KAY (101 "Teenage Ball")...200-300 58
BO-KAY (103 "Rock-N-Bones")...300-500 58
(Counterfeits exist of this release.)

DIFFERENT PARTS
Singles: 7-inch
AMS (101 "Why")...25-35

DIFFERENT STROKES
Singles: 7-inch
OKEH...3-6 69

DIFFERENT STROKES
Singles: 7-inch
LUV (165 "Imaginary Street")...5-10 60s
Also see TIM TAM & TURN-ONS

DIFFIE, Joe *C&W '90*
Singles: 7-inch
EPIC...3-4 90-92

DIFFORD & TILBROOK *LP '84*
Singles: 7-inch
A&M...3-4 84
LPs: 10/12-inch
A&M...5-10 84
Members: Chris Difford; Glenn Tilbrook.
Also see SQUEEZE

DIFOSCO *R&B '76*
(Difosco Erwin)
Singles: 7-inch
EARTHQUAKE...3-5 71
ROXBURY...3-5 76
20TH FOX...3-5 78
Also see IRWIN, Big Dee

DIGA RHYTHM BAND
LPs: 10/12-inch
ROUND...10-15 76
Member: Mickey Hart.
Also see HART, Mickey

DIGGERS: see BLUE JAYS

DIGGS, David
Singles: 7-inch
PAJ...3-4
LPs: 10/12-inch
PBR...8-10 76

DIGITAL SEX
Singles: 7-inch
POST-AMBIENT MOTION...3-5 83
LPs: 10/12-inch
POST-AMBIENT MOTION...8-10 85
Member: Steve Sheehan; John Tingle; Dereck Higgins.
Also see SHEEHAN, Steve

DIGITAL UNDERGROUND *P&R/LP '90*
LPs: 10/12-inch
TOMMY BOY...5-8 90-91

DIKES
Singles: 78 rpm
FEDERAL (12249 "Light Me Up")...50-75 55
Singles: 7-inch
FEDERAL (12249 "Light Me Up")...150-250 55

DILCHER, Cheryl
Singles: 12-inch
BUTTERFLY...4-6 79
Singles: 7-inch
A&M...3-5 73
BUTTERFLY (Black vinyl)...3-5 77
BUTTERFLY (Colored vinyl)...4-8 77
(Promotional issues only.)
Picture Sleeves
BUTTERFLY...3-5 77
LPs: 10/12-inch
A&M...8-10 74
AMPEX...8-10 70
BUTTERFLY...8-10 73-77

DILL, Danny
Singles: 78 rpm
ABC-PAR...15-25 56
Singles: 7-inch
ABC-PAR (9734 "Hungry for Your Lovin' ")...20-30 56
CUB...5-10 59
LPs: 10/12-inch
LIBERTY...20-30 63
MGM...15-25 58

DILLARD, Bobby
Singles: 7-inch
CHI (110 "Spider")...10-20 61

DILLARD, Linda
Singles: 7-inch
POLYDOR...3-5 79

DILLARD, Moses, & Dynamic Showmen
Singles: 7-inch
MARK V (26 "Pretty As a Picture")...20-30 60s

DILLARD, Varetta *R&B '52*
(With the Roamers; with Four Students; with El Venos; with Nitecaps)
Singles: 78 rpm
GROOVE...15-35 55-56
RCA...10-20 57
SAVOY...10-20 52-55
Singles: 7-inch
CUB (9073 "Teaser")...15-20 60
CUB (9083 "Little Bitty Tear")...15-20 61
CUB (9091 "You Better Come Home")...15-20 61
GROOVE (0139 "Darling, Listen to the Words of This Song")...25-40 56
GROOVE (0159 "Got You on My Mind")...20-30 56
GROOVE (0167 "I Miss You Jimmy")...30-40 56
GROOVE (0177 "One More Time")...40-60 56
RCA (6869 "Pray for Me Mother")...20-30 57
RCA (6936 "Time Was")...20-30 57
RCA (7057 "Undecided")...20-30 57
RCA (7285 "What'll I Do")...20-30 58
SAVOY (859 "Them There Eyes") 20-30 52
SAVOY (871 "I Cried and Cried") .20-30 52
SAVOY (1160 "You're the Answer to My Prayer")...30-50 55
SAVOY (1166 "I'll Never Forget You")...25-40 55
TRIUMPH (608 "Scorched")...15-25 59
Also see COOKIES
Also see
Also see FOUR STUDENTS
Also see NITECAPS
Also see ROAMERS

DILLARD & CLARK
LPs: 10/12-inch
A&M...10-15 68-69
Members: Doug Dillard; Gene Clark.
Also see CLARK, Gene
Also see DILLARDS

DILLARDS *P&R '71*
Singles: 7-inch
ANTHEM...3-5 71-72
CAPITOL...4-6 65
ELEKTRA...4-8 63-69
POPPY...3-5 74
U.A....3-5 75
WHITE WHALE...3-5 70
LPs: 10/12-inch
ANTHEM...6-10 72
ELEKTRA (200 series)...20-30 63-65
(Gold label.)
ELEKTRA (7-200 series)...20-30 63-65
(Gold label.)
ELEKTRA (7-200 series)...10-15
(Brown label.)
ELEKTRA (74000 series)...8-12 68
FLYING FISH...5-10 77-81
POPPY...8-12 73
20TH FOX...8-12 73
Members: Doug Dillard; Rodney Dillard; Dean Webb; Mitch Jayne; Joe Osborn.
Also see CEYLEIB PEOPLE
Also see DILLARD & CLARK
Also see NELSON, Rick

DILLARDS & JOHN HARTFORD
LPs: 10/12-inch
FLYING FISH...5-10 77-80s
Also see DILLARDS
Also see HARTFORD, John

DILLINGER
LPs: 10/12-inch
LOVE...5-10 79
MANGO...8-10 76
U.A....8-10 77
LPs: 10/12-inch
MANGO...8-12 76

DILLINGHAM, Craig *C&W '83*
Singles: 7-inch
MCA/CURB...3-4 83-86
Also see HINOJOSA, Tish, & Craig Dillingham

DILLMAN BAND *LP '78*
(Daisy Dillman Band)
Singles: 7-inch
RCA...3-4 81
U.A....3-5 77-78
LPs: 10/12-inch
RCA...5-10 81
U.A....5-10 78
Members: Steve Seamans; Steve Solmonson; Tom Eckhoff.
Also see NEILSEN WHITE BAND

DILLON, Dean *C&W '79*
Singles: 7-inch
ATLANTIC...3-4 91-92
CAPITOL...3-4 88-89
RCA...3-5 79-83
Also see STEWART, Gary, & Dean Dillon

DILLON, Zig
Singles: 7-inch
R (501 "On Down the Line")...15-25 64
R (512 "Bird Song Boogie")...10-20 62

DILLONS
Singles: 7-inch
IMPRESSION...4-8 65

DILLY SISTERS
Singles: 7-inch
GORDO....10-20 69

DIMARKEE, Tommy
Singles: 7-inch
TIC-TOC (13996 "Lost Love")....5-10

DIMENSIONS (on Mohawk): see DEMENSIONS

DIMENSIONS
Singles: 7-inch
HBR (1477 "She's Boss")....5-10 66
PANORAMA (25 "She's Boss")....20-30 66
PANORAMA (41 "Baby What Do You Say")....20-30 66

DIMENSIONS
LPs: 10/12-inch
EVA (10218 "From All Dimensions")....10-15 80s
SAHARA ("From All Dimensions")....300-500 66
Members: Barry Probst; Jim Sebastian; Steve Purnell; Jack Brunsfield.

DIMENSIONS
Singles: 7-inch
CARRAM (105 "Surfside")....15-25 60s
WASHINGTON SQUARE....4-6

DI MEOLA, Al LP '76
(Al Di Meola Project)
Singles: 12-inch
COLUMBIA....4-6 84
Singles: 7-inch
COLUMBIA....3-4 76-84
LPs: 10/12-inch
COLUMBIA....5-10 76-83
EMI....5-10 88
Also see RETURN to FOREVER

DI MILO, Cardella
Singles: 7-inch
CLARIDGE....3-5 77
D-TOWN....3-4 82

DIMINISHED 5TH
Singles: 7-inch
HUSH....5-10

DI MONE, Annmarie
Singles: 7-inch
DEE DEE....5-10 59

DIMPLES
Singles: 7-inch
CAMEO....4-8 64
DORE....8-12 59
ERA....4-8 62

DIMPLES (Richard Fields): see FIELDS, Richard "Dimples"

DIMPLES & HAROLD
Singles: 7-inch
DENA....4-8 61

DING-A-LINGS
Singles: 7-inch
CAPITOL....5-10 60

DING DONGS
(Bobby Darin)
Singles: 7-inch
BRUNSWICK (55073 "Early in the Morning")....100-150 58
(This same track was reissued as by "The Rinky Dinks" and later by "Bobby Darin & the Rinky Dinks.")
Also see DARIN, Bobby

DING DONGS
Singles: 7-inch
TODD (1043 "Lassie Came Home")....10-15 60

DING DONGS
Singles: 7-inch
ELDO (109 "Ding Dong")....15-20 60

DING DONGS
LPs: 10/12-inch
MOTOWN....10-12 70

DINGEY FIGNUS
Singles: 7-inch
COLUMBIA....3-4 85

DINGOES
(With Joe Johnson's Combo)
Singles: 7-inch
DALLAS (2001 "What Would You Do")....300-500 57

DINGOES
Singles: 7-inch
A&M....3-5 77
LPs: 10/12-inch
A&M....8-10 77

DINGUS, Bob
Singles: 7-inch
FLORENTINE (100 "Step It Up and Go")....15-25

DINKINS, Curlee
Singles: 7-inch
JAY-TONE....10-15
VEE TONE....5-10 60

DINKS
Singles: 7-inch
SULLY (914 "Nina-Kocha-Nina")....8-12 66
SULLY (925 "Ugly Girl")....8-12 66

DINNER, Michael
Singles: 7-inch
FANTASY....3-5 74-76
LPs: 10/12-inch
FANTASY....8-10 74-76

DINNING, Mark P&R '59
Singles: 78 rpm
MGM....10-20 57
Singles: 7-inch
CAMEO....4-8 64
HICKORY....4-8 65-66
MGM (Except 12775 & 12980)....5-10 57-63
MGM (12775 "Cutie Cutie")....10-15 59
MGM (12980 "Top 40, News, Weather and Sports")....15-20 61
(With mention of Patrice Lumumba in lyrics.)
MGM (12980 "Top 40, News, Weather and Sports")....5-10 61
(With no mention of Patrice Lumumba in lyrics.)
MGM GOLDEN CIRCLE....3-5
U.A....3-5 67-68
Picture Sleeves
MGM....10-15 60
LPs: 10/12-inch
MGM (E-3828 "Teen Angel")....40-60 60
(Monaural.)
MGM (SE-3828 "Teen Angel")....50-75 60
(Stereo.)
MGM (E-3855 "Wanderin' ")....40-60 60
(Monaural.)
MGM (SE-3855 "Wanderin' ")....50-75 60
(Stereo.)

DINNING SISTERS
Singles: 78 rpm
CAPITOL....4-6 50
DECCA....3-6 54
ESSEX....3-6 55
Singles: 7-inch
CAPITOL....5-10 50
DECCA....5-10 54
ESSEX....5-10 55
Also see FORD, Tennessee Ernie, & Dinning Sisters
Also see HALEY, Bill

DINO
(With the Ex-Teens; Don De Carlo)
Singles: 7-inch
DINO (79920 "Cathy")....10-15 60s
HONEY BEE (101 "Tearing My Heart Out")....10-15 61
Also see DE CARLO, Don

DINO P&R '88
Singles: 7-inch
4TH & BROADWAY....3-4 88-89
ISLAND....3-4 90
Picture Sleeves
4TH & BROADWAY....3-4 89
LPs: 10/12-inch
4TH & BROADWAY....5-8 89
ISLAND....5-8 90

DINO, Bobby
Singles: 7-inch
RIDGECREST (1203 "You Rock Me, Jean")....25-40 59

DINO, Kenny P&R '61
Singles: 12-inch
KDK PRODUCTIONS ("Love Songs for Seka")....15-25 80
(Picture disc. Has photo of adult-film star, Seka.)
Singles: 7-inch
COLUMBIA (43062 "Betty Jean")....5-10 64
DOT (16207 "Just a Little Bit")....8-12 61
MUSICOR (1013 "Your Ma Said You Cried in Your Sleep Last Night")....10-15 61
MUSICOR (1015 "Rosie, Why Do You Wear My Ring")....8-12 62
MUSICOR (1021 "What Good Are Dreams")....8-12 62
RADNOR (311 "Sha La La")....5-10 60s
SMASH....4-8 63-64

DINO, Paul P&R '61
Singles: 7-inch
ENTRE....4-8 63
PROMO....5-10 60-61

DINO, Richy
Singles: 7-inch
KENCO....5-10 60

DINO & ALADDINS: see LENNY & CONTINENTALS

DINO & CALIFORNIA CAFE CHOIR
Singles: 7-inch
STAX....3-5 74

DINO, DESI & BILLY P&R/LP '65
Singles: 7-inch
COLUMBIA (44975 "Let's Talk It Over")....4-8 69
UNI (55127 "Someday")....4-8 69
REPRISE (0324 "Since You Broke My Heart")....10-15 65
REPRISE (0367 "I'm a Fool")....5-10 65
REPRISE (0401 "Not the Lovin' Kind")....5-10 65
REPRISE (0426 "Please Don't Fight It")....5-10 65
REPRISE (0444 "Superman")....5-10 66
REPRISE (0462 "It's Just the Way You Are")....5-10 66
REPRISE (0496 "Look Out Girls")....5-10 66
REPRISE (0529 "I Hope She's There Tonight")....5-10 66
REPRISE (0544 "Pretty Flamingo")....5-10 67
REPRISE (0579 "Two in the Afternoon")....5-10 67
REPRISE (0619 "Kitty Doyle")....5-10 67
REPRISE (0653 "My What a Shame")....5-10 67
REPRISE (0698 "Tell Someone You Love Them")....5-10 68
REPRISE (0965 "Lady Love")....10-15 70
Picture Sleeves
REPRISE (0367 "I'm a Fool")....8-12 65
REPRISE (0401 "Not the Lovin' Kind")....8-12 65
REPRISE (0426 "Please Don't Fight It")....8-12 65
REPRISE (0653 "My What a Shame")....10-15 67
LPs: 10/12-inch
REPRISE (6176 "I'm a Fool")....15-25 65
REPRISE (6194 "Our Time's Coming")....15-25 66
REPRISE (6198 "Memories Are Made of This")....15-25 65
REPRISE (6224 "Souvenir")....25-40 66
(With bonus wallet-sized photos.)
REPRISE (6224 "Souvenir")....15-25 66
(Without bonus photos.)
UNI (73056 "Follow Me")....15-20 69
Members: Dino Martin; Desi Arnaz Jr; Billy Hinsche.
Also see ARNAZ, Desi, Jr.

DINO & DELL-TONES
Singles: 7-inch
COBRA....5-10 65

DINO & DIPLOMATS
Singles: 7-inch
LAURIE (3103 "I Can't Believe")....20-30 61
VIDA (100 "Homework")....20-30 61
VIDA (102 "Such a Fool")....20-30 62

DINO & HEARTSPINNERS
Singles: 7-inch
BARRIER....3-5 76
LPs: 10/12-inch
FIRST BORN (8300 "Believe It Or Not")....12-18 83

DINO & SUSPICIONS
Singles: 7-inch
SCORE....5-10 64

DINOS
Singles: 7-inch
FOX (101 "Darling Oh Darling")....150-250 62

DINOS
(With the Kounts)
Singles: 7-inch
FINE (001 "It's So Good to Know")....25-50 60s
Member: Abraham Quintanilla.

DINOS
Singles: 7-inch
FUN (101 "Our Love's About Over")....300-500

DINOSAUR
Singles: 7-inch
SIRE....3-4 78

DINOSAUR JR.
LPs: 10/12-inch
SIRE/W.B....5-8 91

DINWIDDIE COLORED QUARTET
Singles: 78 rpm
MONARCH (1714 "Down on the Old Camp Ground")....300-500 02
MONARCH (1715 "Poor Mourner")....400-600 02
MONARCH (1716 "Steal Away")....400-600 02
MONARCH (1724 "My Way Is Cloudy")....400-600 02
MONARCH (1725 "Gabriel's Trumpet")....300-500 02
MONARCH (1726 "We'll Anchor Bye-and-Bye")....300-500 02
VICTOR (1714 "Down the Old Camp Ground")....200-300 05
VICTOR (1715 "Poor Mourner")....300-400 05
VICTOR (1716 "Steal Away")....300-400 05
VICTOR (1724 "My Way Is Cloudy")....300-400 05
VICTOR (1725 "Gabriel's Trumpet")....300-400 05
VICTOR (1726 "We'll Anchor Bye-and-Bye")....300-400 05
From the turn of the century, these were thick, single-sided discs which actually played at about 75 revolutions per minute. They are believed to be the earliest black vocal group recordings.
Members: Sterling Rex; Clarence Meredith; James Thomas; Harry Cruder.

DIO: see DIO, Ronnie

DIO, Andy
(With the Hi-Ways)
Singles: 7-inch
CRUSADE (1023 "Bonnie Jean")....20-40 61
GONE (5038 "Daisy Belle")....35-50 58
JOHNSON (114 "Satellite")....10-20 62
JOY (283 "Daisy Belle")....25-40 64
MUSICOR (1118 "Shout")....5-8 65
THOR (104 "Rough and Bold")....50-75 59

DIO, Ronnie LP '83
(With the Redcaps; with Prophets; Dio)
Singles: 7-inch
ATLANTIC (2145 "Love Pains")....20-40 62
JOVE....15-25 63
KAPP (697 "Say You're Mine Again")....5-10 65
KAPP (725 "Dear Darlin' ")....5-10 65
LAWN (218 "Gonna Make It Alone")....15-25 63
PARKWAY....4-8 67
SENCA....25-50 61
SWAN (4165 "Mr. Misery")....10-20 63
W.B....3-4 83-86
LPs: 10/12-inch
JOVE ("Dio at Domino's")....50-100 63
W.B....5-10 83-87
Members: Ronnie James Dio; Vinny Appice; Jimmy Bain; Vivian Campbell; Claude Schell; Craig Goldie;Rowan Robertson; Jen Johansson; Simon Wright; Terry Cook.
Also see AC/DC
Also see BLACKMORE'S RAINBOW
Also see HEAR 'N AID
Also see MALMSTEEN, Yngwie J.

DIOBOLICS
Singles: 7-inch
TOGETHERNESS (1001 "I Bet That You Never Knew I Followed You")....15-25

DION P&R '60
(Dion DiMucci)
Singles: 7-inch
ARISTA....3-4 89
BIG TREE/SPECTOR....3-5 76
COLUMBIA (3-42662 "Ruby Baby")....25-35 62
(Compact 33 single.)
COLUMBIA (4-42662 "Ruby Baby")....5-10 62
COLUMBIA (42776 "This Little Girl")....5-10 63
COLUMBIA (42810 "Be Careful of Stones You Throw")....5-10 63
(Black vinyl.)
COLUMBIA (42810 "Be Careful of Stones You Throw")....25-50 63
(Colored vinyl. Promotional issue only.)
COLUMBIA (42852 "Donna the Prima Donna")....5-10 63
(Black vinyl.)
COLUMBIA (42852 "Donna the Prima Donna")....25-50 63
(Colored vinyl. Promotional issue only.)
COLUMBIA (42917 thru 44719)....5-10 63-68
DAY SPRING (642 "Hearts Made of Stone")....3-5 81
LAURIE (100 series)....3-5
LAURIE (3000 & 3100 series)....8-15 60-63
LAURIE (3400 series)....5-10 68-69
LIFESONG....3-5 78-79
MYRRH....3-5 85
SPECTOR....3-5 75
W.B. (Except 814)....3-6 69-79
W.B. (814 "The Wanderer")....5-10 79
(Promotional issue only.)
W.B./SPECTOR....3-5 75
Picture Sleeves
ARISTA....3-4 89
COLUMBIA (Except 42662)....10-20 64-66
COLUMBIA (42662 "Ruby Baby")....30-50 62
(Promotional sleeve for *Ruby Baby*, but does not show title or number. Simply reads, "Dion Is Now on Columbia Records.")
COLUMBIA (42662 "Ruby Baby")....10-15 62
(Commercially issued sleeve.)
LAURIE....10-20 60-62
LPs: 10/12-inch
ARISTA....6-12 77-89
COLLECTABLES....6-8 83-87
COLUMBIA....15-25 63-73
DAY SPRING....5-10 80-86
LAURIE (2004 "Alone with Dion")....20-30 61
LAURIE (2009 "Runaround Sue")....20-30 61
(Black vinyl.)
LAURIE (2009 "Runaround Sue")....75-100 61
(Colored vinyl.)
LAURIE (2012 "Lovers Who Wander")....20-30 62
LAURIE (2015 "Love Came to Me")....20-30 63
LAURIE (2017 "Dion Sings to Sandy and All Other Girls")....20-30 63
LAURIE (2019 "15 Million Sellers")....20-30 63
LAURIE (2022 "More of Dion's Greatest Hits")....20-30 63
LAURIE (2047 "Dion")....15-20 68
LAURIE (4000 series)....8-15 70s
LIFESONG....5-10 78
PAIR....10-12 86
REALM....5-10
W.B....10-15 69-76
Also see ADAMS, Bryan
Also see DEE, Joey, & Starliters / Dion
Also see EDMUNDS, Dave
Also see LANG, K.D.
Also see REED, Lou
Also see SIMON, Paul
Also see SMYTH, Patty

DION / Glen Stuart Chorus
LPs: 10/12-inch
ABEL....8-12 60s

DION & BELMONTS P&R/R&B '58
(Featuring Dion DiMucci)
Singles: 7-inch
ABC (10868 "My Girl the Month of May")....5-10 66
ABC (10896 "For Bobbie")....5-10 67
COLLECTABLES....3-4 80s
LAURIE (3013 "I Wonder Why")....25-50 58
(Gray label.)
LAURIE (3013 "I Wonder Why")....15-25 58
(Blue label.)
LAURIE (3013 "I Wonder Why")....10-15 59
(Red and white label.)
LAURIE (3015 "No One Knows")....20-30 58
(Blue label.)
LAURIE (3015 "No One Knows")....10-15 58
(Red and white label.)
LAURIE (3021 "Don't Pity Me")....15-25 58
LAURIE (3027 "A Teenager in Love")....10-20 59
(Monaural.)
LAURIE (S-3027 "A Teenager in Love")....25-50 59
(Stereo.)
LAURIE (3035 "Every Little Thing I Do")....10-20 59
LAURIE (3044 "Where Or When")....10-20 59
LAURIE (3052 "Wonderful Girl")....10-20 60
LAURIE (3059 "In the Still of the Night")....10-20 60
LAURIE DOUBLE GOLD....3-5 78
MOHAWK (107 "Tag Along")....30-40 57
REO (8363 "A Teenager in Love")....15-25 59
(Canadian.)
ROCK'N MANIA....3-5
Picture Sleeves
LAURIE (3035 "Every Little Thing I Do")....20-30 59
LAURIE (3044 "Where Or When")....20-30 59
LAURIE (3052 "Wonderful Girl")....20-30 60
LAURIE (3059 "In the Still of the Night")....20-30 60
EPs: 7-inch
LAURIE (301 "Their Hits")....50-100 59
LAURIE (302 "Where Or When")....50-75 59
LPs: 10/12-inch
ABC (599 "Together Again")....15-25 67
ARISTA....8-12 84
COLLECTABLES....5-10 83
GRT....8-10 75
JUKE BOX (95140 "A Teenager in Love")....20-30 70s
(Boxed, four-disc set. Also includes Dion solo tracks.)
LAURIE (1002 "Presenting Dion and the Belmonts")....100-200 59
LAURIE (2002 "Presenting Dion and the Belmonts")....100-200 60
(Monaural.)
LAURIE (2002 "Presenting Dion and the Belmonts")....300-500 60
(Stereo.)
LAURIE (2006 "Wish Upon a Star")....50-75 60
LAURIE (2013 "Dion Sings His Greatest Hits - with the Belmonts")....50-75 62
LAURIE (2016 "By Special Request")....30-50 62
LAURIE (4002 "Everything You Always Wanted to Hear")....10-15 76
LAURIE (6000 "60 Greatest")....15-20
(Standard cover.)
LAURIE (6000 "60 Greatest")....20-30
(Boxed edition.)
PICKWICK....8-10 75
RHINO....5-10 87
W.B....10-15 73
Also see BELMONTS

DION & BELMONTS / Belmonts
LPs: 10/12-inch
MIASOUND (001 "Half & Half")....15-20 81

DION & TIMBERLANES
(Featuring Dion DiMuci)
Singles: 7-inch
JUBILEE (5294 "Chosen Few")....15-25 57
MOHAWK (105 "Chosen Few")....30-35 57
VIRGO....3-5 73
Also see DION

DION, Celine LP '91
Singles: 7-inch
EPIC....3-4 91
LPs: 10/12-inch
EPIC....5-8 88

DION & WANDERERS
Singles: 7-inch
COLUMBIA....8-12 65-68

DIONNE & FRIENDS P&R/R&B '85
Singles: 7-inch
ARISTA....3-4 85
Picture Sleeves
ARISTA....3-4 85
Members: Dionne Warwick; Elton John; Stevie Wonder; Gladys Knight.
Also see JOHN, Elton
Also see KNIGHT, Gladys
Also see WONDER, Stevie

DIONNE & KASHIF P&R/R&B '87
Singles: 7-inch
ARISTA....3-4 87
Members: Dionne Warwick; Kashif.
Also see KASHIF
Also see WARWICK, Dionne

DIPLOMATS P&R/R&B '64
Singles: 7-inch
AROCK (1004 "Here's a Heart")....10-20 64
AROCK (1008 "Help Me")....10-20 64
DYNAMO (Except 122)....5-10 68-69
DYNAMO (122 "I Can Give You Love")....15-20
HOLIDAY (106 "Point of No Return")....10-20 61
MAY (105 "Let's Be in Love")....20-30 61
MINIT....8-12 66
WAND....8-12 65

DIPLOMETTES
Singles: 7-inch
DIPLOMACY....4-8

DIPPERS
Singles: 7-inch
DIPLOMACY (4 "Goin' Ape")....10-20 64

DIPPERS QUINTET
(With Van Perry's Combo)
Singles: 7-inch
FLAYR (500 "It's Almost Christmas") ... 3500-5000 55

DIPSY & DOODLES
Singles: 7-inch
MAY ... 10-15 63

DIRE STRAITS P&R/LP '79
Singles: 12-inch
W.B. ... 4-6 83
Singles: 7-inch
W.B. ... 3-4 79-88
Picture Sleeves
W.B. ... 3-4 79-86
LPs: 10/12-inch
W.B. ... 5-10 78-88
Member: Mark Knopfler.
Also see KNOPFLER, Mark

DIRECT CURRENT R&B '79
Singles: 7-inch
T.E.C. ... 3-5 79

DIRKSEN, Senator Everett McKinley P&R '66
Singles: 7-inch
CAPITOL ... 3-6 66
Picture Sleeves
CAPITOL ... 4-8 66
LPs: 10/12-inch
BELL ... 5-10 70
CAPITOL ... 10-15 66-67

DIRT, Phil, & Dozers
Singles: 7-inch
("Charlie Brown Christmas") ... 4-8
(No label name or number used. Colred vinyl.)
LPs: 10/12-inch
PHIL DIRT ... 10-15

DIRT BAND: see NITTY GRITTY DIRT BAND

DIRTE FOUR
Singles: 7-inch
CHARAY (34 "On the Move") ... 10-20 65
MERCURY (72885 "On the Move") 8-12 68
SOFT (1027 "I Want to Give You All My Love") ... 15-25 69
Also see HOBBS, Willie

DIRTY ANGELS
Singles: 7-inch
A&M ... 3-5 78
PRIVATE STOCK ... 3-5 76-77
SIRE ... 3-5 75
LPs: 10/12-inch
A&M ... 8-10 78
PRIVATE STOCK ... 10-12 76-77
SIRE ... 10-12 75
Member: Charlie Karp.
Also see KARP, Charlie

DIRTY BLUES BAND
Singles: 7-inch
BLUESWAY ... 4-8 68
LPs: 10/12-inch
BLUESWAY ... 10-12 68

DIRTY ELBOWS
Singles: 7-inch
SOLID GOLD (10 "To Carry On") ... 15-25

DIRTY FILTHY MUD
Singles: 7-inch
WOREX (2340 "Forest of Black") ... 20-30 67
EPs: 7-inch
WOREX ("Dirty Filthy Mud") ... 250-350 67
(Selection number not known.)

DIRTY HALF DOZEN
Singles: 7-inch
FUN ... 4-8

DIRTY LOOKS LP '88
LPs: 10/12-inch
ATLANTIC ... 5-8 88-89
STIFF ... 5-10 80

DIRTY OLD MEN
Singles: 7-inch
NOCTURNE ... 4-6 69
LPs: 10/12-inch
NOCTURNE ... 12-15 69

DIRTY RED
(Nelson Wilborn)
Singles: 78 rpm
ALADDIN (194 "Mother Fuyer") ... 75-125 47
ALADDIN (207 "Hotel Boogie") ... 40-60 48

DIRTY SHAMES
Singles: 7-inch
IMPRESSION (112 "I Don't Care") ... 10-20 66
PHILIPS ... 8-12 67

DIRTY TRICKS
LPs: 10/12-inch
POLYDOR ... 8-10 76-77

DIRTY WURDS
Singles: 7-inch
CHESS (1983 "Midnight Hour") ... 8-12 67
MARINA (502 "Why") ... 100-125 65

DISCAYNES
Singles: 7-inch
VEEP ... 10-20 66

DISCHORDS
Singles: 7-inch
BONNEVILLE (205 "Wipe Out") ... 25-35 63

DISCHORDS
Singles: 7-inch
MARK (4000 "Age of Caesar") ... 10-15 71
Also see DYNAMIC DISCHORDS

DISCIPLES
Singles: 7-inch
FEATURE (9427 "It's Over") ... 25-35 67
FOUNDATION (709 "Darlin' ") ... 15-20

DISCIPLES OF BLUES
Singles: 7-inch
ACTION ... 4-8

DISCIPLES OF SHAFTESBURY
Singles: 7-inch
INTERNATIONAL ARTISTS ... 8-12 66

DISCIPLES OF SOUL
Singles: 7-inch
PHANTOM ... 5-10

DISCO CHICKEN
Singles: 7-inch
CIRCUS ... 3-5

DISCO CIRCUS
LPs: 10/12-inch
COLUMBIA ... 5-10 79

DISCO FOUR R&B '82
Singles: 12-inch
PROFILE ... 4-6 83
Singles: 7-inch
PROFILE ... 3-4 82-83

DISCO GETTERS
LPs: 10/12-inch
EXACT ... 5-10 80
GRIT ... 5-10 79

DISCO KIDS
Singles: 12-inch
MUSICOR ... 4-8 77

DISCO 3 R&B '84
Singles: 12-inch
SUTRA ... 4-6 83
Singles: 7-inch
SUTRA ... 3-4 84
Members: Darren Robinson; Mark Morales; Damon Wimbley.
Also see FAT BOYS

DISCOTAYS / Guess Who: see GUESS WHO / Discotays

DISCO-TEX & HIS SEX-O-LETTES P&R/R&B '74
Singles: 7-inch
CHELSEA ... 3-5 74-76
LPs: 10/12-inch
CHELSEA ... 8-10 75-76
MUSICOR ... 5-10 79
Also see ROCK, Monti, III

DI SENTRI, Turner
(Bob Gaudio)
Singles: 7-inch
TOPIX (6001 "10,000,000 Tears") ... 25-35 61
Also see 4 SEASONS
Also see ROYAL TEENS

DISHAW, Tommy
Singles: 7-inch
D&C (500 "We're Gonna Rock") ... 30-50 59
GLORY (299 "Angela") ... 10-15 59

DISILLUSIONED YOUNGER GENERATION
Singles: 7-inch
DYG ... 4-6 68

DISRAELI
Singles: 7-inch
MANTRA ... 4-8 68

DISSENSION
Singles: 7-inch
METALSTORM (8815 "We the Fooled") ... 10-20 89
(Picture disc, packaged in a metal can. 500 made.)

DISSONAIRES
Singles: 7-inch
ALTAIR (101 "One Love") ... 30-50 59
(Reissued as by the Penetrators.)
Also see PENETRATORS

DISTANT COUSINS
Singles: 7-inch
DATE ... 10-15 66
DYNO VOICE ... 10-15 65

DISTANT GALAXY
Singles: 7-inch
VERVE ... 4-6 68
LPs: 10/12-inch
VERVE ... 10-15 68

DISTANT SOUNDS
Singles: 7-inch
CITATION ("It Reminds Me") ... 10-20 66

DISTANTS
(With "Vocal By Richard Strick")
Singles: 7-inch
NORTHERN (3732 "Come On") ... 200-300 60
WARWICK (546 "Come On") ... 50-75 60
WARWICK (577 "Always") ... 75-125 60
Members: Richard Street [Strick]; Otis Williams; Melvin Franklin; Eldridge Bryant.
Also see STREET, Richard, & Distants
Also see TEMPTATIONS

DISTEL, Sacha, & Brigitte Bardot
Singles: 7-inch
POLYDOR ... 4-6 73
Also see BARDOT, Brigitte

DISTORTERS
Singles: 7-inch
CLARK (364 "Distortion") ... 10-20 64

DISTORTIONS
Singles: 7-inch
CAPITOL ... 8-12 68
SEA ... 5-10 60s
SMASH ... 5-10 66

DISTURBERS
Singles: 7-inch
HEAD ... 10-20 60s

DITALIANS
Singles: 7-inch
SAXONY (1011 "Philly Dog New Breed") ... 8-10 66
TRIP (1013 "I Gotta Go") ... 5-10 67
Also see TRADITIONS / DITALIANS

DITTOS
Singles: 7-inch
W.B. ... 4-8 61

DIVIDENDS
Singles: 7-inch
BONANZA ... 4-8 62

DIVINE D&D '83
LPs: 10/12-inch
O ... 5-10 83

DIVINE SOUNDS R&B/D&D '84
Singles: 7-inch
SPECIFIC ... 3-4 84

DIVING for PEARLS P&R '89
Singles: 7-inch
EPIC ... 3-4 89

DIVINYLS LP '85
Singles: 12-inch
CHRYSALIS ... 4-6 85
Singles: 7-inch
CHRYSALIS ... 3-4 83-86
VIRGIN ... 3-4 91
Picture Sleeves
CHRYSALIS ... 3-4 85
LPs: 10/12-inch
CHRYSALIS ... 5-10 83-86
VIRGIN ... 5-8 91
Members: Christina Amphlett; Mark McEntee; Rick Grossman.
Also see HOODOO GURUS

DIVISION
Singles: 7-inch
TRANSACTION (710 "Not Fade Away") ... 15-25 69

DIVITO, Buddy, & Meadowlarks
Singles: 78 rpm
CHANCE ... 10-15 54
Singles: 7-inch
CHANCE (Black vinyl) ... 10-15 54
CHANCE (Colored vinyl) ... 15-25 54

DIVOTS
Singles: 7-inch
MARK ... 4-8
SAVOY ... 10-15 61

DIXIE BLUES BOYS
(With Vocal by Dee Dee)
Singles: 78 rpm
FLAIR (1072 "Monte Carlo") ... 25-50 55
Singles: 7-inch
FLAIR (1072 "Monte Carlo") ... 75-100 55

DIXIE CUPS P&R/R&B/LP '64
Singles: 7-inch
ABC-PAR (10692 "That's Where It's At") ... 8-12 65
ABC-PAR (10715 "I'm Not That Kind of Girl") ... 8-12 65
ABC-PAR (10755 "ABC Song") ... 8-12 65
ABC-PAR (10855 "Daddy Said No") 8-12 66
ANTILLES ... 3-4 87
LANA ... 3-6 60s
RED BIRD (001 "Chapel of Love") ... 8-12 64
RED BIRD (006 "People Say") ... 8-12 64
RED BIRD (012 "You Should Have Seen the Way He Looked at Me") ... 8-12 64
RED BIRD (017 "Little Bell") ... 10-20 65
RED BIRD (024 "Iko Iko"/"Gee Baby, Gee") ... 10-15 65
RED BIRD (024 "Iko Iko"/"I'm Gonna Get You Yet") ... 8-10 65
RED BIRD (032 "Gee the Moon Is Shining Bright") ... 8-12 65
TRIP ... 3-5 70s
Picture Sleeves
ANTILLES ... 3-5 87
EPs: 7-inch
ABC-PAR (525 "Riding High") ... 15-25 65
(Juke box issue only. Includes title strips. Stereo.)
LPs: 10/12-inch
ABC-PAR (ABC-525 "Riding High") ... 25-30 65
(Monaural.)
ABC-PAR (ABCS-525 "Riding High") ... 30-40 65
(Stereo.)
BACK-TRAC ... 8-12
(Colored vinyl.)
RED BIRD (RB-100 "Chapel of Love") ... 35-45 64
(Monaural.)
RED BIRD (RBS-100 "Chapel of Love") ... 50-75 64
(Stereo.)
RED BIRD (RB-103 "Iko Iko") ... 35-55 64
(Monaural.)
RED BIRD (RBS-103 "Iko Iko") ... 60-80 64
(Stereo.)
Members: Barbara Hawkins; Rosa Hawkins; Joan Johnson.

DIXIE DREGS LP '78
(Dregs)
Singles: 12-inch
CAPRICORN ... 4-6 79
Singles: 7-inch
ARISTA ... 3-4 80-82
CAPRICORN ... 3-4 77-79
LPs: 10/12-inch
ARISTA ... 5-10 80-82
CAPRICORN ... 5-10 78-79
Members: Steve Morse; Rog Morganstein; T. Lavitz; Andy West; Alan Sloan.
Also see MORSE, Steve, Band

DIXIE DRIFTER
(Jimmy Dawson)
Singles: 7-inch
CUCA (1186 "Little Hero") ... 5-10 64
Also see DAWSON, Jimmy

DIXIE DRIFTER P&R/R&B '65
(Enoch Gregory)
Singles: 7-inch
AMY ... 4-6 68
CIRRUS (91775 "Hard Times '75") ... 4-6 75
IX CHAINS ... 3-5 74
ROULETTE (4641 "Soul Heaven") ... 4-8 65

DIXIE DRIFTER
Singles: 7-inch
PLATINUM ... 3-5

DIXIE FLIERS
Singles: 7-inch
GUYDEN (2055 "Nail It") ... 10-20 61
LARK (452 "Yellow Dog Blues") ... 5-8

DIXIE GUITARS
Singles: 7-inch
SHELLEY (1004 "Dixieland Guitars") ... 10-20 59

DIXIE HOOTS
Singles: 7-inch
TIVOLI (101 "Russian Roulette") ... 8-12

DIXIE HUMMINGBIRDS R&B '73
Singles: 78 rpm
OKEH ... 4-8 53
Singles: 7-inch
ABC ... 3-5 73-74
OKEH ... 5-10 53
PEACOCK ... 3-6 59-74
LPs: 10/12-inch
CONSTELLATION ... 5-10 64
GOSPEL ROOTS ... 5-10 80
PEACOCK ... 5-10 59-78
Members: Ira Tucker; James Walker; James Davis; Willie Bobo; Beechie Thompson; Howard Carroll.
Also see BOBO, Willie
Also see SIMON, Paul

DIXIEAIRES R&B '48
(Dixie-Aires)
Singles: 78 rpm
EXCLUSIVE ... 15-25 48-49
GOTHAM ... 15-25 48
HARLEM ... 25-50 55
LENOX ... 15-25 49
SITTIN' IN WITH ... 15-25 50
Singles: 7-inch
HARLEM (2326 "Traveling All Alone") ... 100-150 55
Members: Joe Van Loan; Clyde Reddick; Henry Owens; Conrad Frederick; Arlandus Wilson; Willie Ray; Joe Floyd; John Hines; Bob Kornegay; J.C. Giuyard.
Also see BELLS
Also see DU DROPPERS
Also see GOLDEN GATE QUARTET
Also see VALIANTS
Also see VAN LOAN, Joe

DIXIEBELLES P&R/R&B '63
Singles: 7-inch
MONUMENT ... 3-5 72
SOUND STAGE 7 ... 4-8 63-64
EPs: 7-inch
SOUND STAGE 7 ... 15-20 63
LPs: 10/12-inch
SOUND STAGE 7 ... 20-30 63
MONUMENT ... 15-20 65
Also see SMITH, Jerry

DIXIELANDERS
Singles: 7-inch
DO-RE-ME ... 15-25 59-60

DIXIES
Singles: 7-inch
AUTUMN ... 8-12 65

DIXON, Billy, & Topics
Singles: 7-inch
TOPIX (6002 "I Am All Alone") ... 50-75 60
TOPIX (6008 "Lost Lullabye") ... 75-125 60
Also see 4 SEASONS
Also see TOPICS

DIXON, Dave
Singles: 78 rpm
ACE ... 15-25 57
SAVOY ... 8-12 54
Singles: 7-inch
ACE (519 "I'm Not Satisfied") ... 20-30 57
HOME of the BLUES (108 "You Don't Love Me No More") ... 10-15 60
HOME of the BLUES (120 "Hey Hey Pretty Baby") ... 10-15 61
SAVOY (1126 "My Plea") ... 20-30 54

DIXON, Diane
Singles: 7-inch
SMASH ... 5-8 63

DIXON, Dick, & Roommates
Singles: 7-inch
KAPP (292 "Caterpillar Crawl") ... 10-20 59

DIXON, Dizzy
Singles: 78 rpm
VEE JAY ... 10-15 56
Singles: 7-inch
SPARKLE ... 15-25
VEE JAY ... 15-25 56

DIXON, Don LP '87
LPs: 10/12-inch
ENIGMA ... 5-10 87

DIXON, Errol
LPs: 10/12-inch
LONDON ... 10-15 69

DIXON, Floyd R&B '49
(Floyd Dixon's Trio)
Singles: 78 rpm
ALADDIN (3073 "She's Understanding") ... 20-30 50
ALADDIN (3074 "San Francisco Blues") ... 20-30 50
ALADDIN (3078 "Let's Dance") ... 20-30 51
ALADDIN (3083 "Rockin' at Home") ... 20-30 51
ALADDIN (3084 "Don't Cry Now Baby") ... 20-30 51
ALADDIN (3111 "Too Much Jelly Roll") ... 20-30 51
ALADDIN (3135 thru 3151) ... 20-30 52
CASH (1057 "Oh Baby") ... 15-25 57
CAT (106 "Moonshine") ... 15-25 54
CAT (114 "Hey Bartender") ... 15-25 55
MODERN (653 "Dallas Blues") ... 15-25 49
MODERN (664 "That'll Get It") ... 15-25 49
MODERN (700 "Drafting Blues") ... 15-25 49
MODERN (724 "Milky White Way") ... 15-25 49
MODERN (725 "Cow Town") ... 15-25 49
MODERN (727 "Gloomy Baby") ... 15-25 50
MODERN (744 "People Like Me") . 15-25 50
MODERN (761 "It's Gettin' Foggy") ... 15-25 50
MODERN (776 "Playboy Blues") ... 15-25 50
MODERN (797 "You Made a Fool Out of Me") ... 15-25 51
PEACOCK (1528 "Let's Dance") ... 15-25 50
PEACOCK (1544 "She's Understanding") ... 15-25 50
QUALITY (1288 "Moonshine") ... 15-25 54
(Canadian.)
SUPREME (1528 "Houston Jump") ... 20-30 49
SUPREME (1535 "Broken Hearted") ... 20-30 49
SUPREME (1546 "You Need Me Now") ... 20-30 49
SUPREME (1547 "Worries") ... 20-30 50
SWING TIME (261 "Houston Jump") ... 15-25 51
SWING TIME (287 "You Need Me Now") ... 15-25 51
Singles: 7-inch
ALADDIN (3135 "Wine Wine Wine") ... 100-150 52
ALADDIN (3144 "Red Cherries") ... 75-125 52
(Black vinyl.)
ALADDIN (3144 "Red Cherries") ... 200-300 52
(Colored vinyl.)
ALADDIN (3151 "Tired, Broke and Busted") ... 100-150 52
BOXER (101 "I Been Waiting") ... 15-25
CASH (1057 "Oh Baby") ... 20-30 57
CAT (106 "Moonshine") ... 50-75 54
CAT (114 "Hey Bartender") ... 50-75 54
CHATTAHOOCHEE (652 "There Goes My Heart") ... 8-12 64
CHATTAHOOCHEE (697 "Don't Leave Me Baby") ... 8-12 65
CHECKER (857 "Alarm Clock Blues") ... 20-30 58
DODGE (807 "Daisy") ... 10-15 61
EBB (105 "Ooh Little Girl") ... 20-30 57
IMPERIAL (5849 "Tired, Broke and Busted") ... 8-12 62
INCULCATION (47192 "I Think of You Babe") ... 4-8
JELLO ... 10-15 60
KENT (311 "Change Your Mind") ... 10-20 58
PEARL (25 "For Mother") ... 10-15
QUALITY (1288 "Moonshine") ... 50-75 54
(Canadian.)
REVA (7 "Late Freight") ... 10-15 62
SPECIALTY (468 "Hard Living Alone") ... 50-75 53
(Black vinyl.)
SPECIALTY (468 "Hard Living Alone") ... 100-200 53
(Red vinyl.)
SPECIALTY (477 "Hole in the Wall") ... 50-75 53
(Black vinyl.)
SPECIALTY (477 "Hole in the Wall") ... 100-200 53
(Red vinyl.)
SPECIALTY (486 "Ooh-Eee Ooh-Eee") ... 50-75 54
(Black vinyl.)
SPECIALTY (486 "Ooh-Eee Ooh-Eee") ... 100-200 54
(Red vinyl.)

SWINGIN' (626 "Tight Skirts")........10-15 60
LPs: 10/12-inch
INCULCATION 8-10
Session: Roy Hayes; Eddie Williams; Nat McFay; Willie Dixon; Fred Below; Robert Lockwood Jr.
Also see DIXON, Willie
Also see LOCKWOOD, Robert, Jr.
Also see WILLIAMS, Eddie

DIXON, Floyd, & Johnny Moore's Three Blazers
Singles: 78 rpm
ALADDIN (3069 "Girl Fifteen").......20-30 50
ALADDIN (3074 "Empty Stocking Blues")......................................20-30 50
ALADDIN (3075 "Real Lovin' Mama")...20-30 50
ALADDIN (3083 "Unlucky Girl") 20-30 51
ALADDIN (3101 "Do I Love You") ..20-30 51
ALADDIN (3121 "Blues for Cuba") .20-30 52
ALADDIN (3166 thru 3230) 20-30 52-54
Singles: 7-inch
ALADDIN (3101 "Do I Love You")..50-100 51
ALADDIN (3166 "Broken Hearted Traveller")................................50-100 53
ALADDIN (3196 "Married Woman")....................................50-100 53
ALADDIN (3221 "Bad Neighborhood")..........................50-100 54
ALADDIN (3230 "You Need Me Now")......................................50-100 54
Also see DIXON, Floyd
Also see MOORE, Johnny

DIXON, Helene
(Helen Dixon)
Singles: 78 rpm
EPIC... 6-12 54-55
VIK 6-12 56
Singles: 7-inch
EPIC (9078 "I'm Too Busy Crying").. 8-12 54
EPIC (9113 "Heaven Came Down to Earth")....................................10-20 55
EPIC (9121 "Por Favor")................ 8-12 55
PEACH (753 "It Can't Stop My Heart").. 5-10 62
VIK (0212 "Roll Over Beethoven") .15-25 56
VIK (0228 "The Opposite Sex")......10-20 56

DIXON, Hugh
Singles: 7-inch
CLICK (26 "All Gone")................... 8-12

DIXON, James
Singles: 7-inch
CHECKER (1017 "It's Nobody's Business if I Do").. 8-12 62

DIXON, Jim, & Regence
Singles: 7-inch
GOLDEN ARROW (718 "Natural Beauty")....................................10-20 60s

DIXON, Joe, Orchestra
Singles: 7-inch
HERALD 5-10 58

DIXON, Luther
Singles: 7-inch
CHESS.. 8-12 58

DIXON, Mason: see MASON DIXON

DIXON, Mason, & Redskins
Singles: 78 rpm
METEOR..................................25-35 56
Singles: 7-inch
METEOR (5028 "Don't Worry 'Bout Nuthin"....................................40-60 56

DIXON, Richie
Singles: 7-inch
DORSET 10-20 61

DIXON, Walter
Singles: 7-inch
ERWIN (211 "Goodbye, She's Gone")..20-30 57

DIXON, Webb
Singles: 78 rpm
CHECKER.................................... 5-10 55-56
Singles: 7-inch
ASTRO (101 "Rock Awhile") 40-60 59
ASTRO (102 "Rock and Roll Angel")..50-70 59

DIXON, Willie *R&B '55*
Singles: 78 rpm
CHECKER....................................15-25 55-56
Singles: 7-inch
CHECKER (822 "Walkin the Blues")...50-75 55
CHECKER (828 "Crazy for My Baby")..50-75 55
CHECKER (851 "Twenty-Nine Ways")..50-75 56
LPs: 10/12-inch
BLUE HORIZON..........................10-15 70
COLUMBIA....................................10-15 70
OVATION 8-10 74-76
ROOTS N' BLUES......................... 5-8 90
SPIVEY 8-10
YAMBO 8-10
Session: Lafayette Leake; Ollie Crawford; Harold Ashby; Fred Below; Al Duncan.
Also see BOYD, Eddie
Also see DIDDLEY, Bo
Also see DIXON, Floyd
Also see GUY, Buddy
Also see LITTLE WALTER
Also see EMERSON, Billy
Also see FIVE BREEZES
Also see HOWLIN' WOLF
Also see REED, Jimmy
Also see RUSH, Otis
Also see TAYLOR, Koko
Also see WASHBOARD SAM
Also see WATERS, Muddy
Also see WELLS, Junior
Also see WILLIAMSON, Sonny Boy
Also see WITHERSPOON, Jimmy

DIXON, Willie, & Memphis Slim
Singles: 7-inch
PRESTIGE BLUESVILLE 5-10 62
LPs: 10/12-inch
BATTLE..20-40 63
FOLKWAYS 8-12
PRESTIGE BLUESVILLE (1003 "Willie's Blues")..25-35 60
VERVE (3007 "Blues Every Which Way")..25-35 61
Also see BIG THREE TRIO
Also see DIXON, Willie
Also see MEMPHIS SLIM
Also see SELLERS, Johnny

DIXON, Wyle, & Wheels
(Willie Dixon & the Big Wheels)
Singles: 7-inch
ACE...3-5 75
CCHY-TOWN (101 "Sweet Pea")...10-15 65
CHECKER (1164 "How Long Must I Wait")..5-10 67
CONDUC (103 "Sweet Pea") 10-15 65
FEDERAL (12524 "Our Kind of Love")...8-12 64
JERMA (104 "Sweet Pea")...............8-12
TODDLIN' TOWN (105 "Gotta Hold On")..5-10 68
Also see SIMMONS, Simtec, & Wylie Dixon

DIXON HOUSE BAND
Singles: 7-inch
A&M..3-5 81
INFINITY 3-5 79
LPs: 10/12-inch
A&M..5-10 81

DJANGO
Singles: 7-inch
MR. PEACOCK (110 "Nothing for Me")..8-12 62

D'LEON, Oscar
LPs: 10/12-inch
TOP HITS (001 "Con la Salsa De") 5-10 80
(Picture disc.)

DO RAY ME TRIO: see DO-RAY-ME TRIO

DO's & DONT's
Singles: 7-inch
ZORCH (106 "Woman")....................8-12 60s

DO'A
LPs: 10/12-inch
PHILO 6-12 80

DOBBIN, Joseph, & Four Cruisers / Four Cruisers
Singles: 78 rpm
CHESS.......................................100-150 53
Singles: 7-inch
CHESS (1547 "On Account of You")..250-300 53

DOBBINS, Jimmy
Singles: 7-inch
CRASH.. 4-8

DOBKINS, Carl, Jr. *P&R/R&B '59*
Singles: 7-inch
ATCO 4-8 64
CHALET 3-6 69
COLPIX 4-8 65
DECCA.. 5-10 59-62
FRATERNITY................................. 5-10 58
MCA 3-4 73
Picture Sleeves
DECCA.. 5-10 59-60
EPs: 7-inch
DECCA (2664 "My Heart Is an Open Book")...50-75 59
LPs: 10/12-inch
DECCA (8938 "Carl Dobkins Jr.") ..40-50 59
(Monaural.)
DECCA (7-8938 "Carl Dobkins Jr.")...50-65 59
(Stereo.)
Also see LEE, Brenda / Carl Dobkins Jr.

DOBRO, Jimmie
(James Burton)
Singles: 7-inch
PHILIPS (40137 "Swamp Surfer")..30-40 63
Also see BURTON, James

DOBRO, Lon
(Lon Dobro Combo)
Singles: 7-inch
4 STAR (1754 "All the Time") 30-40 61
TROY (1003 "Undercurrent") 15-25 63

DOBSON, Dobby
Singles: 7-inch
TRANQUILITY (30 "What Love Has Joined Together")..10-15

DOBYNE, Bob, & Barefacts
Singles: 7-inch
CROWN LTD.....................................5-10

DOC & DOLPHINS
Singles: 7-inch
DINO (2 "Something About You Darling")..250-350

DOC & INTERNS
Singles: 7-inch
NOW 5-10 65

DOC & ROUNDY
Singles: 7-inch
CUCA (6759 "Not Your Kind").......15-25 67

DOC BOX & B. FRESH *P&R '90*
Singles: 7-inch
MOTOWN 3-4 90

DOC HOLLIDAY
LPs: 10/12-inch
METROMEDIA 10-15 73

DOC ROCKIT
LPs: 10/12-inch
P.S. 5-10 80

DOC SAUSAGE & HIS MAD LADS *R&B '50*
Singles: 78 rpm
REGAL..5-10 50

DOCKERY, Chuck
Singles: 7-inch
NEW SONG (123 "Baby Let's Dance")..50-75 59
NEW SONG (129 "Rock While We Ride")...25-50 59

DOCKETT, Jimmy *R&B '73*
Singles: 7-inch
FLO FEEL 3-5 73
HULL...4-8 64-65

DR. AMERICA *R&B '82*
Singles: 7-inch
ELEKTRA...3-4 82

DOCTOR & PATIENT
Singles: 7-inch
DORE...5-10 60

DOCTOR & MEDICS *P&R/LP '86*
Singles: 7-inch
I.R.S. 3-4 86
Picture Sleeves
I.R.S. 3-4 86
LPs: 10/12-inch
I.R.S. 5-8 86

DR. BOP & HEADLINERS
LPs: 10/12-inch
CHICKEN (1001 "Live")..................35-50

DR. BUZZARD'S ORIGINAL SAVANNAH BAND *P&R/R&B/LP '76*
Singles: 7-inch
RCA 3-5 76-80
LPs: 10/12-inch
ELEKTRA..5-10 79
PASSPORT..5-10
RCA 8-10 76-80
Members: August Darnell; Stony Browder Jr.; Cora Daye; Mickey Sezilla; Andy Hernandez.
Also see DAYE, Cory
Also see KID CREOLE & COCONUTS

DOCTOR CLAYTON: see CLAYTON, Doctor

DOCTOR CLAYTON'S BUDDY
(Albert Luandrew)
Singles: 78 rpm
RCA 5-10 47-48
Also see SUNNYLAND SLIM

DOCTOR FEELGOOD *P&R '62*
(Doctor Feelgood & Interns)
Singles: 7-inch
COLUMBIA..4-8 65-66
EPIC..3-5 70s
MASTER SOUND.................................4-8 67
OKEH 5-10 62-63
1-3-4..4-8 68
LPs: 10/12-inch
OKEH (12101 "Doctor Feelgood")..25-35 62
(Monaural.)
OKEH (14101 "Doctor Feelgood")..35-45 62
(Stereo.)
NUMBER ONE 15-20
Also see JOHNSON, Roy Lee
Also see PIANO RED

DOCTOR FEELGOOD
LPs: 10/12-inch
COLUMBIA...10-12 76-77
STIFF AMERICA 5-10 81

DOCTOR GADDY: see GADDY, Doctor

DR. HEP CAT
(Lavada Durst)
Singles: 78 rpm
UPTOWN ("Hattie Green") 75-100 48
Also see DURST, L.

DR. HOOK *P&R/LP '72*
(With the Medicine Show)
Singles: 7-inch
CAPITOL (4000 series)......................3-5 75-80
CAPITOL (8220 "The Stimu") 4-8 75
(Promotional issue only.)
CASABLANCA 3-4 80-82
COLUMBIA..3-5 71-74
Picture Sleeves
CAPITOL (4000 series)......................3-5 75-80
CAPITOL (8220 "The Stimu") 8-10 75
(Promotional issue only.)
CASABLANCA 3-4 82
COLUMBIA..3-5 71-72
LPs: 10/12-inch
CAPITOL 8-10 75-81
CASABLANCA 5-10 80-82
COLUMBIA (Except 34147)...............15-20 72-74
COLUMBIA (34147 "Best of Dr. Hook")..5-10 76
Also see BEACH BOYS
Also see SAWYER, Ray

DR. HORSE
Singles: 7-inch
FIRE...5-10 62
FLASHBACK..3-6 60s

DOCTOR J.R. KOOL & OTHER ROXANNES *LP '85*
Singles: 12-inch
COMPLEAT 4-6 85
Singles: 7-inch
COMPLEAT 3-4 85
LPs: 10/12-inch
COMPLEAT 5-10 85

DR. JECKYLL & MR. HYDE *R&B '82*
Singles: 12-inch
PROFILE..4-6 83-86
Singles: 7-inch
PROFILE...3-4 83-86
LPs: 10/12-inch
PROFILE...5-10 84-86

DR. JOHN *LP '71*
(Mac Rebennack)
Singles: 7-inch
ATCO 3-5 72-74
COLUMBIA...3-4 82
HORIZON...3-4 79
RCA 3-4 78
STREETWISE...3-4 84
W.B. 3-4 81
EPs: 7-inch
ATCO (4521 "Dr. John") 5-10 72
(Promotional issue only.)
LPs: 10/12-inch
A&M..8-10 79
ACCORD..5-10 81
ACE...10-12
ALLIGATOR 5-8 80s
ATCO (Except 200 & 300 series).....8-12 72-74
ATCO (200 & 300 series)................12-15 68-71
BAROMETER...10-12 74
CLEANCUTS...5-10 82-84
HORIZON...5-10 79
KARATE...8-10 78
SPRINGBOARD.......................................10-12 72
TRIP..8-10 75-76
U.A. 8-10 75
W.B. 5-10 89
Also see BLOOMFIELD, Mike, Dr. John & John Paul Hammond
Also see DICKINSON, James Luther
Also see GUY, Buddy, Dr. John & Eric Clapton / Buddy Guy & J. Geils Band
Also see REBENNACK, Mac
Also see SAHM, Doug
Also see SIMPSONS

DR. JOHN & CHRIS BARBER'S JAZZ & BLUES BAND
LPs: 10/12-inch
GREAT SOUTHERN 8-10 90
Also see BARBER, Chris

DR. JOHN & LIBBY TITUS
Singles: 7-inch
W.B. 3-4 81
Also see DR. JOHN
Also see TITUS, Libby

DR. K'S BLUES BAND
LPs: 10/12-inch
WORLD PACIFIC.....................................10-12 70

DOCTOR MARIGOLD'S PRESCRIPTION
LPs: 10/12-inch
ALSHIRE...10-12 69

DR. OTTO & His Patients
Singles: 12-inch
EPIC...4-6 84

DOCTOR ROCK
Singles: 78 rpm
CARAVAN..15-25 56
Singles: 7-inch
CARAVAN (15610 "One Way of Livin' ")...35-50 56

DOCTOR ROCKIT
LPs: 10/12-inch
PERFECT CIRCLE.....................................10-12 83

DOCTOR ROSS: see ROSS, Doctor

DR. SPEC'S OPTICAL ILLUSION
Singles: 7-inch
FLAMBEAU (103 "She's the One")...20-30 67

DR. STRUT
Singles: 7-inch
MOTOWN 3-4 79-80
LPs: 10/12-inch
MOTOWN 5-10 79-80
Members: David Woodford; Kevin Bassinson; Tim Weston; Peter Frieberger; Claude Pepper; Everett Bryson.

DR. T. & UNDERTAKERS
Singles: 7-inch
TARGET (101 "Undertaker's Theme")..15-25 60s
TARGET (4610 "Times Have Changed")..15-25 60s

DR. WEST'S MEDICINE SHOW & JUNK BAND *P&R '66*
Singles: 7-inch
GO GO (100 "The Eggplant That Ate Chicago")..5-10 66
GO GO (102 "Playboys & Bums")....5-10 67
GO GO (104 "You Can Fly")............5-10 67
GREGAR 4-8 68
ROWE/AMI 4-8 66
("Play Me" Sales Stimulator promotional issue.)
Picture Sleeves
GO GO (102 "Playboys & Bums")...10-20 67
LPs: 10/12-inch
GO GO (002 "The Eggplant That Ate Chicago")..20-30 67
GREGAR 15-20 60s
Also see GREENBAUM, Norman

DOCTOR WHO
LPs: 10/12-inch
GEMCOM (22002 "Doctor Who") ..20-25 85
(Picture disc.)
GEMCOM (22004 "Doctor Who") ..20-25 85
(Picture disc.)

DR. ZINGRR
(Bob Smith)
Singles: 7-inch
HUGGABOOM 3-5 76
Also see THORNDIKE PICKLEDISH

DOCTORS OF MADNESS
LPs: 10/12-inch
U.A. 10-12 78

DODD, Dick
Singles: 7-inch
ATTARACK.......................................8-10 60s
TOWER 8-10 68
LPs: 10/12-inch
TOWER (5142 "First Evolution of Dick Dodd")..30-40 68
Also see STANDELLS

DODD, Jimmy
Singles: 78 rpm
ABC-PAR 5-10 55-56
Singles: 7-inch
ABC-PAR 8-12 55-56
LPs: 10/12-inch
DISNEYLAND 10-20 63
WORD 10-12 63
Also see ANNETTE
Also see MOUSEKETEERS

DODD SISTERS
Singles: 7-inch
GOLD TONE 4-8 62

DODDS, Billy
Singles: 7-inch
PRIME (2601 "Praying for You")....15-25 61

DODDS, Johnny
(Gene Autry)
Singles: 78 rpm
OKEH (45317 "Railroad Boomer") 25-75 30s
OKEH (45417 "Frankie and Johnny")..25-75 30s
OKEH (45462 "No One to Call Me Darling")..25-75 30s
OKEH (45472 "Slu Foot Lou") 25-75 30s
OKEH (45560 "Cowboy Yodel")..25-75 30s
Also see AUTRY, Gene

DODDS, Malcolm
(With the Tunedrops)
Singles: 7-inch
AMY 5-10 61
AURORA...4-8 62
DECCA (30653 "Your Voice").........10-20 58
DECCA (30857 "Deep Inside").........10-20 59
DECCA (30922 "Somehow")............10-20 59
DECCA (30970 "Only for You") 10-20 59
END (1000 "It Took a Long Time")...25-50 57
END (1004 "Can't You See") 30-60 57
END (1010 "Unspoken Love")..........25-50 57
MGM 4-8 61
RAMROD 5-10 60
LPs: 10/12-inch
CAMDEN..10-20 64
Also see TUNEDROPS

DODDS, Nella *P&R/R&B '64*
Singles: 7-inch
WAND (167 "Come See About Me")..8-12 64
WAND (171 thru 187).......................5-10 64
WAND (1111 "Gee Whiz")...............10-15 65
WAND (1136 "Honey Boy") 50-75 65

DODDS, Troy
Singles: 7-inch
BAYTOWN...5-10 64
DAYTONA...10-20 60s
EL CAMINO (701 "Try My Love")..75-150 66
PENT HOUSE (002 "Down in Tennessee")......................................10-20 62
W.B. (5309 "Down in Tennessee")...8-12 62

DODGE, Tony
Singles: 7-inch
SQUARE 5-10 60

DODGER & Johnny Angel
Singles: 7-inch
SKYWAY (117 "Boogie Man") 100-125 58

DODGERS
Singles: 78 rpm
ALADDIN...50-75 54

Singles: 7-inch
ALADDIN (3259 "Let's Make a Whole Lot of Love") ... 100-200 54
ALADDIN (3271 "Cat Hop") ... 100-200 54
Member: Thomas Fox.

DODGERS
Singles: 7-inch
TOP RANK ... 5-10 59

DODGERS
Singles: 7-inch
ISLAND ... 3-5 76
POLYDOR ... 3-4 78
LPs: 10/12-inch
POLYDOR ... 5-10 78
Member: Tom Evans.
Also see BADFINGER

DODO, Joe, & Groovers
Singles: 7-inch
RCA ... 10-20 58

DODSON, Darrell C&W '77
Singles: 7-inch
SCR ... 3-5 77

DODSON, Herb
Singles: 7-inch
STACY ... 4-8 62

DODSON, Marge
Singles: 7-inch
APT ... 4-8 60s

DODSON, Tommy
Singles: 7-inch
DODSON ... 8-12
MAIN SOUND ... 8-12
UPTOWN ... 5-10 60s

DODSON, Venus
Singles: 7-inch
W.B. ... 3-5 79

DOE, John LP '90
LPs: 10/12-inch
DGC ... 5-8 90
Also see X

DOG SOLDIER
LPs: 10/12-inch
U.A. ... 10-12 75

DOGG, Redd
Singles: 7-inch
DEL-FI ... 5-10 61

DOGGETT, Bill P&R/R&B '56
Singles: 78 rpm
KING ... 5-10 53-57
Singles: 7-inch
ABC-PAR ... 3-6 64
CHUMLEY ... 3-4 74
COLUMBIA ... 4-8 62-63
GUSTO ... 3-4 80s
KING (4000 series) ... 10-20 53-56
(Black vinyl.)
KING (4000 series) ... 20-40 50s
(Colored vinyl. We're not yet sure how many different releases came on colored plastic.)
KING (5000 series) ... 6-15 56-65
KING (6000 series) ... 3-8 66-71
ROULETTE ... 3-6 67
SUE ... 4-6 64
W.B. ... 4-8 60-61
Picture Sleeves
COLUMBIA ... 5-10 62
EPs: 7-inch 33/45
KING ... 8-15 53-59
LPs: 10/12-inch
ABC-PAR ... 10-15 65
COLUMBIA ... 10-20 62-63
HARMONY ... 10-15 67
KING (82 thru 118) ... 20-40 52-55
(10-inch LPs.)
KING (500 thru 900 series) ... 12-25 56-66
ROULETTE ... 10-15 66
STARDAY ... 5-10
W.B. ... 12-20 61-62
Session: Howard Tate; Bill Butler; Clifford Scott.
Also see BOSTIC, Earl, & Bill Doggett
Also see BROWN, Wini
Also see DAVIS, Eddie "Lockjaw"
Also see FITZGERALD, Ella, & Bill Doggett
Also see HARLEMAIRES
Also see HUMES, Helen
Also see JACQUET, Illinois
Also see PAGE, Hot Lips
Also see SCOTT, Clifford
Also see TATE, Howard

DOGGETT, Ray
Singles: 78 rpm
DECCA ... 25-35 57
SPADE ... 50-75 56
Singles: 7-inch
DECCA (30295 "It Hurts the One Who Loves You") ... 25-50 57
KEN-LEE (101 "Beach Party") ... 15-25
PEARL (716 "No Doubt About It") ... 100-200 58
SPADE (1928 "Go Go Heart") ... 100-200 56
SPADE (1932 "It Hurts the One Who Loves You") ... 40-60 56
TNT (159 "Whirlpool of Love") ... 25-50 58
TOP RANK (2025 "Can I Be the One") ... 15-25 59

DOHENY, Ned
LPs: 10/12-inch
ASYLUM ... 5-10 73
COLUMBIA ... 5-10 76

DOHERTY, Denny
Singles: 7-inch
COLUMBIA ... 3-5 73
EMBER ... 3-5 75
LPs: 10/12-inch
DUNHILL ... 10-15 70
EMBER ... 8-10 75
Also see HASKELL, Jimmy
Also see MAMAS & PAPAS
Also see MUGWUMPS

DOJO
LPs: 10/12-inch
ECLIPSE (7309 "Down for the Last Time") ... 20-30 71

DOKKEN LP '83
(Don Dokken)
Singles: 7-inch
ELEKTRA ... 3-4 83-88
Picture Sleeves
ELEKTRA ... 3-4 87
LPs: 10/12-inch
ELEKTRA ... 5-10 83-88
GEFFEN ... 5-8 90
Also see HEAR 'N AID

DOLAN, Madonna C&W '88
Singles: 7-inch
TRUE ... 3-4 88

DOLAN, Ramblin' Jimmie C&W '51
Singles: 78 rpm
CAPITOL ... 5-10 51-54
Singles: 7-inch
CAPITOL ... 10-20 51-54

DOLBY, Thomas P&R/R&B/D&D/LP '83
Singles: 12-inch
CAPITOL ... 4-6 83-84
Singles: 7-inch
CAPITOL ... 3-4 83-84
HARVEST ... 3-4 82
Picture Sleeves
CAPITOL ... 3-4 83-84
LPs: 10/12-inch
CAPITOL ... 5-10 83-84
EMI ... 5-8 88
HARVEST ... 5-10 83
Also see DOLBY'S CUBE

DOLBY'S CUBE
(Thomas Dolby)
Singles: 12-inch
CAPITOL ... 4-6 84
Singles: 7-inch
CAPITOL ... 3-4 84
Also see DOLBY, Thomas

DOLCE, Joe P&R/LP '81
Singles: 7-inch
MCA ... 3-5 81
METROMEDIA ... 3-4 81
LPs: 10/12-inch
MCA ... 5-8 81

DOLES, Peter
Singles: 7-inch
ACE ... 4-8 62

DOLENZ, Micky P&R '67
(Mickey Dolenz)
Singles: 7-inch
CHALLENGE (59353 "Don't Do It") ... 10-20 66
CHALLENGE (59372 "Huff Puff") ... 10-20 67
MGM ... 8-12 71-72
ROMAR ... 8-10 73-74
Picture Sleeves
CHALLENGE (59353 "Don't Do It") ... 10-20 66
CHALLENGE (59372 "Huff Puff") ... 20-30 67
LPs: 10/12-inch
CHRYSALIS ... 8-10 79
Also see MONKEES
Also see NILSSON

DOLENZ, Micky, Davy Jones & Peter Tork
Singles: 7-inch
CHRISTMAS RECORDS ... 8-12 76
(Fan club, mail-order issue. Issued with special poster.)
Members: Micky Dolenz; David Jones; Peter Tork.
Also see MONKEES

DOLENZ, JONES, BOYCE & HART
Singles: 7-inch
CAPITOL (4180 "I Remember the Feeling") ... 10-15 75
CAPITOL (4271 "I Love You") ... 10-15 75
LPs: 10/12-inch
CAPITOL ... 10-15 76
Members: Micky Dolenz; David Jones; Tommy Boyce; Bobby Hart.
Also see BOYCE, Tommy, & Bobby Hart
Also see DOLENZ, Micky
Also see JONES, Davy, & Micky Dolenz

DOLL, Andy
Singles: 7-inch
AD ... 10-15 59-61
CUCA ... 4-8 65
JAY JAY ... 4-8 64
MASTERTONE (1014 "Muskrat Ramble") ... 15-25 50s
STARDAY (345 "That's Life") ... 10-20 57

DOLL, Kery
LPs: 10/12-inch
ERIKA/KRYPT KICKER (51459 "Til Death Do Us Part") ... 5-8 83
(Picture disc. Promotional issue only.)

DOLL CONGRESS
Singles: 12-inch
ENIGMA ... 4-6

DOLL HOUSE
Singles: 7-inch
LIVING LEGEND ... 10-20

DOLLAR P&R '79
Singles: 7-inch
CARRERE ... 3-5 79

DOLLAR, Beau
(With the Coins)
Singles: 7-inch
FRATERNITY (960 "Soul Serenade") ... 4-8 66
KING ... 4-6 69
PRIME (1157 "Soul Serenade") ... 8-12 66

DOLLAR, Johnny C&W '66
(Johnny $ Dollar)
Singles: 7-inch
CHART ... 3-6 68-70
COLUMBIA ... 4-8 66
D (1011 "Walking Away") ... 10-20 58
DATE ... 4-6 67-68
DOT ... 4-6 67
LPs: 10/12-inch
CHART ... 10-15 69
DATE ... 15-20 67

DOLLAR, Norville
Singles: 7-inch
NUGGET ... 5-8 64

DOLLAR BILL
Singles: 7-inch
TAHOE (2539 "Mr. Cool") ... 20-30

DOLLS
Singles: 7-inch
OKEH ... 5-10 59
TEENAGE (1010 "Just Before You Leave") ... 500-750 58

DOLLS
(With the Henry Hayes Orchestra)
Singles: 7-inch
KANGAROO (101 "Tell Me Now") ... 50-75 60s
MALTESE (100 "This Is Our Day") ... 25-50 65
MALTESE (107 "Airplane Song") ... 200-300 65
Member: Norma Jenkins.
Also see JENKINS, Norma

DOLLS
Singles: 7-inch
LOMA ... 8-12 66

DOLLS
Singles: 7-inch
MERCURY ... 3-5 76
Also see NEW YORK DOLLS

DOLLY
(With the Fashions)
Singles: 7-inch
IVANHOE (5019 "Just Another Fool") ... 10-15 65
TRI DISC ... 10-15 64

DOLLY & DEANS
(With the Karol-Thorn Orchestra)
Singles: 7-inch
THORNETT (1008 "The Happiest Years") ... 50-100 50s

DOLPHINS P&R '64
Singles: 7-inch
EMPRESS (102 "Rainbow's End") 10-20 61
FRATERNITY (937 "Hey-Da-Da-Dow") ... 8-12 64
FRATERNITY (940 "Little Donna") ... 8-12 65
GEMINI (501 "Pony Race") ... 5-10 62
LAURIE (3202 "Hang On") ... 5-10 63
SHAD (5020 "Tell-Tale Kisses") ... 20-30 60
Members: Carl Edmonson; Paul Singleton; Marvin Lockhard.

DOLPHINS
Singles: 7-inch
YORKSHIRE (125 "Surfing East Coast") ... 15-20 66

DOLTON, Billy
Singles: 7-inch
KAYBO ... 4-8

DOMANE, Dick
Singles: 7-inch
WYE ... 4-8 61

DOMANI, Dick
Singles: 7-inch
U.A. (50054 "Space Walk") ... 4-8 66

DOMESTIC HELP
Singles: 7-inch
ACTA (805 "Bad Seed") ... 15-25 66

DOMINATRIX D&D '84
Singles: 12-inch
STREETWISE ... 4-6 84

DOMINEERS
Singles: 7-inch
ROULETTE (5245 "Nothing Can Go Wrong") ... 10-15 60

DOMINGO, Placido P&R/LP '81
Singles: 7-inch
CBS ... 3-4 81-84
LPs: 10/12-inch
CBS ... 5-10 81-84
EMI ... 5-8 91
RCA ... 5-10 82
Also see DENVER, John, & Placido Domingo

DOMINGOS
Singles: 7-inch
CHELSEA ... 4-8 62

DOMINICO, Michael
Singles: 7-inch
GONE ... 4-8 62

DOMINO
Singles: 7-inch
20TH FOX (2198 "Have You Had a Little Happiness Lately") ... 15-25 75
Member: Tony Burrows.
Also see BURROWS, Tony

DOMINO, Bobby
Singles: 7-inch
DONNA ... 20-25 61

DOMINO, Fats R&B '50
Singles: 78 rpm
IMPERIAL (5058 thru 5477) ... 30-60 50-57
IMPERIAL (5492 "Yes, My Darling") ... 50-75 58
IMPERIAL (5515 "Sick & Tired") ... 50-75 58
IMPERIAL (5526 "Little Mary") ... 50-75 58
Singles: 7-inch
ABC ... 3-5 73
ABC-PAR (455 "I Got a Right to Cry") ... 10-20 63
(Stereo Compact 33.)
ABC-PAR (10000 series) ... 5-10 63-64
BROADMOOR ... 4-8 67
IMPERIAL (001 thru 007) ... 5-8 62
(Back-to-Back Hits series.)
IMPERIAL (5099 "Korea Blues") ... 400-500 52
IMPERIAL (5167 "You Know I Miss You") ... 150-200 52
IMPERIAL (5180 "Goin' Home") ... 100-150 52
IMPERIAL (5197 "Poor Poor Me") ... 50-100 52
IMPERIAL (5209 "How Long") ... 50-100 52
(Black vinyl.)
IMPERIAL (5209 "How Long") ... 150-250 52
(Colored vinyl.)
IMPERIAL (5220 "Nobody Loves Me") ... 50-100 53
(Black vinyl.)
IMPERIAL (5220 "Nobody Loves Me") ... 150-250 53
(Colored vinyl.)
IMPERIAL (5231 "Going to the River") ... 50-100 53
(Black vinyl.)
IMPERIAL (5231 "Going to the River") ... 150-250 53
(Colored vinyl.)
IMPERIAL (5240 "Please Don't Leave Me") ... 40-80 53
(Black vinyl.)
IMPERIAL (5240 "Please Don't Leave Me") ... 150-250 53
(Colored vinyl.)
IMPERIAL (5251 "You Said You Love Me") ... 40-80 53
IMPERIAL (5262 "Something's Wrong") ... 25-50 53
(Black vinyl.)
IMPERIAL (5262 "Something's Wrong") ... 100-200 53
(Colored vinyl.)
IMPERIAL (5272 "Little School Girl") ... 20-50 54
IMPERIAL (5283 "Baby, Please") ... 20-50 54
IMPERIAL (5301 "You Can Pack Your Suitcase") ... 20-50 54
IMPERIAL (5313 "Love Me") ... 20-50 54
IMPERIAL (5323 "I Know") ... 20-50 54
IMPERIAL (5340 "Don't You Know") ... 20-40 55
IMPERIAL (5348 "Ain't It a Shame") ... 15-25 55
IMPERIAL (5357 "All By Myself") ... 15-25 55
IMPERIAL (5369 "Poor Me") ... 15-25 55
IMPERIAL (5357 "Poor Me") ... 15-25 55
IMPERIAL (5375 "Bo Weevil") ... 15-25 56
IMPERIAL (5386 "I'm in Love Again") ... 15-25 56
IMPERIAL (5396 "So Long") ... 15-25 56
IMPERIAL (5407 "Blueberry Hill") ... 15-25 56
(Black vinyl.)
IMPERIAL (5407 "Blueberry Hill") ... 100-200 56
(Colored vinyl.)
IMPERIAL (5417 "What's the Reason I'm Not Pleasing You") ... 10-20 56
IMPERIAL (5428 "I'm Walkin' ") ... 10-20 57
IMPERIAL (5442 "Valley of Tears") ... 10-20 57
IMPERIAL (5454 "When I See You") ... 10-20 57
IMPERIAL (5467 "Wait & See") ... 10-20 57
IMPERIAL (5477 "The Big Beat") ... 10-20 57
IMPERIAL (5492 "Yes, My Darling") ... 10-20 58
(Black vinyl.)
IMPERIAL (5492 "Yes, My Darling") ... 100-150 58
(Colored vinyl.)
IMPERIAL (5515 "Sick & Tired") ... 10-20 58
IMPERIAL (5526 "Little Mary") ... 10-20 58
IMPERIAL (5537 "Young School Girl") ... 10-20 58
IMPERIAL (5553 "Whole Lotta Loving") ... 10-20 58
IMPERIAL (5569 "Telling Lies") ... 10-20 59
IMPERIAL (5585 "I'm Ready") ... 10-20 59
IMPERIAL (5606 "I Want to Walk You Home") ... 10-20 59
IMPERIAL (5629 "Be My Guest") ... 10-20 59
IMPERIAL (5675 "Walking to New Orleans") ... 10-20 60
IMPERIAL (5687 "Three Nights a Week") ... 10-20 60
IMPERIAL (5704 "Natural Born Lover") ... 10-20 60
IMPERIAL (5723 "What a Price") ... 10-15 61
IMPERIAL (5734 "Shu Rah") ... 10-15 61
IMPERIAL (5753 "It Keeps Rainin' ") ... 10-15 61
IMPERIAL (5764 "Let the Four Winds Blow") ... 10-15 61
IMPERIAL (5779 "What a Party") ... 10-15 61
IMPERIAL (5816 "You Win Again") ... 10-15 62
IMPERIAL (5833 "My Real Name") ... 10-15 62
IMPERIAL (5863 "Nothing New") ... 10-15 62
IMPERIAL (5875 "Did You Ever See a Dream Walking") ... 10-15 62
IMPERIAL (5895 "Won't You Come Back") ... 10-15 62
IMPERIAL (5909 "Hum Diddy Doo") ... 10-15 63
IMPERIAL (5937 "Trouble Blues") 10-15 63
IMPERIAL (5959 "Isle of Capri") ... 10-15 63
IMPERIAL (5980 "One Night") ... 10-15 63
IMPERIAL (5999 "Goin' Home") ... 10-15 63
IMPERIAL (66000 series) ... 6-12 63-64
IMPERIAL GOLDEN SERIES ... 3-5 70s
MERCURY (72463 "I Left My Heart in San Francisco") ... 8-10 65
MERCURY (72485 "It's Never Too Late") ... 8-10 65
REO (8026 "Ain't That a Shame") ... 40-60 55
(Canadian.)
REO (8117 "Blueberry Hill") ... 40-60 56
(Canadian. Has the same pitch error found on U.S. issues.)
REPRISE ... 4-8 68-70
TOOT TOOT (001 "My Toot Toot") ... 3-5 85
(With Doug Kershaw.)
U.A. ... 3-5 74
W.B. ... 3-5 80
Picture Sleeves
IMPERIAL (5428 "I'm Walkin' ") ... 20-30 57
IMPERIAL (5477 "The Big Beat") ... 20-30 57
IMPERIAL (5606 "I Want to Walk You Home") ... 15-25 59
IMPERIAL (5629 "Be My Guest") ... 15-25 59
MERCURY (72485 "It's Never Too Late") ... 20-30 65
EPs: 7-inch
ABC-PAR (455 "Here Comes Fats Domino") ... 15-25 63
(Juke box issue only. Includes title strips.)
ABC-PAR (479 "Fats on Fire") ... 15-25 64
(Juke box issue only. Includes title strips.)
ABC-PAR (510 "Getaway") ... 15-25 65
(Juke box issue only. Includes title strips.)
IMPERIAL (138 "Fats Domino") ... 40-60 56
IMPERIAL (139 "Fats Domino") ... 40-60 56
IMPERIAL (140 "Fats Domino") ... 40-60 56
IMPERIAL (141/142/143 "Rock 'n Rollin' with Fats Domino") ... 40-60 56
(Price for any of three volumes.)
IMPERIAL (144/145/146 "This Is Fats Domino") ... 40-60 56
(Price for any of three volumes.)
IMPERIAL (147 "Here Comes Fats") ... 40-60 57
IMPERIAL (148/149/150 "Here Stands Fats Domino") ... 40-60 57
(Price for any of three volumes.)
IMPERIAL (151 "Cookin' with Fats") ... 40-60 57
IMPERIAL (152 "Rockin' with Fats") ... 40-60 57
IMPERIAL (127 "Fats Domino—America's Outstanding Piano Stylist") ... 75-125 53
(Red, script logo label.)
IMPERIAL (127 "Fats Domino—America's Outstanding Piano Stylist") ... 40-60 56
(Maroon label.)
MERCURY ("Fats Domino '65") ... 15-25 65
(Juke box issue only. Includes title strips. Selection number not known.)
LPs: 10/12-inch
ABC-PAR (455 "Here Comes Fats Domino") ... 20-40 63
ABC-PAR (479 "Fats on Fire") ... 20-40 64
ABC-PAR (510 "Getaway") ... 20-40 65
AUDIO FIDELITY ... 10-15 84
(Picture disc.)
CANDLELITE (13197 "Legendary Music Man") ... 15-20 76
(Two discs.)
EVEREST ... 8-10 74-77
GRAND AWARD (267 "Fats Domino") ... 10-15 60s
HARLEM HITPARADE (5005 "Fats' Hits") ... 10-15 75
HARMONY (11343 "When I'm Walking") ... 10-15 69
IMPERIAL (9004 "Rock 'n Rollin' ") ... 100-200 56
(Maroon label.)
IMPERIAL (9004 "Rock 'n Rollin' ") ... 50-75 58
(Black Label.)
IMPERIAL (9009 "Fats Domino Rock 'n Rollin' ") ... 100-200 56
(Maroon label.)
IMPERIAL (9009 "Fats Domino Rock 'n Rollin' ") ... 50-75 58
(Black label.)
IMPERIAL (9028 "This Is Fats Domino") ... 100-200 57
(Maroon label.)

IMPERIAL (9028 "This Is Fats Domino") 50-75 58
(Black label.)
IMPERIAL (9038 "Here Stands Fats Domino") 100-200 57
(Maroon label.)
IMPERIAL (9038 "Here Stands Fats Domino") 50-75 58
(Black label.)
IMPERIAL (9040 "This Is Fats") .100-200 57
(Maroon label.)
IMPERIAL (9040 "This Is Fats") 50-75 58
(Black label.)
IMPERIAL (9055 "The Fabulous Mr. 'D' ") 50-100 58
IMPERIAL (9062 "Fats Domino Swings") 50-100 59
IMPERIAL (9065 "Let's Play Fats Domino") 50-100 59
IMPERIAL (9103 "Million Record Hits") 50-100 60
IMPERIAL (9127 "A Lot of Dominos") 50-75 60
(Monaural.)
IMPERIAL (9138 "I Miss You So")..50-75 61
IMPERIAL (9153 "Let the Four Winds Blow") 40-60 61
(Monaural.)
IMPERIAL (9164 "What a Party")...40-60 61
IMPERIAL (9170 "Twistin' the Stomp") 30-50 62
IMPERIAL (9195 "Million Sellers") .30-50 62
IMPERIAL (9208 "Just Domino")....30-50 62
IMPERIAL (9227 "Walkin' to New Orleans") 30-50 63
IMPERIAL (9239 "Let's Dance")......30-50 63
IMPERIAL (9248 "Here He Comes Again") 30-50 63
IMPERIAL (12066 "A Lot of Dominos") 40-60 60
(Stereo.)
IMPERIAL (12073 "Let the Four Winds Blow") 40-60 61
(Stereo.)
IMPERIAL (12091 "Fats Domino Swings") 20-40 64
IMPERIAL (12103 "Fats Domino") 20-40 64
LIBERTY 5-10 80-81
MERCURY (21039 "Fats Domino '65") 15-25 65
(Monaural.)
MERCURY (61039 "Fats Domino '65") 15-25 65
(Stereo.)
PICKWICK 8-12 70s
REPRISE (6304 "Fats Is Back") 20-30 68
REPRISE (6439 "Fats") 300-500 71
SILVER EAGLE 5-8 86
SUNSET (5103 "Fats Domino") 10-15 66
SUNSET (5158 "Stompin' ")..........10-15 66
SUNSET (5200 "Trouble in Mind") .10-15 68
SUNSET (5299 "Ain't That a Shame") 10-15 70
TOMATO 10-20 89
U.A. (104 "Legendary Masters")......15-25 73
(Edited tracks. Promotional issue only.)
U.A. (233 "Very Best") 8-12 74
U.A. (380 "Very Best") 5-10 75
U.A. (9958 "Legendary Masters")...15-25 71
Members (Band): Dave Bartholomew; Ernest McLean; Herbert Hardesty; Clarence Hall; Alvin "Red" Tyler; Joe Harris; Salvador Doucette; Lee Allen.
Also see ALLEN, Lee
Also see BARTHOLOMEW, Dave
Also see PRICE, Lloyd
Also see WILLS, Oscar

DOMINO, Renaldo

Singles: 7-inch

BLUE ROCK (4061 "Just Say the Word") 20-30 60s
SMASH (2127 "I'm Getting Nearer to Love") 10-20 68
SMASH (2160 "You Don't Love Me No More") 10-20 68
TWINIGHT 5-10

DOMINOES — *R&B/P&R '51*

Singles: 78 rpm

DELUXE (309 "Sixty Minute Man"/"Chicken Blues") 300-500 51
(Canadian. Note different flip than U.S. issue.)
FEDERAL (12001 "Do Something for Me") 100-150 50
FEDERAL (12010 "Harbor Lights") 250-350 50
(Original 45s of #12010 are not known to exist.)
FEDERAL (12022 "Sixty Minute Man") 100-150 51
FEDERAL (12039 "I Am with You") 50-100 51
FEDERAL (12059 "That's What You're Doing to Me") 50-100 52
FEDERAL (12068 "Have Mercy Baby") 50-100 52
FEDERAL (12072 "Love, Love, Love") 50-100 52

Singles: 7-inch

FEDERAL (12001 "Do Something for Me") 750-1000 50
FEDERAL (12022 "Sixty Minute Man") 400-600 51
FEDERAL (12039 "I Am with You") 500-750 51
FEDERAL (12059 "That's What You're Doing to Me") 500-750 52
FEDERAL (12068 "Have Mercy Baby") 300-400 52
FEDERAL (12072 "Love, Love, Love") 300-400 52
For later Federal singles — as well all EPs and LPs — see the Billy Ward & Dominoes section.
GUSTO 3-5 80s
Members: Billy Ward; Clyde McPhatter; Charlie White; William Lamont; Bill Brown.
Also see CHECKERS
Also see GREENWOOD, Lil, & Dominoes
Also see LITTLE ESTHER & DOMINOES
Also see McPHATTER, Clyde
Also see WARD, Billy, & Dominoes

DOMINOES

Singles: 7-inch

MELBOURNE 5-10 62

DON & BLUE DIAMONDS

Singles: 7-inch

SKYLARK 5-10 61

DON & BOB

Singles: 7-inch

ARGO (5373 "Little Red Schoolhouse") 15-25 60
ARGO (5400 "Good Morning Little School Girl") 15-25 60
SPEEDWAY (1000 "The Only Girl") 35-55 64
Member: Don Ciccone.
Also see CICCONE, Don

DON & CHEVELLS

Singles: 7-inch

SPEEDWAY (1000 "Inner Limits") 10-20 64

DON & DARLENE

Singles: 7-inch

DOT 10-15

DON & DAVE

Singles: 7-inch

PEARCE (5808 "If I Were the Wind") 10-20 60s

DON & DEWEY

(With the Titans)

Singles: 78 rpm

SHADE (1000 "Miss Sue") 10-20 56
SPECIALTY (599 thru 631)...........10-15 57-58
SPECIALTY (639 "The Letter")........20-25 58
SPECIALTY (659 "Farmer John") ..25-50 59
SPOT 10-15 56

Singles: 7-inch

FIDELITY 10-15 60
HIGHLAND (1050 "Don't Ever Leave Me") 8-12 62
RUSH (1003 "Don't Ever Leave Me") 10-15 62
(First issue.)
SHADE (1000 "Miss Sue") 25-35 56
SPECIALTY (SPBX series)............15-25 86
(Boxed set of six colored vinyl 45s.)
SPECIALTY (599 "Jungle Hop") 10-20 57
SPECIALTY (610 "I'm Leavng It All Up to You") 15-25 57
(Label makes no mention of Don & Dewey LP.)
SPECIALTY (610 "I'm Leavng It All Up to You") 4-6 80s
(On A-side only, reads "From the Specialty LP *Don and Dewey*.")
SPECIALTY (617 "Just a Little Lovin' ") 10-20 57
SPECIALTY (631 "Justine")............10-20 58
SPECIALTY (639 "The Letter")........10-20 58
SPECIALTY (659 "Farmer John") ...10-20 59
SPECIALTY (691 "Annie Lee") 10-20 61
SPOT (101 "Fiddlin' the Blues") 15-25 56

LPs: 10/12-inch

SPECIALTY (2131 "They're Rockin' Till Midnight") 10-15 70
(Black and gold label.)
SPECIALTY (2131 "They're Rockin' Till Midnight") 5-10 88
(Black and white label.)
Members: Don Harris (a.k.a. Don Bowman); Dewey Terry. Session: Blossoms
Also see BLUEJAYS
Also see BLOSSOMS
Also see HARRIS, Don "Sugar Cane"
Also see SHARPS
Also see SQUIRES
Also see TERRY, Dewey
Also see TITANS

DON & DOMINOS

Singles: 7-inch

CUCA (1088 "Just Let Me Be") 10-15 62
CUCA (1109 "Weary Blues") 10-15 62
CUCA (1143 "Domino Theme") 10-15 63
Also see DON & HARRY

DON & DOVES

Singles: 7-inch

DYNAMIC (107 "I Need You") 15-25 60s

DON & EDDIE

Singles: 7-inch

DECCA 5-10 61

DON & GALAXIES

Singles: 7-inch

FOX-FIDEL 5-10 60

Picture Sleeves

FOX-FIDEL 10-20 60

DON & GOODTIMES — *P&R/LP '67*

(Don Gallucci)

Singles: 7-inch

BURDETTE (3 "Colors of Life")......10-20 66
DUNHILL 5-10 65
EPIC 5-10 67-68
JERDEN 8-12 66
PICCADILLY 5-10 60s
WAND 5-10 64

Picture Sleeves

EPIC (10199 "Happy & Me") 10-20 67

LPs: 10/12-inch

BURDETTE (300 "Greatest Hits") ..40-50 66
EPIC (24311 "So Good") 15-20 67
(Monaural.)
EPIC (26311 "So Good") 15-20 67
(Stereo.)
PANORAMA (104 "Harpo")............30-40
PICCADILLY (3394 "Goodtime Music") 5-10 82
WAND (679 "Where the Action Is") 25-35 67
Members: Don Gallucci; Jeff Hawks; Joe Newman.
Also see KINGSMEN
Also see TOUCH
Also see VALLEY, Jim

DON & HARRY

Singles: 7-inch

CUCA (1062 "Wabash Cannonball") 10-20 61
Also see DON & DOMINOS

DON & HIS ROSES

(Don Guess)

Singles: 7-inch

DOT (15755 "Right Now") 15-25 58
DOT (15784 "Leave Those Cats Alone") 125-150 58
Also see GUESS, Don
Also see HOLLY, Buddy
Also see ROSES

DON & JERRY

Singles: 7-inch

FABOR (140 "In the Cover of the Night") 10-15 65
HIDE-N-JOY 5-10 66

DON & JUAN — *P&R '62*

Singles: 7-inch

BIG TOP (3079 "What's Your Name") 10-20 62
BIG TOP (3106 "Two Fools Are We") 10-20 62
BIG TOP (3121 "Magic Wand") 20-30 62
BIG TOP (3145 "True Love Never Runs Smooth") 10-20 63
ERIC 3-4 70s
MALA (469 "Lonely Man") 8-12 63
MALA (484 "Sincerely") 8-12 63
MALA (509 "Heartbreaking Truth") 15-25 65
TERRIFIC 3-5 70s
TWIRL (2021 "Because I Love You") 15-25 66
Members: Roland Trone: Claude Johnson.
Also see GENIES

DON & LEE

Singles: 78 rpm

ROYAL ROOST 10-15 53

Singles: 7-inch

ROYAL ROOST (631 "Sweet Honey Dew") 15-25 53

DON & MARTY

Singles: 7-inch

CANDIX (309 "Mandolin Rock") 10-20 60

DON & UPBEATS

Singles: 7-inch

LANA (6042 "Night Train") 5-10

DON CLAIRS

Singles: 7-inch

AMP 3 (1001 "I Lost My Job") 20-25 58

DON, DICK N' JIMMY — *P&R '54*

Singles: 78 rpm

CROWN 5-10 54-55
DOT 5-10 54

Singles: 7-inch

CROWN 8-15 54-55
DOT 8-15 54

LPs: 10/12-inch

CROWN (5005 "Spring Fever") 25-35 57
DOT 15-25 59
MODERN (1205 "Spring Fever")....35-50 56
VERVE 15-25 59
Members: Don Sutton; Dick Rock; Jimmy Cook.

DON GILS

(Don Gils Group)

Singles: 7-inch

ACCENT 4-8 66

DON JUAN — *C&W '88*

Singles: 7-inch

MAXX 3-4 88
Members: Stu Stewart; Ed Allen; Toby Strause.

DON JUANS

Singles: 7-inch

ONEZY (101 "The Girl of My Dreams") 1000-2000 59

DON Q

(Don Q's Band Featuring Clenest Gant)

Singles: 78 rpm

BULLET 5-10 40s
KIT (884 "Jump-Jump-Hi Ho") 10-15 56

Singles: 7-inch

KIT (884 "Jump-Jump-Hi Ho") 15-25 56
Also see GANT, Clentt

DON RAYS: see HERMAN, Cleve / Don Rays

DONAHUE, Billy

Singles: 7-inch

COED 5-10 59

DONAHUE, Troy

Singles: 7-inch

W.B. 5-10 63

DONALD & DELIGHTERS — *P&R '63*

(Donald Jenkins & Daylighters)

Singles: 7-inch

BLACK BEAUTY (302 "Elephant Walk") 8-10
CHEST (2001/2002 "Elephant Walk"/"Cool Breeze") 10-20 60s
(*Cool Breeze*, is by the Daylighters.)
CORTLAND (109 "Elephant Walk") 20-25 63
(Credits: "Donald Jenkins & the Daylighters.")
Note: When we learn the year of release for the Black Beauty and Chest discs, we'll know more about how they relate to the Cortland release of *Elephant Walk*.
CORTLAND (109 "Elephant Walk") 10-15 63
(Credits: "Donald & the Delighters.")
CORTLAND (112 "Adios") 15-25 64
CORTLAND (116 "I've Settled Down") 15-25 64
DUCHESS (104 "Happy Days") 10-20 65
THOMAS (806 "Fighting for My Baby") 20-30 60s
Members: Donald Jenkins; Walter Granger; Daylighters.
Also see DAYLIGHTERS

DONALDSON, Bo, & Heywoods — *P&R '72*

(Heywoods)

Singles: 7-inch

ABC 3-5 73-75
CAPITOL 3-5 76
FAMILY 3-5 72-74
PLAYBOY 3-5 77

Picture Sleeves

ABC 3-5 74

LPs: 10/12-inch

ABC 5-10 74
CAPITOL 5-8 76
FAMILY 8-12 72

DONALDSON, Craig — *C&W '76*

Singles: 7-inch

GREAT AMERICAN 3-5 76

DONALDSON, Lou — *LP '63*

(Lou Donaldson Quintet)

Singles: 78 rpm

BLUE NOTE 3-8 52-57

Singles: 7-inch

ARGO 4-6 63-65
BLUE NOTE (100 thru 300 series).....3-5 73-74
BLUE NOTE (1500 & 1600 series)...5-10 52-58
BLUE NOTE (1700 thru 1900 series) 4-8 58-72

LPs: 10/12-inch

ARGO 15-25 63-65
BLUE NOTE 8-15 64-80
(Label shows Blue Note Records as a division of either Liberty or United Artists.)
BLUE NOTE (1500 series)..............50-75 57-58
(Label gives New York street address for Blue Note Records.)
BLUE NOTE (1500 series)...............30-40 58
(Label reads "Blue Note Records Inc. - New York, USA.")
BLUE NOTE (1500 series)...............15-20 66
(Label shows Blue Note Records as a division of either Liberty or United Artists.)
BLUE NOTE (4000 & 84000 series) 15-25 58-63
(Label reads "Blue Note Records Inc. - New York, U.S.A.")
BLUE NOTE (5000 series)...........50-100 52-54
(10-inch LPs.)
BLUE NOTE (5000 series)...........50-100 52-54
(10-inch LPs.)
CADET 8-12 65-71
COTILLION 5-10 76-77
SUNSET 5-10 69-71
TRIP 5-10 79

DONATO, Mike

(With the Tridels)

Singles: 7-inch

PM (0101 "Summertime Love") ... 50-100

DONAYS

Singles: 7-inch

BRENT (7033 "Devil in His Heart") 20-25 62

DONDI

Singles: 7-inch

CHALLENGE (59305 "S&L")............5-10 65

DONDMAN & SKYLARKS

Singles: 7-inch

THUNDERBIRD 4-8 63

DONEGAN, Lonnie — *P&R '56*

(With His Skiffle Group)

Singles: 78 rpm

LONDON 5-10 56
MERCURY 5-10 56

Singles: 7-inch

ABC 3-5 76
APT 5-10 62
ATLANTIC (2058 "My Old Man's a Dustman") 10-20 60
ATLANTIC (2081 "Junco Partner").10-15 61
ATLANTIC (2108 "Have a Drink on Me") 10-15 61
DOT 8-12 61
FELSTED (8630 "Rock Island Line") 8-12 61
HICKORY 4-8 64-65
LONDON (1650 "Rock Island Line") 10-20 56
MCA 3-4
MERCURY (70872 "Lost John")......10-20 56
PYE (5256 "My Old Man's a Dustman") 10-20 60
(Canadian.)

LPs: 10/12-inch

ABC-PAR 15-20 63
ATLANTIC 20-30 60
DOT (3159 "Lonnie Donegan") 25-40 59
DOT (3394 "Lonnie Donegan") 20-30 61
MERCURY 25-40 57
U.A. 10-12 77

DONELL, Delmar

Singles: 7-inch

LAVE HE 5-10 64
NEW SOUND 10-20

DONLEY, Jimmy

Singles: 7-inch

CHESS (1843 "Think It Over").......10-15 62
DECCA (30574 "Please Baby Come Home") 15-25 58
DECCA (30308 "Come Along")......50-75 59
TEAR DROP (3005 Honey, Stop Twistin' ") 8-12 62

LPs: 10/12-inch

CRAZY CAJUN 10-15 70s
STARFLITE (2002 "Born to Be a Loser") 20-35 70s

DONN, Larry

(With the Killer Possum Band)

Singles: 7-inch

ALLEY 5-10 62
RIMROCK 4-6 72
SHELBY 3-5 79
THREE SUNS (1 "The Great American Superstar") 3-5 89
VADEN (113 "Honey Bun")........200-300 59

LPs: 10/12-inch

SHELBY 5-10 72-78
Also see BROWN, Bobby
Also see BURGESS, Sonny, & Larry Donn
Also see COTILLIONS
Also see LEE, Joe
Also see OWENS, Kenny, & Travelers
Also see RILEY, Billy Lee

DONNA

(Donna Ludwig)

Singles: 7-inch

POP (1103 "Lost Without You").....20-30 59

DONNA, Darlene

Singles: 7-inch

KAPP 4-8 65

DONNA, Vic

(With the Parakeets)

Singles: 78 rpm

ATLAS 40-60 57

Singles: 7-inch

ABC-PAR 5-10 62
ATLAS (1071 "Teenage Rose") ... 50-100 57
(Atlas man logo at 9:00 on label. Reads "Atlas Records")
ATLAS (1071 "Teenage Rose") 40-60 57
(Atlas man logo at 11:00 on label. Reads "Atlas Angeltone Records at bottom")
ATLAS (1075 "Love Was a Stanger to Me") 50-100 57
CARLTON 10-20 59
LIDO 10-20 59
TIGER 5-10 64
Also see PARAKEETS QUINTET

DONNA & ARNIE

Singles: 7-inch

VALIANT 4-8 64

DONNA & DAVE

Singles: 7-inch

MELO-DEE 5-10

DONNA & DEES

Singles: 7-inch

BCS 15-20

DONNA & PERSUASIONS

Singles: 7-inch

BLUE SKY 3-5 73
Also see PERSUASIONS

DONNA LEE: see LEE, Donna

DONNA LYNN: see LYNN, Donna

DONNA MARIE

Singles: 7-inch

COLUMBIA 4-6 68
CORAL 4-8 65

Picture Sleeves

COLUMBIA 4-8 68
Also see LA DONNA, Maria

DONNELL, Doug, & Hot Rods

Singles: 7-inch

ALTON 8-12 59

DONNELS

Singles: 7-inch

ALPHA (001 "Here Comes the Bride") 15-25 63

DONNELS, Johnny

Singles: 7-inch

ALPHA 10-20

DONNER, Ral — *P&R '61*

(With the Starfires; with Scotty Moore, D.J. Fontana & Jordanaires)

Singles: 7-inch

ABC 3-5 73
CHICAGO FIRE 8-10 74
END (19 "You Don't Know What You've Got") 10-20 63
FONTANA (1502 "Poison Ivy League") 10-20 64
FONTANA (1515 "Good Lovin' ")...10-20 65

GONE (5102 "Girl of My Best Friend") 30-40 60
(Black label.)
GONE (5100 series, except 5108 & 5119) 10-15 61-62
(Multi-color labels.)
GONE (5108 "To Love"/"And Then") 15-25 61
(Shortly after this release, *You Don't Know What You've Got* was issued using the same selection number.)
GONE (5108 "You Don't Know What You've Got") 10-15 61
GONE (5114 "Please Don't Go") 8-12 61
GONE (5119 "School of Heartbreakers") 30-40 61
GONE (5121 "She's Everything"/"Because We're Young") 10-20 61
GONE (5121 "She's Everything"/"Will You Love Me in Heaven") 15-25 61
(Though credited to "Ral Donner," *Will You Love Me in Heaven* is by a thus far unidentified girl group.)
GONE (5125 "To Love Someone"/"Will You Love Me in Heaven") 10-15 61
(*Will You Love Me in Heaven* is credited to and sung by Ral Donner.)
GONE (5129 "Loveless Life") 10-15 62
GONE (5133 "To Love") 10-15 61
MJ (222 "My Heart Sings") 4-8 70
MID-EAGLE 4-8 68-76
RED BIRD (057 "Love Isn't Like That") 100-150 66
REPRISE (20135 "Christmas Day") 20-30 62
REPRISE (20141 "I Got Burned") 20-30 63
REPRISE (20192 "Run Little Linda") 20-30 63
RISING SONS 5-10 68
ROULETTE 3-5 71
SCOTTIE (1310 "Tell Me Why") 200-300 59
SMASH (34774 "Good Lovin'") 25-35 65
(Promotional issue only.)
STARFIRE (100 "Wait a Minute Now") 5-10 78
STARFIRE (103 "Christmas Day") 5-10 78
STARFIRE (114 "Rip It Up") 5-10 79
(Black vinyl.)
STARFIRE (114 "Rip It Up") 10-25 79
(Picture disc.)
SUNLIGHT 8-10 72
TAU (105 "Lonliness of a Star") 35-50 63
(Blue label. First issue—1,000 made.)
TAU (105 "Lonliness of a Star") 20-30 63
(Yellow label. 2,000 made.)
THUNDER (7801 "The Day the Beat Stopped") 4-6 78
(Clear vinyl.)

Picture Sleeves
MJ (222 "My Heart Sings") 5-10 70
REPRISE (20141 "I Got Burned") 50-75 63
STARFIRE 5-10 78-79

LPs: 10/12-inch
AUDIO RESEARCH 12-15 80
GONE (5012 "Takin' Care of Business") 100-200 61
GONE (5033 "Elvis Scrapbook") 10-15
GYPSY 8-12 79
MIDEAGLE (7902 "1935-1977 - Been Away for a While Now") 40-60 79
MURRAY HILL 5-10 88
STARFIRE (1004 "An Evening with Ral Donner") 10-15 82
(Multi-color vinyl.)
STARFIRE (1004 "An Evening with Ral Donner") 10-20 82
(Picture disc.)
Session: Scotty Moore; Jordanaires.
Also see FONTANA, D.J., Band
Also see JORDANAIRES
Also see MOORE, Scotty
Also see PRESLEY, Elvis

DONNER, Ral / Ray Smith / Bobby Dale

LPs: 10/12-inch
CROWN 15-20 63
Also see SMITH, Ray

DONNER, Ral / Zantees

Singles: 7-inch
EVA-TONE/GOLDMINE 3-4 79
(Soundsheet.)
Also see DONNER, Ral
Also see ZANTEES

DONNIE & COR-VETS

Singles: 7-inch
AERTAUN 5-10 65

DONNIE & DARLINGTONS

Singles: 7-inch
ABC-PAR 10-20 65

DONNIE & DEL CHORDS

(Donnie Huffman)
Singles: 7-inch
EPIC 5-10 62
TAURUS 10-15 61-63
LPs: 10/12-inch
TAURUS (1000 "Donnie and the Del Chords") 200-300 63
Also see HUFFMAN, Donnie

DONNIE & DIANE

Singles: 7-inch
DJB (115 "Hotrod Weekend") 10-20 64

DONNIE & DREAMERS — *P&R '61*

Singles: 7-inch
DECCA (31312 "Carole") 40-60 61
(Multi-color label.)
DECCA (31312 "Carole") 50-100 61
(Pink label. Promotional issue only.)

WHALE (500 "Count Every Star") 15-25 61
WHALE (505 "My Memories of You") 25-35 61
Also see KENNY & WHALERS

DONNY & BI-LANGOS

Singles: 7-inch
COLTON (101 "I'm Not a Know It All") 20-30

DONNY & DUKE

Singles: 7-inch
MGM 5-10 58

DONNIE & RONNIE

Singles: 7-inch
ASSOCIATED ARTISTS 5-10 65

DONNY BOY & HIS GUITAR

Singles: 7-inch
DART 35-50

DONNYBROOKS

Singles: 7-inch
CALICO 5-10 59

DONOFRIO, Vince

Singles: 7-inch
WORLD PACIFIC 4-6

DONOMAN

Singles: 7-inch
TROCADERO (100 "I'm the One") 10-20

DONOVAN — *P&R/LP '65*

(Donovan P. Leitch)
Singles: 12-inch
ALLEGIANCE (1437 "Donovan") 5-10 83
Singles: 7-inch
ALLEGIANCE 3-4 83
ARISTA 3-5 77
EPIC 4-8 66-76
(Black vinyl.)
EPIC (10045 "Sunshine Superman") 10-15 66
(Colored vinyl. Promotional issue only.)
EPIC MEMORY LANE 3-5
HICKORY 8-15 65-68
Picture Sleeves
EPIC 5-10 66-71
LPs: 10/12-inch
ALLEGIANCE 5-10 83
ARISTA 8-10 77
BELL 10-12 73
COLUMBIA 5-10 73
EPIC (Except 26439) 10-20 66-76
EPIC (BXN-26439 "Greatest Hits") 15-20 69
(Gatefold cover. Includes booklet.)
EPIC (PE-26439 "Greatest Hits") 5-10 77
(Standard cover. No booklet.)
HICKORY (123 "Catch the Wind") 20-40 65
HICKORY (127 "Fairy Tale") 20-40 65
HICKORY (135 "The Real Donovan") 20-40 66
HICKORY (143 "Like It Is") 20-40 68
HICKORY (149 "The Best of Donovan") 20-40 69
JANUS 10-12 70-71
KORY 5-10 77
PYE 8-10 76

DONOVAN & JEFF BECK GROUP — *P&R '69*

Singles: 7-inch
EPIC 4-8 69
Also see BECK, Jeff
Also see DONOVAN

DONS

Singles: 7-inch
HEARTBEAT 4-8

DONTELLS

Singles: 7-inch
VEE JAY 4-8 65

DONTELS

Singles: 7-inch
BELTONE (2040 "Lovers Reunion") 175-225 63

DOO, Dicky: see DICKY DOO & DON'TS

DOO & DIDDITS

Singles: 7-inch
TEMPO 15-20
Member: Doo Hickman.

DOO RON RON & O.J. PLAYERS

Singles: 7-inch
(EUREKA (101 "O.J. Meets the King") 3-5 95
(Red vinyl.)

DOOBIE BROTHERS — *P&R/LP '72*

Singles: 12-inch
W.B. 4-8 79
Singles: 7-inch
ASYLUM 3-4 80
CAPITOL 3-4 89
SESAME STREET 3-4 81
W.B. 3-6 71-83
Picture Sleeves
CAPITOL 3-4 89
SESAME STREET 3-4 81
W.B. 3-5 79-83
EPs: 7-inch
W.B. 10-20 74
(Juke box issue.)
LPs: 10/12-inch
CAPITOL 5-8 89-91
MFSL (122 "Takin' It to the Streets") 20-30 84
NAUTILUS (5 "Captain and Me") 25-35 80
(Half-speed mastered.)
NAUTILUS (18 "Minute By Minute") 15-20 81
(Half-speed mastered.)
PICKWICK 6-10 80
W.B. 6-12 71-83
Members: Tom Johnston; Patrick Simmons; John Hartman; Tiran Porter; Jeff "Skunk" Baxter; Michael McDonald; John McFee; Chet McCracken;
Also see BUMPUS, Cornelius
Also see GARDNER, Ron
Also see HELP
Also see McDONALD, Michael
Also see SIMMONS, Patrick
Also see SOUTHERN PACIFIC

DOOBIE BROTHERS, JAMES HALL & JAMES TAYLOR

Singles: 7-inch
ASYLUM 3-4 80
Also see TAYLOR, James

DOOBIE BROTHERS & NICOLETTE LARSON

Singles: 7-inch
W.B. 3-5 79
Also see LARSON, Nicolette

DOOBIE BROTHERS / Kate Taylor & Simon-Taylor Family

Singles: 7-inch
W.B. 3-4 80
Picture Sleeves
W.B. 3-4 80
Also see DOOBIE BROTHERS
Also see SIMON SISTERS
Also see TAYLOR, James
Also see TAYLOR, Kate
Also see TAYLOR, Livingston

DOODLERS

Singles: 7-inch
JONES (1002 "The Dangerous Dangeroo") 10-15

DOODLES

Singles: 7-inch
HIT 5-15 64

DOOLEY, Dottie

Singles: 7-inch
MONITOR (1244 "I'll Always Have Memories of You") 40-60

DOOLEY, Tom

(With the Lovelights)
Singles: 7-inch
HICKORY 5-8 66-67
SAXONY (1006 "Printer's Alley [Before Midnight]"/"Printer's Alley [After Midnight]") 10-15 63
TRX 4-6 68-70

DOOLEY, Tom / Steve Greenberg

Singles: 7-inch
SAXONY (2008 "Printer's Alley [After Midnight]"/"Run to You") 4-8 97
(*Run to You* is the flip side of Greenberg's *Big Bruce*. 1,000 made.)
Also see DOOLEY, Tom
Also see GREENBERG, Steve

DOOLEY SISTERS

Singles: 78 rpm
TAMPA 8-10 55
Singles: 7-inch
R-DELL ("Spider in the Web") 20-30 58
(Selection number not known.)
TAMPA 10-15 55

DOOLITTLE BAND — *P&R '80*

(Dandy & Doolittle Band)
Singles: 7-inch
COLUMBIA 3-4 80

DOOMSDAY MACHINE

Singles: 7-inch
DOT 4-6 69

DOONE, Lorna

Singles: 7-inch
RCA (8532 "Dangerous Town") 15-25

DOOR NOBS

Singles: 7-inch
VIV 4-8

DOORS — *P&R/LP '67*

Singles: 7-inch
ELEKTRA (12400 "The End") 5-10 80
ELEKTRA (45611 "Break on Through") 15-25 67
(Yellow label with Elektra Girl logo.)
ELEKTRA (45611 "Break on Through") 10-15 67
(Standard Elektra logo – no girl pictured.)
ELEKTRA (45615 "Light My Fire") 15-25 67
(Yellow label with Elektra Girl logo. Canadian copies with this label have been verified. First pressings credit Allied Records; second, Kinney Music, and third, WEA. Confirmation of U.S. issues is pending.)
ELEKTRA (45615 "Light My Fire") 5-10 67
(Standard Elektra logo – no girl pictured.)
ELEKTRA (45621 "People Are Strange") 5-10 67
ELEKTRA (45624 "Love Me Two Times") 5-10 67
ELEKTRA (45628 "The Unknown Soldier") 5-10 68
ELEKTRA (45635 "Hello, I Love You") 5-10 68
ELEKTRA (45646 "Touch Me") 5-10 68
ELEKTRA (45656 "Wishful Sinful") 5-10 69
ELEKTRA (45663 "Tell All the People") 5-10 69
ELEKTRA (45675 "Runnin' Blue") 5-10 69
ELEKTRA (45685 "You Make Me Real") 5-10 70
ELEKTRA (45726 "Love Her Madly") 5-10 71
ELEKTRA (45738 "Riders on the Storm") 5-10 71
ELEKTRA (45757 "Tightrope Ride") 5-10 71
ELEKTRA (45768 "Ships with Sails") 10-20 72
ELEKTRA (45793 "Get Up and Dance") 10-20 72
ELEKTRA (45807 "The Mosquito") 5-10 72
ELEKTRA (45825 "Good Rockin' ") 10-20 72
ELEKTRA (69770 "Gloria") 5-10 83
Promotional Singles
ELEKTRA (45611 "Break on Through") 15-20 67
ELEKTRA (45615 thru 45757) 10-15 67-71
ELEKTRA (45768 "Ships with Sails") 15-25 72
ELEKTRA (45793 "Get Up and Dance") 15-25 72
ELEKTRA (45807 "The Mosquito") 10-15 72
ELEKTRA (45825 "Good Rockin' ") 15-25 72
ELEKTRA (69770 "Gloria") 8-12 83
Picture Sleeves
ELEKTRA (45621 "People Are Strange") 15-25 67
ELEKTRA (45628 "The Unknown Soldier") 30-40 68
ELEKTRA (45663 "Tell All the People") 30-40 69
LPs: 10/12-inch
ELEKTRA (500 series) 5-10 78-80
ELEKTRA (4007 "The Doors") 20-35 67
(Monaural.)
ELEKTRA (4014 "Strange Days") 15-25 67
(Monaural.)
ELEKTRA (5035 "Best of the Doors") 15-20 73
ELEKTRA (EKS-6001 "Weird Scenes Inside the Gold Mine") 12-15 72
ELEKTRA (8E-6001 "Weird Scenes Inside the Gold Mine") 8-12 73
ELEKTRA (9002 "Absolutely Live") 15-20 70
(Red label.)
ELEKTRA (60000 series) 5-10 83-91
ELEKTRA (60269 "Alive, She Cried") 10-15 83
(Promotional issue.)
ELEKTRA (74007 "The Doors") 20-25 67
(Gold label.)
ELEKTRA (74014 "Strange Days") 15-25 67
(Gold label.)
ELEKTRA (74024 "Waiting for the Sun") 15-20 68
(Gold label.)
ELEKTRA (75005 "The Soft Parade") 10-20 69
(Red label.)
ELEKTRA (75007 "Morrison Hotel/Hard Rock Cafe") 12-15 70
(Red label.)
ELEKTRA (74079 "Doors 13") 10-20 70
(Includes poster.)
ELEKTRA (75011 "L.A. Woman") 25-35 71
(With die-cut cover.)
ELEKTRA (75011 "L.A. Woman") .... 5-10 Re
(With standard cover.)
ELEKTRA (75017 "Other Voices") 8-12 71
ELEKTRA (75038 "Full Circle") 8-12 72
MFSL (051 "The Doors") 50-70 81
Members: Jim Morrison; Robbie Krieger; Ray Manzarek; John Densmore.
Also see DENSMORE, John, & Robby Krieger
Also see KRIEGER, Robby
Also see MANZAREK, Ray

DOOTONES

Singles: 78 rpm
DOOTONE (366 "Teller of Fortune") 50-75 55
Singles: 7-inch
DOOTONE (366 "Teller of Fortune") 100-150 55
DOOTONE (470 "Strange Love Affair") 15-25 62
DOOTONE (471 "Sailor Boy") 15-25 62
Member: Ronald Barrett.
Also see JULIAN, Don, & Meadowlarks
Also see PENGUINS / Meadowlarks / Medallions / Dootones

DOR & CONFEDERATES

(With the Jack Hansen Orchestra & Chorus)
Singles: 7-inch
BRUNSWICK (55159 "4-D Man") 10-15 59
Session: Rod McKuen.
Also see McFADDEN, Bob
Also see McKUEN, Rod

DORADOS, El: see EL DORADOS

DORAY, Johnny

Singles: 7-inch
PROFILE (4001 "One of These Days") 8-12 58
PROFILE (4003 "Judgement") 20-30 59

DO-RAY-ME TRIO — *R&B '48*

(Do-Re-Mi-Trio; "Featuring Buddy Hawkins"; Do Ray & Me)
Singles: 78 rpm
BRUNSWICK 5-15 53
COMMODORE 10-20 47-48
CORAL 5-15 54
IVORY 10-15 49-50
RAINBOW 5-15 52
VARIETY 5-15 57
Singles: 7-inch
BRUNSWICK 15-25 53
CORAL 15-25 54
IVORY (001 "Let's Go Down Town") 20-30 50
RAINBOW (181 "She Would Not Yield") 20-30 52
REET 5-10 50s
STEREO CRAFT (112 "Saturday Night Fish Fry") 30-50 59
VARIETY 8-10 57
LPs: 10/12-inch
STEREO CRAFT (508 "That Wonderfully Musically Do Ray Mi Trio") 30-45 59
Also see HAWKINS, Buddy, & Do Re Me Trio
Also see RUSSELL, Al

DORCHESTERS

Singles: 7-inch
ABC-PAR 4-8 64

DORE, Charlie — *P&R/LP '80*

Singles: 7-inch
CHRYSALIS 3-4 81
ISLAND 3-4 80-81
LPs: 10/12-inch
ISLAND 5-10 80-81

DORE, Rusty

Singles: 7-inch
LUCK 5-10 60

DORELLS

Singles: 7-inch
ATLANTIC (2244 "Beating of My Heart") 8-12 64
GEL (4401 "Beating of My Heart") 15-25 64

DOREMUS, John

(Doremus)
Singles: 7-inch
CUCA (1303 "What Is a Boy") 10-15 66

DOREN, Van

Singles: 7-inch
HICKORY (1262 "Surfin' Lisa") 10-20 64

DORETY, Dee Dee

Singles: 7-inch
FREEDOM (44021 "Billy Billy") 10-20 60s
MAGNET 5-10 60

DORFF, Steve, & Friends

Singles: 7-inch
REPRISE 3-4 88
Picture Sleeves
REPRISE 3-4 88

DORI, Donna

Singles: 7-inch
20 CENTURY-FOX 5-10 60

DORIAN

Singles: 7-inch
TODD 5-10 59

DORIANS

Singles: 7-inch
BIG TREE 8-10 70

DORIES

Singles: 7-inch
DORE 5-10 59-62

DORIS & KELLEY

Singles: 7-inch
BRUNSWICK 3-5 67

DORITA

Singles: 7-inch
SYCAMORE 5-10 59

DORMAN, Harold — *P&R/R&B '60*

Singles: 7-inch
ABC 3-5 73
COLLECTABLES 3-4
RITA 10-20 60
SANTO 8-12 62
SUN 10-20 61-62
TINCE 10-15 60

DORN, Georgie

Singles: 7-inch
KING 4-8 61

DORN, Jerry

Singles: 7-inch
ARWIN 5-10 59
FLING (711 "Rocking Chair Rock") 30-50 59
KING (Except 4932) 10-15 56-57
KING (4932 "Wishing Well") 25-40 56
(With the Hurricanes.)
Also see HURRICANES

DORO — *LP '89*

LPs: 10/12-inch
MERCURY 5-8 89

DOROTHY & HESITATIONS

Singles: 7-inch
JAMIE 4-8 68

DORRELLES

Singles: 7-inch
RSVP 5-10 65

DORS, Diana

Singles: 7-inch
FONTANA 4-8 64
LPs: 10/12-inch
COLUMBIA (1436 "Swinging Dors") 25-35 60
(Monaural.)
COLUMBIA (8232 "Swinging Dors") 35-45 60
(Stereo.)

DORSAL FINN
Singles: 7-inch
SUNNYBEACH (6183 "Jowls") 4-6 75

DORSALS & GATORMEN
Singles: 7-inch
CAMELOT (120 "Namu") 10-15 66
Also see GATORMEN

DORSETS
Singles: 7-inch
ASNES 5-8 61

DORSEY, Dee Dee
Singles: 7-inch
NAME 8-12 60

DORSEY, Gerry
Singles: 7-inch
HICKORY (1337 "Baby, Turn Around") 8-12 65
Also see HUMPERDINCK, Engelbert

DORSEY, Jack, Big Band
Singles: 7-inch
PARKWAY 4-8 64

DORSEY, Jimmy, Orchestra & Chorus *P&R '35*
(With Bob Eberly)
Singles: 78 rpm
BELL 3-5 54
COLUMBIA 3-5 50-52
CORAL ("60M" Series) 10-15 50
(Boxed, four-disc sets.)
DECCA 2-6 35-57
FRATERNITY 3-5 57
MGM 3-5 54
OKEH 10-15 29
Singles: 7-inch
ABC 3-4 73
BELL 3-5 54
COLUMBIA 3-6 50-52
DECCA 3-6 51-67
DOT 3-4 63
EPIC 3-4 59
FRATERNITY 3-5 57-60
MGM 3-4 54
EPs: 7-inch
COLUMBIA 4-8 52-56
LPs: 10/12-inch
COLUMBIA 10-20 55-56
CORAL 10-20 54
DECCA 10-20 57-66
EPIC 8-12 59
FRATERNITY 10-20 57
HINDSIGHT 5-10 81
LION 10-20 56
MCA 5-10 75
Also see CROSBY, Bing, & Jimmy Dorsey
Also see MARTIN, Dean / Bob Eberly / Gordon MacRae

DORSEY, Lee *P&R/R&B '61*
Singles: 7-inch
ABC 3-4 78
ABC-PAR (10192 "Lotti Mo") 8-12 61
ACE 10-20 61
AMY 4-8 65-69
BELL 5-8
CONSTELLATION 10-20 64
FLASHBACK 3-5 65
FURY 8-15 61-63
GUSTO 3-4 80s
POLYDOR 3-4 70-72
REX (1005 "Rock") 15-25 58
ROULETTE 3-5 70s
SANSU 5-10 67
SMASH 4-8 63
SPRING 3-5 71
VALIANT (1001 "Lotti Mo") 20-30 58
LPs: 10/12-inch
ABC (1048 "Night People") 8-12 78
AMY (8010 "Ride Your Pony") 20-30 66
AMY (8011 "New Lee Dorsey") 20-30 66
ARISTA 5-10 85
FURY (1002 "Ya Ya") 100-200 62
POLYDOR 10-12 70
SPHERE SOUND (7003 "Ya Ya") 15-25 67
Also see JAMES, Tommy & Shondells / Lee Dorsey

DORSEY, Lee, & Betty Harris
Singles: 7-inch
SANSU (474 "Love Lots of Lovin' ") 8-12 67
Also see DORSEY, Lee
Also see HARRIS, Betty

DORSEY, Mel
Singles: 78 rpm
ORBIT 20-30 56
Singles: 7-inch
BLACK JACK 10-20 59
ORBIT (106 "I Ain't Gonna Take It No More") 35-50 56

DORSEY, Mel, & Vince Wallace
Singles: 7-inch
BLACK JACK 5-10 59
Also see DORSEY, Mel

DORSEY, Tommy, Orchestra *P&R '35*
(Starring Warren Covington)
Singles: 78 rpm
BELL 4-8 54
(7-inch disc.)
BLUEBIRD 3-6 40
DECCA 3-5 52-64
OKEH 10-15 29
RCA 3-5 41-57
VICTOR 3-6 35-48
Singles: 7-inch
DECCA 5-10 52-64
MCA 3-4 73
RCA 5-10 50-57
EPs: 7-inch
COLUMBIA 5-10 52-56
DECCA 5-10 52-63
RCA 5-10 51-61
WALDORF 5-10 50s
LPs: 10/12-inch
ACCORD 5-10 82
BRIGHT ORANGE 5-10 73
CAMDEN (Except 200 series) 5-10 61-73
CAMDEN (200 series) 10-20 53-55
COLPIX 10-20 58-63
COLUMBIA 10-20 58
CORAL 5-10 73
CORONET 5-10 60s
DECCA 10-20 52-60
GOLDEN MUSIC SOCIETY 15-20 56
HARMONY 5-10 65-72
MCA 5-10 75-81
MOVIETOWN 8-10 67
RCA 10-20 51-82
SPIN-O-RAMA 5-10 60s
SPRINGBORAD 5-10 77
20TH FOX 10-15 59-73
Also see GARLAND, Judy / Tommy Dorsey
Also see SINATRA, Frank

DO'S & DON'TS
Singles: 7-inch
RED BIRD 5-10 66

DOSS, Bob
(Bobby Doss)
Singles: 78 rpm
STARDAY 15-25 56
Singles: 7-inch
LYNN (505 "I've Got You") 15-25 60
STARDAY (265 "Don't Be Gone Long") 30-50 56

DOSS Jr., Earther
Singles: 7-inch
ABC-PAR 4-8 63

DOSS, Kenny *R&B '80*
Singles: 7-inch
BEARSVILLE 3-5 80
LPs: 10/12-inch
BEARSVILLE 5-10 80

DOSWELL, Kittie "Miss Soul"
Singles: 7-inch
DONNA 5-10 61

DOTS
Singles: 78 rpm
CADDY 25-50 56
Singles: 7-inch
CADDY (101 "I Confess") 50-75 56
CADDY (107 "I Lost You") 50-75 57
CADDY (111 "Good Luck to You") 50-75 57
REV (3512 "Ring Chimes") 1000-1500 57
Member: Jeanette Baker.
Also see BAKER, Jeanette

DOTSON, "Big Bill," & His Guitar
Singles: 78 rpm
BLUES & RHYTHM (7004 "Dark Old World") 50-100 50
(There are no original 45s of this, other than bootlegs.)

DOTSON, Jimmy
(With the Blues Boys)
Singles: 7-inch
HOME of the BLUES 8-12 62
MERCURY (72801 "Heartbreak Avenue") 20-30 68
ROCKO 10-20 60
VOLT (4013 "I Used to Be a Loser") 40-60 69
ZYNN 10-20 62

DOTSON BROTHERS
Singles: 7-inch
LORAN (1027 "Orbit") 15-25

DOTTIE & KATHY
Singles: 7-inch
CHARTER 4-8 63

DOTTIE & RAY *R&B '65*
Singles: 7-inch
LE SAGE 4-8 65

DOTTIE JEAN
Singles: 7-inch
OKEH 4-8 67

DOTTIE MAE
Singles: 7-inch
YALE 5-10 59

DOTTSY *C&W '75*
Singles: 7-inch
RCA 3-5 75-79
TANGLEWOOD 3-4 81
LPs: 10/12-inch
RCA 5-10 76-79
Session: Waylon Jennings.
Also see JENNINGS, Waylon

DOUBLE *P&R/LP '86*
Singles: 12-inch
A&M 4-8 86
Singles: 7-inch
A&M 3-4 86
Picture Sleeves
A&M 3-4 86
LPs: 10/12-inch
A&M 5-10 86
Members: Kurt Maloo; Felix Haug.

DOUBLE DATES
Singles: 7-inch
LUCK 15-20 59

DOUBLE ENTENTE *D&D '84*
Singles: 12-inch
COLUMBIA 4-6 84
Singles: 7-inch
COLUMBIA 3-4 84

DOUBLE EXPOSURE *P&R/R&B/LP '76*
Singles: 12-inch
GOLD COAST 4-6 81
Singles: 7-inch
SALSOUL 3-4 76-79
LPs: 10/12-inch
SALSOUL 8-10 76-79
Members: James Williams; Joseph Harris; Leonard Davis; Charles Whittington.

DOUBLE FEATURE
Singles: 7-inch
DERAM 10-20 66

DOUBLE IV
Singles: 7-inch
CAPITOL 4-8 63

DOUBLE IMAGE
Singles: 7-inch
AMY 4-8 67

DOUBLE IMAGE *P&R '83*
Singles: 7-inch
CBS ASSOCIATED 3-4 83
CURB 3-4 83
LPs: 10/12-inch
ECM 5-10 79

DOUBLE NAUGHT SPYS
LPs: 10/12-inch
ROCKADELIC (65 "Goin' Nowhere") 8-12 92

DOUBLE SIX
Singles: 7-inch
PHILIPS (40192 "Hallelujah, I Love Her So") 10-20 64
PHILIPS (40220 "Lonely Avenue") 10-20 64

DOUBLE SOUL
Singles: 7-inch
MINARET (133 "Blue Diamonds") 10-15 67

DOUBLE VISION *D&D '84*
Singles: 12-inch
PROFILE 4-6 84

DOUCET, Suzanne
Singles: 7-inch
INTERPHON 4-8 64

DOUCETTE *P&R/LP '78*
(Jerry Doucette)
Singles: 7-inch
MUSHROOM 3-4 77-79
LPs: 10/12-inch
MUSHROOM 5-10 78-79

DOUD, Earle
(With Alen Robin)
LPs: 10/12-inch
ATCO 10-15 68
CADET CONCEPT 8-12 71

DOUG & CORKY
Singles: 7-inch
ULTIMA 4-8 64

DOUG & FREDDY
(With the Pyramids)
Singles: 7-inch
FINER ARTS (1001 "Take a Chance on Love") 300-400 61
(Company has a Denver address.)
FINER ARTS (1001 "Take a Chance on Love") 300-400 61
(Company has a Hollywood address. We're not sure which label came first, though it's possible Denver might precede Hollywood.)
K&G (100 "Need Your Love") 50-75 61
RENDEZVOUS (111 "Lover's Plea") 10-20 59
Members: Doug Salma; Freddy Ruiz.

DOUG & SLUGS
Singles: 7-inch
RCA 3-4 81-83
RITDONG (101 "Too Bad") 4-6 80
(Identification number shown since no selection number is used.)
Picture Sleeves
RITDONG (101 "Too Bad") 5-8 80
LPs: 10/12-inch
RCA 5-8 81-83
Members: Doug Bennet; Steve Bosley; John Burton; Rick Baker; Simon Kendall; John Wally Watson.
Also see SLUGS

DOUG E. FRESH & GET FRESH CREW *R&B/D&D '85*
Singles: 12-inch
REALITY 4-6 85
Singles: 7-inch
REALITY 3-4 85-88
LPs: 10/12-inch
REALITY 5-8 88

DOUGHBOYS
Singles: 7-inch
BELL (662 "Rhoda Mendelbaum") 10-15 67
SUE (780 "Copy Cat") 10-15 63

DOUGHERTY, Big Bob
(Bob Dougherty)
Singles: 78 rpm
COSMOPOLITAN 25-50
DECCA 10-15 53
Singles: 7-inch
DECCA (48276 "Big Bob's Boogie") 15-25 53
GOLDEN CREST (517 "Honky") 15-25 59
WESTPORT (137 "Movin'") 15-25 58
WESTPORT (139 "Teen-age Flip") 15-25 58

DOUGIE & DOLPHINS
Singles: 7-inch
ANGLE TONE (542 "Yesterday's Dream") 20-30 62

DOUGIE & DUDE
Singles: 7-inch
AMY 15-25 63
KEITH 5-10 61
Also see DOUGLAS, Freddy

DOUGLAS *C&W '81*
(Douglas Block)
Singles: 7-inch
DOOR KNOB 3-5 81
Also see BLOCK, Doug

DOUGLAS, Bob
Singles: 78 rpm
ACE 6-12 56
Singles: 7-inch
ACE 10-15 56

DOUGLAS, Bobby, & Conspiracy
Singles: 7-inch
CONSPIRACY 3-5 73
LPs: 10/12-inch
CONSPIRACY 10-15 73

DOUGLAS, Carl *P&R/R&B/LP '74*
(With the Big Stampede)
Singles: 7-inch
ERIC 3-4 70s
OKEH 5-10 66-67
20TH FOX 4-6 74-75
LPs: 10/12-inch
20TH FOX 10-15 74

DOUGLAS, Carol *P&R/R&B '74*
Singles: 12-inch
MIDSONG INT'L 4-6 78
Singles: 7-inch
MIDLAND INT'L 3-5 74-79
RCA 3-5 76
20TH FOX 3-4 81
Picture Sleeves
MIDLAND INT'L 3-5 77-88
LPs: 10/12-inch
MIDLAND INT'L 8-10 75-80

DOUGLAS, Craig
Singles: 7-inch
BETHLEHEM 4-8 63
JARO 5-10 60
TCF 4-8 65

DOUGLAS, Dean
Singles: 7-inch
ROULETTE 5-10 59

DOUGLAS, Dwight, & Jaywalkers
Singles: 7-inch
ASTRA 15-20 65

DOUGLAS, Freddy
Singles: 7-inch
KEITH 5-10 61
Also see DOUGIE & DUDES

DOUGLAS, Gary
Singles: 7-inch
ANTIQUE 5-10 60

DOUGLAS, Joe
Singles: 7-inch
PLAYHOUSE (1000 "Crazy Things") 25-35 60s
(At least one source reports this number as 1008. We're not sure yet which is correct, or if there are two different issues.)

DOUGLAS, Joe *C&W '79*
Singles: 7-inch
D 3-5 79
FOXY CAJUN 3-5 80-81

DOUGLAS, Johnny
Singles: 7-inch
MURBO 4-8 66
LPs: 10/12-inch
CAMDEN 10-15 65

DOUGLAS, K.C.
Singles: 78 rpm
DOWN TOWN (2004 "Mercury Boogie") 25-50 48
GILT EDGE (5042 "Mercury Boogie") 20-30 48
HOLLYWOOD 25-50 54
RHYTHM 50-75 54
Singles: 7-inch
ARHOOLIE (504 "I Know You Didn't Want Me") 8-12 63
HOLLYWOOD (1040 "Lonely Blues") 50-75 54
RHYTHM (1780 "Lonely Blues") 75-100 54
LPs: 10/12-inch
ARHOOLIE 8-12
COOK (5002 "Road Recordings") 300-400 56
PRESTIGE BLUESVILLE (1023 "K.C.'s Blues") 40-60 61
PRESTIGE BLUESVILLE (1050 "Big Road Blues") 30-50 63

DOUGLAS, Lew
(Lew Douglas & His Orchestra; Lou Douglas)
Singles: 78 rpm
BALLY (1025 "Levi Lullaby") 10-15 57
Singles: 7-inch
B&F (1329 "Mary Ann's Rock") 10-20 59
B&F (1331 "Heavenly") 10-15 60
(First issue.)
BALLY (1025 "Levi Lullaby") 15-20 57
CARLTON (533 *"From the Terrace* Love Theme") 10-15 60
DOT (15918 "Rhoom Ba-Cha") 20-30 59
MERCURY (71593 "Heavenly") 5-10 60
TODD (1029 "After Hours") 10-15 59
VASSAR 5-10
LPs: 10/12-inch
CARLTON (126 "Themes from Motion Pictures & TV") 15-25 60
Also see PEPPER & RED HOTS

DOUGLAS, Maurice: see MALLARD, Earl, & His Web Feet of Rhythm

DOUGLAS, Mel
Singles: 7-inch
SAN (1506 "Cadillac Boogie") 50-100 59

DOUGLAS, Mike *P&R '65*
Singles: 7-inch
BANANA 5-10
BLUE RIVER 4-6 66
DECCA 3-6 69
EPIC 4-6 65-67
IMAGE 3-5 77
MGM 3-4 71-73
PROJECT 3 3-5 68
STAX 3-5 74
Picture Sleeves
EPIC 4-8 65-66
LPs: 10/12-inch
ATLANTIC 5-10 76
EPIC 10-15 65-67
HARMONY 8-12 68
Also see BAILEY, Pearl, & Mike Douglas

DOUGLAS, Ron
Singles: 7-inch
SMASH (2206 "First Time Around") 10-20 69

DOUGLAS, Ronny *P&R '61*
Singles: 7-inch
DECCA 4-8 63
EPIC 4-8 65
EVEREST 5-10 61

DOUGLAS, Ronny, & Bobby Lonero
Singles: 7-inch
COLUMBIA 3-5 71-72

DOUGLAS, Samuel, & Continentals
Singles: 7-inch
VEEP 4-8 68

DOUGLAS, Scott
Singles: 7-inch
APOGEE 10-15 64
TOLLIE 4-8 65

DOUGLAS, Shy Guy
(Thomas Douglas)
Singles: 78 rpm
CHANE 10-15 54
EXCELLO 10-20 53
Singles: 7-inch
CHANE (517 "Yankee Doodle") 20-30 54
EXCELLO (2008 "Detroit Arrow") 50-75 53
EXCELLO (2024 "I'm Your Country Man") 50-75 54
EXCELLO (2032 "No Place Like Home") 50-75 54
EXCELLO (2200 series) 4-8 66
SUR-SPEED 4-8
TODD 4-8 66

DOUGLAS, Steve
(With the Snowplows; with Rebel Rousers)
Singles: 7-inch
CAPITOL 4-8 65
GRAPEVINE (601 "Rockin' Green Sleeves") 10-15 61
MGM 4-8 64
PHILLES (104 "Yes Sir, That's My Baby") 10-20 62
TANDEM (7000 "Magic Sound") 10-15 61
LPs: 10/12-inch
CROWN 15-25 62
Also see CATALINAS
Also see EDDY, Duane
Also see FOGERTY, John
Also see GOOD GUYS
Also see KICKSTANDS
Also see KNIGHTS
Also see KUSTOM KINGS
Also see PETERSEN, Paul
Also see SUPER STOCKS / Hot Rod Rog / Shutdown Douglas
Also see TYLER, Kip
Also see VETTES
Also see YORK, Dave, & Beachcombers

DOUGLAS, Steve *C&W '80*
Singles: 7-inch
DEMON 3-5 80
DORMAN 3-4 89-90

DOUGLAS, Tony *C&W '63*
(With His Shrimpers)
Singles: 7-inch
COCHISE 3-4 82
D 5-8 61
DOT 3-5 72-73
PAULA 3-6 67-69
20TH CENTURY 3-5 75
VEE JAY 4-8 63
LPs: 10/12-inch
DOT 8-12 73
PAULA 10-15 67-69
SIMS 15-25 64-66
Also see SHRIMPERS

DOUGLAS, Wayne
(Doug Sahm)
Singles: 7-inch
MERCURY ...15-20 70
Also see SAHM, Doug

DOUGLAS FIR
LPs: 10/12-inch
QUAD ...15-20

DOUGLASS, Harry: see DEEP RIVER BOYS

DOUGLASS, Roger
Singles: 7-inch
DOT ... 4-8 65
MERCURY ... 4-8 61-62
PHIL TONE ... 5-10 60

DOUMA, Danny
LPs: 10/12-inch
W.B. ... 5-10 79

DOVAL, Jim
(With the Gauchos)
Singles: 7-inch
ABC-PAR ... 5-10 65
DIPLOMACY ...10-20 64-65
DOT ... 5-10 63-64
LPs: 10/12-inch
ABC-PAR (ABC-506 "The Gauchos Featuring Jim Doval") ...25-35 65
(Monaural.)
ABC-PAR (ABCS-506 "The Gauchos Featuring Jim Doval") ...35-45 65
(Stereo.)
Members: Jim Doval; Joe Silva; Marty Murilly; Al Lopez; Al Hernandez; Kelly Smith.
Also see SANDOVAL, Jimmy, & Gauchos

DOVALE, Debbie *P&R '63*
Singles: 7-inch
ROULETTE ...10-15 63-64

DOVE, Jerry, & Stringmasters
(With Vocal by Bob Martin)
Singles: 78 rpm
TNT (122 "Stand Still") ...15-25 55
Singles: 7-inch
TNT (122 "Stand Still") ...25-50 55
TNT (141 "Pink Bow Tie") ...75-125 59

DOVE, Ronnie *P&R '64*
(With the Beltones)
Singles: 7-inch
ABC ... 3-4 74
DECCA (31288 "Party Doll") ...10-15 61
DECCA (32000 & 33000 series) ... 3-5 71-73
DIAMOND (100 & 200 series) ... 4-8 64-70
DIAMOND (300 series) ... 3-4 87
ERIC ... 3-4 70s
HITSVILLE ... 3-5 76
JALO (1406 "Saddest Song") ...25-50 62
MC ... 3-4 78
MCA ... 3-4 73
MELODYLAND ... 3-5 75-76
MOTION ... 3-4 81
MOON SHINE ... 3-4 83
SWAN (4231 "Happy") ... 5-10 63
WRAYCO ... 3-5 71
Picture Sleeves
DIAMOND ... 5-10 66
LPs: 10/12-inch
CERTRON ...10-12 70
DESIGN (186 "Swingin' Teen Sounds") ...10-15 64
(Four tracks by Dove; six by Terry Phillips.)
DIAMOND ...15-25 65-70
MCA ... 8-10 72-73
POWER PAK ... 8-12 75

DOVELLS *P&R/R&B '61*
Singles: 7-inch
ABKCO ... 3-4 83
COLLECTABLES ... 3-4 80s
DECCA ... 3-6 70
EVENT ... 3-6 70-74
MGM ... 4-6 66-73
PARKWAY (Except 819 & 827) ... 5-10 62-63
PARKWAY (819 "No No No") ...10-15 61
PARKWAY (827 "Bristol Stomp"/"Out in the Cold") ...10-15 61
PARKWAY (827 "Bristol Stomp"/"Letters of Love") ... 5-8 61
(Note different flip.)
SWAN ... 4-8 65
VERVE ... 3-5 73
Picture Sleeves
PARKWAY ... 5-10 62-63
LPs: 10/12-inch
DOVCO ... 5-10 76
PARKWAY (7006 "The Bristol Stomp") ...30-50 61
PARKWAY (7010 "All the Hits of the Teen Groups") ...40-60 62
PARKWAY (7021 "For Your Hully Gully Party") ...50-75 63
PARKWAY (7025 "You Can't Sit Down") ...30-50 63
WYNCOTE ...10-20 65
Members: Len Barry; Arnie Satin; Jerry Summers; Danny Brooks; Mike Dennis.
Also see BARRY, Len
Also see CHRISTIE, Lou / Len Barry & Dovells / Bobby Rydell / Tokens
Also see MAGISTRATES
Also see ORLONS / Dovells

DOVERS
Singles: 7-inch
DAVIS (465 "Sweet As a Flower") 25-35 59
NEW HORIZON (501 "Devil You May Be") ...20-30 61
Members: Miriam Grate; Eddie Quintone; Wyndon Porter; James Sneed.
Also see GRATE, Miriam, & Dovers

DOVERS
(With Billy Mure & Orchestra)
Singles: 7-inch
VALENTINE (1000 "A Lonely Heart") ...150-250 62
Also see MURE, Billy

DOVERS
Singles: 7-inch
MIRAMAR (118 "She's Gone") ...35-45 65
MIRAMAR (121 "I Could Be Happy") ...40-60 66
MIRAMAR (123 "Third Eye") ...35-45 66
MIRAMAR (124 "She's Not Just Anybody") ...35-45 66
REPRISE (0439 "I Could Be Happy") ...10-20 66

DOVES
Singles: 7-inch
BIG TOP ...10-20 60

DOW, Johnny
Singles: 7-inch
ASSAULT ... 4-8 62

DOWD, Ken
Singles: 7-inch
RCA ... 4-8 63

DOWD, Larry, & Rockatones
Singles: 7-inch
SPINNING (6009 "Blue Swingin' Mama") ...50-75 59
Members: Loren Dowd; Ivan Reaseu; Mick Montgomery; Don Archer; Ron Fiscle.
Also see FIRST GARRISON

DOWD, Tommy
Singles: 7-inch
RED BIRD ... 8-10 64

DOWE, Brent
Singles: 12-inch
REAL AUTHENTIC SOUND ... 4-6

DOWELL, Joe *P&R '61*
Singles: 7-inch
JOURNEY ... 3-5 73
MONUMENT ... 4-6 66
SMASH ... 4-8 61-63
Picture Sleeves
JOURNEY ... 3-5 73
SMASH ... 5-10 61-62
LPs: 10/12-inch
SMASH ...15-25 61-62
WING ...10-15 66

DOWELL, Paul & Dolphins
Singles: 7-inch
SIRE ... 4-6 69

DOWLANDS
Singles: 7-inch
TOLLIE ... 5-10 64

DOWN BEATS
Singles: 7-inch
CONN (201 "Amor") ... 8-10 60

DOWN BEATS
Singles: 7-inch
ENTENTE (001 "Again") ...50-75 61

DOWN BEATS
Singles: 7-inch
DAWN (1031 "Why Do You Love Another") ...10-20

DOWN CHILDREN
Singles: 7-inch
PHILIPS ... 4-8 67

DOWN FEATURE
Singles: 7-inch
DERAM ... 4-8 67

DOWN 5
Singles: 7-inch
PARROT ...15-20 67

DOWN HOMERS *C&W '49*
(Kenny Roberts & the Downhomers; Wowo Down Homers)
Singles: 78 rpm
CORAL ... 4-8 49-50
VOGUE (736 "Who's Gonna Kiss You When I'm Gone") ...200-300 46
(Picture disc.)
VOGUE (786 "Boogie Woogie Yodel") ...300-500 47
(Picture disc.)
LPs: 10/12-inch
SOMERSET (22400 "The Downhomers") ...15-20 60s
Members: Bob Mason; Bill Haley; Shorty Cook; Guy Campbell; Lloyd Cornell.
Also see HALEY, Bill
Also see ROBERTS, Kenny

DOWN TOWN TRIO
Singles: 78 rpm
DOWN TOWN (2017 "Make Love to Me Baby") ...50-75 48

DOWNBEATS
(Down Beats)
Singles: 7-inch
GEE (1019 "My Girl") ...100-150 56
(Red and black label.)
GEE (1019 "My Girl") ...15-25 60
(Gray label.)
PEACOCK (1679 "So Many Tears") ...25-50 57
PEACOCK (1689 "You're So Fine") ...20-30 59
SAFARI (1010 "Here") ...75-125 58
SAFARI (1014 "Jelly Bean") ...25-50 58
Session: Sonny Woods.
Also see WOODS, Sonny

DOWNBEATS
("Vocal by Charles Lighteard & Chorus")
Singles: 7-inch
SARG (168 "Darling of Mine") ...25-35 59
SARG (173 "I Need Your Love") ...25-35 59
SARG (186 "Oh Please") ...25-35 59
SARG (223 "Greyhound") ...10-20 66
SARG (228 "Grant's Soul Blues") ...10-20 67
SARG (233 "Soul Bag") ...10-20 69
Member: O.S. Grant.
Also see GRANT, O.S., & Downbeats

DOWNBEATS
Singles: 7-inch
ARDENT (101 "The Hucklebuck") 10-20 60

DOWNBEATS
Singles: 7-inch
DIAMOND ... 5-10 60s
DYNAMIC (1011 "Rug Cuttin'") ...10-20 62
(At least one source shows this label as Dynamite. We're not sure yet which is right.)
WILCO ...10-15 60

DOWNBEATS
Singles: 7-inch
HAMPSHIRE (1002 "Growing Love") ...15-25 61

DOWNBEATS
Singles: 7-inch
TAMLA (54056 "Request of a Fool") ...30-50 62
(Tamla logo in circular letters at top.)
TAMLA (54056 "Request of a Fool") ...20-30 62
(Tamla logo in straight letters at top.)
V.I.P. (25029 "Put Yourself in My Place") ...100-150 65
Members: Cleo Miller; Robert Flemming; John Dawson.
Also see ELGINS
Also see FIVE EMERALDS

DOWNBEATS
Singles: 7-inch
DOWNBEAT (1029 "Dedicated to the One I Love") ...10-20 65

DOWNBEATS
Singles: 7-inch
HAMPSHIRE (1002 "Growing Love") ...15-25 61

DOWNCHILD
(Downchild Blues Band)
Singles: 7-inch
BELL (455 "Flip, Flop and Fly") ... 5-8 74
LPs: 10/12-inch
ADELPHI ... 5-10 79

DOWNES, Jack E., & His Friends
Singles: 7-inch
JEDCO (5001 "Surfin' Way Out") ...15-25 63
JEDCO (5002 "Strictly Drums") ...15-20 63
(Retitled reissue of *Surfin' Way Out*.)

DOWNES, Vinnie
Singles: 7-inch
TRANSCONTINENTAL (1011 "Foolish Pride") ...40-60 59

DOWNEY, Morton, Jr.
(With the Terrytones)
Singles: 7-inch
CADENCE ... 5-10 61
LAKE ERIE ... 4-6 60s
IMPERIAL ... 4-8 60s
MAGIC LAMP ... 4-8 64
PERSONALITY ... 4-8 63
WYE ... 5-10 61
Also see TERRYTONES

DOWNEY, Sean *C&W '81*
(Shawn Downey; Shawn Morton Downey; Morton Downey Jr.)
Singles: 7-inch
BULL DOG ... 5-10 59
CUB ... 8-12 58
ESO ... 3-5 81
Also see DOWNEY, Morton, Jr.

DOWNING, Al *P&R '63*
("Big" Al Downing)
Singles: 7-inch
CARLTON (489 "Miss Lucy") ...30-50 58
CARLTON (507 "It Must Be Love") 20-40 59
CHALLENGE (59006 "Down on the Farm") ...20-40 58
CHESS (1000 series) ... 5-10 62
CHESS (2000 series) ... 3-5 75
COLUMBIA ... 4-8 64
DOOR KNOB ... 3-4 89
HOUSE of the FOX ... 3-5 71
JANUS ... 3-5 74
KANSOMA ... 5-10 62
LENOX ... 4-8 63
POLYDOR ... 3-5 76
SILVER FOX ... 4-8 69
TEAM ... 3-4 82-84
V-TONE ... 5-10 61
VINE ST. ... 3-4 87
W.B. ... 3-5 78-80
WHITE ROCK (1111 "Down on the Farm") ...50-100 58
WHITE ROCK (1113 "Miss Lucy") ...50-100 58
LPs: 10/12-inch
TEAM ... 5-10 83-85
Also see LITTLE ESTHER & Big Al Downing

DOWNING, Don *R&B '73*
Singles: 7-inch
ABNER ... 4-8 62
CHAN ... 4-8 62
ROADSHOW ... 3-5 73
SCEPTER ... 3-5 74
LPs: 10/12-inch
ROADSHOW ... 5-10 79

DOWNING, Will *R&B '88*
Singles: 7-inch
ISLAND ... 3-4 88

DOWNLINERS SECT
Singles: 7-inch
SMASH ... 8-10 65

DOWNS, Bobbie
Singles: 7-inch
CORREC-TONE (3807 "It Won't Be Long") ...50-75 60s

DOWNS, Kerri
Singles: 7-inch
EPIC ... 4-8 63-64
U.A. ... 4-8 66
VEL-V-TONE ... 4-8 63

DOWNS, Laverne *C&W '60*
Singles: 7-inch
PEACH ... 5-10 60

DOWNSET
Singles: 7-inch
THEOLOGIAN ... 3-5 90s
(Colored vinyl.)
LPs: 10/12-inch
MERCURY ... 5-10 94
Members: Ray Oropeza;; James Morris; Rogelio Lozano; Brian Schwager; Chris Lee.

DOWNSET / Shootyz Groove
Singles: 7-inch
INDIVISION ... 3-5 90s
(Colored vinyl.)
Also see DOWNSET

DOYLE, Bobby
(Bobby Doyle Three)
Singles: 7-inch
BACK BEAT (528 "Pauline") ...10-15 59
BACK BEAT (531 "Hot Seat") ...15-25 60
TOWNHOUSE ... 4-6
LPs: 10/12-inch
COLUMBIA (1858 "In a Most Unusual Way") ...20-35 62
(Monaural.)
COLUMBIA (8658 "In a Most Unusual Way") ...25-40 62
(Stereo.)
Members: Bobby Doyle; Kenny Rogers.
Also see BLOOD, SWEAT & TEARS
Also see ROGERS, Kenny

DOYLE, Dicky
Singles: 7-inch
VIKING (4226 "Little Baby Lee") ...50-75 59
WYE (1009 "My Little Angel") ...50-75 61

DOYLE, Jimmie
Singles: 7-inch
POP ... 4-8

DOYLE, Mike
LPs: 10/12-inch
FLEETWOOD (3018 "Secrets of Surfing") ...20-30 63

DOZIER, Gene, & Brotherhood *R&B '67*
Singles: 7-inch
MINIT ... 4-8 67-68
LPs: 10/12-inch
MINIT ...10-15 67

DOZIER, Lamont *P&R/R&B '72*
Singles: 12-inch
M&M ... 4-6 82
W.B. ... 4-8 79
Singles: 7-inch
ABC ... 3-5 73-76
COLUMBIA ... 3-4 81
INVICTUS ... 3-5 72-73
M&M ... 3-4 82
MEL-O-DY (102 "Dearest One") ..75-100 62
LPs: 10/12-inch
ABC ... 8-10 73-74
COLUMBIA ... 5-10 81
INVICTUS ... 8-12 74
M&M ... 5-10 82
W.B. ... 8-10 76-79
Also see ANTHONY, Lamont
Also see HOLLAND, Eddie, & Lamont Dozier
Also see ROMEOS
Also see VOICE MASTERS

DOZIER, Rudy
Singles: 7-inch
TEEN TIME (108 "Wicked") ...30-40 62

DOZIER BOYS
Singles: 78 rpm
ARISTOCRAT (409 "She's Gone") ...25-50 50
ARISTOCRAT (3001 "She Only Fools with Me") ...25-50 49
ARISTOCRAT (3002 "Big Time Baby") ...25-50 49
CHESS (1436 "You Got to Get It") ...25-50 50
FRATERNITY ...40-60 57
UNITED ...50-100 53
Singles: 7-inch
APT (25014 "My Heart Is Yours") ...25-50 58
FRATERNITY (767 "Early Morning Blues") ...40-60 57
JANIE (457 "Wondering Lover") ...25-50 60
UNITED (143 "I Keep Thinking of You") ...100-200 53
UNITED (163 "Early Morning Blues") ... 200-300 53
Also see TIBBS, Andrew, & Dozier Boys

DOZY, BEAKY, MICK & TICH
(DBMT)
Singles: 7-inch
BELL ... 4-6 70
COTILLION ... 4-6 70
Picture Sleeves
COTILLION ... 4-8 70
Also see DEE, Dave, Dozy, Beaky, Mick & Tich

DRABOLIQUES
Singles: 7-inch
MERRI ... 5-8 64

DRAFI *P&R '66*
(Drafi Deutscher)
Singles: 7-inch
LONDON ... 4-8 66-67

DRAG KINGS
(Sonny & Demons)
Singles: 7-inch
U.A. (676 "Nitro") ... 5-10 64
WAYNE WAY (105 "Midnight Drag of Paul Revere") ...35-45 60s
Also see SONNY & DEMONS

DRAGON *P&R/D&D '84*
Singles: 12-inch
POLYDOR ... 4-6 84
Singles: 7-inch
POLYDOR ... 3-4 83-84
PORTRAIT ... 3-5 78-79
LPs: 10/12-inch
POLYDOR ... 5-10 83
PORTRAIT ... 5-10 78

DRAGON, Carmen *LP '62*
LPs: 10/12-inch
CAPITOL ...10-20 62

DRAGON, Paul
(With the Jordanaires)
Singles: 7-inch
BELLE MEADE ... 5-10 77
STARFIRE (109 "Mean Woman Blues") ... 4-6 79
STARFIRE (117 "Memphis Blue Streak") ... 4-6 79
(Colored vinyl.)
Picture Sleeves
STARFIRE (117 "Memphis Blue Streak") ... 4-8 79
LPs: 10/12-inch
BELLE MEADE (1002 "Golden Memories") ...15-25 77
Session: Scotty Moore; D.J. Fontana; Bob Moore; Dale Sellars; Little Willie Rainsford; Jordanaires.
Also see FONTANA, D.J., Band
Also see JORDANAIRES
Also see MOORE, Bob
Also see MOORE, Scotty

DRAGONFLY
LPs: 10/12-inch
MEGAPHONE (1202 "Dragonfly") ...200-300 68
Also see LEGEND

DRAGONS
Singles: 7-inch
CAPITOL ... 5-10 64
Member: Daryl Dragon.
Also see CAPTAIN & TENNILLE

DRAGSTERS
LPs: 10/12-inch
MERCURY ...25-30 64

DRAKE, Charlie *P&R '62*
Singles: 7-inch
CAPITOL (72015 "My Boomerang Won't Come Back") ...15-25 61
(Canadian. Longer version than on U.A. With "Practiced till I was BLACK in the face" lyrics.)
U.A. (Except 398) ... 5-10 61-62
U.A. (398 "My Boomerang Won't Come Back") ...15-25 61
(With "Practiced till I was BLACK in the face" lyrics.)
U.A. (398 "My Boomerang Won't Come Back") ... 5-10 61
(With "Practiced till I was BLUE in the face" lyrics.)

DRAKE, Eddie
Singles: 7-inch
GAR (320 "Duck Soup") ...10-15 67
JUKE (2024 "Guitar") ... 5-10 73
TOWER ... 4-8 60s

DRAKE, George
Singles: 7-inch
HEARTBEAT ... 5-8

DRAKE, Guy *C&W/P&R '70*
(With Tom Johnson)
Singles: 7-inch
MALLARD ... 3-5 71
ROYAL AMERICAN ... 3-5 70
TRIP UNIVERSAL ... 3-5 70s
LPs: 10/12-inch
OVATION ... 5-10 74
ROYAL AMERICAN ...15-20 70
TRIP UNIVERSAL ... 8-12 70s

DRAKE, Joe
Singles: 7-inch
SHAMLEY ... 5-8

DRAKE, Johnny, & Kitten
Singles: 7-inch
ERA....5-10 60

DRAKE, Larry
Singles: 78 rpm
FABLE (576 "Boppin' Baby")....35-50 57
Singles: 7-inch
FABLE (576 "Boppin' Baby")....35-50 57

DRAKE, Lenny
Singles: 7-inch
RATED X (6970 "Love Eyes")....40-50

DRAKE, Mann
Singles: 7-inch
BETHLEHEM (86682 "Vampire's Ball")....4-8 62

DRAKE, Nick
LPs: 10/12-inch
ANTILLES....8-10 73
ISLAND....10-15 71-72

DRAKE, Pete P&R/LP '64
(With His Talking Steel Guitar)
Singles: 7-inch
SMASH....4-8 62-65
STARDAY....3-6 66
STOP....3-5 68-70
LPs: 10/12-inch
CANAAN....8-12 68
CUMBERLAND....12-20 63
PICKWICK/HILLTOP....8-12 67
MOUNTAIN DEW....8-10
SMASH....10-15 64-65
STARDAY....15-25 62-65
STOP....6-10 70
Also see TUBB, Ernest

DRAKE & EN SOLIDS
Singles: 7-inch
ALTEEN (8652 "I'll Always Be There")....10-20

DRAKE SISTERS
Singles: 7-inch
CHATTAHOOCHEE....4-8 64

DRAKES
("Featuring K.L. Jett - Accom. Skip Chavis"; with Nick Kurlas & Buddy Cahn & Orchestra)
Singles: 7-inch
OLIMPIC (252 "I Made a Wish") 100-150 65

DRAKES with J.J. Macambo / J.J. Macambo
Singles: 7-inch
CONQUEST (1001 "Oo Wee So Good")....350-450 58

DRAMATICS R&B '67
(Ron Banks & Dramatics)
Singles: 7-inch
ABC....3-6 75-77
BELL (5 "Toy Soldier")....20-30 60s
CADET....3-6 74
CAPITOL....3-4 82
CRACKERJACK (4015 "Toy Soldier")....50-75 63
FANTASY....3-4 86
MAINSTREAM....3-6 75
MCA....3-4 79-80
SPORT (101 "All Because of You")....40-60 67
VOLT....4-8 71-73
WINGATE (22 "Baby I Need You")....25-35 67
LPs: 10/12-inch
ABC....8-10 75-78
CADET....8-12 74
CAPITOL....5-10 82
FANTASY....5-10 86
MCA....5-10 80
STAX....8-10 77-78
VOLT....10-15 72-74
Members: Ron Banks; Elbert Wilkins; L.J. Reynolds; William Howard; Larry Demps; Lenny Mayes; Carl Smalls; Willie Ford.
Also see BANKS, Ron
Also see DELLS & DRAMATICS
Also see DYNAMICS
Also see REYNOLDS, L.J.
Also see UNDISPUTED TRUTH

DRAPELS
Singles: 7-inch
VOLT (114 "Please Don't Leave")..10-20 64
VOLT (119 "Young Man")....8-12 64

DRAPER, Rusty C&W/P&R '53
Singles: 78 rpm
MERCURY (Except 70921)....5-10 52-57
MERCURY (70921 "Pink Cadillac")....10-15 56
Singles: 7-inch
KL....3-5 80
MERCURY (Except 70921)....5-15 52-62
MERCURY (70921 "Pink Cadillac")....15-25 56
MONUMENT....4-8 63-70
EPs: 7-inch
MERCURY....10-15 54-56
LPs: 10/12-inch
GOLDEN CREST....5-10 73
HARMONY....5-10 72
MERCURY....15-30 54-62
MONUMENT....8-12 65-75
WING....8-12 63-64
Also see DEE, Lola, & Rusty Draper

DRAPERS
Singles: 7-inch
UNICAL (3001 "Merry-Go-Round").50-75 60
VEST (831 "Best Love")....15-25 61
Members: Wilbur Paul; Richard Lewis; Dock Green; Leroy Brown; Jesse Facing.
Also see DUVALS

DRAPERS
Singles: 7-inch
GEE (1081 "I Know Your Love Has Gone Away")....40-60 62
Members: Johnny Moore; Charles Hughes; Dock Green; Tommy Evans.
Also see DRIFTERS

DREAD ZEPPELIN LP '90
LPs: 10/12-inch
I.R.S. 5-8 90

DREAM ACADEMY P&R/LP '85
Singles: 7-inch
W.B. 3-4 85-86
Picture Sleeves
W.B. 3-4 85-86
LPs: 10/12-inch
REPRISE....5-10 87
W.B. 5-10 85

DREAM EXPRESS
Singles: 12-inch
MCA....4-6 79
Singles: 7-inch
MCA....3-5 79
LPs: 10/12-inch
MCA....5-10 79

DREAM GIRLS
Singles: 7-inch
BIG TOP....10-15 60
CAMEO....10-15 59
METRO....10-15 59-60
TWIRL (1002 "Oh This Is Why")....25-40 59
Also see SMITH, Bobbie, & Dream Girls

DREAM KINGS
Singles: 78 rpm
CHECKER (858 "M.T.Y.L.T.T.")...50-100 57
Singles: 7-inch
CHECKER (858 "M.T.Y.L.T.T.").100-200 57

DREAM LOVERS see DREAMLOVERS

DREAM MERCHANTS
Singles: 7-inch
LONDON (1015 "Rattler")....5-10 67
Also see MERCHANTS of DREAM

DREAM POLICE
Singles: 7-inch
DERAM....5-10

DREAM SYNDICATE LP '84
LPs: 10/12-inch
A&M....5-10 84
SLASH....5-10
Also see RAIN PARADE
Also see TEXTONES

DREAM WEAVERS P&R '55
(Featuring Wade Buff)
Singles: 78 rpm
DECCA....10-15 55-56
Singles: 7-inch
DECCA....15-25 55-56
EPs: 7-inch
DECCA....20-40 56
Member: Wade Buff.

DREAMBOY R&B/LP '84
Singles: 7-inch
QWEST....3-4 83-84
LPs: 10/12-inch
QWEST....5-10 83-84

DREAMER
Singles: 7-inch
TIKI....4-8

DREAMERS
Singles: 78 rpm
ALADDIN....50-75 55
JUBILEE....75-125 51
MERCURY....50-75 52
Singles: 7-inch
ALADDIN (3303 "My Plea")....100-150 55
JUBILEE (5053 "These Things I Miss")....150-250 51
MERCURY (5843 "I'm Gonna Hate Myself in the Morning")....100-150 52
MERCURY (70019 "Walkin' My Blues Away")....100-150 52
Members:Warren Suttles; Harriet Callendar; Freddy Francis; Percy Green.
Also see BROWN, Wini
Also see COBB, Arnett
Also see RAVENS

DREAMERS
Singles: 78 rpm
DREAM....100-150 53
GRAND....100-150 55
ROLLIN....100-150 55
Singles: 7-inch
DREAM (101 "Seconds")....300-400 53
GRAND (131 "Tears in My Eyes")....300-400 55
(Glossy yellow label. Rigid disc. No company address shown.)
GRAND (131 "Tears in My Eyes")....50-100 61
(Yellow label. Flexible disc. No company address shown.)
GRAND (131 "Tears in My Eyes")....15-25 60s
(Yellow label. Company address is shown.)
ROLLIN'(1001 "No Man Is an Island")....1000-2000 55
(Outer edge of disc is fairly sharp.)
ROLLIN'(1001 "No Man Is an Island")....50-100
(Outer edge of disc is blunt, or squared off.)

DREAMERS
Singles: 78 rpm
ABC-PAR....10-15 56
Singles: 7-inch
ABC-PAR (9746 "The Right Time for Love")....20-30 56

DREAMERS
Singles: 78 rpm
FLIP (319 "Do Not Forget")....10-20 56
Singles: 7-inch
FLIP (319 "Do Not Forget")....15-25 56
FLIP (354 "Do Not Forget")....10-15 61
Also see BERRY, Richard

DREAMERS
Singles: 78 rpm
MANHATTAN....50-100 56
Singles: 7-inch
MANHATTAN (503 "Lips Were Meant for Kissing")....200-300 56

DREAMERS
Singles: 7-inch
EVENT (4270 "Ding Dong")....25-50 58

DREAMERS
Singles: 7-inch
NUGGET (1000 "Don't Cry")....50-75 59

DREAMERS
Singles: 7-inch
APT (25053 "I Sing This Song")....20-30 60
COUSINS (1005 "Because of You")....50-75 61
DREAM (1223 "This I Swear")....4-8 87
GOLDISC (3015 "Teenage Vows of Love")....15-25 61
GUARANTEED (219 "Canadian Sunset")....15-25 60
MAY (133 "Because of You")....20-40 61
LPs: 10/12-inch
DREAM....8-12 87
Members: Frank Cammarata; John Trancynger; Frank Nicholas; Tony Frederico; Bruce Goldie.

DREAMERS / Temptations
Singles: 7-inch
ROULETTE....3-5 70s
Also see DREAMERS
Also see TEMPTATIONS

DREAMERS
Singles: 7-inch
BLUE STAR (8001 "I Really Love You")....15-25 61

DREAMERS
Singles: 7-inch
FAIRMOUNT....10-15 63

DREAMERS
Singles: 7-inch
U.A. 4-8 65

DREAMERS
Singles: 7-inch
BELL....4-8

DREAMERS
Singles: 7-inch
BLUE STAR....20-25

DREAMERS
Singles: 7-inch
SOUND HOUSE (702 "Road Runner")....5-10

DREAMETTES
Singles: 7-inch
U.A. 10-15 65

DREAMLINERS
Singles: 7-inch
JOX....5-8 65

DREAMLINES
Singles: 78 rpm
SIESTA (6311 "Easy Rockin'")....10-15 55
Singles: 7-inch
SIESTA (6311 "Easy Rockin'")....20-30 55

DREAMLOVERS P&R '61
Singles: 7-inch
CAMEO (326 "Oh Baby Mine")....10-15 64
CASINO (1308 "Amazons and Coyotes")....10-20 64
COLLECTABLES....3-4 82
COLUMBIA (42698 "Sad Sad Boy")....15-20 63
COLUMBIA (42752 "Sad Sad Boy")....10-15 63
COLUMBIA (42842 "Pretty Little Girl")....30-40 63
DOWN (2004 "If I Should Lose You")....250-500 61
END (1114 "If I Should Lose You")....15-25 62
HERITAGE (102 "When We Get Married")....15-25 61
HERITAGE (104 "Welcome Home")....15-25 61
HERITAGE (107 "Zoom Zoom Zoom")....25-50 62
LEN (1006 "For the First Time")....550-650 60
LOST NITE....4-8
MERCURY (72595 "Bless Your Soul")....10-15 66
MERCURY (72630 "Calling Jo Ann")....20-30 66
SWAN (4167 "Amazons and Coyotes")....20-30 63
(White label.)
SWAN (4167 "Amazons and Coyotes")....10-20 63
(Black label.)
V-TONE (211 "Anabelle Lee")....10-20 60
V-TONE (229 "May I Kiss the Bride")....10-20 61
W.B. (5619 "You Gave Me Somebody to Love")....10-20 65
LPs: 10/12-inch
COLLECTABLES ("Dreamlovers")....5-10 82
(Selection number not known.)
COLLECTABLES (5005 "Volume Two")....10-15 82
(Picture disc.)
COLUMBIA (2020 "The Bird")....20-40 63
(Monaural.)
COLUMBIA (8820 "The Bird")....25-50 63
(Stereo.)
HERITAGE....8-12 79
Members: Tommy Ricks; Cleveland Hammock; Cliff Dunn; Morris Gardner; Ray Dunn.
Also see CHECKER, Chubby

DREAMS
Singles: 78 rpm
SAVOY....50-75 54-55
Singles: 7-inch
SAVOY (1130 "Darlene")....100-150 54
(Black vinyl.)
SAVOY (1130 "Darlene")....200-300 54
(Colored vinyl.)
SAVOY (1140 "Under the Willow")....75-125 54
SAVOY (1157 "I'll Be Faithful")....50-100 55
Members: George Tindley; Bernard Harris Wes Hayes; Bobby Henderson; Steve Pressbury.
Also see STARLITES
Also see TINDLEY, George

DREAMS
(With the Frank Perry & Orchestra)
Singles: 7-inch
SMASH (1748 "Too Late")....20-30 62
TALENT (1 "I Love You")....100-200 58

DREAMS LP '70
Singles: 7-inch
COLUMBIA....3-5 71-72
D.C. 4-6 69
LPs: 10/12-inch
COLUMBIA....10-15 70-71
Also see BRECKER BROTHERS

DREAMS & ILLUSIONS
LPs: 10/12-inch
VERVE/FORECAST....10-12

DREAMS SO REAL LP '88
LPs: 10/12-inch
ARISTA....5-8 88
FATHER'S HOUSE....8-10 86
I.R.S. 5-10 87
Members: Barry Marler; Drew Worsham; Trent Allen.

DREAM-TIMERS
(With the Flippin' Teens Orchestra)
Singles: 7-inch
FLIPPIN' (107 "An Invitation")....15-25 61
Also see HENRY, Stacy, & Flip-Jacks Orch.

DREAMTONES
Singles: 78 rpm
MERCURY....5-10 57
Singles: 7-inch
MERCURY....8-15 57

DREAMTONES
(With the Tommy Wilson Orchestra)
Singles: 7-inch
ASTRA (551 "A Lover's Answer")...25-50 59
EARLY BIRD (1005 "Stand Beside Me")....4-6 96
(Colored vinyl.)
EXPRESS (501 "Praying for a Miracle")....150-250 59
KLIK (8505 "Stand Beside Me").400-600 58
SOLD....3-5 75
Member: Major Branch.
Also see MITLO SISTERS

DREGS: see DIXIE DREGS

DRENNON, Eddie, & B.B.S. Unlimited R&B '75
Singles: 7-inch
FRIENDS & CO. 3-5 75

DRESSER, Lee C&W '78
Singles: 7-inch
AIR INT'L....3-4 83
CAPITOL....3-5 78
Also see KRAZY KATS

DRESSLAR, Len P&R '56
(Len Dresslar Singers)
Singles: 78 rpm
MERCURY....4-8 56
Singles: 7-inch
CAPITOL....3-6 63
MERCURY....5-15 56
UNIVERSAL (76936 "Cubs' Song")....5-10

DREW, David
Singles: 7-inch
KING....3-5 71

DREW, Jimmy
Singles: 7-inch
DECCA....5-10 61

DREW, Malvereen
Singles: 7-inch
VIN....4-8 60

DREW, Patti P&R/R&B '67
(With the Drew-Vels)
Singles: 7-inch
CAPITOL....4-8 67-69
INNOVATION....3-5 75
QUILL....4-8 65
LPs: 10/12-inch
CAPITOL (Except 408)....10-20 69-70
CAPITOL (408 "Wild Is Love")....60-90 79
(Picture disc. Promotional issue only. With plastic cover.)
CAPITOL (408 "Wild Is Love")....80-100 79
(Picture disc. Promotional issue only. With cardboard album jacket.)
Also see DREW-VELS

DREW-VELS P&R '63
("Featuring Patti Drew")
Singles: 7-inch
CAPITOL....8-12 63-64
LPs: 10/12-inch
CAPITOL (2804 "Tell Him")....20-30 67
Members: Patti Drew; Erma Drew; Lorraine Drew; Carlton Black.
Also see DREW, Patti
Also see DUVALS

DREWS, J.D. P&R '80
Singles: 7-inch
UNICORN....3-4 80

DREXEL, Steve, & Cut-Ups
Singles: 7-inch
RIP (131 "Baby Blue")....15-25 58

DRIFTER, Dixie: see DIXIE DRIFTER,

DRIFTERS
Singles: 78 rpm
CORAL....100-200 50
EXCELSIOR (1314 "Honey Chile")....150-250 51
Singles: 7-inch
CORAL (65037 "I'm the Caring Kind")....300-400 50
CORAL (65040 "I Had to Find Out for Myself")....300-400 50

DRIFTERS R&B '53
(Clyde McPhatter & the Drifters)
Singles: 78 rpm
ATLANTIC (1006 thru 1161)....15-35 53-57
ATLANTIC (1187 "Drip Drop")....50-100 58
ATLANTIC (2025 "There Goes My Baby")....100-200 59
CROWN....50-75 54
Singles: 7-inch
ANDEE (0014 "Black Silk")....10-15 60s
ATLANTIC (1006 "Money Honey")....50-75 53
ATLANTIC (1019 "Such a Night")...30-60 54
ATLANTIC (1029 "Honey Love")....30-60 54
ATLANTIC (1043 "Bip Bam")....25-50 54
ATLANTIC (1048 "White Christmas")....25-50 54
ATLANTIC (1055 "Whatcha Gonna Do")....20-30 55
ATLANTIC (1078 "Adorable")....20-30 55
ATLANTIC (1089 "Ruby Baby")....20-30 56
ATLANTIC (1101 "I Got to Get Myself a Woman")....20-30 56
ATLANTIC (1123 "Fools Fall in Love")....20-30 57
ATLANTIC (1141 "Hypnotized")....20-30 57
ATLANTIC (1161 "I Know")....20-30 57
ATLANTIC (1187 "Drip Drop")....15-25 58
ATLANTIC (2025 "There Goes My Baby")....15-25 59
ATLANTIC (2040 "Dance with Me")....15-25 59
ATLANTIC (2050 "This Magic Moment")....15-25 60
ATLANTIC (2062 "Lonely Winds")....15-25 60
ATLANTIC (2071 "Save the Last Dance for Me")....15-25 60
ATLANTIC (2087 "I Count the Tears")....15-25 60
ATLANTIC (2096 "Some Kind of Wonderful")....15-25 61
ATLANTIC (2105 "Please Stay")....10-20 61
ATLANTIC (2117 "Sweets for My Sweet")....10-20 61
ATLANTIC (2127 "Room Full of Tears")....10-20 61
ATLANTIC (2134 thru 2786)....5-15 62-71
ATLANTIC OLDIES SERIES....3-5 70s
BELL (320 "I'm Feeling Sad")....4-6 73
BELL (387 "Like Sister & Brother")....4-6 73
BELL (600 "I'm Feeling Sad")....3-5 74
CROWN (108 "The World Is Changing")....100-150 54
Picture Sleeves
ATLANTIC (2260 "Saturday Night at the Movies")....10-20 64
ATLANTIC (2261 "The Christmas Song")....15-25 64
EPs: 7-inch
ATLANTIC (534 "The Drifters Featuring Clyde McPhatter")....75-100 55
ATLANTIC (592 "The Drifters")....40-60 58
LPs: 10/12-inch
ARISTA....8-12 76
ATCO (375 "Their Greatest Recordings")....10-15 71
ATLANTIC (8003 "Clyde McPhatter and the Drifters")....150-250 57
(Black label.)
ATLANTIC (8003 "Clyde McPhatter and the Drifters")....40-60 59
(Red label.)

ATLANTIC (8022 "Rockin' and Driftin' ")...100-200 59
(Black label.)
ATLANTIC (8022 "Rockin' and Driftin' ")...100-200 59
(White label.)
ATLANTIC (8022 "Rockin' and Driftin' ")...30-50 59
(Red label.)
ATLANTIC (8041 "The Drifters' Greatest Hits")...50-75 60
ATLANTIC (8059 "Save the Last Dance for Me")...50-75 62
(Monaural.)
ATLANTIC (SD-8059 "Save the Last Dance for Me")...60-80 62
(Stereo.)
ATLANTIC (8073 "Up on the Roof")...30-50 63
(Monaural.)
ATLANTIC (SD-8073 "Up on the Roof")...40-50 63
(Stereo.)
ATLANTIC (8093 "Biggest Hits")...30-40 64
(Monaural.)
ATLANTIC (SD-8093 "Biggest Hits")...40-50 64
(Stereo.)
ATLANTIC (8099 "Under the Boardwalk")...40-60 64
(Monaural. With black and white group photo.)
ATLANTIC (8099 "Under the Boardwalk")...20-30 64
(Monaural. With color group photo.)
ATLANTIC (SD-8099 "Under the Boardwalk")...50-70 64
(Stereo. With black and white group photo.)
ATLANTIC (SD-8099 "Under the Boardwalk")...25-35 64
(Stereo. With color group photo.)
ATLANTIC (8100 series)...20-30 65-68
CANDLELITE...10-15 70s
CLARION...15-20 64
51 WEST...5-10
GUSTO...5-10 80
MUSICOR...5-10 74
TRIP...5-10 76
Members: Clyde McPhatter; Johnny Moore; Ben E. King; Rudy Lewis; Bobby Hendricks; Johnny Williams; Elsbeary Hobbs; William Anderson; David Baldwin; James Johnson; Charlie Hughes; Charlie Thomas; Bill Pinckney; Andrew Thrasher; Gerhart Thrasher; Willie Ferbie; Walter Adams; Jimmy Milner; Reggie Kimber; Jimmy Oliver; David Baughn; Tommy Evans; Eugene Pearson; Billy Davis (Abdul Samad); Tommy Evans; Dock Green; Johnny Terry; Butch Leak; Grant Kitchings; Bill Fredericks; Butch Mann.
Also see ALSTON, Shirley
Also see CLEFTONES
Also see COASTERS / Drifters
Also see CROWNS
Also see DARROW, Johnny
Also see DRAPERS
Also see DUVALS
Also see FLOATERS
Also see HARMONY GRITS
Also see HENDRICKS, Bobby
Also see HORNETS
Also see JOHN, Little Willie / Drifters
Also see KING, Ben E.
Also see LEWIS, Rudy
Also see LITTLE DAVID & HARPS
Also see McPHATTER, Clyde
Also see MOONGLOWS
Also see ORIGINAL DRIFTERS
Also see PINKNEY, Bill
Also see SPRITES
Also see THOMAS, Charlie, & Drifters
Also see VEE, Bobby / Diamonds / Drifters

DRIFTERS / Lesley Gore / Roy Orbison / Los Bravos

EPs: 7-inch
SWINGERS for COKE...50-75 66
(Promotional issue only. Each artist sings a song about Coca Cola. Has paper cover.)
Also see GORE, Lesley
Also see LOS BRAVOS
Also see ORBISON, Roy

DRIFTERS / Little Joey & Flips

Singles: 7-inch
GRAY'S FERRY...3-5
Also see DRIFTERS
Also see LITTLE JOEY & FLIPS

DRIFTERS

Singles: 7-inch
STEELTOWN...8-10 69

DRIFTERS / Grady K. & Kuhfuss Band

Singles: 7-inch
QUALITY CHEKD (82592 "Cherry Chocolate Twist")...25-35 62
(Promotional issue only.)

DRIFTIN' SLIM

(Elmon Mickle; Driftin' Smith)
Singles: 78 rpm
MODERN (849 "My Little Machine")...50-75 51
RPM (370 "Good Morning Baby")...50-75 52
LPs: 10/12-inch
MILESTONE (93004 "Driftin' Slim & His Blues Band")...20-25 68
Also see MICKLE, Elmon

DRIFTIN' SMITH: see DRIFTIN' SLIM

DRIFTING COWBOYS — C&W '78

(With Jim Owen)
Singles: 78 rpm
MGM...4-8 53-54
Singles: 7-inch
MGM...5-10 53-54
LPs: 10/12-inch
DELTA...5-10
STANDING STONE...5-10 80
Members: Jerry Rivers; Bob McNett; H.B. Butrum; Don Helms.
Also see OWEN, Jim
Also see WILLIAMS, Hank

DRIFTWOOD, Jimmy — C&W '59

Singles: 7-inch
CD...8-12
RCA...5-10 59-60
EPs: 7-inch
RCA...10-20 59
LPs: 10/12-inch
MONUMENT...10-20 63-76
RCA (1635 "Newly Discovered Early American Folk Songs")...45-65 58
RCA (1994 thru 2443)...20-50 59-62
RACKENSACK...8-12
RIMROCK...8-12

DRIFTWOODS

Singles: 7-inch
FAN JR. (5080 "Have You Ever Had the Blues")...15-25 64
LEAF (8973 "Have You Ever Had the Blues")...15-25 62
Members: Pete Sorce; Al Babicky; Dick Aulbaencher; Mike Tezaloff; Nick Fera; Wayne Walters; Steve Olson.
Also see SOURCE, Pete

DRIFTWOODS

Singles: 7-inch
LAURIE (3198 "Ferndoc Street")...10-20 63

DRIFTWOODS

Singles: 7-inch
DBS (163 "Wobble Willie")...30-40

DRIGGERS, Hal, & Key Brothers

Singles: 7-inch
ATLANTIC...4-8 67

DRINK SMALL: see SMALL, Drink

DRINKARD, Cissy: see SWEET INSPIRATIONS

DRISCOLL, Julie

LPs: 10/12-inch
MARMALADE...10-15 68

DRISCOLL, Julie, & Brian Auger

Singles: 7-inch
ATCO...4-6 69
Also see DRISCOLL, Julie
Also see AUGER, Brian

DRIVER

Singles: 7-inch
A&M...3-5 77
LPs: 10/12-inch
A&M...5-10 77

DRIVER, Cliff, & Drivers

(Cliff Driver Combo)
Singles: 7-inch
J&S...10-20
NEPTUNE...4-6 59

DRIVERS

Singles: 78 rpm
DELUXE (6094 "Smooth, Slow and Easy")...25-50 56
DELUXE (6104 "My Lonely Prayer")...50-100 56
DELUXE (6117 "Oh, Miss Nellie")...50-75 57
RCA (7023 "Blue Moon")...30-50 57
Singles: 7-inch
DELUXE (6094 "Smooth, Slow and Easy")...50-100 56
DELUXE (6104 "My Lonely Prayer")...150-200 56
(Black label.)
DELUXE (6104 "My Lonely Prayer")...200-225 56
(White label with bio. Promotional issue only.)
DELUXE (6117 "Oh, Miss Nellie")...50-75 57
RCA (7023 "Blue Moon")...30-50 57
Members: Charlie Harris; Leroy Harmshaw; Carl Rogers; Leroy Smith; Willie Price.

DRIVERS

Singles: 7-inch
COMET (2142 "High Gear")...15-25 61
LIN (1002 "A Man's Glory")...250-500 58

DRIVERS

Singles: 7-inch
KING (5645 "Dry Bones Twist")...10-15 62

DRIVERS

Singles: 7-inch
DRIVE (101 "No One for Me")...150-200 50s

DRIVERS & SPACEMEN

Singles: 7-inch
ALTON (252 "Doe Doe")...20-30 59

DRIVIN' 'N' CRYIN' — LP '88

LPs: 10/12-inch
ISLAND...5-8 88-91
688 RECORDS...5-10 86
Members: Kevin Kinney; Tim Nielsen; Paul Lenz.

DRIVIN' DYNAMICS

Singles: 7-inch
SULLY...5-10 65

DRIVING STUPID

Singles: 7-inch
KR (116 "Horror Asparagus Stories")...25-35 66

DRIVING WHEELS

Singles: 7-inch
PAN AM (4001 "One Year Ago Today")...15-25 66

DRNWYN

LPs: 10/12-inch
WILDERLAND (31778 "Gypsies in the Mist")...50-75 78

D'RONE, Frank

Singles: 7-inch
CAMEO...4-8 63
COLUMBIA...4-6 65-66
MERCURY...4-8 62

DRONGOS

Singles: 7-inch
WHITE WHALE...4-8 66

DROOGS

LPs: 10/12-inch
SKYCLAD...8-10 90
Members: Ric Albin; Roger Clay; Dave Provost; Brian Hudson.

DRU, Jeanie

Singles: 7-inch
INTERLUDE...4-8 65

DRUIDS

Singles: 7-inch
COLUMBIA...10-15 65
SELECT...10-15 64
THUNDERBIRD...15-20 66

DRUIDS

Singles: 7-inch
MNO (101 "Sorry's Not Enough")...15-25 66
SELECT (743 "I Can't Leave You")...5-10 64

DRUIDS

Singles: 7-inch
BROAD COVETTAN HAVEN...5-10

DRUIDS OF STONEHENGE

Singles: 7-inch
UNI (55021 "Painted Woman")...10-15 67
LPs: 10/12-inch
UNI (3004 "Creation")...40-60 67
(Monaural.)
UNI (73004 "Creation")...50-75 67
(Stereo.)
Members: Carl Hauser; Dave Budge; Tom Workman; Bill Tracy; Steve Tindall.

DRUMM, Don — C&W '74

Singles: 7-inch
CHART...3-5 74
CHURCHILL...3-5 78

DRUPI — P&R '73

Singles: 7-inch
A&M...3-5 73

DRUSKY, Roy — C&W '60

Singles: 78 rpm
COLUMBIA...5-10 55-56
STARDAY...5-10 55
Singles: 7-inch
CAPITOL...3-5 74-76
COLUMBIA...8-12 55-56
DECCA...5-10 60-64
MERCURY...3-8 63-73
PLANTATION...3-4 79-80
SCORPION...3-5 77
STARDAY (185 "Such a Fool")...10-15 55
EPs: 7-inch
DECCA...4-8 61-63
LPs: 10/12-inch
BUCKBOARD...5-10
CAPITOL...5-10 76
DECCA...12-20 61-62
HARMONY...10-12 65
MCA...5-8 80s
MERCURY...10-20 64-72
MOUNTAIN DEW...5-10
PICKWICK...5-10 70s
PICKWICK/HILLTOP...8-12 70s
PLANTATION...5-10 79-80
SCORPION...5-10 76
VOCALION...8-12 70
WING...10-15 64-66
Also see WELLS, Kitty, & Roy Drusky

DRUSKY, Roy, & Priscilla Mitchell — C&W '67

Singles: 7-inch
MERCURY...4-6 65-68
LPs: 10/12-inch
MERCURY...8-15 65-68
Also see DRUSKY, Roy
Also see MITCHELL, Priscilla

DRY CITY SCAT BAND

LPs: 10/12-inch
ELEKTRA...15-20

DRY DOCK COUNTY

LPs: 10/12-inch
MERCURY...10-12 70

DRY GINS

Singles: 7-inch
MONTEL...4-8 65

DRY JACK

LPs: 10/12-inch
INNER CITY...5-10 80

DRYSDALE, Don

Singles: 7-inch
REPRISE (20162 "Give Her Love")...5-10 63
Picture Sleeves
REPRISE (20162 "Give Her Love")...10-20 63
Also see BASEBALL ("HOW TO" SERIES)

DUAL TONES

Singles: 7-inch
SABRE (104 "I'll Belong to You")...20-30 60

DUALS

Singles: 7-inch
FURY (1013 "Forever and Ever")...25-35 57

DUALS

Singles: 7-inch
ARC...10-15 59

DUALS — P&R '61

Singles: 7-inch
COLLECTABLES...3-4 80s
INFINITY (032 "Big Race")...20-30 64
JUGGY (321 "Big Race")...10-15 62
STAR REVUE (1031 "Stick Shift")...50-75 61
SUE (745 "Stick Shift")...10-15 61
SUE (758 "Travelin' Guitar")...10-15 61
LPs: 10/12-inch
SUE (2002 "Stick Shift")...50-80 61
Members: John Lagemann; Henry Bellinger.

DU'AMBRA, Joey

Singles: 7-inch
ABC-PAR...15-25 58

DUANE, Dick

Singles: 78 rpm
ABC-PAR...8-12 55-56
Singles: 7-inch
ABC-PAR...15-25 55-56

DUANE & GONDOLIERS

Singles: 7-inch
MAVERICK (606 "Lonesome Night")...4-8 60s

DU BATS, Rose

Singles: 7-inch
RAYNARD...4-8 62

DUBLIN, Sonny

Singles: 7-inch
CUB...4-6 70s

DUBLINERS

LPs: 10/12-inch
EPIC...12-15 67
MGM...15-25 64
TRADITION...5-10 83
VANGUARD...10-20 65

DUBOFF, Steve

Singles: 7-inch
COTILLION...3-6 69

DUBOY, Donna

Singles: 7-inch
SOUNDWAVES (Black vinyl)...3-4
SOUNDWAVES (Colored vinyl)...3-5
(Promotional issue only.)

DU BOY, Jess

(With the Hitchhikers)
Singles: 78 rpm
ABC-PAR...10-20 57
Singles: 7-inch
ABC-PAR...10-20 57
BROOKE...4-8
BRUNSWICK...4-8 64

DUBS — P&R '57

(Richard Blandon & Dubs)
Singles: 78 rpm
GONE (5002 "Don't Ask Me")...50-100 57
GONE (5020 "Beside My Love")...50-100 58
Singles: 7-inch
ABC-PAR (10056 "Early in the Morning")...20-30 59
ABC-PAR (10100 "Don't Laugh at Me")...40-60 60
ABC-PAR (10150 "For the First Time")...20-30 60
ABC-PAR (10198 "If I Only Had Magic")...25-50 61
ABC-PAR (10269 "Lullaby")...25-50 61
CLASSIC ARTISTS...4-6 90
CLIFTON...4-8 73
END (1108 "This to Me Is Love")...50-75 62
GONE (5002 "Don't Ask Me")...50-100 57
(With double image, shadow-like lettering.)
GONE (5002 "Don't Ask Me")...40-60 57
(With normal lettering.)
GONE (5011 "Could This Be Magic")...50-100 57
GONE (5020 "Beside My Love")...50-100 58
GONE (5034 "Be Sure My Love")...50-100 58
GONE (5046 "Chapel of Dreams")...50-100 58
(Black label.)
GONE (5046 "Chapel of Dreams")...25-50 60
(Multi-color label.)
GONE (5138 "Is There a Love for Me")...50-100 62
(Black label.)
JOHNSON (97 "Connie")...4-8 73
JOHNSON (98 "Somebody Goofed")...4-8 73
JOHNSON (102 "Don't Ask Me")...1000-2000 57
JOSIE (911 "This I Swear")...30-50 63
LANA...4-8 64
MARK-X (8008 "Be Sure My Love")...15-25 60
OLDIES 45...4-8 64
REO (8186 "Could This Be Magic")...50-75 57
(Canadian.)
ROULETTE...3-5 70s
VICKI (229 "Lost in the Wilderness")...10-20 62
WILSHIRE (201 "Just You")...25-40 63
ZIRKON (5002 "Chapel of Dreams")...5-10
LPs: 10/12-inch
CANDLELITE...10-15 73
MURRAY HILL...5-10 88
Members: Richard Blandon; Billy Carlisle; Cleveland Still; James Miller; Tom Gardner; Tom Grate; Cordell Brown; Dave Shelley.
Also see BOPCHORDS
Also see 5 WINGS
Also see LARKTONES / Dubs
Also see MARVELS
Also see SCALE-TONES

DUBS / Actuals

Singles: 78 rpm
CANDLELITE (438 "We Three")...5-10 72
Also see VOCALAIRES / Actuals

DUBS / Shells

LPs: 10/12-inch
CANDLELITE...8-10 70s
JOSIE (4001 "The Dubs Meet the Shells")...100-150 62
Also see DUBS
Also see SHELLS

DUBSET — D&D '84

Singles: 12-inch
ELEKTRA...4-6 84

DUCANES

Singles: 7-inch
GOLDISC (3024 "I'm So Happy")...25-30 61
LOST-NITE (245 "I'm So Happy")...5-10 60s
Members: Jeff Breny; Eddie Brian; Rick Scrofani; Ron Nagel; Louie Biscardi; Dennis Buckley.

DUCES of RHYTHM & TEMPO TOPPERS

(Featuring Little Richard)
Singles: 78 rpm
PEACOCK...25-50 53-54
Singles: 7-inch
PEACOCK (1616 "Fool at the Wheel")...50-75 53
PEACOCK (1628 "Always")...50-75 54
Also see LITTLE RICHARD
Also see TEMPO TOPPERS

DUCEY, A.C.

Singles: 7-inch
W.B....4-8 62

DUCEY, Chris

LPs: 10/12-inch
W.B....8-10 75

DUCHESS / Jake Porter

Singles: 7-inch
COMBO (2 "The Monkey")...50-75 53
Also see PORTER, Jake

DUCHESSES

Singles: 7-inch
CHIEF (7019 "Why")...15-25 60
CHIEF (7023 "Will I Ever Make It")...15-25 60
Also see FOUR DUCHESSES

DUCHIEN, Armand — D&D '84

Singles: 12-inch
A&M...4-6 84

DUCK & BEAR

Singles: 7-inch
ATLANTIC...3-6 69

DUCKBUTTER

LPs: 10/12-inch
WIZARD...5-10 78

DUCKETT, Sam, & Stringbusters

Singles: 7-inch
WHIRL...4-8

DUCKS

Singles: 7-inch
JUST SUNSHINE...4-8 73
LPs: 10/12-inch
JUST SUNSHINE...10-12 73
Also see SHAGS

DUCKS DELUXE

Singles: 7-inch
RCA...3-5 71
LPs: 10/12-inch
RCA...8-10 78

"Ducks Flying Backward": see VOLK BROTHERS

DUD, Bo, & Johnny Twist

Singles: 7-inch
T.D.S. (4715 "Honky Tonk")...10-20 62

DUDADS

Singles: 78 rpm
DELUXE...25-50 55
Singles: 7-inch
DELUXE (6083 "I Heard You Call Me Dear")...50-75 55

DUDEK, Les — LP '77

Singles: 7-inch
COLUMBIA...3-5 77-78

LPs: 10/12-inch
COLUMBIA....8-12 75-81
Also see ALLMAN BROTHERS BAND
Also see BLACK ROSE
Also see MASON, Dave / Les Dudek / Southside Johnny & Asbury Jukes / Walter Egan

DUDES
Singles: 7-inch
SUE....6-12 59-60

DUDES
Singles: 7-inch
GAIETY (12 "Let's Not Pretend")....15-25 66

DUDES
Singles: 7-inch
COLUMBIA....3-5 75
LPs: 10/12-inch
COLUMBIA....8-10 75

DUDLEY
Singles: 7-inch
ARVEE....5-10 60
GO....10-20 60
Also see NORMAN, Jimmy

DUDLEY, Bo
Singles: 7-inch
F-M....10-15

DUDLEY, Dave *C&W '61*
(With Charlie Douglas)
Singles: 78 rpm
KING....5-10 55-56
Singles: 7-inch
CIRCLE DOT....8-12 60
COLUMBIA....3-4 78
CURIO....4-8
GOLDEN RING (3030 "Cowboy Boots")....5-10 63
GOLDEN WING (3020 "Six Days on the Road")....5-10 63
(Black vinyl.)
GOLDEN WING (3020 "Six Days on the Road")....15-25 63
(Colored vinyl.)
JUBILEE (5436 "Please Let Me Prove")....5-10 62
KING (1508 "Cry Baby Cry")....10-20 55
KING (4866 "Ink Dries Quicker Than Tears")....10-20 55
KING (4933 "Rock & Roll Nursery Rhyme")....20-30 56
KING (5792 "Ink Dries Quicker Than Tears")....5-8 63
MERCURY....3-8 63-73
NRC (024 "I Won't Be Just Your Friend")....8-12 59
NEW STAR (6420 "Please Let Me Prove")....10-15 62
(First issue.)
PELHAM....5-10 63
RICE....3-5 73-78
STARDAY....10-15 58-60
SUN (Black vinyl)....3-5 79-80
SUN (Colored vinyl)....4-6 79-80
U.A.....3-5 75-76
VEE (7003 "Maybe I Do")....10-20 61
LPs: 10/12-inch
CORONET/PREMIER....8-12 60s
CROWN....8-12 60s
DESIGN....8-12 60s
GOLDEN RING (110 "Six Days on the Road")....25-35 63
GUEST STAR....8-12
HILLTOP....8-12
MERCURY....10-15 64-73
MOUNTAIN DEW....8-12 69
NASHVILLE....8-12 68
PICKWICK....5-10 70s
PLANTATION....5-10 81
RICE....3-4 78
SPIN-O-RAMA....5-10 60s
SUN....5-10 80
U.A.....8-12 75-76
WING....8-12 68
Also see JAMES, Sonny / Dave Dudley / Sunny Williams

DUDLEY, Dave, & Tom T. Hall *C&W '70*
Singles: 7-inch
MERCURY....3-5 70
Also see HALL, Tom T.

DUDLEY, Dave, & Karen O'Donnal *C&W '72*
Singles: 7-inch
MERCURY....3-5 72

DUDLEY, Dave / Link Wray
LPs: 10/12-inch
GUEST STAR....15-25 63
Also see DUDLEY, Dave
Also see WRAY, Link

DUDLEY, James, & Dee Jays
Singles: 7-inch
CHESS....4-8 60s

DUDLEY, Kay
Singles: 7-inch
TEEN ED....4-8 61

DU DROPPERS *R&B '53*
Singles: 78 rpm
GROOVE....25-50 53-55
RCA....20-30 53
RED ROBIN....50-100 52-53
Singles: 7-inch
GROOVE (0001 "Dead Broke")....40-60 54
GROOVE (0013 "Just Whisper")....50-75 54
GROOVE (0036 "Let Nature Take It's Course")....30-40 54
GROOVE (0104 "Talk That Talk")..20-40 55
GROOVE (0120 "You're Mine Already")....20-40 55
RCA (5229 "I Wanna Know")....25-35 53
RCA (5321 "I Found Out")....25-30 53
RCA (5425 "Whatever You're Doin'")....25-30 53
RCA (5504 "Don't Pass Me By")....25-30 53
RCA (5543 "The Note in the Bottle")....25-30 53
RED ROBIN (108 "Can't Do Sixty No More")....100-125 52
(Black vinyl.)
RED ROBIN (108 "Can't Do Sixty No More")....200-300 52
(Colored vinyl.)
RED ROBIN (116 "Come On and Love Me Baby")....100-125 53
EPs: 7-inch
GROOVE (2 "Talk That Talk")...100-200 55
GROOVE (5 "Tops in Rhythm & Blues")....100-200 55
Members: Julius Ginyard; Willie Ray; Eddie Hashaw; Harvey Ray; Bob Kornegay; Prentice Moreland; Joe Van Loan; Charlie Hughes.
Also see BELLS
Also see DIXIEAIRES
Also see GALE, Sunny, & Du Droppers
Also see VAN LOAN, Joe

DU-ETTES
Singles: 7-inch
LOST NITE....4-6 65
MAR-V-LUS....4-8 65
M-PAC....4-8 63
MECCA....8-12 59
ONE-DERFUL....4-8 64
Members: Barbara Livsey; Mary Francis Hayes.
Also see BARBARA & UNIQUES

DUFAY, Rick
LPs: 10/12-inch
POLYDOR....5-10 80

DUFF, Arlie *C&W '53*
Singles: 78 rpm
DECCA....5-10 56
STARDAY....5-10 53-55
Singles: 7-inch
DECCA....10-20 56
STARDAY....10-15 53-55

DUFFETT, Johnny
Singles: 7-inch
BRUNSWICK (55145 "Baby, Oh Baby")....10-12 59

DUFFILL, Tamson
(Tam Duffill)
Singles: 7-inch
GROOVE (0004 "Cooly Dooly")....30-40 62

DUFFY
Singles: 7-inch
DIAL (4097 "Come Back, Come Back")....10-15 67

DUFFY, Kathryn, & Enemies List
Singles: 7-inch
TAKOMA....4-8 74

DUGAN, Jeff *C&W '87*
Singles: 7-inch
W.B.....3-4 87-88

DUGAS, Jay, & Four Kings
Singles: 7-inch
QQ (302 "Fireball Mail")....10-20 63

DUGOSH, Eddie
Singles: 78 rpm
SARG....15-25 56
Singles: 7-inch
AWARD (116 "One Mile")....15-25 58
SARG (135 "Strange Kind of Feeling")....30-40 56

DUHON, James Kelly
Singles: 7-inch
JUDE (741 "In School")....10-20

DU-KANES
Singles: 7-inch
HSH (501 "Our Star")....15-25 64

DUKAYS *P&R '61*
Singles: 7-inch
JERRY-O (105 "Jerk")....10-15 64
NAT (4001 "The Girl's a Devil")....15-20 61
NAT (4002 "Nite Owl")....15-20 61
OLDIES 45....4-6 60s
VEE JAY (430 "Nite Owl")....10-20 62
VEE JAY (442 "Please Help")....10-20 62
VEE JAY (460 "I Never Knew")....10-20 62
Members: Eugene "Gene Chandler" Dixon; James Lowe; Earl Edwards; Ben Broyles; Shirley Jones; Charles Davis; Claude McRae.
Also see ARTISTICS
Also see CHANCE, Nolan
Also see CHANDLER, Gene

DUKE, Billy
(Billy Duke & His Dukes; Bill Duke)
Singles: 78 rpm
CASINO (138 "Flip, Flop & Fly")....15-25 56
CORAL (61203 "I Cried")....8-12 54
Singles: 7-inch
CAPITOL (4784 "New Orleans")....5-10 62
CAPITOL (4831 "Summer at the Shore")....5-10 62
CAPITOL (4907 "Goodbye Stranger")....5-10 63
CAPITOL (5012 "Echoes")....8-12 63
CASINO (138 "Flip, Flop & Fly")....40-60 56
CORAL (61203 "I Cried")....10-20 54
DATE....10-15 58
PEAK (104 "Chalypso")....15-25 57
SEVILLE (132 "I'm the Lonesomest Guy in Town")....5-10 64
TEEN (112 "Rocky Piano")....20-30 57
20TH FOX (242 "This Is What I Ask")....5-10 61
20TH FOX (276 "Be a Dreamer")....5-10 61
20TH FOX (296 "Amen")....5-10 62
20TH FOX (301 "Ain't She Pretty")..5-10 62

DUKE, David
Singles: 7-inch
HI....4-6 70

DUKE, Denver
Singles: 78 rpm
MERCURY....15-25 56
Singles: 7-inch
MERCURY (70970 "Rock and Roll Blues")....25-50 56

DUKE, Doris *P&R/R&B '70*
Singles: 7-inch
CANYON....4-8 70
MANKIND....3-5 72
RRG....3-5
SAM....3-5

DUKE, George *LP '75*
Singles: 12-inch
ELEKTRA....4-6 85-86
EPIC....4-6 83
Singles: 7-inch
ELEKTRA....3-4 85-86
EPIC....3-4 77-83
LPs: 10/12-inch
ELEKTRA....5-10 85-86
EPIC....5-10 77-83
MPS/BASF....8-10 74-76
Also see CLARKE, Stanley, & George Duke
Also see COBHAM, Billy
Also see MOTHERS of INVENTION

DUKE, Patty *P&R/LP '65*
Singles: 7-inch
U.A.....4-8 65-68
Picture Sleeves
U.A.....8-10 65
LPs: 10/12-inch
U.A.....15-20 65-68

DUKE, Roy
Singles: 78 rpm
DECCA....8-12 56-57
REJECT....10-20 56
Singles: 7-inch
DECCA....10-20 56-57
REJECT (1002 "Behave")....20-30 56

DUKE & AMBERS
Singles: 7-inch
STROLL (109 "Joanie")....10-15 60

DUKE & DRIVERS *P&R '75*
Singles: 7-inch
ABC....3-5 75
LPs: 10/12-inch
ABC....8-10 76

DUKE & LEONARD
Singles: 7-inch
CALLA ("Just Do the Best You Can")....8-12 60s
(Selection number not known.)
STOMP TOWN (101 "Just Do the Best You Can")....15-25 60s

DUKE & NULL
Singles: 7-inch
GUITAR (777 "Blue, Blue, Blue")...50-80

DUKE BAYOU
(Champion Jack Dupree)
Singles: 78 rpm
APOLLO....25-50 50
Also see DUPREE, Champion Jack

DUKE EKUD
Singles: 7-inch
SPEC (101 "Please Believe Me")....5-10

DUKE JUPITER *P&R '82*
Singles: 7-inch
COAST to COAST....3-4 82
MOROCCO....3-4 84-85
(Black vinyl.)
MOROCCO....4-6 84
(Colored vinyl. Promotional issue only.)
LPs: 10/12-inch
COAST TO COAST....5-10 82-83
MERCURY....5-10 80
MOROCCO....5-10 84
Members: Marshall James Styler; Rickey Ellis; Greg Walker; David Corcoran; George Barrahas.

DUKE OF EARL *P&R '62*
(Gene Chandler)
Singles: 7-inch
VEE JAY (440 "Walk on with the Duke")....8-10 62
Also see CHANDLER, Gene

DUKE OF IRON
LPs: 10/12-inch
PRESTIGE....15-20 63

DUKES
Singles: 78 rpm
IMPERIAL....50-75 56
SPECIALTY....25-50 54
Singles: 7-inch
FLIP (343 "Looking for You")....25-35 59
FLIP (345 "I Love You")....35-50 59
IMPERIAL (5401 "Teardrop Eyes")....150-250 56
IMPERIAL (5408 "Lovin' You")....100-150 56
IMPERIAL (5415 "Wini Brown")..100-150 56
SPECIALTY (543 "Ooh Bop She Bop")....50-100 54
Also see MIGHTY DUKES
Also see PRICE, Lloyd

DUKES
Singles: 7-inch
SIGNETT (326 "First Time I Saw Her")....10-15 66

DUKES
LPs: 10/12-inch
W.B.....5-10 80

DUKES
Singles: 7-inch
DUKES (68003 "Meet Me at Mary's Place")....10-15

DUKES, Aggie
(Agnes Dukes)
Singles: 78 rpm
ALADDIN (3388 "John John")....25-50 57
Singles: 7-inch
ALADDIN (3388 "John John")....25-50 57

DUKES OF DIXIELAND *LP '57*
LPs: 10/12-inch
AUDIO FIDELITY....5-15 55-61
COLUMBIA....5-10 62
EPIC....5-15 56
RCA VICTOR....5-10 59

DUKES OF RHYTHM
Singles: 7-inch
LA JOY....5-10 60

DUKES OF STRATOSPHERE
Singles: 12-inch
GEFFEN (2840 "Vanishing Girl")....5-10 87
(Promotional issue only.)
LPs: 10/12-inch
GEFFEN....5-10 87
Also see XTC

DULFER, Candy *LP '91*
LPs: 10/12-inch
ARISTA....5-8 91

DU MAURIERS
Singles: 78 rpm
FURY (1011 "Baby, I Love You")...50-75 57
Singles: 7-inch
FURY (1011 "Baby, I Love You")...50-75 57

DUMB GUYS
Singles: 12-inch
TOMMY BOY....4-6 84

DUMONTS
Singles: 7-inch
KING....10-15 61

DUNAVAN, Terry
Singles: 7-inch
FANFARE (727 "Rock It on Mars")....200-300

DUNAWAY, Shelton
Singles: 7-inch
JIN....4-8 69
KHOURY'S....10-20 60
LYRIC....4-8 62

DUNAWAY, Shelton, & Cupcakes / Lil Alfred & Cupcakes
Singles: 7-inch
JIN....5-10 68
Also see DUNAWAY, Shelton

DUNBAR, Aynsley
(Aynsley Dunbar Retaliation)
LPs: 10/12-inch
BLUE THUMB....12-15 68-70
Also see JEFFERSON STARSHIP
Also see JOURNEY
Also see WHITESNAKE

DUNCAN, Al
Singles: 7-inch
STACY....5-10 61-62

DUNCAN, Cleve
Singles: 7-inch
DOOTO (451 "To Keep Our Love")....15-20 59
(With the Radiants.)
DOOTO (456 "You're an Angel")....10-15 59
(With the Penguins.)
ELDO....8-12 61
ORIGINAL SOUND....5-8 63-65
Also see PENGUINS

DUNCAN, Darryl *R&B '88*
Singles: 7-inch
MOTOWN....3-4 88

DUNCAN, Doodle
Singles: 7-inch
LIN....5-10 61

DUNCAN, Don
Singles: 7-inch
VENTURE (111 "Something Special")....75-100 59

DUNCAN, Dorinda
LPs: 10/12-inch
U.A.....12-15 65

DUNCAN, Ferrell
Singles: 7-inch
KIM (100 "Flying Saucer")....15-25 58

DUNCAN, Herbie
Singles: 7-inch
MAR-VEL (1400 "Hot Lips Baby")..50-75 58
GLENN (1401 "Escape")....40-60 59
GLENN (1402 "That's All")....40-60 60

DUNCAN, James
(With the Duncan Trio)
Singles: 7-inch
FEDERAL (928 "My Baby Is Back")...3-6 76
FEDERAL (12549 "Money Can't Buy True Love")....5-8 69
FEDERAL (12552 "I've Got It Made")....5-8 69
KING....10-20 64-66

DUNCAN, Jamie
Singles: 7-inch
SOUTHERN GOLD....3-4 86

DUNCAN, Jimmy
Singles: 78 rpm
KING (5028 "I'm on the Outside")...10-20 57
Singles: 7-inch
BACK BEAT (527 "Doll House")....10-20 59
BRUNSWICK (55077 "I Close the Door")....15-25 58
DECCA (30455 "Run Little Joey")....8-12 58
KING (5028 "I'm on the Outside")..15-25 57

DUNCAN, Johnny *C&W '67*
Singles: 7-inch
COLUMBIA....3-6 67-81
LEADER (807 "Bring Your Heart")....20-30 60
LEADER (812 "Freddy and His Go-Cart")....10-20 60
LEADER (814 "Raindrops")....10-15 61
PHAROAH....3-4 86
LPs: 10/12-inch
COLUMBIA....5-10 69-80
HARMONY....5-10 73
PHAROAH....5-10 86
Session: Janie Fricke.

DUNCAN, Johnny, & Janie Fricke *C&W '77*
Singles: 7-inch
COLUMBIA....3-5 77
LPs: 10/12-inch
COLUMBIA....5-10 80
Also see FRICKE, Janie

DUNCAN, Johnny, & June Stearns *C&W '69*
Singles: 7-inch
COLUMBIA....3-5 69
LPs: 10/12-inch
COLUMBIA....5-10 69
Also see DUNCAN, Johnny
Also see STEARNS, June

DUNCAN, Lanny
Singles: 7-inch
CANDIX....5-10 60-62
GOLDEN STATE....4-8 65

DUNCAN, Lesley
(with the Jokers)
Singles: 7-inch
JERDEN....4-8 65
MERCURY....4-8 64

DUNCAN, Lesley
Singles: 7-inch
COLUMBIA....3-5 71-73
DATE....3-5 70
MCA....3-5 75
LPs: 10/12-inch
COLUMBIA....8-12 71
MCA....8-10 75-77
Also see JOHN, Elton

DUNCAN, Tommy *C&W '49*
(With His Western All Stars)
Singles: 78 rpm
CAPITOL....4-8 48-50
CORAL....4-6 53-54
Singles: 7-inch
CAPITOL....8-12 50
CHEYENE....10-15
CORAL....5-10 53-54
FALEW (104 "Dance, Dance, Dance")....15-25 64
FALEW (107 "Too Much Time")....15-25 64
LPs: 10/12-inch
LONGHORN....5-10 83-84
Also see WILLS, Bob

DUNCAN, Tommy
Singles: 78 rpm
FIRE....20-30 56
Singles: 7-inch
FALEW (104 "Dance Dance Dance")....15-25
FALEW (107 "Too Much Time")....15-25
FIRE (101 "Daddy Loves Mommy-O")....35-50 56
SMASH (2073 "Let Me Take You Out")....15-25 66

DUNCAN BROTHERS
Singles: 7-inch
CAPITOL (5711 "Make Me What You Want Me to Be")....10-20 66

DUNCAN SISTERS *R&B '79*
Singles: 12-inch
EAR MARC....4-6 79
Singles: 7-inch
EAR MARC....3-5 79-80
HI....4-8 75

DUNDAS, David *P&R '76*
Singles: 7-inch
CHRYSALIS....3-5 76-77
LPs: 10/12-inch
CHRYSALIS....8-10 77

DUNDEES
("Featuring Carlyle Dundee")
Singles: 78 rpm
SPACE (201 "Never") 200-300 54
Singles: 7-inch
SPACE (201 "Never") 800-1200 54

DUNE, Lorna
Singles: 7-inch
DORE 4-8 61
SELECT 4-8 64

DUNES
Singles: 7-inch
MADISON 10-20 61

DUNGAREE DARLINGS
(With the Al Sears Orchestra; Dungaree Dolls)
Singles: 7-inch
KAREN (1005 "Boy of My Dreams") 50-75 59
Also see DUNGAREE DOLLS
Also see SEARS, Al

DUNGAREE DOLLS
(With the Al Sears Orchestra)
Singles: 7-inch
REGO (1003 "Boy of My Dreams") 150-200 58
(Reissued as by the Dungaree Darlings.)
Also see DUNGAREE DARLINGS
Also see SEARS, Al

DUNGEON OF FUSION
Singles
AZRA (36 "Digital Darkness") 25-35 89
(Woman shaped, also square car shaped picture disc. 25 made of each shape.)
AZRA (36 "Digital Darkness") 10-20 89
(Square shaped picture disc. 500 made.)

DUNHAM, Andrew
Singles: 78 rpm
SENSATION (23 "Sweet Lucy") 40-60 49

DUNHAM, Jackie
Singles: 7-inch
IMPERIAL 4-8 61

DUNHILLS
Singles: 7-inch
ROYAL (110 "Sound of the Wind") 25-50 61

DUNKIRK, Dick, & Strangers
BANGAR (652 "Don't You Believe Them") 10-20 64
SOMA (1424 "Don't You Believe Them") 8-12 65
Also see VEE, Bobby

DUNLAP, Ernie
Singles: 7-inch
CIN-KAY 3-5
Picture Sleeves
CIN-KAY 8-10

DUNLAP, Gene
Singles: 7-inch
HITT (182 "Made in the Shade") 30-50 58

DUNLAP, Gene R&B '81
(With the Ridgeways)
Singles: 12-inch
CAPITOL 4-6 82
Singles: 7-inch
CAPITOL 3-4 81-83
LPs: 10/12-inch
CAPITOL 5-10 81-83
Also see AYERS, Roy
Also see WYNNE, Philippe

DUNLAP, Norman, & Melodettes
Singles: 78 rpm
ALADDIN 25-50 53
Singles: 7-inch
ALADDIN (3213 "A Dream and a Prayer") 50-75 53

DUNN, Bobby
Singles: 7-inch
LOGO 4-8 63
ORDELL 4-8 62
U.A. 4-8 62
WARWICK 4-8 61

DUNN, Bobby, & Les Cooper
LPs: 10/12-inch
PALACE 10-15
Also see COOPER, Les
Also see DUNN, Bobby

DUNN, David
Singles: 7-inch
LORI (9541 "I'll Never Let You Go") 25-35 60s

DUNN, Elaine
Singles: 7-inch
RCA 5-15 59

DUNN, Fred
(With His Barrelhouse Rhythm)
Singles: 78 rpm
JIFFY (100 "Fred's Boogie Woogie") 200-300 47
SIGNATURE (1026 "Fred's Boogie Woogie") 25-50 47
SIGNATURE (32010 "Railroad Blues") 25-50 48

DUNN, Holly C&W '85
Singles: 7-inch
MTM 3-4 85-88
W.B. 3-4 89-91
LPs: 10/12-inch
MTM 8-10 80s
Also see MURPHEY, Michael Martin, & Holly Dunn
Also see ROGERS, Kenny, & Holly Dunn
Also see TOMORROW'S WORLD

DUNN, Johnny
Singles: 7-inch
DOUBLE L 4-8 63
HULL 4-8 64-65
VEEP 4-8 66

DUNN, Joyce
Singles: 7-inch
BLUE ROCK (4081 "The Push I Need") 10-20 69

DUNN, Leona
LPs: 10/12-inch
HALLMARK 10-15

DUNN, Ronnie C&W '83
Singles: 7-inch
CHURCHILL 3-5 83-84
Also see BROOKS & DUNN

DUNN & BRUCE STREET R&B '82
Singles: 7-inch
DEVAKI 3-4 81-82
Members: Dunn Pearson; Bruce Gray

DUNN & McCASHEN P&R '70
Singles: 7-inch
CAPITOL 3-6 69-70
LPs: 10/12-inch
CAPITOL 10-12 69-70
COLUMBIA 12-15 71
Members: Don Dunn; Tony McCashen.

DUNNE, Hap
Singles: 7-inch
BRUNSWICK 4-8 63

DUNTON, Pete
Singles: 7-inch
RCA 10-15 74

DUPAN, Sunny
Singles: 7-inch
GOLDBAND 8-12
TEK (102 "Looney and Goon") 15-25

DUPONT, Ann, & Four Blues
Singles: 78 rpm
DELUXE 10-20 45
Also see FOUR BLUES

DU PONT, Shelley, & Calendars
Singles: 7-inch
TRIBUNE (1001 "Share My Love") 20-30 60s

DUPONTS
(Little Anthony Gourdine & Duponts)
Singles: 78 rpm
ROYAL ROOST 20-40 56
WINLEY 20-40 56
Singles: 7-inch
ROYAL ROOST (627 "Prove It Tonight") 50-100 56
SAVOY (1552 "Must Be Falling in Love") 25-50 58
WINLEY (212 "Must Be Falling in Love") 50-100 56
Members: Anthony Gourdine; Bill Dokery; Bill Delk; Bill Bracey.
Also see LITTLE ANTHONY & IMPERIALS

DUPONTS
Singles: 7-inch
ROULETTE (4060 "Screamin' Ball") 15-25 58

DUPRE, Dave
(Dave Burgess)
Singles: 7-inch
CHALLENGE 10-20 57
Also see BURGESS, Dave

DUPREE, Champion Jack R&B '55
Singles: 78 rpm
ALERT 15-25 46
APOLLO 15-25 49-50
CELEBRITY 15-25 46
CONTINENTAL 15-25 45
JOE DAVIS 15-25 46
KING 10-20 53-56
RED ROBIN 25-75 53-54
VIK 15-25 57
Singles: 7-inch
ATLANTIC 5-10 61
EVERLAST 4-8 64
FEDERAL 5-10 61
GUSTO 3-4 80s
KING (4695 "Walkin' Upside Your Head") 15-25 53
KING (4706 "Rub a Little Boogie") 15-25 53
KING (4812 "Walking the Blues") 15-25
KING (4938 "Big Leg Emma's") 15-25 56
RED ROBIN (109 "Stumblin' Block Blues") 150-200 53
RED ROBIN (112 "Highway Blues") 150-200 53
RED ROBIN (130 "Drunk Again") 150-200 54
VIK (260 "Dirty Woman") 20-30 57
VIK (279 "Old Time Rock & Roll") .20-30 57
LPs: 10/12-inch
ARCHIVE OF FOLK MUSIC 10-15 68
ATLANTIC (8019 "Blues from the Gutter") 75-100 59
(Green label.)
ATLANTIC (8019 "Blues from the Gutter") 40-60 59
(Black label.)
ATLANTIC (8019 "Blues from the Gutter") 40-60 59
(White label.)
ATLANTIC (8019 "Blues from the Gutter") 20-30 59
(Red label.)
ATLANTIC (8045 "Natural and Soulful Blues") 30-40 61
(Monaural.)
ATLANTIC (SD-8045 "Natural and Soulful Blues") 40-50 61
(Stereo.)
ATLANTIC (8056 "Champion of the Blues") 30-40 61
(Monaural.)
ATLANTIC (SD-8056 "Champion of the Blues") 40-50 61
(Stereo.)
ATLANTIC (8255 "Blues from the Gutter") 8-10 70
BLUE HORIZON 10-15 69
EVEREST 8-12
FOLKWAYS (3825 "Women Blues of Champion Jack Dupree") 20-30 61
GNP 8-12 74
JAZZMAN 5-10 82
KING (735 "Champion Jack Dupree Sings the Blues") 50-60 61
KING (1084 "Walking the Blues") 10-15 70
LONDON 10-15 69
OKEH (12103 "Cabbage Greens") 50-75 63
STORYVILLE 5-10 82
Members: Jack Dupree; Larry Dale; Al Lucas; Gene Moore; Stick McGhee; Willie Jones; Pete Brown.
Also see BROTHER BLUES & Back Room Boys
Also see DUKE BAYOU
Also see DUPREE, Jack, & Mr. Bear
Also see JOHNSON, Blind Boy, & His Rhythms
Also see JOHNSON, Meat Head
Also see JORDAN, Willie, & His Swinging Five
Also see LIGHTNIN' JR. & EMPIRES
Also see McGHEE, Brownie
Also see McGHEE, Stick
Also see RUSHING, Jimmy, & Jack Dupree

DUPREE, Champion Jack, & Mickey Baker
LPs: 10/12-inch
SIRE 10-15 69
Also see BAKER, Mickey

DUPREE, Jack, & Mr. Bear
Singles: 78 rpm
GROOVE 10-15 56
KING 10-20 55
Singles: 7-inch
GROOVE (0171 "Lonely Road Blues") 15-25 56
KING (4812 "Walking the Blues") 15-25 55
Members: Jack Dupree; Teddy "Mr. Bear" McRae; Larry Dale; Al Lucas; Gene Moore.
Also see DALE, Larry
Also see DUPREE, Champion Jack

DU PREE, Florence
(With the Elliot Carpenter Orchestra)
Singles: 7-inch
SKYWAY (130 "Shakin' Hands") 10-15 60s

DUPREE, Lebron
Singles: 7-inch
SPANN 5-10 59

DUPREE, Lillian
Singles: 7-inch
D-TOWN (1051 "Hide & Seek") 40-60 66

DUPREE, Nelson
Singles: 7-inch
PALM (201 "Lost") 15-25

DUPREE, Omar
Singles: 7-inch
JEWEL 5-8

DUPREE, Robbie P&R/R&B/LP '80
Singles: 7-inch
ELEKTRA 3-4 80-81
Picture Sleeves
ELEKTRA 3-4 80
LPs: 10/12-inch
ELEKTRA 5-10 80-81

DUPREE, Simon, & Big Sound
Singles: 7-inch
TOWER 3-5 69
LPs: 10/12-inch
TOWER (5097 "Without Reservations") 15-25 68
Also see GENTLE GIANT

DUPREES P&R/LP '62
Singles: 7-inch
COED (569 thru 580) 10-20 62-63
COED (584 "Why Don't You Believe Me"/"The Things I Love") 25-35 63
COED (584 "Why Don't You Believe Me"/"My Dearest One") 10-15 63
(Note different flip.)
COED (585 thru 596) 10-15 63-65
COLLECTABLES 3-4 80
COLUMBIA 8-12 65-67
ERIC 3-4 70s
1ST CHOICE 3-5 89
HERITAGE 4-8 68-70
LOST-NITE 4-6 70s
(Black vinyl.)
LOST-NITE 10-15
(Colored vinyl.)
RCA 3-6 75
Picture Sleeves
COLUMBIA 10-20 66
HERITAGE 4-8 68
LPs: 10/12-inch
COED (905 "You Belong to Me") .75-125 62
COED (906 "Have You Heard") ...75-125 63
COLLECTABLES 5-10 80
(Black vinyl.)
COLLECTABLES 10-15 82
(Picture disc.)
1ST CHOICE 10-15 87
HERITAGE (35002 "Total Recall") 20-30 68
PICCADILLY 8-12 80
POST (1000 "The Duprees Sing") ..15-25
POST (11000 "The Duprees Sing, Vol. 2") 15-20
Members: Joey "Vann" Canzano; Mike Arnone; Tom Bialaglow; John Salvato; Joe Santollo; Richie Rosato.
Also see ITALIAN ASPHALT & Pavement Company
Also see VANN, Joey

DUPREES / RIVIERAS
LPs: 10/12-inch
LOST NITE (122 Jerry Blavat Presents Drive-In Sounds") 10-15 70s
Also see BLAVAT, Jerry
Also see DUPREES
Also see RIVIERAS

DUPRIES
Singles: 7-inch
TEST (100 "Baby Doll") 25-35 65
THUNDER (106 "Baby Doll") 25-35 65
Members: Dick Schulz; Annie Duprey Schulz; Joanie Duprey Rousseau; Carol Duprey; Dave Pilz; Dave Parpovich.
Also see CANDY & CORALS

DUPRIEST & WHITE
Singles: 7-inch
JOYBIRD 3-4 80
Picture Sleeves
JOYBIRD 3-4 80

DUQUESNAY, Ann
Singles: 7-inch
CAPITOL 5-10 69

DURAIN, Johnny, & Cytones
Singles: 7-inch
BIG CITY (300 "About to Lose My Mind") 8-12 60s
BIG CITY (301 "I'll Show You") 8-12 60s
DORE (624 "My Last Love") 5-10 62

DURAND, Ruth
Singles: 78 rpm
POST (2012 "I'm Wise") 8-12 56
Singles: 7-inch
POST (2012 "I'm Wise") 25-35 56

DURAN DURAN P&R/LP '82
(Duranduran)
Singles: 12-inch
CAPITOL 4-8 82-87
Singles: 7-inch
CAPITOL (Except 12352) 4-8 82-87
CAPITOL (12352 "The Reflex") 10-20 84
(Picture disc.)
Singles: 7-inch
CAPITOL (Black vinyl) 3-4 82-90
CAPITOL (Colored vinyl) 5-10 86-87
(Promotional issues only.)
HARVEST 3-4 81-82
Picture Sleeves
CAPITOL (Except 5345) 3-4 83-89
CAPITOL (5345 "The Reflex") 3-4 84
(Poster sleeve.)
CAPITOL (5438 "Save a Prayer") 5-10 82
(Promotional issue only.)
HARVEST 3-4 82
EPs: 7-inch
HARVEST 15-20 82
LPs: 10/12-inch
CAPITOL 5-10 82-90
HARVEST (12158 "Duran Duran") 8-12 82
MFSL (110 "Rio") 25-35 84
MFSL (182 "Seven and the Ragged Tiger") 25-35 87
Members: Nick Rhodes; Roger Taylor; John Taylor, Andy Taylor; Simon LeBon; Warren Cuccurullo.
Also see ARCADIA
Also see BAND AID
Also see MISSING PERSONS
Also see POWER STATION
Also see TAYLOR, Andy
Also see TAYLOR, John

DURANGO
Singles: 7-inch
UNI 4-6 70

DURANT, Teddy
Singles: 7-inch
IMPRESSION 4-8 65

DURANTE, Jimmy P&R '34
Singles: 78 rpm
BRUNSWICK 5-10 34
DECCA 4-8 44-57
Singles: 7-inch
DECCA 4-8 51-59
W.B. 3-4 63-70
EPs: 7-inch
DECCA 5-10 54-56
MGM 5-10 53-55
VARSITY 5-10 55
LPs: 10/12-inch
DECCA (9000 series) 15-25 54-56
DECCA (78000 series) 8-12 70
HARMONY 8-12 68
LIGHT 5-10 71
LION 15-20 56
MGM (3200 series) 15-25 55
MGM (4200 series) 10-15 64
ROULETTE 15-20 61
W.B. 10-15 63-67
Also see GOLDSBORO, Bobby / Jimmy Durante
Also see KAYE, Danny, Jimmy Durante, Jane Wyman & Groucho Marx
Also see MARTIN, Dean
Also see PRESLEY, Elvis

DURBIN, Mark
Singles: 7-inch
VEGAS 4-6 67

DURDEN, Tommy
Singles: 7-inch
D (1076 "Deep in the Heart of a Fool") 8-12 59
SOUND (272 "Heartbreak Hotel") 5-10
WESTBOUND (55404 "Elvis") 5-10 77
(With insert.)

DURETTES
Singles: 7-inch
SVR (1006 "Sweet, Sweet Love") ..30-50 60s

DURHAM, Bobby C&W '88
Singles: 7-inch
HIGHTONE 3-4 88

DURHAM, Judith
LPs: 10/12-inch
A&M 10-12 75

DURHAM, Paul
Singles: 7-inch
McDOWELL (507 "Mean Woman") 25-50
SANDSPUR (15302 "She Lied") 25-50

DURHAM, Ricky
Singles: 7-inch
JUBILEE 5-10

DURKEE, Ray
Singles: 7-inch
JUBILEE (5422 "Cosmonaut") 5-10 62

DUROCS
Singles: 7-inch
CAPITOL 3-5 79
LPs: 10/12-inch
CAPITOL 10-15 79

DURON, Mario, & Wig-Wags
Singles: 7-inch
WIG-WAG (101 "Ooh-Woo-Wee") ..8-12

DURRENCE, Sam C&W '73
Singles: 7-inch
RIVER 3-5 73

DURST, L.
(Lavada Durst)
Singles: 78 rpm
PEACOCK (1509 "Hattie Green") ..20-30 49
Also see DR. HEP CAT

DURY, Ian, & Blockheads LP '78
Singles: 7-inch
STIFF (Except 23 & 1179) 3-5 79-81
STIFF/COLUMBIA (23 "Sweet Gene Vincent") 5-10 78
(Yellow vinyl. Promotional issue only.)
STIFF (1179 "Hit Me with Your Rhythm Stick") 4-8 79
(Bonus issued with the *Do It Yourself* LP. Promotional issue only.)
Picture Sleeves
STIFF/EPIC (Except 1179) 3-5 79-81
STIFF/COLUMBIA (23 "Sweet Gene Vincent") 4-8
(Yellow vinyl.)
STIFF/EPIC (1179 "Hit Me with Your Rhythm Stick") 4-8 78
(Bonus issue with the *Do It Yourself* LP. Promotional issue only.)
LPs: 10/12-inch
POLYDOR 5-10 81
STIFF/EPIC (Except 36104) 5-10 78-82
STIFF/EPIC (36104 "Do It Yourself") 10-15 79
(Includes bonus single *Hit Me with Your Rhythm Stick*.)
Also see JANKEL, Chas

DUSHON, Jean
(Jean Du Shon)
Singles: 7-inch
ABC-PAR 4-8 60
ATCO (6198 "Talk to Me") 25-35 61
CHESS 4-8 60s
LENNOX 4-8 63
OKEH 4-8 62
LPs: 10/12-inch
ARGO 10-20

DUSK P&R '71
Singles: 7-inch
BELL 4-6 71-72
Member: Peggy Santiglia.
Also see ANGELS

DUST
Singles: 7-inch
KAMA SUTRA 3-5 73
YAS 4-6
LPs: 10/12-inch
KAMA SUTRA (2041 "Dust") 15-20 71
(Pink label.)
KAMA SUTRA (2041 "Dust") 10-15 71
(Blue label.)
KAMA SUTRA (2059 "Hard Attack") 15-20 72
(With gatefold cover.)
KAMA SUTRA (2059 "Hard Attack") 8-10 72
(With standard cover.)
Members: Richie Wise; Marc Bell; Kenny Aaronson.

Also see DERRINGER, Rick

DUST
LPs: 10/12-inch
MYRRH ... 8-10 72

DUST & ASHES
LPs: 10/12-inch
AVANT GARDE ... 8-10 71-72

DUSTERS
(With Jimmy Binkley's Orchestra)
Singles: 78 rpm
ARC (3000 "Give Me Time") ... 75-125 56
Singles: 7-inch
ARC (3000 "Give Me Time") ... 200-300 56
Member: Tommy Tucker.
Also see TUCKER, Tommy

DUSTERS
Singles: 7-inch
ABC-PAR (9886 "Pretty Girl") ... 10-20 58
CUPID (5003 "Rock at the Hop") ... 40-60 58
GLORY (287 "Darling Love") ... 35-40 58
Members: Robert Mansfield; Robert Wentworth; Donald Emilian; Lee de Felice.
Also see BUCCANEERS

DUSTERS
Singles: 12-inch
REPTILE ... 8-10 88

DUSTY CHAPS
Singles: 7-inch
SILVER SPUR ... 3-5 74
LPs: 10/12-inch
BANDOLIER ... 12-15
CAPITOL ... 8-10 78
Member: George Hawke.
Also see MOUSE

DUTONES
Singles: 7-inch
COLUMBIA ... 4-8 62-63

DUVALL, Huelyn — P&R '59
Singles: 78 rpm
CHALLENGE ... 25-50 58
Singles: 7-inch
CHALLENGE (1012 "Comin' Or Goin' ") ... 25-35 58
(Blue label.)
CHALLENGE (1012 "Comin' Or Goin' ") ... 10-20 58
(Maroon label.)
CHALLENGE (59002 "Humdinger") ... 10-20 58
CHALLENGE (59014 "Little Boy Blue") ... 20-40 58
CHALLENGE (59025 "Juliette") ... 10-20 58
CHALLENGE (59069 "Pucker Paint") ... 15-25 59
STARFIRE (600 "It's No Wonder") ... 30-35 59
TWINKLE (506 "Beautiful Dreamer") ... 40-60 50s

DUVALS
(Five Crowns)
Singles: 7-inch
LOST NITE ... 3-6 70s
RAINBOW (335 "You Came to Me") ... 100-200 57
(Yellow label.)
RAINBOW (335 "You Came to Me") ... 25-35 62
(Blue label.)
Members: Wilbur Paul; Jesse Facing; Richard Lewis; Dock Green; William Bailey.
Also see DRAPERS
Also see DRIFTERS
Also see FIVE CROWNS

DUVALS
Singles: 78 rpm
GEE (1003 "Guide Me") ... 25-35 56
Singles: 7-inch
GEE (1003 "Guide Me") ... 40-60 56

DUVALS
Singles: 7-inch
PRELUDE (110 "The Last Surf") ... 20-30 63

DUVALS
Singles: 7-inch
BOSS ... 5-10 63
RED ROCKET ... 5-10 63
Members: Carlton Black; Charles Perry; Charles Woolridge; Arthur Cox; Andy Thomas.
Also see DREW-VELS
Also see NATURALS

DUVELLS
Singles: 7-inch
RUST (5045 "How Come") ... 25-35 63

DWARVES
LPs: 10/12-inch
BOMP ... 5-10

DWEEZIL: see ZAPPA, Dweezil & Moon

DWELLERS
(With the Jap Curry Blazers)
Singles: 7-inch
CONROSE (101 "Lonely Guy") ... 100-200 58
HOWARD (503 "Tell Me Why") ... 100-150 63
OASIS (101 "Oh Sweetie") ... 100-200 59

DWIGHT, Susan, & Minks
Singles: 7-inch
ERMINE ... 5-10 61

DYCE, Billy / Hugh Roy
Singles: 7-inch
TYPHOON (113 "Be My Guest") ... 8-12

DYCKE, Jerry — C&W '80
Singles: 7-inch
CHURCHILL ... 3-4 80-81

DYCUS, Connie
Singles: 7-inch
MERCURY ... 8-12 58

DYER, Ada — R&B '88
Singles: 7-inch
MOTOWN ... 3-4 88

DYESS, David Wayne
Singles: 7-inch
ACE ... 4-8 59

DYKE, Jerry, & Ventells
Singles: 7-inch
SATURN (5010 "Mean Woman Blues") ... 10-15

DYKE & BLAZERS — P&R/R&B/LP '67
Singles: 7-inch
ARTCO ... 8-10 67
ORIGINAL SOUND ... 4-8 67-70
LPs: 10/12-inch
ORIGINAL SOUND (8876 "Funky Broadway") ... 30-35 67
ORIGINAL SOUND (8877 "Dyke's Greatest Hits") ... 20-30 67
Member: Arlester "Dyke" Christian.

DYLAN, Bob — LP '63
(With the Band)
Singles: 7-inch
ASYLUM ... 3-6 74
COLUMBIA (10106 "Tangled Up in Blue") ... 8-12 75
COLUMBIA (10217 "Million Dollar Bash") ... 8-12 75
COLUMBIA (10245 "Hurricane") ... 3-5 75
COLUMBIA (10298 "Mozambique") ... 3-5 75
COLUMBIA (10454 "Rita Mae") ... 8-12 77
COLUMBIA (10805 "Baby Stop Crying") ... 4-8 78
COLUMBIA (10851 "Changing of the Guards") ... 8-12 78
COLUMBIA (11000 series) ... 3-5 79-80
COLUMBIA (13-0000 series) ... 3-4
COLUMBIA (18-0000 series) ... 3-4 81
COLUMBIA (38-0000 thru 0400) ... 3-4 84-86
COLUMBIA (42656 "Mixed Up Confusion") ... 500-1000 63
COLUMBIA (42856 "Blowin' in the Wind") ... 150-250 63
COLUMBIA (43242 "Subterranean Homesick Blues") ... 10-20 65
(Gray label.)
COLUMBIA (43242 "Subterranean Homesick Blues") ... 4-8 65
(Red label.)
COLUMBIA (43346 "Like a Rolling Stone") ... 4-8 65
COLUMBIA (43389 "Positively 4th Street") ... 10-20 65
(Gray label.)
COLUMBIA (43389 "Positively 4th Street") ... 4-8 65
(Red label.)
COLUMBIA (43477 "Can You Please Crawl Out Your Window") ... 10-12 65
COLUMBIA (43683 "I Want You") ... 4-8 66
COLUMBIA (43541 "One of Us Must Know") ... 8-12 66
COLUMBIA (43592 "Rainy Day Women #12 and 35") ... 4-8 66
COLUMBIA (43792 "Just Like a Woman") ... 4-8 66
COLUMBIA (44069 "Leopard-Skin Pill-Box Hat") ... 8-12 67
COLUMBIA (44826 "I Threw It All Away") ... 8-10 69
COLUMBIA (44926 "Lay Lady Lay") ... 4-8 69
COLUMBIA (45004 "Tonight I'll Be Staying Here with You") ... 8-10 69
COLUMBIA (45199 "Wigwam") ... 5-10 69
COLUMBIA (45409 "Watching the River Flow") ... 5-10 71
COLUMBIA (45516 "George Jackson") ... 8-10 71
COLUMBIA (45913 "Knockin' on Heaven's Door") ... 3-5 73
COLUMBIA (45982 "A Fool Such As I") ... 3-5 73
MCA (52811 "Band of the Hand") ... 4-6 86
Picture Sleeves
COLUMBIA (02510 "Heart of Mine") ... 4-8 81
COLUMBIA (04301 "Sweetheart Like You") ... 4-6 84
COLUMBIA (04933 "Tight Connection to My Heart") ... 4-6 85
COLUMBIA (10245 "Hurricane") ... 25-50 75
COLUMBIA (11235 "Slow Train") ... 5-10 80
COLUMBIA (43242 "Subterranean Homesick Blues") ... 300-500 65
(Promotional issue only.)
COLUMBIA (43242 "Subterranean Homesick Blues") ... 40-60 65
(Columbia "Hit Pack" picture sleeve.)
COLUMBIA (43389 "Positively 4th Street") ... 25-35 65
COLUMBIA (43683 "I Want You") ... 20-25 66
MCA (52811 "Band of the Hand") ... 4-6 86
Promotional Singles
ASYLUM ... 8-12 74
COLUMBIA (25 "All the Tired Horses") ... 30-40 70
COLUMBIA (1039 "If Not for You") ... 30-40 71
COLUMBIA (10106 "Tangled Up in Blue") ... 10-20 75
COLUMBIA (10245 "Hurricane") ... 15-20 75
COLUMBIA (10245 "Hurricane") ... 20-30 75
(Compact 33 Single.)
COLUMBIA (10298 "Mozambique") ... 8-10 75
COLUMBIA (10454 "Rita Mae") ... 10-20 77
COLUMBIA (10805 "Baby Stop Crying") ... 10-20 78
COLUMBIA (11000 series) ... 4-8 79-80
COLUMBIA (18-0000 series) ... 3-6 81
COLUMBIA (38-0000 thru 0400) ... 3-5 84-86
COLUMBIA (42656 "Mixed Up Confusion") ... 500-750 63
COLUMBIA (42856 "Blowin' in the Wind") ... 200-300 63
(Add $100 to $200 if accompanied by "Rebel with a Cause" letter-insert, which introduces Bob Dylan.)
COLUMBIA (43242 "Subterranean Homesick Blues") ... 40-60 65
(Black vinyl.)
COLUMBIA (43242 "Subterranean Homesick Blues") ... 75-125 65
(Red vinyl.)
COLUMBIA (43346 "Like a Rolling Stone") ... 40-60 65
(Black vinyl. Labels may show identification numbers "JZSP-110939/110940," but not selection number, 43346.)
COLUMBIA (43346 "Like a Rolling Stone") ... 75-125 65
(Red vinyl.)
COLUMBIA (43389 "Positively 4th Street") ... 30-40 65
(Black vinyl.)
COLUMBIA (43389 "Positively 4th Street") ... 75-125 65
(Colored vinyl.)
COLUMBIA (43389 "Positively 4th Street") ... 100-150 65
(Outtake promo. Has an alternate take of *Can You Please Crawl Out Your Window*.)
COLUMBIA (43477 "Can You Please Crawl Out Your Window") ... 40-60 65
COLUMBIA (43683 "I Want You") ... 30-45 66
(Black vinyl.)
COLUMBIA (43683 "I Want You") ... 75-125 66
(Red vinyl.)
COLUMBIA (43541 "One of Us Must Know") ... 40-55 66
COLUMBIA (43592 "Rainy Day Women #12 and 35") ... 30-40 66
COLUMBIA (43792 "Just Like a Woman") ... 30-40 66
(Black vinyl.)
COLUMBIA (43792 "Just Like a Woman") ... 50-100 66
(Red vinyl.)
COLUMBIA (44069 "Leopard-Skin Pill-Box Hat") ... 30-40 67
COLUMBIA (44826 "I Threw It All Away") ... 15-25 69
COLUMBIA (44926 "Lay Lady Lay") ... 15-25 69
COLUMBIA (45004 "Tonight I'll Be Staying Here with You") ... 15-25 69
COLUMBIA (45199 "Wigwam") ... 15-25 69
COLUMBIA (45409 "Watching the River Flow") ... 15-25 71
COLUMBIA (45516 "George Jackson") ... 15-25 71
COLUMBIA (45913 "Knockin' on Heaven's Door") ... 10-20 73
COLUMBIA (45982 "A Fool Such As I") ... 10-20 73
COLUMBIA (75606 "Blowin' in the Wind") ... 250-400 63
("Special Album Excerpt.")
EPs: 7-inch
COLUMBIA (319 "Step Lively") ... 200-300 65
COLUMBIA (9128 "Bringing It All Back Home") ... 200-300 65
(Juke box issue only. Includes title strips.)
COLUMBIA/PLAYBACK ... 75-100 73
(Promotional issue only. Contains four tracks by four different artists.)
LPs: 10/12-inch
ASYLUM (201 "Before the Flood") ... 10-15 74
ASYLUM (1003 "Planet Waves") ... 15-20 74
(Without cut corner.)
ASYLUM (1003 "Planet Waves") ... 8-10 74
(With cut corner.)
ASYLUM (EQ-1003 "Planet Waves") ... 15-20 74
(Quadrophonic.)
COLUMBIA (C2L-41 "Blonde on Blonde") ... 40-60 66
(Monaural. With "female photos" on inside of jacket.)
COLUMBIA (C2L-41 "Blonde on Blonde") ... 15-25 66
(Monaural. With Dylan photo replacing female photos.)
COLUMBIA (C2S-841 "Blonde on Blonde") ... 40-60 66
(Stereo. With "female photos" on inside of jacket.)
COLUMBIA (C2S-841 "Blonde on Blonde") ... 15-25 66
(Stereo. With Dylan photo replacing female photos.)
COLUMBIA (CL-1779 "Bob Dylan") ... 125-175 62
(Monaural. Red and black label with six Columbia "eye" boxes.)
COLUMBIA (CL-1779 "Bob Dylan") ... 20-30 62
(Monaural. Red label, without six Columbia "eye" boxes.)
COLUMBIA (CL-1986 "The Freewheelin' Bob Dylan") ... 10000-15000 63
(Monaural. With *Let Me Die in My Footsteps, Talkin' John Birch Society Blues, Gamblin' Willie's Dead Man's Hand,* and *Rocks and Gravel,* which may also be shown as *Solid Gravel.* We suggest verification of the above tracks by listening to the LP, rather than accepting the information printed on the label. In fact, some copies of the rare pressing have reissue labels. Identification numbers of this press are XLP-58717-1A and XLP-58718-1A.)
COLUMBIA (CL-1986 "The Freewheelin' Bob Dylan") ... 20-30 63
(Monaural. With the above tracks replaced by four others.)
COLUMBIA (CL-2105 "The Times They Are A-Changin' ") ... 20-30 64
(Monaural.)
COLUMBIA (CL-2193 "Another Side of Bob Dylan") ... 15-20 64
(Monaural.)
COLUMBIA (CL-2328 "Bringin' It All Back Home") ... 15-25 65
(Monaural.)
COLUMBIA (CL-2389 "Highway 61 Revisited") ... 150-200 65
(Monaural. With alternate take of *From a Buick 6.* The alternate take begins with a harmonica riff. This pressing has a "-1" at the end of the identification number, stamped in the vinyl trailoff.)
COLUMBIA (CL-2389 "Highway 61 Revisited") ... 10-15 65
(Monaural.)
COLUMBIA (KCL-2663 "Bob Dylan's Greatest Hits") ... 15-25 67
(Monaural.)
COLUMBIA (CL-2804 "John Wesley Harding") ... 60-100 68
(Monaural.)
COLUMBIA (CS-8579 "Bob Dylan") ... 150-200 62
(Stereo. Red and black label with six Columbia "eye" boxes.)
COLUMBIA (CS-8579 "Bob Dylan") ... 25-40 62
(Stereo. Red label, without six Columbia "eye" boxes. Some—perhaps all—Canadian pressings fail to list *Don't Think Twice, It's Alright* on the back cover, though the song is on the disc—Side 2, Track 1.)
COLUMBIA (PC-8579 "Bob Dylan") ... 5-10
COLUMBIA (CS-8786 "The Freewheelin' Bob Dylan") ... 20-30 63
(Stereo.)
COLUMBIA (PC-8786 "The Freewheelin' Bob Dylan") ... 5-10
COLUMBIA (CS-8905 "The Times They Are A-Changin' ") ... 20-30 64
(Stereo.)
COLUMBIA (CS-8993 "Another Side of Bob Dylan") ... 15-25 64
(Stereo.)
COLUMBIA (CS-9128 "Bringin' It All Back Home") ... 15-25 65
(Stereo.)
COLUMBIA (PC-9128 "Bringin' It All Back Home") ... 5-10 70s
COLUMBIA (CS-9189 "Highway 61 Revisited") ... 100-150 65
(Stereo. With alternate take of *From a Buick 6.* The alternate take begins with a harmonica riff. This pressing has a "-1" at the end of the identification number, stamped in the vinyl trailoff.)
COLUMBIA (CS-9189 "Highway 61 Revisited") ... 10-20 65
(Stereo.)
COLUMBIA (KCS-9463 "Bob Dylan's Greatest Hits") ... 15-25 67
(Stereo.)
COLUMBIA (CS-9604 "John Wesley Harding") ... 20-30 68
(Stereo.)
COLUMBIA (KCS-9825 "Nashville Skyline") ... 8-12 69
COLUMBIA (C2X-30050 "Self Portrait") ... 50-60 70
(With "360-Degree Stereo" at bottom of label.)
COLUMBIA (C2X-30050 "Self Portrait") ... 10-15 70
(Without "360-Degree Stereo" at bottom of label.)
COLUMBIA (KC-30290 "New Morning") ... 8-10 70
COLUMBIA (KC-31120 "Greatest Hits, Vol. 2") ... 10-12 71
COLUMBIA (KC-32460 "Pat Garrett and Billy the Kid") ... 8-10 73
(Soundtrack.)
COLUMBIA (KC-32747 "Dylan") ... 8-10 73
COLUMBIA (CQ-32872 "Nashville Skyline") ... 40-60 74
(Quadrophonic.)
COLUMBIA (PC-33235 "Blood on the Tracks") ... 25-35 75
(With mural pictured on the back cover.)
COLUMBIA (PC-33235 "Blood on the Tracks") ... 8-12 75
(With liner notes on the back cover.)
COLUMBIA (PC2-33682 "The Basement Tapes") ... 10-12 75
COLUMBIA (PC-33893 "Desire") ... 8-10 76
COLUMBIA (PCQ-33893 "Desire") ... 25-35 76
(Quadrophonic.)
COLUMBIA (PC-34349 "Hard Rain") ... 8-10 76
COLUMBIA (JC-35453 "Street Legal") ... 8-10 78
COLUMBIA (PC2-36067 "Bob Dylan at Budokan") ... 8-10 79
COLUMBIA (FC-36120 "Slow Train Comin' ") ... 8-10 79
COLUMBIA (FC-36553 "Saved") ... 8-10 80
COLUMBIA (FC-37496 "Shot of Love") ... 8-10 81
COLUMBIA (PC-38819 "Infidels") ... 8-10 83
COLUMBIA (C5X-38830 "Biograph") ... 20-30 85
(Boxed, five-disc set. includes 36-page booklet.)
COLUMBIA (FC-39944 "Real Live") ... 5-10 84
COLUMBIA (FC-40110 "Empire Burlesque") ... 5-10 85
COLUMBIA (OC-40439 "Knocked Out Loaded") ... 5-10 86
COLUMBIA (OC-40957 "Down in the Groove") ... 5-10 88
COLUMBIA (HC-43235 "Blood on the Tracks") ... 20-30 83
(Half-speed mastered.)
COLUMBIA (45281 "Oh Mercy") ... 5-10 89
COLUMBIA (46794 "Under the Red Sky") ... 5-10 90
COLUMBIA (47382 "The Bootleg Series Volumes 1 - 3") ... 15-20 89
COLUMBIA (HC-49825 "Nashville Skyline") ... 20-30 81
(Half-speed mastered.)
FOLKWAYS (5322 "Bob Dylan Vs. A.J. Weberman") ... 100-175
ISLAND (1 "Before the Flood") ... 25-30 74
MFSL (114 "The Times They Are A-Changing") ... 10-15
Promotional LPs
ASYLUM (201 "Before the Flood") ... 25-40 74
ASYLUM (1003 "Planet Waves") ... 25-40 74
COLUMBIA (422 "Renaldo and Clara") ... 25-35 76
(Soundtrack.)
COLUMBIA (798 "Saved") ... 25-35 80
COLUMBIA (1259 "Dylan London Interview") ... 25-35 80
COLUMBIA (1263 "Shot of Love") ... 25-35 81
COLUMBIA (1471 "Electric Lunch") ... 15-25 83
COLUMBIA (1770 "Infidels") ... 10-20 83
COLUMBIA (C2L-41 "Blonde on Blonde") ... 60-75 66
(Monaural. With "female photos" on inside of jacket.)
COLUMBIA (C2S-841 "Blonde on Blonde") ... 60-75 66
(Stereo. With "female photos" on inside of jacket.)
COLUMBIA (CL-1779 "Bob Dylan") ... 200-300 62
(Monaural.)
COLUMBIA (CL-1986 "The Freewheelin' Bob Dylan") ... 10000-15000 63
(Monaural. With *Let Me Die in My Footsteps, Talkin' John Birch Society Blues, Gamblin' Willie's Dead Man's Hand,* and *Rocks and Gravel,* which may also be shown as *Solid Gravel.* We suggest verification of the above tracks by listening to the LP, rather than accepting the information printed on the label. In fact, some copies of the rare pressing have reissue labels. Identification numbers of this press are XLP-58717-1A and XLP-58718-1A.)
COLUMBIA (CL-1986 "The Freewheelin' Bob Dylan") ... 75-100 63
(Monaural. With the above tracks replaced by four others.)
COLUMBIA (CL-2105 "The Times They Are A-Changin' ") ... 75-100 64
COLUMBIA (CL-2193 "Another Side of Bob Dylan") ... 60-75 64
(Monaural.)
COLUMBIA (CL-2328 "Bringin' It All Back Home") ... 60-75 65
(Monaural.)
COLUMBIA (CL-2389 "Highway 61 Revisited") ... 60-75 65
(Monaural.)
COLUMBIA (KCL-2663 "Bob Dylan's Greatest Hits") ... 60-75 67
(Monaural.)
COLUMBIA (CL-2804 "John Wesley Harding") ... 50-60 68
(Monaural.)
COLUMBIA (CS-8579 "Bob Dylan") ... 200-300 62
(Stereo.)
COLUMBIA (CS-8786 "The Freewheelin' Bob Dylan") ... 75-100 63
(Stereo.)
COLUMBIA (CS-8905 "The Times They Are A-Changin' ") ... 75-100 64
(Stereo.)
COLUMBIA (CS-8993 "Another Side of Bob Dylan") ... 60-75 64
(Stereo.)
COLUMBIA (CS-9128 "Bringin' It All Back Home") ... 60-75 65
(Stereo.)
COLUMBIA (CS-9189 "Highway 61 Revisited") ... 60-75 65
(Stereo.)
COLUMBIA (KCS-9463 "Bob Dylan's Greatest Hits") ... 60-75 67
(Stereo.)
COLUMBIA (KCS-9825 "Nashville Skyline") ... 50-60 69
COLUMBIA (30050 "Self Portrait") ... 50-60 70
COLUMBIA (31120 "Greatest Hits Vol. 2") ... 10-20 71
COLUMBIA (32460 "Pat Garrett and Billy the Kid") ... 15-25 73
(Soundtrack.)
COLUMBIA (32747 "Dylan") ... 10-15 73
COLUMBIA (33235 "Blood on the Tracks") ... 20-25 75
COLUMBIA (33682 "The Basement Tapes") ... 10-15 75
COLUMBIA (33893 "Desire") ... 10-15 76
COLUMBIA (34349 "Hard Rain") ... 10-15 76
COLUMBIA (35453 "Street Legal") ... 10-15 78
(With programmer's timing strip.)

COLUMBIA (36067 "Bob Dylan at Budokan") 10-20 79
COLUMBIA (36120 "Slow Train Comin' ") 10-15 79
COLUMBIA (36553 "Saved") 10-15 80
COLUMBIA (37496 "Shot of Love") 10-15 81
COLUMBIA (38819 "Infidels") 10-15 83
COLUMBIA (39944 "Real Live") 10-15 84
COLUMBIA (40110 "Empire Burlesque") 10-15 85
COLUMBIA (40439 "Knocked Out Loaded") 10-15 86
COLUMBIA (43235 "Blood on the Tracks") 25-50 83
(Half-speed mastered.)
COLUMBIA (49825 "Nashville Skyline") 25-35 81
(Half-speed mastered.)
COLUMBIA (67000 "Unplugged") 10-15 90s
FOLKWAYS (5322 "Bob Dylan Vs. A.J. Weberman") 75-100
ISLAND (1 "Before the Flood") 25-35 74
MFSL (114 "The Times They Are A-Changin' ") 20-30 80s
Session: Michael Bloomfield; Al Kooper; Paul Griffin; Bobby Gregg; Charlie McCoy; Frank Owens; Russ Savakus; Harvey Goldstein.
Also see BAND
Also see BELAFONTE, Harry
Also see BLOOMFIELD, Mike
Also see GREGG, Bobby
Also see HARRISON, George
Also see HESTER, Carolyn
Also see KOOPER, Al
Also see McCOY, Charlie
Also see RIVERA, Scarlet
Also see SAHM, Doug
Also see SWEATHOG / Free Movement / Bob Dylan / Edgar Winter's White Trash
Also see THREE KINGS AND A QUEEN
Also see TRAVELING WILBURYS
Also see U.S.A. for AFRICA

DYLAN, Bob, & Grateful Dead — *LP '89*
LPs: 10/12-inch
COLUMBIA (45056 "Dylan and the Dead") 5-10 89
Also see GRATEFUL DEAD

DYLAN, Bob, & Heartbreakers / Michael Rubini
Singles: 7-inch
MCA 3-4 86
Also see DYLAN, Bob
Also see PETTY, Tom, & Heartbreakers

DYNAMIC BREAKERS — *R&B '85*
Singles: 12-inch
SUNNYVIEW 4-6 85
Singles: 7-inch
SUNNYVIEW 3-4 85

DYNAMIC CORVETTES — *R&B '75*
Singles: 7-inch
ABET 5-10 75
RU JAC 3-5

DYNAMIC DISCHORDS
Singles: 7-inch
IGL (150 "Passageway to Your Heart") 40-60 67
Also see DISCHORDS

DYNAMIC DRIFTERS
Singles: 7-inch
BANGAR 10-20 60s
Picture Sleeves
BANGAR 25-35 60s

DYNAMIC 5
Singles: 7-inch
CHANT 5-10

DYNAMIC FIVE
LPs: 10/12-inch
U.A. 5-10 78

DYNAMIC HEARTBEATS
Singles: 7-inch
P.S. (1781 "Danger") 10-20 60s

DYNAMIC HURSMEN
Singles: 7-inch
IGL (135 "Love Is a Beautiful Thing") 10-20 67

DYNAMIC NUTONES
Singles: 7-inch
SIMS 15-20 67

DYNAMIC SOUL SUPERIORS
LPs: 10/12-inch
SAVOY 5-10 78

DYNAMIC SUPERIORS — *P&R/R&B '74*
Singles: 12-inch
MOTOWN 4-6 77
Singles: 7-inch
MOTOWN 3-5 74-77
LPs: 10/12-inch
MOTOWN 8-10 74-77
Members: Tony Washington; Maurice Washington; Michael McCalpin; George Spann; George Peterback.

DYNAMIC TINTS
Singles: 7-inch
TWINIGHT (123 "Package of Love") 15-25 69
TWINIGHT (145 "Falling in Love") 15-25 71

DYNAMIC UPSETTERS
Singles: 7-inch
CPI 3-4 82

DYNAMICS
Singles: 7-inch
CINDY (3005 "Gone Is My Love") 50-100 57

DYNAMICS
(With the Hutch Davie Orchestra)
Singles: 7-inch
DYNAMIC SOUND (504 "The Girl I Met Last Night") 15-25 59

DYNAMICS
(Dynamics with Jimmy Hanna)
Singles: 7-inch
BOLO 8-15 62-65
GUARANTEED (201 "Aces Up") 15-25 59
JERDEN 5-10 66
PENGUIN (1005 "Aces Up") 30-50 59
(First issue.)
PANORAMA 5-10 67
SEAFAIR 10-20 60-62
LPs: 10/12-inch
BOLO (8001 "The Dynamics with Jimmy Hanna") 25-35 64
Members (1959-'60): Terry Afdem; Dave Williams; Larry Smith; Tom Larson; Jeff Afdem; Pete Borg. (1961-'64): Terry Afdem; Ron Woods; Mark Doubleday; Harry Wilson; Pete Borg; Larry Coryell; Gary Snyder; Jimmy Hanna; Randi Green.
Also see CHANTEURS
Also see ELEVENTH HOUSE
Also see GALLAHADS
Also see HANNA, Jimmy
Also see SPRINGFIELD RIFLE

DYNAMICS
(Dynamic's)
Singles: 7-inch
ARC (4450 "Enchanted Love") 35-50 59
CAPRI (104 "No One But You") 200-300 59
(First issue.)
DELTA (1002 "Blue Moon") 20-40 59
IMPALA (501 "Moonlight") 75-125 58
LAVERE (186 "Wrap Your Troubles in Dreams") 15-25 61
LIBAN (1006 "Blind Date") 50-100 62
LIBERTY (55628 "Chapel on a Hill") 25-35 63
REPRISE (20183 "So Fine") 10-15 63
SEECO (6008 "Moonlight") 25-50 59
WARNER RECORDS (1016 "A Hundred Million Lies") 50-100 59

DYNAMICS
(Zerben R. Hicks & the Dynamics; with Royal Playboys)
Singles: 7-inch
DYNAMIC ("Darling") 250-300 62
(No selection number used. Reissued as by the "Dynamo's.")
DYNAMIC (109 "Don't Be Late") 25-50 59
(We're not sure if 109 is the selection number or an identification number.)
DYNAMIC (579 "Dream Girl") 50-75 62
(Identification number shown since no selection number is used.)
DYNAMIC (1001 "Don't Leave Me") 35-55 59
DYNAMIC (1002 "Delsinia") 25-50 59
RCA (9084 "Love Me") 30-40 67
RCA (9278 "You Make Me Feel Good") 25-50 67
TOP TEN (100 "Yes I Love You Baby") 50-75 60s
TOP TEN (9409 "Love to a Guy") 40-60 60s
WINGATE (18 "Bingo") 25-50 66
Also see DRAMATICS

DYNAMICS
Singles: 7-inch
FARRALL (694 "Later On") 15-20 60

DYNAMICS
Singles: 7-inch
DECCA 5-10 60-62
DOUGLAS 15-25 61

DYNAMICS
Singles: 7-inch
CUCA (1081 "Come Go with Me") 15-25 62
Members: Bobby Price; Don Anderson; Dick Ford; John Thompson; Jack Rygg; John Murray; Dennis Murphy.
Also see PRICE, Bobby, & Dynamics

DYNAMICS
Singles: 7-inch
DO-KAY-LO (101 "Oh, Night of Nights") 20-30 63

DYNAMICS — *P&R/R&B '63*
Singles: 7-inch
BIG TOP 10-15 63-64
BLACK GOLD 4-8 73-74
COTILLION 5-10 68-69
LPs: 10/12-inch
BLACK GOLD 8-10 73
COTILLION 12-15 69
Members: Sam Stevenson; Zeke Harris; Fred Baker; George White.

DYNAMICS
Singles: 7-inch
U.S.A. (769 "Summertime") 15-20 64
Members: Norman Welch; Danny Michel; Roger Maltz; Peter Logan.

DYNAMICS Featuring Tony Maresco
(Anthony & the Sophmores)
Singles: 7-inch
HERALD (569 "Forever") 200-400 61
Also see ANTHONY & SOPHMORES
Also see TONY & TWILIGHTS

DYNAMITE, Johnny
Singles: 7-inch
MINARET (141 "The Night the Angels Cried") 8-12 68

DYNAMITES
Singles: 7-inch
ELBRIDGE (92261 "92261 "Easy Pickin") 10-20 61

DYNAMITES
Singles: 7-inch
PAY (209 "Let's Try") 15-25 60s
PAY (210 "Don't Leave Me This Way") 15-25 60s

DYNAMO, Skinny
Singles: 78 rpm
EXCELLO 10-20 56
Singles: 7-inch
EXCELLO (2097 "So Long, So Long") 15-25 56

DYNAMOS
(Dynamo's)
Singles: 7-inch
AZUZA (1002 "Darling") 100-150 64
(First issued as by the Dynamics.)

DYNAMOS
Singles: 7-inch
CUB 10-15 61
PRESS (101 "Teen Blues") 10-20 61

DYNAMOS
Singles: 7-inch
DYNAMOS 5-10

DYNA-SORES — *P&R '60*
Singles: 7-inch
RENDEZVOUS 8-12 60
Member: Jimmy Norman.
Also see NORMAN, Jimmy

DYNASTY
Singles: 7-inch
ROYAL COURT (262 "I've Gotta Shout") 100-125 66
WESTCHESTER (1155 "Flying on the Ground Is Wrong") 12-18 68
Members: Jack Casper; Mark Casper; Ken Clark; Fred Anderson; Dan Egnash; Mike Polaski.

DYNASTY — *R&B '79*
Singles: 7-inch
SOLAR 3-4 79-88
LPs: 10/12-inch
SOLAR 5-10 79-82
Members: Kevin Spencer; Nidra Beard; Linda Carriere; Leon Sylvers.
Also see DE BLANK
Also see STARFIRE
Also see SYLVERS

DYNASTY FIVE
Singles: 7-inch
BUFF 10-15

DYNASTYS
(Dynasty's)
Singles: 7-inch
COULEE (108 "Go Gorilla") 25-35 64
(Black vinyl.)
COULEE (108 "Go Gorilla") 30-40 64
(Colored vinyl.)
FAN JR (9347 "I'll Be Forever Loving You") 100-200 64
(Identification number shown since no selection number is used.)
JERDEN (783 "It's Been a Long Long Time") 10-20 66

DYNATONES
Singles: 7-inch
BOMARC (300 "Steel Guitar Rag") 25-50 58
BOMARC (303 "Steel Guitar Rag") 20-30 59
BOMARC (305 "Moon Shot") 20-30 59
QUALITY ("Steel Guitar Rag") 20-30 59

DYNATONES — *P&R/R&B '66*
Singles: 7-inch
HBR 4-8 66
ST. CLAIR 8-10 66
LPs: 10/12-inch
HBR 20-25 66

DYNATONES
Singles: 7-inch
ALTO 4-8 66

DYNELL, Johnny, & New York 88 — *D&D '83*
Singles: 12-inch
ACME 4-6 83-84

DYNELS
(Dynells)
Singles: 7-inch
ATCO (6638 "Call On Me") 10-15 68
BLUEBERRY 5-10 68
DOT 5-10 62
NATURAL 10-20 64

DYNETTES
Singles: 7-inch
CONSTELLATION 4-8 65

DYNOMITERS
Singles: 7-inch
EPIC 3-5 76

DYSFUNCTION
LPs: 10/12-inch
METALSTORM (8816 "The $235,000 Demo") 10-20 88
(Picture disc. 500 made.)

DYSON, Clifton — *R&B '82*
Singles: 12-inch
MOTOWN 4-8 79
Singles: 7-inch
MOTOWN 3-4 79
NETWORK 3-4 82
LPs: 10/12-inch
AFTER HOURS 5-10 82
NETWORK 5-10 82

DYSON, Joe, & His Orchestra
(With Luther Hill)
Singles: 78 rpm
ACE (531 "Marie") 10-15 57
CHAMPION (102 "Merc-O-Matic Boogie") 15-25 49
Singles: 7-inch
ACE (531 "Marie") 10-15 57

DYSON, Ronnie — *P&R/R&B/LP '70*
Singles: 12-inch
COTILLION 4-6 83
Singles: 7-inch
COLUMBIA 3-5 69-78
COTILLION 3-4 82-83
Picture Sleeves
COLUMBIA 3-5 73-75
LPs: 10/12-inch
COLUMBIA 8-10 70-79
COTILLION 5-10 82-83

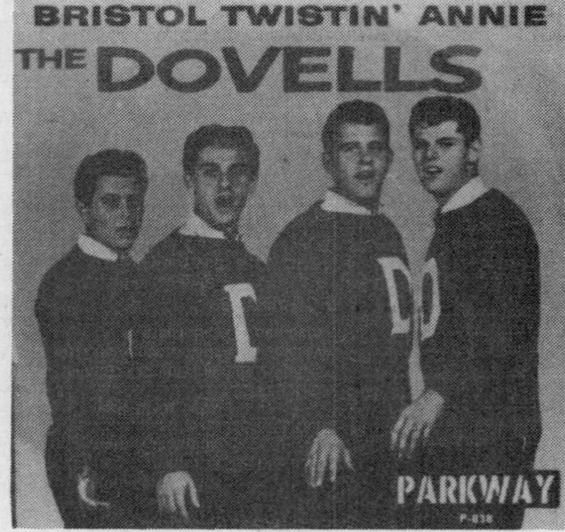

THE DRIFTERS
SATURDAY NIGHT AT THE MOVIES
SPANISH LACE

SANDRA DEE
Dear Johnny
When I Fall In Love
DECCA

Thor
T 104
Time: 2:05
45 RPM
ZTSP 60438
PROMOTIONAL RECORD
NOT FOR SALE
ROUGH AND BOLD
(Andy Dio)
ANDY DIO
and The Hi-Ways

BOXER
PROMOTIONAL COPY
B-101-A
Time 2:48
NOT FOR SALE
I BEEN WAITING
(Mark Hurley)
FLOYD DIXON
Prod. by Riggins and Dixon
1050 W. 49th St.

45 RPM
ATCO
STEREO
VOCAL
SD-58C-459
SD-45-6133
Pub., Rumbalero,-
Fern-Progressive, BMI
Time: 1:56
PLAIN JANE
(Pomus-Shuman)
BOBBY DARIN
Division of ATLANTIC RECORDS, New York, N.Y.

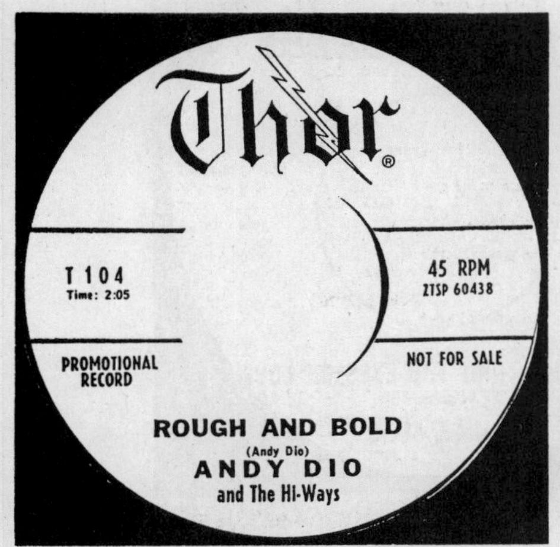

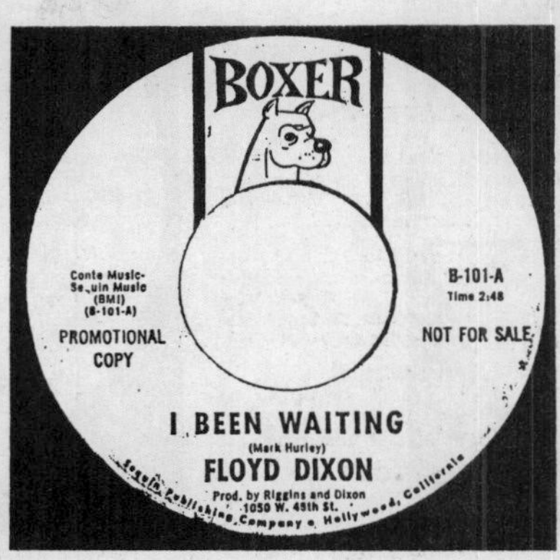

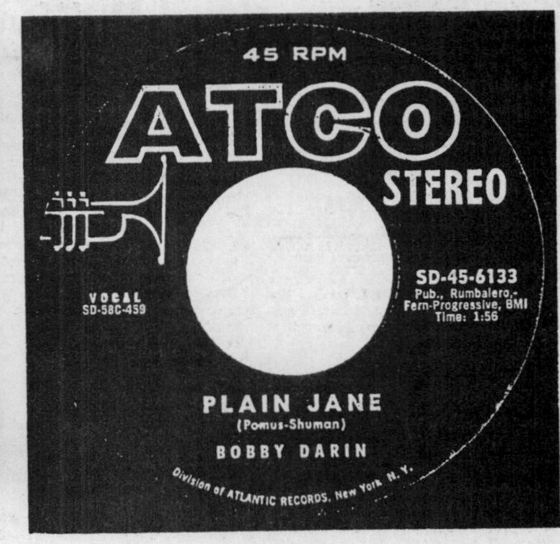

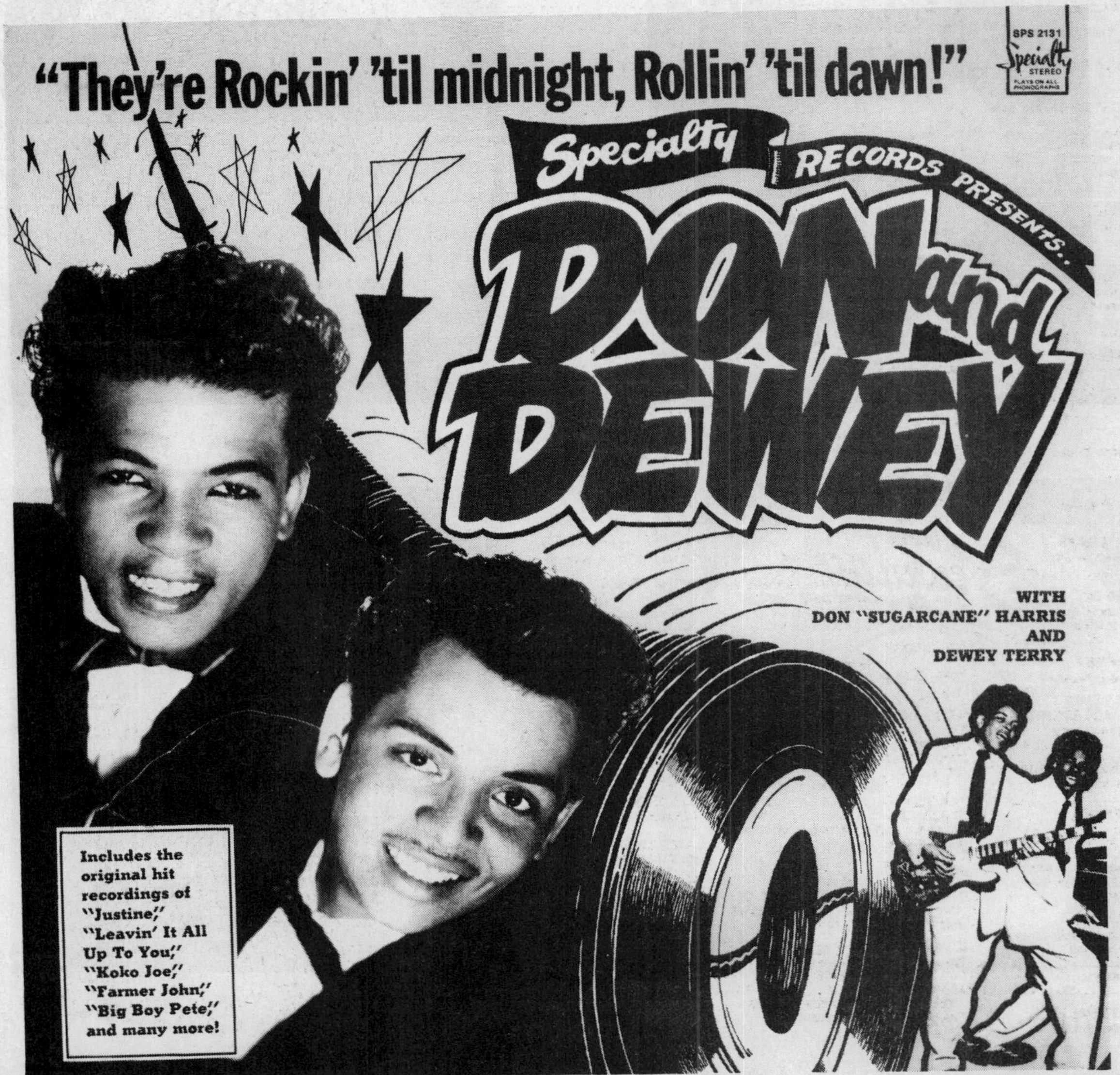

"They're Rockin' 'til midnight, Rollin' 'til dawn!"
SPS 2131
Specialty
STEREO
Specialty RECORDS PRESENTS..
DON and DEWEY
WITH
DON "SUGARCANE" HARRIS
AND
DEWEY TERRY
Includes the original hit recordings of "Justine," "Leavin' It All Up To You," "Koko Joe," "Farmer John," "Big Boy Pete," and many more!

20TH Century
GOTHAM RECORD CORP.
PHILADELPHIA, PENNA.
UNBREAKABLE
45 R.P.M.
Pub. Andrea Music
SESAC
RECORD NO.
TC1204
DMHC3
HOP SCOTCH!
(Russell)
DAISY MAE
& THE HEPCATS

Hip-Delic
314-A
© FISC MUSIC
B.M.I.
(H-D 314-ARKG)
3:30
Prod. by
TOM CROSS
for Hip-Delic
Prod. Inc.
LOOKING THRU THE EYES OF LOVE
(T. Cross-J. Ellis)
JIMMIE ELLIS

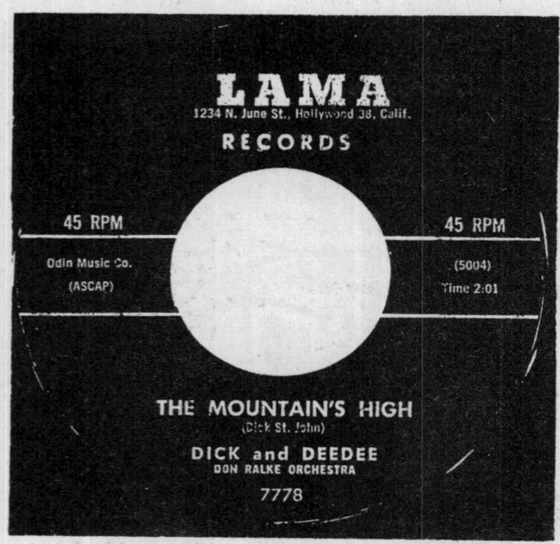
LAMA
1234 N. June St., Hollywood 38, Calif.
RECORDS
45 RPM
45 RPM
Odin Music Co.
(ASCAP)
(5004)
Time 2:01
THE MOUNTAIN'S HIGH
(Dick St. John)
DICK and DEEDEE
DON RALKE ORCHESTRA
7778

Herald
45 RPM
45 RPM
H-5000
Brunswick Music
BMI
POP
SERIES
Vocal Group
ALL THROUGH THE YEARS
(Tennyson-Laverne)
By The
DAY, DAWN, DUSK TRIO
Acc. By Chas. Laverne Orch.
H-1000

Starday
RECORDS
45-242
2441
Starrite-BMI
Vocal By
Link Davis
GRASSHOPPER ROCK
(Davis)
LINK DAVIS

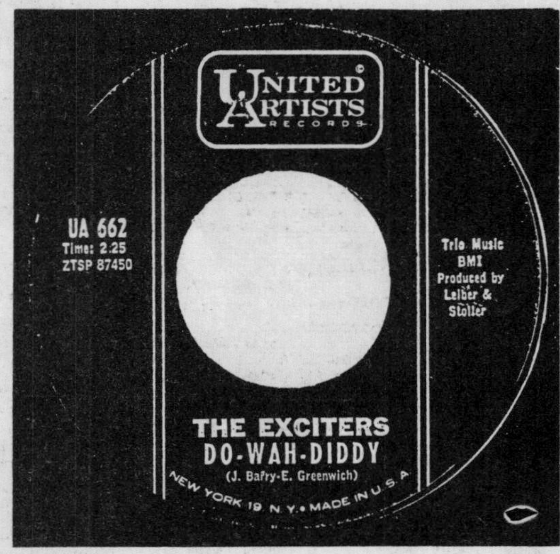
UNITED ARTISTS
RECORDS
UA 662
Time: 2:25
ZTSP 87450
Trio Music
BMI
Produced by
Leiber &
Stoller
THE EXCITERS
DO-WAH-DIDDY
(J. Barry-E. Greenwich)
NEW YORK 19 N. Y. • MADE IN U.S.A.

E

E., Sheila: see SHEILA E.

E PLURIBUS UNAM
Singles: 7-inch
ABC 3-6 70s

EBN/OZN *D&D '83*
(EBN-OZN)
Singles: 12-inch
ELEKTRA 4-6 83-84
Singles: 7-inch
ELEKTRA 3-4 84
LPs: 10/12-inch
ELEKTRA 5-10 84
Members: Ebn; Ozn.

EBO *R&B '85*
Singles: 12-inch
DOMINO 4-6 85
Singles: 7-inch
DOMINO 3-4 85

ED O.G. & Da Bulldogs
LPs: 10/12-inch
PWL/MERCURY 5-8 91

E.G., Rob
Singles: 7-inch
BIGTOP (3154 "Stage to Cimmaron") 10-20 63

E*I*E*I*O
LPs: 10/12-inch
FRONTIER 5-8 86-88
Members: Steve Summers; Mike Hoffmann; Rob Harding; Richard Szeluga; Tommy Ciaccio; Scott Gorsuch.

E.J. & ECHOES
Singles: 7-inch
DIAMOND JIM (8787 "Put a Smile on Your Face") 15-25 60s
DIAMOND JIM (8789 "If You Just Love Me") 15-25 60s
RANGER (410 "Say You're Mine") . 15-25 60s

E.J.'s LTD.
Singles: 7-inch
BACK BEAT 3-6 69

ELO: see ELECTRIC LIGHT ORCHESTRA

EME *C&W '81*
Singles: 7-inch
EPI 3-5 81

EMF *LP '91*
LPs: 10/12-inch
EMI 5-8 91

E.P.M.
Singles: 7-inch
COTILLION 3-4 84
LPs: 10/12-inch
COTILLION 5-10 84

EPMD *R&B/LP '88*
LPs: 10/12-inch
FRESH 5-8 88-89
RAL/COLUMBIA 5-8 91
Members: Erick Sermon; Parrish Smith.

EQ
Singles: 7-inch
ATLANTIC 3-4 85
Singles: 12-inch
ATLANTIC 4-6 86

ESB
Singles: 7-inch
IN ARTS (102 "Mushroom People") 30-40 67
Members: George Caldwell; Richard Fortunato; Pat Burke; Steve Lagana.

E.S.P.
Singles: 7-inch
RED ROOSTER 3-4 83

ET: see TOWNS, Eddie

ETC BAND: see CONLEY, Earl Thomas

E.U. *R&B '88*
(Experience Unlimited)
Singles: 7-inch
ISLAND 3-4 86
MANHATTAN 3-4 88
Picture Sleeves
MANHATTAN 3-4 88
LPs: 10/12-inch
ISLAND 5-10 86
VIRGIN 5-8 89

E.W.B. *C&W '81*
Singles: 7-inch
PAID 3-5 81

EADY, Ernestine
Singles: 7-inch
JUNIOR 10-15 63-65

EAGER, Brenda Lee *R&B '73*
(With the Peaches)
Singles: 12-inch
PRIVATE I 4-6 84
Singles: 7-inch
MERCURY 3-5 72-74
PLAYBOY 3-5 75
PRIVATE I 3-4 84
Also see BUTLER, Jerry, & Brenda Lee Eager

EAGER, Jimmy, & His Trio
(Tampa Red)
Singles: 78 rpm
SABRE 50-75 53
Singles: 7-inch
SABRE (100 "Please Mr. Doctor") 100-150 53
Also see TAMPA RED

EAGER, Johnny
Singles: 7-inch
DESIGN (818 "Join Me Baby") 35-50 58
END 8-12 59

EAGER, Vince
LPs: 10/12-inch
AVENUE 10-15

EAGLE
(Beacon Street Union)
Singles: 7-inch
JANUS 3-6 70
LPs: 10/12-inch
JANUS 10-20 70
Also see BEACON STREET UNION

EAGLE, Bill
Singles: 7-inch
REATA PASS 4-8

EAGLES
Singles: 78 rpm
MERCURY 8-12 54
PREP 5-10 57
Singles: 7-inch
MERCURY (70391 "Trying to Get to You") 25-35 54
MERCURY (70464 "Such a Fool") 25-35 54
MERCURY (70524 "What a Crazy Feeling") 25-35 54
PREP (118 "Kiss Them for Me") 10-15 57

EAGLES
Singles: 7-inch
SMASH (1837 "Stalactite") 5-10 63
W.B. 4-8 65

EAGLES *P&R/LP '72*
Singles: 12-inch
ASYLUM (11402 "Please Come Home for Christmas & Funky New Year") 5-10 78
(Promotional issue only.)
Singles: 7-inch
ASYLUM 3-5 72-80
FULL MOON 3-4 81
Picture Sleeves
ASYLUM 3-5 78
LPs: 10/12-inch
ASYLUM 8-12 72-82
MFSL (126 "Hotel California") 25-35 84
Members: Don Felder; Glenn Frey; Don Henley; Randy Meisner; Timothy B. Schmit; Joe Walsh; Bernie Leadon.
Also see BOLD
Also see FELDER, Don
Also see FREY, Glenn
Also see HENLEY, Don
Also see LEADON, Bernie
Also see LEE, Johnny / Eagles
Also see MEISNER, Randy
Also see NEWMAN, Randy
Also see POCO
Also see RONSTADT, Linda
Also see SCHMIT, Timothy B.
Also see SIMMONS, Patrick
Also see VITALE, Joe
Also see WALSH, Joe

EAGLIN, Ford
Singles: 7-inch
IMPERIAL 5-10 60-63
Also see EAGLIN, Snooks

EAGLIN, Snooks
(Ford Eaglin; Blind Snooks Eaglin)
LPs: 10/12-inch
FANTASY 10-12 73
FOLKWAYS 20-25 59
GNP 5-10 79
PRESTIGE BLUESVILLE 20-25 62
Also see EAGLIN, Ford
Also see WILLIAMS, Robert Pete, & Snooks Eaglin

EARDANCE
LPs: 10/12-inch
TOUCH 5-10 83

EARGAZM
LPs: 10/12-inch
EARRESISTIBLE 15-20 81
Members: Peter Parkhurst; Roger Anderson; David Thomas Stanton; K. Paul Wichterman-West; Mark Killion; Randal Nelson.

EARL, Handsome: see HANDSOME EARL

EARL, Johnny
Singles: 7-inch
GYRO (102 "Pull It Man") 35-50

EARL, Kenny *C&W '81*
Singles: 7-inch
KARI 3-5 81
KIK 3-6 81
Also see WOLFPACK

EARL, Little Billy
Singles: 7-inch
GOLDBAND 15-25 58

EARL, Robert
Singles: 7-inch
CAROL (103 "Say You'll Be Mine") 10-20

EARL & DUKES
Singles: 7-inch
DOUBLE H 4-8 64

EARL OF CRICKLEWOOD
Singles: 7-inch
PAGE ONE 3-6 69

EARLAND, Charles *LP '70*
(Charles Earland's Odyssey; Charlie Earland Jr.)
Singles: 7-inch
COLUMBIA 3-4 81-82
MERCURY 3-5 76
PRESTIGE 3-5 70-74
QUAKER TOWN 4-8 64
LPs: 10/12-inch
COLUMBIA 5-10 80
MERCURY 5-10 76-78
MUSE 5-10 80
PRESTIGE 5-10 70-75
RARE BIRD 5-10 71
TRIP 5-10 73

EARLE, Billy
(With Jerry Tucker's Orchestra)
Singles: 7-inch
NOLTA 4-8 62

EARLE, Steve *C&W '83*
(With the Dukes)
Singles: 12-inch
MCA 4-6 86
Singles: 7-inch
EPIC 3-4 83-85
MCA 3-4 86-90
UNI 3-4 88
Picture Sleeves
EPIC 3-4 84
EPs: 7-inch
LSI 5-10 82
LPs: 10/12-inch
MCA 5-10 86-90
UNI 5-8 88

EARLES
Singles: 7-inch
TEE TI (802 "What Would Your Daddy Say") 20-25

EARLINGTON, Lyn
Singles: 7-inch
JAMIE (1259 "Don't Make My Heart Bleed") 5-10 63
LE MONDE1501 "Love Drops") 15-25 62
SOUTHERN SOUND 8-12 61

EARL-JEAN *P&R '64*
(Earl Jean McCree)
Singles: 7-inch
COLPIX 4-8 64
Also see COOKIES
Also see KING, Ben E.
Also see RAELETTES

EARLS
Singles: 78 rpm
GEM (221 "Believe Me My Love") 100-200 54
Singles: 7-inch
GEM (221 "Believe Me My Love") 300-500 54
GEM (227 "My Marie") 8-12

EARLS *P&R '62*
(Larry Chance & the Earls)
Singles: 12-inch
WOODBURY 10-15 76-77
Singles: 7-inch
ABC 5-10 68
ATLANTIC 3-5
BARRY 4-8 63
CLIFTON (47 "Dreams Come True") 4-8 74
COLLECTABLES 3-4 80s
COLUMBIA 3-5 75
HARVEY (100 "Teenager's Dream") 8-12 75
MEMORIES 3-5
MR. "G" 5-10 67
OLD TOWN (1130 "Remember Then") 40-60 62
(Blue label. Publisher credit is "January Music." Artist credit is in serif style typeface [i.e. THE EARLS], title is sans-serif [REMEMBER THEN.)
OLD TOWN (1130 "Remember Then") 25-50 62
(Blue label. Publisher credit is "Maureen Music." Both title & artist credit is sans-serif.)
OLD TOWN (1130 "Remember Then") 15-25 63
(Multi-color label.)
OLD TOWN (1133 "Never") 25-50 63
(Blue label.)
OLD TOWN (1133 "Never") 15-25 63
(Multi-color label.)
OLD TOWN (1141 "Look My Way") 15-25 63
OLD TOWN (1145 "Kissin' ") 15-25 63
OLD TOWN (1149 "I Believe") 25-50 63
(Blue label.)
OLD TOWN (1149 "I Believe") 15-25 63
(Multi-color label.)
OLD TOWN (1169 "Ask Anybody") 15-25 64
OLD TOWN (1181 "Remember Me Baby") 30-50 65
(Promotional issue only.)
OLD TOWN (1182 "Remember Me Baby") 15-25 65
ROADHOUSE (1021 "I'm All Alone") 4-6
(Colored vinyl.)
ROME (101 "Life Is But a Dream"/"It's You") 100-150 61
ROME (101 "Life Is But a Dream"/"Without You") 40-50 61
(Note different flip side title.)
ROME (102 "Lookin' for My Baby") 30-50 61
ROME (112 "Little Boy and Girl") 3-5 76
ROME (114 "All Through Our Teens") 5-10 76
(Black vinyl.)
ROME (114 "All Through Our Teens") 10-15 76
(Colored vinyl.)
ROME (5117 "My Heart's Desire") 20-40 62
(Black vinyl.)
WOODBURY (101 "Tonight") 8-10 77
EPs: 7-inch
CRYSTAL BALL 5-10
LPs: 10/12-inch
CHANCE (1001 "Today") 8-12 83
CRYSTAL BALL 8-10 82
OLD TOWN (104 "Remember Me Baby") 200-400 63
(Counterfeits exist but can be identified by their 1/2-inch vinyl trail-off and poor fidelity. Originals have a 3/4-inch trail-off and excellent fidelity.)
RAINBOW (1001 "Live") 8-12 87
WOODBURY (104 "Remember Me Baby") 15-20 76
(Red label.)
WOODBURY (104 "Remember Me Baby") 10-15 77
(Green and brown label.)
Members: Larry Chance; Robert Del Din; Jack Wray; Ed Harder; Larry Polumbo.
Also see CEE, Jimmy, & Earls
Also see CHANCE, Larry
Also see DEL & ESCORTS
Also see LASER
Also see SMOKESTACK

EARLS / Pretenders
Singles: 7-inch
ROME/POWER MARTIN 3-5 76
Also see EARLS
Also see PRETENDERS

EARLS, Jack, & Jimbos
Singles: 78 rpm
SUN (240 "Slow Down") 25-50 56
Singles: 7-inch
SUN (240 "Slow Down") 50-75 56

EARLY, Bernie
Singles: 7-inch
MGM 8-12 58

EARLY, Sammy
Singles: 7-inch
MARLIN 15-25

EARLY AMERICANS
Singles: 7-inch
PARIS TOWER (106 "Night After Night") 15-25 67

EARLY FACES
LPs: 10/12-inch
PRIDE 8-10 72

EARLYWINE
LPs: 10/12-inch
AWARD 8-10 77

EARONS *R&B '83*
Singles: 12-inch
ISLAND 4-6 84
Singles: 7-inch
BOARDWALK 3-4 83
ISLAND 3-4 84
Members: Earon .28; Earon .18; Earon .22; Earon .33; Earon .69.

EARTH & FIRE
LPs: 10/12-inch
RED BULLET 10-12

EARTH BORN
Singles: 7-inch
L.C.R. (10104 "Universe of Love") . 15-25 60s

EARTH BOYS
Singles: 7-inch
CAPITOL 5-10 58

EARTH BROTHERS
Singles: 7-inch
HAPPY TIGER 3-5 70s

EARTH ISLAND
LPs: 10/12-inch
PHILLIPS 10-12 70

EARTH OPERA *P&R/LP '69*
Singles: 7-inch
ELEKTRA 4-8 67-69
LPs: 10/12-inch
ELEKTRA 10-15 68-69
Members: Peter Rowan; Paul Dillon; Dave Grishman; Bill Stevenson; John Nagy; Billy Mundi; John Cale.
Also see CALE, John
Also see RHINOCEROS

EARTH QUAKE: see EARTHQUAKE

EARTH, WIND & FIRE *P&R/R&B/LP '71*
Singles: 12-inch
COLUMBIA 4-8 75-83
Singles: 7-inch
ARC 3-4 78-82
COLUMBIA 3-5 73-90
W.B. 3-5 71
Picture Sleeves
ARC 3-4 80
COLUMBIA 3-5 74-88
LPs: 10/12-inch
COLUMBIA (Except 47000 series) ... 8-15 72-90
COLUMBIA (47000 series) 15-20 81-82
(Half-speed mastered.)
COLUMBIA/ARC (Except 35647) 8-15 75-81
COLUMBIA/ARC (35647 "Best of Earth, Wind & Fire") 8-10 79
COLUMBIA/ARC (35647 "Best of Earth, Wind & Fire") 15-20 79
(Picture disc. Promotional issue only.)
MFSL (159 "That's the Way of the World") 20-30 85
W.B. 10-15 71-74
Members: Philip Bailey; Maurice White; Verdine White; Ronnie Laws; Fred White; Andy Woolfolk; Larry Dunn; Ralph Johnson; Al McKay; Johnny Graham; Wade Flemons.
Also see BAILEY, Philip
Also see FLEMONS, Wade
Also see LAWS, Ronnie
Also see LEWIS, Ramsey
Also see SALTY PEPPERS

EARTH, WIND & FIRE & THE EMOTIONS *P&R/R&B '79*
Singles: 12-inch
ARC 4-8 79
Singles: 7-inch
ARC 3-4 79-80
LPs: 10/12-inch
ARC 5-10 79
Also see EMOTIONS

EARTH, WIND & FIRE & RAMSEY LEWIS *R&B '74*
Singles: 7-inch
COLUMBIA 3-5 74-75
Also see EARTH, WIND & FIRE
Also see LEWIS, Ramsey

EARTHMEN
Singles: 7-inch
RIM (2025 "Space Mood") 10-20 67
TROPICAL (123 "She's Mine") 20-30

EARTHQUAKE *LP '69*
(Earth Quake)
Singles: 7-inch
A&M 3-5 72
BESERKLEY 3-5 76-77
LPs: 10/12-inch
A&M 10-12 71-78
BESERKLEY 8-10 76-80
Also see KIHN, Greg, Band / Earthquake / Modern Lovers / Rubinoos
Also see KIHN, Greg, Band / Earthquake / Rubinoos / Jonathan Richman
Also see RICHMAN, Jonathan / Earthquake

EARTHQUAKES
(With the Rhythm Kings; with Armando King)
Singles: 7-inch
FORTUNE (534 "Darling Be Mine") 40-60 59
FORTUNE (538 "This Is Really Real") 50-75 60
FORTUNE (549 "Baby, Only You") 20-30 62

EARTHQUIRE
LPs: 10/12-inch
NATURAL RESOURCES 10-15 72
Also see VEGA, Tata

EARTHWORMS
Singles: 7-inch
BOBBIN 5-10 62

EARTHY SIDE
LPs: 10/12-inch
P.I.P. 10-15 71

EARWOOD, Mundo *C&W '72*
(Mundo Ray)
Singles: 7-inch
EPIC 3-5 75-76
EXCELSIOR 3-4 81
GMC 3-5 78-80
GRT 3-5 74
PEGASUS 3-4 89
PRIMERO 3-4 82
ROYAL AMERICAN 3-5 72
TRUE 3-5 77
LPs: 10/12-inch
EXCELSIOR 5-10 81
GMC 5-10 79
TRUE 6-12 77
Session: Larry Gatlin; Tompall Glaser; Chuck Glaser; Jim Glaser; Mel Tillis.
Also see GATLIN, Larry
Also see GLASER, Chuck
Also see GLASER, Jim
Also see GLASER, Tompall
Also see TILLIS, Mel

EASLEY, Benny
Singles: 7-inch
WORLDS (123 "Say You Love Me") 15-20 63

EASLEY, Clyde
Singles: 7-inch
ENTERPRISE 10-20 59

EAST
Singles: 7-inch
CAPITOL 3-5 72

LPs: 10/12-inch
CAPITOL....................................10-15 72

EAST, Lyndel C&W '78
Singles: 7-inch
NSD...3-5 78

EAST, Thomas R&B '69
(With the Fabulous Playboys)
Singles: 7-inch
LION...3-5 73
MGM...3-5 73
TODDLIN' TOWN..............................4-8 68-69

EAST BAY SOUL BRASS
Singles: 7-inch
RAMPART..3-6 68

EAST COAST R&B '79
Singles: 7-inch
RSO...3-5 79
Members: Gregory Johnson; Larry Blackmon; Gary Dow; Eric Rurham; Anthony Lockett; Arnett Leftenant; Nathan Leftenant.
Also see CAMEO

EAST COAST LEFT
Singles: 7-inch
INTREPID..4-8
KAPP..4-8 68

EAST L.A. CAR POOL P&R '75
Singles: 7-inch
GRC..3-5 75

EAST OF EDEN
Singles: 7-inch
DERAM...3-6 69
LPs: 10/12-inch
DERAM...10-15 69-70
HARVEST.......................................10-12 71

EAST RIVER BOYS
Singles: 7-inch
TOWER...4-8 65

EAST SIDE KIDS
Singles: 7-inch
ORANGE-EMPIRE...............................5-10 67
PHILIPS...5-10 65
UNI..4-8 69
VALHALLA..5-10 67
W.B...5-10 66
LPs: 10/12-inch
UNI (73032 "Tiger & Lamb")..........15-25 68
Member: Joe Madrid.

EASTBOUND EXPRESSWAY R&B '79
Singles: 7-inch
AVI...3-6 78-79
LPs: 10/12-inch
AVI (6068 "Eastbound Expressway")..............................5-10 79

EASTER, Jim
(With the Artistics)
Singles: 7-inch
CHA CHA (720 "Here I Go Again")...30-50 60
CHA CHA (721 "Stroll & Boogie")..30-50 60

EASTER, Monte
Singles: 78 rpm
STERLING...10-15
Singles: 7-inch
SWINGIN' (636 "Weekend Blues")..10-20 61

EASTERHOUSE P&R '89
Singles: 7-inch
COLUMBIA..3-4 89
Members: Andy Perry; Ivor Perry.

EASTERLING, James, & Blue Notes
Singles: 7-inch
RENO (133 "Angel of Mine")..........10-20

EASTERLING, Skip
(With Huey Smith)
Singles: 7-inch
INSTANT..5-10 60
Also see SMITH, Huey

EASTERN ALLIANCE
Singles: 7-inch
WRIGA (124 "Love Fades Away")..10-20 66

EASTERN SCENE
Singles: 7-inch
AMY...4-8 66

EASTFIELD MEADOWS
LPs: 10/12-inch
VMC..10-15 69

EASTIN, Nadine
Singles: 7-inch
ANDINE..3-4

EASTMAN BLUES BAND
Singles: 7-inch
CUCA (6766 "I Found a New World")..15-25 67
Members: Gerry Smith; John Kondos; James Hanns Walner; Tom Jones; Curt Vandenhuevel; Nick Kondos.

EASTMEN
Singles: 7-inch
MERCURY (71434 "Lover, Come Back")...25-35 59

EASTON, Amos, & His Orchestra
Singles: 78 rpm
SPECIALTY (410 "Strange Angel")..20-30 51
Also see BUMBLE BEE SLIM
Also see KING BUMBLE BEE SLIM & His Pacific Coast Senders

EASTON, Billy
Singles: 7-inch
DISPO (700 "I Was a Fool")...........10-20

EASTON, Elliot LP '85
Singles: 7-inch
ELEKTRA..3-4 85
LPs: 10/12-inch
ELEKTRA...5-10 85
Also see CARS

EASTON, Sheena P&R/LP '81
Singles: 12-inch
EMI AMERICA...................................4-6 81-86
Singles: 7-inch
EMI AMERICA...................................3-4 81-86
LIBERTY...3-4 81
MCA..3-4 88-91
RCA..3-4 89
Picture Sleeves
EMI AMERICA...................................3-6 81-86
RCA..3-4 89
LPs: 10/12-inch
EMI AMERICA...................................5-10 81-86
MCA..5-8 88-91
Also see PRINCE & Sheena Easton
Also see ROGERS, Kenny, & Sheena Easton

EASTSIDE KIDS
Singles: 7-inch
PHILLIPS (40295 "Subway Train")..10-20 65

EASTWOOD, Clint
Singles: 7-inch
CAMEO (240 "Rowdy")......................10-20 63
CERTRON...4-6 70
GNP (177 "Get Yourself Another Fool")..15-25 65
GOTHIC (005 "Unknown Girl")..........10-20 61
PARAMOUNT......................................4-8 69
W.B...3-4 81
Picture Sleeves
CAMEO (240 "Rowdy")......................30-50 63
CERTRON...5-8 70
GNP (177 "Get Yourself Another Fool")..50-75 65
GOTHIC (005 "Unknown Girl")........10-20 61
LPs: 10/12-inch
CAMEO (1056 "Cowboy Favorites")..75-125 63
Also see CHARLES, Ray, & Clint Eastwood
Also see HAGGARD, Merle, & Clint Eastwood
Also see MARVIN, Lee / Lee Marvin & Clint Eastwood
Also see SHEPPARD, T.G., & Clint Eastwood

EASY RIDERS
(With Terry Gilkyson)
Singles: 78 rpm
COLUMBIA..4-8 57
Singles: 7-inch
COLUMBIA...5-10 57
LPs: 10/12-inch
EPIC..10-15 63
Also see GILKYSON, Terry

EASY STREET P&R '76
Singles: 7-inch
CAPRICORN.......................................3-5 76
LPs: 10/12-inch
CAPRICORN......................................8-10 76-77

EASYBEATS P&R/LP '67
Singles: 7-inch
ASCOT..8-12 66
RARE EARTH......................................4-8 69
U.A...5-8 67-69
Picture Sleeves
ASCOT...10-20 66
LPs: 10/12-inch
RARE EARTH (517 "Easy Ridin' ").10-20 70
RHINO...5-10 85
U.A. (3588 "Friday on My Mind")....30-40 67
(Monaural.)
U.A. (6588 "Friday on My Mind")....30-40 67
(Stereo.)
U.A. (6667 "Falling off the Edge of the World")..30-40 68
Members: Steve Wright; Harry Vanda; George Young; Dick Diamonde.
Also see FLASH & PAN

EATON, Connie C&W '70
Singles: 7-inch
ABC...3-5 75
CHART...3-5 70-71
DUNHILL...3-5 75
ENTERPRISE.......................................3-5
MUSIC TOWN......................................3-5
LPs: 10/12-inch
ABC/DOT..6-10 75
CHART..8-12 70-71

EATON, Connie, & Dave Peel C&W '70
Singles: 7-inch
CHART...3-5 70
LPs: 10/12-inch
CHART..8-12 70
Also see EATON, Connie
Also see PEEL, Dave

EATON, Sally
Singles: 7-inch
PARAMOUNT......................................3-5 73

EATON, Steve
Singles: 7-inch
MOUNTAIN BLUEBIRD.......................3-5 70s
LPs: 10/12-inch
CAPITOL...8-12 74
MOUNTAIN BLUEBIRD ("Steve Eaton")..10-15 75
(No selection number used.)

EAY, Eddie
Singles: 7-inch
ECHO...5-10

EAZY-E LP '88
LPs: 10/12-inch
RUTHLESS...5-8 88

EBB TIDE R&B '75
(Ebb K. Harrison, Sr.)
Singles: 7-inch
SOUND GEMS......................................3-5 75-76

EBB TIDES
Singles: 7-inch
ACME (720 "Darling, I'll Love Only You")...5-75 57

EBB TIDES
Singles: 7-inch
R&R (303 "Low Tide")......................15-25 63

EBB TIDES
Singles: 7-inch
MALA (480 "Automatic Reaction")..10-20 64
Members: Nino Aiello; Vince Drago; Tony DeLesio.
Also see EBBS
Also see NINO & Ebb Tides

EBB TIDES
Singles: 7-inch
MONUMENTAL (520 "Come on and Cry")..150-250 66

EBB TIDES
Singles: 7-inch
ARCO (107 "My Baby's Gone")......15-25 66
Also see TANGERINE ZOO

EBB TONES
Singles: 7-inch
BEE...10-15 61

EBBONAIRS
Singles: 78 rpm
COMBO (110 "Doodle Doo Doo")..15-25 55
COMBO (111 "You")..........................25-50 55
COMBO (126 "Rosetta")....................25-50 56
Singles: 7-inch
COMBO (110 "Doodle Doo Doo")..25-35 55
COMBO (111 "You")..........................50-75 55
COMBO (126 "Rosetta")....................50-75 56

EBBS
Singles: 7-inch
DORE (521 "Vickie Sue")................10-20 59
Also see EBB TIDES
Also see NINO & Ebb Tides

EBBTIDES
Singles: 7-inch
TEEN (121 "What is Your Name Dear")......................................2000-3000 58

EBBTIDES
Singles: 7-inch
JAN LAR (101 "Love Doctor")....150-200 59
Members: Carl White; Al Frazier; Sonny Harris; Turner Wilson.
Also see RIVINGTONS

EBBTIDES
Singles: 7-inch
MONUMENTAL (520 "Come on and Cry")..25-35 60

EBBTIDES
Singles: 7-inch
DUANE (1022 "Star of Love")......................................2500-3500 64

EBB-TONES
Singles: 78 rpm
CREST..25-75 56-57
Singles: 7-inch
CREST (1016 "I Want You Only")..50-100 56
CREST (1024 "Baby")........................25-50 56
(Black vinyl.)
CREST (1024 "Baby")......................50-100 56
(Colored vinyl.)
CREST (1032 "Dust off the Bible")..25-50 57

EBBTONES
Singles: 78 rpm
EBB (100 "I've Got a Feeling").....75-100 57
Singles: 7-inch
EBB (100 "I've Got a Feeling").....75-100 57

EBBTONES
Singles: 7-inch
PORT...10-20 61

EBBTONES
Singles: 7-inch
DOT..5-10 64

EBERLY, Bob, & Sunshine Serenaders C&W '49
Singles: 78 rpm
DECCA..5-10 48-49

EBERT, Lee
Singles: 7-inch
ROCKET (801 "Let's Jive It")......150-250 58

EBLING, Barry, & Invaders
Singles: 7-inch
NORMAN (581 "I Can Make It Without You")..20-30 67

EBONAIRES
Singles: 78 rpm
ALADDIN...100-200 54
HOLLYWOOD...................................100-150 55
MGM (1036 "Come in Mr. Blues")..50-75 49
MODERN (656 "Song of the Wanderer")......................................35-55 49
MODERN (711 "That Lucky Old Sun")..35-55 49
MONEY..15-25 56
Singles: 7-inch
ALADDIN (3211 "Three O'Clock in the Morning").....................................300-400 53
ALADDIN (3212 "You're Nobody Till Somebody Loves You")..................................300-400 54
COLONIAL (117 "We're in Love")..75-100 59
HOLLYWOOD (1046 "Love for Christmas")....................................200-300 55
HOLLYWOOD (1062 "Let's Kiss and Say Hello Again")..200-300 55
LENA (1001 "Love Call")..............100-150 59
LOST-NITE (118 "Love Call")..........5-10 60s
MONEY (220 "Very Best Luck in the World")...40-60 56

EBONAIRES / Camelots
Singles: 7-inch
CAMEO (334 "Love Call")...............25-35 64
Also see CAMELOTS
Also see EBONARIES

EBONEE WEBB R&B/LP '81
(Ebony Web)
Singles: 7-inch
CAPITOL..3-4 81-84
HI..3-5 70-73
LPs: 10/12-inch
CAPITOL..5-10 81-84

EBONETTES
Singles: 7-inch
EBB (147 "All Alone")......................25-35 58

EBONI BAND
Singles: 7-inch
EBONI USA..4-8 79
Member: Art Stewart.

EBONIERS
Singles: 7-inch
PORT (70013 "Hand in Hand").......25-50 59

EBONIES
Singles: 7-inch
MIDWEST...5-8

EBONISTICS
Singles: 7-inch
GROOVEY..10-15

EBON-KNIGHTS
Singles: 7-inch
STEPHENY..15-25 58
LPs: 10/12-inch
STEPHENY (4001 "First Date")...750-1000 59

EBONY D&D '83
Singles: 12-inch
QUALITY/RFC......................................4-6 83-84

EBONY BROTHERS
Singles: 7-inch
KEM..5-10 61

EBONY, IVORY & JADE R&B '75
Singles: 7-inch
COLUMBIA...3-5 75

EBONY JAM
Singles: 7-inch
AMOS..3-6 69

EBONY MOODS
Singles: 78 rpm
THERON (108 "I've Got News for You")..75-100 55

EBONY MOUNTAIN MAN
LPs: 10/12-inch
DURHAM (6487 "Tribute to the World's Grand Champions")..................................15-20 81
(Picture disc.)

EBONY RHYTHM FUNK CAMPAIGN R&B '75
Singles: 7-inch
INNOVATION...3-5 75
MCA...3-5 72
LPs: 10/12-inch
UNI...5-10 72

EBONY SILHOUETTE
LPs: 10/12-inch
51 WEST..5-10 80s

EBONY THREE
Singles: 78 rpm
DECCA...25-50 38

EBONY WEB: see EBONEE WEBB

EBONYS P&R/R&B '71
Singles: 7-inch
BUDDAH..3-5 76
PHILADELPHIA INT'L..........................3-5 71-74
SOUL CLOCK...3-5 70s
LPs: 10/12-inch
PHILADELPHIA INT'L.........................8-10 73
Members: Jenny Holmes; David Beasley; James Tuten; Clarence Vaughn.
Also see CREME D'COCOA

EBSEN, Buddy
Singles: 7-inch
MGM...3-6 64
REPRISE...4-8 65
Picture Sleeves
MGM...4-6 64
LPs: 10/12-inch
REPRISE..10-15 65
Also see PARKER, Fess

ECCENTRICS
Singles: 7-inch
APPLAUSE...8-12 64

ECCENTRICS
Singles: 7-inch
SHANE (60 "Baby, I Need You")....20-30 66

E-CELLENTS: see X-CELLENTS

ECHO & BUNNYMEN LP '81
Singles: 12-inch
SIRE..5-10 81-86
Singles: 7-inch
SIRE..3-4 81-87
Picture Sleeves
SIRE..3-4 87
LPs: 10/12-inch
SIRE..5-10 81-87

ECHOES
Singles: 78 rpm
ROCKIN'...25-50 53
Singles: 7-inch
ROCKIN' (523 "All That Wine Is Gone")...200-300 53
(The Echoes on Deluxe 6001, *Please Come Back*, is a bootleg.)

ECHOES
Singles: 78 rpm
GEE..30-50 57
SPECIALTY...15-25 57
Singles: 7-inch
GEE (1028 "Ding Dong")...............50-100 57
(Red and black label.)
GEE (1028 "Ding Dong")..................25-50 60
(Gray label.)
SPECIALTY (601 "Over the Rainbow")...15-25 57

ECHOES
Singles: 78 rpm
COMBO (128 "My Little Honey")....25-35 57
Singles: 7-inch
COMBO (128 "My Little Honey")....30-50 57

ECHOES
Singles: 7-inch
EDCO (510 "Teenage Love")......150-250 58

ECHOES
Singles: 7-inch
ANDEX (22101 "Time")....................25-50 59
Members: Darron Stankey; Al Candaleria; Jim West.
Also see INNOCENTS
Also see KENJOLAIRS

ECHOES
Singles: 7-inch
SWAN...10-15 58

ECHOES P&R '61
Singles: 7-inch
ASCOT (2188 "I Love Candy")........20-30 65
COLUMBIA (41549 "Do I Love You")..10-15 59
COLUMBIA (41709 "Ecstasy")........10-15 60
FELSTED (8614 "Angel of Love")...30-40 61
SRG (101 "Baby Blue")................150-200 60
SEG-WAY (103 "Baby Blue")..........15-25 61
SEG-WAY (106 "Sad Eyes")............15-25 61
SEG-WAY (1002 "Angel of My Heart")..20-30 62
ZIRCON (1044 "Baby Blue")............30-40 60
(Canadian.)
EPs: 7-inch
CRYSTAL BALL....................................5-10
LPs: 10/12-inch
CRYSTAL BALL....................................8-12 84
Members: Harry Doyle; Tom Morrissey; Tom Duffy.

ECHOES / Four Esquires
Singles: 7-inch
ROULETTE GOLDEN GOODIES......3-5 70s
Also see ECHOES
Also see FOUR ESQUIRES

ECHOES
Singles: 7-inch
DOLTON (18 "Born to Be with You")..10-15 60
Members: Bonnie Guitar; Don Robertson.
Also see GUITAR, Bonnie
Also see ROBERTSON, Don

ECHOES
Singles: 7-inch
ACE (657 "Restless")......................10-20 62

ECHOES
Singles: 7-inch
SMASH..5-10 62-63

ECHOES
Singles: 7-inch
PULSE..5-8

ECHOES OF CARNABY STREET
Singles: 7-inch
THAMES (105 "No Place")............15-25 67

ECHOLETTES
Singles: 7-inch
IMPERIAL..5-10 63

ECHOMEN
Singles: 7-inch
SOMA (1197 "My Maria")................25-35 62

ECHOMEN
Singles: 7-inch
FOX (1 "Long Green")...50-75 66
Also see BEDLAM FOUR

ECHOMORES
(Featuring Lee Wagoner)
Singles: 7-inch
ROCKET (1042 "Cute Chick")...75-100 59
ROCKET (1048 "How Does It Feel to Be Lonely")...40-60 59

ECHOS
(Echo's)
Singles: 7-inch
HI-TIDE (106 "Angel of Love")...250-500 61
(Black vinyl.)
HI-TIDE (106 "Angel of Love") 750-1000 61
(Green vinyl.)

ECHOS
Singles: 7-inch
ART (198 "Every Second Day")... 8-12
SAGE (323 "Haunted")... 8-12

ECHOTONES
Singles: 7-inch
DART (1009 "So in Love")...15-25 59

ECKSTINE, Billy R&B '44
Singles: 78 rpm
DELUXE...10-15 45
EMARCY...5-10 54
MGM...5-10 47-56
NATIONAL...5-10 45-48
RCA...4-8 56
Singles: 7-inch
A&M...3-5 76
EMARCY...5-10 54
ENTERPRISE...3-5 70-74
MGM...8-15 50-56
MGM GOLDEN CIRCLE (100 series)...3-6 60s
MERCURY...4-8 59-64
MOTOWN...8-15 65-68
RCA...8-12 56
ROULETTE...5-10 59-60
Picture Sleeves
MERCURY...5-10 62
EPs: 7-inch
EMARCY...10-20 54-55
KING...10-20 53
MGM...10-20 50-56
MOTOWN (60632 "Prime of My Life")...15-25 65
RENDITION...15-25 50
LPs: 10/12-inch
AUDIO LAB (1549 "Mr. B")...30-40 60
EMARCY (26025 "Blues for Sale")...50-100 54
(10-inch LP.)
EMARCY (26027 "Love Songs of Mr. B")...50-100 54
EMARCY (36010 "I Surrender Dear")...30-60 55
EMARCY (36029 "Blues for Sale")...25-50 55
EMARCY (36030 "Love Songs of Mr. B")...50-100 55
EMARCY (36129 "Eckstine's Imagination")...25-50 55
ENTERPRISE...5-10 71-74
KING (12 "The Great Mr. B")...75-125 52
(10-inch LP.)
MGM (219 "Tenderly")...30-50 53
(10 Inch LP.)
MGM (257 "I Let a Song Go Out of My Heart")...40-60 55
(10 Inch LP.)
MGM (3176 "Mr. B with a Beat")...15-25 55
MGM (3209 "Rendezvous")...15-25 55
MGM (3275 "That Old Feeling")...15-25 55
MERCURY...15-25 57-64
METRO...10-15 65
MOTOWN (632 "Prime of My Life")...15-25 65
MOTOWN (646 "My Way")...15-25 66
MOTOWN (677 "For Love of Ivy") 10-20 69
NATIONAL (2001 "Billy Eckstine Sings")...75-125 50
(10-inch LP.)
REGENT...20-40 56-57
ROULETTE...15-25 60
SAVOY...8-10 76-79
TRIP...5-10 75
WING...8-12 67
Also see BASIE, Count, & Billy Eckstine
Also see DAMITA JO & Billy Eckstine
Also see FOUR BLUES

ECKSTINE, Billy, & Woody Herman
Singles: 78 rpm
MGM...4-8 51
Singles: 7-inch
MGM...5-10 51
Also see HERMAN, Woody, & Orch.

ECKSTINE, Billy, & Quincy Jones
Singles: 7-inch
MERCURY...3-6 62
LPs: 10/12-inch
MERCURY...15-25 62
Also see JONES, Quincy

ECKSTINE, Billy /Arthur Prysock
LPs: 10/12-inch
GUEST STAR...5-10 64
Also see PRYSOCK, Arthur

ECKSTINE, Billy, & Sarah Vaughan
Singles: 78 rpm
MGM...4-8 52
Singles: 7-inch
MGM...5-10 52
MERCURY...5-10 57-59
EPs: 7-inch
MGM (1002 "Dedicated to You")...10-15 52
LPs: 10/12-inch
GUEST STAR...5-10 64
LION...15-25 59
MERCURY (20316 "Best of Irving Berlin")...20-30 57
Also see ECKSTINE, Billy
Also see VAUGHAN, Sarah

ECLECTIC MOUSE
Singles: 7-inch
CAPITOL...3-6 69

ECLECTION
LPs: 10/12-inch
ELEKTRA...10-15 68

ECLIPSE
Singles: 7-inch
CASABLANCA...3-4 77
LPs: 10/12-inch
CASABLANCA...8-10 77

ECOLOGY, ENVIRONMENT, EVOLUTION
Singles: 7-inch
HAPPY TIGER...5-10 73

ECSTASIES
Singles: 7-inch
AMY (853 "That Lucky Old Sun")...20-25 62

ECSTASY, PASSION & PAIN P&R/R&B '74
Singles: 12-inch
ROULETTE...4-6 84
Singles: 7-inch
ROULETTE...3-4 74-76
LPs: 10/12-inch
ROULETTE...8-10 74
Members: Barbara Roy; Bill Gardner; Joseph Williams Jr.; Althea Smith; Alan Tizer.
Also see ROY, Barbara

ECUADORS
Singles: 7-inch
ARGO (5353 "Say You'll Be Mine")...15-25 59

EDDIE, Jason, & Centermen
Singles: 7-inch
CAPITOL...4-8 66

EDDIE, John P&R/LP '86
Singles: 7-inch
COLUMBIA...3-4 86
Picture Sleeves
COLUMBIA...3-4 86
LPs: 10/12-inch
COLUMBIA...5-10 86

EDDIE, Lee
Singles: 7-inch
DONDEE...4-8 64

EDDIE & BETTY P&R '59
Singles: 7-inch
LARK...5-10 59
SIX THOUSAND...10-15 57
W.B....5-10 59
LPs: 10/12-inch
W.B....20-30 59
Members: Eddie Cole; Betty Cole.

EDDIE & CHUCK
Singles: 7-inch
CHANCE (107 "Boogie the Blues")...35-40

EDDIE & CRUISERS P&R '83
(John Cafferty & Beaver Brown Band)
Singles: 7-inch
SCOTTI BROTHERS...3-4 83
Also see CAFFERTY, John

EDDIE & DE HAVELONS
Singles: 7-inch
PEACOCK...8-12 62

EDDIE & DUTCH P&R '70
Singles: 7-inch
IVANHOE...3-5 70
Members: Eddie Mascari; Dutch Wenzloff.

EDDIE & EMPIRES
Singles: 7-inch
COLPIX (112 "Tears in My Eyes")...75-125 59

EDDIE & ERNIE R&B '65
(Ernie & Eddie)
Singles: 7-inch
CHECKER (1057 "Who's That Knocking at My Door")...10-20 63
CHECKER (1086 "Time Waits for No One")...10-20 64
CHESS...4-8 66
EASTERN (602 "Time Waits for No One")...5-10 65
EASTERN (603 "I'm a Young Man") 5-10 65
EASTERN (606 "I'm Going for Myself")...5-10 65
EASTERN (608 "I'm Gonna Always Love You")...5-10 65
EASTERN (609 "I Can't Do It")...5-10 66
REVUE...4-8 69
Members: Eddie Campbell; Ernie Johnson.
Also see CAMPBELL, Eddie C.
Also see JOHNSON, Ernie

EDDIE & EVERGREENS
(Sha Na Na)
Singles: 7-inch
KAMA SUTRA...4-8 72
Also see SHA NA NA

EDDIE & FIVE DREAMERS: see BANKS, Eddie

EDDIE & FREDDIE R&B '77
Singles: 7-inch
OCTOBER...3-5 77

EDDIE & HOT RODS
Singles: 7-inch
ISLAND...3-5 77-78
LPs: 10/12-inch
EMI AMERICA...5-10 80
ISLAND...8-10 77

EDDIE & JIMMIE
Singles: 7-inch
DELUXE (6179 "Hold the Kiss")...30-50 58

EDDIE & MARY
Singles: 7-inch
PASTEL...4-8 64
STA-SET...4-8 64

EDDIE & PLAYERS
Singles: 7-inch
PLANTATION (206 "Space Invaders")...4-6 81
Member: Eddie Phillips.

EDDIE & SHOWMEN
Singles: 7-inch
LIBERTY (55566 "Toes on the Nose")...10-20 63
LIBERTY (55608 "Squad Car")...10-20 63
LIBERTY (55659 "Mr. Rebel")...10-20 64
LIBERTY (55695 "Far Away Places")...10-20 64
LIBERTY (55720 "Young & Lonely")...10-20 64
EPs: 7-inch
MOXIE...5-10 80
Members: Eddie Bertrand; Phil Pruden; Dick Dodd; Bob Knight; Robert Edwards; Fred Buxton.
Also see BAYMEN
Also see BELAIRS
Also see CHALLENGERS

EDDIE & STARLITES
(With Al Browne Orchestra)
Singles: 7-inch
ALJON (1260 "Come on Home")...25-35 72
SCEPTER (1202 "To Make a Long Story Short")...40-50 59
(White label.)
SCEPTER (1202 "To Make a Long Story Short")...20-25 59
(Red label.)
VINTAGE...3-5 73
Also see STARLITES

EDDIE & TEDDY: see EDDY & TEDDY

EDDIE & TERRI
Singles: 7-inch
DUNES (802 "There's No Other")...5-10 63

EDDIE & TIDE P&R '85
(Eddie Rice)
Singles: 12-inch
SPIN...4-8 88
(Promotional only.)
Singles: 7-inch
ATCO...3-4 85
Picture Sleeves
ATCO...3-4 87

EDDIE & TROPICS
Singles: 7-inch
JOSIE (930 "Don't Monkey with Another Monkey's Monkey")...10-15 65

EDDIE & UPSETS
Singles: 7-inch
DEKTR (41666 "El Mosquito")...10-20 66

EDDIE D. R&B '85
(Eddie Drummond)
Singles: 12-inch
PHILLY WORLD...4-6 85
Singles: 7-inch
PHILLY WORLD...3-4 85

EDDIE THE HAWK
Singles: 7-inch
PRYCE...3-6 69

EDDY, Don
Singles: 7-inch
RONA...20-30 59

EDDY, Duane P&R/C&W/R&B '58
(With the Rebels; with Rebelettes; with His Rock-a-billies; with His Twangy Guitar)
Singles: 78 rpm
FORD (500 "Ramrod")...75-125 57
JAMIE (1101 "Moovin' N' Groovin'")...50-75 58
(Pink label.)
JAMIE (1101 "Moovin' N' Groovin' ")...25-50 58
(Yellow label.)
JAMIE (1104 "Rebel-'Rouser")...25-50 58
JAMIE (1109 "Ramrod")...25-50 58
JAMIE (1111 "Cannonball")...25-50 58
JAMIE (1117 "The Lonely One")...50-75 59
JAMIE (1122 "Yep!")...50-100 59
Singles: 7-inch
BIG TREE...5-10 72
CAPITOL...3-4 87
COLPIX...5-10 65-66
CONGRESS...3-5 70
ELEKTRA...3-5 77
FORD (500 "Ramrod")...75-125 57
(Credits Duane Eddy, but is by Al Casey.)
GREGMARK (5 "Caravan")...5-10 61
(Credits Duane Eddy, but is by Al Casey.)
JAMIE (73 "Peter Gunn")...25-50 61
(Compact 33 single.)
JAMIE (1100 series)...10-20 58-61
(Monaural.)
JAMIE (1100 series)...20-40 59-60
(Stereo.)
JAMIE (1200 series)...8-15 61-62
RCA (Except 8507)...8-15 61-65
RCA (8507 "Moon Shot")...25-35 65
REPRISE...5-15 66-68
UNI...4-6 70
Picture Sleeves
CAPITOL...3-5 87
COLPIX (788 "House of the Rising Sun")...25-40 66
JAMIE...15-25 59-61
RCA...10-15 62-64
EPs: 7-inch
JAMIE...35-75 59-60
RCA/WURLITZER DISCOTHEQUE MUSIC...15-25 64
LPs: 10/12-inch
CAMDEN...8-15
CAPITOL...8-10 87
COLPIX (490 "Duane A-Go-Go")...25-30 65
COLPIX (494 "Duane Eddy Does Bob Dylan")...25-30 65
JAMIE (3000 "Have Twangy Guitar Will Travel")...50-80 58
(White cover.)
JAMIE (3000 "Have Twangy Guitar Will Travel")...25-50 58
(Red cover.)
JAMIE (3006 "For You")...40-60 59
JAMIE (3009 "The 'Twang's' the Thing")...40-60 59
JAMIE (3011 "Songs of Our Heritage")...100-200 60
(Red vinyl.)
JAMIE (3011 "Songs of Our Heritage")...40-60 60
(Gatefold cover. Black vinyl.)
JAMIE (3011 "Songs of Our Heritage")...20-40 61
(Standard cover. Black vinyl.)
JAMIE (3014 "$1,000,000 Worth of Twang")...40-60 61
JAMIE (3019 "Girls! Girls! Girls!")..20-30 61
JAMIE (3021 "$1,000,000 Worth of Twang, Vol. 2")...40-60 62
JAMIE (3022 "Twistin' with Duane Eddy")...30-50 62
JAMIE (3024 "Surfin' with Duane Eddy")...30-50 63
JAMIE (3025 "In Person")...20-30 63
JAMIE (3026 "16 Greatest Hits")...20-30 64
RCA (2525 thru 2648)...25-50 62
RCA (2671 "Pure Gold")...5-10 78
RCA (2681 thru 3477)...20-40 63-66
REPRISE...15-20 66-67
SIRE...10-15 75
Session: Duane Eddy; Al Casey; Corki Casey; Donnie Owens; Plas Johnson; Steve Douglas; Ike Clanton; Mike Bermani; Waylon Jennings; Willie Nelson; Kin Vassy.
Also see ART of NOISE
Also see BLOSSOMS
Also see BURTON, James
Also see CASEY, Al
Also see CLANTON, Ike
Also see CLARK, Sanford, & Duane Eddy
Also see DOUGLAS, Steve
Also see FOGERTY, John
Also see JENNINGS, Waylon
Also see JIMMY & DUANE
Also see JOHNSON, Plas
Also see NELSON, Willie
Also see OWENS, Donnie
Also see PORTER, Frank
Also see ROBINSON, Mark
Also see SHARPE, Ray
Also see SHARPS
Also see THOMAS, B.J.
Also see VASSY, Kin

EDDY, Duane & Mirriam
Singles: 7-inch
REPRISE (0622 "Guitar on My Mind")...10-15 67
Also see EDDY, Duane
Also see JOHNSON, Mirriam

EDDY, Jim
(With Carl Stevens & Orchestra)
Singles: 78 rpm
MERCURY...5-10 57
Singles: 7-inch
DORE (537 "Teen Age Angel")...10-15 59
MERCURY (71171 "I Have No Sweetheart")...8-12 57
SOMA (1091 "Livin' Doll")...15-25 58
SPINNING...8-15

EDDY, Jim, & Highlights
Singles: 7-inch
PLAY...20-25 58
Also see HIGHLIGHTS

EDDY, Link: see LINK - EDDY COMBO

EDDY, Sam, & Revels
Singles: 7-inch
ACCENT (1085 "Skip to My Lou")...8-12 62
DACO (702 "Skip to My Lou")...10-20 62
(First issue.)
Also see REVELS

EDDY & CENTURIES
Singles: 7-inch
SHERRY...10-20

EDDY & TEDDY
(Eddie & Teddy)
Singles: 7-inch
MALA...5-10 61

EDDYS
Singles: 7-inch
DEEP WATER...3-4 84

EDE, Dave, & Rabin Band
Singles: 7-inch
LAURIE (3056 "Easy On")...10-20 60
RUST (5047 "Twistin' Those Meeces to Pieces")...10-15 62

EDELL & T-BIRDS
Singles: 7-inch
MOON...10-20

EDELMAN, Randy P&R '75
Singles: 7-inch
ARISTA...3-5 77-79
LION...3-5 73
MGM...3-5 73
SUNFLOWER...3-5 71-72
20TH FOX...3-5 74-76
LPs: 10/12-inch
ARISTA...5-10 77-79
LION...8-10 72
SUNFLOWER...8-12 71
20TH FOX...8-10 74-78

EDEN, Barbara
Singles: 7-inch
DOT...4-6 67
PLANTATION...4-8 78
(Colored vinyl.)
Picture Sleeves
DOT...10-15 67
LPs: 10/12-inch
DOT (3795 "Miss Barbara Eden")..25-30 67
(Monaural.)
DOT (25795 "Miss Barbara Eden")...30-40 67
(Stereo.)

EDEN, Chance
Singles: 7-inch
BIRTHSTONE...5-10
ROULETTE...4-6 66
Picture Sleeves
BIRTHSTONE...10-15

EDEN, Jack, & Dimensions
Singles: 7-inch
JULENE (1000 "Betty Lou")...40-50

EDEN, Jack, & Sundowners
Singles: 7-inch
T.J. (600 "Come Back Baby")...25-35 66

EDEN, Jimmie, & Revelers
Singles: 7-inch
HARAL (779 "Goddess of Love")...200-300 64

EDEN ROCKERS
Singles: 7-inch
CANNADY...5-10 59

EDEN ROCS
Singles: 7-inch
NUGGET...5-10 59

EDEN'S CHILDREN LP '68
Singles: 7-inch
ABC 11053 "Goodbye Girl")...5-10 68
LPs: 10/12-inch
ABC (624 "Eden's Children")...20-30 68
ABC (652 "Sure Looks Real")...15-25 68

EDGAR, Jim
(With the Roadrunners)
Singles: 7-inch
BISMARK (1011 "What Is One to Do")...10-15 67
DISCOVERY (1001 "The Place")...8-12 66
HAMA (1002 "Hey Little Girl")...10-15 66
POMPEII (66684 "Artificial Army")...8-12 69
SCEPTER (12147 "Tennessee Stud")...5-10 66

EDGE
Singles: 7-inch
ENITH (1011 "Something New")...20-30 65

EDGE
Singles: 7-inch
CASABLANCA...3-5 80
LPs: 10/12-inch
NOSE (48003 "Edge")...20-30 70
Members: Dave Novogroski; Richard Barcellona; John Keith; Gallen Murphy.
Also see AMERICAN REVOLUTION
Also see BOSTON TEA PARTY

EDGE, Bobby
Singles: 7-inch
B&F (1330 "Gambler's Guitar")...5-10

EDGE, Graeme LP '75
(Graeme Edge Band; with Adrian Gurvitz)
Singles: 7-inch
LONDON...3-5 77
THRESHOLD...3-5 74
LPs: 10/12-inch
LONDON (686 "Paradise Ballroom") 8-12 77
THRESHOLD (15 "Kick off Your Muddy Boots")...10-15 75
Also see AVENGERS
Also see GURVITZ, Adrian
Also see MOODY BLUES

EDGE, Kathy C&W '87
Singles: 7-inch
NSD...3-4 87

EDGE OF DARKNESS
Singles: 7-inch
JAMIE...10-20 68

EDGEWOOD
LPs: 10/12-inch
TMI....10-12 72

EDGEWOODS
Singles: 7-inch
EPIC (10275 "Those Golden Oldies")....15-25 68

EDIE & CHANNELS
Singles: 7-inch
HERALD....10-20 63

EDISON ELECTRIC BAND
LPs: 10/12-inch
COTILLION....10-12 70

EDISON
Singles: 7-inch
PHILIPS (40698 "Everybody Knows")....10-15 70

EDISON LIGHTHOUSE P&R '70
Singles: 7-inch
BELL.... 4-8 70-71
FLASHBACK.... 3-5 70s
Member: Tony Burrows.
Also see BURROWS, Tony

EDITORS
Singles: 7-inch
DEXTER....10-15 64

EDMOND, Lee
Singles: 7-inch
ROWE.... 4-8 63
SOLAR.... 4-8 66

EDMONDSON, Carl
Singles: 7-inch
FRATERNITY.... 4-8 63-65

EDMONDSON, Travis
Singles: 7-inch
REPRISE.... 4-6 62
LPs: 10/12-inch
HORIZON....10-15 62
REPRISE....10-15 62
Also see BUD & TRAVIS
Also see GATEWAY SINGERS

EDMUND, Lada, Jr.
Singles: 7-inch
DECCA (31937 "Once Upon a Time")....10-20 66
DECCA (32007 "Soul A-Go-Go")...50-75 66
ROULETTE (4449 "I Want a Man".. 5-10 62

EDMUNDSON, Wayne
Singles: 7-inch
I.M.M.C.O..... 3-5 79

EDMUNDS, Dave P&R '70
Singles: 12-inch
COLUMBIA (Except 1725).... 4-8 85-87
(Promotional issue only.)
COLUMBIA (1725 "Information")....15-20 84
(Picture disc. Promotional issue only.)
Singles: 7-inch
ARISTA (522 "Slipping Away").... 3-5 83
(Clear vinyl.)
COLUMBIA.... 3-5 80-85
MAM (3601 "I Hear You Knocking").. 5-8 70
(Black label.)
MAM (3601 "I Hear You Knocking").. 3-6 70
(Blue label.)
MAM (3608 "I'm Coming Home").... 3-6 71
RCA.... 3-6 73-74
SWAN SONG.... 3-5 77-81
Promotional Singles
COLUMBIA (1576 "Run Rudolph Run").... 4-6 82
(Compact 33 single.)
COLUMBIA (03428 "Run Rudolph Run").... 3-5 82
Picture Sleeves
COLUMBIA.... 3-4 85
SWAN SONG.... 3-5 81
LPs: 10/12-inch
ATLANTIC (320 "College Network")....35-45
(Promotional issue only.)
CAPITOL.... 5-8 90
COLUMBIA (Except 1725).... 5-10 80-87
COLUMBIA (1725 "Information")....15-25 83
(Picture disc. Promotional issue only.)
MAM (3 "Rockpile")....30-40 72
RCA (4238 "Subtle As a Flying Mallet").... 5-10 82
RCA (5003 "Subtle As a Flying Mallet")....10-12
SWAN SONG.... 8-10 77-81
Also see CARTER, Carlene, & Dave Edmunds
Also see DION
Also see EDMUNDS, Dave
Also see HARRISON, George / Jeff Beck / Dave Edmunds
Also see LEWIS, Huey, & News
Also see LOVE SCULPTURE
Also see LOWE, Nick, & Dave Edmunds

EDSELS P&R '61
Singles: 7-inch
ABC.... 3-5 75
CAPITOL....10-20 61-62
DOT (16311 "My Whispering Heart")....15-20 62
DUB (2843 "Lama Rama Ding Dong")....40-60 58
(Black and gold label. Copies with black and silver labels are counterfeits. Humorously, fakes have the 1961 Twin label track, which is noticeably different than the Dub one.)
DUB (2843 "Rama Lama Ding Dong")....10-20 58
(Note title correction.)
EMBER (1078 "Three Precious Words")....10-20 61
LOST-NITE.... 4-6 70s
MUSICTONE....5-10 64
REGENCY ("Rama Lama Ding Dong")....10-20 61
(Canadian. Has the Twin track.)
ROULETTE (4151 "Do You Love Me")....15-20 59
TAMMY (1010 "What Brought Us Together")....30-40 60
TAMMY (1014 "Three Precious Words")....30-40 61
TAMMY (1023 "The Girl I Love") ...25-35 61
TAMMY (1027 "Count the Tears") 25-35 61
TWIN (700 "Rama Lama Ding Dong")....10-20 61
(This track is noticeably different than the one previously issued on Dub.)
Members: George Jones Jr; Larry Green; James Reynolds; Marshall Sewell; Harry Green.

EDWARD BEAR P&R '70
Singles: 7-inch
CAPITOL.... 3-6 70-74
CAPITOL STARLINE (22007 "You, Me and Mexico").... 4-8 72
(Canadian.)
Picture Sleeves
CAPITOL.... 3-6 72-73
LPs: 10/12-inch
CAPITOL....8-10 70-73

EDWARD BROTHERS
Singles: 7-inch
MUSIC WORLD.... 4-8 65

EDWARD TWINS
Singles: 7-inch
TWISTIME.... 4-8 62

EDWARD'S HAND
LPs: 10/12-inch
GRT....10-15 69
RCA....10-12 70

EDWARDS, Alton R&B '82
Singles: 12-inch
COLUMBIA.... 4-6 82
Singles: 7-inch
COLUMBIA.... 3-4 82

EDWARDS, Alvis
Singles: 7-inch
ENALL (80 "Real Gone Baby")....60-85

EDWARDS, Bobby P&R/C&W '61
Singles: 7-inch
BLUEBONNET....5-10 59
CAPITOL.... 4-8 61-63
CHART.... 4-6 68
CREST....5-10 61
MANCO.... 4-8 62
MUSICOR.... 4-8 65
POLARIS.... 3-5

EDWARDS, Brent
Singles: 7-inch
KAREN....8-12 61-63

EDWARDS, Chuck
(With the Five Crowns)
Singles: 78 rpm
DUKE (163 "I'm Wondering")....15-25 57
Singles: 7-inch
ALANNA (557 "If I Were King")....30-40 60
DUKE (163 "I'm Wondering")....15-25 57
RENE (7001 "Bullfight")....10-20 66
(First issue.)
RENE (20013 "Bullfight #2")....10-15
ROULETTE (4705 "Bullfight")....8-12 66

EDWARDS, Danny
Singles: 7-inch
TEEN MUSIC.... 4-8

EDWARDS, Dave
Singles: 7-inch
BERTRAM INT'L....5-10 60
CAMEO.... 4-8 63

EDWARDS, Dee R&B '79
Singles: 12-inch
COTILLION.... 4-6 79
Singles: 7-inch
COTILLION.... 3-6 78-80
D TOWN (1024 "He Told Me Lies")....20-40 65
D TOWN (1031 "What a Party")....10-20 66
D TOWN (1048 "His Majesty My Love")....15-25 66
D TOWN (1063 "All the Way Home")....20-40 66
RCA....5-10 72
TUBA....10-20 62
LPs: 10/12-inch
COTILLION....5-10 80

EDWARDS, Dennis P&R/R&B/LP '84
Singles: 12-inch
GORDY.... 4-6 84
Singles: 7-inch
GORDY.... 3-4 84-85
INT'L SOULVILLE (100 "I Didn't Have to But I Did")....400-600
MOTOWN.... 3-4
LPs: 10/12-inch
GORDY....5-10 84-85
Also see CONTOURS
Also see TEMPTATIONS

EDWARDS, Dewey
Singles: 7-inch
CAMEO (364 "Come on Over to My Place")....10-15 65

EDWARDS, Gary
Singles: 7-inch
DOVER....3-5

EDWARDS, Gary, & Abominable Snow-Men
Singles: 7-inch
GENUINE (154 "I Can't Believe")...10-20

EDWARDS, Gary, & Embers
Singles: 7-inch
FRATERNITY....4-8 68

EDWARDS, George
Singles: 7-inch
DUNWICH....4-8 66

EDWARDS, Gloria
Singles: 7-inch
DELUXE....5-8
JET STREAM....5-8
KING....5-8

EDWARDS, Honeyboy
(David Edwards)
Singles: 78 rpm
ARTIST (102 "Build a Cave")....75-125 51

EDWARDS, J.D.
Singles: 78 rpm
IMPERIAL (5245 "Cryin'")....25-50 53
Singles: 7-inch
IMPERIAL (5245 "Cryin'")....50-100 53

EDWARDS, Jack
Singles: 7-inch
MICHELE (508 "All Night Long")....15-20

EDWARDS, Jackie
(With the Soulmakers)
Singles: 7-inch
DARAN....5-10 68-69
VEEP....4-8 68
LPs: 10/12-inch
VEEP....10-20 68

EDWARDS, Jayne D&D '83
Singles: 12-inch
PROFILE....4-6 83-84
Singles: 7-inch
PROFILE....3-4 83-84
LPs: 10/12-inch
PROFILE....5-10 84

EDWARDS, Jimmy C&W '57
(Jimmie Edwards)
Singles: 78 rpm
MERCURY....10-20 57
Singles: 7-inch
MERCURY (71209 "Love Bug Crawl")....20-30 57
RCA (7597 "Your Love Is a Good Love")....15-25 59
RCA (7717 "Rosie Lee")....10-20 60
RCA (7773 "What Do You Want from Me")....10-20 60

EDWARDS, Joey
Singles: 7-inch
LILLY (501 "Shirley, Shirley")....100-200 60

EDWARDS, John R&B '73
Singles: 7-inch
AWARE....4-8 73-74
BELL (45205 "Look on Your Face")....25-50 72
COTILLION....3-6 76-77
LPs: 10/12-inch
AWARE....5-10 74
CREED....5-10 75
GENERAL/GRC....5-10 74

EDWARDS, Johnny & White Caps
Singles: 7-inch
NORTHLAND (7002 "Rock & Roll Saddle")....200-300 57
(White label. Shown as by the White Caps.)
NORTHLAND (7002 "Rock & Roll Saddle")....100-200 57
(Maroon label. Credits Johnny Edwards & the White Caps.)
NORTHLAND (7002 "Rock & Roll Saddle")....75-125 57
(Maroon label. Shown as by the White Caps.)
Members: Ricky Lee Smolinski; Jerry Stengl; Jack Gardner; Duke Wright; Denny Noie.

EDWARDS, Jonathan P&R/LP '71
Singles: 7-inch
ATCO....3-5 72-73
CAPRICORN....3-5 71
W.B.....3-4 77
LPs: 10/12-inch
AMERICAN MELODY....5-8
ATCO....8-10 72-74
CAPRICORN....10-12 71
REPRISE....8-10 74
W.B.....8-10 77

EDWARDS, Jonathan C&W '88
Singles: 7-inch
MCA/CURB....3-4 88-89

EDWARDS, Jonathan & Darlene
(Paul Weston & Jo Stafford)
LPs: 10/12-inch
COLUMBIA (1024 "Piano Artistry")....25-40 57
COLUMBIA (1513 "In Paris")....20-30 60
(Monaural.)
COLUMBIA (8313 "In Paris")....25-35 60
(Stereo.)
CORINTHIAN....5-10
RCA (LPM-2495 "Sing Along")....15-25 61
(Monaural.)
RCA (LSP-2495 "Sing Along")....20-30 61
(Stereo.)
Also see STAFFORD, Jo
Also see WESTON, Paul, Orchestra

EDWARDS, Lee, & Continentals
Singles: 7-inch
LANTIC GOLD ("On the Rebound")....8-12

EDWARDS, Lucky
Singles: 7-inch
NU KAT....5-10 59

EDWARDS, Michael
Singles
AZRA (A9-6 "You Oughta Be In Pictures")....15-20 84
(Star-, building-, and nude-shaped picture discs. 25 to 50 made of each.)
AZRA (A9-6 "You Oughta Be In Pictures")....8-12 84
(Clipboard-shaped picture disc. 500 made.)

EDWARDS, Michael, Band
Singles: 7-inch
LAURIE (3661 "Tell Me")....5-8 77

EDWARDS, Millard
(Mill Edwards)
Singles: 7-inch
BUNKY (7761 "Use What You Got")....10-20 68
CONSTELLATION (170 "Things Won't Be the Same")....10-20 66
CUTLASS....5-10 72
Also see ESQUIRES

EDWARDS, Monte
(With Bob Ross & His Orchestra)
Singles: 7-inch
ROSCO (409 "Oh! I Never Knew")....50-75

EDWARDS, Pat
Singles: 7-inch
COLONIAL (7013 "Before Long")....5-10 60

EDWARDS, Shirley
Singles: 7-inch
SHRINE (110 "It's Your Love")...100-150 66

EDWARDS, Sonny
Singles: 7-inch
CEVETONE (508 "Toy Balloon") ...15-25 63
CEVETONE (516 "I Love You Tenderly")....15-25 63

EDWARDS, Stoney C&W '71
Singles: 7-inch
CAPITOL....3-5 70-76
JMI....3-5 78
MUSIC AMERICA....3-4 80
LPs: 10/12-inch
BOOT....5-10 83
CAPITOL....10-20 71-76
MUSIC AMERICA....5-10 81

EDWARDS, Tibby
Singles: 7-inch
TODD (1065 "Teenage Troubles") 10-20 60s

EDWARDS, Tom P&R '57
Singles: 78 rpm
CORAL....5-10 57
Singles: 7-inch
CORAL....5-10 57

EDWARDS, Tommy P&R/R&B '51
Singles: 78 rpm
MGM (10000 & 11000 series)....5-15 51-55
MGM (12000 series)....15-25 58
TOP....10-20 49-50
Singles: 7-inch
MGM (10000 & 11000 series)....10-20 51-55
MGM (12000 & 13000 series)....5-15 55-65
MGM (50000 series)....20-30 59
(Stereo.)
Picture Sleeves
MGM....8-12 60
EPs: 7-inch
MGM (1003 "It's All In the Game") 20-30 52
MGM (1614 "It's All In the Game") 10-20 58
MGM (1666/1667/1668 "For Young Lovers")....10-15 59
(Monaural. Price is for any of three volumes.)
MGM (SX-1666/1667/1668 "For Young Lovers")....10-20 59
(Stereo. Price is for any of three volumes.)
LPs: 10/12-inch
LION....15-25 59
MGM....20-40 58-63
METRO....8-12 65
REGENT (6096 "Tommy Edwards Sings")....20-30 58

EDWARDS, Vern
Singles: 78 rpm
PROBE (100 "Cool Baby Cool")....50-75 53
Singles: 7-inch
PROBE (100 "Cool Baby Cool")....100-150 53

EDWARDS, Vincent P&R/LP '62
(Vince Edwards)
Singles: 7-inch
CAPITOL....4-8 62
COLPIX....4-8 65
DECCA (31000 series)....4-8 62-63
DECCA (34039 "Open End Interview")....8-12 62
(Promotional issue only.)
DECCA (34074 "Unchained Melody")....5-10 62
(Stereo 33.)
KAMA SUTRA....4-6 67
RUSS-FI (1 "Oh Babe")....5-10 59
RUSS-FI (7001 "Why Did You Leave Me")....4-8 62
Picture Sleeves
COLPIX....4-8 65
DECCA (4311 "Vincent Edwards Sings")....10-20 62
(Monaural.)
DECCA (7-4311 "Vincent Edwards Sings")....15-25 62
(Stereo.)
KAMA SUTRA....4-8 67
EPs: 7-inch
DECCA....8-10 62
LPs: 10/12-inch
DECCA....10-20 62-63

EDWARDS, Wade
Singles: 7-inch
SHANDALA (1001 "Big Bruce")....5-10

EDWARDS BROTHERS
Singles: 7-inch
MUSIC WORLD (106 "Keep On Knockin' ")....10-20

EDWARDS' GENERATION
(Chuck Edwards)
Singles: 7-inch
TIGHT (302 "I Want You Girl")....10-15
LPs: 10/12-inch
TIGHT (401 "In San Francisco—The Street Thang")....10-20

EDWIN, Donald
Singles: 7-inch
ZENITH....10-15 63

EEE, Don
Singles: 7-inch
CMI (102 "Stop At the Hop")....25-35

EEK-A-MOUSE
LPs: 10/12-inch
REAL AUTHENTIC SOUND....5-10 83

EGAN, Joe
Singles: 7-inch
ARIOLA AMERICA....3-4 79
Also see STEALERS WHEEL

EGAN, Walter P&R/LP '77
Singles: 7-inch
BACKSTREET....3-4 83
COLUMBIA....3-4 77-79
Picture Sleeves
BACKSTREET....3-4 83
LPs: 10/12-inch
BACKSTREET....5-8 83
COLUMBIA....5-10 77-80
Also see BUCKINGHAM, Lindsey
Also see MASON, Dave / Les Dudek / Southside Johnny & Asbury Jukes / Walter Egan
Also see NICKS, Stevie

EGANS, Willie
Singles: 78 rpm
DASH....50-100 57
MAMBO....20-40 55
VITA....20-40 56
Singles: 7-inch
DASH (55001 "Rock & Roll Fever")....50-100 57
MAMBO (102 "What a Shame")....50-75 55
MAMBO (106 "Sad Sad Feeling")..50-75 55
MAMBO (107 "Treat Me Right")....50-75 55
MAMBO (111 "Oh, Baby")....50-75 55
VITA (119 "Willie's Blues")....50-75 56
Also see LLOYD & WILLIE
Also see WILLIE & RUTH

EGG
LPs: 10/12-inch
DERAM....10-15 70-71
Also see ARZACHEL
Also see FISCHER & EPSTEIN

EGG CREAM Featuring Andy Adams LP '77
Singles: 7-inch
PYRAMID....3-5 77
LPs: 10/12-inch
PYRAMID....5-10 77
Member: Andy Adams.

EGGHEADS
Singles: 7-inch
DECCA....5-8 60

EGGHEADS
Singles: 7-inch
BELL (601 "Foolin' Around")....5-10 65

EGGINS, Willie, & Orchestra
(Willie Eagins)
Singles: 78 rpm
MAMBO (102 "What a Shame")....10-20 55
Singles: 7-inch
MAMBO (102 "What a Shame")....40-60 55

EGGLESTON, Cozy
Singles: 78 rpm
STATES....10-15 53
Singles: 7-inch
CO-EGG (3621 "Joker's Wild")....10-20
STATES (133 "Big Heavy")....40-60 53
(Black vinyl.)
STATES (133 "Big Heavy")....100-150 53
(Colored vinyl.)

EGGS OVER EASY
LPs: 10/12-inch
A&M ... 10-12 72

EGYPTIAN COMBO
Singles: 7-inch
MGM ... 5-10 66
NORMAN ... 5-10 64-65

EGYPTIAN KINGS
Singles: 7-inch
NANC (1120 "Give Me Your Love") ... 25-50 61
(Has company address under label name.)
NANC (1120 "Give Me Your Love") ... 10-15 61
(Has "Dist. By Swingin' Records" under name.)
Members: Morris Wade; Leo Blakely; Pete Oden; Paul Moore; Sylvester Moore.
Also see COLUMBUS PHARAOHS
Also see 4 PHARAOHS
Also see KING PHARAOH & EGYPTIANS

EGYPTIAN LOVER *R&B '84*
Singles: 12-inch
EGYPTIAN ... 4-6 84-86
Singles: 7-inch
EGYPTIAN ... 3-4 84-86
FREAK BEAT ... 3-4 84
LPs: 10/12-inch
EGYPTIAN ... 5-10 85

EGYPTIANS
Singles: 7-inch
BIGTOP (0001 "The Wiggle") ... 10-20 62
DANAE (1002 "That's Alright") ... 20-30
MAH'S (0001 "The Party Stomp") ... 20-40 60
PRIME TIME (202 "Turn Around") ... 35-55

EGYPTIANS
Singles: 7-inch
CHANCE (100 "My Little Girl") ... 15-25 65

EHRET, Bob
Singles: 78 rpm
ALADDIN ... 75-125 57
Singles: 7-inch
ALADDIN (3377 "Stop the Clock") ... 75-125 57

"8"
Singles: 7-inch
COLUMBIA (44956 "The King's Birthday Party") ... 4-6 69

EIGHT BALLS
Singles: 7-inch
ALEXIS (8300 "Got a Hot Rod Baby") ... 3-5 84
Picture Sleeves
ALEXIS (8300 "Got a Hot Rod Baby") ... 3-5 84

EIGHT BELLS
(With Jimmy Carroll & Orchestra)
Singles: 78 rpm
BELL (1060 "Dream") ... 10-15 54
Singles: 7-inch
BELL (1060 "Dream") ... 15-25 54

801
LPs: 10/12-inch
EDITIONS E.G ... 5-10 86
Members: Phil Manzanera; Brian Eno.
Also see ENO, Brian
Also see MANZANERA, Phil

805
Singles: 7-inch
RCA ... 3-4 82
LPs: 10/12-inch
RCA ... 5-10 82

EIGHT MINUTES
Singles: 7-inch
JAY PEE (130 "Will You Be Mine") ... 10-15 60s
JAY PEE (200 "Let's Sign a Peace Treaty") ... 10-15 60s
PERCEPTION ... 4-6

EIGHT SECONDS *P&R '87*
Singles: 7-inch
POLYDOR ... 3-4 87
Picture Sleeves
POLYDOR ... 3-4 87

18TH CENTURY CONCEPTS
LPs: 10/12-inch
SIDEWALK ... 10-15 67

8TH DAY *P&R/R&B/LP '71*
(Eighth Day)
Singles: 7-inch
A&M ... 3-4 83
INVICTUS ... 3-5 71-72
KAPP ... 4-8 67-69
Picture Sleeves
KAPP ... 5-8 68
LPs: 10/12-inch
A&M ... 5-10 83
INVICTUS ... 8-10 71-73
KAPP ... 10-15 68
Members: Melvin Davis; Tony Newton; Bruce Nazarion; Michael Anthony; Anita Sherman; Carole Stallings; Lynn Harter.

EIGHTH WONDER *P&R '88*
Singles: 7-inch
WTG ... 3-4 88-89
Picture Sleeves
WTG ... 3-4 88
Members: Patsy Kensit; Jamie Kensit.

88s
Singles: 7-inch
ENGRAM ... 5-10 81
Picture Sleeves
ENGRAM ... 5-10 81

EIH, Damin, A.L.K. & Brother Clark
LPs: 10/12-inch
DEMELOT (7310 "Never Mind") ... 100-150 73
Members: Damin Eih; A.L. Katzner; Brother Clark Dircz.

EINZELGANGER
(Giorgio Moroder)
LPs: 10/12-inch
OASIS ... 5-10 75
Also see MORODER, Giorgio

EIRE APPARENT
Singles: 7-inch
BUDDAH ... 10-15 69
LPs: 10/12-inch
BUDDAH (5031 "Sunrise") ... 25-35 69

EISENHOWER, General Dwight
Singles: 7-inch 78 rpm
PICTUREPLAS ("I Like Ike") ... 40-50 52
(Promotional issue for Presidential campaign. Words and music by Irving Berlin. Includes envelope mailer.)

EITONES
("ElTones")
Singles: 78 rpm
CHIEF ... 100-150 55
Singles: 7-inch
CHIEF (45-8 "I Won't Be Your Fool") ... 300-500 55

EKHOES
Singles: 7-inch
LEMANS ... 3-5
Picture Sleeves
LEMANS ... 4-6

EKSEPTION
Singles: 7-inch
FONTANA ... 5-10 69
LPs: 10/12-inch
PHILLIPS ... 10-12 70

EKUD, Duke: see DUKE EKUD

ELAINE
Singles: 7-inch
CORVAIR (902 "Inside of Me") ... 10-15 62
LAURIE (3093 "Baby, I Need You Now") ... 8-12 61
ROULETTE (4499 "Look But Don't Touch") ... 8-12 63
ROULETTE (4514 "There's Danger Ahead") ... 8-12 63

ELAINE & DEREK
Singles: 7-inch
PARROT ... 5-10 64-65
VEE JAY ... 8-12 62

ELAINE & ELLEN *R&B '80*
Singles: 7-inch
OVATION (1148 "Fill Me Up") ... 3-5 80

ELASTIC OZ BAND: see ELLIOT, Bill, & Elastic Oz Band

ELASTIC PRISM
Singles: 7-inch
KUSTOM (101 "In the Garden") ... 35-50 69
JANA (6969 "Red Purple & Blue") ... 10-20 70
JANA (7235 "Going Down") ... 10-20 71
Members: Terry Atwell; Donnie Atwell.

ELASTIK BAND
Singles: 7-inch
ATCO ... 10-15 68
KAPP ... 10-15 68

ELBERT, Donnie *P&R/R&B '57*
Singles: 78 rpm
DELUXE ... 15-25 57
Singles: 7-inch
A-O ... 3-5 75
ALL PLATINUM ... 3-5 72
AVCO ... 3-5 72
CHECKER (1062 "Everything to Me") ... 10-15 63
COMMAND PERFORMANCE ... 3-5
CUB (9125 "Don't Cry My Love") ... 10-15 63
DELUXE (6143 "Believe It Or Not") ... 20-30 57
DELUXE (6161 "My Confession of Love") ... 30-40 58
DELUXE (6164 "Someone Made You for Me") ... 20-30 58
DELUXE (6168 "I Want to Be Near You") ... 20-30 58
ELBERT ... 4-6
GATEWAY ... 4-8 64-65
GUSTO ... 3-4 80s
JALYNNE (107 "Mommies' [sic] Gone") ... 15-25 60
JALYNNE (110 "Lucille") ... 5-10 62
PARKWAY ... 5-10 62
RARE BULLET ... 3-5 70
RED TOP (122 "Hey Baby") ... 15-25
RED TOP (130 "Someday") ... 15-25
TRIP ... 3-5
UP STATE ... 5-8
VEE JAY (336 "Hey Baby") ... 10-15 60
VEE JAY (353 "Half As Old") ... 10-15 60
VEE JAY (370 "I Beg of You") ... 10-15 60
LPs: 10/12-inch
ALL PLATINUM ... 10-15 71
DELUXE ... 10-15 71
KING (629 "The Sensational Donnie Elbert Sings") ... 100-200 59
SUGARHILL ... 5-10 81
TRIP ... 8-10 72
Also see VIBRAHARPS

ELBOW BENDERS
Singles: 7-inch
HANOVER ... 5-10 59

ELBOW BONES & RACKETEERS *D&D '83*
Singles: 12-inch
EMI AMERICA ... 4-6 83
Singles: 7-inch
EMI AMERICA ... 3-4 84
Members: Ginchy Dan; Stephanie Fuller.

EL BOY
(With the Ralph Sayho Calypso Singers)
Singles: 78 rpm
RAMA (220 "Jack, Jack, Jack") ... 5-10 57
Singles: 7-inch
RAMA (220 "Jack, Jack, Jack") ... 10-20 57

EL CAPRIS
("Featuring Sam Crumby")
Singles: 78 rpm
BULLSEYE ... 25-50 56
Singles: 7-inch
ARGYLE (1010 "Ooh But She Did") ... 20-30 61
BULLSEYE (102 "Ooh But She Did") ... 150-200 56
BULLSEYE (102 "Oh But She Did") ... 100-150 56
(We know of copies on Big City 1502; but have yet to learn their value, or when issued.)
FEE BEE (216 "Your Star") ... 30-40 57
HI-Q (5006 "Girl of Mine") ... 50-100 57
(Blue label.)
HI-Q (5006 "Girl of Mine") ... 25-50 57
(Yellow label.)
PARIS (525 "They're Laughing At Me") ... 25-35 58
RING-O (308 "Quit Pulling My Woman") ... 15-25 60
Member: Sam Crunby.

EL CHICANO *P&R/R&B/LP '70*
Singles: 7-inch
GORDO ... 3-6 70
KAPP/GORDO ... 3-6 70-72
MCA ... 3-5 73-75
RFR ... 3-4 82
SHADYBROOK ... 3-5 77-78
LPs: 10/12-inch
KAPP ... 10-12 70-72
MCA ... 8-10 73-74
Members: Jerry Salas; Mickey Lespron; Fred Sanchez; Bob Espinosa; Andre Baeza.
Also see TIERRA

ELCHORDS
("Featuring Butchy Saunders")
Singles: 78 rpm
GOOD (544 "Peppermint Stick") ... 50-100 58
Singles: 7-inch
GOOD (544 "Peppermint Stick") ... 50-75 58
(Has straight horizontal lines on label. Shows publisher as "Don Music" on both sides of label.)
GOOD (544 "Peppermint Stick") ... 40-60 62
(Red vinyl.)
GOOD (544 "Peppermint Stick") ... 10-20 62
(Has sawtooth horizontal lines on label.)
GOOD (544 "Peppermint Stick") ... 8-12 62
(No lines on label. Shows publisher as "Dan Publishers.")
Members: Butchy Saunders; Ron Talbert; David Ballot.
Also see SAUNDERS, Little Butchie

EL CLOD
Singles: 7-inch
CHALLENGE (9159 "Tijuana Border") ... 8-12 62
MERCURY (72082 "He's Not a Rebel") ... 5-10 63
VEE JAY (647 "Gringo") ... 5-10 65

EL COCO *P&R/R&B '76*
(Coco)
Singles: 12-inch
A.V.I. ... 4-8 76-85
Singles: 7-inch
A.V.I. ... 3-5 75-85
LPs: 10/12-inch
A.V.I. ... 5-10 75-85

EL DAMONTS
Singles: 7-inch
SCOTTY (640 "Over Easy") ... 10-20 65

ELDAROS
(With Ray Parratore & Rhythm Rockaways)
Singles: 7-inch
VESTA (102 "Please Surrender") ... 300-500 58

EL DEBARGE: see DE BARGE, El

EL DEENS
Singles: 7-inch
FEDERAL (12347 "My Love for You") ... 25-35 59
FEDERAL (12356 "Where Are You") ... 25-35 59

ELDEES
Singles: 7-inch
DYNAMICS (1013 "Don't Be Afraid to Love") ... 15-25

ELDER, Billy
Singles: 7-inch
CAPITOL ... 5-10 60

ELDER, Marcia
Singles: 7-inch
GEOVISION ... 3-4 84
Picture Sleeves
GEOVISION ... 3-4 84

ELDERBERRY JAK
LPs: 10/12-inch
ELECTRIC FOX ("Long Overdue") ... 15-25 75
(Selection number not known.)
FOREST ("Elderberry Jak") ... 50-75 69
(Selection number not known.)

EL DOMINGOES
Singles: 7-inch
KAPPA (206 "I'm Not Kidding You") ... 250-500 58

EL DOMINGOS
Singles: 7-inch
CANDLELIGHT (418 "Made in Heaven") ... 10-20 62
CHELSEA (1009 "Made in Heaven") ... 100-150 62
KARMIN (1001 "Are You Ready") ... 100-150 64

ELDORADO
Singles: 7-inch
THOR ... 3-6 79
Picture Sleeves
THOR ... 4-8 79

EL DORADOS *P&R/R&B '55*
Singles: 78 rpm
VEE JAY (115 "Baby I Need You") ... 25-50 54
VEE JAY (118 "Annie's Answer") ... 25-50 54
(With Hazel McCollum.)
VEE JAY (127: "One More Chance") ... 50-100 54
VEE JAY (147 thru 302) ... 20-50 56-57
Singles: 7-inch
COLLECTABLES ... 3-4
VEE JAY (115 "Baby I Need You") ... 50-100 54
(Black vinyl.)
VEE JAY (115 "Baby I Need You") ... 550-650 54
(Red vinyl.)
VEE JAY (118 "Annie's Answer") ... 50-100 54
(Black vinyl. With Hazel McCollum.)
VEE JAY (118 "Annie's Answer") ... 400-500 54
(Red vinyl.)
VEE JAY (127 "One More Chance") ... 150-250 54
VEE JAY (147 "At My Front Door") ... 50-75 55
VEE JAY (165 "I'll Be Forever Lovin' You") ... 50-75 55
VEE JAY (180 "Now That You've Gone") ... 40-60 56
VEE JAY (197 "A Fallen Tear") ... 40-60 56
VEE JAY (211 "Bim Bam Boom") ... 50-75 56
VEE JAY (250 "Tears on My Pillow") ... 25-50 57
VEE JAY (263 "Three Reasons Why") ... 75-125 58
VEE JAY (302 "Lights Are Low") ... 75-125 58
LPs: 10/12-inch
COLLECTABLES (20 "Best of the El Dorados") ... 8-10 80s
(10-inch LP.)
LOST-NITE ... 8-12 81
SOLID SMOKE ... 5-10 82
VEE JAY (1001 "Crazy Little Mama") ... 300-500 58
(Maroon label.)
VEE JAY (1001 "Crazy Little Mama") ... 200-300 58
(Black label.)
Note: Vee Jay 1001 also contains two tracks by the Magnificents.
Members: Pirkle Lee Moses Jr; Arthur Bassett; Louis Bradley; James Maddox; Jewel Jones; Richard Nickens; Johnny Carter; Ted Long; John McCall; Douglas Brown.
Also see DELEGATES
Also see THOSE FOUR ELDORADOS
Also see KOOL GENTS
Also see MAGNIFICENTS
Also see TEMPOS

EL DORADOS
Singles: 7-inch
ROCK-HIGHLAND ("Linda Lee") ... 200-300 60
Members: Robert Henderson; John Westling; Johnny Dee; Bob Henderson.

EL DORADOS
Singles: 7-inch
PORT ... 8-12 65
TORRID (100 "In Over My Head") 15-25 60s

EL DORADOS
Singles: 7-inch
PAULA ... 4-6 72

ELDORAYS
Singles: 7-inch
BUD (114 "Nights of Ecstasy") ... 25-35 61

ELDRED, Lee
Singles: 7-inch
ARCHIVES (67 "Leave Me Your Love") ... 5-10 69

ELDRIDGE, Billy
(With the Fire Balls)
Singles: 7-inch
UNART (2011 "Let's Go Baby") ... 50-75 59
VULCO (1501 "Let's Go Baby") ... 75-125 59

ELDRIDGE, Marvin
Singles: 7-inch
KIM ... 4-6 86

ELECTRAS
Singles: 7-inch
INFINITY (012 "You Lied") ... 30-40 61
INFINITY (016 "The Stomp") ... 10-15 62
Member: Billy Storm.
Also see STORM, Billy

ELECTRAS
Singles: 7-inch
LOLA (100 "Can't You See It in My Eyes") ... 20-30 62

ELECTRAS / Surgeons
Singles: 7-inch
CEE JAM (100 "You Know") ... 10-15 63
Also see ELECTRAS

ELECTRAS
Singles: 7-inch
RUBY DOO (2 "Little Girl of Mine") .8-10 66
SCOTTY (11A " 'Bout My Love") ... 30-40 65
(Second issue—improved quality pressing.)
SCOTTY (6194 "'Bout My Love") 75-125 65
SCOTTY (6351 "Dirty Old Man"/"Courage To Cry") ... 50-75 66
SCOTTY (6511 " 'Bout My Love") .. 25-35 65
(First release—poor fidelity.)
SCOTTY (6613 "Soul Searchin") ... 75-125 66
SCOTTY (6621 "Dirty Old Man") ... 20-30 66
SCOTTY (6720 "Action Woman") ... 500-750 67
SCOTTY (6720 "I'm Not Talkin' ") ... 75-125 67
(Same selection number used twice.)
Members: Earl Bulinski; Bill Bulinski; Jerry Fink; Gary Omerza; Tim Elving.
Also see TWAS BRILLIG

ELECTRAS
Singles: 7-inch
DEE LITE ... 3-5 70

ELECTRATONES
Singles: 7-inch
GONE (7005 "Guitar Bossa Nova") ... 30-40

ELECTRIC BLUES
Singles: 7-inch
MGM ... 4-8 67

ELECTRIC BOYS *P&R/LP '90*
Singles: 7-inch
ATCO ... 3-4 90
LPs: 10/12-inch
ATCO ... 5-8 90

ELECTRIC COMPANY
Singles: 7-inch
TITAN ... 4-8 66

ELECTRIC EXPRESS *P&R/R&B '71*
Singles: 7-inch
AVCO ... 4-8
KEY-VAC (2930 "Hearsay") ... 40-60
LINCO ... 4-8 71

ELECTRIC FLAG *LP '68*
(Electric Flag Music Band)
Singles: 7-inch
ATLANTIC ... 3-5 74-75
COLUMBIA ... 4-8 67
SIDEWALK ... 8-12 67
Picture Sleeves
COLUMBIA ... 5-10 67
LPs: 10/12-inch
ATLANTIC ... 8-10 74
COLUMBIA ... 10-15 68-71
Also see BLOOMFIELD, Mike, & Nick Gravenites
Also see GRAVENTES, Nick
Also see MILES, Buddy, Express

ELECTRIC HAND BAND
Singles: 7-inch
CERTRON (10009 "Electric Blues") ... 10-20 66

ELECTRIC INDIAN *P&R/R&B/LP '69*
Singles: 7-inch
MARMADUKE ... 5-10 69
U.A. ... 3-6 69
LPs: 10/12-inch
U.A. ... 10-15 69
Also see MFSB

ELECTRIC JOHNNY
Singles: 7-inch
FELSTED ... 5-10 61

ELECTRIC JUNGLE
Singles: 7-inch
NIKE ... 10-20

ELECTRIC JUNKYARD
Singles: 7-inch
RCA ... 4-6 69
LPs: 10/12-inch
RCA ... 10-15 69

ELECTRIC LIGHT ORCHESTRA *LP '72*
(ELO)
Singles: 12-inch
JET (Black vinyl) ... 10-15 76-78
JET (137 "Livin' Thing") ... 15-25 76
(Blue vinyl. Promotional issue only.)
Singles: 7-inch
JET/CBS ... 3-5 77-86
JET/U.A. (Black vinyl) ... 3-5 77
JET/U.A. (1000 "Telephone Line") ... 4-8 77
(Green vinyl. Promotional issue only.)

JET/U.A. (1145 "Sweet Talkin' Woman") 4-8 77
(Purple vinyl. Promotional issue only.)
MCA 3-5 80
U.A. 4-6 72-77
Picture Sleeves
JET 3-6 78-79
JET/CBS 3-5 86
JET/U.A. 3-6 77
MCA 3-6 80
U.A. 4-6 74-77
LPs: 10/12-inch
CBS 8-10 86
JET/CBS (Except FZ-35769, 36966 & 40000 series) 5-10 78-86
JET/CBS (FZ-35769 "Discovery") 20-30 79
(Promotional issue only.)
JET/CBS (36966 "Box of Their Best") 20-25 80
(Boxed, three-disc set. Includes *Out of the Blue, A New World Record,* and *Discovery,* plus a bonus single, *Doin' That Crazy Thing.*)
JET/CBS (40000 series) 20-25 80-83
(Half-speed mastered.)
U.A. (Except 546) 10-15 72-76
U.A. (546 "Face the Music") 25-30 75
(Banded for airplay.Promotional issue only.)
U.A./JET (Black vinyl) 8-12 76-77
U.A./JET (123 "Olé ELO") 25-35 76
(Gold vinyl. Promotional issue only.)
U.A./JET (123 "Olé ELO") 25-35 76
(Colored vinyl – any color other than gold, including red, white, and blue. Promotional issues only.)
U.A./JET (679 "A New World Record") 10-20 76
(Colored vinyl.)
U.A./JET (823 "Out of the Blue") 30-40 76
(Blue vinyl. Promotional issue only.)
Also see LYNNE, Jeff
Also see NEWTON-JOHN, Olivia, & Electric Light Orchestra
Also see VIOLINSKI
Also see WOOD, Roy

ELECTRIC LOVE
Singles: 7-inch
CHARAY (40 "This Seat Is Saved") 15-20 68

ELECTRIC MIND — D&D '83
Singles: 12-inch
EMERGENCY 4-6 83

ELECTRIC PEACE
LPs: 10/12-inch
BIG K (109 "Electric Peace") 5-10 83
(Picture disc.)

ELECTRIC PRUNES — P&R '66
Singles: 7-inch
REPRISE (PRO-277 "Sanctus") 35-45 67
(Promotional issue only.)
REPRISE (PRO-0305 "Help Us") 25-35 68
(Promotional issue only.)
REPRISE (0473 "Little Olive") 25-35 66
REPRISE (0532 "I Had Too Much to Dream") 10-15 66
REPRISE (0564 "Get Me to the World on Time") 10-20 67
REPRISE (0594 "Dr. Do Good") 10-20 67
REPRISE (0607 "The Great Banana Hoax") 10-20 67
REPRISE (0652 "You Never Had It Better") 20-30 68
REPRISE (0805 "Hey Mr. President") 10-20 69
REPRISE (0833 "Violet Rose") 25-35 69
REPRISE (0858 "Love Grows") 15-20 69
LPs: 10/12-inch
REPRISE (6248 "I Had Too Much to Dream") 20-30 67
REPRISE (6262 "Underground") 30-40 67
REPRISE (6257 "Mass in F Minor") 20-30 67
REPRISE (6262 "Release of an Oath") 15-25 68
REPRISE (6342 "Just Good Rock 'N' Roll") 15-25 69

ELECTRIC RUBAYAT
Singles: 7-inch
INTERNATIONAL ARTISTS (124 "If I Was a Carpenter") 15-25 67

ELECTRIC SCOUNDRALS
LPs: 10/12-inch
PREMIER 10-15 60

ELECTRIC TOILET
Singles: 7-inch
NASCO (9004 "In the Hands of Karma"/"Revelations") 150-250 70
(No selection number used. Promotional issue only.)
LPs: 10/12-inch
NASCO (9004 "In the Hands of Karma") 250-300 70
Member: Dave Hall.

ELECTRIC TOMORROW
Singles: 7-inch
WORLD PACIFIC 4-8 66

ELECTRIC UNDERGROUND
LPs: 10/12-inch
PREMIER (9060 "Guitar Explosion") 50-75 67

ELECTRIFIED PEOPLE
Singles: 7-inch
RED LITE (113 "One Thousand Dimension in Blue") 10-15 66
Member: Jimmy Peterson.

ELECTRIFYING CASHMERES
Singles: 7-inch
SOUND STAGE 7 (1500 "What Does It Take") 10-20 72

ELECTRONAIRES
Singles: 7-inch
COUNT (505 "One Lonely Night") 50-100 59
Also see RANADO, Chuck

ELECTRONIC — P&R '90
Singles: 7-inch
W.B. 3-4 90
LPs: 10/12-inch
W.B. 5-8 91
Members: Bernard Sumner; John Marr; Neil Tennant; David Palmer; Anne Dudley.
Also see ART of NOISE
Also see NEW ORDER
Also see PET SHOP BOYS

ELECTRONIC CONCEPT ORCHESTRA — LP '69
LPs: 10/12-inch
LIMELIGHT 5-10 69
MERCURY 5-10 70
Member: Eddie Higgins.

ELECTRONS
Singles: 7-inch
DATE (1575 "It Ain't No Big Thing") 10-20 67
LAGUNA (103 "For Sale") 50-75 64
(First issued as by the Wright Sounds.)
SHOCK (290 "Turn on Your Lovelight") 20-30 60s
Also see WRIGHT SOUNDS

ELECTROSONIKS
LPs: 10/12-inch
PHILIPS 10-15 62

ELEGANT 4
Singles: 7-inch
COUSINS (1005 "Time to Say Goodbye") 20-25 65
MERCURY (72518 "Time to Say Goodbye") 8-12 65

ELEGANT TASTE
Singles: 7-inch
MAGNA-GLIDE 3-5 75

ELEGANTES
Singles: 7-inch
LAURIE 5-8 65

ELEGANTS — P&R/R&B '58
(Vito & Elegants)
Singles: 78 rpm
SPARTON/ABC-PAR (620 "Little Star") 50-100 58
(Canadian.)
Singles: 7-inch
ABC (2404 "Little Star") 3-5 73
ABC-PAR (10219 "Tiny Cloud") 20-30 61
APT (25005 "Little Star") 35-50 58
(Silver print on black label. No mention of ABC-Paramount on label.)
APT (25005 "Little Star") 25-35 58
(Silver print on black label. Reads: "A Product of AM-PAR Record Corp.")
APT (25005 "Little Star") 15-25 58
(White or multi-color label.)
APT (25017 "Goodnight") 25-35 58
APT (25029 "Payday") 15-25 59
BIM BAM BOOM (121 "Lonesome Weekend") 10-15 74
(Black vinyl.)
BIM BAM BOOM (121 "Lonesome Weekend") 8-10 74
(Colored vinyl.)
CRYSTAL BALL 4-8 81
HULL (732 "Little Boy Blue") 35-45 60
LAURIE (3283 "Barbara Beware") 15-25 65
LAURIE (3298 "Wake Up") 20-30 65
LAURIE (3324 "Belinda") 10-15 65
MCA 3-4
PHOTO (2662 "A Dream Can Come True") 15-25 63
PLANET (2727 "Human Angel") 3-5
(Colored vinyl.)
ROULETTE 3-4 71
SPARTON/ABC-PAR (620 "Little Star") 25-50 58
(Canadian.)
U.A. (230 "Speak Low") 10-20 60
U.A. (295 "Happiness") 10-20 61
Picture Sleeves
CRYSTAL BALL 4-8
PHOTO (2662 "A Dream Can Come True") 25-35 63
(Add $10 to $20 if accompanied by printed insert.)
LPs: 10/12-inch
CRYSTAL BALL 8-10 82
MURRAY HILL (210 "Little Star") 8-10 86
Members: Vito Picone; Frank Tardagno; Carman Romano; Jimmy Moschella; Artie Venosa.
Also see BARBARIANS
Also see CORDELL, Pat
Also see PICONE, Vito

ELEGANTS / Poni-Tails
Singles: 7-inch
ROULETTE 3-5 73
Also see ELEGANTS
Also see PONI-TAILS

ELEGANTS
Singles: 7-inch
BANGAR (613 "Minor Chaos") 20-30 64

ELEKTRA FYD REVIEW
Singles: 7-inch
N 20-30

ELEKTRAS
Singles: 7-inch
END 5-10 60
U.A. 5-10 63

ELEKTRICS
Singles: 7-inch
CAPITOL 3-4 80-81
Picture Sleeves
CAPITOL 3-4 80
LPs: 10/12-inch
CAPITOL 5-10 80-81

ELEKTRIK DRED — R&B '83
Singles: 7-inch
SOUNDS of FLORIDA 3-4 83

ELEKTRO, Eve — D&D '84
Singles: 12-inch
BLACK SUIT 4-6 84

ELEMENTS
Singles: 7-inch
TITAN (1708 "Lonely Hearts Club") 200-300 60
Members: Kenneth Sinclair.
Also see SIX TEENS

ELEMENTS
Singles: 7-inch
SARU (1224 "Just to Be with You") 20-40

ELENA
Singles: 7-inch
ROULETTE 8-12 65

ELENA MARIE
Singles: 7-inch
GEEBEE (1 "Soldier Boy") 50-100 61

ELEPHANT
LPs: 10/12-inch
CAPITOL 8-12 73
MOONWATCHER 8-12 74

ELEPHANT CANDY
LPs: 10/12-inch
UNI 15-20 69

ELEPHANTS MEMORY — LP '69
Singles: 7-inch
APPLE (1854 "Liberation Special"/"Madness") 5-10 72
APPLE (1854 "Liberation Special"/"Power Boogie") 300-400 72
(Note different flip side.)
BUDDAH 4-8 69
METROMEDIA 3-6 70-71
RCA 3-5 74
Promotional Singles
APPLE (1854 "Liberation Special") 20-25 72
Picture Sleeves
APPLE (1854 "Liberation Special") 8-10 72
METROMEDIA 4-8 70
LPs: 10/12-inch
APPLE (3389 "Elephants Memory") 10-15 72
BUDDAH 10-15 69-74
METROMEDIA 10-12 70
MUSE 8-10 70s
RCA 8-10 74
Also see LENNON, John

ELEVATION
Singles: 7-inch
CROWN TOWN 8-12

ELEVATORS
LPs: 10/12-inch
ARISTA 8-10 80

ELEVENTH HOUR — P&R '74
Singles: 7-inch
BELL (153 "Nothin' Comes Easy") 5-8 71
20TH FOX 3-5 74-76
LPs: 10/12-inch
ARISTA 6-10 75
20TH FOX 8-10 74-76

ELEVENTH HOUSE — LP '74
(With Larry Coryell)
Singles: 7-inch
VANGUARD 3-5 74
LPs: 10/12-inch
ARISTA 5-10 75
VANGUARD (40036 "Introducing the Eleventh House with Larry Coryell") 10-20 74
(Quadrophonic.)
VANGUARD (79342 "Introducing the Eleventh House with Larry Coryell") 8-12 74
Members: Larry Coryell; Kenny Nolan.
Also see APPLETREE THEATRE CO.
Also see CORYELL, Larry
Also see DYNAMICS
Also see MOUZON, Alphonse, & Larry Coryell

ELEY, Jack, & Courtmen
(Jack Eely)
Singles: 7-inch
BANG (520 "Louie Louie '66") 10-15 66
BANG (534 "Louie Go Home") 10-15 66
Also see KINGSMEN
Also see LEE, Jack E., & Squires

ELF
Singles: 7-inch
EPIC 3-5 72
MGM 3-5 71
LPs: 10/12-inch
EPIC 12-15 72
MGM 10-12 74-75
Also see BLACKMORE'S RAINBOW

ELFMAN, Danny
Singles: 12-inch
MCA 4-6 84
LPs: 10/12-inch
MCA 5-10 84
For a complete listing of soundtracks by this artist, consult *The Official Price Guide to Movie/TV Soundtracks and Original Cast Albums.*
Also see OINGO BOINGO

ELFSTONE
Singles: 7-inch
WORLD PACIFIC 4-8 67

ELGART, Larry — P&R/LP '82
(With His Manhattan Swing Orchestra)
Singles: 78 rpm
DECCA 3-5 54-55
Singles: 7-inch
DECCA 3-8 54-55
MGM 3-5 61-62
RCA 3-6 59-83
EPs: 7-inch
BRUNSWICK 5-10 54
DECCA 5-10 54-55
LPs: 10/12-inch
BRUNSWICK 15-25 54
(10-inch LPs.)
CAMDEN 5-10 60-73
DECCA 10-20 54-55
MGM 8-12 60-62
RCA 5-10 59-83

ELGART, Les, Orchestra — P&R/LP '56
Singles: 78 rpm
COLUMBIA 3-5 53-57
Singles: 7-inch
COLUMBIA (40000 series, except 40180) 3-8 53-62
COLUMBIA (40180 "Bandstand Boogie") 15-20 54
COLUMBIA (56767 "Bandstand Twist") 5-10 62
(Promotional issue only.)
GOLD-MOR 3-4 73
EPs: 7-inch
COLUMBIA 5-10 53-59
LPs: 10/12-inch
COLUMBIA 10-20 53-62
HARMONY 5-10 66

ELGART, Les & Larry — LP '64
Singles: 7-inch
COLUMBIA 3-4 64-68
SWAMPFIRE 3-4 69
Picture Sleeves
COLUMBIA 3-5 65
LPs: 10/12-inch
COLUMBIA (Except 38000 series) 8-15 57-68
COLUMBIA (38000 series) 5-10 82
HARMONY 5-10 68-73
SWAMPFIRE 5-10 70
Also see ELGART, Larry
Also see ELGART, Les

ELGIN, Johnny
Singles: 7-inch
KA$H (1010 "My Worst Habit") 3-5 70s

ELGINS
(With Stanley Applebaum Orchestra)
Singles: 7-inch
MGM (12670 "Mademoiselle") 100-200 58

ELGINS
Singles: 7-inch
FLIP (353 "Uncle Sam's Man") 25-35 60

ELGINS
Singles: 7-inch
A-B-S (113 "Pretending") 50-100 61

ELGINS
Singles: 7-inch
JOED (716 "Once Upon a Time") 500-750 62

ELGINS
Singles: 7-inch
LUMMTONE (109 "Finally") 30-40 62
LUMMTONE (109 "Johnny, I'm Sorry") 15-25 62
LUMMTONE (110 "Johnny, I'm Sorry") 15-25 62
LUMMTONE (112 "Finally") 15-25 63
LUMMTONE (113 "Your Lovely Ways") 15-25 64
TITAN (1724 "My Illness") 200-250 62
TITAN (1724 "Heartache Heartbreak") 150-200 62
(No. 1724 issued twice, but with same flip.)
Members: Kenneth Sinclair; Jimmy Smith.
Also see LITTLE TOMMY & ELGINS
Also see SIX TEENS

ELGINS
Singles: 7-inch
DOT (16563 "Cheryl") 35-55 63

ELGINS
Singles: 7-inch
CONGRESS (214 "The Times We've Wasted") 15-25 64
CONGRESS (225 "Here in My Arms") 15-25 64
VALIANT (712 "Street Scene") 15-25 65

ELGINS — P&R/R&B '66
Singles: 7-inch
V.I.P. 10-20 66-71
LPs: 10/12-inch
V.I.P. (400 "Darling Baby") 50-100 66
Members: Saundra Mallet; Cleo Miller; Robert Flemming; John Dawson; Norbert McClean.
Also see DOWNBEATS
Also see FIVE EMERALDS
Also see MALLET, Saundra

ELI'S SECOND COMING — R&B '76
Singles: 7-inch
SILVER BLUE 3-5 76-78
Members: Bobby Eli.
Also see MFSB

ELIAS, Al
Singles: 7-inch
PAYSON 10-15 58
RCA 8-12 58

ELIAS, Jean
Singles: 7-inch
BACK BEAT (623 "You Made Me an Anybody's Woman") 4-8 71

ELIGIBLES
Singles: 7-inch
CAPITOL 5-10 59-60
COURTNEY (712 "Big Day") 10-15 63
MERCURY 4-8 62
W.B. 4-8 63
EPs: 7-inch
CAPITOL 10-15 60
LPs: 10/12-inch
CAPITOL (1310 "Along the Trail") 20-35 60
CAPITOL (1411 "Love Is a Gamble") 20-35 60
MERCURY (20710 "Live at Vegas") 15-20 62

ELIJAH
LPs: 10/12-inch
MCA/SOUNDS of the SOUTH 8-10 73
U.A. 10-12 72

ELIMINATORS
Singles: 7-inch
TE 10-20 60s
LPs: 10/12-inch
LIBERTY (3365 "Liverpool, Dragsters, Cycles and Surfing") 20-30 64
(Monaural.)
LIBERTY (3365 "Liverpool, Dragsters, Cycles and Surfing") 25-30 64
(Stereo.)

ELLIOTT, Shawn: see ELLIOTT, Shawn

ELITE
Singles: 7-inch
CHARAY (17 "One Potato, Two Potato") 5-10 65
CHARAY (31 "My Confusion") 15-25 66
CHARAY (56 "Bye Bye Baby") 5-10 67

ELITES
Singles: 7-inch
ABEL (225 "In the Little Chapel") 30-40 59

ELITES
Singles: 7-inch
HI-LITE (106 "You Mean So Much to Me") 50-75 60

ELITES
Singles: 7-inch
CHIEF (7028 "Dapper Dan") 45-65 61
CHIEF (7032 "Jack the Ripper") 20-30 61

E'LITES
Singles: 7-inch
EGS (001 "Restless") 10-20 62

ELITES
Singles: 7-inch
ABC-PAR (10460 "Tree of Love") 10-15 63

ELIZABETH
Singles: 7-inch
VANGUARD (35070 "Mary Anne") 8-12 68
Picture Sleeves
VANGUARD 8-12 68
LPs: 10/12-inch
VANGUARD (6501 "Elizabeth") 50-75 68
Members: Bob Patterson; Steve Weingart; Steve Bruno; Hank Ransome; Jim Dahme.
Also see GOOD GOD

ELJAYS
Singles: 7-inch
CB (5008 "I Wonder") 50-100 62

ELKINS, Bill
Singles: 7-inch
BLANK (103 "You Made Me Mad") 25-35

ELL, Carl, & Buddies
Singles: 7-inch
COMBO (154 "Bobby My Love") 25-35 59
Also see LAMPLIGHTERS
Also see RIVINGTONS
Also see SHARPS

ELLA & FELLA
Singles: 7-inch
ZENITH 4-8 62

ELLEDGE, Jimmy — P&R '61
Singles: 7-inch
4 STAR 3-5 75
HICKORY 4-8 65-67
LITTLE DARLIN' 4-6 68
RCA (Except 7910 & 8012) 6-12 61-64
RCA (7910 "Swanee River Rocket") 25-35 61
RCA (8012 "Can't You See It in My Eyes") 10-20 62
SIMS 4-8 64

Picture Sleeves
RCA 10-15 62-63
LPs: 10/12-inch
LITTLE DARLIN' 8-12 68

ELLEN, Lori: see LORI ELLEN

ELLEN, Mary: see MARY ELLEN

ELLEN & SHANDELS
Singles: 7-inch
LA SALLE (25 "Gypsy") 10-20

ELLERINE
LPs: 10/12-inch
MAINSTREAM 8-10 72

ELLIE GAYE: see GREENWICH, Ellie

ELLIE POP
Singles: 7-inch
MAINSTREAM (686 "Can't Be Love") 10-15 68
LPs: 10/12-inch
MAINSTREAM (6115 "Ellie Pop") 30-50 68

ELLIMAN, Yvonne P&R '71
Singles: 7-inch
DECCA 3-5 71-72
MCA 3-4
RSO 3-5 74-79
Picture Sleeves
RSO 3-5 78
LPs: 10/12-inch
DECCA 10-15 72
MCA 8-12 73
RSO 6-10 77-79
Also see BISHOP, Stephen, & Yvonne Elliman

ELLIMAN, Yvonne / Carl Anderson
Singles: 7-inch
MCA 3-5 73
Also see ANDERSON, Carl
Also see ELLIMAN, Yvonne

ELLINGSON, Dave
Singles: 7-inch
BELL 3-5 72

ELLINGTON, Duke P&R '27
Singles: 78 rpm
CAPITOL 3-8 53-56
COLUMBIA 3-8 50-53
RCA 3-8 51-55
Singles: 7-inch
BELL 3-4 73
BETHLEHEM 5-10 58-60
CAPITOL (2000 series) 5-15 53-56
COLUMBIA (33000 series) 3-4 76
COLUMBIA (39000 series) 8-15 50-53
COLUMBIA (40000 thru 42000 series) 4-8 58-61
COLUMBIA PRICELESS EDITION. 5-10
RCA (0300 series) 3-5 74
RCA (4000 thru 6000 series) 8-15 51-55
REPRISE 4-8 67
EPs: 7-inch
BRUNSWICK 10-20 54
CAPITOL 10-20 53-56
COLUMBIA 10-20 50-56
RCA 10-20 52-60
ROYALE 10-20 50s
LPs: 10/12-inch
ALLEGIANCE 5-8 84
ALLEGRO 25-50 54
(10-inch LPs.)
ATLANTIC 5-10 71-82
BASF 5-10 73
BETHLEHEM 15-30 56-57
BRIGHT ORANGE 5-10 73
BRUNSWICK (54000 series) 15-30 56
BRUNSWICK (58000 series) 30-50 54
(10-inch LPs.)
CAMDEN (400 series) 15-25 58
CAPITOL (400 series) 25-50 53
(With "H" prefix. 10-inch LPs.)
CAPITOL (400 thru 600 series) 25-40 55-57
CAPITOL (1600 series) 10-20 61
(With "T" prefix.)
CAPITOL (11000 series) 5-10 72-77
CAPITOL (16000 series) 4-6 81
COLUMBIA (27 "The Ellington Era, Volume 1") 25-40 63
COLUMBIA (39 "The Ellington Era, Volume 2, 1927-1940") 25-40 66
COLUMBIA (500 thru 900 series) 20-30 54-57
COLUMBIA (1085 thru 2029 except 1360) 15-30 57-63
(Monaural.)
COLUMBIA (1360 "Anatomy of a Murder") 35-50 59
(Soundtrack. Monaural.)
COLUMBIA (4000 series) 25-50 55
COLUMBIA (6000 series) 30-60 50
(10-inch LPs.)
COLUMBIA (8053 thru 9600, except 8166) 10-20 57-68
(Stereo.)
COLUMBIA (8166 "Anatomy of a Murder") 45-60 59
(Soundtrack. Stereo.)
COLUMBIA (14000 series) 5-10 79
(Columbia Special Products series.)
COLUMBIA (32000 thru 38000 series) 5-10 73-82
COLUMBIA SPECIAL PRODUCTS 8-10 82
DECCA 8-15 67-70
DOCTOR JAZZ 5-8 84
EVEREST 5-10 70-73
FANTASY 6-12 71-75
FLYING DUTCHMAN 5-10 69
HARMONY 5-10 67-71
IMPULSE (Except 9200 series) 15-20 62
IMPULSE (9200 series) 8-12 73
MOSAIC (160 "Complete Capitol Recordings of Duke Ellington") 100-120 90s
(Boxed, eight-disc set. 5000 made.)
ODYSSEY 8-12 68
PABLO 5-10 76-80
PRESTIGE 6-12 73-77
RCA (500 series) 10-20 64-69
RCA (0700 thru 2000 series) 5-8 75-78
(With "ANL1" or "APL1" prefix.)
RCA (1000 series) 25-40 54
(With "LJM" or "LPT" prefix.)
RCA (1300 thru 2800 series) 10-30 57-66
(With "LPM" or "LSP" prefix.)
RCA (3000 series) 25-50 52-53
(10-inch LPs.)
RCA (3500 thru 3900 series) 8-15 66-68
RCA (4000 series) 8-10 81
RCA (6009 "The Indispensible Duke Ellington") 20-30 61
RCA (6042 "This Is Duke Ellington") 10-15 71
REPRISE 10-20 63-68
RIVERSIDE (Except 100 series) 10-20 62-64
RIVERSIDE (100 series) 15-30 56-59
RON-LETTE 15-30 58
SOLID STATE 5-10 70
SUNSET 5-10 69
TRIP 5-10 75-76
U.A. (Except 14000 & 15000 series) 5-10 72
U.A. (14000 & 15000 series) 15-25 62
VERVE 10-15 67
"X" (3037 "Duke Ellington") 25-50 55
(10-inch LP.)
Also see ANDERSON, Ivie
Also see ARMSTRONG, Louis, & Duke Ellington
Also see BASIE, Count, & Duke Ellington
Also see BREWER, Teresa, & Duke Ellington
Also see CARROLL, Diahann, & Duke Ellington Orchestra
Also see CLOONEY, Rosemary, & Duke Ellington
Also see FITZGERALD, Ella, & Duke Ellington
Also see HIBBLER, Al, & Duke Ellington
Also see JACKSON, Mahalia, & Duke Ellington
Also see SINATRA, Frank, & Duke Ellington

ELLINGTON, Duke, & Boston Pops Orchestra LP '66
LPs: 10/12-inch
RCA 10-15 66
Also see BOSTON POPS ORCHESTRA

ELLINGTON, Duke, & John Coltrane
LPs: 10/12-inch
IMPULSE 15-25 63
Also see COLTRANE, John

ELLINGTON, Duke, & Johnny Hodges
LPs: 10/12-inch
PRESTIGE 8-10 81
VERVE (Except 8800 series) 15-30 59-60
VERVE (8800 series) 8-12 73
Also see ELLINGTON, Duke
Also see HODGES, Johnny

ELLINGTON, Harvey
LPs: 10/12-inch
STEPHENY (4010 "I Can't Hide the Blues") 25-30 59

ELLINGTON, Marc
Singles: 7-inch
AMPEX 4-6 71
LPs: 10/12-inch
AMPEX 10-15 71

ELLINGTON, Ron
Singles: 7-inch
ERA 5-10 63

ELLIOT, Bern, & Fenmen
Singles: 7-inch
LONDON 5-10 64

ELLIOT, Bill, Combo
Singles: 7-inch
IMPERIAL 8-10 61

ELLIOT, Bill, & Elastic Oz Band / Elastic Oz Band
(With John Lennon)
Singles: 7-inch
APPLE (1835 "God Save Us") 5-10 71
Promotional Singles
APPLE (1835 "God Save Us") 20-25 71
Picture Sleeves
APPLE (1835 "God Save Us") 8-12 71
Also see LENNON, John
Also see SPLINTER

ELLIOT, Cass P&R/LP '68
(Mama Cass)
Singles: 7-inch
DUNHILL 3-6 68-70
RCA 3-5 71-73
LPs: 10/12-inch
DUNHILL 10-20 68-72
PICKWICK 8-12
RCA 10-15 72-73
Also see BIG THREE
Also see MAMAS & PAPAS
Also see MASON, Dave, & Mama Cass
Also see MUGWUMPS

ELLIOT, Chet
Singles: 7-inch
SEECO 5-10 59

ELLIOT, Linda
Singles: 7-inch
JOSIE (958 "Little Girl Grew Up a Little Last Night") 15-25 66

ELLIOT, Mike, & Bud Latour
Singles: 7-inch
MCA 3-4 86
(Promotional issues only.)
TRI-FIVE 3-4 86

ELLIOT, Ron
LPs: 10/12-inch
W.B. 10-15 69
Also see BEAU BRUMMELS
Also see CLARK, Petula
Also see COODER, Ry
Also see GIANTS
Also see JOYOUS NOISE
Also see MORRISON, Van
Also see NEWMAN, Randy
Also see PAN
Also see PARTON, Dolly
Also see VALENTINO, Sal

ELLIOTT, Bob
LPs: 10/12-inch
CAEDMON 5-10
Also see BOB & RAY

ELLIOTT, Shawn
(Shawn Eliott)
Singles: 7-inch
DOUBLE-L (721 "I Found a New Baby") 10-20 63
ROULETTE 5-10 64-66
LPs: 10/12-inch
ROULETTE 15-25 65

ELLIS
Singles: 7-inch
EPIC 3-5 72
LPs: 10/12-inch
EPIC 8-10 73

ELLIS, Alfred
Singles: 7-inch
KING 10-15

ELLIS, Alton, & Flames
Singles: 7-inch
TREASURE ISLE (7010 "Duke of Earl") 15-25

ELLIS, Anita / Albert Ammons
Singles: 78 rpm
MERCURY/SAV-WAY (3059 "Ask Anyone Who Knows") 100-150 47
(Picture disc. Promotional issue only.)

ELLIS, Anita / Glen Gray & His Orchestra
Singles: 78 rpm
MERCURY/SAV-WAY (3059 "Ask Anyone Who Knows") 100-150 47
(Picture disc. Promotional issue only.)
Also see ELLIS, Anita / Albert Ammons
Also see GRAY, Glen, & Casa Loma Orchestra

ELLIS, Big Boy
(Wilbert Ellis)
Singles: 78 rpm
LENOX (521 "Dices Dices") 15-25 49
Also see BIG CHIEF TRIO

ELLIS, Cindy
Singles: 7-inch
LAURIE 4-8 60
Picture Sleeves
LAURIE 5-10 60

ELLIS, Dolan
Singles: 7-inch
CAPQ 3-5 72
EPs: 7-inch
WESTERN SAVINGS ("Arizona's Balladeer") 10-15 67
LPs: 10/12-inch
ARLIS (1387 "Man from the Big Country") 15-25 65
CAPQ 8-15 72-78
COMMENTARY 15-20 61
REPRISE 10-20 62

ELLIS, Don, & Royal Dukes
Singles: 7-inch
BEE (201 "Party Doll") 10-20 61
BEE (1110 "Blue Diamonds") 25-35 58
BEE (1111 "Come in World") 50-75 59
BEE (1114 "Half of Me") 75-125 59
(Bee 1114 is also the number of a Bunny Sigler release.)
Also see SIGLER, Bunny

ELLIS, Dorothy
Singles: 78 rpm
FEDERAL 15-25 52
Singles: 7-inch
FEDERAL (12070 "Drill Daddy Drill") 40-60 52

ELLIS, Herb, & Vince Megna
Singles: 7-inch
EMP (1001 "Poinciana") 10-20 65
Also see CONTINENTALS

ELLIS, Jimmy
Singles: 7-inch
BLANK LABEL (1142 "That's All Right") 10-15 79
(Gold vinyl. Label has no printing. Identification number – from vinyl trail-off – shown since no selection number is used. Promotional issue only. Includes insert letter from Shelby Singleton.)
BOBLO 5-10 77-78
CENTURY CITY (511 "Looking Through the Eyes of Love") 10-15 60s
CHALLENGER 4-6 73
DRADCO 8-12 64
GOLDBAND 5-10 60s
KRISTAL 3-4 85
MCA 3-5 73
SSS/SUN 3-8 72-77
SOUTHERN TRACKS 3-4 86-87
TONY LAWRENCE 3-4 83-84
Picture Sleeves
BOBLO (536 "I'm Not Trying to Be Like Elvis") 10-20 78
EPs: 7-inch
JIMMY ELLIS FAN CLUB ("Merry Christmas") 4-6 81
(No selection number used. Promotional issue only.)
LPs: 10/12-inch
BOBLO (829 "By Request, Ellis Sings Elvis") 75-125 77
ROLLER SKATE 8-10 82
Also see LEWIS, Jerry Lee, Carl Perkins & Charlie Rich
Also see MISTY / Jimmy Ellis
Also see ORION
Also see SILVER, Steven

ELLIS, Jimmy "Preacher"
(Jim "Preacher" Ellis & the Centuries)
Singles: 7-inch
CROSS ROAD 5-10 60s
HIP-DELIC (313 "That's the Way I Am") 8-12 60s
HIP-DELIC (314 "Looking Thru the Eyes of Love") 8-12 60s
JEWEL 5-10 66
ROMARK (116 "I Can't Work and Watch You") 5-10
SPACE 5-10 60s

ELLIS, Johnny
Singles: 7-inch
FREEDOM 5-10 59

ELLIS, LaBert
Singles: 7-inch
A&M 4-8 66

ELLIS, Larry
Singles: 7-inch
MOONDOG 5-8
ROULETTE 5-10 60

ELLIS, Lloyd
Singles: 78 rpm
MERCURY 10-15 54
Singles: 7-inch
MERCURY (70463 "Yo-Yo Boogie") 15-25 54
MERCURY (70520 "Boogie Blues") 15-25 54

ELLIS, Lorraine
(With the Crows; with Ray Barrow & His Orchestra)
Singles: 78 rpm
BULLSEYE (100 "Perfidia") 10-15 55
GEE (1 "Perfidia") 25-35 54
Singles: 7-inch
BULLSEYE (100 "Perfidia") 35-50 55
GEE (1 "Perfidia") 150-200 54
Also see CROWS

ELLIS, Mike C&W '78
Singles: 7-inch
CIN KAY 3-5 78

ELLIS, Ray, Orchestra P&R '60
Singles: 78 rpm
COLUMBIA 3-8 57
Singles: 7-inch
COLUMBIA 3-8 57
MGM 3-5 59-60
RCA 3-5 61
EPs: 7-inch
COLUMBIA 5-10 57
LPs: 10/12-inch
COLUMBIA 10-20 57
HARMONY 10-15 59
MGM 10-15 59-60
RCA 10-15 61
Also see CRYSTALS

ELLIS, Rex
Singles: 7-inch
RIVERMONT (1160 "Bog Hop Jamboree") 150-200 59

ELLIS, Ronnie
Singles: 7-inch
VAN 15-25

ELLIS, Sheila
Singles: 7-inch
SAN 5-10

ELLIS, Shirley P&R/R&B '63
Singles: 7-inch
COLUMBIA 4-8 67
CONGRESS 5-10 63-65
MCA 3-5 73
Picture Sleeves
CONGRESS 5-10 64-65
LPs: 10/12-inch
COLUMBIA 15-20 67
CONGRESS 20-25 64-65
Also see ELLISTON, Shirley
Also see METRONOMES
Also see SHIRLEE MAY

ELLIS, Steve, & Starfires
Singles: 7-inch
DECIMA (2001 "Walking Around") 25-35 65
LPs: 10/12-inch
IGL (105 "Steve Ellis Songbook") 800-1200 67
Members: Steve Ellis; Jimmy Groth; Clem Hatting; Dean Senfner; Barry Hanson.

ELLIS, Stu
Singles: 7-inch
MADISON 5-8 61

ELLIS BROTHERS
Singles: 7-inch
ABC-PAR (9954 "Sneaky Alligator") 10-20 58

ELLISON, John
(With the Soul Brothers Six; Willie John Ellison; W.J. Ellison)
Singles: 7-inch
GRT (01 "I Think I'm Falling in Love") 4-8 77
(Canadian.)
GRT (128 "Dazz") 4-8 76
(Canadian.)
PHIL L.A. of SOUL (337 "You've Got to Have Rhythm") 5-10 70
PHIL L.A. of SOUL (341 "All I Want Is Your Love") 5-10 71
PHIL L.A. of SOUL (355 "Funky Funky Way of Makin' Love") 5-10 72
Also see ELLISON, Willie John
Also see SOUL BROTHERS SIX

ELLISON, Lorraine R&B '65
Singles: 7-inch
LOMA (2083 "When Love Flies Away") 5-10 67
MERCURY 5-10 65-66
SHARP (635 "Open Up Your Heart") 10-15 63
W.B. 4-6 66-69
LPs: 10/12-inch
W.B. (1000 series) 15-20 67-69
W.B. (2000 series) 8-10 74

ELLISON, Perline
Singles: 78 rpm
DECCA 8-12 44

ELLISON, W.J.: see ELLISON, John

ELLISON, Willie John: see ELLISON, John

ELLISTON, Shirley
Singles: 7-inch
SHELL (307 "Beautiful Love") 10-15 61
Also see ELLIS, Shirley

ELLUSIONS
Singles: 7-inch
LAMON (2004 "You Didn't Have to Leave") 20-30 60s

ELLWANGER, Sandy C&W '89
Singles: 7-inch
DOOR KNOB 3-4 89

EL MARADAS
Singles: 7-inch
RADAX (90711 "Marada Rock") 5-10

ELMER GANTRY'S VELVET OPERA
LPs: 10/12-inch
EPIC (26415 "Elmer Gantry's Velvet Opera") 25-30 68

ELMO, Sunnie, & Minor Chords
Singles: 7-inch
FLICK (009 "Let Me") 20-30 60
Also see MINOR CHORDS

ELMO & ALMO P&R '67
Singles: 7-inch
DADDY BEST 4-6 67

ELMO 'N' PATSY C&W '84
Singles: 7-inch
ELMO 'N' PATSY 3-5 79
EPIC 3-4 84
OINK 3-4 80
SOUNDWAVES 3-4 81
Picture Sleeves
EPIC 3-4 84
LPs: 10/12-inch
OINK 5-10 80
Members: Elmo Shropshire; Patsy Trigg.

ELMORE, Johnny, & Silver-Tones
Singles: 7-inch
JAR (105 "War Chant Boogie") 100-150

ELOISE
Singles: 7-inch
WAND 4-8 62

ELOPERS
Singles: 7-inch
RLW (1287 "Music to Smoke Banana Peels By") 10-20

ELOY
LPs: 10/12-inch
JANUS 8-10 74-75

EL PASO PETE
Singles: 7-inch
TWINKLE 5-10

EL PAULING
(El Pauling & Royalton; El Pauling & Royal Abbit)
Singles: 7-inch
FEDERAL (12383 "Solid Rock") 10-20 60
FEDERAL (12396 "Now Baby, Don't Do It") 15-25 61
FEDERAL (12398 "Please, Please Be Mine") 10-20 61

FEDERAL (12431 "Jail Bird")........10-20 61
FEDERAL (12464 "Send Me Somebody") 10-20 62
Session: Loman Pauling Jr.; Royal J. Abbit.
Also see 5 ROYALES

EL POLLOS
Singles: 7-inch
NEPTUNE (1001 "School Girl")....75-125 58
STUDIO (999 "High School Dance") 550-650 58

EL POOKS
Singles: 7-inch
ORIVIOUS (11129 "Trisha")..........25-35

ELQUIN'S
Singles: 7-inch
ROGO (1026 "Up's And Downs") ...10-20 61

EL RAYS
(With Willie Dixon & Orchestra)
Singles: 78 rpm
CHECKER 200-400 54
Singles: 7-inch
CHECKER (794 "Darling I Know")................................1000-1500 54
Members: Marvin Junior; Vern Allison; Mike McGill; Charles Barksdale.
Also see DELLS
Also see DIXON, Willie

EL RAYS
Singles: 7-inch
MM (104 "Till the End of Time").....25-50 63

EL RAY & NIGHT BEATS
Singles: 7-inch
REVIVE (103 "My Secret")............15-25 63
Member: Raymond Ojeda; Dick Whitstone; Gerald Bartelmas; Ron Kurtz; Bruce Rudan; Tom Montez; Jack Staumbeil; Terry Thuemling; Jack Gebhardt.
Also see LANE, Tommy
Also see NIGHT BEATS

EL REYES
Singles: 7-inch
JADE (501 "Mr. Moonglow")....1000-2000 58

EL REYS
Singles: 7-inch
IDEAL (94706 "Diamonds and Pearls") 20-30 64
(Identification number shown since no selection number is used.)
IDEAL (95388 "Angalie")................20-30 65
(Identification number shown since no selection number is used.)

EL-RICH TRIO & COMBO
Singles: 7-inch
ELCO (1 "This I Swear") 20-30 66

EL ROACHO
LPs: 10/12-inch
COLUMBIA.....................................10-12 73

ELROY & EXCITEMENTS
Singles: 7-inch
ALANNA (565 "My Love Will Never Die")..50-100 61

ELSHIRE, Patsy Ruth
Singles: 78 rpm
CAPITOL....................................... 5-10 54
Singles: 7-inch
CAPITOL.......................................10-15 54

EL SIERROS
Singles: 7-inch
TIMES SQUARE (29 "Love You So")...15-20 64
YUSSELS (7702 "Sunday Kind of Love") 15-25 63
Also see YOUNG ONES / EL SIERROS

EL TEMPOS
Singles: 7-inch
VEE JAY..................................... 5-10 63-64

ELTMAN, Eddie
Singles: 7-inch
TIN PAN ALLEY 5-10 59

ELTON & ROCKIN' ELTRADORS
Singles: 7-inch
LANOR (501 "I Love My Baby") 15-25 58

ELTONES
Singles: 7-inch
CUB (9011 "Like Mattie") 10-20 58

EL TORO & BANLONS
Singles: 7-inch
TRIANGLE (60-30 "I Love You Baby")......................................100-150 63

EL TORROS
Singles: 78 rpm
DUKE (175 "Dance with Me").........20-40 57
Singles: 7-inch
DUKE (175 "Dance with Me").........25-50 57
DUKE (194 "You Look Good to Me")..40-60 58
DUKE (321 "What's the Matter") 25-50 60
DUKE (333 "Two Lips")..................20-30 61
DUKE (353 "Mama's Cookin' ") 20-30 62

EL TORRROS
Singles: 7-inch
FRATERNITY (811 "Love Is Love")..75-125 58

EL TRIO DEL PUEBLO
Singles: 7-inch
PUEBLO...4-6 79
Members: Joe Vargas; Ray Baradat; Henry.

ELUSION R&B '81
Singles: 7-inch
COTILLION 3-4 81
LPs: 10/12-inch
COTILLION 5-10 81

ELUSIVES
Singles: 7-inch
PHILIPS 4-8 66

EL VENOS
(El Vinos)
Singles: 78 rpm
GROOVE 20-30 56
VIK..40-60 57
Singles: 7-inch
GROOVE (0170 "Now We're Together")..40-60 56
RCA (8303 "My Heart Beats Faster")...10-20 64
VIK (0305 "My Heart Beats Faster")...40-60 57
Also see DILLARD, Varetta

ELVES
Singles: 7-inch
DECCA...8-12 69

EL VINOS: see EL VENOS

ELVIRA & VI-TONES
Singles: 12-inch
RHINO..5-10 82

EL VIREOS
Singles: 7-inch
REVELLO (1002 "First Kiss").......75-125 59

ELVIS & ROADRUNNERS
Singles: 7-inch
ATLANTIC.. 4-8 66

ELVIS BROTHERS
Singles: 12-inch
PORTRAIT 4-6 83
Singles: 7-inch
PORTRAIT 3-4 83
LPs: 10/12-inch
PORTRAIT 5-10 83

ELY, Joe C&W '77
Singles: 7-inch
MCA.. 3-4 77-81
SOUTHCOAST................................. 3-4 81
EPs: 7-inch
SOUTHCOAST (1736 "Texas Special") 4-8 81
LPs: 10/12-inch
MCA..5-10 77-81
SOUTHCOAST.................................5-10 81
Also see SEXTON, Charlie

ELY, Rick
LPs: 10/12-inch
RCA...5-10 70

ELYSIAN FIELD
Singles: 7-inch
IMPERIAL....................................... 4-8 68-69
Members: Frank Bugbee; Jim Settle; Marvin Maxwell.
Also see SOUL INCORPORATED

EMANON FOUR
Singles: 78 rpm
FLASH (106 "Oh! That Girl")..........20-30 56
Singles: 7-inch
FLASH (106 "Oh! That Girl")..........40-60 56

EMANONS
Singles: 78 rpm
GEE (1005 "Change of Time").....50-100 56
JOSIE (801 "Blue Moon") 20-30 56
Singles: 7-inch
GGS (443 "Know I Miss You").....150-200
GEE (1005 "Change of Time").....75-100 56
JOSIE (801 "Blue Moon") 50-75 56
Members: Robert Coleman; Carl White; James Hill; Jim Dukes; Ralph Steeley.
Also see CONCEPTS & EMANONS

EMANONS
Singles: 7-inch
ABC-PAR (9913 "Dear One")..........8-12 58
WINLEY (226 "Dear One")..............15-25 58
Members: Jim Danella; Phil DeVito; Mike Buono; Joe Buono.
Also see 3 FRIENDS

EMANONS
Singles: 7-inch
DELBERT (5290 "Emanons Rock")..10-15 59
DOLL ("Stomper")..........................15-25 59
(Selection number not known.)

EMANONS
Singles: 7-inch
PHIL L.A. of SOUL 4-6 68

EMBER GLOWS
Singles: 7-inch
FINK..20-30

EMBERGLOWS
Singles: 7-inch
AMAZON (1005 "Make Up Your Mind") 10-15 62
DORE (591 "Have You Found Someone New")..15-25 61

EMBERMEN FIVE
(Embermen)
Singles: 7-inch
BANGAR (0628 "I'm Gonna Marry Mary")..20-25 65
CENTURY (30851 "Do You Have to Be So Cruel")...10-20 60s

SOMA (1429 "Karen").....................25-35 65
STUDIO CITY (1053 "Fire In My Heart") 25-35 66
STUDIO CITY (1062 "That's Why I Need You")..20-25 67
STUDIO CITY ("My Love for You Won't Die")..25-35 67
(No selection number used.)
Picture Sleeves
CENTURY (30851 "Do You Have to Be So Cruel")...25-35 60s

EMBERS
(With Vi Hamilton Trio)
Singles: 78 rpm
COLUMBIA (40287 "Sweet Lips") ..15-25 54
EMBER (101 "Paradise Hill") 100-200 53
HERALD (410 "Paradise Hill") 25-50 53
Singles: 7-inch
COLUMBIA (40287 "Sweet Lips") ..25-35 54
EMBER (101 "Paradise Hill") 400-500 53
HERALD (410 "Paradise Hill") 200-300 53
(Black label.)
HERALD (410 "Paradise Hill") 50-100 53
(Yellow label.)
HERALD (410 "Paradise Hill") 200-300 53
(Colored vinyl.)
Member: Eugene Pearson.
Also see DRIFTERS
Also see RIVILEERS

EMBERS
Singles: 7-inch
WYNNE...5-10 59

EMBERS
Singles: 7-inch
DOT 10-15 60
Also see SANDERS, Willis

EMBERS
Singles: 7-inch
COLLECTABLES 3-4 80s
EMPRESS (101 "Solitaire") 10-20 61
EMPRESS (104 "I Won't Cry Anymore")......................................10-20 61
EMPRESS (107 "Abigail")...............10-20 62
EMPRESS (108 "What a Surprise")..15-20 62
Picture Sleeves
EMPRESS (101 "Solitaire") 30-40 61

EMBERS
Singles: 7-inch
ARA...5-10
SUEMI..5-10 63

EMBERS
Singles: 7-inch
ATLANTIC..10-15 69
BELL (664 "It Ain't Necessary")......15-20 67
EEE...10-20
JCP (1008 "In My Lonely Room")....30-50 64
JCP (1028 "A Fool in Love") 50-100 64
JCP (1034 "First Time")..................40-60 65
JCP (1054 "It Ain't Necessary")......20-30 65
LIBERTY (55944 "Evelyn")...............5-10 67
MGM (14167 "Watch Out Girl") 15-25 70
LPs: 10/12-inch
EEE..10-15 80-82
JCP (2006 "Rock & Roll") 100-150 65
RIPETE 5-10 82
Members: Jackie Hamilton Gore; Bobby Tomlison; Johnny Hopkins; Craig Woolard; Gerald Davis; Doug Strange; Johnny Barker.
Also see SWINGING EMBERS

EMBERS
Singles: 7-inch
ACT IV (94147 "Forever")............75-125 65
(Identification number shown since no selection number is used. Previously issued as by the Seminoles.)
Also see SEMINOLES

EMBERTONES
(With Tony Agbay & Continentals)
Singles: 7-inch
BAY (203 "I Remember")..........100-200 62

EMBLEMS
Singles: 7-inch
BAYFRONT (107 "Would You Still Be Mine")..50-75 62
(Has straight, parallel horizontal lines.)
BAYFRONT (107 "Would You Still Be Mine")..20-30 62
(With wavy, parallel horizontal lines, or no lines at all.)
BAYFRONT (108 "Bang, Bang, Shoot 'Em, Daddy")..50-75 62
(Black vinyl.)
BAYFRONT (108 "Bang, Bang, Shoot 'Em, Daddy")..15-25
(Colored vinyl.)

EMBLEMS
Singles: 7-inch
OHMY 4-8 62

EMBLEMS
Singles: 7-inch
CAMEO..4-8 64

EMBRACEABLES
("Featuring Herman Bracey")
Singles: 7-inch
CY (1004 "My Foolish Pride") 10-20 62
DOVER (4100 "A Wall Between Us")...20-30 62
DOVER (4101 "Come Back")..........20-30 62
SANDY (1025 "From Someone Who Loves You")..75-125 59

EMBRACEABLES
Singles: 7-inch
SIDRA 4-8 68

EMBRY, Jerry
Singles: 7-inch
EBONY (03 "Jackie's Goodbye") ...40-60 63

EMBRY, Ted
Singles: 7-inch
ACCENT (1057 "New Shoes") 30-50 58

EMBRYO
LPs: 10/12-inch
BASF...8-10 74-75

EMCEES
(Tommy McCleland & Emcees)
Singles: 7-inch
CIMARRON (4041 "Ific")................20-30 60
CIMARRON (4044 "Hot Rock")......20-30 60

EMERALD CITY BANDITS
Singles: 7-inch
PHILIPS 10-15 64
Members: Don Drowty.
Also see DANTE

EMERALD ENTERTAINMENT
Singles
EMERALD (36 "Dungeon of Fusion") 15-20 89
(Diamond-shaped picture disc. 100 made.)

EMERALDS
Singles: 78 rpm
KICKS (3 "Sally Lou")....................50-75 54
Singles: 7-inch
ALLIED (10002 "Sally Lou")...........25-35 58
KICKS (3 "Sally Lou") 100-125 54

EMERALDS
Singles: 78 rpm
FEDERAL (12279 "I Cry")...............25-50 56
Singles: 7-inch
FEDERAL (12279 "I Cry")...........75-125 56
Also see BOND, Luther

EMERALDS
Singles: 7-inch
ABC-PAR (9889 "You Belong to My Heart")...15-25 58
ABC-PAR (9948 "I'm Dreaming")....15-25 58
TOY (7734 "Roadrunner")..............10-20 61
YALE (232 "Trapped")....................10-20 60

EMERALDS
Singles: 7-inch
BOBBIN' (107 "That's the Way It's Got to Be")...50-100 59
BOBBIN' (121 "Lover's Cry")........50-100 60
Member: Billy Davis.
Also see DAVIS, Billy

EMERALDS
Singles: 7-inch
REX (1004 "All the Time") 20-30 59
REX (1013 "I Kneel At Your Throne")..20-30 60
VENUS (1002 "The Lover") 100-200 59
VENUS (1003 "Marsha")............100-200 59

EMERALDS
Singles: 7-inch
JUBILEE..5-10 64

EMERALDS
Singles: 7-inch
DC (179 "Emerald Surf")................15-25 64
MOONGLOW (228 "Sittin' Bull")....15-25 63
MOONGLOW (232 "Moonlight Surf")..15-25 64
(Black vinyl.)
MOONGLOW (232 "Moonlight Surf")..40-50 64
(Green vinyl.)
RIVIERA (714 "Search for Love") ..15-25 64

EMERALDS
Singles: 7-inch
KING (6078 "Promises")................10-15 67

EMERALDS (on Hillside): see GEARS / Emeralds / Dedicated Followers / Internal Canitery Sin

EMERALDS
Singles: 7-inch
TOD 10-20

EMERALDS
Singles: 7-inch
DEE-JAY SPECIAL (18108 "Earthquake")..................................30-40
(Colored vinyl.)
Picture Sleeves
DEE-JAY SPECIAL 10-20

EMERALDS
Singles: 7-inch
NE HONEY 5-10

EMERALS
Singles: 7-inch
TIMES SQUARE (111 "Please Don't Crush My Dreams")..20-30 64
TRIPLE X (100 "Please Don't Crush My Dreams")..150-250 58
Member: Tony Pabon.

EMERGENCY EXIT
Singles: 7-inch
DUNHILL..10-15 67
RU-RO 10-15 66
RCA 10-15 60s
(Canadian.)
Picture Sleeves
RU-RO 10-15 66

EMERSON, Billy
(Billy "The Kid" Emerson; with Willie Dixon's Band)
Singles: 78 rpm
SUN (195 "No Teasin' Around") .150-250 54
SUN (203 "The Woodchuck") 100-200 54
SUN (214 "When It Rains It Pours")...50-100 55
SUN (219 "Red Hot")..................50-100 55
SUN (233 "Little Fine Healthy Thing")...25-50 55
VEE JAY 20-30 56-57
Singles: 7-inch
CHESS (1728 "Believe Me")..........10-20 59
CHESS (1740 "I'll Get to You") 10-20 59
MAD...10-15 60-61
M-PAC (7207 "The Whip")...............5-8 63
SUN (195 "No Teasin' Around") . 300-350 54
SUN (203 "The Woodchuck") 250-300 54
SUN (214 "When It Rains It Pours")...75-125 55
SUN (219 "Red Hot")..................75-125 55
SUN (233 "Little Fine Healthy Thing")...50-75 55
TARPON (6606 "When It Rains It Pours")...10-20 60
U.S.A. (751 "I Get That Feeling").....5-10 63
U.S.A. (777 "When It Rains It Pours")..5-10 64
VEE JAY (219 "Tomorrow Never Comes")..20-30 56
VEE JAY (247 "Somebody Show Me")...20-30 57
VEE JAY (261 "You Never Miss the Water")..20-30 57
Also see DIXON, Willie
Also see TURNER, Ike

EMERSON, Billy "The Kid" / Smokey Joe
Singles: 7-inch
SSS/SUN 5-10 80
Also see EMERSON, Billy
Also see SMOKEY JOE

EMERSON, Keith LP '81
LPs: 10/12-inch
BACKSTREET 5-10 81

EMERSON, Keith, & Nice
Singles: 7-inch
MERCURY......................................3-5 72
LPs: 10/12-inch
MERCURY....................................12-15 72
Also see EMERSON, Keith
Also see EMERSON, LAKE & PALMER
Also see NICE

EMERSON, Lee, & Marty Robbins
Singles: 78 rpm
COLUMBIA 8-12 56
Singles: 7-inch
COLUMBIA (40868 "Where D'ja Go")...10-20 56
Also see ROBBINS, Marty

EMERSON, LAKE & PALMER P&R/LP '71
Singles: 7-inch
ATLANTIC.......................................3-5 77-80
COTILLION.....................................4-6 71-72
MANTICORE (2003 "Brain Salad Surgery")..3-5 78
MANTICORE (2003 "Brain Salad Surgery")..5-10 78
(Promotional issue only.)
POLYDOR (885101 "Touch & Go")....3-4 86
Picture Sleeves
MANTICORE (2003 "Brain Salad Surgery")..10-20 78
(Promotional issue only.)
POLYDOR (885101 "Touch & Go")....3-5 86
LPs: 10/12-inch
ATLANTIC (Except 281)................8-10 77-80
ATLANTIC (281 "Emerson, Lake & Palmer")..12-15 77
(With the London Philharmonic Orchestra. Also contains interviews with the three members. Promotional issue only.)
COTILLION 12-15 71-72
MFSL (031 "Pictures at an Exhibition")......................................25-40 79
MFSL (203 "Tarkus")....................20-25 94
MFSL (218 "Trilogy") 20-25 94
MANTICORE..................................10-12 73-74
Members: Keith Emerson; Greg Lake; Carl Palmer.
Also see ASIA
Also see EMERSON, LAKE & POWELL
Also see 3

EMERSON, LAKE & POWELL P&R/LP '86
Singles: 7-inch
POLYDOR.......................................3-4 86
Picture Sleeves
POLYDOR.......................................3-4 86
LPs: 10/12-inch
POLYDOR.......................................5-10 86
Members: Keith Emerson; Greg Lake; Cozy Powell.
Also see EMERSON, Keith
Also see EMERSON, LAKE & PALMER
Also see LAKE, Greg
Also see POWELL, Cozy

EMERSON'S OLD TIMEY CUSTARD-SUCKIN' BAND
LPs: 10/12-inch
ESP...10-12 70s

EMERSONS
Singles: 7-inch
CUB 8-12 59

NEWPORT (7004 "Joannie, Joannie")....15-20 58
U.A. (379 "Lonliness")....10-20 61
Members: Eddie Jones; Thomas Cook; Frank Cook; Joe Caines. Session: King Curtis.
Also see DEMENS
Also see KING CURTIS

EMERY, Ralph *C&W '61*
Singles: 7-inch
LIBERTY.... 5-10 61-63

EMIGRE
LPs: 10/12-inch
CHRYSALIS.... 5-10 79

EMILY
Singles: 7-inch
CHALLENGE.... 8-15 60

EMJAYS
Singles: 7-inch
GREENWICH....10-15 58
PARIS....10-15 59
Members: Jimmy Curtis; Mike Fox; Judy Lloyd.

EMMERSON, Les *P&R '73*
Singles: 7-inch
LION.... 3-5 73
Also see FIVE MAN ELECTRICAL BAND

EMMETT, Ray, & Superiors
Singles: 7-inch
JOY....15-25 65

EMMETT & JADES
Singles: 7-inch
RUSTONE (1404 "They Tell Me")..25-35 60
RUSTONE (1405 "No One")....15-25 61

EMMONS, Bobby
Singles: 7-inch
ATLANTIC (2124 "This Is What's Happening")....10-20 61
HI (2090 "Blue Organ")....10-20 65
LPs: 10/12-inch
HI (024 "Blues with a Beat")....20-30 65

EMMONS, Little Bobby, & Crosstones
LPs: 10/12-inch
PHYDEAUX.... 8-12 80

EMMY LOU
Singles: 7-inch
LUTE (6018 "I Wanna Know")....100-125 61

EMORY & DYNAMICS
Singles: 7-inch
PEACHTREE (120 "A Love That Is Real")....50-75 69

EMOTIONALS
Singles: 7-inch
ROBIN (189 "Out of Sight, Out of Mind")....25-35 67
Members: Mike Polaski; Jim Van Puymbrouck; Bob Davern; Rick Davern; Skip Anderson; Dick Shaul.

EMOTIONS
Singles: 7-inch
FLIP (356 "I Ran to You")....15-25 61
Also see CALHOUN, Lena, & Emotions

EMOTIONS
Singles: 7-inch
CARD (600 "Silvery Moon")....100-150 62
FURY (1010 "It's Love")....20-40 58

EMOTIONS *P&R '62*
(With the Billy Mure Orchestra)
Singles: 7-inch
BRAINSTORM.... 4-8 68
CALLA.... 5-10 65
CRYSTAL BALL.... 4-8 90
JASON SCOTT.... 4-8
KAPP (490 "Echo")....15-25 62
KAPP (513 "L-o-v-e")....20-30 63
KARATE.... 5-10 64
LAURIE (3167 "Starlit Night")....10-15 63
20TH FOX (430 "Story Untold")....10-20 63
20TH FOX (452 "Rainbow")....10-20 63
20TH FOX (478 "I Love You Madly")....10-20 64
VARDAN (201 "Love of a Girl")....20-40 65
LPs: 10/12-inch
CRYSTAL BALL.... 5-10 90
MAGIC CARPET.... 5-10 82
Members: Joe Favale; Tony Maltese; Don Colluri; Larry Cusamanno; Joe Nigro; Sal Covais.
Also see BLUE EMOTIONS
Also see HI TONES
Also see MOTIONS
Also see MURE, Billy
Also see RUNAROUNDS
Also see SHY-TONES

EMOTIONS
Singles: 7-inch
EMO (2709 "Spur of the Moment").. 8-12 65
JONSAL (79043 "Ebb Tide").... 8-12 60s

EMOTIONS *P&R/R&B '69*
Singles: 12-inch
RED LABEL.... 4-6 84
Singles: 7-inch
ARC.... 3-4 80-81
COLUMBIA.... 3-5 76-81
STAX.... 3-4 77-79
MOTOWN.... 3-4 85
RED LABEL.... 3-4 84
TWIN STACKS.... 4-8 68
VOLT.... 3-6 69-74
LPs: 10/12-inch
ARC.... 5-8 79-81
COLUMBIA.... 5-10 76-81
MOTOWN.... 5-10 85
RED LABEL.... 5-10 84
STAX.... 5-10 77-79
VOLT.... 10-20 69-74
Members: Sheila Hutchinson; Wanda Hutchinson; Jeanette Hutchinson.
Also see EARTH, WIND & FIRE with the EMOTIONS

EMOTIONS
Singles: 7-inch
CENTURY (24742 "Sometimes")....15-20

EMOTIONS
Singles: 7-inch
SOUTH PARK.... 4-8
Also see ORIGINAL EMOTIONS

EMPALA SIX
Singles: 7-inch
BLUE MOON (417 "Double Time")....15-25
BLUE MOON (419 "Sweet and Sour")....15-25

EMPALAS
Singles: 7-inch
MARK V (501 "It's Been a Long Time")....150-200 58

EMPALLOS
Singles: 7-inch
DRUM (009 "Hi-Cups")....100-200 59

EMPEROR
Singles: 78 rpm
ARGO (5264 "Tough De Times")....10-15 57
Singles: 7-inch
ARGO (5264 "Tough De Times")....10-15 57

EMPEROR
(Bob Hudson)
Singles: 7-inch
CURRENT.... 4-8 66
RPR.... 4-8 60s
Also see HUDSON & LANDRY

EMPEROR
Singles: 7-inch
PRIVATE STOCK.... 3-5 77
RCA.... 3-5 77
LPs: 10/12-inch
PRIVATE STOCK....8-10 77

EMPEROR'S FRIENDS
Singles: 7-inch
RPR.... 4-6 69

EMPERORS
Singles: 7-inch
3-J (121 "No Regrets")....50-100 58

EMPERORS
Singles: 7-inch
OLIMPIC (245 "In the Moonlight") 20-30 64
WICKWIRE....5-10 64
Also see STEVE & EMPERORS

EMPERORS
Singles: 7-inch
SABRA (5555 "I Want My Woman")....25-35 60s
TWO PLUS TWO....5-10 66

EMPERORS *P&R/R&B '66*
Singles: 7-inch
BRUNSWICK.... 4-8 67
MALA....5-10 66-67

EMPERORS WITH RHYTHM
Singles: 78 rpm
HAVEN....300-500 54
Singles: 7-inch
HAVEN (511 "I May Be Wrong")....2000-2500 54
(Black vinyl.)
HAVEN (511 "I May Be Wrong")....3000-5000 54
(Red vinyl.)

EMPIRES
Singles: 78 rpm
AMP 3....75-100 57
HARLEM....50-100 54
WHIRLIN' DISC....20-30 56
WING....15-25 55
Singles: 7-inch
AMP 3 (132 "If I'm a Fool")....75-100 57
HARLEM (2325 "Corn Wiskey") 200-300 54
HARLEM (2333 "Make Me Or Break Me")....200-300 55
HARLEM (2326 "Traveling All Alone")....100-150 55
WHIRLIN' DISC (104 "Linda")....50-75 56
WING (90023 "I Want to Know")....35-50 55
WING (90050 "Tell Me, Pretty Baby")....25-40 55
WING (90080 "My First Discovery")....20-30 55
Members: Les Cooper; Bobby Dunn.
Also see COOPER, Les
Also see LIGHTNIN' JR. & EMPIRES
Also see PRESTOS
Also see WHIRLERS

EMPIRES
Singles: 7-inch
CALICO....10-20 61
CANDI (1026 "Love You So Bad") 25-40 62
CANDI (1033 "You're on Top")....35-50 63
CHAVIS (1026 "Love You So Bad")....10-20 62
COLPIX (680 "Everyone Knew But Me")....10-20 63
DCP....5-10 64
LAKE (711 "Over the Summer Vacation")....15-25 62
OLYMPIC (245 "Darling, in the Moonlight")....30-40 64
Also see FRIEND, Eddie, & Empires

EMPIRES
Singles: 7-inch
EPIC (9527 "Time and a Place")....25-35 62
Member: Jay Black.
Also see BLACK, Jay

EMPRESS
Singles: 7-inch
PRELUDE....3-4 81

EMPTY SET
Singles: 7-inch
CARDINAL....8-12 66
IGL....8-12 67

EMULATIONS
Singles: 7-inch
EMULATE....8-12

EN VOGUE
Singles: 7-inch
ATLANTIC....3-4 90
EAST WEST....3-4 92

ENALOUISE & HEARTS
Singles: 7-inch
ARGYLE (1635 "From a Cap and a Gown")....25-35

ENCHANTED FIVE
Singles: 7-inch
CVS (1002 "Try a Little Love")....10-20 61

ENCHANTED FOREST
Singles: 7-inch
AMY....5-10 67

ENCHANTERS
Singles: 78 rpm
JUBILEE....50-100 52
Singles: 7-inch
JUBILEE (5072 "Today Is Your Birthday")....150-200 52
JUBILEE (5080 "I've Lost")....100-150 52
Also see SUGAR-TONES

ENCHANTERS
(With Maurice King & Orchestra)
Singles: 78 rpm
CORAL....20-40 56-57
MERCER....100-150 56
Singles: 7-inch
CORAL (61756 "True Love Gone")....50-75 56
CORAL (61832 "There Goes")....50-100 57
(Complete version. Identification number is 100974.)
CORAL (61832 "There Goes")....20-30 57
(Edited version. Identification number is 102966.)
CORAL (61916 "Bottle Up and Go")....25-50 57
CORAL (62373 "True Love Gone")....15-25 63
CORAL (65610 "True Love Gone")....10-15 67
MERCER (1674 "True Love Gone")....1000-2000 56

ENCHANTERS *P&R '61*
(With the Dave McRae Orchestra)
Singles: 7-inch
BALD EAGLE (3001 "Come on Baby, Let's Do the Stroll")....15-25 58
BAMBOO (513 "Touch of Love")....10-20 61
CANDELITE (432 "Oh Rose Marie")....10-15 64
EP-SOM (103 "I Need Your Love")....200-300 62
J.J.&M. (1562 "Oh Rose Marie")....100-200 62
MUSITRON (1072 "I Lied to My Heart")....30-40 61
ORBIT (532 "Touch of Love")....25-50 59
SHARP (105 "We Make Mistakes")....10-20 60
STARDUST (102 "Spellbound By the Moon")....1000-2000 58
TOM TOM (301 "Surf Blast")....25-35 63

ENCHANTERS *P&R/R&B '64*
Singles: 7-inch
LOMA....4-8 65-66
W.B.....5-10 64
Members: Samuel Bell; Charles Boyer; Zola Pearnell.
Also see MIMMS, Garnet, & Enchanters

ENCHANTERS
Singles: 7-inch
GOLDEN EAR (100 "A Fool Like Me")....10-20
TURFSIDE (401 "Like a Love I Never Had")....10-20

ENCHANTERS
Singles: 7-inch
CONFEDERATE....8-12

ENCHANTERS
Singles: 7-inch
MAL (1019 "Lost You")....5-10

ENCHANTMENT *R&B '76*
Singles: 7-inch
COLUMBIA....3-4 82-84
DESERT MOON....3-5 76
RCA....3-4 80
ROADSHOW....3-5 77-78
U.A.....3-5 76-77
LPs: 10/12-inch
COLUMBIA....5-10 82
RCA....5-10 80
ROADSHOW....8-10 77-79
U.A.....8-10 77
Members: Bobby Green; Mickey Clanton; Joe Thomas; Davis Banks; Emanuel Johnson.

ENCHANTMENTS
Singles: 7-inch
DOYLE ("Why Can't We Fall in Love")....50-75
(No selection number used.)
FARO (620 "I'm in Love with Your Daughter")....50-75 64
GONE (5130 "Sherry")....15-20 62
RITZ (17003 "I Love My Baby")..150-250 63

ENCHANTMENTS
Singles: 7-inch
ROGUE....3-5
LPs: 10/12-inch
ROGUE....10-12

ENCHANTMENTS Featuring Leroy
(With Jim Drake Orchestra)
Singles: 7-inch
ROMAC (1001 "Lonely Heart")....75-125 62

ENCHANTONES
Singles: 7-inch
POPLAR (116 "My Picture of You")....100-150 62

ENCHORDS
Singles: 7-inch
LAURIE (3089 "Zoom Zoom Zoom")....20-40 61

ENCORES
Singles: 78 rpm
CHECKER (760 "When I Look at You")....250-500 52
Singles: 7-inch
CHECKER (760 "When I Look at You")....3000-4000 52

ENCORES
Singles: 78 rpm
MGM....5-10 55
Singles: 7-inch
MGM....5-10 55

ENCORES
Singles: 78 rpm
LOOK....100-150 55
Singles: 7-inch
LOOK (105 "Time Is Moving On")....200-300 55
BOW (302 "Barbara")....50-75 58
VEE EIGHT....10-15 59

ENCOUNTERS
Singles: 7-inch
LOST NITE ("Don't Stop")....5-8
SWAN (4205 "Don't Stop")....75-125 65

ENCOUNTERS
Singles: 7-inch
AUBURN (500 "The U.T. Train")....8-12

END
Singles: 7-inch
LONDON....5-10 67
PHILIPS....5-10 65
LPs: 10/12-inch
LONDON (560 "Introspection")....20-25 69

END
Singles: 7-inch
CAROL (218 "Valley of Love")....20-30 61

END
Singles: 7-inch
CHA CHA (746 "Not Fade Away") 25-35

END GAME
Singles: 7-inch
ROUNDTABLE (151 "Piccadilly Circus Clown")....25-35

END RESULTS
Singles: 7-inch
MOTION CITY....8-12

ENDD
Singles: 7-inch
SEASCAPE (500 "So Sad")....20-30 65
SEASCAPE (501 "Out of My Mind")....20-30 66
SEASCAPE (504 "Come on in to My World")....20-30 67

ENDEAVORS
Singles: 7-inch
STOP....8-12

ENDELLS
Singles: 7-inch
HEIGH-HO (605 "Vicky")....20-30 63

ENDGAMES *D&D '83*
Singles: 12-inch
FLIP....4-6 83
MCA....4-6 83
Singles: 7-inch
MCA....3-4 84
LPs: 10/12-inch
MCA....5-10 84

ENDINGS
Singles: 7-inch
BARRIER (Black vinyl)....3-4 74-77
BARRIER (Colored vinyl)....5-10 77
Members: Ralph Figueroa; Mickey Castaneda; Walter Figueroa; Joe Miranda; Angel Anglero.

ENDINGS
LPs: 10/12-inch
CHRIS MIKE....10-12

ENDLE ST. CLOUD: see ST. CLOUD, Endle

ENDLESS
Singles: 7-inch
CARDINAL (521 "Prevailing Darkness")....25-35 66

ENDLESS PULSE
Singles: 7-inch
LAURIE....4-8 68-69
Member: Carlo Mastrangelo.
Also see CARLO

ENDORSERS
Singles: 7-inch
MOON (109 "Crying").... 1000-2000 59

ENDS
Singles: 7-inch
VIN....4-8 60

ENDSLEY, Melvin
Singles: 78 rpm
RCA....25-50 57-58
Singles: 7-inch
HICKORY....5-8
RCA....10-20 57-58

ENDSLEY, Melvin / Doree Post
Singles: 7-inch
RCA (DJ-58 "Dealer Prevue")....15-25 57
(Promotional issue only.)
Also see POST, Bill & Doree

ENEMYS
Singles: 7-inch
MGM....4-8 66
Also see HUTTON, Danny
Also see WELLS, Corey

ENERGETICS *R&B '79*
Singles: 7-inch
ATLANTIC....3-5 79
TIP TOP....4-6
LPs: 10/12-inch
ATLANTIC....5-10 79

ENERGIES
Singles: 7-inch
COBRA (185 "How Many Tears")....4-8

ENERGIZERS
(Magic Triplets)
Singles: 7-inch
KEF (4458 "That's What Simon Says")....5-10 74
Also see MAGIC TRIPLETS

ENERGY *R&B '74*
Singles: 7-inch
SHOUT....3-5 74

ENERGY PACKAGE
Singles: 7-inch
LAURIE....10-20 67

ENFIELDS
Singles: 7-inch
RICHIE (669 "Eyes of the World")..15-25 66
RICHIE (670 "She Already Has Somebody")....15-25 66
RICHIE (671 "Face to Face")....15-25 66
RICHIE (675 "Time Card")....15-25 66
Members: Mac Morgan; Ted Munda; Robin Eaton; John Bernard; Bill Gallery; John Rhodes.

ENFIELDS / Friends of the Family
LPs: 10/12-inch
DISTORTIONS (1003 "Enfields & Early Friends of the Family")....8-10 91
Also see ENFIELDS

ENFORCERS
Singles: 7-inch
VIVA....3-4 84

ENGEL, Gary
(With the Top Hatters)
Singles: 7-inch
KP (1010 "Kimmy Lee")....100-150 60
PEE BEE (1001 "Money Honey")...20-30

ENGEL, Joanne
Singles: 7-inch
AMY....5-10 64-65
DANCE ALONG (6051 "The Parachute Jump")....5-10
SABRINA (508 "Set Me Free")....8-12 63
SABRINA (516 "Party Time")....8-12 63
SUITE 16 (101 "Hurry Back")....50-75 61

ENGEL, Scott
(Scotty Engel)
Singles: 78 rpm
RKO UNIQUE....15-25 57
Singles: 7-inch
CHALLENGE (2004 "Devil Surfer")....15-20 63
LIBERTY....8-12 62
MARTAY (2004 "Devil Surfer")....25-35 63
ORBIT (506 "The Livin' End")....8-12 58
ORBIT (511 "Charley Bop"/"All I Do Is Dream of You")....8-12 58
(B-side selection is No. 512.)
ORBIT (512 "Blue Bell"/"Paper Doll")....8-12 58
(B-side selection is No. 511.)
ORBIT (537 "Golden Rule of Love")....8-12 59
ORBIT (545 "Comin' Home")....8-12 59
RKO UNIQUE....10-15 57

Picture Sleeves
ORBIT (506 "The Livin' End") 20-30 58
ORBIT (511 "Charley Bop") 20-30 58
ORBIT (512 "Blue Bell") 20-30 58
ORBIT (537 "Golden Rule of Love") 20-30 59
ORBIT (545 "Comin' Home") 20-30 59
Also see WALKER, Scott

ENGEL, Scott, & John Stewart
Singles: 7-inch
TOWER (218 "I Only Came to Dance with You") 10-15 66
(Shown as by "John Stewart & Scott Engel, Now Known As the Walker Brothers.")
LPs: 10/12-inch
TOWER (5026 "I Only Came to Dance with You") 30-50 66
Also see CHOSEN FEW
Also see DALTON BROTHERS
Also see ENGEL, Scott
Also see NEWPORTERS
Also see MOONGOONERS
Also see WALKER BROTHERS

ENGEMANN, Bobby
Singles: 7-inch
CAPITOL 3-5 69
LPs: 10/12-inch
CAPITOL 10-15 69
Also see LETTERMEN

ENGLAND, Benny
Singles: 7-inch
SNAP (400 "Eloping") 30-50 59

ENGLAND DAN & JOHN FORD COLEY *P&R/LP '76*
Singles: 7-inch
A&M 3-5 71-77
BIG TREE 3-5 76-80
MCA 3-4 80
LPs: 10/12-inch
A&M 10-12 71-73
BIG TREE 8-10 76-79
MCA 5-10 80
Members: Dan Seals; John Ford Coley.
Also see ABBA / Spinners / Firefall / England Dan & John Ford Coley
Also see COLEY, John Ford
Also see SEALS, Dan
Also see SOUTHWEST F.O.B.

ENGLE, Butch, & Styx
Singles: 7-inch
LOMA (2065 "I Like Her") 10-20 66
MEA 10-15 60s
ONYX (2200 "Hey I'm Lost") 20-30 67
Also see STYX

ENGLE, Priscilla
LPs: 10/12-inch
FRONTLINE 5-10 86

ENGLEBERG, Fred
LPs:10/12-inch
CRESTVIEW 15-25

ENGLER, Jerry, & Four Ekkos
Singles: 78 rpm
BRUNSWICK (55037 "Sputnik") 40-50 57
Singles: 7-inch
BRUNSWICK (55037 "Sputnik") 60-80 57
CLASSIC EDITION (55037 "What a You Gonna Do") 3-4 92
Picture Sleeves
CLASSIC EDITION (55037 "What a You Gonna Do") 3-4 92
(Sleeve pictures Buddy Holly and Jerry Engler.)
Members: Jerry Engler; Buddy Holly; Dale Masters; Stew Love; Harvey Possamato; Bryan Williams; Jimmy Symonds.
Also see FOUR EKKOS
Also see HOLLY, Buddy

ENGLISH, Anna
Singles: 7-inch
FELSTED 15-25 58

ENGLISH, Barbara *R&B '73*
(Barbara Jean English)
Singles: 7-inch
ALITHIA 4-6 73-74
AURORA (155 "Sittin' in the Corner") 50-75 65
MALA (488 "Easy Come Easy Go") 10-20 64
REPRISE (290 "I've Got a Date")...10-20 65
REPRISE (349 "Small Town Girl") 10-20 65
ROULETTE (4428 "We Need Them") 20-30 62
W.B. (5685 "All Because I Love Somebody") 10-15 65
LPs: 10/12-inch
ALITHIA 8-10 73
Also see FASHIONS

ENGLISH, Jackie *P&R '80*
Singles: 7-inch
VENTURE 3-4 80

ENGLISH, John, III
Singles: 7-inch
MOONGLOW 4-8 66

ENGLISH, Raina
Singles: 7-inch
TREND '61 ....4-8 61

ENGLISH, Scott *P&R '64*
(With the Accents; with Dedications)
Singles: 7-inch
DOT (16099 "White Cliffs of Dover") 15-25 60
JANUS (171 "Brandy") 8-12 71
JANUS (192 "Woman in My Life") 3-6 72
JOKER (777 "Ugly Pills") 15-25 62
SPOKANE (4003 "High on a Hill") 15-25 64
SPOKANE (4007 "Here Comes the Pain") 15-25 64
SULTAN (4003 "High on a Hill")....30-50 63
Also see ACCENTS

ENGLISH BEAT *LP '80*
Singles: 12-inch
I.R.S. 4-6 83-85
Singles: 7-inch
I.R.S. 3-4 83-85
LPs: 10/12-inch
I.R.S. 5-10 82-85
SIRE 5-10 80-81
Members: Andy Cox; David Steele; Roger Charley; Dave Wakeling.
Also see FINE YOUNG CANNIBALS
Also see GENERAL PUBLIC

ENGLISH CONGREGATION *P&R '72*
Singles: 7-inch
ATCO 3-5 72
SIGNPOST 3-5 73
LPs: 10/12-inch
SIGNPOST 8-10 73

ENGLISH HOUSE
Singles: 7-inch
MGM 5-8 72

ENGLISH MUFFINS
Singles: 7-inch
GAMA (702 "Leave or Stay") 20-30 67

ENGLISH SETTERS
Singles: 7-inch
GLAD-HAMP (2029 "Tragedy")......15-25 66
GLAD-HAMP (2033 "Someday You'll See") 15-25 66
JUBILEE (5560 "Wake Up") 5-10 66

ENGLISHMEN
Singles: 7-inch
BRITISH LION (415 "Long Ago") 15-25 60s

ENID
LPs: 10/12-inch
BUK 8-10

ENIGMA *LP '91*
LPs: 10/12-inch
CHARISMA 5-8 91

ENJOYABLES
Singles: 7-inch
CAPITOL (5321 "Push a Little Harder") 5-10 64
SHRINE (118 "Shame") 250-350 66
Members: James Johnson; Carl Kidd; William Britton; Gerald Richardson.

ENNIS, Ethel *LP '64*
Singles: 78 rpm
JUBILEE 4-8 56
Singles: 7-inch
JUBILEE 5-10 56
RCA 5-10 64
EPs: 7-inch
CAPITOL 5-10 57
LPs: 10/12-inch
CAPITOL 15-25 58
JUBILEE 20-40 56-63
RCA 15-25 64

ENO, Brian *LP '74*
(Eno)
Singles: 7-inch
ISLAND 3-5 72
LPs: 10/12-inch
ANTILLES 8-10 73-78
EDITIONS E.G. 5-10 81-82
ISLAND 8-10 73-78
PVC 5-10 79
SIRE 5-10 81
Also see BYRNE, David
Also see 801
Also see FRIPP & ENO
Also see ROXY MUSIC

ENOIS, Lucky, Quintet
(Vocal by Jimmy Waters)
Singles: 78 rpm
MODERN 10-15 53
Singles: 7-inch
MODERN (905 "Crazy Man Crazy") 20-30 53
MODERN (912 "K.C. Limited") 20-30 53

ENSENATORS: SEE ENSENEDAS

ENSENEDAS
(Ensenators)
Singles: 7-inch
TARX (1001 "Just Like Before") 100-200 62
TARX (1005 "Love I Beg of You") 100-200 62

ENSLEY, Art, & Fabulous Echoes Band
Singles: 7-inch
SHIPTOWN 4-6

ENTERTAINERS
Singles: 7-inch
CATCH (101 "Marianne") 8-10 63
MOHAWK (141 "Ginza") 4-8 65
SYMBOL (212 "Love in My Heart") ... 4-8 65

ENTERTAINERS
Singles: 7-inch
DEMAND (2932 "Danny Boy") 10-20 63

ENTERTAINERS
Singles: 7-inch
JCP (1033 "Mr. Pitiful") 15-25 64

ENTERTAINERS
Singles: 7-inch
CHESS (1951 "Too Much") 5-10 66

ENTERTAINERS
Singles: 7-inch
OVIDE (238 "Why") 8-10 67

ENTERTAINERS
Singles: 7-inch
IT WILL STAND 4-6 81

ENTERTAINERS IV *R&B '66*
Singles: 7-inch
DORE 4-8 66

ENTERTAINMENT UNLIMITED / Cornelius & Carol
Singles: 7-inch
ENTERTAINMENT ENT. 5-10
Member: Cornelius Crawford.

ENTICERS
Singles: 7-inch
COTILLION 3-6 71

ENTOUCH *P&R/LP '90*
(Featuring Keith Sweat)
Singles: 7-inch
VINTERTAINMENT 3-4 90
LPs: 10/12-inch
VINTERTAINMENT 5-8 90
Members: Eric McCaine; Free.
Also see SWEAT, Keith
Also see TOUCH

ENTWISTLE, John *LP '71*
(John Entwistle's Rigor Mortis; John Entwistle's Ox)
Singles: 7-inch
DECCA 3-5 72
TRACK 3-5 73
LPs: 10/12-inch
ATCO 5-10 81
DECCA 10-15 71-72
MCA/TRACK 8-10 72-75
Also see TOWNSHEND, Pete, & Ronnie Lane
Also see WHO

ENUFF Z'NUFF *P&R/LP '89*
Singles: 7-inch
ATCO 3-4 89-90
Picture Sleeves
ATCO 3-4 89
LPs: 10/12-inch
ATCO 5-8 89-91

EN VOGUE *P&R/LP '90*
LPs: 10/12-inch
ATLANTIC 5-8 90

ENVOYS
Singles: 7-inch
CRYSTAL BALL 4-8

ENYA *P&R/LP '89*
Singles: 7-inch
GEFFEN 3-4 89
Picture Sleeves
GEFFEN 3-4 89
LPs: 10/12-inch
GEFFEN 5-8 89

EON *R&B '78*
Singles: 7-inch
ARIOLA AMERICA 3-4 78
LPs: 10/12-inch
ARIOLA AMERICA 5-10 78
SCEPTER 8-10 73

EPAE, Jay
Singles: 7-inch
CAPITOL 10-20 63
MERCURY 5-10 62

EPIC FIVE
Singles: 7-inch
LOVE ("Humpty Dumpty") 20-30 66
(Selection number not known.)

EPIC SPLENDOR *P&R '67*
Singles: 7-inch
HOT BISCUIT 4-8 67-68
Picture Sleeves
HOT BISCUIT (1452 "It Could Be Wonderful") 8-10 68

EPICS
Singles: 7-inch
BANDERA (2512 "Summer's Coming") 15-25 60
ERIC (7001 "Wishing You Were Mine") 50-100 62
LYNN (510 "Girl By the Wayside") 30-50 61
LYNN (516 "The Magic Kiss") 50-100 61
LYNN (516 "Most of All") 50-100 61
(Same Lynn selection number used twice. Both have the same flip: *Last Night I Dreamed.*)
SABRA (516 "The Magic Kiss") 30-50 62
(Reissue uses same Lynn number.)

EPICS
Singles: 7-inch
KIM (101 "Wild One") 75-100 62
(500 made.)

EPICS
Singles: 7-inch
ATHENS (202 "On the Rocks") 10-20 62

EPICS
Singles: 7-inch
FULLER 4-8 65
JONI 4-8 63-64
MERCURY 20-25 64
ZEN 4-8 65

EPICS
Singles: 7-inch
BRIDGETOWN 8-12

EPICS
Singles: 7-inch
LIFETIME (1004 "Lonely") 100-150

EPICS
Singles: 7-inch
DOLPHIN 5-10

EPICS Featuring Jeannie
Singles: 7-inch
DANTE (3004 "So Many Times") ...25-50 60

EPICUREANS
Singles: 7-inch
IGL 20-25 66
UA 8-12 69
Also see HIGHWAY

EPIKS
Singles: 7-inch
PROCESS 4-8 65

EPISODE SIX
Singles: 7-inch
CHAPTER ONE (2902 "Lucky Sunday") 20-30 60s
COMPASS 4-8 67
ELEKTRA 4-8 67
W.B. 4-8 66

EPISODES
Singles: 7-inch
FOUR SEASONS (1014 "Where Is My Love") 75-125 65
(Identification number shown since no selection number is used.)

EPITAPH
LPs: 10/12-inch
BILLINGSGATE 8-10 74

EPITOME
(Epitome of Sound)
Singles: 7-inch
MONA LEE 5-10 68
SANDBAG (101 "You Don't Love Me") 25-35 60s

EPKONS
Singles: 7-inch
DEE'S 8-12

EPOQUE, Belle: see BELLE EPOQUE

EPP, Al
Singles: 7-inch
WILDCAT (0018 "Breakin' My Heart") 15-25 59

EPPERSON, Don
Singles: 7-inch
SIDEWALK (933 "Please Mrs. Peckingpaw") 10-20 67

EPPERSON, Minnie
Singles: 7-inch
PEACOCK 4-8 68

EPPS, Arthur
Singles: 7-inch
SPARK 5-10 61

EPPS, Charles
Singles: 7-inch
BROSH 4-8 62
HILLTOP 4-8

EPPS, Preston *P&R '59*
("Lord Preston Epps")
Singles: 7-inch
ADMIRAL 4-8 65
EMBASSY 5-10 62
JO JO 4-6 69
MAJESTY (1300 "Bongo Boogie") ...5-10 60
ORIGINAL SOUND (4 "Bongo Rock") 10-20 60
(Monaural.)
ORIGINAL SOUND (4 "Bongo Rock") 25-40 60
(Stereo.)
ORIGINAL SOUND (9 thru 17) 8-15 60-61
POLO (218 "Bongo Rock 1965") 5-10 65
TOP RANK (2067 "Blue Bongo") ...10-15 60
TOP RANK (2091 "Bongo Hop") 10-15 60
EPs: 7-inch
ORIGINAL SOUND (1001 "Bongo Rock") 15-25 60
LPs: 10/12-inch
CROWN 10-20 60s
ORIGINAL SOUND (5002 "Bongo Bongo Bongo") 30-40 60
(Monaural.)
ORIGINAL SOUND (8851 "Bongo Bongo Bongo") 30-50 60
(Stereo.)
ORIGINAL SOUND (5009 "Surfin' Bongos") 25-40 63
(Monaural.)
ORIGINAL SOUND (8872 "Surfin' Bongos") 25-50 63
(Stereo.)
TOP RANK (349 "Bongola") 30-50 61
Also see SKYLINERS / Preston Epps

EPSILONS
Singles: 7-inch
HEM (1003 "Mind in a Bind") 35-50 60s
SHRINE (106 "Mad at the World") 150-250 66

EPSILONS
Singles: 7-inch
STAX 4-8 70
Members: Lloyd Parkes; Gene McFadden; John Whitehead.
Also see MELVIN, Harold, & Blue Notes
Also see McFADDEN & WHITEHEAD
Also see TALK of the TOWN

EQUADORS
EPs: 7-inch
RCA (4286 "Equadors") 25-35 58
(Issued with paper sleeve.)

EQUADORS
Singles: 7-inch
ARGO (5353 "Say You'll Be Mine") 20-40 59
MIRACLE (7 "You're My Desire") 150-200 62

EQUALLOS
("Featuring Willie Logan")
Singles: 7-inch
M&M (30 "Beneath the Sun"). 1000-2000 62

EQUALOS
Singles: 7-inch
MAD (1296 "Patty Patty") 15-25 59

EQUALS *P&R '68*
Singles: 7-inch
BANG 5-10 70
PRESIDENT 5-10 67-68
RCA 4-8 68
LPs: 10/12-inch
LAURIE (2045 "Unequalled") 20-25 67
PRESIDENT 15-25 68-69
RCA 10-15 68
Members: Eddy Grant; Derv Gordon.
Also see GRANT, Eddy

EQUATIONS
Singles: 7-inch
ALL PLATINUM 3-5 71

EQUIPE 84
Singles: 7-inch
IMPERIAL 10-15 67

ERA OF SOUND
Singles: 7-inch
DELTA (2255 "Girl in the Mini Skirt") 15-25 67

ERADICATORS
Singles: 7-inch
PYRAMID (7232 "Reputation") 30-50 66

ERAMUS HALL *R&B '84*
Singles: 12-inch
CAPITOL 4-6 84
Singles: 7-inch
CAPITOL 3-4 84
LPs: 10/12-inch
CAPITOL 5-10 84
Members: Michael Gatherright; Joe Anderson; James Wilkerson; William Tillery; Marvin Williams; Bernard Provost; Bill Dorsey.

ERASURE *LP '87*
Singles: 7-inch
MUTE 3-5 97
SIRE 3-4 82-89
Picture Sleeves
SIRE 3-4 88
LPs: 10/12-inch
SIRE 5-10 82-89
Members: Vince Clarke; Andy Bell.
Also see DEPECHE MODE
Also see YAZ

ERIC
(With the Plazas & Ralph Casals Trio)
Singles: 7-inch
PRODUCTION (612 "I Wish...") 500-750 63
(Black vinyl.)
PRODUCTION (612 "I Wish...") 4-6 91
(Purple vinyl.)

ERIC *D&D '84*
Singles: 12-inch
MEMO 4-6 84

ERIC, John
(With Isoscelles Popcicles)
Singles: 7-inch
STAX 3-5 73
U.S.A. 4-8 69
VERVE 4-8 68

ERIC, Mark
Singles: 7-inch
REVUE 3-5 69
LPs: 10/12-inch
REVUE 10-12 69

ERIC, Wreckless: see WRECKLESS ERIC

ERIC & CHESSMEN
Singles: 7-inch
KAMA (777 "You Don't Want My Loving") 10-20 65

ERIC & NORSEMEN
Singles: 7-inch
CHROME (103 "Get It On") 15-25 67

ERIC & VIKINGS
Singles: 7-inch
SOULHAWK (10 "Vibrations") 10-20 60s

ERIC B. & RAKIM R&B '86
Singles: 7-inch
4TH & BROADWAY 3-4 87-88
ZAKIA... 3-4 86
LPs: 10/12-inch
4TH & BROADWAY 5-10 87
MCA 5-8 90
UNI 5-8 88

ERICA
LPs: 10/12-inch
ESP (1099 "You Used to Think") 100-200 68

ERICKSON, Del
Singles: 7-inch
RAY NOTE (10011 "Two")............. 8-12

ERICKSON, Roky
(With the Aliens)
Singles: 7-inch
DYNAMIC... 3-4 85
RHINO.. 3-5 77
Picture Sleeves
RHINO... 3-5 77
LPs: 10/12-inch
415 RECORDS............................... 5-10 81
SKYCLAD... 5-10 90
Also see 13TH FLOOR ELEVATORS

ERICKSONS
Singles: 7-inch
AGE of AQUARIUS (1557 "Talk of Love") 5-10 70s

ERIK
(With the Vikings)
Singles: 7-inch
COLISEUM... 3-6
EDEN 3-6 73
GAMBIT 4-8
GENERAL INT'L.................................. 4-8 65-66
GORDY 3-5 73
KARATE 4-8 65
LPs: 10/12-inch
KARATE...15-20 65
VANGUARD 12-15 67

ERIK & SMOKE PONIES
Singles: 7-inch
KAMA SUTRA (227 "I'll Give You More")..10-15 67

ERIKA
LPs: 10/12-inch
ESP (1099 "You Used to Think")..50-100 68
Members: Erica Pomerance; Ron Price; D. Cooper Smith; Bill Mitchell; Tom Moore; Richard Heisler; Michael Ephraim; Lanny Brooks; Dion Brody; Craig Justin; Gail Pollard; Trevor Koehler.

ERKHARD, Tommy
Singles: 7-inch
EBB.. 5-10 59

ERLENE & GIRLFRIENDS
Singles: 7-inch
OLD TOWN.......................................10-15 63

ERMINES: see GUNTER, Cornell

ERNIE / Sesame Street Kids P&R '79
(Jim Henson as "Ernie")
Singles: 7-inch
COLUMBIA.. 3-5 70
Also see HENSON, Jim

ERNIE & EDDIE: see EDDIE & ERNIE

ERNIE & EMPERORS
Singles: 7-inch
REPRISE (414 "Got a Lot I Want to Say").. 5-10 65
Also see ERNIE'S FUNNYS

ERNIE & HALOS
Singles: 7-inch
BURG (5801 "Girl from Across the Sea")... 4-5
GUYDEN (2085 "Girl from Across the Sea")...20-30 63

ERNIE & PETIE
Singles: 7-inch
ACE... 5-10 62

ERNIE'S FUNNYS
("Formerly Ernie & the Emperors")
Singles: 7-inch
YARDBIRD.. 4-8 60s
Also see ERNIE & EMPERORS

ERNIE'S NUTTY GUITAR
Singles: 7-inch
HEARTBEAT (54 "Don't Fence Me In")..10-20 63

EROTIC EXOTIC
Singles: 7-inch
ATLANTIC... 3-4 86

ERRISSON, King
LPs: 10/12-inch
WESTBOUND....................................... 5-10 77

ERSKINE, Joe
Singles: 7-inch
ARROW (728 "I Love You So, Oh")..20-30 58
GLOW-HILL (506 "Weak for You Baby")..15-25 59
Also see LONG, Bobby

ERUPTION P&R/R&B/LP '78
Singles: 12-inch
ARIOLA AMERICA 4-8 78
HANSA... 4-8 70s
Singles: 7-inch
ARIOLA AMERICA 3-4 78
LPs: 10/12-inch
ARIOLA AMERICA 5-10 78
Member: Precious Wilson.
Also see WILSON, Precious

ERVIN, Blue Grass: see BLUE GRASS ERVIN

ERVIN, Dee
(Big Dee Ervin & Pastels)
Singles: 7-inch
ASTRA (1024 "I Can't Help It").........5-10 66
HULL (738 "I Can't Help It") 10-20 60
SIGNPOST (70009 "Darling, Please Take Me Back") 3-6 72

ERVIN, Frankie
(With the Spears; "Lead Singer of the Shields")
Singles: 7-inch
CONTENDER (1316 "Wilhemina").20-30 59
DON (202 "Why Did It End")......100-150 61
GUYDEN (2010 "Believe Me").......10-15 59
HART (1691 "Some Other Guy")...250-350 60
RENDEZVOUS (112 "The Story")..30-50 59
RENDEZVOUS (126 "You Hurt Me")...50-75 60
Also see SHIELDS

ERVIN, Leroy
Singles: 78 rpm
GOLD STAR (628 "Rock Island Blues")..20-35 47
SWING (415 "Rock Island Blues") .40-60 47

ERVIN, Odie
Singles: 78 rpm
BIG TOWN...15-25 54
Singles: 7-inch
BIG TOWN (111 "She's a Bad Bad Woman")..25-50 54

ERVIN, Senator Sam J., Jr.
Singles: 7-inch
COLUMBIA... 4-8 73

ERVIN, Sid
(Sid King)
Singles: 78 rpm
STARDAY 15-25 54
Singles: 7-inch
STARDAY (147 "Who Put the Turtle in Myrtle's Girdle")..30-40 54

ERVIN SISTERS
Singles: 7-inch
TRI PHI (1014 "Do It Right") 30-50 62
TRI PHI (1022 "Every Day's a Holiday")..40-60 62

ERWIN, Dee
(Difosco Erwin; Big Dee Erwin)
Singles: 7-inch
CUB.. 5-8 68
PHIL-LA of SOUL 10-15
ROULETTE 5-8 65
Also see DIFOSCO
Also see ERVIN, Dee
Also see IRWIN, Big Dee

ERWIN, Bill
(With the 4 Jacks)
Singles: 7-inch
FAIRLANE...10-15 62
PEL 10-15 60

ERWIN, Frankie
Singles: 7-inch
INDIGO 4-8 62

ESCAPADES
Singles: 7-inch
POPPY (1002 "Rockin' the Blues") 10-15 59

ESCAPADES
Singles: 7-inch
ARBET (1010 "She's the Kind").........20-30 66
VERVE (10415 "Mad Mad Mad") 10-20 66
XL (356 "She's the Kind")...............20-30 66

ESCAPADES
("Escapade's")
Singles: 7-inch
GLOW (87895 "No Body Know's") 25-50
(Identification number shown since no selection number is used.)

ESCAPE CLUB P&R/LP '88
Singles: 7-inch
ATLANTIC... 3-4 88-91
Picture Sleeves
ATLANTIC... 3-4 88-89
LPs: 10/12-inch
ATLANTIC... 5-8 88-91

ESCORTS
("With Kay")
Singles: 78 rpm
ESSEX (372 "Oh, Honey")..............10-15 54
Singles: 7-inch
ESSEX (372 "Oh, Honey")...............15-25 54

ESCORTS
Singles: 78 rpm
RCA..10-20 57
Singles: 7-inch
JUDD (1014 "My First Year") 10-20 59
RCA..10-15 57-63
SCARLET (4005 "I Will Be Home Again")..30-50 60
SCEPTER (1201 "Why Why Why")..20-30 58
SOMA (1144 "The Main Drag")........10-20 61
WELLS (102 "One More Kiss Good Night")..40-60 59

ESCORTS
Singles: 7-inch
TAURUS (351 "You're for Me")......50-75 61
Also see DEL & ESCORTS

ESCORTS
Singles: 7-inch
CORAL (62302 "Gloria")...................25-50 62
CORAL (62317 "Guadamus") 25-50 62
CORAL (62336 "Somewhere")..........15-25 62
CORAL (62385 "My Heart Cries for You")..15-25 63

ESCORTS
Singles: 7-inch
BOOMERANG (621 "Little Big Horn")..15-25 62

ESCORTS
Singles: 7-inch
FONTANA..5-10 64-65

ESCORTS
Singles: 7-inch
DATE 5-10 68
TEO...5-10 66
SOUL-O 5-10 60s
LPs: 10/12-inch
TEO (5000 "Bring Down the House")..40-60 66
(Shown on cover as also being issued in stereo [LPS-5000], but no stereo copies have been verified.)

ESCORTS R&B '73
Singles: 7-inch
ALITHIA...3-5 73-74
LPs: 10/12-inch
ALITHIA...8-10 73-74
Members: Reginald Hayes; Robert Arrington; Laurence Franklin; Stephen Carter; William Dugger; Frank Heard; Marion Murphy.

ESCORTS
Singles: 7-inch
DE'VOICE 5-10
LONE WOLF...5-10

ESCORTS
(Featuring Roger Booth)
Singles: 7-inch
FREDLO (6311 "I Found Love").....15-25 60s
SOMA 20-25 60
ZORCH (101 "Space Walk")..........25-50 60s
Also see DO's & DON'Ts

ESCOS
("Vocal By Lonnie Carter. Background: George Carter, Wilbert Bell and Winfred Gerald. Music By the Swingin' Rocks")
Singles: 7-inch
ESTA (100 "I'm Lonesome for You")..550-650 59
(Same number also used for a Joe Caldwell release.)
FEDERAL (12380 "Diamonds and Pearls")...25-50 60
FEDERAL (12430 "Golden Rule of Love")...25-50 61
FEDERAL (12445 "Yes I Need Someone")...25-50 62
FEDERAL (12493 "That's Life") 20-40 63
Members: Lonnie Carter; Don Peark; Joe Renn; Richard Parker; Roland Bradley.
Session: George Carter; Wilbert Bell; Winfred Gerald; Swingin' Rocks.
Also see CALDWELL, Joe
Also see CHARMS
Also see FERGUSON, H-Bomb / Escos / Mascots

ESCOVEDO, Coke P&R/LP '76
Singles: 7-inch
MERCURY 3-5 76-77
LPs: 10/12-inch
MERCURY 5-10 76-77
Also see AZTECA
Also see SANTANA

ESKERETTES
Singles: 7-inch
HERMITAGE (776 "Southern Style")..5-10

ESKO AFFAIR
Singles: 7-inch
MERCURY 10-20 68-69

ESKRIDGE, Murrie
Singles: 7-inch
APEX...4-8

ESMERALDA, Santa: see SANTA ESMERALDA

ESMERELDY & HER NOVELTY BAND C&W '48
Singles: 78 rpm
MUSICRAFT...5-8 48

ESOTERIC CIRCLE
LPs: 10/12-inch
FLYING DUTCHMAN 10-12 71

ESPERANTO
LPs: 10/12-inch
A&M...8-10 73-75

ESPOSITO
(Tony Esposito)
LPs: 10/12-inch
PETERS INT'L.....................................8-10 76

ESPOSITO, Joe "Bean" P&R '83
Singles: 7-inch
CASABLANCA 3-4 83
Also see BRANIGAN, Laura, & Joe Esposito
Also see BROOKS, Pattie, & Joe Esposito
Also see BROOKLYN DREAMS
Also see RUSSELL, Brenda

ESQUERITA
Singles: 7-inch
CAPITOL (1075 "Hey Miss Lucy")..25-50 58
(Promotional issue only.)
CAPITOL (4007 "Oh Baby")............25-40 58
CAPITOL (4058 "Rockin' the Joint")...30-50 58
CAPITOL (4145 "Laid Off")............20-40 59
LPs: 10/12-inch
CAPITOL (1186 "Esquerita")......500-700 59
Also see REEDER, Eskew

ESQUIRE LP '87
LPs: 10/12-inch
GEFFEN 5-10 87

ESQUIRE, Kenny, & Starlites
Singles: 78 rpm
EMBER 40-60 57
Singles: 7-inch
EMBER (1011 "They Call Me a Dreamer")..50-100 57
EMBER (1021 "Tears Are Just for Fools")..50-100 57
Also see STARLITES

ESQUIRE BOYS P&R '53
Singles: 78 rpm
DOT 8-10 55
GUYDEN..8-10 54
MEDIA..8-12 55
NICKELODEON 8-10 53
RAINBOW...10-15 52-53
Singles: 7-inch
DOT 10-15 55
FRANSIL 5-10 61
GUYDEN...10-15 54
MEDIA (1004 "Play Me Boogie")....10-20 55
NICKELODEON (102 "Guitar Boogie Shuffle")..10-15 53
RAINBOW (100 & 200 series) 10-20 52-53
(Black vinyl.)
RAINBOW (100 & 200 series) 20-35 52-53
(Colored vinyl.)
20TH FOX (110 "Taboo")................8-10 58
Also see SQUIRES

ESQUIRES
(Five Tinos)
Singles: 78 rpm
EPIC (9024 "If You Only Knew What a Three Cent Stamp Could Do")...............200-300 54
HI-PO 300-400 56
Singles: 7-inch
HI-PO (1003 "Only the Angels Know")...................................1000-2000 56
Also see FIVE TINOS

ESQUIRES
Singles: 7-inch
CAPITOL (72126 "Atlantis")..........10-20 63
(Canadian.)
CAPITOL (72137 "Man from Adano")...10-20 63
(Canadian.)

ESQUIRES
Singles: 7-inch
DURCO (1001 "Flashin'" Red")......20-30 64
Members: Rick Clingman; Durby Wheeler; Marv Gillum; Jim Thompson.
Also see LAUGHING GRAVY

ESQUIRES
Singles: 7-inch
SALEM (003 "Shake a Tail Feather")..8-12 65
Member: Brewster Harding.

ESQUIRES P&R/R&B '67
Singles: 7-inch
B&G 4-8 69
BUNKY...5-10 67-68
CAPITOL...3-6 69
HOT LINE...3-5 72
JU-PAR 3-5 76
LAMAR...3-5 71
LASCO 4-8 79
NEW WORLD (101 "Let Me Build You a New World")..5-10 74
ROCKY RIDGE 3-5 71
WAND...4-8 68-69
LPs: 10/12-inch
BUNKY (300 "Get on Up and Get Away")..20-25 68
Members: Millard Evans; Gilbert Alvis; Betty Moorer; Sam Pace; Harvey Scales; Sean Taylor; Gilbert Moorer; Alvis Moorer; .Sam Davidson; John Bursey; Danny Reed; Ortez Guzman; Clint Mosley.
Also see BOYD, Tim, & Esquires
Also see EDWARDS, Millard
Also see SCALES, Harvey
Also see MOORE, Betty
Also see MOORER, Betty
Also see SHEPPARDS
Also see TAYLOR, Sean

ESQUIRES
Singles: 7-inch
ALLEY (650 "Sadie's Ways") 20-30 65
(We have also seen this number as 996 and as 1023. We don't yet know which is right.)

ESQUIRES
Singles: 7-inch
CFP (2 "Heartaches Stay the Night")..10-20 65
TOWER 5-10 65

ESQUIRES
Singles: 7-inch
GLENVALLEY (103 "Come On") ...20-30 66
GLENVALLEY (104 "Time Don't Mean So Much")..20-30 66
GLENVALLEY (105 "These Are the Tender Years")..20-30 66

ESQUIRES / Mike St. Shaw & Prophets / Thunder Frog Ensemble
LPs: 10/12-inch
AUDIO FIDELITY (2168 "Where It's At: Live at the Cheetah")....................................30-50 66
Members: (Esquires) Jeff Ginman; Dante Renzi; Jay Savino; Danny Mahony; Mike Rubin. (Mike St. Shaw & Prophets) Mike St. Shaw; Ray Garcia; Harold Logan; Danny Taylor; Chuck Hatfield. (Thunder Frog Ensemble) Nichael Orrell; John Porsche; Jack Van Osten; Mark Gauche; Glen Wayne.
Also see ST. SHAW, Mike

ESQUIRES
Singles: 7-inch
COLUMBIA (43815 "It's a Dirty Shame")...10-20 66

ESQUIRES
Singles: 7-inch
DOT (16954 "She's My Woman") ..10-15 66

ESQUIRES
Singles: 7-inch
RAVEN (3 "What Made You Change Your Mind")..15-25 66
ROCKY RIDGE (403 "Dancin' a Hole in the World")..10-20 60s

ESQUIRES
Singles: 7-inch
FEATURE 5-10 67

ESQUIRES
Singles: 7-inch
CIGAR MAN (79880 "The Show Ain't Over")..5-8 80
PHALANX (1002 "Crazy Horse")......15-25 60s
SCRATCH...10-20 60s

ESQUIRES
Singles: 7-inch
RITE..8-12
STONEWAY 8-12

ESQUIRES
Singles: 7-inch
SMOG CITY...4-6
TEXAN...4-6

ESQUIRES III
Singles: 7-inch
CAMARO (3460 "18 Yellow Roses")..3-5 72

ESSENCE R&B '75
Singles: 7-inch
EPIC 3-6 75-77
RONN (70 "Broken Promises")......10-15 73
LPs: 10/12-inch
SAVOY..8-12 78
Members: Marzette Griffith; Anthony Redmond.
Also see TURBULATIONS

ESSEX
Singles: 7-inch
BEST (101 "Cemetery Stomp")......20-30 63

ESSEX P&R/R&B/LP '63
Singles: 7-inch
BANG...4-8 66
ROULETTE 5-8 63-64
LPs: 10/12-inch
ROULETTE (25234 "Easier Said Than Done")..25-35 63
ROULETTE (25235 "A Walkin' Miracle")..20-35 63
ROULETTE (25246 "Young and Lively")..20-30 64
Members: Anita Humes; Walter Vickers; Rodney Taylor; Billie Hill; Rudolph Johnson.

ESSEX, David P&R '73
Singles: 7-inch
COLUMBIA 3-5 73-76
RSO 3-4 79
UNI...4-8 67
Picture Sleeves
COLUMBIA 3-5 73-75
UNI..5-10 67
LPs: 10/12-inch
COLUMBIA (CQ-32560 "Rock On")..15-25 74
(Quadrophonic)
COLUMBIA (KC-32560 "Rock On")..15-20 73
COLUMBIA (33289 "David Essex") 8-15 74
COLUMBIA (33813 "All the Fun of the Fair")..8-15 75
MERCURY 5-10 83

ESSEX, Herb, & Walters Sisters
Singles: 7-inch
J-REE..8-12 60

ESSO TRINIDAD STEEL BAND
LPs: 10/12-inch
W.B. 8-10 72

ESSQUIRES
Singles: 7-inch
MERIDIAN (6282 "Mission Bells") 75-125 63
(Identification number shown since no selection number is used.)

ESTABLISHMENT
Singles: 7-inch
EXCLUSIVE 10-15 60s
LPs: 10/12-inch
KING 8-10 71

ESTEFAN, Gloria P&R/LP '89
Singles: 7-inch
EPIC.... 3-4 89-91
LPs: 10/12-inch
EPIC.... 5-8 89-91
Also see MIAMI SOUND MACHINE

ESTER, Sidney
Singles: 7-inch
DANGOLD....10-20 58
DART (114 "Reach and Get It") 15-25 59

ESTES, Don
Singles: 7-inch
COLUMBIA.... 6-12 58

ESTES, John
(Sleepy John Estes)
Singles: 78 rpm
CHAMPION 10-15
DECCA.... 8-15
BLUEBIRD.... 5-10
VICTOR.... 8-15
LPs: 10/12-inch
DELMARK 10-15 66-69

ESTES, Lindy
Singles: 7-inch
FRATERNITY (872 "Where Will I Go") 20-30 60

ESTER, Sidney
Singles: 7-inch
DANGOLD.... 5-10 58

ESTRADA, Roy, & Rocketeers
Singles: 7-inch
KING 5-10 60
Also see G.T.O.

ESTUS
LPs: 10/12-inch
COLUMBIA.... 8-10 73

ESTUS, Deon LP '89
Singles: 7-inch
MIKA 3-4 89
LPs: 10/12-inch
MIKA 5-8 89

ESTUS, Deon, & George Michael P&R '89
Singles: 7-inch
MIKA 3-4 89
Picture Sleeves
MIKA (871538 "Heaven Help Me") 5-8 89
(With George Michael's name.)
MIKA (871538 "Heaven Help Me") 3-4 89
(Without George Michael's name.)
Also see ESTUS, Deon
Also see MICHAEL, George

ETERNAL FLAME
Singles: 7-inch
VIVA.... 4-8 67

ETERNALS P&R '59
Singles: 7-inch
COLLECTABLES.... 3-4
HOLLYWOOD (68 "Rockin' in the Jungle") 40-60 59
(White label.)
HOLLYWOOD (68 "Rockin' in the Jungle") 30-50 59
(Blue label. Has label name at bottom.)
HOLLYWOOD (68 "Rockin' in the Jungle") 20-40 60s
(Blue label. Has label name at top.)
HOLLYWOOD (68 "Rockin' in the Jungle") 10-20 60s
(Yellow label. Label name is changed slightly to "Transphonic Hollywood Productions.")
HOLLYWOOD (70 "Babalu's Wedding Day") 25-50 59
(Red label.)
HOLLYWOOD (70 "Babalu's Wedding Day") 15-25 59
(Blue label.)
LOST NITE.... 3-5
MUSICTONE (1110 "Babalu's Wedding Day") 8-12 62
MUSICTONE (1111 "Rockin' in the Jungle") 8-12 62
WARWICK (611 "Blind Date") 15-25 60
Members: Charles Girona; Alex Miranda; Fred Hodge; Ernie Sierra; Arnold Torres; George Villanueva.

ETERNALS
Singles: 7-inch
QUALITY (1922 "Hideaway") 15-25 59
(Canadian.)

ETERNITY'S CHILDREN P&R '68
Singles: 7-inch
A&M.... 5-8 67
LIBERTY 4-6 70
TOWER.... 4-6 68-69
Picture Sleeves
TOWER.... 5-10 68
LPs: 10/12-inch
TOWER (5123 "Eternity's Children") 20-25 68
TOWER (5144 "Timeless") 20-25 68
Member: Bruce Blackman.
Also see ALLAN, Davie / Eternity's Children / Main Attraction / Sunrays
Also see KORONA
Also see STARBUCK

ETHEL & SHAMELESS HUSSIES C&W '88
Singles: 7-inch
MCA 3-4 88-89
Members: Gayle Zeiler; Valerie Hunt; Becki Fogle.
Also see ZEILER, Gayle

ETHERIDGE, Melissa LP '88
Singles: 7-inch
ISLAND 3-4 89
Picture Sleeves
ISLAND 3-4 89
LPs: 10/12-inch
ISLAND 5-8 89

ETHICS R&B '69
Singles: 7-inch
GOLDEN FLEECE.... 4-8 74
PHALANX....10-20
VENT....8-12 68-69
Member: Ronald Tyson.
Also see LOVE COMMITTEE

ETHICS
Singles: 7-inch
DYNAMIC SOUND (2001 "A Whole Lot of Confusion") 15-25 66
Members: Don Gruender; Mark Miller; Mike Jablonski; Gene Peranich.
Also see INVASION

ETHICS
Singles: 7-inch
GRAVES (1099 "It's Okay") 15-25
UPTIGHT ("Can't You See") 25-35

ETHICS
Singles: 7-inch
WALE....10-15

ETHIER, Ray
Singles: 7-inch
MERCURY 5-10 59

ETHOS
LPs: 10/12-inch
CAPITOL....8-10 77

ETONS
Singles: 7-inch
U.S.A. 4-8 64

ETRIS, Barry
Singles: 7-inch
SIMS 4-6 64
Picture Sleeves
SIMS 5-8 64

ETTA & AMELIA
Singles: 7-inch
JO ANN 4-8 61

ETTA & HARVEY P&R/R&B '60
Singles: 7-inch
CHESS (1760 "If I Can't Have You") 10-20 60
CHESS (1771 "Spoonful") 10-20 60
Members: Etta James; Harvey Fuqua.
Also see HARVEY
Also see JAMES, Etta

E-TYPES
Singles: 7-inch
DOT (16864 "I Can't Do It") 5-10 66
LINK (1 "I Can't Do It") 20-25 66
SUNBURST (001 "Love of the Love") 15-20 66
TOWER (325 "Put the Clock Back on the Wall") 10-20 67
UPTOWN (754 "Big City") 10-20 67

ETZEL, Jack
Singles: 7-inch
MONUMENT 10-20 62-64
RAT (45 "Meanwhile at the Convention") 10-15 64

ETZEL, Roy LP '65
(With the Jupiter Serenaders)
Singles: 7-inch
HICKORY.... 4-8 63
MGM 4-6 65-67
PRESIDENT.... 4-8 61
TIME 4-8 61
LPs: 10/12-inch
MGM 8-12 65

EUBANKS, Jack P&R '61
Singles: 7-inch
MONUMENT 4-8 61-64
LPs: 10/12-inch
MONUMENT 10-20 66

EUCLID
LPs: 10/12-inch
FLYING DUTCHMAN/ AMSTERDAM....10-12 70

EUCLID BEACH BAND P&R '79
Singles: 7-inch
EPIC/CLEVELAND INT'L.... 3-4 78-79
SCENE.... 4-6 78
LPs: 10/12-inch
EPIC....5-10 79

EUGENE & CYCLONES
Singles: 7-inch
BRYTE 10-20 62

EUGENE & TRAVELLS
Singles: 7-inch
SOLID GOLD 8-12

EUNICE
(With the Earl Palmer Combo; Eunice Russ Frost)
Singles: 7-inch
CLASSIC ARTISTS (108 "Talk About That") 4-6 89
Also see GENE & EUNICE

EUNIQUES
Singles: 7-inch
JASON SCOTT 4-8
620 (1003 "Pretty Baby") 35-45 63
620 (1006 "Cry, Cry, Cry") 40-50 63

EUPHONIOUS WAIL
LPs: 10/12-inch
KAPP (3668 "Euphonius Wail") 35-45 73
Members: Susie Rey; Doug Hoffman; Bart Libby; Gary Violetti; Steve Tracey.

EUPHORIA
Singles: 7-inch
BAND BOX (393 "Somebody Listen") 20-25 60s
MAINSTREAM (655 "Hungry Women") 10-15 68
Also see WILDFLOWER / Harbinger Complex / Euphoria / Other Side

EUPHORIA
Singles: 7-inch
HERITAGE (831 "You Must Forget") 10-15 69
LPs: 10/12-inch
HERITAGE (35005 "Euphoria") 30-40 69
Member: Tom Pacheco.

EUPHORIA
LPs: 10/12-inch
CAPITOL (363 "A Gift from Euphoria") 40-60 69
Members: William Lincoln; Hamilton Watt.

EUPHORIA
LPs: 10/12-inch
RAINBOW (1003 "Lost in a Trance") 200-300 73

EUPHORIA'S ID
Singles: 7-inch
EADIT (201,365 "Hey Joe") 25-35 67

EUROGLIDERS P&R/LP '84
Singles: 7-inch
COLUMBIA....3-4 84-86
Picture Sleeves
COLUMBIA....3-4 86
LPs: 10/12-inch
COLUMBIA....5-10 84
Member: Grace Knight.

EUROPE LP '86
Singles: 12-inch
EPIC....4-8 86
(Promotional only.)
Singles: 7-inch
EPIC....3-4 86-88
Picture Sleeves
EPIC....3-4 87-88
LPs: 10/12-inch
EPIC....5-10 86-88
Members: Joey Tempest; John Leven; Mic Michaeli; Kee Marcello; Ian Haughland.

EUROPEANS
Singles: 12-inch
A&M....4-6 84
Singles: 7-inch
A&M....3-4 84
LPs: 10/12-inch
A&M....5-10 84

EURYTHMICS P&R/D&D/LP '83
Singles: 12-inch
RCA 4-6 83-86
Singles: 7-inch
ARISTA....3-4 89-91
RCA 3-6 83-88
Picture Sleeves
ARISTA....3-4 89
RCA 3-6 83-88
LPs: 10/12-inch
ARISTA....5-8 89-91
RCA 5-10 83-88
Members: Annie Lennox; Dave Stewart.
Also see LENNOX, Annie, & Al Green
Also see TOURISTS

EURYTHMICS & ARETHA FRANKLIN P&R/D&D '85
Singles: 12-inch
RCA 4-6 85
Singles: 7-inch
RCA 3-4 85
Also see EURYTHMICS
Also see FRANKLIN, Aretha

EVALINE
Singles: 7-inch
SOUND STAGE 7....4-8 63-64

EVAN & EMPERORS
Singles: 7-inch
IMPACT....4-8 63

EVANS, Ashley C&W '90
Singles: 7-inch
DOOR KNOB 3-4 89-90

EVANS, Barbara
Singles: 7-inch
PIONEER....4-6
RCA (7519 "Souvenirs") 10-15 59
RCA (7634 "Beatnik Daddy") 10-15 59

EVANS, Dale
LPs: 10/12-inch
ALLEGRO (4116) 15-25 50s
(10-inch LP.)
CAPITOL....8-15 67
EVON....10-15 50s
WORD 5-8
Also see ROGERS, Roy

EVANS, Dave
Singles: 7-inch
SUNRISE 4-8
LPs: 10/12-inch
ALSHIRE....8-10 70

EVANS, Dean
Singles: 7-inch
DAPT 4-8 61

EVANS, Emily
Singles: 7-inch
DOT 4-8 61
JAMIE 4-8 63

EVANS, Frank
Singles: 7-inch
NUGGET (1001 "Got to Get Some Money") 35-50 59

EVANS, Gene
(With the Beavers)
Singles: 7-inch
TREND '61 ....5-10 61

EVANS, Jack
Singles: 7-inch
ENVOY 3-6
KAYO....5-10
Picture Sleeves
KAYO....8-15

EVANS, Jackie
Singles: 7-inch
VIDA....5-8 63

EVANS, Jeff
Singles: 7-inch
GRANDSTAND 3-4 76

EVANS, Jerry
(With the Off Keys & Deans; with Rhythmairs; with Rhythmaires)
Singles: 7-inch
BUBBLE....10-15 62
DREAM (5533 "Still In Love with You") 50-75 65
PENNY (201 "Green, Green Grass of Home") 5-10
ROWE (001 "Oh Little Girl") 100-200 62
ROWE (002 "Oh Little Girl") 75-125 62
(Reissue, re-recorded version.)
STARFIRE 10-15 62
Also see OFF KEYS

EVANS, Jimmy
(With the Jesters)
Singles: 7-inch
CAVEMAN (502 "The Joint's Really Jumpin' ") 500-750 55
CLEARMONT (502 "The Joint's Really Jumpin' ") 300-500 55
REBEL ACE 5-10 65
RIVER....5-10 65
RIVERTOWN....3-6 79
SHIMMY (1054 "Messy Bessy") 150-300 60

EVANS, Kay
Singles: 7-inch
WHIP 4-6

EVANS, Joey
Singles: 7-inch
DOLA....5-8 62

EVANS, Larry
(James Wayne)
Singles: 78 rpm
FABOR....10-20 54-56
Singles: 7-inch
FABOR (4001 "Patricia") 25-50 54
FABOR (4008 "Henpecked") 25-50 56
FABOR (4009 "Junco Returns") 25-50 56
Also see WAYNE, James

EVANS, Larry
Singles: 7-inch
MOD....4-6
Also see RIDDLE, Jimmy

EVANS, Leon
Singles: 7-inch
DE'BESTH (1111 "Satellite Beep Bop") 10-20 60s

EVANS, Linda R&B '79
Singles: 7-inch
ARIOLA....3-5 79
WATTSOUND....3-5 73
Also see CHANSON
Also see CHARMS
Also see QUOTATIONS

EVANS, Margie R&B '73
Singles: 7-inch
ICA....3-5 77
U.A. 3-5 73

EVANS, Mark
Singles: 7-inch
TAB (28 "Gang's House") 350-450
(Pink label.)

EVANS, Marty
Singles: 7-inch
CORAL....5-10 60-61

EVANS, Mike
Singles: 7-inch
A&M....8-12 67

EVANS, Mill
Singles: 7-inch
CONSTELLATION (170 "Things Won't Be the Same") 10-15 66
SHARP (6041 "Don't Forget About Me") 10-20 60s

EVANS, Mimi
Singles: 7-inch
EPIC 4-8 65
Also see EVANS, Paul & Mimi

EVANS, Nate
Singles: 7-inch
TWINIGHT 3-5 71

EVANS, Nora / Duke Hazlett
Singles: 78 rpm
BROADWAY 4-8 54
Singles: 7-inch
BROADWAY....6-12 54

EVANS, Paul P&R '59
(With the Curls)
Singles: 7-inch
ATCO....8-12 59-60
BIG TREE 3-5 75
CARLTON 8-15 61-62
CINNAMON INT'L 3-4 80
COLLECTABLES....3-4 80s
COLUMBIA....3-6 68
DECCA....5-10 58
DOT 3-5 73
EPIC....4-8 64-65
GUARANTEED 10-20 59-60
KAPP 5-10 62-63
LAURIE 3-5 71
MERCURY 3-5 74-75
MUSICOR 3-5 77
RCA 10-20 57
RANWOOD....3-5 72
SPRING 3-5 78-79
EPs: 7-inch
KAPP (1346 "21 Years in a Tennessee Jail") 8-12 64
(Promotional issue only.)
LPs: 10/12-inch
CARLTON (129 "Hear Paul Evans in Your Home Tonight") 20-30 61
(Monaural.)
CARLTON (129 "Hear Paul Evans in Your Home Tonight") 25-35 61
(Stereo.)
CARLTON (130 "Folk Songs of Many Lands") 15-25 61
(Monaural.)
CARLTON (130 "Folk Songs of Many Lands") 20-30 61
(Stereo.)
GUARANTEED (1000 "Fabulous Teens") 20-40 60
(Monaural.)
GUARANTEED (1000 "Fabulous Teens") 30-40 60
(Stereo.)
KAPP (1346 "21 Years in a Tennessee Jail") 15-25 64
(Monaural.)
KAPP (1475 "Another Town, Another Jail") 15-25 66
(Monaural.)
KAPP (3346 "21 Years in a Tennessee Jail") 20-30 64
(Stereo.)
KAPP (3475 "Another Town, Another Jail") 20-30 66
Also see CARTEY, Ric / Paul Evans

EVANS, Paul & Mimi
Singles: 7-inch
EPIC 4-8 64
Also see EVANS, Mimi
Also see EVANS, Paul

EVANS, Paula C&W '77
Singles: 7-inch
AUTUMN....3-5 77

EVANS, Rusty
Singles: 7-inch
BRUNSWICK....10-15 58
EAGLE 10-20 58
RIBBON 5-10 60
Also see DEAN, Jimmy / Marvin Rainwater / Rusty Evans

EVANS, Sandy
Singles: 7-inch
DWAIN....5-10 59

EVANS, Sherman
Singles: 7-inch
MANCO....4-8 62-63

EVANS, Skip
Singles: 7-inch
QUALITY (1765 "Dusty Road") 10-20 64
QUALITY (1824 "Lemon Merangue") 10-20 64
(Canadian.)
TWIRL (2019 "Dusty Road") 10-20 64
(U.S.A. release.)

EVANS, Sticks, & House Rockets
Singles: 7-inch
ZEBRA (118 "Zulu's Court") 15-25 57

EVANS, Sue
(With the Solitaires)
Singles: 7-inch
CADILLAC (2001 "Hey Shorty") 20-30 60
MADISON 8-12 61

20TH FOX ... 10-15 60

EVANS, Tony
Singles: 7-inch
CAMERON (1 "I'm Looking Over") .50-75

EVANS, Vicki
Singles: 7-inch
TUXEDO ... 4-8

EVANS, Vince
Singles: 7-inch
BRAVE ... 3-6 69

EVANS, Warren R&B '45
Singles: 78 rpm
NATIONAL ... 10-15 45
Also see JOHNSON, Buddy

EVAROS
Singles: 7-inch
ROULETTE ... 5-10

EVASIONS R&B '81
Singles: 7-inch
SAM ... 3-5 81
SOIF (1000 "Son of Surf") ... 10-15 82
(Picture disc. 500 made.)

EVE
LPs: 10/12-inch
LHI ... 10-12 70

EVE ELEKTRO: see ELEKTRO, Eve

EVELS
Singles: 7-inch
TRA=X (14 "The Magic of Love") ... 25-50

EVENTUALS
Singles: 7-inch
OKEH ... 10-15 61
Picture Sleeves
OKEH ... 15-25 61

EVER-READY SINGERS
Singles: 78 rpm
CAPITOL ... 10-15 54
Singles: 7-inch
CAPITOL (2763 "One Day When I Was Walking") ... 15-25 54
CAPITOL (2867 "This Heart of Mine") ... 15-25 54
CAPITOL (2984 "I Don't Care What the World May Do") ... 20-30 54

EVERET TRIPLETS
Singles: 7-inch
LEADER ... 5-10 60

EVERETT, Betty P&R/R&B '63
Singles: 7-inch
ABC ... 4-6 66-67
C.J. (619 "Your Lovin' Arms") ... 15-25 61
(Credits Earl Hooker, Al Perkins & Betty Everett.)
C.J. (619 "Happy I Long to Be") ... 8-12 64
(Credits Betty Everett.)
COBRA (5019 "My Life Depends on You") ... 20-30 57
COLLECTABLES ... 3-4 80s
DOTTIE (1126 "Tell Me Darling") ... 15-25
ERIC ... 3-4 70s
FANTASY ... 3-6 70-74
OLDIES 45 ... 3-6 60s
ONE-DERFUL (4806 "Your Love Is Important to Me") ... 10-15 62
ONE-DERFUL (4823 "I'll Be There") ... 10-15 63
UNI ... 4-8 68-69
VEE JAY ... 8-12 63-65
LPs: 10/12-inch
FANTASY ... 8-10 75
SUNSET ... 10-15 68
UNI ... 10-15 69
VEE JAY (1077 "Betty Everett") ... 35-50 63
VEE JAY (1122 "The Very Best of Betty Everett") ... 25-35 65
Session: Blossoms; Earl Hooker All Stars.
Also see BLOSSOMS
Also see BUTLER, Jerry, & Betty Everett
Also see DAYLIGHTERS
Also see HOOKER, Earl, Al Perkins, & Betty Everett
Also see PERKINS, Al

EVERETT, Betty, & Daylighters
Singles: 7-inch
C.J. (611 Please Come Back") ... 15-25 61
Also see DAYLIGHTERS

EVERETT, Betty / Ketty Lester
LPs: 10/12-inch
GRAND PRIX ... 10-15 64
Also see LESTER, Ketty

EVERETT, Betty / Impressions
LPs: 10/12-inch
CUSTOM ... 10-15 64
Also see EVERETT, Betty
Also see IMPRESSIONS

EVERETT, Bracy
Singles: 7-inch
ATLANTIC ... 5-10 59
Session: King Curtis.
Also see KING CURTIS

EVERETT, Chad
Singles: 7-inch
MARINA ... 3-5 71
Picture Sleeves
MARINA ... 3-5 71

EVERETT, Dewell
Singles: 7-inch
JED (0001 "Janie Mae") ... 25-50 62

EVERETT, Keith
Singles: 7-inch
MERCURY ... 8-12 68
TMP-TING ... 10-20

EVERETT, Vince
(Marvin Benefield)
Singles: 7-inch
ABC-PAR (10313 "Such a Night") .. 30-50 62
ABC-PAR (10360 "I Ain't Gonna Be Your Low Down Dog") ... 30-40 62
ABC-PAR (10472 "Baby Let's Play House") ... 30-40 63
ABC-PAR (10624 "To Have, to Hold and Let Go") ... 20-30 64
SAGA (1002 "Don't Worry") ... 25-50 58
TOWN (1964 "Buttercup") ... 10-20 60
EPs: 7-inch
ROCKIN' (005 "The Presley Sound of Vince Everett") ... 10-20
Also see BENEFIELD, Marvin

EVERETTE, Leon C&W '77
Singles: 7-inch
ORLANDO ... 3-4 79-86
RCA ... 3-4 80-84
TRUE ... 5-10 77
LPs: 10/12-inch
ORLANDO ... 5-10 86
RCA ... 5-10 81-84
TRUE (1002 "Goodbye King of Rock & Roll") ... 15-25 77
(With 18" x 23" bonus poster of Elvis Presley.)
TRUE (1002 "Goodbye King of Rock & Roll") ... 10-15 77
(Without poster.)

EVERGLADES
Singles: 7-inch
BVP (112577 "While Sitting in the Chapel") ... 75-150 63

EVERGREEN BLUE SHOES
Singles: 7-inch
AMOS ... 4-8 69
LPs: 10/12-inch
AMOS ... 10-20 69
MUSIC FACTORY ... 10-20 68
Member: Chet McCracken.
Also see HELP

EVERGREEN BLUES
(Ever-Green Blues)
Singles: 7-inch
ABC ... 3-6 69
MERCURY ... 4-8 67-68
Picture Sleeves
MERCURY (72756 "Midnight Confessions") ... 8-12 67
LPs: 10/12-inch
ABC ... 10-15 69
MERCURY ... 10-20 68

EVERGREENS
Singles: 78 rpm
CHART (605 "Very Truly Yours") ... 20-40 55
Singles: 7-inch
CHART (605 "Very Truly Yours") ... 100-200 55

EVERGREENS
Singles: 7-inch
BIRTHSTONE ... 3-5

EVERHART, Bobby
Singles: 7-inch
MONUMENTAL (515 "Boney Maronie") ... 30-50 65

EVERLY, Don C&W '76
Singles: 7-inch
ABC/HICKORY ... 4-8 75-77
HICKORY/MGM ... 4-8 76
ODE ... 4-8 70-74
LPs: 10/12-inch
ABC/HICKORY ... 8-12 76-77
ODE ... 8-12 70-74
Also see HARRIS, Emmylou
Also see KIMBERLY, Adrian

EVERLY, Phil C&W '80
Singles: 7-inch
CAPITOL ... 3-4 83
CURB ... 3-4 80-81
ELEKTRA ... 3-4 79
PYE ... 3-5 73-76
RCA ... 3-5 73
LPs: 10/12-inch
ELECTRA ... 5-10 79
PYE ... 8-10 75-76
RCA ... 8-10 73

EVERLY BROTHERS P&R/R&B/C&W '57
Singles: 78 rpm
CADENCE (1315 thru 1355) ... 40-80 57-58
CADENCE (1364 "Poor Jenny") ... 50-100 59
COLUMBIA (21496 "The Sun Keeps Shining") ... 50-100 56
Singles: 7-inch
BARNABY ... 3-6 70-76
CADENCE (1315 "Bye Bye Love") .15-25 57
CADENCE (1337 "Wake Up Little Susie") ... 15-25 57
CADENCE (1342 "This Little Girl of Mine") ... 15-25 58
CADENCE (1348 "All I Have to Do Is Dream") ... 15-25 58
(Silver and maroon label.)
CADENCE (1348 "All I Have to Do Is Dream") ... 10-20 61
(Red label with black print.)
CADENCE (1350 "Bird Dog") ... 15-25 58
CADENCE (1355 "Problems") ... 15-25 58
CADENCE (1364 "Poor Jenny") ... 15-25 59
CADENCE (1369 "I Kissed You") ... 15-25 59
CADENCE (1376 "Let It Be Me") ... 15-25 60
CADENCE (1380 "When Will I Be Loved") ... 15-25 60
CADENCE (1388 "Like Strangers") ... 15-25 60
CADENCE (1429 "I'm Here to Get My Baby Out of Jail") ... 15-25 62
COLUMBIA (21496 "The Sun Keeps Shining") ... 150-250 56
(Red label.)
COLUMBIA (21496 "The Sun Keeps Shining") ... 100-150 56
(White label. Promotional issue only.)
ERIC ... 3-4 70s
MERCURY ... 3-4 84-86
RCA ... 3-6 72-73
W.B. (5151 "Cathy's Clown") ... 8-10 60
(Monaural.)
W.B. (S-5151 "Cathy's Clown") ... 20-30 60
(Stereo.)
W.B. (5163 thru 5833) ... 5-10 60-69
W.B. (5857 "Fifi the Flea") ... 15-25 67
(Credits "Don Everly Brother" on one side, and "Phil Everly Brother" on the flip.)
W.B. (5901 thru 7425) ... 4-8 67-70
Promotional Singles
BARNABY ... 4-6 70-76
CADENCE (1315 thru 1342) ... 20-30 57
CADENCE (1348 "All I Have to Do Is Dream") ... 20-30 57
(Black vinyl.)
CADENCE (1348 "All I Have to Do Is Dream") ... 50-75
(Colored vinyl.)
CADENCE (1350 thru 1429) ... 10-20 58-62
COLUMBIA (21496 "The Sun Keeps Shining") ... 150-250 56
MERCURY ... 3-5 84-86
RCA ... 4-8 72-73
W.B. (5151 "Cathy's Clown") ... 40-60 60
(Gold vinyl.)
W.B. (5163 "So Sad") ... 40-60 60
(Gold vinyl.)
W.B. (5199 "Ebony Eyes") ... 40-60 61
(Gold vinyl.)
Picture Sleeves
CADENCE (1337 "Wake Up Little Susie") ... 50-100 57
CADENCE (1355 "Problems") ... 20-40 58
CADENCE (1369 "Till I Kissed You") ... 20-40 59
CADENCE (1376 "Let It Be Me") ... 20-40 60
W.B. (5151 "Cathy's Clown") ... 40-60 60
W.B. (5163 "So Sad") ... 40-60 60
W.B. (5199 "Ebony Eyes") ... 40-60 61
W.B. (5220 "Temptation") ... 15-25 61
W.B. (5250 "Crying in the Rain") ... 15-25 62
W.B. (5273 "That's Old Fashioned") ... 15-25 62
W.B. (5297 "Don't Ask Me to Be Friends") ... 15-25 62
MERCURY ... 3-6 84
EPs: 7-inch
CADENCE (3 "Rockin' with the Everly Brothers") ... 25-35 61
(Has single sheet cardboard insert/cover. Compact 33.)
CADENCE (4 "Dream with the Everly Brothers") ... 25-35 61
(Has single sheet cardboard insert/cover. Compact 33.)
CADENCE (104 "Everly Bros., Vol. 1") ... 30-50 57
CADENCE (105 "Everly Bros., Vol. 2") ... 30-50 57
CADENCE (107 "The Everly Brothers") ... 30-50 58
CADENCE ("Songs Our Daddy Taught Us") ... 100-150 58
(White, typewritten label. No selection number shown, only identification numbers "K80H-1718/20." Labeled "Cadence Disc Jockey Pressing." Promotional issue only.)
CADENCE (108/109/110 "Songs Our Daddy Taught Us") ... 25-50 58
(Price is for any of three volumes.)
CADENCE (111 "The Everly Brothers") ... 25-50 59
CADENCE (118 "The Everly Brothers") ... 25-35 59
CADENCE (121 "Very Best of The Everly Brothers") ... 25-35 60
W.B. (120 "Everly Brothers Show") ... 15-25 70
(Juke box issue only. Includes title strips.)
W.B. (1381-1 "Foreverly Yours") ... 15-25 60
(Black vinyl.)
W.B. (1381-1 "Foreverly Yours") ... 35-50 60
(Colored vinyl. Promotional issue only.)
W.B. (1381-2 "Especially for You") ... 15-25 60
W.B. (1471 "Golden Hits") ... 15-25 62
(Juke box issue only. Includes title strips.)
W.B. (5501 "The Everly Brothers Plus Two Oldies") ... 15-25 61
LPs: 10/12-inch
ARISTA ... 8-12 84
BARNABY (350 "Original Greatest Hits") ... 10-15 70
BARNABY (30260 "End of an Era") ... 10-15 71
BARNABY (4000 series) ... 6-10 77
BARNABY (6006 "Greatest Hits") ... 8-12
CADENCE (3003 "The Everly Brothers") ... 75-125 58
CADENCE (3016 "Songs Our Daddy Taught Us") ... 50-75 58
CADENCE (3025 "The Everly Brothers' Best") ... 75-100 59
(Blue cover.)
CADENCE (3040 "The Fabulous Style of the Everly Brothers") ... 50-75 60
CADENCE (3059 "Folk Songs") ... 35-40 63
CADENCE (3062 "15 Everly Hits") ... 45-65 63
CADENCE (25040 "The Fabulous Style of the Everly Brothers") ... 75-100 60
(Stereo.)
CADENCE (25059 "Folk Songs") ... 35-40 63
(Stereo.)
CADENCE (25062 "15 Everly Hits") ... 45-65 63
(Stereo.)
CANDLELITE ... 10-15 76
EXCELSIOR ... 5-10
HARMONY ... 10-12 68-70
HAPPY DAYS ... 5-10
MERCURY ... 5-10 84-86
PAIR ... 8-12 84
PASSPORT ... 5-12 84-86
RCA ... 8-12 72
RHINO (214 "All They Had to Do Was Dream") ... 5-10 85
RHINO (258 "Heartache and Memories") ... 8-10 85
(Picture disc.)
RONCO ... 8-10
TIME-LIFE ... 10-15 86
W.B. (1381 "It's Everly Time") ... 30-50 60
W.B. (1395 "A Date with the Everly Brothers") ... 50-100 60
(With gatefold cover and eight "wallet pix" cut-out photos.)
W.B. (1395 "A Date with the Everly Brothers") ... 20-40 61
(With standard cover.)
W.B. (1418 "Songs for Both Sides of an Evening") ... 20-40 61
W.B. (1430 "Instant Party") ... 20-40 62
W.B. (1471 "Golden Hits") ... 20-40 62
W.B. (1483 "Christmas with the Everly Brothers") ... 20-40 61
W.B. (1513 "Great Country Hits") .. 20-40 63
W.B. (1554 "Very Best of the Everly Brothers") ... 20-40 64
(Yellow cover. Gray label.)
W.B. (1554 "Very Best of the Everly Brothers") ... 10-15 70
(Blue cover. Gray label.)
W.B. (1554 "Very Best of the Everly Brothers") ... 8-12 72
(Blue cover. "Skyline" label.)
W.B. (1578 "Rock 'N Soul") ... 20-35 65
W.B. (1585 "Gone Gone Gone") ... 20-35 65
W.B. (1605 "Beat and Soul") ... 15-25 65
W.B. (1620 "In Our Image") ... 35-45 66
W.B. (1646 "Two Yanks in London") ... 15-25 66
(With the Hollies.)
W.B. (1676 "The Hit Sound of the Everly Brothers") ... 15-20 67
W.B. (1708 "Everly Brothers Sing") ... 15-25 67
W.B. (1752 "Roots") ... 15-25 68
W.B. (1858 "The Everly Brothers Show") ... 12-15 70
Promotional LPs
W.B. (134 "The Everly Brothers") ... 100-200 61
(Single-sided, 10-inch LP with five tracks from *The Everly Brothers - Both Sides of an Evening* [WB 1418]. Promotional issue only.)
W.B. (135 "Souvenir Sampler") . 100-125 61
(Don and Phil discussing *The Everly Brothers - Both Sides of an Evening*. Has an LP discount coupon on sleeve. Promotional issue only.)
W.B. (1381 "It's Everly Time") ... 50-100 60
W.B. (1395 "A Date with the Everly Brothers") ... 75-100 60
(With gatefold cover and eight "wallet pix" cut-out photos.)
W.B. (1418 "Both Sides of an Evening") ... 50-75 61
W.B. (1430 "Instant Party") ... 50-75 62
W.B. (1471 "Golden Hits") ... 50-75 62
W.B. (1483 "Christmas with the Everly Brothers") ... 50-75 61
W.B. (1513 "Great Country Hits") .. 40-60 63
W.B. (1554 "Very Best of the Everly Brothers") ... 40-60 64
(Yellow cover.)
W.B. (1578 "Rock 'N Soul") ... 40-60 65
W.B. (1585 "Gone Gone Gone") ... 40-60 65
W.B. (1605 "Beat 'N Soul") ... 35-50 65
W.B. (1620 "In Our Image") ... 35-50 66
W.B. (1646 "Two Yanks in London") ... 35-50 66
W.B. (1676 "The Hit Sound of the Everly Brothers") ... 35-50 67
W.B. (1708 "The Everly Brothers Sing") ... 35-50 67
W.B. (1752 "Roots") ... 25-40 68
W.B. (1858 "The Everly Brothers Show") ... 25-35 70
Members: Don Everly; Phil Everly. Session: Chet Atkins.
Also see ATKINS, Chet
Also see CASH, Johnny, Rosanne Cash & Everly Brothers
Also see EVERLY, Don
Also see EVERLY, Phil
Also see HOLLIES

EVERLY BROTHERS & BEACH BOYS
Singles: 7-inch
CAPITOL (44297 "Don't Worry Baby") ... 3-5 88
Picture Sleeves
CAPITOL (44297 "Don't Worry Baby") ... 3-5 88
Also see BEACH BOYS

EVERPRESENT FULLNESS
Singles: 7-inch
WHITE WHALE ... 5-10 66-67
LPs: 10/12-inch
WHITE WHALE (7132 "Everpresent Fullness") ... 20-30 70
Member: Paul Johnson.

Also see BELAIRS

EVERY DAY PEOPLE
Singles: 7-inch
ABNAK ... 4-8 69
(Black vinyl.)
ABNAK ... 8-10 69
(Colored vinyl. Promotional issue only.)

EVERY FATHER'S TEENAGE SON P&R '67
Singles: 7-inch
BUDDAH ... 4-8 67

EVERY MOTHER'S NIGHTMARE LP '70
LPs: 10/12-inch
ARISTA ... 5-8 90

EVERY MOTHER'S SON P&R/LP '67
Singles: 7-inch
MGM ... 4-8 67-68
POLYDOR ... 3-4
Picture Sleeves
MGM ... 4-8 67
LPs: 10/12-inch
MGM ... 10-20 67

EVERYDAY HUDSON
(Hudson Brothers)
Singles: 7-inch
DECCA ... 4-6 70
Also see HUDSON BROTHERS

EVERYDAY PEOPLE
Singles: 7-inch
PEOPLE ... 4-8 69
ROULETTE ... 3-6 69
VALANE (1936 "Double Lovin' ") ... 4-6
LPs: 10/12-inch
PARAMOUNT ... 8-10 72

EVERYMAN
Singles: 7-inch
MAINLINE ... 4-8 67
ATLANTIC ... 5-8 90

EVERYTHING BUT THE GIRL LP '90
LPs: 10/12-inch
ATLANTIC ... 5-8 90
SIRE ... 5-8

EVERYTHING IS EVERYTHING P&R '69
Singles: 7-inch
VANGUARD APOSTOLIC ... 4-6 69
LPs: 10/12-inch
VANGUARD ... 15-20 69
Members: Chris Hill; Danny Weiss.

EVIL
Singles: 7-inch
BRIDGE SOCIETY ... 10-15
CAPITOL (2038 "Whatcha Gonna Do") ... 10-20 67
LIVING LEGEND (108 "Whatcha Gonna Do") ... 20-40 67
Members: John Doyle; Stan Kinchen; Al Banyai; Doug Romanella; Larry O'Connell; George Hall; Mike Hughes.

EVIL ENCORPORATED
Singles: 7-inch
SCENE (101 "Hey You") ... 15-25 67
SCENE (102 "Baby It's You") ... 15-25 67

EVIL "I"
Singles: 7-inch
BRIDGE SOCIETY (25-66 "Can't Live Without You") ... 15-25 60s

EVOLUTION REVOLUTION
Singles: 7-inch
GET HIP ... 3-5 90

EWING, Skip C&W '88
Singles: 7-inch
MCA ... 3-4 88-90

EX SAVEYONS
Singles: 7-inch
SMOKE (600 "I Don't Love You No More") ... 15-25 60s
SMOKE (609 "Where Do I Go from Here") ... 15-25 60s

EXCALIBURS
Singles: 7-inch
TRENT TOWN (1001 "Xmas Dreaming") ... 100-200

EXCELLENTS P&R '62
Singles: 7-inch
BLAST (205 "Coney Island Baby") ... 20-30 62
(Red label.)
BLAST (205 "Coney Island Baby") ... 10-20 62
(Red and white label.)
BLAST (205 "Coney Island Baby") ... 50-75 62
(White label.)
(Promotional issue only.)
BLAST (205 "Coney Island Baby") ... 15-25 65
(Purple label.)
COLLECTABLES ... 3-4
MERMAID (106 "Love No One But You") ... 75-125 61
(Label pictures a mermaid.)
MERMAID (106 "Love No One But You") ... 25-50 64
(Mermaid not pictured.)
OLD TIMER ... 4-8 64
LPs: 10/12-inch
ON the CORNER (135 "Excellents Go Bob Bob Bobbin' Along") ... 10-15 90

Also see EXCELLONS

EXCELLENTS
(Ultimates)
Singles: 7-inch
BLAST (207 "I Hear a Rhapsody") ... 35-55 63
(Not the same artist as on the preceding Blast issues. This group is really the Ultimates.)
Also see ULTIMATES

EXCELLONS
(Excellents)
Singles: 7-inch
BOBBY (601 "Helene") ... 35-50 64
(First issue.)
OLD TIMER (601 "Helene") ... 15-25 64
Also see EXCELLENTS

EXCELLS
Singles: 7-inch
BOYD ... 5-10 64

EXCELS
Singles: 78 rpm
CENTRAL ... 25-35 57
Singles: 7-inch
CENTRAL (2601 "You're Mine Forever") ... 25-35 57

EXCELS P&R '61
Singles: 7-inch
GONE (5094 "My Foolish Heart") ... 15-25 60
RSVP (111 "Can't Help Lovin' That Girl of Mine") ... 20-30 61

EXCELS
Singles: 7-inch
CARLA ... 10-20 66-68

EX-CELS
Singles: 7-inch
CORAL ... 10-15 68

EXCELS
Singles: 7-inch
GIBSON (210 "Let's Dance") ... 15-25 65

EXCELSIOR NORFOLK QUARTETTE
Singles: 78 rpm
BLACK SWAN (2060 "Jelly Roll Blues") ... 50-100 22
PARAMOUNT (12131 "Jelly Roll Blues") ... 50-100 22
Member: James C. Brown.
Also see EXCELSIOR QUARTETTE

EXCELSIOR QUARTETTE
Singles: 78 rpm
GENNETT (4881 "Jelly Roll Blues") ... 50-100 22
OKEH (8033 "Roll Them Bones") ... 50-75 22
OKEH (8035 "Over the Green Hill") ... 50-75 22
OKEH (8038 "If Hearts Win") ... 50-75 22
OKEY (Except 4881) ... 15-25
OKEY (4881 "Jelly Roll Blues") ... 25-50
STARR (9250 "Jelly Roll Blues") ... 25-50
Member: James C. Brown.
Also see EXCELSIOR NORFOLK QUARTETTE

EXCENTRICS
Singles: 7-inch
GOLITE ... 10-20

EXCEPTIONAL THREE
Singles: 7-inch
WAY OUT ... 10-15

EXCEPTIONALS
Singles: 7-inch
GRT ... 3-5 76
RED COACH (814 "Gotta Let Some Sunshine in My Life") ... 4-8 75

EXCEPTIONALS
Singles: 7-inch
JULENE (1001 "Sea of Tranquility") ... 8-12

EXCEPTIONS
Singles: 7-inch
CAMEO (378 "Down by the Ocean") ... 15-25 65
PRO (1 "Down by the Ocean") ... 40-60 65
Member: Jimmy Ellis.
Also see MOODS
Also see TRAMMPS

EXCEPTIONS
Singles: 7-inch
CAPITOL (2046 "Business As Usual") ... 8-12 67
CAPITOL (2120 "You Always Hurt Me") ... 8-12 67
CAPITOL (5982 "Girl from New York") ... 8-12 67
MERCURY (72562 "Ask Me if I Care") ... 8-12 66
QUILL (114 "Girl from New York") ... 15-25 67
TOLLIE (9007 "Searchin' ") ... 10-15 64
TOLLIE (9043 "Come on Home") ... 10-15 64
Members: Peter Cetera; Marty Grebb; Kal David; Jimmy Vincent; Billy Herman.
Also see BUCKINGHAMS
Also see CETERA, Peter
Also see DAVID, Kal, & Exceptions

EXCEPTIONS
EPs: 7-inch
FLAIR (6444 "Rock & Roll Mass") ... 20-30 67

EXCEPTIONS
Singles: 7-inch
TRUMP (354 "Still on the Run") ... 15-25

EXCHEQUERS
Singles: 7-inch
BOOM (115 "Is There Some Girl") ... 20-40 65
(Colored vinyl.)
Members: Arnie Bacon; Tom Hake; Rick Blomquist; Dan Woodard.

EXCITERS P&R/R&B '62
Singles: 7-inch
BANG (515 "A Little Bit of Soap") ... 5-10 66
BANG (518 "Weddings Make Me Cry") ... 15-25 66
LIBERTY ... 3-5
ROULETTE (4591 "I Want You to Be My Boy") ... 5-10 64
ROULETTE (4594 "Are You Satisfied") ... 5-10 65
ROULETTE (4614 "My Father") ... 5-10 65
ROULETTE (4632 "There They Go") ... 5-10 65
RCA (9633 "If You Want My Love") ... 15-25 68
RCA (9723 "Blowing Up My Mind") ... 15-25 68
SHOUT (205 "You Got Love") ... 5-10 66
SHOUT (214 "Soul Motion") ... 5-10 67
TODAY ... 4-8 70
U.A. (544 "Tell Him") ... 5-10 62
U.A. (572 "He's Got the Power") ... 5-10 63
U.A. (604 "Get Him") ... 5-10 63
U.A. (662 "Do-Wah-Diddy") ... 5-10 63
U.A. (721 "Having My Fun") ... 5-10 64
Picture Sleeves
ROULETTE (4591 "I Want You to Be My Boy") ... 10-20 64
LPs: 10/12-inch
RCA (4211 "Caviar & Chitlins") ... 20-30 69
ROULETTE (25326 "The Exciters") ... 15-25 66
SUNSET ... 10-12 70
TODAY (1001 "Black Beauty") ... 10-15 71
U.A. (3264 "Tell Him") ... 30-40 63
(Monaural.)
U.A. (6264 "Tell Him") ... 40-50 63
(Stereo.)
Members: Brenda Reid; Herb Rooney; Carol Johnson; Lillian Walker.
Also see BRENDA & HERB
Also see MASTERETTES

EXCITING INVICTAS
(Exciting Invicta's)
Singles: 7-inch
KINGSTON (427 "I Don't Care") ... 200-250 60
Members: Jimmy Noon; Ron Brennan; Jim Baumbauch; Don Humble; Emmett Smith.
Also see DEL CHONTAYS
Also see INTENTIONS

EXCITING VOICES
Singles: 7-inch
BEL CANTO ... 3-5

EXCLUSIVES
(With the Arcs)
Singles: 7-inch
K&C (102 "My Girl Friend") ... 100-150 58

EXEARTIVES
Singles: 7-inch
EDSEL ... 3-6

EXECS
Singles: 7-inch
FARGO (1055 "Walking in the Rain") ... 250-350 64

EXECUTIONERS
Singles: 7-inch
ACTION (500 "Don't Put Me On") ... 20-30 65
ACTION (502 "Dead End") ... 10-20 65
SUNBURST (108 "Guillotine") ... 10-20 65
SWAN ... 5-10 66

EXECUTIVE R&B '81
Singles: 7-inch
20TH FOX ... 3-4 81

EXECUTIVE FOUR
(With the Jesse Powell Orchestra)
Singles: 7-inch
LU MAR (202 "You Are") ... 75-125 60s
Also see POWELL, Jesse

EXECUTIVE SUITE R&B '73
Singles: 7-inch
BABYLON (1109 "I'm a Winner Now") ... 8-15 73
BABYLON (1111 "When the Fuel Runs Out") ... 5-10 74
BABYLON (1113 "Your Love Is Paradise") ... 8-15 74
JUBILEE ... 5-10 69
NORTH BAY ... 3-5
U.A. ... 3-5 75

EXECUTIVES
Singles: 7-inch
BLACK HOLE (1981 "A Girl Like You") ... 25-45 60s
EXPLOSIVE (3621 "River of Tears") ... 200-300 63
(Reissued as by the Challengers.)
REVENGE (5003 "Why") ... 500-1000 63
(First issue.)
Also see CHALLENGERS

EXECUTIVES
Singles: 7-inch
DERBY ... 5-10 64
PRINCETON (112 "My Special Angel") ... 25-50 60s
SCEPTER ... 4-6 73
U.A. ... 5-10 68

EXILE P&R '77
Singles: 7-inch
ARISTA ... 3-4 89-91
ATCO ... 3-5 77
COLUMBIA ... 3-6 69-70
EPIC ... 3-4 83-88
MCA/CURB ... 3-4 85-86
W.B./CURB ... 3-4 78-81
WOODEN NICKEL ... 3-5 72-73
LPs: 10/12-inch
EPIC ... 5-10 83-88
MCA/CURB ... 5-8 85-86
RCA ... 5-10 78
W.B. ... 5-10 78-81
WOODEN NICKEL ... 8-10 73
Members: J.P. Pennington; Les Taylor; Sonny LeMaire; Marlon Hargis; Steve Goetzman.
Also see PENNINGTON, J.P.
Also see TAYLOR, Les

EXILES
Singles: 7-inch
REM (358 "Stay with Me") ... 50-75 65

EXILES
Singles: 7-inch
COLUMBIA ... 4-6 69
DATE ... 5-10 67-69
JIMBO ... 10-20 67

EXILES
Singles: 7-inch
CAMPUS (1111 "Take It Off") ... 30-40

EXITS R&B '67
Singles: 7-inch
GEMINI ... 5-10 67
KAPP (2028 "I'm So Glad") ... 15-25 69

EXODUS
(Four Epics)
Singles: 7-inch
WAND (11241 "M&M") ... 100-125 72
(Black and white label. Promotional issue only.)
WAND (11241 "M&M") ... 30-50 72
(Multi-color label.)
Also see FOUR EPICS

EXODUS LP '87
LPs: 10/12-inch
ARISTA ... 5-10 87
CAPITOL ... 5-8 90
COMBAT ... 5-8 87-89

EXOTIC GUITARS LP '68
Singles: 7-inch
RANWOOD ... 3-5 68-70
LPs: 10/12-inch
RANWOOD ... 5-10 68-70
Member: Al Casey.
Also see CASEY, Al
Also see PLATTERS / Exotic Guitars

EXOTICS
Singles: 7-inch
BOLO (722 "Oasis") ... 5-10 61
JERDEN (106 "Four Banger") ... 15-20 60
SEAFAIR ... 4-8 62-65

EXOTICS
Singles: 7-inch
SPRINGBOARD (101 "Lorraine") ... 20-30 63
Picture Sleeves
SPRINGBOARD (101 "Lorraine") ... 50-80 63

EXOTICS
Singles: 7-inch
CORAL ... 10-20 61-64
EXCELLO ... 6-12 67-68

EXOTICS
Singles: 7-inch
MONUMENT (984 "Fire Engine Red") ... 5-10 67
NUNSUCH ("Hey Little Girl") ... 5-10 66
(No selection number used.)
TAD (2410 "Come with Me") ... 15-25 66
TAD (6701 "Queen of Shadows") ... 15-25 67

EXPLORATIONS
LPs: 10/12-inch
U.A. ... 8-10 78

EXPLORERS
Singles: 7-inch
CORAL (62147 "Vision of Love") ... 25-50 59
CORAL (62175 "Don't Be a Fool") ... 40-60 60
CORAL (62295 "Remember") ... 25-50 60
CORAL (65575 "Don't Be a Fool") ... 10-20 63
Also see DENNIS & EXPLORERS

EXPLOSIONS
Singles: 7-inch
BURTON (101 "Gee Baby") ... 8-12 60s
GOLD CUP ... 5-10 60s
IMPERIAL ... 5-10 65

EXPLOSIVE DYNAMIKS
Singles: 7-inch
LEMCO ... 4-8 66

EXPORT
LPs: 10/12-inch
EPIC ... 5-10 84
Member: Harry Shaw, Steve Morris, Chris Alderman, Lou Rosenthal.

EXPORTS
Singles: 7-inch
KING ... 10-20 64-65

EXPOSE D&D '85
Singles: 12-inch
ARISTA ... 4-6 85-89
Singles: 7-inch
ARISTA ... 3-4 85-90
Picture Sleeves
ARISTA ... 3-4 87-89
LPs: 10/12-inch
ARISTA ... 5-10 86-89
Members: Jeanette Jurado; Gioia Bruno; Ann Curless.

EXPRESS
Singles: 7-inch
MGM ... 4-8 67
PICCADILLY (226 "Long Green") ... 10-15 66

EXPRESSIONS
Singles: 7-inch
TEEN (101 "Now That You're Gone") ... 100-200 59

EXPRESSIONS
Singles: 7-inch
WOW! (2621 "Daydream") ... 10-20 61

EXPRESSIONS
Singles: 7-inch
ARLISS (1012 "My Love, My Love") ... 20-30 62
FEDERAL ... 4-8 64
GUYDEN ... 4-8 65
PARKWAY ... 4-8 63
REPRISE ... 8-10 65
SMASH ... 4-8 63
Members: Bobby Bloom; Phil Agtuca; Richie Le Causi.
Also see IMAGINATIONS

EXPRESSIONS
Singles: 7-inch
EXP (1002 "Temptation") ... 20-30

EXPRESSMEN
Singles: 7-inch
WESTCHESTER ... 20-25 60s

EXPRESSOS
Singles: 7-inch
CHAMP (2 "Straightaways") ... 10-20 62
TRANS AMERICAN (600 "Teenage Express") ... 10-20 60
Member: Aki Aleong.
Also see ALEONG, Aki
Also see SURFMEN

EXQUISITES
Singles: 7-inch
AVENUE D (0012 "Dedicated to the One I Love") ... 10-15 85
(Red vinyl. Reportedly 200 made.)
AVENUE D (0013 "Chapel of Dreams") ... 10-20 85
(Red vinyl. Reportedly 98 made.)

EXTENSIONS
Singles: 7-inch
NICKEL (111 "This Love of Mine") ... 10-20 60s
SUCCESS (109 "I Want to Know") ... 10-20 63

EXTERMINATORS
Singles: 7-inch
CHANCELLOR (1148 "Beetle Bomb") ... 10-20 64
GOLDEN WEST (1002 "Beatle Wig Party") ... 10-20 64
Members: Del Katcher; Jimmie Maddin.

EXTRA Ts R&B '82
Singles: 7-inch
SUNNYVIEW ... 3-4 82

EXTREME LP '89
LPs: 10/12-inch
A&M ... 5-8 89-90

EXTREMES
Singles: 7-inch
EVERLAST (5013 "Come Next Spring") ... 100-150 58
PARO (733 "The Bells") ... 200-300 62
Member: Bobby Sanders.
Also see BOBBY & VELVETS

EXTREMES
Singles: 7-inch
RCA ... 4-8 66

EXUMA
Singles: 7-inch
KAMA SUTRA ... 3-5 72
LPs: 10/12-inch
INAGUA ... 5-10 80
KAMA SUTRA ... 8-10 71-73
MERCURY ... 8-12 70

EXZELS
Singles: 7-inch
CROSS FIRE (228 "Canadian Sunset") ... 20-40 62

EYE TO EYE P&R/LP '82
Singles: 7-inch
W.B. ... 3-4 82-83
LPs: 10/12-inch
W.B. ... 5-10 82-83
Also see MARSHALL-HAIN

EYE ZOOMS
Singles: 7-inch
ATILA (213 "She's Gone") ... 10-15 66

EYE-FUL TOWER
Singles: 7-inch
SSS INT'L ... 4-6 67

EYES OF BLUE
Singles: 7-inch
DERAM ... 5-8 67
MERCURY ... 4-6 69
LPs: 10/12-inch
MERCURY ... 10-15 68-69
Also see ANCIENT GREASE

EYES OF MIND
LPs: 10/12-inch
VOXX ... 5-10

EZBA, Denny
(With the Goldens; Ezba)
Singles: 7-inch
C.A. ("Go Somewhere and Cry") ... 25-50 58
(Selection number not known.)
DOME ... 3-5 71
JAMIE ... 10-15 69
JOX (064 "Cleo's Back") ... 10-20 62
RENNER ... 5-10 62-65
TEXAS RE-CORD CO. ... 3-4 77
Members: Denny Ezba; Augie Meyers; Keith Allison; Harvey Kagan; Marty Kagan. Session: Michael Nesmith
Also see ALLISON, Keith
Also see GOLDENS
Also see MEYERS, Augie
Also see PUSH BUTTON & DIALTONES
Also see SAHM, Doug

EZO LP '87
LPs: 10/12-inch
GEFFEN ... 5-10 87

EZRA & IVIES
Singles: 7-inch
U.A. ... 5-10 59

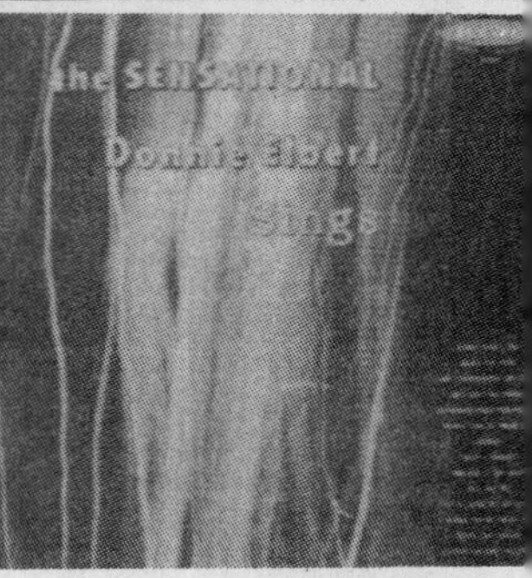

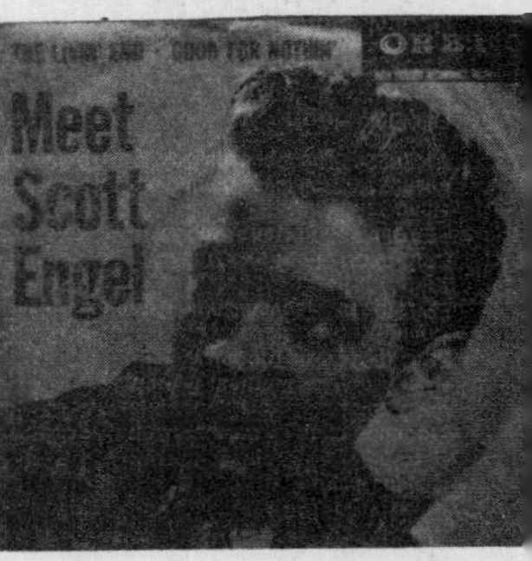

F

F WORD
LPs: 10/12-inch
POSH BOY ... 5-10 78

F., Simon P&R '87
(Simon Fellowes)
Singles: 7-inch
CHRYSALIS ... 3-4 86-87
REPRISE ... 3-4 87
Picture Sleeves
CHRYSALIS ... 3-4 86-87

FCC P&R/LP '79
(Funky Communication Committee)
Singles: 7-inch
FREE FLIGHT (Black vinyl) ... 3-4 79
FREE FLIGHT (Colored vinyl) ... 3-5 79
(Promotional issue only.)
LPs: 10/12-inch
FREE FLIGHT ... 5-8 79
RCA ... 5-10 80

F.F. & Z.
Singles: 7-inch
EPIC ... 3-5 72

F.J. BABIES
Singles: 7-inch
APT ... 4-8 62

FLB: see FAT LARRY'S BAND

FM
LPs: 10/12-inch
PASSPORT ... 5-10 79-81
VISA ... 5-10

F.R. DAVID: see DAVID, F.R.

FSQ
Singles: 7-inch
RAYNARD (10079 "A Girl Named Mae") ... 15-25 66

FAAN BAND
(Feed Africa & Arizona Now)
Singles: 7-inch
FAAN BAND ... 3-4 85
Picture Sleeves
FAAN BAND ... 3-4 85
Members: Patrice Agliata; Dennis Alexander; Phil Allen; Pat Gibbons; Bruce Babbitt; Hattie Babbitt; Randy Baker; Bob Boze Bell; Tommy Bell; Peter Billingsley; Jack Blades; Rabbia Mark Bisman; Roye Bourke; Hal Brice; Joni Heil-Brice; Joani Calapina; Linda Calwell; Glen Campbell; Shorty Campbell; Cantor Caplan; Steve Chanen; Allan Chilcoat; Tim Cullison; Mark Curtis; Jan D'atri; Kent Dana; Rita Davenport; Howard Dean; Mike Del Rosso; Bill Denny; Don DeWolf; John Dixon; Liane Eagan; Dolan Ellis; Mike Farrell; Pat Finn; Nancy Gerber; John Giese; Steve Goddard; Doug Gondeck; Tim Hattrick; Dave Hilker; Ron Hoon; Dewey Hopper; Dan Horn; Susan Huff; Diane Hunter; Carolyn (Wood) Imbrie; Nancy Jackson; Curtiss Johnson; Bil Keane; Chaz Kelly; Dr. Lynn Kitel; Frank Kush; Keith Larson; Vince Leonard; Ann Martinez; Dennis McBroom; John McCain; Cindy McCain; Megan McCain; Pat McMahon; Andrew Means; Dana Metzger; Mellissa Michaelson; Dr. Art Mollen; Bill Mosely; Jim Mulsin; Dave Munsey; Randy Murray; Jenny Nichols; Ron Nix; Hans Olson; Anita Padilla; Jeff Parets; Cheryl Parker; Tom Parras; Dave Patterson; Steve Pascente; Keith Passon; Big Pete Pearson; Debroah Pyburn; Carmela Ramirez; Dennis Reece; Suzan Rivera; Bill Rocz; Tim Rose; Diane Ryan; Michael Sarna; Preson Scott; Chris Shebel; Lin Sue Shepperd; Smokey; Tom Sneva; Roger Steen; Alice Tatum; Tonya Townsend; Stu Tracey; Steve Trella; Linda Turley; Wallace & Ladmo; Mary Jo West; Warren Williams; Danny Zelisko; Luis Zendejas. Also includes the following groups: Catch 22; Curfew; Listen; Living Dolls; Surgical Steel; Last Word.
Also see BROOKLYN BRIDGE
Also see CAMPBELL, Glen
Also see GODDARD, Steve
Also see HUB KAP & WHEELS
Also see NIGHT RANGER
Also see TUBES

FAB FOUR
Singles: 7-inch
BRASS ... 10-15 65-66
PEARCE (5842 "River Days") ... 15-25 60s

FABARES, Shelley P&R/LP '62
Singles: 7-inch
COLPIX (Except 721) ... 5-10 62-64
COLPIX (721 "Football Season's Over") ... 50-100 64
DUNHILL (4001 "My Prayer") ... 15-25 65
DUNHILL (4041 "See Ya 'Round on the Rebound") ... 15-25 65
ERIC ... 3-4
VEE JAY (632 "Lost Summer Love") ... 15-25 64
Picture Sleeves
COLPIX (621 "Johnny Angel") ... 50-100 62
COLPIX (636 "Johnny Loves Me") 40-60 62
LPs: 10/12-inch
COLPIX (426 "Shelley") ... 35-45 62
(Monaural.)
COLPIX (426 "Shelley") ... 45-55 62
(Stereo.)
COLPIX (431 "The Things We Did Last Summer") ... 35-45 62
(Monaural.)
COLPIX (431 "The Things We Did Last Summer") ... 45-55 62
(Stereo.)
Session: Sally Stevens.
Also see DARREN, James / Shelley Fabares / Paul Petersen
Also see PETERSEN, Paul, & Shelley Fabares

FABIAN P&R/R&B/LP '59
(With the Fabulous Four)
Singles: 7-inch
ABC ... 3-5 74
CHANCELLOR (1020 "I'm in Love") ... 15-25 58
CHANCELLOR (1024 "Be My Steady Date") ... 15-25 58
CHANCELLOR (1029 "I'm a Man") ... 15-25 58
(Monaural.)
CHANCELLOR (1029 "I'm a Man") ... 25-50 58
(Stereo.)
CHANCELLOR (1033 "Turn Me Loose") ... 15-25 59
(Monaural.)
CHANCELLOR (1033 "Turn Me Loose") ... 25-50 59
(Stereo.)
CHANCELLOR (1037 "Tiger") ... 15-20 59
(Monaural.)
CHANCELLOR (1037 "Tiger") ... 25-50 59
(Stereo.)
CHANCELLOR (1041 "Come on and Get Me") ... 10-20 59
(Monaural.)
CHANCELLOR (1041 "Come on and Get Me") ... 25-50 59
(Stereo.)
CHANCELLOR (1044 "Hound Dog Man") ... 10-20 59
(Monaural.)
CHANCELLOR (1044 "Hound Dog Man") ... 25-50 59
(Stereo.)
CHANCELLOR (1047 "String Along") ... 10-20 60
(Monaural.)
CHANCELLOR (1047 "String Along") ... 25-50 60
(Stereo.)
CHANCELLOR (1051 "I'm Gonna Sit Right Down and Write Myself a Letter") 10-15 60
CHANCELLOR (1055 "King of Love") ... 10-20 60
CHANCELLOR (1061 "Kissin' & Twistin' ") ... 10-20 60
CHANCELLOR (1067 "Hold On") ... 10-20 60
CHANCELLOR (1072 "David & Goliath") ... 10-15 61
CHANCELLOR (1079 "You're Only Young Once") ... 10-15 61
CHANCELLOR (1084 "Dream Factory") ... 10-15 61
CHANCELLOR (1086 "Kansas City") ... 10-15 61
CHANCELLOR (1092 "Wild Party") ... 10-15 61
COLLECTABLES ... 3-4 80s
CREAM ... 3-5 77
DOT (16413 "Break Down & Cry") ... 8-12 62
ERIC ... 3-4 70s
Picture Sleeves
CHANCELLOR (1029 "I'm a Man") ... 20-30 58
CHANCELLOR (1033 "Turn Me Loose") ... 20-30 59
CHANCELLOR (1037 "Tiger") ... 20-30 59
CHANCELLOR (1041 "Come on and Get Me") ... 15-25 59
CHANCELLOR (1044 "Hound Dog Man") ... 15-25 59
CHANCELLOR (1047 "String Along") ... 15-25 60
CHANCELLOR (1051 "Strollin' in the Springtime") ... 15-25 60
CHANCELLOR (1055 "King of Love") ... 15-25 60
CHANCELLOR (1061 "Kissin' and Twistin' ") ... 15-25 60
CHANCELLOR (1067 "Hold On") ... 15-25 61
CHANCELLOR (1079 "You're Only Young Once") ... 15-25 61
CHANCELLOR (1084 "A Girl Like You") ... 15-25 61
CHANCELLOR (1092 "Wild Party") ... 15-25 61
CREAM ... 4-6 77
EPs: 7-inch
CHANCELLOR (301 "Hound Dog Man") ... 20-40 60
CHANCELLOR (5003 "Hold That Tiger!") ... 20-40 59
(Black label. Price for any of three volumes.)
CHANCELLOR (5003 "Excerpts from *Hold That Tiger!*") ... 30-50 59
(With paper sleeve. White label. Promotional issue only.)
CHANCELLOR (5005 "The Fabulous Fabian") ... 20-40 60
CHANCELLOR (5012 "The Good Old Summertime") ... 20-40 60
(Black label. Price is for any of three volumes.)
CHANCELLOR (9802 "Young and Wonderful") ... 20-40 60
LPs: 10/12-inch
ABC ... 10-12 73
CHANCELLOR (5003 "Hold That Tiger") ... 50-75 59
(Monaural.)
CHANCELLOR (5003 "Hold That Tiger") ... 50-100 59
(Stereo.)
CHANCELLOR (5005 "The Fabulous Fabian") ... 40-60 59
(Monaural.)
CHANCELLOR (5005 "The Fabulous Fabian") ... 50-75 59
(Stereo.)
CHANCELLOR (5012 "The Good Old Summertime") ... 40-60 60
(Monaural.)
CHANCELLOR (5012 "The Good Old Summertime") ... 50-75 60
(Stereo.)
CHANCELLOR (5019 "Rockin' Hot") ... 50-75 61
CHANCELLOR (5024 "16 Fabulous Hits") ... 50-75 62
CHANCELLOR (69802 "Young and Wonderful") ... 40-60 60
EVEREST ... 5-10 83
MCA ... 5-10 85
TRIP ... 8-10 77
U.A. ... 10-15 75
Also see FABULOUS FOUR
Also see 4 DATES

FABIAN / Frankie Avalon
Singles: 7-inch
CHANCELLOR/WIBG 99 ("When the Saints Go Marchin' In") ... 25-50 61
(Colored vinyl. Radio station special products issue. No selection number used. Flip is by the Live Five, who were the WIBG dee jays.)
LPs: 10/12-inch
CHANCELLOR (5009 "The Hit Makers") ... 75-100 60
MCA ... 5-10 85
Also see AVALON, Frankie
Also see FABIAN

FABIANS
Singles: 7-inch
BLUE ROCKET (315 "Confidential") ... 20-40

FABIO & BRUNO
Singles: 7-inch
VIM ... 4-8

FABLES
Singles: 7-inch
ELGO ... 15-20 62

FABRIC, Bent P&R/LP '62
Singles: 7-inch
ATCO ... 4-8 62-65
Picture Sleeves
ATCO (6226 "Alley Cat") ... 10-15 62
EPs: 7-inch
ATCO (164 "Organ Grinder's Swing") ... 8-12 60s
(Stereo. Juke box issue. Includes title strips.)
LPs: 10/12-inch
ATCO (148 "Alley Cat") ... 10-20 62
ATCO (155 "Happy Puppy") ... 10-20 63
Also see BILK, Mr. Acker, & Bent Fabric

FABRIQUE, Tina D&D '84
Singles: 12-inch
PRISM ... 4-6 84

FABS
Singles: 7-inch
COTTON BALL (1005 "That's the Bag I'm In") ... 20-30 66

FABULAIRES
Singles: 78 rpm
EAST WEST ... 100-150 57
Singles: 7-inch
EAST WEST (103 "While Walking") ... 200-300 57
MAIN LINE (103 "While Walking") ... 150-200 58

FABULAIRES
Singles: 7-inch
CHELSEA (103 "Wedding Song") .. 50-75 63
(White label. Promotional issue.)
CHELSEA (103 "Wedding Song") .. 35-55 63
(Black label.)

FABULEERS
(With the Joe Shaw Orchestra)
Singles: 7-inch
KENCO (5002 "If I Had Another Chance") ... 30-50 59

FABULETTES
Singles: 7-inch
MONUMENT ... 4-8 65

FABULONS
Singles: 7-inch
BENSON (100 "Connie") ... 15-25 63
BENSON-RITCO (100 "Connie") ... 25-50 63
(First issue.)
EMBER (1069 "Smoke from Your Cigarette") ... 20-30 60
(White label.)
EMBER (1069 "Smoke from Your Cigarette") ... 10-20 60
(Black label.)

FABULONS
Singles: 7-inch
TOWER ... 5-10 66
Members: Ron Ferrante; Terry McKinley; Mike Roholt; John Chassaign; John Goldman; Dan Shillings; John Duval; Jim Wilson; Gary Welk; Bill Higginbotham.
Also see TIKIS & FABULONS

FABULOUS APOLLOS
Singles: 7-inch
VALTONE (105 "Some Good in Everything Bad") ... 10-20

FABULOUS APOLLOS
Singles: 7-inch
SHANA ... 5-10

FABULOUS BLENDS
Singles: 7-inch
CASA GRANDE (3039 "Graduation Time") ... 4-6 89
(Black vinyl.)
CASA GRANDE (3039 "Graduation Time") ... 4-6 89
(Colored vinyl.)
CASA GRANDE (5001 "Hey Little Fool") ... 25-35 61
(Colored vinyl.)

FABULOUS BROTHERS
Singles: 7-inch
VOSS ... 5-10 59

FABULOUS CAPRICES
Singles: 7-inch
CAMARO (3442 "My Love") ... 15-25 60s

FABULOUS CAPRIS
Singles: 7-inch
CEPRO ... 8-12

FABULOUS CHANCELLORS
Singles: 7-inch
CHANDEL ("Pharaoh") ... 25-35 63
(First issue. Selection number not known.)
DOT (16535 "Blackout") ... 10-15 63

FABULOUS CHIMES
("With Bobby Bell & Satalites Inst. Accomp.")
Singles: 7-inch
INVINCIBLE ("Faithful to Me") ... 50-75 64
(No selection number used.)

FABULOUS CLOVERS
Singles: 7-inch
WINLEY (265 "Be My Baby") ... 15-25 62
Members: Buddy Bailey; Harold Winley.
Also see CLOVERS

FABULOUS COBRAS
Singles: 7-inch
JCP (1051 "I Was a Fool") ... 10-20 65

FABULOUS CONTINENTALS
Singles: 7-inch
CB (5003 "Undertow") ... 15-25 63
CB (5007 "Let's Get Goin' ") ... 10-20 64
RORI (709 "Venus") ... 10-20 60s
SIOUX (42061 "Rockinental") ... 10-20 61
Also see ROCKINENTALS

FABULOUS COUNTS R&B '69
Singles: 7-inch
HIGHLAND (1171 "So Far Away") 25-50 66
KIM (811 "Money") ... 5-10 60s
MOIRA ... 3-6 68-70
LPs: 10/12-inch
COTILLION ... 10-12 69

FABULOUS CRYSTALS
Singles: 7-inch
DELANO (11032 "Left Front Row") ... 50-100

FABULOUS CYCLONES
Singles: 7-inch
BAND BOX ... 4-8 60

FABULOUS DENOS
Singles: 7-inch
KING ... 5-10 64-65

FABULOUS DESIRES
Singles: 7-inch
ERA ... 4-8 64

FABULOUS DIALS
Singles: 7-inch
D n B (1000 "Forget Me Not") ... 50-75 63
JOY (276 "Forget Me Not") ... 20-30 63

FABULOUS DIMENSIONS
Singles: 7-inch
EMM ... 8-12 67
Picture Sleeves
EMM ... 10-20 67

FABULOUS DINOS
Singles: 7-inch
MUSICOR (1025 "Where Have You Been") ... 10-20 62
SABER (105 "Retreat") ... 10-15 60s
SABER (1009 "Instant Love") ... 20-30 64

FABULOUS DOWN BEATS
Singles: 7-inch
POISION RING ... 4-8 68

FABULOUS DUDES
Singles: 7-inch
PRESENCE ... 3-5 89
Member: Paul Payton.
Also see PAYTON, Paul

FABULOUS ECHOES
Singles: 7-inch
LIBERTY ... 5-10 64-65

FABULOUS EGYPTIANS
Singles: 7-inch
CINDY (96749 "End of Time") ... 20-30 65
(Identification number shown since no selection number is used.)

FABULOUS ENCHANTERS
Singles: 7-inch
FINER ARTS (1007 "Why Are You Crying") ... 75-100 61

FABULOUS FABULIERS
Singles: 7-inch
ANGLE TONE (539 "She's the Girl for Me") ... 50-75 59

FABULOUS FAKES
Singles: 7-inch
COLUMBIA ... 4-8 67

FABULOUS FALCONS
Singles: 7-inch
WHITE CLIFFS ... 4-8 66

FABULOUS FARQUAHR LP '70
(Farquahr)
Singles: 7-inch
ELEKTRA ... 3-5 71
VERVE/FORECAST ... 4-8 68-69
W.B. ... 3-6 70
LPs: 10/12-inch
ELEKTRA ... 8-10 70
VERVE/FORECAST ... 10-15 69

FABULOUS FIDELS
Singles: 7-inch
JAA DEE (106 "Westside Boy Meets Eastside Girl") ... 10-20

FABULOUS FIESTAS
Singles: 7-inch
RCA ... 3-5 70

FABULOUS FIVE
Singles: 7-inch
KING ... 10-15 59

FABULOUS FIVE FLAMES
Singles: 7-inch
TIME (1023 "Lonely Lover") ... 20-30 60

FABULOUS FLAMES
(With the Original Sunglows)
Singles: 7-inch
BAY-TONE (102 "Do You Remember") ... 40-60 60
(White label. Credits "B Flat" Publishing.)
BAY-TONE (102 "Do You Remember") ... 30-50 60
(Yellow label. Credits "Bay Tone" Publishing.)
BAY-TONE (105 "Lover") ... 30-50 60
HARLEM (114 "I'm Gonna Try to Live My Life All Over") ... 1000-2000 60
REX (3000 "Josephine") ... 100-150 58
Also see FLAMES
Also see WILLIS, Robert

FABULOUS FLAMES
Singles: 7-inch
ARK ... 8-12

FABULOUS FLARES
Singles: 7-inch
HIT (102 "You Love Her More Than I") ... 10-20 64

FABULOUS FLIPPERS
Singles: 7-inch
CAMEO ... 10-20 66-67
FONA ... 12-18 66
LARIM ASSOCIATON ... 6-10 73
QUILL ... 10-20 65
LPs: 10/12-inch
VERITAS (2570 "Something Tangible") ... 15-25 70
Also see MAG. SANCTUARY BAND
Also see TERRY & FLIPPERS

FABULOUS FOUR
(With Jerry Ragavoy Orchestra)
Singles: 7-inch
CHANCELLOR (1062 "In the Chapel in the Moonlight") ... 15-25 60
CHANCELLOR (1068 "Let's Try Again") ... 15-25 60
CHANCELLOR (1078 "Why Do Fools Fall in Love") ... 30-40 61
CHANCELLOR (1085 "Betty Ann") ... 50-100 61
CHANCELLOR (1090 "I'm Coming Home") ... 15-25 61
CHANCELLOR (1098 "Everybody Knows") ... 10-20 61
CHANCELLOR (1102 "Forever") ... 25-35 62
LPs: 10/12-inch
CRYSTAL BALL ... 8-12 84
Members: Joe Prolia; Joe Mollera; Jimmy Finzino; James Testa.
Also see FABIAN
Also see FOUR Js

FABULOUS FOUR
(With the Maxwell Davis Orchestra)
Singles: 7-inch
MELIC (4114 "Welcome Me Home") ... 25-50 62
Also see DAVIS, Maxwell

FABULOUS FOUR
Singles: 7-inch
BALLAD ... 4-8 69
BRASS ... 5-10 64
CORAL ... 5-10 66

FABULOUS FUTURAS
Singles: 7-inch
IKON ("La Do Da Da") ... 8-12
(No selection number used.)

FABULOUS GARDENIAS
Singles: 7-inch
LIZ (1004 "It's You, You, You") ... 50-75 62
Also see GARDENIAS

FABULOUS GO-GOs
Singles: 7-inch
BISCAYNE...4-8

FABULOUS IDOLS
Singles: 7-inch
KENCO (5011 "Baby")...50-75 60

FABULOUS IMPACS
Singles: 7-inch
BOMB (3017 "I'll Be Crying")...50-100

FABULOUS IMPACTS
Singles: 7-inch
DAD...10-15 67
Picture Sleeves
DAD...20-30 67

FABULOUS IMPERIALS
Singles: 7-inch
IMPRA ("Weird")...20-30 58
(First issue. Selection number not known.)
MGM (12687 "Weird")...10-20 58

FABULOUS JADES
Singles: 7-inch
RIKA ("Come On and Live")...20-30 60s

FABULOUS JETS
Singles: 7-inch
KIM (809 "Ball & Chain of Love")...10-20

FABULOUS JOKERS
Singles: 7-inch
LINCOLN (708 "Little Rain Drops")...100-200 61

FABULOUS LITTLE JOE
Singles: 7-inch
EDEN...5-10 62

FABULOUS MAD LADS: see MAD LADS

FABULOUS MAJESTICS
Singles: 7-inch
TEE VEE (2508 "Early Bird")...10-20 67

FABULOUS MARCELS
Singles: 7-inch
ST. CLAIR...3-5 75
Also see MARCELS

FABULOUS McCLEVERTYS
Singles: 78 rpm
VERVE...10-15 57
Singles: 7-inch
VERVE (10029 "Don't Blame It on Elvis")...15-25 57
LPs: 10/12-inch
VERVE (2034 "Calypso!")...40-60 57
Members: Carl McCleverty; Johnny McCleverty; Gus McCleverty; David McCleverty; Cornelius McCleverty.

FABULOUS MUSTANGS
Singles: 7-inch
STANG (2001 "I Won't Let You Go")...25-35 65

FABULOUS NU-TONES
Singles: 7-inch
WHITEHOUSE (5002 "I'm Not Worthy of Your Love")...50-75
Picture Sleeves
WHITEHOUSE (5002 "I'm Not Worthy of Your Love")...75-125

FABULOUS PACK
Singles: 7-inch
LUCKY ELEVEN...8-12 65
WINGATE...10-15 65
Picture Sleeves
LUCKY ELEVEN...10-15 65
Also see PACK

FABULOUS PEARL DEVINES
Singles: 7-inch
ALCO (1016631 "You've Been Gone")...200-300 63
(Identification number shown since no selection number is used.)

FABULOUS PEARLS
Singles: 7-inch
COLLECTABLES...3-5
DOOTO (448 "My Heart's Desire")...75-125 59

FABULOUS PEPS
Singles: 7-inch
D-TOWN (1065 "My Love Looks Good on You")...30-50 66
GE GE (503 "She's Going to Leave You")...25-35 65
PREMIUM STUFF (1 "I Can't Get It Right")...20-30 60s
PREMIUM STUFF (3 "So Fine")...20-30 60s
PREMIUM STUFF (7 "Gypsy Woman")...20-30 60s
WEE 3 (1001 "With These Eyes") 15-25 67
WHEELSVILLE...8-10
Also see OHIO UNTOUCHABLES
Also see PEPS
Also see STORM, Tom, & Peps

FABULOUS PERSIANS
Singles: 7-inch
BOBBY-O...5-10

FABULOUS PHARAOHS
Singles: 7-inch
THREE STAR (2668 "Church Key")...15-25 60s

FABULOUS PLAIDS
Singles: 7-inch
DIXIE (1110 "I'm Coming Home to You")...10-15 65
Picture Sleeves
DIXIE (1110 "I'm Coming Home to You")...15-25 65

FABULOUS PLATEAUS
Singles: 7-inch
SHOUT (5001 "Rear Back")...10-20 60s

FABULOUS PLAYBOYS
Singles: 7-inch
APOLLO (758 "Forget the Past")...20-30 61
APOLLO (760 "Tears Tears Tears")...20-30 61
COUTOUR (4 "I Fooled You")...20-30 60s
DACO (1001 "Forget the Past")...50-75 61
Also see FALCONS

FABULOUS PLAYBOYS
Singles: 7-inch
CATALINA (1069 "Cheater Stomp")...10-20 62

FABULOUS POODLES *P&R/LP '79*
Singles: 7-inch
EPIC...3-5 79
LPs: 10/12-inch
EPIC...5-10 76-79

FABULOUS QUIET FIVE
Singles: 7-inch
CASA GRANDE...5-10 65

FABULOUS RAIDERS
Singles: 7-inch
DOLLY (21694 "Harmonica Rock")...10-20 60
DOLLY (21703 "Bootblack Blues")...10-20 60
WYE (147 "C.C. Rider")...10-20 62

FABULOUS RAINDROPS
Singles: 7-inch
INFAL (147 "El Putty")...8-12

FABULOUS RHINESTONES *P&R/LP '72*
Singles: 7-inch
JUST SUNSHINE...3-5 72
Picture Sleeves
JUST SUNSHINE...3-5 72
LPs: 10/12-inch
JUST SUNSHINE...8-10 72-73

FABULOUS ROYALS
Singles: 7-inch
AEGIS...4-8

FABULOUS RUMBLES
Singles: 7-inch
SOMA (1448 "Echoing Past")...15-25 65
Members: Richard Clayton; Bud Phillips.
Also see CLAYTON, Rich, & Rumbles
Also see RUMBLES LTD.

FABULOUS SHADOWS
Singles: 7-inch
SHADOW (1256 "Puff Stuff")...8-12

FABULOUS SHALIMARS
Singles: 7-inch
COTILLION...4-8 68

FABULOUS SILVER TONES
Singles: 7-inch
WEST COAST ("Hey Sally Mae")...15-25 60s
(Selection number not known.)

FABULOUS SPLENDORS
("Music By Howard Biggs")
Singles: 7-inch
O-GEE (105 "Your Change of Heart")...50-75 60

FABULOUS SWINGTONES
Singles: 7-inch
ABC-PAR...10-20 58

FABULOUS TABLE TOPPERS
Singles: 7-inch
REM (309 "My Wild Irish")...10-20 61

FABULOUS 3 + 1
Singles: 7-inch
T&L (1039 "Bad Girl")...50-75

FABULOUS THUNDERBIRDS *LP '81*
Singles: 7-inch
CBS ASSOCIATED...3-4 86-89
CHRYSALIS...3-5 79-81
ELEKTRA...3-4 88
Picture Sleeves
CBS ASSOCIATED...3-4 86-87
LPs: 10/12-inch
CBS ASSOCIATED...5-10 86-89
CHRYSALIS...5-10 79-81
TAKOMA...10-15 79
Members: Kim Wilson; Jimmie Vaughan; Preston Hubbard; Fran Christina.
Also see SANTANA
Also see VAUGHAN BROTHERS

FABULOUS TRAITS
Singles: 7-inch
TELE-PHONIC (1001 "Lonely Man")...10-20

FABULOUS TRENIERS
Singles: 7-inch
HERMITAGE...5-10 63
Also see TRENIER, Skip, & Fabulous Treniers
Also see TRENIERS

FABULOUS TRUBADORES With Marv Duncan
Singles: 7-inch
NIGHT OWL (1535 "Tribute to Jimi Hendrix")...5-10 70s

FABULOUS TONES
("George Garabedian Presents the Fabulous Tones")
Singles: 7-inch
MARK 56 (819 "I'll Never Cry Again")...50-100 59
Also see GARABEDIAN, George

FABULOUS TRAITS
Singles: 7-inch
TELE-PHONIC (1001 "Lonely Man")...10-20

FABULOUS TYNSIONS 5
Singles: 7-inch
NATCHEZ-JOE (101 "Lone Ranger Man")...20-30

FABULOUS UPTONES
Singles: 7-inch
TULIP (100 "New Love I Have Found")...200-300 62

FABULOUS VALIENTS
(With the Del Reys)
Singles: 7-inch
HOLIDAY (61005 "Your Golden Teardrops")...400-600 62

FABULOUS VERBS
Singles: 7-inch
CAMARO (3384 "Let Me Be the Man")...15-25 60s

FABULOUS VERSATONES
Singles: 7-inch
D.W....5-10

FABULOUS VOLTS
Singles: 7-inch
BARCO...10-20

FABULOUS WUNZ
Singles: 7-inch
PYRAMID...10-20 66

FABUS, Ray, & Strikes
Singles: 7-inch
SOMA (1158 "Camel Walk")...10-20 61

FACE DANCER
Singles: 7-inch
CAPITOL...3-4 79-80
LPs: 10/12-inch
CAPITOL...5-10 79-80

FACE TO FACE *P&R/D&D/LP '84*
Singles: 12-inch
EPIC...4-6 84
PORTRAIT...4-6 84
Singles: 7-inch
EPIC...3-4 84
MERCURY...3-4 88
PORTRAIT...3-4 84
Picture Sleeves
EPIC...3-4 84
LPs: 10/12-inch
EPIC...5-10 84
MERCURY...5-8 88

FACENDA, Tommy *P&R/R&B '59*
Singles: 7-inch
ATLANTIC (2051 "High School U.S.A. [Virginia]")...15-25 59
ATLANTIC (2052 "High School U.S.A. [New York City Area]")...15-25 59
ATLANTIC (2053 "High School U.S.A. [North Carolina – South Carolina]")...15-25 59
ATLANTIC (2054 "High School U.S.A. [Washington D.C. Area]")...15-25 59
ATLANTIC (2055 "High School U.S.A. [Philadelphia Area]")...15-25 59
ATLANTIC (2056 "High School U.S.A. [Detroit Area]")...15-25 59
ATLANTIC (2057 "High School U.S.A. [Pittsburgh Area]")...15-25 59
ATLANTIC (2058 "High School U.S.A. [Minneapolis – St. Paul Area]")...15-25 59
ATLANTIC (2059 "High School U.S.A. [Florida]")...15-25 59
ATLANTIC (2060 "High School U.S.A. [Newark Area]")...15-25 59
ATLANTIC (2061 "High School U.S.A. [Boston Area]")...15-25 59
ATLANTIC (2062 "High School U.S.A. [Cleveland Area]")...15-25 59
ATLANTIC (2063 "High School U.S.A. [Buffalo Area]")...15-25 59
ATLANTIC (2064 "High School U.S.A. [Hartford Area]")...15-25 59
ATLANTIC (2065 "High School U.S.A. [Nashville Area]")...15-25 59
ATLANTIC (2066 "High School U.S.A. [Indiana]")...15-25 59
ATLANTIC (2067 "High School U.S.A. [Chicago Area]")...15-25 59
ATLANTIC (2068 "High School U.S.A. [New Orleans Area]")...15-25 59
ATLANTIC (2069 "High School U.S.A. [St. Louis – Kansas City Area]")...15-25 59
ATLANTIC (2070 "High School U.S.A. [Alabama -- Georgia]")...15-25 59
ATLANTIC (2071 "High School U.S.A. [Cincinnati Area]")...15-25 59
ATLANTIC (2072 "High School U.S.A. [Memphis Area]")...15-25 59
ATLANTIC (2073 "High School U.S.A. [Los Angeles Area]")...15-25 59
ATLANTIC (2074 "High School U.S.A. [San Francisco Area]")...15-25 59
ATLANTIC (2075 "High School U.S.A. [Texas]")...15-25 59
ATLANTIC (2076 "High School U.S.A. [Seattle – Portland Area]")...15-25 59
ATLANTIC (2077 "High School U.S.A. [Denver Area]")...15-25 59
ATLANTIC (2078 "High School U.S.A. [Oklahoma]")...15-25 59
LEGRANDE (1001 "High School U.S.A.")...10-20 59
(We have yet to learn how to positively identify original pressings, sinch many reissues exist.)
NASCO...10-20 58
Session: King Curtis.
Also see KING CURTIS
Also see VINCENT, Gene

FACES
Singles: 7-inch
IGUANA (601 "Christmas")...50-100 65
REGINA (1326 "What Is This Dream")...8-12 65
REGINA (1328 "I'll Walk Alone")...8-12 65

FACES *LP '70*
Singles: 7-inch
W.B....3-6 71-75
Picture Sleeves
W.B....3-6 73
LPs: 10/12-inch
MERCURY...8-12 73
W.B....10-20 70-76
Members: Rod Stewart; Ron Wood; Ronnie Lane.
Also see McLAGAN, Ian
Also see SMALL FACES
Also see STEWART, Rod
Also see WOOD, Ron

FACETS
Singles: 7-inch
TERRIBLE TOMMY (2672 "Johnny B. Goode")...8-12

FACHIN, Eria *P&R '88*
Singles: 7-inch
CRITIQUE...3-4 88
Picture Sleeves
CRITIQUE...3-4 88

FACINATORS
Singles: 7-inch
QUEEN BEE (1001 "Love Will Conquer All")...75-125

FACTORY
Singles: 7-inch
UNI...5-10 67
Members: Lowell George; Martin Kibbee; Warren Klein; Richard Hayward; Dallas Taylor.
Also see FRATERNITY of MAN
Also see GEORGE, Lowell

FACTORY
Singles: 7-inch
U.S.A. (922 "High Blood Pressure")...10-20 68

FACTS OF LIFE
Singles: 7-inch
FRANA (59 "I've Seen Darker Nights")...10-15 67

FACTS OF LIFE *R&B '76*
Singles: 7-inch
KAYVETTE...3-5 76-77
LPs: 10/12-inch
KAYVETTE...8-10 77
Members: Jean Davis; Keith William; Chuck Carter.

FAD, J.J.: see J.J. FAD

FADS
Singles: 7-inch
MERCURY (72542 "Just Like a Woman")...20-40 66

FAFARA, Frank
Singles: 7-inch
MCI...8-12 60
MASCOT...8-12

FAGAN, Dick
Singles: 7-inch
SARG (155 "Love Like the Sun")...30-40 58

FAGAN, Jim
Singles: 7-inch
WEBCORE...3-5 77

FAGAN, Scott
Singles: 7-inch
BANG...4-8 66
RCA...3-5 76
LPs: 10/12-inch
ATCO...10-15 68

FAGAN BROTHERS
Singles: 7-inch
ADAIRE...5-10 61
SWAN...4-8 63

FAGEN, Donald *P&R/R&B/LP '82*
Singles: 7-inch
W.B....3-4 82-88
Picture Sleeves
W.B....3-4 82-88
LPs: 10/12-inch
MFSL (120 "Nightfly")...20-30 84
W.B....5-10 82-88
Also see JAY & AMERICANS
Also see STEELY DAN

FAGEN, Donald, & Walter Becker
LPs: 10/12-inch
PVC...5-10 85
Also see FAGEN, Donald

FAGIN, Joe *P&R '82*
Singles: 7-inch
MILLENNIUM...3-4 82

FAHEY, John
LPs: 10/12-inch
REPRISE...8-10 72-73
RIVERBOAT...10-12
TAKOMA...10-15 59-81
VANGUARD...10-15 67-74
Also see KOTTKE, Leo, John Fahey & Peter Lang

FAIA, Tommy, & True Blue Facts
Singles: 7-inch
A&M...3-6 68

FAILE, Tommy
Singles: 7-inch
CHOICE...4-6
DOT...4-8 66
LAWN...10-20 60
NOB...4-8 63
SILVER STAR...4-8 66

FAINE JADE
Singles: 7-inch
PROVIDENCE (820 "It Ain't True") 15-25 66
RSVP (1130 "Introspection")...10-20 68
LPs: 10/12-inch
RSVP (8002 "Introspection")...300-500 68
Also see RUSTILS

FAIOLA BROTHERS
Singles: 7-inch
BUDDAH...4-8 67

FAIR, Carlo
Singles: 7-inch
EXPRESS (801 "Beetle Bounce")...10-15 64

FAIR, Frankie
Singles: 7-inch
ACE...5-10 62

FAIR, Yvonne *R&B '74*
Singles: 7-inch
DADE...5-10 63
KING...5-10 62
MOTOWN...3-5 74-76
SMASH...5-10 66
SOUL (Black vinyl)...3-6 70
SOUL (Colored vinyl)...5-10 70
(Promotional issue only.)
LPs: 10/12-inch
MOTOWN...5-10 76

FAIR WARNING
Singles: 7-inch
MCA...3-4 81
LPs: 10/12-inch
MCA...5-10 81

FAIRBURN, Werly
(With the Delta Boys; with Whirlybirds)
Singles: 78 rpm
CAPITOL...5-10 54-55
COLUMBIA (Except 21528)...5-15 56
COLUMBIA (21528 "Everybody's Rockin' ")...20-30 56
DIAMOND...15-25 53
FAIR-LEW...5-10
SAVOY...5-10 56-57
TRUMPET...15-25 53
Singles: 7-inch
CAPITOL...15-25 54-55
COLUMBIA (21432 "I Guess I'm Crazy")...15-25 56
COLUMBIA (21483 "Stay Close to Me")...15-25 56
COLUMBIA (21528 "Everybody's Rockin' ")...50-75 56
FAIR-LEW...5-10 65
MILESTONE...5-10 62
PAULA...4-8 68
SAVOY...10-20 56-57
TRUMPET...20-30 50s

FAIRCHILD
Singles: 7-inch
SEANIE...8-12 60s

FAIRCHILD
Singles: 7-inch
MARJON (520 "I'd Like to Make You Mine")...8-12

FAIRCHILD, Barbara *C&W '69*
Singles: 7-inch
CAPITOL...3-4 86
COLUMBIA...3-4 69-78
DOWN HOME...3-4 80
KAPP...3-5 68
LPs: 10/12-inch
AUDIOGRAPH...5-10 82
COLUMBIA...8-12 70-78
PAID...5-10 81
Session: Jordanaires.
Also see JORDANAIRES
Also see WALKER, Billy, & Barbara Fairchild

FAIRCHILD, Johnny
Singles: 7-inch
ACE...15-25 59-60

FAIRCHILDS
Singles: 7-inch
A&M...4-8 67

FAIRE, Johnny
(Donnie Brooks)
Singles: 7-inch
FABLE (601 "If I'm a Fool"/"You Gotta Walk That Line")...40-50 57

FABLE (601 "If I'm a Fool"/"Make Up Your Mind Baby")....................40-50 57
(Note different flip.)
SURF (5019 "Bertha Lou")............40-50 58
SURF (5024 "Betcha I Getcha").....20-30 58
Also see BROOKS, Donnie

FAIRFIELD FOUR
Singles: 7-inch
OLD TOWN.............................. 8-12 59

FAIRGROUND ATTRACTION P&R '88
Singles: 7-inch
RCA.. 3-4 88-89
Picture Sleeves
RCA.. 3-4 88
LPs: 10/12-inch
RCA.. 5-8 88
Members: Eddi Reader; Mark Nevin.

FAIRLANES
Singles: 7-inch
ARGO (5357 "Little Girl")...............20-30 60
DART (109 "Just for Me")............50-100 59
LUCKY SEVEN (102 "Seventeen Steps")..............................50-75 59
MINARET (103 "I'm Not That Kind of Guy")..10-20 62
RADIANT (101 "Baby Baby") 150-250 64

FAIRLANES
Singles: 7-inch
CONTINENTAL (1001 "Writing This Letter")..............................200-300 61

FAIRLANES
Singles: 7-inch
REPRISE (20213 "Surf Train").......10-20 63

FAIRMOUNT SINGERS
Singles: 7-inch
DOT.. 5-10 62

FAIRMOUNTS
Singles: 7-inch
PLANET (053 "Times & Places") ...30-40 62

FAIRPORT CONVENTION LP '71
Singles: 7-inch
A&M 3-5 71-72
LPs: 10/12-inch
A&M 10-12 69-74
COTILLION 10-15 70
VARRICK/ROUNDER 5-10 86
ISLAND 8-10 74-75
Also see DENNY, Sandy
Also see MATTHEWS, Ian
Also see THOMPSON, Richard

FAIRWEATHER
(Andy Fairweather-Low)
LPs: 10/12-inch
NEON.. 8-10 71
Also see FAIRWEATHER-LOW, Andy

FAIRWEATHER-LOW, Andy P&R '75
Singles: 7-inch
A&M.. 3-5 75-77
LPs: 10/12-inch
A&M 8-10 74-76
W.B. 5-10 80
Also see AMEN CORNER
Also see FAIRWEATHER
Also see WILLIE & Poor Boys

FAISON, Joyce
LPs: 10/12-inch
ERECT 5-10 81

FAITH
LPs: 10/12-inch
BROWN BAG.............................10-15 73
Also see FAITH BAND
Also see LIMOUSINE

FAITH, Adam P&R '65
Singles: 7-inch
AMY 4-8 64-65
CAPITOL.................................. 4-8 65-66
CUB... 5-10 59
DOT... 4-8 62
LPs: 10/12-inch
AMY (8005 "Adam Faith")..............20-30 65
MGM (3951 "England's Top Singer")...................................25-30 61
W.B. 8-12 74

FAITH, Elena
Singles: 7-inch
VASSAR.................................. 5-10

FAITH, Gene R&B '70
Singles: 7-inch
VIRTUE 3-6 69-70
Also see VOLCANOS

FAITH, Percy, Orchestra P&R '50
Singles: 78 rpm
COLUMBIA................................ 3-4 50-57
Singles: 7-inch
COLUMBIA................................ 3-10 50-76
Picture Sleeves
COLUMBIA................................ 5-10 60
EPs: 7-inch
COLUMBIA................................ 5-10 50-59
ROYALE 5-10 50s
LPs: 10/12-inch
COLUMBIA................................ 5-15 51-82
HARMONY 5-10 68-72
Also see SANDERS, Felicia

FAITH, Percy, Orchestra / Johnny Mathis
Singles: 7-inch
COLUMBIA................................ 5-10
Also see FAITH, Percy, Orchestra
Also see MATHIS, Johnny

FAITH BAND P&R '78
Singles: 7-inch
AZRA ("Can't Say Goodbye")...........6-12 88
(Mickey Mouse-shaped picture disc. No selection number used.)
MERCURY 3-5 78-79
VILLAGE 3-6 78
LPs: 10/12-inch
BROWN BAG.............................10-12 73
MERCURY..................................5-10 78-79
VILLAGE....................................6-12 77
Also see CHOSEN FEW

FAITH ESTATE
Singles: 7-inch
VIRGO...................................... 3-5

FAITH, HOPE & CHARITY P&R/R&B '70
Singles: 7-inch
MAXWELL................................. 3-5 70
RCA... 3-5 75-77
SUSSEX................................... 3-5 72
20TH FOX................................. 3-4 78-80
LPs: 10/12-inch
RCA...8-10 75
SUSSEX...................................8-10 72
20TH FOX.................................5-10 80
Members: Brenda Hilliard; Albert Bailey; Zulema Crusseaux; Daine Destry.
Also see ZULEMA

FAITH NO MORE P&R/LP '90
Singles: 7-inch
SLASH 3-4 90
LPs: 10/12-inch
SLASH 5-8 90
Members: Chuck Moseley; Roddy Bottum; Bill Gould; Mike Bordin; Jim Martin; Mike Patton.

FAITHFULL, Marianne P&R '64
Singles: 12-inch
ISLAND 4-6 83
Singles: 7-inch
ISLAND (49121 "Broken English"/"Brain Drain")... 3-5 79
ISLAND (94997 "Why D'Ya Do It"/"Broken English")...................................12-25 79
(Full-length [6:35] track. Promotional issue only.)
LONDON (Except 1022) 4-8 64-72
LONDON (1022 "Sister Morphine")..................................75-100 69
(With the Rolling Stones.)
Picture Sleeves
LONDON...................................5-10 65
LPs: 10/12-inch
ISLAND.....................................5-10 79-90
LONDON...................................15-25 65-69
Also see ROLLING STONES

FALANA, Fluffy
Singles: 7-inch
ALPHA (007 "Hangover from Love")..25-50 67

FALANA, Lola R&B '75
Singles: 7-inch
AMOS....................................... 3-5
RCA... 3-4 75
REPRISE..................................5-10 67

FALCO D&D/LP '83
Singles: 12-inch
A&M 4-6 82-86
Singles: 7-inch
A&M 3-4 82-86
SIRE.. 3-4 87
Picture Sleeves
A&M 3-4 86
SIRE.. 3-4 87
LPs: 10/12-inch
A&M 5-10 83-86

FALCO, Tav: see TAV FALCO

FALCON
Singles: 7-inch
CRUSADER 4-8 65

FALCON, Billy
Singles: 7-inch
MANHATTAN 3-5 78
LPs: 10/12-inch
MANHATTAN 5-10 78

FALCON, Max
Singles: 7-inch
FRATERNITY (903 "Money Back Guarantee")..............................15-25 60

FALCONE, Tommy, & Centuries
Singles: 7-inch
DESIGN 10-15 61
Also see CENTURIES

FALCONER, Roderick
Singles: 7-inch
U.A. 3-5 76-77
Picture Sleeves
U.A. 3-5 76
LPs: 10/12-inch
U.A. 8-12 76

FALCONS
Singles: 78 rpm
CASH.......................................100-150 55
FLIP...50-100 54
Singles: 7-inch
CASH (1002 "Tell Me Why") 250-350 55
FLIP (301 "Stay Mine") 150-250 54
Also see RIVERS, Candy, & Falcons

FALCONS P&R/R&B '59
(With Al Smith's Orchestra; "Musical Direction Sax Kari")
Singles: 78 rpm
SILHOUETTE 200-300 57
Singles: 7-inch
ANNA (1110 "Just for Your Love")..100-150 60
ATLANTIC (2153 "Darling") 10-20 62
ATLANTIC (2175 "Take This Love")..10-20 63
ATLANTIC (2207 "Oh Baby")..........10-20 63
BIG WHEEL 5-10 66
CHESS (1743 "Just for Your Love")..20-30 59
FALCON (1006 "Now That It's Over")..150-250 57
FLICK (001 "You're So Fine") 150-250 59
FLICK (008 "You Must Know I Love You")......................................100-150 60
KUDO (661 "This Heart of Mine")......................................300-400 58
LIBERTY 3-4
LU PINE (103 "I Found a Love")....30-50 62
LU PINE (124 "Lonely Nights").....50-100 62
LU PINE (1003 "I Found a Love") ..10-20 62
LU PINE (1024 "Lonely Nights").....20-40 62
MERCURY (70940 "Baby That's It")..50-75 56
SILHOUETTE (522 "Can This Be Christmas") 250-350 57
(Flip, *Sent Up*, is Silhouette 521, a number also used for a Charmers release.)
UNART (2013 "You're So Fine") 20-30 59
UNART (2013-S "You're So Fine")......................................50-100 59
(Stereo—albeit reprocessed.)
UNART (2022 "Country Shack") 15-25 59
U.A. (229 "The Teacher")..............15-25 60
U.A. (255 "Wonderful Love")..........15-25 60
U.A. (289 "Working Man's Song") ..15-25 60
U.A. (420 "You're So Fine") 10-15 62
EPs: 7-inch
U.A. (10010 "The Falcons") 250-350 59
Members: Wilson Pickett; Joe Stubbs; Eddie Floyd; Arnet Robinson; Ben Rice; Lance Finnie; Sonny Monroe.
Also see CHARMERS
Also see FIVE SCALDERS
Also see FLOYD, Eddie
Also see KARI, Sax
Also see KIRKLAND, Eddie
Also see OHIO UNTOUCHABLES
Also see 100 PROOF Aged in Soul
Also see PICKETT, Wilson
Also see SMITH, Al
Also see STUBBS, Joe

FALKONS
Singles: 7-inch
FUJIMO (2521 "Why Marianne")....10-15

FALL
Singles: 7-inch
I.R.S. 3-4 79
LPs: 10/12-inch
I.R.S. 5-10 79

FALL GUYS
Singles: 7-inch
ROSEMONT (9161 "Teen Age Fool")..10-20 60

FALLEN ANGELS
Singles: 7-inch
TOLLIE (9049 "Up on the Mountain")......................................10-15 65

FALLEN ANGELS
Singles: 7-inch
LAURIE (3343 "Everytime I Fall in Love")..15-20 66
LAURIE (3369 "Have You Ever Lost a Love")..15-20 66
ROULETTE (4770 "Room at the Top")..10-15 67
ROULETTE (4785 "Hello Girl") 10-15 67
SUN DREAM (704 "Everything Would Be Fine")..10-15 60s
LPs: 10/12-inch
ROULETTE (25358 "The Fallen Angels")......................................50-100 68
ROULETTE (42011 "It's a Long Way Down")......................................30-60 68
Members: Jack Bryant; Jack Lauritsen; Wally Cook; Richard Kumer; Howart Danchik.
Also see MAD HATTERS

FALLEN ANGELS
Singles: 7-inch
ECEIP (1003 "Bad Woman") 40-60 70

FALLEN ANGELS
Singles: 7-inch
ARISTA.....................................3-5 75

FALLENROCK
LPs: 10/12-inch
CAPRICORN.............................8-10 74

FALLIN, Johnny
Singles: 7-inch
CAPITOL..................................10-20 59

FALLING PEBBLES
(Buckinghams)
Singles: 7-inch
ALLEY CAT (201 "Lawdy Miss Clawdy"..12-18 60s
Also see BUCKINGHAMS

FALLING STARS
Singles: 7-inch
BLACK 4-8 66

FALLOWS, Scott, & Ebbtones
Singles: 7-inch
DOT 15-20 64

FALLS, Ruby C&W '75
Singles: 7-inch
50 STATES 3-5 75-80
EPs: 7-inch
50 STATES 4-6 80
LPs: 10/12-inch
50 STATES 5-10 80

FALTERMEYER, Harold P&R/R&B '85
Singles: 7-inch
MCA 3-4 85
Picture Sleeves
MCA 3-4 85
LPs: 10/12-inch
MCA 5-10 85
Also see LABELLE, Patti, & Harold Faltermeyer

FALTERMEYER, Harold / Glenn Frey
Singles: 7-inch
MCA 3-4 84
Also see FREY, Glenn

FALTERMEYER, Harold, & Steve Stevens
Singles: 12-inch
COLUMBIA 4-8 86
(Promotional issue only.)
Singles: 7-inch
COLUMBIA 3-4 86
Also see FALTERMEYER, Harold

FALTSKOG, Agnetha P&R/LP '83
Singles: 7-inch
POLYDOR..................................3-4 83
Picture Sleeves
POLYDOR..................................3-5 83
LPs: 10/12-inch
POLYDOR..................................5-10 83
Also see ABBA

FALTSKOG, Agnetha, & Peter Cetera P&R '88
Singles: 7-inch
ATLANTIC..................................3-4 88
Picture Sleeves
ATLANTIC..................................3-4 88
Also see CETERA, Peter
Also see FALTSKOG, Agnetha

FAME: see KIDS from "FAME"

FAME, Georgie P&R/LP '65
(With the Blue Flames)
Singles: 7-inch
EPIC...3-6 68-70
IMPERIAL 4-8 65-67
ISLAND 3-5 75
EPs: 7-inch
EPIC...5-10 68
(Juke box issues only.)
LPs: 10/12-inch
EPIC...10-20 68-70
IMPERIAL 15-20 65-66
ISLAND 8-10 75
Also see FAME & PRICE – Price & Fame Together

FAME, Herb
Singles: 7-inch
DATE 4-8 66
Also see PEACHES & HERB

FAME & PRICE – Price & Fame Together
Singles: 7-inch
REPRISE 3-5 71
Members: Georgie Fame; Alan Price.
Also see FAME, Georgie
Also see PRICE, Alan

FAME GANG
Singles: 7-inch
ATLANTIC..................................4-8 68
FAME..3-6 69
LPs: 10/12-inch
FAME..10-12 69

FAMEN
Singles: 7-inch
DELTA (157 "If You Want Me") 35-50 65
X-POSE ("Crackin' Up")................35-50 66
(No selection number used.)

FAMES
Singles: 7-inch
PYRAMID (6897 "Drinkin' Wine Spo-Dee-O-Dee")..15-25 60s

FAMILY
Singles: 7-inch
U.S.A. (886 "Face the Autumn") 10-20 67
U.S.A. (894 "Without You")............10-20 68

FAMILY LP '72
Singles: 7-inch
LITTLE CITY...............................3-5 77
U.A. 3-5 71-73
LPs: 10/12-inch
REPRISE 15-20 68-70
U.A. 10-12 71-73
Members; Rick Grech; John Weider.
Also see BLIND FAITH
Also see WEIDER, John

FAMILY P&R/R&B/D&D/LP '85
Singles: 12-inch
PAISLEY PARK...........................4-6 85
Singles: 7-inch
PAISLEY PARK...........................3-4 85
Picture Sleeves
PAISLEY PARK...........................3-4 85
LPs: 10/12-inch
PAISLEY PARK...........................5-10 85
Members: Paul Peterson; Jerome Benton; Susannah Melvoin; Jellybean Johnson.
Also see ST. PAUL
Also see TIME

FAMILY AFFAIR
Singles: 7-inch
AUTHENTIC................................3-6
RCA 3-5 79
SMASH 3-6 69

FAMILY ALBUM
Singles: 7-inch
COLUMBIA 4-6 68
DECEMBER 4-8 67

FAMILY AT MAX
Singles: 7-inch
SOUND ODYSSEY 4-6 73
Members: Duane Stuermer; Warren Wiegratz.
Also see MUSTARD MEN

FAMILY BROWN C&W '81
Singles: 7-inch
OVATION 3-5 81
RCA 3-4 82-86
LPs: 10/12-inch
RCA 8-10 80s

FAMILY CIRCLE
Singles: 7-inch
SKY DISC (642 "Changes")............5-10 72
SKY DISC (644 "I Hope You Really Love Me")..5-10 72

FAMILY DOGG
Singles: 7-inch
BELL 4-8 69
LPs: 10/12-inch
BUDDAH 10-15 72
Members: Albert Hammond; Steve Rowland; Mike Hazlewood; Gary Taylor; Ireen Sheer; Sue Lynn.
Also see HAMMOND, Albert
Also see ROWLAND, Steve

FAMILY DREAM R&B '87
Singles: 7-inch
MOTOWN 3-4 87

FAMILY JEWELS
Singles: 7-inch
HARBOUR (306 "You Baby You") 15-25

FAMILY OF APOSTOLIC
LPs: 10/12-inch
VANGUARD (79301 "Family of Apostolic")..................................20-30 69
Members: John Townley; Gil Townley; Lyn Hardy.
Also see TOWNLEY, John, & Apostolic Family

FAMILY PLANN R&B '75
Singles: 7-inch
DRIVE 3-5 75

FAMILY PLAYERS
LPs: 10/12-inch
MCA 5-10 82

FAMILY PLOT
Singles: 7-inch
DMC (102 "Love Show") 15-25 68

FAMILY TREE
Singles: 7-inch
MIRA 10-20 66
PAULA 4-8 68
RCA 4-8 67-68
LPs: 10/12-inch
RCA 15-20 68

FAMILY VIBES
Singles: 7-inch
U.A. 4-6 72
LPs: 10/12-inch
U.A. 10-12 72

FAMOUS HEARTS
Singles: 7-inch
GUYDEN (2073 "Isle of Love") .. 150-200 62
Also see ANDREWS, Lee
Also see HEARTS

FANANDOS
(With Emmet Carter Combo; Fanando's)
Singles: 7-inch
CARTER (2050 "The One I Love")....................................500-1000 57
Also see ROCKERS

FANATICS
Singles: 7-inch
BACK BEAT 4-8 65
SKYWAY 10-15 61

FANATICS
Singles: 7-inch
GINA (1118 "Be Mine")..................20-30 65
Also see FORD, Neal, & Fanatics

FANCY P&R '74
Singles: 7-inch
BIG TREE 3-5 74
POISON RING 3-6 71
RCA 3-5 76-79
LPs: 10/12-inch
BIG TREE 8-10 74
POISON RING 12-20 71
RCA 5-10 79
Members: Al Ranaudo; Billy Durso.

FANCY D&D '85
Singles: 12-inch
PERSONAL.................................4-6 85

FANDANGO
Singles: 12-inch
RCA (3024 "Last Kiss")..................15-20 79
(Picture disc. Promotional issue only.)
Singles: 7-inch
RCA 3-5 78-79

Picture Sleeves

RCA ... 3-5 78

LPs: 10/12-inch

RCA (Except 2696) ... 5-10 77-80
RCA (2696 "Last Kiss") ... 20-30 79
(Picture disc. Promotional issue only.)

FANELLI, Frankie

Singles: 7-inch

ABC ... 4-6 67
BEVERLY HILLS ... 4-8
RCA ... 4-6 64

LPs: 10/12-inch

RCA ... 10-15 64

FANKHAUSER, Merrell

(With H.M.S. Bounty; with Maui Band; Murl Fankhauser)

Singles: 7-inch

D-TOWN ... 3-4 85
FREE SPIRIT ... 3-5 79
SHAMLEY (44006 "Things") ... 8-12 68
SHAMLEY (44008 "I'm Flying Home") ... 8-12 69

Picture Sleeves

FREE SPIRIT ... 3-5 79

LPs: 10/12-inch

CHERRY RED ... 8-10 85
D-TOWN ... 8-10 86
DISC MELOCOTON (001 "Back This Way Again") ... 15-25 90
MAUI (101 "Merrell Fankhauser") ... 40-50 76
OCEAN ... 5-10 88
SHAMLEY (701 "Things Going Round in My Mind") ... 50-75 68
SOURCE (2 "A Day in Paradise") ... 8-10 85
UIP (2250 "Fapardokly") ... 800-1200 67
(Only title is shown on cover—no artist credited. Has tracks recorded by Merrell & Exiles. *Fapardockly* combines portions of each band member's name: FAnkhauser-PARrish-DOdd-dicK LEe.)
Session: Merrell Fankhauser; Dan Parrish; Bill Dodd; Dick Lee; Peter Noone; Mary Lee; Jimmy Dillon; Bill Berg; Ben Benay; Colin Cameron; Bill Cuomo; Gary Malabar; John Cipollina; Jim Murray; John "Drumbo" French.
Also see IMPACTS
Also see MERRELL & EXILES
Also see MU
Also see NOONE, Peter
Also see QUICKSILVER
Also see SENTINELS
Also see ZAPPA, Frank

FANNIE FLAGG: see FLAGG, Fannie

FANNING, Jay

Singles: 7-inch

ACME ... 8-12 60-61

FANNY P&R/LP '71

Singles: 7-inch

CASABLANCA ... 3-5 74-75
REPRISE ... 3-5 70-73

LPs: 10/12-inch

CASABLANCA ... 8-10 74
REPRISE ... 10-12 70-73
Members: Jean Millington; June Millington; Alice de Buhr; Nickey Barclay; Patti Quatro; Wendy Haas; Brie Howard.
Also see BARCLAY, Nickey
Also see MILLINGTON

FANNY ADAMS

LPs: 10/12-inch

KAPP ... 10-15 71

FANO, Nick

Singles: 7-inch

OVO ... 4-8 64

FANS

Singles: 7-inch

DOT ... 10-12 64

FANS

Singles: 7-inch

STRAWBERRY FIELDS (5294 "John Lennon Epitaph") ... 4-6 85

FANTAISIONS

Singles: 7-inch

SATELLITE ... 4-8 65

FANTASIA

Singles: 7-inch

MALA ... 4-8 67

FANTASTIC BAGGYS

Singles: 7-inch

IMPERIAL (66047 "Tell 'Em I'm Surfin' ") ... 15-25 64
IMPERIAL (66072 "Anywhere the Girls Are") ... 15-25 64
IMPERIAL (66092 "Alone on the Beach") ... 15-25 65

LPs: 10/12-inch

IMPERIAL (9270 "Tell 'Em I'm Surfin' ") ... 75-125 64
(Black label with five stars under logo. Monaural.)
IMPERIAL (9270 "Tell 'Em I'm Surfin' ") ... 50-75 64
(Multi-color label. Monaural.)
IMPERIAL (9270 "Tell 'Em I'm Surfin' ") ... 75-125 64
(White label. Promotional issue only.)
IMPERIAL (12270 "Tell 'Em I'm Surfin' ") ... 100-150 64
(Black label with five stars under logo. Stereo.)
IMPERIAL (12270 "Tell 'Em I'm Surfin' ") ... 60-85 64
(Multi-color label. Stereo.)
LIBERTY ... 5-10 82
Members: Phil Sloan; Steve Barri.
Also see BARRI, Steve
Also see IMAGINATIONS
Also see INNER CIRCLE
Also see LIFEGUARDS
Also see PHILIP & STEPHEN
Also see RALLY PACKS
Also see RIP CHORDS
Also see SLOAN, P.F.
Also see STREET CLEANERS
Also see THEMES, INC.

FANTASTIC DEE-JAYS

Singles: 7-inch

FLEETWOOD (1096 "Love Is So Tuff") ... 20-30 65
RED FOX (102 "You're the One") ... 15-25 65
SHERRY (309 "Apache") ... 20-30 65
TRI-POWER (421 "Fight Fire") ... 15-25 66
STONE (044 "Love Is So Tuff") ... 15-20 66

LPs: 10/12-inch

STONE (4003 "The Fantastic Dee Jays") ... 400-600 66
Members: Dick Newton; Denny Nicholson; Bob Hocko.
Also see SWAMP RATS

FANTASTIC EPICS

Singles: 7-inch

TORIES ... 4-6 69

FANTASTIC FIVE KEYS

Singles: 7-inch

CAPITOL ... 5-10 62
Also see FIVE KEYS

FANTASTIC FOUR P&R/R&B '67

Singles: 7-inch

EASTBOUND ... 3-5 73-74
RIC-TIC (Except 113 & 121) ... 10-20 66-68
RIC-TIC (113 "Can't Stop Looking for My Baby") ... 100-200 66
RIC-TIC (121 "Can't Stop Looking for My Baby") ... 50-75 67
SOUL ... 8-15 68-70
WESTBOUND ... 3-5 75-79

LPs: 10/12-inch

SOUL (717 "Best of the Fantastic Four") ... 25-40 69
20TH FOX/WESTBOUND ... 8-10 76
WESTBOUND ... 8-10 75-78
Members: Joe Pruitt; James Epps; Robert Pruitt; Toby Childs; Ernest Newsome; Cleveland Horn.

FANTASTIC FOUR / Wingate's Love-in Strings

Singles: 7-inch

RIC-TIC ... 4-8 67
Also see FANTASTIC FOUR
Also see FLAMING EMBERS / Wingate's Love-in Strings

FANTASTIC JOHNNY C. P&R/R&B '67

(Johnny Corley)

Singles: 7-inch

BRANDING IRON (170 "Let's Do It Together") ... 10-20
KAMA SUTRA ... 3-5 70
PHIL L.A. of SOUL ... 4-8 67-73

LPs: 10/12-inch

PHIL L.A. of SOUL ... 15-20 68

FANTASTIC RHYTHMS

Singles: 7-inch

B&B (1435 "The Girlin Lace") ... 20-25 67

FANTASTIC SHAKERS

Singles: 7-inch

STALLINGS-SCHRONCE ... 3-4 82

LPs: 10/12-inch

STALLINGS-SCHRONCE ... 5-10 82
Member: Bo Schronce.

FANTASTIC VIRTURES: see VIRTURES

FANTASTIC VONTASTICS

Singles: 7-inch

TUFF ... 4-8 65
Also see VONTASTICS

FANTASTIC ZOO

Singles: 7-inch

DOUBLE SHOT (105 "This Calls for a Celebration") ... 10-20 66
DOUBLE SHOT (109 "Light Show") ... 10-20 67
Members: Don Cameron; Erik Karl.

FANTASTICS

Singles: 7-inch

PARK AVE. (309 "Dancing Doll") ... 5-10 90s
(Colored vinyl.)
RCA (7572 "There Goes My Love") ... 35-50 59
(RCA dog at top of label.)
RCA (7572 "There Goes My Love") ... 15-25 65
(RCA dog at left side of label.)
RCA (7664 "I Got a Zero") ... 25-50 59
U.A. (309 "Dancing Doll") ... 50-100 61
Members: Bill Forrest; Bill Sutton; Sam Strain; Fred Warner; Larry Lawrence.

FANTASTICS

Singles: 7-inch

COPA (8005 "High Note") ... 15-25
DONNA (1313 "Blabbermouth") ... 15-25 59
SCORPIO ... 4-8 66
SOUND STAGE 7 ... 5-10 66

FANTASTICS P&R '72

Singles: 7-inch

BELL ... 10-20 71-72
DERAM ... 5-10 69
Members: Jerome Ramos; Don Haywoode; John Cheatdom; Rich Pitts.
Also see VELOURS

FANTASTICS / Jalopy Five: see JALOPY FIVE

FANTASY P&R/LP '70

Singles: 7-inch

IMPERIAL ... 3-6 69
LIBERTY ... 3-5 70

LPs: 10/12-inch

LIBERTY ... 10-15 70

FANTASY R&B '81

Singles: 12-inch

QUALITY ... 4-6 83

Singles: 7-inch

PAVILLION ... 3-4 81

LPs: 10/12-inch

PAVILLION ... 5-10 81-82

FANTASY HILL

LPs: 10/12-inch

PRODIGAL ... 5-10 78

FANTASYS

Singles: 7-inch

GUYDEN (2029 "Why Oh Why") ... 50-75 60

FANTASYS

Singles: 7-inch

SHIRLE (4 "Surf's Up") ... 20-30 60s
Member: Scott Hicks

FANTAYZEE, Haysi: see HAYSI FANTAYZEE

FANTOM

Singles: 7-inch

SULLY (911 "Baby Come Home") ... 15-25 65

FANTOMES

LPs: 10/12-inch

KAPP ... 10-15 64

FANZ

LPs: 10/12-inch

ILLUSION ... 8-10 77
Also see PINERA, Mike

FAPARDOKLY: see FANKHAUSER, Merrell

FAR CORPORATION P&R '86

Singles: 7-inch

ATCO ... 3-4 86

Picture Sleeves

ATCO ... 3-4 86

LPs: 10/12-inch

ATCO ... 5-10 86
Members: Robin McAuley; Bobby Kimball; Steve Lukather; Dave Paich.
Also see McAULEY SCHENKER GROUP
Also see TOTO

FAR CRY

Singles: 7-inch

VANGUARD (35085 "Shapes") ... 5-10 69

LPs: 10/12-inch

VANGUARD (6510 "Far Cry") ... 20-30 69
Members: Dave Perry; Paul Lenart; Dick Martin; Sean Hutchinson.

FAR EAST FAMILY BAND

LPs: 10/12-inch

ALL EARS ... 8-10 77
MULAND ... 10-12

FARAGHER BROTHERS P&R '79

Singles: 7-inch

ABC ... 3-5 76-77
POLYDOR ... 3-4 79

LPs: 10/12-inch

ABC ... 5-10 79
POLYDOR ... 5-10 78-79
Members: Jimmy Faragher; Dan Faragher; Tom Faragher; Dave Faragher.
Also see BONES

FARDON, Don P&R '68

Singles: 7-inch

CHELSEA ... 3-5 73
GNP ... 4-8 68

LPs: 10/12-inch

DECCA ... 10-12 70
GNP ... 15-20 68

FARGO

Singles: 7-inch

PARAMOUNT ... 3-6 70
RCA ... 4-8 69

LPs: 10/12-inch

RCA ... 10-15 69
Members: Dean Wilder; Tony Decker.

FARGO, Donna C&W/P&R/LP '72

Singles: 7-inch

ABC ... 3-4 78
ABC/DOT ... 3-5 74-77
CHALLENGE (59387 "Daddy") ... 5-10 68
CHALLENGE (59391 "Wishful Thinking") ... 5-10 68
CLEVELAND INT'L ... 3-4 84-91
COLUMBIA ... 3-4 83
DECCA (33001 "Daddy") ... 4-6 72
DOT ... 3-5 72-74
MCA ... 3-4 81
MERCURY ... 3-4 86-87
RCA ... 3-4 82
RAMCO (1982 "You Make Me Feel Like a Woman") ... 8-12 67
RAMCO (1988 "Whose Been Playing House") ... 8-12 67
RAMCO (1988 "Whose Been Sleeping on My Bed") ... 8-12 67
(Note change in title.)
RAMCO (1991 "Kinda Glad I'm Me") ... 8-12 67
SONGBIRD ... 3-4 81
W.B. ... 3-5 76-81

Picture Sleeves

DOT ... 3-6 72-74
W.B. ... 3-5 76-80

LPs: 10/12-inch

ABC/DOT ... 5-10 74-77
DOT ... 8-12 72-73
MCA ... 5-8 80s
MERCURY ... 5-10 86
PICKWICK/HILLTOP ... 5-10 70s
RCA ... 5-10 83
SONGBIRD ... 4-8 81
W.B. ... 5-10 76-80
Session: Jordanaires.
Also see BARE, Bobby / Donna Fargo / Jerry Wallace
Also see JORDANAIRES

FARGO, Donna, & Billy Joe Royal C&W '87

Singles: 7-inch

MERCURY ... 3-4 87
Also see FARGO, Donna
Also see ROYAL, Billy Joe

FARINA, Sandy

LPs: 10/12-inch

MCA ... 5-10 80

FARLOW, Stan

Singles: 7-inch

CHECKER ... 3-5 70

LPs: 10/12-inch

CHECKER ... 10-15 70

FARLOWE, Chris

(With the Thunderbirds)

Singles: 7-inch

IMMEDIATE ... 4-8 67-68
MGM ... 5-10 66
POLYDOR ... 3-5 70

LPs: 10/12-inch

COLUMBIA ... 15-20 67
IMMEDIATE ... 15-20 68
POLYDOR ... 10-12 70
Also see ATOMIC ROOSTER
Also see COLOSSEUM

FARM BAND

(Tennessee Farm Band; Stephen & Farm Band)

Singles: 7-inch

FARM ... 4-6 75

Picture Sleeves

FARM ... 4-6 75

LPs: 10/12-inch

FARM ... 10-20 73-77
MANTRA (777 "Farm Band") ... 20-30 72
Members: Walter Rabideau; David Chalmers.
Also see FRANTIC
Also see TOMORROW'S CHILDREN

FARMER, Donny

Singles: 7-inch

ROULETTE ... 5-10 59
SPECTRUM ... 5-10 60

FARMER, Gene

LPs: 10/12-inch

DORE ... 8-10 72-73

FARMER, Wayne

Singles: 7-inch

DODGE ... 5-10

FARMER BOYS

Singles: 78 rpm

CAPITOL ... 5-10 56

Singles: 7-inch

CAPITOL ... 10-20 56

FARNER, Mark

(Mark Farner Band)

Singles: 7-inch

ATLANTIC ... 3-5 77-78
LUCKY ELEVEN (352 "Down in the Valley") ... 10-20 67

LPs: 10/12-inch

ATLANTIC ... 5-10 77-78

FARNER, Mark, & Don Brewer

Singles: 7-inch

LUCKY ELEVEN (366 "Does It Matter to You Girl") ... 10-20 67

Picture Sleeves

LUCKY ELEVEN (366 "Does It Matter to You Girl") ... 20-30 67

LPs: 10/12-inch

QUADICO (7401 "Monumental Funk") ... 5-10 79
QUADICO (7401 "Monumental Funk") ... 20-25 79
(Limited edition, numbered picture disc.)
Also see FARNER, Mark
Also see GRAND FUNK RAILROAD

FARNHAM, John P&R '90

(Johnny Farnham)

Singles: 7-inch

CAPITOL ... 4-6 67
RCA ... 3-4 90
Also see LITTLE RIVER BAND

FARON'S FLAMINGOS: see STORM, Rory, & Hurricanes

FAROS

Singles: 7-inch

TARGET (103 "I'm Crying") ... 20-40 66
Members: Gary Daily; Steve Berg; Chris Wyman; Dan Meredith.

FAR-OUT UNDERGROUND ACID ROCK FEET OF HARRY ZONK

Singles: 7-inch

CRAZY HORSE ... 3-6 69

FARQUAHR: see FABULOUS FARQUAHR

FARR, Frankie

Singles: 7-inch

I-NEZZ ... 5-10 61

FARR, Gary

(With the T-Bones)

Singles: 7-inch

EPIC ... 4-8 65

LPs: 10/12-inch

ATCO ... 8-10 73

FARR, Little Joey

(Joey Farr)

Singles: 7-inch

BAND BOX (286 "Rock & Roll Santa") ... 30-50 61
EAGLE (1002 "Movin' on Down") ... 20-30 58

FARRAR, John

LPs: 10/12-inch

COLUMBIA ... 5-10 80

FARRAR, Lucien

(With the Lifesavers & Don Abney Orchestra)

Singles: 7-inch

JUPITER (1 "Didn't You Know") ... 550-650 57
JUPITER (2 "Tomorrow Night") ... 550-650 57
ROULETTE (4331 "My Dream") ... 15-25 61

FARRAR, Tony

Singles: 7-inch

TRANS ATLAS (001 "A Blast from the Past") ... 15-25 61
(Opens with *In the Still of the Nite*, by the Five Satins.)
Also see FIVE SATINS

FARREL, Lee

LPs: 10/12-inch

TMS (101 "Hard Times") ... 40-50 78
(Boxed picture disc set. Includes bonus autographed photo.)
TMS (101 "Hard Times") ... 30-40 78
(Picture disc.)

FARREL & FLAMES

Singles: 7-inch

FRANSIL (14 "Dreams and Memories") ... 250-350 61

FARRELL, Billy R&B '49

(Bill Farrell)

Singles: 78 rpm

EPIC ... 15-25 57
IMPERIAL ... 8-12 54
MGM ... 10-15 49
MERCURY ... 8-12 56

Singles: 7-inch

CUB ... 5-10 59
DATE ... 10-20 58
EPIC ... 10-20 57
IMPERIAL ... 15-25 54
MERCURY ... 10-20 56
TEL (1000 "You Were Only Fooling") ... 15-25 58

FARRELL, Eileen LP '61

Singles: 7-inch

LONDON ... 3-5 65

LPs: 10/12-inch

COLUMBIA ... 10-20 60-63
HARMONY ... 5-10 68

FARRELL, Ernie, & His Paper Music Band

Singles: 7-inch

COLPIX (775 "Candy Camera") ... 4-8 65

Picture Sleeves

COLPIX (775 "Candy Camera") ... 5-10 65

FARRELL, Leon

Singles: 7-inch

NATION (92767 "Pure Unadulterated Love") ... 10-20

FARRELL, Mickey, & Dynamics

Singles: 7-inch

BETHLEHEM ... 10-15 63-64

FARRELL, Pat, & Believers

Singles: 7-inch

DIAMOND (236 "War Baby") ... 10-20 68
DIAMOND (239 "All My Love") ... 10-20 68
Also see RAZOR'S EDGE
Also see TRIUMPHS

FARRELL, Tony

Singles: 7-inch

TIME ... 5-10 58

FARRENHEIT LP '87

Singles: 12-inch

W.B. ... 4-8 87
(Promotional only.)

Singles: 7-inch

W.B. ... 3-4 87

LPs: 10/12-inch

W.B. ... 5-10 87

FARRO, Johnny

Singles: 7-inch

MONIQUE ... 4-8 63

FARROW, Cee P&R/R&B '83

Singles: 7-inch

ROCSHIRE ... 3-4 83

Picture Sleeves

ROCSHIRE ... 3-4 83

FASCINATES

Singles: 7-inch

PORT ... 5-10 59

FASCINATIONS
Singles: 7-inch
ABC-PAR (10443 "You're Gonna Be Sorry")..........10-20 63
DORE (593 "If I Had Your Love")...20-30 61
PAXLEY (750 "If I Had Your Love")..........50-100 61
SURE (106 "It's Midnight")..........150-250 60
SURE (106 "Midnight")..........75-125 60
(Note slight title change.)

FASCINATIONS R&B '66
Singles: 7-inch
A&G (101 "Since You Went Away")..........25-40 65
MAYFIELD..........5-10 66-67
Members: Bernadine Boswell Smith; Shirley Walker; Fern Bledsoe; Joanne Levell.
Also see FASINATIONS

FASCINATORS
Singles: 78 rpm
YOUR COPY (1135 "The Bells of My Heart")..........75-125 54
YOUR COPY (1136 "My Beauty, My Own")..........75-125 55
Singles: 7-inch
YOUR COPY (1135 "The Bells of My Heart")..........500-1000 54
(Black vinyl.)
YOUR COPY (1135 "The Bells of My Heart")..........1000-2000 54
(Red vinyl.)
YOUR COPY (1136 "My Beauty, My Own")..........500-1000 55
Members: Jerry Potter; Donald Blackshear; Bob Rivers; Clarence Smith; Earl Richardson.

FASCINATORS
Singles: 78 rpm
BLUE LAKE (112 "Can't Stop")..150-200 55
Singles: 7-inch
BLUE LAKE (112 "Can't Stop")..300-450 55
Member: Andrew Smith.
Also see MAPLES

FASCINATORS
Singles: 7-inch
DOOTO (441 "Teardrop Eyes")......50-60 58
KING (5119 "Cuddle Up with Carolyn")..........40-50 58

FASCINATORS
(With Sid Bass & His Orchestra)
Singles: 7-inch
BIM BAM BOOM..........3-5 70s
CAPITOL (4053 "Chapel Bells")...75-125 58
(Purple label.)
CAPITOL (4053 "Chapel Bells") 100-150 58
(Yellow label. Promotional issue only.)
CAPITOL (4053 "Chapel Bells")...50-100 58
(White label. Promotional issue only.)
CAPITOL (4137 "Come to Paradise")..........100-125 59
(Purple label.)
CAPITOL (4137 "Come to Paradise")..........125-175 59
(White label. Promotional issue only.)
CAPITOL (4247 "Oh Rose Marie")..........100-125 59
(Purple label.)
CAPITOL (4247 "Oh Rose Marie")..........125-175 59
(Blue label. Promotional issue only.)
CAPITOL (4544 "Chapel Bells")....35-40 61
(Purple label.)
CAPITOL (4544 "Chapel Bells")....45-50 58
(Yellow label. Promotional issue only.)
SPOT HITS (11 "Oh Rose Marie") 10-15 63
Members: Tony Passalaqua; Nick Trivatto; Angelo LaGrecca; Ed Wheeler; George Cernaeck.
Also see ARCHIES

FASCINATORS
Singles: 7-inch
TRANS ATLAS (688 "You're to Blame")..........10-20 62

FASCINATORS
Singles: 7-inch
BURN (845 "I'll Be Gone")..........15-25 65

FASHION
Singles: 12-inch
EPIC..........4-6 84
Singles: 7-inch
EPIC..........3-4 84
I.R.S...........3-4 79
LPs: 10/12-inch
EPIC..........5-10 84
I.R.S...........5-10 79

FASHIONEERS
Singles: 7-inch
BLUE ROCK..........4-8 65

FASHIONETTES
Singles: 7-inch
GNP..........5-8 64

FASHIONS
Singles: 7-inch
CAMEO..........4-8 64
COLLECTABLES..........3-4 80s
ELMOR (301 "Please Let It Be Me")..........10-20 61
EMBER..........5-10 62
V-TONE (202 "I'm Dreaming of You"/"Lonesome Road")..........25-30 59
(Orange label.)
V-TONE (202 "I'm Dreaming of You"/"I Love You So")..........20-25 59
(Orange label.)
V-TONE (202 "I'm Dreaming of You")..........10-20 59
(Blue label.)
WARWICK..........10-15 61
Members: Barbara English; Frankie Brunson.
Also see ENGLISH, Barbara
Also see PEOPLE'S CHOICE

FASHIONS
Singles: 7-inch
IPG (1001 "Trampoline")..........10-20 63

FASHIONS
Singles: 7-inch
FELSTED (8689 "Surfers Memories")..........15-25 63
GREYBAR (201 "Surfers Memories")..........40-60 63
(First issue.)

FASHIONS
Singles: 7-inch
20TH FOX..........4-8 68

FASHIONS
Singles: 7-inch
PHIL-L.A. of SOUL..........3-5 72

FASINATIONS
Singles: 7-inch
ABC-PAR..........5-10 62-63
Also see FASCINATIONS

FAST ANNIE
LPs: 10/12-inch
CHELSEA..........8-10 77

FAST BACKS
Singles: 7-inch
ARA..........10-20

FAST FLOYD & HIS FAMOUS FIREBIRDS
Singles: 7-inch
KING PIN (666 "Tiger Man")..........4-6 83
(Gold vinyl.)
Picture Sleeves
KING PIN (666 "Tiger Man")..........5-8 83
EPs: 7-inch
KADILLAK (501 "Bizarre")..........8-10 77
(With paper sleeve.)
KADILLAK (501 "Bizarre")..........10-15 77
(With cardboard sleeve.)
KADILLAK (501 "Bizarre")..........15-20 77
(Colored vinyl.)
LPs: 10/12-inch
KING PIN..........12-20 83
Session: Fast Floyd; Franco St. Andrew; Bobby Mack; Lance Campbell; Chris Campbell.
Also see SPIDERS

FAST FONTAINE
Singles: 7-inch
EMI-AMERICA..........3-4 81
LPs: 10/12-inch
EMI-AMERICA..........5-10 81

FAST RADIO D&D '83
Singles: 12-inch
RADAR..........4-6 83

FASTBACKS
Singles: 7-inch
POPLLAMA (6 "They Don't Care")....3-4 92
(Lavender vinyl.)
Picture Sleeves
POPLLAMA (6 "They Don't Care")....3-4 92
(Cardboard stock sleeve.)
Members: Kim; Kurt; Lulu; Floopy Rusty; Posy Mike.

FASTELLS
Singles: 7-inch
NIGHT OWL (6781 "So Much")......15-25 67

FASTER PUSSYCAT LP '87
Singles: 7-inch
ELEKTRA..........3-4 87-90
Picture Sleeves
ELEKTRA..........3-4 88
LPs: 10/12-inch
ELEKTRA..........5-10 87-90
Members: Taime Downe; Brent Muscat; Greg Steele; Mark Michals; Eric Stacy; Brett Bradshaw.

FASTEST GROUP ALIVE
Singles: 7-inch
TEEN (100 "The Bears")..........20-30 67
VALIANT (754 "The Bears")..........10-20 67
VALIANT (759 "Lullabye 5:15 Sports")..........10-20 67
Member: Davie Allan.
Also see ALLAN, Davie

FASTWAY LP '83
Singles: 12-inch
COLUMBIA (1727 "Easy Living")...10-12 83
(Picture disc. Promotional issue only.)
Singles: 7-inch
COLUMBIA..........3-4 83-86
LPs: 10/12-inch
COLUMBIA..........5-10 83-86
GWR..........5-8 89
Members: "Fast" Eddie Clarke; Jerry Shirley; David King; Charles McCracken.
Also see HUMBLE PIE

FAT
Singles: 7-inch
RCA..........3-5 70
LPs: 10/12-inch
DREAM MERCHANT..........5-10
RCA..........8-12 70

FAT ALBERT
Singles: 7-inch
TETRAGAMMATON..........4-8 68
LPs: 10/12-inch
WARNER..........5-10 73

FAT BOYS R&B '84
Singles: 12-inch
EMPEROR..........4-6 92
SUTRA..........4-6 84-86
Singles: 7-inch
SUTRA..........3-4 84-86
TIN PAN APPLE..........3-4 87-89
Picture Sleeves
TIN PAN APPLE..........3-5 88
LPs: 10/12-inch
SUTRA..........5-10 84-87
TIN PAN APPLE..........5-10 87-89
Members: Darren Robinson; Mark Morales; Damon Wimbley.
Also see DISCO 3
Also see KING DREAM CHORUS & Holiday Crew
Also see KRUSH GROVE ALL STARS

FAT BOYS & BEACH BOYS P&R/R&B '87
Singles: 12-inch
TIN PAN APPLE (885-960 "Wipeout")..........5-8 87
Singles: 7-inch
TIN PAN APPLE (885-960 "Wipeout")..........4-6 87
(Shown only as by the "Fat Boys.")
TIN PAN APPLE (885-960 "Wipeout")..........3-4 87
(Credits "Fat Boys and the Beach Boys.")
Picture Sleeves
TIN PAN APPLE (885960 "Wipeout") 3-5 87
Also see BEACH BOYS

FAT BOYS & CHUBBY CHECKER P&R/R&B '88
Singles: 7-inch
TIN PAN APPLE..........3-4 88
Picture Sleeves
TIN PAN APPLE..........3-4 88
Also see CHECKER, Chubby
Also see FAT BOYS

FAT CHANCE
Singles: 7-inch
RCA..........3-5 72
LPs: 10/12-inch
RCA..........8-10 72

FAT CITY
Singles: 7-inch
PARAMOUNT..........3-5 72
PROBE..........3-5 69
LPs: 10/12-inch
ABC/PROBE..........15-20 69
PARAMOUNT..........12-15 72
Members: Bill Danoff; Taffy Nivert.
Also see BILL & TAFFY
Also see DENVER, John
Also see STARLAND VOCAL BAND

FAT DADDY
Singles: 7-inch
JONNA..........4-8 64

FAT DADDY
Singles: 7-inch
MERCURY..........3-5 72

FAT FRED & KAPE MEN
LPs: 10/12-inch
CALIFORNIA..........12-15

FAT JACK BAND
Singles: 7-inch
DOUBLE B (10 "Hey! It's Summer")..........10-15
DOUBLE B (156 "Beach Fever")....10-15

FAT LARRY'S BAND R&B '78
(FLB)
Singles: 12-inch
WMOT..........4-6 78-79
Singles: 7-inch
FANTASY..........3-4 79-82
OMMI..........3-4 86
STAX..........3-5 77
WMOT..........3-4 78-82
LPs: 10/12-inch
FANTASY..........5-10 80
OMMI..........5-10 86
STAX..........8-10 77
WMOT..........5-10 78-82
Members: Larry James; Art Capehart; Doug Jones; Jimmy Lee; Erskine Williams; Ted Cohen; Darryl Grant; Larry Labes.

FAT MAN
Singles: 78 rpm
J.O.B. (103 "You've Got to Stop This Mess")..........100-125 50
NASHBORO (516 "You've Got to Stop This Mess")..........75-100 50

FAT MAN HUMPHRIES: see HUMPHRIES, Fat Man

FAT MAN'S MUSIC FESTIVAL
Singles: 7-inch
SCEPTER..........3-6 69
Member: John Carter.

FAT MATTRESS LP '69
LPs: 10/12-inch
ATCO..........10-20 69-70

FAT WATER
Singles: 7-inch
MGM..........4-8 69
LPs: 10/12-inch
MGM..........10-15 69
Also see ONE EYED JACKS

FATBACK R&B '73
(Fatback Band)
Singles: 12-inch
SPRING..........4-6 83-84
Singles: 7-inch
COTILLION..........3-4 83-85
EVENT..........3-5 74-76
PERCEPTION..........3-5 72-74
POLYDOR..........3-4 79
SPRING..........3-5 76-85
LPs: 10/12-inch
COTILLION..........5-10 83-85
EVENT..........8-10 74-76
PERCEPTION..........8-10 72
POLYDOR..........5-10 79
SPRING..........5-10 76-84
Members: Bill Curtis; Johnny King; George Williams; Johnny Flippin; Earl Shelton; George Adam; Fred Demerey; George Victory; Gerry Thomas.
Also see CHRISTIE, Janice

FATES WARNING LP '87
Soundsheet
EVATONE (103504 "Anarchy Devine")..........4-6 88
LPs: 10/12-inch
ENIGMA..........5-10 87
METAL BLADE (Except 73330)..........5-8 88-89
METAL BLADE (73330 "No Exit")..10-12 88
(Picture disc. Promotional issue only.)

FATHER & SONS
Singles: 7-inch
MINIT..........4-8 66

FATHER M.C. LP '90
LPs: 10/12-inch
UPTOWN..........5-8 90

FATHER YOD: see YA HO WA 13

FATHER'S CHILDREN
LPs: 10/12-inch
MERCURY..........5-10 79

FATIMAS
Singles: 7-inch
ORIGINAL SOUND..........4-8 67

FATMAN, Lloyd: see LLOYD "FATMAN"

FATS JR.
(Fats, Jr.)
Singles: 7-inch
D&H (4021 "Little Mary")..........20-30 60s

FATSO & FLAIRS
(Fatso Theus)
Singles: 78 rpm
ALADDIN..........50-75 56
Singles: 7-inch
ALADDIN (3324 "Be Cool, My Heart")..........100-150 56

FAUBUS, Ray, & Strikes
Singles: 7-inch
SOMA (1191 "Please")..........15-25 61

FAUCETT, Dawnett C&W '89
Singles: 7-inch
STEP ONE..........3-4 89

FAULKCON, Lawrence, & Sounds
Singles: 7-inch
CHECK MATE (1004 "My Girl and My Friend")..........30-50 61
MAH'S (0007 "My Girl and My Friend")..........50-100 61

FAULKNER, Clem, & Robert Oakes Jordan
Singles: 7-inch
ORBIT..........5-10 59

FAULT LINE
Singles: 7-inch
RCA..........3-6 69

FAUN
Singles: 7-inch
GREGAR (7000 "I Asked My Mother")..........10-20 69
GREGAR (7001 "Son of a Literate Man")..........10-20 69
LPs: 10/12-inch
GREGAR (7000 "Faun")..........50-75 69
Members: Ross Vallory; James Trumbo; Lynn Chatwin; George Tickner.
Also see FRUMIOUS BANDERSNATCH

FAWCET, Farrah: see: MAJORS, Farrah Fawcet

FAWNS
Singles: 7-inch
APT (25015 "Until I Die")..........15-20 58
CAPACITY (105 "Wish You Were Here with Me")..........10-15 67
TEC (3015 "Girl in Trouble")..........8-12 60s

FAUTHEREE, Jimmy
Singles: 7-inch
PAULA (239 "Box Full of Git")..........10-20 66

FAWNS
Singles: 7-inch
APT (25015 "Until I Die")..........15-20 58
CAPACITY (105 "Wish You Were Here with Me")..........10-15 67
RCA..........3-5 71
TEC (3015 "Girl in Trouble")..........8-12 60s
Picture Sleeves
RCA..........3-5 71

FAX
(With Alex Campbell; Fax / Lost & Founds)
Singles: 7-inch
TRANSACTION (701 "Her Love") 20-30 66
TRANSACTION (702 "Just Walking in the Rain")..........20-30 66
TRANSACTION (704 "I'll Go Crazy")..........20-30 67
Picture Sleeves
TRANSACTION (704 "I'll Go Crazy")..........20-30 67
Members: Mike Palmer; Greg Fritsch; Steve Noffke; Greg Haskell.
Also see LADDS
TRANSACTION (704 "I'll Go Crazy")..........20-30 67

FAX, Tony R&B '68
Singles: 7-inch
CALLA (151 "Lean on Me")..........10-15 68

FAY, Johnny, & Blazers
Singles: 7-inch
DANI (1539 "Cindy")..........100-150

FAYARD, Al
Singles: 7-inch
ALON (9020 "Doin' Sumpin' ")..........6-12 65
Also see STOKES

FAYARD, Bill
Singles: 7-inch
ALON (9028 "I Don't Know")..........6-12 65
Also see STOKES

FAYE, Alma R&B '79
Singles: 12-inch
CASABLANCA..........4-6 79
Singles: 7-inch
CASABLANCA..........3-4 79

FAYE, Boots
Singles: 7-inch
RCA (8211 "Tip Toes")..........5-10 63

FAYE, Frances
Singles: 78 rpm
CAPITOL..........4-6 52-54
Singles: 7-inch
CAPITOL..........5-10 52-54

FAYE, Judy
Singles: 7-inch
RCA..........8-12 57

FAYERWETHER
LPs: 10/12-inch
GANGSTER (11491 "Fayerwether")..........10-15 82
(Picture disc. Promotional issue only. 1000 made.)

FAYNE, Chuck
Singles: 7-inch
CREST (1094 "Tokyo Stomp")..........10-20 62

FAYE, Rita
(With the Teddy Bears)
Singles: 78 rpm
MGM..........4-8 57
Singles: 7-inch
MGM..........5-10 57
MELRON..........4-8 63

FAYNE, Wally
Singles: 7-inch
HI-FIRE..........10-15 59

FAYROS
Singles: 7-inch
RCA (37-7914 "Skokiaan")..........15-25 61
(Compact 33 Single.)
RCA (47-7914 "Skokiaan")..........8-12 61

FAYTE
Singles: 7-inch
AMERICAN..........5-10 73

FAYTE, Kevin, & Rocket 8
LPs: 10/12-inch
WISEGUY..........10-15 85

FAZE-O R&B/LP '78
Singles: 7-inch
SHE..........3-5 77-79
LPs: 10/12-inch
SHE..........5-10 77-79
Members: Keith Harrison; Ralph Aikens; Roger Parker; Tyrone Crum; Robert Neal Jr.

FEAGANS, Jimmy, & Jap Curry Blazers
Singles: 7-inch
HOWARD (501 "Saturday Night")..25-35 63

FEAR ITSELF
Singles: 7-inch
DOT..........4-6 69
LPs: 10/12-inch
DOT..........15-20 69

FERIS WHEEL
Singles: 7-inch
MAGENDA (5653 "Best Part of Breaking Up")..........10-15 65

FEARNS FOUNDRY
Singles: 7-inch
PARROT..........5-8 68

FEARON, Phil R&B '86
Singles: 7-inch
COOLTEMPO..........3-4 86
ISLAND..........3-4 86

FEARSOME FIVE
Singles: 7-inch
FEARSOME (101 "It's Alright")......15-25

FEARSOME FOURSOME
Singles: 7-inch
CAPITOL ... 5-8 65
Picture Sleeves
CAPITOL ... 10-20 65
Members: Merlin Olson; Roosevelt Greer; Deacon Jones; Lamar Lundy.

FEATHER P&R '70
Singles: 7-inch
WHITE WHALE ... 3-5 70
LPs: 10/12-inch
COLUMBIA ... 10-12 70

FEATHERBED
(Barry Manilow)
Singles: 7-inch
BELL (133 "Could It Be Magic") ... 15-25 71
BELL (971 "Amy") ... 15-25 71
Also see MANILOW, Barry

FEATHERS
(Johnny Staton & Feathers; with Johnny Moore's Blazers)
Singles: 78 rpm
ALADDIN ... 50-75 55
HOLLYWOOD ... 150-200 56
SHOWTIME ... 50-75 54
Singles: 7-inch
ALADDIN (3267 "Johnny Darling") ... 100-125 54
ALADDIN (3277 "I Need a Girl") 125-150 55
CLASSIC ARTISTS ... 4-6 89-90
HOLLYWOOD (1051 "Dear One") ... 300-350 56
SHOW TIME (1104 "Nona") ... 75-125 54
SHOW TIME (1105 "Why Don't You Write Me"/"Busy As a Bee") ... 100-200 55
SHOW TIME (1105 "Why Don't You Write Me"/"Where Did Caledonia Go") .. 75-125 55
(Note different flip side.)
SHOW TIME (1106 "Love Only You") ... 75-125 55
Members: Johnny Staton; Mitchell Alexander.
Also see BELVIN, Jesse, & Five Keys / Feathers
Also see CHARGERS
Also see MOORE, Johnny
Also see MOY, June
Also see STATON, Johnny, & Feathers / Jaguars

FEATHERS
Singles: 7-inch
KAPP ... 3-6 68
TEAM ... 4-8 68
VEEP ... 4-8 64

FEATHERS, Charlie
(With Jody & Jerry)
Singles: 78 rpm
FLIP (503 "I've Been Deceived") ... 200-300 55
KING ... 50-100 56
METEOR ... 100-200 56
SUN (231 "Defrost Your Heart") 100-200 56
SUN (503 "I've Been Deceived") ... 200-300 55
Singles: 7-inch
FEATHERS ... 3-5 80
FLIP (503 "I've Been Deceived") ... 300-500 55
HOLIDAY INN (114 "Deep Elm Blues") ... 100-200 62
KAY (1001 "Jungle Fever") ... 100-200 58
KING (4971 "Everybody's Lovin' My Baby") ... 200-400 56
KING (4997 "One Hand Loose") ... 300-500 56
(Blue label.)
KING (4997 "One Hand Loose") ... 350-550 56
(White bio label. Promotional issue only.)
KING (5022 "Nobody's Woman") ... 200-300 56
KING (5043 "Too Much Alike") ... 200-300 56
MEMPHIS (103 "Wild Wild Party") ... 50-75 62
METEOR (5032 "Tongue Tied Jill") ... 600-800 56
(Maroon label.)
METEOR (5032 "Tongue Tied Jill") ... 300-500 56
(Black label.)
PHILWOOD ... 4-8
POMPADOUR ... 3-5 74
ROLLIN' ROCK ... 3-5 78
SUN (231 "Defrost Your Heart") 200-400 56
SUN (503 "I've Been Deceived") ... 400-600 55
LPs: 10/12-inch
BARRELHOUSE ... 8-10 78
Session: Jody Chastain; Jerry Huffman.
Also see BURLISON, Paul
Also see MORGAN, Charlie
Also see SELF, Mack, & Charlie Feathers

FEDERAL DUCK
LPs: 10/12-inch
MUSICOR (3162 "Federal Duck") .. 15-20 68

FEDERAL RESERVE
Singles: 7-inch
R-JAY ... 10-20 60s

FEDERALS
Singles: 78 rpm
DELUXE ... 20-30 57
FURY ... 30-50 57
Singles: 7-inch
DELUXE (6112 "Come Go with Me") ... 75-125 57
FURY (1005 "While Our Hearts Are Young") ... 100-150 57
FURY (1009 "Dear Loraine") ... 75-125 57
Members: Rudy Anderson; James Pender; Ken Fox; Lorenzo Cook.
Also see WHEELS

FEDERALS
Singles: 7-inch
CAPITOL ... 4-8 65

FEE WAYBILL: see WAYBILL, Fee

FEEBEEZ
Singles: 7-inch
STRANGE (2216 "Walk Away") ... 10-15

FEEL R&B '82
Singles: 12-inch
SUTRA ... 4-6 82-83
Singles: 7-inch
SUTRA ... 3-4 82-83

FEELGOOD, DR: see DR. FEELGOOD

FEELIES
Singles: 7-inch
JERDEN (904 "Louie Louie") ... 10-20 68
JERDEN (910 "Happy") ... 5-10 69

FEELIES LP '88
LPs: 10/12-inch
A&M ... 5-8 88

FE-FI FOUR + TWO
Singles: 7-inch
LANCE (101 "I Wanna Come Back [From the World of LSD]") ... 100-150 66
ODEX (1042 "Mr. Sweet Stuff") ... 10-15 67

FEGAN, Johnny
Singles: 7-inch
GET IT (104 "Problem Child") ... 15-25

FEGER, Don, & Embers
Singles: 7-inch
EBONY (102 "Don't Be Mad") ... 25-40 58
EBONY (103 "Look Out Baby") ... 25-40 58

FELDER, Don P&R '81
Singles: 7-inch
ASYLUM ... 3-4 83
FULL MOON/ASYLUM ... 3-4 81
MCA ... 3-4
Picture Sleeves
FULL MOON/ASYLUM ... 3-4 81
LPs: 10/12-inch
ASYLUM ... 5-10 83
ELEKTRA ... 5-8 83
Also see EAGLES
Also see PURE PRAIRIE LEAGUE
Also see RAVYNS / Don Felder

FELDER, Wilton R&B/LP '78
Singles: 7-inch
ABC ... 3-4 78
MCA ... 3-4 79-85
LPs: 10/12-inch
ABC ... 5-10 78
MCA ... 5-10 80-85
PACIFIC JAZZ ... 8-12 69
Also see JAZZ CRUSADERS
Also see TASTE of HONEY

FELDER, Wilton, & Bobby Womack R&B '85
Singles: 7-inch
MCA ... 3-4 80-85
Picture Sleeves
MCA ... 3-4 80-85
Also see FELDER, Wilton
Also see WOMACK, Bobby

FELDERS ORIOLES
Singles: 7-inch
MERCURY ... 8-12 65

FELDMAN, Victor P&R '62
(Victor Feldman All Stars; Trio; Quartet; Vic Feldman)
Singles: 7-inch
AVA ... 3-5 63
INFINITY ... 3-5 62
PACIFIC JAZZ ... 3-5 66
VEE JAY ... 3-5 64
LPs: 10/12-inch
AVA ... 10-20 63
CONTEMPORARY ... 15-25 58-60
INTERLUDE ... 15-20 59
MODE ... 20-30 58
NAUTILUS ... 10-20 82
(Half-speed mastered.)
PACIFIC JAZZ ... 10-15 67-68
PALTO ALTO ... 5-10 83-84
RIVERSIDE ... 15-20 61
VEE JAY ... 15-25 59-65
WORLD PACIFIC ... 15-25 62

FELICIANO, Jose P&R/R&B/LP '68
Singles: 7-inch
ALA ... 3-4 80
MOTOWN ... 3-4 81-83
PRIVATE STOCK ... 3-5 76-77
RCA ... 3-6 64-75
LPs: 10/12-inch
CAMDEN ... 8-10 72
MOTOWN ... 5-10 81
PRIVATE STOCK ... 6-10 76-77
RCA ... 8-15 65-76
Also see CUBA, Joe
Also see SCHUUR, Diane

FELICIANO, Jose / Petula Clark
EPs: 7-inch
TK (334 "Mackenna's Gold") ... 10-20 69
Also see CLARK, Petula

FELICIANO, Jose, & Quincy Jones
LPs: 10/12-inch
RCA (4096 "Mackenna's Gold") ... 15-25 69
(Soundtrack.)
Also see FELICIANO, Jose
Also see JONES, Quincy

FELICITY
Singles: 7-inch
WILSON (101 "Hurtin' ") ... 20-30 67
Also see FREY, Glenn

FELIX, Julie
Singles: 7-inch
RAK ... 3-5 73
LPs: 10/12-inch
FONTANA ... 12-15 67

FELIX, Mike
Singles: 7-inch
JERDEN ... 4-8 66

FELIX & ESCORTS
Singles: 7-inch
JAG (685 "The Syracuse") ... 25-40 62
Members: Felix Cavaliere; Mike Esposito.
Also see BLUES MAGOOS
Also see CAVALIERE, Felix
Also see CRITTERS / Young Rascals / Lou Christie

FELIX & FABULOUS CATS
("With His Fabulous Guitar")
Singles: 7-inch
AUL (1 "Puerto Rican Riot") ... 15-25 59
ENITH (1272 "Savage Girl") ... 10-20 65
Also see GARCIA, Felix

FELIX & JARVIS R&B '82
Singles: 7-inch
RFC/QUALITY ... 3-4 82-83

FELIX HARP
LPs: 10/12-inch
GUINESS ... 10-15 77
WESTERN WORLD ... 10-20
Member: Eric Beam.

FELL, Terry C&W '54
(With the Fellers)
Singles: 78 rpm
RCA ... 3-8 56
"X" ... 3-8 54-55
Singles: 7-inch
RCA ... 5-10 56
"X" ... 5-10 54-55

FELLER, Dick C&W '73
Singles: 7-inch
ASYLUM ... 3-5 74-75
U.A. ... 3-4 72-80
LPs: 10/12-inch
ASYLUM ... 6-10 74-75
AUDIOGRAPH ALIVE ... 5-10 84
U.A. ... 8-12 73

FELLER, Herman, Jr.
Singles: 7-inch
CUCA (1007 "Swiss Teen Song") ... 15-25 60

FELLINI, Suzanne P&R '80
Singles: 7-inch
CASABLANCA ... 3-4 80
LPs: 10/12-inch
CASABLANCA ... 5-10 80

FELLOWS
Singles: 7-inch
SOLID HIT ... 10-20
TOTO ... 8-10

FELONY P&R/LP '83
Singles: 7-inch
ROCK & ROLL ... 3-4 83-84
LPs: 10/12-inch
ROCK & ROLL ... 5-10 83

FELT
LPs: 10/12-inch
NASCO (9006 "Felt") ... 150-250 71
Members: Mike Neel; Mike Jackson; Tom Gilstrap; Stan Lee; Al Dalrymple.

FELTS, Derrell
Singles: 7-inch
DIXIE (2008 "Playmates") ... 75-100 58
OKEH ... 10-20 59

FELTS, Narvel P&R '60/C&W '73
Singles: 78 rpm
MERCURY ... 10-20 57
Singles: 7-inch
ABC ... 3-5 78
ABC/DOT ... 3-5 75-77
ACTION ... 4-8 70
ARA ... 5-10 64-65
CELEBRITY CIRCLE ... 4-8 65
CINNAMON ... 3-5 73-74
COLLAGE ... 3-5 79
COMPLEAT ... 3-4 82-83
CONE ... 3-4 92
DOT ... 3-5 75-77
EVERGREEN ... 3-4 82-91
GMC ... 3-4 81
GROOVE ... 5-10 63
HI (2100 series) ... 4-8 67
HI (2300 series) ... 3-5 76
HI COUNTRY (8000 series) ... 4-6 72-73
KARI ... 3-4 80
LOBO ... 3-4 82
MCA ... 3-4 79
MERCURY (71140 "Kiss a Me Baby") ... 20-30 57
MERCURY (71249 "Dream World") ... 20-30 57
MERCURY (77190 "Cry Baby Cry") ... 20-30 57
PINK ... 10-20 59-60
RENAY ... 5-10 62-65
RENEGADE ... 2-4 91
STARLINE ... 8-12 62
Picture Sleeves
CONE ... 3-4 92
LPs: 10/12-inch
ABC ... 5-10 78-79
ABC/DOT ... 8-10 75-77
ACTION ... 30-40 70
CINNAMON ... 8-10 73-74
MCA ... 5-8 80s
HI ... 8-10 76
Also see WOLFPACK

FELTS, Narvel / Red Sovine / Mel Tillis
LPs: 10/12-inch
POWER PAK ... 5-10 77
Also see SOVINE, Red
Also see TILLIS, Mel

FELTS, Narvel, & Sharon Vaughn C&W '74
Singles: 7-inch
CINNAMON ... 3-5 74
Also see FELTS, Narvel
Also see VAUGHN, Sharon

FEMALE BEATLES
Singles: 7-inch
20TH FOX ... 10-20 64

FEMALE BODY INSPECTORS
Singles: 12-inch
W.B. ... 4-6 86
Singles: 7-inch
W.B. ... 3-4 86

FEMININE COMPLEX
Singles: 7-inch
ATHENA ... 3-5 3-6
LPs: 10/12-inch
ATHENA ... 15-20 69

FEMME FATALE LP '89
LPs: 10/12-inch
MCA ... 5-8 89

FENCEMEN
Singles: 7-inch
LIBERTY (55509 "Bach N' Roll") ... 10-20 62
LIBERTY (55535 "Sunday Stranger") ... 10-20 63
Member: David Gates.
Also see GATES, David

FENDER, Freddy C&W/P&R/LP '75
(Baldemar Huerta)
Singles: 7-inch
ABC ... 3-4 76-79
ABC/DOT ... 4-6 75-77
ARV INT'L ... 4-8 75
ARGO ... 10-15 60
DISCOS DOMINANTE ... 5-10
DUNCAN ... 10-20 59
FALCON ... 5-10
GRT ... 4-8 75-76
GOLDBAND ... 5-10 60s
GOLDIES 45 ... 3-5 74
IDEAL ... 10-20 60s
IMPERIAL ... 8-12 60
MCA ... 3-4 82
NORCO ... 5-10 63-65
STARFLITE ... 3-4 79-80
W.B. ... 3-4 83
LPs: 10/12-inch
ABC ... 5-10 78-79
ABC/DOT ... 8-10 75-77
ACCORD ... 5-10 81
BIRCHMONT ... 5-10 80s
BRYLEN ... 5-10 82
51 WEST ... 5-10 79
GRT ... 8-10 75
PICCADILLY ... 5-10 81
PICKWICK ... 5-10 70s
POWER PAK ... 5-10 75-80s
STARFLITE ... 5-10 80
SUFFOLK MARKETING ... 5-10 76
Also see HUERTA, Baldemar
Also see WAYNE, Scotty

FENDER, Freddy, & Tommy McLain
LPs: 10/12-inch
CRAZY CAJUN ... 5-10 78
Also see FENDER, Freddy
Also see McLAIN, Tommy

FENDER, Freddy, & Sir Douglas
LPs: 10/12-inch
CRAZY CAJUN ... 5-10 78
Also see SAHM, Doug

FENDER, Freddy, & Noel Vill
Singles: 7-inch
NORCO (107 "The Magic of Love") 5-10 65
SOCK-O (101 "The Magic of Love") ... 10-20 65
(First issue.)
Also see FENDER, Freddy

FENDER BENDERS
Singles: 7-inch
CHICORY ... 5-10 66
VERMILLION ... 10-20 64

FENDERBENDERS
(Sherwin Linton & Fenderbenders)
Singles: 7-inch
AGAR ... 8-12 60s
RAKO ... 10-20 62
LPs:10/12-inch
RISE ... 5-10 65
SMIGER ... 8-12 66
Also see LINTON, Sherwin
Also see TREBUS, Bob, & Fender Benders

FENDER IV
Singles: 7-inch
IMPERIAL ... 10-20 64-66
Member: Randy Holden.
Also see HOLDEN, Randy

FENDER GUITAR SLIM
Singles: 7-inch
ENRICA ... 8-12 61

FENDERMEN P&R/C&W '60
Singles: 78 rpm
APEX (76683 "Mule Skinner Blues") ... 100-150 60
(Canadian.)
Singles: 7-inch
APEX (21802 "Mule Skinner Blues") ... 10-15 60s
(Canadian. Reissue)
APEX (76683 "Mule Skinner Blues") ... 20-30 60
(Canadian.)
COLLECTABLES ... 3-4 80s
CUCA (1003 "Mule Skinner Blues") ... 50-100 60
DAB (102 "Rain Drop") ... 15-25 58
ERA ... 3-5 72
ERIC ... 3-5 70s
KOALA ... 3-5
SOMA ... 10-15 60-61
LPs: 10/12-inch
POINT (213 "Mule Skinner Blues") ... 200-300 61
SOMA (1240 "Mule Skinner Blues") ... 800-1200 60
(Solid black vinyl.)
SOMA (1240 "Mule Skinner Blues") ... 1000-1500 60
(Vinyl is clearer and appears colored when held to a light.)
Members: Phil Humphrey; Jimmy Sundquist; John Hauer; Denny Dale Gudin.
Also see DALE, Denny, & Honeymoons
Also see HUMPHREY, Phil
Also see MULESKINNERS
Also see SUN, Jimmy, & Radiants

FENIANS
Singles: 7-inch
DEE GEE ... 4-8 65

FENNELLY, Michael
Singles: 7-inch
EPIC ... 3-5 74
MERCURY ... 3-5 75
LPs: 10/12-inch
EPIC ... 8-10 74
MERCURY ... 8-10 75
Also see CRABBY APPLETON
Also see MILLENNIUM

FENNEMAN, George
Singles: 7-inch
CAPITOL ("The Capitol Record") ... 8-12 50s
(Excerpts of late '50s Capitol product. No selection number used. Promotional issue only.)

FENSTER, Zoot C&W '75
(Jack Barlow)
Singles: 7-inch
ANTIQUE (23 "Who Wrote That Word") ... 3-5 70s
ANTIQUE (1408 "Man on Page 602") ... 5-10 75
Also see BARLOW, Jack

FENTION & Castle Rockers: see ROBINSON, Fention

FENTON, Shane, & Fentones
Singles: 7-inch
LAURIE ... 4-8 65
20TH FOX ... 4-8 63

FENWAYS
Singles: 7-inch
BEV MAR (401 "Nothing to Offer You") ... 15-25 64
BEV MAR (402 "Be Careful Little Girl") ... 15-25 64
BLUE CAT (116 "Hard Road Ahead") ... 10-15 65
CHESS (1901 "Nothing to Offer You") ... 10-15 64
CO & CE ... 5-10 66-67
IMPERIAL (66082 "The Walk") ... 8-12 64
RICKY "C" (106 "Nothing to Offer You") ... 150-200 64
ROULETTE (4573 "Nothing to Offer You") ... 15-25 64
Members: Sonny DiNuzio; Joey Covington.
Also see JEFFERSON AIRPLANE
Also see RACKET SQUAD
Also see VIBRA-SONICS

FENWYCK
Singles: 7-inch
CHALLENGE (59369 "I'm Spinning") ... 15-25 67
PROGRESSIVE SOUNDS (103 "Lye") ... 15-25 67
Also see RAYE, Jerry / Fenwyck

FERG, Johnny
Singles: 7-inch
DECCA ... 5-10 58

FERGERSON, Charlie (Little Jazz)
Singles: 78 rpm
TIMELY (1008 "Low Lights") ... 8-12 54
Singles: 7-inch
TIMELY (1008 "Low Lights") ... 15-25 54

FERGERSON, Dottie
(With Five Stars; Dottie Ferguson)
Singles: 78 rpm
KERNEL (003 "Slow Burn")....25-50 57
MERCURY....15-25 57
Singles: 7-inch
KERNEL (003 "Slow Burn")....25-50 57
MERCURY (71129 "Slow Burn")....15-25 57
MERCURY (71182 "Darling It's Wonderful")....10-15 57

FERGUSON, Dottie: see FERGERSON, Dottie

FERGUSON, H-Bomb
(With His Mad Lads; Robert Ferguson)
Singles: 78 rpm
ARC (9001 "Little Tiger")....50-75 57
SAVOY....20-30 52
Singles: 7-inch
ARC (9001 "Little Tiger")....50-75 57
ATLAS (1250 "I Love My Baby")....10-20 61
BIG BANG (103 "No-Sackie Sack")....15-25 58
FEDERAL (12399 "Boo Hoo")....10-20 61
FEDERAL (12411 "I'm So Lonely") 10-20 61
SAVOY (830 "Slowly Goin' Crazy")....25-50 52
SAVOY (836 "Bookie's Blues")....25-50 52
SAVOY (848 "Preachin' the Blues")....25-50 52
Also see PARKER, Jack "The Bear"

FERGUSON, H-Bomb / Escos / Mascots
LPs: 10/12-inch
AUDIO LAB (1567 "A Little Rock & Roll for Everybody")....800-1200 61
Also see ESCOS
Also see MASCOTS

FERGUSON, Helena P&R/R&B '67
Singles: 7-inch
COMPASS....4-8 67-68

FERGUSON, Jay P&R '77
Singles: 7-inch
ASYLUM....3-5 77-79
CAPITOL....3-4 82
LPs: 10/12-inch
ASYLUM....8-10 76-79
CAPITOL....5-10 80-82
Also see JO JO GUNNE
Also see SPIRIT

FERGUSON, Johnny P&R '60
Singles: 7-inch
DECCA (30731 "Last Date")....10-20 58
MGM (12789 "Afterglow")....10-20 59
MGM (12855 "Angela Jones")....10-20 60
MGM (12905 "I Understand")....10-20 60
MGM (12960 "Valley of Love")....10-20 60

FERGUSON, Junior
Singles: 7-inch
SUMMIT....5-10 59

FERGUSON, Leon
Singles: 7-inch
GALAXY (737 "Stokin' ")....10-20 65

FERGUSON, Maynard LP '73
(Maynard Ferguson Sextet)
Singles: 78 rpm
CAPITOL....3-8 50-51
EMARCY....3-8 54
MERCURY....3-8 55
Singles: 12-inch
COLUMBIA....4-6 79
Singles: 7-inch
CAMEO....3-5 63
CAPITOL....8-15 50-51
COLUMBIA....3-5 71-82
EMARCY....8-12 54
MAINSTREAM....3-5 71-72
MERCURY....8-12 55
ROULETTE....5-10 59-62
EPs: 7-inch
EMARCY....10-20 54-57
LPs: 10/12-inch
BETHLEHEM....5-10 78
CAMEO....15-25 63
COLUMBIA....5-10 71-82
EMARCY (400 series)....5-10 76
EMARCY (1000 series)....5-10 81
EMARCY (26017 "Hollywood Party")....75-125 54
(10-inch LP.)
EMARCY (26024 "Dimensions")..75-125 54
(10-inch LP.)
EMARCY (36000 series)....20-40 55-57
ENTERPRISE....8-12 68
MAINSTREAM (300 series)....6-12 71-72
MAINSTREAM (6000 series)....15-25 64
(Stereo.)
MAINSTREAM (56000 series)....10-20 64
(Monaural.)
MERCURY....20-30 60
MOSAIC (156 "Complete Roulette Recordings of Maynard Ferguson")....200-225 90s
(Boxed 14 audiophile LP set. 5000 made.)
PALTO ALTO....5-10 83
PRESTIGE....8-12 69
ROULETTE....10-30 58-72
SKYLARK (17 "Great Jazz Solos")....50-75 53
TRIP....5-10 74
WYNCOTE....5-10 60s
Also see AXIDENTALS
Also see BASIE, Count, & Maynard Ferguson
Also see CARPENTER, Ike
Also see KENTON, Stan
Also see MANN, Herbie / Maynard Ferguson

FERGUSON, Maynard, & Chris Connor
Singles: 7-inch
ATLANTIC....4-6 61
LPs: 10/12-inch
ATLANTIC (8049 "Double Exposure")....25-35 61
(Monaural.)
ATLANTIC (SD-8049 "Double Exposure")....35-45 61
(Stereo.)
ROULETTE (52068 "Two's Company")....40-60 58
Also see CONNOR, Chris
Also see FERGUSON, Maynard

FERGUSON, Sheila
Singles: 7-inch
LANDA (706 "How Did That Happen")....15-25 65
SWAN (4217 "Don't")....20-30 65
SWAN (4225 "And in Return")....15-25 65
SWAN (4234 "Heartbroken Memories")....20-30 65

FERGUSON, Troy
Singles: 7-inch
SHARP....4-8

FERGUSON, DAVIS & JONES
Singles: 7-inch
EPIC (10592 "I Think I'm Gonna Cry")....10-15 70

FERGUSON FOUR
Singles: 7-inch
TITAN....5-10 60

FERGUSON TRACTOR
Singles: 7-inch
MTA....4-8

FERKO STRING BAND P&R '48
Singles: 78 rpm
MEDIA....3-5 55
PALDA....4-6 48
SAVOY....3-5 55
Singles: 7-inch
ARGO....3-5 63
FERKO....4-8 50s
MEDIA....4-8 55
SAVOY....4-8 55
LPs: 10/12-inch
ABC-PAR....10-15 63
ALSHIRE....4-6 76
REGENT....12-20 56-59
SURE....6-12 65-73

FERN, Bill
Singles: 7-inch
SPORT....8-12 61

FERN, Mike
Singles: 7-inch
DEMO (4 "A Bomb Pop")....100-150

FERNANDEZ, Pepe
Singles: 7-inch
20TH FOX....4-8 67

FERNANDO 100% MARVELOUS & Half Nelson
Singles: 7-inch
NLT....3-4 87

FERRA, Tina
Singles: 7-inch
LIMELIGHT....8-10 64

FERRANTE & TEICHER P&R/R&B '60
Singles: 78 rpm
COLUMBIA....3-5 53
ENTRE....3-6 53
Singles: 7-inch
ABC-PAR....3-6 58-62
COLUMBIA....4-8 53
ENTRE....5-10 53
U.A.....3-5 59-79
Picture Sleeves
U.A. (Except 231 to 300)....4-8 63-69
U.A. (231 to 300)....5-10 60-61
EPs: 7-inch
ABC-PAR....4-8 58-60
MGM....10-20 54
U.A.....4-8 69
LPs: 10/12-inch
ABC....5-10 73-76
ABC-PAR....8-15 58-66
AVANT GARDE....5-10
COLUMBIA....8-15 55-73
DORAL....10-20
(Promotional mail-order issue, from Doral cigarettes.)
GUEST STAR....4-8 64
HARMONY....5-10 64-70
LIBERTY....5-10 81-84
MGM....20-40 54
METRO....5-10 66
MISTLETOE....4-6 75
SUNSET....5-10 70-71
WESTMINSTER....12-20 55-58
UNART....5-10 67
U.A.....5-15 60-80
URANIA....4-8
Members: Arthur Ferrante; Louis Teicher.
Also see BELL, Vincent

FERRARA
LPs: 10/12-inch
MIDSONG INT'L....5-10 79

FERRARA, Peter, & Bobby Pickett
Singles: 7-inch
PIZZERIA....5-10
POLYDOR....3-5 76
Also see PICKETT, Bobby

FERRARI R&B '82
Singles: 12-inch
SUGAR HILL....4-6 82
Singles: 7-inch
SUGAR HILL....3-4 82

FERRARI, C.W. C&W '88
Singles: 7-inch
SOUTHERN SOUND....3-4 88

FERRARI'S OF CANADA
Singles: 7-inch
DCP....15-25 64

FERRELL, Eddie
Singles: 7-inch
ASTA....10-20 61

FERRELL, Fancy
Singles: 7-inch
CENTAURI....5-10

FERRELL, Garland
Singles: 7-inch
BRW....3-6 69

FERRELL, Lee
LPs: 10/12-inch
TMS....5-10 79

FERRELL FAMILY
Singles: 7-inch
CENTAUR....10-20 59

FERRER, Jose P&R '54
(With the Ferrers)
Singles: 78 rpm
COLUMBIA....3-5 54-55
Singles: 7-inch
COLUMBIA....4-8 54-55
EPIC....3-5 68
RCA....4-6 60
Picture Sleeves
RCA....4-6 60
LPs: 10/12-inch
MGM....8-12 62-65
Also see CLOONEY, Rosemary, & Jose Ferrer

FERRIER, Al
(With His Boppin' Billies)
Singles: 78 rpm
EXCELLO (2105 "Hey! Baby!")....30-50 57
GOLDBAND....15-25 56-57
Singles: 7-inch
EXCELLO (2105 "Hey! Baby!")....30-50 57
GOLDBAND....15-25 56-61
ROCKO (502 "Kiss Me Baby")....35-45
ZYNN (510 "Chisholm Trail Rock")....15-25 58
LPs: 10/12-inch
JIN....5-10 90

FERRIER, Gerry
Singles: 7-inch
ACADEMY....8-10 64

FERRIS & WHEELS
Singles: 7-inch
BAMBI (801 "Chop Chop")....20-30 61
U.A. (458 "Moments Like This")....35-40 62

FERRIS WHEEL
Singles: 7-inch
PHILIPS....5-8 68
LPs: 10/12-inch
UNI....10-12 70

FERRO, Talya
Singles: 7-inch
MGM....4-6 68

FERROS
Singles: 7-inch
HI-Q (5008 "Come Home My Love")....20-25 58

FERRY, Bryan P&R/LP '76
Singles: 12-inch
W.B.....4-6 85
Singles: 7-inch
ATLANTIC....3-4 74-79
REPRISE....3-4 88
W.B.....3-4 85
Picture Sleeves
REPRISE....3-4 88
LPs: 10/12-inch
ATLANTIC....10-12 72-78
REPRISE....5-10 87
W.B.....5-10 85
Also see TANGERINE DREAM / Jon Anderson / Bryan Ferry

FERRY, Bryan, & Roxy Music LP '89
LPs: 10/12-inch
REPRISE....5-10 89
Also see FERRY, Bryan
Also see ROXY MUSIC

FESTIVAL P&R/LP '80
Singles: 7-inch
RSO....3-4 79
LPs: 10/12-inch
RSO....5-10 79

FESTIVALS R&B '70
Singles: 7-inch
BLUE ROCK....3-6 69
COLOSSUS....3-5 70-71
GORDY....3-5 72
SMASH....4-8 66-68

FETCHIN' BONES LP '89
LPs: 10/12-inch
CAPITOL....5-8 89

FETCHIT, Stepin': see STEPIN' FETCHIT

FEVA, Sandra R&B '79
Singles: 7-inch
CATAWBA....3-4 87
KRISMA....3-4 86
VENTURE....3-5 79-81
LPs: 10/12-inch
VENTURE....5-10 81

FEVER R&B '79
Singles: 12-inch
FANTASY....4-6 79-82
JDC....4-6 85
Singles: 7-inch
FANTASY....3-4 79-82
LPs: 10/12-inch
FANTASY....5-10 79-80
Member: Clydene Jackson.

FEVER TREE P&R/LP '68
Singles: 7-inch
AMPEX....10-20 70
MAINSTREAM....5-10 67
UNI (Except 55060)....10-20 68-69
UNI (55060 "San Francisco Girls")...8-12 68
(Black vinyl.)
UNI (55060 "San Francisco Girls")..20-40 68
(Colored vinyl. Promotional issue only.)
LPs: 10/12-inch
AMPEX....12-20 70
MCA....8-10 76
UNI (73024 "Fever Tree")....20-30 68
UNI (73040 "Another Time, Another Place")....15-25 68
UNI (73067 "Creation")....15-25 70
Members: Dennis Keller; Rob Landes; E.E. Wolfe; John Tuttle. Session: Frank Davis.
Also see TRAVEL AGENCY

FEW
Singles: 7-inch
MAESTRO (4977 "Escape")....10-20 67

FIATS
Singles: 7-inch
UNIVERSAL....4-8 64

FIBONACCIS
Singles: 12-inch
ENIGMA....4-6 84
Singles: 7-inch
ENIGMA....3-4 84

FIDELITONES
Singles: 7-inch
ALADDIN (3442 "The Game of Love")....40-60 58

FIDELITONES
Singles: 7-inch
MARLO (1518 "Playboy")....25-35 63

FIDELITYS P&R '58
(With Sammy Lowe & Orchestra)
Singles: 7-inch
BATON (252 "The Things I Love")....10-15 58
BATON (256 "Memories of You")...10-15 58
BATON (261 "My Greatest Thrill")....10-15 58
SIR (271 "Marie")....10-20 59
SIR (274 "Only to You")....10-20 59
SIR (276 "Where in the World")....10-20 60
SIR (277 "Wishing Star")....20-30 60
Member: Buddy Miles.
Also see LOWE, Sammy, Orchestra
Also see MILES, Buddy

FI-DELLS
Singles: 7-inch
IMPERIAL (5780 "What Is Love")..25-35 61

FI-DELLS
Singles: 7-inch
WARNER RECORDS (1014 "No Other Love")....10-20 58
LPs: 10/12-inch
JU-PAR....8-10 77

FI-DELLS
Singles: 7-inch
BARDO (529 "Why Do I Love You")....200-300 50s

FI DELLS QUARTET
("With Rhythm Accompaniment")
Singles: 7-inch
INDIA (2663 "Hey Senorita")....150-250 61

FIDELS
Singles: 7-inch
DORE (761 "I'm Givin' You Notice")....15-25 66
MAVERICK....4-8 69

FI-DELS
Singles: 7-inch
KEYMEN (106 "Try a Little Harder")....25-50 60s
UNITED SOUTHERN....10-15

FIDELTONES
Singles: 7-inch
ALADDIN (3442 "Game of Love")....100-200 58
POOP DECK (101 "For Your Love")....75-125 60

FIEDLER, Arthur: see BOSTON POPS ORCHESTRA

FIELD, Claudia
Singles: 7-inch
ROULETTE....3-5 77
Picture Sleeves
ROULETTE....3-5 77

FIELD, Elysian: see ELYSIAN FIELD

FIELD, Jerry
(With the Lawyers; with Philadelphia Lawyers)
Singles: 7-inch
PARKWAY (801 "The Trial")....15-25 59

FIELD, Sally P&R/LP '67
Singles: 7-inch
COLGEMS....4-6 67-68
Picture Sleeves
COLGEMS....4-8 67
LPs: 10/12-inch
COLGEMS....10-20 67

FIELDS
Singles: 7-inch
UNI....3-6 69
LPs: 10/12-inch
UNI....10-12 69

FIELDS, Alvin
LPs: 10/12-inch
A&M....5-10 82

FIELDS, Bobby
Singles: 78 rpm
ACE (504 "Pity Poor Me")....15-25 55
Singles: 7-inch
ACE (504 "Pity Poor Me")....30-50 55

FIELDS, Ernie P&R/R&B '59
(With His Orchestra)
Singles: 78 rpm
FRISCO (3 "Thursday Evening Blues")....15-20 47
GOTHAM (273 "Butch's Blues")....10-20 52
Singles: 7-inch
CAPITOL....5-10 64
GOTHAM (273 "Butch's Blues")....20-30 52
HIGHLAND....8-12
JAMIE (1102 "Annie's Rock")....10-15 58
RENDEZVOUS....10-15 59-62
LPs: 10/12-inch
RENDEZVOUS (1309 "In the Mood")....40-60 60
Also see WALLS, Ann, & Ernie Fields

FIELDS, Irving, Orchestra
(Irving Fields Trio)
Singles: 78 rpm
ABC-PAR....3-4 56
FALCON....3-4 55
FIESTA....3-5 55
RCA....3-5 49
TICO....3-4 56
Singles: 7-inch
ABC-PAR....3-5 56
FALCON....3-5 55
FIESTA....3-5 55
POCKET....4-8
RCA....3-5 49
TICO....3-5 56
EPs: 7-inch
KING....10-15
LPs: 10/12-inch
ABC-PAR....15-25 56
CAMDEN....10-20 57
EVEREST....15-20 61
RCA (38 "Fields Favorites")....20-40 50
(10-inch LP.)

FIELDS, Kim R&B '84
Singles: 12-inch
CRITIQUE....4-6 84
Singles: 7-inch
CRITIQUE....3-4 84

FIELDS, Lee R&B '86
Singles: 7-inch
ANGLE 3....3-5 79
BDA....3-4 86
NORFOLK....3-5
SOUND PLUS....3-5

FIELDS, Lilly
Singles: 7-inch
SPECTRUM (101 "How You Give Me Love")....10-15 60s

FIELDS, Linda
Singles: 7-inch
BRUNSWICK....5-10 59
GOLD EAGLE....4-8 61
TOP RANK....5-10 60

FIELDS, Richard
Singles: 7-inch
CORDON (101 "Devoted")....50-75

FIELDS, Richard "Dimples" R&B/LP '81
(Dimples)
Singles: 12-inch
RCA....4-6 84-85
Singles: 7-inch
BOARDWALK....3-4 81-83
COLUMBIA....3-4 87
RCA....3-4 84-85
LPs: 10/12-inch
BOARDWALK....5-10 81-82
RCA....5-10 84

FIELDS, Venetta
Singles: 7-inch
SONY....4-8 63
Also see TURNER, Nate, & Mirettes

FIELDS, W.C. LP '69
LPs: 10/12-inch
AMERICAN....5-10 75
BLUE THUMB....8-12
COLUMBIA....6-10 69-77
DECCA....8-12 68
HARMONY....6-10 70
HUDSON....15-25 60
JAY (2001 "Temperance Lecture")....15-25 50s
(10-inch LP.)

MARK '56 (571 "Original Radio Broadcasts")....10-15 73
MARK '56 (571 "Nostalgia")....70-90 78
(Picture disc. Two variations made, one with full photo of Fields standing, other shows only his upper body. Original Radio Broadcasts.)

FIELDS, W.C., & Mae West
LPs: 10/12-inch
HARMONY....6-10 70
PROSCENIUM....15-20 60
Also see FIELDS, W.C.
Also see WEST, Mae

FIELDS, W.C., Memorial Electric String Band
Singles: 7-inch
HBR....4-8 66
MERCURY....5-10 66

FIELDS-MADERA ORCHESTRA
Singles: 7-inch
CATALINA....5-10

FIENDS
Singles: 7-inch
DANNY D....5-10 65
GNP....4-8 65
Member: Billy Barnett.
Also see BARNETT, Billy

FIESTA R&B '78
Singles: 7-inch
ARISTA....3-5 78

FIESTA FOLK SINGERS
Singles: 7-inch
FAN (99 "Fisherman's Fiesta")....4-8 60s
Members: Phil Richards; Joe O'Hara.

FIESTAS P&R/R&B '59
Singles: 7-inch
CHIMNEYVILLE (10216 "Tina, the Disco Queen")....10-15 77
CHIMNEYVILLE (10221 "Is That Long Enough for You")....10-15 78
COLLECTABLES....3-4 80s
OLD TOWN (1062 "So Fine")....35-50 59
(With piano intro. Identification number is "ZTSP 29364.")
OLD TOWN (1062 "So Fine")....15-25 59
(No piano intro. Identification number is "920.")
OLD TOWN (1069 "Our Anniversary")....15-25 59
OLD TOWN (1074 "Good News")....15-25 59
OLD TOWN (1080 "Dollar Bill")....15-25 60
OLD TOWN (1090 "So Nice")....15-25 60
OLD TOWN (1104 "Mr. Dillon, Mr. Dillon")....15-25 61
OLD TOWN (1111 "Hobo's Prayer")....35-50 59-60
OLD TOWN (1122 "Broken Heart")....15-25 62
OLD TOWN (1127 "I Feel Good All Over")....15-25 62
OLD TOWN (1134 "The Gypsy Said")....10-20 63
OLD TOWN (1140 "The Party's Over)....10-20 63
OLD TOWN (1143 "Foolish Dreamer)....10-20 63
OLD TOWN (1166 "All That's Good")....50-75 64
OLD TOWN (1178 "Think Smart")....50-75 65
OLD TOWN (1189 "Ain't She Sweet")....10-15 65
RESPECT....3-5 75
STRAND (25046 "Julie")....20-30 61
VIGOR (712 "So Fine")....3-5 74
Members: Tom Bullock; Eddie Morris; Sam Ingalls; Preston Lane.
Also see ROBERT & JOHNNY / Fiestas

FIESTAS
Singles: 7-inch
COTILLION (44117 "Broken Heart")....15-25 71

FIFTH AMENDMENT
Singles: 7-inch
NEW YORK SOUND....3-5 71

FIFTH ANGEL LP '88
Soundsheet
EVATONE (103537)....4-6 88
(No song titles used.)
LPs: 10/12-inch
EPIC....5-8 88

FIFTH AVE. R&B '87
Singles: 7-inch
PARADISE....3-4 87

FIFTH AVENUE BAND
Singles: 7-inch
REPRISE....3-6 69
LPs: 10/12-inch
REPRISE....10-15 69
Member: Peter Gallaway.

5TH AVENUE BUSSES
Singles: 7-inch
20TH FOX....4-8 66
LPs: 10/12-inch
MOVIETOWN....15-20 66

FIFTH DIMENSION P&R/LP '67
(5th Dimension)
Singles: 7-inch
ABC....3-5 75-76
ARISTA....3-5 75
BELL....3-5 70-74
MOTOWN....3-4 78-79
SOUL CITY....4-8 66-70
SUTRA....3-4 83
Picture Sleeves
SOUL CITY....4-8 67-69
LPs: 10/12-inch
ABC....8-10 75
ARISTA....8-10 75
BELL....8-12 70-74
KORY....8-10 77
MOTOWN....5-10 78-79
RHINO....5-10 86
SOUL CITY....10-15 67-70
Members: Marilyn McCoo; Billy Davis Jr; Lamonte McLemore; Florence LaRue; Ron Townson; Danny Miller Beard; Terri Bryant; Michel Bell.
Also see DAVIS, Billy, Jr.
Also see GOLDENROD
Also see HI-FIs
Also see INTERVALS
Also see MAMAS & PAPAS / Association / Fifth Dimension
Also see McCOO, Marilyn, & Billy Davis Jr.

FIFTH ESTATE P&R '67
Singles: 7-inch
JUBILEE....5-10 67-69
RED BIRD (064 "Love Is All a Game")....10-15 66
LPs: 10/12-inch
JUBILEE (JGM-8005 "Ding Dong the Witch Is Dead")....20-30 67
(Monaural.)
JUBILEE (JGS-8005 "Ding Dong the Witch Is Dead")....25-35 67
(Stereo.)
Members: Wayne Wadhams; Rick Engler; Doug Ferrara; Bill Shute; Ken Evans.
Also see D MEN

FIFTH GENERATION
Singles: 7-inch
FONE BOOTH (1001 "If I See Her")....5-10
IGL (155 "Carolyn")....15-25 68

FIFTH ORDER
Singles: 7-inch
COUNTERPART (2571 "Goin' Too Far")....15-25 66
COUNTERPART (2595 "Thousand Devils")....15-25 67
DIAMOND (212 "Goin' Too Far")....10-15 66
LAURIE (3404 "Thousand Devils")....5-10 67

FIFTY FOOT HOSE
(50 Foot Hose)
Singles: 7-inch
GET HIP....3-5 90
Picture Sleeves
GET HIP....3-5 90
LPs: 10/12-inch
LIMELIGHT (86062 "Cauldron")....50-100 68
Members: Nancy Blossom; Larry Evans; David Blossom.

50 GUITARS OF TOMMY GARRETT LP '61
Singles: 7-inch
LIBERTY....3-5 66-68
LPs: 10/12-inch
LIBERTY....5-15 61-71
MUSICOR....5-10 76-78
U.A.....5-8 73
Also see GARRETT, Tommy

52ND STREET D&D '83
Singles: 12-inch
A&M....4-6 83
MCA....4-6 85-87
PROFILE....4-6 84
Singles: 7-inch
MCA....3-4 85-86
LPs: 10/12-inch
MCA....5-10 86

FIG LEAF FIVE
Singles: 7-inch
DELTONE (5027 "Always Be Mine")....10-15 63

FIG, Lincoln: see LINCOLN FIG

FIGURES ON THE BEACH D&D '84
Singles: 12-inch
METRO AMERICAN....4-6 84
Singles: 7-inch
SIRE....3-4 89
Picture Sleeves
SIRE....3-4 89

FILE 13 D&D '84
Singles: 12-inch
PROFILE....4-6 84

FILET OF SOUL
Singles: 7-inch
MERCURY....10-20 60s

FILET OF SOUND
Singles: 7-inch
DYNAMIC SOUND....10-20 69
FILET of SOUND....3-5 77
ZAP....8-12 70
EPs: 7-inch
ZAP....5-10 77
LP: 10/12-inch
FILET of SOUND....8-12 77
MONIQUID SOUND....10-15 70
Also see ATTILA & HUNS
Also see PEACE, Mike

FILETS OF SOUL
Singles: 7-inch
SAVOY (1630 "C'mon Let's Dance")....10-20 68
LPs: 10/12-inch
SQUID (4857 "Freedom")....75-100 68

FILLER, Marty
Singles: 7-inch
TAURUS....5-10 62

FILLINGANE, H.
Singles: 7-inch
TRIBUTE....3-5 77

FINA, Jack
Singles: 78 rpm
MERCURY/SAV-WAY (5047 "Rhapsody in Blue")....100-150 47
(Picture disc. Promotional issue only.)
Singles: 7-inch
MGM....5-10 50s
LPs: 10/12-inch
MERCURY (20084 "Jack Fina")....20-40 55
(10-inch LP.)

FINAL APPROACH
Singles: 7-inch
GLEN ("Come Love Me Too")....10-20
(Selection number not known.)

FINAL ASSAULT
Singles
AZRA (26 "Final Assault")....15-20 87
(Promotional only, logo-shaped picture disc. 100 made)
AZRA (26 "Final Assault")....8-12 87
(Promotional only, scroll-shaped picture disc. 500 made)

FINCH
Singles: 7-inch
MONTAGE....5-10 70s

FINCHLEY BOYS
LPs: 10/12-inch
GOLDEN THROAT (200-19 "Everlasting Tribute")....150-200 72
Members: George Faver; J. Michael Powers.

FINDERS KEEPERS
Singles: 7-inch
CHALLENGE....10-15 66-67
FONTANA....8-12 68

FINE YOUNG CANNIBALS P&R/LP '86
Singles: 12-inch
I.R.S.....4-6 86-89
Singles: 7-inch
I.R.S.....3-4 86-90
Picture Sleeves
I.R.S.....3-4 86-89
LPs: 10/12-inch
I.R.S.....5-10 86-90
Members: Roland Gift; Danny Cox; David Steele.
Also see ENGLISH BEAT

FINESSE & SYNQUIS
LPs: 10/12-inch
MCA....5-8 88

FINGER LICKIN' GOOD
Singles: 7-inch
SOUND PATTERNS (90 "Bless You")....10-20 60s

FINGERPRINTS
LPs: 10/12-inch
TWIN/TONES....5-10

FINGERPRINTZ
LPs: 10/12-inch
VIRGIN....5-10 79-80

FINGERS
LPs: 10/12-inch
RCA....5-10 79

FINGERS, Rollie
Singles
AMERICAN AUDIOGRAPHICS ("Milwaukee Spells Relief")....10-15 80s
(Square postcard picture disc. No selection number used.)

FINGUS, Digney
Singles: 7-inch
COLUMBIA....3-4 85

FINISHED TOUCH R&B '78
Singles: 7-inch
MOTOWN....3-5 78
LPs: 10/12-inch
MOTOWN....5-10 78
Members: Harold Johnson; Kenny Stover; Mike Sutton; Brenda Sutton; Michael McGloiry.
Also see DEVASTATING AFFAIR
Also see SUTTON, Mike & Brenda

FINK MUNCX
Singles: 7-inch
PRISM (1907 "Coffee, Tea or Me")....5-10

FINKY FUZZ
Singles: 7-inch
EPIC....5-10 68

FINN, Lee
Singles: 7-inch
WESTPORT....15-25 58

FINN, Mickey
(With the Blue Men)
Singles: 7-inch
CHATTAHOOCHEE....8-10 65
WORLD ARTISTS....8-10 65

FINN, Tim LP '83
Singles: 7-inch
A&M....3-4 83
LPs: 10/12-inch
A&M....5-10 83
Also see SPLIT ENZ

FINN & SHARKS
Singles: 12-inch
PARK PLACE (1001 "Finn and the Sharks")....40-50 81
REBEL....15-20 81
Singles: 7-inch
HME....4-8 85
Picture Sleeves
HME....4-8 85
Also see BROADCASTERS

FINNEGAN, Larry P&R '62
Singles: 7-inch
CORAL....4-8 62
OLD TOWN....5-10 62-63
RIC....8-10 64

FINNEGAN, Mike
Singles: 7-inch
COLUMBIA....3-4 78
W.B.....3-5 76

FINNEGAN, Mike, & Surfs
Singles: 7-inch
PARKWAY....15-20 66

FINNEY, Albert LP '77
Singles: 7-inch
MOTOWN....3-4 77
LPs: 10/12-inch
MOTOWN....5-10 77

FINNEY, Chick
Singles: 7-inch
CHICK'S....4-8 64

FINNEY, Maury C&W '76
Singles: 7-inch
SOUNDWAVES....3-5 75-80
LPs: 10/12-inch
SOUNDWAVES....5-10 76-78
Also see CHARMS

FINNEY – MO
Singles: 7-inch
JELLO-JIM (102 "My Baby's Gone")....15-25 63
ROULETTE (4518 "My Baby's Gone")....8-12 63

FINNICUM
Singles: 7-inch
RUFF....10-20 66

FINNIGAN, Mike, & Serfs
Singles: 7-inch
R&S....5-10

FINNIGAN & WOOD
LPs: 10/12-inch
BLUE THUMB....10-12 72

FINSTER, Howard
LPs: 10/12-inch
FOLKWAYS....10-20

FINSTER, Werbley
(Jose Feliciano)
Singles: 7-inch
RCA....5-10 69
Also see FELICIANO, Jose

FIONA P&R/LP '85
(Fiona Flanagan; with Kip Winger)
Singles: 7-inch
ATLANTIC....3-4 84-89
Picture Sleeves
ATLANTIC....3-4 84-89
LPs: 10/12-inch
ATLANTIC....5-10 84-89

FIORILLO, Elisa P&R/LP '88
Singles: 7-inch
CHRYSALIS....3-4 88-90
Picture Sleeves
CHRYSALIS....3-4 88
LPs: 10/12-inch
CHRYSALIS....5-8 88
Also see JELLYBEAN & Elisa Fiorillo

FIRE
Singles: 7-inch
LONDON....5-10 67

FIRE
LPs: 10/12-inch
ABC....10-12 69

FIRE
Singles: 7-inch
BAY TOWN....4-8

FIRE & BRIMSTONE
Singles: 7-inch
DECCA....5-10 68

FIRE & ICE
(Fire & Ice Ltd.)
Singles: 7-inch
CAPITOL....3-6 69
LPs: 10/12-inch
CAPITOL....12-15 66

FIRE & ICE
LPs: 10/12-inch
BUTTERFLY....5-10 79

FIRE & RAIN P&R '73
Singles: 7-inch
MERCURY....3-5 73
LPs: 10/12-inch
MERCURY....8-10 73

FIRE ESCAPE
Singles: 7-inch
GNP (384 "Blood Beat")....5-10 67
LPs: 10/12-inch
GNP (2034 "Psychotic Reaction")....25-35 67

FIRE INC. P&R '84
Singles: 7-inch
MCA....3-4 84
Picture Sleeves
MCA....3-4 84

FIRE over GIBRALTAR
Singles: 7-inch
KIM (103 "Epitath of Tomorrow")....75-100 65
(500 made.)

FIRE TOWN
LPs: 10/12-inch
ATLANTIC....5-10 87-89
Members: Butch Vig; Phil Davis; Doug Erikson; Tom LaVarda.

FIREBALLET LP '75
Singles: 7-inch
PASSPORT....3-5 75-76
LPs: 10/12-inch
PASSPORT....8-10 75-76

FIREBALLS P&R '59
Singles: 7-inch
ASTRA (1021 "Torquay")....4-8 66
ATCO....4-8 67-70
DOT....4-8 63-67
HAMILTON (5036 "Tuff-A-Nuff")....10-20 63
KAPP (248 "Fireball")....75-100 59
QUALITY (048 "Quite a Party")....10-15 61
(Canadian.)
TOP RANK (2008 "Torquay")....10-15 59
TOP RANK (2026 "Bulldog")....10-15 59
(Monaural.)
TOP RANK (2026-ST "Bulldog")....15-25 59
(Stereo.)
TOP RANK (2038 "Foot Patter")....10-15 60
(Monaural.)
TOP RANK (2038-ST "Foot Patter")....15-25 60
(Stereo.)
TOP RANK (2054 "Vaquero")....10-15 61
TOP RANK (2081 "Sweet Talk")....10-15 61
TOP RANK (3003 "Rik-A-Tik")....10-15 61
WARWICK (630 "Rik-A-Tik")....8-10 61
WARWICK (644 "Quite a Party")....8-10 61
EPs: 7-inch
TOP RANK (1000 "The Fireballs")....50-75 60
LPs: 10/12-inch
ATCO....10-20 68-69
TOP RANK (324 "The Fireballs")....50-75 60
TOP RANK (343 "Vaquero")....50-75 60
(Monaural.)
TOP RANK (643 "Vaquero")....75-125 60
(Stereo.)
WARWICK (2042 "Here Are the Fireballs")....50-75 61
Members: Chuck Tharp; George Tomsco; Dan Trammell; Eric Budd; Stan Lark; Doug Roberts; Jimmy Gilmer; Keith McCormick.
Also see DALE, Dick / Surfaris / Fireballs
Also see GILMER, Jimmy
Also see GUITARS INC.
Also see LUPE
Also see PEBBLES & FIREBALLS
Also see ROBERTS, Doug, and Stu Mitchell
Also see STRING-A-LONGS
Also see TOMSCO, George

FIREBIRDS
Singles: 7-inch
DMD....4-8 64
EXCELLO....3-6 69
FENTON....8-12 59
SUPER K....4-8 68

FIREFALL P&R/LP '76
Singles: 7-inch
ATLANTIC....3-5 76-82
Picture Sleeves
ATLANTIC....3-5 78-79
LPs: 10/12-inch
ATLANTIC....5-10 76-83
Members: Rick Roberts; Jack Bartley; Larry Burnette; Mike Clarke; Scott Kirkpatrick; Dave Muse; Mark Andes; Peter Graves.
Also see ABBA / Spinners / Firefall / England Dan & John Ford Coley
Also see FLYING BURRITO BROTHERS
Also see MANILOW, Barry / Firefall
Also see ROBERTS, Rick
Also see SPIRIT

FIREFLIES P&R '59
Singles: 7-inch
CANADIAN AMERICAN (117 "Give All Your Love to Me")....15-25 60
ERIC....3-5 70s
HAMILTON....4-8 63
RIBBON (6901 "You Were Mine")....15-25 59
RIBBON (6904 "I Can't Say Goodbye")....15-25 59
RIBBON (6906 "My Girl")....15-25 60
TAURUS (355 "You Were Mine")....10-20 62
TAURUS (366 "My Prayer for You")....10-20 62
TAURAUS (376 "Could You Mean More")....10-20 62
LPs: 10/12-inch
TAURUS (1002 "You Were Mine")....100-150 61
(Monaural.)
TAURUS (1002 "You Were Mine")....250-350 61
(Stereo.)
Members: Ritchie Adams; Lee Reynolds; John Viscelli; Paul Giacolone.
Also see CASINOS / Fireflies

FIREFLY P&R/R&B '75
Singles: 7-inch
A&M....3-5 75

FIREFLY R&B '81

Singles: 7-inch

EMERGENCY 3-5 81

FIREFLYS

Singles: 7-inch

ROULETTE (4098 "The Crawl") 15-25 58

FIREHOUSE LP '91

LPs: 10/12-inch

EPIC 5-8 91

FIREMEN

Singles: 7-inch

LE CAM (13 "Jaywalk") 10-20 60s
LE CAM (951 "Louie's Theme") 10-20 62

FIRESIDE SINGERS

Singles: 7-inch

HERALD (582 "Darlin' Come Home") 10-20 63

FIRESIDERS

Singles: 7-inch

SWAN 10-15 61

FIRESIGN THEATRE LP '69

Singles: 7-inch

COLUMBIA (Except 34) 3-6 69
COLUMBIA (34 "This Side") 4-8 70
(Single-sided, promotional disc.)
RHINO (904 "Fighting Clowns") 6-12 80
(Picture disc.)
RHINO (904 "Fighting Clowns") 10-15 80
(Picture disc with 12-inch card.)

Picture Sleeves

COLUMBIA (34 "This Side") 5-10 70

LPs: 10/12-inch

BUTTERFLY 5-10 77
COLUMBIA 8-15 69-74
EPIC 5-10 74
MORWAY 5-8 85
RHINO 5-10 79-82
Members: Philip Proctor; Phil Austin; David Ossman; Peter Bergman.

FIRESTONE, Johnny

Singles: 7-inch

ELMONT (1003 "Is It Love") 150-250 58

FIREWORKS

LPs: 10/12-inch

MCA 5-10 82

FIRK, Backwards Sam

LPs: 10/12-inch

ADELPHI 8-10 74
Also see TOWNSEND, Henry, & Backwards Sam Firk

FIRM, The P&R/LP '85

Singles: 7-inch

ATLANTIC 3-4 85-86

Picture Sleeves

ATLANTIC 3-4 85-86

LPs: 10/12-inch

ATLANTIC 5-10 85-86
Members: Jimmy Page; Paul Rodgers; Tony Franklin; Chris Slade.
Also see AC/DC
Also see BAD COMPANY
Also see BLUE MURDER
Also see MANN, Manfred
Also see PAGE, Jimmy
Also see RODGERS, Paul

FIRST, Carl, & Showmen

Singles: 7-inch

LAWN (223 "I'm Still in Love with You") 20-25 63
Member: Carl "First" Falso (aka Kal Dee).
Also see SERMON
Also see SIR MEN

1ST CENTURY

Singles: 7-inch

CAPITOL 3-6 68

FIRST CHOICE P&R/R&B/LP '73

Singles: 12-inch

FIRST CHOICE 4-6 83
SALSOUL 4-6 84

Singles: 7-inch

GOLD MINE 3-5 77-79
PHILLY GROOVE 3-5 73-74
WAND 3-5 72
W.B. 3-5 76

LPs: 10/12-inch

GOLD MINE 5-10 77-80
KORY 8-10 77
PHILLY GROOVE 8-10 73-74
Members: Rochelle Fleming; Annette Guest; Joyce Jones; Wardell Piper.
Also see PIPER, Wardell

FIRST CIRCLE R&B '87

Singles: 7-inch

EMI AMERICA 3-4 87

FIRST CLASS R&B '74

Singles: 7-inch

ALL PLATINUM 3-5 76-77
EBONY SOUNDS 3-5 75
TODAY 3-5 74

LPs: 10/12-inch

ALL PLATINUM 5-10 76
PARK-WAY 5-10 80
SUGARHILL 5-10 81
Members: Harold Bell; Fred Marshall; Sylvester Redditt.

FIRST CLASS P&R '74

Singles: 7-inch

PRIVATE STOCK/UK 3-5 76
UK 3-5 74-75

LPs: 10/12-inch

UK 8-10 74

Members: Tony Burrows; John Carter; Charles Mills; Del John; Spencer James; Eddie Richards; Robin Shaw; Clive Barrett.
Also see BURROWS, Tony

FIRST CROW TO THE MOON

Singles: 7-inch

ROULETTE (4774 "The Sun Lights Up Shadows of Your Mind") 15-25 67

FIRST EDITION P&R/LP '68

Singles: 7-inch

REPRISE 4-8 67-68

LPs: 10/12-inch

INTERMEDIA/QUICKSILVER (5056 "The First Edition") 10-15 84
(Picture disc.)
REPRISE 12-25 67-68
Members: Kenny Rogers; Mike Settle; Thelma Lou Camacho; Terry Williams; Mickey Jones.
Also see CAMACHO, Thelma
Also see NEW CHRISTY MINSTRELS
Also see ROGERS, Kenny, & First Edition
Also see WILLIAMS, Terry

FIRST FAMILY R&B '74

Singles: 7-inch

POLYDOR 3-5 74

FIRST FIRE

LPs: 10/12-inch

TORTOISE INT'L 5-10 78

FIRST FOUR

Singles: 7-inch

CLARIDGE 4-8
STRATA 4-8 65

FIRST GARRISON

Singles: 7-inch

DAMION (6532 "Tell Me No Lies") 15-25 65
Also see DOWD, Larry, & Rockatones

FIRST GEAR

LPs: 10/12-inch

MYRRH 8-10 72

FIRST GRADE

Singles: 7-inch

FROG (767 "Please Come Back") 15-25 60s

FIRST LOVE R&B '80

Singles: 12-inch

CHYCAGO INT'L 4-6 82

Singles: 7-inch

CHYCAGO INT'L 3-4 82
CIM 3-4 83
DAKAR 3-4 80

LPs: 10/12-inch

CHYCAGO INT'L 5-10 82
Members: Yvonne Gage.
Also see GAGE, Yvonne

FIRST NATIONAL BAND

Singles: 7-inch

TENER 15-25

1ST NATIONAL BAND

Singles: 7-inch

MONUMENT 8-12 67

FIRST PLATOON

Singles: 7-inch

S.P.Q.R. (3303 "Ten Ways") 50-75 62

FISCHER, Bobby

Singles: 7-inch

DIAL 4-8 66-68
JAB 4-8 67

FISCHER, Lisa LP '91

LPs: 10/12-inch

ELEKTRA 5-8 91

FISCHER, Wild Man

LPs: 10/12-inch

BIZARRE (6332 "An Evening with Wild Man Fischer") 20-30 69
(With Frank Zappa & Mothers of Invention.)
RHINO 5-10 81
Also see MOTHERS of INVENTION

FISCHER & EPSTEIN

LPs: 10/12-inch

GREENE BOTTLE 8-10 72
Member: Jack Fischer; Bruce Epstein.
Also see EGG

FISCHER-Z

Singles: 7-inch

U.A. 3-4 79-80

LPs: 10/12-inch

U.A. 8-10 79-80

FISCHOFF, George P&R '74

(George Fischoff Keyboard Komplex; with the Peppers; with Luv Ens)

Singles: 7-inch

COLUMBIA 3-5 77
DRIVE 3-4 79
HERITAGE 3-4 81
P.I.P. 3-5 75
RANWOOD 3-5 76
REWARD 3-4 84
U.A. 3-5 72-74

FISHBONE LP '88

Singles: 7-inch

COLUMBIA 3-4 85

LPs: 10/12-inch

COLUMBIA 5-8 88-91

FISCHOFF, George C&W '79

Singles: 7-inch

DRIVE 3-5 79

FISHER, Al, & Lou Marks

LPs: 10/12-inch

CAMEO 12-15 64
SWAN (514 "It's a Beatle World") .. 15-25 64

FISHER, Bob

(With Joe Fisher & the Bonnevilles)

Singles: 7-inch

ESTRELLA 4-8 61

FISHER, Brien

Singles: 7-inch

SPANGLE (2001 "Fingertips") 50-100 59
U.A. (115 "It's Up to You") 40-60 58

FISHER, Chip

Singles: 7-inch

ADDISON 10-15 59
ESCO 5-10 59
RCA (7308 "Sugar Bowl Rock") 15-25 58
20TH FOX 5-10 60

LPs: 10/12-inch

RCA (LPM-1797 "Chipper at the Sugar Bowl") 20-30 58
(Monaural.)
RCA (LSP-1797 "Chipper at the Sugar Bowl") 30-40 58
(Stereo.)

FISHER, Eddie P&R '50

Singles: 78 rpm

RCA 5-10 50-57

Singles: 7-inch

ABC-PAR 5-10 61
DOT 4-8 65-66
MUSICOR 3-6 69
RCA (47-3000 thru 47-6000 series) 10-20 50-57
RCA (WP-3025 "Eddie Fisher Sings") 25-50 50s
(Boxed, four-disc set.)
RCA (7000 thru 9000 series) 5-15 57-68
RAMROD 5-10 60-63
7 ARTS 5-10 61
TRANS ATLAS 4-8 62

Picture Sleeves

RCA (5000 series) 15-25 53-55
RCA (6000 series) 10-15 55-57
RAMROD 8-12 60

EPs: 7-inch

RCA 10-20 51-58
RCA/COCA-COLA 10-20 50s

LPs: 10/12-inch

CAMDEN 6-10 63
CROWN 8-12
DOT 10-15 65-67
FAMOUS TWINSETS 8-12 74
HAMILTON 6-10 66
RCA (1024 thru 2504) 15-30 55-62
RCA (3025 thru 3231) 20-35 52-54
(10-inch LPs.)
RCA (3375 "Best of Eddie Fisher") 10-15 65
RCA (3700 & 3800 series) 10-20 66-67
RAMROD (1 "At the Winter Garden") 10-20 63
RAMROD (6001 "Scent of Mystery") 50-60 60
(Soundtrack. Monaural.)
RAMROD (6001 "Scent of Mystery") 75-85 60
(Soundtrack Stereo.)
Also see COMO, Perry, & Eddie Fisher

FISHER, Eddie / Vic Damone / Dick Haymes

LPs: 10/12-inch

ALMOR 10-15
Also see DAMONE, Vic
Also see HAYMES, Dick

FISHER, Eddie, & Debbie Reynolds

EPs: 7-inch

RCA (4018 "Bundle of Joy") 15-25 56
(Soundtrack.)

LPs: 10/12-inch

RCA (1399 "Bundle of Joy") 40-50 56
(Soundtrack.)
Also see FISHER, Eddie
Also see REYNOLDS, Debbie

FISHER, Eddie

Singles: 7-inch

STANG 3-5 77

LPs: 10/12-inch

STANG 5-10 77

FISHER, Fern

Singles: 7-inch

HI 5-10 59

FISHER, Gene, & Mystics

Singles: 7-inch

PLATEAU (101 "Remember, You're My Girl") 20-30 62

FISHER, Herb, Trio R&B '50

Singles: 78 rpm

MODERN 5-15 50

FISHER, Jerry

Singles: 7-inch

PROJECT 3 3-5
Also see BLOOD, SWEAT & TEARS

FISHER, Jesse

Singles: 7-inch

WAY OUT (Except 104) 8-12
WAY OUT (104 "You're Not Loving a Beginner") 10-20

FISHER, Johnny

Singles: 7-inch

PARK AVE (125 "Tan Dan") 15-20 63

FISHER, Lola

Singles: 7-inch

WARWICK 8-12 59

FISHER, Mary Ann P&R '61

Singles: 7-inch

FIRE 5-10 59-60
IMPERIAL 4-8 62
SEG-WAY 4-8 61

FISHER, Matthew

LPs: 10/12-inch

RCA 8-10 73
Also see PROCOL HARUM

FISHER, Miss Toni: see FISHER, Toni

FISHER, O'Brien

Singles: 7-inch

SPANGLE 8-12 57

FISHER, Sonny

Singles: 78 rpm

STARDAY 50-75 55

Singles: 7-inch

PEACOCK 5-8 67
STARDAY (179 "Rockin' Daddy") 50-100 55
STARDAY (190 "Sneaky Pete") ... 50-100 55
STARDAY (207 "Rockin' and a Rollin' ") 50-100 55
STARDAY (244 "Pink & Black") ... 50-100 56

FISHER, Tee Bee

Singles: 7-inch

JET STREAM 4-8 64

FISHER, Terry

(Terry Fischer)

Singles: 7-inch

DECCA 4-6 71
Also see CARNIVAL
Also see MURMAIDS

FISHER, Tommy

Singles: 7-inch

B&D 4-8 62

FISHER, Toni P&R '59

(Miss Toni Fisher)

Singles: 7-inch

BIG TOP 5-10 62
CAPITOL 4-8 67
COLLECTABLES 3-4 80s
COLUMBIA 5-10 61
ERA 3-5 72
SIGNET 5-10 59-64
SMASH 4-8 63

LPs: 10/12-inch

SIGNET (509 "The Big Hurt") 30-50 60

FISHER, Tricia Leigh P&R '90

Singles: 7-inch

ATCO 3-4 90

FISHER, Vigor

(With the Fisherman)

Singles: 7-inch

ANGIE 5-10 63
MALA 5-10 61-62

FISHER, Willie R&B '77

Singles: 7-inch

TIGRESS 3-5 77

FISHER BROTHERS

Singles: 7-inch

COLUMBIA 4-8 62
ERA 4-8 64

FIST

LPs: 10/12-inch

A&M 5-10 80-82

FIT R&B '88

Singles: 7-inch

A&M 3-4 88
Members: Vince Ebo; Chuck Gentry.
Also see SWEET INSPIRATIONS

FITE, Buddy

Singles: 12-inch

CYCLONE (6 "For Once in My Life") 5-10 69
(Labeled "The World's First 12-inch Single.")

Singles: 7-inch

CYCLONE 3-5 69-70

LPs: 10/12-inch

CYCLONE 6-10 69-70

FI-TONES

(Fi-Tones Quintette; Fi-Tone Featuring Lloyd Davis)

Singles: 78 rpm

ATLAS 25-50 55-56
OLD TOWN (1042 "My Heart") .. 100-200 57

Singles: 7-inch

ANGLE TONE (525 "You'll Be the Last") 50-75 58
ANGLE TONE (530 "What Am I Gonna Do") 40-60 58
ANGLE TONE (536 "Deep in My Heart") 30-50 59
ATLAS (1050 "Foolish Dreams") 200-300 55
(Atlas man logo at 11:00 on label. Reads "Atlas Record Company.")
ATLAS (1050 "Foolish Dreams") 50-75 55
(Atlas man logo at 9:00 on label. Reads "Atlas Records.")
ATLAS (1051 "It Wasn't a Lie") 50-75 55
ATLAS (1052 "I Call to You") 50-75 56
ATLAS (1055 "I Belong to You") 50-75 56
ATLAS (1056 "Waiting for Your Call") 50-75 56
OLD TOWN (1042 "My Heart") .. 300-500 57

LPs: 10/12-inch

RELIC 8-10
Members: Lloyd Davis; Gene Redd; Lowe Murray; Cecil Holmes; Ron Anderson.
Also see CAVERLIERS QUINTETTE
Also see FIVE CHIMES

FITONES

Singles: 7-inch

STROLL (101 "I Love You Judy") .. 15-25 59

FITZ & STARTZ

Singles: 7-inch

CAPITOL 8-12 65

FITZGERALD, Ella P&R '36

(With the Andy Love Quintet)

Singles: 78 rpm

DECCA (800 thru 3000 series) 10-15 36-41
DECCA (18000 thru 29000 series) ... 5-10 42-54
VERVE 3-5 54-57

Singles: 7-inch

CAPITOL 4-8 67-68
DECCA (27000 & 28000 series) 15-25 50-53
DECCA (29000 series) 10-20 54-56
DECCA (30000 series except 30405) 5-15 56-67
DECCA (30405 "Goody Goody") 15-25 57
PABLO 3-4 75
PRESTIGE 4-6 69
REPRISE 3-6 69-71
SALLE 4-6 68
VERVE (10000 series) 8-12 56-59
VERVE (10100 thru 10300 series, except 10340) 4-8 60-65
VERVE (10340 "Ringo Beat") 8-12 64

Picture Sleeves

VERVE 10-20 59-60

EPs: 7-inch

DECCA 15-30 50-58
VERVE 10-25 56-61

LPs: 10/12-inch

ATLANTIC 5-10 72
BAINBRIDGE 5-10 81
CAPITOL (2000 series) 8-15 67-68
CAPITOL (11000 series) 5-10 78
CAPITOL (16000 series) 4-6 82
COLUMBIA 5-12 73
CORAL 4-8 73
DECCA (156 "The Best of Ella Fitzgerald") 25-45 58
(Black label with silver print.)
DECCA (156 "The Best of Ella Fitzgerald") 15-20 65
(Black label with horizontal rainbow band.)
DECCA (4000 series) 10-20 61-67
DECCA (5084 "Souvenir Album") 75-125 49
(10-inch LP.)
DECCA (5300 "Gershwin Songs") 75-125 51
(10-inch LP.)
DECCA (8000 series) 20-40 55-59
EVEREST 5-10 73
MCA 5-10 76-82
MGM 5-10 70
MPS 5-10 72
METRO 10-15 65-66
OLYMPIC 5-10 74
PABLO 5-10 75-83
REPRISE 8-12 69-71
VERVE (29 "Ella Fitzgerald Sings the George & Ira Gershwin Songbook") 30-50 64
(Boxed, five-disc reissue of Verve 4029.)
VERVE (2500 & 2600 series) 5-10 76-82
(Reads "Manufactured By MGM Record Corp.," or mentions either Polydor or Polygram at bottom of label.)
VERVE (4001 thru 4009) 50-75 56
(Reads "Verve Records, Inc." at bottom of label.)
VERVE (4010 "Ella Fitzgerald Sings the Duke Ellington Song Book") 100-125 56
(Boxed, four-disc set.)
VERVE (4013 thru 4015) 30-50 57
(Reads "Verve Records, Inc." at bottom of label.)
VERVE (4019 "Ella Fitzgerald Sings the Irving Berlin Songbook") 30-50 58
VERVE (4020 thru 4028) 25-50 58-59
(Reads "Verve Records, Inc." at bottom of label.)
VERVE (4029 "Ella Fitzgerald Sings the George & Ira Gershwin Songbook") 50-100 59
(Boxed, five-disc set, containing individual LPs 4024 thru 4028.)
VERVE (4036 thru 4071) 10-20 59-66
VERVE (6000 series) 25-50 57-59
(Reads "Verve Records, Inc." at bottom of label.)
VERVE (6100 series) 15-25 60
(Reads "Verve Records, Inc." at bottom of label.)
VERVE (8200 series) 20-40 58
(Reads "Verve Records, Inc." at bottom of label.)
VERVE (64036 thru 64071) 15-30 59-66
VERVE (67000 & 68000 series) 8-15 67-73
VERVE (2610000 series) 20-30 83
VOCALION 6-10 67
Also see CAMPBELL, Glen / Lettermen / Ella Fitzgerald / Sandler & Young
Also see RIDDLE, Nelson

FITZGERALD, Ella, & Louis Armstrong R&B '46

Singles: 78 rpm

DECCA 3-6 53

EPs: 7-inch

VERVE 15-30 56

LPs: 10/12-inch

MFSL (248 "Ella & Louie Again") ... 25-30
METRO 5-10 67
..RVE (4003 "Ella & Louis") 50-100 56

VERVE (4006 "Ella & Louis Again")........50-100 56
VERVE (4011 "Porgy & Bess").......40-60 57
(Monaural.)
VERVE (6040 "Porgy & Bess").....50-100 57
(Stereo.)
VERVE (8811 "Ella & Louis")..........5-10 72
Also see ARMSTRONG, Louis

FITZGERALD, Ella, & Count Basie
LP '63

LPs: 10/12-inch

PABLO........5-10 79
VERVE........15-20 63
Also see BASIE, Count

FITZGERALD, Ella / Bill Doggett

Singles: 78 rpm

DECCA........3-5 53

Singles: 7-inch

DECCA........8-12 53

LPs: 10/12-inch

VERVE........15-25 62
Also see DOGGETT, Bill

FITZGERALD, Ella, & Duke Ellington

Singles: 7-inch

VERVE........4-6 66

LPs: 10/12-inch

VERVE........10-20 65-67
Also see ELLINGTON, Duke

FITZGERALD, Ella / Billie Holiday

LPs: 10/12-inch

MCA........5-10 76
VERVE (6022 "At Newport").........40-60 58
(Stereo.)
VERVE (8234 "At Newport").........30-50 58
(Monaural.)

FITZGERALD, Ella / Billie Holiday / Lena Horne

EPs: 7-inch

COLUMBIA (2531 "Ella, Lena & Billie")........25-45 56

LPs: 10/12-inch

COLUMBIA (2531 "Ella, Lena & Billie")........75-100 56
(10-inch LP.)
Also see HOLIDAY, Billie
Also see HORNE, Lena

FITZGERALD, Ella, & Ink Spots

Singles: 78 rpm

DECCA (18000 series)........4-8 44-45

EPs: 7-inch

DECCA (2040 "Ella Fitzgerald and the Ink Spots")........10-20 53
Also see INK SPOTS

FITZGERALD, Ella, & Antonio Carlos Jobim

LPs: 10/12-inch

PABLO........5-10 81
Also see JOBIM, Antonio Carlos

FITZGERALD, Ella, & Louis Jordan
R&B '46

Singles: 78 rpm

DECCA (23000 series)........4-8 46
Also see JORDAN, Louis

FITZGERALD, Ella, & Peggy Lee
LP '55

LPs: 10/12-inch

DECCA (8166 "Pete Kelly's Blues")........40-60 55
Also see LEE, Peggy

FITZGERALD, Ella, & Mills Brothers
P&R '37

Singles: 78 rpm

DECCA........4-8 37
Also see MILLS BROTHERS

FITZGERALD, Ella, & Oscar Peterson

LPs: 10/12-inch

PABLO........5-10 76
Also see PETERSON, Oscar

FITZGERALD, Ella / Teddy Wilson / Lena Horne

EPs: 7-inch

COLUMBIA (1672 "Floor Show")....10-20 56
Also see FITZGERALD, Ella
Also see HORNE, Lena
Also see WILSON, Teddy

FITZGERALD, Felder

Singles: 7-inch

PAULA (423 "Real CB Savage").......4-6 70s
Session: Dale Hawkins.
Also see HAWKINS, Dale

FITZHUGH, Sammy

Singles: 7-inch

ATCO........5-10 60
POPLAR........5-10 59

5, The

Singles: 7-inch

JB (106 "I'm No Good")........15-25

FIVE AMERICANS
P&R/LP '66

Singles: 7-inch

ABC-PAR (10686 "Love Love Love")........5-10 65
ABNAK (Except 109)........10-15 67-69
(Black vinyl.)
ABNAK (Except 109)........15-25 67-69
(Colored vinyl.)
ABNAK (109 "I See the Light")......15-25 65
(Black vinyl.)
ABNAK (109 "I See the Light").......15-25 65
(Colored vinyl.)
HBR........5-10 65-66
JETSTAR (104 "It's You Girl")........10-15 65
JETSTAR (105 "Slippin' & Slidin' ")........15-20 65
PHILCO/FORD (10 "Western Union")........10-20 67
("Hip-Pocket" flexi-disc.)

Picture Sleeves

ABNAK (125 "Stop Light")........10-15 67
ABNAK (126 "Guided Tour")........10-15 68
HBR (468 "Evol–Not Love")........10-20 66

LPs: 10/12-inch

ABNAK........20-30 67-68
HBR (8503 "I See the Light")........30-35 66
(Monaural.)
HBR (9503 "I See the Light")........35-40 66
(Stereo.)
Members: Michael Rabon; Jimmy Wright; John Durrill.
Also see PEDESTRIANS / Association / Five Americans / Soulblenders
Also see RABON, Michael

FIVE & DIME

Singles: 7-inch

LAURIE........4-8 68

5 ARCADES

Singles: 7-inch

ANTRELL (104 "Ruby Lee")........10-15 80s
(Red vinyl.)
SACTO (101 "Ruby Lee")........15-20 70s

FIVE ARROWS: see BASCOMB, Paul, & Five Arrows

FIVE BARS

Singles: 78 rpm

MONEY (224 "Stormy Weather")...30-50 57

Singles: 7-inch

MONEY (224 "Stormy Weather")...40-60 57

FIVE BELLS

Singles: 7-inch

CLOCK (1017 "It's You")........15-25 60

FIVE BELLS

Singles: 7-inch

STOLPER........5-8

FIVE BILLS
(With Orchestra)

Singles: 78 rpm

BRUNSWICK........100-200 53

Singles: 7-inch

BRUNSWICK (84002 "Can't Wait for Tomorrow")........200-400 53
BRUNSWICK (84004 "Till Dawn and Tomorrow")........200-400 53

FIVE BIRDS: see HEADEN, Willie

FIVE BLACKS

Singles: 7-inch

B&C (100 "Forever in Love")........25-50 61
(Previously issued as by Herman Willis.)

FIVE BLAZES

Singles: 78 rpm

ARISTOCRAT (201 "Dedicated to You")........15-25 47
ARISTOCRAT (202 "All My Geets Are Gone")........15-25 47

FIVE BLIND BOYS OF MONTANA / Sparktones

Singles: 7-inch

VINTAGE........3-6 72

FIVE BLOBS
P&R '58

Singles: 7-inch

COLUMBIA (41250 "The Blob")......15-20 58
JOY........10-15 59
Member: Bernie Nee (only member).

FIVE BLUE FLAMES

Singles: 78 rpm

COLUMBIA (39407 "My Love Has Gone")........100-200 51
OKEH (6818 "The Masquerade Is Over")........50-100 51
OKEH (6875 "Ida Red")........25-50 52
OKEH (6900 "Blue Boy")........25-50 52

Singles: 7-inch

COLUMBIA (39407 "My Love Has Gone")........350-400 51
OKEH (6818 "The Masquerade Is Over")........150-250 51
OKEH (6875 "Ida Red")........50-75 52
OKEH (6900 "Blue Boy")........50-75 52

FIVE BLUE NOTES

Singles: 78 rpm

SABRE (103 "My Gal Is Gone")..150-200 54
SABRE (108 "The Beat of Our Hearts")........150-200 54

Singles: 7-inch

ONDA (108 "My Special Prayer")...50-75 59
ONDA (888 "My Special Prayer")........100-125 58
(First issue.)
SABRE (103 "My Gal Is Gone")........300-500 53
(Black vinyl.)
SABRE (103 "My Gal Is Gone")........500-1000 53
(Red vinyl.)
SABRE (108 "The Beat of Our Hearts")........500-750 54
(White label.)
Members: Fleming Briscoe; Andy Magruder; Jackie Shedrick; Bob Stroud; Moise Vaughan; Louis Smalls.

FIVE BOB-O-LINKS

Singles: 78 rpm

OKEH ("Trying")........150-250 53
(Selection number not known. May have been a promotional only issue.)
Members: Gerald Fields; Charles Perry; Len Henry; Charles Johnston.
Also see RIVIERAS

FIVE BOPS

Singles: 7-inch

HAMILTON (50023 "Unforgotten Love")........15-25 59

FIVE BOROUGHS

Singles: 7-inch

AVENUE D (0015 "Sunday Kind of Love")........10-15 89
(Red vinyl. Reportedly 100 made.)
CLASSIC ARTISTS (119 "One Too Many Lies")........4-6 90
MONA (31866 "Recess in Heaven")...4-6 91
(Colored vinyl.)

EPs: 7-inch

TELE-MEDIA ("Don't Say Goodnight")........5-10
(No selection number used.)
Members: Frank Iovino; Dave Strum; Geno Radicello; Charlie Notobartolo; Bruce Goldie.

FIVE BREEZES

Singles: 78 rpm

BLUEBIRD (8590 "Sweet Louise")........40-50 40
BLUEBIRD (8614 "Return Gal O' Mine")........40-50 41
BLUEBIRD (8679 "What's the Matter with Love")........40-50 41
BLUEBIRD (8710 "Laundry Man") .40-50 41
Member: Willie Dixon.
Also see DIXON, Willie

FIVE BUCKS

Singles: 7-inch

AFTON (1701 "No Use in Trying") 15-25 66
USA (882 "Breath of Time")........5-10 67

FIVE BUCS

Singles: 7-inch

OMNIBUS (1001 "So Wrong").......20-30

FIVE BUDDS
(With Bert Keys Orchestra)

Singles: 78 rpm

RAMA........200-300 53

Singles: 7-inch

RAMA (1 "I Was Such a Fool")........750-1000 53
RAMA (2 "I Guess It's All Over Now")........750-1000 53

FIVE BY FIVE
P&R '68

Singles: 7-inch

PAULA........5-15 67-70

LPs: 10/12-inch

PAULA........15-20 69

FIVE Cs
(Five C's)

Singles: 78 rpm

UNITED........50-75 55

Singles: 7-inch

UNITED (172 "Tell Me")........150-250 54
(Black vinyl.)
UNITED (172 "Tell Me")........300-400 54
(Colored vinyl.)
UNITED (180 "My Heart's Got the Blues")........150-250 55
(Black vinyl.)
UNITED (180 "My Heart's Got the Blues")........300-400 55
(Colored vinyl.)

FIVE Cs

Singles: 7-inch

GOLDWAX........5-10 68

5 CAMPBELLS

Singles: 78 rpm

MUSIC CITY (794 "Hey Baby")....50-100 56

Singles: 7-inch

MUSIC CITY (794 "Hey Baby")..250-350 56

FIVE CANADIANS

Singles: 7-inch

DOMAR (1120 "Goodnight")........30-40 66
DOMAR (1121 "Never Alone")........30-40 66
DOMAR (1123 "Don't Tell Me")........30-40 66

FIVE CARDS STUD
(Five Card Stud)

Singles: 7-inch

RED BIRD (802 "Be-Bop-a-Lula")..10-15 66
SMASH (2080 "Beg Me")........10-15 67

FIVE CASHMERES
(V Cashmeres)

Singles: 7-inch

GOLDEN LEAF (108 "Walkin' Through the Jungle")........100-200 62

FIVE CATS

Singles: 78 rpm

RCA........10-15 54-55

Singles: 7-inch

RCA (6012 "Rockin' Chair")........20-30 54
RCA (6081 "I Was Wrong")........25-50 54

FIVE CHANCELLORS

Singles: 7-inch

PORT (5000 "Tell Me You Love Me")........50-75 58
(Also issued as by the Chancellors.)

FIVE CHANCES
(Featuring Johnny Jones; "Music by Julis Cain")

Singles: 78 rpm

BLUE LAKE (115 "All I Want")...100-150 55
CHANCE (1157 "I May Be Small")........300-400 54
FEDERAL (12303 "My Days Are Blue")........150-250 57
STATES (156 "Gloria")........200-300 56

Singles: 7-inch

ATOMIC (2494 "Make Love to Me")........8-12
BLUE LAKE (115 "All I Want")...500-750 55
(Black vinyl.)
BLUE LAKE (115 "All I Want")........750-1000 55
(Colored vinyl.)
CHANCE (1157 "I May Be Small")........750-1000 54
FEDERAL (12303 "My Days Are Blue")........400-500 57
PS (1510 "Is This Love")........200-300 61
STATES (156 "Gloria")........500-750 56
(Black vinyl.)
STATES (156 "Gloria")........750-1000 56
(Colored vinyl.)
Members: Johnny Jones; John Austell; Darnell Austell; Reggie Smith; Howard Pitman; Harold Jones.
Also see BLUENOTES / Five Echoes / Five Chances
Also see CULLENS, Tommy
Also see MAPLES

5 CHANELS
P&R '58
(Chanels)

Singles: 7-inch

DEB (500 "The Reason")........15-25 58
(Previously issued as by the Chanels.)
Also see CHANELS

FIVE CHAVIS BROTHERS

Singles: 7-inch

CORAL (62270 "Old Time Rock and Roll")........35-50 61
HEADLINE (1015 "Walk with Me Baby")........10-15 62

FIVE CHESTNUTS

Singles: 7-inch

ELGIN (003 "My Kind of Baby") 200-300 59
Also see BASKERVILLE, Hayes, & Five Chestnuts / Norveen Baskerville & Five Chestnuts

FIVE CHIMES

Singles: 78 rpm

BETTA........200-300
ROYAL ROOST........200-300 55

Singles: 7-inch

BETTA (2011 "Rosemarie")........500-600
ROYAL ROOST (577 "A Fool Was I")........500-600 55
Members: Gene Redd; Gary Morrison; Pat Gaston; John Murray; Arthur Crier.
Also see FI-TONES
Also see PRE-HISTORICS

FIVE CHORDS
("Featuring Johnny Jones")

Singles: 78 rpm

JAMIE (1110 "Don't Just Stand There")........50-75 58

Singles: 7-inch

JAMIE (1110 "Love Is Like Music")........35-55 58

FIVE CHORDS
(5 Chords)

Singles: 7-inch

CUCA (1031 "Red Wine")........30-50 61
MACON (104 "Sally")........15-25
SOMA (1151 "I Need Your Lovin' ")........10-20 60

LP: 10/12-inch

BOOM (4949 "Wild Are the Five Chords")........50-75 60s

FIVE CHUMS

Singles: 7-inch

BLENDA ("Give Me a Chance") 100-200
(Selection number not known.)
EXCELLO (2123 "High School Affair")........40-60 58

FIVE CLASSICS
("5 Classic's")

Singles: 7-inch

A (317 "My Imagination")........20-30 61
ARC (317 "My Imagination")........25-50 61
(First issue.)
MEDIEVAL (204 "Magic Star")......15-25 64
POVA (6142 "Love Me")........30-40 61
(First issued as by the Suburbans.)
RODE (101 "Magic Star")........100-200 63
Also see SUBURBANS

FIVE COOKIES

Singles: 7-inch

EVEREST........5-10 62

FIVE COUNTS

Singles: 7-inch

BRENT........8-12 63
VISTAR........4-8

FIVE CROWNS
(5 Crowns; with Orchestra)

Singles: 78 rpm

CARAVAN........15-25 55
OLD TOWN (790 "You Could Be My Love")........75-125 53
OLD TOWN (792 "Lullaby of the Bells")........100-200 53
RAINBOW........100-200 52-56
RIVIERA (990 "You Came to Me")........200-300 55
TRANS-WORLD........25-50 55

Singles: 7-inch

CARAVAN (15609 "I Can't Pretend")........50-100 55
OLD TOWN (790 "You Could Be My Love")........300-500 53
(Black vinyl.)
OLD TOWN (790 "You Could Be My Love")........500-1000 53
(Red vinyl.)
RAINBOW (179 "A Star")........300-500 52
(Black vinyl.)
RAINBOW (179 "A Star")........500-1000 52
(Red vinyl.)
RAINBOW (202 "Keep It a Secret")........350-550 53
RAINBOW (281 "I Was Wrong")........350-550 53
RAINBOW (335 "You Came to Me")........150-250 56
(Reissued the following year but credited to the Duvals.)
RIVIERA (990 "You Came to Me")........800-1200 55
TRANS-WORLD (717 "I Can't Pretend")........150-200 55
(First issue.)
Members: Wilbur Phar; Nicky Clark; John Clark; Jim "Papa" Clark; Dock Green; Jesse Facing; Ben E. King; William Bailey; Bernard Ward; Elsberry Hobbs.
Also see CADILLACS
Also see CROWNS
Also see DUVALS

FIVE CROWNS
(With Jimmy Wright & His Orchestra)

Singles: 78 rpm

GEE (1001 "God Bless You").......50-100 55
(Vocal.)
GEE (1001 "God Bless You")........20-40 55
(Instrumental.)

Singles: 7-inch

GEE (1001 "God Bless You").....150-200 55
(Vocal.)
GEE (1001 "God Bless You")........60-80 55
(Instrumental.)
Also see

FIVE CROWNS
(With the Chuck Danzie Orchestra)

Singles: 7-inch

DE'BESTH (1122 "Memories of Yesterday")........300-350 59
(Flip side number is 1121.)
DE'BESTH (1123 "I Want You") 300-350 59

FIVE CROWNS

Singles: 7-inch

FIVE-O (503 "Just a Part of Life")........15-25

FIVE CRYSTALS

Singles: 7-inch

KANE (25592 "Hey, Landlord")....50-100 59

5 CRYSTELS

Singles: 7-inch

DELCRO (827 "Path of Broken Hearts")........50-100 60
MUSIC CITY (821 "Path of Broken Hearts")........100-200 58

FIVE DAPPS
(With the Band of Joe Hunter)

Singles: 7-inch

BRAX (208 "Doo Whop a Do")...300-400 58

FIVE DEBONAIRES

Singles: 78 rpm

HERALD........100-150 57

Singles: 7-inch

HERALD (509 "Whispering Blues")........100-150 57

FIVE DELIGHTS

Singles: 7-inch

ABEL (228 "The Thought of Losing You")........250-350 59
NEWPORT (7002 "There'll Be No Goodbye")........100-200 58
UNART (2003 "There'll Be No Goodbye")........50-75 58

FIVE DIAMONDS

Singles: 78 rpm

TREAT........100-150 55

Singles: 7-inch

LOST NITE........4-8
TREAT (501 "The Ten Commandments of Love")........200-250 55

FIVE DIPPS

Singles: 78 rpm

ORIGINAL........100-150 54

Singles: 7-inch

ORIGINAL (1005 "Teach Me Tonight")........200-300 54

FIVE DIPS: see ALLEN TRIO

FIVE DISCS
(Mario & the Five Discs)

Singles: 7-inch

CALO (202 "Adios")........150-200 61
(Green label. Has double lines above and below hole.)
CALO (202 "Adios")........75-125 61
(Green label. Has single lines above and below hole.)
CALO (202 "Adios")........75-125 61
(White label.)
CANDLELITE........8-10 60s

CHEER (1000 "Never Let You Go") ...100-150 63
(White label. Promotional issue.)
CHEER (1000 "Never Let You Go") ...50-75 63
(Red label.)
CHEER (4002 "Never Let You Go") ...150-250 62
(White label. Promotional issue.)
CHEER (4002 "Never Let You Go") ...50-100 62
(Black label.)
COLLECTABLES ... 3-4 80s
CRYSTAL BALL ... 5-10 78
DOWNSTAIRS (1001 "Roses") ... 5-10
DWAIN (803 "Roses") ...300-400 59
(Credits: "Mario & the Five Discs.")
DWAIN (803 "Roses") ...250-300 59
(Credits: "Five Discs.")
DWAIN (6072 "Roses") ...2000-3000 59
EMGE (1004 "I Remember") ...150-200 58
LAURIE (3601 "Rock & Roll Revival") ... 8-12 71
MELLOMOOD (1002 "Roses") ...15-25 64
OUR OWN (001 "Zu Zu") ... 3-5 91
(Colored vinyl.)
PYRAMID (166 "Let's Fall in Love") .. 4-6
RUST (5027 "I Remember") ...15-25 63
VIK (0327 "I Remember") ...50-100 58
YALE (240 "When Love Comes Knocking") ...200-300 60
YALE (244 "Come on Baby") ...200-300 60

Picture Sleeves

CRYSTAL BALL ... 5-10
OUR OWN (001 "Zu Zu") ... 3-5 91

LPs: 10/12-inch

CRYSTAL BALL (119 "Unchained") ...10-15 80s
MAGIC CARPET (1002 "The Five Discs Sing Again") ...10-15 80
Members: Mario deAndrade; Andy Jackson; Paul Albano; Joe Barsalona; Charles DiBella; Frank Amone; Ed Pardocchi; Tony Basil; Bobby Stewart.
Also see ALLEN, Adrienne
Also see BOYFRIENDS
Also see DAWN
Also see GEE, Frankie
Also see IMPALAS
Also see LEE, Davey
Also see MARTIN, Steve
Also see STEWART, Bobby

FIVE DISCS / Devotions

Singles: 7-inch

ROBIN HOOD ... 3-5
Also see DEVOTIONS
Also see FIVE DISCS

FIVE DOLLAR SHOES

LPs: 10/12-inch

NEIGHBORHOOD ... 8-10 72

FIVE DOLLARS

Singles: 78 rpm

FORTUNE ...15-25 55-57

Singles: 7-inch

FORTUNE (821 "Harmony of Love") ...50-100 55
FORTUNE (826 "So Strange") ...50-100 56
FORTUNE (830 "I Will Wait") ...50-100 56
FORTUNE (833 "You Fool") ...40-60 57
FORTUNE (854 "That's the Way It Goes") ...25-50 60
Also see LITTLE EDDIE & Five Dollars
Also see WILLIAMS, Andre

FIVE DOTS

Singles: 78 rpm

DOT ...50-75 54
NOTE ...50-75 55

Singles: 7-inch

DOT (1204 "The Other Night") ...75-125 54
NOTE (1003 "I Just Love the Things She Do") ...200-300 55

FIVE DREAMERS

Singles: 78 rpm

PORT (5001 "Beverly") ...40-50 57

Singles: 7-inch

PORT (5001 "Beverly") ...40-50 57

FIVE DREAMS

Singles: 78 rpm

MERCURY ...35-50 57

Singles: 7-inch

MERCURY (71150 "You Are My Only") ...35-50 57

FIVE DUKES OF RHYTHM

(With Gene Moore & His Combo)

Singles: 78 rpm

FORTUNE ...50-75 54
RENDEZVOUS ...200-300 54

Singles: 7-inch

FORTUNE (812 "Soft, Sweet and Really Fine") ...100-200 54
RENDEZVOUS (812 "Soft, Sweet and Really Fine") ...1000-1500 54

FIVE DU-TONES — P&R/R&B '63

Singles: 7-inch

LOST NITE ... 4-8
ONE-DERFUL ... 5-10 63-65
Members: Andrew Butler; Frank McCurrey; Willie Guest; LeRoy Joyce; Andy Butler.
Also see SOUTH SHORE COMMISSION

FIVE ECHOES

(Five Echos)

Singles: 78 rpm

SABRE ...200-300 53-54
VEE JAY ...100-150 54-55

Singles: 7-inch

SABRE (102 "Lonely Mood") ...400-600 53
(Black vinyl.)
SABRE (102 "Lonely Mood") .. 1000-1500 53
(Red vinyl.)
SABRE (105 "So Lonesome") ...400-600 54
(Black vinyl.)
SABRE (105 "So Lonesome") ...1000-1500 54
(Red vinyl.)
VEE JAY (129 "Tell Me Baby") ..200-300 54
VEE JAY (156 "Fool's Prayer") ..150-250 55
Members: Johnny Taylor; Wally Spreegs.
Also see BLUENOTES / Five Echoes / Chances
Also see HUNT, Tommy
Also see SPRIGGS, Walter
Also see TAYLOR, Johnny

5 EMBERS

Singles: 78 rpm

GEM ...100-200 54

Singles: 7-inch

GEM (224 "Please Come Home") ...300-500 54

5 EMBERS

(Featuring Richard Brown; featuring Charles Brown)

Singles: 7-inch

ROYCE (0006 "I'm Free") ...300-400 60
X-BAT (1006 "I'm Free") ... 3-5 95
(Colored vinyl.)

Picture Sleeves

X-BAT (1006 "I'm Free") ... 3-5 95
Members: Richard Brown; Charles Brown; Raymond Johnson; Melvin Smith; Sonny Rates.
Also see BROWN, Charles

5 EMERALDS

(Five Emeralds)

Singles: 78 rpm

S-R-C ...200-300 54

Singles: 7-inch

S.R.C. (106 "I'll Beg") ...800-1200 53
(Credits "5 Emeralds." Blue label. Logo has dots between letters.)
S-R-C (106 "I'll Beg") ...750-1000 53
(Credits "Five Emeralds." Maroon label. Has hyphens between letters.)
S-R-C (107 "Darling") ...800-1200 54
Also see DOWNBEATS
Also see ELGINS

FIVE EMPREES — P&R '65

(Five Empressions)

Singles: 7-inch

FREEPORT ...5-10 65-66
GOLD STANDARD (262 "Little Miss Sad") ...10-20 60s
(Colored vinyl.)
SMASH ... 4-8 66

LPs: 10/12-inch

FREEPORT (3001 "The Five Emprees [Little Miss Sad]") ...35-45 65
(Monaural.)
FREEPORT (3001 "Little Miss Sad") ...20-30 66
(Reissue.)
FREEPORT (4001 "The Five Emprees [Little Miss Sad]") ...30-40 65
(Stereo.)
FREEPORT (4001 "Little Miss Sad") ...25-35 66
(Reissue.)
Also see FIVE EMPRESSIONS

FIVE EMPRESSIONS

(Five Emprees)

Singles: 7-inch

FREEPORT (1001 "Little Miss Sad") ...10-20 65
Also see FIVE EMPREES

FIVE ENCHANTERS

Singles: 7-inch

RPM (1009 "RnR ers Never Gather Moss") ...10-20 60
RPM (1010 "Who's Breaking Whose Heart Now") ...10-20 60

FIVE ENCORES

Singles: 78 rpm

RAMA ...10-20 55-56

Singles: 7-inch

RAMA (180 "Double Date") ...20-40 55
RAMA (185 "Quaker Ben") ...15-25 55
RAMA (187 "Dance with the Rock") ...20-40 56

FIVE FABULOUS DEMONS

Singles: 7-inch

KING (5761 "You Better Come Home") ...15-25 63

FIVE FASHIONS

Singles: 7-inch

CATAMOUNT (102 "Pennies from Heaven") ...10-15 65
CATAMOUNT (103 "Solitaire") ...10-15 65

FIVE FELLOWS

Singles: 7-inch

MELOCLASS ...5-10 60
Member: Richard House.

FIVE FINKS

Singles: 7-inch

BERTRAM INT'L (226 "Crying Guitar") ...15-25 64
Also see LAWRENCE, Bill, & Five Finks

FIVE FLEETS

Singles: 7-inch

FELSTED (8513 "I Been Crying") ..15-20 58
FELSTED (8522 "Slight Case of Love") ...20-25 58
SEVILLE ...10-15 61

FIVE FLIGHTS UP — P&R '70

Singles: 7-inch

T.A. ...3-5 70-71

5 FORTUNES

Singles: 7-inch

RANSOM (103 "You Are My Love") ...800-1200 58

FIVE G's

Singles: 7-inch

WASHINGTONIAN (200,042 "Forget Her") ...200-400 59

5 "GENTS"

Singles: 7-inch

CREST (51657 "I Never Told You") ...750-1000 58

FIVE GENTS

Singles: 7-inch

VEIKING (101 "Baby Doll") ...150-200

5 GLOW TONES

Singles: 7-inch

JAX (101 "At a Dance") ...25-50 58

FIVE GRANDS

Singles: 7-inch

BRUNSWICK (55059 "Kiss Me") ...20-30 58

FIVE GUYS

Singles: 7-inch

QUILL (1546 "You-Eff-Oh") ...5-10 66

FIVE GUYS FROM UNCLE

Singles: 7-inch

SWAN ...4-8 65

FIVE HEARTS

Singles: 78 rpm

FLAIR ...100-200 54

Singles: 7-inch

FLAIR (1026 "Please, Please Baby") ...300-400 54
Members: Cornell Gunter; Richard Berry; Young Jessie; Beverly Thompson; Tom Fox.
Also see FIVE HOLLYWOOD BLUEJAYS
Also see FLAIRS

FIVE HEARTS

Singles: 7-inch

ARCADE (107 "Unbelievable") ..150-250 59

FIVE HEARTS / Lord Luther & Esquires

Singles: 7-inch

MUSIC CITY (833 "Tell Ya What") ...100-150 60

FIVE HOLLYWOOD BLUEJAYS

Singles: 78 rpm

RECORDED in HOLLYWOOD ..200-300 52

Singles: 7-inch

RECORDED in HOLLYWOOD (162; "Put a Nickle in the Juke box") ...500-600 52
Members: Cornell Gunter; Richard Berry; Young Jessie; Beverly Thompson; Tom Fox.
Also see FIVE HEARTS
Also see HOLLYWOOD BLUEJAYS

FIVE HUNDREDS

Singles: 7-inch

MERCURY ...8-12 64

FIVE HUNGRY MEN

Singles: 7-inch

MELMAR (122 "Bustin' Rocks") ...15-25 64

FIVE Js

Singles: 7-inch

FULTON (2454 "My Darling") ...50-75 58

FIVE JADES

Singles: 7-inch

DUKE (188 "Without Your Love") ..25-35 58

FIVE JADES

(5 Jades)

Singles: 7-inch

KELWAY ...3-5 72
YOUR CHOICE ...5-10 65

LPs: 10/12-inch

GOLDEN ACAPPELLA ...8-10 80
RELIC ...8-10
Members: Manuel Hernandez; Spencer Jackson; Junior Roman; Dennis Cerrato; Ray Goodwin.

FIVE JADES / Playground

LPs: 10/12-inch

CLIFTON ...5-10 83
Also see FIVE JADES

FIVE JAYS

Singles: 7-inch

CHANT ...10-20 60s

FIVE JETS

Singles: 78 rpm

DELUXE ...50-75 53-54
FORTUNE (833 "Bacon Fat") ...50-75 57

Singles: 7-inch

DELUXE (6018 "I Am in Love") ...50-100 53
DELUXE (6053 "I'm Stuck") ...50-100 54
DELUXE (6058 "Tell Me You're Mine") ...100-125 54
DELUXE (6064 "Crazy Chickens") ...35-50 54
DELUXE (6071 "Down Slow") ...50-100 54
FORTUNE (833 "Bacon Fat") ...50-75 57
Members: Billy Davis; Joe Murphy; John Dorsey; Carl Stewart.
Also see THRILLERS

FIVE JETS

Singles: 7-inch

JEWEL ...10-15 64

FIVE JINKS

Singles: 78 rpm

BLUEBIRD (6857 "I'm Moaning All Day For You") ...40-60 37
BLUEBIRD (6905 "Cushion Foot") ...40-60 37
BLUEBIRD (6951 "Dirt-Dishing Daisy") ...40-60 37

5 JOHNSON BROTHERS

Singles: 7-inch

CARRIE ("Sleep with a Dream") ...30-40
(Selection number not known.)
FULTON (2455 "Sleep with a Dream") ...50-75 58
(First issue.)

FIVE KEEYS

Singles: 7-inch

BANGAR (661 "Run Around") ...25-35 60s
Also see RAVONS

FIVE KEYS — R&B '51

(Rudy West & the Five Keys; "Featuring Rudy West"; 5 Keys)

Singles: 78 rpm

ALADDIN (3085 "With a Broken Heart") ...100-200 51
ALADDIN (3099 "The Glory of Love") ...100-200 51
ALADDIN (3113 "It's Christmas Time") ...100-200 51
ALADDIN (3118 "Yes Sir, That's My Baby") ...100-200 52
ALADDIN (3127 "Red Sails in the Sunset") ...100-200 52
ALADDIN (3131 "Mistakes") ...100-200 52
ALADDIN (3136 "I Hadn't Anyone 'Til You") ...100-200 52
ALADDIN (3158 "I Cried for You") ...100-200 52
ALADDIN (3167 "Can't Keep from Crying") ...100-200 53
ALADDIN (3175 "There Ought to Be a Law") ...100-200 53
ALADDIN (3190 "These Foolish Things") ...100-200 53
ALADDIN (3204 "Teardrops in Your Eyes") ...100-200 53
ALADDIN (3214 "My Saddest Hour") ...100-200 53
ALADDIN (3228 "Someday Sweetheart") ...100-200 54
ALADDIN (3245 "Deep in My Heart") ...100-200 54
ALADDIN (3263 "My Love") ...100-200 55
ALADDIN (3312 "Story of Love") ...50-100 56
CAPITOL ...15-25 54-57
GROOVE (0031 "I'll Follow You") ...500-1000 51

Singles: 7-inch

ALADDIN (3099 "The Glory of Love") ...800-1200 51
ALADDIN (3113 "It's Christmas Time") ...800-1200 51
ALADDIN (3118 "Yes Sir, That's My Baby") ...800-1200 52
ALADDIN (3127 "Red Sails in the Sunset") ...800-1200 52
ALADDIN (3131 "Mistakes") ...800-1200 52
ALADDIN (3136 "I Hadn't Anyone 'Til You") ...800-1200 52
ALADDIN (3158 "I Cried for You") ...800-1200 52
ALADDIN (3167 "Can't Keep from Crying") ...500-1000 53
ALADDIN (3175 "There Ought to Be a Law") ...500-1000 53
ALADDIN (3190 "These Foolish Things") ...800-1200 53
ALADDIN (3204 "Teardrops in Your Eyes") ...500-1000 53
ALADDIN (3214 "My Saddest Hour") ...700-1000 53
(Flat blue label.)
ALADDIN (3214 "My Saddest Hour") ...500-750 53
(Glossy blue label.)
ALADDIN (3228 "Someday Sweetheart") ...500-1000 54
ALADDIN (3245 "Deep in My Heart") ...500-1000 54
ALADDIN (3263 "My Love") ...400-800 55
ALADDIN (3312 "Story of Love") ...400-800 56
CAPITOL (828 "Just for a Thrill") ...50-75 57
(Promotional issue only.)
CAPITOL (2945 "Ling Ting Tong") ...25-50 54
CAPITOL (3032 "Close Your Eyes") ...25-50 55
CAPITOL (3127 "The Verdict") ...25-50 55
CAPITOL (3185 "I Wish I'd Never Learned to Read") ...25-50 55
CAPITOL (3267 "Gee Whittakers") ...25-50 55
CAPITOL (3318 "What Goes On") ...25-50 56
CAPITOL (3392 "I Dreamt I Dwelt in Heaven") ...25-50 56
(Standard 45rpm hole.)
CAPITOL (3392 "I Dreamt I Dwelt in Heaven") ...50-75 56
(LP-size, 1/4-inch hole. Purple label.)
CAPITOL (3392 "I Dreamt I Dwelt in Heaven") ...50-75 56
(LP-size, 1/4-inch hole. White label. Promotional issue only.)
CAPITOL (3455 "Peace and Love") ...25-50 56
CAPITOL (3502 "Out of Sight, Out of Mind") ...25-50 56
CAPITOL (3597 "Wisdom of a Fool") ...25-50 56
CAPITOL (3660 "Let There Be You") ...25-50 57
CAPITOL (3710 "Four Walls") ...25-50 57
CAPITOL (3738 "This I Promise You") ...25-50 57
CAPITOL (3786 "Face of an Angel") ...20-40 57
CAPITOL (3830 "Do Anything") ...20-40 57
CAPITOL (3861 "From Me to You") ...20-40 58
CAPITOL (3948 "With All My Heart") ...20-40 58
CAPITOL (4009 "Handy Andy") ...20-40 58
CAPITOL (4092 "Our Great Love") ...20-40 58
CAPITOL (6000 series) ...10-15 64
CLASSIC ARTISTS (115 "I Want You for Christmas") ...4-6 89
GUSTO ...3-5
IMPERIAL (016 "The Glory of Love") ...5-10 62
INFERNO (4500 "No Matter") ...10-20 67
KEY (62 "Wisdom of a Fool") ...5-10
KEY (63 "The Verdict") ...5-10
KING (5221 "I Took Your Love for a Toy") ...25-50 59
KING (5273 "Dream On") ...15-25 59
KING (5302 "How Can I Forget You") ...15-25 59
KING (5330 "Rosetta") ...15-25 60
KING (5358 "I Didn't Know") ...15-25 60
KING (5398 "Valley of Love") ...15-25 60
KING (5446 "You Broke the Only Heart") ...15-25 61
KING (5496 "Stop Your Crying") ...15-25 61
KING (5877 "I Can't Escape from You") ...10-20 64
LANDMARK (101 "Goddess of Love") ...5-8 73
OWL ...3-5 73
SEG-WAY (1008 "Out of Sight Out of Mind") ...10-20 62
U.A. (0150 "Glory of Love") ...5-10 60s

EPs: 7-inch

CAPITOL (572 "The Five Keys") ...100-200 55
CAPITOL (828 "The Five Keys on Stage") ...250-400 57
(Pictures one group member's thumb in a phallic-like position.)
CAPITOL (828 "The Five Keys on Stage") ...100-200 57
(Reworked cover, with offending thumb removed from picture.)
CRYSTAL (101 "Five Keys") ...10-15

LPs: 10/12-inch

ALADDIN (806 "Best of the 5 Keys") ...2000-4000 56
(Maroon label. Bootlegs have the Score reissue cover art but using the Aladdin name and number. There is no original Aladdin LPs titled *On the Town*.)
CAPITOL (828 "The Five Keys on Stage") ...500-750 57
(In cover photo, group member on left is holding his right hand in a phallic-like position.)
CAPITOL (828 "The Five Keys on Stage") ...100-200 57
(Reworked cover, with offending hand removed from the picture.)
CAPITOL (1769 "The Fantastic Five Keys") ...100-200 62
(With "T" prefix.)
CAPITOL (1769 "The Fantastic Five Keys") ...8-12 77
(With "M" prefix.)
GREAT GROUP CLASSICS ...8-12 70s
HARLEM HITPARADE ...10-15 72
KING (688 "The Five Keys") ...200-400 60
KING (692 "Rhythm & Blues Hits: Past and Present") ...200-300 60
SCORE (4003 "On the Town") ...500-750 57
(Repackage of *Best of the 5 Keys*, Aladdin 806. See that listing for bootleg information.)
Members: Rudy West; Ripley Ingram; Maryland Pierce; Dickie Smith; Ray Loper; Bernie West; Ulysses Hicks; Thomas Threat.
Also see BELVIN, Jesse, & Five Keys / Feathers
Also see FANTASTIC FIVE KEYS
Also see TEAGARDEN, Jack
Also see SMITH, Dickie
Also see WEST, Rudy

FIVE KEYS / Ferlin Husky

EPs: 7-inch

CAPITOL (503 "Five Keys/Ferlin Husky") ...60-80 57
Also see FIVE KEYS
Also see HUSKY, Ferlin

FIVE KIDS

Singles: 78 rpm

MAXWELL (101 "Carolyn") ...300-500 55

Singles: 7-inch

MAXWELL (101 "Carolyn") ...2000-3000 55

FIVE KINGS

Singles: 78 rpm

MANOR (1061 "I Can't Get Up the Nerve to Miss You") ...25-50 47
MANOR (1062 "Meet Me at No Special Place") ...25-50 47
MANOR (1066 "Sincerely Yours") 25-50 47
Also see CHURCHILL, Savannah

FIVE KINGS
(With Band of Purvis Henson)
Singles: 7-inch
YVETTE (101 "Here Comes My Baby")....30-50 60

FIVE KINGS
Singles: 7-inch
COLUMBIA (43060 "Light Blub")....25-30 64

FIVE KNIGHTS
(With John Johnson's Invaders)
Singles: 7-inch
BUMP'S (1504 "Dark Was the Night")....20-30 61
MINIT (626 "Let Me In")....15-25 61
SPECIALTY....10-15 59
Also see TAYLOR, Tommy, & Five Knights

FIVE KNIGHTS
(With the Dukes)
Singles: 7-inch
TAU (104 "Take Me in Your Arms")....100-200 59

FIVE LARKS
(Larks)
Singles: 78 rpm
APOLLO (1177 "My Heart Cries for You")....50-100 51
Also see LARKS

FIVE LETTERS
Singles: 7-inch
IVY (102 "Your First Love")....150-250 58

FIVE LORDS
Singles: 7-inch
D&S (2078 "Oo-La-La")....200-300 60

FIVE LYRICS
Singles: 78 rpm
MUSIC CITY....100-200 56
Singles: 7-inch
MUSIC CITY (799 "I'm Traveling Light")....250-500 56

FIVE MAN ELECTRICAL BAND *P&R/LP '71*
Singles: 7-inch
CAPITOL.... 4-8 68-69
LION.... 3-5 72-73
LIONEL.... 3-5 71
MGM.... 4-8 70
POLYDOR.... 3-5 74
LPs: 10/12-inch
CAPITOL....15-20 69
LION....10-12 73
LIONEL....10-15 70-71
MGM....10-15 70
PICKWICK.... 5-10 70s
Member: Les Emmerson.
Also see EMMERSON, Les
Also see STACCATOS

FIVE MASKS
Singles: 7-inch
JAN (101 "Forever and a Day")....25-50 58
(Time is on left side of hole.)
JAN (101 "Forever and a Day")....20-40 58
(Time is on right side of hole.)
Members: Al Braggs; Cal Valentine.
Also see BRAGGS, Al "TNT"
Also see 5 NOTES

FIVE MASQUERADERS: see SCOTT, Seaphus, & Five Masqueraders

FIVE MASTERS & ORCHESTRA
Singles: 7-inch
BUMBLE BEE (502 "We Are Like One")....40-60 59
Also see SATINTONES

FIVE MOORE
Singles: 7-inch
PARROT....10-20 67

FIVE MORE
Singles: 7-inch
TONDY.... 5-10

5 NOTES
(With the Hamil-Tones; Five Notes)
Singles: 78 rpm
CHESS....25-50 55
JEN D....100-200 55
JOSIE....25-50 55
SPECIALTY....50-100 53
Singles: 7-inch
CHESS (1614 "Show Me the Way")....100-150 55
JEN D (4185 "You Are So Beautiful")....250-500 55
(Identification number shown since no selection number is used.)
JOSIE (784 "You Are So Beautiful")....50-75 55
SPECIALTY (461 "Thrill Me, Baby")....150-200 53
(Black vinyl.)
SPECIALTY (461 "Thrill Me, Baby")....300-500 53
(Red vinyl.)
Members: Al Braggs; Cal Valentine.
Also see BRAGGS, Al "TNT"
Also see FIVE MASKS

5 O'CLOCK NEWS
Singles: 7-inch
DYNAMO.... 3-6 68
MUSICOR.... 4-6 68

FIVE OF A KIND
Singles: 7-inch
SIDRA (9003 "The Other Side")....35-55
VANDAN (3668 "Never Again")....15-25 65

FIVE OF US
Singles: 7-inch
CURRENT (110 "Hey You")....10-15 66

FIVE OWLS
(With the Vulcan Orchestra)
Singles: 7-inch
VULCAN (1025 "Pleading to You")....200-300 55

FIVE PALMS
Singles: 78 rpm
STATES....20-30 57
Singles: 7-inch
STATES (163 "Little Girl of Mine")....25-50 57
Also see WILKINS, Artie, & Palms

FIVE PASTELS
Singles: 7-inch
DOME (249 "You're Just an Angel")....250-350 62

FIVE PEARLS
Singles: 78 rpm
ALADDIN....50-75 54
Singles: 7-inch
ALADDIN (3265 "Please Let Me Know")....100-150 54
Members: Howard Guyton; Derek Martin.
Also see GUY, Bobby
Also see MARTIN, Derek
Also see PEARLS

FIVE PENNIES
Singles: 78 rpm
SAVOY....10-20 56
Singles: 7-inch
SAVOY (1182 "Mr. Moon")....25-35 56
SAVOY (1190 "Mr. Heart Trembles")....25-35 56
Members: Benjamin Washington; James Myers; Herb Myers; Clifford Curry; Charles Holloway.
Also see BIG MILLER
Also see CURRY, Clifford

FIVE PLAYBOYS
(5 Playboys)
Singles: 78 rpm
DOT....15-25 57
FEE BEE....25-50 57
Singles: 7-inch
DOT (15605 "When We Were Young")....20-40 57
FEE BEE (213 "When We Were Young")....75-125 57
MERCURY (71269 "Why Be a Fool")....20-30 58
PETITE (504 "Mr. Echo")....50-100 58

FIVE PYRAMIDS
Singles: 7-inch
NILE (101 "It's Wonderful")....15-25

FIVE QUAILS
Singles: 78 rpm
MERCURY....25-50 57
Singles: 7-inch
MERCURY (71154 "Jungle Baby")....25-50 57

FIVE QUAILS
Singles: 7-inch
HARVEY (114 "Been a Long Time")....30-60 62
Member: Harvey Fuqua.
Also see HARVEY
Also see QUAILS

FIVE REASONS
Singles: 7-inch
CUB (9006 "Go to School")....30-50 58

FIVE RED CAPS *P&R/R&B/C&W '44*
(5 Red Caps)
Singles: 78 rpm
BEACON....15-25 43-45
GANNETT....15-25 43-45
JOE DAVIS....15-25 43-45
DAVIS....10-20 46
MGM....10-20 48
Members: Steve Gibson; Jim Springs; Romaine Brown; Dave Patillo; Emmett Matthews.
Also see GIBSON, Steve

FIVE ROGUES
Singles: 7-inch
RAZORBACK (127 "Tab Top")....10-20 65

FIVE ROSES
(With the Lil Walters Band)
Singles: 7-inch
CLIFTON.... 4-8 70s
NU KAT (100 "Romance in the Spring")....100-200 59

5 ROVERS
Singles: 78 rpm
MUSIC CITY....50-75 56
Singles: 7-inch
MUSIC CITY (798 "Down to the Sea")....100-200 56
Also see ROVERS

FIVE ROYALES *R&B '53*
("5" Royales; 5 Royals)
Singles: 78 rpm
APOLLO....50-75 51-55
KING....25-75 54-57
Singles: 7-inch
ABC-PAR (10348 "Catch That Teardrop")....10-15 62
ABC-PAR (10368 "I Want It Like That")....10-15 62
APOLLO (441 "Courage to Love")....75-125 52
(Black vinyl.)
APOLLO (441 "Courage to Love")....300-500 52
(Colored vinyl.)
APOLLO (443 "Baby Don't Do It")....75-125 52
(Black vinyl.)
APOLLO (443 "Baby Don't Do It")....300-500 52
(Red vinyl.)
APOLLO (446 "Help Me, Somebody")....75-125 53
APOLLO (448 "Laundromat Blues")....100-150 53
APOLLO (449 "I Want to Thank You")....75-125 53
APOLLO (452 "I Do")....50-100 54
APOLLO (454 "Cry Some More")....50-100 54
APOLLO (458 "What's That")....50-100 54
APOLLO (467 "With All Your Heart")....50-100 55
GUSTO....3-5 80s
HOME of the BLUES (112 "Please, Please, Please")....10-20 60
HOME of the BLUES (218 "If You Need Me")....10-20 61
HOME of the BLUES (232 "Not Going to Cry")....10-20 61
HOME of the BLUES (234 "They Don't Know")....10-20 61
HOME of the BLUES (257 "Catch That Teardrop")....10-20 62
KING (4740 "I'm Gonna Run It Down")....50-75 54
KING (4744 "Monkey Hips and Rice")....50-75 54
KING (4762 "One Mistake")....50-75 54
KING (4785 "Mohawk Squaw")....50-75 55
KING (4806 "When I Get Like This")....40-60 55
KING (4819 "Do Unto You")....40-60 55
KING (4830 "Someone Made You for Me")....40-60 55
KING (4869 "Right Around the Corner")....40-60 56
KING (4901 "I Could Love You")....40-60 56
KING (4952 "Come on and Save Me")....40-60 56
KING (4973 "Just As I Am")....40-60 56
KING (5032 "Tears of Joy")....25-50 57
KING (5053 "Think")....25-50 57
KING (5082 "Messin' Up")....25-50 57
KING (5098 "Dedicated to the One I Love")....25-50 57
KING (5131 "The Feeling Is Real")....20-30 58
KING (5141 "Double Or Nothing") 20-30 58
KING (5153 "Don't Let It Be in Vain")....20-30 58
KING (5162 "The Real Thing")....20-30 59
KING (5191 "Miracle of Love")....20-30 59
KING (5237 "Tell Me You Care")....20-30 59
KING (5266 "It Hurts Inside")....20-30 59
KING (5329 "I'm with You")....15-25 60
KING (5357 "Why")....15-25 60
KING (5453 "Dedicated to the One I Love")....15-25 61
KING (5756 "Dedicated to the One I Love")....10-20 63
KING (5892 "I Need You Lovin' Baby")....10-20 64
SMASH (1936 "I Like It Like That")....10-20 64
SMASH (1963 "Faith")....10-20 65
TODD (1086 "Doin' Everything")....10-20 63
TODD (1088 "Baby Don't Do It")....10-20 63
VEE JAY (412 "Much in Need")....10-20 61
VEE JAY (431 "Talk About My Woman")....10-20 61
WHITE CLIFFS (224 "I'm on the Right Road Now")....10-15 60s
LPs: 10/12-inch
APOLLO (488 "The Rockin' 5 Royales")....1500-2000 59
(Green cover.)
APOLLO (488 "The Rockin' 5 Royales")....800-1200 59
(Yellow cover.)
KING (580 "Dedicated to You")....350-500 58
KING (616 "The 5 Royales Sing for You")....200-300 59
KING (678 "The 5 Royales")....200-300 60
KING (955 "24 All Time Hits")....50-75 66
Members: Johnny Tanner; Eugene Tanner; Lowman Pauling; Clarence Pauling; Jim Moore; Otto Jeffries; Obadiah "Scoop" Carter; Eudell Graham; Bobby Burris.
Also see EL PAULING
Also see JOHN, Little Willie / 5 Royales / Earl (Connelly) King / Midnighters
Also see PAUL, Clarence
Also see ROYAL SONS QUINTET

FIVE SATANS
Singles: 7-inch
JCP (1014 "Here's to You")....10-20 64

FIVE SATINS *P&R/R&B '56*
(5 Satins; Featuring Fred Parris; "Featuring Dick Arnold")
Singles: 78 rpm
EMBER....50-100 56-57
REO (8463 "In the Still of the Nite")....50-75 56
(Canadian.)
STANDORD (100 "All Mine")....200-400 57
STANDORD (200 "In the Still of the Nite")....300-500 56
Singles: 7-inch
ABC....3-5 73
ANOTHER FIRST (104 "When Your Love Comes Along")....30-50 59
(First issue. Reissued on "First" label.)
CANDLELITE (411 "She's Gone") 15-25 63
CHANCELLOR (1110 "The Masquerade Is Over")....20-30 62
CHANCELLOR (1121 "Do You Remember")....20-30 62
COLLECTABLES....3-4 80s
CUB (9071 "Your Memory")....25-35 60
CUB (9077 "These Foolish Things")....25-35 60
CUB (9090 "Can I Come Over Tonight")....25-35 60
EMBER (1005 "In the Still of the Nite")....200-300 56
(Has Ember label pasted over Standord label. Can be identified by the identification number 6106 in the vinyl trail-off.)
EMBER (1005 "In the Still of the Nite")....25-50 56
EMBER (1005 "[I'll Remember] in the Still of the Nite")....100-200 56
(White label. Promotional issue.)
EMBER (1005 "[I'll Remember] in the Still of the Nite")....50-75 59
(Red label. Reads "Special Demand Release.")
EMBER (1005 "In the Still of the Nite")....25-35 60
(Multi-color "logs" label. May also have full title, with "I'll Remember.")
EMBER (1005 "[I'll Remember] in the Still of the Nite")....15-25 60s
(Black label. Some pressings read *In the Still of the Night*, instead of "Nite.")
EMBER (1008 "Wonderful Girl")....25-50 56
EMBER (1014 "Oh, Happy Day")....25-50 57
EMBER (1019 "To the Aisle")....25-50 57
EMBER (1025 "Our Anniversary") 25-50 57
(Red label.)
EMBER (1025 "Our Anniversary") 20-25 57
(Black label.)
EMBER (1028 "Million to One")....25-50 58
EMBER (1038 "A Night to Remember")....25-35 58
EMBER (1056 "Shadows")....25-35 58
EMBER (1061 "I'll Be Seeing You")....25-35 60
EMBER (1066 "Candlelight")....25-35 60
EMBER (1070 "Wishing Ring")....25-35 61
ELEKTRA (47411 "Memories of Days Gone By")....15-25 82
FIRST (104 "When Your Love Comes Along")....20-30 59
(First issued on "Another First.")
FLASHBACK....5-8 65
KIRSHNER....5-10 73-74
KLIK....5-10 73
LANA....5-8 64
LOST NITE....4-8
MUSICTONE (1108 "To the Aisle")....10-15 61
NIGHTRAIN....4-8 70
RCA....4-8 71-87
REGENCY ("In the Still of the Nite")....8-12 60s
(Canadian. Selection number not known.)
REO (8463 "In the Still of the Nite")....75-125 56
(Canadian.)
ROULETTE (4563 "You Can Count on Me")....8-12 64
SAMMY (103 "No One Knows")....50-75
S.G....3-5 90
STANDORD (100 "All Mine")....500-1000 56
(Red label. Copies on a maroon-brown label are unauthorized reissues.)
STANDORD (200 "In the Still of the Nite")....1000-2000 56
(Red label. Reads "Produced By Martin Kuegull.")
STANDORD (200 "In the Still of the Nite")....500-1000 56
(Red label.)
STANDORD (5051 "All Mine")....250-500 57
STANDORD (7107 "The Time")....4-6 90s
(Colored vinyl.)
TIME MACHINE....4-8 62
TIMES SQUARE (4 "All Mine")....20-30 63
(BLue vinyl.)
U.A. (368 "Til the End")....15-20 61
W.B. (5367 "Remember Me")....8-12 63
EPs: 7-inch
EMBER (100 "The Five Satins Sing")....50-100 60
(Red label.)
EMBER (100 "The Five Satins Sing")....25-50 61
(Black or multi-color label.)
EMBER (101 "The Five Satins Sing, Vol. 2")....50-100 60
(Red label.)
EMBER (101 "The Five Satins Sing, Vol. 2")....25-50 61
(Black or multi-color label.)
EMBER (102 "The Five Satins Sing, Vol. 3")....50-100 60
(Red label.)
EMBER (102 "The Five Satins Sing, Vol. 3")....25-50 61
(Black or multi-color label.)
EMBER (104 "In the Still of the Night")....250-350 61
LPs: 10/12-inch
CELEBRITY SHOWCASE....10-12 70
COLLECTABLES....5-10 83
EMBER (100 "The Five Satins Sing")....250-500 57
(Red label. Group is pictured on front cover.)
EMBER (100 "The Five Satins Sing")....100-200 58
(Multi-color label. Black vinyl.)
EMBER (100 "The Five Satins Sing")....500-1000 58
(Multi-color label. Colored vinyl.)
EMBER (100 "The Five Satins Sing")....50-100 60
(Black label.)
EMBER (401 "The Five Satins Encore")....50-100 60
(Black label.)
EMBER (401 "The Five Satins Encore")....40-60 61
(Multi-color label.)
LOST-NITE....8-12 81
MT. VERNON (108 "The Five Satins Sing")....20-30
RELIC....8-10
Members: Fred Parris; Louis Peebles; Stan Dortch; Jim Freeman; Nate Moseley; Bill Baker; Jimmy Curtis; Nate Marshall; Ed Martin; John Brown; Tom Killebrew; Al Denby; Jess Murphy; Wes Forbes; Richard Freeman; Dick Arnold.
Also see ALSTON, Shirley
Also see BAKER, Bill
Also see BLACK SATIN
Also see CARYL, Naomi
Also see CHAMPLAINS
Also see FARRAR, Tony
Also see FREDDIE & LOU
Also see GRANAHAN, Gerry
Also see HIGGINS, Ben
Also see NEW YORK CITY
Also see NEW YORKERS
Also see PARRIS, Fred
Also see ROMANS
Also see SCARLETS
Also see SOUTHSIDE JOHNNY & Asbury Dukes
Also see STARLARKS
Also see WILDWOODS

FIVE SATINS / Merry Clayton
Singles: 7-inch
RCA (6986 "In the Still of the Night")....3-5
Also see CLAYTON, Merry

FIVE SATINS / Gerry Granahan & Five Satins
Singles: 7-inch
X-BAT (1000 "When the Swallows Come Back to Capistrano")....3-4 95
(Red vinyl. 500 made.)
Picture Sleeves
X-BAT (1000 "When the Swallows Come Back to Capistrano")....3-4 95
(500 made.)
Also see GRANAHAN, Gerry
Also see WILDWOODS

FIVE SATINS / Pharotones
Singles: 7-inch
TIMES SQUARE (21 "Paradise on Earth")....15-25 63
TIMES SQUARE (94 "Paradise on Earth")....10-20 64
Also see PHAROTONES

FIVE SATINS / Youngtones / Youngsters / Shells
EPs: 7-inch
NEW YORK CITY (1002 "Gus Gossert Presents")....10-15 71
Also see FIVE SATINS
Also see SHELLS
Also see YOUNGSTERS
Also see YOUNGTONES

FIVE SCALDERS
(With "Bill Moore Tenor Sax")
Singles: 78 rpm
DRUMMOND....200-300 56
SUGAR HILL....300-400 56
Singles: 7-inch
DRUMMOND (3000 "If Only You Were Mine")....800-1200 56
DRUMMOND (3001 "Girl Friend")....800-1200 56
(Blue label.)
DRUMMOND (3001 "Girl Friend")....500-1000 56
(Maroon label.)
SUGAR HILL (3000 "If Only You Were Mine")....2000-3000 56
Members: Mack Rice; Johnny Mayfield; Sol Tilman; Gerald Young; James Bryant.
Also see FALCONS
Also see RICE, Mack

FIVE SCAMPS
Singles: 78 rpm
COLUMBIA (30157 "Chicken Shack Boogie")....25-50 49
OKEH (7049 "With All My Heart")..25-50 54
Singles: 7-inch
OKEH (7049 "With All My Heart")....50-100 54

FIVE SCRIPTS
Singles: 7-inch
LONGFIBER (201 "The Clock")....15-25 66

FIVE SECRETS
Singles: 78 rpm
DECCA....20-30 57
Singles: 7-inch
DECCA (30350 "See You Next Year")....50-75 57
Also see SECRETS

FIVE SHADES
Singles: 7-inch
EMBER (1074 "Mary Had a Little Man")....10-20 61
MGM....5-10 61

FIVE SHADES
Singles: 7–inch
VEEP.. 8-12 65

FIVE SHADOWS
Singles: 7–inch
FROSTY (1 "Blue Moon") 150-250 60

FIVE SHADOWS
Singles: 7–inch
MELLOMOOD (011 "Don't Say Goodnight")................................10-15 65

FIVE SHARKS
Singles: 7–inch
AMBER (852 "The Lion Sleeps Tonight") 8-12 66
OLD TIMER (604 "Gloria")............15-20 65
OLD TIMER (605 "Stand By Me") ..10-20 65
OLD TIMER (611 "Gloria").............. 8-12 65
(Black vinyl.)
OLD TIMER (611 "Gloria")............10-20 65
(Colored vinyl.)
SIAMESE (404 "Gloria") 5-10 65
TIMES SQUARE (35 "Stormy Weather")..................................20-30 64
Also see GOLD BUGS
Also see SHARKS

FIVE SHARPS
Singles: 78 rpm
JUBILEE (5104 "Stormy Weather")...........................7500-10000 52
No original 45s of this have been verified.. Bootleg 45s are common, but can be identified by their lighter shade of blue paper than was used by Jubilee in the '50s. They also have thicker horizontal lines than originals.
Singles: 7–inch
BIM BAM BOOM 4-8 72
Members: Ron Cuffey; Clarence Bassett; Mickey Owens; Robert Ward; Tom Ducket.
Also see VIDEOS

FIVE SHARPS
Singles: 7–inch
JUBILEE (5478 "Stormy Weather") 5-10 64
(A completely different recording than issued on Jubilee 5104.)

FIVE SHILLINGS
Singles: 7–inch
DECCA (30722 "Letter to an Angel")..40-60 58

FIVE SHITS
(5 Shits Formerly the Miracles)
Singles: 7–inch
CHANCE (1163 "My Pretty Little Girl") 10-15 74
(Colored vinyl.)
LOST-CAUSE (100 "Dreaming of You")..10-20 74
(Colored vinyl.)

FIVE SMOOTH STONES
Singles: 7–inch
CHISA (8006 "I Will Never Love Another")...50-75 69
(Black vinyl.)
CHISA (8006 "I Will Never Love Another")...20-30 69
(Colored vinyl.)

FIVE SOUNDS
(With the Julius Dixon Orchestra)
Singles: 7–inch
DEB (1006 "Greatest Gift of All")................................100-200 58

5 SOUNDS
Singles: 7–inch
BARITONE (0940 "That's When I Fell in Love") 30-40 60

FIVE SOUNDS
Singles: 7–inch
EPIC...10-20 65-66

FIVE SOUNDS / Cecil Buffalo & Prophets
Singles: 7–inch
LAKESIDE (2001 "Clumsy Dragon")...................................10-15 60
Also see BUFFALO, Cecil, & Prophets

FIVE SPARKS
Singles: 7–inch
JIMBO (1 "A Million Tears") 75-100 59

FIVE SPECIAL P&R/R&B/LP '79
Singles: 7–inch
ELEKTRA.. 3-4 79-80
LPs: 10/12–inch
ELEKTRA.. 5-10 79
Member: Byran Banks.

5 SPEEDS
("Narr. By Ducky DeCoy")
Singles: 7–inch
WIGGIE (131 "Tell Me") 50-100 59

5 SPENDERS
Singles: 7–inch
VERSATILE (113 "No Hard Feelings")..................................15-25 60
Also see REGENTS

FIVE SPIRITS OF RHYTHM
Singles: 78 rpm
BRUNSWICK (6728 "My Old Man")...30-50 33

FIVE SPLENDORS
Singles: 7–inch
STROLL (106 "Your Dog Hates Me") 10-20 60

FIVE SPOTS
Singles: 7–inch
FUTURE (2201 "Get with It") 30-50 59

FIVE SPOTS
Singles: 7–inch
APEX..20-25 60s
FUTURE (2201 "Get with It") 30-50 59
SOMA (1147 "Black Rock")............15-25 60

FIVE STAIRSTEPS P&R/R&B '66
(Stairsteps; with Cubie)
Singles: 7–inch
BUDDAH 4-6 67-68
COLLECTABLES.................................. 3-4 80s
CURTOM... 4-6 68-69
GOLD.. 4-6
WINDY C.. 4-8 66-67
Picture Sleeves
BUDDAH 4-8 67-68
LPs: 10/12–inch
BUDDAH.......................................10-12 68-70
COLLECTABLES.................................. 6-8 85
CURTOM..8-10 69
WINDY C..10-15 67
Members: Clarence Burke Jr.; James Burke; Keni Burke; Dennis Burke; Cubie Burke; Aloha Burke.
Also see BURKE, Cubie
Also see BURKE, Keni
Also see INVISIBLE MAN'S BAND
Also see ISLEY BROTHERS / Brooklyn Bridge
Also see STAIRSTEPS

FIVE STAR P&R/R&B/D&D/LP '85
Singles: 12–inch
RCA... 4-6 85-86
Singles: 7–inch
RCA... 3-4 85-87
Picture Sleeves
RCA... 3-4 86
LPs: 10/12–inch
RCA..5-10 85-86

FIVE STARS
Singles: 78 rpm
SHOW TIME 25-50 54
Singles: 7–inch
SHOW TIME (1102 "Where Did Caldonia Go")..50-100 54

FIVE STARS
Singles: 78 rpm
TREAT 100-200 55
Singles: 7–inch
TREAT (505 "Let's Fall in Love") 400-500 55

FIVE STARS
Singles: 78 rpm
ATCO (6065 "Take Five")............10-20 56
Singles: 7–inch
ABC-PAR 10-20 58
ATCO (6065 "Take Five")...............15-25 56

FIVE STARS
(With Millard Lee & Orchestra)
Singles: 78 rpm
BLUES BOYS KINGDOM..........100-150 57
Singles: 7–inch
BLUES BOYS KINGDOM (106 "So Lonely, Baby")......................................150-250 57

FIVE STARS
Singles: 7–inch
COLUMBIA (42056 "Baby Baby") ..25-50 61
DOT (15579 "Atom Bomb Baby")...10-20 57
END (1028 "Baby Baby")..............50-75 58
KERNEL (002 "Atom Bomb Baby")..75-125 57
MARK-X (7006 "Dead Wrong") 50-100 57
Members: Walter Gaines; C.P. Spencer.
Also see ORIGINALS
Also see THRILLERS

FIVE STARS
Singles: 7–inch
HUNT (318 "Dreaming") 10-15 58
NOTE (10011 "Dreaming").............20-30 58
(First issue.)
NOTE (10016 "My Paradise") 30-50 58
NOTE (10031 "Am I Wasting My Time")...20-30 58

FIVE STEPS
Singles: 7–inch
DADE 10-15 65

FIVE STRING SINGERS
Singles: 7–inch
PAULA 4-8 66

FIVE STRINGS: see KING, Sid

FIVE SUPERIORS
Singles: 7–inch
GARPAX (44170 "There's a Fool Born Every Day")..100-200 62
Session: Gary Paxton.
Also see PAXTON, Gary

5 SWANS
Singles: 78 rpm
MUSIC CITY......................................50-100 56
Singles: 7–inch
MUSIC CITY (795 "Lil Girl of My Dreams")...250-350 56

FIVE TECHNIQUES
Singles: 7–inch
IMPERIAL (5742 "Heaven Above")...10-20 61

FIVE TEENBEATS
Singles: 7–inch
BIG TOP...10-15 60
Also see DICK & TEENBEATS

FIVE TRADEWINDS, INC.
Singles: 7–inch
ARIOLA...6-12
FOX..8-12 66
FRANKLIN.......................................12-18 68
REACTION (1006 "While I'm Away")..25-35 67
Picture Sleeves
ARIOLA...10-15

5000 VOLTS P&R '75
Singles: 7–inch
PHILIPS 3-5 75
PRIVATE STOCK...............................3-5 76

FIVE THRILLS
Singles: 78 rpm
PARROT (796 "My Baby's Gone") 300-500 54
PARROT (800 "Gloria") 300-500 54
Singles: 7–inch
LOST NITE..4-8
PARROT (796 "My Baby's Gone") 750-1000 54
PARROT (800 "Gloria") 750-1000 54
(Black vinyl.)
PARROT (800 "Gloria") 2000-3000 54
(Red vinyl.)
Members: Levi Jenkins; Gilbert Warren; Oscar Robinson; Fred Washington; Obie Washington; Leon Pace.

FIVE TINOS
Singles: 78 rpm
SUN 300-500 55
Singles: 7–inch
SUN (222 "Sitting by My Window") 800-1200 55
(Counterfeits exist of this release.)
Also see ESQUIRES

5 TROJANS
Singles: 7–inch
TENDER (516 "Don't Ask Me to Be Lonely")......................................50-100 58
(Reissued as by the Trojans.)
Also see TROJANS

FIVE TROJANS
Singles: 7–inch
EDISON INT'L (412 "Little Doll")....25-40 59
Also see ST. CLAIR, Nicky, & Five Trojans

FIVE TRUMPETS
Singles: 78 rpm
GOTHAM 15-25 51-52
RCA 15-25 49
SAVOY...5-10 56
Singles: 7–inch
GOTHAM (681 "Stand by Me") 20-40 51
GOTHAM (693 "My Chains Fell Off")..20-40 52
GOTHAM (696 "No Not One") 20-40 52
RCA (0014 "O Lord")..................25-45 49
(Colored vinyl.)
RCA (0034 "Swing Low Sweet Chariot")..25-45 49
(Colored vinyl.)
RCA (0064 "Preach My Word").......25-45 49
(Colored vinyl.)
RCA (0080 "When the Saints Go Marchin' In")...25-45 50
(Colored vinyl.)
SAVOY...8-12 56

FIVE VETS
Singles: 78 rpm
ALLSTAR (713 "You're in Love") ...50-75 56
Singles: 7–inch
ALLSTAR (713 "You're in Love") 100-150 56

FIVE WAGERS
(V Wagers)
Singles: 7–inch
NATION TIME (1013 "You're My World")...15-25 60s
SALEM (1013 "Lucky I Found You")...15-25 60s
TIARA 10-15

FIVE WHISPERS
Singles: 7–inch
DOLTON 8-15 62-64

5 WILLOWS
(With Don Archer & Orchestra; with Le Roy Kirkland Orchestra)
Singles: 78 rpm
ALLEN (1000 "My Dear, Dearest Darling").....................................100-200 53
ALLEN (1002 "Delores") 100-200 53
ALLEN (1003 "White Cliffs of Dover")......................................150-250 53
HERALD..50-75 55
PEE DEE (290 "Love Bells")......100-200 53
Singles: 7–inch
ALLEN (1000 "My Dear, Dearest Darling")......................................300-500 53
ALLEN (1002 "Delores")..............300-500 53
ALLEN (1003 "White Cliffs of Dover")......................................400-600 53
HERALD (433 "Baby, Come a Little Closer")..200-300 54
HERALD (442 "Look Me in the Eyes")..200-300 55
LOST-NITE 5-10
PEE DEE (290 "Love Bells")......400-500 53
Members: Tony Middleton; Richard Davis; Joe Martin; John Steele; Ralph Martin.
Also see MIDDLETON, Tony
Also see WILLOWS

5 WINGS
Singles: 78 rpm
KING 50-75 55
Singles: 7–inch
KING (4778 "Johnny Has Gone") 100-150 55
KING (4781 "Teardrops Are Falling") 150-200 55
(Reissued in 1959 as by the Checkers.)
Members: Jackie Rue; Frank Edwards; Billy Carlisle; Melvin Flood; Tom Grate; Kenny "Butch" Hamilton; Richard Blandon.
Also see BOP CHORDS
Also see CHECKERS
Also see DUBS
Also see JACKIE & STARLIGHTS
Also see SCALE-TONES
Also see SONICS
Also see VOCALTONES

FIVE WINGS
(Billy Nelson & Five Wings)
Singles: 78 rpm
SAVOY (1183 "Walk Along") 10-20 56
Singles: 7–inch
SAVOY (1183 "Walk Along") 15-25 56

FIXX P&R/LP '82
Singles: 12–inch
MCA...4-6 82-86
Singles: 7–inch
MCA...3-5 82-90
RCA 3-4 89
Picture Sleeves
MCA...3-5 83-84
RCA 3-4 89
LPs: 10/12–inch
MCA (Except 8642) 5-10 82-91
MCA (8642 "Talkabout") 8-12 80s
(Interviews with Fixx. Promotional issue only.)
RCA 5-8 89
Members: Cy Curnin; Adam Woods; Danny Brown; Alfi Agies; Jamie West; Rupert Greenall.
Also see PORTRAITS

FIZZY QWICK R&B '86
Singles: 7–inch
MOTOWN..3-4 86

FLACK, Roberta LP '70
Singles: 7–inch
ATLANTIC..3-5 69-88
MCA...3-4 81
VIVA...3-4 83
Picture Sleeves
ATLANTIC..3-4 78-82
LPs: 10/12–inch
ATLANTIC..5-10 69-88
VIVA...5-10 83
Also see CHIC / Leif Garrett / Roberta Flack / Genesis
Also see McCANN, Les
Also see WATANABE, Sadao, & Roberta Flack

FLACK, Roberta, & Peabo Bryson R&B/LP '80
Singles: 7–inch
ATLANTIC..3-4 80
CAPITOL..3-4 83
Picture Sleeves
CAPITOL..3-4 83
LPs: 10/12–inch
ATLANTIC..5-10 80
CAPITOL..5-10 83
Also see BRYSON, Peabo
Also see FLACK, Roberta

FLACK, Roberta, & Donny Hathaway R&B/LP '72
Singles: 7–inch
ATLANTIC..3-5 71-80
LPs: 10/12–inch
ATLANTIC..5-10 72-80
Also see HATHAWAY, Donny

FLACK, Roberta, & Eric Mercury R&B '83
Singles: 7–inch
ATLANTIC..3-4 83
Also see FLACK, Roberta
Also see MERCURY, Eric

FLAG OF CONVENIENCE
Singles: 12–inch
PVC..4-6

FLAGG, Bill
(With His Rockabillies)
Singles: 78 rpm
TETRA 50-100 56
Singles: 7–inch
MGM (12637 "Doin' My Time") 50-75 58
TETRA (4445 "Go Cat, Go") 75-125 56
TETRA (4448 "Guitar Rock") 75-125 57
EPs: 7–inch
FLUKE (1002 "Bill Flagg & His Rockabillies") ....??
(Since we do not know the year of this EP, we cannot yet price it. Also, having seen only the disc, we are not certain it came with a cover. Readers?)

FLAGG, Fannie LP '67
LPs: 10/12–inch
RCA 10-15 66

FLAGG, Paul
("Sir Raggedy")
Singles: 7–inch
ATLANTIC..4-8 67
COLUMBIA 4-8 68

FLAGMEN
Singles: 7–inch
LIMELIGHT (3104 "Drag Strip USA")...10-20 64
Members: Lloyd Hugo; Jimmy Lenten; Greg Coby; Jay Milhelich.

FLAHARTY, Sonny
(With the Mark V)
Singles: 7–inch
DECCA 4-6 62
EPIC...4-8 60
FALCON 4-6 63
HURON (2204 ("Teenage War Chant")..15-25 61
PHILIPS..10-15 67
SPANGLE (2011 "My Baby's Casual")...30-50 58

FLAIM BROTHERS
Singles: 7–inch
SCARLOTT.......................................4-8 62

FLAIR & Flat Foots
Singles: 7–inch
S.P.Q.R. (1007 "Hey Boy Hey Girl")..5-10 66
(Some copies of *Something Stupid*, by Frank & Nancy Sinatra, mistakenly had this label.)
Also see SINATRA, Frank & Nancy

FLAIRS
Singles: 78 rpm
ABC (9698 "She Loves to Rock")...15-25 56
FLAIR...50-100 53-55
Singles: 7–inch
ABC (9698 "She Loves to Rock")....25-45 56
ANTLER (4005 "I'd Climb the Hills and Mountains") 50-100 59
FLAIR (1012 "I Had a Love") 250-500 53
FLAIR (1019 "Tell Me You Love Me")..250-500 53
FLAIR (1028 "Love Me, Girl") 250-500 54
FLAIR (1041 "You Were Untrue")..250-500 54
FLAIR (1044 "This Is the Night for Love")..250-500 54
FLAIR (1056 "I'll Never Let You Go")..250-500 55
FLAIR (1067 "My Darling, My Sweet")..250-500 55
LPs: 10/12–inch
CROWN (356 "The Flairs")...........40-60 63
(Reprocessed Stereo.)
CROWN (5356 "The Flairs").........50-100 63
(Monaural.)
Members: Cornell Gunter; Richard Berry; Young Jessie; Beverly Thompson; Tom Fox; George Hollis; Patience Valentine.
Also see BERRY, Richard
Also see CHIMES
Also see FIVE HEARTS
Also see GUNTER, Cornell, & Flairs
Also see GUNTER, Shirley, & Flairs
Also see HAYES, Linda
Also see HOLLYWOOD BLUEJAYS
Also see HUNTERS
Also see JAMES, Etta
Also see RAMS
Also see VALENTINE, Patience
Also see WHIPS
Also see YOUNG JESSIE

FLAIRS
(Redwoods)
Singles: 7–inch
EPIC (9447 "Shake Shake Sherry")..20-30 61
(Also issued as by the Redwoods.)
Also see REDWOODS

FLAIRS
Singles: 7–inch
PALMS (726 "Roll Over Beethoven")....................................25-50 61
(Reissued as by the Velaires.)
Also see VELAIRES

FLAIRS
Singles: 7–inch
RAP (007 "You Got to Steal It").....15-25 60s

FLAKES
Singles: 7–inch
NAME...5-8 62

FLAKES
Singles: 7–inch
MAGIC DISC....................................10-20

FLAKES
Singles: 7–inch
SALSOUL...3-4 80-81
LPs: 10/12–inch
SALSOUL...5-10 81

FLAMBEAUS
Singles: 7–inch
OLD TOWN (2001 "Darling, I'm with You")...10-20 66

FLAME P&R '70
Singles: 7–inch
BROTHER.......................................10-15 70-71
LPs: 10/12–inch
BROTHER (2500 "The Flame") 20-30 70
(Includes bonus poster.)
Members: Rick Fataar; Terry "Blondie" Chaplin; Steve Fataar; Brother Fataar.
Also see CHAPLIN, Blondie
Also see RUTLES

FLAME LP '77
Singles: 7–inch
RCA 3-4 78

LPs: 10/12-inch
RCA.. 5-10 77-78
Members: Marge Raymond; Jim Crespo; Frank Ruby.

FLAME "N" KING
Singles: 7-inch
RAINES.. 4-8 65

FLAME 'N' KINGS
Singles: 7-inch
HSP.. 3-6 70

FLAMES
Singles: 78 rpm
ALADDIN..50-75 53
SELECTIVE (113 "Young Girl")..........50-75 50
7-11..50-200 53
SPIN..50-200 54
Singles: 7-inch
ALADDIN (3198 "Sorrowful Heart")..100-150 53
ALADDIN (3280 "Shtiggy Boom")..75-125 53
7-11 (2106 "Keep on Smiling")....350-500 53
7-11 (2107 "Together")..............300-400 53
SPIN (101 "Cryin' for My Baby")..300-400 54
Members: Bobby Byrd; Willie Rockwell; David Ford; Curley Dinkins; Curtis Williams; Leon Hughes.
Also see BYRD, Bobby
Also see HOLLYWOOD FLAMES
Also see PATTI ANNE & FLAMES

FLAMES
Singles: 7-inch
BERTRAM INT'L (203 "Crazy")......25-50 57

FLAMES
(Fabulous Flames)
Singles: 7-inch
DOT (15813 "The Scramble")........15-25 58
GAITY (168 "Rockin' with the Blues")..10-15 59
HARLEM (114 "So Long My Darling")..450-550 60

FLAMES
Singles: 7-inch
VENTURAL (727 "Going Home")...10-20 62

FLAMES
Singles: 7-inch
CUCA (64111 "The Bird")..............15-25 64

FLAMES
Singles: 7-inch
HOT SPOT (101 "Scorched Earth")..10-20 65
HOT SPOT (103 "Williams Estate")..10-20 65

FLAMES
Singles: 7-inch
PEOPLE..10-15 71

FLAMETHROWERS
Singles: 7-inch
CLIX (7 "The Knight's Capers")....... 8-12

FLAMETTES
Singles: 7-inch
LAURIE (3109 "You You You")......15-25 61

FLAMIN' GROOVIES LP '76
Singles: 7-inch
BOMP.. 3-5 74
EPIC.. 4-6 69-70
KAMA SUTRA.. 3-5 71
SIRE.. 4-6 76-79
Picture Sleeves
BOMP.. 4-8 74
EPs: 7-inch
SKYDOG.. 5-10
LPs: 10/12-inch
BUDDAH..10-12 77
EPIC (26487 "Supernazz")..........35-45 69
KAMA SUTRA (2021 "Flamingo")..15-25 70
(Pink label.)
KAMA SUTRA (2021 "Flamingo")..10-15 70s
(Blue label.)
KAMA SUTRA (2031 "Teenage Head")..15-25 71
(Pink label.)
KAMA SUTRA (2031 "Teenage Head")..10-15 70s
(Blue label.)
SIRE..10-12 76-79
SNAZZ (2371 "Sneakers")............60-80 68
(10-inch LP.)
VOXX.. 5-10
Members: Roy Loney; Cyril Jordan; George Alexander; Tim Lynch; Danny Mihm; Chris Wilson; James Farrell; David Wright.
Also see GROUP "B"
Also see LONEY, Roy

FLAMIN' OHS
LPs: 10/12-inch
FAT CITY.. 5-10 80
Also see PRODIGY

FLAMING EMBER P&R '69
Singles: 7-inch
HOT WAX.. 4-8 69-70
LPs: 10/12-inch
HOT WAX..10-15 70-71
Members: Joe Sladich; Jerry Plunk; Bill Ellis; Jim Bugnel.
Also see FLAMING EMBERS

FLAMING EMBERS
Singles: 7-inch
FORTUNE (868 "You Can Count On Me")..15-25 65
FORTUNE (869 "Gone Gone Gone")..25-50 65
FORTUNE (870 "Rain Go Away")..25-50 65

FLAMING EMBERS / Al Kent
Singles: 7-inch
RIC TIC..10-15 68

FLAMING EMBERS / Wingate's Love-in Strings
Singles: 7-inch
RIC TIC..10-15 67
Also see FANTASTIC FOUR / Wingate's Love-in Strings
Also see FLAMING EMBER
Also see FLAMING EMBERS

FLAMING HEARTS
(With the Tornadoes)
Singles: 7-inch
VULCO (1 "Baby")................1000-1500 58

FLAMING KING & DESYREENS
Singles: 7-inch
AMAKER.. 4-8 63

FLAMING LIPS
LPs: 10/12-inch
RESTLESS..5-10 90
(Colored vinyl.)

FLAMING RED LIGHTNING BOLTS
Singles: 7-inch
DMC (101 "Wine Wine Wine")......10-20 65

FLAMING YOUTH
LPs: 10/12-inch
UNI (73075 "Ark 2")..................25-50 69
Member: Phil Collins.

FLAMINGO, Chuck
(Chuck Jackson)
Singles: 7-inch
BELTONE (1004 "Tonight Is Gone")..20-30 61
Also see JACKSON, Chuck

FLAMINGO, Johnny
(Johnny Flamingo Orchestra)
Singles: 78 rpm
ALADDIN..10-15 56
CADDY..10-15 56
Singles: 7-inch
ALADDIN (3385 "When I Lost You")..25-50 57
CADDY (112 "Make Me a Present of You")..25-50 57
CANTON (1785 "I")....................40-60 60
DIADON (103 "This Was Really Love")..10-15 61
DONNA (1357 "You're Mine")........40-60 62
DUB-TONE (2580 "I Just Cry")..........25-50
MALYNN (101 "United")..............50-100 59
SPECIALTY (640 "Paradise Hill")..15-25 58

FLAMINGOS R&B '56
(With Red Holloway's Orchestra)
Singles: 78 rpm
CHANCE (1133 " If I Can't Have You")..100-200 53
CHANCE (1140 "That's My Desire")..100-200 53
CHANCE (1145 "Golden Teardrops")..200-300 53
CHANCE (1149 "Plan for Love")..100-200 53
CHANCE (1154 "Cross Over the Bridge")..100-200 54
CHANCE (1162 "Blues in the Letter")..100-150 54
CHECKER..15-30 55-57
DECCA..15-25 57
END (1035 "Lovers Never Say Goodbye")..500-750 58
END (1046 "I Only Have Eyes for You"/ "At the Prom")..500-750 59
Note: Though possibly made but not yet confirmed on 78 are End 1035 (*Please Wait for Me*), End 1040 and End 1044.
PARROT (808 "Dream of a Lifetime")..100-150 54
PARROT (812 "I'm Yours")........150-200 55
Singles: 7-inch
ABC.. 3-5 73
CHANCE (1133 "If I Can't Have You")..500-750 53
(Black vinyl.)
CHANCE (1133 "If I Can't Have You")..1000-2000 53
(Red vinyl.)
CHANCE (1140 "That's My Desire")..500-750 53
(Black vinyl.)
CHANCE (1140 "That's My Desire")..1000-2000 53
(Red vinyl.)
CHANCE (1145 "Golden Teardrops")..500-750 53
(Black vinyl.)
CHANCE (1145 "Golden Teardrops")..2000-3000 53
(Red vinyl.)
CHANCE (1149 "Plan for Love")..500-750 53
(Yellow and black label.)
CHANCE (1149 "Plan for Love")..300-500 53
(Blue and silver label.)
CHANCE (1154 "Cross Over the Bridge")..500-750 54
CHANCE (1162 "Blues in the Letter")..250-500 54
CHECKER (815 "When")..........50-75 55
(Maroon label, checkerboard design at top.)
CHECKER (815 "When")..........15-25 57
(Maroon label, "Checker" logo vertical on left.)
CHECKER (821 "Please Come Back Home")..50-75 55
(Maroon label, checkerboard design at top.)
CHECKER (821 "Please Come Back Home")..15-25 57
(Maroon label, "Checker" logo vertical on left.)
CHECKER (830 "I'll Be Home")......50-75 56
(Maroon label, checkerboard design at top.)
CHECKER (830 "I'll Be Home")......15-25 57
(Maroon label, "Checker" logo vertical on left.)
CHECKER (830 "I'll Be Home")........4-8 60s
(Blue label.)
CHECKER (837 "A Kiss from Your Lips")..50-75 56
(Maroon label, checkerboard design at top.)
CHECKER (837 "A Kiss from Your Lips")..15-25 57
(Maroon label, "Checker" logo vertical on left.)
CHECKER (846 "The Vow")...........50-75 56
(Maroon label, checkerboard design at top.)
CHECKER (846 "The Vow")...........15-25 57
(Maroon label, "Checker" logo vertical on left.)
CHECKER (853 "Would I Be Crying")..50-75 56
(Maroon label, checkerboard design at top.)
CHECKER (853 "Would I Be Crying")..15-25 57
(Maroon label, "Checker" logo vertical on left.)
CHECKER (915 "Dream of a Lifetime")..20-40 59
CHECKER (1084 "Lover Come Back to Me")..10-20 64
CHECKER (1091 "Goodnight Sweetheart")..10-20 64
CHESS..3-5 73
COLLECTABLES..3-4 80s
DECCA (30335 "The Ladder of Love")..20-30 57
DECCA (30454 "Helpless")..........20-30 57
DECCA (30687 "Rock & Roll March")..20-30 58
DECCA (30880 "Kiss-A-Me")........20-30 58
DECCA (30948 "Hey Now")..........20-30 59
END (1035 "Please Wait for Me")..30-50 58
(Title later changed to *Lovers Never Say Goodbye*.)
END (1035 "Lovers Never Say Goodbye")..10-20 58
END (1040 "I Shed a Tear at Your Wedding")..10-20 58
END (1044 "At the Prom")............10-20 58
END (1046 "I Only Have Eyes for You"/ "At the Prom")..10-20 59
END (1046 "I Only Have Eyes for You"/ "Goodnight Sweetheart")..............15-25 59
(Note different flip.)
END (1046 "I Only Have Eyes for You")..40-50 59
(Stereo.)
END (1055 "Love Walked In")..........8-12 59
(Monaural.)
END (1055 "Love Walked In")........35-45 59
(Stereo.)
END (1062 thru 1124)....................8-12 59-62
JULMAR (506 "Dealin' ")....................4-8 69
LOST NITE..4-8
OLDIES 45..4-8 64
PARROT (808 "Dream of a Lifetime")..500-1000 54
(Black vinyl.)
PARROT (808 "Dream of a Lifetime")..2000-3000 54
(Rred vinyl.)
PARROT (811 "I Really Don't Want to Know")..1000-2000 55
(Black vinyl.)
PARROT (811 "I Really Don't Want to Know")..3000-5000 55
(Red vinyl.)
PARROT (812 "I'm Yours")........250-300 55
(Black vinyl.)
PARROT (812 "I'm Yours")......750-1000 55
(Red vinyl.)
PHILIPS (40308 "Temptation")......10-15 65
PHILIPS (40347 "Boogaloo Party") 10-15 66
PHILIPS (40452 "It Keeps the Doctor Away")..10-15 67
PHILIPS (40496 "Oh Mary, Don't You Worry")..10-15 67
POLYDOR (14019 "Buffalo Soldier"/"Buffalo Soldier")..4-6 70
POLYDOR (14019 "Buffalo Soldier, Part 1"/"Buffalo Soldier, Part 2")..........3-5 72
POLYDOR (14044 "Lover Come Back to Me")..3-5 74
RONZE (111 "Welcome Home")........4-6 71-76
RONZE (115 "Heavy Hips")..............3-6 75
RONZE (116 "Love Keeps the Doctor Away")..3-6 75
ROULETTE (4524 "Ol Man River")...5-10 63
TIMES SQUARE (102 "A Lovely Way to Spend an Evening")..10-20 64
VEE JAY (384 "Golden Teardrops")..10-15 61
WORLDS (103 "Think About Me").....3-6 75
EPs: 7-inch
END (205 "Goodnight Sweetheart")..40-60 59
(Monaural.)
END (205 "Goodnight Sweetheart")..50-85 59
(Stereo.)
LPs: 10/12-inch
CHECKER (1433 "Flamingos")....75-125 59
(Monaural.)
CHECKER (3005 "Flamingos")......25-50 66
(Stereo.)
CHESS..6-12 76-84
CONSTELLATION..15-20 64
EMUS..5-10 79
END (304 "Flamingo Serenade") .50-100 59
(Monaural.)
END (304 "Flamingo Serenade") .75-125 59
(Stereo.)
END (307 "Flamingo Favorites")....40-60 60
(Monaural.)
END (307 "Flamingo Favorites")....50-75 60
(Stereo.)
END (308 "Requestfully Yours").....40-60 60
(Monaural.)
END (308 "Requestfully Yours")....50-75 60
(Stereo.)
END (316 "The Sound of the Flamingos")..40-60 62
(Monaural.)
END (316 "The Sound of the Flamingos")..50-75 62
(Stereo.)
LOST-NITE..8-12 81
MEKA..10-15
PHILIPS..15-25 66
RONZE..10-15 72-73
ROULETTE..8-10 81-84
SOLID SMOKE..5-10 82
Members: Sollie McElroy; John Carter; Zeke Carey; Jake Carey; Paul Wilson; Nate Nelson; Tommy Hunt; Terry Johnson.
Also see ALSTON, Shirley
Also see HUNT, Tommy
Also see McELROY, Sollie
Also see NELSON, Nate
Also see STARGLOWS

FLAMINGOS / Moonglows
Singles: 7-inch
TRIP..3-5
LPs: 10/12-inch
VEE JAY (1052 "The Flamingos Meet the Moonglows")..30-50 62
Also see FLAMINGOS
Also see MOONGLOWS

FLANAGAN, Ralph P&R '49
Singles: 78 rpm
BLUEBIRD..3-6 49
RCA..3-5 50-57
Singles: 7-inch
CORAL..3-6 61
IMPERIAL..3-8 59
RCA..4-8 50-57
EPs: 7-inch
CAMDEN..4-8 54
RCA..5-10 51-57
LPs: 10/12-inch
CAMDEN..10-20 54
GOLDEN ERA..4-8 76
IMPERIAL..8-15 58-59
RCA..10-20 51-57

FLANAGAN BROTHERS
Singles: 7-inch
BRUNSWICK (55078 "Salton City")..150-200 58

FLANDERS, Tommy
Singles: 7-inch
VERVE/FOLKWAYS..3-6 69
LPs: 10/12-inch
VERVE/FORECAST..10-12 69

FLANERY, Dave
Singles: 7-inch
SIMS..4-8 64

FLANNELS
Singles: 78 rpm
TAMPA (121 "Hey Rube")..............20-30 56
Singles: 7-inch
TAMPA (121 "Hey Rube")..............30-60 56

FLARES P&R/R&B '61
Singles: 7-inch
COLLECTABLES..3-4 80s
FELSTED (8604 "Loving You")........8-12 60
FELSTED (8607 "Jump & Bump")....8-12 60
PRESS (2800 "Rock & Roll Heaven")..5-10 62
PRESS (2802 "Doing the Hully Gully")..5-10 62
PRESS (2803 "Mad House")............5-10 62
PRESS (2807 "Do It with Me")..........5-10 63
PRESS (2808 "Hand Clappin' ")........5-10 63
PRESS (2810 "Monkey Walk")..........5-10 63
Picture Sleeves
FELSTED (8607 "Jump & Bump")..20-30 60
LPs: 10/12-inch
PRESS (73001 "Encore of Foot Stompin' Hits")..30-50 61
(Monaural.)
PRESS (83001 "Encore of Foot Stompin' Hits")..50-75 61
(Stereo.)
Members: Aaron Collins; Willie Davis; Tom Miller; Randy Jones.
Also see CADETS
Also see COLLINS, Aaron
Also see JACKSON, Cookie
Also see PEPPERS

FLARES / Ramrocks
Singles: 7-inch
FELSTED (8624 "Foot Stompin' ")...8-10 61
Also see FLARES
Also see RAMROCKS

FLASH P&R/LP '72
Singles: 7-inch
CAPITOL..3-5 72
LPs: 10/12-inch
CAPITOL (11000 series)..............5-10 77
(With "SM" prefix.)
CAPITOL (11000 series)...............8-10 72-73
(With "SMAS" or "ST" prefix.)
Also see BANKS, Peter

FLASH & BOARD OF DIRECTORS
Singles: 7-inch
MALA..4-8 68

FLASH & PAN P&R/LP '79
Singles: 12-inch
EPIC..4-6 81-83
Singles: 7-inch
EPIC..3-4 79-83
LPs: 10/12-inch
EPIC..5-10 79-82
Members: Harry Vanda; George Young.
Also see EASYBEATS

FLASH CADILLAC & CONTINENTAL KIDS P&R '74
Singles: 7-inch
EPIC..4-8 72-74
PRIVATE STOCK..4-6 74-77
LPs: 10/12-inch
EPIC..10-12 72-74
PRIVATE STOCK..8-10 75
Also see WOLFMAN JACK

FLASH GORDON & NUDE HOLLYWOOD ARGYLES
Singles: 7-inch
PARAMOUNT (0289 "Super Streaker")..8-10 70s

FLASHCATS
Singles: 7-inch
BOGUS..3-4 86
Also see JACKSON, Bull Moose

FLASHER BROTHERS
Singles: 78 rpm
ALADDIN..50-75 52
Singles: 7-inch
ALADDIN (3156 "The Lord Gave You to Me")..150-200 52
ALADDIN (3186 "The Last Thing I Do")..75-125 52

FLASHES: see FLYNN, Freddie, & Flashes

FLASHLIGHT
Singles: 7-inch
PHILLY GROOVE..3-4 78
LPs: 10/12-inch
PHILLY GROOVE..5-10 78

FLAT EARTH SOCIETY
LPs: 10/12-inch
FLEETWOOD (3027 "Waleeco")..200-300 68
Members: Jack Kerivan; Paul Carter; Phil Dubuque; Curt Girard.

FLATT, Lester, & Bill Monroe
LPs: 10/12-inch
RCA..5-10 74-81
Also see MONROE, Bill

FLATT, Lester, & Earl Scruggs C&W '52
(With the Foggy Mountain Boys; Flatt & Scruggs)
Singles: 78 rpm
COLUMBIA..5-15 51-57
MERCURY..5-10 49-53
Singles: 7-inch
COLUMBIA (20000 & 21000 series)..8-15 51-56
COLUMBIA (40000 thru 42000 series)..5-10 56-63
COLUMBIA (43000 thru 45000 series)..4-8 64-67
MERCURY..10-15 50-53
Picture Sleeves
COLUMBIA..4-8 62-68
MERCURY..4-6 68
EPs: 7-inch
COLUMBIA..10-20 57-60
LPs: 10/12-inch
CBS..5-10
COLUMBIA (30 "Flatt & Scruggs")..8-12 75
COLUMBIA (400 series)................10-15 69
COLUMBIA (1000 & 2000 series, except 1019)..10-25 60-68
COLUMBIA (1019 "Foggy Mountain Jamboree")..30-50 57
COLUMBIA (8000 & 9000 series)..10-25 60-70
(With "CS" prefix.)
COLUMBIA (8000 & 9000 series)....5-10
(With "PC" prefix.)
COLUMBIA (10000 series)..............6-12 73
COLUMBIA (30000 thru 37000 series)..5-12 70-82
COPPER CREEK..5-10
COUNTY..5-10
EVEREST..5-10 71-82
51 WEST..5-10 80s
HARMONY..8-15 60-71
MERCURY (20000 series).............20-40 58-63
(Monaural.)
MERCURY (60000 series)..............20-30 63
(Stereo.)
MERCURY (61000 series)..............10-15 68
NASHVILLE..8-10 70
PICKWICK/HILLTOP..8-12 68
POWER PAK..5-10
ROUNDER..5-8
WING..8-12 68
Members: Lester Flatt; Earl Scruggs; Mac Wiseman; Jim Shoemate; Cedric Rainwater.
Also see SCRUGGS, Earl
Also see SOME OF CHET'S FRIENDS
Also see STUART, Marty

FLATT, Lester, Earl Scruggs & Jim & Jesse
LPs: 10/12-inch
STARDAY..15-20 66

FLATT, Lester, Earl Scruggs & Bill Monroe
LPs: 10/12-inch
ROUNDER ... 5-8 80s
Also see MONROE, Bill

FLATT, Lester, Earl Scruggs, & Doc Watson
LPs: 10/12-inch
COLUMBIA ... 10-15 67
Also see FLATT, Lester, & Earl Scruggs
Also see WATSON, Doc

FLAVOR P&R '68
Singles: 7-inch
COLUMBIA ... 4-6 68
Picture Sleeves
COLUMBIA ... 4-6 68
LPs: 10/12-inch
JU-PAR ... 8-10 77

FLAVOUR, La: see LA FLAVOUR

FLEAS
Singles: 7-inch
CHALLENGE (9115 "Scratchin' ") .. 20-30 61
Members: Dave Burgess; Glen Campbell; Jerry Fuller; Ricky Nelson.
Also see BURGESS, Dave
Also see CLAMPBELL, Glen
Also see FULLER, Jerry
Also see NELSON, Rick

FLEAS
Singles: 7-inch
BACK BEAT ... 4-8 64-67

FLEET & FREDDY
Singles: 7-inch
ARLEN ... 10-15 61
PROTONE ... 10-20 59

FLEETONES
Singles: 7-inch
BANDERA (2511 "Please Tell Me") ... 20-30 61

FLEETS
Singles: 7-inch
H.I.P. ... 4-6
VOLT ... 10-20 64

FLEETWOOD, Jimmy
(Jimmy Johnson)
Singles: 78 rpm
JAB ... 10-20 54
Singles: 7-inch
JAB ... 35-50 54
(Title and selection number not known.)
Also see JOHNSON, Jimmy

FLEETWOOD, Mick LP '81
LPs: 10/12-inch
RCA (4080 "The Visitor") ... 5-10 81
Also see BOW STREET RUNNERS
Also see FLEETWOOD MAC
Also see ZOO

FLEETWOOD MAC LP '68
Singles: 12-inch
W.B. (652 "Go Your Own Way") ... 15-25 76
(Promotional issue only.)
W.B. (2688 "Big Love") ... 15-25 87
(Promotional issue only.)
W.B. (2728 "Tango in the Night") ... 15-25 87
(Promotional issue only.)
W.B. (20842 "Family Man") ... 8-12 87
Singles: 7-inch
BLUE HORIZON ... 4-8 70
DJM ... 4-8 73
EPIC (10351 "Black Magic Woman") ... 5-10 68
EPIC (10368 "Stop Messin' Around") ... 5-10 68
EPIC (10436 "Albatross") ... 4-6 69
EPIC (11029 "Albatross") ... 3-5 73
EPIC (139609 "Albatross") ... 5-8
(Promotional issue only.)
REPRISE ... 3-6 69-76
W.B. (Except 8304) ... 3-4 77-90
W.B. (8304 "Go Your Own Way") ... 8-12 76
Picture Sleeves
EPIC (139609 "Albatross") ... 8-10 69
(Promotional issue only.)
W.B. ... 3-6 77-88
LPs: 10/12-inch
BLUE HORIZON (3801 "Fleetwood Mac in Chicago") ... 20-25 70
BLUE HORIZON (4803 "Blues Jam in Chicago, Vol. 1") ... 20-25 70
BLUE HORIZON (4805 "Blues Jam in Chicago, Vol. 2") ... 20-25 70
BLUE HORIZON (66227 "Blues Jam at Chess") ... 20-25 69
BLUE HORIZON (83110 "Mr. Wonderful") ... 20-25
COLUMBIA SPECIAL PROD. ... 8-12 73
EPIC (26402 "Peter Green's Fleetwood Mac") ... 20-30 68
EPIC (26446 "English Rose") ... 20-25 69
EPIC (30632 "Black Magic Woman") ... 15-25 71
(Repackage of *Fleetwood Mac* and *English Rose*.)
EPIC (33740 "English Rose") ... 10-15 73
EPIC (33740 "Fleetwood Mac/English Rose") ... 10-15 74
(Repackage of *Black Magic Woman*.)
MFSL (012 "Fleetwood Mac") ... 60-80 78
MFSL (119 "Mirage") ... 25-35 84
NAUTILUS (8 "Rumours") ... 25-35 80
(Half-speed mastered.)
REPRISE (Except 6368) ... 8-15 70-77
REPRISE (6368 "Then Play On") ... 15-25 69
(Without *Oh Well*.)
REPRISE (6368 "Then Play On") ... 10-15 69
(With *Oh Well*.)
SIRE ... 8-10 75-77
VARRICK ... 5-10 85
W.B. ... 8-12 77-90
Members: Mick Fleetwood; John McVie; Peter Green; Jeremy Spencer; Danny Kirwin; Christine McVie; Bob Welch; Bob Weston; Dave Walker; Lindsay Buckingham; Stevie Nicks; Rick Vito; Billy Burnette.
Also see BUCKINGHAM, Lindsay
Also see BURNETTE, Billy
Also see FLEETWOOD, Mick
Also see GREEN, Peter
Also see GRILL, Rob
Also see KIRWIN, Danny
Also see MAYALL, John
Also see McVIE, Christine
Also see NICKS, Stevie
Also see SPANN, Otis, & Fleetwood Mac
Also see SPENCER, Jeremy
Also see WELCH, Bob

FLEETWOOD MAC / Danny Kirwan
Singles: 7-inch
DJM ... 4-8 73
Also see FLEETWOOD MAC
Also see KIRWAN, Danny

FLEETWOODS P&R/R&B '59
Singles: 7-inch
DOLPHIN (1 "Come Softly to Me") . 15-25 59
(No mention of distribution by Liberty.)
DOLPHIN (1 "Come Softly to Me") . 10-20 59
(Reads: "Distributed by Liberty Record Sales Co.")
DOLTON (3 "Graduation's Here") ... 5-10 59
(Monaural.)
DOLTON (S3 "Graduation's Here") 15-25 59
(Stereo.)
DOLTON (5 thru 315) ... 5-15 59-66
LIBERTY (55188 "Come Softly to Me") ... 8-12 59
(Monaural.)
LIBERTY (77188 "Come Softly to Me") ... 10-20 59
(Stereo.)
QUALITY ... 10-20
(Canadian.)
U.A. ... 3-5 74
Picture Sleeves
DOLTON (22 "Runaround") ... 10-15 60
EPs: 7-inch
DOLTON (502 "The Fleetwoods") .. 20-30 60
LPs: 10/12-inch
DOLTON (2001 "Mr. Blue") ... 25-35 59
(Monaural.)
DOLTON (8001 "Mr. Blue") ... 30-40 59
(Stereo.)
DOLTON (2002 thru 2039) ... 20-30 60-65
(Monaural.)
DOLTON (8002 thru 8039) ... 20-35 60-65
(Stereo.)
LIBERTY ... 5-10 82-83
SUNSET ... 10-15 66
U.A. ... 8-10 75
Members: Gary Troxel; Barbara Ellis; Gretchen Christopher.
Also see TROXEL, Gary
Also see VEE, Bobby / Johnny Burnette / Ventures / Fleetwoods

FLEISCHMAN, Robert
Singles: 7-inch
ARISTA ... 3-4 79
LPs: 10/12-inch
ARISTA ... 5-10 79

FLEMING, Ann
Singles: 7-inch
COOKIN' (605 "Beside You") ... 40-60

FLEMING, Carol
Singles: 7-inch
WGW ... 4-8 62

FLEMING, Frank
Singles: 7-inch
LAURIE ... 4-8 62

FLEMING, Frankie, Jr.
Singles: 7-inch
AMY ... 4-8 63

FLEMING, Jim, & Casuals
Singles: 78 rpm
MCI ... 50-75 56
Singles: 7-inch
MCI (1020 "Don't You Just Know It") ... 100-200 56

FLEMING, King
Singles: 78 rpm
CHESS ... 10-20 56
Singles: 7-inch
CHESS (1633 "Please Come Back") ... 20-30 56

FLEMING, Rhonda
LPs: 10/12-inch
COLUMBIA (1080 "Rhonda") ... 20-30 57

FLEMING, Sherwood
Singles: 7-inch
KENT ... 3-5 70
Picture Sleeves
KENT ... 3-5 70

FLEMONS, Wade P&R/R&B '58
(With the Newcomers; Wade Flemmons)
Singles: 7-inch
RAMSEL (1001 "Jeannette") ... 10-20
VEE JAY (Maroon label) ... 15-25 58-59
VEE JAY (Black label, except 368) ... 10-20 60-63
VEE JAY (368 "I'll Come Running") ... 20-30 60
LPs: 10/12-inch
VEE JAY (1011 "Wade Flemons") 50-100 59
(Maroon label.)
VEE JAY (1011 "Wade Flemons") 25-50 61
(Black label.)
Also see EARTH, WIND & FIRE
Also see SALTY PEPPERS
Also see SKYLINERS / Wade Flemons

FLENER, Charlie
Singles: 7-inch
TEMPTOOD (1034 "Moon in My Window") ... 50-75

FLENNOY TRIO
Singles: 78 rpm
EXCELSIOR ... 10-20 44-45
MELODISC ... 10-20 45

FLENNOY TRIO & Joe Turner
Singles: 78 rpm
EXCELSIOR ... 15-25 49
Also see FLENNOY TRIO
Also see TURNER, Joe

FLENOY, Julian R&B '86
Singles: 7-inch
KMA ... 3-4 86

FLESH for LULU LP '87
Singles: 12-inch
MCA ... 4-6 85
Singles: 7-inch
MCA ... 3-4 85
LPs: 10/12-inch
CAPITOL ... 5-10 87
MCA ... 5-10 85
Members: Nick Marsh; James Mitchell; Rocco Barker; Kevin Mills; Derek Grenning.

FLESH GORDON: see GORDON, Flesh

FLESHTONES LP '82
Singles: 7-inch
I.R.S. ... 3-4 81-82
LPs: 10/12-inch
I.R.S. ... 5-10 81-82
Members: Jonithan Weiss; Marek Pakulski; Keith Streng; Bill Milhiser; Peter Zaremba.
Also see VIPERS

FLETCHER, Darrow P&R/R&B '66
Singles: 7-inch
ATLANTIC ... 3-5 81
CONGRESS ... 3-5 70
CROSSOVER ... 3-4 75-79
GROOVY ... 5-10 66
REVUE ... 5-10 68
UNI ... 3-5 70-71

FLETCHER, Dusty R&B '47
Singles: 78 rpm
NATIONAL ... 10-15 47
Singles: 7-inch
SAVOY ... 5-10 60

FLETCHER, Lois P&R '74
Singles: 7-inch
PLAYBOY ... 3-5 74

FLETCHER, Maria Beale
Singles: 7-inch
MONUMENT ... 4-6 62
Picture Sleeves
MONUMENT ... 5-10 62

FLETCHER, Sam
Singles: 7-inch
CUB (9032 "No Such Luck") ... 15-25 59
CUB (9048 "Only Heaven Knows") 15-25 59
METRO (20013 "Torn Between Two Loves") ... 10-20 59
METRO (20022 "If You Love Me") 10-20 59
RCA (7676 "Take Me in Your Arms") ... 15-25 60
RCA (7817 "Far Away from
RCA (8027 "My Girl") ... 15-25 62
RCA (8076 "Me and the One I Love") ... 15-25 62
TOLLIE (9012 "I'd Think It Over") .. 25-50 64
VAULT (934 "Look of Love") ... 8-12 67
VEE JAY (623 "Guess Who") ... 5-10 64
W.B. (5384 "As Time Goes By") ... 10-15 63
LPs: 10/12-inch
VAULT (116 "The Look of Love, the Sound of Soul") ... 15-25 67
VEE JAY (1094 "Sam Fletcher Sings") ... 25-35 64

FLETCHER, Tee
Singles: 7-inch
JOSIE ... 4-8 67

FLETCHER, Vicky C&W '74
Singles: 7-inch
COLUMBIA ... 3-5 74
MUSIC ROW ... 3-5 76

FLEX, M.C., & FBI Crew D&D '84
Singles: 12-inch
POSSE ... 3-4 84

FLIES
Singles: 7-inch
CAPITOL ... 4-6 69

FLIGHT
Singles: 7-inch
MOTOWN ... 3-4 80
LPs: 10/12-inch
MOTOWN ... 5-10 80

FLINT
Singles: 7-inch
COLUMBIA ... 3-5 78
LPs: 10/12-inch
COLUMBIA ... 5-10 78
Members: Don Brewer; Craig Frost; Chuck Rowe; Mel Schacher.
Also see GRAND FUNK RAILROAD

FLINT, Jimmy, & Stones
Singles: 7-inch
W.B. (5236 "Piasano") ... 10-20 61

FLINT, Shelby P&R '60
Singles: 7-inch
CADENCE ... 5-10 58
QUANTUM ... 4-6
VALIANT ... 4-8 60-66
LPs: 10/12-inch
MCA ... 8-12 73
VALIANT (401 "Shelby Flint") ... 25-40 61
VALIANT (403 "Shelby Flint Sings Folk") ... 25-35 61
(Monaural.)
VALIANT (WS-403 "Shelby Flint Sings Folk") ... 35-50 61
(Stereo.)
VALIANT (5003 "Cast Your Fate to the Wind") ... 15-25 66
(Monaural.)
VALIANT (25003 "Cast Your Fate to the Wind") ... 20-30 66
(Stereo.)

FLINTALES
Singles: 7-inch
FLICK ... 8-12 60

FLINTONES
Singles: 7-inch
CAREER (1601 "Unforgettable You") ... 300-500

FLINTS
(Flint's)
Singles: 7-inch
HEART (100 "Why Did You Go") ... 200-300 62
OKEH (7126 "People Say") ... 50-100 59
PETITE (101 "Over the Ocean") ... 150-250 59

FLINTSTONE, Fred
Singles: 7-inch
B-H ... 5-10 62
EPIC ... 5-10 61

FLIP BACK
Singles: 7-inch
JUBILEE ... 5-10 63

FLIP CARTRIDGE: see CARTRIDGE, Flip

FLIPPERS
Singles: 78 rpm
FLIP ... 50-75 55
Singles: 7-inch
FLIP (305 "My Aching Heart") ... 100-150 55

FLIPS
Singles: 7-inch
MERCURY (71426 "Gone Away") 15-25 59

FLIPSIDE
Singles: 7-inch
FLIPSIDE ... 3-5 81

FLIRTATIONS
Singles: 7-inch
FESTIVAL (705 "Stronger Than Her Love") ... 25-50 67
JOSIE (956 "Natural Born Lover") ... 8-12 66

FLIRTATIONS P&R '69
Singles: 7-inch
DERAM ... 4-6 69
PARROT ... 4-8 68
LPs: 10/12-inch
DERAM ... 15-20 69
Members: Ernestine Pearce; Shirley Pearce; Viola Billups.
Also see GYPSIES

FLIRTATIONS D&D '83
Singles: 12-inch
D&D ... 4-6 83

FLIRTS D&D '84
Singles: 12-inch
CBS ASSOCIATES ... 4-6 86
TELEFON ... 4-6 84
Singles: 7-inch
CBS ASSOCIATES ... 3-4 86
O RECORDS ... 3-4 82
LPs: 10/12-inch
CBS ASSOCIATES ... 5-10 86
O RECORDS ... 5-10 82

FLO & EDDIE
Singles: 7-inch
COLUMBIA ... 4-6 74-77
REPRISE (1142 "Afterglow") ... 4-6 73
REPRISE (1160 "You're a Lady") ... 4-6 73
EPs: 7-inch
REPRISE (564 "Flo & Eddie Meet the Wolfman") ... 10-20 73
(Promotional issue only.)
LPs: 10/12-inch
COLUMBIA (33554 "Illegal, Immoral & Fattening") ... 8-12 75
COLUMBIA (34262 "Moving Target") ... 8-12 76
EPIPHANEY ... 8-10 81
REPRISE (2141 "Flo & Eddie") ... 10-15 73
Members: Howard Kaylan; Marc Volman.
Also see KAYLAN, Howard, & Marc Volman
Also see MOTHERS of INVENTION
Also see TURTLES

FLOATERS
Singles: 7-inch
B.E.B. (1001 "Walkin' on a Rainbow") ... 10-15 66
Members: Tommy Evans; Dock Green; Wilbur Paul.
Also see DRIFTERS

FLOATERS P&R/R&B/LP '77
Singles: 7-inch
ABC ... 3-4 77-79
Picture Sleeves
ABC ... 3-4 77
LPs: 10/12-inch
ABC ... 5-10 77-79
Members: Charles Clark; Paul Mitchell; Ralph Mitchell; Larry Cunningham; Jonathan Murray.

FLOATING BRIDGE
Singles: 7-inch
VAULT ... 5-10 68-69
LPs: 10/12-inch
VAULT (124 "The Floating Bridge") ... 20-30 69
Members: Rick Dangel; Jo Johansen.

FLOATING HOUSE BAND
LPs: 10/12-inch
TAKOMA ... 10-12 69

FLOATING OPERA
Singles: 7-inch
FONTANA ... 4-6 69
LPs: 10/12-inch
EMBRYO ... 10-12 71

FLOCK, The LP '69
Singles: 7-inch
COLUMBIA ... 4-6 69-70
DESTINATION ... 5-10 66-67
U.S.A. ... 4-8 68
LPs: 10/12-inch
COLUMBIA ... 10-15 69-71
MERCURY ... 8-10 75
Members: Jerry Goodman; John Billings.
Also see MICHAEL & MESSENGERS

FLOCK OF SEAGULLS P&R/LP '82
Singles: 12-inch
JIVE ... 4-6 82-83
Singles: 7-inch
ARISTA ... 3-4
JIVE ... 3-4 82-86
Picture Sleeves
ARISTA ... 3-4
JIVE ... 3-4 82-84
LPs: 10/12-inch
JIVE ... 5-10 82-86

FLOCK-ROCKER
("The Crown Prince of the Blues")
Singles: 78 rpm
PLANET (100 "Political Prayer Blues") ... 20-40 57
Singles: 7-inch
PLANET (100 "Political Prayer Blues") ... 20-40 57

FLOOD
Singles: 7-inch
BACKWATER ... 5-10 70s

FLOOD, Dick P&R '59
(With the Pathfinders)
Singles: 7-inch
EPIC ... 4-8 61-62
KAPP ... 3-6 65
MONUMENT ... 5-10 59-60
NASCO ... 3-5 71-72
NUGGET ... 4-6 68
TOTEM ... 4-6 67

FLOOR ROCKERS
Singles: 7-inch
PACIFIC (365 "Summer Time Beat") ... 10-15 65

FLOOR TRADERS
Singles: 7-inch
MTA (136 "Live a Little") ... 20-30 67

FLORENCE, Sab
Singles: 7-inch
BAND BOX (389 "I Need Your Love") ... 8-12 60s

FLORES, Bobby
Singles: 7-inch
WHIZ (604 "Everyday I Have to Cry") ... 10-20 68

FLORES, Danny
Singles: 7-inch
RPM (491 "Trying to Forget") ... 15-25 57
Also see ATWOOD, Eddie, & His Goodies
Also see RIO, Chuck

FLORES, Jane, & Bonet Band
Singles: 7-inch
FABULOUS (747 "Symphony on Wheels") ... 4-8 79

FLORES, Ree
Singles: 7-inch
M&H (9343 "Look into My Heart") .. 40-60

FLORES, Rosie C&W '87
Singles: 7-inch
REPRISE ... 3-4 87-88

FLORESCENTS
Singles: 7-inch
ABC-PAR (10317 "Twist Beat") ... 10-20 62
BETHLEHEM ... 10-15 63

FLORIDIANS
Singles: 7-inch
ABC-PAR ... 25-35 61

FLOS R&B '87
Singles: 7-inch
SUPERSTAR I...3-4 87

FLOTSAM & JETSAM LP '88
Singles: 12-inch
ELEKTRA...4-8 88
(Promotional only.)
Singles: 7-inch
ELEKTRA...3-4 88
LPs: 10/12-inch
ELEKTRA...5-8 88
MCA...5-8 90
METAL BLADE (72208 "Doomsday for the Deceiver")...10-15 87
(Picture disc.)

FLOW
LPs: 10/12-inch
CTI...10-12 70

FLOWER
Singles: 7-inch
U.A. ...3-4 77-78
LPs: 10/12-inch
MCA...5-10 79
MONTAGE...5-10 82
U.A. ...8-10 78

FLOWER CHILDREN
Singles: 7-inch
CASTIL...5-8 67

FLOWER COMPANY
Singles: 7-inch
COCONUT GROOVE (2033 "Did You Love Me from the Start")...40-50

FLOWER ISLAND
Singles: 7-inch
SCEPTER...4-8 69

FLOWER POT
Singles: 7-inch
VAULT...5-10 67

FLOWER POWER
Singles: 7-inch
TUNE-KEL (608 "You Make Me Fly")...15-25 67
TUNE-KEL (611 "Bye Bye Baby")..15-25 68
TUNE-KEL (612 "Trivialities")...15-25 68
TUNE-KEL (613 "Don't Burn My Wings")...15-25 69
TUNE-KEL (614 "Stop!")...15-25 69

FLOWER SHOPPE
Singles: 7-inch
SPRING...4-8

FLOWERPOT MEN
(Flower Pots)
Singles: 7-inch
DERAM (7513 "Let's Go to San Francisco")...10-15 67
DERAM (7516 "Walk in the Sky")..10-15 67
DERAM (85051 "I a Moment of Madness")...8-12 60s
Members: Tony Burrows; Pete Nelson; Roger Greenaway; Roger Cook.
Also see IVY LEAGUE
Also see STAMFORD BRIDGE
Also see WHITE PLAINS

FLOWERS, Lester, & Cougars
Singles: 7-inch
HIT ("I Wonder")...10-20

FLOWERS, Pat
Singles: 7-inch
DOT (15469 "Rock, Sock the Boogie")...15-25 56

FLOWERS, Phil
Singles: 78 rpm
EMPIRE...10-5 51
Singles: 7-inch
A&M...4-8 69
ALMANAC (803 "C'mon Dance with Me")...10-20 64
DOMINO...8-12 62
DOT...5-10 67-69
EMPIRE...15-25 51
HOLLYWOOD (108 "You Stole My Heart")...30-50
JOSIE...5-10 62
SWAY...10-20 61
U.A. ...5-10 60
WING (2100 "No Kissin' at the Hop")...35-45 58
LPs: 10/12-inch
DOT...10-15 68
GUEST STAR (1456 "I Am the Greatest")...25-35 64
GUEST STAR (1457 "Phil Flowers Sings a Tribute")...25-35 64
MOUNT VERNON (154 "Rhythm 'N' Blues")...15-25
Also see COLE, Nat "King" / Phil Flowers
Also see FUNHOUSE Starring Phil Flowers
Also see HALEY, Bill / Phil Flowers
Also see HOLLYWOOD ARGYLES / Phil Flowers

FLOWERS, Vancie
Singles: 7-inch
CREST (1073 "You Taught Me to Love You")...8-12 59
PIKE (5901 "What a Man")...10-20 60

FLOWERZ
Singles: 7-inch
KINGSTON (1967 "I Need Your Love Now")...10-20 67
(Selection number seems incompete, since other Kingston issues have one or two digits following the year – "1967" in this case.)
KINGSTON (19684 "Flyte")...10-20 68

FLOYD, Billy
Singles: 7-inch
20TH FOX (6678 "Sweeter Than Candy")...10-15

FLOYD, Bobby
Singles: 7-inch
MUSIC HALL (100 "It Gives Me Chills")...15-25

FLOYD, Bonnie, & Original Untouchables
Singles: 7-inch
BRIGHT YELLOW...4-8 69

FLOYD, Eddie P&R/R&B '66
Singles: 7-inch
ATLANTIC...8-12 65
LU-PINE (115 "Set My Soul on Fire")...15-25 63
LU-PINE (122 "I'll Be Home")...15-25 63
MALACO...3-6 77
MERCURY...3-6 78
SAFICE (334 "Never Get Enough of Your Love")...10-15 64
STAX...4-8 66-75
LPs: 10/12-inch
ATCO...8-10 74
MALACO...5-10 77
STAX...10-20 67-79
Also see FALCONS
Also see MOORE, Dorothy, & Eddie Floyd
Also see REDDING, Otis / Carla Thomas / Sam & Dave / Eddie Floyd

FLOYD, Eddie, & Mavis Staples
Singles: 7-inch
STAX...3-6 69
Also see FLOYD, Eddie
Also see STAPLES, Mavis

FLOYD, Fast: see FAST FLOYD

FLOYD, Frank
Singles: 7-inch
F&L (100 "Monkey Love")...200-300 57
Also see HARMONICA FRANK

FLOYD, Jessie
Singles: 7-inch
DIXIE...10-15

FLOYD, King: see KING FLOYD

FLOYD & JERRY
(With the Counterpoints)
Singles: 7-inch
DOUBLE SHOT...4-8 67
PRESTA...4-8 66

FLUDD
Singles: 7-inch
W.B. ...3-5 72
LPs: 10/12-inch
W.B. ...8-10 72

FLUFF
Singles: 7-inch
ROULETTE...3-5 72
LPs: 10/12-inch
ROULETTE...8-10 72

FLUFFER, Jive M.
Singles: 7-inch
BLADE (001 "Waterbladder")...4-6 72

FLUID: see NIRVANA / The Fluid

FLUKE & O'NEAL
(Fluke & Liz)
Singles: 7-inch
DECEMBER...3-5
TE ME...3-5 79

FLUORESCENTS
Singles: 7-inch
CANDLELITE (420 "The Facts of Love")...8-10 63
HANOVER (4520 "The Facts of Love")...50-100 59

FLY BI NIGHTS
Singles: 7-inch
TIFFANY (564 "Found Love")...20-40 67

FLYBOYS
Singles: 7-inch
FRONTIER...3-5 79

FLYER
Singles: 7-inch
INFINITY...3-4 79
LPs: 10/12-inch
INFINITY...5-10 79

FLYERS
Singles: 78 rpm
ATCO (6088 "On Bended Knee")...20-30 57
Singles: 7-inch
ATCO (6088 "On Bended Knee")...20-30 57
Members: Bobby Hendricks; Bill Pinckney; Dee Bailey; Bill Kennedy.
Also see HENDRICKS, Bobby
Also see PINKNEY, Bill

FLYING BURRITO BROTHERS LP '69
Singles: 7-inch
A&M...3-6 69-70
COLUMBIA...3-5 76
REGENCY...3-4 80
LPs: 10/12-inch
A&M...10-15 69-76
COLUMBIA...8-10 75-76
REGENCY...5-10 80
Members: Gram Parsons; Chris Hillman; Bernie Leadon; Al Perkins; Rick Roberts; Mike Clarke; Pete Battin; "Sneaky" Pete Kleinow; Greg Harris; Ed Ponder; Floyd "Gib" Guilbeau; John Beland
Also see BATTIN, Skip
Also see BURRITO BROTHERS
Also see FIREFALL
Also see GUILBEAU, Floyd "Gib"
Also see HILLMAN, Chris
Also see PARSONS, Gram
Also see SHILOH
Also see SNEAKY PETE & SNEAKERS

FLYING CIRCUS
Singles: 7-inch
GNP...4-6 69
MTA (130 "Green Eyes")...15-25 67
LPs: 10/12-inch
CAPITOL...10-15 73-74

FLYING COLOR
LPs: 10/12-inch
FRONTIER...5-10 87
Members: Richard Chase; Dale Duncan; John Stuart; Hector Peñalosa.

FLYING GIRAFFE
Singles: 7-inch
BELL...4-8 69

FLYING LIZARDS P&R '79
Singles: 7-inch
VIRGIN...3-4 79
Picture Sleeves
VIRGIN...3-4 79
LPs: 10/12-inch
VIRGIN...5-10 80

FLYING MACHINE
Singles: 7-inch
RAINY DAY...5-10 67

FLYING MACHINE
Singles: 7-inch
NIGHT OWL (1493 "I'll Find You Anyway")...15-25 68

FLYING MACHINE P&R/LP '69
Singles: 7-inch
CONGRESS...4-8 69-70
JANUS...4-8 69
LPs: 10/12-inch
JANUS...10-15 69
Members: Tony Newman; Stuart Coleman; Steve Jones; Paul Wilkinson.
Also see TAYLOR, James

FLYNN, Freddy, & Flashes
Singles: 7-inch
LYRIC (107 "Hazel")...5-10 59

FLYNN, Smitty, Band
Singles: 7-inch
IT WILL STAND...3-5 81

FLYS
Singles: 7-inch
MYSKATONIC (100 "Reality Composition")...15-25 66
MYSKATONIC (101 "Be What You Is")...15-25 66

FOAM, Freddy
Singles: 7-inch
R&R...4-8

FOAMY BRINE
Singles: 7-inch
BRINE (101 "Tell Her")...40-50 67

FOCAL POINT
Singles: 7-inch
BAN...3-4 85

FOCUS P&R/LP '73
Singles: 7-inch
ATCO...3-5 75
SIRE...3-5 73
LPs: 10/12-inch
ATCO...8-10 74-75
SIRE...8-10 72-77
Also see AKKERMAN, Jan

FOCUS R&B '87
Singles: 7-inch
EMI AMERICA...3-4 87

FOCUS & P.J. PROBY
LPs: 10/12-inch
HARVEST...5-10 78
Also see FOCUS
Also see PROBY, P.J.

FOGCUTTERS
Singles: 7-inch
CARTHAY (777 "Cry Cry Cry")...25-30 65
CHARTER (1217 "Casting My Spell")...10-20 65
CHARTER (1218 "It's My World")..15-20 66
LIBERTY (55793 "Cry Cry Cry")...10-15 65

FOGELBERG, Dan LP '74
Singles: 7-inch
COLUMBIA...4-6 73
EPIC...3-5 74-75
FULL MOON/EPIC...3-5 75-82
FULL MOON...3-4 82-87
Picture Sleeves
FULL MOON/EPIC...3-4 80-87
LPs: 10/12-inch
COLUMBIA...10-15 72
EPIC...8-10 74-78
EPIC/FULL MOON...8-10 75-82
FULL MOON...5-10 82-90
Also see FOOLS GOLD

FOGELBERG, Dan, & Tim Weisberg LP '78
Singles: 7-inch
FULL MOON/EPIC...3-4 78-80
LPs: 10/12-inch
FULL MOON/EPIC...5-10 78
Also see FOGELBERG, Dan
Also see WEISBERG, Tim

FOGERTY, John P&R '72
Promotional Singles: 12-inch
W.B. (2234 "Old Man Down the Road")...5-10 84
W.B. (2267 "Rock & Roll Girls")...5-10 85
W.B. (2337 "I Can't Help Myself")...5-10 85
W.B. (2362 "Vanz Kant Danz")...5-10 85
W.B. (2363 "Vanz Kant Danz-Edit") 5-10 85
W.B. (2514 "Eye of the Zombie")...5-10 86
Singles: 7-inch
ASYLUM...3-5 75-76
FANTASY...3-6 73
W.B. ...3-4 84-86
Picture Sleeves
W.B. (Except 291007)...3-5 84-87
W.B. (29100 "The Old Man Down the Road")...3-5 84
(With blue pictures.)
W.B. (29100 "The Old Man Down the Road")...5-8 84
(With black pictures.)
LPs: 10/12-inch
ASYLUM (1046 "John Fogerty")...5-10 75
W.B. (25203 "Centerfield")...10-15 84
(Last track is mistitled, *Zanz Kant Danz*.)
W.B. (25203 "Centerfield")...5-8 85
(Last track is *Vanz Kant Danz*.)
W.B. (25449 "Eye of the Zombie")...5-8 85
Also see BLUE RIDGE RANGERS
Also see CREEDENCE CLEARWATER REVIVAL
Also see EDDY, Duane

FOGERTY, Tom LP '72
(With the Blue Velvets; with Blue Violets)
Singles: 7-inch
FANTASY...3-5 71-82
ORCHESTRA ("Now You're Not Mine")...35-50 62
(Selection number not known.)
ORCHESTRA (1010 "Have You Ever Been Lonely")...35-50 61
ORCHESTRA (6177 "Come on Baby")...35-50 61
(Despite the higher number, this is the first Orchestra single.)
Picture Sleeves
FANTASY...3-5 71
LPs: 10/12-inch
FANTASY...8-10 72-81
Members: Tom Fogerty; John Fogerty; Doug Clifford; Stuart Cook.
Also see CREEDENCE CLEARWATER REVIVAL
Also see RUBY
Also see SAUNDERS, Merl

FOGGY NOTIONS
Singles: 7-inch
GINNY (904 "Need a Little Lovin' ")...20-30 66

FOGHAT P&R/LP '72
Singles: 12-inch
BEARSVILLE (725 "Stone Blue")...5-10 78
(Promotional issue only, colored vinyl.)
Singles: 7-inch
BEARSVILLE...3-5 72-80
MARK-O HILDENEN ("Goin' Home for Christmas '86")...3-4 86
Picture Sleeves
BEARSVILLE...3-5 79
MARK-O HILDENEN ("Goin' Home for Christmas '86")...3-4 86
LPs: 10/12-inch
BEARSVILLE...5-10 72-83
Members: Dave Peverett; Roger Earl; Rod Price; Tony Stevens; Erik Cartwright; Nick Jameson.
Also see JAMESON, Nick
Also see SAVOY BROWN
Also see WISHBONE ASH

FOLAND, Bill, & Surfs
Singles: 7-inch
TISHMAN (903 "Surfin' Trumpets")...25-35 63

FOLDY, Peter
Singles: 7-inch
NIGHTFLITE (Black vinyl)...3-4 82
NIGHTFLITE (Colored vinyl)...4-8 82
(Promotional issue only.)
POLYDOR...3-5 76

FOLEY, Betty C&W '54
Singles: 78 rpm
DECCA...4-8 54-55
Singles: 7-inch
BANDERA...4-8 59
DECCA...5-10 54-55

FOLEY, Brian
Singles: 7-inch
KAPP...4-6 67-68
Picture Sleeves
KAPP...4-6 67

FOLEY, Ellen P&R/LP '79
Singles: 7-inch
EPIC/CLEVELAND INT'L...3-4 79-83
Picture Sleeves
EPIC/CLEVELAND INT'L...3-5 80
LPs: 10/12-inch
EPIC/CLEVELAND INT'L...5-10 79-83
Also see MEAT LOAF

FOLEY, Jim
(With the Big Beats)
Singles: 7-inch
BLUE ORCHID (8642 "My Isle of Golden Dreams")...200-300 68
BLUE ORCHID (306012 "My Isle of Golden Dreams")...4-6 81
LUCKY (1001 "Goodbye Train")...1000-2000 60
(Lucky also used the number 1001 on a release by Ronny & Johnny.)
Also see BADWATER BLUES REVIVAL
Also see 1959
Also see RONNY & JOHNNY

FOLEY, Red C&W '44
(With the Cumberland Valley Boys; with His Log Cabin Quartet; with Betty Foley; with Anita Kerr Singers; with Grady Martin & His Slew Foot Five)
Singles: 78 rpm
BANNER...10-15
DECCA (Except 30067 & 30674)...4-10 42-57
DECCA (30067 "Rock 'N Reelin' ") 10-20 56
DECCA (30674 "Crazy Little Guitar Man")...10-20 58
MELOTONE...10-15
ORIOLE...10-15
Singles: 7-inch
DECCA (25000 series)...4-8 61-67
DECCA (27000 thru 29000 series)...10-20 50-56
DECCA (30000 series, except 30067 & 30674)...10-20 56-59
DECCA (30067 "Rock 'N Reelin' ") 25-35 56
DECCA (30674 "Crazy Little Guitar Man")...25-35 58
DECCA (31000 thru 32000 series)...4-8 60-67
DECCA (46411 "Lonely Mile")...4-6 68
MCA...3-5 73
EPs: 7-inch
DECCA...10-20 53-59
LPs: 10/12-inch
CORAL...5-8 73
COUNTRY MUSIC...6-10 76
DECCA (100 series)...15-25 64
DECCA (4000 series, except 4140)...10-25 61-67
DECCA (4140 "Company's Comin' ")...10-20 61
DECCA (5303 "The Red Foley Souvenir Album")...40-60 51
(10-inch LP.)
DECCA (5338 "Lift Up Your Voice")...40-60 51
(10-inch LP.)
DECCA (7100 series)...15-25 64
DECCA (8294 "The Red Foley Souvenir Album")...20-30 56
DECCA (8296 "Beyond the Sunset")...15-25 56
DECCA (8767 "He Walks with Thee")...10-20 58
DECCA (8806 "My Keepsake Album")...20-30 58
DECCA (8847 "Let's All Sing with Red Foley")...15-25 59
DECCA (8903 "Let's All Sing to Him")...10-20 59
DECCA (74000 & 75000 series)...8-12 68-69
DECCA/DICKIES ("Red Foley's Dickies Souvenir Album")...50-100 58
(Special Products issue for the Dickies company.)
MCA...5-8 80s
PICKWICK/HILLTOP...8-12 66
VOCALION...6-12 65-71
Also see KERR, Anita
Also see KNIGHT, Evelyn, & Red Foley
Also see MARTIN, Grady, & His Slew Foot Five
Also see WELK, Lawrence, & His Orchestra
Also see WELLS, Kitty, & Red Foley

FOLEY, Red, & Andrews Sisters
Singles: 78 rpm
DECCA...4-8 54
Also see ANDREWS SISTERS

FOLEY, Red / Jimmie Davis
LPs: 10/12-inch
GREEN VALLEY...6-12 76
Also see DAVIS, Jimmie

FOLEY, Red, & Little Foleys
Singles: 78 rpm
DECCA...4-8 50
Singles: 7-inch
DECCA...10-15 50
Picture Sleeves
DECCA...20-30 50
Members: Red Foley; Shirley Foley, Julie Foley; Jenny Foley.
Also see FOLEY, Red

FOLEY, Red, & Ernest Tubb
EPs: 7-inch
DECCA...10-20 52-56
LPs: 10/12-inch
DECCA (8298 "Red & Ernie")...30-50 56

FOLEY, Webb
Singles: 78 rpm
EMERALD...25-50 56
Singles: 7-inch
EMERALD (2013 "Bee Bop Baby")...50-75 56
EPs: 7-inch
EMERALD (750 "Little Bitty Mama")...150-250 56

FOLGER, Dan
Singles: 7-inch
ELF (90004 "Crossword Puzzle")...10-20

FOLKSTON, Johnny
Singles: 7-inch
DAVCO.............................. 5-10 60

FOLKSWINGERS LP '63
Singles: 7-inch
WORLD PACIFIC.............................. 4-6 66
LPs: 10/12-inch
WORLD PACIFIC.............................. 10-20 63-66
Members: Glen Campbell; Tut Taylor; Harihar Rao.
Also see CAMPBELL, Glen
Also see SHANK, Bud

FONDA, Peter
(Bobby Ogden alias Peter Fonda; with Susan Saint James)
Singles: 7-inch
CAPITOL (4465 "Outlaw Blues").............. 3-5 77
Picture Sleeves
CAPITOL (4465 "Outlaw Blues").............. 4-6 77
LPs: 10/12-inch
CAPITOL.............................. 8-10 77

FONDETTES
Singles: 7-inch
ARHOOLIE.............................. 5-10 64

FONG, Oden
LPs: 10/12-inch
FRONTLINE.............................. 5-10 86

FONTAIN, Maurice
Singles: 7-inch
DECCA (30713 "I'm Frantic")........30-50 58

FONTAINE, Eddie P&R '58
(With the Excels; Eddie Reardon)
Singles: 78 rpm
DECCA.............................. 10-20 56-57
JALO.............................. 25-50 56
VIK.............................. 10-15 56
"X".............................. 10-20 54-56
Singles: 7-inch
ARGO.............................. 10-15 58-59
CHANCELLOR.............................. 15-25 58
DECCA.............................. 10-20 56-57
JALO (102 "Where Is Da Woman").............................. 50-75 56
LIBERTY.............................. 5-10 65
SUNBEAM (105 "Nothing Shakin' ").............................. 30-50 58
VIK.............................. 10-20 56
W.B.............................. 8-12 62-63
"X" (0096 "Rock Love").............. 25-50 54
"X" (0108 "On Bended Knee")........ 25-50 54
Also see REARDON, Eddie

FONTAINE, Eddie, & Karen Chandler
Singles: 78 rpm
DECCA.............................. 5-10 57
Singles: 7-inch
DECCA.............................. 5-10 57
Also see CHANDLER, Karen

FONTAINE, Eddie, & Gerry Granahan
Singles: 7-inch
SUNBEAM.............................. 10-15 58
Also see FONTAINE, Eddie
Also see GRANAHAN, Gerry

FONTAINE, Frank
Singles: 78 rpm
MGM (12129 "Everybody Rocks") .15-25 55
Singles: 7-inch
MGM (12129 "Everybody Rocks") .25-50 55

FONTAINE, Frankie LP '63
(Frank Fontaine)
Singles: 7-inch
ABC-PAR.............................. 3-6 62-65
CAPITOL.............................. 3-6 63
Picture Sleeves
ABC-PAR.............................. 5-8 62
CAPITOL.............................. 5-8 63
LPs: 10/12-inch
ABC-PAR.............................. 10-20 62-66
MGM.............................. 6-10 67

FONTAIN, Maurice: see FONTAIN, Maurice

FONTAINE, Vic: see PAT the CAT

FONTANA, Arlene
Singles: 7-inch
PARIS.............................. 5-10 58

FONTANA, D.J., Band
EPs: 7-inch
DSP (14195 "The D.J. Fontana Band").............................. 5-8
Also see COLTIN, R.J.
Also see DONNER, Ral
Also see DRAGON, Paul
Also see PRESLEY, Elvis
Also see SANFORD, Sandy
Also see SAUCEDO, Rick

FONTANA, Wayne
Singles: 7-inch
BRUT.............................. 3-5 73
MGM.............................. 4-8 66-67
METROMEDIA.............................. 4-6 69
LPs: 10/12-inch
MGM (4459 "Wayne Fontana")......15-25 67

FONTANA, Wayne, & Mindbenders P&R/LP '65
Singles: 7-inch
FONTANA.............................. 5-10 65
LPs: 10/12-inch
FONTANA (27542 "The Game of Love").............................. 30-35 65
(Monaural.)
FONTANA (67542 "The Game of Love").............................. 35-40 65
(Stereo.)
Members: Wayne Fontana; Graham Gouldman; Bob Land; Paul Hancox; Eric Stewart; Rick Rothwell; James O'Neil.
Also see FONTANA, Wayne
Also see GOULDMAN, Graham
Also see MINDBENDERS

FONTANE, Tony
Singles: 78 rpm
MERCURY.............................. 3-8 51
Singles: 7-inch
MERCURY.............................. 5-10 51

FONTANE SISTERS P&R '51
Singles: 78 rpm
DOT.............................. 5-15 54-57
RCA.............................. 5-10 51-54
Singles: 7-inch
DOT.............................. 5-15 54-60
RCA.............................. 10-20 51-54
Picture Sleeves
RCA (5524 "Kissing Bridge")..........15-25 54
EPs: 7-inch
DOT.............................. 10-20 56-57
LPs: 10/12-inch
DOT (Except 108).............................. 20-40 56-63
DOT (108 "The Fontane Sisters")...25-50 55
(10-inch LP.)
EVON.............................. 10-15 50s
Members: Bea Fontane; Marge Fontane; Geri Fontane.
Also see BOONE, Pat
Also see COMO, Perry, & Fontane Sisters

FOO FIGHTERS LP '95
EPs: 7-inch
ROSWELL (58530 "Big Me").......... 5-8 96
LPs: 10/12-inch
ROSWELL (The Colour and the Shape").............................. 5-10 97
(Selection number not known.)
ROSWELL (34027 "Foo Fighters")...5-10 95
Members: Dave Grohl; Pat Smear; William Goldsmith; Nate Mendel.
Also see NIRVANA

FOOD
LPs: 10/12-inch
CAPITOL (304 "Forever Is a Dream").............................. 20-30 69
Member: Steve White.

FOOL, The
Singles: 7-inch
MERCURY.............................. 4-8 68-69
EPs: 7-inch
MERCURY (91 "The Fool")...........10-20 68
(Promotional issue only.)
LPs: 10/12-inch
MERCURY (61178 "The Fool")......20-30 68
Members: Barry Finch; M. Koker; J. Leeger.

FOOLS, The P&R/LP '80
Singles: 12-inch
PVC.............................. 4-6
Singles: 7-inch
EMI AMERICA (Except 9324).......... 3-5 80-81
EMI AMERICA (9324 "It's a Night for Beautiful Girls").............................. 5-10 80
(Picture disc. Promotional issue only.)
Picture Sleeves
EMI AMERICA.............................. 3-5 80
LPs: 10/12-inch
EMI AMERICA (Except 9393)........5-10 80-81
EMI AMERICA (9393 "April Fools Day").............................. 10-15 80
(Promotional issue only.)

FOOL'S FACE
LP: 10/12-inch
TALK.............................. 5-8 81-83

FOOLS GOLD P&R/LP '76
Singles: 7-inch
COLUMBIA.............................. 3-5 77
MORNING SKY.............................. 3-5 76
LPs: 10/12-inch
COLUMBIA.............................. 8-10 77
MORNING SKY.............................. 8-10 76
Also see FOGELBERG, Dan

FOOT IN COLD WATER
Singles: 7-inch
ELEKTRA.............................. 3-5 74
LPs: 10/12-inch
ELEKTRA.............................. 8-12 74
Members: Hugh Leggat; Danny Taylor; Paul Naumann; Bob Horne.
Also see NUCLEUS

FOOT LUCY
Singles: 7-inch
MUSHROOM ("Airplane").............. 3-5 81
(No selection number used.)
Picture Sleeves
MUSHROOM ("Airplane").............. 3-5 81
EPs: 7-inch
DASH (10596 "Heartbeep").............. 5-8 83
Members: Brian Brown; Christy Wilkins; Doug Ash; Rich Samore; Rob Petrie; Alex Sheldon.

FOOTE, Chuck
Singles: 7-inch
ROULETTE.............................. 4-8 63
SONCRAFT.............................. 5-8 61
20TH FOX.............................. 4-8 62

FOOTMAN, John
Singles: 7-inch
BEATLE.............................. 3-5 75

FOOTPRINTS
Singles: 7-inch
CAPITOL (2052 "Never Say Die")....6-12 67

FORBERT, Steve P&R/LP '79
Singles: 7-inch
GEFFEN.............................. 3-4 88
NEMPEROR.............................. 3-5 79-82
Picture Sleeves
GEFFEN.............................. 3-4 88
LPs: 10/12-inch
NEMPEROR.............................. 5-10 79-82

FORBES, Dr. Edvard, & Mr. X
Singles: 7-inch
S.I.N.A. (507 "A Trip to the Moon")...5-10

FORBES, Dorothy
(With David Clowney Orchestra)
Singles: 7-inch
WINLEY (217 "I Still Want You")....10-20 57

FORBES, Graham, & Trio
LPs: 10/12-inch
PHILLIPS INT'L (1955 "The Matini Set").............................. 500-750 59

FORBES, Walter
Singles: 7-inch
RCA (8163 "Jack Daniel").............. 5-8 63

FORBIDDEN FIVE
Singles: 7-inch
CAPITOL (4205 "Enchanted Farm").............................. 15-25 59

FORBIDDEN FRUIT
Singles: 7-inch
PLAYBOY.............................. 3-5 74

FORCE
Singles: 7-inch
LIFESONG (45031 "Star Wars Stars").............................. 4-6 77

FORCE
Singles: 7-inch
PHILADELPHIA INT'L.............................. 3-4 81
LPs: 10/12-inch
PHILADELPHIA INT'L.............................. 5-10 81

FORCE, Gale: see GALE FORCE

FORCE 5
Singles: 7-inch
ASCOT.............................. 10-15 66
LPs: 10/12-inch
MONTAGE.............................. 5-10 82

FORCE M.D.s R&B/LP '84
Singles: 12-inch
TOMMY BOY.............................. 4-6 84-86
Singles: 7-inch
TOMMY BOY.............................. 3-4 84-88
W.B.............................. 3-4 86
Picture Sleeves
TOMMY BOY.............................. 3-4 86-88
W.B.............................. 3-4 86
LPs: 10/12-inch
TOMMY BOY.............................. 5-10 84-87

FORCE OF NATURE
Singles: 7-inch
TOMMY.............................. 3-5 73
LPs: 10/12-inch
TOMMY.............................. 8-10 74

FORCEP, Bent, & Patients
Singles: 7-inch
ORIGINAL SOUND.............................. 5-10 63

FORD, Ann
(Ann Alford)
Singles: 7-inch
APOLLO (532 "The Fool").............. 20-30 59
Also see ALFORD, Annie

FORD, Billy
(With the Thunderbirds)
Singles: 78 rpm
JOSIE.............................. 10-20 55
UNITED.............................. 10-20 53-54
VIK.............................. 10-20 57
Singles: 7-inch
JOSIE (775 "Stop Lying on Me")....20-30 55
REPRISE.............................. 4-8 64
UNITED (142 "Smooth Rockin' ")....15-25 53
UNITED (167 "Old Age")..............15-25 54
VIK (0263 "How Can I Be Sure")....25-35 57
Note: Billy Ford & the Thunderbirds tracks may be found on the flip of Swan releases by Billy & Lillie. See that section for those.
Also see AUGUST, Joseph
Also see BILLY & LILLIE
Also see SHAW, Joan, & Billy Ford

FORD, Billy, & Thunderbirds / Ron Corby
EPs: 7-inch
VIK (5 "Billy Ford & the Thunderbirds").............................. 25-50 57
(Promotional issue only. Not issued with cover.)
Also see CORBY, Ron
Also see FORD, Billy

FORD, Bobby, & Blazers
Singles: 7-inch
LUCK (105 "Grasshopper")............10-20 64

FORD, Carol
Singles: 7-inch
FEDERAL.............................. 4-8 64

FORD, Clinton
Singles: 7-inch
ROULETTE.............................. 5-10 67

FORD, Danby
Singles: 7-inch
ACCENT.............................. 4-8 66

FORD, Dave, & Hollywood Flames: see HOLLYWOOD FLAMES

FORD, David, & Ebbtides
Singles: 7-inch
SPECIALTY (588 "My Confession").............................. 25-35 56

FORD, Dee Dee
(D.D. "Foots" Ford; D.D. Ford)
Singles: 7-inch
ABC-PAR (10503 "Just Like a Fool").............................. 8-10 63
GLOW HILL (500 "D.D.'s Bounce").............................. 10-15 61
POTOMAC (902 "D.D.'s Madison").............................. 10-20 60
Also see GARDNER, Don, & Dee Dee Ford

FORD, Eddie
Singles: 7-inch
SABRINA (332 "The Drag")..........15-25 59
(Reissued as by the Mar-Villes, then again as by Rick & Rick-A-Shays.)
Also see MAR-VILLES
Also see RICK & Rick-A-Shays

FORD, Emile, & Checkmates
Singles: 7-inch
ANDIE.............................. 8-12 60

FORD, Ernie: see FORD, Tennessee Ernie

FORD, Frankie P&R/R&B '59
Singles: 78 rpm
ACE (549 "Cheatin' Woman")........25-50 58
ACE (554 "Sea Cruise")..........200-300 59
Singles: 7-inch
ABC.............................. 3-4 73-74
ACE.............................. 8-15 58-60
BRIARMEADE.............................. 3-5
CINNAMON.............................. 3-5
COLLECTABLES.............................. 3-4 81
CONSTELLATION.............................. 4-8 63
DOUBLOON.............................. 4-8 67
IMPERIAL.............................. 5-10 60-62
PAULA.............................. 3-5 71
SYC.............................. 3-4 82
20TH FOX.............................. 4-8 60s
Picture Sleeves
ACE (592 "Chinatown")..............15-25 60
EPs: 7-inch
ACE (105 "Best of Frankie Ford")..50-75 59
LPs: 10/12-inch
ACE (1005 "Let's Take a Sea Crusie").............................. 75-125 59
BRIARMEADE.............................. 8-10 76
Also see CLANTON, Jimmy / Frankie Ford / Jerry Lee Lewis / Patsy Cline
Also see SMITH, Huey

FORD, Fred
Singles: 7-inch
COVER.............................. 8-12

FORD, Gloria
Singles: 7-inch
ARRAWAK.............................. 4-8 65

FORD, Jim
Singles: 7-inch
DRUMFIRE (2 "The Story of Elvis Presley").............................. 10-20 60
SUNDOWN.............................. 3-5
Also see CHECK-MATES
Also see MANHATTANS
Also see MOHAWKS
Also see STARFIRES
Also see SHAMROCKS

FORD, Jimmy
(Jimmy Forde)
Singles: 7-inch
FLICK CITY.............................. 8-12
MUSTANG.............................. 4-8 67
STYLO (2102 "You're Gonna Be Sorry").............................. 30-50 59
STYLO (2105 "We Belong Together").............................. 30-50 59

FORD, Joy C&W '78
Singles: 7-inch
COUNTRY INT'L.............................. 3-5 78-88

FORD, Kenny, & Jubilaires
Singles: 7-inch
HEART.............................. 10-15

FORD, Kitty
Singles: 7-inch
SMASH.............................. 4-8 61

FORD, Lita LP '84
Singles: 7-inch
MERCURY.............................. 3-5 84
RCA.............................. 3-4 88-90
Picture Sleeves
RCA.............................. 3-4 88-90
LPs: 10/12-inch
MERCURY.............................. 5-10 84
RCA.............................. 5-8 88-90
Also see RUNAWAYS

FORD, Lita, & Ozzy Osbourne
Singles: 7-inch
RCA.............................. 3-4 89
Picture Sleeves
RCA.............................. 3-4 89
Also see FORD, Lita
Also see OSBOURNE, Ozzy

FORD, Lori & Carl
Singles: 7-inch
CARLTON.............................. 5-10 59

FORD, Mac & Sandy
Singles: 7-inch
CUCA (6767 "I Don't Love You Anymore").............................. 8-12 67

FORD, Mary: see PAUL, Les, & Mary Ford

FORD, Neal, & Fanatics
(Neal Ford Factory)
Singles: 7-inch
ABC.............................. 5-10 69
HICKORY.............................. 5-15 67-68
TANTARA (1101 "Don't Tie Me Down").............................. 15-25 66
TANTARA (1104 "Searchin' ")..........15-25 66
TANTARA (1107 "I Will if You Want").............................. 15-25 66
LPs: 10/12-inch
HICKORY (141 "Neal Ford and the Fanatics").............................. 20-30 68
Also see FANATICS

FORD, Nick: see NICK, Ford

FORD, Pennye R&B '84
Singles: 12-inch
TOTAL EXPERIENCE.............................. 4-6 84-85
Singles: 7-inch
TOTAL EXPERIENCE.............................. 3-4 84-85
LPs: 10/12-inch
TOTAL EXPERIENCE.............................. 5-10 85

FORD, Peter
(With Davie Allan)
Singles: 7-inch
PHILIPS.............................. 4-8 65
Also see ALLAN, Davie

FORD, Robben LP '88
LPs: 10/12-inch
W.B.............................. 5-8 88

FORD, Rocky Bill
Singles: 78 rpm
GILT EDGE.............................. 10-20 51

FORD, Ted
Singles: 7-inch
GAYE (34 "You Don't Love Me")......8-10
SOUND STAGE 7 (2594 "Pretty Girls Everywhere").............................. 10-20 68
SOUND STAGE 7 (2604 "You're Gonna Need Me").............................. 10-20 68

FORD, Tennessee Ernie C&W/P&R '49
(With the Green Valley Singers & Orchestra; Tennessee Ernie)
Singles: 78 rpm
CAPITOL (1 "Sixteen Tons")..........5-10 69
(Promotional "Special Commemorative Pressing" for Ford's 20th year on Capitol.)
CAPITOL (1200 thru 2900 series)......5-15 50-57
CAPITOL (40000 series)..............5-10 49-50
Singles: 7-inch
CAPITOL (1275 thru 2900 series)..10-30 50-54
(Purple labels. Ford's many "Boogie" titles represent the higher end of this price range.)
CAPITOL (2000 thru 4100 series).......3-5 70-75
(Orange labels.)
CAPITOL (3000 thru 4400 series, except 3343).............................. 5-15 54-60
CAPITOL (3343 "Bright Lights & Blond-Haired Women").............................. 15-25 56
CAPITOL (4500 thru 5700 series)......3-6 61-67
Picture Sleeves
CAPITOL.............................. 10-20 55-60
EPs: 7-inch
CAPITOL (Except 413)..............5-10 55-61
CAPITOL (413 "Backwoods Boogie and Blues").............................. 20-30 53
GREEN GIANT (2566 "When Pea-Pickers Get Together").............................. 10-15
(Mail order offer. Add $3 to $5 if accompanied by special mailer/sleeve. Promotional issue made for the Green Giant Co.)
LPs: 10/12-inch
CAPITOL (Except 888)..............5-15 56-80
CAPITOL (888 "Ol' Rockin' Ern")....25-50 57
EVEREST.............................. 5-10 70s
LONGINES.............................. 5-10
PICKWICK.............................. 5-10 70s
READER'S DIGEST (241 "Tennessee Ernie Ford").............................. 20-40
(Boxed, eight-disc set. With booklet.)
Session: Jordanaires.
Also see HUTTON, Betty, & Tennessee Ernie Ford
Also see JORDANAIRES
Also see LAWRENCE, Steve / Tennessee Ernie Ford
Also see LEE, Brenda / Tennessee Ernie Ford
Also see OWENS, Buck / Tennessee Ernie Ford
Also see STARR, Kay, & Tennessee Ernie Ford

FORD, Tennessee Ernie, & Glen Campbell
LPs: 10/12-inch
CAPITOL.............................. 10-12 75
Also see CAMPBELL, Glen

FORD, Tennessee Ernie, & Joe "Fingers" Carr C&W '51
Singles: 78 rpm
CAPITOL.............................. 4-8 51
Singles: 7-inch
CAPITOL.............................. 5-10 51
Also see CARR, Joe "Fingers"

FORD, Tennessee Ernie, & Dinning Sisters
Singles: 78 rpm
CAPITOL....4-8 50s
Singles: 7-inch
CAPITOL....5-10 50s
Also see DINNING SISTERS

FORD, Tennessee Ernie, & Andra Willis C&W '75
Singles: 7-inch
CAPITOL....3-5 75
Also see FORD, Tennessee Ernie
Also see WILLIS, Andra

FORD THEATRE
Singles: 7-inch
ABC....5-10 68-69
LPs: 10/12-inch
ABC (658 "Trilogy")....20-30 68
ABC (681 "Time Changes")....15-25 69
Members: Joey Scott; John Mazzarelli.

FORDE, Jimmy: see FORD, Jimmy

FORDHAM, Julia LP '88
Singles: 7-inch
VIRGIN....3-4 88-89
Picture Sleeves
VIRGIN....3-4 88-89
LPs: 10/12-inch
VIRGIN....5-8 88-90

FORECAST R&B '80
Singles: 12-inch
RCA....4-6 83
Singles: 7-inch
ARIOLA....3-4 80
RCA....3-4 83
LPs: 10/12-inch
RCA....5-10 83

FOREHAND, Eddie "Buster"
Singles: 7-inch
JOSIE....4-8 68

FOREIGN INTRIGUE
Singles: 7-inch
E.M....8-12
LAURIE....4-8 77
Members: Ernie Maresca; Del Satins.
Also see DEL SATINS
Also see MARESCA, Ernie

FOREIGNER P&R/LP '77
Singles: 7-inch
ATLANTIC (Black vinyl)....3-5 77-90
ATLANTIC (3543 "Blue Morning, Blue Day")....4-8 78
(Colored vinyl. Promotional issue only.)
ATLANTIC/W.B....3-5 79
Picture Sleeves
ATLANTIC....3-5 78-88
LPs: 10/12-inch
ATLANTIC....5-10 77-91
GEFFEN....5-10 85
MFSL (052 "Double Vision")....25-50 81
Members: Lou Gramm; Rick Wills; Mick Jones; Dennis Elliott; Ian McDonald; Al Greenwood.
Also see BAD COMPANY
Also see FRASER, Andy
Also see NEW JERSEY MASS CHOIR
Also see SPYS
Also see WALKER, Junior

FOREMAN, Jan
Singles: 7-inch
MEADOWBROOK....8-12

FOREMOST AUTHORITY
Singles: 7-inch
GNP....4-8 68

FORERUNNERS
Singles: 7-inch
LIBERTY (55852 "Magic of a Girl")....15-25 65

FOREST
LPs: 10/12-inch
HARVEST....10-12 70

FOREST, Earl: see FORREST, Earl

FOREST, Jimmy R&B '52
(Jimmy Forrest)
Singles: 78 rpm
DOT....5-10 55
UNITED....5-15 52-55
Singles: 7-inch
DOT (15340 "Night Train Mambo")....10-15 55
PRESTIGE....5-10 61-62
TRIUMPH....8-12 59
UNITED (Except 113)....10-20 52-55
UNITED (110 "Night Train")....15-25 52
(Black vinyl.)
UNITED (110 "Night Train")....35-50 52
(Colored vinyl.)
LPs: 10/12-inch
NEW JAZZ (8250 "Forrest Fire")....25-50 60
NEW JAZZ (8293 "Soul Street")....25-50 62
PRESTIGE....20-30 61-62
(Yellow label.)
PRESTIGE....10-20 64
(Blue label.)
UNITED 002 "Night Train")....75-100 57
(10-inch LP.)
Also see DAVIS, Miles

FOREST CITY JOE
(Joe Pugh)
Singles: 78 rpm
ARISTOCRAT (3110 "Memory of Sonny Boy")....50-75 49

FORESTER SISTERS C&W '85
Singles: 7-inch
W.B....3-4 84-91
LPs: 10/12-inch
W.B....5-8 85-91
Members: Kathy Forester; Kim Forester; June Forester; Christy Forester.
Also see BELLAMY BROTHERS & Forester Sisters

FORETELLS
Singles: 7-inch
CATAMOUNT (109 "Return to Me")....10-15 65
(Black vinyl.)
CATAMOUNT (109 "Return to Me")....15-20 65
(Colored vinyl.)

FOREVER CHILDREN
Singles: 7-inch
ABC....4-8 67

FOREVER MORE LP '70
Singles: 7-inch
RCA....3-5 69-70
LPs: 10/12-inch
RCA....10-15 69-70
Also see AVERAGE WHITE BAND

FOREVERS
Singles: 7-inch
APT....10-15 58

FORGE, Val E.
Singles: 7-inch
STRAND....5-10 60

FORGOTTEN TYMES
Singles: 7-inch
NIGHT OWL....5-8 67

FORMAN, Peggy C&W '77
Singles: 7-inch
DIMENSION....3-4 80-81
MCA....3-5 77

FORMATION
LPs: 10/12-inch
ARIES....15-20 71
Members: Joe Vece; Phil Vallie; Ray Francis; Phil Sargent.
Also see PREMIERS
Also see ROCK FORMATION

FORMATIONS P&R '68
Singles: 7-inch
BANK (1007 "At the Top of the Stairs")....20-30 67
MGM (13899 "At the Top of the Stairs")....5-8 68
MGM (13963 "Love's Not Only for the Heart")....10-20 68
MGM (14009 "Don't Get Close")....8-12 68
Members: Victor Drayton; Jerry Akines; Reginald Turner; Ernie Brooks; Johnny Bellman.
Also see CORNER BOYS
Also see HOT ICE
Also see SILENT MAJORITY

FORMERLY FAT HARRY
LPs: 10/12-inch
CAPITOL....10-12 72

FORMINX
Singles: 7-inch
LONDON....4-8 65

FORMULA 1
Singles: 7-inch
W.B....4-8 65

FORMULA V
LPs: 10/12-inch
BURLINGUEN....15-20
MIAMI....15-20
20TH FOX....5-10 77

FORMULA 5
Singles: 12-inch
MALACO....4-6 83
Singles: 7-inch
MALACO....3-4 83
LPs: 10/12-inch
MALACO....5-10 83

FORREST D&D '83
Singles: 12-inch
PROFILE....4-6 83

FORREST, Andrea / Plastic Ice Cube
Singles: 7-inch
WARICK (6750 "Sooner or Later") 15-25 67

FORREST, Carole
Singles: 7-inch
ATCO....4-8 64

FORREST, Earl R&B '53
("Earl "Whoopin' & Hollerin' " Forrest; Earl Forest)
Singles: 78 rpm
DUKE (Except 103)....15-25 52
DUKE (103 "Rock the Bottle")....40-60 52
METEOR....50-75 53
Singles: 7-inch
DUKE (108 "Whoopin' and Hollerin' ")....25-35 52
DUKE (113 "Last Night's Dream")....20-30 53
DUKE (121 "Out on a Party")....20-30 54
DUKE (130 "Your Kind of Love")....20-30 54
DUKE (349 "Memphis Twist")....10-20 62
DUKE (363 "The Duck")....10-20 63
METEOR (5005 "I Wronged a Woman")....50-100 53
Also see ACE, Johnny / Earl Forrest

Also see KING, B.B.

FORREST, Gene, & Four Feathers
(With Chuck Higgins & His Orchestra)
Singles: 78 rpm
ALADDIN (3224 "Dubio")....20-30 54
Singles: 7-inch
ALADDIN (3224 "Dubio")....40-60 54
Also see GENE & EUNICE
Also see HIGGINS, Chuck

FORREST, Jackie
Singles: 7-inch
HITSVILLE (1138 "Breakin' Your Heart for Fun")....50-75 62

FORREST, Jimmy: see FOREST, Jimmy

FORREST, Nick
Singles: 78 rpm
FORTUNE....20-30 55
Singles: 7-inch
FORTUNE (513 "I Can't Fall in Love")....30-40 55
TEEN LIFE ("Let Me Be")....50-100
(No selection number used.)

FORREST, Sonny
Singles: 7-inch
ATCO (6157 "Diddy Bop")....10-15 60
RED TOP (128 "Mama, Keep My Wife at Home")....15-25 60

FORREST, Sylvia C&W '89
Singles: 7-inch
DOOR KNOB....3-4 89

FORSAKEN
Singles: 7-inch
MTA....4-8 66

FORSE, Beanon
Singles: 7-inch
RODNEY (514 "You Better Go Now")....30-50

FORSTON, Robby
Singles: 7-inch
PZAZZ ("Are You for Real")....15-20
(Selection number not known.)

FORSYTH, Bruce
Singles: 7-inch
BLUE CAT....5-10 65

FORSYTH, Ed
Singles: 7-inch
CHESS....5-8 63
JEWEL....5-10 64

FORT, Ruben
(Rubien Fort)
Singles: 7-inch
ANNA (1117 "So Good")....20-30 60
CHECK MATE (1007 "I'll Do the Best I Can")....20-30 61

FORT MUDGE MEMORIAL DUMP
LPs: 10/12-inch
MERCURY (61256 "The Fort Mudge Memorial Dump")....20-30 70

FORT WORTH DOUGHBOYS
Singles: 78 rpm
BLUEBIRD (5257 "Nancy Jane")....150-250 30s
Also see WILLS, Bob

FORTE, Joe
Singles: 7-inch
HI-MAR....5-10

FORTE, Nicky
Singles: 7-inch
HARRISON (100 "Rockin' Guitar")....15-25 57

FORTE FOUR
Singles: 7-inch
DECCA....5-10 66

FORTELLS
Singles: 7-inch
CATAMOUNT....4-8 66

FORTES
Singles: 7-inch
CURRENT (103 "Waiting for My Baby")....50-75 64

FORTNOX
Singles: 7-inch
EPIC....3-4 82
LPs: 10/12-inch
EPIC....5-10 82

FORTRESS
Singles: 7-inch
ATLANTIC....3-4 81
LPs: 10/12-inch
ATLANTIC....5-10 81

FORTUNATO, Joe
Singles: 7-inch
FORTUNE (481 "Little Angel")....5-8 62

FORTUNE
Singles: 7-inch
BEAR BROTHERS....3-4 80
Members: Bobby Aycock; Jimmy Ogburn.

FORTUNE P&R '85
Singles: 7-inch
MCA/CAMEL....3-4 85
Picture Sleeves
MCA/CAMEL....3-4 85
LPs: 10/12-inch
MCA/CAMEL....5-10 86

FORTUNE, Billy
Singles: 78 rpm
EXCELLO....10-20 57
Singles: 7-inch
DICE (478 "Listen to Your Heart")....150-200
(Reissued as by Billy Jones & Squires.)
EXCELLO....20-30 57
Also see JONES, Billy, & Squires

FORTUNE, Diane
Singles: 7-inch
BRUNSWICK....5-10 58

FORTUNE, Gayle, & Terrytones
Singles: 7-inch
WYE....10-15 61
Also see TERRYTONES

FORTUNE, Jessie
Singles: 7-inch
U.S.A....8-12 63

FORTUNE, Johnny
Singles: 7-inch
ARENA....10-15 63
ARHAVEN....10-20 62
BEAVER....5-10 66
CRUSADER....5-10 64
CURRENT....5-10 64-65
EMMY....10-20 59-60
PARK AVE....10-20 63
U.A....5-10 64
VAULT....4-8 70
LPs: 10/12-inch
PARK AVE (401 "Soul Surfer")....30-50 63
(Monaural.)
PARK AVE (401 "Soul Surfer")....40-60 63
(Stereo.)
Session: Johnny Fortune; Joe Sudetta; Jim O'Keith.
Also see SWEET SOULS

FORTUNE, Lance
Singles: 7-inch
SIGNATURE....5-10 60

FORTUNE, Mickey
Singles: 7-inch
LOGAN (3110 "It's Gonna Hurt Me More")....50-100 59

FORTUNE, Rick
Singles: 7-inch
RAN-DEE....5-8 63

FORTUNE, Robb
Singles: 7-inch
NOW (2 "Crazy Feelin' ")....10-20

FORTUNE BROTHERS
Singles: 7-inch
ACCENT....10-20 65

FORTUNE COOKIES
Singles: 7-inch
SMASH....4-8 65

FORTUNE SEEKERS
Singles: 7-inch
TRIDENT (9966 "Why I Cry")....20-40 66

FORTUNE TELLERS
Singles: 7-inch
MUSIC MAKERS....5-10 61
SHERYL....10-15 61

FORTUNE TELLERS
Singles: 7-inch
ATLANTIC....5-10 63

FORTUNE TELLERS
Singles: 7-inch
FESTIVAL (3702 Gypsy Rock")....10-20 67

FORTUNEERS
Singles: 7-inch
SKYTONE (1000 "Look A' There")....15-25 63
Session: Teacho Wiltshire; Prince Eddie McDowell.
Also see WILTSHIRE, Teacho

FORTUNES
Singles: 78 rpm
CHECKER (818 "Believe in Me")....20-30 55
Singles: 7-inch
CHECKER (818 "Believe in Me")....50-75 55

FORTUNES
(With the Eddie Beale Orchestra)
Singles: 7-inch
DECCA (30541 "Who Cares")....75-125 58
DECCA (30688 "How Clever of You")....50-75 58
Member: Don Wyatt.
Also see COLTS
Also see CREATIVE SOURCE

FORTUNES
Singles: 7-inch
ARGO (5364 "Congratulations")....25-50 60
QUEEN (24010 "Nothing Matters Anymore")....10-20 62
TOP RANK (2019 "Steady Vows")255-40 59
YUCCA (168 "The Laugh of the Town")....20-30 64
YUCCA (170 "This Is Love")....30-40 64

FORTUNES
Singles: 7-inch
LAKE (704 "Runnin")....10-20 61

FORTUNES
(Fortune's; with the Max Davis Orchestra)
Singles: 7-inch
DRA (320 "Tell Me")....200-300 62

FORTUNES
Singles: 7-inch
CUB (9123 "You Don't Know")....10-15 63

FORTUNES
Singles: 7-inch
CUCA (1173 "You Got the Right") 15-25 64

FORTUNES P&R '65
Singles: 7-inch
CAPITOL....3-5 71-74
COLLECTABLES....3-4 80s
LONDON....3-4
PRESS (9773 "You've Got Your Troubles")....10-15 65
(White label, commercial issue.)
PRESS (9773 "You've Got Your Troubles")....5-10 65
(Color label.)
PRESS (9798 "Here It Comes Again")....10-15 65
(White label, commercial issue.)
PRESS (9798 "Here It Comes Again")....10-15 65
(Red or orange labels.)
PRESS (9811 "This Golden Ring")..5-10 66
U.A....4-8 67-68
WORLD PACIFIC....3-5 70
LPs: 10/12-inch
CAPITOL....8-10 71-73
COCA-COLA (21904 "It's the Real Thing")....30-40 60s
(Special products issue.)
PRESS (73002 "The Fortunes")....20-25 65
(Monaural.)
PRESS (83002 "The Fortunes")....25-30 65
(Stereo.)
WORLD PACIFIC....8-10 70
Members: Glen Dale; Barry Pritchard; Shel MacRae.
Also see DALE, Glen

FORTUNES
Singles: 7-inch
BISHOP (1005 "This Is Love")....10-15

45 GRAVE
Singles: 12-inch
ENIGMA....4-6 84
Singles: 7-inch
ENIGMA....3-4 84
LPs: 10/12-inch
ENIGMA....5-10 84

FORTY-SEVEN TIMES ITS OWN WEIGHT
Singles: 7-inch
FABLE (101 "Cumulo Nimbus")....25-50

49TH PARALLEL
Singles: 7-inch
BARRY (3518 "I Need You")....15-25 60s
(Canadian.)
MAVERICK (1004 "Close the Barn Door")....15-20 68
MAVERICK (1011 "Come On Little Child and Talk to Me")....15-20 69
MAVERICK (1101 "Now That I'm a Man")....15-20 69
RCA (3447 "She Says")....8-12 60s
(Canadian.)
RCA (9293 "You Do Things")....8-12 67
VENTURE (612 "Missouri")....15-25 60s
(Canadian.)
VENTURE (1004 "Twilight Woman")....15-25 60s
(Canadian.)
LPs: 10/12-inch
MAVERICK (7001 "49th Parallel")....150-250 69

FORUM P&R '67
Singles: 7-inch
MIRA....10-15 67
PENTHOUSE....10-20 66
LPs: 10/12-inch
MIRA....15-20 67
Members: Phil Campos; Rene Nole; Riselle Vaine.

FORUM QUORUM
Singles: 7-inch
DECCA....4-8 68-69
LPs: 10/12-inch
DECCA....10-12 68

FORUMS
Singles: 7-inch
PRISM (1235 "Bring It on Back")....15-25

FORWAYS
Singles: 7-inch
BAY TOWN....4-8 66

FORWOOD, Shirley
Singles: 78 rpm
DOT (15487 "Two Hearts")....8-12 56
Singles: 7-inch
DOT (15487 "Two Hearts")....10-15 56

FOSTER, Betty
Singles: 7-inch
CREST (1092 "Easier Said Than Done")....5-10 62

FOSTER, Bruce P&R '77
Singles: 7-inch
MILLENIUM....3-5 77
Picture Sleeves
MILLENIUM....5-10 77
LPs: 10/12-inch
MILLENIUM....8-15 77

FOSTER, Cell, & Audios
Singles: 78 rpm
ULTRA (105 "Honest I Do")....50-100 56

Singles: 7-inch
ULTRA (105 "Honest I Do")........200-300 56
(Yellow label.)
ULTRA (105 "Honest I Do")........100-200 56
(Maroon label.)
Also see AUDIOS

FOSTER, Chick
Singles: 7-inch
D&J 5-10 64
Also see BELL, Joey, & Chick Foster

FOSTER, Chuck
LPs: 10/12-inch
PHILLIPS INT'L (1965 "Chuck Foster at the Hotel Peabody") 100-200 60

FOSTER, David P&R '85
Singles: 7-inch
ATLANTIC 3-4 85-88
Picture Sleeves
ATLANTIC 3-4 85-88
LPs: 10/12-inch
ATLANTIC 5-10 86-88
MFSL (123 "The Best of Me") 15-25 84
Also see SKYLARK

FOSTER, David, & Olivia Newton-John P&R '86
Singles: 7-inch
ATLANTIC 3-4 86
Also see FOSTER, David
Also see NEWTON-JOHN, Olivia

FOSTER, Eddie
Singles: 7-inch
IN (6311 "I Never Knew") 15-25
LUCK...10-15 60
LYONS 10-15

FOSTER, Helen
(With the Chapters; with Rovers)
Singles: 78 rpm
REPUBLIC.....................................50-100 52-53
Singles: 7-inch
REPUBLIC (7013 "You Belong to Me")..................................200-300 52
REPUBLIC (7037 "Somebody, Somewhere")........................300-400 53
Also see CHAPTERS

FOSTER, Ian R&B '87
Singles: 7-inch
MCA 3-4 87

FOSTER, J.D., & Union Gospel Singers
Singles: 7-inch
LUCKY (9000 "Late in the Evening") 15-25

FOSTER, Jamie
Singles: 7-inch
WUFF (1201 "Yeah, Pretty Baby") .25-35

FOSTER, Jerry C&W '73
(With Tennessee Tornado)
Singles: 7-inch
BACK BEAT 5-10 59-61
CINNAMON....................................... 3-5 73
HITSVILLE 3-5 76
METROMEDIA 3-5 70
MONUMENT 3-5 78
SPAR 10-15 64
TCF 4-8 66

FOSTER, Jim
Singles: 7-inch
RIVER 10-15

FOSTER, Jimmy
Singles: 7-inch
DEL-FI.. 5-10 63

FOSTER, John, & Sons Ltd.
(Black Dyke Mills Band)
Singles: 7-inch
APPLE (1800 "Yellow Submarine")............................100-125 68

FOSTER, Leroy, & Muddy Waters
Singles: 78 rpm
ARISTOCRAT (12334 "Locked Out Boogie")..................................50-75 49
Also see BABY FACE
Also see WATERS, Muddy

FOSTER, Little Bobby
Singles: 7-inch
STEVENS.................................... 5-10 59

FOSTER, Little Willie
Singles: 78 rpm
BLUE LAKE 50-75 53
COBRA...50-75 57
PARROT 50-75 53
Singles: 7-inch
BLUE LAKE (113 "Falling Rain Blues")..................................100-150 53
(Black vinyl.)
BLUE LAKE (113 "Falling Rain Blues")..................................150-250 53
(Colored vinyl.)
COBRA (5011 "Crying the Blues")..50-75 57
PARROT (813 "Falling Rain Blues")..75-125 53

FOSTER, Lloyd David C&W '82
Singles: 7-inch
COLUMBIA....................................... 3-4 84-85
MCA 3-4 82-83

FOSTER, Millie
Singles: 7-inch
PRESIDENT (826 "Love Wheel")...10-15 62
PRESIDENT (829 "What a Thrill") 10-15 63

FOSTER, Nat
Singles: 7-inch
POWELL... 4-8 64

FOSTER, Pat
LPs:10/12-inch
RIVERSIDE (654 "Gold Rush Songs")......................................35-45
Session: Dick Weissman)

FOSTER, Pat, & Quintones
Singles: 7-inch
LEE (1114 "In the Doorway Crying")..20-30 60
Also see QUINTONES

FOSTER, Phil
Singles: 7-inch
CORAL...10-20 54
EPs: 7-inch
CORAL...15-25 54
LPs: 10/12-inch
CORAL...20-30 54
Also see ALLEN, Steve

FOSTER, Ray
Singles: 7-inch
PJ 4-8 63

FOSTER, Reb
Singles: 7-inch
LOMA... 4-8 64

FOSTER, Walter
Singles: 7-inch
LOMA... 4-8 65

FOSTER, Zena
Singles: 7-inch
VEEP... 4-8 65

FOSTER & LLOYD C&W '87
Singles: 7-inch
RCA... 3-4 87-90
LPs: 10/12-inch
RCA... 5-10 86-90
Members: Radney Foster; Bill Lloyd.
Also see TOMORROW'S WORLD

FOSTER BROTHERS
(With Lefty Guitar Bates & His Band; Foster Bros.)
Singles: 7-inch
B&F (1333 "Revenge")....................15-25 60
DILLIE (101 "Land of Love") 15-25 60
EL BEE (161 "Tell Me Who") 20-30 57
HI MI (3005 "Never Again")............50-75
MERCURY (71360 "Show Me") 25-35 58
PROFILE (4004 "Trust in Me").......15-25 59
Members: Laverne Gayles; George Lattimore; Lindsay Langston; Donald Clay; Ray Pettis.
Also see BATES, Lefty Guitar

FOTHERINGAY
Singles: 7-inch
A&M 3-5 70
LPs: 10/12-inch
A&M 10-15 70
Also see DENNY, Sandy

FOTO-FI-FOUR
Singles: 7-inch
FOTO-FI (107 "Stand Up and Holler")..10-15 64
Picture Sleeves
FOTO-FI (107 "Stand Up and Holler")..20-30 64
Member: Harry Nilsson.
Also see NILSSON

FOTOMAKER P&R/LP '78
Singles: 7-inch
ATLANTIC 3-5 78-79
LPs: 10/12-inch
ATLANTIC 5-10 78-79
Members: Gene Cornish; Dino Dannelli; Wally Bryson.
Also see CORNISH, Gene
Also see RASCALS
Also see RASPBERRIES

FOUCHA, Jerry
Singles: 7-inch
NOLA (736 "Come On Baby")........10-20 67
TRAJON (101 "If It's Better")..........10-20 60s

FOUL DOGS
LPs: 10/12-inch
RHYTHM SOUND (481 "No. 1")..250-350 66

FOUNDATIONS P&R '67
Singles: 7-inch
ERIC (912 "Build Me Up Buttercup"). 3-4 70s
(True stereo.)
UNI 3-6 67-71
LPs: 10/12-inch
UNI 15-20 68-69
Members: Clem Curtis; Colin Young.
Also see YOUNG, Colin

FOUNTAIN, Morris
Singles: 78 rpm
SAVOY... 4-8 54
Singles: 7-inch
SAVOY...8-10 54

FOUNTAIN, Pete P&R/LP '60
Singles: 7-inch
CORAL... 3-5 58-62
LPs: 10/12-inch
CORAL... 5-15 59-69
FIRST AMERICAN 4-8 78
GUEST STAR 5-10 64
SOUTHLAND (215 "New Orleans to L.A.")..15-25 56
Also see HIRT, Al, & Pete Fountain
Also see LEE, Brenda, & Pete Fountain

FOUNTAIN, Roosevelt, & Pens of Rhythm P&R '63
Singles: 7-inch
PRINCE-ADAMS 10-20 62-63

FOUNTAIN OF YOUTH
Singles: 7-inch
COLGEMS 10-20 67-69
SUR-SPEED (223 "Hard Woman") ..8-12
Also see CROSSFIRES

FOUR
(The Four)
Singles: 7-inch
CLARK (225 "Lonely Surfer Boy")..20-30 65

FOUR ACES
Singles: 78 rpm
TRILON (143 "I Wonder, I Wonder, I Wonder")......................................15-25 46
TRILON (145 "There's a Rumor Going Around")......................................15-25 47
TRILON (153 "Richard Ain't Gonna Open That Door")..15-25 47
TRILON (178 "I'll Never Let You Go Again")..15-25 47
TRILON (179 "I'm Crying All the Time")..15-25 47
TRILON (180 "Ain't It a Crying Shame")..15-25 47
Also see ORIGINAL FOUR ACES

FOUR ACES P&R '51
Singles: 78 rpm
DECCA..5-15 51-57
FLASH (103 "Who's to Blame") 15-25 50
MERION (104 "Wanted") 15-25 52
VICTORIA (Black Plastic) 10-15 51
VICTORIA (101 "Sin")....................20-30 51
(Colored Plastic.)
Singles: 7-inch
ABC-PAR 5-10 60
DECCA (25000 series).......................4-8 61-64
DECCA (27000 & 28000 series).....10-20 51-53
DECCA (29000 thru 31000 series)..5-15 54-60
FLASH (103 "Who's to Blame") 15-25 50
MERION (104 "Wanted") 10-20 52
VICTORIA (101 "Sin")....................15-25 51
(Black vinyl.)
VICTORIA (101 "Sin")....................40-60 51
(Colored vinyl.)
VICTORIA (102 "There's a Christmas Tree in Heaven")..15-25 51
Picture Sleeves
ABC-PAR 5-10 60
EPs: 7-inch
DECCA 10-20 52-59
LPs: 10/12-inch
ACCORD...5-10 81-82
CRANE NOTTIS.................................8-10 77
DECCA (4013 "The Golden Hits")..15-25 60
DECCA (5429 "The Four Aces") 20-40 52
(10-inch LP.)
DECCA (8122 thru 8693) 15-30 55-58
DECCA (8766 "Swingin' Aces")........15-25 58
(Monaural.)
DECCA (8766 "Swingin' Aces")......20-30 58
(Stereo. With "DL-7" prefix.)
DECCA (8855 "Hits from Broadway")......................................15-25 59
(Monaural.)
DECCA (8855 "Hits from Broadway")......................................20-30 59
(Stereo. With "DL-7" prefix.)
DECCA (8944 "Beyond the Blue Horizon")......................................10-20 59
(Monaural.)
DECCA (8944 "Beyond the Blue Horizon")......................................15-25 59
(Stereo.)
MCA..5-10 74
U.A. 10-15 61
VOCALION...5-10 69
WESTOWN...5-8
Members: Al Alberts; Louis Silvestri; Dave Mahoney; Sol Vocarro.
Also see ALBERTS, Al
Also see LEE, Brenda / Bill Haley & Comets / Kalin Twins / Four Aces

FOUR ACES / Four Lads / Four Preps
LPs: 10/12-inch
EXACT 5-10 80
Also see FOUR ACES
Also see FOUR LADS
Also see FOUR PREPS

FOUR ACES
Singles: 7-inch
RADNOR...4-6 68-69
LPs: 10/12-inch
RADNOR...8-12 69

4 AFTER 5s
Singles: 7-inch
ALL TIME (9076 "Hello, Schoolteacher")............................25-50 61
Members: Carl White; Al Frazier; Sonny Harris; Turner Wilson.
Also see RIVINGTONS

FOUR AIMS
Singles: 78 rpm
GRADY 200-250 56
Singles: 7-inch
GRADY (012 "If Only I Had Known")..400-500 56
Also see FOUR TOPS

FOUR ARCS
Singles: 78 rpm
BOULEVARD 100-200 54
Singles: 7-inch
BOULEVARD (102 "Life of Ease")..250-350 54
(This exact same track was also issued by the Imperials.)
Also see IMPERIALS

FOUR AVALONS
Singles: 7-inch
OVIDE...25-35 60s

FOUR Bs
Singles: 7-inch
D (1013 "Love Eternal")..................25-35 58

FOUR BARONS
Singles: 78 rpm
REGENT (1026 "Lemon Squeezer")..25-50 50
Also see LARKS

FOUR BARS
Singles: 78 rpm
BULLET (1009 "I'm All Dressed Up with a Broken Heart")...................................25-50 47
BULLET (1010 "Deep in My Heart")..25-50 47
JOSIE...150-250 54-55
REPUBLIC......................................100-200 54
Singles: 7-inch
CADILLAC (2006 "Love Me Forever")......................................150-200 60
DAYCO (101 "Try Me One More Time")..150-250 62
(First issue.)
JOSIE (762 "Grief By Day, Grief By Night")..100-200 54
JOSIE (768 "If I Give My Heart to You")..100-125 54
JOSIE (783 "Let Me Live").........500-600 55
REPUBLIC (7101 "Memories of You")..400-600 54
SHELLEY (180 "Try Me One More Time")..150-250 62
TIME (4 "Why Did You Do It")..........50-75 58
Member: Jimmy Sweeney.
Also see DAYE, Eddie
Also see HUNTER, Shane, & Four Bars
Also see SWEENEY, Jimmy
Also see WILSON, Betty, & Four Bars

FOUR BARS
("Featuring Betty Wilson")
Singles: 7-inch
FALEW! (108 "I've Got to Move")..25-35 64

FOUR BARS & A MELODY
Singles: 78 rpm
SAVOY (657 "Near You") 30-50 48

FOUR BEAUS
Singles: 7-inch
TODD..5-10 59

FOUR BEL'AIRES
Singles: 7-inch
M.Z. (006 "Can I Be in Love")....200-400 59
(Reissued as *Stolen Love* and credited to Larry Lee.)
RELIC 4-8
X-TRA (113 "Tell Me Why").....800-1200 58
Also see LEE, Larry

FOUR BELLS
Singles: 78 rpm
BELL 5-10 54
Singles: 7-inch
BELL 10-15 54

FOUR BELLS
(With Fred Norman & Orchestra)
Singles: 78 rpm
GEM...100-200 54
Singles: 7-inch
GEM (207 "Please Tell It to Me")..300-500 53
GEM (220 "Only a Miracle").......300-500 54

FOUR BELOW ZERO
Singles: 7-inch
DOUBLE SHOT................................10-20 67
JERDEN...8-15 68

FOUR BITS
Singles: 7-inch
ART (160 "Don't Call Me") 10-15

FOUR BLACKAMOORS
Singles: 78 rpm
DECCA...15-25 41

FOUR BLADES
Singles: 78 rpm
GATEWAY 15-25 56
Singles: 7-inch
GATEWAY (1170 "I Want You to Be My Girl")..25-50 56
GATEWAY (1174 "Church Bells May Ring")..25-50 56

FOUR BLADES
Singles: 7-inch
ALERT 15-25 63

FOUR BLADES
EPs: 7-inch
4 HITS...5-10

FOUR BLAZERS
Singles: 7-inch
SURE 5-10 61

FOUR BLAZERS
Singles: 7-inch
BUDDY (143 "Buddy")......................15-25

FOUR BLAZES R&B '52
Singles: 78 rpm
UNITED...10-20 52-55
Singles: 7-inch
UNITED (114 "Mary Jo").................30-50 52
(Black vinyl.)
UNITED (114 "Mary Jo")..............75-100 52
(Colored vinyl.)
UNITED (125 "Night Train")............15-25 52
UNITED (127 "Stop Boogie Woogie")..15-25 52
UNITED (146 "Not Any More Tears")..15-25 53
UNITED (158 "Ella Louise")............15-25 53
UNITED (168 "My Great Love Affair")..15-25 54
UNITED (177 "Do the Do") 15-25 54
UNITED (191 "She Needs to Be Loved")..15-25 55
(Reissued as by the Blasers.)
Member: Tommy Braden.
Also see BLASERS
Also see BRADEN, Tommy, & His Flames
Also see HOLLYWOOD'S FOUR BLAZES

FOUR BLUEBIRDS / Johnny Otis & His Orchestra
Singles: 78 rpm
EXCELSIOR (540 "My Baby Done Told Me")..50-100 49
Member: Bobby Nunn.
Also see NUNN, Bobby
Also see OTIS, Johnny

FOUR BLUEJACKETS
Singles: 78 rpm
MERCURY 15-25 46-47

FOUR BLUES
Singles: 78 rpm
APOLLO (398 "It Takes a Long Tall Brownskinned Gal")........................25-50 48
APOLLO (1145 "Re Bop De Boom")..25-50 50
APOLLO (1160 "Missing You") 25-50 50
DECCA (8517 "Easy Does It") 25-50 41
DECCA (8637 "Bluer Than Bluer Than Blue")..25-50 42
DELUXE (1000 "I'm Gone") 25-50 45
DELUXE (1001 "Chittlins and Pigs Feet")..25-50 48
DELUXE (1002 "Things You Want Most of All")..25-50 45
DELUXE (1003 "I Got a Date with Rhythm")..25-50 45
DELUXE (1004 "When the Old Gang's Back on the Corner") 25-50 45
DELUXE (1005 "Study War No Mo")..25-50 45
DELUXE (3195 "Am I Asking Too Much")..25-50 48
Member: Carroll Jones.
Also see DUPONT, Ann, & Four Blues
Also see ECKSTINE, Billy

FOUR BROTHERS & A COUSIN
Singles: 78 rpm
JAGUAR 100-200 54
Singles: 7-inch
JAGUAR (3003 "Trust in Me") ...250-350 54
JAGUAR (3005 "Whispering Winds")......................................300-400 54

FOUR BUDDIES R&B '51
(With Lefty Bates Orchestra)
Singles: 78 rpm
SAVOY...50-75 50-53
Singles: 7-inch
CORAL (62217 "Hurt")....................15-25 60
CORAL (62325 "The Light")............15-25 62
IMPERIAL (66018 "I Want to Be the Boy You Love")..50-75 64
PHILIPS (40122 "Lonely Summer")..10-20 63
SAVOY (769 "I Will Wait")..........300-500 50
SAVOY (779 "Don't Leave Me Now")..300-500 51
SAVOY (789 "My Summer's Gone")..200-400 51
SAVOY (817 "Heart & Soul") 200-400 51
SAVOY (845 "You're Part of Me")..200-400 52
SAVOY (866 "What's the Matter with Me")..200-400 52
SAVOY (888 "My Mother's Eyes")..200-400 53
SAVOY (891 "I'd Climb the Highest Mountain")....................................200-400 53
Members: Leon Harrison; Greg Carroll; Bert Palmer; Tommy Smith.
Also see BARONS
Also see COOPER, Dolly
Also see FOUR BUDS
Also see GREENE, Rudy, & Four Buddies

FOUR BUDDIES
Singles: 78 rpm
CLUB 51...75-125 55-56
Singles: 7-inch
CLUB 51 (103 "You Mean Everything to Me")..150-250 55
CLUB 51 (105 "Delores")............150-250 56
(Black vinyl.)
CLUB 51 (105 "Delores") 2000-4000 56
(Red vinyl.)
Also see JAMES, Bobbie, & Four Buddies

FOUR BUDS
Singles: 78 rpm
SAVOY...100-200 50
Singles: 7-inch
SAVOY (769 "I Will Wait").........250-350 50
(Second pressings shown as by the Four Buddies.)
Also see FOUR BUDDIES

4 BY FOUR *P&R/R&B/LP '87*

Singles: 7-inch

CAPITOL 3-4 87

Picture Sleeves

CAPITOL 3-4 87

LPs: 10/12-inch

CAPITOL 5-10 87

FOUR C's

Singles: 7-inch

CHRISTY (141 "Scottish Rock") 10-20 61

FOUR CAL-QUETTES

Singles: 7-inch

CAPITOL (4574 "Starbright") 10-20 61
CAPITOL (4657 "Most of All") 10-20 61
CAPITOL (4725 "Again") 10-20 62
LIBERTY (55549 "I Cried") 10-20 63
Also see FOUR COQUETTES

FOUR CASTS

Singles: 7-inch

ATLANTIC 5-10 64

FOUR CHALLENGERS

Singles: 7-inch

IDEAL (11111 "Rayburn Street") 5-10 60s

FOUR CHAPS

Singles: 78 rpm

SHERATON (51 "Night Train") 25-50 55

Singles: 7-inch

SHERATON (51 "Night Train") 50-75 55
(Later issued as by the Owens Brothers.)
Members: John Owens; Bob Owens; Bill Owens; D.J. Owens.
Also see OWENS BROTHERS

FOUR CHAPS

Singles: 78 rpm

RAMA (195 "Completely Yours") 10-15 56

Singles: 7-inch

RAMA (195 "Completely Yours") 20-40 56

FOUR CHAPS

Singles: 7-inch

CO & CE 4-8 65

FOUR CHECKERS

Singles: 7-inch

ACE (129 "Broken Heart") 50-75 59

FOUR CHECKS

Singles: 7-inch

TRI DISC 8-12 61

FOUR CHEERS

Singles: 7-inch

END (1034 "Fatal Charms of Love") 150-200 58

FOUR CHELLOWS

Singles: 7-inch

HIT 5-15 62

FOUR CHESSMEN

EPs: 7-inch

RONDO 10-20

FOUR CHEVELLES

Singles: 7-inch

BAND BOX (357 "This Is Our Wedding Day") 25-50 64
(Publishing company shown as "Valjean.")
BAND BOX (357 "This Is Our Wedding Day") 10-20 60s
(Publishing company shown as "Band Box.")
DELFT (6408 "This Is Our Wedding Day") 500-750 64
(Identification number shown since no selection number is used.)
GATEWAY 5-10 64

FOUR CHICADEES

Singles: 78 rpm

CHECKER (849 "Ding Dong") 10-20 56

Singles: 7-inch

CHECKER (849 "Ding Dong") 25-50 56

FOUR CHICKS & CHUCK

Singles: 78 rpm

JUBILEE 4-8 53

Singles: 7-inch

JUBILEE 5-10 53

FOUR CHORDS

Singles: 78 rpm

SITTIN' IN WITH (516 "Again") 20-30 49

FOUR CHYMES: see CHYMES

FOUR CLASSMATES

Singles: 78 rpm

KING 4-8 55

Singles: 7-inch

KING 5-10 55

FOUR CLEFS

Singles: 78 rpm

BLUEBIRD 10-20 39-42
BULLET 10-15 48
RCA 15-25 45-52

Singles: 7-inch

RCA (4507 "Dig These Blues") 25-35 52
Also see CATS & FIDDLE

4 CLEFS

(Consorts)

Singles: 7-inch

B-J (1000 "Please Be Mine") 10-20 66
Also see CONSORTS

FOUR CLIPPERS

(With the Band of Lucky Lee)

Singles: 78 rpm

FOX 75-125 57

Singles: 7-inch

FOX (961 "You Can't Trust a Woman") 75-125 57
Members: Bobby Martin; Hershel Hunter.

FOUR CLOSURES

Singles: 7-inch

SPECIALTY 8-10 58

FOUR COACHMEN

(With "Chorus & Orchestra")

Singles: 7-inch

ADONIS (102 "That Thing Called a Girl") 10-20 60
CASTLE (507 "If You Believe") 10-20 59
DOT (16297 "Swamp Legend") 5-10 61
STELLAR (712 "Swamp Legend") 10-20 61

4 COACHMEN

Singles: 7-inch

MGM 4-6

FOUR COINS *P&R '54*

(With Joe Sherman & Orchestra)

Singles: 78 rpm

EPIC 5-10 54-59

Singles: 7-inch

COLUMBIA 4-6 67
EPIC 5-10 54-59
JOY 4-8 64
JUBILEE 4-8 61-62
MGM 5-10 60-61
VEE JAY 4-8 62-63

Picture Sleeves

EPIC (9258 "My Baby Loves Me") . 10-15 57

EPs: 7-inch

EPIC 10-20 55-58

LPs: 10/12-inch

EPIC (1104 "The Four Coins") 20-30 55
(10-inch LP.)
EPIC (3445 "In Shangri-La") 15-25 58
MGM (3944 "Greek Songs") 10-20 61
ROULETTE (25288 "Greek Songs Mama Never Taught Me") 10-15 65
Members: George Mantalis; George Mahramas; Michael Mahramas; Jim Gregorakis.
Also see SHERMAN, Joe, & His Orchestra

FOUR COQUETTES

Singles: 7-inch

CAPITOL (4534 "Sparkle and Shine") 15-25 61
Also see FOUR CAL-QUETTES

FOUR CORNERS

Singles: 7-inch

PHILIPS (40488 "It's So Right") 10-20 60s

FOUR COUNTS

Singles: 7-inch

CHAM (003 "I Love You with All My Heart") 15-25 58
JOSIE (840 "Cuckoo") 10-15 58

FOUR COUNTS

Singles: 7-inch

DART (1014 "Young Hearts") 10-20 58

FOUR COUNTS

Singles: 7-inch

ACE (597 "Heavenly") 10-20 60

FOUR COUNTS

("Vocal Phil Trunzo with the Tomlinson Sisters")

Singles: 7-inch

FINE (2562 "Graduation") 100-200 62

FOUR COUSINS

Singles: 78 rpm

20TH CENTURY 20-30 55

Singles: 7-inch

20TH CENTURY (75020 "Time and Time Again") 35-50 55

FOUR CRUISERS: see DOBBIN, Joseph, & Four Cruisers

FOUR DARLINGS

Singles: 7-inch

FORTE (1105 "Give Me Love") 50-100

FOUR DATES *P&R '58*

Singles: 7-inch

CHANCELLOR 8-12 58
Also see FABIAN

FOUR DEALS

Singles: 78 rpm

CAPITOL 15-25 50

Singles: 7-inch

CAPITOL (1313 "It's too Late Now") 25-50 50

EPs: 7-inch

TOPS (240 "Sh-Boom") 15-25 55

FOUR DEEP TONES

Singles: 78 rpm

CORAL 50-75 51

Singles: 7-inch

CORAL (65061 "Just in Case You Change Your Mind") 100-150 51
CORAL (65062 "The Night You Said Goodbye") 100-150 51

FOUR DEUCES

Singles: 78 rpm

MUSIC CITY 20-30 56

Singles: 7-inch

MUSIC CITY (796 "Down It Went") 35-55 56

FOUR DEUCES / Mr. Undertaker

Singles: 78 rpm

MUSIC CITY (790 "W-P-L-J") 25-35 55
(Maroon label.)
MUSIC CITY (790 "W-P-L-J") 15-25 55
(Black label.)

Singles: 7-inch

MUSIC CITY (790 "W-P-L-J") 75-125 55
(Maroon label.)
MUSIC CITY (790 "W-P-L-J") 30-50 55
(Black label.)
MUSIC CITY (790 "W-P-L-J") 50-75 57
(Red vinyl.)
Also see FOUR DEUCES

FOUR DIMENSIONS

Singles: 7-inch

GOLDUST (5013 "Sand Surfin' ") ... 20-30 64
KISKI (2069 "Moe's Cast") 10-20 65

IV DIMENSIONS

Singles: 7-inch

SARA (6644 "My Babe") 15-25 66

4 DIRECTIONS

Singles: 7-inch

CORAL (61456 "Tonight We Love") 40-60 64

FOUR DIRECTIONS

Singles: 7-inch

DIRECTIONS! LTD. (73003 "Lovely Way") 50-75 60s

FOUR DOLLS

Singles: 78 rpm

CAPITOL 8-12 57

Singles: 7-inch

CAPITOL 8-12 57-58

FOUR DOTS

Singles: 78 rpm

DOT (1043 "My Dear") 40-60 51
Member: George Davis.

FOUR DOTS

("Featuring Fletcher Williams")

Singles: 78 rpm

BULLSEYE 15-30 56

Singles: 7-inch

BULLSEYE (103 "Rita") 50-100 56
BULLSEYE (104 "Peace of Mind"/"Kiss Me, Sugar Plum") 50-100 56
BULLSEYE (104 "Peace of Mind"/"My Dear") 35-50 56
Also see HEARTBREAKERS

FOUR DOTS

(Featuring Jerry Stone & Jewel Akins)

Singles: 7-inch

FREEDOM (44002 "It's Heaven") 50-100 58
FREEDOM (44005 "Pleading for Your Love") 50-100 58
Members: Jewel Akens, Jerry Stone; Eddie Cochran.
Also see AKENS, Jewel
Also see COCHRAN, Eddie

FOUR DOTS

("Featuring Deek Watson formerly of the Ink Spots")

Singles: 7-inch

CASTLE (2006 "Strange As It Seems") 100-200 50s
(Black vinyl.)
CASTLE (2006 "Strange As It Seems") 250-500 50s
(Colored vinyl.)
Also see BROWN DOTS
Also see INK SPOTS

FOUR DUCHESSES

Singles: 7-inch

CHIEF (7014 "Cry For My Baby") ... 15-25 60
Also see DUCHESSES

4 DUKES

(With Al Browne Orchestra)

Singles: 78 rpm

DUKE 100-200 53

Singles: 7-inch

DUKE (116 "Crying in the Chapel") 400-600 53
Member: Billy Dawn Smith.
Also see DAWN, Billy, Quartet
Also see HERALDS
Also see MIGHTY DUKES

FOUR DUKES

Singles: 7-inch

IMPERIAL (5653 "Baby Won't You Please Come Home") 15-25 60

FOUR EKKOS

(Four Ekko's)

Singles: 7-inch

LABEL (2022 "Hand in Hand") ... 200-400 59
RIP (12558 "My Love I Give") 10-20 58
Also see ENGLER, Jerry, & Four Ekkos
Also see CAMPBELL, Bernie

FOUR ELDORADOS: see THOSE FOUR ELDORADOS

FOUR 'EM

Singles: 7-inch

ROLLO (5905 "While I'm Away") ... 10-20 65

FOUR EMBERS

Singles: 7-inch

SMASH (1846 "But Beautiful") 10-15 64

FOUR EPICS

Singles: 7-inch

COLLECTABLES 3-4 80s
HERITAGE (109 "I'm on My Way to Love") 75-125 62
LAURIE (3155 "Again") 15-25 63
LAURIE (3183 "How I Wish I Was Single Again") 15-25 63

LPs: 10/12-inch

CRYSTAL BALL 8-12 82
Also see EXODUS
Also see VESPERS

FOUR ESCORTS

Singles: 78 rpm

RCA 5-10 54

Singles: 7-inch

RCA 10-15 54
SKYLA 10-15 61

FOUR ESQUIRES *P&R '56*

Singles: 78 rpm

CADENCE 5-10 55
PARIS 10-20 57
PILGRIM 5-10 56

Singles: 7-inch

CADENCE 5-10 55
PARIS 10-15 57
PILGRIM 5-10 56
TERRACE 4-8 63
Also see CAPONE, Susan
Also see ECHOES / Four Esquires

FOUR EVERS: see FOUR-EVERS

FOUR EXCEPTIONS

Singles: 7-inch

PARKWAY (986 "You Got the Power") 20-40 66

FOUR FELLOWS

Singles: 78 rpm

TRI-BORO (101 "Stop Crying") 40-60 53
Members: Cas Bridges; Bill Carey.
Also see CLEFTONES
Also see DANLEERS

FOUR FELLOWS *R&B '55*

(With the Abie Baker Orchestra)

Singles: 78 rpm

DERBY 100-200 54
GLORY 20-40 55-57

Singles: 7-inch

DERBY (862 "I Tried") 200-300 54
GLORY (231 "I Wish I Didn't Know You") 50-100 55
GLORY (234 "Soldier Boy") 50-75 55
GLORY (236 "Angels Say") 50-75 55
GLORY (238 "Fallen Angel") 50-75 56
GLORY (242 "Darling You") 50-100 56
GLORY (244 "I Sit in My Window") 50-75 56
GLORY (248 "You Don't Know Me") 50-75 56
GLORY (250 "Give Me Back My Broken Heart") 50-75 57
GLORY (263 "You're Still in My Heart") 50-75 57
NESTOR (27 "Remember") 150-250 58
Members: David Jones; Ted Williams; Larry Banks; Jim McGowan.
Also see DECOYS / Four Fellows
Also see McLAURIN, Bette

FOUR FELLOWS

Singles: 7-inch

AD-LIB/POP LINE 10-15 62

FOUR FIFTHS

Singles: 7-inch

HUDSON (8101 "Come on Girl") 150-250 63
(Black vinyl.)
HUDSON (8101 "Come on Girl") 500-1000 63
(Blue vinyl.)

FOUR FIFTHS

Singles: 7-inch

COLUMBIA (43913 "If You Still Want Me") 10-15 66

LP: 10/12-inch

VICTORY (2258 "Clap Your Hands") 15-25 67

450 SL *R&B '85*

Singles: 7-inch

GOLDEN BOY 3-4 85

FOUR FINKS

Singles: 7-inch

ANTLER (4024 "Wiki Wiki Woo") 5-10 61
KERNEL (107 "Ka-Bongin") 15-25 63

FOUR FLARES

Singles: 7-inch

EDISON INT'L 10-15 58

FOUR FLAMES

(Hollywood Flames)

Singles: 78 rpm

FIDELITY (3001 "Tabarin") 150-250 51
(First issued as by the Hollywood Four Flames.)
SPECIALTY (423 "Wheel of Fortune") 200-300 52
Also see HOLLYWOOD FLAMES
Also see HOLLYWOOD FOUR FLAMES

FOUR FLAMES / Sherman Williams Orchestra

Singles: 78 rpm

FIDELITY (3002 "Bounce") 100-150 51
Also see FOUR FLAMES

FOUR FLICKERS

(With Perry Wilson Orchestra)

Singles: 7-inch

LEE (1002 "Is There a Way") 25-50 59

440

Singles: 7-inch

SONA (103 ""It's Just Your Mind") 20-30 67

FOUR FRESHMEN *P&R '52*

Singles: 78 rpm

CAPITOL 5-10 50-57

Singles: 7-inch

CAPITOL 5-15 50-65
DECCA 4-6 67
LIBERTY 4-6 68

Picture Sleeves

CAPITOL 5-10 63

EPs: 7-inch

CAPITOL 10-20 54-59

LPs: 10/12-inch

CAPITOL (With "SM" prefix) 5-10 75-79
CAPITOL (522 thru 992) 20-40 54-58
(With "T" prefix.)
CAPITOL (1000 & 2000 series) 10-25 58-64
(With "T" or "ST" prefix.)
CREATIVE WORLD 5-10 72
LIBERTY 5-10 68-82
PHONORAMA 5-8 82
SUNSET 5-10 70
Members: Don Barbour; Ross Barbour; Ken Errair; Bob Flanagan; Hal Kratzsch; Bill Comstock; Ken Albers.

FOUR FRESHMEN / Kirby Stone Four / University Four

LPs: 10/12-inch

CORONET 5-10 60s
Also see FOUR FRESHMEN
Also see STONE, Kirby, Four

FOUR FRIENDS

Singles: 7-inch

FEE BEE 10-15 59

FOUR FROGS

Singles: 7-inch

FROGDEATH (2 "Mr. Big") 5-10 66

Picture Sleeves

FROGDEATH (2 "Mr. Big") 20-30 66

FOUR FROLICS

Singles: 7-inch

CHEX (1001 "Frolic") 10-20 62

FOUR GABRIELS

Singles: 78 rpm

WORLD (2505 "Gloria") 25-50 48

FOUR GEMS

Singles: 7-inch

SANDERS (106 "Gloria") 100-150 64
Member: Charlie Bellizzi.

FOUR GEMS

Singles: 7-inch

BROADCAST (4 "Darling You Know") 30-40
(Colored vinyl.)

4 GENERATIONS

Singles: 7-inch

IVA (101 "Not Coming Back") 20-30

FOUR GENTS

Singles: 7-inch

PARK (114 "On Bended Knee") . 250-350 57

FOUR GENTS

Singles: 7-inch

NITE OWL (50 "Please Don't Ask Me") 30-40 62
Also see GENTS

4 GENTS

("Featuring Jimmy Mana")

Singles: 7-inch

VIDA (0120 "Far Away at Sea") . 100-200 64
VIDA (0123 "I Refuse to Try") 100-200 64

FOUR GENTS

Singles: 7-inch

HBR (509 "Soul Sister") 10-20 66
LIBERTY (50013 "He Got Soul") 10-20 68

FOUR GENTS

Singles: 7-inch

ONCORE (63 "Young Girls Beware") 400-600

FOUR GIRLS

Singles: 78 rpm

CAPITOL 5-10 56
CORAL 5-10 57

Singles: 7-inch

CAPITOL 10-15 56
CORAL 10-15 57

EPs: 7-inch

CORAL (81106 "Make a Joyful Noise Unto the Lord") 20-30 57

LPs: 10/12-inch

CORAL (57158 "Make a Joyful Noise Unto the Lord") 40-60 57
Members: Jane Russell; Connie Haines; Della Russell; Beryl Davis.
Also see RUSSELL, Jane

FOUR GLEAMS: see GLEAMS

FOUR GRADUATES

Singles: 7-inch

CRYSTAL BALL 4-8 78
RUST (5062 "Lovely Way to Spend an Evening") 100-200 63
RUST (5084 "Candy Queen") 150-250 64
Members: Robert Miranda; Tom Guliano; Ralph DeVito; Dave Libert.
Also see HAPPENINGS

FOUR GUYS

("Featuring Larry Austin")

Singles: 78 rpm

CORAL 5-10 54
KENT 10-15 53
MERCURY 5-10
WING 5-10 55

Singles: 7-inch
CORAL 8-12 54
KENT (113 "You Don't Have to Tell Me") 15-25 53
(Black vinyl.)
KENT (113 "You Don't Have to Tell Me") 25-50 53
(Colored vinyl.)
MERCURY (70452 "Tonight's the Night") 8-12 54
WING (90036 "May This Be Your Life") 15-20 55
Member: Larry Austin.

FOUR GUYS
Singles: 7-inch
BARRON (5001 "Tear Drops from My Eyes") 50-75 63
STRIDE (5001 "Tear Drops from My Eyes") 50-75 63
(Aside from the name and a different publishing company credited, Barron and Stride labels are nearly identical. Both have the same address and phone #. We don't know which came first.)

FOUR GUYS C&W '74
Singles: 7-inch
COLLAGE 3-5 79
JNB 3-4 82
RCA 3-5 74

4 HAVEN KNIGHTS
(Haven Knights)
Singles: 78 rpm
ATLAS 100-150 57
JOSIE 20-30 57
Singles: 7-inch
ANGLETONE (1066 "In My Lonely Room") 25-50 58
ANGLETONE (1092 "Why Go on Pretending") 25-50 58
ATLAS (1066 "In My Lonely Room") 100-150 57
ATLAS (1092 "Why Go on Pretending") 100-150 57
JOSIE (824 "In My Lonely Room") 20-30 57
Members: LeRoy Gomes; Robert Johnson; Tom Griffin; Everett Johnson; Carl Haley.

FOUR HAVENS
Singles: 7-inch
VEEP 4-8 65

FOUR HI'S
Singles: 7-inch
VERVE (10450 "Pretty Little Face") 10-15 66

FOUR HITS & A MISS
Singles: 7-inch
FLAMINGO 10-15 62

FOUR HOLIDAYS
Singles: 7-inch
U.A. (163 "Who Can Say") 15-25 59

FOUR HOLIDAYS
Singles: 7-inch
VERVE 5-10 60

FOUR HOLLIDAYS
Singles: 7-inch
MARKIE (109 "Grandma Bird") 30-40 63
MARKIE (115 "I'll Walk Right Out the Door") 40-60 63
Member: Jimmy Ruffin.
Also see RUFFIN, Jimmy

FOUR HORSEMEN
Singles: 7-inch
U.A. (134 "My Heartbeat") 200-300 58

FOUR HUES
Singles: 78 rpm
CROWN (115 "Rock-A-Bye") 10-20 56
Singles: 7-inch
CROWN (115 "Rock-A-Bye") 25-40 56

FOUR HUNKS
Singles: 7-inch
SYMBOL 5-10 61

FOUR IMPERIALS
Singles: 7-inch
CHANT (101 "Teen Age Fool") 25-50 58
DIAL (101 "Valley of Tears") 150-250 59
DOT (15737 "Lazy Bonnie") 25-50 58
FOX (102 "Look Up and Live") 50-100 58
LORELEI (4444 "Lazy Bonnie") 75-125 58
TWIRL (2005 "Seven Lonely Days") 50-75 60

FOUR IMPS
Singles: 7-inch
CIMARRON (4053 "Wabash Blues") 15-25 60

FOUR-IN-LEGION
Singles: 12-inch
CBS ASSOCIATED 4-6 84
Singles: 7-inch
CBS ASSOCIATED 3-4 84
LPs: 10/12-inch
CBS ASSOCIATED 5-10 84

FOUR IN THE MORNING
Singles: 7-inch
CROSSROAD 5-10

FOUR INTERNS
Singles: 78 rpm
FEDERAL 20-30 55
Singles: 7-inch
FEDERAL (12239 "I'm Troubled") 50-75 55

FOUR Js
Singles: 7-inch
CONGRESS 4-6 69
4-J 5-10 63
HERALD 10-15 58
JAMIE 10-20 63-64
U.A. 15-25 58
Members: James Testa; Joseph Prolia; Jimmy Finzino; Joe Mollera.
Also see FABULOUS FOUR

FOUR JACKS R&B '49
Singles: 78 rpm
ALADDIN 50-75 55
ALLEN (21000 "I Challenge Your Kiss") 25-50 49
FEDERAL (12075 "You Met a Fool") 50-100 52
FEDERAL (12087 "The Last of the Good Rockin' Men") 20-40 52
GOTHAM (219 "Take Me") 25-50 50
Singles: 7-inch
ALADDIN (3274 "Tired of Your Sexy Ways") 200-300 55
FEDERAL (12075 "You Met a Fool") 500-1000 52
FEDERAL (12087 "The Last of the Good Rockin' Men") 300-500 52
Also see BURNEY, Mac, & Four Jacks
Also see HAVEN, Shirley, & Four Jacks
Also see SHAY, Janet
Also see WILLIAMS, Cora, & Four Jacks

FOUR JACKS / Allen Trio
Singles: 78 rpm
ALLEN (21001 "Carless Love") 25-50 49
Also see FOUR JACKS

FOUR JACKS
Singles: 78 rpm
MGM 5-10 52
Singles: 7-inch
MGM (11179 "You're in Love with Someone Else") 15-25 52

FOUR JACKS
Singles: 78 rpm
GATEWAY PARADE of HITS 4-8 56
TOP TUNES 4-8 56
Singles: 7-inch
GATEWAY PARADE of HITS 5-10 56
TOP TUNES 5-10 56
EPs: 7-inch
TOPS 10-15 56
(Issued with paper sleeve.)

FOUR JACKS
Singles: 7-inch
REBEL (1313 "Becky Ann") 50-75 58

FOUR JACKS
Singles: 7-inch
PEL (601 "I've Waited Long Enough") 25-50 60

FOUR JACKS & A JILL
Singles: 78 rpm
FORTUNE 10-15 54
Singles: 7-inch
FORTUNE 15-25 54

FOUR JACKS & A JILL P&R/LP '68
Singles: 7-inch
RCA 4-8 68
LPs: 10/12-inch
RCA 10-15 68

FOUR JAYS & FABULOUS IMPERIALS
Singles: 7-inch
IMPRA (1268 "Class Ring") 50-75 58
(Identification number, which is nearly identical to MGM number, is shown since no selection number is used.)
MGM (12687 "Class Ring") 15-25 58

FOUR JETS
(Shadows)
Singles: 7-inch
CAPITOL (4270 "Driftin' ") 10-20 59
Also see SHADOWS

FOUR JEWELS
Singles: 7-inch
CHECKER 10-15 61-64
START (638 "Loaded with Goodies") 20-30 63
START (638 "Someone Special") 15-25 63
(The same number, #638, is used twice.)
START (641 "All That's Good") 15-25 64
TEC (3007 "Baby It's You") 10-20 64
Members: Sandra Bears; Margie Clark; Carrie Mingo; Martha Harvin; Grace Ruffin.
Also see JEWELS

FOUR JOES
Singles: 78 rpm
MGM 8-12 54-56
Singles: 7-inch
DARL (1005 "Lifetime of Happiness") 15-25 57
MGM (11857 "In Your Loving Care") 15-25 54
MGM (11911 "Oh How I Miss You") 20-40 55
MGM (12147 "Honey, My Little Honey") 15-25 55
MGM (12259 "Sometimes") 15-25 56
MGM (12316 "My Heart Says Thanks to You") 15-25 56

FOUR JOKERS
Singles: 78 rpm
MGM (11815 "Tell Me Now") 8-12 54
Singles: 7-inch
MGM (11815 "Tell Me Now") 15-25 54

FOUR JOKERS
Singles: 78 rpm
DIAMOND (3004 "Transfusion") 15-25 56
Singles: 7-inch
DIAMOND (3004 "Transfusion") 20-30 56
Member: Jimmy "Nervous Norvus" Drake.
Also see NERVOUS NORVUS

FOUR JOKERS
Singles: 7-inch
SUE (703 "Written in the Stars") 40-60 58

FOUR JOKERS
Singles: 7-inch
CORAL 5-10 59
CRYSTALETTE 5-10 59

FOUR JOKERS
Singles: 7-inch
AMY 10-15 62

FOUR JUMPS OF JIVE
Singles: 78 rpm
MERCURY (2001 "Satchel Mouth Baby") 20-40 46
MERCURY (2015 "Boo Boo Fine Jelly") 20-40 46

FOUR KINGS
(With the All Stars)
Singles: 78 rpm
FORTUNE (517 "Rose of Tangier") 25-50 55
FORTUNE (811 "You Don't Mean Me Right") 100-200 53
Singles: 7-inch
FORTUNE (517 "Rose of Tangier") 100-200 55
FORTUNE (811 "You Don't Mean Me Right") 500-750 53

FOUR KINGS
Singles: 7-inch
JAX (323 "You Never Knew") 150-250 54
Also see KINGS

FOUR KINGS
Singles: 78 rpm
FRATERNITY (752 "Willingly") 5-8 56
Singles: 7-inch
FRATERNITY (752 "Willingly") 8-12 56

FOUR KINGS
Singles: 7-inch
M.O.C. 5-10 63

FOUR KINGS
Singles: 7-inch
CEE=JAY (580 "Guess Who") 35-50 60

FOUR KINGS
Singles: 7-inch
CANADIAN AMERICAN (173 "One Night") 20-30 64
(Single-sided.)
CANADIAN AMERICAN (173 "One Night"/"Lonely Lovers") 25-50 64

FOUR KNIGHTS P&R '51
Singles: 78 rpm
CAPITOL 10-30 51-57
CORAL 10-20 49
DECCA 15-25 46-47
LANG-WORTH 10-20 40s
(16-inch transcriptions.)
Singles: 7-inch
CAPITOL (346 "Spotlight Songs") 30-50 52
(Boxed set of three singles.)
CAPITOL (1587 thru 1914) 15-30 51-52
CAPITOL (1930 thru 2517) 10-20 52-53
CAPITOL (2654 "Oh Baby Mine") 20-30 53
CAPITOL (2654 "I Get So Lonely") 8-12 53
(Note title change.)
CAPITOL (2782 thru 3730) 8-12 54-57
CORAL (61936 thru 62110) 5-10 58-59
DECCA (48018 "He'll Understand and Say Well Done") 50-75 52
SOUVENIR 4-8 62
EPs: 7-inch
CAPITOL (346 "Spotlight Songs") 50-75 52
(Two-EP set.)
CAPITOL (414 "The Four Knights Sing") 40-60 53
CAPITOL (506 "I Get So Lonely") 40-60 54
LPs: 10/12-inch
CAPITOL (H-346 "Spotlight Songs") 100-200 52
(10-inch LP.)
CAPITOL (T-346 "Spotlight Songs") 100-200 55
CORAL (57221 "Four Knights") 50-100 58
CORAL (57309 "Million Dollar Baby") 30-60 60
(Monaural.)
CORAL (757309 "Million Dollar Baby") 50-75 60
(Stereo.)
Members: Gene Alford; John Wallace; Clarence Dixon; Oscar Broadway.
Also see COLE, Nat "King"
Also see HUNT, Pee Wee

FOUR LABELS
Singles: 7-inch
GRA LOW (5524 "Susie") 25-50 59

FOUR LADS P&R '52
Singles: 78 rpm
COLUMBIA 4-8 52-58
OKEH 4-8 52
Singles: 7-inch
COLUMBIA 10-20 52-60
DOT 4-8 62
FONA 3-5 77-78
KAPP 5-10 60-61
OKEH 5-10 52
U.A. 4-6 63-69
Picture Sleeves
COLUMBIA 10-15 56-59
KAPP 5-10 60
EPs: 7-inch
COLUMBIA 5-15 55-59
LPs: 10/12-inch
AC 8-10
COLUMBIA (912 "On the Sunny Side") 20-30 56
COLUMBIA (1045 "The Four Lads Sing Frank Loesser") 20-30 57
COLUMBIA (1111 "Four on the Aisle") 15-25 58
(Monaural.)
COLUMBIA (1223 "Breezin' Along") 15-25 58
(Monaural.)
COLUMBIA (1235 "Greatest Hits") 15-25 58
COLUMBIA (1299 thru 1550) 10-20 59-60
(Monaural.)
COLUMBIA (2576 "Stage Show") 20-30 56
(10-inch LP.)
COLUMBIA (6329 "Stage Show") 25-40 54
(10-inch LP.)
COLUMBIA (8035 "Breezin' Along") 20-30 58
(Stereo.)
COLUMBIA (8047 "Four on the Aisle") 20-30 58
(Stereo.)
COLUMBIA (8106 thru 8350) 15-25 59-60
(Stereo.)
DOT 10-15 62-63
ENCORE 5-8 86
FONA 8-12 76-77
KAPP 10-15 61
HARMONY 5-10 69
U.A. 8-12 64
VIKING 5-10
Members: Frankie Busseri; Jimmy Arnold; Connie Coderini; Bernie Toorish.
Also see FOUR ACES / Four Lads / Four Preps
Also see LAINE, Frankie, & Four Lads
Also see RAY, Johnnie

FOUR LARKS
Singles: 7-inch
TOWER (364 "You and Me") 15-25 67
TOWER (402 "Groovin' at the Go-Go") 30-40 67
TOWER (450 "I've Got Plenty") 4-8 67
UPTOWN (748 "You and Me") 25-35 67
Members: Irma McDougal; Weldon McDougal III.

FOUR LETTER WORDS
Singles: 7-inch
PARIS TOWER (107 "Quadruple Feature") 25-30 67

FOUR LOVERS P&R '56
Singles: 78 rpm
EPIC (9255 "My Life for Your Love") 250-300 57
RCA 15-30 56-57
Singles: 7-inch
EPIC (9255 "My Life for Your Love") 250-300 57
MAGIC CARPET 3-5
RCA (6518 "You're the Apple of My Eye") 25-35 56
RCA (6519 "Honey Love") 25-35 56
RCA (6646 "Jambalaya") 15-25 56
RCA (6768 "Happy Am I") 15-25 57
RCA (6812 "Shake a Hand") 20-30 57
RCA (6819 "Night Train") 15-25 57
EPs: 7-inch
RCA (869 "The Four Lovers") 150-200 56
RCA (871 "Joyride") 400-500 56
LPs: 10/12-inch
RCA (1317 "Joyride") 500-750 56
Members: Frankie Valli; Tom Devito; Nick Devito; Hank Majewski.
Also see 4 SEASONS
Also see VALLI, Frankie

FOUR LOVERS / Homer & Jethro
EPs: 7-inch
RCA (47 "The Four Lovers/Homer & Jethro") 30-50 56
(Promotional only. Not issued with cover.)
Also see HOMER & JETHRO

FOUR LOVERS / Teddi King
EPs: 7-inch
RCA (64 "The Four Lovers/Teddi King") 30-50 56
(Promotional only. Not issued with cover.)

FOUR LYRICS
Singles: 7-inch
PHILIPS 4-8 64

FOUR MARKSMEN
Singles: 7-inch
RADIO (107 "Birth of Love") 10-15

FOUR MILES HIGH
Singles: 7-inch
CALLA 3-6 69

FOUR MINTS
Singles: 78 rpm
DECCA (30464 "Ruby Baby") 10-15 57
LIN (5001 "Alone") 15-25 56
Singles: 7-inch
BRONCO 3-5 63
DECCA (30464 "Ruby Baby") 10-15 57
LIN (5001 "Alone") 30-40 56
NRC 10-15 58-59
LPs: 10/12-inch
AZTEC (1002 "The Fabulous Four Mints") 200-250 63
Also see MINTS

FOUR MINTS
Singles: 7-inch
CHOCTAW (8002 "What 'Cha Gonna Do") 50-75 59

FOUR MINTS R&B '73
Singles: 7-inch
CAPSOUL 8-15 73
HOLIDAY 10-20 73
LPs: 10/12-inch
CAPSOUL 10-20 73

FOUR MORE
Singles: 7-inch
DEE GEE 10-20 65

FOUR MORE
Singles: 7-inch
FAIRCHILD (1001 "Problem Child") 20-30 66

4 MOST
Singles: 78 rpm
DAWN 4-8 56
Singles: 7-inch
DAWN 5-10 56

4 MOST
Singles: 7-inch
MILO (107 "The Breeze and I") 25-50 59
(Black vinyl.)
MILO (107 "The Breeze and I") 15-25 61
(Colored vinyl.)
RELIC (501 "The Breeze and I") 8-10 63

FOUR NATURALS
Singles: 7-inch
RED TOP (119 "I Hear a Rhapsody") 25-40 59
RED TOP (125 "Long, Long Ago") 150-200 60
Also see NATURALS

FOUR NORTHMEN
Singles: 7-inch
SOMA 5-10 66

FOUR NOTES
Singles: 78 rpm
INTERNATIONAL 10-15
PARADISE 10-15
PREMIER 10-15

4 NOTES: see SMITH, Gene

FOUR NUGGETS
Singles: 7-inch
DOT 4-8 63

FOUR OF A KIND
Singles: 7-inch
BOMARC 5-10 59
CAMEO 5-10 58
LAURIE 4-8 65
MELBA 10-15 57

4 OF US
Singles: 7-inch
BRUNSWICK 5-10 65

4 OF US
Singles: 7-inch
HIDEOUT (1003 "You Gonna Be Mine"/"Free Fall") 25-30 65
HIDEOUT (1003 "You Gonna Be Mine"/"Batman") 20-25 65
(Note different flip.)
HIDEOUT (1012 "I Feel a Whole Lot Better") 15-25 66

FOUR ON THE FLOOR
LPs: 10/12-inch
CASABLANCA 5-10 79

4 OUT OF 5 DOCTORS
Singles: 78 rpm
NEMPEROR (911 "4 Out of 5 Doctors") 5-10 81
(Single-sided, promotional issue.)
Singles: 7-inch
NEMPEROR 3-4 81-82
LPs: 10/12-inch
NEMPEROR 5-10 81-82

IV PACK
Singles: 7-inch
HIPPIE (2019 "Whatzit") 10-20 60s

FOUR PAGES
Singles: 7-inch
PLATEAU 10-15 62

FOUR PALMS
Singles: 7-inch
ALADDIN (3411 "Consideration") 15-25 58

FOUR PALS
Singles: 78 rpm
ROYAL ROOST 10-20 55-56
Singles: 7-inch
ROYAL ROOST (610 "If I Can't Have the One I Love") 15-20 55
ROYAL ROOST (616 "No One Ever Loved Me") 20-25 56

FOUR PALS
Singles: 7-inch
ROULETTE 8-12 59

FOUR PEARLS
Singles: 7-inch
DOLTON (26 "Look at Me") 150-200 60

FOUR PENNIES P&R '63
Singles: 7-inch
LAURIE 3-5

RUST (5070 "When the Boy's Happy")..15-25 63
RUST (5071 "My Block")................15-25 63
Members: Judy Craig; Barbara Lee; Patricia Bennett; Sylvia Peterson.
Also see CHIFFONS

FOUR PENNIES
Singles: 7-inch
BRUNSWICK (55304 "You Have No Time to Lose")... 8-10 66
BRUNSWICK (55324 "Shake a Hand")..15-25 67
PHILIPS.. 8-15 64-65

FOUR PERSUASIONS
Singles: 7-inch
PAY-4-PLAY (100 "Echo") 4-6 72

4 PHARAOHS
("4" Pharaohs)
Singles: 7-inch
PARADISE (109 "Give Me Your Love") 75-125 58
RANSOM (101 "Give Me Your Love")..300-500 58
RANSON (100 "Pray for Me") 300-500 58
(Label name is Ranson on 100 and Ransom on 101.)
Members: Morris Wade; Bobby Taylor; Ron Wilson; Bernard Wilson; Tommy Willis;
Also see CALDWELL, Joe
Also see COLUMBUS PHARAOHS
Also see EGYPTIAN KINGS
Also see KING PHARAOH & EGYPTIANS
Also see SUPREMES
Also see TAYLOR, Bobby

FOUR PIPS & POP
("Four Pip's & a Pop Featuring Pop with Orchestra")
Singles: 7-inch
MERCEDES (5001 "For You") 75-125 59

FOUR PLAID THROATS
Singles: 78 rpm
MERCURY (70143 "My Inspiration")...........................200-300 53
Singles: 7-inch
MERCURY (70143 "My Inspiration")...........................500-1000 53

FOUR PLAYBOYS
Singles: 7-inch
S.R.C. ("Rave On")...................75-100 59
SOUVENIR (1002 "Stay with Me")..30-50 60

FOUR PREPS — *P&R '56*
Singles: 78 rpm
CAPITOL.. 5-10 56-57
Singles: 7-inch
CAPITOL (3576 thru 5074, except 4568).. 5-10 56-63
CAPITOL (4568 "Dream Boy, Dream")..20-30 61
CAPITOL (5143 "A Letter to the Beatles")..15-25 64
CAPITOL (5178 thru 5921) 4-8 64-67
Picture Sleeves
CAPITOL.. 8-12 61-62
EPs: 7-inch
CAPITOL (862 "Dreamy Eyes") 10-20 56
CAPITOL (994 "Four Preps") 10-20 57
CAPITOL (1015 "26 Miles") 10-20 58
LPs: 10/12-inch
CAPITOL.......................................15-30 58-67
Members: Bruce Belland; Glen Larson; Marv Ingraham; Ed Cobb; Don Clarke.
Also see BELLAND & SOMERVILLE
Also see FOUR ACES / Four Lads / Four Preps
Also see KINGSTON TRIO / Four Preps

FOUR PROS
Singles: 7-inch
CARLA 4-8 66-67

FOUR PUZZLES
Singles: 7-inch
FAT BACK....................................10-15 67
Also see PUZZLES

FOUR QUEENS
Singles: 7-inch
ABC-PAR 5-8 63
TERON.. 4-8 64

FOUR REPUTATIONS
Singles: 7-inch
MILLAGE (105 "Call on Me") 15-25 60s

FOUR ROCKETS
Singles: 78 rpm
ALADDIN (3007 "Little Red Wagon")..20-30 48
ALADDIN (3017 "Little Brown Jug") 20-30 48

FOUR ROMANS
Singles: 7-inch
WYNNE..10-20 59

FOUR SAINTS
Singles: 7-inch
W.B. 4-6 62-63
LPs: 10/12-inch
W.B. 10-20 62
Members: Doug Evans; John Howell; Bob Erickson; Jerry Duchene.

4-SALE
Singles: 7-inch
HIGHLAND (1205 "Baby Please Don't Tease") 5-10

FOUR SEASONS
Singles: 7-inch
ALANNA (555 "I'm Still in Love with You")..35-55 58
ALANNA (555 "Don't Sweat It Baby")..30-50 59
ALANNA (558 "Hot Water Bottle")..20-30 60
ROBBEE (106 "Mirage") 100-150 60

4 SEASONS — *P&R/R&B/LP '62*
(Four Seasons; Frankie Valli & 4 Seasons)
Singles: 7-inch
AURAVISION (6724 "Big Man's World")..20-30 64
(Cardboard flexi-disc, one of six by six different artists. Columbia Record Club "Enrollment Premium." Set came in a special paper sleeve.)
BOB CREWE PRESENTS 10-15 70
(Promotional issue only.)
COLLECTABLES (Except 9)............ 3-4 81
COLLECTABLES (9 "Greatest Hits")..30-40 81
(Boxed, six-disc set. Colored vinyl.)
CREWE (333 "And That Reminds Me").. 4-8 69
GONE (5122 "Bermuda")...............35-55 61
MCA/CURB 3-5 85-86
MOTOWN 5-10 73
MOWEST..5-10 72
OLDIES 45 ....5-10 62-63
PHILIPS (40166 thru 40662)..........5-10 64-69
PHILIPS (40688 "Lay Me Down")...15-25 70
PHILIPS (40694 "Where Are My Dreams")..20-25 70
PHILIPS DOUBLE-HIT 4-8
RAINBOW.......................................5-10 62
SEASONS 3-5 75
SEASONS 4-EVER (Black vinyl) ... 4-6 71
SEASONS 4-EVER (Colored vinyl)..10-15 71
VEE JAY (456 thru 562)..................10-15 62-63
VEE JAY (576 "Stay"/"Peanuts")......40-50 63
VEE JAY (582 "Stay"/"Goodnight My Love")..10-15 64
VEE JAY (597 "Alone") 10-20 64
(Yellow label.)
VEE JAY (597 "Alone")....................8-12 64
(Black label.)
VEE JAY (597 "Alone")....................5-10 64
(Multi-color label.)
VEE JAY (608 thru 719)..................10-15 64-66
VEE JAY (901 "Peanuts") 100-150 63
(Single-sided. Promotional issue only.)
WABC RADIO (77 "Cousin Brucie Go Go")..75-125 64
(Special products custom pressing. Colored vinyl.)
WXYZ-DETROIT (121003 "Jody Reynolds' Theme")..50-75 65
(Special products custom pressing.)
W.B. 3-5 75-80
WIBBAGE (WIBG "Jody Reynolds' Theme")..50-75 65
(Special products custom pressing.)
Picture Sleeves
CREWE (333 "And That Reminds Me")..10-15 69
PHILIPS (Except 40542)..............10-20 64-70
PHILIPS (40542 "Saturday's Father")..20-30 68
(Fold-out sleeve.)
PHILIPS (40542 "Saturday's Father")..5-10 68
(Standard sleeve.)
PHILIPS DOUBLE-HIT 4-8
VEE JAY (539 "Candy Girl") 40-60 64
VEE JAY (597 "Alone")...................40-60 64
VEE JAY (626 "I Saw Mommy Kissing Santa Claus")..25-35 64
EPs: 7-inch
MAGIC CARPET 4-8
PHILIPS (2704 "Genuine Imitation Life Gazette")..20-30 68
(Juke box issue only. Includes title strips.)
PHILIPS (2705 "Edizone D'Oro") 20-30 68
(Juke box issue only. Includes title strips.)
VEE JAY (901 "Peanuts + 3")...........20-35 64
VEE JAY (902 "Alone + 3")..............20-35 64
LPs: 10/12-inch
ARISTA 8-12 84
CANDLELITE (151 "Complete Musical Treasury")..35-45 82
(Boxed, five-disc set.)
CANDLELITE (151B "Souvenirs in Gold")..10-15 82
(Bonus LP, offered to buyers of the above set.)
ERA..5-10 82
FBI 10-15 84
GUEST STAR (1481 "Bermuda & Spanish Lace")..15-20 64
(Also has tracks by the Barrons, a.k.a. the Crescendos.)
KOALA 5-10 80
K-TEL...15-20 77
LONGINES (95833 "Greatest Hits of Frankie Valli & 4 Seasons")..25-35
(Boxed, four-disc set. TV mail-order offer.)
LONGINES (95833 "Greatest Hits of Frankie Valli & 4 Seasons")..20-30
(Gatefold, four-disc set. TV mail-order offer.)
MCA 5-10 85
MCA/CURB 5-10 88
MOTOWN 5-10 80
MOWEST......................................10-12 72
PHILIPS (2-6501 "Edizone D'Oro")..20-25 68
PHILIPS (200124 "Dawn and 11 Other Great Hits")..15-20 64
(Monaural.)
PHILIPS (200129 "Born to Wander")..15-20 64
(Monaural.)
PHILIPS (200146 "Rag Doll").........15-20 64
(Monaural.)
PHILIPS (200164 "The 4 Seasons Entertain You")..15-20 65
(Monaural.)
PHILIPS (200193 "Big Hits by Burt Bacharach, Hal David & Bob Dylan")...............50-65 65
(Photos of group on front and back cover. Monaural.)
PHILIPS (200193 "Big Hits by Burt Bacharach, Hal David & Bob Dylan")...............15-20 65
(No group photos on cover. Monaural.)
PHILIPS (200196 "Gold Vault of Hits")..15-20 65
(Monaural.)
PHILIPS (200201 "Working My Way Back to You")..15-20 66
(Monaural.)
PHILIPS (200221 "2nd Gold Vault of Hits")..15-20 66
(Monaural.)
PHILIPS (200222 "Lookin' Back") ..15-20 66
(Monaural.)
PHILIPS (200223 "Christmas Album")..15-25 66
(Stereo.)
PHILIPS (200243 "New Gold Hits")..15-20 67
(Monaural.)
PHILIPS (600124 "Dawn and 11 Other Great Hits")..15-20 64
(Stereo.)
PHILIPS (600129 "Born to Wander")..15-20 64
(Stereo.)
PHILIPS (600146 "Rag Doll").........15-20 64
(Stereo.)
PHILIPS (600164 "The 4 Seasons Entertain You")..15-20 65
(Stereo.)
PHILIPS (600193 "Big Hits by Burt Bacharach, Hal David & Bob Dylan")...............50-65 65
(Photos of group on front and back cover. Stereo.)
PHILIPS (600193 "Big Hits by Burt Bacharach, Hal David & Bob Dylan")...............15-20 65
(No group photos on cover. Stereo.)
PHILIPS (600196 "Gold Vault of Hits")..15-20 65
(Stereo.)
PHILIPS (600201 "Working My Way Back to You")..15-20 66
(Stereo.)
PHILIPS (600221 "2nd Gold Vault of Hits")..15-20 66
(Stereo.)
PHILIPS (600222 "Lookin' Back") ..15-20 66
(Stereo.)
PHILIPS (600223 "Christmas Album")..15-25 66
(Stereo.)
PHILIPS (600243 "New Gold Hits")..15-20 67
(Stereo.)
PHILIPS (600290 "Genuine Imitation Life Gazette")..35-45 69
(Yellow cover.)
PHILIPS (600290 "Genuine Imitation Life Gazette")..10-15 69
(White cover.)
PHILIPS (600341 "Half and Half")..10-15 70
PICKWICK 8-10 70
PRIORITY 8-10 86
PRIVATE STOCK..............................10-12 75
RHINO (Except 72998)........................6-12
RHINO (72998 "25th Anniversary")..15-25 87
(Four-disc set.)
SEARS (609 "Brotherhood of Man")..20-30 70
TIME-LIFE (15 "Rock & Roll Era") .15-20 87
VEE JAY (1053 "Sherry")................30-40 62
(Monaural.)
VEE JAY (1053 "Sherry")................50-75 62
(Stereo.)
VEE JAY (1055 "Four Seasons Greetings")..30-40 62
VEE JAY (1056 "Big Girls Don't Cry")..30-40 63
VEE JAY (1059 "Ain't That a Shame")..30-40 63
VEE JAY (1065 "Golden Hits").......30-40 63
VEE JAY (1082 "Folk-Nanny").......40-50 64
VEE JAY (1082 "Stay and Other Great Hits")..20-30 64
(Repackage of *Folk-Nanny*.)
VEE JAY (1088 "More Golden Hits")..25-35 64
VEE JAY (1121 "We Love Girls")...25-35 64
VEE JAY (1154 "Recorded Live on Stage")..25-35 65
WCI (502 "Silver Anniversary")......15-25 85
(Three-disc set.)
W.B. 8-12 75-81
Members: Frankie Valli; Tom Devito; Nick Devito; Hank Majewski; Bob Gaudio; Charlie Calello; Nick Massi; Joe Long; Don Ciccione; Bill Deloach; Paul Wilson; Jerry Corbetta.
Also see BEACH BOYS with Frankie Valli & 4 Seasons
Also see BEATLES / 4 Seasons
Also see CABBOT, Johnny
Also see CICCONE, Don
Also see CORBETTA, Jerry
Also see COREY, John
Also see CRESCENDOS
Also see CREWE, Bob
Also see DISENTRI, Turner
Also see DIXON, Billy, & Topics
Also see FOUR LOVERS
Also see HALO, Johnny
Also see HAYES, Tommy
Also see JAN & DEAN / Roy Orbison / 4 Seasons / Shirelles
Also see KOKOMOS
Also see LARRY & LEGENDS
Also see MASSI, Nick
Also see MATTHEWS, Shirley
Also see MILLER, Hal
Also see RASCALS / Buggs / Four Seasons / Johnny Rivers
Also see RIVERS, Johnny / 4 Seasons / Jerry Butler / Jimmy Soul
Also see ROYAL TEENS
Also see SANTOS, Larry
Also see SIMON, Paul
Also see TOPICS
Also see TREVOR, Van
Also see VALLI, Frankie
Also see VILLAGE VOICES
Also see WONDER WHO

4 SEASONS / Connie Francis / Barbara Brown & Buggs
LPs: 10/12-inch
CORONET (244 "At the Hop").........15-25 64
PREMIER (9052 "At the Hop").......15-25
Also see FRANCIS, Connie

4 SEASONS / Little Royal
Singles: 7-inch
GORDA..4-8 65

4 SEASONS / Scarlets
Singles: 7-inch
OLDIES 45 ....5-10 63
Also see SCARLETS

4 SEASONS / Neil Sedaka / J Brothers / Johnny Rivers
LP: 10/12-inch
DESIGN...10-20 60s
Also see J BROTHERS
Also see RIVERS, Johnny
Also see SEDAKA, Neil

4 SEASONS / Ray Stevens
Singles: 7-inch
OLDIES 45 ....5-10 63
Also see 4 SEASONS
Also see STEVENS, Ray

FOUR SENSATIONS
Singles: 78 rpm
RAINBOW.......................................10-15 52
Singles: 7-inch
RAINBOW (157 "Heaven Knows")..15-20 52
(Black vinyl.)
RAINBOW (157 "Heaven Knows")..20-40 52
(Colored vinyl.)

FOUR SHADES OF RHYTHM
Singles: 78 rpm
CHANCE 50-100 52
OLD SWINGMASTER.........................10-20 49
Singles: 7-inch
CHANCE (1126 "Yesterdays") ... 200-300 52

FOUR SHARPS
(Delta Rhythm Boys)
Singles: 78 rpm
ATLANTIC (875 "Don't Ask Me Why")..25-50 49
Members: Traverse Crawford; Karl Jones; Kelsey Pharr; Lee Gaines.
Also see DELTA RHYTHM BOYS

FOUR SHARPS
Singles: 7-inch
DARROW (512 "Safari")...............15-25 58

FOUR SHARPS
Singles: 7-inch
DONNA (1330 "Church Key") 15-25 61
(Same single also issued as by the Gonzos.)
Also see GONZOS

FOUR SHARPS
Singles: 7-inch
SHARP (5064 "Surf Guitar")..........15-25 63

FOUR SHARPS
Singles: 7-inch
CAMEO..4-8 66

FOUR SHARPS
Singles: 7-inch
GALE 10-15

FOUR SHELLS
Singles: 7-inch
VOLT..4-8 66

FOUR SHILLINGS
Singles: 7-inch
LIMELIGHT 5-10 64

FOUR SHOTS
Singles: 78 rpm
CADILLAC......................................50-100 55
Singles: 7-inch
CADILLAC (159 "Love Hit Me and I Hollered")..150-250 55

FOUR SHY GIRLS
Singles: 7-inch
PIONEER...5-10 61

FOUR SINGING AVALONS
Singles: 7-inch
ATCO (6585 "She's My Woman, She's My Girl")..10-20 68

FOUR SISTERS
Singles: 7-inch
HERMITAGE....................................8-12 64

FOUR SONICS — *P&R/R&B '68*
Singles: 7-inch
SPORT (110 "You Don't Have to Say You Love Me")..6-12 68
SPORT (111 "Easier Said Than Done")..10-15 68
Members: Eddy Daniels; James Johnson; Steve Gaston; Willie Frazier.

FOUR SONICS PLUS ONE
Singles: 7-inch
SEPIA 4-8 68

FOUR SONS
Singles: 7-inch
LINCO 5-10 60

FOUR SOUNDS
(With the Lawrence Keyes Trio)
Singles: 7-inch
CELESTE (3010 "Afraid")......... 300-400 57

FOUR SOUNDS
Singles: 7-inch
FEDERAL (12421 "Someone to Show Me the Way")..25-50 61
TUFF (1 "The Ring")......................15-25 60

FOUR SOUTHERNERS
Singles: 78 rpm
DECCA (7291 "Dan the Back Door Man")..50-100 37

FOUR SPARKS
Singles: 7-inch
CLEFF=TONE (151 "Key to My Heart")..50-75 58

FOUR SPARKS
Singles: 7-inch
ABC-PAR (9906 "Out of This World")..10-15 58

FOUR SPEEDS
Singles: 78 rpm
DELUXE...20-30 54
Singles: 7-inch
DELUXE (6070 "I Need You, Baby")..40-60 54

FOUR SPEEDS
Singles: 7-inch
CHALLENGE (9187 "R.P.M.") 20-30 63
CHALLENGE (9202 "Four on the Floor")..20-30 63
Member: Gary Usher; Chuck Girard; Richard Burns; Dennis Wilson.
Also see HONDELLS
Also see SUNSETS
Also see USHER, Gary
Also see WILSON, Dennis

FOUR SPORTSMEN — *P&R '61*
SUNNYBROOK (1 "Surrender")......30-50 60
SUNNYBROOK (2 "Lucille") 15-25 61
SUNNYBROOK (4 "Pitter Patter") 15-25 61
SUNNYBROOK (5 "Sixty Minute Man")..15-25 61
SUNNYBROOK (6 "If Your Heart Can Take It")..20-30 61

FOUR STARS
("Piano: Milton Harris Jr.")
Singles: 7-inch
KAY-Y (66781 "The Chapel By the Sea")..400-500 58

FOUR STARS
Singles: 7-inch
BAMBOO...5-10 61
ERA (3021 "Blue Dawn") 4-8 60
(Black vinyl.)
ERA (3021 "Blue Dawn") 8-12 60
(Colored vinyl. Promotional issue only.)
GRAY..5-10

FOUR STEPS
Singles: 7-inch
MARLIN (16022 "Same Ole Beat") ..5-10

FOUR STRANGERS
Singles: 7-inch
ASTOR (7042 "Pearl Diver")............5-10

FOUR STUDENTS
Singles: 78 rpm
GROOVE 15-25 55
Singles: 7-inch
GROOVE (0110 "So Near and Yet So Far")..35-55 55
Also see ALLEN, Sue
Also see CALHOUN, Charles, & Four Students
Also see DILLARD, Varetta, & Four Students
Also see GREER, Big John, & Four Students
Also see MAYS, Zilla
Also see McKENZIE, Lil, & Four Students

FOUR TEENS
Singles: 7-inch
CHALLENGE (59021 "Go Little Go-Cat")..50-60 58

FOUR TEES
Singles: 7-inch
KENT (4530 "One More Chance") .10-15 70
KENT (4536 "I Could Never Love Another")..10-15 71
VEE JAY (627 "I Said, She Said") ...5-10 64

FOUR TEMPOS
Singles: 7-inch
RAMPART..4-6 67-69

FOUR TEMPTATIONS
Singles: 7-inch
ABC-PAR (9920 "Cathy")..............15-25 58

FOUR THOUGHTS
Singles: 7-inch
WOMAR (103 "When I'm with You")..............50-75 60s

FOUR TONES
Singles: 78 rpm
PREVIEW..............15-25 45

4 TONES
(With Jimmy Stella & His Orchestra)
Singles: 7-inch
LA STELLA.............. 5-10

FOUR TOPHATTERS
Singles: 78 rpm
CADENCE.............. 4-8 55
Singles: 7-inch
CADENCE.............. 5-10 55
EXCLUSIVE.............. 5-10 59

FOUR TOPS P&R/R&B '64
Singles: 12-inch
ABC.............. 4-8 77-78
MOTOWN.............. 4-8 80
Singles: 78 rpm
CHESS (1623 "Could It be You")..............75-125 56
Singles: 7-inch
ABC/DUNHILL.............. 3-5 75-79
ARISTA.............. 3-4 88
CASABLANCA.............. 3-4 81-82
CHESS (1623 "Could It be You")..............100-200 56
COLUMBIA (41755 "Lonely Summer")..............50-75 60
COLUMBIA (43356 "Lonely Summer")..............15-25 65
DUNHILL.............. 3-5 72-74
MOTOWN (Colored vinyl).............. 8-12 70
(Promotional issue only.)
MOTOWN (400 series).............. 3-4
MOTOWN (1062 thru 1254).............. 5-10 64-72
MOTOWN (1706 thru 1854).............. 3-4 83-86
MOTOWN/TOPPS (5 "I Can't Help Myself")..............50-75 67
(Topps Chewing Gum promotional item. Single-sided, cardboard flexi, six-inch picture disc. Issued with generic paper sleeve.)
MOTOWN/TOPPS (9 "Baby I Need Your Loving")..............50-75 67
(Topps Chewing Gum promotional item. Single-sided, cardboard flexi, six-inch picture disc. Issued with generic paper sleeve.)
RSO.............. 3-4 82
RELIANT.............. 3-4 88
RIVERSIDE (4534 "Pennies from Heaven")..............50-75 62
Picture Sleeves
ARISTA.............. 3-4 88
MOTOWN (1073 "Ask the Lonely")..............50-75 64
MOTOWN (1098 "Reach Out I'll Be There")..............20-40 66
MOTOWN (1164 "It's All in the Game").............. 8-10 70
MOTOWN (1175 "Just Seven Numbers").............. 8-10 71
RSO.............. 3-5 82
EPs: 7-inch
MOTOWN (60647 "On Top")..............25-50 66
LPs: 10/12-inch
ABC.............. 8-10 75-78
ARISTA.............. 5-8 88
CASABLANCA.............. 5-10 81-82
COMMAND..............10-12 74
DUNHILL.............. 8-10 72-74
GORDY.............. 5-10 85
MOTOWN (100 & 200 series).............. 5-10 82-84
MOTOWN (622 "Four Tops")..............20-30 64
MOTOWN (634 "Second Album")..............15-25 65
MOTOWN (647 "On Top")..............15-20 66
MOTOWN (654 "Live")..............15-25 66
MOTOWN (662 "Greatest Hits")..............12-20 67
MOTOWN (669 "Yesterday's Dream")..............12-20 68
MOTOWN (675 thru 748)..............10-20 69-72
MOTOWN (764 "Best of the Four Tops")..............10-15 73
MOTOWN (6000 series).............. 5-8 83-86
MOTOWN (9809 "Anthology")..............15-20 74
MOTOWN (M9809 "Anthology")..............10-15 86
PICKWICK.............. 5-8 74
NATURAL RESOURCES.............. 8-10 78
WORKSHOP (217 "Breaking Through")..............1000-1500 62
WORKSHOP (217 "Jazz Impressions by the Four Tops")..............500-1000 62
(Retitled reissue.)
Members: Levi Stubbs; Lawrence Payton; Abdul "Duke" Fakir; Obie Benson.
Also see CARROLL, Delores, & Four Tops
Also see FOUR AIMS
Also see HAYES, Carolyn, & Four Tops
Also see HOLLAND - DOZIER
Also see PAYTON, Lawrence
Also see SUPREMES & Four Tops

FOUR TOPS / Temptations
LPs: 10/12-inch
SILVER EAGLE.............. 6-10 87
Also see FOUR TOPS
Also see TEMPTATIONS

FOUR TOTS
Singles: 7-inch
PS (9010 "Tender Years")..............10-20 60s

FOUR TOWNSMEN
Singles: 7-inch
ART-FLOW (145 "It Wasn't So Long Before")..............150-250 60

FOUR TROYS
Singles: 7-inch
FREEDOM (44013 "In the Moonlight")..............20-30 59

FOUR TRUMPS
Singles: 7-inch
MIRA (2050 "I've Waited All My Life for You")..............400-600 58
(Identification number shown since no selection number is used.)

FOUR TUNES P&R/R&B '53
("Featuring Jimmie Nabbie")
Singles: 78 rpm
ARCO.............. 5-15 50
COLUMBIA.............. 5-15 48
JUBILEE..............10-20 53-57
MANOR..............10-20 46-49
RCA..............10-20 49-53
Singles: 7-inch
CROSBY (3 "Never Look Down")..............15-20 60
CROSBY (4 "Twinkle Eyes")..............25-35 60
(Colored vinyl.)
JUBILEE (5128 "Marie")..............25-50 53
JUBILEE (5132 "I Understand")..............20-30 54
JUBILEE (5135 "My Wild Irish Rose")..............10-20 54
JUBILEE (5152 "Lonesome")..............10-20 54
JUBILEE (5165 "Don't Cry Darling")..............20-30 54
JUBILEE (5174 "Let Me Go Lover")..............20-30 54
JUBILEE (5183 "I Close My Eyes")..............20-30 55
JUBILEE (5200 "Time Out for Tears")..............20-30 55
JUBILEE (5212 "Brooklyn Bridge")..............10-20 55
JUBILEE (5218 "You Are My Love")..............10-20 55
JUBILEE (5232 "Our Love")..............10-20 56
JUBILEE (5239 "I Gotta Go")..............10-20 56
JUBILEE (5245 "Far Away Places")..............10-20 56
JUBILEE (5255 "The Ballad of James Dean")..............20-30 56
JUBILEE (5276 "Cool Water")..............10-20 57
JUBILEE (6000 "Marie").............. 5-10 59
KAY-RON (1000 "I Want to Be Loved")..............25-50 54
KAY-RON (1005 "I Understand")..............25-50 54
RCA (0008 "You're Heartless")..............150-250 49
(Colored vinyl.)
RCA (0016 "My Last Affair")..............150-250 49
(Colored vinyl.)
RCA (0042 "I'm Just a Fool in Love")..............150-250 49
(Colored vinyl.)
RCA (0072 "Am I Blue")..............100-200 50
(Colored vinyl.)
RCA (0085 "Old Fashioned Love")..............100-200 50
(Colored vinyl.)
RCA (0131 "May That Day Never Come")..............100-150 51
RCA (3881 "Do I Worry")..............50-75 50
RCA (3967 "Cool Water")..............50-75 50
RCA (4102 "Wishing You Were Here Tonight")..............40-60 51
RCA (4241 "I Married an Angel")..............40-60 51
RCA (4280 "It's No Sin")..............40-60 51
RCA (4305 "Early in the Morning")..............40-60 51
RCA (4427 "I'll See You in My Dreams")..............40-60 51
RCA (4489 "Come What May")..............20-40 52
RCA (4663 "I Wonder")..............20-40 52
RCA (4828 "They Don't Understand")..............20-40 52
RCA (4968 "I Don't Want to Set the World on Fire")..............25-50 52
RCA (5532 "Don't Get Around Much Anymore")..............25-50 53
VIRGO.............. 3-5 72
EPs: 7-inch
RCA (586 "Four Tunes")..............100-150 54
LPs: 10/12-inch
JUBILEE (1039 "12 x 4")..............100-200 57
Members: Jim Nabbie; Danny Owens; William "Pat" Best; Jimmy Gordon; Deek Watson.
Also see CHURCHILL, Savannah
Also see HALL, Juanita, & Four Tunes
Also see NABBIE, Jimmie
Also see SENTIMENTALISTS

FOUR TUNES / Shadows
LPs: 10/12-inch
CHICAGO.............. 8-10 88
Also see FOUR TUNES

4 UNIQUES
(The "4" Uniques with the Stereos Combo)
Singles: 7-inch
ADAM (9002 "Too Young")..............100-150 61
ADAM (9004 "She's the Only Girl")..............100-150 62
DEER (3002 "Good Luck Charm")..............100-200 61

4 UNIQUES
Singles: 7-inch
U.S.A. (753 "Endlessly")..............30-40 64

FOUR UNKNOWNS
Singles: 7-inch
MIDA (112 "Fearless")..............15-20 59

FOUR UPSETTERS
Singles: 7-inch
SUN..............10-20 62-63

Members: George Webb; John Guthrie; Luke Wright; William Felts.

FOUR VAGABONDS P&R/R&B '43
Singles: 78 rpm
APOLLO (1030 "Kentucky Babe")..............20-40 47
APOLLO (1039 "Do You Know What It means to Miss New Orleans")..............20-40 47
APOLLO (1055 "Dreams Are a Dime a Dozen")..............20-40 47
APOLLO (1057 "P.S. I Love You")..............20-40 47
APOLLO (1060 "Ask Anyone Who Knows")..............20-40 47
APOLLO (1075 "Choo-Choo")..............20-40 47
APOLLO (1076 "The Gang That Sang Heart of My Heart")..............20-40 47
ATLAS (111 "I Can't Make Up My Mind")..............20-40 45
BLUEBIRD (0810 "I Had the Craziest Dream")..............30-50 43
BLUEBIRD (0811 "Rose Ann of Charing Cross")..............30-50 43
BLUEBIRD (0815 "It Can't Be Wrong")..............30-50 43
BLUEBIRD (11519 "Slow & Easy")..............30-50 42
LLOYDS (102 "P.S. I Love You")..............50-100 53
MERCURY (2050 "Taking My Chance with You")..............15-25 46
MIRACLE (141 "My Heart Cries")..............15-25 49
RCA (1677 "If I Were You")..............20-30 45
Singles: 7-inch
LLOYDS (102 "P.S. I Love You")..............300-400 53
EPs: 7-inch
LLOYDS (706 "Four Vagabonds")..............400-500 54
Members: Johnny Jordan; Robert O'Neal; Ray Grant; Norval Taborn.
Also see VAGABONDS

FOUR VANNS
Singles: 78 rpm
VIK (0246 "So Young & Pretty")..............10-15 56
Singles: 7-inch
VIK (0246 "So Young & Pretty")..............15-25 56

FOUR VIBES
Singles: 7-inch
SWA=RAY (1001 "You're All I Live For")..............20-30 60s
Session: Jesse Herring.

FOUR VOICES P&R '56
Singles: 78 rpm
COLUMBIA.............. 5-10 55-57
Singles: 7-inch
ABC-PAR.............. 5-10 61
COLUMBIA.............. 8-15 55-60
PEACOCK.............. 5-10 62
VOICE (1112 "Your Love Is Getting Stronger")..............10-20
VOICE (1113 "Summer Kind of Love")..............10-20

FOUR WHEELS
Singles: 7-inch
DELEWARE (1703 "Ratchet")..............20-30 64
SOMA (1428 "Central High Playmate")..............10-20 64
Also see BOYS NEXT DOOR

FOUR WINDS
Singles: 78 rpm
MIDDLETONE..............40-60 56
Singles: 7-inch
MIDDLETONE (008 "I Promise")..............75-125 56
MIDDLETONE (013 "Living in a Dream")..............75-125 56

FOUR WINDS
(With Their Teenage Friends & Eddie Platt's Band)
Singles: 7-inch
CHATTAHOOCHEE (655 "Down & Out")..............10-15 64
DECOR (175 "Five Minutes More")..............15-25 57
DERY (10022 "Jennifer")..............15-25 63
DIAL (3006 "Promised Land").............. 8-12 62
EXPLORER ("Five Minutes More")..............25-35 57
(Selection number not known. Opinions vary as to whether this label preceded or followed Decor. Readers?)
EXPLORER (713 "Doin' the Stroll")..............25-35 57
SHERLUCK (1027 "Ol' Man River")..............40-60
VIK (0221 "Find Someone New")..............10-15 56
WARWICK (633 "Daddy's Home")..............25-50 61
WESTLAND.............. 4-8 66
Also see PLATT, Eddie, & Orchestra

FOUR WINDS
(4 Winds; Tokens)
Singles: 7-inch
B.T. PUPPY.............. 5-10 69
CRYSTAL BALL.............. 4-8 77
SWING..............10-20 64
Also see TOKENS

FOUR Xs
Singles: 7-inch
LOST (101 "I'll Remember")..............25-40 60

4U & HIM
Singles: 7-inch
FENTON ("Back Door Man")..............75-100 60s
(Selection number not known.)

FOUR YOUNG MEN
(Young Men Four)
Singles: 7-inch
CREST.............. 5-8 61-62
DELTA.............. 4-8 63
DORE.............. 8-12 61

FOUR-EVERS P&R '64
(Four Evers)
Singles: 7-inch
CHATTAHOOCHEE.............. 4-8 64
COLUMBIA (42303 "You Belong to Me")..............30-50 62
COLUMBIA (42303 "You Belong to Me")..............75-100 62
(With "3" prefix. Compact 33 Single.)
COLUMBIA (43886 "A Lovely Way to Say Goodbye")..............30-50 66
CONSTELLATION..............10-15 65
CRYSTAL BALL.............. 4-8
JAMIE.............. 5-10 63
JASON SCOTT.............. 4-8
RED BIRD..............10-15 66
SMASH (1853 "It's Love")..............10-15 63
SMASH (1887 "Please Be Mine")..............10-20 63
SMASH (1887 "Be My Girl")..............10-20 64
(Same selection number used on both issues above.)
SMASH (1921 "Doo Be Dum")..............10-15 63
LPs: 10/12-inch
MAGIC CARPET.............. 8-10

FOURGONE CONCLUSION
Singles: 7-inch
COLUMBIA.............. 4-6 69

FOURLANES
Singles: 7-inch
REPRISE.............. 5-10 63

FOURMOST
Singles: 7-inch
LU PINE (105 "Twist-A-Tast")..............15-20 62

FOURMOST
Singles: 7-inch
ATCO (6280 "Hello Little Girl")..............10-20 63
ATCO (6285 "Respectable")..............10-15 64
ATCO (6307 "If You Cry")..............10-15 64
ATCO (6317 "How Can I Tell Her")..............10-15 64
CAPITOL (5591 "Why Do Fools Fall in Love").............. 8-12 66
CAPITOL (5738 "Here, There and Everywhere")..............15-20 66

FOURMOST AUTHORITY
Singles: 7-inch
GNP.............. 4-8 67-68

FOURPLAY LP '91
LPs: 10/12-inch
W.B.............. 5-8 91
Members: Bob James; Lee Ritenour; Harvey Mason; Nathan East.
Also see JAMES, Bob
Also see RITENOUR, Lee

FOURTEEN KARAT SOUL
Singles: 7-inch
CATAMOUNT (Black vinyl).............. 3-4 79
CATAMOUNT (Colored vinyl).............. 3-5 79

4TH AMENDMENT
Singles: 7-inch
CONSTITUTION (5109 "Always Blue")..............10-15 67
4 SONS..............10-15 60s

FOURTH CEKCION
LPs: 10/12-inch
SOLAR (110 "Fourth Cekcion")..............25-35 70

FOURTH DIMENSION
Singles: 7-inch
COLUMBIA.............. 4-8 66

FOURTH GENERATION
Singles: 7-inch
TEEN TOWN (1001 "I'm So Happy")..............10-20 73

FOURTH ST. EXIT
Singles: 7-inch
ROWENA.............. 4-8

FOURTH WAY
Singles: 7-inch
CAPITOL.............. 4-8 69
SOUL CITY.............. 4-8 68
LPs: 10/12-inch
HARVEST..............10-15 70-71
CAPITOL..............15-20 69

FOUR-UM
LPs: 10/12-inch
LIBRA (7008 "Just Us")..............10-15

FOWLER, Jimmy
Singles: 7-inch
DART.............. 5-10 59

FOWLER, Ken C&W '86
Singles: 7-inch
DEJA VU.............. 3-4 86

FOWLER, T.J.
Singles: 78 rpm
GOTHAM.............. 8-12 52
SAVOY.............. 5-10 52-53
SENSATION..............10-20
STATES.............. 5-10 53
Singles: 7-inch
BOW (309 "Milk Shake")..............15-25 57
GOTHAM (254 "Hot Sauce")..............15-25 52
SAVOY..............15-25 52-53
STATES (132 "The Queen")..............15-25 53

FOWLER, Wally C&W '84
(With the Tennessee Valley Boys)
Singles: 7-inch
DOVE (100 "A New Star in Heaven").............. 5-10 77
MERCURY..............10-15 47

NASHWOOD.............. 3-4 84
SONGS OF FAITH.............. 3-4
EPs: 7-inch
DECCA.............. 5-10 60
LPs: 10/12-inch
DECCA..............12-20 60
DOVE (1000 "A Tribute to Elvis Presley")..............15-20 77
KING..............20-30 60
NASHWOOD.............. 5-10
PICKWICK.............. 6-12
PICKWICK/HILLTOP.............. 8-12 65
STARDAY..............15-25 60-64
VOCALION..............10-15 67
Session: J.D. Sumner & Stamps; D.J. Fontana; Charlie McCoy; Harold Bradley; with Anita Kerr Singers; with Oak Ridge Quartet.
Also see KERR, Anita
Also see McCOY, Charlie
Also see OAK RIDGE BOYS
Also see PRESLEY, Elvis
Also see SUMNER, J.D., & Stamps Quartet

FOWLEY, Kim LP '69
Singles: 7-inch
CAPITOL.............. 4-6 72-73
CREATIVE FAMILY..............15-25
IMPERIAL.............. 5-10 68-69
LIVING LEGEND..............10-15 65-66
LOMA.............. 5-10 66
ORIGINAL SOUND.............. 4-8 60s
REPRISE.............. 5-10 67
TOWER.............. 5-10 67
LPs: 10/12-inch
CAPITOL (11075 "I'm Bad")..............15-25 72
CAPITOL (11159 "International Heroes")..............10-20 73
CAPITOL (11248 "Automatic")..............10-20 74
IMPERIAL (12413 "Born to Be Wild")..............15-25 68
IMPERIAL (12423 "Outrageous")..............15-25 69
IMPERIAL (12443 "Good Clean Fun")..............15-20 69
PVC (7906 "Sunset Boulevard").............. 8-12 79
TOWER (5080 "Love Is Alive and Well")..............25-30 67
Also see BELFAST GYPSIES
Also see BERRY, Richard
Also see KING LIZARD
Also see PAUL & VICTORS / Kim Fowley
Also see ROCKY & Border Kings

FOWLKES, Doug, & Airdales
LPs: 10/12-inch
ATCO..............10-12 62

FOWLS
Singles: 7-inch
ROTTEN RAT.............. 5-10

FOX
LPs: 10/12-inch
CREWE..............10-12 70

FOX P&R '75
(Noosha Fox)
Singles: 7-inch
ARIOLA/GTO.............. 3-5 75
GTO.............. 3-5 74
LPs: 10/12-inch
ARIOLA AMERICA.............. 8-10 75

FOX
(The Fox—High Priest Smoking Bear)
Singles: 7-inch
RINGS of SATURN (1000 "The Man, the Man")..............200-300

FOX
Singles: 7-inch
STUDIO 10.............. 4-6
Members: G. Pihl; J. Vemazza; R. Garcia.

FOX, Britny: see BRITNY FOX

FOX, Charles P&R '81
Singles: 7-inch
HANDSHAKE.............. 3-4 81

FOX, Charlie
Singles: 7-inch
AMBASSADOR.............. 4-6 66
Picture Sleeves
AMBASSADOR.............. 4-8 66

FOX, Damon
Singles: 7-inch
FAIRMOUNT (1021 "Packin' Up")..............10-20 67

FOX, Dolly C&W '78
Singles: 7-inch
ARTIC.............. 3-5 78

FOX, Eugene
(The Fox; Sly Fox)
Singles: 78 rpm
CHECKER..............20-30 54
RPM..............25-50 54
SPARK..............25-50 54
Singles: 7-inch
CHECKER (792 "Sinner's Dream")..............30-50 54
RPM (421 "The Dream")..............50-75 54
SPARK (108 "Hoodoo Say")..............50-75 54
SPARK (112 "My Four Women")..............50-75 54

FOX, Jack
Singles: 7-inch
SURE (0001 "John Wayne").............. 3-4 81
Picture Sleeves
SURE (0001 "John Wayne").............. 3-4 81

FOX, Johnny, & Foxes
Singles: 7-inch
NEW TIME..............10-15 62

FOX, Kent C&W '73
Singles: 7-inch
MCA 3-5 73
MERCANTILE 3-5 77

FOX, Lance, & Bloodhounds
Singles: 7-inch
BANG 10-20 66

FOX, Neal
LPs: 10/12-inch
RCA 5-10 77

FOX, Norman, & Rob-Roys
("Rob Roys featuring Norman Fox"; with Sid Bass Orchestra)
Singles: 78 rpm
BACK BEAT 50-75 57-58
Singles: 7-inch
BACK BEAT (499 "Lover Doll") 10-20 80s
BACK BEAT (500 "Rainy Day Bells") 5-10 90s
BACK BEAT (501 "Tell Me Why") 35-55 57
(White label.)
BACK BEAT (501 "Tell Me Why") 20-30 57
(Red label.)
BACK BEAT (508 "Dance Girl Dance") 30-40 58
CAPITOL (4128 "Dream Girl") 200-300 59
(Purple label.)
CAPITOL (4128 "Dream Girl") 250-350 59
(Yellow label. Promotional issue only.)
HAMMER (544 "Pizza Pie") 15-25
Members: Norman Fox; Andre Lilli; Bob Thirer; Bob Trotman; Buzz Halford.

FOX, Orville
Singles: 7-inch
ELLIS (101 "Honey, You Talk Too Much") 100-125

FOX, Samantha P&R/LP '86
Singles: 12-inch
JIVE 4-6 86
Singles: 7-inch
JIVE 3-4 86-89
Picture Sleeves
JIVE 3-4 86-89
LPs: 10/12-inch
JIVE 5-10 86-88

FOX, Tony
Singles: 7-inch
CALLA 5-10 68
EMERALD CITY 3-5 80
TRI-SPIN (004 "Why Did You Lie to Me") 8-12

FOX, Virgil LP '71
LPs: 10/12-inch
DECCA 10-12 71

FOX & HUNTAHS
Singles: 7-inch
MALCOLM Z (45004 "Love Minus Zero") 20-30 66

FOX HOLLAND
Singles
IRON WORKS (1019 "Do You Know") 8-12 87
(Rectangular picture disc.)

FOXALL, Art, Combo
Singles: 7-inch
DOT (15732 "Potato Chips") 10-20 62

FOXES
Singles: 7-inch
ABC-PAR 8-12 63
BRIDGEVIEW 4-8
PICKWICK 4-6
TITANIC 10-15 63

FOXETTES
Singles: 7-inch
DON-EL 10-20 62

FOXFIRE C&W '79
Singles: 7-inch
ELEKTRA 3-5 80
NSD 3-5 79

FOXX, Freddie
Singles: 7-inch
MCA 3-4 90

FOXX, Inez P&R/R&B '63
(With Charlie Foxx)
Singles: 7-inch
DYNAMO 4-6 67-70
LANA 3-6 60s
MUSICOR 4-8 66-68
SUE 4-8 65
SYMBOL 5-10 63-64
VOLT 3-5 72-73
U.A. 3-5 74
LPs: 10/12-inch
DYNAMO 10-15 67
SUE (1037 "Inez & Charlie Foxx") 20-40 65
(Monaural.)
SUE (1037 "Inez & Charlie Foxx") 25-50 65
(Stereo.)
SYMBOL (4400 "Mockingbird") 100-150 63
VOLT 8-10 73
Also see PLATTERS / Inez & Charlie Foxx / Jive Five / Tommy Hunt

FOXX, Redd LP '72
(With Hattie Noel)
Singles: 78 rpm
DOOTO (Except 416) 5-10 57
DOOTO (416 "Real Pretty Mama") 10-15 57
DOOTONE 3-5 56-57
SAVOY 5-10 46
Singles: 7-inch
DOOTO (Except 416) 5-10 57-61
DOOTO (416 "Real Pretty Mama") 15-25 57
DOOTONE 8-12 56-57
EPs: 7-inch
DOOTO 5-10 57-61
DOOTONE 5-10 56-57
LPs: 10/12-inch
ATLANTIC 5-10 75
AUTHENTIC 15-25 55-56
DOOTO 5-15 60-74
DOOTONE 10-20 57
KING 5-10 69-71
LAFF 5-10 79
LOMA 8-12 66-68
MF 5-8
RCA 5-10 72
W.B. 8-10 69

FOXY R&B '70
Singles: 7-inch
DASH 3-5 76-80
DOUBLE SHOT 3-6 69
LPs: 10/12-inch
DASH 5-10 78-80
Members: Ish Ledesma; Richie Puente; Arnold Pasiero; Joe Galdo; Charlie Murciano.
Also see OXO

FOXY & SEVEN HOUNDS
Singles: 7-inch
WISE WORLD 15-20

FOY, Will
(With Lucky Seven)
Singles: 7-inch
20TH FOX 4-8 61

FOZZIE BEAR: see KERMIT / Fozzie Bear

FRACTION
Singles: 7-inch
ANGELUS (5005 "Sanc Divided") 40-60 71
LPs: 10/12-inch
ANGELUS (571 "Moon Blood") 800-1200 71
Members: Jim Beach; Don Swanson; Vic Hemme; Curt Swanson.

FRADY, Garland C&W '73
Singles: 7-inch
COUNTRYSIDE 3-5 73
GNP 3-5 70s
PAULA 3-5 72
LPs: 10/12-inch
COUNTRYSIDE 8-10 73

FRAGILE & EGGS
Singles: 7-inch
LONG VIEW (8010 "If You See Kay") 4-8
Picture Sleeves
LONG VIEW (8010 "If You See Kay") 4-8
(Printed paper sleeve with hole—no picture.)

FRAGILE LIME
Singles: 7-inch
METROMEDIA 3-5 72
REPRISE 4-6 70
THUNDER TUMMY 5-10
Member: Dan Hook.

FRAGILE ROCK VALLEY
Singles: 7-inch
EARTH 5-10

FRALEY, Toad
Singles: 7-inch
ALLIED (10009 "Rock & Roll Music Box") 25-40 59

FRAMPTON, Peter LP '72
Singles: 7-inch
A&M (Except 1988) 3-5 74-81
A&M (1988 "Tried to Love") 3-6 77
(With Mick Jagger.)
A&M (1988 "Tried to Love") 10-15 77
(White label. Promotional issue only.)
ATLANTIC 3-4 86
Picture Sleeves
A&M (Except 1988) 3-5 74-81
A&M (1988 "Tried to Love") 4-6 77
ATLANTIC 3-4 86
LPs: 10/12-inch
A&M (3619 "Somethin's Happening") 8-12 74
A&M (3703 "Frampton Comes Alive") 10-15 76
(Two discs.)
A&M (3703 "Frampton Comes Alive") 10-15 79
(Picture disc.)
A&M (3710 "Where I Should Be") 8-12 79
A&M (3722 "Breaking All the Rules") 5-10 81
A&M (4348 "Wind of Change") 8-15 72
A&M (4512 "Frampton") 8-12 75
A&M (4704 "I'm in You") 8-10 77
A&M (4704 "I'm in You") 15-25 77
(Picture disc. Promotional issue only.)
A&M (4905 "The Art of Control") 5-10 82
ATLANTIC (848 "Frampton Is Alive") 10-15 86
(Promotional issue only.)
ATLANTIC (81290 "Premonition") 5-10 86
ATLANTIC (82030 "When All the Pieces Fit") 5-10 89
Also see FRAMPTON'S CAMEL
Also see JAGGER, Mick
Also see STARR, Ringo
Also see TAGES

FRAMPTON BROTHERS
Singles: 7-inch
BOGUS (102692 "Like an Oliver Stone") 3-4 93
Picture Sleeves
BOGUS (102692 "Like an Oliver Stone") 3-4 93
Also see CYNICS / FRAMPTON BROTHERS

FRAMPTON'S CAMEL
(Peter Frampton)
Singles: 7-inch
A&M 5-10 72-73
LPs: 10/12-inch
A&M (4389 "Frampton's Camel") 10-20 73
Also see FRAMPTON, Peter
Also see HERD
Also see HUMBLE PIE

FRAN, Carol
Singles: 7-inch
EXCELLO 8-12 57-60
FEDERAL 5-10 60s
PORT 4-8 65

FRANCE, Steve, & Varatons
Singles: 7-inch
KAY 5-10

FRANCE JOLI: see JOLI, France

FRANCES, Aileen
Singles: 7-inch
ROULETTE 8-12 64

FRANCETTES
(Fran-Cettes)
Singles: 7-inch
BESCHE (100 "Cradle Love") 15-25 63
CHALLENGE 5-10
WOLFIE (104 "I'm Leaving You") 25-50 63
Member: Frances Gray.

FRANCHI, Sergio LP '62
(With Anna Moffo)
Singles: 7-inch
LAX 3-4 79
METROMEDIA 3-4 71-72
RCA 3-6 62-67
U.A. 3-5 69-70
LPs: 10/12-inch
FOUR CORNERS 6-10 66
RCA 5-15 62-77
U.A. 5-10 70

FRANCIS, Bobby
Singles: 7-inch
CENTAUR 4-8 64

FRANCIS, Connie P&R/R&B '58
Singles: 78 rpm
MGM 20-50 55-58
Singles: 7-inch
GSF 3-5 73
IVANHOE 3-5 70s
MGM CELEBRITY SCENE (CS6-5 "Connie Francis") 30-40 66
(Boxed, five-disc set with bio insert and title strips.)
MGM (9 "Rock-a-Bye Your Baby with a Dixie Melody") 20-30 60
(Stereo.)
MGM (10 "I Almost Lost My Mind") 20-30 60
(Stereo.)
MGM (3000 series) 3-5 71
MGM (12015 "Freddy") 25-50 55
MGM (12056 "Oh, Please Make Him Jealous") 25-50 55
MGM (12122 thru 12555) 15-25 55-57
MGM (12588 thru 13116) 5-15 58-63
MGM (13127 thru 14091 except 13550) 5-10 64-69
MGM (13550 "A Nurse in the U.S. Army Corp") 20-25 66
(Promotional issue only.)
MGM (14500 series) 3-5 81
MGM (50117 "My Happiness") 20-30 58
(Stereo.)
MGM (50129 "You're Gonna Miss Me") 20-30 59
(Stereo.)
MGM (50133 "Among My Souvenirs") 20-30 59
(Stereo.)
POLYDOR 3-4 83
Picture Sleeves
MGM (12000 series except 12738) 5-15 58-61
MGM (12738 "My Happiness") 10-15 58
(Pink sleeve.)
MGM (12738 "My Happiness") 15-25 58
(Black and white sleeve.)
MGM (13000 series, except 13505 & 13773) 5-10 61-68
MGM (13505 "Empty Chapel") 10-20 66
MGM (13773 "My Heart Cries for You") 10-20 67
MGM (14000 series, except 14058 & 14091) 3-6 68-69
MGM (14058 "Gone Like the Wind") 10-20 69
MGM (14091 "Mr. Love") 10-20 69
EPs: 7-inch 33/45
MGM 10-20 58-62
LPs: 10/12-inch
LEO 12-15 60s
LION (70126 "Fun Songs for Children") 40-50 59
MGM (100 series) 10-15 70
MGM (E-3686 "Who's Sorry Now") 30-40 58
(Yellow label. Monaural.)
MGM (SE-3686 "Who's Sorry Now") 15-25 60
(Reprocessed stereo.)
MGM (E-3761 "Exciting Connie Francis") 25-35 58
(Yellow label. Monaural.)
MGM (SE-3761 "Exciting Connie Francis") 30-40 58
(Yellow label. Stereo.)
MGM (E-3776 thru E-3969) 20-30 59-61
(Monaural.)
MGM (SE-3776 thru SE-3969) 20-35 59-61
(Stereo.)
MGM (E-4000 series, except E-4023) 15-25 62-68
(Monaural.)
MGM (SE-4000 series) 15-30 62-69
(Stereo.)
MGM (E-4023 "Fun Songs for Children") 20-40 62
MGM (5400 series) 5-10
MGM (10000 series) 8-12 71
MGM (90000 series) 10-15 60s
(Capitol Record Club series.)
MATI-MOR (8002 "Brylcreem Presents Sing Along with Connie Francis") 10-20 61
(Promotional issue, made for Brylcreem.)
METRO 10-15 65-66
MGM/SESSIONS 10-12 75
POLYDOR 5-10 83
SUFFOLK 8-12
Session: Jordanaires; Boots Randolph.
Also see CRAMER, Floyd
Also see 4 SEASONS / Connie Francis / Barbara Brown & Buggs
Also see JORDANAIRES
Also see RANDOLPH, Boots
Also see SOUL, Jimmy, & Belmonts / Connie Francis

FRANCIS, Connie, & Marvin Rainwater
Singles: 78 rpm
MGM (12555 "Majesty of Love") 10-20 57
Singles: 7-inch
MGM (12555 "Majesty of Love") 15-25 57
Also see FRANCIS, Connie
Also see RAINWATER, Marvin

FRANCIS, Connie, & Hank Williams Jr.
LPs: 10/12-inch
MGM (4251 "Great Country Favorites") 15-25 64
Also see FRANCIS, Connie
Also see WILLIAMS, Hank, Jr.

FRANCISCANS
Singles: 7-inch
JIMBO (1 "Mother Please Answer Me") 30-40 60s

FRANCISCO
(Francisco Lupica)
LPs: 10/12-inch
COSMIC BEAM ("Cosmic Beam Experience") 50-75 76

FRANCISCO, Don
Singles: 7-inch
W.B. 4-6 73

FRANCOIS & ANGELOS
Singles: 7-inch
ROMULUS 4-8

FRANK, Barry
Singles: 7-inch
CALVALCADE 4-8
MOHAWK 4-8 64
Also see ADAMS, Bruce / Barry Frank

FRANK, Harmonica: see HARMONICA FRANK

FRANK, Joe, & Knights
Singles: 7-inch
ABC-PAR (10782 "Can't Find a Way") 15-20 66
EL JAY (100463 "Five Elephants in a Volkswagon") 10-20 64

FRANK, Johnny
Singles: 78 rpm
HERALD (453 "Li'l Lover") 10-15 55
Singles: 7-inch
HERALD (453 "Li'l Lover") 20-30 55

FRANK, Lenny
Singles: 7-inch
A.B.S. (214 "Let's Go Steady for the Summer") 10-15 63

FRANK, Stanley
Singles: 7-inch
ATTIC (130 "S'Cool Days") 10-20 76

FRANK & FLIPS
Singles: 7-inch
NO MAR (107 "Maxine's Place") 10-20 61
SAVOY (1602 "Devil Dog Rock") 10-20 62

FRANK & JACK
(With the Monulanes)
Singles: 7-inch
BERGEN (100 "Twas the Night Before Christmas") 25-30 57
EMBLEM (108 "Count On Me") 10-20
JOZIE (827 "Twas the Night Before Christmas") 10-15 57

FRANKE & KNOCKOUTS P&R/LP '81
Singles: 7-inch
MCA 3-4 84
MILLENNIUM 3-4 81-82
LPs: 10/12-inch
MCA 5-10 84
MILLENNIUM 5-10 81-82

FRANKIE & C-NOTES
Singles: 7-inch
RICHIE (2 "Forever and Ever") 1000-2000 61

FRANKIE & C-NOTES / Montels
Singles: 7-inch
TIMES SQUARE (10 "Forever and Ever") 10-20 63
Also see FRANKIE & C-NOTES
Also see MONTELS

FRANKIE & CLASSICALS
Singles: 7-inch
CALLA 8-10 66

FRANKIE & CORVETTES
Singles: 7-inch
ROXAN 3-5

FRANKIE & DAMONS
Singles: 7-inch
JCP (1031 "Everybody's Time") 10-20 67
JCP (1057 "I Hope You Find the Way") 10-20 67

FRANKIE & ECHOS
Singles: 7-inch
SAVOY (1544 "Come Back Baby") 15-20 58

FRANKIE & FASHIONS
Singles: 7-inch
AVENUE D (0019 "Linda") 4-6 93
AVENUE D (0021 "Blame It on Another Rainy Day") 4-6 94
(Black vinyl.)
AVENUE D (0021 "Blame It on Another Rainy Day") 8-12 94
(Clear vinyl.)

FRANKIE & FLIPS
Singles: 7-inch
SAVOY (1602 "Pop Eye Twist") 5-10 61

FRANKIE & JOHNNY
Singles: 7-inch
BLAST OFF 4-8
LIBERTY 5-10 61
LIDO (604 "Together Tonight") 10-15 59
MERCURY 4-8 69
SABRINA (331 "My First Love") 10-15 59
Members: Frankie Sardo; Johnny Sardo.
Also see SARDO, Frankie

FRANKIE & JOHNNY
Singles: 7-inch
INTERNATIONAL ARTIST 10-15

FRANKIE & MARGIE
Singles: 7-inch
WARWICK 5-10

FRANKIE & MATADORES
Singles: 7-inch
PEERLESS (9012 "With a Girl Like You") 20-30

FRANKIE & SPINDELS R&B '68
(Franky & Spindles)
Singles: 7-inch
CANYON 3-5
FUNNY 4-8
ROC-KER 4-8 68

FRANK & TEL STARS
Singles: 7-inch
ARLEN 5-10 63

FRANKIE & TIMEBREAKERS
Singles: 7-inch
MERCURY 4-8 68

FRANKIE & UPSETTERS
Singles: 7-inch
UNIVERSITY ARTIST 4-8 65

FRANK & VALUCHA
LPs:10/12-inch
PHILIPS 10-20

FRANKIE GOES TO HOLLYWOOD P&R/D&D/LP '84
Singles: 12-inch
ISLAND 4-6 84-86
Singles: 7-inch
ISLAND 3-4 84-86
Picture Sleeves
ISLAND 3-4 84-85
LPs: 10/12-inch
ISLAND 5-10 84-86
Members: Holly Johnson; Paul Rutherford.
Also see JOHNSON, Holly

FRANKLIN, Alan, Explosion
LPs: 10/12-inch
ALADIN ("Come Home Baby") 50-100 68
(Selection number not known.)
HOME ("Blues Climax") 30-50 70
(Selection number not known.)

FRANKLIN, Aretha R&B '60
(With Rev. C.L. Franklin.)
Singles: 78 rpm
CHECKER 10-20 57
J-V-B (47 "Never Grow Old") 25-50 56
Singles: 12-inch
ARISTA 4-8 84-86
Singles: 7-inch
ARISTA (Black vinyl) 3-5 80-91
ARISTA (9528 "Jumpin' Jack Flash") 5-8 86
(Colored vinyl.)
ATLANTIC (2000 series) 3-6 67-74
ATLANTIC (3000 series) 3-4 74-79
ATLANTIC (13000 series) 3-4
BATTLE (45000 series) 4-6 62
CHECKER (800 series) 10-20 57

CHECKER (900 series)................... 8-12 60
COLUMBIA (Except 44000 series).. 5-10 60-67
COLUMBIA (44000 series)............... 3-6 67-68
CHESS.. 3-5 73
J-V-B (47 "Never Grow Old") 250-350 56

Picture Sleeves

ARISTA...................................... 3-4 85-87
COLUMBIA................................. 5-10 62-63

EPs: 7-inch

ATLANTIC (8176 "Lady Soul").......10-20 68
(Stereo. Juke box issue only.)
ATLANTIC (33093 "Let It Be")........10-15 70
(Promotional issue only.)
COLUMBIA.................................10-15 64
(Juke box issues.)

LPs: 10/12-inch

ARISTA 5-10 80-89
ATLANTIC (Except "QD" series)..... 8-15 67-79
ATLANTIC ("QD" series)..............15-20 73
(Quadrophonic.)
BATTLE.......................................5-15
CANDLELITE 8-10 77
CHECKER...................................15-20 65
COLUMBIA (12 "Aretha Franklin") 10-15 68
COLUMBIA (1612 thru 2281).........12-25 61-64
(Monaural.)
COLUMBIA (2300 thru 2700
series).......................................10-20 65-67
(Monaural.)
COLUMBIA (8402 thru 9081).........15-30 61-64
(With "CS" prefix. Stereo.)
COLUMBIA (9100 thru 9700
series).......................................10-20 65-69
(With "CS" prefix. Stereo.)
COLUMBIA (10000 series)............. 5-10 73
COLUMBIA (30000 series)............. 5-10 72-82
HARMONY..................................10-12 68-71
UPFRONT 5-10 79
Also see CLEMONS, Clarence
Also see EURYTHMICS & Aretha Franklin
Also see REVERE, Paul, & Raiders / Simon & Garfunkel / Byrds / Aretha Franklin
Also see SANTANA
Also see SIMON, Paul
Also see SWEET INSPIRATIONS
Also see WOLF, Peter

FRANKLIN, Aretha, & George Benson P&R/R&B '81

Singles: 7-inch

ARISTA....................................... 3-4 81

Picture Sleeves

ARISTA....................................... 3-4 81
Also see BENSON, George

FRANKLIN, Aretha, with James Cleveland & Southern California Community Choir

EPs: 7-inch

ATLANTIC (1025 "Amazing
Grace").. 4-8 72
(Promotional issue only.)

LPs: 10/12-inch

ATLANTIC.................................. 6-10 72

FRANKLIN, Aretha, & Larry Graham

Singles: 7-inch

ARISTA....................................... 3-4 87
Also see GRAHAM, Larry

FRANKLIN, Aretha, & Whitney Houston P&R '89

Singles: 7-inch

ARISTA 3-4 89

Picture Sleeves

ARISTA 3-4 89
Also see HOUSTON, Whitney

FRANKLIN, Aretha, & Elton John P&R '89

Singles: 7-inch

ARISTA....................................... 3-4 89

Picture Sleeves

ARISTA....................................... 3-4 89
Also see JOHN, Elton

FRANKLIN, Aretha, & George Michael P&R/R&B '87

Singles: 7-inch

ARISTA....................................... 3-4 87

Picture Sleeves

ARISTA....................................... 3-4 87
Also see MICHAEL, George

FRANKLIN, Aretha / Union Gap / Blood, Sweat & Tears / Moby Grape

EPs: 7-inch

COLUMBIA (791 "The Tipalet
Experience")...............................25-35 68
(Columbia Special Products issue for Tipalet cigars. Reportedly 500 made.)
Also see BLOOD, SWEAT & TEARS
Also see FRANKLIN, Aretha
Also see MOBY GRAPE
Also see PUCKETT, Gary

FRANKLIN, Bobby R&B '75
(With Insanity; with Friend)

Singles: 7-inch

BABYLON 3-5 75
COLUMBIA................................. 3-5 76
FEE 3-5
LAKESIDE.................................. 3-5 72
THOMAS.................................... 4-8 69

FRANKLIN, Carolyn R&B '69

Singles: 7-inch

RCA.. 3-5 69-73

LPs: 10/12-inch

RCA..10-12 69-73

FRANKLIN, Doug P&R '58
(With the Bluenotes)

Singles: 7-inch

COLONIAL 10-20 58-59
Also see BLUENOTES
Also see FRANKLIN BROTHERS

FRANKLIN, Erma P&R/R&B '67

Singles: 7-inch

BRUNSWICK 5-8 69
EPIC...10-20 61-63
SHOUT (221 "Piece of My Heart")...8-12 67

LPs: 10/12-inch

BRUNSWICK 10-15 69
EPIC (619 "Her Name Is Erma")....30-40 62
(Stereo.)
EPIC (3824 "Her Name Is
Erma")..20-30 62
(Monaural.)

FRANKLIN, Ernest

Singles: 7-inch

CHI TOWN..................................5-10

FRANKLIN, Gene
("Vocal By Texas Ray"; with His House Rockin' Spacemen; with Spacemen)

Singles: 7-inch

ALTON (400 "Hackensack")...........15-20 60
(Reissued as by Texas Ray.)
KAYDEE (50001 "Itchin' &
Twistin")....................................15-25 60
Also see TEXAS RAY

FRANKLIN, Joe
(With the Mimosa Boys)

Singles: 78 rpm

MGM (11612 "Hillbilly Boy")..........15-25 53

Singles: 7-inch

MGM (11612 "Hillbilly Boy")..........30-50 53
MERCURY 8-12 58
RENOWN....................................5-10 60

FRANKLIN, Mabel

Singles: 7-inch

RITZY..10-15 65

FRANKLIN, Marie

Singles: 7-inch

MAVERICK (1002 "You Ain't
Changed")..................................... 4-8
RESIST (507 "I'll Forget About
You")...10-20 60s
STAGE MUSIC (306 "Move On
Love").. 4-8
TANGERINE 4-8
360 DEGREES 5-10 60s
TRECOR (101 "Bad, Bad Woman").. 4-8
VENTURE 5-10 69
WESTBOUND (5021 "Bad, Bad
Woman")...................................... 3-6 76
Also see GARRETT, Vernon, & Marie Franklin

FRANKLIN, Pete

Singles: 78 rpm

RCA (0012 "Casey Brown Blues") 30-50 47

LPs: 10/12-inch

PRESTIGE BLUESVILLE 15-20 63

FRANKLIN, Ray

Singles: 7-inch

CHRIS (1020 "Swamp Stomp")........8-12

FRANKLIN, Rev. C.L.: see FRANKLIN, Aretha

FRANKLIN, Rodney R&B/LP '80

Singles: 7-inch

COLUMBIA.................................. 3-4 80-86

LPs: 10/12-inch

COLUMBIA.................................5-10 80-86

FRANKLIN, Roy

Singles: 78 rpm

EMPIRE (502 "Joni") 10-20 50

Singles: 7-inch

EMPIRE (502 "Joni").....................20-30 50

FRANKLIN, Sammy, Orchestra

Singles: 7-inch

CASH (1049 "Chicken Scratch") 15-25 57

FRANKLIN, Sonny Boy

Singles: 78 rpm

EDDIE'S 20-30 49

FRANKLIN BROTHERS

Singles: 7-inch

BLUE SKY (735 "Oh, Laura").....100-200 59
COLONIAL (7000 "So Real") 20-30 59
Also see FRANKLIN, Doug

FRANKLIN CIRCLE

Singles: 7-inch

LAURIE 4-8 70

FRANKS, Michael P&R/LP '76

Singles: 7-inch

JOHN HAMMOND......................... 3-5 83
REPRISE.................................... 3-5 76
W.B. 3-4 77-83

Picture Sleeves

JOHN HAMMOND......................... 3-5

LPs: 10/12-inch

JOHN HAMMOND.........................5-10 83
REPRISE....................................5-10 76-90
W.B. 5-10 77-87

FRANKS, Tillman C&W '63
(With the Cedar Grove Three; Tillman Franks Singers)

Singles: 78 rpm

GOTHAM 10-15 51

Singles: 7-inch

GOTHAM (7412 "Hi-Tone
Poppa")......................................25-35 51
STARDAY 4-8 63-64

LPs: 10/12-inch

PICKWICK/HILLTOP......................8-12 65
Session: Faron Young.
Also see YOUNG, Faron

FRANTIC

Singles: 7-inch

LIZARD (20002 "Shady Sam").........8-12 70

LPs: 10/12-inch

LIZARD (20103 "Conception") 15-25 71
Members: Max Byfuglin; Kim Sherman; Phil Head; Jim Haas; Dennis Devlin.
Also see FARM BAND

FRANTICS P&R '59

Singles: 7-inch

BOLO (728 "Pony Maronie").........15-20 62
DOLTON (2 "Straight Flush") 15-20 59
DOLTON (6 "Fog Cutter") 15-20 59
DOLTON (13 "Werewolf"/
"Checkerboard")..........................15-25 60
DOLTON (16 "Werewolf"/"No
Werewolf")..................................10-20 60
DOLTON (24 "Delilah")..................10-20 60
DOLTON (31 "Yankee Doodlin' ") ..10-20 61
DOLTON (33 "San Antonio Rose").10-20 61
REO (8468 "Werewolf")................10-20 61
(Canadian.)
SEAFAIR (111 "San Francisco
Swim")..5-10 64
VIBRA-SONIC 5-10 60s
Members: Ron Petersen; Dick Goodman; Jim Manolides; Chuck Schoning; Bob Hosko.
Also see ACCENTS
Also see MOBY GRAPE

FRANTICS FOUR
("Vocal By Bobby Shane")

Singles: 7-inch

GULFSTREAM (1000 "T.V.
Mama") 100-200

FRANTIQUE

Singles: 7-inch

PHILADELPHIA INT'L....................3-4 80

LPs: 10/12-inch

PHILADELPHIA INT'L....................5-10 79

FRASER, Andy P&R '84

Singles: 7-inch

ISLAND 3-4 84

Picture Sleeves

ISLAND 3-4 84
Also see FREE

FRASER, Jan

Singles: 7-inch

LONDON (1976 "Night Train") 10-20 60

FRASER, Jeri Lynne

Singles: 7-inch

ABC-PAR.....................................4-8 63
COLUMBIA..................................5-10 60-61

FRASER, Johnny

Singles: 7-inch

STAR-X......................................10-15 58

FRASER & De Bolt

LPs: 10/12-inch

COLUMBIA..................................10-12 71

FRASIER, Ron

Singles: 7-inch

VIN...4-8 60

FRATERNITY BROTHERS

Singles: 78 rpm

CADENCE....................................4-8 56
VERVE..15-20 57

Singles: 7-inch

CADENCE....................................5-10 56
DATE 5-10 60
VERVE..15-20 57

FRATERNITY OF MAN

Singles: 7-inch

ABC...4-6 68

LPs: 10/12-inch

ABC (647 "Fraternity of Man") 15-25 68
DOT (25955 "Get It On")................10-20 69
Members: Larry Wagner; Martin Kibbee; Warren Klein; Richard Hayward; Elliot Ingber.
Also see FACTORY

FRATS

Singles: 7-inch

COCONUT GROOVE (2030 "Do You Love
Me")..25-35
WASHINGTON SQUARE (2030 "Do You Love
Me")..15-25

FRAZE, Ron

Singles: 7-inch

YOLK (103 "Baby Hold Me")..........10-20 61

FRAZIER, Billy

Singles: 7-inch

LIBERTY.......................................4-8 62
TOGO 4-8 63

FRAZIER, Brenda C&W '80

Singles: 7-inch

TYRO...3-5 80

FRAZIER, Calvin

Singles: 78 rpm

J-V-B...50-75 56
NEW SONG (121 "Got Nobody to Tell My
Troubles To") 400-500
SAVOY.......................................25-50 52

Singles: 7-inch

CHECKER (908 "Have Blues Must
Travel").....................................50-75 58
J-V-B (49 "Rock House")............75-100 56
J-V-B (86 "Have Blues Must
Travel")....................................75-100 58

SAVOY (858 "Got Nobody to Tell My Troubles
To")...50-75 52

FRAZIER, Coleen

Singles: 7-inch

FABLE (614 "Your Mama's
Here") 25-40 58

FRAZIER, Dallas P&R '66/C&W '67

Singles: 78 rpm

CAPITOL.....................................5-10 54

Singles: 7-inch

AUDAN...4-8 60s
CAPITOL (2000 thru 2400 series)......4-8 67-69
CAPITOL (2800 & 2900 series)......10-15 54
CAPITOL (5500 series)....................4-8 65
JAMIE 8-12 59
MERCURY 4-8 64
MUSIKON 5-10 61
RCA..3-5 71-73
20TH FOX......................................3-5 75

LPs: 10/12-inch

CAPITOL....................................10-20 66-67
RCA..8-12 70-71
Also see HOLLYWOOD ARGYLES
Also see SOME of CHET'S FRIENDS

FRAZIER, Dallas, & Joe "Fingers" Carr

Singles: 78 rpm

CAPITOL......................................3-5 54

Singles: 7-inch

CAPITOL......................................5-10 54

EPs: 7-inch

CAPITOL......................................8-12 54
Also see CARR, Joe "Fingers"
Also see FRAZIER, Dallas

FRAZIER, Frank

Singles: 7-inch

OUR (502 "Lovin' One")................30-40

FRAZIER, Joe

Singles: 7-inch

KNOCKOUT (711 "My Way") 4-6 71

FRAZIER, Ray
(With the Lovers; with Moonrays; with Shades of Madness)

Singles: 78 rpm

EXCEL 10-15 55-56

Singles: 7-inch

CARRIAGE TRADE..........................4-8
COMBO (161 "Darling")................25-35 59
EXCEL (111 "Turn Me On") 20-40 55
EXCEL (112 "All My Love") 20-40 56

FRAZIER, Tim, & Ron dela Vega

Singles: 7-inch

CRAZY HORSE 3-4 81

FREAK SCENE

Singles: 7-inch

COLUMBIA (44056 "A Million Grains of
Sand").......................................10-20 67

LPs: 10/12-inch

COLUMBIA (2656 "Psychedelic
Psoul")......................................50-75 67
(Monaural.)
COLUMBIA (9456 "Psychedelic
Psoul")....................................75-100 67
(Stereo.)
Members: David Bromberg; Rusty Evans; David Rubinson.
Also see BROMBERG, David
Also see DEEP, The

FREAKY FUKIN WEIRDOZ

LPs: 10/12-inch

FFW (SB "Extra Play") 5-10 91
(Colored vinyl.)

FREBERG, Stan P&R '51
(Stan Freberg Show; with Dick Roberts & Red Rountree; with Billy May's Orchestra; with Les Baxter's Orchestra; with Jud Conlon Chorale; with Daws Butler & June Foray; with the Toads; with George Burns Quintet)

Singles: 78 rpm

CAPITOL.....................................20-40 50-57

Singles: 7-inch

BELFAST SPARKLING WATER (1515
"Invisible Bubbles") 50-75
(Product commercials for radio use.)
BUBBLE UP (2227 "Music to Bubble Up
By")...20-30 60s
(Product commercials for radio use.
BUTTERNUT COFFEE (2000 "Instant Sales for Instant Butternut by Instant
Freberg")...................................40-50 60s
(Product commercials for radio use.
BUTTERNUT COFFEE (2237 "Amazing
Butternut Coffee") 25-35 60s
(Product commercials for radio use.)
CAPITOL (303 "The Do-It-Yourself
Dragnet") 50-100 53
(Capitol in-house, record sales promotional issue only.)
CAPITOL (1356 "John & Marsha") .20-30 51
CAPITOL (1711 "I've Got You Under My
Skin")..20-30 51
CAPITOL (1962 "Tele Vee Shun") .20-30 52
CAPITOL (2029 "Try")..................20-30 52
CAPITOL (2125 "Abe Snake for
President")..................................35-45 52
CAPITOL (2279 "The World Is Waiting for the
Sunrise") 20-30 52
CAPITOL (2596 "St. George and the
Dragonet")..................................20-30 53
CAPITOL (2671 "Christmas
Dragnet") 20-30 53
CAPITOL (2677 "C'est Si Bon") 20-30 53
CAPITOL (2929 "Sh-Boom")..........20-30 53
CAPITOL (2986 "Yulnet") 15-25 54
(Reissue of *Christmas Dragnet*.)

CAPITOL (3138 "The Lone
Psychiatrist")................................30-40 55
CAPITOL (3249 "The Yellow Rose of
Texas")......................................15-25 55
CAPITOL (3280 "Nuttin' for
Christmas")................................15-25 55
(Add $15 to $25 if accompanied by cartoon insert.)
CAPITOL (3396 "The Great
Pretender") 15-25 56
CAPITOL (3480 "Heartbreak
Hotel")......................................25-35 56
CAPITOL (3503 "Green
Chritma")................................15-25 56
CAPITOL (3687 "Banana Boat") 15-25 57
(Add $25 to $35 if accompanied by banner insert.)
CAPITOL (3815 "Wun'erful,
Wun'erful")................................15-25 57
CAPITOL (3892 "Ya Got Trouble") 10-20 58
CAPITOL (4097 "Green
Chritma")................................10-20 58
CAPITOL (4239 "The Old Payola Roll
Blues").......................................10-20 60
CAPITOL (4433 "Comments for Our
Time").......................................10-20 60
CAPITOL (5726 "Flackman and
Reagan")...................................10-15 66
COCA COLA BOTTLING CO. (2227 Music to
Bubble-Up By") 30-50 60s
(Product commercials for radio use.)
CONTADINA (2574 "Pizza
Anyone")...................................15-25 60s
(Product commercials for radio use.)
CONTADINA (4476/4471 "The Whole Peeled
Bounce"/"Little Bitty Ballad") 35-50
(Product commercials for radio use. With the Hi Lo's.)
CONTADINA (4476/4477 "The Whole Peeled
Bounce"/"Program Notes") 35-50
(Product commercials for radio use. Note different flip.)
MILKY WAY (23300 "Tom Sweet and His
Electric Milky Way Machine")........35-50
PITTSBURGH PAINT (1/2 "Four Pittsburgh
Paint Commercials") 20-30
(Product commercials for radio use.)
RADIO (2225 "Who Listens to
Radio")......................................25-40
(Promotional spots for advertising with radio.)
SOUTHERN BAPTIST CHURCH (101578
"Southern Baptist Radio and TV
Commission") 15-20
(Product commercials for radio use.)
STAINLESS STEEL (1369 "Stainless
Steel")......................................35-50
(Product commercials for radio use.)
STAN FREBERG on COMMERCIALS
("Rubblemeyer Farms")...............40-60 70s
(Promotional issue only. Commercial parodies, comparing right and wrong production of radio spots.)
TERMINIX (3540 "Floor Show, Now Going on
at Your House").........................30-40
(Product commercials for radio use.)
UNITED PRESBYTERIAN CHURCH (1401
"Three More Radio Messages for Our
Time").......................................10-20
(Product commercials for radio use.)
UNITED PRESBYTERIAN CHURCH (101578
"The Presbyterian Church")...........15-20
(Product commercials for radio use.)
ZEE (2020 "Zee with Freberg - Hey You Up
There")......................................35-50
(Product commercials for radio use.)
ZEE (4108 "Z-E-E Spells Zee").......30-35
(Product commercials for radio use.)
ZEE (24005 "Zee Spot
Commercials") 35-50
(Product commercials for radio use.)

Picture Sleeves

BUBBLE UP (2227 "Music to Bubble Up
By")..85-100 60s
(Gatefold sleeve.)
CAPITOL (415 "Wun'erful
Wun'erful")................................15-20 57
(Promotional issue only.)
CAPITOL (4097 "Green
Christmas")..................................8-12 58
CAPITOL (4329 "The Old Payola Roll
Blues").......................................15-20 60
CAPITOL (5726 "Flackman and
Reagan")...................................10-15 66
H.I.S. (122667 "Funny Record by Stan Freberg
for H.I.S.")................................35-50
(Product commercials for radio use.)
PITTSBURGH PAINT (1/2 "Four Pittsburgh
Paint Commercials") 20-30
(Reads: "The Stations Representatives Assn. presents: Some Exciting new commercials for Radio!")
RADIO (2225 "Who Listens to
Radio").....................................25-40
(Promotional spots for using radio advertising.)
SOUTHERN BAPTIST CHURCH (101578
"Southern Baptist Radio & TV
Commission") 15-20
(Product commercials for radio use.)
TERMINIX (3540 "Floor Show").....10-20
(Product commercials for radio use.)
ZEE (2020 "Zee Here, Mr.
Freberg")....................................35-50
(Product commercials for radio use.)

EPs: 7-inch

CAPITOL (415 "Wun'erful
Wun'erful")................................15-25 57
(Single-sided, two track promotional issue. Add $10 to $20 if accompanied by "Two Sides of Bubbling Hilarity" insert. Issued with generic Capitol paper sleeve.)
CAPITOL (496 "Any Requests")......20-30 54
CAPITOL (628 "Real St. George").15-25 55

CAPITOL (731 "Elderly Man River")..........40-50 58
(Promotional issue only.)
CAPITOL (1101 "Omaha")..........15-25 59
CAPITOL (1589 "Stan Freberg")....25-40 61
(Compact 33.)
CAPITOL (3192 "Ugly Duckling")...15-25
CAPITOL (4097 "The Meaning of Christmas – Stan Freberg Presents His Favorite Carols")..........30-50
(Promotional issue only.)
SWIMSUITSMANSHIP (2080 "Swimsuitsmanship")..........100-125
(Promotional issue only. Cover reads: "Fit Facts and Figures, You and Rose Marie Reid.")
UNITED PRESBYTERIAN CHURCH (1400 "Is God Dead?")..........30-45
(Product commercials for radio use.)

LPs: 10/12-inch

BEKINS (27713 "Bekins Presents the Sound of Moving")..........35-50
(Product commercials for radio use.)
BIG SOUND (2 "Jockey's Little Helper")..........35-50
(Product commercials for radio use.)
BUTTERNUT COFFEE (2000 "Instant Butternut Coffee")..........40-60 60s
(Product commercials for radio use.)
CAPITOL (777 "A Child's Garden of Freberg")..........20-40 57
CAPITOL (1035 "The Best of the Stan Freberg Shows")..........40-60 58
CAPITOL (1242 "Stan Freberg with the Original Cast")..........20-35 59
(With "T" prefix.)
CAPITOL (1242 "Stan Freberg with the Original Cast")..........12-20 69
(With "DT" prefix.)
CAPITOL (1242 "Stan Freberg with the Original Cast")..........5-10 75
(With "SM" prefix.)
CAPITOL (1573 "Stan Freberg Presents the United States of America, Volume 1 - the Early Years")..........25-25 61
(With "W" or "SW" prefix.)
CAPITOL (1694 "Face the Funnies")..........25-35 62
CAPITOL (1816 "Madison Avenue Werewolf")..........25-35 62
CAPITOL (2020 "Best of Stan Freberg")..........15-25 64
CAPITOL (2551 "Freberg Underground")..........15-25 66
(With "T" or "ST" prefix.)
CAPITOL (2551 "Freberg Underground").......... 5-10 75
(With "SM" prefix.)
CAPITOL (3264 "Mickey Mouse's Birthday Party")..........15-25 63
CAPITOL (11000 series).......... 5-10 78
CAPITOL (80700 "Uncle Stan Wants You")..........60-80 61
(Promotional issue for the LP series, *Stan Freberg Presents the United States of America.*)
COCA COLA (2468 "The Freedle Family Singers")..........175-200
COLUMBIA (105947 "Hey, Look Us Over")..........60-75
(Label lists shows. Promotional issue only. With booklet.)
COLUMBIA (105948 "Hey, Look Us Over")..........60-75
(Label does not list shows. Promotional issue only. With booklet.)
ESSKAY (59-2 "Esskay Commercials")..........60-75
(Four one-minute spots.)
ESSKAY (2161 "Second Helping – More Rare Esskay Commercials")..........60-75
(Single-sided. Product commercials for radio use.)
ESSKAY (2249 "Still More Expensive Cuts – Esskay Quality Meats")..........60-75
(Single-sided. Product commercials for radio use.)
FREBERG LTD. (2343 "Woburn-Salada Tea")..........35-50
(Product commercials for radio use.)
KAISER FOIL ("Message to Grocers")..........35-50
(10-inch LP. Single-sided.)
KAISER FOIL (22077 "A Kaiser Foil Salesman Faces Life")..........125-175
(10-inch LP. Product commercials for radio use.)
GUARDIAN MAINTENANCE (2581 "Spring Commercials")..........25-35 64
(Single-sided. Product commercials for radio use.)
MEADOWGOLD (2152 "Meadowgold Dairies")..........85-100
(Product commercials for radio use.)
OREGON (2039 "Oregon Soundtrack")..........125-150
(Product commercials for radio use. Includes press kit.)
RAB ("More Here Than Meets The Ear")..........75-125
(Promotional issue only.)
RADIO (3 "Radio Briefings")..........35-50
(Promotional spots for using radio advertising.)
RADIO (1499 "More Here Than Meets the Ear")..........30-45
(Promotional spots for using radio advertising.)
RADIO (2226 "Who Listens to Radio")..........35-50
(Promotional spots for using radio advertising.)
TV GUIDE (2889 "TV Guide Spots")..........60-75
(Product commercials for radio use.)
Note: Advertising agency discs containing commercials for radio station use are listed by product name, since there are no other label names used.
Members: Stan Freberg; Daws Butler; June Foray; George Burns; Jesse White; Peter Leeds; Paul Frees; Billy May.

FRECKLES
Singles: 7-inch
MADISON..........5-10 61

FRED
Singles: 7-inch
ARPEGGIO..........5-10

FRED, John P&R '59
(With His Playboy Band)
Singles: 7-inch
BELL..........3-5 73
JEWEL..........5-10 64-65
MONTEL..........10-15 59-62
N-JOY..........8-12
PAULA..........4-8 65-69
UNI..........3-6 69-70
LPs: 10/12-inch
PAULA..........15-25 66-68
UNI..........10-15 70

FRED & NEW J.B.s
(Fred Wesley)
Singles: 7-inch
PEOPLE..........3-5 75
LPs: 10/12-inch
PEOPLE..........5-10 75
Also see WESLEY, Fred

FREDDIE
Singles: 7-inch
BANDBOX..........10-20

FREDDIE & DREAMERS P&R/LP '65
Singles: 7-inch
CAPITOL (5053 "I'm Telling You Now")..........15-20 63
CAPITOL (5137 "You Were Made for Me")..........15-20 63
ERIC..........3-4 70s
MERCURY..........4-8 64-65
SUPER K..........3-6 70
TOWER (125 "I'm Telling You Now")..........5-10 65
Picture Sleeves
MERCURY..........5-10 65
EPs: 7-inch
MERCURY (74 "Interview with the Dreamers")..........20-30 65
(Promotional issue only.)
MERCURY (661 "Fun Loving Freddie and the Dreamers")..........20-30 65
(Juke box issue only.)
LPs: 10/12-inch
CAPITOL..........8-10 76-79
MERCURY..........20-30 65-66
TOWER (5003 "I'm Telling You Now"): see Various Artists
Members: Derek Quinn; Roy Crewdson; Pete Birrell; Bernie Dwyer; Freddie Garrity.
Also see JONES, Tom / Freddie & Dreamers / Johnny Rivers

FREDDIE & DREAMERS / Beat Merchants P&R '65
Singles: 7-inch
TOWER (127 "You Were Made for Me")..........5-10 65
Also see FREDDIE & DREAMERS

FREDDIE & DREAMERS / Just Four Men
Singles: 7-inch
TOWER (163 "Send a Letter to Me")..........5-10 65
Also see FREDDIE & DREAMERS
Also see JUST FOUR MEN

FREDDIE & FISHSTICKS
Singles: 7-inch
MCA..........4-8 81
Session: Jordanaires.
Also see JORDANAIRES

FREDDIE & FREELOADERS
(Freddy & Freeloaders)
Singles: 7-inch
CROSSROAD (104 "Octopus Song")..........20-30
I & I..........10-20 73
LAURIE (3334 "Patty")..........15-25 66
REDD HEDD..........15-25 72
3 0 9..........3-4
Member: Fred Halls.

FREDDIE & HEARTACHES
Singles: 7-inch
DOT (16247 "Mule Train")..........10-15 61
SCOTT (1206 "Womp-Womp")..........20-30 61

FREDDIE & HITCHHIKERS
Singles: 7-inch
BAND BOX (251 "Mop Flop")..........10-20 60

FREDDIE & LOU
Singles: 7-inch
ASTRA (1003 "You'll Be Mine Tonight")..........10-15 65
THUNDERHEAD (2150 "You'll Be Mine Tonight")..........35-45 61
Members: Fred Parris; Lou Peeples.
Also see FIVE SATINS

FREDDIE & PARLIAMENTS
Singles: 7-inch
TWIRL (1003 "Darlene")..........40-50 59
Also see JOHNNY & HURRICANES

FREDDIE & QUANTRILS
Singles: 7-inch
KAREM (1904 "If I Give My Heart to You")..........500-1000 64

FREDDIE & SOUNDS OF SOUL
Singles: 7-inch
PEARLTONE..........4-8 67

FREDDIE & SWINGIN' BACHELORS
Singles: 7-inch
KNOLL ("You Had Your Chance")..20-30
(Selection number not known.)

FREDDIE & VOXPOPPERS
Singles: 7-inch
WARWICK..........5-10 60

FREDDIE THE FLEA
Singles: 7-inch
NIK NIK..........5-8 73

FREDDY & CLAIRE
Singles: 7-inch
REPRISE..........5-10 62
Member: Freddy Dame.
Also see DAME, Freddy

FREDDY & KINFOLK
Singles: 7-inch
DADE (2016 "Blabbermouth")..........10-20 68

FREDDY & FAT BOYS
Singles: 7-inch
FAT MAN (101 "Why Do Fools Fall in Love")..........15-20

FREDDY & FREELOADERS: see FREDDIE & FREELOADERS

FREDDY & JADES
Singles: 7-inch
RCA..........4-8 65

FREDDY & KINFOLK
Singles: 7-inch
DADE..........4-8 68

FREDDY & LONNIE
(Freddy & Lonie)
Singles: 7-inch
LA RAE (501 "Hot Doggin")..........20-30 63
WED ("Another Love")..........10-20 62
(Selection number not known.)
WESTERN (21 "Allen's Way")..........10-20 62
Members: Freddy Countryman; Lonnie Allen.
Also see COUNTRYMAN, Freddy

FREDDY & RAVENS
Singles: 7-inch
WED (24 "Big Itch")..........8-10 62
Member: Fred Countryman.
Also see COUNTRYMAN, Fred

FREDDY FROGS: see FROGS, Freddy

FREDERICK R&B/D&D '85
Singles: 12-inch
HEAT..........4-6 85
Singles: 7-inch
HEAT..........3-4 85

FREDERICK, Dotty
Singles: 7-inch
20TH FOX..........10-15 58

FREDERICK, Jesse
LPs: 10/12-inch
BEARSVILLE..........8-12 71

FREDERICK, Tommy, & Hi-Notes
Singles: 7-inch
CARLTON..........8-12 58

FREDERICK II R&B '71
Singles: 7-inch
VULTURE..........3-5 71

FREDRIC
Singles: 7-inch
EVOLUTION (1001 "5 O'Clock Traffic")..........15-25 68
FORTE (3001 "5 O'Clock Traffic")..15-25 68
LPs: 10/12-inch
FORTE (80461 "Phases and Faces")..........750-1000 68
Members: Joe McCarger; Ron Bera; Steve Thrall.
Also see ROCK GARDEN

FREE
Singles: 7-inch
ATCO..........4-8 69
MARQUE (448 "Day of Decision for Lost Soul Blues")..........15-25 69

FREE LP '69
Singles: 7-inch
A&M..........3-6 70-71
ISLAND..........3-5 72
Picture Sleeves
A&M..........4-6 70
LPs: 10/12-inch
A&M..........8-15 69-75
ISLAND (Except 7)..........8-10 73
ISLAND (7 "The Free Story")..........25-30 73
(Includes booklet. Promotional issue only.)
Members: Andy Fraser; Paul Rodgers; Simon Kirke; Paul Kossoff.
Also see BACK STREET CRAWLER
Also see BAD COMPANY
Also see FRASER, Andy
Also see KOSSOFF, Paul
Also see RODGERS, Paul
Also see WILLIE & Poor Boys

FREE, Johnny C&W '79
Singles: 7-inch
SABRE..........3-5 79

FREE, Scott
(With the Kerry Bell Voices)
Singles: 7-inch
ALANNA (561 "It Seemed to Me")...5-10 62
LAURIE (3346 "Come on Down to Earth")..........5-10 66

FREE, Slim
Singles: 7-inch
D (1187 "Scratchin' Off")..........5-10 61

FREE, Stan
Singles: 7-inch
AMY (896 "Like Lazy")..........4-8 64
LPs: 10/12-inch
OLD TOWN (2002 "Piano a la Percussion")..........10-20 61

FREE BAND
Singles: 7-inch
VANGUARD..........10-12 69

FREE BEER
Singles: 7-inch
RCA..........3-5 76-77
SOUTHWIND..........3-6 76
Picture Sleeves
RCA..........3-5 77
LPs: 10/12-inch
RCA..........8-12 76-77
SOUTHWIND..........8-12 75
Members: Michael Packer; Caleb Potter; Ned Albright; Sandy Allen; Richard Crooks; Joe Dube; Brendan Harkin; Larry Gonsky; Richard Harbart; Jon Harris; Bernard Purdie; Eric Weissberg; Don Francisco.
Also see PAN

FREE EXPRESSION R&B '81
Singles: 7-inch
VANGUARD..........3-4 81

FREE FARE
Singles: 7-inch
SHOWCASE..........5-10 74

FREE for ALL
Singles: 7-inch
CHALLENGE (59339 "Show Me the Way")..........10-15 66

FREE LIFE R&B '79
Singles: 7-inch
EPIC..........3-5 78
LPs: 10/12-inch
EPIC..........5-10 78

FREE MEN
Singles: 7-inch
MGM..........4-8 68

FREE MIND
Singles: 7-inch
TWIN TOWN..........4-8 60s

FREE MOVEMENT P&R/R&B '71
Singles: 7-inch
COLUMBIA..........3-5 71
DECCA..........3-5 71
LPs: 10/12-inch
COLUMBIA..........8-10 72
Also see SWEATHOG / Free Movement / Bob Dylan / Edgar Winter's White Trash

FREE MOVEMENT / Love Unlimited
Singles: 7-inch
MCA..........3-5 73
Also see FREE MOVEMENT
Also see LOVE UNLIMITED

FREE REIGN
Singles: 7-inch
DIAL..........4-8 68

FREE SAMPLE
Singles: 7-inch
ORIGINAL SOUND..........8-12 67

FREE SPIRITS
Singles: 7-inch
ABC..........4-8 66-67
LPs: 10/12-inch
ABC..........10-20 67

FREE THINKERS
Singles: 7-inch
MALA..........10-15 65

FREEBEES
Singles: 7-inch
MUSITRON (1061/2 "Seymour The Beatnik Elf")..........10-20 60

FREEBEEZ
Singles: 7-inch
STRANGE (2216 "Walk Away")..........15-25 66

FREEBORNE
LPs: 10/12-inch
MONITOR (607 "Peak Impression")..........75-125 67
Members: Nick Castolin; Bob Margolin; Dave Codd.

FREED, Al: see GLITTERS / Al Freed

FREED, Alan
(With His Rock 'N Roll Band)
Singles: 78 rpm
CORAL..........10-30 56-58
Singles: 7-inch
CORAL (61626 "Right Now, Right Now")..........15-25 56
CORAL (61660 "Camel Rock")..........15-25 56
CORAL (61749 "Rock & Roll Boogie")..........15-25 56
CORAL (61818 "Sentimental Journey")..........10-20 58
EPs: 7-inch
CORAL (81136 "Rock 'N Roll Dance Party")..........30-50 56
LPs: 10/12-inch
BRUNSWICK (54043 "The Alan Freed Rock 'N Roll Show")..........75-100 59
(With "Guests" Buddy Holly & Crickets, Jackie Wilson & Terry Noland.)
CORAL (57063 "Rock 'N Roll Dance Party, Vol. 1")..........40-60 56
(With the Modernaires.)
CORAL (57115 "Rock 'N Roll Dance Party, Vol. 2")..........40-60 56
(With Jimmy Cavello & His House Rockers.)
CORAL (57177 "TV Record Hop")..........40-60 57
CORAL (57213 "Rock Around the Block")..........40-60 58
CORAL (57216 "Alan Freed Presents the King's Henchmen")..........40-60 58
(With King Curtis, Sam "The Man" Taylor, Count Hastings, Kenny Burrell, Everett Barksdale, Ernie Hayes.)
Also see CAVELLO, Jimmy, & His House Rockers
Also see KING CURTIS
Also see HOLLY, Buddy
Also see NOLAND, Terry
Also see TAYLOR, Sam "The Man
Also see WILSON, Jackie

FREED, Alan, Steve Allen, Al "Jazzbo" Collins & Modernaires
Singles: 78 rpm
CORAL (61693 "The Space Man")...8-12 56
Singles: 7-inch
CORAL (61693 "The Space Man")..15-25 56
Also see COLLINS, Al
Also see FREED, Alan

FREEDLAND, Nat
LPs: 10/12-inch
U.A...........12-15 73

FREEDOM R&B '79
Singles: 7-inch
ABC..........3-5 70
BUDDAH..........3-5 75
FREEDOM..........15-25
MALACO..........3-4 79
LPs: 10/12-inch
ABC..........10-12 70
COTILLION..........10-12 71

FREEDOM, Johnny
Singles: 7-inch
ALERT..........5-10 59

FREEDOM EXPRESS
LPs: 10/12-inch
MERCURY..........10-12 70

FREEDOM HILL
Singles: 7-inch
LAURIE (3683 "Love Is Like a Merry-Go-Round")..........5-8 80

FREEDOM MACHINE
Singles: 7-inch
ALARM..........3-5

FREEDOM RIDERS
LPs: 10/12-inch
DAUNTLESS..........10-20

FREEDOM SINGERS
LPs: 10/12-inch
MERCURY..........15-25

FREEDOMS
Singles: 7-inch
CONSTELLATION..........4-8 64

FREEEZ R&B/D&D '83
Singles: 12-inch
STREETWISE..........4-6 83
Singles: 7-inch
STREETWISE..........3-4 83
LPs: 10/12-inch
STREETWISE..........5-10 83
Also see ROCCA, John

FREEFALL THREE
Singles: 7-inch
CUCA (1174 "616")..........15-25 64
Members: Doug Tank; Roy Malvitz; Lee Breest.

FREELANCERS
Singles: 7-inch
FREELANCE (20 "High School Flame")..........75-125
(Also issued as by Dan Williams & the Freelancers.)
Member: Dan Williams.
Also see WILLIAMS, Dan, & Freelancers

FREELOADERS
Singles: 7-inch
A&M (1148 "I Who Have Nothing")....4-8 69
Members: Fred Bliffert; Tom McCutcheon; Jimmy Gaskill; Peter Leshin; Sam Friedman; Stan Kellicut; Barry Biehoff; Jeff Irwin.
Also see BLIFFERT, Fred
Also see HENRY, Freddy

FREEMAN, Arthur
(Art Freeman)
Singles: 7-inch
DADE (1852 "Shirley")..........10-15 62
EXCELLO (2322 "Played Out Playgirl")..........10-20 67

FAME (1008 "I Can't Get You Out of My Mind")....................20-40 66
FAME (1012 "Piece of My Heart") .10-20 66
Also see TRAVIS, McKinley

FREEMAN, Benny
Singles: 7-inch
SOUNDEX.................................. 4-8 62

FREEMAN, Bo
Singles: 7-inch
PURL (901 "The Girl for Me").....400-600 60s

FREEMAN, Bobby P&R/R&B '58
Singles: 78 rpm
JOSIE (835 "Do You Want to Dance")..........................100-150 58
JUBILEE (835 "Do You Want to Dance")..........................100-150 58
(Canadian.)
JUBILEE (841 "Betty Lou Got a New Pair of Shoes")..........................100-150 58
(Canadian. U.S. Josie 78 of 841 has not yet been verified.)
Singles: 7-inch
ABC.................................. 3-5 73
AUTUMN.................................. 6-12 63-64
DOUBLE SHOT.................................. 4-8 69-70
GUSTO.................................. 3-5 80s
JOSIE (835 "Do You Want to Dance")..........................20-30 58
JOSIE (841 "Betty Lou Got a New Pair of Shoes")..........................20-30 58
JOSIE (844 "Need Your Love")......20-30 58
JOSIE (855 "When You're Smiling")..........................15-25 59
JOSIE (863 "Mary Ann Thomas")...15-25 59
JOSIE (867 "My Guardian Angel")..........................15-25 59
JOSIE (872 "Ebb Tide")..........15-25 59
JOSIE (879 "I Need Someone").....15-25 60
JOSIE (886 "Miss You So")..........10-20 61
JOSIE (887 "Mess Around")..........10-20 61
JOSIE (889 "She Wants to Dance")..........................10-20 61
JOSIE (896 "Love Me")..........10-20 62
JOSIE (928 "Mess Around")..........6-12 64
KING (5373 "Shimmy Shimmy") 15-20 60
KING (5900 series).................. 6-12 64
LOMA.................................. 5-10 67
PARKWAY (875 "Whip It Up Baby")..........................6-12 63
RNOR.................................. 3-5
TOUCH (101 "Everything's Love") 3-6 73
VIRGO.................................. 3-5 72
Picture Sleeves
RNOR.................................. 5-10
LPs: 10/12-inch
AUTUMN (102 "C'mon & Swim")....20-30 64
JOSIE (4007 "Get in the Swim") 15-25 65
JUBILEE (1086 "Do You Wanna Dance")..........................50-100 59
(Monaural.)
JUBILEE (1086 "Do You Wanna Dance")..........................100-150 59
(Stereo.)
JUBILEE (5010 "Twist with Bobby Freeman")..........................25-40 62
KING (930 "The Lovable Style of Bobby Freeman")..........................100-200 65
Also see ROMANCERS

FREEMAN, Bobby, & Chuck Jackson
LPs: 10/12-inch
GRAND PRIX..........................15-20 64
Also see FREEMAN, Bobby
Also see JACKSON, Chuck

FREEMAN, Bobby
Singles: 7-inch
KIMRAY.................................. 3-6 77

FREEMAN, Eddie
Singles: 7-inch
KEM (2747 "Bullwhip")..........15-25 57

FREEMAN, Ernie R&B '56
(Ernie Freeman Combo)
Singles: 78 rpm
CASH.................................. 5-10 56
IMPERIAL.................................. 8-12 57
MAMBO.................................. 8-12 55
Singles: 7-inch
AVA.................................. 4-8 64
CASH.................................. 8-12 56
IMPERIAL (Except 5752)............ 8-15 57-62
IMPERIAL (5752 "Theme from Igor")..........................10-20 61
KING.................................. 5-10 60
LIBERTY.................................. 4-8 62
MAMBO (107 "Poor Fool")..........10-20 55
EPs: 7-inch
DOOTONE (209 "Jazz Organ")......10-15 56
LPs: 10/12-inch
DUNHILL..........................10-15 67
IMPERIAL..........................20-30 57-62
LIBERTY..........................10-20 62-63
Members: Ernie Freeman; Irvin Ashby; Joe Comfort; R. Martinez.
Also see ASHBY, Irving
Also see B. BUMBLE & STINGERS
Also see JOINER, ARKANSAS JUNIOR HIGH SCHOOL BAND
Also see NELSON, Willie
Also see OTIS, Johnny
Also see RAIN DROPS
Also see RELF, Bobby
Also see ROUVAUN
Also see SIR CHAUNCEY
Also see VOICES
Also see WITHERSPOON, Jimmy

FREEMAN, Ernie, & Scooby Doo All Stars
Singles: 7-inch
ZEPHYR (006 "Ernie's Journey") 5-10 60s

FREEMAN, Evelyn
(With the Exciting Voices)
Singles: 7-inch
DOT (15726 "Come to Me My True Love")..........................15-25 58
IMPERIAL (5967 "Didn't It Rock") 5-10 63
U.A. (406 "Didn't It Rain")..........10-15 62
WHITE WHALE (317 "I Heard the Voice")..........................4-8 69
LPs: 10/12-inch
BEL CANTO..........................15-25 60s
(Colored vinyl.)
U.A. (3178 "Didn't It Rain")..........15-25 62

FREEMAN, Gaffney
Singles: 7-inch
COLUMBIA.................................. 3-5 80

FREEMAN, George
Singles: 7-inch
EPIC (10668 "Stop Now").................. 4-6 71
GARDENA (129 "Sugar Lips") 10-20 62
OKEH (7333 "All Right Now") 8-12 69
SHOUT (201 "Why Are You Doing This to Me")..........................15-25 66
VALIANT (6039 "Down and Out")...50-75 63
VALIANT (6057 "One Last Dance")..........................15-25 64

FREEMAN, Jimmy
LPs: 10/12-inch
HIDEOUT (1007 "The Game of Rock & Roll")..........................10-15 75
(Includes board game cards: Rock Cards, Roll Cards, and Record Cards.)

FREEMAN, John R&B '77
Singles: 7-inch
DAKAR.................................. 3-5 77

FREEMAN, Michele
LPs: 10/12-inch
POLYDOR..........................5-10 79

FREEMAN, Roger
Singles: 7-inch
R (1512 "All Shook Up")..........15-25 67

FREEMAN, Von
Singles: 7-inch
MARKIE (103 "When You Love Someone")..........................10-20 63

FREEMAN BROTHERS
Singles: 7-inch
MALA (485 "I'm Counting on You")..........................15-25 64
MALA (553 "I'm Counting on You")..........................10-15 67
SOUL (35011 "My Baby") 20-30 65

FREEMAN SOUND
Singles: 7-inch
STARSHINE..........................5-10

FREENIE, Ortin
Singles: 7-inch
LUTE.................................. 4-8 62

FREEPORT
LPs: 10/12-inch
MAINSTREAM..........................10-12 70

FREES, Paul
Singles: 7-inch
MGM.................................. 4-8 68
SINGLETTE.................................. 4-8 64
LPs: 10/12-inch
MGM..........................10-15 68

FREESTYLE R&B '84
(Freestyle Express)
Singles: 7-inch
MUSIC SPECIALISTS.................. 3-4 84-86
Member: Tony Butler.
Also see TRINERE / Freestyle / Debbie Deb

FREEWAYS
Singles: 7-inch
HIBACK (107 "Goffin Goffin") 20-40 66

FREEWHEELERS
Singles: 7-inch
EPIC.................................. 4-8 64

FREEWHEELIN'
LPs: 10/12-inch
FORCE..........................5-10 80

FREEZE
Singles: 7-inch
ARATRON (7806 "Walking Wounded")..........................3-5 82
Picture Sleeves
ARATRON (7806 "Walking Wounded")..........................3-5 82

FREEZE, Sonny, & Unchained
Singles: 7-inch
MAGIC TOUCH (2075 "White Snowflake–Blue Christmas")..........................5-10 69

FREHLEY, Ace P&R/LP '78
Singles: 7-inch
MEGAFORCE.................................. 3-5 87
CASABLANCA.................................. 3-5 78
Picture Sleeves
MEGAFORCE.................................. 3-5 87
LPs: 10/12-inch
CASABLANCA (7121 "Ace Frehley")..........................12-20 78
(With poster order form.)
CASABLANCA (7121 "Ace Frehley")..........................8-12 78
(Without poster order form.)
CASABLANCA (PIX-7121 "Ace Frehley")..........................50-60 79
(Picture disc.)
MEGAFORCE..........................5-10 87-89
Also see FREHLEY'S COMET
Also see KISS

FREHLEY'S COMET LP '88
LPs: 10/12-inch
MEGAFORCE..........................5-8 88
Also see FREHLEY, Ace

FREISEN, David
LPs: 10/12-inch
INNER CITY..........................8-10 77-80
STEEPLE CHASE..........................5-10 80

FRENCH, Don P&R '59
Singles: 7-inch
LANCER..........................5-10 59

FRENCH, Irlton
Singles: 78 rpm
OKEH..........................15-25 51
Singles: 7-inch
OKEH (6816 "My Run Around Baby")..........................30-50 51

FRENCH, Jeanne
LPs: 10/12-inch
COLUMBIA..........................5-10 80

FRENCH, Steve
Singles: 7-inch
G&G..........................5-10 59

FRENCH CHURCH
Singles: 7-inch
PRINCETON (101 "Without Crying")..........................15-25 66

FRENCH FRIES
Singles: 7-inch
EPIC..........................10-15

FRENCH KISS
Singles: 7-inch
POLYDOR..........................3-4 79
LPs: 10/12-inch
POLYDOR..........................5-10 79

FRENCH REVOLUTION
Singles: 7-inch
TOWER..........................3-6 69

FRENCHMEN
Singles: 7-inch
PINCUS..........................5-10

FRENCHY & CHESSMEN
Singles: 7-inch
TEMPLE (2081 "Beetle Bebop") 10-15 64

FRESANDOS
("Fresando's with Eddie Bartell & His Dukes of Rhythm")
Singles: 78 rpm
STAR-X (501 "Your Last Goodbye")..........................100-200 57
Singles: 7-inch
STAR-X (501 "Your Last Goodbye")..........................200-300 57

FRESH
Singles: 7-inch
RCA..........................3-5 70
LPs: 10/12-inch
RCA..........................10-12 70

FRESH
Singles: 7-inch
EPIC (10844 "Swanee River") 4-8 72

FRESH
Singles: 7-inch
PRODIGAL..........................3-4 78
LPs: 10/12-inch
MCA..........................5-10 77
PRODIGAL..........................5-10 78
Members: Fred Allen; Bill Pratt; Milo Martin; Paul Marshall; Frank Savino; Elaine Mayo; George England.

FRESH, Doug, E.: see DOUG E. FRESH & Get Fresh Crew

FRESH AIR
Singles: 7-inch
COLUMBIA..........................3-5 70
LPs: 10/12-inch
COLUMBIA..........................8-10 70

FRESH AIRE
Singles: 7-inch
ATLANTIC..........................3-5 78

FRESH BAND D&D '84
Singles: 12-inch
ARE 'N BE..........................4-6 84

FRESH START
Singles: 7-inch
DUNHILL..........................3-5 74
LPs: 10/12-inch
DUNHILL..........................8-10 74

FRESH 3 MCs R&B '84
Singles: 12-inch
PROFILE..........................4-6 84
Singles: 7-inch
PROFILE..........................3-4 84
LPs: 10/12-inch
PROFILE..........................5-10 84
Also see PUMPKIN & Profile All-Stars

FRETTS
Singles: 7-inch
BLUE MOON..........................5-10 59

FREY, Glenn P&R/LP '82
Singles: 12-inch
MCA..........................4-6 84-85
Singles: 7-inch
ASYLUM..........................3-4 82
MCA..........................3-4 84-89
Picture Sleeves
ASYLUM..........................3-4 82
MCA..........................3-4 84-88
LPs: 10/12-inch
ASYLUM..........................5-10 82
MCA..........................5-10 84-89
Also see EAGLES
Also see FALTERMEYER, Harold / Glenn Frey
Also see FELICITY
Also see HAMMER, Jan / Glenn Frey
Also see LONGBRANCH PENNYWHISTLE
Also see SEGER, Bob

FRIAR, Hugh
Singles: 7-inch
CLIX (805 "I Can't Stay Mad at You")..........................40-50

FRIAR TUCK
Singles: 7-inch
BANSHEE..........................8-12 60s
MERCURY..........................5-10 67
LPs: 10/12-inch
MERCURY (21111 "Friar Tuck & His Psychedelic Guitar")..........................15-25 67
(Monaural.)
MERCURY (61111 "Friar Tuck & His Psychedelic Guitar")..........................20-30 67
(Stereo.)
Members: Curt Boetcher; Jim Bell; Michelle O'Malley; Sandy Salisbury; Dottie Holmberg; Sharon Olson; Dyann King; Alicia Vigil; Bob Turner; Mike Deasy; Ben Benay; Mike Henderson; Jim Troxel; Jerry Scheff; Toxie French; Butch Parker; Jim Healms.
Also see BENAY, Ben
Also see BOETCHER, Curt
Also see GOLDENROD

FRIARS FOUR
Singles: 7-inch
DECCA..........................15-25 62

FRICKE, Janie C&W '77
(Janie Frickie)
Singles: 7-inch
COLUMBIA..........................3-5 77-89
LPs: 10/12-inch
CBS (99-1535 "On Tour")..........50-75 82
(Picture disc. Promotional issue only.)
COLUMBIA..........................5-10 78-84
Session: Benny Wilson; Larry Gatlin; Steve Gatlin; Ricky Skaggs.
Also see BANDY, Moe
Also see DUNCAN, Johnny, & Janie Fricke
Also see GATLIN, Larry, & Janie Frickie
Also see GOSDIN, Vern
Also see HAGGARD, Merle, & Janie Fricke
Also see MANDRELL, Barbara
Also see RICH, Charlie, & Janie Fricke
Also see RUSSELL, Johnny
Also see SKAGGS, Ricky
Also see WILSON, Benny

FRID, Jonathan
Singles: 7-inch
PHILIPS..........................3-6 69

FRIDA P&R/LP '82
(Anni-Frid Lyngstad)
Singles: 7-inch
ATLANTIC..........................3-5 82
LPs: 10/12-inch
ATLANTIC..........................5-10 82
Also see ABBA

FRIDAY, Charles
Singles: 7-inch
EXCELLO..........................4-8 66

FRIDAY, Maxwell
Singles: 7-inch
ROADSHOW/RCA..........................3-4 79

FRIDAY & WEEKENDS
Singles: 7-inch
DYNAMIC SOUND (2008 "You Baby")..........................15-25 67

FRIDAY KNIGHTS
Singles: 7-inch
STRAND..........................5-10 60

FRIEDLES
(Fried Brothers)
Singles: 7-inch
BAT (1004 "She Can Go")..........15-20 66
SCOPE (4818 "I Lost Her")..........15-20 65
HANNA (1001 "I Lost Her")..........5-10 65

FRIEDMAN, Dean P&R/LP '77
Singles: 7-inch
LIFESONG..........................3-4 77-78
LPs: 10/12-inch
LIFESONG..........................5-10 77-78
RECORD CO-OP..........................5-10 82

FRIEDMAN, Kinky C&W '73
Singles: 7-inch
ABC..........................3-5 75
EPIC..........................3-4 76-85
SOUND FACTORY..........................3-4 81
SUNRISE..........................3-4 83
VANGUARD..........................3-5 73
LPs: 10/12-inch
ABC..........................5-10 74
EPIC..........................5-10 76
SUNRISE..........................5-8 83
VANGUARD..........................5-10 73

FRIEL, Bill, & Fabulous Furies
Singles: 7-inch
JOKER (1009 "Ft. Lauderdale U.S.A.")..........................30-40 59

FRIEL, Brian
LPs: 10/12-inch
PYE..........................8-10 75

FRIEND
(A Friend)
Singles: 7-inch
HOLLYWOOD (1123 Macon")..........5-10 59
THUNDER TUMMY (1002 "The Ballad of Sonny Sixkiller")..........................5-10

FRIEND, Eddie, & Empires
(With Phil Medley & Orchestra)
Singles: 7-inch
COLPIX (112 "Tears in My Eyes")..........................75-125 59
Also see EMPIRES

FRIEND & LOVER P&R '68
Singles: 7-inch
ABC..........................4-8 67
CADET CONCEPT..........................3-5
VERVE/FORECAST..........................4-8 68
LPs: 10/12-inch
VERVE/FORECAST..........................12-15 68
Members: James Post; Cathy Post.

FRIEND SOUND
LPs: 10/12-inch
RCA..........................10-15 69

FRIENDLY GHOSTS
Singles: 7-inch
BELLAIRE..........................4-8 63

FRIENDLY ROOM
Singles: 7-inch
DELCREST (1005 "Follow Me Back to Louisville")..........................10-20 60s

FRIENDLY TORPEDOS
Singles: 7-inch
ORIGINAL SOUND..........................10-20 68
Member: Sean Bonniwell.
Also see BONNIWELL'S MUSIC MACHINE

FRIENDS
LPs: 10/12-inch
MGM..........................8-10 73
OBLIVION..........................8-10 72

FRIENDS OF DISTINCTION P&R/R&B/LP '69
Singles: 7-inch
RCA..........................3-5 69-73
LPs: 10/12-inch
COLLECTABLES..........................5-10 88
RCA..........................10-15 69-73
Members: Floyd Butler; Jessica Cleaves; Harry Elston; Charlene Gibson; Barbara Jean Love.
Also see HI-FIs

FRIENDS OF WHITNEY SUNDAY
Singles: 7-inch
CAPITOL..........................4-8 69

FRIENDSHIP
Singles: 7-inch
(27044 "Chains")..........................8-12 60s
(No label name used.)
LPs:10/12-inch
FRIENDSHIP..........................15-25 60s
Also see UNBELIEVABLE UGLIES

FRIENDSHIP
Singles: 7-inch
BIG TREE..........................3-5 70
LPs: 10/12-inch
ELEKTRA..........................5-10 79

FRIGO, John
Singles: 7-inch
USA (1311 "Rock Em Sock Em")...10-20 60s
LPs: 10/12-inch
CORAL (57088 "Dick Marx & John Frigo")..........................15-25 56

FRIJID PINK P&R/LP '70
Singles: 7-inch
LION..........................4-8 72
LONDON..........................3-5
PARROT..........................5-10 69-71
LPs: 10/12-inch
FANTASY (9464 "All Pink Inside") 10-15 74
LIONEL (1004 "Earth Omen")........10-20 72
PARROT (71033 "Frijid Pink")........15-25 70
PARROT (71041 "Defrosted")........15-25 70

FRINGE BENEFIT
Singles: 7-inch
CAPRICORN..........................3-4 78
LPs: 10/12-inch
CAPRICORN..........................8-10 77

FRINGE BENEFITS
Singles: 7-inch
NEW AGE..........................3-5 69

FRIPP, Robert LP '79
LPs: 10/12-inch
EDITIONS E.G...........................5-10 79-81
POLYDOR..........................5-10 79-81
Also see GILES, GILES & FRIPP
Also see KING CRIMSON

FRIPP, Robert, & Andy Summers — *LP '82*
LPs: 10/12-inch
A&M ... 5-10 82-84
Also see FRIPP, Robert
Also see POLICE

FRIPP & ENO
LPs: 10/12-inch
ANTILLES ... 8-10 73
Members: Robert Fripp; Brian Eno.
Also see ENO, Brian
Also see FRIPP, Robert

FRISKY
LPs: 10/12-inch
VANGUARD ... 5-10 79

FRITH, Fred
LPs: 10/12-inch
RALPH ... 5-10 81
Also see ART BEARS

FRITTS, Donnie
LPs: 10/12-inch
ATLANTIC ... 8-10 74

FRITZ, Hal, & Playboys
Singles: 7-inch
SOMA (1089 "Three Bad Habits") ... 100-200 58

FRITZ, Joe — *R&B '50*
(Joe "Papoose" Fritz)
Singles: 78 rpm
MODERN ... 5-15 50
PEACOCK ... 10-20 51-54
SITTIN' IN WITH ... 15-25 50-51
Singles: 7-inch
JET STREAM ... 4-8 66
PEACOCK (1606 "Real Fine Girl") 20-40 52
PEACOCK (1627 "Honey Honey") 20-40 53
PEACOCK (1640 "Cerelle") ... 20-40 55
SITTIN' IN WITH (559 "Please Get Off My Mind") ... 50-75 50

FRITZ & JERRY
Singles: 7-inch
RIP (202 "Pad") ... 10-20 59

FRIZZELL, Allen — *C&W '81*
Singles: 7-inch
EPIC ... 3-4 85
SOUND FACTORY ... 3-5 81

FRIZZELL, David — *C&W '70*
Singles: 7-inch
CAPITOL ... 3-5 73-74
CARTWHEEL ... 3-5 71
COLUMBIA ... 3-5 70
COMPLEAT ... 3-4 87
NASHVILLE AMERICA ... 3-4 86
MCA ... 3-4 83
RSO ... 3-5 76
VIVA ... 3-4 83-85
W.B. ... 3-4 81-82
LPs: 10/12-inch
MCA ... 5-8 83
VIVA ... 5-8 81-84
W.B. ... 5-10 82-83
Also see HAGGARD, Merle

FRIZZELL, David, & Shelly West — *C&W '81*
(Frizzell & West)
Singles: 7-inch
VIVA ... 3-4 83-85
W.B. ... 3-4 81-83
LPs: 10/12-inch
VIVA ... 5-8 81-84
W.B. ... 5-10 81-83

FRIZZELL, Lefty — *C&W '50*
Singles: 78 rpm
COLUMBIA ... 5-15 50-57
Singles: 7-inch
ABC ... 3-5 73-76
COLUMBIA (20000 & 21000 series) ... 10-20 50-56
COLUMBIA (40000 & 41000 series) ... 5-15 56-61
COLUMBIA (42000 thru 45000 series, except 42924) ... 3-8 61-72
COLUMBIA (42924 "Saginaw, Michigan") ... 4-6 64
(Black vinyl.)
COLUMBIA (42924 "Saginaw, Michigan") ... 10-15 64
(Colored vinyl. Promotional issue only.)
EPs: 7-inch
COLUMBIA ... 15-35 51-59
LPs: 10/12-inch
ABC ... 8-12 73-77
COLUMBIA (1342 "The One and Only Lefty Frizzell") ... 15-25 59
COLUMBIA (2169 "Saginaw, Michigan") ... 15-25 64
COLUMBIA (2386 "The Sad Side of Life") ... 15-25 65
COLUMBIA (2488 "Lefty Frizzell's Greatest Hits") ... 15-25 66
(Monaural.)
COLUMBIA (2772 "Puttin' On") ... 15-25 67
COLUMBIA (8969 "Saginaw, Michigan") ... 15-25 64
COLUMBIA (9019 "Songs of Jimmie Rodgers") ... 75-100 51
(10-inch LP.)
COLUMBIA (9021 "Listen to Lefty") ... 75-100 52
(10-inch LP.)
COLUMBIA (9186 "The Sad Side of Life") ... 20-25 65
COLUMBIA (9288 "Lefty Frizzell's Greatest Hits") ... 20-25 66
(Stereo. With "CS" prefix.)
COLUMBIA (9288 "Lefty Frizzell's Greatest Hits") ... 5-10
(With "PC" prefix.)
COLUMBIA (9572 "Puttin' On") ... 20-25 67
COLUMBIA (10000 series) ... 5-12 73-83
COLUMBIA (30000 series) ... 5-12 75-82
HARMONY (7241 "Songs of Jimmie Rodgers") ... 15-25 60
HARMONY (11000 series) ... 8-15 66-68
MCA ... 8-12 82
ROUNDER ... 5-10 80-83
2X4 (111 "Lefty Frizzell Story") ... 5-10 80
Also see AGNES & ORVILLE
Also see BOND, Johnny, & Lefty Frizzell
Also see PRICE, Ray / Lefty Frizzell / Carl Smith
Also see SMITH, Carl / Lefty Frizzell / Marty Robbins

FROG, Wynder K.
(Mick Weaver)
Singles: 7-inch
U.A. ... 5-10 67-70
LPs: 10/12-inch
U.A. ... 10-20 70

FROGATT, Raymond
Singles: 7-inch
JET ... 3-4 79

FROGG, John
Singles: 7-inch
LEGRAND ... 4-8

FROGGIE BEAVER
LPs: 10/12-inch
FROGGIE BEAVER (7301 "From the Pond") ... 50-75 73
Members: John Troia; John Fischer; Rick Brown; Ed Stazko.

FROGMEN — *P&R '61*
Singles: 7-inch
ASTRA (1009 "Underwater") ... 5-10 65
ASTRA (1010 "Beware Below") ... 5-10 65
CANDIX (314 "Underwater") ... 15-25 61
CANDIX (326 "Beware Below") ... 15-25 61
SCOTT (101 "Tioga") ... 25-40 61
(First issue.)
SCOTT (102 "Underwater") ... 25-40 61
(First issue.)
TEE JAY (131 "Sea Haunt") ... 15-25 64
(Black vinyl.)
TEE JAY (131 "Sea Haunt") ... 25-50 64
(Colored vinyl.)

FROGS, Freddy
LPs: 10/12-inch
OFF the WALL ... 10-15 85

FROLK HEAVEN
LPs: 10/12-inch
LRS (6032 "At the Apex of High") ... 400-500 70s
Members: Stewart Copeland; Charles Ostman; Bailey Pendergrass.
Also see COPELAND, Stewart

FROMAN, Jane — *P&R '34*
Singles: 78 rpm
CAPITOL ... 3-8 52-56
DECCA ... 5-10 34
Singles: 7-inch
CAPITOL ... 5-10 52-56
EPs: 7-inch
CAPITOL ... 5-15 52-56
ROYALE (254 "Linger in My Arms a Little Longer Baby") ... 10-20 50s
(Red vinyl.)
LPs: 10/12-inch
CAPITOL ... 15-25 52-56
STAR-TONE ... 10-15
Also see MARTIN, Dean / Jane Froman

FROME, Ethan, & Then Some
Singles: 7-inch
HAPPY TIGER ... 3-5 70

FROMHOLTZ, Steve
Singles: 7-inch
COUNTRYSIDE ... 3-5 73

FRONGE
Singles: 7-inch
REDD HEDD ... 4-8 71

FRONT, The — *LP '90*
LPs: 10/12-inch
COLUMBIA ... 5-8 90

FRONT END
Singles: 7-inch
SMASH ... 4-8 68

FRONT LINE
Singles: 7-inch
ATLANTIC ... 4-8 65
TITAN (2001 "Saigon Girl") ... 15-25 67
YORK (9000 "I Don't Care") ... 8-12 65

FRONT OFFICE
Singles: 7-inch
MIJJI (3007 "Girl") ... 15-25 67

FRONT PAGE NEWS
Singles: 7-inch
DIAL (4052 "Thoughts") ... 10-20 66

FRONT PORCH
Singles: 7-inch
JUBILEE (5720 "Wonderful Summer") ... 5-10 67

FRONTERA, Tommy
Singles: 7-inch
HI-LITE (84952 "Be Mine") ... 10-20
(Identification number shown since no selection number is used.)
PALMER (5015 "Street of Shame") ... 15-25
REM (103 "After Tonight") ... 150-250 60
Session: Dennis Coffey.
Also see COFFEY, Dennis

FRONTIERS
(New Frontiers)
Singles: 7-inch
KING ... 8-12 61-62

FRONTIERS
Singles: 7-inch
MGM ... 5-8 67
PHILIPS ... 8-10 63-64
Members: Roger Koob; Andy Smith; Fred Maffeo; Skippy Bianco; Phil Vallie; Jerry Warner.
Also see BETTER DAYS
Also see KOOB, Roger

FROST — *LP '69*
Singles: 7-inch
VANGUARD ... 5-8 69-70
LPs: 10/12-inch
VANGUARD ... 10-20 69-70
Members: Dick Wagner; Don Hartman; Gordy Garris; Bob Riggs.
Also see COOPER, Alice
Also see WAGNER, Dick

FROST, Frank — *R&B '66*
(With the Night Hawks)
Singles: 7-inch
JEWEL (765 "My Back Scratcher") .5-10 66
JEWEL (765 "My Back Scratcher") .5-10 66
JEWEL (778 "Ride with Your Daddy Tonight") ... 5-10 67
PHILLIPS INT'L (3578 "Jelly Roll King") ... 10-20 61
LPs: 10/12-inch
JEWEL (5013 "Frank Frost") ... 10-20 74
PHILLIPS INT'L. (1975 "Hey Boss Man!") ... 1000-2000 61
Also see JOHNSON, Jack, Frank Frost & Sam Carr

FROST, Max, & Troopers — *P&R '68*
Singles: 7-inch
SIDEWALK ... 8-12 68
TOWER ... 8-12 68-69
Picture Sleeves
TOWER (419 "Shapes of Things to Come") ... 10-15 68
TOWER (478 "Paxton Quigley's Had the Course") ... 10-15 68
LPs: 10/12-inch
TOWER (5147 "Shape of Things to Come") ... 25-35 68
Member: Davie Allan.
Also see ALLAN, Davie

FROST, Thomas & Richard — *P&R '69*
Singles: 7-inch
IMPERIAL ... 3-6 69
UNI ... 3-6 72
LPs: 10/12-inch
UNI ... 8-10 72

FROSTED FLAKES
Singles: 7-inch
KAMA SUTRA ... 4-6 68

FROSTED FLAYKES
Singles: 7-inch
MIDNIGHT ... 4-8

FROSTY & DIAMONDS
Singles: 78 rpm
COMBO (122 "Destination Mars") 10-15 56
Singles: 7-inch
COMBO (122 "Destination Mars") 20-25 56

FROZEN GHOST — *P&R/LP '87*
Singles: 7-inch
ATLANTIC ... 3-4 87
LPs: 10/12-inch
ATLANTIC ... 5-10 87
Members: Wolf Hassel; Arnold Lanni.
Also see SHERIFF

FRUGAL SOUND
Singles: 7-inch
RED BIRD ... 5-10 66

FRUMIOUS BANDERSNATCH
EPs: 7-inch
MUGGLES GRAMOPHONE WORKS ("Frumious Bandersnatch") ... 400-600 60s
(No selection number used. Disc shows purple vinyl when held to a light.)
Members: Jimmy Warner; Bob Winkleman; Jackson King; David Denny; Ross Valory; Jack Notestein.
Also see FAUN
Also see JOURNEY
Also see MILLER, Steve

FRUMMOX
Singles: 7-inch
PROBE ... 3-6 69-70
LPs: 10/12-inch
PROBE ... 12-15 69
Members: Steve Fromholz; D. McCrimmon.

FRUMPY
LPs: 10/12-inch
BILLINGSGATE ... 10-12 73

FRUSHAY, Ray — *C&W '79*
Singles: 7-inch
WESTERN PRIDE ... 3-4 79-80
LPs: 10/12-inch
CASINO ... 6-12 76
WESTERN PRIDE ... 5-10 79

FRUT OF LOOM
(Frut)
Singles: 7-inch
LOOM (1001 "One Hand in the Darkness") ... 10-15
LPs: 10/12-inch
TRASH ... 10-20 71
WESTBOUND ... 10-15 70-72

FRY, Bobby
Singles: 7-inch
DORE ... 5-10 59

FRY, James
Singles: 7-inch
HI (2142 "Still Around") ... 10-20 68

FRYE, David — *LP '69*
LPs: 10/12-inch
BUDDAH ... 5-10 71-72
ELEKTRA ... 8-12 69-71

FUDDY BUDDIES
Singles: 7-inch
MELOCLASS ... 4-8 63

FUGITIVE FIVE
Singles: 7-inch
CELL ... 15-20

FUGITIVES
Singles: 7-inch
ARVEE (5014 "Freeway") ... 10-20 60
SIMS (115 "Freeway") ... 30-50 60

FUGITIVES
Singles: 7-inch
COLUMBIA (43261 "Mean Woman") ... 10-15 65
MALA (533 "Your Girl's a Woman") .5-10 66

FUGITIVES
Singles: 7-inch
D-TOWN (1034 "A Fugitive") ... 15-25 65
D-TOWN (1044 "On Trial") ... 15-25 65
WESTCHESTER (1002 "You Can't Make Me Lonely") ... 10-15 65
LPs: 10/12-inch
HIDEOUT (1001 "The Fugitives at Dave's Hideout") ... 750-1000 65
Members: Gary Quackenbush; Glen Quackenbush; Elmer Clawson.
Also see SRC

FUGITIVES/ Oxford Five / Lourds / Individuals
LPs: 10/12-inch
WESTCHESTER (1005 "Friday at the Cage A-Go-Go") ... 1000-1500 65
(Distributed at the Cage A-Go-Go club and other locations. Some copies have a sticker on labels showing title as *Long Hot Summer*. Not issued with a cover.)
Also see FUGITIVES

FUGITIVES
Singles: 7-inch
SHOESTRING ... 5-10 65

FUGITIVES
Singles: 7-inch
MIDNIGHT (101 "Easy Come, Easy Go") ... 15-25 65

FUGITIVES
Singles: 7-inch
FENTON (2075 "I'll Hang Around") ... 50-75 66

FUGITIVES
Singles: 7-inch
TREND (101 "Come On and Clap") ... 15-25 66
Member: Dick Moulder.

FUGITIVES
Singles: 7-inch
CLEVELAND (128 "This Is It") ... 15-25 60s
ROULETTE ... 5-10 67

FUGITIVES
LPs: 10/12-inch
JUSTICE (141 "On the Run") ... 300-400 67

FUGITIVES
Singles: 7-inch
PATH (251 "I Love You More Than Anything") ... 15-25 60s
PATH (252 "I Love You More Than Ever") ... 15-25 60s
SANDMAN (701 "Good Lovin' if You Can Get It") ... 15-25 60s

FUGS — *LP '66*
(Village Fugs)
Singles: 7-inch
ESP ... 5-10 66
LPs: 10/12-inch
BROADSIDE (304 "Ballads of Contemporary Protest, Point of Views, and General Dissatisfaction") ... 300-400 65
(Double slot cover; one for disc and one for quarter-folded insert.
ESP (1018 "Fugs First Album") ... 30-50 65
(Reissue of Broadside 304.)
ESP (1028 "The Fugs") ... 25-40 66
ESP (1038 "Virgin Fugs") ... 25-40 67
ESP (2018 "Fugs Four") ... 20-25 67
PVC ... 5-10 82
REPRISE (6280 "Tenderness Junction") ... 15-25 67
REPRISE (6305 "It Crawled Into My Hand, Honest") ... 15-25 67
REPRISE (6359 "The Belle of Avenue A") ... 10-20 69
REPRISE (6396 "Golden Filth") ... 10-20 70
Members: Ed Saunders; John Anderson; Lee Crabtree; Pete Kearney; Tuli Kupferberg; Vinny Leary; Ken Weaver; Pete Stampfel; Steve Weber.
Also see HOLY MODAL ROUNDERS
Also see SANDERS, Ed, & Hemptones

FUGS
Singles: 7-inch
PERRY (44 "Savage") ... 8-12

FUHRMAN, Micki — *C&W '78*
Singles: 7-inch
LOUISIANA HAYRIDE ... 3-5 77-78
MCA ... 3-4 79-84
LPs: 10/12-inch
DAYSPRING ... 5-10 81
LOUISIANA HAYRIDE ... 5-10 77-78

FUKANO, Eddy
Singles: 7-inch
DOT (17067 "It's Lonesome") ... 5-8 68

FULL FORCE — *R&B/D&D '85*
Singles: 12-inch
COLUMBIA ... 4-6 85-86
Singles: 7-inch
COLUMBIA ... 3-4 85-87
Picture Sleeves
COLUMBIA ... 3-4 87-88
LPs: 10/12-inch
COLUMBIA ... 5-10 85-87
Also see LISA LISA

FULL MOON
LPs: 10/12-inch
DOUGLAS ... 10-12 72
W.B. ... 5-10 82

FULL SWING
LPs: 10/12-inch
PLANET ... 5-10 82

FULLER, Blind Boy
Singles: 78 rpm
COLUMBIA ... 15-25 46

FULLER, Bobby — *P&R/LP '66*
(Bobby Fuller Four; with Jim Reese & Embers; with Fanatics)
Singles: 7-inch
ABC ... 3-5 73
HI-TONE ... 4-8
DONNA (1403 "Our Favorite Martian") ... 75-125 65
EASTWOOD (0345 "Not Fade Away") ... 15-25 62
ERIC ... 3-4 70s
EXETER (122 "Wine, Wine, Wine") ... 100-150 64
EXETER (124 "I Fought the Law") ... 100-150 64
EXETER (126 "Fool of Love") ... 75-125 64
LIBERTY (55812 "Let Her Dance") ... 15-25 65
MUSTANG (3004 "Take My Word") ... 15-25 66
MUSTANG (3006 "Let Her Dance") ... 15-25 65
MUSTANG (3011 "Never to Be Forgotten") ... 15-25 65
MUSTANG (3012 "Let Her Dance") ... 15-25 65
MUSTANG (3014 "I Fought the Law") ... 8-12 65
MUSTANG (3016 "Love's Made a Fool of You") ... 15-25 66
MUSTANG (3018 "My True Love") ... 15-25 66
REGENCY (965 "I Fought the Law") ... 15-25 65
(Canadian.)
TODD (1090 "Saturday Night") ... 50-100 63
YUCCA (140 "Guess We'll Fall in Love") ... 50-100 62
YUCCA (141 "You're in Love") ... 50-100 62
YUCCA (144 "My Heart Jumped") ... 50-100 62
LPs: 10/12-inch
MUSTANG (900 "KRLA King of the Wheels") ... 50-100 66
(Monaural.)
MUSTANG (900 "KRLA King of the Wheels") ... 75-125 66
(Stereo.)
MUSTANG (901 "I Fought the Law") ... 35-55 66
(Monaural.)
MUSTANG (901 "I Fought the Law") ... 45-65 66
(Stereo.)
RHINO ... 5-10 81
VOXX ... 5-10 84
Members: Bobby Fuller; Randy Fuller; Duane Quirico; Jim Reese; Dalton Powell; Johnny Barbata.
Also see BARBATA, Johnny
Also see FULLER, Randy
Also see HORTON, Jay
Also see SHINDIGS

FULLER, Bobby / Seeds
Singles: 7-inch
TRIP ... 3-6 70s
Also see FULLER, Bobby
Also see SEEDS

FULLER, Cheré
Singles: 7-inch
BRYKAS ... 3-5 90
LPs: 10/12-inch
BRYKAS ... 10-15 90

FULLER, Craig, & Eric Kaz
Singles: 7-inch
COLUMBIA ... 3-4 78

Also see KAZ, Eric

FULLER, Curtis

Singles: 7-inch

WARWICK (655 "Chant of the Congo") ... 10-20 61

FULLER, Donna

Singles: 7-inch

COLPIX ... 4-8 63
DCP ... 4-8 65

LPs: 10/12-inch

DCP ... 12-15 65

FULLER, Irving, & Corvettes

Singles: 7-inch

EMERY (121 "I Can't Stop") ... 50-100 60

FULLER, Jerry P&R '59

Singles: 7-inch

ABC ... 3-5 78
BELL ... 4-6 72
CHALLENGE (9100 series) ... 10-20 61
CHALLENGE (59052 "Betty My Angel") ... 20-30 59
CHALLENGE (59057 "Tennessee Waltz") ... 15-25 59
CHALLENGE (59085 thru 59269) .. 10-20 60-65
CHALLENGE (59279 "I Got Carried Away") ... 20-30 65
CHALLENGE (59307 "Don't Look at Me Like That") ... 5-10 65
CHALLENGE (59329 "Double Life") ... 15-25 66
COLUMBIA ... 3-5 70
LIN (5011 "Blue Memories") ... 15-25 58
LIN (5012 "Teenage Love") ... 15-25 58
LIN (5015 "Angel from Above") ... 15-25 58
LIN (5016 "The Door Is Open") ... 15-25 58
LIN (5019 "Lipstick & Rouge") ... 15-25 59
MCA ... 3-5 79

LPs: 10/12-inch

LIN (100 "Teenage Love") ... 25-35 60
MCA ... 5-10 79

Also see FLEAS
Also see FULLER BROTHERS
Also see NELSON, Rick

FULLER, Jerry, & Diane Maxwell

Singles: 7-inch

CHALLENGE (59074 "Above and Beyond") ... 10-15 60

Also see FULLER, Jerry
Also see MAXWELL, Diane

FULLER, Jesse

LPs: 10/12-inch

CAVALIER (5006 "Frisco Bound") 50-75 55
CAVALIER (6009 "Frisco Bound") 35-50 57
FANTASY ... 8-10
GOOD TIME JAZZ ... 15-25 61
PRESTIGE ... 15-20 62
WORLD SONG (1 "Working on the Railroad") ... 60-100 54
(10-inch LP.)

FULLER, Joe

Singles: 7-inch

HI ... 5-10 59

FULLER, Johnny

Singles: 78 rpm

ALADDIN ... 20-40 55
HOLLYWOOD ... 20-40 55
IRMA (110 "First Stage of the Blues") ... 35-50 58
MONEY (206 "I Walk All Night") ... 15-25 55
RHYTHM (1767 "Fool's Paradise") ... 20-40 54
RHYTHM (1773 "Train, Train Blues") ... 20-40 55
RHYTHM (1777 "Lovin' Lovin' Man") ... 20-40 56
RHYTHM (1779 "Mean Old World") ... 20-40 55

Singles: 7-inch

ALADDIN (3278 "Johnny Ace's Last Letter") ... 40-60 55
ART TONE ... 5-10 62
CHECKER ... 8-12 58
FLAIR (1054 "Buddy") ... 50-100 55
HOLLYWOOD (1043 "Train, Train Blues") ... 40-60 55
HOLLYWOOD (1057 "Mean Old World") ... 40-60 55
HOLLYWOOD (1063 "Roughest Place in Town") ... 40-60 55
HOLLYWOOD (1084 "Sunny Road") ... 40-60 55
HOLLYWOOD (1077 "My Mama Told Me") ... 40-60 55
HOLLYWOOD (1084 "Sunny Road") ... 40-60 55
IMPERIAL ... 10-20 59-60
IRMA (110 "First Stage of the Blues") ... 40-60 58
IRMA (112 "All Night Long") ... 30-50 58
MONEY (206 "I Walk All Night") ... 30-50 55
SPECIALTY ... 10-20 59
VELTONE ... 10-20 60

Also see PRETTY BOY

FULLER, Little Boy

Singles: 78 rpm

SAVOY ... 15-25 47

FULLER, Mary Ann

Singles: 7-inch

IMPERIAL (5853 "It's a Man's World") ... 10-20

FULLER, Playboy

(Iverson Minter)

Singles: 78 rpm

FULLER (171 "Sugar Cane Highway") ... 200-300 52

Also see FULLER, Rocky

FULLER, Randy

Singles: 7-inch

MUSTANG (3020 "Wolfman") ... 10-20 66
SHOW TOWN (466 "It's Love") ... 10-20 69
SHOW TOWN (482 "1000 Miles") 10-20 69

Picture Sleeves

SHOW TOWN (466 "It's Love") ... 15-20 69

Also see FULLER, Bobby
Also see SHINDIGS

FULLER, Rocky

(Iverson Minter)

Singles: 78 rpm

CHECKER (753 "Soon One Morning") ... 50-75 52

Also see FULLER, Playboy

FULLER, Ronnie

Singles: 7-inch

JOLI ... 4-8 65

FULLER, Ronnie

Singles: 7-inch

ECR ... 3-4

LP: 10/12-inch

ECR ... 5-10

Also see BESAW, Ron, & Mojo Men

FULLER, Tiny

(With His Combo)

Singles: 7-inch

MARLIN (6301 "Cat Walk") ... 10-20 63
TAP (1000 "Cockleur") ... 10-20 61

FULLER, Tommy

Singles: 7-inch

GIANT (1005 "Soul Twist") ... 10-20 62

FULLER, Walter

(With Club Royale Band.)

Singles: 78 rpm

KICKS ... 25-35

FULLER, Zen

Singles: 7-inch

ACAMA ... 10-20

FULLER, Tiny, & His Combo

Singles: 7-inch

MARLIN (6301 "Cat Walk") ... 8-12 63

FULLER BROTHERS

Singles: 7-inch

CHALLENGE ... 5-10 61-62

Members: Jerry Fuller; Bill Fuller.
Also see FULLER, Jerry

FULLER BROTHERS

Singles: 7-inch

MONUMENT ... 4-8 66

FULLER BROTHERS

Singles: 7-inch

SOUL CLOCK (101 "Let Me Love You") ... 10-15 69

FULLYLOVE, Leroy

(With the Buffs)

Singles: 7-inch

ELKO (2 "I Want to Know") ... 200-400
JO-REE ... 15-25 60
(Title and number not known.)
TANDEM (7002 "I'm So Lonely") ... 100-200 61

FULSON, Lowell R&B '48

(With the Ful-Tones; with His Trio; with His Guitar; with Jon Blue & Band; Lowell Folsom; Lowel Fulsom)

Singles: 78 rpm

ALADDIN ... 25-50 51
BIG TOWN (1068 "Crying Blues") .. 20-40 46
BIG TOWN (1070 "Miss Katie Lee Blues") ... 20-40 46
BIG TOWN (1072 "San Francisco Blues") ... 20-40 46
BIG TOWN (1074 "Trouble Blues") ... 20-40 46
BIG TOWN (1077 "Black Widow Spider Blues") ... 20-40 46
CASH (1051 "Blue Shadows") ... 15-25 57
CAVATONE (250 "Stormin' & Rainin' ") ... 15-25 49
CHECKER (804 thru 865) ... 10-25 54-57
CHECKER (882 "I Want to Make Love to You") ... 20-30 57
CHECKER (937 "It Took a Long Time") ... 25-50 59

Note: Checker 937 may be the last 78 with the checkerboard design at top, as opposed to 45s which switched designs beginning with #876. Also, 78s as early as #900 have Checker name vertically on left side.

CHECKER (952 "Have You Changed Your Mind") ... 150-250 60
COLONIAL (122 "I'm Prison Bound") ... 20-30 49
DOWN BEAT ... 10-20 46-47
DOWN TOWN (2002 "Three O'Clock Blues") ... 20-30 49
GILT EDGE (5041 "Miss Katie Lee Blues") ... 20-30 51
GILT EDGE (5050 "Rambling Blues") ... 20-30 51
HOLLYWOOD ... 10-20 55
PARROT ... 25-50 53
RPM (305 "I'm Prison Bound") ... 20-30 50
SCOTTY'S RADIO (101 "Scotty's Blues") ... 20-40 46
SWING TIME ... 15-30 46-53
TRILON (185 "Jelly Jelly") ... 20-40 47
TRILON (186 "Thinkin' Blues") ... 20-40 47
TRILON (192 "Tryin' to Find My Baby") ... 20-40 48
TRILON (193 "Highway 99") ... 20-40 48

Singles: 7-inch

ALADDIN (3088 "Double Trouble Blues") ... 75-125 53
ALADDIN (3104 "Night & Day") ... 75-125 51
ALADDIN (3104 "Stormin' and Rainin' ") ... 50-100 53
(Black vinyl.)
ALADDIN (3104 "Stormin' and Rainin' ") ... 150-200 53
(Colored vinyl.)
ALADDIN (3217 "Don't Leave Me, Baby") ... 50-75 53
ALADDIN (3233 "Blues Never Fail") ... 50-75 53
CASH (1051 "Blue Shadows") ... 20-40 57
CHECKER (804 "Reconsider Baby") ... 40-60 54
CHECKER (812 "Loving You") ... 30-40 55
CHECKER (820 "Lonely Hours") ... 30-40 55
CHECKER (829 "Trouble Trouble") ... 30-40 55
CHECKER (841 "It's All Your Fault Baby") ... 30-40 56
CHECKER (854 "Baby Please Don't Go") ... 30-40 56
CHECKER (865 "You're Gonna Miss Me") ... 25-35 57
CHECKER (882 "I Want to Make Love to You") ... 25-35 57
CHECKER (937 "It Took a Long Time") ... 15-25 59
CHECKER (952 "Have You Changed Your Mind") ... 15-25 60
CHECKER (959 "I'm Glad You Reconsidered") ... 15-25 60
CHECKER (972 "I Want to Know") 10-20 60
CHECKER (992 "So Many Tears") . 10-20 61
CHECKER (1027 "Shed No Tears") ... 10-20 62
CHECKER (1046 "Trouble with the Blues") ... 10-20 62
GRANITE ... 3-5 76
HOLLYWOOD (242 "The Original Lonesome Christmas") ... 35-55 53
(Shiny red label stock.)
HOLLYWOOD (242 "The Original Lonesome Christmas") ... 15-25 55
(Flat maroon label stock.)
HOLLYWOOD (242 "The Original Lonesome Christmas") ... 4-8 70s
(Black label stock.)
HOLLYWOOD (1029 "Rocking After Midnight") ... 30-50 55
HOLLYWOOD (1103 "Guitar Shuffle") ... 10-20 62
JEWEL ... 3-6 69-73
KENT ... 4-8 64-70
MOVIN' (128 "Baby") ... 8-12 64
PARROT (787 "I've Been Mistreated") ... 75-125 53
(Black vinyl.)
PARROT (787 "I've Been Mistreated") ... 150-250 53
(Red vinyl.)
PROWLIN' (128 "Baby") ... 8-12
SWING TIME (289 "Let's Live Right") ... 40-60 51
SWING TIME (295 "Guitar Shuffle") ... 40-60 51
SWING TIME (301 "The Highway Is My Home") ... 40-60 51
SWING TIME (308 "Black Widow Spider") ... 40-60 51
SWING TIME (315 "Raggedy Daddy Blues") ... 40-60 52
SWING TIME (320 "Ride Until the Sun Goes Down") ... 40-60 52
SWING TIME (325 "Upstairs") ... 40-60 52
SWING TIME (330 "I Love My Baby") ... 40-60 52
SWING TIME (335 "Cash Box Boogie") ... 40-60 53
SWING TIME (338 "I've Been Mistreated") ... 40-60 52

Picture Sleeves

KENT (463 "Make a Little Love") ... 8-10 67

LPs: 10/12-inch

ARHOOLIE ... 10-12 62
BIG TOWN ... 5-10 78
CHESS (205 "Lowell Fulson") ... 15-25 76
CHESS (408 "Hung Down Head") .. 10-12 74
JEWEL ... 8-10 70-73
KENT ... 10-20 65-71
UNITED ... 8-12

Session: Lloyd Glenn; Earl Brown; Bob Harvey; Bill Hadnott; David "Fathead" Newman; Phillip Gibeaux; Julian Beasley; Choker Campbell; Fats Morris; Paul Drake; Leroy Cooper; Chick Booth.
Also see BROWN, Earl
Also see CAMPBELL, Choker
Also see CHARLES, Ray
Also see GLENN, Lloyd
Also see JAMES, Ulysses / Lowell Fulson
Also see MEMPHIS SLIM & LOWELL FULSON
Also see TURRENTINE, Stanley

FULTON, Bobby

Singles: 7-inch

SOULVILLE (1004 "It's All Over") ... 5-10

FULTON, Sonny

(Sunny Fulton & the Mixmasters)

Singles: 7-inch

BIG DADDY ... 8-10
CHELSEA (533 "Honest I Do") ... 50-75 59
(White label.)
CHELSEA (533 "Honest I Do") ... 30-50 59
(Black label.)
SUNBEAM (125 "Fingerprints") .. 100-150 59
U.A. (426 "Simple Things") ... 10-15 62

FUMBLE

LPs: 10/12-inch

RCA ... 8-10 75
SOVEREIGN/CAPITOL ... 8-10 72

FUN & GAMES P&R '69

Singles: 7-inch

UNI ... 5-10 68

LPs: 10/12-inch

UNI (73042 "Elephant Candy") ... 15-25 68

Members: Paul Guille; Joe Romano; Rick Romano; Sam Irwin; Joe Dugan; Carson Graham.
Also see SIXPENTZ

FUN & GAMES

Singles: 7-inch

RON-RON ... 3-5 78

Member: Bob Barian.
Also see COMIC BOOKS

FUN BAND

Singles: 7-inch

ABC ... 4-8 68

Member: Charlie Karp.
Also see KARP, Charlie.

FUN BOY THREE LP '83

Singles: 7-inch

CHRYSALIS ... 3-4 82-83

LPs: 10/12-inch

CHRYSALIS ... 5-10 82-83

Also see SPECIALS

FUN FUN D&D '84

Singles: 12-inch

TSR ... 4-6 84-85

FUN SONS

Singles: 7-inch

CAMEO (478 "Hang Ten") ... 10-20 67

FUNARO, Tobi

Singles: 7-inch

VITA ... 5-10 59

FUN-ATICS

("Vocal by Billy Lee")

Singles: 7-inch

VERSAILLES (100 "Wise Guy") 200-300 62

FUNDAMENTALS

Singles: 7-inch

OKEH ... 5-8 67

FUNHOUSE Starring Phil Flowers

Singles: 7-inch

EPIC (10956 "In Whose Eyes") ... 4-6 73

Also see FLOWERS, Phil

FUNICELLO, Annette: see ANNETTE

FUNK, Professor: see PROFESSOR FUNK

FUNK INC.

LPs: 10/12-inch

PRESTIGE ... 8-10 71-74

FUNK BAND INC.

LPs: 10/12-inch

GRIT ... 5-10 79

FUNK DELUXE R&B/D&D '84

Singles: 7-inch

SALSOUL ... 3-4 83-84

LPs: 10/12-inch

SALSOUL ... 5-10 83

FUNKADELIC P&R/R&B '69

(Featuring George Clinton)

Singles: 7-inch

W.B. ... 3-6 78-79
WESTBOUND ... 3-8 69-76

Picture Sleeves

W.B. ... 3-6 78-81

EPs: 7-inch

W.B. (3209 "One Nation Under a Groove") ... 10-15 78

LPs: 10/12-inch

20TH CENTURY/WESTBOUND ... 8-15 75
W.B. ... 5-10 76-81
WESTBOUND (215 "Let's Take It to the Stage") ... 30-50 75
WESTBOUND (227 "Tales of Kidd Funkadelic") ... 30-50 76
WESTBOUND (1001 "Standing on the Verge") ... 30-50 74
WESTBOUND (1004 "Greatest Hits") ... 25-35 75
WESTBOUND (2000 "Funkadelic") ... 40-50 70
WESTBOUND (2001 "Free Your Mind") ... 30-50 70
WESTBOUND (2007 "Maggot Brain") ... 40-60 71
WESTBOUND (2020 "America Eats Its Young") ... 30-50 72
WESTBOUND (2022 "Cosmic Slop") ... 30-50 73

Also see JUNIE
Also see PARLIAMENT
Also see PARLIAMENTS

FUNKADELIC R&B/LP '81

Singles: 7-inch

LAX ... 3-4 81

LPs: 10/12-inch

LAX ... 5-10 81

Members: Clarence Haskins; Calvin Simon; Grady Thomas.
Also see FUNKADELIC (Featuring George Clinton)

FUNKAPOLITAN

Singles: 7-inch

PAVILLION ... 3-4 82

LPs: 10/12-inch

PAVILLION ... 5-10 82

FUNKATEERS

Singles: 7-inch

CHOCOLATE CITY ... 3-5 77

FUNKHOUSE EXPRESS

Singles: 7-inch

ROXBURY ... 3-5 77

FUNKY COMMUNICATION COMMITTEE: see FCC

FUNKY FIVE

(C.C. Riders)

Singles: 7-inch

DAZEY (1001 "Turn Me Loose") ... 8-12 67

Member: Wayne Hurst.
Also see ROCKIN' CAPRIS

FUNKY KINGS P&R '76

Singles: 7-inch

ARISTA ... 3-5 76

LPs: 10/12-inch

ARISTA ... 5-10 76

Also see JULES & Polar Bears

FUNN R&B '81

Singles: 7-inch

MAGIC ... 3-5 81

FUNNY BUNNIES

Singles: 7-inch

DORE ... 5-10 60

FUNKY PEOPLE

Singles: 7-inch

ROULETTE ... 3-5 75

FUNZONE

Singles: 7-inch

FIRST ARTISTS ... 3-4 77

LPs: 10/12-inch

FIRST ARTISTS ... 5-10 77

FURAY, Richie LP '76

Singles: 7-inch

ASYLUM ... 3-4 77-79

LPs: 10/12-inch

ASYLUM ... 5-10 76-82

Also see AU GO-GO SINGERS
Also see BUFFALO SPRINGFIELD
Also see POCO
Also see SOUTHER-HILLMAN-FURAY

FURE, Tret

Singles: 7-inch

MCA ... 3-5 72

FURIOUS FIVE R&B '84

Singles: 12-inch

SUGAR HILL ... 4-6 84-85

Singles: 7-inch

ATLANTIC ... 3-4
SUGAR HILL ... 3-4 84-85

Picture Sleeves

ATLANTIC ... 3-4

FURIOUS FIVE & SUGARHILL GANG R&B '81

Singles: 12-inch

SUGAR HILL ... 4-6 81

Singles: 7-inch

SUGAR HILL ... 3-4 81

Also see FURIOUS FIVE
Also see SUGARHILL GANG

FURNACEMEN

Singles: 7-inch

JUBILEE ... 4-8 68

FURNESS BROTHERS

Singles: 7-inch

MGM ... 10-20 52
RAE COX ... 10-20 60

Also see BERRY, Al, & Furness Bros.

FURNITURE

Singles: 7-inch

STATURE ... 15-25 60s

FURTER, Frank

Singles: 7-inch

UPTOWN ... 5-10 60

Picture Sleeves

UPTOWN ... 5-10 60

FURY, Billy

Singles: 7-inch

LONDON ... 4-8 59-65
MALA ... 4-8 68
PARROT ... 4-8 64
U.A. ... 4-8 66

FURY, Charlie, & Rebel Rockets

Singles: 7-inch

AL-BE (167 "Reptile") ... 20-30 61

FURY, Ron

Singles: 7-inch

DART ... 5-10 60
SESSION ... 5-10 59

FURY FOUR / New Yorkers

Singles: 7-inch

SANTANA ... 5-10

FURYS

Singles: 7-inch

CUCA (1010 "This Way Out") ... 15-25 60

Members: Wally Henel; Steve Getschou; Dennis Radloff; Joel Jetzer.

FURYS

Singles: 7-inch

DEE JAY (1097 "Run to Him") ... 15-25 62

Member: Jimmy Delwood.

FURYS P&R '63

Singles: 7-inch

MACK IV (112 "Zing! Went the Strings of My Heart")....20-30 62
MACK IV (114 "If There's a Next Time")....20-30 63
Member: Jerome Evans.

FURYS

Singles: 7-inch

AURA....5-10 63
FLEETWOOD....15-25 62
LIBERTY (55719 "Dream")....10-20 64
MANOR (51621 "Lost Caravan")....20-30 63
WORLD PACIFIC (386 "Anything for You")....10-20 63

FURYS

Singles: 7-inch

D&D (31563 "Furyous")....10-20 63

FURYS

Singles: 7-inch

DIAMOND....4-8 68
LAURIE....4-8 67

FURYS

Singles: 7-inch

LAVENDER (1805 "Parchman Farm")....10-15 62
LAVENDER (1926 "Maryann")....10-15 63

FURYS

Singles: 7-inch

STUDIO CITY....20-25 60s

FURYS

(With Jerry DeMarr)

Singles: 7-inch

KAY BEE....10-20 60s

FUSE

Singles: 7-inch

EPIC (10514 "Hound Dog")....8-12 69

LPs: 10/12-inch

EPIC (26502 "Fuse")....30-35 70
Members: Rick Neilsen; Joe Sunberg; Craig Myers; Tom Peterson.
Also see CHEAP TRICK

FUSE ONE LP '82

LPs: 10/12-inch

CTI....5-10 82

FUSION

LPs: 10/12-inch

ATCO....12-15 69

FUT

Singles: 7-inch

BEACON....4-6 70
FUT....3-5 76
Members: Steve Kipner; Maurice Gibb.
Also see GIBB, Maurice

FUTURAS

Singles: 7-inch

RAMPRO (119 "Signed, Sealed & Delivered")....40-60 66

Picture Sleeves

RAMPRO (119 "Signed, Sealed & Delivered")....50-100 66
Members: Jerry Mallon; Gary Josing; Jack Edwards Strucel; Gary Dee Bareman; Al James.

FUTURAS

Singles: 7-inch

ARJAY (115 "Mile Zero")....15-25
WARWICK ("Hurt")....15-25 60s
(Selection number not known. May be the flip side of *Sally*.)
WARWICK (130 "Sally")....15-25 60s

FUTURE

Singles: 7-inch

SHAMLEY....3-6 69
UNI....4-6 68

LPs: 10/12-inch

SHAMLEY....8-10 69

FUTURE R&B '88

Singles: 7-inch

HOUSTON INT'L....3-4 87

FUTURE FLIGHT

LPs: 10/12-inch

CAPITOL....5-10 81

FUTURE SHOCK

Singles: 12-inch

SALSOUL....4-6 84

FUTURES R&B '73

Singles: 7-inch

AVALANCHE....3-4
GAMBLE....3-5 73
PHILADELPHIA INT'L....3-4 81

LPs: 10/12-inch

PHILADELPHIA INT'L....5-10 81
Members: James King; Kenny Crewe; Harry McGilkerry; Frank Washington; John King.
Also see MASON, Barbara

FUTURETONES

Singles: 7-inch

TRESS (2 "I Know")....300-600 59
Member: Edwin Starr.
Also see STARR, Edwin

FUZZ P&R/R&B/LP '71

Singles: 7-inch

CALLA....3-5 71
ROULETTE....3-5 70s

LPs: 10/12-inch

CALLA....10-12 71

Members: Sheila Young; Barbara Gilliam; Val Williams.

FUZZTONES

Singles: 12-inch

MIDNIGHT....4-6 85

Singles: 7-inch

MIDNIGHT....3-4 85
Also see HAWKINS, Screamin' Jay, & Fuzztones

FUZZY BUNNIES

Singles: 7-inch

DECCA (32420 "Make Us One")....4-8 68

Picture Sleeves

DECCA (32420 "Make Us One")....8-10 68

FUZZY QUICK

Singles: 7-inch

MOTOWN....3-4 86

FYRE

LPs: 10/12-inch

STONE POST GYRE....5-10 78

FYREBIRDS

Singles: 7-inch

GREAT LAKES (2528 "Can't Get No Ride")....10-15 67

G

G., Kenny: see KENNY G.

G - CLEFS P&R/R&B '56
(With Jay Raye & Orchestra)
Singles: 78 rpm
PARIS 10-20 57
PILGRIM 10-20 56
Singles: 7-inch
DITTO (503 "I'll Remember") 15-25 62
LOMA 5-10 66
PARIS (502 "Symbol of Love") 15-25 57
PARIS (502 "Symbol of Love") 10-20 57
PILGRIM (715 "Ka Ding Dong") 15-25 56
(Purple label, no pilgrims.)
PILGRIM (715 "Ka Ding Dong") 8-12 56
(Red label with pilgrims.)
PILGRIM (720 "Cause You're Mine") 10-20 56
REGINA (1314 "I Believe in All I Feel") 10-20 64
REGINA (1319 "Angel, Listen to Me") 15-25 64
ROULETTE 3-5 70s
TERRACE 5-10 61-63
VEEP 5-10 65-66
Also see CANNON, Freddy

G - MEN
Singles: 7-inch
GROOVE (0009 "Raunchy Twist") 10-20 61
Member: Johnny Kongos.
Also see KONGOS, Johnny

G - NOTES
Singles: 7-inch
GUYDEN (2012 "Johnny Johnny") 10-15 59
FORM (102 "Say You're Mine") 15-25 59
JACKPOT (48000 "Ronnie") 10-20 58
TENDER (510 "Ronnie") 20-30 58

G's
Singles: 7-inch
YOUNG GENERATIONS (104 "There's a Time") 15-25 66

GF & FRIENDS R&B '77
Singles: 7-inch
MONUMENT 3-5 77

G.L.O.B.E. & WHIZ KID R&B '83
Singles: 12-inch
TOMMY BOY 4-6 83
Singles: 7-inch
TOMMY BOY 3-4 83

G MEN: see G-MEN

GQ P&R/R&B/LP '79
Singles: 7-inch
ARISTA 3-5 79-82
LPs: 10/12-inch
ARISTA 5-10 79-81

G.T. R&B '83
(Gary Taylor)
Singles: 12-inch
A&M 4-6 83
Singles: 7-inch
A&M 3-4 83
LPs: 10/12-inch
A&M 5-8 83

G.T.O.
(G.T.O.'s; Girls Together Outrageously)
Singles: 7-inch
STRAIGHT (104 "Circular Circulation") 15-25 69
LPs: 10/12-inch
REPRISE 10-15 70
REPRISE (6390 "Permanent Damage") 20-30 70
STRAIGHT (1059 "Permanent Damage") 40-60 69
Members: Rod Stewart; Jeff Beck; Frank Zappa; Nicky Hopkins; Jimmy Carl Black.
Also see BECK, Jeff
Also see BLACK, Jimmy Carl
Also see ESTRADA, Roy, & Rocketeers
Also see HOPKINS, Nicky
Also see STEWART, Rod
Also see ZAPPA, Frank

G.T.O.s
Singles: 7-inch
CLARIDGE 10-15 66
PARKWAY 5-10 66
Also see JOEY & CONTINENTALS

GTR P&R/LP '86
Singles: 12-inch
ARISTA 4-6 86
Singles: 7-inch
ARISTA 3-4 86
Picture Sleeves
ARISTA 3-4 86
LPs: 10/12-inch
ARISTA 5-10 86
Members: Max Bacon; Steve Howe; Steve Hackett; Phil Spalding; Jonathan Mover.
Also see HACKETT, Steve
Also see HOWE, Steve, Band
Also see MARILLION

GABBART & HOLT
Singles: 7-inch
SAGE (287 "Hey Baby") 50-75 59

GABLE, Guitar: see GUITAR GABLE

GABLEAIRES
Singles: 7-inch
SONG BIRD (1087 "Search Me Lord") 4-6

GABOR SZABO: see SZABO, Gabor

GABREYS
Singles: 7-inch
SOFT (984 "Down at the Go Go") 10-20 65

GABRIEL P&R '78
Singles: 7-inch
ABC 3-5 76-77
EPIC 3-4 78-79
LPs: 10/12-inch
ABC 8-10 75-76
EPIC 5-10 78
Members: Terry Lauber; Frank Butorac.

GABRIEL C&W '81
(Gabriel Farago)
Singles: 7-inch
NSD 3-4 81
RODGETOP 3-4 81

GABRIEL
(Gabriel Maciocia)
Singles: 7-inch
SLACK ("Somewhere Elvis Is Smiling") 5-10 88
(Colored vinyl. Includes booklet and poster. No selection number used.)
Picture Sleeves
SLACK ("Somewhere Elvis Is Smiling") 5-10 88
EPs: 7-inch
SLACK ("Somewhere Elvis Is Smiling") 10-15 88

GABRIEL, Peter P&R/LP '77
Singles: 12-inch
GEFFEN 4-6 82-86
Singles: 7-inch
ATCO 3-5 77
ATLANTIC 3-5 78
GEFFEN 3-4 82-90
MERCURY 3-4 80
WTG 3-4 89
W.B. 3-4 86
Picture Sleeves
ATLANTIC 4-6 78
GEFFEN 3-5 86
MERCURY 3-5 80
LPs: 10/12-inch
ATCO 10-12 77
ATLANTIC 8-10 78
GEFFEN 5-10 82-90
MERCURY 5-10 80
Also see GENESIS

GABRIEL, Peter, & Kate Bush P&R '87
Singles: 7-inch
GEFFEN 3-4 87
Picture Sleeves
GEFFEN 3-4 87
Also see BUSH, Kate

GABRIEL & ANGELS P&R '62
Singles: 7-inch
AMY (802 "Chumba") 15-25 60
AMY (823 "Zing Went the Strings of My Heart") 25-35 61
AMY (35802 "Chumba") 10-20 60
NORMAN 8-12 61-62
SWAN 8-12 62-63

GABRIEL & TEENAGE CHOIR
Singles: 7-inch
DUNHILL 4-8 66

GABRIEL BONDAGE
LPs: 10/12-inch
DHARMA (804 "Angel Dust") 30-40 75
DHARMA (808 "Another Trip to Earth") 10-15 77
(Colored vinyl.)

GABRIEL GLADSTAR
LPs: 10/12-inch
FLYING GUITAR 5-10 73
Members: Michael Gwinn; Phillip Morgan; Jim Zeiger.

GADABOUTS P&R '56
Singles: 78 rpm
MERCURY 5-10 54-56
WING 5-10 55
Singles: 7-inch
JARO 5-10 60
MERCURY 10-15 54-56
WING 5-15 55

GADDY, Bob
(With His Alley Cats; with His Keys)
Singles: 78 rpm
HARLEM 25-50 52
JACKSON 40-60 52
Singles: 7-inch
HARLEM (2330 "Blues Has Walked in My Room") 75-100 52
JACKSON (2303 "I (Believe You Got a Sidekick)") 125-200 52
(Colored vinyl.)
JAX (308 "No Help Wanted") 125-200 52
(Red vinyl.)
OLD TOWN (1000 series) 15-25 57-60
OLD TOWN (1100 series) 5-10 64
Session: Sonny Terry; Brownie McGhee; Jack Dupree; Joe Ruffin; Al Hall; Gene Brooks; Jimmy Spruill; Willie Jones; Pete Brown.
Also see GADDY, Doctor, & His Orchestra
Also see McGHEE, Brownie, & Sonny Terry

GADDY, Doctor, & His Orchestra
(Bob Gaddy)
Singles: 78 rpm
DOT (1185 "Evil Man Blues") 20-30 53
Singles: 7-inch
DOT (1185 "Evil Man Blues") 50-75 53
Also see GADDY, Bob

GADSON, James R&B '72
Singles: 7-inch
CREAM 4-6 72
Also see SOUL RUNNERS

GADSON, Mel P&R '60
Singles: 7-inch
BIG TOP (3034 "Comin' Down with Love") 10-20 60

GAGE, Cheri
Singles: 7-inch
MARTIAN 3-4 81

GAGE, Yvonne R&B '84
Singles: 12-inch
CIM (05095 "Virginity") 5-8 84
(Promotional issue only.)
Singles: 7-inch
ATLANTIC 3-5 81
CIM 3-4 84
Also see FIRST LOVE

GAGNON, Andre P&R '76
Singles: 7-inch
LONDON 3-5 76

GAIL, Sunny: see GALE, Sunny

GAIL & SANDRA
Singles: 7-inch
RADIO (103 "Bill") 40-60

GAILLARD, Slim P&R/R&B '46
(Slim Gaillard Trio)
Singles: 78 rpm
ATOMIC 10-15 46
BEL-TONE 10-15 45
CADET 10-15 46
CLEF 5-10 53-54
COLUMBIA 5-10 40s
4 STAR 5-10 46
MAJESTIC 10-15 46
OKEH 5-15 40-42
20TH CENTURY 10-15 46
VOCALION 10-20 38-40
Singles: 7-inch
CLEF 10-20 53-54
DOT (15919 "Down By the Station") 10-15 59
ELGO (3001 "Angel") 25-50 62
EPIC 5-10 68
EPs: 7-inch
CLEF 10-20 53
KING 10-20 54
NORGRAN 10-20 54
ROYALE 10-20 50s
LPs: 10/12-inch
CLEF (126 "Mish Mash") 25-50 53
CLEF (138 "Slim Cavorts") 25-50 53
DOT (3190 "Slim Gaillard Rides Again") 20-30 59
(Monaural.)
DOT (25190 "Slim Gaillard Rides Again") 25-40 59
(Stereo.)
KING (80 "Boogie") 50-75 50s
(10-inch LP.)
NORGRAN (13 "Slim Gaillard") 25-40 54
VERVE (2013 "Smorgasbord") 20-40 56
Also see GILLESPIE, Dizzy, & Slim Gaillard

GAILTONES
Singles: 7-inch
DECCA (30726 "Lover Boy") 20-25 58

GAINES, Alvin, & Themes
Singles: 7-inch
FIDELITY ("Cross My Heart") 150-200 60
(No selection number used.)

GAINES, Earl R&B '66
(Earl Gains)
Singles: 7-inch
ACE (3010 "Drownin' on Dry Land") 3-6 75
CHAMPION (1001 "Now Do You Hear") 15-25 58
CHAMPION (1004 "Love You So") 10-20 60
DELUXE 5-10 68-69
EXCELLO (2217 "Baby, Baby, What's Wrong") 10-20 62
HBR 5-10 66
HOLLYWOOD (1117 "Fruit from Another Man's Tree") 5-10 67
KING (6408 "Don't Deceive Me") 3-5 73
SEVENTY SEVEN 3-6 73
LPs: 10/12-inch
DELUXE 10-15 69
HBR 10-20 66

GAINES, Eddie
Singles: 7-inch
SUMMIT (101 "Be-Bop Battling Ball") 600-750 58
SUMMIT (104 "Out of the Shadows") 15-25 58

GAINES, Fats, Band
("Presents Lou Washington Vocalist")
Singles: 7-inch
AVAMAR (105 "For Your Precious Love") 10-15
Also see WASHINGTON, Lou

GAINES, Lenny
Singles: 7-inch
COLUMBIA 5-10 67

GAINES, Peggy
Singles: 7-inch
HIT (19 "Gravy") 5-8 62
HIT (45 "Tell Him") 5-8 62

GAINES, Rosie R&B '85
Singles: 7-inch
EPIC 3-4 85

GAINES, Roy
Singles: 78 rpm
CHART (600 "Loud Mouth Lucy") 15-25 55
DELUXE 10-20 57
Singles: 7-inch
BELL (915 "Lay Lady Lay") 4-6 70
CHART (600 "Loud Mouth Lucy") 25-50 55
CU-BE-AR (58 "Don't Deceive Me") 10-15
DEL-FI 5-10 61
DELUXE 10-20 57
GROOVE (0146 "Right Now, Baby") 15-25 56
GROOVE (0161 "Worried 'Bout You, Baby") 15-25 56
RCA (7243 "Skippy Is a Sissy") 40-60 58

GAINES, Steve
Singles: 7-inch
MCA 3-5 88
LPs: 10/12-inch
MCA (42154 "One in the Sun") 5-8 88
Also see LYNYRD SKYNYRD

GAINORS
Singles: 7-inch
CAMEO (151 "The Secret") 10-20 58
CAMEO (156 "You Must Be an Angel") 75-125 59
MERCURY 10-15 59-60
RED TOP (110 "You Must Be an Angel") 150-250 58
TALLY-HO 10-15 61
Members: Garnet Mimms; Sam Bell; Howard Tate; Willie Combo; John Jefferson.
Also see MIMMS, Garnet
Also see TATE, Howard

GAINSBOROUGH GALLERY
Singles: 7-inch
EVOLUTION 4-8 70
LPs: 10/12-inch
EVOLUTION 10-12 70

GAITLEY & FITZGERALD
Singles: 7-inch
BORNWIN 4-6

GALABOOCHIES
Singles: 7-inch
STAFF (188 "It'll Never Work Out") 20-30 66

GALACTIC FORCE BAND
LPs: 10/12-inch
SPRINGBOARD 5-10 78

GALACTUS
LPs: 10/12-inch
AIRSHIP ("Cosmic Force Field") 20-30 71
Member: Bob Hocko.
Also see SWAMP RATS

GALAHAD, Johnny
Singles: 7-inch
DECCA (31564 ""29 Model-A") 10-15 63

GALAHADS
LPs: 10/12-inch
LIBERTY (3371 "Hello Galahads") 15-20 64
(Monaural.)
LIBERTY (7371 "Hello Galahads") 15-25 64
(Stereo.)

GALAXIES
Singles: 7-inch
DARBO (1595 "If You Want to Be My Baby") 150-200
GUARANTEED (216 "My Tattle Tale") 25-50 60

GALAXIES
Singles: 7-inch
CHESS (1757 "This Rock & Roll") 10-20 60

GALAXIES
Singles: 7-inch
CAPITOL (4427 "The Big Triangle") 10-20 60
DOT (16212 "Tremble") 10-20 61
RICHIE (458 "Dear Someone") 100-200 61

GALAXIES
Singles: 7-inch
SEAFAIR 5-10 64

GALAXIES
Singles: 7-inch
RONNIE 3-5 76

GALAXIES / Regulars
Singles: 7-inch
EPIC (9427 "Get Bent") 8-12 60

GALAXIES IV
Singles: 7-inch
MOHAWK (169 "Piccadilly Circus") 10-15 66
RCA (9235 "Don't Lose Your Mind") 10-15 67
VEEP (1211 "Til Then You'll Cry") 10-15 65

GALAXY
LPs: 10/12-inch
SKY QUEEN (1677 "A Day Without the Sun") 100-200 76

GALAXY
LPs: 10/12-inch
IMPORT 5-10 78

GALAXYS
Singles: 7-inch
CARTHAY (103 "A Lover's Prayer") 300-500 59

GALBRAITH, Rob
LPs: 10/12-inch
COLUMBIA 8-10 70
RCA 5-10 76

GALE, Arlyn
LPs: 10/12-inch
ABC 5-10 78

GALE, Barbara
Singles: 7-inch
JAMCO 8-12

GALE, Barbara, & Larks
Singles: 78 rpm
LLOYDS 50-100 54
Singles: 7-inch
LLOYDS (111 "When You're Near") 150-250 54
LLOYDS (115 "Johnny Darlin' ") 150-250 54
Also see GALE, Barbara
Also see LARKS

GALE, Billy: see GAYLES, Billy

GALE, E., & Ad's
Singles: 7-inch
PHONA (709 "444") 10-20 62

GALE, Eric LP '77
Singles: 7-inch
COLUMBIA 3-5 78-80
LPs: 10/12-inch
COLUMBIA 5-10 77-80
ELEKTRA 5-10 83
KUDU 8-10 73
Also see GRUSIN, Dave

GALE, J.J.
Singles: 7-inch
LIBERTY 4-8 65

GALE, Jack
Singles: 7-inch
COLUMBIA (41665 "The Medicine") 8-10 60

GALE, Jimmy
(Jimmy Gale Quartet)
Singles: 7-inch
SOMA (1431 "School Is Over") 40-60 60s

GALE, Len
Singles: 7-inch
GOLDEN WING 4-8 60s
STUDIO CITY 8-12 64

GALE, Sunny P&R '52
(With the Saints & Sinners Dixieland Band; with Ralph Burns Orchestra; Sunny Gail)
Singles: 78 rpm
DECCA 3-8 56-57
DERBY 3-6 52
RCA 3-6 52-56
Singles: 7-inch
BLAINE 3-5 65
CANADIAN AMERICAN 3-6 63-64
DECCA 5-10 56-59
DERBY (700 series) 10-20 52
(Colored vinyl.)
RCA (4000 thru 6000 series) 6-12 52-56
RCA (9000 series) 3-5 68
RIVERSIDE 3-5 63
STAGE 4-8 62
TERRACE 3-6 62
THIMBLE 3-4 74
WARWICK 4-8 60-61
EPs: 7-inch
KING 5-10
RCA 5-10 56
LPs: 10/12-inch
CANADIAN AMERICAN 10-20 64
RCA (1277 "Sunny and Blue") 20-30 56
WARWICK (2018 "Sunny") 15-25 60
Also see WILCOX, Eddie, Orchestra

GALE, Sunny, & Du Droppers
Singles: 78 rpm
RCA 10-15 53
Singles: 7-inch
RCA (5543 "The Note in the Bottle") 15-25 53
Also see DU DROPPERS
Also see GALE, Sunny

GALE, Terry
Singles: 7-inch
LARRY BEE (1107 "Voodoo") 15-25 65
LAS VEGAS STRIP (1001 "Betty Jean") 15-25 63
PRO-GRESS 5-10 74
WATER ST. 5-10 75

GALE FORCE
Singles: 7-inch
FANTASY 3-5 77
LPs: 10/12-inch
FANTASY 5-10 78

GALENS P&R '63
Singles: 7-inch
CHALLENGE 5-8 63-65

GALES
Singles: 78 rpm
J.O.B. 50-100 56
J-V-B. 200-300 55
Singles: 7-inch
J.O.B. (3001 "Darling Patricia")..150-250 56
J-V-B. (34 "Don't Let the Sun Catch You Crying") 200-300 55
J-V-B. (35 "Darling Patricia")....500-1000 55
MEL-O (111 "Guiding Angel") ..500-1000 58
MEL-O (113 "If I Could Forget") 300-500 58
WINN (916 "I Love You") 400-600 60

GALES
Singles: 7-inch
DEBRA (1002 "Tommy") 20-30 63

GALES, Billy
Singles: 7-inch
SHOCK (200 "I'm Hurting") 10-20

GALES OF JOY
Singles: 7-inch
NASHBORO 4-8

GALLA, Tony, & Rising Sons
Singles: 7-inch
SWAN (4275 "In Love") 50-75 66

GALLAGHER, James
Singles: 78 rpm
DECCA (29984 "Crazy Chicken")...50-75 56
Singles: 7-inch
B&G (222 "Are You the One") 10-15
DECCA (29984 "Crazy Chicken") 75-100 56

GALLAGHER, Rory LP '72
LPs: 10/12-inch
ATCO 10-12 71-72
CHRYSALIS 5-10 75-80
MERCURY 5-10 82
POLYDOR 8-10 72-75
SPRINGBOARD 8-12 76
Also see TASTE

GALLAGHER & LYLE P&R '76
Singles: 7-inch
A&M 3-4 73-78
LPs: 10/12-inch
A&M 8-10 73-78
CAPITOL (SM-10000 series) 5-10 77
CAPITOL (ST-11000 series) 8-12 72
Members: Ben Gallagher; Graham Lyle.
Also see McGUINNESS FLINT

GALLAHADS P&R '56
Singles: 78 rpm
CAPITOL 5-10 55
JUBILEE 5-10 56
VIK 5-10 57
Singles: 7-inch
CAPITOL 10-20 55
JUBILEE 10-20 56
VIK 10-20 57

GALLAHADS
Singles: 7-inch
BEECH WOOD (3000 "Keeper of Dreams") 75-125 60
DEL-FI (4137 "Lonely Guy")....40-60 60
(Green label.)
DEL-FI (4137 "Lonely Guy") 20-30 60
(Black label.)
DEL-FI (4148 "I'm Without a Girlfriend") 35-50 60
(Green label.)
DEL-FI (4148 "I'm Without a Girlfriend") 20-30 60
(Black label.)
DONNA (1322 "Lonely Guy") 60-80 60
LOST NITE 4-8
NIGHT OWL (20 "Gone") 30-40 60
RENDEZVOUS (153 "Why Do Fools Fall in Love") 20-30 61
STARLA (15 "Keeper of Dreams") 20-30 60
Members: "Tiny" Tony Smith; James Pipkin.
Also see DYNAMICS
Also see PIPKIN, Jimmy, & Gallahads
Also see TINY TONY & STATICS

GALLAHADS
(With the Counts)
Singles: 7-inch
SEA CREST (6005 "Have Love Will Travel") 25-40 64

GALLANT, Billy
(With the Roulettes)
Singles: 7-inch
DEE DEE (501 "Thinking, Hoping, Wishing") 40-60 61
GOLDISC (6 "Thinking, Hoping, Wishing") 20-30 62
Also see ROULETTES

GALLANT, Bobby
Singles: 7-inch
LEVEE (706 "Run Boy Run") 10-20 61

GALLANT, Rodney
Singles: 7-inch
SCOOPO (019 "My Life with You") 15-25

GALLANT, Ronnie
Singles: 7-inch
ATLANTIC 5-10 62
W.B. 5-10 62

GALLANT MEN
Singles: 7-inch
FORD 10-20 62

GALLANTS
Singles: 7-inch
CAPITOL 4-8 65-66
LPs: 10/12-inch
CAPITOL 15-20 64

GALLAWAY, Pearl
Singles: 7-inch
AMP 3 ....15-25 58

GALLEGOS, Chuck, & Fabulous Cyclones
Singles: 7-inch
CBG 4-8 63-64

GALLEONS
Singles: 7-inch
VITA (184 "I Played the Fool") 50-75 59

GALLERY
Singles: 7-inch
MIRA 4-6 68

GALLERY P&R/LP '72
Singles: 7-inch
SUSSEX 3-5 72
Picture Sleeves
SUSSEX (239 "I Believe in Music")... 4-6 72
LPs: 10/12-inch
SUSSEX 10-12 72-73
Member: Jim Gold.
Also see GOLD, Jim

GALLIMORE, Byron C&W '80
Singles: 7-inch
LITTLE GIANT 3-5 80
Picture Sleeves
LITTLE GIANT 5-10 80

GALLION, Bob C&W '58
Singles: 78 rpm
MGM (Except 12195) 5-15 56-57
MGM (12195 "My Square Dancin' Mama") 25-50 56
Singles: 7-inch
HICKORY 4-8 60-63
MGM (Except 12195 & 12628) 10-15 55-59
MGM (12195 "My Square Dancin' Mama") 75-100 56
MGM (12628 "Baby, Love Me") 15-25 58
U.A. 4-6 68
LPs: 10/12-inch
HICKORY (159 "Bob Gallion") 8-12 70
Also see POWELL, Pati, Bob Gallion

GALLIS, Paul Orchestra
(Featuring Tommy Shepard)
Singles: 7-inch
GLEN (5011 "Hoot 'N' Switch") 5-10 63
HEARTBEAT (5 "Boogie Twist") 10-20 62

GALLO, Pat
Singles: 7-inch
CHARLIE PARKER (209 "Arabian Camel Walk") 10-20 62

GALLO, Robert
(Robert John Gallo)
Singles: 7-inch
FORD 5-10 61
MANDALA 3-5 72
LPs: 10/12-inch
MANDALA 8-10 72

GALLOP, Frank P&R '58
(With Don Costa & His Orchestra; with Lou Jacobi & Betty Walker; Frank Gallup)
Singles: 7-inch
ABC-PAR (9931 "Got a Match") 10-15 58
KAPP (745 "Ballad of Irving") 4-8 66
MUSICOR (1191 "Son of Irving") 4-8 66
Picture Sleeves
MUSICOR (1191 "Son of Irving") 8-10 66
LPs: 10/12-inch
KAPP (4506 "When You're in Love") 10-15 66
(Monaural.)
KAPP (5506 "When You're in Love") 10-15 66
(Stereo.)
MUSICOR (2110 "Frank Gallop Sings") 10-15 66
(Monaural.)
MUSICOR (3110 "Frank Gallop Sings") 10-15 66
(Stereo.)
Also see COSTA, Don, Orchestra

GALLUP, Frank: see GALLOP, Frank

GALLOW'S POLE
LPs: 10/12-inch
AZRA (7886 "Gallow's Pole") 10-15 87
(Picture disc. Promotional issue only. 500 made.)

GALLOWAY, Ken
Singles: 7-inch
HONEY 5-10

GALLOWAY, Leata R&B '88
Singles: 7-inch
COLUMBIA 3-4 88

GALLOWAY, Pearl
Singles: 7-inch
AMP 10-15

GALLWAY, Peter
Singles: 7-inch
REPRISE 3-6 71
LPs: 10/12-inch
REPRISE 8-12 72
Also see CHILD'S GARDEN OF GRASS
Also see FIFTH AVENUE BAND
Also see OHIO KNOX

GALORE, Mamie
Singles: 7-inch
ST. LAWRENCE 8-12 65-66
THOMAS 5-10 66

GALS & PALS
LPs: 10/12-inch
FONTANA 15-20 65-66

GALT, James
Singles: 7-inch
AURORA ("Don't Put Out the Fire") 15-25 66
(Selection number not known.)
AURORA (158 "With My Baby") 10-20 66

GALWAY, James LP '79
Singles: 7-inch
RCA 3-4 81
LPs: 10/12-inch
RCA 5-8 79-80
Also see LAINE, Cleo, & James Galway

GALWAY, James, & Sylvia C&W '83
Singles: 7-inch
RCA 3-4 83
Also see GALWAY, James
Also see SYLVIA

GAMARIK
Singles: 7-inch
LAG 4-6

GAMBLE, Dee Dee Sharp: see SHARP, Dee Dee

GAMBLE, Kenny
(With the Romeos)
Singles: 7-inch
ARCTIC (114 "Ain't It Baby") 100-150 65
ARCTIC (123 "The Joke's on You") 100-150 65
ATCO (6470 "Hard to Find the Right Girl") 10-15 67
COLUMBIA (43132 "Our Love") 10-20 64
EPIC (9636 "Standing in the Shadows") 10-20 63
MARK II 5-8 65
Also see MFSB
Also see ROMEOS

GAMBLER
LPs: 10/12-inch
EMI AMERICA 5-10 79-80

GAMBLERS
Singles: 7-inch
LAST CHANCE (2 "Teen Machine") 25-35 61
LAST CHANCE (108 "Teen Machine") 20-30 62
WORLD PACIFIC (815 "Moon Dawg") 15-25 60
Members: Larry Taylor; Elliot Ingber; Darry Weaver; Bruce Johnston; Sandy Nelson.
Also see ASCOTS
Also see CANNED HEAT
Also see HOLLYWOOD GAMBLERS
Also see JOHNSTON, Bruce
Also see MOTHERS of INVENTION
Also see NELSON, Sandy
Also see RENEGADES
Also see WEAVER, Darry

GAMBLERS
Singles: 7-inch
GAS-LITE (807 "Ooh-Poo-Pah Doo") 10-20 66

GAMBLERS
Singles: 7-inch
CORAL 5-8 67

GAMBRELLS
Singles: 7-inch
CUB 10-15 68

GAME
LPs: 10/12-inch
EVOLUTION 8-12 70-71
FAITHFUL VIRTUE 15-20 69

GAME THEORY
EPs: 7-inch
ENIGMA 4-6 82-86
LPs: 10/12-inch
ENIGMA 5-10 82-86
Members: Scott Miller; Gil Ray; Shelley LaFreniere; Guillaume Gassuan; Donteet Thayer.

GAMINS
Singles: 7-inch
SOMA 10-15 65
Member: Gunner Olness.
Also see OLNESS, Gunner

GAMMA LP '79
Singles: 7-inch
ELEKTRA 3-4 79-82
LPs: 10/12-inch
ELEKTRA 5-10 79-82
Members: Dave Pattison; Ronnie Montrose; Denny Carmassi.
Also see HEART
Also see MONTROSE

GAMMA GOOCHEE
Singles: 7-inch
COLPIX 10-20 65-66
MGM 8-15 67
Picture Sleeves
COLPIX (786 "The Gamma Goochee") 20-30 65

GANDALF
Singles: 7-inch
CAPITOL (2400 "Golden Earring")..10-20 69
LPs: 10/12-inch
CAPITOL (121 "Gandalf") 100-200 69
Members: Peter Sando; Bob Muller; Davy Bauer; Frank Hubach.

GANDALF THE GREY
LPs: 10/12-inch
GWR (7 "Grey Wizard Am I") 200-400 72

GANDHARVA
LPs: 10/12-inch
SADHU 8-10 77

GANDY, Jack, Trio
Singles: 78 rpm
KING (1388 "Isn't It a Shame") 8-12 54
Singles: 7-inch
KING (1388 "Isn't It a Shame") 10-20 54

GANDY, Little Jimmy
Singles: 7-inch
ROULETTE 10-15 69

GANEY, Jerry
(With the Break of Dawn)
Singles: 7-inch
BI-TRUCKIN' (12345 "Just for Us")..5-10
MGM (13697 "Hi Heel Sneakers")..10-20 67
VERVE (10454 "Who Am I") 50-75 66

GANG OF FOUR LP '81
Singles: 12-inch
W.B. 4-6 80-84
Singles: 7-inch
W.B. 3-4 80-84
LPs: 10/12-inch
W.B. 5-10 80-83
Also see SHRIEKBACK

GANG STARR LP '91
LPs: 10/12-inch
CHRYSALIS 5-8 91

GANG'S BACK R&B '82
Singles: 7-inch
HANDSHAKE 3-4 82

GANGSTER
Singles: 7-inch
HOMETOWN 3-5 80

GANGSTERS R&B '79
Singles: 7-inch
HEAT 3-4 79-81
MONTAGE 3-4 82
LPs: 10/12-inch
MONTAGE 5-10 82

GANGSTERS OF LOVE
Singles: 7-inch
CAPITOL 3-5 73
LPs: 10/12-inch
CAPITOL 8-12 73

GANIP GANOP
Singles: 7-inch
COLOSSUS 3-5 69

GANN, Don
Singles: 7-inch
HOUSTON (1001 "Have You Ever Been Loved") 25-35 69
HOUSTON (1002 "Wildcat Willie") 35-45 70

GANT, Cecil R&B '44
(Pvt. Cecil Gant "The G.I. Sing-Sation"; with His Trio; Cecil Grant)
Singles: 78 rpm
BOP 15-20
BRONZE 10-20 44
BULLET 10-20 46
DOT (1000 series) 5-15 50-51
DOWN BEAT 5-15 49
4 STAR 5-15 47-52
GILT-EDGE (500 "I Wonder") 75-100 45
(Cardboard picture disc. Add $10 to $15 for mailer.)
IMPERIAL 5-15 50-51
IMPERIAL 5-15 50-51
KING 10-15 47
NATIONAL 5-15 44
SWING TIME 5-10 49
Singles: 7-inch
DECCA (30320 "I Wonder") 10-20 57
DECCA (48171 "Someday You'll Be Sorry") 20-30 50
DECCA (48185 "It's Christmas Time Again") 20-30 50
DECCA (48191 "Train Time Blues, No. 2") 20-30 50
DECCA (48200 "Shot Gun Boogie") 25-40 51
DECCA (48212 "Don't You Worry") 20-30 51
DECCA (48231 "Owl Stew") 20-30 50
DECCA (48249 "God Bless My Daddy") 20-30 50
DOT (1121 "Train Time Blues") 20-30 52
GILT-EDGE (5090 "I Wonder") 20-30 55
LPs: 10/12-inch
KING (671 "The Incomprable Cecil Gant") 40-50 60
RED MILL ("Piano and Voice") 50-100
(No selection number used. Colored vinyl.)
SOUND (601 "The Incomprable Cecil Gant") 75-100 57
Also see CARR, Gunter Lee

GANT, Clenest: see DON Q

GANT, Clentt
Singles: 7-inch
CHANSON (1003 "Stormy Weather") 10-20 60
DUKE 5-10 62
Also see DON Q

GANT, Don
Singles: 7-inch
COLPIX 4-8 63
Picture Sleeves
COLPIX 5-10 63

GANT, Ray
(With the Arabian Knights; with Arabians)
Singles: 7-inch
JAY WALKING 5-10 71
SIVAD 5-10

GANTRY, Chris
Singles: 7-inch
RCA 5-10 66
LPs: 10/12-inch
ABC 8-10
MAGIC CARPET 10-12
MONUMENT 10-15 68

GANTRY, Elmer: see ELMER GANTRY'S VELVET OPERA

GANTS
Singles: 78 rpm
ALADDIN 30-50 57
Singles: 7-inch
ALADDIN (3387 "My Unfaithful Love") 30-50 57

GANTS P&R '65
Singles: 7-inch
LIBERTY 10-15 65-67
STATUE (605 "Road Runner") 30-40 65
LPs: 10/12-inch
LIBERTY 15-25 65-66

GANZBERG, Jimmy
Singles: 7-inch
JET (1419 "Rebel Yell") 25-35 58
JET (5434 "White Saddle Shoes") 25-35 58
JET (5436 "Jo-Ellen") 25-35 58

GAP, Billy & Baby: see BILLY & Baby Gap

GAP BAND R&B '77
Singles: 12-inch
PASSPORT 4-6 83
TOTAL EXPERIENCE 4-6 82-86
Singles: 7-inch
A&M 3-5 75
ARISTA 3-4 89
CAPITOL 3-4 89
MEGA 3-4 84
MERCURY 3-4 79-84
PASSPORT 3-4 83
RCA 3-4 87
SHELTER 3-5 74
TATTOO 3-5 77
TOTAL EXPERIENCE 3-4 82-87
Picture Sleeves
ARISTA 3-4 89
TOTAL EXPERIENCE 3-4 82
LPs: 10/12-inch
CAPITOL 5-8 89
MERCURY 5-10 79-80
PASSPORT 5-10 83
SHELTER 8-10 74
TATTOO 8-10 77
TOTAL EXPERIENCE 5-10 82-86
Members: Charles Wilson; Ronnie Wilson; Robert Wilson.
Also see BILLY & Baby Gap
Also see YOUNG, Val

GARABEDIAN, George
(George Garabedian Players; Troubadours)
Singles: 7-inch
MARK 56 ....10-15 58-59
Also see FABULOUS TONES

GARCIA, Al, & Rhythm Kings
Singles: 7-inch
VELPA (100 "Simply Jane") 4-8 77
LPs: 10/12-inch
ACEMGA (10001 "Al Garcia and the Rhythm Kings") 10-15 80
Also see LINK - EDDY COMBO
Also see RHYTHM KINGS

GARCIA, Augie
(Augie Garcia Quintet)
Singles: 7-inch
KIRK (133 "Ivy League Baby") 80-120 50s
NO. STAR (2023 "Drinking Wine") 80-120 58
NO. STAR (2025 "Hi Yo Silver")..80-120 58
NO. STAR (2065 "Ring-A-Ling")..80-120 50s

GARCIA, Felix
Singles: 7-inch
R DELL (104 "Summer Love") 10-20 58
Also see FELIX & FABULOUS CATS

GARCIA, Jerry P&R/LP '72
(Jerry Garcia Band)
Singles: 7-inch
DOUGLAS 4-8 73
ROUND 4-8 72-74
W.B. 4-8 72
LPs: 10/12-inch
ARISTA 5-10 78-82
ROUND 8-10 74-75
U.A. 8-10 76
W.B. (2582 "Garcia") 35-45 72
Also see DYLAN, Bob, & Grateful Dean
Also see GRATEFUL DEAD
Also see HART, Mickey

Also see IT'S a BEAUTIFUL DAY
Also see JAMES & Good Brothers
Also see JEFFERSON AIRPLANE
Also see LAMB
Also see OLD and in the WAY
Also see ROWANS
Also see SAUNDERS, Merl
Also see WALES, Howard, & Jerry Garcia

GARCIA, Jerry, & Robert Hunter
Singles: 7-inch
ROUND (102 "Sampler for Dead Heads")....50-75 74
(Includes letter about the Grateful Dead LP, *The Mars Hotel,* and some miniature LP covers. Promotional fan club issue.)
ROUND (102 "Sampler for Dead Heads")....25-35 74
(Price for disc without inserts.)
Also see GARCIA, Jerry
Also see GRATEFUL DEAD
Also see HUNTER, Robert

GARCIA, Lt: see LT. GARCIA

GARCIA, Marco
Singles
AZRA ("You")....4-6 89
(Heart-shaped picture disc. No selection number used. 500 made.)

GARCIA, Vic
Singles: 7-inch
MANCO (1003 "Black Shadows")....8-12

GARCIA BROTHERS
Singles: 7-inch
RULY....4-8 64
LPs: 10/12-inch
BULLSEYE....5-10 82

GARDENIAS
Singles: 78 rpm
FEDERAL....25-50 56
Singles: 7-inch
FEDERAL (12284 "Flaming Love")....75-125 56

GARDENIAS
Singles: 7-inch
FAIRLANE (21019 "It's You, You, You")....15-20 62
Also see FABULOUS GARDENIAS

GARDEN OF EDEN
Singles: 7-inch
VERVE....4-8 67

GARDNER, Al: see GARNER, Al

GARDNER, Dave P&R '57
(Brother Dave Gardner)
Singles: 7-inch
DECCA (30627 "Slick Slacks")....15-30 58
OJ....5-10 57
RCA....3-8 59-61
LPs: 10/12-inch
CAMDEN....5-10 73
CAPITOL....15-25 63
RCA....15-25 60-64
TOWER....10-20 67

GARDNER, Don
(With His Sonotones)
Singles: 78 rpm
BRUCE....20-30 54-55
DELUXE....10-20 57
Singles: 7-inch
BRUCE (105 "How Do You Speak to an Angel")....40-60 54
BRUCE (127 "It's a Sin to Tell a Lie")....30-40 55
DELUXE (6155 "I Don't Want to Go Home")....15-25 57
DELUXE (6133 "A Dagger in My Chest")....15-25 57
JUNIOR (393 "High School Baby")....20-30 57
JUNIOR (394 "Dark Alley")....15-25 57
JUBILEE (5484 "The Bitter with the Sweet")....5-10 64
JUBILEE (5493 "Little Girl Blue")....5-10 64
KAISER (399 "Ask Anything")....10-20 59
MR. G (824 "Your Love Is Driving Me Crazy")....
SEDRICK....15-25
TRU-GLO-TOWN....6-10 66
VAL-UE (214 "Glory of Love")....10-20 60
VERVE (10582 "You Babe")....5-10
Also see SMITH, Dickie

GARDNER, Don, & Dee Dee Ford P&R/R&B '62
Singles: 7-inch
COLLECTABLES....3-4
FIRE (508 "I Need Your Lovin' ")....8-15 62
FIRE (513 "Don't You Worry")....8-15 62
FIRE (517 "Lead Me On")....8-15 62
FLASHBACK....3-5 65
KC (106 "Glory of Love")....8-12 62
LUDIX (104 "You Upset My Soul")....5-10 63
RED TOP (6501 "People Sho' Act Funny")....5-10 63
LPs: 10/12-inch
FIRE (105 "Need Your Lovin' ")....50-100 62
SUE (1044 "Don Gardner & Dee Dee Ford in Sweden")....20-30 66
Also see FORD, Dee Dee
Also see GARDNER, Don
Also see WASHINGTON, Baby, & Don Gardner

GARDNER, J.
Singles: 7-inch
BLUE ROCK....4-8 65

GARDNER, Joanna R&B '85
Singles: 7-inch
PHILLY WORLD....3-4 85

GARDNER, Leon
Singles: 7-inch
CHATTAHOOCHEE (667 "You're Gonna Cry")....10-20 65
IGLOO (101 "Tell Me Why")....10-20 60s
IGLOO (316 "Stay Here")....10-20 60s
VAULT (915 "Cain't Stop Now")....8-12 65

GARDNER, Reggie R&B '71
Singles: 7-inch
CAPITOL....3-5 71

GARDNER, Ron
LPs: 10/12-inch
MCA....8-10 74
Also see DOOBIE BROTHERS

GARDNER, Sammy, & Mound City 6
LPs: 10/12-inch
NORMAN....12-15 62

GARDNER, Tommy
Singles: 7-inch
KEESON....5-10 65

GARDNER, Taana R&B '81
Singles: 7-inch
WEST END....3-4 81

GARDNERS
LPs:10/12-inch
PRESTIGE INT'L....20-30 60s

GARFIELD
Singles: 7-inch
CAPRICORN....3-4 78
MERCURY....3-5 76
LPs: 10/12-inch
CAPRICORN....5-10 78
MERCURY....8-10 76

GARFUNKEL, Art P&R/LP '73
Singles: 7-inch
COLUMBIA (Except SQ-45926)....3-4 73-88
COLUMBIA (SQ-45926 "All I Know")....5-10 73
(Quadraphonic. Promotional issue only.)
Picture Sleeves
COLUMBIA....3-4 81
LPs: 10/12-inch
COLUMBIA (30000 series)....8-12 73-81
(With "FC," "JC," "KC" or "PC" prefix.
COLUMBIA (30000 series)....10-20 73-75
(With "CQ" or "PCQ" prefix. Quad issues.)
COLUMBIA (40000 series)....5-8 88
COLUMBIA (47000 series)....10-20 78
(Half-speed mastered.)
Also see GARR, Artie
Also see SIMON & GARFUNKEL

GARFUNKEL, Art / Amy Grant
LPs: 10/12-inch
COLUMBIA (40212 "Animals' Christmas")....8-10 86
(Includes booklet.)
Also see GRANT, Amy

GARFUNKEL, Art, James Taylor & Paul Simon P&R '78
Singles: 7-inch
COLUMBIA....3-5 78
Also see GARFUNKEL, Art
Also see SIMON, Paul
Also see TAYLOR, James

GARI, Frank P&R '60
Singles: 7-inch
ATLANTIC....5-8 62
CAPITOL....4-6 68
CRUSADE....6-12 60-62
RIBBON....6-12 59
Picture Sleeves
CRUSADE....10-20 61-62

GARI & PRISTINES
Singles: 7-inch
CAMEO....4-8 66

GARLAND, Dickie
Singles: 7-inch
PIKE....4-8 61

GARLAND, Gabe
Singles: 7-inch
WYNNE....5-10 59

GARLAND, Hank
LPs: 10/12-inch
COLUMBIA....15-25 61-62
HARMONY....15-25 60
Also see PRESLEY, Elvis

GARLAND, Judy P&R '39
Singles: 78 rpm
CAPITOL....3-8 56-57
COLUMBIA....3-8 53-54
DECCA (Except 2000 through 4000 series)....5-15 42-55
DECCA (2000 thru 4000 series)....10-20 39-42
Singles: 7-inch
ABC....3-5 67
CAPITOL....5-10 56-63
COLUMBIA (40000 series)....8-15 53-54
DECCA (25000 series)....4-8 65
DECCA (29000 series)....8-10 55
MCA....3-5 73-78
MGM GOLDEN CIRCLE....3-5 69
W.B....3-5 63
Promotional Singles
CAPITOL ("After You've Gone"/"When You're Smiling")....10-20 59
Picture Sleeves
CAPITOL ("After You've Gone"/"When You're Smiling")....15-25 59
(Sleeve reads "Two of the Top Tunes from *Garland at the Grove.*")
EPs: 7-inch
CAPITOL (676 "Miss Show Business")....10-20 55
CAPITOL (734 "Judy")....10-20 56
CAPITOL (835 "Alone")....10-20 57
CAPITOL (1569 "Judy at Carnegie Hall")....10-15 62
COLUMBIA (1201 "A Star Is Born")....15-20 54
(Soundtrack.)
COLUMBIA (2598 "Judy Garland")....20-30 57
COLUMBIA (7621 "Born in a Trunk")....25-50 56
DECCA (620 "Judy Garland at the Palace/ Greatest Performances")....10-20 55
DECCA (661 "The Wizard of Oz")....15-25 51
DECCA (2050 "Judy Garland, Volume 2")....12-20 53
MGM (40 "Easter Parade")....30-50 50
(Gatefold cover.)
MGM (268 "If You Feel Like Singing, Sing")....10-20 54
MGM (1038 "Get Happy")....10-20 55
MGM (1116 "Look for the Silver Lining")....10-20 55
MGM (1122 "Judy Garland")....10-20 55
LPs: 10/12-inch
ABC (620 Judy Garland at Home at the Palace")....10-15 67
ABC (30007 "Judy Garland the ABC Collection")....5-10 76
AEI (3101 "Meet Me in St. Louis"/"The Harvey Girls")....10-15
(Soundtrack. Reissue.)
ACCESSOR....8-15
AUDIOFIDELITY (311 "Judy Garland")....15-20 83
(Picture disc.)
C.I.T....8-12
CAPITOL (676 "Miss Show Business")....30-40 55
(With "W" prefix.)
CAPITOL (676 "Miss Show Business")....10-20 63
(With "SW" prefix.)
CAPITOL (734 "Judy")....25-35 56
(With "T" prefix.)
CAPITOL (734 "Judy")....10-20 63
(With "DT" prefix.)
CAPITOL (835 "Alone")....25-35 57
(With "T" prefix.)
CAPITOL (835 "Alone")....10-20 63
(With "DT" prefix.)
CAPITOL (1036 "Judy in Love")....20-35 58
CAPITOL (1118 "Garland at the Grove")....40-60 59
CAPITOL (1188 "The Letter")....25-35 59
(With John Ireland.)
CAPITOL (1467 "Judy - That's Entertainment")....20-35 60
CAPITOL (1569 "Judy at Carnegie Hall")....20-35 61
CAPITOL (1710 "The Garland Touch")....20-30 62
CAPITOL (1861 "I Could Go On Singing")....25-30 63
(Soundtrack. With "W" prefix.)
CAPITOL (1861 "I Could Go On Singing")....35-40 63
(Soundtrack. With "SW" prefix.)
CAPITOL (1941 "Our Love Letter")....15-20 63
(With John Ireland.)
CAPITOL (1999 "The Hits of Judy Garland")....20-30 64
(With "T" or "ST" prefix.)
CAPITOL (1999 "The Hits of Judy Garland")....5-10 75
(With "SM" prefix.)
CAPITOL (2062 "Just for Openers")....15-25 64
CAPITOL (2988 "Judy Garland Deluxe Set")....20-35 68
CAPITOL (11763 "Alone")....5-10 78
CAPITOL (11876 "Judy - That's Entertainment")....5-10 79
CAPITOL (12034 "Just for Openers")....5-10 80
CAPITOL (16175 "The Hits of Judy Garland")....4-6 81
COLUMBIA (762 "Born in a Trunk")....50-100 56
(10-inch LP.)
COLUMBIA (1101 "A Star Is Born")....20-25 58
(Soundtrack.)
COLUMBIA (1201 "A Star Is Born")....35-45 54
(Soundtrack. Deluxe boxed edition.)
COLUMBIA (8740 "A Star Is Born")....20-30 63
(Soundtrack.)
COLUMBIA (10011 "A Star Is Born")....6-12 73
(Soundtrack.)
COLUMBIA/CSP (8740 "A Star Is Born")....5-10
(Soundtrack.)
COMPUNSONIC....8-12
DRG....10-20
DECCA (5 "Collector's Items: 1936-1945")....15-25 70
DECCA (172 "The Best of Judy Garland")....15-20 63
(Monaural.)
DECCA (7-172 "The Best of Judy Garland")....15-20 63
(Stereo.)
DECCA (4199 "The Magic of Judy Garland")....15-20 61
DECCA (5152 "Wizard of Oz")....25-50 52
(Soundtrack. 10-inch LP.)
DECCA (6020 "Judy Garland at the Palace")....35-45 55
DECCA (8190 "Judy Garland - Greatest Performances")....35-45 55
DECCA (8387 "The Wizard of Oz")....20-35 56
(Soundtrack. One side, *The Song Hits from Pinocchio,* does not feature Judy.)
DECCA (8498 "Meet Me in St. Louis"/"The Harvey Girls")....60-70 57
(Soundtrack. Different show on each side.)
DECCA (75150 "Judy Garland's Greatest Hits")....8-12 69
DECCA (78387 "Wizard of Oz")....10-15 67
(Soundtrack.)
51 WEST....5-10
HARMONY (11366 "A Star Is Born")....10-15 69
(Soundtrack.)
JUNO (1000 "Judy-London 1969")....6-12 69
MCA (4003 "The Best of Judy Garland")....10-15 73
MFSL (048 "Live at London Palladium")....30-40 80
MGM (1 "Golden Years at MGM")....15-25 69
MGM (21 "The Pirate")....50-75 51
(Soundtrack. With Gene Kelly. 10-inch LP.)
MGM (82 "Judy Garland Sings")....50-100 51
MGM (113 "Judy Garland")....8-12 70
MGM (3149 "Judy Garland")....35-45 54
MGM (3234 "The Pirate")....25-30 55
(Soundtrack. With Gene Kelly.)
MGM (3464 "The Wizard of Oz")....35-45 61
(Soundtrack.)
MGM (3771 "Words and Music")....15-25 60
MGM (3989 "The Judy Garland Story, Vol. 1")....15-20 61
MGM (3996 "The Wizard of Oz")....15-20 61
(Soundtrack.)
MGM (4005 "The Judy Garland Story, Vol. 2")....15-20 61
MGM (4204 "The Very Best of Judy Garland")....12-20 64
MARK 56 (632 "Live In San Francisco")....125-150 79
(Picture disc.)
METRO (505 "Judy Garland")....10-15 65
METRO (581 "Judy Garland in Song")....10-15 66
PARAGON....5-10
PHOENIX 10....8-12
PICKWICK....5-10 70s
RADIANT....6-12
RADIOLA....5-10
SPRINGBOARD....5-10
STANYAN....5-10 74
STAR TONE....5-10
TRIP (9 "16 Greatest Hits")....5-10 76
TROPHY....5-10
Also see CROSBY, Bing, & Judy Garland
Also see HAYMES, Dick, & Judy Garland
Also see MARTIN, Dean
Also see YOUNG, Victor

GARLAND, Judy / Tommy Dorsey
Singles: 78 rpm
VOGUE ("The Trolley Song")....750-1000 46
(Picture disc.)
Also see DORSEY, Tommy

GARLAND, Judy, & Liza Minnelli LP '65
Singles: 7-inch
CAPITOL....4-8 65
LPs: 10/12-inch
CAPITOL (2295 "Live at the London Palladium")....15-20 65
CAPITOL (11191 "Live at the London Palladium")....5-10 73
MFSL (048 "Live at the London Palladium")....20-35 81
TROLLEY CAR....5-10
Also see GARLAND, Judy
Also see MINNELLI, Liza

GARLAND, Willie
Singles: 7-inch
KENT....4-8 66

GARLAND THE GREAT
Singles: 78 rpm
SPARK (121 "Hello Miss Simms")....8-12 55
Singles: 7-inch
SPARK (121 "Hello Miss Simms")....20-25 55

GARLOW, Clarence R&B '50
Singles: 78 rpm
ALADDIN....25-50 52
FEATURE....20-30 51-54
FLAIR....25-50 54
FOLK STAR....15-25 54
GOLDBAND....10-20 56-57
LYRIC....10-20 51
MACY'S....10-15 49
Singles: 7-inch
ALADDIN (3179 "New Bon Ton Roula")....50-75 52
ALADDIN (3225 "You Got Me Crying")....50-75 52
FEATURE (3005 "If I Keep on Worrying")....40-60 54
FLAIR (1021 "Crawfishin' ")....50-75 54
FOLK STAR (1130 "Za Belle")....25-40 54
FOLK STAR (1199 "No No Baby")....25-40 54
GOLDBAND....20-25 56-57

GARNER, Al
(Al Gardner)
Singles: 7-inch
DELTA....8-12
EXCELLO (2199 "I Wonder")....10-15 61
EXCELLO (2208 "Disgusted")....10-15 61
GROOVESVILLE (777 "I'll Get Along")....30-50 64
LUPINE (121 "I'll Get Along")....20-30 64
SIR-RAH (504 "Watch Yourself")....10-20 60s

GARNER, Big Bill
(With Roy & Buddy)
Singles: 7-inch
CROSSROADS....4-6

GARNER, Billy
Singles: 7-inch
MOJO....4-8 61

GARNER, Emmett, Jr.
Singles: 7-inch
MAXWELL (802 "Check Out What You've Got")....15-25 60s

GARNER, Erroll R&B '49
(Erroll Garner Trio)
Singles: 78 rpm
BLACK & WHITE (16 "Movin' Around")....6-12 45
COLUMBIA....4-8 53-54
MERCURY....4-8 54
SAVOY....4-8 45-49
Singles: 7-inch
ABC-PAR....5-8 61-62
ATLANTIC (600 series)....15-25 50-52
COLUMBIA (40000 & 41000 series)....10-15 53-54
MGM....4-6 66-69
MERCURY (70000 series)....5-10 54
MERCURY (72000 & 73000 series)....3-8 63-71
REPRISE....4-6 63
SAVOY....5-10 50s
Picture Sleeves
ABC-PAR....5-10 61-62
MGM....4-6 67
EPs: 7-inch
ATLANTIC....10-15 56
BRUNSWICK....10-15 53
COLUMBIA....10-15 50-59
EMARCY....10-15 56
KING....10-15 54
MERCURY....10-15 54-56
SAVOY....10-15 51-55
LPs: 10/12-inch
ABC-PAR....15-25 61
ATLANTIC (109 "Rhapsody")....50-100 49
(10-inch LP.)
ATLANTIC (112 "Piano Solos")....50-100 50
(10-inch LP.)
ATLANTIC (128 "Passport to Fame")....50-100 51
(10-inch LP.)
ATLANTIC (138 "Piano Solos")....50-100 52
ATLANTIC (1227 "Greatest Garner")....30-40 56
BARONET....15-25 61
BLUE NOTE (5000 series)....20-40 52-53
(10-inch LP.)
COLUMBIA (535 "At the Piano")....45-65 53
(Red and gold label.)
COLUMBIA (535 "At the Piano")....30-50 56
(Red and black label.)
COLUMBIA (583 "Gems")....40-60 54
(Red and gold label.)
COLUMBIA (583 "Gems")....30-50 56
(Red and black label.)
COLUMBIA (617 "Gonest")....40-60 55
(Red and gold label.)
COLUMBIA (617 "Gonest")....30-50 56
(Red and black label.)
COLUMBIA (651 "Music for Tired Lovers")....25-50 55
(Red and gold label.)
COLUMBIA (883 "Concert by the Sea")....25-50 56
COLUMBIA (939 thru 1587)....15-35 57-61
COLUMBIA (2540 "Garnerland")....30-50 56
(10-inch LP.)
COLUMBIA (6139 "Piano Moods")....50-75 50
COLUMBIA (6173 "Gems")....50-75 51
COLUMBIA (8000 series)....15-25 60
COLUMBIA (9000 series)....6-12 70
COLUMBIA SPECIAL PRODUCTS....5-8 79
DIAL (205 "Garner Trio")....75-100 50
(10-inch LP.)
DIAL (902 "Gaslight Session")....60-80 50
(10-inch LP.)
EMARCY (26000 series)....20-40 54
(10-inch LP.)
EMARCY (36000 series)....20-30 55-56
ENRICA....15-25 59
EVEREST....5-10 70
GRAND AWARD....20-35 56
HARMONY....8-12 68
JAZZTONE....20-35 57
KING (265-17 "Erroll Garner")....50-75 54
(10-inch LP.)
KING (540 "Erroll Garner")....25-35 58
LONDON....8-12 72-73
MGM....10-20 65-68
MERCURY (20009 "At the Piano")....50-75 50
MERCURY (20055 "Mambo")....40-60 54
MERCURY (20063 "Solitaire")....40-60 54
MERCURY (20090 "Afternoon of an Elf")....40-60 55
MERCURY (20662 thru 20859)....15-25 62-63
(Monaural.)
MERCURY (25117 "At the Piano")....50-75 51
(10-inch LP.)
MERCURY (25157 "Gone with Garner")....50-75 51
(10-inch LP.)
MERCURY (60662 thru 60859)....20-30 62-63
(Stereo.)
MERCURY (61000 series)....8-12 70
REPRISE....12-25 63

RONDO-LETTE 15-25 58
ROOST (10 "Piano Magic") 40-60 52
(10-inch LP.)
ROOST (2213 "Giants") 25-40 56
SAVOY (1100 series) 5-10 78
SAVOY (2000 series) 5-10 76
SAVOY (12002 "Erroll Garner") 30-50 55
SAVOY (12003 "Erroll Garner, Vol. 2") 30-50 55
SAVOY (12008 "Erroll Garner") 30-50 55
SAVOY (15000 "At the Piano") 75-125 49
(10-inch LP.)
SAVOY (15001 "At the Piano, Vol. 2") 75-125 50
(10-inch LP.)
SAVOY (15002 "At the Piano, Vol. 3") 75-125 50
(10-inch LP.)
SAVOY (15004 "At the Piano, Vol. 4") 75-125 50
(10-inch LP.)
SAVOY (15026 "At the Piano, Vol. 5") 75-125 50
(10-inch LP.)
TRIP 5-10 74
WING 10-20 62
Also see STARR, Kay / Erroll Garner

GARNER, Johnny
Singles: 7-inch
IMPERIAL (5536 "Kiss Me Sweet") 15-20 58
IMPERIAL (5548 "Diddi Diddi") 20-30 58

GARNER, Larry
Singles: 7-inch
CAPITOL 3-5 73

GARNER, Merlene
Singles: 7-inch
DAVCO (102 "You're It") 15-25 60s
DAVCO (106 "Will You Remember Mine") 20-30 60s

GARNER, Pam
Singles: 7-inch
CORAL 5-10 58

GARNER, Reggie
Singles: 7-inch
CAPITOL (3042 "Traces") 5-10 71

GARNER, Russ
Singles: 7-inch
DUAL TONE 4-8 61

GARNER, Stu
(Stu Gardner)
Singles: 7-inch
A&M 4-8 66
CHISA (Black vinyl) 4-8 69
CHISA (Colored vinyl) 8-12 69
REVUE 5-10 67
LPs: 10/12-inch
REVUE 10-15 67

GARNETT, Gale P&R/C&W/LP '64
Singles: 7-inch
RCA 5-10 64-67
Picture Sleeves
RCA 8-12 64
LPs: 10/12-inch
RCA 10-20 64-66

GARNETT, Gale, & Gentle Reign
Singles: 7-inch
COLUMBIA 4-6 68
LPs: 10/12-inch
COLUMBIA 8-12 68-69
Also see GARNETT, Gale
Also see GENTLE REIGN

GARON, Jesse "Elvis"
Singles: 7-inch
SUN RIZE (127 "That's Alright Mama") 4-6 80s

GARR, Artie
(Art Garfunkel)
Singles: 7-inch
OCTAVIA (8002 "Private Love") 20-30 61
WARWICK (515 "Beat Love") 20-30 59
Also see GARFUNKEL, Art

GARRAFFA, Donna D&D '85
Singles: 12-inch
ARTIST INT'L 4-6 85

GARRET, Tambi
Singles: 7-inch
ASCOT (2208 "Let Her") 4-8 66

GARRETT, Bobby
(Bobby Byrd; Bobby Relf)
Singles: 7-inch
E&M (1602 "Short Skirts") 25-35 63
MIRWOOD 5-10 65-66
Also see BYRD, Bobby
Also see RELF, Bobby

GARRETT, Bobby, & Comanches
Singles: 7-inch
TROPHY (501 "Bobcat") 15-25 58

GARRETT, Burke, Orchestra / Keith Mirick & Burke Garrett Orchestra
Singles: 7-inch
NOLTA 4-8 64

GARRETT, Holly
Singles: 7-inch
MEGA 3-5 70
Picture Sleeves
MEGA 3-5 70

GARRETT, Jo Ann
(With the Rock)
Singles: 7-inch
CHESS (1959 "Whole New Plan") 20-30 66
CHESS (1992 "I'm So Afraid") 10-15 67
CHESS (2031 "Just Say When") 10-15 67
CHESS (2097 "We Can Learn Together") 10-15 67
DUKE (475 "Under Your Control") 3-6 73
DUO 4-8 69-70
SCORPIO (101 "Your Faithful Love") 3-6

GARRETT, Johnny, & Rising Signs
Singles: 7-inch
UNI 4-6 69

GARRETT, Kelly
Singles: 7-inch
AVA (137 "Baby, It Hurts") 8-12 63
PALOMAR (2207 "The Boy on the Drums") 5-10 65
RCA 3-6 76
SMASH (2195 "Knowing When to Leave") 50-75 68
SMASH (2216 "Nothing Left to Give") 15-20 68
WIZDOM 3-6

GARRETT, Lee P&R/R&B '76
Singles: 7-inch
CHRYSALIS 3-5 76

GARRETT, Leif P&R/LP '77
Singles: 7-inch
ATLANTIC 3-5 77-78
SCOTTI BROS 3-4 78-81
Picture Sleeves
ATLANTIC 3-5 77-78
SCOTTI BROS 3-4 78-81
LPs: 10/12-inch
ATLANTIC 5-10 77
SCOTTI BROS 5-10 78-81
Also see CHIC / Roberta Flack / Leif Garrett / Genesis

GARRETT, Mel
Singles: 7-inch
REDD-E 8-10 59

GARRETT, Pat C&W '77
Singles: 7-inch
COMPLEAT 3-4 86
GOLD DUST 3-5 80-81
KANSA 3-5 77
MDJ 3-4 87

GARRETT, Robert
Singles: 7-inch
EXCELLO 4-8 62

GARRETT, Robin
Singles: 7-inch
MUTUAL 5-10 64

GARRETT, Scott P&R '59
(Scott Garret)
Singles: 7-inch
LAURIE (3023 "House of Love") 10-15 59
LAURIE (3029 "Love Story") 20-30 59
(With the Mystics.)
LAURIE (3034 "Where Are You) 10-15 59
OKEH 8-10 60
Session: Mystics.
Also see MYSTICS

GARRETT, Siedah R&B/D&D '85
Singles: 12-inch
QWEST 4-6 85
Singles: 7-inch
QWEST 3-4 85-88
Picture Sleeves
QWEST 3-4 85-88
Also see JACKSON, Michael

GARRETT, Tommy
(Tommy Garrett & 25 Pianos)
LPs: 10/12-inch
LIBERTY 8-15 62
Also see 50 GUITARS OF TOMMY GARRETT

GARRETT, Vernon R&B '69
(With His Cross Road Band)
Singles: 7-inch
GATOR (1201 "Think People") 5-10
GLOW HILL ("Johnny Walker Red") 10-15
(No selection number used.)
GLOW HILL (517 "I Got to Get Over") 10-15
ICA 3-6 77
KAPP 4-8 70
KENT (459 "Shine It On") 10-15 64
KENT (476 "Running Out") 10-15 65
L.A. WEST (001 "I Learned My Lesson") 5-10
MODERN (1026 "If I Could Turn Back the Hands of Time") 20-30 57
OPEN.G (401 "Cave Man") 8-12
(Not a typo – label name is correct.)
SAFE (101 "Drowning in the Sea of Love") 5-10
VENTURE 5-10 69
WATTS U.S.A. (054 "I Made My Own World") 5-10
WATTS U.S.A. (0006 "Don't Do What I Do") 5-10
Also see BIGGIE RATT
Also see JACQUET, Russell, Orchestra, & Vernon Garrett
Also see VERNON & JEWELL

GARRETT, Vernon, & Marie Franklin
Singles: 7-inch
VENTURE 3-6 76
Also see GARRETT, Vernon
Also see FRANKLIN, Marie

GARRETT'S CREW R&B '83
Singles: 7-inch
CLOCKWORK 3-4 83

GARRIGAN, Eddie
Singles: 7-inch
FONTANA (1575 "I Wish I Was") 25-35 66

GARRISON, Al C&W '87
Singles: 7-inch
MOTION 3-4 87

GARRISON, Glen C&W '67
Singles: 7-inch
CREST (1047 "Lovin' Lorene") 35-50 58
IMPERIAL 4-8 67-68
LODE (106 "Pony Tail Girl") 35-50 59
LPs: 10/12-inch
IMPERIAL 10-15 67-68

GARRISON, Red, & Zodiacs
Singles: 7-inch
RMP 5-10 60

GARRISON & Van Dyke
LPs: 10/12-inch
ATCO 5-10 79

GARRITY, Hughie, & Hollywood Playboys
Singles: 7-inch
DUEL 15-25 63

GARRON, Jess C&W '79
Singles: 7-inch
CHARTA 3-5 79

GARROWAY, Dave
(Dave Garroway's Orchestra)
LPs: 10/12-inch
CAMEO 15-30 58
RCA 15-30 57

GARRY & LARRY
Singles: 7-inch
GOLIATH (600 "Garlic Bread") 10-20 62

GARSON, Mort
Singles: 7-inch
G-NOTE (2001 "Bowl-A-Game Stomp") 8-12

GARTELL, Dee Dee
(Delia Gartell; Dee Dee Gartrell; Delia Gartrell)
Singles: 7-inch
BAHITH 5-10
MAVERICK (1006 "Would It Break Your Heart") 10-20 60s
RIGHT ON 4-6

GARTHWAITE, Terry
(With Bobby Louise Hawkins & Rosalie Sorrels)
Singles: 7-inch
ARISTA 3-5 75-76
CAPITOL 3-5 73
LPs: 10/12-inch
ARISTA 5-10 75
FANTASY 5-10 78
FLYING FISH 5-10
Also see BROWN, Toni, & Terry Garthwaite
Also see JOY of COOKING

GARTIN, Jimmy
Singles: 7-inch
HI-Q (14 "Gonna Ride That Satellite") 50-75

GARTRELL, Delia R&B '71
Singles: 7-inch
RIGHT ON 3-6 71-72

GARVETTE, Ray
Singles: 7-inch
LA VETTE 5-10

GARVEY, Nick
Singles: 7-inch
VIRGIN 3-4 82
Picture Sleeves
VIRGIN 3-4 82

GARVIN, Rex, & Mighty Cravers
Singles: 7-inch
CHIEFTAIN (4000 "Strange Happening") 10-20 64
EPIC (9437 "Emulsified") 10-20 61
LIKE (301 "Sock It to 'Em J.B.") 10-20 66
OKEH (7174 "Emulsified") 10-20 63
TOWER (374 "Queen of the Go-Go") 10-20 68
ZORRO 10-15 63
LPs: 10/12-inch
TOWER (5130 "Raw Funky Earth") 20-30 68
Also see CRAVERS
Also see HEARTS
Also see MARIE & REX
Also see MIGHTY CRAVERS

GARY, Clyde, & His Orchestra
Singles: 7-inch
SHAD (5016 "Tami's Dance") 10-20 60
Also see GARY & CLYDE
Members: Gary Paxton; Clyde Batton.
Also see GARY & CLYDE

GARY, John LP '63
Singles: 7-inch
ACE 3-5 62
BIG B 3-5 64
FRATERNITY 3-6 59-66
RCA 3-5 63-71
ST. JAMES 3-5 63
EPs: 7-inch
RCA (2804 "John Gary") 4-8 63
(Stereo Compact 33.)
LPs: 10/12-inch
CAMDEN 5-10 68
CHURCHILL 4-8 77
METRO 5-10 65
RCA 5-15 63-78
SPIN-O-RAMA 5-10 60s
WYNCOTE 5-10 60s
Also see ANN-MARGRET & John Gary
Also see DESMOND, Johnny / John Gary / Gordon MacRae

GARY, Phil
(With the Catalinas; with Rock & Roll Zoo)
Singles: 7-inch
BRAVO 5-10
COUNTERPOINT 5-10
TRIODEX (106 "Bobby Lane") 10-20 61
Also see PHIL & CATALINAS

GARY, Richard
Singles: 7-inch
CJ 8-12

GARY, Rickey
Singles: 7-inch
ORCHESTRA (6131 "Cajun Hop") 10-20 61

GARY, Sam
LPs:10/12-inch
TRANSITION 10-20

GARY & BILLY
Singles: 7-inch
20TH FOX 8-12 59

GARY & CASUALS
Singles: 7-inch
VANDAN (609 "My One Desire") 50-100 62

GARY & CHUCK
Singles: 7-inch
ON BEAT 10-15 59

GARY & CLYDE
Singles: 7-inch
REV (3523 "Why Not Confess") 20-30 59
Members: Gary Paxton; Clyde Batton.
Also see GARY, Clyde, & His Orchestra
Also see PAXTON, Gary
Also see PLEDGES
Also see SKIP & FLIP

GARY & DAVE P&R '73
Singles: 7-inch
LONDON 3-5 73
Members: Gary Weeks; Dave Beckett.

GARY & FRIENDS
Singles: 7-inch
JOSIE 5-10 61

GARY & GARY
Singles: 7-inch
HEIDI 4-8
VEE JAY 4-8 62

GARY & GREEN
(With the Rhythm Aces Band)
Singles: 7-inch
CAPRI (101 "All Around the World") 5-10

GARY & HORNETS
Singles: 7-inch
SMASH (2061 "Hi Hi Hazel") 10-15 66
SMASH (2078 "A Kind of Hush") 8-12 67
SMASH (2090 "Baby It's You") 8-12 67
SMASH (2145 "Turn the World On") 8-12 67
Picture Sleeves
SMASH (2061 "Hi Hi Hazel") 15-20 66
SMASH (2078 "A Kind of Hush") 10-15 67

GARY & Knight Lites: see GARY & Nite Lites

GARY & LUVLYTES
Singles: 7-inch
BOOM 5-10 66

GARY & NITE LITES
(Gary & Knight Lites)
Singles: 7-inch
BELL (643 "Lonely Soldier's Pledge") 10-15 66
PRIMA (1016 "Will You Go Steady") 50-75 59
SEEBURG JUKE BOX (3016 "Sweet Little 16") 25-35 65
SEEBURG JUKE BOX (3017 "Bony Maronie") 25-35 65
U.S.A. (833 "I Don't Need Your Help") 15-25 66
Also see AMERICAN BREED
Also see DAYLIGHTERS
Also see LITE NITES

GARY & RAY
Singles: 7-inch
20TH FOX 4-8 67
Member: Ray Molina.

GARY & UNIVERSALS
Singles: 7-inch
CSS (669/670 "Fifth Dimensions") 10-20 64

GARY & WOMBATS
Singles: 7-inch
REGINA 4-8 63

GARY LEE: see LEE, Gary

GARY O' P&R '81
(Gary O'Connor)
Singles: 7-inch
RCA 3-4 85
Picture Sleeves
RCA 3-4 85
LPs: 10/12-inch
CAPITOL 5-10 81

GARY, PHIL, & Rock 'N' Roll Zoo
Singles: 7-inch
BRAVO 4-8

GARY'S GANG P&R/R&B/LP '79
Singles: 12-inch
COLUMBIA 4-8 79
RADAR 4-6 83
Singles: 7-inch
COLUMBIA 3-5 79
RADAR 3-4 83
LPs: 10/12-inch
COLUMBIA 5-10 79
Members: Gary Turnier; Eric Matthew.

GAS & FUNK FACTORY
Singles: 7-inch
BRUNSWICK (55434 "Goodnight Song") 15-25 70

GAS COMPANY
Singles: 7-inch
MIRWOOD 4-8 65
REPRISE 4-8 66-67

GAS LANTERN
Singles: 7-inch
RISING SONS (717 "Mach 1") 10-20 68
Member: Charlie McCoy.
Also see MCCOY, Charlie

GAS MASK
LPs: 10/12-inch
TONSIL 15-20 70

GASCA, Luis LP '72
LPs: 10/12-inch
BLUE THUMB 8-10 72

GASLIGHT SINGERS
LPs: 10/12-inch
MERCURY 12-15 63-64

GASLIGHT UNION
Singles: 7-inch
TOWER 4-8 68

GASOLINE POWERED CLOCK
Singles: 7-inch
GPC (1001 "Forest Fire on Mail Street") 30-40 67

GASS CO.
Singles: 7-inch
PRO (400 "First I Look at the Purse") 5-10 67

GASSAWAY, Senator Bolivar E.
Singles: 7-inch
RCA 4-8 60
Picture Sleeves
RCA 5-10 60

GASSERS
("Gassers & Orchestra")
Singles: 78 rpm
CASH (1035 "Tell Me") 25-50 56
Singles: 7-inch
CASH (1035 "Tell Me") 100-150 56
ENCINO (1011 "Dody Mighty") 50-100 57

GASTON, Charlie
Singles: 78 rpm
BARCLAY 4-8 55
Singles: 7-inch
BARCLAY 15-20 55

GATEMEN
Singles: 7-inch
MAY (141 "Goodnight Irene") 10-15 63

GATES
(Golden Gate Quartet)
Singles: 78 rpm
COLUMBIA (30149 "I'm Just a Dreamer") 15-25 48
Also see GOLDEN GATE QUARTET

GATES Featuring Bobby Ferguson
Singles: 7-inch
PEACH (0628 "Letter to Dick Clark") 300-500 59
(Identification number shown since no selection number is used.)
PEACH (716 "Wedding Bells Gonna Ring") 500-1000 59

GATES, David P&R/LP '73
(With the Accents)
Singles: 7-inch
ARISTA 3-4 81
DEL-FI (4206 "No One Really Loves a Clown") 10-20 63
EAST WEST (123 "Walkin' and Talkin'") 75-100 59
ELEKTRA 3-5 73-80
MALA (413 "You'll Be My Baby") 60-80 60
MALA (418 "Happiest Man Alive") 40-50 61
MALA (427 "Jo-Baby") 40-50 61
PERSPECTIVE ("Jo-Baby") 50-100 58
(No selection number used. 1200 made.)
PLANETARY (108 "Once Upon a Time") 10-15 65
ROBBINS (1008 "Jo-Baby") 35-45 61
Picture Sleeves
ELEKTRA 3-5 77
LPs: 10/12-inch
ARISTA 5-10 81

ELEKTRA................................. 8-15 73-80
Also see ASHLEY, Del
Also see AVALANCHES
Also see BREAD
Also see COUNTY BOYS
Also see DAVID & LEE
Also see FENCEMEN
Also see JENNIE & JAY
Also see MANCHESTERS
Also see PETERSEN, Paul
Also see PICKETT, Bobby
Also see ROBERDS, Smokey
Also see VIBES

GATES, Ed "Great" *R&B '49*
(Great Gates; Ed [The Great] Gates; Edward White)
Singles: 78 rpm
ALADDIN................................ 8-12 55
RECORDED in HOLLYWOOD 15-25 52
SELECTIVE................................10-20 49
Singles: 7-inch
ALADDIN...................................15-25 55
4 STAR (1712 "You Are My Love") 10-20 57
ROBINS NEXT (103 "Can You Feel It")..10-20 62
SPECIALTY................................10-15 59

GATES, Hen, & Orchestra
(With His Gaters)
Singles: 78 rpm
TREAT (503 "Flash") 15-25 55
Singles: 7-inch
TREAT (503 "Flash") 25-35 55
LPs: 10/12-inch
MASTERSEAL (700 "Let's Go Dancing to Rock & Roll")...................................20-25 56
PALACE (P-700 "Let's All Dance to Rock & Roll")...................................20-30 58
(Monaural.)
PALACE (PST-700 "Let's All Dance to Rock & Roll")...................................25-35 58
(Stereo.)
PALACE ("Rock & Roll") 20-30 50s
PARIS (101 "Rock & Roll Festival")..................................20-30 58
PLYMOUTH (144 "Rock & Roll")....30-50 50s
PLYMOUTH (149 "Rock & Roll, No. 2")..30-50 50s

GATES, Jackie
Singles: 7-inch
SKYWAY (128 "I Want Love") 15-25 61

GATES, Kelly
(With Dez & Larry)
Singles: 7-inch
NOLTA 4-8 62

GATES, Walter
Singles: 7-inch
SWAN 4-8 64-65

GATES OF EDEN
Singles: 7-inch
JUBILEE..................................... 4-8 67
W.B. 4-8 67

GATEWAY SINGERS
Singles: 78 rpm
DECCA...................................... 3-8 56-57
Singles: 7-inch
DECCA..................................... 5-10 56-58
MGM 4-8 60-63
W.B. 4-8 59
LPs: 10/12-inch
DECCA (8413 "Puttin' on the Style")....................................20-30 56
DECCA (8671 "The Gateway Singers at the Hungry i")...........................15-25 58
DECCA (8742 "The Gateway Singers in Hi-Fi") 20-30 58
MGM 12-20 61-63
W.B. 15-20 59
Members: Travis Edmondson; Jerry Walter; Lou Gottlieb; Elmerlee Thomas.
Also see EDMONDSON, Travis
Also see LIMELITERS
Also see GATEWAY TRIO

GATEWAY TRIO
Singles: 7-inch
CAPITOL 10-20 63-64
LPs: 10/12-inch
CAPITOL..................................10-20 63-64
Members: Jerry Walter; Milt Chapman; Betty Mann.
Also see GATEWAY SINGERS

GATLIN, June
Singles: 7-inch
REVUE (11021 "Baby Cakes").......10-20 60s

GATLIN, Larry *C&W '73*
(With the Gatlin Brothers Band; with Family & Friends; Gatlin Quartet)
Singles: 7-inch
CAPITOL.. 3-4 90
COLUMBIA..................................... 3-5 79-88
MONUMENT 3-5 73-78
UNIVERSAL 3-4 89
LPs: 10/12-inch
COLUMBIA.................................... 5-10 79-86
HITSVILLE 5-10 76
MONUMENT 5-10 74-78
SWORD & SHIELD (9009 "The Old Country Church")...................................25-50 61
(By the Gatlin Quartet, which included sister Donna.)
Members: Larry Gatlin; Steve Gatlin; Rudy Gatlin.
Also see EARWOOD, Mundo
Also see NELSON, Willie
Also see SHEPPARD, T.G.

GATLIN, Larry, & Janie Frickie *C&W '87*
(With the Gatlin Brothers)
Singles: 7-inch
COLUMBIA..................................... 3-4 87
Also see FRICKE, Janie

GATOR FAMILY
Singles: 7-inch
HOR D'OEUVRE 3-6 80
Members: French Acers; John Lee Barton; Chris Dannemainer; Sally Norvell; Phil Otken.

GATORCREEK
LPs: 10/12-inch
MERCURY 10-12 70

GATORMEN
Singles: 7-inch
CAMELOT....................................10-15 66
Also see DORSALS with the Gatormen

GATORS
(Chuck Lechner 'N' His Gators)
Singles: 7-inch
GATOR ("Your [sic] a Thousand Miles Away")..............................2000-2500 57

GATORS
Singles: 7-inch
DOT (16252 "Sunburst") 10-20 61

GATORVETTES
("Vocal by Hugh Bowers;" "Vocal by Lawrence Johnson")
Singles: 7-inch
BOCALDUN (1001 "If It's Tonight")...................................50-100 59
THUNDER (1001 "If It's Tonight") 150-250 59
Members: Hugh Bowers; Lawrence Johnson.

GATTON, Danny *LP '91*
(Danny Gatton Band; with Billy Windsor)
Singles: 7-inch
NRG.. 3-4 87-90
Picture Sleeves
NRG.. 3-4 90
LPs: 10/12-inch
ELEKTRA...................................... 5-8 91
NRG... 5-10 87
Members: Danny Gatton; Billy Windsor; John Previti; Dave Elliot; Jim Cavanaugh; Randy Hart.
Also see DANNY & Fat Boys
Also see NOAH'S ARC

GATURS
Singles: 7-inch
ATCO 3-5 72
GATUR... 3-5

GAUCHOS: see DOVAL, Jim

GAUDET, De Dee
Singles: 7-inch
DODGE (805 "What Is the Law") ...15-20

GAUDET, John, & Laurels
Singles: 7-inch
MARY GLEN (1001 "Your Name Shall Be Remembered")............................50-100 61

GAUFF, Willie
(With the Kind Brothers; with Love Brothers)
Singles: 7-inch
EUREKA.. 4-8 69
KENT..5-10 68
WATTS WAY (201 "It Hurt So Bad")..15-25 60s

GAULT, Lenny *C&W '78*
Singles: 7-inch
KING COAL.................................. 3-5 79
MRC 3-5 78-79

GAUNGA DINS
Singles: 7-inch
BUSY-B (2 "Stick with Her")..........20-30 67
BUSY-B (4 "No One Cares") 20-30 67

GAVIN, Jimmy
Singles: 78 rpm
CAMEO...5-10 57
Singles: 7-inch
CAMEO...5-10 57

GAVIN, Tony
Singles: 7-inch
20TH FOX (228 "Ever Lovin' Baby")..20-30 61

GAWRONSKI, Dave, 5
Singles: 7-inch
MARK (11166 "Hey!")......................5-10
Picture Sleeves
MARK (11166 "Hey!").....................10-15

GAY, Ben, & Silly Savages
Singles: 7-inch
ELM.. 4-6 73

GAY, Betsy
(With Jack Fascinato & Orchestra)
Singles: 78 rpm
DECCA (29340 "Cool Man") 5-10 54
Singles: 7-inch
DECCA (29340 "Cool Man") 10-20 54

GAY, Bobby
Singles: 7-inch
GAYBAR (1005 "It's Too Late")......30-45
MIDA (104 "Let's Dance") 30-45 58

GAY, Elaine
(With the Five Harmonaires; "With String Band")
Singles: 78 rpm
DELUXE.......................................10-20 54
Singles: 7-inch
DELUXE (2022 "Am I the One to Blame")......................................15-20 54
DELUXE (2029 "Ebony Eyes").......25-35 54

GAY, Frank, & Gay Blades
Singles: 7-inch
CUCA (1138 "Down Bound Train")...10-20 60s

GAY, Johnny, Combo
Singles: 7-inch
RMP (1017 "Let's Go Twist")............8-10 62

GAY, Marvin: see GAYE, Marvin

GAY, Paula
Singles: 7-inch
SIOUX..4-8 61

GAY CHARMERS
Singles: 78 rpm
G&M (2021 "Honky Tonk")...........10-15 56
Singles: 7-inch
G&M (2021 "Honky Tonk")...........15-25 56
GRAND (2001 "What Can I Do")....15-25 59
SAVOY 5-10 58-59
SWAN (4032 "What Can I Do").........8-12 59

GAY CROSS: see CROSS, Gay

GAY JAYS
Singles: 7-inch
JOSIE...5-8 62

GAY KNIGHTS
Singles: 7-inch
PET (801 "Angel") 25-40 58

GAY NOTES
Singles: 78 rpm
DREXEL.......................................100-200 55
Singles: 7-inch
DREXEL (905 "For Only a Moment")...................................300-500 55

GAY NOTES
Singles: 78 rpm
POST (2006 "Hear My Plea").........20-30 55
Singles: 7-inch
POST (2006 "Hear My Plea")..........40-60 55

GAY NOTES
Singles: 7-inch
VIM (501 "Cherie")...........................30-50 59

GAY POPPERS
Singles: 7-inch
FIRE (1026 "I Want to Know") 15-25 60
FIRE (1039 "Please Mr. Cupid").....15-25 60
SAVOY (1573 "I Need Your Love")...15-25 59

GAY TUNES
Singles: 78 rpm
TIMELY...200-400 53
Singles: 7-inch
TIMELY (1002 "Thrill of Romance")..............................2500-3000 53
(Red vinyl.)
Members: Earl Kirton; Wayman Corey; Leroy Williams; Fred Davis; Henry Pinchback.

GAY TUNES
(With Sammy Lowe Orchestra)
Singles: 7-inch
DOME (502 "Don't Go")............200-300 58

GAY-TUNES
Singles: 7-inch
BROADCAST 3-5 73

GAYDEN, Mac, & Skyboat
LPs: 10/12-inch
ABC...8-10 76

GAYE, Barbie
Singles: 78 rpm
DARL..4-8 56
Singles: 7-inch
DARL..8-12 56

GAYE, Ellie
(Ellie Greenwich)
Singles: 7-inch
RCA ("Silly Isn't It")....................15-25 50s
(Selection number not known.)
Also see GREENWICH, Ellie

GAYE, Marvin *P&R/R&B '62*
(With the Love Tones)
Singles: 12-inch
COLUMBIA (Except 40133)..............4-6 83-85
COLUMBIA (40133 "Sanctified Lady") 10-15 85
(Picture disc.)
MOTOWN 4-8 78
Singles: 7-inch
COLUMBIA...3-4 82-85
DETROIT FREE PRESS ("The Teen Beat Song")..50-100 66
(Promotional issue only.)
JOBETE (1 "Save the Children") ...20-30
MOTOWN 3-4
MOTOWN/TOPPS (6 "How Sweet It Is to Be Loved by You") 50-75 67
(Topps Chewing Gum promotional item. Single-sided, cardboard flexi, picture disc. Issued with generic paper sleeve.)
TAMLA ("Witchcraft") 300-500 61
(Promotional issue only. No selection number used. Credited to "Marvin Gay.")
TAMLA ("My Way") 30-50 65
(Promotional issue only. No selection number used.)
TAMLA (1800 series).........................3-4 86
TAMLA (54041 "Let Your Conscience Be Your Guide")...............................50-75 61
TAMLA (54055 "Sandman")...........45-55 62
TAMLA (54063 "Soldier's Plea") 25-30 62
(Credits only Marvin Gaye.)
TAMLA (54063 "Soldier's Plea") 15-25 62
(Credits Marvin Gaye and "Love Tones.")
TAMLA (54068 "Stubborn Kind of Fellow")..15-25 62
TAMLA (54075 thru 54185)..............5-15 63-69
TAMLA (54190 "Gonna Give Her All the Love I've Got")..4-8 69
(Black vinyl.)
TAMLA (54190 "Gonna Give Her All the Love I've Got")......................................10-15 69
(Colored vinyl. Promotional issue only.)
TAMLA (54195 thru 54280)...............3-6 70-77
(Black vinyl.)
TAMLA (54000 series) 5-10 72-76
(Colored vinyl. Promotional issues only.)
Picture Sleeves
TAMLA (1800 series).........................3-4 86
TAMLA (54095 "Try It Baby")..........20-40 64
TAMLA (54101 "Baby, Don't You Do It")..20-40 64
TAMLA (54138 "Little Darlin I Need You")..30-50 66
TAMLA (54280 "Got to Give It Up") 4-8 77
EPs: 7-inch
MOTOWN (2016 "Marvin Gaye")...15-25 60s
TAMLA (60252 "Greatest Hits") 20-30 66
(Stereo. Juke box issue only. Includes title strips.)
LPs: 10/12-inch
COLUMBIA 5-10 82-85
KORY...8-10 76-77
MOTOWN 8-12 64-83
NATURAL RESOURCES 5-10 78
TAMLA (221 "Soulful Moods") ...400-600 61
TAMLA (239 "That Stubborn Kind of Fella")..300-400 63
TAMLA (242 "On Stage")...............50-100 63
TAMLA (251 "When I'm Alone I Cry")..50-100 64
TAMLA (252 "Greatest Hits") 20-40 64
TAMLA (258 "How Sweet It Is") 20-40 65
TAMLA (266 "Moods") 50-75 66
TAMLA (278 thru 299) 15-30 67-69
TAMLA (300 series)..........................8-15 70-81
TAMLA (6100 series) 5-10 86
Also see BURNS, Eddie
Also see CHARADES
Also see MARQUEES
Also see MARTHA & VANDELLAS
Also see MARVELETTES / Mary Wells / Miracles / Marvin Gaye
Also see MOONGLOWS

GAYE, Marvin / Gladys Knight & Pips
Singles: 7-inch
MOTOWN 4-8 68
Also see KNIGHT, Gladys

GAYE, Marvin, & Diana Ross *LP '73*
Singles: 7-inch
MOTOWN 3-5 73-74
LPs: 10/12-inch
MOTOWN 8-12 73
Also see ROSS, Diana

GAYE, Marvin, & Tammi Terrell *P&R '67*
Singles: 7-inch
TAMLA (Black vinyl).........................4-8 67-70
TAMLA (54192 "Onion Song") 8-12 69
(Colored vinyl. Promotional issue only.)
LPs: 10/12-inch
MOTOWN 5-10 80-82
TAMLA..10-15 67-70
Also see TERRELL, Tammi

GAYE, Marvin, & Mary Wells *P&R/R&B/LP '64*
Singles: 7-inch
MOTOWN 5-10 64
Picture Sleeves
MOTOWN (1057 "What's the Matter with You Baby")..20-40 64
LPs: 10/12-inch
MOTOWN (613 "Together")...........40-50 64
Also see WELLS, Mary

GAYE, Marvin, & Kim Weston *P&R/R&B '64*
Singles: 7-inch
TAMLA..5-10 64-67
LPs: 10/12-inch
TAMLA (270 "Marvin Gaye & Kim Weston")..20-25 66
Also see GAYE, Marvin
Also see WESTON, Kim

GAYE SISTERS
Singles: 7-inch
GLENN...5-10 59

GAYLADS
Singles: 7-inch
AUDAN...4-8 61

GAYLARKS
(With John Heartsman Band; Gaylarks/Lord Luther)
Singles: 78 rpm
MUSIC CITY 50-100 57
Singles: 7-inch
MUSIC CITY (793 "Romantic Memories") 200-300 56
Note: Music City 792, *Tell Me, Darling*, is in the next section: GAYLARKS/Rovers.
MUSIC CITY (805 "My Greatest Sin")..100-200 57
MUSIC CITY (809 "Church on the Hill")..200-300 57
MUSIC CITY (812 "Somewhere in This World")..100-200 57
(No company address shown.)
MUSIC CITY (812 "Somewhere in This World") 50-75 57
(Has company address under logo.)
MUSIC CITY (819 "Ivy League Clothes")..50-75 58
Also see LORD LUTHER

GAYLARKS / Rovers
Singles: 78 rpm
MUSIC CITY 50-100 56
Singles: 7-inch
MUSIC CITY (792 "Tell Me, Darling")..200-300 56
Also see GAYLARKS
Also see HEARTSMAN, Johnny
Also see ROVERS

GAYLE, Crystal *C&W '70*
Singles: 7-inch
COLUMBIA 3-5 79-82
DECCA 4-6 70-72
ELEKTRA...3-4 82
MCA..3-4 77
U.A. 3-5 74-80
W.B. 3-4 83-90
Picture Sleeves
COLUMBIA 3-5 79-82
U.A. 4-8 77
LPs: 10/12-inch
COLUMBIA 5-10 79-83
ELEKTRA..5-10 82
LIBERTY 5-10 80-82
MCA..5-10 78
MFSL (043 "We Must Believe in Magic")..20-40 80
U.A. (Except "Somebody Loves You" picture disc)..5-10 75-80
U.A. ("Somebody Loves You").....50-100 78
(Picture disc. Promotional issue only. One of a four-artist, four-LP set. 250 made.)
W.B. 5-10 83-90
Also see BUTLER, Larry, & Friends
Also see CAMPBELL, Glen / Anne Murray / Kenny Rogers / Crystal Gayle
Also see RABBITT, Eddie, & Crystal Gayle

GAYLE, Crystal, & Gary Morris *C&W '88*
Singles: 7-inch
W.B. 3-4 85-88
Also see MORRIS, Gary

GAYLE, Crystal, & Tom Waits
LPs: 10/12-inch
COLUMBIA..5-10 82
Also see GAYLE, Crystal
Also see WAITS, Tom

GAYLE, Jeanne
Singles: 78 rpm
CAPITOL..4-8 52
Singles: 7-inch
CAPITOL (2222 "Butterflies") 8-12 52
DISNEYLAND 5-10 59

GAYLE, Linda
(With the Duke of Coventry)
Singles: 7-inch
COLUMBIA.......................................10-20 65-66
POMPEII 4-8

GAYLE, Melvin
Singles: 7-inch
CASTLE 4-8 62

GAYLES
Singles: 78 rpm
ABC-PAR 10-15 56
KING 8-12 55
Singles: 7-inch
ABC-PAR 10-20 56
KING 10-15 55

GAYLES, Billy
(Billy Gale)
Singles: 78 rpm
FEDERAL...10-20 56
FLAIR (1038 "Night Howler") 20-30 53
Singles: 7-inch
FEDERAL (12265 "I'm Tore Up")...20-30 56
FEDERAL (12272 "Take Your Fine Frame Home")..20-30 56
FEDERAL (12282 "Do Right, Baby")..20-30 56
FEDERAL (12287 "Just One More Time")..20-30 57
FLAIR (1038 "Night Howler") 50-75 53

GAYLES, Joanne
Singles: 7-inch
BRIGHT STAR (12269 "Meet Me Half Way")...5-10 69
(Identification number shown; however, 12269 may *also* be used as the selection number.)

GAYLETTS
Singles: 7-inch
HOUR GLASS (005 "That's How Strong My Love Is") 5-10

GAYLORD, Ronnie *P&R '54*
Singles: 78 rpm
MERCURY 4-8 54-55
WING 4-8 55-56
Singles: 7-inch
MERCURY 5-10 54-55
WING..5-10 55-56
EPs: 7-inch
MERCURY 5-10 55

Also see GAYLORD & HOLIDAY

GAYLORD & HOLIDAY LP '76
Singles: 7-inch
NATURAL RESOURCES.................. 3-5 77
PALMER.............................. 4-8 67
PRODIGAL............................ 3-5 76
TIME................................ 4-8 63
VERVE............................... 4-8 66
LPs: 10/12-inch
NATURAL RESOURCES.................. 5-10 76
PRODIGAL............................ 5-10 75
VMI................................. 5-10 72
Members: Ronnie Gaylord; Burt Holiday.
Also see GAYLORD, Ronnie
Also see GAYLORDS

GAYLORDS P&R '52
Singles: 78 rpm
MERCURY............................. 5-15 52-57
Singles: 7-inch
MERCURY............................. 10-20 52-62
TIME................................ 5-10 64
EPs: 7-inch
MERCURY............................. 15-25 54-56
LPs: 10/12-inch
MERCURY (Except 25198)............ 15-35 55-63
MERCURY (25198 "By Request") 25-50 55
(10-inch LP.)
TIME................................ 10-15 64
WING................................ 10-20 59-64
Members: Ronnie Gaylord; Don Rea; Burt (Holiday) Bonaldi; Billy Christ.
Also see GAYLORD & HOLIDAY
Also see DEL-VIKINGS / Diamonds / Big Bopper / Gaylords

GAYNELS
Singles: 7-inch
OKEH (7114 "Chubby")............... 25-35 59

GAYNOR, Bob
Singles: 7-inch
MILESTONE........................... 5-10 59

GAYNOR, Gloria P&R '74
Singles: 12-inch
POLYDOR............................. 4-6 78
SILVER BLUE......................... 4-6 83
Singles: 7-inch
COLUMBIA............................ 3-5 73
JOCIDA.............................. 4-8 65
MGM................................. 3-5 74-75
POLYDOR............................. 3-5 76-81
SILVER BLUE......................... 3-4 83
LPs: 10/12-inch
ATLANTIC............................ 5-10 82
MGM................................. 8-10 75
POLYDOR............................. 5-10 76-80

GAYNOR, Mel R&B '55
Singles: 78 rpm
MODERN.............................. 5-10 55
Singles: 7-inch
MODERN.............................. 10-15 55

GAYNOR, Mitzi
Singles: 78 rpm
DECCA............................... 3-5 56
Singles: 7-inch
DECCA............................... 5-10 56
LAURIE.............................. 4-6 60
Picture Sleeves
LAURIE.............................. 5-10 60
EPs: 7-inch
DECCA............................... 5-15 56
LPs: 10/12-inch
DECCA............................... 20-30 56
VERVE............................... 12-25 60

GAYNOR, Steve
Singles: 7-inch
MGM................................. 5-10 59

GAYNOTES
(Gay Notes)
Singles: 7-inch
ZYNN (504 "Waiting in the Chapel")........................ 50-100 58
(Credits "Gaynotes." Previously issued as by Little Clem & Dewdrops.)
ZYNN (504 "Waiting in the Chapel")........................ 15-25 60
(Credits "Gay Notes.")
Also see LITTLE CLEM & DEWDROPS

GAYNOTES
Singles: 7-inch
ALADDIN (3424 "Once He Loved Me")............................. 15-25 58

GAYS
Singles: 7-inch
DECCA............................... 5-10 59-61
POOR BOY............................ 5-10 59

GAYTEN, Paul R&B '47
Singles: 78 rpm
ARGO................................ 15-25 57
CHECKER............................. 10-15 55-56
DELUXE.............................. 10-15 47-49
OKEH................................ 10-15 52-55
REGAL............................... 10-15 49-51
Singles: 7-inch
ANNA................................ 10-20 59-60
ARGO................................ 15-25 57-58
CHECKER............................. 10-20 55-58
OKEH................................ 15-25 52-55
Also see HENRY, Clarence
Also see NEWSOM, Chubby, & Her Hip Shakers
Also see TUNE WEAVERS
Also see WILLIAMS, Charles
Also see WILLS, Oscar / Paul Gayten

GAYTONES
Singles: 7-inch
VAL................................. 10-20

GAYTUNES
Singles: 78 rpm
JOYCE (101 "I Love You")......... 50-100 57
Singles: 7-inch
JOYCE (101 "I Love You")......... 100-200 57
(With the oversize letter "Y" in the Joyce logo.)

GAZELLES
Singles: 78 rpm
GOTHAM (315 "Honest")............. 40-60 56
Singles: 7-inch
GOTHAM (315 "Honest")............. 100-200 56

GEARS / Emeralds / Dedicated Followers / Internal Canitery Sin
EPs: 7-inch
HILLSIDE (1967 "We're Through").. 20-30 67
(Since we've seen only the disc, there may not be a special cover. No EP title is given, so we use the Gears' track. Promotional issue only.)

GEARS
LPs: 10/12-inch
PLAYGEMS (6471 "Rockin' at Ground Zero").............................. 8-12 80
Members: Axxel G. Reese; Dave Drive; Kidd Spike; Brian Redz; Crazy Ruben; Gabriel Shock.

GEATER
Singles: 7-inch
HOUSE of ORANGE ("Breathtaking Girl")............................... 25-35 60s
(Selection number not known.)

GEDDES, David P&R '75
Singles: 7-inch
ATCO................................ 3-5 75
BIG TREE............................ 3-5 75
H&L................................. 3-5 77
ZODIAC.............................. 3-5 77
LPs: 10/12-inch
BIG TREE............................ 8-10 75

GEDDINS, Bob / Sherman's Trio
(Louis Sherman)
Singles: 78 rpm
CAVA-TONE (5 "Thinkin' & Thinkin' ")........................ 40-60 49
(First issue.)
MODERN (685 "Thinkin' & Thinkin' ")........................ 20-30 49

GEDDINS, Bob / Turner Willis
(With His Cavaliers; Bob Geddins' Cavaliers)
Singles: 78 rpm
BIG TOWN (1058 "Irma Jean")...... 15-25 45
TRILON (1058 "Irma Jean")......... 30-50 45
(First issue.)
Also see GEDDINS, Bob / Sherman's Trio

GEDDINS & SONS
Singles: 7-inch
JUMPING............................. 10-20

GEE, Billy
(With Mark Reynolds Orchestra & Chorus)
Singles: 7-inch
CORONET (1303 "King of Hearts")............................. 25-50 59

GEE, Bobby
(With the Celestials)
Singles: 7-inch
STACY (922 "Julie Is Mine")....... 20-40 59
XYZ (611 "Sealed with a Kiss")... 10-20 61

GEE, Don
Singles: 7-inch
MOTIF (014 "Station Break")........ 5-10
(Identification number shown since no selection number is used.)

GEE, Ellie
(Ellie Greenwich)
Singles: 7-inch
MADISON (160 "Red Corvette").... 15-25 61
Also see GREENWICH, Ellie

GEE, Frankie
Singles: 7-inch
CHANNEL (101 "Mixed Up, Shook Up Boy").............................. 10-20 64
CLARIDGE............................ 10-15 60s
LIPSTICK............................ 5-10
Also see FIVE DISCS

GEE, Jesse
Singles: 78 rpm
GEE................................. 5-10 56
Singles: 7-inch
BARRY............................... 5-8 67
GEE (1019 "Don't Mess with My Money")............................ 10-20 56

GEE, Jay
Singles: 7-inch
STACY (916 "The Slouch")........... 10-20 62

GEE, Joey
(With the Bluetones)
Singles: 7-inch
SARA (6451 "Don't You Just Know It")................................ 8-12 64
SARA (6599 "She's Mean")........... 8-12 65
Members: Joe Giannunzio; Craig Sorensen; Billy Morrison; Rickey Bates; Vaughn Ryan.

GEE, Joey, & Come-Ons
Singles: 7-inch
ABC-PAR (10781 "Don't Blow Your Cool")............................. 10-20 66

GEE, Johnny
Singles: 7-inch
BIL-LON............................. 4-8 60s
EMIT................................ 4-8 62
NU-CHILD............................ 5-10

GEE, Lenny
Singles: 7-inch
BAYE (577 "I Need Your Love")..... 50-75 60

GEE, Marsha
Singles: 7-inch
UPTOWN.............................. 4-8 65

GEE, Ray
Singles: 7-inch
PLANET (54 "Hootenanny Baby") 10-15 62

GEE, Ricky
Singles: 7-inch
CONDUC (102 "I Will Get You There")............................. 4-8 65

GEE, Roy, & Hitmakers
Singles: 7-inch
HITMAKER............................ 3-5

GEE, Sonny, & Standels
Singles: 7-inch
ARLEN............................... 5-10 63

GEE, Spoonie: see SPOONIE GEE

GEE, Tony
Singles: 7-inch
TIME................................ 4-8

GEE, Ziggy, & Stu Black
Singles: 7-inch
GLEN................................ 10-20

GEE CEES
Singles: 7-inch
CREST (1088 "Buzzsaw"/"Annie Had a Party").............................. 30-40 61
(Glen Campbell plays guitar on *Buzzsaw*. Eddie Cochran plays on *Annie Had a Party*, first issued as *Annie Has a Party*, by the Kelly Four.)
Also see CAMPBELL, Glen
Also see COCHRAN, Eddie
Also see KELLY FOUR

GEE CHORDS
Singles: 7-inch
ROMANTIC RHYTHM.................... 4-6

GEE SISTERS
Singles: 7-inch
HICKORY............................. 4-8 62
PALETTE............................. 4-8 62

GEERS
Singles: 7-inch
SSS INT'L........................... 10-15 68

GEES
(Gee's)
Singles: 7-inch
PORT (3011 "It's All Over")........ 15-25 66

GEESIN & WATERS
LPs: 10/12-inch
HARVEST/EMI (4008 "Music from the Body")............................. 25-35 73
IMPORT.............................. 8-10 77
Members: Ron Geesin; Roger Waters.
Also see WATERS, Roger

GEE-TONES: see HOWARD, Gregory

GEEZINSLAW BROTHERS C&W '66
Singles: 7-inch
CAPITOL............................. 4-6 66-67
COLUMBIA............................ 4-8 63
LPs: 10/12-inch
CAPITOL............................. 10-15 66-67
COLUMBIA............................ 15-20 63
LONE STAR........................... 8-12 79

GEFILTE JOE & FISH
LPs: 10/12-inch
RHINO............................... 5-10 82

GEILS, J., Band P&R/LP '71
(Geils)
Singles: 12-inch
EMI AMERICA (Except 9133).......... 4-8 82-84
EMI/AMERICA (9133 "Wildman").. 10-20 78
(Colored vinyl. Promotional issue only.)
Singles: 7-inch
ATLANTIC............................ 3-5 71-78
EMI AMERICA (Black vinyl).......... 3-4 78-84
EMI AMERICA (Colored vinyl)........ 5-8 78
(Promotional issue only.)
EMI AMERICA (8119 "Centerfold")........................ 10-15 81
(Potato head-shaped picture disc.)
PRIVATE I........................... 3-4 85
Picture Sleeves
ATLANTIC............................ 3-5 73-78
EMI AMERICA......................... 3-4 78-84
PRIVATE I........................... 3-4 85
EPs: 7-inch
EMI AMERICA (9801 "Angel In Blue")............................. 10-15 81
(Potato head-shaped picture disc. Promotional issue only.)
LPs: 10/12-inch
ATLANTIC (Black vinyl)............. 8-12 70-82
ATLANTIC (Colored vinyl)........... 15-20 73
EMI AMERICA......................... 5-10 78-84
NAUTILUS (25 "Love Stinks")....... 15-20 82
(Half-speed mastered.)
Also see GUY, Buddy, with Dr. John & Eric Clapton / Buddy Guy with the J. Geils Band
Also see WOLF, Peter

GELDOF, Bob P&R '86
Singles: 7-inch
ATLANTIC............................ 3-4 86
Picture Sleeves
ATLANTIC............................ 3-4 86
LPs: 10/12-inch
ATLANTIC............................ 5-10 86
Also see BAND AID
Also see BOOMTOWN RATS

GEM D&D '84
Singles: 12-inch
STREETKING.......................... 4-6 84
Singles: 7-inch
STREETKING.......................... 3-4 84

GEM, Frankie
Singles: 7-inch
U.S.A. (713 "Crystal Rock")........ 15-25 61

GEM TONES
Singles: 7-inch
SCARLET (4219 "War Chant")...... 10-20 60

GEMENI TWINS
Singles: 7-inch
HARCO............................... 4-8 64

GEMINI 6
Singles: 7-inch
IGL (142 "Two-Faced Girls")........ 20-25

GEMINILES
Singles: 7-inch
SANDBAG (781 "Thinkin' About My Baby")............................... 15-25 60s

GEMINIS
Singles: 7-inch
RCA................................. 4-8 66-67

GEMS
Singles: 78 rpm
DREXEL.............................. 75-150 54-57
Singles: 7-inch
DREXEL (901 "Deed I Do")........ 200-300 54
(Black vinyl.)
DREXEL (901 "Deed I Do") 500-1000 54
(Red vinyl.)
DREXEL (903 "I Thought You'd Care")............................... 150-250 54
(Black vinyl.)
DREXEL (903 "I Thought You'd Care")............................... 250-350 54
(Red vinyl.)
DREXEL (904 "You're Tired of Love")............................... 150-250 54
(Black vinyl.)
DREXEL (904 "You're Tired of Love")............................... 250-350 54
(Red vinyl.)
DREXEL (909 "One Woman Man")................................ 200-300 56
DREXEL (915 "Till the Day I Die").............................. 175-250 57
Members: Ray Pettis; Bobby Robinson; Wilson James; Dave Taylor; Rip Reed.

GEMS
Singles: 7-inch
RECORTE (407 "Waiting")......... 50-100 58
WIN (701 "The Night Is Over")... 100-120 58

GEMS
Singles: 7-inch
VALOR ("Shutdown")................. 15-25 59
(Selection number not known.)

GEMS
Singles: 7-inch
MERCURY (71819 "Crazy Chicken")............................ 10-20 61

GEMS
(With the Ted McCrae Orchestra)
Singles: 7-inch
PAT (101 "There's No One Like You")............................... 25-50 61

GEMS
Singles: 7-inch
VIRGELLE (711 "Punch Happy")... 10-20 61

GEMS
Singles: 7-inch
CHESS............................... 5-10 63-71
RIVERSIDE (4590 "I'll Be There").. 10-20 67

GEMS
Singles: 7-inch
UPTOWN (1001 "Slave Girl")........ 20-30 61

GENE, Joe
Singles: 7-inch
ANTIQUE............................. 5-10

GENE, Sonny
Singles: 7-inch
RIP (101 "Just Be Good").......... 10-20 57
RIP (109 "You Tear Me Up")........ 8-12 57

GENE & AL'S SPACEMEN
(Gene & Al's Spacemonks)
Singles: 7-inch
ACE................................. 5-10 59

GENE & BILLY
Singles: 78 rpm
SPARK (120 "It's Hot")............ 15-25 55
Singles: 7-inch
SPARK (120 "It's Hot")............ 25-50 55

GENE & DEAN
Singles: 7-inch
MAUREEN (1001 "Eruption")........ 10-20

GENE & DEBBE P&R '67
Singles: 7-inch
HICKORY............................. 3-5 70
SAN (1519 "Go with Me")........... 10-20 67
TRX................................. 4-8 67-69
LPs: 10/12-inch
TRX (1001 "Here and Now")........ 15-25 68
Members: Gene Thomas; Debbe Nevills.
Also see THOMAS, Gene

GENE & EDDIE
Singles: 7-inch
RU JAC.............................. 3-6 69

GENE & ESQUIRES
Singles: 7-inch
GNP (345 "Space Race")............ 10-20 65

GENE & EUNICE R&B '55
Singles: 78 rpm
ALADDIN............................. 10-15 55
COMBO............................... 10-15 55
Singles: 7-inch
ALADDIN (3276 "Ko Ko Mo")........ 25-40 55
ALADDIN (3282 "This Is My Story")............................... 25-50 55
ALADDIN (3292 "Flim Flam")........ 25-50 55
ALADDIN (3305 "Have You Changed Your Mind")............................... 25-50 56
ALADDIN (3315 "Hootchy Kootchy")............................. 25-50 56
ALADDIN (3321 "Let's Get Together")............................ 25-50 56
ALADDIN (3351 "Bom Bom Lulu").. 25-50 56
ALADDIN (3374 "Strange World").. 25-50 57
ALADDIN (3376 "Don't Treat Me This Way")................................ 25-50 57
ALADDIN (3414 "The Angels Gave Me You")................................ 25-50 58
CASE (1001 "Poco Loco")........... 15-25 59
CASE (1002 "Ah Ah")............... 15-25 59
CASE (1005 "Without Love")........ 15-25 59
CASE (1007 "Sugar Babe")......... 15-25 60
COLLECTABLES........................ 3-4
COMBO (64 "Ko Ko Mo")............. 40-60 55
ERA................................. 3-5 72
IMPERIAL............................ 4-6 64
LILLY (512 "Got a Right to Know")... 8-12 62
U.A................................. 3-5
EPs: 7-inch
CASE (100 "Gene & Eunice")....... 25-50 59
(Issued with paper sleeve.)
Members: Gene Forrest; Eunice Levy.
Also see EUNICE
Also see FORREST, Gene, & Four Feathers

GENE & EUNICE / Shirley & Lee
Singles: 7-inch
TRIP................................ 3-5
Also see GENE & EUNICE
Also see SHIRLEY & LEE

GENE & GARE & VELVET TONES
Singles: 7-inch
VELVET TONE......................... 8-12 65
Member: Jimmy Tennant.
Also see TENNANT, Jimmy

GENE & JEANNE
Singles: 7-inch
BOBBY............................... 4-8 63
KAPP................................ 4-8 65

GENE & JERRY
Singles: 7-inch
DIAL (3012 "Did You Ever")........ 8-12 63

GENE & JERRY
Singles: 7-inch
ROULETTE (4537 "Hootenanny Christmas")......................... 4-8 63
LPs: 10/12-inch
ROULETTE............................ 10-15 64

GENE (Chandler) & JERRY (Butler): see CHANDLER, Gene, & Jerry Butler

GENE & RUTH
Singles: 7-inch
KING................................ 5-10 61
SPARK (120 "It's Hot")............ 20-25 55

GENE & TEAM BEATS
Singles: 7-inch
LEATHERWOOD (2096 "Apple Fuzz")............................... 10-20 65

GENE & TEENBEATS
Singles: 7-inch
RAVEN (2011 "Here I Stand")...... 10-15

GENE & TOMMY
Singles: 7-inch
ABC................................. 4-8 67
Members: Terry Cashman; Tommy West.
Also see CASHMAN & WEST

GENE & WENDELL R&B '61
(With the Sweethearts)
Singles: 78 rpm
SPECIALTY (613 "Lula Baby")...... 20-30 57
Singles: 7-inch
PHILIPS............................. 5-10 62-63
RAY STARR........................... 8-12 61-62
SPECIALTY (613 "Lula Baby")...... 10-20 57

GENE LOVES JEZEBEL LP '86
Singles: 12-inch
GEFFEN.............................. 4-6 86
Singles: 7-inch
GEFFEN.............................. 3-4 86-90
Picture Sleeves
GEFFEN.............................. 3-4 88
LPs: 10/12-inch
GEFFEN.............................. 5-10 86-90
Members: Michael Aston; Jay Aston; James Stevenson; Chris Bell; Peter Rizzo.

Also see GENERATION X
Also see THOMPSON TWINS

GENE THE HAT
Singles: 7-inch
CHECKER (960 "Ram-Bunk-Sush") ... 8-12 61
DEAUVILLE ... 4-8 62
GEE ... 4-8 62
PURL (903 "Big Cigar") ... 10-20 61
WALDEN (101 "Ram-Bunk-Sush") ... 15-25 61
(First issue.)

GENELLS
Singles: 7-inch
DEWEY (101 "Linda, Please Wait") ... 40-60 63

GENERAL ASSEMBLY
Singles: 7-inch
DESTINY ... 4-8 79

GENERAL CAINE: see CAINE, General

GENERAL CROOK
Singles: 7-inch
CAPITOL ... 3-5 70
DOWN to EARTH ... 3-5 71

GENERAL ELEKTRIK
Singles: 7-inch
DECCA ... 3-5 70

GENERAL JOHNSON: see JOHNSON, General

GENERAL KANE R&B '86
Singles: 12-inch
MOTOWN ... 5-10 86
Singles: 7-inch
MOTOWN ... 3-4 86-87
LPs: 10/12-inch
MOTOWN ... 5-10 86

GENERAL PUBLIC P&R/D&D/LP '84
Singles: 12-inch
I.R.S. ... 4-6 84-86
Singles: 7-inch
I.R.S. ... 3-4 84-86
Picture Sleeves
I.R.S. ... 3-4 84
LPs: 10/12-inch
I.R.S. ... 5-10 84-86
Members: Roger Charley; Dave Wakeling.
Also see ENGLISH BEAT

GENERAL SOUL ASSEMBLY
Singles: 7-inch
SCARAB (1001 "Happy Song") ... 15-25 60s

GENERALS
Singles: 7-inch
TAMMY (1009 "Never Too Late") ... 30-40 60

GENERALS
Singles: 7-inch
PYRAMID ... 10-20 66

GENERALS
Singles: 7-inch
GENERAL (6167 "Without You") ... 10-20 60s

GENERATION
Singles: 7-inch
MOCKINGBIRD (1010 "Hold On") ... 20-30

GENERATION X
Singles: 7-inch
CHRYSALIS ... 3-5 78
LPs: 10/12-inch
CHRYSALIS ... 5-10 78
Members: Billy Idol; Tony James; James Stevenson.
Also see CHELSEA
Also see GENE LOVES JEZEBEL
Also see IDOL, Billy
Also see SIGUE SIGUE SPUTNIK

GENESIS
Singles: 7-inch
RIPCHORD (004 "Window of Sand") ... 15-25 67

GENESIS
Singles: 7-inch
MERCURY (72806 "Angeline") ... 5-10 68
MERCURY (72869 "Gloomy Sunday") ... 5-10 68
LPs: 10/12-inch
MERCURY (61175 "In the Beginning") ... 15-25 68
Members: Sue Richman; Jack Tanna; Bob Metke; Kent Henry; Fred Rivera.
Also see CHARITY

GENESIS LP '73
Singles: 12-inch
ATLANTIC ... 4-6 86
Singles: 7-inch
ATCO ... 3-5 76-77
ATLANTIC ... 3-4 78-91
CHARISMA ... 4-6 73
PARROT (3018 "Silent Sun") ... 10-15 68
(Promotional issue only.)
Promotional Singles
ATCO ... 3-5 76-77
ATLANTIC ... 3-4 78-86
CHARISMA ... 4-8 73
PARROT ... 10-15 68
Picture Sleeves
ATLANTIC ... 3-5 80-87
EPs: 7-inch
ATLANTIC (1800 "Spot the Pigeon") ... 5-10 77
(Promotional issue only.)
LPs: 10/12-inch
ABC ... 8-10 74
ATCO ... 8-15 74-77
ATLANTIC ... 5-10 78-86
BUDDAH (5659 "Best of Genesis") ... 10-15 76
CHARISMA ... 8-12 72-79
IMPULSE ... 15-25 70
LONDON (600 series) ... 10-15 74
LONDON (50000 series) ... 5-10 77
MCA ... 5-10 78
MFSL (062 "Trick of the Tail") ... 40-60 82
Members: Phil Collins; Peter Gabriel; Tony Banks; Steve Hackett; Anthony Phillips; Mike Rutherford.
Also see AMERICAN CHEESE
Also see BANKS, Tony
Also see CHIC / Roberta Flack / Leif Garrett / Genesis
Also see COLLINS, Phil
Also see GABRIEL, Peter
Also see HACKETT, Steve
Also see PHILLIPS, Anthony
Also see RUTHERFORD, Mike

GENESIS
Singles: 7-inch
BUDDAH (132 "Journey to the Moon") ... 5-10 69
LPs: 10/12-inch
BUDDAH ("Journey to the Moon") ... 10-20 69
(Selection number not known.)

GENESIS
Singles: 7-inch
SCEPTER ... 3-4 71

GENEVIEVE
(With Johnny Tillotson)
Singles: 7-inch
CADENCE ... 10-15 58
Also see TILLOTSON, Johnny

GENGO & GREGORIO
Singles: 12-inch
ONE WORLD (200 "Happy Birthday Rock 'N' Roll") ... 5-10 85
Members: Robert Gengo; M. Gregorio.

GENIES P&R '59
Singles: 7-inch
ERIC ... 3-4 70s
HOLLYWOOD ... 10-15 59
SHAD (5002 "Who's That Knocking") ... 10-15 59
(Pink label.)
SHAD (5002 "Who's That Knocking") ... 5-10 59
(Blue label.)
WARWICK ... 8-12 60-61
Members: Eugene Pitt; Roy Charles Hammond; Claude Johnson; Roland Trone; Jay Washington.
Also see DON & JUAN
Also see JIVE FIVE
Also see ROY C.

GENIES
Singles: 7-inch
LENOX ... 5-10 63

GENIES
Singles: 7-inch
KING ... 5-10
Also see WILSON, G., & Genies

GENIES
Singles: 7-inch
RONN ... 3-5 71

GENO, Bobby (Mr. Big Guitar)
Singles: 7-inch
DORSET (5003 "Nothing") ... 10-20 60
FIRST (101 "The Shawnee") ... 10-20 59

GENO & ENCORES / Revels
Singles: 7-inch
MGW ... 10-15

GENOS
(With the Blue Rays Orchestra)
Singles: 7-inch
SUNDANCE (202 "Wishful Dreaming") ... 100-200 59

GENOTONES
Singles: 7-inch
CASINO (52261 "Counting Stars") ... 250-350 58
WGW (3003 "Midnight Walk") ... 10-20 62

GENOVA, Tommy
(With the Precisions)
Singles: 7-inch
BELLA ... 10-20 61-64
DEBRA (1007 "The Whole World In My Arms") ... 10-15 63
WHITE ROCK (361 "I Loved and I Lost") ... 20-30 61
Also see LANZO, Mike, & Blue Counts

GENTEELS
Singles: 7-inch
CAPITOL (4798 "Take It Off") ... 10-20 62
STAG (2930 "Take It Off") ... 20-30 62
STAG (4949 "Force of Gravity") ... 20-30 62
Member: Lenny Angelo.

GENTLE GIANT LP '72
Singles: 7-inch
CAPITOL ... 3-5 74-78
COLUMBIA ... 3-5 72-73
LPs: 10/12-inch
CAPITOL ... 5-10 74-80
COLUMBIA ... 8-10 72-73
VERTIGO ... 10-15 71
Members: Derek Shulman; Ray Shulman; Phil Shulman; Gary Green; Kerry Minnear; Tony Visconti; John Weathers; Martin Smith.
Also see DUPREE, Simon, & Big Sound

GENTLE MEN
Singles: 7-inch
CAMEO ... 10-15 66

GENTLE PERSUASION P&R '83
Singles: 7-inch
CAPITOL ... 3-4 83
W.B. ... 5-10 78

GENTLE REIGN
LPs: 10/12-inch
VANGUARD ("Gentle Reign") ... 15-25 68
(Selection number not known.)
Also see GARNETT, Gale, & Gentle Reign

GENTLE SOUL
Singles: 7-inch
EPIC ... 4-6 69
LPs: 10/12-inch
EPIC ... 10-20 69

GENTLE TOUCH
Singles: 7-inch
KAPP (882 "Be Young, Be Foolish, Be Happy") ... 10-120 68

GENTLEHOOD
LPs: 10/12-inch
COLUMBIA ... 8-10 73

GENTLEMAN JIM
(With the Horsemen)
Singles: 7-inch
FOX ... 15-25 66
JERDEN (732 "Soul Searchin' ") ... 10-15 60s
TERA (3007 "If You Don't Like My Apples") ... 30-45
Members: Jim Dunlap; Doug Morrison; Ross Alamang; Chuck Jameson; Herb Hamilton; Bob Edwards; Larry Roberts; Bob Bailee.

GENTLEMEN
Singles: 78 rpm
APOLLO ... 40-60 54
Singles: 7-inch
APOLLO (464 "Something to Remember You By") ... 75-100 54
APOLLO (470 "Don't Leave Me Baby") ... 75-100 55

GENTLEMEN
Singles: 7-inch
SPIRIT (5791 "I Really Love You") ... 15-25 65
Members: Shane Todd; Bob Kenison; Robert Cardwell; David Kenison; Jon St. John; Bruce Shaw; Chuck Scalia.

GENTLEMEN
Singles: 7-inch
VANDAN (8303 "It's a Cry'n Shame") ... 30-50 66

GENTLEMEN & Their Ladies R&B '74
Singles: 7-inch
JEAN ... 3-5 74

GENTLEMEN FOUR
Singles: 7-inch
WAND (1184 "It Won't Hurt Baby") ... 40-60 67

GENTLEMEN WILD
Singles: 7-inch
NWI (2694 "You Gotta Leave") ... 10-15 65

GENTONES
Singles: 7-inch
CASINO (52261 "City Lights") ... 550-650 61

GENTRY
Singles: 7-inch
VENTURE ... 5-10

GENTRY, Art
Singles: 7-inch
ABET (9446 "Wonderful Dream") ... 10-20 74

GENTRY, Beau
Singles: 7-inch
FEATURE (202 "Just in Case") ... 15-25 67

GENTRY, Bo, & Ritchie Cordell
Singles: 7-inch
COLUMBIA ... 4-6 69
Also see CORDELL, Ritchie

GENTRY, Bobbie P&R/C&W/R&B/LP '67
Singles: 7-inch
BRUNSWICK ... 3-5 75
CAPITOL ... 3-6 67-76
W.B. ... 3-5 76-78
Picture Sleeves
CAPITOL ... 3-6 67-72
W.B. ... 3-5 76
LPs: 10/12-inch
CAPITOL (Except "SM" series) ... 8-15 67-71
CAPITOL ("SM" series) ... 5-10 81
W.B. ("Ode to Billie Joe: Radio Salute to Bobbie Gentry") ... 15-20 76
(Promotional issue only.)
Also see CAMPBELL, Glen, & Bobbie Gentry
Also see REYNOLDS, Jody, & Bobbie Gentry

GENTRY, Donny
Singles: 7-inch
ROMULUS (3000 "From This Day On") ... 30-50 63

GENTRY, Gary C&W '81
Singles: 7-inch
ELEKTRA ... 3-4 81

GENTRY, Jim
Singles: 7-inch
DAWN (1117 "Shufflin' to St. Louis") ... 5-10

GENTRY, Ray
Singles: 7-inch
MAVERICK (614 "Willie Was a Bad Boy") ... 200-400 58

GENTRY, Steve
Singles: 7-inch
BLAST ... 4-8 64

GENTRYS P&R/LP '65
Singles: 7-inch
BELL ... 4-8 68
CAPITOL ... 3-5 72
MGM (Except 13690) ... 4-8 65-67
MGM (13690 "There's a Love") ... 8-10 67
STAX ... 3-5 74
SUN (1108 thru 1122) ... 4-6 70-71
(Black vinyl, whether commercial or promo.)
SUN (1108 thru 1122) ... 10-15 70-71
(Colored vinyl. Promotional issues only.)
SUN (1126 "God Save Our Country") ... 10-20 71
YOUNGSTOWN (600 "Little Drops of Water") ... 15-25 65
YOUNGSTOWN (601 "Keep on Dancing") ... 15-25 65
Picture Sleeves
MGM ... 5-10 65
LPs: 10/12-inch
MGM ... 20-30 65-70
SUN ... 20-30 70
Members: Larry Raspberry; Jimmy Johnson; Bruce Bowles; Pat Neal; Jimmy Hart.
Also see RASPBERRY, Larry, & Highsteppers

GENTRYS
Singles: 7-inch
KADO ... 5-10

GENTS
Singles: 7-inch
ALL BOY ... 5-10 62
EVE (5153 "Surfin' All Day") ... 20-30 60s
NITE OWL (10 "Moonlight Surf") ... 20-25 60
Also see FOUR GENTS

GENTS / Teen 5
Singles: 7-inch
TIMES SQUARE (2 "I'll Never Let You Go") ... 10-20 64
(Colored vinyl.)
TIMES SQUARE (98 "I'll Never Let You Go") ... 10-20 64
TIMES SQUARE (3 "Island of Love") ... 20-30 64
(Colored vinyl.)
TIMES SQUARE (99 "Island of Love") ... 10-20 64

GENTS
Singles: 7-inch
DELAWARE ... 10-20 64-65
DUANE ("If You Don't Come Back") ... 15-25 66
NORMANDY (91067 "I Wonder Why") ... 15-20 67

GENTS
LPs: 10/12-inch
("Dallas, Texas 1962") ... 400-500 60s
(No label name or selection number used.)

GENTY R&B '80
Singles: 7-inch
VENTURE ... 3-5 80

GENUINE JOHN
Singles: 7-inch
CAPITOL ... 4-8 70

GEORDIE
Singles: 7-inch
MGM ... 3-5 73
SPECTOR (4 "Treat Her Like a Lady") ... 5-10 80
LPs: 10/12-inch
MCA ... 5-10 81
MGM (4903 "Hope You Like It") ... 15-25 73

GEORGE, Allen
Singles: 7-inch
IDEAL ... 4-8 64

GEORGE, Barbara P&R/R&B '61
Singles: 7-inch
AFO ... 8-15 61-62
HEP'ME ... 5-10
SUE ... 5-10 62-63
U.A. ... 3-5 74
LPs: 10/12-inch
AFO (5001 "I Know") ... 50-75 62

GEORGE, Brenda
Singles: 7-inch
GATOR (501 "I'm Not Trying to Make You Pay") ... 10-20 60s
MESA (101 "I'm Not Trying to Make You Pay") ... 20-30 60s

GEORGE, Cassietta
Singles: 7-inch
AUDIO ARTS (6023 "Reach Out and Touch Me") ... 10-20 69

GEORGE, Curious: see CURIOUS GEORGE

GEORGE, Johnny
Singles: 7-inch
COED ... 8-12 61
MUSIC CITY (818 "Music City Hop") ... 10-20 57

GEORGE, Lloyd
Singles: 7-inch
IMPERIAL ... 10-15 62
POST ... 10-15 63

GEORGE, Lowell LP '79
Singles: 7-inch
W.B. ... 3-5 78-79
LPs: 10/12-inch
W.B. ... 5-10 78-79
Also see FACTORY
Also see LITTLE FEAT
Also see MOTHERS of INVENTION

GEORGE, Morton
Singles: 7-inch
AMY (858 "Come On In") ... 5-8 62

GEORGE, Robin P&R '85
Singles: 7-inch
BRONZE ... 3-4 85
Picture Sleeves
BRONZE ... 3-4 85

GEORGE, Terry
Singles: 7-inch
COMET (2144 "My Love, My Dreamy Eyes") ... 15-20

GEORGE, Wally
Singles: 7-inch
ACCENT (1060 "Drag Strip") ... 25-35 58

GEORGE & BABS
Singles: 7-inch
DOT (18667 "You Don't Need Me") ... 10-15 66
Members: George Tomsco; Babs Tomsco.
Also see TOMSCO, George

GEORGE & CO.
Singles: 7-inch
VEEP ... 4-8 67

GEORGE & EARL
Singles: 78 rpm
MERCURY (70632 "Goin' Steady with the Blues") ... 10-15 55
MERCURY (70852 "Done Gone") ... 10-20 56
Singles: 7-inch
MERCURY (70632 "Goin' Steady with the Blues") ... 15-25 55
MERCURY (70852 "Done Gone") ... 30-40 56

GEORGE & GENE
Singles: 7-inch
BARONET ... 5-10 62

GEORGE & GENE (Jones & Pitney): see JONES, George, & Gene Pitney

GEORGE & GREER
Singles: 7-inch
GOLDWAX (313 "You Didn't Know It But You Had Me") ... 15-25 60s
(Also issued as by George Jackson & Dan Greer.)
Also see JACKSON, George, & Dan Greer

GEORGE & GWEN
Singles: 7-inch
ALSTON ... 4-8 69
Members: George McCrae; Gwen McCrae.
Also see McCRAE, George & Gwen

GEORGE & LOUIS
(George & Louis / Jerry Lee Lewis)
Singles: 7-inch
SUN (301 "Return of Jerry Lee"/"Lewis Boogie") ... 15-25 58
(*Lewis Boogie* is by Jerry Lee Lewis.)
SUN (301 "Return of Jerry Lee Part 1"/"Return of Jerry Lee Part 2") ... 10-20 58
Member: George Klein.
Also see KLEIN, George
Also see LEWIS, Jerry Lee

GEORGE & TEDDY
(With the Condors)
Singles: 7-inch
PHILIPS ... 4-8 66-67
Picture Sleeves
PHILIPS ... 4-8 66
LPs: 10/12-inch
MAMMOTH ... 10-12

GEORGE K BAND
LPs: 10/12-inch
PRIVATE STOCK ... 5-10 78

GEORGETTES
Singles: 78 rpm
EBB ... 10-15 57
Singles: 7-inch
CHALLENGE (59012 "Dizzy Over You") ... 15-20 58
EBB (125 "Oh Tonight") ... 15-25 57
GOLDISC (3006 "Forget Me Not") ... 10-20 60
JACKPOT (48001 "Dizzy Over You") ... 20-30 58
(First issue.)
U.A. (237 "Pair of Eyes") ... 10-15 60

GEORGIA
Singles: 7-inch
EPIC ... 3-5 71

GEORGIA PROPHETS
Singles: 7-inch
DOUBLE SHOT ... 4-8 69
CAPRICORN ... 3-6 70

LPs: 10/12-inch
CUSTOM 8 (77 "Georgia Prophets") 10-15 71
Members: Tommy Witcher; Barbara Scott; Fred Williamson; Janet Helm; Billy Scott; David Benson.
Also see CREATION
Also see PROPHETS
Also see SCOTT, Billy
Also see THREE PROPHETS

GEORGIA SATELLITES *P&R/LP '86*
Singles: 12-inch
ELEKTRA 4-8 89
(Promotional only.)
Singles: 7-inch
ELEKTRA 3-4 86-89
Picture Sleeves
ELEKTRA 3-4 86-87
LPs: 10/12-inch
ELEKTRA 5-10 86-89
Members: Dan Baird; Rick Richards; Rich Price.

GEORGIA SOUL TWISTERS
Singles: 7-inch
MAINSTREAM 4-8 67

GEORGIE BOY
Singles: 7-inch
SSS INT'L 4-6 68-69

GEORGIE PORGIE & CRY BABIES
Singles: 7-inch
GEEP (995 "Crocodile") 10-15 60s
GEORGIE PORGIE 8-12 65-66
JUBILEE 5-10 67

GEORGIO *P&R/R&B/LP '87*
Singles: 7-inch
MACOLO 3-4 87
MOTOWN 3-4 87
Picture Sleeves
MOTOWN 3-4 87
LPs: 10/12-inch
MOTOWN 5-10 87

GEORGY
Singles: 7-inch
UNI 3-5 71

GEORGY & VELVET ILLUSIONS: see VELVET ILLUSIONS
Singles: 7-inch
METRO VIDEO 4-8 67

GERACE, Carlo
Singles: 7-inch
CHANCELLOR 4-8 61

GERACI, Sonny
Singles: 7-inch
CAPITOL 4-8 69
Also see CLIMAX
Also see OUTSIDERS

GERARD, Danyel *P&R '72*
Singles: 7-inch
COLUMBIA 4-6 72
MGM/VERVE 3-5 72
LPs: 10/12-inch
VERVE 8-12 71

GERARD, Jackie
Singles: 7-inch
RAY STAR 5-10 61

GERARDI, Bob, & Classics 4
Singles: 7-inch
RECORTE 5-10 60
Also see ROCKIN' CHAIRS

GERARDO *LP '91*
LPs: 10/12-inch
INTERSCOPE 5-8 91

GERBER, Alan
LPs: 10/12-inch
SHELTER 8-10 71

GERBER, Vince
Singles: 7-inch
JERDEN (726 "Cyclone") 10-20 64
Also see VINCE & VICTORS

GERDES, George
LPs: 10/12-inch
U.A. 8-10 72

GERDSDEN, Ray
Singles: 7-inch
TREY 10-20

GERLD, Gino
Singles: 7-inch
MAJOR 10-20 58

GERMAINE, Denise
(With the Delmonicos)
Singles: 7-inch
ABC-PAR 5-10 65
AKU (6139 "Teenage Idol") 150-200 61
U.A. 5-10 64
Also see DELMONICOS

GERMZ
Singles: 7-inch
VERTIGO (8001 "Boy-Girl Love") 10-15 67
Also see KING, Carole

GERONIMO & APACHES
Singles: 7-inch
GALIKO 8-12 66

GERONIMO BLACK
Singles: 7-inch
UNI 5-10 72
LPs: 10/12-inch
HELIOS 5-10 80
UNI 10-20 72
Members: Ray Collins; Jimmy Carl Black; Denny Walley; Bunk Gardner; Buzz Gardner; Tjay Contrelli; Andy Cahan; Tom Leavey; Murray Roman.
Also see BLACK, Jimmy Carl
Also see LOVE
Also see MOTHERS of INVENTION

GERRARD, Donny *P&R '76*
Singles: 7-inch
GREEDY 3-5 76-77
ROCKET 3-5 76
LPs: 10/12-inch
GREEDY 8-10
Also see SKYLARK

GERRI & SHERRI
Singles: 7-inch
RCA 5-10 62

GERRY & GEMS / Ambassadors
Singles: 7-inch
BAY (210 "I Remember"/"Oh Nancy") 5-8 80s
(Colored vinyl.)

GERRY & GEMS / Tyrone & Nu Ports
Singles: 7-inch
WAX TRAX 3-5 90s
(Colored vinyl.)
Also see GERRY & GEMS / Ambassadors
Also see TYRONE & NU PORTS

GERRY & LESLIE
Singles: 7-inch
HUSH (229 "Me Love Am Gone") 20-30 60

GERRY & PACEMAKERS *P&R/LP '64*
Singles: 7-inch
ERIC 3-4 70s
LAURIE (3196 "I Like It") 10-15 63
LAURIE (3233 "How Do You Do It") 8-12 64
LAURIE (3251 thru 3370) 5-10 64-67
LPs: 10/12-inch
ACCORD 5-10 81
CAPITOL 5-10 79
LAURIE 15-25 64-66
LAURIE/CAPITOL 8-10 81
(Label reads "Mfd. by Capitol Records." Record club issue.)
U.A. 20-25 65
Member: Gerry Marsden.
Also see MARSDEN, Gerry
Also see MARTIN, George, & His Orchestra

GERRY & PAUL
Singles: 7-inch
FATBACK 4-8 68

GESTICS
Singles: 7-inch
SURFER (106 "Let's Go Trippin' ") 20-30 63
SURFER (114 "Rockin' Fury") 20-30 63
Member: Jon Gest.

GESTURES *P&R '64*
Singles: 7-inch
APEX 10-15 60s
SOMA (Black vinyl) 8-12 64-65
SOMA (1417 "Run Run Run") 25-35 64
(Colored vinyl.)
Member: Dale Menton.
Also see BUCKWHEAT
Also see CASTAWAYS / Gestures
Also see MADHATTERS
Also see MENTEN, Dale
Member: Dale Menton.

GET WET *P&R '81*
Singles: 7-inch
BOARDWALK 3-4 81
Picture Sleeves
BOARDWALK 3-4 81
LPs: 10/12-inch
BOARDWALK 5-10 81

GETO BOYS *LP '90*
(Ghetto Boys)
LPs: 10/12-inch
DEF AMERICAN 5-8 90
RAP-A-LOT 5-8 90

GETTO KITTY
Singles: 7-inch
STROUD 5-10

GETTYSBURG ADDRESS
Singles: 7-inch
FRANKLIN 15-25 60s

GETZ, Stan *LP '92*
(Stan Getz Quintet)
Singles: 78 rpm
CLEF 3-8 53-54
DAWN 3-8 54
MERCURY 3-8 53
NORGRAN 3-8 54-55
PRESTIGE 3-8 50-53
ROOST 3-8 50-53
Singles: 7-inch
CLEF 5-10 53-54
COLUMBIA 3-4 75-80
DAWN 5-10 54
MGM 3-5 65
MERCURY 5-10 53
NORGRAN 5-10 54-55
PRESTIGE 5-10 50-53
ROOST 5-10 50-53
VERVE 3-8 60-72
EPs: 7-inch
CLEF 10-20 53
DALE 15-25 51
NORGRAN (11 thru 155) 20-30 53-55
NORGRAN (2000-6 "At the Shrine") 50-100 55
(Boxed, six-disc set.)
PRESTIGE (1309 "Stan Getz") 20-40 52
ROOST 15-25 50-53
LPs: 10/12-inch
A&M 5-8 90
AMERICAN RECORDING SOCIETY 20-30 57
BARONET 10-20 62
BLUE RIBBON 10-20 61
CLEF (137 "Stan Getz Plays") 75-100 53
(10-inch LP.)
CLEF (143 "Artistry of Stan Getz") 75-100 53
(10-inch LP.)
COLUMBIA 5-10 74-82
CONCORD JAZZ 5-10 81
CROWN (5002 "Groovin' High") 25-50 57
DALE (21 "Retrospect") 100-150 51
(10-inch LP.)
INNER CITY 5-10 78
JAZZ MAN 5-10 82
JAZZTONE 20-30 57
MGM (Except 4312) 5-10 70
MGM (4312 "Mickey One") 12-20 65
(Soundtrack.)
METRO 10-15 65
MODERN (1202 "Groovin' High") 35-50 56
NEW JAZZ 15-25 59
NORGRAN (4 "Stan Getz") 100-150 53
(10-inch LP.)
NORGRAN (1000 "Interpretations") 50-100 54
NORGRAN (1008 "Interpretations, Vol. 2") 50-100 54
NORGRAN (1029 "Interpretations, Vol. 3") 50-100 55
NORGRAN (1032 "West Coast Jazz") 40-60 55
NORGRAN (1087 "Stan Getz '57") 40-60 57
NORGRAN (2000-2 "At the Shrine") 100-200 55
(With booklet.)
PICKWICK 8-12 70s
PRESTIGE (102 "Stan Getz") 100-200 52
(10-inch LP.)
PRESTIGE (7002 thru 7022) 25-50 56
(Yellow label.)
PRESTIGE (7252 thru 7256) 25-50 56
(Yellow label.)
PRESTIGE (7000 series) 8-18 64-68
(Blue label.)
PRESTIGE (24000 series) 8-12 72-79
ROOST (103 "Stan Getz Years") 30-40 64
ROOST (402 "Stan Getz") 100-150 50
(10-inch LPs)
ROOST (404 "Stan Getz and the Swedish All Stars") 100-125 51
(10-inch LPs)
ROOST (407 "Jazz at Storyville") 75-100 53
(10-inch LPs)
ROOST (411 "Jazz at Storyville, Vol. 2") 75-100 54
(10-inch LP.)
ROOST (420 "Jazz at Storyville, Vol. 3") 75-100 54
(10-inch LP.)
ROOST (417 "Chamber Music") 75-100 54
(10-inch LP.)
ROOST (2207 "Sounds of Stan Getz") 25-40 56
ROOST (2249 thru 2258) 20-30 63
ROULETTE 8-12 71-72
SAVOY (1100 series) 5-10 77
SAVOY (9004 "All Star Series") 100-150 51
(10-inch LPs)
SEECO (7 "Highlights in Modern Jazz") 75-125 54
(10-inch LP.)
VSP 8-12 66-67
VERVE 25-50 57-60
(Reads "Verve Records, Inc." at bottom of label.)
VERVE 15-30 61-72
(Reads "MGM Records - a Division of Metro-Goldwyn-Mayer, Inc." at bottom of label.)
VERVE 5-10 73-84
(Reads "Manufactured By MGM Record Corp.," or mentions either Polydor or Polygram at bottom of label.)
Also see BENNETT, Tony
Also see GILLESPIE, Dizzy, & Stan Getz
Also see HAMPTON, Lionel, & Stan Getz
Also see HOLIDAY, Billie, & Stan Getz
Also see SHEPHERD, Cybil
Also see TJADER, Cal, & Stan Getz

GETZ, Stan, & Laurindo Almeida
Singles: 7-inch
VERVE 4-6 66
LPs: 10/12-inch
VERVE 10-15 66
Also see ALMEIDA, Laurindo

GETZ, Stan, & Boston Pops Orchestra
LPs: 10/12-inch
RCA 10-20 67
Also see BOSTON POPS ORCHESTRA

GETZ, Stan, & Charlie Byrd *P&R/LP '62*
Singles: 7-inch
MGM 3-4 78
VERVE 3-5 62
LPs: 10/12-inch
VERVE 15-25 62
Also see BYRD, Charlie

GETZ, Stan, & Oscar Peterson
LPs: 10/12-inch
VERVE 20-40 57-60
(Reads "Verve Records, Inc." at bottom of label.)
VERVE 10-25 61-72
(Reads "MGM Records - a Division of Metro-Goldwyn-Mayer, Inc." at bottom of label.)
Also see PETERSON, Oscar

GETZ & GILBERTO
(With Joao & Astrud Gilberto) *P&R/LP '64*
Singles: 7-inch
MGM 3-4 78
VERVE 4-6 64-65
LPs: 10/12-inch
MFSL (208 "Getz & Gilberto") 20-25 94
VERVE (8545 "Getz & Gilberto") 20-30 64
Also see GETZ, Stan
Also see GILBERTO, Astrud

GHENT, Tom
Singles: 7-inch
KAPP 3-5
TETRAGRAMMATON 3-6 69
LPs: 10/12-inch
TETRAGRAMMATON 10-12 69

GHETTO BOYS: see GETO BOYS

GHETTO CHILDREN
Singles: 7-inch
COLUMBIA 10-15 73

GHETTO-PACIFIC
Singles: 7-inch
CHALLENGE 4-8 67

GHIGGS, Ray
Singles: 7-inch
AMBER 3-5

GHOST RIDERS
Singles: 7-inch
NEWLAND (1001 "Ghost Riders Theme") 20-30 65

GHOST RIDERS
LPs: 10/12-inch
ANTHEM 5-10 81

GHOSTERS
Singles: 7-inch
GHOST (102 "Traveling Light") 20-30
GHOST (105 "I Get a Little Bit Lonely") 10-20
GHOST (21518 "Drums and Then Some") 10-20

GHOSTWRITERS
Singles: 7-inch
ARMADA (107 "Sunday School Rock Is Sinking") 10-15 60s
Members: Sam McCue; Mike Larsheid.

GHOULS
(Super Stocks)
LPs: 10/12-inch
CAPITOL (T-2215 "Dracula's Deuce") 40-60 65
(Monaural.)
CAPITOL (ST-2215 "Dracula's Deuce") 50-75 65
(Stereo.)
Also see SUPER STOCKS

GIAMO, Joey, & Nobelmen
Singles: 7-inch
KLIK 10-20 58

GIANOTTA, Sonny
Singles: 7-inch
ABC-PAR 10-20 62

GIANT *P&R/LP '89*
Singles: 7-inch
A&M 3-4 89-90
LPs: 10/12-inch
A&M 5-8 89
MERCURY 8-10 70
Members: Dann Huff; David Huff.

GIANT, Ethan
Singles: 7-inch
MARK (141 "Where's My Baby") 100-200 59

GIANT, Jimmy
Singles: 7-inch
VEE JAY 5-10 60

GIANT CRAB
Singles: 7-inch
CORBY 5-10 67
UNI 4-8 68-69
LPs: 10/12-inch
UNI 10-15 68-69

GIANT JELLYBEAN COPOUT
Singles: 7-inch
POPPY 4-8 68

GIANT STEPS *P&R/LP '88*
Singles: 7-inch
A&M 3-4 88-89
LPs: 10/12-inch
A&M 5-8 88

GIANT SUNFLOWER
Singles: 7-inch
ODE 4-8 67
TAKE "6" 4-8 67

GIANTS
Singles: 7-inch
SPINDLETOP (101 "Loose Juice") 8-15 61
T-BIRD (103 "Loose Juice") 10-20 61
(First issue.)

GIANTS
Singles: 7-inch
CASABLANCA 3-5 76
LPs: 10/12-inch
CASABLANCA 8-10 76
Members: Ron Elliott; Bruce Gary; Karl Rucker; Laurie Cohen; John Cohen; John Platania.
Also see ELLIOTT, Ron
Also see KNACK

GIANTS
LPs: 10/12-inch
LAX 5-10 79

GIB & WAYNE
Singles: 7-inch
STARFIRE (100 "World of Dreams") 15-25 65
Members: Floyd "Gib" Guilbeau; Wayne Moore.
Also see GUILBEAU, Floyd "Gib"

GIBB, Andy *P&R/R&B/LP '77*
Singles: 7-inch
RSO 3-4 77-81
Picture Sleeves
RSO 3-4 77-78
LPs: 10/12-inch
RSO 5-10 77-80
Also see BEE GEES
Also see NEWTON-JOHN, Olivia, & Andy Gibb

GIBB, Andy, & Victoria Principal *P&R '81*
Singles: 7-inch
RSO 3-5 81
Picture Sleeves
RSO 5-10 81
Also see GIBB, Andy

GIBB, Barry *P&R '80*
Singles: 12-inch
MCA 4-6 84
Singles: 7-inch
ATCO (6786 "One Bad Thing") 100-150 69
MCA 3-4 84
Picture Sleeves
MCA 3-4 84
LPs: 10/12-inch
MCA 5-10 84
Also see BEE GEES
Also see STREISAND, Barbra, & Barry Gibb
Also see WARWICK, Dionne

GIBB, Maurice
Singles: 7-inch
ATCO 3-5 70
Also see BEE GEES

GIBB, Robin *P&R '78*
Singles: 12-inch
MIRAGE 4-6 84
Singles: 7-inch
ATCO 3-5 69-71
EMI AMERICA 3-4 85
MIRAGE 3-4 84
POLYDOR 3-4 83
RSO 3-5 78
SESAME STREET 3-5 78
Picture Sleeves
EMI AMERICA 3-4 85
MIRAGE 3-4 84
POLYDOR 3-4 83
SESAME STREET 3-5 78
LPs: 10/12-inch
ATCO 8-10 70
MIRAGE 5-10 84
POLYDOR 5-10 83
Also see BEE GEES
Also see LEVY, Marcy, & Robin Gibb

GIBBONS, Lloyd
Singles: 78 rpm
GLOBE 15-25 47

GIBBONS, Steve, Band *P&R '76*
Singles: 7-inch
MCA/GOLD HAWKE 3-5 76-78
POLYDOR 3-5 78
LPs: 10/12-inch
MCA 8-10 76-77
POLYDOR 5-10 78-80
Also see DALTREY, Roger, & Steve Gibbons

GIBBS, Bill
Singles: 7-inch
ODESSA (308 "Rodney's Blues") 10-20 61
Also see BOYD, Tim, & Esquires

GIBBS, Doug *R&B '72*
Singles: 7-inch
OAK 3-5 72

GIBBS, Georgia *P&R '50*
Singles: 78 rpm
CORAL 5-10 50-51
MERCURY 5-10 51-57
Singles: 7-inch
BELL 4-8 64-66
CORAL 10-20 50-51
EPIC (Except 9606) 4-8 63-64
EPIC (9606 "Tater Poon") 10-15 63
IMPERIAL 5-10 60
KAPP 5-10 59
MERCURY 10-20 51-57
RCA (Except 6922 & 7047) 5-15 57-67
RCA (6922 "I'm Walking the Floor Over You") 15-25 57
RCA (7047 "Fun Lovin' Baby") 15-25 57
ROULETTE 5-10 58-59
EPs: 7-inch
MERCURY 10-20 54-56

ROYALE (239 "Georgia Gibbs Sings") ... 10-20 50s
(Colored vinyl.)
LPs: 10/12-inch
BELL ... 10-15 66
CORAL (56037 "Ballin' the Jack") ... 30-50 51
(10-inch LP.)
CORAL (57183 "Her Nibs") ... 20-40 57
EMARCY (36103 "Swingin' with Gibbs") ... 20-40 57
EPIC ... 10-20 63
GOLDEN TONE (14093 "Her Nibs") ... 10-15 50s
IMPERIAL ... 10-20 60
MERCURY (20071 "Music and Memories") ... 20-40 55
MERCURY (20114 "Song Favorites of Georgia Gibbs") ... 20-40 56
MERCURY (20170 "Swingin' with Her Nibs") ... 20-40 56
MERCURY (25175 "Georgia Gibbs Sings Oldies") ... 40-60 53
(10-inch LP.)
MERCURY (25199 "The Man That Got Away") ... 40-60 54
(10-inch LP.)
RONDO ... 8-12
SUNSET ... 8-12 66
TOPPS ... 10-20
Also see DIAMONDS / Georgia Gibbs / Sarah Vaughan / Florian Zabach

GIBBS, Sherri, & Quovans
Singles: 7-inch
PHILLY SOUNDS ("Oh My Baby") ... 25-35 60
(No selection number used.)

GIBBS, Terri — C&W '80
Singles: 7-inch
HORIZON ... 3-4 87
MCA ... 3-4 80-83
TEM ... 3-4 82
W.B. ... 3-4 85
LPs: 10/12-inch
HORIZON ... 5-8 87
MCA ... 5-10 81-83
PHONORAMA ... 5-8 84
W.B. ... 5-8 85
Also see MATTEA, Kathy

GIBRALTARS
Singles: 7-inch
A&W (100 "Side by Side") ... 20-30

GIBSON, Beverly Ann — R&B '59
Singles: 7-inch
DEB ... 5-10 59
JUBILEE ... 4-8 63
LANDA ... 4-8 61

GIBSON, Billy
Singles: 7-inch
COLUMBIA ... 3-4 79

GIBSON, Bob
Singles: 7-inch
DECCA ... 4-8 63
ELEKTRA ... 5-10 59
GIBSON (6003 "B-52") ... 10-15 59
LPs: 10/12-inch
ELEKTRA ... 15-25 59-63
MARK 56 (7177 "Ski Songs") ... 20-30 59
RIVERSIDE (802 "Offbeat Folk Songs") ... 30-40 56
RIVERSIDE (806 "Folk Songs") ... 25-40 57
RIVERSIDE (816 "Carnegie Hall Concert") ... 25-40 57
RIVERSIDE (1111 "There's a Meetin' Here Tonight") ... 25-35 58
(Stereo.)
RIVERSIDE (7000 series) ... 15-20 63

GIBSON, Bob, & Bob Camp
LPs: 10/12-inch
ELEKTRA ... 15-25 61
Also see CAMP, Hamilton
Also see GIBSON, Bob

GIBSON, Bobby, & Voyagers
Singles: 7-inch
GIBSON (6003 "B-52") ... 25-30 61

GIBSON, Buddy, & Vanguards
(With Jesters; with Vanguards)
Singles: 7-inch
SPRY (118 "To Be Or Not to Be") ... 10-20
SWINGIN' (615 "Just a Game") ... 100-200 59

GIBSON, Byron
Singles: 7-inch
LAURIE ... 10-15 61

GIBSON, Cindy
Singles: 7-inch
GENERAL (700 "A Lovely Summer Night") ... 10-20

GIBSON, Curly
(Curly Gibson's Sunshine Playboys)
Singles: 7-inch
LEO (1824 "Hillbilly Hop") ... 10-20 57

GIBSON, Daddyo
Singles: 7-inch
CHECKER ... 5-10 58

GIBSON, Debbie — P&R/LP '87
Singles: 7-inch
ATLANTIC ... 3-4 87-90
Picture Sleeves
ATLANTIC ... 3-4 87-90
LPs: 10/12-inch
ATLANTIC ... 5-10 87-89

GIBSON, Don — C&W '56
Singles: 78 rpm
COLUMBIA ... 5-10 52-54
MGM ... 15-35 55-56
RCA ... 8-12 51
Singles: 7-inch
ABC/HICKORY ... 3-5 75-78
COLUMBIA (20000 series) ... 8-15 52-54
HICKORY ... 3-5 70-72
MCA ... 3-5 79
MGM (12109 "Run Boy") ... 15-25 55
MGM (12194 "Sweet Dreams") ... 15-25 56
MGM (12290 "I Ain't Gonna Waste My Time") ... 20-30 56
MGM (12331 "I Believed in You") ... 15-25 56
MGM (12393 "I'm Gonna Fool Everybody") ... 20-30 57
MGM (12494 "I Ain't A-Studying You Baby") ... 25-35 57
RCA (0400 series) ... 10-20 51
RCA (4300 & 4400 series) ... 10-20 51-52
RCA (7000 series, except 7762) ... 8-15 58-61
RCA (47-7762 "Legend in My Time") ... 6-10 60
(Monaural.)
RCA (61-7762 "Legend in My Time") ... 15-20 60
(Stereo.)
RCA (8000 & 9000 series) ... 4-8 62-70
W.B./CURB ... 3-4 80
Picture Sleeves
RCA ... 5-10 63
EPs: 7-inch
COLUMBIA ... 15-20 57
RCA ... 10-20 58-59
LPs: 10/12-inch
ABC/HICKORY ... 6-10 75-78
CAMDEN ... 10-15 65-74
HARMONY (7300 series) ... 15-20 65
HARMONY (31000 series) ... 5-10 72
HICKORY ... 8-12 70-72
HICKORY/MGM ... 6-10 73-75
LION (70069 "Songs by Don Gibson") ... 25-50 58
MGM ... 8-12 70
METRO ... 12-18 65
RCA (1743 thru 2878) ... 15-30 58-63
(With "LPM" prefix. Monaural.)
RCA (1743 thru 2878) ... 20-40 58-63
(With "LSP" prefix. Stereo.)
RCA (3376 thru 4378) ... 10-20 63-70
(With "LPM" or "LSP" prefix.)
Session: Jordanaires.
Also see JORDANAIRES
Also see WEST, Dottie, & Don Gibson

GIBSON, Don, & Sue Thompson — C&W '71
Singles: 7-inch
HICKORY ... 3-5 71-76
LPs: 10/12-inch
HICKORY ... 8-12 73
HICKORY/MGM ... 5-10 75
Also see GIBSON, Don
Also see THOMPSON, Sue

GIBSON, Douglas, with the Sweet & Sours
Singles: 7-inch
TANGERINE ... 10-20 67

GIBSON, Fred
Singles: 78 rpm
TOPS ... 5-10 55
Singles: 7-inch
TOPS ... 8-12 55

GIBSON, Ginny — P&R '53
Singles: 78 rpm
ABC-PAR ... 4-8 56
DERBY ... 4-8 52
JUBILEE ... 4-8 53
MGM ... 4-8 51-55
Singles: 7-inch
ABC-PAR ... 8-12 56
DERBY ... 8-12 52
JUBILEE ... 8-12 53
MGM ... 8-12 51-55
EPs: 7-inch
JD ... 8-12

GIBSON, Grandpappy
(Clifford Gibson)
Singles: 7-inch
BOBBIN (124 "It's Best to Know Who You're Talking To") ... 25-35 60
BOBBIN (127 "The Monkey Likes to Boogie") ... 25-35 60

GIBSON, Hal — C&W '89
Singles: 7-inch
SUNDIAL ... 3-4 89

GIBSON, Harry "The Hipster"
Singles: 7-inch
MILE ... 3-5 76
LPs: 10/12-inch
SUTTON ... 15-20

GIBSON, Jill
Singles: 7-inch
IMPERIAL (66068 "It's As Easy As 1, 2, 3") ... 40-50 64
(Black label.)
IMPERIAL (66068 "It's As Easy As 1, 2, 3") ... 20-30 64
(White label. Promotional issue only.)
Also see MATADORS

GIBSON, Joe D.
Singles: 7-inch
TETRA (4450 "Good Morning Captain") ... 15-20 59

GIBSON, Johnny — P&R '62
(Johnny Gibson Trio)
Singles: 7-inch
BIG TOP (3088 "Midnight") ... 10-20 62
BIG TOP (3118 "After Midnight") ... 10-20 62
BIG TOP (3149 "Ooh Poo Pah") ... 10-20 63
LAURIE (3256 "Beachcomber") ... 8-12 64
TWIRL (2012 "Beachcomber") ... 10-20 64
(First issue.)
Also see JOHNNY & HURRICANES

GIBSON, Jon
LPs: 10/12-inch
FRONTLINE ... 5-10 86

GIBSON, Paul
Singles: 7-inch
ACE ... 4-8 61

GIBSON, Steve — P&R '48
(With the Red Caps; with Original Red Caps; Red Caps; "Vocal Solo By George Tinley")
Singles: 78 rpm
ABC-PAR ... 10-25 56-57
BEACON ... 15-25 44
MERCURY ... 25-50 47-54
RCA ... 20-30 51-55
Singles: 7-inch
ABC-PAR (9702 "Love Me Tender") ... 15-25 56
ABC-PAR (9750 "Write to Me") ... 15-25 56
ABC-PAR (9796 "You May Not Love Me") ... 15-25 57
ABC-PAR (9856 "Silhouettes") ... 15-25 57
BAND BOX (325 "No More") ... 10-15 62
CASA BLANCA (5505 "Where Are You") ... 100-200 59
(First issue.)
HI LO (101 "I Want to Be Loved") ... 25-50 58
HI LO (103 "It's Love") ... 25-50 58
HUNT (326 "Cheryl Lee") ... 25-35 59
HUNT (330 "Where Are You") ... 20-30 59
JAY DEE (796 "It Hurts Me But I Like It") ... 50-100 54
MERCURY (1253 "I Don't Want to Set the World on Fire") ... 100-200 49
MERCURY (1255 "Blueberry Hill") ... 100-200 49
MERCURY (5380 "I'll Never Love Anyone Else") ... 100-200 50
MERCURY (8038 "San Antonio Rose") ... 50-100 51
MERCURY (8069 "Wedding Bells") ... 50-100 51
MERCURY (8146 "Blueberry Hill") ... 50-100 51
MERCURY (70389 "Wedding Bells") ... 40-60 54
RCA (0127 "I'm to Blame") ... 50-100 51
RCA (0138 "Would I Mind") ... 50-100 51
RCA (3986 "The Thing") ... 75-125 50
RCA (4076 "Three Dollars and Ninety-Eight Cents") ... 30-60 51
RCA (4294 "Shame") ... 30-60 51
RCA (4670 "Two Little Kisses") ... 30-60 52
RCA (4835 "I Went to Your Wedding") ... 30-60 52
RCA (5103 "Truthfully") ... 30-60 52
RCA (5130 "Big Game Hunter") ... 30-60 53
RCA (6096 "Feelin' Kinda Happy") ... 25-50 55
RCA (6345 "How I Cry") ... 25-50 55
ROSE (555 "My Heart Belongs to Only You") ... 15-25 59
ROSE (5534 "Bless You") ... 15-25 60
STAGE (3001 "Blueberry Hill") ... 15-25
EPs: 7-inch
MERCURY (3215 "Blueberry Hill") ... 200-300 52
LPs: 10/12-inch
MERCURY (25115 "You're Driving Me Crazy") ... 300-400 52
(10-inch LP. Title on label is *Harmony Time*.)
MERCURY (25116 "Blueberry Hill") ... 300-400 52
(10-inch LP. Title on label is *Singing & Swinging*.)
Member: George Tinley.
Also see DAMITA JO with Steve Gibson & Red Caps
Also see FIVE RED CAPS
Also see GIBSON, Steve
Also see GREGG, Bobby
Also see JENKINS, Duke, & Roulettes
Also see MODERN RED CAPS
Also see TOPPERS

GIBSON, Steve, & His Red Caps / Damita Jo with Steve Gibson & the Red Caps
Singles: 78 rpm
RCA (5987 "My Tzatskele") ... 15-25 55
Singles: 7-inch
RCA (5987 "My Tzatskele") ... 30-50 55
Also see DAMITA JO with Steve Gibson & Red Caps
Also see GIBSON, Steve

GIBSON, Virginia
Singles: 7-inch
CABOT (118 "Teenage Dance") ... 5-10 58

GIBSON BROTHERS — P&R/R&B/LP '79
Singles: 12-inch
ISLAND ... 4-6 79
Singles: 7-inch
ISLAND ... 3-4 79
LPs: 10/12-inch
HOMESTEAD ... 5-8 90
ISLAND ... 5-8 79

GIBSONS
Singles: 7-inch
DERAM ... 4-8 67

GIDEA PARK — P&R '82
(Featuring Adrian Baker)
Singles: 7-inch
PROFILE ... 3-4 82

GIDEON, Tony
Singles: 7-inch
CHESS (1776 "The Way You Move Me Baby") ... 15-25 60

GIDEON & POWER
LPs: 10/12-inch
BELL ... 8-10 72

GIFTS
Singles: 7-inch
BALLAD ... 8-12 66-69

GIGI
Singles: 7-inch
DOT ... 4-6 66
SEG-WAY ... 8-10 61

GIGI & CHARMAINES
Singles: 7-inch
COLUMBIA ... 4-8 66-67
Also see CHARMAINES

GIGOLOS
Singles: 7-inch
CHESS (1715 "Luna Rock") ... 15-25 59

GIGOLOS
(Gigolo's)
Singles: 7-inch
DAYNITE (1 "Swingin Saints") ... 20-30 60
Members: Don Cole; Bob Taylor.

GIGOLOS
Singles: 7-inch
BROADWAY (1000 "Movin' Out") ... 10-15 61
ENTERPRISE (5000 "Movin' Out") ... 5-10 64
Also see COE, Jamie

GIGUERE, Russ
Singles: 7-inch
W.B. ... 3-5 71
LPs: 10/12-inch
W.B. ... 10-15 71
Also see ASSOCIATION

GIL, Scooter
Singles: 7-inch
RIVER ("Phanton Wheels") ... 15-25
(Selection number not known.)

GIL & EARL
Singles: 7-inch
FRATERNITY ... 4-8 66

GIL & JOHNNY
Singles: 7-inch
WORLD PACIFIC ... 4-8 66

GILBERT, Jewell
(With Mac McCray's Band)
Singles: 78 rpm
HI-PO ... 15-25 57
Singles: 7-inch
HI-PO (1002 "Mad Nervous Woman") ... 20-40 57

GILBERT, Jimmy
Singles: 7-inch
DARN-L (5264 "Believe What I Say") ... 100-200

GILBERT, Marty
EPs: 7-inch
COLD SPOT ... 5-8 86

GILBERT, Regina, & Jan Midkiff
Singles: 7-inch
FOUNTAIN ... 3-5 86
Members: Regina Gilbert; Jan Midkiff; Don Capps; Randy Foushee; Daniel Shumate.

GILBERT, Ronnie
LPs:10/12-inch
MERCURY ... 15-25 60s

GILBERT, Tim
Singles: 7-inch
UNI ... 4-8 67
Also see RAINY DAZE

GILBERTO, Astrud — LP '65
Singles: 7-inch
CTI ... 3-5 71
VERVE ... 3-5 65-70
LPs: 10/12-inch
IMAGE ... 5-10 78
PERCEPTION ... 5-10 72
VERVE ... 10-15 65-70
Also see GETZ & GILBERTO
Also see JOBIM, Antonio Carlos
Also see JONES, Quincy
Also see WANDERLEY, Walter

GILBERTO, Astrud, & Stanley Turrentine
LPs: 10/12-inch
CTI ... 5-10 71
Also see GILBERTO, Astrud
Also see TURRENTINE, Stanley

GILBERTSON, Leroy
Singles: 7-inch
CUCA (1082 "Russian Rumble") ... 10-20 62

GILDER, Nick — P&R/LP '78
Singles: 7-inch
CHRYSALIS ... 3-5 76-79
RCA ... 3-4 85
Picture Sleeves
CHRYSALIS ... 3-5 78
RCA ... 3-4 85
LPs: 10/12-inch
CASABLANCA ... 5-10 80
CHRYSALIS ... 5-10 77-79
Also see SWEENY TODD

GILES, Eddy
Singles: 7-inch
MURCO ... 5-10 60-62
SILVER FOX (9 "That's How Strong My Love Is") ... 5-10

GILES, GILES & FRIPP
LPs: 10/12-inch
DERAM (18019 "The Cheerful Insanity of Giles, Giles & Fripp") ... 25-35 68
Members: Mike Giles; Peter Giles; Robert Fripp; Nicky Hopkins.
Also see FRIPP, Robert
Also see HOPKINS, Nicky
Also see McDONALD & GILES

GILFORD, Jimmy
(Jimmy Guilford)
Singles: 7-inch
SOLID HIT (103 "I Want to Be Your Baby") ... 10-15
THELMA (501 "Too Late to Cry") ... 15-25 65
WHEELSVILLE (101 "I Want to Be Your Baby") ... 20-40 65

GILKYSON, Terry — P&R '57
(With the Easy Riders; with South Coasters)
Singles: 78 rpm
COLUMBIA ... 4-8 54-57
DECCA ... 4-8 51-52
Singles: 7-inch
COLUMBIA ... 5-10 54-57
DECCA ... 5-10 51-52
Picture Sleeves
COLUMBIA (40817 "Marianne") ... 10-15 57
EPs: 7-inch
COLUMBIA ... 5-15 57
DECCA ... 5-15 53
LPs: 10/12-inch
DECCA (5263 "Folk Songs by a Solitary Singer") ... 20-40 50
DECCA (5305 "Solitary Singer") ... 25-50 51
(10-inch LP.)
DECCA (5457 "Golden Minutes of Folk Music") ... 25-50 53
(10-inch LP.)
KAPP ... 10-20 60-63
Members: Terry Gilkyson; Rich Dehr.
Also see EASY RIDERS
Also see LAINE, Frankie, & Easy Riders
Also see MARTIN, Dean
Also see WEAVERS & Terry Gilkyson

GILL, Johnny — R&B '83
Singles: 7-inch
COTILLION ... 3-4 83-85
MOTOWN ... 3-4 90
Picture Sleeves
COTILLION ... 3-4 85
MOTOWN ... 3-4 90
LPs: 10/12-inch
COTILLION ... 5-10 83-85
MOTOWN ... 5-8 90-91
Also see LATTISAW, Stacy, & Johnny Gill
Also see NEW EDITION

GILL, Robert
(With Band)
Singles: 78 rpm
REPUBLIC ... 10-15 54
Singles: 7-inch
REPUBLIC (7076 "Let's Have Some Fun") ... 40-60 54
WONDER (109 "Baby, That's Alright") ... 20-40 58

GILL, Ronnie, & Pastel Keys
Singles: 7-inch
EXPEDITE (2853 "Geraldine") ... 75-125 58
RIP (108 "Geraldine") ... 50-75 58
Also see LOVE NOTES

GILL, Scooter
Singles: 7-inch
RIVER (1313 "Phantom Wheels") ... 20-30

GILL, Vince — C&W '84
Singles: 7-inch
MCA ... 3-4 89-91
RCA ... 3-4 84-89
LPs: 10/12-inch
MCA ... 5-8 90-91
RCA ... 5-8 84-89
Also see GRANT, Amy, & Vince Gill
Also see PURE PRAIRIE LEAGUE
Also see TOMORROW'S WORLD

GILLAN, Ian — LP '80
(Gillan)
Singles: 7-inch
OYSTER ... 3-5 76
LPs: 10/12-inch
ISLAND ... 5-10 77-78
OYSTER ... 8-10 76
VIRGIN ... 5-10 80
Also see DEEP PURPLE

GILLEN, Jack
Singles: 7-inch
ABCO ... 4-8 66

GILLESPIE, Dana
Singles: 7-inch
JERDEN ... 4-8 66
LPs: 10/12-inch
LONDON ... 10-12 68

GILLESPIE, Darlene
Singles: 7-inch
CORAL ... 5-10 59

LPs: 10/12-inch
DISNEYLAND (3010 "Darlene of the Teens") 40-50 57
DISNEYLAND/MICKEY MOUSE (32 "Songs from *Sleeping Beauty*") 25-35 59
Also see MOUSEKETEERS

GILLESPIE, Dizzy P&R '45
(With His All Star Quintet)
Singles: 78 rpm
ATLANTIC 5-10 52-53
CONTEMPORARY 5-10 53
GUILD 5-10 45
NORGRAN 5-10 54-56
PRESTIGE 5-10 51
RCA 5-10 48-52
Singles: 7-inch
ATLANTIC 10-20 52-53
CONTEMPORARY 10-20 53
LIMELIGHT 4-8 65-67
NORGRAN 10-20 54-56
PERCEPTION 4-8 69
PHILIPS 4-6 64
SOLID STATE 3-6 69
VERVE 5-10 57-62
EPs: 7-inch
ATLANTIC (514/521 "Dizzy Gillespie") 25-50 52
CLEF (153 "Dizzy with Strings") 25-50 53
CLEF (291/292/293/294 "Roy and Diz") 20-40 55
(Price is for any volume.)
DEE GEE (4000/4003/4004 "Dizzy Gillespie") 40-60 51
(Price is for any volume.)
DISCOVERY (13 "Dizzy Plays") 25-50 50
GNP (1/2/3 "Dizzy Gillespie") 25-50 50
(Price is for any volume.)
NORGRAN (114/115 "Big Band") ...25-50 55
(Price is for either volume.)
RCA (432 "Dizzier and Dizzier") 20-40 54
LPs: 10/12-inch
ALLEGRO (3017 "Dizzy Gillespie Plays") 50-100 52
(10-inch LP.)
ALLEGRO (3083 "Dizzy Gillespie") 50-100 52
(10-inch LP.)
ALLEGRO (4023 "Dizzy Gillespie") 50-100 53
(10-inch LP.)
AMERICAN RECORDING SOCIETY (405 "Jazz Creations") 75-125 55
AMERICAN RECORDING SOCIETY (423 "Big Band Jazz") 75-125 55
ATLANTIC (138 "Dizzy Gillespie") 200-300 52
(10-inch LP.)
ATLANTIC (142 "Dizzy Gillespie, Vol. 2") 200-300 52
ATLANTIC (1257 "Dizzy at Home and Abroad") 75-100 57
(Black label, silver print.)
BARONET (105 "A Handful of Modern Jazz") 20-40 61
BLUE NOTE (5017 "Horn of Plenty") 150-200 52
(10-inch LP.)
CLEF (136 "Dizzy with Strings") 125-150 53
(10-inch LP.)
CLEF (641 "Roy & Diz") 75-100 55
(With Roy Eldridge.)
CLEF (671 "Roy & Diz, Vol. 2") 75-100 55
CLEF (730 "Trumpet Kings") 75-100 56
CLEF (731 "Trumpet Battle") 75-100 56
CONTEMPORARY (2504 "Dizzy in Paris") 100-150 53
(10-inch LP.)
DEE GEE (1000 "Dizzy Gillespie") 200-250 51
(10-inch LP.)
DIAL (212 "Modern Trumpets") 75-125 52
(10-inch LP.)
DISCOVERY (3013 "Dizzy Plays") 150-200 50
(10-inch LP.)
GNP (4 "Dizzy Gillespie") 100-200 50
(10-inch LP.)
GNP (23 "Dizzy Gillespie") 50-75 57
IMPULSE 10-20 67
LIMELIGHT 15-25 64-67
MERCURY 15-25 66
NORGRAN (1003 "Afro Dizzy") 75-100 54
NORGRAN (1023 "Big Band") 75-100 55
NORGRAN (1083 "Jazz Recital") 75-100 56
NORGRAN (1084 "World Statesman") 75-100 56
NORGRAN (1090 "Big Band") 60-80 56
PHILIPS 20-30 62-65
RCA (530 "Dizzy Gillespie") 15-25 66
RCA (1009 "Dizzier and Dizzier") 50-75 54
RCA (2398 "The Greatest") 30-50 61
REGENT (6043 "School Days") 50-75 57
RON-LETTE (11 "Dizzy Gillespie") 25-50 58
ROOST (106 "Diz and Bird") 75-100 59
(Boxed, two-disc set.)
ROOST (414 "Dizzy Over Paris") 150-200 53
ROOST (2214 "Concert in Paris") 50-75 57
ROOST (2234 "Diz and Bird in Concert") 50-75 59
SAVOY (12000 series) 25-50 55-57
SOLID STATE 10-20 68-69
TRIBUTE 10-15 69
VSP 15-25 66
VERVE (6047 "Have Trumpet, Will Excite") 50-75 59
(Stereo.)
VERVE (6068 "Ebullient") 50-75 59
(Stereo.)
VERVE (6117 "Greatest Trumpet") 50-75 60
(Stereo.)
VERVE (8000 series) 15-30 62-67
(With "MGM Records - a Division of Metro-Goldwyn-Mayer, Inc." at bottom of label.)
VERVE (8015 "Jazz from Paris") ...50-75 57
(Reads "Verve Records, Inc." at bottom of label.)
VERVE (8017 "Dizzy in Greece") ...50-75 57
(Reads "Verve Records, Inc." at bottom of label.)
VERVE (8109 "Trumpet Kings") 50-75 57
(Reads "Verve Records, Inc." at bottom of label.)
VERVE (8110 "Trumpet Battle") 50-75 57
(Reads "Verve Records, Inc." at bottom of label.)
VERVE (8173 "Jazz Recital") 50-75 57
(Reads "Verve Records, Inc." at bottom of label.)
VERVE (8174 "World Statesman") .50-75 57
(Reads "Verve Records, Inc." at bottom of label.)
VERVE (8178 "Big Band") 50-75 57
(Reads "Verve Records, Inc." at bottom of label.)
VERVE (8191 "Afro Dizzy") 50-75 57
(Reads "Verve Records, Inc." at bottom of label.)
VERVE (8198 "For Musicians Only") 50-75 58
(Reads "Verve Records, Inc." at bottom of label.)
VERVE (8208 "Mantecia") 50-75 58
(Reads "Verve Records, Inc." at bottom of label.)
VERVE (8214 "Dizzy & Stuff") 40-60 58
(Reads "Verve Records, Inc." at bottom of label.)
VERVE (8260 "Duets") 50-75 58
(Reads "Verve Records, Inc." at bottom of label.)
VERVE (8262 "Sunny Side Up") 50-75 58
(Reads "Verve Records, Inc." at bottom of label.)
VERVE (8313 "Have Trumpet, Will Excite") 50-75 59
(Monaural. Reads "Verve Records, Inc." at bottom of label.)
VERVE (8328 "Ebullient") 50-75 59
(Monaural. Reads "Verve Records, Inc." at bottom of label.)
VERVE (8352 "Greatest Trumpet") 50-75 60
(Monaural. Reads "Verve Records, Inc." at bottom of label.)
VERVE (8386 "Portrait") 50-75 60
(Monaural. Reads "Verve Records, Inc." at bottom of label.)
VERVE (8394 "Gillespiana") 50-75 61
(Monaural. Reads "Verve Records, Inc." at bottom of label.)
VERVE (68386 "Portrait") 50-75 60
(Stereo. Reads "Verve Records, Inc." at bottom of label.)
VERVE (68394 "Gillespiana") 50-75 61
(Stereo. Reads "Verve Records, Inc." at bottom of label.)

GILLESPIE, Dizzy, & Slim Gaillard
LPs: 10/12-inch
ULTRAPHONIC (50273 "Gaillard & Gillespie") 30-50 58
Also see GAILLARD, Slim

GILLESPIE, Dizzy, & Stan Getz
EPs: 7-inch
NORGRAN (3/4 "Dizzy Gillespie & Stan Getz Sextet") 40-60 53
(Price is for either volume.)
NORGRAN (32 "Dizzy Gillespie & Stan Getz Sextet [Vol. 2]") 40-60 53
LPs: 10/12-inch
NORGRAN (2 "Dizzy Gillespie & Stan Getz Sextet") 150-250 53
(10-inch LP.)
NORGRAN (18 "Dizzy Gillespie & Stan Getz Sextet [Vol. 2]") 150-250 53
NORGRAN (1050 "Dizzy Gillespie & Stan Getz Sextet") 75-125 56
VERVE (8141 "Dizzy Gillespie & Stan Getz Sextet") 50-75 57
VERVE (68141 "Diz & Getz") 15-25 66
Also see GETZ, Stan
Also see GILLESPIE, Dizzy

GILLESPIE, Gary
Singles: 7-inch
DELTA (520 "Honest I Do") 15-25 62

GILLESPIE, Wesley
Singles: 7-inch
ROME 3-5 77

GILLETTE, Bill, & Collegians
Singles: 7-inch
CAPA 5-10

GILLETTE, Gin
Singles: 7-inch
MUSIKON (102 "Train to Satanville") 5-10

GILLETTE, Guy & Pipp
Singles: 7-inch
BIG DADDY (55 "No Butts, No Maybes") 10-15 82

GILLETTE, Ray, & Elegants
Singles: 7-inch
ELEGANTS 4-8 64

GILLETTE, Steve, & Jennifer Warnes C&W '80
Singles: 7-inch
REGENCY 3-5 80
LPs: 10/12-inch
REGENCY 5-10 80

GILLETTES
Singles: 7-inch
J&S 10-15 64

GILLEY, Mickey C&W '68
(With the Urban Cowboy Band)
Singles: 7-inch
ACT 1 .... 4-8 66
ASYLUM 3-4 80
ASTRO (Except 100 series) 3-5 71-73
ASTRO (100 series) 10-20 63-65
DARYL 4-8 63
DOT (15706 "Call Me Shorty") 50-75 58
EPIC 3-4 78-86
ERIC 4-6 64
GOLDBAND 4-8 64
GRT 3-5 70
KHOURY'S (712 "Drive-In Movie") 15-20 59
LYNN 10-20 60-61
MINOR (106 "Ooh Wee") 60-80 57
PAULA (Except 400 series) 6-12 66-68
PAULA (400 series) 3-5 74-84
PLAYBOY 3-5 74-77
POTOMAC 10-15 60
PRINCESS 8-12 62
RESCO 3-5 74
REX (1007 "Grapevine") 20-25 58
SABRA 10-15 61
SAN 10-15 63
SUPREME 8-12 62
TCF HALL 4-8 65
LPs: 10/12-inch
ASTRO (Except 101) 8-10 73-78
ASTRO (101 "Lonely Wine") 75-150 64
EPIC 5-10 79-86
51 WEST 5-10 79
PAULA (Except 2000 series) 5-10 81
PAULA (2195 "Down the Line") 20-25 67
PAULA (2224 "Mickey Gilley at His Best") 10-12 74
PAULA (2234 "Mickey Gilley") 8-10 78
PLAYBOY 8-12 74-78
Also see CHARLES, Ray, & Mickey Gilley
Also see HAGGARD, Merle / Mickey Gilley / Willie Knight

GILLEY, Mickey, & Barbi Benton C&W '75
Singles: 7-inch
PLAYBOY 3-5 75
Picture Sleeves
PLAYBOY 3-5 75
Also see BENTON, Barbi

GILLEY, Mickey, & Johnny Lee
Singles: 7-inch
EPIC 3-4 81
Also see LEE, Johnny
Also see NELSON, Willie / Johnny Lee / Mickey Gilley

GILLEY, Mickey, & Charly McClain C&W '84
(Charly McClain & Mickey Gilley)
Singles: 7-inch
EPIC 3-4 83-84
LPs: 10/12-inch
EPIC 5-8 84
Also see GILLEY, Mickey

GILLIAM, Earl
Singles: 7-inch
SARG 5-10

GILLIAM, Johnny
Singles: 7-inch
MODERN (1052 "Baby Take Me Back") 15-25 68
PAULA 3-5 74

GILLIAN ROW
LP: 10/12-inch
PRISM 15-25 66

GILLS, Don
Singles: 7-inch
ACCENT (1199 "Bad Bass Boogie") 10-20 66

GILLUM, Jazz
(William Gillum)
Singles: 78 rpm
BLUEBIRD 10-20 45-46
GROOVE 20-30 54
RCA 10-20 46-49
Singles: 7-inch
GROOVE (5002 "Key to the Highway") 30-50 54
RCA (0004 "Signifying Woman") .50-100 49
(Colored vinyl.)
RCA (0017 "Take One More Chance with Me") 50-100 49
(Colored vinyl.)
RCA (0035 "Gonna Be Some Shooting") 50-100 49
(Colored vinyl.)
Also see BROONZY, Bill
Also see SYKES, Roosevelt

GILMER, Jimmy P&R/R&B/LP '63
(With the Fireballs)
Singles: 7-inch
ABC 3-5 74
ATCO 5-10 68
DECCA 10-15 59
DOT 5-10 63-66
HAMILTON (55037 "It Won't Be Long") 10-15 63
WARWICK (547 "True Love Ways") 10-20 60
LPs: 10/12-inch
ATCO 10-15 68-69
CROWN 15-20 63
DOT (3512 "Torquay") 15-25 63
(Monaural.)
DOT (3545 "Sugar Shack") 15-25 63
(Monaural.)
DOT (3577 "Buddy's Buddy") 40-50 64
(Monaural.)
DOT (3643 "Lucky 'Leven") 15-25 63
(Monaural.)
DOT (3668 "Folkbeat") 15-25 63
(Monaural.)
DOT (3709 "Campusology") 15-25 63
(Monaural.)
DOT (25512 "Torquay") 20-30 63
(Stereo.)
DOT (25545 "Sugar Shack") 20-30 63
(Stereo.)
DOT (25577 "Buddy's Buddy") 75-100 64
(Stereo.)
DOT (25643 "Lucky 'Leven") 20-30 63
(Stereo.)
DOT (25668 "Folkbeat") 20-30 63
(Stereo.)
DOT (25709 "Campusology") 20-30 63
(Stereo.)
DOT (25856 "Firewater") 20-30 63
Also see FIREBALLS
Also see JIM & MONICA
Also see SEDAKA, Neil, & Tokens / Angels / Jimmy Gilmer and the Fireballs

GILMORE, Boyd
Singles: 78 rpm
MODERN 50-75 52
Singles: 7-inch
MODERN (860 "Ramblin' on My Mind") 100-200 52
MODERN (872 "All in My Dreams") 100-200 52

GILMORE, Boyd /Houston Boines / Charlie Booker
LPs: 10/12-inch
UNITED (7786 "Mississippi Blues") ..8-12
Also see BOINES, Houston
Also see BOOKER, Charlie
Also see GILMORE, Boyd

GILMORE, Dolly
Singles: 7-inch
DOVE (35467 "Sweet, Sweet Baby") 15-20

GILMORE, Geoff / Sheiks
Singles: 7-inch
JAMIE (1132 "Tres Chic") 5-10 59
Also see SHEIKS

GILMORE, Geoff & France
Singles: 7-inch
PATTERN 5-10
Also see GILMORE, Geoff / Sheiks

GILMORE, Jimmie Dale C&W '88
Singles: 7-inch
HIGHTONE 3-4 88-89

GILMOUR, David LP '78
Singles: 12-inch
COLUMBIA 4-6 84-86
Singles: 7-inch
COLUMBIA 3-4 84-86
Picture Sleeves
COLUMBIA 3-4 84
LPs: 10/12-inch
COLUMBIA 5-10 78-85
Also see PINK FLOYD

GILREATH, James P&R/R&B '63
(Jimmy Gilreath)
Singles: 7-inch
JOY (274 "Little Band of Gold") 10-20 63
JOY (278 "Lollipops, Lace and Lipstick") 20-30 63
JOY (286 "Blue Is My Color") 8-12 64
STATUE ("Little Band of Gold") ...75-125 63
(First issue. Approximately 300 made. Selection number not known.)
VEE-EIGHT ("Time Hasn't Helped") 75-125 62
(Selection number not known.)
Session: Johnny Mihalic.
Also see MAHALIC, Johnny

GILSON, Patti
Singles: 7-inch
GOLDEN WORLD (6 "Don't You Tell a Lie") 15-25 64

GILSTRAP, Jim P&R/R&B/LP '75
Singles: 7-inch
BELL 3-5 74
ROXBURY 3-5 75-76
LPs: 10/12-inch
ROXBURY 5-10 75-76

GIMICKS
Singles: 7-inch
ENSIGN (4028 "Naughty Rooster") 15-25 58

GIN & GENTS
Singles: 7-inch
ELDORADO (102 "Boy and Girl") ..10-15
MISS THING ("Dreams for Sale") ..20-30
(Selection number not known.)

GIN BLOSSOMS
Singles: 7-inch
A&M 3-4 93

GINA GO-GO P&R '89
Singles: 7-inch
CAPITOL 3-4 89

GINGER
(Sandra Glantz)
Singles: 7-inch
TITAN (1717 "Dry Tears") 25-50 61
Also see GINGER & SNAPS
Also see HONEYS
Also see USHER, Gary

GINGER ALE
Singles: 7-inch
WHITE WHALE 4-6 70

GINGER & CHIFFONS
Singles: 7-inch
GROOVE (0003 "She") 15-25 62

GINGER & JOHNNY
Singles: 7-inch
ARCADE 10-20 61-62

GINGER & SNAPS
Singles: 7-inch
MGM (13413 "Growing Up Is Hard to Do") 25-50 65
TORE (1008 "Love Me the Way I Love You") 50-75 61
Member: Ginger Blake.
Also see GINGER

GINGER VALLEY
Singles: 7-inch
INTERNATIONAL ARTIST (142 "Country Life") 15-25
(Colored vinyl.)

GINGERSNAPS
Singles: 7-inch
KAPP 10-15 58

GINGERSNAPS
Singles: 7-inch
JUPITER (305 "Remembering") 10-20 60s
WINDOW (1115 "Bald Headed Papa") 10-20 59

GINIE LYNN: see LYNN, Ginie

GINNY & GALLIONS
Singles: 7-inch
DOWNEY 5-10 63
LPs: 10/12-inch
DOWNEY (D-1003 "Two Sides") ...20-30 64
(Monaural.)
DOWNEY (DS-1003 "Two Sides") .25-40 64
(Stereo.)

GINO
Singles: 7-inch
FURY (1025 "Right from the Start") 15-25 59
GOLDEN CREST (581 "It's Only a Paper Moon") 25-35 63
PARNASO 10-20 63
Also see GINO & DELLS

GINO, Marty
Singles: 7-inch
AMY 4-8 62
R&M (616 "That Feelin' ") 15-25
TIME 5-10 59
WINK 4-8 61

GINO & BARONS
(With the Ramblers)
Singles: 7-inch
LARSEN (100 "Peggy") 100-200 59

GINO & DELLS
Singles: 7-inch
GOLDEN CREST (567 "Altar of Dreams") 250-350 62
GOLDEN CREST (576 "We'll Make It Someday") 25-35 62
Also see GINO

GINO & GINA P&R/R&B '58
Singles: 7-inch
BRUNSWICK 4-8 61
MERCURY 10-15 58
WARWICK 5-10 60
Members: "Gino" Giosasi; Irene Giosasi.

GINOS
Singles: 7-inch
CHALLENGE 4-8 62

GINSBURG, Arnie
EPs: 7-inch
VELVET VOICE ("Meet Arnie Ginsburg") 40-60 58
(WBOS radio/Mal's clothier promotional issue only. With the Three Ds.)
Also see JAN & ARNIE

GIORDANO, Lou
Singles: 7-inch
BRUNSWICK (55115 "Stay Close to Me") 500-600 59
(Maroon label.)
BRUNSWICK (55115 "Stay Close to Me") 250-400 59
(Yellow label. Promotional issue.)
Session: Buddy Holly (guitar).
Also see HOLLY, Buddy

GIORGIO: see MORODER, Giorgio

GIOVANNI, Nikki, & New York Community Choir LP '71
LPs: 10/12-inch
RIGHT-ON 4-8 71

GIPSON, Slick, & Sliders
(Byron "Slick" Gipson)
Singles: 78 rpm
SPECIALTY (566 "One I Love") 25-50 55
Singles: 7-inch
SPECIALTY (566 "One I Love") 50-75 55

GIPSON, Wild Child
(With Freddie Tieken & Rockers; with the Katz & Jammers)
Singles: 7-inch
ASTRA (1008 "Uncle John") 15-25 65
IT'S a HIT (2001 "Uncle John") 50-100 58
Note: the Katz & Jammers were actually Freddie Tieken & Rockers.
Also see TIEKEN, Freddie, & Rockers

GIPSY KINGS LP '88
LPs: 10/12-inch
MUSICIAN 5-8 88-89

GIPSY LOVE
LPs: 10/12-inch
MPS 8-10 72

GIRARD, Chuck
LPs: 10/12-inch
GOOD NEWS (Except 8110).......... 5-10 78-80
GOOD NEWS (8110 "Take a Hand") 15-20 79
(Picture disc.)
Also see CASTELLS
Also see DEVONS
Also see HONDELLS
Also see KNIGHTS
Also see LOVESONG
Also see REVELLS
Also see SURFARIS
Also see TIMERS

GIRL
LPs: 10/12-inch
JET 5-10 80-82

GIRLFRIENDS P&R '63
Singles: 7-inch
COLPIX 10-15 63-64
MELIC 5-10 63
PIONEER 10-15 60
Members: Carolyn Willis; Gloria Goodson; Nannette Jackson.
Also see HONEY CONE

GIRLS
Singles: 7-inch
CAPITOL 10-20 65
20TH FOX 10-15 66

GIRLS
Singles: 7-inch
SCEPTER 4-8 68

GIRLS CAN'T HELP IT D&D '83
LPs: 10/12-inch
SIRE 5-10 83-84

GIRLS FROM SYRACUSE
Singles: 7-inch
PALMER (5001 "You Could Have Had Me All Along") 20-30

GIRLS NEXT DOOR C&W '86
Singles: 7-inch
ATLANTIC 3-4 89-90
MTM 3-4 86-88

GIRLS TAKE OVER
Singles: 7-inch
PENTAGON 10-20 69

GIRLS THREE
Singles: 7-inch
CHESS 4-8 66

GIRLS TOGETHER OUTRAGEOUSLY: see G.T.O.

GIRLSCHOOL LP '82
Singles: 7-inch
MERCURY 3-4 82
LPs: 10/12-inch
MERCURY 5-10 82
STIFF AMERICA 5-10 82

GIRLTALK D&D '84
Singles: 7-inch
GEFFEN 3-4 84

GIST, Bruce
Singles: 7-inch
CONQUEST (1001 "Tarantula").....15-25 59

GITTINS, Louis
Singles: 7-inch
KAT (100 "My Hot Mama")............50-75 58

GIUFFRIA P&R/LP '84
Singles: 12-inch
MCA 4-8 84
(Promotional only.)
Singles: 7-inch
MCA 3-4 84-85
MCA/CAMEL 3-4 85-86
Picture Sleeves
MCA 3-4 84-85
LPs: 10/12-inch
MCA 5-10 84-85
MCA/CAMEL 5-10 85-86
Members: Gregg Giuffria; David Glen Eisley; Craig Goldy; Chuck Wright; Lanny Cordola; David Sikes; Alan Krigger.
Also see ANGEL
Also see HEAR 'N AID
Also see HOUSE of LORDS

GIVENS FAMILY R&B '85
Singles: 7-inch
PJ 3-4 86
SUGAR HILL 3-4 85

GLACIERS
LPs: 10/12-inch
MERCURY 15-25 64

GLAD
Singles: 7-inch
ABC 5-10 68
EQUINOX 10-15 67-68
LPs: 10/12-inch
ABC (655 "Feelin' Glad") 15-25 69
Members: Timothy Schmidt; Tom Phillips; George Hullin; Ron Flogel.
Also see POCO
Also see REDWING

GLAD, Julian
Singles: 7-inch
SMASH 4-8 62

GLAD RAGS
Singles: 78 rpm
EXCELLO (2121 "My China Doll")..25-35 57
Singles: 7-inch
EXCELLO (2121 "My China Doll")..25-35 57
O-GEE 5-10 62

GLAD-A-BOUTS Featuring Henri Aubin
Singles: 7-inch
HURRICANE (102 "If You Love Me") 50-75 59

GLADIATORS
(With the Johnny Otis Orchestra)
Singles: 78 rpm
DIG (135 "Girl of My Heart") 100-200 57
Singles: 7-inch
DIG (135 "Girl of My Heart") 250-350 57
Also see OTIS, Johnny

GLADIATORS
Singles: 7-inch
DONNIE (701 "I Need You") 250-350 58
(At least one source pegs this as a mid-'60s release, with a value of $15 to $25 to garage band collectors for the flip, *Turning to Stone.*)

GLADIATORS
Singles: 7-inch
BRITISH LION (525 "I'm Gonna Cry") 15-25

GLADIATORS
LPs: 10/12-inch
NIGHT HAWK 5-10 82

GLADIOLAS P&R/R&B '57
Singles: 78 rpm
EXCELLO 15-25 57
Singles: 7-inch
EXCELLO (2101 "Little Darlin'") 25-50 57
EXCELLO (2110 "Run, Run Little Joe") 25-50 57
EXCELLO (2120 "I Wanta Know") 25-50 57
EXCELLO (2136 "Say You'll Be Mine") 20-40 58
Members: Maurice Williams; Norman Wade; Bill Massey; Willie Jones; Earl Gainey; Bobby Robinson.
Also see WILLIAMS, Maurice, & Zodiacs

GLADNESS, Marie
Singles: 7-inch
ABNER (7004 "I'm Anxious") 20-30 62
BRAND-X 15-25 60s

GLADSTAR, Gabriel: see GABRIEL GLADSTAR

GLADSTONE P&R '72
Singles: 7-inch
ABC 3-5 72
LPs: 10/12-inch
ABC 8-10 72-73
Members: H.L. Voelker; Michael Rabon; Doug Rhone.
Also see RABON, Michael

GLAHE, Will, & His Orchestra P&R '39
Singles: 78 rpm
LONDON 3-5 55-57
RCA 3-5 48
VICTOR 3-5 39-40
Singles: 7-inch
LONDON 4-8 55-60
LPs: 10/12-inch
LONDON 10-15 55-60

GLAS MANAGERIE
Singles: 7-inch
ROMAIN (1009 "Natasha")............15-25 66

GLASCO, Dee
Singles: 7-inch
RSVP 4-8 62

GLASER, Chuck C&W '74
Singles: 7-inch
MGM 3-5 74
Also see EARWOOD, Mundo
Also see TOMPALL & GLASER BROS.

GLASER, Jim C&W '68
(Jim Glaser Singers)
Singles: 7-inch
MCA 3-5 76-86
MGM 3-5 73-75
NOBLE VISION 3-4 82-84
RCA 4-6 68-69
LPs: 10/12-inch
MCA 5-8 86
NOBEL VISION 5-8 84
STARDAY (149 "Old Time Christmas Singing") 50-75 60
STARDAY (158 "Just Looking for a Home") 40-60 61
WYNCOTE (9069 "Country Spectacular") 10-20 64
Also see EARWOOD, Mundo
Also see NEOPHONIC STRING BAND
Also see TOMPALL & GLASER BROS.

GLASER, Ken
Singles
AZRA (101 "Vicious Circles") 35-50 84
(Nine square picture disc set.)
AZRA (101 "Vicious Circles") 4-6 84
(Any of the individual discs.)

GLASER, Tompall C&W '73
(With His Outlaw Band)
Singles: 7-inch
ABC 3-5 77-78
MGM 3-5 73-75
POLYDOR 3-5 76
LPs: 10/12-inch
ABC 8-10 77
MGM 8-12 73-76
U.A. 25-35 66
Also see EARWOOD, Mundo
Also see TOMPALL & GLASER BROS.

GLASS, Charles
Singles: 7-inch
MAGNET 35-40

GLASS, Dawn
Singles: 7-inch
ABC-PAR 6-12 64

GLASS, Dick
Singles: 7-inch
RCA 4-8 66
WINGATE 10-15 65

GLASS, Dick, & Rick Derringer & McCoys
LP: 10/12-inch
L.A. INT'L (58005 "Glass Derringer") 10-15 76
Also see GLASS, Dick
Also see DERRINGER, Rick

GLASS, Philip LP '82
LPs: 10/12-inch
ANTILLES 8-12 83
CBS 5-20 82-86
(Prices at the high end of range are multi-disc sets.)
VIRGIN 5-10 77
Session: Laurie Anderson; Linda Ronstadt; Suzanne Vega; David Byrne; Paul Simon.
Also see ANDERSON, Laurie
Also see BYRNE, David
Also see RONSTADT, Linda
Also see SIMON, Paul
Also see VEGA, Suzanne

GLASS BOTTLE P&R '71
Singles: 7-inch
AVCO 3-5 71
AVCO EMBASSY 3-5 70
LPs: 10/12-inch
AVCO 8-12 71
Member: Gary Criss.

GLASS CANDLE
Singles: 7-inch
TARGET (1004 "Light the Glass Candle") 20-30 69

GLASS FAMILY R&B '78
Singles: 7-inch
SIDEWALK (920 "Teenage Rebellion") 10-20 67
W.B. (309 "Guess I'll Let You Go") 10-15 69
(Promotional issue only.)
W.B. (7262 "Guess I'll Let You Go") 5-10 69
LPs: 10/12-inch
W.B. (1776 "Electric Band")..........15-25 69
Members: Ralph Parrett; Gary Green.

GLASS FAMILY
Singles: 7-inch
JDC 3-5 78
LPs: 10/12-inch
JDC 5-10 78

GLASS HARP LP '71
Singles: 7-inch
DECCA 4-8 71-72
UNITED AUDIO 8-12
LPs: 10/12-inch
DECCA 10-20 71-72
MCA 5-10
Members: Phil Keaggy; Dan Pecchio; John Ferra.
Also see KEAGGY, Phil

GLASS HOUSE P&R/R&B '69
Singles: 7-inch
INVICTUS 3-6 69-72
LPs: 10/12-inch
INVICTUS 8-10 71-72
KIRSHNER 8-10 71
Members: Scherrie Payne; Ty Hunter; Larry Mitchell; Pearl Jones; Eric Dunham.
Also see HUNTER, Ty
Also see PAYNE, Scherrie

GLASS MANAGERIE
Singles: 7-inch
REVOLVO 4-6

GLASS MOON LP '80
Singles: 7-inch
RADIO 3-4 82
LPs: 10/12-inch
RADIO 5-10 80-82

GLASS OPENING
Singles: 7-inch
DONDEE 20-25 60s
NEW WORLD (101 "My Heart Is Heavy") 25-35 60s
Also see GLASS OPENING / MAJOR SIX

GLASS PRISM
LPs: 10/12-inch
RCA 10-12 69-70

GLASS SUN
Singles: 7-inch
SOUND PATTERNS (139 "Silence of the Morning") 40-50
SOUND PATTERNS (150 "Stuck Over You") 40-50

GLASS TIGER P&R/LP '86
Singles: 12-inch
MANHATTAN 4-6 86
Singles: 7-inch
EMI/MANHATTAN 3-4 88
MANHATTAN 3-4 86-87
Picture Sleeves
EMI/MANHATTAN 3-4 88
MANHATTAN 3-4 86-87
LPs: 10/12-inch
EMI/MANHATTAN 5-8 88
MANHATTAN 5-10 86

GLASS WALL
Singles: 7-inch
FRATERNITY 3-4 70

GLASSER, Dick
Singles: 7-inch
ARGO 8-12 58
COLUMBIA (Except 41472) 5-10 60
COLUMBIA (41472 "Crazy Alligator") 20-25 59
RCA 5-10 56

GLAZER, Tom P&R/LP '63
(With the Children's Do-Re-Mi Chorus; with Dotty Evans & Robin Morgan)
Singles: 78 rpm
COLUMBIA 5-10 53-55
CORAL 5-10 56
Singles: 7-inch
COLUMBIA 5-10 53-55
CORAL 5-10 56
KAPP 4-8 63-64
U.A. 4-8 66-67
Picture Sleeves
KAPP 5-10 63
LPs: 10/12-inch
CAMDEN 5-10 64-65
KAPP 10-20 63-64
COLUMBIA 20-30 55
HARMONY 10-20 59
MERCURY 15-25 55
MOTIVATION 5-10 62
RIVERSIDE 10-20 61
U.A. 10-20 66
WASHINGTON 10-20 59
WONDERLAND 10-20 63

GLASSCOCK, Joanne
LPs: 10/12-inch
A&M 8-10 74

GLEAMS
(Four Gleams)
Singles: 7-inch
J-V (101 "Bad Boy") 150-250 60
KAPP (565 "Mr. Magic Moon") 20-30 63
KIP (236 "You Broke My Heart") 20-30 61
RIBBON (6902 "Put That Tear Back") 50-100 59

GLEASON, Jackie P&R '53
(Jackie Gleason's Orchestra)
Singles: 78 rpm
CAPITOL 3-5 52-57
DECCA (27000 series) 3-5 51
Singles: 7-inch
CAPITOL 5-10 52-62
DECCA (27000 series) 4-8 51
EPs: 7-inch
CAPITOL (Except 511) 5-15 53-60
CAPITOL (511 "And Awa-a-ay We Go") 50-75 54
(Double EP set.)
CAPITOL (511 "And Awa-a-ay We Go") 75-100 54
(With "EBF" prefix. Boxed, two-disc set.)
LPs: 10/12-inch
CAPITOL (Except 511) 5-15 53-69
CAPITOL (511 "And Awa-a-y We Go") 75-100 54
(10-inch LP. Has songs by Jackie, sung in character by: Joe the Bartender; The Loud Mouth; Ralph Kramden; Fenwick Babbitt; Reggie Van Gleason III, & the Poor Soul.)
Also see MARTIN, Dean / Jackie Gleason

GLEAVES, Cliff
Singles: 7-inch
DORE 5-10 62
LIBERTY (55263 "Long Black Hearse") 10-15 60
PARK AVE. 5-10 62
SUMMER (501 "Love Is My Business") 35-50 58
Picture Sleeves
SUMMER (501 "Love Is My Business") 50-100 58
(Sleeve has die-cut hole in center to display label.)

GLEEMS
Singles: 7-inch
PARKWAY 15-20 63

GLEEPERS
Singles: 7-inch
DACO (101 "You're Nice to Hold") 30-60

GLENCOVES P&R '63
Singles: 7-inch
SELECT 5-8 63-64

GLENDON, Chris
Singles: 7-inch
GRC (1016 "My Fellow Americans") .. 4-6 73

GLENDOWN, Cerf
Singles: 7-inch
PIONEER 4-8

GLENN, Darrell C&W/P&R '53
Singles: 78 rpm
DOT 4-8 56
RCA 4-8 54
VALLEY 4-8 53
Singles: 7-inch
ARLEN 8-10 60s
COLUMBIA 4-6 66-67
DOT 10-20 56
FASHION 5-10 60
LONGHORN 4-8 65
NRC 10-15 58
POMPEII 3-6 68-69
RCA 10-20 54
ROBBIE 4-6 64
TWINKLE (505 "That's Right") 30-50 58
VALLEY 10-20 53
Picture Sleeves
LONGHORN (546 "The Ways of the World") 8-10 65
LPs: 10/12-inch
NRC (5 "Crying in the Chapel") 20-35 59

GLENN, Garry R&B '87
Singles: 7-inch
(With Soul Set)
Singles: 7-inch
CO & CE 5-8 60s
MOTOWN 3-4 87
PPL 3-4

GLENN, Garry, & Jeweltones
Singles: 7-inch
COVE (284-12 "I Want to Do It") 25-50
STONE ("I Want to Do It") 15-25
(Selection number not known.)

GLENN, Glen
Singles: 7-inch
DORE (523 "Goofin' Around") 8-12 59
ERA (1061 "Everybody's Movin'") 40-50 57
ERA (1074 "One Cup of Coffee") 30-40 58
ERA (1086 "Blue Jeans and a Boy's Shirt") 15-25 59

GLENN, Howdy C&W '77
Singles: 7-inch
W.B. 3-5 77-78

GLENN, Jerry
Singles: 7-inch
CHECKER (949 "Just Take Me Like I Am") 10-15 60

GLENN, Lloyd R&B '50
Singles: 78 rpm
ALADDIN 5-10 56-57
HOLLYWOOD 5-10 54
SWING TIME 5-15 52-54
Singles: 7-inch
ALADDIN 8-12 56-59
HOLLYWOOD 10-15 54
IMPERIAL 4-8 62
SWING TIME 20-30 52-54
LPs: 10/12-inch
ALADDIN (808 "Chica-Boo") 100-150 56
(Black vinyl.)
ALADDIN (808 "Chica-Boo") 250-500 56
(Red vinyl.)
BLACK & BLUE 8-10 77
IMPERIAL (9174 "Chica-Boo") 30-50 62
(Monaural.)
IMPERIAL (12174 "Chica-Boo") 30-50 62
(Stereo.)
SCORE (4006 "Piano Stylings") .100-150 56
SCORE (4020 "After Hours") 100-150 57
SWING TIME (1901 "Lloyd Glenn") 100-200 54
(10-inch LP.)
Also see BROWN, Charles / Lloyd Glenn
Also see FULSON, Lowell
Also see MILLER, Red, Trio
Also see WALKER, T-Bone

GLENNEL & JONELL
Singles: 7-inch
DOT 5-10 57

GLENNS
Singles: 7-inch
HERMITAGE (777 "Flip-End") 10-20 61
RENDEZVOUS 5-10 60

GLENRAYS
Singles: 7-inch
GAITY (111 "Easy Rhythm") 25-35 60
PERRY (601 "When You're Smiling") 25-35 60

GLENS
(With Bill Perry)
Singles: 7-inch
LAITINI (6666 "Cherrish My Love") 100-200 60
RO-NAN (1002 "Image of Love") 100-200
SUDDEN ("Cherrish My Love") 20-40 61
(Selection number not known.)

GLENTELLS
Singles: 7-inch
S&R (302 "Uprisin'") 10-20 62

GLENWOODS
Singles: 7-inch
JUBILEE (5402 "Elaine")................20-30 60

GLIDE SOUND
Singles: 7-inch
W.B. 4-8 67

GLIDERS
Singles: 7-inch
SOUTHERN SOUND (103 "School Days")..............................500-1000 62

GLIDERS / Uniques
Singles: 7-inch
STOOP SOUNDS (501 "School Days"/"Silvery Moon") 100-150 96
(Limited edition. Estimates range from less than 10 to a few dozen made.)
Also see GLIDERS
Also see UNIQUES

GLIDFER
LPs: 10/12-inch
U.A. 8-10 77

GLIEDEN, Mike
(With the R.K.s; with Rhythm Kings; Mike Gliden Trio)
Singles: 7-inch
BANGAR 10-20 60s
LITTLE CROW 8-12 60s
SOMA (1188 "The Bash")................10-20 63
LPs:10/12-inch
TRIPLE CROWN............................ 5-10 74
Also see ONLY ONES

GLITTER, Gary P&R/LP '72
(With the Glitter Band)
Singles: 7-inch
ARISTA 3-5 75
BELL 3-5 72-74
LPs: 10/12-inch
BELL 8-10 72
EPIC... 6-10 81
Also see GLITTER BAND

GLITTER BAND P&R/R&B '76
Singles: 7-inch
ARISTA 3-5 75-76
LPs: 10/12-inch
ARISTA 8-10 76
Member: Pete Gill.
Also see GLITTER, Gary
Also see MOTORHEAD

GLITTERHOUSE
Singles: 7-inch
DYNOVOICE 5-10 68
LPs: 10/12-inch
DYNOVOICE (31905 "Color Blind")....................................15-20 68

GLITTERS
Singles: 7-inch
JENERO (104 "Fireball")................10-20 63

GLITTERS
Singles: 7-inch
BIG C 5-10
POWER..................................... 5-10

GLITTERS
Singles: 7-inch
RUBÁIYÁT (413 "You Don't Know") 50-75

GLITTERS
Singles: 7-inch
J&S (1391 "Same Identical Thing")......................................15-20

GLITTERS / Al Freed
Singles: 7-inch
YOU (6 "Sherry") 8-12 62

GLOBE TROTTERS
Singles: 78 rpm
KING 8-12 53
Singles: 7-inch
KING (1188 "Darktown Strutter's Ball")......................................10-20 53
KING (1210 "My Gal Sal")..............10-20 53

GLOBELITERS
Singles: 7-inch
GUYDEN (2119 "Turn It On").........10-20 64
PHILTOWN (40003 "The Way You Do")..5-10 66
VAN DYK (601 "I Know") 400-800 60

GLOBETROTTERS
Singles: 7-inch
KIRSHNER (5006 "Gravy")........... 5-10 70
KIRSHNER (5008 "Rainy Day Bells") 8-12 70
KIRSHNER (5012 "Duke of Earl") ... 5-10 71
KIRSHNER (5016 "ESP") 5-10 71
Picture Sleeves
KIRSHNER..................................10-15 70
LPs: 10/12-inch
KIRSHNER..................................10-20 70

GLOBETROTTERS / Robert John
Singles: 7-inch
RIPETE (15673 "Rainy Day Bells") ... 3-5
Also see GLOBTROTTERS
Also see JOHN, Robert

GLORIES P&R/R&B '67
Singles: 7-inch
DATE (1553 "I Stand Accused")...... 5-10 67
DATE (1559 "Sing Me a Love Song")......................................10-20 67
DATE (1593 "Stand By")...............10-20 68
DATE (1615 "I Worship You Baby")......................................20-40 67
DATE (1622 "No News") 10-20 67
Members: Yvonne Gearing; Betty Stokes; Mildred Vaney.
Also see QUIET ELEGANCE

GLORIEUX, Francois
LPs: 10/12-inch
VANGUARD 6-12 78

GLORY
LPs: 10/12-inch
TEXAS REVOLUTION (69 "Meat Music")......................................75-125 69
Member: Linden Hudson.

GLORY
LPs: 10/12-inch
AVALANCHE (148 "Glory")............10-15 73

GLORYTONES
Singles: 78 rpm
EPIC...20-30 57
Singles: 7-inch
EPIC (9243 "You Only Came Back to Hurt Me")......................................20-30 57

GLOVER, Clarence
Singles: 7-inch
LYNDELL (797 "Keep Your Promise") 5-10

GLOVER, Clay, Combo
Singles: 7-inch
BROWNFIELD (17 "Drivin' On Ice")......................................10-20 63

GLOVER, Helen
Singles: 7-inch
NELBER (105 "Just Like That")......10-20 60s

GLOVER, Henry
Singles: 78 rpm
KING 4-6 53
Singles: 7-inch
KING 5-10 53
EPs: 7-inch
KING (278 "Soft")........................40-50 54
Also see DAVIS, Eddie "Lockjaw"

GLOVER, Linda
Singles: 7-inch
WARWICK 5-10 60

GLOVER, Roger LP '76
Singles: 7-inch
21 .... 3-4 84
UK 8-10 75
LPs: 10/12-inch
POLYDOR...................................5-10 78
21 ....5-10 84
U.K. 8-10 75
Also see DEEP PURPLE
Also see RAINBOW

GLOWTONES
Singles: 7-inch
EASTWEST (101 "Girl I Love").....20-30 57

GLYNN, Richard
Singles: 7-inch
DOT 5-10 59

GO BETWEENS
Singles: 7-inch
CHEER (1011 "Have You for My Own")......................................10-15 65

GO BETWEENS
Singles: 7-inch
ROUGH TRADE 4-8
LPs: 10/12-inch
BIG TIME 5-10 87
Members: Robert Vickers; Lindy Morrison; Amanda Brown; Grant McLennan; Robert Foster.

GO BOYS
Singles: 7-inch
DC (0418 "Ramble")....................10-15 59

GO TO BLAZES
Singles: 7-inch
DIESEL ONLY (8442 "Why I Drink") . 3-5 92
(Blue vinyl.)

GO TOGETHERS: see GO-TOGETHERS

GO WEST P&R/R&B/D&D/LP '85
Singles: 12-inch
CHRYSALIS 4-6 85
Singles: 7-inch
CHRYSALIS 3-4 85-87
Picture Sleeves
CHRYSALIS 3-4 85-87
LPs: 10/12-inch
CHRYSALIS 5-10 85-87
Members: Peter Cox; Richard Drummie.

GO ZOO BAND
Singles: 7-inch
GO GO 5-8 66
LPs: 10/12-inch
GO GO 12-15 67

GOANNA P&R/LP '83
Singles: 7-inch
ATCO 3-4 83
Picture Sleeves
ATCO 3-4 83
LPs; 10/12-inch
ATCO 5-10 83

GOBBLEHOOF
Singles: 7-inch
NEW ALLIANCE............................ 3-4
EPs: 7-inch
NEW ALLIANCE 4-8
Members: Tim Aaron; Jens; J. Mascis; Charlie Nakajima.

GOBER, Capt. Hershel
(Major Hershel Gober)
Singles: 7-inch
BUDDAH (152 "Pictures of a Man") 8-12 60s
TEE PEE (33/34 "Pictures of a Man")......................................15-25 67

GO-CARTS
Singles: 7-inch
HOPE...5-10 61
ATCO 3-4 83
LPs: 10/12-inch
ATCO 5-10 83

GOD SQUAD
LPs: 10/12-inch
RARE EARTH 8-10 72

GODCHAUX, Keith & Donna: see KEITH & DONNA

GODDARD, Geoff
Singles: 7-inch
LAWN...4-8 64

GODDARD, Steve
Singles: 7-inch
CALIFORNIA SUN 3-5 75

GODDARD, Steve
Singles: 7-inch
CHATON 3-4 82
Picture Sleeves
CHATON 3-5 82
Also see BRANDMIER, Jonathan
Also see FANN BAND

GODER, Ron
Singles: 7-inch
POLYDOR...................................3-4 80
LPs: 10/12-inch
POLYDOR...................................5-10 80

GODFATHER
Singles: 7-inch
COLUMBIA..................................3-5 72

GODFATHERS LP '88
LPs: 10/12-inch
EPIC..5-8 88-89

GODFREY
Singles: 7-inch
CEE JAM (3 "Let's Take a Trip")....10-20 60s

GODFREY, Arthur P&R '47
Singles: 78 rpm
COLUMBIA..................................3-5 50-56
DECCA (29000 series)...................3-5 55
Singles: 7-inch
COLUMBIA..................................5-10 50-56
CONTEMPO.................................3-6 63-64
DECCA (29000 series)...................5-8 55
MGM 3-6 66
MTA 3-5 69
PILGRIM 4-8
SIGNATURE 4-8 60
VEE JAY 3-6 65
Picture Sleeves
MGM 5-10 66
EPs: 7-inch
COLUMBIA..................................8-15 52-56
LPs: 10/12-inch
ADMIRAL 8-12 67
CAMDEN.....................................8-12 66-67
CAPITOL.....................................8-15 62
COLUMBIA..................................10-20 53-61
CONTEMPO.................................8-15
HARMONY...................................10-15 59
RCA 5-10 73
SIGNATURE 8-15 60
Also see MARINERS

GODFREY, Arthur, with Archie Bleyer
EPs: 7-inch
CADENCE....................................10-20 54
LPs: 10/12-inch
CADENCE (540 "Christmas with Godfrey and the Little Godfreys") 30-40 54
(10-inch LP.)
Also see BLEYER, Archie

GODFREY, Arthur /Carmel Quinn / Frank Parker / Janette Davis
(With Will Rowland & His Orchestra)
EPs: 7-inch
COLUMBIA ("Arthur Godfrey & His Friends") 8-10 50s
(No selection number used.)
Also see GODFREY, Arthur
Also see QUINN, Carmel

GODFREY, John, Trio R&B '51
Singles: 78 rpm
CHESS.......................................5-10 51
HILLTOP 5-10 51

GODFREY, Lulu
Singles: 7-inch
FINCH (2002 "Stop Cheatin' on Me")..5-10

GODFREY, Ray C&W '60
Singles: 7-inch
ABC...4-8 67
COLUMBIA..................................4-8 67
J&J (001 "The Picture") 10-15 60
PEACH.......................................10-15 62
SAVOY.......................................5-10 62
SIMS 4-8 62-63
SPRING 4-6 70
TOLLIE 5-10 65
YONAH 5-10 61

GODLEY, Kevin, & Lol Creme P&R/D&D/LP '85
(Godley & Creme)
Singles: 12-inch
POLYDOR...................................4-8 85
Singles: 7-inch
MERCURY 3-5 77
MIRAGE 3-4 82
POLYDOR...................................3-4 85
Picture Sleeves
POLYDOR...................................3-4 85
LPs: 10/12-inch
MERCURY 10-15 77
MIRAGE 5-10 82
POLYDOR...................................5-10 85
Also see SCAFFOLD
Also see 10CC

GODMOMA
Singles: 7-inch
ELEKTRA....................................3-4 81
LPs: 10/12-inch
ELEKTRA....................................5-10 81

GOD'S GIFT TO WOMEN
Singles: 7-inch
A-1 4-8

GODS
LPs: 10/12-inch
IMPORT......................................8-10 77

GODSPELL P&R '72
(Robin Lamont & Original "Godspell" Cast)
Singles: 7-inch
BELL 3-5 72

GODWIN, Peter D&D '83
Singles: 12-inch
POLYDOR...................................4-6 83

GODZ
Singles: 7-inch
ESP 4-8 66-67
LPs: 10/12-inch
ESP 12-15 66

GODZ LP '78
Singles: 7-inch
MILLENIUM.................................3-5 78
LPs: 10/12-inch
CASABLANCA 5-10 78
MILLENIUM/CASABLANCA 5-10 78
Also see CAPITOL CITY ROCKETS

GOFFIN, Gerry
Singles: 7-inch
ADELPHI....................................3-5 73
LPs: 10/12-inch
ADELPHI....................................8-10 73

GOFFIN, Louise P&R/LP '79
Singles: 7-inch
ASYLUM 3-5 79
ELEKTRA....................................3-5 79
SIRE (22821 "Surrender")..............3-5
Picture Sleeves
SIRE (22821 "Surrender")..............4-6
LPs: 10/12-inch
ASYLUM 5-10 79-81

GOGGINS, Curby
Singles: 7-inch
CARNIVAL (510 "Leave Me if You Want To")...10-20

GOGGINS, Delma, & Yo-Yos
Singles: 7-inch
VIBRO 5-10 61

GOGGLES
Singles: 7-inch
AUDIO FIDELITY 3-5 71
LPs: 10/12-inch
AUDIO FIDELITY 8-12 71

GO-Gos
(Go-Go's)
Singles: 7-inch
RCA (8370 "Chicken of the Sea") ..10-20 64
RCA (8435 "Saturday's Hero") 10-20 64
LPs: 10/12-inch
RCA (LPM-2930 "Swim with the Go-Gos")......................................20-30 64
(Monaural.)
RCA (LSP-2930 "Swim with the Go-Gos")......................................25-35 64
(Stereo.)
Also see ISLEY BROTHERS / Go-Gos

GO-GOs P&R/LP '81
Singles: 12-inch 33/45
I.R.S. 4-8 82-84
Singles: 7-inch
I.R.S. (Except 8001) 3-5 81-85
I.R.S. (8001 "We Got the Beat") 4-8 82
(Picture disc.)
Picture Sleeves
I.R.S. 3-5 81-85
LPs: 10/12-inch
I.R.S. 5-10 81-90
Members: Belinda Carlisle; Charlotte Caffey; Jane Wiedlin; Margot Olaverria; Elissa Bello; Gina Schook; Kathy Valentine.
Also see CARLISLE, Belinda
Also see GRACES
Also see TEXTONES
Also see VENTURES
Also see WIEDLIN, Jane

GOINS, Herbie, & Nightriders
Singles: 7-inch
CAPITOL.....................................4-8 67

GOLD
LPs: 10/12-inch
A&M 8-10 74

GOLD
Singles: 7-inch
GOLDEN STATE...........................4-8
PARAMOUNT 4-8

GOLD, Andrew P&R/LP '76
Singles: 7-inch
ASYLUM 3-5 76-78
Picture Sleeves
ASYLUM 3-5 77-78
LPs: 10/12-inch
ASYLUM 5-10 75-80
Also see SIMPSONS
Also see WAX

GOLD, Angie D&D '85
Singles: 12-inch
PASSION 4-6 85

GOLD, Jack, Chorus
(Jack Gold Orchestra & Chorus)
Singles: 7-inch
ASCOT.......................................5-8 66
COLUMBIA..................................4-6 69

GOLD, Jim
Singles: 7-inch
JET EYE 3-5 86
TABU 3-5 79
LPs: 10/12-inch
TABU 8-10 77
Also see GALLERY

GOLD, Johnny
Singles: 7-inch
LIN (5020 "Because I Love You") 8-12 59

GOLD, Lynn
Singles: 7-inch
W.B. (1405 "Lynn Gold") 10-15 63

GOLD, Marty, & His Orchestra LP '63
Singles: 7-inch
KAPP 3-5 58-59
RCA 3-5 60-61
RCA/BLUEBIRD............................3-5
EPs: 7-inch
KAPP 4-8 59
VIK 5-10 56-57
LPs: 10/12-inch
KAPP 8-12 59
RCA 8-12 59-63
VIK 10-20 56-57

GOLD BUGS
Singles: 7-inch
CORAL (62453 "Stop the Wedding")......................................20-30 65
Also see FIVE SHARKS

GOLD COASTERS
Singles: 7-inch
BLUE RIVER................................5-8 64

GOLD NUGGETS
Singles: 7-inch
RHOMA (101 "Gold Dollar") 15-25 58

GOLD STARS
Singles: 7-inch
M.M.I. 10-15 58

GOLDBERG, Barry
Singles: 7-inch
BUDDAH.....................................4-6 68
TMP-TING...................................5-8
LPs: 10/12-inch
ATCO...8-10 74
BUDDAH.....................................10-12 68-71
EPIC 15-20 66
RECORD MAN..............................8-12 72
Also see KGB

GOLDBERG, Barry / Harvey Mandell / Charlie Musselwhite / Neil Merryweather
LPs: 10/12-inch
CHERRY RED (5104 "Blues from Chicago")......................................8-12
Also see MERRYWEATHER, Neil
Also see MUSSELWHITE, Charles

GOLDBERG - MILLER BLUES BAND
Singles: 7-inch
EPIC (Except 9865)......................5-10 65-66
EPIC (9865 "Mother Song") 15-20 65
(Colored vinyl. Promotional issue only.)
Picture Sleeves
EPIC (9865 "Mother Song") 10-15 65
Members: Barry Goldberg; Steve Miller.
Also see GOLDBERG, Barry
Also see MILLER, Steve

GOLDCOAST SINGERS
LPs:10/12-inch
WORLD-PACIFIC 20-25 60s

GOLDDIGGERS LP '69
Singles: 7-inch
METROMEDIA..............................3-5 69
RCA 3-5 72
LPs: 10/12-inch
METROMEDIA..............................8-12 69
RCA 5-10 71
Member: Jimmi Cannon.
Also see CANNON, Jimmi
Also see MARTIN, Dean

GOLDE, Frannie P&R '79
Singles: 7-inch
ATLANTIC...................................3-5 76-77
BIG TREE 3-5 76
PORTRAIT..................................3-5 79

LPs: 10/12-inch
ATLANTIC 8-10 76-79
PORTRAIT 5-10 79

GOLDEBRIARS
Singles: 7-inch
EPIC 4-8 64
LPs: 10/12-inch
EPIC 10-15 64
Members: Curt Boetcher; Dotti Holmberg; Cathi Holmberg; Ron Neilson.
Also see BOETCHER, Curt

GOLDEN, Annie: see LOVE, Darlene / Annie Golden

GOLDEN, Artie, & Mighty Trojans
Singles: 7-inch
DODGE 5-10

GOLDEN, Jeff C&W '88
Singles: 7-inch
MGA 3-4 88-89
SOUNDWAVES 3-4 89

GOLDEN, John
(With the Indexes; Johnny Golden)
Singles: 7-inch
DOUGLAS (101 "Take a Chance") 50-75 61
W.B. (5660 "Angel on Earth") 10-15 65

GOLDEN, Kaye
Singles: 7-inch
HI 5-10 58
TEMPWOOD 4-8 62

GOLDEN, Lee, & Trio Tres Bien
Singles: 7-inch
BALLAD 5-10 55

GOLDEN, Lotti
Singles: 7-inch
ATLANTIC 3-5 69
LPs: 10/12-inch
ATLANTIC 10-12 69
GRT 8-12

GOLDEN, Sandy
Singles: 7-inch
MASTERPIECE ("Your Love Is Everything") 20-30 60s

GOLDEN, William Lee C&W '86
Singles: 7-inch
MCA 3-4 86
Also see OAK RIDGE BOYS
Also see TOMORROW'S WORLD

GOLDEN BAND
Singles: 7-inch
DELUXE 5-10

GOLDEN BELLS
(With the Gems of Rhythm Band)
Singles: 7-inch
SURE (1002 "Pretty Girl") 500-750 59

GOLDEN BOYS
Singles: 7-inch
MAINSTREAM 10-20 65

GOLDEN CATALINAS: see CATALINAS

GOLDEN CRUSADERS
Singles: 7-inch
EPIC (9773 "Hey Good Lookin'") 10-20 60s

GOLDEN DAWN
LPs: 10/12-inch
INT'L ARTISTS (4 "Power Plant") 100-125 68
Members: George Kinney; Bob Rector; Tom Ramsey; Bill Hallman; Jim Bird.

GOLDEN EARRING P&R/LP '74
Singles: 7-inch
ATLANTIC 3-5 70
DWARF (2000 "Back Home") 10-20 69
MCA 3-5 76-78
POLYDOR (2000 series) 3-4 79
POLYDOR (14000 series) 3-6 69
TRACK 3-5 74-75
21 3-4 82-86
Picture Sleeves
DWARF (2000 "Back Home") 15-25 69
21 3-5 84
LPs: 10/12-inch
ATLANTIC 15-20 69
CAPITOL (164 "Miracle Mirror") 30-35 69
CAPITOL (2823 "Winter Harvest") 30-35 67
CAPITOL (11315 "Golden Earring") 10-12 74
DWARF 10-20
MCA 6-10 75-81
POLYDOR 5-10 79-80
TRACK (396 "Moontan") 20-25 73
(With nude showgirl on cover.)
TRACK (396 "Moontan") 10-12 73
(Showgirl not nude on cover.)
TRACK (2139 "Switch") 8-12 75
21 5-10 82-86

GOLDEN GATE QUARTET
Singles: 78 rpm
BLUEBIRD 10-20 37-40
CAPITOL 5-10 48
COLUMBIA 5-15 47-49
LANG-WORTH 10-20 40s
(16-inch transcriptions.)
MERCURY 5-10 49-51
MONTGOMERY WARD 5-10
OKEH (Except 6897) 5-15 41-52
OKEH (6897 "Rain Is the Teadrops of Angels") 25-50 52
RCA 5-10 41-48
SITTIN' IN WITH 5-10 52
Singles: 7-inch
COLUMBIA (39000 series) 10-15 51
OKEH (6897 "Rain Is the Teadrops of Angels") 100-150 52
LPs: 10/12-inch
CAMDEN (308 "Golden Gate Quartet") 25-35 56
COLUMBIA (6102 "Golden Gate Spirituals") 75-100 50
(10-inch LP.)
HARMONY (7018 "Golden Chariot") 25-35 57
MERCURY (25063 "Spirituals") 50-75 51
(10-inch LP.)
Members: Willie Johnson; Henry Owens; Bill Langford; Clyde Riddick; Orlandus Wilson; Cliff Givens; Alton Bradley; Caleb Ginyard; Orville Brooks
Also see DIXIEAIRES
Also see GATES

GOLDEN GATE STRINGS LP '67
(With Stu Phillips)
Singles: 7-inch
EPIC 3-5 67
EPs: 7-inch
EPIC (26158 "Bob Dylan Song Book") 10-15 67
Also see HOLLYRIDGE STRINGS

GOLDEN HARMONEERS
Singles: 7-inch
MOTOWN (1015 "I Am Bound") 20-40 61

GOLDEN HIGHLIGHTERS
Singles: 7-inch
HANOVER (4509 "The Wail") 10-15 58

GOLDEN HORIZON
Singles: 7-inch
FONTANA 4-6 69

GOLDEN NUGGETS
(With Rocky Rhodes & California Versatones)
Singles: 7-inch
FUTURA (1691 "I Was a Fool") 750-1000 59

GOLDEN NUGGETS
Singles: 7-inch
HAWK (105 "Everybody Bird") 20-30 63

GOLDEN PALOMINOS
Singles: 7-inch
CELLULOID (56 "Omaha") 3-5 85
Picture Sleeves
CELLULOID (56 "Omaha") 4-6 85
Member: J. Michael Stripe.
Also see R.E.M.

GOLDEN TOADSTOOL
Singles: 7-inch
MINARET (138 "Silly Savage") 10-15 68

GOLDEN TONES
(With Johnny Guitar & Band)
Singles: 7-inch
HUSH (101 "Little Island Girl") 15-20 59
HUSH (102 "You Left Me Here to Cry Alone") 15-20 59
Member: Joe Simon.
Also see SIMON, Joe

GOLDEN TONES
Singles: 7-inch
JEFF (801 "Swerve") 10-20 59

GOLDEN VOICES
Singles: 7-inch
RCA 3-5 66

GOLDENAIRES
Singles: 7-inch
ANGELUS ("What He Said") 10-20
(Selection number not known.)
RON (325 "My Only Girl") 75-125 59
RON (332 "Love Letter") 25-50 60

GOLDENROD
LPs: 10/12-inch
CHARTMAKER (1101 "Goldenrod") 75-125 68
Members: Jerry Scheff; Toxie French; Ben Benay.
Also see BENAY, Ben
Also see DARIUS
Also see FIFTH DIMENSION
Also see FRIAR TUCK
Also see PRESLEY, Elvis

GOLDENRODS
Singles: 7-inch
VEE JAY (307 "Wish I Was Back in School") 500-750 58

GOLDENS
(Denny Ezba & Goldens)
Singles: 7-inch
BIG STAR 25-50 60
Also see EZBA, Denny

GOLDENS C&W '88
Singles: 7-inch
EPIC 3-4 88
Members: Chris Golden; Rusty Golden.
Also see BOYS BAND
Also see CEDAR CREEK
Also see TOMORROW'S WORLD

GOLDENTONES
(Golden Tones)
Singles: 78 rpm
JAY DEE (806 "Meaning of Love") 25-50 55
RAINBOW (351 "She's Funny That Way") 50-75 56
SAMSON (107 "I'm Wrong") 50-75 55
Singles: 7-inch
BEACON (560 "Meaning of Love") 15-25 61
JAY DEE (806 "Meaning of Love") 50-75 55
RAINBOW (351 "She's Funny That Way") 100-150 56
SAMSON (107 "I'm Wrong") 100-150 55
Members: Vernon Harris; Millie Harris; Harold Holman; Lee McCall; Melvin Johnson.

GOLDIE, Don
Singles: 7-inch
TEARDROP 15-20 66
Also see SIR DOUGLAS QUINTET

GOLDIE & ESCORTS
Singles: 7-inch
CORAL (62302 "Gloria") 10-20 62
CORAL (62317 "As I Love You") 10-20 62
CORAL (62336 "Submarine Race Watching") 10-20 62
CORAL (62349 "One Hand, One Heart") 15-25 62
CORAL (62372 "Back Home Again") 20-30 63
CORAL (62385 "My Heart Cries for You") 10-20 63

GOLDIE & GINGERBREADS
Singles: 7-inch
ATCO (6354 "That's Why I Love You") 10-15 65
ATCO (6427 "Please Please") 10-15 66
ATCO (6475 "Walking in Different Circles") 10-15 67
Member: Genya Ravan.
Also see RAVAN, Genya

GOLDRUSH / Black Diamond
Singles: 78 rpm
JAXSON (6 "All My Money Is Gone") 50-75 48

GOLDSBORO, Bobby P&R '62
Singles: 7-inch
CURB 3-4 80-82
EPIC 3-5 77
LAURIE 5-8 62-63
U.A. (Except 672 thru 980) 4-6 66-73
U.A. (672 thru 980) 5-8 63-66
VISTA 3-5 74
Picture Sleeves
U.A. (Except 710) 4-8 66-74
U.A. (710 "Whenever He Holds You") 8-12 64
LPs: 10/12-inch
CURB 5-10 80-82
DORAL 15-25
(Promotional mail-order issue, from Doral cigarettes.)
EPIC 8-10 77
K-TEL 5-10
LIBERTY 5-10 81
SUNSET 8-12 60s
U.A. 10-20 64-76
Also see ORBISON, Roy
Also see REEVES, Del, & Bobby Goldsboro
Also see WEBS

GOLDSBORO, Bobby / Jimmy Durante
Singles: 7-inch
LIGHT (608 "We Gotta Start Lovin' ") 4-8 71
Also see GOLDSBORO, Bobby
Also see DURANTE, Jimmy

GOLDSMITH, Glen
Singles: 7-inch
RCA 3-4 88

GOLDTONES
Singles: 7-inch
COLONIAL (52 "High Dive into Love") 100-200 50s

GOLDTONES
Singles: 7-inch
Y-R-S (1001 "If I Had the Wings of an Angel") 200-300 61
Y-R-S (1002 "Journey Bells") 100-200 62

GOLDTONES
(Randy Seol & Goldtones)
Singles: 7-inch
A&R (714 "Strike") 20-30 63
Picture Sleeves
A&R (714 "Strike") 30-50 63
LPs: 10/12-inch
LA BREA (8011 "The Goldtones Featuring Randy Seol") 30-50 64
Members: Randy Seol; Cindy Mac; Glenn Campbell; Bill Ewing; Wayne Purvis; Ken Naylor; Al Doss; Mike Peters; Steve Green.
Also see JUICY LUCY
Also see MISUNDERSTOOD
Also see STRAWBERRY ALARM CLOCK

GOLDTONES
Singles: 7-inch
JCP (1015 "I Can't Help Loving You") 10-20 64

GOLDWATER, Barry
Singles: 7-inch
IMPACT (1 "Discrimination") 10-15 64
(Colored vinyl. Flip has Efrem Zimbalist Jr., Walter Brennan, Ronald Reagan, Robert Stack, and others, speaking on behalf of presidential candidate Goldwater.)
LPs: 10/12-inch
AMERICAN UNITED 10-20 64
Also see BRENNAN, Walter
Also see REAGAN, Ronald

GOLIATH
Singles: 7-inch
ABC 3-6 69
LPs: 10/12-inch
ABC 10-12 69

GOLLIWOGS
Singles: 7-inch
FANTASY (590 "Don't Tell Me No Lies") 40-60 64
FANTASY (597 "You Came Walking") 40-60 65
FANTASY (599 "You got Nothing on Me") 30-50 65
SCORPIO (404 "Brown Eyed Girl") 30-50 65
SCORPIO (405 "Fragile Child") 30-50 66
SCORPIO (408 "Walking on the Water") 30-50 66
SCORPIO (412 "Porterville") 40-60 67
LPs: 10/12-inch
FANTASY (9474 "Pre-Creedence") 10-15 75
Members: John Fogerty; Tom Fogerty; Doug Clifford; Stuart Cook.
Also see CREEDENCE CLEARWATER REVIVAL

GOMEZ, Johnny Ray, & U-Neeks
Singles: 7-inch
APPLAUSE (1000 "Romp Out") 15-25 64
APPLAUSE (1001 "Kick Off") 15-25 64

GOMEZ, Vicky
Singles: 7-inch
ABC-PAR 4-8 65

GOMEZ, Yvonne
(With Eddie C. Campbell & His Studio Band)
Singles: 7-inch
HAWAII (127 "Ease the Pain") 15-25 60s
(We have not yet verified this number; however, we are certain about #6333.)
HAWAII (6333 "Ease the Pain") 15-25 60s

GOMM, Ian P&R/LP '79
Singles: 7-inch
STIFF 3-5 79
LPs: 10/12-inch
STIFF 5-10 79-80
Also see SCHWARZ, Brinsley

GONE ALL STARS P&R '58
Singles: 7-inch
GONE 10-15 58
ROULETTE 3-5 71
EPs: 7-inch
GONE (101 "Dancin' Bandstand") 35-55 58
Member: Buddy Lucas.
Also see LUCAS, Buddy

GONE IN SIXTY SECONDS
LPs: 10/12-inch
GET HIP 5-8 92
Members: Lonnie Spillane; Brother E.; Special K.; Steve Smith; Andy Wendler.

GONG
LPs: 10/12-inch
ARISTA 5-10 78-80
VIRGIN 8-10 74-77
Member: Buddy Lucas.
Also see LUCAS, Buddy

GONG SHOW SYMPHONY
Singles: 7-inch
GONG SHOW 3-5 78

GONGETTES
Singles: 7-inch
ORIGINAL SOUND 5-10 62

GONN
Singles: 7-inch
EMIR (9217 "Blackout of Gretley") 300-500 66
EMIR/MCCM (88-9217 "Blackout of Gretley") 3-5 88
(Black vinyl.)
EMIR/MCCM (88-9217 "Blackout of Gretley") 5-10 88
(Colored vinyl.)
MERRY JAINE (2316 "You're Looking Fine") 100-200 67
Members: Brent Colvin; Rex Garrett; Larry LaMaster; Gary Stepp; Gerry Gable; Dave Johnson; Craig Moore.
Also see ILMO SMOKEHOUSE
Also see MOORE, Craig
Also see TIEKEN, Freddie, & Rockers

GONZALES, Babs
Singles: 78 rpm
BRUCE 5-10 54
ESSEX 5-10 54
KING 8-12 55
OKEH 15-25 57
Singles: 7-inch
ATLAS 5-10 59
BRUCE 15-20 54
CRAZY 3-5 60
ESSEX 10-20 54
KING 10-15 55
OKEH (7079 "And About This Rock & Roll") 15-25 57
(Promo copies of this have no selection number on the label.)
LPs: 10/12-inch
JARO 15-20 59

GONZALES, Frank, & Palisades
Singles: 7-inch
F-G (1001 "Let's Make Up") 200-300 61

GONZALES, Terri R&B '82
Singles: 7-inch
BECKET 3-4 82

GONZALEZ P&R/R&B/LP '79
Singles: 12-inch
CAPITOL 4-6 79
Singles: 7-inch
CAPITOL 3-5 78-79
LPs: 10/12-inch
CAPITOL 5-10 78-80

GONZALEZ, Bobby
Singles: 7-inch
KAPP 4-8 62

GONZALEZ, Rudy, & Reno Boys
Singles: 7-inch
TEAR DROP (3057 "All I Could Do Is Cry") 10-20 63

GONZOS
Singles: 7-inch
DONNA (1330 "Church Key") 15-25 61
(Same single also issued as by the Four Sharps.)
Also see FOUR SHARPS

GOOBERS
Singles: 7-inch
SURF (1001 "Hawaiian Holiday") 20-30 63

GOOD, Bobby
Singles: 7-inch
BELL CREST (385 "Crawl Back") 10-20
BELL CREST (386 "Wicked Baby") 10-20

GOOD, Lemme B.
Singles: 7-inch
COLUMBIA (41939 "Dancing Angel") 10-15 61
MERCURY 4-8 64-65

GOOD, Tommy
Singles: 7-inch
GORDY (7034 "Baby I Miss You") 20-30 64

GOOD, BAD & SISTER UGLY
Singles: 7-inch
SISTER UGLY'S 4-8

GOOD, BAD & UGLY
LPs: 10/12-inch
MERCURY 8-10 70
Members: Joe Pipps; Bubba Goode; Kenny Yetman.

GOOD & PLENTY
Singles: 7-inch
SENATE 4-8 67
LPs: 10/12-inch
SENATE 10-15 67

GOOD BUDDY & HIS ROCKIN' BAND
(Buddy Lucas)
Singles: 7-inch
TETRA (4451 "Rockin with the Duke") 15-25 59
Also see LUCAS, Buddy

GOOD EARTH TRIO
LPs: 10/12-inch
DYNOVOICE 10-15 68
Members: Bill Oliver Swofford; Bob Hinkle; Dan Shepherd.
Also see OLIVER

GOOD FEELING
Singles: 7-inch
EAGLE (122 "Tale of Man") 15-25 66

GOOD FEELIN'S
Singles: 7-inch
LIBERTY (55981 "I'm Captured") 10-15 67
ROCK-IT (1007 "I'm Captured") 20-30 67
ROCK-IT (2000 "I'm Lost") 20-30 67

GOOD GIRLS
Singles: 7-inch
COUNSEL 5-10 63

GOOD GOD
LPs: 10/12-inch
ATLANTIC 8-12 72
Member: Hank Ransome.
Also see ELIZABETH

GOOD GUYS
Singles: 7-inch
COUNSEL (123 "Perry's Theme") 10-20 63
Member: Perry Botkin.
Also see McCOY BOYS

GOOD GUYS
Singles: 7-inch
GNP (326 "Asphalt Wipe-Out") 15-25 64
SAN-DEE (1007 "I Love My Baby") 25-35 64
LPs: 10/12-inch
GNP (2001 "Sidewalk Surfing") 25-35 64
U.A. 20-30 64
Members: Jim Roberts; Steve Douglas; Hal Blaine; John Anderson; Art Fisher.
Also see BELAIRS
Also see BLAINE, Hal
Also see DOUGLAS, Steve

GOOD GUYS
Singles: 7-inch
SYLVANIA (8226 "Topsy '66") 8-12 66

GOOD IDEA
Singles: 7-inch
GOOD IDEA (2889 "Inside, Outside") 25-35 60s

GOOD INTENTIONS
Singles: 7-inch
BREWTOWN 5-10 70s
Also see SOURCE, Pete

GOOD JELLY BESS
Singles: 7-inch
HERMITAGE ... 4-8 62

GOOD QUESTION P&R '88
Singles: 7-inch
PAISLEY PARK ... 3-4 88
Picture Sleeves
PAISLEY PARK ... 3-4 88

GOOD RATS
Singles: 7-inch
JESTER (22001 "You're All I Need to Get By") ... 15-25 73
KAPP ... 5-10 68
PASSPORT ... 3-4 79
RAT CITY ... 4-8 76
SMK ("Don't Hate the Ones") ... 20-30 60s
(No label name shown. "SMK" is etched in the trail-off. Distributed at the group's concerts.)
LPs: 10/12-inch
GREAT AMERICAN ... 5-10 81
KAPP (3580 "The Good Rats") ... 35-50 69
PASSPORT (Except 20) ... 5-10 78
PASSPORT (20 "Rats the Way You Like It") ... 40-60 78
(Promotional issue only.)
RAT CITY ... 10-12 76-80
W.B. (2813 "Tasty") ... 20-25 74
Members: Peppi Marchello; John Gatto; Joe Franco; Larry Kotke; Mickey Marchello.

GOOD ROCKIN' SAM
Singles: 78 rpm
EXCELLO ... 10-20 55
Singles: 7-inch
EXCELLO (2059 "Baby, I'm Fool Proof") ... 20-40 55

GOOD ROCKIN' SAMMY T.
Singles: 7-inch
JUNIOR ... 15-25 60

GOOD SEED
LPs: 10/12-inch
VILLAGE ... 8-10 76

GOOD SHIP LOLLIPOP
Singles: 7-inch
EMBER ... 3-6 69
METROMEDIA ... 3-6 69

GOOD TIME BANJO BOYS
Singles: 78 rpm
GOOD TONE ... 3-5 72
Picture Sleeves
GOOD TONE ... 3-5 72

GOOD TIME FOUR
Singles: 7-inch
NEWMAN ... 4-6 66

GOOD TIME SINGERS
LPs:10/12-inch
CAPITOL ... 10-20 60s

GOOD TIMERS
Singles: 7-inch
ATLANTIC ... 3-6 68

GOOD TIMES
Singles: 7-inch
KAMA SUTRA ... 4-8 66-68
LPs: 10/12-inch
KAMA SUTRA ... 12-15 66
Member: Dave Kennedy.
Also see KENNEDY, Dave

GOOD VIBRATIONS
LPs: 10/12-inch
MILLENNIUM ... 5-10 78

GOODE, B., & Goodband
Singles: 7-inch
GEM (0100 "Sabotage") ... 10-20 61

GOODE, Ronnie
Singles: 7-inch
DEMON ... 10-15 58

GOODE, Roy
Singles: 7-inch
VEL-TONE (25 "Stupid Heart") ... 75-125 59

GOODEES P&R '68
Singles: 7-inch
HIP ... 4-8 68-69
LPs: 10/12-inch
HIP ... 10-15 69

GOODFELLOWS
Singles: 7-inch
SUN-NEL (535 "Another Chance") ... 100-200 58

GOODIE R&B '82
Singles: 12-inch
TOTAL EXPERIENCE ... 4-6 82-84
Singles: 7-inch
TOTAL EXPERIENCE ... 3-4 82-84
LPs: 10/12-inch
TOTAL EXPERIENCE ... 5-10 83

GOODIES
Singles: 7-inch
CHESS ... 5-10 59

GOODIES
Singles: 7-inch
BLUE CAT ... 8-10 65

GOODIES P&R '75
Singles: 7-inch
20TH FOX ... 3-5 75

GOODING, Cuba R&B/D&D '83
Singles: 12-inch
STREETWISE ... 4-8 83
Singles: 7-inch
MOTOWN ... 3-5 78-79
STREETWISE ... 3-4 83
LPs: 10/12-inch
MOTOWN ... 5-10 78-79
Also see MAIN INGREDIENT

GOODLY, Miss Ann, & Zydeco Bros.
LPs: 10/12-inch
MAISON de SOUL ... 5-8 90

GOODMAN, Benny, Orch. P&R '31
(Benny Goodman Sextet)
Singles: 78 rpm
CAPITOL ... 3-6 40s
COLUMBIA (Except 2856) ... 5-15 33-56
COLUMBIA (2856 "Your Mother's Son-In-Law") ... 30-50 34
(Colored plastic. Vocal by Billie Holiday.)
MELOTONE ... 10-20 31
VICTOR (Except 25808) ... 5-15 36-58
VICTOR (25808 "Popcorn Man") ... 750-1000 39
Singles: 7-inch
CAPITOL ... 4-8 49
CHESS ... 4-6 59
COLUMBIA (Except 250) ... 4-8 50-56
COLUMBIA (250 "1938 Carnegie Hall Concert") ... 25-45 50s
(Boxed, two-disc set.)
COMMAND ... 3-5 67
DECCA ... 3-5 62
RCA ... 4-8 50-59
EPs: 7-inch
BRUNSWICK ... 5-10 54
CAPITOL ... 5-10 55-56
COLUMBIA ... 5-10 50-58
DECCA (798 "The Benny Goodman Story") ... 10-15 56
MGM ... 4-8 59
RCA ... 5-10 50-59
LPs: 10/12-inch
ABC ... 5-10 76
BRIGHT ORANGE ... 5-10 73
BRUNSWICK ... 10-20 54
CAMDEN ... 5-10 63-65
CAPITOL ... 5-15 55-78
CENTURY ... 5-10 79
CHESS ... 5-15 59
COLPIX ... 8-12 62
COLUMBIA (Except 160) ... 5-15 50-82
COLUMBIA (160 "The Famous 1938 Carnegie Hall Concert") ... 25-40
(Boxed, two-disc set. Includes cardboard inner sleeves.)
COMMAND ... 5-10 67
DECCA (188 "The Benny Goodman Story, Volumes 1 & 2") ... 25-35
DECCA (8252 "The Benny Goodman Story, Volume 1") ... 20-30 56
DECCA (8253 "The Benny Goodman Story, Volume 2") ... 20-30 56
DECCA (7-8252 "The Benny Goodman Story, Volume 1") ... 15-20 59
(Reprocessed stereo.)
DECCA (7-8253 "The Benny Goodman Story, Volume 2") ... 15-20 59
(Reprocessed stereo.)
EVEREST ... 5-10 73
HARMONY ... 5-10 59-60
LONDON ... 5-10 72-78
LONDON/PHASE 4 ... 5-10 71-72
MCA ... 5-10 80
MGM ... 5-15 59
MARK 56 ... 5-10 77
MEGA ... 5-10 72-74
MUSICMASTERS ... 5-10
PAUSA ... 5-10 83
PRESTIGE ... 5-10 69
QUINTESSENCE ... 4-8 79
RCA (Except 6703) ... 5-15 50-78
(Includes 10- & 12-inch LPs.)
RCA (6703 "The Golden Age of Swing") ... 15-20 55
SUNBEAM ... 5-10 73
TIME-LIFE (354 "Into the '70s" ... 10-20 72
(Boxed, three-disc set. Includes booklet.)
WESTINGHOUSE ("World Favorites") ... 20-30 58
((No selection number used.)
"X" ... 10-15 54
Also see BASIE, Count, & Benny Goodman
Also see HOLIDAY, Billie
Also see LEE, Peggy

GOODMAN, Benny, Trio, with Rosemary Clooney
Singles: 78 rpm
COLUMBIA ... 3-5 50-56
Singles: 7-inch
COLUMBIA ... 5-10 56
LPs: 10/12-inch
COLUMBIA ... 15-25 56
Also see CLOONEY, Rosemary

GOODMAN, Benny / Lionel Hampton
Singles: 78 rpm
RCA VICTOR (1 "Jumpin' Jive") ... 10-15
(7-inch 78rpm single. Made for Colgate-Palmolive Co.
Also see GOODMAN, Benny, Orchestra
Also see HAMPTON, Lionel

GOODMAN, Dickie P&R '61
Singles: 7-inch
AUDIO SPECTRUM (75 "Presidential Interview") ... 10-20 64
CASH (451 "Mr. Jaws") ... 4-6 75
COTIQUE (158 "On Campus") ... 4-8 69
COTIQUE (173 "Luna Trip") ... 4-8 69
DIAMOND (119 "Ben Crazy") ... 10-15 62
EXTRAN (601 "Hey E.T.") ... 5-10 82
(First issue.)
GOLDISC ... 8-12 61
GOODNAME (7100 "Safe Sex Report") ... 3-5 88
HOTLINE (1017 "Energy Crisis '79") ... 4-6 79
J.M.D. (001 "Ben Crazy") ... 20-25 62
(First issue.)
JANUS (271 "Star Warts") ... 4-6 77
M.D. (101 "Shmonanza") ... 10-20 61
MARK-X (8009 "The Touchables") ... 10-20 61
MARK-X (8010 "The Touchables in Brooklyn") ... 10-20 61
MONTAGE (1220 "Hey E.T.") ... 3-5 82
PRELUDE (8018 "Election '80") ... 3-5 80
RAINY WEDNESDAY (202 "Watergrate") ... 4-8 73
RAINY WEDNESDAY (204 "Purple People Eater") ... 4-8 73
RAINY WEDNESDAY (205 "The Constitution") ... 4-8 74
RAINY WEDNESDAY (206 "Energy Crisis '74") ... 4-8 74
RAINY WEDNESDAY (207 "Mr. President") ... 4-8 74
RAINY WEDNESDAY (208 "Gerry Ford – A Special Report") ... 4-8 75
RAINY WEDNESDAY (209 "Inflation in the Nation") ... 4-8 75
RAMGO (501 "Speaking of Ecology") ... 8-12 70
RED BIRD (058 "Batman and His Grandmother") ... 10-15 66
RHINO (19 "Radio Russia") ... 3-5 84
RORI (601 "Horror Movies") ... 10-15 61
RORI (602 "Berlin Top Ten") ... 10-15 61
RORI (701 "Santa and the Touchables") ... 10-15 61
SHARK (1002 "Super Superman") ... 4-6 79
SHELL (711 "Election '84") ... 3-5 84
SHOCK (6 "Kong") ... 4-6 77
20TH FOX (443 "Senate Hearing") ... 10-15 63
TWIRL (2015 "James Bomb") ... 10-15 66
WACKO (1001 "Mr. President") ... 3-5 81
WACKO (1002 "Super Duper Man") ... 3-5 81
WACKO (1381 "America '81") ... 3-5 81
Z-100 (100 "Attack of the Z Monster") ... 3-5 84
LPs: 10/12-inch
CASH (6000 "Mr. Jaws") ... 25-30 75
COMET (69 "My Son the Joke") ... 20-30 64
IX CHAINS ... 12-15 73
RHINO ... 5-10 83
RORI (3301 "The Many Heads of Dickie Goodman") ... 50-75 62
Also see BUCHANAN & GOODMAN
Also see CASUAL THREE
Also see JEKYLL & HYDE
Also see PENNSYLVANIA PLAYERS
Also see RAMAL, Bill
Also see SPENCER & SPENCER

GOODMAN, George, & Headliners
Singles: 7-inch
VAL (1 "Let Me Love You") ... 20-30 65
(Some reissues credit only the Headliners.)
VAL (3 "I'm So Tired") ... 8-12 66
VAL (5 "Secret Love") ... 10-15 66
VAL (6 "Need You") ... 10-15 66
VAL (1000 "Let Me Love You") ... 8-12 66
W.B. (5632 "Let Me Love You") ... 10-15 65
Also see HEADLINERS

GOODMAN, Irv
Singles: 7-inch
WHIZ (607 "Colonel Bogey") ... 8-12

GOODMAN, Jerry, & Jan Hammer
LPs: 10/12-inch
NEMPEROR ... 8-10 74
Also see HAMMER, Jan

GOODMAN, Jimmy, & Belmonts
Singles: 7-inch
CAMARO (3385 "Lonliness Is a Word") ... 15-25

GOODMAN, Steve LP '75
Singles: 7-inch
ASYLUM ... 3-5 75-81
BUDDAH ... 3-5 72-73
LPs: 10/12-inch
ASYLUM ... 5-10 75-80
BUDDAH ... 8-12 71-76
RED PAJAMAS ... 5-10 83-87

GOODMAN, Steve, & Phoebe Snow
Singles: 7-inch
ASYLUM ... 3-4 80
Also see GOODMAN, Steve
Also see SNOW, Phoebe

GOODNESS & MERCY
LPs: 10/12-inch
MGM ... 8-10 70
Members: Dave Talisman; Peter Martin; Joe Bellamy; Ric Miller; Elvio Ditta; John Trombatore; Harry Kim; Jerry Grant; Steve Davis.

GOODNIGHT, Gary C&W '80
Singles: 7-inch
DOOR KNOB ... 5-10 80-82
SOUNDWAVES ... 3-4 82
LPs: 10/12-inch
DOOR KNOB ... 5-10 81

GOODNIGHT, Terri
Singles: 7-inch
PHELECTRON (701 "They Didn't Know") ... 250-350 60s

GOODNIGHT KISSES
Singles: 7-inch
ATCO ... 4-8 65

GOODSON, C.L. C&W '75
Singles: 7-inch
ISLAND ... 3-5 75

GOODSON, Hal, & Raiders
Singles: 7-inch
SOLO ... 5-10

GOODSON, Lloyd C&W '76
Singles: 7-inch
U.A. ... 3-4 76

GOODSON, Mitch C&W '80
Singles: 7-inch
PARTRIDGE ... 3-4 80

GOODTHINGS
Singles: 7-inch
CONDOR ... 4-8 65

GOODTHUNDER
Singles: 7-inch
ELEKTRA ... 3-5 72
LPs: 10/12-inch
ELEKTRA ... 8-10 72
Also see L.A. JETS

GOODTIME CHARLIE
Singles: 7-inch
ACE ... 4-8 61

GOODTIME WASHBOARD THREE
Singles: 7-inch
FANTASY ... 5-10 64
LPs:10/12-inch
FANTASY (3361 "Goodtime Washboard Three") ... 25-35 64

GOODTIMERS P&R '61
Singles: 7-inch
ARNOLD (1002 "Pony Time") ... 8-12 61
EPIC (9484 "It's Twistin' Time") ... 5-10 61
Member: Don Covay.
Also see COVAY, Don

GOODWIN, Bill C&W '63
Singles: 7-inch
BAND BOX ... 4-8 62
VEE JAY ... 4-8 63

GOODWIN, Don P&R '73
Singles: 7-inch
SILVER BLUE ... 3-5 73

GOODWIN, Ron P&R '57
Singles: 78 rpm
CAPITOL ... 3-5 56-57
Singles: 7-inch
CAPITOL ... 5-10 56-59
KING ... 4-6 61
LPs: 10/12-inch
CAPITOL ... 8-15 57-60
Also see VINCENT, Gene / Frank Sinatra / Sonny James / Ron Goodwin

GOODY GOODY P&R/R&B '78
Singles: 7-inch
ATLANTIC ... 3-5 78
LPs: 10/12-inch
ATLANTIC ... 5-10 78

GOOFERS
Singles: 78 rpm
CORAL ... 5-10 54-56
Singles: 7-inch
CORAL ... 10-15 54-56

GOOFERS
Singles: 7-inch
PORT ... 10-15 58
TIARA ... 5-10 59

GOOGIE & McCRARY
Singles: 7-inch
CLASS of '74 ... 5-8 75
Member: Googie Rene.
Also see RENE, Googie

GOOGY & JOE'S WORKSHOP
Singles: 7-inch
PARKWAY ... 4-8 67

GOON, Peter / Bab Boon
Singles: 7-inch
POLEESE (100 "The Whistler") ... 20-25 75

GOON SQUAD R&B/D&D '85
Singles: 12-inch
EPIC ... 4-6 85
Picture Sleeves
EPIC ... 3-4 85
Singles: 7-inch
EPIC ... 3-4 85

GOOSE CREEK SYMPHONY P&R/LP '72
(Goose Creek)
Singles: 7-inch
CAPITOL ... 3-6 70-72
LPs: 10/12-inch
CAPITOL (444 "Est. 1970") ... 10-15 70
CAPITOL (690 "Welcome to Goose Creek") ... 10-15 72
CAPITOL (11044 "Words of Earnest") ... 10-15 73
COLUMBIA (32918 "Do Your Thing, But Don't Touch Mine") ... 8-12 74
Members: Charles R. Gearheart; Mike McFadden; Ed Black Paul Spradlin
Also see HART, Ritchie
Also see SUPERFINE DANDELION

GOOSE ISLAND RAMBLERS
Singles: 7-inch
CUCA (Except 1257) ... 4-8 64-66
CUCA (1257 "The Hurley Hop") ... 8-10 65

GORD'S HORDE
Singles: 7-inch
HODAG ("I Don't Care") ... 25-50 66
Members: Gordy Gillman; Phil Van Goethen; Dan Nordall; Dale Smith; Tom Price; Cliff Fellows.

GORDIAN KNOT
Singles: 7-inch
VERVE ... 5-10 69
LPs: 10/12-inch
VERVE ... 10-12 69

GORDON
Singles: 7-inch
PICCADILLY (234 "Greensleeves") ... 5-10 66
UPTOWN ... 4-8 67

GORDON, Alan
Singles: 7-inch
CAPITOL ... 3-5 78
RCA ... 3-5 76
LPs: 10/12-inch
CAPITOL ... 5-10 78

GORDON, Anita
Singles: 7-inch
RCA (8201 "Tommy") ... 8-12 63

GORDON, Barry P&R '55
(With Art Mooney & His Orchestra)
Singles: 78 rpm
MGM ... 4-8 55-56
Singles: 7-inch
ABC ... 4-6 68
CAPITOL ... 3-8 65-71
CADENCE ... 5-10 62
DUNHILL ... 4-6 68
ERA ... 5-10 59
MGM ... 8-15 55-56
MERCURY ... 5-10 61
U.A. ... 4-8 64-66
Picture Sleeves
MGM (12092 "Nuttin' for Christmas") ... 10-20 56
MGM (12367 "I Like Christmas") ... 10-20 56
LPs: 10/12-inch
U.A. ... 8-15 66
Also see MOONEY, Art, & His Orchestra

GORDON, Benny, & Soul Brothers
Singles: 7-inch
DELUXE (145 "Sugar Mama") ... 3-6 73
ENRICA (1015 "Kansas City Woman") ... 15-25 64
ESTILL (1000 "Sugar Mama") ... 50-100 60s
RCA (8953 "Up and Down") ... 8-12 66
RCA (9144 "Greyhound Blues") ... 8-12 67
RCA (9194 "What Is Soul") ... 8-12 67

GORDON, Big Mike
(Big Mike)
Singles: 78 rpm
BATON ... 5-10 54
SAVOY ... 5-10 54
Singles: 7-inch
BATON (219 "Walkin' Slippin' and Slidin'") ... 15-20 54
SAVOY (1152 "Down in New Orleans") ... 15-20 54

GORDON, Bill "Bass," & Colonials
Singles: 78 rpm
GEE (12 "Two Loves Have I") ... 200-300 54
Singles: 7-inch
GEE (12 "Two Loves Have I") ... 1000-2000 54
Also see COINS / Colonials

GORDON, Claude
Singles: 7-inch
W.B. ... 5-10 59-63
Picture Sleeves
W.B. (5091 "Brassmen's Holiday") ... 8-12 59

GORDON, Curtis
Singles: 78 rpm
MERCURY ... 10-20 57
RCA ... 8-12 53
Singles: 7-inch
DOLLIE ... 3-5 66
DUKE of COUNTRY ... 3-5
MERCURY (70800 thru 71000 series) ... 20-40 56-57
MERCURY (71100 series) ... 10-15 57
RCA ... 15-25 53

GORDON, Dave, & Reb-Tides
Singles: 7-inch
PRESS ... 4-8 66

GORDON, Diane
Singles: 7-inch
ARCY ... 5-10 60

GORDON, Don
Singles: 7-inch
FREEDOM ... 10-20 60s

GORDON, Flesh, & Nude Hollywood Argyles
Singles: 7-inch
PARAMOUNT ... 3-6 74

GORDON, Gary
Singles: 7-inch
FLEETWOOD (1002 "No One") ... 20-25 59

GORDON, Gus
(With the Darnels)
Singles: 7-inch
BANA (525 "My Little Homing Pigeon") ... 15-20 57
IPS ... 5-10 60

GORDON, Jim
(Jimmy Gordon)
Singles: 7-inch
CHALLENGE ... 4-8 63-66

GORDON, Junior
(With Huey "Piano" Smith's Orchestra)
Singles: 78 rpm
ACE (522 "Blow Wind, Blow")........10-15 56
Singles: 7-inch
ACE (522 "Blow Wind, Blow")........20-30 56
JAY-O-PEE 5-10 62
Also see SMITH, Huey

GORDON, Justin
LPs: 10/12-inch
DOT (3214 "Justin Gordon Swings")........................30-50 59

GORDON, Kelly
Singles: 7-inch
CAPITOL.................................. 3-6 69
MERCURY 4-8 63
Picture Sleeves
CAPITOL (2442 "He Ain't Heavy") 5-8 69
MERCURY 5-8 63
LPs: 10/12-inch
CAPITOL.................................. 8-12 69

GORDON, Larry
Singles: 7-inch
MERCURY (72273 "Lefty Louie")...10-20 64

GORDON, Larry "T-Bird"
Singles: 7-inch
HI 3-5 79

GORDON, Lena / Sax Kari
Singles: 78 rpm
CHECKER.................................. 8-12 54
Singles: 7-inch
CHECKER (803 "Mama Took the Baby")..............................15-25 54

GORDON, Little Joe
Singles: 7-inch
JIN..................................10-15 60

GORDON, Luke C&W '58
Singles: 7-inch
ISLAND 5-10 58
NASHVILLE................................ 4-6
LPs: 10/12-inch
L&C.. 5-10
MOUNT VERNON 5-10

GORDON, Mike, & Agates
Singles: 7-inch
DORE (681 "Rumble at Newport Beach")..................................15-20 63
DORE (780 "Curfew on the Strip") 10-15 66

GORDON, Mike, & El Tempos
Singles: 78 rpm
CAT..15-25 54
Singles: 7-inch
CAT (101 "Why Don't You Do Right")..................................20-40 54

GORDON, Phil
(With the Page Cavanaugh Trio; with Beales)
Singles: 78 rpm
DECCA.....................................10-20 56
HUB of HOLLYWOOD..................15-25 53
Singles: 7-inch
DECCA (29787 "Down the Road a Piece")..................................15-25 56
HUB of HOLLYWOOD (1105 "Good Morning Judge")..................................25-50 53
HUB of HOLLYWOOD (1108 "Drunk")..................................25-50 53

GORDON, Ramsey
Singles: 7-inch
TAHOE (2530 "Down in the Cellar")..................................15-25 63

GORDON, Robert P&R/LP '77
(With Link Wray)
Singles: 12-inch
PRIVATE STOCK.......................10-15 78
RCA....................................... 8-12 81
(Promotional issue only.)
Singles: 7-inch
PRIVATE STOCK........................ 4-6 77-78
RCA (Black vinyl) 3-5 79-81
RCA (Colored vinyl).................. 8-12 79-81
(Promotional issue only.)
Picture Sleeves
PRIVATE STOCK (45203 "Fire") 5-10 79
RCA (11471 "It's Only Make Believe")..................................5-10 79
LPs: 10/12-inch
PRIVATE STOCK........................ 8-10 77-78
RCA (Except 3294)..................... 6-12 79-82
RCA (3294 "Rockbilly Boogie") 8-12 79
(Black vinyl.)
RCA (3294 "Rockbilly Boogie") 20-30 79
(White vinyl.)
Promotional LPs
RCA (3411 "Robert Gordon"/"Live from Paradise in Boston")......................35-45 79
Also see WRAY, Link

GORDON, Roscoe R&B '51
Singles: 78 rpm
CHESS (1487 "Booted") 50-100 52
DUKE (101 "Tell Daddy")..............50-75 52
DUKE (106 thru 129)....................20-50 53-54
FLIP (227 "Just Love Me Baby") ..50-100 55
FLIP (237 "The Chicken") 20-40 56
RPM 20-50 50-53
SUN (227 "Just Love Me Baby")..................................100-200 55
SUN (237 "The Chicken") 75-125 56
SUN (257 "Shoobie Oobie")...........25-50 56
Singles: 7-inch
ABC-PAR (10351 "Girl to Love")..... 8-12 62
ABC-PAR (10407 "I Want Revenge")..................................8-12 63
CALLA (145 "Just a Little Bit") 4-8 68
CHESS (1487 "Booted") 200-300 52
COLLECTABLES............................ 3-4 81
DUKE (106 "T-Model Boogie").......40-60 53
DUKE (109 "Too Many Women")....25-50 53
DUKE (114 "Ain't No Use")............25-50 53
DUKE (129 "Three Cent Love")......25-50 54
DUKE (320 "Dilly Bop")..................10-20 60
FLIP (227 "Just Love Me Baby")..................................200-300 55
FLIP (237 "The Chicken") 20-30 56
OLD TOWN (1167 "Just a Little At a Time")..................................5-10 64
RPM (324 "Saddle the Cow").....250-350 50
RPM (336 "Dime a Dozen") 100-200 50
RPM (344 "Booted")....................50-100 51
RPM (350 "No More Doggin'")........50-75 51
RPM (358 "New Orleans Wimmen")..................................50-75 51
RPM (365 "What You Got on Your Mind")..................................50-75 51
RPM (369 "Trying")......................40-60 52
RPM (373 "Lucille").......................40-60 52
RPM (379 "Just in from Texas")......40-60 52
RPM (384 "We're All Loaded")........40-60 52
SUN (227 "Just Love Me Baby")..................................400-500 55
SUN (237 "The Chicken") 100-200 56
SUN (257 "Shoobie Oobie")............40-60 56
SUN (305 "Sally Jo")......................25-50 58
VEE JAY (316 "No More Doggin' ") 15-25 59
VEE JAY (332 "Just a Little Bit")....15-25 59
VEE JAY (348 "What You Do to Me")..................................15-25 60
VEE JAY (385 "Let 'Em Try")..........15-20 61
Also see ROSCOE & BARBARA

GORDON, Steve
Singles: 7-inch
ADVENTURE (101 "Come on Baby, Let's Dance")..................................10-15

GORDON, Stomp
Singles: 78 rpm
CHESS.....................................15-25 54
DECCA.....................................15-25 52
MERCURY 15-25 53
SAVOY.....................................10-15 56
Singles: 7-inch
CHESS (1601 "The Grind")............25-50 54
DECCA (48287 "Damp Rag")..........25-50 52
DECCA (48289 "Ooh Yes")............25-50 52
DECCA (48290 "Devil's Daughter")..................................25-50 52
DECCA (48297 "Pennies from Heaven")..................................25-50 52
MERCURY (70223 "Slow Daddy Blues")..................................25-50 53
MERCURY (70246 "What's Her Whimsey, Dr. Kinsey")..................................25-50 53
SAVOY.....................................15-20 56

GORDON & STARLINERS
Singles: 7-inch
STAR (200 "Ding Bat")..................10-20 63

GORDON & SUE & ALGONQUINS
Singles: 7-inch
CARLTON (595 "Surfin' Sal & Charmin' Willie")..................................15-25 63

GORDON 'N ROGERS' INTER-URBAN ELECTRIC A&E PIT CREW & RHYTHM BAND
LPs: 10/12-inch
CAPITOL..................................10-15 69

GORE, Charlie, & Louis Innis
Singles: 78 rpm
KING 10-15 53
Singles: 7-inch
KING (1212 "[You Ain't Nothin' But a Female] Hound Dog")..................................20-30 53

GORE, Judy
Singles: 7-inch
FRATERNITY (1014 "What People Say")..................................4-8 60s

GORE, Lesley P&R/R&B/LP '63
Singles: 7-inch
A&M 3-6 75-76
CREWE..................................... 3-6 70-71
MERCURY (72119 thru 72206).......5-10 63
MERCURY (72245 "Je Ne Sais Plus")..................................10-20 64
MERCURY (72259 thru 72726).......6-12 64-67
MERCURY (72842 thru 72969).....10-15 68-69
MOWEST..................................... 4-6 72
Picture Sleeves
A&M 5-10 75-76
MERCURY 10-15 63-67
LPs: 10/12-inch
A&M 8-10 75
MERCURY (8000 series)..............5-10 80
MERCURY (20000 & 60000 series)..................................20-30 63-68
MOWEST....................................8-12 72
POLYDOR...................................5-10 85
WING 10-20 67-69
Also see BILLY & SUE
Also see DRIFTERS / Leslie Gore / Roy Orbison / Los Bravos

GORE, Leslie, & Lou Christie
Singles: 7-inch
MANHATTAN (50039 "Since I Don't Have You")..................................5-8 86
Also see CHRISTIE, Lou
Also see GORE, Leslie

GORE, Martin L. LP '89
LPs: 10/12-inch
SIRE.. 5-8 89

GORE, Michael P&R '84
Singles: 7-inch
CAPITOL.....................................3-4 84

GORE, Rufus
Singles: 78 rpm
KING 10-15 55
Singles: 7-inch
KING 15-20 55

GORGEOUS BILL
(Bill Yates)
Singles: 7-inch
SUN 4-8 65
Also see YATES, Bill

GORGEOUS GEORGE
Singles: 7-inch
HALE (501 "Cross Every Mountain")..................................50-100 62
NEPTUNE (125 "Will You Love Me")..................................15-25 61
PEACHTREE (105 "Love's Not a Hurtin' Thing")..................................25-50 66
STAX (165 "Sweet Thing")............10-20 65

GORGONI, Martin, & Taylor
Singles: 7-inch
BUDDAH 3-5 72
LP: 10/12-inch
BUDDAH (5089 "Gotta Get Back to Cisco")..................................8-12 71
Members: Trade Martin; Chip Taylor.
Also see MARTIN, Trade
Also see TAYLOR, Chip

GORKY PARK LP '89
Singles: 7-inch
MERCURY...................................3-4 90
LPs: 10/12-inch
MERCURY...................................5-8 89

GORL, Robert D&D '84
Singles: 12-inch
ELEKTRA.................................... 4-6 84
Singles: 7-inch
ELEKTRA.................................... 3-4 84

GORMAN, Barbara, & Sister Viv
Singles: 7-inch
ARROW (715 "8 O'clock Date").....40-60

GORMAN, Cliff
Singles: 7-inch
ROULETTE 4-8 63

GORMAN, Freddie
Singles: 7-inch
MIRACLE (11 "The Day Will Come")..................................25-50 62
RIC TIC 10-20 64-65
Also see ORIGINALS
Also see SATINTONES
Also see VOICE MASTERS

GORMAN SISTERS
Singles: 7-inch
JOY (222 "Sock Hop") 10-15 58

GORME, Eydie P&R '54
Singles: 78 rpm
ABC-PAR 3-5 55-62
Singles: 7-inch
ABC-PAR 4-8 55-62
CALENDAR..................................3-6 67
COLUMBIA..................................3-8 62-68
(Black vinyl.)
COLUMBIA (43082 "I Want You to Be My Baby")..................................5-10 64
(Colored vinyl.)
CORAL.......................................5-10 53-55
GALA 3-5 76
MGM 3-5 71-73
RCA 3-5 69-70
U.A. 3-6 60-76
Picture Sleeves
COLUMBIA..................................4-8 62-63
LPs: 10/12-inch
ABC-PAR 15-25 57-65
APPLAUSE 4-6 81
COLUMBIA..................................10-20 63-73
GALA 5-8 76
HARMONY 5-10 68-71
MGM 5-10 71
RCA 5-10 68-70
U.A. 10-20 61-62
VOCALION..................................8-15 63
Also see LAWRENCE, Steve, & Eydie Gorme

GORSEN, Irv
Singles: 7-inch
ROCK IT....................................4-8 63

GORSHIN, Frank
Singles: 7-inch
A&M 4-8 66
BRAND.......................................4-8
Picture Sleeves
A&M 5-10 66
BRAND.......................................5-10

GORTON'S PANTHERS
Singles: 7-inch
PANTHER 4-8 64

GOSDIN, Rex C&W '79
Singles: 7-inch
GRAPE VINE 3-5 80
MRC..3-5 79
SUN 3-4 83
Also see GOSDIN BROTHERS

GOSDIN, Rex, & Tommy Jennings C&W '80
Singles: 7-inch
SABRE 3-5 80
Also see GOSDIN, Rex
Also see JENNINGS, Tommy

GOSDIN, Vern C&W '76
Singles: 7-inch
AMI 3-4 82-83
COLUMBIA 3-4 87-91
COMPLEAT 3-4 83-86
ELEKTRA.....................................3-5 76-79
OVATION 3-5 81
LPs: 10/12-inch
AMI 5-10 83
COLUMBIA 5-10 87-91
COMPLEAT 5-10 83-84
ELEKTRA.....................................5-10 76-79
OVATION 5-8 81
PHONORAMA 5-8 84
Session: Curtis Wright; Janie Fricke; Emmylou Harris; Roger McGuinn.
Also see FRICKE, Janie
Also see GOSDIN BROTHERS
Also see HARRIS, Emmylou
Also see TUBB, Ernest
Also see WRIGHT, Curtis

GOSDIN BROTHERS C&W '67
Singles: 7-inch
BAKERSFIELD INT'L 4-8 67
LPs: 10/12-inch
CAPITOL....................................10-15 68
Members: Vern Gosdin; Rex Gosdin.
Also see GOSDIN, Rex
Also see GOSDIN, Vern

GOSEY, Johnny
(With Alex Jones & Nite Hawks)
Singles: 7-inch
MOA (1001 "Fools Will Take Chances")..................................150-250 50s

GOSH, Bobby
Singles: 7-inch
POLYDOR....................................3-5 72
ZOO YORK 3-4 85
Picture Sleeves
POLYDOR....................................3-5 72
ZOO YORK 3-4 85
LPs: 10/12-inch
POLYDOR....................................8-10 72

GOSH, Byron, Group
Singles: 7-inch
GOLDEN CREST 5-8

GOSPEL STARS
Singles: 7-inch
DIVINITY (99006 "Have You Any Time for Jesus")..................................15-25 60s
TAMLA (54037 "He Lifted Me")....75-100 61
(With horizontal lines.)
TAMLA (54037 "He Lifted Me")........40-60 61
(With Tamla globe logo.)
LPs: 10/12-inch
TAMLA (222 "Great Gospel Stars")..................................500-750 61

GOSPELAIRES
Singles: 7-inch
JORDAN 3-6 71
LPs: 10/12-inch
JORDAN 8-12 71
Members: Freddie Hall; Eddie Hall; Curt Beasley; John Carruthers; Willie Johnican; Ozzie Johnican; George Jimson Jr; Charles Walker; Tommy Davis.

GOSSERT, Gus
Singles: 7-inch
PENNY ARCADE (100 "Return of the Flying Saucer")..................................10-12 72

GOSSETT, Lou
Singles: 7-inch
POWERTREE 4-8 64
W.B. 4-8 68

GOSSIP
Singles: 7-inch
GOSSIP (102268 "No One's Standing in Your Way")..................................8-12 68

GOTHAM
LPs: 10/12-inch
AURUM 5-10 80
DREAM..5-10 78
NATURAL RESOURCES 8-10 72

GOTHAM CITY CRIME FIGHTERS
Singles: 7-inch
BATWING (1001 "That's Life").......15-25 66

GOTHAM CITY TEENS
Singles: 7-inch
RMT 5-10 66

GOTHAM'S FOUR NOTES
Singles: 78 rpm
GOTHAM 25-35 48

GOTHICS
(With the Sal Ditroia Orchestra; Gothic's)
Singles: 7-inch
CAROL (4115 "My Dream") 100-200 61
DYNAMIC (101 "Marilyn")..........250-350 59

GO-TOGETHERS
Singles: 7-inch
COAST (100 "Time After Time")....25-45

GOTROE, Jackie
Singles: 7-inch
KEEN 10-20 58
RHYTHM (111 "Raised on Rock and Roll")..................................75-125 58
VORTEX (102 "Lobo Jones")......100-200 57

GOUDREAU, Barry LP '80
Singles: 7-inch
PORTRAIT....................................3-4 79
LPs: 10/12-inch
PORTRAIT....................................5-10 79
Also see BOSTON

GOULD, Sandra
Singles: 7-inch
PHILIPS 8-12 63

GOULDMAN, Graham
Singles: 7-inch
RCA (9453 "Impossible Years").......5-10 68
RCA (9584 "Pamela Pamela")..........5-10 68
LPs: 10/12-inch
RCA (3954 "Thing") 25-35 68
Also see FONTANA, Wayne, & Mindbenders
Also see 10CC
Also see WAX

GOULET, Robert P&R/LP '62
Singles: 7-inch
ABC 3-5 74
ARTISTS of AMERICA.....................3-5 75
COLUMBIA (Black vinyl) 3-6 61-70
COLUMBIA (Colored vinyl)...............5-10 63
MGM 3-5 73
MERLIN 3-5 71
PARAMOUNT 3-5 74
Picture Sleeves
ABC 3-6 74
COLUMBIA (Except 59227)...............3-6 62-65
COLUMBIA (59227 "The Moon Was Yellow")..................................5-10 63
(Promotional issue only.)
EPs: 7-inch
COLUMBIA 4-8 65
(Juke box issues.)
LPs: 10/12-inch
ARTISTS of AMERICA.....................5-10 76
COLUMBIA 5-15 61-73
HARMONY 5-10 71-72
MERLIN 5-10 71
ORINDA 5-10 78

GOVE
Singles: 7-inch
TEX (5024 "Death Letter Blues")....10-15 71
UNI (55335 "Carry On")..................5-10 72
LPs: 10/12-inch
TEX (1002 "Heavy Cowboy").........20-30 71

GOVINDA
(Makunda Das Adhikary)
Singles: 7-inch
APPLE (Except 5067)......................8-10 69
APPLE (5067 "Radha Krishna Temple")..................................10-15 69
(Promotional issue only.)

GOWANS, Sammy
Singles: 7-inch
U.A. (114 "Rockin' by Myself")......75-125 58

GOWDY, Curt
Singles: 7-inch
MAGNAVOX ("Hank Arron #715") 10-15 74

GOZA, Gene
(With the Blazers)
Singles: 7-inch
BACK BEAT 4-8 66
COTTON 4-8

GRABEAU, Bobby
Singles: 7-inch
CREST...5-10 59

GRACE, Fredi, & Rhinestone R&B '82
Singles: 7-inch
RCA 3-4 82

GRACE, Jimmie
Singles: 7-inch
DOT 5-8 66

GRACE, Leda R&B '81
Singles: 7-inch
POLYDOR.....................................3-4 81

GRACES P&R/LP '89
LPs: 10/12-inch
A&M 5-8 89
Members: Charlotte Caffey; Meredith Brooks; Gia Ciambotti.
Also see GO-GOs

GRACIE, Charlie P&R/R&B '57
Singles: 78 rpm
CADILLAC....................................25-50 53-54
CAMEO..15-30 57
20TH CENTURY 15-25 55
Singles: 7-inch
ABKCO 3-5 75
CADILLAC (141 "Boogie Woogie Blues")..................................75-125 53
CADILLAC (144 "Rockin' and Rollin' ")..................................75-125 54
CAMEO..12-25 57-59
CORAL...10-15 59
DIAMOND 10-20 65
FELSTED......................................5-10 61
PRESIDENT...................................5-10 62
SOCK & SOUL 4-6 70
ROULETTE 5-10 59-61
20TH CENTURY (5035 "Honey Honey")..................................40-60 55
LPs: 10/12-inch
REVIVAL (0001 "Early Recordings")..................................10-20

GRACIOUS
Singles: 7-inch
CAPITOL.......................................4-6 70

LPs: 10/12-inch
CAPITOL....10-12 70

GRADDOCK, Billy: see CRADDOCK, Billy

GRADIE JOE: see JOE, Gradie

GRADS
Singles: 7-inch
A&M.... 4-8 66
MGM.... 4-8 64
MERCURY....10-15 64
VALIANT.... 5-10 62
Session: Davie Allan.
Also see ALLAN, Davie
Also see SANDPIPERS

GRADUATES P&R '59
Singles: 7-inch
CORSICAN (0058 "What Good Is Graduation")....20-30 59
SHAN-TODD (0055 "Ballad of a Girl and Boy")....15-25 59
Picture Sleeves
CORSICAN (0058 "What Good Is Graduation")....30-50 59

GRADUATES
Singles: 7-inch
GNP.... 5-10 68
RISING SONS (712 "If I Ever Get Out of This Mess I'm In")....15-25 68

GRADY, Don
Singles: 7-inch
CANTERBURY (501 "The Children of St. Monica")....8-12 66
CANTERBURY (507 "Impressions with Syvonne")....8-12 67
CAPITOL....8-12 64-65
CHALLENGE....8-12 66
ORANGE-EMPIRE (91647 "Summertime Game")....10-15 65
Picture Sleeves
CANTERBURY (501 "The Children of St. Monica")....10-15 66
CANTERBURY (507 "Impressions with Syvonne")....10-15 67
Also see AGRATI, Don
Also see PALACE GUARD
Also see YELLOW BALLOON

GRADY, Jim
LPs: 10/12-inch
CHANTERELLE.... 5-10 79
RCA.... 5-10 75
20TH FOX.... 8-10 73

GRADY, Leigh
Singles: 7-inch
APPALOOSA.... 3-5 77

GRADY, Paul
Singles: 7-inch
GLAIZE (109 "Darlin,' I Understand")....75-125 63

GRADY & BRADY
Singles: 7-inch
PLANETARY.... 4-8 65
Members: Grady Sneed; Brady Sneed.
Also see SNEED, Brady & Grady

GRAF
LPs: 10/12-inch
PRECISION.... 5-10 81

GRAFFITI
Singles: 7-inch
ABC-PAR (11123 "He's Got the Knack")....10-15 68
LPs: 10/12-inch
ABC-PAR (663 "Graffiti")....20-30 68

GRAFFITI ORCHESTRA
Singles: 7-inch
PRODIGAL.... 3-5 78

GRAHAM, Billy, & Escalators
Singles: 7-inch
ATLANTIC (2372 "Oop-Poo-Pa-Doo")....15-25 66

GRAHAM, Bobby
Singles: 7-inch
FONTANA (1501 "Zoom, Widge & Wag")....10-20 64

GRAHAM, Bonnie
Singles: 7-inch
SURE SHOT.... 4-8 66

GRAHAM, C., Quintet
Singles: 7-inch
JILL-ANN....10-20 60s

GRAHAM, D., & Crackers
Singles: 7-inch
DYMO DY (4263 "False Love")....10-20 62

GRAHAM, Davy
LPs: 10/12-inch
LONDON....10-12 68

GRAHAM, Jaki R&B '85
Singles: 12-inch
CAPITOL.... 4-6 86
Singles: 7-inch
CAPITOL.... 3-4 86
Picture Sleeves
CAPITOL.... 3-4 86
LPs: 10/12-inch
CAPITOL.... 5-10 86

GRAHAM, Jaki, & David Grant R&B '86
Singles: 12-inch
CAPITOL.... 4-6 86
Singles: 7-inch
CAPITOL.... 3-4 86
Also see GRAHAM, Jaki
Also see GRANT, David

GRAHAM, Jimmy
Singles: 7-inch
REVUE.... 4-8 65

GRAHAM, Joe, & Rubies
Singles: 7-inch
JCP (1023 "So What")....10-20 64

GRAHAM, Larry P&R/LP '74
(Graham Central Station; with Graham Central Station)
Singles: 7-inch
ARISTA.... 3-4 87
W.B.... 3-5 74-83
Picture Sleeves
W.B.... 3-5 80-82
LPs: 10/12-inch
W.B.... 5-10 73-83
Also see FRANKLIN, Aretha, & Larry Graham
Also see SLY & Family Stone

GRAHAM, Lou
Singles: 78 rpm
GOTHAM....10-20 51
Singles: 7-inch
CLYMAX (318 "Wee Willie Brown")....50-75 57
CORAL (61931 "Wee Willie Brown")....15-25 58
GOTHAM (7416 "Long Gone Daddy")....35-50 51

GRAHAM, Ralph
Singles: 7-inch
SUSSEX.... 3-5 74

GRAHAM, Sonny
Singles: 78 rpm
RCA.... 4-8 55
Singles: 7-inch
RCA.... 5-10 55

GRAHAM COUNTY
Singles: 7-inch
KAPP.... 4-8 71-72

GRAINGERS R&B '81
Singles: 7-inch
BC.... 3-4 81

GRAINS OF SAND
Singles: 7-inch
GENESIS (101 "Goin' Away Baby")....30-50 66
PHILIPS (40469 "Drop Down Sometime")....10-15 67
VALIANT (736 "That's When Happiness Begins")....15-25 66

GRAMM, Lou P&R/LP '87
Singles: 7-inch
ATLANTIC.... 3-4 87-90
Picture Sleeves
ATLANTIC.... 3-4 87
LPs: 10/12-inch
ATLANTIC.... 5-10 87-89
Also see BLACK SHEEP
Also see FOREIGNER

GRAMMER, Billy P&R/R&B '58/C&W '59
Singles: 78 rpm
MONUMENT (400 "Gotta Travel On")....40-60 59
Singles: 7-inch
DECCA.... 4-8 61-66
EPIC.... 4-6 66-67
EVEREST.... 5-8 60
MERCURY.... 3-6 68-69
MONUMENT (Except 400 series).... 3-5 75-76
MONUMENT (400 series)....5-15 59-63
RICE (5025 "Mabel")....5-10 67
STOP.... 3-6 69
EPs: 7-inch
DECCA....5-10 64
LPs: 10/12-inch
CLASSIC CHRISTMAS....5-10 77
DECCA....10-15 62-64
EPIC....8-12 67
MONUMENT (4000 "Travelin' On")....20-30 59
(With *Lost in a Small Cafe.*)
MONUMENT (8039 "Travelin' On")....10-15 66
(*Lost in a Small Cafe* is replaced with *Gotta Travel On.*)
SKYLITE.... 5-8
STONEWAY....5-10 75
VOCALION....6-12 68
Also see CASH, Johnny / Billy Grammer / Wilburn Brothers
Also see TUBB, Ernest

GRAMMER, Billy / Judy Lynn / Link Wray
LPs: 10/12-inch
GUEST STAR....10-15 60s
Also see GRAMMER, Billy
Also see JUDY LYNN
Also see WRAY, Link

GRANAHAN, Gerry P&R '58
(With the Hutch Davie Orchestra; Granahan-Quintal Band)
Singles: 12-inch
DOWNTOWN.... 5-8 87
Singles: 7-inch
ATCO (6122 "Sweet Affection")....15-25 58
CANADIAN AMERICAN (116 "In My Heart")....5-10 60
CANADIAN AMERICAN (119 "Where's the Girl")....5-10 60
CAPRICE (106 "Dancing Man")....5-10 61
CAPRICE (108 "Dance Girl Dance")....50-75 61
(With the Wildwoods, a.k.a. the Five Satins.)
COLLECTABLES.... 3-4
GONE....8-12 59-60
SUNBEAM (102 "No Chemise, Please")....15-25 58
SUNBEAM (108 "Baby Wait")....15-25 58
SUNBEAM (122 "King Size")....15-25 59
SUNBEAM (127 "A Ring, a Bracelet, a Heart")....15-25 59
20TH FOX....5-10 63
VEEP....4-8 65
Picture Sleeves
GONE (5081 "Look for Me")....25-50 60
Also see DICKY DOO & DON'TS
Also see FIVE SATINS
Also see FIVE SATINS / Gerry Granahan & Five Satins
Also see FONTAINE, Eddie, & Gerry Granahan
Also see GRANT, Jerry, & Rockabilly Bandits

GRANATA, Rocca, & International Quintet P&R '59
Singles: 7-inch
LAURIE....3-6 59
Picture Sleeves
LAURIE....5-8 59

GRANATI BROTHERS
LPs: 10/12-inch
A&M....5-10 79

GRANBY ST. REDEVELOPMENT
Singles: 7-inch
LEGRAND....10-20 67

GRAND, K.C., & SHADES
Singles: 7-inch
MATT (0003 "Lookie Lookie Lookie")....30-40 61

GRAND CANYON
Singles: 7-inch
FAITHFUL VIRTUE....3-5 70

GRAND CANYON P&R '74
Singles: 7-inch
BANG (713 "Evil Boll-Weevil")....4-6 74
Members: Ed Crown; Jeff McKee.

GRAND FUNK RAILROAD P&R/LP '69
(Grand Funk)
Singles: 7-inch
CAPITOL (Black vinyl)....3-6 69-76
CAPITOL (Colored vinyl)....5-8 73
(Promotional issue only.)
FULL MOON....3-4 81
MCA....3-5 76-77
Picture Sleeves
CAPITOL....3-6 71-76
FULL MOON....3-4 81
MCA....3-5 76
LPs: 10/12-inch
CAPITOL (307 thru 853)....8-15 69-71
CAPITOL (11000 series, except 11207)....6-12 72-76
CAPITOL (11207 "We're an American Band")....6-10 73
(Black vinyl.)
CAPITOL (11207 "We're an American Band")....20-30 73
(Colored vinyl. Promotional issue only.)
CAPITOL (12000 & 16000 series)....5-10 80-81
FULL MOON....5-10 81-83
MCA....8-10 76
Members: Mark Farner; Don Brewer; Mel Schacher; Craig Frost.
Also see FARNER, Mark, & Don Brewer
Also see FLINT
Also see KNIGHT, Terry, & Pack

GRAND PREES
("Featuring Bernice Marsh")
Singles: 7-inch
CANDI (1020 "Sit and Cry")....20-40 61
GO GO (101 "Heartbreak Hotel")....15-25 60s
GOLDEN GROOVE (101 "Sit and Cry")....15-25 62
HARAL (780 "Alone")....20-40 64
SCOTTY (825 "No Time to Lose") 15-25 60s

GRAND PRIX
Singles: 7-inch
VAULT (906 " '41 Ford")....10-15 63
Also see QUADS / Grand Prix / Customs

GRAND PRIX MACHINE
Singles: 7-inch
LAURIE....4-6 69

GRAND PRIXS
Singles: 7-inch
BIG MACK (2942 "I See Her Pretty Face")....25-50 60s
PONCHO (10 "Late Summer Love")....500-1000 63

GRAND PRIXS
(Grand Prix's)
Singles: 7-inch
SARA (6354 "San Jose")....10-20 63
Members: Rick Berkanovic; Kenny Knoll; Don Longhurst; Jeff Hammer; Bruce Cole.

GRANDMA'S ROCKERS
LPs: 10/12-inch
FREDLO ("Homemade Apple Pie & Yankee Ingenuity")....1000-1500 66
(500 made.)
Members: Jim Marousis; Brain Haas; Jamie Farnum; Dave Lange.
Also see GUYS WHO CAME UP from DOWNSTAIRS

GRANDMASTER FLASH & FURIOUS FIVE R&B '80
(With the Furious Five; with Melle Mel; Grandmaster Flash)
Singles: 12-inch 33/45
ATLANTIC....4-6 84
ELEKTRA....4-6 84-86
SUGAR HILL....4-6 80-85
Singles: 7-inch
ATLANTIC....3-4 84
ELEKTRA....3-4 84-87
MCA....3-4 85
SUGAR HILL....3-5 80-85
Picture Sleeves
ATLANTIC....3-4 84
ELEKTRA....3-4 84
LPs: 10/12-inch
ELEKTRA....5-10 86-88
SUGAR HILL....5-10 82-85
Also see JACKSON, Rebbie
Also see KHAN, Chaka
Also see KING DREAM CHORUS & HOLIDAY CREW
Also see MELLE MEL & DUKE BOOTEE

GRANDMIXER D. ST. R&B/D&D '83
Singles: 12-inch
ISLAND....4-6 83
Singles: 7-inch
ISLAND....3-4 83

GRANDMOTHERS
LPs: 10/12-inch
PANDA (001 "Grandmothers")....12-18 83
(Picture disc.)
RHINO....8-10 80-82
Members: Jimmy Carl Black; Don Preston; Elliot Ingber; James Sherwood; Buzz Gardner; Bunk Gardner; Tom Fowler; Walt Flower.
Also see MOTHERS of INVENTION

GRANFALLOON
LPs: 10/12-inch
TAKOMA (9021 "Laser Pace")....25-35 73
Member: Maureen O'Connor.

GRANGER, Gerri
(Jerri Granger)
Singles: 7-inch
ADDIT....5-8
BELL (969 "I Go to Pieces")....15-25 71
BIG TOP....8-12 62-64
DOUBLE L....8-12 65

GRANICUS
LPs: 10/12-inch
RCA (0321 "Granicus")....25-35 73

GRANMAX
LPs: 10/12-inch
PACIFIC....8-10 76
PANAMA....5-10 78

GRANNY
Singles: 7-inch
OBSCURITY (300 "Granny's Holiday Fruitcake")....5-10

GRANNY & JIM
LPs: 10/12-inch
PHILLIPS....10-12 63

GRANT, Al
(Al Cernick)
Singles: 78 rpm
KING (15004 thru 15045)....10-20 49-50
Also see MITCHELL, Guy

GRANT, Amy P&R/LP '85
Promotional 12-inch Singles
A&M (75161 "Heart in Motion")....5-10 91
A&M (23821 "Good for Me")....6-12 91
A&M (83311 "Lucky One")....5-10 94
Promotional Singles
A&M....4-8 85-91
Singles: 7-inch
A&M....3-4 85-91
COLLECTABLES....3-4 90s
MYRRH....3-5 80-85
Picture Sleeves
A&M....3-4 85-88
EPs: 7-inch
MYRRH (001 "Ageless Medley")....4-8 83
LPs: 10/12-inch
A&M (Black vinyl)....5-10 85-92
A&M ("Home for Christmas")....40-80 92
(Picture disc. Promotional issue only. Selection number not known.)
MYRRH (Except 901644158)....5-10 80-85
MYRRH (901644158 "Collection") 20-30 86
(Picture disc. Promotional issue only.)
Also see CETERA, Peter, & Amy Grant
Also see GARFUNKEL, Art / Amy Grant

GRANT, Amy, & Vince Gill
Singles: 7-inch
A&M....3-5 94
Also see GILL, Vince
Also see GRANT, Amy

GRANT, Barry C&W '79
Singles: 7-inch
CSI....3-5 79-80
Also see AMARILLO
Also see BREAKFAST BARRY

GRANT, Carrie, & Grandeors
Singles: 7-inch
NEW ART....4-8
NEWTOWN....5-10 63

GRANT, Cary
Singles: 7-inch
COLUMBIA (44377 "Christmas Lullaby")....4-8 67

GRANT, David R&B/D&D '83
Singles: 12-inch
CHRYSALIS....4-6 83
Singles: 7-inch
CAPITOL....3-4 86
CHRYSALIS....3-4 83
Also see GRAHAM, Jaki, & David Grant
Also see LINX

GRANT, Earl P&R/R&B '58
Singles: 78 rpm
PRINCE....4-8 56
Singles: 7-inch
DECCA....3-8 58-70
PRINCE (1201 "One-Way Street")...5-10 56
(Black vinyl.)
PRINCE (1201 "One-Way Street")....10-20 56
(Colored vinyl.)
EPs: 7-inch
DECCA....5-10 59-62
LPs: 10/12-inch
DECCA....8-18 59-70
MCA....5-10 76
VOCALION....5-10 69-70

GRANT, Eddy R&B '79
Singles: 12-inch
EPIC....4-6 80-82
PORTRAIT....4-6 83-85
Singles: 7-inch
EPIC....3-4 79-80
PORTRAIT....3-4 83-85
Picture Sleeves
PORTRAIT....3-4 84
LPs: 10/12-inch
EPIC....5-10 79-80
PORTRAIT....5-10 83-85
Also see EQUALS

GRANT, Eleanor R&B '76
Singles: 7-inch
CBS ASSOCIATED....3-4 84-85
CATAWBA....3-4 83
COLUMBIA....3-4 76

GRANT, George, & Castelles: see CASTELLES

GRANT, Gogi P&R '55
Singles: 78 rpm
ERA....8-15 55-56
RCA....5-10 52-57
Singles: 7-inch
CHARTER....4-8 63
ERA....10-20 55-56
LIBERTY....5-10 60-61
MONUMENT....4-6 66-67
PETE....4-6 68-69
RCA....10-20 52-58
20TH FOX....4-6 61-62
Picture Sleeves
20TH FOX....5-10 61
EPs: 7-inch
ERA....10-20 56
RCA (Except 1030)....5-10 57-58
RCA (4112 "Helen Morgan Story")..15-25 57
(Soundtrack.)
LPs: 10/12-inch
CHARTER....8-12 64
ERA (106 "The Wayward Wind")...10-20 60s
ERA (20001 "Suddenly There's Gogi Grant")....25-40 56
(Black vinyl.)
ERA (20001 "Suddenly There's Gogi Grant")....50-100 56
(Colored vinyl.)
LIBERTY....10-20 60
PETE....6-10 68-70
RCA (Except 1030)....15-25 57-59
RCA (1030 "Helen Morgan Story")....60-70 57
(Soundtrack.)
Also see PRESLEY, Elvis / Vaughn Monroe / Gogi Grant / Robert Shaw

GRANT, Jane: see GRANT, Janie

GRANT, Janie P&R '61
(Jane Grant)
Singles: 7-inch
CAPRICE....10-15 61-62
DOT....10-15 57
PARKWAY (982 "My Heart, Your Heart")....15-25 66
STEPHANY (1821 "Pinball Machine")....15-25 58
U.A....5-10 63-65
Session: James Ray.
Also see RAY, James

GRANT, Jerry, & Rockabilly Bandits
(Gerry Granahan)
Singles: 7-inch
ATCO (6100 "Talkin' About Love")....20-30 57
Also see GRANAHAN, Gerry

GRANT, Johnny
Singles: 7-inch
PANORAMA....5-8

GRANT, Lola
Singles: 7-inch
TOP TEN (252 "Susie")....10-20

GRANT, O.S., & Downbeats
Singles: 7-inch
SARG (197 "Falling Stars")............20-35 56
SARG (200 "You Did Me Wrong") 20-35 56
Also see DOWNBEATS

GRANT, Tom C&W '79
Singles: 7-inch
ELEKTRA.. 3-4 82
REPUBLIC....................................... 3-5 79
Also see SMITH, Margo, & Tom Grant

GRANT, Tom R&B '81
Singles: 7-inch
WMOT... 3-5 81

GRANT'S BLUE BOYS
Singles: 7-inch
GARLAND (2014 "If I Were a Carpenter")..............................20-40 69

GRANTHAM, Needom Carrol
Singles: 7-inch
STAX.. 3-5 73

GRANTS, Little Guy
Singles: 7-inch
LAWN (103 "So Young")...........125-150 59

GRAPEFRUIT P&R '68
Singles: 7-inch
EQUINOX....................................... 4-8 68
LPs: 10/12-inch
DUNHILL......................................10-12 68
RCA...10-12 69

GRAPES OF WRATH
Singles: 7-inch
VITA (006 "Cauz It Was Her")........10-20 60s

GRAPES OF WRATH
LPs: 10/12-inch
CAPITOL...................................... 5-10 86-88
Members: Kevin Kane; Tom Kane; Hooper Kane.

GRAPEVINE
Singles: 7-inch
MGM... 4-8 68
Also see CARMEL

GRAPPELLI, Stephane
LP: 10/12-inch
ATLANTIC (1391 "Finesse + Feeling = Jazz")...10-20

GRAPPELLI, Stephane, & David Grisman
LPs: 10/12-inch
W.B. 5-10 81
Also see GRISMAN, David

GRAPPELLI, Stephane, & Barney Kessel
LPs: 10/12-inch
MFSL (111 "I Remember Django")..............................30-40 84
Also see GRAPPELLI, Stephane, & David Grisman
Also see NELSON, Rick

GRASS
Singles: 7-inch
GOLDUST (5016 "I'm Gettin' Tired")......................................15-25 67

GRASS, Dick, & Hoppers
Singles: 7-inch
ARROW.. 4-8

GRASS ROOTS P&R '66
(Rob Grill & the Grass Roots)
Singles: 7-inch
ABC.. 3-5 70
DUNHILL (4013 "Mr. Jones") 8-12 65
DUNHILL (4029 thru 15006).......... 4-8 66-74
DUNHILL OLDIES............................ 3-5 70s
HAVEN... 3-5 75-76
MCA.. 3-4 82
OAK... 4-6
ROULETTE..................................... 3-5 70s
Picture Sleeves
DUNHILL (4094 "Things I Should Have Said").. 8-12 67
DUNHILL (4237 "Baby Hold On")..... 5-10 70
DUNHILL (4249 "Come on and Say It")... 5-10 70
EPs: 7-inch
DUNHILL (165 "Grass Roots") 8-12 71
(Promotional issue only.)
LPs: 10/12-inch
ABC.. 8-10 76
ABC/COMMAND (40013 "Their 16 Greatest Hits")..15-25 74
(Quadraphonic.)
DUNHILL.......................................10-20 66-73
GUSTO... 5-8 78
HAVEN... 8-10 75
MCA.. 5-10 81-82
PICKWICK...................................... 5-10 78
Members: Rob Grill; Warren Entner; Creed Bratton; Erik Coonce. Session: Denny Provisor; Joel Larson; Joe Osborn; P.F. Sloan; Reid Kailing.
Also see DESTINATIONS
Also see GRILL, Rob
Also see JIM & JOE
Also see MERRY-GO-ROUND
Also see PROVISOR, Denny
Also see SLOAN, P.F.

GRASSFIRE
Singles: 7-inch
STEAMBOAT (48250 "Smell of Incense")................................10-20 69

Members: Jerry Edwards; Bill Forseth; Gary Lynn; Roger Lynn; Ed Gallagher.

GRASSHOPPER, J.W.
Singles: 7-inch
BROWN DOG (9003 "Ali Shuffle")...5-10 60s

GRASSHOPPERS
Singles: 7-inch
KAPP...10-15 61
SUNBURST (104 "Twin Beat").......10-20 65
SUNBURST (105 "Pink Champagne")...................................10-20 65
W.B. (5607 "Twin Beat")................10-20 65

GRASSHOPPERS
Singles: 7-inch
FOX...20-25 67
Also see CAIN

GRASSHOPPERS Featuring Eddie Maynard
LPs: 10/12-inch
PIROUETTE (56 "Sing Along") 10-20 59

GRASSI, Lucy Ann, & Del-Aires
Singles: 7-inch
VOLCANIC (1002 "Boy Crazy")..................................2000-3000 64

GRATE, Miriam, & Dovers
Singles: 78 rpm
APOLLO (472 "My Angel")..........50-100 55
Singles: 7-inch
APOLLO (472 "My Angel").........150-250 55
Also see DOVERS

GRATEFUL DEAD LP '67
Singles: 12-inch
ARISTA..5-10 88
Singles: 7-inch
ARISTA (Black vinyl) 3-5 77-88
ARISTA (Colored vinyl) 4-6 87
FLASHBACK.................................... 3-4 80
GRATEFUL DEAD............................8-15 73-76
SCORPIO (201 "Don't Ease Me In")..75-150 66
W.B. 10-15 67-73
Promotional Singles
ARISTA 4-6 77-87
GRATEFUL DEAD............................12-20 73-76
W.B. 10-20 67-73
Picture Sleeves
ARISTA (0519 "Alabama Getaway") . 4-6 80
ARISTA (9606 "Touch of Grey") 3-5 87
GRATEFUL DEAD (03 "U.S. Blues") 15-20 74
W.B. (7186 "Dark Star")..................35-55 68
EPs: 7-inch
W.B. (226 "American Beauty").......20-30 70
(Juke box issue only.)
W.B. (438 "American Beauty")...100-200 70
(Radio Spots.)
W.B. (544 "Europe 72")..................20-30 72
(Juke box issue only.)
LPs: 10/12-inch
ARISTA..5-10 77-90
DIRECT-DISK.................................10-15 79
GRATEFUL DEAD (01 "Wake of the Flood")...20-25 73
(No mention on cover of distribution by United Artists.)
GRATEFUL DEAD (01 "Wake of the Flood")...15-20 70s
(Reads "Distribution by United Artists" on cover.)
GRATEFUL DEAD (102 "Mars Hotel")..20-25 74
(No mention on cover of distribution by United Artists.)
GRATEFUL DEAD (102 "Mars Hotel")...10-15 70s
(Reads "Distribution by United Artists" on cover.)
GRATEFUL DEAD (494 "Blues for Allah")...20-25 75
GRATEFUL DEAD (620 "Steal Your Face")...25-30 76
GRATEFUL DEAD (40132 "One from the Vault")..5-10 91
MFSL (014 "American Beauty") 60-80 78
MFSL (172 "From the Mars Hotel")...40-60 85
PAIR...6-12 84
PRIDE..12-20 73
SUNFLOWER (5001 "Vintage Dead")...25-35 70
SUNFLOWER (5004 "Historic Dead")...25-35 71
W.B. (W-1689 "Grateful Dead") 40-60 67
(Monaural. Gold label.)
W.B. (WS-1689 "Grateful Dead")...25-35 67
(Stereo. Gold label.)
W.B. (1689 "Grateful Dead")..........20-30 67
(With Warner Bros. - Seven Arts "W7" label.)
W.B. (1689 "The Grateful Dead")...10-20 71
(With Warner Bros. "Arrowhead" label. Cover has copyright date on back.)
W.B. (1749 "Anthem of the Sun") ..20-30 68
(Background cover color is purple. With Warner Bros. - Seven Arts "W7" label.)
W.B. (1749 "Anthem of the Sun") ..10-20 71
(Background cover color is white. With Warner Bros. "Arrowhead" logo on label.)
W.B. (1790 "Aoxomoxoa") 20-30 69
(With Warner Bros. - Seven Arts "W7" label.)
W.B. (1790 "Aoxomoxoa")...............10-20 71
(With Warner Bros. "Arrowhead" label. Cover has copyright date on back.)
W.B. (1830 "Live Dead")...................25-35 69
(With Warner Bros. - Seven Arts "W7" label. Issued with bonus pamphlet.)
W.B. (1830 "Live Dead") 15-20 71
(With Warner Bros. "Arrowhead" label. Cover has copyright date on back.)
W.B. (1869 "Workingman's Dead")..20-30 70
(With Warner Bros. - Seven Arts "W7" label.)
W.B. (1869 "Workingman's Dead")..10-15 71
(With Warner Bros. "Arrowhead" label. Cover has copyright date on back.)
W.B. (1893 "American Beauty").....15-25 70
(With Warner Bros. - Seven Arts "W7" label.)
W.B. (1893 "American Beauty").....10-15 71
(With Warner Bros. "Arrowhead" label. Cover has copyright date on back.)
W.B. (1893 "American Beauty").......5-10 75
(With Warner Blvd./street and trees label.)
W.B. (1935 "Skull & Roses")..........15-25 71
(Title shown is commonly used to describe what is actually an untitled LP. Includes bonus sticker picturing cover art.)
W.B. (2668 "Europe '72")................15-25 72
W.B. (2721 "History of the Grateful Dead, Vol. 1")...10-15 73
W.B. (2764 "Skeletons from the Closet")..8-12 74
W.B. (3091 "What a Strange Trip It's Been")...8-10 77
Promotional LPs
ARISTA (35 "Grateful Dead Sampler")..40-50 78
ARISTA (7001 "Terrapin Station")...20-25 77
(The lengthy *Terrapin Station* track is banded for radio station airplay.)
U.A. (SP-114 "For Dead Heads") ...25-50 75
Members: Jerry Garcia; Ron McKernan; Bob Weir; Bill Kreutzman; Phil Lesh; Mickey Hart; Tom Constanten; Ned Lagin; Robert Hunter; Keith Godchaux; Donna Godchaux; Brent Mydland.
Also see BROMBERG, David
Also see CLEMENTS, Vassar
Also see CROSBY, David
Also see GARCIA, Jerry
Also see GARCIA, Jerry, & Robert Hunter
Also see HART, Mickey
Also see HUNTER, Robert
Also see KANTER, Paul, & Grace Slick
Also see KEITH & DONNA
Also see KELLY, Mike
Also see KESEY, Ken
Also see NEW RIDERS of the Purple Sage
Also see SILVER
Also see WEIR, Bob

GRATEFUL DEAD / Elvin Bishop Group
Singles: 7-inch
W.B. (7627 "Johnny B. Goode").....10-20 72
Also see BISHOP, Elvin
Also see GRATEFUL DEAD

GRAVELY, Junior
Singles: 7-inch
VELATONE.....................................5-8 59

GRAVEN IMAGE
Singles: 7-inch
V.O.L. (134 "Take a Bite of Life")...20-30
LPs: 10/12-inch
AZRA (1 "Graven Image") 8-12 87
(Picture disc.)

GRAVENITES, Nick
LPs: 10/12-inch
COLUMBIA......................................10-15 69
Also see BIG BROTHER & Holding Company
Also see ELECTRIC FLAG

GRAVES, Billy P&R '59
Singles: 7-inch
MONUMENT (Except 401) 4-8 59-66
MONUMENT (401 "The Shag")........8-12 59

GRAVES, Carl P&R/R&B '74
Singles: 7-inch
A&M 3-5 74
ARIOLA AMERICA 3-5 75-77
Also see SKYLARK

GRAVES, Joe
Singles: 7-inch
PARKWAY......................................10-15 65

GRAVES, Lee
Singles: 78 rpm
MERCURY.......................................5-10 51
Singles: 7-inch
MERCURY.......................................10-15 51

GRAVES, Teresa
Singles: 7-inch
CALENDAR..3-5 69
Picture Sleeves
CALENDAR..4-6 69
LPs: 10/12-inch
KIRSHNER...8-10 70

GRAVESTONE FOUR
Singles: 7-inch
DANI (7749 "Ad Lib Beat")............10-20 63

GRAVITY ADJUSTERS EXPANSION BAND
LPs: 10/12-inch
NOCTURNE (302 "One")..........200-300 73

GRAVY
Singles: 7-inch
GRT..3-5

GRAVY TRAIN
Singles: 7-inch
BELT (102 "I'm Lonely")..................20-25 60s

GRAVYTRAIN
LPs: 10/12-inch
BELL 8-10 73

GRAVEYARD 5
Singles: 7-inch
STANCO (102 "Marble Orchard") 250-300 66

GRAY, Arvella
Singles: 7-inch
GRAY...4-8 65

GRAY, Barry, & Spacemakers
Singles: 7-inch
ABC-PAR 5-10 63

GRAY, Billy
(With His Western Okies)
Singles: 78 rpm
DECCA (29271 "We Just Don't See Things Alike")...5-10 54
DECCA (29800 "Tennessee Toddy")..10-20 56
Singles: 7-inch
DECCA (29271 "We Just Don't See Things Alike")..10-15 54
DECCA (29800 "Tennessee Toddy")..25-40 56
Also see JACKSON, Wanda, & Billy Gray

GRAY, Bobby
Singles: 7-inch
JODY 30-50 50s
OKEH..15-25 58

GRAY, Carol
Singles: 7-inch
RHYTHM (126 "Cha Cha Bop") 100-200 59

GRAY, Charles
Singles: 7-inch
CHOICE (843 "Just Because")...........5-10
VILLAGE..5-10

GRAY, Charlie
Singles: 7-inch
CLYMAX (2 "Completely Satisfied")..20-40

GRAY, Claude C&W '60
(With the Graymen)
Singles: 7-inch
COLUMBIA...4-6 64-66
COUNTRY INT'L....................................3-4 81-86
D..5-10 59-60
DECCA...3-6 66-71
GRANNY..3-5 76-82
MERCURY...4-8 60-64
MILLION..3-5 72-73
MINOR...8-12
LPs: 10/12-inch
DECCA...8-12 67-68
MERCURY...15-25 62
MILLION..5-10 72
PICKWICK/HILLTOP..............................8-12 67

GRAY, Claude, & Norma Jean C&W '82
Singles: 7-inch
GRANNY WHITE 3-4 82
Also see GRAY, Claude
Also see NORMA JEAN

GRAY, Dave
Singles: 7-inch
MARK..8-10 59

GRAY, Diva, & Oyster R&B '80
Singles: 7-inch
COLUMBIA..3-4 79-80
LPs: 10/12-inch
COLUMBIA..5-10 79
Also see ROUNDTREE

GRAY, Dobie P&R '63
Singles: 12-inch
INFINITY...5-8 79
Singles: 7-inch
ARISTA...3-4 83
CAPITOL (5853 "River Deep, Mountain High")...5-8 67
CAPITOL (44126 "Love Letters")...........3-4 87
CAPRICORN..3-5 76-77
CHARGER (105 "The 'In' Crowd").........4-8 64
CHARGER (107 "See You at the Go-Go")..4-8 65
CHARGER (109 "In Hollywood")............4-8 65
CHARGER (113 "Monkey Jerk")............4-8 65
CHARGER (115 "Out on the Floor") ..4-8 66
COLLECTABLES 3-4 81
CORDAK (1602 "Look at Me")...........8-12 62
CORDAK (1605 "Feelin' in My Heart")..8-12 63
CORDAK (1701 "My Shoes Keep Walkin' Back to You")..8-12 64
DECCA...3-5 73
ERIC..3-4 70s
GUSTO...3-4 85
INFINITY..3-5 78-79
JAF (2504 "Be a Man")..........................8-12 63
MCA..3-4 73-75
REAL FINE (835 "Tears Keep Falling on My Tears")...8-12 62
ROBOX..3-4 81
STRIPE (827 "To Be Wanted")......10-15 60
STRIPE (828 "Rags to Riches").....10-15 60
STRIPE (829 "Love Has a Way")...10-15 60
STRIPE (831 "Love Has a Way")....10-15 61
STRIPE (832 "Kissin' Doll") 10-15 61
WHITE WHALE (300 "Rose Garden")...4-8 69
WHITE WHALE (330 "Do You Really Have a Heart"/"What a Way to Go")........100-200 69
WHITE WHALE (330 "Do You Really Have a Heart"/"Do You Really Have a Heart")..50-75 69
(Promotional issue only.)
WHITE WHALE (342 "Honey, You Can't Take It Back")..25-50 70

LPs: 10/12-inch
CAPITOL...5-10 86
CAPRICORN..8-10 76
CHARGER 15-20 65
DECCA..8-10 73
INFINITY..6-10 79
MCA...8-10 73-74
ROBOX..5-10 81
STRIPE...10-12

GRAY, Dolores
Singles: 78 rpm
CAPITOL..5-10 57
DECCA..3-8 51-55
Singles: 7-inch
CAPITOL..5-10 57
DECCA..5-10 51-55
LPs: 10/12-inch
CAPITOL (897 "Warm Brandy") 15-25 57

GRAY, Dori Anne
Singles: 78 rpm
MERCURY...5-10 56
Singles: 7-inch
MERCURY (70801 "Heartbreak Alley")..10-15 56

GRAY, Eddie
Singles: 7-inch
VIM ("Let Me Hold Your Hand") 10-20
(Selection number not known.)

GRAY, Gene, & Stingrays
Singles: 7-inch
DOT (16478 "Surf Bunny") 10-15 63
LINDA (110 "Surf Bunny") 20-30 63
(First issue.)

GRAY, Glen, & Casa Loma Orchestra P&R '31
Singles: 78 rpm
CAPITOL..3-5 56-57
DECCA...3-5 55
MERCURY...3-5 47
Singles: 7-inch
CAPITOL..4-8 56-58
DECCA...4-8 55
EPs: 7-inch
CAPITOL..5-10 56-58
LPs: 10/12-inch
CAPITOL..5-15 56-63
Also see ELLIS, Anita / Glen Gray & His Orchestra

GRAY, Henry, & His Bayou Buddies
Singles: 7-inch
SUN LAND (106 "Tell Me Baby").......3-4 92
(Black vinyl.)
SUN LAND (106 "Tell Me Baby").......5-6 92
(Colored vinyl.)

GRAY, Jan C&W '80
Singles: 7-inch
CYPRESS...3-4 86
JAMEX..3-4 82-84
PAID...3-5 80

GRAY, Jimmy
Singles: 7-inch
GLOBE (006 "Two Timer") 10-20 59
SHASTA..5-10 60

GRAY, Johnny
Singles: 7-inch
TODD..5-10 60
Also see PUDDLE JUMPERS

GRAY, Linda
Singles: 7-inch
KARATE..4-8 65

GRAY, Louis
Singles: 7-inch
ERA...5-8 61

GRAY, Mark C&W '83
Singles: 7-inch
COLUMBIA..3-4 83-86
Picture Sleeves
COLUMBIA (04610 "Diamond in the Dust")..3-4 84

GRAY, Mark, & Bobbi Lace C&W '88
Singles: 7-inch
615...3-4 88
Also see LACE, Bobbi

GRAY, Mark, & Tammy Wynette C&W '85
Singles: 7-inch
COLUMBIA..3-4 85
615...3-4 88
Also see GRAY, Mark
Also see WYNETTE, Tammy

GRAY, Maureen P&R '62
Singles: 7-inch
CHANCELLOR (1082 "Crazy Over You")...10-20 61
CHANCELLOR (1091 "I Don't Want to Cry")..10-20 61
CHANCELLOR (1100 "There Is a Boy")..25-45 62
LANDA (689 "Dancin' the Strand")...10-20 62
LANDA (692 "People Are Talking")..10-20 62
MERCURY...6-12 63-64

GRAY, Pearlean
(With the Passengers)
Singles: 7-inch
DCP (1125 "For Your Love")..............8-12 65
DCP (1143 "Don't Rush Me Baby")...8-12 65
GREEN-SEA (104 "Love of My Man")..10-20 66

GRAY, Phil
Singles: 7-inch
ROBBINS (1002 "Somebody's Got My Baby") 35-50 58

GRAY, Ron, & Countdowns
Singles: 7-inch
N-JOY (1013 "No More") 8-12 65

GRAY, Rudy
(Rudy Grayzell)
Singles: 78 rpm
CAPITOL 10-20 55
Singles: 7-inch
CAPITOL (2946 "There's Gonna Be a Ball") 20-30 55
CAPITOL (3044 "You Better Believe It") 20-30 55
CAPITOL (3149 "Please Big Mama") 20-30 55
Also see GRAYZELL, Rudy

GRAY, Wardell, Quintet
Singles: 7-inch
VEE JAY 10-20 55

GRAY, Wayne
Singles: 7-inch
GOLD CIRCLE (1002 "Space Man's Guitar") 15-25 58

GRAY, Willie Charles
Singles: 7-inch
SSS INT'L 5-10

GRAY THINGS
Singles: 7-inch
LAURIE 10-15 67

GRAYCO, Helen
Singles: 78 rpm
VIK 4-8 56
"X" 4-8 54-55
Singles: 7-inch
VIK 10-15 56
"X" 8-12 54-55

GRAYGHOST C&W '89
Singles: 7-inch
MERCURY 3-4 89
Also see RAZORBACK

GRAYSON, Ann
Singles: 7-inch
RCA 5-8 59

GRAYSON, Bobby, & His Orbits
Singles: 7-inch
JAMCO (105 "Look Over Here Girl") 20-40 63

GRAYSON, Calvin
Singles: 7-inch
CAPITOL 5-10 65

GRAYSON, Jack C&W '79
(With Blackjack; "Blackjack" Jack Grayson; Jack Lebsock)
Singles: 7-inch
AMI 3-4 83-84
CHURCHILL 3-5 79
HITBOUND 3-5 79-80
JOE-WES 3-4 82
KOALA 3-4 80-81
LPs: 10/12-inch
JOE-WES 5-8 82
Also see LEBSOCK, Jack

GRAYSON, Joel
Singles: 7-inch
RIVERSIDE (4557 "My True Story") 40-60 63

GRAYSON, Kim C&W '87
Singles: 7-inch
SOUNDWAVES 3-4 87-88
Picture Sleeves
SOUNDWAVES 3-4 87

GRAYSON, Milton
(With Herb Alpert: Milt Grayson)
Singles: 7-inch
ARWIN (1005 "Don't Blame Me") 15-25 59
COLPIX (626 "Reward") 30-40 62
DERBY (1007 "Your Old Standby") 15-25 63
KEEN (2007 "Beggar Boy") 10-20 58
KEEN (5-2007 "Beggar Boy") 30-40 58
(Stereo. Colored vinyl.)
KEEN (2010 "No Greater Love") 15-25 58
KEEN (2020 "I Want You to Know") 10-15 59
KEEN (2102 "It Ain't Necessarily So") 10-15 59
MGM ((13699 "Hurry Sundown") 10-15 67
Also see ALPERT, Herb

GRAYTONES
Singles: 7-inch
EMPIRE STUDIOS (1001 "Weird One") 10-20 61

GRAYZELL, Rudy
(With His Thunderbirds; with Sparkels; Rudy "Tutti" Grazell)
Singles: 78 rpm
MERCURY 25-50 57
STARDAY 30-60 56-57
Singles: 7-inch
AWARD (130 "You'll Be Mine") 15-25 59
MERCURY (71138; "Let's Get Wild") 25-50 57
STARDAY (229 "The Moon Is Up") 20-30 56
STARDAY (241 "Duck Tail") 40-60 56
STARDAY (270 "Jig-Ga-Lee-Ga") 40-60 56
STARDAY (229 "The Moon Is Up") 40-60 56
STARDAY (321 "Let's Get Wild") 40-60 57
SUN (290 "Judy") 20-30 58
Also see GRAY, Rudy

GRAZIANO, Rocky
Singles: 78 rpm
RAMA 10-15 55
Singles: 7-inch
RAMA (178 "Back in My Old Neighborhood") 15-25 55

GREAN, Charles P&R/LP '69
(Charles Randolph Grean Sounde)
Singles: 7-inch
DOT 3-6 67
RANWOOD 3-5 69-79
LPs: 10/12-inch
RANWOOD 6-12 69-70

GREASE
Singles: 7-inch
USA (921 "Spoonful") 15-25 68
Members: Jim Krueger; Junior Olson; Larry Byrne; Jim Denk; Andy Pigeon; Paul Kowalski; Mike Larsheid; Mark La Que.

GREASE
Singles: 7-inch
LION 3-5 72-73

GREASE BAND LP '71
Singles: 7-inch
SHELTER 3-5 71
LPs: 10/12-inch
SHELTER 8-10 71
Member: Henry McCullough.
Also see COCKER, Joe
Also see McCARTNEY, Paul

GREASERS
Singles: 7-inch
JAYE JOSEPH (1002 "Movin' Out") 20-30 63
Member: Larry Bright.
Also see BRIGHT, Larry

GREAT BEAR
LPs: 10/12-inch
SCEPTER 8-10 71

GREAT BELIEVERS
Singles: 7-inch
CASCADE (365 "Comin' Up Fast") 40-60 66
Member: Johnny Winter.
Also see WINTER, Johnny

GREAT BUILDINGS
Singles: 7-inch
COLUMBIA 3-4 81
Picture Sleeves
COLUMBIA 3-5 81
LPs: 10/12-inch
COLUMBIA 5-10 81
Member: Ian Ainsworth, Richard Sandford, Philip Solem, Danny Wilde.

GREAT EXPECTATIONS
Singles: 7-inch
PHIL-L.A. OF SOUL 3-5

GREAT GATES: see GATES, Ed "Great"

GREAT IMPOSTERS
Singles: 7-inch
DADS (6398 "Who Do Your Love") 20-25 66
Picture Sleeves
DADS (6398 "Who Do Your Love") 25-35 66

GREAT GATES
Singles: 78 rpm
4 STAR 10-20
MILTONE 20-30
SELECTIVE 20-25

GREAT JONES
LPs: 10/12-inch
TONSIL 8-10 70

GREAT NATHANIEL
Singles: 7-inch
VANN 5-10 61

GREAT PLAINS C&W '91
Singles: 7-inch
COLUMBIA 3-4 91
Members: Michael Young; Russ Pahl; Denny Dadmum-Bixby.
Also see JOHNSON, Michael

GREAT PRETENDER & TENNESSEE TWO & A HALF
(Mitchell Torok")
Singles: 7-inch
COLUMBIA 10-15 58
Also see TOROK, Mitchell
Singles: 7-inch

GREAT PRIDE
Singles: 7-inch
CASTLE (113 "The Other Rock'n Roll") 15-20

GREAT SCOTS
(Great Scotts)
Singles: 7-inch
EPIC (9805 "Don't Want Your Love") 10-15 65
EPIC (9866 "That's My Girl") 20-30 65
LONDON (17348 "Ball & Chain") 10-20 66
(Canadian.)
TRIUMPH (66 "Ball & Chain") 15-25 66
TRIUMPH (67 "Light Hurts My Eyes") 15-25 67

GREAT!! SOCIETY!!
Singles: 7-inch
COLUMBIA (44583 "Sally Go 'Round the Roses") 10-15 68
NORTHBEACH (1001 "Someone to Love") 100-150 66
Member: Grace Slick.
Also see JEFFERSON AIRPLANE
Also see SLICK, Grace

GREAT SEBASTIAN
(Wayne Cochran)
Singles: 7-inch
REBEL (1333 "The Naughty Coo") 50-100 57
Also see COCHRAN, Wayne

GREAT SPACE COASTER
LPs: 10/12-inch
COLUMBIA 5-10 82

GREAT SPECKLED BIRD
LPs: 10/12-inch
AMPEX 5-10

GREAT TRAIN ROBBERY
Singles: 7-inch
ABC 4-6 69
Member: Chuck Trois.

GREAT WHITE LP '84
Singles: 7-inch
CAPITOL 3-4 86-90
EMI AMERICA 3-4 84
Picture Sleeves
CAPITOL 3-4 86-89
LPs: 10/12-inch
CAPITOL 5-10 86-91
EMI AMERICA 5-10 84
ENIGMA 5-8 88
GREENWORLD 5-10 85
Members: Jack Russell; Mark Kendall; Michael Ardie; Audie Desbrow; Tony Montana.

GREATER EXPERIENCE
Singles: 7-inch
COLONY (2572 "Don't Forget to Remember") 15-25 60s

GREATER HARVEST BAPTIST CHURCH CHOIR
Singles: 7-inch
SHARP 5-10 62
LPs: 10/12-inch
SHARP 15-25 62
Members: Maurice McAlister; Leonard Caston; Barbara Caston; Richard Dickerson; Green McLaurin.
Also see RADIANTS

GREATEST LITTLE SOUL BAND IN THE LAND
Singles: 7-inch
CONGRESS (6002 "Something for My People") 5-10 69
Member: J.J. Jackson.
Also see JACKSON, J.J.

GREATEST SHOW ON EARTH
LPs: 10/12-inch
HARVEST 8-10 70

GREATS
Singles: 7-inch
EBB (145 "Marching Elvis") 20-25 58

GREAVES, R.B. P&R/R&B '69
Singles: 7-inch
ATCO 3-5 69-70
BAREBACK 3-5 77
MGM 3-5 73
MIDSONG 3-4 80
SUNFLOWER 3-5 72
20TH FOX 3-5 74
LPs: 10/12-inch
ATCO 15-20 69

GREBENSHIKOV, Boris LP '89
LPs: 10/12-inch
COLUMBIA 5-8 89

GRECCO, Cyndi P&R '76
Singles: 7-inch
PRIVATE STOCK 3-5 76-77
LPs: 10/12-inch
PRIVATE STOCK 5-8 76

GRECCO, Johnny, & Devies
Singles: 7-inch
SONIC (813 "Hogwalk") 10-20 63

GRECCO, Tony: see GRECO, Tony

GRECH, Rick LP '73
Singles: 7-inch
RSO 3-5 73
LPs: 10/12-inch
RSO 5-10 73

GRECO, Buddy P&R '47
(Buddy Greco Trio)
Singles: 78 rpm
CORAL 3-8 51-55
KAPP 3-8 56
Singles: 7-inch
CORAL 5-15 51-55
EPIC 5-15 58-67
HERALD 5-10 59
KAPP 5-10 56
MGM 3-5 71-72
REPRISE 4-8 66-68
SCEPTER 4-6 69
Picture Sleeves
EPIC 5-10 64-65
EPs: 7-inch
CORAL 5-15 55
LPs: 10/12-inch
CORAL 15-25 55
EPIC 10-15 60-66
HARMONY 8-12 68
KAPP 10-15 61
MVM 10-15 60s
SCEPTER 5-10 69-73
VOCALION 8-12 64

GRECO, Johnny
(With the Davies; with Vandells)
Singles: 7-inch
FAR-MEL (1 "Gloria") 200-300 63
PAGEANT (602 "Rocket Ride") 75-125 63
SONIC (813 "High School Dance") 50-75 59

GRECO, Juliette
Singles: 7-inch
COLUMBIA (41011 "Si") 5-10 57
Picture Sleeves
COLUMBIA (41011 "Si") 10-15 57

GRECO, Leo
Singles: 7-inch
MMIRROR 10-15 59

GRECO, Tony
(With the Free Fall 3; Tony Grecco)
Singles: 7-inch
BIG BEAT 10-15 62
BUZZ 5-10 64
CUCA (1053 "Say Mama") 10-15 62

GREEK FOUNTAINS
Singles: 7-inch
BOFUZ 10-20 60s
MONTEL 10-15 66
PHILIPS 10-15 66
LPs: 10/12-inch
MONTEL (110 "Requests") 50-75 66

GREELEY, George LP '61
Singles: 7-inch
W.B. 3-5 59-62
Picture Sleeves
W.B. 3-5 62
EPs: 7-inch
CAPITOL 5-10 56
LPs: 10/12-inch
CAPITOL 5-15 56
RAVE 10-20 56
W.B. 5-10 59-61

GREEN
Singles: 7-inch
ATCO 3-6 70-71
LPs: 10/12-inch
ATCO 10-12 69-71

GREEN, Al P&R/R&B '67
(With the Soul Mates; Al Greene)
Singles: 7-inch
A&M 3-5 87-89
BELL 4-6 72-73
FLASHBACK 3-5 70s
HI 4-8 69-78
HOT LINE (15000 "Back Up Train") 10-15 67
HOT LINE (15002 "I'll Be Good to You") 10-15 68
MOTOWN 3-5 82-85
Picture Sleeves
A&M (2919 "Everything's Gonna Be Alright") 3-5 87
HI (77505 "Belle") 4-8 77
HI (78522 "Wait Here") 4-8 78
LPs: 10/12-inch
A&M 5-10 87
BELL 8-10 72
CAPITOL (Black vinyl) 5-8 90s
CAPITOL (Colored vinyl) 10-15 90s
HI (6004 "Belle Album") 8-10 77
HI (27121 "Let's Stay Together") 8-10 95
(Colored vinyl.)
HI (27127 "I'm Still in Love with You") 8-10 95
(Colored vinyl.)
HI (32000 series) 10-20 69-78
HOT LINE (1500 "Back Up Train") 20-40 67
KORY 8-10 77
MELODY 5-10
MOTOWN 5-10 82-85
MYRRH 5-10 80-83
RIGHT STUFF (27121 "Let's Stay Together") 10-12 95
(Colored vinyl.)
RIGHT STUFF (27627 "I'm Still in Love with You") 10-12 95
(Colored vinyl.)
Also see LENNOX, Annie, & Al Green

GREEN, Barbara: see GREENE, Barbara

GREEN, Bernie, & Stereo Mad-Men
LPs: 10/12-inch
RCA (1929 "Musically Mad") 30-50 58

GREEN, Betty
Singles: 7-inch
CRACKERJACK (4018 "He's Down on Me") 10-15 60s
CLARA (111 "He's Down on Me") 8-12 60s

GREEN, Big Charles
Singles: 7-inch
HITT (180 "Rockin' on the Moon Tonight") 35-50 58

GREEN, Bill C&W '76
Singles: 7-inch
PHONO 3-5 76
NSD 3-5 78

GREEN, Birdie: see GREEN, Byrdie

GREEN, Bob, & Missiles
Singles: 7-inch
SOMA (1163 "Above and Beyond") 20-25 61

GREEN, Bobby
Singles: 7-inch
OAK (4429 "Little Heart Attacks") ..50-60

GREEN, Boy
Singles: 78 rpm
REGIS (120 "A & B Blues") 50-100 44

GREEN, Byrdie
Singles: 7-inch
END (1117 "Tremblin' ") 8-12 62
HALLMARK 5-10
PRESTIGE 5-10
20TH FOX (422 "Don't Take Your Love from Me") 15-25 63

GREEN, Cal
Singles: 7-inch
FEDERAL (12318 "The Big Push") 10-15 58
MUTT & JEFF 5-10

GREEN, Carl, Orchestra
Singles: 78 rpm
METEOR (5002 "My Best Friend") 25-50 53
METEOR (5009 "Boogie Freight") 25-50 53

GREEN, Clarence
(With the High Type Five; with Rhythmaires)
Singles: 78 rpm
EDDIE'S 15-25 48
Singles: 7-inch
AQUARIUS 3-5
BRIGHT STAR 10-20
C&P 10-20 59
CHESS (1732 "Mary My Darling") 20-30 59
DUKE 5-10 66
GOLDEN EAGLE 10-20
MASTER 10-20 60
SHOMAR 10-15 61
Also see GREEN, Galveston

GREEN, Claude
Singles: 7-inch
ABC-PAR 5-10

GREEN, Darren R&B '73
Singles: 7-inch
RCA 3-5 73-74

GREEN, Denny
LPs: 10/12-inch
MIDSONG 5-10 79

GREEN, DeRoy
(With the Cool Gents)
Singles: 7-inch
CEE=JAY (584 "At the Teen Center") 100-150 61
SOOZEE (111 "At the Teen Center") 50-100 62

GREEN, Fred
Singles: 7-inch
BOBBIN (111 "Wham Slam Bam") 50-75 59
BOBBIN (123 "Don't Make a Fool of Me") 50-75 59

GREEN, Fred, & Mellards
(With Emmett Carter's Combo)
Singles: 78 rpm
BALLAD 50-100 55
Singles: 7-inch
BALLAD (1012 "You Can't Keep Love in a Broken Heart") 200-250 55
BALLAD (1016 "Love Me Crazy") 100-150 55
Also see GREEN, Fred

GREEN, Galveston
(Clarence Green)
Singles: 78 rpm
ESSEX 10-20 52
Also see GREEN, Clarence

GREEN, Garland P&R/R&B '69
Singles: 7-inch
CASINO 3-5 76
COTILLION 3-6 71
GAMMA 20-40 67
OCEAN FRONT 3-4 83
RCA 3-6 77
REVUE 5-10 67-68
SPRING 5-10 74-75
UNI 4-8 69
LPs: 10/12-inch
OCEAN FRONT 5-10 83
RCA 8-10 74-78
UNI 10-12 70

GREEN, George
Singles: 78 rpm
CHANCE (1135 "Finance Man") 25-50 53
Singles: 7-inch
CHANCE (1135 "Finance Man") ..75-100 53

GREEN, George "Stardust"
(Stardust Green)
Singles: 7-inch
GATEWAY (751 "All Alone") 5-10 65
TEMPUS (1509 "Hug My Pillow") ..10-15 59

GREEN, Grant LP '71
LPs: 10/12-inch
BLUE NOTE 15-25 61-65
(Label reads "Blue Note Records Inc. - New York, U.S.A.")
BLUE NOTE 10-15 66-71
(Label reads "Blue Note Records - a Division of Liberty Records Inc.")

VERVE ... 10-18 65
VERSATILE ... 5-10 78
Also see KESSEL, Barney / Grant Green / Oscar Moore / Mundell Lowe

GREEN, Griz, & Happy Timers
Singles: 7-inch
TAMPA ... 4-8 58

GREEN, Guitar Slim
(Norman Green)
Singles: 7-inch
GEENOTE (907 "Rock the Nation") ... 15-25 57
LPs: 10/12-inch
UNITED ... 10-15
Also see GREEN, R., & Turner
Also see GREEN, Slim

GREEN, Gwen & Don
Singles: 7-inch
SUNSHINE ... 5-8

GREEN, Hattie
Singles: 7-inch
ANGEL TONE (1081 "Green Light Baby") ... 15-25 50s

GREEN, Hazell
Singles: 7-inch
KIT KAT (712 "Heartless Lover") ... 15-25

GREEN, Howard, & Gay Clefs
Singles: 7-inch
SPRY ... 8-12 60

GREEN, Jack LP '80
Singles: 7-inch
RCA ... 3-4 80
LPs: 10/12-inch
RCA ... 5-10 80
Also see PRETTY THINGS
Also see T. REX

GREEN, Jane
LPs: 10/12-inch
SUPERBATONE ... 8-12 89

GREEN, Janice
(The "Oh Julie" Girl)
Singles: 7-inch
NASCO ... 10-20 58
(Janice was labeled the "Oh Julie" girl for her vocal assist on the Crescendos' *Oh Julie.*)
Also see CRESCENDOS

GREEN, Jerry
(With the Passengers; with Wildweeds)
Singles: 7-inch
ATLANTIC ... 4-8 64
COLPIX ... 5-10 61
Also see PASSENGERS

GREEN, Jerry C&W '77
Singles: 7-inch
CONCORDE ... 3-5 77

GREEN, Jimmy
Singles: 7-inch
MAH'S (0005 "Hey Little Girl") ... 8-10 61

GREEN, Johnny, Combo
Singles: 7-inch
GEE ... 10-15 61

GREEN, Johnny "Rockhouse"
(Johnny Green Combo)
Singles: 7-inch
DELUXE (6192 "Green Champagne") ... 10-20 61
GEE (1066 "Lonesome Road") ... 10-20 61
ON THE SQUARE (315 "Little Eva") ... 15-25 59

GREEN, Johnny, & Greenmen
(Greenmen)
Singles: 7-inch
EMERALD (2001 "Something You Got") ... 15-25 65
KAPP (619 "I've Had It") ... 15-25 64
RANWOOD (838 "Poor Little Fat Girl") ... 10-20 69
LP: 10/12-inch
AVI ("Seven Over from Mars") ... 10-20 67
(Selection number not known.)
EDMAR (1140 "When You're Green You're Clean") ... 8-12 74
Member: Johnny Green Pavlick; Joyce Bowers; Howard Wales; Tommy Lee; Bobby Van Holten; Dorin Miller; Denny Lee Sesso; Russ Harding; John Frost Trombatore; Marilyn Winters; Dick Person; John Stratford; George Eberdt.
Also see GREEN MEN
Also see ROSCOE & LITTLE GREEN MEN

GREEN, Keith
Singles: 7-inch
DECCA ... 10-20 66
ERA/HAPPY TIGER ... 3-6 70
LPs: 10/12-inch
PRETTY GOOD ... 5-10 80
SPARROW ... 5-10 77-78

GREEN, L.C.
(With His Guitar)
Singles: 78 rpm
DOT (1103 "When the Sun Is Shining") ... 40-60 52
DOT (1128 "Little School Girl") ... 40-60 52
DOT (1147 "Little Machine") ... 40-60 52
VON (42 "Going Down to the River Blues") ... 250-500 52

GREEN, Larry
(With Pete Wade)
Singles: 7-inch
MOVIN' ... 5-10 66
PARIS (510 "The Stars Look Down") ... 10-20 58
PARIS (517 "Look Homeward Angel") ... 10-20 58
SOUL ... 5-10
LPs: 10/12-inch
BOOT ... 5-8 80
CHART ... 10-15 68-70
GRT ... 5-10 77
LITTLE DARLIN' ... 10-20 66-69
MID-LAND ... 8-12 76
MONUMENT ... 8-12 73-75
MGM ... 10-15 70
PRIZE ... 8-12 71
TIME ... 10-20 64
Also see PARKER, Bobby / Larry Green

GREEN, Laura: see GREENE, Laura

GREEN, Lil: see GREENE, Lil

GREEN, Linda
Singles: 7-inch
RCA ... 5-10 61

GREEN, Lloyd C&W '73
Singles: 7-inch
BIG A (102 "Panic a Trip") ... 10-20 67
CHART ... 10-15 69
MONUMENT ... 3-5 72-74
OCTOBER ... 3-5 76
PRIZE ... 4-8 71
Also see LEE, Bobby

GREEN, Lorne: see GREENE, Lorne

GREEN, Marlin: see GREENE, Marlin

GREEN, Mike: see GREENE, Mike

GREEN, Nick
Singles: 7-inch
GARDENA ... 5-10 60

GREEN, Nick, & Don Jackson
Singles: 7-inch
SPRAY (1007 "San Antonio Rock") ... 10-20 60
Also see GREEN, Nick

GREEN, Peter LP '80
Singles: 7-inch
SAIL ... 3-5 79
LPs: 10/12-inch
REPRISE ... 8-10 71
SAIL ... 5-10 79-80
Also see BOYD, Eddie
Also see FLEETWOOD MAC

GREEN, R., & Turner
(Norman Green)
Singles: 78 rpm
J&M FULLBRIGHT (123 "Alla Blues") ... 50-75 48
Also see GREEN, Guitar Slim
Also see GREEN, Slim

GREEN, Rodger
Singles: 7-inch
DEBONAIR (193 "Betty Mae") ... 50-100

GREEN, Rudy: see GREENE, Rudy

GREEN, St. John
LPs: 10/12-inch
FLICK DISC (001 "St. John Green") ... 50-75

GREEN, Slim
(Norman Green)
Singles: 78 rpm
CANTON (1789 "Shake 'Em Up") ... 25-50 57
MURRAY (501 "Baby, I Love You") ... 50-75 48
Singles: 7-inch
CANTON (1789 "Shake 'Em Up") ... 20-40 57
Also see GREEN, Guitar Slim
Also see GREEN, R., & Turner
Also see SIMMONS, Al, & Slim Green

GREEN, Sonny R&B '73
Singles: 7-inch
FULLER (8156 "I Can Ketch But I Can't Hold") ... 10-20
HILL (339 "Don't Write a Check with Your Mouth") ... 4-6 73
MHR ... 5-10
UNITED ARTISTS ... 3-5

GREEN, Stardust: see GREEN, George "Stardust"

GREEN, Tom
Singles: 7-inch
T GREEN (5037 "Little Sister–Get Back") ... 5-10 70s

GREEN, Vernon, & Medallions
(Medallions; Vernon Greene)
Singles: 78 rpm
DOOTO ... 20-30 57
DOOTONE ... 25-50 54-56
Singles: 7-inch
CHELAN (2001 "Please, Please, Please") ... 4-6 75
CLASSIC ARTISTS ... 4-6 89-90
DOOTO (419 "For Better Or for Worse") ... 50-75 57
DOOTO (425 "Lover's Prayer") ... 50-75 57
DOOTO (446 "Magic Mountain") ... 50-75 58
DOOTO (454 "Behind the Door") ... 30-60 59
DOOTONE (347 "The Letter") ... 75-125 54
(Red label.)
DOOTONE (347 "The Letter") ... 25-50 54
(Black label.)
DOOTONE (357 "The Telegram") ... 50-100 54
(Maroon label.)
DOOTONE (357 "The Telegram") 25-50 54
(Blue label.)
DOOTONE (364 "Edna") ... 50-100 55
DOOTONE (379 "Dear Darling") .. 50-100 55
DOOTONE (393 "I Want a Love") ... 50-100 56
DOOTONE (400 "Push Button Automobile") ... 50-100 56
DOOTONE (407 "Did You Have Fun") ... 50-75 56
DOOTONE (479 "Can You Talk") ... 3-5 73
MINIT (32034 "Look at Me, Look at Me") ... 15-25 68
PAN WORLD (71 "Dear Ann") ... 25-50 62
EPs: 7-inch
DOOTO ... 75-125 60s
DOOTONE (202 "Medallions") ... 150-250 56
LPs: 10/12-inch
DOOTO (200 series) ... 5-10
DOOTO (800 series) ... 8-12
(Counterfeits exist of most Dootone releases.)
Also see BEL-AIRES
Also see PENGUINS / Meadowlarks / Medallions / Dootones
Also see TWOVOICE, Johnny, & Medallions
Also see VERNON & CLIFF

GREEN, Vernon, & Phantoms
Singles: 78 rpm
SPECIALTY ... 15-25 56
Singles: 7-inch
SPECIALTY (581 "Sweet Breeze") ... 40-60 56
Also see GREEN, Vernon, & Medallions

GREEN BEANS
Singles: 7-inch
MERCURY ... 5-10 65
TOWER ... 5-10 66
Session: Davie Allan.

GREEN BERETS R&B '70
Singles: 7-inch
UNI ... 3-5 70

GREEN BROTHERS
Singles: 7-inch
TORTOISE (11130 "Sweet Lovin' Woman") ... 15-25 60s

GREEN BULLFROG
LPs: 10/12-inch
DECCA (75269 "Green Bullfrog") ... 15-25 71

GREEN DAY
LPs: 10/12-inch
CAROLINE ... 8-10 90s
W.B. ... 8-10 90s

GREEN GANG
Singles: 7-inch
BRAGG (226 "She Means That Much to Me") ... 10-20 60s

GREEN LYTE SUNDAY
LPs: 10/12-inch
RCA ... 8-10 70

GREEN MEN
Singles: 7-inch
GOLDEN WING ... 5-10 60s
Members: Roscoe Wharton; Johnny Green; Denny Lee
Also see GREEN, Johnny, & Greenmen
Also see ROSCOE & LITTLE GREEN MEN

GREEN ON RED LP '86
LPs: 10/12-inch
ENIGMA ... 5-10 85
MERCURY ... 5-10 86

GREEN PAJAMAS
LPs: 10/12-inch
BOMP ... 5-8 89

GREEN RIVER
Singles: 7-inch
ICP (01 "Together We'll Never") ... 15-25 86
(Colored vinyl. 800 made.)
ICP (01 "Together We'll Never") ... 5-10 86
(Black vinyl.)
EPs: 7-inch
SUB POP (11 "Dry As a Bone") ... 5-10 87
SUB POP (15 "Rehab Doll") ... 20-30 88
(Colored vinyl. 1000 made.)
SUB POP (15 "Rehab Doll") ... 10-15 88
(Black vinyl.)
LP: 10/12-inch
HOMESTEAD (031 "Come on Down") ... 20-30 85
(Colored vinyl.)
HOMESTEAD (031 "Come on Down") ... 10-15 85
(Black vinyl.)
Members: Bruce Fairweather, Mark Arm, Jeff Ament, Alex Vincent, Stone Gossard.
Also see PEARL JAM

GREEN RIVER BOYS: see CAMPBELL, Glen

GREEN SLIME
Singles: 7-inch
MGM ... 4-6 69
Picture Sleeves
MGM ... 5-8 69

GREENBAUM, Norman P&R/LP '70
Singles: 7-inch
GREGAR ... 4-6 69-70
REPRISE ... 3-5 70-71
Picture Sleeves
REPRISE ... 5-8 69
LPs: 10/12-inch
GREGAR ... 15-20 70
REPRISE ... 12-15 69-72
Also see DR. WEST'S MEDICINE SHOW & Junk Band

GREENBEATS
Singles: 7-inch
JERDEN ... 5-10 66

GREENBERG, Steve P&R '69
Singles: 7-inch
TRIP (3000 "Big Bruce") ... 4-6 69
Also see DOOLEY, Tom / Steve Greenberg

GREENE, Al: see GREEN, Al

GREENE, Barbara P&R/R&B '68
Singles: 7-inch
ATCO (6250 "Long Tall Sally") ... 25-30 62
RENEE ... 8-10 68
VIVID ... 4-8 64
Also see DELLS

GREENE, Claude "Fats"
Singles: 7-inch
CAMILLE (109 "Fat's Shake Up") ... 5-10

GREENE, Hazel, & Dick Baker
Singles: 7-inch
KIT KAT (712 "Heartless Lover") . 50-100
Also see BAKER, Dick, Combo

GREENE, Jack C&W '65
(With the Jolly Green Giants)
Singles: 7-inch
DECCA ... 3-8 65-72
EMH ... 3-4 83-84
FRONTLINE ... 3-5 80
MCA ... 3-5 73-74
LPs: 10/12-inch
CORAL ... 4-8 73
DECCA ... 8-18 66-71
EMH ... 5-10 80
51 WEST ... 5-10 84
FRONTLINE ... 5-10 80
GUSTO ... 5-10 83
HILLTOP/PICKWICK ... 5-10 83
MCA ... 5-10 73
PICKWICK ... 5-10 70s
VOCALION ... 5-10 72
Also see COCHRAN, Hank

GREENE, Jack, & Jeannie Seely C&W '72
Singles: 7-inch
DECCA ... 3-5 69-72
LPs: 10/12-inch
DECCA ... 8-12 70-72
GUSTO ... 5-8
MCA ... 4-6 73
PINNACLE ... 5-10 78
RDS ... 5-10 79
Also see GREENE, Jack
Also see SEELY, Jeannie

GREENE, Kellie
Singles: 7-inch
20TH FOX ... 10-20

GREENE, Laura R&B '69
(With Johnny McKinnis)
Singles: 7-inch
EPIC (50317 "You Take My Heart Away") ... 3-5 77
RCA (9164 "Love Is Strange") ... 10-20 67
SILVER FOX (1 "Pledging My Love") ... 4-6 69
SOUND TREK (104 "Let Me Blow Your Whistle") ... 3-5 80

GREENE, Lil P&R '40
Singles: 78 rpm
ALADDIN ... 25-50 50
ATLANTIC (951 "Every Time") ... 25-50 51
BLUEBIRD ... 12-25 39-46
GROOVE ... 8-15 56
RCA ... 10-20 46-48
Singles: 7-inch
ATLANTIC (951 "Every Time") ... 50-100 51
GROOVE (5004 "Why Don't You Do Right") ... 10-20 56
LPs: 10/12-inch
ROSETTA ... 5-10 86

GREENE, Lorne P&R/C&W/LP '64
Singles: 7-inch
COLUMBIA ... 3-6 69
GRT ... 3-5 70-71
RCA ... 5-10 62-66
Picture Sleeves
RCA ... 5-10 63-65
EPs: 7-inch
RCA (2843 "Welcome to the Ponderosa") ... 5-10 64
(Juke box issue only. Includes title strips.)
LPs: 10/12-inch
CAMDEN ... 5-10 70
MGM ... 5-10 71
RCA ... 10-20 63-66

GREENE, Marlin
Singles: 7-inch
DELTA ... 5-8
PHILIPS ... 4-8 62-63
RCA (7161 "Walkin' to the Dance") 10-15 58
U.A. ... 5-10 60
LPs: 10/12-inch
ELEKTRA ... 8-10 72

GREENE, Mike, Band
LPs: 10/12-inch
GRC ... 8-10 75
MERCURY ... 8-10 75

GREENE, Nick
Singles: 78 rpm
CAPITOL ... 5-10 57
Singles: 7-inch
CAPITOL ... 5-10 57

GREENE, Rudy
(Rudy Green)
Singles: 78 rpm
BULLET ... 15-25 47
CHANCE ... 25-50 52
EMBER ... 15-25 57
EXCELLO ... 10-20 55
Singles: 7-inch
CHANCE (1139 "Love Is a Pain") ... 50-100 52
CHANCE (1146 "The Letter") ... 50-100 52
CHANCE (1151 "I Had a Feeling") ... 50-100 52
(Black vinyl.)
CHANCE (1151 "I Had a Feeling") ... 200-300 52
(Colored vinyl.)
EMBER (1012 "You're the One for Me") ... 20-30 57
EMBER (1020 "Lonesome") ... 20-30 57
EXCELLO (2074 "Good Lovin' Mama") ... 25-35 55
EXCELLO (2090 "Teeny Weeny Baby") ... 25-35 55

GREENE, Rudy
(With the Four Buddies)
Singles: 78 rpm
CLUB 51 ... 50-75 56
Singles: 7-inch
CLUB 51 (103 "You Mean Everything to Me") ... 300-500 56
Also see FOUR BUDDIES
Also see GREENE, Rudy

GREENE, Rudy / Tony La Mar
Singles: 7-inch
SEAFAIR (3 "Oh Baby") ... 3-5 90s
Also see GREENE, Rudy
Also see LA MAR, Tony

GREENE, Vernon: see GREEN, Vernon

GREENE TWINS
Singles: 7-inch
COVER ... 5-10 59

GREENFIELD
LPs: 10/12-inch
RCA ... 8-10 73

GREENLEE, Lee
Singles: 7-inch
BRENT ... 8-12 59

GREENMEN
Singles: 7-inch
JR (91166 "Hold On, I'm Coming") .. 8-12 66

GREENSLADE
LPs: 10/12-inch
MERCURY ... 10-12 74-75
W.B. ... 10-12 73
Members: Dave Greenslade; Andy McCulloch; Tony Reeves; Martin Briley; Dave Lawson; Jill Mackintosh.
Also see BRILEY, Martin

GREENSTREET, Carl
Singles: 7-inch
ACE ... 5-10 60
DUKE ... 5-8 62

GREENSTREETS
Singles: 7-inch
CORSAIR (400 "Moon Shot") ... 20-30 64

GREENWICH, Ellie P&R '67
Singles: 7-inch
BELL ... 5-10 69
RED BIRD (034 "Baby") ... 20-30 65
U.A. ... 8-12 67
VERVE ... 5-10 70-73
LPs: 10/12-inch
U.A. (6648 "Ellie Greenwich Composes, Produces and Sings") ... 30-40 68
VERVE ... 10-15 73
Also see ARCHIES
Also see BONDS, Gary "U.S."
Also see BUTTERFLYS
Also see CROCE, Jim
Also see GAYE, Ellie
Also see GEE, Ellie
Also see MEANTIME
Also see RAINDROPS

GREENWOOD, Johnny, & Islanders
LPs: 10/12-inch
U.A. ... 12-15 63

GREENWOOD, Lee C&W '81
(Lee Greenwood Affair)
Singles: 7-inch
DOT ... 3-6 69
MCA ... 3-4 81-88
PARAMOUNT ... 3-5 71
Picture Sleeves
MCA ... 3-4 83
LPs: 10/12-inch
MCA (Except 5305) ... 5-10 83-88
MCA (5305 "Inside and Out") ... 10-15 82
(Slightly incorrect title used.)
MCA (5305 "Inside Out") ... 5-10 82
(Title corrected.)
Also see MANDRELL, Barbara, & Lee Greenwood

GREENWOOD, Lil, & Dominoes
Singles: 78 rpm
FEDERAL ... 50-100 52

Singles: 7-inch
FEDERAL (12158 "I'll Go") 200-400 52
FEDERAL (12165 "All Is Forgiven") 150-300 52

GREENWOOD, Lil, & Four Jacks
Singles: 78 rpm
FEDERAL........50-100 52
Singles: 7-inch
FEDERAL (12082 "My Last Hour")........200-400 52
FEDERAL (12093 "Never Again")........200-400 52
Also see DOMINOES
Also see GREENWOOD, Lil, & Dominoes

GREENWOOD, Mick
LPs: 10/12-inch
DECCA........8-10 71

GREENWOOD, Paul
Singles: 7-inch
ALLENBERRY (1 "Picture of a Girl")........10-15

GREENWOOD COUNTY SINGERS P&R '64
(Greenwoods)
Singles: 7-inch
DECCA........4-6 64-66
KAPP........4-6 64-66
Picture Sleeves
KAPP........4-6 64
LPs: 10/12-inch
DECCA........10-15 64
KAPP........10-15 64-66
RCA........8-12 70

GREENWOODS: see GREENWOOD COUNTY SINGERS

GREER, Big John, & Four Students
Singles: 78 rpm
GROOVE........10-20 55
KING........10-15 56-57
Singles: 7-inch
GROOVE (0131 "A Man and a Woman")........25-50 55
KING (5006 "Midnight Ramble")....15-25 56
KING (5057 "Duck Walk")........15-25 57
Also see FOUR STUDENTS
Also see GREER, John

GREER, Bonnie
Singles: 7-inch
LENOX........5-10 63

GREER, Cortez
(With the Lifters)
Singles: 7-inch
LIFTER (1001 "Yolanda")........10-20
LIFTER (59424 "Beautiful Things for You")........10-20
VIOLET (101 "Very Strong on You")........10-20
LPs: 10/12-inch
GARNER (1970 "Live at Scarlet O'Hara's")........40-60

GREER, Dan
Singles: 7-inch
BIGBEAT (149 "My Baby's Got a New Way")........10-20
SOUNDS OF MEMPHIS........5-10
Also see JACKSON, George, & Dan Greer

GREER, Dr. Douglas
Singles: 7-inch
REPRISE........4-8 66

GREER, John R&B '52
(Big John Greer; with Rhythm Rockers)
Singles: 78 rpm
GROOVE........15-25 54
KING........8-12 56
RCA........20-30 49-53
Singles: 7-inch
GROOVE (002 "Bottle It Up and Go")........20-30 54
KING (4878 "Record Hop")........10-20 56
RCA (0007 "Drinkin' Wine Spoo-Dee-O-Dee")........35-50 49
(Colored vinyl.)
RCA (0029 "If I Told You Once")....35-50 49
(Colored vinyl)
RCA (0051 "Rocking Jenny Jones")........35-50 50
(Colored vinyl)
RCA (0076 "I'll Never Do That Again")........35-50 50
(Colored vinyl.)
RCA (0096 "Cheatin'")........35-50 50
(Colored vinyl.)
RCA (0104 "Red Juice")........35-50 50
(Colored vinyl.)
RCA (0108 "Once There Lived a Fool")........15-25 51
RCA (0113 "Why Did You Go")........15-25 51
RCA (0125 "Clambake Boogie")........15-25 51
RCA (0137 "Rockin' with Big John")........15-25 51
RCA (4293 "Have Another Drink")........15-25 51
RCA (4348 "Got You on My Mind")........15-25 51
RCA (4484 "Strong Red Whiskey")........15-25 52
RCA (5037 "I'm the Fat Man")........15-25 52
RCA (5170 "You Played on My Piano")........15-25 53
RCA (5259 "Ride Pretty Baby")........15-25 53
RCA (5531 "Drinkin' Fool")........15-25 53
Also see ALLEN, Annisteen
Also see GREER, Big John, & Four Students

GREER, Paula
Singles: 7-inch
WORKSHOP JAZZ (2003 "So in Love")........15-25 63
WORKSHOP JAZZ (2007 "Falling in Love with Love")........15-25 63
LPs: 10/12-inch
WORKSHOP JAZZ (203 "Introducing Miss Paula Greer")........100-200 63

GREER, Paula, & Johnny Griffith Trio
LPs: 10/12-inch
WORKSHOP JAZZ (204 "Detroit Jazz")........100-200 63
Also see GREER, Paula
Also see GRIFFITH, Johnny, Trio

GREER BROTHERS
Singles: 7-inch
DUKE........8-12

GREG & PAUL
Singles: 7-inch
CASABLANCA........3-5 77
LPs: 10/12-inch
CASABLANCA........5-10 77
Members: Greg Evigan; Paul Shaefer.

GREG & UNKNOWNS
Singles: 7-inch
VICKI ("Red Beats")........10-20 65
(Selection number not known.)

GREGG, Bobby P&R/R&B '62
(With His Friends; Bobby Grego)
Singles: 7-inch
COTTON........10-15 62
EPIC........8-12 62-66
LPs: 10/12-inch
EPIC (24051 "Let's Stomp and Wild Weekend")........20-25 63
(Monaural.)
EPIC (26051 "Let's Stomp and Wild Weekend")........25-30 63
(Stereo.)
Also see BUCHANAN, Roy
Also see DYLAN, Bob
Also see GIBSON, Steve

GREGG, Julie
Singles: 7-inch
UNI (55014 "Sunshine")........15-20 67

GREGORY, Bobby, & Cardinals
Singles: 7-inch
KIP (403 "Precious One")........50-100 59
Also see SHANNON, Bobby

GREGORY, Clinton C&W '91
Singles: 7-inch
STEP ONE........3-4 91-92

GREGORY, Dale, & Shouters
Singles: 7-inch
B-SHARP (271 "I Remember")..150-175 66
Also see THOSE OF US

GREGORY, Dick LP '61
Singles: 7-inch
VEE JAY........4-8 62
LPs: 10/12-inch
COLPIX........10-20 61-64
POPPY........8-15 69-73
VEE JAY........10-20 62-64

GREGORY, Don, & Soul Trainers
Singles: 7-inch
APT (26013 "Soul Line")........4-8 60s

GREGORY, Ed / Kit Fleming
Singles: 7-inch
TWIN HITS........4-6

GREGORY, Harrison
(With Paul Simon)
Singles: 7-inch
CORDELLA (047 "Twistin' Raindrops")........20-30
Also see SIMON, Paul

GREGORY, Ivan, & Blue Notes
Singles: 78 rpm
G&G (110 "Elvis Presley Blues")....50-75 56
Singles: 7-inch
G&G (110 "Elvis Presley Blues")..75-125 56

GREGORY, Steve
Singles: 7-inch
KENCO........15-20 60

GREGORY, Terry C&W '81
Singles: 7-inch
HANDSHAKE........3-5 81-82
SCOTTI BROTHERS........3-4 84-85

GREGORY, Tony
Singles: 7-inch
ALSTON........4-6

GREMLINS
Singles: 7-inch
TEEN TOWN (101 "Sometimes I Feel")........15-25 67
Members: Fred Regenfuss; Jim Eide; Dale Pax; Tom Marach; Robin Hauber; George Shuput.

GREMLINS
Singles: 7-inch
D&H ("We've Found a Love")........4-8
(Selection number not known.)

GRESHAM, Jimmy
Singles: 7-inch
BARBARY COAST........8-12
KITTY (005 "Nothing I Can Do About It")........15-25
KITTY (105 "Now That I Have You")........8-12
RIGHT GROOVE........8-12

GRETSCHMEN
Singles: 7-inch
TIMELY........3-5

GREY, Al
Singles: 78 rpm
KING........10-15 54
PEACOCK........10-15 53
Singles: 7-inch
ARGO........4-8 64
KING (4650 "Goofa Nut")........15-25 54
PEACOCK (1609 "Over and Over")........15-25 53

GREY, Buddy
Singles: 7-inch
CHESS........5-8 60

GREY, Chuck
Singles: 7-inch
FABLE (616 "Push the Panic Button")........75-100 58

GREY & HANKS R&B '78
Singles: 7-inch
RCA........3-5 78-80
LPs: 10/12-inch
RCA........5-10 79-80
Members: Zane Grey; Len Hanks

GREYHOUND
Singles: 7-inch
A&M........3-5 72

GRIECO, Frank
Singles: 7-inch
FHG (101 "To Love Again")........300-500

GRIER, Frankie, Quartet
Singles: 7-inch
SWAN (4019 "Oh Gloria")........250-350 58
Note: Is this the same man as Frank Grieco?

GRIER, Roosevelt
(Rosie Grier; Rosy Grier)
Singles: 7-inch
A........10-20 59-60
A&M........4-6 74
ABC........4-6 70
AGP........3-6 69
AMY........5-10 68
BELL........4-8 74
D-TOWN (1058 "Pizza Pie Man")..20-30 60s
BATTLE........10-20 63
LIBERTY........8-12 61-62
MGM........3-5
RIC........10-20 64
SPINDLE TOP........10-15 61
20TH FOX........3-5 75
U.A........3-6 72
LPs: 10/12-inch
RIC........15-25 64

GRIEVES, Grant
Singles: 7-inch
BIG K........10-15
CRACKER BOX........5-10
INJUN........5-10

GRIFF, Ray C&W '67
Singles: 7-inch
ABC/DOT........3-5 75
CAPITOL........3-5 75-77
DOT........3-6 68-74
GROOVE (0054 "Don't Lead Me On")........5-10 64
GROOVE (0063 "Tongue Twistin' Time")........5-10 64
MGM........4-6 67
RCA........3-4 83-86
ROYAL AMERICAN........3-5 70-72
VISION........3-4 81-82
LPs: 10/12-inch
ABC/DOT........8-12 74
DOT........8-12 73
BOOT........5-10 79-81
CAPITOL........6-12 76
DOT........8-15 68-73
ROYAL AMERICAN........8-12 72

GRIFF, Zaine
LPs: 10/12-inch
W.B........5-10 80

GRIFFIN
LPs: 10/12-inch
ABC........10-15 68

GRIFFIN
LPs: 10/12-inch
ROMAR........8-10 72

GRIFFIN
Singles: 7-inch
QWEST........3-4 84

GRIFFIN, Bill
Singles: 7-inch
NAPTOWN (904 "Try to Run a Game on Me")........20-30 60s

GRIFFIN, Billy R&B '83
Singles: 7-inch
ATLANTIC........3-4 86
COLUMBIA........3-4 83-86
LPs: 10/12-inch
COLUMBIA........5-10 84-86
Also see MIRACLES

GRIFFIN, Buck
Singles: 7-inch
LIN........10-20 54
MGM........15-25 56

Singles: 7-inch
HOLIDAY INN (109 "Pretty Lou")....15-25 63
LIN (1005 "Meadowlark Boogie")....30-50 54
LIN (1015 "Ballin' and Squallin' ")....40-60 54
LIN (1016 "Go, Stop-O")........60-70 54
LIN (5030 "First Man on the Moon")........10-20 59
METRO (20007 "The Party")........15-25 58
MGM (12284 "Stutterin' Papa")......60-75 56
MGM (12439 "Bow My Back")........50-60 57
MGM (12597 "Jessie Lee")........50-60 57
LPs: 10/12-inch
LONDON........50-75
(Canadian.)

GRIFFIN, Buddy: see SWANN, Claudia

GRIFFIN, C.C.
Singles: 7-inch
ALLEGRO........10-20 63
JOYCE........10-20 61

GRIFFIN, Curley
Singles: 78 rpm
ATOMIC........50-75 56
Singles: 7-inch
ATOMIC (305 "Got Rockin' on My Mind")........75-100 56

GRIFFIN, George, & Ensembles
Singles: 7-inch
SEAFAIR (102 "I'll Be at Your Side")........25-50 61

GRIFFIN, Herman
(With the Mello-Dees; with Rayber Voices; with Gerry Jackson; with Boys in the Band; with Boys)
Singles: 7-inch
ANNA (1115 "Hurry Up and Marry Me")........20-30 60
COLUMBIA (41951 "It's You")........10-20 61
DOUBLE L (718 "Never Trust Your Girl Friend")........20-30 63
HOB (112 "I Need You")........20-40 60
MAGIC TOUCH (007 "Are You for Me Or Against Me")........15-25 68
MERCURY (72401 "Dream Girl")....35-55 65
MOTOWN (1028 "Sleep")........25-40 62
STEPP (237 "Hurry Up and Marry Me")........50-75 60
STONE BLUE (101 "The Right Direction")........100-200
TAMLA (54032 "It's You")........25-40 60
Also see HOLLAND, Eddie
Also see PLAYERS
Also see TWENTIE GRANS

GRIFFIN, James
(James Arthur Griffin; Jimmy Griffin)
Singles: 7-inch
IMPERIAL........5-10 65-66
POLYDOR........3-5 73-75
REPRISE........10-15 62-64
SHOE........3-4 82
VIVA........4-8 67-70
LPs: 10/12-inch
REPRISE (6091 "Summer Holiday")........20-25 63
POLYDOR (6018 "James Griffin and Co.")........8-12 73
Also see BLACK TIE
Also see BREAD
Also see REMINGTONS

GRIFFIN, Little Jimmy
Singles: 7-inch
R........5-10 62

GRIFFIN, Merv P&R '51
(With the Griffin Family Singers; with Percy Faith Orchestra)
Singles: 78 rpm
COLUMBIA........3-5 53
RCA........3-5 51-52
Singles: 7-inch
CAMEO........3-5 63-64
CARLTON........4-8 61
COLUMBIA........5-10 53-56
CORAL........3-6 66
DECCA........10-20 50s
DOT........3-5 68
GRIFFIN........3-5 73
MGM........4-6 65-67
MERCURY........4-6 62
METROMEDIA........3-5 70
RCA........5-10 51-52
EPs: 7-inch
RCA (3000 series)........5-10 52
LPs: 10/12-inch
CAMEO........8-15 64
CARLTON........10-20 61
MGM........8-15 65-66
METROMEDIA........5-10 69
RCA (3000 series)........15-25 52
(10-inch LPs.)
Also see MARTIN, Freddy, & His Orchestra

GRIFFIN, Paul
Singles: 7-inch
GOLDEN CREST........5-10 58
Picture Sleeves
GOLDEN CREST........10-20 58

GRIFFIN, Reggie, & Technofunk R&B '82
Singles: 7-inch
SWEET MOUNTAIN........3-4 82
Also see MANCHILD
Also see WEST STREET MOB

GRIFFIN BROTHERS R&B '50
(Featuring Tommy Brown; featuring Margie Day)
Singles: 78 rpm
DOT........10-20 50-52
Singles: 7-inch
DOT (1070 "Stubborn As a Mule")........25-50 51
DOT (1071 "Weeping & Crying")....25-50 51
DOT (1094 "It'd Surprise You")......20-40 51
DOT (1095 "The Teaser")........20-40 51
DOT (1104 "I'm Gonna Jump in the River")........20-40 52
DOT (1105 "Coming Home")........20-40 52
DOT (1108 "Ace in the Hole")........25-50 52
DOT (1114 "My Story")........20-30 53
DOT (1117 "I Wanna Go Back")......20-30 53
DOT (1144 "My Story")........20-30 53
DOT (1145 "Black Bread")........20-30 53
DOT (16000 series)........10-15 60
Members: Jimmy Griffin; Edward "Buddy" Griffin.
Also see DAY, Margie

GRIFFINS
Singles: 78 rpm
MERCURY........20-40 55
WING (90067 "Forever More")......50-75 56
Singles: 7-inch
MERCURY (70558 "I Swear by All the Stars Above")........75-100 55
MERCURY (70650 "Bad Little Girl")........75-100 55
MERCURY (70913 "My Baby's Gone")........25-30 56
WING (90067 "Forever More")....75-125 56
Members: Bill Ross; Bill Alford; Larry Tate; Josh Bright; Lewis Thompson.
Also see HEARTBREAKERS

GRIFFITH, Andy P&R '54
(Deacon Andy Griffith)
Singles: 78 rpm
CAPITOL........5-15 53-57
COLONIAL (3 "What It Was—Was Football")........8-12 53
Singles: 7-inch
CAPITOL (2500 series)........4-6 69
CAPITOL (2600 thru 3600 series)..12-25 53-57
CAPITOL (4000 & 5000 series)........5-10 59-63
(Purple or orange/yellow swirl labels.)
CAPITOL (4000 series)........3-5 76
(Orange labels.)
COLONIAL (3 "What It Was—Was Football")........15-25 53
COLUMBIA........5-10 72
EPs: 7-inch
CAPITOL........20-30 54-61
LPs: 10/12-inch
CAPITOL (872 "A Face in the Crowd")........35-50 57
(Soundtrack.)
CAPITOL (962 "Just for Laughs")..35-45 58
CAPITOL (1100 thru 1600 series)...30-40 59-61
CAPITOL (2000 series)........15-25 64-67
COLUMBIA........5-10 72

GRIFFITH, Bill
Singles: 7-inch
BELFAIR........10-15 66

GRIFFITH, Emile
Singles: 7-inch
TRC (983 "Goin' Goin' Gone")........15-20 68

GRIFFITH, Gayle
Singles: 78 rpm
EMERALD........20-40 55
Singles: 7-inch
EMERALD (2003 "Rockin' and Knockin' ")........50-75 55
SAGA (1001 "Rocket Rock & Roll")........15-25 58

GRIFFITH, Glenda C&W '78
Singles: 7-inch
ARIOLA AMERICA........3-5 78

GRIFFITH, Joe
Singles: 7-inch
REELFOOT (1250 "Crazy Sack")..20-30 58
Picture Sleeves
REELFOOT (1250 "Crazy Sack")..30-50 58

GRIFFITH, Johnny, Inc. R&B '73
Singles: 7-inch
RCA........3-5 73

GRIFFITH, Johnny, Trio
Singles: 7-inch
WORKSHOP JAZZ (2005 "I Did")..10-15 63
LPs: 10/12-inch
WORKSHOP JAZZ (205 "Jazz")...30-50 63
Also see GREER, Paula, & Johnny Griffith Trio

GRIFFITH, Nanci C&W '86
Singles: 7-inch
B.F. DEAL........4-8 77
MCA........3-4 87-91
PHILO........3-5 86
LPs: 10/12-inch
MCA........5-8 89-91

GRIFFITH, Peggi
Singles: 7-inch
DOLTON........5-10 60
NOW (1008 "Rockin the Blues")....20-25 58

GRIFFITH, Wes
Singles: 7-inch
BELLA........10-15 59

GRIFFITH HARTER UNION
Singles: 7-inch
JIM-KO........10-20

GRIFFITHS, Marcia P&R '89
Singles: 7-inch
MANGO........3-4 89

GRIFFITHS, Shirley
Singles: 7-inch
PRESTIGE BLUESVILLE 5-10 61
LPs: 10/12-inch
PRESTIGE BLUESVILLE 15-20 61

GRIFS
Singles: 7-inch
AMG (1002 "In My Life") 20-30 66
5-D (007 "In My Life") 20-30 66
PALMER (5025 "Keep Dreamin' ") 20-30 67

GRIGGS, Bobby
Singles: 7-inch
TOWER 10-15 65

GRIGGS, Sammy, & Coronets
("Vocal Charles Carothers")
Singles: 7-inch
JOB (100 "Footsteps") 300-500 60

GRIGGS, Sir Robert Charles
LPs: 10/12-inch
BLUE GOOSE 10-12
CAPITOL 8-10 73

GRILL, Rob
Singles: 7-inch
MERCURY 3-5 79
LPs: 10/12-inch
MERCURY 5-10 79
Also see FLEETWOOD MAC
Also see GRASS ROOTS

GRIM REAPER LP '84
Singles: 7-inch
RCA/EBONY 3-4 80s
RCA/EBONY/EVA-TONE 5-10 85
(Soundsheet. Promotional issue only.)
RCA (Except 715001) 3-4 85
RCA (715001 "Rock You to Hell") 4-6 87
(Square cardboard picture disc.)
Picture Sleeves
RCA/EBONY 3-4
LPs: 10/12-inch
RCA 5-10 84-87

GRIM REAPERS
Singles: 7-inch
SMACK (15 "Cruisin' for Burgers") .. 8-12 60s
Picture Sleeves
SMACK (15 "Cruisin' for Burgers") .10-20 60s
Member: Rick Nielsen.
Also see CHEAP TRICK

GRIM REEPERS
Singles: 7-inch
CHALON (1003 "Two Souls") 15-25 66

GRIMES, Herman
Singles: 7-inch
BOOT HEEL 4-6
MUSICLAND U.S.A. 4-6 67
RED BIRD 5-8 67

GRIMES, Paula
Singles: 7-inch
TURF 4-8

GRIMES, Scott
Singles: 7-inch
JAMEX 3-5
Picture Sleeves
JAMEX 3-5

GRIMES, Tiny R&B '48
(Tiny Grimes Quintet; Swingtet)
Singles: 78 rpm
APOLLO 5-10 53
ATLANTIC 10-25 48-52
BLUE NOTE 5-15 47
GOTHAM 5-10 49-56
RED ROBIN 10-20 52
SAVOY 5-15 46-48
Singles: 7-inch
APOLLO 10-15 53
ATLANTIC (990 "Begin the Beguine") 20-30 52
B&F 4-8 59
GOTHAM 10-20 50-56
PRESTIGE 8-12 59
RED ROBIN (123 "Juicy Fruit") 15-25 52
UNITED 10-20 55
LPs: 10/12-inch
PRESTIGE SWINGSVILLE 15-25 60
U.A. 10-20 62
Also see PRYSOCK, Red

GRIMMS
Singles: 7-inch
DJM 8-10 73

GRIN LP '71
Singles: 7-inch
A&M 3-5 74
SPINDIZZY 3-5 71-72
THUNDER 3-5
LPs: 10/12-inch
A&M 8-10 73
COLUMBIA 5-10
SPINDIZZY 8-10 71-73
Member: Nils Lofgren.
Also see LOFGREN, Nils

GRINDERSWITCH LP '77
Singles: 7-inch
ATCO 3-5 77-78
LPs: 10/12-inch
ATCO 8-10 77
CAPRICORN 8-10 74-76

GRINER, Linda
Singles: 7-inch
MOTOWN (1037 "Good-by Cruel World") 200-300 63
MOTOWN (1037 "Good-by Cruel Love") 100-150 63
(Note title correction: "Love" not "World.")

GRINGO
LPs: 10/12-inch
DECCA 8-10 71
U.A. 5-10 78

GRINGOS
Singles: 7-inch
DOT 15-25 61

GRISHAM, Marlon
Singles: 7-inch
COVER (5982 "Ain't That a Dilly") 25-35 62

GRISMAN, David LP '80
LPs: 10/12-inch
HORIZON 5-10 79
ROUNDER 5-8 83
W.B. 5-10 80-81
Also see GRAPPELLI, Stephane, & David Grisman

GRISSOM, Dan
(With the Ebb Tones; with Buddy Harper's Orchestra)
Singles: 78 rpm
JEWEL 10-20 48
MILLION 25-50 56
Singles: 7-inch
MILLION (2011 "Recess in Heaven") 75-125 56

GRISSOM, Jimmy R&B '51
(With the Red Callender Sextet)
Singles: 78 rpm
HOLLYWOOD 5-10 51
Singles: 7-inch
ARGO 4-8 64
LPs: 10/12-inch
ARGO 10-15 64

GRISSON, Jimmy
Singles: 78 rpm
RECORDED in HOLLYWOOD 20-25

GRITZBACH, George
LPs:10/12-inch
KICKING MULE 10-20

GRIZZARD, Lewis
Singles: 7-inch
SOUTHERN TRACKS (009 "Let's Have a Party") 5-10 86

GROCE, Larry P&R/C&W/LP '76
Singles: 7-inch
PEACEABLE 3-5 75
W.B. 3-5 75
LPs: 10/12-inch
DAYBREAK 8-10 71-72
W.B. 8-10 76

GRODECK WHIPPERJENNY
LPs: 10/12-inch
PEOPLE (3000 "Grodeck Whipperjenny") 50-100 67
Members: Kenny Poole; Mary Ellen Bell; Dave Matthews; Mike Moore; Jim Madison.

GRODES
Singles: 7-inch
IMPRESSION (114 "What They Say About Love") 15-25 67
RALLY (505 "Love Is a Sad Song") 20-30 66
SPLITSOUND (4 "Give Me Some Time") 15-25 67
TRI-M (1001 "Uh Huh Girl") 10-20 65
TRI-M (1002 "Cry a Little Longer") .10-20 66
Also see SPRING FEVER
Also see TONGUES of TRUTH / Grodes

GROGAN, Toby
Singles: 7-inch
VEE JAY (560 "Angel") 10-20 63

GRONENTHAL, Max
Singles: 7-inch
CHRYSALIS 3-5 79
Picture Sleeves
CHRYSALIS 3-5 79
LPs: 10/12-inch
CHRYSALIS 5-10 79-80

GROOMS, Sherry C&W '77
Singles: 7-inch
ABC (10875 "Night Fall") 15-25 67
PARACHUTE 3-5 78
Also see STEVENS, Even, & Sherry Grooms

GROOP
Singles: 7-inch
JAMIE 5-10 67-69

GROOTNA
Singles: 7-inch
COLUMBIA 3-6 71-72
LPs: 10/12-inch
COLUMBIA 8-10 71

GROOVE, The
Singles: 7-inch
20TH FOX 5-10 66
WAND 5-10 67

GROOVENEERS / Norma Lee King
Singles: 78 rpm
DECCA 10-20 42

GROOVERS
Singles: 7-inch
MINIT 5-8 66
T.C.B. (417 "Don't Fight It") 8-12 60s

GROOVIE GOOLIES
Singles: 7-inch
RCA 3-6 70
LPs: 10/12-inch
RCA 8-10 70

GROOV-U
LPs: 10/12-inch
GATEWAY 12-15

GROOVY FIVE
(Groovy Trio)
Singles: 78 rpm
GROOVY 10-20 49
Member: Willie Johnson.
Also see JOHNSON, Willie

GROPUS CACKUS
Singles: 7-inch
BELL 3-6 72
JAGUAR 4-8

GROSS, Felix R&B '49
Singles: 78 rpm
DOWN BEAT 15-25 54-49
SAVOY 15-25 49

GROSS, Henry P&R/LP '75
Singles: 7-inch
A&M 3-5 74-75
LIFESONG 3-5 76-78
LPs: 10/12-inch
ABC-PAR 8-10 71
A&M 8-10 73-75
CAPITOL 5-10 81
LIFESONG 8-10 76-78
Also see SHA NA NA

GROSS, Jimmie
Singles: 7-inch
TOLLIE 4-8 65

GROSS SISTERS
Singles: 7-inch
CHECKER (932 "Oom Baby") 20-30 59

GROSVENOR, Luther
LPs: 10/12-inch
ISLAND 8-10 71
Also see SPOOKY TOOTH
Also see WIDOWMAKER

GROTESQUE MOMMIES
Singles: 7-inch
PIECE (1002 "One Night Stand") ...25-35

GROUND FLOOR PEOPLE
Singles: 7-inch
MERCURY 10-20 67

GROUND HOG R&B '74
(Joe Richardson)
Singles: 7-inch
GEMIGO 3-5 74
Also see TENDER SLIM

GROUNDHOGS
Singles: 7-inch
INTERPHON 4-8 65
EPs: 7-inch
U.A. 10-12 71
CLEVE (82871 "Groundhogs") 35-40 60s
(With John Lee Hooker & John Mayall.)
IMPERIAL 15-20 69
LIBERTY 8-10 70
U.A. 10-12 71-76
WORLD PACIFIC (21892 "Scratchin the Surface") 25-40 68
Session: Bruce Kulick.
Also see HOOKER, John Lee
Also see JOHN LEE
Also see KISS
Also see MAYALL, John

GROUNDSPEED
Singles: 7-inch
DECCA (32344 "In a Dream") 15-20 68

GROUP, The
LPs: 10/12-inch
BELL 10-15 69
RCA 12-18 63
U.A. 10-15 69

GROUP, The
Singles: 7-inch
FREAK (9240 "Why Does My Head Go Boom") 15-25 60s
W.B. 5-10 66

GROUP AXIS
Singles: 7-inch
ATCO (6642 "Not Fade Away") 10-15 69

GROUP "B"
Singles: 7-inch
SCORPIO (402 "Stop Calling Me") 10-20 66
SCORPIO (406 "I Know Your Name Girl") 10-20 67
Members: Dick Peterson; Jerri Peterson; Danny Mihm.
Also see BLUE CHEER
Also see FLAMIN' GROOVIES

GROUP 87
LPs: 10/12-inch
COLUMBIA 5-10 80
Also see ZAPPA, Frank

GROUP FROM QUEENS
Singles: 7-inch
VEEP (1232 "Boss Man") 10-15 66

GROUP IMAGE
Singles: 7-inch
COMMUNITY 8-12 68
LPs: 10/12-inch
COMMUNITY (101 "A Mouth in the Clouds") 15-25 68

GROUP INC.
Singles: 7-inch
FREPORT (1008 "Like a Woman") 10-15 66
STAFF (177 "Like a Woman") 15-25 66

GROUP LOVE CORP.
Singles: 7-inch
PRIDE (8450 "Love Corporation") ..30-40

GROUP NINE
Singles: 7-inch
BEECH (501 "Nothing But Love") ..10-15

GROUP 1
LPs: 10/12-inch
RCA 10-15 66

GROUP THERAPY
Singles: 7-inch
CANTERBURY 5-10 67
SALMAR (101 "Take Me Back") 10-15
LPs: 10/12-inch
PHILLIPS 10-12 69
RCA 10-12 68

GROUP WITH NO NAME
Singles: 7-inch
CASABLANCA 3-5 77
ELEKTRA 3-5 77
LPs: 10/12-inch
CASABLANCA 5-10 76

GROUPIES
Singles: 7-inch
ATCO (6393 "Primitive") 15-25 66

GROUPIES
LPs: 10/12-inch
EARTH 10-12

GROVE, Bobby
Singles: 7-inch
KING 5-8 63-64
LPs: 10/12-inch
KING (831 "It Was For You") 20-35 63

GROVE, Harry, Trio
Singles: 78 rpm
LONDON 3-5 52
Singles: 7-inch
LONDON 4-6 52
LPs: 10/12-inch
LONDON 10-20 52

GROVES, Big Boy
Singles: 78 rpm
MONEY 10-15 56
SPARK 5-10 55
VITA 5-10 56
Singles: 7-inch
GME 5-8 62
MONEY (217 "The Solid Rock") 15-25 56
SPARK 10-15 55
VITA 10-15 56

GROVES, Carl
Singles: 7-inch
MUSICALE (116 "Canteen Baby") 35-50 59

GROVES, Edgel C&W '81
Singles: 7-inch
SILVER STAR 3-4 81

GROWING CONCERN
Singles: 7-inch
MAINSTREAM (685 "Tomorrow Has Been Canceled") 10-20 68
LPs: 10/12-inch
MAINSTREAM (6108 "The Growing Concern") 50-100 68
Members: Mary Gartski; Bonnie MacDonald; Pete Guerino; Dan Passaglia.

GROWING SOCIETY
Singles: 7-inch
DUNHILL (4093 "The Red Fuzz") 8-15 67
MR. BONES ("The Big Red Tomato") 10-20 67
(Selection number not known.)

GROWL
LPs: 10/12-inch
DISCREET 8-10 74

GRUBBS, Jimmy, & His Music Makers
Singles: 7-inch
MAC (468 "Let's Rock To-Night") 750-1000

GRUBSTAKE
LPs: 10/12-inch
BISCUIT CITY 8-10 77

GRUMP
Singles: 7-inch
MAGIC CARPET 4-8 69

GRUNION HUNTERS
Singles: 7-inch
HIGHLAND (1035 "Four-Eyed, Tongue-Tied, Swimmin' Surfer") 20-30 63

GRUNIONS
Singles: 7-inch
JOCKO (505 "Surfin Psycho") 25-30 63

GRUPPO SPORTIVO
EPs: 7-inch
SIRE 4-8 79
LPs: 10/12-inch
SIRE 5-10 79

GRUSIN, Dave LP '80
(Dave Grusin Quintet; Dave Grusin & NY/LA Dream Band)
Singles: 7-inch
DECCA 3-6 68-69
EPIC 4-8 63
W.B. 3-4 83
LPs: 10/12-inch
COLUMBIA 10-20 65
EPIC 15-25 62
GRP 5-10 80-89
POLYDOR 5-10 77
SHEFFIELD LAB 8-15 77-82
VERSATILE 5-10 78
Also see BISHOP, Stephen
Also see GALE, Eric

GRUSIN, Dave, & Lee Ritenour LP '85
LPs: 10/12-inch
GRP 5-10 85
Also see GRUSIN, Dave
Also see RITENOUR, Lee

GRUSSETT, Larry
Singles: 7-inch
MATT 4-8 60s

GRUVE
Singles: 7-inch
LIBERTY (5603 "Said I Wasn't Gonna Tell") 20-40 68

GRYPHON
LPs: 10/12-inch
BELL (1316 "Red Queen to Gryphon Three") 15-25 74
NR (12497 "Gryphon") 50-75 70s
Member: Geoff Gibor.

GUADALCANAL DIARY LP '88
Singles: 7-inch
ELEKTRA 3-5 88
Picture Sleeves
ELEKTRA (69816 "Always Saturday") 3-5 88
LPs: 10/12-inch
ELEKTRA 5-10 86-89
Members: Rhett Crowe; Murray Attaway; John Poe; Jeff Walls.

GUARALDI, Vince P&R '62
(Vince Guaraldi Trio)
Singles: 7-inch
FANTASY 4-6 62-66
LPs: 10/12-inch
FANTASY (3200 series) 20-30 56-58
FANTASY (3300 series) 15-25 62-66
FANTASY (8000 series) 15-25 62
FANTASY (8300 series) 10-20 63-66
MFSL (112 "Jazz Impressions of Black Orpheus") 20-40 84
W.B. 8-12 68-69

GUARD, Dave, & Whiskeyhill Singers
Singles: 7-inch
CAPITOL 4-8 62
LPs: 10/12-inch
CAPITOL 15-20 62
Members: Dave Guard; Cyrus Faryar; Judy Hensky; David "Buck" Wheat.
Also see HENSKEY, Judy
Also see KINGSTON TRIO
Also see MFQ

GUARDSMEN
Singles: 7-inch
GOLDCREST (163 "The Weasel") .10-20 61

GUARNIR, Johnny
Singles: 7-inch
MAGNIFIQUE 8-12 64

GUCKENHEIMER
Singles: 7-inch
ABNAK (143 "Why Can't the People See") 4-6 69
(Black vinyl.)
ABNAK (143 "Why Can't the People See") 5-10 69
(Colored vinyl. Promotional issue only.)

GUCCI CREW II LP '89
LPs: 10/12-inch
GUCCI 5-8 89

GUERCIO, James William
Singles: 7-inch
COLUMBIA 3-5 70
Also see CHICAGO

GUERILLAS
Singles: 7-inch
DONNA (1406 "Lonely") 10-15 65

GUERNEY, Crip
Singles: 7-inch
HI 3-6 69

GUERRERO, Lalo
(Lalo "Pancho Lopez" Guerrero)
Singles: 78 rpm
L&M 10-20 56
REAL 10-20 55
Singles: 7-inch
CAP/LATINO 3-5
DISCOS CLAVE 3-5
L&M (1000 "Pound Dog") 20-30 56
L&M (1001 "Elvis Perez") 20-30 56
L&M (1003 "Pancho Claus") 10-20 56
REAL (1301 "Pancho Lopez") 15-25 55

REAL (1303 "Mickey Mouse Mambo") ... 10-20 55

GUESS, Don

Singles: 7-inch

BRUNSWICK ... 10-20 58
PROFILE ... 5-10 59
RORO ... 4-8
YUCCA ... 8-12 59
Also see DON & His Roses
Also see ROSES
Also see TUCKER, Rick

GUESS, George

Singles: 7-inch

PEARL HARBOR (45704 "Do It to Death") ... 3-6 73

GUESS, Lenis

Singles: 7-inch

LEGRAND (1042 "Just Ask Me") ... 8-15 66
(First issue.)
LEGRAND (1044 "In My Room") ... 8-15 66
PEANUT COUNTRY (1002 "Thank Goodness Gotta Good Woman") ... 8-12 66
S.P.Q.R. (1102 "Just Ask Me") ... 5-10 66

GUESS & ABNER

Singles: 7-inch

KAPP ... 4-8 70

GUESS WHO P&R '65

Singles: 7-inch

AMY ... 10-20 67
FONTANA ... 10-15 69
HILLTAK ... 3-5 78-79
QUALITY ... 10-20 65-68
(Canadian.)
RCA ... 3-6 69-76
RCA RECORDING SERVICES (55829 "Two Wheel Freedom") ... 4-8
SCEPTER (1295 "Shakin' All Over") ... 8-12 65
SCEPTER (12000 series) ... 10-20 65-66

Picture Sleeves

RCA ... 8-12 70

LPs: 10/12-inch

HILLTAK ... 5-10 79
MGM ... 12-15 69
PICKWICK ... 8-10 72
PIP ... 8-10 71
PRIDE ... 8-10 73
RCA (Except "AYL1" & LSP-4000 series) ... 8-12 73-80
RCA ("AYL1" series) ... 5-10 80
RCA (LSP-4141 thru LSP-4830) ... 12-25 69-72
RCA (1004 "Best of the Guess Who") ... 10-20 71
(With bonus, black light poster.)
RCA (1004 "Best of the Guess Who") ... 8-12 71
(Without poster.)
SCEPTER ... 8-10 73
SPRINGBOARD ... 8-10 72
WAND ... 12-15 69
Members: Chad Allen; Burton Cummings; Randy Bachman; Domenic Troiano.
Also see ALLEN, Chad
Also see BACHMAN, Randy
Also see CUMMINGS, Burton
Also see TROIANO, Domenic
Also see WOLFMAN JACK

GUESS WHO / Discotays

Singles: 7-inch

SCEPTER (1295 "Shakin' All Over") ... 15-20 65
Also see GUESS WHO

GUEST, Chris

Singles: 7-inch

BANANA ... 4-8
Also see NATIONAL LAMPOON

GUEVARA, Ruben

Singles: 7-inch

BIG 7 (002 "Star Spangled Banner") ... 10-15
Also see APOLLO BROTHERS
Also see RUBEN & JETS

GUGEL, Les Barney

Singles: 7-inch

CUCA (6551 "My Hog's Gone Wild") ... 15-25 65
CUCA (6552 "Devil Woman") ... 15-25 65

GUIDED TOUR

Singles: 7-inch

SOUND 80 (42-1448 "In a World Full of Fright") ... 25-35 60s

GUIDES

Singles: 7-inch

GUYDEN (2023 "How Long Must a Fool Go On") ... 30-40 59
(First pressings mistakenly credit the Swallows.)
Also see DANDEVILLES
Also see SWALLOWS
Also see UPTONES

GUIDRY, Greg P&R/LP '82

Singles: 7-inch

COLUMBIA ... 3-4 82

LPs: 10/12-inch

COLUMBIA/BADLAND ... 5-10 82

GUIDRY, Johnny

Singles: 7-inch

MERCURY ... 4-8 61
SCOPE (101 "High School Dance") ... 15-25 59

GUILBEAU, Floyd "Gib"

Singles: 7-inch

A&S (4544 "What Kind of Flower") ... 8-12 76
Also see FLYING BURRITO BROTHERS
Also see GIB & WAYNE
Also see GUILBEAU & PARSONS

GUILBEAU & PARSONS

Singles: 7-inch

BAKERSFIELD INT'L (1001 "Louisiana Rain") ... 30-40 68
Members: Floyd "Gib" Guilbeau; Gram Parsons.
Also see FLYING BURRITO BROTHERS
Also see GUILBEAU, Floyd "Gib"
Also see PARSONS, Gram

GUILD

Singles: 7-inch

ELEKTRA ... 3-5 72
PHILIPS (40403 "You Can See the Trees") ... 4-6 66

Picture Sleeves

PHILIPS (40403 "You Can See the Trees") ... 5-8 66

GUILFORD, Jimmy: see GILFORD, Jimmy

GUILLORY, Isaac

LPs: 10/12-inch

ATLANTIC ... 8-10 74

GUILLOTEENS

Singles: 7-inch

COLUMBIA (43852 "Wild Child") ... 8-12 66
COLUMBIA (44089 "I Love That Girl") ... 5-10 66
HBR (446 "I Don't Believe") ... 8-12 65
HBR (451 "For My Own") ... 8-12 65
HBR (486 "I Sit and Cry") ... 10-15 66

Picture Sleeves

COLUMBIA (43852 "Wild Child") ... 20-30 66
(Promotional issue only.)
HBR (451 "For My Own") ... 10-20 65
Members: Louis Paul Jr.; Loddie Hutcherson; Joe Davis.

GUILLOTINE

LPs: 10/12-inch

AMPEX ... 8-10 71

GUION, King

Singles: 7-inch

CANADIAN-AMERICAN ... 4-6 64
CITATION ... 4-8 59
DOT ... 4-8 59

Picture Sleeves

CANADIAN-AMERICAN ... 4-8 64

LPs: 10/12-inch

ABC-PAR (172 "Emotion Inc.") ... 25-45 56

GUISE

Singles: 7-inch

MUSICLAND ... 10-20 67

GUITAR, Billy, & Night Hawks

Singles: 7-inch

APEX (76185 "Here Comes the Night") ... 25-30 58
DECCA (30634 "Here Comes the Night") ... 40-60 58

GUITAR, Bobby: see BENNETT, Bobby "Guitar"

GUITAR, Bonnie C&W/P&R '57

Singles: 78 rpm

DOT ... 10-15 57
FABOR (Except 4018) ... 5-10 55-56
FABOR (4018 "Dark Moon") ... 15-25 57
4 STAR ... 5-10 56

Singles: 7-inch

ABC ... 3-5 74
CHARTER ... 4-6
COLUMBIA ... 3-5 72
DOLTON ... 5-10 59
DOT (15000 series) ... 8-15 57-59
DOT (16000 & 17000 series) ... 4-6 66-69
FABOR (138 "Ra Ta Ta Ta") ... 4-8 64
FABOR (4013 "If You See My Love Dancing") ... 10-20 55
FABOR (4017 "Clinging Vine") ... 10-20 56
FABOR (4018 "Dark Moon") ... 20-30 57
4 STAR (1003 "Honey on the Moon") ... 3-5 80
4 STAR (1006 "I Want to Spend My Life with You") ... 10-20 56
JERDEN ... 5-10 63
MCA ... 3-5 74
PARAMOUNT ... 3-5 70
PLAYBACK ... 3-4 89
RCA ... 10-20 61-62
RADIO ... 5-10 58

LPs: 10/12-inch

CAMDEN ... 6-12 69
DOT (Except 3069 & 3385) ... 10-15 59-68
DOT (3069 "Moonlight and Shadows") ... 15-25 57
DOT (3385 "Dark Moon") ... 15-20 63
HAMILTON ... 8-12 65
PARAMOUNT ... 8-12 70
PICKWICK ... 6-12 70
Also see BONNIE & BUDDY
Also see ECHOES

GUITAR, Buddy

Singles: 7-inch

BERTRAM INT'L (223 "Much Too Young") ... 8-12 63

GUITAR, Jeff

Singles: 7-inch

CREOLE (1762 "Wait a Minute Baby") ... 60-80
ROCKET (502 "Jump & Shout") ... 50-75

GUITAR, Johnny

Singles: 7-inch

CONTESTE (1 "Track Seven") ... 15-25 58

GUITAR, Johnny, & Rhythm Rockers

EPs: 7-inch

BARON ... 4-8 79

GUITAR, Sonny

Singles: 7-inch

YUCCA ... 8-12 61

GUITAR CRUSHER

Singles: 7-inch

BETHLEHEM ... 4-8 62-63
KING ... 4-8 63
COLUMBIA ... 5-10 67
T&S (101 "Cuddle Up") ... 15-20

GUITAR DAVE

Singles: 7-inch

CENTRAL ... 5-10 61

GUITAR FRANK

Singles: 7-inch

BRIDGES MUSIC DEN ("Wild Track") ... 20-25 60
(Selection number not known.)

GUITAR GABLE

Singles: 7-inch

EXCELLO ... 10-15 57-59

GUITAR JR.
(Lee Baker)

Singles: 7-inch

GOLDBAND ... 5-10 59
MERCURY ... 5-10 60

LPs: 10/12-inch

CAPITOL ... 10-12 69
Also see BROOKS, Lonnie
Also see McDOWELL, Mississippi Fred / Guitar Junior

GUITAR MURPHY

Singles: 7-inch

EMERSON (5555 "Sufferin' Soul") ... 10-20 64

GUITAR NUBBITT

Singles: 7-inch

BLUESTOWN ... 10-20 62-64

GUITAR RAMBLERS

Singles: 7-inch

COLUMBIA ... 10-15 64

LPs: 10/12-inch

COLUMBIA (2067 "Happy, Youthful New Sounds") ... 15-25 64
(Monaural.)
COLUMBIA (8867 "Happy, Youthful New Sounds") ... 25-35 64
(Stereo.)

GUITAR RAY

Singles: 7-inch

SHAGG (711 "You're Gonna Wreck My Life") ... 20-30

GUITAR RED
(Paul Johnson)

Singles: 7-inch

CHECKER ... 5-10 61
EXCELLO (2085 "Hot Potato") ... 15-25 57
EXCELLO (2086 "Chili Pot") ... 20-30 57
FORMAL (1007 "Red Hot Devil") ... 15-25 58
Also see JOHNSON, Paul

GUITAR SHORTY

Singles: 7-inch

COBRA (5017 "You Don't Treat Me Right") ... 50-75 57
PULL (301 "Hard Life") ... 15-25 59

GUITAR SLIM P&R/R&B '54
(Eddie Jones)

Singles: 78 rpm

ATCO ... 10-15 56
IMPERIAL ... 15-25 54
SPECIALTY ... 10-15 55

Singles: 7-inch

ATCO (6072 "Oh Yeah") ... 20-30 56
ATCO (6097 "It Hurts to Love Someone") ... 15-25 57
ATCO (6108 "I Don't Mind at All") ... 15-25 58
IMPERIAL (5278 "Woman Troubles") ... 40-50 54
IMPERIAL (5310 "New Arrival") ... 40-50 54
SPECIALTY (482 "The Things That I Used to Do") ... 20-30 55
SPECIALTY (490 "The Story of My Life") ... 20-30 54
SPECIALTY (527 "Later for You, Baby") ... 15-25 56
SPECIALTY (536 "Sufferin' Mind") ... 15-25 55
SPECIALTY (542 "Our Only Child") ... 15-25 55
SPECIALTY (551 "I Got Sumpin' for You") ... 15-25 55
SPECIALTY (557 "Quicksand") ... 15-25 56
SPECIALTY (569 "Sum'thin' to Remember You By") ... 15-25 56

LPs: 10/12-inch

SPECIALTY ... 8-10 70-88
Also see CHARLES, Ray
Also see JONES, Eddie

GUITAR SLIM
(Johnny Winter)

Singles: 7-inch

DIAMOND JIM (204 "Crying in My Heart") ... 100-150 62
(Reissued as by Texas "Guitar" Slim.)
Also see TEXAS "GUITAR" SLIM
Also see WINTER, Johnny

GUITAR SLIM (Alec Seward): see BLUES BOY

GUITAR TWINS

Singles: 7-inch

STAR ... 5-10

GUITARS INC.

Singles: 7-inch

W.B. (5049 "Guy Dad, It's Early") ... 15-25 59

GUITARS INC.

Singles: 7-inch

HAMILTON (50035 "Holiday Love") ... 15-25 63
Also see FIREBALLS

GULF

Singles: 7-inch

LE CAM ... 3-5
Members: Sonny Threatt; Phyllis Brown-Threatt.
Also see SONNY & PHYLLIS

GULF COAST QUARTET

Singles: 78 rpm

COLUMBIA ... 10-20 24

GULLIORY, Steve

Singles: 7-inch

GARRETT ... 5-10 66

GULLIVER

Singles: 7-inch

ELEKTRA ... 3-6 70

LPs: 10/12-inch

ELEKTRA (74070 "Gulliver") ... 20-30 70
Members: Daryl Hall; Tim Moore.
Also see HALL, Daryl

GULLIVER

Singles: 7-inch

COLUMBIA ... 3-4 79

LPs: 10/12-inch

COLUMBIA ... 6-10 79

GUM DROPS

Singles: 78 rpm

KING ... 8-15 55-56

Singles: 7-inch

CORAL ... 5-10 58-59
DECCA ... 5-10 58
KING ... 15-20 55-56

GUMBALL

Singles: 7-inch

GET HIP (146 "Girl Don't Tell Me") ... 3-4 92

Picture Sleeves

GET HIP (146 "Girl Don't Tell Me") ... 3-4 92

LPs: 10/12-inch

EPIC ... 8-10 90s

GUMINA, Tommy

Singles: 7-inch

CONTINENTAL (5615 "Charmine") ... 5-10 56
DECCA (30265 "Theme from Paliacci") ... 5-10 57

GUN

Singles: 7-inch

EPIC ... 5-10 69-70

LPs: 10/12-inch

EPIC ... 15-25 69-70
Members: Adrian Gurvitz; Ben Gurvitz.
Also see BAKER-GURVITZ ARMY
Also see GURVITZ, Adrian

GUN LP '90

LPs: 10/12-inch

A&M ... 5-8 90
Members: Mark Rankin; Giuliano Gizzi; Dante Gizzi; Scott Shields; Baby Stafford.

GUN, Tommy: see TOMMY GUN

GUN CLUB

LPs: 10/12-inch

ANIMAL ... 5-10 82
RUBY ... 5-10 81
SLASH ... 5-10

GUNHILL ROAD P&R '73

Singles: 7-inch

KAMA SUTRA ... 3-5 73
MERCURY ... 3-5 72

LPs: 10/12-inch

KAMA SUTRA ... 8-10 72
MERCURY ... 8-10 71

GUNN, J.W. C&W '82

Singles: 7-inch

PRIMERO ... 3-5 82

GUNN, Ray, & His Blasters

LPs: 10/12-inch

PARADE ... 8-12 62

GUNS & BUTTER

LPs: 10/12-inch

COTILLION ... 8-10 72

GUNS 'N' ROSES LP '87

Singles: 12-inch

GEFFEN ... 4-8 89

Singles: 7-inch

GEFFEN ... 3-4 88-92

Picture Sleeves

GEFFEN ... 3-4 88-89

EPs: 7-inch

UZI SUICIDE ("Live Like a Suicide") ... 150-200 86

LPs: 10/12-inch

GEFFEN (Except 24148 & 24617) ... 5-10 88-89
GEFFEN (24148 "Appetite for Destruction") ... 50-75 87
(With robot/rape painting on cover.)
GEFFEN (24148 "Appetite for Destruction") ... 5-8 87
(With skulls and cross cover.)
GEFFEN (24617 "Spaghetti Incident") ... 10-15 93
(Colored vinyl.)
Members: Axl Rose; Slash; Duff McKagan; Saul Hudson; Steve Adler; Izzy Stradlin; Matt Sorum; Dizzy Reed; Gilby Clarke; Matt Sorum.
Also see CULT

GUNTER, Arthur R&B '55

Singles: 78 rpm

EXCELLO ... 15-30 54-57

Singles: 7-inch

EXCELLO (2047 "Baby Let's Play House") ... 30-50 54
EXCELLO (2053 "She's Mine, All Mine") ... 25-40 55
EXCELLO (2058 "Honey Babe") ... 25-40 55
EXCELLO (2073 "Trouble with My Baby") ... 20-30 56
EXCELLO (2084 "Hear My Plea Baby") ... 20-30 57
EXCELLO (2125 "Baby Can't You See") ... 20-30 58
EXCELLO (2137 "Ludella") ... 15-25 59
EXCELLO (2147 "Don't Leave Me Now") ... 15-25 59
EXCELLO (2164 "No Naggin', No Draggin' ") ... 15-25 59
EXCELLO (2191 "Little Blue Jeans Woman") ... 15-25 60
EXCELLO (2201 "My Heart's Always Lonesome") ... 15-25 61
EXCELLO (2204 "Workin' for My Baby") ... 15-25 61

LPs: 10/12-inch

EXCELLO (8017 "Black & Blues") ... 10-15 71

GUNTER, Cornell
(With the Flairs; with Ermines)

Singles: 78 rpm

ABC-PAR ... 10-20 56
DOT ... 10-20 57
EAGLE ... 15-25 57
LOMA ... 25-50 55-56

Singles: 7-inch

ABC-PAR (9689 "She Loves to Rock") ... 25-50 56
ABC-PAR (9740 "Aladdin's Lamp") ... 25-50 56
CHALLENGE (59281 "Wishful Thinking") ... 15-25 64
DOT (15654 "You Send Me") ... 15-25 57
EAGLE (301 "Baby Come Home") ... 20-40 57
LOMA (701 "True Love") ... 50-100 55
LOMA (703 "You Broke My Heart") ... 50-100 56
LOMA (704 "Keep Me Alive") ... 50-75 56
LOMA (705 "I'm Sad") ... 50-100 56
W.B. (5266 "Lift Me Up Angel") ... 10-20 62
Members: Cornell Gunter; Ken Byle; Tommy Miller; George Hollis; Robbie Robinson; Beverley Harris.
Also see COASTERS
Also see FLAIRS
Also see JAC-O-LACS
Also see PENGUINS
Also see PLATTERS

GUNTER, Dennis

Singles: 7-inch

GO (103 "Our Love") ... 5-10

GUNTER, Hardrock
(Hardrock & Rhythm Rockers with the Buddy Durham Singers)

Singles: 78 rpm

BAMA (9 "Birmingham Bounce") ... 20-40 51
DECCA ... 10-15 52-53
EMPEROR ... 50-100 57
KING ... 10-15 55
SUN (201 "Gonna Dance All Night") ... 200-250 54

Singles: 7-inch

DECCA ... 10-20 52-53
EMPEROR (112 "Whoo! I Mean Whee!") ... 50-100 57
KING ... 10-20 55
SUN (201 "Gonna Dance All Night") ... 550-650 54
Also see RHYTHM ROCKERS

GUNTER, Launa, with Queen City Ramblers

Singles: 7-inch

EXCELLENT (807 "He's My Man") ... 100-150 58

GUNTER, Shirley R&B '54
(With the Flairs; with Queens)

Singles: 78 rpm

FLAIR (Except 1076) ... 8-15 54-55
FLAIR (1076 "How Can I Tell You") ... 20-30 55
MODERN ... 8-12 56

Singles: 7-inch

FLAIR (Except 1076) ... 15-25
FLAIR (1076 "How Can I Tell You") ... 30-60 55
MODERN ... 10-20 56
TANGERINE ... 4-8 65
Members: Shirley Gunter; Lula Bea Kinney; Lula Mae Suggs; Zola Taylor.
Also see FLAIRS
Also see TAYLOR, Zola

GUNTHER, Gloria

Singles: 7-inch

ARCH ... 15-20

GURLEY, Randy C&W '78

Singles: 7-inch

ABC ... 3-5 78
RCA ... 3-5 79

LPs: 10/12-inch

ABC ... 8-10 78

GURUS
Singles: 7-inch
U.A. ... 4-8 66-67
Picture Sleeves
U.A. (50089 "Come Girl") ... 15-20 66

GURVITZ, Adrian
Singles: 7-inch
JET ... 3-5 79
Also see BAKER-GURVITZ ARMY
Also see EDGE, Graeme
Also see GUN
Also see PARRISH & GURVITZ

GUS
LPs: 10/12-inch
NEMPEROR ... 5-10 80

GUSSIE
Singles: 7-inch
ERIC ... 3-5

GUTENBERGER, Lou
Singles: 7-inch
SEESAW (8400 "Student Protest") ... 5-8 68

GUTHRIE, Arlo LP '67
Singles: 7-inch
REPRISE ... 3-6 67-77
LPs: 10/12-inch
REPRISE ... 8-10 67-76
U.A. ... 10-15 69
W.B. ... 5-10 77-81
Also see SEEGER, Pete, & Arlo Guthrie

GUTHRIE, Gwen R&B '82
Singles: 12-inch
GARAGE ... 4-6 85
ISLAND ... 4-6 83-85
Singles: 7-inch
GARAGE ... 3-4 85
ISLAND ... 3-4 82-85
POLYDOR ... 3-4 86-87
W.B. ... 3-4 88
Picture Sleeves
ISLAND ... 3-4 85
POLYDOR ... 3-4 86
LPs: 10/12-inch
GARAGE ... 5-10 85
ISLAND ... 5-10 85
POLYDOR ... 5-8 86
Also see HOWARD, George
Also see LIMIT

GUTHRIE, Gene
Singles: 7-inch
MANCO ... 4-8 61-62

GUTHRIE, Jack C&W '45
Singles: 78 rpm
CAPITOL ... 10-20 45-47
LPs: 10/12-inch
CAPITOL (2456 "Greatest Songs") ... 25-35 66

GUTHRIE, Woody
(With Cisco Houston)
LPs: 10/12-inch
COLUMBIA ... 8-12 72
FOLKWAYS ... 12-25
STINSON ... 20-30 52-54
VERVE ... 15-20
W.B. ... 10-20 72

GUY R&B/LP '88
Singles: 7-inch
MCA ... 3-4 90
UPTOWN/MCA ... 3-4 88-89
Picture Sleeves
UPTOWN/MCA (53300 "Groove Me") ... 3-4 88
LPs: 10/12-inch
MCA ... 5-8 90
UPTOWN/MCA ... 5-8 88
Also see RILEY, Teddy, & Guy

GUY, Art
Singles: 7-inch
VALIANT (762 "Where You Gonna Go") ... 15-25 67

GUY, Billy
(With the Coasters)
Singles: 7-inch
ABC-PAR ... 4-8 62
DOUBLE L ... 4-8 63
SAL/WA ... 4-8 60s
VERVE ... 4-8 66
Also see COASTERS

GUY, Bob
(Frank Zappa)
Singles: 7-inch
DONNA (1380 "Letter from Jeepers") ... 50-75 61
Also see ZAPPA, Frank

GUY, Bobby
(Howard Guyton)
Singles: 7-inch
APT (25052 "A Vow") ... 15-20 60
Also see FIVE PEARLS
Also see GUYTON, Howard
Also see HOWIE & SAPPHIRES
Also see PEARLS
Also see POWELL, Jessie

GUY, Browley, & Skyscrapers
Singles: 78 rpm
CHECKER ... 50-75 54
MIRACLE (137 "Knock Me a Zombie") ... 20-30 49
STATES (107 "Blues Train") ... 50-75 52
Singles: 7-inch
CHECKER (779 "Watermelon Man") ... 100-200 54
(Black vinyl.)
CHECKER (779 "Watermelon Man") ... 300-500 54
(Red vinyl.)
Also see SKYSCRAPERS

GUY, Buddy R&B '62
Singles: 7-inch
ARTISTIC (1501 "Sit and Cry") ... 20-30 58
ARTISTIC (1503 "You Sure Can Do") ... 20-30 58
CHESS (1735 "I Got My Eyes on You") ... 15-25 60
CHESS (1759 "Slop Around") ... 10-20 60
CHESS (1784 "Let Me Love You Baby") ... 10-20 61
CHESS (1812 "Stone Crazy") ... 10-20 62
CHESS (1838 "When My Left Eye Jumps") ... 10-20 62
CHESS (1878 "It's Hard But It's Fair") ... 10-20 63
CHESS (1936 "Crazy Music") ... 10-20 65
CHESS (1974 "My Mother") ... 10-20 66
LPs: 10/12-inch
BLUE THUMB ... 8-10 70
BLUES BALL ... 15-25
CHESS ... 10-15 69
VANGUARD ... 12-18 68
Session: Otis Spann; Jerret Gibson; Donald Hankins; Leonard Caston; Jack Meyers; Clifton James; Lafayette Leake; Al Duncan; Fred Below; Willie Dixon; Bob Neely.
Also see DIXON, Willie
Also see SPANN, Otis
Also see TAYLOR, Koko
Also see WELLS, Junior, & Buddy Guy

GUY, Buddy, with Dr. John & Eric Clapton / Buddy Guy with the J. Geils Band
Singles: 7-inch
ATCO (6890 "Man of Many Words") . 4-8 72
Also see CLAPTON, Eric
Also see DR. JOHN
Also see GEILS, J., Band

GUY, Dewey
Singles: 7-inch
RIDGECREST ... 10-15 60

GUY, Jasmine LP '90
LPs: 10/12-inch
W.B. ... 5-8 90

GUY, Vernon
Singles: 7-inch
ELECTRIC LAND (3 "Ooh Vernon") .. 4-6 80
SONJA (2007 "Anything to Make It with You") ... 20-30 63
TEENA (1703 "They Ain't Lovin' You") ... 30-40 63
Also see SHARPEES
Also see TURNER, Ike & Tina

GUY & RALNA C&W '75
Singles: 7-inch
RANWOOD ... 3-5 75
LPs: 10/12-inch
BIRCHWOOD ... 5-10
RANWOOD ... 5-10 75

GUYS
Singles: 7-inch
ORIGINAL SOUND ... 4-8 65

GUYS & DOLLS
Singles: 7-inch
APOSTROPHE ... 8-12
MELLOW (1006 "You Left Me") ... 10-20 60s
TODDLIN' TOWN (132 "Let's Push and Pull") ... 8-12
TODDLIN' TOWN (135 "Heartaches") ... 10-20 60s

GUYS FIVE
Singles: 7-inch
ARA ... 8-12 68

GUYS FROM UNCLE
Singles: 7-inch
SWAN (4240 "The Spy") ... 10-15 65

GUYS WHO CAME UP FROM DOWNSTAIRS
Singles: 7-inch
DISC-GUYS (6836 "Growth") ... 50-100 66
(Reportedly 200 made.)
Also see GRANDMA'S ROCKERS

GUYTON, Howard
Singles: 7-inch
VERVE (10386 "I Watched You Slowly Slip Away") ... 50-75 66
Also see GUY, Bobby

GUYTONES
Singles: 78 rpm
DELUXE ... 20-30 57
Singles: 7-inch
DELUXE (6144 "You Won't Let Me Go") ... 50-75 57
DELUXE (6152 "She's Mine") ... 50-75 57
DELUXE (6159 "This Is Love") ... 50-75 57
DELUXE (6163 "Baby, I Don't Care") ... 40-60 58
DELUXE (6169 "Tell Me") ... 40-60 58

GYPSIES
Singles: 78 rpm
GROOVE ... 5-10 55
Singles: 7-inch
GROOVE ... 10-15 55

GYPSIES
Singles: 78 rpm
ATLAS (1073 "Why") ... 40-60 57
Singles: 7-inch
ATLAS (1073 "Why") ... 40-60 57

GYPSIES R&B '65
Singles: 7-inch
CAPRICE ... 5-10 66
OLD TOWN (1168 "Blue Bird") ... 10-20 64
OLD TOWN (1180 "Jerk It") ... 10-20 65
OLD TOWN (1184 "It's a Woman's World") ... 40-60 65
OLD TOWN (1193 "Oh I Wonder Why") ... 10-20 66
Members: Betty Pearce; Ernestine Pearce; Shirley Pearce; Lestine Johnson.
Also see FLIRTATIONS

GYPSY P&R/LP '70
Singles: 7-inch
COGNITO ... 3-5
DORE (907 "Don't Stop for Nothin' ") ... 20-30
METROMEDIA ... 3-5 70
RCA ... 3-5 71-72
LPs: 10/12-inch
METROMEDIA ... 8-12 70-71
RCA ... 8-12 72-73
Also see AMERICAN GYPSY
Also see UNDERBEATS
Also see WALSH, James, Gypsy Band

GYPSY
(English Gypsy)
LPs: 10/12-inch
DECCA ... 10-12 71

GYPSY TRIPS
Singles: 7-inch
WORLD PACIFIC (77809 "Rock & Roll Gypsies") ... 15-25 65
Members: Roger Tillison; Terry Tillison.
Also see LEATHERCOATED MINDS

GYROS
LPs: 10/12-inch
FAKE DOOM ... 8-10

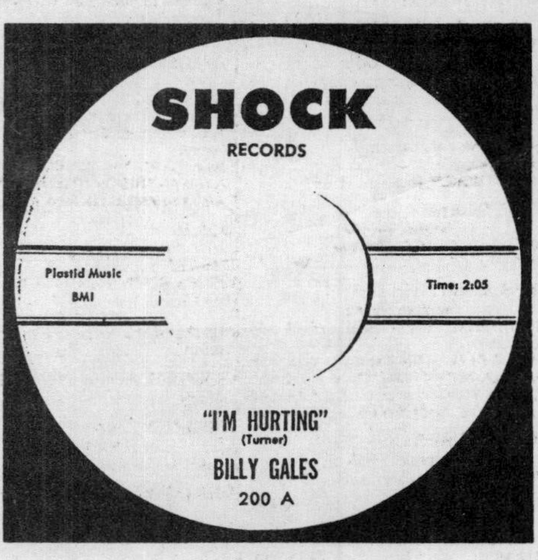

SHOCK
RECORDS
Plastid Music
BMI
Time: 2:05
"I'M HURTING"
(Turner)
BILLY GALES
200 A

Neptune
RECORDS
SUITE 207, 1650 BROADWAY, NEW YORK CITY, NEW YORK
UNBREAKABLE
45 R.P.M.
RECORD NO.
125
(0364)
Prigan Music
BMI — 2:42
WILL YOU LOVE ME
(WHEN I'M OLD)
(Gorgeous George)
GORGEOUS GEORGE

SPARK
RECORD CO.
BMI
Quintet Music Co.
(LS-59)
Harmonica Instr.
HELLO MISS SIMMS
(Leiber - Stoller - Emanuel)
GARLAND THE GREAT
121—45

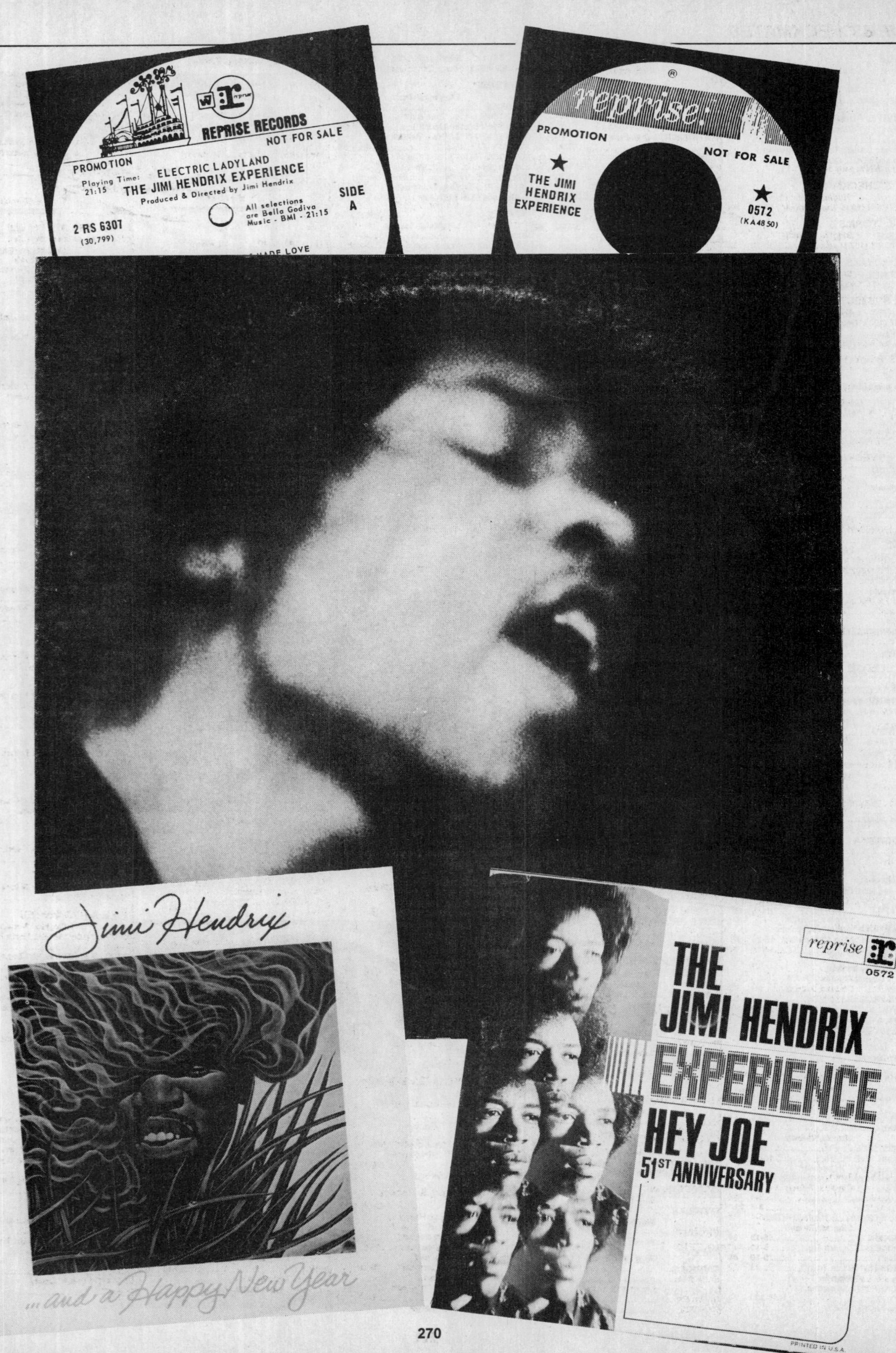
REPRISE RECORDS
NOT FOR SALE
PROMOTION
ELECTRIC LADYLAND
Playing Time: 21:15
THE JIMI HENDRIX EXPERIENCE
Produced & Directed by Jimi Hendrix
SIDE A
All selections are Bella Godiva Music - BMI - 21:15
2 RS 6307
(30,799)
reprise
PROMOTION
NOT FOR SALE
THE JIMI HENDRIX EXPERIENCE
0572
(KA4850)
Jimi Hendrix
...and a Happy New Year
reprise
0572
THE JIMI HENDRIX EXPERIENCE
HEY JOE
51ST ANNIVERSARY
PRINTED IN U.S.A.

H

H., JOHNNY: see JOHNNY H.

H.B. & CHECKMATES
Singles: 7-inch
LAVENDER (1936 "Summertime") 15-25 60s

H.I. & STORMS
Singles: 7-inch
TREND '63 (107 "Twister")............10-20 63

H.M. ROYALS
Singles: 7-inch
ABC (10957 "Old Town") 15-25 67

H.M. SUBJECTS
Singles: 7-inch
SAINT (1001 "Don't Bring Me Down") 5-10 66
Also see MONTELLS

H.M.S. BOUNTY: see FANKHAUSER, Merrell

H.P. & GRASS ROUTE MOVEMENT
Singles: 7-inch
BBTC ("You Don't Know Like I Know") 10-20 60s
(No selection number used.)
HIDEOUT (1232 "Heavy Music")..... 8-12 60s

H.P. LOVECRAFT
(Lovecraft)
Singles: 7-inch
MERCURY 4-6 75-76
PHILLIPS............................... 5-10 67-68
REPRISE.................................. 4-8 70
Picture Sleeves
PHILLIPS (40491 "Wayfaring Stranger")..........................10-20 67
LPs: 10/12-inch
MERCURY (1041 "We Love You").10-15 76
PHILLIPS (200252 "H.P. Lovecraft") 20-30 67
(Monaural.)
PHILLIPS (600252 "H.P. Lovecraft") 25-35 67
(Stereo.)
PHILLIPS (600279 "Lovecraft II")...20-30 68
REPRISE (6419 "Valley of the Moon") 10-12 70

H.Y. SLEDGE
LPs: 10/12-inch
SSS INT'L (22 "Bootleg Music") 15-25 71
Members: Jan Pulver; Richard Porter; Mike Ewbank.

HA HA'S
Singles: 7-inch
DINO 3-5 70

HAAS, Jimmie
Singles: 7-inch
U.A. 5-8 64

HAAS, Wayne
Singles: 7-inch
CHOICE (5607 "Betty Ann")..........30-50 57

HABIBAYYA
LPs: 10/12-inch
ISLAND 8-10 72

HACIENDAS
Singles: 7-inch
PACIFIC CHALLENGER (1001 "Sherry Stole My XKE") 20-30 64

HACKAMORE BRICK
LPs: 10/12-inch
KAMA SUTRA 10-12 71

HACKERT, Veline
(Buddy Covelle)
Singles: 7-inch
BRUNSWICK (55151 "Billy Boy")...................................75-100 59
Also see COVELLE, Buddy

HACKETT, Bobby
Singles: 7-inch
PACEMAKERS............................ 4-8

HACKETT, Buddy P&R '53
Singles: 78 rpm
CORAL..................................... 3-5 53-56
Singles: 7-inch
CORAL..................................... 5-10 53-56
LAUREL 4-8 60
LPs: 10/12-inch
CORAL..................................... 8-15 65
DOT..10-15 59

HACKETT, Steve LP '76
Singles: 7-inch
CHARISMA............................... 3-4 80
CHRYSALIS 3-5 76-79
EPIC.. 3-4 81
LPs: 10/12-inch
CHARISMA............................... 5-10 80
CHRYSALIS 5-10 76-79
EPIC.. 5-10 81
Also see GTR
Also see GENESIS

HADDAD, Eddie
Singles: 7-inch
MGM 3-5 74

HADDIX, Travis
LPs: 10/12-inch
ICHIBAN....................................5-10

HADDOCK, Durwood C&W '74
Singles: 7-inch
CAPRICE 3-5 74
COUNTRY INT'L 3-5 78-79
EAGLE INT'L............................ 3-5 77-80
MONUMENT 3-6 68-69

HADLEY, Red
Singles: 78 rpm
METEOR................................40-60 56
Singles: 7-inch
METEOR (5017 "Brother That's All") 75-125 56

HAFF-TONES
Singles: 7-inch
TWILIGHT (001 "I Need You").....75-125 64

HAFNER, Dick
Singles: 7-inch
VALIANT 4-8 64

HAGAN, Sammy, & Viscounts
Singles: 78 rpm
CAPITOL..................................20-30 57
Singles: 7-inch
CAPITOL (3772 "Out of Your Heart") 20-30 57
CAPITOL (3818 "Don't Cry")..........20-30 57
CAPITOL (3885 "Tail Light") 20-30 58

HAGAR, Ernie
Singles: 7-inch
SAND (400 "Surf 'N Sand")............10-20 63
SAND (402 "Spindrift")..................10-20 63

HAGAR, Sammy P&R/LP '77
Singles: 7-inch
CAPITOL.................................. 3-5 76-79
COLUMBIA................................ 3-4 87
GEFFEN (Except 29246) 3-4 82-87
GEFFEN (29246 "Two Sides of Love") 3-4 84
(Black vinyl.)
GEFFEN (29246 "Two Sides of Love") 4-8 84
(Colored vinyl.)
Picture Sleeves
CAPITOL.................................. 3-5 79
COLUMBIA................................ 3-4 87
GEFFEN................................... 3-4 82-87
LPs: 10/12-inch
CAPITOL..................................5-10 77-82
GEFFEN...................................5-10 82-87
Also see HAGAR, SCHON, AARONSON, SHRIEVE
Also see JUSTICE V
Also see MONTROSE
Also see VAN HALEN

HAGAR, SCHON, AARONSON, SHRIEVE P&R/LP '84
Singles: 7-inch
GEFFEN.................................. 3-4 84
Picture Sleeves
GEFFEN.................................. 3-4 84
LPs: 10/12-inch
GEFFEN..................................5-10 84
Members: Sammy Hagar; Neal Schon; Ken Aaronson; Michael Shrieve.
Also see HAGAR, Sammy
Also see SCHON, Neal, & Jan Hammer
Also see SANTANA

HAGE, David & Dennis
LPs: 10/12-inch
DOUBLE TAKE 5-10 84

HAGEN, Don
Singles: 7-inch
SEA GULL (103 "Surfin' Son of a Gun") 15-25 60s

HAGEN, Earl
Singles: 7-inch
CAPITOL.................................. 4-5 61
COLPIX.................................... 4-8 64

HAGEN, Nina LP '82
(Nina Hagen Band)
Singles: 12-inch
COLUMBIA............................... 4-6 84-85
Singles: 7-inch
COLUMBIA............................... 3-4 80-85
LPs: 10/12-inch
COLUMBIA...............................5-10 80-83

HAGER, Charley C&W '89
Singles: 7-inch
KILLER.................................... 3-4 89

HAGER, Don, & Hot Tots
Singles: 7-inch
OAK (357 "Bebop Boogie") 150-200
OAK (358 "Liza Jane Bop")........100-150

HAGER, Joan
Singles: 78 rpm
DECCA.................................... 4-8 56
Singles: 7-inch
DECCA....................................8-12 56

HAGERS C&W '69
Singles: 7-inch
CAPITOL.................................. 3-6 69-71
ELEKTRA................................. 3-5 74
LPs: 10/12-inch
BARNABY 6-12 72
CAPITOL..................................8-15 70-71
ELEKTRA.................................6-12 74
Members: Jim Hager; John Hager.

HAGGARD, Jay
Singles: 7-inch
DAJA......................................15-25 58-59

HAGGARD, Marty C&W '81
Singles: 7-inch
DIMENSION 3-5 81
MTM..3-4 86-88
Also see HAGGARD, Merle

HAGGARD, Merle C&W '63
(With the Strangers)
Singles: 7-inch
CAPITOL..................................3-8 65-77
COLUMBIA...............................3-4 83
CURB......................................3-4 90
EPIC..3-4 81-89
MCA..3-5 77-85
MERCURY................................3-4 83
TALLY 10-20 63-65
Picture Sleeves
CAPITOL..................................4-8 67-71
MCA..3-5 77-80
EPs: 7-inch
CAPITOL..................................8-15 71
(Juke box issues only.)
LPs: 10/12-inch
ALBUM GLOBE (9005 "Melody Ranch Featuring Merle Haggard & Friends") 40-50 80s
CAPITOL (168 thru 735)..................8-15 69-71
(With "T," "ST," "STBB" or "SWBB" prefix.)
CAPITOL (168 thru 735).................4-8 69-71
(With "SKA0" or SM" prefix.)
CAPITOL (796 "Merle Haggard's Strangers and Friends Honky Tonkin'").........20-30 71
CAPITOL (803 "Land of Many Churches") 30-50 71
(With "SWBO" prefix.)
CAPITOL (835 "Someday We'll Look Back")...................................8-12 71
CAPITOL (882 "Let Me Tell You About a Song")....................................8-12 72
CAPITOL (2373 thru 2972)...........15-25 65-68
(With "T," "ST" or, in the case of 2951, an "SKAO" prefix.)
CAPITOL (2702 thru 2972) 5-10 80s
(With "SM" prefix.)
CAPITOL (11000 thru 16000 series)...................................5-10 72-82
EPIC.......................................5-10 81-86
MCA..4-8 77-84
MERCURY................................5-10 83
PICKWICK/HILLTOP..................8-12 60s
RADIANT 5-10 81
RONCO.....................................5-8
SONGBIRD 5-10 81
SPARTON 30-60
(Canadian.)
TEE VEE 5-10 77
Session: Biff Adam; Norm Hamlet; Dennis Hromek; Roy Nichols; Bobby Wayne; Johnny Gimble; Jordanaires; James Burton; Marty Haggard; Ronnie Reno; Bonnie Owens; Carter Family.
Also see ANDERSON, John
Also see BANDY, Moe
Also see BURTON, James
Also see COCHRAN, Hank
Also see FRIZZELL, David
Also see HAGGARD, Marty
Also see JORDANAIRES
Also see MADDOX, Rose
Also see NASHVILLE SUPERPICKERS
Also see PAYCHECK & HAGGARD
Also see RENO, Ronnie
Also see TUBB, Ernest
Also see WAYNE, Bobby
Also see WILLS, Bob

HAGGARD, Merle / Patsy Cline
LPs: 10/12-inch
OUT of TOWN DIST 5-10 82
Also see CLINE, Patsy

HAGGARD, Merle, & Clint Eastwood C&W '80
Singles: 7-inch
ELEKTRA.................................3-4 80
Picture Sleeves
ELEKTRA.................................3-4 80
Also see EASTWOOD, Clint

HAGGARD, Merle, & Janie Fricke C&W '84
Singles: 7-inch
EPIC.......................................3-4 84
Also see FRICKE, Janie

HAGGARD, Merle / Mickey Gilley / Willie Knight
LPs: 10/12-inch
OUT of TOWN DIST 5-10 82
Also see GILLEY, Mickey

HAGGARD, Merle / Sonny James
LPs: 10/12-inch
CAPITOL..................................10-15 60s
Also see JAMES, Sonny

HAGGARD, Merle, & George Jones C&W/LP '82
(George Jones & Merle Haggard)
Singles: 7-inch
EPIC (03405 "C.C. Waterback") 3-4 82
EPIC (03405 "C.C. Waterback") 40-50 82
(Picture disc. Autographed.)
EPIC (03405 "C.C. Waterback") 10-15 82
(Picture disc. Not signed.)
LPs: 10/12-inch
EPIC.......................................5-10 82
Also see JONES, George

HAGGARD, Merle, & Willie Nelson C&W/LP '83
(Willie Nelson & Merle Haggard)
Singles: 7-inch
EPIC.......................................3-4 83-87
LPs: 10/12-inch
EPIC.......................................5-10 83
Also see NELSON, Willie

HAGGARD, Merle, & Bonnie Owens C&W '64
TALLY (181 "Just Between the Two of Us")....................................10-20 64
LPs: 10/12-inch
CAPITOL (2453 "Just Between the Two of Us")....................................20-30 66
Also see OWENS, Bonnie

HAGGARD, Merle, & Leona Williams C&W '78
Singles: 7-inch
CAPITOL..................................3-5 78
MERCURY................................3-4 83
LPs: 10/12-inch
MERCURY 5-10 83
Also see WILLIAMS, Leona

HAGGETT, Jimmy
(With the Daydreamers)
Singles: 78 rpm
METEOR...............................100-200 57
SUN (236 "No More") 100-200 56
Singles: 7-inch
CAPROCK 10-20 58
METEOR (5043 "Gonna Shut You Off Baby").................................100-200 57
SUN (236 "No More") 250-300 56

HAHN, Carol D&D '83
Singles: 12-inch
NICKLE 4-6 83

HAHN, Jerry, Brotherhood
LPs: 10/12-inch
COLUMBIA 8-12 70
Members: Jerry Hahn; George Marsh; Mike Finnigan; Clyde Graves.

HAHN, Joyce P&R '57
Singles: 78 rpm
CADENCE..................................4-8 57
Singles: 7-inch
CADENCE..................................4-8 57

HAHN, Tommy, & Mojo Men
Singles: 7-inch
TIDE (2001 "Mojo Workout") 8-12 64
Members: Tom Hahn; Doug Weiss; Duane Smith; Gary Myers.
Also see DARNELLS
Also see MOJO MEN
Also see MYERS, Gary
Also see WEISS, Doug

HAIG, Ronnie
(With the Monograms; Ron Hege)
Singles: 7-inch
ABC-PAR (9912 "Don't You Hear Me Calling, Baby")....................................40-60 58
ABC-PAR (10209 "Don't You Hear Me Calling, Baby")....................................10-20 61
ASTRA......................................5-10
NOTE (10010 "Don't You Hear Me Calling, Baby")....................................20-30 58
NOTE (10014 "Rocking with Rhythm and Blues")...................................75-100 58
SILVERBALL (1 "Pork's Chop Boogie")...................................4-8 93
(Pink vinyl. 200 made.)
SILVERBALL (1 "Pork's Chop Boogie")...................................4-8 93
(White vinyl. 300 made.)
SILVERBALL (101 "Open House ")....4-8 92
(Black vinyl. 900 made.)
SILVERBALL (101 "Open House ")..10-15 92
(Colored vinyl. 100 made for promotional use only.)
SILVERBALL (103 "Just One Kiss")...4-6 93
(Colored vinyl.)
SILVERBALL (105 "Mucho Fine ")....3-4 94
(Colored vinyl.)
Picture Sleeves
SILVERBALL (105 "Mucho Fine ")...3-4 94
EPs: 7-inch
GET HIP (4 "Ronnie Haig")...............4-8 94
(Promotional copies of this three-track EP are credited to the Hoosier Hotshots.)
Also see HEGE, Ron
Also see HOOSIER HOTSHOTS

HAINES, Connie
Singles: 7-inch
MOTOWN (1092 "What's Easy for Two Is Hard for One")............................15-25 66

HAINES, Gary
(With the Five Sequins)
Singles: 7-inch
KAPP (383 "Another Girl Like You").....................................15-25 61
SOUND (110 "Keep On Going") 25-35

HAIR
Singles: 7-inch
RCA 3-4 79

HAIRCUT ONE HUNDRED P&R/LP '82
Singles: 7-inch
ARISTA....................................3-4 82
LPs: 10/12-inch
ARISTA....................................5-10 82
Member: Nick Heyward.
Also see HEYWARD, Nick

HAIRCUTS
Singles: 7-inch
PARKWAY (899 "She Loves You")...................................10-20 64
Picture Sleeves:
PARKWAY (899 "She Loves You")...................................20-30 64

HAIRCUTS & IMPOSSIBLES
LPs: 10/12-inch
SOMERSET 10-15 66
STEREO FIDELITY....................10-15 66

HAIRPOWER
Singles: 7-inch
EPIC 3-5 70

HAIRSTON, Brother Will
("Hurricane of the Motor City)
Singles: 78 rpm
JVB (44 "The Alabama Bus").......50-100 56
Singles: 7-inch
JVB (44 "The Alabama Bus").....100-200 56
KNOWLES...............................10-20

HAIRSTON, Curtis D&D '83
Singles: 12-inch
PRETTY PEARL 4-6 83
Singles: 7-inch
ATLANTIC.................................3-4 87
PRETTY PEARL 3-4 84-85

HAIRSTON, Forrest
Singles: 7-inch
VINEY (01 "We Go to Pieces") 20-30

HAIRSTON, Jackie
Singles: 7-inch
ATCO (6464 "Monkey on My Back")..................................10-15 67

HAL & HIS PALS
Singles: 7-inch
DC...5-10 62

HAL & JEAN
Singles: 7-inch
CAPITOL...................................5-10 63

HAL & PROPHETS
Singles: 7-inch
SCEPTER..................................10-15 64

HAL HOPPERS
Singles: 78 rpm
KEM (2733 "More Love") 50-100 55
Singles: 7-inch
KEM (2733 "More Love") 125-175 55
Member: Hal Hopper.

HALE, Billy Jack
Singles: 7-inch
DECCA (30447 "Your Eyes") 20-25 57

HALE, Larry
Singles: 7-inch
DIAMOND..................................10-20 66
FONTANA....................................4-6
U.A. 3-5 75

HALE, Michael
Singles: 7-inch
MGM 5-10 58

HALE, Rex
RHYTHM..................................20-30 49
Singles: 7-inch
RHYTHM (303 "Big Mama's House")..................................250-350 49

HALE, Ricky
Singles: 7-inch
FRANKIE 10-15 57

HALE & HAYDEN
Singles: 7-inch
ABC-PAR 4-8 62

HALE & HUSHABYES
Singles: 7-inch
APOGEE (104 "Yes Sir, That's My Baby")...................................50-100 65
REPRISE (0299 "Yes Sir, That's My Baby")...................................20-40 64
(Reissued in 1967 as by a Date with Soul.)
Members: Brian Wilson; Sonny & Cher; Blossoms; Jack Nitzsche; Jackie DeShannon; Darlene Love; Edna Wright; Albert Stone.
Also see A DATE with SOUL
Also see BLOSSOMS
Also see DE SHANNON, Jackie
Also see HONEY CONE
Also see LOVE, Darlene
Also see NITZSCHE, Jack
Also see SONNY & CHER
Also see WILSON, Brian

HALEY, Bill P&R '53
(With His Comets; with Saddlemen; with Saddle Men; with Four Aces of Western Swing; with Reno Browne & Her Buckaroos)
Singles: 78 rpm
ATLANTIC (727 "I'm Gonna Dry Ev'ry Tear with a Kiss")................................250-350 50
COWBOY (1201 "Too Many Parties Too Many Pals")...................................300-500 48
COWBOY (1202 "Candy Kisses")..................................300-500 49
COWBOY (1203 "The Covered Wagon Rolled Right Along")...........................250-300 49
COWBOY (1204 "Behind the Eight Ball")....................................250-300 50
COWBOY (1205 "Candy Kisses")..................................250-350 50
COWBOY (1701 "Candy Kisses")..................................250-350 49

COWBOY (1701 "My Palomino and I")....250-350 49
(By "Reno Browne & Her Buckaroos featuring Bill Haley." The Cowboy 1701 number is used twice.)
DECCA (29124 "Rock Around the Clock")....50-100 54
(Black label with gold print.)
DECCA (29124 "Rock Around the Clock")....25-50 54
(Black label with silver print. Decca multi-color labels are $4 to $8 reissues.)
DECCA (29204 "Shake, Rattle & Roll")....50-80 54
(Black label with gold print.)
DECCA (29204 "Shake, Rattle & Roll")....25-50 54
(Black label with silver print.)
DECCA (29317 thru 30530)....20-50 54-57
DECCA (30592 thru 30781)....20-40 58
DECCA (30844 "I Got a Woman")..25-50 59
DECCA (30873 "A Fool Such As I")....40-60 59
DECCA (30926 "Caldonia")....50-75 59
DECCA (30956 "Ooh, Look-a-There Ain't She Pretty")....50-100 59
ESSEX....30-40 52-55
HOLIDAY (105 "Rocket 88")....100-150 51
HOLIDAY (108 "Green Tree Boogie")....100-150 51
HOLIDAY (111 "A Year Ago This Christmas")....100-150 51
HOLIDAY (113 "Juke box Cannonball")....100-150 51
KEYSTONE (5101 "Deal Me a Hand")....750-1000 50
KEYSTONE (5102 "Susan Van Dusan")....750-1000 50
QUALITY (Except 1082)....30-40 53-54
(Canadian.)
QUALITY (1082 "Rocking Chair on the Moon")....100-200 52
(Canadian. First Haley disc on Quality.)

Singles: 7-inch

APT (25081 "Burn That Candle")...15-20 65
APT (25087 "Haley A-Go-Go")....15-20 65
ARZEE.... 8-12 77
DECCA (29000 series)....20-35 54-56
(Silver lines on both sides of the name Decca.)
DECCA (29000 series)....10-20 54-56
(Star and silver lines under the name Decca.)
DECCA (30000 series)....10-20 56-59
DECCA (31000 series)....5-10 60-64
DECCA (72000 series).... 4-6 69
ESSEX (102 "Rock Around the Clock")....10-20 60s
ESSEX (303 "Rock the Joint")....500-750 52
(Colored vinyl.)
ESSEX (303 "Rock the Joint")....65-75 52
(Black vinyl. Block style logo.)
ESSEX (303 "Rock the Joint")....55-65 52
(Black vinyl. Script style logo.)
ESSEX (305 "Rocking Chair on the Moon")....50-100 52
ESSEX (310 "Real Rock Drive")...50-100 52
ESSEX (321 "Crazy Man Crazy")...50-75 53
ESSEX (327 "Fractured")....30-40 53
ESSEX (332 "Live It Up")....25-35 53
ESSEX (340 "Ten Little Indians")...25-35 53
ESSEX (348 "Chattanooga Choo-Choo")....20-30 54
ESSEX (374 "Juke box Cannonball")....50-75 54
ESSEX (381 "Rocket 88")....100-125 55
ESSEX (399 "Rock the Joint")....50-75 55
GONE (5111 "Spanish Twist")....15-25 61
GONE (5116 "Riviera")....15-25 61
HOLIDAY (113 "Juke box Cannonball")....300-400 51
JANUS (162 "Traveling Band").... 8-12 71
JUKE BOX.... 3-4 90
KAMA SUTRA.... 5-10 70
MCA.... 3-5 73-80
NEWTOWN (5013 "Tenor Man")...10-15 63
NEWTOWN (5014 "Midnight in Washington")....10-15 63
NEWTOWN (5024 "Dance Around the Clock")....10-15 63
NEWTOWN (5025 "Tandy")....10-15 63
OLD GOLD.... 3-5 82
QUALITY (1082 "Rocking Chair on the Moon")....150-250 52
(Canadian. First Haley disc on Quality.)
QUALITY (1120 "Crazy Man, Crazy")....50-100 53
(Canadian.)
QUALITY (1145 "Fractured")....40-60 53
(Canadian.)
QUALITY (1168 "Live It Up")....40-60 53
(Canadian.)
QUALITY (1399 "Rock the Joint")....50-100 54
(Canadian.)
RADIO ACTIVE.... 4-8 70
TRANSWORLD (381 "Rocket 88").60-80 54
TRANSWORLD (718 "Real Rock Drive")....50-75 53
U.A. (50483 "That's How I Got to Memphis").... 5-10 69
W.B. (5145 "Candy Kisses")....15-25 60
W.B. (5154 "Chick Safari")....15-25 60
W.B. (5171 "So Right Tonight")....15-25 60
W.B. (5228 "Flip, Flop & Fly")....15-25 60
W.B. (7124 "Rock Around the Clock")....10-15 68

Picture Sleeves

ARZEE.... 8-12 77
DECCA (30314 "Billy Goat")....40-60 57
DECCA (30530 "Mary Mary Lou") .25-35 58

EPs: 7-inch

ARZEE (137 "Bill Haley Sings")....20-30 77
CLAIRE (4779 "Bill Haley and the Comets")....15-20 78
DECCA (2168 "Shake, Rattle & Roll")....40-60 54
DECCA (2209 "Dim, Dim the Lights")....40-60 55
DECCA (2322 "Razzle Dazzle")....40-60 56
DECCA (2398/2399/2400 "He Digs Rock & Roll")....40-60 56
(Price is for any of three volumes.)
DECCA (2416/2417/2418 "Rock'n Roll Stage Show")....40-50 56
(Price is for any of three volumes.)
DECCA (2532 "Rockin' the Oldies")....30-40 57
DECCA (2533 "Rock 'N' Roll Party")....30-40 57
DECCA (2534 "Rockin' & Rollin' ") 30-40 57
DECCA (2564 "Rockin' Around the World")....30-40 57
DECCA (2576 "Rockin' Around Europe")....30-40 57
DECCA (2577 "Rockin' Around the Americas")....30-40 57
DECCA (2615/2616 "Rockin' the Joint")....30-40 58
(Price is for either of two volumes.)
DECCA (2638 "Bill Haley's Chicks")....30-40 58
DECCA (2670 "Bill Haley and His Comets")....30-40 59
DECCA (2671 "Strictly Instrumental")....30-40 59
DECCA (72638 "Bill Haley's Chicks")....50-75 59
(Stereo.)
DECCA (72670 "Bill Haley and His Comets")....50-75 59
(Stereo.)
DECCA (72671 "Strictly Instrumental")....50-75 59
(Stereo.)
ESSEX (102 "Dance Party")....50-100 54
ESSEX (117/118/119 "Rock with Bill Haley and the Comets")....50-100 54
(Price is for any of three volumes.)
SOMERSET (460 "Rock with Bill Haley and the Comets")....40-60 55
TRANSWORLD (117/118/119 "Rock with Bill Haley & Comets")....50-100 54
(Price is for any of three volumes. May be titled *For Your Dance Party.*)

LPs: 10/12-inch

AEI (3106 "Rock Around the Clock")....8-12 82
ACCORD....5-10 81-82
ALSHIRE....8-10 79
AMBASSADOR....8-15 70-87
BUDDAH....5-10 84
CORAL....8-10 73
DECCA (5560 "Shake, Rattle & Roll")....300-400 54
(10-inch LP.)
DECCA (7211 "Golden Hits")....12-18 72
DECCA (8225 "Rock Around the Clock")....75-125 55
(All black label with silver print.)
DECCA (8225 "Rock Around the Clock")....20-40 60
(Black label with rainbow color stripe. Reads "M'F'D by Decca Records Inc. New York, U.S.A.")
DECCA (8225 "Rock Around the Clock")....15-20 68
(Black label with rainbow color stripe. Reads "Mfr'd by Decca Records, a Div. of MCA Inc. New York, U.S.A.")
DECCA (8315 "He Digs Rock & Roll")....100-200 56
DECCA (8345 "Rock'n Roll Stage Show")....100-200 56
DECCA (8569 "Rockin' the Oldies")....100-200 57
DECCA (8692 "Rockin' Around the World")....50-100 58
DECCA (8775 "Rockin' the Joint")....50-100 58
DECCA (8821 "Bill Haley's Chicks")....50-75 58
DECCA (8964 "Strictly Instrumental")....40-60 60
DECCA (75027 "Greatest Hits")....15-20 68
DECCA (78225 "Rock Around the Clock")....50-100 59
(All black label with silver print.)
DECCA (78225 "Rock Around the Clock")....50-100 59
(Black label with rainbow color stripe.)
DECCA (78692 "Rockin' Around the World")....20-40 62
DECCA (78821 "Bill Haley's Chicks")....50-100 58
DECCA (78964 "Strictly Instrumental")....50-75 60
ESSEX (202 "Rock with Bill Haley and the Comets")....300-500 54
EXACT....5-10 80
51 WEST....5-10 83
GNP....8-12 74-76
GREAT NORTHWEST....8-12 81
GUEST STAR....12-20 65
JANUS....15-25 72
JOKER....5-10 81
KAMA SUTRA (2014 "Bill Haley's Scrapbook")....20-30 70
KOALA....8-10 79
MCA....6-10 73-88
PAIR.... 5-8 86
PHOENIX....5-10 81
PICKWICK....8-10 71-74
ROULETTE....15-20 62
SILHOUETTE....5-10 83
SOMERSET (1300 "Rock & Roll Dance Party"): see Various Artists section
SOMERSET (4600 "Rock with Bill Haley & Comets")....75-125 58
SPRINGBOARD....8-10 77
SUN....10-15 80
TRANSWORLD (202 "Rock with Bill Haley and the Comets")....200-300 56
VOCALION....15-25 63
W.B. (W-1378 "Bill Haley & His Comets")....25-35 60
(Monaural.)
W.B. (WS-1378 "Bill Haley & His Comets")....35-45 60
(Stereo.)
W.B. (W-1391 "Haley's Juke Box")....25-35 60
(Monaural.)
WARNER (WS-1391 "Haley's Juke Box")....35-45 60
(Stereo.)
W.B. (1831 "Rock & Roll Revival") ..8-12 70
Members: Bill Haley; Rudy Pompilli; Bill Miller; Ray Crawley; Buddy Dee.
Also see BROWNE, Reno, & Her Buckaroos
Also see CARSON, Ken
Also see CLIFTON, Johnny, & His String Band
Also see DOWN HOMERS
Also see KINGSMEN
Also see LEE, Brenda / Bill Haley & Comets / Kalin Twins / Four Aces
Also see LIFEGUARDS
Also see LOPEZ, Trini / Scott Gregory
Also see MERRI-MEN
Also see RANDOLPH, Boots / Bill Haley
Also see WELZ, Joey

HALEY, Bill / Phil Flowers

Singles: 7-inch

KASEY (7006 "ABC Boogie")....10-15 61

Picture Sleeves

KASEY (7006 "ABC Boogie")....25-35 61
Also see FLOWERS, Phil

HALEY, Bill / Lionel Hampton / Sal Salvador Quartet / Lenny Dee

EPs: 7-inch

DECCA (38088 "Webcor High Fidelity Demonstration Record")....15-25 59
(Special products issue, made for Webcor Phonographs. Not issued with special cover.)
Also see DEE, Lenny
Also see HAMPTON, Lionel

HALEY, Bill / Bunny Paul / Dinning Sisters

EPs: 7-inch

SOMERSET (460 "Rock and Roll Dance Party")....30-40 55
Also see DINNING SISTERS
Also see HALEY, Bill
Also see PAUL, Bunny, & Harptones

HALF A SIXPENCE

Singles: 7-inch

MIKE....8-12 66

HALF BROTHERS

Singles: 7-inch

MERCURY (71299 "My Foolish Fling")....20-30

HALF DOZEN

Singles: 7-inch

DUNWICH....4-8 66
SOMA....4-8 66

HALF JAPANESE

LPs: 10/12-inch

LSR (8-1 "The Band That Would Be King")....8-10 89
Members: Jad Fair; Don Fleming; J. Rice; Scott Jarvis; Rob Kennedy.

HALF LIFE

Singles: 7-inch

SKYCLAD....5-8 89
Members: Jeff Lamm; Troy Mezzio; Ron Volpe; Rick Dowdle.

HALF PINT & FIFTHS

Singles: 7-inch

ORLYN (6018 "Orphan Boy")....5-10

HALF SISTERS

Singles: 7-inch

CHATTAHOOCHEE....4-8 64

HALFNELSON

LPs: 10/12-inch

BEARSVILLE....15-20 72
Members: Ron Mael; Russell Mael.
Also see SPARKS

HALIFAX THREE

Singles: 7-inch

EPIC....4-6 62-64

Picture Sleeves

EPIC....4-8 63

LPs: 10/12-inch

EPIC....5-15 62-64

HALL, Alberta

Singles: 78 rpm

SPECIALTY....15-25 55

Singles: 7-inch

SPECIALTY (562 "Oh How I Need Your Love")....25-35 55

HALL, Arch, Jr.

Singles: 7-inch

FAIRWAY INT'L....5-10 63
SIGNATURE (12014 "Konga Joe")....20-30

HALL, Baby Terry

Singles: 7-inch

PHILIPS....4-8 65

HALL, Ben

Singles: 7-inch

FAYETTE....4-8 64

HALL, Betty

Singles: 7-inch

EMBER....10-15 63

HALL, Bill, & Sonnetts

Singles: 7-inch

CHECKER (884 "Three Wishes")....300-400 58

HALL, Billy

(With the Arabs)

Singles: 7-inch

GLENN (1006 "Good Bye Angel")..25-35 63
GLENN (1007 "I Need Some Lovin' ")....25-35 64
GLENN (1008 "Ooga-Booga Boo Boo")....25-35 64
GLENN (1009 "Move Over, Rover")....20-30 64
MAR-VEL (1002"Move Over, Rover")....50-75 57

HALL, Bobby, & Kings

Singles: 78 rpm

HARLEM....50-100 54

Singles: 7-inch

HARLEM (2322 "Fire in My Heart")....200-300 54
(Black vinyl.)
HARLEM (2322 "Fire in My Heart").... 1500-2000 54
(Red vinyl.)
Also see KINGS

HALL, Brenda

Singles: 7-inch

LOMA....8-12 65

HALL, Buck C&W '89

Singles: 7-inch

TRACK....3-4 89

HALL, Carl

Singles: 7-inch

COLUMBIA....3-6
LOMA....4-8 68
MERCURY (72547 "He Gets Everything He Wants")....30-40 66

HALL, Carol

Singles: 7-inch

COLUMBIA....4-6 62

LPs: 10/12-inch

ELEKTRA....8-10 72

HALL, Chuck, & Hallmarks

Singles: 7-inch

NU-TOP....4-8 65

HALL, Connie C&W '60

Singles: 7-inch

DECCA....4-8 60-63
MERCURY....4-8 60

LPs: 10/12-inch

DECCA....15-25 62
VOCALION....10-20 65
Also see SKINNER, Jimmie

HALL, Daryl LP '80

(With Gulliver)

Singles: 7-inch

AMY....4-8 69
CHELSEA....3-6 76
RCA....3-4 80-87

Picture Sleeves

RCA....3-4 80-87

LPs: 10/12-inch

RCA....5-10 80-86
Also see COSTELLO, Elvis
Also see GULLIVER
Also see KNIGHT, Holly
Also see TEMPTONES
Also see U.S.A. for AFRICA

HALL, Daryl, & Ruth Copeland

Singles: 7-inch

RCA....3-4 76
Also see COPELAND, Ruth
Also see HALL, Daryl

HALL, Daryl, & John Oates P&R/LP '74

(Hall & Oates)

Singles: 12-inch

RCA (Except 13705)....4-8 78-85
RCA (13705 "Jingle Bell Rock")....30-40 83
(Picture disc. Promotional issue only.)

Singles: 7-inch

ARISTA....3-4 88-90
ATLANTIC....3-5 72-77
CHELSEA....3-5 76
RCA....3-5 76-84
SIRE....3-4
RCA GOLD STANDARD....3-4 83-84

Picture Sleeves

ARISTA....3-4 88
RCA....3-5 77-85
SIRE....3-4

Picture Sleeves

ARISTA....3-4 88
RCA....3-5 77-85

Promotional Singles

RCA (Colored vinyl)....5-8 85
(One side by Daryl Hall and one side by John Oates.)

EPs: 7-inch

ATLANTIC (265 "She's Gone")....8-12 73
(Promotional issue only.)

LPs: 10/12-inch

ARISTA....5-8 88-90
ATLANTIC....8-12 72-77
CHELSEA....10-12 76
MFSL (069 "Abandoned Luncheonette")....25-35 82
RCA (Black vinyl)....5-10 75-84
RCA (Colored vinyl)....10-15 78

Promotional LPs

RCA ("Special Radio Series")....15-25 81
Also see PRINE, John / Daryl Hall & John Oates / Barnaby Bye / Delbert & Glen
Also see WHOLE OATS

HALL, Daryl, John Oates, David Ruffin & Eddie Kendrick P&R/R&B/LP '85

Singles: 7-inch

RCA....3-4 85

Picture Sleeves

RCA....3-4 85

LPs: 10/12-inch

RCA....5-8 85
Also see KENDRICK, David
Also see RUFFIN, David

HALL, Delores

Singles: 7-inch

KEYMEN (111 "W-o-m-a-n")....10-20

LPs: 10/12-inch

CAPITOL....5-10 79

HALL, Dickson, & Wayfarers

Singles: 7-inch

EPIC (9262 "Cowboy")....5-10 58

Picture Sleeves

EPIC (9262 "Cowboy")....15-25 58

HALL, Dora

(Dorothy Hall)

Singles: 7-inch

CALAMO....5-10 63
COZY....5-8 60s
PREMORE (1025 "Rockin' Around the Christmas Tree")....5-8 60s
REINBEAU (1016 "Time to Say Goodbye")....5-8 65

Picture Sleeves

PREMORE (1025 "Rockin' Around the Christmas Tree")....8-12 60s

LPs: 10/12-inch

CALAMO (1000 "Adult-Teen Pop")....15-25 63
(Promotional issue only.)
COZY....10-15 60s
PREMORE....10-15 60s

HALL, Ellis, Jr. R&B '83

Singles: 7-inch

H.C.R.C....3-4 83

HALL, Fox

Singles: 7-inch

LIMELIGHT (3003 "Do the Rock and Roll")....35-50 58

HALL, Freddie

(With the Night Rockers; with Carl Jones & Orchestra)

Singles: 78 rpm

ABCO (103 "Can This Be Mine")...25-40 56
CHANCE....25-50 54

Singles: 7-inch

ABCO (103 "Can This Be Mine")...50-75 56
C.J. (602 "Little Baby's Rock")....50-75 59
C.J. (610 "Love and Affection")....25-50 59
CHANCE (1159 This Crooked World")....75-100 54
Members: Freddie Hall; Bill; Ike; Joe.

HALL, Gene

Singles: 7-inch

ARK....10-20

HALL, Gerri

(Geri Hall)

Singles: 7-inch

ACE....4-8 62
ATCO....4-8 63
HOT LINE....10-15 60s

HALL, Jennifer

Singles: 7-inch

W.B....3-4

Picture Sleeves

W.B....3-4

HALL, Jim, & His Radio Pals

Singles: 7-inch

BONEY (204 "Old Fort Smith")....10-15
PROCESS (107 "Hydrogen, Nitrogen Potassium")....25-40

HALL, Jimmy

Singles: 7-inch

HICKORY (1209 "Cathy's Clown") 10-20 63

HALL, Jimmy P&R/LP '80

Singles: 7-inch

EPIC....3-5 80-82

LPs: 10/12-inch

EPIC....5-10 80
Also see BECK, Jeff
Also see WET WILLIE

HALL, Jimmy, & Hi-Lighters

Singles: 7-inch

CANNON....10-20 59

HALL, Joanie

Singles: 7-inch

SAND....4-8 66

HALL, Joe

Singles: 7-inch

GLOBAL....5-10 59

HALL, Joey

Singles: 7-inch

TALOS....10-20
Also see BEETHOVENS

HALL, John P&R/LP '81
(John Hall Band)
Singles: 7-inch
ASYLUM...3-5 78
COLUMBIA...3-5 79
EMI AMERICA...3-4 81-83
LPs: 10/12-inch
ASYLUM...5-10 78
COLUMBIA...8-10 70
EMI AMERICA...5-10 81-82
Also see KANGAROO
Also see ORLEANS

HALL, Juanita
Singles: 7-inch
COUNTERPOINT (008 "You're No Good for Me")...10-15
EPs: 7-inch
VARSITY...10-20 50
LPs: 10/12-inch
COUNTERPOINT (556 "Juanita Hall Sings the Blues")...30-45
VARSITY (8 "Stephen Foster Songs")...20-40 50
(10-inch LP.)

HALL, Juanita / Eric Silver
LPs: 10/12-inch
HALO...10-20 50s

HALL, Juanita, & Four Tunes
Singles: 78 rpm
RCA...15-25 50
Singles: 7-inch
RCA (3149 "I'm in the Mood for Love")...40-50 50
Also see FOUR TUNES
Also see HALL, Juanita

HALL, Lani P&R '81
Singles: 7-inch
A&M...3-5 71-85
Picture Sleeves
A&M...3-5 72-85
LPs: 10/12-inch
A&M...5-10 72-85
Also see MENDES, Sergio

HALL, Lani, & Herb Alpert
Singles: 7-inch
A&M...3-4 81
Also see ALPERT, Herb
Also see HALL, Lani

HALL, Larry P&R '59
Singles: 7-inch
BARREL (621 "Sandy")...20-30 59
(Canadian.)
EVER GREEN (1001 "Sandy")...25-35 59
GOLD LEAF...8-12 62
HOT (1 "Sandy")...15-25 59
STRAND...10-15 59-62
LPs: 10/12-inch
STRAND (1005 "Sandy")...40-60 60

HALL, Linda
Singles: 7-inch
CUCA (1044 "You Don't Have a Wooden Heart")...10-20 61
CUCA (1070 "Almost Always True")...10-20 62

HALL, Linda
Singles: 7-inch
ARTCRAFT (7 "Beach Boy")...20-30 65
COLUMBIA...4-8 60s

HALL, Linda / Mat Mathews Orchestra
Singles: 7-inch
COLUMBIA...4-8 64
Also see HALL, Linda

HALL, Pam
Singles: 7-inch
ABC-PAR...4-8 64

HALL, Randy R&B '84
Singles: 7-inch
MCA...3-4 84-88
LPs: 10/12-inch
MCA...5-10 84

HALL, Rebecca C&W '85
Singles: 7-inch
CAPITOL...3-4 85

HALL, Reggie
Singles: 7-inch
RIP/CHESS (1816 "The Joke")...10-15 62
WHITE CLIFFS (255 "Please, Please Phone")...15-25 60s

HALL, René
(René Hall Trio)
Singles: 78 rpm
DECCA...4-8 51
RCA...5-10 53
SPECIALTY...5-10 57
Singles: 7-inch
ALLIED...4-8 60
ARVEE...4-8 60
CASTILE (101 "Turf")...10-15 59
DECCA...10-12 51
DEL-FI...5-10 60
RCA (5407 "Two Guitar Boogie")...10-20 53
SPECIALTY...5-10 57
Also see BOB & EARL
Also see COOKE, Sam
Also see HUGHES, Ben
Also see LIONS
Also see SUGAR & SPICES
Also see TANGENTS
Also see TRONICS

HALL, Rona
Singles: 7-inch
BIG TREE...3-5 75

HALL, Roy
(With His Cohutta Mountain Boys)
Singles: 78 rpm
DECCA...15-25 56
FORTUNE...20-45 49-56
HI-Q...25-35 56
Singles: 7-inch
DECCA (29697 "Whole Lotta Shakin' Goin' On")...50-75 55
DECCA (29786 "See You Later Alligator")...50-75 56
DECCA (29880 "Blue Suede Shoes")...30-50 56
DECCA (30060 "Three Alley Cats")...30-50 56
FORTUNE (170 "Going Down That Road")...35-50 53
FORTUNE (521 "Corrine Corrina")...35-50 56
HI-Q (5045 "Three Alley Cats")...50-75 56
PIERCE (1918 (One Monkey Don't Stop the Show")...75-125 50s
STRATE 8 (1508 "Rockin' the Blues")...20-30 59
Also see DAVIS SISTERS / Roy Hall
Also see HUNT SISTERS

HALL, Royce, & Lucky Four
Singles: 7-inch
NU TRYL...3-6 77-78
RAYNARD (1068 "That's My Life")...10-20 67
Members: Billy Woods; Mark Sands; Richard Kermesey.

HALL, Sammy C&W '84
Singles: 7-inch
DREAM...3-4 84

HALL, Sidney
Singles: 7-inch
SHRINE (109 "The Weekend")...250-350 66

HALL, Sonny, & Echoes
Singles: 7-inch
D (1009 "My Big Fat Baby")...50-75 58
D (1035 "Men Do Cry")...10-20 59
INT'L ARTISTS (131 "Poor Planet Earth")...10-20

HALL, Thomas
Singles: 7-inch
DIAMOND...4-8 65

HALL, Tom T. C&W '67
(With the Storytellers)
Singles: 7-inch
MERCURY (Except 70000 series)...3-5 77-86
MERCURY (70000 series)...3-8 67-77
RCA...3-5 77-81
LPs: 10/12-inch
K-TEL...5-10 77
MERCURY (500 thru 1100 series)...5-10 73-77
MERCURY (5000 thru 8000 series)...5-10 78-84
MERCURY (61000 series)...8-15 69-71
MERCURY (80000 series)...5-10 83-86
OUT of TOWN DIST...5-10 82
RCA...5-10 78-81
Session: Johnny Rodriguez; Gary Sargeants.
Also see DUDLEY, Dave, & Tom T. Hall
Also see PAGE, Patti, & Tom T. Hall
Also see RODRIGUEZ, Johnny
Also see SARGEANTS, Gary

HALL, Tom T., & Earl Scruggs C&W '82
Singles: 7-inch
COLUMBIA...3-4 82
LPs: 10/12-inch
COLUMBIA...5-10 82
Also see FLATT, Lester, & Earl Scruggs
Also see HALL, Tom T.

HALL, Vi
Singles: 7-inch
CT (1 "It's Graduation Time")...5-10

HALL & OATES: see HALL, Daryl, & John Oates

HALL BROTHERS
Singles: 7-inch
ARC...10-20 58
4 STAR...5-10 62

HALLADAY, Chance
Singles: 7-inch
BULLDOG (51 "Lucky Me")...25-50 59
BULLDOG (103 "Home Run")...50-75 59
GENE NORMAN PRESENTS (171 "Thirteen Women")...40-50 62

HALLEY, Bob
Singles: 7-inch
COLUMBIA...4-8 62
REGATTA...4-8 61

HALLEMAN, Dick
Singles: 7-inch
SUMMIT (189-10 "Pajama Top")...10-20 60s

HALLIQUINS
Singles: 7-inch
EARLY BIRD (1004 "Confession of Love")...4-6 96
(Colored vinyl.)
JUANITA (102 "Confession of Love")...1000-1500 58

HALLMAN, Victoria C&W '87
Singles: 7-inch
EVERGREEN...3-4 87

HALLMARK, Roger, & Thrasher Brothers C&W '79
Singles: 7-inch
VULCAN...3-6 79
Also see THRASHER BROTHERS

HALLMARKS
Singles: 7-inch
DOT...10-15 62
EPIC...4-8 64

HALLMARKS
Singles: 7-inch
SMASH (2115 "Psychedelic Sally")...15-25 67

HALLORAN, Jack, Singers P&R '62
Singles: 7-inch
DOT...3-5 63

HALLOWAY, Larry
Singles: 7-inch
PARKWAY (903 "Beatle Teen Beat")...10-20 64

HALLOWEEN
Singles: 7-inch
MERCURY...3-4 79
LPs: 10/12-inch
MERCURY...5-10 79

HALLYDAY, David P&R '87
Singles: 7-inch
SCOTTI BROS...3-4 87
Picture Sleeves
SCOTTI BROS...3-4 87

HALLYDAY, Johnny
Singles: 7-inch
PHILIPS (40014 "Hold Back the Sun")...10-20 62
PHILIPS (40024 "Be Bop a Lula")...10-20 62
PHILIPS (40043 "Hey Little Girl")...10-20 62
Picture Sleeves
PHILIPS (40024 "Be Bop a Lula")...20-30 62
LPs: 10/12-inch
PHILIPS (200019 "America's Rockin' Hits")...30-40 62
(Monaural.)
PHILIPS (600019 "America's Rockin' Hits")...35-45 62
(Stereo.)

HALO, Johnny
Singles: 7-inch
ANGLE TONE (538 "Little Annie")...30-40 59
ANGLE TONE (541 "It Hurts Me")...30-40 59
SOUTHERN SOUND...10-15 62
TOPIX (6004 "Betty Jean")...35-50 62
(With the 4 Seasons.)
Also see 4 SEASONS

HALOS P&R '61
Singles: 7-inch
7 ARTS (709 "Nag")...10-20 61
7 ARTS (720 "Come On")...10-20 62
TRANS ATLAS (690 "Village of Love")...8-12 62
LPs: 10/12-inch
WARWICK (2046 "The Halos")...200-400 62
Member: Arthur Crier.
Also see KING, Ben E.
Also see LEE, Curtis
Also see MANN, Barry
Also see PRE-HISTORICS

HALOS
Singles: 7-inch
CONGRESS...4-8 65

HAM BROTHERS
LPs: 10/12-inch
ARIOLA...8-10 77

HAMAMURA, Michiko
EPs: 7-inch
RCA (4190 "With a Beat")...40-60 58

HAMBER, Kenny
Singles: 7-inch
ARCTIC (131 "Ain't Gonna Cry")...150-250 66
ARCTIC (139 "Looking for a Love")...100-150 67
(Single-sided. Promotional issue only.)
ARCTIC (139 "Looking for a Love"/"These Arms of Mine")...50-100 67
DE JAC (1234 "Show Me Your Monkey")...10-20 64
MEAN (200 "Camel Walk")...15-25 60s
SPAR (101 "Tears in My Eyes") 150-250 60

HAMBLEN, Stuart C&W '49
Singles: 78 rpm
COLUMBIA...4-8 49-57
Singles: 7-inch
BLUEBIRD...5-10 59
COLUMBIA...5-10 50-62
CORAL...4-8 59
ELECTRADISK...25-50 30s
(Made for sale through Woolworth Stores.)
KAPP...4-8 66
LAMB & LION...3-5 74
RCA (0500 series)...3-5 71
RCA (5000 & 6000 series)...5-15 54-56
EPs: 7-inch
COLUMBIA...5-10 58-59
RCA...5-15 54-60
LPs: 10/12-inch
CAMDEN...5-15 59-66
COLUMBIA...5-15 61-62
CORAL...12-25 60
HURRAH...5-10
KAPP...15-20 66
LAMB & LION...5-8 74
RCA...15-30 54-57
SACRED...5-8
VOSS...10-15
WORD...5-8

HAMBONE
Singles: 7-inch
SALSOUL...3-4 81
LPs: 10/12-inch
SALSOUL...5-10 81

HAMBRIC, Billy
Singles: 7-inch
DRUM (1204 "She Said Goodbye")...15-25 60s
FURY (5000 "Talk to Me Baby")...10-20 63
FURY (5006 "This Is My Prayer")...10-20 63
JOVIAL (730 "Someone to Love") 15-25 64
LEE (5001 "New York City Baby") 8-12 60s
SOHO (5001 "New York City Baby")...15-25 60s

HAMBY, Bill
Singles: 7-inch
CONGRESSIONAL...4-6

HAMEL, Gerry
Singles: 7-inch
MAYPOLE...10-15

HAMES SISTERS
Singles: 7-inch
FELSTED...5-10 59

HAMILL, Claire
LPs: 10/12-inch
ISLAND...8-10 72

HAMILTON, Big John
Singles: 7-inch
MINARET (124 "Big Bad John")...8-12 66
MINARET (129 "I Have No One")...8-12 66
MINARET (136 "Big Fanny")...8-12 67
MINARET (139 "Pretty Girls")...8-12 68
MINARET (143 "Love Comes and It Goes")...8-12 68
MINARET (148 "If You're Looking for a Fool")...8-12 69
SSS INT'L (413 "I Have No One")...4-6 70s
SSS INT'L (835 "I Finally Caught Up with Jody")...5-8 71

HAMILTON, Big John, & Doris Allen
Singles: 7-inch
MINARET (156 "Let a Little Love In")...8-12 70s
MINARET (159 "Bright Star")...8-12 70s
Also see ALLEN, Doris
Also see HAMILTON, Big John

HAMILTON, Bill
Singles: 7-inch
BIG K...3-5

HAMILTON, Billy
Singles: 7-inch
BETHLEHEM...4-8 62

HAMILTON, Bobby P&R '58
Singles: 7-inch
APT...8-12 58-59
DECCA...5-10 59
DIANA...5-10 59

HAMILTON, Bobby J.
Singles: 7-inch
EMERSON...3-5 72
Picture Sleeves
EMERSON...8-12 72

HAMILTON, Chico LP '64
(Chico Hamilton Trio; Quartet; Quintet; with Players)
Singles: 7-inch
COLUMBIA...4-6 61
CORAL...4-6 62
ENTERPRISE...3-5 74
IMPULSE...5-8 64-67
PACIFIC JAZZ (600 series)...8-15 54-55
PACIFIC JAZZ (88000 series)...4-6 66
EPs: 7-inch
DECCA...15-25 57
PACIFIC JAZZ...20-40 55-56
LPs: 10/12-inch
BLUE NOTE...5-10 75
COLUMBIA...15-25 60-62
CROWN...10-20 63
DECCA (8614 "Jazz from Sweet Smell of Success")...25-40 57
DISCOVERY...5-8 81
ELEKTRA...5-8 80
EVEREST...5-8 79
FLYING DUTCHMAN...8-10 71
IMPULSE...10-20 63-71
INSTANT...10-20 64
MERCURY...5-10 77
ODYSSEY...10-20 68
PACIFIC JAZZ (17 "The Chico Hamilton Trio")...75-100 55
(10-inch LP.)
PACIFIC JAZZ (39 "Spectacular Chico Hamilton")...15-25 62
PACIFIC JAZZ (1209 "Chico Hamilton Quintet")...50-75 55
PACIFIC JAZZ (1216 "In Hi Fi")...50-75 56
PACIFIC JAZZ (1220 "Chico Hamilton Trio")...50-75 57
PACIFIC JAZZ (1225 "Chico Hamilton Quintet")...50-75 57
PACIFIC JAZZ (20000 series)...10-20 68
REPRISE...15-25 63
SESAC...35-55 59
SOLID STATE...10-15 68-69
SUNSET...8-15 68
W.B. (1245 "With Strings Attached")...50-75 58
W.B. (1271 "Goings East")...50-75 58
W.B. (1344 "Three Faces of Chico")...40-60 59
WORLD PACIFIC (1000 & 1200 series)...25-40 58-60
Also see ALMEIDA, Laurindo / Chico Hamilton

HAMILTON, Chico, & Charles Lloyd
LPs: 10/12-inch
COLUMBIA...10-15 68
Also see HAMILTON, Chico
Also see LLOYD, Charles, Quartet

HAMILTON, Danny
Singles: 7-inch
REGENCY...10-20 64

HAMILTON, Dave
(With His Peppers)
Singles: 7-inch
FORTUNE (861 "Beatle Walk")...20-30 64
HI-Q (5019 "Donna's Cha-Cha")...20-30 60
WORKSHOP JAZZ (2004 "Late Freight")...10-20 63
LPs: 10/12-inch
WORKSHOP JAZZ (206 "Blue Vibrations")...40-60 63

HAMILTON, Edward
(With the Arabians; with Fifes; Edw. Hamilton)
Singles: 7-inch
CARRIE (9 "I'm Gonna Love You")...15-25
JAMECO (2008 "Call Me")...20-30
LANROD (1605 "I Love You So")...50-100 60
MARY JANE (1005 "Baby Don't You Weep")...30-50 60s
MARY JANE (1006 "My Darling Baby")...30-50 60s
Also see ARABIANS

HAMILTON, George
Singles: 7-inch
ABC-PAR...4-8 65
MGM...4-8 63
Picture Sleeves
ABC-PAR (10734 "Loneliness")...5-10 65
MGM (13178 "Don't Envy Me")...5-10 63
EPs: 7-inch
ABC-PAR (535 "George Hamilton")...8-12 65
(Juke box issue.)
LPs: 10/12-inch
ABC-PAR (535 "George Hamilton")...15-25 65

HAMILTON, George, IV P&R '56/C&W '60
(With the Country Gentlemen; with Arthur Smith)
Singles: 78 rpm
ABC-PAR...10-20 56-57
COLONIAL (420 "A Rose and a Baby Ruth")...30-40 56
COLONIAL (451 "Sam")...10-20 56
Singles: 7-inch
ABC...3-5 78
ABC/DOT...3-5 77
ABC-PAR (9000 series)...10-20 56-59
ABC-PAR (10000 series)...5-15 59-65
COLONIAL (420 "A Rose and a Baby Ruth")...25-40 56
COLONIAL (451 "Sam")...20-30 56
GRT...3-5 76
MCA...3-5 79-80
RCA...3-8 61-74
EPs: 7-inch
ABC-PAR (220 "On Campus")...15-25 58
LPs: 10/12-inch
ABC...8-10 72-77
ABC-PAR (ABC-220 "On Campus")...20-40 58
(Monaural.)
ABC-PAR (ABCS-220 "On Campus")...25-50 58
(Stereo.)
ABC-PAR (ABC-251 "Sing Me a Sad Song")...20-40 58
(Monaural.)
ABC-PAR (ABCS-251 "Sing Me a Sad Song")...25-50 58
(Stereo.)
ABC-PAR (ABC-461 "Big 15")...20-30 63
(Monaural.)
ABC-PAR (ABCS-461 "Big 15")...25-35 63
(Stereo.)
CAMDEN...8-10 68-73
GRAND AWARD...5-10
HARMONY...8-10 70
MCA...5-10 80
RCA ("APL1" series)...8-10 74-76
RCA ("LPM" & "LSP" series)...10-20 61-73
Also see ANKA, Paul, George Hamilton IV & Johnny Nash
Also see BLUENOTES
Also see DAVIS, Skeeter, & George Hamilton IV
Also see SOME of CHET'S FRIENDS

HAMILTON, George, IV / Arthur Smith
LPs: 10/12-inch
LAMB & LION...5-8 74
Also see HAMILTON, George, IV
Also see SMITH, Arthur

HAMILTON, George, V C&W '88
Singles: 7-inch
MTM...3-4 88

HAMILTON, Gil
Singles: 7-inch
CAPITOL...5-8 62
VEE JAY...5-8 62
Also see THUNDER, Johnny

HAMILTON, Jimmy
("Mighty Man of the Tenor Sax")
Singles: 78 rpm
STATES (113 "Big Fifty") 5-10 52
Singles: 7-inch
STATES (113 "Big Fifty") 15-25 52

HAMILTON, Joel
Singles: 7-inch
ROULETTE 3-5 62

HAMILTON, Judd
Singles: 7-inch
AMERICAN INT'L 4-8 60s
DOLTON (80 "Dream") 20-30 63

HAMILTON, Little Johnny, & Creators
Singles: 7-inch
DORE (754 "Oh How I Love You") 25-50 66
DORE (760 "Keep on Movin' ") 8-12 66
Also see CREATORS

HAMILTON, Penny C&W '79
Singles: 7-inch
DOOR KNOB 3-5 79

HAMILTON, Peter
Singles: 7-inch
JAMIE (1338 "Hey Girl") 15-25 66

HAMILTON, Professor: see PROFESSOR HAMILTON

HAMILTON, Roy P&R/R&B '54
Singles: 78 rpm
EPIC 5-10 54-57
Singles: 7-inch
AGP 8-12 69
CAPITOL 4-8 67
EPIC (9015 thru 9354) 10-20 54-59
EPIC (9372 thru 9538) 5-10 60-63
EPIC (70464 "Don't Let Go") 25-50 61
(Stereo.)
EPIC MEMORY LANE 4-6 63-64
MGM (13138 thru 13175) 5-10 63
MGM (13217 "The Panic Is On") 25-35 64
MGM (13247 "Unchained Melody") 5-10 64
MGM (13291 "You Can Count on Me") 25-35 64
MGM (13315 "Sweet Violet") 5-10 65
RCA (8641 thru 8841) 5-10 65-66
RCA (8960 "Crackin' Up Over You") 15-25 66
RCA (9061 "I Taught Her Everything She Knows") 8-12 67
RCA (9171 "So High My Love") 25-45 67
Picture Sleeves
EPIC 10-20 60-62
EPs: 7-inch
EPIC 10-20 54-59
LPs: 10/12-inch
CBS 5-8
EPIC (518 "With All My Love") 25-35 58
(Stereo.)
EPIC (525 "Why Fight the Feeling") 20-30 59
(Stereo.)
EPIC (530 "Come Out Swingin' ") 20-30 59
(Stereo.)
EPIC (535 "Have Blues Must Travel") 20-30 59
(Stereo.)
EPIC (551 "Spirituals") 20-25 60
(Stereo.)
EPIC (578 "Soft 'N Warm") 20-25 60
(Stereo.)
EPIC (595 "You Can Have Her") 20-25 61
(Stereo.)
EPIC (610 "Only You") 20-25 61
(Stereo.)
EPIC (632 "You'll Never Walk Alone") 10-20 65
(Stereo.)
EPIC (1023 "You'll Never Walk Alone") 50-100 54
(10-inch LP.)
EPIC (1103 "The Voice of Roy Hamilton") 50-100 55
(10-inch LP.)
EPIC (3176 "Roy Hamilton") 25-50 57
EPIC (3294 "You'll Never Walk Alone") 50-75 54
EPIC (3364 "Golden Boy") 30-40 57
EPIC (3519 "With All My Love") 15-25 58
(Monaural.)
EPIC (3545 "Why Fight the Feeling") 15-25 59
(Monaural.)
EPIC (3561 "Come Out Swingin' ") 15-25 59
(Monaural.)
EPIC (3580 "Have Blues Must Travel") 15-25 59
(Monaural.)
EPIC (3628 "At His Best") 15-25 60
(Monaural.)
EPIC (3654 "Spirituals") 15-25 60
(Monaural.)
EPIC (3717 "Soft 'N Warm") 15-25 60
(Monaural.)
EPIC (3775 "You Can Have Her") 15-25 61
(Monaural.)
EPIC (3807 "Only You") 15-25 61
(Monaural.)
EPIC (24000 "Mr. Rock & Soul") 15-25 62
(Monaural.)
EPIC (24009 "Greatest Hits") 15-25 63
(Monaural.)
EPIC (24316 "Greatest Hits, Vol. 2") 10-20 67
(Monaural.)
EPIC (26000 "Mr. Rock & Soul") 20-25 62
(Stereo.)
EPIC (26009 "Greatest Hits") 15-25 63
(Stereo.)
EPIC (26316 "Greatest Hits, Vol. 2") 10-20 67
(Stereo.)
MGM (4139 "Warm Soul") 15-25 63
MGM (4233 "Sentimental, Lonely and Blue") 15-25 64
RCA (3532 "Impossible Dream") 15-25 66
SEAGULL 8-12

HAMILTON, Russ P&R/R&B '57
Singles: 78 rpm
KAPP 5-10 57
Singles: 7-inch
KAPP 5-10 57-64
MGM 4-8 60
LPs: 10/12-inch
KAPP (1076 "Rainbow") 45-55 57

HAMILTON, Walter
Singles: 7-inch
FORTUNE 8-10 59

HAMILTON, Willie
Singles: 7-inch
CONTOUR (500 "I'm So Glad You're Mine") 15-25 60
HRP (001 "Cheer Up") 10-15 60s

HAMILTON FACE BAND
LPs: 10/12-inch
BELL 8-10 70
PHILLIPS 10-12 69

HAMILTON, JOE FRANK & DENNISON P&R '76
Singles: 7-inch
PLAYBOY 3-5 76-77
Picture Sleeves
PLAYBOY 3-5 76
LPs: 10/12-inch
PLAYBOY 8-10 76-77
Members: Dan Hamilton; Joe Frank Carollo; Alan Dennison.

HAMILTON, JOE FRANK & REYNOLDS P&R/LP '71
Singles: 7-inch
ABC 3-5 72
DUNHILL 3-5 71
PLAYBOY 3-5 75-76
Picture Sleeves
PLAYBOY 3-5 76
LPs: 10/12-inch
DUNHILL 8-10 71-72
PICKWICK 5-8 70s
PLAYBOY 8-10 75-77
Members: Dan Hamilton; Joe Frank Carollo; Tom Reynolds.
Also see HAMILTON, JOE FRANK & DENNISON
Also see T-BONES

HAMILTON SISTERS
Singles: 78 rpm
COLUMBIA 5-10 54
Singles: 7-inch
COLUMBIA 10-15 54

HAMILTON STREETCAR
Singles: 7-inch
LHI 10-15 67
DOT 5-10 69
LPs: 10/12-inch
DOT (25939 "Hamilton Streetcar") 15-25 69

HAMLET
Singles: 7-inch
CAPITOL 3-5 73
LPs: 10/12-inch
CAPITOL 8-10 73

HAMLISCH, Marvin P&R/LP '74
Singles: 12-inch
U.A. 4-6 77
Singles: 7-inch
A&M 3-5 74-76
ARISTA 3-4 79
MCA 3-5 74-83
PLANET 3-4 80
U.A. 3-4 71-77
LPs: 10/12-inch
MCA 5-10 74
SOUTHERN CROSS 5-10 83

HAMMACK, Bobby
Singles: 7-inch
CAPITOL (4193 "Little Child") 5-10 59
(Monaural.)
CAPITOL (4193 "Little Child") 10-15 59
(Stereo.)

HAMMAN, Jeff, & Surf Teens
Singles: 7-inch
WESTCO (9 "Moment of Truth") 15-20 63
(Black vinyl.)
WESTCO (9 "Moment of Truth") 30-40 63
(Colored vinyl.)

HAMMEL, Karl, Jr. P&R '61
(Carl Hammel)
Singles: 7-inch
ARLISS (1007 "Summer Souvenirs") 10-20 61
ARLISS (1011 "Sittin' Alphabetically") 30-40 61
GONE (5059 "My Broken Heart") 10-15 59
LAURIE 5-10 63
20TH FOX 4-8 66

HAMMER
LPs: 10/12-inch
SAN FRANCISCO (203 "Hammer") 10-20 70

HAMMER
Singles: 7-inch
ASYLUM 3-5 79
LPs: 10/12-inch
ASYLUM 5-10 79

HAMMER, Jack
Singles: 78 rpm
DECCA 3-8 56
Singles: 7-inch
DECCA 5-10 56
KAPP 4-8 60
MILESTONE 5-10 59
RONNEX 4-8 62
ROULETTE 5-10 58

HAMMER, Jan P&R/R&B/D&D '85
(Jan Hammer Group)
Singles: 12-inch
MCA 4-6 85
Singles: 7-inch
ASYLUM 3-4 79
MCA 3-4 85
NEMPEROR 3-5 76-78
Picture Sleeves
MCA 3-4 85
LPs: 10/12-inch
ECM 5-10
MPS 5-10 76
NEMPEROR 5-10 74-86
VANGAURD 5-10 77
Also see BECK, Jeff
Also see GOODMAN, Jerry, & Jan Hammer
Also see SCHON, Neal, & Jan Hammer

HAMMER, Jan, / Glenn Frey
LPs: 10/12-inch
MCA (6150 "Miami Vice Theme") 4-8 85
(Picture disc.)
Also see FREY, Glenn

HAMMER, M.C. LP '88
(Hammer; Stanley Burrell)
Singles: 7-inch
CAPITOL 3-4 88-90
LPs: 10/12-inch
CAPITOL 5-8 88-90
Also see OAKTOWN'S 3-5-7

HAMMERR, Franklinn, Band
Singles: 7-inch
NDR 10-15

HAMMERSMITH
Singles: 7-inch
MERCURY 3-5 75-76
LPs: 10/12-inch
MERCURY 8-10 75-76

HAMMILL, Peter
LPs: 10/12-inch
FAMOUS CHARISMA 8-10 72

HAMMOND, Albert P&R/LP '72
Singles: 7-inch
EPIC 3-5 76
MUMS 3-5 72-75
LPs: 10/12-inch
COLUMBIA 5-10 81-82
EPIC 8-10 77
MUMS 8-10 72-74
Also see FAMILY DOGG
Also see MAGIC LANTERNS
Also see SPRINGSTEEN, Bruce / Albert Hammond / Loudon Wainwright, III / Taj Mahal
Also see STEVE & ALBERT

HAMMOND, Clay
Singles: 7-inch
DUO-DISC 5-10 65
EVEJIM 3-4 88
GALAXY 10-15 63
KENT 5-10 69
KEYMEN 8-12 67
LIBERTY 5-10 65
MERCURY 3-5 73
RAUSHAN 3-4 82
RONN 3-5 70
TAG 10-20 62
VERSEPTO 3-4 82
Also see HAMMOND BROTHERS

HAMMOND, Clay, with Johnnie Young & Celebritys
Singles: 78 rpm
CAROLINE 150-250 56
Singles: 7-inch
CAROLINE (2302 "We Made Romance") 500-750 56
Also see CELEBRITYS
Also see HAMMOND, Clay

HAMMOND, Jack
Singles: 7-inch
TYGON 10-15

HAMMOND, Jay, & Rhythm Kings
(With the Golden Voices)
Singles: 7-inch
HI-Q (5015 "I'll Be Your Fool") 15-25 60

HAMMOND, John
(With the Nighthawks)
Singles: 7-inch
ATLANTIC 4-8 69
COLUMBIA 3-5 71
ITZY 4-8
RED BIRD (047 "I Wish You Would") 10-15 66
LPs: 10/12-inch
ATLANTIC 10-15 68-69
CAPRICORN 8-10 75
COLUMBIA 8-10 71-72
VANGUARD 6-12 64-79
Also see BLOOMFIELD, Mike, Dr. John & John Paul Hammond Jr.
Also see HELM, Levon
Also see JEFFERSON AIRPLANE
Also see WINTER, Johnny / Argent / Chambers Brothers / John Hammond
Also see WYMAN, Bill

HAMMOND, Johnny LP '71
(John Hammond)
Singles: 7-inch
MILESTONE 4-8 75
LPs: 10/12-inch
KUDU 8-12 71-72

HAMMOND, Little Walter
Singles: 7-inch
DUO-DISC 5-10 65

HAMMOND, Roy, & Genies
Singles: 7-inch
FORUM (701 "Mama, Blow Your Top") 15-25 61

HAMMOND, Stick Horse
Singles: 78 rpm
J.O.B. (100 "Gambling Man") 35-55 50
J.O.B. (105 "Highway 51") 35-55 50
GOTHAM 20-30 50
ROYALTY (906 "Highway 51") 35-55 50

HAMMOND, Tommy
Singles: 7-inch
KOOL (1011 "Forget We Ever Met") 50-100

HAMMOND, Wayne, & Starfires
Singles: 7-inch
GALA (105 "Can't See Why") 15-25 59

HAMMOND BROTHERS
Singles: 7-inch
ABNER 5-10 62
Members: Clay Hammond; Walter Hammond.

HAMMONDS, George
Singles: 7-inch
ME-O 4-8 65

HAMOD, Oscar, & Majestics
Singles: 7-inch
SCORE 10-20 64
SOULFUL 8-12 60s
Members: Oscar Hamod; Sam Hamod; Robert Wheeler; John Toda; Vince Jimkimzak.
Also see OSCAR & MAJESTICS

HAMP, Monti
Singles: 7-inch
PRESTIGE BLUESVILLE 4-8 61
LPs: 10/12-inch
PRESTIGE BLUESVILLE 20-30 61

HAMPSHIRE, Keith P&R '72
(With the Ladys)
Singles: 7-inch
A&M 3-5 72-74
RCA 3-5 71

HAMPTON, Duke
Singles: 78 rpm
KING 10-20 53
Singles: 7-inch
KING (4625 "Please Be Good to Me") 30-50 53

HAMPTON, John, & Hamptones
Singles: 78 rpm
UNITED (210 "Honey Hush") 50-100 57
Singles: 7-inch
UNITED (210 "Honey Hush") 75-100 57

HAMPTON, Johnny
Singles: 7-inch
DOTTY'S (1001 "Not My Girl") 20-30 60s
ROSE (003 "Beatle Dance") 10-20 64

HAMPTON, Junior / Brother Jackson
Singles: 78 rpm
MURRAY (500 "J.H. Stomp") 25-50 48
Also see JACKSON, Louis

HAMPTON, Lionel P&R '37
(With the Hamptones)
Singles: 78 rpm
CLEF 4-8 55
DECCA 5-10 42-53
MGM 4-8 51-56
NORGREN 4-8 56
VICTOR 5-15 37-41
Singles: 7-inch
CLEF 5-10 55
BRUNSWICK 3-5 74
COLUMBIA 3-4 76
DECCA (Except 140 & 154) 5-10 50-53
DECCA (140 "Moonglow") 15-25 51
(Boxed, four-disc set)
DECCA (154 "Just Jazz") 15-25 53
(Boxed, four-disc set)
GLAD 4-6 60s
GLAD HAMP 4-6 60-67
IMPULSE 4-6 65
MGM 5-10 51-61
NORGREN 5-10 56
EPs: 7-inch
CAMDEN 10-15 50s
CLEF 15-30 53-56
COLUMBIA 10-20 56
DECCA 10-20 51-53
EMARCY 10-20 56
EPIC 10-20 56
GLAD HAMP 5-10 62
MGM 10-20 56
MERCURY 10-20 55
NORGREN 10-30 55
RCA 10-20 54-57
LPs: 10/12-inch
AMERICAN RECORDING SOCIETY (403 "Swinging Jazz") 100-150 56
(Includes booklet.)
AUDIO FIDELITY 20-40 57-59
BLUENOTE (5046 "Rockin' and Groovin' ") 100-150 53
(10-inch LP.)
BRUNSWICK 5-10 74
CAMDEN (400 & 500 series) 20-30 58-59
CLEF (142 "Lionel Hampton Quartet") 75-125 53
(10-inch LP.)
CLEF (611 "Lionel Hampton Quartet") 50-100 53
CLEF (628 "Lionel Hampton Quintet") 50-100 54
CLEF (642 "Lionel Hampton Quintet") 50-100 54
CLEF (667 "Quartet/Quintet") 50-100 55
CLEF (670 "Big Band") 50-100 55
CLEF (673 "Big Band") 50-100 55
CLEF (735 "Flying Home") 50-100 56
CLEF (736 "Swingin' with Hamp") 50-100 56
CLEF (744 "Hamp's Big Four") 50-100 56
CLEF (709 "Lionel Hampton Trio") 50-100 56
COLUMBIA (711 "Wailin' at the Trianon") 50-100 56
COLUMBIA (1304 thru 1661) 20-40 59-61
(Monaural.)
COLUMBIA (8110 thru 8461) 25-50 59-61
(Stereo.)
CONTEMPORARY (3502 "Lionel Hampton Swings in Paris") 50-100 55
CORAL 15-25 63
DECCA (4000 series) 20-40 61-63
(Monaural.)
DECCA (7-4000 series) 25-50 61-63
(Stereo.)
DECCA (5230 "Boogie Woogie") 50-100 51
(10-inch LP.)
DECCA (7013 "Just Jazz") 50-100 53
(10-inch LP.)
DECCA (8200 series) 40-60 56
DECCA (9000 series) 25-50 58
DECCA (79000 series) 10-15 69
EMARCY (26037 "In Paris") 50-100 53
(10-inch LP.)
EMARCY (26038 "Crazy Hamp") 50-100 53
(10-inch LP.)
EMARCY (36032 "In Paris") 50-75 53
EMARCY (36034 "Crazy Hamp") 50-75 56
EPIC (3190 "Lionel Hampton Apollo Hall Concert 1954") 50-75 56
EPIC (16027 "Many Splendored Vibes") 20-40 62
(Monaural.)
EPIC (17027 "Many Splendored Vibes") 25-50 62
(Stereo.)
GNP (15 "Lionel Hampton with the Jazz All Stars") 50-100 57
GLAD HAMP (1001 thru 1009) 15-25 61-65
GLAD HAMP (1020 & 1021) 5-10 80
GLAD HAMP (3000 series) 15-25 62
HARMONY (7000 series) 20-35 58-61
HARMONY (32000 series) 5-10 73
IMPULSE 15-25 65
LAURIE 5-10 78
MCA 5-8 75-82
MGM (285 "Oh Rock") 75-125 51
(10-inch LP.)
MGM (3386 "Oh Rock") 50-75 56
MUSE 5-8 79
NORGREN (1080 "Lionel Hampton and His Giants") 50-100 55
PERFECT (12002 "Hampton Swings") 40-60 59
RCA (1000 "Hot Mallets") 50-100 54
RCA (1422 "Jazz Flamenco") 50-75 57
RCA (LPM-2318 "Swing Classics") 25-40 61
(Monaural.)
RCA (LSP-2318 "Swing Classics") 35-55 61
(Stereo.)
RCA (3900 series) 10-15 68
RCA (5536 "The Complete Lionel Hampton") 50-75 76
(Boxed, six-disc set.)
SUTRA 5-10 81
VERVE (2018 "Lionel Hampton Plays Love Songs") 50-100 56
VERVE (2500 series) 5-10 82
VERVE (8019 thru 8228) 40-60 57-58
WHO'S WHO in JAZZ 5-10 78-81
Also see BOSTIC, Earl
Also see BROWN, Wini
Also see CARTER, Betty
Also see COLE, Cozy
Also see GOODMAN, Benny / Lionel Hampton
Also see HALEY, Bill / Lionel Hampton / Sal Salvador Quartet / Lenny Dee
Also see JACQUET, Illinois

HAMPTON, Lionel & Stan Getz
LPs: 10/12-inch
NORGREN (1037 "Hamp and Getz") 75-100 55
VERVE (8128 "Hamp and Getz") 40-60 57
Also see GETZ, Stan

HAMPTON, Lionel & Dinah Washington R&B '44
Singles: 78 rpm
DECCA 5-15 44-47
LPs: 10/12-inch
DECCA (8088 "All American Award Concert") 40-60 54
Also see HAMPTON, Lionel
Also see WASHINGTON, Dinah

HAMPTON, Paul
Singles: 7-inch
BATTLE.......4-8 63
CAMEO.......5-10 61
COLUMBIA.......10-20 58-59
DECCA.......4-8 66
DOT.......5-10 60-63
W.B. 4-8 62-63
Picture Sleeves
BATTLE.......5-10 63

HAMPTON GREASE BAND
LPs: 10/12-inch
COLUMBIA.......8-10 71

HAMPTONS
Singles: 7-inch
LEGRAND (1007 "I Know Why Dreamers Cry").......15-25 61

HANCHEY, Donald, & Marauders
Singles: 7-inch
MI-TIA (1001 "Hang Loose").......8-12

HANCOCK, Billy
(With the Tennessee Rockets)
Singles: 7-inch
RIPSAW.......3-5 78-85
LPs: 10/12-inch
RIPSAW.......5-10 85
SOLID SMOKE.......5-10 78
Also see RUBINOWITZ, Tex

HANCOCK, Conni, & Supernatural Family Band
LPs: 10/12-inch
AKASHIC.......5-10 86
Also see HANCOCK, Tommy, & Supernatural Family Band

HANCOCK, Herbie *LP '67*
Singles: 12-inch
COLUMBIA (Except 39913).......4-6 79-85
COLUMBIA (39913 "Rock It").......10-15 84
(Picture disc.)
Singles: 7-inch
BLUE NOTE.......3-6 62-65
COLUMBIA.......3-5 74-88
W.B. 3-5 69-72
LPs: 10/12-inch
BLUE NOTE.......15-25 62-65
(Label reads "Blue Note Records Inc. - New York, U.S.A.")
BLUE NOTE.......8-15 66-71
(Label shows Blue Note Records as a division of either Liberty or United Artists.)
COLUMBIA.......6-12 67-85
UPFRONT.......5-10
W.B. 8-15 70-74
Also see SANTANA
Also see SUMMERS, Bill

HANCOCK, Herbie, & Willie Bobo
LPs: 10/12-inch
BLUE NOTE.......5-10 73
Also see BOBO, Willie
Also see HANCOCK, Herbie

HANCOCK, Herbie, & Chick Corea *LP '79*
LPs: 10/12-inch
COLUMBIA.......5-10 79
POLYDOR.......8-10 79
Also see COREA, Chick
Also see HANCOCK, Herbie

HANCOCK, Tommy, & Supernatural Family Band
LPs: 10/12-inch
AKASHIC.......5-10 86
Members: Tommy Hancock; Conni Hancock; Traci Lamar; Joaquin Hancock; John Reed.
Also see HANCOCK, Conni, & Supernatural Family Band
Also see LAMAR, Traci

HAND, Bassett: see BASSETT HAND

HAND OF GLORY
LPs: 10/12-inch
SCREAMIN' SKULL.......5-10 91
Members: Joe Doerr; Bill Anderson; Tim Swingle; Rey Washam.

HANDCLAPPERS
Singles: 7-inch
COLLIER (2500 "Three Gassed Rats").......10-20 61

HANDICAPPERS
Singles: 7-inch
ADVANCE (6250 "I Got a Little Girl").......25-50 60s

HANDS OF DOCTOR TELENY
Singles: 7-inch
RCA.......4-6 60s

HANDS OF TIME
Singles: 7-inch
SIDEWALK (903 "Got to Get You into My Life").......10-20 66
Members: Mike Curb; Davie Allan.
Also see ALLAN, Davie

HANDSOME EARL
Singles: 7-inch
VIN.......8-12 58

HANDY, Cap'n John
LPs: 10/12-inch
GHB.......8-12
RCA.......10-12 68
Session: Kid Thomas Valentine; Jim Robinson; Sammy Rimmington; Bill Sinclair; Dick Griffith; Dick McCarthy; Sammy Penn.

HANDY, Cheryl *C&W '84*
Singles: 7-inch
AUDIOGRAPH.......3-4 84
COMPLEAT.......3-4 87
RCM.......3-4 87

HANDY, John
(Gene Autry)
Singles: 78 rpm
BENNETT (7290 "Hobo Bill's Last Ride").......25-75
BENNETT (7310 "Dust Pan Blues").......25-75
RADIEX.......25-75
Also see AUTRY, Gene

HANDY, John *P&R/R&B/LP '76*
(John Handy Quartet; Quintet)
Singles: 7-inch
IMPULSE.......3-5 76-77
COLUMBIA.......4-6 66-69
LPs: 10/12-inch
IMPULSE.......5-10 76-77
COLUMBIA.......10-15 66-68
RCA.......10-15 67
ROULETTE (52000 series).......15-25 60
ROULETTE (52100 series).......10-15 66-67
W.B. 5-10 78

HANDY, John, III
LPs: 10/12-inch
ROULETTE (100 series).......5-10 76
ROULETTE (52000 series).......15-25 60
ROULETTE (52100 series).......10-20 66-67

HANDY, Mary, & Butterflies
Singles: 7-inch
L&J (50 "Life Is Not Worth Living").......25-50

HANDY, Roy
(With the Parlets)
Singles: 7-inch
MARTON (1001 "What Did He Do").......20-30
STEPHAYNE (234 "Baby, That's a Groove").......20-30

HANDY, Wayne
Singles: 7-inch
DIAL.......5-10 61
PARKWAY.......5-10 60
RENOWN.......10-20 57-59
TREND.......10-15 58

HANDY & HANDY
Singles: 7-inch
JCP.......10-20 60s

HANEY, Bill
(With His Dixie Buddies)
Singles: 7-inch
BRIAR.......5-10 62
DOT (16731 "Leavin' Town").......10-15 65
JIM DANDY (1013 "Crawdad Song").......30-45
RAV.......5-8 77

HANEY, Bill, & Ken Meggs
Singles: 7-inch
DEE-BEE (69 "Wild Party Twist").......10-20 62
Also see HANEY, Bill

HANEY, Jack, & Nikiter Armstrong
Singles: 7-inch
MEL-O-DY (107 "The Interview").......10-20 63

HANEY, Sally
Singles: 7-inch
VULCAN (153 "I'm in a Green M&M Mood Tonight").......4-6
(Colored vinyl, green of course.)

HANGMEN
Singles: 7-inch
SHOWCASE.......4-8 63

HANGMEN
Singles: 7-inch
MONUMENT (910 "What a Girl Can't Do").......10-15 65
MONUMENT (951 "Faces").......10-15 66
LPs: 10/12-inch
MONUMENT (8077 "Bitter Sweet").......20-30 67
(Monaural.)
MONUMENT (18077 "Bitter Sweet").......25-35 67
(Stereo.)
Also see REEKERS

HANGMEN OF FAIRFIELD COUNTY
Singles: 7-inch
HIGH CASTLE (401 "Stacey").......15-25 66

HANK & CAROLEE
Singles: 7-inch
MALA (424 "Go On and Go").......25-30 60
Members: Hank Davis; Kenny Burrell.
Also see DAVIS, Hank

HANK & ELECTRAS
Singles: 7-inch
DAUPHIN (106 "Get Lost Baby").......175-225 58
(Identification number used since no selection number is shown.)
Members: Hank Davis; Barry Kaplan; Mike Kantor; Gerry Greenwald.
Also see DAVIS, Hank

HANK & FRANK
Singles: 78 rpm
COLUMBIA.......8-15 50
Singles: 7-inch
COLUMBIA (20675 "I Offer You My Second Hand Heart").......15-25 50
(33 1/3 single.)
XYZ (101 "The Rockabilly Walk").......15-25 57
Members: Johnny Bond; Bert Dodson.

HANK & ROVER
Singles: 7-inch
OKEH.......4-8 66

HANK & SUGAR PIE
Singles: 78 rpm
FEDERAL.......10-15 55
Singles: 7-inch
FEDERAL (12217 "I'm So Lonely").......20-30 55
Member: Hank Huston; Umpeylia Balinton.
Also see CUFF LINKS
Also see DE SANTO, Sugar Pie
Also see LOVE, Preston
Also see LOVE BUGS

HANK THE COWHAND
Singles: 7-inch
COZY (27322 "Would You Care").......25-35

HANK'S HOUNDS: see JALOPY FIVE

HANKINS, Hank
Singles: 7-inch
REKA (298 "Kentucky Home Rock").......10-20 60

HANKINS, John C.
Singles: 7-inch
LOUIS ("K.C. Twist").......10-20 62
(Selection number not known.)

HANKINS, "Tall" Paul
Singles: 7-inch
BISCAYNE (001 "The Turnpike").......10-20 65
BISCAYNE (003 "Hot Spot").......10-20 65

HANKS, Kamryn *C&W '89*
Singles: 7-inch
COUNTRY PRIDE.......3-4 89

HANKS, Mickey: see HAWKS, Mickey

HANKS, Mike
(With the Del-Phis; with Del-Fi's; with Contours)
Singles: 7-inch
AL-JACK'S (0001 "I Cried").......75-125
BRAX (22-1 "Christine").......100-200 59
MAH'S (1003 "The Hawk").......50-75 60
MAH'S (1004 "I Think About You").......50-75 61
MAH'S (1014 "J.F.K.").......15-25 63
SPARTAN (401 "The Hawk").......75-125 61
Also see CONTOURS
Also see DEL-FIS
Also see DEL-PHIS

HANLEY, Pete
Singles: 78 rpm
OKEH.......5-10 53
Singles: 7-inch
EPIC (9155 "I Look at You").......10-20 60s
OKEH (6956 "Big Mamou").......10-20 53

HANLEY, Tye Tongue
Singles: 7-inch
JVB (88 "You Got My Nose Wide Open").......50-60 57

HANNA, Jimmy
(With the Dynamics & Chanteurs; with Blues Band; Jimmy Hanna Big Band +1)
Singles: 7-inch
BOLO (737 "Genevieve").......8-15 66
BOLO (747 "Busybody").......8-15 66
SEAFAIR BOLO (752 "Leaving Here").......8-15 66
SEAFAIR BOLO (756 "The Happy Hour").......8-15 67
LPs: 10/12-inch
BOLO (8003 "Memory Bank of Early Northwest Sounds").......8-10 83
BOLO (8004 "Leaving Here").......8-10 84
Members: Jimmy Hanna; Larry Coryell; Terry Afdem; Jeff Afdem; Ron Woods; Harry Wilson; Marcus Doubleday; Gary Snyder; Mike Mandell; Pete Borg; Valerie Rosa; Nancy Claire; Billy Burns; Steve Fischler.
Also see CHANTEURS
Also see DYNAMICS

HANNAN, Jimmy
Singles: 7-inch
ATLANTIC.......10-15 64

HANNIBAL
(James T. Shaw)
Singles: 7-inch
KING (5706 "Baby Please Change Your Mind").......10-20 62
KING (5720 "Ain't That Love").......10-20 62
KING (5780 "Help Me").......10-20 63
MEXI (101 "What About You Baby").......15-25 62
MY RECORD KOMPANY.......3-5 81
PAN WORLD (517 "Please Take a Chance on Me").......10-20 60
PAN WORLD (521 "Mother Goose Breaks Loose").......10-20 60
SUE (751 "I Need a Woman").......10-20 61
Also see KING HANNIBAL
Also see MIGHTY HANNIBAL

HANNIBAL, Sonny
Singles: 7-inch
LITE.......5-10

HANNON, Beau
Singles: 7-inch
DIONYSAN (102 "Who's Got the Right of Way").......8-12

HANNS, James, & Soul Entertainers
Singles: 7-inch
RAYNARD (1004 "It's a Fine Thing").......15-25 66
Members: James Hanns Walner; Patrick McCarthy; Tom Jones; Gene Roceb; Curt Vandenhuevel; Doc Mathias; Tom Cody; Dennis Reeves Regowsky.

HANOI ROCKS
LPs: 10/12-inch
CBS.......5-8 84

HANS NAUGHTY
Singles
IRON WORKS ("Tears in the Night").......8-12 89
(Picture disc in shape of singer. No selection number used.)
IRON WORKS ("Tears in the Night").......10-15 89
(Logo-shaped picture disc. No selection number used.)
LPs: 10/12-inch
IRON WORKS (1022 "Paint the Town Red").......8-12 89
(Picture disc. Promotional issue only.)

HANSEN, Doug
(With the Hot Doggers)
Singles: 7-inch
DORE.......4-8 60
EVA (104 "Surfin' Movies").......15-25 63

HANSEN, Randy
LPs: 10/12-inch
SHARPNEL.......8-10 83

HANSEN, Rudy
Singles: 7-inch
DECCA.......5-10 58

HANSEN BROTHERS,
(Paul Hansen & the Hansen Brothers)
Singles: 7-inch
AAA-ARON.......5-10 77
CRYSTAL BALL.......4-6 80-81
DUCK.......3-6 75
JAZZY BEBOPPER.......3-6 76
PAUL!!.......3-5 82
PAUL, DALE, TOM & RAY.......5-10 77
EPs: 7-inch
STARFIRE.......4-8 78
SURF DAZE/BEACH DAYS.......3-5 79
LPs: 10/12-inch
KATHY KELLEY.......15-20
Members: Paul Hansen; Dale Hansen; Tom Hansen; Ray Hansen.

HANSON
(Junior Hanson)
Singles: 7-inch
MANTICORE.......3-5 73
LPs: 10/12-inch
MANTICORE.......8-10 73-74

HANSON, Connie, & Friend *C&W '82*
(With Darrell McCall)
Singles: 7-inch
SOUNDWAVES.......3-4 82
Also see McCALL, Darrell

HANSON, Jerry
Singles: 7-inch
COLPIX.......4-8 60

HANSON & DAVIS *D&D '85*
Singles: 12-inch
FRESH.......4-6 85-86
Singles: 7-inch
FRESH.......3-4 86

HANSSON, Bo *LP '73*
Singles: 7-inch
CHARISMA.......3-5 73
SIRE.......3-5 76-77
LPs: 10/12-inch
FAMOUS CHARISMA.......8-10 72-73
PVC.......5-10 79
SIRE.......8-10 76-77

HA'PENNYS
LPs: 10/12-inch
FERSCH (1110 "Love Is Not the Same").......50-75 68

HAPPENINGS *P&R/LP '66*
Singles: 7-inch
ABC.......3-4 73
B.T. PUPPY (Except 181).......4-8 66-69
B.T. PUPPY (181 "Have Yourself a Merry Little Christmas").......20-30 67
(Promotional issue only.)
BIG TREE.......3-5 72
ERIC.......3-4
JUBILEE.......3-6 69-71
MIDLAND INT'L.......3-5 77
MUSICORE.......3-5 72
TRIP.......3-5
VIRGO.......3-4 72
Picture Sleeves
B.T. PUPPY.......5-15 67-69
LPs: 10/12-inch
B.T. PUPPY (1001 "Happenings") 15-25 66
B.T. PUPPY (1003 "Psycle").......15-25 67
B.T. PUPPY (1004 "Golden Hits") 25-35 68
JUBILEE (8028 "Piece of Mind").......15-20 69
JUBILEE (8030 "Greatest Hits").......15-20 69
POST.......8-12 70s
Member: Bob Miranda; Tom Guliano; Ralph DeVito; Dave Libert; Bernie Laporte; Mike LaNeue.
Also see 4 GRADUATES
Also see HONOR SOCIETY
Also see MIRANDA, Bob
Also see TOKENS / Happenings

HAPPY CADAVERS
EPs: 7-inch
UNDEFINED (28109 "I Saw My Baby in the Meat Section").......20-25

HAPPY DAY
Singles: 7-inch
UNI.......3-5 71

HAPPY DAYS REVUE
Singles: 7-inch
RIBBON (109 "Baby Let's Wait").......3-6 70s
Also see RICOCHETTES

HAPPY DRAGON BAND
LPs: 10/12-inch
FIDDLERS ("Happy Dragon Band").......40-60 78
(Selection number not known.)

HAPPY ELVES
Singles: 7-inch
GARLIN.......5-8 60

HAPPY FRENCHMEN
Singles: 7-inch
OKEH.......4-8 60

HAPPY HOSS
Singles: 7-inch
STARK (0015 "Call Me Baby").......15-25

HAPPY JESTERS
Singles: 78 rpm
DOT (15566 "Just Because").......8-12 57
Singles: 7-inch
DOT (15566 "Just Because").......10-15 57

HAPPY LOUIE
Singles: 7-inch
MGM.......4-8 66

HAPPY MONDAYS *LP '91*
LPs: 10/12-inch
ELEKTRA (60854 "Bummed").......10-12 89
(With "nude" inner sleeve.)
ELEKTRA (60854 "Bummed").......5-10 89
(Without "nude" inner sleeve.)
ELEKTRA (60986 "Pills & Thrills and Bellyaches").......5-10 91

HAPPY RETURN
Singles: 7-inch
CADET (5651 "To Give You Lovin'").......6-10 69
STACK (510 "Longed For").......10-15

HAPPY TEENS
Singles: 7-inch
PARADISE.......4-8 60

HAPPY TONES
Singles: 7-inch
COLPIX (693 "Summertime Nights").......10-15 63

HAPSHASH & COLOURED COAT
LPs: 10/12-inch
IMPERIAL.......12-15 68-69

HARBIN, Tommy
Singles: 7-inch
VALIANT.......10-15

HARBINGER COMPLEX
Singles: 7-inch
BRENT.......4-8 66
Also see WILDFLOWER / Harbinger Complex / Euphoria / Other Side

HARBINGERS
Singles: 7-inch
COLUMBIA.......5-10 67

HARBOR, Pearl: see PEARL HARBOR

HARBOR LIGHTS
(Harbor Lites)
Singles: 7-inch
JARO (77020 "What Would I Do Without You").......25-35 60
MALA (422 "Angel of Love").......20-30 60
Members: Kenny Vance; Sandy Deane.
Also see JAY & AMERICANS

HARBORSIDE
LPs: 10/12-inch
CLIFTON.......5-10 85

HARBOUR LITES
Singles: 7-inch
FONTANA.......4-8 66

HARBUS
LPs: 10/12-inch
EVOLUTION.......8-10 73

HARD, Randy, & Hi-Lites
Singles: 7-inch
NRC (013 "Honey Doll").......25-50 58

HARD MEAT
LPs: 10/12-inch
W.B. 10-12 69-70

HARD ROCK
Singles: 7-inch
SWEEPSTAKE.......4-8 61

HARD STUFF
LPs: 10/12-inch
MERCURY.......8-10 73

HARD TIMES
Singles: 7-inch
GRAY ANT (107 "Can't Wait 'Til Friday").......10-15 60s

HARDCASTLE, Paul R&B/D&D '84
Singles: 12-inch
CHRYSALIS 4-6 85-86
PROFILE 4-6 84
Singles: 7-inch
CHRYSALIS 3-4 85-86
PROFILE 3-4 84-85
Picture Sleeves
CHRYSALIS 3-4 85
LPs: 10/12-inch
CHRYSALIS 5-10 86
PROFILE 5-10 85

HARDEN, Arlene C&W '67
Singles: 7-inch
CAPITOL 3-5 74-75
COLUMBIA 3-6 67-73
ELEKTRA 3-5 77-78
LPs: 10/12-inch
CAPITOL 5-10 75
COLUMBIA 5-12 68-70
Also see ROBBINS, Marty

HARDEN, Arlene, & Bobby C&W '68
(Hardens)
Singles: 7-inch
COLUMBIA 4-6 68
Also see HARDEN, Arlene
Also see HARDEN, Bobby
Also see HARDEN TRIO

HARDEN, Bobby C&W '75
Singles: 7-inch
MEGA 3-5 70-71
U.A. 3-5 75
Picture Sleeves
MEGA 3-5 70
LPs: 10/12-inch
STARDAY 6-12 69
Also see HARDEN TRIO

HARDEN, Doug
Singles: 78 rpm
HUMMINGBIRD 20-30 56
LIBERTY BELL 10-20 56
REV 10-20 57
Singles: 7-inch
HUMMINGBIRD ("Dig That Ford") 75-100 56
LIBERTY BELL (9006 "Dig That Ford") 30-50 56
REV (3502 "Foolin' Me") 10-20 57

HARDEN, Robbie
Singles: 7-inch
PLANTATION 3-5 70
Also see HARDEN TRIO

HARDEN TRIO P&R/C&W/LP '66
Singles: 7-inch
COLUMBIA 3-4 65-68
PAPA JOE 3-4 72
LPs: 10/12-inch
COLUMBIA 10-15 66-68
HARMONY 8-12 70
Members: Arlene Harden; Bobby Harden; Robbie Harden. Session: Karen Wheeler.
Also see HARDEN, Arlene
Also see HARDEN, Bobby
Also see HARDEN, Robbie
Also see WHEELER, Karen

HARDESTY, Herb
Singles: 7-inch
FEDERAL (12410 "Beatin' and Blowin'") 10-20 61
FEDERAL (12444 "Just a Little Bit of Everything") 10-20 61
FEDERAL (12460 "Chicken Twist") 10-20 62
MUTUAL (1001 "Beatin' and Blowin'") 15-25 60

HARDIE, Celest
Singles: 7-inch
LOADSTONE (3931 "You Touched the Inner Part of Me") 10-20 78
REYNOLDS (200 "You're Gone") 10-20

HARDIER, John
Singles
CONDOR CLASSIX ("Dean 55") 8-12 89
(Selection number not known. Oval-shaped picture disc. 500 made.)

HARDIN, "Big" George
Singles: 7-inch
RECORTE (403 "Up the Harlem Way") 20-30 58

HARDIN, Ed: see JALOPY FIVE

HARDIN, Gus C&W '83
(Carolyn Ann Hardin)
Singles: 7-inch
RCA 3-4 83-86
LPs: 10/12-inch
RCA (Except 1-8603) 5-10 83-84
RCA (1-8603 "Interview with Gus Hardin") 8-12 83
(Promotional issue only.)

HARDIN, Gus, & Earl Thomas Conley C&W '84
Singles: 7-inch
RCA 3-4 84
Also see CONLEY, Earl Thomas

HARDIN, Gus, & Dave Loggins C&W '85
Singles: 7-inch
RCA 3-4 85
Also see HARDIN, Gus
Also see LOGGINS, Dave

HARDIN, Jim, & Musical Erupters
Singles: 7-inch
VOLCANO (100 "High Stepping Woman") 40-60 58

HARDIN, Pete
Singles: 7-inch
PEACH 5-8 61

HARDIN, Rink
Singles: 7-inch
U.A. 4-6 64-67

HARDIN, Tim P&R/LP '69
Singles: 7-inch
COLUMBIA 3-5 69-72
VERVE/FOLKWAYS 3-5 66-70
VERVE/FORECAST 3-5 67-71
LPs: 10/12-inch
ANTILLES 5-10 73
ATCO 8-15 67
COLUMBIA (9787 "Suite for Susan Moore and Damian") 20-30 69
COLUMBIA (30551 "Bird on a Wire") 15-20 70
COLUMBIA (37164 "Shock of Grace") 5-10 81
MGM 6-10 70-74
POLYDOR 5-10 81
VERVE/FORECAST 10-20 66-69
(May show "Verve/Folkways" on spine. Some have a silver sticker covering that name with "Verve/Folkways.")

HARDIN, Wes, & Roxsters
Singles: 7-inch
AFS (302 "Anyway") 300-400 58
PERFECT (110 "Honky Tonk Man") 40-50 57
Also see ROXSTERS

HARDIN & YORK
LPs: 10/12-inch
BELL 8-10 70
LONDON 8-10 71

HARDIN BROTHERS
Singles: 78 rpm
DECCA 10-20 41

HARDING, Chip
Singles: 7-inch
RSO 3-4 80

HARDING, Gayle C&W '78
Singles: 7-inch
ROBCHRIS 3-5 78-79

HARDISON, Bernie
(With Band)
Singles: 78 rpm
EXCELLO 15-25 53
REPUBLIC (7111 "Too Much") 20-40 55
Singles: 7-inch
EXCELLO (2020 "Yeah, It's True") 40-50 53
REPUBLIC (7111 "Too Much") 50-75 55

HARDLE, Joe, & Orchids
Singles: 7-inch
DERY (10016 "Confusion") 10-20 61

HARDLY WORTHIT DELEGATES
Singles: 7-inch
PRUNE (13 "Disco Press Conference") 4-6 70s

HARDLY WORTHIT PLAYERS P&R '67
(Featuring Senator Bobby & Senator McKinley)
Singles: 7-inch
PARKWAY 4-8 66-67
LPs: 10/12-inch
PARKWAY 10-20 66-67
Also see SENATOR BOBBY

HARDROCK
Singles: 7-inch
MARK (142 "A Hit Record") 10-15
Member: Dave Williams.

HARDROCK & Rhythm Rockers: see GUNTER, Hardrock

HARDSELL, Harold
Singles: 7-inch
DECCA 3-6 71
DUNHILL (4384 "Speaking of Streaking") 4-8 74

HARDTIMES P&R '66
Singles: 7-inch
WORLD PACIFIC 5-10 66-68
LPs: 10/12-inch
WORLD PACIFIC 15-25 66-68
Members: Lee Kiefer; Rudy Romero; Bob Morris; Bill Richardson.
Also see NEW PHOENIX
Also see STEPPENWOLF
Also see T.I.M.E.

HARDWATER
Singles: 7-inch
CAPITOL 5-10 68
LPs: 10/12-inch
CAPITOL 15-25 68

HARDY, Francoise
Singles: 7-inch
4 CORNERS 4-8 65
REPRISE 4-8 69
LPs: 10/12-inch
4 CORNERS 10-15 65

HARDY, Hagood P&R '75
Singles: 7-inch
CAPITOL 3-5 75-78
HERITAGE 3-5 71
LPs: 10/12-inch
CAPITOL 4-8 75-76

HARDY, Hal
Singles: 7-inch
HOLLYWOOD (1116 "House of Broken Hearts") 15-25 59

HARDY, Hank
Singles: 7-inch
COLONIAL 5-10 60s

HARDY, Johnny
Singles: 7-inch
ACE 8-12 61
J&J 5-10 61

HARDY, Lavell
Singles: 7-inch
ROJAC 4-6

HARDY, Ulyces
Singles: 7-inch
BEVERLY (752 "Fussin' Women") 15-25 59

HARDY BOYS LP '69
Singles: 7-inch
RCA 4-8 69-70
LPs: 10/12-inch
RCA 10-15 69-70
Members: Frank Hardy; Joe Hardy. Session: Chubby Morton; Wanda Key; Pete Jones.

HAREWOOD, Dorian
Singles: 7-inch
EMERIC 3-4 88
LPs: 10/12-inch
EMERIC 5-8 88

HARGETT, Johnnie
Singles: 7-inch
CHERRY (1016 "Rock the Town Tonight") 50-75 60

HARGO, Charles
(With Bob Fonville Orchestra & Chorus)
Singles: 7-inch
DAB (101 "Baby Oh Baby") 75-125 59

HARGRAVE, Don
Singles: 7-inch
SILVER SLIPPER ("Fee-Fi-Fo Fum") 15-25
(Selection number not known.)

HARGRAVE, Don, & Jack Merrill
Singles: 7-inch
CANJO 4-8 64
Also see HARGRAVE, Don

HARGRAVE, Ron
Singles: 78 rpm
MGM (Except 12422) 5-15 56-58
MGM (12422 "Latch on") 20-30 57
Singles: 7-inch
CUB 5-10 59
MGM (Except 12422) 5-15 56-58
MGM (12422 "Latch On") 20-30 57

HARGRO, Charles
Singles: 7-inch
DAB (101 "Baby Oh Baby") 50-75 59

HARGROVE, Danny C&W '78
Singles: 7-inch
CHECKER (1009 "Seven Wonders of My World") 5-10 62
50 STATES 3-5 78

HARGROVE, Linda C&W '74
Singles: 7-inch
CAPITOL 3-5 75-77
ELEKTRA 3-5 74
RCA 3-5 78
LPs: 10/12-inch
CAPITOL 5-10 75-77
ELEKTRA 5-10 73-74

HARINGTON, Jackie
Singles: 7-inch
MUSICTONE (1120 "Reach Out") 10-20 64

HARKEY, Fred
Singles: 7-inch
HILLCREST 5-10

HARKNESS, Sam
Singles: 7-inch
COLPIX 5-10 61

HARLAN, Billy
Singles: 7-inch
BRUNSWICK (55066 "I Wanna Bop") 100-150 58

HARLAND BROTHERS
Singles: 7-inch
KUSTOM (4167 "Rockin' at Midnight") 15-20 60s

HARLEM GLOBETROTTERS
Singles: 7-inch
HARLEM GLOBETROTTERS 4-6

HARLEM RIVER DRIVE R&B '75
(Featuring Eddie Palmieri)
Singles: 7-inch
ARISTA 3-5 75
ROULETTE 3-5 70-72
LPs: 10/12-inch
ROULETTE 8-10 71
TICO 5-10 72
Members: Eddie Palmieri; Jimmy Norman.
Also see NORMAN, Jimmy

HARLEM STARS
Singles: 78 rpm
E&W (100 "All Right, Baby") 25-50 51
Member: Willie Mae Thornton.
Also see THORNTON, Willie Mae

HARLEMAIRES
Singles: 78 rpm
ATLANTIC (856 "If You Mean What You Say") 40-60 48
Members: Dottie Smith; Chester Slater; Bill Butler; Percy Doell.
Also see BENNET, Connie, Bill Smyth, & Harlem-Aires
Also see DOGGETT, Bill

HARLEQUIN
LPs: 10/12-inch
COLUMBIA 5-10 80-82

HARLEQUINS
Singles: 7-inch
COLLIER 4-8 61
ENTREE 4-8 65

HARLESS, Ogden C&W '87
Singles: 7-inch
DOOR KNOB 3-4 87-88
MSC 3-4 88

HARLEY, Rufus
LPs: 10/12-inch
ATLANTIC 12-15 66-68

HARLEY, Steve P&R '76
(With Cockney Rebel)
Singles: 7-inch
CAPITOL 3-5 78
EMI 3-5 75-77
LPs: 10/12-inch
CAPITOL 5-10 78
EMI 5-10 75-77

HARLEY & NIGHT RIDERS
Singles: 7-inch
EMI 3-5 74-75
MANHATTAN 8-12 67

HARLOWE, Ray, & Gyp Fox
LPs: 10/12-inch
WATER WHEEL (711 "First Rays") 20-30 78

HARMAN, Bobby
Singles: 7-inch
DECCA (29872 "Kingfish Blues") ... 15-25 56

HARMAN, Buddy, Combo
Singles: 7-inch
MERCURY (72100 "Diamonds") 10-20 63
W.B. 5-8 60-61

HARMAN, James, Band
LPs: 10/12-inch
RIVERA 8-10 90
Members: James Harman; Michael Mann; David Ramos; Stephen Hodges; William Campbell.

HARMON, Bob
(With the T Tones; with His Band)
Singles: 78 rpm
REPUBLIC 15-25 55
Singles: 7-inch
REPUBLIC (7114 "Shake Rag Shuffle") 30-40 55
SALEM (523 "Song of Caroline") ... 15-25 50s

HARMON, Clinton
Singles: 7-inch
NOTE 5-10

HARMON, Jeannie
Singles: 7-inch
RING-A-DING 4-8 63

HARMON, Larry
Singles: 7-inch
DORE 4-8 60

HARMON, Lucky
Singles: 7-inch
RUST (5026 "Date Bait") 8-12 60

HARMONAIRES
Singles: 78 rpm
MAJESTIC 10-20 48
ROYALE 4-8
Singles: 7-inch
ROYALE 5-10

HARMONAIRES
Singles: 78 rpm
KAYBEE ("Get on Board") 10-20

HARMONAIRES
Singles: 7-inch
HOLIDAY (2602 "Lorraine") 200-300 57
(Black label.)
HOLIDAY (2602 "Lorraine") 50-75 60
(Glossy red label. Has double horizontal lines.)
HOLIDAY (2602 "Lorraine") 15-25 60s
(Flat red label. Has single horizontal line.)
LOST NITE 4-8
Also see CHARTS / Bop - Chords / Ladders / Harmonaires

HARMONAIRES MALE QUARTET
LPs: 10/12-inch
VARSITY (6915 "Spirituals") 50-75 50s
(10-inch LP.)

HARMONICA BLUES KING
Singles: 78 rpm
EBONY 50-75 56
Singles: 7-inch
EBONY (1003 "I Need You Pretty Baby") 100-200 56

HARMONICA FATS
Singles: 7-inch
DARCEY (5000 "I Get So Tired") 15-25 63
DARCEY (5003 "Mama Mama Talk to Your Daughter for Me") 10-20 63
DOT (16978 "Drive Way Blues") ... 10-20 66
KRIS (8092 "Mind Your Own Business") 15-25

HARMONICA FRANK
(Frank Floyd)
Singles: 78 rpm
CHESS (1494 "Howlin' Tomcat") 150-250 51
CHESS (1475 "Swamp Root") ... 150-250 51
SUN (205 "Rockin Chair Daddy") 300-500 54
Singles: 7-inch
SUN (205 "Rockin Chair Daddy") 1000-1500 54
LPs: 10/12-inch
ADELPHI 8-10 76
PURITAN 8-10
Also see FLOYD, Frank

HARMONICA HARRY
(Elmon Mickle)
Singles: 7-inch
SOULIN' 4-6 64
Also see MICKLE, Elmon

HARMONICA IMPS
Singles: 7-inch
HALIFAX (104 "Steel Guitar Rag"). 10-20 64

HARMONICA JOE
Singles: 7-inch
SKYMAC 5-10 64

HARMONICA KING
(George Smith)
Singles: 78 rpm
LAPEL (103 "All Last Night") 20-30 55
Singles: 7-inch
LAPEL (103 "All Last Night") 40-60 55
Also see ALLEN, George
Also see LITTLE WALTER JR.
Also see SMITH, George

HARMONICA SLIM
(Travis Blaylock)
Singles: 78 rpm
ALADDIN 10-20 56
SPRY 10-20 56
VITA 10-20 57
Singles: 7-inch
ALADDIN (3317 "Mary Helen") 20-30 56
CENCO (1001 "I'll Take Love") 5-10
SPRY (103 "Thought I Didn't Love You") 25-35 56
VITA (138 "My Girl Won't Quit Me") 25-35 57
VITA (146 "Drop Anchor") 25-35 57
LPs: 10/12-inch
BLUESTIME 10-15

HARMONICATS P&R '47
(Jerry Murad's Harmonicats)
Singles: 78 rpm
MERCURY 3-5 50-57
UNIVERSAL 3-6 48
VITACOUSTIC 4-8 47
Singles: 7-inch
COLUMBIA 3-6 61-67
MERCURY 5-10 50-60
Picture Sleeves
COLUMBIA 5-10 60
EPs: 7-inch
MERCURY 5-10 50-61
LPs: 10/12-inch
COLUMBIA 8-15 61-67
HARMONY 5-10 66
MERCURY 5-15 50-69
WING 5-10 59-64
Members: Jerry Murad; Al Fiore; Don Les.

HARMONY BLAZERS
LPs: 10/12-inch
HARMONY (7126 "Rock & Roll Vol. II") 25-35 59
HARMONY (7200 "Big Ten") 25-35 59
Also see BLAZERS

HARMONY BROTHERS
Singles: 7-inch
BOBBIN 5-10 59

HARMONY GRASS
Singles: 7-inch
RCA 4-6 69

HARMONY GRITS
Singles: 7-inch
END (1051 "Am I to Be the One") .. 10-15 59
END (1063 "Gee") 10-15 59
Members: Bill Pinkney; Gerhart Thrasher.
Also see DRIFTERS

HARMONY HOUNDS
Singles: 78 rpm
COLUMBIA 15-25 26

HARMONY KINGS
Singles: 7-inch
CASH 4-8 58

HARMONY TWIN
Singles: 7-inch
UNITED SOUND (2727 "Barnyard Rock & Roll") 25-35 60s

HARMS, Joni C&W '89
Singles: 7-inch
UNIVERSAL 3-4 89

HARNELL, Joe, His Orchestra P&R '62
(With His Trio)
Singles: 7-inch
COLUMBIA 3-6 66-68
EPIC 5-10 59-60
KAPP 4-8 61-65
MCA 3-4 78
MEDALLION 4-8 61-62
MOTOWN 4-8 69-70
Picture Sleeves
KAPP 5-10 63
LPs: 10/12-inch
CAPITOL 5-8 77
COLUMBIA 5-10 66
EPIC 5-15 59-63
KAPP 5-15 63-66
MEDALLION 5-15 61
MOTOWN (698 "Moving On") 25-45 70

HARNELL, Vernon
Singles: 7-inch
SCORE 8-12

HARNER, Bill
(With the Expressions; Billy Harner)
Singles: 7-inch
ATLANTIC (2351 "A Message to My Babe") 5-10 66
DEBORAH (100 "Pretty Little Girl") 8-12 62
KAMA SUTRA 4-8 67
LAWN (239 "Whatcha Gonna Do") 10-15 64
OPEN 8-10 66
OR (1253 "Fool Me") 10-20 60s
OR (1255 "Watch Your Step") 10-20 60s
SOUND GEMS (1007 "I Get It from Heaven") 10-20 60s
V-TONE (1000 "A Message to My Babe") 15-25 66
(First issue.)

HARNEY, Ben, & Sheryl Lee Ralph R&B '83
Singles: 7-inch
GEFFEN 3-4 83
Also see RALPH, Sheryl Lee

HAROLD, Prince: see PRINCE HAROLD

HAROLD & BOB
Singles: 7-inch
DELTA (503 "Spitfire") 15-25 59

HAROLD & CASUALS
Singles: 7-inch
SCOTTY (628 "Darling Do You Love Me") 150-250 59

HAROLD & CONNIE
Singles: 7-inch
CARNIVAL (519 "Boogaloo Party") 10-20 68

HAROLD & OFFBEATS
Singles: 7-inch
HAPPY HEARTS 15-20 61
HICKORY 5-10 62

HARP, Felix: see FELIX HARP

HARP, Lloyd, & His Hoosier Boys
Singles: 7-inch
YORK (102 "Slow Boogie Rock") 100-200 61

HARP, Martha Lou
Singles: 78 rpm
PREP 10-15 57
Singles: 7-inch
PREP 10-15 57
W.B. 5-10 59

HARPE, Neil
LPs: 10/12-inch
ADELPHI 5-10

HARPER, Ben, & Cincos
Singles: 7-inch
TALENT 5-8 60

HARPER, Billy
Singles: 7-inch
KAMA SUTRA 4-6 67-68
MEL OMEGA 4-6 60s
NEROC 4-6 60s

HARPER, Bud
Singles: 7-inch
PEACOCK (1932 "Wherever You Were") 20-30 64
PEACOCK (1939 "Mr. Soul") 8-12 65
SARG 8-12 60s

HARPER, Chuck
Singles: 7-inch.
FELSTED 10-15 62
Also see REGENTS

HARPER, Janice P&R '57
Singles: 7-inch
CAPITOL 5-10 58-60
PREP 5-10 57
RCA 4-6 66
LPs: 10/12-inch
CAPITOL 15-20 58-60

HARPER, Jeanette
Singles: 7-inch
20TH FOX (668 "Put Me in Your Pocket") 25-35 66

HARPER, Paul
Singles: 7-inch
FEDORA 4-8 61

HARPER, Reed
(With the Three Notes; with Notes; Reed Harper Trio; with Walter Francis Orchestra)
Singles: 7-inch
INTERNATIONAL 10-15
LUCK 10-15 60
PYRAMID (4012 "Oh Elvis") 25-35 57
TERRY 5-10 63
RCA (7426 "Shaky Little Baby") 15-25 58
SMART (1001 "I Miss You So 25-50 58
VIK (328 "I Miss You So") 15-25 58

HARPER, Ric
Singles: 78 rpm
ABBEY (1028 "I'm a Sixty Minute Rocket Man") 25-50 51

HARPER, Roy
Singles: 7-inch
EPIC 5-10 67
LPs: 10/12-inch
CHRYSALIS (Except 620) 8-10 71-77
CHRYSALIS (620 "Introducing Roy Harper") 15-25 76
(Includes interviews with Paul McCartney, Jimmy Page and others, plus the Led Zeppelin song *Hat's off to Harper.* Promotional issue only.)
HARVEST 8-12 70
SUNSET 15-20 69
WORLD PACIFIC 8-10 72
Also see LED ZEPPELIN
Also see McCARTNEY, Paul

HARPER, Sonny
Singles: 7-inch
BALL 5-10 62
Also see AMOS, Ira

HARPER, Toni R&B '48
(With the Eddie Beale Sextet)
Singles: 78 rpm
COLUMBIA 5-10 48
Singles: 7-inch
RCA 5-10 60-61
LPs: 10/12-inch
RCA 15-20 60
Also see LIMELITERS

HARPER, Walt
Singles: 7-inch
GATEWAY (724 "School Days") 5-10 64

HARPER, Willie
Singles: 7-inch
ALON 5-10 62

HARPER - BRINSON BAND
Singles: 78 rpm
SPECIALTY 10-15 57
Singles: 7-inch
SPECIALTY 10-15 57
Member: Buddy Harper.

HARPER & ROWE
Singles: 7-inch
WORLD PACIFIC 5-10 68
LPs: 10/12-inch
WORLD PACIFIC 10-15 68

HARPERS BIZARRE P&R/LP '67
Singles: 7-inch
FOREST BAY CO 3-5 76
W.B. 3-6 67-72
EPs: 7-inch
W.B. 4-8 68
(Juke box issues only.)
LPs: 10/12-inch
FOREST BAY CO 8-10 76
W.B. 10-20 67-68
Members: Ted Templeman; John Petersen; Dick Yount; Dick Scoppettone; John Peterson. Session: Van Dyke Parks.
Also see OTHER TIKIS
Also see PARKS, Van Dyke
Also see TIKIS

HARPO, Slim P&R/R&B '61
Singles: 78 rpm
EXCELLO 15-25 57
Singles: 7-inch
ABC 3-5 73
EXCELLO (2113 "I'm a King Bee") 50-75 57
(Orange & blue label. Company address at top.)
EXCELLO (2113 "I'm a King Bee") 50-75 57
(White label. Promotional issue only.)
EXCELLO (2113 "I'm a King Bee") 20-30 60
(Orange & blue label. Company address at bottom.)
EXCELLO (2138 "Wondering and Worrying") 25-50 58
(Orange & blue label. Company address at top.)
EXCELLO (2138 "Wondering and Worrying") 20-40 58
(White label. Promotional issue only.)
EXCELLO (2138 "Wondering and Worrying") 15-25 60
(Orange & blue label. Company address at bottom.)
EXCELLO (2162 "One More Day") 15-25 59
(Orange & blue label.)
EXCELLO (2162 "One More Day") 15-25 59
(White label. Promotional issue only.)
EXCELLO (2171 "Buzz Me Babe") 15-25 60
(Counterfeits exist, but all we've seen have the hole off-center. Originals do not.)
EXCELLO (2184 "Blues Hang Over") 15-25 60
EXCELLO (2194 "Rainin' in My Heart") 15-25 61
EXCELLO (2239 thru 2309) 5-15 63-70
EXCELLO (2316 "Rainin' in My Heart") 5-8 71
(Remixed, overdubbed version.)
Note: Any Slim Harpo singles with a yellow and blue Excello label are counterfeits.
LPs: 10/12-inch
EXCELLO (Except 8003 & 8005) 10-20 68-70
EXCELLO (8003 "Raining in My Heart") 30-50 61
(Orange and blue label.)
EXCELLO (8003 "Raining in My Heart") 5-10 95
(Blue label. Reprocessed stereo.)
EXCELLO (8005 "Baby, Scratch My Back") 20-30 66

HARPS
Singles: 7-inch
LAURIE (3239 "Daddy's Going Away") 25-35 64

HARPSICHORDS
Singles: 7-inch
ASCOT 4-8 66

HARPTONES P&R '61
(Harp-Tones; "Featuring Willie Winfield"; with Morty Croft, His Orchestra and Chorus)
Singles: 78 rpm
ANDREA 20-40 56
BRUCE 25-50 53-55
GEE 25-50 57
PARADISE 25-50 56
RAMA 20-40 56-57
TIP TOP 25-50 56
Singles: 7-inch
AMBIENT SOUND 5-10 82
ANDREA (100 "What Is Your Decision") 40-60 56
(White label. Has rope-like horizontal lines.)
ANDREA (100 "What Is Your Decision") 20-30 56
(Pink label. Has straight horizontal lines.)
BRUCE (101 "A Sunday Kind of Love") 300-500 53
(Has "Bruce" in script lettering.)
BRUCE (101 "A Sunday Kind of Love") 50-75 56
(Has "Bruce" in block lettering. With straight horizontal lines.)
BRUCE (101 "A Sunday Kind of Love") 25-50 61
(Has "Bruce" in block lettering. With jagged horizontal lines.)
BRUCE (102 "My Memories of You"/"It Was Just for Laughs") 100-200 54
(With straight horizontal lines.)
BRUCE (102 "My Memories of You"/"The Laughs [sic] on You") 50-100 56
(Note different title on flip label. Actual track is identical to *It Was Just for Laughs*)
BRUCE (102 "My Memories of You") 20-30 61
(With jagged horizontal lines.)
BRUCE (102 "My Memories of You"/"It Was Just for Laughs") 60-80 54
(Has straight horizontal lines on A-side, but jagged lines on B-side.)
BRUCE (104 "I Depended on You") 100-125 54
BRUCE (109 "Forever Mine") 75-100 54
(With the Shytans. Has "Mfg. By Nu-Way Enterprises, Inc." at top.)
BRUCE (109 "Forever Mine") 75-100 54
(With the Shytans. Has "Mfg. By Nu-Way Enterprises, Inc." on side.)
BRUCE (113 "Since I Fell for You") 100-125 54
(Reads "Mfg. By Nu-Way Enterprises, Inc.")
BRUCE (113 "Since I Fell for You") 20-40
(No mention of "Mfg. By Nu-Way.")
BRUCE (123 "Loving a Girl Like You") 25-45 61
(Colored vinyl. "Collectors Series" issue.)
BRUCE (128 "I Almost Lost My Mind") 50-100 55
(Reads "Mfg. By Nu-Way Enterprises, Inc.")
BRUCE (128 "I Almost Lost My Mind") 20-40 55
(No mention of "Mfg. By Nu-Way.")
COED (540 "Answer Me My Love") 15-25 60
COMPANION (102 "All in Your Mind") 40-60 61
COMPANION (103 "What Will I Tell My Heart") 75-100 61
CUB (9097 "Devil in Velvet") 25-35 61
GEE (1045 "Cry Like I Cried") 50-75 57
(Red label.)
GEE (1045 "Cry Like I Cried") 15-25 61
(Gray label.)
KT (201 "Sunset") 50-75 63
OLDIES 45 4-8 60s
PARADISE (101 "Life Is But a Dream") 100-200 56
(Maroon label.)
PARADISE (101 "Life Is But a Dream") 50-75 56
(Purple label.)
PARADISE (103 "My Success [It All Depends on You]") 200-400 56
PARADISE (103 "It All Depends on You") 100-200 56
(Maroon label. Note slight title change.)
PARADISE (103 "It All Depends on You") 50-75 56
(Purple label.)
RAMA (203 "Three Wishes") 50-100 56
RAMA (214 "The Masquerade Is Over") 50-100 56
RAMA (221 "The Shrine of Saint Cecilia") 50-100 57
RAVEN (8001 "Sunday Kind of Love") 20-30 62
(Has bird at the top of label, over logo.)
RAVEN (8001 "Sunday Kind of Love") 15-25 62
(No bird on label.)
ROULETTE GOLDEN GOODIES 4-6 71
TIP TOP (401 "My Memories of You") 50-100 56
WARWICK (500 "Laughing on the Outside") 35-45 59
("Warwick" is in sans-serif, or block style type.)
WARWICK (500 "Laughing on the Outside") 25-35 59
("Warwick" is in serif style type.)
WARWICK (512 "Love Me Completely") 25-35 59
WARWICK (551 "No Greater Miracle") 25-35 59
EPs: 7-inch
BRUCE (201 "The Sensational Harptones") 8000-12000 54
LPs: 10/12-inch
AMBIENT SOUND (37718 "Love Needs") 8-12 82
HARLEM HITPARADE (5006 "The Harptones") 10-15 70s
MURRAY HILL 5-8 88
RARE BIRD 8-10
RELIC 8-10 70s
Members: Willie Winfield; Nicky Clark; Bill Brown; Bill Dempsey; Bill "Dicey" Galloway; Raoul Cita; Jimmy Beckum; Lynn Daniels; Vicki Burgess; Margaret Moore; Fred Taylor.
Also see BLADES, Carol
Also see JOYTONES
Also see PAUL, Bunny, & Harptones
Also see RAPIDTONES
Also see SOOTHERS
Also see WOODSIDE SISTERS

HARPTONES / Cleftones
Singles: 7-inch
ROULETTE 3-5 71
Also see CLEFTONES

HARPTONES / Crows
LPs: 10/12-inch
ROULETTE (114 "Echoes of a Rock Era") 15-20 72
(Two LPs, one by each group.)
Also see CROWS

HARPTONES / Paragons
LPs: 10/12-inch
MUSICNOTE 20-30 64

HARPTONES / Paragons / Jesters / Clovers
LPs: 10/12-inch
GRAND PRIX 10-20 60s
Also see CLOVERS
Also see HARPTONES
Also see JESTERS
Also see PARAGONS

HARRALL, Hank
Singles: 7-inch
CAPROCK 15-25 57-59

HARRELL, Doug
Singles: 7-inch
COLONIAL 10-15
Members: Jim Crisp; Joe Tanner; Henry Heitman.

HARRELL, Grady R&B '85
Singles: 7-inch
MCA 3-5 85
Also see PAPA'S RESULTS

HARRELL, Vernon
Singles: 7-inch
CALLA (136 "Can't Take the Hurt") 15-25 67
DECCA (31721 "All That's Good") 15-25 64
SCORE (1008 "Your Love") 10-20

HARRELL & SCOTT C&W '89
Singles: 7-inch
ASSOCIATED ARTISTS 3-4 89

HARRIET, Judy
Singles: 7-inch
AMERICAN INT'L 10-15 59
COLUMBIA 8-10 61
SURF (5023 "Nuff Said") 15-20 58
SURF (5027 "Tall Paul") 15-20 58

HARRINGTON, Bill
(With the Jones Boys)
Singles: 7-inch
ANCHOR (24 "Ace in the Hole") 8-12
JUBILEE (5359 "Don't Bug Me Baby") 8-12 59

HARRINGTON, Carly C&W '88
Singles: 7-inch
OAK 3-4 88

HARRINGTON, Rick
Singles: 7-inch
BIG B (501 "Pore Ole Ruben") 5-10
HITT 5-10 59

HARRIS, Ace
Singles: 78 rpm
STERLING 20-40 48

HARRIS, Allen, Band
LPs: 10/12-inch
COLUMBIA/TAPPAN ZEE (35364 "Oceans Between Us") 5-10 78

HARRIS, Anita
Singles: 7-inch
COLUMBIA 4-8 67
W.B. 4-8 65

HARRIS, Betty P&R/R&B '63
Singles: 7-inch
JUBILEE 8-12 63-69
PROM 3-4
SSS INT'L 4-8 69
SANSU 5-10 66-68
Also see DORSEY, Lee, & Betty Harris

HARRIS, Bill
Singles: 7-inch
STRAND 5-8 60
W.B. 3-5 71

HARRIS, Bill, & Continentals
Singles: 7-inch
EAGLE (1002 "I'm So Glad") 200-250 58

HARRIS, Bob
(Little Bobby Harris)
Singles: 78 rpm
DERBY 10-20 51
JACKSON 100-200 52
PAR 10-20 52
Singles: 7-inch
JACKSON (2301 "Friendly Advice") 400-500 52

HARRIS, Bobby R&B '65
Singles: 7-inch
ATLANTIC 4-8 65
Also see LUNDY, Pat, & Bobby Harris

HARRIS, Bobby
Singles: 7-inch
MOON 8-12
SHOUT (203 "Mr. Success") 15-25 66
SHOUT (210 "The Love of My Women") 10-20
TURNTABLE (715 "The Password is Love") 15-25
TURNTABLE (716 "Lonely Intruder") 15-25

HARRIS, Brenda Jo R&B '68
Singles: 7-inch
BETTER 5-10 60s
ROULETTE 4-6 68

HARRIS, Chris, & Invaders
Singles: 7-inch
DIAL (4075 "So Much Soul") 5-10 68

HARRIS, Coatsville
Singles: 7-inch
RHYTHM 5-10 64

HARRIS, Damon R&B '79
Singles: 12-inch
WMOT 4-6 78-79
Singles: 7-inch
WMOT 3-5 78-79
LPs: 10/12-inch
WMOT 5-10 78
Also see IMPACT
Also see TEMPTATIONS

HARRIS, Dave
Singles: 7-inch
TOWN (2004 "Elvis and the Unmentionables") 8-12 76

HARRIS, Dave / Catman & Toenail
Singles: 7-inch
FUN-E-BONE (816 "Elvis and the Unmentionables") 5-8 76
Also see HARRIS, Dave

HARRIS, Dave, & Power House Five
LPs: 10/12-inch
DECCA 15-20 61

HARRIS, David R&B '74
Singles: 7-inch
PLEASURE 3-5 74

HARRIS, Dimples, & Orchestra
Singles: 78 rpm
CREST (1013 "If You'll Be True") 10-15 56
Singles: 7-inch
CREST (1013 "If You'll Be True") 20-40 56

HARRIS, Dinky
Singles: 7-inch
FAD 5-10 60

HARRIS, Don "Sugar Cane"
LPs: 10/12-inch
BASF 8-10 72-74
EPIC 10-12 70
Also see DON & DEWEY
Also see SUGARCANE & His Violin

HARRIS, Donna C&W '66
Singles: 7-inch
ABC 4-6 66

HARRIS, Ed: see JALOPY FIVE

HARRIS, Eddie P&R/R&B/LP '61
Singles: 7-inch
ABC 3-5 73
ATLANTIC 3-6 65-77
COLUMBIA 4-6 64
VEE JAY 5-8 61-63
W.B. 3-4 81
LPs: 10/12-inch
ANGELACO 5-10 81
ATLANTIC 6-12 65-81
BUDDAH 8-12 69
COLUMBIA 10-20 64-68
CRUSADERS 5-10 82
GNP 5-10 73
HARMONY 5-10 72

RCA....................5-10 78
SUNSET....................5-10 69
TRIP....................5-10 73
VEE JAY (3016 thru 3028)....................20-35 61-62
VEE JAY (3031 thru 3034)....................15-25 63
Also see McCANN, Les, & Eddie Harris
Also see MOORE, Shelly, & Eddie Harris

HARRIS, Eddie, & John Klemmer
LPs: 10/12-inch
CRUSADERS....................5-8 82
Also see HARRIS, Eddie
Also see KLEMMER, John

HARRIS, Emmylou *C&W/P&R '75*
(With Her Hot Band; with Cheryl White & Sharon White)
Singles: 7-inch
JUBILEE....................5-10 69-70
REPRISE (Except 1341)....................3-5 75-77
REPRISE (1341 "Light of the Stable")....................4-6 75
W.B....................3-5 77-86
Picture Sleeves
REPRISE....................3-5 75-77
WARNER....................3-4 80-86
LPs: 10/12-inch
EMUS....................10-20 79
JUBILEE (8031 "Gliding Bird")....................60-80 69
MFSL (015 "Quarter Moon in a Ten-Cent Town")....................30-40 78
REPRISE....................8-10 75
W.B....................5-10 77-87
Members: James Burton; Glen D. Hardin; Emory Gordy; Ronnie Tutt.
Also see ANDERSON, John
Also see BURTON, James
Also see CASH, Johnny
Also see CASH, Rosanne
Also see CONLEY, Earl Thomas, & Emmylou Harris
Also see CRICKETS
Also see CROWELL, Rodney
Also see DENVER, John, & Emmylou Harris
Also see EVERLY, Don
Also see GOSDIN, Vern
Also see JENNINGS, Waylon
Also see KENDALLS
Also see LITTLE FEAT
Also see LOUVIN, Charlie, & Emmylou Harris
Also see MADDOX, Rose
Also see NELSON, Willie
Also see ORBISON, Roy, & Emmylou Harris / Craig Hundley
Also see OWENS, Buck, & Emmylou Harris
Also see PARSONS, Gram
Also see PARTON, Dolly
Also see PARTON, Dolly, Linda Ronstadt, & Emmylou Harris
Also see PEDERSEN, Herb
Also see PRESLEY, Elvis
Also see RONSTADT, Linda, & Emmylou Harris
Also see SOUTHERN PACIFIC
Also see TUCKER, Tanya
Also see WHITES
Also see WINCHESTER, Jesse
Also see YOUNG, Neil

HARRIS, Emmylou, & Don Williams *C&W '81*
Singles: 7-inch
W.B....................3-4 81
Also see WILLIAMS, Don

HARRIS, Erline
Singles: 78 rpm
DELUXE....................10-15 49

HARRIS, Ernie
Singles: 7-inch
DUKE....................5-10 60
OKEH....................4-8 64

HARRIS, Frank
Singles: 7-inch
MAB-JAB (1002 "A Sweet Dream")....................100-150 62

HARRIS, Frosty, & Kool-Tones
(Bruce Harris)
Singles: 7-inch
DON (200 "Big Noise from L.A.")....................20-30 60
DOT (16171 "Big Noise from L.A.")....................10-15 60

HARRIS, Gayle
Singles: 7-inch
CARLTON....................4-8 63
DCP....................4-8 65

HARRIS, Gene *R&B '74*
(With the Three Sounds)
Singles: 7-inch
BLUE NOTE....................3-5 71-77
LPs: 10/12-inch
BLUE NOTE....................5-10 71-77
Also see THREE SOUNDS

HARRIS, Genee
Singles: 7-inch
ABC-PAR (9900 "Bye Bye Elvis")....................15-25 58

HARRIS, Georgia
(With Lyrics; with Hy-Tones; with Steve Samuel's Orchestra)
Singles: 7-inch
HY-TONE (117 "Let's Exchange Hearts for Xmas")....................300-400 58
HY-TONE (121 "Let Me Hold Your Hand")....................150-200 58
Also see HY-TONES
Also see LYRICS

HARRIS, Huey "Baby" *R&B '85*
Singles: 7-inch
PROFILE....................3-4 85

HARRIS, Jack, & Arabians
Singles: 7-inch
WITCH....................8-12

HARRIS, Jet
(With Tony Meehan)
Singles: 7-inch
LONDON....................8-12 63
SRT (75355 "Theme for a Fallen Idol")....................8-12
SRT (73389 "The Guitar Man")....................8-12
Also see SHADOWS

HARRIS, Jill
Singles: 7-inch
CAPITOL....................6-12 64-65

HARRIS, Johnny Ray
Singles: 7-inch
RAY (100 "Doggone")....................15-25

HARRIS, Joyce
Singles: 7-inch
DOMINO....................15-25 61
INFINITY....................10-15 62

HARRIS, Kurt
Singles: 7-inch
DIAMOND (158 'Go On")....................50-80 63
JOSIE....................5-15 62-63

HARRIS, Lee
Singles: 7-inch
JACKPOT....................8-12 58

HARRIS, Leslie
Singles: 7-inch
SHAD....................5-8 60

HARRIS, Little Bobby: see HARRIS, Bob

HARRIS, Major *P&R/R&B/LP '75*
(Major Harris Boogie Blues Band)
Singles: 7-inch
ATLANTIC....................4-6 75-76
OKEH (7314 "Just Love Me")....................15-25 68
OKEH (7327 "Like a Rolling Stone")....................30-60 69
POP ART....................3-4 83
WMOT....................3-5 76-81
LPs: 10/12-inch
ATLANTIC....................8-10 75
RCA....................5-10 78
WMOT....................8-10 76
Also see DELFONICS

HARRIS, Mike
(With the Hi-Tides)
Singles: 7-inch
DORE....................4-8 63
EPIC....................4-8 64
KRIMMIE (24 "I'm So Proud")....................20-30 63
LIBERTY....................10-20 64
SIDEWALK....................4-8 66
ZUMA....................5-10 60s

HARRIS, Nick, & Soundbarriers
Singles: 7-inch
FLEETWOOD (7004 "Freeway Hot Rod")....................20-30 63
NORTHWEST SOUND....................10-15 60s
TEE PEE....................5-10 61

HARRIS, Odessa
Singles: 7-inch
CAPITOL....................4-8 62
UPTOWN....................4-8 65-66

HARRIS, Peppermint: see PEPPERMINT HARRIS

HARRIS, Phil *P&R '33*
Singles: 78 rpm
ARA....................4-8 46
COLUMBIA....................4-8 33
DECCA....................4-6 35
RCA....................5-10 47-54
Singles: 7-inch
COLISEUM....................3-5 68
MEGA....................3-4 73
MONTCLARE....................3-4 76
RCA....................10-20 50-54
REPRISE....................3-5 62
VISTA....................3-5 67-70
Picture Sleeves
MONTCLARE....................3-5 76
EPs: 7-inch
RCA....................5-10 53-60
LPs: 10/12-inch
CAMDEN....................8-12 63
MEGA....................5-10 72-74
RCA (1900 series)....................10-20 59
RCA (3000 series)....................20-30 53-54
ZODIAC....................5-10 77
Also see BELL SISTERS
Also see SHORE, Dinah, Tony Martin, Betty Hutton & Phil Harris

HARRIS, Quinn
Singles: 7-inch
MLF ("I'll Always Love You")....................15-25
(Selection number not known.)

HARRIS, Ralph
Singles: 7-inch
EXCELLO....................5-10 60

HARRIS, Ray
Singles: 78 rpm
SUN....................20-50 56-57
Singles: 7-inch
SUN (254 "Come On Little Mama")....................30-60 56
SUN (272 "Greenback Dollar, Watch and Chain")....................25-50 57
Session: Charlie Rich.
Also see RICH, Charlie

HARRIS, Rene, & Terrans
Singles: 7-inch
GRAHAM (801 "Moonrise")....................75-125 63
(Previously issued as by the Terrans.)
Also see TERRANS

HARRIS, Richard *P&R/LP '68*
Singles: 7-inch
ATLANTIC....................3-5 74-75
DUNHILL....................3-6 68-75
Picture Sleeves
DUNHILL (Except 4134)....................4-8 70-72
DUNHILL (4134 "MacArthur Park")....................3-6 68
DUNHILL (4134 "MacArthur Park")....................8-12 68
(Special promotional sleeve, labeled as such.)
EPs: 7-inch
DUNHILL....................4-6 68
(Juke box issues only.)
LPs: 10/12-inch
ATLANTIC....................6-10 74-75
DUNHILL....................8-15 68-74
PICKWICK....................5-8 78

HARRIS, Rolf *P&R/R&B/LP '63*
Singles: 7-inch
EPIC (Except 9721)....................4-8 63-66
EPIC (9721 "Ringo for President")....................10-15 64
MGM....................3-5 70
20TH FOX....................8-12 60-61
Picture Sleeves
EPIC....................8-12 63-64
LPs: 10/12-inch
EPIC....................20-30 63-64

HARRIS, Sam *P&R/D&D/LP '84*
Singles: 12-inch
MOTOWN....................4-6 84-86
Singles: 7-inch
MOTOWN....................3-4 84-86
Picture Sleeves
MOTOWN....................3-4 84-86
LPs: 10/12-inch
MOTOWN....................5-10 84-86

HARRIS, Shaky Jake
LPs: 10/12-inch
POLYDOR....................8-10 72

HARRIS, Shaun
Singles: 7-inch
CAPITOL....................4-6 73
LPs: 10/12-inch
CAPITOL....................10-15 73
Also see WEST COAST POP ART EXPERIMENTAL BAND

HARRIS, Slim, & His Sterophonixs
Singles: 7-inch
FRAN....................4-8

HARRIS, Ted
Singles: 7-inch
RCA....................8-12 58

HARRIS, Thurston *P&R/R&B '57*
(With the Sharps)
Singles: 78 rpm
ALADDIN....................10-15 57
Singles: 7-inch
ALADDIN....................15-25 57-61
CUB....................4-8 62
DOT....................4-8 62-63
IMPERIAL....................4-8 63
REPRISE....................4-8 64
Also see SHARPS

HARRIS, Tony *P&R '57*
Singles: 78 rpm
EBB....................5-15 56-57
Singles: 7-inch
EBB....................10-15 56-57

HARRIS, Tony, & Woodies
Singles: 7-inch
DEE GEE....................10-15 66
TRIUMPH (60 "Go Go Little Scrambler")....................15-25 65

HARRIS, Wee Willie
Singles: 7-inch
CHARLIE PARKER....................4-8 63

HARRIS, Willard
Singles: 78 rpm
EKKO....................20-30 55
Singles: 7-inch
EKKO (20001 "Straighten Up Baby")....................40-60 55

HARRIS, Wynonie *R&B '46*
(With Lucky Millinder)
Singles: 78 rpm
ALADDIN....................20-30 47
APOLLO....................20-30 45-46
ATCO....................10-20 56
BULLET....................15-25 46
HAMP-TONE....................15-25 45
KING....................20-40 47-57
PHILO....................15-25 45
QUALITY/KING (4074 "Bloodshot Eyes")....................200-300 51
(Canadian.)
Singles: 7-inch
ATCO (6081 "Destination Love")....................25-40 56
KING (4210 "Good Rockin' Tonight")....................50-100 52
KING (4461 "Bloodshot Eyes")....................50-100 51
KING (4468 "I'll Never Give Up")....................50-100 51
KING (4485 "Lovin' Machine")....................50-100 51
(Black vinyl.)
KING (4485 "Lovin' Machine")....................200-300 51
(Colored vinyl.)
KING (4507 "My Playful Baby's Gone")....................50-100 51
KING (4526 "Keep on Churnin'")....................50-100 52
KING (4555 "Night Train")....................50-100 52
KING (4565 "Adam, Come and Get Your Rib")....................50-100 52
KING (4592 "Greyhound")....................50-100 52
KING (4593 "Bad News, Baby")....................50-100 52
KING (4620 "Wasn't That Good")....................50-100 53
KING (4635 "The Deacon Don't Like It")....................50-100 53
KING (4662 "Tremblin' ")....................50-75 53
KING (4668 "Please, Louise")....................50-75 53
KING (4685 "Quiet Whiskey")....................50-75 53
KING (4716 "Shake That Thing")....................50-75 54
KING (4724 "Don't Take My Whiskey Away from Me")....................50-75 54
KING (4763 "Christina")....................25-50 54
KING (4774 "Good Mambo Tonight")....................25-50 54
KING (4789 "Mr. Dollar")....................25-50 54
KING (4814 "Drinkin' Sherry Wine")....................25-50 54
KING (4826 "Wine, Wine, Sweet Wine")....................25-40 54
KING (4839 "Shotgun Wedding")....................25-40 54
KING (4900 & 5000 series)....................15-30 56-57
KING (5050 "Big Old Country Fool")....................10-20 57
KING (5073 "There's No Substitute for Love")....................10-20 57
KING (5100 thru 5400 series)....................5-10 58-60
KING (6011 "Bloodshot Eyes")....................10-15
ROULETTE (4291 "Bloodshot Eyes")....................10-15 60
EPs: 7-inch
KING (260 "Wynonie Harris")....................300-400 54
LPs: 10/12-inch
KING (1086 "Good Rockin' Blues")....................10-15 72
Also see MILBURN, Amos / Wynonie Harris / Crown Prince Waterford
Also see MILLINDER, Lucky, & His Orchestra

HARRIS, Wynonie / Roy Brown
LPs: 10/12-inch
KING (607 "Battle of the Blues")....................100-200 58
KING (627 "Battle of the Blues, Vol. 2")....................100-200 58

HARRIS, Wynonie / Roy Brown / Eddie Vinson
LPs: 10/12-inch
KING (668 "Battle of the Blues, Vol. 4")....................200-300 60
Also see BROWN, Roy
Also see HARRIS, Wynonie
Also see VINSON, Eddie

HARRIS SISTERS
Singles: 78 rpm
CAPITOL....................5-8 55
Singles: 7-inch
CAPITOL....................8-12 55
SMASH (2002 "Don't Let Me Fall in Love")....................10-20

HARRISON
Singles: 7-inch
VISION of SOUND....................3-6 70

HARRISON, B.J. *C&W '80*
Singles: 7-inch
TELESONIC....................3-5 80

HARRISON, Bob "Lil" Elvis
Singles: 7-inch
LIL' ELVIS WORLD....................3-5 77
LPs: 10/12-inch
LIL' ELVIS WORLD....................10-15 77

HARRISON, Danny
(With the Count Victors)
Singles: 7-inch
CORAL....................4-8 63-66
DENEBA....................3-6 69
EVENT (4273 "Rockabilly Boogie")....................40-60 58
EVENT (4278 "Have You Ever Been Lonely")....................5-10 59
U.A....................4-8 68
LPs: 10/12-inch
DENEBA....................10-15 69

HARRISON, Danny, & Benny Reed
Singles: 7-inch
COOL....................5-10 60
Also see HARRISON, Danny

HARRISON, Dixie *C&W '82*
Singles: 7-inch
AIR INT'L....................3-4 82

HARRISON, Don, Band *P&R/LP '76*
Singles: 7-inch
ATLANTIC....................4-8 76
MERCURY....................4-8 77
LPs: 10/12-inch
ATLANTIC....................8-10 76
MERCURY....................8-10 77
Members: Don Harrison; Doug Clifford; Stu Cook.
Also see CREEDENCE CLEARWATER REVIVAL

HARRISON, Eddy
Singles: 7-inch
LIBERTY....................5-8 66

HARRISON, George *LP '69*
Singles: 12-inch
DARK HORSE (949 "All Those Years Ago")....................25-30 81
(Promotional issue only. Includes title sleeve.)
DARK HORSE (1075 "Wake Up My Love")....................20-30 82
(Promotional issue only. Includes title sleeve.)
DARK HORSE (2845 "Got My Mind Set on You")....................20-30 87
(Promotional issue only. Includes picture cover.)
DARK HORSE (2885 "When We Was Fab")....................20-30 88
(Promotional issue only.)
DARK HORSE (2889 "Devil's Radio")....................20-30 87
(Promotional issue only. Includes picture cover.)
Singles: 7-inch
APPLE (1828 "What Is Life")....................10-15 71
(With black star on label.)
APPLE (1828 "What Is Life")....................5-8 71
(No black star on label.)
APPLE (1836 "Bangla Desh")....................15-25 71
(With black star on label.)
APPLE (1836 "Bangla Desh")....................5-8 71
(No black star on label.)
APPLE (1862 "Give Me Love")....................5-8 73
APPLE (1877 "Dark Horse")....................8-10 74
APPLE (1879 "Ding Dong Ding Dong")....................5-8 74
(Black with *white* tint photo label.)
APPLE (1879 "Ding Dong Ding Dong")....................200-250 74
(Black with *blue* tint photo label.)
APPLE (1884 "You")....................5-8 75
APPLE (1885 "This Guitar")....................20-25 75
APPLE (2995 "My Sweet Lord")....................30-40 70
(With black star on label.)
APPLE (2995 "My Sweet Lord")....................5-8 70
(No black star on label. Does not have "All Rights Reserved, etc." print on label.)
APPLE (2995 "My Sweet Lord")....................15-25 70
(With "All Rights Reserved, etc." on label.)
CAPITOL (Orange label)....................25-35 76
CAPITOL (Tan "Starline" label)....................5-8 77
CAPITOL (Purple label)....................5-8 78
CAPITOL (Black label, except 6245)....................10-15 83
CAPITOL (Tan or purple label)....................4-6 88
CAPITOL (6245 "Dark Horse")....................30-40 87
DARK HORSE (0410 "All Those Years Ago")....................4-6 81
(Tan label.)
DARK HORSE (0410 "All Those Years Ago")....................4-6 91
(White or cream label.)
DARK HORSE (8294 "This Song")....................5-10 76
DARK HORSE (8313 "Crackerbox Palace")....................4-6 77
DARK HORSE (8763 "Blow Away")....................4-6 79
(Tan label with "Loka Productions" print on label.)
DARK HORSE (8763 "Blow Away")....................15-20 79
(Tan label without "Loka Productions" print on label.)
DARK HORSE (8844 "Love Comes to Everyone")....................5-10 79
DARK HORSE (27913 "This Is Love")....................3-5 88
DARK HORSE (28131 "When We Was Fab")....................3-5 88
DARK HORSE (28178 "Got My Mind Set on You")....................3-5 87
DARK HORSE (29744 "I Really Love You")....................20-25 83
DARK HORSE (29864 "Wake Up My Love")....................5-10 82
DARK HORSE (49725 "All Those Years Ago")....................3-5 81
DARK HORSE (49785 "Teardrops")....................5-10 81
W.B. (22807 "Cheer Down")....................10-15 89
Picture Sleeves
APPLE (1828 "What Is Life")....................30-40 71
APPLE (1836 "Bangla Desh")....................15-20 71
APPLE (1877 "Dark Horse")....................50-75 74
APPLE (1879 "Ding Dong Ding Dong")....................10-15 74
APPLE (1884 "You")....................10-15 75
APPLE (2995 "My Sweet Lord")....................30-40 70
DARK HORSE (8294 "This Song")....................20-30 76
DARK HORSE (8294 "This Song")....................60-80 76
(Special promotional sleeve issued with promo single. Price includes insert flyer with "The Story Behind *This Song*," which represents about $30-$40 of the value.)
DARK HORSE (8763 "Blow Away")....................4-6 79
DARK HORSE (8844 "Love Comes to Everyone")....................700-800 79
DARK HORSE (27913; "This Is Love")....................3-5 88
DARK HORSE (28131 "When We Was Fab")....................3-5 88
DARK HORSE (28178 "Got My Mind Set on You")....................3-5 87
DARK HORSE (49725 "All Those Years Ago")....................3-4 81
W.B. (22807 "Cheer Down")....................10-15 89
Promotional Singles
APPLE (1862 "Give Me Love")....................35-45 73
APPLE (1879 "Ding Dong Ding Dong")....................25-30 74
APPLE (1877 "Dark Horse")....................40-60 74
APPLE (1879 "Ding Dong Ding Dong")....................25-35 74
APPLE (1884 "You")....................25-35 75
APPLE (1885 "This Guitar")....................35-45 75

APPLE/20TH FOX (791 "Concert for Bangla Desh") ... 700-750 71
(Four radio spots. Issued only to radio stations.)
DARK HORSE (8294 "This Song") ... 15-25 76
DARK HORSE (8313 "Crackerbox Palace") ... 10-15 77
DARK HORSE (8763 "Blow Away") ... 10-15 79
DARK HORSE (8844 "Love Comes to Everyone") ... 10-15 79
DARK HORSE (27913 "This Is Love") ... 10-15 88
DARK HORSE (28131 "When We Was Fab") ... 10-15 88
DARK HORSE (28178 "Got My Mind Set on You") ... 10-15 87
DARK HORSE (29744 "I Really Love You") ... 10-15 83
DARK HORSE (29864 "Wake Up My Love") ... 10-15 82
DARK HORSE (49725 "All Those Years Ago") ... 10-15 81
DARK HORSE (49785 "Teardrops") ... 10-15 81
W.B. (22807 "Cheer Down") ... 150-200 89

LPs: 10/12-inch

APPLE (639 "All Things Must Pass") ... 30-40 70
(Boxed, three-disc set. Includes bonus poster. Disc does not have "S" in trail-off area.)
APPLE (639 "All Things Must Pass") ... 50-75 88
(Boxed, three-disc set. Includes bonus poster. Disc has "S" in trail-off area.)
APPLE (3350 "Wonderwall Music") ... 20-30 68
(Apple label without Capitol logo.)
APPLE (3350 "Wonderwall Music") ... 100-125 68
(Apple lable with Capitol logo.)
APPLE (3385 "Concert for Bangla Desh") ... 40-50 71
(Boxed, three-disc set. Includes 64-page booklet. Also has Eric Clapton, Bob Dylan, Ringo Starr, Leon Russell, Ravi Shankar, and others.)
APPLE (3410 "Living in the Material World") ... 10-15 73
APPLE (3418 "Dark Horse") ... 15-20 73
APPLE (3420 "Extra Texture") ... 10-15 75
CAPITOL (639 "All Things Must Pass") ... 20-30 76-78
(Boxed, three-disc set. Orange or purple labels. Includes bonus poster.)
CAPITOL (639 "All Things Must Pass") ... 70-90 83
(Black label. Boxed, three-disc set. Includes bonus poster.)
CAPITOL (3410 "Living in the Material World") ... 10-15 80
CAPITOL (3420 "Extra Texture") ... 15-25 80
CAPITOL (11578 "The Best of George Harrison") ... 10-15 76
(Custom label with six photos of Harrison. Also contains tracks by the Beatles that feature George.)
CAPITOL (11578 "The Best of George Harrison") ... 125-150 77
(Orange label.)
CAPITOL (11578 "The Best of George Harrison") ... 8-10 78
(Purple label with "Mfd. by Capitol, etc." on perimeter print.)
CAPITOL (11578 "The Best of George Harrison") ... 15-25 83
(Black label or apple label.)
CAPITOL (11578 "The Best of George Harrison") ... 50-75 89
(Purple label with "Manufactured by Capitol, etc." on perimeter print.)
CAPITOL (12248 "Concert For Bangla Desh") ... 300-350 82
(Two-disc set.)
CAPITOL (16000 series) ... 10-20 81
DARK HORSE (3005 "Thirty-Three and 1/3") ... 8-10 76
DARK HORSE (3255 "George Harrison") ... 8-10 79
DARK HORSE (3255 "George Harrison") ... 30-40 79
(Columbia Record Club issue.)
DARK HORSE (3492 "Somewhere in England") ... 5-10 81
DARK HORSE (23734 "Gone Troppo") ... 8-12 82
DARK HORSE (25643 "Cloud Nine") ... 10-15 87
DARK HORSE (25726 "Best of Dark Horse") ... 15-25 89
ZAPPLE (3358 "Electronic Music") ... 20-30 69

Promotional LPs

DARK HORSE ("Dark Horse Radio Special") ... 250-300 74
DARK HORSE (649 "A Personal Music Dialogue with George Harrison at 33⅓") ... 30-40 76
DARK HORSE (23734 "Gone Troppo") ... 20-25 82
(Audiophile Quiex II vinyl pressing.)
Also see BEATLES
Also see BROMBERG, David
Also see CLAPTON, Eric
Also see DYLAN, Bob
Also see HODGE, Chris
Also see RUSSELL, Leon
Also see SCOTT, Tom
Also see SHANKAR, Ravi
Also see SPLINTER
Also see TRAVELING WILBURYS

HARRISON, George / Jeff Beck / Dave Edmunds

Singles: 12-inch

COLUMBIA (2034 "I Don't Want to Do It") ... 10-20 85
(Has one song by each artist. Promotional issue only.)
COLUMBIA (2085 "I Don't Want to Do It") ... 10-20 85
(Promotional issue only. Has the Harrison song on both sides.)

Singles: 7-inch

COLUMBIA (04887 "I Don't Want to Do It") ... 3-4 85

Promotional Singles

COLUMBIA (04887 "I Don't Want to Do It") ... 8-12 85
(Has the Harrison song on both sides.)
Also see BECK, Jeff
Also see EDMUNDS, Dave
Also see HARRISON, George

HARRISON, Jerry — *LP '88*

(With the Casual Gods)

LPs: 10/12-inch

FLY/SIRE ... 5-8 90
SIRE ... 5-8 88
Also see MODERN LOVERS
Also see TALKING HEADS

HARRISON, Jim & Bob

(With Jimmy Spruill's Band)

Singles: 7-inch

CLOCK ... 15-25 61
SMASH ... 4-8 63
Also see SPURILL, Wild Jimmy

HARRISON, Jimmy

Singles: 7-inch

ATCO ... 5-8 59

HARRISON, John, & Hustlers

Singles: 7-inch

IDEAL (10 "Don't Ask Me Why") ... 10-15 65

HARRISON, Mike

Singles: 7-inch

ISLAND ... 3-5 75

LPs: 10/12-inch

ISLAND ... 8-10 72-75
Also see SPOOKY TOOTH

HARRISON, Noel — *P&R '65*

Singles: 7-inch

LONDON ... 4-8 65-67
REPRISE ... 3-6 67-70

LPs: 10/12-inch

LONDON ... 15-20 66-67
REPRISE ... 10-15 67-69
RIVERSIDE ... 10-12 60s

HARRISON, Reggie: see HIPPIES / Reggie Harrison

HARRISON, Sterling

Singles: 7-inch

ASTROSCOPE ... 3-5 73
SMASH ... 4-8 63-64
V ... 4-8 62

HARRISON, Wes — *LP '63*

(With Eddie Gale)

Singles: 78 rpm

LIN (5002 "There Y'Are") ... 10-15 56

Singles: 7-inch

LIN (5002 "There Y'Are") ... 15-25 56
PHILIPS ... 8-12 63

LPs: 10/12-inch

PHILIPS ... 15-25 63

HARRISON, Wilbert — *P&R/R&B '59*

(With the Roamers; with His Kansas City Playboys; "Wilbert Harrison One Man Band"; Wilburt Harrison; Wilbur Harrison)

Singles: 78 rpm

CHART ... 10-20 56
DELUXE ... 20-30 52-53
FURY (1023 "Kansas City") ... 100-200 59
SAVOY ... 10-20 54

Singles: 7-inch

ABC ... 3-4 73
BARREL ... 5-10
BELL (869 "Since I Fell for You") ... 4-6 70
BRUNSWICK ... 3-5 74
CHART (626 "Calypso Man") ... 20-30 56
CONSTELLATION (122 "Mama, Mama, Mama") ... 8-10 64
DEE-SU (301 "Clementine") ... 5-8 66
DELUXE (6002 "This Woman of Mine") ... 40-50 52
DELUXE (6031 "Gin and Coconut Milk") ... 40-50 53
DOC (1002 "Off to School Again") ... 5-10 62
ERIC ... 3-5 73
FURY (1023 "Kansas City") ... 10-20 59
FURY (1027 "Cheating Baby") ... 10-20 59
FURY (1028 "Goodbye Kansas City") ... 10-20 59
FURY (1031 "C.C. Rider") ... 8-15 60
FURY (1037 "Little School Girl") ... 8-15 60
FURY (1041 "Da-De-Ya") ... 8-15 61
FURY (1047 "Happy in Love") ... 8-15 61
FURY (1055 "My Heart Is Yours") ... 8-15 61
FURY (1059 "Let's Stick Together") ... 10-20 62
FURY (1063 "Let's Stick Together") ... 8-12 62
GLADES (603 "Gonna Tell You a Story") ... 10-15 59
HOT LINE (101 "Get It While You Can") ... 4-6 72
HOUSE of SOUND ... 4-6
NEPTUNE (123 "After Graduation") 8-12 61
PORT (3003 "Baby Move On") ... 5-10 65
PORT (3009 "Sugar Lump") ... 5-10 65
ROCKIN' (526 "This Woman of Mine") ... 75-100 52
ROULETTE ... 3-6 67
SSS INT'L (830 "My Heart Is") ... 4-8 71
(Black vinyl.)
SSS INT'L (830 "My Heart Is") ... 5-10 71
(Colored vinyl. Promotional issue only.)
SAVOY (1138 "Don't Drop It") ... 20-30 54
SAVOY (1149 "Women & Whiskey") ... 15-25 55
SAVOY (1164 "Darling, Listen to This Song") ... 15-25 55
SAVOY (1517 "My Love Is True") ... 10-20 57
SAVOY (1531 "My Love for You Lingers On") ... 10-20 58
SAVOY (1571 "Don't Drop It") ... 10-20 59
SEA HORN (502 "Near to You") ... 8-10 63
SUE (11 "Let's Work Together") ... 10-20 69
(No company address shown.)
SUE (11 "Let's Work Together") ... 5-10 69
(Company address at bottom of label.)
SUE (11 "Let's Work Together") ... 4-8 69
(Company address at top or on either side.)
WET SOUL (4 "My Heart Is Yours") ... 3-5 70

LPs: 10/12-inch

BUDDAH ... 10-18 71
CHELSEA ... 8-10 77
FURY ... 5-8
JUGGERNAUT ... 15-25 71
RELIC ... 5-10 90
RES IPSA ... 10-15
SPHERE SOUND ... 25-40 65
SUE ... 15-25 70
WET SOUL ... 10-15 70
Also see ROAMERS

HARRISON & TYLER

LPs: 10/12-inch

DORE ... 10-12 72

HARROD, Chuck

Singles: 7-inch

CHAMPION (1013 "They Wanna Fight") ... 30-50 59

HARRY, Debbie — *P&R/R&B/LP '81*

(Deborah Harry)

Singles: 12-inch

CHRYSALIS ... 4-6 81-83
GEFFEN ... 4-6 85-86

Singles: 7-inch

CHRYSALIS ... 3-5 81-88
GEFFEN ... 3-4 85-87

Picture Sleeves

CHRYSALIS ... 3-5 81-88
GEFFEN ... 3-4 86-87

LPs: 10/12-inch

CHRYSALIS ... 5-10 81
GEFFEN ... 5-10 86
SIRE ... 5-8 89
Also see BLONDIE
Also see WIND IN THE WILLOWS

HARRY & CROC-O-DOLLS / Croc-o-dolls

Singles: 7-inch

RCA ... 5-10 63

HARRY & KEYAVAS

Singles: 7-inch

I.P.G. (1011 "Tears") ... 15-25 64

HARRY HEPCAT: see HEPCAT, Harry, & Boogie Woogie Band

EPs: 7-inch

AETERNUS ... 5-10

HARRY M. & MARVELS

Singles: 7-inch

ABC-PAR ... 5-10 61-64
Also see MARVELS

HARSHMAN, Robert Luke

(Bobby Hart)

Singles: 7-inch

GUYDEN (2022 "Is You Is Or Is You Ain't My Baby") ... 15-25 59
RADIO (122 "Love Whatcha Doin' to Me") ... 20-30 59
Also see HART, Bobby

HART, Billy & Don

(With the Downbeats)

Singles: 7-inch

ROULETTE (4133 "Rock-A Bop-A-Lina") ... 30-40 59
ROULETTE (4172 "Checkmated and Bingoed") ... 15-25 59
Also see HART, Don

HART, Bobby

Singles: 7-inch

BAMBOO (507 "Girl I Used to Know") ... 15-25 61
CHELSEA ... 3-5 72
DCP ... 10-20 64-66
ERA (3039 "Girl in the Window") ... 5-10 61
INFINITY ... 5-10 62
REEL (100 "Girl in the Window") ... 15-25 60
W.B. ... 3-5 74
W.B./CURB ... 3-4 79
Also see BOYCE, Tommy, & Bobby Hart
Also see HARSHMAN, Robert Luke

HART, Bonnie

Singles: 7-inch

BADGER ... 3-5 88

HART, Cajun: see CAJUN HART

HART, Casey

Singles: 7-inch

CHOICE ... 4-8 61

HART, Clay — *C&W '69*

Singles: 7-inch

METROMEDIA ... 3-5 69-70

LPs: 10/12-inch

METROMEDIA ... 6-12 69
RANWOOD ... 5-10 74-75

HART, Corey — *P&R/D&D/LP '84*

Singles: 7-inch

EMI AMERICA ... 3-4 84-87
EMI MANHATTAN ... 3-4 88

Picture Sleeves

EMI AMERICA (Except 8268) ... 3-4 84-86
EMI AMERICA (8268 "Never Surrender") ... 4-6 85
(Poster sleeve.)
EMI MANHATTAN ... 3-4 88

LPs: 10/12-inch

EMI AMERICA ... 5-10 84-86
EMI MANHATTAN ... 5-8 89

HART, Danny

Singles: 7-inch

TUXEDO ... 5-10 59

HART, Don

(With the Fyve; with James Shorter)

Singles: 7-inch

COOLSCHOOL (2001 "It's in My Mind") ... 75-125 50s
COOLSCHOOL (2002 "Soldier, Come Home") ... 75-125 50s
COOLSCHOOL (2003 "I Can Make It") ... 75-125 50s
RESERVE (118 "Presley on Her Mind") ... 40-60 57
Also see HART, Billy & Don
Also see HEART, Don

HART, Freddie — *C&W '59*

(With the Heartbeats)

Singles: 78 rpm

CAPITOL ... 5-10 53-55
COLUMBIA (Except 21512) ... 5-15 56-57
COLUMBIA (21512 "Dig Boy Dig") . 15-25 56

Singles: 7-inch

CAPITOL (2500 thru 3000 series) ... 5-10 53-55
(Purple labels.)
CAPITOL (2600 thru 4600 series) ... 3-5 70-79
(Orange labels.)
COLUMBIA (Except 21512) ... 5-10 56-63
COLUMBIA (21512 "Dig Boy Dig") ... 25-35 56
KAPP ... 3-8 65-72
MCA ... 3-5 73
MONUMENT ... 4-6 63-64
SUNBIRD ... 3-4 80-81

Picture Sleeves

KAPP ... 4-6 68
SUNBIRD ... 3-5 80

LPs: 10/12-inch

BRYLEN ... 5-10 84
CAPITOL ... 5-10 70-79
COLUMBIA (1700 series) ... 20-25 62
COLUMBIA (13000 series) ... 10-12 72
CORAL ... 5-8 73
HARMONY ... 8-12 67-73
KAPP ... 8-15 65-69
MCA ... 8-12 75
PICKWICK ... 5-10 70s
PICKWICK/HILLTOP ... 8-12 70s
SUNBIRD ... 5-10 80
VOCALION ... 8-10 72

HART, Freddie / Sammi Smith / Jerry Reed

LPs: 10/12-inch

HARMONY ... 6-10 72
Also see HART, Freddie
Also see REED, Jerry
Also see SMITH, Sammi

HART, Haze

Singles: 7-inch

SWINGIN' ... 10-20 62

HART, J.D. — *C&W '89*

Singles: 7-inch

UNIVERSAL ... 3-4 89

HART, Judy

Singles: 7-inch

GOLD LEAF ... 5-10 62
STACCATTO ... 8-12 62
Also see HENSKE, Judy

HART, Kelly

Singles: 7-inch

OKEH ... 5-10 59
SWAN ... 4-8 64
TOP RANK ... 4-8 60
XYZ (606 "Boy Crazy") ... 15-25 60

HART, Larry

Singles: 78 rpm

OKEH ... 8-12 57

Singles: 7-inch

OKEH ... 8-12 57

HART, Mickey — *LP '72*

Singles: 7-inch

W.B. ... 4-8 71-72

LPs: 10/12-inch

RELIX (Except 2026) ... 5-10 85
RELIX (2026 "Rolling Thunder") ... 25-30 87
(Picture disc.)
W.B. ... 10-20 72
Also see BUFFALO, Norton
Also see DIGA RHYTHM BAND
Also see GRATEFUL DEAD
Also see RHYTHM DEVILS
Also see WOLFF, Henry, Nancy Hennings & Mickey Hart

HART, Mickey, Airto & Flora Purim

LPs: 10/12-inch

REFERENCE ... 8-10 83
Also see HART, Mickey
Also see MOREIRA, Airto
Also see PURIM, Flora

HART, Rita — *D&D '84*

Singles: 12-inch

ENVELOPE ... 4-6 84

HART, Ritchie

(With the Heartbeats; Charles R. Gearheart)

Singles: 7-inch

FELSTED (8593 "The Great Duane") ... 15-25 59
MCI (1025 "I Want You") ... 10-20 60
RAMCO ("If You Can't, Don't Worry") ... 5-10 62
(Selection number not known.)
RAMCO (3707 "Her Singing Idol") ... 5-10 61
RAMCO (3709 "Phyllis") ... 5-10 61
RAMCO (3716 "Love Is") ... 5-10 62
Also see GOOSE CREEK SYMPHONY

HART, Robin

Singles: 7-inch

CHALLENGE ... 8-12 64

HART, Rocky

Singles: 7-inch

BIG TOP (3069 "Crying") ... 10-20 61
CUB (9052 "Every Day") ... 10-20 59
GLO (5216 "I Play the Part of a Fool") ... 300-500 61
GOLDEN WORLD (105 "When a Teenager Gets Blue") ... 15-25 62
Also see APOLLOS
Also see PASSIONS

HART, Rod — *C&W/P&R '76*

Singles: 7-inch

IBC ... 3-4 80
PHOENIX SUN ... 3-6 68
PLANTATION ... 3-5 76-77

LPs: 10/12-inch

PLANTATION ... 5-10 76

HART, Ron

Singles: 7-inch

COLUMBIA ... 4-8 63

HART, Ronny, & Dynamic Encores

Singles: 7-inch

BARC ... 4-8 64

HART, Sally June — *C&W '75*

Singles: 7-inch

BUDDAH ... 3-5 75

HART, Susan

Singles: 7-inch

MGM ... 4-8 70-72
TOWER ... 4-8 69

Picture Sleeves

TOWER ... 4-8 69

HARTER, Griffith, Union see GRIFFITH HARTER UNION

HARTFIELD, Pete

Singles: 7-inch

BABY (610 "Mighty Man") ... 25-50
MIRACLE (8 "Love Me") ... 40-60 60

HARTFORD, Chapin — *C&W '78*

Singles: 7-inch

LS ... 3-5 78

HARTFORD, John — *C&W '67*

Singles: 7-inch

AMPEX ... 3-5 71
FLYING FISH ... 3-4 84
RCA ... 4-8 66-70

LPs: 10/12-inch

FLYING FISH ... 5-10 76-84
RCA ... 8-15 67-70
W.B. ... 8-12 71-72
Also see DILLARDS & John Hartford

HARTFORD, Ken

(With Frankie Valli)

Singles: 7-inch

SOUTHERN SOUND (119 "Jay Walker") ... 15-25 63
Also see VALLI, Frankie

HARTLEY, Al

(With the Heartbeats)

Singles: 7-inch

HERMITAGE ... 10-15
IMPERIAL ... 10-20 63
LIMELIGHT ... 10-15 59
SCARLET ... 10-15 59

HARTLEY, Keef, Band — *LP '70*

Singles: 7-inch

DERAM ... 3-5 70-73

LPs: 10/12-inch

DERAM ... 10-12 69-73
Also see MAYALL, John

HARTMAN, Dan — *P&R/R&B/LP '78*

Singles: 12-inch

BLUE SKY ... 4-6 78-81
MCA ... 4-6 84-85

Singles: 7-inch

BLUE SKY ... 3-5 76-81
MCA ... 3-4 84-85
PORTRAIT ... 3-4 81

Picture Sleeves

MCA ... 3-4 84-85

LPs: 10/12-inch

BLUE SKY (Except 246) ... 5-10 76-81
BLUE SKY (246 "Who Is Dan Hartman") ... 8-15 75
(Promotional issue only.)
MCA ... 5-10 84-85
Also see LEGENDS
Also see WINTER, Edgar

HARTMAN, Dan / Blasters
Singles: 7-inch
MCA 3-4 84
Picture Sleeves
MCA 3-4 84
Also see BLASTERS
Also see HARTMAN, Dan

HARTMAN, Lisa
Singles: 7-inch
ATLANTIC 3-4 87-88
KIRSHNER 3-5 76-79
RCA 3-4 84
Picture Sleeves
ATLANTIC 3-4 87-88
LPs: 10/12-inch
KIRSHNER (34109 "Lisa Hartman") 25-35 76
KIRSHNER (35685 "Hold On") 10-15 79
RCA (8014 "Letterock") 5-8 82

HARTSMAN, Johnny: see HEARTSMAN, Johnny

HARTSOOK, Jimmy C&W '74
Singles: 7-inch
RCA 3-5 74

HARTT, Dolly C&W '88
Singles: 7-inch
KASS 3-4 88

HARUMI
LPs: 10/12-inch
VERVE/FORECAST (3030 Harumi") 15-20 68

HARVELL, Nate C&W '78
Singles: 7-inch
REPUBLIC 3-5 78-79

HARVES, Cleo
Singles: 78 rpm
O.T. (105 "Skinny Woman Blues") .20-40 49

HARVEST, Barclay James: see BARCLAY JAMES HARVEST

HARVEST, King: see KING HARVEST

HARVEY
("Former Lead of the Moonglows"; Harvey Fuqua)
Singles: 7-inch
CHESS (1713 "I Want Somebody") 20-30 59
CHESS (1725 "Twelve Months of the Year") 20-30 59
CHESS (1749 "Blue Skies") 10-20 60
TRI-PHI (1010 "She Loves Me So") 20-30 62
TRI-PHI (1017 "She Loves Me So") 20-30 62
TRI-PHI (1024 "Come On and Answer Me") 25-40 63
Also see ETTA & HARVEY
Also see FIVE QUAILS
Also see HARVEY & ANN
Also see HARVEY & MOONGLOWS
Also see HARVEY & SPINNERS
Also see NEW BIRTH

HARVEY
Singles: 7-inch
NASTY 3-5 71
Members: Joe Mele; Bob Mele; Tom Harper; Paul Saffioti; Dick Liso.

HARVEY, Alex LP '75
(Sensational Alex Harvey Band)
Singles: 7-inch
ATLANTIC 3-5 75
CAPITOL 3-5 72
VERTIGO 3-5 73-75
LPs: 10/12-inch
CAPITOL 8-12 72
ATLANTIC 8-10 75
VERTIGO 8-10 73-75

HARVEY, Laurence
Singles: 7-inch
ATLANTIC 4-6 62
COLUMBIA 4-6 61
LPs: 10/12-inch
ATLANTIC (1367 "This Is My Beloved") 25-50 62

HARVEY, Phil
(Phil Spector)
Singles: 7-inch
IMPERIAL (5583 "Bumbershoot") ..50-75 59
Also see HARVEY & DOC & DWELLERS
Also see RONETTES / Crystals / Darlene Love / Bob B. Soxx & Blue Jeans
Also see TEDDY BEARS

HARVEY, Steve D&D '84
Singles: 12-inch
LONDON 4-6 84
Singles: 7-inch
LONDON 3-4 84

HARVEY, Tina
Singles: 7-inch
UK 3-5 72-73
LPs: 10/12-inch
UK 8-10 73

HARVEY & ANN
Singles: 7-inch
HARVEY (121 "What Can You Do Now") 20-30 63
Members: Harvey Fuqua; Ann Bogan.
Also see HARVEY
Also see LOVE, PEACE & HAPPINESS

HARVEY & DOC & DWELLERS
(Phil Spector)
Singles: 7-inch
ANNETTE (1002 "Oh Baby") 50-100 64
Also see HARVEY, Phil

HARVEY & MOONGLOWS
(Harvey Fuqua)
Singles: 7-inch
CHESS (1705 "Ten Commandments of Love") 15-25 58
CHESS (1738 "Mama Loocie") 10-20 59
Also see HARVEY
Also see MOONGLOWS

HARVEY & SEVEN SOUNDS
(Harvey Scales)
Singles: 7-inch
CUCA (1155 "New York City") 4-8 63
Also see SCALES, Harvey

HARVEY & SPINNERS
("Harvey [Former Lead of the Moonglows] & the Spinners")
TRI-PHI (1010 "She Loves Me So") 30-50 62
(Reissued sans credit to the Spinners.)
Also see HARVEY
Also see SPINNERS

HARVEY AVERNE DOZEN
Singles: 7-inch
UP-TITE 4-6 69

HARVEY BOYS P&R '57
Singles: 78 rpm
CADENCE 5-10 57
Singles: 7-inch
CADENCE 5-10 57

HASH BROWN: see BROWN, Hash

HASHIM D&D '84
Singles: 12-inch
CUTTING EDGE 4-6 84

HASKELL, Jack
(With the Honey Dreamers)
Singles: 7-inch
CAPRICE 5-8 58
THUNDERBIRD 6-12
LPs: 10/12-inch
STRAND (1020 "Jack Haskell Swings for Jack Parr") 20-30 60

HASKELL, Jimmie
(Jimmie Haskell Orchestra)
Singles: 78 rpm
IMPERIAL 10-15 57
Singles: 7-inch
CAPITOL 4-6 63
IMPERIAL 10-15 57-58
LPs: 10/12-inch
CAPITOL 15-25 63
Also see JIMMIE & NIGHT HOPPERS

HASKELL, Jimmy
Singles: 7-inch
ABC 3-5 71
LPs: 10/12-inch
ABC 8-12 71
Members: Denny Doherty; Jimmy Witherspoon; Merry Clayton; Clydie King.
Also see CLAYTON, Merry
Also see DOHERTY, Denny
Also see KING, Clydie
Also see WITHERSPOON, Jimmy

HASKELL, May
Singles: 7-inch
SUNDOWN (102 "Party Line") ...150-200 58

HASKINS, Al
Singles: 7-inch
SURE SHOT 4-8 66

HASLAM, Annie LP '77
Singles: 7-inch
SIRE 3-5 78
LPs: 10/12-inch
SIRE 8-12 77
Also see RENAISSANCE

HASSAN, Ali
(Al Pousan)
Singles: 7-inch
PHILLIES (103 "Chop Stick") 10-20 62

HASSAN & 7-11 R&B/D&D '84
Singles: 7-inch
EASY STREET 3-4 84

HASSELHOFF, David
Singles: 7-inch
SILVER BLUE 3-4 84
Picture Sleeves
SILVER BLUE 3-4 84
LPs: 10/12-inch
SILVER BLUE 5-10 84

HASSILEV, Alex
Singles: 7-inch
RCA 6-12 65

HASSLES
Singles: 7-inch
U.A. 8-12 67-69
Picture Sleeves
U.A. 10-12 67-69
LPs: 10/12-inch
LIBERTY 8-10 81
U.A. (6631 "The Hassles") 20-30 68
U.A. (6699 "Hour of the Wolf") 20-30 68
Members: William (Billy) Joel; Howard Blauvelt; Johathan Small; Richard McKenner; John Dizek.
Also see JOEL, Billy

HASTINGS, Count
Singles: 78 rpm
DARL (1006 "The Count") 8-10 56
Singles: 7-inch
DARL (1006 "The Count") 10-20 56

HATCH, Tony
Singles: 7-inch
LONDON 4-8 62

HATCHER, Harley
Singles: 7-inch
MGM 3-5 73
NEW CELEBRITY 3-6 69
PHILIPS 3-6 69
SIDEWALK (2 "All I Need Is You") 5-8 65
(With Davie Allan.)
LPs: 10/12-inch
MGM 8-15 73
SMASH 12-15 69
Also see ALLAN, Davie

HATCHER, Roger R&B '76
(Little Roger Hatcher)
Singles: 7-inch
BROWN DOG 3-5 76
DOTTY'S 5-10 64
EXCELLO (2297 "Sweetest Girl in the World") 15-25 68

HATCHER, Will
(Willie Hatcher)
Singles: 7-inch
COLUMBIA (44259 "Good Things Come to Those Who Wait") 30-40 67
KING (6360 "Head Over Heels") 15-25 70
THELMA 15-20 63

HATFIELD, Bobby P&R '69
Singles: 7-inch
MOONGLOW (220 "I Need a Girl") 10-15 63
VERVE 5-10 68-69
W.B. 3-5 72
LPs: 10/12-inch
MGM 10-15 71
Also see RIGHTEOUS BROTHERS

HATFIELD, Chuck
Singles: 7-inch
FORTUNE (175 "Steel Wool") 15-25 58

HATFIELD, David
Singles: 7-inch
FRATERNITY 3-5 80

HATFIELD, Dixie
Singles: 7-inch
MARK E (2511 "Skool Daze") 10-15 63

HATFIELD, Jean
Singles: 7-inch
CAMEO 10-20 60s
PHAROAH 8-12

HATFIELD, Overton
(Gene Autry)
Singles: 78 rpm
Columbia (15987 "A Gangster's Warning") 50-75 30s
Also see AUTRY, Gene

HATFIELD, Vince & Diane C&W '81
Singles: 7-inch
SOUNDWAVES 3-4 81-83

HATFIELD & NORTH
LPs: 10/12-inch
VIRGIN 8-10 73
Also see CARAVAN

HATFIELDS
Singles: 7-inch
WYE 5-8 63

HATFIELDS
Singles: 7-inch
CHA CHA (754 "Yes I Do") 50-75 67
CHA CHA (760 "The Kid from Cincy") 50-75 67

HATFUL OF RAIN
Singles: 7-inch
SENTAR 5-8 67

HATHAWAY, Donny P&R/R&B '70
Singles: 7-inch
ATCO 3-6 69-78
LPs: 10/12-inch
ATCO 8-10 70-78
ATLANTIC 5-10 80
Also see FLACK, Roberta, & Donny Hathaway

HATHAWAY, Donny, & June Conquest P&R '72
Singles: 7-inch
CURTOM (1971 "I Thank You") 3-5 72
(Previously issued as by June & Donnie.)
Members: Donny Hathaway; June Conquest.
Also see CONQUEST, June
Also see JUNE & DONNIE

HATHAWAY, Donny, & Margie Joseph
Singles: 7-inch
ATCO 3-5 72
Also see HATHAWAY, Donny
Also see JOSEPH, Margie

HATHAWAY, Lalah LP '90
LPs: 10/12-inch
VIRGIN 5-8 90

HATHAWAY, Maggie: see ROBINS

HATTON, Gene
Singles: 7-inch
KING 4-8 65

HAUCK, Tim
LPs: 10/12-inch
COLUMBIA 8-10 70

HAUNTED
Singles: 7-inch
AMY (959 "1-2-5") 25-35 66
MARK II (7001 "Vapeur Mauve") ...15-25 68
QUALITY (1814 "1-2-5") 25-50 66
(Canadian.)
QUALITY (1840 "I Can Only Give You Everything") 25-50 66
(Canadian.)
TRANS-WORLD (1674 "Searching for My Baby") 25-50 67
(Canadian.)
TRANS-WORLD (1682 "Come On Home") 25-50 67
(Canadian.)
TRANS-WORLD (1702 "Land of Make Believe") 25-50 68
(Canadian.)
LPs: 10/12-inch
EVA (12029 "Vapeur Mauve") 10-20 84
TRANSWORLD (6701 "The Haunted") 600-800 66
(Canadian.)
VOXX 5-10
Members: Dave Wynne; Bob Burgess.
Also see INFLUENCE
Also see ORIGINAL HAUNTED

HAUSER, Bruce, & Sawmill Creek Band C&W '85
Singles: 7-inch
COWBOY 3-4 85-86
Also see SAWMILL CREEK

HAVANA 3 A.M. LP '91
LPs: 10/12-inch
I.R.S. 5-8 91

HAVEN, Marc, & Aquarians
Singles: 7-inch
VILLA-YORE (201 "Janice") 250-350

HAVEN, Shirley, & Four Jacks
Singles: 78 rpm
FEDERAL 50-100 52
Singles: 7-inch
FEDERAL (12092 "Troubles of My Own") 200-400 52
Also see FOUR JACKS
Also see WILLIAMS, Cora, & Four Jacks / Shirley Haven & Four Jacks

HAVEN KNIGHTS: see 4 HAVEN KNIGHTS

HAVENS
Singles: 7-inch
POPLAR (123 "Want You") 15-25 63

HAVENS, Bobby, & Country Company C&W '78
Singles: 7-inch
CIN KAY 3-5 78

HAVENS, Don, & Hi-Fi's
Singles: 7-inch
TONE-CRAFT (205 "Bread and Butter") 10-20 60s

HAVENS, Richie LP '68
Singles: 7-inch
A&M 3-5 77
DOUGLAS 4-8 68
ELEKTRA 3-4 80
MGM 3-5 70
ODE '70 .... 3-5 72
STORMY FOREST 3-5 70-74
VERVE/FOLKWAYS 4-8 66-68
VERVE/FORECAST 4-8 68-69
LPs: 10/12-inch
A&M 8-10 76
DOUGLAS 12-15 68
ELEKTRA 5-10 80
MGM 8-10 70
ODE '70 .... 8-10 73
RBI 5-10 87
STORMY FOREST 10-12 69-74
VERVE/FOLKWAYS 12-15 67-68
VERVE/FORECAST 12-15 67-69

HAWK
Singles: 7-inch
SUNBURST 3-6 73
Also see DEE, Joey

HAWK, The
(Jerry Lee Lewis)
Singles: 7-inch
PHILLIPS INT'L (3559 "In the Mood") 15-25 60
Also see LEWIS, Jerry Lee

HAWK, Tommy
Singles: 7-inch
NAP 4-6
RITA 5-10 61

HAWK & RANDELAS
Singles: 7-inch
RIVERTON 8-12 65

HAWKETTS
Singles: 78 rpm
CHESS 25-50 55
Singles: 7-inch
CHESS (1591 "Mardi Gras Mambo") 50-75 55
Also see MOONBEEMS / Hawkettes

Also see NEVILLE BROTHERS

HAWKEYE
Singles: 7-inch
BEANTOWN 3-5

HAWKINS, Bobby
Singles: 7-inch
CUCA (1256 "Root Beer") 15-25 66
CUCA (6533 "White Lightnin' ") 10-20 65
CUCA (6563 "Hawaiian War Chant") 15-25 65
CUCA (6681 "Just Between the Two of Us") 10-20 66
WHITE LIGHTNIN' (500 "Root Beer") 15-25 60s

HAWKINS, Buddy, & Do Re Me Trio
Singles: 7-inch
CARLTON 8-10 58
Also see DO-RE-ME TRIO

HAWKINS, Dale P&R/R&B '57
(With the Escapades)
Singles: 78 rpm
CHECKER (843 "See You Soon Baboon") 20-30 56
CHECKER (863 "Suzi-Q") 20-30 57
CHECKER (876 "Baby, Baby") 20-30 57
CHECKER (892 "Little Pig") 25-50 58
CHECKER (900 "La-Do-Dada") 25-50 58
CHECKER (906 "A House, a Car, and a Wedding Ring") 40-60 58
CHECKER (913 "Someday One Day") 50-75 58
CHECKER (923 "Ain't That Lovin' You Baby") 50-100 59
Note: Checker 78s as late as #937 exist with the checkerboard design at top, as opposed to 45s which switched designs beginning with #876. Also, 78s as early as #900 have Checker name vertically on left side.
Singles: 7-inch
ABC-PAR (10668 "La La Song") 8-12 65
ATLANTIC (1022 "Peaches") 10-20 61
ATLANTIC (2126 "Stay at Home Lulu") 10-20 61
ATLANTIC (2150 "What a Feeling") 10-20 62
BELL (807 "Little Rain Cloud") 5-10 69
CHECKER (843 "See You Soon Baboon") 30-40 56
(Maroon label, checkerboard design at top.)
CHECKER (843 "See You Soon Baboon") 15-25 57
(Maroon label, "Checker" logo vertical on left.)
CHECKER (863 "Suzi-Q") 20-30 57
(Maroon label, checkerboard design at top.)
CHECKER (863 "Suzi-Q") 10-20 57
(Maroon label, "Checker" logo vertical on left.)
CHECKER (876 "Baby, Baby") 25-35 57
(Maroon label, checkerboard design at top.)
CHECKER (876 "Baby, Baby") 10-20 57
(Maroon label, "Checker" logo vertical on left.)
CHECKER (892 "Little Pig") 20-30 58
(Maroon label.)
CHECKER (900 "La-Do-Dada") 20-30 58
(Maroon label.)
CHECKER (906 "A House, a Car, and a Wedding Ring") 20-30 58
(Maroon label.)
CHECKER (913 "Someday One Day") 20-30 58
(Maroon label.)
CHECKER (914 "Take My Heart") .15-25 59
(Maroon label.)
CHECKER (916 "Class Cutter") 20-25 59
(Maroon label.)
CHECKER (916 "Yea-Yea [Class Cutter]") 15-20 59
(Maroon label. Note title variation.)
CHECKER (923 "Ain't That Lovin' You Baby") 15-25 59
(Maroon label.)
CHECKER (929 "Our Turn") 10-20 59
(Maroon label.)
CHECKER (934 "Back to School Blues") 10-20 59
(Maroon label.)
CHECKER (940 "Hot Dog") 10-20 60
(Maroon label.)
CHECKER (944 "Poor Little Rhode Island") 10-20 60
(Maroon label.)
CHECKER (962 "Linda") 10-20 61
(Maroon label.)
CHECKER (970 "I Want to Love You") 10-20 61
(Maroon label.)
CHECKER (Blue label) 5-10 60s
(Reissues.)
LINCOLN (002 "Baby We Had It") ...8-12
TILT (781 "Money Honey") 10-20 61
TILT (783 "Wish I Hadn't Called Home") 10-20 61
ZONK (1002 "Gotta Dance") 10-20 62
Picture Sleeves
CHECKER (944 "Poor Little Rhode Island") 150-250 60
LPs: 10/12-inch
BELL (6036 "L.A., Memphis and Tyler, Texas") 20-30 69
CHESS (1429 "Suzy-Q") 500-1000 58
ROULETTE (R-25175 "Let's All Twist at Miami Beach Peppermint Lounge") 50-100 62
(Monaural.)
ROULETTE (SR-25175 "Let's All Twist at Miami Beach Peppermint Lounge") 75-125 62
(Stereo.)
Also see BUCHANAN, Roy
Also see BURTON, James
Also see FITZGERALD, Felder

HAWKINS, Debi C&W '75
Singles: 7-inch
W.B. ... 3-5 75-77

HAWKINS, Dolores
(With Don Costa & Orchestra)
Singles: 78 rpm
EPIC ... 4-8 55-57
OKEH ... 4-8 57
Singles: 7-inch
EPIC ... 5-10 55-57
OKEH ... 5-10 57
EPs: 7-inch
EPIC ... 10-20 55-57
LPs: 10/12-inch
EPIC (1119 "Meet Delores Hawkins") ... 20-30 55
EPIC (3250 "Dolores") ... 20-30 57
Also see COSTA, Don
Also see MELLO-LARKS & Delores Hawkins

HAWKINS, Edwin, Singers P&R/R&B/LP '69
Singles: 7-inch
BUDDAH ... 3-5 71-72
PAVILION ... 3-6 69
LPs: 10/12-inch
BUDDAH ... 8-12 71-72
PAVILION ... 10-12 69
Members: Edwin Hawkins; Walter Hawkins; Tramaine Hawkins; Daniel Hawkins; Elaine Kelley; Norma King; Dorothy Morrison; Barbara Gill; Shirley Miller; Edwin Miller; Donald Henderson.
Also see ISLEY BROTHERS / Brooklyn Bridge
Also see MELANIE
Also see MORRISON, Dorothy

HAWKINS, Erskine P&R '36
(Erskine Hawkins Quintet)
Singles: 78 rpm
BLUEBIRD ... 5-15 39-44
BRUNSWICK ... 5-10 53
DECCA ... 5-10 56
CORAL ... 5-10 50-54
KING ... 5-10 51-52
VICTOR/RCA ... 5-10 45-52
VOCALION ... 5-15 36-37
Singles: 7-inch
BRUNSWICK ... 10-20 53
DECCA ... 10-20 56
CORAL ... 10-20 52-54
KING (4514 "Steel Guitar Rag") ... 15-25 52
(Black vinyl.)
KING (4514 "Steel Guitar Rag") ... 30-50 52
(Colored vinyl.)
KING (4522 "Down Home Jump") .. 15-25 52
(Black vinyl.)
KING (4522 "Down Home Jump") .. 30-50 52
(Colored vinyl.)
KING (4574 "New Gin Mill Special") ... 15-25 52
KING (4597 "The Way You Look Tonight") ... 15-25 52
KING (4671 "My Baby Please") ... 15-25 53
RCA (0169 "After Hours") ... 10-15 59
(Gold Standard Series.)
EPs: 7-inch
RCA (5095 "After Hours") ... 15-25 59
(Gold Standard Series.)
LPs: 10/12-inch
CORAL (56051 "After Hours") ... 50-100 54
DECCA (4081 "Hawk Blows at Midnight") ... 20-30 61
IMPERIAL (9191 "25 Golden Years of Jazz") ... 20-30 62
(Monaural.)
IMPERIAL (9197 "25 Golden Years of Jazz, Vol. 2") ... 20-30 62
(Monaural.)
IMPERIAL (12191 "25 Golden Years of Jazz") ... 25-35 62
(Stereo.)
IMPERIAL (12197 "25 Golden Years of Jazz, Vol. 2") ... 25-35 62
(Stereo.)
RCA (2227 "After Hours") ... 30-4 60
Also see DASH, Julian

HAWKINS, Erskine, & Four Hawks
Singles: 78 rpm
KING (4671 "My Baby, Please") ... 25-50 53
KING (4686 "Double Shot") ... 15-25 53
Singles: 7-inch
KING (4671 "My Baby, Please") ... 50-100 53
KING (4686 "Double Shot") ... 50-75 53
Also see HAWKINS, Erskine

HAWKINS, Hawkshaw C&W '48
Singles: 78 rpm
KING ... 4-8 46-53
RCA ... 4-8 55-57
Singles: 7-inch
COLUMBIA ... 4-8 59-62
KING (900 thru 1100 series) ... 5-10 50-53
KING (5000 series) ... 4-8 60-64
RCA ... 5-10 55-59
STARDAY ... 3-5 71
EPs: 7-inch
KING ... 8-12 53
LPs: 10/12-inch
CAMDEN ... 10-15 64-66
HARMONY ... 10-15 63
KING (587 "Hawkshaw Hawkins, Vol. 1") ... 40-60 58
KING (592 "Hawkshaw Hawkins Sings Grand Ole Opry Favorites, Vol. 2") ... 40-60 58
KING (599 "Hawkshaw Hawkins") ... 40-60 59
KING (808 "All New Hawkshaw Hawkins") ... 20-40 63
KING (858 "Taken From Our Vaults, Vol. 1") ... 15-20 63
KING (858 "Taken From Our Vaults, Vol. 2") ... 15-20 63
KING (858 "Taken From Our Vaults, Vol. 3") ... 15-20 64
KING (1043 "Lonesome 7-7203") ... 8-12 69
LA BREA (8020 "Hawkshaw Hawkins") ... 25-50 60s
NASHVILLE ... 8-12 69
STARDAY ... 5-10 77
Also see CLINE, Patsy / Cowboy Copas / Hawkshaw Hawkins
Also see COPAS, Cowboy / Hawkshaw Hawkins

HAWKINS, Hillary
Singles: 7-inch
STONEWAY ... 10-15

HAWKINS, Jalacy
(Jay Hawkins)
Singles: 7-inch
MERCURY (70549 "This Is All") ... 50-75 55
TIMELY (1004 "Baptize Me in Wine") ... 50-75 54
TIMELY (1005 "Please Try to Understand") ... 50-75 54
WING (90005 "Well, I Tried") ... 20-30 55
WING (90055 "Even Though") ... 20-30 56
Also see HAWKINS, Screamin' Jay

HAWKINS, Jennell R&B '61
Singles: 7-inch
AMAZON ... 8-12 61-63
DYNAMIC ... 8-12 61
DYNAMITE ... 8-12 61
OLDIES 45 ... 4-6
LPs: 10/12-inch
AMAZON (AM-1001 "Many Moods of Jenny") ... 25-50 61
(Monaural.)
AMAZON (AS-1001 "Many Moods of Jenny") ... 40-60 61
(Stereo.)
AMAZON (AM-1002 "Moments to Remember") ... 25-50 62
(Monaural.)
AMAZON (AS-1002 "Moments to Remember") ... 40-60 62
Also see RICKIE & JENNELL

HAWKINS, Jerry
Singles: 7-inch
EBB ... 5-10 59

HAWKINS, Jimmy
Singles: 7-inch
KEM (2751 "Sure Do") ... 10-15 57
(Colored vinyl.)
Picture Sleeves
KEM (2751 "Sure Do") ... 10-20 57

HAWKINS, Nippy, & Nip-Tones
("The Nation's Most Promising Group")
Singles: 7-inch
LORRAINE (1001 "Angie") ... 30-50 65

HAWKINS, Ronnie P&R/R&B '59
(With the Hawks)
Singles: 7-inch
COTILLION ... 3-5 70-71
HAWK ... 5-10
MONUMENT ... 3-5 72-73
QUALITY ... 10-20
(Canadian.)
ROULETTE (4154 "Forty Days") ... 10-15 59
ROULETTE (SSR-4154 "Forty Days") ... 25-50 59
(Stereo.)
ROULETTE (4177 "Mary Lou") ... 10-15 59
ROULETTE (SSR-4177 "Mary Lou") ... 25-50 59
(Stereo.)
ROULETTE (4209 thru 4502) ... 5-10 59-63
YORKVILLE ... 8-12
LPs: 10/12-inch
ACCORD ... 5-10 83
COTILLION ... 10-15 70-71
MONUMENT ... 8-12 72-75
ROULETTE (25078 "Ronnie Hawkins") ... 75-125 59
(Black vinyl. Monaural.)
ROULETTE (SR-25078 "Ronnie Hawkins") ... 100-200 59
(Black vinyl. Stereo.)
ROULETTE (25078 "Ronnie Hawkins") ... 300-400 59
(Red vinyl.)
ROULETTE (25102 "Mr. Dynamo") ... 75-125 60
(Black vinyl. Monaural.)
ROULETTE (SR-25102 "Mr. Dynamo") ... 100-200 60
(Black vinyl. Stereo.)
ROULETTE (25102 "Mr. Dynamo") ... 300-400 60
(Red vinyl.)
ROULETTE (25120 "Folk Ballads") ... 50-100 60
(Monaural.)
ROULETTE (SR-25120 "Folk Ballads") ... 100-200 60
(Stereo.)
ROULETTE (25137 "Songs of Hank Williams") ... 50-100 60
(Monaural.)
ROULETTE (SR-25137 "Songs of Hank Williams") ... 100-200 60
(Stereo.)
ROULETTE (25255 "Ronnie Hawkins") ... 75-125
(Canadian.)
ROULETTE (25390 "Mojo Man") . 50-100
(Canadian.)
ROULETTE (42045 "Best of Ronnie Hawkins") ... 25-35 70
U.A. ... 5-10 79
Also see BAND
Also see LENNON, John
Also see LEVON & HAWKS
Also see ROCKIN' RONALD & REBELS

HAWKINS, Roy R&B '50
Singles: 78 rpm
DOWN TOWN (2018 "Christmas Blues") ... 15-25 48
DOWN TOWN (2020 "It's Too Late to Change") ... 15-25 48
DOWN TOWN (2024 "Forty Jim") . 15-25 48
DOWN TOWN (2025 "Quarter to One") ... 15-25 48
MODERN ... 15-25 48-54
RPM ... 15-25 54
Singles: 7-inch
KENT ... 5-10 62
MODERN (826 "The Thrill Is Gone") ... 40-60 51
MODERN (852 "Gloom and Misery All Around") ... 40-60 51
MODERN (853 "I Don't Know Just What to Do") ... 40-60 51
MODERN (859 "Highway 59") ... 25-40 52
MODERN (869 "Doin' All Right") ... 25-40 52
MODERN (898 "Bad Luck Is Falling") ... 25-40 54
RPM (440 "Is It Too Late") ... 25-30 54
RHYTHM (120 "I Hate to Be Alone") ... 30-50 58
Also see ROYAL HAWK

HAWKINS, Sam R&B '65
Singles: 7-inch
ARNOLD ... 4-8 63
BLUE CAT (112 "Hold on Baby") ... 5-10 65
DECCA ... 8-12 59-61
EPIC (10520 "Dream Lover") ... 4-8 69
GONE (5042 "King of Fools") ... 15-25 58
GONE (5054 "When Nobody Loves You") ... 15-25 59
SHELL ... 4-8
Session: Ronnie Bright; J.R. Bailey; Freddie Barksdale.
Also see BAILEY, J.R.
Also see HO-DADS

HAWKINS, Screamin' Jay
(Jalacy Hawkins)
Singles: 78 rpm
APOLLO ... 10-20 56-57
GRAND ... 10-20 57
OKEH ... 10-20 56-57
Singles: 7-inch
APOLLO ... 10-20 56-58
DECCA (32100 "I Put a Spell on You") ... 25-35 67
ENRICA ... 5-10 62
EPIC ... 5-10 63
GRAND ... 10-20 57
OKEH ... 10-20 56-57
PHILIPS ... 3-5 70
PROVIDENCE ... 4-8
QUEEN BEE ... 3-5 73
RCA ... 3-5 74
LPs: 10/12-inch
EPIC (3448 "At Home with Screamin' Jay Hawkins") ... 150-250 56
EPIC (3457 "I Put a Spell on You") ... 100-150 57
EPIC (26457 "I Put a Spell on You") ... 15-25 69
HOT LINE (10024 "Portrait of a Man and His Woman") ... 15-25
MIDNIGHT ... 5-10 88
PHILIPS (600319 "What That Is") ... 15-25 69
PHILIPS (600336 "Screamin' Jay Hawkins") ... 15-25 70
SOUNDS of HAWAII (5015 "A Night at Forbidden City") ... 20-30
VERSATILE ... 8-10 78
Also see HAWKINS, Jalacy

HAWKINS, Screamin' Jay / Lillian Briggs
LPs: 10/12-inch
CORONET ... 10-15
Also see BRIGGS, Lillian

HAWKINS, Screamin' Jay, & Pat Newborn
Singles: 7-inch
CHANCELLOR ... 4-8 62
Also see HAWKINS, Screamin' Jay

HAWKINS, Screamin' Jay, & Fuzztones
LPs: 10/12-inch
MIDNIGHT ... 5-10
Also see FUZZTONES

HAWKINS, Walter & Selah
Singles: 7-inch
FANTASY ... 3-5 72

HAWKLORDS
LPs: 10/12-inch
CHARISMA ... 5-10 79

HAWKS
Singles: 78 rpm
IMPERIAL ... 50-75 54-55
MODERN ... 50-75 56
POST ... 100-200 55
Singles: 7-inch
IMPERIAL (5266 "Joe the Grinder") ... 200-300 54
IMPERIAL (5281 "She's All Right") ... 150-250 54
IMPERIAL (5292 "It Ain't That Way") ... 75-125 54
IMPERIAL (5306 "Nobody But You") ... 50-100 54
IMPERIAL (5317 "All Women Are the Same") ... 50-100 54
IMPERIAL (5332 "It's too Late Now") ... 50-100 55
MODERN (990 "It'a All Over") ... 200-300 56
POST (2004 "Why Oh Why") ... 500-750 55

HAWKS
Singles: 7-inch
DEL-FI (4108 "Fussy") ... 20-30 58
Members: Don Cole; Loy Clingman.
Also see CLINGMAN, Loy
Also see COLE, Don

HAWKS
Singles: 7-inch
MALA (401 "Cupcake") ... 15-25 59

HAWKS
Singles: 7-inch
ABC-PAR (10116 "Grissle") ... 20-30 60

HAWKS P&R '81
Singles: 7-inch
COLUMBIA ... 3-4 81
LPs: 10/12-inch
COLUMBIA ... 5-10 81

HAWKS, Billy
LPs: 10/12-inch
PRESTIGE ... 12-15 67

HAWKS, Mickey C&W '89
(With Moon Mullins & His Night Raiders; "Night Raiders Featuring Mickey Hanks")
Singles: 7-inch
C-HORSE ... 3-4 89
HUNCH (347 "Hidi Hidi Hidi") ... 25-50 61
PROFILE (4002 "Bip Bop Boom") ... 75-125 58
PROFILE (4007 "Hidi Hidi Hidi") .. 75-125 59
(Some copies mistakenly credit "Mickey Hanks.")
PROFILE (4010 "Screamin' Mimi Jeanie") ... 50-75 59
Also see MULLINS, Moon

HAWKWIND LP '73
Singles: 7-inch
ATCO ... 3-5 75
U.A. ... 3-5 71-73
LPs: 10/12-inch
ATCO ... 8-10 75
SIRE ... 5-10 78
U.A. ... 10-15 71-74
Also see MOTORHEAD

HAWLEY, Deane P&R '60
(With the Crystals)
Singles: 7-inch
DORE ... 8-12 59-61
LIBERTY ... 8-12 61-62
SUNDOWN ... 4-8
VALOR (2003 "Don't Keep Me Guessin' ") ... 25-35 59
W.B. ... 4-8 64

HAWLEY, Linda
Singles: 7-inch
EXCALIBUR (110 "Use Your Head") ... 10-20

HAWN, Goldie
Singles: 7-inch
REPRISE ... 3-5 72
Picture Sleeves
REPRISE ... 4-8 72
LPs: 10/12-inch
REPRISE ... 8-12 72

HAWTHORNE, Jim "Specs"
Singles: 7-inch
BINGO ... 5-10 59

HAY, Colin James P&R/LP '87
(Colin Hay Band)
Singles: 7-inch
COLUMBIA ... 3-4 87
Picture Sleeves
COLUMBIA ... 3-4 87
LPs: 10/12-inch
COLUMBIA ... 5-10 87
MCA ... 5-10 90
Also see MEN AT WORK

HAY, Timothy
Singles: 7-inch
RCA ... 4-8 61

HAYDEN, Gil
Singles: 7-inch
V-TONE ... 8-12

HAYDEN, Ronnie
Singles: 7-inch
CAMAY ... 4-8 61-62
JOSIE ... 5-10 59

HAYDEN, Willie: see HEYDEN, Willie

HAYDEN SISTERS
Singles: 7-inch
ROYCE (0007 "Silent Tears") ... 20-30 60
TILT ... 5-10 61
Member: Martha Hayden.

HAYDOCK, Ron, & Boppers
Singles: 7-inch
CHA CHA (701 "Be-Bop-a Jean") ... 50-100 59
(Red label.)
CHA CHA (704 "Baby Say Bye-Bye") ... 50-100 59
CHA CHA (785 "Be-Bop-A Jean") ... 100-200 59
(White label.)
CHA CHA (1002 "In the Mood") ... 20-30 59

HAYDON, Bob
Singles: 7-inch
KNIGHT (1046 "Suzanne") ... 10-15

HAYES, Barnie
Singles: 7-inch
DOUBLE SOUL ... 5-10

HAYES, Bernie
Singles: 7-inch
BRIGHT STAR (500 "Soul Pearl") ... 8-12 67
VOLT ... 4-8 70

HAYES, Bill
(Henry Hayes)
Singles: 78 rpm
JADE (211 "Just") ... 10-20 50
SITTIN' IN WITH (551 "I Want to Cry") ... 15-25 50
SITTIN' IN WITH (560 "I'm Sorry I Was Reckless") ... 15-25 50
Also see HAYES, Henry

HAYES, Bill P&R '55
(With the Archie Bleyer's Orchestra)
Singles: 78 rpm
ABC-PAR ... 8-12 57
CADENCE ... 5-8 55-56
MGM ... 3-6 55
Singles: 7-inch
ABC-PAR (Except 9895) ... 10-15 57
ABC-PAR (9895 "Bop Boy") ... 40-60 58
ABLE ... 4-8
BARNABY ... 3-5 76
CADENCE ... 10-20 55-56
DAYBREAK ... 3-5 74
KAPP ... 5-10 59
MGM ... 5-10 55
SHAW ... 4-6 65
Picture Sleeves
ABC-PAR ... 8-12 57
CADENCE (1/1256 "Ballad of Davy Crockett") ... 20-30 55
(Sleeve is numbered CCS-1 ["Cadence Children's Series], disc is 1256.)
EPs: 7-inch
MGM (312 "Bill Hayes") ... 10-20 55
LPs: 10/12-inch
ABC-PAR (194 "Bill Hayes Sings the Best of Walt Disney") ... 25-50 57
DAYBREAK ... 5-10 74
KAPP ... 10-20 60
Also see BLEYER, Archie

HAYES, Bruce
Singles: 7-inch
DWAIN (812 "Sing with Bruce Hayes") ... 5-10 60

HAYES, Carolyn, & Four Tops
Singles: 78 rpm
CHATEAU ... 25-50 55
Singles: 7-inch
CHATEAU (2001 "Baby Say You Love Me") ... 50-100 55
Also see CARROLL, Delores, & Four Tops
Also see FOUR TOPS

HAYES, Edgar, & Stardusters
Singles: 78 rpm
EXCLUSIVE ... 10-20 49

HAYES, Gabby
Singles: 78 rpm
CORAL (1312 "Tall Tales") ... 5-8 54
Singles: 7-inch
CORAL (1312 "Tall Tales") ... 6-12 54
Picture Sleeves
CORAL (1312 "Tall Tales") ... 10-20 54

HAYES, Gini
Singles: 7-inch
NRC ... 4-8 60

HAYES, Henry
(Henry Hayes' Four Kings)
Singles: 78 rpm
ALADDIN (157 "All Alone Blues") .. 15-25 46
ALADDIN (158 "Angel Child Blues") ... 15-25 46
GOLD STAR (633 "Bowlegged Angeline") ... 15-25 48
SWING (414 "Bowlegged Angeline") ... 15-25 48
Singles: 7-inch
KANGAROO ... 10-15 61
ZEBRA ... 8-12 59
Also see BROWN, James "Widemouth"
Also see CAMPBELL, Carl
Also see HAYES, Bill
Also see KING TUT
Also see NIXON, Elmore

HAYES, Isaac P&R/R&B/LP '69
(Isaac Hayes Movement)
Singles: 12-inch
COLUMBIA ... 4-6 85-86
Singles: 7-inch
ABC ... 3-5 77
BRUNSWICK ... 4-8 64
COLUMBIA ... 3-4 85-87
ENTERPRISE ... 3-6 69-74
HBS ... 3-5 75-76
POLYDOR ... 3-4 78-80
SAN AMERICAN ... 3-5 70
STAX ... 3-6 78
YOUNGSTOWN ... 15-25 60s
(Title and selection number not known.)
LPs: 10/12-inch
ABC-PAR ... 8-10 75-77
ATLANTIC ... 8-10 72
COLUMBIA ... 5-10 86
ENTERPRISE ... 10-12 68-75
HBS ... 8-12 75-77
POLYDOR ... 5-10 77-81
STAX ... 5-10 77-82

Also see REDDING, Otis

HAYES, Isaac, & Millie Jackson R&B/LP '79
Singles: 7-inch
POLYDOR.... 3-4 79-80
LPs: 10/12-inch
POLYDOR.... 5-10 79
Also see JACKSON, Millie

HAYES, Isaac, & David Porter R&B '72
Singles: 7-inch
ENTERPRISE.... 3-5 72
Also see PORTER, David

HAYES, Isaac, & Dionne Warwick R&B/LP '77
Singles: 7-inch
ABC.... 3-5 77
LPs: 10/12-inch
ABC.... 10-15 77
Also see HAYES, Isaac
Also see WARWICK, Dionne

HAYES, Jay
Singles: 7-inch
SOLID GOLD (715 "Tellin' Lies") ...40-60

HAYES, Jerry
Singles: 7-inch
CAPITOL.... 4-6 69
CRAZY HORSE.... 3-5 70

HAYES, Jimmy
Singles: 7-inch
HAPPY HEARTS (141 "Tom Cat Boogie").... 20-30 62

HAYES, Jimmy, & Soul Surfers
Singles: 7-inch
IMPERIAL (5986 "Summer Surfin' ").... 10-20 63

HAYES, Linda R&B '53
(With the Platters; with Tony Williams; with Flairs; with Red Callender Sextet; with Twigs)
Singles: 78 rpm
ANTLER.... 10-20 56
DECCA.... 10-20 55
HOLLYWOOD (Except 1032).... 10-20 52-55
HOLLYWOOD (1032 "Our Love Is Forever Blessed").... 20-30 55
KING.... 10-20 55
Singles: 7-inch
ANTLER (4000 "I Had a Dream")...30-40 56
DECCA (29644 "Our Love's Forever Blessed").... 20-30 55
HOLLYWOOD (200 "I've Tried So Hard").... 25-50 52
HOLLYWOOD (244 "Yes I Know") .20-30 53
HOLLYWOOD (246 "Big City").... 20-30 53
HOLLYWOOD (407 "What's It to You, Jack").... 20-30 53
HOLLYWOOD (1003 "Take Me Back").... 20-30 53
HOLLYWOOD (1009 "No Next Time").... 20-30 54
HOLLYWOOD (1016 "Play It Right").... 20-30 54
HOLLYWOOD (1019 "Non Cooperation").... 20-30 54
HOLLYWOOD (1027 "Darling Angel").... 20-30 55
HOLLYWOOD (1032 "Our Love Is Forever Blessed").... 40-60 55
KING (4752 "My Name Ain't Annie").... 50-100 54
KING (4773 "Please Have Mercy").... 35-50 55
Also see FLAIRS
Also see MOORE, Johnny, & Linda Hayes
Also see PLATTERS
Also see HUGHES, Ben
Also see WOODS, Sonny

HAYES, Malcolm
Singles: 7-inch
CHATTAHOOCHEE (686 "Searchin' for My Baby").... 50-75 65
LIBERTY (55943 "It's Not Easy").... 10-15 67
OKEH (7299 "Baby Please Don't Leave Me").... 10-15 67

HAYES, Marcel
EPs: 7-inch
GUYDEN.... 5-10

HAYES, Otis, Trio
Singles: 7-inch
TANGERINE (954 "Gettin' It").... 8-12

HAYES, Peter Lind P&R '49
Singles: 78 rpm
DECCA.... 4-6 49
Singles: 7-inch
DOT.... 4-8 59

HAYES, Peter Lind, & Mary Healy
Singles: 7-inch
COLUMBIA.... 4-8 55
ESSEX.... 4-8 53
KAPP.... 4-8 56
Also see HAYES, Peter Lind

HAYES, Richard P&R '49
Singles: 78 rpm
MERCURY.... 5-10 49-55
Singles: 7-inch
ABC-PAR.... 15-25 56
COLUMBIA.... 10-20 60-61
CONTEMPO.... 4-6 64
DECCA.... 4-6 61
MERCURY.... 10-20 50-55
EPs: 7-inch
MERCURY.... 15-25 54
LPs: 10/12-inch
MERCURY.... 20-30 55

HAYES, Richard, & Kitty Kallen P&R '51
Singles: 78 rpm
MERCURY.... 4-8 50-51
Singles: 7-inch
MERCURY.... 5-10 50-51
Also see HAYES, Richard
Also see KALLEN, Kitty

HAYES, Tommy
(With the 4 Seasons)
Singles: 7-inch
PHILIPS (40259 "Trance").... 20-30 65
Also see 4 SEASONS

HAYMAN, Richard, Orchestra P&R '53
(With Jan August)
Singles: 78 rpm
MERCURY.... 3-6 50-57
Singles: 7-inch
COMMAND.... 3-5 69
MGM.... 3-6 65
MERCURY.... 3-8 50-62
MUSICOR.... 3-5 73
EPs: 7-inch
MERCURY.... 4-8 51-59
LPs: 10/12-inch
ASCOT.... 5-10 64
COMMAND.... 5-10 69
MAINSTREAM.... 5-10 67
MERCURY.... 10-20 51-64
TIME.... 5-10 63-64
WING.... 5-10 62-64
Also see AUGUST, Jan

HAYMARKET RIOT
Singles: 7-inch
STATURE.... 10-20 60s

HAYMARKET RIOT
Singles: 7-inch
COCONUT GROOVE (204068 "Nine O'Clock").... 20-30 68

HAYMARKET SQUARE
LPs: 10/12-inch
CHAPARRAL (201 "Magic Lantern").... 500-1000 68
(Opinions vary as to whether "Magic Lantern" is the group name, or "Haymarket Square" is. Perhaps someone who's certain can tell us.)
Members: Gloria Lambert; Marc Swenson; Robert Homa; John Kowslowski.

HAYMES, Dick P&R/R&B '43
Singles: 78 rpm
CAPITOL.... 3-5 56
DECCA.... 4-8 43-54
Singles: 7-inch
CAPITOL.... 5-10 56
GNP.... 3-5 75
DECCA.... 5-10 50-54
WARWICK.... 3-6 60
EPs: 7-inch
CAPITOL.... 5-10 56
DECCA.... 5-10 50-54
LPs: 10/12-inch
AUDIOPHILE.... 5-10 78
CAPITOL.... 10-20 56
CORAL.... 4-6 73
DAYBREAK.... 5-10 74
DECCA.... 10-20 50-54
GLENDALE.... 5-10 84
MCA.... 5-10 76-83
WARWICK.... 8-15 60
Also see CLOONEY, Rosemary, & Dick Haymes
Also see CROSBY, Bing, Dick Haymes & Andrews Sisters
Also see FISHER, Eddie / Vic Damone / Dick Haymes
Also see JAMES, Harry, & Dick Haymes
Also see MERMAN, Ethel, Dick Haymes

HAYMES, Dick, & Andrews Sisters P&R '48
Singles: 78 rpm
DECCA.... 4-6 48
Also see ANDREWS SISTERS

HAYMES, Dick, & Judy Garland P&R '47
Singles: 78 rpm
DECCA.... 4-6 47
Also see GARLAND, Judy
Also see HAYMES, Dick

HAYNES, Earl
Singles: 7-inch
RON.... 4-8 60

HAYNES, Walter
Singles: 7-inch
JACK O' DIAMONDS (1008 "Tear Time").... 10-20 67

HAYNESS, Gayle
Singles: 7-inch
BANG (535 "Johnny Ander").... 4-8 66

HAYS, Larry
Singles: 7-inch
FABBRI.... 4-8 61

HAYSI FANTAYZEE P&R '83
Singles: 7-inch
RCA.... 3-4 83
Picture Sleeves
RCA.... 3-4 83
LPs: 10/12-inch
RCA.... 5-10 83
Members: Kate Garner; Jeremiah Healy.

HAYSLIP, F. Lee
Singles: 7-inch
ALBINO.... 10-20

HAYSTACKS BALBOA
LPs: 10/12-inch
POLYDOR.... 10-12 70

HAYWARD, Jerry
Singles: 7-inch
SYMBOL.... 4-8 63

HAYWARD, Justin P&R '75
Singles: 7-inch
COLUMBIA.... 3-5 78
DERAM.... 3-5 77
LPs: 10/12-inch
DERAM (4801 "Night Flight").... 8-12 80
DERAM (18073 "Songwriter").... 10-20 77
Also see MOUSKOURI, Nana

HAYWARD, Justin, & John Lodge P&R/LP '75
Singles: 7-inch
THRESHOLD.... 3-5 75
Picture Sleeves
THRESHOLD.... 3-5 75
LPs: 10/12-inch
THRESHOLD (14 "Blue Jays").... 10-15 75
THRESHOLD (101 "Blue Jays").... 15-25 75
(Promotional issue only. Interview with script.)
Also see HAYWARD, Justin
Also see LODGE, John
Also see MOODY BLUES

HAYWARD LEE: see LEE, HAYWARD

HAYWARD, Leon: see HAYWOOD, Leon

HAYWARD, Susan
Singles: 7-inch
MGM.... 5-10 55-56
Picture Sleeves
MGM (12148 "Happiness Is a Thing Called Joe").... 20-30 55
EPs: 7-inch
MGM.... 10-20 55

HAYWOOD, Ann
Singles: 7-inch
BROUGHAM.... 3-5 78

HAYWOOD, Joe
Singles: 7-inch
ENJOY (2013 "Warm and Tender Love").... 15-25 64
FURY (5052 "Debt of Love").... 10-20 63

HAYWOOD, Leon P&R/R&B '65
(Leon Hayward)
Singles: 12-inch
CASABLANCA.... 4-6 83
MCA.... 4-8 79
20TH FOX.... 4-6 80
Singles: 7-inch
ATLANTIC.... 3-5 71-72
CAPITOL.... 10-15 69-70
CASABLANCA.... 3-4 83
COLUMBIA.... 3-5 76-77
DECCA.... 4-6 67-68
EPIC.... 3-4 80-81
EVEJIM.... 4-8
FANTASY (581 "The Truth About Money").... 10-20 64
FAT FISH (8005 "Soul Cargo").... 15-25 66
GALAXY.... 4-6 67
IMPERIAL.... 5-15 65-66
MCA.... 3-5 77-79
MODERN.... 3-4 84
20TH FOX.... 3-5 74-80
LPs: 10/12-inch
CASABLANCA.... 5-10 83
DECCA.... 8-12 67
GALAXY.... 8-12 67
MCA.... 5-10 78-79
20TH FOX.... 5-10 73-80

HAZA, Ofra LP '89
LPs: 10/12-inch
SIRE.... 5-8 89-90

HAZARD C&W '83
Singles: 7-inch
W.B.... 3-4 83
Members: Bernie Faulkner; Wayne Davis; Bruce Dees.

HAZARD, Donna C&W '81
Singles: 7-inch
EXCELSIOR.... 3-4 81-82

HAZARD, Robert P&R/LP '83
Singles: 7-inch
RCA.... 3-4 83
LPs: 10/12-inch
RCA.... 5-10 83

HAZARDS
Singles: 7-inch
GROOVE (502 "Hey Joe").... 15-25 66
UNICORN ("Tinted Green").... 15-25
(Selection number not known.)

HAZE R&B '75
Singles: 7-inch
ASI.... 3-5 75
MOONSPELL.... 5-8 78
LPs: 10/12-inch
ASI.... 8-10 74

HAZEL, Eddie
Singles: 7-inch
W.B.... 3-5 77
LP: 10/12-inch
W.B.... 5-10 77
Also see PARLIAMENT

HAZELTONES
Singles: 7-inch
REALM.... 10-20

HAZLEWOOD, Eddie
Singles: 78 rpm
IMPERIAL.... 5-15 49

HAZLEWOOD, Lee
Singles: 7-inch
CAPITOL.... 3-5 72
JAMIE.... 5-10 60
LHI.... 4-6 68
MCA.... 3-4 79-80
MGM.... 4-6 66-67
REPRISE.... 4-6 65-68
SMASH.... 5-8 61
LPs: 10/12-inch
CAPITOL.... 8-10 72
HARMONY.... 8-12 67
MGM.... 10-15 66-67
MERCURY.... 10-20 63
REPRISE.... 10-15 64-65
Also see ANN-MARGRET & Lee Hazlewood
Also see S&H Scamps
Also see SHACKLEFORDS
Also see SINATRA, Nancy, & Lee Hazlewood
Also see WOODCHUCKS

HAZZARD, Tony
Singles: 7-inch
UNI.... 3-5 73
LPs: 10/12-inch
UNI.... 8-10 72

HEAD
LPs: 10/12-inch
BUDDAH (5062 "Head").... 30-40 70
NOVA SOL.... 10-12

HEAD, Don
Singles: 7-inch
DUB (2840 "Goin' Strong").... 40-60 58

HEAD, Harry
Singles: 7-inch
KING.... 4-8 61

HEAD, Jim, & His Del Rays
LPs: 10/12-inch
H.P. (22893 "Jim Head & His Del Rays").... 50-75 63
(Monaural.)
H.P. (22893 "Jim Head & His Del Rays").... 75-100 63
(Stereo.)

HEAD, Murray P&R '70
(With the Trinidad Singers; Murry Head)
Singles: 12-inch
CHESS.... 4-6 85
Singles: 7-inch
A&M.... 3-5 76
CAPITOL.... 4-6 67
CHESS.... 3-4 84-85
DECCA.... 3-6 69-71
RCA.... 3-4 85
Picture Sleeves
CHESS.... 3-4 85
DECCA.... 3-6 70-71
RCA.... 3-4 85
LPs: 10/12-inch
A&M.... 8-10 76
COLUMBIA.... 5-10 72

HEAD, Roy P&R/R&B/LP '65
(With the Traits)
Singles: 7-inch
ABC.... 3-5 73-79
ABC/DOT.... 3-5 76-77
AVION.... 3-4 83
BACK BEAT.... 5-10 65-67
CHURCHILL.... 3-4 81
DUNHILL.... 3-5 70
ELEKTRA.... 3-4 79-80
MEGA.... 3-5 74
MERCURY.... 4-6 68
NSD.... 3-4 82
SCEPTER.... 4-8 65-66
SHANNON.... 3-5 75
SUAVE.... 10-20
TMI.... 3-5 71-73
TNT.... 8-12 65
TEXAS CRUDE.... 3-4 85
LPs: 10/12-inch
ABC.... 5-10 73-78
CRAZY CAJUN.... 5-10 77
DUNHILL.... 8-12 70
ELEKTRA.... 5-10 79-80
SCEPTER (532 "Treat Me Right") 15-25 65
(Monaural.)
SCEPTER (532 "Treat Me Right") 20-30 65
(Stereo. With an "SS" prefix.)
TMI (1000 "Dismal Prisoner").... 8-10 72
TNT (101 "Roy Head and the Traits").... 100-150 65
(Counterfeits can be identified by their content. They include *Treat Her Right*, as well as other later Head tracks on side two. Originals do not have these.)
TEXAS CRUDE.... 5-10 85
Also see ROY - SARAH & TRAITS
Also see TRAITS

HEAD & HARES
Singles: 7-inch
H&H PRODUCTIONS (200,891 "I Won't Come Back").... 20-30 65

HEAD EAST P&R/LP '75
Singles: 7-inch
A&M.... 3-5 75-79
Picture Sleeves
A&M.... 3-5 78
LPs: 10/12-inch
A&M.... 5-10 75-80
ALLEGIANCE.... 5-10 83
Members: John Schlitt; Mike Sommerville; Roger Boyd; Steve Huston.

HEAD, HANDS & FEET
Singles: 7-inch
ATCO.... 3-5 73
LPs: 10/12-inch
ATCO.... 8-10 73
CAPITOL.... 8-10 71-72
Also see LEE, Albert

HEAD LYTERS
(Headlyters)
Singles: 7-inch
PHALANX (1010 "The Girl Down the Street").... 25-35 60s
WAND (199 "Better Come Home").... 15-25 65

HEAD OVER HEELS
LPs: 10/12-inch
CAPITOL.... 10-12 71-72

HEAD SHOP
LPs: 10/12-inch
EPIC (26476 "Head Shop").... 30-40 69

HEADBOYS P&R/LP '79
Singles: 7-inch
RSO.... 3-5 79
LPs: 10/12-inch
RSO.... 5-10 79

HEADCOATS
Singles: 7-inch
SUB POP.... 3-5 90
Picture Sleeves
SUB POP.... 3-5 90

HEADEN, Willie
(With the Five Birds; Willie Hayden)
Singles: 78 rpm
AUTHENTIC (410 "Let Me Cry").... 20-30 56
AUTHENTIC (703 "I Wanna Know").... 15-25 56
DOOTONE (410 "Let Me Cry").... 15-25 56
Singles: 7-inch
AUTHENTIC (410 "Let Me Cry").. 75-125 56
AUTHENTIC (703 "I Wanna Know").... 60-80 56
DOOTO (410 "Let Me Cry").... 20-30 59
DOOTO (417 "Everybody Has a Fool").... 25-50 57
DOOTO (427 "Cool Cat").... 25-50 57
DOOTO (437 "Real Fine Daddy").... 25-50 58
DOOTO (703 "Back Home Again").... 20-30 58
DOOTONE (410 "Let Me Cry").... 50-100 57
KENT.... 4-8 68
EPs: 7-inch
DOOTO (457 "Willie Headen").... 20-30 60
LPs: 10/12-inch
DOOTO (293 "Willie Headen").... 50-100 60

HEADHUNTERS
Singles: 7-inch
FENTON (2518 "Times We Share").... 15-25 69

HEADHUNTERS LP '75
LPs: 10/12-inch
ARISTA.... 5-10 75-78

HEADLINERS
Singles: 7-inch
KENO (1002 "Back to School Again").... 20-30 60s
V.I.P. (25011 "You're Bad News")... 20-30 64
V.I.P. (25026 "We Call It Fun").... 15-20 65

HEADLINERS
Singles: 7-inch
A&M (1011 "Let Me Love You").... 5-10 68
VAL (1 "Let Me Love You").... 10-15 68
(First issued as by George Goodman & the Headliners.)
Also see GOODMAN, George, & Headliners

HEADLINERS
Singles: 7-inch
VAUGHN LTD.... 5-10

HEADLYTERS: see HEAD LYTERS

HEADPINS P&R '83
Singles: 7-inch
ATCO.... 3-5 82
SOLID GOLD.... 3-5 83
Picture Sleeves
SOLID GOLD.... 3-5 83
LPs: 10/12-inch
ATCO.... 5-10 82
SOLID GOLD.... 5-8 83
Member: Darby Mills.

HEADROOM, Max
Singles: 7-inch
CHRYSALIS.... 3-4 86
Picture Sleeves
CHRYSALIS.... 3-4 86
Also see ART of NOISE & Max Headroom

HEADS
Singles: 7-inch
LIBERTY.... 5-10 68
LPs: 10/12-inch
LIBERTY.... 15-25 68

HEADS OF THE FAMILY
LPs: 10/12-inch
ALSHIRE.... 10-12 69

HEADSTONE
LPs: 10/12-inch
STARR (1056 "Still Looking").... 75-125 71

Members: Dave Applegate; Tom Applegate; Barry Applegate; Bruce Flynn.

HEADSTONE

LPs: 10/12-inch

DUNHILL 8-10 74
20TH FOX 8-10 75

HEADSTONES

Singles: 7-inch

PHARAOH (147 "Wish She Were Mine") 15-25 66
PHARAOH (152 "Bad Day Blues") 15-25 66
Members: Dave Williams; Paul Veale; Winston Logan.

HEALEY, Debra, & Magic Tones

Singles: 7-inch

CHRYSLER (701 "Can't Erase My Old Lover's Face") 8-12

HEALEY, Jeff *LP '88*

(Jeff Healey Band)

Singles: 7-inch

ARISTA 3-4 89-90
FORTE (001 "Adrianna") 8-10 86

Picture Sleeves

ARISTA 3-4 89
FORTE (001 "Adrianna") 10-15 86

LPs: 10/12-inch

ARISTA 5-8 89-90
Members: Jeff Healey; Joe Rockman; Tom Stephen.

HEAP, Jimmy *P&R/C&W '56*

(With the Melody Masters & Perk Williams)

Singles: 78 rpm

CAPITOL 5-15 53-55
IMPERIAL 8-12 50-52

Singles: 7-inch

CAPITOL 10-20 53-55
D 8-10 59
DART 5-10 60
FAME (502 "Little Jewel") 200-250 58
FAME (509 "Night Cap") 8-15 61
FAME (510 "Go Get Em") 8-15 61
FAME (511 "Flint Rock") 8-15 61
IMPERIAL (8325 "When They Operated on Papa They Opened Mama's Male") 5-10 60

HEAPS, George

LPs:10/12-inch

SUNNY MOUNTAIN 20-30

HEAR & NOW

Singles: 7-inch

POMPEI 3-5 71

LPs: 10/12-inch

POMPEI 8-10 71

HEAR 'N AID *LP '86*

Singles: 7-inch

MERCURY 3-4 85

LPs: 10/12-inch

MERCURY/POLYGRAM 5-10 85
Members: Tommy Aldridge; Dave Alford; Carmine Appice; Vinny Appice; Jimmy Bain; Frankie Banali; Eric Bloom; Mick Brown; Vivian Campbell; Carlos Cavazo; Amir Derakh; Ronnie James Dio; Don Dokken; Kevin Dubrow; Brad Gillis; Craig Goldy; Chris Hager; Rob Halford; Chris Holmes; Blackie Lawless; Geroge Lynch; Yngwie Malmsteed; Mick Mars; Dave Meniketti; Dave Murray; Vince Neil; Ted Nugent; Eddie Ojeda; Jeff Pilson; Donald Roeser; Rudy Sarzo; Chaude Schnell; Neal Schon; Paul Shortino; Adrian Smith; Spinal Tap; Mark Stein; Geoff Tate Matt Thor.
Also see APPICE, Carmine
Also see DIO, Ronnie
Also see DOKKEN
Also see GIUFFRIA
Also see MALMSTEEN, Yngwie J.
Also see NUGENT, Ted
Also see QUIET RIOT
Also see SPINAL TAP

HEARD

Singles: 7-inch

AUDITION (6107 "Stop It Baby") 15-25 66
FEATURE (203 "Stop It Girl") 8-12 67
Also see WYLDE HEARD

HEARD

Singles: 7-inch

ONE WAY (01 "Exit 9") 15-25 67

HEARD

Singles: 7-inch

GARLAND 10-15

HEARD, Buddy

Singles: 7-inch

RED TOP (501 "Rock with Me") 40-60

HEARD, Lonnie

Singles: 7-inch

ARLISS 10-15 61

HEARD, Oma

Singles: 7-inch

V.I.P. (25008 "Mr. Lonely Heart") 75-150 64
Also see UTMOSTS

HEARNS, Mitch

Singles: 7-inch

DOT (16438 "Miss You So") 10-20 62

HEARSEMEN

Singles: 7-inch

WHEELS (3619 "Christy Ann") 10-15

HEART

Singles: 7-inch

HEART 3-5 70
LOOK 3-6 69-70

LPs: 10/12-inch

KING 10-12 70
LOOK 10-12 69
NATURAL RESOURCES 8-10 72

HEART *P&R/LP '76*

Singles: 12-inch

CAPITOL 4-6 85
MUSHROOM 4-8 76
PORTRAIT 4-8 77-79

Promotional 12-inch Singles

MUSHROOM (7023 "Dreamboat Annie") 8-10 76
PORTRAIT (16445 "Straight On") 8-10 78

Singles: 7-inch

CAPITOL 3-4 85-90
EPIC 3-5 81-83
MUSHROOM 3-6 76-79
PORTRAIT 3-5 77-79

Picture Sleeves

CAPITOL 3-4 85-90
EPIC (Except 04047) 3-5 82-83
EPIC (04047 "How Can I Refuse") 3-5 83
EPIC (04047 "How Can I Refuse") 8-10 83
(Promotional sleeve. Labeled: "Demonstration Only—Not for Sale.)

LPs: 10/12-inch

CAPITOL 5-10 85-90
CAPITOL RADIO STAR ("Audio Cue Card") 10-15 87
(Radio interview. Promotional issue only.)
EPIC 5-10 80-83
MUSHROOM (MRS-5005 "Dreamboat Annie") 8-12 76
MUSHROOM (MRS-5008 "Magazine") 50-75 77
(First issue. Last track on Side One is *Magazine*.
MUSHROOM (MRS-5008 "Magazine") 5-10 77
(Second issue. First track on Side Two is *Magazine*. There are also other differences in song order.)
MUSHROOM (MRS-5008 Magazine") 50-75 78
(Promotional only picture disc.)
MUSHROOM (MRS-1-SP "Magazine") 15-25 78
(Picture Disc.)
MUSHROOM (MRS-2-SP "Dreamboat Annie") 20-30 79
(Picture Disc.)
NAUTILUS 20-25 80
(Half-speed mastered.)
PORTRAIT (30000 series) 5-10 77-81
PORTRAIT (40000 series) 12-15 81
(Half-speed mastered.)
Members: Nancy Wilson; Ann Wilson; Howard Leese; Steve Fossen; Roger Fisher; Mike Derosier; Mark Andes; Denny Carmassi.
Also see BORDERSONG
Also see GAMMA
Also see SPIRIT
Also see WILSON, Ann & Daybreaks
Also see WILSON, Nancy / Red Hot Chili Peppers

HEART, Buddy

Singles: 7-inch

DECCA 5-10 59

HEART, Don

(Don Hart)

Singles: 7-inch

D-TOWN (1022 "A Telegram with Love") 15-25 64
D-TOWN (1030 "I'm Gonna Make a Comeback") 15-25 64
MAH'S (11 "Just Say You Care") 20-30 63
Also see HART, Don

HEART & SOUL *P&R/R&B '77*

(Heart & Soul Orchestra)

Singles: 7-inch

CASABLANCA 3-5 77

HEART ATTACKS

Singles: 7-inch

REMUS (5000 "Babby Diddy Baby") 10-20

HEART BEATS QUINTET

("Russell Jacquet & His Orch. - The Heart Beats Quintet")

Singles: 10-inch

CANDLELITE (437 "Tormented") 20-30 72
(Colored vinyl 45 rpm.)
CANDLELITE (437 "Tormented") 10-20 72
(Black vinyl 45 rpm.)

Singles: 7-inch

CANDLELITE (1135 "Tormented") 3-5 76
NETWORK (71200 "Tormented") 100-150 55
(Black vinyl. Pastel yellow label.)
NETWORK (71200 "Tormented") 50-100
(Black vinyl. Bright yellow label.)
NETWORK (71200 "Tormented") 15-25
(Colored vinyl.)
Members: James Sheppard; Albert Crump; Vernon Walker; Wally Roker; Rob Adams.
Also see HEARTBEATS
Also see JACQUET, Russell

HEART BREAKERS

("Vocal By Lisa Tomasulo)

Singles: 7-inch

P&M (402 "Who Do You Love") 50-100 65

HEART OF GOLD BAND

LPs: 10/12-inch

RELIX 5-10 86
Members: Keith Godchaux; Donna Godchaux.
Also see KEITH & DONNA

HEART OF NASHVILLE *C&W '85*

Singles: 7-inch

COMPLEAT 3-4 85

HEARTBEATS

Singles: 78 rpm

JUBILEE (5202 "Finally") 8-12 55

Singles: 7-inch

JUBILEE (5202 "Finally") 10-20 55
Members: Frank Starro; Al Rosenberg; Flo Guida; Joe Sucamenle; Tony Grochowski.
Also see 3 FRIENDS

HEARTBEATS *P&R/R&B '56*

Singles: 78 rpm

GEE 25-50 57
HULL 25-50 55-56
RAMA 25-50 56-57
ROULETTE (4054 "Down on My Knees") 40-60 58

Singles: 7-inch

COLLECTABLES 3-4
GEE (1043 "When I Found You") 25-50 57
GEE (1047 "After New Year's Eve") 25-50 57
(Red label.)
GEE (1047 "After New Year's Eve") 15-25 57
(Gray label.)
GEE (1061 "People Are Talking") 15-25 60
GEE (1062 "Darling, How Long") 15-25 60
GUYDEN (2011 "One Million Years") 20-40 59
(Yellow label.)
GUYDEN (2011 "One Million Years") 15-25 59
(Purple label.)
HULL (711 "Crazy for You") 300-400 55
(White label. Promotional issue only.)
HULL (711 "Crazy for You") 250-350 55
(Pink label.)
HULL (711 "Crazy for You") 100-125 55
(Black label.)
HULL (713 "Darling How Long") 150-250 56
HULL (716 "People Are Talking") 150-250 56
HULL (720 "A Thousand Miles Away") 200-300 56
(Black label.)
HULL (720 "A Thousand Miles Away") 75-100 56
(Red label.)
RAMA (216 "A Thousand Miles Away") 75-100 56
RAMA (222 "I Won't Be the Fool Anymore") 50-100 57
RAMA (231 "Everybody's Somebody's Fool") 50-100 57
ROULETTE (4054 "Down on My Knees") 15-25 58
ROULETTE (4091 "One Day Next Year") 15-25 58
ROULETTE (4194 "Crazy for You") 15-25 58

LPs: 10/12-inch

EMUS 5-10 79
ROULETTE (25107 "A Thousand Miles Away") 100-200 60
ROULETTE (59019 "A Thousand Miles Away") 5-10 81

LPs: 10/12-inch

EMUS 8-10 79
ROULETTE (25107 "A Thousand Miles Away") 75-125 60
ROULETTE (59019 "A Thousand Miles Away") 8-10 81
Members: James Sheppard; Albert Crump; Vernon Walker; Wally Roker; Rob Adams.
Also see HEART BEATS QUINTET
Also see SHEP & LIMELIGHTS

HEARTBEATS / Shep & Limelights

LPs: 10/12-inch

ROULETTE (115 "Echoes of a Rock Era") 40-60 72
Also see HEARTBEATS
Also see SHEP & LIMELIGHTS

HEARTBEATS

Singles: 7-inch

BROADCAST (1125 "Have Rock Will Roll") 5-10

HEARTBREAKERS

Singles: 78 rpm

RCA 75-150 51-52

Singles: 7-inch

RCA (4327 "Heartbreaker") 400-500 51
RCA (4508 "I'm Only Fooling My Heart") 400-500 52
RCA (4662 "Why Don't I") 200-300 52
RCA (4849 "There Is Time") 200-300 52
Members: Robert Evans; Lawrence Green; Jim Rose; Junior Davis; Larry Tate.
Also see FOUR DOTS
Also see GRIFFINS

HEARTBREAKERS

("Vocal Lead: Paul Himmelstein")

Singles: 78 rpm

VIK 50-100 57

Singles: 7-inch

VIK (0261 "Without a Cause") 100-150 57
VIK (0299 "My Love") 150-250 57
Member: Paul Himmelstein.

HEARTBREAKERS

Singles: 7-inch

DONNA (1381 "Every Time I See You") 50-100 63
Member: Frank Zappa (guitar).
Also see ZAPPA, Frank

HEARTBREAKERS

Singles: 7-inch

ATCO (6258 "The Willow Wept") 15-25 63
BRENT (7037 "I'm Leaving It All Up to You") 25-35 62
DERBY CITY (101 "I've Got to Face It") 15-25 60s
LINDA (114 "Please Answer") 10-20 64
MARKAY (106 "Since You Been Gone") 50-75 62
MIRACLE (101 "I Found a New Lover") 20-30 60s

HEARTBREAKERS

Singles: 7-inch

MGM (13129 "It's Hard Being a Girl") 10-15 63

HEARTBREAKERS

Singles: 7-inch

SWAN (4242 "Baby Baby") 5-10 66
TOMI 5-10 60s

HEARTLAND *C&W '88*

Singles: 7-inch

TRA-STAR 3-4 88-89

HEARTS

Singles: 78 rpm

APOLLO 50-75 52

Singles: 7-inch

APOLLO (444 "Angel Baby") 150-250 52
(Black vinyl.)
APOLLO (444 "Angel Baby") 550-650 52
(Red vinyl.)
Member: Bill Austin.

HEARTS *R&B '55*

Singles: 78 rpm

BATON 10-20 55-56

Singles: 7-inch

BATON (208 "Lonely Nights") 25-50 55
BATON (211 "All My Love Belongs to You") 25-50 55
BATON (215 "Gone Gone Gone") 25-50 55
BATON (222 "Going Home to Stay") 15-25 56
BATON (228 "I Had a Guy") 15-25 56
J&S (1002 "If I Had Known") 15-25 57
J&S (1180 "You Weren't Home") 25-50 57
J&S (1626 "I Want Your Love Tonight") 25-50 58
J&S (1657 "Dancing in a Dream World") 25-50 57
J&S (1660 "So Long Baby") 25-50 57
J&S (4571 "Goodbye Baby") 20-30
LAVENDER (1008 "Lonely Nights") 8-12 62
TUFF (370 "Dear Abby") 8-12 63
ZELLS (3377 "I Feel Good") 15-20 63

LPs: 10/12-inch

ZELLS (337 "I Feel Good") 200-300 63
Members: Justine "Baby" Washington; Rex Garvin; Pat Ford; Joyce Peterson; Zell Sanders.
Also see GARVIN, Rex, & Mighty Cravers
Also see JAYNETTS
Also see WASHINGTON, Baby

HEARTS

Singles: 7-inch

CHANCELLOR (1057 "On My Honor") 15-25 60
Also see ANDREWS, Lee, & Hearts
Also see FAMOUS HEARTS

HEARTS & FLOWERS

Singles: 7-inch

CAPITOL 5-10 67-68

LPs: 10/12-inch

CAPITOL 15-25 67-68
Members: Rick Cunha; Larry Murray; Dave Lawson; Bernie Leadon; David Jackson.
Also see CUNHA, Rick

HEARTS OF STONE

Singles: 7-inch

V.I.P. 4-8 70-71

LPs: 10/12-inch

V.I.P. (404 "Stop the World") 20-40 71

HEARTSFIELD *P&R '74*

Singles: 7-inch

MERCURY 3-5 74

LPs: 10/12-inch

COLUMBIA 5-10 77
MERCURY 8-10 73-75

HEARTSMAN, Johnny *R&B '57*

(With the Gaylarks; Johnny Hartsman Band)

Singles: 78 rpm

MUSIC CITY 10-15 57
RHYTHM 10-15 53

Singles: 7-inch

BIG J (101 "Syrup Sopping") 15-25
MUSIC CITY (807 "Johnny's House Party") 10-20 57
MUSIC CITY (811 "Johnny's Thunderbird") 10-20 57
TRIAD (501 "One More Time") 8-12
WORLD PACIFIC (372 "Sizzlin") 10-20 63

LPs: 10/12-inch

CAT 'N HAT 10-15
Also see SIMON, Joe

HEARTSPINNERS

Singles: 7-inch

X-TRA (109 "Oh So Much") 200-250 58

HEARTSPINNERS

Singles: 7-inch

BIM BAM BOOM 4-6 72

HEARTSPINNERS / Admirations

Singles: 7-inch

TIMES SQUARE 8-12 63

HEARTSTOPPERS

Singles: 7-inch

ALL PLATINUM 3-5 71

LPs: 10/12-inch

ALL PLATINUM 8-10 71

HEART-THROBS

Singles: 78 rpm

ALADDIN (3394 "So Glad") 20-30 57
LAMP (2010 "So Glad") 20-30 57

Singles: 7-inch

ALADDIN (3394 "So Glad") 20-30 57
LAMP (2010 "So Glad") 20-30 57

HEARTWOOD

LPs: 10/12-inch

GRC 8-10 75
L&M 8-10 73

HEAT *R&B '80*

Singles: 7-inch

MCA 3-5 79-81

LPs: 10/12-inch

MCA 5-10 79-81

HEAT, Reverend Horton

Singles: 7-inch

SUB POP ("Psychobilly Freakout") 3-5 90
(Colored vinyl.)

Picture Sleeves

SUB POP ("Psychobilly Freakout") 3-5 90

HEATERS

Singles: 7-inch

COLUMBIA (Black vinyl) 3-5 80
COLUMBIA (Colored vinyl) 8-15 80

LPs: 10/12-inch

ARIOLA AMERICA 5-10 78
COLUMBIA 5-10 80

HEATH, Boyd *C&W '45*

Singles: 78 rpm

BLUEBIRD 5-10 45

HEATH, Jimmy

Singles: 7-inch

MEGA (2261 "Little Darlin' ") 100-150

HEATH, Joyce

(Joyce Heath & Priviteers)

Singles: 7-inch

AGON (1003 "Honor Roll of Love") 30-40 62
(Also issued as by Joyce & Priviteers.)
DRAGON (415 "I Wouldn't Dream of It") 10-20 61
LAURIE 5-10 60
MAY 5-10 61
RCA 5-10 59
Also see JOYCE & PRIVITEERS

HEATH, Ted *P&R '56*

Singles: 78 rpm

LONDON 3-4 50-61

Singles: 7-inch

LONDON 3-6 50-61

EPs: 7-inch

LONDON 4-8 51-56

LPs: 10/12-inch

LONDON 5-15 50-62
RICHMOND 5-10 62

HEATH, Walter *R&B '74*

Singles: 7-inch

BUDDAH 3-5 74

HEATH BROTHERS *R&B '81*

Singles: 7-inch

COLUMBIA 3-5 79-81

LPs: 10/12-inch

COLUMBIA 5-10 79-81

HEATHENS

Singles: 7-inch

VIBRA (104 "The Other Way Around") 15-25 67

HEATHER

Singles: 7-inch

CHATHAM 5-10

HEATHER BLACK

LPs: 10/12-inch

AMERICAN PLAYBOY 25-30
DOUBLE BAYOU 15-20

HEATHERTON, Joey *P&R/LP '72*

Singles: 7-inch

CORAL (62422 "That's How It Goes") 10-20 64
CORAL (62451 "Hullabaloo") 10-20 65
CORAL (62459 "But He's Not Mine") 10-20 65
DECCA (31962 "When You Call Me Baby") 25-50 66
MGM 5-10 72-73

Picture Sleeves

CORAL (62422 "That's How It Goes") 15-25 64
MGM 5-10 72

LPs: 10/12-inch

MGM 10-15 72

HEATS

Singles: 7-inch

ALBATROSS (2002 "Rivals") 3-5 81
HRRR (001 "I Don't Like Your Face") 3-5 80

Picture Sleeves

ALBATROSS (2002 "Rivals") 3-5 81
HRRR (001 "I Don't Like Your Face") 3-5 80

LPs: 10/12-inch

ALBATROSS (1001 "The Heats") 15-20 80
SUSHI (1801 "Burnin' Live") 5-10 83

Members: Keith Lilly; Don Short; Steve Pearson; Kenny Deans; Wayne Clack; Rick Burgoin.

HEATWAVE P&R/R&B/LP '77
(Heat Wave)
Singles: 12-inch
EPIC.......... 4-8 77-82
Singles: 7-inch
EPIC.......... 3-5 77-82
LPs: 10/12-inch
EPIC.......... 5-10 77-82
Member: Keith Wilder; Rod Temperton; Ernie Berger; John Wilder; Eric Johns.

HEATWAVES
Singles: 7-inch
JOSIE.......... 10-20 65
PHILTOWN.......... 10-20 60s
Member: Billy Carl.
Also see BILLY & ESSENTIALS

HEAVEN
Singles: 7-inch
COLUMBIA.......... 3-4 82
LPs: 10/12-inch
COLUMBIA.......... 5-10 82

HEAVEN & EARTH R&B '76
Singles: 7-inch
OVATION.......... 3-5 72-73
LPs: 10/12-inch
OVATION.......... 8-10 73

HEAVEN & EARTH
Singles: 7-inch
GEC.......... 3-5 76
MERCURY.......... 3-5 78-80
TEC.......... 3-4 80
WMOT.......... 3-4 81
LPs: 10/12-inch
MERCURY.......... 5-10 78-79
WMOT.......... 5-10 81
Members: Dwight Dukes; Dean Williams; James Dukes; Keith Steward.

HEAVEN BOUND P&R '71
(With Tony Scotti)
Singles: 7-inch
MGM.......... 3-5 71
LPs: 10/12-inch
MGM.......... 8-12 72
Members: Joan Medora; Eddie Medora; Michael Lloyd; Tom Oliver.

HEAVEN'S EDGE LP '90
LPs: 10/12-inch
COLUMBIA.......... 5-8 90

HEAVEN 17 P&R/D&D/LP '83
Singles: 12-inch
ARISTA.......... 4-6 83-84
Singles: 7-inch
ARISTA.......... 3-4 83-84
LPs: 10/12-inch
ARISTA.......... 8-10 83
VIRGIN.......... 5-10 87
Members: Glenn Gregory; Craig Marsh; Martyn Ware.
Also see BAND AID
Also see HUMAN LEAGUE

HEAVENER, David C&W '81
Singles: 7-inch
BRENT.......... 3-4 81-82

HEAVY BALLOON
LPs: 10/12-inch
ELEPHANT (104 "16 Ton").......... 50-75 69

HEAVY CRUISER
Singles: 7-inch
FAMILY.......... 3-5 72
LPs: 10/12-inch
FAMILY.......... 12-15 72-73
TIGER LILY.......... 5-10
Member: Neil Merryweather.
Also see MERRYWEATHER, Neil

HEAVY D. & BOYZ R&B '86
Singles: 12-inch
MCA.......... 4-6 86
Singles: 7-inch
MCA.......... 3-4 86-88
LPs: 10/12-inch
MCA.......... 5-10 86-87
UPTOWN.......... 5-8 89

HEAVY MANNERS
LPs: 10/12-inch
DISTURBING.......... 5-10 82

HEAVY METAL KIDS
(Kids)
LPs: 10/12-inch
ATCO.......... 5-10 74-80

HEAVY REGGAE MACHINE
LPs: 10/12-inch
REGGAE.......... 8-10 70

HEBB, Bobby P&R/R&B/LP '66
Singles: 7-inch
BOOM.......... 4-8 66
CADET.......... 3-6 72
FM.......... 5-10 61
LAURIE.......... 3-5 75
PHILIPS.......... 5-10 66-67
RICH.......... 10-20 60
SCEPTER.......... 4-8 66
Picture Sleeves
PHILIPS.......... 5-10 66
LPs: 10/12-inch
EPIC.......... 10-12 70
PHILIPS.......... 15-20 66
Also see BOBBY & SYLVIA

HEBB, Bobby / Billy Sha-Rae
Singles: 7-inch
LAURIE.......... 3-4
Also see HEBB, Bobby
Also see SHA-RAE, Billy

HEBEL, Ray
Singles: 7-inch
ENCORE.......... 3-5 77

HECK, Tommy, Quintet
Singles: 7-inch
CHARIOT (513 "Lost World").......... 15-25

HECKEL, Beverly C&W '77
Singles: 7-inch
RCA.......... 3-5 77-78
Also see HECKELS
Also see RUSSELL, Johnny

HECKELS, The C&W '76
Singles: 7-inch
RCA.......... 3-5 76
Members: Beverly Heckel; Susie Heckel; Denny Franks.
Also see HECKEL, Beverly

HEDGEHOPPERS ANONYMOUS P&R '65
Singles: 7-inch
PARROT.......... 5-8 65-66
Also see KING, Jonathan

HEDLEY & LEE
Singles: 7-inch
CHALLENGE.......... 5-8 63

HEDREN, Tippi
Singles: 7-inch
CHALLENGE (59345 "If You Were a Carpenter").......... 5-8 66

HEFTI, Neal LP '55
(With His Orchestra; Neal Hefti Quintet; with Mello-Larks)
Singles: 78 rpm
CORAL.......... 3-5 51-57
EPIC.......... 3-5 55-56
Singles: 7-inch
COLUMBIA.......... 3-5 65
CORAL.......... 4-6 51-59
DOT.......... 3-5 67-68
EPIC.......... 4-6 55-56
RCA.......... 3-5 66
REPRISE.......... 3-5 62
U.A. 3-5 65-66
Picture Sleeves
RCA.......... 4-8 66-67
RCA GOLD STANDARD SERIES.......... 3-4 89
EPs: 7-inch
CORAL.......... 5-10 52-56
EPIC.......... 5-10 56
"X".......... 5-10 55
LPs: 10/12-inch
COLUMBIA.......... 8-15 60
CORAL.......... 10-20 52-60
EPIC.......... 10-15 56
RCA (3621 "Hefti in Gotham City").......... 10-20 66
REPRISE.......... 8-15 62
20TH FOX.......... 8-12 64
U.A. (573 "Definitely Hefti").......... 8-15 67
X.......... 10-20 55
For a complete listing of soundtracks by this artist, consult *The Official Price Guide to Movie/TV Soundtracks and Original Cast Albums.*

HEFTI, Neal / Tom Glazer
Singles: 7-inch
WONDERLAND (2101 "Batman Theme"/"Superman Song").......... 10-20 60s
Also see GLAZER, Tom
Also see HEFTI, Neal

HEFTY, Jack, & Rusty
Singles: 7-inch
COULEE.......... 5-10 70s

HEGE, Ron
Singles: 7-inch
ACTS.......... 4-8 83
Member: John Magee.
Also see HAIG, Ronnie

HEGEL, Bob
Singles: 7-inch
RCA.......... 3-5 74-80

HEGGENESS & WEST
Singles: 7-inch
CLOWD (7302 "Dr. Gorrie's Labratory").......... 4-6 73
CLOWD (7403 "Dr. Gorrie's Press Conference").......... 4-6 69
Picture Sleeves
CLOWD (7302 "Dr. Gorrie's Labratory").......... 8-10 73
Members: Fred Heggeness; Frank Wataschke.

HEIDT, Horace, Jr., & Tradewinds
("James Austin - Vocal")
Singles: 7-inch
MAGNOLIA (4 "What Can I Do").......... 15-25
Member: James Austin.

HEIGHT, Donald R&B '66
Singles: 7-inch
DAKAR.......... 3-5 76
JUBILEE.......... 5-10 63-69
KING.......... 10-20 60
OLD TOWN.......... 10-20 64-65
RCA.......... 5-10 65
ROULETTE.......... 5-10 65
SHOUT.......... 5-10 66-68
SOOZEE.......... 8-12 62
Also see HOLLYWOOD FLAMES

HEIGHT, Ronnie P&R '59
Singles: 7-inch
BAMBOO.......... 5-10 61
DORE.......... 8-12 59
ERA.......... 5-10 59-61

HEINDORF, Ray
(With the Warner Bros. Orchestra)
Singles: 78 rpm
COLUMBIA (Except 40574).......... 3-5 55-56
COLUMBIA (40574 "Theme from *East of Eden* and *Rebel Without a Cause* – Tribute to James Dean").......... 5-10 56
Singles: 7-inch
COLUMBIA (Except 40574).......... 3-6 55-56
COLUMBIA (40574 "Theme from *East of Eden* and *Rebel Without a Cause* – Tribute to James Dean").......... 5-10 56
Picture Sleeves
COLUMBIA (40574 "Theme from *East of Eden* and *Rebel Without a Cause* - Tribute to James Dean").......... 25-40 56
EPs: 7-inch
COLUMBIA.......... 3-8 55-56
LPs: 10/12-inch
COLUMBIA (Except 940).......... 5-15 55-57
COLUMBIA (940 "Tribute to James Dean").......... 25-40 56

HEINTJE LP '70
Singles: 7-inch
MGM.......... 3-6 70
LPs: 10/12-inch
MGM.......... 8-10 70

HEINZ
(Heinz Burt)
Singles: 7-inch
TOWER.......... 10-15 64-66
Also see TORNADOES

HEINZ, Charles
Singles: 7-inch
SATELLITE.......... 8-12 59-60

HEIRS
Singles: 7-inch
PANORAMA (39 "Do You Want Me").......... 10-15 66

HELDER, Eddie
Singles: 7-inch
CUIMS.......... 4-8 60s
Picture Sleeves
CUIMS.......... 4-8 60s
Also see PRINCE & PAUPERS

HELIX LP '83
LPs: 10/12-inch
CAPITOL.......... 5-10 83-87
GRUDGE.......... 5-8 90

HELL, Richard, & Voidoids
Singles: 7-inch
SIRE.......... 4-6 77
EPs: 7-inch
SHAKE (101 "Time").......... 5-8 80
LPs: 10/12-inch
SIRE.......... 15-20 77
Members: Richard Hell; Ivan Julian; Robert Quine; Xavier Sessive; James Morrison; Tom Verlaine; Kitty Summerall.
Also see NEON BOYS
Also see VERLAINE, Tom

HELLCATS
LPs: 10/12-inch
RADIO.......... 5-10 82
Also see RANNO, Richie

HELLEMS, Hollie, & Rhythm Kings
Singles: 7-inch
MAJOR.......... 4-8 67

HELLER, Jackie / Glenn Miller
Singles: 78 rpm
PHILCO/VOGUE ("Rum and Coca-Cola").......... 500-700 45
(Picture disc. Promotional issue only. No selection number used.)

HELLERS
LPs: 10/12-inch
COMMAND (934 "Singers, Talkers, Players, Swingers & Doers").......... 25-50 68
Member: Hugh Heller.

HELLFIELD
LPs: 10/12-inch
EPIC.......... 5-10 78

HELLION
LPs: 10/12-inch
NEW RENAISSANCE.......... 5-10 85

HELLO PEOPLE LP '74
Singles: 7-inch
ABC/DUNHILL.......... 3-5 75-76
PHILIPS.......... 4-6 68
Picture Sleeves
PHILIPS.......... 5-8 68
LPs: 10/12-inch
ABC/DUNHILL.......... 8-10 74
ABC-PAR.......... 8-10 75
MEDIARTS.......... 12-15 70
PHILIPS.......... 15-20 68

HELLOWEEN LP '87
Singles: 7-inch
NOISE/RCA (5223 "Halloween").......... 20-25 87
(Pumpkin-shaped disc. Promotional issue only.)
LPs: 10/12-inch
MX.......... 10-15 86
RCA.......... 5-10 87-89

HELM, Carl
Singles: 7-inch
CANADIAN AMERICAN.......... 8-12

HELM, Levon LP '77
(With the RCO All-Stars)
Singles: 7-inch
A&M.......... 3-4 80
ABC.......... 3-5 78
CAPITOL.......... 3-4 82
MCA.......... 3-4 80
LPs: 10/12-inch
ABC-PAR (Except 4-5).......... 5-10 77-78
ABC-PAR (4-5 "Levon Helm").......... 15-20 78
(Picture disc. Promotional issue only.)
A&M.......... 5-10 80
CAPITOL.......... 5-10 82
MCA.......... 5-10 80
Also see BAND
Also see HAMMOND, John
Also see LEVON & HAWKS

HELM, Levon, Johnny Cash, Emmylou Harris & Charlie Daniels
LPs: 10/12-inch
A&M.......... 5-10 80
Also see CASH, Johnny
Also see DANIELS, Charlie
Also see HARRIS, Emmylou
Also see HELM, Levon

HELMET BOY
LPs: 10/12-inch
ASYLUM.......... 5-10 80

HELMS, Bobby C&W/P&R/R&B '57
Singles: 78 rpm
DECCA.......... 5-15 56-57
Singles: 7-inch
BLACK ROSE.......... 3-4 83-84
CAPITOL.......... 3-5 70
CERTRON.......... 3-5 70
COLUMBIA.......... 4-8 64
DECCA (Except 29947).......... 8-15 57-62
DECCA (29947 "Tennessee Rock and Roll").......... 20-30 56
GUSTO.......... 3-5 74
KAPP.......... 4-6 65-67
LARRICK.......... 3-5 75
LITTLE DARLIN'.......... 3-6 67-79
MCA.......... 3-4
MILLION.......... 3-5 72
MISTLETOE.......... 3-5 74
PLAYBACK.......... 3-4
Picture Sleeves
CERTRON.......... 4-6 70
DECCA ("New Singing Sensation").......... 10-20 57
(Pictures Helms, but no number or title shown. With die-cut center hole.)
DECCA (30194 "Fraulein").......... 15-20 57
DECCA (30513 "Jingle Bell Rock").......... 10-15 57
EPs: 7-inch
DECCA (2555 "Bobby Helms Sings to My Special Angel").......... 15-25 57
DECCA (2586 "Tonight's the Night").......... 10-20 58
DECCA (2629 "Bobby Helms").......... 10-20 59
LPs: 10/12-inch
CERTRON.......... 8-10 70
COLUMBIA.......... 12-15 63
DECCA (8638 "Bobby Helms Sings to My Special Angel").......... 30-50 57
HARMONY.......... 10-12 67
HOLIDAY.......... 5-10 80
KAPP.......... 10-15 66
LITTLE DARLIN'.......... 10-12 68
MCA.......... 5-10 83
MISTLETOE.......... 5-10 74
VOCALION.......... 10-12 65
Session: Anita Kerr Singers.
Also see KERR, Anita

HELMS, Don
Singles: 7-inch
SMASH (1781 "Fire Ball Mail").......... 10-20 62

HELMS, Jimmie
Singles: 7-inch
EAST WEST (114 "It Was Ours").......... 20-30 58
FOREST.......... 4-8 63
SCOTTIE.......... 10-15 59
SYMBOL.......... 4-8 63

HELMS, Jimmy R&B '73
Singles: 78 rpm
CAPITOL.......... 5-10 55
Singles: 7-inch
CAPITOL.......... 10-15 55
DATE.......... 4-8 67
MGM.......... 3-5 73

HELP
Singles: 7-inch
DECCA (32879 "Good Time Music").......... 5-10 71
LPs: 10/12-inch
DECCA (75257 "Help").......... 20-30 71
DECCA (75304 "Second Coming").......... 20-30 71
Members: Chet McCracken; Jack Merrill; Rob Rochan.
Also see DOOBIE BROTHERS
Also see EVERGREEN BLUE SHOES

HELP, TRUTH & PORTRAITS
Singles: 7-inch
TRUE LOVE.......... 8-10

HELP YOURSELF
LPs: 10/12-inch
U.A. 8-10 72-73

HEMLOCK
Singles: 7-inch
W.B. 3-5 79

HEMLOCKS
Singles: 78 rpm
FURY (1004 "Cora Lee").......... 50-75 57
Singles: 7-inch
FURY (1004 "Cora Lee").......... 75-100 57

HEMPHILL, Jessie Mae
LPs: 10/12-inch
HIGH WATER.......... 5-10 90

HEMPHILL, Neal
Singles: 7-inch
HEMPHILL (1003 "Little Booga from Chatanooga").......... 10-20 60s

HENCHMEN
Singles: 7-inch
GUILLOTINE.......... 10-20 65-66
LEAF (6684 "Love Till the End of Time").......... 15-25 67
MONUMENT.......... 5-10 60s
SWAN (4249 "Baby, What's Wrong").......... 10-15 66
SWAN (4264 "James Brown").......... 8-12 66
TOUCHE (2007 "She's a Big Girl Now").......... 10-20 60s

HENCHMEN
Singles: 7-inch
PUNCH (1009 "Please Tell Me").......... 20-30 66

HENCHMEN
Singles: 7-inch
NIGHT OWL (67102 "The Secret").......... 15-25 67
Also see SCARLET HENCHMEN

HENCHMEN VI
Singles: 7-inch
CUCA (6731 "All of the Day").......... 15-25 67
LEAF (6684 "Love Till the End of Time").......... 15-25 66
NIGHT OWL (67102 "The Secret").......... 15-25 67
Members: Scott Keinski; Joe DeHut; Bob Durant; Jay Jackson; Art Moinlenen.

HENDERSON, Al
Singles: 7-inch
EAST WEST.......... 8-12 58
KING (5612 "Lemon Twist").......... 5-10 62
Picture Sleeves
KING (5612 "Lemon Twist").......... 10-15 62

HENDERSON, Big Bertha, & Al Smith Orchestra
Singles: 78 rpm
CHANCE.......... 75-125 52
SAVOY.......... 10-20 54
Singles: 7-inch
CHANCE (1143 "Rock Daddy, Rock").......... 200-300 52
SAVOY (1119 "Little Daddy").......... 25-40 54
Also see SMITH, Al

HENDERSON, Bill
Singles: 7-inch
VEE JAY.......... 5-10 60
VERVE.......... 5-10
LP: 10/12-inch
VEE JAY (1031 "Bill Henderson").......... 10-20 61

HENDERSON, Bob
Singles: 78 rpm
STAR.......... 5-10 53
Singles: 7-inch
STAR.......... 10-15 53

HENDERSON, Brice C&W '83
Singles: 7-inch
UNION STATION.......... 3-4 83

HENDERSON, Bugs
(Bugs Henderson Group)
LPs: 10/12-inch
ARMADILLO (1 "At Last").......... 30-50 78
Also see NITZINGER

HENDERSON, C., & Minor Chords
Singles: 7-inch
FLICK.......... 10-20 59
Also see MINOR CHORDS

HENDERSON, Carl
Singles: 7-inch
OMEN.......... 8-12 65
RENFRO.......... 5-10

HENDERSON, Chuck
Singles: 7-inch
OZARK (959 "Rock & Roll Baby").......... 150-200 58

HENDERSON, Duke
(With King Perry & His Orchestra)
Singles: 78 rpm
EXCELSIOR.......... 10-15 48
U.A. 5-10

HENDERSON, Eddie, Quintet
Singles: 7-inch
ENTERPRISE.......... 3-6 68

HENDERSON, Finis R&B '83
Singles: 7-inch
MOTOWN.......... 3-4 83
LPs: 10/12-inch
MOTOWN.......... 5-10 83
Also see TEMPTATIONS / Finis Henderson
Also see WEAPONS of PEACE

HENDERSON, Floyd
Singles: 7-inch
TRIANGLE.......... 8-10 59-60

HENDERSON, Jesse
Singles: 7-inch
GOLD DUST (001 "The Gator") 15-25

HENDERSON, Joe P&R/R&B/LP '62
("Fantastic" Joe Henderson)
Singles: 7-inch
ABC 3-5 73
FONTANA 5-10 67
KAPP 5-10 64
RIC 5-10 64
TODD 5-10 62-63
VIRGO 3-5 72
LPs: 10/12-inch
FONTANA (27590 "Hits Hits Hits") 20-30 67
(Monaural.)
FONTANA (67590 "Hits Hits Hits") 25-35 67
(Stereo.)
TODD (2701 "Snap Your Fingers").30-40 62

HENDERSON, Michael R&B/LP '76
Singles: 12-inch
EMI AMERICA 4-6 86
Singles: 7-inch
BUDDAH 3-5 76-83
EMI AMERICA 3-4 86
LPs: 10/12-inch
ACCORD 5-10
BUDDAH 8-12 76-83
EMI AMERICA 5-10 86
Also see CONNORS, Norman
Also see HYMAN, Phyllis, & Michael Henderson

HENDERSON, Ron, & Choice of Colour R&B '77
Singles: 7-inch
CHELSEA 3-5 77

HENDERSON, Sam "High Pockets"
Singles: 78 rpm
GROOVE (0121 "Go Mother, Go").. 5-10 55
Singles: 7-inch
GROOVE (0121 "Go Mother, Go").10-20 55

HENDERSON, Skitch LP '65
Singles: 7-inch
COLUMBIA 3-6 65-66
EPs: 7-inch
CAPITOL 10-20 50-54
DECCA 5-15 56
RCA 5-10 57-58
LPs: 10/12-inch
CAPITOL (H-110 "Keyboard Sketches") 25-45 50
(10-inch LP.)
CAPITOL (502 "A Man and His Music") 15-25 54
COLUMBIA 5-15 65-66
DECCA (8000 series) 15-25 56
RCA 15-25 57-58
SEECO (62 "Skitch Henderson")....25-45 50s
SEECO (401 "Latin Favorites")....20-35 56

HENDERSON, Tobias Wood
LPs: 10/12-inch
PULSAR 8-10

HENDERSON, Wayne R&B '78
(With the Freedom Sounds)
Singles: 7-inch
POLYDOR 3-5 78-79
LPs: 10/12-inch
ABC 5-10 77
ATLANTIC 8-12 67-68
POLYDOR 5-10 78-79
Also see AYERS, Roy, & Wayne Henderson

HENDERSON, Wes
Singles: 7-inch
RARE EARTH 3-6 69
Also see TAYLOR, Bobby

HENDERSON, Willie P&R/R&B '70
(With the Soul Explosions)
Singles: 7-inch
BRUNSWICK 3-6 70
PLAYBOY 3-5 74
LPs: 10/12-inch
BRUNSWICK 10-12 69-74

HENDLEY, John
Singles: 7-inch
MUTT & JEFF (2401 "My Baby Came from Out of Nowhere") 15-25

HENDRICKS, Belford
Singles: 7-inch
CAPITOL (5021 "Crazy 'Bout My Baby") 10-20 63
LPs: 10/12-inch
WING 10-15 60s

HENDON, R.D.
Singles: 78 rpm
4 STAR (1644 "Blues Boogie")........ 8-12 53
Singles: 7-inch
4 STAR (1644 "Blues Boogie").......15-25 53

HENDRICKS, Belford
Singles: 7-inch
CAPITOL (5021 "Crazy 'Bout My Baby") 10-20 63
MERCURY (71276 "Rockin' the Stroll") 15-25 58

HENDRICKS, Bobby P&R/R&B '58
Singles: 7-inch
MGM 10-20 63
MERCURY 5-10 61
SUE 10-20 58-60
Also see COASTERS
Also see DRIFTERS
Also see FLYERS
Also see VELVIT, Jimmy

HENDRICKS, James
Singles: 7-inch
MGM 3-5 71
SOUL CITY 4-6 68
STARCREST 3-5 76
Picture Sleeves
STARCREST 3-5 76
LPs: 10/12-inch
MGM 8-10 71
SOUL CITY 10-12 68
Also see MUGWUMPS

HENDRICKS, James & Vanessa
Singles: 7-inch
CHATTAHOOCHEE 4-8 65
Also see HENDRICKS, James

HENDRICKS, Lloyd
Singles: 7-inch
MALA (12007 "Your Cold Cold Heart Just Burns Me Up") 10-20 68
STATUE ("Your Cold Cold Heart Just Burns Me Up") 25-50 68
(First issue. Selection number not known.)

HENDRICKS, Nat
Singles: 7-inch
SEW CITY 4-8 66

HENDRIX, Al
(With Jolly Jody & His Go Daddies)
Singles: 78 rpm
ABC-PAR 15-25 57
TALLY 50-75 57
Singles: 7-inch
ABC-PAR (9901 "Rhonda Lee").....25-35 57
LEGREE (701 "Young and Wild") 75-100 60
TALLY (119 "Rhonda Lee").........50-100 57

HENDRIX, Jimi P&R/LP '67
(Jimi Hendrix Experience)
Singles: 12-inch
REPRISE (840 "Jimi Hendrix") 50-100 79
(Brown label. Includes cover. Promotional issue only.)
Singles: 7-inch
AUDIO FIDELITY (167 "No Such Animal") 10-20
REPRISE (1000 "Freedom")..........10-15 71
REPRISE (1044 "Dolly Dagger").....10-15 71
REPRISE (1082 "Johnny B. Goode") 15-25 72
REPRISE (1118 "The Wind Cries Mary") 15-25 72
REPRISE (0572 "Hey Joe") 50-75 67
REPRISE (0597 "Purple Haze").....10-15 67
REPRISE (0641 "Foxey Lady")......10-15 67
REPRISE (0665 "Up from the Skies") 15-25 68
REPRISE (0767 "All Along the Watchtower") 10-15 68
REPRISE (0792 "Crosstown Traffic") 10-15 68
REPRISE (0853 "Stone Free")........15-25 69
REPRISE (0905 "Stepping Stone") 75-125 70
REPRISE BACK-TO-BACK 4-6 70s
TRIP (3002 "Suspicious") 5-10 72
Promotional Singles
REPRISE (1000 "Freedom")..........15-25 71
REPRISE (1044 "Dolly Dagger").....15-25 71
REPRISE (1082 "Johnny B. Goode") 15-25 72
REPRISE (1118 "The Wind Cries Mary") 15-25 72
REPRISE (0572 "Hey Joe") 50-75 67
REPRISE (0597 "Purple Haze").....10-20 67
REPRISE (0641 "Foxey Lady")......10-20 67
REPRISE (0665 "Up from the Skies") 20-30 68
REPRISE (0767 "All Along the Watchtower") 10-20 68
REPRISE (0792 "Crosstown Traffic") 10-20 68
REPRISE (0853 "Stone Free")........20-30 69
REPRISE (0905 "Stepping Stone") 75-100 70
Picture Sleeves
AUDIO FIDELITY (167 "No Such Animal") 15-25
REPRISE (0572 "Hey Joe") 400-800 67
EPs: 7-inch
REPRISE (595 "And a Happy New Year") 100-200 74
(Promotional issue only. Issued with paper sleeve.)
LPs: 10/12-inch
ACCORD (7101 "Before London") ...8-10 81
ACCORD (7112 "Free Sprit") 8-10 81
ACCORD (7139 "Cosmic Feeling") ..8-10 81
AUDIO FIDELITY (320 "Jimi Hendrix") 10-20 84
(Picture disc.)
CRAWDADDY (5-1975 "Jimi Hendrix Interview LP") 200-300 75
PHOENIX 10 (320 "Rare Hendrix") ..8-10 80s
PICKWICK (3528 "Jimi") 10-15 75
NUTMEG (1001 "High, Live 'N Dirty") 15-20 78
(Colored vinyl.)
RCA (68233 "Storm") 10-15 90s
(Picture disc.)
REPRISE (2025 "Smash Hits") 20-30 69
(Orange and brown label. Add $20 to $30 if accompanied by 28" x 20" bonus poster.)
REPRISE (2025 "Smash Hits") 50-100 71
(White label. Promotional issue only. Add $20 to $30 if accompanied by 28" x 20" bonus poster.)
REPRISE (2025 "Smash Hits") 10-15 71
(Brown label.)
REPRISE (2029 "Historic Performances") 10-15 70
REPRISE (2029 "Historic Performances") 15-25 70
(White label. Promotional issue only.)
REPRISE (2034 "The Cry of Love") 10-15 70
(Brown label.)
REPRISE (2034 "The Cry of Love") 300-400 70
(Orange label.)
REPRISE (2034 "The Cry of Love") 15-25 70
(White label. Promotional issue only.)
REPRISE (2040 "Rainbow Bridge") 10-15 71
REPRISE (2040 "Rainbow Bridge") 15-25 71
(White label. Gatefold cover has titles/timing sticker. Promotional issue only.)
REPRISE (2049 "In the West") 10-15 72
REPRISE (2049 "In the West") 15-25 72
(White label. Promotional issue only.)
REPRISE (2103 "War Heroes") 10-15 72
REPRISE (2103 "War Heroes") 15-25 72
(Promotional issue only.)
REPRISE (2204 "Crash Landing") 10-15 75
REPRISE (2204 "Crash Landing") 15-25 75
(White label. Promotional issue only.)
REPRISE (2229 "Midnight Lightning") 10-15 75
REPRISE (2229 "Midnight Lightning") 15-25 75
(White label. Promotional issue only.)
REPRISE (2245 "Essential Jimi Hendrix") 10-15 78
(Two discs.)
REPRISE (2245 "Essential Jimi Hendrix") 15-25 78
(Two discs. White label. Promotional issue only.)
REPRISE (2276 "Smash Hits") 8-12 77
REPRISE (2293 "Essential Jimi Hendrix, Vol. 2") 20-50 79
(Includes the bonus *Gloria*, extended version. Prices vary even more widely than the range shown here – from less than $10 to nearly $100. Egad!)
REPRISE (2293 "Essential Jimi Hendrix, Vol. 2") 30-60 79
(White label. Promotional issue only.)
REPRISE (2293 "Essential Jimi Hendrix, Vol. 2") 8-15 79
(Without the bonus single.)
REPRISE (2299 "Nine to the Universe") 8-12 80
REPRISE (2299 "Nine to the Universe") 15-20 80
(White label. Promotional issue only.)
REPRISE (R-6261 "Are You Experienced") 50-75 67
(Monaural. Green, pink and yellow label.)
REPRISE (R-6261 "Are You Experienced") 200-400 67
(White label. Promotional issue only.)
REPRISE (RS-6261 "Are You Experienced") 50-75 67
(Stereo. Green, pink and yellow label.)
REPRISE (6261 "Are You Experienced") 15-25 68
(Orange and brown label.)
REPRISE (6261 "Are You Experienced") 8-12 71
(Brown label.)
REPRISE (R-6281 "Axis: Bold As Love") 300-500 68
(Monaural. Orange and brown label.)
REPRISE (R-6281 "Axis: Bold As Love") 1000-1500 68
(White label. Promotional issue only.)
REPRISE (RS-6281 "Axis: Bold As Love") 20-30 68
(Stereo. Green, pink and yellow label.)
REPRISE (RS-6281 "Axis: Bold As Love") 8-12 71
(Brown label.)
REPRISE (6307 "Electric Ladyland") 15-25 68
(Two discs. Orange and brown label.)
REPRISE (6307 "Electric Ladyland") 100-150 68
(Two discs. White label. Promotional issue only. Cover has "Promotion – Not for Sale" sticker. Stereo. Mono is not known to exist.)
REPRISE (6307 "Electric Ladyland") 8-12 71
(Brown label.)
REPRISE (6481 "Sound Track Recordings from the film *Jimi Hendrix*") 15-20 73
(Two discs. Soundtrack.)
REPRISE (6481 "Sound Track Recordings from the film *Jimi Hendrix*") 20-30 73
(Two discs. White label. Pink "Not for Sale" sticker on cover. Promotional issue only.)
REPRISE (22306 "Jimi Hendrix Concerts") 8-12 82
(Two discs.)
REPRISE (22306 "Jimi Hendrix Concerts") 15-20 82
(Two discs. White label. Promotional issue only.)
REPRISE (25119 "Kiss the Sky").....8-10 84
REPRISE (25119 "Kiss the Sky")...15-20 84
(White label. Promotional issue only.)
REPRISE (25358 "Jimi Plays Monterey") 8-10 86
REPRISE (25358 "Jimi Plays Monterey") 15-20 86
(White label. Promotional issue only.)
RHINO (254 "Interview") 15-20 82
(Picture disc.)
RYKO 10-15 87-88
SHOUT (502 "In the Beginning")....10-15 72
(White label with red and blue printing.)
SHOUT (502 "In the Beginning")......8-10
(Yellow label.)
SPRINGBOARD (4031 "In Concert") 8-10 72
TRIP (3505 "Superpak") 15-25 74
TRIP (3509 "Superpak") 15-25 74
(Same title but different tracks than Trip 3505.)
TRIP (9500 "Rare Hendrix")..........15-25 72
(Gatefold cover. Includes Hendrix poster.)
TRIP (9500 "Rare Hendrix")..........10-15 72
(Standard cover.)
TRIP (9501 "Roots of Hendrix") 10-15 72
TRIP (9523 "Genius of Jimi Hendrix") 10-15 74
U.A. (505 "Very Best of the World of Jimi Hendrix") 8-12 75
Session: Al Kooper; Buddy Miles; Mike Finnigan; Freddie Smith; Larry Faucette; Stevie Winwood; Jack Cassidy; Chris Wood.
Also see BROOKS, Rosa Lee
Also see REDDING, Noel, Band
Also see REDDING, Otis / Jimi Hendrix

HENDRIX, Jimi, & Isley Bros.
LPs: 10/12-inch
T-NECK (3007 "In the Beginning") 10-20 71
Also see ISLEY BROTHERS

HENDRIX, Jimi, & Curtis Knight
LPs: 10/12-inch
CAPITOL (659 "Flashing") 8-10 70
CAPITOL (2856 "Get That Feeling") 10-15 67
CAPITOL (2894 "Flashing")..........10-15 68
51 WEST 5-10 82
Also see KNIGHT, Curtis

HENDRIX, Jimi, & Lightnin' Rod
Singles: 12-inch
CELLULOID (166 "Doriella Du Fontaine") 5-10 84

HENDRIX, Jimi, & Little Richard
(Little Richard - Jimi Hendrix)
Singles: 7-inch
ALA (1175 "Goodnight Irene")..........5-10 72
LPs: 10/12-inch
ALA (1972 "Friends from the Beginning") 10-15 72
EVEREST (296 "Roots of Rock")........8-10 74
PICKWICK (3347 "Together")..........8-10 73
Also see LITTLE RICHARD

HENDRIX, Jimi, & Buddy Miles
(With Billy Cox)
LPs: 10/12-inch
CAPITOL (472 "Band of Gypsies"). 10-20 70
CAPITOL (12416 "Band of Gypsies 2") 5-10 86
(Mini-LP. Shows three tracks correctly on Side 2.)
CAPITOL (12416 "Band of Gypsies 2") 75-125 86
(Has four tracks on Side 2 – all different than the three listed on label.)
CAPITOL (16319 "Band of Gypsies") 8-10 86
CAPITOL (96414 "Band of Gypsies") 10-15 95
(Limited numbered edition.)
Also see MILES, Buddy

HENDRIX, Jimi, & Lonnie Youngblood
(Lonnie Youngblood with Jimi Hendrix) LP '71
Singles: 7-inch
FAIRMOUNT 10-20 65
LPs: 10/12-inch
MAPLE (6004 "Two Great Experiences Together") 20-25 71
Also see HENDRIX, Jimi
Also see YOUNGBLOOD, Lonnie

HENDRIX, Margie
Singles: 78 rpm
LAMP 5-10 56
Singles: 7-inch
LAMP 10-15 56
MERCURY 4-6 65-68
SOUND STAGE 7 .... 3-6 69
TANGERINE 4-6 64
Also see CHARLES, Ray
Also see RAELETTES

HENDRIX, Patti R&B '78
Singles: 7-inch
HILLTAK 3-5 78
20TH FOX 3-5 74

HENDRYX, Nona P&R/R&B/D&D/LP '83
Singles: 12-inch
RCA 4-6 83-86
Singles: 7-inch
EMI AMERICA 3-4 87
EPIC 3-5 77
RCA 3-4 83-87
Picture Sleeves
EMI AMERICA 3-4 87
LPs: 10/12-inch
EMI AMERICA 5-8 87
EPIC 5-10 77
RCA 5-10 83-87
Also see LABELLE, Patti

HENHOUSE FIVE PLUS TOO P&R '77
Singles: 7-inch
W.B./AHAB 3-5 76-77
Member: Ray Stevens.
Also see STEVENS, Ray

HENKE, Mel
Singles: 7-inch
CUCA (1460 "Woman in Space").....5-10 69

HENLEY, Don P&R/LP '82
Singles: 12-inch
GEFFEN 4-6 85
Singles: 7-inch
ASYLUM 3-4 82-83
GEFFEN 3-4 84-90
Picture Sleeves
ASYLUM 3-4 82
GEFFEN 3-4 84-89
LPs: 10/12-inch
ASYLUM 5-10 82-83
GEFFEN 5-10 84-89
Also see EAGLES
Also see HORNSBY, Bruce
Also see NICKS, Stevie, & Don Henley
Also see SHILOH

HENLEY, Larry
Singles: 7-inch
ATCO 4-8 68
CAPRICORN 3-5 74
HICKORY 5-10 63-66
LPs: 10/12-inch
CAPRICORN 6-10 74
VIKING 8-10 71
Also see NEWBEATS

HENN, Rick
Singles: 7-inch
EPIC 4-6 74
Also see RANGERS
Also see RENEGADE V
Also see SUNRAYS

HENRI, Adrian, & Roger McGough
LPs: 10/12-inch
EPIC 12-15 67

HENRIETTA
(With the Hairdooz)
Singles: 7-inch
LIBERTY (Except 55606) 8-12 63
LIBERTY (55606 "I Love Him")......20-25 63

HENRY, Andrea
Singles: 7-inch
MGM (13893 "I Need You Like a Baby") 10-20 68

HENRY, Audie C&W '85
Singles: 7-inch
CANYON CREEK 3-4 85

HENRY, Clarence P&R/R&B '56
(Clarence "Frogman" Henry)
Singles: 78 rpm
ARGO 10-20 56-57
Singles: 7-inch
ARGO (5200 series) 15-20 56-58
ARGO (5300 & 5400 series) 8-15 59-63
CADET 4-8 66
DIAL 4-8 67
PARROT 4-8 64-66
CHESS 3-5 73
ERIC 3-5 73
MAISON DE SOUL 3-5 77
LPs: 10/12-inch
ARGO (4009 "You Always Hurt the One You Love") 75-125 61
CFH (101 "Bourbon St. New Orleans") 15-20
CADET (4009 "You Always Hurt the One You Love") 20-30 65
(Cadet 4009 LPs can be found in Argo 4009 covers.)
ROULETTE (42039 "Clarence 'Frogman' Henry Is Alive & Well") 15-25 69
Also see GAYTEN, Paul

HENRY, Earl
Singles: 7-inch
DOT (15756 "What'cha Gonna Do") 30-40 58

HENRY, Edd
Singles: 7-inch
BIG MACK (1286 "Crooked Woman") 100-200
NU-SOUND (180 "I Love Only You") 50-100

HENRY, Freddy
(Freddy Bliffert)
LP: 10/12-inch
CLOUDS 8-12 79
Also see BLIFFERT
Also see FREELOADERS

HENRY, Freddy, & Betty Wright
Singles: 7-inch
TK (1045 "Tell Her") 3-4 81
Member: Freddy Bliffert.
Also see WRIGHT, Betty

HENRY, Haywood
Singles: 7-inch
MERCURY (71674 "Midnight Alley") 10-20 60

HENRY, Ja Neen
Singles: 7-inch
BLUE ROCK (4010 "Baby Boy") 15-25

HENRY, James
(With the Olympics)
Singles: 7-inch
JERDEN 4-8 65

HENRY, John, & Steel Drivers
Singles: 7-inch
ARLINGTON (108 "Sweet and Neat") 20-30

HENRY, John, III
Singles: 7-inch
COUNTRY BLUES 3-5

HENRY, John "Rootman"
Singles: 7–inch
AMBER ANTIQUE.. 4-6 72
BROWNSTONE 10-15

HENRY, Robert
Singles: 78 rpm
KING (4624 "Miss Anna B") 150-200 53
KING (4646 "Old Battle Ax") 150-200 53
Singles: 7–inch
KING (4624 "Miss Anna B") 550-650 53
KING (4646 "Old Battle Ax") 550-650 53

HENRY, Stacy, & Flip Jacks Orchestra
Singles: 7–inch
FLIPPIN' (108 "Sweetest Darling") .10-15
FLIPPIN' (203 "Magic Was the Night")..10-15 60
(With the Dream-Timers.)
Also see DREAM-TIMERS

HENRY, Thomas
Singles: 7–inch
HIT (73 "So Much in Love") 5-10 63

HENRY & FRIENDS
Singles: 7–inch
ORIGINAL SOUND........................... 4-8 63

HENRY & MAMIE
Singles: 7–inch
AMY 5-10 60

HENRY COW
LPs: 10/12–inch
VIRGIN.. 8-10 74
Member: Fred Frith.

HENRY PAUL: see PAUL, Henry, Band

HENRY IX
Singles: 7–inch
SHOWCASE 4-6 66

HENRY TREE
Singles: 7–inch
MAINSTREAM................................... 5-10 70
LPs: 10/12–inch
MAINSTREAM (6129 "Electric Holy Man")..20-30 70

HENSKE, Judy
Singles: 7–inch
ELEKTRA....................................... 5-10 63
MERCURY 4-8 65
REPRISE.. 4-8 66
STRAIGHT 5-10 68
LPs: 10/12–inch
ELEKTRA....................................... 15-20 63
MERCURY 10-20 65
REPRISE....................................... 10-20 66
Also see COFFEE HOUSE
Also see GUARD, Dave, & Whiskeyhill Singers
Also see HART, Judy

HENSKE, Judy, & Jerry Yester
LPs: 10/12–inch
REPRISE....................................... 8-12 68
STRAIGHT 15-20 68
Also see HENSKE, Judy
Also see ROSEBUD
Also see YESTER, Jerry

HENSLEE, Gene
Singles: 78 rpm
IMPERIAL (8227 "Dig'n & Datin' ") 15-25 54
Singles: 7–inch
IMPERIAL (8227 "Dig'n & Datin' ") 35-50 54
LE CAM.. 3-5 73
MEL-O-DY (110 "Beautiful Woman")......................................10-15 64
U.A. 5-8 65

HENSLEY, Ken *LP '73*
Singles: 7–inch
MERCURY 3-5 73
LPs: 10/12–inch
MERCURY 8-10 73
W.B. 8-10 75
Also see TOE FAT
Also see URIAH HEEP

HENSLEY, Ronnie, & Co.
Singles: 7–inch
VICTIM ("Hang Down Your Head John Hinckley")................................. 5-8 82
(No selection number used.)

HENSLEY, Tari *C&W '83*
Singles: 7–inch
MERCURY 3-4 83-86

HENSON
Singles: 7–inch
FAME 3-5 74
LPs: 10/12–inch
FAME 5-10 74

HENSON, Curley
Singles: 7–inch
GULF REEF 5-10 61

HENSON, Jim *P&R '70*
(Jim Henson's Muppets)
Singles: 7–inch
COLUMBIA....................................... 3-5 72
SIGNATURE..................................... 5-8 60
Singles: 12–inch
COLUMBIA....................................... 5-10 71
Also see ERNIE
Also see KERMIT / Fozzie Bear
Also see MUPPETS

HENTSCHEL, David
Singles: 7–inch
RING O'.. 3-5 75
LPs: 10/12–inch
RING O'.. 6-10 75

HEP CATS
Singles: 7–inch
DEL-FI (4159 "What in the World Can I Do")...25-50 61

HEP STARS
Singles: 7–inch
CAMEO 10-15 65

HEP STARS
Singles: 7–inch
CHARTMAKER 8-10 69
DUNHILL... 12-15 66
Member: Benny Andersson.
Also see ABBA
Also see BJORN & BENNY

HEPCAT, Dr: see DURST, L.

HEPCAT, Harry, & Boogie Woogie Band
Singles: 7–inch
GRAFFITI 3-5 72
EPs: 7–inch
AETERNUS...................................... 5-10

HEPSTERS
Singles: 78 rpm
RONEL... 50-100 55
Singles: 7–inch
RONEL (107 "I Had to Let You Go")..250-350 55
RONEL (110 "I Gotta Sing the Blues")..200-300 56

HEPTONES
Singles: 78 rpm
ABBCO (401 "I'm So in Love Tonight")......................................150-250 56
Singles: 7–inch
ABBCO (401 "I'm So in Love Tonight")....................................500-1000 56
(Serial numbers "105"/"106," are more prominent on label than selection no. "401.")

HEPTONES
LPs: 10/12–inch
U.A. 5-10 77

HERALDS
Singles: 78 rpm
HERALD (435 "Eternal Love") 50-75 54
Singles: 7–inch
HERALD (435 "Eternal Love") ...100-200 54
Member: Billy Dawn Smith.
Also see DAWN, Billy, Quartet
Also see FOUR DUKES

HERALDS
Singles: 7–inch
TAMBORINE (2 "Wonder Boy").......8-10

HERB & CRONIES
Singles: 7–inch
TOP NOTCH 4-8 66

HERB & JERRY
Singles: 7–inch
DOT 5-8 62

HERB B. LOU: see LOU, Herb B.

HERB THE "K" *R&B '85*
Singles: 7–inch
PRIVATE I... 3-4 85

HERB'S HALLUCINATIONS
Singles: 7–inch
MGM (13735 "Birds, Fish & Chips")...10-15 67

HERBERT, Johnny, & Cavaliers
Singles: 7–inch
TED.. 5-10 73

HERBIE & CLASS CUTTERS
Singles: 7–inch
RCA... 8-12 59

HERBIE'S PEOPLE
Singles: 7–inch
OKEH 4-6 66

HERBS, The
Singles: 7–inch
SMOKE (602 "Never Never").........15-25 60
SMOKE (612 "There Must Be an Answer")......................................15-25 60

HERBST, Jack
Singles: 7–inch
DEL-FI (4228 "Jimmy's Party") 10-15 63

HERBY JOE
Singles: 78 rpm
ABCO 15-25 56
Singles: 7–inch
ABCO (101 "Smokestack Lightning")......................................30-50 56

HERD
Singles: 7–inch
FONTANA 4-8 67-68
LPs: 10/12–inch
FONTANA 15-25 68
Also see FRAMPTON, Peter

HERD
Singles: 7–inch
OCTOPUS (257 "Things Won't Change")..20-30 67

HERDER, Pervis
(With the Combo Kings)
Singles: 7–inch
IMPERIAL 5-10 63
JAMIE 5-10 63
Also see COMBO KINGS

HERE & NOW
Singles: 7–inch
MONUMENT 10-15 69

HERETICS
Singles: 7–inch
GET HIP.. 3-5 90
LPs: 10/12–inch
GET HIP.. 5-10 90
Members: Steve Fabian; Mike Michalski; Rube; Joel Timulak.

HERITAGE
Singles: 7–inch
PIP 8-12 60s

HERMAN, Bonnie
Singles: 7–inch
COLUMBIA.. 4-6 66-67
Picture Sleeves
COLUMBIA.. 4-6 66
Also see SINGERS UNLIMITED

HERMAN, Cleve / Don Rays
Singles: 7–inch
CAPCO (103 "In This Corner").......10-20 63

HERMAN, Keith *P&R '79*
Singles: 7–inch
RADIO.. 3-5 79

HERMAN, Pee-Wee
Singles: 7–inch
COLUMBIA.. 3-4 87
Picture Sleeves
COLUMBIA.. 3-4 87
Also see WILLIS, Allee

HERMAN, Sticks
Singles: 78 rpm
HOLLYWOOD.................................. 25-50 57
Singles: 7–inch
HOLLYWOOD (1085 "Wipe the Tears from Your Eyes")..................................25-50 57
TIC TOC (103 "Give Me Your Love")..10-20

HERMAN, Woody, Orchestra *P&R '37*
Singles: 78 rpm
CAPITOL.. 3-5 54-56
COLUMBIA.. 3-6 45-48
DECCA... 4-6 37-45
MARS... 3-5 52-53
Singles: 7–inch
CADET... 3-5 69
CAPITOL.. 4-8 54-56
CENTURY... 3-4 79
CHURCHILL...................................... 3-4 79
COLUMBIA.. 3-5 65-76
FANTASY.. 3-5 73-74
MCA... 3-5 73
MARS... 4-8 52-53
PHILIPS.. 3-5 62
EPs: 7–inch
CAPITOL.. 5-10 55-56
COLUMBIA.. 8-12 52-54
DECCA... 5-10 56
MGM.. 5-10 52-55
LPs: 10/12–inch
ACCORD.. 5-10 82
ATLANTIC (1300 series)................ 10-20 60
ATLANTIC (90000 series)................ 5-10 82
BRIGHT ORANGE............................. 5-10 73
CADET... 8-12 69-71
CAPITOL.. 5-10 72-75
(With "M" or "SM" prefix.)
CAPITOL.. 10-25 55-62
(With "T" or "ST" prefix.)
CENTURY... 5-10 78
CHESS... 5-10 76
COLUMBIA (500 series) 15-25 55
COLUMBIA (2300 & 2400 series) 5-15 65-66
COLUMBIA (2500 series) 15-25 52-54
(10–inch LPs.)
COLUMBIA (6000 series) 15-25 49-55
COLUMBIA (9000 series) 5-15 65-67
COLUMBIA (32000 series) 5-10 74
CONCORD JAZZ 5-10 81-83
CROWN... 10-15 59
DECCA (4000 series) 8-15 64
DECCA (8000 series) 10-25 56
EVEREST (Except 200 & 300 series)... 10-20 59-63
EVEREST (200 & 300 series) 5-10 74-78
FPM 5-10 75
FANTASY... 5-10 71-81
HARMONY....................................... 5-10 72
JAZZLAND 10-20 60
MGM 10-25 55
METRO 5-12 65
PHILIPS... 10-15 62-65
ROULETTE 10-20 59
SURREY 8-12 66
TREND.. 5-10 81
TRIP 5-10 75
VSP 8-12 66-67
VERVE... 8-15 63-68
WHO'S WHO in JAZZ 5-10 78
WING 5-10
Also see BYRD, Charlie, & Woody Herman
Also see CLOONEY, Rosemary
Also see ECKSTINE, Billy, & Woody Herman
Also see WISEMAN, Mac

HERMAN'S HERMITS *P&R '64*
Singles: 7–inch
ABKCO... 3-4
BUDDAH 3-5 74-76
MGM 4-6 64-69
PRIVATE STOCK............................... 3-5 75
Picture Sleeves
MGM 5-12 65-67
LPs: 10/12–inch
ABKCO... 5-10 73-76
CAPITOL (90646 "Hold On!") 10-20 66
(Soundtrack. Record club issue.)
MGM (E-4000 series, except 4478).. 10-20 65-67
(Monaural.)
MGM (SE-4000 series, except 4478).. 8-15 65-68
MGM (E-4478 "Blaze")................... 35-45 67
(Monaural.)
MGM (SE-4478 "Blaze")................... 8-15 67
(Stereo.)
Members: Peter Noone; Derek Leckenby; Karl Green; Keith Hopwood; Barry Whitwham.
Also see ALSTON, Shirley
Also see NOONE, Peter
Also see PAGE, Jimmy

HERMETO
LPs: 10/12–inch
BUDDAH 8-10 72

HERMON & ROCKIN' TONICS
Singles: 7–inch
ROYAL (2871 "Been So Long") . 100-200

HERN, Sheila
Singles: 7–inch
CHART 4-6 68

HERNANDEZ, Danny, & Ones
Singles: 7–inch
RARE EARTH (5018 "As Long As I've Got You")..5-10 70
(Black vinyl.)
RARE EARTH (5018 "As Long As I've Got You")..10-15 70
(Colored vinyl. Promotional issue only.)
LPs: 10/12–inch
SPIRIT (2003 "Back Home at the Brewery")..10-15 72
Also see ONES, The

HERNANDEZ, Patrick *P&R/LP '79*
Singles: 12–inch
COLUMBIA.. 4-6 79
Singles: 7–inch
COLUMBIA.. 3-4 79
LPs: 10/12–inch
COLUMBIA.. 5-10 79

HERO
Singles: 7–inch
LIFESONG 3-5 75
20TH FOX 3-4 78
LPs: 10/12–inch
MERCURY 8-10 77
20TH FOX 5-10 78

HEROES
Singles: 12–inch
RCA... 4-8 87
Singles: 7–inch
RCA... 3-4 87
LPs: 10/12–inch
POLYDOR.. 5-10 80
RCA... 5-10 87

HEROES OF CRANBERRY FARM
Singles: 7–inch
JAMIE (1386 "Big City Miss Ruth Ann").. 8-10 70
LANCELOT 5-10

HERON, Mike
LPs: 10/12–inch
ELEKTRA.. 15-20 71

HERRERA, Little Julian
(With the Tigers; with Jim Balcom Orchestra; Ron Gregory)
Singles: 78 rpm
DIG 25-50 56-57
Singles: 7–inch
DIG (118 "Lonely Lonely Nights") 75-125 56
DIG (137 "Here in My Arms") 50-100 57
ELDO (118 "Lonely Lonely Nights")..15-25 62
EMMO (3302 "You Will Cry")......... 15-25 60s
ESSAR (1012 "Lonely Lonely Nights")..15-25 63
STARLA (6 "I Remember Linda")... 50-75 58
Also see BALCOM, Bill

HERRING, Red *C&W '60*
Singles: 7–inch
COUNTRY JUBILEE 5-10 60

HERRINGS, Harry, & Radials
Singles: 7–inch
HIGHLAND ("A Crystal Ship")........20-30
(Selection number not known.)

HERROLD, Dennis
Singles: 78 rpm
IMPERIAL 40-60 57
Singles: 7–inch
IMPERIAL (5482 "Hip Hip Baby") .. 40-60 57

HERSHEY, Bill, & Almonds
Singles: 7–inch
GULF 5-10 60

HERVEY, Pat
Singles: 7–inch
RCA... 5-10 62-64

HESITATIONS *R&B '67*
Singles: 7–inch
GWP (504 "Yes I'm Ready") 15-25 69
KAPP 8-15 66-68
LPs: 10/12–inch
KAPP 10-20 67-68
Members: George Scott; Fred Deal; Leonard Veal.
Also see METROTONES
Also see TURNER, Sonny, & Sound Ltd.

HESS, Bennie
(Big Ben Hess)
Singles: 7–inch
MAJOR (1001 "Wild Hog Hop") ... 75-125 58
MUSICODE (5693 "Wild Hog Hop").. 40-60
SHOWLAND 3-5 78
SPADE (2202 "Elvis Presley Boogie")... 50-75 58
TAP (1016 "Tennessee Mama Blues")....................................... 75-100 60

HESS, Chuck
Singles: 7–inch
AMIGO (103 "Tijuana Guitar") 10-20 66

HESS, Fred: see JALOPY FIVE

HESS, Troy
Singles: 7–inch
SHOW LAND 8-10

HESSLER, Fred, & the U.C.L.A. Basketball Team
LPs: 10/12–inch
DOT (9501 "Perfect Season") 10-20 64

HESTER, Carolyn
Singles: 7–inch
DOT 4-8 64
LPs: 10/12–inch
COLUMBIA (1796 "Carolyn Hester")..25-50 62
(Monaural.)
COLUMBIA (2032 "This Life I'm Living")..10-20 63
COLUMBIA (8596 "Carolyn Hester")..30-60 62
(Stereo. Has six "eye" logo boxes—three on each side.)
COLUMBIA (8596 "Carolyn Hester")..15-25 65
(Stereo. No "eye" logo boxes.)
DOT 10-15 64-65
Session: Bob Dylan (harmonica on 1962 Columbia LP.)
Also see DYLAN, Bob

HESTOR, Hoot *C&W '79*
Singles: 7–inch
LITTLE DARLING.............................. 3-5 79

HESTOR, Tony
(Tony Hester)
Singles: 7–inch
GIANT (707 "Watch Yourself") .. 100-150 66
KARATE (523 "Watch Yourself") ... 50-75 66
LUCK 5-10 66

HEVY GUNZ
LPs: 10/12–inch
ENTERPRISE 10-12 72

HEW
LPs: 10/12–inch
JAM... 6-12

HEWETT, Howard *R&B '85*
Singles: 7–inch
ARISTA 3-4 88
ELEKTRA.. 3-4 85-90
Picture Sleeves
ELEKTRA.. 3-4 86
LPs: 10/12–inch
ELEKTRA.. 5-8 85-90
Also see SHALAMAR
Also see WARWICK, Dionne, & Howard Hewett

HEWITT, Ben
Singles: 7–inch
MERCURY (Except 71472 and 71612) 10-20 58-59
MERCURY (71472 "For Quite Awhile").. 5-10 59
MERCURY (71612 "Whirlwind Blues").. 20-30 60

HEWITT, Dolph *C&W '49*
Singles: 78 rpm
RCA... 5-10 49

HEXORCIST
Singles: 7–inch
DUNHILL.. 3-5 74
LPs: 10/12–inch
DUNHILL.. 8-10 74
Members: Gary Owens; Dick Gautier; Pat Paulsen; Jaye P. Morgan; Jack DeLeon; Patti Deutsch; Joan Gerber; Gary Miller; Dennis Flanigan; John Rappaport.
Also see MORGAN, Jaye P.
Also see OWENS, Gary
Also see PAULSEN, Pat

HEYBURNERS
Singles: 7–inch
TITANIC (5009 "Speedway") 10-20 63
Session: Davie Allan; Mike Curb.

HEYES, Mark
LPs: 10/12–inch
GOOD SOUNDS 10-12

HEYETTES *P&R '76*
Singles: 7–inch
LONDON.. 3-5 76
Picture Sleeves
LONDON.. 5-10 76

LPs: 10/12-inch
LONDON ... 5-10 76

HEYMAN, Richard X.
LPs: 10/12-inch
CYPRESS ... 5-10 90

HEYWARD, Nick LP '84
Singles: 7-inch
ARISTA ... 3-4 83-84
LPs: 10/12-inch
ARISTA ... 5-10 83
Also see HAIRCUT ONE HUNDRED

HEYWARD, Sammy
Singles: 78 rpm
COLUMBIA (40884 "Honey Man")... 5-10 57
Singles: 7-inch
COLUMBIA (40884 "Honey Man")... 5-10 57

HEYWOOD, Eddie P&R '45
Singles: 78 rpm
DECCA ... 3-5 45-53
MERCURY ... 3-5 55-57
Singles: 7-inch
DECCA ... 4-6 51-53
LIBERTY ... 3-5 61-63
MERCURY ... 3-6 55-61
20TH FOX ... 3-5 63
EPs: 7-inch
COLUMBIA ... 4-8 52
DECCA ... 4-8 56
MERCURY ... 4-8 55-56
LPs: 10/12-inch
BRUNSWICK ... 10-15 55
CAPITOL ... 5-10 67-69
COLUMBIA ... 10-20 52
CORAL ... 10-15 55
DECCA ... 10-15 56
EPIC ... 10-15 56
LIBERTY ... 8-12 62-63
MERCURY ... 10-15 55-60
RCA ... 10-12 59
SUNSET ... 5-10 66
VOCALION ... 5-10 66
WING ... 8-12 59-64
Also see HOLIDAY, Billie, & Eddie Heywood
Also see WINTERHALTER, Hugo, & His Orchestra

HEYWOOD, Ann
Singles: 7-inch
HONDO (100 "Crook His Little Finger") ... 10-20

HEYWOODS: see DONALDSON, Bo, & Heywoods

HEZEKIAH
Singles: 7-inch
CASUAL (001 "Do You Feel the Beat") ... 10-15 79

HEZEKIAH & HOUSE ROCKERS
LPs: 10/12-inch
HIGH WATER ... 8-10 90

HI FIVES
Singles: 78 rpm
FLAIR-X ... 10-20 56
Singles: 7-inch
FLAIR-X (3000 "Throwing Pebbles in the Pond") ... 25-45 56

HIATT, John LP '87
Singles: 12-inch
A&M ... 4-8 87
(Promotional only.)
GEFFEN ... 4-8 85
(Promotional only.)
Singles: 7-inch
A&M ... 3-4 87-90
ATLANTIC ... 3-4 85
GEFFEN ... 3-4 85
MCA ... 3-4 79-90
Picture Sleeves
A&M ... 3-4 87
LPs: 10/12-inch
A&M ... 5-10 87-90
GEFFEN ("Riot with Hiatt") ... 25-35
(Promotional issue only.)
MFSL (210 "Bring the Family") ... 20-25 94
Also see COSTELLO, Elvis

HI-BALLERS
(Hi Ballers)
Singles: 7-inch
SUN STATE (103 "Day Train") ... 10-20 62

HIBBLER, Al R&B '48
Singles: 78 rpm
ALADDIN ... 4-8 56
ATLANTIC ... 5-10 50
CHESS ... 5-10 51
CLEF ... 4-6 54
COLUMBIA ... 4-6 50
DECCA ... 4-8 55-57
MERCURY ... 4-6 52-56
MIRACLE ... 5-10 48
NORGRAN ... 4-6 54-55
ORIGINAL ... 4-8 55
Singles: 7-inch
ALADDIN ... 5-10 56
ATLANTIC (925 "The Blues Came Tumbling Down") ... 30-40 51
ATLANTIC (932 "Travelin' Light") ... 30-40 51
ATLANTIC (945 "This Is Always") ... 30-40 51
ATLANTIC (1071 "Danny Boy") ... 15-25 55
CLEF ... 4-8 54
COLUMBIA ... 5-10 50
DECCA ... 4-8 55-59
MCA ... 3-4 74
MERCURY ... 4-8 52-56
NORGRAN ... 4-8 54-55
ORIGINAL ... 5-10 55
REPRISE ... 4-6 61-62
SATIN ... 3-6 66
TOP RANK ... 4-6 60
VEGAS ... 3-6 67
EPs: 7-inch
CLEF ... 10-20 51
DECCA ... 10-20 55-57
NORGRAN ... 10-20 53
RCA ... 10-15 55
LPs: 10/12-inch
ATLANTIC ... 25-50 56
CLEF ... 25-50 54
DECCA (8000 series) ... 20-40 56-59
DECCA (75000 series) ... 5-10 69
LMI ... 8-12 65
MCA ... 5-10 76
NORGRAN (4 "Favorites") ... 25-50 53
REPRISE ... 10-15 61
TRIP ... 4-8 77
VERVE ... 10-20 55
Also see HOLIDAY, Billie, & Al Hibbler
Also see McSHANN, Jay
Also see RUSHING, Jimmy, & Al Hibbler

HIBBLER, Al, & Duke Ellington
Singles: 7-inch
COLUMBIA (33000 series) ... 3-4 76
LPs: 10/12-inch
COLUMBIA ... 15-25 56
Also see ELLINGTON, Duke
Also see HIBBLER, Al

HI-BOYS
Singles: 7-inch
MALA ... 5-10 59
WOODRICH (1250 "So Good") ... 10-20 60s

HI-BREDS
Singles: 7-inch
MAGIC CIRCLE ... 4-8 63

HICKEY, Ersel P&R '58
Singles: 7-inch
APOLLO (761 "Upside Down Love") ... 15-25 62
BLACK CIRCLE ... 3-5 72
EPIC ... 10-15 58-60
JANUS ... 3-5 71
KAPP ... 8-12 61
LAURIE ... 8-12 63
MAGNUM ... 3-4 84
RAMESES ... 3-5 76
TOOT ... 8-12
UNIFAX ... 3-5 74
EPs: 7-inch
EPIC (7206 "Ersel Hickey in Lover's Land") ... 75-100 58

HICKEY, Sara "Honeybear" C&W '83
Singles: 7-inch
PCM ... 3-4 83

HICKMAN, Dwayne
Singles: 7-inch
ABC-PAR (9908 "School Dance") ... 5-10 58
CAPITOL ... 5-10 60
Picture Sleeves
ABC-PAR (9908 "School Dance") .. 10-20 58
LPs: 10/12-inch
CAPITOL (T-1441 "Dobie!") ... 15-25 60
(Monaural.)
CAPITOL (ST-1441 "Dobie!") ... 25-40 60
(Stereo.)

HICKORIES
Singles: 7-inch
BELL (125 "Teen Beat") ... 15-25 59

HICKORY WIND
LPs: 10/12-inch
GIGANTIC ("Hickory Wind") ... 500-1000 69
(Reportedly 100 made. Number not known.)
Members: Mike McGuyer; Alan Jones; Bob Strehl.

HICKOX, Jack
Singles: 7-inch
CONSTELLATION ... 3-5 77

HICKS, Bob
(Bobby Hicks)
Singles: 7-inch
MIRASONIC (1001 "Rock, Baby, Rock") ... 100-200 59
SKYWAY (116 "Hassle It Jack") ... 25-50

HICKS, Clair, & Love Exchange D&D '84
Singles: 12-inch
KN ... 4-6 84

HICKS, Dan, & His Hot Licks LP '71
Singles: 7-inch
BLUE THUMB ... 3-5 73-74
LPs: 10/12-inch
BLUE THUMB ... 8-10 71-73
EPIC ... 10-12 69
W.B. ... 5-10 78
Also see CHARLATANS

HICKS, Joe
Singles: 7-inch
ENTERPRISE ... 3-5 73
LPs: 10/12-inch
ENTERPRISE ... 8-10 73

HICKS, Jimmy
Singles: 7-inch
BIG DEAL ... 10-15

HICKS, Johnny
Singles: 78 rpm
COLUMBIA (21064 "Pick Up Blues") ... 10-20 53
COLUMBIA (21135 "I Swear") ... 8-12 53
COLUMBIA (21240 "Hey Now Honey") ... 8-12 54
Singles: 7-inch
COLUMBIA (21064 "Pick Up Blues") ... 25-50 53
COLUMBIA (21135 "I Swear") ... 10-20 53
COLUMBIA (21240 "Hey Now Honey") ... 10-20 54

HICKS, Zerben, & Dynamics: see DYNAMICS

HIDDEN STRENGTH R&B '76
Singles: 7-inch
U.A. ... 3-5 76

HIDE-A-WAYS
Singles: 78 rpm
MGM ... 100-200 55
RONNI ... 300-500 54
Singles: 7-inch
LOST-NITE ... 5-10
MGM (55004 "Cherie") ... 250-350 55
RONNI (1000 "Can't Help Loving That Girl of Mine") ... 4000-6000 54

HIDEAWAYS
Singles: 7-inch
DUEL ... 10-15 63
MIRWOOD ... 4-6 66

HIDER & O'NEILL
Singles: 7-inch
MERCURY ... 4-8 65

HI-FI FEATURING DAVID SURKAMP & IAN MATTHEWS
Singles: 7-inch
SP&S ... 4-8 81
LPs: 10/12-inch
SP&S ... 10-15 81
Also see PAVLOV'S DOG
Also see MATTHEWS, Ian

HI-FIDELITIES
Singles: 7-inch
HI-Q (5000 "Street of Lonliness") ... 100-200 57
Also see CONTOURS
Also see PARKS, Gino

HI-FI-DELS
Singles: 7-inch
ATLANTIC ... 8-12 61

HI-FI FOUR P&R '56
Singles: 78 rpm
KING ... 5-10 56
Singles: 7-inch
KING ... 10-20 56

HI-FIs
Singles: 78 rpm
LIBERTY ... 5-10 56
Singles: 7-inch
LIBERTY ... 10-15 56
Members: Marilyn McCoo; La Monte McLemore; Floyd Butler; Harry Elston.
Also see FIFTH DIMENSION
Also see FRIENDS of DISTINCTION

HI-FIs
("Hi-Fi's")
Singles: 7-inch
MONTEL (1005 "My Dear") ... 200-300 59
Also see SINGLETON, Jimmy, & Royal Satins

HI-FIs
Singles: 7-inch
CAMEO ... 10-15 65
INTERFON ... 10-15 64
U.A. ... 10-15 67

HI-FIVE LP '90
LPs: 10/12-inch
JIVE ... 5-8 90

HI-FIVES
Singles: 7-inch
STAR-X (507 "The Hen Cackle") ... 15-25 57

HI-FIVES
Singles: 7-inch
BINGO (1006 "Felicia") ... 15-20 60
DECCA (30576 "My Friend") ... 20-30 58
DECCA (30657 "Dorothy") ... 50-100 58
(Pink label. Promotional issue only.)
DECCA (30657 "Dorothy") ... 50-100 58
(Black label. Has "Unbreakable 45 rpm Record" on right side. No star under middle "C" in Decca.)
DECCA (30657 "Dorothy") ... 30-50 58
(Black label. No "Unbreakable 45 rpm Record" on label. Has a star under middle "C" in Decca.)
DECCA (30744 "Lonely") ... 20-30 58
Members: Dave Brigatti; Ron Menhardt; Peter Grieco; Howard Lanza; Rudy Jezerak; Joey Dee.
Also see DEE, Joey

HI-FIVES
Singles: 7-inch
BELL (634 "Son of Raunchy") ... 10-20 66
HIT (0003 "Mo-Shun") ... 10-20 60
JERDEN (730 "Going Away") ... 10-15 64

HI-FIVES
Singles: 7-inch
BELL (634 "Julie") ... 30-50 66

HIGDON, Curt
Singles: 7-inch
JUBILEE ... 8-12 58

HIGGINS, Ben
Singles: 7-inch
JAMIE ... 10-20 62
Also see FIVE SATINS

HIGGINS, Bertie P&R '81
Singles: 7-inch
CBS ASSOCIATED ... 3-4 85
KAT FAMILY ... 3-4 81-82
SOUTHERN TRACKS ... 3-4 87-89
LPs: 10/12-inch
KAT FAMILY ... 5-10 82
Also see ROEMANS

HIGGINS, Bertie, & Roy Orbison
Singles: 7-inch
SOUTHERN TRACKS (2010 "Leah") .3-5 89
Also see HIGGINS, Bertie
Also see ORBISON, Roy

HIGGINS, Chuck
(With His Mellotones)
Singles: 78 rpm
ALADDIN ... 5-10 53
CADDY ... 10-15 57
COMBO (Except 12) ... 5-10 54-55
COMBO (12 "Pachuko Hop") ... 10-15 53
DOOTONE ... 8-15 55-57
LOMA ... 5-15 56
LUCKY ... 5-10 53
MONEY ... 5-15 56
R&B ... 5-10 55
SPECIALTY ... 10-20 52-53
Singles: 7-inch
ALADDIN ... 15-25 53
CADDY ... 10-20 57
COMBO (Except 12) ... 10-20 54-65
COMBO (12 "Pachuko Hop") ... 20-40 53
DOOTONE ... 15-25 55-57
KICKS (6F "Groove") ... 15-20
LOMA (706 "Double Dip") ... 15-20 56
LUCKY ... 10-20 53
MONEY (214 "Rock & Roll") ... 15-20 56
R&B ... 10-20 55
ROLLIN' ROCK (011 "Big Bop Boom") ... 3-5 73
ROXBURY ... 3-5 75
SPECIALTY ... 15-30 52-53
EPs: 7-inch
COMBO (2 "Chuck Higgins") ... 35-50 55
LPs: 10/12-inch
COMBO (300 "Pachuko Hop") ... 200-300 55
(Cover pictures a woman wearing only a scarf.)
COMBO (300 "Pachuko Hop") ... 75-100 55
(Cover pictures Higgins and a saxophone.)
ROLLIN' ROCK ... 8-10
Also see FORREST, Gene, & Four Feathers

HIGGINS, Chuck / Roy Milton
EPs: 7-inch
DOOTO (208 "Rock 'N' Roll vs. Rhythm & Blues") ... 10-20 57
DOOTONE (208 "Rock 'N' Roll vs. Rhythm & Blues") ... 25-40 57
LPs: 10/12-inch
AUTHENTIC/DOOTO (223 "Rock 'N' Roll vs. Rhythm & Blues") ... 10-15
DOOTONE (223 "Rock 'N' Roll vs. Rhythm & Blues") ... 75-125 57
Members (Mellotones): John Watson; Eli Toney; Joe Ursery.
Also see HIGGINS, Chuck
Also see MILTON, Roy

HIGGINS, Chuck, & Mellomoods
Singles: 78 rpm
MONEY (214 "Beautiful Love") ... 15-25 56
Singles: 7-inch
MONEY (214 "Beautiful Love") ... 30-50 56
Also see MELLOMOODS

HIGGINS, Monk R&B '66
(With the Specialties)
Singles: 7-inch
BUDDAH ... 3-5 74
CHESS ... 3-6 67
SOLID STATE ... 3-6 68
ST. LAWRENCE ... 4-6 66
U.A. ... 3-5 72-73
LPs: 10/12-inch
BUDDAH ... 5-10 74
SOLID STATE ... 8-12 69
U.A. ... 8-10 72
Also see MASON, Barbara

HIGGINS, Sharon
Singles: 7-inch
KAPP ... 5-10

HIGGS & WILSON
Singles: 7-inch
TIME (1028 "Manny, Oh") ... 5-10 61

HIGH, Bobby, & Gang on 29th Street
Singles: 7-inch
KAMA SUTRA (261 "Turn on the Oven") ... 3-5 74

HIGH, Don
Singles: 7-inch
APT ... 4-8 65
P.I.P. ... 3-5 76

HIGH, Martha
Singles: 7-inch
SALSOUL ... 3-4 80

HIGH, Scot, & Highlanders
Singles: 7-inch
FONO GRAF (1236 "Toy Balloons") ... 8-12 63
Member: Billy Mure.
Also see MURE, Billy

HIGH & MIGHTY
Singles: 7-inch
ABC ... 4-8 66
Also see REFLECTIONS

HIGH COUNTRY
Singles: 7-inch
W.B. ... 3-5 72

HIGH FASHION R&B '82
Singles: 7-inch
CAPITOL ... 3-4 82
LPs: 10/12-inch
CAPITOL ... 5-10 82

HIGH INERGY P&R/R&B/LP '77
Singles: 12-inch
GORDY ... 4-6 83
Singles: 7-inch
GORDY (Black vinyl) ... 3-5 77-83
GORDY (Colored vinyl) ... 4-8 78
(Promotional only.)
LPs: 10/12-inch
GORDY ... 5-10 77-83
Members: Barbara Mitchell; Vernessa Mitchell; Linda Howard; Michelle Martin.
Also see ROBINSON, Smokey, & Barbara Mitchell

HIGH KEYES P&R '63
Singles: 7-inch
ATCO ... 10-20 63-64
Members: Troy Keyes; Jim Williams; Bob Haggard; Cliff Rice.
Also see KEYES, Troy

HIGH KEYS
Singles: 7-inch
VERVE (10423 "Living a Lie") ... 50-75 66

HIGH NUMBERS
Singles: 7-inch
OCEAN (8855 "I'm a Man") ... 8-12 60s

HIGH NUMBERS
Singles: 7-inch
POLYDOR (570 "I'm the Face") ... 3-5 80
(Promotional issue only.)
Picture Sleeves
POLYDOR (570 "I'm the Face") ... 3-5 80
(Promotional issue only.)
Also see WHO

HIGH PERFORMANCE
Singles: 12-inch
NASTYMIX ... 4-8 90

HIGH RIDERS
Singles: 7-inch
SUE ... 5-10 59

HIGH ROLLERS
Singles: 7-inch
SHO-BOAT (101 "Big Thing") ... 20-30

HIGH SCHOOLERS
Singles: 7-inch
QUILL (108 "Graduation Song") ... 10-20 66

HIGH SEAS
Singles: 7-inch
D-M-G (4000 "We Go Together") ... 50-100 60
Member: Adrian Torres.
Also see SATELLITES

HIGH SIERRA
Singles: 7-inch
JCS ... 3-4 84

HIGH SPIRITS
Singles: 7-inch

HIGH SPIRITS
Singles: 7-inch
APEX (76972 "Love Light") ... 20-30 65
(First issue.)
SOMA (1436 "Love Light") ... 10-20 65
SOMA (1446 "I Believe") ... 40-60 66

HIGH TENSIONS & TOMMY DAE
Singles: 7-inch
HITT (591 "Tampico Rage") ... 20-30 64
HITT (6601 "You Got It Made") ... 10-15 66
HITT (6603 "Poor Man") ... 10-15 66

HIGH TIDE
LPs: 10/12-inch
LIBERTY ... 10-15 69

HIGH TREASON
LPs: 10/12-inch
ABBOTT (1209 "High Treason") ... 50-75 68
Members: Joe Cleary; Marcie Rauer; Sam Goodman.

HIGH VOLTAGE
Singles: 7-inch
COLUMBIA ... 3-5 72
LPs: 10/12-inch
COLUMBIA ... 8-10 72

HIGHBAUGH, Rev. John
Singles: 78 rpm
KING ... 10-20 53
Singles: 7-inch
KING (4652 "Do What the Lord Says Do") ... 20-40 53

HIGHBROWS
Singles: 7-inch
ROCK HIGHLAND ... 4-8 60

HIGHER ELEVATION
Singles: 7-inch
LIBERTY (56035 "Summer Skies") .. 5-10 68
Also see DIAMOND, Dave

HIGHFILL, George C&W '87
Singles: 7-inch
W.B. ... 3-4 87

HIGHLANDERS
Singles: 7-inch
RAYS (36 "Sunday Kind of Love") 1000-2000 57

HIGHLIFES
Singles: 7-inch
PIT (403 "No One to Tell Her") 15-25 65

HIGHLIGHTERS
(With Fred Harris' Red Tops Organ Trio)
Singles: 7-inch
NEW SONG (115 "Flang Dang Do") 30-50 50s

HIGHLIGHTS P&R '56
(Featuring Frank Pizani)
Singles: 78 rpm
BALLY 10-20 56-57
Singles: 7-inch
BALLY (1016 "City of Angels") 15-25 56
BALLY (1027 "Will I Ever Know") ...15-25 57
Also see PIZANI, Frank

HIGHLIGHTS
Singles: 7-inch
LODESTAR 20-25 59
PLAY (1004 "Ah, So") 20-25 58
Also see EDDY, Jim & Highlights

HIGHLIGHTS
Singles: 7-inch
ARCADE 5-8 64

HIGHMINDED
Singles: 7-inch
RAIO & RAIO (1006 "The New E") 15-25

HIGHTOWER, Dean, & Twangin' Fools
Singles: 7-inch
ABC-PAR 5-10 59
LPs: 10/12-inch
ABC-PAR (312 "Guitar-Twangy with a Beat") 25-35 59
(Monaural.)
ABC-PAR (S-312 "Guitar-Twangy with a Beat") 35-45 59
(Stereo.)

HIGHTOWER, Donna
(Little Donna Hightower; with Sid Feller Orchestra)
Singles: 7-inch
CAPITOL 8-12 59
DECCA 10-20 52
RPM 10-20 55-58
EPs: 7-inch
CAPITOL (1316 "Selections from *Gee, Baby ... Ain't I Good to You*") 20-30 59
(Promotional issue only.)
LPs: 10/12-inch
CAPITOL (1133 "Take One") 25-50 59
CAPITOL (1273 "Gee, Baby ... Ain't I Good to You") 25-50 59

HIGHTOWER, Jimmy "Okera"
Singles: 7-inch
20TH CENTURY-WESTBOUND 3-5 75

HIGHTOWER, Willie R&B '69
Singles: 7-inch
ADVENTURE ONE (8502 "Tell Me What You Want") 5-8
CAPITOL (2226 "It's a Miracle") 5-10 68
CAPITOL (2651 "It's Too Late") 4-6 69
ENJOY (2019 "Too Late") 8-12 65
FAME (1465 "Walk a Mile in My Shoes") 4-8 70
FAME (1474 "I Can't Live Without You") 4-8 70
FAME (1477 "Poor Man") 4-8 71
FURY (5002 "If I Had a Hammer") 10-20 63
FURY (5004 "I Love You") 10-20 63
SOUND STAGE 7 (2503 "Chicago, Send Her Home") 4-6 76
(This same number is used on a 1963 release by Don Owens.)
Also see OWENS, Don

HIGHWAY
LPs:10/12-inch
HIGHWAY 12-18 74
Also see EPICUREANS

HIGHWAY
Singles: 7-inch
RSO 3-4 79
LPs: 10/12-inch
RSO 5-10 79
Members: Daryl Braithwaite; Harvey James; Tony Mitchell; Garth Porter.
Also see SHERBET

HIGHWAY
Singles: 7-inch
HARE 8-12

HIGHWAY 101
Singles: 7-inch
ROCKET 3-5 77

HIGHWAY 101 C&W '87
Singles: 7-inch
W.B. 3-4 86-92
LPs: 10/12-inch
W.B. 5-10 86-92
Members: Paulette Carlson; Jack Daniels; Scott Moser; Curt Stone; Nikki Nelson.
Also see CARLSON, Paulette
Also see TOMORROW'S WORLD

HIGHWAY ROBBERY
LPs: 10/12-inch
RCA 10-15 72

Members: Don Francisco; John Tunison; Michael Stevens.
Also see PAN

HIGHWAYMEN P&R/LP '61
Singles: 7-inch
ABC-PAR 5-10 65-66
LIBERTY 3-5 81
U.A. 5-15 61-64
LPs: 10/12-inch
ABC-PAR 10-15 66
LIBERTY 5-8 82
U.A. 15-30 61-65
Members: Steve Butts; Chan Daniels; Gil Robbins; Dave Fisher.

HIGNEY, Kenneth
LPs: 10/12-inch
KERBRUTNEY ("Attic Demonstration") 50-75 76

HI-HATS
(Hi Hats)
Singles: 7-inch
EVERLAST (5012 "Hoppin' ") 15-25 58
HI HAT (123 "Big Wake") 8-12

HI-HATS
Singles: 7-inch
HI-HAT (123 "The Big Wake") 30-40

HI-JACKS
Singles: 78 rpm
ABC-PAR 5-10 56
Singles: 7-inch
ABC-PAR 10-15 56

HI-LADS
Singles: 7-inch
CABOT (132 "Ain't You Surprised") 10-15

HI-LARKS
(Hi Larks)
Singles: 7-inch
BEAT (50 "Mine") 150-250 59

HILDEBRAND, Ray
Singles: 7-inch
PHILIPS 4-6 65
LPs: 10/12-inch
MYRRH 5-10 73
TEMPO 5-10 76
WORD 5-10 68-71
Also see JILL & RAY
Also see PAUL & PAULA
Also see RON-DELS

HI-LIGHTERS
Singles: 7-inch
CANNON (369 "Jeannie") 25-35 59
CANNON (372 "Sweet Little Baby of Mine") 20-30 59

HI-LITERS
Singles: 78 rpm
WEN DEE 20-30 55
Singles: 7-inch
WEN DEE (1927 "Baby, Don't Treat Me That Way") 40-60 55

HI-LITERS
Singles: 78 rpm
CELESTE (3005 "Ain't Giving Up Nothing") 50-100 56
Singles: 7-inch
CELESTE (3005 "Ain't Giving Up Nothing") 200-300 56

HI-LITERS
Singles: 78 rpm
VEE JAY (184 "Hello Dear") 100-200 56
Singles: 7-inch
VEE JAY (184 "Hello Dear") 500-750 56

HI-LITERS
Singles: 7-inch
HANOVER 5-10 58

HI-LITERS
(With the Hamiltones; with King Bassie & Three Aces)
Singles: 7-inch
HICO (2432 "Let Me Be True to You") 75-125 58
HICO (2433 "Over the Rainbow") 100-125 58
Member: Ben Vereen.

HI-LITES
(With Leroy Kirkland & Orchestra)
Singles: 78 rpm
OKEH (7046 "I Found a Love") 50-75 54
Singles: 7-inch
OKEH (7046 "I Found a Love") ..100-150 54

HI-LITES
(Hi Lites)
Singles: 78 rpm
MERCURY 5-10 56
Singles: 7-inch
BRUNSWICK (55102 "Friday Night, Go, Go") 10-15 58
JET (501 "The Pony") 10-15 61
JET (502 "4,000 Miles Away") 20-30 61
JULIA (1105 "Gloria") 100-150 62
MERCURY (70987 "The Next Four Years") 10-20 56
RENO (1030 "Please Believe I Love You") 100-200
SCOTTY (301 "The Party's Over") .10-15
TWISTIME (12 "Twistin' Time") 10-15 62
WASSEL 5-10 65

HI-LITES
Singles: 7-inch
AUDIODISC ("Extinction") 10-20 61
(Selection number not known. Promotional issue only.)

HI-LITES
Singles: 7-inch
MONOGRAM (119 "Everybody's Somebody's Fool") 5-8 76
MONOGRAM (120 "To the Aisle") 5-8 76
MONOGRAM (121 "Maybe You'll Be There") 5-8 76
(Colored vinyl.)
RECORD FAIR (500 "I'm Falling in Love") 30-50 61
RECORD FAIR (501 "For Your Precious Love") 30-50 62
LPs: 10/12-inch
DANDEE (206 "For Your Precious Love") 100-200 62
Members: William Tucker; Shelton Highsmith; James Hodge; Eugene Hodge; Allen Gant.

HI-LITES
(Chi-Lites)
Singles: 7-inch
DARAN (011 "You Did That to Me") 50-100 64
DARAN (222 "I'm So Jealous") 50-100 64
Also see CHI-LITES

HILKA C&W '80
(Hilka Cornelius)
Singles: 7-inch
IBC 3-5 79-80

HILKA & JEBRY C&W '79
Singles: 7-inch
IBC 3-5 79-80
Members: Hilka Cornelius; Jebry Lee Briley.
Also see BRILEY, Jebry Lee
Also see HILKA

HILL, The
Singles: 7-inch
IMMEDIATE 4-6 69

HILL, Barbata, Ethridge
LPs: 10/12-inch
ATCO 10-12 71

HILL, Billy: see BILLY HILL

HILL, Bobby R&B '69
Singles: 7-inch
LOLO (2305 "The Children") 5-8 69
LOLO (2307 "To the Bitter End") 25-50 70

HILL, Bunker P&R/R&B '62
Singles: 7-inch
MALA (451 "Hide & Go Seek") 5-10 62
MALA (457 "Nobody Knows") 5-10 62
MALA (464 "The Girl Can't Dance") 8-12 63
Also see MIGHTY CLOUDS of JOY

HILL, Dan LP '75
Singles: 7-inch
COLUMBIA 3-4 87
EPIC 3-4 80-81
20TH FOX 3-5 75-79
Picture Sleeves
20TH FOX 3-5 78
LPs: 10/12-inch
EPIC 5-10 80-81
20TH FOX 5-10 75-80

HILL, Dan, & Vonda Sheppard P&R '87
Singles: 7-inch
COLUMBIA 3-4 87
LPs: 10/12-inch
COLUMBIA 5-10 87
Also see HILL, Dan

HILL, Dave
Singles: 7-inch
APOGEE (106 "Only Boy on the Beach") 20-30 64

HILL, David P&R '59
Singles: 78 rpm
ALADDIN 5-10 57
RCA 5-10 57
Singles: 7-inch
ALADDIN 10-15 57
KAPP 10-15 59
RCA 10-15 57-58

HILL, Delores
Singles: 7-inch
COMPANION (104 "Roller Coaster") 15-25
COMPANION (105 "What He Used to Tell Me") 15-25

HILL, Eddie
Singles: 7-inch
GE GE (502 "I Can't Help It") 15-25 60s
M&S (207 "Nothin' Sweeter Than You Girl") 35-55 68
THELMA (105 "You Got the Best of Me") 50-100 64

HILL, Elaine
Singles: 7-inch
RSVP 4-8 63

HILL, Farris, & Madison Bros.
Singles: 7-inch
V-TONE (231 "Did We Go Steady Too Soon") 25-75 62

HILL, Goldie C&W '53
(Goldie Hill Smith; The Golden Hillbilly)
Singles: 78 rpm
DECCA 4-8 52-57
Singles: 7-inch
DECCA 5-12 52-59
EPs: 7-inch
DECCA 6-12 55-61
LPs: 10/12-inch
DECCA 10-25 60-62
EPIC 10-20 68-69
VOCALION 6-12 67-69
Also see SOVINE, Red, & Goldie Hill

HILL, Goldie, & Justin Tubb C&W '54
(Justin Tubb & Goldie Hill)
Singles: 78 rpm
DECCA 4-8 54-55
Singles: 7-inch
DECCA 6-12 54-55
Also see TUBB, Justin

HILL, Harvey
(Harvey Hill String Band)
Singles: 7-inch
SRC (104 "Boogie Woogie Woman") 150-250 51

HILL, Henry
Singles: 78 rpm
FEDERAL 15-25 51-52
Singles: 7-inch
FEDERAL (12030 "Wandering Blues") 75-100 51
FEDERAL (12037 "Hold Me, Baby") 75-100 51
FEDERAL (12044 "If You Love Me") 75-100 51
FEDERAL (12083 "My Baby's Back Home") 75-100 52

HILL, J.C.
Singles: 7-inch
ARGO 4-8 58

HILL, Jackie
Singles: 7-inch
MAR-BRIT 5-10 63

HILL, Jaycee
Singles: 78 rpm
EPIC (Except 9185) 10-25 56-57
EPIC (9185 "Romp Stompin' Boogie") 10-20 56
Singles: 7-inch
EPIC (Except 9185) 20-40 56-57
EPIC (9185 "Romp Stompin' Boogie") 35-50 56

HILL, Jessie P&R/R&B '60
Singles: 7-inch
BLUE THUMB 5-10
CHESS (1999 "My Children, My Children") 8-12 67
DOWNEY 8-12 64
KERWOOD 10-15
MINIT (607 "Ooh Poo Pah Doo") 10-20 60
MINIT (611 "Whip It on Me") 10-20 60
MINIT (616 "Scoop Scoobie Doobie") 10-20 60
MINIT (622 "I Got Mine") 10-20 61
MINIT (628 "My Love") 10-20 61
MINIT (638 "Sweet Jelly Roll") 10-20 61
MINIT (646 "Can't Get Enough") 10-20 62
YOGI-MAN (607 "Hey Now Mama") 10-15 65
LPs: 10/12-inch
BANDY (70016 "Jessie Hill") 10-15 70s
BLUE THUMB 10-20 72

HILL, Jim, & Jerry Miller
(With the New Mexico Playboys)
Singles: 7-inch
RAZORBACK (110 "Blues at Midnight") 5-10 63

HILL, Joel
(With the Strangers; with Invaders)
Singles: 7-inch
MONOGRAM 8-12 63-65
TRANS-AMERICAN (519 "Little Lover") 35-55 60
Also see CANNED HEAT
Also see MONTEZ, Chris
Also see STRANGERS

HILL, John
Singles: 7-inch
AMY (972 "Get It") 10-20 67

HILL, John, & Piemen
Singles: 7-inch
OTTY 5-10

HILL, Lance
Singles: 7-inch
BANG BANG (4811 "Make My Love a Hurting Thing") 10-20

HILL, Lindel
Singles: 7-inch
BRIGHT STAR (144 "Crush on You") 8-12 65

HILL, Lonnie R&B '84
Singles: 7-inch
URBAN SOUND 3-4 84-85
LPs: 10/12-inch
URBAN SOUND 5-10 85

HILL, Maddy
Singles: 7-inch
COLUMBIA 4-8 64

HILL, Marty
Singles: 7-inch
CAPRICE (103 "Wanting You") 10-15 61

COLUMBIA (41936 "Mr. Oracle of Love") 20-40 61

HILL, Michael
Singles: 7-inch
CAPITOL (4504 "Beatnik Boogie") .10-20 61

HILL, Murray
Singles: 7-inch
STAY (914 "Ooh Ginny Lou") 25-40

HILL, Raymond
Singles: 78 rpm
SUN (204 "The Snuggle") 100-200 54
Singles: 7-inch
SUN (204 "The Snuggle") 250-350 54

HILL, Sam
(Gene Autry)
Singles: 78 rpm
GREYBULL (4281 "My Oklahoma Home") 25-50
GREYBULL (4310 "No One to Call Me Darling") 25-50
GREYBULL (4314 "Stay Away from My Chicken House") 25-50
VAN DYKE (5001 "Why Don't You Come Back Home") 25-50
VAN DYKE (7481 "My Oklahoma Home") 25-50
VAN DYKE (84310 "No One to Call Me Darling") 25-50
Also see AUTRY, Gene

HILL, Sylvia
Singles: 7-inch
CAPITOL 4-8 61-62

HILL, Tessie
Singles: 7-inch
PEACOCK 3-5 75-76

HILL, Tiny, & His Orchestra C&W '46
Singles: 78 rpm
MERCURY 5-10 46-54
Singles: 7-inch
MERCURY 5-15 51-54
EPs: 7-inch
MERCURY 10-15 51-54
LPs: 10/12-inch
MERCURY (25126 "Tiny Hill") 20-35 52
(10-inch LP.)

HILL, Tom
Singles: 7-inch
DREEM (4465 "Stroll Through the Night with Me") 25-35

HILL, Tutti
Singles: 7-inch
AROCK 5-10

HILL, Vernell
Singles: 7-inch
TUFF 4-8 64

HILL, Vicki
Singles: 7-inch
CONGRESS 4-8 64

HILL, Wendy
Singles: 7-inch
ERA 8-12 61-62
LIBERTY 5-8 65

HILL, Windy
Singles: 7-inch
RCA 10-15 57

HILL, Z.Z. P&R/R&B '64
Singles: 7-inch
ATLANTIC 4-8 69-70
AUDREY 4-8 71-72
COLUMBIA 3-5 77-78
HILL 3-6 71-73
KENT 5-15 64-71
M.H. 5-10 63
M.H.R. 4-8 75
MALACO 3-4 82-84
MAILBU 3-4
MESA 8-12 64
MANKIND 4-6 71-72
QUINCY 4-6 70
RARE BULLET 3-4 84
U.A. 3-6 73-75
LPs: 10/12-inch
COLUMBIA 5-10 78-79
KENT 10-20 69-71
MALACO 5-10 82-84
MANKIND 8-12 71
U.A. 8-10 72-75

HILL CITY C&W '85
Singles: 7-inch
MOON SHINE 3-4 85

HILL SISTERS
Singles: 7-inch
ANNA (103 "Hit & Run Away Love") 250-350 59
ANNA (1103 "Hit & Run Away Love") 25-50 59
SPACE (309 "My Lover") 10-20 60s

HILLAGE, Steve LP '77
Singles: 7-inch
ATLANTIC 3-5 76-77
LPs: 10/12-inch
ATLANTIC 8-10 76-77
VIRGIN 8-10 75
Also see ARZACHEL

HILLARD STREET
Singles: 7-inch
CAPITOL (4080 "River Love") 20-40 58
REPRISE (20052 "Indian Giver") ...10-15 62

HILLMAN, Chris LP '76
Singles: 7-inch
ASYLUM.................................3-5 76-77
LPs: 10/12-inch
ASYLUM.................................5-10 76-77
SUGAR HILL.............................5-10 82-84
Session: James Burton; Herb Pedersen; Bennie Leadon; Byron Berline.
Also see BURTON, James
Also see BYRDS
Also see DESERT ROSE BAND
Also see FLYING BURRITO BROTHERS
Also see McGUINN, CLARK & HILLMAN
Also see PEDERSEN, Herb
Also see SOUTHER - HILLMAN - FURAY BAND

HILLMAN, Chris, & Roger McGuinn C&W '89
Singles: 7-inch
UNIVERSAL..............................3-4 89
Members: Roger McGuinn; Chris Hillman.
Also see HILLMAN, Chris
Also see McGUINN, Roger

HILLOW HAMMET
LPs: 10/12-inch
HOUSE of FOX (2 "Hammer").....75-150 68
L&BJ...................................5-10 78

HILLS, Clayton
Singles: 7-inch
LINCO (1319 "Rock, City,Rock")....35-50 61

HILLSIDE SINGERS P&R '71
Singles: 7-inch
METROMEDIA.............................3-5 71-72
LPs: 10/12-inch
METROMEDIA.............................8-12 71

HILLSIDERS
Singles: 7-inch
MEL-O-DY (120 "You Only Pass This Way One Time")..............................10-20 65

HILLTOPPERS P&R '52
(Hill Toppers)
Singles: 78 rpm
DOT....................................5-10 52-57
Singles: 7-inch
ABC....................................3-4 74
DOT (15000 series).....................5-15 52-60
DOT (16000 series).....................4-6 63
3-J....................................3-6 66
EPs: 7-inch
DOT....................................10-15 54-56
LPs: 10/12-inch
DOT (105 "The Hilltoppers")..........30-40 54
(10-inch LP.)
DOT (106 "The Hilltoppers")..........30-40 54
(10-inch LP.)
DOT (3003 "Tops in Pops")............20-30 55
DOT (3029 "Towering Hilltoppers")......................20-30 56
DOT (3073 "The Hilltoppers").........20-30 57
SOUVENIR...............................8-15 73
Members: Jimmy Sacca; Billy Vaughn; Don McGuire; Seymour Spiegelman.
Also see SACCA, Jimmy
Also see VAUGHN, Billy

HILMONT COMBO / Danfords
Singles: 7-inch
DOUBLE A...............................5-10

HI-LOs P&R '54
Singles: 78 rpm
COLUMBIA...............................5-10 57
STARLITE...............................3-8 55-56
TREND..................................3-8 54
Singles: 7-inch
COLUMBIA...............................5-10 57-60
REPRISE................................4-8 62
STARLITE...............................5-12 55-56
TREND..................................8-15 54
EPs: 7-inch
COLUMBIA...............................5-15 57-58
KAPP...................................5-15 56
STARLITE...............................10-20 56
TREND (514 "The Hi-Los")..............10-20 54
LPs: 10/12-inch
COLUMBIA...............................15-25 57-60
KAPP...................................15-25 56-60
STARLITE (6004 "The Hi-Los")......20-30 55
STARLITE (6005 "The Hi-Los I Presume").............................20-30 56
STARLITE (7005 "Under Glass")....20-30 56
Members: Clark Burroughs; Don Shelton; Bob Morse; Gene Puerling.
Also see CLOONEY, Rosemary, & Hi-Los

HILTON, Denny C&W '81
Singles: 7-inch
OAK....................................3-5 81
ROSEBRIDGE.............................3-4 82-83

HILTON, Jerry, & Diadems
Singles: 7-inch
GOODIE (207 "My Little Darling")...........................250-350 63
Also see DIADEMS

HIM
Singles: 7-inch
TEAR DROP..............................10-20 66
Also see SAHM, Doug

HIM, HE & ME
LPs: 10/12-inch
METROMEDIA.............................8-10 70

HIMES, Vernon
Singles: 7-inch
ARTIST.................................3-5 78

HINDSIGHT
Singles: 7-inch
HI.....................................3-5 75

HINDSIGHT R&B '88
Singles: 7-inch
VIRGIN.................................3-4 88
Picture Sleeves
VIRGIN.................................3-4 88

HINDU LOVE GODS LP '90
Singles: 7-inch
I.R.S..................................3-4 86
Picture Sleeves
I.R.S..................................3-4 86
LPs: 10/12-inch
GIANT..................................5-8 90
Members: Bill Berry Peter Buck; Mike Mills; Warren Zevon.
Also see R.E.M.
Also see ZEVON, Warren

HINDUS
Singles: 7-inch
DARDEAU................................4-8

HINE, Eric
Singles: 7-inch
MONTAGE................................3-4 81

HINE, Graham
LPs: 10/12-inch
BLUE GOOSE.............................8-10 73-76

HINE, Rupert, & David McIver
LPs: 10/12-inch
CAPITOL/PURPLE.........................10-12 72

HINES, Billy
Singles: 7-inch
WA-TUSI................................4-8 64

HINES, Debbie
Singles: 7-inch
KECK...................................3-5 75

HINES, Donald
(Don Hines & Ben Branch Band)
Singles: 7-inch
HI.....................................5-10 62-63
STARMAKER (1001 "Going Crazy")................................50-60
Also see BIG AMOS / Big Lucky / Don Hines

HINES, Ernie
Singles: 7-inch
STAX...................................4-6 69
U.S.A..................................4-8 67

HINES, Gregory R&B '88
Singles: 7-inch
EPIC...................................3-4 87-88
Also see VANDROSS, Luther, & Gregory Hines

HINES, J., & Fellows R&B '73
(With the Boys)
Singles: 7-inch
DELUXE.................................4-8 73
NATION-WIDE (100 "Funky Funk")................................15-20
NATION-WIDE (105 "Going Down for the Last Time")...............................15-20

HINES, Jackie
("E. [Jackie] Hines")
Singles: 7-inch
COSMIC.................................4-6 75
VIRGITONE (101 "I'm So Glad")........5-8

HINES, Jimmie
Singles: 7-inch
VIVA...................................4-8 60

HINES, Mimi
(With Phil Ford)
Singles: 7-inch
DECCA..................................4-8 67
RCA....................................10-15 59

HINES, Ray
Singles: 7-inch
RNH....................................10-20

HINES, Ronnie
Singles: 7-inch
ROCKET.................................10-15

HINES, Sonny
Singles: 7-inch
AIRTOWN (2005 "Nothing Like Your Love")................................15-25
DECCA (31045 "It's Not a Game").15-25 60
TERRY (113 "All My Love Belongs to You")................................15-25

HINES, Willie
Singles: 7-inch
DEMON..................................5-10 59

HINES, HINES & DAD
Singles: 7-inch
COLUMBIA...............................3-5 67
Picture Sleeves
COLUMBIA...............................4-6 67

HINGE
Singles: 7-inch
TEE PEE (75/76 "Come on Up").....15-25 68

HINKLE, Kenny
Singles: 7-inch
WESTCO (5 "The Bee")..................10-20 63
(First issued as by the Sentinals.)
Also see CALIFORNIA MUSIC
Also see KARTER, Kenny
Also see SENTINALS

HINOJOSA, Tish C&W '89
Singles: 7-inch
A&M....................................3-4 89

HINOJOSA, Tish, & Craig Dillingham C&W '86
Singles: 7-inch
MCA/CURB...............................3-4 86
Also see DILLINGHAM, Craig
Also see HINOJOSA, Tish

HI-NOONS
Singles: 7-inch
HI-NOON................................10-15

HINSHAW, Skip, & In-Men Ltd., see In-MEN LTD.

HINSON, Don
(With the Rigamorticians)
Singles: 7-inch
CAPITOL................................5-10 64
STARBURST..............................10-20 66
TREVA..................................10-15 66
LPs: 10/12-inch
CAPITOL................................15-20 64

HINTON, Don
Singles: 7-inch
PHILLIPS INT'L.........................5-10 60

HINTON, Eddie
Singles: 7-inch
PACEMAKER..............................8-10
LPs: 10/12-inch
CAPRICORN..............................5-10 78

HINTON, Joe P&R/R&B '63
(Little Joe Hinton)
Singles: 78 rpm
BACK BEAT (519 "I Know")...........40-60 58
Singles: 7-inch
ARVEE (5028 "My Love Is Real")..10-15 61
ARVEE (5029 "Let's Start a Romance").............................10-15 61
BACK BEAT (519 "I Know")...........15-25 58
BACK BEAT (526 "Pretty Little Mama")...............................10-20 59
BACK BEAT (532 "If You Love Me")..................................10-20 60
BACK BEAT (537 "Lovesick Blues")...............................8-12 63
BACK BEAT (539 "Better to Give Than to Receive")............................8-12 64
BACK BEAT (540 "You're My Girl")..................................8-12 64
BACK BEAT (541 thru 594)...........5-10 64-68
HOTLANTA...............................8-10 74
SOUL (35080 "You Are Blue").........5-10 71
(Black vinyl.)
SOUL (35080 "You Are Blue").........15-20 71
(Colored vinyl. Promotional issue only.)
Picture Sleeves
BACK BEAT (526 "Pretty Little Mama")...............................15-25 59
LPs: 10/12-inch
BACKBEAT (60 "Funny")...............20-25 65
DUKE...................................8-10 73

HINTON, Otis
Singles: 78 rpm
TIMELY.................................50-100 53
Singles: 7-inch
TIMELY (1003 "Walkin' Downhill")..........................200-250 53

HINTON, Sam
LPs: 10/12-inch
DECCA (8108 "Singing Across the Land")...............................20-30 55

HINTON, Van
LPs: 10/12-inch
EARMARC................................5-10 80

HINZE, Chris
LPs: 10/12-inch
COLUMBIA...............................8-10 74

HIP POCKET
Singles: 7-inch
TEAM...................................5-10

HIPPIES / Reggie Harrison P&R '63
Singles: 7-inch
PARKWAY (863 "Memory Lane")..15-20 63
Also see STEREOS
Also see TAMS

HIPPY DIPPYS
Singles: 7-inch
UNI....................................5-10 67

HIPSTER IMAGE
Singles: 7-inch
AMY....................................5-10 65

HIPSWAY P&R/LP '87
Singles: 7-inch
COLUMBIA...............................3-4 87
Picture Sleeves
COLUMBIA...............................3-4 87
LPs: 10/12-inch
COLUMBIA...............................5-10 87
Member: John McElhone.
Also see TEXAS

HI-ROLLERS
Singles: 7-inch
VAN....................................4-8

HIROSHIMA LP '79
Singles: 12-inch
EPIC...................................4-6 85
Singles: 7-inch
ARISTA.................................3-4 80-84
EPIC...................................3-4 85
LPs: 10/12-inch
ARISTA.................................5-10 79-84
EPIC...................................5-10 83-89
MFSL (525 "Hiroshima")..............15-25 79

HIRT, Al LP '61
Singles: 7-inch
CORAL..................................3-5 65
GWP....................................3-5 69-70
MONUMENT...............................3-4 74
RCA....................................3-6 61-68
Picture Sleeves
RCA....................................4-8 61-66
EPs: 7-inch
RCA....................................4-8 62
LPs: 10/12-inch
ACCORD.................................4-8 82
AUDIO FIDELITY.........................10-15 59-61
CAMDEN.................................5-10 67-71
CORAL..................................8-15 65
GWP....................................5-10 70-71
LONGINES SYMPHONETTE...................5-10
METRO..................................5-10 65
MONUMENT...............................5-8 74
RCA (Except 3309)......................5-15 61-78
RCA (LPM-3309 "Best of Al Hirt")..10-15 65
(Monaural. Has Ann-Margret on one track.)
RCA (LSP-3309 "Best of Al Hirt")...15-20 65
(Stereo. Has Ann-Margret on one track.)
VOCALION...............................5-10 70
Also see ANN-MARGRET & Al Hirt

HIRT, Al, & Boston Pops Orchestra
LPs: 10/12-inch
RCA....................................10-15 64
Also see BOSTON POPS ORCHESTRA

HIRT, Al, & Pete Fountain LP '62
Singles: 7-inch
CORAL..................................3-6 61
EPs: 7-inch
CORAL..................................4-8 62
LPs: 10/12-inch
CORAL..................................8-15 61-62
MGM....................................8-15 64
MONUMENT...............................5-10 75
VERVE..................................10-20 61
Also see FOUNTAIN, Pete

HIRT, Al / Henry Mancini / Perez Prado
LPs: 10/12-inch
RCA....................................8-15 63
Also see MANCINI, Henry
Also see PRADO, Perez

HIRT, Al, & Hugo Montenegro
LPs: 10/12-inch
RCA (4275 "Viva Max")...............15-20 70
(Soundtrack.)
Also see MONTENEGRO, Hugo

HIRT, Al, & Boots Randolph
Singles: 7-inch
MONUMENT...............................3-5 75
Also see HIRT, Al
Also see RANDOLPH, Boots

HI-SPEEDS
Singles: 7-inch
SAN WAYNE (1142 "Drag Race") 10-20 63
Member: Bob Tucker.

HIT PACK
Singles: 7-inch
COLPIX (745 "Summer Fever").....10-20 64
SOUL (35010 "Let's Dance")..........15-25 65

HIT PARADE
Singles: 7-inch
RCA....................................3-6 69

HITCHCOCK, Robyn LP '88
(With the Egyptians)
Singles: 7-inch
A&M....................................3-4 88-90
LPs: 10/12-inch
A&M....................................5-8 88-90
RELATIVITY.............................5-10 86

HITCHCOCK, Russell
Singles: 7-inch
ARISTA.................................3-4 88
LPs: 10/12-inch
ARISTA.................................5-10 88
Also see AIR SUPPLY

HITCHCOCK, Stan C&W '67
Singles: 7-inch
CINNAMON...............................3-5 73-74
EPIC...................................3-6 67-70
GRT....................................3-5 70
MMI....................................3-5 78-79
RAMBLIN'...............................3-4 81
LPs: 10/12-inch
AUDIOGRAPH ALIVE.......................5-10 82
CINNAMON...............................8-12 73
EPIC...................................10-15 65-69
GRT....................................8-12 70

HITCHCOCK, Stan, & Sue Richards C&W '79
Singles: 7-inch
MMI....................................3-5 79
Also see HITCHCOCK, Stan
Also see RICHARDS, Sue

HITCHHIKERS
Singles: 7-inch
TEAR DROP..............................4-8 64

HITCH-HIKERS
Singles: 7-inch
HH (1 "Beaver Shot")...................20-30
HH (008 "S-O-M-F")....................20-30

HI-TENSION
Singles: 7-inch
ISLAND.................................3-5 79
LPs: 10/12-inch
ISLAND.................................5-10 79

HI-TENSIONS
(With the Downbeats; Hi Tensions)
Singles: 7-inch
AUDIO (201 "The Clock")..........100-150 60
K&G (101 "The Clock")..............50-75 61
K&G (9000 "The Clock")..............40-60 61

HI-TENSIONS
(Hi Tensions)
Singles: 7-inch
MILESTONE (2018 "Ebbing of the Tide")..............................50-100 63
WHIRLYBIRD (2005 "She'll Break Your Heart")...........................75-125 64
Also see PEELS, Leon

HI-TEX 3 Featuring Ya Kid K P&R '90
Singles: 7-inch
SBK....................................3-4 90

HI-TIMERS
(Hi Timers)
Singles: 7-inch
SONIC (1502 "You're Everything")......................150-250 59

HITMAKERS
Singles: 7-inch
ANGLE TONE (1104 "I Can't Take It Anymore")............................50-75 59
ORIGINAL SOUND (1 "Chapel of Love")...............................80-100 58
(Flat black label.)
ORIGINAL SOUND (1 "Chapel of Love")...............................40-50 58
(Glossy black label with outer color band.)
Also see NUGGETS

HITMAKERS
Singles: 7-inch
DORE...................................8-12 65

HITMEN
LPs: 10/12-inch
COLUMBIA...............................5-10 80-81

HI-TOMBS
Singles: 7-inch
CANNON (832 "Sweet Rockin' Mama")..........................100-150 58

HI-TONES
(Hi Tones; Shy-Tones; with Madaro White & Orchestra)
Singles: 7-inch
CANDIX (307 "The Special Day")..10-20 60
EON (101 "What Was the Cause of It All")..........................100-150 61
FONSCA (201 "Lovers Quarrel")....40-60 61
(First issued as by the Shy-Tones.)
FONSCA (202 "No More Pain")...75-125 61
KING (5414 "Fool Fool Fool").......15-25 60
SEG-WAY (105 "Sure As the Flowers")..........................100-200 61
Members: Graham True; Al Seavozzo; Fred Alvarez; Sal Covais; Bill Scarpa.
Also see EMOTIONS
Also see SHY-TONES
Also see TRENTONS

HI-TONES
LPs: 10/12-inch
HI (12011 "Raunchy Tones")........15-20 63
(Monaural.)
HI (32011 "Raunchy Tones")........20-25 63
(Stereo.)

HI-TONES
Singles: 7-inch
BELL ("You Don't Even Know My Name")..............................15-25 60s
(Selection number not known.)
SOUTHERN ARTISTS (2023 "You Don't Even Know My Name")...................25-35 60s

HI-TONES
Singles: 7-inch
ALLANDALE (3669 "Especially for You")................................4-8 72

HI-TONES
LPs: 10/12-inch
L&M (223 "I'm So Sorry")..........100-200

HIX, Chuck, & Count Downs
Singles: 7-inch
FLAIR (101 "Loretta")...............10-15 61
VERVE (708 "Sandy")................20-25 59
(Stereo.)
VERVE (10169 "Sandy")...............10-15 59
(Monaural.)
VERVE (10190 "Is You Is")...........10-15 59

HO, Don P&R/LP '66
(With the Aliis)
Singles: 7-inch
HEL....................................3-5 77
MEGA...................................3-5 74-75
REPRISE................................3-6 65-71
Picture Sleeves
HEL....................................3-5 77
LPs: 10/12-inch
MEGA...................................4-8 74
REPRISE................................5-15 65-70

HOBAN, Bob, & Midniters
Singles: 7-inch
MIDNITE (010 "Indian Boogie")......8-12

HOBART
Singles: 7-inch
VAULT (944 "Say Listen")..............10-20 67

HOBIE CAT
Singles: 7-inch
96X (9600 "Mr. Gums")................ 4-6 75

HOBIN, Todd
Singles: 7-inch
ARIES 3-4 83
LPs: 10/12-inch
ARIES 8-10 83

HOBBIE, Margie
Singles: 7-inch
TERON.................................... 4-8 64

HOBBIT
Singles: 7-inch
TUBE....................................... 5-10 67

HOBBITS
Singles: 7-inch
DECCA..................................... 5-10 68
LPs: 10/12-inch
DECCA (4920 "Down to Middle Earth")..............................20-25 68
DECCA (74920 "Down to Middle Earth")..............................20-30 67
DECCA (75009 "Men and Doors")..15-25 67
Also see CURTISS, Jimmy

HOBBS, Becky C&W '78
Singles: 7-inch
EMI AMERICA.......................... 3-4 84-85
LIBERTY 3-4 84
MCA....................................... 3-5 74
MTM...................................... 3-4 88
MERCURY 3-5 78-81
RCA....................................... 3-4 89
TATTOO.................................. 3-5 76-77
LPs: 10/12-inch
MCA....................................... 5-10 74
TATTOO.................................. 5-10 76-77
Also see BANDY, Moe, & Becky Hobbs

HOBBS, Bud, & His Trail Herders C&W '48
Singles: 78 rpm
MGM 4-8 48-49

HOBBS, Lou C&W '81
Singles: 7-inch
KIK 3-5 81

HOBBS, Pam C&W '81
Singles: 7-inch
50 STATES 3-5 81

HOBBS, Randy
Singles: 7-inch
APT.. 8-12 61
GATOR (1000 "You Better Run")................................75-100 60
EMBER.................................... 5-10 64

HOBBS, Willie
Singles: 7-inch
BANDIT.................................... 4-8 70s
CHARAY (38 "Gloria") 10-15 60s
LECAM (333 "Cry Cry Cry")............15-25
SEVENTY-SEVEN......................... 4-8
SOFT (1018 "Under the Pines").....10-20 69
SOUND STAGE 7........................ 4-8
Also see DIRTE FOUR

HOBBY HORSE
Singles: 7-inch
BELL 3-5 72

HOBECK, Curtis
Singles: 7-inch
LU (508 "China Rock")..................40-60 59
TENNESSEE (301 "Tom Dooley Rock and Roll").....................................40-60 59

HOBOS
Singles: 7-inch
KAPP...................................... 4-8 65

HOBSON, Emmett, & Rag-Muffins
Singles: 78 rpm
CENTRAL..................................50-75 53
GROOVE...................................15-25 55
Singles: 7-inch
CENTRAL (1001 "Looka Here, Mattie Bee")................................125-150 53
GROOVE (0124 "Mattie Bee") 25-50 55

HOBSON, George
Singles: 7-inch
SOUND CITY ("Let It Be Real") 15-25

HOCKADAYS
Singles: 7-inch
SYMBOL (918 "Fairytales")............10-20 62

HO-DADS
(With Sam Hawkins)
Singles: 7-inch
DEE JAY 15-25
IMPERIAL.................................10-20 63-64

HODGE, Bobby
Singles: 7-inch
CUCA (1140 "It's Almost Tomorrow")............................. 8-12 63
CUCA (1066 "Sitting on Top of the World")..................................30-50 62
CUCA (68101 "Blue Christmas")..... 8-12 68
GOLDEN WING 4-8 63
NASHVILLE (5014 "Carolina Bound").................................10-20 61
STATURE.................................. 8-12 60s
STOP 5-10 68-69
VOLUNTEER.............................. 5-10

HODGE, Catfish: see CATFISH

HODGE, Chris P&R '72
(With George Harrison)
Singles: 7-inch
APPLE (1850 "We're on Our Way").......................................5-10 72
APPLE (1858 "Goodbye Sweet Lorraine")...............................5-10 73
RCA.. 3-5 73-75
Picture Sleeves
APPLE (1850 "We're on Our Way").......................................5-10 72
Also see HARRISON, George

HODGE, Gary
Singles: 7-inch
DOLTON 8-12 59

HODGE, Gaynel
Singles: 7-inch
RCA (7964 "The Door Is Still Open")......................................8-12 61
XEDO (202 "Follow the Fox")..........8-12
Also see ATLANTICS
Also see HOLLYWOOD ARGYLES
Also see HOLLYWOOD FLAMES
Also see JETS
Also see JONES, J.J.
Also see MO & JO
Also see OTIS, Johnny
Also see RIVINGTONS
Also see RUBIES
Also see SOLID GOLD
Also see SPARKLETTES
Also see TRI-LITES
Also see TURKS

HODGES, Charles R&B '70
Singles: 7-inch
ALTO (2016 "There Is Love").........10-15 65
ALTO (2022 "Who's Crying Now")...10-15 65
CALLA..................................... 4-6 70
Also see HUNT, Geraldine, & Charlie Hodges

HODGES, Eddie P&R '61
Singles: 7-inch
AURORA................................... 4-6 65-66
BARNABY.................................. 3-5 76
CADENCE.................................8-15 61-62
COLUMBIA................................ 4-8 62-63
DECCA.....................................5-10 59
MGM.. 4-8 64
Picture Sleeves
CADENCE.................................10-15 61
COLUMBIA.................................5-10 63
EPs: 7-inch
CADENCE (33-6 "Eddie Hodges") .15-25 61
("Cadence Little LP." With cardboard insert in clear cover.)
Also see DE SHANNON, Jackie / Bobby Vee / Eddie Hodges
Also see MILLS, Hayley, & Eddie Hodges
Also see MILLS, Hayley, & Burl Ives

HODGES, Jesse
Singles: 7-inch
FABLE (609 "Until")......................8-10 58

HODGES, Johnny P&R '37
(J. Hodges)
Singles: 78 rpm
BLUEBIRD 5-8 40-44
CLEF 4-6 53-56
COLUMBIA................................ 4-6 51
GROOVE 4-6 56
MERCURY 4-6 51-53
NORGRAN 4-6 54-56
VARIETY...................................5-10 33
VOCALION.................................5-10 37
Singles: 7-inch
CLEF..5-15 53-56
COLUMBIA.................................5-15 51
GROOVE 5-15 56
MERCURY 5-15 51-53
NORGRAN 5-15 54-56
VMC 3-6 68
VARIETY....................................5-15 33
VERVE..................................... 4-8 57-67
EPs: 7-inch
ATLANTIC..................................20-30 54
EPIC...15-25 55
NORGRAN..................................25-50 54
RCA (3000 "Alto Sax")..................50-75 52
LPs: 10/12-inch
AMERICAN RECORDING (421 "Johnny Hodges & Ellington All Stars").......40-60 57
CLEF (111 "Johnny Hodges Collates")...............................100-200 52
(10-inch LP.)
CLEF (128 "Johnny Hodges Collates, Vol. 2")..............................100-200 52
(10-inch LP.)
ENCORE....................................10-15 68
EPIC (3105 "Hodge Podge") 50-75 55
EPIC (22000 series)........................8-12 74
IMPULSE....................................10-20 65
INSTANT....................................15-20 64
MCA..5-10 82
NORGRAN (1 "Swing with Johnny Hodges")..............................150-250 53
(10-inch LP.)
NORGRAN (1004 "Memories of Ellington")............................100-200 54
NORGRAN (1009 "More Johnny Hodges")..............................100-200 54
NORGRAN (1024 "Dance Bash")...................................100-200 55
NORGRAN (1045 "Creamy") 100-200 56
NORGRAN (1048 "Castle Rock")...................................100-200 56
NORGRAN (1055 "Ellingtonia") 75-150 56
NORGRAN (1059 "In a Tender Mood")......................................75-150 56
NORGRAN (1060 "Used to Be Duke")......................................75-150 56
NORGRAN (1061 "The Blues")....75-150 56
PABLO 5-10 78
RCA (500 series) 10-20 66
RCA (3000 "Alto Sax")...............200-300 52
(10-inch LP.)
RCA (3800 series) 10-20 67
VSP..10-20 66-67
VERVE (8179 "Perdido") 50-100 57
VERVE (8180 "In a Mellow Tone").......................................50-100 57
VERVE (8203 "Duke's in Bed") 50-100 57
VERVE (8271 "Big Sound") 50-100 58
(Reads "Verve Records, Inc." at bottom of label.)
VERVE (8271 "Big Sound") 15-25
(Reads "MGM Records - A Division Of Metro-Goldwyn-Mayer, Inc." at bottom of label.)
VERVE (8314 thru 8358)...............25-45 59-60
(Reads "Verve Records, Inc." at bottom of label.)
VERVE (8314 thru 8358) 15-25 61-69
(Reads "MGM Records - A Division Of Metro-Goldwyn-Mayer, Inc." at bottom of label.)
VERVE...8-15 74-79
(Reads "Manufactured By MGM Record Corp.," or mentions either Polydor or Polygram at bottom of label.)
Also see ELLINGTON, Duke, & Johnny Hodges
Also see MULLIGAN, Gerry, & Johnny Hodges

HODGES, Johnny, & Lawrence Welk
LPs: 10/12-inch
DOT 10-20 66
Also see WELK, Lawrence

HODGES, Johnny, & Wild Bill Davis LP '65
LPs: 10/12-inch
RCA 10-20 65-67
VERVE..15-30 61-66
Also see HODGES, Johnny

HODGES, Ralph
Singles: 7-inch
WHISPERING PINES (101 "Honey Talk").......................................30-50 58

HODGES, Russ
Singles: 78 rpm
("The Giants Win the Pennant").....10-15 52
(No label name or selection number used.)
Singles: 7-inch
("The Giants Win the Pennant").....15-25 52
(No label name or selection number used.)

HODGES, Sonny
Singles: 7-inch
GLOBAL (404 "Jamie")...................35-50
LARRY (802 "Shake a Leg")........75-125 59
MYRL 5-10 61

HODGES, JAMES & SMITH P&R/R&B '77
Singles: 12-inch
LONDON..4-8 79
Singles: 7-inch
LONDON..3-5 76-79
PEOPLE...3-5 70s
20TH FOX......................................3-5 75
LPs: 10/12-inch
LONDON..5-10 78
Members: Pat Hodges; Denita James; Jessica Smith.
Also see DAMION & DENITA

HODGSON, Roger P&R/LP '84
Singles: 7-inch
A&M..3-4 84
LPs: 10/12-inch
A&M..5-10 84-87
Also see SUPERTRAMP

HOEHN, Rick: see THUNDERMEN

HOEHN, Tommy
LPs: 10/12-inch
LONDON..8-10 78
POWER PLAY 8-10 81
Members: Tommy Hoehn; Gene Nunez; John Hampton; Keith Young; Joe Hardy; Jack Holder.

HOENIG, Michael
Singles: 7-inch
W.B. 3-5 78
Picture Sleeves
W.B. 3-5 78
LPs: 10/12-inch
W.B. 5-10 78

HOFFAR, Gary
Singles: 7-inch
JEMKL (3294 "Hank's 715th")...........4-6 76

HOFFMAN, Abbie
LPs: 10/12-inch
BIG TOE 15-20

HOFFMAN, Danny
Singles: 7-inch
BETH 4-8

HOFFMAN, Steve
Singles: 7-inch
MCA..3-5 73

HOFFS, Susanna LP '91
LPs: 10/12-inch
COLUMBIA......................................5-8 91
Also see BANGLES

HOFMAN, Peter
LPs: 10/12-inch
COLUMBIA 5-10 83

HOFNER, Adolph
(With the San Antonians)
Singles: 7-inch
SARG (Except 207) 10-15 57-62
SARG (207 "Milk Cow Blues") 15-25 62
EPs: 7-inch
DECCA (2227 "Dance-O-Rama")....40-50
LPs: 10/12-inch
COLUMBIA (9017 "Dude Ranch Dances")......................................40-50 51
(10-inch LP.)
DECCA (5564 "Dance-O-Rama")....40-50 55
(10-inch LP.)
Also see HOFNER, Bash

HOFNER, Bash
Singles: 78 rpm
SARG (131 "Tickle Toe Song")........5-10 56
SARG (138 "Rockin' & a-Boppin' ") 20-30 56
Singles: 7-inch
SARG (131 "Tickle Toe Song").......10-20 56
SARG (138 "Rockin' & a-Boppin' ") 40-60 56
Also see HOFNER, Adolph

HOG HEAVEN P&R '71
Singles: 7-inch
ROULETTE..3-5 71
LPs: 10/12-inch
ROULETTE...10-12 71
Members: Ron Rosman; Mike Vale; Peter Lucia; Eddie Gray.
Also see JAMES, Tommy, & Shondells

HOGAN, Billy
Singles: 7-inch
VENA (101 "Shake It Over Sputnik")..75-125 58

HOGAN, Carl, & Miracles
Singles: 78 rpm
FURY (1001 "I Love You So").... 100-200 57
Singles: 7-inch
FURY (1001 "I Love You So").... 150-200 57

HOGAN, Cha-Cha
Singles: 78 rpm
STAR TALENT 15-25 50
Singles: 7-inch
SOULVILLE (1017 Just Because You've Been Hurt")...5-10 60s

HOGAN, Mal: see MOORE, Johnny

HOGAN, Mike, & Microwave
Singles: 7-inch
LE CAM...4-8

HOGAN, Silas
Singles: 7-inch
EXCELLO...4-8 63-66
LPs: 10/12-inch
EXCELLO..10-15 72

HOGG, Andrew
Singles: 78 rpm
EXCLUSIVE (89 "He Knows How Much We Can Bear")......................................30-40 47
Also see HOGG, Smokey

HOGG, John
Singles: 78 rpm
MERCURY (8230 "Got a Mean Woman")......................................20-40 51
OCTIVE (705 "Black Snake Blues")...20-40 51
OCTIVE (706 "West Texas Blues")...20-40 51

HOGG, Smokey R&B '48
(Andrew Hogg)
Singles: 78 rpm
BULLET...20-40 48
COLONY..25-50 50
COMBO...25-50 52
CROWN..10-20 54
DECCA...30-50 37
EXCLUSIVE...25-50 47
FEDERAL..15-25 53
FIDELITY..10-20 52
IMPERIAL..20-30 50-53
INDEPENDENT......................................15-25 49
JADE..25-35 51
MACY'S..20-30 49
MERCURY 20-30 51
METEOR..30-50 54
MODERN...20-30 48-52
RAY'S RECORD 30-50 52
RECORDED in HOLLYWOOD 10-20 52
SHOW TIME 20-30 54
SITTIN' IN WITH 10-20 51-52
SPECIALTY (300 series) 10-15 49
TOP HAT 15-25 52
Singles: 7-inch
COMBO (11 "Believe I'll Change Towns")..75-125 52
CROWN (122 "I Declare") 50-100 54
EBB...10-20 58
FEDERAL (12109 "Keep A-Walking").......................................50-75 53
FEDERAL (12117 "Your Little Wagon")...50-75 53
FEDERAL (12127 "Gone, Gone, Gone")...50-75 53
IMPERIAL (5269 "When I've Been Drinkin' ")..50-75 53
IMPERIAL (5290 "My Baby's Gone")...50-75 53
MERCURY (8235 "Miss Georgia")..50-75 51
MERCURY (8228 "She's Always on My Mind")..50-75 51
METEOR (5021 "I Declare") 50-75 54
MODERN (884 "Baby Don't You Tear My Clothes")..50-75 51
MODERN (896 "Too Late, Old Man")..50-75 51
MODERN (924 "Can't Do Nothin' ")..50-75 52
RAY'S RECORD (33 "Penitentiary Blues")..75-100 52
RAY'S RECORD (35 "I've Been Happy")..75-100 52
SHOW TIME (1101 "Ain't Gonna Play Second No Mo'")..50-75 54
LPs: 10/12-inch
CROWN (5526 "Smokey Hogg Sings the Blues")..20-30 62
KENT...10-15
TIME (6 "Smokey Hogg")...............40-50 62
UNITED..5-10
Also see HOGG, Andrew

HOGMAN MAXEY: see MAXEY, Hogman

HOGS
Singles: 7-inch
HBR (511 "Blues Theme") 25-50 66
Also see CHOCOLATE WATCH BAND
Also see ZAPPA, Frank

HOGSED, Roy C&W '48
Singles: 78 rpm
CAPITOL...5-10 48
COAST...20-30 47

HO-HOs
(Peter Roberts with "Orchestra Beat UP by Sid Ramin")
Singles: 7-inch
THUNDERBIRD (1956 "The Ho-Ho Rock and Roll")..5-10 60s
Also see RAMIN, Sid, & Orchestra
Also see ROBERTS, Peter

HOKE, Billy
(With James Wayne & Nighthaws)
Singles: 7-inch
D.W...10-15 65
Also see WAYNE, James

HOKIS POKIS
Singles: 7-inch
SHIELD 5-10

HOKUM BOYS
LP: 10/12-inch
YAZOO 15-25

HOKUM, Suzi Jane C&W '67
Singles: 7-inch
LHI 4-6 69
Also see WARNER, Virgil, & Suzi Jane Hokum

HOKUS POKUS
Singles: 7-inch
ROMAR..3-5 72
LPs: 10/12-inch
ROMAR..10-15 72

HOLA PISTOLA
Singles: 7-inch
LAETRILE (001 "Hit Him with My First Shot")...6-12 81

HOLBEN, Pat
(Pat Holben Trio)
Singles: 7-inch
FORTUNE...4-8 64

HOLBROOK, Jay
Singles: 7-inch
ARZEE..8-10

HOLBROOK, Tom
Singles: 7-inch
COUNTRYSIDE 4-6 73

HOLCOLM, Manuel B.
Singles: 7-inch
DIAMOND JIM (900 "Kick Out").......5-10 70

HOLDEN, Dave
Singles: 7-inch
BOLO...8-10 61
CEMELOT...8-12
HEMLOCK 8-12

HOLDEN, Lorenzo
(With His Tenor Sax)
Singles: 78 rpm
CROWN..10-15 54
FLASH 10-15 56
Singles: 7-inch
CROWN (103 "Cry of the Wounded Juke Box")..20-30 54
CROWN (105 "East Chester Flats")...20-30 54
FLASH (108 "Walking Down Swing Street")..15-25 56

HOLDEN, Lula, & Mighty Blasters
Singles: 7-inch
LANOR..5-10 60

HOLDEN, Mark
Singles: 7-inch
SCOTTI BROS. 3-4 79

HOLDEN, Randy
LPs: 10/12-inch
HOBBIT (5002 "Population II")......75-125 68
Session: Chris Lockhead.
Also see BLUE CHEER
Also see FENDER IV
Also see KAK
Also see OTHER HALF

HOLDEN, Rebecca C&W '89
Singles: 7-inch
TRA-STAR 3-4 89

HOLDEN, Ron P&R/R&B '60
(With the Thunderbirds; with Twiliters)
Singles: 7-inch
ABC 3-5 73
APEX (76645 "Love You So") 15-25 59
(Canadian.)
BARONET (3 "Things Don't Happen That Way") 150-250 62
CHALLENGE (59360 "I Tried") 20-30 67
COLLECTABLES 3-4
DONNA (1315 "Love You So") 15-25 59
(Blue or Green label.)
DONNA (1315 "Love You So") 10-20 60
(Black label.)
DONNA (1324 thru 1335) 10-20 60-62
ELDO 10-20 61
LANA 3-6 60s
LOST NITE 4-8
NITE OWL (10 "Love You So") 50-75 60
NOW 3-6 74
RAMPART 5-10 65
LPs: 10/12-inch
DONNA (DLP-2111 "Love You So") 75-125 60
(Monaural.)
DONNA (DLPS-2111 "Love You So") 150-200 60
(Stereo.)
Session: Bruce Johnston.
Also see JOHNSTON, Bruce
Also see LITTLE CAESAR & ROMANS / Ron Holden

HOLDER, Ace
Singles: 7-inch
LULU 5-10 64
MOVIN' 5-10 66
PIONEER INT'L 10-12 61
VANESSA 8-10 62

HOLDER, Pervis / Leon Huff
Singles: 7-inch
JAMIE 4-6 65
Also see HUFF, Leon

HOLDER, Ram Jam
LPs: 10/12-inch
PHILLIPS 12-15 69

HOLE IN THE WALL
Singles: 7-inch
EPIC 5-10 67

HOLIDAY, Billie P&R '35
(With Teddy Wilson & His Orchestra)
Singles: 78 rpm
BRUNSWICK 10-20 35-38
CAPITOL 5-10 42
CLEF 5-10 53-55
COLUMBIA 5-10 51-52
COMMODORE 10-15 39
DECCA 10-20 45-52
MERCURY 5-10 52-53
OKEH 10-10 41
VOCALION 10-15 36-38
Singles: 7-inch
CLEF 10-20 53-55
COLUMBIA (30000 series) 10-20 51-52
DECCA (250 "Lover Man") 30-50 52
(Boxed set of four singles.)
DECCA (27000 series) 10-20 50-52
DECCA (48000 series) 10-20 51-52
KENT 3-5 73
MCA 3-5 73
MGM 8-12 59
MERCURY (89000 series) 10-20 52-53
U.A. 3-5 72
VERVE 8-12 59-62
Picture Sleeves
MGM (12813 "Just One More Chance") 15-25 59
EPs: 7-inch
CLEF 20-30 53-54
COLUMBIA 15-25 54-58
DECCA 5-15 56
LPs: 10/12-inch
AJ 10-20
ALADDIN 50-75 56
(Title and selection number not known.)
AMERICAN RECORDING SOCIETY (409 "Billie Holiday Sings") 50-100 56
AMERICAN RECORDING SOCIETY (431 "Lady Sings the Blues") 50-100 56
ATLANTIC 5-10 72
AUDIO FIDELITY (312 "Billie Holiday") 10-20 84
(Picture disc.)
CLEF (118 "Favorites") 150-250 53
(10-inch LP.)
CLEF (144 "Evening with Billie") 150-250 54
(10-inch LP.)
CLEF (161 "Billie Holiday") 150-250 54
(10-inch LP.)
CLEF (169 "Jazz at the Philharmonic") 100-250 55
CLEF (669 "Music for Torching") 30-50 55
CLEF (686 "A Recital") 100-150 56
CLEF (690 "Solitude") 100-150 56
CLEF (713 "Velvet Moods") 100-150 56
CLEF (718 "Jazz Recital") 100-150 56
CLEF (721 "Lady Sings the Blues") 100-150 56
COLUMBIA (21 "The Golden Years") 50-75 62
(Boxed, three-disc set.)
COLUMBIA (40 "The Golden Years, Vol. 2") 25-35 66
(Boxed, three-disc set.)
COLUMBIA (637 "Lady Day") 100-150 54
(Red label with gold printing. Includes tracks from CL-6040.)
COLUMBIA (637 "Lady Day") 50-75 56
(Red label with black and white printing.)
COLUMBIA (2600 series) 8-15 67
COLUMBIA (6040 "Teddy Wilson Featuring Billie Holiday") 150-200 49
(10-inch LP. Reissued as part of CL-637.)
COLUMBIA (6129 "Billie Holiday Sings") 150-200 50
(10-inch LP.)
COLUMBIA (6163 "Billie Holiday Favorites") 150-200 51
(10-inch LP.)
COLUMBIA (1157 "Lady in Satin") 30-50 58
COLUMBIA (30000 series, except 32134) 8-15 72-73
COLUMBIA (32134 "Billie Holiday Story, Vol. 2") 50-100 73
(Two discs.)
DECCA (100 series) 10-20 65-72
DECCA (5345 "Lover Man") 150-250 52
(10-inch LP.)
DECCA (8215 "The Lady Sings") 50-100 56
DECCA (8701 "Blues Are Brewin' ") 50-100 58
DECCA (75000 series) 8-15 68
ESP 8-12 71-73
EVEREST 5-10 73-75
HARMONY 5-10 73
JAZZTONE (1209 "Billie Holiday Sings") 30-40 56
JOLLY ROGER (5020 "Billie Holiday") 75-100 54
KENT 5-10 73
MCA 5-10 73
MFSL (201 "In Rehearsal") 25-35 87
MFSL (247 "Body & Soul") 20-25 95
MGM (100 series) 6-10 70
MGM (3700 series) 25-50 59
MGM (4900 series) 5-10 74
MAINSTREAM 10-20 65
METRO 10-20 65
MONMOUTH-EVERGREEN 5-10 72
PARAMOUNT 5-10 73
PICKWICK 5-10
RIC 10-20 64
SCORE 25-50 57
SOLID STATE 8-12 69
TRIP 5-10 73
U.A. (5600 series) 5-10 72
U.A. (14000 & 15000 series) 20-30 62
VSP 8-15 66
VERVE 25-50 57-60
(Reads "Verve Records, Inc." at bottom of label.)
VERVE 10-25 61-72
(Reads "MGM Records - a Division of Metro-Goldwyn-Mayer, Inc." at bottom of label.)
VERVE 5-10 73-84
(Reads "Manufactured By MGM Record Corp.," or mentions either Polydor or Polygram at bottom of label.)
Also see FITZGERALD, Ella / Billie Holiday / Lena Horne

HOLIDAY, Billie, & Stan Getz
LPs: 10/12-inch
DALE (25 "Billie & Stan") 150-250 51
(10-inch LP.)
Also see GETZ, Stan
Also see GOODMAN, Benny, Orchestra
Also see LYNNE, Gloria / Nina Simone / Billie Holiday

HOLIDAY, Billie, & Eddie Heywood
LPs: 10/12-inch
COMMODORE (20005 "Billie Holiday, Vol. 1") 100-200 50
(10-inch LP.)
COMMODORE (20006 "Billie Holiday, Vol. 2") 100-200 50
(10-inch LP.)
COMMODORE (30008 "Billie Holiday, Vol. 1") 50-75 59
COMMODORE (30011 "Billie Holiday, Vol. 2") 50-75 59
Also see HEYWOOD, Eddie

HOLIDAY, Billie, & Al Hibbler
LPs: 10/12-inch
IMPERIAL 20-30 62
SUNSET 8-15 67
Also see HIBBLER, Al
Also see HOLIDAY, Billie

HOLIDAY, Buddy
Singles: 7-inch
HI 5-10 59

HOLIDAY, Chico P&R '59
(Chico)
Singles: 7-inch
CORAL 5-10 61-63
KARATE 5-10 65
NEW PHOENIX 8-12 61
RCA 5-10 59
SHAMLEY 4-8 69
EPs: 7-inch
RAYNARD (10065 "What Did I Do") 15-25 58
LP: 10/12-inch
ASEPH 5-8 89
EAGLE WING 5-8 89
MELODYLAND 10-20 75-78
SONGSPIRATION 5-10 73
Also see VERLIN, Chico

HOLIDAY, Connie
Singles: 7-inch
CAPITOL 6-12 65
SMASH 4-8 62

HOLIDAY, Danny
Singles: 7-inch
NOLTA 5-10 66

HOLIDAY, Doc
Singles: 7-inch
CAYTON 4-8 78
7 ARTS 5-10

HOLIDAY, Jay, & Giants
Singles: 7-inch
CMI (1001 "The Stalk") 8-12

HOLIDAY, Jim, & Futuretones
Singles: 7-inch
4 STAR (1720 "All I Want Is You") 50-75 58

HOLIDAY, Jimmy P&R/R&B '63
(Jimmy Holliday)
Singles: 7-inch
DIAL (1004 "Sing a Song of Love") 4-8 71
DIPLOMACY (340 "New Breed") 8-12 65
EVEREST (2022 "How Can I Forget") 10-15 63
EVEREST (2027 "Don't Laugh") 8-12 63
EVEREST (2034 "Country Girl") 8-12 63
EVEREST (2038 "I Lied") 8-12 64
EVEREST (2049 "One More Thing") 8-12 64
EVEREST (2056 "Old Man River") 8-12 65
KT 5-10
KENT 5-10 68
MINIT 6-12 66-68
OLDIES 45 4-6 60s
TIP (1019 "A Friend of Mine") 8-12
LPs: 10/12-inch
MINIT (24005 "Turning Point") 20-30 66

HOLIDAY, Jimmy, & Clydie King
Singles: 7-inch
MINIT 8-10 67
Also see HOLIDAY, Jimmy
Also see KING, Clydie

HOLIDAY, Joe
EPs: 7-inch
KING 10-20 53

HOLIDAY, Jon E.
Singles: 7-inch
ATLANTIC 10-15 61

HOLIDAY, Johnny
Singles: 7-inch
LAWN 8-12 63

HOLIDAY, Marva
Singles: 7-inch
GNP (411 "It's Written All Over Your Face") 10-20 68

HOLIDAY, Willie
Singles: 78 rpm
PEACOCK 5-15 49

HOLIDAYS
Singles: 78 rpm
KING 10-15 56
Singles: 7-inch
KING 15-20 56

HOLIDAYS
Singles: 78 rpm
SPECIALTY (522 "Irene") 15-25 54
Singles: 7-inch
SPECIALTY (522 "Irene") 50-75 54

HOLIDAYS
Singles: 7-inch
BRUNSWICK 5-10 58
MARK IV (725 "Down By the Shore") 50-75 60s
MELBA (112 "The Robin") 100-150 57
NIX (537 "One Little Kiss") 40-60 61
(No "Pgh, Pa." on label.)
NIX (537 "One Little Kiss") 20-30 61
(Has "Pgh, Pa." under label name.)
PAM (111 "Refreshing") 150-250 61
ROBBEE (103 "Miss You") 35-55 60
ROBBEE (107 "Lonely Summer") 30-40 60
WONDER (115 "My Heart Never Knows") 75-125 59

HOLIDAYS
Singles: 7-inch
ANDIE (5019 "The Stars Will Remember") 30-50 60
BRENT (7018 "Come Back to Me") 20-30 61
GALAXY (714 "Send Back My Love") 25-35 62
(Black vinyl.)
GALAXY (714 "Send Back My Love") 40-60 62
(Colored vinyl. Promotional issue only.)

HOLIDAYS
Singles: 7-inch
MONUMENT 8-12 60
TRACK 8-12 62

HOLIDAYS
Singles: 7-inch
CORAL (62430 "Love & Learn") 10-15 65

HOLIDAYS P&R/R&B '66
Singles: 7-inch
GOLDEN WORLD (36 "I Love You Forever") 10-20 66
GOLDEN WORLD (47 "No Greater Love") 10-20 66
GROOVE CITY (206 "Easy Living") 50-75 60s
REVILOT (205 "Never Alone") 15-25 67
REVILOT (210 "I Know She Cares") 15-25 67
Members: Edwin Starr; Steve Mancha; J.J. Barnes.
Also see BARNES, J.J., & Steve Mancha
Also see STARR, Edwin

HOLIDAYS
Singles: 7-inch
DIXIE (1156 "Little Miss Hurt") 15-25 60
SANTO (500 "Desparate") 8-12 63

HOLIDAYS
Singles: 7-inch
WILJER (6002 "Love That's True") 20-30

HOLIEN, Danny P&R '72
Singles: 7-inch
MOUNTAIN 3-5 71
TUMBLEWEED 3-5 72
Also see MIDWEST
Also see SHADES

HOLLADAY, Dave C&W '86
Singles: 7-inch
STEP ONE 3-4 86

HOLLAND
Singles: 7-inch
ATLANTIC 3-4 85

HOLLAND, Amy P&R/LP '80
Singles: 7-inch
CAPITOL 3-4 80-83
Picture Sleeves
CAPITOL 3-4 80
LPs: 10/12-inch
CAPITOL 5-10 80-83
Also see CHRISTIAN, Chris
Also see McDONALD, Michael

HOLLAND, Brian R&B '72
(Briant Holland with the Band)
Singles: 78 rpm
KUDO (667 "In Nature Boy") 100-200 58
Singles: 7-inch
INVICTUS 4-6 72-73
KUDO (667 "In Nature Boy") 300-500 58
Also see HOLLAND, Eddie
Also see HOLLAND - DOZIER
Also see SATINTONES

HOLLAND, Eddie P&R/R&B '62
(With the Rayber Voices)
Singles: 7-inch
MERCURY (71290 "You") 75-100 58
MOTOWN (Except 1049) 15-25 61-64
MOTOWN (1049 "I'm on the Outside Looking In") 50-100 64
TAMLA (102 "Merry-Go-Round") 100-200 59
U.A. (172 "Merry-Go-Round") 15-25 59
U.A. (191 "Because I Love Her") 15-25 59
U.A. (207 "Magic Mirror") 15-25 60
U.A. (280 "Last Laugh") 15-25 61
Picture Sleeves
MOTOWN (1030 "If Cleopatra Took a Chance") 30-50 62
LPs: 10/12-inch
MOTOWN (604 "Eddie Holland") 50-75 63
Members (Rayber Voices): Brian Holland; Raynoma Gordy; Robert Bateman; Sonny Sanders; Gwen Murray.
Also see GRIFFIN, Herman
Also see HOLLAND, Brian
Also see JOHNSON, Marv
Also see REMUS, Eugene
Also see SATINTONES
Also see STRONG, Barrett

HOLLAND, Eddie, & Lamont Dozier
Singles: 7-inch
MOTOWN 8-12 63
Also see DOZIER, Lamont
Also see HOLLAND, Eddie
Also see HOLLAND - DOZIER

HOLLAND, Jimmy
Singles: 7-inch
SYCO (2001 "Sugar Baby") 10-20 65

HOLLAND, Jools, & Millionaires
Singles: 7-inch
I.R.S. 3-4 84
LPs: 10/12-inch
I.R.S. 5-10 84
Also see SQUEEZE

HOLLAND, Lee
Singles: 7-inch
KING 4-8 63

HOLLAND, Ray
Singles: 7-inch
AERTAUN 5-10 66
MARGO (101 "Surfboard Stag") 20-30 63
SAM 15-25

HOLLAND – DOZIER P&R '72
(With the Andantes & Four Tops; featuring Lamont Dozier)
Singles: 7-inch
INVICTUS 3-5 72-73
MOTOWN 15-20 63
Members: Brian Holland; Lamont Dozier
Also see FOUR TOPS
Also see HOLLAND, Brian
Also see HOLLAND, Eddie, & Lamont Dozier
Also see KENT, Billy, & Andantes

HOLLANDER, Xaviera
LPs: 10/12-inch
MILIDOMO 15-20 73

HOLLENBECK, Sheridan
Singles: 7-inch
INTERPHON 8-12 64

HOLLER, Dick
(With His Rockets; with Holidays)
Singles: 7-inch
ACE (540 "Uh Uh Baby") 20-30 58
COMET (913 "Hey Little Fool") 15-25 60s
COMET (2152 "Double Shot") 15-25 62
HERALD 8-12 61
VITAL (108 "Rumble") 10-20 65
LPs: 10/12-inch
ATLANTIC 8-15 70

HOLLERS, Wayne
Singles: 7-inch
DEL-FI 10-15 59

HOLLEY, Peanut
Singles: 7-inch
K&C 5-10 59

HOLLIDAY, Doc
LPs: 10/12-inch
A&M 5-10 81

HOLLIDAY, Jay
Singles: 7-inch
EAST WEST 5-10 57
GIANT 10-20 57

HOLLIDAY, Jennifer P&R/R&B '82
Singles: 12-inch
GEFFEN 4-6 83-86
Singles: 7-inch
GEFFEN 3-4 82-87
Picture Sleeves
GEFFEN 3-4 85-86
LPs: 10/12-inch
GEFFEN 5-10 82-86

HOLLIDAY, Johnny
Singles: 7-inch
ROULETTE 5-8 61

HOLLIDAY, Judy
LPs: 10/12-inch
COLUMBIA 10-20

HOLLIDAY, Sonny
Singles: 7-inch
CONSTELLATION 4-8 63

HOLLIDAYS
(With the Gerald Wilson Orchestra)
Singles: 7-inch
PREP (136 "I'm Not Ashamed") 30-50 58

HOLLIDAYS
(With the Blazers Band)
Singles: 7-inch
LYONS (107 "Got My Letter") 200-300 61
Also see BLAZERS

HOLLIER, Jill C&W '86
Singles: 7-inch
W.B. 3-4 86-89

HOLLIER, Tom
LPs: 10/12-inch
IMPERIAL 10-12 69

HOLLIES P&R '64
Singles: 12-inch
ATLANTIC (502 "Stop in the Name of Love") 6-12 83
(Promotional issue only.)
EPIC (08157 "Draggin' My Heels") 8-10 77
Singles: 7-inch
ATLANTIC (89819 "Stop in the Name of Love") 3-4 83
EPIC (2000 series) 3-5 71
(Reissue series.)
EPIC (10180 thru 10613) 4-8 67-70
EPIC (10677 "Dandelion Wine") 5-10 70
EPIC (10716 "Survival of the Fittest") 8-12 71
EPIC (10754 "Row the Boat Together") 5-10 71
EPIC (10842 "The Baby") 5-10 72
EPIC (10871 thru 11100) 3-8 72-74
EPIC (50000 series) 3-5 75-78
IMPERIAL (66026 thru 66070) 10-20 64-65
IMPERIAL (66099 "Yes I Will") 20-40 65
IMPERIAL (66119 thru 66258) 5-10 66-68
IMPERIAL (66271 "If I Needed Someone") 20-40 65
LIBERTY (55674 "Stay") 25-40 64
Picture Sleeves
ATLANTIC (89819 "Stop in the Name of Love") 3-5 83
EPIC (10180 "Carrie-Anne") 8-12 67
EPIC (10234 "King Midas in Reverse") 8-12 67
EPIC (10251 "Dear Eloise") 8-12 67
IMPERIAL (66231 "On a Carousel") 8-12 67
LPs: 10/12-inch
ATLANTIC (81905 "Buster") 5-10 83
CAPITOL (16056 "Greatest") 6-10 80
EMI (92882 "Best of the Hollies") 5-10 80s
EPIC (24315 "Evolution") 25-35 67
(Monaural.)
EPIC (24344 "Dear Eloise/King Midas in Reverse") 25-35 67
(Monaural.)
EPIC (26315 "Evolution") 15-25 67
(Stereo.)
EPIC (26344 "Dear Eloise/King Midas in Reverse") 15-25 67
(Stereo.)
EPIC (26538 "He Ain't Heavy He's My Brother") 10-20 70
EPIC (30255 "Moving Finger") 10-20 71
EPIC (KE-30958 "Distant Light") 10-20 72
EPIC (AL-30958 "Distant Light") 5-10 77
EPIC (31000 thru 35000 series) 6-12 73-78
IMPERIAL (9265 "Here I Go Again") 125-175 64
(Monaural. Black label with five stars under

"Imperial" and straight lines from "10" to "2" [if label were a clock race].)
IMPERIAL (9265 "Here I Go Again") ... 50-75 64
(Monaural. Multi-color label.)
IMPERIAL (9299 "Hear! Here!") ... 40-60 65
(Monaural.)
IMPERIAL (9312 "The Hollies [Beat Group]") ... 35-50 66
(Monaural.)
IMPERIAL (9330 "Bus Stop") ... 35-50 66
(Monaural.)
IMPERIAL (9339 "Stop! Stop! Stop!") ... 35-50 67
(Monaural.)
IMPERIAL (9350 "Greatest Hits") ... 40-60 67
(Monaural.)
IMPERIAL (12265 "Here I Go Again") ... 75-125 64
(Stereo. Black "Imperial Stereo" label.)
IMPERIAL (12299 "Hear! Here!") ... 30-50 65
(Stereo.)
IMPERIAL (12312 "The Hollies [Beat Group]") ... 25-50 66
(Stereo.)
IMPERIAL (12330 "Bus Stop") ... 25-50 66
(Stereo.)
IMPERIAL (12339 "Stop! Stop! Stop!") ... 25-50 67
(Stereo.)
IMPERIAL (12350 "Greatest Hits") ... 25-50 67
(Stereo.)
LIBERTY ... 5-10 84
U.A. (329 "Very Best") ... 8-12 75
Members: Allan Clarke; Graham Nash; Bobby Elliott; Tony Hicks; Terry Sylvester.
Also see BAMBOO
Also see CLARKE, Allan
Also see EVERLY BROTHERS
Also see NASH, Graham
Also see PARSONS, Alan, Project
Also see SPRINGSTEEN, Bruce / Johnny Winter / Hollies
Also see SYLVESTER, Terry
Also see TREMELOES / Hollies

HOLLIES / Peter Sellers
Singles: 7-inch
U.A. (50079 "After the Fox") ... 10-20 66
LPs: 10/12-inch
U.A. (286 "After the Fox") ... 8-10 74
(Soundtrack.)
U.A. (4148 "After the Fox") ... 15-25 66
(Soundtrack. Monaural.)
U.A. (5148 "After the Fox") ... 25-35 66
(Soundtrack. Stereo.)
Also see HOLLIES
Also see SELLERS, Peter

HOLLIMAN, Earl
Singles: 7-inch
CAPITOL (3983 "A Teenager Sings the Blues") ... 10-20 58
CAPITOL (4042 "La La La Lovable") ... 8-15 58
PREP (127 "Nobody Knows How I Feel") ... 10-20 58

HOLLINS, Tony
Singles: 78 rpm
DECCA ... 15-25 52
Singles: 7-inch
DECCA (48288 "Wine-O-Woman") ... 50-75 52
DECCA (48300 "Fishin' Blues") ... 50-75 52

HOLLINS & STAR
Singles: 7-inch
OVATION ... 3-5 71
LPs: 10/12-inch
OVATION ... 5-10 71

HOLLIS, Pat
LPs: 10/12-inch
CASABLANCA ... 5-10 77

HOLLISTER, Bobby, & Rialtos
Singles: 7-inch
PIKE ... 10-15 61
Also see RIALTOS

HOLLOW MEN
LPs: 10/12-inch
ARISTA ... 5-8 91
EVENSONG ... 5-10 90
Members: David Ashmoore; Choque; Jonny Cragg; Brian Roberts; Howard Taylor.

HOLLOWAY, Alden
Singles: 7-inch
DIXIE ... 5-10 59

HOLLOWAY, Bobby
Singles: 7-inch
SMASH ... 4-8 67

HOLLOWAY, Brenda — *P&R/R&B '64*
(With the Carrolls)
Singles: 7-inch
BREVIT ... 5-10 63
CATCH (109 You're My Only Love") ... 15-25 64
DONNA (1358 "Echo") ... 20-40 62
TAMLA ("Play It Cool, Stay in School") ... 300-500 60s
(No selection number used. Promotional issue only.)
TAMLA (54094 "Every Little Bit Hurts") ... 5-10 64
TAMLA (54099 "I'll Always Love You") ... 10-15 65
TAMLA (54099 "I'll Always Love You") ... 50-100 65
(Single-sided. Promotional issue only.)
TAMLA (54111 "When I'm Gone") .. 5-10 65
TAMLA (54115 thru 54137) ... 10-20 65-66
TAMLA (54144 "Til Johnny Comes") ... 100-200 67
TAMLA (54148 "Just Look What You've Done") ... 10-20 67
TAMLA (54155 "You've Made Me So Very Happy") ... 10-20 67
Picture Sleeves
TAMLA (54111 "When I'm Gone") 20-40 65
LPs: 10/12-inch
MOTOWN (5242 "Every Little Bit Hurts") ... 5-10 80s
(Stereo.)
TAMLA (257 "Every Little Bit Hurts") ... 100-200 65
Also see BARBARA & BRENDA
Also see DAVIS, Hal

HOLLOWAY, Brenda, & Jess Harris
Singles: 7-inch
BREVIT ("Never Knew You Looked") ... 25-35 63
(Selection number not known.)
Also see HOLLOWAY, Brenda

HOLLOWAY, Loleatta — *R&B '73*
(With the Salsoul Orchestra)
Singles: 12-inch
SALSOUL ... 4-8 83
STREETWISE ... 4-8 84
Singles: 7-inch
AWARE ... 3-5 73-75
GRC ... 3-5 73
GALAXY ... 3-5 71
GOLD MINE ... 3-5 76-77
SALSOUL ... 3-4 77-83
LPs: 10/12-inch
GOLD MINE ... 5-10 77
Also see SALSOUL ORCHESTRA

HOLLOWAY, Loleatta, & Bunny Sigler — *P&R/R&B '78*
Singles: 7-inch
GOLD MINE ... 3-5 78
Also see HOLLOWAY, Loleatta
Also see SIGLER, Bunny

HOLLOWAY, Patrice
Singles: 7-inch
CAPITOL (5680 "Stolen Hours") ... 50-75 66
CAPITOL (5778 "Love & Desire") ... 30-60 66
CAPITOL (5985 "Stay with Your Own Kind") ... 25-50 67
TASTE (125 "Do the Del Viking") ... 20-30 63
Also see JOSIE & PUSSYCATS

HOLLOWAY, Stanley
Singles: 78 rpm
COLUMBIA ... 10-15

HOLLOWAY, Stevie
Singles: 7-inch
MOONGLOW ... 4-8 66

HOLLOWAY, Vikki
Singles: 7-inch
ATLANTIC ... 3-5 79

HOLLOWELL, Terri — *C&W '78*
Singles: 7-inch
CON BRIO ... 3-5 78-79

HOLLOWS
Singles: 7-inch
RENDEVOUS (141 "Revival Stomp") ... 10-20 61

HOLLY, Buddy — *P&R/R&B '57*
(With the Crickets; with Three Tunes; with Picks)
Singles: 12-inch
SOLID SMOKE ... 10-20 79
(Picture disc.)
Singles: 78 rpm
BRUNSWICK (55009 "That'll Be the Day") ... 100-200 57
BRUNSWICK (55035 "Oh Boy") 100-200 58
BRUNSWICK (55053 "Maybe Baby") ... 100-200 58
BRUNSWICK (55072 "Think It Over") ... 100-200 58
BRUNSWICK (55094 "It's So Easy") ... 100-200 58
CORAL (61852 "Words of Love") ... 150-250 57
CORAL (61885 "Peggy Sue") ... 100-200 57
CORAL (61947 "Listen to Me") .. 100-200 58
CORAL (61985 "Rave On") ... 100-200 58
CORAL (62006 "Early in the Morning") ... 100-200 58
CORAL (62051 "Heartbeat") ... 100-200 58
DECCA (29854 "Blue Days – Black Nights") ... 100-200 56
DECCA (30166 "Modern Don Juan") ... 100-200 56
DECCA (30434 "That'll Be the Day") ... 100-200 57
DECCA (30543 "Love Me") ... 100-200 58
DECCA (30650 "Ting-A-Ling") ... 100-200 58
Singles: 7-inch
BRUNSWICK (55009 "That'll Be the Day") ... 25-50 57
BRUNSWICK (55035 "Oh Boy") ... 25-50 58
BRUNSWICK (55053 "Maybe Baby") ... 20-40 58
BRUNSWICK (55072 "Think It Over") ... 20-40 58
BRUNSWICK (55094 "It's So Easy") ... 20-40 58
CORAL (61852 "Words of Love") ... 200-300 57
CORAL (61885 "Peggy Sue") ... 20-30 57
CORAL (61947 "Listen to Me") ... 20-30 58
CORAL (61985 "Rave On") ... 20-30 58
CORAL (62006 "Early in the Morning") ... 20-30 58
CORAL (62051 "Heartbeat") ... 20-30 58
CORAL (62074 "It Doesn't Matter Anymore") ... 20-30 59
CORAL (62134 "Peggy Sue Got Married") ... 30-40 59
(Orange label.)
CORAL (62134 "Peggy Sue Got Married") ... 10-20 62
(Yellow label.)
CORAL (62210 "True Love Ways") ... 30-40 60
CORAL (62329 "Reminiscing") ... 20-30 62
CORAL (62352 "Bo Diddley") ... 25-35 63
CORAL (62369 "Brown Eyed Handsome Man") ... 25-35 63
CORAL (62390 "Rock Around with Ollie Vee") ... 30-40 64
CORAL (62407 "Maybe Baby") ... 30-40 64
CORAL (62448 "Slippin' & Slidin'") ... 50-75 65
CORAL (62554 "Rave On") ... 25-35 68
CORAL (62558 "Love Is Strange") 15-25 69
CORAL (65618 "That'll Be the Day") ... 15-25 69
DECCA (29854 "Blue Days – Black Nights") ... 100-150 56
(With silver lines on both sides of the name Decca.)
DECCA (29854 "Blue Days – Black Nights") ... 75-100 56
(With silver star and lines under the name Decca.)
DECCA (30166 "Modern Don Juan") ... 100-150 56
(With silver lines on both sides of the name Decca.)
DECCA (30166 "Modern Don Juan") ... 75-100 56
(With silver star and lines under the name Decca.)
DECCA (30434 "That'll Be the Day") ... 100-150 57
(With silver lines on both sides of the name Decca.)
DECCA (30434 "That'll Be the Day") ... 75-100 57
(With silver star and lines under the name Decca.)
DECCA (30543 "Love Me") ... 100-150 58
(With silver lines on both sides of the name Decca.)
DECCA (30543 "Love Me") ... 75-100 58
(With silver star and lines under the name Decca.)
DECCA (30650 "Ting-A-Ling") ... 100-150 58
(With silver lines on both sides of the name Decca.)
DECCA (30650 "Ting-A-Ling") ... 75-100 58
(With silver star and lines under the name Decca.)
MCA ... 3-6 73-78
MEMORY LANE ... 3-5
Promotional Singles
BRUNSWICK (55009 "That'll Be the Day") ... 50-100 57
BRUNSWICK (55035 "Oh Boy") .. 50-100 58
BRUNSWICK (55053 "Maybe Baby") ... 50-100 58
BRUNSWICK (55072 "Think It Over") ... 50-100 58
BRUNSWICK (55094 "It's So Easy") ... 50-100 58
CORAL (61852 "Words of Love") ... 150-200 57
CORAL (61885 "Peggy Sue") ... 100-150 57
CORAL (61947 "Listen to Me") ... 50-100 58
CORAL (61985 "Rave On") ... 50-100 58
CORAL (62006 "Early in the Morning") ... 50-75 58
CORAL (62051 "Heartbeat") ... 50-75 58
CORAL (62074 "It Doesn't Matter Anymore") ... 50-75 59
CORAL (62134 "Peggy Sue Got Married") ... 50-75 59
CORAL (62210 "True Love Ways") ... 50-75 60
CORAL (62329 "Reminiscing") ... 50-75 62
CORAL (62352 "Bo Diddley") ... 50-75 63
CORAL (62369 "Brown Eyed Handsome Man") ... 50-75 63
CORAL (62390 "Rock Around with Ollie Vee") ... 50-75 64
CORAL (62407 "Maybe Baby") ... 50-75 64
CORAL (62448 "Slippin' & Slidin'") ... 50-75 65
CORAL (62554 "Rave On") ... 40-60 68
CORAL (62558 "Love Is Strange") ... 40-60 69
(Price doubles if accompanied by dee jay insert sheet.)
CORAL (65618 "That'll Be the Day") ... 40-60 69
DECCA (29854 "Blue Days - Black Nights") ... 100-150 56
DECCA (30166 "Modern Don Juan") ... 100-150 56
DECCA (30434 "That'll Be the Day") ... 100-150 57
DECCA (30543 "Love Me") ... 100-150 58
DECCA (30650 "Ting-A-Ling") ... 100-150 58
Picture Sleeves
CORAL (62558 "Love Is Strange") ... 10-15 69
MCA ... 3-5 78
EPs: 7-inch
BRUNSWICK (71036 "The Chirping Crickets") ... 300-350 57
(With printed back cover.)
BRUNSWICK (71036 "The Chirping Crickets") ... 350-450 57
(With blank back cover.)
BRUNSWICK (71038 "The Sound of the Crickets") ... 100-200 58
CORAL (81169 "Listen to Me") .. 200-300 58
CORAL (81182 "The Buddy Holly Story") ... 150-250 59
CORAL (81191 "Buddy Holly") ... 150-250 62
CORAL (81193 "Brown Eyed Handsome Man") ... 100-200 63
DECCA (2575 "That'll Be the Day") ... 500-750 58
(With liner notes on the back cover.)
DECCA (2575 "That'll Be the Day") ... 400-600 58
(With EP ads on the back cover.)
LPs: 10/12-inch
BRUNSWICK (54038 "The Chirping Crickets") ... 400-800 57
CORAL (8 "Best of Buddy Holly") ... 75-125 66
CORAL (57210 "Buddy Holly") ... 150-200 58
(Maroon label.)
CORAL (57210 "Buddy Holly") ... 25-50 63
(Black label.)
CORAL (57279 "The Buddy Holly Story") ... 100-150 59
(Maroon label. With red and black print on the back cover.)
CORAL (57279 "The Buddy Holly Story") ... 75-125 59
(Maroon label. With black print on the back cover.)
CORAL (57279 "The Buddy Holly Story") ... 30-40 63
(Black label. With pictures of other LPs, or black print, on the back cover.)
CORAL (57326 "The Buddy Holly Story, Vol. II") ... 100-200 60
(Maroon label.)
CORAL (57326 "The Buddy Holly Story, Vol. II") ... 25-50 63
(Black label.)
CORAL (57405 "Buddy Holly and the Crickets") ... 50-100 62
(Maroon label.)
CORAL (57405 "Buddy Holly and the Crickets") ... 25-45 63
(Black label.)
CORAL (57426 "Reminiscing") ... 50-75 63
(Maroon label.)
CORAL (57426 "Reminiscing") ... 20-40 63
(Black label.)
CORAL (57450 "Showcase") ... 40-50 64
CORAL (57463 "Holly in the Hills") ... 75-100 65
CORAL (57492 "Buddy Holly's Greatest Hits") ... 75-100 67
CORAL (757279 "The Buddy Holly Story") ... 25-35 63
(Stereo.)
CORAL (757405 "Buddy Holly and the Crickets") ... 50-75 62
(Maroon label. Stereo.)
CORAL (757405 "Buddy Holly and the Crickets") ... 25-45 63
(Black label. Stereo.)
CORAL (757463 "Holly in the Hills") ... 40-60 65
(Stereo.)
CORAL (757504 "Giant") ... 40-80 69
(Stereo.)
CREATIVE RADIO ("The Day the Music Died") ... 25-30
(Two-LP set, includes poster.)
DECCA (207 "A Rock & Roll Collection") ... 15-20 72
DECCA (8707 "That'll Be the Day") ... 250-350 58
(Black label.)
DECCA (8707 "That'll Be the Day") ... 150-250 61
(Multi-color label.)
LIFE (8707 "That'll Be the Day") ... 150-250 61
(Multi-color Decca label, but with "Life" on label instead of Decca. Cover shows Decca, not Life.)
MCA (Except 6-80000) ... 8-15 75-85
MCA (6-80000 "The Complete Buddy Holly") ... 30-40 81
(Boxed six-disc set.)
VOCALION (3811 "The Great Buddy Holly") ... 90-110 67
(Monaural.)
VOCALION (73811 "The Great Buddy Holly") ... 20-30 67
(Reprocessed stereo.)
VOCALION (73923 "Good Rockin' Buddy Holly") ... 100-125 71
(Reprocessed stereo.)
Promotional LPs
BRUNSWICK (54038 "The Chirping Crickets") ... 300-400 57
CORAL (Except 757504) ... 50-75 58-65
CORAL (757504 "Giant") ... 35-45 69
DECCA (8707 "That'll Be the Day") ... 400-500 58
(Pink label.)
PICK (1111 "Buddy Holly and the Picks") ... 10-12 86
Also see BEATLES / Beach Boys / Buddy Holly
Also see CRICKETS
Also see CURTIS, Sonny
Also see DAVIS, Sherry
Also see DON & His Roses
Also see ENGLER, Jerry, & Four Ekkos
Also see FREED, Alan
Also see GIORDANO, Lou
Also see HUDDLE, Jack
Also see JENNINGS, Waylon
Also see KING, Ben E.
Also see MONTGOMERY, Bob
Also see PETTY, Norman, Trio
Also see PHILLIPS, Charlie
Also see PICKS
Also see PRESLEY, Elvis / Buddy Holly
Also see ROBINSON, Jim
Also see TUCKER, Rick

HOLLY, Doyle — *C&W '72*
(With the Vanishing Breed)
Singles: 7-inch
BARNABY ... 3-5 72-74
LPs: 10/12-inch
BARNABY ... 10-20 73
PICKWICK ... 5-10 70s

HOLLY, Little Brenda
Singles: 7-inch
BRITE STAR ... 5-10 59

HOLLY, Pete, & Looks
Singles: 7-inch
BOMP ... 3-4 87
Picture Sleeves
BOMP ... 3-4 87

HOLLY, Wes
Singles: 7-inch
IOWANA (809 "Shufflin' Shoes") ... 20-30 58
WES HOLLY ("Hop Rock") ... 15-25 50s
(Selection number not known.)

HOLLY & ITALIANS — *LP '81*
(Featuring Holly Beth Vincent)
Singles: 7-inch
OVAL ... 3-5
VIRGIN ... 3-4 82
Picture Sleeves
OVAL ... 3-5
LPs: 10/12-inch
VIRGIN ... 5-10 81-82
Also see VINCENT, Holly Beth

HOLLY TWINS
Singles: 78 rpm
LIBERTY ... 15-25 57
Singles: 7-inch
LIBERTY (55048 "I Want Elvis for Christmas") ... 15-25 57
(With Eddie Cochran.)
RENDEZVOUS ... 4-8 62
Also see COCHRAN, Eddie

HOLLYHAWKS
Singles: 7-inch
JUBILEE (5441 "I Cry All the Time") ... 50-75 63
Members: Niki Sullivan; Gene Evans.
Also see SULLIVAN, Niki

HOLLYHOCKS
Singles: 78 rpm
NASCO ... 15-25 57
Singles: 7-inch
NASCO (6001 "Don't Say Tomorrow") ... 15-25 57

HOLLYRIDGE STRINGS — *P&R/LP '64*
(Stu Phillips & Hollyridge Strings)
Singles: 7-inch
CAPITOL ... 3-6 61-68
EPs: 7-inch
CAPITOL (2626 "Selections from *Beatles Songbook*") ... 5-10 64
(Promotional issue only.)
LPs: 10/12-inch
CAPITOL ... 5-15 64-78
Also see GOLDEN GATE STRINGS
Also see PHILLIPS, Stu

HOLLYWOOD ALLSTARS
Singles: 7-inch
ADMIRAL (501 "Justine") ... 20-30 61

HOLLYWOOD ARGYLES — *P&R/R&B '60*
Singles: 7-inch
ABC ... 3-5 74
CHATTAHOOCHEE (691 "Longhair, Unsquare Dude Called Jack") ... 5-8 65
ERA ... 3-5 72
FELSTED (8674 "Bossynover") ... 5-10 63
FINER ARTS (1002 "Morning After") ... 5-10 61
LUTE (5905 "Alley-Oop") ... 10-15 60
LUTE (6002 "Hully Gully") ... 10-15 60
PAXLEY (751 "You Been Torturing Me") ... 8-12 61
LPs: 10/12-inch
LUTE (9001 "Alley Oop") ... 250-350 60
Members: Gary Paxton; Dallas Frazier; Buddy Mize; Scotty Turner. Session: Gary Webb; Bobby Rey; Gaynel Hodge; Ronnie Caleco; Harper Cosby; Sandy Nelson; Marshall Leib; Deary Weaver.
Also see ARGYLES
Also see FRAZIER, Dallas
Also see HODGE, Gaynel
Also see NEW HOLLYWOOD ARGYLES
Also see NELSON, Sandy
Also see PAXTON, Gary
Also see REY, Little Bobby

HOLLYWOOD ARGYLES / Phil Flowers
Singles: 7-inch
WHAT ... 3-5
Also see FLOWERS, Phil
Also see HOLLYWOOD ARGYLES

HOLLYWOOD ARIST-O-KATS
(With the Red Callender Sextette)
Singles: 78 rpm
RECORDED in HOLLYWOOD .. 200-300 53
Singles: 7-inch
RECORDED in HOLLYWOOD (406 "I'll Be Home Again") ... 1000-2000 53

HOLLYWOOD BLUEJAYS
(Flairs)
Singles: 78 rpm
RECORDED in HOLLYWOOD (185 "Cloudy and Raining") ... 50-100 52

RECORDED in HOLLYWOOD (396 "I Had a Love") ... 50-100 53
Singles: 7-inch
RECORDED in HOLLYWOOD (396 "I Had a Love") ... 300-500 53
Also see FIVE HOLLYWOOD BLUEJAYS
Also see FLAIRS

HOLLYWOOD CHAMBER JAZZ GROUP
EPs: 7-inch
RCA (4199 "Stakeout") ... 25-35 58
(Soundtrack.)

HOLLYWOOD CHICKS
Singles: 7-inch
CLASS ... 8-10 62

HOLLYWOOD FLAMES P&R/R&B '57
(Dave Ford & Hollywood Flames; "with Orchestra Acc.")
Singles: 78 rpm
DECCA ... 20-30 54-55
EBB ... 50-100 57-58
LUCKY (001 "One Night with a Fool") ... 100-150 54
LUCKY (006 "Peggy") ... 100-150 54
LUCKY (009 "Let's Talk It Over") ... 50-100 54
MONEY (202 "I'm Leaving") ... 100-150 54
SWING TIME (345 "Let's Talk It Over") ... 100-200 53
Singles: 7-inch
ATCO (6155 "If I Thought You Needed Me") ... 15-20 59
ATCO (6164 "Ball & Chain") ... 10-20 60
ATCO (6171 "Devil Or Angel") ... 15-20 60
ATCO (6180 "Money Honey") ... 15-20 60
CHESS (1787 "Gee") ... 15-20 61
DECCA (29285 "Peggy") ... 50-100 54
DECCA (48331 "Let's Talk It Over") ... 50-100 55
EBB (119 "Buzz, Buzz, Buzz") ... 15-25 57
EBB (131 "Give Me Back My Heart") ... 15-25 58
EBB (144 "Strollin' on the Beach") 15-25 58
EBB (146 "Chains of Love") ... 15-25 58
EBB (149 "A Star Fell") ... 15-25 58
EBB (153 "Just for You") ... 15-25 58
EBB (158 "So Good") ... 15-25 58
EBB (162 "Now That You've Gone") ... 15-25 59
EBB (163 "In the Dark") ... 15-25 59
GOLDIE (1101 "Believe in Me") ... 10-15 62
LUCKY (001 "One Night with a Fool") ... 500-750 54
LUCKY (006 "Peggy") ... 500-750 54
LUCKY (009 "Let's Talk It Over") ... 300-500 54
MONA-LEE (135 "Buzz, Buzz, Buzz") ... 15-25 59
MONEY (202 "I'm Leaving") ... 500-750 54
SWING TIME (345 "Let's Talk It Over") ... 500-750 53
SYMBOL (211 "Dance Senorita") ... 10-20 65
SYMBOL (215 "I'm Coming Home") ... 10-20 66
VEE JAY (515 "Letter to My Love") ... 10-20 63
LPs: 10/12-inch
SPECIALTY ... 8-10 88
Members: David Ford; Bobby Byrd; Gaynel Hodge; Clyde Tillis; Earl Nelson; Curtis Williams; Donald Height; Ray Brewster; John Berry; George Home.
Also see BOB & EARL
Also see BREWSTER, Ray
Also see BYRD, Bobby
Also see FLAMES
Also see FOUR FLAMES
Also see HEIGHT, Donald
Also see HODGE, Gaynel
Also see HOLLYWOOD FOUR FLAMES
Also see JETS
Also see NELSON, Earl
Also see QUESTION MARKS
Also see SATELLITES
Also see TANGIERS
Also see TURKS

HOLLYWOOD FLAMES / Question Marks
Singles: 78 rpm
SWING TIME (346 "Go and Get Some More") ... 100-200 54

HOLLYWOOD FOUR FLAMES
(Hollywood Flames)
Singles: 78 rpm
RECORDED IN HOLLYWOOD (164 "I'll Always Be a Fool") ... 200-400 52
RECORDED IN HOLLYWOOD (165 "Young Girl") ... 200-400 52
UNIQUE (003 "Dividend Blues") 250-500 51
UNIQUE (005 "Tabarin") ... 250-500 51
(Reissued as by the Four Flames.)
UNIQUE (015 "Please Say I Am Wrong") ... 200-400 51
Also see FOUR FLAMES
Also see HOLLYWOOD FLAMES

HOLLYWOOD GAMBLERS
Singles: 7-inch
DON (201 "Moon Katt") ... 10-15 61
Also see GAMBLERS

HOLLYWOOD GUITARS
LPs: 10/12-inch
MTA ... 8-10 70

HOLLYWOOD HURRICANES
Singles: 7-inch
PRIMA (1009 "Beavershot") ... 10-20 64

HOLLYWOOD PERSUADERS
Singles: 7-inch
ORIGINAL SOUND (39 "Grunion Run") ... 20-30 63
(First pressings credited to the Persuaders.)
ORIGINAL SOUND (44 "Juarez") ... 8-12 63
ORIGINAL SOUND (50 "Drums A-Go-Go") ... 8-12 64
ORIGINAL SOUND (58 "Hollywood A-Go-Go") ... 10-20 65
LPs: 10/12-inch
ORIGINAL SOUND (8874 "Drums A-Go-Go") ... 20-25 65
Also see PERSUADERS
Also see ZAPPA, Frank

HOLLYWOOD PLAYBOYS
Singles: 7-inch
SURE (105 "Ding Dong School Is Out") ... 20-30 60
Member: Nick Massi.
Also see MASSI, Nick

HOLLYWOOD PRODUCERS
Singles: 7-inch
PARKWAY (993 "You're Not Welcome") ... 30-50 66
(Previously issued as by Jan Davis.)
Also see DAVIS, Jan

HOLLYWOOD REBELS
Singles: 7-inch
IMPACT (18 "Rebel Stomp") ... 15-20 64

HOLLYWOOD SAXONS
Singles: 7-inch
ELF (101 "Everyday's a Holiday") .. 25-50 62
ELF (103 "It's You") ... 25-50 62
HARECO (102 "Everyday Holiday" ... 1000-2000 62
(Note slight title variation on reissues.)
SWINGIN' (631 "Everyday's a Holiday") ... 15-25 61
SWINGIN' (651 "It's You") ... 15-25 61
20TH FOX (312 "Everyday's a Holiday") ... 75-100 63
Also see BEVERLY, Stan, & Hollywood Saxons
Also see PORTRAITS
Also see SAXONS

HOLLYWOOD SOUL COMFORTERS
Singles: 78 rpm
HOLLYWOOD ... 20-30 55
Singles: 7-inch
HOLLYWOOD (1042 "Silent Night") ... 50-75 55

HOLLYWOOD SPECTRUM
LPs: 10/12-inch
COTILLION ... 10-12 70

HOLLYWOOD STARS P&R '77
Singles: 7-inch
ARISTA ... 3-5 77
LPs: 10/12-inch
ARISTA ... 8-10 77
Also see ANTHONY, Mark
Also see KINKS / Hollywood Stars

HOLLYWOOD STUDIO ORCHESTRA LP '61
Singles: 7-inch
U.A. ... 4-8 59
LPs: 10/12-inch
U.A. ... 10-15 61

HOLLYWOOD SUNSETS BAND
(With the Sunset Choraliers)
EPs: 7-inch
RAINBOW (1001 "Teenage World of Music") ... 25-35 64
Also see ADRIAN & SUNSETS

HOLLYWOOD SURFERS / Dick Dale
LPs: 10/12-inch
DUB-TONE ... 15-30 60s
Also see DALE, Dick

HOLLYWOOD TORNADOES
Singles: 7-inch
AERTAUN ... 10-20 62-63
ORIGINAL SOUND ... 5-10 64
Also see TORNADOES

HOLLYWOOD VINES
Singles: 7-inch
CAPITOL ... 8-12 61

HOLLYWOOD'S FOUR BLAZES
Singles: 78 rpm
EXCELSIOR ... 15-25 45-46
LAMPLIGHTER ... 15-25 46
Also see FOUR BLAZES

HOLM, Johnny C&W '77
Singles: 7-inch
ASI ... 3-5 77

HOLM, Michael P&R '74
Singles: 7-inch
MERCURY ... 3-5 74

HOLMAN, Eddie R&B '65
Singles: 7-inch
ABC ... 5-10 69-71
AGAPE ... 3-5 82
ASCOT (2142 "Laughing at Me") ... 10-20 63
BELL ... 10-20 68
CAMEO (253 "Crossroads") ... 15-25 63
DON-EL (124 "She's Beautiful") ... 15-25 60s
GSF ... 3-6 73
LEOPARD (5001 "I'm Counting Every Tear") ... 20-30 60s
PARKWAY ... 10-20 65-67
SALSOUL ... 3-5 77
SILVER BLUE ... 3-6 74
LPs: 10/12-inch
ABC-PAR (701 "I Love You") ... 10-15 70
SALSOUL (5511 "Night to Remember") ... 5-10 77

HOLMAN, Eddie / Lamplighters
Singles: 7-inch
SCRIPT (12212 "Never Let Go") ... 10-20
(Colored vinyl. Promotional issue only.)
Also see HOLMAN, Eddie
Also see LAMPLIGHTERS

HOLMAN, Jay
Singles: 7-inch
EMBER ... 5-10 61
FALEW! (106 "Love Is a Sweet Thing") ... 10-20

HOLMAN, Rocky, & Romancers
Singles: 7-inch
FLIP (355 "My Precious Love") ... 20-30 61

HOLMBERG, Jim
LPs: 10/12-inch
ESP ... 10-12

HOLMES, Carl
(With the Commanders)
Singles: 7-inch
ATLANTIC ... 4-8 62
PARKWAY ... 4-8 64
VERVE ... 4-8 67
LPs: 10/12-inch
ATLANTIC ... 25-35 62
Carl Holmes; Marco King; Sports Lewis; Tommy Howard; Calvin Irons; John Holmes.

HOLMES, Cecil
(Cecil Holmes' Soulful Sounds)
Singles: 7-inch
BUDDAH ... 3-5 73
LPs: 10/12-inch
BUDDAH ... 6-12 73

HOLMES, Christine
Singles: 7-inch
MERCURY ... 4-8 65

HOLMES, Clint P&R/LP '73
Singles: 7-inch
ATCO ... 3-5 74
EPIC ... 3-5 73
PRIVATE STOCK ... 3-5 76-79
LPs: 10/12-inch
EPIC ... 10-12 73

HOLMES, Eldridge
Singles: 7-inch
ALON ... 6-12 62-65
DEESU (305 "Lovely Woman") ... 15-25 60s
DEESU (320 "Now I've Lost You") 15-25 60s
DECCA ... 8-10
DEESU (305 "Lovely Woman") ... 15-25 67
DEESU (320 "Now I've Lost You") 15-25 68
JET SET (765 "Gone, Gone, Gone") ... 15-25
JETSET (1006 "I Like What You Do") ... 15-25
SANSU (469 "Without a Word") ... 5-10

HOLMES, Elmer
Singles: 7-inch
MARLO (1524 "Stuck with Blues") ... 8-12 62

HOLMES, Fat Daddy
Singles: 7-inch
JET (505 "Chicken Rock") ... 25-35 60

HOLMES, Jake P&R/LP '70
Singles: 7-inch
COLUMBIA ... 3-5 71-72
POLYDOR ... 3-5 70
TOWER ... 4-6 67
Picture Sleeves
TOWER ... 4-6 67
LPs: 10/12-inch
POLYDOR ... 8-12 70
TOWER ... 10-15 67

HOLMES, Jan R&B '85
Singles: 7-inch
JAY JAY ... 3-4 85

HOLMES, Johnny
Singles: 7-inch
STRAND ... 4-8 61

HOLMES, Leon, & His Georgia Ramblers
Singles: 7-inch
PEACH (597 "She's My Baby") ... 2500-3000 59
PEACH (730 "Tears on My Pillow") ... 25-50 60

HOLMES, Leroy, Orchestra P&R '54
Singles: 78 rpm
MGM ... 3-5 51-57
Singles: 7-inch
MGM ... 4-8 51-61
METRO ... 3-6 59
U.A. ... 3-5 67-68
Picture Sleeves
U.A. ... 4-8 67
EPs: 7-inch
MGM ... 4-8 52-56
U.A. (10041 "Leroy Holmes and His Orchestra") ... 4-8 67
(Promotional issue only.)
LPs: 10/12-inch
LION ... 5-10 59-60
MGM ... 5-15 52-62
U.A. ... 4-8 67-68

HOLMES, Marvin
(With the Uptights; with Justice)
Singles: 7-inch
BROWN DOOR (6574 "Tell the Truth") ... 10-20
UNI (55111 "Ooh Ooh the Dragon") ... 5-10 69
UNI (55177 "You're My Girl") ... 10-20 69
UNI (55233 "Sweet Talk") ... 10-20 69
LPs: 10/12-inch
UNI (73046 "Ooh Ooh the Dragon") ... 15-25 69

HOLMES, Monty C&W '89
Singles: 7-inch
ASHLEY ... 3-4 89

HOLMES, Richard "Groove" P&R/R&B/LP '66
Singles: 7-inch
BLUE NOTE ... 3-5 71
FLYING DUTCHMAN ... 3-5 76
PACIFIC JAZZ ... 4-8 61-69
PRESTIGE ... 3-6 66-69
LPs: 10/12-inch
BLUE NOTE ... 5-10 71
FLYING DUTCHMAN ... 5-10 75-76
GROOVE MERCHANT ... 5-10 72-75
LOMA ... 10-15 66
MUSE ... 5-10 78-80
PACIFIC JAZZ (Except 20000 series) ... 15-25 61-62
PACIFIC JAZZ (20000 series) ... 8-15 68-69
PRESTIGE ... 8-15 66-70
VERSATILE ... 5-10 78
W.B. ... 10-20 64
WORLD PACIFIC JAZZ ... 8-12 70
Also see AMMONS, Gene, & Richard "Groove" Holmes
Also see JONES, Brenda, & "Groove" Holmes
Also see McGRIFF, Jimmy
Also see WITHERSPOON, Jimmy

HOLMES, Richard "Groove," & Les McCann
LPs: 10/12-inch
PACIFIC JAZZ ... 15-25 62
Also see HOLMES, Richard "Groove"
Also see McCANN, Les

HOLMES, Rupert P&R '78
Singles: 7-inch
EPIC ... 3-6 74-76
INFINITY (50035 "Escape") ... 3-5 79
(May also be found on exact same label, but with MCA instead of Infinity.)
MCA ... 3-5 80-81
PRIVATE STOCK ... 3-5 78
Picture Sleeves
EPIC ... 3-4 75
LPs: 10/12-inch
ELEKTRA ... 5-10 81
EPIC ... 8-12 74-75
EXCELSIOR ... 5-8 80-81
INFINITY ... 5-10 79
MCA ... 5-10 80
PRIVATE STOCK ... 5-10 78
Also see CUFF LINKS
Also see STREET PEOPLE

HOLMES, Sherlock
Singles: 7-inch
BRUNSWICK ... 5-10 64
PART III ("Standing at a Standstill") ... 10-20 60s
(Selection number not known.)

HOLMES, Sonny Boy
Singles: 78 rpm
RECORDED in HOLLYWOOD (223 "Walking and Crying Blues") ... 25-50 52
RECORDED in HOLLYWOOD (225 "I Got Them Blues") ... 25-50 52

HOLMES, Tommy
Singles: 7-inch
CHERRY (112 "Wa-Chic-Ka-Naka") ... 150-250 58
CHERRY (113 "Witch Doctor's Wedding") ... 150-250 58

HOLMES, Wright
Singles: 78 rpm
GOTHAM (508 "Good Road Blues") ... 15-25 47
GOTHAM (511 "Alley Special") ... 25-50 47
MILTONE (5221 "Alley Special") ... 20-40 47

HOLOCAUST
Singles: 7-inch
RED ROBB (2025 "Savage Affection") ... 30-40

HOLT, Darrell C&W '87
Singles: 7-inch
ANOKA ... 3-4 87-89

HOLT, Davey, & Hubcaps
Singles: 7-inch
U.A. ... 10-15 58
Also see SNOW MEN

HOLT, Dennis I.
Singles: 7-inch
A&A ("King of Rock & Roll") ... 5-10 78
(No actual label name or number used.)

HOLT, Jim
Singles: 7-inch
GULFSTREAM (1061 "Paralyzed") ... 75-125 50s
GULFSTREAM (1062 "Money") ... 75-125 50s
GULFSTREAM (1064 "Money") ... 75-125 50s

HOLT, Katherine
Singles: 7-inch
BOOKER (510 "My Love") ... 10-15

HOLT, Lonnie
Singles: 7-inch
BREEZE (552 "Will It Mean a Broken Heart") ... 8-12 60s

HOLT, Will
Singles: 78 rpm
CORAL ... 4-8 54
Singles: 7-inch
CORAL ... 8-12 54

HOLTON, Bennie, Trio
Singles: 7-inch
STAFF (800 "Bennie's Boogie") ... 15-25 50s

HOLTS, Roosevelt
(With Boogie Bill)
Singles: 7-inch
BLUESMAN (100 "Down the Big Road") ... 6-12 60s
LPs: 10/12-inch
BLUE HORIZON ... 10-12 69

HOLY GHOST RECEPTION COMMITTEE #9
LPs: 10/12-inch
PAULIST PRESS ("Songs for Liturgical Worship") ... 50-75 68
(Selection number not known.)
PAULIST PRESS (4436 "Torchbearers") ... 50-75 69

HOLY LIGHTS
LPs: 10/12-inch
SAVOY ... 8-10 72

HOLY MACKEREL
LPs: 10/12-inch
REPRISE ... 10-15 68
Members: Paul Williams; Mentor Williams; Michael Cannon; Cynthia Ann Fitzpatrick; George Hiller; Jeremiah Scheff.
Also see WILLIAMS, Paul

HOLY MODAL ROUNDERS
Singles: 7-inch
METROMEDIA ... 4-8 71
LPs: 10/12-inch
ESP (1068 "Indian War Whoop") ... 25-35 68
ELEKTRA (74026 "Moray Eels Eat the Holy Modal Rounders") ... 20-30 68
FANTASY (24711 "Stampfel and Weber") ... 15-20 72
METROMEDIA (1039 "Good Taste") ... 15-25 71
PRESTIGE (7410 "Holy Modal Rounders 2") ... 20-30 65
PRESTIGE (7451 "Holy Modal Rounders") ... 20-30 66
PRESTIGE (7720 "Holy Modal Rounders") ... 20-25 69
PRESTIGE (14031 "The Holy Modal Rounders") ... 25-35 64
ROUNDER ... 5-10
Members: Steve Weber; Pete Stampfel; Richard Tyler; Michael Hurley; Ken Crabtree.
Also see FUGS

HOLY MOSES
Singles: 7-inch
RCA ... 3-5 71
LPs: 10/12-inch
RCA ... 8-10 71

HOLY SISTERS OF GAGA DADA
LPs: 10/12-inch
BOMP ... 8-10 87

HOMBRES P&R/LP '67
Singles: 7-inch
SUN ... 4-8 69
VERVE/FORECAST (Except 5058) ... 4-8 67-68
VERVE/FORECAST (5058 "Let It All Hang Out") ... 5-10 67
VERVE/FORECAST (5058 "Let It Out") ... 4-8 67
(Note shortened title.)
LPs: 10/12-inch
VERVE/FORECAST ... 15-20 67

HOMBS, Jimmie / Twinkletones
(With the Invictas & Hollywood Rebels)
Singles: 7-inch
JACK BEE (1004 "Voo Doo Dolly") ... 30-40 59
Also see INVICTAS

HOME
Singles: 7-inch
COLUMBIA ... 3-5 71
EPIC ... 3-5 72
LPs: 10/12-inch
EPIC ... 10-12 72
Member: Mike Stubbs.

HOME SWEET HOME
LPs: 10/12-inch
CAPITOL ... 8-10 71

HOMEGAS
LPs: 10/12-inch
TAKOMA ... 10-12 71

HOMEMADE THEATER
Singles: 7-inch
A&M ... 3-5 76

HOMER
Singles: 7-inch
UNITED (123-6 "I Never Cared for You") ... 10-20 69
UNITED (123-8 "Texas Lights") ... 10-20 70

UNITED (123-10 "Dandelion Wine")....10-20 70
LPs: 10/12-inch
UNITED (101 "Grown in USA")...100-150 70
Members: Phil Bepko; Frank Coy; Gene Coleman; Howard Gloor; Galen Niles.

HOMER, Chris
Singles: 7-inch
KICK (285 "Little Bull and Buttercup")....50-75

HOMER, Dennis
Singles: 7-inch
TRI-STATE ("Mean Woman Blues")....35-50
(Selection number not known.)

HOMER & JETHRO *C&W/P&R '49*
Singles: 78 rpm
KING....5-15 46-53
FEDERAL....8-15 51
RCA....5-15 50-58
Singles: 7-inch
BLUEBIRD....4-8 59
KING....3-6 63
RCA (0100 series)....30-50 50
(Colored vinyl.)
RCA (0100 thru 0468)....15-30 50-51
(Black vinyl.)
RCA (0500 series)....3-5 71
RCA (4290 thru 7704)....10-20 51-59
RCA (47-7744 "Sink the Bismarck")....8-12 60
(Monaural.)
RCA (61-7744 "Sink the Bismarck")....15-25 60
(Stereo.)
RCA (7790 thru 9922)....4-8 60-70
Picture Sleeves
RCA (5000 series)....8-12 53
RCA (8000 series)....3-6 64
EPs: 7-inch
AUDIO LAB....10-20 59
KING....15-25 53-54
RCA....15-25 53-57
LPs: 10/12-inch
AUDIO LAB (1513 "Musical Madness")....25-50 58
CAMDEN....10-20 62-71
DIPLOMAT....8-12
GUEST STAR....10-15 63
KING (639 "They Sure Are Corny")....20-30 59
KING (800 series)....10-20 63
KING (1000 series)....8-12 67
NASHVILLE....8-12 69
RCA (1412 "Barefoot Ballads")....20-40 57
RCA (1516 "Worst of Homer & Jethro")....20-40 57
RCA (LPM-1880 "Life Can Be Miserable")....20-30 58
(Monaural.)
RCA (LSP-1880 "Life Can Be Miserable")....25-35 58
(Stereo.)
RCA (2100 thru 2900 series)....15-25 60-64
(Monaural. With "LPM" prefix.)
RCA (2100 thru 2900 series)....20-30 60-64
(Stereo. With "LSP" prefix.)
RCA (3112 "Homer & Jethro Fracture Frank Loesser")....30-60 53
(10-inch LP.)
RCA (3300 thru 4600 series)....15-30 65-72
Members: Henry "Homer" Haynes; Kenneth "Jethro" Burns.
Also see ANN-MARGRET
Also see COUNTRY ALL STARS
Also see FOUR LOVERS / Homer & Jethro
Also see JONES, Spike

HOMER & JETHRO WITH JUNE CARTER *C&W '49*
Singles: 78 rpm
RCA....5-10 49
Also see CARTER, June
Also see HOMER & JETHRO

HOMER T.
Singles: 7-inch
RAVEN....4-8 66

HOMER THE GREAT
(Pee Wee Crayton)
Singles: 78 rpm
HOLLYWOOD....15-25 54
Singles: 7-inch
HOLLYWOOD (1055 "Steppin' Out")....35-50 54
Also see CRAYTON, Pee Wee

HOMESICK JAMES
(James Williamson)
Singles: 7-inch
BLUESVILLE....5-10 64
COLT....10-20 62
PRESTIGE....4-8 64
USA....10-20 62
LPs: 10/12-inch
BLUES ON BLUE....8-10
BLUESWAY....8-10 73
PRESTIGE....15-20
Also see WILLIAMSON, James

HOMESTEAD
Singles: 7-inch
ODYSSEY (962 "School Jive")....10-20 72
Members: Mike Fenech; Gary Herrewig; Gary Cox; Steve Brigida.
Also see ARTFUL DODGER

HOMESTEADERS
Singles: 7-inch
END (1017 "Riff Rock")....10-20 58

HOMESTEADERS *C&W '66*
Singles: 7-inch
LITTLE DARLIN'....4-6 66-68
LPs: 10/12-inch
HOMESTEADERS....5-10
LITTLE DARLIN'....10-15 67
Members: Frank Evans; Jerry Rivers; Bob Leftridge.

HOMETOWN BAND
Singles: 7-inch
A&M....3-5 76
LPs: 10/12-inch
A&M....8-10 76-77

HOMETOWNERS
Singles: 7-inch
FRATERNITY....8-12 59
LPs: 10/12-inch
PALACE....10-20

HONDAS
Singles: 7-inch
EDEN (4 "Twelve Feet High")....20-30 62

HONDELLS *P&R/LP '64*
Singles: 7-inch
AMOS....4-8 69-70
COLUMBIA....5-10 67-68
MERCURY (72324 "Little Honda")..10-15 64
MERCURY (72366 "My Buddy Seat")....10-15 64
MERCURY (72405 "Little Sidewalk Surfer Girl")....8-12 65
MERCURY (72443 "Sea of Love")...8-12 65
MERCURY (72479 "Sea Cruise")....5-10 65
MERCURY (72523 "Follow Your Heart")....5-10 66
MERCURY (72563 "Younger Girl")..5-10 67
MERCURY (72605 "Kissin' My Life Away")....5-10 67
Promotional Singles
MERCURY (72324 "Hot Rod High")....20-25 64
(Shows *Hot Rod High* as the "A" side.)
MERCURY (72324 "Little Honda")..15-20 64
(Shows *Little Honda* as the "A" side.)
MERCURY (72366 "My Buddy Seat")....15-20 64
MERCURY (72405 thru 72605)....8-12 65-67
Picture Sleeves
MERCURY (72366 "My Buddy Seat")....10-20 64
MERCURY (72479 "Sea Cruise")...10-20 65
LPs: 10/12-inch
MERCURY (20940 "Go, Little Honda")....20-25 64
(Monaural.)
MERCURY (60940 "Go, Little Honda")....25-30 64
(Stereo.)
MERCURY (20982 "Hondells")....20-25 64
(Monaural.)
MERCURY (20982 "Hondells")....25-30 65
(Stereo.)
Members: Chuck Girard; Richard Burns; Brian Wilson; Wayne Edwards; Glen Campbell; Joe Kelly; Bruce Johnston; Terry Melcher; Jerry Naylor; Gary Usher. Session: Davie Allan.
Also see ALLEN, Davie
Also see BRUCE & TERRY
Also see CAMPBELL, Glen
Also see FOUR SPEEDS
Also see GIRARD, Chuck
Also see NAYLOR, Jerry
Also see PENDLETONS
Also see SUNSETS
Also see USHER, Gary
Also see WILSON, Brian

HONDELLS / Del Shannon / Martha & Vandellas
EPs: 7-inch
PEPSI-COLA (8256 "Pepsi-Cola Ad Radio Youth Market, 1966")....15-20 66
(Promotional issue only.)
Also see MARTHA & VANDELLAS
Also see SHANNON, Del

HONDELLS / Dusty Springfield
Singles: 7-inch
COLLECTABLES....3-4 86
Also see HONDELLS
Also see SPRINGFIELD, Dusty

HONEST ABE & JACKIE
Singles: 7-inch
RIC....4-8 65

HONEST JOHN & TORNADOES
Singles: 7-inch
SWINGIN'....8-12 61

HONEST MEN
Singles: 7-inch
V.I.P. (25047 "Cherie")....15-25 68

HONEY & BEES
Singles: 7-inch
PENTAGON (500 "Please Go Away")....40-60 59

HONEY & BEES
Singles: 7-inch
ACADEMY....5-10 65
ARCTIC (141 "Go Now")....5-10 68
ARCTIC (149 "Love Addict")....5-10 69
ARCTIC (158 "Baby Do That Thing")....5-10 68
BELL....4-6 72
JOSIE....4-8 70
LPs: 10/12-inch
JOSIE....12-18 70
Members: Nadine Felder; Gwen Oliver; Ann Wooten; Jean Davis.

HONEY & DEW-DROPS
Singles: 7-inch
MMC (005 "Come My Little Baby")....50-100 59
Members: Scotty Stuart Cameron; Sandy Stuart Cameron; Jack Bieulisbach; Walter Roberts; Frank Zitske.
Also see STUART, Scotty

HONEY & TEARDROPS
Singles: 7-inch
VAL (202 "You Are the One")....50-100 62
(Black vinyl.)
VAL (202 "You Are the One")....150-250 62
(Colored vinyl.)

HONEY BEARS
Singles: 78 rpm
CASH (1004 "Cucamonga")....25-50 55
SPARK....25-50 54
Singles: 7-inch
CASH (1004 "Cucamonga")....75-100 55
SPARK (104 "It's a Miracle")....75-100 54
SPARK (111 "I Shall Not Fail")....75-100 54

HONEY BEES
Singles: 78 rpm
IMPERIAL (5400 "Endless")....15-20 56
Singles: 7-inch
IMPERIAL (5400 "Endless")....25-50 56

HONEY BEES
Singles: 7-inch
FONTANA (1939 "She Don't Deserve You")....10-20
GARRISON (3005 "Never in a Million Years")....100-150 60s
SMASH....5-10 64
VEE JAY....10-20 64
WAND....5-10 66

HONEY BOY
(Frank Patt)
Singles: 78 rpm
SPECIALTY....20-30 54
Singles: 7-inch
SPECIALTY (476 "Bloodstains on the Wall")....50-75 54
Also see PATT, Frank

HONEY BOYS
Singles: 78 rpm
MODERN....12-25 56
Singles: 7-inch
MODERN (980 "Never Lose Faith in Me")....25-50 56

HONEY BROWN: see BROWN, Honey

HONEY CONE *P&R/R&B '69*
Singles: 7-inch
HOT WAX....3-6 69-76
LPs: 10/12-inch
HOT WAX....8-10 70-72
Members: Edna Wright; Carolyn Willis; Shellie Clark; Sharon Cash.
Also see BEAS
Also see BOB B. SOXX & Blue Jeans
Also see CASH, Sharon
Also see GIRLFRIENDS
Also see WYNNS, Sandy

HONEY DEWS
Singles: 7-inch
SUE (746 "Someone")....30-40 61

HONEY DREAMERS
Singles: 78 rpm
CAMDEN....4-8 56
COLUMBIA....4-8 55-56
Singles: 7-inch
CAMDEN....10-20 56
COLUMBIA....10-20 55-56
CORONADO....5-10 59

HONEY JUG
Singles: 7-inch
H.I.P....4-8 67-69

HONEY LANE: see LANE, Honey

HONEY LTD.
Singles: 7-inch
LHI....4-6 68

HONEYBEES
(Featuring "La La")
Singles: 7-inch
BEE (1101 "Kiss Me My Love")..250-350 58

HONEYBEES
Singles: 7-inch
FONTANA (1939 "One Wonderful Night")....15-20 65
Also see KING, Carole

HONEYBIRDS
Singles: 7-inch
CORAL....8-12 64

HONEYBROOKS
Singles: 7-inch
WASP....4-6

HONEYBUS
Singles: 7-inch
DERAM....5-8 68

HONEYCOMBS
Singles: 7-inch
TIDE....4-8 62

HONEYCOMBS *P&R '64*
Singles: 7-inch
INTERPHON....5-10 64-65
W.B....5-10 65-66
Picture Sleeves
INTERPHON (7713 "I Can't Stop")....10-20 64
LPs: 10/12-inch
INTERPHON (88001 "Here Are the Honeycombs")....20-30 64
VEE JAY (88001 "Here Are the Honeycombs")....35-45 64
Members: Honey Lantree; John Lantree; Martin Murray; Denis D'Ell; Alan Ward.

HONEYCONES *P&R '58*
Singles: 7-inch
EMBER....8-12 58-59

HONEYCUTT, Glenn
Singles: 78 rpm
SUN....15-25 57
Singles: 7-inch
BLACK GOLD (100 "Right Gal, Right Time")....20-30 57
FERNWOOD (142 "Campus Love")....75-100 62
SUN (264 "I'll Be Around")....20-30 57
Also see BURLISON, Paul

HONEYCUTT, Johnny
Singles: 7-inch
FURY (6000 "Love Theme")....4-6 74
TRIODE....15-25 60s

HONEYCUTT, Miki *R&B '77*
Singles: 7-inch
PAULA....3-5 77

HONEYDREAMERS
Singles: 78 rpm
COLUMBIA....4-6 55-56
FANTASY....4-6 55
JUNIOR....4-6 51
MGM....4-6 56
MOOD....4-6 54
RCA....4-6 50
Singles: 7-inch
COLUMBIA....5-10 55-56
FANTASY....5-10 55
JUNIOR....5-10 51
MGM....5-10 56
MOOD....5-10 54
RCA....5-10 50
LPs: 10/12-inch
RKO UNIQUE....10-20

HONEYDREAMERS
Singles: 7-inch
DOUBLE AA....4-8

HONEYDRIPPERS *P&R/LP '84*
Singles: 7-inch
ESPARANZA....3-4 84-85
Picture Sleeves
ESPARANZA....3-4 84-85
LPs: 10/12-inch
ESPARANZA....5-10 84
Members: Jeff Beck; Jimmy Page; Robert Plant; Nile Rodgers.
Also see BECK, Jeff
Also see CHIC
Also see PAGE, Jimmy
Also see PLANT, Robert
Also see RODGERS, Nile

HONEYMAN
Singles: 7-inch
RED BIRD....4-8 68

HONEYMOON SUITE *P&R/LP '84*
Singles: 7-inch
W.B....3-4 84-88
Picture Sleeves
W.B....3-4 84-88
LPs: 10/12-inch
W.B....5-10 84-88

HONEYS
Singles: 7-inch
CAPITOL (2454 "Tonight You Belong to Me")....30-50 69
CAPITOL (4952 "Surfin' Down the Swanee River")....75-125 63
CAPITOL (5034 "Pray for Surf") 100-125 63
CAPITOL (5093 "The One You Can't Have")....100-125 63
RHINO....4-6 83
W.B. (5430 "He's a Doll")....50-100 64
LPs: 10/12-inch
RHINO (851 "Ecstasy")....8-10 83
Picture Sleeves
CAPITOL (4952 "Surfin' Down the Swanee River")....200-300 63
Members: Ginger Blake; Diane Rovell; Marilyn Rovell.
Also see ANNETTE
Also see BEACH BOYS
Also see CASEY, Al
Also see DAVE & MARKSMEN
Also see GINGER
Also see PETERSEN, Paul
Also see SHARON MARIE
Also see SPRING
Also see SURFARIS
Also see USHER, Gary

HONEYSTROLLERS
Singles: 7-inch
GLORY (272 "Honeystrollin")....15-25 58

HONEYTONES
Singles: 78 rpm
MERCURY....5-10 55
WING (90013 "False Alarm")....10-15 55
Singles: 7-inch
MERCURY....15-20 55
WING (90013 "False Alarm")....20-25 55

HONEYTONES
Singles: 7-inch
BIG TOP....10-15 58

HONG KONG
Singles: 7-inch
PEPPER (906 "Chinese Bandit")....8-12

HONG KONG WHITE SOX
Singles: 7-inch
TRANS-WORLD (6906 "Cholley Oop")....10-15 60

HONG KONGS
Singles: 7-inch
COUNSEL (50 "Surfin' in the China Sea")....15-25 63
MELODY MILL (303 "Surfin' in the China Sea")....15-25 63

HONK
LPs: 10/12-inch
EPIC....8-10 74
20TH FOX....8-10 73

HONKERS
Singles: 7-inch
OKEH....5-10 59

HONOR SOCIETY
Singles: 7-inch
JUBILEE....5-10 70
Also see HAPPENINGS

HONORABLES
Singles: 7-inch
HONOR (100 "Castles in the Sky")....50-100 61
HONOR (102 "Sunday Stroll")....15-25 62

HOOCHIE & Coochie Coos
Singles: 7-inch
FRATERNITY....4-8 61

HOOD
Singles: 7-inch
BELL....5-8 74

HOOD, Bobby *C&W '81*
Singles: 7-inch
CHUTE....3-4 78-81
PLANTATION....3-5 78

HOOD, Darla
(With Bill Baker's Orchestra)
Singles: 7-inch
ACAMA (122 "No Secret Now")....20-30 60
ENCINO (1007 "No Secret Now")..50-75 57
Also see BAKER, Bill

HOOD, Robin: see ROBIN HOOD

HOOD, Robbin
Singles: 78 rpm
MGM....10-20 57
Singles: 7-inch
MGM....10-20 57

HOODS
Singles: 7-inch
DIONYSUS....3-4 91
Picture Sleeves
DIONYSUS....3-4 91
Members: Jay Wiseman; John Chilson; Ron Swart; Mike Stax; Xavier Anaya.

HOODOO GURUS *LP '86*
Singles: 7-inch
A&M....3-4 85
RCA....3-4 89-90
LPs: 10/12-inch
A&M....5-10 85
ELEKTRA....5-10 86-87
RCA....5-8 89-91
Members: David Faulkner; Rick Grossman.
Also see DIVINYLS

HOODOO RHYTHM DEVILS
Singles: 7-inch
BLUE THUMB....3-5 74
CAPITOL....3-5 71
FANTASY....3-4 78
LPs: 10/12-inch
BLUE THUMB....8-10 73
CAPITOL....8-10 72
FANTASY....5-10 77-78
Members: Joe Crane; Roger Clark; John Rewind; Glenn Walters; Dexter Plates; Suzy Storm.
Also see POINTER SISTERS

HOOK
Singles: 7-inch
UNI....4-6 68-69
LPs: 10/12-inch
UNI (73023 "The Hook Will Grab You")....20-25 68
UNI (73038 "Hooked")....20-25 68
Members: Bob Arlin; Craig Boyd; Dale Loyola; Buddy Skylar; Denny Provisor.
Also see ARLIN, Bob
Also see PROVISOR, Denny

HOOK, Dr: see DR. HOOK

HOOK, Marcus, Roll Band
Singles: 7-inch
CAPITOL....8-10 73
LPs: 10/12-inch
CAPITOL....5-10 79-80

HOOKER, D.R.
LP: 10/12-inch
XLP....10-20

HOOKER, Earl
(With His Roadmasters; with Earlettes; with Soul Twisters; with Soul Thrillers)
Singles: 78 rpm
KING (4600 "Race Track") 50-75 53
ROCKIN' (513 "On the Hook") 50-75 52
ROCKIN' (519 "Sweet Angel") 50-75 52
Singles: 7-inch
AGE (29106 "Blue Guitar") 20-30 62
AGE (29111 "How Long Can This Go On") 20-30 62
AGE (29114 "That Man") 20-30 63
ARGO (5265 "Frog Hop") 20-30 57
ARHOOLIE (521 "Wah Wah Blues") 10-20 70
BEA & BABY (106 "Dynamite") 15-20 60
BLUE THUMB (103 "Boogie, Don't Blot") 5-10 69
CHECKER (1025 "Tanya") 10-20 62
CHIEF (7031 "Rockin' with the Kid") 15-25 60
CHIEF (7039 "Messing with the Kid") 15-25 61
C.J. (613 "Do the Chicken") 15-25 61
C.J. (643 "Chicken") 8-12 65
CUCA (1194 "Bertha") 30-40 64
CUCA (1445 "Dust My Broom") 10-15 69
CUCA (6793 "Dynamite") 10-15 67
JIM KO 10-15 65
KING (4600 "Race Track") 300-400 53
MEL (1005 "Messing with the Kid") 10-20 64
MEL-LON (1000 "Want You to Rock") 10-20 64
MEL-LON (1001 "The Leading Brand") 10-20 64
ROCKIN' (513 "Sweet Angel") 300-400 52
SUE (392 "Calling All Blues") 10-15 65
LPs: 10/12-inch
ARHOOLIE 8-10 70-73
BLUES ON BLUE 8-10
BLUESWAY 8-10 73
BLUE THUMB 12-18 68
CUCA (4100 "Genius of Earl Hooker") 10-15 65
Session: Earl Tidwell; Freddie Roulette.
Also see EVERETT, Betty
Also see MEMPHIS SLIM
Also see ROULETTE, Freddie
Also see TAYLOR, Hound Dog / Robert Nighthawk / John Littlejohn / Earl Hooker
Also see WATERS, Muddy

HOOKER, Earl, & A.C. Reed
Singles: 7-inch
AGE (29101 "This Little Voice") 15-25 61
Also see REED, A.C.

HOOKER, Earl, & Bobby Saxton
Singles: 7-inch
CHECKER (947 "Trying to Make a Living") 10-20 60

HOOKER, Earl / Junior Wells
Singles: 7-inch
CHIEF (7016 "Blues in D Natural") 10-20 60
CHIEF (7021 "Universal Rock") 10-20 60
Also see HOOKER, Earl
Also see WELLS, Junior

HOOKER, Frank, & Positive People R&B '79
Singles: 7-inch
PANORAMA 3-4 79-80

HOOKER, John Lee R&B '49
Singles: 78 rpm
CHART 10-20 53
CHESS (1505 "High Priced Woman") 50-75 52
CHESS (1513 "Sugar Mama") 25-50 52
CHESS (1562 "It's My Own Fault") 20-30 54
JVB 20-30 53
MODERN 20-30 48-56
REGAL 20-30 50-51
SENSATION 25-40 49-50
SPECIALTY 15-25 54
VEE JAY 10-20 55-60
Singles: 7-inch
ABC 3-5 71-73
BATTLE (45901 "No More Doggin'") 8-12 62
BLUESWAY 4-8 67-69
CHART (609 "Goin' South") 25-50 53
CHART (614 "Misbelieving Baby") 25-50 53
CHESS (1505 "High Priced Woman") 200-300 52
CHESS (1513 "Sugar Mama") 50-100 52
CHESS (1562 "It's My Own Fault") 100-150 54
CHESS (1965 "In the Mood") 5-8 66
ELMOR (303 "Blues for Christmas") 10-20
FEDERAL (12377 "Late Last Night") 10-20 60
FORTUNE (853 "Cry Baby") 10-20 60
GALAXY (716 "I Lost My Job") 8-12 63
HI-Q (5018 "609 Boogie") 10-20 61
IMPULSE (242 "Honey") 5-8 66
JVB (30 "Boogie Rambler") 100-150 53
JEWEL 3-5 70-77
KENT (332 "Boogie Chillen") 8-12 60
KING 3-5 70
LAUREN 4-8 61
MODERN (835 "How Can You Do It") 30-60 51
MODERN (862 "Cold Chills All Over Me") 30-60 52
MODERN (886 "Bluebird Blues") 30-60 52
MODERN (893 "New Boogie Chillen") 30-60 52
MODERN (897 "Rock House Boogie") 30-60 53
MODERN (901 "It's a Stormin' and Rainin'") 25-50 53
MODERN (908 "Love Money Can't Buy") 25-50 53
MODERN (916 "Too Much Boogie") 25-50 53
MODERN (923 "Down Child") 25-50 54
MODERN (931 "I Wonder Little Darling") 25-50 54
MODERN (935 "I Tried Hard") 20-40 54
MODERN (942 "Cool Little Car") 20-40 54
MODERN (948 "Half a Stranger") 20-40 55
MODERN (958 "You Receive Me") 20-40 55
MODERN (966 "Hug and Squeeze") 20-40 55
MODERN (978 "Lookin' for a Woman") 20-40 56
PLANET (114 "Don't Be Messing with My Bread") 5-8 66
SPECIALTY (528 "Everybody's Blues") 20-40 54
STARDAY 3-5 70
STAX 4-8 69
VEE JAY (164 "Mambo Chillen") 20-30 55
VEE JAY (188 "Every Night") 20-30 56
VEE JAY (205 "Baby Lee") 20-30 56
VEE JAY (233 "I'm So Worried, Baby") 15-25 57
VEE JAY (245 "I'm So Excited") 15-25 57
VEE JAY (255 "Little Wheel") 15-25 57
VEE JAY (265 "You Can Lead Me, Baby") 15-25 58
VEE JAY (293 "I Love You Honey") 15-25 58
VEE JAY (308 "Maudie") 15-25 59
VEE JAY (319 "Tennessee Blues") 15-25 59
VEE JAY (331 "Hobo Blues") 15-25 59
VEE JAY (349 "No Shoes") 15-25 60
VEE JAY (366 "Dusty Road") 15-25 60
VEE JAY (397 "Want Ad Blues") 15-25 60
VEE JAY (438 "Boom Boom") 10-15 62
VEE JAY (453 "She's Mine") 10-15 62
VEE JAY (493 "Frisco Blues") 10-20 63
VEE JAY (538 thru 708) 8-15 63-65
EPs: 7-inch
IMPULSE 8-10 66
(Juke box issue only. Includes title strips.)
LPs: 10/12-inch
ABC 10-20 71-74
ARCHIVE of FOLK MUSIC 10-12 68
ATCO (151 "Don't Turn Me from Your Door") 20-25 63
(Monaural.)
ATCO (SD-151 "Don't Turn Me from Your Door") 25-30 63
(Stereo.)
ATLANTIC 8-10 72
BATTLE (6113 "John Lee Hooker") 30-50 60
BLUESWAY 15-30 66-73
BRYLEN 5-10 84
BUDDAH 12-15 69
CHAMELEON 5-8 89
CHESS (1438 "House of the Blues") 50-100 61
CHESS (1454 "John Lee Hooker Plays and Sings the Blues") 50-100 61
CHESS (1500 series) 15-20 66
CHESS (9000 series) 8-10
CHESS (60011 "Mad Man Blues") 10-15
CROWN (5157 "The Blues") 25-35 60
CROWN (5232 "John Lee Hooker Sings the Blues") 20-30 62
CROWN (5295 "Folk Blues") 15-25 63
CROWN (5353 "The Great John Lee Hooker") 15-25 63
CUSTOM 10-15
EVEREST 5-10 79-83
EXODUS 8-10
FANTASY 8-10 72-77
FORTUNE 20-30 69
GNP 8-10 74
GALAXY (201 "John Lee Hooker") 20-30 63
GREEN BOTTLE 10-12 72
IMPULSE 12-15 66
JEWEL 10-12 71
KENT 10-12 71
KING (727 "John Lee Hooker Sings Blues") 50-75 61
KING (1000 series) 10-12 70
MCA 5-10 83
MUSE 5-10 80
SPECIALTY 10-15 70
(Black and gold label.)
SPECIALTY 5-10 88
(Black and white label.)
STAX (2000 series) 10-12 69
STAX (4000 series) 8-10 77
TOMATO 5-10 78
TRADITION 10-12 69
TRIP 8-10 73-78
UNITED 10-12
U.A. 12-15 71-73
VEE JAY (1007 "I'm John Lee Hooker") 40-60 59
(Maroon label.)
VEE JAY (1007 "I'm John Lee Hooker") 20-30 61
(Black label.)
VEE JAY (1023 thru 1043) 25-40 60-62
VEE JAY (1049 thru 1078) 15-25 62-64
VEE JAY (8502 "Is He the World's Greatest Blues Singer") 25-35
VERVE/FOLKWAYS 10-15 66
WAND 10-12 70
Also see BIRMINGHAM SAM & His Magic Guitar
Also see BOOGIE MAN
Also see BOOKER, John Lee
Also see COOKER, John Lee
Also see COTTON, Sylvester
Also see DELTA JOHN
Also see GROUNDHOGS
Also see JOHN LEE
Also see JOHNNY LEE
Also see LITTLE PORK CHOPS
Also see MARTHA & VANDELLAS
Also see McGHEE, Sticks / John Lee Hooker
Also see MEMPHIS SLIM
Also see TEXAS SLIM
Also see WILLIAMS, Johnny

HOOKER, John Lee, & Canned Heat LP '71
Singles: 7-inch
U.A. 3-5 71
LPs: 10/12-inch
LIBERTY 10-15 71
RHINO 5-10 82
TRIP 5-10 74
Also see CANNED HEAT

HOOKER, John Lee / Lightnin' Hopkins / J. Carroll
LPs: 10/12-inch
GUEST STAR 15-20 64
Also see HOPKINS, Lightnin'

HOOKER, John Lee, & Little Eddie Kirkland
Singles: 78 rpm
MODERN 15-25 52
Singles: 7-inch
MODERN (876 "It's Hurts Me So") 30-60 52

HOOKER, John Lee / Eddie Kirkland / Eddie Burns / Sylvester Cotton
LPs: 10/12-inch
UNITED (7783 "Detroit Blues") 10-20
Also see BURNS, Eddie
Also see COTTON, Sylvester
Also see HOOKER, John Lee
Also see KIRKLAND, Eddie

HOOKFOOT
Singles: 7-inch
A&M 3-5 71-73
LPs: 10/12-inch
A&M 8-10 71-73

HOOKS, Willie
Singles: 7-inch
SOUL WORLD 5-10

HOOKS BROTHERS
Singles: 7-inch
HOOKS (526 "Natural Blues") 10-20 66
(Colored vinyl.)

HOOLEY, John
Singles: 7-inch
G-CLEF (710 "Kathleen") 5-10 65

HOOPER, Jess, & Daydreamers
Singles: 78 rpm
CHERRY 20-40 55
METEOR 15-25 55
Singles: 7-inch
CHERRY (602 "All Messed Up") 300-400 55
(First issue.)
METEOR (5025 "All Messed Up") 150-200 55

HOOPER, Larry
(Lawrence Welk Presents Larry Hooper)
Singles: 78 rpm
BRUNSWICK 5-10 57
CORAL (61763 "Roger Boom") 10-15 56
Singles: 7-inch
BRUNSWICK 5-10 57
CORAL (61763 "Roger Boom") 15-25 56
(Orange label.)
CORAL (61763 "Roger Boom") 25-45 56
(Blue label. Promotional issue only.)
Also see WELK, Lawrence, & His Orchestra

HOOPER, Les
LPs: 10/12-inch
ITI 5-8 89

HOOPER, Stix LP '79
Singles: 7-inch
MCA 3-4 79-82
LPs: 10/12-inch
MCA 5-10 79-82
Also see BUTLER, Jerry, & Stix Hooper
Also see CRUSADERS

HOOPER TWINS
Singles: 7-inch
AZALEA 5-10 60

HOOSIER HOT SHOTS C&W '44
(With Sally Foster; with Two Ton Baker)
Singles: 78 rpm
BANNER 3-5 30s
CONQUEROR 3-5 30s
DECCA 3-5 44-47
MELOTONE 3-5 30s
ORIOLE 3-5 30s
VOCALION 3-5 30s
LPs: 10/12-inch
DOT 15-30 64
GOLDEN TONE 10-20
SPIN-O-RAMA 10-20 60s
SUNBEAM 10-20 75
TOPS 10-20
Members: Hezzie Trietsch; Nathan Harrison; Gabe Ward; Keith Milheim.

HOOSIER HOTSHOTS
(Ronnie Haig)
EPs: 7-inch
MALTSHOP (1 "The Hoosier Hotshots") 10-15 94
(Promotional issue only. 100 made. Commercial issues of this three-track EP are credited to Ronnie Haig.)
Also see HAIG, Ronnie)

HOOTCH
LPs: 10/12-inch
PROGRESS (4844 "Hootch") 200-300 74

HOOTERS P&R/LP '85
Singles: 7-inch
ANTENNA (84 "Hanging on to a Heartbeat") 4-6 84
COLUMBIA 3-4 85-89
88 PERCENT (80 "Fightin' on the Same Side") 5-10 81
88 PERCENT (82 "All You Zombies") 5-10 82
MONTAGE 3-4 83
Picture Sleeves
ANTENNA (84 "Hanging on to a Heartbeat") 4-8 84
COLUMBIA 3-4 85-87
88 PERCENT (80 "Fightin' on the Same Side") 5-10 81
88 PERCENT (82 "All You Zombies") 5-10 82
LPs: 10/12-inch
COLUMBIA 5-10 85-89
Members: Rob Hyman; Eric Bazillian.
Also see CONWELL, Tommy, & Young Rumblers
Also see LAUPER, Cyndi

HOOVEN, Jeff
Singles: 7-inch
TREY 5-10 60

HOOVER
Singles: 7-inch
MONUMENT 4-6 68
LPs: 10/12-inch
EPIC 8-10 70

HOP, Poppy: see POPPA HOP

HOPE
Singles: 7-inch
A&M 4-6 72
COULEE 4-6 71
PEACE (944 "Greenhouse") 25-35 70
RSA 3-6
LPs: 10/12-inch
A&M 8-15 72
Members: Wayne McKibbon; Jeff Cozy.
Also see JESTERS III

HOPE, Billy, & Badmen
Singles: 7-inch
BONANZA 8-12 61
SAVOY 8-12 58

HOPE, Bob LP '76
Singles: 78 rpm
CAPITOL 3-5 52
RCA 3-5 56
("The Paleface") 75-100 44
(Label name and selection number not known. Santa Claus-shaped cardboard. Promotional issue only for the film *The Paleface*.)
Singles: 7-inch
CAPITOL 5-10 52
RCA 5-10 56
LPs: 10/12-inch
CAPITOL 5-10 76
DECCA 10-20 63
RCA 15-25 60
Also see BACKUS, Jim
Also see CROSBY, Bing, & Bob Hope
Also see MARTIN, Dean

HOPE, Bob, & Eydie Adams
Singles: 7-inch
U.A. 4-6 63
Picture Sleeves
U.A. 4-8 63

HOPE, Bob, & Rosemary Clooney
Singles: 7-inch
RCA 4-8 59
Also see HOPE, Bob
Also see CLOONEY, Rosemary

HOPE, Dee D.
Singles: 7-inch
JOLUM (100 "California Surfer") 30-40 63

HOPE, Eddie, & Mannish Boys
Singles: 78 rpm
MARLIN (804 "A Fool No More") 50-75 56
Singles: 7-inch
MARLIN (804 "A Fool No More") 100-200 56

HOPE, Ellie D&D '83
Singles: 12-inch
QUALITY 4-6 83

HOPE, Lynn R&B '50
(Lynn Hope Quintet)
Singles: 78 rpm
ALADDIN 15-25 54-56
CHESS (1499 "Stardust") 5-10 52
PREMIUM (851 "Song of the Wanderer") 5-10 50
PREMIUM (861 "Poinciana") 5-10 50
PREMIUM (862 "Mona Lisa") 5-10 50
Singles: 7-inch
ALADDIN 15-35 51-56
CHESS (1499 "Stardust") 15-25 52
KING 10-15 60
EPs: 7-inch
ALADDIN (505 "Lynn Hope") 20-40 55
ALADDIN (512 "Lynn Hope") 20-40 55
LPs: 10/12-inch
ALADDIN (707 "Lynn Hope & His Tenor Sax") 150-250 55
(10-inch LP.)
ALADDIN (850 "Lynn Hope") 100-150 56
IMPERIAL (9177 "Tenderly") 15-25 62
(Monaural.)
IMPERIAL (12177 "Tenderly") 20-30 62
(Stereo.)
KING (717 "Maharaja of the Saxophone") 20-40 61
SCORE (4015 "Tenderly") 50-100 57

HOPEFUL
Singles: 7-inch
MERCURY 4-8 66

HOPELESS, Homer
Singles: 78 rpm
GOLDBAND 30-50 57
Singles: 7-inch
GOLDBAND (1040 "New Way of Rockin'") 30-50 57

HOPKIN, Mary P&R '68
(Mary Hopkins)
Singles: 7-inch
APPLE/AMERICOM (238 "Those Were the Days") 250-350 69
(Four-inch flexi, "pocket disc.")
APPLE 5-10 68-72
ESKEE 4-8 66
RCA 3-5 76
Promotional Singles
ESKEE 4-8 66
RCA 3-5 76
Picture Sleeves
APPLE 5-10 68-70
LPs: 10/12-inch
AIR 8-10 72
APPLE 15-25 69-72
APPLE/CAPITOL RECORD CLUB (5-3351 "Postcard") 30-40 69

HOPKINS, Claude, Quartet
Singles: 78 rpm
RAINBOW 10-15 45

HOPKINS, Clyde
Singles: 7-inch
BLACK GOLD 4-8 66

HOPKINS, Don
Singles: 7-inch
DART (147 "Tiddley Diddley") 75-100 61
VANDAN (8030 "Evening in Paris") 10-20 60s
VANDAN (8351 "That's No Way to Treat a Girl") 10-20 60s

HOPKINS, Ford
Singles: 7-inch
APEX (7757 "She Was Not My Kind") 10-20

HOPKINS, Lightnin' R&B '49
(With "His Guitar"; "Singing and Accompanying Himself on Guitar"; Lightning Hopkins; Sam "Lightnin'" Hopkins.)
Singles: 78 rpm
ACE 10-20 56
ALADDIN 25-50 47-54
CHART 10-15 55
DECCA 10-15 53
GOLD STAR 20-40 47-50
HARLEM 20-30 54-55
HERALD 25-35 54-55
LIGHTNING 100-150 55
MERCURY 15-25 52
MODERN 20-40 47-49
RPM 20-40 52-54
SITTIN' IN WITH 25-50 51-53
TNT 50-75 53-54
Singles: 7-inch
ACE (516 "My Little Kewpie Doll") 20-30 56
ALADDIN (3063 "Shotgun Blues") 100-200 50
ALADDIN (3077 "Moonrise Blues") 100-200 50
ALADDIN (3096 "Abilene") 100-200 51
ALADDIN (3117 "You Are Not Going to Worry My Life Anymore") 100-200 52
ALADDIN (3262 "My California") 50-100 54
ARHOOLIE (508 "Mama's Fight") 5-10 65
BLUESVILLE (813 "Got to Move Your Baby") 10-20 61
BLUESVILLE (814 "Sail On") 10-20 61
BLUESVILLE (817 "Back to New Orleans") 10-20 62
BLUESVILLE (820 "Happy Blues for John Glenn") 8-12 62
BLUESVILLE (821 "Last Night Blues") 8-12 63
BLUESVILLE (822 "Angel Child") 8-12 63
BLUESVILLE (823 "Wake Up Old Lady") 8-12 63
CANDID (603 "Mister Charlie") 8-12 62
CHART (636 "Walkin' the Streets") 15-25 55
DART (123 "Unsuccessful Blues") 10-20 60
DECCA (28841 "War Is Over") 15-25 53
DECCA (48306 "Merry Christmas") 15-25 53
DECCA (48312 "Highway Blues") 15-25 53
DECCA (48321 "I'm Wild About You, Baby") 15-25 53
FIRE (1034 "Mojo Hand") 10-20 61
FLASHBACK (18 "Mojo Hand") 5-10 65
HARLEM (2321 "Contrary Mary") 100-150 54
HARLEM (2324 "Lightnin's Boogie") 100-150 54
HARLEM (2331 "Fast Life") 100-150 55

HARLEM (2336 "Old Woman Blues") 100-150 55
HERALD (425 "Lightnin's Boogie") 25-50 54
HERALD (428 "Lightnin's Special") 25-50 54
HERALD (436 "Sick Feeling Blues") 25-50 54
HERALD (443 "Nothin' But the Blues") 25-50 54
HERALD (449 "They Wonder Who I Am") 25-50 55
HERALD (471 "Hopkins' Sky Hop") 25-50 55
HERALD (476 "Grandma's Boogie") 25-50 56
HERALD (542 "Let's Move") 20-30 59
HERALD (547 "Gonna Change My Ways") 20-30 60
IMPERIAL (5834 "Feel So Bad") 10-15 62
IMPERIAL (5852 "Picture on the Wall") 10-15 62
IVORY 8-12 61
JAX (315 "No Good Woman") 150-250 53
(Red vinyl.)
JAX (318 "Automobile") 150-250 53
(Red vinyl.)
JAX (321 "Contrary Mary") 150-250 54
(Red vinyl.)
JAX (661 "Down to the River") 150-250 53
(Red vinyl. Jax label has a Sittin' in With number.)
JEWEL 3-6 68-72
KENT 3-5
KIMBERLEY (2017 "If You Steal My Chickens, You Can't Make 'Em Lay") 10-20 60
LIGHTNING (104 "Unsuccessful Blues") 250-350 55
MERCURY (70081 "Ain't It a Shame") 50-75 52
MERCURY (70191 "My Mama Told Me") 50-75 52
MERCURY (8274 "Sad News from Korea") 50-75 52
MERCURY (8293 "Gone with the Wind") 50-75 52
PRESTIGE (326 thru 452) 5-10 6-67
RPM (337 "Beggin' You to Stay") 50-75 51
RPM (346 "Jake Head") 50-75 52
RPM (351 "Don't Keep My Baby Long") 50-75 52
RPM (359 "Needed Time") 50-75 52
RPM (378 "Another Fool in Town") 50-75 53
RPM (388 "Black Cat") 50-75 53
RPM (398 "Sante Fe") 50-75 54
SHAD (5011 "Hello Central") 10-20 59
SITTIN' IN WITH (621 "New York Boogie") 150-250 51
(Red vinyl.)
SITTIN' IN WITH (635 "Coffee Blues") 150-250 52
(Red vinyl.)
SITTIN' IN WITH (642 "You Caused My Heart to Weep") 50-75 52
(Black vinyl.)
SITTIN' IN WITH (644 "Jailhouse Blues") 150-250 52
(Red vinyl.)
SITTIN' IN WITH (647 "Dirty House") 150-250 52
(Red vinyl.)
SITTIN' IN WITH (652 "Papa Bones Boogie") 150-250 52
(Red vinyl.)
SITTIN' IN WITH (658 "Broken Hearted Blues") 150-250 53
(Red vinyl.)
SITTIN' IN WITH (660 "I've Been a Bad Man") 150-250 53
(Red vinyl.)
TNT (8002 "Late in the Evening") 200-300 54
TNT (8003 "Leavin' Blues") 200-300 54
TNT (8010 "Moanin' Blues") 200-300 55
VAULT 3-5 70

Note: There is some confusion regarding Jax and Sittin' in With singles. Some shown here as red vinyl may also exist as black. We have confirmed 642 as black. Additional information will appear as it becomes available.

LPs: 10/12-inch

ARHOOLIE (1034 "The Texas Bluesman") 10-15 68
ARHOOLIE (2007 "Early Recordings") 8-12
BARNABY 8-10 71
BULLDOG (1010 "Live at the Bird Lounge") 12-18 65
CANDID (8010 "Lightnin' in New York") 20-30 61
(Monaural.)
CANDID (9010 "Lightnin' in New York") 25-40 61
(Stereo.)
COLLECTABLES 6-8 88
CROWN (5224 "Lightnin' Hopkins Sings the Blues") 20-30 61
DART 10-15
EVEREST (241 "Lightnin' Hopkins") 10-15 69
EVEREST (342 "Autobiography in Blues") 5-10 79
FANTASY 8-12 72-81
FIRE (104 "Mojo Hand") 75-100 62
GUEST STAR (1459 "Live at the Bird Lounge") 15-20 64
HARLEM HITPARADE 5-10
HERALD (1012 "Lightnin' and the Blues") 400-600 60
IMPERIAL (9180 "On Stage") 25-50 62
IMPERIAL (9186 "Lightnin' Hopkins Sings the Blues") 25-50 62
IMPERIAL (9211 "And Then Blues") 25-50 62
INT'L ARTISTS (6 "Free Form Patterns") 50-100 68
JAZZ MAN 5-10 82
JEWEL 10-12 67-70
MAINSTREAM 8-10 71-74
MOUNT VERNON (104 "Nothin' But the Blues") 15-20
OLYMPIC 8-10 73
PICKWICK 8-10
POPPY (60002 "Lightnin' ") 15-20 69
(Two discs.)
PRESTIGE (7370 "Lightnin' Hopkins") 20-25 65
(Two discs.)
PRESTIGE (7377 thru 7811) 10-20 66-70
PRESTIGE (14021 "Hootin' the Blues") 10-20 64
PRESTIGE/BLUESVILLE (1019 "Lightnin' ") 20-30 61
PRESTIGE/BLUESVILLE (1045 "Blues in My Bottle") 20-30 62
PRESTIGE/BLUESVILLE (1057 "Lightnin' Hopkins") 20-30 62
PRESTIGE/BLUESVILLE (1070 "Smokes Like Lightning") 15-25 63
PRESTIGE/BLUESVILLE (1073 "Goin' Away") 15-25 64
PRESTIGE/BLUESVILLE (1084 "Greatest Hits") 15-25 64
PRESTIGE/BLUESVILLE (1086 "Down Home Blues") 15-25 64
RHINO 5-10 82
SCORE (4022 "Lightnin' Hopkins Strums the Blues") 200-400 59
SOUL PARADE 8-10
TIME (1 "Blues & Folk") 20-30 61
TIME (3 "More Blues & Folk") 20-30 61
TIME (70004 "Last of the Great Blues Singers") 25-35 60
TOMATO 5-10 77
TRADITION (1035 "Country Blues") 20-40 59
TRADITION (1040 "Autobiography in Blues") 20-40 60
TRADITION (1056 thru 2103) 10-15 67-72
TRIP 5-10 71-78
UNITED 10-15
UPFRONT 8-12
VAULT (129 "California Mudslide") 10-15 69
VEE JAY (1044 "Lightnin' Hopkins") 20-30 62
VERVE (8453 "Fast Life Woman") 20-30 62
VERVE/FOLKWAYS (3013 "Something Blue") 10-15 67
VERVE/FOLKWAYS (9000 "Roots") 12-18 65
VERVE/FOLKWAYS (9022 "Lightnin' Strikes") 12-18 65
Also see HOOKER, John Lee / Lightnin' Hopkins / Johnny Carroll
Also see THOMAS, Andrew

HOPKINS, Lightnin,' & Sonny Terry

Singles: 7-inch

PRESTIGE BLUESVILLE 4-8 61

LPs: 10/12-inch

PRESTIGE BLUESVILLE 15-20 61-63
Also see TERRY, Sonny

HOPKINS, Lightnin' / Brownie McGhee & Sonny Terry

LPs: 10/12-inch

HORIZON (WP-1617 "Blues Hoot") 20-25 63
(Monaural.)
HORIZON (ST-1617 "Blues Hoot") 25-30 63
(Stereo.)
Also see McGHEE, Brownie, & Sonny Terry

HOPKINS, Lightnin,' & Thunder Smith

Singles: 78 rpm

ALADDIN (165 "West Coast Blues") 75-100 47
ALADDIN (167 "Katie Mae Blues") 75-100 47
ALADDIN (168 "Feel So Bad") 75-100 47
Also see HOPKINS, Lightnin'
Also see SMITH, Thunder

HOPKINS, Linda

Singles: 12-inch

COLUMBIA 4-8 77

Singles: 7-inch

AMPEX 3-5 71
ATCO (6154 "Sentimental Fool") 10-15 59
BRUNSWICK 6-12 61-65
COLUMBIA 3-5 75
FEDERAL (12365 "Danny Boy") 10-15 59

LPs: 10/12-inch

COLUMBIA 5-10 76
PALO ALTO 5-10 83
RCA 8-10 72
Also see WILSON, Jackie, & Linda Hopkins

HOPKINS, Lyman, & Chestnuts: see CHESTNUTS

HOPKINS, Nicky — *LP '72*

Singles: 7-inch

COLUMBIA 3-5 72
DECCA (32139 "Mr. Pleasant") 5-10 67

LPs: 10/12-inch

COLUMBIA 8-10 73
ROLLING STONE 10-15 72
Session: Mick Jagger; Bill Wyman; Charlie Watts; Ry Cooder.
Also see BECK, Jeff
Also see COODER, Ry
Also see GILES, GILES & FRIPP
Also see JEFFERSON AIRPLANE
Also see LORD SUTCH
Also see NERVOUS EATERS
Also see NIGHT
Also see QUICKSILVER
Also see ROLLING STONES

HOPPER, Bristow

Singles: 7-inch

KO-MAT (2000 "Hate That Bear") 5-10 61
Also see CLANTON, Jimmy / Bristow Hopper

HOPPI & BEAU HEEMS

Singles: 7-inch

LAURIE (3411 "So Hard") 15-20 68
LAURIE (3439 "When I Get Home") 10-20 68

HORAN, Eddie — *R&B '78*

Singles: 7-inch

HDM 3-5 78
MGM 3-5 74

HORIZON

Singles: 7-inch

CAPITOL 3-5 72
JUBILEE 3-5

HORIZONS

Singles: 7-inch

REGINA 10-20 64

HORLICK, Maynard, & Hep Teens

Singles: 7-inch

V·I·R (7163 "Rollin' on Down the Street") 300-400 57
Also see MAYNIE & HOWIE

HORMEL, Geordie

(With Bill Hitchcock & Orchestra)

Singles: 78 rpm

CORAL 4-8 53

Singles: 7-inch

CORAL (60943 "Sweet Georgia Brown") 5-10 53
ZEPHYR (001 "Need Me") 8-12 50s
(May have been promotional only.)
ZEPHYR (005 "Gonna Wander") 8-12 50s
(May have been promotional only.)

HORN, DeAnne — *C&W '78*

Singles: 7-inch

CHARTWHEEL 3-5 78

HORN, Paul — *R&B '78*

Singles: 7-inch

MUSHROOM 3-5 78

LPs: 10/12-inch

COLUMBIA (36803 "Jingle Bell Jazz") 5-8 85
COLUMBIA (1677 thru 2050) 20-30 61-63
(Monaural.)
COLUMBIA (8477 thru 8850) 25-35 61-63
(Stereo.)
DOT (3091 "House of Horn") 40-60 57
DOT (9002 "Plenty of Horn") 40-60 58
EPIC 6-12 69-76
EVEREST 5-10 75
GPB 5-8 87
HI-FI JAZZ (615 "Something Blue") 30-50 60
IMPULSE 5-10 78
KUCKUCK 5-10 80-88
MUSHROOM 5-10 77-78
OVATION 8-12 70
RCA (3414 thru 3613) 15-25 65-66
(With "LPM" prefix. Monaural.)
RCA (3414 thru 3613) 15-30 65-66
(With "LSP" prefix. Stereo.)
SHELTER 8-12 71
WHO'S WHO in JAZZ 5-8 86-88
WORLD PACIFIC (Except 1266) 10-20 67-68
WORLD PACIFIC (1266 "Impressions") 30-50 59

HORN, Red

Singles: 7-inch

JALYN 10-15

HORN, Sam

LPs: 10/12-inch

COLUMBIA 10-15 66

HORN, Sam / Elise Britten

Singles: 78 rpm

BELL (90 "Rebel Rouser") 8-12 58

Singles: 7-inch

BELL (90 "Rebel Rouser") 8-12 58
Also see HORN, Sam

HORN, Trevor, Paul Morley & Art of Noise

Singles: 7-inch

ISLAND 3-4 86
Also see ART of NOISE

HORNE, Jimmy "Bo" — *R&B '75*

Singles: 12-inch

SUNSHINE SOUND 4-8 79

Singles: 7-inch

ALSTON 3-5 75-77
DADE (235 "I Can't Speak") 35-55 60s
(At least one source shows this number as 2031. We don't know yet who's right.)
SUNSHINE SOUND 3-5 77-80

LPs: 10/12-inch

SUNSHINE SOUND 5-10 78-80

HORNE, Lena — *P&R '43*

Singles: 78 rpm

RCA 3-5 52-57

Singles: 7-inch

BUDDAH 3-5 71
CHARTER 4-6 63
DRG 3-4 86
GRYPHON 3-5 76
MCA 3-4 78
RCA (4000 thru 7000 series) 5-10 52-61
20TH FOX 4-6 63-64
U.A. 3-6 65-66

Picture Sleeves

RCA 4-8 62

EPs: 7-inch

MGM 5-10 54-55
RCA 5-10 56-59

LPs: 10/12-inch

BUDDAH 5-10 71
CAMDEN 10-20 56
CHARTER 10-15 63
CORONET 5-10
DRG 5-10 86
GOLDEN TONE 5-10
GRYPHON 5-10 75-76
LIBERTY 5-8 81
MFSL (094 "Lady & Her Music") 25-40 82
MGM 15-30 54-55
POLYDOR 4-8
QWEST 5-10 81
RCA (Except 4300 series) 10-30 52-63
RCA (4300 series) 4-8 81
RADIO CRAFTSMEN 10-20
SPRINGBOARD 4-8 77
TOPS 15-30 56
20TH FOX 8-15 64
U.A. 8-15 65-66
Also see BELAFONTE, Harry, & Lena Horne
Also see FITZGERALD, Ella / Billie Holiday / Lena Horne
Also see FITZGERALD, Ella / Teddy Wilson / Lena Horne

HORNE, Lena, & Michel Legrand

LPs: 10/12-inch

GRYPHON 5-10 75
Also see LEGRAND, Michel

HORNE, Lena, & Gabor Szabo — *LP '70*

(Lena & Gabor)

Singles: 7-inch

SKYE (4523 "Rocky Raccoon") 4-6 70

LPs: 10/12-inch

SKYE (15 "Lena & Gabor") 8-15 70
Also see HORNE, Lena
Also see SZABO, Gabor

HORNETS

(Hornets & Orchestra)

Singles: 78 rpm

STATES (127 "I Can't Believe") 1000-2000 53

Singles: 7-inch

STATES (127 "I Can't Believe") 4000-6000 53
(Black vinyl.)
STATES (127 "I Can't Believe") 7500-10000 53
(Red vinyl.)
The wide price range here reflects both one known sale of, and one offer which was declined for the red vinyl pressing – though our valuation isn't quite as high as the 1988 sale price.
Members: James "Sonny" Long; Johnny Moore; Ben Iverson; Gus Miller.
Also see DRIFTERS

HORNETS

Singles: 78 rpm

FLASH (125 "Crying Over You") 50-100 57

Singles: 7-inch

FLASH (125 "Crying Over You") 200-300 57

HORNETS

Singles: 7-inch

REV (3515 "Slow Dance") 35-50 58

HORNETS

Singles: 7-inch

LIBERTY 10-15 64

LPs: 10/12-inch

LIBERTY 25-35 63-64

HORNETS

Singles: 7-inch

COLUMBIA (42999 "Fruit Cake") 15-25 64
V.I.P. (25004 "She's My Baby") 25-35 64

HORNETS

Singles: 7-inch

EMERALD (501 "Runt") 20-30

HORNSBY, Bruce, & Range — *P&R/C&W/LP '86*

Singles: 7-inch

RCA 3-4 86-90

Picture Sleeves

RCA 3-4 87-88

LPs: 10/12-inch

RCA 5-10 86-90
Also see HENLEY, Don

HORSEHAIRS

LPs: 10/12-inch

SHOWTOWN 8-10 69

HORSES

Singles: 7-inch

WHITE WHALE 3-5 70

LPs: 10/12-inch

WHITE WHALE 8-10 70

HORSLIPS — *LP '78*

Singles: 7-inch

DJM (Except 1036) 3-5 77-79
DJM (1036 "Sure the Boy Was Green") 4-8 77
(Colored vinyl.)
MERCURY 3-5 79
RCA 3-5 75

LPs: 10/12-inch

ATCO 10-12 73-74
DJM 5-10 77-79
MERCURY 5-10 79-80
RCA 8-10 74
Members: Eamon Carr; John Fean; Jim Lockhart; Barry Devlin; Charles O'Connor.

HORTON, Big Walter, & His Combo

Singles: 78 rpm

COBRA 20-30 54
STATES 25-50 54

Singles: 7-inch

COBRA (5002 "Have a Good Time") 75-100 54
STATES (145 "Hard Hearted Woman") 75-100 54

LPs: 10/12-inch

ALLIGATOR 10-20 72
ARGO 15-20 68
Also see BELL, Carey
Also see BIG WALTER
Also see HORTON, Shakey
Also see JIMMY & WALTER
Also see MUMBLES
Also see SHINES, Johnny, & Big Walter Horton
Also see SUNNYLAND SLIM
Also see TAYLOR, Koko
Also see WATERS, Muddy

HORTON, Bill

(With the Silhouettes: with Dawns; Billy Horton)

Singles: 7-inch

ACE (563 "Evelyn") 10-20 59
KAYDEN (403 "I Wanna Know") 10-20
LAWN (241 "Like to See You in That Mood") 30-50 64
Also see SILHOUETTES

HORTON, Billie Jean — *C&W '61*

Singles: 7-inch

FOX 5-8 61

HORTON, J.D.

Singles: 78 rpm

BULLET (350 "Cadillac Blues") 50-100 52

HORTON, Jamie — *P&R '60*

Singles: 7-inch

ERIC 3-5 68
JOY 8-12 59-61

HORTON, Jay

Singles: 7-inch

MUSTANG (3010 "I Trip on You Girl") 20-25 65
Also see FULLER, Bobby

HORTON, Johnny — *C&W '56*

Singles: 78 rpm

ABBOTT 15-25 51-52
COLUMBIA 10-25 56-57
CORMAC 25-50 51
MERCURY 10-20 54-55

Singles: 7-inch

ABBOTT (100 "Candy Jones") 20-30 51
ABBOTT (101 "Happy Millionaire") 20-30 51
ABBOTT (102 "Plaid & Calico") 20-30 51
ABBOTT (103 "Birds and Butterflies") 20-30 51
ABBOTT (104 "Go and Wash") 20-30 51
ABBOTT (105 "Shadows on the Old Bayou") 20-30 51
ABBOTT (106 "Words") 20-30 51
ABBOTT (107 "Long Rocky Road") 20-30 52
ABBOTT (108 "Somebody's Rockin' My Broken Heart") 20-30 52
ABBOTT (109 "Rhythm in My Baby's Walk") 20-30 52
ABBOTT (135 "Plaid & Calico") 15-20 53
CORMAC (1193 "Plaid & Calico") 75-100 51
CORMAC (1197 "Birds and Butterflies") 75-100 51
COLUMBIA (21504 "Honky Tonk Man") 15-25 56
COLUMBIA (21538 "I'm a One-Woman Man") 10-20 56
COLUMBIA (40813 "I'm Coming Home") 15-25 57
COLUMBIA (40919 "She Knows Why") 10-15 57
COLUMBIA (40986 "I'll Do It Every Time") 10-15 57
COLUMBIA (41043 "Lover's Rock") 15-25 57
COLUMBIA (41110 "Honky Tonk Hardwood Floor") 30-50 58
COLUMBIA (41210 "All Grown Up") 10-15 58
COLUMBIA (41308 thru 44156) 5-10 58-67
DOT (15996 "Plaid & Calico") 8-12 59
MERCURY (6412 "The Devil Sent Me You") 15-25 52
MERCURY (6418 "The Rest of Your Life") 15-25 52
MERCURY (70014 "I Won't Forget") 15-25 52
MERCURY (70100 "Tennessee Jive") 15-25 53
MERCURY (70156 "S.S. Lureline") 15-25 53
MERCURY (70198 "You You You") 15-25 53
MERCURY (70227 "All for the Love of a Girl") 15-25 53
MERCURY (70325 "Move Down the Line") 15-25 54
MERCURY (70399 "The Door of Your Mansion") 15-25 54
MERCURY (70462 "No True Love") 15-25 54
MERCURY (70636 "Ridin' the Sunshine Special") 15-25 55

MERCURY (70707 "Big Wheels Rollin' ")..15-25 55

Picture Sleeves

COLUMBIA (Except 41308)..........10-15 59-64
COLUMBIA (41308 "When It's Springtime in Alaska")..15-20 59
(Blue and white sleeve. Promotional only.)
DOT...10-15 59

EPs: 7-inch

COLUMBIA (2130 "Honky Tonk Man") 25-50 57
COLUMBIA (13621/22/23 "The Spectacular Johnny Horton ") 20-40 60
(Price is for either volume.)
COLUMBIA (14781/82/83 "Johnny Horton Makes History") 20-40 60
(Price is for either volume.)
MERCURY (3091 "Requestfully Yours")..25-50 55
SESAC (1201 "Free and Easy Songs")...30-50 59

LPs: 10/12-inch

BRIAR INT'L (104 "Done Rovin' ") 100-150 60s
COLUMBIA (CL-1362 "The Spectacular Johnny Horton ") 20-30 60
(Monaural.)
COLUMBIA (CL-1478 "Johnny Horton Makes History")...20-30 60
(Monaural.)
COLUMBIA (CL-1596 "Johnny Horton's Greatest Hits")..20-30 61
(Monaural. Add $15 to $25 if accompanied by bonus photo.)
COLUMBIA (CL-1721 "Honky Tonk Man")..20-30 62
(Monaural.)
COLUMBIA (CL-2566 "Johnny Horton on the Louisiana Hayride")..............................20-25 66
(Monaural.)
COLUMBIA (CL-2566 "Johnny Horton on Stage")..10-20 66
(Monaural. Repackage of *Johnny Horton on the Louisiana Hayride*.)
COLUMBIA (CS-8167 "The Spectacular Johnny Horton ") 25-35 60
(Stereo.)
COLUMBIA (CS-8269 "Johnny Horton Makes History")..25-35 60
(Stereo.)
COLUMBIA (CS-8396 "Johnny Horton's Greatest Hits")..25-35 61
(Stereo. Add $15 to $25 if accompanied by bonus photo.)
COLUMBIA (PC-8396 "Johnny Horton's Greatest Hits")............................... 5-10
COLUMBIA (CS-8779 "Honky Tonk Man")..25-35 62
(Stereo.)
COLUMBIA (CS-9099 "I Can't Forget You")...15-20 65
(Stereo.)
COLUMBIA (CS-9366 "Johnny Horton on the Louisiana Hayride")..............................20-25 66
(Stereo.)
COLUMBIA (CS-9366 "Johnny Horton on Stage")..10-15 66
(Stereo. Repackage of *Johnny Horton on the Louisiana Hayride*.)
COLUMBIA (CS-9940 "Johnny Horton on the Road")..10-15 69
COLUMBIA (KG-30884 "The World of Johnny Horton")..15-20 71
COLUMBIA (CG-30884 "The World of Johnny Horton")..10-15
COLUMBIA HOUSE (6418/19 "Johnny Horton, the Legend")..10-15 75
CROWN 10-20 63
CUSTOM...10-15 60s
DOT (3221 "Johnny Horton") 30-50 59
(Monaural.)
DOT (25221 "Johnny Horton")............20-30 66
(Stereo.)
HARMONY (11291 "The Unforgettable Johnny Horton")..10-15 70
HARMONY (11384 "The Legendary Johnny Horton")..10-15 70
HARMONY (30394 "The Battle of New Orleans")...10-15 71
JUKE BOX.. 5-10
MERCURY (20478 "The Fantastic Johnny Horton")..35-50 59
PICKWICK/HILLTOP (6060 "All for the Love of a Girl")..10-15 65
PICKWICK/HILLTOP (6012 "The Voice of Johnny Horton")................................10-15 68
SEARS (110 "Legend of Johnny Horton")..10-15 60s
SESAC (1201 "Free and Easy Songs")..75-125 59
Also see CLINE, Patsy / Cowboy Copas / Johnny Horton
Also see DEAN, Jimmy / Johnny Horton
Also see PRICE, Ray / Johnny Horton / Carl Smith / George Morgan

HORTON, Johnny / Sonny James

LPs: 10/12-inch

CUSTOM.. 6-12
Also see JAMES, Sonny

HORTON, Johnny / Texas Slim

LPs: 10/12-inch

CROWN 6-12 60s
Also see HORTON, Johnny

HORTON, Little Willie

Singles: 7-inch

BUSH LEAGUE 4-6

HORTON, Shakey

(Walter Horton)

Singles: 7-inch

ARGO... 4-8 64

LPs: 10/12-inch

ARGO (4037 "The Soul of Blues Harmonica")....................................25-35 64
Also see HORTON, Big Walter, & His Combo

HORTON, Steven Wayne — C&W '89

Singles: 7-inch

CAPITOL.. 3-4 89

HORTON, Walter: see HORTON, Big Walter, & His Combo

HORTON, Willie

(With the Supremes)

Singles: 7-inch

CITY of DETROIT (1900 "Detroit Is Happening") 100-200 67
(Promotional issue only.)
Also see SUPREMES

HORTON BROTHERS

Singles: 7-inch

FEDORA 5-10

HORWITZ, Bill

Singles: 7-inch

ESP... 3-5 75

LPs: 10/12-inch

ESP..10-12 75

HOSANNA — R&B '76

Singles: 7-inch

CALLA 3-5 76

HOSEA

Singles: 7-inch

A&M 3-5 75

HOSEA, Don

Singles: 7-inch

CRYSTAL (501 "Everlasting Love") 100-150 58
RITA...8-10 60
SUN..8-10 61

HOSELL, Coward

Singles: 7-inch

ANTICS (1001 "Super Steelers '76") . 4-6 76

HOSFORD, Larry — C&W '74

Singles: 7-inch

SHELTER.. 3-5 74-76

HOSS, Charlie, & Ponies

Singles: 7-inch

COLUMBIA...8-10 60

HOT — P&R/R&B/LP '77

Singles: 7-inch

BIG TREE 3-5 77-79

LPs: 10/12-inch

BIG TREE 5-10 77-79
Members: Gwen Owens; Cathy Carson; Juanita Curiel.

HOT BUTTER — P&R/LP '72

Singles: 7-inch

MUSICOR 3-5 72

LPs: 10/12-inch

MUSICOR 8-10 72-74
Members: Steve Jerome; Bill Jerome; Johnny Abbott; Stan Free; Dave Mullaney.

HOT CHOCOLATE — P&R/R&B '75

(Hot Chocolate Band)

Singles: 7-inch

APPLE...5-10 69
BELL 3-5 74
BIG TREE 3-5 75-77
EMI AMERICA.................................... 3-4 82
INFINITY 3-5 78-79
RAK.. 3-5 72-73

LPs: 10/12-inch

BIG TREE 8-10 74-77
EMI AMERICA.....................................5-10 82
INFINITY 5-10 78-79
Members: Errol Brown; Tony Wilson; Harvey Hinsley; Larry Ferguson; Tony Conner; Patrick Olive.
Also see WILSON, Tony

HOT CHOCOLATE MUSIC CO., LTD.

Singles: 7-inch

CORAL.. 3-6 69

HOT CUISINE — R&B '81

Singles: 7-inch

PRELUDE 3-4 81

HOT DOG STAND

Singles: 7-inch

MALA (12014 "C'mon Summer's Happening")..10-20

HOT DOGGERS

LPs: 10/12-inch

EPIC (24054 "Surfin' U.S.A.")..........40-50 63
(Monaural.)
EPIC (26054 "Surfin' U.S.A.")..........50-75 63
(Stereo.)
Member: Bruce Johnston.
Also see JOHNSTON, Bruce

HOT DOGS

LPs: 10/12-inch

ARDENT...10-12 73
Also see JOHNSON, Robert

HOT FOOD TO GO

Singles

ERIKA (68 "Frogs Are Fun") 10-15 83
(French fries-shaped picture disc.)

HOT HALF DOZEN

Singles: 7-inch

DUNWICH (134 "Angels Listened In")..40-60 65
SOMA...12-18 65
Also see DONN E. & KOSTIRS

HOT ICE

Singles: 7-inch

TEE PEE (101 "I'm Your Fool")........5-10 69
Members: Larry Watson; Steve Gove; Rudy Passonno; Dennis La Plant; Jerry Watson; Steve "Kink" Curnett.

HOT ICE

Singles: 7-inch

ATLANTIC... 3-5 70s

LPs: 10/12-inch

RADIO...5-10 79
RAGE..5-10 77
Members: Victor Drayton; Jerry Akines; Reginald Turner; Ernie Brooks; Johnny Bellman.
Also see FORMATIONS

HOT KNIVES

Singles: 7-inch

K.O. 3-5

HOT LINE — R&B '74

Singles: 12-inch

MEMO... 4-6 84

Singles: 7-inch

RED COACH 3-5 74

HOT PEPPER

LPs: 10/12-inch

KMA 5-10 82
Members: Joey Miraglia; Tony Piazza; David Norcross; Bob Strunk.

HOT PEPPERS

Singles: 7-inch

BISCAYNE (001 "The Turnpike")...10-20 63
SEA-HORN (501 "New Orleans Surf")..15-25 63

HOT POOP

LPs: 10/12-inch

HOT POOP (3072 "Hot Poop Does Their Stuff")..50-100 75

HOT PROPERTY

(Magnificents)

Singles: 7-inch

CREW ("Too Hard to Handle").......15-20 68
(Promotional issue only.)
Also see MAGNIFICENTS

HOT ROD HAPPY

(James Bledsoe)

Singles: 78 rpm

PACEMAKER (1014 "Hot Rod Boogie")..75-125 50
Also see COUNTRY JIM

HOT RODDERS

LPs: 10/12-inch

CROWN 15-25 63

HOT SAUCE — P&R/R&B '72

Singles: 7-inch

VOLT..5-10 72-74

HOT SHOT LOVE: see LOVE, Hot Shot

HOT SHOTS

Singles: 78 rpm

SAVOY...5-8 53

Singles: 7-inch

SAVOY...8-12 53

HOT SHOTS

LPs: 10/12-inch

MCA..5-10 80

HOT SOUP

Singles: 7-inch

RAMA RAMA (7775 "You Took Me by Surprise")..10-15 69

LPs: 10/12-inch

RAMA RAMA ("Hot Soup") 25-35 69
(Selection number not known.)

HOT STREAK — D&D '83

Singles: 12-inch

EASY STREET.................................... 4-6 83

HOT TAMALES

Singles: 7-inch

ALPINE 5-10 60
DETROIT 4-8 64
DIAMOND 4-8 66
PAC (3501 "Hot Tamale")..................5-10 61

HOT TODDYS — P&R '59

(Featuring Bill Pernell; Hot-Toddys)

Singles: 7-inch

BARREL (602 "Rockin' Crickets") ..20-30 59
(Canadian.)
CORSICAN (0056 "Rockin' Crickets")..15-25 59
SHAN-TODD (0056 "Rockin' Crickets") 15-25 59
STRAND (25001 "Hoe-Down")........10-15 60
(Issued with two different flip sides.)
SWAN (4140 "Rockin' Crickets").....10-20 63
Also see ROCKIN' REBELS
Also see VINCENT, Rudy, Jr.

HOT TUNA — LP '70

Singles: 7-inch

GRUNT 3-6 71-76

Picture Sleeves

GRUNT 4-8 72

LPs: 10/12-inch

GRUNT 10-20 72-78
RCA (3000 series)..............................5-10 81
RCA (4000 series)..............................10-15 70-71
RELIX ("Acoustic Hot Tuna Splashdown")...................................10-15 84
(No selection number used.)
RELIX (2004 "Tuna Splashed").........25-30 84
(Picture disc.)
Members: Jack Casady; Jorma Kaukonen; Papa John Creach; Sammy Piazza.
Also see CLEMENTS, Vassar
Also see CREACH, Papa John
Also see JOPLIN, Janis / Hot Tuna
Also see KAUKONEN, Jorma

HOTBOX — R&B/D&D '84

Singles: 12-inch

POLYDOR...4-6 84

Singles: 7-inch

POLYDOR...3-4 84

HOTEL — P&R '78

Singles: 7-inch

MCA..3-4 79-80
MERCURY 3-5 78

LPs: 10/12-inch

MCA..5-10 79-80

HOTHOUSE FLOWERS — LP '88

Singles: 7-inch

LONDON..3-4 88-90

LPs: 10/12-inch

LONDON..5-10 88-90
Members: Liam O'Maonlai; Fiachna O'Braonain; Peter O'Toole; Leo Barnes.

HOTLEGS — P&R '70

Singles: 7-inch

CAPITOL (Except 3043) 3-5 70-71
CAPITOL (3043 "Run Baby Run")..10-15 71

LPs: 10/12-inch

CAPITOL...15-20 71
Members: Eric Stewart; Kevin Godley; Lol Cream.
Also see 10CC

HOTSHOTS

Singles: 7-inch

MERCURY (73409 "Snoopy Versus the Red Baron")..5-10 73

HOTSPUR

LPs: 10/12-inch

COLUMBIA 8-10 73

HOT-TODDYS: see HOT TODDYS

HOULE BROTHERS

Singles: 7-inch

CIRCLE DOT (1013 "Dream Night")....................................150-250

HOUND, Huckleberry: see BUTLER, Daws

HOUND DOG CROWNS

Singles: 7-inch

UNI 10-15 67

HOUND DOGS

Singles: 7-inch

DEE DEE (733 "I'm Beginning to Understand Them")...50-100 64

HOUNDS

Singles: 7-inch

LARK..5-10 60

HOUNDS

Singles: 7-inch

COLUMBIA 3-5 79

LPs: 10/12-inch

COLUMBIA 5-10 78-79
Also see SINCEROS / Hounds / The Beat / Jules & Polar Bears

HOUR GLASS

(Greg Allman & Hour Glass)

Singles: 7-inch

LIBERTY (56002 "Nothing But Tears")..10-15 68
LIBERTY (56029 "Power of Love") 10-15 68
LIBERTY (56091 "I've Been Trying")..10-15 69

Picture Sleeves

LIBERTY (56002 "Nothing But Tears")..40-60 68

LPs: 10/12-inch

LIBERTY 15-20 67-68
U.A. 10-15 73
Members: Duane Allman; Gregg Allman.
Also see ALLMAN BROTHERS BAND

HOUSE

LPs: 10/12-inch

LIBERTY 8-10 70

HOUSE, David — C&W '82

Singles: 7-inch

DOOR KNOB 3-4 82

HOUSE, Dickson

(Dickson House Band)

LPs: 10/12-inch

INFINITY 5-10 79

HOUSE, James — C&W '89

Singles: 7-inch

MCA..3-4 89-90

HOUSE, Son

LPs: 10/12-inch

BLUE GOOSE.....................................10-15
COLUMBIA 10-20 65
EDSEL 5-10 86

HOUSE, Son, & J.D. Short

LPs: 10/12-inch

VERVE/FOLKWAYS 10-15 66
Also see HOUSE, Son

HOUSE OF FREAKS — LP '89

LPs: 10/12-inch

RHINO 5-8 89

HOUSE OF LORDS

Singles: 7-inch

BVA (101 "Last Stand") 15-25 67

HOUSE OF LORDS — LP '88

Singles: 7-inch

RCA/SIMMONS....................................3-4 89

Picture Sleeves

RCA/SIMMONS....................................3-4 89

LPs: 10/12-inch

RCA/SIMMONS....................................5-8 88
SIMMONS 5-8 90
Members: James Christian; Gregg Giuffria; Chuck Wright; Lanny Cordola; Ken Mary.
Also see GIUFFRIA

HOUSE OF LOVE — LP '88

LPs: 10/12-inch

FONTANA 5-8 90
RELATIVITY..5-8 88

HOUSE OF SHOCK

Singles: 7-inch

CAPITOL...3-4 88

Picture Sleeves

CAPITOL...3-4 88

HOUSE ROCKERS

Singles: 7-inch

CLIFTON (1 "Times Square Stomp")...8-12

HOUSEBAND

Singles: 7-inch

MIDLAND 3-5

HOUSEHOLD SPONGE

Singles: 7-inch

MURBO (1017 "Scars") 15-25 67

HOUSEMARTINS — LP '87

LPs: 10/12-inch

ELEKTRA 5-10 87-88
Member: Norman Cook.
Also see BEATS INTERNATIONAL

HOUSTON

Singles: 7-inch

SSS INT'L 3-5 71

LPs: 10/12-inch

SSS INT'L 8-10 71

HOUSTON, Bee

LPs: 10/12-inch

ARHOOLIE..8-10 69

HOUSTON, Cissy — R&B '70

(Sissie Houston; Cissie Houston)

Singles: 7-inch

COLUMBIA 3-4 79-80
COMMONWEALTH UNITED.............3-5 70
CONGRESS (268 "Bring Him Back")..30-50 66
JANUS 3-5 71
KAPP (814 "Don't Come Running to Me")..15-25 67
PRIVATE STOCK 3-5 77-78

LPs: 10/12-inch

COLUMBIA 5-10 79-80
JANUS 8-10 70
PRIVATE STOCK 5-10 77-78
Also see BOWIE, David
Also see MANN, Herbie, & Cissy Houston
Also see SWEET INSPIRATIONS

HOUSTON, Dale

Singles: 7-inch

MONTEL..5-10 62
Also see DALE & GRACE

HOUSTON, David — C&W '63

(With Calvin Crawford; with Sherri Jerrico)

Singles: 78 rpm

IMPERIAL 8-12 55
RCA (6611 "Sugar Sweet")................8-12 56
RCA (6696 "Blue Prelude")................8-12 56
RCA (6927 "One and Only")...............15-25 57
RCA (7001 "Teenage Frankie and Johnny")..15-25 57

Singles: 7-inch

BLACK ROSE 3-4 82
COLONIAL..3-5 78
COUNTRY INT'L..................................3-4 80
DERRICK 3-4 79
ELEKTRA 3-5 78-79
EXCELSIOR 3-4 81
EPIC 3-8 63-76
IMPERIAL 10-20 55
NRC (005 "Waited So Long").............25-35 58
NRC (047 "It's Been So Long")..........20-25 59
PHILLIPS INT'L 5-10 61
RCA (6611 "Sugar Sweet")................10-20 56
RCA (6696 "Blue Prelude")................10-20 56
RCA (6927 "One and Only")...............30-40 57
RCA (7001 "Teenage Frankie and Johnny")..15-25 57
SOUNDWAVES 3-4 83
STARDAY 3-5 77
SUN (400 series)................................5-10 66
SUN (1100 series)..............................3-5 72

Picture Sleeves

EPIC 5-8 66-69

LPs: 10/12-inch

CAMDEN...8-12 66
COLUMBIA 6-10 73
DELTA 5-10 82
EPIC 5-15 64-76
EXACT 5-10 80
EXCELSIOR 5-10 81
51 WEST 5-10 84
GUEST STAR 6-12 64
GUSTO 5-10 78
HARMONY..8-12 70-72
STARDAY 6-10 77
Session: Jordanaires.
Also see DEAN, Jimmy / David Houston /

Warner Mack / Autry Inman
Also see JAMES, Sonny / David Houston
Also see JERRICO, Sherri
Also see JORDANAIRES
Also see JONES, George / Buck Owens / David Houston / Tommy Hill.

HOUSTON, David, & Barbara Mandrell C&W '70
Singles: 7-inch
EPIC.......3-5 70-74
LPs: 10/12-inch
EPIC.......8-15 72-75
Also see MANDRELL, Barbara

HOUSTON, David, & Tammy Wynette C&W '68
Singles: 7-inch
EPIC.......4-6 67
LPs: 10/12-inch
EPIC.......8-12 67
51 WEST.......5-10 82
Also see HOUSTON, David
Also see WYNETTE, Tammy

HOUSTON, Don
Singles: 7-inch
THUNDER.......5-10 59

HOUSTON, Eddie
Singles: 7-inch
CAPITOL (2170 "That's How Much").......15-25 68
CAPITOL (2397 "I Won't Be the Last to Cry").......15-25 69
OVATION (1051 "Knock and the Door Shall Be Opened").......8-10 78

HOUSTON, Freddie
Singles: 7-inch
CAPTAIN (692 "Willing to Try").......10-20 62
CARLTON (542 "Do You Feel It").......10-20 61
CARLTON (550 "Only Me").......10-20 61
OLD TOWN (1153 "Chills and Fever").......10-20 63
OLD TOWN (1156 "Only the Lonely One").......25-50 64
TOTO (101 "Soft Walkin'").......15-25 62
WHIZ-ON (7 "True").......15-25 60s

HOUSTON, Jimmy, & Alamos
Singles: 7-inch
CLEVELAND (104 "Summer Souvenir").......35-45 60

HOUSTON, Joe R&B '52
(With His Rockets; Mighty Joe Houston; Fabulous Joe Houston; Joe Houston Orchestra)
Singles: 78 rpm
BAYOU.......10-15 53
CASH.......10-15 55
COMBO.......10-20 53-57
CROWN.......10-20 56
FREEDOM (1526 "It's Really Wee Wee Hours").......30-40 49
FREEDOM (1535 "Jumping the Blues").......30-40 50
IMPERIAL.......10-20 52-55
LUCKY.......10-20 54
MACY'S (5017 "Cornbread and Cabbage Greens").......20-30 51
MERCURY.......10-20 51
MODERN.......10-15 51-52
MONEY.......10-15 55
RPM.......10-15 55
RECORDED in HOLLYWOOD.......10-20 54
SPHINX (122 "Worry, Worry, Worry").......25-35 51
Singles: 7-inch
BAYOU (004 "Moody").......15-25 53
BAYOU (012 "Chittlin'").......15-25 53
BAYOU (015 "Blues Jump the Rabbit").......15-25 53
BAYOU (017 "Scramble").......15-25 53
BIG TOWN.......4-6 79
CASH (1013 "Flying Home").......15-25 55
CASH (1014 "Hey Now").......15-25 55
CASH (1018 "Rockin' 'N' Boppin'").......15-25 55
COMBO (19 "Vino").......15-25 53
COMBO (54 "Drag Race").......15-25 54
COMBO (136 "We're Gonna Rock & Roll").......15-25 57
COMBO (185 "Lightnin'").......15-25 65
CROWN (102 "Hum Bug").......15-25 56
CROWN (109 "Dear Mom").......15-25 56
DOOTO (439 "Shindig").......15-25 58
IMPERIAL (5183 "Jumping the Blues").......20-30 52
IMPERIAL (5196 "Hurricane").......20-30 52
IMPERIAL (5201 "Earthquake").......20-30 52
IMPERIAL (5213 "Atom Bomb").......20-30 53
IMPERIAL (5334 "Tough Enough").......20-30 55
KEM (2761 "Ko Ko Mo").......8-12 61
KEM (2762 "Hush Your Mouth").......8-12 61
KENT (366 "Doing the Twist").......8-12 62
LUCKY (004 "Go, Joe, Go").......20-30 54
MAGNUM.......10-20 64-65
MERCURY (8248 "Worry, Worry, Worry").......25-35 51
MODERN (830 "Blow Joe, Blow").......30-50 51
MODERN (850 "Have a Ball").......20-30 52
MODERN (863 "Doin' the Lindy Hop").......20-30 52
MODERN (879 "Boogie Woogie Woman").......20-30 52
MODERN (917 "Blowin' Crazy").......20-30 52
MONEY (203 "All Nite Long").......15-25 55
MONEY (207 "Celebrity Club Stomp").......15-25 55
RONNEX (1103 "All Night Long").......15-25 55
RPM (422 "Celebrity Club Stomp").......10-20 55
RPM (426 "Joe's Gone").......15-25 55
RPM (427 "Riverside Rock").......15-25 55
RECORDED in HOLLYWOOD (423 "Jay's Boogie").......20-30 54
EPs: 7-inch
COMBO (3 "Joe Houston").......50-75 54
COMBO (10 "Joe Houston").......50-75 55
MODERN/RPM (200 "The Fabulous Joe Houston").......50-75 55
(Cover shows Modern, but label shows RPM.)
TOPS (607 "Rock & Roll Party").......50-75 56
LPs: 10/12-inch
BIG TOWN (1004 "Kicking Back").......8-12 78
COMBO (100 "Joe Houston").......300-400 55
(Cover has titles and color photo of Houston)
COMBO (100 "Joe Houston").......100-200 56
(No photo or titles on cover. Has a saxophone as the "J" in Joe. No artist or title shown on label.)
COMBO (400 "Rockin' at the Drive-In").......200-300 55
CROWN (313 "Surf Rockin'").......15-30 63
CROWN (5006 "Joe Houston Rocks All Nite Long").......50-100 56
CROWN (5203 "Wild Man of the Tenor Sax").......25-35 62
CROWN (5319 "Limbo").......20-30 63
GOLD AWARD (8033 "Rock & Roll").......30-40
(Colored vinyl.)
MODERN (1206 "Joe Houston Blows All Night Long").......100-150 56
TOPS (1518 "Rock & Roll with Joe Houston").......50-100 56
Also see REYNOLDS, Teddy, & Twisters / Joe Houston

HOUSTON, Joe / Phantoms
Singles: 7-inch
PICO (2803 "All Night Long").......10-20
Also see HOUSTON, Joe
Also see PHANTOMS

HOUSTON, Johnny, & Playboys
Singles: 7-inch
EVENT (4277 "Playboy").......15-25 59
SURF (1001 "Rockin' on the Range").......15-25 59

HOUSTON, Larry
Singles: 7-inch
HFMP (001 "Let's Spend Some Time Together").......5-10

HOUSTON, Lawyer
Singles: 78 rpm
ATLANTIC (916 "Dallas Be-Bop Blues").......30-50 50
Also see HOUSTON, Soldier Boy

HOUSTON, Penelope, & Her Band
Singles: 7-inch
ILOKI (104 "Glad I'm a Girl").......3-4 92
(Includes insert.)
Picture Sleeves
ILOKI (104 "Glad I'm a Girl").......3-4 92

HOUSTON, Sammy & Alamos
Singles: 7-inch
CLEVELAND (104 "Summer Souvenir").......30-40 60

HOUSTON, Soldier Boy
(Lawyer Houston)
Singles: 78 rpm
ATLANTIC.......50-75 52
Singles: 7-inch
ATLANTIC (971 "Western Rider Blues").......100-200 52

HOUSTON, Thelma P&R '70
(With Pressure Cooker)
Singles: 12-inch
MCA.......4-6 83
Singles: 7-inch
CAPITOL (5767 "Baby Mine").......25-50 66
DUNHILL (Except 11).......4-8 70
DUNHILL (11 "Everybody Gets to Go to the Moon").......10-15 69
(Special Apollo 11 Mission promotional issue.)
MCA.......3-4 83
MOTOWN.......3-4 74-78
MOWEST.......3-6 71-73
RCA.......3-4 80-81
TAMLA.......3-4 76-79
Picture Sleeves
DUNHILL (11 "Everybody Gets to Go to the Moon").......10-15 69
(Special Apollo 11 Mission promotional issue.)
LPs: 10/12-inch
DUNHILL.......10-15 69
MCA.......5-10 83
MOTOWN.......5-10 81-82
MOWEST.......8-12 72
RCA.......5-10 80-81
SHEFFIELD (2 "I've Got the Music in Me").......25-30 74
SHEFFIELD (200 "I've Got the Music in Me").......5-10 82
TAMLA.......5-10 76-79
MYRRH.......8-10 74
Also see REYNOLDS, Art, Singers
Also see BUTLER, Jerry, & Thelma Houston

HOUSTON, Whitney P&R/R&B/LP '85
Singles: 12-inch
ARISTA.......4-6 85-89
Singles: 7-inch
ARISTA.......3-4 85-91
Picture Sleeves
ARISTA.......3-4 85-88
LPs: 10/12-inch
ARISTA.......5-10 85-91
Also see FRANKLIN, Aretha, & Whitney Houston
Also see KING DREAM CHORUS & Holiday Crew
Also see PENDERGRASS, Teddy, & Whitney Houston

HOUSTON FEARLESS
LPs: 10/12-inch
IMPERIAL.......10-12 69

HOUSTON OUTLAWS
Singles: 7-inch
WESTBOUND (179 "Ain't No Telling").......10-20 69

HOUSTONS
Singles: 7-inch
WORLD PACIFIC (77926 "Solar Light").......8-12 69

HOVEN, Beat: see BEAT HOVEN

HOVIS, Larry
Singles: 7-inch
CAPITOL (3873 "Do I Love You").......8-12 58

HOW TO (BAT, PITCH, FIELD, ETC.): see BASEBALL

HOWARD, Annie
Singles: 7-inch
MAGNASONIC (200 "Colors of Blue").......5-10 50s

HOWARD, Buddy
Singles: 7-inch
MIDA (115 "Take Your Hands Off Me, Baby").......40-60 59

HOWARD, Camille R&B '48
(With Her Boy Friends; Camille Howard Trio)
Singles: 78 rpm
FEDERAL.......10-15 53
IMPERIAL.......10-15 53
SPECIALTY.......10-15 48-53
VEE JAY.......8-12 56
Singles: 7-inch
FEDERAL (12125 "Excite Me, Daddy").......20-30 53
FEDERAL (12134 "Hurry Back, Baby").......20-30 53
FEDERAL (12147 "You're Lower Than a Mole").......20-30 53
IMPERIAL.......15-25 53
SPECIALTY (359 "Ferocious Boogie").......30-40 50
SPECIALTY (370 "Fire Ball Boogie").......30-40 51
SPECIALTY (443 "Old Baldy Boogie").......20-30 53
SPECIALTY (449 "Bacarolle Boogie").......20-30 53
VEE JAY.......10-20 56
Members: Camille Howard; Roy Milton; Dallas Bartley.
Also see BROWN, Clarence "Gatemouth" / Camille Howard / Bill Johnson Quartet / Van "Piano Man" Walls
Also see MILTON, Roy

HOWARD, Chuck
Singles: 7-inch
ESA (1017 "Joe Gray").......50-75 57
FLAME (1020 "Gossip").......100-200 59
FRATERNITY.......4-8 64
JOY.......5-10 60
PORT (70002 "Crazy Crazy Baby").......30-50 58
SAND (266 "Crazy Crazy Baby").......75-100 58

HOWARD, Chuck
Singles: 7-inch
APEX (76915 "Johnny Be Good").......25-35 63
(First issue.)
GARRETT (4001 "Johnny Be Goode").......10-20 63

HOWARD, Chuck C&W '80
Singles: 7-inch
NEW STAR.......4-6
W.B.......3-5 80

HOWARD, Danny
Singles: 7-inch
BIRTHSTONE.......8-15
Picture Sleeves
BIRTHSTONE.......10-20

HOWARD, Dave
Singles: 7-inch
CHOREO.......4-8 62
M.M.I. (259 "While We Danced the Tango").......50-100
LPs: 10/12-inch
CHOREO.......10-20 62

HOWARD, Don P&R '52
Singles: 78 rpm
ESSEX.......4-8 52
MERCURY.......3-5 56
TRIPLE A.......10-15 52
Singles: 7-inch
ESSEX (311 "Oh Happy Day").......8-15 52
(Black vinyl.)
ESSEX (311 "Oh Happy Day").......15-25 52
(Colored vinyl.)
MERCURY.......5-10 56
TRIPLE A (2503 "Oh Happy Day").......20-30 52

HOWARD, Eddy P&R '40
Singles: 78 rpm
MAJESTIC.......4-8 46
MERCURY.......3-5 50-57
Singles: 7-inch
MERCURY.......5-10 50-61
MISHAWAKA.......3-5 72
EPs: 7-inch
MERCURY.......5-10 50-59
LPs: 10/12-inch
IMPERIAL.......8-15 61
MERCURY.......10-20 50-65
WING.......5-10 60-63

HOWARD, Edwin
Singles: 7-inch
PHILLIPS INT'L.......5-10 59

HOWARD, Frank
Singles: 7-inch
BARRY (1008 "I'm So Glad").......15-25 67
EXCELLO (2291 "Judy").......10-20 68

HOWARD, George R&B '83
(With Gwen Guthrie)
Singles: 12-inch
MCA.......4-6 86
Singles: 7-inch
MCA.......3-4 86-90
PALO ALTO.......3-4 83
TBA.......3-4 84-86
LPs: 10/12-inch
GRP.......5-8 91
MCA.......5-10 86-90
PALO ALTO.......5-10 83
TBA.......5-10 84-86
Also see GUTHRIE, Gwen

HOWARD, Gregory
Singles: 7-inch
KAPP (536 "When in Love").......100-200 63
(Black label.)
KAPP (536 "When in Love").......50-100 63
(White label. Promotional issue only.)
Copies of *When in Love* on Gee, credited to the Gee-Tones, are boots from the mid-'70s.
Session: Cadillacs.
Also see CADILLACS

HOWARD, Harlan C&W '71
Singles: 7-inch
CAPITOL.......5-10 61
MONUMENT.......4-8 64-65
NUGGET.......3-5 71
RCA.......4-6 67
LPs: 10/12-inch
CAPITOL (1631 "Harlan Howard Sings Harland Howard").......20-40 61
MONUMENT.......15-25 65
NUGGET.......10-20 71
RCA.......15-25 67-68

HOWARD, James Newton
LPs: 10/12-inch
KAMA SUTRA.......8-10 75
SHEFFIELD.......8-10

HOWARD, Jan C&W '60
Singles: 7-inch
CHALLENGE.......5-10 60
CAPITOL.......4-8 63
CON BRIO.......3-5 77-78
DECCA.......4-6 65-72
GRT.......3-5 74
LPs: 10/12-inch
A.V.I.......5-8 83-84
CAPITOL.......15-25 62
CORAL.......5-10 73
DECCA.......10-20 66-72
FIRST GENERATION.......5-10 81
FORUM.......10-15
GRT.......6-12 75-76
PHONORAMA.......5-8 83
PICKWICK/HILLTOP.......6-12 60s
TOWER.......15-20 67-68
WRANGLER.......10-20 62
Session: Jordanaires.
Also see ANDERSON, Bill, & Jan Howard
Also see JORDANAIRES
Also see STEWART, Wynn, & Jan Howard

HOWARD, Jeff
Singles: 7-inch
TITAN.......4-8 61

HOWARD, Jerry
Singles: 7-inch
DITTO.......5-10 61
IMPERIAL.......5-10 59
LPs: 10/12-inch
IMPERIAL.......15-25 60s

HOWARD, Jim C&W '64
Singles: 7-inch
DEL-MAR.......4-6 64

HOWARD, Johnny
Singles: 7-inch
DELUXE (6044 "Vacation Blues").......50-75 53

HOWARD, Johnny
Singles: 7-inch
BASHIE (101 "I Miss My Lady").......4-8

HOWARD, Lenny
Singles: 7-inch
REAL GEORGE (501 "Keep the Faith Baby").......10-20

HOWARD, Meredith
Singles: 7-inch
RCA (0028 "Easy Come, Easy Go Blues").......25-50 49
(Colored vinyl.)
RCA (0044 "Cold Potato").......25-50 49
(Colored vinyl.)

HOWARD, Miki R&B '86
Singles: 7-inch
ATLANTIC.......3-4 86-90
LPs: 10/12-inch
ATLANTIC.......5-10 86-90
Also see SIDE EFFECT

HOWARD, Miki, & Gerald Levert R&B '88
Singles: 7-inch
ATLANTIC.......3-4 88
Also see HOWARD, Miki

HOWARD, Paul, & Ralph Willis
LPs: 10/12-inch
KING.......8-10 70

HOWARD, Paul Mason
Singles
("This Is How the Shrimp Boats Was Born").......15-20 50s
(Square cardboard picture disc. No label name or selection number used.)

HOWARD, Randy C&W '83
Singles: 7-inch
ATLANTIC AMERICA.......3-4 88
W.B.......3-5 83

HOWARD, Rosetta R&B '48
(With the Big Three Trio)
Singles: 78 rpm
COLUMBIA.......8-15 48-55
Singles: 7-inch
COLUMBIA.......15-25 51-55
Also see BIG THREE TRIO

HOWARD, Trustin
Singles: 7-inch
AMERICAN.......4-8 66
REPRISE.......4-8 63

HOWARD, Van
Singles: 78 rpm
IMPERIAL (8245 "My Tears").......10-20 54
Singles: 7-inch
IMPERIAL (8245 "My Tears").......20-30 54

HOWARD, Vince, & Vin-Ettes
Singles: 7-inch
BIG R.......4-8

HOWARD, Willie, & Chordells
Singles: 7-inch
MASCOT (127 "Louise").......250-500 58

HOWARD & HARRY
Singles: 7-inch
GOLDEN EARS (1 "Howard & Harry").......4-6 73

HOWARDS
Singles: 7-inch
ABC-PAR.......8-12 58

HOWDY MOON
Singles: 7-inch
A&M.......3-5 74
LPs: 10/12-inch
A&M.......8-10 74

HOWE, Darrell
Singles: 7-inch
JAMIE.......10-15 59

HOWE, Steve, Band LP '75
Singles: 7-inch
ATLANTIC.......3-5 75-79
LPs: 10/12-inch
ATLANTIC.......5-10 75-79
Also see ASIA
Also see GTR
Also see YES

HOWELL, Loyd
Singles: 7-inch
HI-Q (3756 "Truck Driving Jack").......20-30
NASHVILLE (5028 "Little Froggy").......150-200 61

HOWELL, Ruben
Singles: 7-inch
MOTOWN.......3-5 74

HOWES, O'Neil
Singles: 7-inch
DART.......5-10 59

HOWIE & CRYSTALS
Singles: 7-inch
FLEETWOOD (4521 "Rockin' Hall").......10-20 62

HOWIE & MEL
Singles: 7-inch
ROCK-A-BYE.......4-8 63

HOWIE & SAPPHIRES
Singles: 7-inch
OKEH (7112 "More Than the Day Before").......20-30 59
Member: Howard Guyton.
Also see GUY, Bobby

HOWL THE GOOD
LPs: 10/12-inch
RARE EARTH.......10-12 72

HOWLIN' BANANA
Singles: 7-inch
1-SHOT.......4-8 74

HOWLIN' WOLF R&B '51
("The Howlin' Wolf"; Chester Burnett)
Singles: 78 rpm
CHESS (1479 "Moanin' at Midnight").......25-50 51
CHESS (1497 "Howlin' Wolf Boogie").......25-50 52
CHESS (1515 "Saddle My Pony").......25-50 52
CHESS (1528 thru 1695).......20-30 53-58
CHESS (1712 "I'm Leaving You").......50-75 58
CHESS (1726 "Howlin' Blues").......50-100 59
CHESS (1735 "I've Been Abused").......75-125 59

RPM (333 "Riding in the Moonlight")......50-75 51
RPM (340 "Passing By Blues")......50-75 51
RPM (347 "My Baby Stole Off")......50-75 51

Singles: 7-inch

CADET CONCEPT (7013 "Evil")...... 4-8 69
CHESS (1528 "My Last Affair")....75-100 53
CHESS (1557 "All Night Boogie") ...50-75 53
CHESS (1566 "No Place to Go")...40-60 54
CHESS (1575 "Baby How Long") ...40-60 54
CHESS (1584 "I'll Be Around")......25-50 55
CHESS (1593 "Who Will Be Next")......25-50 55
CHESS (1607 "Come to Me Baby")......15-25 55
CHESS (1618 "Smokestack Lightning")......15-25 56
CHESS (1632 "I Asked for Water")......15-25 56
CHESS (1648 "Going Back Home")......15-25 57
CHESS (1668 "Somebody in My Home")......15-25 57
CHESS (1679 "Sitting on Top of the World")......15-25 57
CHESS (1695 "I Didn't Know")......15-25 58
CHESS (1712 "I'm Leaving You") ..10-20 58
CHESS (1744 "You Gonna Wreck My Life")......10-20 59
CHESS (1750 "Who's Been Talking")......10-20 60
CHESS (1753 "I've Been Abused") 10-20 60
CHESS (1762 "Spoonful")......10-20 61
CHESS (1777 "Back Door Man") ...10-20 61
CHESS (1793 "Little Baby")......10-20 61
CHESS (1804 thru 1968) 8-15 61-66
CHESS (2000 series)...... 4-8 67-71

LPs: 10/12-inch

CADET (319 "New Album")......10-15 69
CHESS (201 "Howlin' Wolf")...... 8-12 76
CHESS (418 "Change My Way") ... 8-12 77
CHESS (1434 "Moaning in the Moonlight")......100-200 58
(Black label.)
CHESS (1469 "Howlin' Wolf")......50-100 62
(Black label.)
CHESS (1469 "Howlin' Wolf")....200-300 62
(White label. Promotional issue only.)
CHESS (1502 "Real Folk Blues")...15-25 66
CHESS (1512 "More Real Folk Blues")......15-25 67
CHESS (1540 "Evil")......15-20 69
CHESS (50002 "Message to the Young")......10-12 71
CHESS (50015 "Live & Cookin'") ..10-12 72
CHESS (50045 "Back Door Wolf")..10-12 74
CHESS (60008 "The London Howlin' Wolf Sessions")......10-12 71
CHESS (60016 "Howlin' Wolf AKA Chester Burnett")......10-12 72
CHESS/MCA (Except 9332) 5-8 89
CHESS/MCA (9332 "Howlin' Wolf")......35-45 91
(Boxed, five-disc set. Includes 32-page booklet.)
CROWN (5240 "Howlin' Wolf Sings the Blues")......15-20 62
CUSTOM (2055 "Big City Blues") ..10-12 60s
KENT (526 "Original Folk Blues")...10-15 67
RPM (340 "Passing By Blues")......1500-2500 51
RPM (347 "My Baby Stole Off") .100-200 51
UNITED (7717 "Big City Blues")...... 8-10
UNITED (7747 "Original Folk Blues")...... 8-10
Session: James Cotton; Ike Turner; Willie Steel; Pat Hare; Willie Johnson; Fred Below; Hubert Sumlin; Lee Cooper; Willie Dixon; Hosea Lee Kennard; Jody Williams; Earl Phillips.
Also see BERRY, Chuck, & Howlin' Wolf
Also see COTTON, James
Also see DIDDLEY, Bo, Howlin' Wolf & Muddy Waters
Also see DIXON, Willie
Also see ROBINSON, Freddy
Also see TURNER, Ike
Also see WATERS, Muddy, & Howlin' Wolf

HOWLIN' WOLF JR.

Singles: 7-inch

FAY...... 8-12

HOYLE, Johnnie

Singles: 7-inch

RAY-BO (105 "What About Me")...15-25

HUANG CHUNG: see WANG CHUNG

HUB

Singles: 7-inch

CAPITOL...... 3-5 76

LPs: 10/12-inch

CAPITOL...... 8-10 75-76
Members: Peter Hoorelbeke; Michael Urso; Gil Bridges.
Also see RARE EARTH

HUB KAPP & WHEELS

Singles: 7-inch

CAPITOL (5215 "Sigh, Cry, Almost Die")...... 8-12 64
TAKE FIVE (631 "Let's Really Hear It")......10-20 63
FRAMAGRATZ......10-15 63

Picture Sleeves

CAPITOL (5215 "Sigh, Cry, Almost Die")......10-20 64
TAKE FIVE (631 "Let's Really Hear It")......15-25 63
Members: Pat McMahon; Michael Condello.
Also see CONDELLO
Also see FAAN

HUBBARD, Freddie — LP '73

Singles: 12-inch

FANTASY...... 4-8 81

Singles: 7-inch

ATLANTIC...... 3-5 69
BLUE NOTE...... 4-8 61-64
COLUMBIA...... 3-7 74-76

LPs: 10/12-inch

ATLANTIC......8-15 67-76
BLUE NOTE......15-25 60-65
(Label reads "Blue Note Records Inc. - New York, U.S.A.")
BLUE NOTE......8-15 66-76
(Label shows Blue Note Records as a division of either Liberty or United Artists.)
CTI......6-12 70-75
COLUMBIA......5-10 74-83
ELEKTRA...... 5-8 82
ENJA...... 5-8 81
FANTASY...... 5-8 81-83
IMPULSE......10-20 63-73
LIBERTY...... 5-8 81
PABLO...... 5-8 82-83
PAUSA...... 5-8 82

HUBBARD, Freddie, & Oscar Peterson

LPs: 10/12-inch

PABLO......5-10 80
Also see PETERSON, Oscar

HUBBARD, Freddie, & Stanley Turrentine

LPs: 10/12-inch

CTI......6-12 74
Also see HUBBARD, Freddie
Also see TURRENTINE, Stanley

HUBBARD, Mother: see MOTHER HUBBARD

HUBBARD, Muvva "Guitar"

Singles: 7-inch

ABC-PAR......5-10 56-58

HUBBARD, Orangie

Singles: 7-inch

KING...... 5-8 68
LEE (4009 "In Search of You")...... 4-6 79
LUCKY (0007 "Look What I Found")......85-100 60

HUBBELL, Hal — C&W '78

Singles: 7-inch

50 STATES...... 3-5 78

HUBBELL, Frank, & Hubbcaps

Singles: 7-inch

TOPIX......10-20 63

HUBBELS

Singles: 7-inch

AUDIO FIDELITY...... 3-6 69

HUBCAPS

Singles: 7-inch

BRUNSWICK......8-12 59

HUBCAPS

Singles: 7-inch

LAURIE (3219 "Hot Rod City")......10-20 65
Members: Ernie Maresca; Tom Bogdany.
Also see MARESCA, Ernie

HUBCAPS

Singles: 7-inch

TSMB...... 3-5 84-89

Picture Sleeves

TSMB...... 3-5 84

LPs: 10/12-inch

TSMB......10-15 84

HUCKLEBERRY HOUND: see BUTLER, Daws

HUDDERSFIELD TRANSIT AUTHORITY

Singles: 7-inch

DECCA...... 3-5 71

HUDDLE, Jack

(With Buddy Holly)

Singles: 7-inch

KAPP (207 "Starlight")......75-125 58
PETSY (1002 "Starlight")......250-350 58
Also see HOLLY, Buddy
Also see JACK & JIM

HUDGINS, Joe

Singles: 7-inch

ANTENNA (6437 "Where'd You Stay Last Night")......20-30 59
DECCA (30854 "Where'd You Stay Last Night")......10-15 59
ROBBINS (1005 "Where'd You Stay Last Night")......40-50 58

HUDMON, R.B., Jr. — R&B '76

Singles: 7-inch

ATLANTIC...... 3-5 76-77
CAPITOL...... 3-5 71
COTILLION...... 3-5 78
1-2-3...... 3-6 68-70

LPs: 10/12-inch

COTILLION......5-10 78

HUDSON

Singles: 7-inch

ELEKTRA...... 3-4 80
LIONEL...... 3-5 71
PLAYBOY...... 3-5 73
ROCKET...... 3-5 73

LPs: 10/12-inch

ELEKTRA......5-10 80
Members: Bill Hudson; Brett Hudson; Mark Hudson.
Also see HUDSON BROTHERS

HUDSON, Al — R&B '76

(With the Soul Partners)

Singles: 12-inch

ABC......4-8 77

Singles: 7-inch

ABC......3-5 76-79
ATCO......3-5 75-76

LPs: 10/12-inch

ABC......8-10 77
Also see ONE WAY

HUDSON, David — P&R/R&B/LP '80

Singles: 7-inch

ALSTON......3-4 80

LPs: 10/12-inch

ALSTON......5-10 80

HUDSON, Doug

Singles: 78 rpm

MGM......5-10 57

Singles: 7-inch

MGM......10-15 57

HUDSON, Eddie

Singles: 7-inch

EXCELLO (2135 "She's Sugar Sweet")......15-20 58

HUDSON, "Emperor" Bob, & Lawrence Welk

Singles: 7-inch

RANWOOD......3-5 72
Also see HUDSON & LANDRY
Also see WELK, Lawrence

HUDSON, G.L., & COMPANY

Singles: 7-inch

GM (15 "Super Rock")......4-8

HUDSON, George, & Kings of Twist

LPs: 10/12-inch

CAPITOL......10-15 61

HUDSON, Glinda

Singles: 7-inch

SMALLTOWN (300 "I'll Wait") 20-30

HUDSON, Helen — C&W '79

Singles: 7-inch

CYCLONE......3-5 79

HUDSON, Jerry

Singles: 7-inch

BIG TREE......3-5 72
Also see ROAD

HUDSON, Joe, & His Rockin' Dukes

Singles: 78 rpm

EXCELLO......10-20 57

Singles: 7-inch

EXCELLO (2112 "Baby Give Me a Chance")......20-30 57

HUDSON, Johnny

Singles: 7-inch

CHALLENGE......5-10 59

HUDSON, Larry G. — C&W '76

Singles: 7-inch

AQUARIAN......3-5 76
LONE STAR......3-5 78-79
MERCURY......3-4 80

HUDSON, Lavine

Singles: 7-inch

VIRGIN......3-4 88

HUDSON, Little: see LITTLE HUDSON

HUDSON, Pookie — P&R '63

(With the Spaniels)

Singles: 7-inch

CHESS......5-10 66
DOUBLE-L (711 "I Know, I Know")......10-20 63
DOUBLE-L (720 "Miracles")......10-20 63
JAMIE (1319 "This Gets to Me") 25-50 66
NEPTUNE (124 "For Sentimental Reasons")......15-20 61
PARKWAY (839 "Turn Out the Lights")......10-15 62
Also see SPANIELS

HUDSON, Ray, & Rhythmaires

Singles: 7-inch

DIXIE (1043 "Jackhammer")......15-25 58

HUDSON, Rock

Singles: 7-inch

DECCA (30966 "Pillow Talk") 5-10 59

Picture Sleeves

DECCA (30966 "Pillow Talk") 10-15 59

LPs: 10/12-inch

STANYAN......10-15 71
Also see MARTIN, Dean / Rock Hudson

HUDSON, Tommy

(With the Savoys)

Singles: 7-inch

D (1073 "Swanee River Gal")......50-75 59
WHITE ROCK (1110 "Rock-It")......50-75 58

HUDSON & COMPANY

Singles: 7-inch

G.M......3-5

HUDSON & LANDRY — P&R/LP '71

Singles: 7-inch

DORE......3-5 71-74

LPs: 10/12-inch

DORE (Except 326)......10-20 71-77
DORE (326 "Losing Their Heads") ...8-12 77
(Picture disc.)
Members: Bob Hudson; Ron Landry.
Also see EMPEROR
Also see HUDSON, "Emperor" Bob, & Lawrence Welk

HUDSON BROTHERS — P&R/LP '74

Singles: 7-inch

ARISTA......3-5 76-78
CASABLANCA......3-5 74
MCA/ROCKET......3-5 74-76

Picture Sleeves

MCA/ROCKET......3-5 75

LPs: 10/12-inch

CASABLANCA......8-10 74
PLAYBOY......8-10 72
MCA/ROCKET......8-10 74-75
Members: Bill Hudson; Brett Hudson; Mark Hudson.
Also see EVERYDAY HUDSON
Also see HUDSON
Also see NEW YORKERS

HUDSON - FORD

Singles: 7-inch

A&M......3-5 73-75

LPs: 10/12-inch

A&M (3652 "Free Spirit")......8-12 74
A&M (4535 "Worlds Collide")......8-12 77
Also see STRAWBS

HUDSON VALLEY BOYS

Singles: 7-inch

SESSION......15-25 60

HUERTA, Baldemar

(El Bebop Kid)

Singles: 7-inch

FALCON (838 "Encaje De Chantilly [Chantilly Lace]")......15-25 58
Also see FENDER, Freddy

HUES CORPORATION — P&R '73

Singles: 7-inch

RCA......3-5 73-75
W.B......3-5 77

LPs: 10/12-inch

RCA......8-10 73-77
W.B......5-10 77-78
Members: St. Clair Lee; H. Ann Kelly; Tommy Brown; Karl Russell; Fleming Williams.

HUESTON, Lou

Singles: 7-inch

AVANT GARDE (101 "Last Kiss I Remember")......5-8 65

HUESTON, Mel

Singles: 7-inch

CHANSON (1179 "Double Confusion")......10-20
Also see UNLIMITED FOUR

HUEY, Richard

Singles: 78 rpm

DECCA......10-15 43

HUEY & CURLEY

Singles: 7-inch

ACE......5-10 63
Member: Huey Smith.
Also see SMITH, Huey

HUEY & JERRY

Singles: 7-inch

VIN (1000 "Little Chickie Wah Wah")......8-12 58
Member: Huey Smith; Jerry Vincent.
Also see SMITH, Huey

HUEYS

Singles: 7-inch

INSTANT......4-6 68

HUFF, Leon — R&B '80

(Leon "Fingers" Huff)

Singles: 7-inch

JAMIE (1254 "Soul City")......15-25 62
PHILLY INT'L......4-6 80-81
Also see HOLDER, Pervis / Leon Huff
Also see MFSB
Also see ROMEOS

HUFF, Luther

Singles: 78 rpm

TRUMPET (132 "Dirty Disposition")......15-25 50
TRUMPET (141 "Rosalie Blues")...15-25 50

HUFF, Terry — R&B '76

(With Special Delivery)

Singles: 7-inch

MAINSTREAM......3-5 76
PHILADELPHIA INT'L......3-4 80

LPs: 10/12-inch

MAINSTREAM......5-10 76
Also see SPECIAL DELIVERY

HUFF, Willie B.

Singles: 78 rpm

BIG TOWN......15-25 53
RHYTHM......15-25 53

Singles: 7-inch

BIG TOWN (105 "I Love You Baby")......50-75 53
RHYTHM (1770 "Beggar Man Blues")......50-75 53

HUFFMAN, Donnie

Singles: 7-inch

TAURUS......8-10 62
Also see DONNIE & DELCHORDS

HUFFMAN, Paul

Singles: 7-inch

WINSTON......15-25 57

HUGGER

LPs: 10/12-inch

COLUMBIA......5-10 84
FINAL VINYL......10-12 80

HUGGY'S ORR

Singles: 7-inch

MINIT ("Help Wanted")......20-30 60s

HUGH, Grayson — LP '88

Singles: 7-inch

RCA......3-4 89-90

Picture Sleeves

RCA......3-4 89

LPs: 10/12-inch

RCA......5-8 88

HUGH, Grayson, & Betty Wright

Singles: 7-inch

RCA......3-4 89
Also see HUGH, Grayson
Also see WRIGHT, Betty

HUGH T. & JOHNNY

Singles: 7-inch

ASTRO (103 "Shirley Shirley") 10-15 60

HUGHES, Ben

(With the Twigs; with René Hall's Orchestra)

Singles: 78 rpm

HOLLYWOOD......15-25
SPECIALTY......20-30 58

Singles: 7-inch

HOLLYWOOD (1014 "Someday, Somewhere, Somewhere")......75-125 54
SPECIALTY (616 "I Need Someone to Love Me")......15-25 58
SPECIALTY (630 "Sack")......15-25 58
TRUE (101 "Crazy Man")......10-20 59
Also see HALL, René
Also see HAYES, Linda
Also see WOODS, Sonny

HUGHES, Bobby, & Pretzels

Singles: 7-inch

HIGHLAND (1010 "Berlin Bounce") 8-10 60

HUGHES, Carol

Singles: 7-inch

CARLTON......4-8 62
RCA......5-10 59
ROULETTE......5-10 58

HUGHES, Fred

Singles: 78 rpm

COLUMBIA......3-5

HUGHES, Fred — P&R/R&B '65

(With the Chevelles; Freddie Hughes)

Singles: 7-inch

BRUNSWICK......4-8 69-71
CADET......5-10 68
COLLECTABLES......3-4 81
EXODUS (2006 "We've Got Love") .5-10 66
HAPPY FOX (504 "Will You Be There")......4-6
MINASA (709 "One Step Too Far")......15-25 65
VEE JAY (684 "Oo Wee Baby, I Love You")......8-12 65
VEE JAY (703 "You Can't Take It Away")......8-12 65
VEE JAY (718 "Don't Let Me Down")......8-12 66
WAND......6-12 68-69
WEE......4-8

LPs: 10/12-inch

BRUNSWICK (754157 "Bad Boy").10-15 70
WAND (664 "Send My Baby Back")......10-20 68

HUGHES, Hollie — C&W '87

Singles: 7-inch

LUV......3-4 87

HUGHES, Jimmy — P&R/R&B '64

Singles: 7-inch

ATLANTIC......5-10 68
COLLECTABLES......3-5 81
FAME......8-12 64-67
GUYDEN......8-12 62
JAMIE (1280 "My Loving Time")....10-15 64
VOA (4002 "I Like Everything About Him")......8-12
VOLT......5-10 69-71

LPs: 10/12-inch

ATCO (209 "Why Not Tonight")......15-20 67
STAX......5-10 85
VEE JAY (1102 "Steal Away") 20-30 64
VOLT (6003 "Something Special").10-20 69

HUGHES, Joe, & His Orchestra

Singles: 7-inch

KANGAROO (106 "Make Me Dance Little Ant")......100-150

HUGHES, Glenn, & D'Lighters

Singles: 7-inch

DYNASTY......5-10 59

HUGHES, Jeff

Singles: 7-inch

KAREN......4-8 62
TILLIS......4-8 62

HUGHES, Joel — C&W '82

Singles: 7-inch

SUNBIRD......3-4 82

HUGHES, Johnny

Singles: 7-inch

UBC......4-8 61

HUGHES, Judy

Singles: 7-inch

CRUSADER (128 "Ocean of Emotion")......40-60 66
VAULT (917 "Crazy for You") 20-30 65

HUGHES, Lynne

Singles: 7-inch

MERCURY......4-6 70

LPs: 10/12-inch
FONTANA 10-12 70
Also see CHARLATANS
Also see STONEGROUND
Also see TONGUE & GROOVE

HUGHES, Marvin
Singles: 7-inch
CAPITOL 4-8 63

HUGHES, Pee Wee, & Delta Duo
Singles: 78 rpm
DELUXE (3228 "Country Boy") 20-40 49

HUGHES, Rhetta R&B '69
Singles: 12-inch
ARIA 4-6 83
Singles: 7-inch
ARIA 3-4 83
COLUMBIA 4-6 67-68
SUTRA 3-4 80
TETRAGRAMMATON 4-6 68-69
LPs: 10/12-inch
SUTRA 5-10 80
TETRAGRAMMATON 10-12 69

HUGHES, Rhetta, & Tennyson Stephens
LPs: 10/12-inch
COLUMBIA 12-18 65
Also see HUGHES, Rhetta
Also see STEPHENS, Tennyson

HUGHES, Sid
Singles: 7-inch
McCARSON COOK 5-8 77
EMBER 5-10 57

HUGHES, Wally
Singles: 78 rpm
EMBER 8-12 57
Singles: 7-inch
COLUMBIA 5-10 58
EMBER 8-12 57

HUGHES - THRALL P&R '82
Singles: 7-inch
BOULEVARD 3-4 82
Members: Glenn Hughes; Pat Thrall.

HUGHLEY, George
Singles: 7-inch
GAYE 5-10 64

HUGO & LUIGI P&R '55
(Hugo & Luigi Chorus)
Singles: 78 rpm
MERCURY 3-5 55-56
Singles: 7-inch
MERCURY 5-10 55-56
RCA 4-8 59-60
ROULETTE 4-8 58
Picture Sleeves
ROULETTE 5-10 58
LPs: 10/12-inch
FORUM 5-10 60
MERCURY 5-15 56
RCA 5-10 60-63
ROULETTE 5-12 59
WING 5-10 60
Members: Hugo Peretti; Luigi Creatore.

HUGO & TONIO
Singles: 7-inch
VIK-TRO (32101 "Hi-Way Ramble") 10-15

HUHN, Billy, & Catalinas
Singles: 7-inch
LESLEY 15-20 63

HULIN, T.K. P&R '63
Singles: 7-inch
SMASH (1830 "I'm Not a Fool Anymore") 4-8 63
L.K. (1001 "Little Bitty Boy") 100-200 60
L.K. (1116 "On Lonely Street") 15-25 62
L.K. (1118 "As You Pass Me By") 15-25 62
L.K. (1119 "Baby, Be My Steady") 15-25 63
LPs: 10/12-inch
STARFLITE 20-30

HULL, Gene
Singles: 7-inch
COLUMBIA 4-6 67
Picture Sleeves
COLUMBIA 4-8 67

HULL, Martha
(With the Steady Jobs; Tex Rubinowitz)
Singles: 7-inch
RIPSAW 3-4 81
EPs: 7-inch
WASP (33 "First Time") 5-10 82
(Selection number not known.)
Members: Martha Hull; Mark Matarese; David Van Allen; Doug Corbin; Michael Vincent.
Also see RUBINOWITZ, Tex

HULL, Terry, & Starfires
Singles: 7-inch
STAFF (103 "Those Pretty Brown Eyes") 500-750

HULLABALOO SINGERS & ORCHESTRA
LPs: 10/12-inch
COLUMBIA 10-15 65

HULLABALOOS P&R '64
Singles: 7-inch
ROULETTE 5-10 64-65
Picture Sleeves
ROULETTE 10-20 64-65
LPs: 10/12-inch
ROULETTE (25297 "England's Newest Singing Sensations") 25-30 65
ROULETTE (25310 "The Hullabaloos on Hullabaloo") 25-30 65

HULLY GULLY BOYS
Singles: 7-inch
AMY (800 "Yabba") 4-8 60

HUMAN BEINGS
Singles: 7-inch
IMPACT ("An Inside Look") 20-30 66
(No selection number used.)
IMPACT (1006 "You're Bad News") 20-30 65
IMPACT (1022 "I Can Tell") 10-15 66
W.B. (5622 "Because I Love Her") 5-10 65

HUMAN BEINZ P&R '67
(Human Beingz; with the Mammals)
Singles: 7-inch
CAPITOL 5-8 67-69
ELYSIAN (3376 "Hey Joe") 15-25 67
ELYSIAN (8687 "My Generation") 15-25 66
GATEWAY (828 "Gloria") 5-10 68
GATEWAY (838 "My Generation") 5-10 68
Picture Sleeves
CAPITOL (2119 "Turn on Your Lovelight") 10-15 68
LPs: 10/12-inch
CAPITOL (2906 "Nobody But Me") 15-25 68
CAPITOL (2926 "Evolutions") 25-35 68
GATEWAY (3012 "Nobody But Me") 25-35 68
Members: Richard Belley; Mel Pachuta; Mike Tatman; Ting Markulin.

HUMAN BODY R&B '84
Singles: 7-inch
BEARSVILLE 3-4 84

HUMAN EXPRESSION
Singles: 7-inch
ACCENT (1214 "Every Night") 25-50 67
ACCENT (1226 "Optical Sound") 25-50 67

HUMAN INSTINCT
Singles: 7-inch
TIME 5-10 69

HUMAN JUNGLE
Singles: 7-inch
DOUBLE SHOT 4-8 67

HUMAN LEAGUE P&R/LP '82
Singles: 12-inch
A&M 4-6 82-86
Singles: 7-inch
A&M 3-4 82-86
Picture Sleeves
A&M 3-4 82-85
LPs: 10/12-inch
A&M 5-10 82-86
Members: Phil Oakey; Craig Marsh; Martyn Ware; Colin Thurston.
Also see HEAVEN 17
Also see LEAGUE UNLIMITED ORCHESTRA
Also see MORODER, Giorgio, & Phil Oakey

HUMAN SEXUAL RESPONSE
Singles: 12-inch
PASSPORT 4-6 84
LPs: 10/12-inch
PASSPORT 5-10 84

HUMAN SWITCHBOARD
LPs: 10/12-inch
FAULTY PRODUCTS 5-10 82

HUMAN ZOO
LPs: 10/12-inch
ACCENT 8-10

HUMANE SOCIETY
Singles: 7-inch
LIBERTY (55968 "Knock Knock") 10-20 67

HUMANS
Singles: 7-inch
AUDITION (6109 "Warning") 20-30 66

HUMANS
LPs: 10/12-inch
I.R.S. 5-10 81

HUMBLE GATHERING
Singles: 7-inch
STANG (5040 "Lora") 4-8 69
LPs: 10/12-inch
STANG ("Humble Gathering") 10-15 69
Members: Brian Humble; Jack Vallati.
Also see INTENTIONS

HUMBLE MIND
Singles: 7-inch
MUDWERK (10001 "African Judy") 25-35 60s
Also see LITTER
Also see STRANGELOVES

HUMBLE PIE P&R/LP '71
Singles: 7-inch
A&M 3-5 71-75
ATCO 3-4 80
IMMEDIATE 4-8 69
Picture Sleeves
A&M 4-8 71-72
LPs: 10/12-inch
A&M 8-12 70-82
ACCORD 5-10 82
ATCO 5-10 80-81
IMMEDIATE 10-15 68-72
Members: Steve Marriott; Peter Frampton; Greg Ridley; B.J. Cole; Jerry Shirley; Lyn Dobson; Dave Clempson.
Also see FASTWAY
Also see FRAMPTON, Peter
Also see MARRIOTT, Steve
Also see NATURAL GAS
Also see SMALL FACES

HUMBLEBUMS
Singles: 7-inch
U.A. 4-6 71
LPs: 10/12-inch
LIBERTY 10-12 70
Members: Bill Connolly; Ron Rae; Tim Harvey; Terry Cox; Gerry Rafferty.
Also see RAFFERTY, Gerry

HUMDINGERS
Singles: 78 rpm
DALE 8-12 57
Singles: 7-inch
DALE 8-12 57

HUMDINGERS
Singles: 7-inch
DONNA 5-10 63
JAYE JOSEPH 10-20 63
Members: Larry Bright; Mike Rubini.
Also see BRIGHT, Larry

HUMES, Anita
(With the Essex)
Singles: 7-inch
ROULETTE 5-15 64-67
LPs: 10/12-inch
ROULETTE 15-20 64
Also see ESSEX

HUMES, Bill
Singles: 7-inch
BEE HIVE (11504 "Bahama Isle") 10-15

HUMES, Helen R&B '45
(With the Bill Doggett Octet)
Singles: 78 rpm
ALADDIN 10-20 45
DECCA 10-15 52
MODERN (779 "I'm Gonna Let Him Ride") 20-40 50
Singles: 7-inch
DECCA (28113 "They Raided the Joint") 20-30 52
MODERN (779 "I'm Gonna Let Him Ride") 50-100 50
LPs: 10/12-inch
COLUMBIA 8-10
Members (Octet): Bill Doggett; Johnny Brown; Bill Moore; Ernest Thompson; Ross Butler; Alfred Moore; Charles Harris; Elmer Warner.
Also see DOGGETT, Bill
Also see MILTON, Roy

HUMMEL, Ray
(Ray Hummel III)
Singles: 7-inch
FENTON (2188 "Fine Day") 15-25 67
RENEGADE 3-5 78-83
Picture Sleeves
FENTON (2188 "Fine Day") 20-30 67
Also see JUJUs

HUMMERS C&W '73
Singles: 7-inch
CAPITOL 3-5 73-74

HUMMINGBIRD
Singles: 7-inch
A&M 3-5 76-77
LPs: 10/12-inch
A&M 8-10 75-77
Members: Madeline Bell; Robert Ahwal.
Also see BELL, Madeline

HUMMINGBIRDS
(Humming Birds)
Singles: 7-inch
CANNON (4600 "You and Me") 15-25 62
PANETTE 5-10 61

HUMMINGBIRDS
(Humming Birds)
Singles: 7-inch
JERDEN 5-8 64

HUMOROUS DIANE
Singles: 7-inch
VELTONE (712 "Interview with Mr. K.") 10-15 62

HUMPERDINCK, Engelbert P&R/LP '67
(Gerry Dorsey)
Singles: 12-inch
EPIC/CBS (35020 "Last of the Romantics") 50-70 76
(Picture disc. Promotional issue only.)
Singles: 7-inch
EH (1 "For My Friends") 10-15
(Promotional issue only.)
EPIC 3-5 76-83
PARROT 3-6 67-73
Picture Sleeves
PARROT 3-6 67-71
EPs: 7-inch
PARROT 5-10 67-69
(Juke box issues.)
LPs: 10/12-inch
EPIC 5-10 76-83
LONDON 5-10 77
PARROT 5-15 67-77
TEE VEE 5-10
(TV mail order offer.)
Also see DORSEY, Gerry

HUMPHREY, Bobbi R&B/LP '74
Singles: 12-inch
EPIC 4-8 78-79
Singles: 7-inch
BLUE NOTE 3-5 71-76
EPIC 3-5 77-79
LPs: 10/12-inch
BLUE NOTE 5-10 71-76
EPIC 5-10 78-79

HUMPHREY, Della P&R/R&B '68
Singles: 7-inch
ARCTIC 4-6 68

HUMPHREY, Paul, & His Cool Aid Chemists P&R/R&B/LP '71
Singles: 7-inch
LIZARD 3-6 70-71
LPs: 10/12-inch
LIZARD 8-12 71

HUMPHREY, Phil
(With the Fendermen)
Singles: 7-inch
DAB (0284 "Raindrops") 10-20 60s
SASSY (0284 "Popeye") 20-25 62
Also see FENDERMEN

HUMPHRIES, Earl
LPs: 10/12-inch
VERVE (V-6136 "Earl Humphries") 40-60 60
(Monaural.)
VERVE (VS-6136 "Earl Humphries") 50-75 60
(Stereo.)

HUMPHRIES, Frank "Fat Man," & 4 Notes
Singles: 78 rpm
JUBILEE (5085 "Lulubell Blues") 50-100 52
Singles: 7-inch
JUBILEE (5085 "Lulubell Blues") 175-225 52
Note: the 4 Notes were actually the Crows.
Also see CROWS

HUMPHRIES, Teddy R&B '59
Singles: 7-inch
KING (5000 series) 10-15 59-61
(Monaural.)
KING (S-5205 "What a Night") 20-30 59
(Stereo.)
Session: Mickey Baker.
Also see BAKER, Mickey

HUMPTY & IVANHOES
Singles: 7-inch
GRAMOPHONE 4-8 65

HUNG JURY
Singles: 7-inch
COLGEMS 4-8 67

HUNGATE, Congressman William, & Watergate Singers
Singles: 7-inch
PERCEPTION 4-8 73

HUNGER
Singles: 7-inch
PUBLIC (101 "Mind Machine") 15-25 68
PUBLIC (103 "No Shame") 15-25 68
PUBLIC (1001 "Colors") 15-25 69
LPs: 10/12-inch
PUBLIC (1006 "Strictly from Hunger") 400-600 69
Members: Mike Parkison; Mike Lane; Bill Daffem; Steve Hansen; Tom Tanory; John Morton.

HUNGRI I's
Singles: 7-inch
PARIS TOWER (127 "Half Your Life") 15-25 67

HUNGRY CHUCK
LPs: 10/12-inch
BEARSVILLE 8-10 72

HUNGRY IV
Singles: 7-inch
ERA 4-8 65

HUNGRY TIGER
Singles: 7-inch
WHITE WHALE 4-6 69
MAGNA GLIDE 3-5 77

HUNLEY, Con C&W '77
Singles: 7-inch
CAPITOL 3-4 84-86
MCA 3-4 83
PRAIRIE DUST (7600 series) 4-6 77
PRAIRIE DUST (84000 series) 3-4 77
W.B. 3-5 78-82
LPs: 10/12-inch
MCA (5423 "Once You Get the Feel of It") 10-15 83
W.B. 5-10 79-82
Session: Porter Wagoner.
Also see WAGONER, Porter

HUNNICUTT, Ed C&W '83
Singles: 7-inch
MCA 3-4 83-84

HUNS
Singles: 7-inch
PYRAMID (6646 "Shakedown") 15-25 66

HUNS
Singles: 7-inch
ROCK 'N' JAZZ (8668 "Destination Lonely") 30-50 66
(Blue label.)
ROCK 'N' JAZZ (8668 "Destination Lonely") 10-20 66
(Red label.)

HUNS OF TIME
Singles: 7-inch
MAGIC TOUCH (2070 "Walking in the Vineyards") 10-15 69
Also see ATTILA & HUNS

HUNT
LPs: 10/12-inch
VISA 5-10 80

HUNT, Clay
Singles: 7-inch
BAY SOUND (67005 "Your Love's Gone Bad") 10-20
LPs: 10/12-inch
POLYDOR 5-10 81

HUNT, D.A.
Singles: 78 rpm
SUN (183 "Lonesome Ol' Jail") 250-500 53

HUNT, Danny
Singles: 7-inch
DYNAMITE (8663 "What's Happening to Our Love Affair") 10-20

HUNT, Dennis
Singles: 7-inch
SAY (12 "A Story Untold") 40-60

HUNT, Geraldine R&B '70
Singles: 7-inch
ABC (10859 "Winner Take All") 15-25 67
BOMBAY (4501 "He's for Real") 50-75 64
CHECKER (1028 "I Let Myself Go") 10-20 62
PRISM 3-4 80
ROULETTE 4-6 70-73
U.S.A. (732 "Sneak Around") 15-25 62
U.S.A. (737 "Sneak Around") 10-20 63

HUNT, Geraldine, & Charlie Hodges
Singles: 7-inch
CALLA 4-6 70
Also see HODGES, Charles
Also see HUNT, Geraldine

HUNT, Granger, & Believers
Singles: 7-inch
JOSIE 5-10 64

HUNT, Lanny, & Themes
Singles: 7-inch
PANORAMA 5-10 66
STAR 20-30 65

HUNT, Pat
Singles: 7-inch
KENT 4-8 62

HUNT, Pee Wee P&R '48
Singles: 78 rpm
CAPITOL 3-5 48-57
Singles: 7-inch
CAPITOL 5-10 50-62
SAVOY 5-10 51
EPs: 7-inch
CAPITOL 5-10 50-56
SAVOY 5-10 51
LPs: 10/12-inch
CAPITOL 4-8 78
(With "SM" prefix.)
CAPITOL 15-30 50-63
(With "T" or "ST" prefix.)
GLENDALE 4-8 78
SAVOY (15042 "Dixieland") 25-35 54
(10-inch LP.)
TOPS 15-25 57
Also see BLANC, Mel
Also see FOUR KNIGHTS

HUNT, Ricky, & Hunters
Singles: 7-inch
KATHY (101 "His Shoulder") 15-25

HUNT, Skipper, Combo
Singles: 7-inch
GLENN (1900 "Scalded") 50-75

HUNT, Slim
Singles: 78 rpm
EXCELLO 50-75 55
Singles: 7-inch
EXCELLO (2005 "Welcome Home, Baby") 125-175 55

HUNT, Tommy P&R/R&B '61
Singles: 7-inch
ATLANTIC 4-8 65
CAPITOL 4-8 66
DYNAMO 4-8 67
SCEPTER 4-8 61-63
LPs: 10/12-inch
DYNAMO (8001 "Greatest Hits") 15-25 67
SCEPTER (506 "I Just Don't Know What to Do with Myself") 25-35 62
Also see FIVE ECHOES
Also see FLAMINGOS
Also see PLATTERS / Inez & Charlie Foxx / Jive Five / Tommy Hunt

HUNT, William
Singles: 7-inch
STREAMSIDE (100 "Would You Believe") 10-20

HUNT SISTERS
(Hunt Sisters & Mark)
Singles: 7-inch
FORTUNE (213 "I'm Not Going to Take It Anymore") 5-10 60
FORTUNE (210 "Elvis Is Rocking Again") 20-35 60
SAMPSON 3-5 61
Also see HALL, Roy

HUNTER, Bob
LPs: 10/12-inch
HUNTER ENTERPRISES 8-10 81

HUNTER, Christine
Singles: 7-inch
ROULETTE 8-12 64

HUNTER, Dean
Singles: 7-inch
CRYSTALETTE ... 5-10 59

HUNTER, Fluffy: see POWELL, Jesse

HUNTER, Herbert
Singles: 7-inch
HIT ... 5-15 60s
(Hit discs here may have other artists, such as Bill Austin or Joe Cash, on the flips.)
PONCELLO (711 "I'm So Satisfied") ... 10-20
SPAR (718 "Twistin' Party") ... 10-15 62
SPAR (723 "I Can't Help It") ... 10-20 62
SPAR (741 "Happy Go Lucky") ... 20-30 63
SPAR (9009 "I Was Born to Love You") ... 20-30

HUNTER, Ian LP '75
Singles: 7-inch
CHRYSALIS ... 3-4 79
COLUMBIA ... 3-5 75-83
LPs: 10/12-inch
CHRYSALIS ... 5-10 79-81
COLUMBIA ... 8-10 75-79
Also see MOTT the HOOPLE

HUNTER, Ian, & Mick Ronson LP '89
LPs: 10/12-inch
MERCURY ... 5-8 89
Also see HUNTER, Ian
Also see RONSON, Mick

HUNTER, Ivory Joe R&B '45
(With the Ivorytones)
Singles: 78 rpm
ATLANTIC ... 20-30 55-58
EXCLUSIVE ... 15-25 45
4 STAR ... 25-50 48-51
KING ... 10-20 47-57
MGM ... 10-15 49-54
PACIFIC ... 15-25 45-47
Singles: 7-inch
ATLANTIC ... 15-30 55-58
CAPITOL ... 5-10 61-62
DOT ... 15-25 58-59
GOLDISC ... 10-15 60
GOLDWAX (307 "Every Little Bit Helps") ... 15-25
JOIE ... 8-12
KING (4424 "False Friend Blues") .. 25-50 51
KING (4443 "She's Gone Blues") ... 25-50 51
KING (4455 "Old Gal and New Gal Blues") ... 25-50 51
KING (5280 "Guess Who") ... 10-15 59
MGM (500 series) ... 3-5 78
MGM (8011 "I Almost Lost My Mind") ... 25-50 49
MGM (10000 & 11000 series) ... 20-30 49-54
MGM (10578 "I Almost Lost My Mind") ... 25-50 49
PARAMOUNT ... 4-6 73
SMASH ... 5-10 63
SOUND STAGE 7 ... 4-8 68
STAX ... 5-10 64
VEE JAY ... 8-12 62
VEEP ... 5-10 67
EPs: 7-inch
ATLANTIC (589 "Ivory Joe Hunter") ... 50-75 58
ATLANTIC (608 "Rock with Ivory Joe Hunter") ... 50-75 58
KING (265 "Ivory Joe Hunter") ... 50-75 54
MGM (1376/7/8 "I Get That Lonesome Feeling") ... 20-40 57
(Price is for any of three volumes.)
LPs: 10/12-inch
ATLANTIC (8008 "Ivory Joe Hunter") ... 100-200 58
(Black Label.)
ATLANTIC (8008 "Ivory Joe Hunter") ... 50-100 59
(Red Label.)
ATLANTIC (8015 "Ivory Joe Hunter Sings the Old and the New") ... 100-150 58
(Black Label.)
ATLANTIC (8015 "Ivory Joe Hunter Sings the Old and the New") ... 50-100 59
(Red Label.)
DOT (3569 "This Is Ivory Joe Hunter") ... 25-35 64
(Monaural.)
DOT (25569 "This Is Ivory Joe Hunter") ... 30-40 64
(Stereo.)
EPIC ... 8-10 71
EVEREST ... 8-10 74
GOLDISC (403 "Fabulous Ivory Joe Hunter") ... 40-60 61
GRAND PRIX ... 10-15
HOME COOKING ... 5-10 89
KING (605 "16 Greatest Hits") ... 75-125 58
LION ... 15-25
MGM (3488 "I Get That Lonesome Feeling") ... 50-100 57
PARAMOUNT ... 8-10 74
SAGE (603 "Ivory Joe Hunter") ... 35-50 59
SMASH ... 15-20 63
SOUND (603 "Ivory Joe Hunter") ... 150-250 57
Also see CHARLES, Ray / Ivory Joe Hunter / Jimmy Rushing
Also see TURNER, Sammy / Ivory Joe Hunter

HUNTER, Ivory Joe / Memphis Slim
LPs: 10/12-inch
STRAND (1123 "The Artistry of Ivory Joe Hunter") ... 15-25
Also see HUNTER, Ivory Joe
Also see MEMPHIS SLIM

HUNTER, John
(Lost John Hunter & Blind Bats; Long John Hunter)
Singles: 78 rpm
4 STAR (1492 "Cool Down Mama") ... 20-40 50
4 STAR (1511 "Y-M and V Blues") ... 20-40 50
Singles: 7-inch
YUCCA (132 "Midnight Stroll") ... 10-15 61
YUCCA (138 "Grandma") ... 10-15 61
YUCCA (159 "Slash") ... 5-10 63
Also see LONG JOHN

HUNTER, John P&R '84
Singles: 7-inch
PRIVATE I ... 3-4 84-85
LPs: 10/12-inch
PRIVATE I ... 5-10 85

HUNTER, Kirk
Singles: 12-inch
AZRA/RPM (627 "Cat's Away") ... 5-10 80s
(Picture disc. 100 made.)

HUNTER, Lee
Singles: 78 rpm
GOLD STAR (651 "Let's Boogie") .. 20-30 48

HUNTER, Lost John: see HUNTER, John

HUNTER, Riverhouse
Singles: 7-inch
ASCOT ... 4-8 63

HUNTER, Robert
Singles: 7-inch
RELIX ... 3-4 86
ROUND ... 5-10 74
LPs: 10/12-inch
RELIX (Except 2002) ... 5-10 80-86
RELIX (2002 "Promontory Rider") 15-20 82
(Picture disc. 1000 made.)
ROUND ... 20-30 74-75
Members: Jerry Garcia; Mickey Hart.
Also see GARCIA, Jerry / Robert Hunter
Also see HART, Mickey
Also see OLD and in the WAY / Keith & Donna / Robert Hunter / Phil Lesh & Ned Lagin

HUNTER, Rod
Singles: 7-inch
LONDON ... 3-5 72

HUNTER, Shane, & Four Bars
Singles: 7-inch
IPS ... 10-20 59
Also see FOUR BARS

HUNTER, Shirlee
Singles: 7-inch
MERCURY ... 4-8 66
SALEM ... 4-8 63-65
TIP TOP ... 5-10 59
TOWER ... 4-8 65

HUNTER, Steve
LPs: 10/12-inch
ATCO ... 8-10 77
Also see BAD BOY

HUNTER, Tab P&R/R&B '57
Singles: 78 rpm
DOT ... 5-15 56-57
HEAR ("Tab Hunter") ... 20-30 56
(Seven-inch, cardboard disc, originally attached to front cover of *Hear* magazine. Double this price for magazine with record intact. Back cover has a similar disc by Jayne Mansfield.)
Singles: 7-inch
DOT ... 10-20 56-62
W.B. (Monaural) ... 8-15 58-59
W.B. (S-5032 "I'll Be with You in Apple Blossom Time") ... 15-25 59
(Stereo.)
W.B. (S-5051 "There's No Fool Like a Young Fool") ... 15-25 59
(Stereo.)
Picture Sleeves
W.B. (5008 "Jealous Heart" ... 10-20 58
W.B. (5093 "Waitin' for Fall" ... 10-20 60
W.B. (5160 "Again") ... 10-20 61
EPs: 7-inch
W.B. (EA-1221 "Tab Hunter") ... 15-25 58
(Monaural. Has one track not found on stereo version.)
W.B. (ESB-1221 "Tab Hunter") ... 20-35 58
(Stereo. Has one track not found on mono version.)
LPs: 10/12-inch
DOT (3370 "Young Love") ... 25-45 61
(Monaural.)
DOT (25370 "Young Love") ... 30-40 61
(Stereo. Includes some tracks originally recorded in mono – and found on 3370 – that were rerecorded in stereo especially for this LP.)
W.B. (1221 "Tab Hunter") ... 30-40 58
(Monaural.)
W.B. (1221 "Tab Hunter") ... 30-50 58
(Stereo.)
W.B. (1292 "When I Fall in Love") ... 30-40 58
(Monaural.)
W.B. (1292 "When I Fall in Love") ... 30-50 58
(Stereo.)
W.B. (1367 "R.F.D.") ... 30-40 60
(Monaural.)
W.B. (1367 "R.F.D.") ... 30-50 60
(Stereo.)
Also see MANSFIELD, Jayne

HUNTER, Tommy C&W '67
Singles: 7-inch
COLUMBIA ... 4-6 67
RCA ... 4-6 60s
LPs: 10/12-inch
COLUMBIA ... 10-20 60s
HARMONY ... 10-25 60s
RCA ... 10-20 60s

HUNTER, Ty R&B '60
(With the Voice Masters)
Singles: 7-inch
ANNA (1114 "Everything About You") ... 20-30 60
ANNA (1123 "Everytime") ... 20-30 60
CHECK MATE (1002 "Memories") . 15-25 61
CHECK MATE (1015 "Lonely Baby") ... 15-25 61
CHESS ... 10-20 62-64
INVICTUS ... 10-15 72
Also see GLASS HOUSE
Also see ORIGINALS
Also see ROMEOS
Also see VOICE MASTERS

HUNTER MUSKETT
LPs: 10/12-inch
BRADLEY (1003 "Hunter Muskett") ... 35-45 73
Members: Danny Thompson; Jim McCarty; Chris George; Doug Morter; Roger Trevit; Terry Hiscock; Mike Giles; Ken Freeman.

HUNTERS
(Flairs)
Singles: 78 rpm
FLAIR ... 25-50 53
Singles: 7-inch
FLAIR (1017 "Down at Hayden's") ... 100-125 53
Also see FLAIRS

HUNTERS
Singles: 7-inch
ERA ... 5-10 64
Also see TOWERS

HUNTERS
Singles: 7-inch
MARLY ... 4-8

HUNTINGTONS
Singles: 7-inch
WASP ... 8-12

HUNTLEY, Chet, & David Brinkley LP '64
LPs: 10/12-inch
RCA ... 8-15 64-66

HUNTSBERRY, Howard
Singles: 7-inch
MCA ... 3-4 88
LPs: 10/12-inch
MCA ... 5-8 88
Also see KLIQUE

HUNTSMEN
Singles: 7-inch
SHUR-SHOT (6704 "So Long") ... 20-30 60s

HURBY'S MACHINE
LPs: 10/12-inch
SOUND CHECK ... 5-8 88

HURD, Debra R&B '83
Singles: 7-inch
GEFFEN ... 3-4 83

HURLEY, Carolyn
Singles: 7-inch
STAX ... 3-5 74

HURLEY, John
Singles: 7-inch
AKA (103 "Lonely Boy") ... 250-350 58

HURLEY, Libby C&W '87
Singles: 7-inch
EPIC ... 3-4 87-88

HURLEY, Michael, & Pals
LPs: 10/12-inch
W.B. ... 10-12 71-72

HURRICANE LP '88
Singles: 7-inch
MCA ... 3-4 87
Picture Sleeves
MCA ... 3-4 87
LPs: 10/12-inch
ENIGMA ... 5-10 85-90
Members: Robert Sarzo; Kelly Hansen; Jay Schellen; Tony Cavazo; Doug Aldrich.

HURRICANE, Al, & Night Rockers
Singles: 7-inch
APT ... 10-15 60
CHALLENGE ... 10-15 61

HURRICANE STRINGS
Singles: 7-inch
ASCOT (2145 "Venus") ... 5-10 64

HURRICANES
(Featuring Bob Gaye)
Singles: 78 rpm
AUDIVOX ... 10-15 54
Singles: 7-inch
AUDIVOX (109 "I Keep Crying") ... 20-40 54
AUDIVOX (112 "I'll Follow You") ... 25-50 54

HURRICANES
Singles: 78 rpm
KING ... 25-75 55-57
Singles: 7-inch
KING (4817 "Poor Little Dancing Girl") ... 100-200 55
KING (4867 "Maybe It's All for the Best") ... 100-200 56
KING (4898 "Raining in My Heart") ... 100-200 56
KING (4926 "Little Girl of Mine") ... 100-200 56
KING (4932 "Sentimental Heaven") ... 75-125 56
KING (4947 "Dear Mother") ... 75-125 56
KING (5018 "Fallen Angel") ... 50-100 57
KING (5042 "Priceless") ... 50-100 57
Members: Henry Auston; James Brown; Frederick Williams; Vernon Britton.
Also see DORN, Jerry
Also see MEMOS
Also see TOPPERS

HURT, Charlotte C&W '78
Singles: 7-inch
COMPASS ... 3-5 78

HURT, Cindy C&W '81
Singles: 7-inch
CHURCHILL ... 3-4 81-83

HURT, Harvey
Singles: 7-inch
MASTER (1226 "Big Dog, Little Dog") ... 100-150

HURT, Jim P&R '80
Singles: 7-inch
SCOTTI BROTHERS ... 3-4 80

HURT, Jimmy, & Del Rios
Singles: 7-inch
DO-RA-ME (1401 "Oh What a Feeling") ... 50-75 59

HURT, Mary, & Lambs
Singles: 7-inch
ZEBRA ... 4-8 64

HURT, Mississippi John
LPs: 10/12-inch
BIOGRAPH ... 10-15
PIEDMONT ... 10-15
VANGUARD ... 10-15 66-72

HURT 'EM BAD & S.C. Band R&B '82
Singles: 7-inch
PROFILE ... 3-4 82

HURVITZ, Sandy
LPs: 10/12-inch
VERVE ... 10-12 68

HUSAK, George
Singles: 7-inch
WIND JAMMER NO. 3 ... 10-20

HUSH
LPs: 10/12-inch
ASI ... 5-10 79

HUSHLEY, George
Singles: 7-inch
GAYE ... 4-8 64

HUSKER DU LP '86
Singles: 12-inch
W.B. ... 4-6 86
Singles: 7-inch
SST ... 3-4 85
W.B. ... 3-4 86
Picture Sleeves
SST ... 3-4 85
LPs: 10/12-inch
SST ... 5-10 85
W.B. ... 5-10 86-87
Members: Bob Mould; Grant Hart; Greg Norton.

HUSKEY, Ferlin: see HUSKY, Ferlin

HUSKEY, Johnny
Singles: 7-inch
TEEN ... 5-10 60

HUSKEY, Kenni C&W '71
Singles: 7-inch
CAPITOL ... 3-5 71-72

HUSKIES
(Featuring Stan Ross)
Singles: 7-inch
IMPERIAL ... 8-12 58
Also see ROSS, Stan

HUSKY, Ferlin C&W '55
(With the Hush Puppies; with Hushpuppies; with Coon Creek Girls; with Bettie Husky; Ferlin Huskey)
Singles: 78 rpm
CAPITOL ... 5-15 52-57
Singles: 7-inch
ABC ... 3-5 73-75
ABC/DOT ... 3-5 75
CAPITOL (2000 thru 3400) ... 3-6 67-72
(Orange labels.)
CAPITOL (2300 thru 4300) ... 8-15 52-60
(Purple labels.)
CAPITOL (4400 thru 5900) ... 4-8 60-67
CACHET ... 3-4 80
FIRST GENERATION ... 3-5 78
KING ... 4-8 60-61
EPs: 7-inch
CAPITOL (609 "Ferlin Husky") ... 25-35 55
CAPITOL (1-2-3 718 "Songs of the Home and Heart") ... 20-40 56
(Price is for any of three volumes.)
CAPITOL (837 "Husky Hits") ... 15-25 57
CAPITOL (1-2-3 880 "Boulevard of Broken Dreams") ... 15-25 57
(Price is for any of three volumes.)
CAPITOL (921 "Songs from Country Music Holiday") ... 15-25 57
CAPITOL (1-2-3 1280 "Ferlin Favorites") ... 10-20 60
(Price is for any of three volumes.)
CAPITOL (1516 "Wings of a Dove") ... 15-25 60
Picture Sleeves
CAPITOL ... 5-10 62-68
LPs: 10/12-inch
ABC ... 5-10 73-75
AUDIOGRAPH ALIVE ... 5-10 82
CAPITOL (718 "Songs of the Home and Heart") ... 30-50 56
CAPITOL (880 "Boulevard of Broken Dreams") ... 25-45 57
CAPITOL (1200 thru 2800 series) .. 10-20 60-68
(With "T" or "ST" prefix.)
CAPITOL (1200 thru 2800 series) ... 5-10 68-75
(With "DT" or "SM" prefix.)
FIRST GENERATION ... 5-10 81
KING (647 "Country Tunes Sung from the Heart") ... 25-35 59
KING (728 "Easy Livin' ") ... 25-35 60
PHONORAMA ... 5-8 83
PICKWICK ... 5-10 70s
PICKWICK/HILLTOP ... 8-12 65
STARDAY ... 5-10 77
Also see CRUM, Simon
Also see FIVE KEYS / Ferlin Husky
Also see OWENS, Buck / Faron Young / Ferlin Husky
Also see PRESTON, Terry
Also see SHEPARD, Jean, & Ferlin Husky
Also see TUBB, Ernest
Also see VINCENT, Gene / Tommy Sands / Sonny James / Ferlin Husky

HUSKY, Ferlin / Pat Boone
Singles: 7-inch
U.S.A.F. ... 5-10 60
(Promotional issue only.)
Also see BOONE, Pat
Also see HUSKY, Ferlin

HUSTLER
Singles: 7-inch
A&M ... 3-5 74-75
LPs: 10/12-inch
A&M ... 8-10 74-75

HUSTLERS
Singles: 7-inch
DOWNEY (118 "Inertia") ... 15-25 63
DOWNEY (125 "Kopout ... 15-25 64
FASCINATION (6570 "Goodbye") . 25-35
FINE ART ... 10-15
HOUSE of NOTE (69 "Barefoot Venture") ... 25-35
ORLYN ... 10-20
RICH (113 "Linda") ... 20-30 65
Also see ORIGINAL HUSTLERS

HUSTLERS 4
Singles: 7-inch
BARCALY (19677 "Kind of Hurt") .. 25-35

HUTCH, Billy
Singles: 7-inch
TIME ... 5-10 63

HUTCH, Willie P&R/R&B/LP '73
Singles: 78 rpm
MODERN ... 8-12 57
Singles: 7-inch
DUNHILL (4012 "The Duck") ... 25-50 65
MAVERICK ... 5-10 68
MODERN (1021 "I Can't Get Enough") ... 20-30 57
MOTOWN ... 3-5 73-82
RCA ... 4-8 69
SOUL CITY ... 4-8
WHITFIELD ... 3-5 78-79
Picture Sleeves
MOTOWN ... 3-5 75
LPs: 10/12-inch
MOTOWN ... 5-10 73-82
RCA ... 10-12 69
WHITFIELD ... 5-10 78-79
Also see PHONETICS

HUTCHINS, Loney C&W '87
Singles: 7-inch
ARC ... 3-4 87

HUTCHINSON, Clark
LPs: 10/12-inch
LONDON/SIRE ... 20-35 69

HUTCHISON, Terry
Singles: 7-inch
TAP ... 3-4

HUTSON, Leroy R&B '73
(With the Free Spirit Symphony)
Singles: 7-inch
CURTOM ... 3-5 73-78
RSO ... 3-5 79
LPs: 10/12-inch
CURTOM ... 8-10 73-78
Also see IMPRESSIONS

HUTTO, J.B.
(With the Hawks; J.B. & His Hawks; with Houserockers)
Singles: 78 rpm
CHANCE ... 25-75 54
Singles: 7-inch
CHANCE (1155 "Now She's Gone") ... 150-250 54
CHANCE (1160 "Pet Cream Man") ... 150-250 54
CHANCE (1165 "Things Are So Slow") ... 150-250 54
LPs: 10/12-inch
DELMARK ... 10-15 72-73

BARON (Black vinyl.)..................10-15 79
BARON (Colored vinyl.)..................15-20 79

HUTTON, Betty P&R '44

Singles: 78 rpm

CAPITOL.....................................4-8 44-56
RCA..4-6 50
VICTOR.......................................4-8 46

Singles: 7-inch

CAPITOL.....................................5-10 50-56

EPs: 7-inch

CAPITOL.....................................10-20 50-54

LPs: 10/12-inch

CAPITOL (256 "Square in a Social Circle")..................30-50 50
(10-inch LP.)
CAPITOL (547 "Satins & Spurs")...20-40 54
W.B. 15-25 59
Also see COMO, Perry, & Betty Hutton
Also see SHORE, Dinah, Tony Martin, Betty Hutton & Phil Harris

HUTTON, Betty, & Tennessee Ernie Ford

Singles: 78 rpm

CAPITOL.....................................4-8 54

Singles: 7-inch

CAPITOL.....................................5-10 54
Also see FORD, Tennessee Ernie
Also see HUTTON, Betty

HUTTON, Bobby

Singles: 7-inch

BLUE ROCK (4055 "That's How Heartaches Are Made")..................10-20
PHILIPS (40601 "Come See What's Left of Me")..................15-20 69
PHILIPS (40657 "I've Got a Memory")..................15-20 70

HUTTON, Danny P&R '65

Singles: 7-inch

HBR...4-8 65
MGM...4-8 66

Picture Sleeves

HBR...10-15 65
MGM...8-12 66

LPs: 10/12-inch

MGM...8-10 70
Also see ENEMYS
Also see SWIFT, Basil, & Seegrams
Also see THREE DOG NIGHT

HUTTON, Neil

Singles: 7-inch

AVA (129 "It's Cold in This Dungeon")..................10-20 63

Picture Sleeves

AVA (129 "It's Cold in This Dungeon")..................15-25 63

HYDE, Paul, & Payolas P&R/LP '85

Singles: 7-inch

A&M...3-4 85
I.R.S. 3-4

Picture Sleeves

A&M...3-4 85
I.R.S. 3-4

LPs: 10/12-inch

A&M...5-10 85
Also see PAYOLAS

HYDRA

LPs: 10/12-inch

CAPRICORN..................................8-10 74-75
POLYDOR....................................5-10 77

HYLAND, Brian P&R/R&B '60

Singles: 7-inch

ABC...3-5 73
ABC-PAR (Except 10400)..............5-10 61-64
ABC-PAR (10400 "If Mary's There")..................5-10 63
(Black vinyl.)
ABC-PAR (10400 "If Mary's There")..................15-20 63
(Colored vinyl. Promotional issue only.)
DOT...4-6 67-69
KAPP..4-8 60-61
LEADER......................................10-15 60
MCA...3-4 73
PHILIPS......................................4-8 64-67
ROWE/AMI..................................5-10 66
("Play Me" Sales Stimulator promotional issue.)
ROULETTE...................................3-4
UNI..3-5 70-72

Picture Sleeves

ABC-PAR....................................8-15 61-63
KAPP (342 "Itsy Bitsy Teenie Weenie Yellow Polkadot Bikini")..................15-20 60
KAPP (352 "Four Little Heels").......20-30 60
(Black and white sleeve. Promotional issue only.)
KAPP (352 "Four Little Heels").......10-20 60
(Color sleeve.)
KAPP (363 "I Gotta Go")..................15-25 60
PHILIPS......................................4-8 64-67

LPs: 10/12-inch

ABC-PAR....................................20-25 61-64
DOT...10-12 69
KAPP (1202 "Bashful Blonde").......25-30 60
(Monaural.)
KAPP (3202 "Bashful Blonde").......30-40 60
PHILIPS......................................15-20 64-66
PICKWICK...................................5-10
PRIVATE STOCK............................5-10 77
RHINO..5-8
UNI..8-10 70
WING..10-12 67

HYLAND, Brian / Jerry Keller

Singles: 7-inch

MCA...3-6 73
Also see HYLAND, Brian
Also see KELLER, Jerry

HYMAN, Dick P&R '54

(Dick Hyman Trio; with His Electric Eclectics)

Singles: 78 rpm

MGM...3-5 54-57

Singles: 7-inch

COLUMBIA..................................3-5 74-75
COMMAND...................................3-8 61-70
EVEREST....................................4-8 60
MGM...5-10 54-62
RCA...4-8 62

Picture Sleeves

MGM (12149 "Mack the Knife")......10-15 55

LPs: 10/12-inch

ATLANTIC....................................5-10 75
COLUMBIA..................................5-10 74
COMMAND...................................5-15 60-73
EVEREST....................................5-10 60
FAMOUS DOOR............................5-10 73
MCA...5-10 77
MGM...10-20 54-63
PROJECT 3..................................5-10 71
RCA...4-8 80-83
SUNSET......................................5-10 66
Also see CLYDE
Also see ROUGH RIDERS
Also see TAYLOR, Sam "The Man," & Dick Hyman

HYMAN, Phyllis R&B '76

Singles: 12-inch

ARISTA.......................................4-6 83

Singles: 7-inch

ARISTA.......................................3-5 78-83
BUDDAH......................................3-5 77
DESERT MOON.............................3-5 76
PHILADELPHIA INT'L....................3-4 86

LPs: 10/12-inch

ARISTA.......................................5-10 79-83
BUDDAH......................................5-10 77
PHILADELPHIA INT'L....................5-10 86

HYMAN, Phyllis, & Michael Henderson

Singles: 7-inch

ARISTA.......................................3-4 81
Also see CONNORS, Norman
Also see HENDERSON, Michael
Also see HYMAN, Phyllis

HYPERIONS

Singles: 7-inch

CHATTAHOOCHEE (669 "Why Do You Wanna Treat Me Like You Do")..............75-125 64

HYPERIONS

Singles: 7-inch

PARIS TOWER (102 "The Truth Always Hurts")..................15-25 67

HYPNOTICS

Singles: 7-inch

REPRISE......................................3-5 73

HYPNOTICS

Singles: 7-inch

WARKEE (905 "Eloise")............150-250 59

HYPO DERMICS

Singles: 7-inch

TITANIC......................................4-8 62

HYSTERIC NARCOTICS

Singles: 7-inch

TREMOR......................................3-4 85

Picture Sleeves

TREMOR......................................3-4 85

HYSTERICAL SOCIETY

Singles: 7-inch

TIPTON (100 "I Put a Spell on You")..................15-25 66
U.A. (50147 "Come with Me")........10-20 67

HYSTERICS

Singles: 7-inch

BING (303 "Everything's There")....15-25 65
SWAN...5-10 66
TOTTENHAM (500 "Won't Get Far")..................20-30 66
Also see LOVE-INS

HYPSTRZ

LPs: 10/12-inch

VOXX...8-12

HYTONES

Singles: 7-inch

A-BET (9415 "Bigger & Better")...50-100 66

HY-TONES

(With Steve Samuel's Orchestra)

Singles: 7-inch

HY-TONE (120 "I'm a Fool")......150-250 58
Session: Frank Anderson.
Also see HARRIS, Georgia, & Hy-Tones

HY TONES

Singles: 7-inch

SOUTHERN ARTISTS (2023 "You Don't Even Know My Name")..................10-20 60s

HYTOWER, Roy

Singles: 7-inch

BRAINSTORM.................................4-8 68
EXPO..6-12

HYTS

Singles: 7-inch

GOLD MOUNTAIN..........................3-4 85

LPs: 10/12-inch

GOLD MOUNTAIN..........................5-10 85

I

I.C.C.

Singles: 7-inch

HY NIBBLE...................................8-12 60s

I DON'T CARE

LPs: 10/12-inch

BUDDAH......................................8-10 76

I LEVEL D&D '83

Singles: 12-inch

VIRGIN.......................................4-6 82-84

Singles: 7-inch

VIRGIN.......................................3-4 82-84

LPs: 10/12-inch

VIRGIN.......................................5-10 83

I.A.& P. CO: see ITALIAN ASPHALT & Pavement Co.

I.M. BROKE & TAXPAYERS

Singles: 7-inch

POVERTY (1 "Wiped Out")...........25-50 60s

I.N.D.

LPs: 10/12-inch

ERECT...5-10 82

I.R.T. D&D '84

(Interboro Rhythm Team)

Singles: 12-inch

RCA...4-6 84

Singles: 7-inch

RCA...3-4 84

I-V-LEAGUERS

(I.V. Leaguers)

Singles: 78 rpm

DOT (15677 "Ring Chimes")..........15-25 57
PORTER (1004 "Ring Chimes")....40-60 57

Singles: 7-inch

DOT (15677 "Ring Chimes")..........25-50 57
NAU-VOO (803 "Jim-Jamin' ")...200-300 59
NAU-VOO (803 "Jim-Jam")........200-300 59
(Note slight title change.)
PORTER (1004 "Ring Chimes") 100-200 57
Also see IVY LEAGUERS

IAMAI

Singles: 7-inch

LEGRAND....................................5-10 60s

IAN, Janis P&R/LP '67

Singles: 7-inch

CAPITOL.....................................3-5 71
CASABLANCA..............................3-4 80
COLUMBIA..................................3-5 74-81
POLYDOR....................................3-5 78
VERVE..3-5
VERVE/FOLKWAYS......................4-8 66-67
VERVE/FORECAST.......................4-6 68-69

Picture Sleeves

COLUMBIA..................................3-6 75

LPs: 10/12-inch

CAPITOL.....................................8-12 71-75
COLUMBIA..................................8-10 74-81
MGM...8-10 70
POLYDOR....................................8-10 75
VERVE/FOLKWAYS......................10-15 67
VERVE/FORECAST.......................10-15 68-69
Members: Paul Arnold; Jerry Cole.
Also see COLE, Jerry

IAN & SYLVIA LP '63

Singles: 7-inch

COLUMBIA..................................3-5 71-72
MGM...4-6 67-69
VANGUARD..................................4-8 63-68
VERVE/FOLKWAYS......................3-6 67

Picture Sleeves

COLUMBIA..................................3-5 71

LPs: 10/12-inch

AMPEX..8-10 70
COLUMBIA..................................6-10 71-73
MGM...8-12 67-70
VANGUARD..................................10-20 63-71
VERVE/FOLKWAYS......................8-15 67
Members: Ian Tyson; Sylvia Fricker.

IAN & ZODIACS

Singles: 7-inch

PHILIPS......................................4-8 64-66

Picture Sleeves

PHILIPS (40291 "So Much in Love with You")..................10-15 65

EPs: 7-inch

PHILIPS (807 "Ian & Zodiacs")......10-20 65

LPs: 10/12-inch

COLUMBIA (2172 "Exciting New Liverpool Sound")..................20-30 64
PHILIPS (200176 "Ian and the Zodiacs")..................15-25 65
(Monaural.)
PHILIPS (600176 "Ian and the Zodiacs")..................15-25 65
(Stereo.)

ICARUS

LPs: 10/12-inch

GRIT..8-10 72

ICE

Singles: 7-inch

BONNY (1212 "Chicago Blues")....10-20 60s

ICE

Singles: 7-inch

UA (50210 "Don't Let Nobody Turn You Around")..................10-15 70

ICE COLD LOVE

Singles: 7-inch

TAMMY.......................................10-15

ICE CREAM

Singles: 7-inch

CAPITOL.....................................4-8 68

ICE CUBE LP '90

LPs: 10/12-inch

PRIORITY....................................5-8 90-91

ICE MAN'S BAND

LPs: 10/12-inch

MERCURY....................................8-10 72
Also see BUTLER, Jerry

ICE-T LP '87

Singles: 7-inch

SIRE...3-4 88-90

Picture Sleeves

SIRE...3-4 88

LPs: 10/12-inch

SIRE...5-10 87-91

ICEBERG

Singles: 7-inch

U.A. 3-5 74

LPs: 10/12-inch

U.A. 8-10 74

ICEHOUSE P&R/LP '81

Singles: 12-inch

CHRYSALIS.................................4-6 81-86

Singles: 7-inch

CHRYSALIS.................................3-4 81-88

Picture Sleeves

CHRYSALIS.................................3-4 81-88

LPs: 10/12-inch

CHRYSALIS.................................5-10 81-88

ICEMEN

Singles: 7-inch

ABC...4-8 68
OLE 9 (1008 "It's Gonna Take Time")..................10-20 60s

ICHABOD & CRANES

Singles: 7-inch

CORAL..8-10 64

ICICLE WORKS P&R/D&D/LP '84

Singles: 12-inch

ARISTA.......................................4-6 84

Singles: 7-inch

ARISTA.......................................3-4 84

LPs: 10/12-inch

ARISTA.......................................5-10 84

ICON LP '84

LPs: 10/12-inch

CAPITOL.....................................5-10 84
Members: Steve Clifford; Dan Wexler; Pat Dixon; John Aquilino; Tracy Wallach; Jerry Harrison.

ID

Singles: 7-inch

JOLLY ROGER (101 "Rotten Apple")..................8-12 60s
RCA...5-10 67

Picture Sleeves

JOLLY ROGER (101 "Rotten Apple")..................10-15 60s

LPs: 10/12-inch

RCA (LPM-3805 "Inner Sounds")....30-40 67
(Monaural.)
RCA (LSP-3805 "Inner Sounds")....35-45 67
(Stereo.)

ID

LPs: 10/12-inch

AURA (1000 "Where Are We Going")..................50-75 75
Members: Gary Oickle; Dave Oickle; Ralph Jenkins; Kevin Orson; James Albert.

IDAHO, Ken

Singles: 7-inch

FAME..5-10 59

IDEALS

Singles: 7-inch

COOL (108 "Do I Have the Right")..................250-350 58
Also see OVATIONS

IDEALS

Singles: 7-inch

DECCA (30720 "My Girl")............25-50 58
DECCA (30800 "Ivy League Lover")..................20-30 58
STARS of HOLLYWOOD (1001 "Always Yours")..................50-75 59

IDEALS R&B '66

Singles: 7-inch

CHECKER (920 "Knee Socks")......15-25 59
CHECKER (979 "Knee Socks").......10-15 61
PASO (6401 "Together")..............30-50 61
PASO (6402 "Magic")..................30-50 61
SATELLITE (2007 "Kissin' ")..........5-10 65
SATELLITE (2009 "You Hurt Me") 10-15 66
SATELLITE (2011 "Kissing Won't Go Out of Style")..................15-25 66
Members: Major Lance; Sam Stewart; Reggie Jackson; Leonard Mitchell.
Also see LANCE, Major

IDEALS

Singles: 7-inch

BOOGALOO (108 "Mighty Lover").15-25 60s
CARLTON (110 "Don Juan")...........10-15 60s
CORTLAND...................................5-10 63-64
DAISY (04 "Thunder Drums").......10-20 64
FARGO (1024 "Trans Zister")..........5-10 62
ST. LAWRENCE (1020 "I Got Lucky")..................10-15 66

IDENTICALS

Singles: 7-inch

FIREBIRD....................................4-8

IDES

Singles: 7-inch

KEN-DEL (5309 "Psychedelic Ride")..................50-100 60s

IDES OF LOVE

Singles: 7-inch

TALMU..4-6 68

IDES OF MARCH P&R '66

Singles: 7-inch

KAPP..4-6 69
PARROT......................................5-10 66-67
RCA...3-5 72-73
W.B. 3-6 69-71

LPs: 10/12-inch

RCA...8-12 72-73
W.B. 10-15 70-71
Members: Jim Peterik; Mike Borch; Ray Herr; Bob Bergland; Chuck Soumar; John Larson; Larry Millas.
Also see PETERIK, Jim

IDIOTS & CO.

Singles: 7-inch

RIVERSIDE..................................4-8 61

LPs: 10/12-inch

RIVERSIDE..................................15-25 61

IDLE RACE

Singles: 7-inch

LIBERTY (55997 "Here We Go Round the Lemon Tree")..................10-15 67

LPs: 10/12-inch

LIBERTY (7603 "Birthday Party")...25-30 69
SUNSET......................................8-12 72
Members: Jeff Lynne; Greg Masters; Roger Spencer; Dave Pritchard.
Also see LYNNE, Jeff
Also see SHERIDAN, Mike, & Nightriders

IDLERS

Singles: 7-inch

AUDIO SPECTRUM.........................5-8 64

IDOL, Billy LP '81

Singles: 12-inch

CHRYSALIS (Black vinyl)..............4-8 81-86
CHRYSALIS (8V8-42719 "Eyes Without a Face")..................10-15 84
(Picture disc.)

Singles: 7-inch

CHRYSALIS.................................3-4 81-90

Picture Sleeves

CHRYSALIS.................................3-5 82-90

LPs: 10/12-inch

CHRYSALIS (1377 "Billy Idol")......10-20 82
(Promotional issue only.)
CHRYSALIS (4000 "Don't Stop")......8-10 81
CHRYSALIS (20000 series)............5-8 90
CHRYSALIS (40000 series)............5-10 82-87
Also see CHELSEA
Also see GENERATION X

IDOLS

Singles: 7-inch

RCA...10-15 58

IDOLS

(With the Luca Trio)

Singles: 7-inch

E.Z (1 "Jeannine")......................35-55 61

IDOLS

Singles: 7-inch

GALAXIE (77 "The Stars Will Remember")..................75-100 61

IDOLS

Singles: 7-inch

L-U-V (201,306 "True Love Gone")..................20-40 66

IDOLS / Swans

Singles: 7-inch

DOT (16210 "Why Must I Cry")......15-25 61
REVEILLE (1002 "Why Must I Cry")..................30-50 61

IDYLLS

Singles: 7-inch

SPINNING (6012 "Annette")...........50-75 60

IF

Singles: 7-inch

CAPITOL.....................................3-5 70-74
METROMEDIA..............................3-5 72

LPs: 10/12-inch

CAPITOL.....................................10-12 69-74
METROMEDIA..............................8-10 72-73
Also see CHELSEA

IFIELD, Frank P&R '62

Singles: 7-inch

CAPITOL.....................................5-10 63-65
HICKORY....................................4-8 66-71
MAM...3-5 71
VEE JAY.....................................5-10 62-63
W.B. 3-5 79

LPs: 10/12-inch

CAPITOL.....................................10-20 63
COLUMBIA..................................10-20
HICKORY....................................10-20 66-68
VEE JAY.....................................10-20 62
Also see BEATLES / Frank Ifield

IGGY & STOOGES: see POP, Iggy

IGLESIAS, Julio — *LP '83*
Singles: 7-inch
ALAHAMBRA ... 3-6 72-75
COLUMBIA ... 3-4 83-89
LPs: 10/12-inch
COLUMBIA (Except 39928) ... 5-10 83-90
COLUMBIA (39928 "1100 Bel Air Place") ... 10-15 84
(Picture disc.)

IGLESIAS, Julio, & Willie Nelson — *C&W/P&R '84*
(Willie Nelson & Julio Iglesias)
Singles: 7-inch
COLUMBIA (Except 04495) ... 3-4 84
COLUMBIA (04495 "As Time Goes By") ... 8-12 84
Picture Sleeves
COLUMBIA (Except 04495) ... 3-4 84
COLUMBIA (04495 "As Time Goes By") ... 10-15 84
Also see NELSON, Willie

IGLESIAS, Julio, & Diana Ross — *P&R '84*
Singles: 7-inch
COLUMBIA ... 3-4 84
Picture Sleeves
COLUMBIA ... 3-4 84
Also see ROSS, Diana

IGLESIAS, Julio, & Stevie Wonder — *P&R '88*
Singles: 7-inch
COLUMBIA ... 3-4 88
Picture Sleeves
COLUMBIA ... 3-4 88
Also see IGLESIAS, Julio
Also see WONDER, Stevie

IGOR & MANIACS
Singles: 7-inch
DOLTON (29 "Big Green") ... 5-10 60

IGUANA
LPs: 10/12-inch
LION ... 8-10 72
U.A. ... 8-10 76

IGUANAS
Singles: 7-inch
DUNHILL ... 4-6 65-66

IGUANAS
Singles: 7-inch
FORTE (201 "Mona") ... 25-35 66
Member: Don Swickerath.
Also see POP, Iggy

IGUANAS
Singles: 7-inch
IGUANA (101 "I Can Only Give You Everything") ... 20-30 67

IGUANAS
LPs: 10/12-inch
MIDNIGHT ... 5-10

IKETTES — *P&R/R&B '62*
(With the Ike & Tina Revue)
Singles: 7-inch
ATCO (6212 "I'm Blue") ... 8-12 61
ATCO (6223 "Troubles on My Mind") ... 8-12 62
ATCO (6232 "Heavenly Love") ... 8-12 62
ATCO (6243 "I Do Love You") ... 8-12 62
INNIS (3000 "Here's Your Heart") ... 8-10 64
MODERN (1003 "Camel Walk") ... 5-8 64
MODERN (1005 "Peaches 'N' Cream") ... 5-8 65
MODERN (1008 "Fine Fine Fine") ... 5-8 65
MODERN (1011 "I'm So Thankful") ... 5-8 65
MODERN (1015 "Lonely for You") ... 5-8 66
PHI-DAN (5009 "Down Down") ... 4-8
POMPEII (66683 "Make 'Em Wait") ... 4-8 68
TEENA (1702 "Prisoner in Love") ... 8-12 63
U.A. (50866 "If You Take a Close Look") ... 4-6 71
U.A. (51103 "I'm Just Not Ready for Love") ... 4-6 72
LPs: 10/12-inch
MODERN (102 "Soul Hits") ... 15-25 65
U.A. ... 8-10 73-75
Members: Delores Johnson; Eloise Hester; Joshie Jo Armstead; Vanetta Fields; Jessie Smith; Robbie Montgomery. Session: Tina Turner.
Also see ARMSTEAD, Joshie Jo
Also see MAXAYN
Also see MIRETTES
Also see TURNER, Ike & Tina

IL GRUPPO
Singles: 7-inch
RCA ... 10-15 67
Member: Ennio Morricone.

ILANA
Singles: 7-inch
VOLT ... 3-6 71

ILFORD SUBWAY
Singles: 7-inch
EQUINOX ... 4-8 67

ILL WIND
Singles: 7-inch
ABC (11107 "In My Dark World") ... 10-20 68
LPs: 10/12-inch
ABC (641 "Flashes") ... 50-100 68
Members: Conny Devanney; Richard Griggs; Carey Mann; Ken Frankel; Dave Kinsman.

ILL WINDS
Singles: 7-inch
REPRISE ... 5-10 65-66
Also see CHANTAYS

ILLEGALS
LPs: 10/12-inch
A&M ... 5-10 83

ILLINOIS SPEED PRESS — *LP '69*
Singles: 7-inch
COLUMBIA ... 4-8 68-70
LPs: 10/12-inch
COLUMBIA ... 10-15 69-70
Members: Paul Cotton; Rob Lewine; Fred Page; Kal David; Mike Anthony; Frank Bartoli.
Also see POCO
Also see ROVIN' KIND

ILLUSION — *P&R/LP '69*
(The Illusion)
Singles: 7-inch
DYNO VOICE ... 4-8 68
STEED ... 4-6 69-71
LPs: 10/12-inch
STEED ... 10-20 69-70

ILLUSION — *LP '77*
Singles: 7-inch
ISLAND ... 3-5 77-78
LPs: 10/12-inch
ISLAND ... 5-10 77-78

ILLUSION — *R&B '82*
Singles: 7-inch
SUGAR HILL ... 3-4 82

ILLUSION
Singles
GEFFEN (2322 "Get It to Go") ... 10-15 85
(Triangular picture disc. Promotional only issue.)

ILLUSIONS
Singles: 7-inch
AXTEL (101 "Better Late Than Never") ... 50-75 60
COLUMBIA ... 5-10 66
CORAL (62173 "The Letter") ... 20-30 60
DIAL ... 5-10 65
DOT ... 10-15 65
EMBER (1071 "Can't We Fall in Love") ... 25-35 61
KAPE ... 5-10
LAURIE (3245 "Maybe") ... 30-40 64
MALI (104 "Hey Boy") ... 150-200 62
NORTH-EAST (801 "Hey Boy") ... 50-75 62
SHERATON (104 "Hey Boy") ... 75-125 62
Also see 3 FRIENDS

ILLUSIONS
Singles: 7-inch
LITTLE DEBBIE (105 "Story of My Life") ... 200-300 64
PAMA (126 "Big Beat '65") ... 10-20 65
ROUND (1018 "Jezebel") ... 15-25 63

ILLUSIONS
Singles: 7-inch
AUDIO UNLIMITED (1000 "The Outcast") ... 25-50 66

ILLUSIONS
Singles: 7-inch
MICHELLE (1 "City of People") ... 15-25 66

ILLUSTRATED MAN — *D&D '84*
Singles: 12-inch
EMI ... 4-6 80s
Singles: 7-inch
CAPITOL ... 3-4 84

ILLUSTRATION
LPs: 10/12-inch
JANUS ... 10-12 69

ILMO SMOKEHOUSE
LPs: 10/12-inch
BEAUTIFUL SOUND (3002 "Ilmo Smokehouse") ... 25-35 71
ROULETTE (3002 "Ilmo Smokehouse") ... 15-20 71
Members: Freddie Tieken; Dennis Tieken; Slink Rand; Gerry Gabel; Craig Moore.
Also see GONN
Also see TIEKEN, Freddie, & Rockers

IMAGE
Singles: 7-inch
TWIN TOWN ... 10-20 60s

IMAGE
Singles: 7-inch
CHAPPAREL (1306 "Witchcraft - 71") ... 5-10 70
JANUS ... 3-5

IMAGINATION
Singles: 7-inch
20TH FOX ... 3-6 74

IMAGINATION — *R&B '82*
Singles: 12-inch
ELEKTRA ... 4-6 84
MCA ... 4-6 83
Singles: 7-inch
ELEKTRA ... 3-4 83
MCA ... 3-4 82-83
RCA ... 3-4 87
LPs: 10/12-inch
MCA ... 5-10 82

IMAGINATIONS
Singles: 7-inch
BACON FAT (101 "I Want a Girl") ... 15-25 61

IMAGINATIONS
Singles: 7-inch
BALLAD (500 "Wait a Little Longer") ... 10-20 63
BO MARC (301"Guardian Angel") ... 20-30 61
DUEL (507 "Guardian Angel") ... 15-20 62
HARVEY ... 4-6 80s
MUSIC MAKERS (103 "Goodnight Baby") ... 30-50 61
MUSIC MAKERS (108 "Guardian Angel") ... 30-50 61
LPs: 10/12-inch
RELIC ... 5-10
Members: Frank Mancuso; Bobby Bloom; Phillip Agtuca; Pete Agtuca; Richie Le Causi.
Also see BLOOM, Bobby
Also see DAY, Darlene
Also see EXPRESSIONS

IMAGINATIONS
Singles: 7-inch
DUNHILL ... 5-10 67
Members: Phil Sloan; Steve Barri.
Also see FANTASTIC BAGGYS

IMAGINATIONS
Singles: 7-inch
FRATERNITY (1001 " I Just Can't Get Over Losing You") ... 15-25 67

IMAGINATIONS
Singles: 7-inch
20TH FOX ... 3-5 74
LPs: 10/12-inch
20TH FOX ... 8-10 74

IMITATION LIFE
LPs: 10/12-inch
SKYCLAD ... 5-10 86
Members: Mars Bonfire; Bruce Joyner; Jay Work; Ethan James; Ed Munoz; Dave Drewry; Marc Platt.
Also see BONFIRE, Mars

IMMIGRANTS
Singles: 7-inch
STARBURST (225 "Blues") ... 8-12

IMMORTALS
Singles: 7-inch
LAURIE (3009 "Moonshine") ... 10-20 61

IMPACS
(Pat Scot & Impacs)
Singles: 7-inch
IMPAC (59 "Lost Love") ... 10-15 61
Members: Pat Scot; Vic Waters.
Also see WATERS, Vic, & Entertainers

IMPACS
Singles: 7-inch
KING ... 5-10 64-65
PARKWAY ... 5-10 63
LPs: 10/12-inch
KING (886 "Impact!") ... 20-35 64
KING (916 "Weekend with the Impacts") ... 20-35 64

IMPACT — *P&R/R&B '76*
Singles: 7-inch
ATCO ... 3-5 76
FANTASY ... 3-5 77-78
LPs: 10/12-inch
ATCO ... 8-10 75
FANTASY ... 5-10 77
Members: Damon Harris; John Simms; Donald Tilghman; Charles Timmons.
Also see HARRIS, Damon

IMPACT EXPRESS
Singles: 7-inch
LAVENDER (2006 "You Get Your Kicks") ... 8-12 67
LAVENDER (2008 "Fly with Me") ... 8-12 68
Members: Henry Brusco; Bruce Farguhar; Dan White; Ron Baldwin; Bill Uhlig; Steve Green: La Donna Lockner.
Also see IMPACTS

IMPACT V
Singles: 7-inch
AGAR (7171 "Island of Love") ... 20-25 63

IMPACTS
Singles: 7-inch
CARLTON (548 "Darling, No You're Mine") ... 50-75 61
("Now" is misspelled.)
CARLTON (548 "Darling, Now You're Mine") ... 25-50 61
("Now" is spelled correctly.)
RCA (7583 "Bobby Sox Squaw") ... 10-20 59
RCA (7609 "Canadian Sunset") ... 20-40 59
WATTS (5599 "Now Is the Time") ... 50-100 59

IMPACTS
LPs: 10/12-inch
DEL-FI (1234 "Wipe Out") ... 20-30 63
OCEAN (8701 "Wipe Out") ... 5-10 88
Members: Merrell Wayne Fankhauser; Joel Rose; Steve Lee Evans; Wayne Marty Brown; Steve Eric Metz.
Also see FANKHAUSER, Merrell

IMPACTS
Singles: 7-inch
KIP ... 10-20 63
MERSEY ... 10-15 64

IMPACTS
(Impact Express)
Singles: 7-inch
DCP ... 5-10 66
LAVENDER (2005 "Don't You Dare") ... 8-12 66
LAVENDER (2007 "Don't You Dare") ... 8-12 67
NWI (2660 "Leavin' Here") ... 10-15 65
Members: Henry Brusco; Bruce Farguhar; Dan White; Ron Baldwin; Bill Uhlig; Steve Green: La Donna Lockner.
Also see IMPACT EXPRESS

IMPACTS
Singles: 7-inch
ANDERSON (104 "Linda") ... 20-30
ANDERSON (201 "Speed Zone") ... 10-20

IMPAKS
Singles: 7-inch
EXPRESS ... 15-20 62

IMPALA SYNDROME
LPs: 10/12-inch
PARALLAX (4002 "Impala Syndrome") ... 25-35 69

IMPALAS
("Featuring Bobby Byrd with Buddy T. & His T-Men")
Singles: 7-inch
CORVET (1017 "Why!") ... 100-200 58
Also see BYRD, Bobby

IMPALAS — *P&R/R&B '59*
("Featuring Joe 'Speedo' Frazier")
Singles: 7-inch
CUB (9022 "I Ran All the Way Home") ... 50-75 59
CUB (9022 "Sorry I Ran All the Way Home") ... 15-25 59
(Note slightly different title.)
CUB (9033 "Oh What a Fool") ... 15-25 59
CUB (9053 "Peggy Darling") ... 15-25 60
HAMILTON (50026 "I Was a Fool") ... 15-25 59
MGM ... 3-6 64-78
U.G.H.A. (17 "My Hero") ... 3-5 82
Picture Sleeves
U.G.H.A. (17 "My Hero") ... 3-5 82
EPs: 7-inch
CUB (5000 "Sorry, I Ran All the Way Home") ... 100-150 59
LPs: 10/12-inch
CUB (CUB-8003 "Sorry, I Ran All the Way Home") ... 150-250 59
(Monaural.)
CUB (CUBS-8003 "Sorry, I Ran All the Way Home") ... 250-350 59
(Stereo.)
Also see SPEEDO & IMPALAS

IMPALAS / Horst Jankowski & His Orchestra
Singles: 7-inch
COLLECTABLES ... 3-4 85
Also see IMPALAS
Also see JANKOWSKI, Horst, & His Orchestra

IMPALAS
("Vocal by Celeste Warren")
Singles: 7-inch
ECHO (6018 "Betty Jean") ... 100-200 50s

IMPALAS
Singles: 7-inch
BUNKY ... 5-10 69
CHECKER ... 8-12 61
SUNDOWN ... 5-10 59
20TH FOX ... 8-12 63

IMPALAS
Singles: 7-inch
BO (001 "Raincheck") ... 10-20 62

IMPALAS
Singles: 7-inch
ELAART ... 3-5 75
FEATURE (107 "Spoonful") ... 10-20 66
PAGE ... 3-5 77
Members: Jeff Moretti; Jerry Morcia; Ron Moen; Gene Schiller; Mike Price; Chuck Loth; Jerry Kueper; Jack Gebhyardt; Steve Keppen; Phil Shields; Donnie Roberts; Emmit Smith.

IMPALAS
Singles: 7-inch
RED BOY ... 10-20 66
RITE-ON ... 10-15
STEADY ... 10-15
Also see FIVE DISCS

IMPAX
Singles: 7-inch
W.B. ... 3-5 60

IMPELLAS
Singles: 7-inch
ALL BOY ... 5-10 63
CONSTELLATION ... 5-10 64
SAN (1515 "Continental Whip") ... 8-15 59
SAN (1519 "Hook-Em") ... 8-15 59

IMPELLITTERI — *LP '88*
LPs: 10/12-inch
RELATIVITY ... 5-8 88

IMPERIAL C's
Singles: 7-inch
PHIL-LA of SOUL ("Someone Tell Her") ... 15-25 60s

IMPERIAL GENTS
Singles: 7-inch
LAURIE ... 8-10 70

IMPERIAL 7
Singles: 7-inch
ATHENS (207 "Midnight Tom") ... 10-20 62

IMPERIAL WONDERS
Singles: 7-inch
BLACK GOLD ... 3-5
BLACK PRINCE (317 "When I Fall in Love") ... 10-20
DAY-WOOD (6901 "Just a Dream") ... 10-20
MUSICOR ... 3-5
SOLID FOUNDATION (101 "You Live Only Once") ... 10-20

IMPERIAL WONDERS
Singles: 7-inch
DAY-WOOD (6901 "Just a Dream") ... 10-20
SOLID FOUNDATION (101 "You Live Only Once") ... 10-20

IMPERIALITES
Singles: 7-inch
IMPERIAL ... 10-15 64

IMPERIALS
Singles: 78 rpm
DERBY ... 50-100 54
GREAT LAKES (1201 "Life of Ease") ... 50-100 54
GREAT LAKES (1212 "You'll Never Walk Alone") ... 100-200 54
(Though Great Lakes 1201 exists on 45 rpm, this release is not yet verified as being on 45.)
Singles: 7-inch
BUZZY (1 "My Darling") ... 10-20 62
(Colored vinyl.)
DERBY (858 "Why Did You Leave Me") ... 200-300 54
GREAT LAKES (1201 "Life of Ease") ... 250-350 54
(This exact same track was also issued by the Four Arcs.)
SAVOY (1104 "My Darling") ... 150-200 54
Members: M. Harris; L. Goodwin; R. Adams; B. Knight.
Also see FOUR ARCS

IMPERIALS — *R&B/P&R '58*
Singles: 7-inch
CAPITOL (4924 "I'm Still Dancing") ... 10-20 63
CARLTON (566 "Faithfully Yours") ... 20-30 61
END (1027 "Tears on My Pillow") ... 25-50 58
(First pressing. Quickly repressed, crediting "Little Anthony & Imperials.")
LIBERTY ... 8-12 58
Also see LITTLE ANTHONY & IMPERIALS

IMPERIALS
(With Richard Barrett)
Singles: 7-inch
NEWTIME (503 "A Short Prayer") ... 10-15 62
NEWTIME (505 "The Letter") ... 10-15 62
Also see BARRETT, Richard

IMPERIALS
Singles: 7-inch
JERDEN (745 "Backyard Compost") ... 15-20 64
Members: Alan Park; Jeff Beals; Dan Denton; Rocky Rhoades; Jeff La Brache; Jim Wolfe; George Mitroff.
Also see CITY LIMITS
Also see ROCKY & His Friends
Also see ROCKY & RIDDLERS

IMPERIALS
Singles: 7-inch
UNITED SOUND (2658 "Avalanche") ... 50-75 60s

IMPERIALS — *R&B '78*
Singles: 7-inch
OMNI ... 3-5 78

IMPERIALS MINUS 2
Singles: 7-inch
IMPERIAL (5787 "A Swingin' Dream") ... 10-20 61

IMPI
Singles: 7-inch
EPIC ... 3-5 71

IMPLACABLES
Singles: 7-inch
KAIN (1004 "Don't Call for Me") ... 1000-2000 61
(Reissued as by Johnny Williams.)
Also see WILLIAMS, Johnny

IMPLEMENTS
Singles: 7-inch
LOMA ... 4-8 68

IMPLICITS
Singles: 7-inch
ATOLL ... 10-15 64
Member: Tom Johnston.
Also see JOHNSTON, Tom

IMPOLLOS: see INMAN, Jimmy

IMPORTED MOODS
Singles: 7-inch
HI ... 3-5 70

IMPOSSIBLES
Singles: 7-inch
BLANCHE (029 "Chapel Bells") ... 300-400 61
RMP (500 "Everywhere I Go") ... 15-25 60
RMP (1030 "Mr. Maestro") ... 15-25 59
REPRISE (305 "Paint Me a Pretty Picture") ... 15-25 64
ROULETTE (4745 "I Wanna Know") ... 10-20 67
Also see NAPOLEON XIV

IMPOSTERS
Singles: 7-inch
FROG DEATH (1 "Wipe In") ... 25-40 63

IMPRESSIONS R&B '58
("Featuring Jerry Butler"; with Riley Hampton's Orchestra)
Singles: 12-inch
20TH FOX 4-8 79
Singles: 78 rpm
ABNER (1017 "Come Back My Love") 50-75 58
Singles: 7-inch
ABC 4-8 66-68
ABC-PAR (Except 10328) 5-15 61-66
ABC-PAR (10328 "Never Let Me Go") 20-30 62
ABNER (1017 "Come Back My Love") 20-30 58
ABNER (1023 "The Gift of Love") .. 20-30 58
ABNER (1025 "Lonely One") 20-30 59
ABNER (1034 "Say That You Love Me") 25-50 59
ADORE (901 "Popcorn Willie") 50-75 64
BANDERA (2504 "Listen") 35-50 59
CHI-SOUND 3-5 81
COTILLION 3-5 76-77
CURTOM 3-6 68-76
ICHIBAN 3-4 94
MCA 3-4 87
PORT 5-10 62
SWIRL (107 "I Need Your Love") .. 20-40 62
20TH FOX 3-5 81
VEE JAY (424 thru 574) 10-15 61-63
(Vee Jay 280, *For Your Precious Love*, appears in the Jerry Butler section.)
VEE JAY (621 "Say That You Love Me") 20-30 64
Picture Sleeves
CURTOM (1932 "Fool for You") 4-8 68
EPs: 7-inch
ABC-PAR (505 "People Get Ready") 10-20 64
(Juke box issue only. Includes title strips.)
CURTOM (20 "Do You Want to Win") 5-10 70
(Promotional issue only.)
LPs: 10/12-inch
ABC 10-20 66-76
ABC-PAR 15-30 63-66
COTILLION 8-10 76
CURTOM 8-10 68-76
EMUS 5-8
MCA 5-10 82
PICKWICK 8-10 75
SCEPTER/CITATION 8-10
SIRE 8-12 76
20TH FOX 5-10 79-81
UPFRONT 8-10
Members: Curtis Mayfield; Sam Gooden; Richard Brooks; Fred Cash; Leroy Hutson; Reggie Torian; Ralph Johnson; Nate Evans.
Also see BRADLEY, Jan
Also see EVERETT, Betty / Impressions
Also see HUTSON, Leroy
Also see MAYFIELD, Curtis
Also see MYSTIQUE
Also see RAMSEY, Gloria

IMPRESSIONS / Jerry Butler
LPs: 10/12-inch
SIRE 5-10 77
Also see BUTLER, Jerry
Also see IMPRESSIONS

IMPRESSORS
Singles: 7-inch
CUB (9010 "Do You Love Her") 25-50 58
ONYX (514 "Is It Too Late") 50-100 57

IMPROPER BOSTONIANS
Singles: 7-inch
CORAL 5-8 67
MINUTEMAN 5-10 67

IMPS
Singles: 7-inch
DO-RA-ME (1414 "That'll Get It") .. 15-20 61
(First issue.)
SCEPTER (1240 "That'll Get It") 8-15 61

IMUS, Don
("Imus in the Morning")
Singles: 7-inch
HAPPY TIGER 4-8 71
RCA 3-6 72-73
LPs: 10/12-inch
RCA 8-15 72

IMUS, Jay Jay, & Freddy Ford
Singles: 7-inch
CHALLENGE 10-15 63

IN
Singles: 7-inch
HICKORY 10-15 66

IN BETWEEN
Singles: 7-inch
HIGHLAND 5-10

IN BETWEEN SET
Singles: 7-inch
RUST 5-10 65

IN CROWD P&R '66
Singles: 7-inch
BRENT 5-10 65
HICKORY 10-15 65
MUSICOR (1111 "Do the Surfer Jerk") 10-20 65
RONN 10-20
SWAN 4-8 65
TOWER 5-8 65-66
VIVA 4-8 66-67

IN CROWD
Singles: 7-inch
ABNAK 4-8 67
Also see JON & ROBIN

IN SET
Singles: 7-inch
CAL OMEN 5-10

IN TRANSIT
LPs: 10/12-inch
RCA 5-10 80

INADEQUATES
Singles: 7-inch
CAPITOL 5-10 59

INCIDENTALS
Singles: 7-inch
FORD (134 "All Night") 15-25 64
FORD (138 "Lucille") 15-25 65
GAR-LO (1000 "Barbara") 15-25 61

INCIDENTALS
Singles: 7-inch
PARIS TOWER (126 "It's in Your Mind") 20-30 67

INCOGNITOS
Singles: 7-inch
ZEE (001 "Dee Jay's Dilemma") 50-75 61

INCONCEIVABLES
Singles: 7-inch
COLUMBIA 4-8 66

INCONQUERABLES
Singles: 7-inch
FLODAVIEUR (803 "Wait for Me") 1500-2500 64

INCREDABLES
Singles: 7-inch
KELRICH (851 "If You Gave a Party") 15-25

INCREDIBLE BONGO BAND P&R/R&B '73
Singles: 7-inch
MGM 3-5 73
PRIDE 3-5 72-74
LPs: 10/12-inch
PRIDE 8-10 73-74

INCREDIBLE BROADSIDE BRASS BED BAND
LPs: 10/12-inch
POISON RING 10-12 71

INCREDIBLE CASUALS
LPs: 10/12-inch
ROUNDER 5-8 88
Member: Joe Spampinato.
Also see NRBQ

INCREDIBLE INVADERS
Singles: 7-inch
PROPHONICS (2028 "Boy Is Gone") 10-20 67
Also see LYN & INVADERS

INCREDIBLE STRING BAND LP '68
LPs: 10/12-inch
ELEKTRA 8-12 67-72
REPRISE 8-12 72-74

INCREDIBLE UPSETTERS
EPs: 7-inch
AUDIO LAB (2 "Incredible Upsetters") 250-350 59

INCREDIBLE VIKINGS
Singles: 7-inch
WINNDCOSK ("Love Will Be Mine") 2000-3000 55
(No selection number used.)

INCREDIBLES R&B '66
Singles: 7-inch
AUDIO ARTS 4-8 66-68
CLASS 4-8 66
TETRAGRAMMATON 3-6 69
LPs: 10/12-inch
AUDIO ARTS 10-12 70

INDECENT OBSESSION P&R/LP '90
Singles: 7-inch
MCA 3-4 90
LPs: 10/12-inch
MCA 5-8 90

INDEEP R&B/D&D '83
Singles: 12-inch
SOUND of NEW YORK 4-6 83-85
Singles: 7-inch
SOUND of NEW YORK 3-4 83-85
LPs: 10/12-inch
SOUND of NEW YORK 5-10 83

INDEPENDENTS P&R/R&B '72
Singles: 7-inch
WAND 3-6 72-74
LPs: 10/12-inch
WAND 8-12 72-74
Members: Chuck Jackson; Maurice Jackson; Eric Thomas; Helen Curry.

INDEX
(The Index)
LPs: 10/12-inch
DC ("The Index") 2500-3000 68
(No selection number used. Reportedly 100 made. Identification number in the trail-off is "DC-71.")
DC ("Index") 1500-2500 68
(No selection number used. Not issued with cover. Reportedly 100 made. Identification number in the trail-off is "DC-4736.")
Members: Jim Valice; John Ford; Gary Ballew.

INDIA D&D '83
Singles: 12-inch
WEST END 4-6 83

INDIAN PUDDIN' & PIPE
LP: 10/12-inch
SAN FRANCISCO SOUND 10-20
Members: Jeff Simmons; Phil Kirby; Peter Larson; Al Malosky; Matthew Katz.

INDIAN SUMMER
LPs: 10/12-inch
RCA/NEON 10-12 71

INDIANA C&W '87
Singles: 7-inch
KILLER 3-4 87

INDIGO
Singles: 7-inch
W.B. 3-5 77
LPs: 10/12-inch
W.B. 8-10 77

INDIGO GIRLS P&R/LP '89
Singles: 7-inch
EPIC 3-4 89-90
LPs: 10/12-inch
EPIC 5-8 89-90

INDIGOS
(With the Cornel Tanassy Orchestra)
Singles: 7-inch
ADMIRAL (906 "Get Up & Go") 8-12 61
ARCADE ("Servant of Love") 50-100 59
(Selection number not known.)
CORNEL (515 "High School Social") 15-25 58
CORNEL (3001 "Servant of Love") 200-300 57
IMAGE (5001 "Girl By the Wayside") 10-20 61

INDIGOS
Singles: 7-inch
COR (6581 "He's Coming Home") 10-20 65

INDIGOS R&B '66
Singles: 7-inch
DATE 4-8 66
VERVE/FOLKWAYS 5-10 65

INDIGOS
Singles: 7-inch
NEPTUNE 4-6 69-70

INDIOS TABAJARAS, Los: see LOS INDIOS TABAJARAS

INDIVIDUAL ACTIVITY
Singles: 7-inch
TEE PEE (73/74 "Ten O'Clock") 10-20 68
Members: Al Blau; Brian Olson; Bill Shaw; Dennis Moore.

INDIVIDUALISTS
Singles: 7-inch
ONDA (110 "A Blue Note") 15-25 57

INDIVIDUALS
(With the Curly Palmer Orchestra)
Singles: 7-inch
CHASE (1300 "Wedding Bells") .300-500 64

INDIVIDUALS
Singles: 7-inch
SHOW TIME (595 "Met Her at a Dance") 35-50 59
SHOW TIME (598 "Dear One") 35-50 59
SPARROW (100 "Without Success") 200-300 59

INDIVIDUALS
Singles: 7-inch
RAVEN (2018 "I Want Love") 15-25
RENDEZVOUS (176 "Crazy Horse") 10-15 62
TEQUILA (101 "La Bamba") 10-20 61
TEQUILA (103 "If You Were the Only Girl") 15-25 61
Also see MERCEEDEES

INDIVIDUALS
Singles: 7-inch
RENDEZVOUS (176 "7 Potato Mash") 10-20 62
Members: Pat Vegas; Lolly Vegas.
Also see VEGAS, Pat & Lolly

INDIVIDUALS R&B '75
Singles: 7-inch
P.I.P. 3-5 75
21 3-5
Also see MAHAFFAY, Chuck, & Individuals

INDIVIDUALS / Andrew Taylor
Singles: 7-inch
MUSIC CITY (838 "Beverly My Darling") 150-250 61
Also see TAYLOR, Andrew

INDUSTRIAL IMAGE
Singles: 7-inch
EPIC 4-8 66

INDUSTRY P&R '83
Singles: 7-inch
CAPITOL 3-4 83

INELIGIBLES
Singles: 7-inch
ANDERSON 10-20 65
CAPELLA (501 "Just the Things That You Do") 25-35 60

INEXPENSIVE HANDMADE LOOK
Singles: 7-inch
BRUNSWICK 10-20 67

INFASCINATIONS
Singles: 7-inch
CLAUWELL (004 "I'm So in Love") 500-750 61
(Polystyrene pressing.)
CLAUWELL (004 "I'm So in Love") 25-50 61
(Vinyl pressing.)

INFATUATORS
Singles: 7-inch
DESTINY (504 "I Found My Love") 100-150 61
VEE JAY (395 "I Found My Love") 20-30 61
Also see LEE, Larry, & Leesures

INFERNAL BLUES MACHINE
Singles: 7-inch
LONDON 3-5 76

INFERNO
Singles: 7-inch
DATE 10-20 66

INFERNOS
Singles: 7-inch
HAWK (13500 "Goin' Cruisin' ") 20-30 63
RUDY 5-10 64

INFINITE STAIRCASE
Singles: 7-inch
BLACK SHEEP (1337 "Long Hair") 20-30

INFINITY R&B '69
(Featuring Billy Butler)
Singles: 7-inch
FOUNTAIN 4-6 69
MERCURY 3-5 70
UNI 3-5 72
Members: Billy Butler; Earl Batts; Jess Tillman; Larry Wade; Phyllis Know.
Also see BUTLER, Billy

INFLAMMABLE, Dan
Singles: 7-inch
WINE (09 "High Flying") 40-60

INFLUENCE
LPs: 10/12-inch
ABC (630 "Influence") 25-35 68
Members: Andrew Keiler; Walter Rossi; Dave Wynne; Jack Geisinger; Louis McKelvey; Bobo Island.
Also see HAUNTED
Also see LUKE & APOSTLES

INFORMATION SOCIETY P&R/LP '88
Singles: 7-inch
TOMMY BOY 3-4 88-90
Picture Sleeves
TOMMY BOY 3-4 88
LPs: 10/12-inch
TOMMY BOY 5-8 88-90

INFORMERS
Singles: 7-inch
DORE (562 "Don't Cry") 20-30 60

INFORMERS
(With Morris Bailey & Orchestra)
Singles: 7-inch
BLACKJACK (1402 "Baby, Set Me Free") 300-500 65
J-RUDE (1400 "If You Love Me") 200-300 65
(Identification number shown since no selection number is used.)
Also see BAILEY, Morris, & Thomas Boys

INGLE, Red, & Natural Seven C&W '47
(With Jo Stafford as "Cinderella G. Stump")
Singles: 78 rpm
CAPITOL 5-10 47-48
Also see JONES, Spike
Also see STAFFORD, Jo

INGLES, David C&W '69
Singles: 7-inch
CAPITOL 3-6 69

INGMANN, Jørgen P&R/R&B '61
Singles: 78 rpm
MERCURY 4-8 56
Singles: 7-inch
ATCO 5-10 60-66
MERCURY 8-12 56
PARROT 4-8 64
U.A. INT'L 4-6 68
LPs: 10/12-inch
ATCO 25-35 62
MERCURY 25-35 56
U.A. INT'L 8-12 68

INGRAM R&B '77
Singles: 7-inch
H&L 3-5 77
LPs: 10/12-inch
H&L 8-10 77

INGRAM, Benny
Singles: 7-inch
BANDERA (1302 "Jello Sal") 75-100 58
TODD 10-20 59

INGRAM, James R&B/D&D/LP '83
Singles: 12-inch
QWEST 4-6 83
Singles: 7-inch
MCA 3-4 87
QWEST 3-4 83-86
W.B. 3-4 90
Picture Sleeves
QWEST 3-4 83-86
LPs: 10/12-inch
QWEST 5-10 83-86
W.B. 5-8 90
Also see AUSTIN, Patti, & James Ingram
Also see JONES, Quincy, & James Ingram
Also see ROGERS, Kenny, Kim Carnes & James Ingram
Also see RONSTADT, Linda, & James Ingram
Also see U.S.A. for AFRICA

INGRAM, James, & Michael McDonald P&R/R&B '83
Singles: 7-inch
QWEST 3-4 83
Also see INGRAM, James
Also see McDONALD, Michael

INGRAM, Luther R&B '69
(With the G-Men)
Singles: 7-inch
DECCA (31794 "Ain't That Nice") 4-8 65
ERIC 3-4 70s
HIB (698 "If It's All the Same to You Babe") 50-75 67
KO KO 5-10 67-78
PROFILE 3-4 86-87
SMASH (2019 "Foxy Devil") 10-15 66
LPs: 10/12-inch
KO KO 8-10 71-76
(May also be shown as Koko—one word.)

INGREDIENTS
Singles: 7-inch
TODDLIN' TOWN (101 "Hey Who") 15-25 67
Also see RUSH HOUR

IN-GROUP
LPs: 10/12-inch
IN (1002 "Swinging 12 String") 15-25 64
Members: Glen Campbell; Leon Russell; Earl Palmer.
Also see CAMPBELL, Glen
Also see RUSSELL, Leon

INITIALS
("As Originated on the Terry Lee Show")
Singles: 7-inch
DEE (1001 "Bells of Joy") 100-150 59
KELLA (100 "Giggling Girl") 200-300
SHERRY (2 "Bells of Joy") 50-75 59
(What appears to the the selection number actually reads "Teen Sound #2.")
VINTAGE 3-5 73

INITIALS
Singles: 7-inch
CONGRESS (207 "School Day") ... 10-15 64
CONGRESS (219 "Dancing on the Sand") 10-15 64

INK SPOTS P&R '39
(Charlie Fuqua's Ink Spots; Charlie Owens & Sensational Ink Spots)
Singles: 78 rpm
BLUEBIRD (6530 "Swingin' on the Strings") 15-25 36
DECCA (800 series) 10-15 36
DECCA (1000 thru 4000 series) 5-15 36-42
DECCA (18000 thru 30000 series) 5-10 42-57
Singles: 7-inch
DECCA 10-20 50-61
GRAND AWARD 8-15 56
VERVE 5-10 60
X-TRA 5-10 60
EPs: 7-inch
DECCA 5-15 54-56
GRAND AWARD 5-15 56
TOPS (606 "Ink Spots") 10-15 59
(Two discs.)
WALDORF MUSIC HALL 5-15 55
LPs: 10/12-inch
AUDITION 15-25 56
COLORTONE 15-25 58
CORAL 4-8 73
CORONET 10-15 60s
CROWN (144 "Greatest Hits") 10-15 59
(Black vinyl.)
CROWN (144 "Greatest Hits") 40-60 59
(Colored vinyl.)
CROWN (175 "The Ink Spots") 10-15 61
(Monaural.)
CROWN (217 "Sensational Ink Spots") 10-15 61
CROWN (448 "If I Didn't Care") 10-15 63
CROWN (5112 "Greatest Hits") 10-15 59
(Monaural.)
CROWN (5142 "The Ink Spots") 10-15 61
(Stereo.)
CROWN (5197 "Sensational Ink Spots") 10-15 62
DECCA (182 "Best of the Ink Spots") 10-20 65
(Monaural. Two discs.)
DECCA (7-182 "Best of the Ink Spots") 10-20 65
(Stereo. Two discs.)
DECCA (4297 "Our Golden Favorites") 10-20 63
(Monaural.)
DECCA (7-4297 "Our Golden Favorites") 10-20 63
(Stereo.)
DECCA (5000 series) 20-40 51-53
(10-inch LPs.)
DECCA (7000 & 8000 series) 15-30 54-59
DESIGN 5-10 60s
DIPLOMAT 5-10 64
EVEREST 5-10 82
EVON 10-20 50s
EXACT 5-10 80
FLAGG (20117 "Someone Loves Someone") 20-25
FORD (115 "Hawaiian Wedding Song") 15-25 62
GOLDEN TONE 5-10

GRAND AWARD 10-25 56-59
HURRAH 10-15 60s
MCA 5-10 73
MAYFAIR 8-15
MODERN (7023 "Fabulous Ink Spots") 75-125
MONTGOMERY WARD'S 10-20
(Colored vinyl.)
PRI (3 "In the Spotlight") 10-15
PAULA 5-10 72
PIROUETTE 10-20
SPIN-O-RAMA 5-10 60s
TOPS (1561 "The Ink Spots") 20-30 57
TOPS (1668 "The Ink Spots, Vol. 2") 15-20 59
VERVE 15-25 56-60
VOCALION 8-15 59-65
WALDORF MUSIC HALL (144 "Spirituals and Jubilees") 30-50 55
WALDORF MUSIC HALL (152 "Spirituals and Jubilees, Vol. 2") 30-50 55
WESCO ("Hawaiian Wedding Song") 25-35 62
(Selection number not known.)
Members: Bill Kenny; Orville Jones; Herb Kenny; Charlie Fuqua; Ivory "Deek" Watson; Bernie Mackey; Cliff Givens; Billy Bowen; Charlie Owens.
Also see BROOKS, George E., & Ink Spots
Also see BROWN DOTS
Also see FITZGERALD, Ella, & Ink Spots
Also see FOUR DOTS
Also see KENNY, Bill
Also see OWENS, Charlie

INK SPOTS
Singles: 78 rpm
KING (1297 thru 1512) 15-25 53-55
KING (4670 "Here in My Lonely Room") 20-30 53
(Blue label.)
KING (4670 "Here in My Lonely Room") 40-60 53
(White label with "Introducing the Ink Spots" bio. Promotional issue only.)
KING (4857 "Command Me") 15-25 55
Singles: 7-inch
KING (1297 "Ebb Tide") 25-50 53
KING (1304 "Stranger in Paradise") 40-60 54
KING (1336 "Melody of Love") 40-60 54
KING (1378 "Yesterday") 25-50 54
KING (1425 "Someone's Rocking My Dreamboat") 25-50 55
KING (1429 "Melody of Love") 20-40 55
KING (1512 "Don't Laugh at Me") 20-40 55
KING (4670 "Here in My Lonely Room") 75-125 53
(Blue label.)
KING (4670 "Here in My Lonely Room") 100-200 53
(White label with "Introducing the Ink Spots" bio. Promotional issue only.)
KING (4857 "Command Me") 20-40 55
EPs: 7-inch
KING (376 "Great Songs of Our Times Sung by Ink Spots") 50-100 56
LPs: 10/12-inch
KING (535 "Something Old, Something New") 100-200 57
KING (642 "Something Old, Something New") 75-125 59
Members: James Holmes; Charlie Fuqua; Harry Jackson; Isaac Royal; Leon Antoine.

INK SPOTS
Singles: 7-inch
FABULOUS (1003 "A Man") 50-75 63
Members: Joe Van Loan; Ray Richardson; Napoleon Allen; Bob Moreland; Al Meyers; George Kelly.
Also see MODERN INK SPOTS
Also see VAN LOAN, Joe

INMAN, Autry — C&W '53
Singles: 78 rpm
DECCA (Except 28629 & 29936) 4-8 53-56
DECCA (28629 "That's All Right") 5-10 56
DECCA (29936 "Be Bop Baby") 5-10 56
Singles: 7-inch
DECCA (Except 28629 & 29936) 5-10 53-56
DECCA (28629 "That's All Right") 15-25 56
DECCA (29936 "Be Bop Baby") 25-50 56
EPIC 4-8 67-69
GLAD 5-10 60
JUBILEE 4-8 65-69
MERCURY 4-8 62
MILLION 3-5 72
RCA 5-10 58
RISQUE (103 "Niteclubbin' ") 5-10 67
RISQUE (105 "The Golf Game") 5-10 67
SIMS 4-8 63-64
U.A. 5-8 60
LPs: 10/12-inch
ALSHIRE 8-12 69
EPIC 10-15 68
GUEST STAR 8-12
JUBILEE 10-20 64-69
MOUNTAIN DEW 15-25 63
SIMS 15-20 64
Also see DEAN, Jimmy / David Houston / Warner Mack / Autry Inman

INMAN, Deryl
LPs: 10/12-inch
L.A. 5-10 77

INMAN, Jerry — C&W '74
Singles: 7-inch
CHELSEA 3-5 74
ELEKTRA 3-5 78-79
LPs: 10/12-inch
COLUMBIA 10-15 68
ELEKTRA 5-10 76

INMAN, Jimmy
(With the Impollos)
Singles: 7-inch
ALADDIN (3426 "I'm So Sorry") 40-60 58
NRC (5004 "Saving My Love") 15-25 59

INMAN, Leroy, & Ira Rogers
LPs: 10/12-inch
MERCURY 10-20 63

IN-MEN LTD.
(Featuring Skip Hinshaw)
Singles: 7-inch
JOKERS THREE ("Voice Your Choice") 20-30 60s
(Selection number not known.)
PYRAMID (7200 "Take a Look at Me Baby") 15-25 66
PYRAMID (7454 "Little Girl") 15-25 60s

INMATES
Singles: 7-inch
COLUMBIA 10-20 67
KOPIT 10-20 66

INMATES
Singles: 7-inch
JCP (1029 "Baby, Come On") 10-20 64

INMATES — P&R/LP '79
Singles: 7-inch
POLYDOR/RADAR 3-5 79
LPs: 10/12-inch
POLYDOR 5-10 79-80

IN-MEN
Singles: 7-inch
PYRAMID (7454 "Little Girl") 15-25

INN CROWD
Singles: 7-inch
20TH FOX 4-8 66

INNER CIRCLE
Singles: 7-inch
DUNHILL (4128 "Goes to Show You") 10-20 68
IMPACT (1019 "Sally Go Round the Roses") 15-25 67
Members: Phil Sloan; Steve Barri.
Also see FANTASTIC BAGGYS

INNER CIRCLE
Singles: 12-inch
ATLANTIC 5-8 91
Singles: 7-inch
CAPITOL 3-5 76-77
ISLAND 3-5 79
MANGO 3-4 80
SALSOUL 3-4 81
LPs: 10/12-inch
CAPITOL 5-10 76-77
ISLAND 5-10 79
MANGO 5-10 80
SALSOUL 5-10 81

INNER CITY — P&R/LP '89
Singles: 7-inch
VIRGIN 3-4 89-90
Picture Sleeves
VIRGIN 3-4 89
LPs: 10/12-inch
VIRGIN 5-8 89

INNER CITY JAM BAND — R&B '77
Singles: 7-inch
BAREBACK 3-5 77

INNER CITY MISSION
Singles: 7-inch
KAMA SUTRA 5-10 70

INNER DIALOGUE
LPs: 10/12-inch
RANWOOD 8-10 70
Members: Lynn Dolin; Ernie McDaniel; Gene Di Novi; Barry Zweig; Kay Cole.

INNER LIFE — R&B '79
Singles: 12-inch
SALSOUL 4-6 83
Singles: 7-inch
PERSONAL 3-4 84
PRELUDE 3-5 79-80
SALSOUL 3-4 83
Member: Jocelyn Brown.
Also see BROWN, Jocelyn

INNER LITE
Singles: 7-inch
SSEXX 4-8
Member: Ritchie Cordell.
Also see CORDELL, Ritchie

INNER THOUGHTS
Singles: 7-inch
PARIS TOWER (105 "1,000 Miles") 20-30 67

INNERVISION — R&B '75
Singles: 7-inch
ARIOLA AMERICA 3-5 77
PRIVATE STOCK 3-5 75

INNES, Dixie Lee
Singles: 7-inch
BELL 3-5 72
LPs: 10/12-inch
BELL 8-12 72
Also see ORIGINAL CASTE

INNKEEPERS
Singles: 7-inch
GALIKO (895 "Wanted") 20-30
SIX CENTS ("A Man Can Tell") 30-40

INNOCENCE — P&R '66
Singles: 7-inch
KAMA SUTRA 4-8 66-67
LPs: 10/12-inch
KAMA SUTRA 15-20 67
Members: Pete Anders; Vinnie Poncia.
Also see ANDERS & PONCIA

INNOCENCE IN DANGER — D&D '84
Singles: 12-inch
EPIC 4-6 84
Singles: 7-inch
EPIC 3-4 84

INNOCENCE MISSION — LP '90
LPs: 10/12-inch
A&M 5-8 90

INNOCENT BYSTANDERS
Singles: 7-inch
ATLANTIC (2766 "Frantic Escape") 8-12 70
PAMELINE (302 "Crime") 10-20

INNOCENTS — P&R '60
Singles: 7-inch
DECCA (31519 "Don't Cry") 15-25 63
ERA 3-5 72
INDIGO (105 "Honest I Do") 15-25 60
INDIGO (111 "Gee Whiz") 15-25 60
INDIGO (116 "Kathy") 15-25 61
INDIGO (124 "Beware") 15-25 61
INDIGO (128 "Donna") 15-25 61
INDIGO (132 "Pains in My Heart") 15-25 61
INDIGO (141 "Time") 10-20 62
PORT (3026 "Gee Whiz") 5-10 60s
REPRISE (20112 "Oh How I Miss My Baby"/"Be Mine") 15-25 62
REPRISE (20125 "Oh How I Miss My Baby"/"You're Never Satisfied") 10-20 62
TRANS WORLD (7001 "Tick Tock") 15-25 60
W.B. (5450 "My Heart Stood Still") 20-30 64
LPs: 10/12-inch
INDIGO (503 "Innocently Yours") 50-100 61
Members: Darron Stankey; Al Candalaria; Jim West. Session: Gary Paxton.
Also see ECHOES
Also see KENJOLAIRS
Also see PAXTON, Gary
Also see SUGAR BEATS
Also see WASHER WINDSHIELD
Also see YOUNG, Kathy

INNOCENTS
LPs: 10/12-inch
BOARDWALK 5-10 82

INNSMEN
Singles: 7-inch
WHEELS (3611 "I Don't Know") 20-30 67

IN-OVATIONS
Singles: 7-inch
ASCOT (2219 "This Ain't Real") 5-8 66

INOVATIONS
Singles: 7-inch
HIT SOUND (889 "Stay on the Case") 5-8 70
HIT SOUND (890 "Just Keep on Loving") 5-8 70

INRHODES
Singles: 7-inch
DUNHILL 5-10 66-67

INSANE
Singles: 7-inch
ALLEN ASSOCIATES (201,347 "I Can't Prove It") 20-30 67

IN-SECT
LPs: 10/12-inch
CAMDEN (909 "Introducing the In-Sect Direct from England") 20-30 65

INSECT FEAR
EPs: 7-inch
MANUFACTURE 3-5 90
(Issued with a paper sleeve.)

INSECT TRUST
Singles: 7-inch
ATCO (6764 "Reciprocity") 5-10 69
DYNAMIC SOUND 5-10 67
LPs: 10/12-inch
ATCO (313 "Hoboken Saturday Night") 20-30 70
CAPITOL (0109 "Insect Trust") 15-25 68
Members: Nancy Jeffries; Luke Faust.

INSECTS: see LITTLE LADY BEATLES / Insects

INSIDE OUT
LPs: 10/12-inch
FREDLO (6834 "Bringing It All Back") 100-200 68

INSIDE-OUTS
Singles: 7-inch
PALMER 5-10

INSIDERS
Singles: 7-inch
RCA (9225 "I'm Just a Man") 10-20 67
RCA (9325 "If You Had a Heart") 10-20 67
RED BIRD (055 "Chapel Bells Are Calling") 8-12 66

INSIDERS — LP '87
Singles: 12-inch
EPIC ("Ghost on the Beach") 4-8 87
(Promotional issue only.)
Singles: 7-inch
EPIC (07352 "Ghost on the Beach") 3-4 87
(Black vinyl.)
EPIC (07352 "Ghost on the Beach") 4-8 87
(Colored vinyl. Promotional issue only.)
Picture Sleeves
EPIC (07352 "Ghost on the Beach") 3-4 87
LPs: 10/12-inch
EPIC (40630 "Ghost on the Beach") 5-10 87

INSIGHT
Singles: 7-inch
CASCADE ("Please Come Home for Christmas") 15-25 64

INSIGHTS
Singles: 7-inch
PALMETTO ARTISTS (9021 "I Need Your Lonliness") 15-25

INSITES
Singles: 7-inch
VAGUE (901 "Nothing Is Wrong with Love") 10-20 66

INSPIRATIONS
(With Fats Gaines & Band)
Singles: 78 rpm
APOLLO (494 "Raindrops") 50-75 56
Singles: 7-inch
APOLLO (494 "Raindrops") 150-250 56
LAMP (2019 "Don't Cry") 75-100 58

INSPIRATIONS
Singles: 78 rpm
JAMIE (1034 "Dry Your Eyes") 25-50 56
Singles: 7-inch
AL-BRITE (1651 "Angel in Disguise") 40-60 59
BELTONE (2037 "The Girl by My Side") 25-50 63
GONE (5097 "Angel in Disguise") 20-40 61
JAMIE (1034 "Dry Your Eyes") 75-125 56
JAMIE (1212 "Dry Your Eyes") 15-25 62
RONDAK (9787 "Ring Those Bells") 1000-2000 61
SPARKLE (102 "Angel in Disguise") 100-200 59
SULTAN (1 "The Genie") 20-30 59
Picture Sleeves
SULTAN (1 "The Genie") 50-75 59

INSPIRATIONS
Singles: 7-inch
RONDACK (9787 "Ring Those Bells") 175-225 63

INSPIRATIONS
Singles: 7-inch
MIDAS (9003 "Your Wish Is My Command") 250-500 64

INSPIRATIONS
Singles: 7-inch
FEATURE (110 "Baby Please Come Home") 25-35 66

INSPIRATIONS
Singles: 7-inch
BLACK PEARL 5-10 67
BREAKTHROUGH ("No One Can Take Your Place") 20-30
(Selection number not known.)

INSPIRATIONS
Singles: 7-inch
PKC (1012 "Watermelon Man") 10-20 68
Members: John Draws; Tom Bloom; Ron Skaluta; Dean Hottinger; Steve Fuchs; Dave Zylka; Bill Tate Tazinsky; Dale Streeter.

INSPIRATIONS
Singles: 7-inch
BIM BAM BOOM 4-8 72

INSPIRATIONS
Singles: 7-inch
BREAKTHROUGH ("No One Can Take Your Place") 20-30
(Selection number not known.)

INSPIRATORS
Singles: 78 rpm
TREAT (502 "If Loving You Is Wrong") 100-200 55
Singles: 7-inch
LOST NITE 4-8
OLD TOWN (1053 "Starlight Tonight") 175-225 58
TREAT (502 "If Loving You Is Wrong") 300-500 55

INSTANT FUNK — P&R/R&B/LP '79
Singles: 12-inch
SALSOUL 4-8 79-83
Singles: 7-inch
SALSOUL 3-5 78-83
TSOP 3-5 75-77
LPs: 10/12-inch
SALSOUL 5-10 79-83
TSOP 5-10 76

INSTANT RALSTON
Singles: 7-inch
SCEPTER 8-12 71

INSTANTS
Singles: 7-inch
RENDEZVOUS (193 "Always Be True") 20-30 62

INSTIGATIONS
Singles: 7-inch
T-BIRD (101 "I Don't Want to Discuss It") 10-15

INSTINCTS
LPs: 10/12-inch
TCS (3952 "Loving Sandwich Live") 10-15

INSTRUCTIONS
LPs: 10/12-inch
RADIO 5-10 82

INSTRUMENTALS
Singles: 7-inch
FORWARD 5-10 59
HANOVER 5-10 58
RED FOX (100 "Chop Suey Rock") 10-15

INTELLECTUALS
Singles: 7-inch
STARK (010 "One True Love") 10-20 60s

INTENSIONS
Singles: 7-inch
BLUELIGHT (1212 "She's My Baby") 25-35
BLUELIGHT (1214 "I Don't Care Anymore") 25-35
BLUELIGHT (1234 "I Don't Get Down Like That") 25-35

INTENTIONS
Singles: 7-inch
JAMIE (1253 "Summertime Angel") 1000-1500 63

INTENTIONS
Singles: 7-inch
UPTOWN 5-10 65

INTENTIONS
Singles: 7-inch
MELRON (5014 "I'm in Love with a Go Go Girl") 150-200 65
Members: Chip Kopaczewski; Tony Avicoll; Charlie Votta; Ed Sachetti.

INTENTIONS
Singles: 7-inch
PHILIPS (40428 "Don't Forget That I Love You") 10-20 67
Members: Brian Humble; Jack Vallati; Dennis Brennan; Ron Brennan; Greg Coates; Rick Smith; Henry Urick; Bob Siverling.
Also see EXCITING INVICTAS
Also see HUMBLE GATHERING

INTENTIONS
Singles: 7-inch
BLACK PEARL 4-8
BLUE LIGHT 3-6

INTENSIVE HEAT
LPs: 10/12-inch
MY DISC 5-10 82

INTERGALACTIC TOURING BAND
LPs: 10/12-inch
PASSPORT 5-10 77

INTERIORS
Singles: 7-inch
WORTHY (1008 "Darling Little Angel") 125-150 61
WORTHY (1009 "Echoes") 50-75 61

INTERLUDE — R&B '80
Singles: 7-inch
STAR VISION INT'L 3-4 80

INTERLUDES
Singles: 7-inch
RCA (7281 "I Shed a Million Tears") 30-50 58
Members: Frankie Anderson; Kenny Loftman; Otha Sonnie; Eddie Adams; Fred Jackson.

INTERLUDES
Singles: 7-inch
HI 10-15 59
VALLEY 10-15 59-60

INTERLUDES
Singles: 7-inch
ABC-PAR (10213 "No. 1 in the Nation") 10-20 61
KING (5633 "Darling I'll Be True") 25-35 62

INTERNAL CANITERY SIN: see GEARS / Emeralds / Dedicated Followers / Internal Canitery Sin

INTERNATIONAL ALL STARS — LP '61
LPs: 10/12-inch
LONDON 5-10 61

INTERNATIONAL BONGO BAND
Singles: 7-inch
CHALLENGE 4-8 65

INTERNATIONAL BOOGIE BAND
Singles: 7-inch
GAME (296 "Drinkin' Wine Spo-Dee-O-Dee") 15-25

INTERNATIONAL BRICK
Singles: 7-inch
CAMELOT 10-15 67

INTERNATIONAL GTO's
Singles: 7-inch
ROJAC (1007 "I Love My Baby") 15-25 60s

INTERNATIONAL POP ORCHESTRA
Singles: 7-inch
CAMEO 5-10 61
LPs: 10/12-inch
WYNCOTE 10-20 60s

INTERNATIONAL SUBMARINE BAND
Singles: 7-inch
ASCOT (2218 "The Russians Are Coming") 10-15 66
COLUMBIA 8-12 66
LHI 5-10 68
Picture Sleeves
ASCOT (2218 "The Russians Are Coming") 25-35 66
LPs: 10/12-inch
LHI (12001 "Safe at Home") 40-60 68
Members: Gram Parsons; Earl Ball; Bob Buchanan; Jon Corneal; John Nuese; J.D. Maness.
Also see PARSONS, Gram

INTERNATIONALS
Singles: 7-inch
ABC-PAR (9964 "Goin' to a Party") 10-20 58

INTERNS
Singles: 7-inch
CAPITOL 4-8 66
UPTOWN 4-8 66

INTERPRETATIONS
Singles: 7-inch
BELL 5-10 69

INTERPRETERS
Singles: 7-inch
A-BET (9425 "Pretty Little Thing") 10-15 67
GEMINI (100 "Stop That Man") 10-20 65
LPs: 10/12-inch
CADET 10-15 66

INTERTAINS
Singles: 7-inch
UPTOWN 5-10 65-66

INTERVAL, Jimmy
Singles: 7-inch
WORLD ARTIST (1018 "One-Sided Love") 5-10 64

INTERVALS
(With Chick Morris & His Band)
Singles: 7-inch
AD (104 "I Still Love That Man") 20-30 58
APT (25019 "I Still Love That Man") 10-20 59
CLASS (304 "Here's That Rainy Day") 75-100 62
Also see FIFTH DIMENSION

INTERVIEW
LPs: 10/12-inch
VIRGIN 5-10 82

INTICERS
Singles: 7-inch
BABY LOV (003 "I've Got to Find My Baby") 15-25

INTIMATES
Singles: 7-inch
AMCAN (402 "Only Girl for Me") 25-45 64
AMCAN (402 "Got You Where I Want You") 15-25 64
EPIC 8-12 64

INTREPIDES
Singles: 7-inch
MASCIO (120 "Golash") 20-30 65

INTREPIDS
Singles: 7-inch
COTILLION (44094 "It's Just a Picture") 10-15 70

INTRIGUES
Singles: 7-inch
BRUNSWICK 4-8 63
JOEY (6152 "Road Race") 10-15 62

INTRIGUES
Singles: 7-inch
PORT 10-20 66

INTRIGUES P&R/R&B '69
Singles: 7-inch
TOOT 4-8 68
YEW 3-6 69-71
LPs: 10/12-inch
YEW 10-15 70

INTRIGUES
Singles: 7-inch
WORLD TRADE 3-4 85

INTRIQUE R&B '87
Singles: 7-inch
COOLTEMPO 3-4 87

INTROS
Singles: 7-inch
JAMIE (1350 "Stop, Look and Listen") 10-20 67

INTRUDER
Singles
IRON WORKS (1024 "Cover Up") 10-15 88
(Monster-shaped picture disc. 500 made.)
IRON WORKS (1024-A "Cover Up") 10-20 88
(Square picture disc. 200 made.)
LPs: 10/12-inch
IRON WORKS (1023 "Live to Die") 10-15 88
(Picture disc. 500 made.)

INTRUDERS P&R '59
(Intruders Trio)
Singles: 7-inch
BELTONE (1009 "Camptown Rock") 5-10 61
FAME (101 "Jeffries Rock") 10-20 59
FAME (313 "Creepin") 10-20 59
FAME (616 "Rock-A-Ma-Roll") 10-20 59
VALTONE (409 "Rockamaroll") 15-25 59

INTRUDERS
Singles: 7-inch
TOAD (27166 "Dis-Tor-Shun") 8-12 63

INTRUDERS P&R/R&B '66
Singles: 7-inch
EXCEL 10-15
GAMBLE 5-10 66-73
GOWEN (1401 "Come Home Soon") 20-40 62
PHILADELPHIA INT'L 3-5 72
RIPETE 3-5 85
TSOP 3-5 74-75
Picture Sleeves
GAMBLE 4-8 66
LPs: 10/12-inch
GAMBLE 10-15 67-73
TSOP 8-10 75
Members: Sam Brown; Eugene Doughtry; Phil Terry; Robert Edwards; Bobby Starr.

INTRUDERS
Singles: 7-inch
ANDERSON (103 "Intruder") 20-30 63
MUSIC VOICE (504 "But You Belong to Me") 15-25 64
SAHARA (101 "Wild Goose") 10-20 63

INTRUDERS
Singles: 7-inch
GALLANTRY 10-15 63
MOXIE 10-20 64
Also see BELOVED ONES
Also see DEARLY BELOVEDS
Also see QUINSTRELS

INTRUDERS
Singles: 7-inch
IT (2312 "She's Mine") 10-20 66
Picture Sleeves
IT (2312 "She's Mine") 20-30 66

INTRUDERS
Singles: 7-inch
CINEMA (6901 "Total Raunch") 25-50 66
MARLO (1545 "That's the Way") 30-40 66
Picture Sleeves
CINEMA (6901 "Total Raunch") 50-100 66

INTRUDERS
Singles: 7-inch
CLAREMONT (665 "Bringing Me Down") 10-20 66

INTRUDERS FIVE
Singles: 7-inch
GROG (2201 "Ain't Comin' Back") 20-30 66

INVADERS
Singles: 7-inch
BAMBOO 10-20 61
EL TORO (503 "Paradise") 25-35 63
INSTRO (1000 "Invasion") 10-15 62
(Also issued as *Surfer's Charge* by the Roulettes.)
MOHAWK 8-12 64
MUSICTONE 5-8 65
OO 4-6
PHILIPS 5-10 64
VAUGHN LTD. 10-20
WHINGDING 10-15
LPs: 10/12-inch
JUSTICE (125 "On the Right Track") 100-200 60s
Also see ROULETTES

INVADERS
Singles: 7-inch
CALENDAR ("I Won't Be Lanly [sic]") 8-12 68
CALENDAR (223 "Invasion") 8-12 68
CAPITOL (2292 "California Sun") 5-10 68
USA (902 "Flower Song") 5-10 68
Members: Dave Dobry; Mark Paulick; Pete Polzak; Jim Sawyer; John Sawyer.

INVADERS
Singles: 7-inch
DELTA (2134 "You Can't Sit Down") 8-12
JCP (1027 "You Really Tear Me Up") 10-20 64
PHALANX (1028 "Set Me Free") 50-100 60s

INVADERS
Singles: 7-inch
20TH FOX (469 "Mr. Guitar") 10-20 64
(Previously issued as *Crazy* by Buchanan & Goodman.)
Also see BUCHANAN & GOODMAN

INVASION
Singles: 7-inch
DYNAMIC SOUND (2004 "Invasion Is Coming") 5-10 67
DYNAMIC SOUND (2009 "Do You Like What You See") 5-10 67
Members: Gene Peranich; Don Gruender; Mark Miller; Mike Jablonski; Tony Menotti; Bob McKenna; Rick Cier; P.T. Pedersen; Gary Frey; Bruce Cole.
Also see ETHICS

INVENTIONS
Singles: 7-inch
UP 8-12 60

INVERTS
Singles: 7-inch
TOWER (324 "Look Out Love") 15-25 67

INVICTAS
(With the Hollywood Rebels; "Featuring Sonny Patterson")
Singles: 7-inch
JACK BEE (1003 "Gone So Long") 50-75 59
VAULT (903 "Gone So Long") 15-25 63
(Also issued on Vault 101, credited to Sonny Patterson & the Invictas.)
Also see HOMBS, Jimmie / Twinkletones
Also see PASTEL SIX
Also see PATTERSON, Sonny, & Invictas

INVICTAS
Singles: 7-inch
20TH FOX (493 "Breakout") 10-15 64
LPs: 10/12-inch
20TH FOX (3132 "The Invictas") 30-40 64

INVICTAS
Singles: 7-inch
SAHARA (107 "The Hump") 5-10 65
SAHARA (110 "Do It") 5-10 65
SAHARA (113 "I'm Alright") 5-10 65
SAHARA (117 "Shake a Tail Feather") 5-10 65
LPs: 10/12-inch
EVA (12016 "A-Go-Go") 10-15 83
SAHARA (101 "A-Go-Go") 50-100 65
Member: Herb McGovern.

INVICTAS
Singles: 7-inch
PIX (1101 "Lest You Forget") 800-1200 60
RAMA RAMA (7779 "New Babe") 15-25

INVICTORS
Singles: 7-inch
BEE (1117 "I'll Always Care for You") 100-200 59

INVICTORS
Singles: 7-inch
TPE (8217 "This Thing Called Love") 50-100 62
TPE (8219 "Don't Take My Love") 50-100 62
TPE (8221 "Where All Lovers Meet") 600-800 62
(Reissued in '63 with a Victorio label added on top of this one, crediting the Vendors.)
TPE (8223 "I Took a Chance") 200-300 62
Also see VENDORS

INVINCIBLE SONGBIRDS: see CONVINCERS

INVINCIBLES
Singles: 7-inch
CHESS (1727 "Mr. Moonglow") 30-40 59
Members: David Richardson; Clifton Knight; Lester Johnson.

INVINCIBLES R&B '65
Singles: 7-inch
DOUBLE SHOT (131 "Keep on Trying") 10-20 66
LOMA (2032 "Can't Win") 10-20 66
LOMA (2057 "How Many Times") 10-20 66
RAMPART (665 "Crystal Blue Persuasion") 5-10 69
STARDOM (3500 "Heart Full of Love 1970") 5-10 70
W.B. (5495 "Heart Full of Love") 15-20 64
W.B. (5636 "My Heart Cries") 15-20 65
W.B. (5667 "I Got Soul") 15-20 65
W.B. (7061 "Git It") 8-12 67
Members: Lester Johnson; David Richardson; Clifton Knight.

INVINCIBLES
Singles: 7-inch
INVINCIBLE (200 "Tonda") 5-10 66

INVISIBLE MAN'S BAND P&R/R&B/LP '80
Singles: 7-inch
BOARDWALK 3-4 81-82
MANGO 3-4 80
MOVE'N GROOVE 3-4 83
LPs: 10/12-inch
BOARDWALK 10-20 81
MANGO 5-8 80
Members: Clarence Burke; Ken Burke; James Burke; Dennis Burke.
Also see FIVE STAIRSTEPS

INVITATIONS
Singles: 7-inch
DIAMOND 5-10 68
DYNO VOICE (206 "Written on the Wall") 15-25 65
DYNO VOICE (210 "What's Wrong with Me Baby") 15-25 65
DYNO VOICE (215 " Skiing in the Snow") 25-50 66
MGM (13574 "The Skate") 5-10 66
OUT of the PAST (9 "Skiing in the Snow") 5-10

INVITATIONS R&B '73
Singles: 7-inch
SILVER BLUE 5-10 73
Members: Herman Colefield; Gary Grant; Bill Morris; Bobby Rivers.

INVITATIONS
Singles: 7-inch
BIG TREE 3-5

INXS P&R/LP '83
Singles: 12-inch
ATCO 4-6 84
ATLANTIC (Except 86563) 4-6 85-86
ATLANTIC (86563 "New Sensation") 10-15 88
(Picture disc.)
ATLANTIC (86563 "New Sensation") 15-20 88
(Picture disc. Promotional issue only.)
Singles: 7-inch
ATCO 3-4 83-85
ATLANTIC 3-4 85-90
Picture Sleeves
ATCO 3-4 83-84
ATLANTIC 3-4 85-90
LPs: 10/12-inch
ATCO 5-10 83-85
ATLANTIC 5-10 85-90
Members: Micheal Hutchence; Tim Farriss; Andrew Farriss; Jon Farriss; Gary Beers; Kirk Pengilly.

INXS & Jimmy Barnes P&R '87
Singles: 7-inch
ATLANTIC 3-4 87
Also see BARNES, Jimmy
Also see INXS

IOTA
Singles: 7-inch
HI 3-5 71

IRBY, Jerry C&W '48
(With His Texas Ranchers)
Singles: 78 rpm
DAFFAN (106 "Time You Started Looking") 10-20 56
DAFFAN (108 "Clickety Clack") 20-30 56
MGM 5-8 48
Singles: 7-inch
DAFFAN (106 "Time You Started Looking") 30-40 56
DAFFAN (108 "Clickety Clack") 50-80 56
JER-RAY (222 "Chantilly Lace") 10-20 60
POLLY (201 "Forty Nine Women") 20-30

IRBY, Jerry & Jeanne
Singles: 7-inch
JER-RAY (222 "Chantilly Lace") 15-25
Also see IRBY, Jerry

IRBY, Joyce "Fenderella" P&R '90
Singles: 12-inch
MOTOWN 4-8 90
Singles: 7-inch
MOTOWN 3-4 90
LPs: 10/12-inch
MOTOWN 5-8 90
Also see KLYMAXX

IRELAND, Bey
Singles: 7-inch
NEWPORT 4-8 66

IRENE, Cookie
Singles: 7-inch
4 STAR 4-6 75

IRENE & SCOTTS
Singles: 7-inch
SMASH (2138 "I'm Stuck on My Baby") 10-20 67

IRIDESCENTS
Singles: 7-inch
HAWK (4001 "Bali Hai") 25-35
HUDSON (8102 "Three Coins in the Fountain") 15-25 63
(Black vinyl.)
HUDSON (8102 "Three Coins in the Fountain") 50-75 63
(Colored vinyl.)
HUDSON (8107 "I Found You") 10-20 63
INFINITY (37 "Bali Hai") 15-25
ULTRASONIC (109 "The Angels Sang") 200-300 60

IRIS, Donnie P&R/LP '80
Singles: 7-inch
HME 3-4 85
MCA 3-4 80-83
Picture Sleeves
HME 3-4 85
MCA 3-4 82-83
LPs: 10/12-inch
HME 5-10 85
MCA 5-10 80-83
MIDWEST 5-10 80
Also see JAGGERZ

IRISH ROVERS P&R/LP '68
Singles: 7-inch
DECCA 3-6 68-70
LPs: 10/12-inch
CLEVELAND INT'L 5-8 81
DECCA 8-15 68-72
MCA 5-10 73-77
SANDCASTLE 5-10 76
Also see ROVERS

IRMA & FASCINATORS
Singles: 7-inch
SCEPTER 5-10 65

IRMA & LARKS
Singles: 7-inch
PRIORITY (322 "Without You Baby") 50-100 60s

IRON BRIGADE QUICKSTEP
Singles: 7-inch
DECCA 3-6 71

IRON BUTTERFLY P&R/LP '68
Singles: 7-inch
ATCO 3-8 68-71
MCA 3-4 75
EPs: 7-inch
ATCO (4524 "Iron Butterfly") 20-30 68
(Promotional issue only. Issued with paper sleeve.)
LPs: 10/12-inch
ATCO (Except 227) 10-15 68-71
ATCO (227 "Heavy") 15-20 68
MCA 8-10 75
Members: Doug Ingle; Mike Pinera; Larry Reinhardt; Ron Bushy; Lee Dorman; Erik Brann.
Also see CAPTAIN BEYOND
Also see PINERA, Mike

IRON CITY HOUSEROCKERS
Singles: 7-inch
MCA 3-4 79-80
MCA ("Love's So Tough") 20-25 79
(Picture disc. Promotional issue only. Selection number not known.)
MCA (8418 "Hideaway") 8-15 79
(Picture disc. Promotional issue only.)
LPs: 10/12-inch
MCA (Except 1813) 5-10 79-81
MCA (8313 "Love's So Tough") 30-35 79
(Promotional only picture disc.)

IRON GATE
Singles: 7-inch
MARBELL (1001 "Feelin' Bad") 15-25 66

IRON GATE
Singles: 7-inch
MOBIE (3529 "Get Ready") 15-25 68

IRON MAIDEN LP '81
Singles: 7-inch
CAPITOL (Except V-15375) 3-4 88
CAPITOL (V-15375 "Can I Play with Madness") 10-20 88
(Shaped picture disc.)
LPs: 10/12-inch
CAPITOL (Except "SEAX" & "SJ" series) 5-10 82-88
CAPITOL (SEAX-12215 "Number of the Beast") 35-45 82
(Picture disc.)
CAPITOL (SEAX-12306 "Piece of Mind") 40-60 83
(Picture disc.)
CAPITOL (SJ-12321 "Powerslave") 8-12
("Special Limited Edition, Virgin Maiden Vinyl Pressing.")
EPIC 5-8 90
HARVEST 5-10 80-82
Members: Bruce Dickinson; Dave Murray; Adrian Smith; Niko Mc Brian; Steve Harris.

IRON TYRANTS
LPs: 10/12-inch
("World Metal Record") 10-15 84
(Picture disc. No label name or selection number used.)

IRONHORSE P&R/LP '79
Singles: 7-inch
SCOTTI BROS 3-4 79-80
LPs: 10/12-inch
SCOTTI BROS 5-10 79-80
Member: Randy Bachman.
Also see BACHMAN, Randy

IRONING BOARD SAM
Singles: 7-inch
ATLANTIC 3-6 69
HOLIDAY INN 5-10
STYLETONE (391 "Non-Support") 10-20 69
(Colored vinyl.)

IRONMEN
LPs: 10/12-inch
REGGAE 8-10

IRRESISTABLES
Singles: 7-inch
IMPERIAL 4-8 66

IRRIDESCENTS
Singles: 7-inch
HAWK (4001 "Bali Ha'i") 25-35 63
INFINITY (037 "Bali Ha'i") 15-25 63
OLDIES 45 (183 "Bali Ha'i") 8-10 63
Also see STRAWBERRY ALARM CLOCK

IRVIN, Curtis, & Sparks
Singles: 78 rpm
RPM (417 "Make a Little Love") 50-75 54
Singles: 7-inch
RPM (417 "Make a Little Love") 100-150 54

IRVINE, Robert
Singles: 7-inch
PRESTO (525 "Fastest Shot in Town") 50-75

IRVING, Gloria, & Sax Kari
Singles: 78 rpm
STATES 10-20 53
Singles: 7-inch
STATES 15-25 53
Also see KARI, Sax

IRVING, Lonnie C&W '60
Singles: 7-inch
LONNIE IRVING 10-15 50s
STARDAY 5-10 60

IRWIN, Big Dee P&R '63
(Difosco Erwin; Dee Irwin; with Little Eva)
Singles: 7-inch
BLISS 5-10
DIMENSION 5-10 63-64
FAIRMOUNT 8-12 66
IMPERIAL 5-10 68
ROTATE 10-20 65
20TH FOX 5-10
Also see DIFOSCO
Also see ERVIN, Dee
Also see ERWIN, Dee
Also see IRWIN, Dee, & Mamie Galore

Also see LITTLE EVA
Also see PASTELLS

IRWIN, Dee
Singles: 7-inch
REDD COACH ... 5-10

IRWIN, Dee, & Mamie Galore
Singles: 7-inch
IMPERIAL ... 4-8 68-69
Also see IRWIN, Big Dee

IRWIN TWINS
Singles: 7-inch
COLUMBIA (42989 "It's All Right") .. 5-10 64

ISAAC, Esau
Singles: 7-inch
SWAN ... 4-8 62

ISAACSON, Peter C&W '83
Singles: 7-inch
UNION STATION ... 3-4 83-84

ISAAK, Chris LP '87
Singles: 12-inch
W.B. (2265 "Dancin") ... 8-12 80s
(Promotional issue.)
Singles: 7-inch
REPRISE ... 3-4 91
W.B. ... 3-4 85
LPs: 10/12-inch
REPRISE ... 5-8 89
W.B. ... 5-10 87

ISAAK, Steve
LPs: 10/12-inch
W.B. ... 5-10 85

ISABELL, Rusty
Singles: 7-inch
BRENT (7001 "Firewater") ... 15-20 59
BRENT (7006 "Manhunt") ... 15-20 59
Also see RIO ROCKERS

ISH
Singles: 7-inch
GEFFEN ... 3-4 85
Picture Sleeves
CLOUDS ... 4-6 79
LPs: 10/12-inch
CLOUDS ... 5-10 79
GEFFEN ... 5-10 85

ISIS
Singles: 7-inch
BUDDAH ... 3-5 74-75
LPs: 10/12-inch
BUDDAH ... 8-10 74-75

ISLANDERS P&R '59
(Featuring Randy Starr)
Singles: 7-inch
MAYFLOWER ... 5-10 59-60
LPs: 10/12-inch
MAYFLOWER ... 20-30 60
Members: Randy Starr; Frank Metis.
Also see BELAFONTE, Harry / Islanders
Also see STARR, Randy
Also see WARRIORS

ISLE, Jimmy
Singles: 78 rpm
BALLY ... 10-15 57
Singles: 7-inch
BALLY ... 10-15 57
EVEREST ... 5-10 59
MALA ... 5-10 63
ROULETTE (4065 "Goin' Wild") ... 20-30 58
SUN ... 8-12 58-59

ISLE, Ronnie
(With the Yo Yos)
Singles: 7-inch
IMAGE ... 10-20 60
MGM (12682 "Wicked") ... 15-25 58
METRO ... 5-10 59
OKEH ... 4-8 62
Also see WOW WOWS

ISLE OF MAN P&R/LP '86
Singles: 7-inch
PASHA ... 3-4 86
Picture Sleeves
PASHA ... 3-4 86
LPs: 10/12-inch
PASHA ... 5-10 86

ISLEY, Ernie LP '90
Singles: 7-inch
ELEKTRA ... 3-4 90
LPs: 10/12-inch
ELEKTRA ... 5-8 90
Also see ISLEY BROTHERS

ISLEY, Ron
Singles: 7-inch
W.B. ... 3-4 89
LPs: 10/12-inch
W.B. ... 5-8 89
Also see ISLEY BROTHERS
Also see STEWART, Rod, & Ronald Isley

ISLEY BROTHERS P&R '59
("Featuring Ronald Isley")
Singles: 78 rpm
TEENAGE (1004 "Angels Cried") ... 200-400 57
Singles: 12-inch
T-NECK ... 4-8 79-83
W.B. ... 4-6 87
Singles: 7-inch
ATLANTIC (2092 "Jeepers Creepers") ... 10-15 61
ATLANTIC (2100 "Standing on the Dance Floor") ... 10-15 61
ATLANTIC (2110 "Your Old Lady") 10-15 61
ATLANTIC (2122 "A Fool for You") 10-15 61
ATLANTIC (2263 "The Last Girl") .. 10-15 64
ATLANTIC (2277 "Wild As a Tiger") ... 10-20 65
CINDY (3009 "Don't Be Jealous") ... 50-100 58
EARLY BIRD (1007 "Don't Be Jealous") ... 4-6 96
(Colored vinyl.)
GONE (5022 "Everybody's Gonna Rock & Roll") ... 25-50 58
GONE (5048 "My Love") ... 25-50 59
MARK-X (7003 "Rockin' MacDonald") ... 25-50 57
MARK-X (8000 "Rockin' MacDonald) ... 15-25 58
RCA (7537 "Turn to Me") ... 15-25 59
RCA (47-7588 "Shout!") ... 15-25 59
(Monaural.)
RCA (61-7588 "Shout") ... 25-50 59
(Stereo.)
RCA (7657 "Respectable") ... 15-25 59
RCA (7718 "He's Got the Whole World in His Hands") ... 15-25 60
RCA (7746 "Open Up Your Heart") 15-25 60
RCA (7787 "Tell Me Who") ... 15-25 60
RCA GOLD STANDARD ... 5-8 61
(Black label, RCA dog on top.)
RCA GOLD STANDARD ... 4-6 65
(Black label, RCA dog on left side.)
T-NECK (Except 501) ... 3-6 69-84
T-NECK (501 "Testify") ... 4-8 64
TAMLA ... 5-15 66-69
TEENAGE (1004 "Angels Cried") ... 200-400 57
U.A. (605 "She's Gone") ... 10-20 63
U.A. (638 "Surf & Shout") ... 10-20 63
U.A. (659 "Please Please Please") . 10-20 63
U.A. (714 "Who's That Lady") ... 10-20 64
V.I.P. (25020 "I Hear a Symphony") ... 300-500 65
VEEP (1230 "Love Is a Wonderful Thing") ... 8-12 66
WAND (118 "Right Now") ... 8-12 62
WAND (124 "Twist & Shout") ... 8-12 62
WAND (127 "Twistin' with Linda") ... 8-12 62
WAND (131 "Nobody But Me") ... 8-12 63
W.B. ... 3-4 85-88
Picture Sleeves
W.B. ... 3-5 87-89
LPs: 10/12-inch
BUDDAH ... 10-12 76
CAMDEN ... 8-10 73-75
COLLECTABLES ... 6-8 88
MOTOWN ... 5-10 80-82
PHILADELPHIA INT'L ... 5-10 78
PICKWICK ... 5-10 77
RCA (LPM-2156 "Shout!") ... 40-60 59
(Monaural.)
RCA (LSP-2156 "Shout!") ... 50-75 59
(Stereo.)
SCEPTER ... 10-20 66
SUNSET ... 8-10 69
T-NECK (Except 137) ... 8-10 69-84
T-NECK (137 "Everything You Always Wanted to Hear") ... 10-15 76
(Promotional issue only.)
TAMLA (269 "This Old Heart of Mine") ... 25-50 66
TAMLA (275 "Soul on the Rocks") 15-25 67
TAMLA (287 "Doin' Their Thing") ... 15-20 69
TRIP ... 8-10 76
U.A. (500 series) ... 8-10 75
U.A. (6000 series) ... 20-25 63
WAND (WD-653 "Twist & Shout") .. 20-30 62
(Monaural.)
WAND (WDS-653 "Twist & Shout") ... 30-40 62
(Stereo.)
W.B. ... 5-10 85-87
Members: Ron Isley; Rudy Isley; O'Kelly Isley; Ernie Isley; Marvin Isley. Session: Jimi Hendrix.
Also see CHRISTIE, Lou, & Classics / Isley Brothers / Chiffons
Also see HENDRIX, Jimi, & Isley Brothers
Also see ISLEY, Ernie
Also see ISLEY, Ron
Also see ISLEY - JASPER - ISLEY
Also see RASCALS / Isley Brothers

ISLEY BROTHERS & DAVE "BABY" CORTEZ
LPs: 10/12-inch
T-NECK ... 8-10 69
Also see CORTEZ, Dave "Baby"

ISLEY BROTHERS / Brooklyn Bridge
LPs: 10/12-inch
T-NECK (3004 "Live at Yankee Stadium") ... 20-30 69
(With guests, Edwin Hawkins Singers; Five Stairsteps, Sweet Cherries, and Judy White.)
Also see BROOKLYN BRIDGE
Also see FIVE STAIRSTEPS
Also see HAWKINS, Edwin, Singers
Also see WHITE, Judy

ISLEY BROTHERS / Go-Go's
EPs: 7-inch
RCA/WURLITZER ... 10-15 64
(Promotional issue only.)
Also see GO-GOs

ISLEY BROTHERS / Marvin & Johnny
LPs: 10/12-inch
CROWN ... 10-20 63
Also see MARVIN & JOHNNY

ISLEY - JASPER - ISLEY R&B '84
Singles: 12-inch
CBS ASSOCIATED ... 4-6 85-86
Singles: 7-inch
CBS ASSOCIATED ... 3-4 85-87
LPs: 10/12-inch
CBS ASSOCIATED ... 5-10 85-86
Members: Marvin Isley; Chris Jasper; Ernie Isley.
Also see ISLEY BROTHERS
Also see JASPER, Chris

ISOM RAY
(Ray Agee)
Singles: 7-inch
RGA (114 "Rock Hard") ... 40-60

ISONICS
Singles: 7-inch
KAMMY (369 "He Needs Her") ... 20-30

ISOTOPE
LPs: 10/12-inch
GULL ... 8-10 75

IT'S A BEAUTIFUL DAY LP '69
(Featuring David LaFlamme)
Singles: 7-inch
COLUMBIA ... 4-8 69-73
SAN FRANCISCO SOUND ... 8-12 70
LPs: 10/12-inch
COLUMBIA (1058 "Marrying Maiden") ... 15-20 70
COLUMBIA (9768 "It's a Beautiful Day") ... 20-30 69
COLUMBIA (30734 "Choice Quality Stuff/Anytime") ... 10-15 71
COLUMBIA (31338 "Live at Carnegie Hall") ... 10-15 72
COLUMBIA (32181 "It's a Beautiful Day Today") ... 10-15 73
COLUMBIA (32660 "1001 Nights") ... 30-40 73
(Promotional issue only.)
SAN FRANCISCO SOUNDS (04800 Marrying Maiden") ... 30-40 80s
(Half-speed mastered.)
SAN FRANCISCO SOUNDS (11790 "It's a Beautiful Day") ... 30-40 80s
(Half-speed mastered.)
Also see GARCIA, Jerry
Also see LA FLAMME, David
Also see PABLO CRUISE

IT'S THEM
Singles: 7-inch
TOY TIGER ... 8-12

IT'S US
Singles: 7-inch
ARAB ("Don't Want Your Lovin' ") .. 25-35

ITALIAN ASPHALT & PAVEMENT COMPANY P&R '70
(Duprees)
Singles: 7-inch
COLOSSUS ... 3-5 70
Picture Sleeves
COLOSSUS ... 4-6 70
LPs: 10/12-inch
COLOSSUS ... 8-10 70
Also see AGEE, Ray
Also see DUPREES

ITALS
LPs: 10/12-inch
NIGHTHAWK ... 5-10 82
Members: Keith Porter; Ronnie Davis; Lloyd Ricketts.

ITELS
Singles: 7-inch
MAGNIFICO (101 "Star of Paradise") ... 25-35 61

ITEMS
Singles: 7-inch
TELEDISC (63 "Foxy Lady") ... 10-20 60s

ITHICAS
Singles: 7-inch
FEE BEE (220 "If You Want My Love") ... 10-20 58

ITHICAS
Singles: 7-inch
VAL (6 "Michael's Madness") ... 10-20 66

ITO, Richie
Singles: 7-inch
STELLAR (711 "Don't Cry Linda") ... 50-100 61

IVALEE
Singles: 7-inch
PEORIA ... 4-8 65

IVAN P&R '58
(Jerry Ivan Allison)
Singles: 7-inch
CORAL (62017 "Real Wild Child") ... 50-100 58
CORAL (62081 "Frankie Frankenstein") ... 50-100 59
CORAL (65607 "Real Wild Child") ... 20-30 67
Also see CRICKETS

IVAN / Johnny Tillotson
Singles: 7-inch
OLDIES 45 ... 5-8 64
Also see IVAN
Also see TILLOTSON, Johnny

IVAN & SABERS
Singles: 7-inch
PRISM ... 4-8 64

IVANAVICH, Ivan
Singles: 7-inch
ELKO (12 "Dear Jimmy") ... 5-8 62

IVERS, Peter
(Peter Ivers Band; Peter Ivers Group)
Singles: 7-inch
EPIC ... 4-8 70
W.B. ... 3-5 74
LPs: 10/12-inch
EPIC (26500 "Knight of the Blue Communion") ... 25-30 70
W.B. ... 8-12 74

IVERSON, Ben, & Hornets
Singles: 7-inch
WAY OUT (4960 "Love Me") ... 150-200 62
(Identification number shown since no selection number is used.)
Also see JOHNSON, Lester, & Hornets

IVES, Burl P&R '48
("The Wayfaring Stranger;" With the Trinidaddies)
Singles: 78 rpm
COLUMBIA ... 10-15 50-51
DECCA ... 10-15 47-57
STINSON (522 "Blue Tail Fly") ... 15-20 47
Singles: 7-inch
BELL ... 3-5 70
BIG TREE ... 3-5 71
BUENA VISTA ... 4-6 63
CAMAY ... 5-10
COLUMBIA (39000 series) ... 5-10 50-51
COLUMBIA (44000 series) ... 3-6 68-69
COLUMBIA (70000 series) ... 3-6 69
CYCLONE ... 3-5 70
DECCA (25000 series) ... 4-8 66-69
DECCA (27000 thru 30000 series) ... 6-12 50-59
DECCA (31000 thru 33000 series) ... 3-8 60-73
DISNEYLAND ... 4-6 64
MCA ... 3-5 73-74
MONKEY JOE ... 3-5 78
Picture Sleeves
BUENA VISTA ... 5-10 63
COLUMBIA ... 5-10
DECCA ... 5-10 62
U.A. ... 5-10 62
EPs: 7-inch
COLUMBIA ... 5-15 51-55
DECCA ... 5-15 49-65
LPs: 10/12-inch
BELL ... 5-10 71
CAEDMON ... 4-6 72
COLUMBIA (628 "Wayfaring Stranger") ... 15-25 55
COLUMBIA (1459 "Return of the Wayfaring Stranger") ... 10-20 60
COLUMBIA (2570 "Children's Favorites") ... 20-35 55
(10-inch LP.)
COLUMBIA (6058 "Wayfaring Stranger") ... 25-40 50
(10-inch LP.)
COLUMBIA (6109 "Wayfaring Stranger, Vol. 2") ... 25-40 51
(10-inch LP.)
COLUMBIA (6144 "Wayfaring Stranger, Vol. 3") ... 25-40 51
(10-inch LP.)
COLUMBIA (9000 series) ... 10-15 68-69
COLUMBIA (30000 series) ... 8-12
CORAL ... 4-8 73
CORONET ... 5-10
DECCA (100 series) ... 15-25 61
DECCA (4000 series) ... 10-20 62-68
(Decca LP numbers in this series preceded by a "7" or a "DL-7" are stereo issues.)
DECCA (5013 "Ballads and Folk Songs") ... 20-40 49
(10-inch LP.)
DECCA (5080 "Ballads and Folk Songs, Vol. 2") ... 20-40 49
(10-inch LP.)
DECCA (5490 "Women—Songs of the Fair Sex") ... 20-30 53
(10-inch LPs)
DECCA (8000 series) ... 10-20 55-59
DISNEYLAND ... 8-12 63-64
EVEREST ... 5-10 78
HARMONY ... 8-15 59-70
MCA ... 5-10 73-75
NATIONAL GEOGRAPHIC ... 10-15
SUNSET ... 5-10 70
UNART ... 6-12 67
U.A. ... 10-20 59-62
WORD ... 5-10 63-66
Session: Anita Kerr Singers.
Also see KERR, Anita
Also see MILLS, Hayley, & Burl Ives

IVES, Burl, with Grady Martin & His Slew Foot Five C&W '52
Singles: 78 rpm
DECCA ... 4-8 52
Singles: 7-inch
DECCA ... 8-12 49
Also see MARTIN, Grady

IVES, Burl, with Captain Stubby & Buccaneers C&W '49
Singles: 78 rpm
DECCA ... 4-8 49
Also see IVES, Burl
Also see STUBBY & BUCCANEERS

IVES, Jimmy
Singles: 7-inch
COMET (21 "My Tumbling Heart") . 15-25 61

IVEY, Chet "Poison"
(With His Fabulous Avengers; Ivy Group; Chet Ivey)
Singles: 7-inch
ABC-PAR ... 5-10 60-61
ATCO ... 5-10 59
BEE CEE ... 10-15
GATOR ... 4-8
SYLVIA ... 3-6
TANGERINE ... 3-6 68

IVEYS P&R '69
(Badfinger)
Singles: 7-inch
APPLE (1803 "Maybe Tomorrow") . 10-15 69
APPLE/AMERICOM (301 "Maybe Tomorrow") ... 150-250 69
(Four-inch flexi, "pocket disc.")
Also see BADFINGER

IVIE, Roger, & Silvercreek C&W '81
Singles: 7-inch
CARDINAL ... 3-4 81
Also see SILVER CREEK

IVIES
Singles: 7-inch
BRUNSWICK (55112 "Sunshine") . 15-25 58
IVY (110 "Sunshine") ... 50-75 58
ROULETTE ... 10-15 59
U.A. ... 4-6 59

IVOLEERS
(With the Bobby Smith Orchestra & Chorus)
Singles: 7-inch
BUZZ (101 "Lovers' Quarrel") ... 100-200 59

IVORIES
(With the Sampson Horton Orchestra)
Singles: 7-inch
JAGUAR (3019 "Alone") ... 300-400 56
JAGUAR (3023 "Alone") ... 100-200 57

IVORIES
Singles: 7-inch
MERCURY (71239 "Me & You") ... 10-20 57

IVORY
LPs: 10/12-inch
PLAYBOY ... 8-10 73
TETRAGRAMMATON ... 10-15 68

IVORY, Jackie
Singles: 7-inch
ATCO ... 4-8 65-66
LPs: 10/12-inch
ATCO ... 12-15 65

IVORY HUNTERS
Singles: 7-inch
PARENT (1001 "Zanzibar") ... 8-12

IVORY JACK C&W '80
Singles: 7-inch
COUNTRY INT'L ... 3-4 81
NSD ... 3-5 80

IVORY TONES
Singles: 7-inch
NORWOOD (101 "Little Fool") .. 200-300 60

IVORYS
(Ivory's)
Singles: 7-inch
DARLA (1000 "Wishing Well") ... 1000-2000 62
(First issue.)
SPARTA (001-BB "Why Don't You Write Me") ... 100-200 62
("BB" used because Sparta 001, without "BB," is *Wishing Well*, credited to the Blue Chips.)
Also see BLUE CHIPS

IVORYTONES
Singles: 7-inch
UNIDAP (448 "Wo Wo Wo Wo") ... 35-50 60

IVY R&B '86
Singles: 7-inch
HEAT ... 3-4 86

IVY, Sir Henry
Singles: 7-inch
FUTURE DIMENSION ("He Left You Standing There") ... 25-35
(Selection number not known.)

IVY, Sonny Joe
Singles: 7-inch
JEWEL (Except 738) ... 5-10 65
JEWEL (738 "Ruby and the Gambler") ... 15-20 65

IVY GROUP: see IVEY, Chet "Poison"

IVY JIVES
Singles: 7-inch
JARO ... 10-20 60

IVY JO
(Ivy Joe; Ivy Jo Hunter)
Singles: 7-inch
V.I.P. (25055 "I Remember When") ... 10-15 70
(Black vinyl.)
V.I.P. (25055 "I Remember When") ... 20-30 70
(Colored vinyl. Promotional issue only.)
V.I.P. (25063 "I'd Still Love You") .. 10-15 70

IVY LEAGUE P&R '65
Singles: 7-inch
CAMEO (356 "Funny How Love Can Be") ... 10-15 65
CAMEO (365 "That's Why I'm Crying") ... 10-15 65
CAMEO (377 "Tossing & Turning") ... 10-15 65
CAMEO (388 "I Could Make You Fall in Love") ... 10-15 65
CAMEO (402 "Rain Rain Go Away") ... 10-15 66
CAMEO (449 "My World Fell Down") ... 10-15 66

LPs: 10/12-inch

CAMEO (2000 "Tossing & Turning") 25-35 65
(Monaural.)
CAMEO (S-2000 "Tossing & Turning") 30-40 65
(Stereo.)
Members: John Carter; Ken Lewis; Perry Ford.
Also see FLOWERPOT MEN
Also see PHILWIT & PEGASUS

IVY LEAGUERS

Singles: 7-inch

FLIP (325 "Beware of Love")..........20-30 57
Also see I.V. LEAGUERS

IVY THREE *P&R/R&B '60*

Singles: 7-inch

SHELL (302 "I Cried Enough for Two")..........50-100 61
SHELL (302 "I Cried Enough for Two")..........20-30 61
SHELL (719 "I'll Walk the Earth")...10-20 60
SHELL (720 "Yogi") 15-20 60
(Blue label.)
SHELL (720 "Yogi") 10-15 60
(Multi-color label.)
SHELL (723 "Alone in the Chapel") 15-25 60

IVY TONES

Singles: 7-inch

RED TOP (105 "Oo-Wee Baby")....15-20 58
(Blue label.)
RED TOP (105 "Oo-Wee Baby")..... 8-12 58
(Red label.)
Members: John Ivy; William Brown; James Green; James Thomas; Little Joe Cook.
Also see COOK, Little Joe
Also see NAKED TRUTH

IVYLIERS

Singles: 7-inch

DONNA (3 "Echo from the Blue")...40-60 57

IVYMEN

Singles: 7-inch

TWIN TOWN (720 "La-Do-Da Da")....................80-120 67

IVYS

Singles: 7-inch

COED (518 "All I Want")................10-15 59

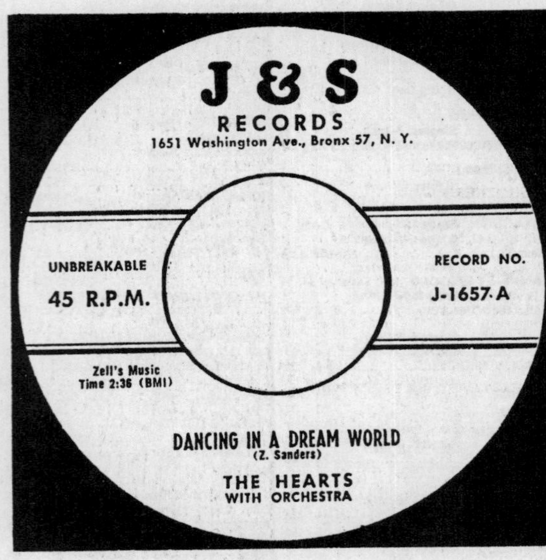

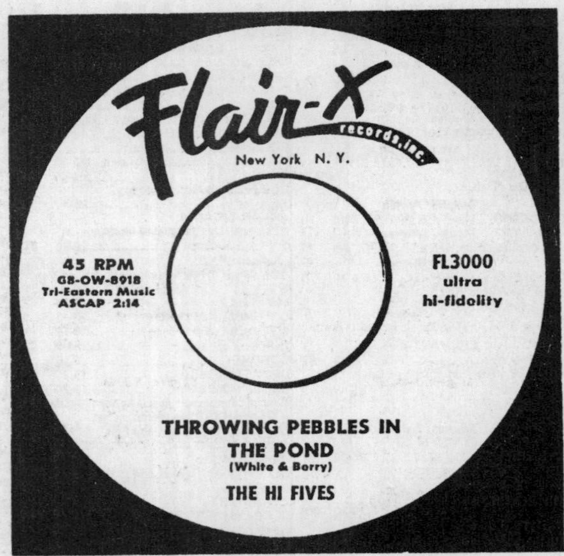

J

J & SABERS
(With the Gents)
Singles: 7-inch
VAVRAY (1003 "Little One") ... 15-25 62

J. BIRD: see BIRD, J.

J. BROTHERS
(With the Belltones)
Singles: 7-inch
MERMAID (3360 "The Girl I Used to Know") ... 75-150 58
Members: John Tirino; Jim Tirino.
Also see 4 SEASONS / Neil Sedaka / J Brothers / Johnny Rivers
Also see JOHN & JIM

J. JERRY
Singles: 12-inch
BLACK DIAMOND ... 4-6 90

J. MERCY BABY: see MERCY BABY

J.A.K.E.
(Just Another Kind of Energy)
Singles: 7-inch
SPHYR A MID ... 3-4 80

J.A.L.N. BAND
LPs: 10/12-inch
U.A. ... 5-8 77

J.B. & His Bayou Boys
(J.B. Lenoir)
Singles: 7-inch
JOB (1008 "The Mountain") ... 50-75 52
JOB (1016 "I'll Die Trying") ... 50-75 52
RCA (3355 "Love, Happiness and Sweet You") ... 10-15
Picture Sleeves
RCA (3355 "Love, Happiness and Sweet You") ... 10-20
Also see LENOIR, J.B.

J.B. & His Hawks: see HUTTO, J.B.

J.B. & V-KINGS
Singles: 7-inch
ZAP-ZING ... 3-6 69

J.B.s P&R '72
(J.B.'s Internationals)
Singles: 7-inch
PEOPLE ... 3-5 72-76
POLYDOR ... 3-5 77-78
LPs: 10/12-inch
PEOPLE ... 5-8 72-75
Also see BROWN, James
Also see WESLEY, Fred

J.B.G. & JULES
(Jules Blattner Group & Jules)
Singles: 7-inch
NORMAN ... 10-15 65
Also see BLATTNER, Jules

JC & B-1 Bombers
Singles: 7-inch
BOMBADIER (007 "You're the One") ... 20-30

J.C.
LPs: 10/12-inch
PERCEPTION ... 8-10 69

J.B.K. FOUR
Singles: 7-inch
QUEST ... 4-8

J.C.W. RATFINKS
Singles: 7-inch
BUDDAH ... 4-8 68
KAMA SUTRA ... 4-8 68
Member: Mark Gutkowski.
Also see 1910 FRUITGUM COMPANY

J.D. & DYNAMICS
Singles: 7-inch
FENTON ... 10-15 64

J.D. & EXPRESSIONS
Singles: 7-inch
GUYDEN ... 4-8 65

J.D. & IMPRESSIONS
Singles: 7-inch
STAR SATELLITE (1021 "Blues Kick") ... 10-20 62

J.D. DREWS: see DREWS, J.D.

J.E. THE P.C. FROM D.C. R&B '87
Singles: 7-inch
PROFILE ... 3-4 87

JFA
Singles: 7-inch
PLACEBO (Black vinyl) ... 3-5 83-85
PLACEBO (Colored vinyl) ... 4-8 83
LPs: 10/12-inch
PLACEBO ... 8-10 83-85

J.J. FAD P&R/R&B/LP '88
Singles: 7-inch
RUTHLESS ... 3-4 88
Picture Sleeves
RUTHLESS ... 3-4 88
LPs: 10/12-inch
RUTHLESS ... 5-8 88
Members: Juana Burns; Dania Birks; Michelle Franklin.

J.K. & CO.
LPs: 10/12-inch
WHITE WHALE ... 10-12 69

J.O.B. ORQUESTRA
LPs: 10/12-inch
GOVINDA ... 5-10

J.P. & REACTORS
(J.P. Megonnell)
Singles: 7-inch
THREE MILE ISLAND ... 3-5 79

J.P. & TURNPIKES
Singles: 7-inch
ECO ... 5-10 61

J.R. & ATTRACTIONS
Singles: 7-inch
HUNCH (928 "I'm Yours") ... 15-25 65

J's WITH JAMIE
Singles: 7-inch
COLUMBIA ... 3-5 62-64
Picture Sleeves
COLUMBIA ... 5-10 63
LPs: 10/12-inch
COLUMBIA ... 15-25 63-64
Members: Tom Jamison; Serena Jamison.
Also see JAMIES

JSD BAND
LPs: 10/12-inch
W.B. ... 8-10 73

J.T. CONNECTION
LPs: 10/12-inch
BUTTERFLY ... 5-8 79
Member: Dennis Tufano.
Also see TUFANO & GIAMMERESE

JTM
LPs: 10/12-inch
MASQUE (8805 "Absence & the Presence") ... 10-15 88
(Picture disc. 500 made.)

JTS BAND
Singles: 7-inch
MERCURY ... 3-5 77
LPs: 10/12-inch
MERCURY ... 5-8 77

J – WALKERS
Singles: 7-inch
EVEREST ... 8-12 62
TIDAL ... 5-10

JABARA, Paul
Singles: 12-inch
CASABLANCA (20129 "Disco Queen") ... 5-10 78
(Single-sided. Promotional issue only.)
Singles: 7-inch
A&M ... 3-5 76
CASABLANCA ... 3-5 78
Picture Sleeves
A&M ... 3-5 76
CASABLANCA ... 3-5 78

JABLONSKI, Sir, & Unknowns
Singles: 7-inch
MAND L ("A Merry Christmas") ... 100-150
(No selection number used.)

JAC & JAY
(With the Tom Toms)
Singles: 7-inch
SHANE (47-2 "Peanut Butter") ... 25-50 65

JACK, Ballin': see BALLIN' JACK

JACK, Bobby
Singles: 7-inch
TOP RANK ... 10-15 59

JACK, Johnny
Singles: 7-inch
DORE ... 5-10 61
GONE (5132 "Beggar That Became King") ... 15-20 62
GREAT ... 8-12 59
RICKY ... 8-10 62
Also see CHRISTIE, Lou

JACK, Jimmy
Singles: 7-inch
BLUE MASQUE ... 4-6 66

JACK, Robin
(Jonathan King)
Singles: 7-inch
UK/MIDLAND INT'L ... 3-5 75
Also see KING, Jonathan

JACK & BEANSTALKS
Singles: 7-inch
LE RON (3601 "Don't Bug Me") ... 75-125 66
REVOLUTION (2914 "A Long Time Coming") ... 75-125 68
Members: Jack Tadych; John Conrath; Robert Kennedy; John Lyons; Pat Glass; Doug Werginz; Jim Dietrich.

JACK & BETTY
Singles: 7-inch
TEEN ... 5-10 55

JACK & BIRDS
Singles: 7-inch
DIANA ... 8-12 59

JACK & DRIFTERS
Singles: 7-inch
B-W ... 5-10 61
MELLOWTONE ... 5-10 61
Member: Jack Sutton.

JACK & JILL
Singles: 78 rpm
IMPERIAL ... 8-10 57
Singles: 7-inch
ARLEN ... 4-8 63
CADDY ... 4-8
IMPERIAL ... 8-10 57
JOSIE ... 4-8 65
MAXX ... 4-8 64
SMASH ... 4-8 63

JACK & JIM
Singles: 7-inch
BRUNSWICK (55141 "Midnight Monsters Hop") ... 40-60 59
Members: Jack Huddle; Jim Robinson.
Also see HUDDLE, Jack
Also see ROBINSON, Jim

JACK & TRINK C&W '78
Singles: 7-inch
NSD ... 3-5 78
Members: Jack Ruthven; Trink Ruthven.

JACK LADS
Singles: 7-inch
KISKI (2050 "Hot Toddy") ... 10-15 63

JACK THE LAD
LPs: 10/12-inch
ELEKTRA ... 8-10 74

JACKALS
Singles: 7-inch
LIBERTY ... 4-6 69

JACKASSES
Singles: 7-inch
BRAY (2626 "Sugaree") ... 10-20

JACKIE & GAYLE
Singles: 7-inch
CAPITOL ... 4-8 64
MAINSTREAM ... 4-8 65
U.A. ... 4-8 66
Picture Sleeves
U.A. ... 8-12 66
Members: Jackie Miller; Gayle Caldwell.
Also see NEW CHRISTY MINSTRELS

JACKIE & GIANTS
Singles: 7-inch
HIT ... 5-15 64

JACKIE & JILL
Singles: 7-inch
CUCA (64112 "I Want the Beatles for Christmas") ... 15-25 64
U.S.A. (791 "I Want the Beatles for Christmas") ... 10-20 65

JACKIE & RAINDROPS
Singles: 7-inch
COLPIX (738 "Down Our Street") ... 15-25 64
Members: Jackie Beadle; Len Beadle; Brian Adams.

JACKIE & RHYTHMS
Singles: 7-inch
CUPID ... 15-20 60

JACKIE & ROY
Singles: 7-inch
VERVE ... 4-8 66

JACKIE & STARLITES R&B '62
Singles: 78 rpm
FIRE & FURY (1000 "They Laughed at Me") ... 500-750 59
Singles: 7-inch
FIRE & FURY (1000 "They Laughed at Me") ... 1000-2000 59
FURY (1057 "I'm Coming Home") ... 20-30 62
HULL (760 "I Cried My Heart Out") ... 25-50 63
MASCOT (128 "For All We Know") ... 35-50 62
(No horseshoe on label.)
MASCOT (128 "For All We Know") ... 25-45 62
(Has horseshoe around hole.)
MASCOT (130 "You Keep Telling Me") ... 25-50 63
MASCOT (131 "Walking from School") ... 25-50 63
SPHERE SOUND ... 8-12
LPs: 10/12-inch
LOST-NITE ... 5-10 81
Member: Jackie Rue; Alton Jones; George Lassu; John Felix; Billy Montgomery; Charles Hudson..
Also see 5 WINGS
Also see STARLITES

JACKIE & TUT
Singles: 7-inch
CHESS (2008 "Hawaii Punch") ... 5-10 66

JACKIE & UMPIRES
Singles: 7-inch
SEW CITY ... 4-6 68

JACKIE LEE: see LEE, Jackie

JACK-O-LANTERNS
Singles: 7-inch
GOLDCREST (163 "Lori Anne") ... 1000-2000

JACKS P&R/R&B '55
Singles: 78 rpm
RPM (Except 428) ... 15-25 55-56
RPM (428 "Why Don't You Write Me"/"Smack Dab in the Middle") ... 50-75 55
RPM (428 "Why Don't You Write Me"/"My Darling") ... 25-35 55
(Note different flip side.)
Singles: 7-inch
KENT (344 "Why Don't You Write Me") ... 10-20 60
RPM (428 "Why Don't You Write Me"/"Smack Dab in the Middle") ... 100-200 55
RPM (428 "Why Don't You Write Me"/"My Darling") ... 50-100 55
(Note different flip side.)
RPM (433 "I'm Confessin' ") ... 50-100 55
RPM (444 "This Empty Heart") ... 50-75 55
RPM (454 "How Soon") ... 50-75 56
RPM (458 "Why Did I Fall in Love") ... 50-75 56
RPM (467 "Let's Make Up") ... 50-75 56
LPs: 10/12-inch
BEST ... 15-25
CROWN (372 "The Jacks") ... 50-75 62
(Stereo.)
CROWN (5021 "Jumpin' with the Jacks") ... 100-200 56
CROWN (5372 "The Jacks") ... 50-75 62
(Monaural.)
RPM (3006 "Jumpin' with the Jacks") ... 250-500 56
RELIC ... 10-15
UNITED ... 8-10 70s
Members: Willie Davis; Ted Taylor; Aaron Collins; Will Jones; Lloyd McCraw; Prentice Moreland.
Also see CADETS
Also see MORELAND, Prentice
Also see ROCKETS
Also see YOUNG JESSIE

JACKS, A., & Cleansers
Singles: 7-inch
CLEAN (110 "Stronger Than Dirt") ... 10-20 65

JACKS, Susan P&R '75
Singles: 7-inch
EPIC ... 3-4 80
MERCURY ... 3-5 75-76
LPs: 10/12-inch
EPIC ... 5-8 80
Also see POPPY FAMILY

JACKS, Terry P&R/LP '74
Singles: 7-inch
BELL ... 3-5 74
FLASHBACK ... 3-5 75
LONDON ... 3-5 73
PRIVATE STOCK ... 3-5 75-76
LPs: 10/12-inch
BELL ... 8-10 74
Also see POPPY FAMILY

JACKS, Warren
Singles: 7-inch
PAPER DRAGON ... 3-5 77

JACKS & JILLS
Singles: 78 rpm
EMPIRE ... 8-12 56
Singles: 7-inch
EMPIRE ... 10-20 56
MGM ... 5-10 58

JACKSON, Alan C&W '89
Singles: 7-inch
ARISTA ... 3-4 89-92
LPs: 10/12-inch
ARISTA ... 5-8 90-91
Also see JONES, George, & Alan Jackson

JACKSON, Barbara
Singles: 7-inch
VEE JAY ... 4-8 63
W.B. ... 4-8 65

JACKSON, Bart
(George Jackson)
Singles: 7-inch
DECCA ... 10-20 68
Also see JACKSON, George

JACKSON, Bill
(Bill Jackson Quintet)
Singles: 78 rpm
BATON ... 25-50 57
Singles: 7-inch
BATON (239 "Traveling Stranger") ... 25-50 57
LPs: 10/12-inch
TESTAMENT ... 10-20 63

JACKSON, Billy
Singles: 7-inch
BRUNSWICK ... 4-6 68

JACKSON, Bobby
Singles: 7-inch
BRUNSWICK (55026 "Wow Man") ... 20-30 57
BRUNSWICK (55060 "Dinah's Party") ... 20-30 58

JACKSON, Brother: see HAMPTON, Junior / Brother Jackson

JACKSON, Bull Moose R&B '46
(With His Buffalo Bearcats; with Flashcats; Moose Jackson)
Singles: 78 rpm
ENCINO ... 25-50 57
KING ... 20-40 45-55
MGM ... 10-20 47
QUEEN ... 10-20 45-46
Singles: 7-inch
BOGUS ... 4-6 85
ENCINO (1004 "Understanding") ... 25-50 57
GUSTO ... 3-5
KING (4181 "I Love You, Yes I Do") ... 25-50 51
KING (4189 "I Want a Bowlegged Woman") ... 50-100 51
KING (4451 "Trust in Me") ... 25-50 51
KING (4462 "Unless") ... 25-50 51
KING (4472 "Cherokee Boogie") ... 25-50 51
KING (4493 "I'll Be Home for Xmas") ... 25-50 51
KING (4524 "Nosey Joe") ... 50-75 52
KING (4535 "Let Me Love You All Night") ... 25-50 52
KING (4551 "Bearcat Blues") ... 25-50 52
KING (4580 "Big Ten-inch Record") ... 100-200 52
KING (4600 thru 4800 series) ... 15-25 53-55
SEVEN ARTS ... 5-10 61
WARWICK ... 5-10 60
Picture Sleeves
BOGUS ... 3-4 85
EPs: 7-inch
KING (211 "Bull Moose Jackson Sings His All-Time Hits") ... 50-100 52
KING (261 "Bull Moose Jackson Sings His All-Time Hits, Vol. 2") ... 50-100 54
LPs: 10/12-inch
AUDIO LAB (1524 "Bullmoose Jackson") ... 100-200 59
BOGUS ... 5-8 85
Also see FLASHCATS

JACKSON, Burt
Singles: 7-inch
JAMIE ... 4-8 63

JACKSON, Carl C&W '84
Singles: 7-inch
COLUMBIA ... 3-4 84-86
LP: 10/12-inch
CAPITOL ... 6-12 73
PRIZE ... 5-10
SUGAR HILL ... 5-10 81

JACKSON, Carl, Marty Stuart & Vicki Cook
LP: 10/12-inch
REBEL ... 5-10 80s
Also see JACKSON, Carl
Also see STUART, Marty

JACKSON, Casey
Singles: 7-inch
BUM STEER ... 4-8 79

JACKSON, Charles: see JACKSON, Chuck

JACKSON, Chubby
LPs: 10/12-inch
ARGO ... 15-25 60-62
EVEREST ... 15-25 62
LAURIE ... 15-25 62
Also see MARSHALL, Maria
Also see MERCURY ALL-STARS

JACKSON, Chuck P&R/R&B '61
(With the Vikings; with Kripp Johnson's Versatiles; Charles Jackson)
Singles: 7-inch
ABC ... 3-6 73-74
ALCAR (209 "Little Man") ... 10-12 63
ALCAR (210 "Never Let Me Go") ... 10-12 63
ALL PLATINUM ... 3-5 75-77
AMY (849 "Come On and Love Me") ... 10-15 62
AMY (868 "I'm Yours") ... 10-15 62
ATCO (6197 "Never Let Me Go" ... 10-20 61
BELTONE (1005 "Mister Pride") ... 10-20 61
CHANNEL (103 "Good Love") ... 5-10
CLOCK (1015 "Come On and Love Me") ... 20-30 59
CLOCK (1022 "I'm Yours") ... 20-30 60
DAKAR (4512 "I Forgot to Tell You") . 4-6 72
EMI AMERICA (8042 "I Want to Give You Some Love") ... 3-5 80
EMI AMERICA (8056 "Let's Get Together") ... 3-5 81
FEE BEE (231 "Girl, Girl, Girl") ... 10-20 59
LOGO (1015 "Come On and Love Me") ... 5-10
MOTOWN (1118 thru 1152) ... 10-15 68-69
MOTOWN (1160 "The Day the World Stood Still") ... 150-250 70
PETITE (502 "Willette") ... 15-25 59
PETITE (503 "Cold Feet") ... 15-25 59
SCEPTER (21000 series) ... 3-5 73
(Reissues of Wand tracks.)
SUGAR HILL (764 "Sometimes When We Touch") ... 3-5 81
VIBRATION ... 3-5 77
V.I.P. (25052 thru 25059) ... 10-15 69-71
V.I.P. (25067 "Who You Gonna Run To") ... 100-200 71
WAND (106 "I Don't Want to Cry") . 10-15 61
(Blue label.)
WAND (106 "I Don't Want to Cry") ... 4-6
(Multi-color label.)
WAND (108 thru 188) ... 8-15 61-65
WAND (1100 series) ... 5-10 65-68
Picture Sleeves
WAND (132 "Tell Him I'm Not Home") ... 10-20 63
LPs: 10/12-inch
ABC (798 "Through All Times") ... 8-12 73
ALL PLATINUM (3014 "Wanting You, Needing You") ... 8-10 76
EMI-AMERICA (17031 "I Wanna Give You Some Love") ... 5-10 80
MOTOWN (667 "Chuck Jackson Arrives") ... 25-40 67
MOTOWN (687 "Goin' Back to Chuck Jackson") ... 20-30 69
SCEPTER ... 8-10 72
SPINORAMA ... 10-15 60s
U.A. ... 8-10 75
V.I.P. (403 "Teardrops Keep Fallin' ") ... 20-40 70

WAND (650 "I Don't Want to Cry") 40-60 62
WAND (654 "Any Day Now") 40-60 62
WAND (655 "Encore") 25-35 64
WAND (658 "On Tour") 25-35 64
WAND (667 "Mr. Everything") 25-35 65
WAND (673 "Tribute to Rhythm & Blues, Vol. 1") 20-30 66
WAND (676 "Tribute to Rhythm & Blues, Vol. 2") 20-30 66
WAND (680 "Dedicated to the King") 25-50 67
WAND (683 "Greatest Hits") 15-25 67
Also see BENTON, Brook / Chuck Jackson / Jimmy Soul
Also see BONDS, Gary "U.S."
Also see FLAMINGO, Chuck
Also see FREEMAN, Bobby, & Chuck Jackson
Also see JOHNSON, Kripp, & Chuck Jackson
Also see SYLVIA & CHUCK JACKSON

JACKSON, Chuck, & Maxine Brown *P&R/R&B '65*
Singles: 7-inch
WAND 5-10 65-67
LPs: 10/12-inch
COLLECTABLES 5-10 88
WAND (669 "Saying Something") 20-30 65
WAND (678 "Hold On, We're Coming") 20-30 67
Also see BROWN, Maxine

JACKSON, Chuck / Percy Sledge
Singles: 7-inch
TRIP 3-5
Also see SLEDGE, Percy

JACKSON, Chuck, & Tammi Terrell
LPs: 10/12-inch
WAND (682 "The Early Show") 20-30 67
Also see TERRELL, Tammi

JACKSON, Chuck / Young Jesse
LPs: 10/12-inch
CROWN (5354 "Chuck Jackson & Young Jesse") 15-25 62
GUEST STAR 10-15 64
Also see JACKSON, Chuck
Also see YOUNG JESSE

JACKSON, Clarence *R&B '85*
Singles: 7-inch
R&R 3-4 85

JACKSON, Cliff, & Naturals
Singles: 7-inch
MIDNIGHT SUN (1 "Blues Walk") 20-30 69
MIDNIGHT SUN (2 "Nine Below Zero") 20-30 69

JACKSON, Cookie
(With the Flares)
Singles: 7-inch
CYCLONE (121 "Hot Dog") 10-20 61
OKEH 5-10 67
PRESS (2814 "Write a Song About Me") 5-10 64
PROGRESS (912 "Blind Love") 15-25 63
UPTOWN (700 "Uptown Jerk") 5-10 65
Also see FLARES

JACKSON, Cordell
Singles: 7-inch
MOON (80 "Rock & Roll Christmas") 40-60 58

JACKSON, Deacon
(Blind Lemon Jefferson)
Singles: 78 rpm
HERWIN (93031 "I Want to Be Like Jesus in My Heart") 150-200 26
(Previously issued as by Deacon L.J. Bates.)
Also see BATES, Deacon L.J.
Also see JEFFERSON, Blind Lemon

JACKSON, Deon *P&R/R&B '66*
Singles: 7-inch
ABC 3-5 75
ATLANTIC 5-10 63-64
CARLA 4-8 66-69
SHOUT (254 "I'll Always Love You") 15-25
LPs: 10/12-inch
ATCO 15-20 66
COLLECTABLES 6-8 88

JACKSON, Dimples
Singles: 7-inch
GARDENA 5-10 60

JACKSON, Earl
(With Kent Harian Orchestra)
Singles: 78 rpm
CARAVAN (15602 "Coyote") 10-15 56
Singles: 7-inch
CARAVAN (15602 "Coyote") 25-35 56

JACKSON, Earl
Singles: 7-inch
ABC (11142 "Self Soul Satisfaction") 15-25 68

JACKSON, Earnest *P&R/R&B '73*
Singles: 7-inch
STONE 3-5 73

JACKSON, Eddie
Singles: 78 rpm
FORTUNE 5-10 56
Singles: 7-inch
FORTUNE 8-12 56

JACKSON, Eddy
Singles: 7-inch
KING (5574 "Don't Call Me") 20-30 61

JACKSON, Freddie *P&R/R&B/D&D/LP '85*
Singles: 12-inch
CAPITOL 4-6 85-86
Singles: 7-inch
CAPITOL 3-4 85-90
Picture Sleeves
CAPITOL 3-4 85-88
LPs: 10/12-inch
CAPITOL 5-8 85-90
Also see LAURENCE, Paul
Also see MOORE, Melba, & Freddie Jackson
Also see MYSTIC MERLIN

JACKSON, Gator Tail
Singles: 7-inch
TRU-SOUND 5-10

JACKSON, George
Singles: 78 rpm
ATLANTIC (1024 "Uh-Huh") 15-25 53
RPM 8-12 55
Singles: 7-inch
ATLANTIC (1024 "Uh-Huh") 25-35 53
RPM 10-20 55

JACKSON, George *R&B '70*
Singles: 7-inch
CHESS 3-6 75
CAMEO 5-10 66
DOT 5-10 65
DOUBLE R 5-10
ER MUSIC 3-5 76
FAME 4-8 69
HAPPY HOOKERS 3-4 85
HI (2100 series) 5-10 67
HI (2200 series) 3-6 72-73
MGM 3-6 73-74
MERCURY 10-20 67-68
MUSCLE SHOALS SOUNDS 3-6 79
PRANN 10-20 63
PUBLIC 10-15 68
VERVE (10658 "Love Highjacker") 15-25 70
WASHATAU 3-4 84
Also see JACKSON, Bart
Also see OVATIONS

JACKSON, George, & Dan Greer
Singles: 7-inch
GOLDWAX (313 "You Didn't Know It But You Had Me") 15-25 60s
(Also issued as by George & Greer.)
Also see GEORGE & GREER
Also see GREER, Dan
Also see JACKSON, George

JACKSON, Gootch
Singles: 7-inch
GATEWAY 10-15

JACKSON, Handy
Singles: 78 rpm
SUN (177 "Got My Application, Baby") 200-250 53

JACKSON, Hard Rock
Singles: 7-inch
VAM 5-10

JACKSON, Harold
Singles: 7-inch
ALADDIN (3410 "Move It on Down the Line") 15-25 57

JACKSON, Irv
Singles: 7-inch
MARIDENE (104 "Cool") 5-10

JACKSON, J.J. *P&R/R&B '66*
(With the Jackels; with Jackals; with Jackaels)
Singles: 7-inch
ABC 3-5 73
CALLA 4-8 66-67
CANDIX 12-18
EVEREST 4-8 62
LOMA 4-8 67-68
MAGNA GLIDE 3-5 75
PRELUDE 10-20 59
STORM 10-15 59
W.B. 4-6 69
LPs: 10/12-inch
CALLA 15-25 67
CONGRESS 15-20 68
PERCEPTION 10-15 69-70
W.B. 10-20 69
Also see GREATEST LITTLE SOUL BAND IN THE LAND

JACKSON, Jackie
Singles: 7-inch
MOTOWN 3-5 73
LPs: 10/12-inch
MOTOWN 5-8 73
Also see JACKSONS

JACKSON, Janet *P&R/R&B/LP '82*
Singles: 12-inch
A&M 4-6 82-90
Singles: 7-inch
A&M 3-4 82-90
Picture Sleeves
A&M 3-4 83-87
LPs: 10/12-inch
A&M 5-8 82-90

JACKSON, Jenny *R&B '76*
Singles: 7-inch
FARR 3-5 76

JACKSON, Jeri, & Kenny Smith
Singles: 7-inch
FRATERNITY 4-8 63
Also see SMITH, Kenny

JACKSON, Jermaine *P&R/R&B/LP '72*
Singles: 12-inch
ARISTA 4-6 84-89
MOTOWN 4-8 80-83
Singles: 7-inch
ARISTA (Black vinyl) 3-4 84-89
ARISTA (9190 "Dynamite") 3-4 84
(Colored vinyl.)
MOTOWN 3-5 72-83
Picture Sleeves
ARISTA 4-6 84-89
MOTOWN 3-5 81
LPs: 10/12-inch
ARISTA 5-8 84-89
MOTOWN 5-8 72-82
Also see DEVO
Also see JACKSONS
Also see ORIGINALS & Jermaine Jackson

JACKSON, Jermaine, & Michael Jackson
Singles: 12-inch
ARISTA 4-6 84
Also see JACKSON, Michael

JACKSON, Jermaine, & Pia Zadora *P&R/R&B '85*
Singles: 7-inch
CURB 3-4 85
Also see JACKSON, Jermaine
Also see ZADORA, Pia

JACKSON, Jerry
Singles: 7-inch
CAPITOL 5-10 68
COLUMBIA 5-10 64-65
KAPP 10-20 61-63
PARKWAY 10-20 66
TOP RANK 8-12 60

JACKSON, Jerry "Count"
Singles: 7-inch
FROLIC 4-8 63
VEE JAY 4-8 63

JACKSON, Jill
Singles: 7-inch
REPRISE (297 "All Over Again") 10-15 64
REPRISE (323 "Pixie Girl") 10-15 64
Also see JILL & RAY
Also see PAUL & PAULA

JACKSON, Jim
Singles: 7-inch
EVEREST (20001 "F-oldin' Money") 10-15 62
FABLE (639 "I Want Your Love") 15-25 58
SANDBAG (102 "Some Love with Soul") 20-30

JACKSON, Jimmy
Singles: 7-inch
BUDDAH 4-8 74-76
LPs: 10/12-inch
BUDDAH 8-12 76

JACKSON, Jimmy
(With All Stars)
Singles: 78 rpm
DERBY 10-15 51
RPM 10-15 52
Singles: 7-inch
DERBY (781 "Piano Boogie") 15-25 51
RPM (349 "Stompin' ") 15-25 52

JACKSON, Joe *P&R/LP '79*
Singles: 12-inch
A&M 4-6 82-86
Singles: 7-inch
A&M (Except 18000) 3-5 79-86
A&M (18000 "I'm the Man") 10-15 79
(Boxed set of five 45s with sleeves and poster. Labeled "The 7-inch Album.")
Picture Sleeves
A&M 3-5 79-86
LPs: 10/12-inch
A&M (3666 "Look Sharp") 10-20 79
(Double 10-inch LP set. Add $4 to $6 if "Look Sharp" button is included.)
A&M (3900 series) 5-8 87
A&M (4000 & 5000 series) 5-10 79-89
A&M (6000 series) 8-12 86-88
MFSL (080 "Night and Day") 25-35 82
VIRGIN 5-8 91

JACKSON, John
Singles: 7-inch
FRANKIE 8-10 58

JACKSON, John
LPs: 10/12-inch
ARHOOLIE 10-15 65

JACKSON, Johnnie, & Blazers
Singles: 7-inch
J-MER 10-20 67

JACKSON, Johnny
Singles: 7-inch
SWAN 4-8 62

JACKSON, Jump
(Jump Jackson Combo; Jump Jackson Orchestra)
Singles: 78 rpm
COLUMBIA 5-10 47
SPECIALTY 5-10 49-50
Singles: 7-inch
FAY 10-20 65
LA SALLE 5-10 61

JACKSON, Jump / Fred Clark
Singles: 78 rpm
GATEWAY (5002 "Red Light Boogie") 10-15
Also see CLARK, Fred
Also see JACKSON, Jump

JACKSON, June
Singles: 7-inch
BELL (45173 "Little Dog Heaven") 10-20 72
IMPERIAL (66185 "It's What's Up Front That Counts") 15-25 66

JACKSON, LaToya *R&B/LP '80*
Singles: 12-inch
LARC 4-6 83
PRIVATE I 4-6 84
Singles: 7-inch
LARC 3-4 83
POLYDOR 3-4 80-81
PRIVATE I 3-4 84-86
Picture Sleeves
PRIVATE I 3-4 84
LPs: 10/12-inch
POLYDOR 5-8 80-81
PRIVATE I 5-8 84
Also see CERRONE & LaToya Jackson

JACKSON, Lee
Singles: 78 rpm
COBRA 25-50 57
Singles: 7-inch
ATLANTIC (2284 "Ad for Love") 5-10 65
CJ (652 "Juanita") 15-25 65
COBRA (5007 "Fishin' in My Pond") 25-50 57
ROBIN RED 3-5
LPs: 10/12-inch
BLUESWAY 8-10 74

JACKSON, Lil' Son *R&B '48*
(With His Rockin' Rollers; Little Son Jackson)
Singles: 78 rpm
GOLD STAR 10-20 48-50
IMPERIAL 20-40 51-57
MODERN 10-20 49
POST 10-20 53
Singles: 7-inch
IMPERIAL (5204 "Journey Back Home") 50-100 52
IMPERIAL (5218 "Black and Brown") 50-100 52
IMPERIAL (5229 "Lonely Blues") 50-100 53
IMPERIAL (5237 "Spending Money Blues") 50-100 53
IMPERIAL (5248 "Movin' to the Country") 50-100 53
IMPERIAL (5259 "Dirty Work") 50-100 53
IMPERIAL (5267 "Thrill Me, Baby") 50-75 53
IMPERIAL (5276 "Big Rat") 50-75 53
IMPERIAL (5286 "Trouble Don't Last Always") 50-75 53
IMPERIAL (5300 "Get High Everybody") 50-75 53
IMPERIAL (5312 "How Long") 50-75 53
IMPERIAL (5319 "My Younger Days") 50-75 54
IMPERIAL (5339 "Sugar Mama") 50-75 54
IMPERIAL (5400 thru 5900 series) 15-25 56-63
POST (2014 "No Money") 25-35 53
EPs: 7-inch
BLACK DIAMOND (450 "Everybody Blues") 20-30
LPs: 10/12-inch
ARHOOLIE (1004 "Lil' Son Jackson") 15-30 60
IMPERIAL (9142 "Rockin' and Rollin' ") 75-100 61
Also see CHARLES, Ray / Arbee Stidham / Li'l Son Jackson / James Wayne.

JACKSON, Lolita *C&W '89*
Singles: 7-inch
OAK 3-4 89

JACKSON, Louis
Singles: 78 rpm
C NOTE 5-10 56
Singles: 7-inch
C NOTE (110 "Tweedle Woofin' Boogie") 10-20 56
Also see HAMPTON, Junior / Brother Jackson
Also see LOUIS & FROSTY

JACKSON, Mahalia *P&R '48*
Singles: 78 rpm
APOLLO 3-5 50-57
COLUMBIA 3-5 55-57
Singles: 7-inch
APOLLO (200 thru 500 series) 5-10 50-59
APOLLO (600 thru 700 series) 4-6 59-62
COLUMBIA 4-8 55-70
GRAND AWARD 4-8 58-59
KENWOOD 3-6 64-69
Picture Sleeves
APOLLO 4-8 62
EPs: 7-inch
APOLLO 5-10 54-59
COLUMBIA 5-10 55-60
LPs: 10/12-inch
APOLLO (201/2 "Spirituals") 15-20 54
APOLLO (482 "No Matter How You Pray") 10-15 59
APOLLO (499 "Mahalia Jackson") 10-15 62
APOLLO (1001 "Command Performance") 10-15 61
AUDIOFIDELITY 4-8
(Reissue of Apollo 499.)
CAEDMON 4-8 73
COLORTONE 5-8
(Reissue of Grand Award 265.)
COLUMBIA (CL-600 thru CL-2100 series) 10-20 55-64
COLUMBIA (CL-2400 thru CL-2600 series) 5-15 66-67
COLUMBIA (CS-8000 thru CS-8900 series) 10-20 59-64
(Stereo.)
COLUMBIA (CS-9200 thru CS-9900 series) 5-15 66-69
(Stereo. Reissues, with a "CSP," "JCS" or "PC" prefix, are in the $5 to $10 range.)
COLUMBIA (10000 series) 4-8 73
COLUMBIA (30000 series) 5-10 71-72
GRAND AWARD (265 "Spirtuals") 5-10 66
(Reissue of Grand Award 326.)
GRAND AWARD (326 "Spirtuals") 15-25 55
HARMONY 5-10 68-72
KENWOOD 5-10 64-73
PRIORITY 4-6 82

JACKSON, Mahalia, & Duke Ellington
LPs: 10/12-inch
COLUMBIA (CL-1162 "Black, Brown and Beige") 25-35 58
(Monaural.)
COLUMBIA (CS-8015 "Black, Brown and Beige") 35-40 58
(Stereo.)
COLUMBIA (JCS-1162 "Black, Brown and Beige") 5-10
Also see ELLINGTON, Duke
Also see JACKSON, Mahalia

JACKSON, Mark
Singles: 7-inch
STARFIRE 4-8 61-63

JACKSON, Marlon *R&B/LP '87*
Singles: 7-inch
CAPITOL 3-4 87
LPs: 10/12-inch
CAPITOL 5-8 87

JACKSON, Mattie
(Mattie Jackson / Ervin Rucker)
Singles: 7-inch
ASTRA (1004 "I Want to Help") 5-10 65
DUPLEX (9001 "I Want to Do It") 15-25
(It's possible these are the same song, with the Astra being a reissue of the Duplex. If so, one of the titles is likely incorrect. Readers?)

JACKSON, Maurice
Singles: 7-inch
CANDLE LITE 10-20 60s
FEDERAL 8-12 63

JACKSON, Michael *P&R/R&B '71*
Singles: 12-inch
EPIC 4-8 79-87
Singles: 7-inch
EPIC (Except 07253) 3-5 79-88
EPIC (07253 "I Just Can't Stop Loving You") 3-5 87
(Black vinyl.)
EPIC (07253 "I Just Can't Stop Loving You") 5-8 87
(Colored vinyl. Promotional issue only.)
MCA (1786 "Someone in the Dark") 25-50 83
(Promotional issue only.)
MOTOWN (Except 1914) 3-5 71-88
MOTOWN (1914 "Twenty Five Miles") 4-8 84
(Colored vinyl. Promotional issue only.)
Picture Sleeves
EPIC 3-5 83-88
MCA (1786 "Someone in the Dark") 25-50 83
(Promotional issue only.)
MOTOWN (1202 "I Wanna Be Where You Are") 3-5 72
MOTOWN (1914 "Twenty Five Miles") 4-8 84
(Promotional issue only.)
LPs: 10/12-inch
EPIC (35000 thru 40000, except 38867 & 44043) 5-8 79-87
EPIC (38867 "Thriller") 15-20 83
(Picture disc.)
EPIC (44043 "Bad") 10-15 87
(Picture disc. Includes poster.)
EPIC (45000 series) 10-15 80s
(Half-speed mastered.)
EPIC (68000 "Blood on the Dance Floor: History in the Mix") 10-15 97
MCA (70000 "E.T.") 50-100 82
(Boxed set with booklet & poster.)
MCA (6145 "E.T.") 50-100 85
(Boxed set with booklet & poster.)
MOTOWN (Except 6099) 5-10 72-85
MOTOWN (6099 "14 Greatest Hits") 10-12 84
(Picture disc. Has poster and glove.)
Also see CROUCH, Andrae
Also see GARRETT, Siedah
Also see JACKSON, Jermaine, & Michael Jackson
Also see JACKSONS
Also see JONES, Quincy
Also see McCARTNEY, Paul, & Michael Jackson
Also see ROCKWELL
Also see ROSS, Diana, & Michael Jackson
Also see U.S.A. for AFRICA
Also see VAN HALEN, Edward
Also see WINANS
Also see WONDER, Stevie, & Michael Jackson

JACKSON, Michael, & Mick Jagger / Jacksons *P&R '84*
Singles: 12-inch
EPIC (5022 "State of Shock") 8-12 84
(With special cover.)
EPIC (05022 "State of Shock") 15-20 84
(Promotional issue with cover.)
Singles: 7-inch
EPIC (4503 "State of Shock") 3-5 84
Picture Sleeves
EPIC (4503 "State of Shock") 3-5 84
Also see JACKSON, Michael

Also see JACKSONS
Also see JAGGER, Mick

JACKSON, Mick P&R '78
Singles: 7-inch
ATCO ... 3-5 78

JACKSON, Millie R&B '71
Singles: 7-inch
GEFFEN ... 3-4 87
JIVE ... 3-4 86-88
MGM ... 3-6 69
SPRING ... 3-5 71-83
LPs: 10/12-inch
JIVE ... 5-8 86
SPRING ... 5-8 73-83
POLYDOR ... 5-8 79
Also see BRANDYE
Also see HAYES, Isaac, & Millie Jackson
Also see JOHN, Elton, & Millie Jackson
Also see WHODINI & Millie Jackson

JACKSON, Monroe "Moe"
Singles: 78 rpm
MERCURY (8127 "Move It on Over") ... 50-100 49

JACKSON, Moose: see JACKSON, Bull Moose

JACKSON, Nisha C&W '87
Singles: 7-inch
CAPITOL ... 3-4 87

JACKSON, Ollie
Singles: 7-inch
MAGNUM (737 "The Day My Heart Stood Still") ... 35-45

JACKSON, Paul, Jr. R&B '88
Singles: 7-inch
ATLANTIC ... 3-4 88

JACKSON, Prentis
Singles: 7-inch
VEE JAY (417 "Be Mine") ... 15-20 62

JACKSON, Preston, & Rhythm Aces
Singles: 7-inch
HERMITAGE (820 "Three Quarter Stomp") ... 10-20 63

JACKSON, Python Lee: see PYTHON LEE JACKSON

JACKSON, Ralph "Soul"
Singles: 7-inch
ATLANTIC ... 3-6 69

JACKSON, Randy R&B '78
Singles: 7-inch
EPIC ... 3-5 78
Also see JACKSONS

JACKSON, Rebbie P&R/R&B/D&D/LP '84
Singles: 12-inch
COLUMBIA ... 4-6 84-86
Singles: 7-inch
COLUMBIA ... 3-4 84-86
Picture Sleeves
COLUMBIA ... 3-4 84
LPs: 10/12-inch
COLUMBIA ... 5-8 84-86
Also see GRANDMASTER FLASH & Furious Five
Also see JACKSONS

JACKSON, Rebbie, & Robin Zander R&B '86
Singles: 7-inch
COLUMBIA ... 3-4 86
Also see JACKSON, Rebbie

JACKSON, Reuben (Tutti)
Singles: 7-inch
WHEEL CITY (05 "Come Home") 10-20 60s

JACKSON, Robert
Singles: 7-inch
JAN (101 "Oh Baby") ... 20-30 58
JAN (102 "You've Got Me Rocking and Rolling") ... 20-30 58

JACKSON, Roddy
Singles: 78 rpm
SPECIALTY (623 "I've Got My Sights Set on Somebody New") ... 10-20 58
Singles: 7-inch
SPECIALTY ... 10-15 58-59

JACKSON, Roy
Singles: 7-inch
MOONGLOW ... 5-10 61

JACKSON, Rudy
(With the Mel-O-Aires)
Singles: 78 rpm
R&B (1310 "I'm Crying") ... 20-40 55
Singles: 7-inch
IMPERIAL (5425 "Teasin' Me") ... 25-50 63
R&B (1310 "I'm Crying") ... 75-125 55
Session: Vera Potts; Hattie Potts; Gladys Jackson; Mel-O-Aires.
Also see JEWELS

JACKSON, Sammy
Singles: 7-inch
ARVEE ... 8-15 60-63
ORBIT (536 "Are You My Baby") ... 10-15 59
ORBIT (583 "Teen Age Miss") ... 10-15 59
Picture Sleeves
ORBIT (536 "Are You My Baby") ... 15-25 59
ORBIT (583 "Teen Age Miss") ... 15-25 59

JACKSON, Scottie
Singles: 7-inch
AVA ... 4-8 64
DORE ... 4-8 62
EMPALA ... 4-8 65
W.B. ... 4-6 69

JACKSON, Shawne R&B '74
Singles: 7-inch
PLAYBOY ... 3-5 74

JACKSON, Shirley
Singles: 7-inch
METRO ... 4-8 60

JACKSON, Skip
(Skippy & Shantons; with Shantons)
Singles: 7-inch
CAPITOL ... 4-6 72
DOT-MAR (324 "I'm on to You Girl") ... 10-15 69
DOT-MAR (575 "Christmas Song") ... 10-15 69
Also see BROWN, Skip, & Shantons

JACKSON, Solid
Singles: 7-inch
CANDIX ... 5-10 60

JACKSON, Stonewall C&W '58
Singles: 7-inch
COLUMBIA (Except 41000 series) ... 3-8 61-73
COLUMBIA (41000 series) ... 4-8 58-61
FIRST GENERATION ... 3-4 81
GRT ... 3-5 74
LITTLE DARLIN' ... 3-5 78-79
MGM ... 3-5 73
PHONORAMA ... 3-4 83
Picture Sleeves
COLUMBIA (41393 "Waterloo") ... 8-10 59
EPs: 7-inch
COLUMBIA ... 5-10 59
LPs: 10/12-inch
AUDIOGRAPH ALIVE ... 5-8 82
COLUMBIA (1391 "The Dynamic Stonewall Jackson") ... 20-30 59
(Monaural.)
COLUMBIA (1700 thru 2700 series) ... 8-15 62-67
(Monaural.)
COLUMBIA (8186 "The Dynamic Stonewall Jackson") ... 25-40 59
(Stereo.)
COLUMBIA (8500 thru 9900 series) . 8-15 62-70
(Stereo.)
COLUMBIA (10000 series) ... 5-8 73
COLUMBIA (30000 series) ... 5-10 70-72
FIRST GENERATION ... 5-10 81
GRT ... 5-10 75-76
HARMONY ... 8-12 66-74
LITTLE DARLIN' ... 5-8 79
MYRRH ... 5-8 76
PHONORAMA ... 5-8 83
SUNBIRD ... 5-8 80
Session: Jordanaires.
Also see JORDANAIRES

JACKSON, Stoney
Singles: 7-inch
MUSICNOTE ... 4-8 64

JACKSON, Tami
Singles: 7-inch
HIT ... 4-8 63

JACKSON, Tommy
Singles: 7-inch
SUN-RAY (131 "Flat-Top Box") ... 25-50

JACKSON, Tony, & Vibrations
Singles: 7-inch
KAPP ... 5-10 64

JACKSON, Walter P&R/R&B '64
Singles: 7-inch
BRUNSWICK ... 3-6 73
CHI-SOUND ... 3-5 76-78
COLUMBIA (02000 series) ... 3-4 81
COLUMBIA (42000 series) ... 10-20 62-63
COTILLION ... 4-8 69
EPIC ... 5-10 66-68
KELLI-ARTS ... 3-6 83
OKEH (Except 7204) ... 5-10 64-67
OKEH (7204 "It's All Over") ... 5-10 64
(Black vinyl.)
OKEH (7204 "It's All Over") ... 15-25 64
(Colored vinyl.)
20TH FOX ... 3-6 79
U.A. ... 3-6 78
USA ... 6-12 60s
WAND ... 3-5 72
Picture Sleeves
OKEH ... 8-12 66-67
LPs: 10/12-inch
CHI-SOUND ... 8-10 76-78
COLUMBIA ... 5-8 81
EPIC ... 8-10 77
OKEH ... 10-20 65-69
20TH FOX ... 5-8 79

JACKSON, Wanda C&W '56
(With the Party Timers)
Singles: 78 rpm
CAPITOL ... 15-40 56-57
DECCA ... 10-20 54-55
Singles: 7-inch
ABC ... 3-5 75
CAPITOL (2000 thru 3000 series) ... 3-8 67-72
(Orange or orange/yellow labels.)
CAPITOL (3400 thru 4600 series) .. 10-25 56-61
(Purple labels.)
CAPITOL (4700 thru 5900 series) ... 5-10 61-67
DECCA (29253 "Right to Love") ... 20-40 54
DECCA (29267 "You'd Be the First One to Know") ... 20-40 54
(Flip is a duet with Billy Gray.)
DECCA (29514 "Tears at the Grand Ole Op'ry") ... 20-40 55
DECCA (29677 "It's the Same World") ... 10-20 55
DECCA (29803 "Wasted") ... 20-40 55
JIN ... 3-6
MYRRH ... 3-4 73-75
Picture Sleeves
CAPITOL ... 5-10 62-66
EPs: 7-inch
CAPITOL (1041 "Wanda Jackson") ... 25-50 58
LPs: 10/12-inch
CAPITOL (100 thru 600 series) ... 15-20 69-71
CAPITOL (1041 "Wanda Jackson") ... 75-150 58
CAPITOL (1384 "Rockin' with Wanda") ... 50-100 60
CAPITOL (1511 "There's a Party Goin' On") ... 40-80 61
(With "T" prefix. Monaural.)
CAPITOL (1511 "There's a Party Goin' On") ... 50-100 61
(With "ST" prefix. Stereo.)
CAPITOL (1596 "Right Or Wrong") ... 25-50 61
(With "T" prefix. Monaural.)
CAPITOL (1596 "Right Or Wrong") ... 30-55 61
(With "ST" prefix. Stereo.)
CAPITOL (1776 "Wonderful Wanda") ... 20-30 62
(With "T" prefix. Monaural.)
CAPITOL (1776 "Wonderful Wanda") ... 25-35 62
(With "ST" prefix. Stereo.)
CAPITOL (1911 "Love Me Forever") ... 20-30 63
(With "T" prefix. Monaural.)
CAPITOL (1911 "Love Me Forever") ... 25-35 63
(With "ST" prefix. Stereo.)
CAPITOL (2030 "Two Sides of Wanda Jackson") ... 25-35 64
(With "T" prefix. Monaural.)
CAPITOL (2030 "Two Sides of Wanda Jackson") ... 30-40 64
(With "ST" prefix. Stereo.)
CAPITOL (2300 thru 2900 series) .. 10-20 65-68
CAPITOL (11000 series) ... 5-8 72-73
DECCA (4224 "Lovin' Country Style") ... 40-50 62
GUSTO ... 5-8 80
MYRRH ... 5-8 73-76
PICKWICK/HILLTOP ... 8-12 65-68
VARRICK/ROUNDER ... 5-8 87
VOCALION ... 8-12 69
WORD ... 4-8 77

JACKSON, Wanda, & Billy Gray C&W '54
Singles: 7-inch
DECCA (29140 "You Can't Have My Love") ... 20-40 54
Also see GRAY, Billy
Also see JACKSON, Wanda

JACKSON, Willie
Singles: 78 rpm
BROADWAY (5050 "Telephone to Glory") ... 100-150
COLUMBIA ... 25-75
CROWN (3326 "Telephone to Glory") ... 40-60
HERWIN (92035 "Telephone to Glory") ... 100-200
HERWIN (93005 "Rock of Ages") ... 50-100

JACKSON, Willis LP '66
(Willis "Gator Tail" Jackson & His Orch.; vocal By the 4'Gaters; with Jack McDuff)
Singles: 78 rpm
APOLLO ... 10-20 50
ATLANTIC ... 20-50 51-53
DELUXE ... 4-8 53
MODERN ... 10-15 52
Singles: 7-inch
ATCO (6089 "Later 'Gator") ... 15-25 57
ATLANTIC (946 "Harlem Nocturne") ... 75-125 51
ATLANTIC (957 "Wine-O-Wine") 75-125 52
ATLANTIC (967 "Rock, Rock, Rock") ... 50-75 52
ATLANTIC (975 "Gator's Groove") ... 40-60 52
ATLANTIC (998 "Shake Dance") ... 40-60 53
CADET ... 4-8 66
COTILLION ... 3-5 76
DELUXE ... 10-15 53
FIRE ... 5-10 59
MODERN (906 "Let's Jump") ... 15-25 52
PAUL WINLEY (1101 "Bow Legged Daddy") ... 10-20 64
PRESTIGE ... 5-10 59-69
TRU-SOUND (410 "Backtrack") ... 10-15 62
TRU-SOUND (410 "That Twistin' Train") ... 8-12 62
(Retitled reissue.)
VERVE ... 4-8 64
LPs: 10/12-inch
ATLANTIC ... 5-8 75
AUDIO-LAB ... 15-25 59
BIG CHANCE ... 5-10 75
CADET ... 10-20 66
COTILLION ... 5-8 76
MGM ... 10-20 64
MOODSVILLE ... 15-20 62
MUSE ... 5-8 76-81
PRESTIGE (2500 series) ... 5-8 82
PRESTIGE (7100 & 7200 series) ... 15-25 59-64
(Yellow label.)
PRESTIGE (7100 & 7200 series) ... 10-20 65
(Blue label.)
PRESTIGE (7300 thru 7800 series) . 8-15 65-71
TRIP ... 5-10 73
VERVE ... 10-20 64-69
Also see BROWN, Ruth
Also see CLOVERS
Also see JENKINS, Bill & Willis Jackson
Also see McDUFF, Brother Jack, & Willis Jackson

JACKSON, Zeke, Show
Singles: 7-inch
GINK ... 3-5 72

JACKSON BROTHERS
Singles: 78 rpm
DECCA (28055 "Wild Side of Life") 8-12 52
Singles: 7-inch
ATCO (6139 "Tell Him No") ... 8-12 59
DECCA (28055 "Wild Side of Life") ... 10-15 52

JACKSON BROTHERS
Singles: 7-inch
CANDY (002 "Baby, Baby") ... 10-20 59
PROVIDENCE (409 "I've Gotta Hear It from You") ... 15-25 65

JACKSON BROTHERS ORCHESTRA
Singles: 7-inch
ARROW (1003 "The Wrong Door") .. 5-10 57

JACKSON HEIGHTS
Singles: 7-inch
MERCURY ... 3-6 70
VERVE ... 3-5 73
LPs: 10/12-inch
MERCURY ... 15-25 70
VERVE ... 10-20 73
Members: Lee Jackson; Charles Harcourt; Mario Enrique; Tom Sloan; Brian Chatton; Mike Giles; Lawrie Wright; Dave Watts.

JACKSON HIGHWAY
LPs: 10/12-inch
CAPITOL ... 5-8 80

JACKSON INVESTMENT CO.
Singles: 7-inch
PARIS TOWER (125 "What Can I Do") ... 15-25 67
(Label error. Actual title: *What Can I Say*.)

JACKSON JILLS
Singles: 7-inch
DOT ... 4-8 63

JACKSON SISTERS R&B '73
Singles: 7-inch
PROPHESY ... 3-5 73

JACKSONS P&R/R&B '69
(Jackson 5; Michael Jackson & Jackson 5)
Singles: 12-inch
EPIC ... 4-8 79-84
MOTOWN ... 5-10 83
Singles: 7-inch
DYNAMO (Except 146) ... 3-5
DYNAMO (146 "You Don't Have to Be Over 21") ... 15-25 71
EPIC ... 3-5 76-81
MCA ... 3-4 87
MOTOWN ("ABC") ... 20-30 70
(Six-inch, cardboard cutout picture disc. No selection number used.)
MOTOWN ("Sugar Daddy") ... 10-20 70
(Six-inch, cardboard cutout picture disc. No selection number used. Artists neither pictured nor credited.)
MOTOWN (1157 "I Want You Back") ... 4-8 69
MOTOWN (1157 "I Want You Back") ... 15-20 69
(Colored vinyl. Promotional issue only.)
MOTOWN (1163 "ABC") ... 4-8 70
MOTOWN (1166 "The Love You Save") ... 4-6 70
(Black vinyl.)
MOTOWN (1166 "I Found That Girl") ... 15-20 70
(Colored vinyl. Same song on both sides. Promotional issue only.)
MOTOWN (1166 "Love You Save") ... 15-20 70
(Colored vinyl. Same song on both sides. Promotional issue only.)
MOTOWN (1171 thru 1310) ... 3-6 70-75
MOTOWN (1177 "Mama's Pearl") 12-18 71
(Colored vinyl. Promotional issue only.)
MOTOWN (1277 "Get It Together") ... 10-15 73
(Colored vinyl. Promotional issue only.)
MOTOWN (1356 "Forever Came Today") ... 3-5 75
(Black vinyl.)
MOTOWN (1356 "Forever Came Today") ... 10-15 75
(Colored vinyl. Promotional issue only.)
STEEL-TOWN (681 "Big Boy") ... 30-40 68
STEEL-TOWN (682 "We Don't Have to Be Over 21") ... 25-35 71
Picture Sleeves
EPIC ... 3-5 76-84
MCA ... 3-4 87
MOTOWN ... 4-6 71-75
EPs: 7-inch
MOTOWN ("Jackson Five") ... 25-50 70
(Five track flexi-disc.)
MOTOWN ("Sugar Daddy") ... 20-40 70s
(Three track, cardboard flexi-disc.)
MOTOWN (60718 "Jackson Five, Third Album") ... 15-25 70
LPs: 10/12-inch
EPIC (30000 series, except picture discs) ... 5-8 76-84
EPIC (SAI-2561 "Kellog's & the Jacksons, for the Taste of Victory") ... 100-200 84
("Victory Tour" picture disc in gatefold cover. Promotional issue, made for Kellog's.)
EPIC (PAL 34835 "Goin' Places") ... 20-25 78
(Picture disc. Promotional issue only. Has same picture on both sides.)
EPIC (PAL 34835 "Goin' Places") ... 200-250 78
(Picture disc. Promotional issue only. Has "Radio Ten Q" logo on one side.)
EPIC (8E8-39576 "Victory") ... 15-25 84
(Picture disc.)
EPIC (40000 series) ... 5-8 89
EPIC (46000 series) ... 10-15 81
(Half-speed mastered.)
MCA ... 5-8 87
MOTOWN (100 series) ... 5-10 80
MOTOWN (700 series, except 713) ... 8-15 69-74
MOTOWN (713 "The Jackson 5 Christmas Album") ... 10-20 70
MOTOWN (800 series) ... 8-15 75-76
MOTOWN (5000 series) ... 5-8
MOTOWN (6000 series) ... 5-8 84
NATURAL RESOURCES ... 8-12 79
(Promotional issues only.)
PHILLY INTL (34229 "The Jacksons") ... 125-150 78
(Picture disc. Promotional issue only.)
PICKWICK ... 5-10 70s
Members: Michael Jackson; Jermaine Jackson; Jackie Jackson; Marlon Jackson; Tito Jackson; Randy Jackson; Rebbie Jackson.
Also see JACKSON, Jackie
Also see JACKSON, Jermaine
Also see JACKSON, Michael
Also see JACKSON, Randy
Also see JACKSON, Rebbie
Also see RIPPLES & WAVES PLUS MICHAEL
Also see ROSS, Diana, & Bill Cosby / Diana Ross & Jackson Five
Also see WONDER, Stevie

JACKY & LEE
Singles: 7-inch
TEEN-AGER (102 "Misery") ... 50-75

JACKYL
Singles: 12-inch
MCA ... 8-12 90s
(Picture Disc.)
Singles: 7-inch
GEFFEN ... 3-4 91
LPs: 10/12-inch
MCA (24710 "Push Comes to Shove") ... 12-18 90s
(Picture Disc.)

JACOBI, Lou LP '66
LPs: 10/12-inch
CAPITOL ... 5-12 66
VERVE ... 5-12 67

JACOBS, Bobby
("Toldeo's Bobby Jacobs Accompanied By Rhythm Rascals")
Singles: 7-inch
("How Deep Is the Ocean") ... 25-50
(No label name used.)

JACOBS, Dale, & Cobra
LPs: 10/12-inch
EPIC ... 5-10 79
Also see PRISM

JACOBS, Debbie R&B/LP '79
Singles: 12-inch
PERSONAL ... 4-6 84
Singles: 7-inch
MCA ... 3-4 79-80
LPs: 10/12-inch
MCA ... 5-10 79-80

JACOBS, Dick, & His Orchestra P&R '56
Singles: 78 rpm
CORAL (Except 61705) ... 4-6 54-62
CORAL (61705 "Ballad of James Dean") ... 15-20 56
Singles: 7-inch
CORAL (Except 61705) ... 5-10 54-62
CORAL (61705 "Ballad of James Dean") ... 20-30 56
EPs: 7-inch
CORAL ... 8-15 56
LPs: 10/12-inch
CORAL ... 10-25 56-60
VOCALION ... 10-15 60
Also see DIAMONDS
Also see ODOM, King

JACOBS, Donnie
Singles: 7-inch
JIN (212 "If You Want Good Lovin' ") ... 15-25 66

JACOBS, Eddie
Singles: 7-inch
BLUE CAT ... 4-8 66

JACOBS, Eddy
Singles: 7-inch
CHESS (2014 "Tired of Being Lonely") ... 10-20 67
KISS-KISS (222 "Was I So Young") ... 8-12 64

JACOBS, Hank P&R/R&B '64
Singles: 7-inch
CALL ME ... 4-6
IMPERIAL (5894 "Sting Ray") ... 10-15 62
SUE ... 5-10 63-64
LPs: 10/12-inch
SUE (1023 "So Far Away") ... 20-30 64

JACOBS, Jay
Singles: 7-inch
SALCO ... 5-10 62

JACOBS, Little Walter: see LITTLE WALTER

JACOBS, Lori C&W '80
Singles: 7-inch
NEOSTAT ... 3-5 80

JACOBS CREEK
LPs: 10/12-inch
COLUMBIA ... 8-10 69
Also see VAN EATON, Lon & Derrek

JACOBSON, Al
Singles: 7-inch
CAVE (555 "I Gotta Do It") ... 20-30
CAVE (18000 "Rockabilly Blues") .. 40-60

JACOBSON & TANSLEY
Singles: 7-inch
FILMWAYS ... 4-8 66

JACOBY, Scott
LPs: 10/12-inch
MIDLAND INT'L ... 5-10 75

JACOBY BROTHERS
Singles: 78 rpm
TNT ... 8-12 53
Singles: 7-inch
TNT ... 10-20 53

JAC-O-LACS
Singles: 78 rpm
TAMPA (103 "Cindy Lou") ... 25-50 55
Singles: 7-inch
TAMPA (103 "Cindy Lou") ... 75-100 55
Member: Cornell Gunter.
Also see GUNTER, Cornell

JACONO, Jim
Singles: 7-inch
KAY-Y (66783 "Take My Money") ... 50-100 58
(Rigid pressing.)
KAY-Y (66783 "Take My Money") .. 25-50 58
(Flexible vinyl pressing.)

JACQUELINE & JILLS
Singles: 7-inch
GOLDISC (3023 "Gee But It's Great to Be in Love") ... 10-20

JACQUES, Rick C&W '78
Singles: 7-inch
CAPRICE ... 3-5 78

JACQUET, Illinois R&B '52
(With His All-Stars; Jacque Rabbit; with Russell Jacquet)
Singles: 78 rpm
ARA ... 5-10 46
ALADDIN ... 5-15 45-54
APOLLO ... 5-10 46-47
MERCURY ... 5-10 52
PHILO ... 5-10 45
RCA ... 5-15 48-51
SAVOY ... 5-10 46
Singles: 7-inch
ALADDIN ... 10-20 53-54
ARGO ... 4-8 63-65
MGM (89001 "One-Nighter Boogie") ... 15-25
MERCURY ... 10-15 52
PRESTIGE ... 3-6 68-69
RCA (0011 "Black Velvet") ... 10-20 49
(Black vinyl.)
RCA (0011 "Black Velvet") ... 20-30 49
(Colored vinyl.)
RCA (0021 "Big Foot") ... 20-30 49
(Colored vinyl.)
RCA (0047 "Blue Satin") ... 20-30 49
(Colored vinyl.)
RCA (0087 "My Old Gal") ... 20-30 49
(Colored vinyl.)
RCA (0097 "Slow Down, Baby") ... 15-20 49
(Colored vinyl.)
VERVE ... 4-8 62
EPs: 7-inch
ALADDIN (504 "Illinois Jacquet and His Tenor Sax") ... 50-75 54
ALADDIN (511 "Illinois Jacquet and His Tenor Sax") ... 50-75 54
APOLLO (602 "Jam Session") ... 50-75 50
CLEF (126 "Illinois Jacquet Collates") ... 25-40 51
CLEF (143 "Illinois Jacquet Collates") ... 25-40 51
CLEF (166 "Illinois Jacquet Collates, No. 2") ... 20-40 52
CLEF (167 "Illinois Jacquet Collates, No. 2") ... 20-40 52
CLEF (207 "Jazz Moods") ... 20-40 54
CLEF (374 "Illinois Jacquet & His Orchestra") ... 20-40 55
RCA (3236 "Black Velvet") ... 40-60 53
SAVOY ... 20-30 50-53
LPs: 10/12-inch
ACCORD ... 5-8 82
ALADDIN (708 "Illinois Jacquet and His Tenor Sax") ... 100-200 54
(10-inch LP.)
APOLLO (104 "Jam Session") ... 150-250 50
ARGO (722 "Message") ... 15-25 63
ARGO (735 "Desert Winds") ... 15-25 64
ARGO (746 "Illinois Jacquet Plays Cole Porter") ... 15-25 65
ARGO (754 "Spectrum") ... 15-25 65
CLEF (112 "Illinois Jacquet Collates") ... 100-125 51
(10-inch LP. Has Mercury label with Clef logo and number.)
CLEF (129 "Illinois Jacquet Collates, No. 2") ... 100-125 52
(10-inch LP. Has Mercury label with Clef logo and number.)
CLEF (622 "Jazz Moods") ... 50-100 54
CLEF (676 "Illinois Jacquet & His Orchestra") ... 50-75 55
CLEF (680 "The Kid & Brute") ... 50-75 55
CLEF (700 "Jazz Moods") ... 40-60 56
CLEF (702 "Groovin' ") ... 40-60 56
CLEF (750 "Swing's the Thing") ... 40-60 56
EPIC (16033 "Illinois Jacquet") ... 15-25 63
(Monaural.)
EPIC (17033 "Illinois Jacquet") ... 15-25 63
(Stereo.)
GRAND AWARD (315 "Uptown Jazz") ... 20-35 56
IMPERIAL (9184 "Flying Home") ... 15-25 62
JRC ... 5-10 79
MOSAIC (165 "Complete Illinois Jacquet Sessions 1945-50") ... 70-90 90s
(Boxed, six-disc audiophile set. 5000 made.)
PRESTIGE ... 8-12 69-75
RCA (3236 "Black Velvet") ... 50-100 53
(10-inch LP.)
ROULETTE ... 20-30 60
SAVOY (15024 "Tenor Sax") ... 50-100 53
(10-inch LP.)
TRIP ... 5-8 79
VERVE (2500 series) ... 5-10 82-87
VERVE (8000 series) ... 25-50 57-58
(Reads "Verve Records, Inc." at bottom of label.)
VERVE (8000 series) ... 10-20 61-65
(Reads "MGM Records - a Division of Metro-Goldwyn-Mayer, Inc." at bottom of label.)
Session: Johnny Otis; Russell Jacquet; Arthur Dennis; Henry Coker; Sir Charles; Ulysses Livingston; William Hadnott; Miles Davis.
Also see COLE, Cozy, & Illinois Jacquet
Also see DAVIS, Miles
Also see DOGGETT, Bill
Also see HAMPTON, Lionel
Also see HEART BEATS QUINTET
Also see **JAZZ** at the Philharmonic
Also see OTIS, Johnny
Also see X-RAYS

JACQUET, Illinois, & Count Basie
LPs: 10/12-inch
CLEF (701 "Port of Rico") ... 40-60 56
Also see BASIE, Count

JACQUET, Illinois / Lester Young
EPs: 7-inch
ALADDIN (501 "Battle of the Saxes") ... 50-100 54
LPs: 10/12-inch
ALADDIN (701 "Battle of the Saxes") ... 150-250 54
(10-inch LP. Black vinyl.)
ALADDIN (701 "Battle of the Saxes") ... 500-1000 54
(10-inch LP. Colored vinyl.)
ALADDIN (803 "Illinois Jacquet & His Tenor Sax") ... 75-100 56
(Eight tracks from *Battle of the Saxes*, plus four others.)
Also see JACQUET, Illinois
Also see YOUNG, Lester

JACQUET, Russell
(With His All Stars; with His Yellow Jackets; with His Bopper Band)
Singles: 78 rpm
GLOBE ... 5-10 45
JEWEL ... 5-10 47
KING ... 5-10 49-50
MODERN MUSIC ... 5-10 46
SENSATION ... 5-10 48
EPs: 7-inch
KING (308 "Russell Jacquet and His All Stars") ... 50-75 53
KING (309 "Russell Jacquet and His All Stars") ... 50-75 53
LPs: 10/12-inch
KING (8 "Russell Jacquet and His All Stars") ... 75-125 53
(10-inch LP.)
Also see HEART BEATS QUINTET
Also see JACQUET, Illinois

JACQUET, Russell, Orchestra, & Vernon Garrett
(Russel Jacquet Orchestra with Vernon & Jewell)
Singles: 7-inch
IMPERIAL (5722 "Sail On") ... 15-25 61
Also see GARRETT, Vernon
Also see JACQUET, Russell
Also see VERNON & JEWELL

JADE
LPs: 10/12-inch
GENERAL AMERICAN (11311 "Faces of Jade") ... 50-75 68

JADE
Singles: 7-inch
JADE (769 "I'm Leaving Here") ... 15-25 60s

JADE
Singles: 7-inch
CENTURY CITY ... 3-6 70
PESANTE ... 3-6 74

JADE, Faine: see FAINE JADE

JADE FOUR
Singles: 7-inch
IVORY ... 4-6 77

JADE WARRIOR LP '72
Singles: 7-inch
VERTIGO ... 3-4 71-72
LPs: 10/12-inch
ANTILLES ... 5-8 78
ISLAND ... 8-10 74-76
VERTIGO ... 10-12 71-72

JADES
Singles: 7-inch
TIME (1002 "So Blue") ... 150-200 58
Member: Lou Reed.

JADES
(With the Pacers Band; with Pacer's Music; with Rocket Flames Band)
Singles: 7-inch
CHRISTY (110 "Oh Why!") ... 300-400 59
CHRISTY (111 "Tell Me Pretty Baby") ... 250-350 59
CHRISTY (112 "Bon Bon Baby") ... 250-350 59
CHRISTY (113 "Don't Be a Fool") ... 300-400 59
CHRISTY (114 "Look for a Lie") ... 750-1000 59
(Reportedly, 100 made.)
CHRISTY (117 "Pretend") ... 100-150 59
EPs: 7-inch
CHRISTY (100 "The Jades") ... 5-8
(Colored vinyl. Issued with paper sleeve.)
Members: Louis Allen; Art Robinson; Ocie Watkins; Leroy Davis; David McShade.
Also see KLINT, Bobby

JADES
(With the Bluetone Orchestra)
Singles: 7-inch
NAU-VOO (807 "Walking All Alone") ... 200-300 59

JADES
Singles: 7-inch
DOT (15822 "I'm Pretending") ... 50-75 58
REO (825 "I'm Pretending") ... 50-75 58
(Canadian.)
REO (831 "I Sit Alone") ... 150-200 58
(Canadian only. Not issued in U.S.)

JADES
Singles: 7-inch
ADONA ... 15-25 62
DORE (687 "When They Ask About You") ... 25-40 63
PONCELLO (7703 "My Loss, Your Gain") ... 25-50 60s

JADES
Singles: 7-inch
PORT (70042 "He's My Guy") ... 10-20 64

JADES
Singles: 7-inch
GAITY (2-23-64 "Surfin' Crow") ... 125-175 64
OXBORO (2002 "Surfin' Crow") ... 100-150 64
OXBORO (2005 "Little Marlene") ... 75-125 64

JADES
Singles: 7-inch
HOLIDAY (101 "I Cried") ... 20-30 65
MGM (13399 "You're So Right for Me") ... 5-10 65

JADES
LPs: 10/12-inch
JARRETT (21517 "Live at the Disco A-Go-Go") ... 35-50 65

JADES
Singles: 7-inch
ECTOR (101 "I'm All Right") ... 20-30 65
EMCEE (012 "Little Girl") ... 10-20 66
STRAWBERRY (10 "I'm Coming Home") ... 10-20 66
LPs: 10/12-inch
CICADELIC ... 5-10 82
Members: Gary Carpenter; Ron Brown; Jack Henry; Larry Earp; Alvin McCool.

JADES
Singles: 7-inch
NITE LIFE ("I'm Where It's At") ... 50-100
(Selection number not known.)
VERVE ... 5-10 66

JADES
Singles: 7-inch
FENTON (2134 "Please Come Back") ... 15-25 67
FENTON (2194 "Twin City Saucer") ... 15-25 67
FENTON (2208 "Surface World") ... 10-20 67
Also see RANK, Ken / Jades

JADES
Singles: 7-inch
CAPITOL ... 4-6 68
CLARK ... 10-20 60s
IMPERIAL ... 4-6 69
UNI ... 4-8 67

JADES
Singles: 7-inch
MODE ("Lucky Fellow") ... 15-25
(Selection number not known.)

JADES LTD
Singles: 7-inch
TOWER ... 10-20 69

JA-DETTS
Singles: 7-inch
DELTONE ... 5-10 64
Session: Davie Allan.
Also see ALLAN, Davie

JADS
Singles: 7-inch
ASHLEY (770 "Miss Pretty") ... 15-25 66

JAE, Judy
(With the Moonglows)
Singles: 7-inch
BROSH ... 4-8 63

JACOB-CARLE ... 4-8 62

JAG PANZER
Singles: 12-inch
AZRA (010 "Tyrants") ... 10-15 83
(Picture disc. 500 made.)
Singles
AZRA (007 "Death Row") ... 10-20 83
(Picture disc. Pictures a girl with a saw.)
AZRA (007 "Death Row") ... 5-10 83
(Picture disc, square with either monster or torture scene.)
AZRA (007 "Death Row") ... 15-25 83
(Two rectangular picture discs. 200 made.)
AZRA (007 "Death Row") ... 25-35 83
(Two tombstone-shaped picture discs. 100 made.)
LPs: 10/12-inch
IRON WORKS (1001 "Ample Destruction") ... 15-20 86
(Picture disc. 250 made.)

JAGGED EDGE
Singles: 7-inch
GALLANT (3017 "You Can't Keep a Good Man Down") ... 15-25
RCA ... 4-8 66
TWIRL (2024 "Midnight-to-Six Man") ... 15-25 66

JAGGER, Chris LP '73
LPs: 10/12-inch
ASYLUM ... 8-10 73-74

JAGGER, Mick P&R/R&B/D&D/LP '85
Singles: 12-inch
ATLANTIC ("Sweet Thing") ... 20-30 93
(Colored vinyl. Promotional issue only. Includes six versions.)
COLUMBIA (2060 "Lucky in Love") ... 4-8 85
(With special cover.)
COLUMBIA (2060 "Lucky in Love") ... 15-20 85
(Promotional issue with special cover.)
COLUMBIA (5181 "Just Another Night") ... 4-8 85
(With special cover.)
COLUMBIA (5181 "Just Another Night") ... 15-20 85
(Promotional issue with special cover.)
COLUMBIA (6926 "Let's Work") ... 5-10 87
COLUMBIA (7492 "Throwaway") ... 5-10 87
EPIC (5931 "Ruthless People") ... 10-15 86
(With special cover.)
Singles: 7-inch
COLUMBIA (04743 "Just Another Night") ... 3-5 85
COLUMBIA (04893 "Lucky in Love") .. 3-5 85
COLUMBIA (07306 "Let's Work") ... 3-5 87
COLUMBIA (07653 "Throwaway") ... 3-5 87
EPIC (06211 "Ruthless People") ... 3-5 86
Picture Sleeves
COLUMBIA (04743 "Just Another Night") ... 3-5 85
COLUMBIA (04893 "Lucky in Love") .. 3-5 85
COLUMBIA (07306 "Let's Work") ... 3-5 87
COLUMBIA (07653 "Throwaway") ... 3-5 87
EPIC (06211 "Ruthless People") ... 3-5 86
Promotional Singles
COLUMBIA (04743 "Just Another Night") ... 8-10 85
COLUMBIA (04893 "Lucky in Love") ... 8-10 85
COLUMBIA (07306 "Let's Work") ... 8-10 87
COLUMBIA (07653 "Throwaway") ... 8-10 87
EPIC (06211 "Ruthless People") ... 5-10 86
LPs: 10/12-inch
COLUMBIA (39940 "She's the Boss") ... 8-10 85
COLUMBIA (40919 "Primitive Cool") ... 8-10 87
EPIC ... 8-12 86
LONDON WAVELENGTH (006 "The Mick Jagger Special") ... 75-100 81
(Promotional issue only.)
ROLLING STONES (164 "Interview with Mick Jagger") ... 75-100 71
(Promotional issue only.)
U.A. (300 "Ned Kelly") ... 10-15 74
(Soundtrack.)
U.A. (5213 "Ned Kelly") ... 15-20 70
(Soundtrack.)
Also see BOWIE, David, & Mick Jagger
Also see FRAMPTON, Peter
Also see JACKSON, Michael, & Mick Jagger
Also see NEON LEON
Also see OR, John
Also see ROLLING STONES
Also see SIMON, Carly
Also see TOSH, Peter, & Mick Jagger
Also see WEST, Leslie
Also see WOLF, Peter, & Mick Jagger

JAGGERS
Singles: 7-inch
EXECUTIVE ("Feel So Good") ... 25-40 66
(No selection number used.)

JAGGERZ P&R/LP '70
Singles: 7-inch
GAMBLE ... 4-8 68
JAGGERZ ... 3-5 74
KAMA SUTRA ... 3-6 70
WOODEN NICKEL ... 3-5 75
LPs: 10/12-inch
GAMBLE (5006 "Introducing the Jaggerz") ... 15-20 69
KAMA SUTRA ... 10-15 70
WOODEN NICKEL ... 8-10 75
Members: Dominic Ierace (a.k.a. Donnie Iris); Jim Pugliano; Jim Ross; Bill Maybray; Ben Faiella.
Also see IRIS, Donnie
Also see Q

JAGIELLO, Walter
Singles: 7-inch
VEE JAY ... 4-8 65

JAGNEAUX, Rufus
JIN ... 3-6 69
Also see RUFUS

JAGS
Singles: 7-inch
LONDON (9507 "Cry Wolf") ... 8-12 61

JAGS
Singles: 7-inch
SOMA (1104 "Lost Woman") ... 40-60 60s

JAGS P&R '80
Singles: 7-inch
ISLAND ... 3-5 79-80
Picture Sleeves
ISLAND ... 3-5 79-80
LPs: 10/12-inch
ISLAND ... 5-8 80-81

JAGUAR
LPs: 10/12-inch
RCA ... 5-8 77

JAGUARS
Singles: 78 rpm
AARDELL ... 20-40 55-56
R-DELL ... 20-40 56-57
Singles: 7-inch
AARDELL (0003 "Rock It Davy, Rock It") ... 25-50 55
AARDELL (0006 "You Don't Believe Me") ... 25-50 56
BARONET (1 "The Way You Look Tonight") ... 50-100 62
CLASSIC ARTISTS ... 4-6 89
EBB (129 "Hold Me Tight") ... 50-100 58
ORIGINAL SOUND (6 "Thinking of You") ... 50-100 59
ORIGINAL SOUND (20 "Thinking of You") ... 25-35 62
ORIGINAL SOUND (59 "The Way You Look Tonight") ... 10-20 65
R-DELL (11 "The Way You Look Tonight"/ "Moonlight and You") ... 200-300 56
(Black vinyl.)
R-DELL (11 "The Way You Look Tonight"/ "Moonlight and You") ... 550-650 56
(Red vinyl.)
R-DELL (11 "The Way You Look Tonight"/ "Baby, Baby, Baby") ... 25-50 56
R-DELL (16 "I Love You Baby") 100-200 57
R-DELL (45 "Rock It Davy, Rock It") ... 50-75 58
R-DELL (107 "Rock It Davy, Rock It") ... 25-50 59
R-DELL (117 "Girl of My Dreams") ... 50-75 60
Member: Val Poliuto; Herman Chaney; Manuel Chavez; Charles Middleton. Session: Tony Allen.
Also see ALLEN, Tony
Also see NUGGETS
Also see STATON, Johnny, & Feathers / Jaguars

JAGUARS
Singles: 7-inch
EPIC (9308 "Jaguar") ... 10-15 59
EPIC (9325 "Drive-In") ... 10-15 59

JAGUARS
Singles: 7-inch
FARO ... 5-10 64
RENDEZVOUS ... 8-12 62
Also see SALAS BROTHERS

JAGUARS
Singles: 7-inch
PIC (604 "Jaguar") ... 10-20 64

JAGUARS
Singles: 7-inch
CUCA (6542 "Boney Maronie") ... 15-25 65
SARA (6583 "Things We Said Today") ... 20-30 65
Members: Tom Sumner; Dave Peterson; Jim Flynn; Paul Nebel; Howie Market; Curt Johnson.
Also see UPSTAIRS

JAGUARS
Singles: 7-inch
DOT (16931 "Gorilla") ... 5-10 66

JAGUARS
Singles: 7-inch
SKOOP (1067 "It's Gonna Be Alright") ... 10-15 66

JAGUARS
Singles: 7-inch
WHIZZ (001 "Middle of a Heartache") ... 10-20 60s

JAGUARS
Singles: 7-inch
SPAY (121 "Rendezvous") ... 25-50

JAGUARS
Singles: 7-inch
ALCO (1006 "The Metropolitan") ... 5-10
AZTEC ... 5-10
JAGUAR ... 5-10

JAGUARS
Singles: 7-inch
ATHENS (211 "Shooting Star") ... 5-10
HAMILTON (1001 "Catwalk") ... 5-10

JAH FISH
Singles: 7-inch
GRAPE (3034 "The Vampire") ... 8-12

JAH WOBBLE
LPs: 10/12-inch
ISLAND 5-8 84
Members: Edge Czukay; Holger Czukay.
Also see PUBLIC IMAGE LTD.

JAIM
Singles: 7-inch
ETHEREAL.. 5-10
LPs: 10/12-inch
ETHEREAL (1001 "Prophesy Fulfilled")..............................30-40 69

JAIMES, DeAnne
Singles: 7-inch
DODE (1004 "Look at Me Mama") 4-8

JAISUN R&B '78
Singles: 7-inch
JETT SETT.. 3-5 78

JAK R&B '85
Singles: 7-inch
EPIC.. 3-4 84-86
LPs: 10/12-inch
EPIC.. 5-8 85

JAKE & FAMILY JEWELS
Singles: 7-inch
POLYDOR... 3-5 72
LPs: 10/12-inch
POLYDOR... 8-10 72
Member: Jake Jacobs.
Also see BUNKY & JAKE
Also see MAGICIANS

JA-KKI P&R '76
Singles: 7-inch
PYRAMID... 3-5 76
WEST END....................................... 3-5

JAKKY BOY & BAD BUNCH
Singles: 7-inch
ATLANTIC.. 3-4 87
LPs: 10/12-inch
ATLANTIC.. 5-8 87

JALOPY FIVE
(Johnny & Jalopy Five)
Singles: 7-inch
HIT 5-15 64-69
TOP POP HITS................................. 4-8 69
Many Hit and Top Pop Hits 45s have other artists on the flip, such as: Jason Allen & Gigolos, Bobby & Connie, Bobby Brooks, Richie Brown, Buchanans, Bugs, Chellows, Chords, Classmates, Cords, Dacrons; Fantastics, Hank's Hounds, Ed Hardin, Wayne Harris, Harris Brothers, Fred Hess, Sandy Holiday, Jack Jones & Jetset Band; Joe King, Mary Sue & Trams, Richard Phillips, Roamers, Kathy Shannon, Bobby Sims, and Fred York.
LPs: 10/12-inch
COMPATIBLE 20-30 65
Also see BROOKS, Bobby
Also see BUGS / Chellows
Also see SIMS, Bobby, & Simmers

JAM
Singles: 7-inch
SIRE.. 4-6 68

JAM LP '80
Singles: 7-inch
POLYDOR... 3-5 78-83
Picture Sleeves
POLYDOR... 3-5 80-83
LPs: 10/12-inch
POLYDOR... 5-8 77-83
Also see STYLE COUNCIL

JAM FACTORY
Singles: 7-inch
EPIC.. 3-5 70
LPs: 10/12-inch
EPIC.. 8-12 70

JAMAICA BOYS R&B '87
Singles: 7-inch
W.B. 3-4 87-88

JAMAICA GIRLS D&D '83
Singles: 12-inch
SLEEPING BAG 4-6 83

JAMAICAN ALL STARS
LPs: 10/12-inch
ATLANTIC.......................................10-12 64

JAMAL, Ahmad R&B/LP '58
(Ahmad Jamal Trio; Quintet)
Singles: 7-inch
ARGO... 4-8 57-65
CADET 3-6 66-68
CHESS 3-5 73
PARROTT 5-10 55
20TH FOX.. 3-5 73-80
EPs: 7-inch
ARGO... 8-15 59-61
LPs: 10/12-inch
ABC.. 8-12 68
ARGO (610 thru 662)......................20-40 56-60
ARGO (667 thru 758)......................15-25 61-65
CADET 10-25 65-73
CATALYST.. 5-10 76
EPIC (600 series)...........................15-30 63-65
EPIC (3212 "Ahmad Jamal Trio")....30-50 56
EPIC (3600 series)..........................20-30 59
IMPULSE...10-20 69-73
MOTOWN 5-10 80
PERSONAL CHOICE 5-8 82
SHUBRA 5-8 83
20TH FOX.. 5-10 73-80
WHO'S WHO in JAZZ 5-10 81

JAMAL, Ahmad, & Larry Gorshin
Singles: 7-inch
ATLANTIC... 3-4 86
Also see JAMAL, Ahmad

JAMBALAYA
LPs: 10/12-inch
A&M 8-10 73

JAMECOS
Singles: 7-inch
JAMECO (2004 "Second Hand Love")..20-30 60s

JAMELLS
Singles: 7-inch
CROSLEY (350 "Beatle March")....15-25 64

JAMES, Atlanta: see ATLANTA JAMES

JAMES, Art
Singles: 7-inch
CODE (711 "Congratulations").......50-75 58

JAMES, Betty
Singles: 7-inch
CEE JAY 10-15 61
CHESS (Except 1801 & 1837) 6-12 61-66
CHESS (1801 "I'm a Little Mixed Up")..15-25
CHESS (1837 "Henry Lee") 10-20 63

JAMES, Bill, & Hex-O-Tones
Singles: 7-inch
MUN RAB (104 "School's Out")..100-200 59

JAMES, Billy, & Crystaltones
Singles: 7-inch
MZ (111 "Meant for Me")............200-300 62
Also see CRYSTAL TONES

JAMES, Billy, & Stenotones
Singles: 7-inch
RUST (5038 "Phyllis")....................40-60 61

JAMES, Bob P&R '74
(Bob James Trio)
Singles: 7-inch
CTI 3-5 74-77
COLUMBIA.. 3-5 79-83
TAPPAN ZEE/COLUMBIA.................. 3-5 77-85
Picture Sleeves
COLUMBIA.. 3-5 79-80
LPs: 10/12-inch
CTI 5-10 74-77
COLUMBIA.. 5-8 83
ESP 10-15 65
MERCURY 15-25 63
TAPPAN ZEE/COLUMBIA..................5-10 77-85
Also see FOURPLAY

JAMES, Bob, & Earl Klugh LP '79
Singles: 7-inch
CAPITOL... 3-4 82
TAPPAN ZEE/COLUMBIA................... 3-5 79
LPs: 10/12-inch
CAPITOL... 5-8 82
MFSL (124 "2 of a Kind") 20-30 84
TAPPAN ZEE/COLUMBIA...................5-10 79
Also see KLUGH, Earl

JAMES, Bob, & David Sanborn LP '86
LPs: 10/12-inch
W.B. 5-8 86-88
Also see JAMES, Bob
Also see SANBORN, David

JAMES, Bobbie, & Four Buddies
Singles: 78 rpm
CLUB 51 (104 "I Need You So").....50-75 56
Singles: 7-inch
CLUB 51 (104 "I Need You So").150-250 56
Also see FOUR BUDDIES

JAMES, Bobby
Singles: 7-inch
INDIGO 5-10 62
JOLUM (102 "Let's Surf")...............15-25
KAROL..8-12
LANT (66009 "Let's Go").................8-12 60s

JAMES, Brian
Singles: 7-inch
I.R.S. 3-5 79

JAMES, Bucky Dee
(With the Nashville Explosion)
LPs: 10/12-inch
SPRINGBOARD 8-12 78

JAMES, Carroll: see BEATLES

JAMES, Charles
Singles: 7-inch
ABC... 4-8 61
LAB 4-8 61
ZAB (102 "Rockin' Chair")...............10-15 62

JAMES, Chick
Singles: 7-inch
PRIDE 8-12 59

JAMES, Chuck
Singles: 7-inch
STADIUM (2266 "Chuckels") 10-20 66

JAMES, Colin
Singles: 7-inch
VIRGIN... 3-4 88
Picture Sleeves
VIRGIN... 3-4 88

JAMES, Chick
Singles: 7-inch
PRIDE 8-12 59

JAMES, D.D.
Singles: 7-inch
SOULTRACK 4-8 68

JAMES, Daniel
Singles: 78 rpm
ALLSTAR (7163 "Rock, Moon, Rock")...200-300 57
Singles: 7-inch
ALLSTAR (7163 "Rock, Moon, Rock")...200-300 57

JAMES, Danny
Singles: 7-inch
GOLDBAND 5-10

JAMES, Denita
Singles: 7-inch
FLIP (364 "Wild Side")....................10-20

JAMES, Deviny
(Jim Pewter)
Singles: 7-inch
BETA (1006 "Little Girl")..................25-35 59
STUDIO CITY (1002 "That's All Right Mama")..10-20 61
Also see PEWTER, Jim

JAMES, Dian
(With the Satisfactions)
Singles: 7-inch
GROOVE 4-8 65
RADIANT 4-8 65

JAMES, Donnie
Singles: 7-inch
GALAHAD 4-8 63

JAMES, Dusty C&W '79
Singles: 7-inch
SRC 3-5 79

JAMES, Elmore R&B '52
(With His Broomdusters; Elmo James)
Singles: 78 rpm
ACE...50-75 53
CHECKER.......................................100-150 53
CHIEF 25-50 57
FLAIR..25-50 54-56
METEOR (5000 "I Believe").........50-100 53
METEOR (5003 "Sinful Woman")....................................50-100 53
MODERN (983 "Wild About You")..25-50 56
TRUMPET (146 "I Believe My Time Ain't Long")...25-50 52
VEE JAY (249 "The 12-Year-Old Boy")..20-30 57
VEE JAY (259 "It Hurts Me Too")....30-50 57
Singles: 7-inch
ACE (508 "My Time Ain't Long") 100-200 53
CHECKER (777 "Country Boogie")..200-400 53
CHESS (1756 "The Sun Is Shining")...20-30 60
CHIEF (7001 "The Twelve Year Old Boy")..35-50 57
CHIEF (7004 "It Hurts Me Too").....35-50 57
CHIEF (7006 "Cry for Me Baby") 35-50 57
CHIEF (7020 "Knocking at Your Door")..25-35 58
ENJOY (2015 "It Hurts Me Too")......10-20 65
FIRE (504 "Fine Little Mama").......10-20 62
FIRE (1011 "Make My Dreams Come True")...10-20 60
FIRE (1016 "The Sky Is Crying")....10-20 60
FIRE (1024 "I'm Worried") 10-20 60
FIRE (1031 "Fine Little Mama") 10-20 61
FIRE (1503 "Anna Lee") 10-20 62
FLAIR (1011 "Early in the Morning")......................................150-200 54
FLAIR (1014 "Can't Stop Lovin' ")...150-200 54
FLAIR (1022 "Strange Kinda Feeling").......................................100-150 55
FLAIR (1031 "Make My Dreams Come True")...100-200 55
FLAIR (1039 "Sho'nuff, I Do") 100-200 55
FLAIR (1048 "Dark and Dreary")...100-200 56
FLAIR (1057 "Standing at the Crossroads").................................100-200 55
FLAIR (1062 "Late Hours at Midnight")......................................75-125 56
FLAIR (1069 "Happy Home")..........75-125 56
FLAIR (1074 "Dust My Blues")......100-150 56
FLAIR (1079 "Blues Before Sunrise")..75-100 56
FLASHBACK......................................3-6 65
JEWEL (764 "Dust My Broom") 4-8 66
JEWEL (783 "Catfish Blues")............4-8 66
(Though credited to Elmo James, the flip sides of Jewel 764 and 783 are actually by Big Boy Crudup.)
KENT 5-15 60-67
METEOR (5000 "I Believe").......200-300 53
METEOR (5003 "Sinful Woman")......................................200-300 53
MODERN (983 "Wild About You")..150-250 56
M-PAC..4-8
S&M 4-8
SOUND 4-8
SPHERE SOUND.................................8-12 65
VEE JAY (249 "The 12-Year-Old Boy")..20-30 57
VEE JAY (259 "It Hurts Me Too")...20-30 57
VEE JAY (269 "Cry for Me Baby") ...20-30 58
LPs: 10/12-inch
BELL 10-12 68-69
BLUE HORIZON.................................10-12
CHESS..10-12 69
COLLECTABLES 6-8 88
CROWN (5168 "Blues After Hours")..50-100 61
CUSTOM...8-12
INTERMEDIA 5-8 84
KENT (5022 "Original Folk Blues")..20-30 64
KENT (9000 series) 10-20 67-69
KENT TREASURE SERIES...............5-8 86
RELIC 5-10 88
SPHERE SOUND (7002 "The Sky Is Crying")...25-35 60s
SPHERE SOUND (7008 "I Need You")..25-35 60s
TRIP 8-10 71-78
UNITED..10-12 60s
UPFRONT...8-10 70s
Also see BROWN, J.T.
Also see CRUDUP, Big Boy
Also see JONES, Little Johnny

JAMES, Elmore, & John Brim
LPs: 10/12-inch
CHESS..10-15 69
Also see BRIM, John
Also see JAMES, Elmore

JAMES, Etta R&B '55
(With the Peaches; Etta "Miss Peaches" James)
Singles: 78 rpm
MODERN 10-20 55-56
Singles: 7-inch
ABC...3-5 74
ARGO 8-15 60-64
CADET 4-8 67-72
CHESS...3-5 73-76
KENT (304 thru 345.......................12-25 58-60
MODERN (947 "The Wallflower") ..25-40 55
MODERN (957 "Hey Henry").........25-40 55
MODERN (962 "Good Rockin' Daddy")..25-40 55
MODERN (972 "That's All") 25-40 55
MODERN (984 "Number One").......25-40 55
MODERN (988 "Shortnin' Bread Rock")..25-40 55
MODERN (998 "Tough Lover")........25-40 55
MODERN (1007 "Then I'll Care") 15-25 57
MODERN (1016 "The Pickup") 15-25 57
MODERN (1022 "Come What May")..15-25 57
REGENCY 10-20
T-ELECTRIC 3-5 80
W.B. 3-5 78
LPs: 10/12-inch
ARGO 20-35 61-65
ARRIVAL..5-10 83
CADET 10-20 67-71
CHESS..10-12 71-76
CROWN (5209 "Miss Etta James")...20-30 61
CROWN (5234 "The Best of Etta James")..20-30 62
CROWN (5250 "Twist with Etta James")...15-25 62
CROWN (5360 "Miss Etta James") 15-25 63
INTERMEDIA 5-8 84
KENT (3002 "Miss Etta James") 20-35 61
(Black vinyl.)
KENT (3002 "Miss Etta James") ..50-100 61
(Colored vinyl.)
T-ELECTRIC 5-8 80
UNITED 10-12
W.B. 5-8 78
WESTBOUND.......................................8-10
Session: Richard Berry; Riley Hampton's Orchestra.
Also see BERRY, Richard
Also see ETTA & HARVEY
Also see FLAIRS

JAMES, Etta, & Sugar Pie DeSanto P&R '65
Singles: 7-inch
CADET 4-8 65-66
Also see DESANTO, Sugar Pie
Also see JAMES, Etta

JAMES, Gary, & Creations
Singles: 7-inch
LIGHT'NING 4-8 64

JAMES, George C&W '79
Singles: 7-inch
JANE...3-5 79

JAMES, Gino
Singles: 7-inch
EPIC...5-10 60

JAMES, Harry, & His Orchestra P&R '38
Singles: 78 rpm
BRUNSWICK 3-6 38
COLUMBIA..3-6 40-57
VARIETY...4-8 40
Singles: 7-inch
COLUMBIA (33000 series) 3-5 76
COLUMBIA (38000 thru 40000 series)..5-8 50-56
DOT 3-6 65-66
GOLD-MOR 3-5 73
MGM 4-6 59-63
EPs: 7-inch
COLUMBIA 5-15 50-56
LPs: 10/12-inch
BAINBRIDGE 5-8 83
BRIGHT ORANGE 5-8 73
CAPITOL (600 thru 1500 series)....15-30 55-61
(With "T" or "ST" prefix.)
CAPITOL (1500 series)...................10-20 62
(With "DT" prefix.)
CAPITOL (1500 series).......................5-8 77
(With "M" prefix.)
COLUMBIA 10-30 50-67
COLUMBIA SPECIAL PRODUCTS 5-8 79
DOT 8-15 66-67
HARMONY 10-20 59-72
LONDON 5-10 68
MGM 10-20 59-65
METRO 8-15 65-67
PICKWICK 5-10 70s
SHEFFIELD LAB..................................5-8 77-79
Also see KALLEN, Kitty
Also see SINATRA, Frank

JAMES, Harry, & Dick Haymes
LPs: 10/12-inch
CIRCLE 5-8 81
Also see HAYMES, Dick
Also see JAMES, Harry, & His Orchestra

JAMES, Homesick: see HOMESICK JAMES

JAMES, Jackie
Singles: 7-inch
ALFA..4-8 62

JAMES, Jesse
Singles: 78 rpm
SITTIN' IN WITH (569 "Forgive Me Blues")..50-100 51
Also see JAMES, Sunny

JAMES, Jesse
Singles: 7-inch
KENT (314 "Red Hot Rockin' Blues")...100-200 58

JAMES, Jesse P&R/R&B '67
(With the Royal Aces; Jessie James)
Singles: 7-inch
BUDDAH..5-10
HIT (6119 "I Call on You") 20-30 60s
HIT (6120 "Believe in Me Baby")....15-25 60s
MUSICOR (1008 "Dreams Never Hurt Nobody")..10-15 61
SHIRLEY (103 "I Will Go") 75-125 61
SHIRLEY (112 "I Wanna Full Time Love")..25-50 63
SHIRLEY (122 "I Want a Girl") 25-50 63
T.T.E.D. 3-5 87
20TH FOX...3-8 67-75
UNI..5-8 69
ZEA (ZAY)...3-5 70-71
LPs: 10/12-inch
20TH FOX...8-10 67
Also see JAMES BOYS

JAMES, Jesseca C&W '76
(Kathy Twitty)
Singles: 7-inch
MCA..3-5 76-77
Also see TWITTY, Kathy

JAMES, Jessica, & Outlaws
Singles: 7-inch
DYNOVOICE 4-8 66

JAMES, Jessie
Singles: 7-inch
KETO (101 "Do the Pony") 5-10 61

JAMES, Jessye
Singles: 7-inch
ARGO 8-12 64

JAMES, Jimmy
Singles: 7-inch
REDSTART 4-8 65

JAMES, Jimmy, & Candy Canes
Singles: 7-inch
COLUMBIA 5-10 58

JAMES, Jimmy, & Vagabonds P&R/R&B '68
Singles: 7-inch
ATCO...4-8 67-68
HBR (496 "Hi Diddley Dee Dum Dum")...10-20 66
PYE..3-5 75-76
LPs: 10/12-inch
ATCO..10-15 67
PYE..5-8 75

JAMES, Joe
(With Bob Rush & Orchestra)
Singles: 7-inch
WAG (213 "A Fool for You") 50-100 59

JAMES, Joni P&R '52
Singles: 78 rpm
MGM (222 "Let There Be Love")..100-200 53
(Four-disc boxed set.)
MGM (234 "Award Winning Album")..100-200 54
(Four disc boxed set.)
MGM (272 "Little Girl Blue") 100-200 54
(Four-disc boxed set.)
MGM (11000 & 12000 series) 10-20 52-58
MGM (30000 series) 5-10 54
SHARP (46 "Let There Be Love") ...25-50 52
SHARP (50 "You Belong to Me") 25-50 52
Singles: 7-inch
MGM (16 thru 19)...........................20-40 59-60
(Stereo compact 33 singles.)
MGM (11223 thru 12660)..................15-25 52-58
MGM (12706 "There Goes My Heart")...10-15 58
(Monaural.)
MGM (12706 "There Goes My Heart")...20-30 58
(Stereo. Unusual numbering—most MGM stereo 45s are in the 50000 series. Billed as the industry's "First Single Stereo Disc.")
MGM (12746 thru 13304)..................10-20 59-64
MGM (13288 "Sentimental Me") 50-75 64
(Promotional issue only.)
MGM (30000 series) 10-20 54
MGM (50111 "There Must Be a Way")..15-25 59
(Stereo.)

MGM/GOLDEN CIRCLE (101 thru 104)....5-10 61
SHARP (46 "Let There Be Love")....150-250 52
SHARP (50 "You Belong to Me")....100-200 52
Picture Sleeves
MGM (12565 "Never Till Now")......10-20 57
MGM (12706 "There Goes My Heart")....25-50 58
MGM (12779 "I Still Get a Thrill")...10-20 59
MGM (12895 "We Know")....10-20 60
MGM (12933 "My Last Date")....10-20 60
MGM (12948 "Be My Love")....10-20 61
MGM (13037 "You Were Wrong") 10-20 62
EPs: 7-inch
MGM (222 "Let There Be Love")....50-75 53
MGM (234 "Award Winning Album")....50-75 54
MGM (272 "Little Girl Blue")....50-75 54
MGM (326 "When I Fall in Love")..20-40 55
(EPs 222 through 326 are two-disc sets.)
MGM (1160 "When I Fall in Love")....10-20 55
MGM (1172 "Have Yourself a Merry Little Christmas")....25-50 55
MGM (1211 thru 1617)....10-20 56-58
MGM (1652/3/4 "Songs of Hank Williams")....10-15 59
(Monaural. Price is for any of three volumes.)
MGM (1652/3/4 "Songs of Hank Williams")....30-40 59
(Stereo. Price is for any of three volumes.)
MGM (1656/7/8 "100 Strings and Joni")....10-15 59
(Monaural. Price is for any of three volumes.)
MGM (1656/7/8 "100 Strings and Joni")....30-40 59
(Stereo. Price is for any of three volumes.)
MGM (1672/3/4 "Joni Swings Sweet")....10-15 59
(Monaural. Price is for any of three volumes.)
MGM (1672/3/4 "Joni Swings Sweet")....30-40 59
(Stereo. Price is for any of three volumes.)
MGM (3328 "In the Still of the Night")....20-35 56
MGM (3533 "Songs by Jerome Kern & Harry Warren")....20-35 57
LPs: 10/12-inch
MGM (222 "Let There Be Love")..75-125 53
(10-inch LP.)
MGM (234 "Award Winning Album")....75-125 54
(10-inch LP.)
MGM (272 "Little Girl Blue")....75-125 54
(10-inch LP.)
MGM (3240 "When I Fall in Love")....30-50 55
MGM (3328 "In the Still of the Night")....30-50 56
MGM (3346 "Award Winning Album, Vol. 1")....30-50 56
MGM (3347 "Little Girl Blue")....30-50 56
MGM (3348 "Let There Be Love")..30-50 56
MGM (3449 "Songs by Victor Young & Frank Losser")....30-50 56
MGM (3468 "Merry Christmas")....30-50 56
MGM (3528 "Give Us This Day")....25-45 57
MGM (3533 "Songs by Jerome Kern & Harry Warren")....25-45 57
MGM (3602 "Among My Souvenirs")....25-45 58
MGM (3623 "Ti Voglio Bene")....25-45 58
MGM (3706 "Award Winning Album, Vol. 1")....25-45 58
MGM (E-3718 "Je T'Aime")....25-45 58
(Monaural.)
MGM (SE-3718 "Je T'Aime")....35-55 58
(Stereo.)
MGM (E-3729 "Songs by Hank Williams")....25-45 59
(Monaural.)
MGM (SE-3729 "Songs by Hank Williams")....35-55 59
(Stereo.)
MGM (E-3749 thru E-4286)....20-30 59-65
(Monaural.)
MGM (SE-3749 thru SE-4286)....20-35 59-65
(Stereo.)

JAMES, Judy
Singles: 7-inch
NORMAN....4-8 62

JAMES, Keef
LPs: 10/12-inch
RARE EARTH....8-10 72

JAMES, Leon
Singles: 7-inch
BUMBLE BEE (501 "Baby, Let's Rock")....50-100

JAMES, Leonard
LPs: 10/12-inch
DECCA (8772 "Boppin' and A-Strollin' ")....40-50 58

JAMES, Marion
Singles: 7-inch
EXCELLO (2280 "That's My Man").. 5-10 66

JAMES, Mark
Singles: 7-inch
BELL....3-5 73
CRS (1-8-35 "Blue Suede Heaven").. 5-8 85
(Black vinyl.)
CRS (1-8-35 "Blue Suede Heaven")....8-15 85
(Colored vinyl.)
JAMIE....4-8 63
LIBERTY....4-8 67
MERCURY....3-5 75
NEW DESIGN....3-5 71
PRIVATE STOCK....3-5 78
SCEPTER....4-8 68
SPOTLIGHT (450 "Writing This Letter")....75-125 60s
Picture Sleeves
CRS (1-8-35 "Blue Suede Heaven")....8-10 85
LPs: 10/12-inch
BELL....8-12 73

JAMES, Mary Kay C&W '74
Singles: 7-inch
AVCO....3-5 75
JMI....3-4 74

JAMES, Melvin LP '87
LPs: 10/12-inch
MCA....5-8 87

JAMES, Nicky
LPs: 10/12-inch
THRESHOLD....10-12 72

JAMES, Peter
Singles: 7-inch
REPRISE....4-8 65-66
W.B.....4-8 66

JAMES, Rick P&R/R&B/LP '78
(With the Stone City Band)
Singles: 12-inch
GORDY....4-6 79-85
MOTOWN....4-6 78-85
Singles: 7-inch
GORDY....3-5 78-85
MOTOWN....3-4 86
REPRISE....3-4 88
Picture Sleeves
GORDY....3-5 79-85
LPs: 10/12-inch
GORDY....5-8 78-86
REPRISE....5-8 88
Also see STONE CITY BAND
Also see TEMPTATIONS & Rick James

JAMES, Rick, & Friend R&B '83
(With Smokey Robinson)
Singles: 7-inch
GORDY....3-5 83

JAMES, Rick, & Smokey Robinson P&R '83
Singles: 7-inch
GORDY....3-5 83
Also see JAMES, Rick
Also see JAMES, Rick, & Friend
Also see ROBINSON, Smokey

JAMES, Rick, & Roxanne Shante R&B '88
Singles: 7-inch
REPRISE....3-4 88
Also see SHANTE, Roxanne

JAMES, Roland: see JANES, Roland

JAMES, Ron
Singles: 7-inch
MAR-VEL (2500 "Please Be Mine")....15-25

JAMES, Ronny
(Ronnie James)
Singles: 7-inch
ENVOY....5-10 61
PAN-OR....5-10
PHILADELPHIA INT'L....3-5 79
UPTITE....4-8

JAMES, S., & Soul Babies
Singles: 7-inch
FARO (628 "Takin' Care of Business")....10-20 60s

JAMES, Sherri
Singles: 7-inch
WHEEL....10-20 60s

JAMES, Skip
LPs: 10/12-inch
BIOGRAPH....10-15 68-69
HISTORICAL....10-15
MELODEAN....10-15
VANGUARD....10-15 66-68

JAMES, Sonny C&W '53
(With the Southern Gentlemen; with Silver; with Tennessee State Prison Band; the Southern Gentleman)
Singles: 78 rpm
CAPITOL....5-15 52-57
Singles: 7-inch
CAPITOL (2000 thru 3900)....3-6 67-74
(Orange labels.)
CAPITOL (2200 thru 3800)....10-20 52-57
(Purple labels.)
CAPITOL (3900 thru 5900)....5-10 58-67
(Purple or orange/yellow swirl labels.)
CAPITOL (6000 series)....4-6 60s
CAPITOL CUSTOM ("Salute to KRAK")....15-25 67
(Promotional issue for a Sacramento radio station.)
COLUMBIA....3-5 72-78
DIMENSION....3-4 81-83
DOT....4-6 62
GROOVE....4-8 61
MONUMENT....3-5 79
NRC....5-8 60
RCA....4-8 61-62
Picture Sleeves
CAPITOL (Except 4268)....4-10 65-71
CAPITOL (4268 "Who's Next in Line")....6-10 59
COLUMBIA....3-5 72-75
DIMENSION....3-5 80s
NRC (050 "Jenny Lou")....10-15 60
EPs: 7-inch
CAPITOL....8-15 57-58
CAPITOL CREATIVE PRODUCTS..5-10 68
LPs: 10/12-inch
ABC....5-8 77
BROOKVILLE....8-12 75
CAMDEN....8-12 60s
CAPITOL (100 thru 800 series)....8-12 68-71
CAPITOL (779 "The Southern Gentleman")....25-35 57
CAPITOL (867 "Sonny")....20-30 57
CAPITOL (988 "Honey")....20-30 58
CAPITOL (1100 series)....15-25 59
CAPITOL (2000 thru 2800 series)....8-15 64-68
CAPITOL (11000 series)....5-8 72-75
COLUMBIA....5-10 72-78
CROWN....8-12 60s
DIMENSION....5-8 82
DOT....15-20 62
GUEST STAR....10-15 64
HAMILTON....8-12 65
MONUMENT....5-8 79
PICKWICK....5-8 76-78
PICKWICK/HILLTOP....8-12 69
SUNRISE MEDIA....5-10
TEE VEE....8-12 79
TVP....8-12 75
WYNCOTE....8-12 60s
Also see HAGGARD, Merle / Sonny James
Also see HORTON, Johnny / Sonny James
Also see SUNSHINE RUBY
Also see VINCENT, Gene / Tommy Sands / Sonny James / Ferlin Husky
Also see VINCENT, Gene / Frank Sinatra / Sonny James / Ron Goodwin

JAMES, Sonny / Dave Dudley / Sunny Williams
LPs: 10/12-inch
DIPLOMAT....5-10 60s
Also see DUDLEY, Dave

JAMES, Sonny / David Houston
LPs: 10/12-inch
PICKWICK/HILLTOP....8-12 67
Also see HOUSTON, David

JAMES, Sonny / Seekers
Singles: 7-inch
CAPITOL (5375 "I'll Keep Holding On"/"I'll Never Find Another You")....4-8 65
(These two tracks were unintentionally pressed back-to-back.)
Also see JAMES, Sonny
Also see SEEKERS

JAMES, Sunny
(Jesse James)
Singles: 78 rpm
DOWN TOWN (2010 "Please Mam, Forgive Me")....50-100 48
Also see JAMES, Jesse

JAMES, Tom
Singles: 78 rpm
RCA....10-20 54
Singles: 7-inch
KLIX (1 "Track Down Baby")....250-500 58
RCA (5695 "Your Kind of Lovin' ") 50-75 54
RCA (5790 "I'm a Pig About Your Lovin' ")....50-75 54

JAMES, Tommy P&R/R&B/LP '66
(With the Shondells)
Singles: 7-inch
ABC....3-5 73
FANTASY....3-4 75-80
MCA....3-5 74
MILLENNIUM....3-5 79-81
PHILCO....10-20 67
("Hip-Pocket" flexi-disc.)
ROULETTE....4-8 66-73
TWENTY-ONE....3-4 83
Picture Sleeves
FANTASY....3-5 76
MILLENNIUM....3-5 71
ROULETTE....5-10 66-67
TWENTY-ONE....3-4 83
LPs: 10/12-inch
FANTASY....8-10 76-80
MILLENNIUM....5-8 80
RHINO....8-12 89
ROULETTE....10-20 66-72
SCEPTER....8-10 73
SCEPTER/CITATION....5-8 82
TWENTY-ONE....5-8 83
Members: Tommy James; Mike Vale; Ed Gray; Ron Rosman; Pete Lucia.
Also see HOG HEAVEN
Also see SHONDELLS

JAMES, Tommy & Shondells / Lee Dorsey
Singles: 7-inch
ROULETTE (4710 "It's Only Love"/"Ya Ya")....5-10 66
(Credits Tommy James & Shondells, but plays Lee Dorsey.)
Also see DORSEY, Lee
Also see JAMES, Tommy

JAMES, Ulysses / Lowell Fulson
Singles: 78 rpm
CAVATONE (250 "Poor Boy")....40-60 48
Also see FULSON, Lowell

JAMES & GARY
Singles: 7-inch
CALGAR (004 "The Godfather's Daughter")....4-6 74

JAMES & GOOD BROTHERS
Singles: 7-inch
COLUMBIA....4-6 71
LPs: 10/12-inch
COLUMBIA....10-20 71
Also see GARCIA, Jerry

JAMES BOYS
Singles: 7-inch
COLPIX....4-8 63
COLUMBIA....4-8 66
EDSEL....15-25 60
GALLIANT (1002 "Back Rub")....40-60 59
KAPP (502 "Stampede")....8-12 63

JAMES BOYS P&R/R&B '68
Singles: 7-inch
PHIL L.A. of SOUL (316 "The Mule")..4-8 68
Member: Jesse James.
Also see JAMES, Jesse
Also see MFSB

JAMES BROTHERS
Singles: 7-inch
DOT....5-10 58

JAMES GANG
Singles: 7-inch
ASCOT....4-8 65-66

JAMES GANG LP '69
Singles: 7-inch
ABC....3-6 70-72
ATCO....3-5 74-75
BLUESWAY....4-8 69
LPs: 10/12-inch
ABC....10-12 70-73
ABC/COMMAND (984 "16 Greatest Hits")....15-25 74
(Quadraphonic. Two discs.)
ATCO....8-10 74-76
BLUESWAY (6034 "Yer' Album")....10-15 69
MCA....5-8
Members: Joe Walsh; Tommy Bolin; Dominic Troiano Dale Peters; Jim Fox..
Also see BOLIN, Tommy
Also see WALSH, Joe

JAMES QUINTET
Singles: 78 rpm
CORAL (60018 "Pleasing You")....20-40 49
CORAL (60022 "Tell Me Why")....20-40 49
CORAL (65002 "Pleasing You")....20-40 49
CORAL (65016 "Tell Me Why")....20-40 49
DECCA....15-25 51
DERBY (726 "I'm Just a Fool")....20-40 49
DERBY (732 "Don't Worry")....20-40 50
Singles: 7-inch
DECCA (48218 "A Neighborhood Affair")....100-150 51
DECCA (48237 "I Could Make You Care")....100-150 51
Also see POWELL, Austin

JAMES T. & WORKERS
Singles: 7-inch
PROPHONICS....4-8

JAMESON
Singles: 7-inch
VERVE....4-8 67
LPs: 10/12-inch
VERVE....10-12 67

JAMESON, Bobby
Singles: 7-inch
BRIT....4-8 65
CURRENT....4-8 64
LONDON (9730 "Each and Everyday")....20-30 65
PENTHOUSE (503 "Gotta Find My Roogalator")....20-30 66
TALAMO (1934 "I'm Lonely")....4-8 64
TALAMO (1934 "I'm So Lonely")....4-8 64
(Note title variation.)
VERVE....4-8 67
LPs: 10/12-inch
GRT....8-10
Also see ROLLING STONES

JAMESON, Cody C&W/P&R '77
Singles: 7-inch
ATCO....3-5 77

JAMESON, Nick P&R '86
Singles: 7-inch
MOTOWN....3-4 86
LPs: 10/12-inch
BEARSVILLE (6972 "Already Free") 8-12 77
MOTOWN....5-8 86
Also see FOGHAT

JAMESTOWN MASSACRE P&R '72
Singles: 7-inch
W.B.....3-5 72

JAMIE
Singles: 7-inch
MUSICOR....4-6 69

JAMIE & BLACKHAWKS
Singles: 7-inch
MGM....4-8 66

JAMIE & JANE
Singles: 7-inch
DECCA (30862 "Strolling")....15-25 59
DECCA (30934 "Faithful Our Love")....15-25 59
Members: Gene Pitney; Ginny Arnell.
Also see ARNELL, Ginny
Also see PITNEY, Gene

JAMIE & JURY
Singles: 7-inch
COLUMBIA....3-5 66-67

JAMIES P&R '58
Singles: 7-inch
EPIC....5-10 58-63
EPIC (11000 series)....3-4 74
U.A.....4-6 59
Picture Sleeves
EPIC (9281 "Summertime Summertime")....15-20 58-63
Members: Tom Jamison; Serena Jamison.
Also see J's with JAMIE

JAMISON, Bob
Singles: 7-inch
BAND BOX....4-8 63

JAMME
Singles: 7-inch
DUNHILL....3-5 70
LPs: 10/12-inch
DUNHILL....10-12 70
Members: Keith Adey; Don Adey.

JAMMERS
Singles: 7-inch
DEARBORN (519 "You're Gonna Love Me Too")....25-35 65

JAMMERS R&B '82
Singles: 7-inch
JUBILEE....4-8 66
LOMA....4-8 67

JAMMERS
Singles: 7-inch
SALSOUL....3-4 82-83

JAMMERS
(Featuring Sonny Stevenson)
Singles: 7-inch
ONDA (108 "The Thunderbird")....15-20 57

JAMMIN' JIM
(Ed Harris)
Singles: 78 rpm
SAVOY (1106 "Shake Boogie")....15-25 52
Singles: 7-inch
SAVOY (1106 "Shake Boogie")....25-50 52
Also see CAROLINA SLIM
Also see COUNTRY PAUL
Also see LAZY SLIM JIM

JAMUL P&R '70
Singles: 7-inch
LIZARD....3-5 70
LPs: 10/12-inch
LIZARD....10-12 70

JAN & ARNIE P&R '58
(With Don Ralke's Orchestra; with Adam Ross Orchestra)
Singles: 78 rpm
ARWIN (108 "Jennie Lee")....150-250 58
QUALITY (1761 "Gas Money")..100-200 58
(Canadian.)
Singles: 7-inch
ARWIN (108 "Jennie Lee")....15-25 58
ARWIN (111 "Gas Money")....15-25 58
ARWIN (113 "I Love Linda")....15-25 58
DOT (16116 "Gas Money")....10-20 58
DORE (522 "Baby Talk")....300-400 59
(By Jan & Dean though shown on first pressings as by Jan & Arnie.)
QUALITY (1761 "Gas Money")....50-75 58
(Canadian.)
EPs: 7-inch
DOT (1097 "Jan & Arnie")....350-450 60
Members: Jan Berry; Arnie Ginsburg.
Also see BERRY, Jan
Also see GINSBURG, Arnie
Also see JAN & DEAN
Also see RALKE, Don
Also see RITUALS

JAN & CHUCK
Singles: 7-inch
NIGHT OWL....5-8 66
Member: Jan Bradley.
Also see BRADLEY, Jan

JAN & DEAN P&R/R&B '59
Singles: 7-inch
AURAVISION (6723 "Linda")....40-60 64
(Cardboard flexi-disc, one of six by six different artists. Columbia Record Club "Enrollment Premium." Set came in a special paper sleeve.)
CAPITOL (89 "Jennie Lee")....3-5 89
(By Jan & Dean instead of Jan & Arnie.)
CHALLENGE (9120 "Wanted: One Girl")....10-20 61
CHALLENGE (9111 "Heart and Soul"/"Those Words")....25-35 61
CHALLENGE (9111 "Heart and Soul"/"Midsummer Night's Dream")....10-20 61
(Note different flip side.)
CHALLENGE (59111 "Heart and Soul")....10-20 61
COLUMBIA (44036 "Yellow Balloon")....15-25 67
DORE....15-25 59-61
J&D (1 "Oh What a Beautiful Morning")....150-200 87
(Private, limited, promotional, red vinyl pressing by Dean Torrence which he used as Christmas gifts. With Chris Farmer and Phil Bardowell.)
J&D (001 "California Lullabye")....20-30 66
J&D (402 "Like a Summer Rain")....20-30 66
JAN & DEAN (10 "Hawaii")....45-60 66
JAN & DEAN (11 "Fan Tan")....50-75 66
LIBERTY (55397 "A Sunday Kind of Love")....10-20 61
LIBERTY (55454 "Tennessee")....10-20 62
LIBERTY (55496 "Who Put the Bomp")....20-30 62
LIBERTY (55522 "She's Still Talkin' Baby Talk")....50-75 62
LIBERTY (55531 "Linda")....8-12 63
LIBERTY (55580 thru 55727)....5-10 63-64

LIBERTY (55766 thru 55923)... 8-12 63-66
MAGIC LAMP (401 "California Lullabye")...15-25 66
ODE (66111 "Fun City")...15-25 75
U.A. ...10-20 72-76
W.B. (7151 "Only a Boy")...35-50 67
W.B. (7219 "I Know My Mind")...30-40 68
Picture Sleeves
DORE (555 "We Go Together")...35-50 60
DORE (576 "Gee")...75-100 60
LIBERTY (Except 55766 & 55849)...15-25 63-65
LIBERTY (55766 "From All Over the World")...80-125 65
LIBERTY (55849 "Folk City")...20-30 65
U.A. (50859 "Jenny Lee")...15-25 71
EPs: 7-inch
ARTISTIC (227 "Original Golden Hits"): see Various Artists section
LPs: 10/12-inch
ARTISTIC (227 "Original Golden Hits"): see Various Artists section
AUDIO ENCORE... 5-8 89
AXIS (45 "Very Best")... 5-10
COLUMBIA (9461 "Save for a Rainy Day")...1500-2000 67
(At least one sale of this LP has been confirmed. It DOES exist but is probably not a U.S. issue. Tracks are remixed from what is heard on the J&D LP of the same title. Does have one track, *Lullaby in the Rain*, which is not on the J&D LP.)
DEADMAN'S CURVE ("Live at Keystone Berkeley")...15-25 78
(With Papa Doo Ron Ron.)
DESIGN/STEREO SPECTRUM...10-20 63
DORE (101 "Jan & Dean")...300-400 60
(With 12"x12" bonus Jan & Dean color photo.)
DORE (101 "Jan & Dean")...200-300 60
(Without bonus photo.)
EMI...10-15 86
EMI/LIBERTY...10-20 90
EXACT... 5-8 80
EXCELSIOR...10-15 80
IMPERIAL HOUSE... 5-8 80
INTERNATIONAL AWARD... 8-10
J&D (101 "Save for a Rainy Day")...200-300 67
K-TEL... 5-10 70-89
LIBERTY (3248 thru 3403)...20-25 62-65
(Monaural.)
LIBERTY (3414 "Pop Symphony Number 1")...40-45 65
(Monaural.)
LIBERTY (3417 thru 3460)...20-25 65-66
(Monaural.)
LIBERTY (7248 thru 7403)...20-30 62-65
(Stereo.)
LIBERTY (7414 "Pop Symphony Number 1")...40-50 65
(Stereo.)
LIBERTY (7417 thru 7460)...20-30 65-66
(Stereo.)
LIBERTY (10000 series)... 8-12 81-82
MAGIC CARPET...10-12
NEON (333006 "Greatest Hits")... 8-10 83
PAIR (1071 "California Gold")...10-15
RHINO (1498 "One Summer Night Live")...25-45 82
SILVER EAGLE (1039 "Silver Summer")...25-35 86
(Mail-order offer.)
SUNDAZED (5022 "Save for a Rainy Day")...15-18 96
(Colored vinyl. Two-discs.)
SUNDAZED (5040 "Jan & Dean")... 8-10 96
(Colored vinyl. Includes poster.)
SUNSET...10-15 67
U.A. ...10-12 71-79
Members: Jan Berry; Dean Torrence. Session: Glen Campbell; Leon Russell; Hal Blaine; Sally Stevens; Carol Kaye; Ray Pholman; Don Randi; Chris Farmer; Phil Bardowell.
Also see BEACH BOYS
Also see BEACH BOYS / Jan & Dean
Also see BERRY, Jan
Also see BLAINE, Hal
Also see CALIFORNIA MUSIC
Also see CAMPBELL, Glen
Also see JAN & ARNIE
Also see KAYE, Carol
Also see LAUGHING GRAVY
Also see LEGENDARY MASKED SURFERS
Also see MATADORS
Also see MIKE & DEAN
Also see OUR GANG
Also see PAPA DOO RON RON
Also see RALLY PACKS
Also see RUSSELL, Leon

JAN & DEAN / Roy Orbison / 4 Seasons / Shirelles
EPs: 7-inch
COKE ("Let's Swing the Jingle for Coca-Cola")...40-60 65
(Coca-Cola radio spots. Issued to radio stations only.)
Also see 4 SEASONS
Also see ORBISON, Roy
Also see SHIRELLES

JAN & DEAN & RANDELL KIRSCH
Singles: 7-inch
JAN & DEAN (1 "Wa Ichi Nichi Show")... 5-10 87
Members: Jan Berry; Dean Torrence; Randell Kirsch; Gary Griffin; Chris Farmer; John Cowsil; Phil Bardowell; Mark Ward; Kevin Leonard; Bill Hollingshead; Dave Hoffman; Sue Nelson; Members of Shangahi audience.

JAN & DEAN / Soul Surfers
LPs: 10/12-inch
L-J (101 "Jan & Dean with the Soul Surfers")...35-45 63
Also see SOUL SURFERS / Delicates

JAN & DEAN / Bobby Vinton / Andy Williams
Singles
AURAVISION (2 "Special Teen Preview Record #2")...12-20 64
(Square cardboard picture disc. Columbia Record Club bonus. Has song excerpts by each artist, plus *Pipeline* by an unknown band.)
Also see JAN & DEAN
Also see VINTON, Bobby
Also see WILLIAMS, Andy

JAN & JERRY
Singles: 7-inch
METRO...10-15 59

JAN & JILL
Singles: 7-inch
20TH FOX... 3-5 76

JAN & KJELD P&R '60
Singles: 7-inch
ALONCA... 4-6 66
IMPERIAL...5-10 59
JARO INT'L...5-10 60
KAPP...5-10 60-61
Picture Sleeves
JARO INT'L...5-10 60
KAPP...5-10 60
LPs: 10/12-inch
KAPP (1190 "Banjo Boy")...20-30 60

JAN & LORRAINE
LPs: 10/12-inch
ABC-PAR (691 "Gypsy People")...15-25 69
Members: Jan Hendin; Lorraine Lefevre.

JAN & MALCOLM C&W '77
Singles: 7-inch
PAULA... 3-5 77

JAN & PHIL
Singles: 7-inch
CRUSADER... 4-8 64

JAN & RADIANTS: see LITTLE JAN & RADIANTS

JANA LOUISE
Singles: 7-inch
DOT... 4-8 64-65
LPs: 10/12-inch
DOT...10-15 64

JANDY
Singles: 7-inch
PLAYGROUND... 3-5 78

JANE
Singles: 7-inch
CAPITOL... 3-5 74
LPs: 10/12-inch
CAPITOL...8-10 74

JANE, B., & Teenettes
Singles: 7-inch
CRUSADER (2440 "Dial L for Love")...10-20 60s

JANE, Baby: see BABY JANE

JANE'S ADDICTION LP '88
LPs: 10/12-inch
TRIPLE X...10-20
(Clear vinyl.)
W.B. ...5-10 88-90

JANERO, Triste
Singles: 7-inch
GPC... 4-8 69
LPs: 10/12-inch
WHITE WHALE (299 "Rene De Marie")... 5-8 69

JANES, Bill
Singles: 7-inch
MUNFAB (104 "School's Out")...25-40

JANES, Roland
(Roland James)
Singles: 7-inch
JUDD (1012 "Guitarville")...10-20 59
RITA (1007 "Down Yonder")...10-15 60
Also see ALTON & JIMMY
Also see ANDERSON, Brother James
Also see BARTON, Ernie
Also see CARAWAY, Bobby
Also see RILEY, Billy Lee
Also see WARREN, Randy

JANET & JAY
Singles: 7-inch
HANOVER...5-10 60
LEADER...5-10 60
Picture Sleeves
LEADER...5-10 60

JANETTES
Singles: 7-inch
GOLDIE...5-10 62

JANEY & DENNIS
Singles: 7-inch
REPRISE... 3-5 70
LPs: 10/12-inch
REPRISE...8-10 70

JANEY & JAY
(Janie & Jays)
Singles: 7-inch
LEADER...5-10 61
HI... 4-8 67

JANGO'S CAROUSEL
Singles: 7-inch
PROBE...3-5 70

JANIANNE
Singles: 7-inch
ASHLEY...4-8 65

JANICE R&B '86
Singles: 7-inch
BORN AGAIN...3-4 80
COTILLION...3-5 76
FANTASY...3-5 75-76
ROULETTE (7083 "I Thank You Kindly")...10-20 70
LPs: 10/12-inch
FANTASY...6-10 75
Also see SADDLER, Reggie

JANICE
Singles: 7-inch
4TH & BROADWAY...3-4 86

JANICE & RUBYS
Singles: 7-inch
SWAN...4-8 63

JANIE
Singles: 7-inch
CAPITOL...5-10 60

JANIS, Johnny P&R '57
Singles: 78 rpm
ABC-PAR...5-10 57
CORAL...5-10 55
Singles: 7-inch
ABC-PAR (9800 "Pledge of Love") 10-20 57
ABC-PAR (9840 "Later Baby")...10-20 57
BOMARC (304 "Willing to Learn")...8-12 59
BOMARC (307 "I Said You")...8-12 60
CARLTON (463 "The Better to Love You")...10-20 58
COLUMBIA (41797 "Gina")...8-12 60
COLUMBIA (41933 "Catch a Falling Star")...8-12 61
COLUMBIA (42040 "I Get Ideas")...8-12 61
CORAL (61552 "Move It Or Lose It")...10-20 55
MONUMENT...4-8 66-68
LPs: 10/12-inch
ABC-PAR (140 "For the First Time")...50-75 57
COLUMBIA (1674 "Start of Something New")...20-30 61
(Monaural.)
COLUMBIA (8474 "Start of Something New")...30-40 61
(Stereo.)
MONUMENT...10-15 65

JANIT & JAYS
Singles: 7-inch
HI...4-8 66

JANKEL, Chas R&B/LP '82
Singles: 12-inch
A&M...4-6 83
Singles: 7-inch
A&M...3-4 82
LPs: 10/12-inch
A&M...5-8 82
Also see DURY, Ian, & Blockheads

JANKOWSKI, Horst, Orchestra P&R/LP '65
Singles: 7-inch
MERCURY...3-6 65-68
Picture Sleeves
MERCURY...4-6 65
LPs: 10/12-inch
MERCURY...5-15 65-69
Also see IMPALAS / Horst Jankowski & His Orchestra

JANO C&W '79
Singles: 7-inch
SCR...3-5 79

JANO, Big Al, & Secret Lover
Singles: 7-inch
HOTTRAX (15009 "Condom Man")...3-5 87
(With insert/sleeve)

JANO, Johnny
Singles: 78 rpm
EXCELLO...20-30 56
Singles: 7-inch
EXCELLO (2099 "Having a Whole Lot of Fun")...50-100 56
GOLDBAND (1062 "Mable's Gone")...20-30 58
GOLDBAND (1087 "Mable's Gone")...15-25 58
HOLLYWOOD (1087 "Mable's Gone")...30-40 58
(First issue.)

JANS, Tom
Singles: 7-inch
COLUMBIA...3-5 76-77
LPs: 10/12-inch
A&M...8-10 74
COLUMBIA...5-8 76

JANSCH, Bert
LPs: 10/12-inch
COUNTRYSIDE...8-10 74
REPRISE...8-10 69-73
VANGUARD...10-15 66-70
Also see PENTANGLE

JANSEN, Gus
Singles: 7-inch
ARVEE...4-8

JANSEN, Jimmy
Singles: 7-inch
ACE...4-8 60

JANSKY, Clifton C&W '85
Singles: 7-inch
AXBAR...3-4 85

JANSSEN, Danny
Singles: 7-inch
STEPHANY (1841 "Mirror on the Wall")...20-30 60

JANSSEN, David
(With the Tradewinds Orchestra)
LPs: 10/12-inch
EPIC...10-20 65

JANUARY TIME
LPs: 10/12-inch
ENTERPRISE...8-10

JANUS
LPs: 10/12-inch
HARVEST (29433 "Gravedigger")...40-60 72

JAPAN
LPs: 10/12-inch
ARIOLA AMERICA...5-8 78
VIRGIN...5-8 82

JAPANESE BEATLES
Singles: 7-inch
GOLDEN CREST...15-20 64

JAPHET, Cliff
EPs: 7-inch
ARZEE...3-5 79

JARETT, Peter, & Fifth Circle
Singles: 7-inch
MGM (13768 "Let's Dance Close")...30-40 67

JARMAIN, Robb
Singles: 7-inch
CHESS...3-6 69

JARMELS P&R/R&B '61
Singles: 7-inch
LAURIE...10-15 61-63
LPs: 10/12-inch
COLLECTABLES...6-8 87
Members: Nate Ruff; Ray Smith; Tom Eldridge; Paul Burnett; Earl Christian; Major Harris.

JARR, Cook E: see COOK E. JARR

JARRARD, Rick
Singles: 7-inch
CHATTAHOOCHEE...10-15 64-67
PLEBE...10-20 62
Also see JEFFERSON AIRPLANE

JARRE, Jean-Michael LP '77
Singles: 12-inch
POLYDOR...4-6 86
Singles: 7-inch
POLYDOR...3-5 78-87
LPs: 10/12-inch
DREYFUS...5-8 85-86
MFSL (212 "Oxygene")...20-25 94
MFSL (227 "Equinoxe")...20-25 95
POLYDOR...5-8 77-87
Also see ANDERSON, Laurie
Also see U.S.A. for AFRICA

JARREAU, Al R&B/LP '76
(Jarreau)
Singles: 7-inch
MCA...3-4 87
RAYNARD (10022 "I'm Not Afraid")...50-100 65
RAYNARD (10024 "Shake Up")...50-100 65
REPRISE...3-5 76-88
W.B. ...3-5 77-86
Picture Sleeves
MCA...3-4 87
W.B. ...3-5 83-84
LPs: 10/12-inch
MFSL (019 "All Fly Home")...40-60 78
REPRISE...5-10 75-88
W.B. ...5-10 77-86
Also see U.S.A. for AFRICA

JARREAU, Al, & Randy Crawford R&B '82
Singles: 7-inch
W.B. ...3-4 82
Also see CRAWFORD, Randy
Also see JARREAU, Al

JARRETT, Keith LP '75
LPs: 10/12-inch
ATLANTIC...8-10 75
ECM...8-12 76-80
IMPULSE...8-10 75-77

JARRETT, Mike, & Gene Herd
Singles: 7-inch
TOWER...5-10 65

JARVIS, Carol P&R '57
Singles: 78 rpm
BALLY...5-10 57
DOT...5-10 57
Singles: 7-inch
BALLY...5-10 57
DOT...5-10 57-59
ERA...5-10 60-61

JARVIS, Felton
(With the Fel-Tones)
Singles: 7-inch
ABC-PAR...5-10 64-65
MGM (12982 "Goin' Downtown")...5-10 61

THUNDER INT'L (1023 "Swingin' Cat")...50-75 60
THUNDER INT'L (1030 "Little Wheel")...25-50 61
VIVA (1001 "Don't Knock Elvis")...15-25 59
Also see PRESLEY, Elvis

JARVIS, Little Richard
Singles: 7-inch
CAPITOL...3-5 73

JARVIS, Marion R&B '74
Singles: 7-inch
ROXBURY...3-5 74

JASMIN D&D '84
Singles: 12-inch
TVI...4-6 84

JASON, Bobby
Singles: 7-inch
CHANCELLOR...4-8 64

JASON, Eddie
Singles: 7-inch
ASCOT...4-8 67
MGM...4-6 69
MERCURY...4-6 69

JASON & SCORCHERS LP '84
(Jason & Nashville Scorchers)
Singles: 7-inch
EMI AMERICA...3-4 84-86
PRAXIS...10-15 83-84
LPs: 10/12-inch
EMI AMERICA...5-8 84-86
Member: Jason Ringenberg.

JASON GARFIELD
Singles: 7-inch
KEF...5-10

JASPER, Bob
Singles: 7-inch
PACER...4-8 67

JASPER, Chris R&B '87
Singles: 7-inch
CBS ASSOCIATED...3-4 87-88
LPs: 10/12-inch
CBS ASSOCIATED...3-4 87
Also see ISLEY - JASPER - ISLEY

JASPER WRATH
Singles: 7-inch
FUTURE MUSIC...4-6 76
SUNFLOWER (107 "It's Up to You")...5-10 71
LPs: 10/12-inch
SUNFLOWER (5003 "Jasper Wrath")...40-60 71

JAVALANS
Singles: 7-inch
EVENT...10-20 58

JAVALONS
(With the Respectable Three)
Singles: 7-inch
DIP (6901 "Took a Chance")...75-100 61
TRU EKO (6901 "Took a Chance")...50-80 61
(Light yellow label.)
TRU EKO (6901 "Took a Chance")...25-50 61
(Gold label.)

JAVAROO
LPs: 10/12-inch
CAPITOL...5-8 80

JAVELINS
Singles: 7-inch
CAPITOL (5050 "Joe the Guitar Man")...10-20 63

JAVELS
Singles: 7-inch
JAIRO (500 "Distant Guitar")...10-20 64

JAWBREAKER
LPs: 10/12-inch
MCA...8-10 90s

JAXON, Bob
(Bob Jaxon & Hi Tones)
Singles: 78 rpm
CADENCE...5-10 55
RCA...10-15 57
Singles: 7-inch
CADENCE (1264 "Why Does a Woman Cry")...8-12 55
RCA (6945 "I'm Hangin' Around")...20-30 57
RCA (7106 "I'm Hurtin' Inside")...20-30 57
20TH FOX (441 "Weep, Mary, Weep")...5-10 63

JAXON SISTERS
Singles: 78 rpm
BIG...10-15 57
Singles: 7-inch
BIG (605 "For a Lifetime")...10-15 57
BIG (606 "Thanks Mr. Moonbeam")...10-15 57

JAY
(Jay Traynor)
Singles: 7-inch
CORAL...8-12 64
MICHELE...8-12 63
Also see JAY & AMERICANS
Also see TRAYNOR, Jay

JAY, Al & Gerry: see THUNDERMEN

JAY, Bee
Singles: 7-inch
CLOCK...4-8 62

JAY, Bobby, & Hawks
EPs: 7-inch
W.B. (1438 "Bobby Jay & the Hawks") ... 8-10 64
LPs: 10/12-inch
W.B. (1562 "Everybody's Doing the Watusi") ... 10-15 64
W.B. (1563 "Everybody's Doing the Ska") ... 10-15 64
W.B. (1564 "Everybody's Doing the Monkey") ... 10-15 64

JAY, Bobby
(With the Runarounds)
Singles: 7-inch
ALTA ... 4-6
EXCELLO (2225 "Tell Me Now") ... 8-12 62
IMPERIAL (5590 "So Lonely") ... 10-20 59
RUSTONE (1407 "Because of You") ... 8-12 61
TOWER (777 "Block Party") ... 4-8 60s
LP: 10/12-inch
W.B. ... 10-15

JAY, Brian
Singles: 7-inch
LAURIE (3228 "Tuff Enuff") ... 10-20 64

JAY, Dale, & Storms
Singles: 7-inch
RAVEN ... 5-10 59

JAY, Dave
Singles: 7-inch
BIG TIME ... 5-10 60

JAY, Dee: see DEE JAY

JAY, Eddie, & Kingmen
Singles: 7-inch
KM ... 5-8

JAY, George, & Rockin' Ravens
Singles: 7-inch
DYNAMIC ("Say That You Love Me") ... 20-30
RAVE (103 "El Gringo") ... 10-20

JAY, Harold
Singles: 7-inch
JOHNNY ... 8-12 64

JAY, Harry, & Group Therapy
Singles: 7-inch
ARCOLIA ... 5-10

JAY, Herbie
Singles: 7-inch
MALA ... 4-8 62

JAY, Ira, II
Singles: 7-inch
SUN ... 8-10 60

JAY, Jazzy: see JAZZY JAY

JAY, Jerry
(Jerry Osborne)
Singles: 7-inch
QUALITY (201 "The King's Country") ... 200-300 66
(Six copies made as gifts.)
Also see OSBORNE, Jerry

JAY, Jimmy
Singles: 7-inch
ALPAC ... 15-25
HICKORY ... 4-8 65
PHILIPS ... 5-10 62-63

JAY, Jimmy
(With the Blue Falcons; with Moon-Reyes)
Singles: 7-inch
BELMONT (4006 "Turbine Drive") 15-25 62
DIXIETONE (1912 "Highleggin' Party") ... 200-300 65
Session: Romans.

JAY, Johnny
Singles: 78 rpm
MERCURY ... 10-20 57-58
Singles: 7-inch
MERCURY ... 10-20 57-58
PLAY ... 10-20 58
STOP ... 10-20 67-68
Also see HUHTA, Johnny

JAY, Johnny, & Gangbusters
Singles: 7-inch
JOSIE ... 4-8 67

JAY, Karl
Singles: 7-inch
MARJON (503 "Unemployment Line") ... 30-40 62

JAY, Kathy
Singles: 7-inch
VEE JAY ... 4-8 63
WARWICK ... 4-8 61

JAY, Lonnie, & Jaynes
Singles: 7-inch
ARLEN (724 "Somewhere") ... 15-25 63

JAY, Morty P&R '63
(With the Surfin' Cats)
Singles: 7-inch
KAYDEN ... 5-10 60s
LEGEND (124 "What Is Surfin'") ... 10-20 63
20TH FOX ... 5-10 63
Picture Sleeves
LEGEND (124 "What Is Surfin'") ... 10-20 63
Also see NORELL, Jerry

JAY, P., & Haystackers
Singles: 7-inch
OAK ... 10-15

JAY, Sammy
Singles: 7-inch
TRIBE ... 4-8 65

JAY, Tommy
Singles: 7-inch
DOVER ... 4-8 63
GOLBE (1258 "Sandie Jane") ... 5-10 60s
HI ... 4-8 65
M.O.C. ... 4-8 64

JAY & AMERICANS P&R '62
Singles: 7-inch
COLLECTABLES ... 3-5 92-93
EEOC (1140 "Things Are Changing") ... 50-100 65
(Equal Employment Opportunity Center promotional issue.)
FUTURA ... 3-5 72
U.A. (353 thru 992) ... 5-10 61-66
U.A. (50000 series) ... 3-6 66-71
U.A. (1600 series) ... 3-4
U.A. SILVER SPOTLIGHT ... 3-5
Picture Sleeves
EEOC (1140 "Things Are Changing") ... 50-100 65
(Equal Employment Opportunity Center promotional issue.)
U.A. ... 5-10 65-66
EPs: 7-inch
AMERICA'S (101 "America's Most Exciting Pop Concert Attraction") ... 20-30 60s
(Promotional issue only.)
LPs: 10/12-inch
PAIR ... 8-10 88
RHINO ... 5-8 86
SUNSET ... 10-12 69-70
UNART ... 8-12 67
U.A. (300 series) ... 5-8 75
U.A. (1000 series) ... 5-8 80
U.A. (3222 "She Cried") ... 20-25 62
(Monaural.)
U.A. (3300 "At the Cafe Wha") ... 20-25 63
(Monaural.)
U.A. (3407 "Come a Little Bit Closer") ... 15-25 64
(Monaural.)
U.A. (3417 thru 3562) ... 15-20 64-67
(Monaural.)
U.A. (6222 "She Cried") ... 20-30 62
(Stereo.)
U.A. (6300 "At the Cafe Wha") ... 20-30 63
(Stereo.)
U.A. (6407 "Come a Little Bit Closer") ... 20-25 64
(Stereo.)
U.A. (6417 thru 6762, except 6671) ... 10-20 64-70
U.A. (6671 "Sands of Time") ... 20-30 69
U.A. (90814 "Greatest Hits") ... 15-20 60s
(Record club issue.)
Members: Jay Traynor; Kenny Vance; Howard Kane; Jay Black; Marty Sanders; Sandy Yaguda.
Also see BLACK, Jay
Also see FAGEN, Donald
Also see JAY
Also see KINGS KOUNTY KARNIVAL
Also see MOONSHINE
Also see TRAYNOR, Jay
Also see VANCE, Kenny

JAY & DEE
Singles: 7-inch
ARLISS ... 5-10 61

JAY & DELTAS
Singles: 7-inch
W.B. (5404 "Bells Are Ringing") ... 20-30 64
Members: Jim Waller; Roy Carlson; Ed Atkinson; Jeff Christensen; Terry Christofferson.
Also see WALLER, Jim, & Deltas

JAY & DRIVING WHEELS
Singles: 7-inch
LANOR (528 "House of the Rising Sun") ... 15-25

JAY & FREDDY
Singles: 7-inch
CHALLENGE ... 4-8 64

JAY & SHUFFLERS
Singles: 7-inch
CRACKERJACK ... 5-10 63

JAY & TECHNIQUES P&R/R&B/LP '67
Singles: 7-inch
EVENT ... 4-6 75-76
GORDY ... 4-6 72
SILVER BLUE ... 4-8 74
SMASH ... 5-8 67-69
Picture Sleeves
SMASH ... 5-10 67-68
LPs: 10/12-inch
EVENT ... 8-12 75
SMASH ... 15-20 67-68
Members: Jay Proctor; John Walsh; Ron Goosly; Chuck Crowl; Dante Dancho; Karl Landis.
Also see SINCERES

JAY BEE & KATS
Singles: 7-inch
BANGAR (606 "Tension") ... 25-35 64
Members: Robert Shaw; Lloyd Nerland; Steven Pugsley; Joe Unzicker.

JAY BEES
Singles: 7-inch
COZY (580 "Good Times") ... 8-12

JAY CEE & INCREDIBLES
Singles: 7-inch
CLASS ... 4-8 66

JAY CEEs
Singles: 7-inch
ENJOY ... 5-10 62

JAY FIVE
Singles: 7-inch
RCA ... 5-10 68

JAY HAWKERS: see JAYHAWKERS

JAY JAY & SELECTONES
Singles: 7-inch
GUEST ... 5-10 62

JAY-MARS
Singles: 7-inch
BANGAR ... 4-8 60s
Also see UNBELIEVABLE UGLIES

JAY WALKER: see WALKER, Jay

JAY WALKERS
Singles: 7-inch
CAMEO ... 5-10 64
LAURIE (3363 "Love at First Sight") ... 10-20 67
SELSOM ... 4-8
SWAN ... 5-10 66
WISTERIA (101 "Olive Oil") ... 5-10 60s

JAYA P&R '89
Singles: 7-inch
LMR ... 3-4 89
Also see STEVIE B

JAYBEES
Singles: 7-inch
RCA ... 10-15 66

JAYE, Jerry
Singles: 7-inch
CARLTON ... 15-25 64
STEPHANY (1320 "Sugar Dumplin'") ... 20-30 58

JAYE, Jerry
Singles: 7-inch
LABEL ... 10-15 59

JAYE, Jerry P&R/LP '67
Singles: 7-inch
COLUMBIA ... 3-5 75
CONNIE (101) ... 10-15 67
(Title not known.)
HI (2100 series) ... 4-8 67-68
HI (2300 series) ... 3-5 76-77
MEGA ... 3-5 71-74
RAINTREE ... 3-5 72
LPs: 10/12-inch
HI (32000 series) ... 15-20 67
HI (32100 series) ... 5-8 76

JAYE, Miles R&B/LP '87
Singles: 7-inch
ISLAND ... 3-4 87-89
LPs: 10/12-inch
BEJAY (1370) ... 20-25 70
BEJAY (300 series) ... 8-10 84
ISLAND ... 5-8 87-89
MCA ... 5-8 87

JAYE SISTERS
Singles: 7-inch
ATLANTIC (1171 "Going to the River") ... 5-10 58
DECCA (30236 "Have You Ever Been Lonely") ... 5-10 57
U.A. (187 "G-3") ... 5-10 59

JAYES
Singles: 7-inch
ARC (4443 "Panic Stricken") ... 15-20 58

JAYHAWKERS
Singles: 7-inch
DELTRON (1227 "Dawn of Instruction") ... 10-15 60s
DELTRON (1228 "To Have a Love") ... 10-15 60s
LUCKY ELEVEN (232 "Come On") ... 8-12 60s
LYKE TIL (7147 "Love Have Mercy") ... 10-15 60s

JAYHAWKS P&R/R&B '56
Singles: 78 rpm
ALADDIN (3393 "Everyone Should Know") ... 50-75 57
FLASH (Except 105) ... 10-20 56
FLASH (105 "Counting My Teardrops") ... 50-75 56
Singles: 7-inch
ALADDIN (3393 "Everyone Should Know") ... 50-100 57
EASTMAN (792 "I Wish the World Owed Me a Living") ... 100-200 59
EASTMAN (798 "New Love") ... 100-200 59
FLASH (105 "Counting My Teardrops") ... 200-300 56
FLASH (109 "Stranded in the Jungle") ... 25-50 56
FLASH (111 "Love Train") ... 25-50 56
OLDIES 45 ... 4-8 60s
Members: James Johnson; Carl Fisher; Dave Govan; Carver Bunkem; Richard Owens.
Also see CURRY, James "King"
Also see MARATHONS
Also see PALMER, Earl
Also see VIBRATIONS

JAYHAWKS
Singles: 7-inch
ARGYLE ... 10-20 61
ASSOCIATED ARTISTS (1064 "Creepin'") ... 10-20 62

JAYHAWKS
LPs: 10/12-inch
W.B. ... 8-10 90s

JAYNE, Betty, & Teenettes
Singles: 7-inch
CARELLEN ... 5-10 61
MONA LEE ... 10-20 59

JAYNES, Harry, & Jaynemen
Singles: 7-inch
JOSIE ... 5-10 65

JAYNELLS
Singles: 7-inch
CAMEO ... 10-15 63
DIAMOND (153 "I'll Stay Home") ... 20-30 63
Also see CREATORS / Jaynells

JAYNETTS P&R/R&B '63
(Jaynetts / Art Butler)
Singles: 7-inch
GOLDIE ... 3-5
J&S ... 5-10 65
TUFF (369 "Sally Go 'Round the Roses") ... 5-10 63
TUFF (370 "Keep an Eye on Her") ... 5-10 63
TUFF (370 "Dear Abby") ... 5-10 63
TUFF (374 "Snowman Snowman, Sweet Potato Nose") ... 5-10 63
TUFF (377 "Johnny Don't Cry") ... 5-10 64
LPs: 10/12-inch
TUFF (13 "Sally, Go 'Round the Roses") ... 150-250 63
(Includes *Dear Abby* by the Hearts.)
Members: Ethel Davis; Johnnie Louise; Mary Sue Wells; Ada Ray; Yvonne Bushnell.
Also see BUTLER, Art
Also see HEARTS
Also see JOHNNIE & JOE

JAYS, Janet
Singles: 7-inch
HI ... 4-8 66-67

JAYTONES
Singles: 78 rpm
TIMELY (1003 "The Bells") ... 200-400 53
Singles: 7-inch
BRUNSWICK (55087 "The Clock") ... 100-150 58
CUB (9057 "My Only Love") ... 50-75 59
TIMELY (1003 "The Bells") ... 1000-2000 53
Also see CENTURIES / Jaytones

JAY-TONES
Singles: 7-inch
PARIS SKY (5000 "Cleopatra Cha-Cha") ... 20-30

JAYWALKER & PEDESTRIANS
Singles: 7-inch
AMY (848 "Never Happen") ... 10-15 62
Member: Peter Antell.
Also see ANTELL, Peter

JAZZ AT PHILHARMONIC R&B '49
Singles: 78 rpm
MERCURY ... 4-6 49
Also see JACQUET, Illonis

JAZZ CRUSADERS P&R '66
Singles: 7-inch
CHISA ... 3-5 70-71
PACIFIC JAZZ ... 4-8 62-68
WORLD PACIFIC ... 4-8 64-65
LPs: 10/12-inch
BLUE NOTE ... 5-10 75-80
CHISA ... 8-12 70
LIBERTY ... 8-12 70
PACIFIC JAZZ (27 thru 87) ... 20-35 61-64
PACIFIC JAZZ (10000 & 20000 series) ... 10-20 65-69
PAUSA ... 5-8 82
WORLD PACIFIC ... 8-15 65
Members: Wilton Felder; Stix Hooper; Wayne Henderson; Joe Sample.
Also see CRUSADERS
Also see FELDER, Wilton

JAZZBOMBERS
("Featuring Bobby Boyd")
Singles: 7-inch
TATTLER (1001 "Bad Boy") ... 100-200

JAZZY
Singles: 12-inch
FADER ... 4-6 92

JAZZY JAY R&B '84
Singles: 7-inch
ATLANTIC ... 3-4 84

JAZZY JEFF & FRESH PRINCE
LPs: 10/12-inch
JIVE (1489 "Code Red") ... 5-10

JEAN, Barbara: see BARBARA JEAN

JEAN, Bobbie: see BOBBIE JEAN

JEAN, Cathy: see CATHY JEAN

JEAN, Dottie: see DOTTIE JEAN

JEAN, Earl: see EARL-JEAN

JEAN, Norma: see NORMA JEAN

JEAN, Vickie: see VICKIE JEAN

JEAN & DARLINGS P&R '67
(Jeannie & Darlings; (Jeanne & Darlings)
Singles: 7-inch
VOLT ... 4-8 67-69

JEANETTE
Singles: 7-inch
LAURIE ... 4-8 61

JEANETTE, JOAN & KAY
Singles: 7-inch
TEEN-ED ... 5-10 61

JEANIE & BOY FRIENDS
Singles: 7-inch
WARWICK (508 "Baby") ... 50-75 59

JEANNE & JANIE
Singles: 7-inch
CAPITOL ... 5-10 62

JEANNIE & DARLINGS: see JEAN & DARLINGS

JEANNIE & MILLER SISTERS
Singles: 7-inch
HULL ... 5-10 62
Also see MILLER SISTERS

JEANS
Singles: 7-inch
ZEFCO (4127 "My Own Time") ... 15-25 68

JEBADIAH
LPs: 10/12-inch
EPIC ... 5-8 78

JECKYLL, Dr: see DR. JECKYLL

JEENS, Jimmy
Singles: 78 rpm
VULCAN ... 8-12 54
Singles: 7-inch
VULCAN (1001 "Ring Bells, Ring") ... 40-50 54

JEFF & ALETA R&B '80
Singles: 7-inch
SRI ... 3-5 80

JEFF & ATLANTICS
Singles: 7-inch
SOUND PATTERNS (2501 "Twistin' Postman") ... 20-30 60s

JEFF & CHARLES
Singles: 7-inch
JUNE ("Janet Ann") ... 20-40
(No selection number used.)
JUNE (100 "Sadie Hawkins Day in Tennessee") ... 20-40

JEFF & GINOS
Singles: 7-inch
MERCURY ... 5-10 63

JEFF & P.J.
Singles: 7-inch
ROYCE (0002 "Mr. Blues") ... 15-25 59

JEFF & SHANNONS
Singles: 7-inch
ARLEN ... 4-8 63

JEFFERIES, Prince
Singles: 7-inch
OLD TOWN ... 4-8 64

JEFFERS, Jimmy
Singles: 7-inch
FRATERNITY (857 "Teardrops from My Eyes") ... 5-10 59
TARGET (850 "Purple Crackle") ... 5-10

JEFFERSON P&R '69
(Geoff Turton)
Singles: 7-inch
DECCA ... 4-6 69
JANUS ... 4-6 69
LPs: 10/12-inch
JANUS ... 10-15 69
Also see ROCKIN' BERRIES

JEFFERSON, Blind Lemon
Singles: 78 rpm
OKEH (8455 "Black Snake Moan") ... 100-200
PARAMOUNT ... 100-200 26-30
LPs: 10/12-inch
BIOGRAPH ... 10-15 68
MILESTONE ... 8-10 74
OLYMPIC ... 8-10 75
RIVERSIDE (1014 "Folk Blues of Blind Lemon Jefferson") ... 100-200 53
(10-inch LP.)
RIVERSIDE (1053 "Blind Lemon's Penitentiary Blues") ... 100-200 55
(10-inch LP.)
RIVERSIDE (125 "Folk Blues Classics") ... 50-75 58
RIVERSIDE (126 "Folk Blues Classics") ... 50-75 58
Also see BATES, Deacon L.J.
Also see JACKSON, Deacon

JEFFERSON, Eddie
(With James Moody & His Orchestra; with Walter Harper Orchestra)
Singles: 78 rpm
CHECKER (855 "Billie's Bounce") ... 8-12 57
HI-LO (1416 "Honeysuckle Rose") ... 8-12 53
Singles: 7-inch
CHECKER (855 "Billie's Bounce") 10-20 57
HI-LO (1416 "Honeysuckle Rose") 20-30 53
(Colored vinyl.)
STAX ... 5-10 64

JEFFERSON, Eugene
Singles: 7-inch
BAY TONE ... 4-8 61-65

JEFFERSON, Hilton
Singles: 7-inch
RCA (7126 "Cole Slaw") ... 15-25 57

JEFFERSON, Morris R&B '77
Singles: 7-inch
PARACHUTE ... 3-5 78
LPs: 10/12-inch
PARACHUTE ... 5-8 78

JEFFERSON, Ron
Singles: 7-inch
NEDWARD ... 10-20

JEFFERSON AIRPLANE LP '66
Singles: 7-inch
ELEKTRA ... 3-4 88
GRUNT (0500 thru 0511) ... 3-5 71-72
GRUNT (10988 "White Rabbit") ... 10-20 77
(Colored vinyl. Promotional issue only.)
RCA (0150 thru 0343) ... 4-6 69-70
RCA (5156 "White Rabbit") ... 4-8 87
(Colored vinyl. Promotional issue only.)
RCA (8769 thru 9644) ... 5-10 66-68
(Dog on side of label.)
RCA (9000 series) ... 3-4 89
(Dog near top of label.)
Picture Sleeves
GRUNT (0500 "Pretty As You Feel") ... 5-10 71
GRUNT (0506 "Long John Silver") ... 10-15 72
RCA (Except 5156) ... 8-12 68-70
RCA (5156 "White Rabbit") ... 4-8 87
(Promotional issue only.)
EPs: 7-inch
RCA (SP33-564 "Jefferson Airplane") ... 30-50 69
(Promotional issue only.)
LPs: 10/12-inch
EPIC ... 5-8 89
GRUNT (0147 "Thirty Seconds Over Winterland") ... 10-15 73
GRUNT (1001 "Bark") ... 30-60 71
GRUNT (1007 "Long John Silver") ... 30-60 72
GRUNT (0437 "Early Flight") ... 10-15 74
GRUNT (4386 "Bark") ... 10-15 82
PAIR ... 8-10 84
RCA (0320 ("Volunteers") ... 15-20 73
(Quadrophonic.)
RCA (1511 "After Bathing at Baxter's") ... 20-30 67
(Black label. With "LPM" or "LSP" prefix.)
RCA (1511 "After Bathing at Baxter's") ... 10-12 70s
(Orange or tan label.)
RCA (3584 "Jefferson Airplane Takes Off") ... 75-125 66
(Has 12 tracks. With "LPM" or "LSP" prefix.)
RCA (3584 "Jefferson Airplane Takes Off") ... 15-25 66
(Has 11 tracks. With "LPM" or "LSP" prefix.)
RCA (3584 "Jefferson Airplane Takes Off") ... 10-15 69
(Orange label.)
RCA (3661 "Worst of Jefferson Airplane") ... 5-10 80
RCA (3739 "Jefferson Airplane Takes Off") ... 5-10 80
RCA (3766 "Surrealistic Pillow") ... 20-30 67
(Black label. With "LPM" or "LSP" prefix.)
RCA (3766 "Surrealistic Pillow") ... 10-12 69
(Orange label.)
RCA (3766 "Surrealistic Pillow") ... 5-8 80s
(With "AYL" prefix.)
RCA (3797 "Crown of Creation") ... 5-10 80
RCA (3798 "Bless Its Pointed Little Head") ... 5-10 80
RCA (3867 "Volunteers") ... 5-10 81
RCA (4058 "Crown of Creation") ... 10-15 68
RCA (4133 "Bless Its Pointed Little Head") ... 10-20 69
(Includes artwork insert.)
RCA (4238 "Volunteers") ... 10-15 69
RCA (4448 "Blows Against the Empire") ... 10-15 70
(Black vinyl. Add $4 to $6 if accompanied by booklet.)
RCA (4448 "Blows Against the Empire") ... 75-100 70
(Clear vinyl. Promotional issue only.)
RCA (LSP-4459 "Worst of Jefferson Airplane") ... 10-15 70
RCA (AFL1-4459 "Worst of Jefferson Airplane") ... 5-10 80s
RCA (5724 "2400 Fulton Street") ... 8-12 87
Members: Signe Anderson; Marty Balin; Paul Kantner; Jack Casady; Jorma Kaukonen; Skip Spence; Grace Slick; Craig Chaquico; Joey Covington; Papa John Creach; Spencer Dryden; Dave Freiberg.
Also see BALIN, Marty
Also see CREACH, Papa John
Also see CROSBY, David
Also see GARCIA, Jerry
Also see GREAT!! SOCIETY!!
Also see HAMMOND, John Paul
Also see HOPKINS, Nicky
Also see JARRARD, Rick
Also see JEFFERSON STARSHIP
Also see KBC BAND
Also see KANTNER, Paul, & Grace Slick
Also see KAUKONEN, Jorma
Also see QUICKSILVER
Also see SLICK, Grace
Also see STILLS, Stephen
Also see VIBRA-SONICS

JEFFERSON COUNTY
Singles: 7-inch
DEE GEE ... 15-20 66

JEFFERSON HANDKERCHIEF
Singles: 7-inch
CHALLENGE ... 10-20 67

JEFFERSON LEE
Singles: 7-inch
ORIGINAL SOUND ... 10-15 67

JEFFERSON STARSHIP LP '74
Singles: 7-inch
GRUNT ... 3-5 74-84
Picture Sleeves
GRUNT ... 3-5 78-87
RCA ... 3-4 87-89
LPs: 10/12-inch
GRUNT (0717 thru 1557) ... 10-15 74-76
GRUNT (1255 "Flight Log, 1966-1976") ... 15-20 77
(With simulated leather cover. Also has Jefferson Airplane, Hot Tuna, Grace Slick and Paul Kanter tracks.)
GRUNT (1255 "Flight Log, 1966-1976") ... 10-20 81
(With standard cover.)
GRUNT (2515 thru 3247) ... 10-15 78-79
GRUNT (3363 "Gold") ... 15-20 79
(Picture disc.)
GRUNT (3452 thru 6413) ... 6-12 79-87
RCA ... 5-8 81-89
Members: Grace Slick; Marty Balin; Paul Kantner; Aynsley Dunbar; Pete Sears; Mickey Thomas; John Barbata.
Note: Cross references that already appear under Jefferson Airplane are not duplicated below.
Also see DUNBAR, Aynsley
Also see HART, Mickey
Also see HOT TUNA
Also see JEFFERSON AIRPLANE
Also see KANTNER, Paul, & Jefferson Starship
Also see STARSHIP
Also see STONEGROUND

JEFFREE R&B '78
Singles: 7-inch
MCA ... 3-5 78-79
LPs: 10/12-inch
MCA ... 5-8 79

JEFFREY, Joe P&R '69
(Joe Jeffrey Group)
Singles: 7-inch
WAND ... 4-6 69
LPs: 10/12-inch
WAND ... 10-15 69

JEFFREY, Wally
Singles: 7-inch
DO-RA-ME (1402 "Oh Yeah") ... 200-300 57

JEFFREYS, Garland LP '77
Singles: 7-inch
A&M ... 3-5 77-79
ARISTA ... 3-5 75
ATLANTIC ... 3-5 73
EPIC ... 3-4 81-83
EPs: 7-inch
EPIC (1223 "Escape Artist") ... 4-8 81
(Promotional issue only.)
LPs: 10/12-inch
A&M ... 5-8 77-79
ATLANTIC ... 8-10 73
EPIC ... 5-8 81-83

JEFFREYS, Garland, & Phoebe Snow
Singles: 7-inch
A&M ... 3-5 78
Picture Sleeves
A&M ... 3-5 78
Also see JEFFREYS, Garland
Also see SNOW, Phoebe

JEFFRIES, Bob
(With "Marcels 123")
Singles: 7-inch
JODY (1048 "Take Me Back") ... 500-1000 58
(Were not quite certain if the "123" has to do with the Marcels, or if it means something else. It does appear, however, that 1048 is the selection number.)
RHYTHM (110 "Never Let Me Go") ... 150-250 57

JEFFRIES, Herb
Singles: 7-inch
MERCURY ... 4-8
LPs: 10/12-inch
BCP (72 "Herb Jeffries") ... 50-75 57
CORAL (56044 "Time on My Hands") ... 25-40 51
(10-inch LP.)

JEKYLL & HYDE
Singles: 7-inch
DCP (1126 "Frankenstein Meets the Beatles") ... 15-20 64
Member: Dickie Goodman.
Also see GOODMAN, Dickie

JEKYLL & HYDES
Singles: 7-inch
G.A.R. (107 "High Heeled Sneakers") ... 10-20 67
Members: John "Jekyll" Lohman; Gary Grimes; Chris Riley.
Also see NORSEMEN

JELLY
Singles: 7-inch
ASYLUM ... 3-5 77
SCEPTER (12386 "Sharpshooter") ... 4-6 73

JELLY & SLIM SEWARD
Singles: 78 rpm
APOLLO (412 "Sorry Women Blues") ... 20-40 47
Members: Louis Hayes; Alec Seward.
Also see SEWARD, Alec, & Fat Boy Hayes

JELLY BEAN BANDITS
Singles: 7-inch
MAINSTREAM (674 "Country Woman") ... 10-15 67
LPs: 10/12-inch
MAINSTREAM (6103 "Jelly Bean Bandits") ... 50-75 67
Members: Bill Donald; John Dougherty; Fred Buck; Mike Raab; Joe Scalfari.

JELLY BEANS P&R/R&B '64
Singles: 7-inch
ESKEE (001 "I'm Hip to You") ... 15-25 65
RED BIRD (003 "I Wanna Love Him So Bad") ... 8-12 64
RED BIRD (011 "Baby, Be Mine") ... 8-12 64
Members: Diane Taylor; Maxine Herbert; Elyse Herbert; Alma Brewer.

JELLY ROLL
Singles: 7-inch
KAPP ... 3-5 71
LPs: 10/12-inch
KAPP ... 10-12 71

JELLY ROLL KINGS
LPs: 10/12-inch
EARWIG ... 5-8 80

JELLYBEAN D&D '84
("Jellybean" Benitez; Featuring Steven Dante)
Singles: 12-inch
EMI AMERICA ... 4-6 84-86
Singles: 7-inch
CHRYSALIS ... 3-4 87
EMI AMERICA ... 3-4 84-86
Picture Sleeves
CHRYSALIS ... 3-4 87
EMI AMERICA ... 3-4 85
LPs: 10/12-inch
CHRYSALIS ... 5-8 87
EMI AMERICA ... 5-8 84-86

JELLYBEAN & ELISA FIORILLO P&R '87
Singles: 7-inch
CHRYSALIS ... 3-4 87
Picture Sleeves
CHRYSALIS ... 3-4 87
Also see FIORILLO, Elisa
Also see JELLYBEAN

JELLYBREAD
LPs: 10/12-inch
BLUE HORIZON ... 10-15 70

JELLYFISH LP '90
LPs: 10/12-inch
CHARISMA ... 5-8 90

JENKINS, Beverly
LPs: 10/12-inch
ABC-PAR ... 10-15
IMPULSE ... 10-20 64

JENKINS, Bill, Quartet
(Bill Jenkins & Al)
Singles: 78 rpm
KING ... 10-15 54
Singles: 7-inch
KING (4760 "Danny Boy") ... 15-25 54
KING (4877 "Day Train") ... 15-25 55
PRESTIGE (175 "Billin' & Bluin' ") ... 10-20 60
Also see JENKINS, Bill, & Willis Jackson

JENKINS, Bill, & Willis Jackson
Singles: 7-inch
KING (5087 "Wishbone") ... 15-25 57
Also see JENKINS, Bill, Quartet
Also see JACKSON, Willis

JENKINS, Bob C&W '82
Singles: 7-inch
LIBERTY ... 3-4 82
PICAP ... 3-4 83
LP: 10/12-inch
20TH FOX ... 6-10 74

JENKINS, Bobby
(With the Jades)
Singles: 7-inch
ASTRO ... 5-10
BECKINGHAM (1080 "Hey Man") ... 8-12 65
HAMILTON ... 10-20 58
NASCO (6006 "My Baby's Gone") ... 10-20 58

JENKINS, Bobby C&W '84
Singles: 7-inch
CONFEDERATE ... 4-6
ZONE 7 ... 3-4 83-85

JENKINS, Bobo
(Bobo Jenkins & Band)
Singles: 78 rpm
CHESS ... 25-50 54
FORTUNE ... 30-60 56
Singles: 7-inch
BIG=STAR (001 "Tell Me Where You Stayed Last Night") ... 10-20
BOXER (202 "Nothing But Love") ... 20-30 59
CHESS (1565 "Democrat Blues") ... 125-150 54
FORTUNE (838 "Baby, Don't You Want to Go") ... 100-125 56
(Orange label.)
FORTUNE (838 "Baby, Don't You Want to Go") ... 15-25
(Red label)

JENKINS, Ceaser L.
Singles: 7-inch
NANCY ... 4-8 61
PO-AB ... 4-8 61

JENKINS, Diane
Singles: 7-inch
CREATIVE FUNK (12002 "Anniversary") ... 4-8 73

JENKINS, Donald: see DONALD & DELIGHTERS

JENKINS, Duke
(With the Roulettes)
Singles: 7-inch
BEE (1175 "Oh Boy") ... 5-10 60s
COBRA (5009 "The Duke Walks") ... 15-25 57
PENNANT (331 "Mambo Blues") ... 10-15 50s
Also see GIBSON, Steve

JENKINS, Ella
LPs:10/12-inch
FOLKWAYS ... 10-15

JENKINS, Gene
Singles: 7-inch
TRINITY ("Short Stuff") ... 15-25 50s
(No selection number used.)

JENKINS, George, & Tune Twisters
Singles: 78 rpm
SKYLARK ... 5-10 54
Singles: 7-inch
SKYLARK (565 "Shufflin' Boogie") ... 10-20 54
TAMPA (113 "Drum Boogie") ... 10-20 56
Also see JOHNSON, Plas

JENKINS, Gordon, & Orchestra P&R '42
Singles: 78 rpm
DECCA ... 3-6 50-56
Singles: 7-inch
COLUMBIA ... 4-6 64
DECCA ... 5-10 50-56
KAPP ... 4-8 60-64
TIME ... 4-6 62
"X" ... 4-8 55
EPs: 7-inch
DECCA ... 5-15 51-56
LPs: 10/12-inch
CAPITOL (700 series) ... 15-25 56
(With "T" prefix.)
CAPITOL (700 series) ... 10-15 61
(With "DT" prefix.)
CAPITOL (700 series) ... 4-8 75
(With "SM" prefix.)
COLUMBIA ... 10-20 62-63
CORAL ... 5-8 73
CUSTOM ... 5-10
DECCA ... 15-30 51-63
(Decca LP numbers in this series preceded by a "7" or a "DL-7" are stereo issues.)
DOT ... 5-10 66
GWP ... 5-10 71
MCA ... 5-8 73-75
SUNSET ... 5-10 67
TIME ... 10-15 62-64
Also see ARMSTRONG, Louis
Also see BOONE, Pat
Also see CARROLL, Bob
Also see CASHMAN & WEST / Gordon Jenkins & His Orchestra
Also see LEE, Peggy
Also see WEAVERS

JENKINS, Gus P&R/R&B '56
(Gus Jinkins)
Singles: 78 rpm
COMBO ... 10-20 54
FLASH ... 10-20 56-57
Singles: 7-inch
CATALINA (711 "New Tricky") ... 10-15 63
COMBO (87 "I Been Working") ... 40-60 54
FLASH (115 "Tricky") ... 20-30 56
FLASH (116 "I Remember Last Xmas") ... 20-30 57
FLASH (123 "Pay Day Shuffle") ... 20-30 57
FLASH (126 "Stand By Me") ... 20-30 57
FLASH (128 "Hit the Road") ... 20-30 58
FLASH (130 "I'm Hurted") ... 20-30 58
FLASH (131 "Slow Down") ... 20-30 58
GENERAL ARTIST ... 8-15 64-69
PIONEER INT'L (101 "Spanky") ... 15-25 59
PIONEER INT'L (1003 "Cuttin' Out") ... 10-20 61
PIONEER INT'L (1006 "You Made Me") ... 10-20 61
PIONEER INT'L (1007 "Let's Talk It Over") ... 10-20 61
PIONEER INT'L (1009 "Off the Road") ... 10-20 61
PIONEER INT'L (10011 "Too Tough") ... 10-20 62
PIONEER INT'L (10013 "Celebrate") ... 10-20 62
SAR (149 "Right Shakey") ... 10-15 64
TOWER (107 "Chittlins") ... 10-15 64
TOWER (122 "Frosty") ... 10-15 64
Also see LITTLE TEMPLE & HIS 88
Also see YOUNG WOLF

JENKINS, Jimmy / Eddie Pollina
Singles: 7-inch
SEATBELTS FASTENED? EP-60 OHIO (102675 "Farewell to the King") ... 4-8 77

JENKINS, Johnny
(With the Pinetoppers)
Singles: 7-inch
ATLANTIC (2144 "Love Twist") ... 8-12 62
CAPRICORN ... 3-6 70
GERALD (1001 "Love Twist") ... 20-30 62
(First issue.)
TIFKO (825 "Love Twist") ... 10-20 62
VOLT ... 4-8 64
LPs: 10/12-inch
CAPRICORN ... 10-15 70
Members: Johnny Jenkins; Otis Redding.
Also see ALLMAN, Duane
Also see REDDING, Otis

JENKINS, Kechia R&B '88
Singles: 7-inch
PROFILE ... 3-4 88

JENKINS, Larry C&W '82
Singles: 7-inch
CAPITOL ... 3-4 82
MCA ... 3-4 84

JENKINS, Marvin
Singles: 7-inch
PALOMAR ... 10-15 65
TANGERINE ... 5-10
LPs: 10/12-inch
PALOMAR ... 10-15 65

JENKINS, Mecie
Singles: 7-inch
CORNUTO ... 4-8 61

JENKINS, Norma R&B '76
Singles: 7-inch
CARNIVAL (528 "Need Someone to Love") ... 15-25 67
DESERT MOON ... 3-5 76
JEAN ... 5-8
Also see DOLLS
Also see KEYES, Troy, & Norma Jenkins

JENKINS, Robert
Singles: 78 rpm
PARKWAY (103 "Steelin' Boogie") ... 100-200 50

JENKINS, Vanda
Singles: 7-inch
CRESCENT (633 "On a Journey") ... 8-12 63

JENKINS, Walter
Singles: 7-inch
FADER KAT (302 "Back in My Life") ... 15-25 75

JENNIE & JAY
Singles: 7-inch
RESCUE (102 "Jo Baby") ... 20-40
(Reissue of David Gates & Accents' 1958 Perspective release.)
Member: David Gates.
Also see GATES, David

JENNIFER
(Jennifer Warnes)
Singles: 7-inch
PARROT ... 4-6 67-70
LPs: 10/12-inch
PARROT ... 10-20 68-70
Also see WARNES, Jennifer

JENNIFER
Singles: 7-inch
REPRISE ... 3-5 72

JENNIFER / Syretta
Singles: 12-inch
MOTOWN ... 4-8 77
Also see SYRETTA

JENNIFER WITH QUEEN BEE
Singles: 7-inch
LUNAR (002 "Crazy Man") ... 5-10

JENNIFER'S FRIENDS
Singles: 7-inch
BUDDAH ... 4-6 68

JENNINGS, Baby Boy, & Satelites
Singles: 7-inch
SAVOY ... 8-12 60

JENNINGS, Bob C&W '64
Singles: 7-inch
SIMS ... 4-8 64

JENNINGS, Lee
Singles: 7-inch
DOTTY'S (347 "Going & Get It") ... 25-35 60s

JENNINGS, Lenny
Singles: 7-inch
ROULETTE (4704 "Last Laugh") ... 10-20 66

JENNINGS, Tommy C&W '75
Singles: 7-inch
MONUMENT ... 3-5 78
PARAGON ... 3-5 75
LPs: 10/12-inch
AUDIOGRAPH ... 5-8 82
Session: Waylon Jennings.
Also see GOSDIN, Rex, & Tommy Jennings
Also see JENNINGS, Waylon

JENNINGS, Waylon C&W '65
(With the Waylors; with Kimberlys; with Crickets; Waylon)
Singles: 7-inch
A&M (739 "Four Strong Winds") ... 10-15 64
A&M (722 "Rave On") ... 10-20 63
A&M (753 "The Race Is On") ... 10-20 64
A&M (762 "The Real House of the Rising Sun") ... 10-20 65
BAT (121639 "Dream Baby") ... 25-35 62
BRUNSWICK (55130 "Jole Blon") ... 100-150 59
(Maroon label. With Buddy Holly & King Curtis.)
BRUNSWICK (55130 "Jole Blon") ... 75-100 59
(Yellow label. Promotional issue only.)
COLUMBIA ... 3-4 83
EPIC ... 3-4 91
RCA (Except 8572 thru 9642) ... 3-6 69-82
RCA (8572 thru 9642) ... 5-10 65-68
RAMCO ... 8-12 67
TREND '61 (102 "Another Blue Day") ... 20-30 61
TREND '63 (106 "The Stage") ... 50-75 63
Picture Sleeves
RCA ... 3-5 79-80
LPs: 10/12-inch
A&M (4238 "Don't Think Twice") ... 25-30 69

BAT (1001 "Waylon Jennings at JD's") 200-300 64
(500 copies were made on Bat, then another 500 were done on Sounds Ltd.)
CAMDEN 8-15 67-76
EPIC 5-8 90
MCA 5-8
PICKWICK 5-10 75
RCA (AFL-1 series) 5-10 78
RCA (0240 thru 3378) 5-10 73-79
RCA (3406 "Greatest Hits") 30-40 79
(Picture disc.)
RCA (3493 "What Goes Around Comes Around") 5-10 79
RCA (3523 "Folk Country") 15-25 66
RCA (3602 "Music Man") 5-10 80
RCA (3620 "Leavin' Town") 20-30 66
RCA (3660 "Waylon Sings Ol' Harlan") 15-20 67
RCA (3663 "Are You Ready for the Country") 5-8 80
RCA (3736 "Nashville Rebel") 15-25 66
(Soundtrack.)
RCA (3737 "Good Hearted Woman") 5-8 80
RCA (3825 "Love of the Common People") 15-25 67
RCA (3897 "Honky Tonk Heroes") 5-8 81
RCA (3918 "Hangin' On") 15-20 68
RCA (3942 "This Time") 5-8 81
RCA (4023 "Only the Greatest") 15-20 68
RCA (4072 "Dreaming My Dreams") . 5-8 81
RCA (4073 "The Ramblin' Man") 5-8 81
RCA (4085 "Jewels") 15-20 68
RCA (4137 "Just to Satisfy You") 15-20 69
RCA (4163 "Waylon Live") 5-8 81
RCA (4164 "I've Always Been Crazy") 5-8 81
RCA (4180 "Country Folk") 15-25 69
RCA (4247 "Black on Black") 5-8 82
RCA (4250 "Music Man") 5-8 82
RCA (4260 "Waylon") 10-15 70
RCA (4341 "Best of Waylon Jennings") 8-10 77
RCA (4418 "Singer of Sad Songs") 10-15 70
RCA (4487 "The Taker/Tulsa") 10-15 71
RCA (4567 "Cedartown Georgia") 10-15 71
RCA (4647 "Good Hearted Woman") 10-15 72
RCA (4673 "It's Only Rock & Roll") ... 5-8 83
RCA (4751 "Ladies Love Outlaws") 10-15 72
RCA (4826 "Waylon & Co.") 5-8 83
RCA (4828 "Best of Waylon Jennings") 5-8 83
RCA (4854 "Lonesome, On'ry and Mean") 10-15 73
RCA (5473 "Collector's Series") 5-10 85
SEAGULL 5-8 83
SOUNDS (1001 "Waylon Jennings at JD's") 200-250 64
(First issued on Bat.)
TIME-LIFE 5-8 81
VOCALION 15-20 69
Session: Buddy Holly; King Curtis; James Burton.
Also see ANDERSON, John
Also see BARE, Bobby
Also see BOWMAN, Don
Also see BURTON, James
Also see CASH, Johnny, & Waylon Jennings
Also see CLARK, Guy
Also see COE, David Allan
Also see CRICKETS
Also see CUNHA, Rick
Also see DAVIS, Skeeter
Also see EDDY, Duane
Also see HARRIS, Emmylou
Also see HOLLY, Buddy
Also see JENNINGS, Tommy
Also see JONES, David Lynn
Also see KIMBERLYS
Also see KING CURTIS
Also see MANDRELL, Barbara
Also see MONROE, Bill
Also see NELSON, Willie
Also see RABBITT, Jimmy, & Renegade
Also see RODRIGUEZ, Johnny
Also see SCHNEIDER, John
Also see SCRUGGS, Earl
Also see SOME of CHET'S FRIENDS
Also see TUBB, Ernest
Also see U.S.A. for AFRICA
Also see WHITE, Tony Joe
Also see YOUNG, Neil

JENNINGS, Waylon, & Anita Carter
C&W '68

Singles: 7-inch

RCA 4-8 68
Also see CARTER, Anita

JENNINGS, Waylon, & Jessi Colter
LP '81

(Waylon & Jessi)

Singles: 7-inch

RCA 3-5 69-71

LPs: 10/12-inch

RCA (3931 "Leather and Lace") 5-10 81
Also see COLTER, Jesse

JENNINGS, Waylon, & Willie Nelson
P&R '77

(Waylon & Willie)

Singles: 7-inch

COLUMBIA 3-4 83
MCA 3-4 86
RCA 3-5 76-86

LPs: 10/12-inch

AURA 5-8 83
COLUMBIA 5-8 83
OUT of TOWN DIST. 5-8 80s
RCA (2686 "Waylon & Willie") 5-10 78
RCA (2686 "Waylon & Willie") 20-25 78
(Colored vinyl. Promotional issue only.)
RCA (4455 "Waylon & Willie II") 5-8 82

JENNINGS, Waylon, Willie Nelson, Jessi Colter, & Tompall Glaser
LP '76

LPs: 10/12-inch

RCA (1321 "The Outlaws") 5-10 76

JENNINGS, Waylon, Willie Nelson, Johnny Cash, & Kris Kristofferson
LP '85

Singles: 7-inch

COLUMBIA 3-4 85-90

LPs: 10/12-inch

COLUMBIA 5-8 85-90
Also see CASH, Johnny
Also see KRISTOFFERSON, Kris
Also see NELSON, Willie

JENNINGS, Waylon / Johnny Paycheck

LPs: 10/12-inch

OUT of TOWN DIST. 5-8 82
Also see PAYCHECK, Johnny

JENNINGS, Waylon, & Jerry Reed

Singles: 7-inch

RCA 3-4 83
Also see REED, Jerry

JENNINGS, Waylon / White Water

Singles: 7-inch

RCA 3-4 81

JENNINGS, Waylon, & Hank Williams Jr.

Singles: 7-inch

RCA 3-4 83
Also see JENNINGS, Waylon
Also see WILLIAMS, Hank, Jr.

JENNINGS BROTHERS

Singles: 7-inch

ATLANTIC (2245 "Believe in Me") .10-20 64

JENNY & HYPHENS

Singles: 7-inch

DOME 15-20 58

JENNY LEE & STARLETS

Singles: 7-inch

CONGRESS 5-10 62
Also see STARLETS

JENNY LYNN: see LYNN, Jenny

JENSEN, Curt

Singles: 7-inch

BIG B 4-8 62
DE WITT 5-10 60
PET (806 "Just for You") 15-25 58
20TH FOX (183 "Meet Me in St. Louis") 10-20 60s

JENSEN, Dick

(With the Imports; with Swamp Men)

Singles: 7-inch

AMBER (7001 "Swamped") 15-25 63
LOMA 4-8 65-66
MAHALO (1012 "Surfin' in Hawaii") 15-25 63
PHILADELPHIA INT'L 3-6 72
PROBE 3-6 69

Picture Sleeves

PROBE 4-8 69

LPs: 10/12-inch

PROBE 10-12 69

JENSEN, Kris
P&R '62

Singles: 7-inch

A&M 3-5 70
COLPIX 5-10 59
HICKORY 5-10 62-65
KAPP 5-10 61
LEADER 10-15 60-61

Picture Sleeves

HICKORY 10-15 62-64

LPs: 10/12-inch

HICKORY (110 "Torture") 40-50 62

JENSEN, Kurt, & His Orchestra

LPs: 10/12-inch

HOLLYWOOD (137 "An Evening with Jayne") 30-50 50s
(Cover pictures Jayne Mansfield, although she is not heard on the disc.)
Also see MANSFIELD, Jayne

JENSON, Jimmy

Singles: 7-inch

PLEASANT (5020 "Ace in the Hole") 5-8

JENSON, Ken

Singles: 7-inch

AVA (158 "Box Cars") 15-25 57

JEREMIAH

Singles: 7-inch

PHILIPS 10-20 65

JEREMIAH

Singles: 7-inch

UNI 3-5 71

LPs: 10/12-inch

UNI 8-10 71

JEREMIAH
C&W '88

Singles: 7-inch

CHARIOT 3-4 88

JEREMY & SATYRS

Singles: 7-inch

REPRISE 5-10 68

LPs: 10/12-inch

REPRISE 10-20 68

JEREMY'S FRIENDS

LPs: 10/12-inch

WARWICK (2019 "Jeremy's Friends") 25-35
Member: Alan Arkin.

JERICHO

Singles: 7-inch

BEARSVILLE 3-5 72

LPs: 10/12-inch

BEARSVILLE 8-10 71

JERICHO, Jerry

(Smilin' Jerry Jericho)

Singles: 78 rpm

4 STAR 5-10 50
STARDAY 10-15 53

Singles: 7-inch

STARDAY (120 "Moanin' in the Morning") 20-30 53
STARDAY (133 "Lovin' Up a Storm") 20-30 53

JERICHO HARP

Singles: 7-inch

U.A. 3-5 77-78

JERMS

Singles: 7-inch

DEL MAR (521 "Since You Went Away") 50-100 60s
JERMS INC. (2079 "Bald Headed Woman") 25-50 60s
SHANA (7195 "Not At All") 10-20 60s

JERMS

Singles: 7-inch

HONOR BRIGADE 4-8 69

JEROME, Henry, & His Orchestra
LP '61

Singles: 7-inch

DECCA 3-5 60-64

EPs: 7-inch

DECCA 4-6 61

LPs: 10/12-inch

DECCA 5-12 60-64
ROULETTE 5-15 59
Also see DALTON BOYS

JEROME, Patti

Singles: 78 rpm

JOSIE (774 "Johnny Has Gone") 5-10 55

Singles: 7-inch

AMERICAN ARTS 5-10 64
JOSIE (774 "Johnny Has Gone") 10-20 55
JOSIE (908 "Only You") 5-10 63
Also see P.J.
Also see PATTI & MICKEY

JEROME, Ralph

Singles: 7-inch

K.P. (1006 "Don't Destroy Me") 40-60 59
K.P. (1007 "Rockhouse") 75-100 59

JEROMES, The

(With the Johm Abbot; The Jerome's)

Singles: 7-inch

DAR (300 "Rocking Chair") 150-250 61

JERRICO, Sherri
C&W '77

Singles: 7-inch

GUSTO/STARDAY 3-5 77

JERRY, Mungo: see MUNGO JERRY

JERRY & ATTACHES

Singles: 7-inch

CRASH 4-8 64

JERRY & CAPRIS

Singles: 7-inch

GLENDALE 10-15

JERRY & CASUALS / Rockin' Tones

Singles: 7-inch

STARS of TOMORROW (2235 "Battle of Three Blind Mice") 25-50 61
BMG (1001"Battle of Three Blind Mice") 25-50 61
Also see PAGE, Jerry
Also see ROCKIN' TONES / Jerry & Casuals
Also see STOREY, Denny

JERRY & CATALINAS

Singles: 7-inch

VEROONA (101 "Away from It All") 10-20 63

JERRY & CONTINENTALS

Singles: 7-inch

NIGHT OWL (6791 "I've Had It") 15-20 67
Members: Jerry Karow; Larry Barden; Jerry Nennig; Tom Roland; Tom Nennig; Dean Packard; Rich Hartley; Mike Jordan.

JERRY & DEBORAH

Singles: 7-inch

EPIC 10-15 66

JERRY & DEL-FIs

Singles: 7-inch

HOUND (102 "Little Suzanne") 30-40

JERRY & DIAMONDS

(Jerry Swallow)

Singles: 7-inch

ARC (7456 "Sea-N-Shore") 15-25 64

JERRY & JEFF

Singles: 7-inch

SUPER K 4-8 68-69

Members: Jerry Kasenetz; Jeff Katz.
Also see KASENETZ - KATZ SINGING ORCHESTRAL CIRCUS
Also see ORLANDO, Tony
Also see SCOTT, Neal

JERRY & JOHNNY

Singles: 7-inch

HEART 5-10 60

JERRY & JULIE

Singles: 7-inch

FINER ARTS 4-8 65

JERRY & LANDSLIDES

Singles: 7-inch

PPX 4-8 66

JERRY & MEL

Singles: 7-inch

W.B. 4-8 61

JERRY & OTHERS

Singles: 7-inch

PRISM 15-25

JERRY & PLAYMATES

Singles: 7-inch

ALVERA ("Want-a Love You") 20-25 66

JERRY & PLEDGES

Singles: 7-inch

CAMPUS (109 "Skins") 10-20
(Colored vinyl.)

JERRY & PORTRAITS: see PORTRAITS

JERRY & RADIANTS

Singles: 7-inch

JOX 4-8 64

JERRY & REGGIE

Singles: 7-inch

M.O.C. 4-8 64

JERRY & RIALTOS

Singles: 7-inch

ALL BOY 4-8 64

JERRY & SILVERTONES

Singles: 7-inch

COULEE (104 "Ce'ny") 8-12 63

Picture Sleeves

COULEE (104 "Ce'ny") 15-25 63
Members: Jerry Grosskopf; Rollie Grosskopf; Calvin Grosskopf; Richard Krause; Tom Perry; Jerry Oliver.
Also see TOWNSMEN

JERRY & UPBEATS

Singles: 7-inch

U.A. 4-8 62

JERRY & WAYNE

Singles: 78 rpm

ABC-PAR 10-15 57

Singles: 7-inch

ABC-PAR (9806 "Baby Baby Baby, Be Mine") 10-15 57
ABC-PAR (9806 "Baby Baby Baby") 10-15 57
(With shortened title.)

JERRY & WILLA

Singles: 7-inch

JERRY 4-8 67

JERRY B. & SOUL AGENTS

Singles: 7-inch

DOUBLE CHECK 5-10 65

JERRY DEE & INTRUDERS

Singles: 7-inch

SARA (6352 "Bo Diddley") 15-25 63
Members: Wes Lamuska; Olie Wahl; Wayne Toske; Mick Zimgible; Mike Schelberger.

JERRY G. & CO.

(With the Statesman)

Singles: 7-inch

CLEVETOWN (240 "She's Gone") 5-10 66

JERRY KELLY

Singles: 7-inch

EPIC 3-5 78

LPs: 10/12-inch

EPIC 5-10 78
Members: Jerry Hludzik; Bill Kelly.
Also see BUOYS

JERRY, MEL & JACK

Singles: 7-inch

DORE 4-8 62

JERRYO
P&R/R&B '67

(Jerry Murray)

Singles: 7-inch

SHOUT 4-8 67
WHITE WHALE 3-6 69
Also see TOM & JERRIO

JERSEY DREAM

LP: 10/12-inch

CLIFTON (1013 "Jersey Dream") 8-10 92

JERVEY, Arden

Singles: 7-inch

CUPID 5-10 59

JESSE & BUZZY

Singles: 7-inch

SAVOY 5-10 58
Member: Jesse Perkins.
Also see PERKINS, Jesse, & Bad Boys

JESSE & JAMES

Singles: 7-inch

CARLTON 4-8 63
EPIC 5-10 59

JESSE & MARVIN
R&B '53

Singles: 78 rpm

SPECIALTY (447 "Dream Girl") 20-30 52

Singles: 7-inch

SPECIALTY (447 "Dream Girl") 50-75 52
(Black vinyl.)
SPECIALTY (447 "Dream Girl"). 100-200 52
(Colored vinyl.)
Members: Jesse Belvin; Marvin Phillips.
Also see BELVIN, Jesse
Also see MARVIN & JOHNNY
Also see PHILLIPS, Marvin

JESSE & ROADRUNNERS

Singles: 7-inch

JARO (77034 "Sentimental") 10-20 60

JESSE J. & BANDITS

Singles: 7-inch

RE CAR (9003 "Stomp Your Feet") 60-80 60s

LPs: 10/12-inch

RE CAR 12-18 65
Also see KING KRUSHER & TURKEYNECKS

JESSE LEE

LPs: 10/12-inch

ETERNAL RAINBOW 8-12 85

JESSE, WOLFF & WHINGS

LPs: 10/12-inch

SHELTER 8-10 72

JESSE'S GANG
D&D '85

Singles: 12-inch

JES SAY 4-6 85

Singles: 7-inch

GEFFEN 3-4 87

Picture Sleeves

GEFFEN 3-4 87

JESSIE & JESSICA

Singles: 7-inch

CM 3-5
Members: Sonny Threatt; Phyllis Brown-Threatt.
Also see SONNY & PHYLLIS

JESSIE & SEQUINS

(With Lefty Bates' Band)

Singles: 7-inch

BOXER (201 "Hold My Hand") 50-75 59
PROFILE (4008 "Hold My Hand") 25-50 59
Also see SEQUINS

JESSIE LEE & RHYTHMAIRES

Singles: 7-inch

MIDA 15-25

JESSUP, Walt

Singles: 7-inch

DARCEY 8-12

JESTER, Charlie

(With the Kilts)

Singles: 7-inch

LANAR (102 "Crazy Baby") 75-100 61
LE CAM (726 "Once There Was a Time") 4-6 70s
Session: Ron-Dels.
Also see RON-DELS

JESTERS
P&R '57

(With David Clowney's Band)

Singles: 78 rpm

WINLEY 25-35 57

Singles: 7-inch

ABC 3-4 73
AMY 3-5 62
COLLECTABLES 3-4 80s
CYCLONE (5011 "I Laughed") 50-75 58
(Title and artist in normal bold print. Songwriting credit is *directly* under title.)
CYCLONE (5011 "I Laughed") 25-50
(Title and artist in narrow, extra bold print. Songwriting credit is approximately centered between title and artist.)
LOST-NITE 4-8 63
WINLEY (218 "So Strange") 50-75 57
(Has "Winley" in 3/8-inch letters.)
WINLEY (218 "So Strange") 20-30 61
(Has "Winley" in 1/4-inch letters.)
WINLEY (221 "I'm Fallin in Love") 50-75 57
WINLEY (221 "I'm Falling in Love") 20-30 61
(Note slight title change.)
WINLEY (225 "The Plea") 40-60 58
(Has "Winley" in 3/8-inch letters.)
WINLEY (225 "The Plea") 20-30 61
(Has "Winley" in 1/4-inch letters.)
WINLEY (242 "The Wind") 40-60 60
WINLEY (248 "That's How It Goes") 100-200 61
(Colored vinyl.)
WINLEY (248 "That's How It Goes") 20-30 61
(Black vinyl.)
WINLEY (252 "Come Let Me Show You") 20-30 61

LPs: 10/12-inch

COLLECTABLES 6-8 86
LOST-NITE 8-12 81
Members: Len McKay; Adam Jackson; Jimmy Smith; Noel Grant; Leo Vincent; Melvin Lewis; Don Lewis.
Also see HARPTONES / Paragons / Jesters / Clovers

JESTERS / Paragons

LPs: 10/12-inch

JOSIE ("Jesters Meet the Paragons") 50-75 60s
(Selection number not known.)
JUBILEE (1098 "Jesters Meet the Paragons") 250-350 59

PAUL WINLEY PROD. (102 "Jesters Meet the Paragons") 20-40 65
WINLEY (6003 "War: Jesters Meet the Paragons") 150-250 60
Also see JESTERS
Also see PARAGONS

JESTERS
Singles: 7-inch
RIO 8-12 61
VIV (1001 "Side Track") 10-20 62

JESTERS
Singles: 7-inch
JERDEN (740 "Amazon") 8-10 64

JESTERS
Singles: 7-inch
FEATURE (101 "Panther Pounce") 20-30 64
ULTIMA (705 "Drag Bike Boogie") 15-25 64
Members: Jim Messina; Dave Archuleta; Bill Beckman; Larry Cundieff.
Also see MESSINA, Jim

JESTERS
Singles: 7-inch
SUN (400 "Cadillac Man") 10-20 66
Members: Jim Dickinson; Teddy Paige; Jerry Phillips; Billy Wulfurs; Eddie Robertson.

JESTERS
Singles: 7-inch
SIDEWALK 5-8 67

JESTERS
Singles: 7-inch
AL-STAN 8-12 60s

JESTERS
LPs: 10/12-inch
PACIFIC ARTS 5-8 79

JESTERS III
Singles: 7-inch
COULEE (114 "Pledge of Love") 8-12 65
Members: Wayne McKibbin; Jim Burkhardt; Tom Eisenman.
Also see HOPE

JESTERS IV
Singles: 7-inch
FULLER (2684 "She Lied") 15-25 66

JESTERS OF DESTINY
LPs: 10/12-inch
DIMENSION 5-10 86

JESTERS OF NEWPORT
Singles: 7-inch
SOLO (700 "Stormy") 15-25 65

JESUS & MARY CHAIN *LP '86*
Singles: 7-inch
W.B. 3-4 87-89
LPs: 10/12-inch
REPRISE 5-8 86
W.B. 5-8 87-89

JESUS JONES *LP '91*
LPs: 10/12-inch
SBK 5-8 91

JESUS LIZARD: see NIRVANA / Jesus Lizard

JET CITY FIVE
Singles: 7-inch
THUMBS DOWN 4-8

JET MEN
Singles: 7-inch
LINCOLN (300 "Mountain Dew") 10-20 60

JET SET
Singles: 7-inch
BLAINE (4000 "Swing, Swing Jet") 10-20 65
CAPITOL (5358 "You Got Me Hooked") 10-20 65
DELTA (5001 "VC 10") 8-12
JET (101 "Super Sport") 8-12

JET STREAM
Singles: 7-inch
SMASH 4-8 67

JET STREAMS
Singles: 7-inch
DECCA (30743 "Who Me") 15-25 58

JET TONES
Singles: 7-inch
CHESS (1723 "Jet Tone Boogie") ... 8-12 59
PIX (1102 "Twangy") 10-20 59
PLAID (102 "Twangy") 15-25 59

JETBOY *LP '88*
LPs: 10/12-inch
MCA 5-8 88

JETE, Le: see LE JETE

JETER, Genobia *R&B '86*
Singles: 12-inch
RCA 4-6 86
Singles: 7-inch
RCA 3-4 86-87
LPs: 10/12-inch
RCA 5-8 86

JETER, Genobia, & Glenn Jones *R&B '87*
Singles: 7-inch
RCA 3-4 87
Also see JONES, Glenn

JETHRO TULL *LP '69*
Singles: 12-inch
CHRYSALIS 4-8 88-89
(Promotional only.)
Singles: 7-inch
CHRYSALIS 3-6 72-88
REPRISE/CHRYSALIS 5-10 69-72
Picture Sleeves
CHRYSALIS 4-6 74
EPs: 7-inch
CHRYSALIS 8-12 71
LPs: 10/12-inch
CHRYSALIS (Except CH4 & V5X series) 5-15 73-89
CHRYSALIS (CH4-1044 "Aqualung") 15-25 73
(Quadrophonic.)
CHRYSALIS (CH4-1067 "War Child") 20-30 74
(Quadrophonic.)
CHRYSALIS (V5X-41653 "Twenty Years of Jethro Tull") 50-75 88
(Boxed, five-disc set.)
MFSL (061 "Aqualung") 30-50 82
MFSL (092 "Broadsword and the Beast") 25-35 82
MFSL (187 "Thick As a Brick") 15-25 80s
REPRISE (1024 "Hymn 43") 10-20 71
REPRISE (2035 "Aqualung") 10-20 71
REPRISE (2071 "Thick As a Brick") 10-20 72
(With color booklet.)
REPRISE (6336 "This Was Jethro Tull") 10-20 69
REPRISE (6360 "Stand Up") 15-25 69
(With pop-up, or "Stand Up" cover.)
REPRISE (6400 "Benefit") 10-15 70
REPRISE/CHRYSALIS (2106 "Living in the Past") 15-20 72
(With color booklet.)
Members: Ian Anderson; Clive Bunker; Glen Cormick; John Evan; Barry Barlow; David Palmer; John Glascock; Jeff Hammond; Mick Abrahams.
Also see ABRAHAMS, Mick, Band
Also see ANDERSON, Ian
Also see WILD TURKEY

JETS
Singles: 78 rpm
RAINBOW (201 "The Lovers") 100-150 53
Singles: 7-inch
RAINBOW (201 "The Lovers") 250-350 53
Members: Buck Mason; Jim Walton; Walt Taylor; John Bowie; Charlie Booker; Herb Fisher.
Also see BACHELORS

JETS
Singles: 78 rpm
ALADDIN 100-150 54
7-11 (2102 "Volcano") 100-150 53
Singles: 7-inch
ALADDIN (3247 "I'll Hide My Tears") 300-500 54
7-11 (2102 "Volcano") 300-500 53
Members: David Ford; Gaynel Hodge; Bobby Byrd; Clyde Tillis.
Also see HOLLYWOOD FLAMES

JETS
Singles: 78 rpm
CAPITOL 5-10 55
Singles: 7-inch
CAPITOL 10-15 55

JETS
Singles: 78 rpm
GEE 250-500 56
Singles: 7-inch
GEE (1020 "Heaven Above Me") 1500-2000 56

JETS
Singles: 7-inch
ARROW (100 "Soul Dinner") 15-25 63
Also see MARCELS

JETS
Singles: 7-inch
PORT (3016 "Everything I Do") 10-20 66

JETS *R&B/D&D '85*
Singles: 12-inch
MCA 4-6 85-88
Singles: 7-inch
MCA 3-4 85-89
Picture Sleeves
MCA 3-4 86-88
LPs: 10/12-inch
MCA 5-8 85-89
Members: Elizabeth Wolfgram; Eugene Wolfgram (a.k.a. Gene Hunt).
Also see BOYS CLUB

JETSONS & TANGIERS / Jetsons
Singles: 7-inch
PUMPKIN 5-10
Also see TANGIERS & Jetson Band

JETSTARS
Singles: 7-inch
JERDEN 5-8 65

JETSTREAM
Singles: 7-inch
SMASH (2095 "All's Quiet on West 23rd St.") 10-20 60s

JETT, Joan *LP '81*
(With the Blackhearts)
Singles: 12-inch
BLACKHEART/CBS 4-8 88
(Promotional only.)
MCA 4-8 83
Singles: 7-inch
BLACKHEART/CBS 3-4 83-90
BOARDWALK 3-5 81-82
MCA 3-5 83
Picture Sleeves
BLACKHEART/CBS 3-4 83-88
BOARDWALK 3-5 81-82
MCA 3-5 83
LPs: 10/12-inch
BLACKHEART 50-75 80
(Red label with black heart. No mention of CBS. Number not known.)
BLACKHEART/CBS 5-8 83-90
BOARDWALK 5-8 81-82
MCA 5-8 83-84
RHINO (250 "Little Lost Girls") 15-20 82
(Picture disc.)
W.B. 8-10 90s
Also see BANGLES / Joan Jett
Also see BARBUSTERS
Also see BEACH BOYS
Also see RUNAWAYS

JETT, Tommy
Singles: 7-inch
JOX (60 "Groovy Little Trip") 15-25 67

JEUJENE & JAYBOPS
Singles: 7-inch
ZERO-O (3279 "Thunderin' Guitar") 200-300 60s
(Colored vinyl. 50 made.)

JEWEL
LPs: 10/12-inch
ERECT 5-8 82

JEWEL & EDDIE
Singles: 7-inch
SILVER 10-20 60
Members: Jewel Akens; Eddie Daniels.

JEWELL, Leonard
(Len Jewell)
Singles: 7-inch
DRANDELL 8-12 63
FONTANA (1599 "Paint Me") 20-30 66

JEWELL, Nancy
Singles: 7-inch
PICKIN' POST 3-5 77

JEWELL & RUBIES
Singles: 7-inch
ABC-PAR 5-10 63
LA LOUISIANNE (8041 "Kidnapper") 15-25 63
Member: Jewell Douglas.

JEWELLS
Singles: 7-inch
KING (6068 "Smokie Joe's") 8-12 67

JEWELS
(Crows)
Singles: 78 rpm
RAMA (10 "Heartbreaker") 200-250 53
Singles: 7-inch
RAMA (10 "Heartbreaker") 500-750 53
(Black vinyl. May show *Heartbreaker* by the Crows and *Call a Doctor* by the Jewels on some labels.)
RAMA (10 "Heartbreaker") 1000-2000 53
(Red vinyl.)
Also see CROWS

JEWELS
Singles: 78 rpm
IMPERIAL 20-30 55-56
R&B 25-50 54
RPM 20-30 56
Singles: 7-inch
ANTLER (1102 "The Wind") 25-50 59
IMPERIAL (5351 "Hearts Can Be Broken") 50-100 55
IMPERIAL (5362 "Natural, Natural Ditty") 50-100 55
IMPERIAL (5377 "How") 50-100 56
IMPERIAL (5387 "My Baby") 50-100 56
ORIGINAL SOUND (38 "Hearts of Stone") 10-20 64
R&B (1301 "Hearts of Stone") 100-200 54
R&B (1303 "A Fool in Paradise") 200-300 54
RPM (474 "She's a Flirt") 50-75 56
Members: Johnny Torrence; Dee Hawkins; James Brown; Rudy Jackson; Vernon Knight.
Also see JACKSON, Rudy
Also see TORRENCE, Johnny

JEWELS
Singles: 7-inch
SHASTA (115 "Are You Comin' to the Party") 10-20 59

JEWELS
Singles: 7-inch
FERN (806 "Space Guitar") 10-20 60

JEWELS
(With Johnny & the Sparks)
Singles: 7-inch
OLIMPIC (244 "Jimmy Lee") 10-20 64
Also see STUDENTS

JEWELS *P&R/R&B '64*
Singles: 7-inch
DIMENSION (1034 "Opportunity") .10-15 65
DIMENSION (1048 "But I Do") 10-15 65
Members: Sandra Bears; Margie Clark; Martha Harvin; Grace Ruffin.
Also see FOUR JEWELS

JEWELS
Singles: 7-inch
DYNAMITE (2000 "Papa Left Mama Holding the Bag") 8-12 65
FEDERAL (12541 "My Song") 10-20 66
KING (6068 "Smokie Joe's") 5-10 66

JEWELS
Singles: 7-inch
MGM (13577 "We Got Togetherness") 10-20 66

JHAMELS
Singles: 7-inch
CELESTIAL 4-8 66
LIBERTY 4-8 67

JIANTS
Singles: 7-inch
CLAUDRA (112 "Tornado") 100-150 59
Jerry Hedges; Andy Anderson; Bill Lee Balsbaugh; Ron Wolfe.
Also see SHONDELL, Troy

JIGGLES & ZANIES
Singles: 7-inch
DORE 4-8 64
Also see ZANIES

JIGSAW *P&R/LP '75*
Singles: 7-inch
CHELSEA 3-5 75-76
20TH FOX 3-5 77-78
LPs: 10/12-inch
CHELSEA 8-10 75
ELEKTRA 5-8 82
20TH FOX 5-8 77

JIGSAW SEEN
Singles: 7-inch
SKYCLAD 3-4 89
Picture Sleeves
SKYCLAD 3-4 89
LPs: 10/12-inch
SKYCLAD 5-8 89

JILL & RAY
Singles: 7-inch
LE CAM (979 "Hey Paula") 25-35 62
Members: Jill Jackson; Ray Hildebrand.
Also see HILDEBRAND, Ray
Also see JACKSON, Jill
Also see PAUL & PAULA

JILLETTES
Singles: 7-inch
AMAZON 8-12 62
PHILIPS 5-10 63

JIM & BILL
Singles: 7-inch
QUARTERCASH 4-8
SMART 4-8

JIM & CATHY
Singles: 7-inch
CADET 4-8 66

JIM & GLENN
Singles: 7-inch
PATTERN (701 "Philadelphia Flyer") 5-10

JIM & INGRID: see CROCE, Jim & Ingrid

JIM & INVICTAS
Singles: 7-inch
MEAN MOUNTAIN 3-4 81
(Black vinyl.)
MEAN MOUNTAIN 4-6 81
(Colored vinyl.)

JIM & JEAN *P&R '68*
Singles: 7-inch
VERVE/FOLKWAYS 5-10 68
LPs: 10/12-inch
VERVE/FOLKWAYS 10-20 68
Members: Jim Glover; Jean Glover

JIM & JESSE *C&W '64*
(With the Virginia Boys; with Sweet Mountain Boys)
Singles: 7-inch
CAPITOL 3-5 3-5
EPIC 3-6 64-70
MSR 3-4 86
LP: 10/12-inch
CAPITOL 15-25 69
CMH 8-12 80
EPIC 15-30 63-75
GATE 10-20 60s
HARMONY 8-12 70
HILLTOP 6-12
MASTERSEAL 10-15
MOUNT VERNON 8-12
OLD DOMINION 10-20
PALACE 10-15
PRIZE 8-12
ULTRA SONIC 8-12
VERNON 8-12
Also see CLEMENTS, Vassar
Also see FLATT, Lester, Earl Scruggs & Jim & Jesse

JIM & JESSE & Charlie Louvin *C&W '82*
Singles: 7-inch
SOUNDWAVES 3-4 82
LP: 10/12-inch
SOUNDWAVES 5-10 82
Also see JIM & JESSE
Also see LOUVIN, Charlie

JIM & JOE
Singles: 7-inch
FABOR (124 "Fireball Mail"/"Bimbo") 25-35 63
FABOR (124 "Fireball Mail"/"Daisy Mae") 20-30 63
Members: James Burton; Joe Osborn.
Also see GRASS ROOTS
Also see NELSON, Rick

JIM & KAY & CHAUNTEYS
Singles: 7-inch
KEYE (11 "Backside") 8-12

JIM & LEE
Singles: 7-inch
SMASH (2112 "Let's Go, Baby") 15-25 67

JIM & LYN
Singles: 7-inch
TIGER 4-8 66-67

JIM & MONICA *P&R '64*
Singles: 7-inch
BETTY 8-12 64
Member: Jimmy Gilmer.
Also see GILMER, Jimmy

JIM & ROD
Singles: 7-inch
CHALLENGE (59034 "Didn't It Rock") 75-125 58

JIM, JEFF & JAN
Singles: 7-inch
CAPITOL 15-20 63

JIM DANDEES
Singles: 7-inch
EXPRESS (105 "Mackey's Twist") ... 8-12 62
STARCREST 5-10 61

JIM DANDIES
Singles: 7-inch
EMPRESS 4-8 62

JIM 'N' I
Singles: 7-inch
MAJI (182 "Reagun's Budget Cuts") ... 3-6 82
Members: Jim Lang; Marc Bird.

JIMAE, Gene
Singles: 78 rpm
DOT 8-12 56
GENIE 10-15 55
Singles: 7-inch
DOT (15478 "Riders in the Sky") ... 10-20 56
GENIE (1301 "Riders in the Sky") 15-25 55

JIMENEZ, Jose: see DANA, Bill

JIMENEZ, Señor
Singles: 7-inch
FEATURE 4-8 64

JIMMIE & NIGHT HOPPERS
Singles: 7-inch
KNIGHT (2006 "Cruising") 15-25 58
Member: Jimmie Haskell.
Also see HASKELL, Jimmie

JIMMY, Bobby, & Critters *R&B/LP '86*
Singles: 12-inch
MACOLA 4-6 86
LPs: 10/12-inch
MACOLA 5-8 86
Member: Russ Parr.

JIMMY & CRESTONES
(With the Al Browne Orchestra)
Singles: 7-inch
AVENUE D (0011 "Angel Maureen") 8-10 85
MARIA (101 "Angel Maureen") 50-100 64
Also see BROWNE, Al

JIMMY & DUANE
Singles: 7-inch
EB X. PRESTON (212 "Soda Fountain Girl") 200-300 55
Members: Jimmy Delbridge; Duane Eddy.
Also see DELL, Jimmy
Also see EDDY, Duane

JIMMY & ENTERTAINERS
Singles: 7-inch
TRODDLIN' TOWN 8-12

JIMMY & FABULOUS EARTHQUAKES
("Vocal By Jimmy Hopkins and the Starfires")
Singles: 7-inch
MERIDIAN (1518 "In the Chapel in the Moonlight") 400-600 60
Member: Jimmy Hopkins.

JIMMY & ILLUSIONS
Singles: 7-inch
JOLYNN (36 "Karen") 15-25 63
MARIA (101 "Angel Maureen") 10-20 64

JIMMY & JACK
Singles: 78 rpm
ACE (507 "Love, Love, Love") 15-25 55
Singles: 7-inch
ACE (507 "Love, Love, Love") 20-40 55

JIMMY & JEAN
Singles: 7-inch
SUE 5-10 61

JIMMY & JOHNNY *C&W '54*
Singles: 78 rpm
CHESS 5-10 54
DECCA (Except 30061) 5-10 56
DECCA (30061 "Sweet Love on My Mind") 10-20 56
Singles: 7-inch
CHESS (4859 "If You Don't, Somebody Else Will") 10-20 54
CHESS (4863 "Love Me") 10-20 54
D (1004 "I Can't Find the Door Knob") 35-55 58
D (1089 "My Little Baby") 10-20 58
DECCA (Except 30061) 10-20 56

DECCA (30061 "Sweet Love on My Mind") 35-50 56
Members: Jimmy Lee Fautheree; "Country" Johnny Mathis
Also see MATHIS, Country Johnny

JIMMY & MUSTANGS
LPs: 10/12-inch
CURB 8-10 84
VANITY 10-12 82

JIMMY & OFFBEATS
Singles: 7-inch
BOFUZ (1113 "Stronger Than Dirt") 15-25

JIMMY & REBELS
Singles: 7-inch
ROULETTE 5-10 59

JIMMY & ROADRUNNERS
Singles: 7-inch
VARMINT 4-8 66

JIMMY & SPARTONS
Singles: 7-inch
SATELLITE 5-10 61

JIMMY & TOWERS
Singles: 7-inch
DEBANN (102 "One More Chance") 50-100

JIMMY & WALTER
Singles: 78 rpm
SUN (180 "Easy") 250-450 53
Singles: 7-inch
SUN (180 "Easy") 750-1000 53
Members: Jimmy DeBerry; Walter Horton.
Also see DE BERRY, Jimmy
Also see HORTON, Big Walter

JIMMY B. & ROCKATONES
CUCA (6481 "Everything I Do") 10-15

JIMMY C. & CHELSEA 5
Singles: 7-inch
ZERO (1003 "Play with Fire") 10-20 65

JIMMY "D" & "D"-LITES
Singles: 7-inch
START (643 "Dream World") 40-60 63

JIMMY G. & TACKHEADS R&B '86
Singles: 7-inch
CAPITOL 3-4 85-86
LPs: 10/12-inch
CAPITOL 5-8 86

JIMMY J & J's
Singles: 7-inch
SALCO (647 "Please Be My Girlfriend") 50-100 61

JIMMY LEE
(Jimmy Lee Robinson)
Singles: 7-inch
BANDERA 15-20 60
Also see LONESOME LEE
Also see ROBINSON, Jimmy Lee

JIMMY LEE & ARTIS: see LEE, Jimmy, & Artis

JIMMY, SANDRA & PAM
Singles: 7-inch
S.P.Q.R. 4-8 63

JIMMY SLIM & BLUES 5
Singles: 7-inch
RIKA (109 "Sweet Chicago") 5-8 67

JINKINS, Gus: see JENKINS, Gus

JINNIE & VELLA
LPs: 10/12-inch
IMPERIAL 10-12 69

JINX
Singles: 7-inch
RI-CATH 4-8 64

JITTERZ
EPs: 7-inch
NOCOPO (7451 "The Jitterz") 5-10 81
Members: Brian Moldawsky; Bruce Erhard; John Zuppa; Bill Zuppa; Rich Bannon.

JIVA
Singles: 7-inch
DARK HORSE 3-5 76
POLYDOR 3-5 78-79
LPs: 10/12-inch
DARK HORSE 8-10 75
POLYDOR 5-8 78

JIVE BOMBERS P&R/R&B '57
(Featuring Clarence "Bad Boy" Palmer; Clarence Palmer & Jive Bombers)
Single: 78 rpm
CITATION 25-40 52
SAVOY 10-20 57
Singles: 7-inch
CITATION (1160 "It's Spring Again") 50-80 52
CITATION (1161 "Brown Boy") 50-80 52
COLLECTABLES 3-4 85
MIDDLE TONE (20 "Anytime") 15-25 64
SAVOY 10-20 57-59
LPs: 10/12-inch
SAVOY 5-8 86
Members: Clarence Palmer; Earl Johnson; Allen Tinney; William Tinney.

JIVE BUNNY & MASTERMIXERS P&R '89
Singles: 7-inch
MUSIC FACTORY 3-4 89-90
LPs: 10/12-inch
MUSIC FACTORY 5-8 89

JIVE CHORDS: see SCHARMEERS / Jive Chords

JIVE FIVE P&R/R&B '61
("Featuring Eugene Pitt"; Jive Fyve; with Horace & Orchestra)
Singles: 7-inch
AMBIENT SOUND 5-10 82
BELTONE (1006 "My True Story") ..10-20 61
BELTONE (1014 "Never Never") 15-25 61
BELTONE (2019 "No Not Again") ..10-20 62
BELTONE (2024 "What Time Is It") 30-40 62
(White label. Vinyl is more brown than black.)
BELTONE (2024 "What Time Is It") 10-20 62
(Orange label.)
BELTONE (2029 "These Golden Rings") 40-50 62
(White label.)
BELTONE (2029 "These Golden Rings") 30-40 62
(Orange label.)
BELTONE (2030 "Lily Marlene") 10-20 62
BELTONE (2034 "Rain") 10-15 63
(Black vinyl.)
BELTONE (2034 "Rain") 20-30 63
(Vinyl color is more brown than black.)
BELTONE (3000 series) 10-15 62
DECCA (32671 "You Showed Me the Light of Love") 5-10 70
DECCA (32736 "I Want You to Be My Baby") 5-10 70
LANA 4-6
LOST-NITE 4-6 70s
MUSICOR (1250 "Crying Like a Baby") 6-12 67
MUSICOR (1270 "No More Tears") 6-12 67
MUSICOR (1305 "Sugar") 6-12 68
OLDIES 45 .... 4-8 60s
RELIC 4-8 75-78
SIR RENDER (007 "Falling Tears") ... 5-8
(Colored vinyl.)
SKETCH (219 "United") 20-30 64
STOOP SOUNDS (101 "Where Do We Go from Here") 100-150 96
(Limited edition. Estimates range from less than 10 to a few dozen made.)
U.A. (807 "United") 10-20 64
U.A. (853 "I'm a Happy Man") 10-20 65
U.A. (936 "A Bench in the Park") 10-20 65
U.A. (50004 "Main Street") 10-20 66
U.A. (50033 "In My Neighborhood") 10-20 66
U.A. (50069 "Ha Ha") 10-20 66
U.A. (50107 "You") 10-20 66
LPs: 10/12-inch
AMBIENT SOUND 8-12 82
AMBIENT SOUND/ROUNDER 5-10 84
COLLECTABLES 6-8 85
RELIC 8-10
Members: Eugene Pitt; Norm Johnson; Richard Harris; Jerry Hannah; Billy Prophet; Johnny Watson; Casey Spencer; Webster Harris.
Also see CORVAIRS
Also see GENIES
Also see JYVE FYVE
Also see PITT, Eugene
Also see PLATTERS / Inez & Charlie Foxx / Jive Five / Tommy Hunt

JIVE M. FLUFFER: see FLUFFER, Jive M.

JIVE TONES
Singles: 7-inch
APT (25020 "Geraldine") 25-50 58
RHYTHM RECORDS (5000 "Geraldine") 75-125 58
Member: James Whittier.
Also see DESIRES

JIVE-A-TONES
Singles: 7-inch
FELSTED (8506 "Flirty Girty") 50-75 57
FOX (1 "Flirty Girty") 100-150 57
FRATERNITY (823 "Wild Bird") 15-25 58

JIVERS
Singles: 78 rpm
ALADDIN (3329 "Cherie") 25-50 56
ALADDIN (3347 "Ray Pearl") 50-100 56
Singles: 7-inch
ALADDIN (3329 "Cherie") 100-150 56
ALADDIN (3347 "Ray Pearl") 150-250 56

JIVERS
Singles: 7-inch
RCA (7478 "I Wonder if You Know") 20-30 59

JIVES
Singles: 7-inch
HOUR (102 "Ubangi Stomp") 25-40 62
Also see CHARLIE & JIVES

JIVIN' FIVE
Singles: 7-inch
NITA (129 "Basin Street Blues") 10-20 62

JIVIN' GENE P&R '59
(With the Jokers)
Singles: 7-inch
ABC 3-5 73
CHESS 5-10 64
HALL WAY 5-10 64
JIN (109 "Going Out with the Tide") 20-30 59
JIN (116 "Breakin' Up Is Hard to Do") 20-40 59
JIN (7331 "Going Out with the Tide") 15-25 59
MERCURY (71485 "Breakin' Up Is Hard to Do") 10-20 59
MERCURY (71561 "Go On, Go On") 10-20 60
MERCURY (71680 "Going Out with the Tide") 10-20 60
MERCURY (71751 "Poor Me") 10-20 61
MERCURY (71802 "Don't Pretend") 10-20 61
MERCURY (71863 "I Cried") 10-20 61
MERCURY (72403 "Memory of You") 10-20 62
TFC/HALL 4-8 65
Member: Gene Bourgeois.
Also see BOURGEOIS, Gene
Also see MIZZELL, Bobby

JIVING JUNIORS
(With Duke Reid & His Group)
Singles: 7-inch
ASNES (103 "Sweet As an Angel") 35-50 61
BLUE BEAT (4 "Dearest Darling") 150-250 61
BLUE BEAT (5 "My Heart's Desire") 150-250 61

JO
Singles: 7-inch
CAPITOL 5-10 62

JO, Betty: see BETTY JO

JO, Damita: see DAMITA Jo

JO, Ivy: see IVY JO

JO, Linda: see LINDA JO

JO, Marcy: see MARCY JOE

JO, Willie: see JOE, Willie

JO, Sami: see SAMI JO

JO, Tammy: see TAMMY JO

JO ANN
Singles: 7-inch
NAME 4-8 64

JO ANN & TROY P&R '64
Singles: 7-inch
ATLANTIC 8-12 64
Members: Jo Ann Campbell; Troy Seals.
Also see CAMPBELL, Jo Ann
Also see SEALS, Troy

JO ELLYN
Singles: 7-inch
ALFA 4-8 62

JO JO
Singles: 7-inch
ACE (113 "To-To-Mo-To") 25-50 57
RENDEZVOUS 5-10 63

JO JO & OUTCASTS
Singles: 7-inch
SOUND-O-RIFFIC (926 "Why Baby") 15-25

JO JO GUNNE P&R/LP '72
Singles: 7-inch
ASYLUM 3-5 72
LPs: 10/12-inch
ASYLUM (Except 5071) 8-10 72-74
ASYLUM (5071 "Jumpin' the Gunne") 10-15 73
(With gatefold cover.)
ASYLUM (5071 "Jumpin' the Gunne") 8-10 73
(With standard cover.)
Member: Jay Ferguson.
Also see FERGUSON, Jay

JO JO WAIL & SOMETHINGS
Singles: 7-inch
SMASH 4-8 63

JO JO ZEP & FALCONS
LPs: 10/12-inch
COLUMBIA 5-8 81

JO MAMA
Singles: 7-inch
ATLANTIC 3-5 71
LPs: 10/12-inch
ATLANTIC 8-10 70-71
Members: Joel Bishop O'Brien; Ralph Schuckett; Abigale Haness; Danny Kootch; Charles Larkey.

JOAN & JOY
Singles: 7-inch
HULL 8-10 58

JOANNE & TRIANGLES
Singles: 7-inch
V.I.P. (25003 "After the Showers Come Flowers") 25-50 64

JOBE, Don
Singles: 7-inch
TAR (1283 "Going to Have a Party") 15-25

JOBETTES
Singles: 7-inch
KENIN 4-8 66

JOBIM, Antonio Carlos LP '65
Singles: 7-inch
A&M 4-6 67
CTI 3-5 70
MCA 3-5 74
VERVE 4-6 63-64
LPs: 10/12-inch
A&M 8-12 67-70
CTI 8-12 70-71
CAPITOL 10-20 64
DISCOVERY 5-8 82
MCA 5-8 73
VERSATILE 5-8 78
VERVE (Except 3000 series) 10-20 63
VERVE (3000 series) 5-8 82
W.B. 8-15 65-80
Also see FITZGERALD, Ella, & Antonio Carlos Jobim
Also see GILBERTO, Astrud
Also see SINATRA, Frank, & Antonio Carlos Jobim

JOBOXERS P&R/LP '83
Singles: 7-inch
RCA 3-4 83
LPs: 10/12-inch
RCA 5-8 83

JOBRIATH
LPs: 10/12-inch
ELEKTRA 8-10 73-74

JOCKO
Singles: 7-inch
WAND 4-8 61

JOCKO J.
Singles: 7-inch
KAMA SUTRA 3-5 75
LPs: 10/12-inch
KAMA SUTRA 8-12 75

JOCKO, Jackie
Singles: 78 rpm
UNIQUE 4-6 56
VIK 4-6 50s
Singles: 7-inch
UNIQUE 5-10 56
VIK 5-10 50s

JODARETTES
Singles: 7-inch
JOCIDA (302 "What's in Da Box") 10-20 60s

JODE
LPs: 10/12-inch
VANGUARD 8-10 71

JODIMARS
Singles: 78 rpm
CAPITOL 5-15 55-57
Singles: 7-inch
CAPITOL 5-15 55-57
PRESIDENT 8-12 58
Member: Chuck Hess.

JODO
LPs: 10/12-inch
DECCA 8-10 70

JODY & BOBBY
Singles: 7-inch
TITAN 4-8 66

JODY & BOOGIEMEN
Singles: 7-inch
TROLLEY 5-10 70
LPs: 10/12-inch
TROLLEY 10-15 70

JODY GRIND
LPs: 10/12-inch
U.A. 10-15 69

JOE, Billy: see BILLY JOE

JOE, Gradie
Singles: 7-inch
BLUE MOON (407 "Rockabilly Music") 150-200 58

JOE, Marcy: see MARCY JOE

JOE, Willie
Singles: 78 rpm
SPECIALTY (618 "Flippin' ") 10-15 56
Singles: 7-inch
SPECIALTY (618 "Flippin' ") 15-25 56

JOE & ANN R&B '60
Singles: 7-inch
ACE 5-10 60-62

JOE & BING
Singles: 7-inch
KIRSHNER 3-5 74

JOE & EDDIE LP '64
Singles: 7-inch
CAPITOL 5-10 59
FLIP (348 "Debbie Jill") 10-15 59
GNP 4-8 62-65
LPs: 10/12-inch
GNP 10-20 63-66
Members: Joe Gilbert; Eddie Brown.

JOE & FURIES
Singles: 7-inch
PARLIAMENT (9770 "Weasel") 15-25

JOE & JUMA
Singles: 7-inch
FREEDOM (44023 "Teenage Heart") 8-12 59
JERDEN (108 "Mr. Wind") 5-10 60

JOE & RAMRODS
Singles: 7-inch
SC 8-10

JOE & RITA
WASP 4-8
Singles: 7-inch

JOE & SATELLITES
Singles: 7-inch
SAFARI (1003 "Say a Prayer") ..150-200 57

JOE BOB C&W '75
(Joe Bob's Nashville Sound Company)
Singles: 7-inch
CAPITOL 3-5 75
LP: 10/12-inch
R.P.A. 5-10 77

JOE JR. & Side Effects
Singles: 7-inch
DIAMOND 5-8 68

JOEL, Billy P&R/LP '74
Singles: 12-inch
COLUMBIA 4-8 83
Singles: 7-inch
COLUMBIA (2628 "She's Got a Way") 4-6 81
(Promotional issue only.)
COLUMBIA (02518 thru 06526) 3-4 81-86
COLUMBIA (10000 & 11000 series) .. 3-5 74-80
COLUMBIA (40000 series) 3-5 73-74
COLUMBIA (70000 series) 3-4 89-94
EPIC 3-4 86
FAMILY (0900 "She's Got a Way") 10-20 73
FAMILY (0906 "Tomorrow Is Today") 10-20 73
Picture Sleeves
COLUMBIA (Except 02628) 3-5 79-87
COLUMBIA (02628 "She's Got a Way") 4-6 81
(Promotional issue only.)
LPs: 10/12-inch
CBS 5-8
COLUMBIA (30000 & 40000 series) 5-10 73-89
(With "FC," "JC," "KC," "OC," "PC," "QC," or "TC" prefix.)
COLUMBIA (30000 series) 10-15 74-76
(With "CQ" or "PCQ" prefix. Quadraphonic.)
COLUMBIA (40000 series) 8-12
(With "C2X" prefix.)
COLUMBIA (HC-40000 series) 10-15 80-87
(Half-speed mastered.)
FAMILY PRODUCTIONS (2700 "Cold Spring Harbor") 35-45 71
Promotional LPs
COLUMBIA (326 "Souvenir") 25-35 77
COLUMBIA (402 "Interchords") 25-35 77
COLUMBIA (452 "Now Playing") 20-30 78
COLUMBIA (1343 "Interview Album") 15-25 81
SKYCLAD (102 "A Tribute to Billy Joel") 6-8 91
(Clear vinyl. Intentionally has no music—by Billy Joel or anyone. Limited edition of 666 copies.)
Also see ATTILA
Also see HASSLES
Also see KHAN, Steve
Also see U.S.A. for AFRICA

JOEL, Billy, & Ray Charles P&R '87
Singles: 7-inch
COLUMBIA (06994 "Baby Grand") 3-4 87
Picture Sleeves
COLUMBIA (06994 "Baby Grand") 3-4 87
Also see CHARLES, Ray

JOEL, Billy / Ricky Van Shelton
Singles: 7-inch
EPIC (74422 "All Shook Up") 3-4 92
Also see JOEL, Billy
Also see SHELTON, Ricky Van

JOEL, Dennis
Singles: 7-inch
TAPE 4-8 62

JOEL & CONCORDS
AMBER 10-15 66

JOEL & DYMENSIONS
Singles: 7-inch
CLASSIC ARTISTS 4-6 90
LPs: 10/12-inch
CLASSIC ARTISTS 8-10 90
Members: Joel Katz; Johnny Maestro; Bobby Jay.
Also see MAESTRO, Johnny

JOESKI LOVE R&B '86
Singles: 7-inch
VINTERTAINMENT 3-4 86

JOEY
(Joey Hall)
Singles: 7-inch
CAMEO 5-10 64
JOY 5-10 60
TAURUS (353 "A Place in Your Heart") 15-20 62
Also see LITTLE JOEY & FLIPS

JOEY & AMBERS
Singles: 7-inch
BIG TOP (3052 "The Treasure in My Heart") 10-15 60

JOEY & CLASSICS
Singles: 7-inch
TEEN 10-15 64

JOEY & CONTINENTALS
Singles: 7-inch
CLARIDGE 10-15 65
KOMET (1001 "Will Love Ever Come My Way") 15-25 65
LAURIE (3294 "Sad Girl") 10-20 65
Member: Joey Porello.
Also see G.T.O.s

JOEY & DANNY WITH ALI BABA & 4 THEIVES
Singles: 7-inch
SWAN (4147 "Rats in My Room")..10-20 63
SWAN (4157 "I Got Rid of the Rats")..........10-20 63
Members: Joey Reynolds; Danny Neaverth.

JOEY & DUAL SONICS
Singles: 7-inch
WGW (3006 "Chicken Back Twist")................ 5-10 62

JOEY & FLIPS: see JOEY

JOEY & HIS FRIENDS
Singles: 7-inch
COLPIX (733 "Farmer's Daughter")... 5-8 64

JOEY & IMPRESSIONS
Singles: 7-inch
CAGG (101 "Lonesome Teenager")..........................40-50

JOEY & LEXINGTONS
Singles: 7-inch
COMET (2154 "Heaven")...........100-200 62
DUNES (2029 "Bobbie")...............75-125 63

JOEY & Original 3 Friends: see VILLA, Joey

JOEY & OVATIONS
Singles: 7-inch
HAWK (153 "I Still Love You")...........................500-1000 64

JOEY & RODGE
(With the Crysteles; "With Guitar & Chorus")
Singles: 7-inch
TABBY (100 "I Should Live So Long")..........................100-200

JOEY & TEENAGERS
(With Herman, Jimmy & Sherman)
Singles: 7-inch
COLUMBIA (3-42054 "What's on Your Mind")..........................100-125 61
(Compact 33 Single.)
COLUMBIA (4-42054 "What's on Your Mind")..........................60-80 61
Members: Joey Pruitt; Jimmy Castor.
Also see CASTOR, Jimmy
Also see TEENAGERS

JOEY & TWISTERS
Singles: 7-inch
DUEL (505 "Mumblin' ")................10-20 61
DUEL (509 "Last Dance")...............10-20 62
Also see TWISTERS

JOEY & V.I.P.s
Singles: 7-inch
SWAN.. 4-8 66

JOGETTES
Singles: 7-inch
MAR (102 "Your Love")..................15-25 62

JOHANNA
Singles: 7-inch
KAPP.. 4-8 60
LEADER.. 5-10 60
Picture Sleeves
KAPP.. 5-10 60

JOHANNES & HIS ORCHESTRA
Singles: 7-inch
ATCO (6249 "Margarita")...............10-20 62

JOHANSEN, David LP '79
Singles: 7-inch
BLUE SKY.. 3-5 78-82
Picture Sleeves
BLUE SKY.. 4-6
LPs: 10/12-inch
BLUE SKY.. 5-8 78-82
Also see NEW YORK DOLLS
Also see POINDEXTER, Buster, & His Banshees of Blue

JOHN, Billy, & Continentals
Singles: 7-inch
JIN.. 4-8 66
N-JOY.. 4-8 62

JOHN, Bobby
Singles: 7-inch
IMPERIAL.. 4-8 62

JOHN, Dr: see DR. JOHN

JOHN, Elton P&R/LP '70
Singles: 12-inch
GEFFEN... 4-8 83-85
(Promotional only.)
MCA... 4-8 78-88
(Promotional only.)
Singles: 7-inch
COLLECTABLES (4900 series)........ 3-5 92
(Colored vinyl.)
CONGRESS (6017 "Lady Samatha")..........................20-30 69
CONGRESS (6022 "Border Song")..........................20-30 70
DJM (70008 "Lady Samatha").......40-60 69
EPIC.. 3-4 87
GEFFEN (Except 2176).................. 3-5 81-86
GEFFEN (2176 "Sasson")............... 5-10 84
(Single-sided. Promotional issue only.)
MCA (40000 thru 40505)................ 3-6 72-76
MCA (40892 thru 40973)................ 3-5 78
MCA (40993 "Song for Guy").......... 4-6 78
(Promotional issue only.)
MCA (41042 thru 41293)................ 3-5 79-80
MCA (53196 thru 53953)................ 3-4 87-90
MCA/ROCKET................................ 3-5 76-77
ROCKET.. 3-5 76-77
UNI (55246 "Border Song")............5-10 70
UNI (55265 thru 55343).................. 4-8 70-72
UNI (55351 "Crocodile Rock").......25-50 72
(Canadian. In error, first issues were on UNI, instead of MCA.)
VIKING (1010 "From Denver to L.A.").........................30-60 69
(Flip is by the Barbara Moore Singers.)
Picture Sleeves
GEFFEN.. 3-5 81-86
MCA (40344 thru 40505)................ 3-6 74-75
MCA (40892 thru 40973)................ 3-6 78
MCA (40993 "Song for Guy").......... 4-8 78
(Promotional issue only.)
MCA (41042 thru 41293)................ 3-6 79-80
MCA (53196 thru 53000 series)........ 3-6 87-88
MCA/ROCKET................................. 3-6 76-77
ROCKET... 3-6 76-77
EPs: 7-inch
MCA (Except 40105)......................8-10 73
(Juke box issues.)
MCA (40105 "Saturday Night's Alright for Fighting")............................... 3-5 73
(Single with two tracks on side two. Not issued with EP cover.)
UNI...10-12 70
(Juke box issue only.)
LPs: 10/12-inch
COLUMBIA SPECIAL PRODUCTS.. 5-8 81
DCC (2004 "Madman Across the Water")..................................10-15 95
(Analog audiophile pressing.)
D.D.L. (16614 "Goodbye Yellow Brick Road")..................................50-75 73
(Half-speed mastered.)
DJLP (403 "Empty Sky")...............20-25 69
(U.K. issue, distributed in the U.S.A.)
GEFFEN... 5-8 81-87
MCA (2015 thru 2130)...................6-10 73-75
(Includes MCA reissues of UNI albums.)
MCA (2142 "Captain Fantastic and the Brown Dirt Cowboy")..........................10-12 75
(Includes poster, lyrics booklet, bio scrapbook and comic insert. Deduct $3 to $5 if these items are missing.)
MCA (2142 "Captain Fantastic")..50-100 79
(Colored vinyl. Promotional issue only.)
MCA (2163 thru 5121)...................5-10 75-80
MCA (6000 series)..........................5-8 88-89
MCA (8000 series)........................10-12 87
MCA (10003 "Goodbye Yellow Brick Road")..................................10-12 73
MCA (13921 "Thom Bell Sessions")..5-10 79
MCA (14591 "A Single Man")........15-20 79
(Picture disc. Both sides have front view of Elton.)
MCA (14591 "A Single Man")........50-60 79
(Promotional picture disc. B-side has back view of Elton.)
MCA (37000 series)........................ 4-8 79
MCA/ROCKET (Except 1953 & 11004)...10-12 76-77
MCA/ROCKET (1953 "Get Up and Dance")......................................20-25 77
(Promotional issue only.)
MCA/ROCKET (11004 "Blue Moves")...8-12 70s
MFSL (160 "Goodbye Yellow Brick Road")......................................30-40 73
(Half-speed mastered.)
NAUTILUS (10003 "Goodbye Yellow Brick Road")......................................30-40 82
(Half-speed mastered.)
PARAMOUNT (6004 "Friends").....10-15 71
(Soundtrack.)
PICKWICK (3598 "Friends")...........8-10 70s
SASSON/GEFFEN (2176 "Sasson Presents Elton John").................................20-30 81
(Single-sided, four-track LP. Promotional issue only.)
UNI (73090 "Elton John")..............15-20 70
(Includes booklet.)
UNI (73096 "Tumbleweed Connection")..................................15-20 71
(Includes booklet.)
UNI (93105 "11-17-70")..................15-20 71
UNI (93120 "Madman Across the Water")..15-20 71
(Includes booklet.)
UNI (93135 "Honky Chateau")........15-20 72
VIKING (105 "The Games").......150-175 70
(Soundtrack. With Francis Lai & Barbara Moore Singers.)
Also see BIRDS of a FEATHER
Also see CHINA
Also see DIONNE & FRIENDS
Also see FRANKLIN, Aretha, & Elton John
Also see LAI, Francis, & His Orchestra
Also see MICHAEL, George
Also see OLSSON, Nigel
Also see RUSH, Jennifer, & Elton John
Also see SEDAKA, Neil
Also see STARR, Ringo
Also see WONDER, Stevie

JOHN, Elton, & Kiki Dee P&R '76
Singles: 7-inch
ROCKET... 3-5 76
Picture Sleeves
ROCKET... 3-5 76
Also see DEE, Kiki

JOHN, Elton, & Lesley Duncan
Singles: 7-inch
MCA (1938 "Love Song")...............15-20 76
(Promotional issue only.)
Also see DUNCAN, Lesley

JOHN, Elton, & Millie Jackson
Singles: 7-inch
GEFFEN... 3-4 85
Picture Sleeves
GEFFEN... 3-4 85
Also see JACKSON, Millie

JOHN, Elton / John Lennon P&R '75
Singles: 7-inch
MCA (40364 "Philadelphia Freedom").......................................3-5 75
Picture Sleeves
MCA (40364 "Philadelphia Freedom").......................................3-5 75
MCA (40364 WFIL radio "Philadelphia Freedom")....................................30-40 75
(Promotional issue only.)
Also see LENNON, John

JOHN, Elton / Tina Turner
Singles: 7-inch
POLYDOR (002 "Pinball Wizard") 25-35 75
(Promotional issue only.)
Also see JOHN, Elton
Also see TURNER, Tina

JOHN, Evan, & H-Bombs
LPs: 10/12-inch
JUNGLE...10-12 85

JOHN, Honest: see HONEST JOHN

JOHN, Johnny Little: see JOHNNY LITTLE JOHN

JOHN, Little Willie R&B '55
Singles: 78 rpm
KING..10-20 56-57
Singles: 7-inch
GUSTO ("Fever")............................3-4 87
(Selection number not known.)
KING (500 series)..........................3-5
KING (4818 thru 5394)................10-20 56-60
KING (5428 thru 5949)..................5-10 61-64
Picture Sleeves
GUSTO ("Fever")............................3-4 87
EPs: 7-inch
KING (423 "Talk to Me")...............25-50 58
KING (767 "The Sweet, the Hot, the Teen-Age Beat")..15-25 61
(Stereo. Juke box issue only.)
KING (802 "At a Recording Session")......................................15-25 62
(Stereo. Juke box issue only.)
LPs: 10/12-inch
BLUESWAY...................................10-15 73
KING (564 "Fever")......................100-200 56
(With brown cover.)
KING (564 "Fever")........................40-60 59
(With blue cover.)
KING (596 "Talk to Me")...............75-125 58
KING (603 "Mr. Little Willie John")..50-100 58
KING (691 "In Action")................100-125 60
KING (739 "Sure Things")...............20-40 61
KING (767 "The Sweet, the Hot, the Teen-Age Beat")..20-40 61
KING (802 "At a Recording Session")......................................20-30 62
KING (895 "These Are My Favorite Songs")..20-30 64
KING (949 "All Originals")............20-30 66
KING (1081 "Free at Last")............20-30 70
Also see WILLIAMS, Paul

JOHN, Little Willie / Hank Ballard & the Midnighters
Singles: 7-inch
KING (5428 "Walk Slow"/"Hoochi Coochi Coo")..10-20 60

JOHN, Little Willie / Drifters
Singles: 7-inch
ATLANTIC (89189 "Fever")...............3-4 89
Picture Sleeves
ATLANTIC (89189 "Fever")...............3-4 89
Also see DRIFTERS

JOHN, Little Willie / 5 Royales / Earl King / Midnighters
EPs: 7-inch
KING (387 "Rock & Roll Hit Parade")...................................75-100 56
Also see 5 ROYALES
Also see JOHN, Little Willie
Also see KING, Earl (Connelly)
Also see MIDNIGHTERS

JOHN, Mable P&R/R&B '66
Singles: 7-inch
MOTOWN (54081 "Who Wouldn't Love a Man Like That")..................................300-400 63
(May have been promotional only. Should have been on Tamla, as selection number indicates.)
STAX..5-15 66-68
TAMLA (54031 "Who Wouldn't Love a Man Like That")..................................75-100 60
TAMLA (54040 "No Love")..............50-100 61
TAMLA (54050 "Take Me")..............30-60 61
TAMLA (54081 "Who Wouldn't Love a Man Like That")..................................50-100 63
Also see RAELETTES

JOHN, Manny
Singles: 7-inch
LOST GOLD (1002 "Spend My Eternity with You")..3-4 90
(Blue vinyl.)
Picture Sleeves
LOST GOLD/ABR (1002 "Spend My Eternity with You")...................................3-4 90

JOHN, Pope: see POPE JOHN

JOHN, R. see R JOHN

JOHN, Robby
Singles: 7-inch
DEL-FI...5-10 59

JOHN, Robert P&R '68
(Bobby Pedrick Jr.)
Singles: 12-inch 33/45
CBS ASSOCIATED............................4-6 84
Singles: 7-inch
A&M...3-5 70-72
ARIOLA..3-5 78
ATLANTIC...3-5 71-73
COLUMBIA (Except 44697)..............4-8 68-69
COLUMBIA (44697 "Can't Stop Loving You")..8-12 68
EMI AMERICA...................................3-4 79-80
MOTOWN..3-4 83
LPs: 10/12-inch
COLUMBIA.......................................10-20 68
EMI AMERICA...................................5-8 79-82
HARMONY..8-10 72
Also see GLOBETROTTERS / Robert John
Also see PEDRICK, Bobby

JOHN, Sammie
Singles: 7-inch
SOFT (1003 "Boss Bag")..................4-8 66
(Also issued as by "Little John" Sammie Myers.)
Also see MYERS, Sammie "Little John"

JOHN, Sheriff: see SHERIFF JOHN

JOHN & ERNEST P&R/R&B '73
Singles: 7-inch
RAINY WEDNESDAY (201 "Super Fly Meets Shaft")..4-8 73
RAINY WEDNESDAY (203 "Soul President Number One")....................................4-8 73
Members: John Free; Ernest Smith.

JOHN & HERB
Singles: 7-inch
DOT..4-6 69

JOHN & JACKIE
Singles: 78 rpm
ALADDIN (3425 "Raging Sea")......40-60 57
Singles: 7-inch
ALADDIN (3425 "Raging Sea")......40-60 57

JOHN & JIM
Singles: 7-inch
TIRINO (1 "The Girl I Used to Know")..10-20 73
TIRINO (101 "The Girl I Used to Know")..4-6 73
Members: John Tirino; Jim Tirino.
Also see J. BROTHERS

JOHN & JUDY
Singles: 7-inch
DORE..5-10 59-60
ELDO..4-8 61

JOHN & PAUL
Singles: 7-inch
TIP..10-15 64

JOHN & PAUL
Singles: 7-inch
SWAN..5-10 65

JOHN DAVID & CINDERS
Singles: 7-inch
W.B. (5825 "No, Not My Heart")......8-12 66
Member: John David Souther.
Also see SOUTHER, J.D.

JOHN DEER: see DEER, John

JOHN LEE
(John Lee Hooker; John Lee's Groundhogs)
Singles: 78 rpm
GOTHAM (515 "Mean Old Train")..15-25 53
Singles: 7-inch
PLANET..5-8 67
Also see GROUNDHOGS
Also see HOOKER, John Lee

JOHN LEE
(John Lee Henley)
Singles: 7-inch
J.O.B. (114 "Rhythm Rockin' Boogie")...................................150-250 58
Also see SPIRES, Big Boy

JOHN R.
Singles: 7-inch
SMASH (1982 "Mojo Blues")............5-10 64
SMASH (2013 "Stag 'O Lee")...........5-10 65
USD (1041 "Keep Your Baby Home")..15-25 60s

JOHN'S CHILDREN
Singles: 7-inch
WHITE WHALE..................................10-15 66
LPs: 10/12-inch
WHITE WHALE (7128 "John's Children")...60-80 70

JOHNNIE & STAN
Singles: 7-inch
KO MAT..4-8 61

JOHNNIE
(Johnnie Louise Richardson)
Singles: 7-inch
J&S (1004 "My Dreams Have Turned to Bubbles")..4-6
J&S (1005 "Why Don't You Stop")......4-6
Also see JOHNNIE & JOE

JOHNNIE & JACK C&W '51
(With the Tennessee Mountain Boys; with Kitty Wells; Johnny & Jack)
Singles: 78 rpm
RCA..5-10 51-57
Singles: 7-inch
DECCA...4-8 62
RCA..8-15 51-59
EPs: 7-inch
DECCA...8-12 62
RCA..10-20 55-57
LP: 10/12-inch
ANTHOLOGY of COUNTRY MUSIC..8-12
CAMDEN..10-20 63-64
COUNTRY CLASSICS........................5-10
DECCA (4308 "Smiles and Tears")...15-25 62
GOLDEN COUNTRY............................5-10
MCA..5-8 80s
RCA (1587 "Tennessee Mountain Boys")...25-35 57
RCA (LPM-2017 "Hits")....................20-30 59
RCA (LSP-2017 "Hits")....................30-50 59
RCA (6022 "All the Best")...............10-20 70
VOCALION..10-15 68
Members: John Wright; Jack Anglin.
Also see WELLS, Kitty
Also see WRIGHT, Johnny

JOHNNIE & JEANNIE
Singles: 7-inch
JOSIE (878 "Kiss You a Thousand Times")..40-60 60

JOHNNIE & JOE P&R/R&B '57
(Johnny & Joe; Johnni & Joe; with Rex Garvin & His Orchestra; with Shytone 5 Orchestra)
Singles: 78 rpm
CHESS...25-50 57
J&S...25-50 57
Singles: 7-inch
ABC-PAR (10079 "I Adore You")....10-20 60
ABC-PAR (10117 "Your Love")........10-20 60
AMBIENT SOUND (03410 "Kingdom of Love")...5-10 82
BLUE ROCK (4084 "My Baby Is So Sweet")...5-8 69
CHESS (1641 "Feel Alright")...........15-25 56
CHESS (1654 "Over the Mountain")...20-30 57
(Silver and blue label.)
CHESS (1654 "Over the Mountain")...10-20 60
(Blue or multi-color label.)
CHESS (1677 "I Was So Lonely")..15-25 57
CHESS (1693 "Why Did She Go") 15-25 58
CHESS (1706 "Darling")..................15-25 58
CHESS (1769 "Across the Sea")....15-25 60
GONE (5024 "Who Do You Love")...15-25 61
J&S (1008 "Over the Mountain, Cross the Sea")..4-6
J&S (1603 "I Was So Lonely").......20-30 57
(First issue.)
J&S (1605 "Trust in Me")..............20-30 57
J&S (1606 "Who Do You Love")....20-30 57
J&S (1630 "Warm Soft & Lovely") 20-30 58
J&S (1631 "False Love Has Got to Go")...20-30 58
J&S (1659 "It Was There")............20-30 57
J&S (1664 "Over the Mountain, Cross the Sea")..35-45 57
(First issue. Though intended as 1654, selection number on label is 1664. Chess reissue has correct number. Has double horizontal lines across label.)
J&S (1664 "Over the Mountain, Across the Sea")..10-15 62
(Without horizontal lines across label.)
J&S (1684 "You're Just Right for the Part")..15-25 60
J&S (1701 "Red Sails in the Sunset")..15-25 59
J&S (1762 "Feel Alright")...............20-40 56
J&S (1763 "I'll Be Spinning")..........20-40 56
(First issue.)
J&S (4420 "The Devil Said No")......5-10 60s
J&S (8718 "False Love Has Got to Go")...4-6 70
J&S (8719 "Tell Me")..........................4-6 70
J&S (42830 "Love Me Now")............5-10 68
J&S (42832 "You're the Loveliest Song I've Ever Heard")..5-10 68
LANA (121 "Over the Mountain, Across the Sea")...5-8 65
OMEGA (237 "Speak Softly")...........8-12 63
OMEGA (967 "My Ideal")..................8-12 63
TUFF (379 "Here We Go Baby")......8-12 64
LPs: 10/12-inch
AMBIENT SOUND..............................8-12 82
Members: Johnnie Louise Richardson; Joe Rivers.
Also see JAYNETTS
Also see JOHNNIE

JOHNNIE & JOE / Jimmy Charles
Singles: 7-inch
TRIP (16 "Over the Mountain, Across the Sea")...3-5 70s
Also see CHARLES, Jimmy

JOHNNIE & JOE / Marcels
Singles: 7-inch
ROYALE (1003 "Over the Mountain, Across the Sea")...3-5 88
Also see JOHNNIE & JOE
Also see MARCELS

JOHNNY
Singles: 7-inch
MERIDIAN..5-10 60

JOHNNY & B.
Singles: 7-inch
RED WING (705 Meaner Than an Alligator")..50-100

JOHNNY & BAA BAAS
Singles: 7-inch
FRANKIE..5-10 59

JOHNNY & BARB

Singles: 7-inch

DECCA (30663 "At the Prom")........10-15 58

JOHNNY & BILL

Singles: 7-inch

FEDERAL.. 4-8 62
TRY ME.. 4-8 63

JOHNNY & BLUE JAYS

Singles: 7-inch

DJ (1001 "Japanese Rock") 10-20 60

JOHNNY & BLUE BEATS

LPs: 10/12-inch

WINSOR (1001 "Smile") 30-40

JOHNNY & BOB

Singles: 7-inch

SATIN... 5-10 60

JOHNNY & CANADIANS

Singles: 7-inch

COLUMBIA....................................10-15 65

JOHNNY & DEBONAIRES

Singles: 7-inch

FENWAY......................................10-15 62

JOHNNY & DIANE

Singles: 7-inch

ARGO... 4-8 61

JOHNNY & DISTRACTIONS *LP '82*

Singles: 7-inch

A&M 3-4 81-82

LPs: 10/12-inch

A&M 5-8 81-82

JOHNNY & DONNA

Singles: 7-inch

TITANIC 4-8 63

JOHNNY & DREAMS

Singles: 7-inch

RICHIE (457 "You're Too Young for Me")....................................200-300 61
(Black vinyl. Orange label.)
RICHIE (457 "You're Too Young for Me")....................................150-250 61
(Black vinyl. Green label.)
RICHIE (457 "You're Too Young for Me")....................................350-500 61
(Colored vinyl.)

JOHNNY & DRIFTERS

Singles: 7-inch

MALFRA (1001 "Rimshot") 8-12

JOHNNY & DUANE / Duane Carter

Singles: 7-inch

HEP (2002 "Can You")...................25-35 60s
Also see CARTER, Duane

JOHNNY & EXPRESSIONS

P&R/R&B '66

Singles: 7-inch

JOSIE.. 5-10 65-66
Member: Johnny Matthews.
Also see SOUL STOPPERS

JOHNNY & HURRICANES *P&R/R&B '59*

Singles: 7-inch

ABC... 3-5 73
ATILA.. 5-10 66-67
BIG TOP....................................... 8-15 60-63
JA-DA.. 8-12
JEFF.. 5-10 64
MALA... 5-10 63
TWIRL (1001 "Crossfire") 30-40 59
WARWICK (502 "Crossfire")............15-25 59
("Warwick" in sans-serif, or block style print.)
WARWICK (502 "Crossfire")...........10-15 59
("Warwick" in serif style print, but does not extend across entire label. "Crossfire" in quotes.)
WARWICK (502 "Crossfire")........... 8-10 59
("Warwick" in serif style print, extending across entire label. No quotes on Crossfire.)
WARWICK (509 "Red River Rock) . 8-10 59
(Monaural.)
WARWICK (509-ST "Red River Rock")......................................20-30 59
(Stereo.)
WARWICK (513 "Reville Rock) 10-15 59
(Monaural.)
WARWICK (513-ST "Reville Rock")......................................20-30 59
(Stereo.)
WARWICK (520 "Beatnik Fly") 10-15 60
("Warwick" in serif style print.)
WARWICK (520 "Beatnik Fly") 5-10 60
(With Warwick horse and scroll logo.)

Picture Sleeves

BIG TOP (3036 "Down Yonder") 10-20 60
BIG TOP (3051 "Rocking Goose") 10-20 60
BIG TOP (3056 "You Are My Sunshine")....................................10-20 60
BIG TOP (3063 "Ja-Da")................10-20 61
BIG TOP (3076 "Old Smokie")........10-20 61
WARWICK (520 "Beatnik Fly") 15-25 60

EPs: 7-inch

WARWICK (700 "Johnny and the Hurricanes") 50-75 59

LPs: 10/12-inch

ATILA (1030 "Live at the Star Club")..75-125 64
(Price includes fan club insert.)
BIG TOP (1302 "The Big Sound of Johnny and the Hurricanes") 45-55 60
(Monaural.)
BIG TOP (ST-1302 "The Big Sound of Johnny and the Hurricanes")....................75-100 60
(Stereo.)
TWIRL (5002 "Beatnik Fly") 70-90 59
WARWICK (W-2007 "Johnny and the Hurricanes") 50-75 59
(Monaural.)
WARWICK (WST-2007 "Johnny and the Hurricanes")..............................75-100 59
(Stereo.)
WARWICK (W-2010 "Stormsville")45-60 60
(Monaural.)
WARWICK (WST-2010 "Stormsville") 55-80 60
(Stereo.)
Members: Johnny Paris; Paul Tesluk; Dave Yorko; Lionel "Butch" Mattice; Bill Savitch; Eddie Fields.
Also see CRAFTSMEN
Also see FREDDIE & PARLIAMENTS
Also see GIBSON, Johnny

JOHNNY & HIGH-KEYS

Singles: 7-inch

JAMIE... 4-8 68

JOHNNY & INTERLUDES

Singles: 7-inch

GREGAR.. 4-6 69

JOHNNY & JACKEY

(Johnny & Jackie)

Singles: 7-inch

ANNA (1108 "Lonely & Blue")........10-20 59
ANNA (1120 "No One Else But You")..10-20 59
TRI-PHI (1002 "Carry Your Own Load")..10-20 61
TRI-PHI (1005 "Someday We'll Be Together")..................................10-20 61
TRI-PHI (1016 "Do You See My Love")..10-20 62
TRI-PHI (1019 "Baby Don'tcha Worry")..10-20 63
Members: Johnny Bristol; Jackey Beavers.
Also see BRISTOL, Johnny

JOHNNY & JACKS

Singles: 7-inch

TIKI 4-8 63

JOHNNY & JAKE

Singles: 7-inch

PHILIPS 5-10 69

JOHNNY & JALOPY FIVE: see JALOPY FIVE

JOHNNY & JAMMERS

Singles: 7-inch

DART (131 "School Day Blues")..200-250 59
Member: Johnny Winter.
Also see WINTER, Johnny

JOHNNY & JAYS

Singles: 7-inch

FAIRBANKS...................................10-20 61

JOHNNY & JERRY

Singles: 7-inch

SILVER SLIPPER (1004 "Cry Baby")..5-10 60

Picture Sleeves

SILVER SLIPPER (1004 "Cry Baby")..10-20 60

JOHNNY & JOE

Singles: 7-inch

JEWEL.. 3-5

JOHNNY & JOKERS

Singles: 7-inch

BELTONE (2028 "I Know") 15-25 62
HARVARD (804 "Why Must It Be")..40-60 59

JOHNNY & JONIE

Singles: 7-inch

CHALLENGE (59024 "Still Going Steady")......................................10-20 58
CHALLENGE (59041 "Tijuana Jail")...8-12 59
Also see MOSBY, Johnny & Jonie

JOHNNY & JUMPER CABLES: see VOODOO DOLLS / Johnny & Jumper Cables

JOHNNY & Leisure Suits: see BRANDMEIER, Jonathan

JOHNNY & LILY

Singles: 7-inch

U.A. 4-6 69
VEEP... 4-6 69

JOHNNY & MARK V / Ron-Dels

Singles: 7-inch

CHARAY (95 "Sands of Malibu")....15-25 68
(First issue.)
REVUE (11056 "Sands of Malibu")..10-15 68
Member: Sonny Threatt.
Also see RON-DELS
Also see SONNY & PHYLLIS

JOHNNY & NITE RYDERS

Singles: 7-inch

PERFECTION (558 "I Had a Girl")..20-30 60s

JOHNNY & SHY GUYS

Singles: 7-inch

CASCADE (1001 "Pretty Baby") 15-25 64
CUCA (1145 "Moon Dawg") 15-25 63
MA (101 "Shorty's Shack")..............15-25 64
REGAL (200 "What I'd Say")..........15-25 64
Members: Rudy Von Ruden; John Bernadot; Larry Ball Gaulke; Les King; Hal Atkinson; Tari Tovsen; Jan Hassman; Danny Baker.
Also see SHY GUYS
Also see VON RUDEN

JOHNNY & SPARK-LETS

Singles: 7-inch

REPRISE 4-8 64

JOHNNY & THUNDERBIRDS

(With the Trends)

Singles: 7-inch

CLOVER (1001 "They Say") 100-200 59
RIC (160 "Fugitive")......................10-20 65

JOHNNY & TOKENS

Singles: 7-inch

WARWICK (658 "Taste of a Tear")...10-15 61
Also see KINGS of the HOT RODS / Tokens / Hal Jones & Wheelers

JOHNNY & VELVETONES

Singles: 7-inch

JERDEN (714 "Hitch Hiking Home")..5-10 63

JOHNNY & VIBRATIONS

Singles: 7-inch

W.B. (5372 "Bird Stompin' ")..........10-20 63

JOHNNY & VOLUMES

Singles: 7-inch

ANGLETONE (552 "Ticker Tape") ...8-12

JOHNNY & WILLIS

Singles: 7-inch

NEWTIME (509 "Run Joe")..............5-10 62

JOHNNY AVERAGE BAND *P/R '81*

Singles: 7-inch

BEARSVILLE 3-5 81

LPs: 10/12-inch

BEARSVILLE 5-8 81
Member: Nikki Wills.

JOHNNY BELL TONES: see BELL, Johnny

JOHNNY C. & BLAZES

Singles: 7-inch

CHATTAHOOCHEE 4-8 64

JOHNNY H. & SINCERES

(With Little Joe & the Latinaires)

Singles: 7-inch

EL ZARAPE (122 "Why Don't You Write Me")......................................350-500 63
(Label is multi-color at top, white on bottom. Has no address under name.)
EL ZARAPE (122 "Why Don't You Write Me")......................................200-250 63
(Label is purple with silver print. Has address under name.)

JOHNNY HATES JAZZ *P&R/LP '88*

Singles: 7-inch

VIRGIN..3-4 88

Picture Sleeves

VIRGIN..3-4 88

LPs: 10/12-inch

VIRGIN..5-8 88

JOHNNY J. & HITMEN

Singles: 7-inch

NITE SHADE...................................5-8 85

JOHNNY JO

Singles: 7-inch

A-B-S 5-8 61

JOHNNY LEE

(John Lee Hooker)

Singles: 78 rpm

DELUXE.......................................30-60 52

Singles: 7-inch

DELUXE (6009 "(I Came to See You Baby")....................................75-100 52
Also see HOOKER, John Lee

JOHNNY LITTLE JOHN

Singles: 7-inch

JOLIET..4-8
MARGARET....................................5-10
TERRELL (6178 "Can't Be Still")....10-20 65

JOHNNY - O

Singles: 7-inch

DORE..5-10 59

JOHNNY T. ANGEL *P&R '74*

Singles: 7-inch

BELL 3-5 74

JOHNNY TWIST: see TWIST, Johnny

JOHNNY TWOVOICE: see TWOVOICE, Johnny

JOHNNY Z.

Singles: 7-inch

DORE (667 "Midnight Beach Party")..10-15 63

JOHNNY'S DANCE BAND

Singles: 7-inch

JAMIE (1405 "I'm Walkin' ")...........5-8 72
WINDSONG.....................................3-5 77-78

LPs: 10/12-inch

WINDSONG.....................................5-8 77-78

JOHNNYS

Singles: 7-inch

W.B. 8-12 67

JOHNS, Johnny

Singles: 7-inch

HI MAR...4-8 61-62

JOHNS, Judi, & Astro Notes

Singles: 7-inch

TROUBADOUR................................4-8 67

JOHNS, Liz

([Liz]Johns)

Singles: 7-inch

POWER (201 "To Prove My Love")..10-15 64

JOHNS, Sammy *C&W/P&R '74*

Singles: 7-inch

ELEKTRA..3-4 81
GRC...3-5 73-75
MCA...3-4 88
REAL WORLD 3-5 80
W.B./CURB......................................3-5 76

LPs: 10/12-inch

GRC...8-10 73
W.B. 5-10 77

JOHNS, Sammy, & DeVilles

Singles: 7-inch

DIXIE (1107 "Making Tracks") 25-50 60
KEDLEN (129 "Making Tracks")...50-100 60
(First issue.)
Also see DEVILLES

JOHNS, Sarah *C&W '75*

Singles: 7-inch

RCA 3-5 75-76

JOHNS, Tricia *C&W '77*

Singles: 7-inch

ELEKTRA..3-4 80-81
W.B. 3-5 77

JOHNSON, Addie

Singles: 7-inch

TCB...5-8 78

JOHNSON, Al

Singles: 7-inch

RIC (967 "Good Lookin' ")..............10-20 60
SOUTH CAMP (7002 "Love Waits for No Man")...20-30

JOHNSON, Al *R&B '80*

Singles: 7-inch

COLUMBIA 3-5 80

LPs: 10/12-inch

COLUMBIA 5-8 80

JOHNSON, Al, & Jean Carn *R&B '80*

Singles: 7-inch

COLUMBIA 3-5 80
Also see CARNE, Jean
Also see JOHNSON, Al

JOHNSON, Alphonso

Singles: 7-inch

EPIC (34869 "Spellbound")..............5-10 77

JOHNSON, Amos, & Rhythm Playboys

Singles: 7-inch

(01 "Rhythm Playboy's Stomp").....10-20
(No label name is shown.)

JOHNSON, Barry

Singles: 7-inch

RIC RAC 3-5 80

JOHNSON, Benny *R&B '73*

Singles: 7-inch

TODAY..3-5 73

JOHNSON, Betty *P&R '54*

Singles: 78 rpm

BALLY...5-10 56-57
BELL...8-15 54
COLUMBIA 5-10 51-52
NEW DISC..8-12 54-55
RCA 5-10 55

Singles: 7-inch

ATLANTIC..10-20 58-60
BALLY...10-20 56-57
BELL...3-5 71
COED..8-12 60
COLUMBIA 10-15 51-52
DOT..8-12 60
NEW DISC (10013 "I Want Eddie Fisher for Christmas")...................................15-25 54
NEW DISC (10018 "Did They Tell You")...15-25 55
RCA (6000 series) 10-15 55
RCA (8000 series) 5-10 63
REPUBLIC 8-12 60-61
SPARTAN 10-20 56-57
(Canadian.)
WORLD ARTISTS...............................5-10 63

EPs: 7-inch

ATLANTIC (611 "The Little Blue Man")...25-50 58
RCA (4059 "Betty Johnson")..........25-50 57

LPs: 10/12-inch

ATLANTIC (8017 "Betty Johnson").......................................25-50 58
ATLANTIC (8027 "Songs You Heard When You Fell in Love")...................................25-35 59
BALLY (12011 "The Touch")...........30-50 57

JOHNSON, Betty, with Three Beaus & a Peep / Anne Lloyd & Carillons

Singles: 7-inch

BELL (1031 "Cross Over the Bridge")...8-12 54
(Seven-inch 78.)
Also see LLOYD, Anne, & Michael Stewart

JOHNSON, Big Jack: see JOHNSON, Jack

JOHNSON, Bill

(With Four Steps of Rhythm)

Singles: 7-inch

JOCIDA...5-10 65
SUN (340 "Bad Times Ahead")......10-15 60
TALOS (402 "You Better Dig It")...150-250 59
Also see BEETHOVEN 4

JOHNSON, Bill, & Musical Notes *R&B '47*

(Bill Johnson Orchestra)

Singles: 78 rpm

ALERT 15-20 46
HARLEM 10-15 46
KING...10-15 46-50
QUEEN 10-15 47
VICTOR 10-15 47-48

Singles: 7-inch

TRU-BLUE (414 "When Your Hair Has Turned to Silver")......................................75-100 54
(Colored vinyl.)

JOHNSON, Bill, Quartet

Singles: 78 rpm

RONNEX..25-50 55

Singles: 7-inch

RONNEX (1001 "I Almost Lost My Mind")..200-300 55

JOHNSON, Billy

Singles: 7-inch

POP SIDE 4-8 62

JOHNSON, Blind Boy, & His Rhythms

(Champion Jack Dupree)

Singles: 78 rpm

LENOX...15-25 46
Also see DUPREE, Champion Jack

JOHNSON, Blind Willie

LPs: 10/12-inch

FOLKWAYS (3585 "The Blues")....20-25 57
RBF/FOLKWAYS...............................15-20 65

JOHNSON, Bob, & Pete Knight

Singles: 7-inch

CHRYSALIS......................................3-5 77

LPs: 10/12-inch

CHRYSALIS......................................5-8 77

JOHNSON, Bobby

Singles: 7-inch

MERCURY (71168 "Flat Tire").......25-35 57

JOHNSON, Brownie

Singles: 7-inch

LARK..5-10
LYNN (101 "The Sun Would Never Shine")..75-125 59

JOHNSON, Bubber *P&R/R&B '55*

(With the Dreamers)

Singles: 78 rpm

KING...10-15 55-57
MERCURY 10-15 52

Singles: 7-inch

KING (4000 series)...........................15-25 55-56
KING (5000 series)...........................10-20 57-60
MERCURY (8285 "Forget if You Can")..35-45 52

LPs: 10/12-inch

KING (569 "Come Home")................40-60 57
KING (624 "Sweet Love Songs") ...30-40 59

JOHNSON, Budd

(Budd Johnson & Orchestra; with the Voices Five)

Singles: 7-inch

CRAFT (113 "Castle Rock")...........15-25 58
(Monaural.)
CRAFT (116 "For Sentimental Reasons")......................................100-200 59
STERE-O-CRAFT (113 "Castle Rock")..30-40 58
(Stereo.)

JOHNSON, Budd

(With the Voices Five; with Boy & Girl)

LPs: 10/12-inch

STERE-O-CRAFT (509 "Big Beat Dance Party")..400-600 58
Also see JOHNSON, Budd

JOHNSON, Buddy *R&B '43*

(Buddy Johnson & His Orchestra)

Singles: 78 rpm

ATLANTIC..4-6 53
COLUMBIA 4-8 48
DECCA 4-8 42-54
MERCURY 4-8 53-56
RCA 4-6 56

Singles: 7-inch

ATLANTIC..5-10 53
DECCA (24996 "You Got to Walk That Chalk Line")...15-25 50
DECCA (28907 "Talkin' About Another Man's Wife")..10-20 53
DECCA (29058 "Handful of Stars") 10-20 54
MERCURY 5-10 53-56
RCA 5-10 56
ROULETTE 4-8 59
WING 10-20 56

LPs: 10/12-inch

FORUM..10-15
MERCURY (20072 "Buddy Johnson Wails")...25-35 58
(Monaural.)
MERCURY (60072 "Buddy Johnson Wails")...35-55 58
(Stereo.)
MERCURY (20209 "Rock 'N' Roll")..30-40 58
MERCURY (20322 "Walkin' ") 20-30 58
WING (1211 "Rock 'N' Roll")..........10-20 63
WING (12005 "Rock 'N' Roll").........35-50 56
Also see BROWN, Ruth
Also see EVANS, Warren
Also see PRYSOCK, Arthur

JOHNSON, Buddy & Ella P&R '60
Singles: 78 rpm
MERCURY ... 4-8 56-57
Singles: 7-inch
MERCURY ... 5-12 56-61
ROULETTE ... 5-10 59
LPs: 10/12-inch
MERCURY (20347 "Swing Me") ... 25-35 58
ROULETTE (R-25085 "Go Ahead and Rock & Roll") ... 20-30 59
(Monaural.)
ROULETTE (SR-25085 "Go Ahead and Rock & Roll") ... 30-40 59
Also see JOHNSON, Ella
Also see JOHNSON, Buddy

JOHNSON, Candy
(Candy Johnson Show; with Her Exciters)
Singles: 7-inch
CANJO ... 5-10 64
LPs: 10/12-inch
CANJO (1001 "The Candy Johnson Show") ... 25-35 64
CANJO (1002 "Bikini Beach") ... 25-35 64
Also see MacRAE, Meredith, with Candy Johnson's Exciters

JOHNSON, Candy, Orchestra
(C. Johnson & Band)
Singles: 78 rpm
D.R.C. DANCELAND (399 "Stompin' ") ... 20-30 49
D.R.C. DANCELAND (401 "Sunset Jump") ... 20-30 49

JOHNSON, Cheryl & Pam
Singles: 7-inch
STAX ... 5-10 64

JOHNSON, Chuck
Singles: 7-inch
SYMBOL ... 4-8 63

JOHNSON, Cliff
Singles: 78 rpm
COLUMBIA ... 20-40 57
Singles: 7-inch
COLUMBIA (40865 "Go 'Way Hound Dog") ... 30-60 57

JOHNSON, Col. Jubilation B.
LPs: 10/12-inch
COLUMBIA ... 10-20 66

JOHNSON, Conrad
Singles: 78 rpm
GOLD STAR ... 15-25 47
Also see CONNIE'S COMBO

JOHNSON, Craig
Singles: 7-inch
CAPITOL ... 3-5 75
Picture Sleeves
CAPITOL ... 3-5 75

JOHNSON, Curtis
Singles: 7-inch
EVENT (4268 "Baby Baby") ... 50-75 57

JOHNSON, Curtis
Singles: 7-inch
PELICAN (1920 "Sho-Nuff the Real Thing") ... 4-6 71

JOHNSON, Dan
Singles: 7-inch
M&J ... 4-8

JOHNSON, Danny R&B '79
Singles: 7-inch
FIRST AMERICAN ... 3-5 79
LPs: 10/12-inch
FIRST AMERICAN ... 5-8 79
Also see CHI-LITES

JOHNSON, Darnell
Singles: 7-inch
DORE ... 4-8 61

JOHNSON, Dave
Singles: 7-inch
APT ... 5-10 60

JOHNSON, Dave
Singles: 7-inch
TRADE WIND ... 4-8 66

JOHNSON, Dave, & Shadows
Singles: 7-inch
SOMA (1154 "Maybe Baby") ... 15-25 60
Also see STRANGERS

JOHNSON, David Earle
LPs: 10/12-inch
VANGUARD ... 8-10 77

JOHNSON, Debb
Singles: 7-inch
MONOLITH ... 4-8
LPs:10/12-inch
MONOLITH ... 8-12 71
Also see RISE & SHINE

JOHNSON, Dee
Singles: 7-inch
DIXIE (2012 "Just Look, Don't Touch") ... 15-25 59

JOHNSON, Deena
Singles: 7-inch
SIMPSON ... 15-20

JOHNSON, Denny
Singles: 7-inch
MSP ... 8-12 60s
Also see JOKERS WILD

JOHNSON, Dolores
Singles: 7-inch
CARNIVAL ... 4-8 62

JOHNSON, Don R&B '49
(Don Johnson Band)
Singles: 7-inch
SPECIALTY ... 4-8 49

JOHNSON, Don
Singles: 7-inch
DOT (15812 "I'm Hypnotized") ... 20-30 58

JOHNSON, Don
Singles: 7-inch
CAPITOL ... 3-5 73

JOHNSON, Don P&R/LP '86
Singles: 7-inch
EPIC ... 3-4 86
Picture Sleeves
EPIC ... 3-4 86
LPs: 10/12-inch
EPIC ... 5-8 86
Also see STREISAND, Barbra, & Don Johnson

JOHNSON, Doug, & Outlaws
Singles: 7-inch
BETHLEHEM ... 4-8 62

JOHNSON, Ella
LPs: 10/12-inch Singles: 78 rpm
MERCURY ... 4-8 54-56
WING ... 4-8 56
Singles: 7-inch
MERCURY ... 5-10 54-56
WING ... 5-10 56
LP: 10/12-inch
MCA ... 5-8
Also see JOHNSON, Buddy & Ella

JOHNSON, Eric LP '90
LPs: 10/12-inch
CAPITOL ... 5-8 90

JOHNSON, Ernie
Singles: 7-inch
ASNES ... 5-10 61
RIDE ... 5-10
RONN ... 3-5 84
STEPH & LEE ... 5-8
Also see ERNIE & EDDIE

JOHNSON, F.D.
Singles: 7-inch
JAN ("Be My Baby") ... 25-50
(Selection number not known.)

JOHNSON, Frank
Singles: 7-inch
JAN ("Be My Baby") ... 25-50
(Selection number not known.)

JOHNSON, Fred
Singles: 7-inch
CAPRI (110 "I Need Love") ... 4-8 72

JOHNSON, Gene
(Gene Autry)
Singles: 78 rpm
TIMELY TUNES (1550 "High Steppin' Mama Blues") ... 25-75
TIMELY TUNES (1551 "Jimmie the Kid") ... 25-75
TIMELY TUNES (1552 "Do Right Daddy Blues") ... 25-75
Also see AUTRY, Gene

JOHNSON, General R&B '76
(With the Chairmen; Norman Johnson)
Singles: 12-inch
ARISTA ... 4-8 78
Singles: 7-inch
ARISTA ... 3-5 76-78
INVICTUS ... 3-5 71
SURFSIDE (Except "Down at the Boondocks") ... 3-5 80
SURFSIDE ("Down at the Boondocks") ... 5-10 80
(Colored vinyl. Promotional issue made for the Boondocks club. Number not known.)
LPs: 10/12-inch
SURFSIDE (1001 "Success") ... 5-10 80
Also see CHAIRMEN of the BOARD
Also see JOHNSON, Norman
Also see SHOWMEN

JOHNSON, Glenn
Singles: 7-inch
OAK (7673 "Run Here Honey") ... 20-30

JOHNSON, Goldie
Singles: 7-inch
MONTCLARE ... 4-6 77

JOHNSON, Harold
Singles: 7-inch
REVUE ... 3-6 69

JOHNSON, Harry "Slick"
Singles: 78 rpm
PEACOCK ... 5-10 51

JOHNSON, Herb
(With the Cruisers; with Impacts)
Singles: 7-inch
ARTIC ... 8-12
BRUNSWICK (55393 "I'm So Glad") ... 15-25 68
COLLECTABLES ... 3-4 82
LEN (1007 "Guilty") ... 20-30 60
SWAN (4186 "Tell Me So") ... 10-20 64
V-TONE (216 "Remember Me") ... 5-10 61

JOHNSON, Holly P&R '89
Singles: 7-inch
UNI ... 3-4 89
Also see FRANKIE GOES to HOLLYWOOD

JOHNSON, Howard
Singles: 7-inch
SHOUT ... 3-6 69-70

JOHNSON, Howard R&B/LP '82
Singles: 12-inch
A&M ... 4-6 82-85
Singles: 7-inch
A&M ... 3-4 82-85
LPs: 10/12-inch
A&M ... 5-8 82-85
Also see NITEFLYTE

JOHNSON, Hoyt
Singles: 7-inch
ERWIN (555 "Eenie Meany Minie Mo") ... 100-200 57
RCA ... 5-10 59-60
SATELLITE ... 5-10 61

JOHNSON, Ike & Dee Dee
Singles: 7-inch
INNIS (3002 "The Drag") ... 10-20 64
(Reportedly Ike Turner.)
Also see TURNER, Ike

JOHNSON, J.
Singles: 7-inch
BELL (953 "Never Let Me Go") ... 3-5 70

JOHNSON, Jack
LPs: 10/12-inch
EARWIG ... 5-8 87

JOHNSON, Jack, Frank Frost, & Sam Carr
LPs: 10/12-inch
EARWIG ... 8-10 79
Also see FROST, Frank
Also see JOHNSON, Jack

JOHNSON, Jackie
Singles: 7-inch
TULANE (106 "Too Late") ... 10-20
WILLAMETTE (102 "Star Light, Star Bright") ... 35-45 59

JOHNSON, James Arthur R&B '86
Singles: 7-inch
TUXEDO MUSIC ... 3-4 86

JOHNSON, Jan
Singles: 7-inch
WAHOO ... 4-8 68

JOHNSON, Janice Marie R&B '84
Singles: 7-inch
CAPITOL ... 3-4 84
Also see TASTE of HONEY

JOHNSON, Jeanie
Singles: 7-inch
RCA ... 4-8 60
Picture Sleeves
RCA ... 4-8 60

JOHNSON, Jena
Singles: 7-inch
D-TOWN ... 3-5 80

JOHNSON, Jess
(Jesse Johnson)
Singles: 7-inch
CROSS ROADS ... 5-10
SYMBOL ... 5-10 59

JOHNSON, Jesse
Singles: 7-inch
OLD TOWN (1195 "Left Out") ... 50-100 66

JOHNSON, Jesse P&R/R&B/D&D/LP '85
(Jesse Johnson's Revue)
Singles: 12-inch
A&M ... 4-6 85-88
(Black vinyl.)
A&M ... 5-8 85-88
(Colored vinyl.)
Singles: 7-inch
A&M ... 3-4 85-88
OLD TOWN ... 3-5 66
Picture Sleeves
A&M ... 3-4 85-88
LPs: 10/12-inch
A&M ... 5-10 85-88
Also see TIME

JOHNSON, Jesse, & Sly Stone P&R/R&B '86
Singles: 7-inch
A&M ... 3-4 86
Also see JOHNSON, Jesse
Also see STONE, Sly

JOHNSON, Jimmy
(Jim Johnson)
Singles: 78 rpm
VIV (3000 "Cat Daddy") ... 50-75 56
Singles: 7-inch
CLASS (237 "Cool, Cool School") ... 15-25 58
MAGNUM ... 8-12
MID WEST (1002 "Mean Woman Blues") ... 175-225
RENDEZVOUS (145 "Cool, Cool School") ... 10-15 61
VIV (3000 "Cat Daddy") ... 150-200 56
LPs: 10/12-inch
ALLIGATOR ... 8-10
DELMARK ... 10-20
Also see FLEETWOOD, Jimmy

JOHNSON, Jimmy R&B '65
(With His Band featuring Hank Alexander)
Singles: 7-inch
MAGNUM ... 4-8 65

JOHNSON, Joe
Singles: 7-inch
A-BET (9417 "Dirty Woman Blues") ... 5-8 66
CASCADE (5909 "Cool Love") ... 15-25 59

JOHNSON, Joe D.
Singles: 7-inch
ACME (45 "First After You") ... 75-100 62
(Black and silver label. Has a large "A" in the middle of the name, like this: "ACAME.")
ACME (45 "First After You") ... 25-35 63
(Black and orange label. Has a large "A" in the middle of the name "Acme.")
ACME (46 "Last Letter") ... 50-75 63
(Black and silver label. Has a large "A" in the middle of the name "Acme.")
ACME (46 "Last Letter") ... 20-30 63
(Black and orange label. Has a large "A" in the middle of the name "Acme.")
ACME (47 "Rattlesnake Daddy") ... 150-200 59
(Red label. No "A" in the middle of the name "Acme.")
ACME (47 "Rattlesnake Daddy") ... 50-75 63
(Black and silver label. Has a large "A" in the middle of the name "Acme.")
ACME (47 "Rattlesnake Daddy") ... 20-30 63
(Black and orange label. Has a large "A" in the middle of the name "Acme.")
ACME (48 "Beneath the Arizona Moon") ... 30-60 64
(Black and silver label. Has a large "A" in the middle of the name "Acme.")
ACME (48 "Beneath the Arizona Moon") ... 20-30 64
(Black and orange label. Has a large "A" in the middle of the name "Acme.")
Members: Joe D. Johnson; Leland Matthew; Dean Narramore; Bob Mack; Rudy Alcorts; David Bittick; Pete Pittman; Beau Pittman; George Edmunds; John Allan; Charlie Murphy; Brent Pace; Herschel Menchue; Joe Flood.
Also see PACE, Brent

JOHNSON, Johnny
Singles: 7-inch
ASSAULT ... 4-8 62

JOHNSON, Johnny, & Bandwagon
Singles: 7-inch
BELL ... 4-6 70
DIRECTION ... 5-8 66
EPIC ... 4-6 69
LPs: 10/12-inch
EPIC ... 10-20 69

JOHNSON, Joshua
Singles: 78 rpm
CAPITOL ... 8-12 50
Singles: 7-inch
CAPITOL (1180 "Pile Driver Boogie") ... 20-30 50

JOHNSON, Kay
Singles: 7-inch
PAMELA ... 5-10 60
WILLAMETTE ... 5-10 59

JOHNSON, Kevin P&R '73
Singles: 7-inch
MAINSTREAM ... 3-5 73

JOHNSON, Kripp
(With the Dell Vikings; Krip Johnson; "Lead Singer of Whispering Bells"; "The Dell Viking Kripp Johnson"; "The Dell Viking Kripp Johnson.")
Singles: 7-inch
DOT (15636 "I'm Spinning") ... 15-25 57
FEE BEE (218-A "I'm Spinning") ... 75-100 57
(Reissued as by the "Dell-Vikings.")
MERCURY (71436 "Everlasting") ... 15-25 59
MERCURY (71486 "A Door That Is Open") ... 15-25 59
Also see BLACK EYED PEAS
Also see RICHIE & RUNAROUNDS

JOHNSON, Kripp, & Chuck Jackson
("The Dell Viking Kripp Johnson and Charles Jackson")
Singles: 7-inch
DOT (15673 "Willette") ... 20-30 57
FEE BEE (221 "Willette") ... 50-100 57
(Reissued as by the "Dell-Vikings.")
Also see DEL-VIKINGS
Also see JACKSON, Chuck
Also see JOHNSON, Kripp

JOHNSON, L.V. R&B '80
Singles: 7-inch
ICA ... 3-4 80-81
LPs: 10/12-inch
ICHIBAN ... 5-10

JOHNSON, Laurie, Orchestra
Singles: 7-inch
COLPIX ... 4-8 64
HBR ... 4-8 66
Picture Sleeves
HBR ... 5-10 66
LPs: 10/12-inch
COLPIX ... 10-15 64

JOHNSON, Larry
Singles: 7-inch
BLUE SOUL ... 5-8 66
LPs: 10/12-inch
PRESTIGE ... 12-15 66

JOHNSON, Larry
Singles: 7-inch
ZORRO ... 4-8

JOHNSON, La Vera
Singles: 7-inch
BELINDA (103 "Foolish Lies") ... 5-10 60s
JULIE (603 "Call My Name") ... 5-10 64

JOHNSON, Lee
Singles: 7-inch
ARNOLD ... 5-10 61

JOHNSON, Len
(With the Hi-Lighters)
Singles: 7-inch
RAY-CO (503 "Sweet Thing") ... 8-12 60s
VENDED (107 "Nobody But You") ... 15-25 61

JOHNSON, Lenny
Singles: 7-inch
BETHLEHEM ... 5-10 62

JOHNSON, Leonard
Singles: 7-inch
ARVEE ... 8-12 59

JOHNSON, Leroy
Singles: 78 rpm
FREEDOM ... 15-25 49
OKEH (6813 "Unlucky Blues") ... 10-15 51
Singles: 7-inch
OKEH (6813 "Unlucky Blues") ... 20-30 51

JOHNSON, Lester, & Hornets
Singles: 7-inch
WAY OUT ("Wedding Day") ... 100-200 62
(No selection number used.)
Also see IVERSON, Ben, & Hornets

JOHNSON, Lil
Singles: 78 rpm
BLUEBIRD ... 15-25
CHAMPION ... 15-25
VOCALION ... 20-40

JOHNSON, Lil' Ernie: see JOHNSON, Ernie

JOHNSON, Lois C&W '69
Singles: 7-inch
COLUMBIA ... 3-6 69
MGM ... 3-5 70-73
POLYDOR ... 3-5 76-78
20TH FOX ... 3-5 74-75
LP: 10/12-inch
20TH FOX ... 8-12 74
Also see WILLIAMS, Hank, Jr., & Lois Johnson

JOHNSON, Lois, & Bill Rice C&W '77
Singles: 7-inch
POLYDOR ... 3-5 77
Also see JOHNSON, Lois
Also see RICE, Bill

JOHNSON, Lonnie P&R/R&B '48
(With Victoria Spivey)
Singles: 78 rpm
ALADDIN ... 15-25 47
ARCO ... 15-25
BLUEBIRD ... 15-25 38-44
DECCA ... 15-25 30s
DISC ... 15-25 46-47
GROOVE ... 10-20 55
HOLIDAY ... 15-25 48
KING ... 15-25 47-57
OKEH ... 25-75
PARADISE ... 15-25 52
RCA ... 15-25 46-50
RAMA ... 10-20 56
SCORE ... 15-25 49
Singles: 7-inch
FEDERAL (12376 "What a Real Woman") ... 10-15 60
GROOVE (5003 "He's a Jelly-Roll Baker") ... 25-50 55
KING (4201 "Tomorrow Night") ... 50-75 51
KING (4400 thru 4600 series) ... 30-60 50-53
KING (4700 thru 4900 series) ... 20-40 54-56
KING (5000 series) ... 10-20 57-65
KING (6000 series) ... 4-6 70
PRESTIGE ... 5-10 60-64
RAMA (9 "My Woman Is Gone") ... 25-50 53
(Black vinyl.)
RAMA (9 "My Woman Is Gone") ... 50-100 53
(Red vinyl.)
RAMA (14 "Stick with Me Baby") ... 30-40 53
RAMA (19 "It's Been So Long") ... 30-40 53
RAMA (20 "This Love of Mine") ... 30-40 53
EPs: 7-inch
KING (267 "Lonnie Johnson") ... 50-100 54
LPs: 10/12-inch
BLUES BOY ... 8-12
COLLECTOR'S CLASSICS (30 "Masters of the Blues") ... 10-15
KING (520 "Lonesome Road") ... 1000-1500 56
KING (958 "12 Bar Blues") ... 15-20 66
KING (1083 "Tomorrow Night") ... 10-15 70
PRESTIGE (7724 "Losing Game") ... 10-15 69
PRESTIGE BLUESVILLE (1007 "Blues By Lonnie") ... 30-50 60
PRESTIGE BLUESVILLE (1024 "Losing Game") ... 30-50 61
PRESTIGE BLUESVILLE (1044 "Idle Hours") ... 30-50 61
PRESTIGE BLUESVILLE (1054 "Woman Blues") ... 20-40 62
PRESTIGE BLUESVILLE (1062 "Another Night to Cry") ... 20-40 63
ROOTS N' BLUES ... 5-8 90
Also see SPIVEY, Victoria
Also see THREE KINGS & A QUEEN

JOHNSON, Lonnie, & Elmer Snowden
LPs: 10/12-inch
PRESTIGE BLUESVILLE (1011 "Blues & Ballads") 30-50 61

JOHNSON, Lonnie / George Dawson's Chocolateers
Singles: 78 rpm
PARADE 5-15 52
Also see JOHNSON, Lonnie

JOHNSON, Lorraine
Singles: 7-inch
ATLANTIC (2967 "Can I Hold You to It") 15-25 73

JOHNSON, Lou P&R/R&B '63
Singles: 7-inch
BIG HILL (Except 554) 4-8 64-66
BIG HILL (554 "Park Avenue") 10-15 65
BIG TOP 6-12 62-67
COTILLION 5-10 68-69
HILLTOP 5-10 64
VOLT 4-6 71
LPs: 10/12-inch
COTILLION 10-15 69
VOLT 8-12 71

JOHNSON, Louis
Singles: 7-inch
PALMS 4-8

JOHNSON, Luther
(Luther Houserocker Johnson)
LPs: 10/12-inch
ICHIBAN 5-10
MUSE 20-30

JOHNSON, Luther, & Muddy Waters Blues Band
LPs: 10/12-inch
DOUGLAS 10-15 68-69

JOHNSON, Mack, Combo
(Mack Johnson Combo)
Singles: 7-inch
SOLAR 10-15 63
XLP 5-10 63

JOHNSON, Marv P&R/R&B '59
(With the Band of Harold "Beans" Bowles; with Rayber Voices)
Singles: 78 rpm
U.A. (160 "Come to Me") 50-75 59
(Canadian.)
Singles: 7-inch
GORDY 8-12 65-68
KUDO (663 "My Baby-O") 200-300 58
TAMLA (101 "Come To Me") 200-300 59
(No company address shown.)
TAMLA (101-G1 "Come to Me") 175-225 59
(Has Gladstone St. Address under "Tamla.")
U.A. 10-25 59-64
EPs: 7-inch
U.A. (10,007 "Marv Johnson") 30-40 60
U.A. (10,009 "Marv Johnson") 30-40 60
LPs: 10/12-inch
U.A. (3081 "Marvelous Marv Johnson") 50-75 60
(Monaural.)
U.A. (3084 "More Marv Johnson") 50-75 60
(Monaural.)
U.A. (3187 "I Believe") 25-50 62
(Monaural.)
U.A. (6081 "Marvelous Marv Johnson") 75-125 60
(Stereo.)
U.A. (6081 "More Marv Johnson") 60-100 60
(Stereo.)
U.A. (6187 "I Believe") 40-60 62
(Stereo.)
Also see HOLLAND, Eddie
Also see PETERS, Nancy

JOHNSON, Marvin, & His Orchestra
(Vocal by Calvin Boze.)
Singles: 78 rpm
G&G (1029 "Safronia Bee") 50-75 47
Also see BOZE, Calvin

JOHNSON, Mary
Singles: 7-inch
FEDERAL (12506 "You Have My Blessings") 5-10 63

JOHNSON, Meat Head
(Champion Jack Dupree)
Singles: 78 rpm
APEX 15-25 50
GOTHAM 10-12 50
Also see DUPREE, Champion Jack

JOHNSON, Michael P&R/R&B/LP '78
Singles: 7-inch
ATCO 3-5 73
EMI AMERICA 3-5 78-80
RCA 3-4 86-88
Picture Sleeves
EMI AMERICA 3-5 78
LPs: 10/12-inch
ATCO 8-10 73
EMI AMERICA 5-8 78-82
Session: Michael Young; Russ Pahl; Denny Dadmum-Bixby.
Also see BACK PORCH MAJORITY
Also see DENVER, BOISE & JOHNSON
Also see GREAT PLAINS
Also see MITCHELL TRIO
Also see SYLVIA & Michael Johnson

JOHNSON, Mirriam
(Miriam Johnson)
Singles: 7-inch
JAMIE (1181 "Young and Innocent") 10-15 61
Picture Sleeves
JAMIE (1181 "Young and Innocent") 15-25 61
Also see COLTER, Jessie
Also see EDDY, Duane & Mirriam

JOHNSON, Neal
Singles: 7-inch
SPECIALTY 5-10 60

JOHNSON, Norman
Singles: 7-inch
INSTANT 8-10 65
Also see JOHNSON, General

JOHNSON, Orlando, & Trance D&D '83
Singles: 12-inch
EASYSTREET 4-6 83

JOHNSON, Paul
(Guitar Red)
Singles: 7-inch
KELLMAC (1009 "Red Rock") 10-20 63
Also see GUITAR RED

JOHNSON, Paul
Singles: 7-inch
SURFSIDE 3-5 81
Also see ALLAN, Davie
Also see P.J. & GALAXIES

JOHNSON, Paul R&B '88
Singles: 7-inch
EPIC 3-4 88

JOHNSON, Pete R&B '45
(Pete Johnson All-Star Orchestra)
Singles: 78 rpm
APOLLO 4-8 46-49
BRUNSWICK 4-8 44
DOWN BEAT 4-6 49
MODERN 4-6 47
NATIONAL 4-6 45-46
Singles: 7-inch
APOLLO 10-20 50s
EPs: 7-inch
APOLLO (608 "Pete Johnson") 15-25 50s
BRUNSWICK 10-20 55
LPs: 10/12-inch
SAVOY (14018 "Pete's Blues") 30-50 58
Also see AMMONS, Albert, & Pete Johnson
Also see BROOKS, Hadda / Pete Johnson
Also see TURNER, Joe

JOHNSON, Pete
Singles: 7-inch
CRYIN' in the STREETS 3-5 77

JOHNSON, Peter C.
LP: 10/12-inch
A&M (4723 "Peter C. Johnson") 5-10 77

JOHNSON, Phil, & Duvals / Royal Notes
(With Floyd Williams & Orchestra)
Singles: 7-inch
KELIT (7032 "Kisses Left Unkissed") 300-500 58
Also see ROYAL NOTES

JOHNSON, Plas
(With George Jenkins Orchestra)
Singles: 78 rpm
BEDFORD (505 "Last Call") 10-15 56
TAMPA 5-15 56-57
Singles: 7-inch
A.F.O. (501 "Lift Off") 8-12 60s
BEDFORD (505 "Last Call") 15-25 56
CAPITOL 10-20 58-61
JET 5-10
TAMPA 15-25 56-57
YANKEE DOODLE 4-8 62
LPs: 10/12-inch
CAPITOL 25-50 59-61
TAMPA (24 "On Tenor Sax") 50-75 57
Session:.
Also see EDDY, Duane
Also see JENKINS, George
Also see JOHNSON, Ray
Also see PETERSEN, Paul
Also see WILLIAMS, Larry

JOHNSON, Ralph
(With the Good Luck Charms)
Singles: 78 rpm
RALPH JOHNSON 50-75 55
Singles: 7-inch
RALPH JOHNSON (639 "Henpecked Daddy") 300-400 55
WEDGE (1007 "Hemphill Mine Blues") 50-100 50s

JOHNSON, Randy
LPs: 10/12-inch
AMARET 10-15 69

JOHNSON, Ray
(With the Hi-Liters; Red Johnson; Ray Johnson Combo)
Singles: 78 rpm
ALADDIN 8-12 57
BLEND 15-25 55
DOT 5-10 56
MERCURY 5-10 52-53
Singles: 7-inch
ALADDIN 10-20 57
BLEND (1002 "Gonna Roll Lucky Seven Tonight") 50-75 55
DOT 10-20 56
FLIP 10-20 58
GOAD (1002 "Cee-Cee Rider") 10-20 62
IMPERIAL (5709 "Miss Mary") 10-15 60
INFINITY (024 "Soul City") 8-10 62
LIBERTY 10-15 58
LOMA 5-8 66
MERCURY 10-20 52-53
RCA (7498 "Baby, Won't You Please Come Home") 10-15 59
RCA (7573 "Prayer of a Fool") 10-15 59
RCA (7737 "Sheik of Araby") 10-15 60
LPs: 10/12-inch
GOAD (1001 "Birth of a Scene") 20-30 62
Session: Plas Johnson.
Also see JOHNSON, Plas

JOHNSON, Red: see JOHNSON, Ray

JOHNSON, Rick
Singles: 7-inch
COMET 5-10 59

JOHNSON, Robert LP '90
Singles: 78 rpm
ORIOLE (7-04-60 "32-20 Blues") 1500-2500 37
VOCALION (03416 "Terraplane Blues") 500-1000 37
VOCALION (03475 "I Believe I'll Dust My Broom") 1000-2000 37
VOCALION (03445 "32/20 Blues") 1000-1500 37
VOCALION (03519 "Crossroads Blues") 1500-2500 37
VOCALION (03563 "Come On in My Kitchen") 1000-2000 37
VOCALION (03601 "Sweet Home Chicago") 1000-1500 37
VOCALION (03623 "Hell Hound on My Trail") 1000-2000 37
VOCALION (03665 "Milkcow's Calf Blues") 1000-2000 37
VOCALION (03723 "Stones in My Passway") 1000-2000 37
VOCALION (04002 "Stop Breakin' Down Blues") 1000-2000 38
VOCALION (04108 "Me and the Devil Blues") 1500-2500 38
VOCALION (04630 "Love in Vain Blues") 2000-3000 38
LPs: 10/12-inch
COLUMBIA (1654 "King of the Delta Blues Singers") 35-50 61
COLUMBIA (30034 "Robert Johnson, Vol. 2") 10-15 70
COLUMBIA (46222 "The Complete Recordings") 8-12 90
ROOTS 'N' BLUES 5-8 90

JOHNSON, Robert LP '79
Singles: 7-inch
INFINITY 3-5 78
LPs: 10/12-inch
INFINITY 5-8 78
Also see HOT DOGS

JOHNSON, Rockheart
Singles: 78 rpm
RCA 10-20 52
Singles: 7-inch
RCA (4967 "Evilest Woman in Town") 30-50 52
RCA (5136 "Black Spider") 30-50 52

JOHNSON, Roland C&W '59
Singles: 7-inch
BRUNSWICK 5-10 59

JOHNSON, Rolling Joe
Singles: 7-inch
NU-CLEAR 5-10 59

JOHNSON, Roy Lee
(With Doctor Feelgood & Interns)
Singles: 7-inch
COLUMBIA (43286 "My Best Just Ain't Good Enough") 15-25 65
COLUMBIA (43529 "Two Doors Down") 25-35 66
EPIC (2250 "Too Many Tears") 8-12 66
OKEH (7160 "Too Many Tears") 15-25 62
1-2-3 ....10-15 60s
JOSIE (965 "Boogaloo No. 3") 10-15 66
PHILIPS (40558 "She Put the Wammy on Me") 10-20 68
STAX 5-8 72
Also see DOCTOR FEELGOOD

JOHNSON, Rozetta P&R/R&B '70
(Rosetta Johnson)
Singles: 7-inch
ATLANTIC (2297 "It's Nice to Know") 40-80 65
CLINTONE 5-8 70-71

JOHNSON, Ruby R&B '66
Singles: 7-inch
NEBS 10-15 65
VOLT 10-20 66
V-TONE 10-20 60

JOHNSON, Sam "Suitcase"
Singles: 78 rpm
SITTIN' IN WITH (608 "Sam's Coming Home") 20-40 51

JOHNSON, Sherman
(With His Clouds of Joy)
Singles: 78 rpm
NASHBORO (507 "Back Alley Boogie") 20-30 51
TRUMPET 15-25 53

JOHNSON, Smokey
(Smokey Johnson & Company)
Singles: 7-inch
INTREPID 4-6 69
NOLA 4-8 66
NOLAN 4-8 60s

JOHNSON, Sonny, & Sunglows
Singles: 7-inch
CARIB (1025 "If You Don't Want My Love") 100-200

JOHNSON, Sonny Boy, & His Blue Blazers
Singles: 78 rpm
MURRAY (505 "Come and Go with Me") 50-100 48
MURRAY (507 "I'm Drinking My Last Drink") 50-100 48

JOHNSON, Spider
Singles: 7-inch
RIVERSIDE 4-8 62

JOHNSON, Stacie: see JOHNSON, Stacy

JOHNSON, Stacy
(Stacie Johnson)
Singles: 7-inch
M-PAC (7230 "Stand Alone") 8-12 66
MODERN (1001 "Consider Yourself") 15-25 64
MOTOWN 4-8 73
SONY (113 "Remove My Doubts") 25-50 63
Also see SHARPEES
Also see TURNER, Ike & Tina

JOHNSON, Stan
Singles: 7-inch
RUBY (100 "Big Black Train") 50-75 55
RUBY (280 "Shimmy & Shake") 50-75 57
RUBY (550 "Baby, Baby Doll") 50-75 58

JOHNSON, Stella
Singles: 7-inch
KRC 8-15 58
VIN 5-10 60

JOHNSON, Susan
Singles: 78 rpm
RCA 5-10 57
Singles: 7-inch
RCA 5-10 57

JOHNSON, Sweetpea
(Billy Strange)
Singles: 7-inch
LIBERTY (55315 "The Crawdad Scene") 15-25 61
Also see STRANGE, Billy

JOHNSON, Syl P&R/R&B '67
Singles: 12-inch
BOARDWALK 4-6 82
Singles: 7-inch
CHA CHA 10-20
EPIC 8-10
FEDERAL 12-25 59-62
HI 3-5 73-79
SHAMA 3-6 77
SPECIAL AGENT (20079 "Do You Know What Love Is") 15-25
TAG LTD. (1 "Surround") 15-25
TMP-TING 8-10 65
TWILIGHT 5-10 67-68
TWINIGHT 5-10 69
LPs: 10/12-inch
HI 8-10 73-75
TWINIGHT 10-15 68

JOHNSON, Terry
Singles: 7-inch
GORDY (7091 "My Springtime") ..50-100 69
GORDY (7095 "What 'Cha Gonna Do") 10-20 69

JOHNSON, Tim C&W '87
Singles: 7-inch
SUNDIAL 3-4 87

JOHNSON, Tommy
Singles: 7-inch
ASTRA 10-15

JOHNSON, Troy R&B '86
Singles: 7-inch
KALLISTA 3-4 86

JOHNSON, Vicki
(With the Vals)
Singles: 7-inch
UNIQUE LABORATORIES ("Bells Are Ringing") 75-100 62
(No selection number used.)
Also see VALS

JOHNSON, Wallace
Singles: 7-inch
A.F.O. 10-20 62
SANSU 5-10 68

JOHNSON, Walt
Singles: 7-inch
TOPPA 4-8 62

JOHNSON, Willie
(Bill Johnson)
Singles: 78 rpm
IMPERIAL (5163 "Tears Come Falling Down") 20-30 51
JADE (201 "Boogie in Blues") 20-30 51
JADE (209 "That Boy's Boogie") 20-30 52
REGAL 20-30 47
SAVOY 15-25 52
SITTIN' IN WITH (570 "Sampson Street Boogie") 20-30 50
SPECIALTY (493 "That Night") 10-20 54
Singles: 7-inch
SAVOY (881 "Here Comes My Baby") 35-50 52
SAVOY (894 "Sometimes I Wonder Why") 35-50 52
SPECIALTY (493 "That Night") 25-35 54
Also see GROOVY FIVE

JOHNSON, White Willie
EPs: 7-inch
BLUES ECONOMIQUE 8-10 79

JOHNSON BROTHERS
Singles: 7-inch
VALOR (2006 "Zombie Lou") 50-75 59

JOHNSON BROTHERS
Singles: 7-inch
CUCA (1014 "Like Rachel") 10-20 61
Members: Cliff Johnson; Chuck Johnson; John Cooke.

JOHNSON BROTHERS
Singles: 7-inch
(106242 "Roll Over Beethoven") 20-25
(No label name used.)

JOHNSON BROTHERS
Singles: 7-inch
IMPERIAL (5550 "Find Another Heart") 10-20 60s

JOHNSON, HAWKINS, TATUM & DURR
Singles: 7-inch
CAPSOUL 4-8

JOHNSON SISTERS
Singles: 7-inch
BROADWAY (400 "I Found My Peace") 10-20
JOSIE 5-10 64
KAPP 5-10 65
SWAN 5-10 62

JOHNSTON, Bruce
Singles: 12-inch 33/45
COLUMBIA (10567 "Pipeline") 8-10 77
Singles: 7-inch
COLUMBIA (10568 "Pipeline") 4-6 77
DEL-FI (4202 "The Original Surfer Stomp") 10-15 63
(First pressings credit the Surf Stompers.)
DONNA (1354 "Do the Surfer Stomp") 15-20 62
(First pressings credit the Surf Stompers.)
DONNA (1364 "Soupy Shuffle Stomp") 15-20 62
DONNA (1374 "The Original Surfer Stomp") 15-20 63
RONDA (1003 "Do the Surfer Stomp") 30-40 62
Picture Sleeves
DONNA (1354 "Do the Surfer Stomp") 40-50 62
LPs: 10/12-inch
COLUMBIA (2057 "Surfin' 'Round the World") 50-100 63
(Monaural.)
COLUMBIA (8857 "Surfin' 'Round the World") 75-150 63
(Stereo.)
COLUMBIA (34459 "Going Public") 10-15 77
DEL-FI (DFLP-1228 "Surfer's Pajama Party") 40-60 63
(Monaural.)
DEL-FI (DFST-1228 "Surfer's Pajama Party") 50-75 63
(Del-Fi 1228 also may be found as by the Centurians—or may credit both Bruce Johnston and the Centurians on the same cover. Copies also exist with one artist's name on the cover and the other on the disc.)
Members (Centurians): Dennis Rose; Ernie Furrow; Jeff Lear; Joe Dominic; Ken Robinson; Pat Gaguebin.
Also see CATALINAS
Also see BEACH BOYS
Also see BOBSLED & TOBAGGANS
Also see BRUCE & TERRY
Also see GAMBLERS
Also see HOLDEN, Ron
Also see HOT DOGGERS
Also see KUSTOM KINGS
Also see SIDEWALK SURFERS
Also see SLED, Bob & Tobbogons
Also see SURF STOMPERS
Also see VETTES

JOHNSTON, Chuck
Singles: 7-inch
BRUNSWICK 10-15 59
HOT (1001 "Weepin' & Wailin' ") 20-30 59

JOHNSTON, Day C&W '88
Singles: 7-inch
ROADRUNNER 3-4 88

JOHNSTON, Don
Singles: 78 rpm
CHIC (1014 "Whistle Bait") 10-20 57
MERCURY 15-25 56
Singles: 7-inch
CHIC (1014 "Whistle Bait") 10-20 57
MERCURY (70991 "Born to Love One Woman") 35-50 56

JOHNSTON, Inez
Singles: 7-inch
BRUNSWICK 5-10 60-61

JOHNSTON, Jay
Singles: 7-inch
FREEDOM 5-10 59
LIBERTY 5-10 59

JOHNSTON, Tom P&R/LP '79
Singles: 7-inch
W.B. 3-5 79-81
LPs: 10/12-inch
W.B. 5-8 79-81
Also see CHARADES
Also see DOOBIE BROTHERS

Also see IMPLICITS

JOHNSTON BROTHERS
Singles: 78 rpm
LONDON 4-6 54
Singles: 7-inch
LONDON (1470 "The Bandit") 8-10 54

JOHNSTONS C&W '87
Singles: 7-inch
HIDDEN VALLEY 3-4 87
TETRAGRAMMATON 4-6 68-69
LPs: 10/12-inch
MERCURY 8-10 72
TETRAGRAMMATON 10-15 69
VANGUARD 8-10 71

JOINER, ARKANSAS JUNIOR HIGH SCHOOL BAND P&R '60
(Ernie Freeman)
Singles: 7-inch
LIBERTY 8-12 60-61
Also see FREEMAN, Ernie

JOINT EFFORT
Singles: 7-inch
JOINT EFFORT (1 "Children") 20-30 67
RUBY DOO (10 "Loving You Could Be Magic") 10-20 60s
SPIRIT (127 "The Square") 10-20 60s

JOINT EFFORT
LPs: 10/12-inch
HOME MADE (11034 "Two-Sided Country Blues") 10-15 71

JOINT EFFORT
LPs: 10/12-inch
AMPHION SEAHORSE (8100 "Cannabis") 50-80 72
Members: Keith Tweedly; Gary Wilkinson; Bob Randell; Tony Rodriguez; Brian Kelly; Lonny Gasperini.

JOINT EFFORT
Singles: 7-inch
DEEEK (104 "Country") 8-12

JOINT VENTURE
Singles: 7-inch
DIAMOND (268 "Sweet Smoke") 4-8 69
HI 3-5 72

JOKERS
Singles: 7-inch
LIN (5027 "Dogfight") 15-25 60
Members: Dave Spencer; Bob Welz; Don Hosek; Joe Cook; Ray Cochran.

JOKERS
(With the Aztec Combo)
Singles: 7-inch
DANCO (117 "I Do") 500-1000 60
Also see DARLENE & JOKERS

JOKERS
Singles: 7-inch
DRUMFIRE (3 "One Million B.C.") 10-20 60

JOKERS
Singles: 7-inch
GRACE (510 "Little Mama") 150-250 61
(At least one source shows this release as Greco 609. Whether it appeared on Grace, Greco, or both, we have yet to confirm.)
WAND (111 "Whisper") 400-600 61
(Black vinyl.)
WAND (111 "Whisper") 500-1000 61
(Colored vinyl.)

JOKERS
Singles: 7-inch
BRUNSWICK 5-8 64

JOKERS
Singles: 7-inch
BRO-KET (101 "Arkansas Twist") 10-20 60s

JOKERS WILD
Singles: 7-inch
METROBEAT (4451 "All I See Is You") 25-35 68
PEAK 25-35 68
Also see COOKIEFOOT
Also see JOHNSON, Denny
Also see RAVE-ONS

JOLAIRS
Singles: 7-inch
DELMAR 3-5

JOLI, France P&R/R&B/LP '79
Singles: 12-inch
EPIC 4-6 83-85
Singles: 7-inch
EPIC 3-4 83-85
PRELUDE 3-5 79-82
LPs: 10/12-inch
EPIC 5-8 83-85
PRELUDE 5-8 79-80

JOLLIVER ARKANSAS
Singles: 7-inch
BELL 3-6 69
LPs: 10/12-inch
BELL 10-15 69
Also see BO GRUMPUS

JOLLY, Clarence
Singles: 78 rpm
COBRA (5016 "Don't Leave Me") 75-100 57

JOLLY, Jack
Singles: 7-inch
MUSIC TOWN (212 "Johnnie Skid Row") 40-60

JOLLY, Pete LP '63
(Pete Jolly Trio & Friends)
Singles: 7-inch
A&M 3-5 68-69
AVA 4-8 63-64
COLUMBIA 3-6 66
MAINSTREAM 3-6 69
LPs: 10/12-inch
A&M 8-12 68-71
AVA 10-20 63-64
CHARLIE PARKER 15-20 62
COLUMBIA 10-20 65
MGM 8-15 63
METROJAZZ 15-25 60
RCA (1100 thru 1300 series) 20-30 55-57
TRIP 5-8 75
Also see MONTEZ, Chris

JOLLY GREEN GIANTS
Singles: 7-inch
REDCOAT (101 "Caught You Red Handed") 15-25 66

JOLLY JACKS
Singles: 7-inch
LANDA 5-10 64
V-TONE (233 "There's Something on Your Mind") 15-25 62

JOLLY JAX
Singles: 7-inch
AIRMASTER 5-10
DASHER 5-10 61
MONTICELLO 5-10 62

JOLLY JESTERS
Singles: 7-inch
CRYSTALETTE 5-10 59

JOLLY JOKER
Singles: 7-inch
RENDEZVOUS 4-8 63

JOLLY OLLIE
Singles: 7-inch
JOHNSON (128 "That's What True Love Can Do") 15-25 63

JOLLY ROCKERS
Singles: 7-inch
MARK X 8-10 60

JOLO D&D '84
Singles: 12-inch
MEGATONE 4-6 84

JOMO
Singles: 7-inch
CHECKER 4-6 68

JON & IN CROWD
(Jon Abnor)
Singles: 7-inch
ABNAK 4-8 68
Also see JON & ROBIN

JON & LYNN C&W '81
Singles: 7-inch
SOUNDWAVES 3-4 81-82
Members: Jon Hargis; Lynn Hargis.

JON & NIGHTRIDERS
EPs: 7-inch
CALIFORNIA (101 "Jon and the Nightriders") 8-12 79
(Black vinyl.)
CALIFORNIA (101 "Jon and the Nightriders") 10-20 79
(Colored vinyl.)
INVASION 5-8 82
LPs: 10/12-inch
NORTON 8-10 90
RAMPART 8-15 80
VOXX 8-10 80-81
Members: John Blair; Nikki Syxx; Dusty Watson; Jeff Nicholson; George White.
Also see MOTLEY CRUE

JON & PAUL
(Jon-Paul Twins)
Singles: 7-inch
PALOMAR 5-10 64

JON & ROBIN P&R '67
(With the In Crowd)
Singles: 7-inch
ABNAK 4-8 67-68
LPs: 10/12-inch
ABNAK 15-20 67-68
Members: Jon Abnor; Robin Abnor.
Also see ABNOR, Jon
Also see JON & In Crowd
Also see ROBIN

JON & VANGELIS P&R/LP '80
Singles: 7-inch
POLYDOR 3-5 77-83
LPs: 10/12-inch
POLYDOR 5-8 80-83
Members: Jon Anderson; Vangelis.
Also see ANDERSON, Jon
Also see VANGELIS

JONAE, Gwen D&D '83
Singles: 12-inch
ARIAL 4-6 83
C&M 4-6 83

JONAH
LPs: 10/12-inch
20TH FOX 8-10 74

JONATHAN & Long Island Sound
Singles: 7-inch
TEAM 8-15

JONES, A.C.
(With the Atomic Aces)
Singles: 7-inch
IMPERIAL (66150 "Hole in Your Soul") 5-10 66
LULA (5587 "Ooh Baby") 15-25 60s
LUAU (5588 "Hole in Your Soul") 10-20 63

JONES, Al
Singles: 7-inch
GLENMAR 4-8 65
JAMIE 4-8 63
POPLAR 5-10 57

JONES, Albert
Singles: 7-inch
KAPP (2100 "It's Going to Be a Lovely Summer") 10-20 70
TRI-CITY 5-10

JONES, Ann C&W '49
Singles: 78 rpm
CAPITOL 5-10 49
KING 4-8 51
SIMS 5-10 55
Singles: 7-inch
KING 5-15 51-61
SIMS (101 "Kind of Love I'm Craving") 15-25 55
LP: 10/12-inch
AUDIO LAB 20-30

JONES, Anthony Armstrong C&W '69
Singles: 7-inch
AIR 3-4 86
CHART 3-6 69-70
EPIC 3-5 73
LP: 10/12-inch
CHART 8-12 69-70
Also see TWITTY, Conway

JONES, Art
(Al Casey)
Singles: 78 rpm
OLD TIMER 4-8
WESTERN JUBILEE 4-8
Singles: 7-inch
OLD TIMER 5-10
WESTERN JUBILEE 5-10
Also see CASEY, Al

JONES, Barry
Singles: 7-inch
DIAL 4-6 68

JONES, Bessie
Singles: 7-inch
A-BET (9424 "No More Tears") 5-10 67

JONES, Beverly
Singles: 7-inch
SWAN 4-8 65

JONES, Billy, & Squires
(Billy Fortune)
Singles: 7-inch
DECK (478 "Listen to Your Heart") 40-60
(Previously issued as by Billy Fortune.)
Also see FORTUNE, Billy

JONES, Billy, & Teenettes
Singles: 7-inch
CARELLEN (102 "Night Angel") 25-50 61
NET (101 "I Would Never Dare") 25-50 61
Also see BETTY JANE & TEENETTES

JONES, Bob
Singles: 7-inch
WEB 5-10

JONES, Bob, & Bobcats
Singles: 7-inch
BO-JO (100 "Tennessee Twister") 10-20 62

JONES, Bobby
(With the Para-monts)
Singles: 7-inch
EXPO 4-8 68
KITTEN 8-12 62
U.S.A. 5-10 67
Also see PAULINE & BOBBY

JONES, Brenda R&B '82
(Brenda Lee Jones)
Singles: 7-inch
FLYING DUTCHMAN 3-5 76
MERCURY 3-5 74
RUST 4-8 66
WAVE 3-4 82
Also see DEAN & JEAN
Also see LEE, Brenda

JONES, Brenda, & "Groove" Holmes
Singles: 7-inch
FLYING DUTCHMAN 3-5 76
Also see HOLMES, Richard "Groove"
Also see JONES, Brenda

JONES, Brian
LPs: 10/12-inch
ROLLING STONES (49100 "Pipes of Pan") 10-15 71
Promotional LPs
ROLLING STONES (49100 "Pipes of Pan") 30-35 71
(Includes poster and cue sheets.)
Also see ROLLING STONES

JONES, Buster
Singles: 7-inch
PHIL. L.A. of SOUL 5-10 69
SURE SHOT 8-18 66-67

JONES, Calvert
Singles: 7-inch
CORAL (65056 "Tra La La") 35-50 51

JONES, Carl
Singles: 7-inch
C.J. 3-5 77

JONES, Chuck
Singles: 7-inch
BELLE MEADE 5-10 60-61

JONES, Commonwealth
(Ronnie Dawson)
Singles: 7-inch
BANNER 15-25 63
COLUMBIA 10-15 62
Also see DAWSON, Ronnie

JONES, Corky
(Buck Owens)
Singles: 78 rpm
DIXIE 50-75 56
PEP 50-100 56
Singles: 7-inch
DIXIE (505 "Rhythm & Booze") 75-125 56
PEP (107 "Hot Dog") 150-250 56
(Rerecorded in 1958, credited to Buck Owens.)
Also see OWENS, Buck

JONES, Curtis
Singles: 78 rpm
CONQUEROR (9030 "You Got Good Business") 25-50 37
OKEH 15-30 36-41
PARROT (782 "Wrong Blues") 50-100 53
VOCALION 10-20 30s
Singles: 7-inch
PARROT (782 "Wrong Blues") 300-400 53
LPs: 10/12-inch
BLUE HORIZON 10-12 69
DELMARK 15-20 63
PRESTIGE BLUESVILLE 15-25 61
Also see MEMPHIS SLIM & Curtis Jones

JONES, David
(With the Dolphins; Davy Jones Quartet)
Singles: 78 rpm
AUDICON (116 "Strictly Polynesian") 8-12 62
(Promotional issue only.)
Singles: 7-inch
APT 10-15 61-62
AUDICON 10-15 62
GLADES (601 "No More Tears") 35-50 59
SHEPHERD (2205 "My Son, the Surfer") 15-25 63
SINCLAIR (1005 "Annabelle Lee") 15-25 61
TOWER 5-10 68
20TH FOX 5-10 61

JONES, David Lynn C&W '87
Singles: 7-inch
MERCURY 3-4 87-88
Session: Waylon Jennings.
Also see JENNINGS, Waylon

JONES, Davy P&R '65
(David Jones)
Singles: 7-inch
BELL 8-10 71-72
COLPIX 10-20 65
MGM 10-15 72-73
MY FAVORITE MONKEE–DAVY JONES SINGS ("A Little Bit Me, a Little Bit You") 50-100 67
(Promotional issue only. No selection number used.)
Picture Sleeves
COLPIX (764 "Dream Girl") 20-30 65
COLPIX (784 "What Are We Going to Do") 20-30 65
COLPIX (789 "Girl from Chelsea") 20-30 65
LPs: 10/12-inch
BELL (6067 "Davy Jones") 15-25 71
COLPIX (CP-493 "David Jones") 20-25 65
(Monaural.)
COLPIX (SCP-493 "David Jones") 25-30 65
(Stereo.)
Also see NILSSON, Harry

JONES, Davy, & Mickey Dolenz
Singles: 7-inch
BELL 8-10 71
MCA 3-5 78
Picture Sleeves
MCA 3-5 78

JONES, Davy, Mickey Dolenz, & Peter Tork
LPs: 10/12-inch
RHINO/FOSHOFF (71110 "20th Anniversary Tour") 20-30 87
Also see JONES, Davy
Also see DOLENZ, Micky
Also see MONKEES

JONES, Deacon Dale
Singles: 78 rpm
COAST 10-20 47
Singles: 7-inch
ABC-PAR 5-10 62

JONES, Dean
Singles: 7-inch
ABC-PAR 8-12 62
LIBERTY 5-8 62

JONES, Dizzy
Singles: 7-inch
NEW BREED 4-8 65-66

JONES, Doc: see JONES, Willie

JONES, Dorothy
Singles: 7-inch
COLUMBIA 4-8 61
Picture Sleeves
COLUMBIA 4-8 61

JONES, E. Rodney
Singles: 7-inch
DOUBLE SOUL 10-20
TUFF 5-8
TWILIGHT 5-8 73
WESTBOUND 8-12

JONES, Eddie
(Eddie "Guitar Slim" Jones; with His Playboys)
Singles: 78 rpm
IMPERIAL 20-40 51
JIM BULLET 40-60 52
Singles: 7-inch
J-B (Black vinyl) 3-5 79
J-B (Colored vinyl) 4-8 79
JIM BULLET (603 "Feelin' Sad") 100-150 52
Also see GUITAR SLIM

JONES, Elaine, & Tri-Dells
Singles: 7-inch
ANGEL-TOWN ("They're Doin' It") 25-35
(Selection number not known.)

JONES, Elmer
Singles: 7-inch
COZY (581 "Lazy Man's Blues") 8-12

JONES, Etta P&R/R&B '60
Singles: 7-inch
KING 4-8 61-62
PRESTIGE 4-8 60-65
20TH FOX/WESTBOUND 3-5 75
LPs: 10/12-inch
GRAND PRIX 8-12 60s
KING (544 "Etta Jones Sings") 40-60 58
KING (707 "Etta Jones Sings") 35-50 61
MUSE 5-8 77-81
PRESTIGE (7100 & 7200 series) 25-50 60-63
(Yellow labels.)
PRESTIGE (7100 & 7200 series) 15-25 65
(Blue labels.)
PRESTIGE (7400 thru 7700 series) 10-20 67-70
ROULETTE 10-20 66
20TH FOX/WESTBOUND 5-10 75
Also see PARKER, Jack, & Etta Jones

JONES, Evon
Singles: 7-inch
DANIELS 4-8 65

JONES, Floyd
(With His Trio)
Singles: 78 rpm
CHESS (1498 "Dark Road") 50-100 52
CHESS (1527 "You Can't Live Long") 50-100 53
JOB (1001 "Big World") 50-100 52
Singles: 7-inch
JOB (1013 "Skinny Mama") 100-200 53
VEE JAY (111 "Schooldays on My Mind") 100-200 55
(Black vinyl.)
VEE JAY (111 "Schooldays on My Mind") 200-400 55
(Colored vinyl.)
VEE JAY (126 "Floyd's Blues") 200-400 55
(Black vinyl.)
VEE JAY (126 "Floyd's Blues") 500-750 55
(Colored vinyl.)

JONES, Gary
Singles: 7-inch
TYFILMS 3-5 79

JONES, Genie
Singles: 7-inch
FELSTED 5-10 59

JONES, George C&W '55
(With the Jones Boys; with Sonny Burns; Tina & Daddy)
Singles: 78 rpm
DIXIE (#534) 25-50 56
(With Sleepy La Beef. Title not known. 78 rpm EP. Not issued with cover.)
DIXIE (#535) 25-50 56
(78 rpm EP. Not issued with cover.)
MERCURY 10-25 57
STARDAY 10-25 54-57
Singles: 7-inch
D 4-8 65-66
EPIC 3-5 72-82
MERCURY (71000 & 72000 series) 5-15 57-64
MUSICOR 3-8 65-71
PROMOTIONAL COPIES ("The Race Is On") 20-25 64
(No label name other than "Promotional Copies," is shown on disc.)
RCA 3-5 72-74
STARDAY (Except 100 & 200 series) 4-8 64-71
STARDAY (100 & 200 series) 10-20 54-57
(Black vinyl.)
STARDAY (264 "Just One More") 30-40 56
(Colored vinyl.)
U.A. 4-8 62-67
Picture Sleeves
MERCURY 8-12 62-64
MUSICOR 5-10 65
U.A. 5-10 62-63
EPs: 7-inch
DIXIE (501 "Why Baby Why") 25-50 56
(Not issued with cover.)
DIXIE (505 "Heartbreak Hotel") 25-50 56
(Not issued with cover.)
DIXIE (516 "Poor Old Me") 25-50 56
(Not issued with cover.)
DIXIE (525 "Don't Do This to Me") 15-25 59
(Has one George Jones track. Not issued with cover.)
MERCURY 10-20 61

RECORD of the MONTH (280 "Heartbreak Hotel") ... 30-40 56
(Colored vinyl.)
STARDAY ... 8-15 65
(Juke box issues. May include title strips.)

LPs: 10/12-inch

ACCORD ... 4-6 82
ALBUM GLOBE ... 5-8 81
ALLEGIANCE ... 4-8 84
AMBASSADOR ... 5-8
AURA ... 5-8 82
BUCKBOARD ... 5-8 76
BULLDOG ... 8-10
CAMDEN ... 5-8 72-74
COLUMBIA ... 5-8 80-83
EPIC ... 10-30 72-82
EVEREST ... 5-8 79
51 WEST ... 5-8 79-82
GRASS COUNTRY ... 8-10 80s
GUEST STAR ... 8-12 63
GUSTO ... 5-8 78-81
I&M ... 5-8 82
KOALA ... 5-8
K-TEL ... 5-8
LIBERTY ... 5-8 82
MCA ... 3-4 91-92
MERCURY (8000 series) ... 5-10 72
MERCURY (20306 "14 Country Favorites") ... 40-60 58
MERCURY (20462 "Country Church Time") ... 40-60 59
MERCURY (20477 "White Lightning") ... 40-60 59
MERCURY (20621 thru 20836) ... 20-30 60-63
(Monaural.)
MERCURY (20906 thru 21048) ... 20-30 64-65
(Monaural.)
MERCURY (60257 thru 60836) ... 25-35 60-63
(Stereo.)
MERCURY (60906 thru 61048) ... 15-25 64-65
(Stereo.)
MOUNTAIN DEW ... 5-8
MUSIC DISC ... 6-10 69
MUSICOR ... 10-20 65-77
MUSICOR/RCA ... 10-20 74-75
NASHVILLE ... 10-20 70-71
PAIR ... 6-10 70s
PHOENIX 10 ... 5-8 81
PHOENIX 20 ... 5-8 81
PICADILLY ... 5-8 81
PICKWICK ... 4-8 80
PICKWICK/HILLTOP ... 8-12 69
POWER PAK ... 5-8 75
RCA ... 10-20 72-75
ROUNDER ... 5-8 82-84
RUBY ... 5-8
SEARS ... 8-12
STARDAY (101 "The Grand Ole Opry's New Star") ... 100-150 58
STARDAY (102 "George Jones") ... 50-75 59
STARDAY (125 "George Jones: Crown Prince of Country Music") ... 50-75 60
STARDAY (150 "George Jones Sings His Greatest Hits") ... 40-60 62
STARDAY (151 "Fabulous Country Music Sound of George Jones") ... 40-60 62
STARDAY (335 "George Jones") ... 25-35 65
STARDAY (344 "Long Live King George") ... 25-35 65
STARDAY (366 "The George Jones Story") ... 25-35 66
(With bonus 8" x 10" color photo.)
STARDAY (366 "The George Jones Story") ... 15-25 66
(Without bonus photo.)
STARDAY (400 series, except 401) ... 15-20 69
STARDAY (401 "George Jones Song Book and Picture Album") ... 35-45 67
(With 32-page song booklet.)
STARDAY (401 "George Jones Song Book and Picture Album") ... 15-25 68
(Without song booklet.)
STARDAY (3000 series) ... 5-8 77
STARDAY (90000 series) ... 8-12
SUNRISE ... 5-8 81
TIME-LIFE ... 5-15 81-82
TRIP ... 5-8 76
TROLLY CAR ... 5-8
UNART ... 8-12 67-68
U.A. (85 "Superpak") ... 10-15 71
U.A. (100 series) ... 5-8 73
U.A. (3000 series) ... 10-20 62-67
(Monaural.)
U.A. (6000 series) ... 12-25 62-69
(Stereo.)
WHITE LIGHTNING ... 12-18
WING ... 8-12 64-68
WING/PICKWICK ... 4-6
Session: Jordanaires; Oak Ridge Boys.
Also see CHARLES, Ray, George Jones & Chet Atkins
Also see DARRELL, Johnny / George Jones / Willie Nelson
Also see HAGGARD, Merle, & George Jones
Also see JONES, Thumper
Also see JORDANAIRES
Also see OAK RIDGE BOYS
Also see PARTON, Dolly / George Jones
Also see SMITH, Hank
Also see TRAVIS, Randy, & George Jones
Also see TUBB, Ernest
Also see WILLIAMS, Hank, Jr.

JONES, George / Benny Barnes

EPs: 7-inch

DIXIE (518 "Stolen Moments") ... 25-50 56
(Not issued with cover.)
Also see BARNES, Benny

JONES, George, & Brenda Lee — *C&W '84*

Singles: 7-inch

EPIC ... 3-4 84
Also see LEE, Brenda

JONES, George, & Brenda Carter — *C&W '68*

Singles: 7-inch

MUSICOR ... 4-6 68

JONES, George, & David Allan Coe

Singles: 7-inch

COLUMBIA ... 3-4 81
Also see COE, David Allan

JONES, George, & Lacy J. Dalton — *C&W '85*

Singles: 7-inch

EPIC ... 3-4 85
Also see DALTON, Lacy J.

JONES, George, & Jeanette Hicks — *C&W '57*

Singles: 7-inch

STARDAY ... 5-8 57

Singles: 7-inch

STARDAY ... 10-20 57

JONES, George, & Alan Jackson

Singles: 7-inch

MCA ... 3-5 90s
Also see JACKSON, Alan

JONES, George, & Shelby Lynne — *C&W '88*

Singles: 7-inch

EPIC ... 3-4 88
Also see LYNNE, Shelby

JONES, George, & Melba Montgomery — *C&W '63*

Singles: 7-inch

CURIO ... 4-8 60s
MUSICOR ... 4-8 66-67
U.A. ... 4-8 63-66

Picture Sleeves

CURIO (7020 "You're in My Heart") ... 8-10 60s

LPs: 10/12-inch

BUCKBOARD ... 5-8 76
GUEST STAR ... 8-10 60s
LIBERTY ... 4-6 82
MUSIC DISC ... 6-10 69
MUSICOR ... 10-20 66-74
MUSICOR/RCA ... 10-20 74
U.A. (200 series) ... 5-8 73
U.A. (3000 series) ... 10-20 63-66
(Monaural.)
U.A. (6000 series) ... 12-25 63-66
(Stereo.)
Also see MONTGOMERY, Melba

JONES, George / Buck Owens / David Houston / Tommy Hill

LPs: 10/12-inch

NASHVILLE ... 10-15 60s
Also see HOUSTON, David
Also see OWENS, Buck

JONES, George, & Johnny Paycheck — *C&W '80*

Singles: 7-inch

EPIC ... 3-5 78-80

LPs: 10/12-inch

EPIC ... 5-8 80
Also see PAYCHECK, Johnny

JONES, George, & Gene Pitney — *C&W/LP '65*

(George & Gene, with the Jordanaires)

Singles: 7-inch

MUSICOR ... 4-8 65-66

Picture Sleeves

MUSICOR ... 5-10 65

LPs: 10/12-inch

DESIGN ... 6-10
INTERNATIONAL AWARD ... 8-10
MUSIC DISC ... 10-12 69
MUSICOR (3044 "George Jones & Gene Pitney") ... 15-25 65
(Front cover shows title as "For the First Time! Two Great Stars, George Jones & Gene Pitney.")
MUSICOR (3044 "George Jones & Gene Pitney") ... 15-20 65
(Front cover shows title as "Recorded in Nashville, Tennessee, George Jones & Gene Pitney.")
MUSICOR (3065 "It's Country Time Again") ... 10-20 65
TS (439 "Country Cousins") ... 5-10
Session: Jordanaires.
Also see JORDANAIRES
Also see PITNEY, Gene

JONES, George, Gene Pitney, & Melba Montgomery

LPs: 10/12-inch

MUSICOR ... 10-20 66
(Contains duets by these artists, but there are no tracks where all three perform together.)
Also see MONTGOMERY, Melba

JONES, George, & Margie Singleton — *C&W '61*

Singles: 7-inch

MERCURY ... 4-8 61-62

LPs: 10/12-inch

MERCURY (20747 "Duets") ... 15-25 62
(Monaural.)
MERCURY (60747 "Duets") ... 20-30 62
(Stereo.)
WING ... 10-15 66
Also see SINGLETON, Margie

JONES, George, & Ernest Tubb

Singles: 7-inch

FIRST GENERATION ... 3-4 81

JONES, George, & Tammy Wynette — *C&W/LP '71*

(George, Tammy & Tina)

Singles: 7-inch

EPIC ... 3-5 71-80

LPs: 10/12-inch

COLUMBIA ... 5-8 81
EPIC ... 8-12 71-81
TEE VEE/CBS ... 5-8 79
Also see JONES, George
Also see WYNETTE, Tammy

JONES, Geraldine

Singles: 7-inch

SONAR (101 "I'm Cracking Up") ... 15-25

JONES, Glenn — *R&B/D&D '83*

Singles: 12-inch

RCA ... 4-6 83-85

Singles: 7-inch

JIVE ... 3-4 87-88
RCA ... 3-4 83-87

Picture Sleeves

JIVE ... 3-4 87

LPs: 10/12-inch

JIVE ... 5-8 87
RCA ... 5-8 83-84
Also see JETER, Genobia, & Glenn Jones
Also see WARWICK, Dionne, & Glenn Jones

JONES, Gloria

Singles: 7-inch

CHAMPION ... 4-8 65
MINIT ... 4-6 68
MOTOWN ... 3-5 73-74
UPTOWN ... 4-8 66

LPs: 10/12-inch

MOTOWN ... 8-10 73
UPTOWN ... 10-20 66

JONES, Grace — *P&R/LP '77*

Singles: 12-inch

ISLAND ... 4-6 83
MANHATTAN ... 4-6 85

Singles: 7-inch

BEAM JUNCTION ... 3-5 76-77
ISLAND ... 3-5 78-83
MANHATTAN ... 3-4 85-86

Picture Sleeves

MANHATTAN ... 3-4 86

LPs: 10/12-inch

ISLAND ... 5-8 77-82
MANHATTAN ... 5-8 85-86

JONES, Grandpa — *C&W '59*

Singles: 78 rpm

KING ... 5-10 44-54
RCA ... 4-8 52-54

Singles: 7-inch

DECCA ... 5-10 59
KING ... 4-8 60-63
MONUMENT ... 4-6 62-67

EPs: 7-inch

DECCA ... 5-10 59
KING ... 5-15 50s

LP: 10/12-inch

CMH ... 5-10 76-81
CORAL ... 5-10 73
DECCA (4364 "Evening with Grandpa Jones") ... 15-25 63
HARMONY ... 6-12 72
KING (554 "Greatest Hits") ... 25-35 58
KING (625 "Strictly Country Tunes") ... 20-30 59
KING (809 "Rollin' Along") ... 15-25 63
KING (822 thru 1042) ... 10-20 63-69
MONUMENT ... 10-20 62-74
POWER PAK ... 5-10 80s
VOCALION ... 8-12 70

JONES, Grandpa / Minnie Pearl

LP: 10/12-inch

CAMDEN ... 5-10 74
Also see JONES, Grandpa
Also see MINNIE PEARL

JONES, Grant — *R&B '51*

(Grant "Mr. Blues" Jones & Brown's Blues Blowers)

Singles: 78 rpm

DECCA ... 15-25 50
STATES ... 15-25 52
UNITED ... 15-25 52

Singles: 7-inch

DECCA (48129 "For You, My Love") ... 50-75 50
DECCA (48133 "Crying Good Morning Blues") ... 50-75 50
DECCA (48163 "Hospitality Blues") ... 50-75 50
DECCA (48169 "It's Been a Long Time, Baby") ... 50-75 50
DECCA (48179 "Night Time Is the Right Time") ... 50-75 50
STATES (114 "Stormy Monday") ... 30-50 52
STEPHENY (1821 "Pinball Machine") ... 15-20 58
UNITED (112 "Strange Man") ... 30-40 52
UNITED (133 "Hello Stranger") ... 30-50 52

JONES, Harrison — *C&W '74*

Singles: 7-inch

GRT ... 3-5 74

JONES, Herman, & Kilts

("Featuring Tony La Mar")

Singles: 7-inch

GAYNOTE (105 "I'll Be True") ... 50-100 58

JONES, Hilliard

Singles: 7-inch

ERMINE (52 "Wish I Were the Wind") ... 15-25 64

JONES, Horace DeBussey

Singles: 7-inch

SATCH (1 "The O.J. Simpson Show") ... 3-6 95

JONES, Howard — *P&R/D&D/LP '84*

Singles: 12-inch

ELEKTRA ... 4-6 83-85

Singles: 7-inch

ELEKTRA ... 3-4 83-89

Picture Sleeves

ELEKTRA ... 3-4 84-89

LPs: 10/12-inch

ELEKTRA ... 5-8 83-89

JONES, Ignatius — *D&D '83*

Singles: 12-inch

W.B. ... 4-6 83

Singles: 7-inch

W.B. ... 3-4 83

JONES, Inez

Singles: 78 rpm

RCA ... 8-12 53

Singles: 7-inch

RCA (5135 "Take a Back Seat Mister Jackson") ... 20-30 53

JONES, J.J.

Singles: 7-inch

EBB ... 10-15 57-59
LITA ... 5-10 62
MOROCCO ... 10-15 58
Also see HODGE, Gaynel
Also see JONES, Jay J.

JONES, Jack — *P&R '62*

Singles: 7-inch

CAPITOL ... 4-8 59-60
KAPP ... 4-6 60-67
POLYDOR ... 3-5 83
RCA ... 3-6 67-77

Picture Sleeves

CAPITOL ... 5-10 59
KAPP ... 4-8 63-69

LPs: 10/12-inch

CAMDEN ... 5-8 73
CAPITOL ... 10-20 59-64
KAPP ... 10-20 61-69
MCA ... 5-8 77
MGM ... 5-8 79
RCA ... 5-10 67-77
SEARS ... 5-10
Also see ANDREWS, Julie & Andre Previn / Vic Damone / Jack Jones / Marian Anderson
Also see ANN-MARGRET

JONES, Jack, & Jetset Band: JALOPY FIVE

JONES, Janie

Singles: 7-inch

JAMA ... 5-10 61
SMASH ... 4-8 66

JONES, January

Singles: 7-inch

ASCOT ... 4-8 65
20TH FOX ... 4-8 64

JONES, Jay J.

Singles: 7-inch

V-TONE (508 "I Don't Know About You") ... 10-15 59
(May well be the same artist as J.J. Jones.)
Also see JONES, J.J.

JONES, Jericho

Singles: 7-inch

TODD ... 5-10 59

JONES, Jesus: see JESUS JONES

JONES, Jill

Singles: 7-inch

PAISLEY PARK ... 3-4 87

Picture Sleeves

PAISLEY PARK ... 3-4 87

JONES, Jim, & Chaunteys

Singles: 7-inch

MANCO (1068 "Kiwi Boogie") ... 10-20 63

LPs: 10/12-inch

SUNGLOW ... 10-15

JONES, Jimmy — *P&R '59*

(With the Jones Boys; with Savoys)

Singles: 7-inch

ARROW (717 "Heaven in Your Eyes") ... 100-200 57
BELL ... 5-8 67
CUB ... 10-20 59-62
DEKE (5413 "I Don't Mind Confessing") ... 5-10
EPIC (9339 "Whenever You Need Me") ... 75-125 59
MGM ... 3-5 78
PARKWAY ... 5-8 66
ROULETTE (4232 "Lover") ... 15-25 60
ROULETTE (4608 "Walkin' ") ... 5-10 64
SAVOY (1586 "Say You're Mine") ... 10-20 60
SAVOY (1586 " Please Say You're Mine") ... 10-15 61
(Rerecorded. Has slightly different title.)
VEE JAY (505 "Mr. Fix-It") ... 8-10 63

Picture Sleeves

CUB (9072 "That's When I Cried") ... 15-20 60

LPs: 10/12-inch

JEN JILLUS ... 5-10 77
MGM (E-3847 "Good Timin' ") ... 35-45 60
(Monaural.)
MGM (SE-3847 "Good Timin' ") ... 45-60 60
(Stereo.)
Also see SAVOYS
Also see SPARKS OF RHYTHM

JONES, Jimmy, & Pretenders

Singles: 78 rpm

RAMA (207 "Lover") ... 50-75 56
RAMA (210 "Lover") ... 30-50 56

Singles: 7-inch

ABC-PAR (10094 "Blue & Lonely") ... 10-15 60
RAMA (207 "Lover") ... 200-300 56
RAMA (210 "Lover") ... 100-200 56
Also see JONES, Jimmy
Also see PRETENDERS

JONES, Jimmy — *R&B '76*

Singles: 7-inch

CONCHILLO ... 3-5 76

JONES, Jimmy, & His Trio

Singles: 78 rpm

HOLIDAY ... 10-20 49

JONES, Joe — *P&R/R&B '60*

Singles: 78 rpm

CAPITOL ... 8-15 54

Singles: 7-inch

ABC ... 3-5 73
CAPITOL ... 10-20 54
RIC ... 10-15 60
ROULETTE ... 5-10 60-61

LPs: 10/12-inch

PRESTIGE ... 10-15 69
ROULETTE (R-25143 "You Talk Too Much") ... 25-30 61
(Monaural.)
ROULETTE (SR-25143 "You Talk Too Much") ... 30-40 61
(Stereo.)

JONES, John Paul

(John Paul Jones Orchestra)

Singles: 7-inch

PARKWAY (915 "Baja") ... 20-30 64

LPs: 10/12-inch

COLUMBIA (32047 "John Paul Jones") ... 20-30 73
Also see LED ZEPPELIN

JONES, John Paul / Rosemary & Howard

Singles: 7-inch

JERDEN (761 "Sound City") ... 5-10 60s

JONES, Johnn "Boris"

(John "Boris" Jones / John Burton)

Singles: 7-inch

DORE (682 "Surfer Smash") ... 15-25 63

JONES, Johnny — *R&B '68*

Singles: 7-inch

BRUNSWICK ... 3-5 70
HERMITAGE ... 4-8
FURY (5050 "Tennessee Waltz") ... 8-10 63

LPs: 10/12-inch

ALLIGATOR ... 10-12

JONES, Johnny, & Billy Boy Arnold

LPs: 10/12-inch

ALLIGATOR ... 5-10
Also see ARNOLD, Billy "Boy"

JONES, Johnny, & Beat Boys

Singles: 7-inch

HOLLYWOOD ... 4-8 67

JONES, Johnny, & Catalinas

Singles: 7-inch

RI ... 4-8

JONES, Jonah — *LP '58*

(Jonah Jones Quartet)

Singles: 78 rpm

GROOVE ... 3-8 56

Singles: 7-inch

BETHLEHEM ... 4-6 59
CAPITOL ... 4-6 58-63
DECCA ... 3-6 65
GROOVE ... 5-10 56
MOTOWN (1144 "For Better Or Worse") ... 50-100 69

EPs: 7-inch

BETHLEHEM ... 5-15 55
CAMDEN ... 5-8 69
CAPITOL ... 5-10 58-59
GROOVE ... 5-15 56
RCA ... 5-10 59

LPs: 10/12-inch

ANGEL ... 20-30 56
BETHLEHEM ... 20-40 55-60
CAPITOL (1000 thru 2800 series) ... 10-25 58-67
(With "T" or "ST" prefix.)
CAPITOL (1600 series) ... 5-8 77
(With "SM" prefix.)
CAPITOL (11000 series) ... 5-8 75
DECCA ... 10-20 65-67
GROOVE ... 30-40 56
INNER CITY ... 5-8 81
MOTOWN (683 "Along Came Jonah") ... 30-50 69
MOTOWN (690 "Dis & Dat") ... 30-50 69
RCA ... 15-25 59-63
Also see CHRISTY, June
Also see SINATRA, Frank / Jonah Jones

JONES, Joyce

Singles: 7-inch

ATCO (6681 "Help Me Make Up My Mind") ... 10-15 69
V-8 (10001 "Help Me Make Up My Mind") ... 15-25

JONES, Jupiter

Singles: 7-inch

SUPERIOR ... 5-10

JONES, Kay Cee *P&R '55*
(Kaycee Jones)
Singles: 78 rpm
AMERICAN....5-10 56
DECCA....5-10 57
MARQUEE....5-10 55
Singles: 7-inch
AMERICAN....8-12 56
CHANCELLOR....5-10 59
DECCA....5-10 57
DOT (15694 "Johnny, Johnny, Johnny")....10-15 58
MARQUEE....5-10 55

JONES, Ken
Singles: 7-inch
ALMONT....5-10 63
DECCA....4-8 63-67
MONUMENT....4-6 66
W.B.....5-10 59
Picture Sleeves
W.B.....5-10 59

JONES, Klinte *D&D '84*
Singles: 12-inch
OH MY....4-6 84

JONES, Kookie
Singles: 7-inch
SHEL....5-10 59

JONES, Lacey
Singles: 7-inch
AVA....4-8 64
RING-A-DING....4-8 63

JONES, Lee
Singles: 7-inch
FLAME (633 "Cool, Cool Daddy")..50-75

JONES, Lee, & Sounds of Soul
Singles: 7-inch
AMY....4-8 68

JONES, Lefty
Singles: 7-inch
CADENCE (1395 "Tennessee Molly")....10-20 61

JONES, Leroy
Singles: 7-inch
GIANT (1001 "Peppermint Twist") 10-15 62
GIANT (1002 "Check Mr. Popeye") 8-12 62
GIANT (1004 "Slow Twistin'")....10-15 62
HIT....5-20 64

JONES, Letha, & Rivals
Singles: 7-inch
ANNA (1113 "I Need You"/"I Got That Feeling")....75-125 60
ANNA (1113 "I Need You"/"Black Clouds")....50-100 60

JONES, Linda *P&R/R&B '67*
(With the Whatnauts)
Singles: 7-inch
ATCO (6344 "I'm Taking Back My Love")....15-25 65
BLUE CAT (128 "Hit Me Like TNT")....15-25 65
COTIQUE....8-12 69
LOMA....5-10 67-68
NEPTUNE....4-8 69
STANG....4-8 72
TURBO....3-6 71-72
W.B. (7278 "My Heart")....15-25 69
LPs: 10/12-inch
LOMA (5907 "Hyptomized")....20-30 67
TURBO....10-15 72
Also see LANE, Linda

JONES, Linda / Bessie Banks
Singles: 7-inch
COTIQUE (177 "Fugitive from Luv"/"Go Now")....10-15 64
Also see BANKS, Bessie
Also see JONES, Linda

JONES, Little Billy
Singles: 7-inch
ARCADIA....5-10 59

JONES, Little Johnny
(Little Johnny & the Chicago Hound Dogs; Little Johnny)
Singles: 78 rpm
ARISTOCRAT (405 "Big Town Playboy")....50-100 50
ATLANTIC (1045 "Hoy, Hoy")....20-40 54
FLAIR....40-60 53
FLAIR (1010 "Sweet Little Woman")....50-75 53
Singles: 7-inch
ATLANTIC (1045 "Hoy, Hoy")....50-75 54
FLAIR (1010 "Sweet Little Woman")....150-250 53
(Credited to Jones but by Elmore James. Jones was Elmore's pianist.)
Session: Muddy Waters; Leroy Foster; J.T. Brown; Odie Payne.
Also see JAMES, Elmore
Also see WATERS, Muddy

JONES, Little Montie
Singles: 7-inch
JENN (100 "You're Just That Kind")....100-150 59

JONES, Little Sonny
Singles: 7-inch
IMPERIAL (5275 "I Got Booted")...50-75 53
IMPERIAL (5287 "Winehead Baby")....50-75 53
SPECIALTY (443 "Everything All Right")....40-60 51

JONES, Little Willie
Singles: 7-inch
VRC (115 "When Will I Stop Loving You")....15-25

JONES, Louis
(Louis "Blues Boy" Jones)
Singles: 7-inch
OKEH....4-8 62
SABRA (519 "I'll Be Your Fool")....5-10 60s

JONES, Luke
Singles: 78 rpm
ATLAS....15-25 46

JONES, Mad Man
Singles: 7-inch
CAMEO....10-15 58
M&M....10-15
MAD (1207 "Oh Henry")....15-25 58

JONES, Michael
LPs: 10/12-inch
NARADA LOTUS....5-8 88

JONES, Mick *LP '89*
LPs: 10/12-inch
ATLANTIC....5-8 89

JONES, Mickey *C&W '79*
Singles: 7-inch
BAYSHORE....3-5 79
STOP HUNGER....3-4 89

JONES, Mike, Group
Singles: 7-inch
JET (4001 "Funny Feelings")....20-30 67

JONES, Mildred
Singles: 78 rpm
PEACOCK....5-10 54
Singles: 7-inch
PEACOCK....10-15 54

JONES, Minnie, & Minuettes
Singles: 7-inch
SUGAR (100 "Shadow of a Memory")....100-125

JONES, Nyles
Singles: 7-inch
GEMINI (101 "Welfare Blues")....15-25

JONES, Old Sam
Singles: 7-inch
GWENN....4-8 63

JONES, Oran "Juice" *P&R/R&B/LP '86*
(Juice)
Singles: 7-inch
DEF JAM....3-4 86-87
LPs: 10/12-inch
DEF JAM....5-8 86

JONES, Palmer
Singles: 7-inch
EPIC (10321 "Dancing Master")....10-15 68

JONES, Paul
Singles: 7-inch
BELL....4-8 69
CAPITOL....4-6 68
LONDON....3-5 72
PRIVATE STOCK....3-5 75
LPs: 10/12-inch
CAPITOL....10-12 67
LONDON....8-10 71
Also see MANN, Manfred

JONES, Quincy *LP '62*
Singles: 7-inch
A&M (Except 9288)....3-5 69-81
A&M (9288 "Quincy Jones")....50-75 78
(Octagon picture disc. Promotional issue only.)
ABC....3-6 68
BELL....3-6 69
COLGEMS....3-6 68
IMPULSE....4-8 62
MERCURY....5-12 59-66
RCA....3-6 69
REPRISE....3-5 72
UNI....3-6 69
U.A.....3-5 70
Picture Sleeves
A&M....3-5 77-81
COLGEMS....4-8 68
LPs: 10/12-inch
A&M....5-10 69-82
ABC (700 series)....8-12 73
ABC-PAR (149 "How I Feel About Jazz")....75-100 56
ABC-PAR (186 "Go West, Man")..75-100 57
ALLEGIANCE....5-8 84
COLGEMS....20-30 68
EMARCY (36083 "Jazz Abroad")....75-100 56
IMPULSE (11 "Quintessence")....15-25 62
IMPULSE (9300 series)....8-12 78
LIBERTY....10-20 67
MFSL (078 "You've Got It Bad")....25-35 82
MERCURY (623 "Ndeda")....15-20 72
MERCURY (2014 "Around the World")....20-30 61
(Monaural.)
MERCURY (20444 "Birth of a Band")....40-50 59
(Monaural.)
MERCURY (20561 "Great, Wide World")....40-50 60
(Monaural.)
MERCURY (20612 "I Dig Dancers")....40-50 60
(Monaural.)
MERCURY (20653 "Quincy Jones at Newport '61")....20-30 61
(Monaural.)
MERCURY (20751 "Big Band Bossa Nova")....20-30 62
(Monaural.)
MERCURY (20799 "Hip Hits")....20-30 63
(Monaural.)
MERCURY (20863 thru 21070)....10-20 64-66
(Monaural.)
MERCURY (6014 "Around the World")....25-35 61
(Stereo.)
MERCURY (60444 "Birth of a Band")....45-60 59
(Stereo.)
MERCURY (60561 "Great, Wide World")....45-55 60
(Stereo.)
MERCURY (60612 "I Dig Dancers")....45-55 60
(Stereo.)
MERCURY (60653 "Quincy Jones at Newport '61")....25-35 61
(Stereo.)
MERCURY (60751 "Big Band Bossa Nova")....25-35 62
(Stereo.)
MERCURY (60799 "Hip Hits")....25-35 63
(Stereo.)
MERCURY (60863 thru 61070)....15-25 64-66
NAUTILUS (52 "The Dude")....15-25 82
PRESTIGE (172 "Sweden-American All Stars")....200-250 53
(10-inch LP.)
QWEST....5-8 89
TRIP....5-8 74-76
U.A.....10-15 70
VERVE....15-20 67
WING....6-12 69
Also see ASHFORD & SIMPSON
Also see AUSTIN, Patti
Also see ECKSTINE, Billy, & Quincy Jones
Also see FELICIANO, Jose, & Quincy Jones
Also see GILBERTO, Astrud
Also see JACKSON, Michael
Also see MAYS, Willie, & Treniers
Also see RIPERTON, Minnie
Also see SINATRA, Frank, with Quincy Jones & His Orchestra
Also see U.S.A. for AFRICA
Also see VAUGHAN, Sarah, & Quincy Jones
Also see WASHINGTON, Dinah

JONES, Quincy, & Brothers Johnson *P&R '75*
Singles: 7-inch
A&M....3-5 75
Picture Sleeves
A&M....3-5 75
Also see BROTHERS JOHNSON

JONES, Quincy, & Tevin Campbell *P&R '90*
Singles: 7-inch
QWEST....3-4 90
Also see CAMPBELL, Tevin

JONES, Quincy, Ray Charles & Chaka Khan *P&R '89*
Singles: 7-inch
QWEST....3-4 89
Picture Sleeves
QWEST....3-4 89
Also see CHARLES, Ray
Also see KHAN, Chaka

JONES, Quincy, & James Ingram *P&R/R&B '81*
Singles: 7-inch
A&M....3-5 81
Also see JONES, Quincy

JONES, Quincy, James Ingram, Al B. Sure, El DeBarge & Barry White *P&R '90*
Singles: 7-inch
QWEST....3-4 90
Picture Sleeves
QWEST....3-4 90
Also see AL B. SURE!
Also see DE BARGE
Also see INGRAM, James
Also see JONES, Quincy, & James Ingram
Also see WHITE, Barry

JONES, Rev. Jim
LPs: 10/12-inch
CHRISTIAN CRUSADERS (2017 "Message for the Total Man")....25-50
("Last Supper")....40-60
(Picture disc. Label name and selection number not known.)

JONES, Rev. P.W.
Singles: 7-inch
NORMAN....4-8 61

JONES, Rickie Lee *P&R/R&B/LP '79*
Singles: 7-inch
W.B.....3-5 79-84
Picture Sleeves
W.B.....3-5 84
EPs: 10-inch
W.B. (23805 "Girl at Her Volcano")....10-15 83
LPs: 10/12-inch
GEFFEN....5-8 89
MFSL (089 "Rickie Lee Jones")....30-50 82
W.B.....5-8 79-84

JONES, Ricky
Singles: 7-inch
HERALD (498 "Hate to Say Goodbye")....10-20 57

JONES, Rocky
Singles: 7-inch
WASP....8-12

JONES, Rodney E., & Friends
Singles: 7-inch
TWINIGHT....4-8

JONES, Romeo
Singles: 7-inch
LITTLE STAR....4-8 62

JONES, Ron
(With the 'C' Notes)
Singles: 7-inch
AURORA....10-15
MOBIE (3419 "Goodbye Linda")....20-30 66

JONES, Ronnie
Singles: 7-inch
PAN-OR (1126 "Falling Tears")....25-35

JONES, Ronnie, & Classmates
Singles: 7-inch
END (1002 "Little Girl Next Door")....100-150 57
END (1014 "Lonely Boy")....100-150 58
END (1125 "Lonely Boy")....25-50 63

JONES, Roy
Singles: 7-inch
GLO-LIGHT (99 "Your Pilot Light Went Out")....50-75

JONES, Roy, & Shells
Singles: 7-inch
SWIRL....10-20 60

JONES, Royal, & Dukes
Singles: 7-inch
FUJIMO ("Do It Now")....8-10
(Selection number not known.)

JONES, Ruby
(Ruby Starr)
Singles: 7-inch
CURTOM....3-5 73
LPs: 10/12-inch
CURTOM....8-10 71
Also see STARR, Ruby

JONES, Rufus
LPs: 10/12-inch
CAMEO....12-15 64

JONES, Sam, Satch Sanders, & K.C. Jones
Singles: 7-inch
CEL (501 "Basketball Twist")....25-35 60s

JONES, Samantha
Singles: 7-inch
U.A.....4-8 65-66
Picture Sleeves
U.A.....4-8 65

JONES, Sammy
Singles: 7-inch
MERCURY....3-6 72

JONES, September
Singles: 7-inch
KAPP (802 "I'm Coming Home")....20-30 66

JONES, Senator
Singles: 7-inch
BELL....4-8 67

JONES, Shirley *R&B/LP '86*
Singles: 7-inch
PHILADELPHIA INT'L....3-4 86-87
LPs: 10/12-inch
PHILADELPHIA INT'L....5-8 86
Also see JONES GIRLS

JONES, Sonny
Singles: 7-inch
CHART (601 "My Baby's Crying")..15-25
MALA (534 "Just Me")....5-10 65

JONES, Spencer *D&D '83*
Singles: 12-inch
NEXT PLATINUM....4-6 83
Singles: 7-inch
NEXT PLATINUM....3-4 83
PROFILE....3-4 86

JONES, Spike *P&R '42*
(With His City Slickers)
Singles: 78 rpm
BLUEBIRD....10-20 42-43
RCA....5-15 46-55
VICTOR....8-12 44-45
Singles: 7-inch
LIBERTY....5-10 59-65
MUSICAL POSTCARD....15-25 50s
(Cardboard picture disc series.)
RCA (0030 "Cocktails for Two")....10-20 50s
(Silver label, "Collector's Issue.")
RCA (0500 series)....3-5 71
RCA (3287-89 "Spike Jones Favorites")....40-60 49
(Boxed, three-disc set.)
RCA (2900 thru 6000 series)....10-20 49-55
(Black vinyl.)
RCA (Colored vinyl)....20-40 50s
(We're not sure yet of which specific numbers are colored vinyl.)
W.B.....5-10 59
Picture Sleeves
RCA (5067 "I Saw Mommy Kissing Santa Claus")....20-30 53
RCA (5742 "I'm in the Mood for Love")....20-30 54
EPs: 7-inch
RCA....20-30 51-59
VERVE....15-25 56-57
LPs: 10/12-inch
GLENDALE....5-8 78
LIBERTY....15-25 60-65
MGM....8-12 70
PICKWICK....8-12
RCA (18 "Spike Jones Plays the Charleston")....50-100 51
RCA (1000 series)....5-10 75
RCA (2200 series)....20-25 60
RCA (2300 series)....5-10 77
RCA (3054 "Bottoms Up")....40-60 52
RCA (3128 "Spike Jones Kids the Classics")....40-60 53
RCA (3200 series)....8-12 71
RCA (3700 series)....4-8 80
RCA (3800 series)....10-15 67
(With "LPM" or "LSP" prefix.)
RCA (3800 series)....5-8 81
(With "AYL1" prefix.)
TIARA....8-12
U.A.....5-10 75
VERVE (Except 8500 series)....20-40 56-59
VERVE (8500 series)....12-20 63
W.B.....15-25 59-60
Session: Homer & Jethro.
Also see HOMER & JETHRO
Also see INGLE, Red, & Natural Seven
Also see KATZ, Mickey, & His Orchestra

JONES, Steve *LP '89*
LPs: 10/12-inch
MCA....5-8 89

JONES, Sunny
Singles: 78 rpm
ORCHID (1211 "Don't Want Pretty Women")....50-100 50

JONES, Sweetie
Singles: 7-inch
FOX (3 "Oh Yeah")....50-75 58
NRC....8-10 58
SCOTTIE....8-12 60

JONES, Tamiko *P&R/R&B '75*
Singles: 12-inch
T.K. (6 "Let It Flow")....10-15 76
Singles: 7-inch
A&M....4-6 68-69
ARISTA....3-5 75
ATLANTIC....4-8 66
ATLANTIS....3-5 77
CONTEMPO....3-5 76
DECEMBER....4-8 67-68
GOLDEN WORLD (40 "I'm Spellbound")....15-25 66
POLYDOR....3-5 79
SUTRA....3-4 86
T.K.....3-5 76
20TH FOX....3-5 74
LPs: 10/12-inch
A&M....10-12 68
DECEMBER....10-12 68
Also see TAMIKO

JONES, Tamiko, & Herbie Mann *P&R '66*
Singles: 7-inch
ATLANTIC....4-6 66
LPs: 10/12-inch
ATLANTIC....8-15 67
Also see JONES, Tamiko
Also see MANN, Herbie

JONES, Tani
Singles: 7-inch
CAMEO....5-10 60
MOSAIC....5-10 61

JONES, Thelma *R&B '67*
Singles: 7-inch
BARRY....4-8 66-68
COLUMBIA....3-5 78

JONES, Thumper
(George Jones)
Singles: 78 rpm
STARDAY (240 "Rock-It")....50-75 56
Singles: 7-inch
STARDAY (240 "Rock-It")....75-100 56
EPs: 7-inch
DIXIE (502 "Thumper Jones")....20-30 58
(Contains three Jones tracks. Not issued with cover.)
LPs: 10/12-inch
TEENAGE HEAVEN....8-12
Also see JONES, George

JONES, Tom *P&R/R&B/LP '65*
Singles: 7-inch
EPIC....3-5 76-80
LONDON....3-5 77
MCA....3-5 79
MERCURY....3-4 81-85
PARROT....3-8 65-75
SYMBOL....5-8 65
TOWER....8-12 65
Picture Sleeves
PARROT (9765 "What's New Pussycat")....5-10 65
PARROT (9787 "With These Hands")....5-10 65
PARROT (9801 "Thunderball")....5-10 65
PARROT (40000 series)....3-8 69-71
EPs: 7-inch
PARROT....5-10
(Juke box issues only. Includes title strips.)
LPs: 10/12-inch
EPIC....8-12 70-77
LONDON....5-8 77

MERCURY 5-8 81-85
PARROT 10-20 65-74
Also see ART of NOISE & Tom Jones
Also see BARRY, John

JONES, Tom / Freddie & Dreamers / Johnny Rivers
LPs: 10/12-inch
TOWER (5007 "Three at the Top") 15-20 65
Also see FREDDIE & DREAMERS
Also see JONES, Tom
Also see RIVERS, Johnny

JONES, Toni
Singles: 7-inch
SMASH 4-8 63

JONES, Van
Singles: 7-inch
CONWAY (50138 "I Want to Groove You") 20-30

JONES, Wade
Singles: 7-inch
RAYBER (1001 "I Can't Concentrate") 200-300 59

JONES, Will, & Cadets
Singles: 78 rpm
MODERN 10-15 57
Singles: 7-inch
MODERN 10-15 57
Also see CADETS

JONES, Willie
(Doc Jones)
Singles: 78 rpm
PEACOCK 10-15 50
Singles: 7-inch
BIG TOP (3050 "Mary") 8-12 60
MR. PEACOCK 5-10 62
SAVOY 10-15 54

JONES & BLUMENBERG
Singles: 7-inch
VOLT 3-5 70

JONES BOYS
(With Ray Heath & His Orchestra)
Singles: 78 rpm
S&G (5007 "The Song Is Ended") 10-15 54
Singles: 7-inch
S&G (5007 "The Song Is Ended") 20-30 54

JONES BOYS
(Featuring Bongo Pete)
Singles: 7-inch
SABRA 8-10 64

JONES BOYS
Singles: 7-inch
ATCO 4-8 66-67

JONES BROTHERS
Singles: 78 rpm
MAJESTIC 15-25 46

JONES BROTHERS
Singles: 7-inch
SEEL (10 "That's All Over Baby") 25-30

JONES BROTHERS
Singles: 78 rpm
SUN (213 "Every Night") 200-400 54
Singles: 7-inch
SUN (213 "Every Night") 600-750 54

JONES GIRLS *P&R/R&B/LP '79*
Singles: 7-inch
CURTOM 3-5 75
EPIC 3-4 81
PARAMOUNT 3-5 74
PHILADELPHIA INT'L 3-5 79-82
RCA 3-4 83
LPs: 10/12-inch
PHILADELPHIA INT'L 5-8 79-81
RCA 5-8 83
Members: Shirley Jones; Brenda Jones; Valorie Jones.
Also see JONES, Shirley

JONESES *P&R/R&B '74*
Singles: 7-inch
MERCURY 3-5 74-83
VMP (00005 "Pretty Pretty") 8-15 72
Picture Sleeves
MERCURY 3-5 75
LPs: 10/12-inch
EPIC 5-8 77
MERCURY 5-8 74-83
Members: Glenn Dorsey; Harold Taylor; Cy Brooks; Ernest Holt; Wendell Noble; Reginald Noble; Larry Noble; Sam White.

JON-PAUL TWINS: see JON & PAUL

JONSEY'S COMBO
Singles: 78 rpm
COMBO 10-15 55
Singles: 7-inch
COMBO (79 "Ting Ting Boom Scat") 15-25 55

JONZUN, Michael *R&B '86*
Singles: 12-inch
A&M 4-6 85
(Black vinyl.)
A&M 5-8 85
(Colored vinyl.)
Singles: 7-inch
A&M 3-4 85
Also see JONZUN CREW

JONZUN CREW *R&B '82*
Singles: 12-inch
A&M 4-6 84-85
TOMMY BOY 4-6 82-85
Singles: 7-inch
A&M 3-4 84-85
TOMMY BOY 3-4 82-85
LPs: 10/12-inch
A&M 5-8 84-85
TOMMY BOY 5-8 83-85
Members: Michael Jonzun; Soni Jonzun; Steve Thorpe; Gordy Worthy.
Also see JONZUN, Michael

JOOK
EPs: 7-inch
BOMP 4-8

JOPLIN, Janis *P&R/LP '69*
(With Big Brother & Full Tilt)
Singles: 7-inch
COLUMBIA 4-8 69-72
SIMON & SHUSTER ("Janis") 3-5
(Soundsheet. Included with the book *Janis*.)
LPs: 10/12-inch
COLUMBIA (KCS-9913 "I Got Dem 'Ol Kozmic Blues Again, Mama") 20-25 69
COLUMBIA (PC-9913 "I Got Dem 'Ol Kozmic Blues Again, Mama") 5-8
COLUMBIA (30000 series) 10-15 71-75
(With "C2," "KC" or "PG" prefix.)
COLUMBIA (30000 series) 12-20 74
(With "CQ" prefix. Quad.)
COLUMBIA (30000 series) 5-8 82-84
(With "PC" prefix.)
MEMORY 5-10
Also see BIG BROTHER & Holding Company

JOPLIN, Janis / Hot Tuna
LPs: 10/12-inch
GRUNT ("The Last Interview") 25-35 72
(Promotional issue only. Includes bonus Joplin home recording.)
Also see HOT TUNA
Also see JOPLIN, Janis

JORDAN: see JORDAN BROTHERS

JORDAN, Bub
Singles: 7-inch
BUCCANEER 8-10

JORDAN, Clifford
LPs: 10/12-inch
VORTEX 8-10 70

JORDAN, Danny
Singles: 7-inch
CLIMAX 20-30 59
LEADER 8-12 60
SMASH 5-8 61

JORDAN, Dave, & Shadows
Singles: 7-inch
SOMA 5-10 60s

JORDAN, Diane
Singles: 7-inch
ABC-PAR 4-8 63

JORDAN, Don
Singles: 7-inch
SHAD 5-10 60

JORDAN, Frank
Singles: 7-inch
A-STREET 3-5 86
Also see JORDAN BROTHERS

JORDAN, Jennie
Singles: 7-inch
JAMIE 4-8 62

JORDAN, Jerry *LP '75*
(Jordans)
Singles: 7-inch
MCA 3-5 75-76
LPs: 10/12-inch
MCA 5-8 75-76

JORDAN, Jill *C&W '88*
Singles: 7-inch
MAXX 3-4 88

JORDAN, Jimmy
Singles: 7-inch
NEW PHOENIX 4-8 62
20TH FOX 4-8 64

JORDAN, Jimmy & Connie
Singles: 7-inch
AGAPE (9002 "Guess I Never Had It So Good") 20-25

JORDAN, Johnny
(Donnie Brooks)
Singles: 7-inch
JOLT (332 "Sweet, Sweet, Sweet") 15-25 59
Also see BROOKS, Donnie

JORDAN, Joy, & Jets
Singles: 7-inch
ORPHEUS (1103 "Keep Cool") 50-100 56
(At least one source shows this number as 1102; however, we have 1102 as being one side of a Bombers release. Confirmation either way would be welcome.)

JORDAN, Juanita
Singles: 7-inch
LAURIE (3235 "Some Sweet Day") 15-25 64
NOR VA JAK (1324 "Some Sweet Day") 25-35 59

JORDAN, King
LPs: 10/12-inch
CORAL 10-15 62

JORDAN, Lee
Singles: 7-inch
CROSSTOWN 4-8 63

JORDAN, Lonnie *R&B '76*
Singles: 7-inch
BOARDWALK 3-4 82
MCA 3-5 78
U.A. 3-5 76-77
LPs: 10/12-inch
MCA 5-8 78
Also see WAR

JORDAN, Lou
(With the Billy Mure Orchestra)
Singles: 7-inch
JOSIE (888 "Paradise for Two") 50-75 61
JOSIE (903 "Just to Look at You") 8-12 62
MUSICNOTE 5-10 64
20TH FOX 5-10 64
Also see CHAPERONES
Also see MURE, Billy

JORDAN, Louis *R&B '42*
(Louis Jordan's Elk Rendezvous Band; with His Tympani 5)
Singles: 78 rpm
ALADDIN 5-10 54
DECCA (7500 thru 8600 series) 5-15 38-43
DECCA (18000 thru 30000 series) 5-10 44-50
VIK 5-10 56
Singles: 7-inch
ALADDIN (3223 "Whiskey Do Your Stuff") 20-30 54
ALADDIN (3227 "Ooo-Wee") 20-30 54
ALADDIN (3242 "A Dollar Down") 25-35 54
ALADDIN (3246 "Messy Bessie") 20-30 54
ALADDIN (3249 "Louis' Blues") 20-30 54
ALADDIN (3264 "Put Some Money in the Pot") 20-30 54
ALADDIN (3270 "Fat Back and Corn Liquor") 20-30 54
ALADDIN (3279 "Gal, You Need a Whippin' ") 20-30 54
DECCA (20000 thru 30000 series) 15-25 50-54
LOU-WA 5-10 60
MERCURY 10-20 56-58
PZAZZ 4-6 68
TANGERINE 4-8 62-66
VIK 8-12 56
WARWICK 5-10 60-61
"X" 8-12 55
EPs: 7-inch
DECCA 15-25 56
MERCURY 15-25 57
LPs: 10/12-inch
CLASSICAL JAZZ 5-8 82
DECCA (5035 "Greatest Hits") 10-20 68
DECCA (8551 "Let the Good Times Roll") 30-40 56
MCA 5-8 75-80
MERCURY (20242 "Somebody Up There Digs Me") 25-30 57
MERCURY (20331 "Man, We're Wailin' ") 25-30 58
SCORE (4007 "Go Blow Your Horn") 75-125 57
TANGERINE 12-15 64
TRIP 8-10 75
WING 15-20 63
Also see CROSBY, Bing, & Louis Jordan
Also see DAVIS, Martha
Also see FITZGERALD, Ella, & Louis Jordan
Also see STURGIS, Rodney

JORDAN, Reva
Singles: 7-inch
AGON 4-8 62-63

JORDAN, Ron, & Volcanoes
Singles: 7-inch
FREDLO (6009 "By My Side") 8-10 60

JORDAN, Stanley *LP '85*
LPs: 10/12-inch
BLUE NOTE 5-8 85-87
EMI 5-8 88

JORDAN, Steve
Singles: 7-inch
FALCON 5-8

JORDAN, Tenita *R&B '85*
Singles: 7-inch
CBS ASSOCIATED 3-4 85

JORDAN, Will
(With the Sickniks)
LPs: 10/12-inch
AMY (2 "Sick, No. 2") 15-25 61
JUBILEE 10-20 59

JORDAN, Willie, & His Swinging Five
(Champion Jack Dupree)
Singles: 78 rpm
ALERT 10-15 46
Also see DUPREE, Champion Jack

JORDAN & FASCINATIONS
(With the Sal Ditroia Orchestra)
Singles: 7-inch
CAROL (4116 "Once Upon a Time") 30-40 61
DAPT (203 "I'll Be Forever Loving You") 30-40 61
(With straight horizontal lines.)
DAPT (203 "I'll Be Forever Loving You") 15-25 61
(With jagged horizontal lines.)
DAPT (207 "Love Will make Your Mind Go Wild") 30-40 61
(With straight horizontal lines.)
JOSIE (895 "If You Love Me, Really Love Me") 30-40 62

JORDAN BROTHERS
(Jordan)
Singles: 7-inch
CAMEO 5-10 65
CHELTENHAM 5-10 65
GOLDEN CHARIOT (7000 series) 5-10 68
GOLDEN CHARIOT (73000 series) 4-8 68
HURRAH 4-6 84
JBP 3-5 80
JAMIE (1112 "Send Me Your Picture") 15-25 58
JAMIE (1125 "Never Never") 10-20 59
JAMIE (1133 "Be Mine") 10-20 59
JAMIE (1169 "Things I Didn't Say") 10-20 60
JAMIE (1176 "Living for the Day") 10-20 60
JAMIE (1205 "Love's Made a Fool of You") 10-20 61
JAMIE (1390 "It's You Girl") 5-10 70
JORDAN (100 "Send Me Your Picture") 15-25 57
JORDAN (102 "Sloe Gin") 10-20 63
JOR-DAN 5-10 66
MER-BRI (101 "Beach Party") 100-200 65
PARKWAY 5-10 65
PHILIPS 4-8 66
RUBY (475 "Revenge") 20-25 64
TURBO 5-8 68
VIM 5-10 64
SSS INT'L 4-8 67
LPs: 10/12-inch
JBP 8-10 80
Members: Joe Jordan; Frank Jordan; Bob Jordan; Lew Jordan.
Also see JORDAN, Frank

JORDAN HARMONIZERS
Singles: 7-inch
TIR-PHI (1009 "Do You Know Him") 20-30 62

JORDANAIRES
Singles: 78 rpm
CAPITOL 3-5 54-58
DECCA 3-5 52-54
RCA 3-5 51-53
"X" 3-5 54
Singles: 7-inch
CAPITOL 5-10 54-60
COLUMBIA (Except 43283) 4-8 64-66
(Columbia 43283, *Malibu Run*, is by another group of Jordanaires—listed in a separate section that follows.)
DECCA 5-10 52-54
SESAC 4-6 59
STOP 3-5 69
RCA 5-10 51-53
"X" 5-10 54
EPs: 7-inch
CAPITOL 5-10 55-59
RCA (3081 "Beautiful City") 15-25 53
LPs: 10/12-inch
CAPITOL 5-15 58-62
CLASSIC 10-15 78
COLUMBIA 5-15 64-66
DECCA 10-15 57
100% MUSIC 8-10 86
RCA (3081 "Beautiful City") 20-30 53
(10-inch LP.)
STEP ONE (0029 "Elvis' Favorite Spirituals") 8-10 90
SESAC 20-30 59
STEP ONE 5-8 87
STOP 5-10
VOCALION 4-8 69
Members: Gordon Stoker; Neal Matthews; Hoyt Hawkins; Hugh Jarrett; Ray Walker; Louis Nunley; Duane West.
Also see ACUFF, Roy
Also see ANDERSON, Bill
Also see ANDERSON, Lynn
Also see BANDY, Moe
Also see BRYANT, Soda, & Jordanaires
Also see CLINE, Patsy
Also see DAMON, Mark, & Jordanaires
Also see DONNER, Ral
Also see DRAGON, Paul
Also see FAIRCHLILD, Barbara
Also see FARGO, Donna
Also see FORD, Tennessee Ernie
Also see FRANCIS, Connie
Also see FREDDIE & FISHSTICKS
Also see GIBSON, Don
Also see HAGGARD, Merle
Also see HOUSTON, David
Also see HOWARD, Jan
Also see JACKSON, Stonewall
Also see JONES, George
Also see JONES, George, & Gene Pitney
Also see LEE, Brenda
Also see LEE, Robin
Also see LOCKLIN, Hank
Also see LYNN, Loretta
Also see MACK, Warner
Also see McDOWELL, Ronnie
Also see MIZE, Billy
Also see NELSON, Rick
Also see PARTON, Dolly
Also see PAYCHECK, Johnny
Also see PRESLEY, Elvis
Also see PROFITT, Randy, & Beachcombers
Also see REEVES, Jim
Also see RICH, Charlie
Also see ROBBINS, Marty
Also see RUSSELL, Johnny
Also see SAUCEDO, Rick
Also see SMITH, Andy Lee
Also see SNOW, Hank
Also see STARR, Frank, & His Rock-Away Boys
Also see TIGRE, Terry
Also see TOLSON, Bill, & Jordanaires
Also see TUBB, Ernest
Also see WEST, Dottie
Also see YOUNG, Faron

JORDANAIRES
Singles: 7-inch
COLUMBIA (43283 "Malibu Run") 10-15 65

JORDANS: see JORDAN, Jerry

JORG, Mark
LPs: 10/12-inch
MOUNT ANGEL ABBEY 10-12 72

JORGENSON, Christine
Singles: 7-inch
JOLT 8-10 59
LPs: 10/12-inch
J ("Christine Jorgensen Reveals") 50-75 57
(No selection number used. Has date, "11-26-57" etched in trail-off.)

JOSEFUS
Singles: 7-inch
HOOKAH 5-10 79
MAINSTREAM (725 "Jimmy Jimmy") 10-15 70
LPs: 10/12-inch
EVA (12010 "Dead Man") 8-12 83
HOOKAH (330 "Dead Man") 150-250 69
MAINSTREAM (6127 "Josefus") 40-60 70
Members: Pete Bailey; Dave Mitchell; Ray Turner; Doug Tull.
Also see STONE AXE

JOSEPH, Alton, & Jokers
Singles: 7-inch
LOMA 4-8 66

JOSEPH, David *R&B/D&D '83*
Singles: 12-inch
MANGO 4-6 83
Singles: 7-inch
MANGO 3-4 83

JOSEPH, Doc Bill
Singles: 7-inch
FLYGHT 4-8 63

JOSEPH, Irving, Orchestra & Chorus
Singles: 7-inch
U.A. 4-8 59
Picture Sleeves
U.A. 10-15 59

JOSEPH, Margie *R&B '70*
(With Blue Magic)
Singles: 12-inch
H.C.R.C. 4-6 83
Singles: 7-inch
ATCO 3-5 75
ATLANTIC 3-5 72-78
COTILLION 3-5 76-84
H.C.R.C. 3-4 82-83
OKEH 4-8 68
VOLT 3-5 68-71
LPs: 10/12-inch
ATLANTIC 8-10 73-74
H.C.R.C. 5-8 83
VOLT 10-12 71
Also see BLUE MAGIC
Also see HATHAWAY, Donny, & Margie Joseph

JOSEPH, Mike: see SKYLITES

JOSEPH CONSORTIUM
Singles: 7-inch
SCEPTER 3-5 71
Picture Sleeves
SCEPTER 3-5 71
LPs: 10/12-inch
SCEPTER 8-10 71

JOSEPHINE XIII
Singles: 7-inch
CAMEO 10-15 66

JOSHUA FOX
Singles: 7-inch
TETRAGRAMMATON 5-10 68
LPs: 10/12-inch
TETRAGRAMMATON (125 "Joshua Fox") 20-30 68
Members: Mike Botts; Larry Hansen; Jo LaManno; Tom Menefee.
Also see BREAD

JOSIAS, Cory *D&D '83*
Singles: 12-inch
SIRE 4-6 83

JOSIE, L.T.
Singles: 7-inch
TOWER 4-6 67
Picture Sleeves
TOWER 4-8 67

JOSIE, Lori
Singles: 7-inch
ARGO (5293 "Why Did You Leave Me") 10-15 58

JOSIE, Lou
Singles: 7-inch
ARGO (5312 "Time's a Wastin' ") 10-15 58
BATON (269 "Lonely Years") 10-20 59
RENDEZVOUS (143 "Talk to the Angels") 50-100 61

JOSIE & PUSSYCATS
Singles: 7-inch
CAPITOL (2900 & 3000 series) 10-20 70-71
CAPITOL CREATIVE PRODUCTS (50 thru 61) 10-20 70
(Kellogg's cereal promotional issues.)

Picture Sleeves
CAPITOL CREATIVE PRODUCTS (50 thru 61) 10-20 70
(Mailing envelope/sleeve from Kellogg's.)
LPs: 10/12-inch
CAPITOL (665 "Josie and the Pussycats") 100-150 70
(TV Soundtrack.)
Members: Patrice Holloway; Cherie Moor (a.k.a. Cheryl Ladd); Cathy Dougher;.
Also see HOLLOWAY, Patrice
Also see LADD, Cheryl

JOURNEY LP '75
Singles: 12-inch
COLUMBIA.................... 5-10 82
Singles: 7-inch
COLUMBIA.................... 3-5 74-87
GEFFEN.................... 3-4 85
Picture Sleeves
COLUMBIA.................... 3-5 81-87
GEFFEN.................... 3-4 85
EPs: 7-inch
CSP.................... 4-6 81
(Nestle's candy promotional issue.)
LPs: 10/12-inch
COLUMBIA ("Captured")..........100-120 81
(10-inch picture disc. No selection number used. Promotional issue only.)
COLUMBIA (662 "Live Sampler") ..12-15 75
(Promotional issue only.)
COLUMBIA (914 "Journey")..........12-15 75
(Promotional issue only.)
COLUMBIA (30000 series)............ 5-10 75-82
COLUMBIA (KC2-37016 "Captured")....................80-100 81
(Picture disc made for promotional use, but, due to a production error, the actual recordings are by unidentified artists.)
COLUMBIA (46000 & 47000 series)....................20-40 81-82
(Half-speed mastered.)
MFSL (144 "Escape")..............100-200 85
Members: Steve Perry; Neal Schon; Aynsley Dunbar; Gregg Rolie; Ross Valory; Jonathan Cain; Robert Fleishman.
Also see BABYS
Also see BAD ENGLISH
Also see CAIN, Jonathan
Also see DUNBAR, Aynsley
Also see FRUMIOUS BANDERSNATCH
Also see PERRY, Steve
Also see SCHON, Neal, & Jan Hammer

JOURNEYMEN
Singles: 7-inch
AMY.................... 4-8 61
CAPITOL.................... 4-8 61-64
LPs: 10/12-inch
CAPITOL....................15-20 61-63
Members: John Phillips; Scott McKenzie; Dick Weissman.
Also see McKENZIE, Scott
Also see PHILLIPS, John
Also see SMOOTHIES

JOURNEYMEN
(Baylanders)
Singles: 7-inch
IONA (1111 "Work Out")................10-20 63
IONA (1115 "Surfers Rule") 10-20 63
(Also issued as by the Baylanders.)
Member: Art Fisher.
Also see BAYLANDERS
Also see CHALLENGERS

JOURNEYMEN
Singles: 7-inch
TEE PEE (57/58 "You're a Better Man Than I")....................50-100 68
Members: Dennis Pharis; Tom Halfpap; Mike Giese; Tobin Kraft; Donald Eastman.

JO-VALS
(Jovals)
Singles: 7-inch
ALWIL (101 "Ballerina")................10-20 64
GROVE (105 "Well It's Alright") 10-15 64
LAURIE (3229 "Sometimes I'm Happy")....................15-20 64

JOVATIONS
Singles: 7-inch
TAURUS....................10-15 63

JOVI, Bon: see BON JOVI

JOVIALETTS
Singles: 7-inch
JOSIE (949 "T'Ain't No Big Thing") 10-20 65

JOY
Singles: 7-inch
PHILIPS.................... 4-6 68-70
LPs: 10/12-inch
PAULA.................... 8-12 72

JOY
Singles: 7-inch
EPIC (10528 "Bah Bah Bah").........10-15 69
Also see BOLTON, Michael

JOY
Singles: 7-inch
LAURIE 4-8 75

JOY, Arlene
Singles: 7-inch
RENDEZVOUS (185 "Too Young") 15-25 62

JOY, Barbara
Singles: 7-inch
TAR-GET (1001 "Twistin' & Stompin' ").................... 5-10 62
U.C.S. (101 "Story of My Life") 25-50 62

JOY, Benny
(With Big John Taylor)
Singles: 7-inch
ANTLER (4011 "Crash the Party")....................100-200 58
DECCA....................8-12 61
DIXIE (2001 "Steady with Betty")....................100-200 58
RAM (1107 "Ittie Bittie Everything")....................100-200 59
TRI DEC (8667 "Spin the Bottle")....................100-200 58
Also see TAYLOR, Big John

JOY, Bobby
Singles: 7-inch
SENTRY (103 "You Sweet Devil You")....................15-25
TANGERINE....................5-10 68

JOY, Carol
Singles: 7-inch
CLOCK....................5-10 59

JOY, Cee Cee
Singles: 7-inch
REGINA (293 "His Buddy's Girl") ...10-15 63
W.B. 4-8 63

JOY, Homer C&W '74
Singles: 7-inch
CAPITOL.................... 3-5 74

JOY, Roddie P&R/R&B '65
Singles: 7-inch
PARKWAY....................5-10 66-67
RED BIRD (021 "Come Back Baby")....................8-12 65
RED BIRD (031 "He's So Easy to Love") 10-20 65
RED BIRD (037 "If There's Anything You Want")....................20-30 66

JOY & BOYS
Singles: 7-inch
SEAFAIR.................... 4-8 61

JOY & SORROWS
Singles: 7-inch
MGM 4-8 65

JOY DIVISION LP '88
Singles: 7-inch
FOCUS.................... 4-8
LPs: 10/12-inch
FACTORY 5-8 81
QWEST.................... 5-8 88
Members: Bernard Sumner; Peter Hook; Gillian Gilbert; Stephen Morris.
Also see NEW ORDER

JOY OF COOKING P&R/LP '71
(The Joy)
Singles: 7-inch
BROWNSVILLE 3-5 71
CAPITOL.................... 3-5 71-73
FANTASY.................... 3-5 77-78
LPs: 10/12-inch
CAPITOL....................8-10 71-72
FANTASY....................5-10 77-78
Members: Terry Garthwaite; Toni Brown; Fritz Kasten; David Garthwaite; Ron Wilson.
Also see BROWN, Toni, & Terry Garthwaite
Also see GARTHWAITE, Terry

JOY ROCKERS
Singles: 7-inch
PENNY (9021 "The Gauster Bop") .10-20 62

JOY UNLIMITED
LPs: 10/12-inch
BASF....................8-10 72
MERCURY 8-12 70

JOY VENDORS
Singles: 7-inch
PAWN (1201 "Popeye Line") 10-20 62

JOYCE, Billy
(Billy Joyce Combo)
Singles: 7-inch
ON the BALL 4-8 62

JOYCE, Brenda C&W '79
Singles: 7-inch
MERCURY 4-8 65
WESTERN PACIFIC

JOYCE, Jo Ann
Singles: 7-inch
CARLTON 4-8 64

JOYCE, Judy
Singles: 7-inch
CUPID (1001 "My Foolish Heart") ..20-30 58

JOYCE & PRIVITEERS
(Joyce Heath)
Singles: 7-inch
AGON (1003 "Honor Roll of Love")....................50-100 62
(Also issued as by Joyce Heath & Priviteers.)
Also see HEATH, Joyce
Also see TREMONTS

JOYE, Col: see COLONEL JOYE

JOYETTES
Singles: 78 rpm
ONYX (502 "Story of Love")...........20-40 56
Singles: 7-inch
ONYX (502 "Story of Love").........50-100 56

JOYFUL NOISE
LPs: 10/12-inch
RCA....................10-12 68

JOYLARKS
Singles: 7-inch
CANDELITE (426 "Betty My Love") 10-15 63
SNAG (107 "Betty My Love") 300-400 59

JOYLETS
Singles: 7-inch
ABC-PAR (10403 "Say Yeah").......10-15 63

JOYOUS NOISE
LPs: 10/12-inch
CAPITOL....................15-20 71
Members: Ron Elliott; Marc McClure; Dennis Dragon.
Also see ELLIOTT, Ron
Also see LEVITT & McCLURE
Also see SURF PUNKS

JOYRIDE
(The Joyride)
Singles: 7-inch
WORLD PACIFIC....................10-15 67-68

JOYRIDE
LPs: 10/12-inch
RCA (4114 "Friend Song")............20-30 69
Also see REVERE, Paul, & Raiders

JOYS
Singles: 7-inch
VALIANT 8-12 64

JOYS OF LIFE
Singles: 7-inch
COLUMBIA (44188 "Descent") 10-20 67

JOYTONES
Singles: 78 rpm
RAMA....................50-100 56
Singles: 7-inch
RAMA (191 "All My Love Belongs to You")....................50-100 56
RAMA (202 "Gee What a Boy") 150-250 56
RAMA (215 "My Foolish Heart")....................400-500 56
STOOP SOUNDS (504 "My Foolish Heart") 100-150 96
(Limited edition. Estimates range from less than 10 to a few dozen made.)
Members: Lynn Middleton; Vicki Burgess; Margaret Moore; Toni Brown.
Also see CHARMERS
Also see HARPTONES

JOY-TONES
Singles: 7-inch
COED....................5-10 65

JUAN, Don: see DON JUAN

JUAREZ
Singles: 7-inch
DECCA....................3-6 70
LPs: 10/12-inch
DECCA....................8-12 70

JUBAL
Singles: 7-inch
ELEKTRA....................3-5 73
LPs: 10/12-inch
ELEKTRA....................8-10 72
Members: Dennis Linde; Alan Rush.
Also see LINDE, Dennis

JUBALAIRES
Singles: 78 rpm
CAPITOL....................5-10 49-51
DECCA....................5-10 44-46
LANG-WORTH....................10-20 40s
(16-inch transcriptions.)
Singles: 7-inch
CAPITOL (845 "That Old Piano Roll Blues")....................20-30 50
CAPITOL (1054 "Little Mr. Big").....20-30 50
CAPITOL (1779 "Living Is a Lie")....20-30 51
CAPITOL (1888 "David & Goliath")....................20-30 51
Members: Julius Ginyard; Ted Brooks; Bill Johnson; John Jennings; George McFadden.
Also see ROYAL HARMONY QUARTET

JUBALAIRES R&B '46
(With Andy Kirk's Orchestra)
Singles: 78 rpm
CORAL....................5-10 49
DECCA....................5-10 46
KING 10-15 49-50
QUEEN (4163 "A Sunday Kind of Love")....................15-25 47
QUEEN (4166 "Jubes Blues")..........15-25 47
QUEEN (4167 "God Almighty's Gonna Cut You Down")....................15-25 47
QUEEN (4168 "My God Called Me This Morning")....................15-25 47
QUEEN (4172 "Icky, Yacky")..........15-25 47
Also see KIRK, Andy, & His Clouds of Joy
Also see ORIGINAL JUBALAIRES

JUDAS JUMP
Singles: 7-inch
CAPITOL....................3-6 70
PRIDE....................3-5 72
LPs: 10/12-inch
CAPITOL....................10-12 70
PRIDE....................8-10 72

JUDAS PRIEST LP '78
Singles: 7-inch
ATLANTIC....................3-4 88
COLUMBIA....................3-5 79-84
Picture Sleeves
COLUMBIA....................3-5 81
LPs: 10/12-inch
COLUMBIA (Except picture discs).....5-8 77-90
COLUMBIA (99-1543 "Screaming for Vengeance")....................15-20 84
(World Tour picture disc.)
COLUMBIA (99-1543 "Screaming for Vengeance")....................20-30 84
(Picture disc that, due to a production error, plays Neil Diamond's *Primitive* album.)
COLUMBIA (99-1851 "Love Bites")....................60-70 84
(Picture disc with bite mark on outer edge.)
COLUMBIA (99-1851 "Love Bites")....................15-25 84
(Picture disc.)
COLUMBIA (39926 "Great Vinyl and Concert Hits")....................25-30 84
(Picture disc.)
JANUS (7019 "Sad Wings of Destiny")....................8-12 76
OVATION (1751 "Sad Wings of Destiny")....................5-10 80
RCA....................5-8 83-84
VISA (7001 "Rocka Rolla")..........15-25 74
(With bottle cap front cover.)
VISA (7001 "Rocka Rolla")..............8-10 74
(No bottle cap on cover.)
Members: Rob Halford; K.K. Downing; Glenn Tipton; Ian Hill; Dave Holland; Scott Travis.
Also see DIAMOND, Neil

JUDD
LPs: 10/12-inch
ASI....................5-8 78-79

JUDDS C&W '83
Singles: 7-inch
CURB/RCA....................3-4 90-91
RCA....................3-5 83-88
RCA/CURB....................3-4 89-89
Promotional Singles
RCA....................5-10 83-88
(Black vinyl.)
RCA (13673 "Had a Dream") 15-20 83
(Colored vinyl.)
RCA (13923 "Why Not Me")...........10-20 84
(Colored vinyl.)
RCA (13673 "Had a Dream") 15-20 83
(Colored vinyl.)
LPs: 10/12-inch
RCA....................5-8 83-88
RCA/CURB....................5-8 89-89
Members: Naomi Judd; Wynonna Judd.

JUDGE, Jimmy
Singles: 7-inch
JEWEL....................5-10 60

JUDGE 'N JURY
Singles: 7-inch
VERVE....................10-15 67

JUDGE DREAD
Singles: 7-inch
20TH FOX 3-5 73

JUDGE'S NEPHEWS
Singles: 7-inch
AUDIO (585 "Without Your Tender Love")....................20-30

JUDY & AFFECTIONS
Singles: 7-inch
DODE (103 "Dum Dum De Dip")....30-40

JUDY & DUETS
Singles: 7-inch
WARE....................8-12 64

JUDY & JADES
Singles: 7-inch
STARBURST (124 "Rooster")........15-20 67

JUDY & JANEY
Singles: 7-inch
BUDDAH (87 "The Reverend") 4-8 69

JUDY & JOYCE
Singles: 7-inch
DECCA....................5-10 58
DOT....................5-10 58

JUDY, JOHNNY, & BILLY
Singles: 7-inch
SILVER (1003 "Beautiful Brown Eyes")....................10-15 59

JUDY LEE & PLAYBOYS
Singles: 7-inch
DARLY (6382 "I Wonder Could It Be")....................20-25
Members: Judy Lee Reeths; Pat Reeths; Dan Helland; Jim Jandrain; Tim Polzak; Dave Parpovich; Mike Larsheid.

JUDY LYNN C&W '62
(Judy Lynn Voiten)
Singles: 7-inch
AMARET....................3-5 71-73
COLUMBIA....................3-6 69
MUSICOR....................4-6 66-67
U.A. 4-8 62-66
W.B./CURB....................3-5 75
LP: 10/12-inch
AMARET....................5-10 71-73
COLUMBIA....................8-12 69
MUSICOR....................10-15 66-67
U.A. 10-20 62-66
UNART....................10-15 67
Also see GRAMMER, Billy / Judy Lynn / Link Wray

JUICE
Singles: 7-inch
FULL CIRCLE 3-4 81
LPs: 10/12-inch
FULL CIRCLE 5-8 81

JUICY R&B '83
Singles: 12-inch
ATLANTIC....................4-8 83-84
PRIVATE I....................4-6 85
Singles: 7-inch
ARISTA....................3-4 83
ATLANTIC....................3-4 83-84
CBS ASSOC 3-4 86
PRIVATE I....................3-4 85-86
LPs: 10/12-inch
ARISTA....................5-8 83
ATLANTIC....................5-8 84
Members: Jerry Barnes; Katreese Barnes

JUICY GROOVE
LPs: 10/12-inch
PAYOLA ("First Taste") 10-15 78
(Picture disc. Up to 50 different graphics/color variations made. Selection number not known.)

JUICY LUCY
Singles: 7-inch
ATCO....................3-6 70-71
LPs: 10/12-inch
ATCO....................10-12 70-71
Member: Glenn Campbell.
Also see GOLDTONES

JUJUS
Singles: 7-inch
FENTON (1004 "You Treat Me Bad")....................35-45 65
UNITED (121570 "Do You Understand Me")....................15-25 66
Picture Sleeves
UNITED (121570 "Do You Understand Me")....................20-30 66
Members: Ray Hummell, Rod Shepard; Bill Gorski; Max Colley; Rick Stevens.
Also see HUMMEL, Ray

JUKES: see SOUTHSIDE JOHNNY

JUKIN' BONE
LPs: 10/12-inch
RCA....................8-10 72

JULES, Jimmy
Singles: 7-inch
ABET....................3-5 74
ATLANTIC (2120 "Talk About You")....................10-20 61
GAMBLE....................10-15

JULES & POLAR BEARS
Singles: 7-inch
COLUMBIA 3-5 79
EPs: 7-inch
COLUMBIA 4-6 80
(Promotional only.)
LPs: 10/12-inch
COLUMBIA 5-8 79
Member: Jules Shear.
Also see FUNKY KINGS
Also see SHEAR, Jules
Also see SINCEROS / Hounds / The Beat / Jules & Polar Bears

JULES, Jimmy
Singles: 7-inch
ATLANTIC (2120 "Talk About You")....................10-20 61

JULIA LEE: see LEE, Julia

JULIAN
Singles: 7-inch
ONYX (519 "Whip")....................15-25 58

JULIAN, Don & Meadowlarks
Singles: 78 rpm
DOOTO....................30-40 57
DOOTONE 20-40 55-56
RPM (399 "Love Only You")..........25-50 54
RPM (406 "LSMFT Blues")...........50-100 54
Singles: 7-inch
CLASSIC ARTISTS (101 "Our Love")....................4-6 89
DOOTO (359 "Heaven and Paradise")....................30-40 57
DOOTO (424 "Blue Moon")............30-40 57
DOOTONE (359 "Heaven and Paradise")....................75-100 55
DOOTONE (367 "Always and Always")....................50-75 55
(Red label.)
DOOTONE (367 "Always and Always")....................50-75 55
(Maroon label.)
DOOTONE (372 "This Must Be Paradise")....................50-75 55
DOOTONE (394 "Please Love a Fool")....................50-75 56
DOOTONE (405 "I Am a Believer")....................50-100 56
DYNAMITE (1112 "Heaven Only Knows")....................15-25 62
JERK (100 "How Can You Be So Foul")....................15-25 60s
ORIGINAL SOUND (3 "Please Say You Want Me")....................20-30 58
ORIGINAL SOUND (12 "There's a Girl")....................15-25 58
RPM (399 "Love Only You") 125-200 54
RPM (406 "LSMFT Blues") 125-200 54
EPs: 7-inch
DOOTO (203 "Don Julian and the Meadowlarks")....................25-50 58
DOOTONE (203 "Don Julian and the Meadowlarks")....................100-150 56
DOOTONE (203 "Don Julian and the Meadowlarks")....................10-20 70s
(Reissues from the '70s, and later, can easily be identified by the "South Hope Street" Dootone address.

Members: Don Julian; Ronald Barrett; Earl Jones; Randy Jones; Glen Reagan; Freeman Bralton; Benny Patricks.
Also see DEL-VIKINGS / Sonnets
Also see DOOTONES
Also see LARKS
Also see PENGUINS / Meadowlarks / Medallions / Dootones

JULIAN'S TREATMENT
(Julian Jay Savarin)
LPs: 10/12-inch
DECCA.......8-10 70

JULIANA
Singles: 7-inch
RCA (7906 "You Can Have Any Boy").......30-50 61

JULIE P&R '76
(Julie Budd)
Singles: 7-inch
A&M.......3-4 84-85
TOM CAT.......3-5 76
Also see BUDD, Julie

JULIETTES
Singles: 7-inch
CHATTAHOOCHEE (634 "I'll Be Forever Loving You").......10-20 64

JULITO & LATIN LADS
(Julio y Latin Lads)
Singles: 7-inch
RICO-VOX (27 "Nunca").......75-125 63
Also see LATIN LADS / Clif-Tones

JULIUS & CAESAR
Singles: 7-inch
WREN.......5-10 60

JULUKA LP '83
Singles: 7-inch
W.B. 3-4 83-84
LPs: 10/12-inch
W.B. 5-8 83-84

JULY
Singles: 7-inch
EPIC.......5-10 69
LPs: 10/12-inch
EPIC.......10-15 69

JULY FOUR
Singles: 7-inch
CAMEO.......10-15 67

JUMBO R&B '77
Singles: 7-inch
PRELUDE.......3-5 77
LPs: 10/12-inch
PYE.......5-8 77

JUMP
LPs: 10/12-inch
JANUS.......10-12 71

JUMP 'N THE SADDLE BAND P&R '83
Singles: 7-inch
ACME.......4-6 82
ATLANTIC.......3-4 83
Picture Sleeves
ATLANTIC.......3-4 83

JUMP STREET BAND
LPs: 10/12-inch
MCA.......5-8 81

JUMPIN' JACKS
Singles: 78 rpm
1-0-1.......25-35 54
DECCA.......10-15 56
Picture Sleeves
DECCA (29973 "You'll Wonder Where the Yellow Went").......20-30 56
101 (100 "Let There Be Rockin' ").......100-200 54

JUMPIN' JAGUARS
Singles: 78 rpm
DECCA.......5-10 56
Singles: 7-inch
DECCA.......10-15 56
Singles: 7-inch
1-0-1 (100 "Let There Be Rockin' ").......75-100 54

JUMPIN' JAY
Singles: 7-inch
TURBAN (101 "Come on Home").......20-25

JUMPIN' JUDGE & HIS COURT / Lafayette Thomas
Singles: 78 rpm
JUMPING (5000 "The Trial").......10-20 55
Singles: 7-inch
JUMPING (5000 "The Trial").......25-35 55
Also see THOMAS, Lafayette

JUMPIN' TONES
Singles: 7-inch
RAVEN (8004 "I Had a Dream")...50-100 64
RAVEN (8005 "Grandma's Hearing Aid").......50-100 64
Also see RAINDROPS

JUMPING JACKS
Singles: 78 rpm
BRUCE (115 "Embraceable You").......100-200 54
LLOYDS (101 "Do Let That Dream Come True").......75-150 53
Singles: 7-inch
BRUCE (115 "Embraceable You").......300-400 54
LLOYDS (101 "Do Let That Dream Come True").......200-300 53

JUMPING JACKS
Singles: 78 rpm
CAPITOL.......4-8 56
DECCA.......8-10 56
Singles: 7-inch
CAPITOL.......5-10 56
DECCA.......8-12 56
Picture Sleeves
DECCA.......10-20 56

JUMPING JACKS
Singles: 7-inch
ABC-PAR.......5-10 58

JUMPING JACKS
Singles: 7-inch
BERTRAM INT'L (221 "Roasted Peanuts").......20-25 61

JUNE, Rosemary
Singles: 7-inch
PARIS.......10-15 58-59
TALENT.......5-10 62
U.A. 5-10 59

JUNE & DONNIE R&B '69
Singles: 7-inch
CURTOM (1935 "I Thank You Baby").......4-8 68
Members: June Conquest; Donny Hathaway.
Also see HATHAWAY, Donny, & June Conquest

JUNE & JOY
Singles: 7-inch
DOT.......5-10 60

JUNGKLAS, Rob LP '86
Singles: 7-inch
MANHATTAN.......3-4 87
Picture Sleeves
MANHATTAN.......3-4 87
LPs: 10/12-inch
MANHATTAN.......5-8 86

JUNGLE BROTHERS
LPs: 10/12-inch
IDLERS.......5-8 88

JUNIE R&B '74
(Walter Morrison; Junie Morrison)
Singles: 7-inch
COLUMBIA.......3-4 81
EASTBOUND.......3-5 74
20TH FOX/WESTBOUND.......3-5 75-76
LPs: 10/12-inch
20TH FOX/WESTBOUND.......5-8 76
Also see FUNKADELIC
Also see MORRISON, Junie
Also see OHIO PLAYERS

JUNIE'S JIVIN' FIVE
Singles: 7-inch
AD.......5-10 60

JUNIOR P&R/R&B/LP '82
(Junior Giscombe)
Singles: 12-inch
LONDON.......4-6 84
MERCURY.......4-6 83
Singles: 7-inch
CASABLANCA.......3-4 83
LONDON.......3-4 84-88
MERCURY.......3-4 82-86
LPs: 10/12-inch
MERCURY.......5-8 82-83

JUNIOR, Carl: see CARL JUNIOR

JUNIOR, Roy
Singles: 7-inch
HICKORY.......5-10 66

JUNIOR & CLASSICS
Singles: 7-inch
BIRDIE.......3-4 82
GROOVE.......5-10 64
MAGIC TOUCH.......5-10 67-68
Member: Junior Brantley; Dennis Madigan; Kent Ivy; Brand Shank; Jerry Sworske; Keith Dreher; Vic Pitts.
Also see FABULOUS THUNDERBIRDS
Also see ROOMFUL of BLUES
Also see SHORT STUFF

JUNIOR & HI-FIVES
Singles: 7-inch
MAYTE.......10-15 60

JUNIOR & HIS FRIENDS
Singles: 7-inch
ABC-PAR (10089 "Who's Our Pet, Annette").......15-25 60

JUNIOR & STAR LITES
Singles: 7-inch
MEX MELODY (121 "Queen of My Heart").......100-200

JUNIOR BLUES
Singles: 78 rpm
RPM (320 "Wiskey Head Woman").......25-50 50

JR. CADILLAC
Singles: 7-inch
GREAT NORTHWEST.......3-5 80
LPs: 10/12-inch
GREAT NORTHWEST.......8-12 80
Member: Ned Neltner.
Also see SEATTLE HELPS the HUNGRY

JUNIOR GORDON: see GORDON, Junior

JUNIOR RAYMEN
LPs: 10/12-inch
NORTON.......5-10 90

Members: Vern Wray Jr.; John Corboo; Roger Atkinson.

JUNIOR'S EYES
LPs: 10/12-inch
A&M.......10-12 69

JUNIORS
Singles: 7-inch
LAURIE.......4-8 63
MGM.......4-8 64
TEXOMA (1900 "Dream Girl").......10-20 60

JUNIORS
Singles: 7-inch
SIT on IT.......5-10 76
Also see DANNY & JUNIORS

JUNKYARD LP '89
LPs: 10/12-inch
GEFFEN.......5-8 89

JUNKYARD ANGELS
Singles: 7-inch
UNICYCLE.......5-10 66

JUNS, Jimmy
Singles: 7-inch
VULCAN.......3-5

JU-PAR UNIVERSAL ORCHESTRA R&B '77
Singles: 7-inch
JU-PAR.......3-5 77

JUPITER, Duke: see DUKE JUPITER

JUPITER RECORD'S FEMALE SINGER / Larry R. Mumford
Singles: 7-inch
M.P.E. (2099 "Goodbye to the Great Elvis").......10-15 79

JURGENS, Dick, & His Orchestra C&W '47
Singles: 78 rpm
COLUMBIA.......4-6 47

JURY
Singles: 7-inch
PORT (3019 "Who Dat").......15-25 66

JUST BROTHERS
Singles: 7-inch
GARRISON (3003 "Carlena").......50-100 60s

JUST FOUR MEN
Singles: 7-inch
TOWER.......4-8 65
Also see FREDDIE & DREAMERS / Just Four Men

JUST - ICE
LPs: 10/12-inch
FRESH FIVE.......5-8 88

JUST LUV
Singles: 7-inch
M-S (216 "Valley of Hate").......30-50 60s

JUST US P&R '66
Singles: 7-inch
ATLANTIC.......3-5 71
COLPIX.......4-8 66
KAPP.......4-8 66-67
MINUTEMAN.......4-8 66
Picture Sleeves
KAPP.......4-8 66
LPs: 10/12-inch
KAPP.......10-15 66
Members: Chip Taylor; Al Gorgoni.
Also see TAYLOR, Chip

JUST US GIRLS
Singles: 7-inch
EPIC/CLEVELAND INT'L.......3-5 79
Also see WAGNER, Dick

JUST WATER
Singles: 7-inch
JUST.......3-5

JUSTICE, Jimmy
Singles: 7-inch
BLUE CAT.......5-10 64
KAPP.......4-8 62-63
LPs: 10/12-inch
KAPP.......15-20 63

JUSTICE DEPARTMENT
Singles: 7-inch
NEW DESIGN (1008 "Let John and Yoko Stay in the U.S.A.").......10-20 72
(A paper insert with the lyrics, originally available with the single, is valued about the same as the record.)

JUSTICE V
Singles: 7-inch
PANORAMA (55 "Things Get Worse").......5-10 67
Members: Bill Church; Mike Mantor; Ron Ryser; Steve Hatley; Paul Manktelow.
Also see HAGAR, Sammy
Also see MORRISON, Van

JUSTIFIERS
Singles: 7-inch
KIM (101 "Lonely Boy").......150-250 58

JUSTIN
Singles: 7-inch
DOWN EAST.......5-10

JUSTIS, Bill P&R/R&B/C&W '57
(With the Jury; Bill Justis Orchestra; with Roger Fakes & Spinners)
Singles: 78 rpm
PHILLIPS INT'L.......15-30 57
Singles: 7-inch
BELL.......3-5 70
MONUMENT.......3-5 76
PHILLIPS INT'L.......8-15 57-59
PLAY ME.......8-12 59
MCA.......3-5 77
MONUMENT.......4-8 66
NRC.......4-8 60
SMASH.......4-8 63-65
Picture Sleeves
SMASH.......5-10 63
LPs: 10/12-inch
HARMONY.......8-10 72
PHILLIPS INT'L (1950 "Cloud 9")...50-75 57
SMASH.......15-20 62-66
SUN.......8-10 69
WING.......10-20 65
Also see POWERS, Johnny

JUSTIS, Bill / Jerry Reed
EPs: 7-inch
MCA (1961 "Music from *Smokey and the Bandit*").......10-15 77
(Promotional issue only.)
Also see JUSTIS, Bill
Also see REED, Jerry

JUVENILES
(With Al Caiola & Combo)
Singles: 7-inch
MODE (1 "Beat in My Heart").......50-100 57
(Black label with white print. Has "45 RPM" on two lines.)
MODE (1 "Beat in My Heart").......25-50 58
(Black label with silver print. Has 45 R.P.M." on one line.)
Also see CAIOLA, Al

JUVENILES
Singles: 7-inch
JERDEN (770 "Bo Diddley").......5-10 65
JERDEN (795 "I've Searched").......5-10 66
PANORAMA (50 "You Gotta Understand").......5-10 66
LPs: 10/12-inch
PICCADILLY (3371 "Bo Diddley")...5-10 80

JUVET, Patrick LP '78
Singles: 12-inch
CASABLANCA.......4-6 78-79
Singles: 7-inch
CASABLANCA.......3-5 78-79
LPs: 10/12-inch
CASABLANCA.......5-8 78-79

J-WALKERS
Singles: 7-inch
EVEREST.......5-10 62
TIDAL.......5-10 61

JYNX PACK
Singles: 7-inch
MERCURY.......5-10 66

JYVE FYVE
Singles: 7-inch
BRUT.......3-5 74
Also see JIVE FIVE
Also see PITT, Eugene, & Jyve Fyve

K

K., Big Buddy: see BIG BUDDY K.

K & D BOOTERY COMPANY
Singles: 7-inch
TEE PEE (1002 "Birthday").......10-20 69

KBC BAND P&R/LP '86
Singles: 7-inch
ARISTA.......3-4 86
Picture Sleeves
ARISTA.......3-4 86
LPs: 10/12-inch
ARISTA.......5-8 86
Members: Paul Kantner; Marty Balin; Jack Casady.
Also see JEFFERSON AIRPLANE

KC & Sunshine Band R&B '73
(KC; Sunshine Band)
Singles: 12-inch
EPIC.......4-6 82
MECA.......4-6 83-85
SUNSHINE SOUND.......4-6 81
Singles: 7-inch
CASABLANCA.......3-4 80-83
EPIC.......3-4 81-83
MECA.......3-4 83-85
SUNSHINE SOUND.......3-4 81
TK.......3-5 73-81
Picture Sleeves
TK.......3-5 77-78
LPs: 10/12-inch
CASABLANCA.......5-8 81
EPIC.......5-8 81-82
MECA.......5-8 84
SUNSHINE SOUND.......5-8 81
TK.......8-10 74-80
Also see DE SARIO, Teri, & K.C.
Also see WRIGHT, Betty

KGB LP '76
Singles: 7-inch
MCA.......3-5 76
LPs: 10/12-inch
MCA.......8-10 76
Members: Ray Kennedy; Rick Grech; Mike Bloomfield; Barry Goldberg; Carmine Appice.
Also see APPICE, Carmine
Also see BLOOMFIELD, Mike
Also see GOLDBERG, Barry
Also see KENNEDY, Ray

K.I.D. R&B '81
Singles: 12-inch
SAM.......4-6 81
Singles: 7-inch
SAM.......3-5 81

K - 9 POSSE LP '89
LPs: 10/12-inch
ARISTA.......5-8 89

KTP: see KISSING the PINK

KACHER, Del
(Del Katcher)
Singles: 7-inch
DENNY (347 "Night Bird").......10-20 62
MERRI (201 "Night Mist Over Highway No. 2").......10-20 60
Also see KACHERS in the RYE

KACHERS IN THE RYE
Singles: 7-inch
W.B. 5-8 66
Member: Del Kacher.
Also see KACHER, Del

KAC-TIES
Singles: 7-inch
ATCO (6299 "Oh What a Night")...10-15 64
KAPE (502 "Smile").......15-25 63
KAPE (503 "Let Your Love Light Shine").......15-25 63
KAPE (702 "Over the Rainbow")....10-15 63
KAPE (515632 "Girl in My Heart") 15-25 63
(Identification number shown since no selection number is used.)
SHELLEY (163 "Let Your Love Light Shine").......15-25 64
SHELLEY (165 "Oh What a Night").......15-25 64

KACT-TIES
Singles: 7-inch
TRANS ATLAS (695 "Walking in the Rain").......200-300 62
(With thunderstorm sound effects at beginning.)
TRANS ATLAS (695 "Walking in the Rain").......50-100 62
(Without thunderstorm effect.)

KADAKS: see KODAKS

KADDO STRINGS
Singles: 7-inch
IMPACT (1005 "Crying Over You").......25-35 66
Also see BROWNER, Duke, & Kaddo Strings
Also see TARTANS with the Kaddo Strings

KADO, Ernie: see K-DOE, Ernie

KADOR, Ernest: see K-DOE, Ernie

KAE, Ronny
(With the Saints)
Singles: 7-inch
BAND BOX.......8-12 59-64
HONEY.......5-10 78
L.E.O. 5-10

KAEMPFERT, Bert, & His Orchestra P&R/R&B/LP '60
Singles: 7-inch
DECCA.......3-8 60-71
Picture Sleeves
DECCA.......4-8 66
EPs: 7-inch
DECCA.......5-8 61
LPs: 10/12-inch
CADENCE.......10-15 61
DECCA.......10-15 59-72
MCA.......5-10 73-76

KAGNY & Dirty Rats
Singles: 7-inch
MOTOWN.......3-4 83
LPs: 10/12-inch
MOTOWN.......5-8 83

KAHANE, Jackie
Singles: 7-inch
RAINTREE.......4-6 77

KAI, Lani
Singles: 7-inch
KEEN.......10-15 59

KAIN, Buddy
Singles: 7-inch
BAND BOX.......4-8 62
MYERS (106 "Jump Rope Hop")...20-30 60
20TH FOX (118 "Spider").......10-20 60s

KAI-RAY
Singles: 7-inch
LODESTAR.......4-8 62

KAJAGOOGOO P&R/D&D/LP '83
(Kaja)
Singles: 12-inch
EMI AMERICA.......4-6 83-85
Singles: 7-inch
EMI AMERICA.......3-4 83-85
Picture Sleeves
EMI AMERICA.......3-4 83

LPs: 10/12-inch
EMI AMERICA ... 5-8 83-85
Also see LIMAHL

KAJANUS - PICKETT
Singles: 7-inch
MCA ... 3-5 73
LPs: 10/12-inch
MCA ... 8-10 73
Also see SAILOR

KAK
Singles: 7-inch
EPIC (10383 "Everything's Changing") ... 10-15 68
EPIC (10446 "Disbelievin' ") ... 10-15 69
LPs: 10/12-inch
EPIC (26429 "Kak") ... 75-125 69
Members: Chris Lockheed; Delmer Patten; Joe Damrell; Gary Yoder.
Also see BLUE CHEER
Also see HOLDEN, Randy

KAKO ORCHESTRA
LPs: 10/12-inch
MUSICOR ... 8-15 68

KALA, Sandy, & Mark Four
Singles: 7-inch
KALA (272 "Your House") ... 5-10

KALAPANA
LPs: 10/12-inch
ABATTOIR ... 8-10 76-77
WMOT ... 5-8 81

KALASANDRO
Singles: 7-inch
W.B. ... 5-8 59

KALB, Buddy
Singles: 7-inch
SCOTTIE ... 10-20 59

KALB, Danny, & Stefan Grossman
LPs: 10/12-inch
COTILLION ... 10-15 69

KALE
LPs: 10/12-inch
PRINCIPLE (6010 "Shambles") ... 8-12 91
Members: David Maricich; Brian Crook.

KALEIDOSCOPE LP '69
Singles: 7-inch
A&M ... 3-5 73
EPIC (10117 "Elevator Man") ... 15-25 67
EPIC (10219 "Little Orphan Nannie") ... 15-25 67
EPIC (10239 "I Found Out") ... 15-25 67
EPIC (10332 "Just a Taste") ... 15-25 68
EPIC (10481 "Lie to Me") ... 15-25 69
EPIC (10500 "Tempe, Arizona") ... 15-25 69
TSOP ... 4-8 75
LPs: 10/12-inch
BACK-TRAC ... 5-8 85
EPIC (24304 "Side Trips") ... 50-100 67
(Monaural.)
EPIC (24333 "Beacon from Mars") ... 50-100 67
(Monaural.)
EPIC (26304 "Side Trips") ... 50-75 67
(Stereo.)
EPIC (26333 "Beacon from Mars") ... 50-100 67
(Stereo.)
EPIC (26467 "Incredible Kaleidoscope") ... 20-40 69
EPIC (26508 "Bernice") ... 15-20 70
PACIFIC ARTS ... 5-10 78
Members: David Lindley; Solomon Feldthouse; John Vidican; John Welsh; Rick O'Neil; Brian Monsour; Chris Darrow.
Also see RODENTS
Also see WILLIAMS, Larry, & Johnny Guitar Watson

KALIN TWINS P&R/C&W/R&B '58
Singles: 78 rpm
DECCA (30642 "When") ... 50-75 58
Singles: 7-inch
AMY ... 4-8 66
DECCA (Except 30642) ... 8-15 58-62
DECCA (30642 "When") ... 15-25 58
(With silver lines on both sides of the name "Decca.")
DECCA (30642 "When") ... 8-15 58
(With a star and silver lines under the name "Decca.")
MCA ... 3-5 73
Picture Sleeves
DECCA (30977 "Why Don't You Believe Me") ... 10-20 59
EPs: 7-inch
DECCA (2623 "Kalin Twins") ... 25-50 58
DECCA (2641 "Forget Me Not") ... 25-50 59
LPs: 10/12-inch
DECCA (8812 "Kalin Twins") ... 50-75 58
VOCALION (73771 "Kalin Twins") ... 30-40 66
Members: Hal Kalin; Herb Kalin.
Also see LEE, Brenda / Bill Haley & Comets / Kalin Twins / Four Aces

KALLABASH CORP
LPs: 10/12-inch
UNCLE BILL (311 "Kallabash Corp") ... 30-50 70
Members: Ted Keaton; Rick Oates.

KALLEN, Kitty P&R '49
Singles: 78 rpm
DECCA ... 4-8 54-57
COLUMBIA ... 4-8 54
MERCURY ... 4-8 51-54
Singles: 7-inch
BELL ... 4-6 67
DECCA ... 5-10 54-59
COLUMBIA (40000 series) ... 5-10 54
COLUMBIA (41000 series) ... 4-8 59-61
MGM ... 4-6 65
MERCURY ... 5-10 51-54
PHILIPS ... 4-6 66
RCA ... 4-8 63
20TH-CENTURY-FOX ... 4-8 64
U.A. ... 4-8 65
Promotional Singles
DECCA (78094 "Personal Introduction by Kitty Kallen to '54 Christmas Seal Song") ... 8-12 54
(Single-sided promotional pressing.)
Picture Sleeves
DECCA (290 "It's Not the Whistle") ... 10-15 55
EPs: 7-inch
DECCA ... 10-15 54-56
COLUMBIA ... 10-15 54
MERCURY ... 10-15 55
LPs: 10/12-inch
COLUMBIA ... 10-20 60-61
DECCA (8397 "It's a Lonesome Old Town") ... 20-30 56
MCA ... 4-8 83
MERCURY (25206 "Pretty Kitty Kallen Sings") ... 30-50 55
(10-inch LP.)
MOVIETONE ... 8-12 67
RCA ... 10-20 63
20TH-CENTURY-FOX ... 10-15 64
VOCALION ... 10-20 59
WING ... 10-15 63
Also see ANN-MARGRET / Kitty Kallen / Della Reese
Also see HAYES, Richard, & Kitty Kallen
Also see JAMES, Harry, & His Orchestra

KALLEN, Kitty, & Georgie Shaw
Singles: 78 rpm
DECCA ... 4-8 55
Singles: 7-inch
DECCA ... 5-10 55
Also see KALLEN, Kitty
Also see SHAW, Georgie

KALLMANN, Gunter, Chorus LP '65
Singles: 7-inch
4 CORNERS ... 4-6 65-68
LPs: 10/12-inch
4 CORNERS ... 8-12 65-68
POLYDOR ... 5-10 70

KALLUM, Johnny
Singles: 7-inch
BANG (730 "The Great Debate") ... 4-6 76
GRT (048 "Patty & Friends") ... 4-6 75

KALYAN R&B/LP '77
Singles: 7-inch
MCA ... 3-5 77
LPs: 10/12-inch
MCA ... 8-10 77

KAMA-DEL-SUTRA
Singles: 7-inch
ZIG ZAG (273 "Come On Up") ... 75-125 67

KAMEN, Michael
LPs: 10/12-inch
ATCO ... 10-12 73
BUDDAH ... 8-10 80

KAMIKAZE D&D '84
Singles: 12-inch
A&M ... 4-6 84
Singles: 7-inch
A&M ... 3-4 84

KAMINSKI, George
Singles: 7-inch
MOST ... 5-8 59

KAMON, Karen P&R '84
Singles: 7-inch
COLUMBIA ... 3-4 84
Picture Sleeves
COLUMBIA ... 3-4 84

KAMPELLS
Singles: 7-inch
SELECT (736 "New Lock on My Door") ... 50-75 63

KAMPUS KIDS
Singles: 7-inch
ENSIGN ... 10-20 58

KAMPUS KINSMEN
Singles: 7-inch
ENSIGN ... 4-8 63

KAN DELLS
Singles: 7-inch
BEAR (1971 "Do You Know") ... 100-125 66
BOSS (6501 "Cry Girl") ... 25-35 65

KANDY, Jim C&W '65
Singles: 7-inch
K-ARK ... 4-8 65

KANDY KOLORED KONSPIRACY
Singles: 7-inch
MEDIA (007 "Konspiracy '68") ... 10-20 68

KANE, Bernie, & Rockin' Rhythms
Singles: 7-inch
TABB ... 8-12 66

KANE, Big Daddy LP '88
Singles: 7-inch
REPRISE ... 3-4 89
Picture Sleeves
REPRISE ... 3-4 89
LPs: 10/12-inch
COLD CHILL ... 5-8 88-90

KANE, Eden
Singles: 7-inch
FONTANA ... 4-8 64
LONDON ... 5-10 61-62
T.A. ... 3-6 70

KANE, Gary
Singles: 7-inch
AMY ... 4-8 63

KANE, General: see GENERAL KANE

KANE, Jerry
Singles: 7-inch
AUDIO ARTISTS ("There's Not Enough Love") ... 10-20
(No selection number used.)

KANE, Kieran C&W '81
Singles: 7-inch
ELEKTRA ... 3-5 81-82
W.B. ... 3-4 83-84
Also see O'KANES

KANE, Madleen P&R '82
Singles: 12-inch
CHALET ... 4-6 82
TSR ... 4-6 85
Singles: 7-inch
CHALET ... 3-4 82
W.B. ... 3-5 78-79
Picture Sleeves
W.B. ... 3-5 78-79
LPs: 10/12-inch
CHALET ... 5-8 82
W.B. ... 5-8 78-79

KANE, Paul
(Paul Simon)
Singles: 7-inch
TRIBUTE (128 "Carlos Dominguez") ... 50-75 63
(Copies crediting "Paul Simon" as the singer are bootlegs.)
Also see SIMON, Paul

KANE, Sandy
Singles: 7-inch
BARE with ME (69 "He Comes and Goes Home.") ... 10-15

KANE, Tommy, & Emeralds
Singles: 7-inch
DEAN ... 5-10 60

KANE & ABEL
Singles: 7-inch
DESTINATION (607 "Man Ain't Supposed to Cry") ... 8-12 65
RED BIRD (10059 "He Will Break Your Heart") ... 8-12 66
Members: Art Herrera; Al Herrera. Session: James Holvay; Gary Beiser.
Also see LITTLE ARTIE & PHAROAHS
Also see MOB

KANE & ABEL
Singles: 7-inch
CORONADO ... 4-8 60s

KANE GANG P&R/LP '87
Singles: 12-inch
LONDON ... 4-6 86
Singles: 7-inch
CAPITOL ... 3-4 87
LONDON ... 3-4 86
Picture Sleeves
CAPITOL ... 3-4 87
LPs: 10/12-inch
CAPITOL ... 5-8 87
LONDON ... 5-8 86
POLYGRAM ... 5-8 85

KANE'S COUSINS
Singles: 7-inch
SHOVE LOVE (069 "Take Your Love and Shove It") ... 10-15 69
(Colored vinyl.)
SHOVE LOVE (500 "Take Your Love and Shove It") ... 5-10 69
(Black vinyl.)
LPs: 10/12-inch
SHOVE LOVE (9827 "Undergum Bubbleground") ... 25-35 69
Also see COUSINS

KANGAROO
Singles: 7-inch
MGM (13960 "I Never Tell Me Twice") ... 5-10 68
LPs: 10/12-inch
MGM (4586 "Kangaroo") ... 10-15 68
Members: Barbara Keith; N.D. Smart; John Hall.
Also see HALL, John
Also see KEITH, Barbara, & Kangaroo
Also see SMART, N.D., & Kangaroo

KANGAS, Les
Singles: 7-inch
KANGAROO ... 5-10 59

KANNIBAL KOMIX
Singles: 7-inch
COLOSSUS ... 3-5 70
Picture Sleeves
COLOSSUS ... 3-5 70
LPs: 10/12-inch
COLOSSUS ... 10-15 70

KANNON, Jackie
Singles: 7-inch
STAGE ... 4-8 63

KANNON, Ray, & Corals
Singles: 7-inch
CUCA (1078 "Muleskinner Twist") ... 10-20 62
CUCA (1106 "Little Baby") ... 10-20 62
CUCA (1122 "Rendezvous") ... 10-20 63
CUCA (1164 "Let's Surf") ... 10-20 64
Member: James Curley Cooke.; Ray Kannonberg; Dick Bartig; Buddy Bradford; Jim Marcotte; Tom Litzer.
Also see CORALS

KANNON, Sandy
Singles: 7-inch
KEF ... 10-15
Also see OVATIONS

KANO R&B '80
Singles: 7-inch
EMERGENCY ... 3-5 80
MIRAGE ... 3-4 81
LPs: 10/12-inch
EMERGENCY ... 5-8 81
MIRAGE ... 5-8 81

KANSAS LP '74
Singles: 12-inch
CBS ASSOCIATED ... 5-10 83
(Promotional only.)
MCA ... 5-8 88
(Promotional only.)
Singles: 7-inch
CBS ASSOCIATED ... 3-4 83
KIRSHNER ... 3-5 74-82
MCA (17290 "Power") ... 3-6 87
(CD mix on vinyl. Promotional issue only.)
MCA (50000 series) ... 3-4 86-87
Picture Sleeves
CBS ASSOCIATED ... 3-4 83
KIRSHNER ... 3-5 82
MCA ... 3-4 86-87
LPs: 10/12-inch
CBS ASSOCIATED ... 5-8 83-84
KIRSHNER (30000 series) ... 8-12 74-82
KIRSHNER (40000 series) ... 15-25 81-82
(Half-speed mastered.)
MCA ... 5-8 86-88
Promotional LPs
BURNS MEDIA ("Two for the Show") ... 15-25 78
KIRSHNER (34929 "Point of Know Return") ... 50-100 79
(Picture disc. Promotional issue only.)
KIRSHNER (35660 "Two for the Show") ... 10-15 78
Members: Dave Hope; Rich Williams; Phil Ehart; Kerry Livgren; Robbie Steinhardt; Steve Walsh; Terry Brock.
Also see LIVGREN, Kerry
Also see MORSE, Steve, Band
Also see STREETS
Also see WALSH, Steve

KANSAS CITY PLAYBOYS
Singles: 7-inch
RSVP ... 4-8 63

KANSAS CITY TOM CATS
Singles: 78 rpm
JOSIE ... 4-8 55-56
Singles: 7-inch
JOSIE ... 5-10 55-56

KANSAS CITY TURNPIKES
Singles: 7-inch
ANGLETONE (537 "Douglas Blues") ... 10-20 59

KANSAS CITY TWISTERS
Singles: 7-inch
APT ... 4-8 62

KANSAS STANDARD
Singles: 7-inch
NOLTA ... 5-10 68

KANT, Klerk
(Klark Kent)
LPs: 10/12-inch
I.R.S. ... 5-8 82

KANTNER, Hillary C&W '84
Singles: 7-inch
RCA ... 3-4 84-85

KANTNER, Paul R&B '79
Singles: 7-inch
MALACO ... 3-5 79
RCA ... 5-10 83

KANTNER, Paul, & Grace Slick LP '71
(With David Freiberg)
Singles: 7-inch
GRUNT ... 3-5 72
Picture Sleeves
GRUNT ... 3-6 72
LPs: 10/12-inch
GRUNT (0100 series) ... 8-10 71-73
GRUNT (2002 "Sunfighter") ... 10-15 71
(Includes booklet.)
GRUNT (4000 series) ... 5-8 82
Also see GRATEFUL DEAD
Also see JEFFERSON AIRPLANE
Also see SLICK, Grace

KANTNER, Paul, & Jefferson Starship LP '70
Singles: 7-inch
RCA ... 3-6 71
Also see KANTNER, Paul
Also see JEFFERSON STARSHIP

KAOMA LP '90
Singles: 7-inch
EPIC ... 3-4 90
LPs: 10/12-inch
EPIC ... 5-8 89

KAPLAN, Gabriel P&R '77
Singles: 7-inch
ABC ... 3-5 74
ELEKTRA ... 3-5 76-77
Picture Sleeves
ELEKTRA ... 3-5 77
LPs: 10/12-inch
ABC ... 8-10 74

KAPP, Hub: see HUB KAPP

KAPP, Johnny
Singles: 7-inch
LAURIE (3182 "I Love Her, She Loves Me") ... 5-10 63

KAPPALIERS
Singles: 7-inch
SHADOW (1229 "Down in Mexicali") ... 500-750 50s

KAPPAS
Singles: 7-inch
WONDER (112 "Sweet Juanita") ... 40-60 59

KAPT. KOPTER & Fabulous Twirly Birds
(Randy California)
Singles: 7-inch
EPIC ... 3-5 73
LPs: 10/12-inch
EPIC (31755 "Kaptain Kopter and the Fabulous Twirly Birds") ... 20-30 72
Also see CALIFORNIA, Randy

KAPTAIN KOOL & KONGS
Singles: 7-inch
EPIC ... 3-5 78
LPs: 10/12-inch
EPIC ... 5-8 78
Members: Michael Lembeck; Debby Clinger; Louise Duart; Mickey McMeel.
Also see CLINGERS

KAPTIONS
Singles: 7-inch
HAM-MIL (1520 "Dreaming of You") ... 15-25
LOST CAUSE ("Dreaming of You") ... 5-10
(Selection number not known.)
Member: Jack Strong.
Also see LYTATIONS

KAPUSTA, Dick, & Troubled Mind
Singles: 7-inch
CUCA (1508 "Forgotten People") ... 5-10 70

KARAS, Anton P&R '50
Singles: 78 rpm
LONDON ... 4-6 50
Singles: 7-inch
LONDON ... 5-10 50
EPs: 7-inch
LONDON (6035 "Anton Karas") ... 15-25 50

KARE TAKERS
Singles: 7-inch
WAM (5970 "Have You Seen My Baby") ... 15-25 67

KAREN, Kenny P&R '73
(Ken Karen)
Singles: 7-inch
BIG TREE ... 3-5 73
COLUMBIA (3-42264 "Oh Susie, Forgive Me") ... 25-35 62
(Compact 33 Single.)
COLUMBIA (3-42452 "To Sandy, with Love") ... 25-35 62
(Compact 33 Single.)
COLUMBIA (3-42638 "16 Years Ago Tonight") ... 25-35 62
(Compact 33 Single.)
COLUMBIA (4-42264 "Oh Susie, Forgive Me") ... 10-20 62
COLUMBIA (4-42452 "To Sandy, with Love") ... 10-20 62
COLUMBIA (4-42638 "16 Years Ago Tonight") ... 10-20 62
STRAND ... 10-15 59-60
Picture Sleeves
COLUMBIA (42264 "Oh Susie, Forgive Me") ... 15-25 62
COLUMBIA (42452 "To Sandy, with Love") ... 15-25 62

KAREN & CUBBY
Singles: 7-inch
DISNEYLAND ... 10-20 58

KAREN SUE
Singles: 7-inch
IMPERIAL ... 5-10 62
U.A. ... 4-8 66

KARI, Harry, & His Six Saki Sippers P&R '53
(Harry Stewart)
Singles: 78 rpm
CAPITOL ... 4-8 53-55
Singles: 7-inch
CAPITOL ... 8-15 53-55
Also see YORGESSON, Yogi

KARI, Sax
(With His Jivin' Jukes and Boogie Bob; Sax Kari Show Starring the Newports)
Singles: 78 rpm
APOLLO (389 "Play It Cool Blues") ... 10-15 47
APOLLO (397 "I'll Never Leave You") ... 10-15 47
GREAT LAKES ... 5-10 54
STATES ... 5-10 53
Singles: 7-inch
AISLE (004 "T.V. Mama") ... 3-5 94
(Black vinyl. 900 made.)
AISLE (004 "T.V. Mama") ... 5-10 94
(Red vinyl. 100 made.)

CONTOUR (301 "Chicky-Chop-Chop")..........10-15 59
FLORIDA ROCK..........4-6 80
GREAT LAKES (1205 "Train Ride")..........25-50 54
JOB (1118 "Chocolate Fizz")..........25-50 57
STATES (115 "Daughter")..........10-20 53
STATES (117 "Henry")..........10-20 53
Picture Sleeves
AISLE (004 "T.V. Mama")..........3-5 94
Also see ALLEY KATS
Also see CANDY YAMS
Also see FALCONS
Also see IRVING, Gloria, & Sax Kari
Also see VON CARL, Jimmy
Also see WARD, Little Sammy
Also see WATKINS, Katie / Texas Red & Jimmy

KARI, Sax / Lena Gordon
Singles: 78 rpm
CHECKER..........10-15 54
Singles: 7-inch
CHECKER (803 "Disc Jockey Jamboree")..........25-35 54
Also see KARI, Sax

KARI, Sax, & Quailtones
Singles: 78 rpm
JOSIE (779 "Tears of Love")..........25-50 55
Singles: 7-inch
JOSIE (779 "Tears of Love")..........100-200 55

KARI, Sax & Rockin' Jukes / Seven Secrets / Tony & Rockin' Orbits
EPs: 7-inch
AISLE (005 "Big Fat Fanny")..........5-8 95
Also see KARI, Sax
Also see SEVEN SECRETS
Also see TONY & ROCKIN' ORBITS

KARL, Frankie P&R/R&B '68
(With the Dreams)
Singles: 7-inch
D.C...........10-15 68
LIBERTY (56164 "Don't Sleep Too Long")..........10-20 70
PHILTOWN (105 "You Should O' Held On")..........5-10

KARLOFF, Boris
Singles: 7-inch
MOL..........4-8 67
EPs: 7-inch
COLUMBIA (1526 "Peter Pan")..........25-50 50
LPs: 10/12-inch
CAEDMON (1088 "Just So Stories")..........20-30 58
CAEDMON (1129 "Fairy Tales")..........15-25 62
CAEDMON (1182 "Let' Listen")..........15-25 63
(With Julie Harris.)
CAEDMON (1221 "Aesop's Fables")..........10-15 68
COLUMBIA (4312 "Peter Pan")..........50-75 50
DECCA (4833 "An Evening with Karloff and Friends")..........10-20 67
MGM (901 "How the Grinch Stole Christmas")..........10-20 66
MERCURY (20815 "Tales of the Frightened, Vol. 1")..........25-50 63
MERCURY (20816 "Tales of the Frightened, Vol. 2")..........25-50 63
MERCURY (60815 "Tales of the Frightened, Vol. 1")..........25-50 63
MERCURY (60816 "Tales of the Frightened, Vol. 2")..........25-50 63
PLAYHOUR (22 "Tales of Mystery and Imagination")..........20-40 61

KARMA R&B '77
Singles: 7-inch
HORIZON..........3-5 79
LPs: 10/12-inch
A&M..........8-10 77

KARMELS
Singles: 7-inch
KARMA..........4-8

KARMEN, Steve
Singles: 7-inch
AUDIO FIDELITY (171 "You've Said It All")..........8-12 68
ELDORADO (510 "Freight Train")..15-25 57

KARNES, Pete, Blooze Band
LPs: 10/12-inch
V8..........8-12

KARP, Charlie
(With the Name Droppers)
LPs: 10/12-inch
GRUDGE..........5-8 87
Members: Charlie Karp; Mark Epstein; Reggy Marks; Tyger MacNeal; John Goldschmid; Dan Aldrich; Roger Ball; Corky Laing; Felix Cavaliere; Frank Sims; Jeff Bova.
Also see AVERAGE WHITE BAND
Also see CAVALIERE, Felix
Also see DIRTY ANGELS
Also see FUN BAND
Also see LAING, Corky
Also see LEE, Arthur
Also see MILES, Buddy
Also see WHITE CHOCOLATE

KAROL, Shirley
Singles: 7-inch
DAKAR (1449 "Just to Make You Happy")..........10-20

KARPETBAGGERS
Singles: 7-inch
TRIG..........4-8 60s

KARR, Eddie
Singles: 7-inch
MEMORY..........3-5 77

KARR, Tim
LP: 10/12-inch
EMI..........5-8 89

KARR, Tyler
Singles: 7-inch
CREST..........4-8 61

KARRIANNS
("Karriann's - Don & Neil with the Playboys")
Singles: 7-inch
PELPAL (118 "Don't Want Your Picture")..........500-750 50s

KARTER, Kenny
(Kenny Hinkle)
Singles: 7-inch
WESTCO (8 "Surfing with Bony Maronie")..........10-20 63
(Black vinyl. First issued as by the Sentinals.)
WESTCO (8 "Surfing with Bony Maronie")..........20-30 63
(Colored vinyl.)
Also see HINKLE, Kenny
Also see SENTINALS

KARTHAGO
LPs: 10/12-inch
BASF..........10-12 74

KARTOON KREW R&B '85
Singles: 7-inch
PROFILE..........3-4 86

KARTUNE KAPERS
Singles: 7-inch
SPACE (11 "Knock on Wood")..........15-25 67

KARTUNES
Singles: 78 rpm
MGM..........10-25 57
Singles: 7-inch
MGM (12598 "Raindrops")..........15-25 57
MGM (12680..........10-20 58

KASANDRA P&R/R&B/LP '68
(With the Midnight Riders; John Anderson)
Singles: 7-inch
CAPITOL..........4-8 68
IMPERIAL..........5-10 60
LPs: 10/12-inch
CAPITOL..........10-15 68

KASEM, Casey
Singles: 7-inch
MGM..........3-4 71
W.B. (5474 "Letter from Elaina")..........10-15 64
LPs: 10/12-inch
SIDEWALK..........10-20 67

KASENETZ - KATZ SINGING ORCHESTRAL CIRCUS P&R '68
(Kasenetz - Katz Super Cirkus; Kasenetz - Katz Fighter Squadron)
Singles: 7-inch
BELL (966 "When He Comes")..........5-10 71
(With 10CC.)
BUDDAH..........4-8 68
EPIC..........3-5 77
MAGNA-GLIDE..........3-5 75
SUPER K..........3-5 69-71
LPs: 10/12-inch
BUDDAH..........10-15 68
Also see LT. GARCIA'S MAGIC MUSIC BOX
Also see MUSIC EXPLOSION
Also see NELSON, Teri
Also see 1910 FRUITGUM COMPANY
Also see OHIO EXPRESS
Also see 10CC

KASHA, Al
Singles: 7-inch
W.B...........5-10 58

KASHIF R&B/D&D/LP '83
Singles: 12-inch
ARISTA..........4-6 83-86
Singles: 7-inch
ARISTA..........3-4 83-88
LPs: 10/12-inch
ARISTA..........5-8 83-87
Also see KENNY G. & Kashif
Also see MOORE, Melba, & Kashif
Also see WARWICK, Dionne, & Kashif

KASHIF & MELI'SA MORGAN R&B '87
Singles: 7-inch
ARISTA..........3-4 87
Also see MORGAN, Meli'sa

KASHMIRS
Singles: 7-inch
WONDER (104 "Heaven Only Knows")..........125-175 58

KASPER, Mary
Singles: 7-inch
MERCURY..........5-10 59

KASS, Steve, & Lovelarks
Singles: 7-inch
CLASS (10X "Darling, My Love")..........200-300 57

KATCHER, Del: see KACHER, Del

KATS
Singles: 7-inch
E&C (1002 "Wear Me Out")..........10-20 63

KATFISH P&R '75
Singles: 7-inch
BIG TREE..........3-5 75

KATHY & CALENDARS
Singles: 7-inch
PORT..........4-8 67

KATHY & CAROL
LPs: 10/12-inch
ELEKTRA..........10-15 65

KATMANDU
LPs: 10/12-inch
MAINSTREAM (6131 "Katmandu")..........30-40 71
Members: Norman Harris; Ken Zale; Bob Jabo; Bob Caldwell.

KATO, Tommy
Singles: 7-inch
FORTUNE..........4-8 64

KATRINA & WAVES P&R/LP '85
Singles: 7-inch
CAPITOL..........3-4 85-86
SBK..........3-4 89
Picture Sleeves
CAPITOL..........3-4 85-86
SBK..........3-4 89
LPs: 10/12-inch
CAPITOL..........5-8 85-86
SBK..........5-8 89
Members: Katrina Leskanich; Kimberley Rew; Alex Cooper; Vince de La Cruz.
Also see SOFT BOYS

KATZ, Fred
LPs: 10/12-inch
WARNER..........10-20 59

KATZ, Mickey, & His Orchestra P&R '50
Singles: 78 rpm
CAPITOL..........4-8 51-57
Singles: 7-inch
CAPITOL..........5-12 51-62
EPs: 7-inch
CAPITOL..........10-20 53-56
LPs: 10/12-inch
CAPITOL (Except SM-298)..........15-35 53-65
CAPITOL (SM-298 "Mickey Katz")..........5-8 78
Also see JONES, Spike

KATZ KRADLE
Singles: 7-inch
SHUR SHOT (6609 "Bad Case of You on My Mind")..........8-12

KATZMAN, Nick
LPs: 10/12-inch
KICKING MULE..........8-10 77

KAUFMAN, Murray
(Murry the "K"; Ludwig Von Kaufman)
Singles: 78 rpm
FRATERNITY..........10-15 55
Singles: 7-inch
FRATERNITY (714 "Out of the Bushes")..........15-25 55
HAN-O-DISC ("A Salute to Murray the K")..........25-35 79
(Picture disc. Promotional issue only.)
RED BIRD..........5-8 65

KAUFMANN, Bob
LPs: 10/12-inch
LHI (12002 "Trip Thru a Blown Mind")..........30-40 67

KAUKONEN, Jorma LP '81
(With Vital Parts)
Singles: 7-inch
GRUNT..........3-5 73
LPs: 10/12-inch
GRUNT..........8-12 73
RCA..........5-10 79-81
RELIX (2027 "Quah")..........10-20 87
(Picture disc.)
Also see HOT TUNA
Also see JEFFERSON AIRPLANE

KAUKONEN, Peter
Singles: 7-inch
GRUNT..........3-5 72-73
LPs: 10/12-inch
GRUNT..........8-10 72

KAVANOVICH, Ivan
Singles: 7-inch
ELKO..........5-10 62

KAVETTES
Singles: 7-inch
OKEH (7194 "I'm Not Sorry for You")..........20-40 64

KAY, Carol
Singles: 78 rpm
RECORDED in HOLLYWOOD..........10-15 54
Singles: 7-inch
RECORDED in HOLLYWOOD..........15-25 54
WRIGHT-SOUND (4479 "This Time You're Wrong")..........10-20

KAY, Eddie
Singles: 7-inch
BETHELEM (3063 "Cindy")..........10-20 63

KAY, Gary
(Billy Carlucci)
Singles: 7-inch
RAN-DEE (116 "Cinderella")..........75-125 63
Session: Andre Williams.
Also see BILLY & ESSENTIALS
Also see WILLIAMS, Andre

KAY, Janet
Singles: 7-inch
CUCA (68111 "The Worst Is Yet to Come")..........5-10 68

KAY, Jerry
Singles: 7-inch
PRESS-LEY..........5-10

KAY, Joey
LPs: 10/12-inch
LA BREA (1816 "Joey Kay")..........15-25 61

KAY, John P&R/LP '72
(With Steppenwolf; with Sparrows)
Singles: 7-inch
DUNHILL..........3-5 72-73
MERCURY..........3-5 78
LPs: 10/12-inch
COLUMBIA..........10-20 69
DUNHILL..........8-10 72-73
MERCURY..........5-8 78
QWIL..........5-8 87
Also see STEPPENWOLF

KAY, Johnny
Singles: 7-inch
A..........5-10 59
TIGER..........10-15
LPs: 10/12-inch
SPIN-O-RAMA..........5-10 60s

KAY, Melissa C&W '88
Singles: 7-inch
REED (Black vinyl)..........3-4 88-89
REED (1119 "After Lovin' You")..........4-6 88
(Colored vinyl.)

KAY, Rick, & Shades of Today
Singles: 7-inch
POLICE..........4-8 76

KAY, Tommy
Singles: 7-inch
EMBERS (1521 "Man Without a Name")..........15-25 60s
SARA (6754 "Oh, My Love")..........15-25 67

KAY GEES: see KAY-GEES

KAYAK LP '76
Singles: 7-inch
JANUS..........3-5 78
MERCURY..........3-4 80
LPs: 10/12-inch
HARVEST..........8-10 74
JANUS..........5-10 75-79
MERCURY..........5-8 80
Also see WERNER, Max

KAYE, Angela C&W '81
Singles: 7-inch
YATAHEY..........3-4 81

KAYE, Barry C&W '78
Singles: 7-inch
MCA..........3-5 78

KAYE, Carol
(Carol Kay)
Singles: 7-inch
CREST (1062 "Time")..........8-12 59
GNP..........5-10 62
TEEN TIME..........5-10 62
Also see DEE, Tommy
Also see JAN & DEAN
Also see MONTEZ, Chris

KAYE, Colleen, & Secrets
Singles: 7-inch
BIG TOP..........5-10 63

KAYE, Danny P&R '47
(Danny Kaye & Co.)
Singles: 78 rpm
COLUMBIA..........4-8 49-54
DECCA..........4-8 50-56
RCA..........4-8 47-48
Singles: 7-inch
COLUMBIA..........3-10 49-70
DECCA..........5-10 50-56
REPRISE..........5-10 62
Picture Sleeves
DECCA (151 "Little White Duck")..........10-15 50s
REPRISE (20105 "D-o-d-g-e-r-s Song")..........8-12 62
EPs: 7-inch
CAPITOL..........5-10 58
COLUMBIA..........10-20 49-54
DECCA..........8-15 54-57
LPs: 10/12-inch
CAMDEN..........15-25 57
CAPITOL..........15-25 58
COLUMBIA (6000 series)..........25-50 49-54
(10-inch LPs.)
DECCA (100 series)..........10-20 63
DECCA (5000 series)..........20-40 54
(10-inch LPs.)
DECCA (8000 series)..........20-40 54-59
DECCA (78000 series)..........10-15 67
GOLDEN..........5-10 62
HARMONY (7000 series)..........15-25 57
HARMONY (7300 series)..........8-15 64
Also see ARMSTRONG, Louis, & Red Nichols, & Danny Kaye

KAYE, Danny, & Louis Armstrong
Singles: 7-inch
DOT..........4-8 59-64
Picture Sleeves
DOT..........5-10 59
Also see ARMSTRONG, Louis

KAYE, Danny, Jimmy Durante, Jane Wyman & Groucho Marx P&R '51
Singles: 78 rpm
DECCA..........3-8 51
Singles: 7-inch
DECCA..........5-10 51
Also see DURANTE, Jimmy
Also see KAYE, Danny
Also see MARX, Groucho

KAYE, Debbie Lori C&W '68
Singles: 7-inch
COLUMBIA..........4-8 65-68
Picture Sleeves
COLUMBIA..........4-8 65

KAYE, Jimmy, & Coachmen
Singles: 7-inch
SOMA (1441 "Gloria")..........25-35 60s

KAYE, Kitty, & Cats
Singles: 7-inch
HAWK (72054 "Can't You Hear the Music")..........15-25

KAYE, Lenny
LPs: 10/12-inch
G.P.S...........5-10 84
Also see SMITH, Patti

KAYE, Lois C&W '79
Singles: 7-inch
OVATION..........3-5 79
LP: 10/12-inch
OVATION..........5-10 79

KAYE, Mary P&R '52
(Mary Kaye Trio)
Singles: 78 rpm
CAPITOL..........3-6 52
DECCA..........3-6 55-56
RCA..........3-6 54
Singles: 7-inch
BLUE-J..........4-8
CAMELOT..........4-6 67
CAPITOL..........5-10 52
DECCA..........5-10 55-56
LECTRON..........4-6 65
RCA..........5-10 54
VERVE..........4-8 60
W.B...........4-8 59
EPs: 7-inch
DECCA..........5-10 56
LPs: 10/12-inch
COLUMBIA..........8-15 62
DECCA..........10-25 56
MOVIETONE..........8-12 67
20TH FOX..........8-15 64
VERVE..........10-15 60-62
W.B...........10-20 59
Also see BYRNES, Edd "Kookie," with Joanie Sommers & Mary Kaye Trio

KAYE, Norman
Singles: 78 rpm
DECCA..........5-10 57
Singles: 7-inch
DECCA..........5-10 57

KAYE, Ritchie
Singles: 7-inch
ABC-PAR..........4-8 65

KAYE, Ronnie
Singles: 7-inch
SCENE..........3-5 77

KAYE, Sammy, & His Orchestra P&R '37
Singles: 78 rpm
COLUMBIA..........3-6 50-57
RCA..........3-6 52-53
Singles: 7-inch
COLUMBIA..........5-10 50-60
DECCA..........4-6 60-70
PROJECT 3..........3-5 72
RCA..........5-10 52-53
EPs: 7-inch
COLUMBIA..........5-15 50-60
DECCA..........4-6 64
RCA..........5-15 52-53
LPs: 10/12-inch
CAMDEN..........10-25 53-56
COLUMBIA..........10-25 50-62
DECCA..........8-15 60-70
HARMONY..........5-10 59-68
MCA..........5-10 74
PROJECT 3..........5-8 72
RCA..........5-10 68-72
VOCALION..........5-10 71
Also see CORNELL, Don

KAYE, Sandra C&W '78
Singles: 7-inch
DOOR KNOB..........3-5 78-79

KAYE, Thomas Jefferson
Singles: 7-inch
DUNHILL..........3-5 74
LPs: 10/12-inch
DUNHILL..........8-10 74

KAYE, Tony
(With the Heartbeats)
Singles: 7-inch
GMC (10004 "Hey, Hey, Little Orphan Annie")..........5-10 60s
HULL..........4-8 66

KAY-GEES R&B '74
Singles: 7-inch
DE-LITE..........3-5 78-79
GANG..........3-5 74-76
LPs: 10/12-inch
DELITE..........5-8 78-79
GANG..........5-10 75

KAYLAN, Howard, & Marc Volman
Singles: 7-inch
REPRISE (1113 "Nikki Hoi")..........4-6 72
LPs: 10/12-inch
REPRISE (2099 "The Phlorescent Leech & Eddie")..........10-15 72
Also see FLO & EDDIE
Also see T. REX

Also see TURTLES
Also see ZAPPA, Frank

KAYLI, Bob P&R '58
(With the Berry Gordy Orchestra; Robert Gordy)
Singles: 7-inch
ANNA (1104 "Never More") 25-35 59
CARLTON (482 "Everyone Was There") 20-30 58
GORDY (7004 "Toodle Loo"/"Hold On Pearl") 30-50 62
GORDY (7008 "Toodle Loo"/"Hold On Pearl") 20-30 62
TAMLA (54051 "Small Sad Sam")..20-30 61

KAYNINES
Singles: 7-inch
AMBER 4-8

KAYO & TRINITIES
Singles: 7-inch
SOUVENIR 10-20 60

KAYS BAND
(Kays; Kays Combo)
Singles: 7-inch
CAS LTD. 3-5
CHOICE (3757 "To Be with You")..10-20
CREATIVE ARTS 3-5 80
HIT 4-8
JCP (1007 "Shout") 10-20 64

KAZ, Eric
Singles: 7-inch
ATLANTIC 3-4 73
LPs: 10/12-inch
ATLANTIC 8-10 73
Also see AMERICAN FLYER
Also see BEAR

KAZ, Eric, & Craig Fuller
LPs: 10/12-inch
COLUMBIA 5-8 78
Also see KAZ, Eric

KAZAN, Lainie
Singles: 7-inch
COLPIX 4-8 65
MGM 4-8 66-68
POMPEII 3-5 71
LPs: 10/12-inch
MGM 12-25 66-69

KAZEECHES
Singles: 7-inch
MURIEL 4-8 65

KAZOOS BROTHERS
LPs: 10/12-inch
RHINO 5-8 80s

KAZY, Harlin, & Ernst Stacy
Singles: 7-inch
RENA 5-8 61

K-DOE: see K-DOE, Ernie

K-DOE, Ernie P&R/R&B '61
(Ernest Kador; Ernie Kado; K-Doe)
Singles: 78 rpm
SPECIALTY (563 "Eternity") 10-20 55
Singles: 7-inch
DUKE 5-10 64-69
EMBER (1050 "My Love for You") 25-35 59
EMBER (1075 "My Love for You") 10-20 61
IMPERIAL (039 "Mother-in-Law") 4-8 60s
INSTANT 5-10 63-64
MINIT (614 "Hello My Lover") 10-20 60
MINIT (623 "Mother-in-Law") 10-20 61
MINIT (634 "I Cried My Last Tear") 10-20 61
MINIT (656 "Lovin' You") 10-20 62
MINIT (661 "Be Sweet") 10-20 63
MINIT (665 "I'm the Boss") 10-20 63
SANSU (1016 "She Gave It All to Me") 10-20
SPECIALTY (563 "Eternity") 20-30 55
SYLA 4-8
U.A. (110 "Mother-in-Law") 3-5
LPs: 10/12-inch
BANDY (70004 "Ernie K-Doe, Vol. 1") 10-15 70s
BANDY (70005 "Ernie K-Doe, Vol. 2") 10-15 70s
JANUS 8-10 71
MINIT (0002 "Mother in Law") 75-100 61
Session: Benny Spellman.
Also see BLUE DIAMONDS
Also see SPELLMAN, Benny
Also see THOMAS, Irma / Ernie K-Doe / Showmen / Benny Spellman.

K-DOE, Ernie / Phil Phillips
Singles: 7-inch
RIPETE 3-4
Also see PHILLIPS, Phil

K-DOE, Ernie / Ray Smith
Singles: 7-inch
COLLECTABLES 3-4
Also see K-DOE, Ernie
Also see SMITH, Ray

KEACK, Alex
LPs: 10/12-inch
CROWN 5-10 60s

KEAGGY, Phil
LPs: 10/12-inch
MYRRH 5-8 78
NEW SONG 5-8 73-79
SPARROW 5-8 80-82
STAR SONG 5-8 78
Also see GLASS HARP

KEAN, Ronnie
Singles: 7-inch
FEDERAL (12424 "Charoit") 10-20 61

KEANE BROTHERS P&R '76
Singles: 12-inch
ABC 4-8 79
Singles: 7-inch
ABC 3-5 79
20TH FOX 3-4 76
LPs: 10/12-inch
ABC 5-8 79

KEARNEY, Christopher, & Pemmican
Singles: 7-inch
CAPITOL 3-5 73
LPs: 10/12-inch
CAPITOL 8-10 73

KEARNEY, Ramsey C&W '85
Singles: 7-inch
CHALLENGE 4-6 66
DARGON 3-4 84
HICKORY 4-6 62-64
JUBAL 3-5 72-73
NASHCO 3-4 85
SAFARI 3-5 74-90
SPOTLIGHT 3-4 81-88
Picture Sleeves
SAFARI 3-4 90
LPs: 10/12-inch
NASHCO 8-10 85
SAFARI 10-20 90

KEARNS, Nick, & His Satellites
Singles: 7-inch
TOBE (1177 "T'was Down in Mexico") 50-100 58
(Identification number shown since no selection number is used.)

KEATON, Johnny, & Twisters
Singles: 7-inch
SPAR 5-10 62

KEATS
Singles: 7-inch
EMI 3-4 84
LPs: 10/12-inch
EMI 5-8 84
Members: Colin Blunstone; Peter Bardens; Ian Bairnson; David Paton; Stuart Elliot.
Also see BARDENS, Peter
Also see BLUNSTONE, Colin
Also see PARSONS, Alan, Project
Also see POWELL, Andrew

KEBEKELEKTRIK
Singles: 7-inch
SALSOUL 3-5 78
LPs: 10/12-inch
SALSOUL 5-8 78

KEEBLER, Danny
Singles: 7-inch
SOUTH 10-15

KEEFER, Brenda
Singles: 7-inch
MARLO (1525 "Down the Line") 10-15 62
Also see KEEFER SISTERS

KEEFER, Rusty, & His Greenlights
Singles: 78 rpm
CORAL 5-10 55
Singles: 7-inch
CORAL 10-20 55

KEEFER SISTERS
Singles: 7-inch
LAWN 10-20 60
SWAN 8-12 58
VIRTUE 4-8
Also see KEEFER, Brenda

KEEGAN, Kathy
Singles: 7-inch
ABC 4-8 66
AL BRITE 5-10 60
COMPASS 4-8 67
DCP 4-8 64-65
MALIBU 4-8 63
LPs: 10/12-inch
ABC 10-15 66
DCP 10-20 64
MALIBU 10-20 63

KEEGAN, Sky
Singles: 7-inch
CLARIDGE 3-5 75

KEEL LP '85
Singles: 7-inch
GOLD MOUNTAIN 3-4 84-85
LPs: 10/12-inch
GOLD MOUNTAIN 5-8 85
MCA 5-8 86-87

KEEN, Billy
(Billy Keene)
Singles: 7-inch
ACCLAIM (1006 "Come a Little Closer") 15-25 61
DOTTIE (1134 "Somebody Please") 10-20
GALAXIE 8-12
KEEN (1922 "Don't Call Me") 30-50 58
KEEN (82123 "Angel") 5-10 61
LESLEY 5-10
PAULA (335 "Cross My Heart") 10-15 70
VAULT 8-12

KEEN, Speedy
Singles: 7-inch
ISLAND 3-5 75
TRACK 3-5 73
LPs: 10/12-inch
ISLAND 8-10 75
TRACK/MCA 8-10 73
Also see NEWMAN, Thunderclap

KEEN STEVE & TEENS
Singles: 7-inch
POLICE 4-8 74

KEENAN, Alex
Singles: 7-inch
COLGEMS 4-6 69

KEENAN, Ronny
Singles: 7-inch
SANDY (1005 "Juke box Queen")..50-75 57

KEENE, Billy: see KEEN, Billy

KEENE, Bob
(Bob Keene Orchestra; Quintet; with His Clarinet)
Singles: 7-inch
DEL-FI 5-10 60
MARAVILLA 4-8 66
MUSTANG 4-8 66
LPs: 10/12-inch
DEL-FI 15-20 59-62

KEENE, Bobby
Singles: 7-inch
CORAL (62290 "Angel or Devil") ...20-25 61

KEENE, Nelson
Singles: 7-inch
CAPITOL 3-5 61

KEENE, Tommy LP '86
Singles: 7-inch
GEFFEN 3-4 86
LPs: 10/12-inch
GEFFEN 5-8 86

KEENE, Verrill
Singles: 7-inch
SHOW TOWN (460 "Velvet Waters") 8-12

KEENEY, Chuck
Singles: 7-inch
FELSTED (8584 "Rockin' March") 15-25 59

KEENOS
Singles: 7-inch
LARK (4513 "Catwalk") 10-20 59
(Colored vinyl.)

KEENOS
Singles: 7-inch
LARK 5-10 59

KEEPER
LPs: 10/12-inch
RCA 5-8 82

KEEPERS
Singles: 7-inch
BRAVURA 4-8 65
CUSTOM 10-20 60s

KEEPERS
LPs: 10/12-inch
PLANET 5-8 80

KEEPERS OF THE LIGHT
Singles: 7-inch
STEED 4-8 67

KEETIE & KATS
Singles: 7-inch
HURON (22007 "Way Out") 8-12 62
K-RECORDS (301 "Move") 10-20 60

KEGGS
Singles: 7-inch
ORBIT (20959 "To Find Out") 200-300 67
(Identification number shown since no selection number is used. Reportedly 75 copies made.)
Note: Originals have "Produced by Yolanda Owens" at right. Counterfeits credit "Yalanda Owens" – Yolanda being misspelled.
Members: Art Lenox; Steve Cool; Bob Rich; Pat Amboyan.

KEITH P&R '66
(James Keefer)
Singles: 7-inch
DISCREET 3-5 71-74
MERCURY 4-8 66-68
RCA 4-6 69
Picture Sleeves
MERCURY 4-8 66-68
LPs: 10/12-inch
MERCURY 15-20 67
RCA 15-25 69
Also see KEITH & ADMIRATIONS
Also see TOKENS

KEITH
Singles: 7-inch
PASTEL (119 "Days Go By") 3-5 74

KEITH, Anne
Singles: 7-inch
MEMO (97 "Lonely Girl") 150-250 59

KEITH, Barbara
Singles: 7-inch
VERVE/FORECAST 4-6 69
LPs: 10/12-inch
VERVE/FORECAST 10-15 69

KEITH, Barbara, & Kangaroo
Singles: 7-inch
MGM (13961 "Daydream Stallion")..5-10 68
Also see KANGAROO
Also see KEITH, Barbara

KEITH, Bryan
Singles: 7-inch
DOT (16532 "Hound Dog") 10-15 63
JOSIE (897 "Always Heartaches") 20-30 62

KEITH, David
Singles: 7-inch
RCA 3-4 88
Picture Sleeves
RCA 3-5 88
Also see PRESLEY, Elvis / David Keith

KEITH, Dusty
Singles: 7-inch
ARK (294 "Fool Over You") 50-75

KEITH, Freeman, & Ramrods
Singles: 7-inch
KEY (15673 "I'll Find a New Love") 10-15

KEITH, Gordon
Singles: 7-inch
CALUMET (682 "Look Ahead") 15-25
STEELTOWN 8-12

KEITH, Larry
Singles: 7-inch
NUMBER ONE 3-5 79
RCA 3-5 80-81

KEITH, Rod
Singles: 7-inch
PRE-VIEW 5-10 70s

KEITH, Ron
Singles: 7-inch
A&M 8-12

KEITH, Ronnie
Singles: 7-inch
EL MONTE 8-12 61

KEITH & ADMIRATIONS
Singles: 7-inch
COLUMBIA (43268 "Dream") 5-10 65
Member: James Keefer.
Also see KEITH

KEITH & DONNA
Singles: 78 rpm
ROUND 4-6 75
LPs: 10/12-inch
RELIX 5-8 86
ROUND 10-20 75
Members: Keith Godchaux; Donna Godchaux.
Also see BROMBERG, David
Also see GRATEFUL DEAD
Also see HEART of GOLD BAND
Also see NEW RIDERS of the Purple Sage
Also see OLD and in the WAY / Keith & Donna / Robert Hunter / Phil Lesh & Ned Lagin

KELL & CHERRY
Singles: 7-inch
GLOWHILL (701 "That's What's Happenin' ") 15-25
Member: Kell Osborne.
Also see OSBORNE, Kell

KELLEM, Manny, & Orchestra P&R/LP '68
Singles: 7-inch
EPIC 4-6 68
METROMEDIA 4-6 69
LPs: 10/12-inch
EPIC 5-10 68

KELLER, Jack
Singles: 7-inch
JUBILEE 5-10 58

KELLER, Jerry P&R '59
Singles: 7-inch
CAPITOL 5-10 61
CORAL 5-10 63-64
JUBILEE 5-10 58
KAPP (K-277 "Here Comes Summer") 8-12 59
(Monaural.)
KAPP (KS-277 "Here Comes Summer") 20-30 59
(Stereo.)
KAPP (310 thru 353) 5-10 59-60
RCA 5-10 67
REPRISE 5-10 65
WEB 5-10 58
Picture Sleeves
KAPP (277 "Here Comes Summer") 10-15 59
KAPP (295 "If I Had a Girl") 10-15 59
LPs: 10/12-inch
KAPP (1178 "Here Comes Jerry Keller") 20-30 59
(Monaural.)
KAPP (3178 "Here Comes Jerry Keller") 25-35 59
(Stereo.)
Also see HYLAND, Brain / Jerry Keller

KELLERMAN, Sally
Singles: 7-inch
DECCA 3-5 73
LPs: 10/12-inch
DECCA 8-10 72

KELLEY, Cathy
Singles: 7-inch
DIXIE 5-10 59

KELLEY, Dean
Singles: 7-inch
CORAL (61969 "If The Shoe Fits") 10-15 58

KELLEY, Emorise
Singles: 7-inch
PEACOCK 4-8 62

KELLEY, John C&W '82
Singles: 7-inch
COMSTAR 3-4 82

KELLEY, Pat
Singles: 7-inch
CHIC 4-6

KELLEY, Peter
Singles: 7-inch
SIRE 3-6 69-71
LPs: 10/12-inch
SIRE 10-15 69

KELLI
Singles: 7-inch
SOUND STAGE 7 .... 4-8 64

KELLIS, Rick
Singles: 7-inch
MALA 4-8 61

KELLOGS
Singles: 7-inch
LAURIE 10-15 69
Member: Vito Balsamo.
Also see VITO & SALUTATIONS

KELLUM, Murry P&R '63
Singles: 7-inch
CINNAMON 3-5 73-74
EPIC 3-5 71-72
MUSIC MILL 3-5 76
PLANTATION 3-5 78
RANWOOD 3-5 76
LPs: 10/12-inch
PLANTATION 5-8 78

KELLUM, Murry, & Alton Lott
Singles: 7-inch
K&M 3-5 61

KELLUM, Murry / Glenn Sutton
Singles: 7-inch
ABC 3-5 73
M.O.C. (Except 658) 10-15 63-64
M.O.C. (658 "I Dreamed I Was a Beatle") 15-20 64
Also see KELLUM, Murry
Also see SUTTON, Glenn

KELLY, Bill
Singles: 7-inch
ARTIST'S RECORDING 3-4 82
Picture Sleeves
ARTIST'S RECORDING 4-6 82

KELLY, Bob, & Bob Kats
Singles: 7-inch
BANGO 4-8 62

KELLY, Calvin
Singles: 7-inch
CAMARO (3455 "I'm Begging You") 10-20

KELLY, Casey P&R '72
Singles: 7-inch
ELEKTRA 3-5 72-73
PRIVATE STOCK 3-5 77
LPs: 10/12-inch
ELEKTRA 8-10 72

KELLY, Clyde
Singles: 7-inch
CUCA (6471 "I'll Cry Tomorrow") ...15-25 64

KELLY, Colette
Singles: 7-inch
VOLT 3-6 69

KELLY, Emmett
LPs: 10/12-inch
ROULETTE (R-25130 "Sing Along with Emmett Kelly") 15-25 61
(Monaural.)
ROULETTE (SR-25130 "Sing Along with Emmett Kelly") 20-30 61

KELLY, George
Singles: 7-inch
WINLEY (237 "Just Rollin' ") 8-12 59

KELLY, George / Earl Knight
Singles: 7-inch
ABC-PAR (10023 "Let It Roll") 8-12 59
Also see KELLY, George
Also see KNIGHT, Earl, & George Kelly

KELLY, Grace: see CROSBY, Bing, & Grace Kelly

KELLY, Herman, & Life R&B '78
Singles: 7-inch
ALSTON 3-5 78

KELLY, Irene C&W '89
Singles: 7-inch
MCA 3-4 89

KELLY, J., & Premiers R&B '74
(J. Kely & Premiers)
Singles: 7-inch
ROADSHOW 3-5 74

KELLY, Jerri C&W '80
Singles: 7-inch
CARRERE 3-4 82
LITTLE GIANT 3-4 80-81
Also see MITCHELL, Price, & Jerri Kelly

KELLY, Jerry: see JERRY KELLY

KELLY, Jimmy
(With the Op Birds; with Rockabeats)
Singles: 78 rpm
IMPERIAL (8275 "Dunce Cap") 10-20 54
Singles: 7-inch
ASTRA (101 "Little Chickie") 15-25 58
CEVETONE (514 "Op Song") 5-10 63
COBRA (5028 "Little Chickie") 40-50 58
EPIC 5-10 63
IMPERIAL (8275 "Dunce Cap") 20-40 54
JIFFY (202 "Dunce Cap") 50-75 53
MERCURY 4-8 66

KELLY, Karen *C&W '70*
Singles: 7-inch
CAPITOL 3-5 70
SOUND STAGE 7 4-8 64-65

KELLY, Lee
Singles: 7-inch
WASP 4-8

KELLY, Leon, & Rhythm Rockers
Singles: 7-inch
SPACE 10-15 59

KELLY, Mike
LPs: 10/12-inch
RELIX 5-8 86
Also see GRATEFUL DEAD
Also see KINGFISH

KELLY, Mike, & Legend
Singles: 7-inch
MEGAPHONE (705 "I Love the Little Girls") 10-15 60s
Also see LEGEND

KELLY, Monty, & His Orchestra *P&R '53*
Singles: 78 rpm
ESSEX 3-5 53-54
Singles: 7-inch
CARLTON 4-8 59-60
ESSEX 5-10 53-54
LPs: 10/12-inch
ALSHIRE 4-8 72
CARLTON 10-20 59

KELLY, Nat / Ron-Dels
Singles: 7-inch
CHARAY (37 "Looking Back") 4-8
Also see KELLY, Nathaniel
Also see RON-DELS

KELLY, Nathaniel
Singles: 7-inch
JUBILEE 4-8 65
Also see KELLY, Nat / Ron-Dels

KELLY, Pat
Singles: 7-inch
CHIC 10-15 57
JUBILEE (5315 "Hey Doll Baby") 35-55 58
JUBILEE (5333 "Patsy") 8-12 58

KELLY, Paul *P&R/R&B '70*
Singles: 7-inch
DIAL 5-10 65-68
HAPPY TIGER 3-6 70
PHILIPS 10-20 66-68
TK 10-20 60
W.B. 3-6 73-76
Picture Sleeves
PHILIPS 10-20 66
LPs: 10/12-inch
HAPPY TIGER 8-10 70
W.B. 8-10 72-76
Also see TEX, Joe
Also see VALADIERS

KELLY, Peter
Singles: 7-inch
RSO 3-5 73

KELLY, Ronnie
Singles: 7-inch
CHARAY (101 "Tough") 4-8 60s
Also see RON-DELS

KELLY, Roy
Singles: 7-inch
MAIL CALL (1003 "Rock & Roll Rock") 100-200 61

KELLY, Tim
Singles: 7-inch
THUNDERBIRD 4-6

KELLY, Walt
LPs: 10/12-inch
SIMON & SCHUSTER ("Songs of the Pogo") 50-75 56
(No selection number used.)

KELLY & GAIL
Singles: 7-inch
COLPIX 4-8 65

KELLY & SOUL EXPLOSIONS
Singles: 7-inch
DYNA MITE (110 "Talkin' 'Bout My Baby's Love") 20-30 60s

KELLY BROTHERS *R&B '66*
Singles: 7-inch
EXCELLO (2286 "You Put Your Touch on Me") 8-12 67
EXCELLO (2290 "That's What You Mean to Me") 8-12 67
EXCELLO (2295 "Haven't I Been Good to You") 8-12 68
EXCELLO (2300 "It Takes Two") 8-12 68
EXCELLO (2308 "My Baby Loves Me") 8-12 69
FEDERAL (12373 "I've Been Striving for So Long") 25-50 60
FEDERAL (12404 "He's All Right") 25-50 60
SIMS (210 "Counting on You") 10-20 65
SIMS (239 "Got the Feeling") 10-20 65
SIMS (247 "Love Time") 10-20 65
SIMS (265 "Falling in Love Again") 10-20 66
SIMS (281 "Make Me Glad") 10-20 66
SIMS (287 "My Love Grows Stronger") 10-20 66
SIMS (293 "Can't Stand It No Longer") 10-20 66
SIMS (310 "If That Will Hold You") 10-20 66
SIMS (313 "Ouch! Oh Baby") 10-20 67
SIMS (317 "You Put Your Touch on Me") 10-20 67
(First issue.)
LPs: 10/12-inch
EXCELLO (8007 "Sweet Soul") 15-25 68
Members: Andrew Kelly; Robert Kelly; Curtis Kelly. Session: Charles Lee; Offe Reese.
Also see KING PINS

KELLY FOUR
Singles: 7-inch
CANDIX (325 "Annie Had a Party") 10-15 63
SILVER (1001 "Strollin' Guitar") 15-25 59
SILVER (1006 "Annie Has a Party") 25-50 59
(Eddie Cochran plays guitar on *Annie Has a Party*, later issued as *Annie Had a Party*, by the Gee Cees. The Candix release is a different take of basically the same song.)
Also see COCHRAN, Eddie
Also see GEE CEES

KELLY MARIE: see MARIE, Kelly

KELLY SISTERS
Singles: 7-inch
COED (602 "Joey") 15-25 65

KELSEY, Rev. *R&B '48*
(Rev. Kelsey's Congregation)
Singles: 78 rpm
SUPER DISC 8-12 48

KELSO, Dave
Singles: 7-inch
ROSE (112 "My Heart Goes Thump") 25-50 58

KELSO, Jackie
Singles: 78 rpm
MAMBO 10-15 55
VITA 10-15 56-57
Singles: 7-inch
CENCO (121 "Baby Elephant Walk") 15-25 62
(First issue.)
MAMBO 15-25 55
RIVIERA (121 "Baby Elephant Walk") 10-15 62
VITA 15-25 56-57

KELTON, Bob
Singles: 7-inch
RHODES WAY 8-12

KELTON, Gene
Singles: 7-inch
AVATAR 3-4 87

KELTON, Robert, & His Trio
Singles: 78 rpm
ALADDIN (3000 series) 10-20 50
Singles: 7-inch
ALADDIN (3187 "No, No, Baby") 20-30 50

KELY, J.: see KELLY, J.

KEMP, Dave *C&W '83*
Singles: 7-inch
SOUNDWAVES 3-4 83

KEMP, Eugene
Singles: 7-inch
EXCELLO (2342 "No Pity in the City") 8-10 74

KEMP, Johnny *R&B '86*
Singles: 7-inch
COLUMBIA 3-4 86-89
Picture Sleeves
COLUMBIA 3-4 86-89
LPs: 10/12-inch
COLUMBIA 5-8 86-89

KEMP, Tara *LP '91*
LPs: 10/12-inch
GIANT 5-8 91

KEMP, Wayne *C&W '69*
Singles: 7-inch
DECCA 3-6 69-72
DOOR KNOB 3-4 83-86
MCA 3-5 73-74
MERCURY 3-4 80-82
U.A. 3-5 76-77
LP: 10/12-inch
DECCA 5-10 71
MCA 5-10 73

KEMP, Wayne, & Bobby G. Rice *C&W '86*
Singles: 7-inch
DOOR KNOB 3-4 86
Also see KEMP, Wayne
Also see RICE, Bobby G.

KEMPER, Jim, & Four Tiers
(With the Renegades)
Singles: 7-inch
LE MANS (002 "Lonely for Kathy") 200-300 64

KEMPY & GUARDIANS
Singles: 7-inch
LUCKY SOUND (1006 "Never") 20-30 60s
ROMUNDA (1 "Never") 20-30 60s

KEN & BUSHMEN
Singles: 7-inch
CAPTAIN 5-10 60s

KEN & CAROL
Singles: 7-inch
COLUMBIA 5-8 65
Session: Davie Allan.
Also see ALLAN, Davie

KEN & FOURTH DIMENSION
Singles: 7-inch
STARBURST (128 "See If I Care") 15-25 66

KENDALL, Jeannie
(Jeanie Kendall)
Singles: 7-inch
DOT 3-5 72-73
Also see KENDALLS

KENDALL SISTERS *P&R/R&B '58*
Singles: 7-inch
ARGO 5-10 57-58
CHECKER 5-10 58

KENDALLS *C&W '70*
(Featuring Jeannie Kendall)
Singles: 7-inch
DOT 3-5 72-73
EPIC 3-4 89
MCA/CURB 3-4 86
MERCURY 3-4 81-85
OVATION 3-5 77-80
STEP ONE 3-4 87-88
STOP 3-6 70
U.A. 3-5 75-76
VARSITY 10-15 69
LPs: 10/12-inch
DOT 8-12 72
GUSTO 5-8 78
MCA/CURB 5-8 86
MERCURY 5-8 81-85
OVATION 5-10 76-80
STOP 10-15 70
PICKWICK 5-8 79
POWER PAK 5-8 74
Members: Jeannie Kendall; Royce Kendall.
Also see HARRIS, Emmylou
Also see KENDALL, Jeannie

KENDRICK, Nat, & Swans *P&R/R&B '60*
Singles: 7-inch
DADE (1804 "Mashed Potatoes") 10-15 59
DADE (1808 "Dish Rag") 10-15 60
DADE (1812 "Slowdown") 10-15 60
DADE (5003 Wobble, Wobble) 8-10 63
DADE (5004 "Mashed Potatoes") 5-10 63
Members: James Brown; King Coleman; J.C. Davis; Bobby Roach; Bernard Odum.
Also see BROWN, James

KENDRICK, Willie
Singles: 7-inch
GOLDEN WORLD (1 "Fine As Wine") 15-25 63
RCA (8947 "You Can't Bypass Love") 20-30 66
RCA (9212 "Change Your Ways") 25-50 67

KENDRICKS, Eddie *P&R/R&B/LP '71*
(Eddie Kendrick)
Singles: 7-inch
ARISTA 3-5 78-80
ATLANTIC 3-4 80-81
CORNER STREET 3-4 84
MOTOWN 3-5 76
RCA 3-4 85-88
TAMLA 3-5 71-77
LPs: 10/12-inch
ARISTA 5-8 78
ATLANTIC 5-8 81
MOTOWN 5-8 75-82
MS. DIXIE 5-8 83
TAMLA 8-10 71-78
Also see HALL, Daryl, John Oates, David Ruffin & Eddie Kendrick
Also see RUFFIN, David, & Eddie Kendricks
Also see TEMPTATIONS

KENDRICKS, Linda *D&D '84*
Singles: 12-inch
AIRWAVE 4-6 84
Singles: 7-inch
AIRWAVE 3-4 84

KENDRIX, Bert
Singles: 7-inch
MARTAY (2003 "Zodico") 10-20 64

KENJOLAIRS
Singles: 7-inch
A&M 5-10 62
Members: Ken; Joe; Larry.
Also see ECHOES
Also see INNOCENTS

KENNARD
Singles: 7-inch
DORE (848 "What Did You Gain by That") 20-30 69

KENNARD & JOHN *C&W '89*
Singles: 7-inch
CURB 3-4 89
Members: Philip Kennard; Ron John.

KENNEBRUEW, Delilah
Singles: 7-inch
LOMA 4-8 66

KENNEDY, Ace
(With the Candies)
Singles: 7-inch
PHILIPS 4-8 63
SWAN 4-8 61
XYZ 4-8 60

KENNEDY, Billy
(Billie Kennedy)
Singles: 7-inch
SILVER (250 "If I Was a Kid") 10-20 60s
THELMA (109 "Groovy Generation") 50-100 64

KENNEDY, Cindy
Singles: 7-inch
BEL FAIR 5-8

KENNEDY, Dave
(With the Blazers)
Singles: 7-inch
APEX (76071 "Joanie") 10-20 60
BOLO (721 "Where Did My Darling Go") 8-12 61
CUCA (1004 "Joanie") 15-20 60
(First issue. Later Cuca releases are by another Dave Kennedy, listed next.)
DINAMO (1002 "Pizza Pie") 10-20 59
JOB (502 "Night Train") 8-12 60s
RAYNARD (1001 "Some Sweet Tomorrow") 15-25 66
RAYNARD (1002 "That Ring on Your Finger") 15-25 66
SOMA (1138 "Joanie") 8-12 60
LPs: 10/12-inch
PAGE 10-12

KENNEDY, Dave
(With Ambassadors; with Blazers; with Super-Phonics; with U.S.A. Band)
Singles: 7-inch
AUDEM 3-4 89
CUCA (1036 "Wooden Heart") 10-20 61
CUCA (1050 "Lili Marlene") 10-20 61
CUCA (1058 "Do Not Forsake Me") 10-20 61
CUCA (1094 "Little Red Rented Rowboat") 10-20 62
CUCA (1107 "Peepin' & Hidin' ") 10-20 62
CUCA (1133 "Zombie Jamboree") 10-20 63
Note: Cuca 1004 is also by a Dave Kennedy, a completely different artist who is listed above.)
Picture Sleeves
CUCA 10-20 61-63
LPs:10/12-inch
COULEE (1001 "Breaking Up Is Hard to Do") 20-40 64
ELI 5-8 80s
Members: Tari Tovsen; Ronnie Rink; Tom Neary; Tom Eisenman; Al Banasik; Chuck Sargeant; Jerry Oliver; George Eberdt.
Also see GOOD TIMES
Also see O'NEAL, Lance
Also see SARGENT, Chuck, & Ambassadors
Also see WALKER, Lonnie

KENNEDY, Dave / Super-Phonics
Singles: 7-inch
LINDY (101 "Me Neither") 10-20 60
Also see KENNEDY, Dave
Also see SUPER-PHONICS

KENNEDY, Edward M.
LPs: 10/12-inch
RCA 8-15 65

KENNEDY, Gene
Singles: 7-inch
HICKORY 4-8 64-66
INTREPID 4-6 69
OLD TOWN 5-10 60-62
VICTORIA 5-8 63

KENNEDY, Gene *C&W '86*
Singles: 7-inch
SOCIETY 3-4 86

KENNEDY, Gene, & Karen Jeglum *C&W '81*
Singles: 7-inch
DOOR KNOB 3-4 81-83
Also see KENNEDY, Gene

KENNEDY, Glory
LPs: 10/12-inch
PATHE 15-20

KENNEDY, Harrison
LPs: 10/12-inch
INVICTUS 8-10 72

KENNEDY, Jacqueline
LPs: 10/12-inch
AUDIO FIDELITY (703 "Jacqueline Kennedy") 15-25 66

KENNEDY, Jerry
Singles: 7-inch
DECCA 10-15 58
SMASH 4-8 63-64
LPs: 10/12-inch
SMASH 15-20 62-65
Also see KENYON, Joe
Also see PRESLEY, Elvis
Also see TIDES
Also see TOM & JERRY

KENNEDY, Jim
Singles: 7-inch
SKOOP 10-15 62

KENNEDY, Joe
Singles: 7-inch
BANG 4-8 66

KENNEDY, John Fitzgerald *LP '63*
LPs: 10/12-inch
CAEDMON 5-10 64
CHALLENGE 8-15 64
COLPIX 10-20 64
COLUMBIA 10-20 65
DECCA 10-20 63
DIPLOMAT 5-15 63
DOCUMENTARIES UNLIMITED 10-20 63
GATEWAY 8-15 64
HARMONIA 8-15 64
LEGACY 10-20 65
PALACE 8-15 64
PHILIPS 8-15 64
PICKWICK 8-12 63
PREMIER 10-20 63
RCA 8-15 64
REGINA 5-15 64
SOMERSET 5-15 63
20TH FOX 10-20 63
Most of the albums listed above are a tribute of some type to President Kennedy after his assassination on November 22, 1963. Most contain excerpts of his speeches.

KENNEDY, John Fitzgerald / Richard M. Nixon
LPs: 10/12-inch
COLUMBIA 10-15 68
Also see KENNEDY, John Fitzgerald
Also see NIXON, Richard

KENNEDY, Jon
Singles: 7-inch
BINGO 4-8 62

KENNEDY, Joyce *R&B/LP '84*
Singles: 7-inch
A&M 3-4 84-85
BLUE ROCK (4016 "I'm a Good Girl") 20-25 65
BLUE ROCK (4023 "Hi-Fi, Albums and I") 15-20 65
FONTANA (1924 "Could This Be Love") 10-15 64
RAN DEE (110 "I Still Love You") 10-20 63
RAN DEE (118 "How Old Is Old") 10-20 63
LPs: 10/12-inch
A&M 5-8 84
Also see MOTHER'S FINEST

KENNEDY, Joyce, & Jeffrey Osborne *R&B '84*
Singles: 7-inch
A&M 3-4 84
Also see KENNEDY, Joyce
Also see OSBORNE, Jeffrey

KENNEDY, Larry Wayne *C&W '85*
Singles: 7-inch
JERE 3-4 85

KENNEDY, Mike *P&R '72*
Singles: 7-inch
ABC 3-5 72
LPs: 10/12-inch
ABC 8-10 72
Also see LOS BRAVOS

KENNEDY, Ray *P&R '80*
Singles: 7-inch
ARC 3-5 80
Picture Sleeves
ARC 3-5 80
LPs: 10/12-inch
CREAM 10-12 72
Also see KGB

KENNEDY, Ray *C&W '90*
Singles: 7-inch
ATLANTIC 3-4 90-91

KENNEDY, Raymond Lewis
Singles: 7-inch
A&M 3-5 73

KENNEDY, Robert Francis *LP '69*
LPs: 10/12-inch
COLUMBIA 8-15 68

KENNEDY, Tiny
Singles: 7-inch
CAPITOL (840 "The Lady with the Black Dress On") 25-40 49
GROOVE (00106 "Country Boy") 30-50 55
GROOVE (00133 "Strange Kind of Feeling") 30-50 55
TRUMPET 15-25 53

KENNER, Chris *R&B '57*
Singles: 78 rpm
BATON 10-20 56
IMPERIAL 10-20 57
Singles: 7-inch
BATON (220 "Don't Let Her Pin That Charge") 30-40 56
HEP ME (115 "We Belong Together") 4-8
IMPERIAL (5448 "Sick & Tired") 25-35 57
IMPERIAL (5488 "Will You Be Mine") 20-30 58
IMPERIAL (5767 "Sick & Tired") 10-15 61
INSTANT (3229 "I Like It Like That") 10-20 61
INSTANT (3234 thru 3257) 10-20 61-63
INSTANT (3263 thru 3290) 8-12 64-68
OLDIES 45 4-8 60s
PRIGAN 10-20 61
RON 10-15 61
TRIP 3-6
UPTOWN 5-10 65
VALIANT (3229 "I Like It Like That") 40-60 61
LPs: 10/12-inch
ATLANTIC (8117 "Land of 1,000 Dances") 20-30 66

BANDY (70015 "The Name of the Place") 10-15 70s

KENNY
Singles: 7-inch
ATCO 3-5 72
MERCURY 3-5 76
UK 3-5 74

KENNY, Bill
(With the Song Spinners)
Singles: 78 rpm
DECCA 4-6 50-53
VIK 4-6 56
"X" 4-6 55
Singles: 7-inch
DECCA 5-10 50-53
MERCURY 5-10 62
TEL 5-10 59
VIK 5-10 56
WARWICK 5-10 60
"X" 5-10 55
LPs: 10/12-inch
DECCA (5333 "Precious Memories") 25-50 51
(10-inch LP.)
MERCURY (20691 "Golden Hits of the Ink Spots") 20-30 62
(Monaural.)
MERCURY (60691 "Golden Hits of the Ink Spots") 25-35 62
(Stereo.)
WING (16266 "Golden Hits of the Ink Spots") 10-20 60s
Also see INK SPOTS

KENNY, FRANK & RAY
Singles: 7-inch
CAMEO (144 "Everybody Loves Saturday Night") 15-25 58
Member: Kenny Bolognese; Frank Cacapardo; Ray Carlisle.
Also see CHANDLER, Kenny

KENNY, G.: see KENNY G.

KENNY, G.W.
Singles: 7-inch
KAMA-SUTRA 3-5 73

KENNY, Gerrard, & New York Band
Singles: 7-inch
INTERNATIONAL COMMITTEE to REUNITE the BEATLES 8-12 76

KENNY, Herb
(With the Comets; with Rockets)
Singles: 78 rpm
FEDERAL (12083 "Only You") 50-100 52
MGM (11332 "My Song") 25-50 52
Singles: 7-inch
FEDERAL (12083 "Only You") 200-400 52
MGM (11332 "My Song") 50-100 52
MGM (11360 "I Don't Care") 50-100 52
MGM (11397 "I Miss You So") 50-100 53
MGM (11487 "But Always Your Friend") 50-100 53

KENNY, Michael
LPs: 10/12-inch
TOM CAT 5-10 76

KENNY, Sue
Singles: 7-inch
TRIBUTE (118 "Look") 250-500 63
Session: Concords.
Also see CONCORDS

KENNY & CADETS
Singles: 7-inch
RANDY (422 "Barbie") 550-650 62
(Black vinyl.)
RANDY (422 "Barbie") 750-1000 62
(Red and yellow vinyl.)
Members: Kenny Doll; Brian Wilson; Carl Wilson; Al Jardine; Audree Wilson.
Also see BEACH BOYS

KENNY & CORKY
Singles: 7-inch
BIG TOP (3031 "Nuttin' for Christmas") 8-10 59
Picture Sleeves
BIG TOP (3031 "Nuttin' for Christmas") 10-20 59

KENNY & DOOLITTLE
Singles: 7-inch
SIMS (123 "Kitty Kat") 100-125 61

KENNY & DRASTICS
Singles: 7-inch
BOLO 5-10 63

KENNY & FIENDS
(Kenny & the Beach Fiends)
Singles: 7-inch
DOT (16568 "House on Haunted Hill") 8-12 63
DOT (16596 "Moon Shot") 8-12 64
POSEA (80 "The Raven") 15-25 63
POSEA (87 "House on Haunted Hill") 15-25 63
PRINCESS (51 "House on Haunted Hill") 15-25 63
(First issue.)
PRINCESS (84 "Last Night") 15-25 63

KENNY & HO-DADDIES
Singles: 7-inch
INDIGO 10-15 62

KENNY & IMPACTS
Singles: 7-inch
DCP (1147 "Wishing Well") 25-35 65

KENNY & JOHNNY R&B '86
Singles: 7-inch
PHILADELPHIA INT'L 3-4 86
Members: Kenny Whitehead; Johnny Whitehead.
Also see WHITEHEAD, Kenny & Johnny

KENNY & KASUALS
Singles: 7-inch
MARK (911 "Nothing Better to Do") 20-25 65
MARK (1002 "Don't Let Your Baby Go") 20-30 66
MARK (1003 "It's All Right") 20-25 66
MARK (1004 "Strings of Time") 20-30 66
MARK (1006 "Journey to Tyme") 25-35 66
MARK (1008 "See-Saw Ride") 20-30 67
U.A. (50085 "Journey to Tyme") 10-15 66
EPs: 7-inch
MARK (400 "Kenny and the Kasuals Are Back") 10-15 79
(Black vinyl.)
MARK (400 "Kenny and the Kasuals Are Back") 10-15 79
(Clear vinyl.)
LPs: 10/12-inch
MARK (5000 "Impact Sound") 250-350 66
MARK (5000 "Impact Sound") 8-12 77
(Cover reads "Reissue, 1977.")
MARK (6000 "Teen Dreams") 100-150 78
(Colored vinyl, signed, numbered limited edition.)
MARK (7000 "Garage Kings") 10-15 79
Members: Kenny Daniel; Tom Nichols; Jerry Smith; Richard Borgens; Paul Roach; David Blackley; Dan Green; Ron Mason; Karl Tomorrow; Greg Daniels.
Also see TRUTH

KENNY & MODADS
Singles: 7-inch
BAYTOWN 4-8

KENNY & MOE
(Blues Boys; Kenny & Mose)
Singles: 78 rpm
DELUXE 10-15 56
Singles: 7-inch
DELUXE (6101 "Can't Help Myself") 15-25 56
JOSIE 10-15 59

KENNY & NIGHT RIDERS
Singles: 7-inch
BRISTOL (102 "Andromeda") 10-20 63

KENNY & SHEPHERDS
Singles: 7-inch
KAPP 4-8 67

KENNY & SOCIALITES
(With the Joe René Orchestra)
Singles: 7-inch
CROSSTOWN (001 "I'll Have to Decide") 100-200 58

KENNY & SULTANS
Singles: 7-inch
GARLLO 10-20 63

KENNY & WHALERS
(With Vince Catalano & Orchestra)
Singles: 7-inch
WHALE (504 "Life Is But a Dream") 100-200 61
Also see DONNIE & DREAMERS

KENNY & YVONNE
Singles: 7-inch
COLUMBIA (43594 "Don't Go to Strangers") 10-15 66
Member: Kenny Rankin.
Also see RANKIN, Kenny

KENNY BEE
(With Rog Winters; with Plainsmen)
Singles: 7-inch
CUCA 8-12 66-67
Also see ART, Bobby, & Plainsmen
Also see WINTERS, Rog, & Plainsmen

KENNY G. R&B/LP '84
(With G Force; Kenny Gorelick)
Singles: 7-inch
ARISTA 3-4 83-89
Picture Sleeves
ARISTA 3-4 87-89
LPs: 10/12-inch
ARISTA 5-10 83-89
Also see LORBER, Jeff
Also see LOVE UNLIMITED

KENNY G. & KASHIF
Singles: 7-inch
ARISTA 3-4 85
Also see KASHIF

KENNY G. & SMOKEY ROBINSON
Singles: 7-inch
ARISTA 3-4 89
Also see ROBINSON, Smokey

KENNY G. & LENNY WILLIAMS
Singles: 7-inch
ARISTA 3-4 83-86
Also see KENNY G.
Also see WILLIAMS, Lenny

KENNY O. C&W '81
Singles: 7-inch
RHINESTONE 3-4 81

KENSINGTON MARKET
Singles: 7-inch
W.B. 4-8 68
LPs: 10/12-inch
W.B. 15-20 68-69

KENT, Al P&R/R&B '67
Singles: 78 rpm
CHECKER (881 "Dat's Why") 25-50 57
Singles: 7-inch
BARITONE (942 "Hold Me") 50-100 60
CHECKER (881 "Dat's Why") 25-50 57
RIC-TIC (127 "You've Got to Pay the Price") 10-20 67
RIC-TIC (133 "Ooh! Pretty Lady") 10-20 68
WINGATE (4 "You Know I Love You") 15-25 65
WIZARD (100 "Hold Me") 75-100 59
Also see FLAMING EMBERS / Al Kent
Also see WEAVER, Joe

KENT, Billy, & Andantes
Singles: 7-inch
MAH'S (0002 "Your Love") 50-100 60
(No mention of Roulette Records.")
MAH'S (0002 "Your Love") 40-60 60
(With "Dist. By Roulette Records.")
Also see HOLLAND – DOZIER

KENT, Bob
Singles: 78 rpm
PAR (1303) 20-30 52
(Title not known.)

KENT, Bobby
Singles: 7-inch
BAY STATE (82159 "Don't Go Away") 30-50
MERCURY 8-12 60

KENT, George C&W '69
(With Diana Duke)
Singles: 7-inch
MERCURY 3-6 69-70
SHANNON 3-5 74-76
SOUNDWAVES 3-5
LPs: 10/12-inch
SHANNON 10-20 75

KENT, Wayne
Singles: 7-inch
INSTRO (1000 "Pam") 50-75

KENT, Willie
LPs: 10/12-inch
BIG BOY 5-10 90

KENT & CANDIDATES
Singles: 7-inch
DOUBLE SHOT 4-8 67-68

KENTON, Stan, & His Orchestra P&R '44
Singles: 78 rpm
CAPITOL 3-6 45-57
Singles: 7-inch
CAPITOL (Purple labels) 5-15 50-61
CAPITOL (Orange & Yellow labels) 4-6 61-68
CAPITOL STARLINE 3-5 60s
Picture Sleeves
CAPITOL ("Stan Kenton Prologue: This Is an Orchestra") 10-20 50s
(Selection number not known.)
EPs: 7-inch
CAPITOL 5-15 50-59
LPs: 10/12-inch
BRIGHT ORANGE 5-8 73
CAPITOL (H-155 "Encores") 50-75 49
(10-inch LP.)
CAPITOL (T-155 "Encores") 25-50 55
CAPITOL (H-167 "Artistry in Rhythm") 50-75 49
(10-inch LP.)
CAPITOL (T-167 "Artistry in Rhythm") 25-50 55
(With "T" prefix.)
CAPITOL (DT-167 "Artistry in Rhythm") 5-10 69
(Stereo.)
CAPITOL (SM-167 "Artistry in Rhythm") 5-8 75
CAPITOL (H-172 "Progressive Jazz") 50-75 50
(10-inch LP.)
CAPITOL (T-172 "Progressive Jazz") 25-50 55
CAPITOL (H-190 "Milestones") 50-75 50
(10-inch LP.)
CAPITOL (T-190 "Milestones") 25-50 55
CAPITOL (H-248 "Stan Kenton Presents") 50-75 50
(10-inch LP.)
CAPITOL (T-248 "Stan Kenton Presents") 25-50 55
CAPITOL (H-353 "City of Glass") 50-75 52
(10-inch LP.)
CAPITOL (T-353 "City of Glass") 25-50 55
CAPITOL (H-358 "Classics") 50-75 52
(10-inch LP.)
CAPITOL (T-358 "Classics") 25-50 55
CAPITOL (H-386 "This Is an Orchestra") 50-75 53
(10-inch LP.)
CAPITOL (T-421 "Popular Favorites By Stan Kenton") 25-50 54
CAPITOL (H-462 "Standards") 50-75 53
(10-inch LP.)
CAPITOL (T-462 "Standards") 25-50 55
CAPITOL (H-525 "Showcase") 50-75 54
(10-inch LP.)
CAPITOL (W-525 "Showcase") 25-75 55
CAPITOL (H-526 "Showcase") 50-75 54
(10-inch LP.)
CAPITOL (W-526 "Showcase") 25-50 55
CAPITOL (305 "Hair") 5-10 69
CAPITOL (600 thru 1200 series) 15-25 56-59
CAPITOL (1300 thru 2900 series) 10-20 60-68
CAPITOL (11000 & 12000 series) 5-8 72-80
CAPITOL (16000 series) 4-6 81
CREATIVE WORLD 5-8 71-80
HINDSIGHT 4-8 84
LONDON 5-8 72-77
MARK 56 ....5-8 77
MFSL (091 "Stan Kenton Plays Wagner") 15-25 82
Also see CHRISTY, June, & Stan Kenton
Also see COLE, Nat "King"
Also see FERGUSON, Maynard

KENTON, Stan, & Tex Ritter
LPs: 10/12-inch
CAPITOL (T-1757 "Stan Kenton & Tex Ritter") 40-60 62
(Monaural.)
CAPITOL (ST-1757 "Stan Kenton & Tex Ritter") 50-75 62
(Stereo.)
Also see KENTON, Stan
Also see RITTER, Tex

KENTONES
(With the Court Jesters)
Singles: 7-inch
SIROC (202 "Marie") 100-200 58

KENTS
Singles: 7-inch
ARGO (5299 "I Found My Girl") 10-20 58
DOME (501 "I Love You So") 150-250 58

KENTT, Klark
Singles: 7-inch
4 STAR 10-15 59

KENTUCKY
Singles: 7-inch
DNS 3-5 82

KENTUCKY EXPRESS
Singles: 7-inch
LIBERTY 3-5 70s
LPs: 10/12-inch
CREAM 10-12 71

KENTUCKY HEADHUNTERS C&W/LP '89
Singles: 7-inch
MERCURY 3-4 89-91
LPs: 10/12-inch
MERCURY 5-8 89-91
Members: Fred Young; Richard Young; Greg Martin; Ricky Lee Phelps; Doug Phelps; Mark Orr; Anthony Kenny.

KENYON, Joe C&W '87
Singles: 7-inch
MERCURY 3-4 87
Members: Jerry Kennedy; David Briggs.
Also see BRIGGS, David
Also see KENNEDY, Jerry

KENYON, Taldo
Singles: 7-inch
SKYWAY 5-10 59

KERMIT P&R '79
(Jim Henson)
Singles: 7-inch
ATLANTIC 3-5 79

KERMIT / Fozzie Bear
(Jim Henson)
Singles: 7-inch
ATLANTIC 3-5 80
Also see KERMIT
Also see HENSON, Jim
Also see MUPPETS

KERNOCHAN, Sarah
LPs: 10/12-inch
RCA 8-10 74

KEROUAC, Jack
LPs: 10/12-inch
HANOVER (5006 "Blues and Haikus") 50-100 60
VERVE (15005 "Readings by Jack Kerouac on the Beat Generation") 75-125 59

KEROUAC, Jack, & Steve Allen
LPs: 10/12-inch
DOT (3154 "Poetry for the Beat Generation") 100-150 59
HANOVER (5000 "Poetry for the Beat Generation") 75-125 59
Also see ALLEN, Steve
Also see KEROUAC, Jack

KERR, Anita LP '69
(Anita Kerr Singers; Quartette)
Singles: 78 rpm
DECCA 3-6 51-57
Singles: 7-inch
AMPEX 3-5 71
DECCA (27000 thru 30000 series) 5-10 51-60
DECCA (31000 thru 33000 series) 3-6 60-72
DOT 3-5 69-70
RCA 3-8 63-75
W.B. 3-6 66-68
Picture Sleeves
DECCA 4-8
EPs: 7-inch
SESAC 10-15 59
(Also has tracks by Buddy Hacket, Elliot Lawrence, and Bill Snyder.)
LPs: 10/12-inch
AMPEX 5-8 71
BAINBRIDGE 4-6 81
CAMDEN 5-10 68
CENTURY 4-8 79
DECCA 8-15 60-69
DOT 5-10 69-70
RCA 8-15 62-77
VOCALION 5-10 70
W.B. 8-12 66
WORD 4-8 75-77
Also see ANDERSON, Bill
Also see ANITA & So-And-So's
Also see ANN-MARGRET
Also see ATKINS, Chet
Also see ATKINS, Chet, Faron Young, & Anita Kerr Singers
Also see BARE, Bobby
Also see CARVER, Johnny
Also see CHARLES, Tommy
Also see CLINE, Patsy
Also see DAVIS, Jimmie
Also see FOLEY, Red
Also see HELMS, Bobby
Also see IVES, Burl
Also see LEE, Brenda
Also see LEE, Robin
Also see LITTLE DIPPERS
Also see MULLICAN, Moon
Also see NELSON, Willie
Also see PRESLEY, Elvis
Also see REEVES, Jim
Also see RICH, Charlie
Also see SHANNON, Pat
Also see SNOW, Hank
Also see WILBURN BROTHERS
Also see WILLIAMS, Lawton
Also see YOUNG, Faron

KERR, Dick, & Sing-Along Teen-Agers
LPs: 10/12-inch
W.B. 15-20 60

KERR, George R&B '70
Singles: 7-inch
ALL PLATINUM 3-5 70
Also see SERENADERS

KERR, Richard
Singles: 7-inch
A&M 3-5 78
EPIC 3-5 76
LPs: 10/12-inch
A&M 5-10 78
EPIC 5-10 76

KERRY'S AKOUSTIKS
Singles: 7-inch
MARKUS (6059 "I Can Tell") 20-30 65

KERSEY, Kenny, Trio
Singles: 78 rpm
MERCURY 10-15 52
Singles: 7-inch
MERCURY (8948 "Jap Boogie") 15-25 52

KERSHAW, Doug C&W '69
Singles: 7-inch
BGM 3-4 88-89
SCOTTI BROS. 3-4 81
W.B. 3-6 69-78
LP: 10/12-inch
BGM 5-8 89
CBS 5-8 79
HICKORY 6-12 72
SCOTTI BROS. 5-8 81
W.B. 6-12 69-78
Also see RUSTY & DOUG

KERSHAW, Doug, & Hank Williams Jr. C&W '88
Singles: 7-inch
BGM 3-4 88
Also see KERSHAW, Doug
Also see WILLIAMS, Hank, Jr.

KERSHAW, Nik P&R/LP '84
Singles: 7-inch
MCA 3-4 84-85
Picture Sleeves
MCA 3-5 84
LPs: 10/12-inch
MCA 5-8 84-85

KERSHAW, Sammy C&W '91
Singles: 7-inch
MERCURY 3-4 91-92

KESEY, Ken
LPs: 10/12-inch
SOUND CITY PROD. (27690 "The Acid Test") 100-150 67
Also see GRATEFUL DEAD

KESSEL, Barney / Grant Green / Oscar Moore / Mundell Lowe
LPs: 10/12-inch
PARKER (826 "Best Plucking in Town") 20-30
Also see GREEN, Grant
Also see NELSON, Ricky

KESSLER, Keith
Singles: 7-inch
MTW (102 "Don't Crowd Me") 15-25 68

KESTRELS
Singles: 7-inch
LAURIE 10-20 60

KETCHUM, Ben
Singles: 7-inch
UBC (1025 "I Don't Wanna") 40-60

KETCHUM, Robert
Singles: 78 rpm
PEACOCK (1623 "Stockade") 10-15 53
Singles: 7-inch
PEACOCK (1623 "Stockade") 15-25 53

KEVIN, Chris
Singles: 7-inch
COLT 5-10 59

KEVIN, Chris, & Comics
Singles: 7-inch
COLT 45 5-10

KEVIN & AUGIE
Singles: 7-inch
KEVIN KAT....3-4 90
Members: Kevin Kosub; Augie Meyers.

KEVIN & BLACKTEARS
(Kevin Kosub; Kevin Y Los Blacktears featuring Augie Meyers; Kevin & Augie with the Blacktears)
Singles: 7-inch
KEVIN KAT....3-4 85-88
Picture Sleeves
KEVIN KAT....3-4 85
LPs: 10/12-inch
KEVIN KAT....5-10 87-88
Also see BLACKTEARS
Also see KEVIN & AUGIE
Also see MEYERS, Augie

KEVIN & GREGG
Singles: 7-inch
ASSOCIATED ARTISTS (116 "Boy You Oughta See Her Now")....8-10 63
ASSOCIATED ARTISTS (464 "I Know Just How You Feel")....8-10 64

KEY, Gary
Singles: 7-inch
RAN-DEE (116 "Cinderella")....50-75 63

KEY, Scott
Singles: 7-inch
PYRAMID (8022 "Town Cryer")....4-6
LPs: 10/12-inch
BLIVET....8-10 76

KEY, Troyce
Singles: 7-inch
W.B. (5007 "Drown in Tears")....15-25 58
W.B. (5035 "Ain't I Cried Enough").20-30 59
W.B. (5070 "Most of All")....20-30 59
Session: Sharps.
Also see COCHRAN, Eddie
Also see MELLOMOODS
Also see SHARPS
Also see VELOURS

KEY BROTHERS
Singles: 7-inch
GARDENA (102 "My Baby Doll")....8-12 60
MAGNET....10-15

KEY LARGO
Singles: 7-inch
MERCURY....3-5 78
LPs: 10/12-inch
MERCURY....5-8 78

KEY MEN
Singles: 7-inch
EM....10-20 64
GOLDUST (5019 "What Am I to Do")....20-30

KEY NOTES
Singles: 7-inch
LIN (1001 "Pyramid")....15-25 58

KEYES
Singles: 7-inch
TOP DOG (2314 "She's the One")....10-20 60s

KEYES, Bert
(With His Trio; with Eddie Combs Quintet; with Teddy McRae & His Orchestra; Burt Keyes)
Singles: 78 rpm
RAMA....5-10 53-54
SAVOY....4-8 51
Singles: 7-inch
AMP 3 (133 "Stop Jivin', Start Drivin'")....10-15 57
CLOCK....4-8 65
CORAL....8-10 58
RAMA (4 "Wandering Blues")....15-25 53
RAMA (6 "After All I've Been to You")....15-25 53
(Black vinyl.)
RAMA (6 "After All I've Been to You")....40-60 53
(Red vinyl.)
RAMA (12 "Lonely")....15-25 53
RAMA (31 "Write Me Baby")....10-20 54
RAMA (32 "You Blame My Heart") 10-20 54

KEYES, Larry
Singles: 7-inch
MASCARA (120 "Beatnik Boogie")....10-20 60

KEYES, Troy P&R/R&B '68
Singles: 7-inch
ABC (11027 "Love Explosion")....4-8 67
ABC (11060 "No Sad Songs")....8-12 68
CHUMLEY....3-5 74
Also see HIGH KEYES

KEYES, Troy, & Norma Jenkins
Singles: 7-inch
ABC (11116 "A Good Love Gone Bad")....10-20 68
Also see JENKINS, Norma
Also see KEYES, Troy

KEYHOLE PEEPERS
Singles: 7-inch
TRIAD (501 "Batman & Robin")....8-10 66

KEYMEN
Singles: 7-inch
ABC-PAR (9977 "Miss You")....5-10 58
ABC-PAR (9977S "Miss You")....15-20 58
(Stereo.)
ABC-PAR (9991 "Gazachstahagen")....5-10 58
ABC-PAR (9991S "Gazachstahagen")....15-20 58
(Stereo.)
ABC-PAR (10039 "Camilia")....5-10 59
EPs: 7-inch
ABC-PAR (258 "Dance with Dick Clark")....15-25 58
LPs: 10/12-inch
ABC-PAR (ABC-258 "Dance with Dick Clark")....20-30 58
(Monaural.)
ABC-PAR (ABCS-258 "Dance with Dick Clark")....25-50 58
(Stereo.)

KEYNOTES
Singles: 78 rpm
DOT (15225 "Who")....10-15 54
Singles: 7-inch
DOT (15225 "Who")....15-25 54

KEYNOTES
Singles: 78 rpm
APOLLO....25-50 55
Singles: 7-inch
APOLLO (478 "Suddenly")....75-125 55
APOLLO (484 "I Don't Know")....75-100 55
APOLLO (493 "Really Wish You Were Here")....75-100 56
APOLLO (498 "Now I Know")....75-100 56
APOLLO (503 "In the Evening")....75-100 56
APOLLO (513 "One Little Kiss")....75-100 57
Members: Floyd Adams; Sam Kearney; Bernard Matthews.

KEYNOTES
(With Rubin & His Boys)
Singles: 7-inch
POP (111 "Congratulations Baby")....100-200 57

KEYNOTES
Singles: 7-inch
TOP RANK (2005 "With These Rings")....15-25 59
LPs: 10/12-inch
SUPERIOR....5-10

KEY-NOTES
Singles: 7-inch
SWAN (4048 "Starlight & You")....10-20 59

KEYS
Singles: 78 rpm
MGM (11168 "Am I in Love")....5-10 52
Singles: 7-inch
MGM (11168 "Am I in Love")....15-25 52

KEYS
Singles: 7-inch
JAM (501 "Barbara")....50-100 64

KEYS
LPs: 10/12-inch
A&M....5-8 81

KEYS, Bobby
Singles: 7-inch
RING O'....3-5 75

KEYSTONERS
(Keystoner's)
Singles: 78 rpm
EPIC (9187 "The Magic Kiss")....5-10 56
G&M (102 "Magic Kiss")....10-20 56
Singles: 7-inch
EPIC (9187 "Magic Kiss")....35-50 56
G&M (102 "Magic Kiss")....100-200 56
RIFF (202 "Sleep & Dream")....100-200 61
OKEH (7210 "Magic Kiss")....10-20 64

KEYTONES
Singles: 78 rpm
OLD TOWN (1041 "Wonder of the World")....100-150 57
OLD TOWN (1041 "Seven Wonders of the World")....50-75 57
Singles: 7-inch
OLD TOWN (1041 "Wonder of the World")....150-250 57
OLD TOWN (1041 "Seven Wonders of the World")....50-100 57
(Note slight title change.)

KEYTONES
(With Billy Costa & Orchestra; Key Tones)
Singles: 7-inch
CHELSEA (101 "I Don't Care"/"La Do Da")....10-20 62
(Some sources show this number for these two tracks. Though we have not confirmed this issue, we are certain about #1004 with its tracks.)
CHELSEA (1002 "Don't Tell William")....8-12 61
CHELSEA (1004 "I Don't Care"/"I Was a Teen-Age Monster")....10-20 62
(See note for Chelsea 101.)
CHELSEA (1013 "Sweet Chariot")....8-12 63
CHESS (1821 "Lover of Mine")....150-250 62
Picture Sleeves
CHELSEA (1004 "I Don't Care"/"I Was a Teen-Age Monster")....25-35 62
(Promotional issue only.)

KEYTONES
Singles: 7-inch
CHESS (1821 "Lover of Mine")....150-250 62

KHAN
LPs: 10/12-inch
PVC....5-8 78

KHAN, Chaka P&R/R&B/LP '78
Singles: 12-inch
W.B....4-6 79-87
Singles: 7-inch
ATLANTIC....3-4 78-87
MCA....3-4 80-86
W.B....3-5 78-88
Picture Sleeves
MCA....3-4 85
W.B....3-5 78-86
LPs: 10/12-inch
ELEKTRA....5-10 70s
W.B....5-8 78-88
Also see BOWIE, David
Also see GRANDMASTER FLASH & Furious Five
Also see JONES, Quincy, with Ray Charles & Chaka Khan
Also see RUFUS
Also see WONDER, Stevie

KHAN, Geno
Singles: 7-inch
ARROW....3-5 79

KHAN, Sajid
Singles: 7-inch
COLGEMS....3-6 69
LPs: 10/12-inch
COLGEMS....10-12 69

KHAN, Steve LP '78
Singles: 7-inch
TAPPAN ZEE....3-5 78
LPs: 10/12-inch
COLUMBIA....5-8 79
NOVAS....5-8 80
TAPPAN ZEE....5-8 78
Also see JOEL, Billy

KHAZAD DOOM
LPs: 10/12-inch
LPL (892 "Level 61/2")....800-1200 70
Members: Jack Eadon; Tom Sievers; Al Yates; Steve Hilkin.

KHEMISTRY R&B '82
Singles: 7-inch
COLUMBIA....3-4 82
LPs: 10/12-inch
COLUMBIA....5-8 82

KIARA R&B '85
Singles: 7-inch
ARISTA....3-4 87
WARLOCK....3-4 85
Picture Sleeves
ARISTA....3-4 87
LPs: 10/12-inch
ARISTA....5-8 88

KIARA & SHANICE WILSON P&R '89
Singles: 7-inch
ARISTA....3-4 89
Picture Sleeves
ARISTA....3-4 89
Also see KIARA
Also see WILSON, Shanice

KICK AXE LP '84
LPs: 10/12-inch
PASHA....5-8 84

KICK LITSCHER
Singles: 7-inch
FENTON....10-15 65

KICKER
Singles: 7-inch
TJ....3-5 82

KICKLIGHTER, Richy
LPs: 10/12-inch
ICHIBAN....5-10

KICKS
Singles: 7-inch
BAMBOO....5-8 61

KICKS & COMPANY
(With Paul Anka)
Singles: 7-inch
RCA....4-6 69
Also see ANKA, Paul

KICKSTANDS
Singles: 7-inch
CHINA....10-20 63
LPs: 10/12-inch
CAPITOL (T-2078 "Black Boots and Bikes")....20-40 64
(Monaural.)
CAPITOL (ST-2078 "Black Boots and Bikes")....25-50 64
(Stereo.)
Session: Gary Usher; Dick Burns; Dennis McCarthy; Jerry Cole; Steve Douglas; Glen Cass; Earl Palmer; William Oden; Stephen LaFever; Frank Capp; Ray Johnson; Benjamin Barrett.
Also see KNIGHTS
Also see USHER, Gary

KID, The
Singles: 7-inch
OKEH (7139 "The Pony")....10-15 60
RUMBLE (1347 "Sleep Tight")....100-200 60

KID, Joey P&R '90
Singles: 7-inch
ATLANTIC....3-4 90
BASSMENT....3-5 90

KID BLAST
LPs: 10/12-inch
CLARIDGE....8-10 76

KID BROTHER
Singles: 7-inch
MCA....3-5 79
LPs: 10/12-inch
MCA....8-10 77

KID CREOLE & COCONUTS LP '81
Singles: 12-inch
ATLANTIC....4-6 84-85
Singles: 7-inch
ANTILLES....3-5 80
ATLANTIC....3-4 84-85
SIRE....3-4 81-82
ZE....3-4 81
LPs: 10/12-inch
ANTILLES....8-10 80
SIRE....5-8 81-82
Also see DR. BUZZARD'S ORIGINAL SAVANNAH BAND
Also see MANILOW, Barry / Kid Creole & Coconuts

KID DYNAMITE
LPs: 10/12-inch
CREAM....8-10 76

KID FROST LP '90
LPs: 10/12-inch
VIRGIN....5-8 90

KID GLOVES
Singles: 7-inch
BUDDAH....3-5 72
LPs: 10/12-inch
BUDDAH....8-10 72

KID 'N PLAY LP '88
Singles: 7-inch
SELECT....3-4 88
LPs: 10/12-inch
SELECT....5-8 88

KID PONIES
Singles: 7-inch
OKEH....4-8 60

KID ROCK
Singles: 7-inch
ARNO (100 "Look What You've Done")....100-150 58

KID SENSATION LP '90
LPs: 10/12-inch
NASTYMIX....5-8 90

KID THOMAS
Singles: 78 rpm
FEDERAL (12298 "The Spell")....50-75 57
Singles: 7-inch
FEDERAL (12298 "The Spell")....50-75 57
TRANSCONTINENTAL (1012 "Rockin' This Joint Tonight")....50-75 57
EPs: 7-inch
DNL (004 "Rockin' This Joint")....15-25

KIDD, Billy
(With the Madisons)
Singles: 7-inch
JANE (107 "Crazy Guitar")....15-25 59
MADISON (153"First Time")....50-100 61

KIDD, Eddie
LPs: 10/12-inch
AZRA (001 "Eddie Kidd")....10-15 85
(Picture disc. 500 made.)

KIDD, Johnny, & Pirates
Singles: 7-inch
APT (25040 "Shakin' All Over")....20-30 60
CAPITOL (5065 "I'll Never Get Over You")....8-12 63
Also see PIRATES

KIDD GLOVE
Singles: 7-inch
MOROCCO....3-4 84
LP: 10/12-inch
MOROCCO....5-8 84
Member: Paul Sabu.
Also see SABU

KIDDIE KA-DEES
Singles: 7-inch
KING (5181 "Ol Grey Goose")....15-25 58

KIDDO R&B '83
Singles: 12-inch
A&M....4-6 83
Singles: 7-inch
A&M....3-4 83-84
LPs: 10/12-inch
A&M....5-8 83

KIDDS
Singles: 78 rpm
IMPERIAL....100-200 55
POST....50-100 55
Singles: 7-inch
IMPERIAL (5335 "Are You Forgetting Me")....500-750 55
POST (2003 "You Broke My Heart")....350-500 55
Also see PELICANS

KIDDS
Singles: 7-inch
BIG BEAT....4-8

KIDNEY STONE TRIO
Singles: 7-inch
SOMA....4-8 61

KIDS
EPs: 7-inch
RCA (4061 "Teenager's Dance the Hop-A-Do")....30-50 57
RCA (4188 "The Kids")....30-50 58

KIDS
Singles: 7-inch
CHROMA (1004 "Flipped Hair and Lace")....8-12 65
Picture Sleeves
CHROMA (1004 "Flipped Hair and Lace")....10-20 65

KIDS
LPs: 10/12-inch
ATCO....8-10 75

KIDS AT WORK R&B '84
Singles: 7-inch
CBS ASSOCIATED....3-4 84
Member: Teddy Riley.
Also see RILEY, Teddy, & Guy

KIDS FROM C.A.P.E.R.
Singles: 7-inch
KIRSHNER....3-5 76
LPs: 10/12-inch
KIRSHNER....8-10 76

KIDS FROM "FAME" LP '82
Singles: 7-inch
RCA....3-4 82-83
Picture Sleeves
RCA....3-4 82-83
LPs: 10/12-inch
RCA....5-8 82-83

KIDS FROM TEXAS
Singles: 7-inch
HANOVER (4500 "Long Legged Linda")....25-50 58

KIDS FROM WISCONSIN
Singles: 7-inch
AMERICAN....5-10

KIDS NEXT DOOR P&R '65
Singles: 7-inch
DECCA....4-8 67
4 CORNERS of the WORLD....4-8 65
Picture Sleeves
4 CORNERS of the WORLD....5-10 65

KIDS THESE DAYS
Singles: 7-inch
SMASH....4-6 69

KIHN, Greg, Band LP '78
(Greg Kihn)
Singles: 12-inch
BESERKLEY....4-8 78-83
Singles: 7-inch
BESERKLEY....3-5 78-83
EMI AMERICA....3-4 85-86
Picture Sleeves
BESERKLEY....3-4 81-82
EMI AMERICA....3-4 85-86
LPs: 10/12-inch
BESERKLEY....8-10 76-84
EMI AMERICA....5-8 85-86

KIHN, Greg, Band / Earthquake / Modern Lovers / Rubinoos
EPs: 7-inch
BESERKLEY (1120 "Great Ideas")....5-8 77
Also see MODERN LOVERS

KIHN, Greg, Band / Earthquake / Rubinoos / Jonathan Richman
LPs: 10/12-inch
BESERKLEY (0044 "Beserkley Chartbusters, Vol. 1")....8-12 77
(Promotional issue only.)
Also see EARTHQUAKE
Also see KIHN, Greg, Band
Also see RICHMAN, Jonathan
Also see RUBINOOS

KILETTES
Singles: 7-inch
CHECKER....4-8 64

KILGORE, Merle C&W '60
(With "Friends")
Singles: 7-inch
COLUMBIA....4-6 67
D....8-12 59
ELEKTRA....3-4 81-82
EPIC....4-6 65-67
IMPERIAL (5300 series)....15-25 56
IMPERIAL (5409 "Ernie")....35-55 56
IMPERIAL (5500 series)....10-15 58-59
IMPERIAL (8200 series)....10-20 54-55
IMPERIAL (8300 "Everybody Needs a Little Lovin'")....30-40 56
MGM....4-8 63-64
MERCURY....5-8 61-62
STARDAY (400 thru 600 series)....6-12 59-61
STARDAY (900 series)....3-5 72
W.B....3-5 74-85
Picture Sleeves
EPIC....8-12 65
LPs: 10/12-inch
PICKWICK....10-20 70s
STARDAY (251 "There's Gold in Them Thar Hills")....20-30 63
STARDAY (479 "Big Merle Kilgore")....8-10 73
WING....10-20 66
Session: Johnny Cash; Hank Williams Jr.

KILGORE, Theola P&R/R&B '63
Singles: 7-inch
CANDIX (311 "The Sound of My Man")....15-25 60
KT....8-12 64
MERCURY....5-10
SEROCK....10-15 63

KILI JACKS
Singles: 7-inch
LONDON (10004 "China Rock").....10-20 62

KILLEBREW, George
Singles: 7-inch
HIT 4-6 64

KILLEN, Billy
(Billy J. Killen)
Singles: 7-inch
KAM (101 "Walkin' Talkin' ") 10-20 60
MERIDIAN (1509 "It Makes No Difference") 25-50 59
MERIDIAN (1511 "Georgia Boy") ...20-30 59

KILLEN, Buddy
Singles: 7-inch
DIAL 4-6 68
SCARLET 4-8 60s
UNIVERSITY 4-8 60

KILLER BEES & CYRIL NEVILLE
Singles: 7-inch
BEEHIVE (1002 "Groovin' ") 3-5 86
Also see NEVILLE, Cyril

KILLER DWARFS LP '88
LPs: 10/12-inch
EPIC 5-8 88

KILLER JOE ORCHESTRA
Singles: 7-inch
ATLANTIC 4-8 65
LPs: 10/12-inch
ATLANTIC 15-25 65

KILLER PUSSY
EPs: 7-inch
SHO-PINK ("Teenage Enema Nurses in Bondage") 25-35 82
(With paper sleeve.)
Members: Lucy LaMode; Gary Russell; John E. Precious; Dash Assult; Robert X. Planet.

KILLING FLOOR
LPs: 10/12-inch
SIRE (97019 "Killing Floor") 15-25 70

KILLING JOKE LP '87
LPs: 10/12-inch
EDITIONS 5-8 81-82
VIRGIN 5-8 87

KILLOUGH, Rock
LPs: 10/12-inch
ELEKTRA 5-8 80
STAX 5-8 79

KILPATRICK, Milt
Singles: 7-inch
CORVETTE (1007 "Come on In") ..10-20 60s

KILTS
Singles: 7-inch
GAYNOTE (105 "I'll Be True") 30-40 58
(Pink label.)
GAYNOTE (105 "I'll Be True") 15-25 58
(Green label.)

KILZER, John LP '88
Singles: 7-inch
GEFFEN 3-4 88
Picture Sleeves
GEFFEN 3-4 88
LPs: 10/12-inch
GEFFEN 5-8 88

KIM, Andy P&R '68
Singles: 7-inch
ABC 3-5 74
CAPITOL 3-5 74-76
RED BIRD 4-8 65
STEED 3-6 68-71
TCF 4-8 64
20TH FOX 4-8 68
UNI 3-5 72-73
U.A. 4-8 63
Picture Sleeves
CAPITOL 3-5 74
STEED 4-6 69-71
LPs: 10/12-inch
CAPITOL 8-12 74-75
DUNHILL 8-12 74
STEED 10-15 68-71
UNI 8-12 72-73
Also see ARCHIES

KIM & CHARACTERS
Singles: 7-inch
KIMLEY (1744 "Sinbad Stomp") 5-10

KIM & DAVE / J.B.'s Pickers
Singles: 7-inch
AMOS 3-6 71

KIM & SKIPPERS
Singles: 7-inch
RUSS FI 4-8 62

KIMBERLY, Adrian P&R '61
(Don Everly)
Singles: 7-inch
CALLIOPE (6501 "Pomp and Circumstance") 10-20 61
CALLIOPE (6503 "Greensleeves") 25-35 61
CALLIOPE (6504 "Draggin' Dragon") 25-35 61
Also see EVERLY, Don

KIMBERLY & TERRIERS
Singles: 7-inch
JERDEN 8-12 65

KIMBERLY SPRINGS C&W '84
Singles: 7-inch
CAPITOL 3-4 84

KIMBERLYS P&R '71
Singles: 7-inch
CANADIAN AMERICAN 4-8 62-63
COLUMBIA 4-8 65-66
HAPPY TIGER 3-5 70-71
RCA 3-5 69
LPs: 10/12-inch
HAPPY TIGER 8-12 70
Also see JENNINGS, Waylon

KIMBLE, Bobby
Singles: 7-inch
FAT FISH 4-8 66

KIMBLE, Neal R&B '68
Singles: 7-inch
TRC 4-6 71
VENTURE 4-8 68

KIMBLE, Paul
Singles: 7-inch
STAT (722 "Big Fat Mama") 10-20

KIMBLE, Quinn, Orchestra
Singles: 78 rpm
RPM 5-10 53
Singles: 7-inch
RPM 10-20 53

KIMBLE, Sam
Singles: 7-inch
MARBLE (124 "Stop and Go") 8-12
TOF (728 "Henry's In") 10-20 64
TOF (1224 "Jerking with the K's") ..10-20 64

KIMBROUGH, Bill
Singles: 7-inch
D 10-15 59

KIME, Warren, & His Brass Impact Orchestra LP '67
LPs: 10/12-inch
COMMAND 5-10 67

KIMMEL, Tom P&R/LP '87
Singles: 7-inch
MERCURY 3-4 87
Picture Sleeves
MERCURY 3-4 87
LPs: 10/12-inch
MERCURY 5-8 87

KIN & CHARACTERS
Singles: 7-inch
KIMLEY 5-10 63

KINCHELOE, Turk
Singles: 78 rpm
VEE JAY 4-8 55
Singles: 7-inch
ABNER 4-8 62
VEE JAY 5-10 55

KIND, Roslyn
LPs: 10/12-inch
RCA (4138 "Give Me You") 8-12 69

KINDLER, Steven
LPs: 10/12-inch
GLOBAL PACIFIC 5-8 88

KINDRED
Singles: 7-inch
W.B. 3-5 71-72
LPs: 10/12-inch
W.B. 8-10 71-72

KINDRED SPIRIT
Singles: 7-inch
INTREPID 3-6 69

KINETIC ENERGY
Singles: 7-inch
AMY 10-15 68

KINETICS
Singles: 7-inch
STUDIO CITY (1033 "I'm Blue") ..75-125 65

KINETICS
Singles: 7-inch
NASHVILLE (5334 "Put Your Loving on Me") 15-25 67
LPs: 10/12-inch
ETIQUETTE 5-8 86
Members: Roger Rogers; Daniel Davison; Roger Baldwin; Denney Goodhew.

KINFOLK
Singles: 7-inch
WHITE WHALE 4-8

KINFOLK V
Singles: 7-inch
KEY (4444 "The Dude") 5-10

KINFOLKS
Singles: 7-inch
DUO-O-DISC (106 "Mustang") 10-20 64
REVIS (1012 "Do You Wanna Dance") 10-20 64

KING P&R/D&D/LP '85
Singles: 12-inch
EPIC 4-6 85
Singles: 7-inch
EPIC 3-4 85
Picture Sleeves
EPIC 3-4 85
LPs: 10/12-inch
ELEKTRA 5-8 80-81
EPIC 5-8 85
Member: Paul King.

KING, Al R&B '66
Singles: 7-inch
KENT 5-10
MODERN 5-10 68
RONN 5-10
SAHARA 5-10 66
SHIRLEY 8-12 64
TRIAD (501 "Reconsider Baby") 10-15
Also see SMITH, Alvin

KING, Albert R&B '61
Singles: 78 rpm
PARROT (798 "Bad Luck Blues") ..25-50 53
Singles: 7-inch
ATLANTIC 4-8 69
BOBBIN 10-15 59-62
COUN-TREE 8-12 65
KING 6-12 61-69
PARROT (798 "Bad Luck Blues") 100-200 53
STAX 4-8 66-74
TOMATO 3-6 78-79
UTOPIA 3-6 76-77
Picture Sleeves
BOBBIN (143 "Old Blue Ribbon") ..15-25 62
LPs: 10/12-inch
ATLANTIC 8-12 69-82
FANTASY 5-8
KING (852 "Big Blues") 50-75 63
KING (1000 series) 10-12 69
PARRALL (202 "At the Blues Festival Live") 8-12 80s
STAX (Except 723 & 2000 series) 8-12 72-81
STAX (723 "Born Under a Bad Sign") 15-25 67
STAX (2000 series) 10-15 68-71
STAX (8000 series) 5-10 90
TOMATO 8-12 77-79
UTOPIA 10-15 76-77
Also see LITTLE MILTON & Albert King
Also see STAPLES, Roebuck

KING, Albert, & Otis Rush
LPs: 10/12-inch
CHESS 10-15 69
Also see KING, Albert
Also see RUSH, Otis

KING, Alex, & Turnpikes
Singles: 7-inch
CENTRAL (314004 "Weightless") ..10-20 63

KING, Anna P&R/R&B '64
Singles: 7-inch
END (1126 "Mama's Got a Bag of Her Own") 15-25 63
LUDIX (103 "Big Change") 20-30 63
MALIBU (1020 "In Between Tears") 10-20 61
RUST 8-12 64
SMASH 5-10 63-65
LPs: 10/12-inch
SMASH (27059 "Back to Soul") 15-20 64
(Monaural.)
SMASH (67059 "Back to Soul") 20-25 64
(Stereo.)

KING, Anna, & Bobby Byrd P&R '64
Singles: 7-inch
SMASH 4-8 64
Also see BYRD, Bobby
Also see KING, Anna

KING, Armando: see EARTHQUAKES

KING, B.B. R&B '51
(With the King's Men; with Vocal Chords; "B.B. 'Blues Boy' King")
Singles: 78 rpm
BULLET (309 "Miss Martha King") 50-100 49
BULLET (315 "Got the Blues") 50-100 49
RPM 10-25 50-57
Singles: 7-inch
ABC 3-8 66-78
ABC-PAR 5-10 62-66
BLUESWAY 4-8 67-70
KENT (300 series) 8-15 58-64
KENT (400 series) 5-10 64-68
KENT (4000 & 5000 series) 3-5
MCA 3-5 79-85
PAULA 3-5 81
RPM (339 "3 O'Clock Blues") 100-200 52
RPM (348 "Fine Looking Woman") 100-150 52
RPM (355 "Shake It Up and Go") 75-125 52
RPM (363 "You Didn't Want Me") ..40-60 52
RPM (360 "Someday, Somewhere") 25-50 52
RPM (380 "Woke Up This Morning") 25-50 53
RPM (374 "Story from My Heart and Soul") 25-50 53
RPM (386 "Please Love Me") 25-50 53
RPM (391 "Neighbourhood Affair") 25-50 53
RPM (395 "Why Did You Love Me") 25-50 53
RPM (403 "Praying to the Lord") 20-40 54
RPM (408 "I Love You Babe") 20-40 54
RPM (411 "Everything I Do Is Wrong") 20-40 54
RPM (412 "When My Heart Beats Like a Hammer") 20-40 54
RPM (416 "You Upset Me Baby") 20-40 54
RPM (421 "Sneakin' Around") 20-40 55
RPM (425 "Lonely and Blue") 20-40 55
RPM (430 "Shut Your Mouth") 20-40 55
RPM (435 "Talkin' the Blues") 20-40 55
RPM (437 "What Can I Do") 20-40 55
RPM (450 "Ruby Lee") 20-40 56
RPM (451 "Crying Won't Help You") 20-40 56
RPM (457 "Did You Ever Love a Woman") 20-40 56
RPM (459 "Dark Is the Night") 20-40 56
RPM (468 "Sweet Little Angel") 20-40 56
RPM (479 "Bim Bam") 20-40 56
RPM (486 "Early in the Morning") 20-40 56
RPM (490 "How Do I Love You") 20-40 57
RPM (492 "I Want to Get Married") 20-40 57
RPM (494 "Quit My Baby") 20-40 57
RPM (498 "I Wonder") 20-40 57
RPM (501 "Key to My Kingdom") 10-20 57
Picture Sleeves
BLUESWAY (61032 "The Thrill Is Gone") 5-8 69
MCA 3-4 85
EPs: 7-inch
ABC-PAR (456 "Mr. Blues") 10-20 63
(Juke box issue only.)
RPM (459 "Disc Jockey Special EP - Dark Is the Night") 75-125 56
(Not issued with cover. Promotional issue only.)
LPs: 10/12-inch
ABC (713 thru 1061) 8-12 70-78
ABC/COMMAND (40022 "Friends") 15-25 74
(Quadraphonic.)
ABC-PAR (456 "Mr. Blues") 20-30 63
ABC-PAR (509 "Live at the Regal") 15-25 65
ABC-PAR (528 "Confessin' the Blues") 15-25 65
ACCORD 5-8 82
("B.B. King Live") 250-500
(Picture disc. No label name or selection number used. Promotional issue only.)
BLUESWAY (6001 thru 6050) 10-20 67-73
CROWN (147 "B.B. King Wails") 20-30 60
(Stereo. Black vinyl.)
CROWN (147 "B.B. King Wails") 100-200 60
(Stereo. Colored vinyl.)
CROWN (152 "Spirtuals") 15-25 60
(Stereo. Black vinyl.)
CROWN (152 "Spirtuals") 100-150 60
(Stereo. Colored vinyl.)
CROWN (195 "King of the Blues") 20-30 61
(Stereo. Black vinyl.)
CROWN (195 "King of the Blues") 100-150 61
(Stereo. Colored vinyl.)
CROWN (309 "Blues in My Heart") 15-25 62
CROWN (359 "B.B. King") 15-25 63
(Mono, or 5000 series, numbers may exist for 309 & 359. If so, we would like to know them.)
CROWN (5020 "B.B. King") 40-60 57
CROWN (5063 "The Blues") 30-50 58
CROWN (5115 "B.B. King Wails") .20-30 60
(Monaural.)
CROWN (5119 "Spirtuals") 15-25 60
(Monaural.)
CROWN (5120 "Singing the Blues") 20-30 60
CROWN (5143 "The Great B.B. King") 20-30 61
CROWN (5167 "King of the Blues") 20-30 61
(Monaural.)
CROWN (5188 "My Kind of Blues") 20-30 61
CROWN (5230 "B.B. King") 20-30 62
CROWN (5248 "Twist") 15-25 62
CROWN (5286 "Easy Listening Blues") 10-20 62
CRUSADERS 5-8 82
CUSTOM 8-10
FANTASY 5-8 81
GALAXY (202 "Best of B.B. King") .15-25 63
KENT 10-20 64-73
MCA 5-10 79-85
MFSL (235 "Lucille") 20-25 94
PICKWICK 5-10
UNITED 10-15
Session: Ike Turner; Willie Mitchell; Hank Crawford; Calvin Newborn; Earl Forest; Floyd Jones; Connie McBooker; George Coleman; Charles Crosby; Ted Curry; Kenny Sands.
Also see BASIE, Count
Also see BLAND, Bobby, & B.B. King
Also see CRAWFORD, Hank
Also see CRUSADERS & B.B. KING
Also see FORREST, Earl
Also see KING, Carole
Also see McBOOKER, Connie
Also see MITCHELL, Willie
Also see SIMPSONS
Also see TURNER, Ike
Also see U2 & B.B. KING

KING, B.B., Jr., & Blues Messengers
Singles: 7-inch
L. BROWN (101 "I'm So Glad It's All Over") 10-15 64

KING, Ben E. P&R '60
Singles: 7-inch
ATLANTIC (Except 89361) 3-5 75-81
ATLANTIC (89361 "Stand By Me Medley") 4-8 86
(Promotional issue only. Has excerpts of nine songs from the film soundtrack, by: Ben E. King, Buddy Holly, Shirley & Lee, Bobbettes, Chordettes, Del Vikings, Coasters, Silhouettes, and Jerry Lee Lewis.)
ATCO (Except 6100 & 6200 series) 4-6 64-69
ATCO (6100 & 6200 series) 4-8 60-64
ELEKTRA 3-5 76
MANDALA 3-5 72-73
MAXWELL 3-6 69
Picture Sleeves
ATLANTIC 3-5 86
LPs: 10/12-inch
ATCO (133 "Spanish Harlem") 20-30 61
(Monaural.)
ATCO (SD-133 "Spanish Harlem") 30-40 61
(Monaural.)
ATCO (137 "For Soulful Lovers") 20-30 62
(Monaural.)
ATCO (SD-137 "For Soulful Lovers") 25-35 62
(Stereo.)
ATCO (142 "Don't Play That Song") 20-30 62
(Monaural.)
ATCO (SD-142 "Don't Play That Song") 25-35 62
(Stereo.)
ATCO (165 "Greatest Hits") 20-30 64
(Monaural.)
ATCO (SD-165 "Greatest Hits") 25-35 64
(Stereo.)
ATCO (174 "Seven Letters") 20-30 65
(Monaural.)
ATCO (SD-174 "Seven Letters") 25-35 65
(Stereo.)
ATLANTIC 8-12 75-81
CLARION (606 "Young Boy Blues") 10-15 60s
KING (3008 "Audio Biography") 10-15
MANDALA 8-12 72
MAXWELL 10-15 70
Also see BAKER, Lavern, & Ben E. King
Also see BOBBETTES
Also see BONDS, Gary "U.S."
Also see CHORDETTES
Also see COASTERS
Also see DEL-VIKINGS
Also see DRIFTERS
Also see EARL-JEAN
Also see HALOS
Also see HOLLY, Buddy
Also see LEWIS, Jerry Lee
Also see LITTLE EVA
Also see SHIRLEY & LEE
Also see SILHOUETTES
Also see SOUL CLAN

KING, Ben E., & Average White Band R&B/LP '77
Singles: 7-inch
ATLANTIC 3-5 77
LPs: 10/12-inch
ATLANTIC 8-10 77
Also see AVERAGE WHITE BAND

KING, Ben E., & Dee Dee Sharp
Singles: 7-inch
ATCO 4-8 68
Also see KING, Ben E.
Also see SHARP, Dee Dee

KING, Billy
("The Singingest Man You've Ever Seen")
Singles: 78 rpm
ABBOTT 10-15 54
Singles: 7-inch
ABBOTT (1001 "Can't Get You Outta' My Mind") 15-25 54

KING, Bobby
(With His Silver Foxx Band)
Singles: 7-inch
FEDERAL 5-10 62
MOS-BE (101 "Hey Lulu") 5-10

KING, Bobby R&B '84
(Featuring Alfie Silas)
Singles: 7-inch
MOTOWN 3-4 84
RODEO 10-15
Also see SILAS, Alfie

KING, Buzzy
Singles: 7-inch
TOP RANK 5-10 59

KING, Carole P&R '62
Singles: 7-inch
ABC 3-5 74
ABC-PAR (9921 "Goin' Wild") 30-40 58
ABC-PAR (9986 "Baby Sittin' ") 30-40 59
ALPINE (57 "Oh, Neil") 50-100 60
ATLANTIC 3-5 82-83
AVATAR 3-5 77-78
CAPITOL 3-5 77-80
COMPANION (2000 "It Might As Well Rain Until September") 75-125 62
DIMENSION (1009 "He's a Bad Boy") 15-25 63
DIMENSION (1004 "School Bells Are Ringing") 15-25 63
DIMENSION (2000 "It Might As Well Rain Until September") 10-20 62
(Purple label. Has black ring around center hole.)
DIMENSION (2000 "It Might As Well Rain Until September") 8-12 62
(Blue label. No black ring around center hole.)
ODE (Except 66112) 3-5 71-76
ODE (66112 "Pierre") 5-10 75
(Compact 33.)
RCA (7560 "Short Mort") 40-60 59
TOMORROW (7502 "A Road to Nowhere") 10-15 66
Picture Sleeves
ATLANTIC 3-5 82
AVATAR 3-5 77
CAPITOL 3-5 77-80
ODE 3-5 71-75
LPs: 10/12-inch
ATLANTIC 5-8 82-83
AVATAR 8-12 78
CAPITOL (Except 11000 series) 5-8 80
CAPITOL (11000 series) 8-10 77-79
EPIC/ODE (30000 series) 5-8 78-80
EPIC/ODE (40000 series) 12-15 80
(Half-speed mastered.)
ODE 10-12 70-78
Also see CITY
Also see COOKIES / Little Eva / Carole King

Also see DACHE, Bertell
Also see GERMZ
Also see HONEYBEES
Also see KING, B.B.
Also see PALISADES
Also see SHIRELLES

KING, Claude *C&W/P&R '61*
Singles: 7-inch
CINNAMON....3-5 74
COLUMBIA....3-8 61-71
DEE JAY (1248 "Run Baby, Run") .30-50 57
TRUE....3-5 77-80
Picture Sleeves
COLUMBIA....4-8 61-69
LPs: 10/12-inch
COLUMBIA....10-20 62-70
GUSTO....5-8 80
HARMONY....8-12 68
TRUE....8-10 77
Also see YOUNG, Faron / Carl Perkins / Claude King

KING, Clyde
Singles: 7-inch
ASSULT....4-8 62-63

KING, Clydie *R&B '71*
(With the Sweet Things)
Singles: 78 rpm
SPECIALTY....10-20 57
Singles: 7-inch
IMPERIAL....10-20 65-66
LIZARD....3-5 71
MINIT....5-10 67-69
PHILIPS....8-12 62-63
SPECIALTY....10-20 57
LPs: 10/12-inch
LIZARD....8-12 71
Also see BLACKBERRIES
Also see BROWN SUGAR
Also see CARTER, Mel, & Clydie
Also see HASKELL, Jimmy
Also see HOLIDAY, Jimmy, & Clydie King
Also see RAELETTS

KING, Curtis
Singles: 7-inch
COLUMBIA (44096 "Bad Habits")....10-20 67

KING, Dave, & Royal Knights
Singles: 7-inch
TEIA (1004 "The Beatle Walk")....10-15 64

KING, Denny
Singles: 7-inch
SARA (5016 "Fate of a Fool")....8-12 61
SPECIALTY....3-5 72
LPs: 10/12-inch
SPECIALTY....8-12 72
Also see DARNELLS

KING, Diane
Singles: 7-inch
TEIA....5-8 64

KING, Don *C&W '76*
Singles: 7-inch
BENCH MARK....3-4 86
CON BRIO....3-5 76-79
EPIC....3-4 80-82
615....3-4 88
LP: 10/12-inch
CON BRIO....5-10 77-78
EPIC....5-8 80-81

KING, Donny *C&W '75*
Singles: 7-inch
W.B.....3-5 75-76

KING, Doris
(With the Versa-Tones)
Singles: 7-inch
HICKORY....4-8 63-64
KING....4-8 66
MAGNA....4-8 63

KING, Earl *R&B '55*
Singles: 78 rpm
ACE....10-25 55-57
SPECIALTY....10-20 54-55
Singles: 7-inch
ACE (509 "Those Lonely, Lonely Nights")....40-60 55
ACE (514 "My Love Is Strong")....35-55 56
ACE (517 "It Must Have Been Love")....35-55 56
ACE (520 "Is Everything Alright")....35-55 56
ACE (529 "Those Lonely, Lonely Feelings")....25-50 57
ACE (543 "I'll Never Get Tired")....25-50 58
ACE (598 "Buddy It's Time to Go")....15-25 60
IMPERIAL (5713 "Come On")....15-25 60
IMPERIAL (5730 "Love Me Now")....15-25 61
IMPERIAL (5750 "Come Along with Me")....15-25 61
IMPERIAL (5774 "You Better Know")....10-15 61
IMPERIAL (5811 "Always a First Time")....10-15 62
IMPERIAL (5858 "We Are Just Friends")....10-15 62
IMPERIAL (5891 "Come Along with Me")....10-15 62
REX (1015 "I Can't Help Myself")....15-25 61
SPECIALTY (495 "I'm Your Best Bet, Baby")....50-75 54
SPECIALTY (531 "Eating and Sleeping")....50-75 54
SPECIALTY (558 "Funny Face")....50-75 55
Also see SMITH, Huey
Also see UNIQUES

KING, Earl, & Roomful of Blues
LP: 10/12-inch
BLACK TOP (1035 "Glazed")....5-10 87
Also see KING, Earl
Also see ROOMFUL of BLUES

KING, Earl
(Earl Connelly King)
Singles: 78 rpm
KING....10-15 55-57
Singles: 7-inch
KING (Except 5670)....15-25 55-57
KING (5670 "Big Blue Diamonds")....10-15 62
Also see JOHN, Little Willie / 5 Royales / Earl (Connelly) King / Midnighters

KING, Eddie
(With the Three Queens)
Singles: 7-inch
BIG WHEEL (170 "I Talk Too Much")....15-25 66
J.O.B.....10-20 60
PARKWAY....5-10 65

KING, Eddie, & Mae B. Mae
Singles: 7-inch
JAY-V....5-8

KING, Evelyn *P&R/R&B/LP '78*
(Evelyn "Champagne" King)
Singles: 12-inch
PRIVATE I....4-6 85
RCA....4-8 78-86
Singles: 7-inch
EMI....3-4 90
EMI-MANHATTAN....3-4 88-86
RCA....3-4 78-86
Picture Sleeves
RCA....3-6 78-86
LPs: 10/12-inch
EMI....5-8 90
EMI-MANHATTAN....5-8 88
RCA....5-8 77-86

KING, Freddie *P&R/R&B '61*
(Freddy King)
Singles: 78 rpm
EL-BEE (157 "Country Boy")....20-30 56
Singles: 7-inch
COTILLION....3-6 68-70
EL-BEE (157 "Country Boy")....50-75 56
FEDERAL....10-20 60-65
GUSTO....3-5 78
KING....3-5 69
EPs: 7-inch
KING (773 "Let's Hide Away and Dance Away")....40-60 61
(Juke box issue only. Includes title strips.)
LPs: 10/12-inch
COTILLION....10-15 69-70
GUSTO (5033 "Hide Away")....10-12 78
KING (762 "Freddy King Sings the Blues")....30-40 61
KING (773 "Let's Hide Away and Dance Away")....35-50 61
KING (821 "Bossa Nova & Blues")....20-30 62
KING (856 "Freddy King Goes Surfin' ")....20-30 63
KING (900 series)....15-20 65-66
KING (1000 series)....10-15 69
MCA....5-8 80s
RSO....8-10 74-77
SHELTER....8-10 71-75
Also see ROGERS, Jimmy, and Freddie King

KING, Freddie, & Lulu Reed
Singles: 7-inch
FEDERAL (12477 "Say Hey, Pretty Baby")....15-25 62

KING, Freddie / Lulu Reed / Sonny Thompson
LPs: 10/12-inch
KING (777 "Boy-Girl-Boy")....20-30 62
Also see KING, Freddie
Also see REED, Lulu
Also see RUSSELL, Leon
Also see THOMPSON, Sonny

KING, Harold
Singles: 7-inch
MERRI (6004 "Buzz Me Baby")....40-60 63

KING, Hial
(Hyle King Movement)
Singles: 7-inch
LIBERTY....4-8 67
MBK (103 "Death Valley")....20-30 63
MBK (104 "Mailbu Sunset")....20-30 63

KING, J.D., & Dick Taylor Orchestra
Singles: 78 rpm
AARDELL (9 "Private Property")....10-15 56
Singles: 7-inch
AARDELL (9 "Private Property")....20-30 56

KING, Jack
Singles: 7-inch
COOL (144 "Dance Everybody")....20-30
4 STAR (1725 "I Just Learned to Rock")....50-75 58

KING, Jayson
Singles: 7-inch
BELL....5-8 64

KING, Jean
Singles: 7-inch
HBR....8-12 66
LPs: 10/12-inch
HBR....10-20 66

KING, Jeanie
Singles: 7-inch
GENERAL AMERICAN....5-10

KING, Jessie Lee, & His Crowns
Singles: 7-inch
PINE (652 "Rock & Roll Rover")....150-250

KING, Jewel *R&B '50*
(With Dave Bartholomew's Orchestra)
Singles: 78 rpm
IMPERIAL....15-25 49
Also see BARTHOLOMEW, Dave

KING, Jimmy
Singles: 7-inch
HERALD (535 "Knocking on Your Door")....35-50 58

KING, Joanne
Singles: 7-inch
CORAL (62463 "My Baby Left Me")....25-35 65
RCA....10-20 58

KING, Joe: see JALOPY FIVE

KING, Johnny
Singles: 78 rpm
MGM (11255 "Where Were You")....5-10 52
Singles: 7-inch
DOT....5-10 58
GUY....4-8 61
MGM (11255 "Where Were You")....10-15 52
MONTICELLO....5-10 59
TIARA....5-10 59

KING, Jonathan *P&R '65*
Singles: 7-inch
PARROT....4-8 65-72
UK....3-5 73-74
UK/BIG TREE....3-5 75
LPs: 10/12-inch
PARROT (71013 "Jonathan King, Or Then Again")....25-30 67
UK....10-20 72-73
Also see HEDGEHOPPERS ANONYMOUS
Also see JACK, Robin
Also see PIGLETS
Also see SOUND 9418

KING, Joy
Singles: 7-inch
RIC....4-8 64

KING, Julius
Singles: 78 rpm
TENNESSEE (123 "I Want a Slice of Your Pudding")....100-150 52

KING, Karl
Singles: 7-inch
EXCELLO....5-10 59

KING, Kenny, & Be Bops
Singles: 7-inch
CUCA (1101 "You're Alright")....20-30 62
Members: Kenny King Jaeger; Ken Kleist; Dan Derfus; Tom Leininger; Rick Leigh.

KING, Kid *R&B '53*
(Kid King's Combo)
Singles: 78 rpm
EXCELLO....8-15 53-57
Singles: 7-inch
EXCELLO....10-20 53-60
Also see BEASLEY, Good Rockin' Sam / Kid King's Combo

KING, Lenore, & Tommy Anderson
Singles: 7-inch
HER MAJESTY....5-8 65

KING, Leonard, & Soul Messengers
Singles: 7-inch
INFERNO....10-20 67

KING, Mabel
Singles: 78 rpm
RAMA....15-25 56
Singles: 7-inch
AMY (874 "Love")....35-45 62
RAMA (200 "Alabama Rock & Roll")....50-75 56
RAMA (204 "Symbol of Love")....50-75 56

KING, Marcel *D&D '84*
Singles: 12-inch
A&M....4-6 84
Singles: 7-inch
A&M....3-4 84

KING, Martin Luther: see KING, Rev. Martin Luther, Jr.

KING, Marva
Singles: 7-inch
TRI-WORLD....3-4 88
Also see CISSEL, Chuck, & Marva King
Also see MADAGASCAR

KING, Maurice
(With the Wolverines)
Singles: 78 rpm
COLUMBIA....5-10 51
OKEH....10-15 51
Singles: 7-inch
COLUMBIA....15-20 51
OKEH (6800 "I Want a Lavender Cadillac")....20-30 51
Also see RAY, Johnnie

KING, Morgana *LP '64*
Singles: 78 rpm
MERCURY....4-6 56
Singles: 7-inch
MAINSTREAM....4-8 64
MERCURY....5-10 56
PARAMOUNT....3-5 73-74
REPRISE....4-6 66-67
20TH FOX....4-8 59
VERVE....4-6 68
WING....5-10 56
Picture Sleeves
PARAMOUNT....3-5 73
LPs: 10/12-inch
ASCOT....15-25 65-66
CAMDEN....15-25 60
EMARCY (36079 "For You, for Me, Forever More")....30-50 56
MAINSTREAM (300 series)....5-10 72
MAINSTREAM (6000 series)....15-25 64-65
MERCURY (20231 "Morgana King Sings the Blues")....30-40 57
MUSE....5-8 79-82
PARAMOUNT....5-10 73
REPRISE....15-25 65-67
TRIP....5-8 74
U.A. (3028 "Folk Songs ala King")....30-40 59
(Monaural.)
U.A. (3028 "Folk Songs ala King")....40-50 59
(Stereo.)
U.A. (30020 "Let Me Love You")....30-40 60
VERVE....10-15 68
WING....10-20 65

KING, Norma Lee: see GROOVENEERS / Norma Lee King

KING, Pee Wee *C&W/P&R '48*
(With Redd Stewart; with His Golden West Cowboys)
Singles: 78 rpm
BLUEBIRD....5-10 49
RCA....4-8 50-55
Singles: 7-inch
BRIAR....4-8 61
JARO....5-10 60
CUCA....5-10 64-68
LANDA....4-8 61
RCA....10-20 50-55
STARDAY....4-6 64-71
TODD....8-12 59
EPs: 7-inch
RCA (797 "Swing West")....15-30 56
RCA (3028 "Country Classics")....15-30 53
RCA (3071 "Western Hits")....15-30 53
RCA (3109 "Country Classics, Vol. 2")....15-30 53
RCA (3280 "Swing West")....15-30 56
LPs: 10/12-inch
BRIAR (102 "Golden Olde-Tyme Dances")....50-70 62
CAMDEN....8-15 65-71
CUCA....20-40 64
DETOUR....5-10
LONGHORN....5-10
RCA (1237 "Swing West")....40-60 56
RCA (2464 "Swing West")....5-8 77
RCA (3071 "Western Hits")....25-50 53
(10-inch LP.)
RCA (3028 "Country Classics")....50-75 53
(10-inch LP.)
STARDAY (284 "Back Again")....15-20 64
STARDAY (900 series)....8-10 75-76
Also see WAYNE, Hal, & Pee Wee King

KING, Peggy *P&R '55*
Singles: 78 rpm
COLUMBIA....3-5 54-56
MGM....3-5 52
Singles: 7-inch
BUENA VISTA....4-8 62
BULLET....3-5 71
COLUMBIA....5-10 54-56
MGM....5-10 52
ROULETTE....4-8 61
Picture Sleeves
BUENA VISTA....4-8 62
EPs: 7-inch
COLUMBIA....8-12 55
LPs: 10/12-inch
COLUMBIA....15-25 55
IMPERIAL....10-20 59
Also see VALE, Jerry, Peggy King & Felicia Sanders

KING, Ramona
Singles: 7-inch
AMY....4-8 67
EDEN....10-20 62-63
W.B.....4-8 64

KING, Randy
Singles: 78 rpm
TNT (108 "Crazy As a Loon")....10-20 54
TNT (9009 "Be-Boppin' Baby")....50-75 57
Singles: 7-inch
TNT (108 "Crazy As a Loon")....25-35 54
TNT (9009 "Be-Boppin' Baby")....50-75 57

KING, Ray
Singles: 7-inch
ACTION (100 "You've Gotta Stand Up")....10-15
KARL (222 "A Date at Eight")....40-60

KING, Red, & Souls
Singles: 7-inch
SPACE....4-8 67

KING, Rev. Martin Luther, Jr. *LP '63*
(Rev. Martin Luther King)
Singles: 7-inch
DOOTO....4-6 68
MERCURY....4-6 68
EPs: 7-inch
GORDY (906 "Speech Excerpts")....15-25 63
LPs: 10/12-inch
AUDIO FIDELITY (343 "Martin Luther King")....15-20 84
(Picture disc.)
BLACK FORUM....5-10 70
BUDDAH....8-15 69
CREED....8-12 68-71
DOTTO....8-15 62-68
EXCELLO....8-15 68
GORDY (906 "The Great March") 25-50 63
GORDY (929 "Free at Last")....15-25 68
MERCURY....8-15 68
MR. MAESTRO....10-15 63
NASHBORO....5-8 72
20TH FOX....8-15 63-68
UNART....8-12 68
These recordings contain speeches or excerpts of speeches by King.
Also see LANDS, Liz / Martin Luther King

KING, Richard, & Orchestra
Singles: 78 rpm
KHOURY'S....10-20 51

KING, Rod
Singles: 7-inch
SPACE (00021 "Don't Be Afraid")..40-60

KING, Ronnie, & Passions
Singles: 7-inch
GATEWAY (786 "Girl, Break Away")....15-25 67

KING, Sammy, & Voltairs
Singles: 7-inch
MGM....5-8 64

KING, Sander
Singles: 7-inch
J.R.M.....5-10

KING, Sandra
Singles: 7-inch
BELL....10-20 65

KING, Saunders *R&B '49*
Singles: 78 rpm
ALADDIN....10-20 49
FLAIR....15-20 54
MODERN....10-20 48
RHYTHM....10-20 42-47
Singles: 7-inch
FLAIR (1035 "My Close Friend")....30-40 54
FLAIR (1045 "Quit Hangin' 'Round Me")....30-40 54
GALAXY (712 "S.K. Blues")....10-20 62
RPM (341 "Lazy Woman")....25-35 51
RPM (375 "New S.K. Blues")....25-35 52
RPM (497 "S.K. Blues")....15-25 56

KING, Sherri *C&W '76*
Singles: 7-inch
U.A.....3-5 76

KING, Sherry
Singles: 7-inch
MCM....3-5 77

KING, Sid
(With the Five Strings; Five Strings)
Singles: 78 rpm
COLUMBIA....15-25 55-57
Singles: 7-inch
COLUMBIA (21361 "I Like It")....30-40 55
COLUMBIA (21403 "Drinkin' Wine Spoli Oli")....40-50 55
COLUMBIA (21449 "Sag, Drag and Fall")....30-40 55
COLUMBIA (21489 "Mama, I Want You")....30-40 56
COLUMBIA (21503 "Blue Suede Shoes")....40-50 56
COLUMBIA (21564 "Good Rockin' Baby")....40-50 55
COLUMBIA (40680 "Oobie Doobie")....25-40 57
COLUMBIA (40833 "It's True, I'm Blue")....25-35 57
COLUMBIA (41019 "I've Got the Blues")....25-35 57
DOT (16293 "Once Upon a Time")....10-15 61
SOUNDWAVES....3-5 80
Members: Sid King; Billy King; Melvin Robinson; Dave White; Kenny Massey.

KING, Sleepy *P&R '61*
Singles: 7-inch
AWAKE (852 "Rock Rock")....25-40
JOY (257 "Pushin' Your Luck")....5-10 61
SYMBOL (904 "Begging")....10-20 59

KING, Solomon: see SOLOMON, King

KING, Susan
Singles: 7-inch
TURNTABLE....4-6

KING, Teddi *P&R '56*
Singles: 78 rpm
RCA....3-5 56-57
Singles: 7-inch
CHAMPION....5-10
RCA....5-10 56-57
LPs: 10/12-inch
CORAL (57278 "All the King's Songs")....40-60 59
(Monaural.)
CORAL (757278 "All the King's Songs")....50-75 59
(Stereo.)
RCA (1147 "Bidin' My Time")....50-75 56
RCA (1313 "From Teddi King")....50-75 57
RCA (1454 "A Girl & Her Songs")....50-75 57
STORYVILLE (302 "'Round Midnight")....100-200 54
(10-inch LP.)
STORYVILLE (314 "Storyville Presents Teddi King")....100-200 54
(10-inch LP.)

STORYVILLE (903 "Now in Vogue")....75-125 56

KING, Toby

Singles: 7-inch

FEDERAL (12573 "Mr. Tuff Stuff")....10-20 65

KING, Tom, & Starfires

(With the Ardells)

Singles: 7-inch

E.M.K. 5-10
PAMA (115 "Ring of Love")....15-25 61
PAMA (116 "I Know")....50-75 61
POP-SIDE 10-15 61
RESCUE (103 "Please Don't Leave Me")....10-15 60s
Also see LEATHERWOOD, Alan

KING, Tommy, & Starlites

Singles: 7-inch

CLAREMONT (661 "I'm Gonna Knock on Your Door")....15-25 66

KING, Will R&B '85

(Willard King)

Singles: 7-inch

CAPITOL 3-5 73
TOTAL EXPERIENCE 3-4 85

KING, Willie

(With the Ike Turner Band.)

Singles: 78 rpm

VITA (123 "Peg Leg Woman")....35-40 56

Singles: 7-inch

VITA (123 "Peg Leg Woman")....50-100 56

KING & BARNES / Loyce Cotton

Singles: 7-inch

PACEMAKER (0000 "Leak at Watergate").... 5-8 74

KING & SHARPETTES

Singles: 7-inch

ALDO (503 "Did He Know")....15-25 62
Member: Windsor King.
Also see CASHMERES
Also see ROYAL SONS

KING ARTHUR & KNIGHTS

Singles: 7-inch

MALA 5-10 60
Also see PASSENGERS

KING BEES

(With Lloyd Price's Orchestra)

Singles: 78 rpm

FLIP....20-30 57
KRC....20-30 57

Singles: 7-inch

CHECKER (909 "Buzzin' ")....40-60 58
FLIP (323 "Puppy Love")....25-50 57
KRC (302 "Can't You Understand")....35-50 57
NOBLE (715 "Tender Love")....150-200 59
Also see MOORE, Jimmy, & Peacocks
Also see PRICE, Lloyd

KING BEES

Singles: 7-inch

PYRAMID (6217 "I Want My Baby")....15-25 66

KING BEES

Singles: 7-inch

RCA.... 5-10 65-66

Picture Sleeves

RCA.... 8-15 65-66
Member: Danny Kortchmar.
Also see KORTCHMAR, Danny

KING BEES

Singles: 7-inch

RSO 3-5 80

LPs: 10/12-inch

RSO 8-10 80-81

KING BEEZ

(King Beezz)

Singles: 7-inch

JET....10-15 67
QUALITY (1792 "Gloria")....15-25 66
(Canadian.)
QUALITY (1817 "I Can't Explain") 15-25 66
(Canadian.)
QUALITY (1860 "Found & Lost")....15-25 66
(Canadian.)

KING BISCUIT BOY LP '70

(With Crowbar)

Singles: 7-inch

EPIC.... 3-5 75
PARAMOUNT.... 3-5 70-73

LPs: 10/12-inch

EPIC.... 8-10 74
PARAMOUNT....10-15 70-73

KING BISCUIT ENTERTAINERS

Singles: 7-inch

BURDETTE (7 "Stormy")....10-15 68
BURDETTE (9 "Take My Thought Away")....10-15 68
KBE (1 "Courtship of Priscilla Brown")....10-15 68
REVUE (11066 "Rollin' Free")....10-15 69
Members: Ray Kennedy.
Also see AMERICAN CHEESE

KING BUMBLE BEE SLIM & HIS PACIFIC COAST SENDERS

(Amos Easton)

Singles: 78 rpm

MARIGOLD ("Twin Beds")....25-50 51
(No selection number used.)
Also see EASTON, Amos, & His Orchestra

KING CHARLES

(With Left Hand Charlie.)

Singles: 7-inch

FOLK STAR (1131 "Bop Cat Stomp")....40-60 54

KING CHARLES & COUNTS

Singles: 7-inch

CRUSADER 10-20 65

KING COBRAS

Singles: 7-inch

IRVANNE (117 "To Hold Your Hand")....1000-2000 59

KING COBRAS

Singles: 7-inch

ABS....5-10 61
CUSTOM SOUND 5-10

KING COLE TRIO: see COLE, Nat "King"

KING COLEMAN

Singles: 7-inch

COLUMBIA.... 4-8 61

KING CONEY: see CONEY, King

KING CRIMSON LP '69

Singles: 12-inch

W.B. 4-6 84

Singles: 7-inch

ATLANTIC.... 3-5 70-74
W.B. 3-4 81-84

LPs: 10/12-inch

ATLANTIC (Except 18000 & 19000 series)....10-20 69-74
ATLANTIC (18000 & 19000 series)..8-10 74-75
EDITIONS 5-10
MFSL (075 "In the Court of the Crimson King")....35-50 82
W.B. 5-8 81-84
WIZARDO 10-12
WORLD RECORD CLUB 12-15
Members: Greg Lake; Robert Fripp; Boz Burrell; Bill Bruford; Adrian Belew; Ian MacDonald; Michael Giles; Peter Sinfield.
Also see BAD COMPANY
Also see BELEW, Adrian
Also see BOZ
Also see BRUFORD, Bill
Also see FRIPP, Robert
Also see LAKE, Greg
Also see SINFIELD, Pete
Also see YES

KING CROONERS

(Little Rico & King Krooners; King Crooner's)

Singles: 7-inch

EXCELLO (2168 "Won't You Let Me Know")....30-40 59
EXCELLO (2187 "Memoirs")....40-50 60
HART (1002 "Lonely Nights")....250-350 59

KING CRUSHER & TURKEYNECKS

Singles: 7-inch

RASSLER (9008 "Fuzzy")....60-80 65
Also see JESSE J. & BANDITS

KING CURTIS P&R/R&B '62

(With the Kingpins; with Nobel Knights; King Curtis Combo; with His Tenor Sax)

Singles: 78 rpm

APOLLO (507 "King's Rock")....10-20 57
GEM (208 "Tenor in the Sky")....10-20 54
GROOVE (0160 "Movin' On")....10-15 56
MONARCH (702 "Wine Head")....20-30 53
RPM (383 "Boogie in the Moonlight")....15-25 53

Singles: 7-inch

ABC-PAR....8-12 60
ALCOR....5-10 62
APOLLO (507 "King's Rock")....15-25 57
ATCO (6100 series)....10-20 58-59
ATCO (6400 thru 6900 series) 4-8 66-71
CAPITOL....5-10 62-65
DELUXE (6142 "Steel Guitar Rag")....10-20 57
DELUXE (6157 "Wicky Wacky")....10-20 57
ENJOY....8-12 62
EVEREST....8-12 61
GEM (208 "Tenor in the Sky")....40-60 54
GROOVE (0160 "Movin' On")....10-20 56
KING....8-12 62
MONARCH (702 "Wine Head")....50-75 53
NEW JAZZ....5-10 61
RPM (383 "Boogie in the Moonlight")....40-60 53
SEG-WAY....10-15 61
TRU-SOUND....8-12 61-63

Picture Sleeves

CAPITOL (5377 "Bill Bailey")....5-10 65

EPs: 7-inch

ATCO (33-266 "Best of King Curtis")....5-10 68
(Stereo. Juke box issue only.)
CAPITOL....8-15 63

LPs: 10/12-inch

ATCO (113 "Have Tenor Sax Will Blow")....75-100 59
(Monaural.)
ATCO (SD-113 "Have Tenor Sax Will Blow")....100-125 59
(Stereo.)
ATCO (189 thru 385)....10-20 66-72
CAMDEN....10-15 68
CAPITOL (2000 series)....10-20 64-68
CAPITOL (11000 series).... 5-8 78-79
CLARION....8-10 60s
COLLECTABLES.... 6-8 88
ENJOY (2001 "Soul Twist")....30-50 62
EVEREST (1121 "Azure")....20-30 61
HARLEM HIT PARADE 8-10 70s
MOUNT VERNON 10-12
NEW JAZZ (8237 "New Scene")....20-30 60
PRESTIGE (7200 series)....15-20 62
PRESTIGE (7700 series)....8-12 69-70
RCA....15-25 60s
TRU-SOUND....15-20 62
Also see BAKER, Lavern
Also see BARRY, Jeff
Also see BENTON, Brook
Also see BOBBETTES
Also see CLOVERS
Also see COASTERS
Also see COMMANDOS
Also see COMSTOCK, Bobby
Also see COOPER, Horace
Also see DARIN, Bobby
Also see EMERSONS
Also see EVERETT, Bracy
Also see FACENDA, Tommy
Also see FREED, Alan
Also see JENNINGS, Waylon
Also see KING PINS
Also see LED ZEPPELIN / King Curtis
Also see MANN, Herbie
Also see McPHATTER, Clyde
Also see MICKEY & SYLVIA
Also see MR. BEAR
Also see MITCHELL, Freddie
Also see NOBLE KNIGHTS
Also see PAT & SATELLITES
Also see PRETTY BOY
Also see RAMRODS
Also see REDDING, Otis / King Curtis
Also see RESTIVO, Johnny
Also see RINKY DINKS
Also see SEDAKA, Neil
Also see SHARPE, Ray
Also see SHIRELLES & KING CURTIS
Also see SUNNYLAND SLIM
Also see TURNER, Joe
Also see TURNER, Sammy
Also see WASHBOARD BILL

KING DAVID & HOUSE ROCKERS

Singles: 7-inch

VERVE (10492 "Baby, You Satisfy Me")....15-25 67

KING DAVIS: see DAVIS, King

KING DIAMOND LP '87

LPs: 10/12-inch

ROADRACER (Except picture discs)....5-8 87-90
ROADRACER (9439 "Conspiracy")....15-20 89
(Picture disc.)
ROADRACER (9517 "Them")....20-25 89
(Picture disc. Promotional issue only.)
ROADRACER (65484 "Halloween")....15-20 80s
(Picture disc.)

KING DREAM CHORUS & HOLIDAY CREW R&B '86

Singles: 12-inch

MERCURY 4-6 86

Singles: 7-inch

MERCURY....3-4 86

Picture Sleeves

MERCURY....3-4 86
Members: Kurtis Blow; El De Barge; Fat Boys; Grandmaster Melle Mel; Whitney Houston; Stacy Lattisaw; Lisa Lisa & Full Force; Teena Marie; Menudo; Stephanie Mills; New Edition; Run-DMC; James Taylor; Whodini; Greg Phillinganes.
Also see BLOW, Kurtis
Also see DE BARGE
Also see FAT BOYS
Also see GRANDMASTER FLASH & Furious Five
Also see HOUSTON, Whitney
Also see LATTISAW, Stacy
Also see LISA LISA & Cult Jam with Full Force
Also see MARIE, Teena
Also see MENUDO
Also see MILLS, Stephanie
Also see NEW EDITION
Also see PHILLINGANES, Greg
Also see RUN-D.M.C.
Also see TAYLOR, James
Also see WHODINI

KING EDWARD & B.D.'s

(With the Bee Dees)

Singles: 7-inch

GROOVE (501 "Girls Are")....15-25
GROOVE (503 "I Do")....15-25
ROGA (69-14 "Working for My Baby")....15-25

KING EDWARD IV & KNIGHTS C&W '77

Singles: 7-inch

SOUNDWAVES 3-5 77-81

KING FAMILY LP '65

Singles: 7-inch

W.B. 3-5 65-66

LPs: 10/12-inch

CAPITOL....5-15 65
W.B. 5-15 65
Also see KING SISTERS

KING V

Singles: 7-inch

FTP (410 "Purple Wall")....10-20 61
(We think this band is King "V," the Roman Numeral, and not "V" as in King Victor.)

KING FLASH

Singles: 78 rpm

COLUMBIA....5-10 57

Singles: 7-inch

COLUMBIA....5-10 57

KING FLEMING: FLEMING, King

KING FLOYD P&R/R&B '70

(With the Three Queens)

Singles: 7-inch

CHIMNEYVILLE 3-5 70-76
ORIGINAL SOUND 4-8 64
PULSAR....4-8
UPTOWN....4-8 66

Picture Sleeves

CHIMNEYVILLE....3-5 71

LPs: 10/12-inch

ATCO....8-10 73
CHIMNEYVILLE 8-10 72
COTILLION 8-12 71
PULSAR....10-15 69
V.I.P. (407 "Heart of the Matter")...20-25 70

KING GEORGE

(With the Fabulous Souls; with Jim Laurro & His Orchestra; King George / Jim Laurro)

Singles: 7-inch

AUDIO ARTS (60015 "Baby, I've Got It")....10-20 60s
END (1023 "Woke Up This Morning")....15-25 58
RCA (8743 "I'm Gonna Be Somebody, Someday")....10-20 66
RCA (8846 "Ah Huh")....8-12 66

KING GEORGE & CHECKMATES

Singles: 7-inch

JERDEN....5-10 65-66
PANORAMA....5-10 65
Also see VANCE, Tommy

KING GUION: see GUION, King

KING HANNIBAL R&B '73

(James T. Shaw)

Singles: 7-inch

AWARE....3-6 73

LPs: 10/12-inch

AWARE....8-12 73
Also see HANNIBAL
Also see MIGHTY HANNIBAL

KING HARRY

LPs: 10/12-inch

HARVEST 5-8 78

KING HARVEST P&R '72

Singles: 7-inch

A&M....3-5 75-76
PERCEPTION 3-5 72-73

LPs: 10/12-inch

A&M....10-15 75
PERCEPTION....8-12 73
Also see LOVE, Mike
Also see WILSON, Carl

KING IVORY LEE

(Ivory Lee)

Singles: 7-inch

ALAMEDA....15-20 54
IVORY....5-10 62
TREY....10-20 58

KING JAMES

Singles: 7-inch

BONANZA (1002 "Goin' Fishin' ")....8-12
HAL (601 "Hunchback")....8-12

KING JAMES & ROYALS

Singles: 7-inch

BELL 4-6 69

KING KEELS

Singles: 7-inch

KING 4-8 65

KING KOBRA

Singles: 7-inch

REQUEST....4-8 63

KING KOBRA

Singles: 12-inch

CAPITOL....4-6 86

Singles: 7-inch

CAPITOL....3-4 86

LPs: 10/12-inch

CAPITOL....5-8 86
Members: Carmine Appice; Mark Free; David Michael Phillips; Johnny Rod; Mick Sweda.
Also see APPICE, Carmine

KING KONG

Singles: 7-inch

HOMESTEAD....5-10 91
Members: Ethan Buckler; Darren Rappa; Rich Schuler; David Pajo.

KING KROONERS: see KING CROONERS

KING LEO & LIONS

Singles: 7-inch

DORAINE (1001 "Daddy's Gone Again")....15-25

KING LIZARD

(Kim Fowley)

Singles: 7-inch

ORIGINAL SOUND 8-12 75
Also see FOWLEY, Kim

KING LOUIE & COURT JESTERS

Singles: 7-inch

MOCKINGBIRD....5-10 68

KING LOUIE'S COURT

Singles: 7-inch

STICKY (145 "King Louie's Glue") 10-15 66

KING MIDAS & MUFFLERS

Singles: 7-inch

CHROME 8-10

KING ODOM: see ODOM, King

KING OF HEARTS

Singles: 7-inch

CAPITOL....3-5 78

LPs: 10/12-inch

CAPITOL....5-8 78

KING PERRY: see PERRY, King

KING PHAROAH & EGYPTIANS

Singles: 7-inch

FEDERAL (12413 "By the Candlelight")....30-40 61
Members: Harold "King Pharoah" Smith; Morris Wade; Bernard Wilson; Pee Wee Lowrey.
Also see EGYPTIAN KINGS
Also see FOUR PHARAOHS

KING PINS

Singles: 7-inch

U.A. (111 "Ungaua")....15-25 58
RADIANT (1507 "Forever Lonely") 10-20 62

KING PINS P&R/R&B '63

(King-Pins; Kingpins)

Singles: 7-inch

ATCO....5-10 67
FEDERAL (12480 "Believe in Me")....15-25 62
FEDERAL (12484 "How Long Will It Last")....15-25 63
FEDERAL (12505 "With the Other Guy")....15-25 63
FEDERAL (12512 "Wonderful One")....15-25 63
FEDERAL (12517 "Two Hearts")....15-25 64
FEDERAL (12519 "I Got the Monkey off My Back")....15-25 64
FEDERAL (12525 "Just Keep on Smiling")....15-25 64
VEE JAY (494 "A Lucky Guy")....15-25 62

LPs: 10/12-inch

KING (865 "It Won't Be This Way Always")....35-50 63
Members: Andrew Kelly; Robert Kelly; Curtis Kelly. Session: Charles Lee; Offe Reese.
Also see KELLY BROTHERS
Also see KING CURTIS
Also see LEE, T.C., & King Pins

KING PINS

Singles: 7-inch

LARSE (101 "Rod Hot Rod")....25-50 66
MGM (13535 "Rod Hot Rod")....10-20 66

KING PLEASURE R&B '52

(Clarence Beeks)

Singles: 78 rpm

ALADDIN....10-15 57
JUBILEE 8-15 55
PRESTIGE....8-15 52-55

Singles: 7-inch

ALADDIN....10-15 57
HI-FI....5-10 60
JUBILEE 10-15 55
PRESTIGE (100 series)....5-10 60
PRESTIGE (800 & 900 series)....10-20 52-55
U.A.....5-10 62

LPs: 10/12-inch

HI-FI (425 "Golden Days")....35-55 60
PRESTIGE (208 "King Pleasure Sings")....75-125 55
(10-inch LP.)
PRESTIGE (7128 "King Pleasure Sings")....50-75 57
U.A. (14031 "Mr. Jazz")....30-40 62
(Monaural.)
U.A. (15031 "Mr. Jazz")....35-50 62
(Stereo.)

KING RICHARD & POOR BOYS

Singles: 7-inch

APOLLO....5-10 61
Also see POOR BOYS

KING RICHARD'S FLUEGEL KNIGHTS LP '68

Singles: 7-inch

MTA 3-6 66-68

LPs: 10/12-inch

MTA 5-10 67-70

KING ROCK

Singles: 7-inch

ZOOM....5-10 59

KING SISTERS C&W '46

(With Alvino Rey & His Orchestra; with Horace Heidt & His Orchestra)

Singles: 78 rpm

ALLIED....4-6 54
BLUEBIRD 4-8 39-44
BRUNSWICK....4-8 37-38
CAPITOL....4-6 47
JUBILEE 4-6 55
MERCURY 4-8 50
RCA VICTOR 4-8
VICTOR 4-8 44-46

Singles: 7-inch

CAPITOL....5-10 57-59
JUBILEE 5-10 55

EPs: 7-inch

CAPITOL....8-12 58

LPs: 10/12-inch

AJAZZ....5-8 80s
CAMDEN....8-15 66
CAPITOL (T-808 thru T-1333)....15-25 57-60
(Monaural.)
CAPITOL (ST-1205 "Warm and Wonderful")....20-30 59
CAPITOL (2397 "TV's Wonderful King Sisters")....10-15 66
CAPITOL CUSTOM 8-12 70
HINDSIGHT 5-8 81-83
JOYCE....5-10 80s

SPIN-O-RAMA ... 8-15 66-67
W.B. ... 8-15 66
Members: Luise King; Donna King; Alyce King; Yvonne King; Marilyn King
Also see KING FAMILY

KING ROCK & KNIGHTS
Singles: 7-inch
ZOOM (005 "Scandal") ... 10-15 59

KING SOLOMAN: see SOLOMAN, King

KING SOUND INTERPRETERS & TIPS
Singles: 7-inch
TALENT of MUSIC (8253 "Hi Note") ... 100-150 66

KING SUN-D MOET R&B '87
Singles: 7-inch
ZAKIA ... 3-4 87

KING SWAMP LP '89
Singles: 7-inch
VIRGIN ... 3-4 89
Picture Sleeves
VIRGIN ... 3-4 89
LPs: 10/12-inch
VIRGIN ... 5-8 89

KING SYAM
Singles: 7-inch
KING ... 4-8 63

KING TEE LP '89
LPs: 10/12-inch
CAPITOL ... 5-8 89-90

KING TONES
Singles: 7-inch
ATCO ... 4-8 69

KING TONES
("Vocal Pete Mervenne")
Singles: 7-inch
MUSITONE (102 "Wish for an Angel") ... 100-200

KING TOPPERS
Singles: 78 rpm
JOSIE ... 40-60 57
Singles: 7-inch
JOSIE (811 "You Were Waiting for Me") ... 40-60 57

KING TUT
Singles: 78 rpm
SITTIN' IN WITH (542 "Lonely Blues") ... 15-25 50
SITTIN' IN WITH (550 "Why Did You Leave Me Baby") ... 15-25 50
Singles: 7-inch
STARLINE ... 5-10 62
Members: Ed Wiley; Henry Hayes; Willie Johnson; Donald Cooks; Ben Turner.
Also see HAYES, Henry
Also see WILEY, Ed

KING USZNIEWICZ & HIS USZNIEWICZTONES
Singles: 7-inch
1-SHOT (175 "Surfin' School") ... 10-15 74
(Yellow/orange label.)
1-SHOT (175 "Surfin' School") ... 4-8 74
(Gold "Oldies Series" label.)
1-SHOT (178 "Wild Little Willie") ... 4-8 76
1-SHOT (180 "Sapphire") ... 4-8 78
(Promotional issue only.)
Also see LOGJAM LURCH & TURKEYNECKS

KING V: see KING 5

KING VICTOR
Singles: 7-inch
MADISON (110 "Boppin' Bobbie Jean") ... 25-35 59

KINGBEES P&R/LP '80
(Nino Tempo & Kingbees)
Singles: 7-inch
RSO ... 3-5 80-81
Picture Sleeves
RSO ... 4-6 80-81
LPs: 10/12-inch
RSO ... 5-10 80-81
Members: Jamie James; Michael; Rex.
Also see TEMPO, Nino

KINGDOM
Singles: 7-inch
SPECIALTY (722 "Seven Fathoms Deep") ... 5-10 70
LPs: 10/12-inch
SPECIALTY (2135 "Kingdom") ... 35-50 70
(Black and gold label.)
Members: John Toyne; Ed Nelson; Tim Potkey; Gary Varga.

KINGDOM BOUND SINGERS
Singles: 7-inch
VEE JAY (874 "I'll Be Standing") ... 10-15 59

KINGDOM COME P&R/LP '88
Singles: 7-inch
POLYDOR ... 3-4 88
Picture Sleeves
POLYDOR ... 3-4 88
LPs: 10/12-inch
POLYDOR ... 5-8 88-89

KINGFISH LP '76
Singles: 7-inch
JET ... 3-5 78
ROUND ... 3-5 76
LPs: 10/12-inch
ACCORD ... 5-8 81
JET ... 8-10 77
ROUND ... 10-20 76
Members: Bob Weir; David Torbert; Matt Kelly.
Also see NEW RIDERS of the Purple Sage
Also see WEIR, Bob

KINGFISH
LPs: 10/12-inch
TOWNHOUSE ... 5-8 81
U.A. ... 8-10 77

KINGLETS
Singles: 78 rpm
CALVERT ... 50-75 56
Singles: 7-inch
BOBBIN (104 "Pretty Please") ... 50-100 59
CALVERT (101 "Six Days a Week") ... 100-200 56

KINGOFTHEHILL LP '91
LPs: 10/12-inch
SBK ... 5-8 91

KINGPINS
Singles: 7-inch
BAMBOO ... 5-10 61

KINGPINS
Singles: 12-inch
HOO-HA (001 "The Kingpins") ... 10-15 82
(With picture cover.)
Singles: 7-inch
HOO-HA ... 4-6 82

KINGS
Singles: 78 rpm
SPECIALTY ... 200-300 54
Singles: 7-inch
SPECIALTY (497 "What Can I Do") ... 800-1200 54

KINGS
("Kings Featuring Bobby Hall"; King's; with Jack Gale Orchestra)
Singles: 78 rpm
GONE (5013 "Don't Go") ... 50-75 57
GOTHAM (316 "God Made You Mine") ... 35-55 56
Singles: 7-inch
EPIC (9370 "I Want to Know") ... 15-25 60
GONE (5013 "Don't Go") ... 100-200 57
GOTHAM (316 "God Made You Mine") ... 100-200 56
JALO (203 "Angel") ... 75-100 58
(Black vinyl.)
JALO (203 "Angel") ... 50-75 60s
(Red vinyl.)
JAX (314 "Why? Oh Why") ... 500-1000 53
(Maroon label. Red vinyl.)
JAX (314 "Why? Oh Why") ... 450-550 53
(Green label. Red vinyl.)
JAX (316 "Baby, Be There") ... 550-650 53
(Red vinyl.)
JAX (320 "Sunday Kind of Love") ... 500-1000 53
(Red vinyl.)
JAY WING (5805 "Surrender") ... 100-150 59
LOOKIE (18 "I Want to Know") ... 50-100 60
RCA (7419 "Till You") ... 50-75 58
RCA (7544 "Your Sweet Love") ... 25-50 59
Members: Robert Hall; Richard Holcomb; Adolphus Holcomb; Gil Wilkes.
Also see FOUR KINGS
Also see HALL, Bobby, & Kings

KINGS
Singles: 7-inch
JOX (045 "It's the LCB") ... 10-20 65
JOX (049 "Baby, You're the One") ... 15-25 65
JOX (052 "I've Got a License") ... 10-20 65

KINGS
Singles: 78 rpm
BATON ... 25-35 57
Singles: 7-inch
BATON (245 "Long Lonely Nights") ... 30-45 57
Members: Joe Van Loan; James Van Loan; Paul Van Loan; Dave Bowers.
Also see RAVENS
Also see VAN LOAN, Joe

KINGS
Singles: 7-inch
U.A. ... 3-5 73

KINGS P&R/LP '80
Singles: 7-inch
ELEKTRA (47006 "Switchin' to Glide") ... 5-10 80
ELEKTRA (47052 "Switchin' to Glide") ... 3-6 80
ELEKTRA (47110 "Don't Let Me Know") ... 3-6 81
ELEKTRA (47213 "All the Way") ... 3-6 81
LPs: 10/12-inch
ELEKTRA (274 "The Kings Are Here") ... 15-25 80
ELEKTRA (543 "Amazon Beach") ... 6-12 81
Members: David Diamond; Aryan Zero; Sonny Keyes; Max Styles.

KINGS & QUEENS
Singles: 7-inch
EVERLAST (5003 "Voices of Love") ... 15-25 57

KINGS & QUEENS
Singles: 7-inch
ASCOT ... 4-8 65
DORE ... 4-8 61

KINGS V
Singles: 7-inch
PALA (300 "Purple Wail") ... 15-20

KING'S COURT
Singles: 7-inch
WHEELS ... 10-15

KING'S HENCHMEN
(King's Henchmen)
Singles: 7-inch
CORAL (61979 "Deep Down and Low") ... 15-25 58
CORAL (61980 "Shufflin") ... 15-25 58

KINGS KOUNTY KARNIVAL
Singles: 7-inch
U.A. ... 4-6 69
Also see JAY & AMERICANS

KINGS LANCERS
Singles: 7-inch
BRAND-X (110 "Lancers Charge") ... 8-10 60s
Member: John King.

KINGS MEN
Singles: 7-inch
CLUB 51 (108 "Don't Say You're Sorry") ... 2000-3000 57

KINGS OF HOT RODS / Tokens / Hal Jones & Wheelers
LPs: 10/12-inch
DIPLOMAT (2308 "King's of the Hot Rods") ... 15-25 64
(The two Tokens tracks on this LP are actually by Johnny & Tokens.)
Also see JOHNNY & TOKENS

KINGS OF SUN P&R/LP '88
Singles: 12-inch
RCA ... 4-8 88-89
Singles: 7-inch
RCA ... 3-4 88-90
Picture Sleeves
RCA ... 3-4 88
LPs: 10/12-inch
RCA ... 5-8 88-90

KINGS RANSOM
Singles: 7-inch
INTEGRA (101 "Shame") ... 10-20 68
INTEGRA (102 "Shadows of Dawn") ... 10-20 68

KING'S X LP '88
Singles: 12-inch
MEGAFORCE ... 4-8 88
(Promotional only.)
LPs: 10/12-inch
MEGAFORCE ... 5-8 88-90

KINGSFIVE
(With the New Redtops Orchestra)
Singles: 7-inch
TROPHY (2 "I Hear the Rain") ... 800-1200 59

KINGSLEY, Christopher
Singles: 7-inch
WINRO ... 4-6 69

KINGSLEY, Gershon
Singles: 7-inch
EPIC (11084 "Kohoutek") ... 4-8 74

KINGSLEY, Pee Wee
(Featuring Sugar Pie De Santo)
Singles: 7-inch
MUSIC CITY (824 "Nickel and a Dime") ... 25-35 58
Also see DE SANTO, Sugar Pie

KINGSLEY, Robin
Singles: 7-inch
JERDEN ... 8-12 65
TOWER ... 5-10 65

KINGSMEN
Singles: 78 rpm
ALL STAR ... 50-75 57
NEIL ... 20-40 56
Singles: 7-inch
ALL STAR (500 "Guardian Angel") ... 50-75 57
NEIL (102 "Stranded Love") ... 35-55 56

KINGSMEN
(Kingsmen Quintet)
Singles: 7-inch
HILLSIDE ... 10-20 58
Members: Bob Shaw; Dick Greenberg; Jerry Swirsky; Hank Sargent; Howard Kurhan.
Also see ACADEMICS

KINGSMEN P&R '58
Singles: 7-inch
EAST WEST (115 "Week End") ... 15-20 58
EAST WEST (120 "Cat Walk") ... 15-20 58
Also see HALEY, Bill

KINGSMEN / Calvin Cool
Singles: 7-inch
ASTRA (1025 "Week End") ... 4-8 66
Also see COOL, Calvin
Also see KINGSMEN

KINGSMEN
Singles: 7-inch
JALYNNE (108 "Ladies Choice") ... 10-12 61

KINGSMEN P&R '63
Singles: 7-inch
CAPITOL ... 3-5 72
EARTH ... 4-6 69
ERIC ... 3-5 70s
JERDEN (712 "Louie Louie") ... 40-60 63
REO (028 "Louie Louie") ... 5-8 66
(Canadian.)
REO (8745 "Louie Louie") ... 25-50 63
(Canadian.)
WAND (Except 1107 & 1115) ... 5-10 63-68
WAND (1107 "It's Only the Dog") ... 10-15 65
WAND (1115 "Killer Joe") ... 8-12 65
Picture Sleeves
WAND (1118 "The Krunch") ... 10-20 66
LPs: 10/12-inch
ARISTA ... 8-10 81
HEAVY WEIGHT ... 20-25 67
PICADILLY ... 5-8 80
RHINO ... 5-8 80s
SCEPTER/CITATION ... 8-12 72
WAND (657 "The Kingsmen in Person") ... 30-35 64
WAND (659 "The Kingsmen, Vol. 2") ... 50-100 64
(Without *Death of an Angel.*)
WAND (659 "The Kingsmen, Vol. 2") ... 25-35 64
(With *Death of an Angel.*)
WAND (662 "The Kingsmen, Vol. 3") ... 25-30 65
WAND (670 thru 681) ... 20-25 65-67
Members: Lynn Easton; Mike Mitchell; Don Gallucci; Norm Sundholm; Gary Abbot; Jack Eley; Barry Curtis; Dick Peterson.
Also see DON & GOODTIMES
Also see ELEY, Jack, & Courtmen

KINGSMEN
Singles: 7-inch
ARNOLD (2106 "Goodnight Sweetheart") ... 75-125 60s

KINGSNAKES
Singles: 7-inch
BLUE WAVE ... 3-5 84
LPs: 10/12-inch
BLUE WAVE ... 8-10 84-86

KINGSTON, Jack
Singles: 78 rpm
QUALITY ... 20-30 56
(Canadian.)
Singles: 7-inch
QUALITY (1491 "I Got the Blues") ... 50-100 56
(Canadian.)

KINGSTON, Larry C&W '74
Singles: 7-inch
JMI ... 4-6 74
W.B. ... 3-5 75

KINGSTON TRIO P&R/R&B/LP '58
Singles: 7-inch
CAPITOL (856 "Merry Minuet") ... 20-30 59
(Promotional issue only.)
CAPITOL (1400 & 1800 series) ... 10-20 60-63
(Compact 33 Singles.)
CAPITOL (2006 "Farewell Adelita") ... 15-25 60
(Special products giveaway for Welgrume Sportswear.)
CAPITOL (2782 "Molly Dee") ... 15-25 59
(Promotional issue only.)
CAPITOL (3970 thru 4114) ... 10-15 58-59
CAPITOL (4167 "Tijuana Jail") ... 10-15 59
CAPITOL (S-4167 "Tijuana Jail") ... 20-30 59
(Stereo.)
CAPITOL (4221 "M.T.A.") ... 10-15 59
CAPITOL (4221 "M.T.A.") ... 25-35 59
(Promotional "Special Preview Record." Label pictures the Trio.)
CAPITOL (4271 "A Worried Man") ... 10-15 59
CAPITOL (4303 "Coo Coo-U") ... 8-12 59
CAPITOL (S-4303 "Coo Coo-U") ... 15-25 59
(Stereo.)
CAPITOL (4338 thru 5166) ... 5-10 59-64
CAPITOL (6000 series) ... 4-6 62-65
CAPITOL/LION OF TROY (2006 "Farewell Adelita") ... 10-20 60
(Capitol Special Products issue for Lion of Troy shirt buyers.)
DECCA ... 5-10 64-66
TETRAGRAMMATON ... 4-6 69
NAUTILUS ... 4-6 79
XERES ... 3-5 82
Picture Sleeves
CAPITOL (2006 "Farewell Adelita") ... 20-30 60
(Special products issue for Welgrume Sportswear.)
CAPITOL (2782 "Molly Dee") ... 20-30 59
(Promotional issue only.)
CAPITOL (4338 "El Matador") ... 15-25 60
CAPITOL (4740 "Scotch & Soda") ... 10-20 62
CAPITOL (4842 "One More Town") ... 10-20 62
CAPITOL/LION OF TROY (2006 "Farewell Adelita") ... 15-25 60
(Capitol Special Products issue for Lion of Troy shirts.)
DECCA (31702 "Hope You Understand") ... 15-25 65
DECCA (31790 "Yes, I Can Feel It") ... 15-25 65
DECCA (31860 "Runaway Song") ... 15-25 65
XERES ... 3-5 82
EPs: 7-inch
CAPITOL ... 15-30 58-61
CAPITOL CUSTOM (2670 "Cool Cargo") ... 30-40 60
(Special products issue for 7 Up.)
LPs: 10/12-inch
CANDLELITE (6971 "Historic Recordings") ... 15-25 70s
CAPITOL (500 series) ... 8-15 70
CAPITOL (T-996 "The Kingston Trio") ... 50-75 58
(Green label. Monaural.)
CAPITOL (T-996 "The Kingston Trio") ... 25-40 58
(Black label. Monaural.)
CAPITOL (DT-996 "The Kingston Trio") ... 10-15 69
(Reprocessed stereo.)
CAPITOL (T-1107 "From the Hungry i") ... 30-40 59
(Monaural.)
CAPITOL (ST-1183 "Stereo Concert") ... 25-35 59
(Stereo.)
CAPITOL (T-1199 "Kingston Trio at Large") ... 25-35 59
(Monaural.)
CAPITOL (ST-1199 "Kingston Trio at Large") ... 30-40 59
(Stereo.)
CAPITOL (T-1258 "Here We Go Again") ... 25-35 59
(Monaural.)
CAPITOL (ST-1258 "Here We Go Again") ... 30-40 59
(Stereo.)
CAPITOL (T-1352 "Sold Out") ... 20-30 60
(Monaural.)
CAPITOL (ST-1352 "Sold Out") ... 25-35 60
(Stereo.)
CAPITOL (T-1407 "String Along ... 20-30 60
(Monaural.)
CAPITOL (ST-1407 "String Along ... 25-35 60
(Stereo.)
CAPITOL (T-1446 thru T-2081) ... 20-30 60-64
(Monaural.)
CAPITOL (ST-1446 thru ST-2081) ... 25-35 60-64
(Stereo.)
CAPITOL (T-2180 "Folk Era") ... 30-40 64
(Monaural. Three-disc set with bound-in booklet.)
CAPITOL (ST-2180 "Folk Era") ... 35-45 64
(Stereo. Three-disc set with bound-in booklet.)
CAPITOL (T-2280 thru T-2614) ... 15-25 65-66
(Monaural.)
CAPITOL (ST-2280 thru ST-2614) ... 15-30 65-66
(Stereo.)
CAPITOL (11000 series) ... 5-8 79
CAPITOL (16000 series) ... 4-6 81
DECCA (4000 series) ... 15-25 64-65
(Monaural.)
DECCA (7-4000 series) ... 15-30 64-65
(Stereo.)
INTERMEDIA ... 5-8 85
NAUTILUS ... 20-25 79
PICKWICK ... 5-10 70s
TETRAGRAMMATON ... 10-15 69
XERES ... 5-10 82
Members: John Stewart; Dave Guard; Nick Reynolds; Bob Shane.
Also see BEATLES / Beach Boys / Kingston Trio
Also see GUARD, Dave, & Whiskeyhill Singers
Also see NEW KINGSTON TRIO
Also see STEWART, John
Also see STEWART, John, & Nick Reynolds

KINGSTON TRIO / Four Preps
Singles: 7-inch
U.S.A.F. (103 "El Matador") ... 20-25 60
(Promotional, radio station issue only.)
Also see FOUR PREPS

KINGSTON TRIO / Dinah Shore
Singles: 7-inch
U.S.A.F. (129 "Everglades") ... 20-25 60
(Promotional, radio station issue only.)
Also see SHORE, Dinah

KINGSTON TRIO / Frank Sinatra
EPs: 7-inch
CAPITOL (2229 "Excerpts from Great New Releases") ... 40-60 62
(Promotional issue only.)
Also see KINGSTON TRIO
Also see SINATRA, Frank

KINGTONES
("Vocal by Pete Mervenne"; King Tones)
Singles: 7-inch
COTILLION (44069 "It Doesn't Matter Anymore") ... 40-50 69
DERRY (101 "Twins") ... 30-50 64
DRUMMOND (105 "The Girl I Love") ... 50-75 67
EUCALYPTUS (002 "It Doesn't Matter Anymore") ... 10-20 69
KITOCO ("A Love I Had") ... 50-75 62
(No selection number used.)
KITOCO (355 "Twins") ... 40-60 63
MUSITONE (102 "Wish for an Angel") ... 30-50 61
Members: Pete Mervenne; Dave Roberts; Phil Roberts, Jr; Bruce Snoap.
Also see ROBERTS, Dave, & Kingtones

KINISON, Sam LP '86
LPs: 10/12-inch
W.B. ... 5-8 86-90

KINKS P&R/LP '64
Singles: 12-inch
ARISTA ... 4-8 79-83
Singles: 7-inch
ARISTA ... 3-6 77-85
CAMEO (308 "Long Tall Sally") ... 75-100 64
CAMEO (345 "Long Tall Sally") ... 40-60 65
CAMEO (348 "You Still Want Me") ... 100-200 65
ERIC ... 3-5
MCA ... 3-5 86
RCA ... 4-6 72-76
REPRISE (0306 thru 0647) ... 5-8 65-67
REPRISE (0691 thru 0863) ... 8-12 68-69
REPRISE (0930 thru 1094) ... 4-8 70-72
Promotional Singles
ARISTA (Except 5) ... 3-6 77-85
ARISTA (5 "Sleepwalker") ... 10-15 77
(Colored vinyl.)
CAMEO (308 "Long Tall Sally") ... 50-75 64
CAMEO (345 "Long Tall Sally") ... 35-45 65

CAMEO (348 "You Still Want Me") 100-150 65
REPRISE (0306 thru 0647) 10-20 65-67
REPRISE (0691 thru 0863) 10-15 68-69
REPRISE (0930 thru 1094) 6-12 70-72

Picture Sleeves

ARISTA 3-5 80-84

EPs: 7-inch

ARISTA (22 "The Kinks Misfit Record") 20-25 78
(Promotional issue only.)
CAMEO 4-6 78
REPRISE (352 "Arthur") 10-20 69
(Promotional issue only.)

LPs: 10/12-inch

ARISTA 6-12 77-86
COMPLEAT 5-8
MCA 5-8 86-89
MFSL (070 "Misfits") 20-30 82
PICKWICK 5-10 72-79
PYE 8-10 75-76
RCA (Except "AYL1" series) 10-15 71-76
RCA VICTOR ("AYL1" series) 5-8 80-82
REPRISE (2127 "The Great Lost Kinks Album") 20-30 73
REPRISE (R-6143 "You Really Got Me") 50-100 64
(Monaural.)
REPRISE (RS-6143 "You Really Got Me") 20-30 64
(Stereo.)
REPRISE (R-6158 "Kinks Size") 50-75 65
(Monaural.)
REPRISE (RS-6158 "Kinks Size") 20-30 65
(Stereo.)
REPRISE (R-6173 "Kinda Kinks") 50-75 65
(Monaural.)
REPRISE (RS-6173 "Kinda Kinks") 20-30 65
(Stereo.)
REPRISE (R-6184 "Kinks Kinkdom") 50-75 65
(Monaural.)
REPRISE (RS-6184 "Kinks Kinkdom") 20-30 65
(Stereo.)
REPRISE (R-6197 "The Kink Kontroversy") 50-75 66
(Monaural.)
REPRISE (RS-6197 "The Kink Kontroversy") 20-30 66
(Stereo.)
REPRISE (R-6217 "The Kinks' Greatest Hits") 50-75 66
(Monaural.)
REPRISE (RS-6217 "The Kinks' Greatest Hits") 20-30 66
(Stereo.)
REPRISE (R-6228 "Face to Face") 50-75 66
(Monaural.)
REPRISE (RS-6228 "Face to Face") 20-30 66
(Stereo.)
REPRISE (R-6260 "Live Kinks") 50-75 67
(Monaural.)
REPRISE (RS-6260 "Live Kinks") 20-30 67
(Stereo.)
REPRISE (R-6279 "Something Else") 50-75 67
(Monaural.)
REPRISE (RS-6279 "Something Else") 20-30 67
(Stereo.)
REPRISE (6327 "Village Green Preservation Society") 25-35 69
REPRISE (6366 "Arthur") 15-20 69
(Price includes lyrics insert.)
REPRISE (6423 "Lola Vs. the Powerman") 12-15 69
(Blue and white cover.)
REPRISE (6423 "Lola Vs. the Powerman") 6-10 69
(Black, blue and white cover.)
REPRISE (6454 "The Kink Kronikles") 8-12 69
(Original Reprise Kinks LPs from the '60s are on a multi-colored label. All 11 of these LPs have been reissued on the brown Reprise label and are valued at $10 to $15.)

Promotional LPs

ARISTA (Except 69) 10-15 77-84
ARISTA (69 "Low Budget Radio Interview") 40-50 79
REPRISE (2127 "The Great Lost Kinks Album") 50-75 73
REPRISE (R-6143 "You Really Got Me") 50-100 64
(White label, monaural.)
REPRISE (R-6158 "Kinks Size") 100-200 65
(White label, monaural.)
REPRISE (R-6173 "Kinda Kinks") 100-200 65
(White label, monaural.)
REPRISE (R-6184 "Kinks Kingdom") 100-200 65
(White label, monaural.)
REPRISE (R-6197 "The Kink Kontroversy") 100-200 66
(White label, monaural.)
REPRISE (R-6217 "The Kinks' Greatest Hits") 100-200 66
(White label, monaural.)
REPRISE (R-6228 "Face to Face") 75-150 66
(White label, monaural.)
REPRISE (R-6260 "Live Kinks") 75-150 67
(White label, monaural.)
REPRISE (R-6279 "Something Else") 75-150 67
REPRISE (RS-6000 series) 30-60 64-72
(White label, stereo.)
W.B. (328 Complete "Kinks Kit"/"Then Now and In-Between") 325-375 69
(Boxed set, includes Then Now and In-Between LP, button, pin, postcard, letter, decal, and other promotional materials.)
W.B. (328 "Then Now and In-Between") 75-100 69
(Price for LP only.)
Members: Ray Davies; Dave Davies; Mick Avory; Peter Quaife; John Dalton; John Gosling; Ian Gibbons; Jim Rodford; Bob Henrit; John Beecham; Mike Cotton.
Also see DAVIES, Dave

KINKS / Hollywood Stars

Singles: 7-inch

ARISTA (5 "Sleepwalker") 8-10 77

Picture Sleeves

ARISTA (5 "Sleepwalker") 10-15 77
Also see HOLLYWOOD STARS
Also see KINKS

KINNEY, Fern *P&R/R&B '79*

Singles: 7-inch

ATLANTIC 4-6 68
MALACO 3-5 79-80

KINNEY, June

Singles: 7-inch

MILKY WAY (001 "The Hands You're Holding Now") 15-25 64
(With Arlie Neaville and Dave Marten.)
MILKY WAY (008 "Look Out Heart") 4-6 66
Also see NEAVILLE, Arlie

KINNEY, Mary

Singles: 7-inch

ANDEX (4031 "Bobby My Love") 25-35 59

KINSEY, Big Daddy, & Kinsey Report

LPs: 10/12-inch

ROOSTER BLUES 5-10 85

KINSMAN DAZZ *R&B '78*

Singles: 7-inch

20TH FOX 3-5 78-79

LPs: 10/12-inch

20TH FOX 5-8 79
Members: Rob Harris; Michael Calhoun; Kenny Pettus; Ike Wiley; Mike Wiley; Ed Meyers; Skip Martin; Pierre De Mudd; Eric Fearman; Kevin Kendrick.
Also see DAZZ BAND

KIP & KEN

Singles: 7-inch

CRUSADER 4-8 65-66

KIPNER, Steve

Singles: 7-inch

ELEKTRA 3-5 79
RSO 3-5 78
Also see TIN TIN

KIPP, Dave

Singles: 7-inch

CORAL (61920 "No Sweat Baby") 15-25 58

KIPPER & EXCITERS

Singles: 7-inch

TORCH (501 "Drum Twist") 5-10 62
Member: Kip Tyler.
Also see KIPSTERS
Also see TYLER, Kip

KIPPINGTON LODGE

Singles: 7-inch

CAPITOL (2236 "Rumors") 10-20 68
Member: Nick Lowe.
Also see LOWE, Nick

KIPSTERS

Singles: 7-inch

TARGET ("Twistin' & Stompin' ") 8-12
Member: Kip Tyler.
Also see KIPPER & EXCITERS
Also see TYLER, Kip

KIRBY, Bruce

Singles: 7-inch

CRYSTALETTE 5-10 59

KIRBY, Buzz

Singles: 7-inch

PARKWAY 4-8 64

KIRBY, Dave *C&W '69*

Singles: 7-inch

DIMENSION 3-4 81
MONUMENT 3-6 69

LP: 10/12-inch

DOT 6-10 74

KIRBY, George

Singles: 7-inch

CADET (5523 "What Can I Do") 40-50 65

KIRBY, Kathy *P&R '65*

Singles: 7-inch

ASCOT 4-6 67
LONDON 4-8 62-65
PARROT 4-8 65-66

KIRBY, Larry

Singles: 7-inch

APOLLO 5-10 58

KIRBY, Monica

Singles: 7-inch

CORAL 4-8 63-64

KIRBY, Ted, & Starliters

Singles: 7-inch

GALA (104 "Pink Petticoat") 8-12 59

KIRBY STONE FOUR: see STONE, Kirby, Four

KIRIAE CRUCIBLE

Singles: 7-inch

NIGHT OWL (6836 "The Salem Witch Trial") 10-20 68
Also see CRUCIBLES

KIRK, Andy, & His Clouds of Joy *R&B '42*

(With the Jubalaires; Andy Kirk & His Orchestra; with 12 Clouds; with June Richmond)

Singles: 78 rpm

CORAL 10-20 49
DECCA 10-20 42-46
Also see JUBALAIRES

KIRK, Eddie *C&W '48*

(With Tex Ritter)

Singles: 78 rpm

CAPITOL 5-10 48-49
Also see RITTER, Tex

KIRK, Eddie

(Eddie Kirkland)

Singles: 7-inch

KING 10-20 64-65
VOLT 10-20 63
Also see KIRKLAND, Eddie

KIRK, James

Singles: 7-inch

GUYDEN (2126 "You Better Come Home") 20-30 65

KIRK, Jim, & TM Singers *P&R '80*

Singles: 7-inch

CAPITOL 3-5 80

Picture Sleeves

CAPITOL 3-5 80

KIRK, Johnny, & Lilly Thomas

Singles: 7-inch

COTIQUE 4-6

KIRK, Paul

(With the Pageants & Sandy Block Orchestra)

Singles: 7-inch

URANIA (5006 "Long Ago") 100-150 59

KIRK, Red *C&W '49*

Singles: 78 rpm

MERCURY 10-20 49-50
Session: Jerry Byrd.
Also see BYRD, Jerry

KIRK, Robie

Singles: 78 rpm

QUEEN 15-25 45

KIRK, Wilbur, & Phil Celia

Singles: 7-inch

PENNY 5-10 59

KIRKLAND, Billy

Singles: 7-inch

ALFA 3-5 82

KIRKLAND, Bo *R&B '75*

Singles: 7-inch

CLARIDGE 3-5 75

KIRKLAND, Bo, & Ruth Davis *R&B '76*

(Bo & Ruth)

Singles: 7-inch

CLARIDGE 3-5 75-78

LPs: 10/12-inch

CLARIDGE 5-10 76
Also see DAVIS, Ruth
Also see KIRKLAND, Bo

KIRKLAND, Danny, & His Band

Singles: 7-inch

J-V-B (60 "They Were Rockin' ") 20-40 57

KIRKLAND, Eddie

(With the Falcons; with His House Rockers; Little Eddie Kirkland)

Singles: 78 rpm

KING 40-60 53
RPM (367 "It's Time") 60-80 52
(7-inch 78rpm.)

Singles: 7-inch

FORTUNE (848 "I Need You, Baby") 25-35 59
KING (4659 "No Shoes") 100-150 53
KING (4680 "Please Don't Think I'm Nosey") 100-200 53
LU PINE (801 "I Tried") 5-10
PRESTIGE 4-8 64
TRU-SOUND 5-10 61-62

LPs: 10/12-inch

LU PINE (8003 "3 Shades of the Blues") 10-20
TRIX 5-10 79
Also see FALCONS
Also see HOOKER, John Lee, & Little Eddie Kirkland
Also see KIRK, Eddie

KIRKLAND, Jimmy

Singles: 7-inch

FOX (918 "Come On Baby") 50-75 57
TEEN LIFE (918 "Come On Baby") 75-100 58

KIRKLAND, Leroy

Singles: 7-inch

APT (25056 "The Diddy Bop") 10-20 60

KIRKLAND, Mike James

Singles: 7-inch

BRYAN 4-6

KIRTON, Lew *R&B '77*

Singles: 7-inch

BELIEVE 3-4 83
MARLIN 3-5 77

KIRWAN, Danny

Singles: 7-inch

DJM 3-5 75-76

LPs: 10/12-inch

DJM 8-10 75-79
Also see FLEETWOOD MAC

KISS *P&R/LP '74*

Singles: 12-inch

CASABLANCA 10-20 78-82
MERCURY 10-20 83-88

Singles: 7-inch

CASABLANCA 4-8 74-82
MERCURY (Except 0002) 3-6 85-88
MERCURY (0002 "World Without Heroes") 15-25 81
(Picture disc.)

Picture Sleeves

CASABLANCA (858 "Flaming Youth") 8-10 75
CASABLANCA (2365 "I Love It Loud") 8-10 81
MERCURY 4-8 85-87

LPs: 10/12-inch

CASABLANCA (7001 "Kiss") 10-20 70s
(Reissue of 9001.)
CASABLANCA (7006 "Hotter Than Hell") 10-15 74
CASABLANCA (7016 "Dressed to Kill") 10-15 75
CASABLANCA (7020 "Alive") 15-20 75
(With 8-page color booklet.)
CASABLANCA (7020 "Alive") 10-15 75
(Without booklet.)
CASABLANCA (7025 "Destroyer") 10-15 75
CASABLANCA (7032 "The Originals") 50-75 76
(With inserts: Army sticker; 16-page booklet; six trading cards.)
CASABLANCA (7032 "The Originals") 10-15 76
(Without inserts.)
CASABLANCA (7037 "Rock & Roll Over") 20-25 76
(With sticker-sheet order form.)
CASABLANCA (7037 "Rock & Roll Over") 10-15 76
(Without sticker-sheet.)
CASABLANCA (7057 "Love Gun") 25-75 77
(With cardboard gun. Apart from the LP unused cardboard gun is valued at $35 to $50. Labels on some pressings have tracks listed in the wrong sequence.)
CASABLANCA (7057 "Love Gun") 10-15 77
(Without cardboard gun.)
CASABLANCA (7076 "Alive II") 250-300 77
(Has three tracks not found on later issues: *Take Me, Hooligan,* and *Do You Love Me.* Reportedly 50 copies made.)
CASABLANCA (7076 "Alive II") 40-50 77
(With 8-page tatoo booklet. Add $20-30 if cover lists the three tracks, *Take Me, Hooligan,* and *Do You Love Me,* that are not on LP.)
CASABLANCA (7076 "Alive II") 10-15 77
(Without tatoo booklet. Add $20-30 if cover lists the three tracks, *Take Me, Hooligan,* and *Do You Love Me,* that are not on LP.)
CASABLANCA (7100 "Double Platinum") 30-40 78
(With platinum award order form.)
CASABLANCA (7100 "Double Platinum") 15-20 78
(Without platinum award order form.)
CASABLANCA (7152 "Dynasty") 8-12 79
CASABLANCA (7225 "Kiss Unmasked") 8-10 80
CASABLANCA (7261 "Music from the Elder") 25-35 81
(With lyric sheet.)
CASABLANCA (7261 "Music from the Elder") 8-12 81
(Without lyric sheet.)
CASABLANCA (7270 "Creatures of the Night") 30-45 82
(With make up.)
CASABLANCA (7270 "Creatures of the Night") 8-10 82
(Without make up.)
DYNASTY (7152 "Dynasty") 15-20 79
(With poster order form.)
DYNASTY (7152 "Dynasty") 8-12 79
(Without poster order form.)
CASABLANCA (9001 "Kiss") 30-50 74
(Does not contain *Kissin' Time.*)
CASABLANCA (9001 "Kiss") 10-20 74
(Contains *Kissin' Time.*)
MERCURY (814297 "Lick It Up") 5-8 83
MERCURY (822495 "Animalize") 5-8 84
MERCURY (826099 "Asylum") 5-8 85
MERCURY (832626 "Crazy Nights") 5-8 86
MERCURY (836887 "Smashes, Thrashes and Hits") 20-30 88
(Picture disc. Gatefold cover.)
MERCURY (836913 "Hot in the Shade") 5-8 89
MERCURY (522123 "Kiss My Ass") 25-30 94
(Colored vinyl, limited edition.)
POLYGRAM ("Kiss Alive III") 20-25 94
(Colored vinyl. Limited edition.)
POLYGRAM (832-903 "Crazy Nights") 20-25 87
(Picture disc.)
UNMASKED (7225 "Kiss Unmasked") 15-20 80
(With poster order form.)
UNMASKED (7225 "Kiss Unmasked") 8-10 80
(Without poster order form.)

Promotional LPs

BURNS MEDIA ("Rock & Roll Over with Kiss") 50-75 76
CASABLANCA ("A Taste of Platinum") 30-50 78
CASABLANCA ("Rock & Roll Over") 30-50 76
CASABLANCA (76 "Kiss Tour Album") 30-50 76
CASABLANCA (7001 "Kiss") 40-60 74
(Without *Kissin' Time.*)
CASABLANCA (7001 "Kiss") 20-30 74
(With *Kissin' Time.*)
CASABLANCA (7032 "The Originals") 100-125 76
(With inserts.)
CASABLANCA (9001 "Kiss") 75-125 74
(Does not contain *Kissin' Time.*)
CASABLANCA (9001 "Kiss") 25-35 74
(Contains *Kissin' Time.*)
CASABLANCA (20137 "Criss, Frehley, Simmons, Stanley") 20-30 78
MERCURY (792-1 "First Kiss, Last Licks") 75-100 90
Members: Gene Simmons; Ace Frehley; Paul Stanley; Peter Criss; Bruce Kulick; Eric Carr; Vinnie Vincent. Session: Mark St. John.
Also see BLACKJACK
Also see CRISS, Peter
Also see FREHLEY, Ace
Also see GROUNDHOGS
Also see SIMMONS, Gene
Also see STANLEY, Paul
Also see VINCENT, Vinnie, Invasion
Also see WHITE TIGER

KISS / Mighty Bosstones

Singles: 7-inch

MERCURY (858894 "Detroit Rock City") 3-6 94
(Colored vinyl.)
Also see KISS

KISSING THE PINK *P&R '83*

(KTP)

Singles: 7-inch

ATLANTIC 3-5 83
MERCURY 3-4 87

Picture Sleeves

MERCURY 3-4 87

LPs: 10/12-inch

ATLANTIC 5-8 83
MERCURY 5-8 87

KISSOON, Katie *D&D '84*

Singles: 12-inch

JIVE 4-6 84

KISSOON, Mac

LPs: 10/12-inch

DECCA 10-20 70

KISSOON, Mac & Katie *P&R '71*

Singles: 7-inch

ABC 3-5 71
BELL 3-5 72
MCA/STATE 3-5 75-76

LPs: 10/12-inch

MCA/STATE 8-12 76
Also see KISSOON, Katie
Also see KISSOON, Mac
Also see WATERS, Roger

KIT & OUTLAWS

Singles: 7-inch

EMPIRE (1 "Mama's Gone") 15-25 66
PHILIPS (40420 "Midnight Hour") 8-12 66
Also see OUTLAWS

KIT KATS

Singles: 7-inch

JAMIE 5-10 66-68
LAURIE 10-15 63
LAWN 8-12 64
PARAMOUNT 4-6 71

LPs: 10/12-inch

JAMIE (3029 "It's Just a Matter of Time") 20-30 67
JAMIE (3032 "The Kit Kats Do Their Thing-Live") 25-35 68
VIRTUE (102067 "Very Best") 30-35 67
Members: Kit Stewart; Carl Von Hausman; John Bradley; Ron Shane.
Also see NEW HOPE
Also see PONCE, Pablo, Four
Also see ROSCOE & Green Men
Also see TAK TIKS

KITAJIMA, Osamu

LPs: 10/12-inch

ANTILLES 8-10 76
ISLAND 8-10 77

KITARO *LP '85*

(Mansanori Takahashi)

Singles: 12-inch

GEFFEN 4-8 86
(Promotional only.)

Singles: 7-inch

GEFFEN 3-4 86

LPs: 10/12-inch

GEFFEN 5-8 85-90
GRAMAVISION 5-8 85-86

KITCHEN CINQ

Singles: 7-inch

DECCA 5-10 68
LHI 5-10 66-67

LPs: 10/12-inch

LHI (1200 "Everything But") 20-30 67
Also see Y'ALLS

KITT, Eartha *P&R '53*

Singles: 12-inch

STREETWISE 4-6 83

Singles: 78 rpm
RCA....................................... 4-8 53-57
Singles: 7-inch
DECCA....................................... 4-8 65
KAPP....................................... 5-10 59-66
RCA....................................... 10-20 53-57
STREETWISE....................................... 3-4 83
Picture Sleeves
RCA....................................... 15-25 54-55
EPs: 7-inch
RCA....................................... 20-30 53-57
LPs: 10/12-inch
CAEDMON....................................... 5-10 69
DECCA....................................... 10-15 65
GNP....................................... 10-15 65
KAPP....................................... 10-20 59-60
MGM....................................... 10-20 62
PHILIPS....................................... 8-15 68
RCA....................................... 25-50 53-57
STANYAN....................................... 5-10 72
SUNNYVIEW....................................... 5-8 84

KITT, Eartha, & Perez Prado
Singles: 78 rpm
RCA....................................... 4-8 50s
Singles: 7-inch
RCA....................................... 10-15 50s
Also see PRADO, Perez
Also see KITT, Eartha

KITT 'N KORY
Singles: 7-inch
WARWICK (523 "First Star") 8-12 60
Member: Jimmy Tennant.
Also see TENNANT, Jimmy

KITTENS
Singles: 7-inch
ABC-PAR....................................... 10-15 65-66
ALPINE (64 "Dark Sunglasses")..... 15-25 60
CHESS....................................... 5-10 67-68
CHESTNUT (203 "I'm Worried") 50-75 63
DON EL (122 "Walter")................. 20-30 63
DON EL (205 "I Need Your Love Tonight")....................................... 20-30 63
IMPERIAL (5728 "Wedding Bells").. 15-25 61
MURBO....................................... 5-10 67
UNART (2010 "Letter to Donna") 30-40 59

KITTENS FIVE
Singles: 7-inch
HERALD....................................... 8-12 64

KITTENS THREE
Singles: 7-inch
NEWARK (215 "I'm Coming Apart at the Seams")....................................... 20-30 60s

KITTRELL, Christine
("With Band")
Singles: 78 rpm
REPUBLIC....................................... 15-25 53-55
TENNESSEE....................................... 20-40 52
Singles: 7-inch
FEDERAL (12540 "Call His Name") 5-10 65
KING (6045 "Call His Name") 4-8 66
REPUBLIC (7026 "Gotta Stop Loving You")....................................... 25-50 53
REPUBLIC (7044 "L&N Special")..... 25-50 53
REPUBLIC (7055 "Evil-Eyed Woman")....................................... 25-50 53
REPUBLIC (7096 "Sittin' Here Drinkin' Again")....................................... 25-50 54
REPUBLIC (7109 "Leave My Man Alone")....................................... 25-50 55
TENNESSEE (128 "Sittin' Here Drinking")....................................... 50-100 52
VEE JAY (399 "Sittin' & Drinkin' ") .. 10-15 61
VEE JAY (444 "I'm a Woman")....... 10-15 62

KITTY & CLAY
Singles: 7-inch
KING (5450 "But I Do") 5-8 61

KITTY & HAYWOODS R&B '77
Singles: 7-inch
MERCURY....................................... 3-5 77
LPs: 10/12-inch
MERCURY....................................... 8-10 77

KITTY & KATS
Singles: 7-inch
COULEE (132 "Windy")................. 10-20 60s

KITTY & LA FETS
Singles: 78 rpm
APOLLO....................................... 100-150 57
Singles: 7-inch
APOLLO (520 "Christmas Letter")....................................... 100-150 57

KITTYHAWK
LPs: 10/12-inch
EMI AMERICA....................................... 5-8 80-81

KIX LP '83
Singles: 7-inch
ATLANTIC....................................... 3-4 81-89
Picture Sleeves
ATLANTIC....................................... 3-4 89
LPs: 10/12-inch
ATLANTIC....................................... 5-8 81-89

KLAATU P&R/LP '77
Singles: 12-inch
CAPITOL....................................... 3-4 80
(Promotional only.)
Singles: 7-inch
CAPITOL....................................... 3-5 77-80
ISLAND....................................... 4-6 75
Picture Sleeves
CAPITOL....................................... 3-5 77
LPs: 10/12-inch
CAPITOL....................................... 8-12 76-80
Members: John Woloschuk; Cary Draper; David Long;; Dino Tome.

KLASSMEN
Singles: 7-inch
MUSICLAND USA (20016 "Can't You Hear the Music")....................................... 15-20 67

KLASSY, Kaye, & Kustoms
Singles: 7-inch
SURE PLAY (1002 "Karate Twist")....................................... 10-20 62

KLAUS, Paddy, & Gibson: see PADDY, KLAUS & GIBSON

KLEEER R&B '79
Singles: 7-inch
ATLANTIC....................................... 3-5 79-85
LPs: 10/12-inch
ATLANTIC....................................... 5-8 79-85
Members: Paul Crutchfield; Richard Lee; Norm Durham.
Also see UNIVERSAL ROBOT BAND

KLEEN-KUTS
Singles: 7-inch
VITALITY....................................... 10-20
Members: Skippy; Mickey; Johnny.

KLEIN, George
Singles: 7-inch
SUN....................................... 5-10 61
Also see GEORGE & LOUIS

KLEIN, Mo
(With the Sergeants)
Singles: 7-inch
CRYSTALETTE (Except 722).......... 5-10 59
CRYSTALETTE (722 "All Right Private Presley")....................................... 15-20 58

KLEIN, Robert LP '73
Singles: 7-inch
BRUT....................................... 4-8 73
CASABLANCA....................................... 3-5 79
LPs: 10/12-inch
BRUT....................................... 8-12 73

KLEIN, Terry, with Dee Jay & Runaways
Singles: 7-inch
SONIC....................................... 10-20 66
STONE....................................... 10-20 66
VILLAGE WEST....................................... 3-4 87
Picture Sleeves
VILLAGE WEST....................................... 3-4 87
Also see DEE JAY & RUNAWAYS

KLEIN & MBO D&D '83
Singles: 12-inch
ATLANTIC....................................... 4-6 83
Singles: 7-inch
ATLANTIC....................................... 3-4 83

KLEMMER, John LP '69
Singles: 7-inch
ABC....................................... 3-5 76
CADET CONCEPT....................................... 4-6 69
LPs: 10/12-inch
ABC....................................... 5-10 75-79
CADET CONCEPT....................................... 8-12 69
CHESS....................................... 8-12 76
ELEKTRA....................................... 5-8 80-83
MCA....................................... 5-10 79-82
NAUTILUS....................................... 5-8 80-81
NOVUS....................................... 5-8 79
Also see HARRIS, Eddie, & John Klemmer

KLEZMORIM
LPs: 10/12-inch
ARHOOLIE....................................... 5-8 83
FLYING FISH....................................... 5-8 82

KLINE, Bobby
Singles: 7-inch
MB (105 "Taking Care of Business")....................................... 100-200 67

KLINE, Joey
Singles: 7-inch
POPLLAMA (57 "Makin' Wishes")..... 3-4 92
(Includes Joey Kline collector card.)
Picture Sleeves
POPLLAMA (57 "Makin' Wishes")..... 3-4 92
Members: Joey Kline; Emily Bishton; Don Pawlak; Craig Ferguson; Chris Friel.

KLINE, Johnny
Singles: 7-inch
JET (101 "Rock Me Mama")............. 4-6 88
(Black vinyl.)
JET (101 "Rock Me Mama")............. 4-8 88
(Red vinyl.)
JET (111 "Memphis")....................... 3-5 90
JET (126 "It's Late")........................ 3-5 91
(Red vinyl.)
TCB (100 "That's All Right")............ 3-5 96
(Colored vinyl.)
TCB (101 "Mystery Train") 3-5 96
(Colored vinyl.)
EPs: 7-inch
JET (109 "Mystery Train")................ 5-8 88
Members: Johnny Kline; Stan Butcler; Jim Cochran.

KLINT, Bobby
(With the Jades)
Singles: 7-inch
CHRISTY (109 "Mona") 20-30 59

KLINT, Pete, Quintet P&R '67
Singles: 7-inch
ATLANTIC....................................... 8-12 68
IGL (127 "Very Last Day")............. 15-25 64
MERCURY....................................... 8-12 67
P.K.Q....................................... 8-12 60s
TWIN SPIN....................................... 12-18 60s

KLIQUE R&B '81
Singles: 12-inch
MCA....................................... 4-6 81-85
Singles: 7-inch
MCA....................................... 3-4 81-85
LPs: 10/12-inch
MCA....................................... 5-8 81-85
Members: Howard Huntsberry; Deborah Hunter; Isaac Suthers.
Also see HUNTSBERRY, Howard

KLIXS
Singles: 7-inch
MUSIC CITY (817 "It's All Over")....................................... 300-500 57
(Black vinyl.)
MUSIC CITY (817 "It's All Over")....................................... 1500-2500 57
(Colored vinyl.)
MUSIC CITY (823 "Elaine") 500-1000 58

KLOCKWISE R&B '84
Singles: 7-inch
SINBAN....................................... 3-4 84-85

KLOWNS P&R/LP '70
Singles: 7-inch
RCA....................................... 3-5 70
Picture Sleeves
RCA....................................... 3-5 70
LPs: 10/12-inch
RCA....................................... 8-10 70

KLUGH, Earl R&B/LP '77
Singles: 7-inch
BLUE NOTE....................................... 3-5 76-77
LIBERTY....................................... 3-4 81
U.A....................................... 3-4 78-79
W.B....................................... 3-4 85
LPs: 10/12-inch
BLUE NOTE....................................... 5-8 76-77
CAPITOL....................................... 5-8 83-84
LIBERTY....................................... 5-8 80-81
MFSL (025 "Finger Paintings")......... 30-40 79
MFSL (UHQR 025 "Finger Paintings")....................................... 50-75 79
(Boxed set.)
MFSL (076 "Late Night")................ 25-35 82
U.A....................................... 5-10 78-80
W.B....................................... 5-8 84-91
Also see BENSON, George, & Earl Klugh
Also see JAMES, Bob, & Earl Klugh
Also see LAWS, Hubert, & Earl Klugh

KLYMAXX R&B '81
Singles: 12-inch
CONSTELLATION....................................... 4-6 84-87
MCA....................................... 4-6 84-86
Singles: 7-inch
CONSTELLATION....................................... 3-4 84-87
MCA....................................... 3-4 84-86
SOLAR....................................... 3-5 81-83
Picture Sleeves
CONSTELLATION....................................... 3-4 85-87
MCA....................................... 4-6 84-86
LPs: 10/12-inch
CONSTELLATION....................................... 5-8 85-87
MCA....................................... 5-8 90
SOLAR....................................... 5-8 81-83
Members: Lorena Hardiman; Ann Williams; Cheryl Coolen; Robbin Grider; Lynn Malsby; Joyce Irby; Bernadette Cooper; Judy Takeuchi.
Also see IRBY, Joyce "Fenderella"

KNACK
Singles: 7-inch
CAPITOL (2000 & 5000 series).......... 4-8 67-68

KNACK P&R/LP '79
Singles: 7-inch
ATCO (7051 "Pick It Up") 3-5 77
CAPITOL (4000 series)................... 3-5 79-81
RCA (62800 "My Sharona") 3-4 94
Picture Sleeves
CAPITOL (4731 "My Sharona")........... 4-8 79
CAPITOL (4771 "Good Girls Don't")... 3-5 79
CAPITOL (4822 "Baby Talks Dirty")....................................... 8-10 80
CAPITOL (5054 "Pay the Devil") 8-10 80
RCA (62800 "My Sharona") 3-4 94
LPs: 10/12-inch
CAPITOL....................................... 8-10 79-81
CHARISMA....................................... 5-8 91
Members: Doug Fieger; Bruce Gary; Berton Averre; Prescott Niles.
Also see GIANTS
Also see SKY
Also see SUNSET BOMBERS

KNACKIN, Tommy, & Four Jets
Singles: 7-inch
CASCADE....................................... 10-15 59

KNAPP, Jack
Singles: 7-inch
ADKORP....................................... 4-6 70

KNAVES
Singles: 7-inch
DUNWICH (147 "Leave Me Alone")....................................... 8-12 67
DUNWICH (164 "Inside Outside").... 8-12 68
GLEN (8303 "Leave Me Alone") 15-25 67

KNAVES
Singles: 7-inch
MITCHELL (101 "Surf-Mad") 10-20 60s

KNEE, Bernie: see Nee, Bernie

KNICKERBOCKERS
(With the Buddy Lucas Band)
Singles: 78 rpm
IT'S a NATURAL....................................... 150-250 53
Singles: 7-inch
IT'S a NATURAL (3000 "You Must Know")....................................... 400-600 53
Also see LUCAS, Buddy

KNICKERBOCKERS P&R '65
Singles: 7-inch
CHALLENGE (59268 "All I Need Is You")....................................... 10-20 65
CHALLENGE (59293 thru 59384) 5-10 65-67
ERIC....................................... 3-5 70s
LANA....................................... 3-6 60s
LPs: 10/12-inch
CHALLENGE (621 "Jerk and Twine Time")....................................... 45-55 66
CHALLENGE (622 "Lies")............... 50-75 66
CHALLENGE (12664 "Lloyd Thaxton Presents the Knickerbockers")....................... 50-75 65
SUNDAZED....................................... 5-10 89
Members: Buddy Randell; Beau Charles; Jimmy Walker; John Charles.
Also see RANDELL, Buddy
Also see THAXTON, Lloyd
Also see WALKER, Jimmy

KNICKERS
LPs: 10/12-inch
RHINO....................................... 5-8

KNICK-KNACKS
Singles: 7-inch
COLUMBIA....................................... 4-8 66
CUB....................................... 10-15 59

KNIGHT, Alan
(Winston Wheaton)
Singles: 7-inch
BAMBOO....................................... 5-10 62
TIDE....................................... 10-20 60-61
Also see WHEATON, Winston

KNIGHT, Baker
(With His Knightmares)
Singles: 7-inch
ANOTHER....................................... 3-5 75
CHALLENGE....................................... 5-10 63-64
CHECKER....................................... 5-10 63
CHESS....................................... 5-10 61
CORAL....................................... 8-12 59
DECCA (Except 30135)................... 10-15 57
DECCA (30135 "Bring My Cadillac Back")....................................... 15-20 56
EVEREST....................................... 5-10 63
JUBILEE....................................... 5-10 57-58
KIT....................................... 30-35 56
RCA (37-7892 "Dum Dum Diddley Dum")....................................... 15-25 61
(Compact 33 Single.)
RCA (47-7892 "Dum Dum Diddley Dum")....................................... 10-15 61
REPRISE....................................... 5-10 65-68
Also see LIMELITERS
Also see SUGAR BEARS
Also see TRONICS

KNIGHT, Bob, Four
Singles: 7-inch
GOAL (4 "Willingly")....................... 15-25 64
JOSIE (899 "Memories")................. 15-25 62
JUBILEE (5451 "Crazy Love") 20-30 63
LAUREL (1020 "Good, Goodby")..... 15-25 61
LAUREL (1023 "For Sale") 15-25 61
LAUREL (1025 "Well I'm Glad") 150-250 61
(Single-sided.)
LAUREL (1030 "Mr. Conscience")........ 3-5 93
TAURUS (100 "So Long")............... 15-25 62
TAURUS (356 "I'm Selling My Heart")....................................... 15-25 62
EPs: 7-inch
NEMO (1009 "Acappella") 5-8 83
(Colored vinyl.)
LPs: 10/12-inch
KAPE (1001 "Greatest Hits")............ 8-10 73
Members: Bob Bovino; John Ropers; Paul Ferrigno; Ralph Garone; Sandy Lynn; Charles Licarta; Frank Ivino.
Also see DELMAR, Eddie

KNIGHT, Catfish, & Blue Express
Singles: 7-inch
VERVE....................................... 4-8 68

KNIGHT, Chris, & Maureen McCormick
LPs: 10/12-inch
PARAMOUNT (6062 "Chris Knight & Maureen McCormick")....................................... 50-100 73
Also see BRADY BUNCH

KNIGHT, Curtis
(With the Squires)
Singles: 7-inch
GULF (31 "That's Why") 15-25 61
HORTON....................................... 5-10 60
RSVP....................................... 4-8 65-66
SHELL....................................... 4-8 62
LPs: 10/12-inch
PARAMOUNT....................................... 10-15 70
Also see HENDRIX, Jimi, & Curtis Knight

KNIGHT, Danny
Singles: 78 rpm
MGM....................................... 3-5 56
Singles: 7-inch
MGM....................................... 5-10 56
Picture Sleeves
MGM....................................... 10-20 56

KNIGHT, Dave
Singles: 7-inch
WASP....................................... 4-8

KNIGHT, Earl, & George Kelly
Singles: 7-inch
WINLEY (238 "Let the Good Times Roll")....................................... 15-25 59
Also see KELLY, George
Also see KELLY, George / Earl Knight

KNIGHT, Evelyn
(With the Ray Charles Singers)
Singles: 78 rpm
DECCA....................................... 4-6 51
Also see CHARLES, Ray, Singers

KNIGHT, Evelyn, & Red Foley C&W '51
Singles: 78 rpm
DECCA....................................... 4-8 51
Singles: 7-inch
DECCA....................................... 5-10 51
Also see FOLEY, Red
Also see KNIGHT, Evelyn

KNIGHT, Frederick P&R/R&B '72
Singles: 7-inch
JUANA....................................... 3-4 81
MAXINE....................................... 4-6 69
1-2-3....................................... 10-15
STAX....................................... 3-5 72
TRUTH....................................... 3-5 75
LPs: 10/12-inch
STAX....................................... 8-10 73

KNIGHT, Gladys P&R/R&B '61
(Pips; with the Pips)
Singles: 12-inch
COLUMBIA....................................... 4-8 79-85
MCA....................................... 4-6 86
Singles: 7-inch
ABC....................................... 3-5 73
BRUNSWICK (55048 "Whistle My Love")....................................... 75-100 58
BUDDAH....................................... 3-5 73-79
CASABLANCA....................................... 3-5 77-78
COLUMBIA....................................... 3-5 79-85
ENJOY....................................... 10-20 64
ERIC....................................... 3-5 78
EVERLAST (5025 "Happiness")...... 15-20 63
FLASHBACK....................................... 3-5 67
FURY (1050 thru 1067) 10-20 61-62
FURY (1073 "Come See About Me")....................................... 20-30 63
HUNTOM (2510 "Every Beat of My Heart")....................................... 300-500 61
MCA....................................... 3-4 86-88
MAXX....................................... 10-20 64-65
SOUL....................................... 6-12 67-74
VEE JAY (386 "Every Beat of My Heart")....................................... 10-15 61
VEE JAY (545 "Queen of Tears") .. 10-20 63
Picture Sleeves
BUDDAH....................................... 3-5 73-75
COLUMBIA....................................... 3-5 81
MCA....................................... 3-4 87
LPs: 10/12-inch
ACCORD....................................... 5-8 81-82
ALLEGIANCE....................................... 5-8 84
BELL....................................... 10-15 68-75
BUDDAH....................................... 8-12 73-78
CASABLANCA....................................... 5-10 77-78
COLUMBIA....................................... 5-8 79-85
51 WEST....................................... 5-8 80s
FURY (1003 "Letter Full of Tears")....................................... 200-300 62
LOST-NITE....................................... 8-12 81
MCA....................................... 5-8 87
MCP....................................... 8-10 76
MAXX (3000 "Gladys Knight and the Pips")....................................... 20-30 64
MOTOWN (Except 792) 5-8 80-82
MOTOWN (792 "Anthology")............ 8-12 74
NATURAL RESOURCES 5-8 78
PICKWICK....................................... 8-10 73
RELIC....................................... 5-10 90
SOUL (706 "Everybody Needs Love")....................................... 20-30 67
SOUL (707 "Feelin' Bluesy").......... 15-25 67
SOUL (711 "Silk 'N' Soul")............. 15-25 69
SOUL (713 "Nitty Gritty") 15-25 69
SOUL (723 thru 744) 8-15 70-75
SPHERE SOUND (7006 "Gladys Knight and the Pips")....................................... 20-30 65
SPRINGBOARD....................................... 8-10 75
TRIP....................................... 8-10 73
U.A....................................... 10-15 75
UPFRONT....................................... 10-12
VEE JAY....................................... 10-15 75
Members: Gladys Knight; Merald Knight; William Guest; Edward Guest.
Also see DIONNE & Friends
Also see GAYE, Marvin / Gladys Knight & Pips
Also see PIPS

KNIGHT, Gladys, & Johnny Mathis
Singles: 7-inch
COLUMBIA....................................... 3-5 80
Also see MATHIS, Johnny

KNIGHT, Gladys, & Bill Medley
Singles: 7-inch
SCOTTI BROS....................................... 3-4 86
Also see KNIGHT, Gladys
Also see MEDLEY, Bill

KNIGHT, Gloria
Singles: 7-inch
EMERSON (2101 "Lonely Girl")...... 10-20 64

KNIGHT, Holly P&R '88
Singles: 7-inch
COLUMBIA....................................... 3-4 88
Picture Sleeves
COLUMBIA....................................... 3-4 88
LP: 10/12-inch
COLUMBIA (44243 "Holly Knight") .. 5-10 88
Session: Nancy Wilson; Daryl Hall.
Also see DES BARRES, Michael, & Holly Knight
Also see DEVICE
Also see HALL, Daryl

Also see SPIDER
Also see WILSON, Nancy / Red Hot Chili Peppers

KNIGHT, James, & Butlers
Singles: 7-inch
CAT (1972 "Baby Please Pretty Please")....10-15 78

KNIGHT, Jean *P&R/R&B/LP '71*
(With Premium)
Singles: 7-inch
CHELSEA....3-5 75
COTILLION....3-5 81-82
DIAL....3-5 74
JETSTREAM....4-8 65
MIRAGE....3-4 85
OLA....3-5 77
OPEN....3-5 76
SOULIN....4-8 81-85
STAFF....5-10 72
STAX....3-5 71-73
TRIBE....5-10 65
Picture Sleeves
MIRAGE....3-4 85
LPs: 10/12-inch
COTILLION....5-8 81
MIRAGE....5-8 85
STAX....10-15 71

KNIGHT, Jerry *R&B/LP '80*
Singles: 7-inch
A&M....3-4 80-83
Picture Sleeves
A&M....3-4 80
LPs: 10/12-inch
A&M....5-8 80-81
Also see OLLIE & JERRY
Also see RAYDIO

KNIGHT, Jim
Singles: 7-inch
FAME (601 "Twist")....25-50 60s
STATUE (72676 "Magnolia Street")....8-10 70s
TEAR DROP (3253 "The Wrong Side of Town")....75-100 60s

KNIGHT, Jimmy
Singles: 7-inch
GOOD (001 "Playmates")....10-20
KANGAROO (27 "Crankshaft")....8-12 64
TOP ROCK (9140 "Flyin' High")....10-15 60

KNIGHT, Johnny
(With the Kingsmen; John Knight)
Singles: 7-inch
CHANCE (568 "Secret Heart")....25-50 62
MOROCCO (1005 "Rock and Roll Guitar")....40-60 58
SSS INT'L....4-6 67
20TH FOX....5-8 64

KNIGHT, K.J.
Singles: 7-inch
SOUND PATTERNS ("Mo-Jo")....15-25 60s
(Selection number not known.)
Also see AMBOY DUKES

KNIGHT, Larry, & Upsetters
Singles: 7-inch
GOLDEN WORLD (37 "Hurt Me")..10-20 66

KNIGHT, Little Sonny
Singles: 7-inch
NEW TEENAGE (5001 "My Darling")....150-200

KNIGHT, Lonnie
LPs: 10/12-inch
FLASHLIGHT....8-10 75
SYMPOSIUM....10-12 74

KNIGHT, Marie *R&B '49*
Singles: 78 rpm
DECCA (Except 48315)....5-15 49-54
DECCA (48315 "You Got a Way of Making Love")....10-20 54
MERCURY....10-15 56
WING....5-10 56
Singles: 7-inch
ADDIT....8-10
DECCA (Except 48315)....10-20 51-54
DECCA (48315 "You Got a Way of Making Love")....25-35 54
DIAMOND....8-12 63
MERCURY....15-20 56
MUSICOR (1076 "Cry Me a River")....10-20 65
MUSICOR (1106 "Say It Again")....25-50 65
MUSICOR (1128 "You Lie So Well")....10-20 65
OKEH....5-10 61-65
WING....10-15 56
Picture Sleeves
OKEH (7141 "Come Tomorrow")....10-15 61
LPs: 10/12-inch
BLUE LABOR....15-25
CARLTON (119 "Lift Every Voice and Sing")....25-50 60
Session: Louisiana Red.
Also see LOUISIANA RED
Also see MARIE & REX
Also see THARPE, Sister Rosetta, & Marie Knight

KNIGHT, Paul
Singles: 7-inch
BETHLEHEM....4-8 62
PLANET....4-8 61
Picture Sleeves
PLANET....5-10 61

KNIGHT, Peter
LPs: 10/12-inch
DERAM....8-12 67
MERCURY....10-20 67

KNIGHT, Richie
Singles: 7-inch
ARC....4-8 63

KNIGHT, Robert *P&R/R&B/LP '67*
Singles: 7-inch
DOT....4-8 61
ELF....4-8 68-69
MONUMENT....3-5 74
PRIVATE STOCK....3-5 75
RISING SONS....4-8 67-68
LPs: 10/12-inch
RISING SONS/MONUMENT (17000 "Everlasting Love")....15-25 67
Also see PARAMOUNTS

KNIGHT, Sonny *P&R '56*
(With the Cleeshays)
Singles: 78 rpm
ALADDIN....15-25 53
DOT....10-20 56
SPECIALTY....15-25 57
VITA....15-25 56
Singles: 7-inch
A&M....5-10 63-64
ALADDIN (3195 "Dear Wonderful")....25-50 53
ALADDIN (3207 "But Officer")....25-50 53
AURA (403 "If You Want This Love")....5-10 64
AURA (4505 "Love Me")....5-10 65
DOT (15507 "Confidential")....30-40 56
(Maroon label.)
DOT (15507 "Confidential")....10-20 57
(Black label.)
EASTMAN (787 "Lipstick Kisses")....20-40 59
FIFO (105 "Small Girl, Big World")....50-75 61
MERCURY (72033 "Just One More Chance")....10-15 62
ORIGINAL SOUND (2 "Once in Awhile")....25-35 58
ORIGINAL SOUND (18 "Those Oldies But Goodies Are Dedicated to You")....10-15 62
SPECIALTY (547 "Keep a Walkin' ")....25-50 55
STARLA (Except 1)....15-25 58-59
STARLA (1 "Dedicated to You")....25-50 57
VITA (137 "Confidential")....40-60 56
WORLD PACIFIC (403 "If You Want This Love")....10-20 64
(Reissued a few months later on Aura 403.)
WORLD PACIFIC (77811 "If I May")....5-10 66
Picture Sleeves
AURA (4505 "Love Me")....10-20 64
LPs: 10/12-inch
AURA (A-3001 "If You Want This Love")....15-25 64
(Monaural.)
AURA (AS-3001 "If You Want This Love")....25-35 64
(Stereo.)
Also see TYRELL, Danny, & Cleeshays

KNIGHT, Terry *P&R/LP '66*
(With the Pack; with Fabulous Pack)
Singles: 7-inch
A&M....5-10 65
ABKCO....3-5 75
CAMEO (482 "Lizbeth Peach")....5-10 67
CAMEO (495 "Come Home Baby")....5-10 67
CAPITOL (2506 "Saint Paul")....8-12 69
FRATERNITY....5-10 67
LUCKY ELEVEN (225 "How Much More")....15-25 66
LUCKY ELEVEN (226 "Better Man Than I")....15-25 66
LUCKY ELEVEN (229 "A Change on the Way")....10-15 66
LUCKY ELEVEN (230 "I")....10-15 66
LUCKY ELEVEN (235 "This Precious Time")....10-15 67
LUCKY ELEVEN (236 "One Monkey Don't Stop No Show")....10-15 67
Note: Label may be shown as either "Lucky 11" or "Lucky Eleven."
SPICE....5-10 60s
LPs: 10/12-inch
ABKCO....10-15 72
CAMEO (2007 "Reflections")....20-30 67
LUCKY ELEVEN (8000 "Terry Knight and the Pack")....25-35 66
LUCKY ELEVEN (8001 "Reflections")....25-35 67
Members: Terry Knapp (a.k.a. Knight); Mark Farner; Don Brewer; Bob Caldwell; Curt Johnson.
Also see GRAND FUNK RAILROAD
Also see PACK

KNIGHT, Tommy
Singles: 7-inch
ATCO....4-8 61
EMERSON....4-8 64

KNIGHT, Toni
Singles: 7-inch
GEE....4-8 61

KNIGHT, Wally
Singles: 7-inch
VEEP....4-8 67

KNIGHT, Whitey
Singles: 78 rpm
DOT....8-10 57
Singles: 7-inch
DART....10-20 59
DOT....8-10 57

KNIGHT BEATS
Singles: 7-inch
CRYSTALETTE....5-10 59

KNIGHT BROTHERS *P&R/R&B '65*
Singles: 7-inch
CHECKER....10-20 63-66
MERCURY....8-15 67-68
Members: Richard Dunbar; Jerry Diggs.

KNIGHT HAWKS
Singles: 7-inch
CONTOUR....5-10 60

KNIGHT KAPS
Singles: 7-inch
RICKY (211 "Mama Loochie")....20-30

KNIGHT RAIDERS: see HAWKS, Mickey

KNIGHT RIDERS
(Featuring Billy Vera)
Singles: 7-inch
1220 CLUB ("My Heart Crys")....30-40
(No selection number used. Labeled "Souvenir Copy.")
U.A. (366 "Annie's Place")....10-20 61
Also see VERA, Billy

KNIGHT RIDERS
Singles: 7-inch
TRAVEL (5303 "Roc-A-Nof")....10-20 66

KNIGHT RYDERS
Singles: 7-inch
CUCA (1197 "They'll Never Guess I'm Lonely")....10-20 60s
CUCA (1264 "Talking in Your Sleep")....10-20 60s
Members: Bill West; Mel West.

KNIGHT SISTERS
Singles: 7-inch
TEMPWOOD....4-8 62

KNIGHT TRAINS
Singles: 7-inch
HART-VAN (126 "Beach Head")....20-30 63

KNIGHTLY, John
Singles: 7-inch
SPAR....10-15 61

KNIGHTMARE II
Singles
AZRA (1 "Razor Love")....20-30 87
(Square picture disc. 25 made.)
MASQUE (1020 "Guillotine")....10-15 88
(Ram-shaped picture disc. 500 made.)
MASQUE (8806 "Down Town Brown")....5-10 89
(Hockey mask shaped picture disc. 500 made.)
LPs: 10/12-inch
MASQUE (8807 "Edge of Knight")..15-20 89
(Picture disc. Promotional issue only. 100 made.)

KNIGHTON, Reggie
Singles: 7-inch
COLUMBIA....3-5 79

KNIGHTS
Singles: 7-inch
RED FEATHER (18401 "Cut Out")..10-20 61
RED FEATHER ("Lonely by the Sea")....10-20 61
(Selection number not known.)

KNIGHTS
Singles: 7-inch
FELSTED (8640 "White Fang")....8-12 62
Member: Jimmy Wisner.
Also see KOKOMO
Also see WISNER, Jimmy

KNIGHTS
Singles: 7-inch
CAPITOL (5302 "Hot Rod High")....10-20 64
LPs: 10/12-inch
CAPITOL (T-2189 "Hot Rod High")....40-50 64
(Monaural.)
CAPITOL (ST-2189 "Hot Rod High")....50-70 64
(Stereo.)
Session: Gary Usher; Chuck Girard; Dick Burns; Joe Kelly; Hal Blaine; Jerry Cole; Glen Campbell; Leon Russell; Steve Douglas; Tommy Tedesco; Bill Pitman; Charles Berghofer; Jay Migliori; Frank Capp.
Also see BLAINE, Hal
Also see CAMPBELL, Glen
Also see COLE, Jerry
Also see DOUGLAS, Steve
Also see GIRARD, Chuck
Also see KICKSTANDS
Also see RUSSELL, Leon
Also see TEDESCO, Tommy
Also see USHER, Gary

KNIGHTS
LPs: 10/12-inch
ACE (4763 "Cold Days, Hot Knights")....200-400 60s
ACE (200854 "Across the Board")....200-400 66
ACE (201302 "Knights 1967")....200-400 67
CO (1269 "Off Campus")....300-500 65

KNIGHTS
Singles: 7-inch
TRAGAR (6806 "The Hump")....10-20 65

KNIGHTS BRIDGE
Singles: 7-inch
SEA-ELL....10-20 68

KNIGHTS BRIDGE QUINTET
Singles: 7-inch
K (101 "Sorrow in Major C")....10-20
MARK VII....10-20 67
SALMAR....10-20

KNIGHTS OF DAY
Singles: 7-inch
TEE PEE (55/56 "Mr. Pitiful")....10-15 68
TOWER....5-10 66

KNIGHTS OF THE ROAD
Singles: 7-inch
LEVE-WAY (4150 "Color of Dream")....10-15 60s

KNIGHTSBRIDGE BRASS
Singles: 7-inch
SHAD....4-8 59

KNIGHTSBRIDGE STRINGS *P&R '59*
Singles: 7-inch
MONUMENT....3-6 66
TOP RANK....4-8 59-60
LPs: 10/12-inch
MONUMENT....5-10 66-69
PURIST....5-10 64
RIVERSIDE....5-12 62-64
SESAC....8-15 59
TOP RANK....5-15 59-60
Also see CAMBRIDGE STRINGS & SINGERS
Also see RANDOLPH, Boots

KNIGHTSMEN
Singles: 7-inch
BOCALDUN (1005 Darling Why")....100-200 59

KNIPP, Lowell
Singles: 7-inch
DEWL....10-15 65
MUSICOR....4-8 65-69

KNOBLOCK, Fred *C&W/P&R/LP '80*
Singles: 7-inch
SCOTTI BROS....3-4 80-82
LPs: 10/12-inch
SCOTTI BROS....5-8 80-82

KNOBLOCK, Fred, & Susan Anton *C&W/P&R '80*
Singles: 7-inch
SCOTTI BROS....3-5 80
Also see ANTON, Susan
Also see KNOBLOCK, Fred

KNOCKOUTS *P&R '59*
Singles: 7-inch
SHAD (5013 "Darling Lorraine")....10-20 59
SHAD (5018 "Rich Boy, Poor Boy")....10-20 60
TRIBUTE (199 "Got My Mojo Working")....8-10 64
TRIBUTE (201 "What's on Your Mind")....10-15 64
TRIBUTE (1039 "Don't Say Goodbye")....8-10 65
LPs: 10/12-inch
TRIBUTE (1202 "Go Ape")....50-60 64
Member: Robert D'Andrea.

KNOCKOUTS
(With Harry Hershey Orchestra)
Singles: 7-inch
COS-DE (1003 "Sweet Talk")....100-150 60

KNOCKOUTS
Singles: 7-inch
MGM (13010 "Fever")....5-10 61

KNOPFLER, David
Singles: 7-inch
FAST ALLEY....3-4 83

KNOPFLER, Mark
Singles: 7-inch
W.B....3-4 83
LPs: 10/12-inch
W.B....5-8 83
Also see ATKINS, Chet, & Mark Knopfler
Also see DIRE STRAITS
Also see SUN FERRY AID

KNOTT SISTERS: see SHADES / Knott Sisters

KNOTTS, Bobby
(With "Choral & Orch. Arr & Conducted by Squeak's")
Singles: 7-inch
GEE CLEF (077 "Too Young")....75-125 61

KNOWBODY ELSE
Singles: 7-inch
FLIP....8-12 69
HIP....10-20 69
LPs: 10/12-inch
HIP (7003 "Knowbody Else")....20-30 69
Member: James Mangrum.
Also see BLACK OAK ARKANSAS

KNOX, Buddy *P&R/R&B '57*
("Lieutenant Buddy Knox"; with the Rhythm Orchids)
Singles: 78 rpm
ROULETTE....15-40 57
Singles: 7-inch
ABC....3-5 73
LIBERTY....6-12 60-64
REPRISE....5-10 65-66
ROULETTE (4002 "Party Doll")....25-35 57
(With roulette wheel circling label. Label may be either red/orange or maroon.)
ROULETTE (4002 "Party Doll")....15-25 57
(With roulette wheel on top half of label.)
ROULETTE (4002 "Party Doll")....10-15 58
(No roulette wheel on label.)
ROULETTE (4009 "Rock Your Little Baby to Sleep")....25-35 57
(With roulette wheel circling label.)
ROULETTE (4009 "Rock Your Little Baby to Sleep")....15-25 57
(With roulette wheel on top half of label.)
ROULETTE (4009 "Rock Your Little Baby to Sleep")....10-15 58
(No roulette wheel on label.)
ROULETTE (4018 thru 4262)....10-20 57-60
RUFF....5-10 65
U.A....4-8 68-71
Picture Sleeves
LIBERTY (55305 "Ling Ting Tong")....15-25 61
EPs: 7-inch
ROULETTE (301 "Buddy Knox")....50-75 57
LPs: 10/12-inch
ACCORD....5-8 82-83
LIBERTY (3251 "Golden Hits")....20-30 62
(Monaural.)
LIBERTY (7251 "Golden Hits")....25-35 62
(Stereo.)
ROULETTE (25003 "Buddy Knox")....75-100 57
U.A....10-15 69
Members (Rhythm Orchids): Buddy Knox; Jimmy Bowen; Dave Alldred; Don Lanier.

KNOX, Buddy / Jimmy Bowen *P&R/R&B '57*
(With the Rhythm Orchids)
Singles: 78 rpm
ROULETTE....20-40 57
TRIPLE-D (797 "Party Doll"/"I'm Stickin' with You")....50-100 57
Singles: 7-inch
ROULETTE (4001 "My Baby's Gone"/"I'm Stickin' with You")....30-50 57
TRIPLE-D (797 "Party Doll"/"I'm Stickin' with You")....300-400 57
LPs: 10/12-inch
MURRAY HILL....5-8 80s
ROULETTE (25048 "Buddy Knox & Jimmy Bowen")....75-125 58
Members (Rhythm Orchids): Buddy Knox; Jimmy Bowen; Dave Alldred; Don Lanier.
Also see BOWEN, Jimmy
Also see KNOX, Buddy

KNOX, George, & Ultra Tones
Singles: 7-inch
EVEREST....15-20 59

KNUDSEN, Kurt
Singles: 7-inch
TRIODEX....4-8 61

KNULL, Ron
Singles: 7-inch
CARROL....15-20

KO KOs
Singles: 78 rpm
COMBO....40-60 57
Singles: 7-inch
COMBO (141 "First Day of School")....40-60 57

KOALA
Singles: 7-inch
CAPITOL (2365 "Don't You Know What I Mean")....8-12 68
LPs: 10/12-inch
CAPITOL (176 "Koala")....15-25 69

KOATS OF MALE
Singles: 7-inch
IGL (134 "Life's Matter")....30-50 60s

KOCK ROBYNS
Singles: 7-inch
MONUMENT (967 "One Kiss Led to Another")....5-10 66
Session: Ray Stevens.
Also see STEVENS, Ray

KOCKY
LPs: 10/12-inch
WINDSONG....5-8 79

KODA, Cub
(With the Points; with Houserockers)
Singles: 7-inch
GARAGELAND....3-5
LOLITA....3-5 85
NEW ROSE....3-5 84
LPs: 10/12-inch
BARON (Black vinyl)....8-10 81
BARON (Colored vinyl)....10-15 81
BLACK ROSE....5-10 84
GARAGELAND....5-10 89-91
SOUNDS INTERESTING....5-10 84
Also see BROWNSVILLE STATION
Also see DEL-TINOS
Also see KODA CORPORATION

KODA CORPORATION (Cub Koda)
Singles: 7-inch
PRINCETON (112 "Let's Hear a Word for the Folks in the Cemetary")....5-10 68
Also see KODA, Cub

KODAKS
(Featuring Pearl McKinnon; with the Joy Vendors; Kadak's; Kodoks)
Singles: 78 rpm
FURY....25-75 57
Singles: 7-inch
FLASHBACK....3-5 65
FURY (1007 "Teenager's Dream")..50-75 57
FURY (1015 "Oh Gee Oh Gosh")..40-60 57
FURY (1019 "My Baby and Me")....50-75 58

FURY (1020 "Guardian Angel") 40-60 58
J&S (1684 "Look Up in the Sky") 200-400 60
(With straight horizontal lines.)
J&S (1684 "Look Up in the Sky") 50-100 60
(With wavy horizontal lines.)
WINK (1004 "Let's Rock") 15-20 61
WINK (1006 "Love Wouldn't Mean a Thing") 20-25 61
LPs: 10/12-inch
LOST-NITE 8-12 81
RELIC 5-10 90
Members: Pearl McKinnon; Jean Miller; Jim Patrick; Bill Franklin; Bill Miller; Larry Davis; Harold Jenkins; Richard Dixon; Renaldo Gamble.
Also see KADAKS
Also see SCHOOLBOYS

KODAKS / Starlites
LPs: 10/12-inch
SPHERE SOUND (7005 "The Kodoks Versus the Starlites 100-150 65
Also see KODAKS
Also see STARLITES

KODIAKS
Singles: 7-inch
SCEPTER 4-8 69

KODOKS: see KODAKS

KOEMPEL, Doug
Singles: 7-inch
CART ACTION 3-5 77

KOENEMANN, Randy, with Midwests Best
Singles: 7-inch
L. PARKS 3-4 87

KOENIG, Freddy, & Jades
Singles: 7-inch
LORI (9548 "Hey Clarice") 75-125 63
(First issue.)
VALERIE (225 "Hey Clarice") 50-100 63

KOERNER, Spider John
LPs: 10/12-inch
ELEKTRA 12-15 65
SWEET JANE 20-25
Also see KOERNER, RAY & GLOVER

KOERNER, Spider John, & Willie Murphy
LPs: 10/12-inch
ELEKTRA 10-15 69

KOERNER, RAY & GLOVER
LPs: 10/12-inch
ELEKTRA 10-15 63-66
MIL CITY 10-15
Members: John Koerner; Dave Ray; Tony Glover.
Also see KOERNER, Spider John

KOFFIE
Singles: 7-inch
PHILIPS 4-8 68

KOFFIE D&D '83
Singles: 12-inch
PAN DISC 4-6 83

KOFFMAN, Moe P&R '58
(Moe Koffman Quartette; Quintet; Septette)
Singles: 7-inch
ABC 3-5 73
ASCOT 4-6 62
ATCO 4-6 65
GOLD EAGLE 4-8 61
JUBILEE 3-8 58-68
PALETTE 4-6 60-63
VIRGO 3-5 72
LPs: 10/12-inch
ASCOT 10-15 62
JANUS 5-8 78
JUBILEE (1000 series) 15-25 57-58
JUBILEE (8000 series) 8-12 68
U.A. 15-25 62-63

KOGIN, Patti
Singles: 7-inch
MGM 4-8 63

KOKI, Sam, & Paradise Islanders
LPs: 10/12-inch
KAPP 10-20 63

KOKO JOE & Job Hunters
Singles: 7-inch
LMI 4-8

KOKOMO P&R '61
(Jimmy Wisner)
Singles: 7-inch
FELSTED 5-10 61-62
FUTURE (1023 "Asia Minor") 10-20 61
Picture Sleeves
FELSTED 8-12 61
LPs: 10/12-inch
FELSTED 15-20 61
Also see KNIGHTS
Also see WISNER, Jimmy

KOKOMO LP '75
Singles: 7-inch
COLUMBIA 3-5 75-76
LPs: 10/12-inch
COLUMBIA 8-10 75-76
Member: Tony O'Malley.
Also see ARRIVAL
Also see 10CC

KOKOMOS
Singles: 7-inch
GONE 8-10 62
JOSIE 5-10 63
Also see 4 SEASONS

KOKO-POP R&B '84
Singles: 7-inch
MOTOWN 3-4 84-85
LPs: 10/12-inch
MOTOWN 5-8 84
Members: Eric O'Neal; Matt Seward; Chris Powell; Recco Philmore; Alexandro.

KOLBY, Diane P&R '70
Singles: 7-inch
COLUMBIA 3-5 70-71

KOLE, Jerry, & Strokers
Singles: 7-inch
HAPPY TIGER 3-5
LPs: 10/12-inch
CROWN 15-20 63
Also see COLE, Jerry

KOLE, Kenny, & Huskies
Singles: 7-inch
KLIK (8205 "Sorry") 35-50 58
Members: Jerry Cole; Ken Kolok; Jack Covert; Ed Hayden; Dave Jones; Dick Crane.
Also see BALLADS

KOLE, Ronnie, Trio
Singles: 7-inch
PAULA 3-5
WHITE CLIFFS 5-10 66

KOLETTES
Singles: 7-inch
BARBARA (1094 "Who's That Guy") 15-20 64
(First issue.)
CHECKER (1094 "Who's That Guy") 5-10 64

KOLLECTION
Singles: 7-inch
HEADS UP (101 "Savage Lost") 15-25

KOLOC, Bonnie
Singles: 7-inch
OVATION 3-5 75
LPs: 10/12-inch
EPIC (35254 "Wild and Recluse") 5-10 80s
OVATION (1438 "You're Gonna Love Yourself in the Morning") 15-25 74
(Quadraphonic.)

KOLOR KORPORATION
Singles: 7-inch
HYPE (1015 "Sunshine on Our Love") 20-40 67
(Not commercially distributed. About 500 were made for sales at the group's concerts.)
Members: Mike Stegall; Wayne Proctor; Bob Pennington; Wayne Corbin; Steve Michaels; Jimmy Chambers.

KOMBINATION
Singles: 7-inch
PRESTIGE 4-8

KOMIKO R&B '82
Singles: 7-inch
SAM 3-4 82

KOMMOTIONS
Singles: 7-inch
BELL (630 "Little Black Egg") 10-15 66

KOMONS
Singles: 7-inch
FEATURE (104 "Caught in the Trap") 15-25 66

KON KAN P&R '88
Singles: 7-inch
ATLANTIC 3-4 88-89
Picture Sleeves
ATLANTIC 3-4 88-89

KONDOS, John, & Galaxies
Singles: 7-inch
GALAXIE (5009 "Hip Snap") 20-30 66
Members: Mike Miller; Nick Kondos; Patrick McCarthy.

KONGAS P&R/LP '78
Singles: 7-inch
POLYDOR 3-5 78
LPs: 10/12-inch
POLYDOR 5-8 78
SALSOUL 5-8 78

KONGOS, John P&R '71
(John T. Kongos; Johnny Kongos)
Singles: 7-inch
ELEKTRA 3-5 71-72
GROOVE 8-12 61
KAPP 4-8 67
RCA 6-12 63
Picture Sleeves
ELEKTRA 3-5 71
LPs: 10/12-inch
ELEKTRA 8-10 72
JANUS 8-10 71
Also see G-MEN

KONK D&D '84
Singles: 12-inch
SLEEPING BAG 4-6 84

KONTRAST
Singles: 7-inch
KONTRAST (101 "Walkin' the Dog") 20-30

KOO KREW
Singles: 7-inch
ASCOT (2225 "Wet and Wild") 15-25 67

KOOB, Roger
(Roger K.)
Singles: 7-inch
BIRTH 4-6 70
Also see DAVID & GOLIATH
Also see FRONTIERS
Also see PREMIERS
Also see ROGER & TRAVELERS

KOOBAS
Singles: 7-inch
CAPITOL 4-8 69
KAPP 8-12 66

KOOKIE
(Kookie & Satalites)
Singles: 7-inch
GMA (8 "Rebel Walk") 10-20 64
MILKY WAY (2586 Ooby Dooby") 25-35 65
(Actually this was Milky Way 005, but that number was omitted from label.)
Also see CARTER, Dean

KOOKIE BEAVERS
Singles: 7-inch
GONE 4-8 60

KOOKIE BIRDS
Singles: 7-inch
P.H.D. 5-10 59

KOOKIE JOE
Singles: 7-inch
NERMEL (846 "Kookie Limbo") 10-20 61

KOOKIE KAT
Singles: 7-inch
ATCO 5-10 59

KOOL, Dr. J.R: see DR. J.R. KOOL

KOOL & GANG P&R/R&B '69
Singles: 12-inch
DE-LITE 4-8 79-85
MERCURY 4-6 86-87
Singles: 7-inch
DE-LITE 3-5 69-85
MERCURY 3-4 86-87
Picture Sleeves
DE-LITE 3-5 85
MERCURY 3-4 86-87
LPs: 10/12-inch
DE-LITE (Except 8502) 8-10 69-87
DE-LITE (8502 "Something Special") 8-10 81
DE-LITE (8502 "History of Kool and the Gang") 15-20 81
(Promotional issue only. With interviews.)
MERCURY 5-8 86-88
Members: Robert "Kool" Bell; Ronald Bell; George Brown; Curtis Williams; Charles Smith; James Taylor.
Also see BAND AID

KOOL BLUES
Singles: 7-inch
CAPSOUL (35 "Keep on Loving You") 15-25

KOOL GENTS
Singles: 78 rpm
VEE JAY 40-60 56
Singles: 7-inch
VEE JAY (173 "This Is the Night") 100-200 55
VEE JAY (207 "You Know") 100-200 56
Members: Dee Clark; Johnny Carter; Ted Long; John McCall; Doug Brown.
Also see CLARK, Dee
Also see DELEGATES
Also see EL DORADOS

KOOL GENTS
Singles: 7-inch
BETHLEHEM (3061 "Picture on the Wall") 75-125 63

KOOL KYLE & Billy Bill
Singles: 12-inch
PROFILE 4-6 86
Singles: 7-inch
PROFILE 3-4 86

KOOL MOE DEE P&R/R&B/LP '87
Singles: 7-inch
JIVE 3-4 87-88
LPs: 10/12-inch
JIVE 5-8 87-91
Also see TREACHEROUS THREE

KOOL RAY
LPs: 10/12-inch
STUFF 5-8 82

KOOL TOPPERS
Singles: 78 rpm
BEVERLY 25-50 55
Singles: 7-inch
BEVERLY (702 "Cause I Love You So") 50-100 55

KOON, Larry
("Parkersburg's Larry Koon")
Singles: 7-inch
COUNTRY MUSIC CITY (50070 "The Heartaches") 3-5 82
HITVILLE (50067 "Easy to Say, Hard to Do") 15-25 66
HITVILLE (50069 "Oh How I Could Love You") 10-20 69

KOOPER, Al LP '69
Singles: 7-inch
AURORA 4-8 67
COLUMBIA 3-6 69-71
VERVE/FOLKWAYS 4-8 66
Picture Sleeves
COLUMBIA 3-5 69
LPs: 10/12-inch
COLUMBIA 10-15 69-82
U.A. 8-10 76
Also see APPALOOSA
Also see BLOOD, SWEAT & TEARS
Also see BLOOMFIELD, Mike, & Al Kooper
Also see BLUES PROJECT
Also see DYLAN, Bob
Also see MUSCLEMEN
Also see ROYAL TEENS

KOOPER, Al / Blood, Sweat & Tears
Singles
AURAVISION ("You've Got It First") 6-12 79
(Square cardboard picture disc from a teen magazine.)
Also see BLOOD, SWEAT & TEARS

KOOPER, Al, & Steve Mills
Singles: 7-inch
COLUMBIA 4-8 68

KOOPER, Al, & Shuggie Otis LP '70
LPs: 10/12-inch
COLUMBIA 10-15 69
Also see KOOPER, Al
Also see OTIS, Shuggie

KOPE, Billy, & Quadrells
Singles: 7-inch
KUDO (662 "It's All My Fault") 250-500
Also see QUADRELLS

KOPPER R&B '86
Singles: 7-inch
KMA 3-4 86-87

KORDS
(Buzz Sears & Kords; "Featuring Sharon LaMaster")
Singles: 7-inch
LAURIE (3403 "Boris the Spider") 5-10 67
NWI (2765 "Mr. Someone") 10-15 60s
NWI (2793 "Worked Hard All My Life") 10-15 60s

KORGIS P&R/LP '80
Singles: 7-inch
ASYLUM 3-5 80
W.B. 3-6 79
LPs: 10/12-inch
ASYLUM 5-8 80
W.B. 5-10 79
Members: Andrew Davis; Jim Warren.
Also see STACKRIDGE

KORMAN, Jerry
Singles: 7-inch
ABC-PAR (10024 "Hurry Back") 20-40 59
MEADOW (1001 "Hurry Back") 100-200 59

KORNEGAY, Big Bob
Singles: 7-inch
STACY (952 "Wowsville") 10-20 63

KORNER, Alexis
Singles: 7-inch
COLUMBIA 3-5 75
LPs: 10/12-inch
COLUMBIA 8-10 75
JUST SUNSHINE 10-12 74
W.B. 10-15 72
Also see C.C.S.
Also see ROCKET 88

KORNERS OF TIME
Singles: 7-inch
REACTION (1009 "Cara Lin") 40-60 60s

KORNERSTONES
Singles: 7-inch
E&M (9774 "The D.J.") 5-10

KORNFELD, Artie
(Artie Kornfeld Circus; Artie Kornfield Tree)
Singles: 7-inch
BELL 4-6 67
NEIGHBORHOOD 3-5 72-73
LPs: 10/12-inch
DUNHILL 8-10 70

KORONA P&R '80
Singles: 7-inch
U.A. 3-5 79-80
LPs: 10/12-inch
U.A. 5-8 80
Members: Bruce Blackman; Bob Gauthier.
Also see ETERNITY'S CHILDREN
Also see STARBUCK

KORTCHMAR, Danny
Singles: 7-inch
ASYLUM 3-4 80
LPs: 10/12-inch
ASYLUM 5-8 80
W.B. 8-10 73
Also see ATTITUDES
Also see CITY
Also see KING BEES
Also see TAYLOR, James

KOSHER CLUB
Singles: 12-inch
RHINO 4-8 84

KOSINEC, Tony
LPs: 10/12-inch
COLUMBIA 10-12 70

KOSSOFF, Paul LP '75
LPs: 10/12-inch
DJM 10-12 77
ISLAND 8-10 73-75
Also see BACK STREET CRAWLER
Also see FREE

KOSSOFF / Kirke / Tetsu / Rabbit
LPs: 10/12-inch
ISLAND 8-10 72
Members: Paul Kossoff; Simon Kirke.
Also see FREE
Also see KOSSOFF, Paul
Also see RABBIT

KOSTELANETZ, Andre, & His Orchestra LP '55
Singles: 78 rpm
COLUMBIA 3-5 50-57
Singles: 7-inch
COLUMBIA 4-8 50-61
EPs: 7-inch
COLUMBIA 5-10 50-59
LPs: 10/12-inch
COLUMBIA 5-15 50-71
HARMONY 5-10
Also see STREISAND, Barbra / Doris Day / Jim Nabors / Andre Kostelanetz

KOSUB, Kevin: see KEVIN & BLACKTEARS

K-OTICS
(K-Ottics)
Singles: 7-inch
BANG (521 "Double Shot") 10-15 66
FORTUNE (1000 "Double Shot") 20-30 66
RICK (10276 "Ooh-Wee") 5-10

KOTTKE, Leo LP '71
Singles: 7-inch
CAPITOL 3-5 75
LPs: 10/12-inch
CAPITOL (Except 16000 series) 8-12 71-76
CAPITOL (16000 series) 5-8 81
CHRYSALIS 5-10 76-81
OBLIVION 15-20
SYMPOSIUM 10-12 70
TAKOMA 8-12 71-74

KOTTKE, Leo, John Fahey & Peter Lang
LPs: 10/12-inch
TAKOMA 8-10 74
Also see FAHEY, John
Also see KOTTKE, Leo
Also see LANG, Peter

KOTTO, Yaphet
Singles: 7-inch
CHISA 3-5

KOTTON KANDIE
Singles: 7-inch
SSS INT'L 3-6 69

KOZ, Dave LP '91
LPs: 10/12-inch
CAPITOL 5-8 91

KRAAN
LPs: 10/12-inch
PASSPORT 8-10 75-76

KRACKER
Singles: 7-inch
DUNHILL 3-5 72-73
LPs: 10/12-inch
DUNHILL 10-15 72-73
PRIMO 8-10 78-79

KRACKER-BARREL-COMPLEX
Singles: 7-inch
PAGE (1087 "My World") 15-25 68

KRAFT, Robert
Singles: 7-inch
RCA 3-4 83

KRAFTONES
Singles: 7-inch
MEDIEVAL (206 "Memories") 30-50 64
(Black vinyl.)
MEDIEVAL (206 "Memories") 75-100 64
(Colored vinyl.)
Also see BEACHCOMBERS

KRAFTWERK P&R/LP '75
Singles: 12-inch
W.B. 4-6 83
Singles: 7-inch
CAPITOL 3-5 76-78
VERTIGO 3-5 75
W.B. 3-4 81-83
Picture Sleeves
W.B. 3-4 81-83
LPs: 10/12-inch
CAPITOL 8-10 75-78
MERCURY 5-8 77
VERTIGO 8-10 73-75
W.B. 5-8 80-86

KRAG, Johnny
Singles: 7-inch
SIGNET 5-10 59

KRAIG, Kathy, & Novas
Singles: 7-inch
FLO 10-20

KRAMER, Billy J., & Dakotas P&R/LP '64
Singles: 7-inch
EPIC 4-8 68
ERIC 3-5
IMPERIAL 4-8 64-66

LIBERTY (55586 "Do You Want to Know a Secret"/"I'll Be on My Way")........ 8-12 63
LIBERTY (55626 "Bad to Me")........ 8-10 64
LIBERTY (55643 "I'll Keep You Satisfied")........ 8-10 64
LIBERTY (55667 "Do You Want to Know a Secret"/"Bad to Me")........ 5-8 64

Picture Sleeves

IMPERIAL (66051 "From a Window")........10-15 64

LPs: 10/12-inch

CAPITOL........ 8-10 78-79
IMPERIAL (9267 "Little Children")..25-35 64
(Monaural.)
IMPERIAL (9273 "I'll Keep You Satisfied")........25-35 64
(Monaural.)
IMPERIAL (9291 "Trains and Boats and Planes")........25-35 65
(Monaural.)
IMPERIAL (12267 "Little Children")........25-40 64
(Stereo.)
IMPERIAL (12273 "I'll Keep You Satisfied")........25-40 64
(Stereo.)
IMPERIAL (12291 "Trains and Boats and Planes")........25-40 65
(Stereo.)
Also see DAKOTAS

KRAMER, Rex *C&W '76*

Singles: 7-inch

COLUMBIA........ 3-5 76
Also see NEW CHRISTY MINSTRELS

KRAMER, Wayne

Singles: 7-inch

PURE & EASY (017 "Negative Girls")........ 4-8 83
Also see MC 5
Also see SINCLAIR, John

KRANZ, George *D&D '83*

Singles: 12-inch

PERSONAL........ 4-6 83

Singles: 7-inch

PERSONAL........ 3-4 83-84

KRAVITZ, Lenny *LP '89*

Singles: 7-inch

VIRGIN........ 3-4 89-90

LPs: 10/12-inch

VIRGIN........ 5-8 89-91

KRAZY KATS

Singles: 7-inch

DAMON (12350 "Beat Out My Love")........20-30 61
(Re-recording of tracks made first in 1959, which existed only on acetate. Has added sax and guitar.)
ECCO-FONIC (1006 "Beat Out My Love")........ 4-6 94
(First record release of 1959 version. Made from original acetate.)

Picture Sleeves

ECCO-FONIC (1006 "Beat Out My Love")........ 5-8 94

LPs: 10/12-inch

DAMON (12478 "Movin' Out")......75-125 64
Members: Lee Dresser; Willie Carig; Fred Fletcher.
Also see DRESSER, Lee

KRAZY KRIS

Singles: 7-inch

KING (4991 "Floyd's Guitar Blues")........15-25 57

KREED

LPs: 10/12-inch

VISION of SOUND (71-56 "Kreed")........1000-1500 71
Members: David Cannon; Reed Boyd; Dean Sack; Doug Parent; Nigel Coff.

KREEG

Singles: 7-inch

LANCE (2229 "How Can I")........15-25 67

KREKEL, Tim

Singles: 7-inch

CAPRICORN........ 3-5 79

KRIDER, Wally

Singles: 7-inch

K&R........ 4-6 70

KRIEGER, Robby

LPs: 10/12-inch

BLUE NOTE........ 8-10 77
PASSPORT........ 5-8 82
Also see DOORS

KRIS, Bobby, & Imperials

Singles: 7-inch

COLUMBIA........ 5-10

KRISENDALE

LPs: 10/12-inch

ASI........ 5-8 78

KRISS, Bobb

Singles: 7-inch

ACTION........ 4-8 60

KRISS, Jimmy

Singles: 7-inch

WINSTON........ 8-10 59

KRISTOFFERSON, Kris *P&R/LP '71*

Singles: 7-inch

A&M........ 3-5 73
COLUMBIA........ 3-5 77-81
EPIC........ 4-8 67
MONUMENT........ 3-5 70-81

Picture Sleeves

A&M........ 3-6 73

EPs: 7-inch

MONUMENT (532 "Kristofferson")...5-10 71
(Promotional issue only.)
MONUMENT (31909 "Jesus Was a Capricorn")........5-10 72
(Juke box issue only. Includes title strips.)

LPs: 10/12-inch

COLUMBIA........ 5-8 77-81
MONUMENT (Except 18139)........8-15 70-76
MONUMENT (18139 "Kristofferson")........25-35 70
(Green and yellow label.)
MONUMENT (18139 "Kristofferson")........15-25 70
(Brown label.)
Session: Larry Gatlin; Rita Coolidge.
Also see COE, David Allan
Also see JENNINGS, Waylon, Willie Nelson, Johnny Cash, & Kris Kristofferson
Also see NELSON, Willie, & Kris Kristofferson
Also see SCAGGS, Boz / Kris Kristofferson

KRISTOFFERSON, Kris, & Rita Coolidge *C&W '73*

Singles: 7-inch

A&M........ 3-5 73-74
MONUMENT........ 3-5 74-75

Picture Sleeves

A&M........ 3-6 73

LPs: 10/12-inch

A&M (Except PR-4690)........8-12 73-79
A&M (PR-4690 "Natural Act")........10-15 79
(Picture disc, numbered edition. Promotional issue only.)
MONUMENT........8-10 74
Also see COOLIDGE, Rita

KRISTOFFERSON, Kris, Willie Nelson, Dolly Parton, & Brenda Lee

LPs: 10/12-inch

Monument........8-12 82
Also see KRISTOFFERSON, Kris
Also see NELSON, Willie
Also see PARTON, Dolly

KRISTYL

LPs: 10/12-inch

("Krystyl")........75-125 75
(No label name or number used.)
Members: Sonny DeVore; Bruce Whiteside; Bob Terrell; David Atherton.

KRIVDA, Ernie

LPs: 10/12-inch

INNER CITY........ 5-8 78

KROKUS *LP '81*

Singles: 7-inch

ARIOLA AMERICA........ 3-4 81
ARISTA........ 3-4 82-86

Picture Sleeves

ARISTA........ 3-4 84-86

LPs: 10/12-inch

ARIOLA AMERICA........ 5-8 81
ARISTA........ 5-8 82-86
MCA........ 5-8 88
Members: Dani Crivelli; Chris Von Rohr; Marc Storace; Fernando Von Arb; Mark Kohler.

KRONDES, John

Singles: 7-inch

TREE TOP........ 4-6

KRUSH GROOVE ALL STARS *R&B '85*

Singles: 12-inch

W.B........ 4-6 85
Also see BLOW, Kurtis
Also see SHEILA E.
Also see FAT BOYS
Also see RUN D.M.C.

KRYSTAL

Singles: 7-inch

MAGIC TOUCH........ 3-5 76
SPRING........ 3-5 79

KRYSTAL GENERATION *R&B '71*

Singles: 7-inch

BUDDAH........ 4-6 69
MR. CHAND........ 3-5 71
Members: Joyce Smith; Darlene Arnold; Mary Shelley; Mary Lead; Wylie Dixon; Walter "Simtec" Simmons.
Also see SIMTEC & WYLIE

KRYSTOL *R&B/D&D '84*

Singles: 12-inch

EPIC........ 4-6 84-86

Singles: 7-inch

EPIC........ 3-4 84-86

LPs: 10/12-inch

EPIC........ 5-8 86

KUBAN, Bob *P&R/LP '66*

(With the In-Men; Bob Kuban Band)

Singles: 7-inch

ERIC........ 3-5 70s
MUSICLAND USA (Except 20001)........5-10 66-67
MUSICLAND USA. (20001 "The Cheater")........10-20 66
("Vocal by Walter Scott" shown on both sides.)
MUSICLAND USA (20001 The Cheater")........5-10 66
("Vocal by Walter Scott" shown only on flip, *Try Me Baby*.)
MUSICLAND USA (20001 "The Cheater")........ 4-8 66
("Vocal by Walter Scott" not on either side.)
NORMAN........ 5-15 65-66
(Walter Scott may be shown as "Little Walter.")
REPRISE........ 4-8 70

LPs: 10/12-inch

MUSICLAND USA (3500 "Look Out for the Cheater")........25-35 66
Members: Walter Scott; Bob Kuban; John Krenski; Greg Hoeltzel.
Also see CASH, J.D., & Bob Kuban Brass
Also see SCOTT, Walter

KUBANEC, David

LPs: 10/12-inch

A&M........5-8 79

KUF-LINX *P&R '58*

("Featuring John Jennings"; Kuff-Linx)

Singles: 78 rpm

CHALLENGE........25-50 57-58

Singles: 7-inch

CHALLENGE (1013 "So Tough")...25-50 57
(Blue or white label.)
CHALLENGE (1013 "So Tough")...15-25 58
(Maroon label.)
CHALLENGE (59004 "Service with a Smile")........15-25 58
CHALLENGE (59015 "Climb Love's Mountain")........25-50 58
Member: John Jennings.

KUHN, Bob

Singles: 7-inch

IMPACT (8 "Rendezvous")........10-15 61
(Colored vinyl.)

KÜK, Kid & Friends

Singles: 7-inch

NO LABEL NAME ("The New 49er Havoc and We Like It That Way"........4-8 85
(Promotional issue only.)

KUKIE KATS

Singles: 7-inch

HANOVER (4524 "Kukie")........10-15 59

KULIS, Charlie *P&R '75*

Singles: 7-inch

PLAYBOY........3-5 75

KUNKEL, Leah

Singles: 7-inch

COLUMBIA........3-5 79

LPs: 10/12-inch

COLUMBIA........5-8 79-80
Also see COTTON CANDY
Also see COYOTE SISTERS
Also see TAYLOR, Livingston, & Leah Kunkel

KUNKEL, Rob

LPs: 10/12-inch

TUMBLEWEED........8-10 73

KUPER, Gary

LPs: 10/12-inch

POLYDOR........8-10 71

KURRYETTES

Singles: 7-inch

KHOURY'S (722 "The Spook")......10-15 60

KURT & KAPERS

Singles: 7-inch

V-LEE (211 "Mongoose")........20-30 60s

KURTZ, John

Singles: 7-inch

ABC........4-6 72

KUSIK-ADAMS

Singles: 7-inch

HOLLYWOOD........4-8

KUSTOM KINGS

Singles: 7-inch

SMASH (1883 "In My '40 Ford")......15-25 64

LPs: 10/12-inch

SMASH (27051 "Kustom City USA")........25-35 64
(Monaural.)
SMASH (67051 "Kustom City USA")........30-40 64
(Stereo.)
Members: Bruce Johnston; Steve Douglas.
Also see DOUGLAS, Steve
Also see JOHNSTON, Bruce

KWAME *LP '89*

(With a New Beginning)

LPs: 10/12-inch

ATLANTIC........5-8 89-90
POLYDOR........5-8 80

KWESKIN, Jim

(Jim Kweskin's Jug Band)

Singles: 7-inch

REPRISE........4-8 67

LPs: 10/12-inch

REPRISE........10-15 67-71
VANGUARD........12-18 66-67
Also see MULDAUR, Geoff & Maria

KWICK *R&B '80*

Singles: 12-inch

CAPITOL........4-6 83

Singles: 7-inch

CAPITOL........3-4 83
EMI AMERICA........3-4 80-82

LPs: 10/12-inch

CAPITOL........5-8 83
EMI AMERICA........5-8 80-81
Members: Terry Bartlett; Bert Brown; William Sumlin; Vince Williams.
Also see NEWCOMERS

KYKS

Singles: 7-inch

RAF (1001 "Where Are You")........10-20 65

Picture Sleeves

RAF (1001 "Where Are You")........20-30 65

KYLE

(Kyle Garrahm)

LPs: 10/12-inch

ABC........8-10 74
MGM........8-10 73
PARAMOUNT........10-12 71

KYM *R&B '84*

Singles: 12-inch

AWARD........4-6 84

Singles: 7-inch

AWARD........3-4 84

KYND

Singles: 7-inch

KYND (103169 "Clouds")........15-20 69

KYNDS

Singles: 7-inch

MO-FROG (101 "Find Me Gone")..10-15

KYPER *P&R/LP '90*

Singles: 7-inch

ATLANTIC........3-4 90

LPs: 10/12-inch

ATLANTIC........5-8 90

DISC JOCKEY SAMPLE
NOT FOR SALE
MGM RECORDS is FIRST!
WITH A SINGLE
STEREO DISC
JONI JAMES
THERE
GOES
MY
HEART
B/W FUNNY
K12706

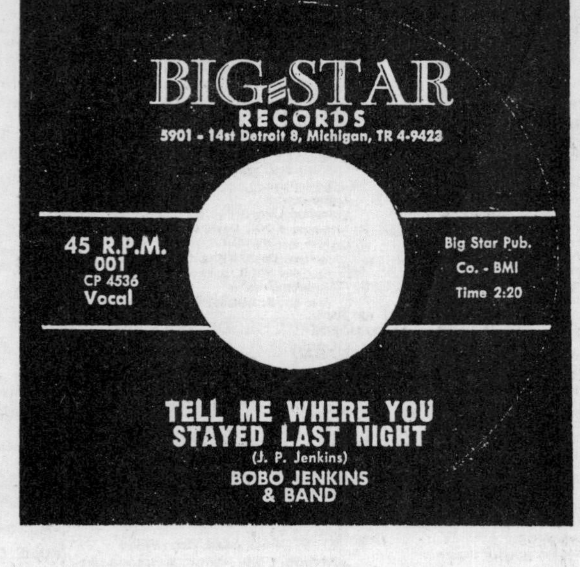
BIG STAR
RECORDS
5901 - 14st Detroit 8, Michigan, TR 4-9423
45 R.P.M.
001
CP 4536
Vocal
Big Star Pub.
Co. - BMI
Time 2:20
TELL ME WHERE YOU
STAYED LAST NIGHT
(J. P. Jenkins)
BOBO JENKINS
& BAND

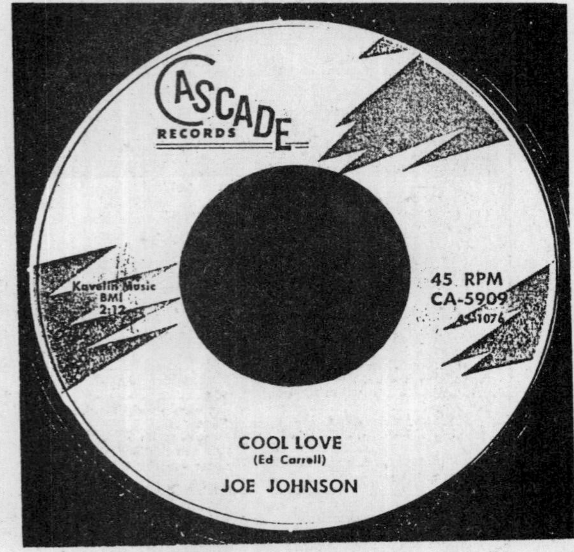
CASCADE
RECORDS
Kavelin Music
BMI
2:12
45 RPM
CA-5909
COOL LOVE
(Ed Carrell)
JOE JOHNSON

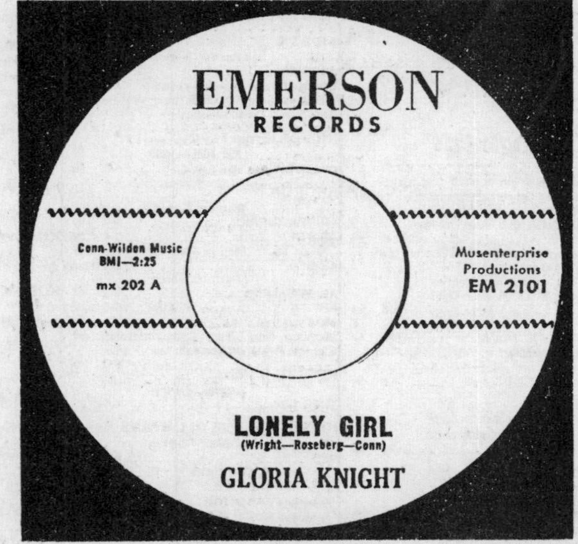
EMERSON
RECORDS
Conn-Wilden Music
BMI—2:25
mx 202 A
Musenterprise
Productions
EM 2101
LONELY GIRL
(Wright—Roseberg—Conn)
GLORIA KNIGHT

RCA VICTOR
45 RPM
47-5135
(E2VW-5371)
TAKE A BACK SEAT MISTER JACKSON
(Inez Loewer–Don Johnson)
Inez Jones
RCA VICTOR DIVISION, RADIO CORPORATION OF AMERICA, CAMDEN, N. J. MADE IN U. S. A.

REPUBLIC
"45"
7044-45
(E3KW-0242)
Babb Music
(BMI)
Vocal:
Christine Kittrell
L & N SPECIAL
(Jarrett–Kittrell)
CHRISTINE KITTRELL
with Band
REPUBLIC RECORDING CO. • NASHVILLE, TENNESSEE

L

L., Dony
Singles: 7-inch
EPITOME 3-5
Picture Sleeves
EPITOME 5-8

L.A.
Singles: 7-inch
RADIO 3-5 81
LPs: 10/12-inch
RADIO 5-10 81

L.A. BOPPERS R&B/LP '80
Singles: 7-inch
MCA 3-4 82
MERCURY 3-5 80-81
LPs: 10/12-inch
MCA 5-8 82
MERCURY 5-10 80-81
Also see SIDE EFFECT

L.A. DREAM TEAM R&B/LP '86
Singles: 12-inch
MCA 4-6 86
Singles: 7-inch
MCA 3-4 86
LPs: 10/12-inch
MCA 5-8 86-87
Members: Rudy Pardee; Chris Wilson.

L.A. EXPRESS LP '76
Singles: 7-inch
CARIBOU 3-5 75-78
LPs: 10/12-inch
CARIBOU 8-10 75-76
Also see MITCHELL, Joni, & L.A. Express
Also see SCOTT, Tom

L.A. GUNS LP '88
LPs: 10/12-inch
VERTIGO 5-8 88-89
Members: Philip Lewis; Tracii Guns; Kelly Nickels; Mick Cripps; Steve Riley.
Also see W.A.S.P.

L.A. JETS P&R '76
Singles: 7-inch
RCA 3-5 76
LPs: 10/12-inch
RCA 8-10 76
Also see GOODTHUNDER

L.A. TEENS
Singles: 7-inch
DECCA 5-10 65
Also see USHER, Gary

L.A.X.
LPs: 10/12-inch
A&M 8-10 75

L.B.J. & BIRDS
Singles: 7-inch
ERA 4-6 67

L.C.
(L.C. Cooke)
Singles: 7-inch
SAR 4-8 64
Also see COOKE, L.C.

L.C.: see CLINGMAN, Loy

L.H. & MEMPHIS SOUNDS
Singles: 7-inch
HOLLYWOOD 4-8 67

L.L. COOL J R&B '85
(Ladies Love Cool James; James Todd Smith)
Singles: 12-inch
COLUMBIA 4-6 85-86
Singles: 7-inch
COLUMBIA 3-4 85-86
DEF JAM 3-4 87-90
MOTOWN 3-4 90
Picture Sleeves
DEF JAM 3-4 88
LPs: 10/12-inch
CAPITOL 5-10 90s
COLUMBIA 5-8 85
DEF JAM 5-10 87-90

LMNOP
LPs: 10/12-inch
BABY SUE (333 "Elemen Opee Elpee") 5-10 86
Members: Stephen Fievet; Steve Lange; Tom Lewis; Ken Sailer.

LRY
LPs: 10/12-inch
CONGRESS of the CROW (8031002 "The LRY Record") 150-250 68

LSD
Singles: 7-inch
MUSICOR (429 "Mystery of the Mystical Invasion") 15-25 67

L7 LP '92
Singles: 7-inch
SUB POP (58 "Shove") 3-6 80s
Picture Sleeves
SUB POP (58 "Shove") 4-8 80s
LPs: 10/12-inch
EPITAPH (86401 "L7") 5-8 88
(With lyrics insert.)
W.B. (45624 "Hungry for Stink") 5-8 90s
W.B. (86401 "L7") 5-8 90s
Members: Suzi Gardner; Jennifer Finch; Donita Sparks; Roy Koutsky; René Lucas.

L.T.D. P&R/R&B/LP '76
(Love, Togetherness & Devotion)
Singles: 7-inch
A&M 3-5 76-80
MONTAGE 3-4 83
Picture Sleeves
A&M 3-5 76-78
LPs: 10/12-inch
A&M 8-10 74-81
MONTAGE 5-8 83
SPRINGBOARD 8-10 77
Members: Jeffrey Osborne; Leslie Ray; Andre Ray.
Also see OSBORNE, Jeffrey

LTG EXCHANGE R&B '74
Singles: 7-inch
FANIA 3-5 74
WAND 3-5 74

LABAN P&R '86
Singles: 7-inch
CRITIQUE 3-4 86

LA BARBARA, Joan
LPs: 10/12-inch
WIZARD 8-10 76

LABAT
LPs: 10/12-inch
BEARSVILLE 8-10 73

LA BEEF, Sleepy C&W '68
(Tommy LaBeef)
Singles: 78 rpm
MERCURY (71112 "I'm Through") 50-100 57
MERCURY (71179 "All the Time") 50-100 57
STARDAY (292 "I'm Through") 50-100 57
Singles: 7-inch
COLUMBIA 4-8 65-68
CRESCENT (102 "Turn Me Loose") 100-200 57
MERCURY (71112 "I'm Through") 50-100 57
MERCURY (71179 "All the Time") 50-100 57
PLANTATION (Except 55) 5-10 70-71
PLANTATION (55 "Too Much Monkey Business") 15-25 70
STARDAY (292 "I'm Through") 50-100 57
(Issued the same month on both Mercury and Starday.)
SUN 3-6 68-78
LPs: 10/12-inch
BARON 10-12 79
ROUNDER 5-8 81
SUN 8-10 74-78

LA BEEF, Tommy
Singles: 78 rpm
PICTURE (1937 "Ride on Josephine") 100-150 57
WAYSIDE (1651 "Ride on Josephine") 150-200 57
WAYSIDE (1654 "Tore Up") 200-300 57
Singles: 7-inch
PICTURE (1937 "Ride on Josephine") 100-150 57
WAYSIDE (1651 "Ride on Josephine") 150-200 57
WAYSIDE (1654 "Tore Up") 200-300 57
Also see LA BEEF, Sleepy

LABELLE, Patti P&R '62
(With the Blue Belles; Pattie La Belle; Labelle; Patty La Belle)
Singles: 12-inch
EPIC 5-10 78-79
MCA 4-6 85
PHILADELPHIA INT'L 4-6 83-85
Singles: 7-inch
ATLANTIC 5-10 65-70
EPIC 3-6 74-80
KING (5777 "Down the Aisle") 15-25 63
MISTLETOE 3-5 73
PHILADELPHIA INT'L 3-5 81-85
MCA 3-4 85-87
NEWTIME (510 "Love Me Just a Little") 10-15 62
NEWTOWN (5006 "I Found a New Love") 10-15 62
NEWTOWN (5007 "Tear After Tear") 10-15 62
NEWTOWN (5009 "When Johnny Comes Marching Home") 10-15 62
NEWTOWN (5019 "Decatur Street") 10-15 63
NEWTOWN (5777 "Down the Aisle") 10-15 63
(Reads "Pressed by King Records.")
NEWTOWN (5777 "Down the Aisle") 5-10 63
(No mention of King Records.)
NICETOWN (5020 "You'll Never Walk Alone"/"Where Are You") 15-20 63
NICETOWN (5020 "You'll Never Walk Alone"/"Decatur Street") 10-15 63
PARKWAY (896 "You'll Never Walk Alone") 8-10 63
PARKWAY (913 "One Phone Call") 8-10 64
PARKWAY (935 "Danny Boy") 8-10 64
RCA 4-6 73
TRIP 3-6 71
W.B. 3-6 71-72
Picture Sleeves
MCA 3-4 85-86
LPs: 10/12-inch
ATLANTIC 15-25 65-67
EPIC 8-10 74-82
MCA 5-8 85-89
MISTLETOE 10-20
NEWTOWN (631 "Sweethearts of the Apollo") 50-100 63
NEWTOWN (632 "Sleigh Bells, Jingle Bells and Blue Bells") 50-100 63
PARKWAY (7043 "On Stage") 30-50 64
PHILADELPHIA INT'L 5-8 81-85
RCA (0200 series) 8-10 73
RCA (4100 series) 5-8 82
TRIP 8-10 71-75
U.A. 8-10 74-75
UPFRONT 10-15
W.B. 8-10 71-72
Also see BLUE BELLES
Also see DASH, Sarah
Also see HENDRIX, Nona
Also see NYRO, Laura
Also see WOMACK, Bobby, & Patti Labelle

LABELLE, Patti, & Bill Champlin
Singles: 7-inch
MCA 3-4 87
Picture Sleeves
MCA 3-4 87
Also see CHAMPLIN, Bill

LABELLE, Patti / Harold Faltermeyer
Singles: 7-inch
MCA 3-4 85
Also see FALTERMEYER, Harold

LABELLE, Patti, & Michael McDonald P&R/R&B '86
Singles: 7-inch
MCA 3-4 86
Picture Sleeves
MCA 3-4 86
Also see McDONALD, Michael

LABELLE, Patti, & Grover Washington Jr. R&B '82
Singles: 7-inch
ELEKTRA 3-4 82
Also see LABELLE, Patti
Also see WASHINGTON, Grover, Jr.

LABOE, Art
Singles: 7-inch
ORIGINAL SOUND 5-10 62

LABOMBAS
Singles: 7-inch
NEW TEENAGE (5000 "Taboo") 25-35 60s

LA BONTE, Nestor
Singles: 7-inch
ARVEE 4-8 62
RENDEZVOUS 4-8 62

LA BOUNTY, Bill P&R '78
Singles: 7-inch
20TH FOX 3-5 75-76
W.B. 3-5 78

LABRADORS
Singles: 7-inch
CHIEF (7009 "When Someone Loves You") 150-200 58

LABYRINTH R&B '85
Singles: 7-inch
21 .... 3-4 85
Member: Julie Loco.

LACE R&B '87
Singles: 7-inch
WING 3-4 87
LPs: 10/12-inch
WING 5-8 87

LACE, Bobbi C&W '86
Singles: 7-inch
GBS 3-4 86
615 .... 3-4 87-89
Also see GRAY, Mark, & Bobbi Lace

LACE, Patty, & Petticoats
Singles: 7-inch
KAPP 4-6 63-65

LACEWING
Singles: 7-inch
MAINSTREAM (731 "Paradox") 8-12 70
LPs: 10/12-inch
MAINSTREAM (6132 "Lacewing") 10-12 70
Members: Mary Stepka; Mark Frazier; Bob Webb; Dave Andress; Jeff Currey.

LA CHORDS
Singles: 7-inch
GAY (629 "To Be") 100-150 62

LACKEY, Joe, & Ramrod Combo
Singles: 7-inch
BRIGHT (511 "Sittin' Alone") 100-200

LA COSTA C&W '74
(La Costa Tucker)
Singles: 7-inch
CAPITOL 3-5 74-80
ELEKTRA 3-4 82
LPs: 10/12-inch
CAPITOL 5-10 74-77

LACOUR, Lenny
Singles: 78 rpm
ACADEMY 75-100 57
Singles: 7-inch
ACADEMY (3571 "Rockin' Rosalie") 75-100 57
ACADEMY (5732 "Jungle Rock") 75-100 57
MAGIC TOUCH 3-5 76
Also see BIG ROCKER

LA CROIX, Helen
Singles: 7-inch
CENTAUR (101 "Abby") 6-10
W.B. 4-8 62

LA CROIX, Jerry
Singles: 7-inch
EPIC 3-5 72
LPs: 10/12-inch
EPIC 8-10 72
MERCURY 8-10 74
Also see DERRINGER, Rick
Also see WINTER, Edgar

LACY, Steve, & Backups
Singles: 7-inch
CAVALCADE (1193 "I Have Her Love Tonight") 10-15

LADD, Cheryl P&R/LP '78
Singles: 12-inch
CAPITOL (8894 "Skinnydippin' ") 10-15 78
(Promotional issue only.)
Singles: 7-inch
CAPITOL 3-5 76-79
Picture Sleeves
CAPITOL 3-5 78-79
W.B. 4-6 74
LPs: 10/12-inch
CAPITOL 8-10 78-79
Also see JOSIE & PUSSYCATS
Also see VALLI, Frankie, & Cheryl Ladd

LADD, David
Singles: 7-inch
DOT 5-10 59

LADD, Gaylan
Singles: 7-inch
MGM (13435 "Think About Me") 10-20 65
PACEMAKER (257 "Repulsive Situation") 25-35 66
VENTURAL (723 "Smokey Places") 15-30 65
VENTURAL (731 "Painted Lady") .. 15-30 65

LADD, Mike
Singles: 7-inch
CONCORD 4-8

LADDERS
Singles: 7-inch
HOLIDAY (2611 "Counting the Stars") 200-300 57
(Glossy red label. Has double horizontal lines.)
HOLIDAY (2611 "Counting the Stars") 50-75 60s
(Flat red label. Has single horizontal line.)
VEST (826 "My Love Is Gone") . 100-150 60
(No stars are around the Vest logo.)
VEST (826 "My Love Is Gone") 25-50 60
(Has 11 stars around the Vest logo.)
Also see CHARTS / Bop - Chords / Ladders / Harmonaires

LADDINS
Singles: 7-inch
ANGIE (85713 "I'll Kiss Your Teardrops Away") 30-50 62
(Blue label. Identification number shown since no selection number is used. First issue.)
ANGIE (1790 "I'll Kiss Your Teardrops Away") 20-40 62
(Red label. Selection number is shown.)
BARDELL (776 "Push, Shake, Kick and Shout") 10-15 63
BUTANE (779 "Dream Baby") 10-15 64
CENTRAL (2602 "Now You're Gone") 550-650 57
(Black label.)
CENTRAL (2602 "Now You're Gone") 250-350 57
(Yellow label.)
CENTRAL (2602 "Now You're Gone") 50-100 57
(Pink label.)
GREY CLIFF (721 "Light a Candle") 20-30 59
GROOVE 8-10 62
ISLE (801 "Come On") 50-75 60
THEATRE (111 "There Once Was a Time") 25-50 61
TIMES SQUARE (3 "Now You're Gone") 10-15 62
(Black vinyl.)
TIMES SQUARE (3 "Now You're Gone") 20-30 62
(Colored vinyl.)
LPs: 10/12-inch
RELIC 10-15
Members: David Coleman; Ernest Gordy; Bob Jeffers; Earl Marcus; John Marcus.

LADDS
Singles: 7-inch
TEEN TOWN (4789 "Goodness Gracious Baby") 10-20 69
TRANSACTION (703 "Keep on Running") 15-25 67
UA (706 "I Found a Girl") 25-35 75
Picture Sleeves
TRANSACTION 25-35 67
UA 40-60 75
Also see FAX
Also see TODAY'S TOMORROW

LADDS from BELLEVUE: see VOODOO DOLLS / Johnny & Jumper Cables

LA DELL SISTERS
Singles: 78 rpm
MERCURY 5-10 56
Singles: 7-inch
MERCURY 10-15 56

LADELLES
Singles: 7-inch
DEBONAIR (309 "Fortrocke") 10-20
DEBONAIR (1218 "Borrowed Time") 10-20

LADIES' CHOICE R&B '83
Singles: 7-inch
STREETWISE 3-4 83

LADNER, Jerry, & Travelers
Singles: 7-inch
FLAME (127 "Give Me Your Love") 15-25

LADNER, Kirby
Singles: 7-inch
CAPA 10-15

LA DONNA, Marie
Singles: 7-inch
GATEWAY 5-10 63-64
TRY ME 5-10 63
Also see DONNA MARIE

LADREW, John
Singles: 7-inch
ROULETTE (4688 "What's the Matter with Me") 10-20 66

LADY
Singles: 7-inch
BARONESS (011 "Live Show Tigers") 5-8 80
(Shaped picture disc. 500 made.)
BARONESS (1 "Live Show Tigers") 5-8 80
(Rectangle picture disc. 100 made.)

LADY R&B '82
Singles: 7-inch
MEGA 3-4 82

LADY & TRAMPS
Singles: 7-inch
U.A. 4-8 60s

LADY BIANCA
Singles: 7-inch
MAGIC O 4-6

LADY BIRDS
(Ladybirds)
Singles: 7-inch
ATCO 5-10 64
LAWN 5-10 64
LEGRAND 5-10 64
MPI 10-15 60s
WICKWIRE 10-15 64

LADY BUGS
(Ladybugs)
Singles: 7-inch
CHATTAHOOCHEE 5-10 64
DEL-FI 10-15 64
LEGRAND 10-15 64

LADY FLASH P&R '76
Singles: 7-inch
RSO 3-5 76
LPs: 10/12-inch
RSO 8-12 76
Members: Monica Burruss; Debra Byrd; Reparata.
Also see DANTE'S INFERNO
Also see MANILOW, Barry
Also see REPARATA

LADY FOX & FOXETTES
Singles: 7-inch
DON-EL (114 "Our Love") 15-25 62
DON-EL (118 "It Must Be Love") 15-25 62

LADY JANE & VERITY
Singles: 7-inch
PALETTE 5-10 59

LADY JEAN
Singles: 7-inch
CJ 5-10 60

LADY LUCK & LULLABIES
Singles: 7-inch
PHILIPS 4-8 63

LADY MARGO
Singles: 7-inch
CYNTHIA 5-8

LADY NELL
(With Sunny's Nu Kat Orchestra)
Singles: 7-inch
NU-KAT (128 "Loving Daddy") 25-50 60

LADY ROSE
Singles: 7-inch
STRAWBERRY 3-5 76

LADY SYLVIA
Singles: 7-inch
FULL MOON 3-4 80

LADY WILDE: see WILDE, Lady

LADYBIRDS: see LADY BIRDS

LADYBUGS: see LADY BUGS

LA FAYETTE & LaSABRES
Singles: 7-inch
PORT (70036 "Free Way") 15-25 63
YOUR-PICK (1005 "Free Way") 50-75 63

LAFAYETTES P&R '62
(With Frank James)
Singles: 7-inch
BONA (1741 "I Lost My Way") 25-50
RCA (8044 "Life's Too Short") 20-30 62
RCA (8082 "Caravan of Lonely Men") 15-25 62
Member: Frank Bonarrigo.

LA FLAMME, David P&R/LP '76
Singles: 7-inch
AMHERST 3-5 76-77
Picture Sleeves
AMHERST 3-5 76
LPs: 10/12-inch
AMHERST 8-10 76-78
Also see IT'S A BEAUTIFUL DAY

LA FLAVOUR R&B '79
Singles: 12-inch
SWEET CITY 8-10 80
Singles: 7-inch
MERCURY 3-5 79
SWEET CITY 3-5 80
LPs: 10/12-inch
SWEET CITY 5-8 80

LaFLEUR, Don C&W '88
Singles: 7-inch
WORTH 3-4 88

LA FONS
Singles: 7-inch
LA FON (16121 "The King") 5-8

LA FORGE, Jack P&R '65
("With His Piano & Orchestra")
Singles: 7-inch
REGINA (Except 284) 4-8 63-66
REGINA (284 "Cleopatra Kick") 8-15 63
RIO 4-6 62
LPs: 10/12-inch
AUDIO FIDELITY 6-12 66
PURPLETONE 8-15 62
REGINA 8-15 63-65

LAGO, Jim
Singles: 7-inch
("Year of the Lobos") 4-6 83
(Label and selection number not known for this break-in novelty.)

LAI, Francis, & His Orchestra P&R '71
Singles: 7-inch
PARAMOUNT 3-5 70
Picture Sleeves
PARAMOUNT 3-5 70
Also see JOHN, Elton
For a complete listing of soundtracks by this artist, consult *The Official Price Guide to Movie/TV Soundtracks and Original Cast Albums.*

LAID BACK D&D '83
Singles: 12-inch
SIRE 4-6 84-85
W.B. 4-6 83
Singles: 7-inch
SIRE 3-4 84-85
W.B. 3-4 83-84
LPs: 10/12-inch
SIRE 5-8 84
Members: Timothy Stahl; John Guldberg.

LAINE, Bette
Singles: 7-inch
CHESS (1666 "Rock a Bye Rock") 20-25 57

LAINE, Brandi
Singles: 7-inch
BLOSSOM (Haight St. Dream") 10-15 67
(No selection number used.)
Picture Sleeves
BLOSSOM ("Haight St. Dream") 15-25 67

LAINE, Cleo LP '74
Singles: 7-inch
RCA 3-5 74-80
LPs: 10/12-inch
BUDDAH 8-10 74
FONTANA 10-15 66
GNP 5-10 74
QUINTESSENCE 5-8 80
RCA 5-10 73-80
Also see CHARLES, Ray, & Cleo Laine

LAINE, Cleo, & James Galway LP '80
LPs: 10/12-inch
RCA 5-8 80
Also see GALWAY, James
Also see LAINE, Cleo

LAINE, Denny
Singles: 7-inch
ARISTA 3-5 80
CAPITOL 4-8 76-77
DERAM 4-8 67
LPs: 10/12-inch
CAPITOL 10-20 77
REPRISE/WIZARD 8-10 74
TAKOMA 5-8 83
Also see BAKER, Ginger
Also see McCARTNEY, Paul
Also see MOODY BLUES

LAINE, Frankie P&R/R&B '47
(With Paul Weston & the Mellomen)
Singles: 78 rpm
ATLAS 10-20 47
MERCURY 8-15 47-51
MERCURY/SAV-WAY (1027 "On the Sunny Side of the Street") 150-200 47
(Picture disc. Promotional issue only.)
MERCURY/SAV-WAY (1028 "West End Blues") 150-200 47
(Picture disc. Promotional issue only.)
MERCURY/SAV-WAY (5059 "Kiss Me Again") 100-200 47
(Picture disc. Promotional issue only.)
COLUMBIA 5-15 51-57
Singles: 7-inch
ABC 3-5 67-69
AMOS 3-5 70-71
CAPITOL 4-8 64-66
COLUMBIA (39367 thru 41486) 10-20 51-59
COLUMBIA (41613 thru 42966) 5-10 60-64
MAINSTREAM 3-5 75
MERCURY (5000 series) 10-20 50-51
SUNFLOWER 3-5 72
W.B. 3-5 74
Picture Sleeves
COLUMBIA 15-25 56-57
EPs: 7-inch
COLUMBIA 10-20 52-59
MERCURY 10-20 51-54
LPs: 10/12-inch
ABC (600 series) 8-15 67-69
ABC (30000 series) 5-8 76
AMOS 8-12 70-71
CAPITOL 10-15 65
COLUMBIA (600 thru 1200 series) 15-30 54-58
COLUMBIA (1300 thru 1900 series) 10-20 59-63
(Monaural.)
COLUMBIA (2500 series) 20-30 56
(10-inch LPs.)
COLUMBIA (6000 series) 20-40 53-54
(10-inch LPs.)
COLUMBIA (8100 thru 8700 series) 10-20 59-63
(Stereo.)
HARMONY 8-15 65-71
HINDSIGHT 4-8 84
MERCURY (20000 series) 20-40 54-61
MERCURY (25000 series) 50-75 51-52
(10-inch LPs.)
MERCURY (60000 series) 15-25 61
PICKWICK 5-10 78
TOWER 8-15 67
TRIP 5-8 75
WING 8-15 60-67
Also see DAY, Doris, & Frankie Laine
Also see MILLER, Mitch

LAINE, Frankie, & Jimmy Boyd P&R '53
Singles: 78 rpm
COLUMBIA 4-8 53
Singles: 7-inch
COLUMBIA 10-20 53
Also see BOYD, Jimmy

LAINE, Frankie, & Easy Riders P&R '57
Singles: 78 rpm
COLUMBIA 4-8 57
Singles: 7-inch
COLUMBIA 10-20 57
Also see GILKYSON, Terry

LAINE, Frankie, & Four Lads P&R '54
Singles: 78 rpm
COLUMBIA 4-8 54
Singles: 7-inch
COLUMBIA 10-20 54
EPs: 7-inch
COLUMBIA 10-20 56
LPs: 10/12-inch
COLUMBIA 20-30 56
Also see FOUR LADS

LAINE, Frankie, & Andre Previn
LP: 10/12-inch
RONDO 8-12
Also see PREVIN, Andre

LAINE, Frankie, & Jo Stafford P&R '51
Singles: 78 rpm
COLUMBIA 4-8 51-53
Singles: 7-inch
COLUMBIA 10-20 51-53
EPs: 7-inch
COLUMBIA 10-20 54
LPs: 10/12-inch
COLUMBIA 20-40 54
Also see LAINE, Frankie
Also see STAFFORD, Jo

LAINE, Jeff
Singles: 7-inch
BATTLE (45906 "Baby, Come Back Home") 10-20 63

LAINE, Linda, & Sinners
Singles: 7-inch
TOWER 8-10 64

LAINER & CO.
LPs: 10/12-inch
LARC 5-8 83

LAING, Corky
Singles: 7-inch
ELEKTRA 3-5 77
LPs: 10/12-inch
ELEKTRA 8-10 76
Also see KARP, Charlie
Also see MOUNTAIN
Also see WEST, BRUCE & LAING

LAKE P&R/LP '77
Singles: 7-inch
CARIBOU 3-5 81
COLUMBIA 3-5 77-79
LPs: 10/12-inch
CARIBOU 5-8 81
COLUMBIA 5-10 77-79
Also see PIERCE ARROW / Lake / Crawler / Ram Jam

LAKE, Arthur
(With the Wheels)
Singles: 78 rpm
PREMIUM 10-20 56
Singles: 7-inch
PREMIUM (406 "May I Count on You") 25-35 56
Also see WHEELS

LAKE, Bobby
Singles: 7-inch
LAP (1003 "Savannah") 20-30 62
(Colored vinyl. Also issued as by Bobby Angel.)
Also see ANGEL, Bobby

LAKE, Don, & Don Juans
Singles: 78 rpm
FORTUNE 15-25 56
Singles: 7-inch
FORTUNE (520 "Ooh, Ooh, Those Eyes") 30-40 56
Also see LITTLE EDDIE & Don Juans
Also see WEAVER, Joe, & Don Juans
Also see WILLIAMS, Andre, & Don Juans

LAKE, Greg P&R '75
Singles: 7-inch
ATLANTIC 3-5 75-77
CHRYSALIS 3-5 81
Picture Sleeves
ATLANTIC 3-5 75
LPs: 10/12-inch
CHRYSALIS 5-10 81
Also see EMERSON, LAKE & PALMER
Also see KING CRIMSON

LAKE, Karen
Singles: 7-inch
ABC-PAR 10-20 60
BIG TOP (3077 "Air Mail Special Delivery") 20-30 61

LAKE, Tony
Singles: 7-inch
HERALD 5-10 59

LAKESIDE R&B '78
Singles: 7-inch
ABC-PAR 3-5 77
ELEKTRA 3-4
SOLAR 3-5 78-87
Picture Sleeves
SOLAR 3-5
LPs: 10/12-inch
ABC-PAR 8-10 77
SOLAR 5-8 77-84
Members: Tiemeyer McCain; Thomas Shelby; Mark Woods; Otis Stokes; Steve Shockley; Marvin Craig; Norman Beavers; Fred Alexander; Fred Lewis.

LAKEWOODS
Singles: 7-inch
ASSOCIATED ARTISTS 4-8 62

LA LA R&B '87
(La Forest Cope)
Singles: 7-inch
ARISTA 3-4 87

LA LA, Prince: see PRINCE LA LA

LA LA & LALARETTS
Singles: 7-inch
ELPECO (2922 "This Day Is Ours") 20-30 63

LALALAND
Singles: 7-inch
GFI (107 "I'll Make Somebody Pay") 3-4 94
(Colored vinyl.)
Picture Sleeves
GFI (107 "I'll Make Somebody Pay") 3-4 94
(With photo insert.)
Members: Phil Marshall; Gary Skinner; Jim Huie; Bill King.

LA LANNE, Jack
LPs: 10/12-inch
LA LANNE ("Glamour Strecher Time") 15-25 59
(Blue vinyl. Selection number not known.)

LALUMIA, Jimi, & Psychotic Frogs
Singles: 7-inch
DEATH (001 "Death to Disco") 4-8 79

LA LUPE
Singles: 7-inch
ROULETTE 3-5 72
LPs: 10/12-inch
ROULETTE 10-12 69

LAM, Tommy
("With Glenn Douglass & His Orchestra & the Monograms")
Singles: 7-inch
NABOR (103 "Speed Limit") 150-250 58
R (303 "Blue Willow") 25-35 61
RANDALL (303 "Blue Willow") 50-75 59
SILVERBALL (102 "Speed Limit ") 4-6 93

LA MARR, Gene
Singles: 7-inch
FLAME (1102 "Just a Stranger") 25-35 60
SPRY (113 "Crazy Little House on the Hill") 100-150 59
SPRY (114 "Count on Me") 100-150 59
SPRY (115 "Close to Me") 25-35 59

LAMAR, Chris
Singles: 7-inch
DON-EL (121 "Love So True") 15-25 63

LAMAR, Lee
Singles: 7-inch
ERA (1041 "Teenage Pedal Pushers") 20-25 57

LA MAR, Tony
Singles: 7-inch
DUCO (5001 "Promises") 200-300 60
FIVE-FOUR 4-6 71
Also see GREENE, Rudy / Tony La Mar

LAMAR, Traci
(With the Supernatural Family Band)
LPs: 10/12-inch
AKASHIC 5-8 82
Also see HANCOCK, Tommy, & Supernatural Family Band

LAMARR, Chico
Singles: 7-inch
FULLER 8-12

LA MARR, Gene
Singles: 7-inch
FLAME (1102 "Just a Stranger") 25-35
SPRY (113 "Crazy Little House on the Hill") 100-150
SPRY (114 "Count on Me") 100-150
SPRY (115 "Close to Me") 25-35

LAMARR, Toni
Singles: 7-inch
BUDDAH (Except 29) 5-10
BUDDAH (29 "I'd Do Anything") 10-20 68

LAMARS
Singles: 7-inch
GOLDWAX (120 "Patsy") 15-25 65

LAMAS, Lorenzo P&R '84
Singles: 7-inch
SCOTTI BROTHERS 3-4 84-85
Picture Sleeves
SCOTTI BROTHERS 3-4 84

LAMASTER, Don C&W '89
Singles: 7-inch
K-ARK 3-4 89

LA MASTER, Sharon: see KORDS

LAMB
LPs: 10/12-inch
FILLMORE 10-20 70
W.B. 10-20 71-72
Also see GARCIA, Jerry

LAMB
LPs: 10/12-inch
SPARROW 5-10 80
Members: Joel Chernoff; Rick "Levi" Coghill.

LAMB, Kevin P&R '78
Singles: 7-inch
ARISTA 3-5 78

LAMBERT, Dave
Singles: 7-inch
POLYDOR 3-5 79
LPs: 10/12-inch
POLYDOR 5-8 79
Also see STRAWBS

LAMBERT, Dennis
Singles: 7-inch
DUNHILL 3-5 72
LPs: 10/12-inch
DUNHILL 8-12 72

LAMBERT, Gloria
Singles: 7-inch
COLUMBIA (41216 "You Only Love Me") 15-25 58
COLUMBIA (41975 "Each Time I Hear, Don't Worry") 10-20 61

LAMBERT, Guy: see PRESLEY, Elvis

LAMBERT, Jerry, & Aces
Singles: 7-inch
K&C (100 "Rockin' Strings") 10-20 60

LAMBERT, Lloyd
Singles: 78 rpm
SPECIALTY 10-20 55
Singles: 7-inch
SPECIALTY 20-40 55

LAMBERT, Rudy
(With the Mondellos)
Singles: 7-inch
RHYTHM (114 "My Heart") 250-500 57
RHYTHM (128 "That Old Feeling") 200-400 57
Also see MONDELLOS

LAMBERT, Tony
Singles: 7-inch
DAWN (232 "Hot Rod Scooter") 30-50 57

LAMBERT, Willy Joe
Singles: 7-inch
THUNDERHEAD 4-8

LAMBERT & NUTTYCOMBE
LPs: 10/12-inch
A&M 10-12 70
20TH FOX 8-10 73

LAMBERTH, Jimmy, with the Saxons
Singles: 78 rpm
METEOR 50-100 56
Singles: 7-inch
METEOR (5044 "Latch on to Your Baby") 150-200 56
REKA (294 "Reelin' & Rockin'") 50-75 61
REKA (400 "Step-Out") 10-20 65

LAMBRETTAS
Singles: 7-inch
ROCKET 3-5 80
LPs: 10/12-inch
ROCKET 5-8 80

LAMEGO, Danny, & Jumpin' Jacks
Singles: 78 rpm
ANDREA 50-75 56
Singles: 7-inch
ANDREA (101 "Hickory Dickory Rock") 75-100 56
LPs: 10/12-inch
FORGET-ME-NOT (105 "Big Weekend") 35-45 64
Also see PEPPERMINT, Danny, & His Jumping Jacks

LAMIE, Tony & Jackie
Singles: 7-inch
SUNSET (706 "Wore to a Frazzle") 100-150

LAMM, Robert
Singles: 7-inch
COLUMBIA 3-5 72
LPs: 10/12-inch
COLUMBIA 8-10 74
Also see CHICAGO

LAMMAR, Denny, & Echos
Singles: 7-inch
APPLAUSE 8-12 65

LAMMON, Tom
Singles: 7-inch
BLACK GOLD (7141 "Little Old Ford") 8-12

LAMOND, George P&R/LP '90
Singles: 7-inch
COLUMBIA 3-4 90
LPs: 10/12-inch
COLUMBIA 5-8 90

LAMONT
LPs: 10/12-inch
UNI 8-10 70

LA MONT, Billy
Singles: 7-inch
CANDELO (376 "Tom Cat") 25-50 58
KING (5403 "Hear Me Now") 10-15 60
OKEH (7125 "Country Boy") 20-30 59
OKEH (7131 "I'm Gonna Try") 20-30 60
SAVOY 10-15 58
THREE D (850 "Country Boy") 75-100 59
(First issue.)

LAMONT, Charles
(With the Extremes; Charles La Mont)
Singles: 7-inch
CHALLENGE (59290 "I've Got to Keep Moving") 20-30 65
REVUE 4-8 69

LAMONT, Lee R&B '65
Singles: 7-inch
BACK BEAT 5-10 64-66

LAMONT, Paula
Singles: 7-inch
LOADSTONE 8-10 64

LAMONT CRANSTON BAND
Singles: 7-inch
WATERHOUSE 3-5 79
LPs: 10/12-inch
SHADOW 8-10 76-77
WATERHOUSE 5-8 78-81

L'AMOUR D&D '84
Singles: 12-inch
BROCCOLLI 4-6 84

LAMP, Buddy
Singles: 7-inch
ABC-PAR (10398 "Promised Land") 8-12 63
D TOWN (1064 "Next Best Thing") 15-25 66
DOUBLE L (716 "My Tears") 10-20 63
DUKE 4-8 68
GONE (5104 "Good News") 8-12 61
PEANUT (1001 "Have Mercy Baby") 10-20 61
PEANUT (1003 "Insanity") 10-20 61
WHEELSVILLE (113 "I Wanna Go Home") 25-50 60s
WHEELSVILLE (120 "Confusion") 15-20 60s
WHEELSVILLE (122 "Save You Love") 25-50 60s

LAMP OF CHILDHOOD
Singles: 7-inch
DUNHILL 4-8 66-67

LAMP SISTERS R&B '68
Singles: 7-inch
DUKE 4-8 68-69

LAMPERT, Rudy
Singles: 7-inch
RHYTHM (128 "Sunday Kind of Love") 100-150 59

LAMPKIN, Tommy
Singles: 78 rpm
EBB (110 "Three Minus One") 10-15 57
IMPERIAL (5361 "Lover's Plea") 15-20 55
Singles: 7-inch
EBB (110 "Three Minus One") 20-30 57
IMPERIAL (5361 "Lover's Plea") 30-50 55

LAMPLIGHTERS
Singles: 78 rpm
FEDERAL (Except 12149) 15-25 53-56

FEDERAL (12149 "Part of Me")...50-100 53
Singles: 7-inch
FEDERAL (12149 "Part of Me") .200-400 53
FEDERAL (12152 "Give Me")....100-200 53
FEDERAL (12166 "Smootchie") 100-200 54
FEDERAL (12176 "Tell Me You Care")..........100-200 54
FEDERAL (12182 "Salty Dog") ..100-200 54
FEDERAL (12192 "Five Minutes Longer")..........100-200 54
FEDERAL (12197 "Yum! Yum!")..........100-200 54
FEDERAL (12206 "I Wanna Know")..........100-200 55
FEDERAL (12212 "Roll On")......100-200 55
FEDERAL (12242 "Don't Make It So Good")..........100-200 55
FEDERAL (12255 "You Were Sent Down from Heaven")..........75-125 56
FEDERAL (12261 "It Ain't Right") 75-125 56
GUSTO 3-5
Members: Al Frazier; Thurston Harris; Carl White; Willie Rockwell; Matthew Nelson.
Also see ELL, Carl, & Buddies
Also see HARRIS, Thurston
Also see HOLMAN, Eddie / Lamplighters
Also see RIVINGTONS
Also see TENDERFOOTS
Also see WITHERSPOON, Jimmy, & Lamplighters

LANA RAE: see RAE, Lana

LANAS
Singles: 7-inch
LAURIE 4-8 63

LANCASTER, Ernest
LPs: 10/12-inch
ICHIBAN.......... 5-10

LANCASTER, J.J.
Singles: 7-inch
DATE..........10-20 68

LANCASTER, Jack, & Robin Lumley
LPs: 10/12-inch
RSO (3020 "Marscape").......... 5-10 76

LANCASTERS
Singles: 7-inch
TITAN.......... 5-8 64

LANCASTRIANS
Singles: 7-inch
CAPITOL..........15-20 65
JERDEN.......... 5-10 66

LANCE, Al
Singles: 7-inch
COLUMBIA (42471 "I'm Walkin' Out")..........10-20 63

LANCE, Bobby
Singles: 7-inch
SQUARE 5-10 60

LANCE, Bobby
(B. Lance)
Singles: 7-inch
ATLANTIC.......... 3-5 72
COTILLION.......... 3-5 71
LPs: 10/12-inch
ATLANTIC.......... 8-10 72
COTILLION.......... 8-10 71

LANCE, Herb R&B '49
(With the Classics; with Roger Sherman & Orchestra)
Singles: 78 rpm
DELUXE..........15-25 57
SITTIN' IN WITH (514 "Close Your Eyes")..........20-40 49
SITTIN' IN WITH (519 "Because") 20-40 49
Singles: 7-inch
DELUXE (6150 "You Can't Be Sure")..........25-35 57
MALA (404 "Like a Baby")..........10-20 59
MALA (405 "Some Love")..........10-20 59
MALA (420 "Deep in My Heart")....10-20 60
PROMO (1010 "Blue Moon")..........20-30 61
LPs: 10/12-inch
CHESS (1506 "Comeback")..........20-30 66
Also see BEAVERS

LANCE, Larry, & Skywriters
Singles: 7-inch
MONKSWELL..........10-15

LANCE, Linda K. C&W '69
(With the Gary Paxon Singers)
Singles: 7-inch
ABC.......... 4-6 67
GAR-PAX.......... 3-5 76
ROYAL AMERICAN.......... 3-6 69-71
TRIUNE.......... 3-5 73
WAYSIDE.......... 3-5 70s
LPs: 10/12-inch
ROYAL AMERICAN.......... 8-12 69
Also see PETERS, Jimmy, & Linda K. Lance

LANCE, Major P&R/R&B/LP '63
Singles: 12-inch
KAT FAMILY.......... 4-6 82
Singles: 7-inch
COLUMBIA.......... 3-5 77
CURTOM.......... 4-6 70
DAKAR.......... 5-10 69
EPIC.......... 4-8 66
KAT FAMILY.......... 3-4 82
MERCURY (71582 "I've Got a Girl")..........20-30 60
OKEH (7168 thru 7197).......... 5-10 63-64
OKEH (7200 "Think Nothing About It")..........25-50 64
OKEH (7203 thru 7266).......... 8-15 64-66
OKEH (7284 "You Don't Want Me No More")..........25-50 67
OKEH (7298 "Forever")..........5-10 67
OSIRIS.......... 3-5 75
PLAYBOY.......... 3-5 74-75
SOUL.......... 3-5 78
VOLT.......... 3-5 72
Picture Sleeves
OKEH..........5-10 63-65
EPs: 7-inch
OKEH..........10-15 64
(Juke box issue only.)
LPs: 10/12-inch
BACK-TRAC.......... 5-8 85
CONTEMPO..........10-12
KAT FAMILY.......... 5-8 83
OKEH..........15-20 63-64
SOUL.......... 5-8 78

LANCE, Ric
Singles: 7-inch
PLAZA.......... 4-8

LANCE & SPIRITS
Singles: 7-inch
GARRETT.......... 4-8 67

LANCELO & TEERS
Singles: 7-inch
PROMENADE.......... 4-8

LANCELOT, Rick
(With the 7 Knights)
Singles: 7-inch
RCA.......... 4-8 65-66
TURBAN.......... 4-8 62
20TH FOX.......... 4-8 65

LANCELOT LINK & EVOLUTION REVOLUTION
Singles: 7-inch
ABC (11278 "Sha La Love You") 4-6 70
LPs: 10/12-inch
ABC..........10-15 70

LANCERS P&R '53
Singles: 78 rpm
CORAL.......... 4-6 54-56
Singles: 7-inch
CORAL..........5-10 54-56
IMPERIAL.......... 5-8 59
LANCELOT.......... 4-8
SWF.......... 4-8 62
TREND..........5-10 54
Picture Sleeves
SWF.......... 4-8 62
EPs: 7-inch
CORAL..........10-20 55
LPs: 10/12-inch
IMPERIAL..........15-25 59
Members: Jerry Meacham; Dick Burr; Bob Porter; Corky Lindgren.
Also see McGUIRE SISTERS / Lancers / Dorothy Collins / Teresa Brewer

LANCERS
Singles: 7-inch
CENTRAL (6001 "The Moocher")...15-25 50s

LANCERS
Singles: 7-inch
LAWN (205 "Oh Little Girl")..........25-35 63
(Also issued as by the Royal Lancers.)
Also see ROYAL LANCERS

LANCERS
Singles: 7-inch
VEE JAY (654 "Hush-A-Bye")..........10-15 65

LANCERS
Singles: 7-inch
CLOUD (500 "Baja")..........20-30 65
OLD TIMER (604 "Baja")..........10-20 65
(Black vinyl.)
OLD TIMER (604 "Baja")..........20-30 65
(Colored vinyl.)
Also see DESTINAIRES / Lancers

LANCERS
Singles: 7-inch
PANTHER (1051 "Alone")..........150-250

LAND, Billy
Singles: 7-inch
ESCO (100 "Shimmy Shake")..........50-75 59
SCOTTIE..........10-20 60
W.B...........10-20 59

LAND, Eddie
Singles: 7-inch
RON (320 "Easy Rockin' ")..........10-15 59

LANDAN SISTERS
Singles: 7-inch
MERCURY..........5-10 59-60

LANDECKER, John
Singles: 7-inch
EVA-TONE ("Press My Conference – Make a Date with Watergate").......... 4-6 74
(Plastic soundsheet. No selection number used.)

LANDERS, Bob, & Willie Joe
Singles: 78 rpm
SPECIALTY..........8-12 56
Singles: 7-inch
SPECIALTY..........15-25 56

LANDERS, Dave C&W '49
Singles: 78 rpm
MGM.......... 4-8 49

LANDERS, Froggy, & Cough Drops
Singles: 7-inch
ENSIGN..........10-15 58

LANDERS, Rich C&W '81
Singles: 7-inch
AMI..........3-4 81-83
OVATION..........3-5 81

LANDERS, Sue
Singles: 7-inch
LANDA..........4-8 61

LANDIS, Jerry P&R '63
(Paul Simon)
Singles: 7-inch
AMY (875 "Lone Teen Ranger")..........25-35 62
CANADIAN AMERICAN (130 "I'm Lonely")..........25-50 61
MGM (12822 "Anna Belle")..........25-50 59
WARWICK (552 "Just a Boy")..........25-50 60
WARWICK (588 "Just a Boy")..........25-50 60
WARWICK (619 "Play Me a Sad Song")..........40-60 61
Also see SIMON, Paul

LANDIS, Richard
Singles: 7-inch
DUNHILL..........4-8 72
LPs: 10/12-inch
DUNHILL..........8-10 72

LANDIS, Tommy
(With the Spinners)
Singles: 7-inch
WYN (1603 "Someone to Love")...40-60 59

LANDLORDS
Singles: 7-inch
REED (1069 "I'll Return")..........8-12

LANDON, Alan
Singles: 7-inch
DANG..........3-5

LANDON, Buddy
(Bud Landon & the Rhythm Masters)
Singles: 7-inch
BELLE (109 "Get Away")..........20-40 59
BELLE (111 "Running Man")..........20-40 59
BELLE (113 "Walking")..........20-40 59
DONNA..........10-20 59
JAGUAR (3026 "Raunchy Little Baby")..........20-30 58
JAGUAR (3028 "Oh Yes")..........20-30 58

LANDON, Michael
Singles: 7-inch
FONO GRAF (1240 "Gimme a Little Kiss")..........25-35 60
Picture Sleeves
FONO GRAF (1240 "Gimme a Little Kiss")..........50-100 60

LANDON, Richard
Singles: 7-inch
MR. MAESTRO..........4-8 63

LANDS, Hoagy
Singles: 7-inch
ABC-PAR..........10-15 60-63
ATLANTIC..........5-10 64
JUDI (054 "Cry Some Tears")..........50-70 60
LAURIE (3349 "Theme from the Other Side")..........10-15 66
LAURIE (3381 "The Next in Line") 10-20 67
MGM..........8-12 61-62

LANDS, Liz
Singles: 7-inch
GORDY (7026 "What He Lived For")..........20-25 63
ONE-DERFUL..........5-10 67
T&L..........5-10

LANDS, Liz / Martin Luther King
Singles: 7-inch
GORDY (7023 "We Shall Overcome")..........15-25 63
Also see KING, Rev. Martin Luther, Jr.

LANDS, Liz, & Temptations
Singles: 7-inch
GORDY (7030 "Keep Me")..........25-50 64
Also see LANDS, Liz
Also see TEMPTATIONS

LANDSLIDE
LPs: 10/12-inch
CAPITOL (11006 "Two Sided Fantasy")..........25-35 72

LANDSLIDES
Singles: 7-inch
HUFF & PUFF (1001)..........4-6 70s
(Title not known.)

LANE, Barry
Singles: 7-inch
ELKO (11 "Doggone Lonesome Town")..........10-15 62
RA-Q..........5-10 60

LANE, Billy
(Billy Lane Quintet)
Singles: 7-inch
ROLLIN' (1003 "The New Night Train")..........20-30
TABA (201 "Beginner in Love")..........400-600 60s

LANE, Bobby
Singles: 7-inch
AMCO (2 "You Shake Me")..........50-100 62

LANE, Bonnie
Singles: 7-inch
GONE..........4-8 62

LANE, Cindy
Singles: 7-inch
REMO..........5-10 60

LANE, Connie
Singles: 7-inch
DYNAMIC (501 "Breaks of the Game")..........10-20

LANE, Cristy C&W '77
Singles: 7-inch
LS (100 series)..........3-5 77-78
LS (1000 series)..........3-4 87
LIBERTY..........3-5 81-83
U.A...........3-5 79-80
LPs: 10/12-inch
LS..........5-10 77-83
LIBERTY..........5-8 80-83
U.A...........5-10 79-80

LANE, Ernest
Singles: 78 rpm
BLUES & RHYTHM (7000 "What's Wrong, Baby")..........25-50 51
Singles: 7-inch
M.J.C. (1 "Slices Apples")..........10-20 61
Also see TURNER, Ike

LANE, Gary & Mad Lads
Singles: 7-inch
CUCA (6494 "Henrietta")..........15-25 64
Also see MAD LADS

LANE, Herb
Singles: 7-inch
VIGOR..........3-5 76

LANE, Honey
(With the Triumphs)
Singles: 7-inch
FEDORA..........4-8 62
REVOLVO..........4-8 61
TOPPA..........4-8 62

LANE, Jack
Singles: 7-inch
ELKO (102 "Mr. Blues")..........10-20
ELKO (107 "Restless")..........10-20
YOLO (12 "King Fool")..........50-100 60

LANE, Jerry C&W '74
(Jerry "Max" Lane)
Singles: 7-inch
ABC..........3-5 74-75
CHART..........3-5 70
STOCKYARD..........3-4 83
LPs: 10/12-inch
CHART..........6-12 70
Also see ANDERSON, Lynn, & Jerry Lane

LANE, Jimmy, & Sugartones
Singles: 7-inch
TIME (6602 "Constantly")..........75-125 59
(Also issued as by Jimmy Bailey. We're not yet sure which came first.)
Also see BAILEY, Jimmy

LANE, Kenny
Singles: 7-inch
STRATE 8 (1504 "Froggy Went A-Courtin' ")..........100-200 59

LANE, Linda
Singles: 7-inch
DOT..........4-8 62

LANE, Linda
(Linda Jones)
Singles: 7-inch
CUB (9124 "Lonely Teardrops").....35-50 63
Also see JONES, Linda

LANE, Lois
Singles: 7-inch
DISNEYLAND..........5-10
WAND (166 "My Only Prayer")......10-20 64

LANE, Mickey
Singles: 7-inch
BRUNSWICK..........10-15 58
LAURIE..........10-20 60

LANE, Mickey Lee P&R '64
Singles: 7-inch
MALA..........5-8 68
SWAN..........5-10 64-66

LANE, Mike
Singles: 7-inch
ACE..........4-8 63
BUDDY..........4-8 65-68

LANE, Penny
Singles: 7-inch
FORD..........4-6

LANE, Ralph
Singles: 7-inch
COWTOWN (811 "You Gotta Show Me")..........50-100 59

LANE, Red C&W '71
Singles: 7-inch
RCA..........3-5 71-72
LPs: 10/12-inch
RCA..........6-12 71
Also see SOME of CHET'S FRIENDS

LANE, Robin, & Chartbusters P&R '80
Singles: 7-inch
W.B...........3-5 80-81
Picture Sleeves
W.B...........3-5 80
LPs: 10/12-inch
W.B...........5-8 80-81
Members: Robin Lane; Leroy Radcliffe; Asa Brebner; Scott Baerenwald; Tim Jackson.

LANE, Rocki, & His Gross Group
Singles: 7-inch
EPIC..........4-6 69

LANE, Rocky
Singles: 7-inch
BELMONT..........3-5 80

LANE, Rocky, & Vernon Miller
Singles: 7-inch
RIDGECREST..........5-10 60

LANE, Ron
Singles: 7-inch
NATIONAL AMERICAN..........5-10 80

LANE, Ronnie
Singles: 7-inch
A&M..........3-5 73
Also see SMALL FACES
Also see TOWNSHEND, Pete, & Ronnie Lane

LANE, Ronnie, & Capers
Singles: 7-inch
CAVALIER (6001 "500 Miles")..........5-10
(Canadian.)

LANE, Rose Lee
Singles: 7-inch
GARDENA..........4-8 62

LANE, Ruby
Singles: 7-inch
COLPIX..........4-8 60

LANE, Rusty
Singles: 7-inch
LAURIE (3031 "Karen")..........150-250 59

LANE, Stacy
Singles: 7-inch
EXCELLO (2302 "No Brags Just Facts")..........8-12 68

LANE, Sunny
Singles: 7-inch
HBR..........4-8 67

LANE, Terri C&W '73
(With Nall)
Singles: 7-inch
MONUMENT..........3-5 73

LANE, Tom
Singles: 7-inch
CABIN TRAIL (01 "Booger Time Blues")..........10-20 80

LANE, Tommy
(With Tommy Sheridan & Orchestra; with El Ray & Night Beats)
Singles: 7-inch
ERRO (201 "Teen Ager's Lament")..........75-100 60s
SURE (502 "Mine Alone")..........100-200 50s
Also see EL RAY & NIGHT BEATS

LANE, Trinity: see TRINITY LANE

LANE, Weldon
Singles: 7-inch
GARY PAXTON RECORDS (1100 "Makin' Me Look Good")..........5-10

LANE, Willie
(Little Brother)
Singles: 78 rpm
STAR TALENT (805 "Prowlin' Ground Hog")..........40-60 49
STAR TALENT (806 "Howling Wolfe Blues")..........40-60 49

LANE BROTHERS P&R '57
Singles: 78 rpm
RCA..........8-15 57
Singles: 7-inch
FXL..........3-5 81
LEADER (804 "Mimi")..........8-12 60
RCA (6810 "Marianne")..........10-20 57
RCA (6900 "Uh-uh Honey")..........20-30 57
RCA (7220 "Boppin' in the Sack")..20-30 58
RCA (7304 "Little Brother")..........20-30 58
EPs: 7-inch
RCA (4175 "The Lane Brothers")....30-50 57
Members: Pete Lane; Arthur Lane; Frank Lane.

LANE BROTHERS / Julius La Rosa
EPs: 7-inch
RCA..........10-20 57
(Promotional issue only.)
Also see LANE BROTHERS
Also see LA ROSA, Julius

LANE SISTERS
Singles: 7-inch
LANDA (672 "Birmingham Rag")...10-20 60s

LANEAR, Donnie
Singles: 7-inch
APT (25073 "I Don't Think U Love Me")..........10-20 62

LANEGAN, Mark
LPs: 10/12-inch
SUB POP (61 "Winding Street")....15-25 90
(Colored vinyl.)
Session: Kurt Cobain; Krist Novoselic.
Also see NIRVANA
Also see SCREAMING TREES

LANES
Singles: 78 rpm
GEE (1023 "You Alone")..........15-25 56
Singles: 7-inch
GEE (1023 "You Alone")..........25-35 56

LANG, Don
Singles: 7-inch
CAPITOL..........5-10 58
KING..........5-10 60-61

LANG, Eddie
Singles: 78 rpm
RPM 8-12 56
Singles: 7-inch
JEWEL 5-10 60s
RPM 10-15 56
RON (324 "Troubles Troubles") 15-25 59

LANG, Judi
Singles: 7-inch
WWM 5-10

LANG, Julie
Singles: 78 rpm
DELUXE 10-20 57
Singles: 7-inch
DELUXE 10-20 57

LANG, K.D. C&W/LP '88
(k.d. lang & the Reclines)
Singles: 7-inch
SIRE 3-4 88-91
W.B. 3-4 90s
Picture Sleeves
SIRE 3-4
LPs: 10/12-inch
SIRE 5-8 88-90
W.B. 8-10 90s
Also see DION
Also see ORBISON, Roy, & K.D. Lang

LANG, Kelly C&W '82
Singles: 7-inch
SOUNDWAVES 3-4 82

LANG, Peter
LPs: 10/12-inch
TAKOMA 8-10 73
Also see KOTTKE, Leo, John Fahey & Peter Lang

LANG, Tony
Singles: 7-inch
SENTRY 4-8

LANG SISTERS
Singles: 7-inch
DORE 4-8 62

LANGAN SISTERS
Singles: 7-inch
RCA 5-10 61
Also see LIMELITERS

LANGDON, Jim, Trio
Singles: 7-inch
CUCA (1129 "Billy Sol") 10-20 63
EPs: 7-inch
CUCA (1149 "Maryann") 15-25 63
LP: 10/12-inch
CUCA (1100 "Jim Langdon Trio") 15-25 63
Members: Bill Lengacher; Don Tollefson; Steve MacEnroth; John Segerstrom; Steve Sperry; Dean Kaul.
Also see SPERRY, Steve

LANGFORD, Billie
(Emperor of the Blues; Billy Langford Combo)
Singles: 78 rpm
HARLEM 10-20 46
LENOX 10-20 45

LANGFORD, Jerry, & Ben Denton Singers
(Jerry Langford)
Singles: 7-inch
DEL-FI (4113 "Still of the Night") 10-20 59
Also see DENTON, Ben, Singers

LANGLEY, Chuck
Singles: 7-inch
CHECKER 4-8 65

LANGLEY, Curley, & His Western All Stars
Singles: 78 rpm
ARCADIA 30-50 56
Singles: 7-inch
ARCADIA (110 "Rockin' and Rollin'") 100-200 56

LANGRAN, Joel
Singles: 7-inch
RORI 8-10 64

LANHAM, Richard
(With the Tempotones; "12 Year Old Richard Lanham")
Singles: 7-inch
ACME (712 "On Your Radio") 35-50 57
("Radio" is spelled right. First pressing.)
ACME (712 "On Your Raido") 50-75 57
("Radio" is misspelled.)
JOSIE 5-10 65
Also see TEMPO-TONES

LANHAM, Roy
Singles: 7-inch
RADIO (104 "Altitude") 15-25 58
RADIO (109 "Boys Out of School") 15-25 58

LANI & BONI
Singles: 7-inch
GARPAX (4084 "Cherry Pie") 8-12 64

LANIER, Don
Singles: 7-inch
GEE 8-12 60

LANIER & CO. P&R/R&B '82
Singles: 7-inch
LARC 3-4 82-83
LPs: 10/12-inch
LARC 5-8 83
Member: Farris Lanier Jr.

LANIN, Lester, & His Orchestra LP '57
Singles: 78 rpm
EPIC 3-5 56-57
Singles: 7-inch
EPIC 4-8 56-62
EPs: 7-inch
EPIC 4-8 56-58
LPs: 10/12-inch
EPIC 5-15 56-62
PHILIPS 5-10 65

LANKFORD, Jessie
Singles: 7-inch
PABLO 4-6

LANO, Mickey
Singles: 7-inch
SINGULAR (718 "I Promise") 100-200 59

LANOIS, Daniel LP '90
LPs: 10/12-inch
W.B./OPAL 5-8 89

LARAND, Johnny
Singles: 7-inch
OCTAVIA 20-30

LANSDOWNE, Jerry C&W '89
Singles: 7-inch
STEP ONE 3-4 89

LANSON, Snooky P&R '48
(With the Ray Noble Orchestra)
Singles: 78 rpm
DECCA 3-6 52
DOT 3-6 55-56
LONDON 3-6 49-51
MERCURY 4-8 48
REPUBLIC 3-6 53
Singles: 7-inch
DECCA 5-10 52
DOT 5-10 55-56
LONDON 5-10 50-51
REPUBLIC 5-10 53
STARDAY 3-6 68
LPs: 10/12-inch
CAMDEN (200 series) 10-20 55
DOT 10-15 60
STARDAY 5-10 68

LANTERNS
Singles: 7-inch
BARON 3-5 76

LANTZ, Barbara
Singles: 7-inch
PHIL TONE 5-10 60

LANZ, David LP '88
(With Paul Speer)
LPs: 10/12-inch
NARADA 5-8 88

LANZA, Mario P&R '50
Singles: 78 rpm
RCA 3-5 50-57
Singles: 7-inch
RCA (0400 series) 3-5 71
RCA (3200 thru 8500 series) 5-10 51-59
RCA (1300 series) 4-6 50
Picture Sleeves
RCA (3300 "The Loveliest Night of the Year") 15-25 51
RCA (4209 "Song of India") 15-25 51
RCA 5-8 50s
(For generic, die-cut paper sleeves with artist photo. Not for any specific release.)
EPs: 7-inch
RCA (Except 1837) 8-15 53-61
RCA (1837 "Student Prince") 15-25 54
(Soundtrack.)
LPs: 10/12-inch
CAMDEN (Except 400 series) 5-15 63
CAMDEN (400 series) 10-20 57
(With "CAL" prefix. Monaural.)
CAMDEN (400 series) 8-15 63
(With "CAS" prefix. Stereo.)
RCA (75 "Toast of New Orleans") 45-60 51
(Soundtrack. (10-inch LP.)
RCA (86 thru 1181) 20-30 51-53
RCA (1750 "Legendary Performer") 5-8 76
RCA (1837 "Student Prince") 35-45 54
(Soundtrack.)
RCA (1860 thru 2090) 15-25 54-57
(Black label.)
RCA (1860 thru 2090) 6-12 68
(Orange label.)
RCA (2211 "Seven Hills of Rome") 20-30 58
(Soundtrack tunes on side one, other Mario Lanza songs on side two.)
RCA (2331 thru 2333) 15-25 59-61
(Black label.)
RCA (2331 thru 2333) 6-12 68
(Orange label.)
RCA (2338 "For the First Time") 20-30 59
(Soundtrack.)
RCA (2339 thru 2790) 10-20 60-64
(Black or Red Seal label.)
RCA (2339 thru 2790) 6-12 68
(Orange or Red Seal label.)
RCA (2800 series) 4-8 78
RCA (2900 thru 3200) 8-15 68-71
RCA (4158 "The Mario Lanza Collection") 35-45 81
(Boxed, five-disc set.)
RCA/TELEHOUSE 5-10 74
(Mail order offer.)
Also see LIMELITERS / Della Reese / Mario Lanza / Norman Luboff Choir

LANZO, Mike, & Blue Counts
Singles: 7-inch
DEBRA (2006 "At the Fair") 100-200 64
Members: Mike Lanzo; Lee Jacobs; Eddie Petro; Billy Sincavage; Spencer Smith; Joe Richards; Don Manzo.
Also see GENOVA, Tommy
Also see MAGICS

LAPELS
Singles: 7-inch
DOT (16129 "Sneakin' Around") 10-20 60
MELKER (103 "Sneakin' Around") 40-60 60
MELKER (104 "I Want a True Friend") 150-250 60

LaPOINTE, Perry C&W '86
Singles: 7-inch
DOOR KNOB 3-4 86-89
Also see RICE, Bobby G., & Perry LaPointe

LA PRADE, Sharon
Singles: 7-inch
PHILIPS 4-8 63

LARA, Sammy
Singles: 7-inch
GAYLO 10-15 58

LARADOS
(With the Band of Lucky Lee)
Singles: 7-inch
FOX (962 "Now the Parting Begins") 200-300 57
MADOG 4-6 80
EPs: 7-inch
MADOG 5-10 81
Members: Ronnie Morris; Don Davenport; Tom Hust; Bernie Turnbull; Bob Broderick; Tony Micale; Gary Banovitz; Rick Benko; John Dean.
Also see ROMEOS
Also see ZELLA, Danny

LARAINE, Little Rita
Singles: 7-inch
BLUE BONNETT (5284 "Stop") 15-25

LARAMIE
Singles: 7-inch
MERCURY 3-5 70
LPs: 10/12-inch
MERCURY 8-10 70

LA RAYS
Singles: 7-inch
ARLEN 5-8 63

LA REINE, La Mar
Singles: 7-inch
CLOUD 10-15

LA RELLS
Singles: 7-inch
LIBERTY 10-15 62
ROBBEE (109 "Everybody Knew") 15-25 61
ROBBEE (114 "I Just Can't Understand") 20-30 61

LARGE
Singles: 7-inch
PREDATOR 3-5 76

LARGE, Billy C&W '66
Singles: 7-inch
COLUMBIA 4-6 66-67
Picture Sleeves
COLUMBIA 4-8 66

LARGOS
Singles: 7-inch
DOT (16292 "I Wonder Why") 15-25 61

LARINO BROTHERS
Singles: 7-inch
FRA-DEL 5-10 63

LARK, Frances
Singles: 7-inch
DORE (730"Get Up and Dance") 25-35 64

LARK, Freddie, & Blue Knights
Singles: 7-inch
INTERNATIONAL 5-10
THANX (52 "Angel from Above") 8-12

LARK, Johnnie
Singles: 7-inch
ACE 5-10 59

LARK, Toby
(Tobi Lark)
Singles: 7-inch
COTILLION 5-10 69
TOPPER (1011 "Talking About Love") 15-20 60s
TOPPER (1015 "Challenge My Love") 15-20 60s

LARKE, Chrys
Singles: 7-inch
DO-RE-MI 5-10 59

LARKIN, Billy LP '66
(With the Delegates)
Singles: 78 rpm
MELODY 20-30 56
Singles: 7-inch
BRYAN 3-5 75
CASINO 3-5 76
MELODY (103 "Rock-it, Davy Crockett") 50-75 56
MERCURY 3-5 78-79
SUNBIRD 3-5 80-81
WORLD PACIFIC 4-8 66
LPs: 10/12-inch
AURA 15-25 65-66
BRYAN 5-10 75
WORLD PACIFIC 10-20 65-69

LARKS R&B '51
Singles: 78 rpm
APOLLO (427 "Eyesight to the Blind") 200-300 51
APOLLO (429 "Little Side Car") 200-300 51
APOLLO (430 "Ooh . . . It Feels So Good") 100-200 51
APOLLO (435 "My Lost Love") 100-200 51
APOLLO (437 "Darlin'") 100-200 52
APOLLO (475 "Honey from the Bee") 50-100 55
APOLLO (1177 "My Heart Cries for You") 150-250 51
APOLLO (1180 "Hopefully Yours") 100-200 51
APOLLO (1184 "My Reverie") 150-300 51
APOLLO (1189 "Shadrack") 100-200 52
APOLLO (1190 "Stolen Love") 100-200 52
APOLLO (1194 "Hold Me") 100-200 52
LLOYDS (108 "Margie") 100-200 54
LLOYDS (110 "If It's a Crime") 100-200 54
LLOYDS (112 "No Other Girl") 100-200 54
LLOYDS (114 "Forget It") 100-200 54
Singles: 7-inch
APOLLO (430 "Ooh, It Feels So Good") 500-750 51
APOLLO (435 "My Lost Love") 500-750 51
APOLLO (475 "Honey from the Bee") 250-350 55
APOLLO (1180 "Hopefully Yours") 500-750 51
(Black vinyl.)
APOLLO (1180 "Hopefully Yours") 2000-4000 51
(Orange vinyl.)
APOLLO (1184 "My Reverie") 1000-2000 51
(Black vinyl)
APOLLO (1184 "My Reverie") 3000-5000 51
(Red vinyl.)
APOLLO (1189 "Shadrack") 500-750 52
APOLLO (1190 "Stolen Love") 500-750 52
(Black vinyl)
APOLLO (1190 "Stolen Love") 2000-4000 52
(Orange vinyl)
APOLLO (1194 "Hold Me") 500-750 52
LLOYDS (108 "Margie") 500-750 54
LLOYDS (110 "If It's a Crime") 400-600 54
LLOYDS (112 "No Other Girl") 400-600 54
LLOYDS (114 "Forget It") 300-500 54
Members: Gene Mumford; Allen Bunn; Ray Barnes; Thermon Ruth; Dave McNeil; Hadie Rowe; Orville Brooks; David Bowers; Isaiah Bing; Glen Burgess.
Also see BUNN, Allen
Also see FIVE LARKS
Also see FOUR BARONS
Also see GALE, Barbara, & Larks
Also see KING ODOM
Also see MUMFORD, Gene
Also see SELAH JUBILEE QUARTET
Also see SOUTHERN HARMONAIRES

LARKS P&R/R&B '61
Singles: 7-inch
CROSS FIRE (74-50 "Fabulous Cars & Diamond Rings") 15-25 62
GUYDEN (2098 "I Want Her to Love Me") 8-12 62
GUYDEN (2103 "Fabulous Cars & Diamond Rings") 8-12 62
JETT (3001 "Love Me True") 75-125 65
SHERYL (334 "It's Unbelievable") 20-30 61
SHERYL (338 "There Is a Girl") 20-30 61
STACY 5-10 63
VIOLET (1051 "I Want Her to Love Me") 15-25 63
LPs: 10/12-inch
SHERYL ("It's Unbelievable") 100-200 62
(Selection number not known.)

LARKS
Singles: 7-inch
R&R (301 "Hippo") 10-20 63

LARKS P&R '64
(Don Julian & the Larks; Meadowlarks)
Singles: 7-inch
ELEKTRA (101 "Mashin' Time") 4-8 60s
JERK (103 "Baby My Love") 4-8 65
JERK (202 "Shorty the Pimp") 4-8
MONEY (106 "The Jerk") 5-10 64
MONEY (110 "Mickey's East Coast Jerk") 5-8 64
MONEY (112 "Heavenly Father") 5-8 65
MONEY (115 "Sad Sad Boy") 5-8 65
MONEY (119 "The Answer Came Too Late") 5-8 66
MONEY (122 "Philly Dog") 5-8 66
MONEY (127 "The Skate") 4-8 67
MONEY (601 "I Want You Back") 5-10 71
MONEY (604 "My Favorite Beer Joint") 5-10 72
NASCO 3-5 72
LPs: 10/12-inch
AMAZON (1009 "Greatest Hits") 45-55 63
MONEY 15-20 65-67
Also see JULIAN, Don, & Meadowlarks
Also see MASON, Barbara, & Larks
Also see SHIRELLES / Don Julian & Larks

LARKS / Masqueraders
Singles: 78 rpm
COBRA 5-10
Also see LARKS
Also see MASQUERADERS

LARKTONES
(With Teacho Wiltshire & Orchestra)
Singles: 7-inch
ABC-PAR (9909 "The Letter") 30-50 58
RIKI (140 "Why Are You Tearing Us Apart") 50-100 60
Also see WILTSHIRE, Teacho

LARKTONES / Dubs
Singles: 7-inch
POPULAR REQUEST 3-6

LA ROC, Dallan
(Dal La Roc)
Singles: 7-inch
ARTEEN (102 "Margo") 10-15 61
ARTEEN (1010 "Stop What You're Doing") 20-30 61

LA ROCCA, Pat
Singles: 7-inch
BELLA (4284 "Rowena") 50-75 59
JAN ELL 10-15 60

LA ROSA, Julius P&R '53
Singles: 78 rpm
CADENCE 3-6 53-55
Singles: 7-inch
ABC 4-6 67
BARNABY 3-5 70
CADENCE (1200 series) 5-10 53-55
CADENCE (1400 series) 4-8 63-64
KAPP 4-8 60-62
MGM 4-6 66
MGM CELEBRITY SCENE (CS5-5 "Julius LaRosa") 10-20 66
(Boxed set of five singles with bio insert and title strips.)
METROMEDIA 3-5 70
RCA (0900 series) 3-5 73
RCA (6000 & 7000 series) 5-10 56-58
ROULETTE 4-8 59
EPs: 7-inch
CADENCE 5-15 54-58
RCA (EPA-841 "Julius LaRosa") 5-10 56
RCA (EPB-1299 "Julius LaRosa") 15-25 56
LPs: 10/12-inch
CADENCE (1007 "Julie's Best") 20-30 55
FORUM 10-15 60
KAPP 10-15 61
MGM 10-15 66-67
METROMEDIA 5-10 71
RCA (1299 "Julius LaRosa") 20-30 56
ROULETTE 10-20 59
Also see LANE BROTHERS / Julius La Rosa

LA ROSA, Julius, & Bob Crewe Generation
Singles: 7-inch
CREWE 3-6 69
Also see CREWE, Bob
Also see LA ROSA, Julius

LARRATT, Iris C&W '79
Singles: 7-inch
INFINITY 3-5 79
LPs: 10/12-inch
INFINITY 8-10 79
RCA 8-10

LARRICE D&D '84
Singles: 12-inch
STREETWISE 4-6 84

LARRY & BLUE NOTES
Singles: 7-inch
CHARAY (20 "Talk About Love") 10-20 65
CHARAY (44 "In and Out") 10-20 65
TIRIS (101 "Night of the Phantom") 20-30 65
20TH FOX (573 "Night of the Phantom") 15-25 65
Also see MARK FIVE
Also see ROQUEMORE, Larry

LARRY & CONSERVATIVES
Singles: 7-inch
LIKE 4-8 63

LARRY & CROSSFIRES
Singles: 7-inch
SEARCY 15-20 65

LARRY & GENTS
Singles: 7-inch
DELAWARE 5-10

LARRY & GREATEST OF EASE
Singles: 7-inch
MINARET (154 "High Flyin' Hazel") 4-8 69

LARRY & HANK
LPs: 10/12-inch
PRESTIGE 10-15 66

LARRY & INMATES
Singles: 7-inch
STYLE 5-10 66

LARRY & JOHNNY
Singles: 7-inch
JOLA (1000 "Beatle Time") 10-15 64
Members: Larry Williams; Johnny "Guitar" Watson.
Also see WILLIAMS, Larry, & Johnny Watson

LARRY & LARKS
Singles: 7-inch
VEEP 4-8 67

LARRY & LEGENDS
(With the 4 Seasons)
Singles: 7-inch
ATLANTIC (2220 "Don't Pick on Me") 10-20 64
Also see 4 SEASONS

LARRY & LENORE
Singles: 7-inch
ABC-PAR 8-12 59
REQUEST (3005 "Sweet Kissin' Baby") 25-35 59

LARRY & LOAFERS
Singles: 7-inch
HEART 5-10 62
SHURFINE 5-10

LARRY & LYNDA
Singles: 7-inch
NUGGET 3-5

LARRY & MIGHTY STORMS
Singles: 7-inch
ATCO 4-8 67

LARRY & MIKE
Singles: 7-inch
ERA (3135 "So Long Little Buddy") 10-15 64
PICADILLY (500 "Queen of the Starlight Dance") 75-125 63

LARRY & MONTCLAIRS
Singles: 7-inch
ZEST (750 "Jumping Rock") 8-12

LARRY & PAPER PROPHETS
Singles: 7-inch
EPIC (10186 "Can't Sit Around") 5-10 67

LARRY & REXETTES
Singles: 7-inch
ZORRO 4-8 66

LARRY & STANDARDS
Singles: 7-inch
LAURIE (3119 "Where Is She") 25-35 62

LARRY & TOM CATS
Singles: 7-inch
RUST 5-10 61

LARRY & UPSETTERS
Singles: 7-inch
GOLDEN WORLD (27 "Hurt Me") 10-15 65

LARRY & VICKY
Singles: 7-inch
FRATERNITY (3406 "Soul Salute to Elvis") 10-15 77

LARRY LEE: see LEE, Larry

LARSEN, Key
(With Frank Slay's Orchestra & Chorus)
Singles: 7-inch
LAWN (106 "A Little Lovin'") 20-30 61
Also see SLAY, Frank, & His Orchestra

LARSEN, Neil LP '79
Singles: 7-inch
A&M 3-5 79
W.B. 3-4 83
LPs: 10/12-inch
A&M 5-8 79
HORIZON 8-10 78-79
W.B. 5-8 83
Also see LARSEN - FEITEN BAND

LARSEN - FEITEN BAND P&R/LP '80
Singles: 7-inch
W.B. 3-5 80
LPs: 10/12-inch
W.B. 5-8 80
Members: Neil Larsen; Buzz Feiten.
Also see LARSEN, Neil
Also see MR. MISTER

LARSON, Duke
Singles: 7-inch
BANGAR 4-8 64

LARSON, Jack
Singles: 7-inch
FRATERNITY 5-10 59-61
Picture Sleeves
FRATERNITY 10-15 61

LARSON, Mike
Singles: 7-inch
CAMELLIA 10-15
TOM TOM (104 "Ghost Guitar") 10-20 60

LARSON, Neil
Singles: 7-inch
HORIZON 3-5 79

LARSON, Nicolette P&R/LP '78
Singles: 7-inch
MCA 3-4 85-86
W.B. 3-5 78-82
Picture Sleeves
W.B. 3-5 80
LPs: 10/12-inch
MCA 5-8 86
W.B. 5-8 78-82
Session: Michael McDonald, Steve Wariner.
Also see DOOBIE BROTHERS & Nicolette Larson
Also see McDONALD, Michael
Also see NITTY GRITTY DIRT BAND
Also see SHAVER, Billy Joe
Also see WARINER, Steve
Also see WINCHESTER, Jesse
Also see YOUNG, Neil

LARSON, Ron
Singles: 7-inch
FOX RIVER (1001 "We'd Have a Better Way") 5-10 70s

LA RUE, D.C. P&R/LP '76
Singles: 12-inch
CASABLANCA 4-6 79-80
PYRAMID 4-8 78-79
Singles: 7-inch
CASABLANCA 3-5 79-80
PYRAMID 4-6 76-79
LPs: 10/12-inch
CASABLANCA 5-8 79-80
PYRAMID 5-10 76-79
Also see CHRISTIE, Lou

LA RUE, J.R.
Singles: 7-inch
PIKE (5915 "I Know Better") 5-8 62

LA RUE, Roc, & 3 Pals
Singles: 78 rpm
RAMA (226 "Teenage Blues") 75-125 57
Singles: 7-inch
RAMA (226 "Teenage Blues") 75-125 57
Also see CARDELL, Johnny, & 3 Pals

LA RUE, Roger
Singles: 7-inch
HOLLAND (7421 "If I Were in Your Shoes") 50-75 58

LAS VEGAS CONVENTION
Singles: 7-inch
HEP ME 3-5

LAS VEGAS NIGHTS
Singles: 7-inch
MAGNA-GLIDE 4-8 77

LA SABERS
Singles: 7-inch
RAYNARD (10011 "Lonely Days") 15-25 65

LA-SABERS / Echoes / Stoney Kilroy
EPs: 7-inch
CO-OP (1001 "Goodbye Johnny") 15-25 64
Members: Bill Meusy; Terry Lee Oman; Ken Erdeman; Dennis Rinzel; David Wenca; Richard Bucholz.

LA SALLE, Denise P&R/R&B '71
Singles: 7-inch
ABC 3-5 77-79
CHESS 4-8 68
MCA 3-5 79-80
MALACO 3-4 81-85
PARKA 4-6
TARPON (6603 "A Love Reputation") 10-20 67
WESTBOUND 3-5 71-75
LPs: 10/12-inch
ABC 8-10 77-78
MCA 5-8 80
MALACO 5-8 81-85
WESTBOUND 8-10 72-75

LA SALLE, John, Quartet
EPs: 7-inch
CAPITOL 5-10 59
LPs: 10/12-inch
CAPITOL 15-25 58-59

LA SALLE, Lynn
Singles: 7-inch
A&M 10-15 67
HY NIBBLE 10-15 60s
Also see DAYBREAK

LA SALLE, Patti
Singles: 7-inch
MCI 5-10 60
MAGENTA 4-8 61

LA SALLES
Singles: 7-inch
MZ 5-10
V.I.P. 5-10 65

LASER
(Larry Chance & the Earls)
Singles: 7-inch
BVM (004 "He's Alive") 4-6 91
Also see EARLS

LA SEINE
LPs: 10/12-inch
ARIOLA AMERICA 8-10 76

LA'SHELL & SHELLETTES
Singles: 7-inch
EAGLE 4-8 66

LASHONS
Singles: 7-inch
VENDED 5-10 63

LASKY, Emanuel
(Emanuel Laskey)
Singles: 7-inch
NPC (303 "I Need Somebody") 30-40 63
THELMA (100 "Welfare Cheese") 15-25 63
THELMA (101 "Welfare Cheese") 15-25 63
THELMA (103 "Lucky to Be Loved") 100-200 64
THELMA (106 "Don't Lead Me On") 15-25 64
THELMA (108 "I'm a Peace Lovin' Man") 15-25 65
THELMA (110 "Run for My Life") 15-25 65
THELMA (2282 "I Need Somebody") 25-35 63
WESTBOUND (143 "More Love") 10-20 66
WILD DEUCE (1003 "Lucky to Be Loved") 20-30 60s

LASLEY, Clyde, & Cadillac Baby Specials
Singles: 7-inch
BEA & BABY (121 "Santa Came Home Drunk") 15-25 60

LASLEY, David P&R/R&B '82
Singles: 12-inch
EMI AMERICA 4-6 84
Singles: 7-inch
EMI AMERICA 3-4 82-84

LA SO
LPs: 10/12-inch
MCA 5-8 77

LA SONE, Jimmy
Singles: 7-inch
CHELSEA (3046 "Black Folks Love Country Music Too") 3-6 76

LASER
(Larry Chance & the Earls)
Singles: 7-inch
BVM (5789 "He's Alive") 3-6 91
Also see EARLS

LA SPADA, Vince
Singles: 7-inch
LAURIE 5-10 59
Also see SMOKEY / Vince La Spada

LASSER, Max
(Max Lasser's Ark)
LPs: 10/12-inch
CBS 5-8 88

LASSIES P&R '56
Singles: 78 rpm
DECCA 5-10 56
Singles: 7-inch
DECCA 8-12 56

LASSITER, Art
Singles: 7-inch
MARBO (0677 "Sum'n Nother") 100-150 62

LAST
Singles: 12-inch
BOMP 10-15 80
Singles: 7-inch
BACKLASH 10-20 78
BOMP 5-8 80
EPs: 7-inch
BOMP 5-8 79
LPs: 10/12-inch
BOMP 8-10 79

LAST, James P&R/LP '72
(James Last Band)
Singles: 7-inch
POLYDOR 3-5 71-82
LPs: 10/12-inch
POLYDOR 5-10 72-81

LAST CALL OF SHILOH
LPs: 10/12-inch
LAST CALL (5136 "Last Call") 100-150

LAST DRAFT
Singles: 7-inch
TRANSACTION (711 "It's Been a Long Time") 10-15 69
Picture Sleeves
TRANSACTION 15-25 69

LAST EPISODE
Singles: 7-inch
A&M 3-5 75

LAST FIVE
Singles: 7-inch
WAND (1122 "Kicking You") 10-20 66

LAST FRIDAY'S FIRE
Singles: 7-inch
L.H.I. 4-8 67

LAST KNIGHT
Singles: 7-inch
ORLYN (3520 "Shadow of Fear") 20-30 67

LAST KNIGHTS
Singles: 7-inch
PARIS TOWER (116 "The Way You Do the Things You Do") 20-30 67

LAST NIKLE
Singles: 7-inch
MAINSTREAM 4-6 69
LPs: 10/12-inch
MAINSTREAM 10-15 69
Also see McDANIEL, Lenny, & Last Nikle

LAST POETS LP '70
Singles: 7-inch
DOUGLAS 3-5 71
LPs: 10/12-inch
BLUE THUMB 8-12 72-73
DOUGLAS 10-15 70-71
Members: David Nelson;Gylan Kain; Felipe Luciano.

LAST RITUAL
Singles: 7-inch
CAPITOL (2495 "Delighted") 10-15 69
LPs: 10/12-inch
CAPITOL (206 "Last Ritual") 30-40 69

LAST WORD P&R '67
(Last Words)
Singles: 7-inch
ATCO 4-8 67-68
BOOM 4-8 66
DOWNEY 5-10 65
LPs: 10/12-inch
ATCO 10-20 68

LA STAZA, Pepe
Singles: 7-inch
EVEREST 3-4
Picture Sleeves
EVEREST 4-6

LATE BRONZE AGE
LPs: 10/12-inch
LANDSLIDE 5-8 81

LATE SHOW
LPs: 10/12-inch
RAVE (801 "Portable Pop") 15-20 80
Members: Mark Moran; Don Main; Rick Clayton; Chris Pyle.

LATEEF, Yusef LP '69
(Yusef Lateef Quintet)
Singles: 7-inch
ATLANTIC 3-5 68-70
IMPULSE 3-6 64
NEW JAZZ 4-8 60
PRESTIGE 3-6 63-69
LPs: 10/12-inch
ATLANTIC 8-15 68-76
CTI 5-8 77-79
CADET 10-15 69
CHARLIE PARKER 20-30 62
EVEREST 5-10 74
IMPULSE (56 thru 9125) 10-20 63-66
IMPULSE (9200 & 9300 series) 5-10 73-78
MILESTONE 8-12 73
MOODSVILLE 25-35 61
NEW JAZZ 25-40 59-61
PRESTIGE (7122 "The Sounds of Yusef Lateef") 50-100 57
(Yellow label.)
PRESTIGE (7400 thru 7800 series) 10-20 66-71
PRESTIGE (24000 series) 8-15 72-74
RIVERSIDE (300 series) 20-30 60
(Monaural.)
RIVERSIDE (3000 series) 10-20 68
RIVERSIDE (9300 series) 25-35 60
(Stereo.)
SAVOY (2200 series) 8-12 76-79
SAVOY (12000 series) 25-50 56-58
SAVOY (13000 series) 25-50 58
TRIP 5-10 73
VERVE (8217 "Before Dawn") 50-100 57
(Reads "Verve Records, Inc." at bottom of label.)
VERVE (8217 "Before Dawn") 25-35 60s
(Reads "MGM Records - a Division of Metro-Goldwyn-Mayer, Inc." at bottom of label.)

LATEERS
Singles: 7-inch
WORLD ARTISTS 4-8 63

LATHAM, Buddy C&W '88
Singles: 7-inch
PRAIRIE DUST 3-4 88

LATHAM, Tommie
(Tommy Latham)
Singles: 7-inch
BANNON 10-15 60s
DOT 4-6 69

LATIMORE, Benny R&B '73
(Latimore)
Singles: 7-inch
ATLANTIC 4-8 69
DADE 5-10 67-68
GLADES 3-6 73-79
HIT 4-6 60s
MALACO 3-4 83-86
LPs: 10/12-inch
GLADES 8-10 73-78
MALACO 5-8 83-86

LATIN LADS / Clif-Tones
Singles: 7-inch
CLIFTON ("Nunca") 4-8
(Selection number not known.)
Also see JULITO & LATIN LADS

LATIN QUARTERS
Singles: 7-inch
RED BIRD 5-10 64

LATIN SOULS
Singles: 7-inch
KAPP 4-8 67-68
LPs: 10/12-inch
KAPP 10-15 67-68

LATONS
Singles: 7-inch
PORT 10-15 62

LATORRE, Johnny
Singles: 7-inch
BLACK GOLD (4613 "Atomic Bounce") 50-75

LATTIMORE
LPs: 10/12-inch
TK DISCO 5-10 78

LATTIMORE, Almetta
Singles: 7-inch
MAINSTREAM (5575 "These Memories") 10-20

LATTIMORE, Carl "Little Rev"
Singles: 7-inch
CAPITOL 4-8 62

LATTISAW, Stacy R&B '79
Singles: 7-inch
COTILLION 3-5 79-84
MOTOWN 3-4 86-88
Picture Sleeves
MOTOWN 3-4 86
LPs: 10/12-inch
COTILLION 5-8 79-84
MOTOWN 5-8 86-88
Also see KING DREAM CHORUS & Holiday Crew

LATTISAW, Stacy, & Johnny Gill R&B/D&D/LP '84
Singles: 7-inch
COTILLION 3-5 84-85
LPs: 10/12-inch
COTILLION 5-8 84
Also see GILL, Johnny
Also see LATTISAW, Stacy

LAUDERDALE, Jim C&W '88
Singles: 7-inch
EPIC 3-4 88

LAUGHING DOGS
Singles: 7-inch
COLUMBIA 3-5 79
LPs: 10/12-inch
COLUMBIA 5-8 79-80

LAUGHING GRAVY
Singles: 7-inch
WHITE WHALE (261 "Vegetables") 30-40 67
Members: Dean Torrance; Rick Clingman; Durby Wheeler.
Also see ESQUIRES
Also see JAN & DEAN

LAUGHING KIND
Singles: 7-inch
HEAT WAVE (102 "Empty Heart") 15-25 67
JOX (66 "Show Me") 10-15 67
JOX (72 "Shotgun") 10-15 68

LAUGHING MATTERS
Singles: 7-inch
FUNTONE USA (23 "Tickets to Heaven") 15-25

LAUGHING SOUP DISH
Singles: 7-inch
VOXX 3-4 87
LPs: 10/12-inch
VOXX 5-8 87

LAUGHING WIND
Singles: 7-inch
TOWER 4-8 66

LAUNCHERS
Singles: 7-inch
CITE (5010 "Space Cowboy") 10-20 64
CITE (5011 "I See Her Face") 10-20 65
Also see LEE, Robin

LAUNDRY, Bill
Singles: 7-inch
SPINDLE 3-5

LAUPER, Cyndi P&R/LP '83
Singles: 12-inch
PORTRAIT 4-6 83-87
Singles: 7-inch
EPIC 3-4 88-89
PORTRAIT 3-4 83-88
Picture Sleeves
EPIC 3-5 88
PORTRAIT 3-4 83-87
LPs: 10/12-inch
PORTRAIT (Except 39610) 5-8 83-86
PORTRAIT (39610 "She's So Unusual") 20-25 83
(Picture disc.)
Also see BLUE ANGEL
Also see HOOTERS
Also see U.S.A. for AFRICA

LAURA
Singles: 7-inch
OVATION 3-5 71
LPs: 10/12-inch
OVATION 8-10 71

LAURA LEE: see LEE, Laura

LAURAN, Niki D&D '83
Singles: 12-inch
WAVE 4-6 83

LAURELS
Singles: 78 rpm
"X" (143 "Truly Truly") 50-75 55
Singles: 7-inch
"X" (143 "Truly Truly") 100-200 55
Member: Bobby Relf.
Also see BYRD, Bobby
Also see PEPPERMINT HARRIS
Also see PORTER, Jake, & Laurels
Also see RELF, Bobby

LAURELS
Singles: 7-inch
ABC-PAR (10048 "Picture of Love") 20-30 59
SPRING (1112 "Baby Talk") 35-50 59

LAUREN, Rod P&R '59
Singles: 7-inch
CHANCELLOR 5-10 62
RCA 8-12 59-62
Picture Sleeves
RCA 10-15 59-60
LPs: 10/12-inch
RCA (LPM-2176 "I'm Rod Lauren") 20-40 61
(Monaural.)
RCA (LSP-2176 "I'm Rod Lauren") 30-50 61
(Stereo.)
Also see COOKE, Sam / Rod Lauren / Neil Sedaka / Browns

LAURENCE, Paul R&B '85
Singles: 12-inch
CAPITOL 4-6 86
Singles: 7-inch
CAPITOL 3-4 85-86
LPs: 10/12-inch
CAPITOL 5-8 86
Also see JACKSON, Freddie
Also see THOMAS, Lillo

LAURENCE, T., & Sherwood Greens
Singles: 7-inch
BANGAR ... 10-20 60s
Also see ROSCOE & HIS LITTLE GREENMEN

LAURENZ, John / Starlighters
Singles: 78 rpm
MERCURY/SAV-WAY (3060 "Here We Are") ... 100-150 47
(Picture disc. Promotional issue only.)

LAURIE, Annie R&B '49
Singles: 78 rpm
DELUXE ... 5-15 47-57
REGAL ... 5-10 49
OKEH ... 5-10 55
SAVOY ... 5-10 56
Singles: 7-inch
DELUXE ... 10-20 57-60
DOVE ... 4-6 68
GUSTO ... 3-5 78
OKEH ... 10-15 55
RITZ ... 4-8 62
SAVOY ... 10-15 56
LPs: 10/12-inch
AUDIO LAB (1510 "It Hurts to Be in Love") ... 100-150 58

LAURIE, Bob
Singles: 7-inch
STEPHENY ... 8-12 58

LAURIE, Linda P&R '59
Singles: 7-inch
ANDIE ... 5-10 60
GLORY ... 5-10 59
KEETCH ... 4-8 64
RECONA ... 4-8 63
RUST ... 4-8 60-63
Also see DEL SATINS

LAURIE, Lou, & Harlequins
Singles: 7-inch
U.A. ... 10-15 61

LAURIE, Lynda
Singles: 7-inch
DYNOVOICE ... 4-8 68

LAURIE & SIGHS
Singles: 7-inch
ATLANTIC ... 3-5 80
LPs: 10/12-inch
ATLANTIC ... 5-10 80

LAURIE SISTERS P&R '55
Singles: 78 rpm
MERCURY ... 4-6 54-55
VIK ... 4-6 56
Singles: 7-inch
MGM ... 5-10 59-60
MERCURY ... 5-10 54-55
PORT ... 4-8 63
VIK ... 5-10 56
LPs: 10/12-inch
CAMDEN (CAL-545 "Hits of the Great Girl Groups") ... 15-25 60
(Monaural.)
CAMDEN (CAS-545 "Hits of the Great Girl Groups") ... 25-35 60
(Stereo.)

LAURRO, Jim
Singles: 7-inch
END (1023 "Jive Train") ... 10-20 58

LA VAH, Camille
Singles: 7-inch
WAX (18 "Let's Steal Away") ... 75-100
(Gold label, colored vinyl.)
WAX (18 "Let's Steal Away") ... 15-25
(Gold label, black vinyl.)
WAX (18 "Let's Steal Away") ... 3-6
(Green label.)

LAVANT, Jackie, & Fashions
Singles: 7-inch
PHIL-LA of SOUL (354 "What Goes Up") ... 8-12 72

LA VELL, Miss: see MISS LA VELL

LAVELLE, Ronnie
Singles: 7-inch
PARKWAY ... 4-8 61

LAVELLS
Singles: 7-inch
MERCURY ... 5-10 63

LAVENDER HILL EXPRESS
Singles: 7-inch
SONOBEAT (102 "Visions") ... 10-20 67
SONOBEAT (105 "Watch Out") ... 10-20 68
SONOBEAT (110 "Outside My Window") ... 10-20 68
Picture Sleeves
SONOBEAT (102 "Visions") ... 10-20 67
SONOBEAT (105 "Watch Out") ... 10-20 68
SONOBEAT (110 "Outside My Window") ... 10-20 68
Also see REASONS WHY

LAVENDER HILL MOB
Singles: 7-inch
U.A. ... 3-5 77
LPs: 10/12-inch
U.A. ... 8-10 77

LAVENDER HOUR
Singles: 7-inch
STEFFEK (619 "Hang Loose") ... 10-15 67
STEFFEK (1929 "So Sophisticated") ... 10-15 67
TRIBE (8323 "Hang Loose") ... 5-10 67
Also see CLIQUE

LAVENDERS
Singles: 7-inch
C.R. (1003 "Angel") ... 30-50 61
DOT ... 5-10 64
LAKE (706 "The Bells") ... 20-30 61
MERCURY (72126 "One More Time") ... 10-20 63

LAVENDERS
Singles: 7-inch
CUCA (1130 "Aw Shucks") ... 15-25 63
CUCA (1152 "Maria") ... 15-25 63
Also see LEE, Robin
Also see ROD & TERRY

LAVERNE, Charles
(Charley LaVerne & Spitfires)
Singles: 78 rpm
MARK ... 8-12 57
Singles: 7-inch
ABEL (224 "Spitfire") ... 10-15 59
LITE (9008 "The Shoot 'Em Up Twist") ... 10-15 62
MARK ... 10-20 57

LAVERNE, Thelma
Singles: 7-inch
NORTHERN ... 8-12

LAVERNE & SHIRLEY P&R '76
Singles: 7-inch
ATLANTIC ... 3-6 76-77
LPs: 10/12-inch
ATLANTIC ... 8-10 76
Members: Penny Marshall; Cindy Williams.

LAVETTE, Betty R&B '62
(Betty Lavett; Bettye LaVette)
Singles: 7-inch
ATCO ... 8-12 72-73
ATLANTIC ... 10-15 62-63
BIG WHEEL ... 5-10 66
CALLA ... 8-12 65
EPIC ... 3-5 75
KAREN ... 5-10 68-69
LUPINE (123 "Witch Craft in the Air") ... 20-30 64
LUPINE (1021 "Witch Craft in the Air") ... 10-20 64
MOTOWN ... 3-5 81-82
SSS INT'L ... 3-5 71
SILVER FOX ... 4-8 69-70
TCA ... 3-5 71
WEST END ... 4-8 78
LPs: 10/12-inch
MOTOWN ... 5-10 81

LA VETTES
Singles: 7-inch
PHILIPS ... 4-8 65

LA VON, Del
Singles: 7-inch
CAVALIER (870 "Rocking Chair Idol") ... 20-30 57

LAVORATO, Al
Singles: 7-inch
FLAME ... 5-10 59

LAW
Singles: 7-inch
MCA ... 3-5 77
LPs: 10/12-inch
GRC ... 10-12 75
MCA ... 8-10 77

LAW, Art
Singles: 7-inch
GULFSTREAM (1050 "Big Train") 50-75 50s
GULFSTREAM (1051 "Kitty Kat Rock") ... 100-200 50s

LAW, Johnny, Four
Singles: 7-inch
PROVIDENCE ... 10-20 67
Also see CORRENTE, Sal

LAW, Pamela
Singles: 7-inch
BOYD ... 4-8 60-62

LAW, Tommy
Singles: 7-inch
CREST (1055 "Cool Juice") ... 15-25 58

LAW BROTHERS & OUTLAWS
Singles: 7-inch
GLENN (3500 "Sweet Little Thing") ... 10-20

LAW FIRM
Singles: 7-inch
IMPERIAL ... 4-8 65

LAWHON, Jan
Singles: 7-inch
BOYD ... 4-8 64

LAWNING, Mike, & Dissonaires
Singles: 7-inch
ALTAIR (101 "One Love") ... 50-75

LAWRENCE, Bernie
Singles: 7-inch
U.A. ... 4-8 61
W.B. ... 4-8 61

LAWRENCE, Bill
(With the Lawrence Brothers)
Singles: 7-inch
BERTRAM INT'L (207 "Hey Baby") ... 100-125 59
BERTRAM INT'L (227 "Please Don't Leave Me") ... 40-60 60
FREEDOM (44004 "Hey Baby") ... 100-150 58
LP: 10/12-inch
TOPS ... 10-20
Also see LAWRENCE BROTHERS COMBO

LAWRENCE, Bill, & Five Finks
Singles: 7-inch
BERTRAM INT'L (227 "Please Don't Leave Me") ... 30-50 64
Also see LAWRENCE, Bill
Also see FIVE FINKS

LAWRENCE, Bob
Singles: 7-inch
MARK-X ... 8-15

LAWRENCE, Eddie P&R '56
Singles: 78 rpm
CORAL ... 3-5 56-57
Singles: 7-inch
CORAL ... 4-8 56-63
EPIC ... 4-6 65
SHASTA ... 4-8 60
SIGNATURE ... 4-8 60
Picture Sleeves
CORAL ... 5-10 56
EPIC ... 4-8 65
LPs: 10/12-inch
CORAL ... 15-25 55-62
EPIC ... 8-15 65
SIGNATURE ... 10-20 59

LAWRENCE, Karen, & Pins
Singles: 7-inch
RCA ... 3-5 81
LPs: 10/12-inch
RCA ... 5-8 81
Promotional LPs
RCA ("Special Radio Series") ... 10-15 81

LAWRENCE, Larry
(With the Hub Caps)
Singles: 7-inch
BALBOA ... 5-10 59-60
KING ... 5-10 59

LAWRENCE, Mark
Singles: 7-inch
JERDEN ... 4-8 60s

LAWRENCE, Robby
Singles: 7-inch
MGM ... 4-8 62

LAWRENCE, Steve P&R '52
Singles: 78 rpm
CORAL ... 5-15 55-57
KING ... 5-10 52-53
Singles: 7-inch
ABC ... 3-5 73
ABC-PAR ... 6-12 58-60
CALENDAR ... 4-8 67-68
COLUMBIA (Black vinyl) ... 5-10 62-68
COLUMBIA (42865 "Walking Proud") ... 15-25 63
(Colored vinyl. Promotional issue only.)
CORAL ... 10-20 55-59
KING (1200 series) ... 10-20 53
KING (5000 series) ... 4-8 60-64
KING (15000 series) ... 10-20 52-53
MGM ... 3-5 71-73
RCA ... 3-6 69-70
ROULETTE ... 3-5 73
STAGE 2 ... 3-4 84
20TH FOX ... 3-5 75-77
U.A. (200 & 300 series) ... 5-10 60-61
U.A. (900 thru 1100 series) ... 3-5 76-78
W.B. ... 3-5 78
Picture Sleeves
COLUMBIA ... 5-10 62-63
STAGE 2 ... 3-4 84
U.A. ... 10-15 60-61
EPs: 7-inch
COLUMBIA ... 5-10 64-69
(Juke box issues only.)
CORAL ... 5-10 60
(Juke box issues only.)
KING ... 10-20 53
RCA ... 4-8 70
LPs: 10/12-inch
ABC-PAR ... 20-30 57-60
APPLAUSE ... 5-10 81
COLUMBIA ... 10-25 63-68
COLUMBIA RECORD CLUB ... 8-15 75
CORAL (57050 "About That Girl") 20-40 56
CORAL (57182 "Songs By Steve Lawrence") ... 20-30 57
CORAL (57204 "Here's Steve Lawrence") ... 20-30 57
CORAL (57268 "All About Love") ... 20-30 58
(Monaural.)
CORAL (57434 "Songs Everybody Knows") ... 12-20 62
(Monaural.)
CORAL (757268 "All About Love") ... 20-40 58
(Stereo.)
CORAL (757434 "Songs Everybody Knows") ... 15-25 62
(Stereo.)
GALA ... 5-10 77
GUEST STAR ... 5-10 64
HARMONY ... 6-12 68-71
KING (593 "Steve Lawrence") ... 25-35 58
MGM ... 5-10 71
RCA ... 6-12 69-70
SESAC ... 10-20 59
SPINORAMA ... 8-15 63
U.A. ... 10-20 61-64
VERSATILE ... 5-8 77
VOCALION ... 5-12 66-69

LAWRENCE, Steve / Tennessee Ernie Ford
LPs: 10/12-inch
CAMAY ... 5-15 60
Also see FORD, Tennessee Ernie

LAWRENCE, Steve, & Eydie Gorme P&R '63
(Steve & Eydie)
Singles: 78 rpm
CORAL ... 5-15 55
Singles: 7-inch
CALENDAR ... 4-6 68
COLUMBIA ... 4-8 62-67
CORAL ... 10-20 55
MGM ... 3-5 72-73
RCA ... 3-5 68-69
EPs: 7-inch
ABC ... 10-15 60
(Juke box issues only.)
ADVERTISING COUNCIL (5071 "Celebrity Spots") ... 15-30
(Promotional issue, with other artists.)
COLUMBIA ... 5-10 64-69
(Juke box issues only.)
CORAL ... 10-20 58
LPs: 10/12-inch
ABC ... 5-10 73-76
ABC/LONGINES ("Romantic Treasury") ... 30-45 67
(Boxed, six-disc set.)
ABC-PAR ... 15-25 59-64
CBS ... 10-15 63
CALENDAR ... 8-15 68
COLUMBIA ... 10-20 63-67
CORAL (57336 "Steve & Eydie") ... 15-25 60
ENCORE ... 5-8 84
HARMONY ... 5-10 64-71
MCA ... 5-10
MGM ... 5-10 72-73
MATI-MOR (8003 "It's Us Again") ... 10-15
(Promotional issue made for Silvikrin Shampoo.)
PICKWICK ... 5-10 70s
RCA ... 6-12 69-72
STAGE 2 ... 5-10 78-84
U.A. ... 10-20 61-62
VOCALION ... 5-12 67
Also see GORME, Eydie
Also see OSMONDS, Steve Lawrence & Eydie Gorme

LAWRENCE, Steve / Trini Lopez
LPs: 10/12-inch
DIPLOMAT ... 10-15 65
Also see LAWRENCE, Steve
Also see LOPEZ, Trini

LAWRENCE, Suzie
Singles: 7-inch
UNITED AMERICAN ... 4-8 64

LAWRENCE, Syd, & Friends / Billy Mure
(With Bill Buchanan)
Singles: 78 rpm
COSMIC ... 10-20 58
Singles: 7-inch
COSMIC (1001 "Answer to Flying Saucer") ... 15-25 58
Also see BUCHANAN, Bill
Also see MURE, Billy

LAWRENCE, Tracy C&W '91
Singles: 7-inch
ATLANTIC ... 3-4 91

LAWRENCE, Vicki P&R/C&W/LP '73
Singles: 7-inch
BELL ... 3-5 73-74
ELF ... 4-6 69
FLASHBACK ... 3-5 74
PRIVATE STOCK ... 3-5 75-76
U.A. ... 3-5 71
LPs: 10/12-inch
BELL ... 8-12 73
WINDMILL ... 5-10 79

LAWRENCE, Walt
Singles: 7-inch
HOLLYWOOD INT'L (2 "Cascade") ... 20-30

LAWRENCE & ARABIANS
Singles: 7-inch
SHOUT ... 8-12 67

LAWRENCE & FIRST LOVES
Singles: 7-inch
PHILIPS ... 4-8 69

LAWRENCE BROTHERS COMBO
Singles: 7-inch
BERTRAM INT'L (213 "Puramid") .. 10-20 59
Member: Bill Lawrence
Also see LAWRENCE, Bill

LAWS, Debra P&R/R&B/LP '81
Singles: 7-inch
ELEKTRA ... 3-5 80-81
LPs: 10/12-inch
ELEKTRA ... 5-8 81

LAWS, Eloise P&R/R&B/LP '78
Singles: 7-inch
ABC ... 3-5 77-78
CAPITOL ... 3-4 82
COLUMBIA ... 4-6 68-70
INVICTUS ... 3-5 75-77
LIBERTY ... 3-5 80-81
MUSIC MERCHANT ... 3-5 72-73
Picture Sleeves
LIBERTY ... 3-5 80
LPs: 10/12-inch
ABC ... 8-10 77-78
CAPITOL ... 5-8 82
INVICTUS ... 5-10 76
LIBERTY ... 5-8 80

LAWS, Hubert R&B/LP '73
Singles: 7-inch
ATLANTIC ... 4-6 65
CTI ... 4-6 70-75
COLUMBIA ... 3-5 78
LPs: 10/12-inch
ATLANTIC ... 8-18 66-81
CTI ... 8-15 70-77
COLUMBIA ... 5-10 76-80

LAWS, Hubert, & Earl Klugh LP '80
LPs: 10/12-inch
COLUMBIA ... 5-10 80
Also see KLUGH, Earl
Also see LAWS, Hubert

LAWS, Lucky
Singles: 7-inch
ONE-DERFUL ... 4-8 64

LAWS, Ronnie R&B/LP '75
(With Pressure)
Singles: 7-inch
BLUE NOTE ... 3-5 75-77
CAPITOL ... 3-4 83-84
LIBERTY ... 3-5 80-81
U.A. ... 3-5 75-80
LPs: 10/12-inch
BLUE NOTE ... 6-12 75-77
CAPITOL ... 5-8 83
LIBERTY ... 5-10 81
U.A. ... 5-10 75-80
Also see EARTH, WIND, & FIRE
Also see PRESSURE

LAWSON, Bobby
Singles: 7-inch
M.R.C. (600 "Baby Don't Be That Way") ... 50-75 58

LAWSON, Chuck
Singles: 7-inch
AWARD ... 10-20 58

LAWSON, Janet C&W '70
Singles: 7-inch
U.A. ... 3-5 70

LAWSON, Jimmie
Singles: 78 rpm
COLUMBIA ... 5-10 47
Singles: 7-inch
FABLE (583 "Fickle Fool") ... 15-25 57
FABLE (584 "Ol' Jack Hammer Blues") ... 15-25 57

LAWSON, Robby
Singles: 7-inch
KYSER (2122 "Burning Sensation") ... 1000-2000

LAWSON, Shirley
Singles: 7-inch
BACK BEAT ... 10-20 66
ENTERPRISE ... 10-20

LAWSON, Teddy, & Lawson Boys
Singles: 7-inch
MANSFIELD (611 "There's No Return from Love") ... 500-750 57

LAWSON & 4 MORE
Singles: 7-inch
ARDENT (107 "Half Way Down the Stairs") ... 25-30

LAWTON, John
Singles: 7-inch
POLYDOR ... 3-5
Picture Sleeves
POLYDOR ... 3-5
LPs: 10/12-inch
RCA ... 5-8 81

LAWTON, Lou
(Moondog Lawton)
Singles: 7-inch
CAPITOL ... 4-8 66
HEART & SOUL ... 4-8 68
WAND ... 4-8 67

LAWTON, Lucius
Singles: 7-inch
LAURIE ... 5-10 63

LAWTON, Luke, & Chickadees
Singles: 7-inch
STARR ("Look What Tears Have Done") ... 35-50 60

LAY, Rodney C&W '81
(With Wild West)
Singles: 7-inch
CHAN ... 10-15 62
CHURCHILL ... 3-4 82-83
EVERGREEN ... 3-5 86
SUN ... 3-5 79-81
LPs: 10/12-inch
CHURCHILL ... 5-8 82
SUN ... 8-10 79-81

LAY, Sam
LPs: 10/12-inch
BLUE THUMB ... 10-15 68

LAYMEN
Singles: 7-inch
RISE ... 3-5

LAYNA, Magda D&D '83
Singles: 12-inch
MEGATONE ... 4-6 83

LAYNE, Herbie
Singles: 7-inch
GATEWAY (1253 "Rebel Rouser") ... 15-25 58

LAYNE, Joy P&R '57

Singles: 78 rpm

MERCURY 5-10 57

Singles: 7-inch

LUCKY FOUR 4-8 61
MERCURY 5-10 57
PHIL TONE 5-10

LAYNE, Sandy

Singles: 7-inch

LOMA 4-8 66

LAYNE, Valerie

Singles: 7-inch

NOLTA 4-8 61

LAYTONAIRS

Singles: 7-inch

TELA-STAR 10-15 63

LAZAR, Billy, & Woody Wagoners

Singles: 7-inch

SCARLETT (1 "Surfin' Around") 30-40 60s

LAZAR, Sam

Singles: 7-inch

CAWTHRON (507 "Space Flight") 10-20 65
CHECKER (1030 "I Ain't Mad at You") 10-20 62

LAZARUS

Singles: 7-inch

AMAZON 3-5 70
BEARSVILLE 3-5 71-73
MIDSONG INT'L 3-5 77

LPs: 10/12-inch

AMAZON 10-20 70
BEARSVILLE 10-15 71-73
MIDSONG INT'L 8-10 77

LAZARUS, Ken

Singles: 7-inch

STEADY 3-5 70

LPs: 10/12-inch

STEADY 8-10 70

LAZER BAND

LPs: 10/12-inch

ERECT 5-8 80-82

LAZY BILL & HIS BLUE RHYTHMS

Singles: 78 rpm

CHANCE 100-200 53

Singles: 7-inch

CHANCE (1148 "She Got Me Walkin' ") 300-500 53
Member: Bill Lucas.

LAZY COWGIRLS

Singles: 7-inch

BOMP 3-4 87

Picture Sleeves

BOMP 3-4 87

LPs: 10/12-inch

BOMP 5-8 87

LAZY EGGS

Singles: 7-inch

ENTERPRISE 4-8 65

LAZY FOUR

Singles: 7-inch

TAURUS 5-10 62

LAZY LESTER

(Leslie Johnson)

Singles: 78 rpm

EXCELLO 10-30 56-57

Singles: 7-inch

EXCELLO (2095 "I'm Gonna Leave You Baby") 30-40 56
(Orange & blue label. Company address at top.)
EXCELLO (2107 "They Call Me Lazy") 25-35 57
(Orange & blue label. Company address at top.)
EXCELLO (2107 "They Call Me Lazy") 15-25 58
(Orange & blue label. Company address at bottom.)
EXCELLO (2107 "They Call Me Lazy") 8-12 60s
(Red, white & blue label. No address shown.)
EXCELLO (2129 "I Told My Little Woman") 20-30 58
(Orange & blue label.)
EXCELLO (2143 "I'm a Lover, Not a Fighter") 20-30 58
(Orange & blue label.)
EXCELLO (2155 "Through the Goodness of My Heart") 50-75 58
(Orange & blue label.)
EXCELLO (2166 "I Love You, I Need You") 15-25 59
(Orange & blue label.)
EXCELLO (2182 "Bye Bye Baby") .15-25 60
(Orange & blue label.)
EXCELLO (2197 "You Got Me Where You Want Me") 15-25 61
(Orange & blue label.)
EXCELLO (2206 "I'm So Glad") 10-20 61
(Orange & blue label.)
EXCELLO (2219 "If You Think I've Lost You") 10-15 62
EXCELLO (2230 "Lonesome Highway Blues") 10-15 63
EXCELLO (2235 "You're Gonna Ruin Me Baby") 10-15 63
EXCELLO (2243 "A Word About Women") 8-12 64
EXCELLO (2274 "Take Me in Your Arms") 8-12 65
EXCELLO (2277 "Because She's Gone") 8-12 66

LPs: 10/12-inch

EXCELLO 10-20 67
Session: Lionel Torrence; Guitar Gable; Bruce Broussard; Katie Webster.
Also see WEBSTER, Katie

LAZY RACER P&R '79

Singles: 7-inch

A&M 3-5 79-80

LPs: 10/12-inch

A&M 5-10 79-80

LAZY SLIM JIM

(Edward Harris)

Singles: 78 rpm

SAVOY 15-25 52

Singles: 7-inch

SAVOY (854 "Georgia Woman") 25-50 52
SAVOY (868 "Slo Freight Blues") ... 25-50 52
SAVOY (887 "Wine Head Baby") 25-50 52
Also see CAROLINA SLIM
Also see COUNTRY PAUL
Also see JAMMIN' JIM

LAZY SMOKE

LPs: 10/12-inch

ONYX (6903 "Corridor of Faces") 1000-1200 67

LAZY SUSANS

Singles: 7-inch

KAPP 4-8 66

L'CAP-TANS

(With the "Go" Boys; L'Captans; with Frank Motley's Orchestra)

Singles: 7-inch

DC (0416 "Say Yes") 40-60 59
HOLLYWOOD (1092 "The Bells Ring Out") 200-300 58
SAVOY (1567 "Say Yes") 15-25 59
Also see CAP-TANS

LEA, Jim, & Inmates

Singles: 7-inch

MICKEY 4-8 69

LEACH, Billy P&R '57

Singles: 78 rpm

BALLY 5-10 57

Singles: 7-inch

BALLY 5-10 57
BREMNER 4-8 56

LEACH, C.J.

Singles: 7-inch

SHEILA 3-6 69

LEACH, Chuck, & XLs

Singles: 7-inch

4 SONS 5-10 63

LEACH, Lillian

(With the Jimmy Brokenshire Orchestra)

Singles: 7-inch

CELESTE (3002 "My "Darling") .400-600 56
Also see MELLOWS

LEADBELLY

(Lead Belly)

Singles: 78 rpm

ASCH 10-20
ATLANTIC (917 "Good Morning Blues") 30-50 50
BLUEBIRD 10-20
CAPITOL 10-15 50s
MUSICRAFT 5-10

Singles: 7-inch

ABC 3-5 76

EPs: 7-inch

CAPITOL (369 "Classics in Jazz") .. 15-25 53

LPs: 10/12-inch

ALLEGRO (4027 "Sinful Songs") ... 30-50
ARCHIVE of FOLK MUSIC 12-15 65
CAPITOL (H-369 "Classics in Jazz") 40-50 53
(10-inch LP.)
CAPITOL (1800 series) 15-25 62
COLUMBIA 8-10 70
ELEKTRA 15-20 66
FANTASY 8-10 73
FOLKWAYS (4 "Memorial Album, Vol. 1: Take This Hammer") 20-35 51
(10-inch LP.)
FOLKWAYS (14 "Memorial Album, Vol. 2: Rock Island Line") 20-40 51
(10-inch LP.)
FOLKWAYS (24 "Memorial Album, Vol. 3") 20-40 51
FOLKWAYS (34 "Memorial Album, Vol. 4") 20-40 51
FOLKWAYS (42 "Last Sessions, Vols. 1 and 2") 20-40 53
FOLKWAYS (2004 "Memorial Album, Vol. 1: Take This Hammer") 15-25 60s
(10-inch LP. With bio insert.)
FOLKWAYS (2014 "Memorial Album, Vol. 2: Rock Island Line") 15-25 60s
(10-inch LP. With bio insert.)
FOLKWAYS (2024 "Memorial Album, Vol. 3") 15-25 60s
(With bio insert.)
FOLKWAYS (2034 "Memorial Album, Vol. 4") 15-25 60s
(With bio insert.)
Note: The four LPs in the 2000 series are difficult to date. Folkways 2014 has, for example, "copyright 1951" on the bio insert; "copyright 1953" on the label; and another insert with a zip code in the address. Zip codes were not in use before 1963.
FOLKWAYS (2900 series) 10-20 63-65
FOLKWAYS (3000 series) 10-15 67-68
OLYMPIC 8-12 73
PLAYBOY 10-20 73-75
RCA (505 "Midnight Special") 15-25 64
STINSON 30-50 53-57
SUTTON 8-10
VERVE/FOLKWAYS 10-20 63-67
Also see WHITE, Josh / Leadbelly / Bill Broonzy

LEADBELLY / Josh White / Sonny Terry

LPs: 10/12-inch

TRADITION 10-12 69
Also see LEADBELLY
Also see TERRY, Sonny
Also see WHITE, Josh

LEADER, Dottie

Singles: 78 rpm

ARCADIA (1951 "I Want a Pardon for Daddy") 15-25 49

LEADERS

(With Abbie Baker Orchestra)

Singles: 78 rpm

GLORY 20-40 55-56

Singles: 7-inch

GLORY (235 "Stormy Weather") ... 40-60 55
GLORY (239 "Nobody Loves Me") 50-75 56
GLORY (243 "Can't Help Lovin' That Girl of Mine") 50-75 56
Members: Harry Burton; Edward Alston; Nelson Shields; Joe Sheppard; Prince McKnight; Charles Simpson; Ronald Judge.
Also see CORVAIRS
Also see WESTSIDERS

LEADERS

Singles: 7-inch

PIV (1014 "Singapore Passage") ... 10-15 50s

LEADERS

Singles: 7-inch

BLUE ROCK 3-5 68

LEADERS

Singles: 7-inch

VOLT 3-6 71-72

LEADERS

Singles: 7-inch

SOUTH STAR 4-8
Member: J.D. Cash.
Also see CASH, J.D.

LEADON, Bernie LP '77

(With the Michael Georgiades Band)

Singles: 7-inch

ASYLUM 3-5 77

LPs: 10/12-inch

ASYLUM 8-10 77
Also see BROOKS, Denny
Also see EAGLES
Also see MAUNDY QUINTET

LEAGUE UNLIMITED ORCHESTRA LP '82

Singles: 7-inch

A&M 3-4 82

LPs: 10/12-inch

A&M 5-8 82
Also see HUMAN LEAGUE

LEAHY, Joe

(With the Teen Starlets; Joe Leahy Orch.)

Singles: 7-inch

FELSTED 5-10 59
MGM 4-8 61
RPC 4-8 61
RING-A-DING 5-10 63
TOWER 4-8 65-66

LPs: 10/12-inch

TOWER 15-25 66-67
Also see LINDEN, Kathy

LEAHY, Joe, & Jeannie Sheffield

LPs: 10/12-inch

SUNSET 4-8 71
Also see LEAHY, Joe

LEAK, Sid / Gary Wayne

Singles: 7-inch

AMERICAN SOUND (81687 "Candlelight Service Prayer") 3-4 87

Picture Sleeves

AMERICAN SOUND (81687 "Candlelight Service Prayer") 3-5 87

LEAKE, Lafayette

Singles: 7-inch

VAL (02 "Disgusted") 15-25 57

LEAL, Joey

Singles: 7-inch

CUB 4-8 62

LEANDROS, Vicky

LPs: 10/12-inch

AVCO 10-20
Also see VICKY

LEAP FROGS

(With Jimmy Johnson; Louis Campbell)

Singles: 78 rpm

EXCELLO (2014 "Dirty Britches") .. 20-30 54

Singles: 7-inch

EXCELLO (2014 "Dirty Britches") 75-125 54
Also see CAMPBELL, Louis

LEAPER, Bob

(With the Prophets)

Singles: 7-inch

REPRISE (0274 "Come and Join Us") 4-8 64

LPs: 10/12-inch

LONDON (3391 "Big Band Beatle Songs") 15-20 64
(Monaural.)
LONDON (44056 "Big Band Beatle Songs") 15-20 64
(Stereo.)

LEAPING FERNS

(Chantays)

Singles: 7-inch

X-P-A-N-D-E-D SOUND (103 "Maybe Baby") 20-30 65
Also see CHANTAYS

LEAPING FLAMES

Singles: 7-inch

MRC (1201 "It's Been So Long") 200-300 60s
MAH'S (8 "Dance Social") 75-125 61

LEAPY LEE C&W/P&R '68

Singles: 7-inch

CADET 4-6 69
DECCA 4-8 68-71
MAM 3-5 72
MCA 3-5 75

Picture Sleeves

MCA 3-5 75

LPs: 10/12-inch

DECCA 10-20 68-70

LEARY, Dr. Timothy, PH.D.

LPs: 10/12-inch

DOUGLAS (1 "You Can Be Anyone This Time Around") 25-35 60s
E.S.P. (1027 "Turn On, Tune In, Drop Out") 35-50 66
MERCURY (21131 "Turn On, Tune In, Drop Out") 20-25 67
(Monaural. Soundtrack.)
MERCURY (61131 "Turn On, Tune In, Drop Out") 25-30 67
(Stereo. Soundtrack.)
PIXIE (1069 "L.S.D.") 50-75 66

LEASEBREAKERS

Singles: 7-inch

U.A. 4-8 65-66

LPs: 10/12-inch

U.A. 15-20 65

LEATHER BOY

(Leather Boy Milan)

Singles: 7-inch

FLOWER (100 "My Prayer") 30-40 66
MGM (13724 "I'm a Leather Boy") 20-30 67
MGM (13790 "On the Go") 20-30 67
PARKWAY (125 "Jersey Thursday") 20-30 66
Also see MILAN

LEATHER PAGES

Singles: 7-inch

BUSY-B ("Accept Me for What I Am") 10-20 68
(Selection number not known.)

LEATHERCOATED MINDS

LPs: 10/12-inch

VIVA (36003 "Trip Down Sunset Strip") 50-75 67
Members: J.J. Cale; Roger Tillison; Terry Tillison.
Also see CALE, J.J.
Also see GYPSY TRIPS

LEATHERWOLF LP '88

LPs: 10/12-inch

ISLAND 5-8 88-89

LEATHERWOOD

Singles: 7-inch

LEMCO (103078 "Midnight Breakdown") 10-20 65

LEATHERWOOD, Alan

LPs: 10/12-inch

MOON 8-10 85-86
Also see CASSARO, Al
Also see KING, Tom, & Starfires

LEATHERWOOD, Bill C&W '60

Singles: 7-inch

COUNTRY JUBILEE 5-8 60

LEATHERWOOD, Patti C&W '76

Singles: 7-inch

EPIC 3-5 76-77

LEAVES P&R/LP '66

Singles: 7-inch

CAPITOL (5799 "Lemon Princess") 8-12 66
MIRA (202 "Too Many People") 10-20 65
MIRA (207 "Hey Joe, Where You Gonna Go") 10-20 65
MIRA (213 "You Better Move On") ... 5-10 66
MIRA (222 "Hey Joe"/"Funny Little World") 5-10 66
MIRA (222 "Hey Joe"/"Girl from the East") 5-10 66
MIRA (227 "Too Many People") 5-8 66
MIRA (231 "Get Out of My Life Woman") 5-10 66
MIRA (234 "You Better Move On") .. 5-10 66
PANDA (1003 "Hey Joe") 8-12 82
(Colored vinyl on one side, picture on flip. Leaf-shaped disc.)

LPs: 10/12-inch

CAPITOL (T-2638 "All the Good That's Happening") 25-50 67
(Monaural.)
CAPITOL (ST-2638 "All the Good That's Happening") 30-60 67
(Stereo.)
MIRA (LP-3005 "Hey Joe") 25-35 66
(Monaural.)
MIRA (LPS-3005 "Hey Joe") 30-40 66
(Stereo.)
Members: John Beck; Bob Arlin; Jim Pons; Tom Ray; Bill Rheinhart; Robert Reiner; Jim Kern.
Also see ARLIN, Bob
Also see MERRY-GO-ROUND
Also see MOTHERS of INVENTION
Also see TURTLES

LEAVES OF GRASS

Singles: 7-inch

PLATINUM (2001 "All This Is Right") 10-20 60s

LEAVES OF GRASS

Singles: 7-inch

MAAD (2668 "Crabs") 60-80 68

LEAVILL, Otis R&B '65

(Otis Leaville)

Singles: 7-inch

BLUE ROCK 8-12 65
BRUNSWICK 5-10 67
COLUMBIA 8-12 66
DAKAR 4-8 69-70
LIMELIGHT (3020 "I'm Amazed") .. 10-20 64
LIMELIGHT (3037 "Jane Girl") 10-20 64
LUCKY (1004 "Got a Right to Cry") 25-40 64
SMASH 4-8 68

LEAVY, Calvin R&B '70

Singles: 7-inch

BLUE FOX (100 "Cummins Prison Farm") 5-10 70
DOWNTOWN 4-6 76
SOUL BEAT 10-20 66
SSS INT'L 4-8
Also see SCOTT, Calvin

LE BAN, Sue

Singles: 7-inch

PROMO (6112 "Slave Girl") 5-8

LeBEAU, Tim C&W '88

Singles: 7-inch

ROSE HILL 3-4 88

LE BLANC

(Mel Blanc as "Pepé Le Pew")

Singles: 78 rpm

CAPITOL 10-15 53

Singles: 7-inch

CAPITOL (2635 "I'm in the Mood for Love") 20-30 53
Also see BLANC, Mel

LE BLANC, Lenny P&R '77

Singles: 7-inch

BIG TREE 3-6 76-77
CAPITOL 3-5 81

LPs: 10/12-inch

BIG TREE 8-12 76-77
CAPITOL 5-10 81
Also see WHALEFEATHERS

LE BLANC & CARR LP '78

Singles: 7-inch

BIG TREE 3-5 77-78

LPs: 10/12-inch

ATLANTIC (003 "Live from the Atlantic Studios") 8-12 78
(Promotional issue only.)
BIG TREE 8-10 77
Members: Lenny LeBlanc; Pete Carr.
Also see CARR, Pete
Also see LE BLANC, Lenny

LE BOEUF BROTHERS

Singles: 7-inch

CHROMA 5-10 63

LE BON, Pierre

Singles: 7-inch

AMY 4-8 62

LEBSOCK, Jack C&W '73

Singles: 7-inch

CAPITOL 3-5 73-74
Also see GRAYSON, Jack

LECEA, Richie

LPs: 10/12-inch

WOODEN NICKEL 8-10 74-75

LECHNER, Chuck, 'N' His Gators: see GATORS

LECTRIC WOODS

Singles: 7-inch

APT 4-6 69

LED ZEPPELIN P&R/LP '69

Singles: 7-inch

ATLANTIC (2613 "Good Times Bad Times") 10-15 69
ATLANTIC (2690 "Whole Lotta Love") 5-8 69
(Edited version [3:12].)
ATLANTIC (2777 "The Immigrant Song"/"Hey Hey, What Can I Do") 15-25 70
(Has "Do What Thou Wilt Shall Be the Whole of the Law" etched in the vinyl trail-off.)
ATLANTIC (2777 "The Immigrant Song"/"Hey Hey, What Can I Do") 10-15 70
(Does not have "Do What Thou Wilt Shall Be the Whole of the Law" etched in the vinyl trail-off.)
ATLANTIC (2849 "Black Dog") 5-10 71
ATLANTIC (2865 "Rock & Roll") 5-10 72
ATLANTIC (2970 "Over the Hills and Far Away") 5-10 73
ATLANTIC (2986 "D'yer Mak'er") 5-10 73
ATLANTIC (13116 "Whole Lotta Love") 4-6 70s
ATLANTIC (13131 "The Immigrant Song") 4-6 70s
ATLANTIC (13129 "Black Dog") 4-6 70s

ATLANTIC (13130 "Rock & Roll") 4-6 70s
Note: Atlantic 13000 numbers are "Oldies Series" reissues.
SWAN SONG (70102 "Trampled Under Foot") 4-6 75
SWAN SONG (70110 "Candy Store Rock") 4-6 76
SWAN SONG (71003 "Fool in the Rain") 4-6 76

Picture Sleeves

ATLANTIC (175 "Stairway to Heaven") 50-75 72
(Promotional issue only.)

Promotional Singles

ATLANTIC (157 "Gallows Pole") 50-75 71
ATLANTIC (175 "Stairway to Heaven") 50-75 72
ATLANTIC (269 "Stairway to Heaven") 20-30 77
ATLANTIC (1019 "Dazed and Confused") 75-100 69
(With picture sleeve.)
ATLANTIC (2613 "Good Times Bad Times") 25-35 69
(Black and white label.)
ATLANTIC (2613 "Good Times Bad Times") 20-30 69
(Red and white label.)
ATLANTIC (2690 "Whole Lotta Love"/"Living Loving Maid") 15-25 69
ATLANTIC (2690 "Whole Lotta Love" [5:33] /Whole Lotta Love" [3:12]) 25-35 69
ATLANTIC (2777 "The Immigrant Song"/"The Immigrant Song") 15-25 70
ATLANTIC (2777 "The Immigrant Song"/ "Blank) 15-25 70
(Single-sided.)
ATLANTIC (2849 "Black Dog") 15-20 71
ATLANTIC (2865 "Rock & Roll") 15-20 72
ATLANTIC (2970 "Over the Hills and Far Away") 10-20 73
ATLANTIC (2986 "D'yer Mak'er") 10-20 73
SWAN SONG (70102 "Trampled Under Foot") 10-15 75
SWAN SONG (70110 "Candy Store Rock") 10-15 76
SWAN SONG (71003 "Fool in the Rain") 10-15 76
(Blue label. Side one runs 6:08; side two is edited [3:20].)
SWAN SONG (71003 "Fool in the Rain") 8-12 76
(White label. Both sides run 6:08.)

EPs: 7-inch

ATLANTIC (7-7208 "Led Zeppelin") 50-75 71
(Juke box issue only.)
ATLANTIC (7-7255 "Houses of the Holy") 50-75 73
(Juke box issue only.)

LPs: 10/12-inch

ATLANTIC (7201 "Led Zeppelin III") 10-15 70
ATLANTIC (7208 "Led Zeppelin IV") 10-15 71
(Their fourth LP though no title is actually shown on cover.)
ATLANTIC (7255 "Houses of the Holy") 15-20 73
(With "Led Zeppelin paper band around cover.)
ATLANTIC (7255 "Houses of the Holy") 10-15 73
(Without "Led Zeppelin paper band around cover.)
ATLANTIC (8216 "Led Zeppelin") 50-100 69
(Pink and brown label.)
ATLANTIC (8216 "Led Zeppelin") .. 10-20 69
(Red and green label.)
ATLANTIC (8236 "Led Zeppelin II") 10-15 69
ATLANTIC (19126 "Led Zeppelin") . 5-10 80s
ATLANTIC (19127 "Led Zeppelin II") 5-10 80s
ATLANTIC (19128 "Led Zeppelin III") 5-10 80s
ATLANTIC (19129 "Led Zeppelin IV") 5-10 80s
ATLANTIC (19130 "Houses of the Holy") 5-10 80s
ATLANTIC (82144 "Led Zeppelin") 50-75
(Boxed, six-disc set. Includes 36-page booklet.)
ATLANTIC MUSIC SERVICE 10-15 69
(Record club issue.)
MFSL (065 "Led Zeppelin II") 25-50 82
SWAN SONG (2-200 "Physical Graffiti") 10-15 75
SWAN SONG (2-201 "The Song Remains the Same") 10-15 76
(Embossed print on cover. With bound-in eight-page booklet. Soundtrack.)
SWAN SONG (2-201 "The Song Remains the Same") 8-12 76
(Standard, not-embossed, cover.)
SWAN SONG (8416 "Presence") 8-12 76
SWAN SONG (16002 "In Through the Out Door") 8-12 79
SWAN SONG (90051 "Coda") 8-10 82

Promotional LPs

ATLANTIC (7201 "Led Zeppelin III") 100-150 70
(White label. Monaural.)
ATLANTIC (7201 "Led Zeppelin III") 100-150 70
(White label. Stereo.)
ATLANTIC (7208 "Led Zeppelin IV") 100-150 71
(White label. No title actually shown on cover; however, it was their fourth LP.)
ATLANTIC (7225 "Houses of the Holy") 100-150 73
(White label. Monaural.)
ATLANTIC (7225 "Houses of the Holy") 100-150 73
(White label. Stereo.)
ATLANTIC (8216 "Led Zeppelin") 100-150 69
(White label.)
ATLANTIC (8236 "Led Zeppelin II") 100-150 69
(White label.)
SWAN SONG (200 "Physical Graffiti") 15-20 75
(With "FT" suffix.)
SWAN SONG (2-201 "The Song Remains the Same") 15-20 76
(With "MO" suffix.)
SWAN SONG (8416 "Presence") 10-20 76
(With "MO" suffix.)
SWAN SONG (16002 "In Through the Out Door") 10-15 79
(With "MO" suffix.)
SWAN SONG (90051 "Coda") 10-12 82
(With designate promo stamping on back cover.)
Members: Robert Plant; Jimmy Page; John Paul Jones; John Bonham.
Also see BAND of JOY
Also see DENNY, Sandy
Also see HARPER, Roy
Also see JONES, John Paul
Also see PAGE, Jimmy
Also see PLANT, Robert

LED ZEPPELIN / King Curtis

Singles: 7-inch

ATLANTIC/ATCO (2690/6779 "Whole Lotta Love") 40-50 71
(Promotional issue only. Atlantic label on Zep side; Atco label on flip, King Curtis' version of same song.)
Also see KING CURTIS
Also see LED ZEPPELIN

LEDERNACKEN D&D '84

Singles: 12-inch

4TH & BROADWAY 4-6 84

LEDFORD, Susan C&W '89

Singles: 7-inch

PROJECT ONE 3-4 89

LEDGENDS

Singles: 7-inch

LOCKET (756 "Fear Not") 15-25

LEDO, Les

(With His Consorts; with Jerry Bruno Orchestra)

Singles: 7-inch

NINA (1601 "Nina") 50-75 59
SHELL (721 "Scarlet Angel") 25-30 60
Members: Les Ledo; Nick Marco; Joe Walsh; Dennis Conboy; Bob Fava.
Also see MARCO, Nick, & Venetians

LeDOUX, Chris C&W '79

Singles: 7-inch

CAPITOL 3-4 90s
LUCKY MAN 3-5 73-80

LPs: 10/12-inch

LUCKY MAN 5-12 73-80

LEE: see MARENO, Lee

LEE, Ada

LPs: 10/12-inch

ATCO 15-25 61

LEE, Addie

Singles: 7-inch

END (1018 "Please Buy My Record") 15-25 58
KAPP 4-8 59
ROULETTE 10-15 57

LEE, Alan

Singles: 7-inch

JEAN (1001 "Broken Hearted Baby") 25-50 58

LEE, Albert

Singles: 7-inch

A&M 3-5 79
BELL 5-10 69
Also see HEAD, HANDS & FEET

LEE, Alvin LP '75

(Alvin Lee & Company; with Ten Years Later)

Singles: 7-inch

COLUMBIA 3-5 74
RSO 3-5 79

LPs: 10/12-inch

ATLANTIC 5-8 80-81
COLUMBIA 10-12 73-75
LONDON 8-10 78
RSO 10-12 77-79
21 RECORDS 5-8 86
Also see TEN YEARS AFTER

LEE, Alvin, & Mylon LeFevre LP '74

Singles: 7-inch

COLUMBIA 3-5 74

LPs: 10/12-inch

COLUMBIA 10-12 73
Also see LEE, Alvin
Also see LE FEVRE, Mylon

LEE, Arthur

Singles: 7-inch

A&M 4-6 72
CAPITOL (4980 "Ninth Wave") 10-15 63

LPs: 10/12-inch

A&M 10-12 72
RHINO 5-8 81
Member: Charlie Karp.
Also see AMERICAN FOUR
Also see KARP, Charlie
Also see LOVE

LEE, Arty

Singles: 7-inch

FARGO (1060 "Shadago") 20-30 60s

LEE, Barry

(With the Actions; Barry Lee Show)

Singles: 7-inch

ASCOT 4-8 67
INDEPENDENCE 4-8 68
REDDA 5-10
VEEP 5-10 64
Also see WHITE, Barry

LEE, Bill

Singles: 7-inch

ACE 5-10 61
STA-SET (404 "Workingman's Prayer") 4-6 64

LEE, Billy

Singles: 7-inch

SELECT (734 "I Don't Wanna Make You Cry") 5-8 64

LEE, Billy, & Ramblers

Singles: 7-inch

NORTHWAY (1003 "Tijuana Stomp") 15-20 59

LEE, Billy, & Rivieras

Singles: 7-inch

CARRIE (1515 "Fool for You") 10-15 60s
HYLAND (3016 "Won't You Dance with Me") 15-25 64
Members: Mitch Ryder; Joe Kubert; Jim McCarty; Earl Elliott.
Also see RYDER, Mitch

LEE, Billy, & Rugbeaters: see BILLY LEE & RUGBEATERS

LEE, Bob

Singles: 7-inch

DOT 12-25
TRAC 5-8 65

LEE, Bob

(Bobby Lee Trammell)

Singles: 7-inch

SKYLA (1117 "You Mostest Girl") .. 10-20 61
Also see TRAMMELL, Bobby Lee

LEE, Bobby

Singles: 7-inch

CUCA 5-10 61-62
MUSTANG 4-8 62

LEE, Bobby R&B '66

Singles: 7-inch

A-B-S (106 "Miss Mary") 150-200
DECCA 5-10 60-61
FALEW 5-10 64
GOLD COAST INT'L 4-8 60s
MUSICOR 4-6 68-69
PORT 4-8 67
RAMCO 4-8 67
SAGE 5-10 60s
SUE 4-8 66
VISTONE 4-8 60s

LPs: 10/12-inch

LITTLE RICHIE 8-12 76
Session: Lloyd Green; Charlie McCoy; Pig Robbins; Bob Moore; Buddy Spicher; Buddy Harmon; Kelso Hersten; Billy Stanford; Nashville Edition.
Also see GREEN, Lloyd
Also see McCOY, Charlie
Also see MOORE, Bob
Also see ROBBINS, Hargus "Pig"

LEE, Booker, Jr.

Singles: 7-inch

FEDERAL (12321 "Rockin' Blues") 35-50 58

LEE, Brenda

(Brenda Lee Jones)

Singles: 78 rpm

APOLLO 10-20 56

Singles: 7-inch

APOLLO (490 "I Ain't Gonna Give Nobody None") 15-25 56
Also see JONES, Brenda

LEE, Brenda P&R/C&W '57

(With the Jordanaires; with Holladays)

Singles: 78 rpm

DECCA 20-50 56-58

Singles: 7-inch

DECCA (30050 "Jambalaya") 25-35 56
DECCA (30107 "Christy Christmas") 20-30 56
DECCA (30198 "One Step at a Time") 25-35 57
DECCA (30333 "Dynamite") 25-35 57
DECCA (30411 "One Teenager to Another") 20-30 57
DECCA (30535 "Rock-A-Bye Baby Blues") 20-30 57
DECCA (30673 "Ring-A My Phone") 25-35 58
DECCA (30776 "Rockin' Around the Christmas Tree") 10-15 58
DECCA (30806 "Bill Bailey") 10-15 59
DECCA (30967 "Sweet Nothin's") 8-12 59
(Price range of 30050 through 30967 is for black, pink or green label originals. Pink and green were promotional only. Decca multi-color labels in that series are $4 to $8 reissues.)
DECCA (31093 thru 32330) 5-10 60-68
DECCA (32428 thru 32975) 4-6 69-72
DECCA (34330 "Interview") 10-20 72
(Promotional issue only.)
DECCA (88215 "I'm Gonna Lasso Santa Claus") 20-30 56
(Decca "Children's Series.")
ELEKTRA 3-5 78
MCA 3-5 73-86

Picture Sleeves

W.B. 3-4 91
DECCA (30776 "Rockin' Around the Christmas Tree") 15-25 59
DECCA (30967 "Sweet Nothin's") .. 25-35 59
DECCA (31093 thru 32428) 5-15 60-69
DECCA (34000 series) 5-10 62
(Compact 33 stereo.)
DECCA (88215 "I'm Gonna Lasso Santa Claus") 30-40 56
(For either 45 or 78 rpm single sleeve.)

EPs: 7-inch

DECCA 10-20 60-65

LPs: 10/12-inch

CORAL 5-10 73
DECCA (4039 thru 4104) 20-35 60-61
(Monaural.)
DECCA (4176 thru 4755) 15-30 61-66
(Monaural.)
DECCA (4757 "10 Golden Years") 15-25 66
(Gatefold cover. Monaural.)
DECCA (4757 "10 Golden Years") 10-15 60s
(Standard cover. Monaural.)
DECCA (4825 thru 4955) 10-20 66-68
(Monaural.)
DECCA (8873 "Grandma, What Great Songs You Sang") 30-40 59
(Monaural.)
DECCA (74039 thru 74104) 25-40 60-61
(Stereo.)
DECCA (74176 thru 74755) 20-35 61-66
(Stereo.)
DECCA (74757 "10 Golden Years") 20-30 66
(Gatefold cover. Stereo.)
DECCA (74757 "10 Golden Years") 10-15 60s
(Standard cover. Stereo.)
DECCA (74825 thru 75232) 10-20 66-70
(Stereo.)
DECCA (78873 "Grandma, What Great Songs You Sang") 35-45 59
(Stereo.)
MCA (Except 700 series) 8-10 73-86
MCA (700 series) 5-8
PICKWICK 5-10 70s
TEE-VEE 5-10 78
VOCALION 10-15 67-70
WARWICK (5083 "Little Miss Dynamite") 5-10 80
(TV mail order offer.)
Session: Anita Kerr; Bob Moore; Boots Randolph; Jordanaires; James "Buzz" Cason.
Also see CASON, Buzz
Also see JORDANAIRES
Also see KERR, Anita
Also see KRISTOFFERSON, Kris, Willie Nelson, Dolly Parton, & Brenda Lee
Also see MOORE, Bob
Also see NELSON, Willie, & Brenda Lee
Also see RANDOLPH, Boots

LEE, Brenda / Carl Dobkins, Jr.

EPs: 7-inch

DECCA (38169 "Datesetters, U.S.A.") 15-25 60
(Celanese Special Products issue.)
Also see DOBKINS, Carl, Jr.

LEE, Brenda / Bill Haley & Comets / Kalin Twins / Four Aces

EPs: 7-inch

DECCA (7-2661 "Top Teen Hits") .. 15-25 59
(Stereo.)
Also see FOUR ACES
Also see HALEY, Bill
Also see KALIN TWINS

LEE, Brenda / Tennessee Ernie Ford

LPs: 10/12-inch

DECCA (9226 "Brenda Lee/Tennessee Ernie Ford Show for Christmas Seals") ... 20-30
(Promotional issue only.)
Also see FORD, Tennessee Ernie

LEE, Brenda, & Pete Fountain LP '68

Singles: 7-inch

DECCA 4-6 68

EPs: 7-inch

DECCA (734528 "Brenda & Pete") ... 5-10 68
(Juke box issue.)

LPs: 10/12-inch

DECCA 10-15 68
PICKWICK 5-10 70s
Also see FOUNTAIN, Pete

LEE, Brenda, & Oak Ridge Boys

Singles: 7-inch

MCA 3-5 82
Also see OAK RIDGE BOYS

LEE, Bryan, & Embers

Singles: 7-inch

TEST 10-20 60s

LEE, Buddy

(With the Satellites)

Singles: 7-inch

BRUNSWICK 5-10 62
COLUMBIA 8-12 64
SCO-INA 8-12 63

LEE, Buzzy

Singles: 7-inch

PAM 5-8

LEE, Byron

(With the Dragonaires; with Dragonairs; with Ska Kings)

Singles: 7-inch

ATLANTIC (2236 "Watermelon Man Ska") 10-20 64
BATA ("Bata Cha-Cha-Cha") 30-60
BRA 4-8
DRAGON 4-6 72
DYNAMIC 4-8
JAD 4-8 68
KING 4-8 67

LPs: 10/12-inch

ATCO 10-20 66
BMN 10-20
DYNAMIC 10-15
JAD 10-20 68
KENTONE 10-20
TOWERS HALL 10-20

LEE, Byron, & Danny Davis

Singles: 7-inch

MGM 4-8 64
Also see LEE, Byron

LEE, Calvin

Singles: 7-inch

JOSIE 4-8 69
MINIT 5-10 62

LEE, Carol

Singles: 7-inch

TRIUMPH 4-8 62
TRU SOUND 4-8 63

LEE, Chandy C&W '79

Singles: 7-inch

ODC 3-5 79

LEE, Curtis P&R '61

(With the KCP's)

Singles: 7-inch

ABC 3-5 74
DUNES (801 "California GL-903") 10-20 60
DUNES (1001 "Pretty Little Angel Eyes") 25-35 60
DUNES (2001 "Special Love") 10-20 60
DUNES (2003 "Pledge of Love") ... 10-20 61
DUNES (2007 "Pretty Little Angel Eyes") 10-20 61
DUNES (2008 "Under the Moon of Love") 10-20 61
DUNES (2010 "Let's Take a Ride") 10-20 61
DUNES (2012 "Just Another Fool") 10-20 62
DUNES (2015 "The Wobble") 10-20 62
DUNES (2017 "Afraid") 10-20 62
DUNES (2020 "Lonely Weekends") 10-20 63
DUNES (2021 "Pickin' Up the Pieces of My Heart") 10-20 63
DUNES (2023 "I'm Sorry") 10-20 63
HOT (7 "Gotta Have You") 25-35 60
MCA 3-4
MIRA (240 "Sweet Baby") 10-20 67
SABRA (517 "Let's Take a Ride") .. 15-25 61
WARRIOR (1555 "With All My Heart") 20-30 59

Picture Sleeves

DUNES (2003 "Pledge of Love") ... 20-30 61
Also see HALOS

LEE, Curtis

Singles: 7-inch

ROJAC (114 "Get in My Bag") 5-10 67

LEE, Damon, & Diablos

Singles: 7-inch

SOMA (1181 "Say Mama") 60-80 61

LEE, Danny

Singles: 7-inch

TIME 5-10 59
U.A. 4-8 62

LEE, Darron

Singles: 7-inch

HIP 4-8 69
MYRL 10-15 61
Also see RILEY, Billy Lee

LEE, Davey

Singles: 7-inch

EMGE (1050 "Need You") 15-25 60s
Also see FIVE DISCS

LEE, Denny

(Denny Lee Incorporated Plus)

Singles: 7-inch

AGE of AQUARIUS (1556 Searchin") 8-12 70
CUCA (1278 "Fortune Teller") 8-12 66
OWL 8-12 63-64

LEE, Denny

Singles: 7-inch

GOLDRUSH 8-12

LEE, Dick P&R '61

(With the Big Action Sound)

Singles: 78 rpm

ESSEX 4-8 54
VIK 4-8 56
"X" 4-8 55

Singles: 7-inch

ABC 4-6 67
ACTION 3-6
BLUE BELL 4-6 61
CAPITOL 4-6 68
CENTAUR 5-8 59
DOT 4-8 66
ESSEX 5-10 54
FELSTED 5-8 60
KAPP 4-6 69
MGM 5-10 59
METRO 4-8 65
ROULETTE 4-8 62-63
20TH FOX 4-8 65
VIK 5-10 56
"X" 5-10 55

Picture Sleeves

FELSTED 8-12 60

LEE, Dickey P&R/R&B/LP '62
(With the Collegiates; Dickie Lee)
Singles: 78 rpm
SUN (280 "Good Lovin' ")...............15-25 57
SUN (297 "Dreamy Nights")............20-30 57
TAMPA (131 "Dream Boy")............15-25 57
Singles: 7-inch
ABC..3-5 73
ATCO......................................4-8 68
DIAMOND..................................4-8 69
DICKIE LEE STORY.................15-20 77
(No label name or number used. Promotional issue only.)
DOT.......................................10-15 60
ERIC..3-5 70s
HALL......................................5-10 64
MERCURY..................................3-5 79-82
OLDIES 45................................4-6 65
RCA...3-5 70-78
RENDEZVOUS (188 "Stay True Baby")...............................15-25 62
SMASH....................................5-10 62-64
SUN (280 "Good Lovin' ")...........15-25 57
SUN (297 "Dreamy Nights")..........20-30 57
TCF..4-8 65
TCF HALL.................................5-10 64-65
TAMPA (131 "Dream Boy")............15-25 57
TRACIE.....................................4-8 67
LPs: 10/12-inch
RCA..6-12 71-76
MERCURY..................................5-8 79-80
SMASH....................................20-30 62
TCF HALL.................................15-20 65
Also see MIZZELL, Bobby
Also see SOME of CHET'S FRIENDS

LEE, Dickey, & Kathy Burdick C&W '81
Singles: 7-inch
MERCURY..................................3-4 81-82
Also see LEE, Dickey

LEE, Don C&W '82
Singles: 7-inch
CRESCENT..................................3-4 82

LEE, Donna
Singles: 7-inch
COLUMBIA..................................4-6 67-68
Picture Sleeves
COLUMBIA..................................4-8 68

LEE, Ed
Singles: 7-inch
HIGHLAND (1161 "Country Boy") ... 8-12 66

LEE, Eddy
Singles: 7-inch
U.A. (459 "There'll Be an Angel") 4-8 62

LEE, Emma Dell
Singles: 78 rpm
KHOURY'S (900 "How Much I Love You")..................................20-30 51

LEE, Floyd
Singles: 7-inch
ENTERPRISE (1234 "Go Boy") .100-150 59

LEE, Frankie
Singles: 7-inch
DORE...4-8 61

LEE, Frankie
Singles: 7-inch
CLARIDGE..................................3-5 75

LEE, Gary
Singles: 7-inch
TIME (1009 "Why")...................10-15 60s

LEE, Gene, & Blues Rockers
Singles: 78 rpm
MUSIC CITY..............................25-50 57
Singles: 7-inch
MUSIC CITY (803 "You're the One")..40-60 57

LEE, George
Singles: 78 rpm
BULLET....................................10-20 49

LEE, George E.
Singles: 7-inch
KAPP...4-8 63

LEE, Georgia
Singles: 7-inch
DECCA......................................5-8 60

LEE, Harold C&W '68
Singles: 7-inch
CARTWHEEL...............................4-6 71
COLUMBIA..................................4-6 68
ESTA (293 "Blond Headed Woman")...............................100-200 58

LEE, Harry
Singles: 7-inch
ACE..5-10 60-61
IGLOO (101 "Rockin' on a Reindeer")...........................150-200 58
VIN (Except 1007)........................8-12 59
VIN (1007 "You Don't Know").........50-75 58

LEE, Hayward
Singles: 7-inch
JAN-ELL....................................4-8 62

LEE, Herbie
Singles: 7-inch
EVENT......................................6-10 58

LEE, Hyapatia
Singles: 7-inch
SRO..3-4 86-88

LEE, Jack E., & Squires
(Jack Eley)
Singles: 7-inch
RCA...5-10 64
Also see ELEY, Jack, & Courtmen

LEE, Jackie
(Jackie Lee Orchestra)
Singles: 78 rpm
CORAL.......................................3-6 53
ESSEX.......................................3-6 53
Singles: 7-inch
CORAL......................................5-10 53
ESSEX......................................5-10 53
FAYETTE...................................5-10 64
OASIS.......................................5-10
SURE..5-10 61
SWAN.......................................5-10 59

LEE, Jackie P&R '59
Singles: 7-inch
SWAN..8-12 59

LEE, Jackie
Singles: 7-inch
SURE...4-8 61-62

LEE, Jackie P&R/R&B '65
(Earl Nelson)
Singles: 7-inch
ABC...10-20 68
FAYETTE...................................5-10 64
KEYMAN...................................5-10 67-68
MIRWOOD..................................5-10 65-66
UNI...3-6 70
LPs: 10/12-inch
MIRWOOD................................15-25 66
Also see BOB & EARL
Also see NELSON, Earl

LEE, Jackie, & Dolores Hall
Singles: 7-inch
MIRWOOD..................................4-8 66
Also see LEE, Jackie

LEE, Jackie
Singles: 7-inch
EPIC..4-8 65-67

LEE, Jackie, & Raindrops
Singles: 7-inch
JAYLEE......................................4-8 62
LONDON.....................................4-8 62

LEE, James Washington
Singles: 7-inch
L&M (1003 "I Need Somebody") 40-60 62

LEE, Jamie
Singles: 7-inch
J-LEE.......................................10-15

LEE, Jennie
Singles: 7-inch
AMY...4-8 62

LEE, Jenny: see JENNY LEE

LEE, Jerry, Trio
Singles: 7-inch
NORTHWAY (1001 "Warpath") 15-25 59

LEE, Jessie: see JESSIE LEE

LEE, Jimmy
(Jimmie Lee)
Singles: 78 rpm
CAPITOL (2491 "How About a Date")......................................10-15 53
FORTUNE..................................50-75 56
Singles: 7-inch
APOLLO......................................8-12 58
CAPITOL (2491 "How About a Date")......................................20-25 53
CLIX (100 "She's Gone")..............20-30
FORTUNE (191 "You Ain't No Good for Me")......................................75-100 56
VIN..10-15 58

LEE, Jimmy
Singles: 7-inch
BANDERA (2506 "Chicago Jump")......................................5-10 60
CANADIAN AMERICAN...................5-10 61

LEE, Jimmy (Robinson): see JIMMY LEE

LEE, Jimmy, & Artis R&B '52
Singles: 78 rpm
MODERN...................................10-20 52
Singles: 7-inch
MODERN (885 "Let's Talk It Over")......................................25-35 52

LEE, Jimmy, & Johnny Mathis
Singles: 78 rpm
CHESS......................................10-20 55
Singles: 7-inch
CHESS (4859 "If You Don't Somebody Else Will")......................................25-35 55
Also see LEE, Jimmy, & Wayne Walker

LEE, Jimmy, & Earls
Singles: 7-inch
BO-P-C.......................................5-8

LEE, Jimmy, & Wayne Walker
Singles: 78 rpm
CHESS (4863 "Love Me")............50-100 55
Singles: 7-inch
CHESS (4863 "Love Me")............150-250 55
Also see LEE, Jimmy, & Johnny Mathis
Also see WALKER, Wayne

LEE, Joe
Singles: 7-inch
ALLEY......................................5-10 63-65
FERNWOOD (108 "Ethel Mae").....15-25 58
FERNWOOD (112 "Hang-Out").....15-25 59
Member: Larry Donn.
Also see DONN, Larry

LEE, John
(John Arthur Lee)
Singles: 78 rpm
FEDERAL (10254 "Down at the Depot")..................................50-100 51
FEDERAL (10289 "Baby Blues")..50-100 51

LEE, John (John Lee Henley/Hooker): see JOHN LEE

LEE, Johnny C&W '75
Singles: 7-inch
ABC/DOT....................................3-5 75
ASTRO.......................................3-5 80
ASYLUM.....................................3-5 80-82
CURB...3-4 89
EPIC..3-5 81
FULL MOON/W.B...........................3-4 80-86
GRT...3-5 76-78
Picture Sleeves
ASYLUM.....................................3-5 80
LPs: 10/12-inch
ACCORD.....................................5-8 83
ASYLUM....................................5-10 80-81
FULL MOON/W.B...........................5-8 80-86
GRT..8-10 77
JMS..8-12
PLANTATION..............................5-10 81
Session: Deborah Allen; Michael Murphey; Charlie Daniels.
Also see DANIELS, Charlie
Also see GILLEY, Mickey, & Johnny Lee
Also see MURPHEY, Michael
Also see NELSON, Willie / Johnny Lee / Mickey Gilley

LEE, Johnny, & Lane Brody C&W '84
Singles: 7-inch
W.B...3-4 84-86

LEE, Johnny / Eagles
Singles: 7-inch
ASYLUM.....................................3-5 80-81
Picture Sleeves
ASYLUM.....................................3-5 80
Also see EAGLES

LEE, Johnny, Michael Martin Murphey, & Charlie Daniels C&W '82
(Johnny Lee & Friends)
Singles: 7-inch
FULL MOON.................................3-4 82
Also see DANIELS, Charlie
Also see LEE, Johnny
Also see MURPHEY, Michael

LEE, Joni C&W '75
Singles: 7-inch
MCA...3-5 75-78
LPs: 10/12-inch
MCA..5-10 76
Also see TWITTY, Conway

LEE, Joyce
Singles: 7-inch
JAYLEE (6601 "Tore Up")............10-15

LEE, Judi: see JUDI LEE

LEE, Judy
Singles: 7-inch
COLE..4-6
WASP...4-6

LEE, Julia R&B '46
(With Her Boy Friends; with Her Scat Cats)
Singles: 78 rpm
CAPITOL....................................10-20 46-52
DAMON (12151 "Scat You Cats")..10-20 53
Singles: 7-inch
CAPITOL (Except 2203)...............15-30 49-52
CAPITOL (2203 "Last Call for Alcohol")..................................35-40 52
DAMON (12151 "Scat You Cats")..15-25 53
EPs: 7-inch
CAPITOL (EBF-228 "Party Time")......................................50-75 50
LPs: 10/12-inch
CAPITOL (H-228 "Party Time")...75-100 50
(10-inch LP.)
CAPITOL (T-228 "Party Time").......50-75 55
Session: Baby Lovett; Tommy Douglas; Jim Daddy Walker; Clint Weaver; Vic Dickenson; Bobby Sherwood; Red Norvo; Red Callender; Dave Cavanaugh; Benny Carter; Jack Marshall.
Also see CALLENDER, Red

LEE, Katie
Singles: 7-inch
SPECIALTY.................................5-10 59
LPs:10/12-inch
HORIZON..................................15-20 60s

LEE, Kimo
Singles: 7-inch
ADDISON...................................5-10 60

LEE, King Ivory: see KING IVORY LEE

LEE, Larry
(With the Four Bel-Aires; with Frankie Valli)
Singles: 7-inch
COLUMBIA..................................3-5 82
GENIUS......................................4-8
M.Z. (006 "Stolen Love")............100-200 59
(First issued as *Can I Be in Love* and credited to the Four Bel'Aires.)
Also see FOUR BEL'AIRES
Also see OZARK MOUNTAIN DAREDEVILS
Also see VALLI, Frankie

LEE, Larry, & Leesures
(With the Infaturators)
Singles: 7-inch
CAMELOT....................................5-10
DESTINY (503 "Desire")............100-150 61
Also see INFATUATORS

LEE, Laura LP '72
Singles: 7-inch
ARIOLA AMERICA.........................3-5 76
ARLEN (732 "What's Done Is Done")......................................15-25 63
CHESS.......................................8-15 67-69
COTILLION..................................5-8 69
HOT WAX....................................3-6 71-73
INVICTUS....................................4-8 74
RIC TIC.....................................10-20 66
LPs: 10/12-inch
CHESS......................................10-20 72
HOT WAX....................................8-12 72-73
INVICTUS....................................8-12 74

LEE, Leapy: see LEAPY LEE

LEE, Leon R&B '74
Singles: 7-inch
CROSSOVER................................3-5 74

LEE, Little Frankie, & Saxons
Singles: 7-inch
GREAT SCOTT.............................5-10 63
PEACOCK....................................4-8 63-68

LEE, Little Mr., & Cherokees
Singles: 7-inch
SURE SHOT.................................4-8 64-65

LEE, Lois
Singles: 7-inch
OKEH (7119 "I've Got It Bad for You Baby")......................................10-15 59
Also see DEE, Joey, & Lois Lee
Also see ROCKETS

LEE, London
Singles: 7-inch
MR. G...4-8 67
LPs: 10/12-inch
PHILIPS.....................................10-15 69

LEE, Lonesome: see LONESOME LEE

LEE, Lonnie
Singles: 7-inch
APT (25071 "Marilyn").................15-25 58

LEE, Lorry: see LORRY LEE

LEE, Mamie
Singles: 7-inch
MGM..4-8 66

LEE, Marva
Singles: 7-inch
ATCO (6367 "If You Can't Be True")......................................15-20 65

LEE, Michele P&R '68
Singles: 7-inch
ABC-PAR.....................................4-8 62-63
COLUMBIA..................................4-8 65-69
LPs: 10/12-inch
COLUMBIA.................................10-20 66-68

LEE, Milliard
Singles: 7-inch
BLUES BOYS KINGDOM (105 "Waughely's Boogie")......................................30-40 57

LEE, Mr: see MR. LEE

LEE, Myron
(With the Caddies)
Singles: 7-inch
ABC-PAR...................................15-25 65
DEL-FI (4180 "Town Girl")............25-35 62
FELSTED (8570 "Rona Baby")......25-35 59
GARRETT (4009 "Summertime Blues")......................................25-35 60s
HEP (2076 "Rona Baby")..............50-75 59
(First issue.)
HEP (2146 "Homicide")..............100-150 60
JARO (77037 "From Now On")......40-60 60
KEEN (2104 "Come Back Baby")...20-25 59
M&L...20-25 62
NOR VA JAK (1326 "Blue Lawdy Blue")..................................100-150 60
QUALITY (1308 "Blue Lawdy Blue")......................................50-75 60
(Canadian.)
SOMA (114 "Mary's Swingin' Lamb")......................................50-75 59
LPs:10/12-inch
ML..8-12 80-83
UNLIMITED.................................5-10 84
Also see WINTER, Cyril

LEE, Nancy
Singles: 7-inch
ACME (711 "So They Say")..........50-75 57
ARC...10-15 63
Also see LOVE LETTERS

LEE, Nickie R&B '68
Singles: 7-inch
DADE..4-8 67
MALA..10-15 68-69

LEE, Notorious Rockin'
Singles: 7-inch
BOBBETTE (371 "My Baby Left Me")......................................5-10
Session: Scotty Moore.
Also see MOORE, Scotty

LEE, Peggy P&R '45
(With Benny Goodman's Orchestra)
Singles: 78 rpm
CAPITOL....................................5-15 41-58
OKEH...5-15 41-42
Singles: 7-inch
A&M..3-5 75
ATLANTIC...................................3-5 74
CAPITOL (801 thru 2000 series).....8-12 49-51
CAPITOL (2100 thru 3400 series).....3-6 68-72
CAPITOL (3800 thru 5900 series).....4-8 58-67
CAPITOL (90000 series)................4-8
COLUMBIA...................................3-5 76
DECCA (25000 series)...................4-6 64
DECCA (28000 & 29000 series)......4-8 52-58
DECCA (30000 series)...................4-8 58-59
EPs: 7-inch
CAPITOL (Except 100 series)........10-20 57-59
CAPITOL (100 series).................20-40 52
COLUMBIA..................................20-40 50-51
DECCA......................................15-30 52-55
LPs: 10/12-inch
A&M..5-8 75
ATLANTIC...................................5-8 74
CAMAY (3003 "Peggy Lee's Greatest")...................................10-15 50s
CAPITOL (183 "A Natural Woman")......................................8-12 69
CAPITOL (H-155 "Rendezvous with Peggy")......................................50-75 52
(10-inch LP.)
CAPITOL (T-155 "Rendezvous with Peggy")......................................25-50 55
CAPITOL (H-204 "My Best to You")......................................50-75 52
(10-inch LP.)
CAPITOL (377 thru 810)................5-10 69-71
CAPITOL (864 "The Man I Love")...20-40 56
CAPITOL (979 "Jump for Joy").......20-40 57
CAPITOL (T-1049 thru T-1969)......15-25 58-63
(Monaural.)
CAPITOL (ST-1049 thru ST-1969).20-30 58-63
(Stereo.)
CAPITOL (T-2096 thru T-2887).....10-20 64-68
(Monaural.)
CAPITOL (ST-2096 thru ST-2887)......................................10-20 64-68
CAPITOL (6600 series).................5-10 70
CAPITOL (11000 series)...............5-10 72-79
CAPITOL (16000 series)................4-8 80
COLUMBIA (6033 "Benny Goodman & Peggy Lee")......................................40-60 50
(10-inch LP.)
DRG..5-8 79
DECCA (DXB-164 "Best of Peggy Lee")......................................15-25 60
(Monaural.)
DECCA (DXSB7-164 "Best of Peggy Lee")......................................10-20 66
(Stereo.)
DECCA (DL-4000 series)..............10-15 64
(Monaural.)
DECCA (DL7-4000 series)............15-20 64
(Stereo.)
DECCA (5482 "Black Coffee").......50-75 53
(10-inch LP.)
DECCA (5539 "Songs in an Intimate Style")......................................50-75 53
(10-inch LPs.)
DECCA (8411 "Dream Street")......30-50 56
DECCA (8358 "Black Coffee")........30-50 57
DECCA (8591 "Sea Shells")..........30-50 58
DECCA (8816 "Miss Wonderful")....20-40 59
EVEREST.....................................5-8 74
GLENDALE..................................4-8 82
HARMONY (7000 series).............15-25 58
HARMONY (30000 series).............5-10 70
HORIZON (1004 "Best of Peggy Lee")......................................25-35 62
MERCURY...................................5-8 77
VOCALION..................................6-12 66-70
Also see CROSBY, Bing, & Peggy Lee
Also see FITZGERALD, Ella, & Peggy Lee
Also see GOODMAN, Benny, Orchestra
Also see JENKINS, Gordon, & His Orchestra

LEE, Peggy, & Dean Martin
Singles: 78 rpm
CAPITOL (15349 "You Was")........20-30 49
Also see MARTIN, Dean

LEE, Peggy, & George Shearing
Singles: 7-inch
CAPITOL......................................4-8 59
LPs: 10/12-inch
CAPITOL (1219 "Beauty and the Beat")......................................20-30 59
(Capitol logo on left side of label.)
CAPITOL (1219 "Beauty and the Beat")......................................10-20 62
(Capitol logo at the top of label.)

LEE, Peggy, & Mel Torme
Singles: 78 rpm
CAPITOL.....................................5-10 49
Singles: 7-inch
CAPITOL....................................10-15 49
Also see LEE, Peggy
Also see TORME, Mel

LEE, Perk
Singles: 7-inch
BOSS (2125 "The Docks")...........25-50 64

LEE, Peter
Singles: 7-inch
TOPAZ.......................................5-10

LEE, Pinky
Singles: 78 rpm
DECCA..5-8 55
Singles: 7-inch
DECCA.......................................6-12 55

Picture Sleeves
DECCA (301 "Yoo-Hoo It's Me") 10-20 55
DECCA (303 "Little Doggie with the Big Woof-Woof")....10-20 55

LEE, Randy
Singles: 7-inch
CUB.... 5-10 60
EVEREST.... 5-10 60-61
PHILIPS.... 4-8 62-63
SPANN.... 5-10 59

LEE, Richard
Singles: 7-inch
PARIS TOWER (104 "Cloudy Cool").... 5-10

LEE, Robert, & Exquisites
Singles: 7-inch
STEELTOWN (687 "Tears Are Falling")....15-25 69

LEE, Roberta *P&R '51*
Singles: 78 rpm
DECCA.... 4-6 51-54
TEMPO.... 4-8 50-51
"X".... 4-6 54
Singles: 7-inch
DECCA.... 5-10 51-54
TEMPO.... 5-10 50-51
TOWER.... 4-6 68
"X".... 5-10 54

LEE, Robin
(With Robins; with Royal Host; with Revels; with Wasau's Night Beats; with Jordanaires; with Anita Kerr Singers)
Singles: 7-inch
BIG SOUND.... 8-12 65-66
CIRCLE DOT (103 "Pretty Patty") 15-25 60
CITATION.... 4-8 65
ESU.... 5-10 72
KARRYE....10-20 61
PRO-GRESS.... 8-12 69
REPRISE.... 4-8 62-63
TEE PEE.... 8-12 68
USA.... 8-12 67
LPs: 10/12-inch
PRO-GRESS....15-25 69
STRAND....15-25 64
Members: Terry Christian; Rodney Means; Bob Oestreich; Jerry Suchomski; Curly Cooke.
Also see JORDANAIRES
Also see KERR, Anita
Also see LAUNCHERS
Also see LAVENDERS
Also see ROYAL HOST
Also see SCHENZEL, Roger, & Flav-o-rites
Also see WINSTON, Roger, & Plaids

LEE, Robin
Singles: 7-inch
DOT.... 5-10 65
LPs: 10/12-inch
DOT....15-25 65

LEE, Robin *C&W '83*
Singles: 7-inch
ATLANTIC.... 3-4 90-91
ATLANTIC AMERICA.... 3-4 88
EVERGREEN.... 3-5 83-86

LEE, Robin, & Lobo *C&W '85*
Singles: 7-inch
EVERGREEN.... 3-4 85
Also see LEE, Robin
Also see LOBO

LEE, Ronni
Singles: 7-inch
EVEREST.... 4-8 61

LEE, Roosevelt
Singles: 78 rpm
EXCELLO (2022 "Lazy Pete")....15-25 54
Singles: 7-inch
EXCELLO (2022 "Lazy Pete")....30-50 54

LEE, Ruby
Singles: 7-inch
POPTONE (1901 "I Believe in You")....15-20

LEE, Samantha
Singles: 7-inch
PEANUT COUNTRY....10-20

LEE, Sammy, & Summits
Singles: 7-inch
RAMPART.... 5-10 66

LEE, Sharon
Singles: 7-inch
JEWEL....10-20

LEE, Soul
Singles: 7-inch
ATLAS.... 4-8 66

LEE, Suzie
Singles: 7-inch
SEECO.... 4-8 59

LEE, T.C., & King Pins
Singles: 7-inch
FEDERAL (12525 "I'm a Lonesome Rooster")....10-20 64
Also see KELLY BROTHERS
Also see KING PINS

LEE, T.L., & Kathy Walker *C&W '87*
Singles: 7-inch
COMPLEAT.... 3-4 87

LEE, Teddy, & Tom Cats
Singles: 7-inch
LIBERTY.... 4-8 67

LEE, Terri, & Swinging 7 Colossal Communicators Chorus
Singles: 7-inch
SHAMROCK.... 4-8

LEE, Terry
Singles: 7-inch
KSWO....5-10 61

LEE, Terry, & Poor Boys
Singles: 7-inch
SOMA (1002 Congo Bongo")....150-250 59

LEE, Thunder
Singles: 7-inch
GROOVE....5-10 62

LEE, Tommy
Singles: 78 rpm
DELTA (403 "Packing Up My Blues")....250-350 53

LEE, Tommy
Singles: 7-inch
TIDE....5-10 60

LEE, Tommy
Singles: 7-inch
STARR....5-10

LEE, Toney *D&D '83*
Singles: 12-inch
RADAR.... 4-6 83
Singles: 7-inch
CRITIQUE.... 3-4 85

LEE, Tony
Singles: 7-inch
DARRYL (723 "Walking Slow")....10-20
FORTUNE (530 "Suicide")....10-20 58
KING (5230 "I Don't Care What You Do")....10-15 59
MERCURY (71511 "Summer Love")....8-12 59

LEE, Veronica, & Moniques
Singles: 7-inch
CENTAUR (106 "Ringo Did It")....15-20 64
Also see MONIQUES

LEE, Vicki
Singles: 78 rpm
SPECIALTY....10-20 55
Singles: 7-inch
COURT.... 4-8 61
DRUM (017 "Cryin' My Heart Out")....100-200 59
SPECIALTY (546 "Tears Keep a Falling")....20-40 55

LEE, Vicki *C&W '86*
Singles: 7-inch
SUNSHINE.... 3-4 86

LEE, Vik. E.
Singles: 7-inch
LIBERTY.... 4-8 63

LEE, Vinnie, & Spunkys
Singles: 7-inch
ABC-PAR (10189 "Mule Train")....10-20 61
LEE ("Bustin' Through")....15-25 58
(Selection number not known.)
OLD TOWN (1061 "Mule Train Rock")....15-25 59
OLD TOWN (1083 "Whipper Snapper")....10-20 60
Also see LEEMEN

LEE, Wally, & Storms
Singles: 7-inch
NOW (1010 "Oh No Daddy")....20-30
SUNDOWN (122 "I Never Felt This Way")....300-500 59

LEE, Warren
(Warren Lee Taylor)
Singles: 7-inch
DEESU....10-20 60s
NOLA (711 "Key to My Heart")....15-25 65
SOUNDEX....10-15 63
WAND....5-10 69

LEE, Wibby
Singles: 7-inch
JALYN (214 "I'm Lost Without Your Love")....100-150

LEE, Wilma: see WILMA LEE

LEE & BART
Singles: 7-inch
U.A. (140 "Knock at My Door")....10-20 58

LEE & DEE & Grand Prees
Singles: 7-inch
LOWERY.... 4-8 65

LEE & LEOPARDS
Singles: 7-inch
FORTUNE (867 "What About Me")....25-40 64
GORDY (7002 "Come Into My Palace")....30-50 62
LAURIE (3197 "Come Into My Palace")....10-20 62
Member: Lee Moore.

LEE & PAUL *P&R '59*
Singles: 7-inch
COLUMBIA....5-10 59-65
Members: Lee Pockriss; Paul Vance.
Also see VANCE, Paul

LEE & SOUNDS
Singles: 7-inch
LIDO (600 "Beautiful Romance")....40-60 59

LEE & VIBRATONES
Singles: 7-inch
DAROW (16013 "Too Cool")....10-20 60

LEE ANNE: see LEE-ANNE

LEE BROTHERS
Singles: 78 rpm
COLUMBIA....5-10 51
Singles: 7-inch
COLUMBIA....10-15 51

LEE-ANNE
(Leeanne Leyden)
Singles: 7-inch
ANN (1000 "Never")....25-50 63

LEE-ANNE, Donna
Singles: 7-inch
DORE....4-8 62

LEED TWINS
Singles: 7-inch
FLAME....10-15 59

LEEDS
Singles: 7-inch
WAND (102 "Heaven Only Knows")....25-50 59

LEEDS, Bobby
Singles: 7-inch
KING....4-8 64

LEEDS, Brad
Singles: 7-inch
SIGNATURE....4-8 60

LEEDS, Mike
Singles: 7-inch
ABC-PAR....5-10 60

LEEDS, Randy
Singles: 7-inch
ROULETTE....10-15 59

LEEMEN
Singles: 7-inch
ABC-PAR....5-10 61
Member: Vinnie Lee.
Also see LEE, Vinnie, & Vibratones

LEEN TEENS
Singles: 7-inch
IMPERIAL (5593 "So Shy")....50-75 59

LEER, Thomas
Singles
ARISTA (2 "Heartbeat")....5-8 85
(Picture disc.)

LEER BROTHERS
Singles: 7-inch
INTREPID (75007 "Love Fever")....4-6
Members: J. Leer; L.D. Leer.

LEERICS
Singles: 7-inch
UN-RELEASED GOLD....3-5

LE FEVRE, Jimmy
Singles: 7-inch
MONOGRAM....4-8 63-64

LE FEVRE, Mylon
(Mylon)
Singles: 7-inch
COLUMBIA....3-5 70
W.B.....3-5 77-79
LPs: 10/12-inch
COLUMBIA....10-20 71-72
W.B.....8-15 78
Also see LEE, Alvin, & Mylon LeFevre

LEFEVRE, Raymond, & Orchestra *P&R '58*
Singles: 7-inch
ATLANTIC....4-6 61
4 CORNERS....4-6 67-68
JAMIE....4-6 60
KAPP....3-8 58-66
MERCURY....4-8 60
VERVE....4-6 62
LPs: 10/12-inch
ATLANTIC....8-15 61
BUDDAH....5-10 71-72
4 CORNERS....5-10 67-68
KAPP....8-15 59-66
MONUMENT....6-12 67

LE FORS, Jeff
Singles: 7-inch
MERRI....5-10 60

LEFT BANKE *P&R '66*
Singles: 7-inch
CON AMERICA....5-8 78
SMASH (Except 2243)....5-10 66-69
SMASH (2243 "Myrah")....30-40 69
Picture Sleeves
SMASH (Except 2243)....10-20 67
SMASH (2243 "Myrah")....30-40 69
LPs: 10/12-inch
RHINO....5-8 85
SMASH (27088 "Walk Away Renee")....20-30 67
(Monaural.)
SMASH (67088 "Walk Away Renee")....25-35 67
(Stereo.)
SMASH (67113 "Left Banke Too") .25-35 69
MERCURY....5-10 81
Members: Michael Brown; George Cameron; Tom Finn; Steve Martin; Rick Brand; Jeff Winfield; Tom Feher.
Also see BECKIES
Also see BROWN, Michael
Also see MAGIC PLANTS
Also see MARTIN, Steve
Also see MONTAGE
Also see STORIES

LEFT END
Singles: 7-inch
POLYDOR....3-5 75
RED (Colored vinyl)....4-6
LPs: 10/12-inch
POLYDOR....8-10 75

LEFTY BOY
Singles: 7-inch
TOPPA....4-8 63

LEGACY *R&B '82*
Singles: 7-inch
BRUNSWICK....3-5 82
PRIVATE I....3-4 85

LEGAL EAGLES
Singles: 7-inch
ARCH (1607 "The Trial")....20-30 58
(Also issued as by Herb. B. Lou & Legal Eagles.)
Also see LOU, Herb B., & Legal Eagles

LeGARDES *C&W '78*
(LeGarde Twins)
Singles: 7-inch
BEAR....3-4 88
BEL CANTO (725 "Hi-Di")....15-25 58
4 STAR....3-5 79
INVITATION....3-5 80
RAINDROP....3-5 78
LPs: 10/12-inch
CAPITOL....10-20
KOALA....8-10
PLATINUM PLATT....8-10

LE GAULT, Hank
Singles: 78 rpm
STARDALE (200 "I Knew")....50-75 56
Singles: 7-inch
STARDALE (200 "I Knew")....100-200 56

LEGEND
LPs: 10/12-inch
BELL....10-15 69

LEGEND
Singles: 7-inch
MEGAPHONE (701 "The Kids Are Alright")....10-15 68
MEGAPHONE (703 "Enjoy Yourself")....10-15 68
LPs: 10/12-inch
MEGAPHONE (101 "Legend")....50-75 70
Also see DRAGONFLY
Also see KELLY, Mike, & Legend

LEGEND, Tobi
Singles: 7-inch
MALA (591 "Heartbreaker")....25-45 68
MALA (12003 "No Good Cry")....10-20 68

LEGEND, Tom
Singles: 7-inch
COLPIX....4-8 62

LEGENDARY MASKED SURFERS
Singles: 7-inch
U.A. (270 "Summer Means Fun")...10-15 73
(Tan label. This track, previously included on the Jan & Dean LPs *The Little Old Lady from Pasadena* and *Popsicle* was mistakenly used for this single.)
U.A. (270 "Summer Means Fun")....10-15 73
(White label, promotional issue. Same incorrect track as noted above.)
U.A. (270 "Summer Means Fun")....100-125 73
(Tan label, promotional issue. Has the intended, new version with added vocal backing, not available elsewhere. Can be identified by playing, or visually by the following letters etched in the vinyl trail-off: Side 1 "BJ/TM/DT." Side 2 "GG/ILY/DOT.")
U.A. (270 "Summer Means Fun")....100-125 73
(White label, promotional issue. Has correct version as described above.)
U.A. (670 "Gonna Hustle You")....10-20 75
(Reissued in 1977.)
U.A. (50958 "Gonna Hustle You")..10-20 72
Picture Sleeves
U.A. (270 "Summer Means Fun")...20-30 73
(Add $5.00 if accompanied by explanatory note from Dean Torrence.)
Members: Jan Berry; Dean Torrece; Brian Wilson; Bruce Johnston; Terry Melcher; Leon Russell; Glen Campbell; Larry Knechtel.
Also see CAMPBELL, Glen
Also see JAN & DEAN
Also see RUSSELL, Leon
Also see WILSON, Brian

LEGENDARY STARDUST COWBOY
(Norman Odam)
Singles: 7-inch
MERCURY....10-20 68-69
PSYCHO-SAUVE (1033 "Paralyzed")....15-25 68
Also see BURNETT, T-Bone

LEGENDS
Singles: 7-inch
HULL (727 "The Legend of Love")....50-75 58
(Red label.)
HULL (727 "The Legend of Love") .15-25 62
(Multi-color label.)
MELBA (109 "I'll Never Fall in Love Again")....75-125 57
(Titles and artists shown in print approximately 1/8-inch letters. Label also has double horizontal lines.)
MELBA (109 "I'll Never Fall in Love Again")....25-35 60s
(Titles and artists shown in print approximately 1/4-inch letters.)

LEGENDS
Singles: 7-inch
COLUMBIA....5-10 61
LPs: 10/12-inch
COLUMBIA....20-30 61
Member: Bill Ramal.
Also see RAMAL, Bill

LEGENDS
Singles: 7-inch
HART-VAN (18003 "Traction")....20-25 62

LEGENDS
Singles: 7-inch
CALDWELL (410 "Go Away with Me")....15-20 62
JAMIE (1228 "Tell the Truth")....10-15 62

LEGENDS
Singles: 7-inch
CAPITOL....10-20 63
DATE....10-15 66
ERMINE....10-20 62-63
KEY (1002 "Lariat")....15-25 61
PARROT....5-8 65
THAMES (104 "Raining in My Heart")....10-15 64
W.B.....4-8 64
Picture Sleeves
ERMINE....15-25 62
LPs: 10/12-inch
CAPITOL (T-1925 "The Legends Let Loose")....50-75 63
(Monaural.)
CAPITOL (DT-1925 "The Legends Let Loose")....75-100 63
(Reprocessed stereo.)
CAPITOL ("Run to the Movies") 100-200 63
(Capitol Custom pressing. No number shown on cover, has RB-2047 on label.)
ERMINE (101 "The Legends Let Loose")....50-100 63
Members: Larry Foster; Sam McCue; Jerry Schils; Jim Sessody. Session: John Rondell; Billy Joe Burnette.
Also see BIRDWATCHERS
Also see BURNETTE, Billy Joe
Also see CROWFOOT
Also see McCUE, Sam

LEGENDS
Singles: 7-inch
FALCO (305 "Well, Darling") . 1000-2000 63

LEGENDS
Singles: 7-inch
DOC HOLIDAY (107 "Surf's Up")...15-25 63
Picture Sleeves
DOC HOLIDAY (107 "Surf's Up")...25-35 63

LEGENDS
Singles: 7-inch
FENTON (2512 "I'll Come Again") 15-25 67

LEGENDS
Singles: 7-inch
UP (2207 "Baby, Get Your Head Screwed On")....20-30 68
RAILROAD HOUSE (12003 "High Towers")....10-15 69
Picture Sleeves
RAILROAD HOUSE (12003 "High Towers")....20-30 69
Also see HARTMAN, Dan

LEGENDS
Singles: 7-inch
EPIC....5-8 73
HEART....10-20 72

LEGENDS
Singles: 7-inch
CHEECO (655 "Baby I Need Your Loving")....15-25
CHEECO (656 "If Ever")....15-25
MAGENTA (2 "You Little Nothing")....15-25
PUMPKIN (103 "Deep Inside")....15-20

LEGGERIORS
Singles: 7-inch
GOLIATH....3-5 63

LEGGS, Price
Singles: 7-inch
GLEN (101 "Teenage Fun")....20-40 58

LEGION OF SUPER HEROES
Singles: 7-inch
AMY....4-8 67

LEGRAND, Michel, & Orchestra *LP '55*
Singles: 7-inch
A&M....3-4 83
BELL....3-5 71-72
COLUMBIA....4-8 55-59
DECCA....3-6 68
FLASHBACK....3-5 73
MCA....3-5 73-76
MGM....3-6 67-68
PHILIPS....4-6 63-66
RCA....3-5 75
20TH FOX....3-5 77
U.A.....3-5 70
W.B.....3-6 68-76
Picture Sleeves
MGM....8-15 67
EPs: 7-inch
COLUMBIA....5-10 56-59
LPs: 10/12-inch
BELL....5-10 72-74
COLUMBIA....10-20 55-71

GRYPHON ... 5-8 75-79
HARMONY ... 5-10 66-74
KORY ... 4-8 77
MCA ... 8-15 73-76
MERCURY ... 8-15 65
PABLO ... 4-8 83
PHILIPS ... 8-15 62-64
SPRINGBOARD ... 4-8 77
20TH FOX ... 5-10 77
U.A. ... 6-12 69
VERVE ... 8-15 68-72
W.B. ... 6-12 71-76
Also see HORNE, Lena, & Michel Legrand
Also see VAUGHAN, Sarah
For a complete listing of soundtracks by this artist, consult *The Official Price Guide to Movie/TV Soundtracks and Original Cast Albums.*

LEGS, Stick: see STICK LEGS

LEGS AKIMBO
Singles: 7-inch
VINDALOO ... 3-4 80
Picture Sleeves
VINDALOO ... 3-4 80

LEGS DIAMOND
Singles: 7-inch
CREAM ... 3-5 78-79
MERCURY ... 3-5 77
LPs: 10/12-inch
CREAM ... 5-8 79
MERCURY ... 8-10 77

LEHMAN, Billy
(With the Penn-Men; with Rock-itts)
Singles: 7-inch
ARP ... 5-10 59

LEHMAN, John
Singles: 7-inch
MERCURY ... 3-5 72

LEHMANN, Frankie
Singles: 7-inch
VJM RUSS (4424 "A Long Day's Flight") ... 10-15 64

LEHR, Zella *C&W '77*
(Zella)
Singles: 7-inch
COLUMBIA ... 3-4 81-83
COMPLEAT ... 3-4 84-85
RCA ... 3-5 77-80
LPs: 10/12-inch
COLUMBIA ... 5-10 82

LEHRER, Tom *LP '65*
Singles: 7-inch
REPRISE ... 3-6 69
EPs: 7-inch
LEHRER (1 "Songs By Tom Lehrer") ... 50-100 52
(Double EP, gatefold cover.)
LPs: 10/12-inch
LEHRER (101 "Songs By Tom Lehrer") ... 50-100 52
(10-inch LP.)
LEHRER (102 "More Songs By Tom Lehrer") ... 30-50 59
LEHRER (202 "An Evening Wasted with Tom Lehrer") ... 30-50 59
REPRISE ... 10-20 65-66

LEIBER, Jerry
LPs: 10/12-inch
KAPP (1127 "Scooby Doo") ... 30-40 59

LEIBER & STOLLER BIG BAND
Singles: 7-inch
U.A. ... 4-8 62
LPs: 10/12-inch
ATLANTIC (847 "Yakety Yak") ... 20-30 61
(Monaural.)
ATLANTIC (SD-847 "Yakety Yak") ... 25-35 61
(Stereo.)
Members: Jerry Leiber; Mike Stoller.
Also see LEIBER, Jerry
Also see STOLLER, Mike, & Stoller System

LEIGH, Andrew
LPs: 10/12-inch
SIRE ... 8-10

LEIGH, Bonnie *C&W '86*
Singles: 7-inch
R.C.P. ... 3-4 86-87

LEIGH, Diane
Singles: 78 rpm
FABOR ... 4-8 55
Singles: 7-inch
FABOR ... 8-12 55
TOWER ... 4-8 65

LEIGH, Linda
Singles: 7-inch
AMERICAN INT'L (540 "My Guy") ... 10-20 59
AMERICAN INT'L (543 "Beri Beri") ... 20-40 59
AMERICAN INT'L (546 "Foolish Dreams") ... 10-15 60
KASH ... 5-10 65
RENDEZVOUS (103 "Move Out") ... 10-15 58
REPRISE ... 4-8 62

LEIGH, Richard *C&W '83*
Singles: 7-inch
CAPITOL ... 3-4 83
U.A. ... 3-4 80
LPs: 10/12-inch
U.A. ... 5-10 80

LEIGH, Rickey, & Shondelles
Singles: 7-inch
SAVOY ... 4-8 63

LEIGH, Shannon *C&W '82*
Singles: 7-inch
AMI ... 3-4 82

LEIGH BELL & CHIMES
Singles: 7-inch
RUST ... 4-8 62

LEIGHTON, Bernie
Singles: 7-inch
COLPIX ... 4-6 63
Picture Sleeves
COLPIX ... 5-8 63

LEISURE LADS
(With Michael Francis & Orchestra)
Singles: 7-inch
DELCO (801 "A Teenage Memory") ... 15-25 59

LE JETE *D&D '83*
Singles: 12-inch
MEGATONE ... 4-6 83

LEKAKIS, Paul *P&R '87*
Singles: 7-inch
ZYX ... 3-4 87

LELAND
(Leland Yoshitsu)
LPs: 10/12-inch
CONTEMPT ... 8-10 76-77

LELAND, George, & Rockets
Singles: 7-inch
ACCA ... 10-20

LEM
LPs: 10/12-inch
WAVEFRONT ... 8-10 77

LEMAIRE, Eddie
Singles: 7-inch
ELKO ... 5-10 60
MCI ... 5-10 60

LEMAN, Charles
Singles: 7-inch
DREW-BLAN ... 5-10 61

LE MEL, Gary
Singles: 7-inch
REV ... 5-10 58
VEE JAY ... 4-8 65

LEMMON, Dave *C&W '83*
Singles: 7-inch
SCP ... 3-4 83

LEMMON, Jack
LPs: 10/12-inch
CAPITOL (T-1943 "Jack Lemmon Plays Piano Selections from *Irma La Douce* ... 30-50 63
(Monaural.)
CAPITOL (ST-1943 "Jack Lemmon Plays Piano Selections from *Irma La Douce*) ... 40-60 63
(Stereo.)
EPIC (LN-523 "Twist of Lemmon") ... 20-30 59
(Monaural.)
EPIC (BN-523 "Twist of Lemmon") ... 25-35 59
(Stereo.)
Also see NELSON, Rick, & Jack Lemmon

LEMMONS, Billy *P&R '77*
Singles: 7-inch
ARIOLA AMERICA ... 3-5 77

LEMON
LPs: 10/12-inch
PRELUDE ... 8-10 78

LEMON, John, Trio
Singles: 7-inch
TALLY (945 "Chilly Willy") ... 8-12 60s
TIMBRE (501 "African Twist") ... 8-12 64
TRUDEL (1002 "Beatle Shuffle") ... 8-12 64
Members: John Lemon; Robert Brooks; James Scott.

LEMON, Meadowlark
Singles: 7-inch
CASABLANCA ... 3-5 79
RSVP ... 4-8 66
Picture Sleeves
RSVP ... 5-10 66

LEMON DROP BAND
Singles: 7-inch
TEEN TOWN (122 "Twist O Lemon") ... 10-20 60s
TEEN TOWN (123 "Chubby Mind") ... 10-20 60s

LEMON DROPS
Singles: 7-inch
ALADDIN ... 5-10 60
CORAL ... 5-10 59
CRYSTALETTE ... 5-10 61
DORE ... 5-10 61

LEMON DROPS
Singles: 7-inch
REMBRANDT (5009 "I Love in the Springtime") ... 15-25 67
LPs: 10/12-inch
CICADELIC ... 8-10 85-87
Members: Dick Sidman; Danny Smola; Jeff Brand; George Sorenson; Rick Erickson.
Also see NUCHEZS

LEMON FOG
Singles: 7-inch
ORBIT (1117 "Lemon Fog") ... 20-30 67
ORBIT (1123 "Summer") ... 20-30 68
ORBIT (1127 "Day by Day") ... 20-30 68

LEMON PIPERS *P&R '67*
Singles: 7-inch
BUDDAH ... 4-8 67-69
CAROL ... 8-12
ERIC ... 3-5 78
Picture Sleeves
BUDDAH ... 5-10 68
LPs: 10/12-inch
BUDDAH ... 12-20 68
Members: Ivan Browne; Bill Bartlett; Paul Lenka; Bill Albaugh; Steve Walmsley; Reg Nave.
Also see 1910 FRUITGUM COMPANY / Lemon Pipers
Also see RAM JAM

LEMONADE CHARADE
Singles: 7-inch
BELL ... 4-8 68
CAPITOL ... 4-6 69
EPIC ... 4-8 67

LEMONGELLO, Peter
Singles: 7-inch
PRIVATE STOCK ... 3-5 76-77
LPs: 10/12-inch
PRIVATE STOCK ... 8-10 76

LEMONS, Bill
Singles: 7-inch
CORT (1313 "Lorene") ... 50-75

LEMONS, George
Singles: 7-inch
GOLD SOUL (102 "Fascinating Girl") ... 1000-2000
(Promotional issue only.)

LEMONS, John
Singles: 7-inch
TIMBRE ... 4-8 62

LEN & GLEN
Singles: 7-inch
COLUMBIA ... 4-8 65-67
Picture Sleeves
COLUMBIA ... 4-8 65-67

LEN & JIM
Singles: 7-inch
DEL-FI ... 5-10 60

LEN & JUDY
Singles: 7-inch
DEER (3001 "I'm Leavin' Town, Baby") ... 50-100 61

LENA & DELTANETTES
Singles: 7-inch
UPTOWN (721 "Turn Around, Baby") ... 4-8 66

LEN-DELLS
Singles: 7-inch
REACH (2 "Mary Ann") ... 50-75 66
Also see LY-DELLS

LENKE, Rod, & Pearls
Singles: 7-inch
PHARAOH (120 "Till the End") ... 8-12

LENNARD, Marty
Singles: 7-inch
JUBILEE ... 5-8

LENNEAR, Claudia
Singles: 7-inch
W.B. ... 3-5 73
LPs: 10/12-inch
W.B. ... 8-10 73
Also see COODER, Ry
Also see TOUSSAINT, Allen

LENNON, Freddie
Singles: 7-inch
JERDEN (792 "That's My Life") ... 20-30 66

LENNON, John *P&R/LP '69*
(John & Yoko; Plastic Ono Band; with Plastic Ono Nuclear Band; with Flux Fiddlers)
Singles: 12-inch
CAPITOL (9585/6 "Imagine"/"Come Together") ... 25-35 86
(Promotional issue only.)
CAPITOL (9894 "Happy Xmas") ... 150-200 86
(Promotional issue only. Black label.)
CAPITOL (9894 "Happy Xmas") ... 40-50 86
(Promotional issue only. Silver label.)
CAPITOL (9917 "Rock & Roll People") ... 50-60 86
(Promotional issue only.)
CAPITOL (9929 "Happy Xmas") ... 35-45 86
(Promotional issue only.)
CAPITOL (79453 "Stand by Me") ... 30-40 88
(Promotional issue only.)
GEFFEN (919 "Starting Over") ... 60-75 80
(Promotional issue only.)
GEFFEN (1079 "Happy Xmas") ... 25-30 82
(Price range includes special sleeve. Promotional issue only.)
POLYDOR (250 "Nobody Told Me") ... 25-30 83
Singles: 7-inch
AMERICOM (435 "Give Peace a Chance") ... 500-750 69
(Plastic "Pocket Disc" soundsheet.)
APPLE (1809 "Give Peace a Chance") ... 4-6 69
APPLE (1813 "Cold Turkey") ... 4-6 69
APPLE (1818 "Instant Karma") ... 15-30 70
(With Capitol logo.)
APPLE (1818 "Instant Karma") ... 5-10 70
(No Capitol logo.)
APPLE (1827 "Mother") ... 8-12 70
(No "Mono" print on label.)
APPLE (1827 "Mother") ... 30-40 70
(With "Mono" on label.)
APPLE (1830 "Power to the People") ... 8-12 71
APPLE (1840 "Imagine") ... 8-12 71
APPLE (1842 "Happy Xmas") ... 10-15 71
(Label pictures John & Yoko.)
APPLE (1842 "Happy Xmas") ... 5-10 71
(Standard Apple label.)
APPLE (1848 "Woman Is the Nigger of the World") ... 5-8 72
(With Elephant's Memory.)
APPLE (1868 "Mind Games") ... 4-6 73
APPLE (1874 "Whatever Gets You Through the Night") ... 4-6 74
APPLE (1878 "#9 Dream") ... 5-8 74
APPLE (1881 "Stand by Me") ... 5-8 75
CAPITOL (Except 1842 & 1878) ... 10-15 76
(Orange labels.)
CAPITOL (1842 "Happy Xmas") ... 40-50 76
CAPITOL (1878 "#9 Dream") ... 30-40 76
CAPITOL ... 5-10 78-88
(Purple or black labels.)
CAPITOL (6244 "Stand by Me") ... 40-50 86
(Blue "Starline" series label.)
CAPITOL (17644 "Happy Xmas") ... 3-4 94
(Colored vinyl, 30th Anniversary juke box issue. Mistakenly has a slash following title: "Happy Xmas (War Is Over)/".)
CAPITOL (17644 "Happy Xmas") ... 3-5 95
(Colored vinyl, 30th Anniversary juke box issue. Erroneous slash removed from title.)
CAPITOL (17783 "Give Peace a Chance") ... 75-100 94
CAPITOL (57849 "Imagine") ... 30-50 92
COLLECTABLES (4307 "Nobody Told Me") ... 15-20 92
GEFFEN (0408 "Starting Over") ... 3-5 81
(Cream color label. Logo has narrow print.)
GEFFEN (0408 "Starting Over") ... 20-30 81
(Cream color label. Logo has bold print.)
GEFFEN (0408 "Starting Over") ... 15-30 80
(Black label.)
GEFFEN (0415 "Watching the Wheels") ... 3-5 81
(Cream color label. Logo has narrow print.)
GEFFEN (0415 "Watching the Wheels") ... 30-40 82
(Cream color label. Logo has bold print.)
GEFFEN (0415 "Watching the Wheels") ... 20-30 86
(Black label without bar code symbol.)
GEFFEN (0415 "Watching the Wheels") ... 5-10 88
(Black label with bar code symbol.)
GEFFEN (29855 "Happy Xmas") ... 3-5 82
GEFFEN (49604 "Starting Over") ... 3-5 80
GEFFEN (49644 "Woman") ... 3-5 80
GEFFEN (49695 "Watching the Wheels") ... 3-4 81
ORANGE PEEL (70078 "Interview") ... 15-20 81
(John is interviewed by David Peel. Picture disc.)
POLYDOR ... 4-8 84-86
Promotional Singles
APPLE (1809 "Give Peace a Chance") ... 8-12 69
APPLE (1813 "Cold Turkey") ... 20-25 69
APPLE (1818 "Instant Karma") ... 150-200 70
APPLE (1827 "Mother") ... 25-35 70
APPLE (1830 "Power to the People") ... 15-25 71
APPLE (1840 "Imagine") ... 10-15 71
APPLE (1848 "Woman Is the Nigger of the World") ... 12-15 72
APPLE (1868 "Mind Games") ... 40-50 73
APPLE (1874 "Whatever Gets You Through the Night") ... 35-45 74
APPLE (1878 "#9 Dream") ... 40-50 74
APPLE (1878 "What You Got") ... 75-100 74
(Two separate promo singles have the same selection number [1878]. On commercial issues these tracks were back to back.)
APPLE (1881 "Stand by Me") ... 40-50 75
APPLE (1883 "Ain't That a Shame") ... 150-200 75
APPLE (1883 "Slippin' and Sliddin') ... 150-200 75
(Two separate promo singles are numbered 1883.)
APPLE (47663/4 "Happy Xmas") ... 600-750 71
(White label with black print.)
CAPITOL (44230 "Jealous Guy") ... 10-15 88
CAPITOL (57849 "Imagine") ... 30-50 92
COTILLION (104/5 "John Lennon on Ronnie Hawkins") ... 30-35 70
(John Lennon promotes a 1970 Ronnie Hawkins Cotillion release.)
EVA-TONE ("John Lennon Radio Play") ... 400-600 69
(Soundsheet only. Originally included with a boxed set issue of *Aspen* Magazine. Price for complete set would be double that of just the Lennon disc.)
EVA-TONE (101075 "The Rock Generation") ... 30-40 76
(Issued with the book *The Rock Generation* Has a brief Lennon interview. Price for book with disc would be double that of just the disc.)
GEFFEN (29855 "Happy Xmas") ... 10-15 82
GEFFEN (49604 "Starting Over") ... 15-20 80
GEFFEN (49644 "Woman") ... 15-20 80
GEFFEN (49695 "Watching the Wheels") ... 15-20 81
KYA ("KYA 1969 Peace Talk") ... 150-200 69
(Radio KYA's Tom Campbell and Bill Holley's telephone interview with John Lennon.)
POLYDOR ... 10-15 84-86
QUAKER ... 10-15 86
(Picture disc soundsheet, issued with Quaker Granola Dipps. See "Great Moments in Rock N Roll" in Picture Disc Chapter for other titles.)
QUAYE/TRIDENT (3419 "Rock-N-Roll") ... 400-500 75
(Contains a one minute radio spot for the "Rock 'N' Roll" LP. For radio stations only.)
WHAT'S IT ALL ABOUT ... 15-20 70s
(Public service disc for radio play.)
Picture Sleeves
APPLE (1809 "Give Peace a Chance") ... 10-15 69
APPLE (1813 "Cold Turkey") ... 50-75 69
APPLE (1818 "Instant Karma") ... 10-15 70
APPLE (1827 "Mother") ... 100-125 70
APPLE (1830 "Power to the People") ... 20-30 71
APPLE (1842 "Happy Xmas") ... 10-20 71
APPLE (1848 "Woman Is the Nigger of the World") ... 15-25 72
APPLE (1868 "Mind Games") ... 10-15 73
CAPITOL (44230 "Jealous Guy") ... 3-5 88
GEFFEN (29855 "Happy Xmas") ... 3-5 82
GEFFEN (49604 "Starting Over") ... 3-4 80
GEFFEN (49644 "Woman") ... 3-4 80
GEFFEN (49695 "Watching the Wheels") ... 3-4 81
POLYDOR ... 3-5 84
LPs: 10/12-inch
ADAM VIII LTD. (8018 "Great Rock & Roll Hits—Roots") ... 750-1000 75
APPLE (3361 "Wedding Album") ... 125-150 69
(Price range is for complete boxed set with all inserts.)
APPLE (3362 "Live Peace in Toronto") ... 30-40 69
(With Capitol logo. Has 16-page photo calendar, valued separately at $20 to $40.)
APPLE (3362 "Live Peace in Toronto") ... 10-20 70
(No Capitol logo. Has 16-page photo calendar, valued separately at $20 to $40.)
APPLE (3372 "John Lennon, Plastic Ono Band") ... 15-20 70
APPLE (3379 "Imagine") ... 15-25 71
(Includes bonus poster and photo card.)
APPLE (3392 "Sometime in New York City") ... 20-30 72
APPLE (3414 "Mind Games") ... 10-20 73
APPLE (3416 "Walls & Bridges") ... 10-20 74
(Includes booklet.)
APPLE (3419 "Rock 'N' Roll") ... 10-20 75
APPLE (3421 "Shaved Fish") ... 10-20 75
APPLE/TETRAGRAMMATON (5001 "Two Virgins") ... 125-150 68
(With brown paper outer sleeve.)
APPLE/TETRAGRAMMATON (5001 "Two Virgins") ... 75-100 68
(Without paper outer sleeve.)
APPLE/TETRAGRAMMATON (5001 "Two Virgins") ... 10-15 85
(Reissue, with brown paper outer sleeve that does NOT cover entire jacket.)
CAPITOL (3362 "Live Peace in Toronto") ... 10-15 82
(Purple label.)
CAPITOL (3362 "Live Peace in Toronto") ... 50-60 83
(Black label.)
CAPITOL (3372 "John Lennon, Plastic Ono Band") ... 10-20 78
(Purple label with "Mfd. by Capitol, etc." print, or black label.)
CAPITOL (3372 "John Lennon, Plastic Ono Band") ... 20-30 78
(Purple label with "Manufactured. by Capitol, etc." print.)
CAPITOL (3379 "Imagine") ... 5-10 78
(Purple label with "Mfd. by Capitol, etc." print.)
CAPITOL (3379 "Imagine") ... 20-30 86
(Black or purple label with "Manufactured by Capitol, etc." print.)
CAPITOL (3392 "Sometime in New York City") ... 20-30 72
CAPITOL (3414 "Mind Games") ... 35-45 78
CAPITOL (3416 "Walls & Bridges") ... 15-30 78
(Purple or black label.)
CAPITOL (3419 "Rock 'N' Roll") ... 25-35 75
CAPITOL (3421 "Shaved Fish") ... 8-12 78
(Purple label. Without Capitol logo on back cover.)
CAPITOL (3421 "Shaved Fish") ... 25-40 78
(Purple or black label. With Capitol logo on back cover.)
CAPITOL (16068 "Mind Games") ... 8-12 78
CAPITOL (16069 "Rock 'N' Roll") ... 8-12 78
CAPITOL (12451 "Live in New York City") ... 10-15 86
CAPITOL (12533 "Menlove Ave.") ... 10-15 86
CAPITOL (91425 "Double Fantasy") ... 15-25 89
GEFFEN (2001 "Double Fantasy") ... 10-15 80
(Cream color label. Logo has narrow print.)
GEFFEN (2001 "Double Fantasy") ... 40-50 80
(Cream color label with bold logo print.)
GEFFEN (2001 "Double Fantasy") ... 25-50 86
(Black label or purple label.)
GEFFEN (2023 "John Lennon Collection") ... 15-20 82
MFSL (153 "Imagine") ... 40-50 85
(Half-speed mastered.)
NAUTILUS (47 "Double Fantasy") ... 50-60 82
(Half-speed mastered.)
POLYDOR (Except colored vinyl) ... 10-20 84

POLYDOR (817160 "Milk and Honey") 100-150 84
(Colored vinyl.)
SILHOUETTE (10014 "Reflections and Poetry") 15-25 84
ZAPPLE (3357 "Life with the Lions") 20-25 69
Promotional LPs
APPLE (3392 "Sometime In New York City") 700-900 72
GEFFEN (2023 "John Lennon Collection") 35-45 82
(Quiex II "Limited Edition Pressing.")
NAUTILUS (47 "Double Fantasy") 50-60 82
(Issued in promotional white cover with blue print. Commercial disc.)
POLYDOR (817 238-1 "Heart Play") 20-30 83
(Includes program notes and copy of a letter from Yoko on her stationary.)
SILHOUETTE (10014 "Reflections and Poetry") 60-75 84
U.A. (671010 "How I Won the War") 200-250 66
(Promotional issue only with radio advertisements.)
Also see BEATLES
Also see ELEPHANT'S MEMORY
Also see ELLIOT, Bill, & Elastic Oz Band
Also see HAWKINS, Ronnie
Also see JOHN, Elton / John Lennon
Also see ONO, Yoko
Also see PEEL, David, & Lower East Side / John Lennon & Yoko Ono

LENNON, Julian — P&R/LP '84
Singles: 12-inch
ATLANTIC 5-8 85
Singles: 7-inch
ATLANTIC 3-5 84-89
Picture Sleeves
ATLANTIC 3-5 84-89
LPs: 10/12-inch
ATLANTIC 5-10 84-89

LENNON, Julian, & Stevie Wonder
Singles: 7-inch
CAPITOL 3-5 80s
Picture Sleeves
CAPITOL 3-5 80s
Also see LENNON, Julian
Also see WONDER, Stevie

LENNON, Sean Ono
Singles: 7-inch
POLYDOR 3-5 84
LPs: 10/12-inch
POLYDOR 5-10 84

LENNON SISTERS — P&R '56
(With Lawrence Welk)
Singles: 78 rpm
BRUNSWICK 4-6 57
CORAL 4-6 56
Singles: 7-inch
BRUNSWICK 5-10 57-59
CORAL 5-10 56
DOT 4-8 58-67
MERCURY 3-6 68
EPs: 7-inch
BRUNSWICK 5-10 57
LPs: 10/12-inch
BRUNSWICK 10-25 57
DOT 5-15 59-67
HAMILTON 5-12 64
MERCURY 8-12 68-69
RANWOOD 4-8 68-81
VOCALION 5-10 69-70
WING 5-10 69
Members: Kathy Lennon; Peggy Lennon; Janet Lennon; Dianne Lennon.
Also see WELK, Lawrence

LENNOX, Annie, & Al Green — P&R '88
Singles: 7-inch
A&M 3-4 88
Picture Sleeves
A&M 3-4 88
Also see EURYTHMICS
Also see GREEN, Al

LENNY & CHIMES
(Lenny Cocco & the Chimes)
Singles: 7-inch
FREEDOM 4-8
TAG 8-12 61
VEE JAY 5-10 64
Also see CHIMES

LENNY & CONTINENTALS
("Featuring Dino & the Aladdins")
Singles: 7-inch
DOMAR (103 "Get Off the Road") 10-20 61
TRIBUTE (119 "Little Joe & Linda Lee") 20-30 63
TRIBUTE (125 "Rosebuds") 100-200 63

LENNY & DICK
Singles: 7-inch
LAURIE 4-8 64

LENNY & M.H.F.R.
Singles: 7-inch
READING 4-8 67

LENNY & SQUIGTONES
LPs: 10/12-inch
CASABLANCA 5-10 79
Also see CREDIBILITY GAP

LENNY & STAR CHIEFS
Singles: 7-inch
MARK (149 "Warpath") 10-20 60

LENNY & STORKS: see WELCH, Lenny

LENNY & THUNDERTONES
Singles: 7-inch
ASTRA (2002 "Homicidal") 25-40 60
COMMA (444 "Thunder Express") 15-25 61
COMMA (445 "On the Loose") 15-25 61
DOT (16137 "Hot Ice") 10-20 60
DOT (16177 "Street Beat") 10-20 61
Member: Lenny Drake.
Also see BROWN, Doug
Also see CARPENTER, Chris
Also see PRESTON
Also see THUNDERTONES

LENOIR, J.B. — R&B '55
(J.B. Lenore; J.B. Lenor; with His African Hunch Rhythm)
Singles: 78 rpm
CHECKER 15-25 56-57
CHESS (1449 "My Baby Told Me") 25-50 51
CHESS (1463 "Deep in Debt Blues") 25-50 51
J.O.B. 25-50 52
PARROT 25-50 54-55
Singles: 7-inch
CHECKER (844 "Let Me Die with the One I Love") 35-50 56
CHECKER (856 "Don't Touch My Head") 35-50 56
CHECKER (874 "Five Years") 25-50 57
CHECKER (901 "Don't Talk to Your Son") 20-40 58
J.O.B. (1012 "The Mojo") 100-150 52
J.O.B. (1016 "I Want My Baby") 100-150 52
J.O.B. (1102 "Play a Little While") 100-150 52
PARROT (802 "Eisenhower Blues") 100-150 54
PARROT (802 "Tax Paying Blues") 100-150 54
(Black vinyl.)
PARROT (802 "Tax Paying Blues") 300-350 54
(Colored vinyl. *Eisenhower Blues* was retitled *Tax Paying Blues* and was issued using the same selection number. They are slightly different recordings.)
PARROT (809 "Mama, Talk to Your Daughter") 100-150 54
PARROT (814 "Mama, Your Daughter Is Going to Miss Me") 100-150 55
PARROT (821 "Fine Girls") 100-150 55
SHAD (5012 "Back Door") 15-25 59
U.S.A. (744 "I Feel So Good") 10-15 63
VEE JAY (352 "Oh Baby") 10-20 60
LPs: 10/12-inch
CHESS (1410 "Natural Man") 50-75 63
POLYDOR (4011 "J.B. Lenoir") 10-15 70
Session: Lorenzo Smith; Joe Montgomery; Al Garvin; Sunnyland Slim; Al Wallace; Junior Wells; Jesse Fowler; Ernest Cotton.
Also see SUNNYLAND SLIM
Also see J.B. & His Bayou Boys
Also see WELLS, Junior

LEO & DUETS
Singles: 7-inch
CO-OP 5-8 65

LEO & LEOPARDS
Singles: 7-inch
FORTUNE 10-15 64

LEO & PROPHETS
Singles: 7-inch
TOTEM (105 "Tilt-A-Whirl") 20-30 66

LEOLA & LOVEJOYS
Singles: 7-inch
TIGER 8-12

LEON, Antoine (Lucky), & Key-Notes
Singles: 7-inch
BELL-O-TONIC (001 "Only in a Dream") 20-30 59

LEON, Eddie
Singles: 7-inch
FLIP 10-15 59

LEON, Greg, Invasion
LPs: 10/12-inch
AZRA (R2R "Invasion") 5-10 83
(Picture disc. 500 made.)

LEON, Randey
Singles: 7-inch
CONTE (824 "4th Dimension") 10-20 62

LEON & BURNERS
Singles: 7-inch
JOSIE (945 "Crack Up") 10-20 65

LEON & CARLOS
Singles: 7-inch
LIBERTY TONE (108 "Rock Everybody") 200-250 58
ROCKIN' STARS (101 "Rock Everybody") .... ??
(Since we do not know the year of this disc, and are not positive it is a legit issue, we cannot yet price it. Readers?)
Member: Carlos Jones.

LEON & DREAMERS
Singles: 7-inch
PARKWAY 8-12 62

LEON & HI-TONES
Singles: 7-inch
AROIN (19169 "Rock & Roll in the Groove") 40-60

LEON & JAMES
Singles: 7-inch
THUNDER (1029 "Ella Rea") 40-50

LEON & METRONOMES
Singles: 7-inch
CARNIVAL 5-10 66

LEON LEE: see LEE, Leon

LEONARD, Ben, & Furys
Singles: 7-inch
REO (1002 "Little Girl") 20-40

LEONARD, Bobby, & Explorers
Singles: 7-inch
UNITY (2114 "Project Venus") 10-15 62

LEONARD, Chuck
Singles: 7-inch
CRACKERJACK 4-8

LEONARD, Deke
LPs: 10/12-inch
U.A. 8-10 73

LEONARD, Harlan, & His Rockets
LPs: 10/12-inch
RCA 10-20 66

LEONARD, Jack
Singles: 7-inch
CUCA 5-10 65
DURA-BAC ("How Not to Lose Your Shirt") 5-10 60s
ROYCE 5-10 59

LEONARD, Jay
Singles: 7-inch
HANOVER (4549 "I Was Wrong") 10-15 60

LEONARD, Johnny
Singles: 7-inch
INVICTA 4-8 63

LEONARD, Tennie
Singles: 7-inch
CORAL 4-8 63

LEONARD FAMILY
Singles: 7-inch
PIP 5-10

LEONDA
LPs: 10/12-inch
EPIC 10-15 69

LEONETTI, Tommy — P&R '55
Singles: 78 rpm
CAPITOL 4-8 54-56
VIK 5-10 57
Singles: 7-inch
ATLANTIC 5-8 60
CAPITOL 5-10 54-56
COLUMBIA 4-6 67-73
DECCA 4-6 68-69
EPIC 3-5 74
RCA 3-8 59-77
20TH FOX 3-5 77
VIK 5-10 57
Picture Sleeves
COLUMBIA 4-8 68
LPs: 10/12-inch
CAMDEN 10-20 59
RCA 10-20 64-67

LEOPARDS
(With the Joe René Orchestra)
Singles: 7-inch
LEOPARD (5006 "Valerie") 350-500 63

LEOPARDS
Singles: 7-inch
VOXX 3-5 85
LPs: 10/12-inch
MOON 15-20 77
VOXX 5-8 87

LEOPOLD, Glenn
Singles: 7-inch
G.A.R. (108 "Someone New") 10-20 67

LE ORME
LPs: 10/12-inch
PETERS INT'L 10-12 74

LE PAMPLEMOUSSE — P&R/R&B '77
Singles: 12-inch
A.V.I. 4-8 78-85
Singles: 7-inch
A.V.I. 3-5 77-85
LPs: 10/12-inch
A.V.I. 5-8 78-85

LEPPARD, Def: see DEF LEPPARD

LE 'ROI BROTHERS — LP '87
EPs: 7-inch
AMAZING 8-10 81
DEMON 4-8 84
LPs: 10/12-inch
JUNGLE 8-10 83
PROFILE 5-8 85-87

LE ROUX — P&R/LP '78
(Louisiana's LeRoux)
Singles: 7-inch
CAPITOL 3-6 78
NEW ORLEANS LADY 5-10
RCA 3-5 82-83
LPs: 10/12-inch
CAPITOL 5-8 78-81
NEW ORLEANS LADY 20-30
RCA 5-8 82

LEROUX, Kelly
Singles: 7-inch
SCORPION (0518 "Teddy Bear") 4-6 78

LEROY & GALAHADS
Singles: 7-inch
PANORAMA 5-8

LEROY & Rocky Fellers
Singles: 7-inch
CAMEO 4-8 61

LEROY & WALLY
Singles: 7-inch
CARLTON 5-10 59

LERTZMAN, Carl: see BO-WEEVELS

LES & GLORIA
Singles: 7-inch
ENJOY 4-8 63

LES CHANSONETTES
Singles: 7-inch
SHRINE (114 "Deeper") 200-300 66

LES COMPAGNONS DE LA CHANSON — P&R '52
Singles: 78 rpm
COLUMBIA 3-6 52
Singles: 7-inch
CAPITOL 4-6 59-60
COLUMBIA 5-8 52

LES FEMMES
Singles: 7-inch
POWER PACK (100 "Closer") 50-100

LES LEDO
Singles: 7-inch
SHELL (721 "Scarlet Angel") 20-30

LES SABRES COMBO
Singles: 7-inch
RCT (1302 "Heaven in My Arms") 10-20 60s

LES SOULES
Singles: 7-inch
KIM (102 "Nobody But You") 75-100 63
(500 made.)

LES SULTANS
LPs: 10/12-inch
EXPRESS (16003 "Les Sultans") 40-60

LES TRES FEMMES
Singles: 7-inch
PHIL-L.A. of SOUL 4-6 69

LES VARIATIONS
LPs: 10/12-inch
BUDDAH 10-15 74-75

LE SABRES
Singles: 7-inch
CO & WI (111 "Summer Nights") 8-12

LESEAR, Anne — R&B '84
Singles: 7-inch
H.C.R.C. 3-5 84

LESH, Phil, & Ned Lagin
LPs: 10/12-inch
ROUND 30-40 75
Also see OLD and in the WAY / Keith & Donna / Robert Hunter / Phil Lesh & Ned Lagin
Also see RHYTHM DEVILS

LESLEE BROTHERS: see LESLIE BROTHERS

LESLEY, Alis
Singles: 78 rpm
ERA 15-25 57
Singles: 7-inch
ERA (1034 "He Will Come Back to Me") 15-25 57

LESLIE, Pat
Singles: 7-inch
CHA CHA (707 "You Played with Love") 10-20 60s

LESLIE, C. Vaughn
Singles: 7-inch
MASTERTONE (4014 "Hold It") 10-20 67

LESLEY, Tom
Singles: 7-inch
ENOLA 8-12

LESLIE, John
Singles: 7-inch
ABC-PAR (10293 "Fortune Teller") 10-15 62

LESLIE, Laura
Singles: 7-inch
HANOVER 5-10 59
PRODUCTION 4-8 63
LPs: 10/12-inch
HANOVER 15-25 59

LESLIE BROTHERS
(Leslee Brothers)
Singles: 78 rpm
BAN 10-20 56
COLUMBIA 10-20 56
Singles: 7-inch
BAN 20-40 56
COLUMBIA (40651 "Ready, Rudy Rock & Roll") 20-40 56

LESLIE SISTERS
Singles: 7-inch
MARBLE 10-15
SCOPE 5-8

LESTER, Bobby
Singles: 7-inch
CHECKER 5-10 59
COLUMBIA 3-5 70
LPs: 10/12-inch
COLUMBIA 10-15 70

LESTER, Bobby, & Moonglows
Singles: 7-inch
CHESS 5-8 62
LPs: 10/12-inch
CHESS (1471 "Best of Bobby Lester and the Moonglows") 30-40 62
Also see MOONGLOWS

LESTER, Bobby, & Moonlighters
Singles: 78 rpm
CHECKER (806 "So All Alone") 20-30 54
Singles: 7-inch
CHECKER (806 "So All Alone") 50-75 54
(Checkerboard top label.)
CHECKER (806 "So All Alone") 10-20 58
(Vertical logo.)
Also see LESTER, Bobby

LESTER, Chester — C&W '79
Singles: 7-inch
CON BRIO 3-5 79

LESTER, Danny
Singles: 7-inch
CHRISTY 5-10 59

LESTER, Jerry
Singles: 78 rpm
CORAL 4-8 50
Singles: 7-inch
CORAL 5-10 50

LESTER, Jimmie
Singles: 7-inch
CANON (224 "Granny Went Rockin' ") 75-100 59

LESTER, John
Singles: 7-inch
C&M (500 "At Last") 10-20 59

LESTER, Ketty — P&R/R&B/LP '62
Singles: 7-inch
COLLECTABLES 3-4 80s
ERA 5-10 62-63
EVEREST 4-8 62
PETE 4-6 68-69
RCA 4-6 64
TOWER 4-6 65-66
LPs: 10/12-inch
AVI 5-8 80
ERA (EL-108 "Love Letters") 25-35 62
(Monaural.)
ERA (ES-108 "Love Letters") 30-40 62
(Stereo.)
MEGA 5-8 85
PETE 10-15 69
RCA 10-20 64-65
SHEFFIELD 8-10 77
TOWER 10-15 66
Also see EVERETT, Betty, & Ketty Lester

LESTER, Larry
Singles: 7-inch
LOMA (2043 "Help Yourself") 50-75 65

LESTER, Lonnie
Singles: 7-inch
NU TONE (210 "You Can't Go") 10-15

LESTER, Lonnie, & Chuck Danzy
Singles: 7-inch
NUTONE (1209 "Ain't That a Shame") 15-25

LESTER, Robie
(With Sy Miller & His Orchestra)
Singles: 78 rpm
LIBERTY 5-8 56
Singles: 7-inch
LANDA 4-8 61
LIBERTY (55033 "With You Where You Are") 10-15 56
LUTE 5-10 60

LESTER, Sonny
Singles: 7-inch
20TH FOX (304 "Creampuff") 10-20 61

LESTER (SMITH) JR. & UPNILONS: see SMITH, Lester, Jr., & Upnilons

LET'S ACTIVE — LP '84
LPs: 10/12-inch
I.R.S. 5-8 84-86

LETTA
Singles: 7-inch
CHISA 3-5 71
LPs: 10/12-inch
A&M 8-10 76
CAPITOL 10-12 68
CHISA 8-12 70
FANTASY 8-10 73

LETTERMEN
Singles: 7-inch
LIBERTY 5-10 58
LONDON 3-5

LETTERMEN — P&R '61
Singles: 7-inch
ALPHA-OMEGA 3-5 78-88
APPLAUSE 3-4 83
CAPITOL 3-8 61-76
W.B. 5-8 60
Picture Sleeves
CAPITOL 5-10 61-71
LPs: 10/12-inch
ALPHA-OMEGA 5-15 77-88
APPLAUSE 5-8 82
CANDELITE 5-10 70s
CAPITOL (138 thru 836 except 577) 5-15 68-71
CAPITOL (577 "The Lettermen") 10-20 62-68
(Boxed, three-disc set.)

CAPITOL (1669 thru 2934) 10-20 62-68
(With "T" or "ST" prefix.)
CAPITOL (2500 & 2700 series)......... 5-8 80s
(With "SM" prefix.)
CAPITOL (11000 series)................. 5-10 71-75
CAPITOL (16000 series)................. 4-8 80-83
CAPITOL (90000 series)................10-20
LONGINES (220 "Time for Us") 15-30
(Boxed, five-disc set.)
LONGINES (220 "From the Lettermen, with Love") 5-8 72
(Bonus LP, issued with the above box set.)
PICKWICK (577 "The Lettermen") .10-15 70
(Three-LP set.)
PICKWICK (3000 series) 5-10 70-77
Members: Tony Butala; James Pike; Bob Engemann; Gary Pike; Donny Pike; Chad Nichols; Don Campo.
Also see BUTALA, Tony
Also see CAMPBELL, Glen / Lettermen / Ella Fitzgerald / Sandler & Young
Also see ENGEMANN, Bob
Also see PETER & GORDON / Lettermen
Also see PIKE, Jim
Also see REUNION
Also see SONNY & CHER / Bill Medley / Lettermen / Blendells
Also see TONY, BOB & JIMMY

LETTERMEN
Singles: 7-inch
MOONGLOW 5-10 61
Also see RHYTHM ROCKETS

LETTIE & JUNIOR
Singles: 7-inch
CUB (9101 "Coming Back Home to You") 8-12 61

LEVEE SONGSTERS
Singles: 7-inch
KAREN 12-18 59

LEVEL 42 *D&D '84*
Singles: 12-inch
A&M 4-6 84
Singles: 7-inch
A&M 3-4 84
POLYDOR.................................. 3-4 82-88
Picture Sleeves
POLYDOR.................................. 3-4 86-87
LPs: 10/12-inch
A&M 5-8 84
POLYDOR.................................. 5-10 82-88
Members: Mark King; Mike Lindup; Phil Gould; Boon Gould; Krys Mach.

LEVENE, Gus, Singers
Singles: 7-inch
CHALLENGE................................ 4-8 60

LEVERETT SISTERS
Singles: 7-inch
KAYDEN..................................... 5-10

LEVERETTE, Chico
(With the Satintones)
Singles: 7-inch
BETHLEHEM (3062 "Baby Don't Leave") 30-50 63
TAMLA (54024 "I'll Never Love Again") 300-500 60
Also see SATINTONES

LEVERT *R&B '85*
Singles: 7-inch
ATLANTIC.................................. 3-4 86-88
TEMPRE 3-5 85
LPs: 10/12-inch
ATLANTIC.................................. 5-8 86-90
Members: Sean Levert; Gerald Levert; Marc Gordon.

LEVETTES
Singles: 7-inch
UNITY (1002 "I'll Try Again")..........25-50 63

LEVI & ROCKATS
Singles: 7-inch
KOOL KAT 8-15 79
Picture Sleeves
KOOL KAT 5-10 79
Member: Levi Dexter.
Also see DEXTER, Levi
Also see ROCKATS

LEVIATHAN
LPs: 10/12-inch
MACH (12501 "Leviathan")............20-25 74

LEVIATHON
Singles
AZRA (013 "Sandy Jean")..............10-15 88
(Square-, heart-, and odd-shaped picture disc variations.)

LEVINE, Hank *P&R '61*
(With the Minature Men)
Singles: 7-inch
ABC-PAR 8-12 61
DOLTON 8-12 62-63
TOPS 8-12 60
Also see AKIM & AKTONES
Also see BACHELOR THREE
Also see CONNORS, Carol
Also see MINIATURE MEN
Also see WAYNE, John

LEVINE, Jeff
Singles: 7-inch
QUESTION MARK (301 "An Economy Package").. 4-6 75
EPs: 7-inch
CHIP (2501 "Wyatt Earp Meets Silly the Kid") 8-15 78
(Blue vinyl.)

LEVINE, Joey
Singles: 7-inch
EARTH 4-6 69
Also see THIRD RAIL

LEVINE & BROWN
Singles: 7-inch
BELL 4-8 74

LEVINS, Roosevelt
Singles: 7-inch
GG (520 "I'll Tell the World")..........35-55

LEVINS, Susan
Singles: 7-inch
DEERO ("Saturday Night")..............25-35
(Selection number not known.)

LEVINSKY & SINCLAIR
Singles: 7-inch
CHARISMA 3-5 79

LEVITT, Estelle
LPs: 10/12-inch
BUDDAH 5-10 75

LEVITT, Rod
LPs: 10/12-inch
RCA...10-15 65

LEVITT & McCLURE
LPs: 10/12-inch
CASABLANCA 8-12
Members: Dan Levitt; Marc McClure.
Also see JOYOUS NOISE

LEVON & HAWKS
(Featuring Levon Helm)
Singles: 7-inch
ATCO (6383 "Stones I Throw") 20-25 65
ATCO (6625 "Go Go Lisa Jane") ...10-20 68
Also see BAND
Also see HELM, Levon
Also see HAWKINS, Ronnie

LEVONS
Singles: 7-inch
COLUMBIA.................................. 8-12 62-63

LEVY, Marcy
Singles: 7-inch
EPIC 3-5 82
LPs: 10/12-inch
EPIC 8-15 82
Also see CLAPTON, Eric

LEVY, Marcy, & Robin Gibb
Singles: 7-inch
RSO 3-4 80
Picture Sleeves
RSO 3-5 80
Also see GIBB, Robin
Also see LEVY, Marcy

LEVY, O'Donnel
Singles: 7-inch
GROOVE MERCHANT.................... 3-5 75

LEWALLEN, Jimmy
Singles: 7-inch
PANORAMA................................. 3-5 70

LEWIE, Jona
Singles: 7-inch
STIFF 3-5 79-80

LEWIE & 7 DAYS
Singles: 7-inch
SKIPPER (0774 "Night Train") 15-20 69
Member: Larry Lee.
Also see OZARK MOUNTAIN DAREDEVILS

LEWIS, Al, & Modernistics / Lord Luther
Singles: 7-inch
MUSIC CITY (829 "What Will the Outcome Be") 60-70 59
Also see LORD LUTHER

LEWIS, Artie
Singles: 7-inch
ATCO 10-15 60
FLING.......................................10-20 59
KENCO 10-15 60
LOMA 10-15 66

LEWIS, Barbara *P&R/R&B '63*
Singles: 7-inch
ATLANTIC.................................. 5-10 62-67
ENTERPRISE.............................. 3-5 70-71
KAREN (313 "My Heart Went Do Dat Da")..15-25 61
REPRISE 3-5 73
LPs: 10/12-inch
ATLANTIC (8086 thru 8173) 20-35 63-68
ATLANTIC (8286 "Best of Barbara Lewis") 10-15 71
COLLECTABLES.......................... 6-8 88
ENTERPRISE..............................10-12 70
SOLID SMOKE............................ 8-10 70s
Also see DELLS

LEWIS, Bart
Singles: 7-inch
OKLAHOMA (5011 "Frankenstein") 10-15

LEWIS, Billy
("Billy" Lewis; Billy Lewis Group)
Singles: 7-inch
FIRE (1025 "Heart Trouble") 15-20 60
FLO LOU (101 "I Won't Tell a Soul") 75-125 56

LEWIS, Bobby *P&R/R&B '61*
(With Dave Hamilton's Peppers)
Singles: 78 rpm
SPOTLIGHT 10-15 56
Singles: 7-inch
ABC-PAR 4-8 64
BELTONE 10-15 61-62
ERIC 3-4 70s
LANA 3-6 60s
MERCURY (71245 "Mumbles Blues") 10-20 57
PHILIPS (40519 "Soul Seekin' ") ...10-20 68
ROULETTE 8-12 59
SPOTLIGHT (394 "Mumbles Blues") 20-40 56
SPOTLIGHT (397 "Solid As a Rock") 50-100 57
LPs: 10/12-inch
BELTONE (4000 "Tossin' and Turnin' ") 50-100 61

LEWIS, Bobby *C&W '66*
Singles: 7-inch
ACE of HEARTS 3-5 73-75
CAPRICORN 3-5 79
GRT 3-5 74
HME 3-4 85
RPA 3-5 76-77
SABER (107 "Forty Dollars a Week") 8-12
U.A. 4-8 66-71
LPs: 10/12-inch
ACE of HEARTS 6-12 73
ALBUM GLOBE............................ 5-8 80s
RPA 6-12 77
U.A. 10-20 66-70

LEWIS, Buddy
(Ernest Lewis)
Singles: 78 rpm
SWING TIME (312 "Lonesome Bedroom")..................................30-50 52
Also see LEWIS, Ernest

LEWIS, Buddy / Barry Frank
Singles: 78 rpm
BELL 5-10 56
Singles: 7-inch
BELL 10-20 56
Also see LEWIS, Buddy

LEWIS, Cappy: see OLYMPICS

LEWIS, Clarence, Jr.
Singles: 78 rpm
RED ROBIN 15-25 55
Singles: 7-inch
FURY 8-12 60
RED ROBIN (136 "Lost Everything") 50-75 55

LEWIS, Dave
Singles: 7-inch
A&M 5-10 63-64
JERDEN 4-8 66
NORTHGATE............................... 4-8 60s
PANORAMA................................ 4-8 68
PICCADILLY 4-8 67
SEAFAIR................................... 5-10 61
LPs: 10/12-inch
A&M 15-25 64
JERDEN 15-25 66
PANORAMA...............................15-25 65

LEWIS, Debra
Singles: 7-inch
VALIANT 4-8 61

LEWIS, Diane
Singles: 7-inch
LOVE (101 "Please Let Me Help You") 10-20 60s
Also see ADORABLES

LEWIS, Donna
Singles: 7-inch
DECCA (Except 31554) 4-8 63
DECCA (31554 "Surfer Boy Blue") 10-15 63

LEWIS, Dorsey, Jr.
Singles: 7-inch
ADVANCE................................... 4-8 66

LEWIS, Doug
Singles: 78 rpm
INTRO (6053 "Ice Worm Boogie") .15-25 52
Singles: 7-inch
INTRO (6053 "Ice Worm Boogie") .30-50 52

LEWIS, Earl, & Channels: see CHANNELS

LEWIS, Ernest
Singles: 78 rpm
PARROT (791 "No More Lovin' ") ..50-75 53
Singles: 7-inch
PARROT (791 "No More Lovin' ") 100-125 53
Also see COUNTRY SLIM
Also see LEWIS, Buddy
Also see WEST TEXAS SLIM

LEWIS, Furry
LPs: 10/12-inch
ADELPHI 10-12 70
AMPEX.....................................10-12 71
BIOGRAPH 10-12 70
BLUE HORIZON..........................10-12
FANTASY..................................10-12 72
PRESTIGE 8-10 70
PRESTIGE BLUESVILLE (1036 "Back on My Feet Again") 25-35 61
SOUTHLAND 8-10 76
Also see ALABAMA STATE TROUPERS

LEWIS, Gary
Singles: 7-inch
EPIC 4-6 75

LEWIS, Gary, & Playboys *P&R '65*
Singles: 7-inch
LIBERTY (Except 56144) 4-8 64-69
LIBERTY (56144 "I Saw Elvis Presley Last Night") 10-15 69
Picture Sleeves
LIBERTY 5-10 65-67
EPs: 7-inch
LIBERTY (227 "Doin' the Flake") ...10-20 65
(Liberty/Kellogg's Premium Record. Issued with paper sleeve.)
LPs: 10/12-inch
GUSTO 5-8 72
LIBERTY (Except 10000 series) 15-30 65-69
LIBERTY (10000 series) 5-8 81
SUNSET....................................12-15 69
U.A. (Except 1000 series) 8-10 75
U.A. (1000 series) 5-8 81

LEWIS, Gene
Singles: 78 rpm
JOSIE.......................................25-35 57
Singles: 7-inch
JOSIE (819 "Too Young to Settle Down")..25-35 57
R-DELL (103 "Crazy Legs") 50-75 58

LEWIS, Grady
Singles: 7-inch
COLONIAL (7010 "Runaway Lover") 10-15 60

LEWIS, Happy
(With Mae Questel)
Singles: 7-inch
JUBILEE.................................... 4-8

LEWIS, Huey, & News *P&R/LP '82*
Singles: 12-inch
CHRYSALIS (Except 8V8-42795)..... 4-8 84-89
CHRYSALIS (8V8-42795 "The Heart of Rock & Roll") 8-12 84
(Picture disc.)
Singles: 7-inch
CHRYSALIS................................ 3-5 80-89
Promotional Singles
CHRYSALIS (2589 "Do You Believe in Love") 8-12 80
(Colored vinyl. With Valentine card. Promotional issue only.)
CHRYSALIS (43065 "Hip to Be Square") 10-15 85
(Four disc set, each of a different color vinyl.)
Picture Sleeves
CHRYSALIS................................ 3-5 82-89
LPs: 10/12-inch
CHRYSALIS................................ 5-8 80-89
MFSL 15-20 85
Members: Huey Lewis; Bill Gibson; Mario Cipollina; Sean Hopper; Chris Hayes; Johnny Colla.
Also see CLOVER
Also see EDMUNDS, Dave
Also see SAN FRANCISCO ALL STARS
Also see U.S.A. for AFRICA

LEWIS, Hugh
Singles: 7-inch
FERN (803 "Rockin' Moon Men") 40-60 61

LEWIS, Hugh X. *C&W '64*
Singles: 7-inch
COLUMBIA................................. 3-6 70
GRT 3-6 70
KAPP 4-6 64-69
LITTLE DARLIN' 3-5 78-79
LPs: 10/12-inch
GUINESS 5-10 77
KAPP 10-20 66-68

LEWIS, J.D. *C&W/R&B '89*
Singles: 7-inch
SING ME 3-4 89

LEWIS, J.G. *R&B '76*
Singles: 7-inch
IX CHAINS 4-6 76

LEWIS, Jack
Singles: 78 rpm
CREST 5-10 57
RPM 5-10 57
Singles: 7-inch
ALLIED..................................... 5-10 59
CREST 5-10 57-58
IMPERIAL 4-8 63
RPM 5-10 57

LEWIS, Jerry *P&R/LP '56*
Singles: 78 rpm
CAPITOL 4-8 50-53
DECCA 4-8 56-57
Singles: 7-inch
CAPITOL 10-20 50-53
DECCA 8-15 56-62
DOT 8-10 60
LIBERTY 5-8 63
EPs: 7-inch
CAPITOL 10-15 56
DECCA 10-15 56
LPs: 10/12-inch
CAPITOL 10-15 64
DECCA 20-30 56
DOT 10-20 60
VOCALION................................. 8-12 66
Also see MARTIN, Dean, & Jerry Lewis

LEWIS, Jerry Lee *P&R/C&W/R&B '57*
(With "His Pumping Piano")
Singles: 78 rpm
SUN 50-100 56-58
Singles: 7-inch
AMERICA SMASH 3-5 86
BUDDAH 3-6 71
ELEKTRA................................... 3-5 79-82
MCA 3-5 82-83
MERCURY 3-6 70-82
POLYDOR.................................. 3-4 89
SCR (386 "Get Out Your Big Roll, Daddy") 3-5 85
(Colored vinyl.)
SSS/SUN 3-5 69-84
(Includes numbers below 100 and over 1000.)
SMASH (1857 "Pen & Paper") 8-12 63
SMASH (1886 "I'm On Fire") 15-25 64
SMASH (1906 "She Was My Baby") 8-12 64
SMASH (1930 "You Went Back on Your Word") 8-12 64
SMASH (1969 "I Believe in You") ..10-20 65
SMASH (1992 "Rockin' Pneumonia & the Boogie Woogie Flu") 8-12 65
SMASH (2006 "You Got What It Takes") 8-12 65
SMASH (2027 "What a Heck of a Mess") 8-12 66
SMASH (2053 "Memphis Beat") 8-12 66
SMASH (2103 thru 2257) 4-8 67-70
SUN (169/213 "Whole Lotta Shakin' Going On"/"Great Balls of Fire") 5-10 94
(Gold vinyl. Promotional issue only.)
SUN (259 "Crazy Arms") 20-40 56
SUN (267 "Whole Lot of Shakin' Going On") 15-25 57
SUN (281 "Great Balls of Fire") 15-25 57
SUN (288 "Breathless") 15-25 58
SUN (296 "High School Confidential") 15-25 58
SUN (303 "Break-Up") 15-25 58
SUN (317 "Lovin' Up a Storm") 15-25 59
SUN (312 "I'll Sail My Ship Alone") 15-25 59
SUN (324 "Let's Talk About Us") 15-25 59
SUN (330 "Little Queenie") 15-25 59
SUN (337 "Baby Baby, Bye Bye") ..10-20 60
SUN (344 "Hang Up My Rock & Roll Shoes") 10-20 60
SUN (352 "Love Made a Fool of Me") 10-20 60
SUN (356 "What'd I Say") 10-20 61
SUN (364 "Cold Cold Heart") 10-20 61
SUN (367 "Save the Last Dance for Me") 10-20 61
SUN (371 "Money") 10-20 61
SUN (374 "I've Been Twistin' ") 10-20 62
SUN (379 "Sweet Little Sixteen") ...10-20 62
SUN (382 "I Can't Trust Me") 10-20 62
SUN (384 "Teenage Letter") 10-20 63
SUN (396 "Carry Me Back to Old Virginia") 10-15 65
Picture Sleeves
POLYDOR.................................. 3-4 89
SUN (281 "Great Balls of Fire") 35-50 57
SUN (296 "High School Confidential") 35-50 57
EPs: 7-inch
MERCURY (6 "Special Radio Cuts from *Would You Take Another Chance on Me*") 15-25 71
(Promotional issues only.)
MERCURY (14 "Special Radio Cuts from *The Killer Rocks On*") 15-25 72
(Promotional issues only.)
SCR 10-15 86
SSS/SUN (108 "Golden Cream of the Country") 15-25 69
(Juke box issue only.)
SSS/SUN (114 "A Taste of Country") 15-25 69
(Juke box issue only.)
SMASH (2 "Jerry Lee Lewis") 20-25 64
SMASH (28 "Open-End Interview") 30-40 64
(Promotional issue only.)
SUN (107 "Great Ball of Fire") 75-125 57
(Issued with a paper sleeve.)
SUN (108 "Jerry Lee Lewis") 50-100 57
(Blue cover. First track listed is *Don't Be Cruel*.)
SUN (109 "Jerry Lee Lewis") 50-100 58
(Yellow cover. First track listed is *Ubangi Stomp*.)
SUN (110 "Jerry Lee Lewis") 50-100 58
(Red cover. First track listed is *High School Confidential*.)
LPs: 10/12-inch
ACCORD.................................... 5-8 81-82
AURA 5-8 82
BUCKBOARD.............................. 8-10 75
ELEKTRA................................... 5-10 79-82
EVEREST 8-12 75
HILLTOP 10-12 72
KOALA 8-15 79
MCA 5-8 82-84
MERCURY (SRM1 series) 8-15 72-78
MERCURY (SRM2-803 "Session") 15-20 73
MERCURY (3 "Southern Roots") ...20-35 73
MERCURY (61318 "In Loving Memories") 30-40 71
MERCURY (61323 "There Must Be More to Love Than This") 8-12 71
MERCURY (61343 "Touching Home") 15-20 71
(Cover is mostly an artist's drawing with a small photo of Lewis on the right side.)
MERCURY (61343 "Touching Home") 12-15 71
(Cover pictures Lewis standing in front of a brick wall.)
MERCURY (61346 "Would You Take Another Chance on Me") 8-12 71
MERCURY (61366 "Who's Gonna Play This Old Piano") 8-12 72
OUT of TOWN DIST 5-8 82
PICKWICK 10-12 70-74

POLYDOR (839516 "Great Ball of Fire") 5-8 89
(Includes tracks by other artists.)
POLYSTAR 8-10
POWER PAK 8-10 74
RHINO (255 "Original Sun Greatest Hits") 10-15 83
(Picture disc.)
SCR 5-10 85
SSS/SUN 5-10 69-84
SEARS 10-15
SMASH (690 "Jerry Lee Lewis Radio Special") 40-50 73
(Promotional issue only.)
SMASH (7001 "Golden Rock Hits") 5-8 82
SMASH (27040 "Golden Hits of Jerry Lee Lewis") 20-30 64
(Monaural.)
SMASH (27056 "Greatest Live Show on Earth") 15-20 64
(Monaural.)
SMASH (27063 "Return of Rock") 20-25 65
(Monaural.)
SMASH (27071 "Country Songs for City Folks") 15-20 65
(Monaural.)
SMASH (27079 "Memphis Beat") 20-25 65
(Monaural.)
SMASH (27086 "By Request") 15-20 66
(Monaural.)
SMASH (27097 "Soul My Way") 20-25 67
(Monaural.)
SMASH (67040 "Golden Hits of Jerry Lee Lewis") 25-35 64
(Stereo.)
SMASH (67040 "Golden Rock Hits of Jerry Lee Lewis") 20-30 60s
(Reissue.)
SMASH (67056 "Greatest Live Show on Earth") 20-25 64
(Stereo.)
SMASH (67063 "Return of Rock") 25-30 65
(Stereo.)
SMASH (67071 "Country Songs for City Folks") 20-25 65
(Stereo.)
SMASH (67071 "All Country") 10-15 69
(Stereo. Reissue.)
SMASH (67079 "Memphis Beat") 25-30 65
(Stereo.)
SMASH (67086 "By Request") 20-25 66
(Stereo.)
SMASH (67097 "Soul My Way") 25-30 67
(Stereo.)
SMASH (67104 thru 67131) 8-15 68-70
SUN (1230 "Jerry Lee Lewis") 75-125 58
SUN (1265 "Jerry Lee's Greatest") 75-125 62
SUNNYVALE 8-10 77
TRIP 8-10 74
WING (125 "The Legend of Jerry Lee Lewis") 20-30 69
WING (12000 series) 12-15 66-67
(Monaural.)
WING (16000 series) 15-20 66-67
(Stereo.)
Also see CLANTON, Jimmy / Frankie Ford / Jerry Lee Lewis / Patsy Cline
Also see GEORGE & LOUIS
Also see HAWK
Also see KING, Ben E.
Also see McDOWELL, Ronnie, & Jerry Lee Lewis
Also see MEYERS, Augie
Also see NELSON, Willie / Jerry Lee Lewis / Carl Perkins / David Allan Coe
Also see TENNESSEE TWO & FRIEND

LEWIS, Jerry Lee / Curly Bridges / Frank Motley
LPs: 10/12-inch
DESIGN 10-15 63

LEWIS, Jerry Lee / Johnny Cash
LPs: 10/12-inch
SSS/SUN 8-10 71
Also see CASH, Johnny
Also see CASH, Johnny / Jerry Lee Lewis / Jeanie C. Riley
Also see PERKINS, Carl, Jerry Lee Lewis, Roy Orbison & Johnny Cash

LEWIS, Jerry Lee, & Friends C&W '79
Singles: 7-inch
SSS/SUN (1139 "Save the Last Dance for Me") 4-6 78
(Gold vinyl. Credits only Jerry Lee Lewis.)
SSS/SUN (1141 "Cold, Cold Heart") 4-6 79
LPs: 10/12-inch
SSS/SUN (1011 "Duets") 8-12 78
(Colored vinyl.)
SSS/SUN (1011 "Duets") 8-12 78
(Black vinyl, even though cover indicates "Special Gold Vinyl." RCA Record Club issue.)
Members: Jerry Lee Lewis; Jimmy Ellis; Charlie Rich.
Also see ORION
Also see RICH, Charlie

LEWIS, Jerry Lee & Linda Gail C&W '69
Singles: 7-inch
SMASH 3-6 69-70
SUN 5-10 63
LPs: 10/12-inch
SMASH 15-25 69

LEWIS, Jerry Lee / Roger Miller / Roy Orbison
LPs: 10/12-inch
PICKWICK 8-10 70s
Also see MILLER, Roger
Also see ORBISON, Roy

LEWIS, Jerry Lee, Carl Perkins & Charlie Rich
LPs: 10/12-inch
SSS/SUN (1018 "Trio +") 8-10 78
(With Jimmy Ellis.)
Also see ELLIS, Jimmy
Also see LEWIS, Jerry Lee, & Friends
Also see PERKINS, Carl

LEWIS, Jerry Lee / Charlie Rich / Johnny Cash
LPs: 10/12-inch
POWER PAK 8-10 80s
Also see CASH, Johnny, Carl Perkins & Jerry Lee Lewis
Also see LEWIS, Jerry Lee

LEWIS, Jim, & Checkers
Singles: 7-inch
BOMP 3-5 80
LPs: 10/12-inch
BOMP 8-10 80

LEWIS, Jimmie
Singles: 7-inch
CYCLONE 5-10 62
LUCK 5-10 60

LEWIS, Jimmy
(Jimmy Lewis Band)
Singles: 78 rpm
ATLANTIC 20-30 51
CAT 10-15 54
RCA (4899 "Cherry Wine") 10-15 52
Singles: 7-inch
ACCENT (1059 "Go Go Go") 50-75 58
ATLANTIC (943 "Let's Get Together and Make Some Love") 50-75 51
CAT 15-25 54
ERA 5-10 65-66
FOUR J 5-10 63
MENT (02 "I Love You") 10-20 60s
MENT (1010 "I've Tried to Please You") 50-100 60s
MINIT 5-10 67-68
RCA (4899 "Cherry Wine") 25-40 52
TANGERINE 4-8 68-69
Also see CHARLES, Ray, & Jimmy Lewis

LEWIS, Jimmy
Singles: 7-inch
VOLT 10-15 73

LEWIS, Jimmy R&B '75
(With the L.A. Street Band)
Singles: 7-inch
HOTLANTA 3-5 75
MCA 3-4 84
LPs: 10/12-inch
HOTLANTA 5-10 74

LEWIS, Jimmy, & Volumes
Singles: 7-inch
IVY (104 "I Saw a Cottage in My Dreams") 25-35 57

LEWIS, Joe "Cannonball"
Singles: 78 rpm
KENTUCKY 20-30 53
Singles: 7-inch
KENTUCKY (574 "You Been Honky Tonkin' ") 25-50 53

LEWIS, Joe "Cannonball" / Eddie Moore
EPs: 7-inch
QUEEN CITY (43 "Big 4 Hits") 20-30 50s
Also see LEWIS, Joe "Cannonball"

LEWIS, Johnnie
LPs: 10/12-inch
ARHOOLIE 10-15

LEWIS, Johnny
(Joe Hill Louis)
Singles: 78 rpm
ROCKIN' (517 "She's Taking All My Money") 100-150 52
Also see LOUIS, Joe Hill

LEWIS, Jon Jon
Singles: 7-inch
WORLD PACIFIC 4-8 66

LEWIS, Junior
Singles: 7-inch
ATCO 4-8 62
COLUMBIA 4-8 61-62
MGM 4-8 67
SCEPTER 4-8 63
Picture Sleeves
COLUMBIA 5-10 61-62

LEWIS, Katherine Handy
LPs: 10/12-inch
FOLKWAYS 10-12

LEWIS, Keni
Singles: 7-inch
DE-VEL (6753 "Ain't Gonna Make It Easy") 10-20 73

LEWIS, Lavenia
(Levenia Lewis; Luvenia Lewis)
Singles: 7-inch
COTILLION 4-6 69
GOLDEN EAGLE 3-5
VELERIE 10-20 64
WETSOUL 4-6

LEWIS, Lenny, & His Orchestra R&B '46
Singles: 78 rpm
QUEEN 4-8 46

LEWIS, Linda R&B '75
Singles: 7-inch
ARISTA 3-5 75-78
REPRISE 3-5 73
LPs: 10/12-inch
REPRISE 8-10 74

LEWIS, Linda Gail C&W '72
Singles: 7-inch
MERCURY 3-5 72
SMASH 4-8 69
LPs: 10/12-inch
SMASH 10-20 69
Also see LEWIS, Jerry Lee & Linda Gail

LEWIS, Little Junior
Singles: 7-inch
FURY 8-12 60

LEWIS, Lovey
Singles: 78 rpm
DUKE (126 "Alright, Baby") 10-15 53
Singles: 7-inch
DUKE (126 "Alright, Baby") 15-25 53

LEWIS, Margaret C&W '68
Singles: 7-inch
CAPITOL 5-10 64-65
RAM (1549 "No No Never") 15-25
SSS INT'L 4-6 68

LEWIS, Marcus
Singles: 7-inch
AEGIS 3-4 88

LEWIS, Marty
Singles: 7-inch
FLAME 5-10 59-60
HOME of the BLUES 5-10 61

LEWIS, Melissa C&W '80
Singles: 7-inch
DOOR KNOB 3-5 80

LEWIS, Mia
Singles: 7-inch
PARROT 4-8 65

LEWIS, Monica, & Ames Bros. P/R '48
Singles: 78 rpm
SIGNATURE 5-10 48
Also see AMES BROTHERS

LEWIS, Paige
Singles: 7-inch
RENDEZVOUS 4-8 63

LEWIS, Pat
Singles: 7-inch
GOLDEN WORLD (42 "Can't Shake It Loose") 10-20 66
SOLID HIT (101 "Look What I Almost Missed") 15-25 66
SOLID HIT (105 "Warning") 15-25 66
SOLID HIT (109 "No One to Love") 200-300 67
Also see ADORABLES

LEWIS, Paul, & Swans
(Paul Lewis "The Mighty Swamba" & Swans)
Singles: 78 rpm
FORTUNE 100-200 55
Singles: 7-inch
FORTUNE (813 "Wedding Bells, Oh Wedding Bells") 500-1000 55
(Purple label.)
Also see SWANS

LEWIS, Pete "Guitar"
(Carl Lewis)
Singles: 78 rpm
FEDERAL 25-50 52
PEACOCK 25-50 53
Singles: 7-inch
FEDERAL (12066 "Louisiana Hop") 50-100 52
FEDERAL (12076 "Harmonica Boogie") 50-100 52
FEDERAL (12103 "Ooh, Midnight") 50-100 52
FEDERAL (12112 "The Blast") 50-100 52
PEACOCK (1624 "Goin' Crazy") 50-100 53

LEWIS, Ramsey LP '62
(Ramsey Lewis Trio; Ramsey Lewis & Co.)
Singles: 12-inch
COLUMBIA 4-6 79-85
Singles: 7-inch
ABC 3-5 74
ARGO 4-8 58-65
CADET 3-6 65-72
CHESS 3-5 73
COLUMBIA 3-5 72-87
EMARCY 4-8 59
EPs: 7-inch
ARGO (687 "Sound of Christmas") 15-25 61
LPs: 10/12-inch
ARGO (611 "Gentleman of Swing") 40-60 58
ARGO (627 "Gentleman of Jazz") 40-60 58
ARGO (642 "Ramsey Lewis Trio with Len Winchester") 30-50 59
ARGO (645 "An Hour with the Ramsey Lewis Trio") 25-50 59
ARGO (665 "Stretching Out") 25-50 60
ARGO (680 "From the Soil") 25-50 61
ARGO (687 "Sound of Christmas") 25-50 61
ARGO (693 "Sound of Spring") 25-35 62
ARGO (700 series) 20-40 62-65
CADET 10-20 65-72
COLUMBIA 6-12 72-85
EMARCY (36150 "Down to Earth") 25-45 59
(Monaural.)
EMARCY (80029 "Down to Earth") 35-60 59
(Stereo.)
TRIP 5-8 75
Members: Ramsey Lewis; Eldee Young; Red Holt; Cleveland Eaton; Maurice White.
Also see DUSHON, Jean, & Ramsey Lewis Trio
Also see EARTH, WIND & FIRE with Ramsey Lewis
Also see YOUNG HOLT UNLIMITED

LEWIS, Ramsey, & Nancy Wilson LP '84
LPs: 10/12-inch
COLUMBIA 5-10 84
Also see LEWIS, Ramsey
Also see WILSON, Nancy

LEWIS, Raymond
Singles: 7-inch
INSTANT 5-10 61-62

LEWIS, Richard
Singles: 78 rpm
ALADDIN 8-12 54-55
Singles: 7-inch
ALADDIN 10-20 54-55

LEWIS, Ricky
Singles: 7-inch
CINDY (100 "Stop, Think and Listen") 15-25
FURY (5051 "Cupid") 10-20 63
MERCURY (72640 "Dance All Night") 15-25 66

LEWIS, Roger
Singles: 7-inch
KARATE 4-8 65

LEWIS, Ross C&W '88
Singles: 7-inch
WOLF DOG 3-4 88-89

LEWIS, Roy
LPs: 10/12-inch
MONTGOMERY WARD (005 "A Tribute to Hank Williams") 10-20 60s

LEWIS, Rudy
Singles: 7-inch
ATLANTIC (2193 "Baby, I Dig Love") 8-12 63
Also see DRIFTERS

LEWIS, Rudy, & Sputniks
Singles: 7-inch
ART (157 "Beer, Beer and More Beer") 15-25 60
(First issue.)
RCA (7792 "Beer, Beer and More Beer") 8-12 60

LEWIS, Sabby
(With the Vibra-Tones; with Uniques)
Singles: 78 rpm
ABC-PAR 10-20 56
Singles: 7-inch
ABC-PAR (9685 "Ding-A-Ling") 15-25 56
ABC-PAR (9697 "Forgive Me My Love") 30-40 56
GONE (5074 "Bwana") 10-20 59

LEWIS, Sammy
Singles: 78 rpm
SUN (218 "I Feel So Worried") 50-75 55
Singles: 7-inch
8TH STREET 5-8
ST. LAWRENCE (704 "Hold On") 15-25
SUN (218 "I Feel So Worried") 100-150 55

LEWIS, Shirley P&R '89
Singles: 7-inch
VENDETTA 3-4 89

LEWIS, Sidney Jo
Singles: 7-inch
ISLAND (6 "Boppin' to Grandfather's Clock") 100-200 58

LEWIS, Smiley R&B '52
Singles: 78 rpm
COLONY (106 "Sad Life") 50-75 52
COLONY (110 "Where Were You") 50-75 52
DELUXE (3099 "Turn Your Volume On, Baby") 50-75 47
IMPERIAL 20-40 50-57
QUALITY 25-50 56
(Canadian.)
Singles: 7-inch
DOT (16674 "I Wonder") 8-12 64
IMPERIAL (5124 "My Baby Was Right") 75-125 52
IMPERIAL (5194 "The Bells Are Ringing") 50-100 52
IMPERIAL (5208 "Gumbo Blues") 50-100 52
IMPERIAL (5224 "Gypsy Blues") 50-100 54
IMPERIAL (5234 "Play Girl") 50-100 53
(Black vinyl.)
IMPERIAL (5234 "Play Girl") 150-200 53
(Colored vinyl.)
IMPERIAL (5241 "Caldonia's Party") 50-100 53
IMPERIAL (5252 "Little Fernandez") 50-100 53
IMPERIAL (5268 "Down the Road") 50-100 54
IMPERIAL (5279 "I Love You for Sentimental Reasons") 50-100 54
IMPERIAL (5296 "Can't Stop Loving You") 50-100 54
IMPERIAL (5316 "Too Many Drivers") 50-100 54
IMPERIAL (5325 "Jailbird") 50-100 54
IMPERIAL (5349 "Real Gone Lover") 50-100 55
IMPERIAL (5356 "I Hear You Knocking") 50-75 55
IMPERIAL (5372 "Queen of Hearts") 50-75 55
IMPERIAL (5380 "One Night") 50-75 56
IMPERIAL (5389 "She's Got Me Hook, Line and Sinker") 50-75 56
IMPERIAL (5404 "Down Yonder We Go Ballin' ") 50-75 56
IMPERIAL (5418 "Shame, Shame, Shame") 50-75 56
IMPERIAL (5431 thru 5820) 15-30 57-62
KNIGHT (2007 "Baby, Please") 10-20 59
KNIGHT (2011 "Lost Weekend") 10-20 59
LOMA (2024 "Bells Are Ringing") 8-10 65
OKEH (7146 "Tore Up") 8-10 62
QUALITY (1497 "She's Got Me Hook, Line and Sinker") 75-100 56
LPs: 10/12-inch
IMPERIAL (9141 "I Hear You Knocking") 150-200 61
Also see BARTHOLOMEW, Dave
Also see THOMAS, B.J., / Smiley Lewis

LEWIS, Tamala
Singles: 7-inch
MARTON (1002 "You Won't Say Nothing") 300-400

LEWIS, Texas Jim, & His Lone Star Cowboys C&W '44
Singles: 78 rpm
DECCA 5-8 44
VOCALION 5-10 37

LEWIS, Thelma
Singles: 7-inch
MAGIC CITY ("Why Weren't You There") 15-25
(No selection number used.)

LEWIS, Tiny
Singles: 7-inch
LINDA 5-10 59
TAP (502 "Too Much Rockin' ") 4-8 61

LEWIS, Vickie
Singles: 7-inch
NORMAR 8-12

LEWIS, Wally
Singles: 78 rpm
DOT 5-10 58
Singles: 7-inch
DOT (15705 "Kathleen") 15-25 58
DOT (157 "White Bobby Sox") 15-25 58
LIBERTY 8-12 59-61
SIMS 5-10 63
TALLY (117 "Kathleen") 25-50 58
(First issue.)

LEWIS, Webster R&B/LP '80
(With the Post-Pop Space Rock Be-Bop Gospel Tabernacle Orchestra & Chorus; with Love Unlimited Orchestra)
Singles: 12-inch
EPIC 4-8 77
UNLIMITED GOLD 4-6 81
Singles: 7-inch
EPIC 3-5 77-81
UNLIMITED GOLD 3-5 81
LPs: 10/12-inch
EPIC 5-10 78-80
UNLIMITED GOLD 5-10 81

LEWIS, Wink
Singles: 78 rpm
TONE 5-10 56
Singles: 7-inch
TONE 10-15 56

LEWIS & CLARKE P&R '67
(Lewis & Clarke Expedition)
Singles: 7-inch
CHARTMAKER 4-8 66
COLGEMS (1006 "I Feel Good") 5-10 67
COLGEMS (1011 "Destination Unknown") 8-12 67
COLGEMS (1022 "Why Need Pretend") 8-12 68
COLGEMS (1028 "Daddy's Plastic Child") 8-12 68
Picture Sleeves
COLGEMS (1006 "I Feel Good") 8-12 67
LPs: 10/12-inch
COLGEMS (105 "Lewis & Clarke Expedition") 20-35 67
Members: Travis Lewis; Boomer Clarke (Castleman); John London. Session: Jim Pewter; Michael Murphey.
Also see CASTLEMAN, Boomer
Also see MIKE, JOHN & BILL
Also see MURPHEY, Michael
Also see PEWTER, Jim

LEWIS CONNECTION
LP: 10/12-inch
("The Lewis Connection") 300-400 79
(No label name nor selection number used. Prince plays guitar and sings backup on *Got to Be Something Here*.)
Member: Sonny Thompson. Session: Prince.
Also see PRINCE

LEWIS SISTERS
("The Singing School Teachers")
Singles: 7-inch
V.I.P. (25018 "He's an Oddball") 15-25 65
V.I.P. (25024 "You Need Me") 15-25 65
Members: Kay Lewis; Helen Lewis.

LEXIA
LPs: 10/12-inch
VERVE 10-12 72

LEXINGTON AVENUE LOCAL
Singles: 7-inch
EPIC (10309 "Along Comes Mary") 8-12 68

LEXINGTON PROJECT
Singles: 7-inch
SONIC (4626 "She Looks Much Older") ... 10-20 67

LEXINGTONS
Singles: 7-inch
EVEREST (19369 "I Found My Baby") ... 10-15 60

LEXINGTONS
Singles: 7-inch
INTERNATIONAL (500 "My Honey Loves Another Girl") ... 20-30 63

LEXONS
Singles: 7-inch
LEXINGTON (100 "Angels Like You") ... 100-200 58

LEYDEN, Jimmy
Singles: 7-inch
BELL ... 4-8

LEYDEN, Leanne
(Lee-Ann Leyden)
Singles: 7-inch
DORE ... 4-8 62
RENDEZVOUS ... 4-8 61

LEYDEN JAR
Singles: 7-inch
A&M ... 3-5 81
LPs: 10/12-inch
A&M ... 5-10 81

LIA
Singles: 7-inch
VIRGIN ... 3-4 88

LIA, Orsa P&R '79
Singles: 7-inch
INFINITY ... 3-5 79
RCA ... 4-6 68

LIAR
Singles: 7-inch
BEARSVILLE ... 3-5 78
LPs: 10/12-inch
BEARSVILLE (738 "Set the World on Fire") ... 10-15 78
(Picture disc. Promotional issue only.)
BEARSVILLE (6982 "Set the World on Fire") ... 5-10 78

LIBBY, Brenda C&W '83
Singles: 7-inch
COMSTOCK ... 3-4 83

LIBBY & SUE
Singles: 7-inch
ERA ... 4-8 61

LIBERACE P&R '52
Singles: 78 rpm
ADVANCE ... 5-8 55
COLUMBIA ... 3-6 52-57
DECCA ... 3-6 52
LIBERACE (25 "Lullaby") ... 10-15
(Senven-inch disc. Made for Ortmeyer Furniture Co.)
Singles: 7-inch
A.V.I. ... 3-5 76-77
COLUMBIA (39000 thru 41000 series) ... 5-10 52-58
COLUMBIA (48000 series) ... 3-6
CORAL ... 4-6 59-61
DECCA (28000 series) ... 5-10 52
DOT ... 4-6 64-67
MGM ... 3-5 73
W.B. ... 3-5 71
Picture Sleeves
COLUMBIA ... 10-15 54
EPs: 7-inch
COLUMBIA ... 5-15 52-56
DECCA ... 10-20 52
LPs: 10/12-inch
ABC ... 5-8 74
A.V.I. (Except 6065) ... 5-8 73-79
A.V.I. (6065 "Liberace") ... 10-20 79
(Picture disc.)
BROOKVILLE ... 8-15
COLUMBIA (589 "Christmas") ... 30-45 54
COLUMBIA (600 "At the Hollywood Bowl") ... 30-45 55
COLUMBIA (645 "Hollywood Bowl Encore") ... 35-45 55
COLUMBIA (661 "By Candlelight") ... 25-45 55
COLUMBIA (800 "Sincerely Yours") ... 25-45 56
COLUMBIA (896 "At Home") ... 20-40 56
COLUMBIA (1000 thru 1200 series) ... 15-25 57-58
COLUMBIA (2516 "Piano Reverie") ... 50-75 56
(10-inch LP.)
COLUMBIA (2592 "Kiddin' on the Keys") ... 50-75 56
(10-inch LP.)
COLUMBIA (6217 "At the Piano") ... 50-100 52
(10-inch LP.)
COLUMBIA (6239 "Evening with Liberace") ... 50-100 53
(10-inch LP.)
COLUMBIA (6269 "Concertos for You") ... 50-100 53
(10-inch LP.)
COLUMBIA (6283 "Dream of Olwen") ... 50-100 54
(10-inch LP.)
COLUMBIA (6327 "Liberace Plays Chopin' ") ... 50-100 54
(10-inch LP.)
COLUMBIA (9800 series) ... 5-10 69
CORAL ... 8-15 59-64
DECCA ... 5-10 72
DOT ... 8-15 63-68
FORWARD ... 5-10 69
HARMONY ... 8-15 59-70
HAMILTON ... 5-10 65
MISTLETOE ... 5-8 74
PARAMOUNT ... 5-10 73-74
TRIP ... 4-8 76
VOCALION ... 5-10 68
W.B. ... 5-10 71
Also see PRESLEY, Elvis

LIBERACE, George
(George Liberace Orchestra)
LPs: 10/12-inch
COLUMBIA ... 15-30 54-55
IMPERIAL (9039 "George Liberace Goes Teenage") ... 30-45 57

LIBERATED BROTHER
Singles: 7-inch
RCA (10187 "Muhammad Ali") ... 4-8 75

LIBERATION
Singles: 7-inch
AM. GRAMAPHONE ... 5-10 71

LIBERATION STREET SINGERS
Singles: 7-inch
PENTAGRAM ... 3-5 70
LPs: 10/12-inch
PENTAGRAM ... 10-12 70

LIBERMAN, Jeff
LPs: 10/12-inch
LIBRAH (1545 "Jeff Liberman") ... 15-25 75
LIBRAH (6969 "Solitude Within") ... 15-25 75
LIBRAH (12157 "Synergy") ... 10-20 78

LIBERTO, Ray
Singles: 7-inch
DOT (15848 "Wicked, Wicked Woman") ... 5-10 58
TNT (156 "Wicked, Wicked Woman") ... 10-20 58

LIBERTY BELL
Singles: 7-inch
BACK BEAT (595 "Thoughts and Visions") ... 5-10 68
BACK BEAT (600 "Naw Naw Naw") ... 5-10 69
CEE BEE (1001 "The Nazz Are Blue") ... 20-30 67
CEE BEE (1002 "That's How It Will Be") ... 20-30 67
CEE BEE (1003 "Al's Blues") ... 20-30 67

LIBERTY BELLES
Singles: 7-inch
SHOUT ... 5-10 67

LIBERTY LADS
Singles: 7-inch
DIXON (111 "Too Much Loving") ... 15-25 60s

LIBERTY PARTY
Singles: 7-inch
JERDEN ... 5-10 66

LIBRARY
Singles: 7-inch
EXCLUSIVE ... 10-15 68

LICHTER, John
Singles: 7-inch
MIDWAY ("Mean-Eyed Cat") ... 30-50

LICK, SLICK & SLIDE
Singles: 78 rpm
SAVOY (1150 "I Got Drunk") ... 40-60 54
Singles: 7-inch
SAVOY (1150 "I Got Drunk") ... 75-100 54

LICORICE SCHTIK
Singles: 7-inch
DOT ... 4-8 68

LIDOS
Singles: 7-inch
BANDBOX (359 "Since I Last Saw You") ... 15-25 64
MERCURY (72080 "Bashanova") ... 8-12 62
PRINCE (6407 "Drivin' Little Dragster") ... 15-20 64

LIEBERMAN, Lori LP '73
Singles: 7-inch
CAPITOL ... 3-5 72-75
MILLENIUM ... 3-5 78
LPs: 10/12-inch
CAPITOL ... 8-12 72-74

LIEBMAN, Dave
LPs: 10/12-inch
ECM ... 8-10 74

LIESELOTTE
LPs: 10/12-inch
REQUEST ... 12-18 64

LT. GARCIA'S MAGIC MUSIC BOX
LPs: 10/12-inch
KAMA SUTRA ... 10-15 68
Also see KASENETZ-KATZ SINGING ORCHESTRAL CIRCUS

LIEUTENANT PIGEON
Singles: 7-inch
LONDON ... 5-8 73

LIFE
Singles: 7-inch
LAURIE ... 3-5 71

LIFE
Singles: 7-inch
ELEKTRA ... 3-5 81
LPs: 10/12-inch
ELEKTRA ... 5-8 81

LIFEGUARDS
Singles: 7-inch
ABC-PAR (10021 "Everybody Out'a the Pool") ... 10-20 59
CASA BLANCA (5535 "Everybody Out'a the Pool") ... 20-30 59
DR (69 "Everybody Out'a the Pool") 8-15 65
LPs: 10/12-inch
WYNCOTE ... 15-25 64
Also see HALEY, Bill

LIFEGUARDS
Singles: 7-inch
CATCH (104 "State Beach") ... 20-30 64
REPRISE (277 "Swim Time") ... 10-20 64
Members: Phil Sloan; Steve Barri.
Also see BARRI, Steve
Also see SLOAN, P.F.

LIFERAFT
LPs: 10/12-inch
AERO SPACE ... 10-12 72

LIFESTYLE R&B '77
Singles: 7-inch
MCA ... 3-5 77
LPs: 10/12-inch
MCA ... 8-10 77

LIFTON, Jimmy
Singles: 7-inch
ATLANTIC ... 3-4 87

LIGGETT, Larry
Singles: 78 rpm
CHESS ... 10-15 54-56
NOTE (1000 "The Flop") ... 10-15 56
Singles: 7-inch
CHESS ... 15-25 54-56
NOTE (1000 "The Flop") ... 15-25 56

LIGGETT, Otis D&D '83
Singles: 12-inch
EMERGENCY ... 4-6 83
Singles: 7-inch
EMERGENCY ... 3-5 83

LIGGINS, Jimmy R&B '48
(With His 3-D Music)
Singles: 78 rpm
ALADDIN ... 15-25 54
SPECIALTY ... 15-25 47-54
Singles: 7-inch
ALADDIN (3250 "I Ain't Drunk") ... 25-50 54
ALADDIN (3251 "No More Alcohol") ... 25-50 54
DUPLEX ... 4-6
SPECIALTY (434 "Brown Skin Baby") ... 25-50 49
SPECIALTY (470 "Drunk") ... 20-40 53
(Black vinyl.)
SPECIALTY (470 "Drunk") ... 50-100 53
(Colored vinyl.)
SPECIALTY (484 "Going Away") ... 25-50 54

LIGGINS, Joe P&R/R&B '45
(With His Honeydrippers)
Singles: 78 rpm
DOT ... 8-15 51-56
EXCLUSIVE ... 15-25 45-48
SMASH ... 10-20 54
SPECIALTY ... 10-20 49-54
Singles: 7-inch
ALADDIN (3368 "Justina") ... 15-25 56
DOT (1031 "The Honey Dripper") ... 15-25 56
DOT (1032 "I've Got a Right to Cry") ... 15-25 56
DOT (1033 "Tanya") ... 15-25 56
MERCURY (70440 "Yeah, Yeah, Yeah") ... 20-30 54
SPECIALTY (338 "The Honey Dripper") ... 20-40 49
SPECIALTY (379 "Little Joe's Boogie") ... 20-40 51
SPECIALTY (392 "Frankie Lee") ... 20-40 51
SPECIALTY (402 "Whiskey, Gin and Wine") ... 20-40 52
SPECIALTY (409 "Louisiana Woman") ... 20-40 52
SPECIALTY (413 "So Alone") ... 20-40 52
SPECIALTY (426 "Boogie Woogie Lou") ... 20-40 52
SPECIALTY (430 "Tanya") ... 20-40 52
SPECIALTY (441 "Goin' Back to New Orleans") ... 20-40 52
SPECIALTY (453 "Freight Train Blues") ... 20-40 53
SPECIALTY (465 "Farewell Blues") ... 20-40 53
SPECIALTY (474 "Everyone's Down on Me) ... 20-40 53
SPECIALTY (529 "Whiskey, Women and Loaded Dice") ... 25-50 54
LPs: 10/12-inch
BLUES SPECTOR ... 15-25
Also see MILTON, Roy / Joe Liggins

LIGHT
Singles: 7-inch
A&M ... 4-8 67

LIGHT, Burt
Singles: 7-inch
CROSSROAD ... 4-8

LIGHT, Enoch, & His Orchestra P&R '37
(Terry Snyder & All-Stars; Command All-Stars; with Light Brigade; with Brass Menagerie)
Singles: 78 rpm
VOCALION ... 4-6 37
Singles: 7-inch
COMMAND ... 4-6 61
LPs: 10/12-inch
COMMAND ... 8-20 59-72
GRAND AWARD ... 10-15 59
PROJECT ... 5-10 67-71
REALISTIC ... 5-10
WALDORF (185 "Melody of Love") ... 35-55 54
(10-inch LP. Cover pictures Tina Louise, although she is not heard on the disc. Also issued credited to Vincent Lopez & His Orchestra.)
WALDORF (193 "Moments to Remember") ... 35-55 54
(10-inch LP. Cover pictures Tina Louise, although she is not heard on the disc. Also issued credited to Vincent Lopez & His Orchestra.)
WALDORF (1214 "Moments to Remember") ... 25-50 57
(Cover pictures Jayne Mansfield, although she is not heard on the disc. Also issued credited to Vincent Lopez & His Orchestra.)
WALDORF (1232 "Melody of Love") ... 20-40 57
(10-inch LP. Cover pictures Tina Louise, although she is not heard on the disc. Also issued credited to Vincent Lopez & His Orchestra.)
WALDORF (1329 "Moments to Remember") ... 20-40 58
(Cover pictures Tina Louise, although she is not heard on the disc. Also issued credited to Vincent Lopez & His Orchestra.)
Members: Enoch Light; Terry Snyder; Charles Magnante; Dick Hyman; Jack Lesberg; Teddy Sommer; Bob Haggart; Tony Mattola; Willie Rodriguez; Moe Wechsler; Urbie Green; Bobby Byrne; Pee Wee Erwin; Artie Marotti; Dominic Cortese; Ezelie Watson; Russ Banzer; Stanley Webb; Milt Yaner; Leonard Calderon; George Dessinger; Bernie Kaufman.
Also see LOPEZ, Vincent, & His Orchestra
Also see MANSFIELD, Jayne
Also see TINA LOUISE

LIGHT, J.J.
(Jim Stallings)
Singles: 7-inch
LIBERTY ... 5-10 69
Also see SIR DOUGLAS QUINTET
Also see STALLINGS, James Michael

LIGHT BROTHERS
Singles: 7-inch
CANADIAN-AMERICA ... 5-10 60
DOT ... 5-10 61

LIGHT DRIVERS
Singles: 7-inch
GEMINI (1021 "Operator") ... 15-25

LIGHT NITES
Singles: 7-inch
DUNWICH (149 "Same Old Thing") ... 10-15 67

LIGHTFOOT, Charlie
Singles: 7-inch
SPOTLIGHT (5010 "Yes, Baby") ... 100-150 60

LIGHTFOOT, Gordon LP '69
(Gord Lightfoot)
Singles: 7-inch
ABC-PAR ... 10-20 62
CHATEAU ... 5-10 65
REPRISE ... 3-5 70-77
U.A. ... 3-8 65-69
W.B. (Except 5621) ... 3-5 78-86
W.B. (5621 "For Lovin' Me") ... 5-10 65
Picture Sleeves
U.A. (50152 "The Way I Feel") ... 5-10 67
W.B. ... 3-4 86
LPs: 10/12-inch
AME ("Early Lightfoot") ... 75-100
(Number not known.)
K-TEL ... 5-8
LIBERTY ... 5-8 80
MFSL (018 "Sundown") ... 25-50 78
PICKWICK ... 5-8 79
REPRISE (Except 93228) ... 5-12 70-76
REPRISE (93228 "Sit Down Young Stranger") ... 10-20 70
U.A. (Except 3400 & 6400 series) ... 5-10 69-74
U.A. (3400 series) ... 10-15 66-69
(Monaural.)
U.A. (6400 series) ... 10-20 66-69
(Stereo.)
W.B. ... 5-8 78-86

LIGHTFOOT, Papa
(Papa George Lightfoot; with His Harmonica; Alexander Lightfoot)
Singles: 78 rpm
ALADDIN (3171 "After-While") ... 50-75 52
ALADDIN (3304 "Blue Lights") ... 40-60 52
IMPERIAL ... 40-60 54
SAVOY (1161 "Mean Old Train") ... 10-15 55
SULTAN ... 40-60 50
Singles: 7-inch
ALADDIN (3171 "After-While") ... 100-150 52
ALADDIN (3304 "Blue Lights") ... 75-125 52
IMPERIAL (5289 "Wine, Women, Whiskey") ... 75-125 54
SAVOY (1161 "Mean Old Train") ... 15-25 55
LPs: 10/12-inch
VAULT ... 10-15 69

LIGHTHOUSE LP '70
Singles: 7-inch
EVOLUTION ... 3-5 71-72
POLYDOR ... 4-6 73-74
RCA ... 3-4 69-70
LPs: 10/12-inch
EVOLUTION ... 10-15 71-72
JANUS ... 8-10 76
POLYDOR ... 8-12 73-74
RCA ... 10-15 69-70
Also see McBRIDE, Bob

LIGHTMAN, Aaron
LPs: 10/12-inch
POPPY ... 10-12 70

LIGHTMYTH
Singles: 7-inch
RCA (219 "Across the Universe") ... 10-20 70
(Promotional issue only.)
RCA (0361 "Across the Universe") ... 3-5 70

LIGHTNIN' BUG
(With Sammy Berk)
Singles: 78 rpm
TRIPLE A ... 10-20 53
Singles: 7-inch
TRIPLE A ... 25-35 53

LIGHTNIN' GUITAR'S BAND
(Sonny Smith; Lonnie Johnson)
LPs: 10/12-inch
MASTERSEAL ... 15-25
Also see SONNY BOY & LONNIE

LIGHTNIN' JR.
(L.C. Williams)
Singles: 78 rpm
GOLD STAR (614 "Trying Trying") ... 25-50 47
Also see WILLIAMS, L.C.

LIGHTNIN' JR. & EMPIRES
(Champion Jack Dupree)
Singles: 78 rpm
HARLEM ... 50-75 55
Singles: 7-inch
HARLEM (2334 "Ragged and Hungry") ... 100-150 55
Also see DUPREE, Champion Jack
Also see EMPIRES

LIGHTNIN' LEON
(Billy Lee Riley)
Singles: 7-inch
RITA ... 10-20 60
Also see RILEY, Billy Lee

LIGHTNIN' ROD
LPs: 10/12-inch
U.A. ... 10-15 73

LIGHTNIN' SLIM R&B '59
(Otis Hicks)
Singles: 78 rpm
ACE (505 "Bad Feeling Blues") ... 50-75 55
EXCELLO ... 15-25 55-57
FEATURE (3006 "Rock Me, Mama") ... 50-75 54
FEATURE (3008 "I Can't Live Happy") ... 10-25 54
FEATURE (3012 "Bugger Bugger Boy") ... 10-25 54
Singles: 7-inch
ACE (505 "Bad Feeling Blues") ... 75-125 55
EXCELLO (2000 series) ... 30-50 55-56
EXCELLO (2100 series) ... 20-30 57-61
EXCELLO (2200 series) ... 10-20 62-67
EXCELLO (2300 series) ... 5-10 68-72
FEATURE (3006 "Rock Me, Mama") ... 100-200 54
FEATURE (3008 "I Can't Live Happy") ... 25-50 54
FEATURE (3012 "Bugger Bugger Boy") ... 25-50 54
LPs: 10/12-inch
EXCELLO (8000 "Rooster Blues") 30-50 60
EXCELLO (8004 "Bell Ringer") ... 15-25 65
EXCELLO (8018 "High and Low Down") ... 10-15 71
EXCELLO (8023 "London Gumbo") ... 10-15 72
QUICKSILVER ... 10-15

LIGHTNING
Singles: 7-inch
P.I.P. ... 10-20 71
LPs: 10/12-inch
P.I.P. (6807 "Lightning") ... 20-30 71
Also see LITTER
Also see WHITE LIGHTING

LIGHTNING
LPs: 10/12-inch
CASABLANCA ... 5-10 79

LIGHTNING SEEDS LP '90
LPs: 10/12-inch
MCA ... 5-8 90

LIL ALFRED & CUPCAKES: see DUNAWAY, Shelton, & Cupcakes

LIL' BOB & LILLIPOPS: see LITTLE BOB & LOLLIPOPS

LIL' BOYS BLUE
Singles: 7-inch
BAT WING (2003 "I'm Not There") ... 20-30 66

LIL DYNAMITE & EXPLOSIONS
Singles: 7-inch
LIL DYNAMITE (578 "Dancing Little Thing") ... 10-20 62

LIL' JUNE & JANUARYS: see LITTLE JUNE & HIS JANUARYS

LIL' LAVAIR & JADES
Singles: 7-inch
LENNAN........................ 8-12

LIL' QUEENIE
Singles: 7-inch
GREAT SOUTH........................ 3-5
Picture Sleeves
GREAT SOUTH........................ 3-5

LIL' RAY: see LITTLE RAY

LIL' SOUL BROTHERS
Singles: 7-inch
D-TOWN (10691 "I've Got Heartaches")........................10-20 66
WHEELSVILLE (111 "I've Got Heartaches")........................15-25 66

LIL' WALLY
(With the Venturas)
Singles: 7-inch
DRUM BOY........................ 5-10 65
JAY JAY........................ 3-8 60s
LPs: 10/12-inch
JAY JAY........................ 5-15
Also see VENTURAS

LILA & RONNIE
Singles: 7-inch
SECCO........................ 8-12

LILE, Bobby
(With the El Montes)
Singles: 7-inch
ALMO (227 "Man of the World")..........15-25 65
CORONA........................ 5-10 64
4 STAR........................ 8-12 58-59
IMPERIAL........................ 8-12 60-61
ROLLO........................ 5-10 65
SAND........................ 5-10 62
SIDEWALK........................ 4-8 67
TRILL........................ 5-10 63
WHITE WHALE........................ 4-8 68

LILITH
LPs: 10/12-inch
GALAXIE........................ 8-10 78

LILLEY, Carol J.
(Carol Jean)
Singles: 7-inch
STARR........................ 3-5 78

LILLY, Lee
Singles: 7-inch
ALCOR........................ 4-8 62

LILY MAE & House Rockers
Singles: 78 rpm
MIRACLE........................15-25 48

LIMAHL P&R/D&D/LP '85
(Chris Hamill)
Singles: 12-inch
EMI AMERICA........................ 4-6 85-86
Singles: 7-inch
EMI AMERICA........................ 3-4 85-86
Picture Sleeves
EMI AMERICA........................ 3-4 85-86
LPs: 10/12-inch
EMI AMERICA........................ 5-8 85-86
Also see KAJAGOOGOO

LIMAR, Ronnie
Singles: 7-inch
BRC (116 "You Mean the World to Me Sweetheart")........................ 8-12 76

LIME
Singles: 7-inch
CHESS (2045 "Hey Girl")..............10-15 68
WESTWOOD ("Love A-Go-Go")........ 5-8 60s
(Selection number not known.)

LIME D&D '83
Singles: 12-inch
PRISM........................ 4-6 83
TSR........................ 4-6 85
Singles: 7-inch
PRISM........................ 3-5 83
LPs: 10/12-inch
PRISM........................ 5-8 83

LIME 3
LPs: 10/12-inch
ULTRASOUND/MATRA (006 "Guilty")........................40-50 83
(Picture disc. Promotional issue only. Canadian.)

LIMELIGHTERS
Singles: 78 rpm
JOSIE (795 "Cabin Hideaway")......40-60 56
Singles: 7-inch
JOSIE (795 "Cabin Hideaway")....75-100 56

LIMELIGHTERS
(With the "Guitar-Billy Davis Orchestra")
Singles: 7-inch
GILCO (213 "This Lonely Boy")...250-350 57

LIMELITERS P&R/LP '61
Singles: 7-inch
ELEKTRA........................ 5-10 60-61
RCA........................ 5-10 61-64
W.B........................ 4-8 68
Picture Sleeves
RCA........................ 8-12 61-63
EPs: 7-inch
RCA ("Introducing . . .")..................10-15 61
(Promotional issue only. Introduces 11 new RCA acts with about 30 seconds of music by: Limeliters, Cables; Toni Harper; Gary Judis; Cleo Jons; Baker Knight; Langan Sisters; Barry Martin; Penny & Jean; Gordon Terry; Universals.)
LPs: 10/12-inch
CAMDEN........................5-10 74
ELEKTRA........................15-25 60-61
LEGACY........................8-10 70
PICKWICK........................ 5-8 72
RCA (Except 2336)........................10-25 61-68
RCA (2336 "Pure Gold")........................ 5-8 77
STAX........................6-10 74
W.B........................8-15 68
Members: Glen Yarbrough; Lou Gottlieb; Alex Hassilev; Ernie Sheldon.
Also see ANN-MARGRET
Also see CABLES
Also see GATEWAY SINGERS
Also see HARPER, Toni
Also see LANGAN SISTERS
Also see PENNY & JEAN
Also see YARBROUGH, Glen

LIMELITERS / Della Reese /Mario Lanza / Norman Luboff Choir
EPs: 7-inch
RCA (33-150 "Headline Hits")..........8-12 61
(Promotional issue, made for Nestle's.)
Also see LANZA, Mario
Also see LIMELITERS
Also see LUBOFF, Norman
Also see REESE, Della

LIMELITERS
Singles: 7-inch
PIC........................ 4-6

LIMELITES
Singles: 7-inch
APT........................15-25 60

LIMEY & YANKS
Singles: 7-inch
LAURIE........................10-20 67
LOMA (2059 "Gather My Things and Go")........................25-40 66
STARBURST (127 "Guaranteed Love")........................35-55 65

LIMEYS
Singles: 7-inch
AMCAN (406 "Somebody Help Me")........................10-20 64
DOT........................8-12 65
SHERWOOD (1715 "Come Back")........................15-25 60s
Members: Andrea Gennard; Stephan Gennard.

LIMEYS
Singles: 7-inch
COULEE........................8-12 65

LIMIT R&B '82
Singles: 12-inch
PORTRAIT........................ 4-6 84
Singles: 7-inch
ARISTA........................ 3-5 82
PORTRAIT........................ 3-4 84
Also see GUTHRIE, Gwen

LIMITATIONS
Singles: 7-inch
BACONE (1011 "I'm Lonely")..........10-20
VOLT........................ 3-5 71

LIMITED WARRANTY P&R '86
Singles: 7-inch
ATCO........................ 3-4 86
Picture Sleeves
ATCO........................ 3-4 86
LPs: 10/12-inch
ATCO........................ 5-8 86

LIMMIE & FAMILY COOKIN' P&R '72
Singles: 7-inch
AVCO........................ 3-6 72

LIMOUSINE
LPs: 10/12-inch
GSF........................15-20 72
Also see FAITH

LINCOLN, Abbey
LPs: 10/12-inch
BARNABY........................8-12 72
INNER CITY........................ 5-8 79

LINCOLN, Philamore
LPs: 10/12-inch
EPIC........................10-15 70

LINCOLN, Victor, & Toybreakers
Singles: 7-inch
MURBO........................ 4-8 66

LINCOLN COUNTY C&W '81
Singles: 7-inch
SOUNDWAVES........................ 3-5 81

LINCOLN FIG & DATES
Singles: 7-inch
WORTHY (1006 "Way Up")..........50-75 58
(Black vinyl.)
WORTHY (1006 "Way Up")..........75-125 58
(Colored vinyl.)
Members: Ivan Figueroa; Steve Aspromonti; Manny Banuchi; Johnny Gigliono; Eddie Cruz.

LINCOLN PARK ZOO
Singles: 7-inch
MERCURY........................ 4-8 67

LINCOLN STREET EXIT
Singles: 7-inch
ECCO (1001 "Bummer")..........10-20 67
LANCE (102 "Paper Place")..........15-25 66
LANCE (109 "Who's Been Driving My Yellow Taxi Cab")........................15-25 66
LPs: 10/12-inch (continued)
MAINSTREAM (722 "Soulful Drifter")........................5-10 69
SOULED OUT (104 "St. Louis Mama")........................5-10 69
EPs: 7-inch
PSYCH OUT (101 "Lincoln Street Exit")........................10-15 83
LPs: 10/12-inch
MAINSTREAM (6126 "Drive It")......30-50 70
Members: Michael Martin.
Also see XIT

LINCOLN TRIO
Singles: 7-inch
BIG TOP........................4-8 60
FASCINATION........................4-8 61

LINCOLNS
Singles: 7-inch
ALJON (113 "I Cried")..........150-200 60
ATLAS (1100 "Don't Let Me Shed Any More Tears")........................100-125 58
MERCURY (71553 "Baby, Please Let Me Love You")........................10-20 59

LINCOLNS
Singles: 7-inch
BUD (113 "Sometime Somewhere")........................10-20 61

LINCOLNS
Singles: 7-inch
MEDALLION........................5-10 62
TRIPP........................4-8 69

LINCOLNS
Singles: 7-inch
ABCO (1001 "Night Drag")..........10-20 64
(Also issued as by the Vagabonds.)
Also see VAGABONDS

LINCOLNS
Singles: 7-inch
DOT (16958 "Pop Kat")..........5-10 66

LINCOLNS QUINTET
Singles: 7-inch
ANGLE TONE (552 "Dream of Romance")........................150-200 58

LIND, Bob P&R/LP '66
Singles: 7-inch
CAPITOL........................3-5 71
VERVE/FOLKWAYS........................4-6 66
WORLD PACIFIC........................4-8 65-66
LPs: 10/12-inch
CAPITOL........................10-15 71
VERVE/FOLKWAYS........................10-20 66
WORLD PACIFIC........................10-20 66

LIND, Cory
Singles: 7-inch
VITA (164 "Billy Loves Me")..........10-15 57

LINDA & DEL RIOS
Singles: 7-inch
CRACKERJACK........................10-15 62

LINDA & EPICS
Singles: 7-inch
BLUE MOON (415 "Memories of Love")........................25-35 59

LINDA & PAUL
Singles: 7-inch
ROULETTE........................4-8 63

LINDA & PRETENDERS
Singles: 7-inch
ASSULT (1879 "Believe Me")..........15-25 63

LINDA & ROBERTO
Singles: 7-inch
SHAD........................8-12 58

LINDA & TEARS
Singles: 7-inch
CHALLENGE (59317 "Good Goodbye")........................30-50 65

LINDA & VISTAS
Singles: 7-inch
SHRINE (100 "She Went Away")........................200-300 65

LINDA JEAN
Singles: 7-inch
FAYETTE........................10-15 65

LINDA DEE: see DEE, Linda

LINDA JO & NOMADS
Singles: 7-inch
JULIAN (103 "Just Like You")..........15-25 60s

LINDA LOU
Singles: 7-inch
CHUCKIE........................5-8 65

LINDA LOU & HITMAKERS
Singles: 7-inch
LAMA (7786 "The Torch Is Out")........................75-125 61

LINDA SUE
Singles: 7-inch
CLARK COUNTRY........................3-5 77

LINDE, Dennis
Singles: 7-inch
ELEKTRA........................3-5 73-74
INTREPID........................3-6 69
MONUMENT........................3-5 76-78
Picture Sleeves
MONUMENT........................4-6 76
LPs: 10/12-inch
ELEKTRA........................8-12 73-74
INTREPID........................12-18 66
MONUMENT........................8-10 77-78
Also see JUBAL

LINDEMAN, Bob, & Continentals
Singles: 7-inch
CUCA (1569 "Stay Near Me")..........8-12 70s
Also see CONTINENTALS

LINDEN, Kathy P&R '58
(With Joe Leahy's Orchestra)
Singles: 7-inch
CAPITOL........................4-8 62-63
FELSTED........................5-15 58-59
MONUMENT........................5-10 60-61
NATIONAL........................4-8 60s
RECORD PROD. CORP........................4-8 61
Picture Sleeves
FELSTED........................10-20 58-59
MONUMENT........................4-8 60-61
EPs: 7-inch
FELSTED (35001 "Hits")..........35-45 58
LPs: 10/12-inch
FELSTED (7501 "That Certain Boy")........................40-60 59
Also see LEAHY, Joe

LINDER, Sy, & Cams / Cams
Singles: 7-inch
INDIE (1303 "Drag Race")..........10-20 60s

LINDISFARNE P&R '72
Singles: 7-inch
ATCO........................3-5 78
ELEKTRA........................3-5 72-73
LPs: 10/12-inch
ATCO........................8-12 78
ELEKTRA........................10-15 71-74

LINDLEY, David LP '81
(With El Rayo)
Singles: 7-inch
ASYLUM........................3-5 81
LPs: 10/12-inch
ASYLUM........................5-10 81
ELEKTRA........................5-8 88
Also see BROWNE, Jackson

LINDSAY, Calvin, & Hysterics
Singles: 7-inch
JOKERS 3 (2143 "So Young and So Innocent")........................15-25

LINDSAY, J.D.
Singles: 7-inch
LITTLETOWN........................4-8 77

LINDSAY, Mark P&R '69
Singles: 7-inch
COLUMBIA........................3-8 69-75
ELKA (310 "Sing Your Own Song")....3-6
GREEDY........................3-6 76
W.B........................3-6 77
LPs: 10/12-inch
COLUMBIA........................10-15 70-71
Also see REVERE, Paul, & Raiders
Also see UNKNOWNS

LINDSAY, Merle
Singles: 7-inch
SHASTA........................5-10 59

LINDSEY, Bennie C&W '76
Singles: 7-inch
PHONO........................3-5 76

LINDSEY, Benny
Singles: 7-inch
GALAXIE........................4-6

LINDSEY, Bobby
Singles: 7-inch
CANADIAN AMERICAN..........4-8 61
Also see BISHOPS

LINDSEY, Bryan
Singles: 7-inch
BOYD........................4-8 63

LINDSEY, Hank
Singles: 7-inch
DEARBORN (614 "Action Speaks Louder Than Words")........................10-20
MSK........................3-5 80

LINDSEY, Judy C&W '89
Singles: 7-inch
GYPSEY........................3-4 89

LINDSEY, LaWanda C&W '69
Singles: 7-inch
CAPITOL........................3-5 73-74
CHART........................3-6 69-72
MERCURY........................3-5 77-78
LPs: 10/12-inch
CAPITOL........................5-10 74
CHART........................6-12 69-71

LINDSEY, LaWanda, & Kenny Vernon C&W '71
Singles: 7-inch
CHART........................3-6 71
LPs: 10/12-inch
CHART........................6-12 70
Also see LINDSEY, LaWanda
Also see VERNON, Kenny

LINDSEY, Lewis
Singles: 7-inch
ALL AMERICAN (104 "So Sweet")........................20-40

LINDSEY, Theresa
Singles: 7-inch
CORRECTONE (1053 "Good Idea")........................10-20 60s
CORRECTONE (5840 "Gotta Find a Way")........................10-20 60s
GOLDEN WORLD (43 "I'll Bet You")........................15-25 66

LINDSEY BROTHERS
Singles: 7-inch
NASCO........................4-8 62

LINDSEY TRIPLETS
Singles: 7-inch
TOP RANK........................8-12 59

LINDY, Johnny
Singles: 7-inch
OPERATORS........................4-8 62

LINDY & LAVELLS
(With the Lindells)
Singles: 7-inch
LAVETTE (5001 "Meet Me Tonight in Your Dreams")........................25-50 64
RED FEATHER ("There's My Baby")........................15-25
(No selection number used.)
Member: Lindy Blaskey.
Also see BLASKEY, Lindy

LINEAR P&R/LP '90
LPs: 10/12-inch
ATLANTIC........................5-8 90

LINER P&R '79
Singles: 7-inch
ATCO........................3-5 79
LPs: 10/12-inch
ATCO........................5-10 79

LINE'S END
Singles: 7-inch
LOMPRI (90599 "Hey Little Girl")...15-25 68
Members: Steve Harkus; Pat James; Rocky Rockwell; Mike Tebeau; Bob Lakas.

LINHART, Buzzy
(With Music)
Singles: 7-inch
BUDDAH........................3-5 72-73
KAMA SUTRA........................3-5 71-72
PHILIPS........................3-5 69
LPs: 10/12-inch
ATCO........................8-10 74
KAMA SUTRA........................10-12 71-72
PHILIPS........................10-12 69

LINK
LPs: 10/12-inch
OUR GANG........................5-10 80

LINK - EDDY COMBO R&B '61
Singles: 7-inch
REPRISE........................8-12 61
Singles: 12-inch
Members: Al Garcia; Fred Mendoza; Vince Bumatay; Art Rodriguez.
Also see RHYTHM KINGS

LINKCHAIN, Hip
LPs: 10/12-inch
TEARDROP........................5-8 82

LINKLETTER, Art LP '66
Singles: 7-inch
CAPITOL........................3-5 69
EPs: 7-inch
COLUMBIA........................5-10 56
WORD........................3-5 69
LPs: 10/12-inch
CAPITOL........................8-15 61
COLUMBIA........................15-25 56
HARMONY........................8-15 59
20TH FOX........................8-15 63-66
WORD........................5-10 68

LINKLETTER, Bob
Singles: 7-inch
CHATTAHOOCHEE (702 "The Out Crowd")........................10-15 65

LINKS
Singles: 7-inch
TEENAGE (1009 "She's the One")........................1000-2000 57
Members: Herb Fisher; James Walton; Wilbert Dobson; Joe Woodley; John Terry.
Also see BACHELORS

LINKS
Singles: 7-inch
BRUNSWICK (55081 "Scraunch") 15-25 58

LINN, Ray
Singles: 7-inch
DOT (16471 "Trumpeter's Dream")........................5-10 63

LINN & GINN
(With the Rocks)
Singles: 7-inch
TNT (9019 "Promise Me")..........400-600 59

LINN COUNTY
(Linn County Blues Band)
Singles: 7-inch
MERCURY........................4-6 68-69
PHILIPS........................4-6 70
Picture Sleeves
PHILIPS........................4-6 70
LPs: 10/12-inch
MERCURY........................10-15 68-69
PHILIPS........................10-15 69

LINNEAS
Singles: 7-inch
DIAMOND........................8-12 68

LINNETTES
Singles: 7-inch
PALETTE........................10-15 60

LINSEY, Bill
Singles: 7-inch
DOT........................4-8 63

LINTON, Sherwin C&W '77
(With the Cotton Kings)
Singles: 7-inch
BLACK GOLD 3-6 68-72
BREAKER 3-4 86
HICKORY 3-5 69
NEW WORLD 4-6 67
SOMA (1405 "Remember Me") 8-12 63
SOUNDWAVES 3-5 77-83
Picture Sleeves
BREAKER (3902 "Santa Got a DWI") 3-5 86
LPs: 10/12-inch
BLACK GOLD 8-12 72

LINTONS
Singles: 7-inch
ENRICA (005 "Lost Love") 15-25

LINUS & LITTLE PEOPLE
Singles: 7-inch
HERITAGE 4-8

LINX R&B/LP '81
Singles: 7-inch
CHRYSALIS 3-4 81
Picture Sleeves
CHRYSALIS 3-4 81
LPs: 10/12-inch
CHRYSALIS 5-8 81
Members: David Grant; Peter Martin.
Also see GRANT, David

LION, Johnny
Singles: 7-inch
COED 10-15 59

LION & LEPRECHAUNS
Singles: 7-inch
LITTLE FORT (8846 "Mouse Trap") 20-30 60s

LIONEL & CLIPPER TRIO
Singles: 7-inch
CARIB 5-10

LION'S DEN
Singles: 7-inch
SIRE 3-4 79

LIONS
(With René Hall Orchestra)
Singles: 7-inch
RENDEZVOUS (116 "Two Timing Lover") 150-250 60
(Red label.)
RENDEZVOUS (116 "Two Timing Lover") 100-200 60
(White label. Promotional issue only.)
Also see HALL, René

LIONS
Singles: 7-inch
EVEREST (19388 "No One") 10-15 60
IMPERIAL (5678 "Hickory Dickory") 5-10 60
MARK IV (1 "No One") 10-15 60

LIONS
LPs: 10/12-inch
METRO 10-20 62
Also see LIVERT, Paul, & Lions

LIONS & GHOSTS LP '87
LPs: 10/12-inch
EMI AMERICA 5-8 87

LIPPS, INC. P&R/R&B/LP '80
Singles: 7-inch
CASABLANCA 3-5 79-83
LPs: 10/12-inch
CASABLANCA 5-8 79-81

LIPS
LPs: 10/12-inch
NEMPEROR 5-10 79

LIPSCOMB, Mance
Singles: 7-inch
REPRISE 4-8 61
LPs: 10/12-inch
ARHOOLIE 5-15 63-86
REPRISE (2012 "Trouble in Mind") 20-25 61
(Monaural.)
REPRISE (R9-2012 "Trouble in Mind") 25-30 61
(Stereo.)
REPRISE (6000 series) 8-12 70

LIPSCOMB, Max K.
Singles: 7-inch
DOT 10-15 62
SQUIRE (102 "Baby, You're So Square") 100-200 62
Also see McKAY, Scotty

LIPSTICK KILLERS
Singles: 7-inch
VOXX 3-5

LIPSTIQUE
LPs: 10/12-inch
TOM 'N JERRY 5-10 78

LIPTON, Holly C&W '89
Singles: 7-inch
EVERGREEN 3-4 89

LIPTON, Peggy
Singles: 7-inch
ODE 4-8 68-69
Picture Sleeves
ODE 5-10 69
LPs: 10/12-inch
ODE 10-20 68

LIQUID GOLD P&R '79
Singles: 12-inch
CRITIQUE 4-6 83
PARACHUTE 4-8 79
Singles: 7-inch
CRITIQUE 3-4 83
PARACHUTE 3-5 79
LPs: 10/12-inch
PARACHUTE 5-10 79

LIQUID LIQUID D&D '83
Singles: 12-inch
99 RECORDS 4-6 83

LIQUID SMOKE P&R '70
Singles: 7-inch
AVCO EMBASSY 4-8 70
LPs: 10/12-inch
AVCO EMBASSY (33005 "Liquid Smoke") 20-30 70
Member: Sandy Dantaleo.

LIQUIDATORS
LPs: 10/12-inch
REGGAE 8-10 70

LIS, Yolanda
Singles: 7-inch
STRAND 4-8 59

LISA D&D '83
Singles: 12-inch
MOBY DICK 5-10 83-84

LISA & LULLABIES
(Concords)
Singles: 7-inch
COED (589 "Why Do I Cry") 15-25 64
Also see CONCORDS

LISA & WAYNE
Singles: 7-inch
SPARKETTE ("Sweet Talk") 8-12
(Selection number not known.)

LISA LISA P&R/R&B/D&D/LP '85
(With Cult Jam & Full Force)
Singles: 12-inch
COLUMBIA 4-6 85-86
Singles: 7-inch
COLUMBIA 3-4 85-89
PENDULUM 3-4
Picture Sleeves
COLUMBIA 3-4 85-89
LPs: 10/12-inch
COLUMBIA 5-8 84-89
Member: Lisa Velez.
Also see FULL FORCE
Also see KING DREAM CHORUS & Holiday Crew

LISEO, Archie, & Cinaways
Singles: 7-inch
CLW (6576 "Homebrew") 8-12

LISI, Ricky
Singles: 7-inch
ROULETTE 5-10 63
Also see CONCORDS

LISS, Tommy, & Matadors
Singles: 7-inch
SAXONY (1005 "Just in Make Believe") 15-25 63
SAXONY (2007 " Just in Make Believe ") 4-8 97
(1,000 made.)
Also see MARTIN, Fred, & Matadors

LISS, Tony
Singles: 7-inch
JAMIE 5-8 66

LISTEN
Singles: 7-inch
COLUMBIA (43967 "You Better Run") 50-75 67
(Red label.)
COLUMBIA (43967 "You Better Run") 40-50 67
(White label. Promotional issue only.)
Member: Robert Plant.
Also see PLANT, Robert

LISTENING
Singles: 7-inch
VANGUARD (35077 "I Can Teach You") 10-15 68
VANGUARD (35094 "Life Stories") 10-15 68
LPs: 10/12-inch
VANGUARD (6504 "Listening") 40-60 68

LISTER, Big Bill
Singles: 78 rpm
CAPITOL 10-15 51
Singles: 7-inch
CAPITOL (1488 "Beer Drinking Blues") 15-25 51

LITE, Tippo, & His All Stars
Singles: 78 rpm
BACK ALLEY (202 "Dark Skin Woman Blues") 25-50 50

LITE NITES
Singles: 7-inch
DUNWICH (149 "One, Two Bugaloo") 10-20 67
Also see AMERICAN BREED
Also see GARY & NITE LITES

LITE STORM
LPs: 10/12-inch
BEVERLY HILLS (1135 "Lite Storm Warning") 40-60 73

LITES, Shirley D&D '83
Singles: 7-inch
ATLANTIC 3-4 85
Singles: 12-inch
WEST END 4-6 83

LITSCHER, Kick: see KICK LITSCHER

LITTER LP '89
Singles: 7-inch
PROBE (461 "Silly People") 15-25 69
PROBE (467 "Blue Ice") 15-25 69
SCOTTY (6710 "Action Woman") 75-100 67
WARICK (6711 "Somebody Help Me") 150-200 67
WARICK (6712 "Action Woman") 100-150 67
LPs: 10/12-inch
EVA (12013 "Rare Tracks") 10-15 83
HEXAGON (681 "$100 Fine") 150-250 69
PROBE (4504 "Emerge the Litter") 30-50 69
WARICK (671 "Distortions") 200-400 68
Members: Dan Rinaldi; Tom Caplan; Denny Waite; Mark Gallagher; Ray Melina; Jim Kane; Tom Murray.
Also see HUMBLE MUD
Also see STRAIGHT UP
Also see WHITE LIGHTNING

LITTERER
LPs: 10/12-inch
CATAMOUNT 8-10 87
Members: Steve Litterer; Dave Litterer; Tom Litterer; Carlene Litterer; Brent Estlund.

LITTERBUGS
Singles: 7-inch
OKEH (7164 "Valerie") 20-30 62

LITTLE, Baby, & Playboys
Singles: 7-inch
WATTS WAY 4-8

LITTLE, Ben, & Four Kings
Singles: 7-inch
REVIVAL (635 "Forever Mine") 50-75 61

LITTLE, Connie
Singles: 7-inch
ELMOR 4-8 61

LITTLE, Dane & Mason
Singles: 7-inch
MERCURY 5-8

LITTLE, Frankie
Singles: 7-inch
ABC-PAR 4-8 63-64
MR. PEACOCK 4-8 62

LITTLE, Horace
(With the Bobby Edwards Band)
Singles: 7-inch
ASCOT (2102 "Texas Stomp") 8-10 62

LITTLE, Lee Roy
Singles: 7-inch
CEE=JAY (579 "Hurry Baby, Please Come Home") 25-50 60

LITTLE, Little Rose
Singles: 7-inch
BLUE ROCK 4-8 65
ROULETTE 4-8 67

LITTLE, Paul
Singles: 7-inch
PEAK (188 "I Want to Walk with You") 50-75

LITTLE, Peggy C&W '69
Singles: 7-inch
DOT 3-6 69-71
EPIC 3-5 73
LPs: 10/12-inch
DOT 10-15 70

LITTLE, Rich LP '82
Singles: 7-inch
BOARDWALK 3-4 82
MERCURY 3-5 71
LPs: 10/12-inch
BOARDWALK 5-8 82
CAEDMON 5-10 72
KARR 8-15 68
MERCURY 8-10 71
PIZZA HUT ("Pizza Hut '73") 15-20 73
(Souvenir of an annual company meeting. Promotional issue only. No selection number used.)

LITTLE, Victor
Singles: 7-inch
RICHLAND ("Papa Lou") 10-20
(Selection number not known.)

LITTLE AL
(Al Gunter)
Singles: 78 rpm
EXCELLO (2098 "No Jive") 20-40 57
Singles: 7-inch
EXCELLO (2098 "No Jive") 25-50 57
(Orange and blue label.)
EXCELLO (2098 "No Jive") 10-15 62
(Red, white and blue label.)
EXCELLO (2128 "Easy Ridin' Buggy") 25-50 58

LITTLE ALFRED
(With the Berry Cup)
Singles: 7-inch
JEWEL 5-10 65
KHOURY'S (726 "Miss Ann") 10-15 60
LYRIC 8-12 62-64
Also see COOKIE & HIS CUPCAKES / Little Alfred

LITTLE ALICE
Singles: 7-inch
FOUR J 5-10 62

LITTLE ALTON & VELVATONES
Singles: 7-inch
J-M-O (1004 "She Said Yeah") 20-30 66

LITTLE AMERICA LP '87
LPs: 10/12-inch
GEFFEN 5-8 87

LITTLE ANGEL
Singles: 7-inch
AWARD (126 "Help Me Baby") 10-20 59

LITTLE ANGELS
Singles: 7-inch
CAPITOL (4490 "Says You") 10-20 60
Also see SYLVERS

LITTLE ANN
Singles: 7-inch
RIC-TIC (142 "Going Down a One-Way Street") 15-25 67
Also see TARHEEL SLIM & LITTLE ANN

LITTLE ANTHONY
LPs: 10/12-inch
MCA/SONGBIRD 5-8 80

LITTLE ANTHONY & IMPERIALS R&B/P&R '58
(Anthony & the Imperials; Imperials)
Singles: 7-inch
APOLLO (755 "The Fires Burn No More") 15-20 61
AVCO 4-6 74-75
DCP 6-12 64-66
END (1027 "Tears on My Pillow") 15-25 58
(First issued as by the Imperials.)
END (1036 "So Much") 15-25 58
END (1038 "The Diary") 15-25 58
END (1039 "When You Wish Upon a Star") 10-20 58
END (1047 "A Prayer and a Juke Box") 10-20 59
(Monaural.)
END (1047 "A Prayer and a Juke Box") 40-50 59
(Stereo.)
END (1053 "I'm Alright") 10-20 59
END (1060 "Shimmy Shimmy Ko-Ko Bop") 10-20 59
END (1067 "My Empty Room") 10-20 60
END (1074 "Only Sympathy") 10-20 60
END (1080 "Limbo") 10-20 60
END (1083 "Formula of Love") 10-20 60
END (1086 "Please Say You Want Me") 10-20 61
END (1091 "Traveling Stranger") 10-20 61
END (1104 "A Lovely Way to Spend an Evening") 10-20 61
JANUS 4-6 71-72
MCA 3-4 80
OLD HIT 3-4
PCM 3-4 83
PURE GOLD 3-5 76
ROULETTE (4379 "It Just Ain't Fair") 10-15 61
ROULETTE (4477 "I've Got a Lot to Offer Darling") 8-12 63
U.A. 4-6 69-70
VEEP 5-10 66-68
Picture Sleeves
DCP (1128 "Hurt So Bad") 10-20 65
VEEP (1228 "Better Use Your Head") 10-20 66
EPs: 7-inch
END (203 "Little Anthony and the Imperials") 50-100 58
END (204 "We Are the Imperials Featuring Little Anthony") 50-100 59
LPs: 10/12-inch
ACCORD (7216 "Tears on My Pillow") 5-10 83
AVCO (11012 "On a New Street") 8-10 73
DCP (3801 "I'm on the Outside Looking In") 20-30 64
(Monaural.)
DCP (3808 "Goin' Out of My Head") 20-30 65
(Monaural.)
DCP (3809 "Best of Little Anthony & the Imperials") 15-25 66
(Monaural.)
DCP (6801 "I'm on the Outside Looking In") 25-40 64
(Stereo.)
DCP (6808 "Goin' Out of My Head") 25-40 65
(Stereo.)
DCP (6809 "Best of Little Anthony & the Imperials") 20-35 66
(Stereo.)
EMUS 5-10 79
END (303 "We Are the Imperials Featuring Little Anthony") 75-125 59
(Monaural.)
END (303 "We Are the Imperials Featuring Little Anthony") 50-100 59
(Reprocessed stereo.)
END (311 "Shades of the '40s") 50-100 60
FORUM CIRCLE (9107 "Their Big Hits") 10-20
LIBERTY (10133 "Best of Little Anthony & the Imperials") 5-10 81
ROULETTE (25294 "Greatest Hits") 20-30 65
SUNSET (5287 "Little Anthony & the Imperials") 10-15 70
U.A. (026 "Legendary Masters") 12-18 73
(Two discs.)
U.A. (255 "Very Best") 10-12 74
U.A. (382 "Very Best") 8-10 74
U.A. (1017 "Out of Sight, Out of Mind") 5-10 80
U.A. (6720 "Out of Sight, Out of Mind") 10-15 69
VEEP (13510 "I'm on the Outside Looking In") 15-20 66
VEEP (13513 "Payin' Our Dues") 15-20 66
(Monaural.)
VEEP (13514 "Reflections") 15-20 67
(Monaural.)
VEEP (13516 "Movie Grabbers") 15-20 67
(Monaural.)
VEEP (16510 "I'm on the Outside Looking In") 15-25 66
(Stereo.)
VEEP (16513 "Payin' Our Dues") 15-25 66
(Stereo.)
VEEP (16514 "Reflections") 15-25 67
(Stereo.)
VEEP (16516 "Movie Grabbers") 15-25 67
(Stereo.)
VEEP (16519 "Best of Little Anthony & the Imperials, Vol. 2") 15-25 68
Members: Anthony Gourdine; Clarence Collins; Sam Strain; Tracy Lord; Ernie Wright; Gloucester Rogers.
Also see CHESTERS
Also see CHIPS
Also see DUPONTS
Also see IMPERIALS
Also see LITTLE ANTHONY
Also see O'JAYS

LITTLE ANTHONY & IMPERIALS / Platters
LPs: 10/12-inch
EXACT (231 "Little Anthony & the Imperials & the Platters") 5-10 80
Also see LITTLE ANTHONY & IMPERIALS
Also see PLATTERS

LITTLE ARCHIE
Singles: 7-inch
DIAL 4-8 68

LITTLE ARTIE & PHAROAHS
Singles: 7-inch
CUCA (1142 "Fox & the Hound") 10-20 63
CUCA (1157 "It Puzzles Me") 10-20 63
CUCA (1162 "Foxy Devil") 10-20 64
Members: Artie Herrera; Mike Morgan; Jim Lombard; Phil Zinos; Dick Baradic; Al Herrera; Pete Psiroupolis; Andy Bakiris; Chuck Matson; Tom Markin; Pat Short Cibarrich.
Also see KANE & ABEL
Also see MOB

LITTLE AUGGIE AUSTIN
Singles: 7-inch
PONTIAC 4-8

LITTLE BEATS
Singles: 7-inch
MERCURY (71155 "Love Is True") 25-35 57

LITTLE BEAVER R&B '72
(Willie Hale)
Singles: 7-inch
CAT 3-5 72-76
OCTAVIA 10-15
PHIL-LA of SOUL 4-8 67
SAADIA 3-5
Also see BIRDLEGS & PAULINE
Also see WRIGHT, Betty

LITTLE BEN & CHEERS
Singles: 7-inch
BELL (731 "I Don't Have to Cry") 5-10 68
LAREDO (2518 "Beggar of Love") 20-30 58
REVIVAL (635 "Forever Mine") 15-25 61
RUSH (601 "Beggar of Love") 10-15 60s
RUSH (603 "It's Love I Need") 10-15 60s
RUSH (604 "I Don't Have to Cry") 10-15 60s

LITTLE BENNY
(With the Stereos; with Dickie Thompson's Orchestra)
Singles: 7-inch
SPOT (106 "My Sweetheart") 10-15 61
TRI-ODE (100 "Astronaut Glenn") 8-12 62

LITTLE BERNIE & BLAZERS
Singles: 7-inch
JOSIE (884 "My Love I Have You") 100-200 61

LITTLE BERNIE & CAVALIERS
Singles: 7-inch
ASCOT (2183 "Do You") 5-10 65
JOVE (100 "Lonely Soldier") 15-25 62

LITTLE BESSIE
Singles: 7-inch
AMY (816 "Broken Hearted") 10-20 61

LITTLE BETTY
Singles: 7-inch
ALTO (2006 "Twistn' School") 5-10 61
SAVOY (1603 "I May Be Wrong") 5-10 61

LITTLE BIG HORN
Singles: 7-inch
CRAZY HORSE 4-8

LITTLE BIG JOHN
Singles: 7-inch
BURDETTE (4 "Rebel Rouser") 8-12

LITTLE BILL: see LITTLE BILL & BLUENOTES

LITTLE BILL & BLUENOTES P&R '59
(With the Adventurers & Shalimars; Little Bill)
Singles: 7-inch
BOLO (725 "Little Angel") 20-30 62

DOLTON (4 "I Love an Angel") 15-25 59
TOPAZ (1303 "Sweet Cucumber") 25-50 60
TOPAZ (1305 "Louie Louie") 50-75 61

LPs: 10/12-inch

CAMELOT (102 "The Fiesta Club Presents Little Bill & the Blue Notes") 100-200 60
Members: Bill Engelhart; Frank Dutra; Tom Giving; Buck Ormsby; Lassie Aanes; Buck England; Tom Morgan.

LITTLE BILLY & ESSENTIALS: see BILLY & ESSENTIALS

LITTLE BIT OF SOUND

Singles: 7-inch

CAROLE (1002 "Incense and Peppermints") 10-15 67
ROULETTE (4744 "Girl Who Paints Designs") 10-15 67

LITTLE BITS

Singles: 7-inch

DYNOVOICE 4-8 69
TIGER EYE (101 "Girl, Give Me Love") 20-25 60s
Member: Karyl Mann.

LITTLE BO: see BO, Little

LITTLE BOB & LOLLIPOPS

Singles: 7-inch

(Lil Bob & Lollipops; Little Bob)

Singles: 7-inch

B&L (1 "Rock the Uke") 10-20 66
DECCA (31412 "Twisting Home") ... 5-10 62
HIGH-UP (101 "Are You Ever Coming Home") 10-20 60s
JIN (222 "I Don't Wanna Cry") 10-20 60s
JIN (225 "You Know It Ain't Right") 10-20 60s
JIN (227 "I Found Someone") 10-20 60s
LA LOUISIANNE 4-8 66
Also see CAMILLE, Bob, & Lollipops
Also see LITTLE BOB

LITTLE BONES

Singles: 7-inch

PRANN 5-8 63

LITTLE BOOKER

(James Booker)

Singles: 78 rpm

IMPERIAL 25-45 54

Singles: 7-inch

ACE (547 "Teen-Age Rock") 15-25 58
IMPERIAL (5293 "Thinkin' 'Bout My Baby") 50-75 54
Also see BOOKER, James

LITTLE BOPPERS

Singles: 7-inch

GLENDALE 10-20

LITTLE BOY BLUEHORN

Singles: 7-inch

SPACE 5-10 63

LITTLE BOY BLUES

Singles: 7-inch

FONTANA (1623 "It's Only You") 5-10 68
IRC (6929 "Look at the Sun") 10-15 66
IRC (6936 "I'm Ready") 15-25 66
IRC (6939 "I Can Only Give You Everything") 15-25 66
RONKO (6996 "The Great Train Robbery") 15-25 67

Picture Sleeves

IRC (6939 "I Can Only Give You Everything") 25-35 66

LPs: 10/12-inch

FONTANA (67578 "In the Woodland of Weir") 15-25 68

LITTLE BROTHER BROWN: see BROWN, Little Brother

LITTLE BUBBER

Singles: 78 rpm

IMPERIAL 25-45 53

Singles: 7-inch

IMPERIAL (5225 "High Class Woman") 50-75 53
IMPERIAL (5238 "Runnin' 'Round") 50-75 53

LITTLE BUCK

Singles: 7-inch

DUKE 5-8 61-62

LITTLE BUDDY

Singles: 7-inch

NRC 8-12 58

LITTLE BUSTER

Singles: 7-inch

JUBILEE 10-20 65-66

LITTLE BUTCH & VELLS

(Butchie Saunders)

Singles: 7-inch

ANGLE TONE (535 "Over the Rainbow") 25-35 58
(Black vinyl.)
ANGLE TONE (535 "Over the Rainbow") 50-75 58
(Colored vinyl.)
Also see SAUNDERS, Little Butchie

LITTLE CAESAR *R&B '52*

(With Maxwell Davis & His Orchestra)

Singles: 78 rpm

BIG TOWN 15-25 53
RPM 15-25 53
RECORDED in HOLLYWOOD 15-25 53

Singles: 7-inch

BIG TOWN (106 "Big Eyes") 25-50 53
BIG TOWN (110 "What Kind of Fool Is He") 25-50 53
RPM (393 "Tried to Reason with You Baby") 25-50 53
RECORDED in HOLLYWOOD (234 "The River") 25-50 52
RECORDED in HOLLYWOOD (235 "Goodbye Baby") 25-50 52
RECORDED in HOLLYWOOD (236 "Talking to Myself") 25-50 53
RECORDED in HOLLYWOOD (237 "Atomic Love") 25-50 53
Also see DAVIS, Maxwell
Also see WILSON, Jimmy / Thrillers / Little Caesar

LITTLE CAESAR

Singles: 7-inch

RCA 10-20 58

LITTLE CAESAR

(With the Ark Angels)

Singles: 7-inch

JACK BEE 8-12 60

LITTLE CAESAR *LP '90*

LPs: 10/12-inch

DGC 5-8 90

LITTLE CAESAR & CONSPIRATORS

Singles: 7-inch

STUDIO CITY (1023 "New Orleans") 40-60 60s

LITTLE CAESAR & CONSULS *P&R '65*

Singles: 7-inch

MALA 8-12 65

LITTLE CAESAR & EMPIRE

Singles: 7-inch

PARKWAY (152 "Everybody Dance Now") 10-20 66

LITTLE CAESAR & ROMANS *P&R/R&B '61*

(Caesar & the Romans; Caesar & Romans)

Singles: 7-inch

DEL-FI (4158 "Those Oldies But Goodies") 10-20 61
DEL-FI (4164 "Hully Gully Again") 10-20 61
DEL-FI (4166 "Memories of Those Oldies But Goodies") 25-50 61
DEL-FI (4170 "Ten Commandments of Love") 20-40 61
DEL-FI (4176 "Popeye One More Time") 10-20 62
ESSAR (7803 "We Belong Together") 4-6 78
HI-NOTE (194 "What's Wrong with You") 5-10
LOST NITE 4-8

LPs: 10/12-inch

DEL-FI (1218 "Memories of Those Oldies But Goodies") 50-75 61
Members: David "Little Caesar" Johnson; Larry Sanders; Johnny Simmons; Carl Burnett.
Also see BLUE JAYS / Little Caesar & Romans
Also see BURNETT, Carl, & Hustlers

LITTLE CAESAR & ROMANS / Ron Holden

Singles: 7-inch

TRIP 3-5 70s
Also see HOLDEN, Ron
Also see LITTLE CAESAR & ROMANS

LITTLE CAL

Singles: 7-inch

GOLDEN CREST (553 "Young School Girl") 15-20 60

LITTLE CAL / Mad Lads

Singles: 7-inch

GOLDEN CREST (533 "Young School Girl") 15-25 59
(Reissued on Golden Crest 553 with Little Cal on both sides.)
Also see LITTLE CAL

LITTLE CAMERON

Singles: 7-inch

STYLO 8-12 59

LITTLE CHARLES

(With the Sidewinders)

Singles: 7-inch

BOTANIC (1001 "Shanty Town") 5-10 68
DECCA (31980 I'm Available") 20-30 66
DECCA (32095 Taste of the Good Life") 10-20 67
DECCA (32233 The Loner") 10-15 67
DECCA (32321 Sweet Lorene") 10-15 68
JEWEL (752 "Give Me a Chance") 10-15 65

LITTLE CHERYL

(Cheryl Williams)

Singles: 7-inch

CAMEO (270 "Heaven Only Knows") 25-35 63
CAMEO (276 "Mama Let the Phone Bell Ring") 8-12 63
CAMEO (292 "Come On Home") 8-12 64
CAMEO (307 "Yeh, Yeh, We Love 'Em All") 10-15 64
REPRISE (20109 "Jim") 8-12 62

LITTLE CINDY

Singles: 7-inch

COLUMBIA 5-10 59

Picture Sleeves

COLUMBIA 8-12 59

LITTLE CINDY & WILLIS SISTERS

Singles: 7-inch

COLUMBIA 5-10 59

Picture Sleeves

COLUMBIA 8-12 59
Also see LITTLE CINDY
Also see WILLIS SISTERS

LITTLE CLEM & DEW DROPS

Singles: 7-inch

ZYNN (504 "Waiting in the Chapel") 100-150 58
(Reissued as by the Gay Notes.)
Also see GAYNOTES

LITTLE CLYDIE & TEENS

Singles: 78 rpm

RPM (462 "A Casual Look") 25-50 56

Singles: 7-inch

RPM (462 "A Casual Look") 50-100 56

LITTLE COOPER & DRIFTERS

Singles: 7-inch

STEVENS (105 "Evening Train") 75-125 59
Member: Sonny Cooper.

LITTLE COQUETTES

Singles: 7-inch

COLPIX 5-10 64

LITTLE CURTIS & BLUES

Singles: 7-inch

VANCO 5-10

LITTLE D & DELIGHTERS

Singles: 7-inch

LITTLE "D" (1010 "Oh My Darling") 200-300 58

LITTLE D & HARLEMS

Singles: 7-inch

JOSIE 5-10 63

LITTLE DANNY

Singles: 7-inch

SHARP 8-12 60

LITTLE DAVID

(David Wylie)

Singles: 78 rpm

REGAL (3271 "Shackels 'Round My Body") 25-50 50

LITTLE DAVID

Singles: 78 rpm

INTERNATIONAL 10-15 52
RPM (371 "Crying Blues") 25-50 52
(7-inch 78rpm.)
RPM (371 "Crying Blues") 10-15 52

LITTLE DAVID

Singles: 7-inch

SYMPHONY 10-15
Also see CORRENTE, Sal

LITTLE DAVID & HARPS

Singles: 78 rpm

SAVOY (1178 "I Won't Cry") 15-25 56

Singles: 7-inch

SAVOY (1178 "I Won't Cry") 30-40 56
Member: David Baughan.
Also see DRIFTERS

LITTLE DAVID & HIS FRAMUS

Singles: 7-inch

DORE (661 "Gypsy Guitar") 8-12 63

LITTLE DEAN'S COMBO

Singles: 7-inch

PEORIA (101 "Happy Bullfrog") 10-20 64

LITTLE DEE

Singles: 7-inch

M&M (451 "Monster") 8-12

LITTLE DENNY

(With the Torkays)

Singles: 7-inch

PERRY (1 "Rock & Roll Blues") .100-150 58
PERRY (2 "I'd Love to Take You Walking") 50-100 58

LITTLE DION

Singles: 7-inch

RCA 4-8 67

LITTLE DIPPERS *P&R '60*

(Anita Kerr Singers)

Singles: 7-inch

DOT 5-10 64
UNIVERSITY 8-12 59-60
Also see KERR, Anita

LITTLE DIXIE

("11 Year-Old International Prince of Rhythm")

Singles: 7-inch

LAS VEGAS STRIP (101 "Be Fair") 100-200 59

LITTLE DOOLEY & FABULOUS TEARS

Singles: 7-inch

BAYLOR (101 "I Love You") 15-25 65
NORTH BAY 5-10
Member: Dooley Silverspoon.
Also see SILVERSPOON, Dooley

LITTLE DOUG

(Doug Sahm)

Singles: 78 rpm

SARG 15-25 55

Singles: 7-inch

SARG (113 "A Real American Joe") 30-50 55
Also see SAHM, Doug

LITTLE DUCK & QUACKERS

Singles: 7-inch

RONN 5-10 68

LITTLE DUCKS & DRAKES

Singles: 7-inch

KINGSTON (419 "Blue Velvet") .150-200 59
PEE VEE (139 "Every Beat of My Heart") 30-50 66
Members: Ronnie Auno; Gordie Snyder.

LITTLE "E" & MELLO-TONE 3

Singles: 7-inch

FALCO (302 "Candy Apple Red Impala") 15-20 61

LITTLE EDDIE

Singles: 7-inch

BIG BEAT 5-10 60s
MONUMENT 5-10 63
REGINALD 10-20 65

LITTLE EDDIE & DON JUANS

Singles: 7-inch

FORTUNE (836 "This Is a Miracle") 10-20 57
Also see LAKE, Don, & Don Juans
Also see LITTLE EDDIE & FIVE DOLLARS

LITTLE EDDIE & FIVE DOLLARS

Singles: 7-inch

FORTUNE (845 "Yellow Moon") 15-25 58
Also see FIVE DOLLARS
Also see LITTLE EDDIE & DON JUANS

LITTLE EDDIE & 5 SANDS

Singles: 7-inch

20TH FOX 4-8 65

LITTLE EDITH

Singles: 7-inch

JESSICA (1602 "I Couldn't Take It") 10-20

LITTLE ELLEN

Singles: 7-inch

SMASH 4-8 61

LITTLE ELLIS & L7s

Singles: 7-inch

CLW (6578 "Barb Wire") 8-12

LITTLE ERNIE

(With the Park Williams Combo)

Singles: 7-inch

SUMIT (0008 "You Lied and I Cried") 75-125 63

LITTLE ESTHER *R&B '50*

(Esther Phillips; Little Esther Phillips; with Earle Warren Orchestra; with Johnny Otis Orchestra)

Singles: 78 rpm

DECCA 15-25 54
FEDERAL 25-50 51
SAVOY 10-20 50-56

Singles: 7-inch

ATLANTIC 8-15 64-67
DECCA (28804 "Talkin' All Out of My Head") 25-50 54
DECCA (48305 "Stop Cryin' ") 25-50 54
DECCA (48314 "He's a No Good Man") 50-75 54
FEDERAL (12023 "I'm a Bad Girl") 75-125 51
FEDERAL (12042 "Crying and Sighing") 75-125 51
FEDERAL (12055 "Crying Blues") 75-125 52
FEDERAL (12063 "Summertime") 75-125 52
FEDERAL (12065 "Better Beware") 75-125 52
FEDERAL (12078 "Aged and Mellow") 75-125 52
FEDERAL (12090 "Ramblin' Blues") 75-125 52
FEDERAL (12126 "Hound Dog") .. 75-125 53
FEDERAL (12142 "Cherry Wine") 75-125 53
GUSTO 3-5
KUDU 4-6 72-76
LENOX 10-15 62-63
MERCURY 3-5 77-79
ROULETTE 4-6 69
SAVOY (731 "Double Crossing Blues") 25-50 50
SAVOY (1100 series) 20-30 56
SAVOY (1500 series) 10-20 58-59
WARWICK 10-20 60-61
WINNING 3-5 83

LPs: 10/12-inch

ATLANTIC (1500 & 1600 series) 8-12 70-76
ATLANTIC (8100 series) 20-30 65-66
KING (622 "Memory Lane") ... 1500-2000 59
KUDU 8-12 72-76
LENOX (227 "Release Me") 30-50 62
MERCURY 5-10 78-81
YORKSHIRE 8-12
Also see ADAMS, Faye / Little Esther / Shirley & Lee
Also see PHILLIPS, Esther, & Joe Beck

LITTLE ESTHER & DOMINOES

(With the Earle Warren Orchestra)

Singles: 78 rpm

FEDERAL 100-200 51

Singles: 7-inch

FEDERAL (12036 "Heart to Heart") 300-400 51
Also see LITTLE ESTHER with the Earle Warren Orchestra (With the Dominoes)
Also see LITTLE ESTHER & Clyde McPhatter

LITTLE ESTHER & BIG AL DOWNING

Singles: 7-inch

LENOX 10-15 63
Also see DOWNING, Al

LITTLE ESTHER & JUNIOR WITH THE JOHNNY OTIS ORCHESTRA / Johnny Otis Orchestra with the Vocaleers

Singles: 78 rpm

SAVOY (824 "Get Together Blues") 25-50 51
Also see VOCALEERS

LITTLE ESTHER & LITTLE WILLIE LITTLEFIELD

Singles: 78 rpm

FEDERAL 40-60 52

Singles: 7-inch

FEDERAL (12108 "Last Laugh Blues") 75-125 52
FEDERAL (12115 "Turn the Lamps Down Low") 75-125 52
Also see LITTLEFIELD, Little Willie

LITTLE ESTHER & CLYDE MCPHATTER

Singles: 7-inch

FEDERAL (12344 "Heart to Heart") 40-60 58
Also see LITTLE ESTHER & DOMINOES
Also see McPHATTER, Clyde

LITTLE ESTHER & BOBBY NUNN

Singles: 78 rpm

FEDERAL 50-100 52-53

Singles: 7-inch

FEDERAL (12100 "Saturday Night Daddy") 250-450 52
FEDERAL (12122 "You Took My Love Too Fast") 250-450 53
Also see NUNN, Bobby

LITTLE ESTHER & MEL WALKER

(With the Johnny Otis Orchestra)

Singles: 78 rpm

FEDERAL 15-25 52
SAVOY 15-25 50

Singles: 7-inch

FEDERAL (12055 "Ring-A-Ding Doo") 100-150 52
SAVOY (735 "Mistrustin' Blues") 100-150 50
SAVOY (759 "Deceivin' Blues") . 100-150 50
Also see OTIS, Johnny
Also see WALKER, Mel

LITTLE ESTHER & EARLE WARREN ORCHESTRA

(With the Dominoes)

Singles: 78 rpm

FEDERAL (12016 "The Deacon Moves In") 150-250 51
FEDERAL (12036 "Heart") 100-200 51

Singles: 7-inch

FEDERAL (12016 "The Deacon Moves In") 400-600 51
FEDERAL (12036 "Heart") 350-500 51
Also see DOMINOES
Also see LITTLE ESTHER & DOMINOES

LITTLE EVA *P&R/R&B/LP '62*

Singles: 7-inch

ABC 3-5 74
AMY 4-8 65-66
BELL 3-5 72
DIMENSION 5-10 62-65
MCA 3-4 80
SPRING 3-5 70
VERVE 4-8 66

Picture Sleeves

DIMENSION (1035 "Makin' with the Magilla") 20-30 64

LPs: 10/12-inch

DIMENSION (DLP-6000 "L-L-L-L-Locomotion") 35-55 62
(Monaural.)
DIMENSION (DLPS-6000 "L-L-L-L-Locomotion") 50-75 62
(Stereo.)
Also see COOKIES / Little Eva / Carole King
Also see IRWIN, Big Dee
Also see KING, Ben E.

LITTLE FAY

Singles: 7-inch

TOP-POP (260 "I Don't Care What the People Say") 75-125 66

LITTLE FEAT *LP '74*

Singles: 7-inch

W.B. 3-6 70-78

LPs: 10/12-inch

MFSL (2-013 "Waiting for Columbus") 75-125 78
NAUTILUS (24 "Time Loves a Hero") 25-35 70s
(Half-speed mastered.)
W.B. (984 "Hoy Hoy") 15-20 81
(Promotional issue only.)
W.B. (1890 thru 2884) 8-15 70-76
W.B. (3015 thru 3538) 6-12 77-81
W.B. (25000 & 26000 series) 5-8 88-90
Members: Lowell George; Ken Gradney; Richard Hayward; Sam Clayton; Fred Tackett; Paul Barrere; Bill Payne; Roy Estrada.
Also see BARRERE, Paul
Also see BRAMLETT, Bonnie
Also see CARTER, Valerie
Also see COODER, Ry
Also see GEORGE, Lowell
Also see HARRIS, Emmylou
Also see MOTHERS of INVENTION
Also see TOWER of POWER
Also see ZEVON

LITTLE FLAYTUS & DREAMAIRES
(Dave Antrell)
Singles: 7-inch
ANTRELL (101 "Buy a Van") 8-10 85
(Red label.)
ANTRELL (101 "Buy a Van") 3-5 85
(Yellow label, black vinyl.)
ANTRELL (101 "Buy a Van") 4-8 85
(Yellow label, colored vinyl.)
Also see ANTRELL, Dave

LITTLE FLORENCE
Singles: 7-inch
EXCELLO 4-8 63

LITTLE FLOYD
Singles: 7-inch
ARLEN 4-8 62

LITTLE FOXES
Singles: 7-inch
OKEH 4-8 68

LITTLE FRANKIE
Singles: 7-inch
CAPITOL 8-12 65
INTERSTATE 5-8 60s
SMASH 5-8 66

LITTLE FREDDIE & GENTS
Singles: 7-inch
SHOWCASE 10-20 65

LITTLE FREDDY & ROCKETS
Singles: 7-inch
CHIEF (33 "All My Love") 250-500 58
Also see WOOD, Brenton

LITTLE GERHARD
Singles: 7-inch
PARIS 5-8 59

LITTLE GIGI
(With Vernon Harrell)
Singles: 7-inch
DECCA (31721 "Baby, Dont'cha Worry") 5-10 64
DECCA (31760 "I Volunteer") 10-20 65
SELECT (731 "I'm Hurt and So Is My Heart") 8-12 64

LITTLE GINO & JINKS
Singles: 7-inch
.007 (101 "Beggar of Love") 15-25 60s

LITTLE GIRL BLUE
Singles: 7-inch
UNIVERSAL 4-8 64

LITTLE GIRLS
LPs: 10/12-inch
LG (1985 "Little Girls") 15-20 85
(Clear vinyl. Promotional issue only. Issued with two 8" x 10" photos and bios. With Clem Burke and Nigel Harrison.)
PVC 5-8 83
Member: Kip Brown.
Also see BLONDIE
Also see CHEQUERED PAST
Also see SHOCK
Also see SILVERHEAD

LITTLE GRACIE
Singles: 7-inch
BAND BOX 4-8 61

LITTLE GUY & GIANTS
Singles: 7-inch
LAWN (103 "So Young") 150-250 60

LITTLE GRANTS & EDDIE
Singles: 7-inch
PRESIDENT 4-8

LITTLE GREGORY & CONCEPTS
Singles: 7-inch
LOMPRI (270 "Go Away") 15-25 69

LITTLE GRIER
Singles: 7-inch
DON-EL 8-12 60s

LITTLE HANK
Singles: 7-inch
SOUND STAGE 7 .... 8-15 65-66

LITTLE HANK & RHYTHM KINGS
Singles: 7-inch
RHYTHM & RANGE (101 "Christene") 20-30

LITTLE HELEN
Singles: 7-inch
SOULTOWN 4-8 67

LITTLE HENRY & SHAMROCKS
Singles: 7-inch
KENT (398 "Come to Me") 10-15 64

LITTLE HERBERT & ARABIANS
Singles: 7-inch
TEEK (4824 "Bouncing Ball") 100-200 61
TEEK (4824 "Pray Tell Me") 100-200 61
(Same Teek number used twice.)
Member: Herbert Reeves.
Also see SHARPEES

LITTLE HERBIE
(With the Sandbags; with Wise Guys)
Singles: 7-inch
BAMBOO (522 "Crab Louie") 8-12 62
CATCH (107 "Crab Louie") 5-8 64
IN-SOUND 4-8 68

LITTLE HERMAN
Singles: 7-inch
ARLEN (749 "One Out of a Hundred") 10-20 64
ARLEN (751 "I'm Gonna Put the Hurt on You") 10-20 64

LITTLE HITE & SOUL ROCKERS
Singles: 7-inch
JA-WES (0116 "Soul Blues") 10-20 60s
JA-WES (3007 "Fine") 10-20 60s

LITTLE HOOKS & KINGS
(With the Sentries)
Singles: 7-inch
CENTURY (1300 "Count Your Blessings") 15-20 63
(Second issue.)
CHESS (1867 "Count Your Blessings") 10-15 63
(Third issue.)
CLARIDGE (303 "Jerk Train") 8-12 65
LITTLE RICK (909 "Count Your Blessings") 25-50 63
(First issue.)
U.A. (50932 "Give the Drummer Some Time") 5-10 72

LITTLE HUDSON & HIS RED DEVIL TRIO
(Hudson Shower)
Singles: 78 rpm
J.O.B. 50-75 53
Singles: 7-inch
J.O.B. (1015 "Rough Treatment") 125-175 53

LITTLE HUGHIE & CONTACTS
Singles: 7-inch
DORE 5-8 63

LITTLE HYMIE
Singles: 7-inch
LIBERTY 5-10 60

LITTLE IKE
Singles: 7-inch
CHAMPION (1011 "She Can Rock") 50-75 59

LITTLE ISIDORE & INQUISTORS
Singles: 7-inch
EARLY BIRD (5000 "Woo Woo Train") 4-6 95
(Colored vinyl.)
EARLY BIRD (5001 "Bongo Stomp") 4-6 95
(Colored vinyl.)

LITTLE IVA & HER BAND
Singles: 7-inch
MIRACLE (2 "When I Needed You") 500-1000 60

LITTLE JAN & RADIANTS
(Jan & Radiants)
Singles: 7-inch
CLOCK (1028 "Is It True") 50-75 60
GOLDISC (15 "If You Love Me") 15-25 63
QUEEN (24007 "If You Love Me") 20-40 61
VIM (507 "If You Love Me") 30-50 60
(Yellow label.)
VIM (507 "If You Love Me") 25-35 60
(Pink label.)

LITTLE JANICE
Singles: 7-inch
PZAZZ 4-6 69
LPs: 10/12-inch
PZAZZ 10-15 69

LITTLE JEANETTE
Singles: 7-inch
GREEN LIGHT (0040 "Crazy Crazy") 15-25

LITTLE JERRY
(Jerry Williams)
Singles: 7-inch
ACADEMY 4-8 63
ALDO 10-15 61
EMBER 4-8 61
Also see WILLIAMS, Jerry
Also see WILLIAMS, Little Jerry

LITTLE JERRY & CHANTS
Singles: 7-inch
ACE 5-10 61

LITTLE JERRY & GEMS
Singles: 7-inch
HASEDEM (501 "Teardrops Are Falling") 5-10 90
(Colored vinyl.)

LITTLE JESSIE
Singles: 7-inch
EBB (136 "Huggin' ") 15-25 58

LITTLE JIMMY
Singles: 7-inch
BIG TOP 5-10 64

LITTLE JIMMY & HOMEWRECKERS
EPs: 7-inch
BARON (505 "I'm on Fire") 10-15
(Colored vinyl.)

LITTLE JIMMY & SPARROWS
Singles: 7-inch
VAL-UE (101 "Two Hearts Together") 75-125 58

LITTLE JIMMY & TOPS
(Little Jimmy Rivers)
Singles: 7-inch
LEN (1011 "Puppy Love") 15-25 61
V-TONE (102 "Puppy Love") 25-35 61
(First issue. First pressings credit only the Tops.)
Member: Jimmy Rivers.
Also see RIVERS, Little Jimmy, & Tops
Also see TOPS

LITTLE JO ANN — P&R '62
Singles: 7-inch
KAPP 8-12 62

LITTLE JOE
(Joe Hill Louis)
Singles: 7-inch
HOUSE of SOUND (500 "Glamour Girl") 75-125 57
Also see LOUIS, Joe Hill

LITTLE JOE
Singles: 7-inch
BRUNSWICK 4-8 68
LPs: 10/12-inch
BRUNSWICK 10-15 68

LITTLE JOE & LATTNAIRS
Singles: 7-inch
TOMI 3-5

LITTLE JOE & MOROCCOS
Singles: 78 rpm
BUMBLE BEE 15-25 58
Singles: 7-inch
BUMBLE BEE (500 "Trouble in the Candy Shop") 20-30 58
Member: Joe Cook.
Also see LITTLE JOE & THRILLERS
Also see PEPS
Also see UNDISPUTED TRUTH

LITTLE JOE & MUSTANGS
Singles: 7-inch
CHALLENGE 10-15 64

LITTLE JOE & RAMRODS
Singles: 7-inch
SOMA 20-25 60s
STUDIO CITY 25-35 60s

LITTLE JOE & THRILLERS — P&R '57
(Little Joe; Little Joe the Thriller)
Singles: 78 rpm
EPIC 15-25 57
OKEH 15-25 56-57
Singles: 7-inch
ENJOY 4-8 64
EPIC (7088 "Peanuts") 15-25 57
(Canadian. Has same number as on Okeh)
EPIC (9292 "It's Too Bad We Had to Say Goodbye") 10-15 58
(Canadian.)
MGM 3-5 70-73
OKEH (7075 "This I Know") 15-25 56
OKEH (7088 "Peanuts") 15-25 57
(Purple label.)
OKEH (7088 "Peanuts") 10-15 57
(Yellow label.)
OKEH (7094 "Echoes Keep Calling Me") 10-20 57
(Yellow label.)
OKEH (7099 "What Happened to Your Halo") 15-25 57
OKEH (7116 thru 7140) 10-15 59-61
PEANUT 5-10
REPRISE 5-8 63
ROSE 5-8 63
TWENTIETH CENTURY (1214 "For Sentimental Reasons") 25-35 61
EPs: 7-inch
EPIC (7198 "Little Joe and the Thrillers") 75-125 58
Members: Joe Cook; Richard Frazier; Farris Hill; Don Burnett; Harry Pascle.
Also see COOK, Little Joe
Also see LITTLE JOE & MOROCCOS

LITTLE JOE & WAYLITES
Singles: 7-inch
RON (4459 "Summertime") 8-12

LITTLE JOE BLUE — R&B '66
(Joe Valery Jr.)
Singles: 7-inch
CHECKER 5-10 66-67
JEWEL 4-6 70-76
KRIS 4-6
MILES AHEAD 5-10
MOVIN' 4-8 66
SOUL SET (103 "Why I Sing the Blues") 4-6 74
RONN 3-5 84
SOUND STAGE 7 .... 4-6 70

LITTLE JOEY & FLIPS — P&R '62
(Joey Hall)
Singles: 7-inch
JOY 8-10 62
Also see DRIFTERS / Little Joey & Flips
Also see JOEY

LITTLE JOHN
Singles: 7-inch
GO GATE (2 "Just Wait and See") 50-100
MARTAY (4508 "Heart Breakin' Time") 20-30 60s

LITTLE JOHN
Singles: 7-inch
EPIC 3-5 70-71
LPs: 10/12-inch
EPIC 10-12 70-71

LITTLE JOHN, Johnny: see JOHNNY LITTLE JOHN

LITTLE JOHN & MONKS
Singles: 7-inch
JERDEN 8-12 65
TORK 8-12

LITTLE JOHN & SHERWOODS
Singles: 7-inch
BANGAR (608 "Movin' Out") 25-35 64
FLEETWOOD 10-20
Member: John Schilling.
Also see SCHILLING, Johnny, & Sherwoods

LITTLE JOHN & TONY
Singles: 7-inch
VOLKANO (5001 "All I Ask") 50-75

LITTLE JOHN & UNFORGETTABLES
Singles: 7-inch
ALAN K (6901 "Funny What a Little Kiss Can Do") 75-100 62
(First issued as by the Untouchables.)
Also see UNTOUCHABLES

LITTLE JOHNNY & INSTEPS
Singles: 7-inch
O-T-O (103 "Do the Muslin") 8-12

LITTLE JOHNNY & RUMBLERS
Singles: 7-inch
DOWNEY 8-12 64
Member: Johnny Kirkland.
Also see RUMBLERS

LITTLE JOSEPH
Singles: 7-inch
BLUE CAT 5-8 64

LITTLE JUAREZ
Singles: 7-inch
NORTH BEACH (1002 "El Jefe") 15-25 66

LITTLE JULIUS
Singles: 7-inch
DIAMOND 4-8 63

LITTLE JUNE & HIS JANUARYS
(Lil' June & January's)
Singles: 7-inch
PROFILE (4009 "Oh My Love") 50-100 59
SALEM (188 "Hello") 1000-2000 63
Member: June Coleman.

LITTLE JUNIOR'S BLUE FLAMES — R&B '53
(Junior Parker)
Singles: 78 rpm
SUN 50-100 53
Singles: 7-inch
SUN (187 "Feelin' Good") 100-200 53
SUN (192 "Love My Baby") 100-200 53
Also see PARKER, Little Junior

LITTLE KIDS
Singles: 7-inch
TOWER (298 "Santa Claus Is Stuck in the Chimney") 10-15 66

LITTLE LADY BEATLES / Insects
Singles: 7-inch
APPLAUSE (1002 "Dear Beatles"). 15-25 64

LITTLE LARRY
Singles: 7-inch
AGON 5-10 61
SUCCESS 5-8 63

LITTLE LATOURS
Singles: 7-inch
FOLK STAR (1205 "Ho Ho Ho Babe") 10-20

LITTLE LEE & JUDY
Singles: 7-inch
LA VETTE 4-8 63

LITTLE LEROY
Singles: 7-inch
CEE JAY 5-10 60
DEVILLE 4-8 61

LITTLE LINDA
Singles: 7-inch
CORAL 8-12 61

LITTLE LISA
(Lisa Miller)
Singles: 7-inch
V.I.P. (25023 "Hang On Bill") 15-25 65
Also see MILLER, Lisa

LITTLE LOU & HIS BAND
LPs: 10/12-inch
BIG TOP 15-25 62
Member: James Gary "Little Lou" Fowler.

LITTLE LOUIE
Singles: 7-inch
SIMS ("Short Trip") 15-25 59
(Selection number not known.)

LITTLE LOUIE & FINGER CYMBALS
Singles: 7-inch
KING KAROL 4-8 71

LITTLE LOUIE & LOVERS
Singles: 7-inch
VISCOUNT 10-15 62

LITTLE LUTHER
Singles: 7-inch
APT 4-8 61
CHECKER 4-8 64
CRISS CROSS 5-8
DOT 4-8 62

LITTLE MAC
(With the Bravadoes; "Mac" McCardle)
Singles: 7-inch
JAYBIRD 15-20
LITTLE MAC 10-15
LUCKY 10-20

LITTLE MAC & BOSS SOUNDS — R&B '65
Singles: 7-inch
ATLANTIC 4-8 65
Member: Ann Mason.

LITTLE MACK
(Little Mac; Little Mack & His Boys; Mack Simmon & His Boys; Mack Simmons)
Singles: 7-inch
BEA & BABY (109 "Time Is Getting Tougher") 20-30 60
BEA & BABY (113 "You Mistreated Me") 20-30 60
BEA & BABY (118 "Let's Hootenanny Blues") 20-30 61
C.J. (606 "Come Back") 20-30 59
C.J. (607 "Jumpin' at the Cadillac") 20-30 59
CHECKER (984 "I Need Love") 10-20 61
DUD SOUND (4220 "Hard Times") 10-20 65
EL SATURN 5-10 67
PACER (1201 "Drivin Wheel") 15-25 61
PALOS (1201 "Drivin' Wheel") 50-75 61
(First issue.)

LITTLE MAN & VICTORS
Singles: 7-inch
TARHEEL 10-15 63

LITTLE MAN HENRY
Singles: 7-inch
CENTRAL (4701 "Wailin' Wildcat") 500-750

LITTLE MARCUS & DEVOTIONS
Singles: 7-inch
GORDIE (1001 "I'll Always Remember") 150-200 64

LITTLE MELVIN
Singles: 7-inch
AMA (502 "Life Is Miserable") 20-30
Also see SHAW, Timmy, & Little Melvin

LITTLE MELVIN & BOLEROS
Singles: 7-inch
VALERIE (4397 "Jealous Lover") 20-30

LITTLE MIGUEL'S GOLDEN FIVE
Singles: 7-inch
DRUMMOND (106 "Garlic Breath") 10-20 67

LITTLE MILTON
(Milton Anderson)
Singles: 78 rpm
DELTA (403 "Little Milton's Boogie") 50-75 53

LITTLE MILTON — R&B '62
(Milton Campbell)
Singles: 78 rpm
METEOR 50-100 57
SUN (194 "Beggin' My Baby") 50-100 53
SUN (200 "If You Love Me") 75-125 54
SUN (220 "Homesick for My Baby") 100-150 55
Singles: 7-inch
BOBBIN (101 "I'm a Lonely Man") 20-30 58
BOBBIN (103 "Long Distance Operator") 20-30 59
BOBBIN (112 "Strange Dreams") 20-30 59
BOBBIN (117 "Hold Me Tight") 20-30 59
BOBBIN (120 "Dead Love") 20-30 60
BOBBIN (125 "Hey Love") 20-30 61
BOBBIN (128 "Cross My Heart") 20-30 61
CHECKER (0124 thru 0252) 4-6 72-76
CHECKER (977 thru 1096) 8-15 61-65
CHECKER (1105 thru 1239) 5-10 65-71
CHESS 3-6 73-76
EAR 3-5 80
GLADES 3-5 76-78
GOLDEN EAR 3-5 80
MCA 3-5 83
MALACO 3-4 84-86
METEOR (5040 "Love at First Sight") 150-250 57
METEOR (5045 "Let My Baby Be") 150-250 57
MIER 3-5 78
STAX 3-6 71-83
SUN (194 "Beggin' My Baby") 200-300 53
SUN (200 "If You Love Me") 250-350 54
SUN (220 "Homesick for My Baby") 300-500 55
LPs: 10/12-inch
CHECKER (2995 "We're Gonna Make It") 20-30 65
CHECKER (3002 "Big Blues") 20-30 66
CHECKER (3011 "Grits Ain't Groceries") 15-20 69
CHECKER (3012 "If Walls Could Talk") 20-30 70
CHESS 10-15 72-76
GLADES 8-10 76-77
GOLDEN 5-10 80
MCA 5-8 83
MALACO 5-8 84-92
STAX 6-12 73-81
Also see CAMPBELL, Little Milton
Also see MANN, Herbie

LITTLE MILTON & ALBERT KING
LPs: 10/12-inch
STAX 5-10 79
Also see KING, Albert

LITTLE MILTON & JACKIE ROSS
Singles: 7-inch
EAR 3-5 80
LPs: 10/12-inch
EAR 5-10 81
Also see LITTLE MILTON
Also see ROSS, Jackie

LITTLE MISS CORNSHUCKS
Singles: 7-inch
CHESS ... 5-10 61
LPs: 10/12-inch
CHESS (1453 "Loneliest Girl in Town") ... 25-40 61

LITTLE MISS JESSIE / Benny Sharp & His Band
Singles: 7-inch
MEL-O (101 "My Baby's Gone") ... 25-50 61
Also see SHARP, Benny, & Sharpees

LITTLE MISTLETONES
Singles: 7-inch
IN ... 8-12

LITTLE MOJO
(With the Jesters; with Caravans; George Buford)
Singles: 7-inch
MOJO (0513 "Paula") ... 200-400 60
(Identification number shown since no selection number is used.)
NORMAN (505 "Paula") ... 50-100 61
Also see BUFORD, Mojo
Also see MOJO

LITTLE MOJO
Singles: 7-inch
INDIGO (139 "Something on Your Mind") ... 10-15 62

LITTLE MUMMY
Singles: 7-inch
FEDERAL ... 8-12 60

LITTLE NAT
Singles: 7-inch
PIK (242 "Do This Do That") ... 10-20 61

LITTLE NAT & ETIQUETTES
Singles: 7-inch
CLOCK (2001 "You're So Close") ... 25-50 65
Member: Nathaniel Burknight.
Also see LITTLE NATE & CHRYSLERS

LITTLE NATALIE & HENRY
(With the Gifts)
Singles: 7-inch
ROULETTE (4540 "Teardrops Are Falling") ... 5-10 64
Member: Henry Ford.

LITTLE NATE & CHRYSLERS
Singles: 7-inch
JOHNSON (318 "Cry Baby Cry") ... 50-75 59
Member: Nathaniel Burknight.
Also see LITTLE NAT & ETIQUETTES
Also see SHELLS

LITTLE OSCAR
(Little O.)
Singles: 7-inch
SHAMA ... 4-8
SUPREME BLUES ... 5-10

LITTLE OTIS
(Otis Hayes)
Singles: 7-inch
TAMLA (54058 "I Out-Duked the Duke") ... 15-25 62

LITTLE PAPA JOE
(Joseph Leon Williams)
Singles: 78 rpm
BLUE LAKE ... 40-60 55
Singles: 7-inch
BLUE LAKE (116 "Lookin' for My Baby") ... 75-100 55
Also see WILLIAMS, Jody
Also see WILLIAMS, Sugar Boy

LITTLE PATRICK & SIG-A-LERTS
Singles: 7-inch
EBB TIDE (416 "Freeway Strut") ... 50-100 62

LITTLE PATTIE & STATESMEN
Singles: 7-inch
WORLD HITS ... 10-20 64

LITTLE PENNY
Singles: 7-inch
CHERRY ... 10-15

LITTLE PEOPLE
Singles: 7-inch
MOHAWK ... 5-10 62

LITTLE PETE & YOUNGSTERS
(With the Aristocrats)
Singles: 7-inch
LESLEY (1925 "You Told Another Lie") ... 50-100 63
Also see YOUNGSTERS

LITTLE PHIL & NIGHTSHADOWS: see NIGHT SHADOWS

LITTLE PIA
(Pia Zadora)
Singles: 7-inch
LAP INT'L (1002 "Bye Bye Boy") ... 20-30
(May have been a promo issue only.)
Also see ZADORA, Pia

LITTLE PORK CHOPS
(John Lee Hooker)
Singles: 78 rpm
D.R.C. DANCELAND (403 "Wayne County Ramblin' Blues") ... 200-300 49
Also see HOOKER, John Lee

LITTLE RALPHIE D
Singles: 7-inch
20TH FOX (6654 "Half Way Lover") ... 10-20 66

LITTLE RAY
(With the Midnighters; Lil' Ray)
Singles: 7-inch
ATCO ... 5-10 65
DORE ... 10-15 61
FARO ... 5-10 64
IMPACT (30 "Loretta") ... 50-75 65
REPRISE ... 5-10 63
Member: Ray Jiminez.

LITTLE RED RYDERS
Singles: 7-inch
LANJO ... 8-12

LITTLE RED WALTER
Singles: 7-inch
LE SAGE ... 10-15 65

LITTLE RICHARD *P&R '56*
Singles: 78 rpm
PEACOCK ... 25-50 53
RCA (4392 "Taxi Blues") ... 50-100 51
RCA (4582 "Get Rich Quick") ... 50-100 52
RCA (4772 "Ain't Nothing Happenin' ") ... 50-75 52
RCA (5025 "Please Have Mercy on Me") ... 50-75 52
SPECIALTY ... 20-40 56-57
Singles: 7-inch
ABC ... 3-5 73
ATLANTIC (2181 "Crying in the Chapel") ... 5-10 63
ATLANTIC (2192 "It Is No Secret") ... 5-10 63
BELL ... 3-5 73
BRUNSWICK ... 5-10 68
CORAL (62366 "Milky White Way") ... 5-10 63
END (1057 "Save Me Lord") ... 10-20 59
END (1058 "Milky White Way") ... 10-20 59
GREEN MOUNTAIN ... 3-5 73
KENT ... 3-5 73
MCA ... 3-4 86
MANTICORE ... 3-5 75
MERCURY (71884 "Joy Joy Joy") ... 5-10 61
MERCURY (71911 "Do You Care") ... 5-10 62
MERCURY (71965 "He Got What He Wanted") ... 5-10 62
MODERN (1018 "Holy Mackeral") ... 5-10 66
MODERN (1019 "Do You Feel It") ... 5-10 66
MODERN (1022 "Directly from My Heart") ... 5-10 66
MODERN (1030 "Slippin' and Sliddin' ") ... 5-10 66
MODERN (1043 "Baby, What You Want Me to Do") ... 5-10 67
MYSTIC VALLEY (551 "Every Night About This Time") ... 10-15
OKEH ... 5-10 66-69
PEACOCK (1658 "Little Richard's Boogie") ... 50-75 53
PEACOCK (1673 "Maybe I'm Right") ... 50-75 54
RCA (4392 "Taxi Blues") ... 200-300 51
(Turqoise label.)
RCA (4582 "Get Rich Quick") ... 200-300 52
(Turqoise label.)
RCA (4772 "Ain't Nothing Happenin' ") ... 100-200 52
(Black label.)
RCA (5025 "Please Have Mercy on Me") ... 100-200 52
(Black label.)
REPRISE ... 3-6 70-72
SPECIALTY (561 "Tutti-Frutti") ... 20-30 56
SPECIALTY (572 "Long Tall Sally") ... 20-30 56
SPECIALTY (579 "Rip It Up") ... 20-30 56
SPECIALTY (584 "Heeby Jebbies") ... 20-30 56
SPECIALTY (591 "All Around the World") ... 20-30 56
SPECIALTY (598 "Lucille") ... 20-30 57
SPECIALTY (606 "Jenny Jenny") ... 20-30 57
SPECIALTY (611 "Keep a Knockin' ") ... 20-30 57
SPECIALTY (624 "Good Golly Miss Molly") ... 20-30 58
SPECIALTY (624 "True Fine Mama"/"Ooh! My Soul") ... 25-45 58
(*True Fine Mama* mis-numbered. *Ooh! My Soul* correctly numbered 633.)
SPECIALTY (633 "Ooh! My Soul"/"True Fine Mama") ... 20-30 58
(Both sides numbered 633.)
SPECIALTY (645 "Baby Face") ... 20-30 58
SPECIALTY (660 "By the Light of the Silvery Moon") ... 20-30 59
SPECIALTY (664 "Kansas City") ... 20-30 59
SPECIALTY (670 "Shake a Hand") ... 15-25 59
SPECIALTY (681 "Baby") ... 10-20 60
SPECIALTY (686 "Directly from My Heart") ... 10-20 60
SPECIALTY (692 "Bama Lama Bama Loo") ... 10-15 64
SPECIALTY (SPBX series) ... 15-20 85
(Boxed sets of six colored vinyl 45s.)
TRIP ... 3-5 71
VEE JAY (612 "Whole Lotta Shakin' Goin' On") ... 5-10 64
VEE JAY (625 "Blueberry Hill") ... 5-10 64
VEE JAY (652 "Cross Over") ... 5-10 65
VEE JAY (665 "Without Love") ... 5-10 65
VEE JAY (698 "I Don't Know What You've Got") ... 15-25 65
W.B. ... 3-5 87
Picture Sleeves
MCA (52780 "Great Gosh A'Mighty") ... 3-4 86
MODERN (1018 "Holy Mackeral") ... 25-35 57
OKEH (7251 "Poor Dog") ... 10-15 66
SPECIALTY (606 "Jenny Jenny") ... 20-40 57
SPECIALTY (611 "Keep a Knockin' ") ... 20-40 57
SPECIALTY (624 "Good Golly Miss Molly") ... 20-40 58
SPECIALTY (633 "Ooh! My Soul") ... 20-40 58
SPECIALTY (736 "All Around the World") ... 4-6 85
EPs: 7-inch
CAMDEN (416 "Little Richard") ... 150-200 56
CAMDEN (446 "Little Richard Rocks") ... 100-150 56
KAMA SUTRA (17 "Little Richard") ... 10-20 70
SPECIALTY (400 "Here's Little Richard") ... 40-60 56
SPECIALTY (401 "Here's Little Richard") ... 40-60 56
SPECIALTY (402 "Here's Little Richard") ... 40-60 56
SPECIALTY (403 "Little Richard") ... 40-60 57
SPECIALTY (404 "Little Richard") ... 40-60 57
SPECIALTY (405 "Little Richard") ... 40-60 57
LPs: 10/12-inch
ACCORD ... 5-10 81
AUDIO ENCORES ... 20-25 80
BUDDAH ... 10-12 69
CAMDEN (420 "Little Richard") ... 150-250 56
CAMDEN (2430 "Every Hour") ... 20-30 70
CORAL ... 20-30 63
CROWN ... 15-25 63
CUSTOM ... 10-12 60s
EPIC ... 10-12 71
EVEREST ... 5-8 82
EXACT ... 5-10 80-81
EXODUS ... 5-10
51 WEST ... 5-8 80s
GNP ... 5-8 90s
GRT ... 5-8 77
GOLD DISC ... 10-15
GUEST STAR ... 10-15 64
KAMA SUTRA ... 10-12 70
KOALA ... 8-15
MERCURY ... 20-30 61
MODERN ... 10-20 66
OKEH ... 10-20 67
PICKWICK ... 10-15 72
REPRISE ... 10-15 70-72
ROULETTE ... 10-15 68
SCEPTER ... 10-15
SPECIALTY (100 "Here's Little Richard") ... 300-500 57
(Reissued as Specialty 2100.)
SPECIALTY (2100 "Here's Little Richard") ... 50-100 57
(Label indicates "Natural Sound.")
SPECIALTY (2100 "Here's Little Richard") ... 25-50 60s
(Label indicates "Stereo Natural Sound.")
SPECIALTY (2103 "Little Richard") ... 50-100 57
SPECIALTY (2104 "The Fabulous Little Richard") ... 50-100 58
SPECIALTY (2111 "Biggest Hits") 20-30 63
SPECIALTY (2113 "Grooviest 17 Original Hits") ... 10-15 68
SPECIALTY (2136 "Well Alright!") ... 8-10
SPECIALTY (2154 "The Essential Little Richard") ... 8-12 84
SPIN-O-RAMA ... 10-15 60s
SPRINGBOARD (6002 "Little Richard") ... 5-10 70s
SUMMIT ... 10-15
TRIP ... 10-15 71-78
20TH FOX (5010 "Gospel Songs") ... 15-25 63
UNITED ... 8-10 70s
U.A. ... 8-10 75
UPFRONT ... 8-10 77
VEE JAY ... 15-25 64-65
VEE JAY/DYNASTY ... 10-12
W.B. ... 5-8 87
WING ... 10-20 64
Session: Lee Allen; Robins; Jimi Hendrix; Billy Preston.
Note: Many Specialty reissues exist, some of which are very similar in appearance to '50s originals. Any with a zip code on covers are obviously post-1963 reissues. Discs from the '50s are heavier than reissues. Many reissues have a raised vinyl ridge around the record's outer edge—originals do not. Any on colored, or semi-transparent vinyl are reissues. Some reissues do have an identifying copyright date.
Also see ALLEN, Lee
Also see BAILEY, Philip, & Little Richard
Also see BEACH BOYS & Little Richard
Also see CANNED HEAT
Also see CHARLES, Ray / Little Richard / Sam Cooke
Also see COOKE, Sam / Lloyd Price / Larry Williams / Little Richard
Also see DUCES of RHYTHM & Tempo Toppers
Also see HENDRIX, Jimi, & Little Richard
Also see McPHATTER, Clyde / Little Richard / Jerry Butler
Also see ROBINS
Also see UPSETTERS
Also see UPSETTERS Featuring Little Richard

LITTLE RICHARD / John Cougar Mellancamp
Singles: 7-inch
ELEKTRA ... 3-5 88
Picture Sleeves
ELEKTRA ... 4-6 88
Also see MELLENCAMP, John Cougar

LITTLE RICHARD / Arthur Crudup / Red Callendar Sextet
LPs: 10/12-inch
CAMDEN (371 "Little Richard, Arthur Crudup & Red Callendar Sextet") ... 75-125 56
Also see CRUDUP, Big Boy

LITTLE RICHARD / Sister Rosetta
LPs: 10/12-inch
GUEST STAR ... 10-15
Also see LITTLE RICHARD
Also see THARPE, Sister Rosetta

LITTLE RICHIE
Singles: 7-inch
SOUND STAGE 7 (2554 "Just Another Heartache") ... 75-125 66
SOUND STAGE 7 (2567 "I Catch Myself Crying ") ... 15-25 66

LITTLE RICK
Singles: 7-inch
MAESTRO ... 4-8 63

LITTLE RICO & King Krooners: see KING CROONERS

LITTLE RIVER BAND *P&R/LP '76*
(LRB)
Singles: 12-inch
CAPITOL ... 4-6 83
Singles: 7-inch
CAPITOL ... 3-4 79-85
HARVEST ... 3-5 76-78
MCA ... 3-4 89-90
Picture Sleeves
CAPITOL ... 3-5 81-85
HARVEST ... 3-5 78
MCA ... 3-4 89
LPs: 10/12-inch
CAPITOL ... 5-8 79-85
HARVEST ... 5-8 75-80
MFSL (036 "First Under the Wire") ... 25-35 79
Member: John Farnham.
Also see FARNHAM, John
Also see SHORROCK, Glen

LITTLE ROBBIE
Singles: 7-inch
RSVP ... 5-10 64

LITTLE ROCK COACHMEN
Singles: 7-inch
MY (2924 "I've Had Enough") ... 10-20 60s

LITTLE ROGER & GOOSEBUMPS
Singles: 7-inch
RICHMOND (5 "Kennedy's Girls") ... 4-8 79
SPLASH (315 "Stairway to Gilligan's Island") ... 5-10 94
SPLASH (901 "Stairway to Gilligan's Island") ... 10-15 78

LITTLE ROMEO & CASANOVAS
Singles: 7-inch
ASCOT ... 8-12 65
Also see OVATIONS

LITTLE RONNIE & CHROMATICS
Singles: 7-inch
EARLY BIRD ... 10-20 60s
H-L-S ... 5-10 60s

LITTLE ROYAL
Singles: 7-inch
(With Swingmasters)
Singles: 7-inch
CARNIVAL (531 "I Can Tell") ... 10-20 67
TRI-US ... 3-6 72-73
EPs: 7-inch
FLAME (1001 "Groovin") ... 25-35 67

LITTLE SAM
(Big Bill Broonzy)
Singles: 78 rpm
HUB ... 15-25 45
Also see BROONZY, Big Bill

LITTLE SAMMY & TONES
Singles: 7-inch
JACLYN (1161 "Christine") ... 30-50 62
(First issued as by Little Sammy Rozzi and the Guys.)
Member: Sammy Rozzi.
Also see ROZZI, Little Sammy, & Guys

LITTLE SAMMY & WHEELETTS
Singles: 7-inch
RIP-COR (6001 "Good By [sic] My Love") ... 40-60 60s

LITTLE SHELTON
(With the Huey P. Smith Band")
Singles: 7-inch
ACE (7101 "What Can I Do") ... 4-6 71
Also see SMITH, Huey

LITTLE SHERMAN & MOD SWINGERS
Singles: 7-inch
ABC-PAR (11233 "The Price of Love") ... 10-15 69
SAGPORT (105 "The Price of Love") ... 25-35 69

LITTLE SHY GUY & HOT RODS
Singles: 78 rpm
CALVERT (107 "My Little Baby") ... 15-25 57
Singles: 7-inch
CALVERT (107 "My Little Baby") ... 30-40 57

LITTLE SISTER *P&R '70*
Singles: 7-inch
STONE FLOWER ... 5-10 70-72
LPs: 10/12-inch
STONE FLOWER ... 10-15 70
Members: Vanetta Stewart; Elva Melton; Mary Rand.

LITTLE SISTERS
(Little Sisters with Chubby Checker)
Singles: 7-inch
MGM ... 3-5 62
PARKWAY ... 8-12 60
WEE ... 5-10
Also see CHECKER, Chubby

LITTLE SONNY
(Aaron Willis)
Singles: 78 rpm
DUKE ... 25-50 58
Singles: 7-inch
DUKE ... 15-25 58
ENTERPRISE ... 4-8 70
EXCELLO ... 10-20 62
JVB ... 15-25 58
REVILOT ... 5-10 66
SPEEDWAY ... 4-8 72
WHEELSVILLE ... 10-20 65

LITTLE SONNY
Singles: 7-inch
ENTERPRISE ... 3-5 70
LPs: 10/12-inch
ENTERPRISE ... 8-12 70

LITTLE STANLEY
Singles: 7-inch
VANCE ... 8-12

LITTLE STEVE
Singles: 7-inch
GUYDEN ... 5-10 62

LITTLE STEVE & SEGO BROTHERS
(Steve Sanders)
Singles: 7-inch
SONGS of FAITH ... 3-5
Also see SANDERS, Steve

LITTLE STEVEN *P&R/LP '82*
(With the Disciples of Soul)
Singles: 7-inch
EMI AMERICA ... 3-5 82-84
LPs: 10/12-inch
EMI AMERICA ... 5-8 82-84
MANHATTAN ... 5-8 87
Also see BEAUVOIR, Jean
Also see SPRINGSTEEN, Bruce

LITTLE STEVIE
Singles: 7-inch
GUYDEN (2060 "I See a Star") ... 100-150 62

LITTLE SUNNY DAY: see DAY, Sonny

LITTLE SUSIE
Singles: 7-inch
ROULETTE ... 4-8 62

LITTLE SUZIE
Singles: 7-inch
BURBANK ... 4-8 61

LITTLE SYLVIA
(With the Heywood Henry Orchestra; Sylvia Vanderpool)
Singles: 78 rpm
CAT (102 "Fine Love") ... 10-20 53
JUBILEE ... 10-20 52
SAVOY (816 "Little Boy") ... 15-25 51
Singles: 7-inch
CAT (102 "Fine Love") ... 15-25 53
JUBILEE (5093 "Drive, Daddy, Drive") ... 25-35 52
Also see MICKEY & SYLVIA
Also see PAGE, Hot Lips
Also see SYLVIA

LITTLE T-BONE
Singles: 78 rpm
MILTONE (5223 "Love's a Gamble") ... 20-40 47

LITTLE TED & NOVAS
Singles: 7-inch
KAY-GEE (440 "All Your Lovin' ") ... 50-75 60s

LITTLE TEMPLE & HIS 88
(Gus Jenkins)
Singles: 78 rpm
SPECIALTY ... 15-25 54
Singles: 7-inch
SPECIALTY (475 "I Ate the Wrong Part") ... 30-50 54
Also see JENKINS, Gus

LITTLE TERRY
Singles: 78 rpm
SAVOY ... 10-15 57
Singles: 7-inch
SAVOY ... 10-15 57

LITTLE THUMPERS
Singles: 7-inch
RCA (47-7440 "Buck Dance") ... 10-15 59
(Monaural.)
RCA (61-7440 "Buck Dance") ... 20-30 59
(Stereo.)

LITTLE TOIANS
Singles: 7-inch
SMALLTOWN ("I Love You") ... 500-750 56
(No selection number used.)

LITTLE TOM & HIS VALENTINES
Singles: 7-inch
MR. BIG (222 "School Girl") ... 25-35 61

LITTLE TOMMY
Singles: 7-inch
JIM-KO ... 15-20
SOUND of SOUL (100 "I'm Hurt") ... 30-60 65
SOUND of SOUL (104 "Baby Can't You See") ... 50-100 66

LITTLE TOMMY & ELGINS
Singles: 7-inch
ABC-PAR (10358 "Never Love Again") ... 20-30 62
ELMAR (1084 "Never Love Again") ... 100-150 62
Also see ELGINS

LITTLE TONY
Singles: 7-inch
LONDON 4-8 61
RENFRO 5-10

LITTLE TOOTSIE
Singles: 7-inch
FIDELITY 5-10 63

LITTLE TOOTSIE / Little Joey
Singles: 7-inch
FIEDLITY 5-10 59
Also see LITTLE TOOTSIE

LITTLE VICTOR
Singles: 7-inch
LANOR (511 "Can't Stop My Loving You") 15-25
(At least one source shows this number as 509. We're not yet sure which is correct.)

LITTLE VICTOR & VISTAS
Singles: 7-inch
RENDEZVOUS (183 "No More") 20-25 62

LITTLE "WALKIN'" WILLIE
Singles: 78 rpm
JAGUAR (3012 "Clayhouse Blues") 20-30 55

LITTLE WALTER *R&B '52*
(With His Jukes; with Night Caps; with Night Cats; Little Walter Trio; Little Walter J., Guitar & Harmonica; Little Walter Jacobs; Marion Walter Jacobs)
Singles: 78 rpm
CHANCE 100-200 52
CHECKER 20-30 52-57
ORA NELLE (711 "Ora Nelle Blues [That's Allright]") 150-250 47
Singles: 7-inch
CHANCE (1116 "That's Allright") 400-600 52
CHECKER (758 "Juke") 35-50 52
CHECKER (764 "Mean Old World") 35-50 52
CHECKER (770 "Off the Wall") 35-50 53
(Black vinyl.)
CHECKER (770 "Off the Wall") 100-200 53
(Colored vinyl.)
CHECKER (780 "Blues with a Feeling") 35-50 53
CHECKER (786 "You're So Fine") 25-50 53
CHECKER (793 "Oh Baby") 25-50 54
CHECKER (799 "You Better Watch Yourself") 25-50 54
(Black vinyl.)
CHECKER (799 "You Better Watch Yourself") 75-125 54
(Colored vinyl.)
CHECKER (805 "Last Night") 20-40 54
CHECKER (811 "My Babe") 20-40 55
CHECKER (817 "Roller Coaster") 20-40 55
CHECKER (825 "Too Late") 20-40 55
CHECKER (833 "Who") 20-40 56
CHECKER (838 "One More Chance with You") 20-40 56
CHECKER (845 "Teenage Beat") 20-40 56
CHECKER (852 "It's Too Late Brother") 20-40 56
CHECKER (859 "Everybody Needs Somebody") 20-40 57
CHECKER (867 "Boom Boom, Out Goes the Lights") 20-40 57
CHECKER (890 "The Toddle") 20-40 58
CHECKER (904 "Key to the Highway") 15-25 58
CHECKER (930 "Everything's Gonna Be Alright") 15-25 59
CHECKER (939 "Break It Up") 15-25 59
CHECKER (945 "Ah'w Baby") 15-25 60
CHECKER (955 "My Babe") 15-25 60
CHECKER (968 "I Don't Play") 15-25 61
CHECKER (986 "Crazy Legs") 15-25 61
CHECKER (1013 thru 1117) 10-20 62-65
LPs: 10/12-inch
CHECKER 20-30
CHESS (202 "Little Walter") 15-25 76
CHESS (416 "Confessin the Blues") 10-12 74
CHESS (1428 "Best of Little Walter") 100-200 57
CHESS (1535 "Hate to See You Go") 15-25 69
CHESS (9000 series) 8-10 80s
CHESS (60014 "Boss Blues Harmonica") 15-20 72
DELMARK 12-25
LE ROI DU BLU 12-25
Session: Louis Myers; Dave Myers; Fred Below; Robert Lockwood Jr.; Leonard Caston; Willie Dixon.
Also see BRIM, John
Also see DIXON, Willie
Also see ROBINSON, Freddy
Also see SUNNYLAND SLIM

LITTLE WALTER
(Leroy Foster)
Singles: 78 rpm
PARKWAY (502 "I Just Keep Loving Her") 100-200 50
Singles: 7-inch
HERALD (403 "I Just Keep Loving Her") 200-300 52
HERALD (404 "Boll Weevil") 200-300 52
Also see BABY FACE

LITTLE WALTER JR.
(George Smith)
Singles: 78 rpm
LAPEL 20-30 55
Singles: 7-inch
LAPEL (100 "Miss O'Mally's Rally") 40-60 55
Also see ALLEN, George
Also see HARMONICA KING

LITTLE WHEELS
Singles: 7-inch
TAB (1016 "Something Special") 10-20 60

LITTLE WHEELS
Singles: 7-inch
DOT (16676 "Four Wheeled, Ball Bearing Surfing Board") 10-20 64
Members: Ray Hildebrand; Jill Jackson.
Also see PAUL & PAULA

LITTLE WILBUR & PLEASERS: see WHITFIELD, Wilbur, & Pleasers

LITTLE WILLIE & ADOLESCENTS
Singles: 7-inch
TENER (1009 "Get Out of My Life") 15-25 66
TENER (1013 "Looking for Love") 15-25 66

LITTLE WILLIE JOHN: see JOHN, Little Willie

LITTLE WILMA
Singles: 7-inch
TRI-X 8-12

LITTLEFIELD, Little Willie *R&B '48*
Singles: 78 rpm
BULLS-EYE 15-25 58
EDDIE'S (1202 "Little Willie's Boogie") 50-75 48
EDDIE'S (1205 "Chicago Bound") 50-75 48
EDDIE'S (1212 "Swanee River") 50-75 49
FEDERAL 25-50 52-57
MODERN 25-50 49-50
RHYTHM (107 "Mistreated") 25-50 57
Singles: 7-inch
ARGYLE ("Easy Go") 10-20 59
(Selection number not known.)
BLUES CONNOISEUR 5-8
BULLS-EYE (1005 "Ruby-Ruby") 25-40 58
FEDERAL (12101 "Sticking on You, Baby") 75-125 52
FEDERAL (12110 "K.C. Loving") 75-125 52
FEDERAL (12137 "The Midnight Hour Was Shining") 75-125 53
FEDERAL (12148 "Miss K.C.'s Fine") 75-125 53
FEDERAL (12163 "Please Don't Go-o-o-o-oh") 75-125 53
FEDERAL (12174 "Falling Tears") 75-125 54
FEDERAL (12221 "Jim Wilson's Boogie") 50-100 55
FEDERAL (12300 series) 15-25 57-59
RHYTHM (107 "Mistreated") 100-200 57
RHYTHM (108 "Ruby-Ruby") 200-300 56
Also see LITTLE ESTHER & Little Willie Littlefield

LITTLEFIELD, Little Willie / Goree Carter
Singles: 78 rpm
FREEDOM (1502 "Littlefield Boogie") 50-75 49
Also see CARTER, Goree
Also see LITTLEFIELD, Little Willie

LITTLES, Hattie
(With the Fayettes)
Singles: 7-inch
GORDY (7004 "Back in My Arms Again") 150-250 63
GORDY (7007 "Here You Come") 15-25 63

LITTLETON, John, & Capistranos
Singles: 7-inch
DUKE (179 "Po Mary") 50-75 58
Members: James Brown; Johnny Littleton.

LITTLETOWN GIRLS
Singles: 7-inch
CARNEY 4-6

LITTRELL, Bubba
Singles: 7-inch
MANCO (1037 "Ain't That Cool") 40-60 62

LITTRELL, Johnny
Singles: 7-inch
CHEVELL 4-8 64

LIVE
Singles: 7-inch
T.S.O.B. 3-5 81

LIVE FIVE
Singles: 7-inch
PANORAMA (31 "Shake a Tail Feather") 10-20 66
PANORAMA (46 "Let's Go") 10-20 66
JERDEN (797 "Shake a Tail Feather") 5-10 66
PICCADILLY 8-12 67

LIVE WIRE
Singles: 7-inch
A&M 3-5 79-81
LPs: 10/12-inch
A&M 5-10 79-81

LIVE WIRES
Singles: 7-inch
CAPITOL 5-8 66
REF (110 "Kick Off") 15-20 62
REF (301 "Love") 20-25 60s

LIVELY GHOULS
Singles: 7-inch
BELLAIRE 5-10 63

LIVELY ONES
Singles: 7-inch
DEL-FI (4184 "Guitarget") 10-20 62
DEL-FI (4189 thru 4217) 5-10 63-64
MGM 4-8 67
SMASH 4-8 64
LPs: 10/12-inch
DEL-FI (DFLP-1200 series) 25-35 63-64
(Monaural.)
DEL-FI (DFST-1200 series) 30-50 63-64
(Stereo.)
MGM 15-25 67
Members: Jim Masener; Ron Griffith; Jim Fitzpatrick; Ed Chiaverini; Joe Willenbring.
Also see SURFMEN

LIVELY SET
Singles: 7-inch
CAPITOL 4-8 66
DECCA 5-10 64
MERCURY 4-8 65
STRAIGHT AHEAD 4-8 60s

LIVELY TIM & PROFITS
Singles: 7-inch
PROFIT (067 "Simon Sez") 15-25 67

LIVERBIRDS
Singles: 7-inch
PHILIPS 5-8 65

LIVERPOOL BEATS
(Beats)
LPs: 10/12-inch
RONDO (2026 "New Merseyside Sound") 25-35 64
(Also issued as by the Beats.)
Also see BEATS

LIVERPOOL ECHO
LPs: 10/12-inch
SPARK 10-15 73

LIVERPOOL EXPRESS
Singles: 7-inch
ATCO 4-6 77
Member: Bill Kinsley.
Also see MERSEYBEATS
Also see ROCKIN' HORSE

LIVERPOOL FIVE *P&R '66*
Singles: 7-inch
RCA 5-10 65-67
LPs: 10/12-inch
RCA (LPM-3583 "The Liverpool Five Arrive") 20-25 66
(Monaural.)
RCA (LSP-3583 "The Liverpool Five Arrive") 20-30 66
(Stereo.)
RCA (LPM-3682 "Out of Sight") 20-25 67
(Monaural.)
RCA (LSP-3682 "Out of Sight") 20-30 67
(Stereo.)
Also see ASTRONAUTS / Liverpool Five

LIVERPOOL KIDS
(Schoolboys)
LPs: 10/12-inch
PALACE (777 "Beatle Mash") 35-45 64
Also issued as by the Schoolboys.)
Also see SCHOOLBOYS

LIVERLPOOL LADS
Singles: 7-inch
ALL LLOYDS 8-12 64

LIVERPOOL SCENE
Singles: 7-inch
RCA 4-8 69
LPs: 10/12-inch
EPIC (24336 "Incredible New Liverpool Scene") 20-25 67
(Monaural.)
EPIC (26336 "Incredible New Liverpool Scene") 20-30 67
(Stereo.)
RCA 15-20 69-70
Also see ROBERTS, Andy

LIVERPOOL SET
Singles: 7-inch
COLUMBIA 4-8 65-66

LIVERPOOL SPINNERS
Singles: 7-inch
FONTANA 4-8 67

LIVERPOOLS
LPs: 10/12-inch
WYNCOTE 15-25 64-65

LIVERS
Singles: 7-inch
CONSTELLATION (118 "Beatle Time") 5-10 64
Member: James Holvay.
Also see MOB

LIVERT, Paul, & Lions
LPs: 10/12-inch
METRO 15-20 62
Also see LIONS

LIVGREN, Kerry
LPs: 10/12-inch
KIRSHNER 5-8 80
Also see AD
Also see KANSAS

LIVIGNI, John *P&R '75*
Singles: 7-inch
RAINTREE 3-5 75

LIVIN' BLUES
LPs: 10/12-inch
DWARF 10-15 71

LIVIN' END
Singles: 7-inch
SOFT 8-12 68-69

LIVIN' ENDS
Singles: 7-inch
ATLANTIC (2622 "I Love You More Than You Know") 10-20 69

LIVIN' PROOF
Singles: 7-inch
JU-PAR 3-5 77
Members: Stan Sheppard; Steven Rice; Sterling Rice.
Also see SKOOL BOYZ
Also see TRIPLE "S" CONNECTION

LIVING CHILDREN
Singles: 7-inch
MTA (140 "Crystalize Your Mind") 10-20 68

LIVING COLOUR *LP '88*
Singles: 7-inch
EPIC 3-4 88-90
LPs: 10/12-inch
EPIC 5-8 88-90
Members: Corey Glover; Vernon Reid; Muzz Skillings; William Calhoun.

LIVING END
Singles: 7-inch
MIRA (215 "Turkey Stomp") 15-25 66

LIVING END
Singles: 7-inch
BOLO 4-8 66
DI VENUS 4-8 67

LIVING ENDS
Singles: 7-inch
HUDSON (707 "I Don't Mind") 15-25 66
Member: Larry Gonsky.
Also see LOOKING GLASS

LIVING IN A BOX *P&R/LP '87*
Singles: 12-inch
CHRYSALIS 4-6 87
Singles: 7-inch
CHRYSALIS 3-4 87
Picture Sleeves
CHRYSALIS 3-4 87
LPs: 10/12-inch
CHRYSALIS 5-8 87

LIVING LEGENDS
Singles: 7-inch
RCA 4-8 66

LIVING PROOF
Singles: 12-inch
FANTASY 4-6 87

LIVING SOULS
Singles: 7-inch
REVUE 4-8 67

LIVING STRINGS *LP '61*
(With the Living Voices)
Singles: 7-inch
COMMAND 3-5 59
GRAND AWARD 3-5 59
LPs: 10/12-inch
CAMDEN 5-15 60-62
COMMAND 5-10 59
GRAND AWARD 5-10 59
RCA 5-8 78

LIVINGSTON, Buddy, & Versatones
Singles: 7-inch
SCOTTIE (1313 "Fumbling") 15-25 59

LIVINGSTON, Patty
Singles: 7-inch
DIMENSION 10-20 64

(LIZ) JOHNS: see JOHNS, Liz

LIZA & JET SET
Singles: 7-inch
CAPITOL 5-10 65

LIZARD, King: see KING LIZARD

LIZARDS
Singles: 7-inch
20TH FOX 10-15 64

LIZZY BORDEN *LP '86*
Soundsheets
EVATONE (1029231CS "Me Against the World") 4-6 87
LPs: 10/12-inch
ENIGMA/METAL BLADE 5-8 86-89

LLOIDS OF LON-DEN
Singles: 7-inch
FENTON (1000 "Girls Can Really Dance") 20-30 65

LLOYD, Adrian
Singles: 7-inch
SUNSET 4-6

LLOYD, Anne, & Carillons: see JOHNSON, Betty / Anne Lloyd & Carillons

LLOYD, Baby: see BABY LLOYD

LLOYD, Carroll
Singles: 7-inch
EARMARC 3-5 79
TOWER 5-10

LLOYD, Charles, Quartet *LP '67*
Singles: 7-inch
ATLANTIC 4-8 67
EAR-MARK 3-5 79
LPs: 10/12-inch
ATLANTIC 10-15 67
Also see HAMILTON, Chico

LLOYD, David
LPs: 10/12-inch
EPIC 12-18 65

LLOYD, Duke
(Harold Lloyd Jr.)
Singles: 7-inch
SURF 5-10 59
LPs: 10/12-inch
CORAL 10-20 63

LLOYD "Fatman"
Singles: 78 rpm
OKEH ("7073 "Where You Been") 10-20 56
Singles: 7-inch
OKEH ("7073 "Where You Been") 25-35 56

LLOYD, Grady
Singles: 7-inch
SMASH 8-12 67

LLOYD, Ian *P&R '79*
Singles: 7-inch
POLYDOR 3-5 76
SCOTTI BROTHERS 3-4 79
LPs: 10/12-inch
POLYDOR 5-10 76
SCOTTI BROTHERS 5-8 79
Also see STORIES

LLOYD, Jack
Singles: 78 rpm
EASTMAN (779 "Real Crazy") 8-12 56
Singles: 7-inch
EASTMAN (779 "Real Crazy") 10-20 56

LLOYD, Jackie
Singles: 7-inch
HERO (342 "Warm Love") 250-300 60

LLOYD, Jerry
Singles: 7-inch
TOP RANK 8-10 60

LLOYD, Jimmy
Singles: 78 rpm
ROULETTE 10-20 57
Singles: 7-inch
AIR (1003 "Baby Won't You Listen") 10-20 59
ROULETTE (4062 "Rocket in My Pocket") 50-75 58
ROULETTE (7001 "Where the Rio De Rosa Flows") 25-50 57

LLOYD, Johnny, & Essentials
Singles: 7-inch
LORRAINE 5-10 65

LLOYD, Leroy, & Swinging Dukes
Singles: 7-inch
CAROL (105 "Party Time") 10-20 67

LLOYD, Linda
Singles: 7-inch
COLUMBIA 4-8 64-65

LLOYD, Leroy, & Dukes
Singles: 7-inch
MINARET (146 "Taste of the Blues") 5-8 68

LLOYD, Melody
Singles: 7-inch
STARR 3-5 77

LLOYD, Michael
Singles: 7-inch
JMT (118 "I'll Go On") 4-6 73
W.B. 3-5 78
Also see COTTON, LLOYD & CHRISTIAN
Also see STARSHIP

LLOYD, Mick, & Jerri Kelly *C&W '81*
Singles: 7-inch
LITTLE GIANT 3-4 81

LLOYD, Sam
LPs: 10/12-inch
CHARTON 10-12

LLOYD & GLEN
Singles: 7-inch
WIRL (159 "What You've Got") 15-25

LLOYD & Village Squires
Singles: 7-inch
JUBILEE 4-8 65

LLOYD & WILLIE
Singles: 78 rpm
MAMBO 20-40 55
Singles: 7-inch
MAMBO (101 "Don't Know Where She Went") 50-75 55
Member: Willie Egans.
Also see EGANS, Willie

LOAD
Singles: 7-inch
OWL (740501 "Wow, We'll Say We Tried") 15-25 60s

LOAD OF MISCHIEF
Singles: 7-inch
HOLIDAY INN (2205 "I'm a Lover") 10-15 68
SUN (407 "I'm a Lover") 75-100 68

LOADING ZONE
Singles: 7-inch
COLUMBIA 5-10 66
RCA 5-10 68
UMBRELLA 5-10 67
LPs: 10/12-inch
RCA (3959 "Loading Zone") 15-25 68
UMBRELLA (101 "One for All") 40-60 67

Members: Linda Tillery; Paul Faverso; Steve Busfield; Steve Downer; George Marsh.
Also see TILLERY, Linda, & Loading Zone

LOADSTONE
LPs: 10/12-inch
BARNABY 10-15 69

LOAF, Meat: see MEAT LOAF

LOAN, Joe Van: see VAN LOAN, Joe

LOBO P&R/LP '71
(Roland Kent Lavole)
Singles: 7-inch
BIG TREE 3-6 71-75
ELEKTRA 3-5 80
EVERGREEN 3-4 85
FLASHBACK 3-5 73
LOBO 3-5 81-82
MCA 3-4 79
MARIANNE 3-5 77
PHILIPS 3-5
W.B. 3-5 76-78
LPs: 10/12-inch
BIG TREE 10-15 71-75
CALUMET 10-15 73
MCA 5-10 79
Also see LEE, Robin, & Lobo
Also see STAFFORD, Jim
Also see WOLFPACK

LOCAL OPERATOR
LPs: 10/12-inch
VIRGIN 5-8 80

LOCKE, Cathy
Singles: 7-inch
SMASH 4-8 63

LOCKETS
Singles: 7-inch
ARGO 5-10 63

LOCKETT, John
Singles: 7-inch
TRIANGLE 4-8 62

LOCKETTES
Singles: 7-inch
FLIP 10-20 58
Also see BERRY, Richard

LOCKETTES
Singles: 7-inch
ABC 5-10 66

LOCKLIN, Hank C&W '49
Singles: 78 rpm
DECCA 5-10 52
4 STAR 5-10 49-54
RCA 5-10 55-57
Singles: 7-inch
COUNTRY ARTISTS 3-4 83
DECCA (29000 series) 10-15 52
4 STAR (1500 & 1600 series) 10-15 52-54
KING (5000 series) 5-8 59
MGM 3-5 74
PLANTATION 3-5 76-77
RCA (0030 thru 0900 series) 3-5 72-74
RCA (6100 thru 7600 series) 8-15 55-59
RCA (7700 thru 9900 series) 4-8 60-71
EPs: 7-inch
RCA 8-15 58-61
LPs: 10/12-inch
ARCADE 5-8
CAMDEN 8-15 62-74
DESIGN 10-15 62
INTERNATIONAL AWARD 8-12 60s
KING (600 & 700 series) 15-25 61
MGM 5-10 75
METRO 10-15 65
PICKWICK/HILLTOP 8-15 65-68
PLANTATION 5-8 77-81
RCA (Except 1673 series) 10-20 62-71
RCA (1673 "Foreign Love") 15-25 58
SEARS 8-12 60s
STEREO SPECTRUM 5-10 60s
WRANGLER 8-12 62
Session: Jordanaires.
Also see CLINE, Patsy / Hank Locklin / Miller Brothers / Eddie Marvin
Also see JORDANAIRES
Also see SNOW, Hank / Hank Locklin / Porter Wagoner
Also see SOME of CHET'S FRIENDS

LOCKLIN, Hank, with Danny Davis & Nashville Brass C&W '70
Singles: 7-inch
RCA 3-6 69-70
LPs: 10/12-inch
RCA 8-10 70
Also see DAVIS, Danny
Also see LOCKLIN, Hank

LOCKMAN, Janet, & Chaperons
Singles: 7-inch
IGL (192 "Tequila") 8-12

LOCKS, James
(Jimmy Locks; James "Blazer Boy" Locks)
Singles: 78 rpm:
REGAL 8-12
SAVOY 8-12 56
Singles: 7-inch
SAVOY 10-20 56

LOCKSMITH R&B '80
Singles: 7-inch
ARISTA 3-5 80
LPs: 10/12-inch
ARISTA 5-10 80

LOCKWOOD, Robert, Jr.
(Robert Jr. Lockwood)
Singles: 78 rpm
J.O.B. (1107 "Aw Aw Baby") 50-75 54
MERCURY (8260 "I'm Gonna Dig Myself a Hole") 50-75 51
Singles: 7-inch
J.O.B. (1107 "Aw Aw Baby") 100-200 54
LPs: 10/12-inch
TRIX 10-15
Also see DIXON, Floyd
Also see SPANN, Otis, & Robert Lockwood Jr.
Also see SUNNYLAND SLIM

LOCO, Joe
LPs: 10/12-inch
GNP 15-25 62
IMPERIAL 15-25 62
SUNSET 10-15 66

LOCOMOTIONS
Singles: 7-inch
GONE 10-15 62
SWAN 4-8 65
Also see MFSB

LOCOMOTIV GT
Singles: 7-inch
ABC 3-6 73-75
LPs: 10/12-inch
ABC (Except 860) 8-12 74-75
ABC (860 "All Aboard") 20-25 75
(Promotional issue only.)

LOCOMOTIVE
Singles: 7-inch
BELL 4-6 69
MGM 4-6 69
LPs: 10/12-inch
MGM 10-15 69

LOCOS
Singles: 7-inch
RCA 4-8 66
20TH FOX 5-10 58

LOCUST
LPs: 10/12-inch
ANNUIT 8-10 77

LODGE, John LP '77
Singles: 7-inch
LONDON 3-5 77
LPs: 10/12-inch
LONDON (683 "Natural Avenue") 10-15 77
Also see HAYWARD, Justin, & John Lodge
Also see MOODY BLUES

LOE & JOE
Singles: 7-inch
HARVEY (112 "Little Ole Boy, Little Ole Girl") 15-25 62
Members: Lorri Rudolph; Joe Charles.
Also see RUDOLPH, Lorri
Also see SATINTONES
Also see SPINNERS

LOFGREN, Nils LP '75
Singles: 7-inch
A&M 3-5 75-77
LPs: 10/12-inch
A&M (Except 8362) 8-10 75-82
A&M (8362 "Authorized Bootleg") 25-30 76
(Promotional issue only.)
BACKSTREET 5-8 81
COLUMBIA 5-8 85
EPIC 8-10 76
RYKODISC 5-8 91
Also see GRIN

LOFTIN, Willie, & Discords
Singles: 7-inch
SMOKE (101 "Bad Habit") 50-100 59

LOFTIS, Bobby Wayne C&W '76
Singles: 7-inch
CHARTA 3-5 76-79

LOFTON, Cripple Clarence
Singles: 78 rpm
SESSION 10-20 43
Also see YANCEY, Jimmy / Cripple Clarence Lofton

LOFTON, Rohny
Singles: 7-inch
IMPACT (4292 "El Diablo") 10-20 61

LOFTON, Verneta
Singles: 7-inch
MACK IV 8-12

LOGAN, Betty
Singles: 7-inch
ABC-PAR 5-10 63
ACADEMY 5-10 63

LOGAN, Bud, & Wilma Burgess C&W '73
Singles: 7-inch
SHANNON 3-5 73-74
LPs: 10/12-inch
SHANNON 10-15 74
Also see BLUE BOYS
Also see BURGESS, Wilma

LOGAN, Chris
Singles: 7-inch
BELMONT 3-4 85
Picture Sleeves
BELMONT 3-4 85

LOGAN, Gene
Singles: 7-inch
ASCOT 5-8

LOGAN, John
(John Logan / Jack Grey & Andrew Jacks)
Singles: 7-inch
CURIO (15 "Working for the Man") 5-10 62
CURIO (20 "Wiggle Wobble") 5-10 62
Also see LOGAN, John / Jack Grey & Andrew Jacks

LOGAN, Josh C&W '88
Singles: 7-inch
CURB 3-4 88-89

LOGAN, Willie & Plaids
Singles: 7-inch
JERRY-O (103 "You Conquered Me") 40-60 64
(Reissued as by Charles McCline.)
Also see McCLINE, Charles

LOGAN SISTERS
Singles: 7-inch
FAIRLANE 4-8 62

LOGAN VALLEY BOYS
Singles: 78 rpm
EXCELLENT 50-75 56
Singles: 7-inch
EXCELLENT (279 "Rock & Roll Country Style") 125-150 56

LOGG R&B '81
Singles: 7-inch
SALSOUL 3-5 81
LPs: 10/12-inch
SALSOUL 5-8 81

LOGGINS, Dave P&R/LP '74
Singles: 7-inch
EPIC 3-5 74-81
VANGUARD 4-6 72-74
LPs: 10/12-inch
CAPITOL 5-8 84
EPIC 8-10 74-81
VANGUARD 8-12 72
Also see HARDIN, Gus, & Dave Loggins
Also see MURRAY, Anne, & Dave Loggins

LOGGINS, Kenny P&R/LP '77
Singles: 12-inch
COLUMBIA 4-8 81-86
Singles: 7-inch
COLUMBIA 3-5 77-88
Picture Sleeves
COLUMBIA 3-4 83-88
LPs: 10/12-inch
COLUMBIA (Except 45387) 6-12 72-88
COLUMBIA (45387 "Nightwatch") 10-15 81
(Half-speed mastered.)
Also see SECOND HELPING
Also see U.S.A. for AFRICA

LOGGINS, Kenny, & Stevie Nicks
Singles: 7-inch
COLUMBIA 3-5 78
Also see NICKS, Stevie

LOGGINS, Kenny, & Steve Perry
Singles: 7-inch
COLUMBIA 3-5 82
Picture Sleeves
COLUMBIA 3-5 82
Also see LOGGINS, Kenny
Also see PERRY, Steve

LOGGINS & MESSINA P&R/LP '72
Singles: 7-inch
COLUMBIA 3-5 72-76
LOS ANGELES KINGS COLUMBIA (10444 "Angry Eyes") 3-5 76
(Promotional issue for "Columbia/Kings Record Night" at the L.A. Forum.)
Picture Sleeves
LOS ANGELES KINGS COLUMBIA (10444 "Angry Eyes") 3-5 76
(Promotional issue for "Columbia/Kings Record Night" at the L.A. Forum.)
LPs: 10/12-inch
COLUMBIA (30000 series) 8-10 72-82
COLUMBIA (44000 series) 10-15 82
(Half-speed mastered.)
DIRECT-DISK (16606 "Full Sail") 15-25 82
(Half-speed mastered.)
Members: Kenny Loggins; Jim Messina.
Session: Larry Sims; Vince Denham; Merle Bregante; Jon Clarke; Don Roberts; Steve Forman.
Also see LOGGINS, Kenny
Also see MESSINA, Jim

LOGGINS & MESSINA / David Bromberg
LPs: 10/12-inch
COLUMBIA 8-15 72
(Promotional only.)
Also see BROMBERG, David
Also see LOGGINS & MESSINA

LOGICS
Singles: 7-inch
EVERLAST (5015 "One Love") 15-25 62
GAIT (1004 "Ain't That a Mess") 50-100 60s

LOGIUDICE, Wayne
Singles: 7-inch
PHILIPS 4-8 66

LOGJAM LURCH & TURKEYNECKS
Singles: 7-inch
1-SHOT 4-8 77
Also see KING USZNIEWICZ & His Uszniewicztones

LOGSDON, Jimmy
Singles: 78 rpm
DECCA 5-10 54
Singles: 7-inch
DECCA 10-15 54
LPs: 10/12-inch
KING (843 "Howdy Neighbors") 15-25 63

LOHMAN & BARKLEY
Singles: 7-inch
MGM 4-6 74
LPs: 10/12-inch
MGM 8-12 74
Members: Al Lohman; Roger Barkley.

LOIS & LOUIS
Singles: 7-inch
SPECIALTY 5-10 60

LOKO
Singles: 7-inch
FUN-E-BONE (99 "The Watergate Report") 4-6 73

LOLITA P&R '60
Singles: 7-inch
4 CORNERS 4-6 65
KAPP 5-8 60-61
Picture Sleeves
KAPP 10-15 61
LPs: 10/12-inch
KAPP 15-25 61

LOLITA & EXOTICS
Singles: 7-inch
LIBRA 8-12 60s

LOLLAR, Bobby
Singles: 7-inch
BENTON (101 "Bad Bad Boy") 200-250 58

LOLLIPOP FANTASY
Singles: 7-inch
ERA 4-8 68

LOLLIPOP, Lukas: see LUKAS LOLLIPOP

LOLLIPOP SHOPPE
Singles: 7-inch
SHAMLEY 5-10 68
UNI 8-12 68
LPs: 10/12-inch
UNI (73019 "Just Colour") 40-60 68
Members: Ron Buzzel; Bob Atkins; Edward Bowen; Fred Cole; Carl Fortina; Tim Rockson.
Also see WEEDS

LOLLIPOP TREE
Singles: 7-inch
B.T. PUPPY 4-8 68

LOLLIPOPS
Singles: 7-inch
W.B. 5-8 59

LOLLIPOPS
Singles: 7-inch
ATCO 3-6 70
GORDY (7089 "Cheating Is Telling on You") 200-300 69
IMPACT (1021 "Loving Good Feeling") 20-30 67
RCA (8344 "Peggy Got Engaged") 15-20 64
RCA (8430 "Big Brother") 10-15 64
SMASH 5-10 66
V.I.P. (25051 "Cheating Is Telling on You") 10-20 69

LOLLIPOPS
Singles: 7-inch
SSS INT'L 10-15 69

LOLLYPOPPERS
Singles: 78 rpm
ALADDIN 10-20 55
HARLEM 10-15 55
Singles: 7-inch
ALADDIN (3291 "A Bottle of Pop and a Lollipop") 15-25 55
HARLEM 15-25 55

LOLLYPOPS
Singles: 7-inch
HOLLAND (7420 "My Love Is Real") 2000-3000 58
UNIVERSAL INT'L (7420 "My Love Is Real") 2000-3000 58
(Were not yet certain which label is the first issue.)

LOLLYPOPS
Singles: 7-inch
JAMIE 8-10 64
KANDEE 8-10

LOMAN, Jack
Singles: 7-inch
J&J (100 "Feet Draggin' Blues") 8-12 69

LOMAN, Laurie
Singles: 7-inch
ABC-PAR 5-10 60

LOMAS, Bobby Joyce
Singles: 7-inch
MICHELLE 4-8 65

LOMAX, Alan
LPs:10/12-inch
KAPP 15-20

LOMAX, Jackie LP '69
Singles: 7-inch
APPLE (1802 "Sour Milk Sea") 15-20 68
APPLE (1807 "New Day") 60-80 69
APPLE (1819 "How the Web Was Woven") 5-10 70
APPLE (1834 "Sour Milk Sea") 5-10 71
CAPITOL 3-5 77
EPIC 4-8 68
W.B. 3-5 71-73
Promotional Singles
APPLE (6240 "Sour Milk Sea") 25-30 68
W.B. (514 "Let the Play Begin") 5-10 72
Picture Sleeves
APPLE (1819 "How the Web Was Woven") 5-10 70
W.B. (514 "Let the Play Begin") 5-10 72
(Promotional only issue.)
LPs: 10/12-inch
APPLE (3354 "Is This What You Want") 12-20 69
CAPITOL 5-10 76-77
W.B. 8-12 71-72
Also see BADGER
Also see CLAPTON, Eric
Also see McCARTNEY, Paul
Also see STARR, Ringo

LOMBARD, Wilbert, & Kartels
Singles: 7-inch
DEB (1002 "That's How It Will Be") 50-60 58

LOMBARDIE, Joe
Singles: 7-inch
NEW ENGLAND (1015 "Let's All Rock & Roll") 25-35

LOMBARDO, Guy P&R '27
(With the His Royal Canadians)
Singles: 78 rpm
BRUNSWICK 4-8 32-34
COLUMBIA 4-8 27-31
DECCA 3-8 34-57
VICTOR 3-6 36-38
Singles: 7-inch
CAPITOL 3-6 59-67
DECCA 3-8 50-73
EPs: 7-inch
CAMDEN 5-10
CAPITOL 5-10 56-59
DECCA 5-10 50-59
RCA 5-10 60
LPs: 10/12-inch
CAMDEN 10-30 54-65
CAPITOL (Except 739 thru 1598) 5-15 61-81
CAPITOL (739 thru 1598) 10-25 56-61
DECCA 10-30 50-67
LONDON 5-8 73
MCA 5-8 75
PICKWICK 5-8
RCA 5-8 72-77
SUFFOLK 5-8
VOCALION 5-10 66-68
Also see ARMSTRONG, Louis, & Guy Lombardo
Also see SMITH, Kate

LOMBARDO, John
Singles: 7-inch
PARAMOUNT 3-5 72

LOMBARDOS
Singles: 7-inch
A 8-12 59

LOMONTE, Tommy
Singles: 7-inch
IMPERIAL (5524 "Yeah, Yeah, Yeah") 15-25 58

LON & DERREK: see VAN EATON, Lon & Derrek

LONDIE & CAMEOS
Singles: 7-inch
ABC-PAR 8-12 63

LONDON, Bob
(With the Mike Stoller & Orchestra)
Singles: 78 rpm
DOT (15442 "Reckless") 5-10 55
SPARK (109 "Lola") 5-10 54
Singles: 7-inch
DOT (15442 "Reckless") 8-12 55
SPARK (109 "Lola") 8-12 54
(Red label.)
SPARK (109 "Lola") 10-15 54
(Blue label. This may be the only blue label Spark release.)
Also see STOLLER, Mike, & Stoller System

LONDON, Bobbie
Singles: 7-inch
DOT 3-6 62

LONDON, Clarence
Singles: 78 rpm
FIDELITY (3009 "Goin' Back to Mama") 25-50 53

LONDON, Dutch
Singles: 78 rpm
FAWN (6003 "Each Day") 200-300

LONDON, Jack, & Sparrows: see SPARROWS

LONDON, Jimmy
Singles: 7-inch
KARATE 4-8 65

LONDON, Johnny
("Alto Wizard")
Singles: 78 rpm
SUN (175 "Drivin' Slow") 1000-2000 52
(First commercial issue on the Sun label.)
Session: Johnny London; Charles Keel; Joe Louis Hall; Julius Drake.

LONDON, Johnny
Singles: 7-inch
KING 5-10 61-62

LONDON, Julie *P&R '55*
(With Barney Kessel, Roy Leatherwood & Felix Slatkin's Orchestra; with Russ Garcia & His Orchestra; with Bobby Troup's Quintet)
Singles: 78 rpm
LIBERTY 5-10 55-57
Singles: 7-inch
BETHLEHEM.......................... 5-10 59
LIBERTY 5-15 55-68
Picture Sleeves
LIBERTY (55269 "Time for Lovers")..................10-15 61
EPs: 7-inch
BETHLEHEM (133 "Julie London")..................10-20 59
LIBERTY (1001 "Cry Me a River") 10-20 56
LIBERTY (1-2-3 3006 "Julie Is Her Name")..................10-20 56
(Price is for any of three volumes.)
LIBERTY (1-2-3 3012 "Lonely Girl") 10-20 56
(Price is for any of three volumes.)
LIBERTY (1-2-3 3060 "Make Love to Me")..................10-20 57
(Price is for any of three volumes.)
LIBERTY (1-2-3 9002 "Calendar Girl")..................10-20 56
(Price is for any of three volumes.)
LPs: 10/12-inch
GUEST STAR.......................... 5-10 64
LIBERTY (3006 "Julie Is Her Name")..................35-50 56
(Monaural.)
LIBERTY (3012 "Lonely Girl") 35-50 56
(Monaural.)
LIBERTY (3043 "About the Blues") 20-40 57
(Monaural.)
LIBERTY (3060 "Make Love to Me")..................20-40 57
(Monaural.)
LIBERTY (3096 "Julie Swings")......20-40 58
(Monaural.)
LIBERTY (3100 "Julie Is Her Name, Vol. 2")..................20-40 58
(Monaural.)
LIBERTY (3105 "London By Night")..................15-30 59
(Monaural.)
LIBERTY (3119 "Swing Me an Old Song")..................15-30 59
(Monaural.)
LIBERTY (3130 "Your Number Please")..................15-30 59
(Monaural.)
LIBERTY (3152 "Julie at Home") ...15-30 60
(Monaural.)
LIBERTY (3164 "Around Midnight")..................15-30 60
(Monaural.)
LIBERTY (3171 "Send for Me") 15-30 61
(Monaural.)
LIBERTY (3192 "Whatever Julie Wants")..................15-30 61
(Monaural.)
LIBERTY (3203 "Sophisticated Lady")..................15-25 62
(Monaural.)
LIBERTY (3231 "Love Letters")......15-25 62
(Monaural.)
LIBERTY (3249 "Love on the Rocks")..................15-25 62
(Monaural.)
LIBERTY (3278 "Latin in a Satin Mood")..................15-25 63
(Monaural.)
LIBERTY (3291 "Golden Hits").......15-25 63
(Monaural.)
LIBERTY (3300 "End of the World")..................15-25 63
(Monaural.)
LIBERTY (3324 "Wonderful World of Julie London")..................15-25 63
(Monaural.)
LIBERTY (3342 "Julie London") 15-25 64
(Monaural.)
LIBERTY (3375 "Julie London in Person at the Americana")..................15-25 64
(Monaural.)
LIBERTY (3392 "Our Fair Lady") ...15-25 65
(Monaural.)
LIBERTY (3416 "Feeling Good") 15-25 65
(Monaural.)
LIBERTY (3478 "For the Night People")..................15-25 66
(Monaural.)
LIBERTY (3493 "Nice Girls Don't Stay for Breakfast")..................15-25 67
(Monaural.)
LIBERTY (3514 "With Body and Soul")..................15-25 67
(Monaural.)
LIBERTY (5501 "Best of Julie")......20-30 62
(Monaural.)
LIBERTY (6601 "Best of Julie")......25-35 62
(Stereo.)
LIBERTY (7012 "About the Blues") 50-75 57
(Stereo.)
LIBERTY (7027 "Julie Is Her Name")..................75-100 60
(Stereo. Colored vinyl.)
LIBERTY (7029 "Lonely Girl") 20-35 60
(Stereo.)
LIBERTY (7060 "Make Love to Me")..................20-35 60
(Stereo.)
LIBERTY (7100 "Julie Is Her Name, Vol. 2")..................20-35 59
(Stereo.)
LIBERTY (7105 "London By Night")..................20-35 59
(Stereo.)
LIBERTY (7119 "Swing Me an Old Song")..................20-35 59
(Stereo.)
LIBERTY (7130 "Your Number Please")..................20-35 59
(Stereo.)
LIBERTY (7152 "Julie at Home") ...20-35 60
(Stereo.)
LIBERTY (7164 "Around Midnight")..................20-35 60
(Stereo.)
LIBERTY (7171 "Send for Me")......20-35 61
(Stereo.)
LIBERTY (7192 "Whatever Julie Wants")..................20-35 61
(Stereo.)
LIBERTY (7203 "Sophisticated Lady")..................20-30 62
(Stereo.)
LIBERTY (7231 "Love Letters")......20-30 62
(Stereo.)
LIBERTY (7249 "Love on the Rocks")..................20-30 62
(Stereo.)
LIBERTY (7278 "Latin in a Satin Mood")..................20-30 63
(Stereo.)
LIBERTY (7291 "Golden Hits").......20-30 63
(Stereo.)
LIBERTY (7300 "End of the World")..................20-30 63
(Stereo.)
LIBERTY (7324 "Wonderful World of Julie London")..................20-30 63
(Stereo.)
LIBERTY (7342 "Julie London") 20-30 64
(Stereo.)
LIBERTY (7375 "Julie London in Person at the Americana")..................20-30 64
(Stereo.)
LIBERTY (7392 "Our Fair Lady") ...20-30 65
(Stereo.)
LIBERTY (7416 "Feeling Good")....20-30 65
(Stereo.)
LIBERTY (7478 "For the Night People")..................20-30 66
(Stereo.)
LIBERTY (7493 "Nice Girls Don't Stay for Breakfast")..................15-25 67
(Stereo.)
LIBERTY (7514 "With Body and Soul")..................15-25 67
(Stereo.)
LIBERTY (7546 "Easy Does It") 15-20 68
LIBERTY (7609 "Yummy, Yummy, Yummy")..................15-20 69
LIBERTY (9002 "Calendar Girl") 40-60 56
SUNSET..................8-15 66-68
U.A. (437 "Very Best of Julie London")..................5-10 75
Session: Barney Kessel; Ray Leatherwood; Bobby Troup; Buddy Collette; Howard Roberts; Bob Enevoldsen; Don Heath.
Also see CONNOR, Chris / Julie London / Carmen McRae

LONDON, Julie, & Bud Shank Quintet
LPs: 10/12-inch
LIBERTY (3434 "All Through the Night")..................10-20 66
(Monaural.)
LIBERTY (7434 "All Through the Night")..................15-25 66
(Stereo.)
Also see LONDON, Julie
Also see SHANK, Bud

LONDON, Laurel
Singles: 7-inch
GULF REEF (1007 "Don't Knock the Rock")..................25-50 62

LONDON, Laurie *P&R/R&B '58*
Singles: 7-inch
CAPITOL..................8-10 58-59
ROULETTE..................5-10 59
EPs: 7-inch
CAPITOL (10182 "Laurie London")..................20-30 58
CAPITOL (10191 "Laurie London")..................20-30 58
LPs: 10/12-inch
CAPITOL (10169 "Laurie London")..................30-50 58

LONDON, Lloyd, & Yachtsmen
Singles: 7-inch
DESTINY (530 "Will There Ever Be a Girl for Me")..................50-75 59
Also see YACHTSMEN

LONDON, Mark
Singles: 7-inch
CAMEO..................8-12 65

LONDON, Mel
Singles: 78 rpm
CHIEF..................10-15 57
Singles: 7-inch
CHIEF..................10-15 57

LONDON, Paul, & Capers
Singles: 7-inch
CHECK MATE (1006 "Sugar Baby")..................20-40 62

LONDON, Robb, & Rogues
Singles: 7-inch
BECKINGHAM (1085 "It Should Have Been Me")..................15-25 65
SUZUKI (1001 "Gloria")..................15-25 60s

LONDON, Seth
Singles: 7-inch
MGM 4-8 66

LONDON & BRIDGES
Singles: 7-inch
DATE (1502 "It Just Ain't Right")......5-10 66
DATE (1517 "Tell It to the Preacher")..................5-10 66
DATE (1535 "Keep Him")..................4-8 67
Picture Sleeves
DATE (1502 "It Just Ain't Right")....10-15 66

LONDON BRIDGE
Singles: 7-inch
CAPITOL..................3-5 73

LONDON CHIMES
Singles: 7-inch
PHILIPS..................4-8 65

LONDON FOG
(With the Continentals)
Singles: 7-inch
COULEE (118 "Mr. Baldi") 15-25 66
GOLD STARS (90852 "Trippin' ")...10-20 68
(First issue.)
IMPERIAL ("Trippin' ") 5-10 68
(Selection number not known.)
LPs: 10/12-inch
POMPEI..................8-12

LONDON KNIGHTS
Singles: 7-inch
MIKE (4200 "Go to Him")..............15-25 66

LONDON PHOGG
Singles: 7-inch
A&M..................3-6 69

LONDON QUIREBOYS *LP '90*
LPs: 10/12-inch
CAPITOL..................5-8 90

LONDON ROCK SYMPHONY
LPs: 10/12-inch
BASF..................10-15 73

LONDON SYMPHONY ORCHESTRA *LP '79*
(With Ian Anderson)
Singles: 7-inch
RCA (14262 "Elegy")..................3-4 86
LPs: 10/12-inch
RCA (4000 series)..................5-8 83
RCA (7067 "A Classic Case") 8-10 86
RSO..................5-8 79
Also see ANDERSON, Ian

LONDON TAXI
Singles: 7-inch
PICADILLY..................8-15 60s

LONDON TEENS
Singles: 7-inch
PIC (112 "Little Suzy")..................8-12

LONDONAIRS
Singles: 7-inch
LONDON..................4-8 68

LONDONS
Singles: 7-inch
PYRAMID (7211 "Old Man")..........10-15 66

LONE JUSTICE *P&R/LP '85*
Singles: 7-inch
GEFFEN..................3-4 85-87
LPs: 10/12-inch
GEFFEN..................5-8 85-86
Member: Tony Gilkyson.
Also see X

LONE STAR
LPs: 10/12-inch
COLUMBIA..................8-10 76-77

LONE TWISTER
Singles: 7-inch
ATLANTIC..................5-10 61

LONE X
Singles: 7-inch
SELF..................5-8

LONELY BOYS
Singles: 7-inch
NU-WAY (555 "My Girl")..................50-75 59

LONELY GUYS
Singles: 7-inch
CADDY (117 "The Way You Look Tonight")..................75-100 58

LONELY KNIGHTS
Singles: 7-inch
L&K (1125 "Do It to It")..................8-12

LONELY ONE
Singles: 7-inch
CAROL (4110 "A Letter to My Love")..................10-15 60s

LONELY ONES
Singles: 7-inch
BATON..................8-10 59
SIR (270 "My Wish")..................10-20 59

LONELY ONES
Singles: 7-inch
RENDEVOUS (125 "Swanee River Fling")..................10-15 60

LONELY ONES
EPs: 7-inch
STUB'S PUB (2277 "Stub's Pub") ..35-50

LONELY RIDERS
Singles: 7-inch
MTA (139 "Lonely Rider")..........10-15 68

LONELY SOULS
Singles: 7-inch
PARIS TOWER..................20-30 67

LONERO, Bobby
Singles: 7-inch
APT..................8-12 60
LIBERTY (55180 "Little Bit")..........15-25 59
SPINETT..................8-12 60

LONESOME DRIFTER
Singles: 78 rpm
K (5812 "Eager Boy")..................250-500 56
Singles: 7-inch
K (5812 "Eager Boy")..................750-1000 56
R.A.M. (1738 "What Do You Think of Me")..................20-30

LONESOME LARRY
Singles: 7-inch
TILT (779 "Cool Today")..................10-20 62

LONESOME LEE
(Jimmy Lee Robinson)
Singles: 7-inch
BANDERA (2501 "Cry Over Me") ..25-35 59
Also see JIMMY LEE
Also see ROBINSON, Jimmy Lee

LONESOME RHODES
Singles: 7-inch
RCA (9305 "Delight of My Day") 10-15 67

LONESOME STRANGER *C&W '89*
HIGHTONE..................3-4 89

LONESOME SUNDOWN
Singles: 7-inch
EXCELLO..................10-20 57-65
LPs: 10/12-inch
ALLIGATOR..................5-10 80
EXCELLO..................10-20 69
JOLIET..................10-15 78

LONESOME SUNDOWN & PHILIP WALKER
LPs: 10/12-inch
ROUNDER..................8-12
Also see LONESOME SUNDOWN
Also see WALKER, Philip

LONETTE
Singles: 7-inch
M-S (208 "Veil of Mystery")..........15-25 68

LONEY, Roy
LPs: 10/12-inch
WAR BRIDE..................8-10 82
Also see FLAMIN' GROOVIES

LONG, Barbara
LPs: 10/12-inch
SAVOY (12161 "Soul")..................15-25 61

LONG, Bobby
(With the Cherrios; with Satelites; Joe Erskine)
Singles: 7-inch
ARROW (727 "Patty")..................20-30 57
CUB (9120 "Flip Flop")..................8-10 63
EVERLAST (5020 "Ooh Poo Pah Doo")..................5-10 63
FOUNTAINHEAD (105 "I Need You")..................10-15 60
GLOW-HILL (503 "Don't You Run")..................15-25 58
GLOW-HILL (504 "Hold Me")..........15-25 59
GLOW-HILL (505 "Calling")..........15-25 59
(First issue.)
SKYMAC (1007 "Just for a Day")......5-10 64
SKYMAC (1011 "I Had to Come Back")..................5-10 64
TEIA (1001 "Jenny Lee")..................5-10 64
UNART (2023 "Calling")..................10-20 59
VEGAS (500 "Mojo Workout")..........5-10 64
VEGAS (700 "Stir It Up")..................5-10 64
ZIP (102 "A Night to Remember")..................150-250 57
Also see ERSKINE, Joe

LONG, Buddy
Singles: 7-inch
DEMON..................5-10 59

LONG, Curtis
Singles: 7-inch
LINCO (1314 "Hootchy Cootchy")..................75-125 59
STARDALE (600 "Goin' Out on the Town")..................50-75 59

LONG, Dewey
Singles: 7-inch
BIG SOUND (22849 "Feelings on Paper")..................30-50

LONG, Huey
Singles: 7-inch
FIDELITY (Except 4055)..................5-10 62
FIDELITY (4055 "Elvis Stole My Gal")..................40-50 62
ROCK-IT..................3-5 77

LONG, Joey
(Joey Longoria)
Singles: 7-inch
ARGO (5563 "I Need Someone")...10-20 60
CRAZY CAJUN..................4-6 77
RUNNING BEAR (8300 "I'm Glad for Your Sake")..................10-15 62
TRIBE (8302 "Hurtin' Inside")..........10-15 62
LPs: 10/12-inch
CRAZY CAJUN..................10-15 77
Also see MEYERS, Augie
Also see SIR DOUGLAS QUINTET

LONG, Johnny
Singles: 78 rpm
CORAL..................4-6 55
Singles: 7-inch
CORAL..................5-10 55
MCA..................3-5 73
LP: 10/12-inch
TOPS..................6-12

LONG, Johnny
Singles: 7-inch
SOMA..................10-20 61
STARDUST..................10-20 60s
TWIN TOWN..................8-12 60s

LONG, Joseph
LPs: 10/12-inch
SCEPTER..................10-15 69

LONG, Shorty *C&W '48*
(With the Santa Fe Rangers; with Searchers)
Singles: 78 rpm
DECCA..................4-8 48
DOLLO..................10-20
Also see WELLINGTON, Rusty

LONG, Shorty *P&R/R&B '66*
Singles: 78 rpm
RCA..................20-50 56
Singles: 7-inch
JAMIE (1315 "Greetings")..................8-12 66
RCA (6572 "Vacation Rock") 40-60 56
RCA (6873 "You Don't Have to Be a Baby to Cry")..................35-50 57
SOUL (35001 "Devil with a Blue Dress")..................20-25 64
SOUL (35005 "It's a Crying Shame")..................15-25 64
SOUL (35021 thru 35064)..................6-12 66-69
SOUL (Colored vinyl)..................10-20 60s
(Promotional only.)
TRI-PHI (1006 "I'll Be There")........25-35 62
TRI-PHI (1015 "Too Smart")..........25-35 62
TRI-PHI (1021 "Going My Way") ...25-35 62
VALLEY (108 "I Got Nine Little Kisses")..................50-100 59
LPs: 10/12-inch
SOUL (709 "Here Comes the Judge")..................10-20 68
SOUL (719 "The Prime")..................10-15 69

LONG, Tom
(Gene Autry)
Singles: 78 rpm
Sunrise (33070 "I'll Be Thinking Of You Little Girl")..................25-75
Also see AUTRY, Gene

LONG, Tommy
Singles: 7-inch
BELLWOOD..................4-8 63

LONG GONE MILES: see MILES, Long Gone

LONG HAIRS
Singles: 7-inch
MEMPHIS (110 "Go Go Go")..........50-75 62

LONG ISLAND SOUNDS
(Long Island Soundes)
Singles: 7-inch
BALBOA (021 "Pancho's Villa") 5-10
DYNO-VOICE (903 "One, Two, Three and I Fell")..................5-10 67
WONDER (165 "Tiger")..................10-15 65
WONDER (166 "Don't Cry Linda") .10-15 65
Members: Tony Pragano; Andelo Frisketti; Tom Hanlon; Jack Russell; Fred O'Brien; Bob Pasternak.

LONG JOHN
(John Hunter)
Singles: 78 rpm
DUKE (122 "Crazy Girl")..........10-20 53
Singles: 7-inch
DUKE (122 "Crazy Girl")..........20-30 53
Also see HUNTER, John

LONG JOHN & SILVERMEN
Singles: 7-inch
WANTED (001 "Heart Filled with Love")..................15-25 66
WANTED (4581 "I'll Come Back") . 10-15 66

LONG MAN BINDER: see BINDER, Dennis

LONG RYDERS
EPs: 7-inch
PVC..................5-8 83
LPs: 10/12-inch
FRONTIER..................8-10
Members: Steve McCarthy; Sid Griffin; Greg Sowders; Tom Stevens.

LONG TALL LESTER
(Lester Foster)
Singles: 7-inch
DUKE..................10-20 58

LONG TALL MARVIN
(Marvin Phillips)
Singles: 78 rpm
MODERN..................20-40 56
Singles: 7-inch
MODERN (993 "Mave Mercy Miss Percy")..................50-75 56
Also see PHILLIPS, Marvin

LONGBRANCH PENNYWHISTLE
Singles: 7-inch
AMOS..................5-10 69
LPs: 10/12-inch
AMOS (7007 "Longbranch Pennywhistle")..................25-40 69
Members: John David Souther; Glen Frey; James Burton; Ry Cooder.
Also see BURTON, James
Also see COODER, Ry
Also see FREY, Glen
Also see SOUTHER, J. D.

FASCINATION 1007— "ROSIE LEE" $12,000

LONGDANCER
Singles: 7-inch
MCA ... 3-5 73
LPs: 10/12-inch
MCA ... 8-10 73

LONGET, Claudine *P&R '66*
Singles: 7-inch
A&M ... 3-6 66-70
BARNABY ... 3-5 70-73
LPs: 10/12-inch
A&M ... 5-12 67-69
BARNABY ... 5-10 70-72

LONGHAIR, Professor: see PROFESSOR LONGHAIR

LONGMIRE, Wilbert *R&B '80*
Singles: 7-inch
TAPPAN ZEE ... 3-5 79-80
WORLD PACIFIC ... 4-6
LPs: 10/12-inch
TAPPAN ZEE ... 5-8 79-80

LONGO, Bobby
Singles: 7-inch
ZIP (102 "A Night to Remember") ... 200-300

LONNIE
(Irving Brofsky)
Singles: 7-inch
MOHAWK (122 "Beeline") ... 10-15 61
Also see LONNIE & CAROLLONS

LONNIE & CAROLLONS
Singles: 7-inch
MOHAWK (108 "Chapel of Tears") ... 35-50 59
(Green label.)
MOHAWK (108 "Chapel of Tears") 10-20 59
(Red label.)
MOHAWK (111 "Trudy") ... 15-25 58
MOHAWK (112 "You Say") ... 15-25 59
MOHAWK (113 "The Gang All Knows") ... 25-35 60
STREET CORNER ... 3-5
Members: Irving Brofsky; Richie Jackson; Eric Nathanson; Jimmy Laffey.
Also see LONNIE
Also see REYNOLDS, Ricky

LONNIE & CAROLLONS / Barons
Singles: 7-inch
MOHAWK (902 "Chapel of Tears") . 8-12 63
Also see BARONS

LONNIE & CAROLLONS / Deans
LPs: 10/12-inch
CRYSTAL BALL ... 5-8
Also see DEANS
Also see LONNIE & CARROLLONS

LONNIE & CRISIS
(With Bob Alfieri & Orchestra)
Singles: 7-inch
UNIVERSAL (103 "Bells in the Chapel") ... 100-150 61

LONNIE & FLOYD
Singles: 7-inch
JEWEL ... 4-8 67

LONNIE & LEGENDS
Singles: 7-inch
IMPRESSION (109 "I Cried") ... 20-30 66
REV (1005 "Penguin Walk") ... 15-25 63

LONNIE B. & VIKI G.
Singles: 7-inch
REVUE ... 4-8 68-69

LONNIE LEE: see LEE, Lonnie

LONNIE THE CAT
Singles: 78 rpm
RPM (410 "I Ain't Drunk") ... 15-25 54
Singles: 7-inch
RPM (410 "I Ain't Drunk") ... 30-50 54

LONNIE'S LEGENDS
Singles: 7-inch
PLAYBOY (108 "Trying So Hard to Forget") ... 10-20 60s

LONNY & ANGELS
Singles: 7-inch
PLEDGE ... 5-10 61

LONZO & OSCAR *C&W '48*
(With the Winston County Pea Pickers)
Singles: 78 rpm
DECCA ... 4-8 53-54
DOT ... 4-8 54
RCA ... 5-10 48
Singles: 7-inch
DECCA ... 5-10 53-54
DOT ... 5-10 54
GRC ... 3-5 74
NUGGET ... 4-6 62-64
STARDAY ... 4-8 60-61
LPs: 10/12-inch
BRYLEN ... 5-10 82
COLUMBIA ... 10-20 68
DECCA ... 15-25 63
GRC ... 6-12 75
NUGGET ... 6-12
PICKWICK/HILLTOP ... 10-20 65
STARDAY (119 "America's Greatest Country Comedians") ... 35-45 60
STARDAY (244 "Country Music Time") ... 25-35 63
Members: Rollin Sullivan; Ken Marvin; John Sullivan; David Hooten.

LOOK
LPs: 10/12-inch
PLASTIC ... 5-8 81-82
QUALITY/RFC ... 5-8 83

LOOKING GLASS
Singles: 7-inch
SUNNY ... 3-6 69
UNI ... 4-8 67
VALIANT ... 4-8 66
W.B. ... 4-8 67

LOOKING GLASS *P&R/LP '72*
Singles: 7-inch
EPIC ... 3-5 72-74
LPs: 10/12-inch
EPIC ... 10-12 72-73
Members: Elliot Lurie; Carolyn Davis; Jeff Grob; Barbara Massey; P. Sweval; Larry Gonsky.
Also see LIVING ENDS
Also see LURIE, Elliot

LOOKING GLASSES
Singles: 7-inch
MEDIA (414 "Visions") ... 20-30 67
Also see CLOUDS

LOOK OUTS
Singles: 7-inch
SEEBURG ... 10-15 65

LOOK UK
LPs: 10/12-inch
MCA ... 5-8 81

LOOMS
Singles: 7-inch
MONTGOMERY (0009 "It's True") ... 25-35 60s

LOOSE
Singles: 7-inch
NOCTURNE ... 4-6 70
LPs: 10/12-inch
NOCTURNE ... 10-15 70

LOOSE CHANGE *R&B '80*
Singles: 7-inch
CASABLANCA ... 3-5 79-80
LPs: 10/12-inch
CASABLANCA ... 5-10 79

LOOSE ENDS
Singles: 7-inch
BELL (671 "Dead End Kid") ... 5-10 66
MALA (538 "He's a Nobody") ... 10-20 66
MEADOW BROOK (69 "Hey Sweet Baby") ... 10-15 69

LOOSE ENDS *P&R/R&B/D&D/LP '85*
Singles: 12-inch
MCA ... 4-6 85-86
Singles: 7-inch
MCA ... 3-4 85-90
Picture Sleeves
MCA ... 3-4 85-88
LPs: 10/12-inch
MCA ... 5-8 85-90

LOOSE ENZ
Singles: 7-inch
VIRTUE (2502 "Easy Rider") ... 10-20 68

LOOSE GRAVEL
Singles: 7-inch
KELLY ... 5-10

LOOSE JOINTS *D&D '84*
Singles: 12-inch
4TH & BROADWAY ... 4-6 84
Singles: 7-inch
4TH & BROADWAY ... 3-4 84

LOOSE WIG
Singles: 7-inch
RESIST (506 "I'll Always Love You Darlin' ") ... 10-20 60s

LOPEZ, Denise *P&R/LP '88*
LPs: 10/12-inch
A&M ... 5-8 88

LOPEZ, Frank, & Travelers: see TRAVELERS

LOPEZ, Trini *P&R/R&B/LP '63*
Singles: 12-inch
ROULETTE ... 5-8 77
Singles: 7-inch
CAPITOL ... 3-5 71-72
D.R.A. ... 5-10 61
GRIFFIN ... 3-5 73-75
KING (5173 "Nola") ... 10-15 59
KING (5187 "Rock On") ... 15-25 59
KING (5198 "Here Comes Sally") ... 10-15 59
KING (5234 thru 5487) ... 8-15 59-61
KING (5800 series) ... 5-10 63-64
KING (6000 series) ... 4-8 65-66
MARIANNE ... 3-5 77
PRIVATE STOCK ... 3-5 75
REPRISE ... 4-8 63-71
ROULETTE ... 3-5 77
UNITED MODERN ... 4-8 64
VOLK (101 "The Right to Rock") ... 15-25 58
Picture Sleeves
REPRISE ... 5-10 62-66
EPs: 7-inch
COLUMBIA/W.B. (124178 "Trini Lopez Sings His Greatest Hits") ... 10-15 67
(Special products issue for Coca-Cola/Fresca.)
KING (483 "Teenage Idol") ... 15-25 63
REPRISE ... 8-12 63-68
LPs: 10/12-inch
CAPITOL ... 5-10 72
CROWN ... 6-12 65
EXACT ... 5-8 81
GRIFFIN ... 8-10 72
HARMONY ... 8-10 70
KING (863 "Teenage Love Songs") ... 20-30 63
KING (877 "More of Trini Lopez") ... 20-30 63
REPRISE ... 10-20 63-69
ROULETTE ... 5-8 78
SILVER EAGLE ... 5-10 82
WEA LATINA ... 5-8 91
Also see BIG BEATS
Also see LAWRENCE, Steve / Trini Lopez
Also see RIVERS, Johnny / Trini Lopez

LOPEZ, Trini / Scott Gregory
LPs: 10/12-inch
GUEST STAR (1499 "Trini Lopez / Scott Gregory [Bill Haley]") ... 30-50 64
Also see HALEY, Bill

LOPEZ, Trini, with the Ventures & Nancy Ames
LPs: 10/12-inch
REPIRSE (6361 "The Trini Lopez Show") ... 10-15 70
Also see AMES, Nancy
Also see LOPEZ, Trini
Also see VENTURES

LOPEZ, Vincent, & His Orchestra
LPs: 10/12-inch
MERCURY ... 15-25 50s
WALDORF (185 "Melody of Love") ... 35-55 54
(10-inch LP. Cover pictures Tina Louise, although she is not heard on the disc. Also issued credited to Enoch Light & His Orchestra.)
WALDORF (193 "Moments to Remember") ... 35-55 54
(10-inch LP. Cover pictures Tina Louise, although she is not heard on the disc. Also issued credited to Enoch Light & His Orchestra.)
WALDORF (1214 "Moments to Remember") ... 25-50 57
(Cover pictures Jayne Mansfield, although she is not heard on the disc. Also issued credited to Enoch Light & His Orchestra.)
WALDORF (1232 "Melody of Love") ... 20-40 57
(10-inch LP. Cover pictures Tina Louise, although she is not heard on the disc. Also issued credited to Enoch Light & His Orchestra.)
WALDORF (1329 "Moments to Remember") ... 20-40 58
(Cover pictures Tina Louise, although she is not heard on the disc. Also issued credited to Enoch Light & His Orchestra.)
Also see LIGHT, Enoch, & His Orchestra
Also see MANSFIELD, Jayne

LOR, Denise *P&R '54*
Singles: 78 rpm
LIBERTY ... 3-5 56
MAJAR ... 4-6 54
MERCURY ... 3-5 55
Singles: 7-inch
LIBERTY ... 4-8 56
MAJAR ... 5-10 54
MERCURY ... 4-8 55
EPs: 7-inch
MERCURY ... 5-10 55

LORAIN, A'Me *P&R '90*
Singles: 7-inch
RCA ... 3-4 90
Picture Sleeves
RCA ... 3-4 90

LORAN, Kenny
Singles: 7-inch
CAPITOL (Except 4276) ... 10-15 59-60
CAPITOL (4276 "Magic Star") ... 30-40 59

LORBER, Alan
Singles: 7-inch
VERVE ... 4-6 60s
LPs: 10/12-inch
MGM ... 10-15 69

LORBER, Jeff *LP '79*
(Jeff Lorber Fusion; with Audrey Wheeler; with Karyn White)
Singles: 12-inch
ARISTA ... 4-6 85
Singles: 7-inch
ARISTA ... 3-5 79-85
INNER CITY ... 3-5 78
W.B. ... 3-4 86
Picture Sleeves
W.B. ... 3-4 86
LPs: 10/12-inch
ARISTA ... 5-8 79-85
INNER CITY ... 5-10 78
W.B. ... 5-8 86
Members: Kenny Gorelick; Karyn White; Michael Jeffries.
Also see KENNY G.
Also see UNLIMITED TOUCH
Also see WHITE, Karyn

LORD, Bobby *C&W '56*
Singles: 78 rpm
COLUMBIA (21000 series, except 21339 & 21539) ... 5-10 55-56
COLUMBIA (21339 "No More, No More") ... 10-15 55
COLUMBIA (21539 "Everybody's Rockin' But Me") ... 10-20 56
COLUMBIA (40000 series) ... 10-15 56
Singles: 7-inch
COLUMBIA (21339 "No More, No More") ... 40-60 55
COLUMBIA (21339 "No More") ... 10-20 55
COLUMBIA (21367 "I'm the Devil Who Made Her That Way") ... 10-20 55
COLUMBIA (21397 "Something's Missing") ... 10-20 55
COLUMBIA (21437 "Hawk-Eye") ... 15-25 55
COLUMBIA (21498 "So Doggone Lonesome") ... 10-20 55
COLUMBIA (21459 "I Can't Do Without You Anymore") ... 10-20 55
COLUMBIA (21539 "Everybody's Rockin' But Me") ... 50-75 56
COLUMBIA (40666 "Fire of Love") 20-30 56
COLUMBIA (40819 "Your Sweet Love") ... 10-20 57
COLUMBIA (40927 "High Voltage") ... 15-25 57
COLUMBIA (41030 "Am I a Fool") 10-20 57
COLUMBIA (41155 "Sack") ... 15-25 58
COLUMBIA (41288 "Walking Alone") ... 10-20 58
COLUMBIA (41352 "Party Pooper") ... 15-25 59
COLUMBIA (41505 thru 42012) ... 15-25 59-61
DECCA ... 3-5 68-71
HICKORY ... 4-6 61-64
LPs: 10/12-inch
DECCA ... 8-10 70
HARMONY ... 10-20 64
HICKORY ... 10-12 65

LORD, Brian, & Midnighters
Singles: 7-inch
CAPITOL (4981 "Big Surfer") ... 20-40 63
VIGAH (0001 "Big Surfer") ... 75-125 63
Members: Brian Lord; Frank Zappa; Ray Collins; Paul Buff; David Aerni.
Also see MOTHERS OF INVENTION
Also see NED & NELDA
Also see ROTATIONS

LORD, C., & L. Doherty
Singles: 7-inch
PILGRIM (702 "The Wedding Is Over") ... 10-20 60s

LORD, C.M. *R&B '82*
Singles: 12-inch
MONTAGE ... 4-6 82-84
WAVE ... 4-6 83
Singles: 7-inch
CAPITOL ... 3-5 76
MONTAGE ... 3-4 82-84
LPs: 10/12-inch
CAPITOL ... 8-10 76
MONTAGE ... 5-8 84

LORD, Dick
Singles: 7-inch
ATCO ... 8-10 64

LORD, Emmett
Singles: 7-inch
ANTEL (520 "Been So Long") ... 5-10 60s
LIBERTY ... 4-8 62

LORD, Jon
LPs: 10/12-inch
CAPITOL ... 10-12 70
U.A. ... 5-8 78
W.B. ... 8-10 73
Also see ASHTON, Tony, & Jon Lord
Also see DEEP PURPLE
Also see WHITESNAKE

LORD, Leige
Singles: 12-inch
IRON WORKS (1006 "Five from Eight") ... 10-15 86
(Picture disc. 250 made.)
Singles
IRON WORKS ("Warrior's Farewell") ... 10-15 87
(Warrior-shaped picture disc. 250 made. No selection number used.)
LPs: 10/12-inch
IRON WORKS (1006 "Freedom's Rise") ... 10-15 86
(Picture disc. 250 made.)

LORD, Mike *C&W '87*
Singles: 7-inch
NSD ... 3-4 87

LORD, Peggy
LPs: 10/12-inch
STEREODDITIES ... 15-20 63

LORD ALAN & SIR RICHARD
Singles: 7-inch
CANNON ... 4-8 64

LORD & FLIES
Singles: 7-inch
U.S.A. (828 "You Made a Fool Out of Me") ... 4-8 66
U.S.A. (857 "Echoes") ... 10-20 66

LORD & HIS BARONS
Singles: 7-inch
FLEETWOOD (4566 "Foolish Lies") ... 15-25 66

LORD AUGUST & VISIONS OF LITE
Singles: 7-inch
A-OK ... 4-8 68
SSS INT'L ... 4-8 68
VOL ... 5-10 67
Member: Augie Meyers.
Also see MEYERS, Augie

LORD BUCKLEY: see BUCKLEY, Lord

LORD DENT & INVADERS
Singles: 7-inch
SHELLEY (1001 "Wolf Call") ... 10-20 60s
SHELLEY (1810 "Wolf Call") ... 10-15 60s
Picture Sleeves
SHELLEY (1001 "Wolf Call") ... 10-20 60s
Member: Clayton "Lord Dent" Watson.

LORD DOUGLAS & SERFS
Singles: 7-inch
HR (606 "Your Turn to Cry") ... 15-25

LORD FLEA
Singles: 78 rpm
CAPITOL ... 5-10 57
Singles: 7-inch
CAPITOL ... 5-10 57

LORD JIM: see SCREAMIN' LORD JIM

LORD JIM & V.I.P.s
Singles: 7-inch
BLUE STAR ... 8-12

LORD JOHN
LPs: 10/12-inch
BOMP ... 5-8 87

LORD KALVERT & RESERVES
Singles: 7-inch
QUEST ... 4-8

LORD LUTHER
(With the Counts; with Garnets; with Kingsmen; Luther McDaniel)
Singles: 7-inch
FRANTIC (112 "Truth") ... 25-40 59
IMPERIAL (5596 "Truth") ... 10-20 59
LUSAN (101 "Two of a Kind") ... 15-25
SCHIRECK (101 "My Mistake") ... 15-25
Also see GAYLARKS
Also see LEWIS, Al, & Modernistics / Lord Luther

LORD ROCKINGHAM'S XI *P&R '58*
Singles: 7-inch
LONDON ... 5-10 58

LORD SITAR
Singles: 7-inch
CAPITOL ... 5-8 67
LPs: 10/12-inch
CAPITOL (2916 "Lord Sitar") ... 10-20 68

LORD SUPERIOR
Singles: 7-inch
CAB ... 4-8 62

LORD SUTCH *LP '70*
(With His Heavy Friends)
LPs: 10/12-inch
COTILLION (9015 "Lord Sutch & His Heavy Friends") ... 20-30 70
COTILLION (9049 "Hands of Jack the Ripper") ... 15-25 72
Member: Daniel Edwards.
Also see BECK, Jeff
Also see BLACKMORE, Ritchie
Also see HOPKINS, Nicky
Also see MOON, Keith
Also see PAGE, Jimmy

LORD THUNDER
Singles: 7-inch
DELUXE ... 4-6 69

LORD WESTBROOK
Singles: 7-inch
BIGTOP (3138 "Quiet Please") ... 10-20 63

LORD WILLIAM & HIS COURT
Singles: 7-inch
APPLAUSE ... 5-10 60

LORDAN, Jerry
Singles: 7-inch
CAPITOL (4389 "Do I Worry") ... 10-15 60

LORDI, Tony
Singles: 7-inch
RCA ... 3-5 72

LORDS
Singles: 7-inch
VALIANT (725 "She Belongs to Me") ... 10-20 66

LORDS
Singles: 7-inch
ALDRICH (1001 "Light Rain") ... 15-25 66

LORDS
Singles: 7-inch
MIKIM ... 4-6 71

LORDS OF LONDON
Singles: 7-inch
APEX (21809 "Candy Rainbow") ... 15-20
(Canadian.)
APEX (77054 "Cornflakes and Ice Cream") ... 15-20 67
(Canadian.)
APEX (77068 "Popcorn Man") ... 15-20 67
(Canadian.)
APEX (77074 "Candy Rainbow") ... 15-20 68
(Canadian.)
DECCA (32196 "Cornflakes and Ice Cream") ... 10-15 67
DOMAIN (1421 "Broken Heart") ... 15-20 65
MGM (13919 "Candy Rainbow") ... 10-15 68

LORDS OF PERCUSSION
Singles: 7-inch
OLD TOWN ... 3-5 74

LORDS OF THE NEW CHURCH *LP '85*
Singles: 12-inch
I.R.S. ... 4-6 83
Singles: 7-inch
I.R.S. ... 3-4 82-85
LPs: 10/12-inch
I.R.S. ... 5-8 82-85
Member: Stiv Bators.
Also see BATORS, Stiv

LORDS OF THE UNDERGROUND
Singles: 7-inch
CAPITOL (30710 "Keepers of the Funk")....10-15 90s

LORDS OF THUNDER
Singles: 7-inch
DAVIS....5-10 64

LORELEIS P&R '55
Singles: 78 rpm
BALLY....5-15 57
DOT....5-10 54
SPOTLIGHT....5-10 55
Singles: 7-inch
BALLY....5-15 57
BRUNSWICK....3-5 64
DOT....5-12 54
SPOTLIGHT....5-15 55

LOREN, Bryan R&B '84
Singles: 12-inch
PHILLY WORLD....4-6 83-84
Singles: 7-inch
PHILLY WORLD....3-4 83

LOREN, Donna
Singles: 7-inch
CAPITOL....8-12 64-65
CHALLENGE....8-12 62-64
CREST....5-10 62
REPRISE....4-8 67
Picture Sleeves
CAPITOL (5250 "Blowing Out the Candles")....10-15 64-65
LPs: 10/12-inch
CAPITOL (T-2323 "Beach Blanket Bingo")....20-25 65
(Monaural.)
CAPITOL (ST-2323 "Beach Blanket Bingo")....20-30 65
(Stereo.)

LOREN, Frankie
Singles: 7-inch
MERCURY....10-15 59
PORTER....10-20 59

LOREN, John
Singles: 7-inch
GEE....5-10 60

LOREN, Johnny
Singles: 7-inch
PHILIPS....4-8 62

LOREN, Keith
Singles: 7-inch
MARK IV (8800 "Born to Ramble")....25-50

LOREN, Kenny
(With the Cordairs)
Singles: 7-inch
DAWN (1113 "My Girl Doesn't Care")....50-100 59

LORENE, Shirley
Singles: 7-inch
JERDEN (919 "You Get to Me")....3-5 70

LOREN, Sophia
Singles: 7-inch
COLUMBIA (41200 "Bing, Bang, Bong")....10-15 58

LORENZ, John / Starlighters
Singles: 78 rpm
MERCURY (3060 "Here We Are")....100-200 47
(Picture disc. Promotional only issue.)

LORENZ, Trey
Singles: 7-inch
EPIC....3-4 92

LORENZO
Singles: 7-inch
SKYLARK....5-8 61

LORENZO & 4 STARS
Singles: 7-inch
KAPP....5-8 61

LORETTA
Singles: 7-inch
VALIANT....4-8 64

LORETTA LYNN: see LYNN, Loretta

LORI, Fran
Singles: 7-inch
CHANCELLOR....5-10 59-60
EMBER....4-8 64
LENOX....4-8 63
SUNNYBROOK....4-8 61

LORI & LANCE
Singles: 7-inch
FEDERAL (12548 "I Don't Have to Worry")....15-25 64

LORI ANN
Singles: 7-inch
MELRON (5004 "The Same Thing Could Happen to You")....10-20 62
MELRON (5007 "Darling")....10-20 63

LORI ELLEN
Singles: 7-inch
BELTONE....4-8 61

LORIE ANN C&W '88
Singles: 7-inch
SING ME....3-4 88-89

LORIN, Tempi, & Candy Girls
Singles: 7-inch
ROTATE (5005 "Runaround")....10-20 64
Also see CANDY GIRLS

LORING, Al & Jet
Singles: 7-inch
SWAN....5-8 60
U.A....4-6 69

LORING, Gloria LP '86
Singles: 7-inch
ATLANTIC....3-4 86
MGM....3-5 72
LPs: 10/12-inch
ATLANTIC....5-8 86

LORING, Gloria, & Carl Anderson P&R '86
Singles: 7-inch
CARRERE....3-4 86
Picture Sleeves
CARRERE....3-4 86
LPs: 10/12-inch
EPIC....5-8 85
Also see ANDERSON, Carl

LORING, Randy
Singles: 7-inch
ROWENA....4-8 64

LORIS & SCHULMAN
Singles: 7-inch
SO-CHAR....4-8

LORNETTES
Singles: 7-inch
GALLIO....10-15 65-66

LORRAINE, Libby
Singles: 7-inch
DORE....4-8 62

LORRAINE & SOCIALITES
Singles: 7-inch
MERCURY....5-10 63

LORRI, Mary Ann
Singles: 7-inch
UNITED INTERNATIONAL....4-8 64

LORRIE, Myrna
LPs: 10/12-inch
HARMONY....20-40

LORRIE, Myrna, & Buddy DeVal C&W '55
Singles: 78 rpm
ABBOTT....4-8 55
Singles: 7-inch
ABBOTT....5-10 55

LORRY & TEMPESTS
Singles: 7-inch
D-H....8-12 60s

LORRY LEE & DELLA
Singles: 7-inch
MECCA (2699 "Let Him Go, Go, Go")....10-20 60s

LORY, Dick
Singles: 78 rpm
DOT (15496 "Cool It Baby")....15-25 56
Singles: 7-inch
COLUMBIA (41224 "Wild Blooded Women")....15-25 58
COLUMBIA (41276 "Crazy Little Daisy")....15-25 58
DOT (15496 "Cool It Baby")....25-50 56
LIBERTY (55306 "The Pain Is Here")....8-15 61
LIBERTY (55319 "Hello Walls")....8-15 61
LIBERTY (55529 "I Got Over You")....8-15 61
LIBERTY (55600 "Crazy Arms")....8-15 63

LOS ADMIRADORES LP '60
LPs: 10/12-inch
COMMAND....8-15 60

LOS ALL STARS
Singles: 7-inch
SCREWBALL (001 "Ballad of Fernando Valenzuela")....5-10 70s

LOS ANGELES
Singles: 7-inch
CARAVAN-FORTY (6601 "I Can Read Between the Lines")....50-100 62

LOS BLUES
Singles: 7-inch
U.A....3-5 71
LPs: 10/12-inch
U.A....8-10 71

LOS BRAVOS P&R/LP '66
Singles: 7-inch
LONDON....3-4 70s
PARROT....4-8 68
PRESS....4-8 66-68
LPs: 10/12-inch
PARROT (71021 "Bring a Little Lovin' ")....20-30 68
PRESS (83003 "Black Is Black")....30-40 66
Member: Mike Kennedy.
Also see DRIFTERS / Lesley Gore / Roy Orbison / Los Bravos
Also see KENNEDY, Mike

LOS CANARIOS
Singles: 7-inch
CALLA....4-8 68

LOS CINCO LATINOS
Singles: 7-inch
COLUMBIA....15-25

LOS DIABLOS
Singles: 7-inch
CRAZY HORSE....3-5

LOSERS
Singles: 7-inch
CONGRESSIONAL ("Saxy Guitar") 8-12
(Selection number not known.)
PARLEY (711 "Snake Eyes")....20-30 63
SPHINX (6109 "Pourquoi")....10-20 65

LOSERS
Singles: 7-inch
ATCO....4-8 65

LOS FRENETICOS
Singles: 7-inch
NORCO (105 "Paradise Stomp")....8-12

LOS GOLEDOS
Singles: 7-inch
ATCO....4-8 67

LOS INDIOS TABAJARAS P&R/LP '63
Singles: 7-inch
RCA....4-8 63-64
LPs: 10/12-inch
ARAVEL....20-30
CAMDEN....8-12
RCA (LPM-1788 "Sweet and Savage")....20-30 58
(Monaural.)
RCA (LSP-1788 "Sweet and Savage")....30-50 58
(Stereo.)
RCA (Except 2800 thru 4649)....5-10
RCA (2800 thru 4649)....10-20 63-66
VOX....10-20
Members: Natalicio; Antenor Moreyra Lima (aka Musaperi & Herundy).

LOS LOBOS LP '84
Singles: 12-inch
SLASH....5-8 86
(Promotional issue only.)
Singles: 7-inch
LOS LOBOS....5-10 81
SLASH....3-4 83-90
Picture Sleeves
SLASH....3-4 85-87
LPs: 10/12-inch
SLASH....5-8 83-90
Member: David Hidalgo.

LOS MOSQUITOS
Singles: 7-inch
CANYON STATE (114 "Wipe Out")....25-35 60s

LOS OXFORDS
Singles: 7-inch
PEERLESS....4-8 60s

LOS POP-TOPS: see POP-TOPS

LOS SILVER ROCKETS
Singles: 7-inch
IDEAL (2538 "Señorita Dizzy Livy [Dizzy Miss Lizzy]")....10-20 58

LOSS, Joe
Singles: 7-inch
RIVERSIDE....4-8 62

LOS STARDUSTERS
(Sunglows)
LPs: 10/12-inch
TEAR DROP (3113 "El Papalote") 10-15 64
Also see SUNGLOWS

LOST
Singles: 7-inch
CAPITOL....8-12 65-66
GARAGE....4-8 66
JANUS....4-8 66

LOST AGENCY
Singles: 7-inch
U.S.A. (881 "One Girl Man")....15-25 67

LOST & FOUND
Singles: 7-inch
INT'L ARTISTS (120 "Everybody's Here")....10-20 67
INT'L ARTISTS (125 "Professor Black")....10-20 67
PINS (1 "Don't Move Girl")....10-20 60s
LPs: 10/12-inch
INT'L ARTISTS (3 "Everybody's Here")....75-100 68
TEMPO....10-15 73
Members: Peter Black; Jim Frost; Steve Webb; James Harrell.

LOST CHILDREN
Singles: 7-inch
TOPAZ....5-8 60s

LOST CHORDS
Singles: 7-inch
VAUGHN LTD. (725 "I Want to Be Her Man")....10-20 66

LOST GENERATION P&R/R&B '70
Singles: 7-inch
BOFUZ....4-8
BRUNSWICK....3-8 70-71
INNOVATION....3-5 74
LPs: 10/12-inch
BRUNSWICK....10-12 70
Members: Lowrell Simon; Fred Simon; Larry Brownlee; Jesse Dean.
Also see C.O.D.s
Also see MYSTIQUE
Also see SIMON, Lowrell

LOST GONZO BAND
LPs: 10/12-inch
MCA....8-10 75

LOST IN SOUND
Singles: 7-inch
SHOWCASE....4-8 66

LOST NATION
LPs: 10/12-inch
RARE EARTH....8-12 70

LOST ONES
Singles: 7-inch
MERSEY (002 "I Can't Believe You")....15-25 66
VALIANT (721 "Trouble in the Streets")....8-12 65

LOST SOUL
Singles: 7-inch
RAVEN (2016 "A Secret of Mine") 15-25
RAVEN (2032 "I'm Gonna Hurt You")....20-30

LOST SOULS
Singles: 7-inch
DAWN (809 "Artifical Rose")....10-15 68
GLORIA (778 "It's Not Fair")....15-20 67
LIBERTY (56024 "Artifical Rose")....10-20 68

LOST SOULS
Singles: 7-inch
BANG (509 "Simple to Say")....15-25 65
GLASCO....10-15 67

LOST SOULS
Singles: 7-inch
LEOPARD (100 "My Girl")....8-12

LOST TRIBE
Singles: 7-inch
U.A....8-12

LOST WEEKEND
Singles: 7-inch
USA (101 "Bridge of Love")....10-20 60s

LOS VALENDAS
Singles: 7-inch
MUNSTER (7022 "Purple Friend")....3-4 92
EPs: 7-inch
MUNSTER (91 "Purple Friend")....3-6 92
Members: Javi Escutia; Tony Noguera; Bajo; Bateria.

LOT
Singles: 7-inch
CHESS....8-12 60s
STANAL....15-20 60s

LOTHAR & HAND PEOPLE
Singles: 7-inch
CAPITOL (2008 "Have Mercy")....15-25 67
CAPITOL (2376 "Milkweed Love") 15-25 68
CAPITOL (2556 "Midnight Ranger")....15-25 69
CAPITOL (5874 "L-o-v-e")....15-25 67
CAPITOL (5945 "Comic Strip")....15-25 68
LPs: 10/12-inch
CAPITOL (247 "Space Hymn")....30-50 69
CAPITOL (ST-2997 "Presenting Lothar and the Hand People")....30-50 68
CAPITOL (SM-2997 "Presenting Lothar and the Hand People")....5-10 77

LOTSA POPPA
(Lots-A-Poppa)
Singles: 7-inch
JET STREAM....10-20 60s
TRIBE....8-12 64

LOTUS
Singles: 7-inch
PHANTOM....3-5 76

LOU, Bonnie: see BONNIE LOU

LOU, Emmy: see EMMY LOU

LOU, Herb B., & Legal Eagles / Legal Eagles
(Herb Alpert)
Singles: 7-inch
ARCH (1607 "The Trial")....20-30 58
(Also issued as by the Legal Eagles.)
Also see ALPERT, Herb
Also see LEGAL EAGLES

LOU, Linda: see LINDA LOU

LOU & GINNY
Singles: 7-inch
HEP (2141 "Do It Right")....15-25 58

LOU MAC: see MAC, Lou

LOUDERMILK, John D. P&R '61
Singles: 7-inch
COLUMBIA....5-10 58-60
MUSIC IS MEDICINE....3-5 78-79
RCA....5-10 61-69
W.B....3-5 71
Picture Sleeves
COLUMBIA (41165 "Yearbook")....10-20 58
RCA (8101 "Road Hog")....5-10 62
LPs: 10/12-inch
MUSIC IS MEDICINE....10-20 78
RCA....15-30 61-69
W.B....8-12 71
Also see DEE, Johnny
Also see SNEEZER, Ebe, & Epidemics
Also see SOME OF CHET'S FRIENDS

LOUDNESS LP '85
LPs: 10/12-inch
ATCO....5-8 85-87

LOUIE & AMBASSADORS
Singles: 7-inch
HILLTOP....5-10 62

LOUIE & LOVERS
Singles: 7-inch
EPIC....4-8 70-72
LPs: 10/12-inch
EPIC....10-15 70

LOUIE LOUIE P&R/LP '90
(Louie Cordero)
Singles: 7-inch
WTG....3-4 90
LPs: 10/12-inch
WTG....5-8 90

LOUIS, Bobby
Singles: 7-inch
CAPITOL (4224 "Adult Western")....15-25 59
CAPITOL (4272 "Call of Love")....15-25 59

LOUIS, Dwain, & Classmates
Singles: 7-inch
CAROLE (111 "That's All Right")....400-600

LOUIS, Jimmy
Singles: 7-inch
PHILLIPS INT'L....5-10 60

LOUIS, Joe Hill
Singles: 78 rpm
BIG TOWN (401 "Hydramatic Woman"....100-150 54
CHECKER (763 "Dorothy Mae")....200-300 52
COLUMBIA (30182 "Railroad Blues")....50-75 49
COLUMBIA (30221 "Don't Trust Your Best Friend")....50-75 49
PHILLIPS (9001 "Gotta Let You Go")....4000-6000 50
MODERN (795 "I Feel Like a Million")....50-75 51
MODERN (813 "Boogie in the Park")....50-75 51
MODERN (822 "Walkin' Talkin' Blues")....50-75 52
MODERN (828 "Eyesight to the Blind")....50-75 51
MODERN (839 "Gotta Go, Baby")....50-75 51
MODERN (856 "Peace of Mind")....50-75 52
SUN (178 "We All Gotta Go Sometime")....200-400 53
Singles: 7-inch
BIG TOWN (401 "Hydramatic Woman"....200-300 54
CHECKER (763 "Dorothy Mae")....500-750 52
Also see CHICAGO SUNNY BOY
Also see LEWIS, Johnny
Also see LITTLE JOE
Also see MEMPHIS MINNIE

LOUIS, Leslie
Singles: 7-inch
ROCKIN' (509 "Ridin' Home")....100-200 52

LOUIS, Tommy, & Rhythm Rockers
Singles: 7-inch
MURIEL....5-10

LOUIS & FROSTY
Singles: 78 rpm
C-NOTE....10-20 55
Singles: 7-inch
C-NOTE....15-25 55
Members: Louis Jackson; William Pyles.
Also see JACKSON, Louis

LOUIS & SCHULMAN
Singles: 7-inch
SO-CHAR ("Broadstreet Bullies")....4-6 70s
(No selection number used.)

LOUISE, Anita
Singles: 7-inch
HICKORY (1334 "Jim Dandy")....10-20 65

LOUISE, Tina: see TINA LOUISE

LOUISIANA RED
(Red Minter)
Singles: 7-inch
ATLAS....5-10 60
GLOVER....5-10 64
ROULETTE....4-8 63
LPs: 10/12-inch
ATCO....10-12 72
ROULETTE (25200 "Lowdown Back Porch Blues")....15-20 63
Also see KNIGHT, Marie

LOUISIANA'S LE ROUX: see LE ROUX

LOUNGE LIZARDS
LPs: 10/12-inch
EDITIONS....5-8 81
ISLAND....5-8

LOUNGERS
Singles: 7-inch
HERALD (534 "Remember the Night")....40-50 58
(Yellow label.)
HERALD (534 "Remember the Night")....30-40 61
(Multi-color label.)

LOUNGERS
Singles: 7-inch
BEACHWOOD....5-10 64

LOUVIN, Charlie C&W '64
Singles: 7-inch
CAPITOL....3-8 64-72
U.A....3-5 74

LPs: 10/12-inch
AUDIOGRAPH ALIVE.................... 5-10 82
CAPITOL.................................. 8-20 65-72
FIRST GENERATION.................... 5-10 81
LITTLE DARLIN'........................ 8-12
MUSIC BOX.............................. 10-20
PHONORAMA............................. 5-8 82
PICKWICK................................. 5-8 70s
THUNDERBIRD.......................... 5-8
U.A.. 6-12 74
Also see JIM & JESSE & Charlie Louvin
Also see LOUVIN BROTHERS

LOUVIN, Charlie, & Roy Acuff *C&W '89*
Singles: 7-inch
HAL KAT.................................. 3-4 89
Also see ACUFF, Roy

LOUVIN, Charlie, & Emmylou Harris *C&W '79*
Singles: 7-inch
LITTLE DARLIN'........................ 3-5 79
Also see HARRIS, Emmylou

LOUVIN, Charlie, & Melba Montgomery *C&W '70*
Singles: 7-inch
CAPITOL.................................. 3-5 70-73
LPs: 10/12-inch
CAPITOL.................................. 10-20 71-75
Also see MONTGOMERY, Melba

LOUVIN, Ira *C&W '65*
Singles: 7-inch
CAPITOL.................................. 4-8 65
LPs: 10/12-inch
CAPITOL (2413 "Unforgettable")....25-35 65
Also see LOUVIN BROTHERS

LOUVIN BROTHERS *C&W '55*
Singles: 78 rpm
CAPITOL.................................. 5-10 55-57
MGM....................................... 8-12 52
Singles: 7-inch
CAPITOL.................................. 5-15 55-63
MGM....................................... 10-20 52
EPs: 7-inch
CAPITOL.................................. 10-20 55-60
LPs: 10/12-inch
ACM.. 5-10
CMF.. 5-10
CAPITOL (T-769 "Tragic Songs of Life")....................................50-100 56
(Monaural.)
CAPITOL (DT-769 "Tragic Songs of Life")....................................25-50 68
(Reprocessed stereo.)
CAPITOL (910 "Ira & Charlie").......30-40 58
CAPITOL (T-1061 "Family Who Prays")...................................20-40 58
(Monaural.)
CAPITOL (DT-1061 "Family Who Prays")...................................10-15 68
(Reprocessed stereo.)
CAPITOL (SM-1061 "Family Who Prays")................................... 5-10
(Reprocessed stereo.)
CAPITOL (1106 "Country Love Ballads")................................30-40 59
CAPITOL (1449 "Tribute to the Delmore Brothers")............................50-75 60
CAPITOL (1547 "Encore")............30-40 61
CAPITOL (1616 "Country Christmas")............................20-40 61
CAPITOL (1721 "Weapon of Prayer")..................................10-20 73
CAPITOL (11000 series)...............10-20 62
CAPITOL (1834 "Keep Your Eyes on Jesus")....................................15-25 63
CAPITOL (2091 "Current Hits")......20-40 64
CAPITOL (2331 "Thank God for My Christian Home")..................................20-40 65
CAPITOL (2827 "The Great Roy Acuff Songs")...................................20-30 67
COUNTRY CLASSICS.................. 5-10
GOLDEN COUNTRY.................... 5-10
GUSTO.................................... 5-10
MGM (3426 "Louvin Brothers")....75-150 57
METRO (598 "The Louvin Brothers")..............................20-40 62
PICKWICK/HILLTOP.................10-15 66-67
ROUNDER.............................. 5-10 79-80s
TOWER (5038 "Two Different Worlds")...................................20-40 66
TOWER (5122 "Country Heart & Soul")......................................20-40 68
Members: Charlie Louvin; Ira Louvin
Also see LOUVIN, Charlie
Also see LOUVIN, Ira

LOVABLES
(Loveables)
Singles: 7-inch
TOOT..................................... 5-10 67-68

LOVATIONS
Singles: 7-inch
CAP CITY................................. 3-6 69
PART III.................................. 3-6 69

LOVE *P&R/LP '66*
Singles: 7-inch
BLUE THUMB........................... 4-6 69-70
ELEKTRA (45603 "My Little Red Book")..................................... 5-8 66
ELEKTRA (45605 "7 & 7 Is")........ 5-8 66
ELEKTRA (45608 "Stephanie Knows Who")....................................10-20 66
ELEKTRA (45608 "She Comes in Colors")................................... 5-8 67
(Same number and flip used again.)
ELEKTRA (45613 "Que Vida").......15-25 67
ELEKTRA (45629 thru 45700)....... 5-10 68-70
RSO.. 4-6 74-75

LPs: 10/12-inch
BLUE THUMB (8822 "False Start")...................................20-30 70
BLUE THUMB (9000 "Out Here")...15-25 69
ELEKTRA (4001 "Love")...............25-40 66
(Monaural.)
ELEKTRA (4005 "Da Capo")..........25-40 66
(Monaural.)
ELEKTRA (4013 "Forever Changes")..............................25-40 67
(Monaural.)
ELEKTRA (74001 "Love")..............25-35 66
(Stereo.)
ELEKTRA (74005 "Da Capo").........25-35 67
(Stereo.)
ELEKTRA (74013 "Forever Changes")...................................20-30 67
(Stereo.)
ELEKTRA (74049 "Four Sail").......20-30 69
(Stereo.)
ELEKTRA (74058 "Revisited").......20-30 70
(Gatefold cover.)
ELEKTRA (74058 "Revisited")......... 5-8 81
(Standard cover.)
MCA.. 5-8 82
RSO.. 8-10 74
RHINO (251 "Love Live")............. 8-10 82
RHINO (251 "Love Live")............10-15 82
(Picture disc.)
RHINO (800 "Best of Love")......... 5-8 80
Members: Arthur Lee; John Echols; John Fleckenstein; Don Conka; Ken Forssi; Al Pfisterer; Michael Stuart; Tjay Contrelli; Bryan Maclean;Gary Rowles.
Also see AMERICAN FOUR
Also see GERONIMO BLACK
Also see LEE, Arthur

LOVE, Billy
Singles: 7-inch
GLEE (1005 "Sweet Talkin' ").........20-30 61
GLEE (1010 "I'll Find My Way")......20-30 62
SMAK..................................... 4-8 67
SMOGVILLE.............................. 4-8 67

LOVE, Billy, & Lovers
Singles: 7-inch
DRAGON (4403 "Legend of Love")....................................50-75 65

LOVE, Billy "Red"
Singles: 78 rpm
CHESS (1508 "Drop Top")............50-75 52
CHESS (1516 "My Teddy Bear Baby")....................................50-75 52

LOVE, Buddy, & Blue Flames
Singles: 7-inch
THUNDER (1 "I Love You").......100-150 62

LOVE, Candace *R&B '69*
Singles: 7-inch
AQUARIUS.............................. 4-8 68

LOVE, Clayton
Singles: 78 rpm
ALADDIN.................................15-25 52
GROOVE..................................10-20 55
MODERN..................................10-20 54
Singles: 7-inch
ALADDIN (3148 "Chained to Your Love")....................................35-55 52
GROOVE (0161 "Mary Lou").........25-50 55
MODERN (929 "Wicked Little Baby")....................................25-50 54

LOVE, Cyndy
Singles: 7-inch
SPACE (00013 "You Never Knew")...................................10-20 67

LOVE, Darlene *P&R '63*
Singles: 7-inch
COLUMBIA............................... 3-5 88
ELEKTRA (79647 "River Deep, Mountain High")..................................... 3-5 85
(Promotional issue only.)
PHILLES (111 "The Boy I'm Gonna Marry"/"My Heart Beat a Little Bit Faster")..........12-18 63
PHILLES (111 "The Boy I'm Gonna Marry"/"Playing for Keeps")..................8-12 63
PHILLES (114 "Wait Till My Bobby Gets Home")...................................10-15 63
PHILLES (117 "A Fine, Fine Boy")...8-15 63
PHILLES (119 "Christmas, Baby Please Come Home")..................................15-25 63
PHILLES (123 "He's a Quiet Guy")....................................30-50 64
PHILLES (125 "Christmas, Baby Please Come Home")..................................15-25 64
REPRISE.................................. 4-8 66
RHINO..................................... 5-8 86
W.B./SPECTOR......................... 3-6 74-77
Picture Sleeves
COLUMBIA............................... 3-5 88
ELEKTRA (79647 "River Deep, Mountain High")..................................... 3-5 85
(Promotional issue only.)
LPs: 10/12-inch
COLUMBIA (40605 "Paint Another Picture")................................... 8-12 88
RHINO (855 "Live at Hop Singh's")..8-10 85
Also see BLOSSOMS
Also see BOB B. SOXX & Blue Jeans
Also see CRYSTALS
Also see HALE & HUSHABYES
Also see MOOSE & PELICANS
Also see RONETTES / Crystals / Darlene Love / Bob B. Soxx & Blue Jeans

LOVE, Darlene / Annie Golden
Singles: 7-inch
ELEKTRA.................................. 3-5 85
Picture Sleeves
ELEKTRA.................................. 3-5 85

LOVE, Darlene / Ronettes
Singles: 7-inch
CHRYSALIS (3202 "Phil Spector's Christmas Mix")..3-5 87
Picture Sleeves
CHRYSALIS (3202 "Phil Spector's Christmas Mix")..3-5 87
Also see LOVE, Darlene
Also see RONETTES

LOVE, Frankie
Singles: 7-inch
LA ROSA.................................. 5-10 62
LOMA...................................... 8-12 66

LOVE, Honey, & Love Notes
Singles: 7-inch
CAMEO.................................... 8-10 65

LOVE, Hot Shot
Singles: 78 rpm
SUN (196 "Wolf Call Boogie")....400-500 54
Singles: 7-inch
SUN (196 "Wolf Call Boogie")..................................800-1200 54

LOVE, Janice
Singles: 7-inch
DCA (100 "Forever Love")...........10-20

LOVE, Johnny
(With the Way Singers)
Singles: 7-inch
MERCURY.................................10-15 59-60
STARTIME (5001 "Chills and Fever")....................................25-35 60
TEE PEE (295 "Consolation")........15-20
Also see LOVE, Ronnie

LOVE, Joyce
Singles: 7-inch
BLUE ANGEL............................ 4-8 63

LOVE, Kitty
Singles: 7-inch
DADE....................................... 4-8 63

LOVE, Le Juan *R&B '88*
Singles: 7-inch
LUKE SKY................................ 3-4 88

LOVE, Lonnie
Singles: 12-inch
PROFILE.................................. 4-6 83
Singles: 7-inch
PROFILE.................................. 3-4 83

LOVE, Marion
Singles: 7-inch
MERCURY.................................10-15 72

LOVE, Mary *R&B '66*
Singles: 7-inch
JOSIE...................................... 4-6 68
MODERN..................................10-20 65-66

LOVE, Mike
Singles: 7-inch
BOARDWALK............................ 3-5 81
LPs: 10/12-inch
BOARDWALK............................ 8-10 81
Also see ASSOCIATION / Bobby Vee / Mike Love / Mary MacGregor
Also see BEACH BOYS
Also see CELEBRATION
Also see MIKE & DEAN
Also see WILSON, Brian, & Mike Love

LOVE, Mike / Dean Torrence: see MIKE & DEAN

LOVE, Monie *LP '90*
LPs: 10/12-inch
W.B... 5-8 90

LOVE, Nancy
Singles: 7-inch
DECCA (32338 "Hangin' On")........10-20 68
VEE JAY (432 "Rescue Me")......... 8-12 62
VEE JAY (458 "Proove It to Me").... 8-12 62

LOVE, Preston
(With the Love Bugs)
Singles: 78 rpm
FEDERAL.................................15-25 52-53
ULTRA......................................10-20 56
Singles: 7-inch
DIG (101 "If You Ever Get Lonesome")..............................15-25 55
DIG (103 "That's All Right Baby")...15-25 55
DIG (110 "Dog-Faced Boy")..........15-25 56
DIG (116 "Country Home")............15-25 56
FEDERAL (12069 "Wango Blues")...................................50-100 52
FEDERAL (12085 "Like a Ship at Sea").....................................50-100 52
FEDERAL (12132 "You Got Me Drinkin'")...............................50-100 53
FEDERAL (12145 "My Love Is Draggin'")...............................50-100 53
KENT...................................... 4-6 68
KING......................................10-15 68
MEXIE (103 "Tough Walk")............15-25 62
("Mexie" is the mother of Preston Love.)
ULTRA (101 "If You Ever Get Lonesome")..............................50-75 55
ULTRA (103 "That's All Right Baby")....................................50-75 55
(Credited to Preston Love, but vocalist is really Johnny Otis.)
LPs: 10/12-inch
KENT......................................10-15 68
Also see HANK & Sugar Pie
Also see LOVE BUGS
Also see OTIS, Johnny, & Preston Love
Also see SAILOR BOY / Preston Love

LOVE, Ronnie *P&R/R&B '61*
Singles: 7-inch
ALMERIA (4001 "Nothing to It").....15-25
D TOWN (1027 "Judy")...............75-125 64
D TOWN (1047 "Judy")................30-50 65
DOT.......................................5-10 60-61
STARTIME (5003 "Shakin' and a Breakin' ")...............................20-30 61
Also see LOVE, Johnny

LOVE, Robert, Jr.
Singles: 7-inch
EMBER..................................... 5-8 64

LOVE, Rudy, & Love Family *R&B '76*
Singles: 7-inch
CALLA...................................... 3-5 76
LPs: 10/12-inch
CALLA...................................... 5-10 76

LOVE, Sybil, & Love Notes
Singles: 7-inch
VALEX (505 "I Love You Darling")..........................250-500 59

LOVE, Tommy
Singles: 7-inch
BAGDAD................................... 4-8 63
DONDEE................................... 4-8 61-62
ORBIT...................................... 4-8 62
REV... 4-8 63
EPs: 7-inch
DONDEE...................................10-20 62

LOVE, Vikki: see NUANCE

LOVE, Wendy
Singles: 7-inch
PALETTE.................................. 4-8 61

LOVE, Willie
(With His Three Aces; Willie Love's Three Aces)
Singles: 78 rpm
TRUMPET.................................20-30 51-53
Singles: 7-inch
TRUMPET (173 "Vanity Dresser Boogie")..................................40-60 52
TRUMPET (174 "Shady Lane Blues")....................................40-60 52
TRUMPET (175 "Nelson Street Blues")....................................40-60 52
TRUMPET (209 "Shout, Brother, Shout")...................................40-60 53

LOVE AFFAIR
Singles: 7-inch
DATE....................................... 4-8 68-69
Picture Sleeves
DATE....................................... 8-12 69
Members: Steve Ellis; Rex Brayley; Mick Jackson; Morgan Fisher; Maurice Bacon.
Also see WIDOWMAKER

LOVE AFFAIR
Singles: 7-inch
RADIO..................................... 3-5 80
LPs: 10/12-inch
RADIO..................................... 5-8 80

LOVE & KISSES *LP '77*
Singles: 7-inch
CASABLANCA............................ 3-5 77-79
LPs: 10/12-inch
CASABLANCA............................ 8-10 77-79

LOVE & MONEY *P&R/LP '89*
Singles: 7-inch
MERCURY................................ 3-4 89
Picture Sleeves
MERCURY................................ 3-4 89
LPs: 10/12-inch
MERCURY................................ 5-8 89
Member: Stuart Kerr.
Also see TEXAS

LOVE & ROCKETS *LP '86*
Singles: 7-inch
BIG TIME.................................. 3-4 86
RCA.. 3-4 89
Picture Sleeves
RCA.. 3-4 89
LPs: 10/12-inch
BEGGARS BANQUET................... 5-8 89
BIG TIME.................................. 5-8 86-87
Members: David Jor; Kevin Haskins; Daniel Ash.
Also see BAUHAUS

LOVE & TEARS
Singles: 7-inch
POLYDOR................................. 4-8

LOVE BROTHERS
Singles: 7-inch
BY LOVE (843 "Baby, I'll Never Let You Go")...................................150-200

LOVE BROTHERS
Singles: 7-inch
NORTHBAY................................ 3-5 73

LOVE BUG STARSKI *D&D '83*
Singles: 12-inch
ATLANTIC................................. 3-4 85
FEVER..................................... 4-6 83

LOVE BUGS
Singles: 78 rpm
FEDERAL..................................25-50 55
Singles: 7-inch
FEDERAL (12216 "Boom Diddy Wawa Baby")..................................50-100 55
Member: Preston Love; Hank Huston; Peylia Balinton.
Also see HANK & Sugar Pie
Also see LOVE, Preston

LOVE CHAIN
Singles: 7-inch
MINIT (32065 "I'm Loving You Baby")....................................15-25 69

LOVE CHILD'S AFRO CUBAN BLUES BAND *P&R/R&B/LP '75*
(Love Child's Latin Soul Afro Blues Band)
Singles: 7-inch
A&M.. 3-6 69
ROULETTE................................ 3-5 75
LPs: 10/12-inch
ROULETTE................................ 5-10 75

LOVE CLUB *D&D '83*
Singles: 12-inch
WEST END................................ 4-6 83

LOVE COLUMN
Singles: 7-inch
DUO (7460 "Can't Get Enough")....20-30

LOVE COMMITTEE *R&B '76*
Singles: 7-inch
ARIOLA AMERICA....................... 3-5 75-76
GOLD MIND............................... 3-5 77-78
Also see ETHICS

LOVE COMPANY
Singles: 7-inch
SRO.. 3-5 80

LOVE EXCHANGE
Singles: 7-inch
UPTOWN (755 "Swallow the Sun")....................................15-25 67
LPs: 10/12-inch
TOWER (1515 "Love Exchange")..15-25 68

LOVE GENERATION *P&R '67*
Singles: 7-inch
IMPERIAL.................................. 4-8 67-68
LPs: 10/12-inch
IMPERIAL..................................12-15 67-68
U.A... 8-10 77
Also see CLIMAX

LOVE / HATE *LP '90*
LPs: 10/12-inch
COLUMBIA................................ 5-8 90

LOVE INC.
Singles: 7-inch
PINK DOLPHIN........................... 5-10

LOVE INS
Singles: 7-inch
CURTIS BROS (101 "Everything's There")...................................15-25 67
LAURIE (3415 "You're Supposed to Be Mine")....................................10-20 67
Also see HYSTERICS

LOVE KITTENS
Singles: 7-inch
MOS-LEY.................................. 5-10

LOVE LETTERS
Singles: 7-inch
ACME (714 "Walking the Streets Alone")...............................100-200 57
Also see LEE, Nancy

LOVE LORDS
Singles: 7-inch
AL KING (11021 "Burning Love")...................................150-250 62

LOVE MACHINE
LPs: 10/12-inch
DESIGN....................................15-25 67

LOVE MACHINE
Singles: 7-inch
ARISTA.................................... 3-5 76

LOVE NOTES
("On Tenor Sax Lucky Warren")
Singles: 78 rpm
IMPERIAL (5254 "Surrender Your Heart")...................................100-200 53
RAINBOW (266 "I'm Sorry").........75-150 54
RIVIERA (970 "I'm Sorry")..........150-250 54
RIVIERA (975 "Since I Fell for You")....................................200-300 54
Singles: 7-inch
IMPERIAL (5254 "Surrender Your Heart")...................................400-500 53
LOST NITE................................ 5-10
RAINBOW (266 "I'm Sorry").........200-250 54
RIVIERA (970 "I'm Sorry")...........500-800 54
RIVIERA (975 "Since I Fell for You")....................................700-900 54
Member: Ronald Gill. Session: Lucky Warren.
Also see GILL, Ronnie, & Pastel Keys

LOVE NOTES / Ronald Gill / Nats Walker Orchestra / Margie Anderson
EPs: 7-inch
FAMILY LIBRARY OF RECORDED MUSIC (1040 "Crawling")................200-300 53
Also see LOVE NOTES

LOVE NOTES *R&B '57*
Singles: 7-inch
HOLIDAY (2605 "United")............30-50 57
(Glossy label stock.)
HOLIDAY (2605 "United")............10-15
(Flat label stock.)
HOLIDAY (2607 "If I Could Make You Mine")....................................20-30 57

LOVE NOTES
(With Vinny Catalano & Orchestra)
Singles: 7-inch
WILSHIRE (200 "Nancy")..............20-40 63
WILSHIRE (203 "Gloria")..............50-75 63

LOVE PATROL R&B '85
Singles: 7-inch
4TH & BROADWAY ... 3-4 85

LOVE, PEACE & HAPPINESS R&B '72
Singles: 7-inch
RCA ... 3-5 71-72
LPs: 10/12-inch
RCA ... 8-10 71
Members: Ann Bogan; Leslie Wilson; Melvin Wilson.
Also see HARVEY & ANN
Also see NEW BIRTH

LOVE POTION
Singles: 7-inch
KAPP ... 5-8 69
TCB ("This Love") ... 8-12 69
(No selection number used.)

LOVE SCULPTURE
Singles: 7-inch
PARROT ... 8-12 68-70
LPs: 10/12-inch
PARROT (71035 "Forms and Feelings") ... 20-25 70
RARE EARTH (505 Blues Helping") ... 20-40 69
(Rounded-top cover.)
RARE EARTH (505 "Blues Helping") ... 15-20 69
(Standard cover.)
Member: Dave Edmunds.
Also see EDMUNDS, Dave

LOVE SOCIETY
Singles: 7-inch
MERCURY (73130 "America") ... 8-12 70
RCA ... 5-10 69-70
SCEPTER ... 5-10 68-69
TARGET (1006 "Let's Pretend") ... 10-20 69
TARGET (1009 "Hey Bulldog") ... 10-20 69
TEE PEE (3878 "Do You Wanna Dance") ... 15-25 68
Members: Dave Steffen; Mike Holdridge; Keith Abler; Steve Giles; Mike Dellger.
Also see SUNBLIND LION

LOVE SPECIAL DELIVERY
Singles: 7-inch
LANCE ("Babe") ... 25-50 60s
(Selection number not known.)

LOVE TRACTOR
LPs: 10/12-inch
BIG TIME ... 5-8 87
I.R.S. ... 5-8 86
Members: Mark Cline; Michael Richmond; Armistead Wellford; Andrew Carter.

LOVE UNLIMITED P&R/R&B/LP '72
(Love Unlimited Orchestra)
Singles: 7-inch
CASABLANCA ... 3-5 70s
MCA ... 3-4
20TH FOX ... 3-5 73-77
UNI ... 3-5 72
UNLIMITED GOLD ... 3-5 77-84
LPs: 10/12-inch
20TH FOX ... 8-10 74-76
UNI ... 5-10 72
UNLIMITED GOLD ... 5-8 77-84
Members: Kenny Gorelick; Glodean James; Linda James; Diane Taylor.
Also see FREE MOVEMENT / Love
Also see KENNY G.
Also see WHITE, Barry

LOVE'S CHILDREN
Singles: 7-inch
CURTOM (1961 "This Is the End") ... 10-20 71

LOVECRAFT, H.P: see H.P. LOVECRAFT

LOVED ONES
Singles: 7-inch
AMBASSADOR (212 "Surprise Surprise") ... 15-25 66
BROOKMONT (556 "Country Club Life") ... 20-30 60s

LOVED ONES
Singles: 7-inch
KAPP ... 5-10 67
MAINSTREAM ... 3-5 66

LOVE-INS
Singles: 7-inch
LAURIE ... 5-10 67

LOVEJOY, Tony
Singles: 7-inch
SCOTT (1001 "Traffic Jam") ... 10-20 61

LOVEJOY, Louie
Singles: 7-inch
CHICO (6305 "Midnight Blues") ... 10-20 63

LOVEJOYS
(Leola & the Lovejoys)
Singles: 7-inch
RED BIRD (10003 "Payin' ") ... 15-25 64
TIGER ... 10-15 63-64

LOVELACE, Paul
Singles: 7-inch
ALLEY ... 4-8 63

LOVELARKS
Singles: 7-inch
MASON'S (070 "Diddle-Le-Bom") ... 800-1200 61
(At least one source gives a 1957 release date for this disc. We don't know yet who's right.)

LOVELESS, Bobby
(With the Night Owls)
Singles: 7-inch
HBR ... 4-8 66
MICHELLE ... 4-8 65
MONTEL ... 4-8 65
STEPHANIE ... 4-8 65

LOVELESS, Patty C&W '85
Singles: 7-inch
MCA ... 3-4 85-92
Also see WHITLEY, Keith

LOVELETS
Singles: 7-inch
LAURIE ... 3-5

LOVELITES
Singles: 7-inch
PHI-DAN ... 10-15 66

LOVELITES R&B '69
(Patti & the Lovelites; Patti Hamilton & Lovelites)
Singles: 7-inch
BANDERA (2515 "I Found Me a Lover") ... 10-15 67
COTILLION (44145 "I'm the One That You Need") ... 3-6 72
COTILLION (44161 "Is That Lovin' in Your Heart") ... 3-6 72
LOCK (723 "How Can I Tell My Mom and Dad") ... 8-10 69
LOVELITE (01 "My Conscience") ... 5-10 70
LOVELITE (02 "Bumpy Road Ahead") ... 4-8 71
LOVELITE (03 "The Way That You Treat Me Baby") ... 4-8 72
LOVELITE (1008 "Oh My Love") ... 4-8 70s
20TH FOX (2068 "Love Is So Strong") ... 4-8 73
UNI (55181 "How Can I Tell My Mom and Dad") ... 4-8 69
UNI (55222 "Oh My Love") ... 4-8 70
LPs: 10/12-inch
UNI (73081 "The Lovelites") ... 10-20 70
Members: Patti Hamilton; Rozena Petty; Barbara Peterman; Dell McDaniel; Joni Berlman; Rhonda Grayson.

LOVELLES
Singles: 7-inch
ATCO (6670 "Pretending Dear") ... 5-8 69

LOVELLS
Singles: 7-inch
BRENT ... 4-8 67

LOVELY, Ike R&B '73
Singles: 7-inch
WAND ... 3-5 73

LOVEMAKER, Jimmy
Singles: 7-inch
DECCA ... 4-8 64

LOVEMASTERS
Singles: 7-inch
JACKLYN ... 5-10
LPs: 10/12-inch
ALIVE/TOTAL ENERGY ... 5-10 95
(10-inch LP.)

LOVENOTES
Singles: 7-inch
PREMIUM (611 "A Love Like Yours") ... 200-400 57
(Reissued almost immediately with artist credit changed to the True Loves.)
Member: David Haywood.
Also see TRUELOVES

LOVER, Joe
Singles: 7-inch
PARLIAMENT ... 5-8 61

"LOVER BOY"
Singles: 78 rpm
RPM (409 "Love Is Scarce") ... 10-15 54
Singles: 7-inch
CRYSTALETTE ... 5-8 63
RPM (409 "Love Is Scarce") ... 20-30 54

LOVER SPEAKS
Singles: 7-inch
A&M ... 3-4 86

LOVERBOY P&R/LP '81
Singles: 7-inch
CBS (651060 "Notorious") ... 5-10 87
(Picture disc. Promotional issue only. Canadian.)
COLUMBIA ... 3-4 81-88
Picture Sleeves
COLUMBIA ... 3-5 81-88
LPs: 10/12-inch
COLUMBIA (Except 169961) ... 5-10 80-89
COLUMBIA (XSM-169961 "Hot Girls In Love") ... 15-20 82
(Picture disc. Promotional issue only.)
Members: Mike Reno; Matthew Frenette; Paul Dean; Doug Johnson; Scott Smith.
Also see RENO, Mike, & Ann Wilson

LOVERDE D&D '83
Singles: 12-inch
MOBY DICK ... 4-6 83

LOVERS P&R/R&B '57
Singles: 78 rpm
DECCA ... 15-25 56
Singles: 7-inch
ALADDIN (3419 "Tell Me") ... 20-30 58
DECCA (29862 "Don't Touch Me") ... 20-30 56
IMPERIAL (5845 "Darling It's Wonderful") ... 10-20 62
IMPERIAL (5960 "Let's Elope") ... 10-20 63
KELLER (101 "Strange As It Seems") ... 100-200 61
LAMP (2005 "Darling It's Wonderful") ... 25-50 58
LAMP (2013 "Let's Elope") ... 25-50 58
LAMP (2018 "Tell Me") ... 25-50 58
POST (10007 "Darling It's Wonderful") ... 10-15 63
Member: Tarheel Slim.
Also see TARHEEL SLIM

LOVERS
Singles: 7-inch
CASINO (103 "Let's") ... 15-25 58

LOVERS
Singles: 7-inch
SUNNY (1 "Temptation") ... 15-25 63

LOVERS
Singles: 7-inch
AGON (1011 "Caravan of Lonely Men") ... 10-20 65
CHECKER ... 5-10 65
GATE (501 "Someone") ... 75-125 65
HERMITAGE (818 "It's Too Late") ... 5-10 60s
PHILIPS (40353 "Someone") ... 15-25 66

LOVERS P&R '77
Singles: 7-inch
MARLIN ... 3-5 77

LOVERS
Singles: 7-inch
FRANTIC ... 8-12

LOVESMITH R&B '83
(Michael Lovesmith)
Singles: 7-inch
MOTOWN ... 3-4 81-85
LPs: 10/12-inch
MOTOWN ... 5-8 81
Also see SMITH CONNECTION

LOVESONG
LPs: 10/12-inch
GOOD NEWS ... 8-10 70s
Also see GIRARD, Chuck

LOVETONES
Singles: 7-inch
BARRIER ... 3-5 74

LOVETONES
Singles: 7-inch
LOVE-TONE (101 "When I Asked My Love") ... 10-20 61
PLUS (108 "Talk to an Angel") ... 300-500 58

LOVETT, Coleen
Singles: 7-inch
BRUNSWICK ... 5-10 59
DOT ... 10-15 58

LOVETT, Coleen, & Ted Phillips
Singles: 7-inch
DRUM BOY ... 8-12 60s
Also see PHILLIPS, Teddy

LOVETT, Lyle C&W '86
(With His Large Band)
Singles: 7-inch
ATLANTIC (1058 Unchained Melody") ... 20-30
CURB/MCA ... 3-4 86-89
LPs: 10/12-inch
CURB/MCA ... 5-10 86-89
Also see CARNES, Kim

LOVETT SISTERS
Singles: 7-inch
TODD ... 5-10 58

LOVETTE, Eddie P&R '69
Singles: 7-inch
STEADY ... 4-8 69
LPs: 10/12-inch
STEADY ... 8-10 70

LOVETTES
Singles: 7-inch
CARNIVAL ... 4-8 66
CHECKER ... 5-10 63
KNIGHT ... 10-15 59

LOVICH, Lene LP '79
Singles: 7-inch
STIFF ... 3-5 79-83
LPs: 10/12-inch
STIFF ... 5-8 79-83
Session: Lene Lovich; Les Chappell; Bobbi Irwin; Ron Francois; Nick Plytas.

LOVIN' COHENS
Singles: 7-inch
MGM ... 4-6 67

LOVIN' FACTOR
Singles: 7-inch
SSS INT'L ... 3-5 74

LOVIN' SPOONFUL P&R/LP '65
Singles: 7-inch
ERIC ... 3-4 78
KAMA SUTRA ... 3-8 65-72
Picture Sleeves
KAMA SUTRA ... 5-10 65-67
EPs: 7-inch
KAMA SUTRA (1 "Nashville Cats") ... 10-15 67
(Promotional issue only.)
LPs: 10/12-inch
AZZURRA (5801 "Anthology") ... 5-10 83
BACK-TRAC ... 5-8 85
BUDDAH ... 8-10 73
EMUS ... 5-8
51 WEST ... 5-8 80s
GRT ... 8-15 76
GUSTO ... 5-8 80s
KAMA SUTRA (750 "24 Karat Hits") ... 10-15 68
KAMA SUTRA (2000 series) ... 8-15 70-76
KAMA SUTRA (8050 thru 8054) ... 15-25 65-66
KAMA SUTRA (8056 "Best of the Lovin' Spoonful") ... 15-25 67
(Add $10 to $20 if accompanied by four color photos.)
KAMA SUTRA (8058 thru 8073) ... 15-25 67-69
KAMA SUTRA (91102 "Best of the Lovin' Spoonful") ... 8-10
Members: John Sebastian; Zalman Yanovsky; Joe Butler; Steve Boone; Jerry Yester.
Also see BUTLER, Joe
Also see SEBASTIAN, John
Also see YANOVSKY, Zalman
Also see YESTER, Jerry

LOVING SISTERS
Singles: 7-inch
PEACOCK ... 4-8 66

LOVING TREE
Singles: 7-inch
VIVA ... 5-10 66

LOVINS
Singles: 7-inch
FONTANA ... 4-8 67

LOW, Andy Fairweather: see FAIRWEATHER-LOW, Andy

LOW, Gary D&D '83
Singles: 12-inch
QUALITY ... 4-6 83

LOW EBB
Singles: 7-inch
PATTEN BENNETT (1001 "Can't Make Up My Mind") ... 15-20

LOW NUMBERS
Singles: 7-inch
BIG SEVEN INCH ... 4-6 76

LOW ROCKS
Singles: 7-inch
SABRE (101 "Blueberry Jams") ... 10-20 61
S.A.K. (1048 "Snooker") ... 10-20 63

LOWE, Bernie P&R '58
(Bernie Lowe Orchestra)
Singles: 7-inch
CAMEO ... 5-10 58-63
LPs: 10/12-inch
CAMEO ... 15-25 62-63

LOWE, Buddy
Singles: 7-inch
CREST (1049 "Kiss Me Goodnight") ... 15-25 58
ENSIGN (4037 "Sherry Lee") ... 10-20 59
IMPERIAL ... 5-10 60

LOWE, Dave
Singles: 7-inch
LIBERTY BELL ... 5-8

LOWE, Jim P&R '53
Singles: 78 rpm
DOT ... 5-15 55-57
MERCURY ... 4-8 53-54
Singles: 7-inch
BUDDAH ... 4-6 68
DECCA ... 4-8 60-61
DOT (15300 thru 16200 series) ... 5-10 55-60
DOT (16600 series) ... 4-8 64
MERCURY ... 5-10 53-54
20TH FOX ... 4-8 63
U.A. ... 4-6 67
EPs: 7-inch
DOT ... 10-20 57
MERCURY ... 10-20 57
LPs: 10/12-inch
DOT (3051 "The Green Door") ... 25-35 57
DOT (3114 "Wicked Women") ... 25-35 58
DOT (3681 "The Green Door") ... 10-20 66
(Monaural.)
DOT (25681 "The Green Door") ... 10-20 66
(Stereo.)
KATS KARAVAN (100 "Old Favorites") ... 50-100 50s
MERCURY (20246 "Door of Fame") ... 25-35 57

LOWE, Nick LP '78
(With Rockpile; with His Cowboy Outfit)
Singles: 7-inch
COLUMBIA ... 3-5 78-86
LPs: 10/12-inch
COLUMBIA ... 5-10 78-86
REPRISE ... 5-8 90
Also see KIPPINGTON LODGE
Also see NICK & ELVIS
Also see SCHWARTZ, Brinsley
Also see WRECKLESS ERIC

LOWE, Nick, & Dave Edmunds
Singles: 7-inch
COLUMBIA ... 3-5 81
EPs: 7-inch
COLUMBIA (1219 "Nick Lowe & Dave Edmunds Sing the Everly Brothers") 5-10 80
(Promotional issue only.)
Also see EDMUNDS, Dave
Also see LOWE, Nick
Also see ROCKPILE

LOWE, Sammy
(Sammy Lowe & Orchestra)
Singles: 7-inch
NEWPORT (7001 "Speak Up") ... 10-20 58
NEWPORT (7003 "Moon Glide") ... 10-20 58
LPs: 10/12-inch
RCA (2770 "Hitsville USA") ... 15-25 63
Also see FIDELITYS
Also see IMPRESSORS
Also see MARQUIS
Also see PEARLS
Also see SPARKS, Milton
Also see VALETS
Also see VELOURS
Also see WANDERERS

LOWE, Virginia
Singles: 78 rpm
MELBA ... 10-20 56
Singles: 7-inch
MELBA (107 "I'm in Love with Elvis Presley") ... 15-25 56

LOWELL, Jackie
Singles: 7-inch
BAND BOX (226 "Rocket Trip") ... 40-60 61

LOWERY, Frankie
Singles: 7-inch
KHOURY'S (716 "Kansas City Train") ... 15-25 61

LOWERY, Frankie
Singles: 7-inch
COLUMBIA ... 5-10 58

LOWERY, Fred, & Big Bo
Singles: 7-inch
COTILLION (44084 "I'll Take Care of You My Love") ... 8-12 70

LOWERY, Sonny
Singles: 78 rpm
SPECIALTY ... 10-20 57-58
Singles: 7-inch
SPECIALTY ... 10-20 57-58

LOWES, The C&W '86
Singles: 7-inch
API ... 3-4 86-87
SOUNDWAVES ... 3-4 86

LOWRELL R&B '78
Singles: 7-inch
AVI ... 3-5 78-80
Also see SIMON, Lowrell

LOWRY, Ron C&W '70
Singles: 7-inch
REPUBLIC ... 3-5 70
LPs: 10/12-inch
REPUBLIC ... 8-12 70

LOYAL OPPOSITION
Singles: 7-inch
TARGET (1002 "Telling Lies") ... 25-35 69
Members: Carl Weinberger; Rick Gustafson; Greg Rakun; Mike Eubank; Steve Hofschield.

LOYAL OPPOSITION
Singles: 7-inch
JAVO ... 5-10 60s

LOYD, Harold
Singles: 7-inch
MODERN AGE ... 3-5 79

LOYD, James, & Whirlwinds
Singles: 7-inch
EMPALA (117 "I Can't Stand Another Broken Heart") ... 30-50 63

LOYD, Jay B.
Singles: 7-inch
ABC-PAR (9922 "You're Just My Kind") ... 100-150 58
HI (2017 "I'm So Lonely") ... 50-75 59
U.A. ... 5-10 61
Also see BLACK, Bill

LOYE, Bobby, Jr.
Singles: 7-inch
EMBER ... 8-12 61
LAURIE (3222 "I'm Startin' Tonight") ... 25-35 63
WILSHIRE (202 "Lovin' Tree") ... 15-25 60s

LOZ NETTO: see NETTO, Loz

L'TRIMM P&R/LP '88
Singles: 7-inch
ATLANTIC ... 3-4 88
LPs: 10/12-inch
ATLANTIC ... 5-8 88

LUBOFF, Norman, Choir LP '55
Singles: 78 rpm
COLUMBIA ... 3-5 54-59
Singles: 7-inch
COLUMBIA ... 3-6 54-59
RCA ... 3-6 62
Picture Sleeves
RCA ... 3-6 62
EPs: 7-inch
COLUMBIA ... 4-8 54-59
LPs: 10/12-inch
COLUMBIA ... 5-15 54-60
HARMONY ... 5-10 61
RCA ... 5-10 61-62
Also see LIMELITERS / Della Reese /Mario Lanza / Norman Luboff Choir

LUBY DUBY DOO & ZANIES
Singles: 7-inch
DORE ... 4-8 65
Also see ZANIES

LUCAS, Al
Singles: 78 rpm
GROOVE ... 5-10 54
JUBILEE ... 5-10 51-52
RCA ... 5-10 53

Singles: 7-inch
CHALLENGE (59042 "She's My Baby") ... 25-35 59
CHALLENGE (59050 "Sweet Tooth for Baby Ruth") ... 25-35 59

LUCAS, Buddy R&B '52
(With His Band of Tomorrow; with Wigglers; with Studio "B" Orchestra)
Singles: 78 rpm
BELL ... 10-15 57
GROOVE ... 10-15 54
JUBILEE ... 10-15 51-52
RCA ... 10-15 53
Singles: 7-inch
BELL ... 10-20 57
CAPRICE ... 5-10 63
CARLTON ... 10-15 59
GONE ... 10-15 58
GROOVE ... 15-25 54
JUBILEE ... 15-25 51-52
LAWN ... 4-8 64
PIONEER ... 4-8
RCA ... 15-25 53
TRU SOUND ... 5-10 62
VIM ... 8-12 59-60
LPs: 10/12-inch
CAMDEN ... 10-15 67
U.A. ... 10-20 66
Also see BUDDY & EDNA
Also see GONE ALL STARS
Also see GOOD BUDDY
Also see KNICKERBOCKERS
Also see McGRIFF, Edna

LUCAS, Carrie P&R/R&B/LP '77
(Carrie)
Singles: 12-inch
CONSTELLATION ... 4-6 84-85
Singles: 7-inch
CONSTELLATION ... 3-4 84-85
SOLAR ... 3-5 79-82
SOUL TRAIN ... 3-5 77
LPs: 10/12-inch
CONSTELLATION ... 5-8 85
SOLAR ... 5-10 79-82
SOUL TRAIN ... 8-10 77

LUCAS, Carrie, & Whispers R&B '85
Singles: 7-inch
CONSTELLATION ... 3-4 85
Also see LUCAS, Carrie
Also see WHISPERS

LUCAS, David
Singles: 7-inch
ARWIN ... 4-8 60

LUCAS, Ernie
Singles: 7-inch
OKEH (7315 "Love Thief") ... 10-20 68
OKEH (7321 "What We Pay for Love") ... 10-20 68

LUCAS, Frank P&R/R&B '77
("The Good Thing Man")
Singles: 7-inch
ICA ... 3-5 77-78

LUCAS, Frankie
Singles: 7-inch
EVEREST ... 5-8 61

LUCAS, Jim
Singles: 78 rpm
REPUBLIC (7123 "Tutti Frutti") ... 5-10 56
Singles: 7-inch
BIG ... 5-10 59
REPUBLIC (7123 "Tutti Frutti") ... 10-15 56

LUCAS, Matt P&R '63
Singles: 7-inch
DOT ... 4-8 63-64
KAREN (2524 "Baby You Better Go") ... 50-75
RENE ... 10-15 63
SMASH ... 4-8 63

LUCAS, Steve
Singles: 7-inch
DEEP SOUTH ... 3-5

LUCAS, Tammy C&W '89
Singles: 7-inch
SOUNDS of AMERICA ... 3-4 89

LUCE, Bob
Singles: 7-inch
LOVE LOCK ... 5-10 60

LUCEY, Chris
LPs: 10/12-inch
SURREY ... 10-15

LUCIA
Singles: 7-inch
APPLAUSE ... 4-8 60

LUCIA & JOHNNY
Singles: 7-inch
JET ... 5-10 60
ROULETTE ... 4-8 60

LUCIANO, Danny
Singles: 7-inch
LU-MAR (121467 "Get in to It") ... 10-20 67

LUCIE, Don
Singles: 7-inch
EMPALA (119 "Just a Walkin' ") ... 10-20 60s

LUCIFER
(Mort Garson)
Singles: 7-inch
INVICTUS ... 3-6 71-73
LPs: 10/12-inch
GALLO ("Lucifer") ... 200-300 70
(Selection number not known.)
INVICTUS ... 5-10 71
UNI ... 10-12 71

LUCIFER'S FRIEND
LPs: 10/12-inch
BILLINGSGATE ... 10-15 73-74
ELEKTRA ... 8-10 78-81
JANUS ... 8-10 76
PASSPORT ... 10-12 75

LUCK, Randy
Singles: 7-inch
ART ... 5-10 58

LUCKY CHARMS
Singles: 7-inch
STARFIRE ... 3-5 81
Picture Sleeves
STARFIRE ... 3-5 81
LPs: 10/12-inch
STARFIRE (1001 "Dedicated to You") ... 8-10 81
(Colored vinyl.)
STARFIRE (1001 "Dedicated to You") ... 12-15 81
(Picture disc.)

LUCKY CHARMS
Singles: 7-inch
RUBBERTOWN (100 "I Want a Love of My Own") ... 40-60

LUCKY SEVEN
LPs: 10/12-inch
ANOTHER ... 8-10 87

LUCKY STARS
Singles: 7-inch
GUYDEN ... 5-10 63

LUDAWAY, Rudy
(Ludaway)
Singles: 7-inch
DUEL ... 5-10 64
GALIKO (102 "What's Wrong Baby") ... 15-25 69
U.A. ... 10-15 70

LUE, Mary, & Temptees
Singles: 7-inch
EVERLAST ... 5-8 63

LUGEE & LIONS
Singles: 7-inch
ROBBEE (112 "The Jury") ... 50-75 61
Members: Lou Christie; Kay Chick; Amy Sacco; Bill Faveck.
Also see CHRISTIE, Lou
Also see CLASSICS

LUGO, Danny, & Destinations D&D '84
Singles: 12-inch
C&M ... 4-6 84

LUJACK, Larry, "Superjock"
Singles: 7-inch
CURTOM ... 4-6 74
Also see UNCLE LAR' & Li'l Tommy

LUKAS LOLLIPOP
Singles: 7-inch
LOMA (2067 "Don't Hold on to Someone") ... 20-30 67

LUKE, Jimmy
Singles: 7-inch
BIG C (1002 "Joanie") ... 20-30
RAZORBACK ... 5-10 63
UNI ... 4-8 67

LUKE, Jimmy, & Bruce Channel
Singles: 7-inch
LE CAM ... 3-5 78
Also see CHANNEL, Bruce
Also see LUKE, Jimmy

LUKE, Robin P&R/R&B '58
Singles: 7-inch
BERTRAM INT'L (206 "Susie Darlin' ") ... 25-50 58
BERTRAM INT'L (208 thru 212) ... 15-25 58-59
DOT ... 10-20 58-61
Picture Sleeves
BERTRAM INT'L (206 "Susie Darlin' ") ... 40-60 58
DOT (16096 "Everlovin' ") ... 10-20 60
EPs: 7-inch
DOT (1092 "Susie Darlin' ") ... 50-75 60
LPs: 10/12-inch
STARFIRE (1002 "Boppin' with Robin Luke") ... 10-15 81

LUKE, Robin, & Roberta Shore
Singles: 7-inch
DOT (16366 "Foggin Up the Windows") ... 5-10 62
Also see LUKE, Robin
Also see SHORE, Roberta

LUKE & APOSTLES
Singles: 7-inch
BOUNTY (105 "Been Burnt") ... 15-25 67
(First issue.)
ELEKTRA (45605 "Been Burnt") ... 8-12 67
TRUE NORTH (101 "You Make Me High") ... 15-25 60s
Members: Walter Rossi; Jack Geisinger.
Also see INFLUENCE
Also see MOONQUAKE

LUKE & DISCIPLES
Singles: 7-inch
FANNIN (1003 "Three") ... 10-20 64

LUKE the Drifter: see WILLIAMS, Hank

LUKE the Drifter Jr.: see WILLIAMS, Hank, Jr.

LUKE WARM
Singles: 7-inch
REPRISE ... 3-6 69

LULLABYES
Singles: 7-inch
DIMENSION (1039 "You Touch Me") ... 10-20 64

LULU P&R '64
(With the Luvers; with Dixie Flyers)
Singles: 7-inch
ALFA ... 3-5 79-82
ATCO ... 3-6 69-72
CHELSEA ... 3-5 73-75
EPIC ... 4-8 67-68
PARROT (9000 series) ... 5-10 64-65
PARROT (40000 series) ... 4-8 67
ROCKET ... 3-5 78
Picture Sleeves
ALFA (7006 "I Could Never Miss You More") ... 4-6 81
(Pictures Lulu without headband.)
ALFA (7006 "I Could Never Miss You More") ... 3-5 81
(Pictures Lulu wearing headband.)
ALFA (7011 "If I Were You") ... 3-4 81
EPIC ... 4-8 67-68
EPs: 7-inch
EPIC (26339 "To Sir with Love") ... 5-10 67
(Juke box issue only. Includes title strips.)
LPs: 10/12-inch
ALFA ... 5-10 81
ATCO ... 10-12 70-72
CAPRICORN ... 8-10 74
CHELSEA ... 10-12 73-77
EPIC ... 10-15 67-70
HARMONY ... 10-12 70
PARROT (61016 "From Lulu with Love") ... 50-100 67
(Monaural.)
PARROT (71016 "From Lulu with Love") ... 50-100 67
(Stereo.)
PICKWICK ... 8-10 73
ROCKET ... 5-8 78
Also see CLARK, Dave, Five / Lulu
Also see MOORE, Jackie

LUMAN, Bob C&W/P&R/R&B '60
Singles: 78 rpm
IMPERIAL ... 20-50 57
Singles: 7-inch
CAPITOL ... 10-20 58
EPIC ... 3-5 68-77
HICKORY (1200 series) ... 4-8 63-64
HICKORY (1300 thru 1500 series) ... 3-5 65-70
IMPERIAL (5705 "Red Cadillac and a Black Mustache") ... 10-20 60
(Black label. Reissue of 8311.)
IMPERIAL (8311 "Red Cadillac and a Black Mustache") ... 35-55 57
(Maroon label.)
IMPERIAL (8313 "Red Hot") ... 40-60 57
(Maroon label.)
IMPERIAL (8313 "Red Hot") ... 30-40 59
(Black label.)
IMPERIAL (8315 "Make Up Your Mind Baby") ... 20-30 57
(Maroon label.)
IMPERIAL (8315 "Make Up Your Mind Baby") ... 10-15 59
(Black label.)
POLYDOR ... 3-5 77-78
W.B. ... 5-15 59-62
Picture Sleeves
W.B. ... 15-25 60-62
EPs: 7-inch
HICKORY (124-006 "Selections from Livin' Lovin' Sounds") ... 25-35 65
(Promotional "Six-Pac" issue only.)
ROLLIN' ROCK (34 "Bob Luman") ... 5-8 80s
W.B. (1396 "Let's Think About Livin' ") ... 50-75 60
W.B. (5506 "Bob Luman") ... 50-75 60
(Promotional issue only.)
LPs: 10/12-inch
EPIC ... 8-15 68-77
HARMONY ... 10-15 72
HICKORY (124 "Livin' Lovin' Sounds") ... 15-25 65
HICKORY (4000 series) ... 8-12 74
POLYDOR ... 8-12 78
W.B. (W-1396 "Let's Think About Livin' ") ... 30-40 60
(Monaural.)
W.B. (WS-1396 "Let's Think About Livin' ") ... 40-60 60
(Stereo.)

LUMAN, Bob, & Sue Thompson
Singles: 7-inch
HICKORY ... 4-8 63
Also see LUMAN, Bob
Also see THOMPSON, Sue

LUMLEY, Rufus
Singles: 7-inch
AFFORD ... 4-8 60s
HOLTON ... 8-12 60s
RCA (9230 "Michelle") ... 5-10 67
RCA (9396 "Annabella") ... 10-20 67
Picture Sleeves
RCA ... 5-10 67
LPs: 10/12-inch
RCA (3898 "Rufus Lumley") ... 40-50 67

LUMPKIN, Henry
(With the Love Tones)
Singles: 7-inch
BUDDAH (55 "Honey Hush") ... 5-10 68
MOTOWN (1005 "We Really Love Each Other") ... 40-60 61
MOTOWN (1013 "Don't Leave Me") ... 20-30 61
MOTOWN (1029 "Mo Jo Hanna") ... 20-30 62
PAGEANT (605 "Make a Change") ... 25-50 63

LUNA
LPs: 10/12-inch
ARHOOLIE ... 8-10 67

LUNA, Recardo
Singles: 7-inch
REVOLVO ... 4-8 62

LUNAR FUNK P&R/R&B '72
Singles: 7-inch
BELL ... 3-5 72

LUNARTICS
Singles: 7-inch
SUNLIGHT (1002 "Mountains of the Moon") ... 8-12 71
Members: Jules Blattner; Warren Groovy.
Also see BLATTNER, Jules

LUNCEFORD, Jimmie, & Orchestra P&R '34
Singles: 78 rpm
DECCA ... 4-8 33-52
MAJESTIC ... 4-6 46
EPs: 7-inch
DECCA ... 10-15 50s
Also see BOSTIC, Earl / Jimmie Lunceford
Also see DELTA RHYTHM BOYS

LUND, Alan, & Diplomats
Singles: 7-inch
MTW ... 4-8

LUND, Art, & His Orchestra P&R '47
Singles: 78 rpm
CORAL ... 3-5 52-57
MGM ... 3-6 47-55
Singles: 7-inch
CORAL ... 4-8 52-58
MGM ... 5-10 50-55
U.A. ... 3-6 65
EPs: 7-inch
MGM ... 5-10 54-55
LPs: 10/12-inch
MGM ... 10-20 55

LUND, Garrett
LPs: 10/12-inch
("Almost Grown") ... 150-250 75
(No label or number used.)

LUND, Kenny, & Roller Coasters
Singles: 7-inch
HOLIDAY INN ... 4-8 60s

LUNDBERG, Victor P&R '67
Singles: 7-inch
LIBERTY ... 4-6 67
LPs: 10/12-inch
LIBERTY ... 10-15 68

LUNDI, Pat: see LUNDY, Pat

LUNDY, Pat R&B '73
(Pat Lundi)
Singles: 7-inch
COLUMBIA ... 4-6 67-68
DELUXE ... 4-6 69
HEIDI ... 4-8 65
LEOPARD ... 3-5
PYRAMID ... 3-5 76
RCA ... 3-5 73
TOTO ... 4-8 62
VIGOR ... 3-5 75
LPs: 10/12-inch
COLUMBIA ... 10-15 68
PYRAMID ... 5-8 76

LUNDY, Pat, & Bobby Harris
Singles: 7-inch
HEIDI ... 4-8 65
Also see HARRIS, Bobby
Also see LUNDY, Pat

LUNN, Judy
Singles: 7-inch
MASCOT ... 4-8 61

LUNSFORD, Mike C&W '75
Singles: 7-inch
EVERGREEN ... 3-4 88
GUSTO ... 3-5 75-80
STARDAY ... 3-5 75-78
LPs: 10/12-inch
STARDAY ... 6-12 75-77

LUNSFORD, Mona
Singles: 7-inch
VAN-DECK (117 "You're No Warden") ... 20-30

LUPE
(Fireballs)
Singles: 7-inch
MGM ... 5-10 65
Also see FIREBALLS

LUREX, Larry
Singles: 7-inch
ANTHEM (104 "I Can Hear Music") ... 40-60 73
Also see MERCURY, Freddie

LURIE, Elliot
Singles: 7-inch
ARISTA ... 3-5 76
LPs: 10/12-inch
EPIC ... 8-10 75
Also see LOOKING GLASS

LUSHUS DAIM & Pretty Vain R&B '85
Singles: 7-inch
MOTOWN ... 3-4 85
LPs: 10/12-inch
MOTOWN ... 5-8 85

LUSSON, Robert, & Some Cast of Characters
Singles: 7-inch
SGL (001 "Free James Brown") ... 4-8 90s
(Single-sided. Promotional issue only.)

LUTCHER, Joe R&B '48
(With His Society Cats)
Singles: 78 rpm
CAPITOL ... 5-10 48
MODERN ... 5-10 49
SPECIALTY ... 5-10 48-51
Singles: 7-inch
SPECIALTY (303 "Rockin' Boogie") ... 50-75 51

LUTCHER, Nellie P&R/R&B '47
(With Her "Rhythm")
Singles: 78 rpm
CAPITOL ... 5-10 47-50
Singles: 7-inch
CAPITOL ... 10-20 50
EPs: 7-inch
CAPITOL (232 "Real Gone") ... 20-40 50
LIBERTY (3014-1/2/3 "Our New Nellie") ... 10-20 56
(Price is for any of three volumes.)
LPs: 10/12-inch
CAPITOL (H-232 "Real Gone!") ... 35-55 50
(10-inch LP.)
CAPITOL (T-232 "Real Gone!") ... 20-30 55
EPIC (1108 "Whee! Nellie") ... 25-35 55
(10-inch LP.)
LIBERTY (3014 "Our New Nellie") ... 20-40 56

LUTCHER, Nellie, & Nat "King" Cole R&B '50
Singles: 78 rpm
CAPITOL ... 5-10 50
Singles: 7-inch
CAPITOL ... 10-20 50
Also see COLE, Nat "King"
Also see LUTCHER, Nellie

LUTHER R&B '76
(Luther Vandross)
Singles: 7-inch
COTILLION ... 3-5 76-77
LPs: 10/12-inch
COTILLION ... 8-10 77
Also see VANDROSS, Luther

LUTHER & LITTLE EVA
Singles: 7-inch
KING (5010 "Ain't Got No Home") ... 15-25 57

LUTHER, Betty
Singles: 7-inch
ALL ... 4-8 63
TOPPA ... 4-8 62

LUTHER, Lord: see LORD LUTHER

LUV
Singles: 7-inch
POLYDOR ... 3-4 79

LUV, Frankie
Singles: 7-inch
CHANCELLOR ... 5-10 63

LUV BANDITS
Singles: 7-inch
PARROT ... 10-15 67

LUV BIRDS
Singles: 7-inch
ABC ... 4-8 66-67

LUV BUGS
Singles: 7-inch
STON-ROC ... 12-18

LUV CO.
Singles: 7-inch
SPRING (705 "Things Are Not the Same") ... 10-20 70

LUV'D ONES
Singles: 7-inch
DUNWICH ... 10-20 66
WHITE OAK (759101 "Up and Down Sue") ... 20-30 60s

LUVS
Singles: 7-inch
STALLION (1002 "We Kiss in the Shadows") ... 100-200 63

LUX
Singles: 7-inch
GAZETTE ... 4-6 69

LYALL, William
LPs: 10/12-inch
EMI ... 5-8 76
Also see PARSONS, Alan, Project
Also see PILOT
Also see RUNNER

LYDELLS
(With the Paul Swain Orchestra)
Singles: 7-inch
LOST-NITE ... 10-15 64
PAM (103 "There Goes the Boy") ... 75-125 59
PARKWAY (897 "There Goes the Boy") ... 15-25 64

LY-DELLS P&R '61
(With Frank Slay & His Orchestra)
Singles: 7-inch
MASTER (111 "Genie of the Lamp") ... 100-150 61

MASTER (251 "Wizard of Love") ... 50-75 61
ROULETTE (4493 "Karen") ... 20-30 63
SCA (18001 "Book of Songs") ... 25-50 62
SOUTHERN SOUND (122 "Hide and Seek") ... 25-35 65
LPs: 10/12-inch
CLIFTON (2002 "Greatest Hits") ... 8-10 81
Also see LEN-DELLS
Also see SLAY, Frank, & His Orchestra

LYERLY, Bill *C&W '81*
Singles: 7-inch
RCA ... 3-5 81

LYKES OF US
Singles: 7-inch
MOLT (6801 "7:30 Said") ... 15-25 68

LYLE
Singles: 7-inch
BELL ... 3-5 74

LYLE, Bobby *R&B '78*
Singles: 7-inch
CAPITOL ... 3-5 78

LYMAN, Arthur *LP '58*
(Arthur Lyman Group)
Singles: 7-inch
GNP ... 3-6 64-75
HI FI ... 4-8 59-69
ORBIT ... 8-12 58
LPs: 10/12-inch
GNP ... 8-15 63-75
HI FI ... 10-20 58-69
OLYMPIC ... 5-8 79

LYMAN, Joni
Singles: 7-inch
REPRISE (378 "Happy Birthday Blue") ... 20-30 65

LYMAN, Tiny, & Jukes
Singles: 7-inch
RUNNIN' WILD (1940 "Left Overs") ... 8-12

LYME & CYBELLE *P&R '66*
Singles: 7-inch
WHITE WHALE ... 5-10 66-67
Also see ZEVON, Warren

LYMON, Frankie *P&R/R&B '56*
(With the Teenagers; with Jimmy Wright & His Orchestra)
Singles: 78 rpm
GEE (1002 "Why Do Fools Fall in Love") ... 30-60 55
(Red label, gold print.)
GEE (1002 "Why Do Fools Fall in Love") ... 15-25 55
(Red label, black print.)
GEE (1012 thru 1039) ... 20-30 56-57
ROULETTE ... 15-25 57
Singles: 7-inch
ABC ... 3-4 73
BIG KAT ... 5-10 68
COLUMBIA (43094 "Somewhere") ... 8-12 64
GEE (1002 "Why Do Fools Fall in Love") ... 400-600 55
(Colored vinyl.)
GEE (1002 "Why Do Fools Fall in Love") ... 75-125 55
(Red label, gold print.)
GEE (1002 "Why Do Fools Fall in Love") ... 30-40 55
(Red label, black print.)
GEE (1012 "I Want You to Be My Girl") ... 30-40 56
GEE (1018 "I Promise to Remember") ... 30-40 56
GEE (1022 "The ABCs of Love") ... 30-40 56
GEE (1032 "Paper Castles") ... 25-35 57
GEE (1035 "Love Is a Clown") ... 25-35 57
GEE (1036 "Out in the Cold Again") ... 25-35 57
GEE (1039 "Goody Goody") ... 35-50 57
(Credits "Frankie Lymon & the Teenagers.")
GEE (1039 "Goody Goody") ... 15-25 59
(No mention of the Teenagers.)
GEE (1052 "Goody Good Girl") ... 15-25 59
MURRAY HILL ... 3-5 80s
RAMA (34 "I Want You to Be My Girl") ... 5-10 64
(Golden Goodies Series.)
ROULETTE (4026 "So Goes My Love") ... 15-25 57
ROULETTE (4068 "Portable on My Shoulder") ... 15-25 58
ROULETTE (4093 "Melinda") ... 15-25 58
ROULETTE (4128 "No Matter What You've Done") ... 10-20 59
ROULETTE (4150 "Before I Fall Asleep") ... 10-20 59
ROULETTE (4257 "Little Bitty Pretty One") ... 10-20 60
ROULETTE (4283 "Buzz Buzz Buzz") ... 10-20 60
ROULETTE (4310 "Silhouettes") ... 10-20 60
ROULETTE (4348 "So Young") ... 10-20 61
ROULETTE (4391 "I Put the Bomp") ... 10-20 61
TCF (11 "To Each His Own") ... 8-12 64
Picture Sleeves
BIG KAT (7008 "I Want You to Be My Girl") ... 5-10 68
EPs: 7-inch
GEE (601 "The Teenagers Go Rockin' ") ... 75-125 56
GEE (601 "The Teenagers Go Romantic") ... 75-125 56
ROULETTE (304 "Frankie Lymon at the London Palladium") ... 50-75 58
LPs: 10/12-inch
ACCORD ... 5-10 82
GEE (701 "The Teenagers Featuring Frankie Lymon") ... 200-300 57
(Red or white label.)
GEE (701 "The Teenagers Featuring Frankie Lymon") ... 50-100 61
(Gray label.)
GUEST STAR ... 5-10
MURRAY HILL (148 "Frankie Lymon and the Teenagers") ... 50-75 80s
(Boxed, five-LP set, with booklet and bonus single.)
ROULETTE (25013 "Frankie Lymon at the London Palladium") ... 100-150 58
ROULETTE (25036 "Rock & Roll") ... 50-100 58
ROULETTE (25250 "Frankie Lymon's Greatest") ... 25-50 64
Members: Frankie Lymon; Herman Santiago; Sherman Games; Jim Merchant; Joe Negroni.
Also see WRIGHT, Jimmy
Also see TEENAGERS

LYMON, Lewis, & Teenchords
(With the Teenchords)
Singles: 78 rpm
END ... 25-50 57
FURY ... 25-50 57
Singles: 7-inch
END (1003 "Too Young") ... 75-125 57
END (1007 "I Found Out Why") ... 50-100 57
END (1113 "Too Young") ... 20-40 62
FURY (1000 "I'm So Happy") ... 100-200 57
(Maroon label.)
FURY (1000 "I'm So Happy") ... 25-50
(Yellow label.)
FURY (1003 "Please Tell the Angels") ... 150-250 57
(Maroon label.)
FURY (1003 "Please Tell the Angels") ... 50-75
(Yellow label.)
JUANITA (101 "Dance Girl") ... 25-50 58
LPs: 10/12-inch
COLLECTABLES ... 6-8 88
LOST-NITE ... 8-12 81
Members: Lewis Lymon; Ralph Vaughan; David Lyttle; Ross Rocco; Lyndon Harold; Jimmy Castor; John Pruitt; Ed Pellegrino.
Also see CASTOR, Jimmy
Also see TOWNSMEN / Louie Lymon

LYN, Ronnie
(Ronnie Lynn Quartet)
Singles: 7-inch
SPANGLE ... 10-15
V.A.C. ... 5-10

LYN & INVADERS
Singles: 7-inch
FENTON (2040 "Secretly") ... 25-35 66
Also see INCREDIBLE INVADERS

LYNAN, Mike, & Little People
Singles: 7-inch
EMANON ... 5-10

LYNCH, Frank
Singles: 7-inch
MY RECORD ... 8-12

LYNCH, Jimmy
(Jimmy "Mr. Motion" Lynch)
LPs: 10/12-inch
LAVAL (869 "There Was a Time") ... 8-12
LAVAL (904 "Tramp Time") ... 15-20 76
LAVAL (904-P "Tramp Time, Volume, Three") ... 8-10 76
(Picture disc.)

LYNCH, Kenny
Singles: 7-inch
ARLEN ... 5-10 64
BIG TOP ... 5-10 63
WHITE WHALE ... 4-8 69

LYNCH, Ray *LP '89*
LPs: 10/12-inch
MUSIC WEST ... 5-10 89

LYNCH MOB *LP '90*
LPs: 10/12-inch
ELEKTRA ... 5-8 90

LYNDELL, Linda *R&B '68*
Singles: 7-inch
VOLT ... 4-8 68

LYNDELL, Liz *C&W '80*
Singles: 7-inch
KOALA ... 3-4 80-81

LYNDEN, Tracy *C&W '85*
Singles: 7-inch
RCA ... 3-4 85

LYNDON, Frank
Singles: 7-inch
BANG (531 "Earth Angel") ... 10-15 66
JAB (1004 "Cry Cry Cry") ... 10-20 60s
LAURIE (3322 "Santa's Jet") ... 8-12 65
SABINA (520 "Earth Angel") ... 15-25 65
STRAWBERRY ... 3-5 80s
UPTOWN ... 10-20 60s
Session: Guy Valari.
Also see BELMONTS
Also see REGENTS

LYNN, Amery
Singles: 7-inch
DART ... 8-10 59

LYNN, Barbara, & Jimmie Clyde
Singles: 78 rpm
DELUXE (1181 "Too Many Kisses") ... 5-10 48

LYNN, Barbara *P&R/R&B '62*
Singles: 7-inch
ATLANTIC ... 4-8 67-72
COLLECTABLES ... 3-4 80s
COPYRIGHT ... 4-8
ERIC (7004 "Dina & Patrina") ... 15-25 62
JAMIE ... 6-12 62-65
JET STREAM ... 5-8
TRIBE (8316 "I'm a Good Woman") ... 15-25 66
TRIBE (8319 "Until I'm Free") ... 8-10 66
TRIBE (8322 "Watch the One") ... 8-10 67
TRIBE (8324 "I Don't Want a Playboy") ... 8-10 67
(Though a higher number, this disc came out about three months before 8322.)
LPs: 10/12-inch
ATLANTIC ... 10-20 68
FONTANA ... 10-20
JAMIE ... 20-30 62-64

LYNN, Barbara, & Lee Maye
Singles: 7-inch
JAMIE ... 5-10 65
Also see LYNN, Barbara
Also see MAYE, Arthur Lee

LYNN, Billy
Singles: 7-inch
AMY (802 "Little Pony Tail") ... 30-50 61

LYNN, Blow Top, & His House Rockers
(With Melvin Smith)
Singles: 78 rpm
RCA ... 15-25 51
Singles: 7-inch
RCA (0110 "School Boy Blues") ... 20-30 51
RCA (0124 "Up on the Hill") ... 20-30 51
RCA (0139 "Rampaging Mama") ... 20-30 51
RCA (4328 "Come Back My Darlin'") ... 20-30 51

LYNN, Bobbi
Singles: 7-inch
ELF (90009 "Earthquake") ... 10-20

LYNN, Cherri
Singles: 78 rpm
APOLLO ... 10-15 54
Singles: 7-inch
APOLLO ... 15-25 54

LYNN, Cheryl *P&R/R&B/LP '78*
Singles: 12-inch
COLUMBIA ... 4-6 78-85
Singles: 7-inch
COLUMBIA ... 3-5 78-85
MANHATTAN ... 3-4 87
PRIVATE I ... 3-4 85
LPs: 10/12-inch
COLUMBIA ... 5-10 78-84

LYNN, Cheryl, & Luther Vandross *R&B '82*
Singles: 7-inch
COLUMBIA ... 3-5 82
Also see LYNN, Cheryl
Also see VANDROSS, Luther

LYNN, Cindy: see CINDY LYNN

LYNN, Debra
(Debbie Lynn)
Singles: 7-inch
FLIGHT (10001 "Fujiyama Mama") ... 20-30 62
SAM ... 5-10 62

LYNN, Delores
Singles: 7-inch
JUNIOR ... 10-15

LYNN, Diana
JIM ("Queen of the Silver Dollar") ... 15-20 83
(Picture disc. No selection number used.)
ERICA (9109 "Turn Down the TV") ... 5-8 82
(Square picture disc.)

LYNN, Donna *P&R '64*
Singles: 7-inch
CAPITOL (Except 5127) ... 5-10 63-65
CAPITOL (5127 "My Boyfriend Got a Beatle Haircut") ... 15-20 64
EPIC ... 4-8 63
PALMER (5016 "Don't You Dare") ... 15-25 67
LPs: 10/12-inch
CAPITOL ... 15-25 64

LYNN, Georgia
Singles: 7-inch
BIG AL ... 4-8 63
CHALLENGE ... 4-8 63

LYNN, Gerrie
Singles: 7-inch
COLUMBIA ... 4-6 66
Picture Sleeves
COLUMBIA ... 4-8 66

LYNN, Ginie *R&B '78*
(Ginny Lynn)
Singles: 7-inch
ABC ... 3-5 78
IN SOUND ... 5-10
MISTY ... 3-5

LYNN, Jeannie, & Friends
Singles: 7-inch
REX (1001 "You Can Dance") ... 15-25 58
REX (1009) ... 10-15 59
(Title not known.)

LYNN, Jeff: see LYNNE, Jeff

LYNN, Jeri: see SANDS, Jeri Lynn

LYNN, Jerry
Singles: 7-inch
D (1041 "Bugger Burns") ... 30-50 59
KRC (102 "Don't Want Your Money Honey") ... 10-20 59

LYNN, Joyce
Singles: 7-inch
WRIMUS ... 5-8 61

LYNN, Judy: see JUDY LYNN

LYNN, Kari
Singles: 7-inch
AUBURN ... 5-10 61-62

LYNN, Kathy
(With the Playboys)
Singles: 7-inch
SWAN (4175 "Rock City") ... 30-50 64
SWAN (4193 "I Got a Guy") ... 30-50 65
Also see ROCKIN' REBELS

LYNN, Lorelei
Singles: 7-inch
AWARD (128 "Rock-a-Bop") ... 20-30 59

LYNN, Loretta *C&W '60*
(With the Coal Miners)
Singles: 7-inch
DECCA (31384 thru 31966) ... 5-10 62-66
DECCA (32045 thru 32851) ... 4-8 66-71
DECCA (32900 "Here in Topeka") ... 10-15 71
DECCA (32900 "One's on the Way") ... 3-6 71
DECCA (32974 thru 33039) ... 3-6 72
MCA ... 3-5 73-86
ZERO (107 "I'm a Honky Tonk Girl") ... 50-75 60
ZERO (110 "New Rainbow") ... 60-100 61
ZERO (112 "The Darkest Day") ... 60-100 61
Picture Sleeves
DECCA (31000 series) ... 8-12 66
DECCA (32000 series) ... 4-6 70
MCA ... 3-5 78
EPs: 7-inch
DECCA ... 10-20 64-65
LPs: 10/12-inch
CORAL ... 5-8 73
COUNTRY MUSIC MAGAZINE ... 15-20 76
(Mail-order LP sold by *Country Music* magazine.)
DECCA (DL-4457 "Loretta Lynn Sings") ... 40-60 63
(Monaural.)
DECCA (DL7-4457 "Loretta Lynn Sings") ... 45-65 63
(Stereo.)
DECCA (DL-4541 "Before I'm Over You") ... 30-40 65
(Monaural.)
DECCA (DL7-4541 "Before I'm Over You") ... 35-45 65
(Stereo.)
DECCA (DL-4620 "Songs from My Heart") ... 30-40 65
(Monaural.)
DECCA (DL7-4620 "Songs from My Heart") ... 35-45 65
(Stereo.)
DECCA (DL-4665 "Blue Kentucky Girl") ... 15-25 65
(Monaural.)
DECCA (DL7-4665 "Blue Kentucky Girl") ... 20-30 65
(Stereo.)
DECCA (DL-4655 "Hymns") ... 15-25 65
(Monaural.)
DECCA (DL7-4655 "Hymns") ... 20-30 65
(Stereo.)
DECCA (DL-4744 "I Like 'Em Country") ... 15-25 66
(Monaural.)
DECCA (DL-4744 "I Like 'Em Country") ... 15-25 66
(Monaural.)
DECCA (DL7-4744 "I Like 'Em Country") ... 15-25 66
(Stereo.)
DECCA (DL-4783 "You Ain't Woman Enough") ... 15-25 66
(Monaural.)
DECCA (DL7-4783 "You Ain't Woman Enough") ... 15-25 66
(Stereo.)
DECCA (DL-4817 "A Country Christmas") ... 15-25 66
(Monaural.)
DECCA (DL7-4817 "A Country Christmas") ... 15-25 66
(Stereo.)
DECCA (DL-4842 "Don't Come Home a Drinkin' ") ... 15-25 67
(Monaural.)
DECCA (DL7-4842 "Don't Come Home a Drinkin' ") ... 15-25 67
(Stereo.)
DECCA (DL-4928 "Who Says God Is Dead") ... 15-25 67
(Monaural.)
DECCA (DL7-4928 "Who Says God Is Dead") ... 15-25 67
(Stereo.)
DECCA (DL-4930 "Singin' with Feeling") ... 15-25 67
(Monaural.)
DECCA (DL7-4930 "Singin' with Feeling") ... 15-25 67
(Stereo.)
DECCA (DL-4997 "Fist City") ... 15-25 68
(Monaural.)
DECCA (DL7-4997 "Fist City") ... 10-20 68
(Stereo.)
DECCA (75000 "Greatest Hits") ... 12-25 68
DECCA (75113 "Woman of the World/To Make a Man") ... 25-35 69
DECCA (75198 "Loretta Lynn Writes 'Em and Sings 'Em") ... 12-25 70
DECCA (75163 "Wings Upon Your Horns") ... 12-25 70
DECCA (75253 "Coal Miner's Daughter") ... 10-20 71
DECCA (75282 "I Want to Be Free") ... 12-25 71
DECCA (75310 "You're Looking at Country") ... 12-25 71
DECCA (75334 "One's on the Way") ... 12-25 72
DECCA (75351 "God Bless America Again") ... 12-25 72
DECCA (75381 "Here I Am Again") ... 12-25 72
DECCA (75084 "Your Squaw Is on the Warpath") ... 25-35 69
(Has *Barney*.)
DECCA (75084 "Your Squaw Is on the Warpath") ... 15-20 69
(Without *Barney*.)
L.L. ... 20-25 76
MCA ... 5-10 73-86
TEE VEE ... 8-12 78
TROLLEY CAR ... 8-10 81
VOCALION ... 8-15 68-72
Promotional LPs
MCA (1934 "Loretta Lynn's Greatest Hits") ... 30-40 74
(Cover shows title as simply *Loretta Lynn*.)
MCA (35013 "Allis-Chalmers Presents Loretta Lynn") ... 30-40 78
MCA (35018 "Crisco Presents Loretta Lynn's Country Classics") ... 30-40 79
Session: Bob Hempker; Chuck Flynn; Ken Riley; Dave Thornhill; Gene Dunlap; Don Ballenger; Jordanaires.
Also see BEATLES / Loretta Lynn
Also see PIERCE, Webb / Loretta Lynn
Also see STARR, Kenny
Also see TUBB, Ernest, & Loretta Lynn
Also see TWITTY, Conway, & Loretta Lynn
Also see WEBB, Jay Lee
Also see WILBURN BROTHERS

LYNN, Loretta, & Conway Twitty *C&W/P&R '71*
Singles: 7-inch
CRLX (7211281"Seasons Greetings") ... 50-100 80s
(Picture disc. Promotional issue only.)
DECCA ... 4-6 71-72
MCA ... 3-5 73-81
LPs: 10/12-inch
DECCA ... 8-15 71-72
MCA ... 5-10 73-84
TVP ... 8-12 76
Also see LYNN, Loretta
Also see TWITTY, Conway

LYNN, Loretta / Tammy Wynette
LPs: 10/12-inch
RADIANT ... 5-8 81
Also see LYNN, Loretta
Also see WYNETTE, Tammy

LYNN, Marcia: see MARCIA LYNN

LYNN, Michelle *C&W '89*
Singles: 7-inch
MASTER ... 3-4 89

LYNN, Micki
Singles: 7-inch
BLUE DIAMOND ... 5-8
REVUE (11042 "In The Meantime") ... 8-10

LYNN, Nita, & Jimmy Parrish
Singles: 7-inch
ALLSTAR ... 5-8 60

LYNN, Ray
Singles: 7-inch
GLEN (2300 "Mean Mean Woman") ... 20-30 60s

LYNN, Rebecca *C&W '78*
Singles: 7-inch
SCORPION ... 3-5 78-79
SUNBIRD ... 3-5 80

LYNN, Robby, & Teens
Singles: 7-inch
CUCA (1086 "The Angel Sent Me") ... 10-15 62
SUNDERLAND (1086 "Angel, You Sent Me") ... 10-20 62

LYNN, Sammi
Singles: 7-inch
SUE ... 5-10 61

LYNN, Sandra
(Sandy Lynn)
Singles: 7-inch
CONSTELLATION ... 5-10 64
LAUREL (1024 "Hurry Home") ... 50-75 61
LEMAY ... 4-8 64
OPERATORS ... 4-8 62
Also see CORVETS

LYNN, Smiling Smokey
Singles: 78 rpm
PEACOCK ... 10-20 51-52
SPECIALTY ... 10-20 49

LYNN, Tami
Singles: 7-inch
ATCO (6342 "I'm Gonna Run Away from You") ... 10-20 65
MOJO (001 "I'm Gonna Run Away from You") ... 5-8 71

LPs: 10/12-inch
COTILLION 10-15 72

LYNN, Trisha C&W '88
(Trish Lynn)
Singles: 7-inch
OAK 3-4 88-89

LYNN, Trudy
Singles: 7-inch
ICHIBAN 3-4 93
LPs: 10/12-inch
ICHIBAN 5-10

LYNN, Vera P&R '48
Singles: 78 rpm
LONDON 3-5 51-57
Singles: 7-inch
ARCO 4-6 67
DJM 4-6 69
LONDON 5-10 51-64
U.A. 4-6 67
EPs: 7-inch
LONDON 10-20 52-56
LPs: 10/12-inch
LONDON 15-30 52-64
MGM 8-12 61
U.A. 5-10 67

LYNN, Vicki
Singles: 7-inch
APPLAUSE 10-15 65
INDIGO 8-12 61

LYNN, Windie
Singles: 7-inch
LACONIC 5-10 61

LYNN & LINDA
Singles: 7-inch
ROULETTE 5-10 59

LYNN & Mersey Maids
Singles: 7-inch
RIC 5-10 65

LYNN DEE: see DEE, Lynn

LYNNE, Connie
Singles: 7-inch
AMERICAN SOUND 3-5 77

LYNNE, Gloria P&R/R&B/LP '61
(Gloria Alleyne)
Singles: 7-inch
CANYON 3-5 70
EVEREST 5-10 59-66
FONTANA 4-6 64-69
HI FI 4-6 66
IMPULSE 3-5 76
MERCURY 3-5 72
SEECO 4-8 61
LPs: 10/12-inch
CANYON 5-10 70
DESIGN 10-15 62
EVEREST (300 series) 5-10 75
EVEREST (1000 series) 20-30 58-65
(Stereo.)
EVEREST (5000 series) 15-25 58-65
(Monaural.)
FONTANA 10-20 64-69
HI FI 10-15 66
IMPULSE 5-10 76
MERCURY 8-12 69-72
PAUL WINLEY 5-10 74
SUNSET 8-15 66-67
UPFRONT 5-10 72
Also see ALLEYNE, Gloria

LYNNE, Gloria / Nina Simone / Billie Holiday
LPs: 10/12-inch
ALMOR 10-15
Also see HOLIDAY, Billie
Also see SIMONE, Nina

LYNNE, Jeff P&R '84
(Jeff Lynn)
Singles: 12-inch
JET 5-8 77
Singles: 7-inch
JET 3-5 77
REPRISE 5-8 90
TWIN-SPIN 10-15 65
VIRGIN 3-4 84
Also see ELECTRIC LIGHT ORCHESTRA
Also see IDLE RACE
Also see MOVE
Also see TRAVELING WILBURYS

LYNNE, Larry, Group
Singles: 7-inch
MAMOUTH 5-10 70
WATER ST. 5-10 69
Members: Larry Lynne Ostricki; Tyler; Famularo; Todd Famularo; Val Dwyer; Mike O'Krongly.
Also see BONNEVILLES
Also see SKUNKS

LYNNE, Shelby C&W '89
Singles: 7-inch
EPIC 3-4 89-91
Also see JONES, George, & Shelby Lynne
Also see TOMORROW'S WORLD

LYNNE, Shelby, & Les Taylor C&W '89
Singles: 7-inch
EPIC 3-4 91
Also see LYNNE, Shelby
Also see TAYLOR, Les

LYNNE, Susan
Singles: 7-inch
CAPITOL 4-8 64
DUEL 4-8 62-63

LYNOTT, Philip
Singles: 7-inch
W.B. 3-5 82
LPs: 10/12-inch
W.B. 5-8 82
Also see THIN LIZZY

LYNTON, Jackie
Singles: 7-inch
MURBO 4-8

LYNX
Singles: 7-inch
THUNDERBALL (135 "You Lie") 20-30 67
THUNDERBALL (137 "Show Me") 20-30 67

LYNX
Singles: 7-inch
A.V.I. 3-5 78
CHRYSALIS 3-4 82
LPs: 10/12-inch
A.V.I. 5-8 78
CHRYSALIS 5-8 82

LYNX
Singles: 7-inch
HARE (2121 "Time and a Word") 8-12

LYNYRD SKYNYRD LP '73
Singles: 7-inch
ATNIA (129 "Need All My Friends") 4-8 78
MCA (Except 1966) 3-6 74-78
MCA (1966 "Gimmie Back My Bullets") 8-12 77
(Promotional concert souvenir issue.)
EPs: 7-inch
MCA 10-15 76
(Promotional issue only.)
LPs: 10/12-inch
MCA (2000 & 3000 series, except 3029) 8-10 75-78
MCA (3029 "Street Survivors") 30-40 77
(Front cover pictures the group in flames.)
MCA (3029 "Street Survivors") 8-10 77
(Pictures the group without flames.)
MCA (5000 series) 5-8 79-82
MCA (6000 series) 10-15 76-81
MCA (8011 "Live at the Fox") 10-15 76
MCA (8027 "Southern by the Grace of God") 8-12 88
MCA (10000 series) 10-15 79-81
MCA (37000 series) 5-8 79-82
MCA (42000 series) 5-8 87
MCA/SOUNDS of the SOUTH (300 & 400 series) 8-15 73-74
Promotional LPs
MCA (1946 "Special Advance Preview *Live* Album") 25-35 76
(White label.)
MCA (1988 "Lynyrd Skynyrd") 25-35 76
(White label.)
MCA (2170 "Gimmie Back My Bullets") 25-35 76
(White label. Concert souvenir copy.)
Members: Ronnie Van Zant; Gary Rossington; Allen Collins; Steve Gaines; Cassie Gaines; Ed King; Rick Medlocke; Greg Walker; Leon Wildeson; Billy Powell; Artimus Pyle; Bob Burns; Johnny Van Zant.
Also see ALIAS
Also see BLACKFOOT
Also see COLLINS, Allen, Band
Also see GAINES, Steve
Also see PYLE, Artimus, Band
Also see ROSSINGTON - COLLINS BAND
Also see STRAWBERRY ALARM CLOCK
Also see VAN ZANT, Johnny, Band

LYON, Bob, & Cubs
Singles: 7-inch
LYON (4721 "Ram Charger") 15-20 61

LYON, Ken
Singles: 7-inch
EPIC (9446 "Fallen Idol") 25-35 61

LYON, Sue
Singles: 7-inch
MGM 8-12 62

LYONS, Barbara
Singles: 7-inch
ABC-PAR 4-8 60

LYONS, Billy
Singles: 7-inch
AVA 4-8 63

LYONS, Cleve
Singles: 7-inch
VIK (0276 "Out of the Closet") 15-25 57

LYONS, Jamie, Group
Singles: 7-inch
LAURIE 4-8 67-69
Also see CAPITOL CITY ROCKETS
Also see MUSIC EXPLOSION

LYONS, Joanie, & Hitchhikers
Singles: 7-inch
STAR 4-8 63

LYONS, Joe, & Arrows
Singles: 7-inch
HIT MAKER (600 "Bob-O-Loop") 50-100 59
Also see ARROWS

LYONS, Lonnie
(Lonnie Lyons Combo)
Singles: 78 rpm
FREEDOM 15-25 49

LYONS, Marie
(Marie "Queenie" Lyons)
Singles: 7-inch
DELUXE 5-10 68-70
LPs: 10/12-inch
DELUXE (12001 "Soul Fever") 15-25 70

LYONS, Queenie
Singles: 7-inch
DELUXE 8-12
SIMS 3-5

LYONS, Ricky
Singles: 7-inch
FEDERAL 5-10 60

LYRES
(Nutmegs)
Singles: 78 rpm
J&G (101 "Ship of Love") 200-400 53
Members: Leroy Griffin; Sonny Griffin; Leroy McNeil; Bill Embery; Walter Singleterry.
Also see NUTMEGS

LYRICS
(With Ray's Combo)
Singles: 7-inch
HY-TONE (111 "I'm in Love") 300-400 57
Also see HARRIS, Georgia

LYRICS
Singles: 7-inch
MARVELS (1005 "Did She Leave You") 15-25 58
MID-SOUTH (1500 "Down in the Alley") 50-75 59
RHYTHM (127 "Every Night") 1000-2000 59
VEE JAY (285 "Come on Home") 40-60 58
Member: Carl Henderson.

LYRICS
Singles: 7-inch
CORAL (62322 "Oh, Please Love Me") 15-25 62
HARLEM (101 "Oh, Please Love Me") 550-650 59
(First issue.)
HARLEM (104 "I Want to Know") 300-400 59
WILDCAT (0028 "Oh, Please Love Me") 50-100 59
LPs: 10/12-inch
HARLEM 8-10 79

LYRICS
Singles: 7-inch
FERNWOOD (129 "Let's Be Sweethearts Again") 200-300 61
FLEETWOOD (233 "Let's Be Sweethearts Again") 200-300 61

LYRICS
(Ida Valentine & Lyrics; Leo Valentine & Lyrics)
Singles: 7-inch
SKYLIGHT (200 "Now That You're Gone") 200-300 62
SKYLIGHT (201 "Baby Doll") 500-750 62
Also see WIGFALL, William, & Lyrics

LYRICS
Singles: 7-inch
ABC-PAR (10560 "So Hard to Get Along") 5-10 64
DAN-TONE (1002 "I Can't Get Along Without You") 10-20 63
GOLDWAX (101 "Darling") 10-20 63
GOLDWAX (105 "So Hard to Get Along") 10-20 63

LYRICS
Singles: 7-inch
J.W.J. (19792 "They Call That Love") 10-20 67

LYRICS
Singles: 7-inch
ERA (3153 "So What") 50-75 65
FEATHER (1968 "Wake Up to My Voice") 15-25 68
GNP (381 "My Son") 8-12 66
GNP (393 "Mr. Man") 8-12 67
Members: Chris Gaylord; Steve Khailer; Michael Allen; Bill Garcia; Gary Neves.
Also see MAGIC MUSHROOM

LYTATIONS
Singles: 7-inch
TIMES SQUARE 10-15 64
Member: Jack Strong.
Also see KAPTIONS

LYTE
Singles: 7-inch
BOLO (761 "It's Gonna Work Out Fine") 10-15 68

LYTELL, Marshall
Singles: 7-inch
CAMEO 5-10 59

LYTHGOE, John, & Tri Five
Singles: 7-inch
VARBEE (2002 "Oh Baby") 10-20 61

LYTLE, Johnny P&R/LP '66
(Johnny Lytle Quintet; J Trio)
Singles: 7-inch
PACIFIC JAZZ 4-6 68
RIVERSIDE 4-8 63
SOLID STATE 4-6 68
TUBA 5-10 65-66
EPs: 7-inch
NEOPHON 10-15
LPs: 10/12-inch
JAZZLAND 15-25 60-62
MILESTONE 5-10 72
MUSE 5-8 78-81
PACIFIC JAZZ 8-15 67
RIVERSIDE 10-20 63-68
SOLID STATE 8-15 67-69

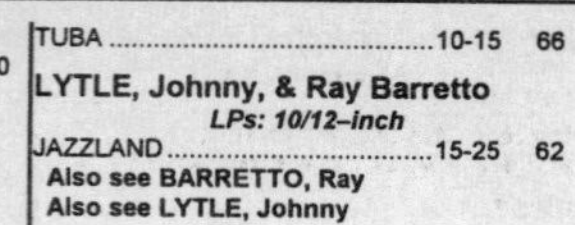
TUBA 10-15 66

LYTLE, Johnny, & Ray Barretto
LPs: 10/12-inch
JAZZLAND 15-25 62
Also see BARRETTO, Ray
Also see LYTLE, Johnny

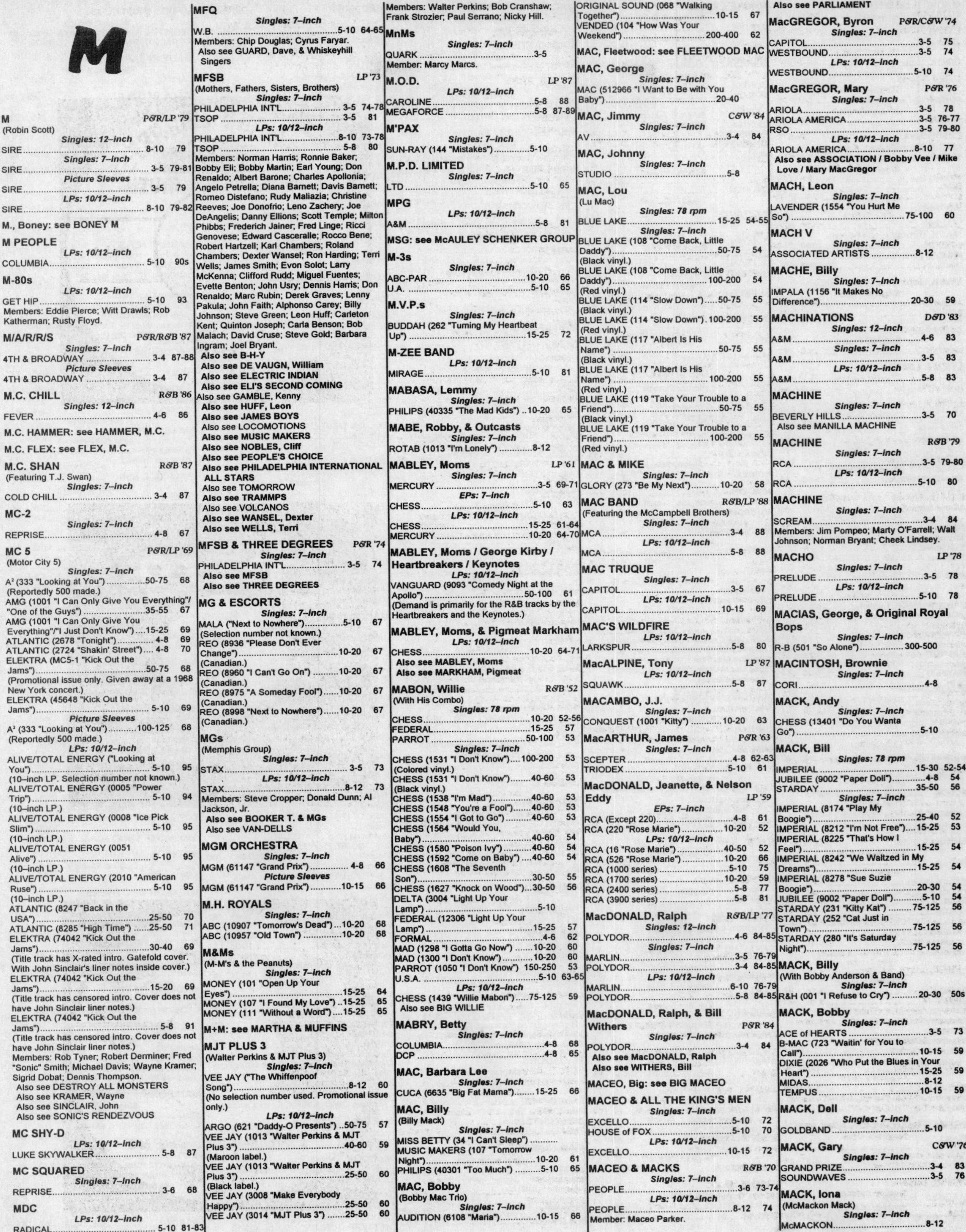

M P&R/LP '79
(Robin Scott)
Singles: 12-inch
SIRE 8-10 79
Singles: 7-inch
SIRE 3-5 79-81
Picture Sleeves
SIRE 3-5 79
LPs: 10/12-inch
SIRE 8-10 79-82

M., Boney: see BONEY M

M PEOPLE
LPs: 10/12-inch
COLUMBIA 5-10 90s

M-80s
LPs: 10/12-inch
GET HIP 5-10 93
Members: Eddie Pierce; Witt Drawls; Rob Katherman; Rusty Floyd.

M/A/R/R/S P&R/R&B '87
Singles: 7-inch
4TH & BROADWAY 3-4 87-88
Picture Sleeves
4TH & BROADWAY 3-4 87

M.C. CHILL R&B '86
Singles: 12-inch
FEVER 4-6 86

M.C. HAMMER: see HAMMER, M.C.

M.C. FLEX: see FLEX, M.C.

M.C. SHAN R&B '87
(Featuring T.J. Swan)
Singles: 7-inch
COLD CHILL 3-4 87

MC-2
Singles: 7-inch
REPRISE 4-8 67

MC 5 P&R/LP '69
(Motor City 5)
Singles: 7-inch
A² (333 "Looking at You") 50-75 68
(Reportedly 500 made.)
AMG (1001 "I Can Only Give You Everything"/"One of the Guys") 35-55 67
AMG (1001 "I Can Only Give You Everything"/"I Just Don't Know") 15-25 69
ATLANTIC (2678 "Tonight") 4-8 69
ATLANTIC (2724 "Shakin' Street") 4-8 70
ELEKTRA (MC5-1 "Kick Out the Jams") 50-75 68
(Promotional issue only. Given away at a 1968 New York concert.)
ELEKTRA (45648 "Kick Out the Jams") 5-10 69
Picture Sleeves
A² (333 "Looking at You") 100-125 68
(Reportedly 500 made.)
LPs: 10/12-inch
ALIVE/TOTAL ENERGY ("Looking at You") 5-10 95
(10-inch LP. Selection number not known.)
ALIVE/TOTAL ENERGY (0005 "Power Trip") 5-10 94
(10-inch LP.)
ALIVE/TOTAL ENERGY (0008 "Ice Pick Slim") 5-10 95
(10-inch LP.)
ALIVE/TOTAL ENERGY (0051 Alive") 5-10 95
(10-inch LP.)
ALIVE/TOTAL ENERGY (2010 "American Ruse") 5-10 95
(10-inch LP.)
ATLANTIC (8247 "Back in the USA") 25-50 70
ATLANTIC (8285 "High Time") 25-50 71
ELEKTRA (74042 "Kick Out the Jams") 30-40 69
(Title track has X-rated intro. Gatefold cover. With John Sinclair's liner notes inside cover.)
ELEKTRA (74042 "Kick Out the Jams") 15-20 69
(Title track has censored intro. Cover does not have John Sinclair liner notes.)
ELEKTRA (74042 "Kick Out the Jams") 5-8 91
(Title track has censored intro. Cover does not have John Sinclair liner notes.)
Members: Rob Tyner; Robert Derminer; Fred "Sonic" Smith; Michael Davis; Wayne Kramer; Sigrid Dobat; Dennis Thompson.
Also see DESTROY ALL MONSTERS
Also see KRAMER, Wayne
Also see SINCLAIR, John
Also see SONIC'S RENDEZVOUS

MC SHY-D
LPs: 10/12-inch
LUKE SKYWALKER 5-8 87

MC SQUARED
Singles: 7-inch
REPRISE 3-6 68

MDC
LPs: 10/12-inch
RADICAL 5-10 81-83

MFQ
Singles: 7-inch
W.B. 5-10 64-65
Members: Chip Douglas; Cyrus Faryar.
Also see GUARD, Dave, & Whiskeyhill Singers

MFSB LP '73
(Mothers, Fathers, Sisters, Brothers)
Singles: 7-inch
PHILADELPHIA INT'L 3-5 74-78
TSOP 3-5 81
LPs: 10/12-inch
PHILADELPHIA INT'L 8-10 73-78
TSOP 5-8 80
Members: Norman Harris; Ronnie Baker; Bobby Eli; Bobby Martin; Earl Young; Don Renaldo; Albert Barone; Charles Apollonia; Angelo Petrella; Diana Barnett; Davis Barnett; Romeo Distefano; Rudy Maliazia; Christine Reeves; Joe Donofrio; Leno Zachery; Joe DeAngelis; Danny Ellions; Scott Temple; Milton Phibbs; Frederich Jainer; Fred Linge; Ricci Genovese; Edward Cascaralle; Rocco Bene; Robert Hartzell; Karl Chambers; Roland Chambers; Dexter Wansel; Ron Harding; Terri Wells; James Smith; Evon Solot; Larry McKenna; Clifford Rudd; Miguel Fuentes; Evette Benton; John Usry; Dennis Harris; Don Renaldo; Marc Rubin; Derek Graves; Lenny Pakula; John Faith; Alphonso Carey; Billy Johnson; Steve Green; Leon Huff; Carleton Kent; Quinton Joseph; Carla Benson; Bob Malach; David Cruse; Steve Gold; Barbara Ingram; Joel Bryant.
Also see B-H-Y
Also see DE VAUGN, William
Also see ELECTRIC INDIAN
Also see ELI'S SECOND COMING
Also see GAMBLE, Kenny
Also see HUFF, Leon
Also see JAMES BOYS
Also see LOCOMOTIONS
Also see MUSIC MAKERS
Also see NOBLES, Cliff
Also see PEOPLE'S CHOICE
Also see PHILADELPHIA INTERNATIONAL ALL STARS
Also see TOMORROW
Also see TRAMMPS
Also see VOLCANOS
Also see WANSEL, Dexter
Also see WELLS, Terri

MFSB & THREE DEGREES P&R '74
Singles: 7-inch
PHILADELPHIA INT'L 3-5 74
Also see MFSB
Also see THREE DEGREES

MG & ESCORTS
Singles: 7-inch
MALA ("Next to Nowhere") 5-10 67
(Selection number not known.)
REO (8936 "Please Don't Ever Change") 10-20 67
(Canadian.)
REO (8960 "I Can't Go On") 10-20 67
(Canadian.)
REO (8975 "A Someday Fool") 10-20 67
(Canadian.)
REO (8998 "Next to Nowhere") 10-20 67
(Canadian.)

MGs
(Memphis Group)
Singles: 7-inch
STAX 3-5 73
LPs: 10/12-inch
STAX 8-12 73
Members: Steve Cropper; Donald Dunn; Al Jackson, Jr.
Also see BOOKER T. & MGs
Also see VAN-DELLS

MGM ORCHESTRA
Singles: 7-inch
MGM (61147 "Grand Prix") 4-8 66
Picture Sleeves
MGM (61147 "Grand Prix") 10-15 66

M.H. ROYALS
Singles: 7-inch
ABC (10907 "Tomorrow's Dead") 10-20 68
ABC (10957 "Old Town") 10-20 68

M&Ms
(M-M's & the Peanuts)
Singles: 7-inch
MONEY (101 "Open Up Your Eyes") 15-25 64
MONEY (107 "I Found My Love") 15-25 65
MONEY (111 "Without a Word") 15-25 65

M+M: see MARTHA & MUFFINS

MJT PLUS 3
(Walter Perkins & MJT Plus 3)
Singles: 7-inch
VEE JAY ("The Whiffenpoof Song") 8-12 60
(No selection number used. Promotional issue only.)
LPs: 10/12-inch
ARGO (621 "Daddy-O Presents") 50-75 57
VEE JAY (1013 "Walter Perkins & MJT Plus 3") 40-60 59
(Maroon label.)
VEE JAY (1013 "Walter Perkins & MJT Plus 3") 25-50 60
(Black label.)
VEE JAY (3008 "Make Everybody Happy") 25-50 60
VEE JAY (3014 "MJT Plus 3") 25-50 60
Members: Walter Perkins; Bob Cranshaw; Frank Strozier; Paul Serrano; Nicky Hill.

MnMs
Singles: 7-inch
QUARK 3-5
Member: Marcy Marcs.

M.O.D. LP '87
LPs: 10/12-inch
CAROLINE 5-8 88
MEGAFORCE 5-8 87-89

M'PAX
Singles: 7-inch
SUN-RAY (144 "Mistakes") 5-10

M.P.D. LIMITED
Singles: 7-inch
LTD 5-10 65

MPG
LPs: 10/12-inch
A&M 5-8 81

MSG: see McAULEY SCHENKER GROUP

M-3s
Singles: 7-inch
ABC-PAR 10-20 66
U.A. 5-10 65

M.V.P.s
Singles: 7-inch
BUDDAH (262 "Turning My Heartbeat Up") 15-25 72

M-ZEE BAND
LPs: 10/12-inch
MIRAGE 5-10 81

MABASA, Lemmy
Singles: 7-inch
PHILIPS (40335 "The Mad Kids") 10-20 65

MABE, Robby, & Outcasts
Singles: 7-inch
ROTAB (1013 "I'm Lonely") 8-12

MABLEY, Moms LP '61
Singles: 7-inch
MERCURY 3-5 69-71
EPs: 7-inch
CHESS 5-10 63
LPs: 10/12-inch
CHESS 15-25 61-64
MERCURY 10-20 64-70

MABLEY, Moms / George Kirby / Heartbreakers / Keynotes
LPs: 10/12-inch
VANGUARD (9093 "Comedy Night at the Apollo") 50-100 61
(Demand is primarily for the R&B tracks by the Heartbreakers and the Keynotes.)

MABLEY, Moms, & Pigmeat Markham
LPs: 10/12-inch
CHESS 10-20 64-71
Also see MABLEY, Moms
Also see MARKHAM, Pigmeat

MABON, Willie R&B '52
(With His Combo)
Singles: 78 rpm
CHESS 10-20 52-56
FEDERAL 15-25 57
PARROT 50-100 53
Singles: 7-inch
CHESS (1531 "I Don't Know") 100-200 53
(Colored vinyl.)
CHESS (1531 "I Don't Know") 40-60 53
(Black vinyl.)
CHESS (1538 "I'm Mad") 40-60 53
CHESS (1548 "You're a Fool") 40-60 53
CHESS (1554 "I Got to Go") 40-60 53
CHESS (1564 "Would You, Baby") 40-60 54
CHESS (1580 "Poison Ivy") 40-60 54
CHESS (1592 "Come on Baby") 40-60 54
CHESS (1608 "The Seventh Son") 30-50 55
CHESS (1627 "Knock on Wood") 30-50 56
DELTA (3004 "Light Up Your Lamp") 5-10
FEDERAL (12306 "Light Up Your Lamp") 15-25 57
FORMAL 4-6 62
MAD (1298 "I Gotta Go Now") 10-20 60
MAD (1300 "I Don't Know") 10-20 60
PARROT (1050 "I Don't Know") 150-250 53
U.S.A. 5-10 63-65
LPs: 10/12-inch
CHESS (1439 "Willie Mabon") 75-125 59
Also see BIG WILLIE

MABRY, Betty
Singles: 7-inch
COLUMBIA 4-8 68
DCP 4-8 65

MAC, Barbara Lee
Singles: 7-inch
CUCA (6635 "Big Fat Mama") 15-25 66

MAC, Billy
(Billy Mack)
Singles: 7-inch
MISS BETTY (34 "I Can't Sleep")
MUSIC MAKERS (107 "Tomorrow Night") 10-20 61
PHILIPS (40301 "Too Much") 5-10 65

MAC, Bobby
(Bobby Mac Trio)
Singles: 7-inch
AUDITION (6108 "Maria") 10-15 66
ORIGINAL SOUND (068 "Walking Together") 10-15 67
VENDED (104 "How Was Your Weekend") 200-400 62

MAC, Fleetwood: see FLEETWOOD MAC

MAC, George
Singles: 7-inch
MAC (512966 "I Want to Be with You Baby") 20-40

MAC, Jimmy C&W '84
Singles: 7-inch
AV 3-4 84

MAC, Johnny
Singles: 7-inch
STUDIO 5-8

MAC, Lou
(Lu Mac)
Singles: 78 rpm
BLUE LAKE 15-25 54-55
Singles: 7-inch
BLUE LAKE (108 "Come Back, Little Daddy") 50-75 54
(Black vinyl.)
BLUE LAKE (108 "Come Back, Little Daddy") 100-200 54
(Red vinyl.)
BLUE LAKE (114 "Slow Down") 50-75 55
(Black vinyl.)
BLUE LAKE (114 "Slow Down") 100-200 55
(Red vinyl.)
BLUE LAKE (117 "Albert Is His Name") 50-75 55
(Black vinyl.)
BLUE LAKE (117 "Albert Is His Name") 100-200 55
(Red vinyl.)
BLUE LAKE (119 "Take Your Trouble to a Friend") 50-75 55
(Black vinyl.)
BLUE LAKE (119 "Take Your Trouble to a Friend") 100-200 55
(Red vinyl.)

MAC & MIKE
Singles: 7-inch
GLORY (273 "Be My Next") 10-20 58

MAC BAND R&B/LP '88
(Featuring the McCampbell Brothers)
Singles: 7-inch
MCA 3-4 88
LPs: 10/12-inch
MCA 5-8 88

MAC TRUQUE
Singles: 7-inch
CAPITOL 3-5 67
LPs: 10/12-inch
CAPITOL 10-15 69

MAC'S WILDFIRE
LPs: 10/12-inch
LARKSPUR 5-8 80

MacALPINE, Tony LP '87
LPs: 10/12-inch
SQUAWK 5-8 87

MACAMBO, J.J.
Singles: 7-inch
CONQUEST (1001 "Kitty") 10-20 63

MacARTHUR, James P&R '63
Singles: 7-inch
SCEPTER 4-8 62-63
TRIODEX 5-10 61

MacDONALD, Jeanette, & Nelson Eddy LP '59
EPs: 7-inch
RCA (Except 220) 4-8 61
RCA (220 "Rose Marie") 10-20 52
LPs: 10/12-inch
RCA (16 "Rose Marie") 40-50 52
RCA (526 "Rose Marie") 10-20 66
RCA (1000 series) 5-10 75
RCA (1700 series) 10-20 59
RCA (2400 series) 5-8 77
RCA (3900 series) 5-8 81

MacDONALD, Ralph R&B/LP '77
Singles: 12-inch
POLYDOR 4-6 84-85
Singles: 7-inch
MARLIN 3-5 76-79
POLYDOR 3-4 84-85
LPs: 10/12-inch
MARLIN 6-10 76-79
POLYDOR 5-8 84-85

MacDONALD, Ralph, & Bill Withers P&R '84
Singles: 7-inch
POLYDOR 3-4 84
Also see MacDONALD, Ralph
Also see WITHERS, Bill

MACEO, Big: see BIG MACEO

MACEO & ALL THE KING'S MEN
Singles: 7-inch
EXCELLO 5-10 72
HOUSE of FOX 5-10 70
LPs: 10/12-inch
EXCELLO 10-15 72

MACEO & MACKS R&B '70
Singles: 7-inch
PEOPLE 3-6 73-74
LPs: 10/12-inch
PEOPLE 8-12 74
Member: Maceo Parker.
Also see PARLIAMENT

MacGREGOR, Byron P&R/C&W '74
Singles: 7-inch
CAPITOL 3-5 75
WESTBOUND 3-5 74
LPs: 10/12-inch
WESTBOUND 5-10 74

MacGREGOR, Mary P&R '76
Singles: 7-inch
ARIOLA 3-5 78
ARIOLA AMERICA 3-5 76-77
RSO 3-5 79-80
LPs: 10/12-inch
ARIOLA AMERICA 8-10 77
Also see ASSOCIATION / Bobby Vee / Mike Love / Mary MacGregor

MACH, Leon
Singles: 7-inch
LAVENDER (1554 "You Hurt Me So") 75-100 60

MACH V
Singles: 7-inch
ASSOCIATED ARTISTS 8-12

MACHE, Billy
Singles: 7-inch
IMPALA (1156 "It Makes No Difference") 20-30 59

MACHINATIONS D&D '83
Singles: 12-inch
A&M 4-6 83
Singles: 7-inch
A&M 3-5 83
LPs: 10/12-inch
A&M 5-8 83

MACHINE
Singles: 7-inch
BEVERLY HILLS 3-5 70
Also see MANILLA MACHINE

MACHINE R&B '79
Singles: 7-inch
RCA 3-5 79-80
LPs: 10/12-inch
RCA 5-10 80

MACHINE
Singles: 7-inch
SCREAM 3-4 84
Members: Jim Pompeo; Marty O'Farrell; Walt Johnson; Norman Bryant; Cheek Lindsey.

MACHO LP '78
Singles: 7-inch
PRELUDE 3-5 78
LPs: 10/12-inch
PRELUDE 5-10 78

MACIAS, George, & Original Royal Bops
Singles: 7-inch
R-B (501 "So Alone") 300-500

MACINTOSH, Brownie
Singles: 7-inch
CORI 4-8

MACK, Andy
Singles: 7-inch
CHESS (13401 "Do You Wanta Go") 5-10

MACK, Bill
Singles: 78 rpm
IMPERIAL 15-30 52-54
JUBILEE (9002 "Paper Doll") 4-8 54
STARDAY 35-50 56
Singles: 7-inch
IMPERIAL (8174 "Play My Boogie") 25-40 52
IMPERIAL (8212 "I'm Not Free") 15-25 53
IMPERIAL (8225 "That's How I Feel") 15-25 54
IMPERIAL (8242 "We Waltzed in My Dreams") 15-25 54
IMPERIAL (8278 "Sue Suzie Boogie") 20-30 54
JUBILEE (9002 "Paper Doll") 5-10 54
STARDAY (231 "Kitty Kat") 75-125 56
STARDAY (252 "Cat Just in Town") 75-125 56
STARDAY (280 "It's Saturday Night") 75-125 56

MACK, Billy
(With Bobby Anderson & Band)
Singles: 7-inch
R&H (001 "I Refuse to Cry") 20-30 50s

MACK, Bobby
Singles: 7-inch
ACE of HEARTS 3-5 73
B-MAC (723 "Waitin' for You to Call") 10-15 59
DIXIE (2026 "Who Put the Blues in Your Heart") 15-25 59
MIDAS 8-12
TEMPUS 10-15 59

MACK, Dell
Singles: 7-inch
GOLDBAND 5-10

MACK, Gary C&W '76
Singles: 7-inch
GRAND PRIZE 3-4 83
SOUNDWAVES 3-5 76

MACK, Iona
(McMackon Mack)
Singles: 7-inch
McMACKON 8-12

MACK, Jack, & Heart Attack
Singles: 7-inch
FULL MOON....3-5 82
LPs: 10/12-inch
FULL MOON....5-10 82

MACK, Jeani
Singles: 7-inch
CLASS....10-20 59

MACK, Jimmie, & Watts
Singles: 7-inch
ELGIN....15-25 60
GEE....10-20 60

MACK, Jimmie
(With the Jumpers)
Singles: 7-inch
BIG TREE....3-5 78-79
RCA....3-5 80
LPs: 10/12-inch
BIG TREE....8-10 78-79
RCA....5-8 80

MACK, Jimmy
Singles: 7-inch
PALMER (5019 "My World Is on Fire")....100-200

MACK, Jimmy, & Music Factory
Singles: 7-inch
ATLANTIC....4-8 68

MACK, Lonnie P&R/R&B/LP '63
(With Pismo)
Singles: 7-inch
ABC....3-5 73
A.M.G....3-6
BARRY....3-5
CAPITOL....3-5 77
COLLECTABLES....3-4 80s
ELEKTRA....3-5 71
FRATERNITY....5-10 63-68
ROULETTE....3-5 75
LPs: 10/12-inch
ALLIGATOR....5-8 85-86
CAPITOL....8-10 77
ELEKTRA....10-20 69-71
FRATERNITY (SF-1014 "Wham of That Memphis Man")....25-50 63
(Monaural.)
FRATERNITY (SSF-1014 "Wham of That Memphis Man")....50-100 63
(Stereo.)
TRIP....8-10 75
Members: Lonnie Mack; Jim Keltner; Tim Drummond.
Also see ALABAMA STATE TROUPERS

MACK, Lonnie, & Rusty York
LPs: 10/12-inch
QCA....10-15 73
Also see MACK, Lonnie
Also see YORK, Rusty

MACK, Melody
Singles: 78 rpm
RAYMOR....5-10 54
Singles: 7-inch
RAYMOR....10-20 54

MACK, Oscar
Singles: 7-inch
STAX....10-20 64
VOLT....8-12 63

MACK, Ronnie
Singles: 7-inch
LONESOME TOWN....3-4 86
ROLLIN' ROCK....3-5 80s
Also see CAMPI, Ray

MACK, Teddy, & Mackinteers
Singles: 7-inch
MONROE ("Is There Any Doubt") 50-100
(No selection number used.)

MACK, Warner C&W/P&R '57
Singles: 78 rpm
DECCA....5-15 57
Singles: 7-inch
DECCA (30301 thru 31684)....5-15 57-64
DECCA (31774 thru 33045)....3-6 65-73
KAPP....5-10 61-62
LOST GOLD....3-5 93
MCA....3-5 73-76
PAGEBOY....3-5 77-81
SCARLET....5-10 60
TOP RANK....5-10 60
EPs: 7-inch
DECCA....5-10 65
LPs: 10/12-inch
CORAL....5-10 73
DECCA....8-18 65-70
KAPP....12-25 61-66
PAGEBOY....5-10
SAPPHIRE....5-10
Session: Jordanaires.
Also see DEAN, Jimmy / David Houston / Warner Mack / Autry Inman
Also see JORDANAIRES

MacKAY, Bruce
LPs: 10/12-inch
ORO....10-15

MacKAY, Rabbit, & Somis Rhythm Band
Singles: 7-inch
UNI....4-6 69
LPs: 10/12-inch
UNI....10-15 68-69

MACKEY, Bobby C&W '82
Singles: 7-inch
MOON SHINE....3-4 82

MACKEY, Linda
Singles: 7-inch
VJ INT'L....4-8
Picture Sleeves
VJ INT'L....5-10

MacKENZIE, Gisele P&R '52
Singles: 78 rpm
CAPITOL....3-5 51-54
VIK....3-5 56
"X"....3-5 55
Singles: 7-inch
CAPITOL....5-10 51-54
EVEREST....4-8 60
MERCURY....4-8 63
VIK....5-10 56
"X"....5-10 55
Picture Sleeves
VIK....5-10 56
"X"....5-10 55
EPs: 7-inch
CAPITOL....5-10 53-69
VIK....5-10 56
LPs: 10/12-inch
CAMDEN....10-20 59
EVEREST....10-20 60
GLENDALE....5-8 78
MERCURY....10-20 63
RCA....10-20 59
SUNSET....8-12 67
VIK....15-25 56

MACKLIN, Danny
Singles: 7-inch
REDD HEDD....4-6 70

MacMURRAY, Fred
Singles: 7-inch
BUENA VISTA (381 "Flubber")....5-10 61
Picture Sleeves
BUENA VISTA (381 "Flubber")....15-25 61
(Sleeve pictures Annette.)
Also see ANNETTE

MacNEISH, Jerry
Singles: 78 rpm
NOR-VA-JAK....4-8 50s
Singles: 7-inch
NOR-VA-JAK....5-10 50s

MACON
Singles: 7-inch
CAPRICORN....3-5 70

MacRAE, Gordon P&R '47
Singles: 78 rpm
CAPITOL....3-5 47-57
Singles: 7-inch
CAPITOL....4-8 50-68
EPs: 7-inch
CAPITOL....5-10 54-57
ROYALE....5-10
LPs: 10/12-inch
CAPITOL....10-25 54-69
EVON....10-15 50s
RONDO-LETTE....15-30
Also see DESMOND, Johnny / John Gary / Gordon MacRae
Also see MARTIN, Dean / Bob Eberly / Gordon MacRae

MacRAE, Gordon, & Jo Stafford P&R '48
Singles: 78 rpm
CAPITOL....4-8 48-50
Singles: 7-inch
CAPITOL....4-8 62
LPs: 10/12-inch
CAPITOL (1600 & 1900 series)....10-20 62-63
CAPITOL (11000 series)....4-8 79
Also see BRYANT, Anita / Jo Stafford & Gordon MacRae
Also see MacRAE, Gordon
Also see STAFFORD, Jo

MacRAE, Johnny
Singles: 7-inch
CANDIX....5-10 60
FELSTED....5-10 62
GARPAX....5-10 63
LANDA....5-10 61
MUSICOR....4-8 65

MacRAE, Meredith, with Candy Johnson's Exciters
Singles: 7-inch
CANJO (103 "Image of a Boy")....8-12 64
Also see JOHNSON, Candy

MACREE, Vincent
Singles: 7-inch
GAME TIME....10-20 57

MAD ANDY'S TWIST COMBO
Singles: 7-inch
ORIGINAL SOUND (85 "Painted Smile")....10-15 68

MAD ANGEL
Singles: 7-inch
BASF (15345 "Can't Run, Can't Hide")....10-15 74

MAD CAPS
Singles: 7-inch
COOL (100 "Chit Chat")....10-20 58
COOL (101 "Jam Sam")....10-20 58

MAD DOCTORS: see PAUL & PACK / Mad Doctors

MAD DOG
LPs: 10/12-inch
FISH HEAD....10-15

MAD ENGLISHMEN & FURYS
Singles: 7-inch
VEE SIX (1023 "Beatle Mania")....10-20 64

MAD HATTERS
Singles: 7-inch
ASCOT (2197 "I Need Love")....10-20 65
FONTANA (1582 "I'll Come Running")....10-15 67
LPs: 10/12-inch
20TH FOX (4141 "At Midnight")....20-30 64
Also see FALLEN ANGELS

MAD HATTERS / Apollos
LPs: 10/12-inch
CICADELIC....8-10 80s

MAD LADS P&R/R&B '65
Singles: 7-inch
MARK-FI (1934 "Why")....20-40 62
CAPITOL....5-10 64
STAX....10-20 64
VOLT (100 series)....5-15 65-68
VOLT (4000 series)....3-8 69-73
LPs: 10/12-inch
COLLECTABLES....6-8 86
VOLT (400 series)....15-25 66
VOLT (6000 series)....10-15 69-73
Members: Julius Green; John Williams; Robert Phillips; Sam Nelson; Cliff Billops Jr.; William Brown.
Also see OLLIE & NIGHTINGALES

MAD LADS
Singles: 7-inch
MARK-FI (1934 "Why")....100-200 62
Session: H.B. Barnum.
Also see BARNUM, H.B.

MAD LADS
(Fabulous Mad Lads)
Singles: 7-inch
CUCA....8-12 68
RAYNARD....5-10 65
Members: Gary Lane; Norm Sherian; Larry Lynne; Paul Frederick; Frank Deaton; Wayne Walters; Jerry Mallon; Al Babicky.
Also see DARNELLS
Also see LANE, Gary & Mad Lads

MAD LADS
(Fabulous Mad Lads)
Singles: 7-inch
IGL....8-12 60s
K-ARK....5-10 60s
TARGET....5-10 68
TEEN TOWN....5-10 60s

MAD LADDS
Singles: 7-inch
TREY (300 "Midnight Terror")....10-20 64

MAD MAN JONES: see JONES, Mad Man

MAD MARTIANS
Singles: 7-inch
SATELLITE (33617 "Outer Space Looters")....20-30 57

MAD MIKE & MANIACS
Singles: 7-inch
HUNCH (345 "Quarter to Four")....10-15 61

MAD MILO
Singles: 7-inch
COMBO (131 "Elvis on Trial")....25-40 57

MAD MILO / Roy Tan & Combo
Singles: 7-inch
MILLION (20018 "Elvis for Christmas")....20-30 57
Also see MAD MILO

MAD MODS
Singles: 7-inch
COBRA (1131 "The Mad Mod")....10-20 65
JOX (69 "No One Like Me")....15-25 65

MAD PERFESSER
Singles: 7-inch
BIG TOP....4-8

MAD PLAIDS
Singles: 7-inch
GOLDEN CREST (533 "Blood Rare")....15-20 59

MAD RIVER LP '69
Singles: 7-inch
CAPITOL....5-10 68-69
EPs: 7-inch
WEE (10021 "Mad River")....25-50 68
LPs: 10/12-inch
CAPITOL (185 "Paradise Bar and Grill")....25-35 69
CAPITOL (2985 "Mad River")....25-35 68
Members: David Robinson; Tom Manning; Lawrence Hammond; Rick Bochner; Greg Dewey; Ron Wilson.

MADADORS
Singles: 7-inch
FEATURE (105 "Girl, Don't Leave Me")....15-25 66
Members: Phil Holzbauer; Larry Black; Jerry Adams; Gene Bell; Nels Christiansen; Jerry Stefani; Ron Buchek.
Also see EASY STREET

MADAGASCAR R&B '81
Singles: 7-inch
ARISTA....3-5 81-82
Members: John Barnes; Marva King.
Also see KING, Marva

MADAM
LPs: 10/12-inch
KENT....10-12 72

MADAME X R&B/LP '87
Singles: 7-inch
ATLANTIC....3-4 87
LORIMAR....3-4 88
LPs: 10/12-inch
ATLANTIC....5-8 87

MADARA, Johnny
(Johnny Madera)
Singles: 78 rpm
PREP (110 "Lovesick")....15-25 57
Singles: 7-inch
BAMBOO....10-15 61
LANDA....10-20 62
MATT....10-15 60
PREP (110 "Lovesick")....15-25 57
PREP (129 "My Big Thrill")....15-25 58
SWAN....10-15 60
Also see SPOKESMEN

MADCATS
LPs: 10/12-inch
BUDDAH....5-8 79

MADDENING CROWD
Singles: 7-inch
PARROT....4-8 68

MADDIN, Eddie
Singles: 7-inch
TAMPA....5-10 59

MADDIN, Jimmy
(Jimmy Madden)
Singles: 7-inch
AMERICAN INT'L (525 "Bird Dog")....20-30 59
AMERICAN INT'L (542 "Tongue Tied")....20-30 59
CONCERT ROOM....5-10 63
DOT....10-20 57
FABOR....8-12 61
FREEDOM....10-15 59
GOLDEN WEST....4-8
IMPERIAL....10-20 58
RADAR....4-8

MADDOX, Johnny P&R '52
(With the Rhythmasters)
Singles: 78 rpm
DOT....3-8 50-57
Singles: 7-inch
ABC....3-5 74
DOT....5-15 50-63
EPs: 7-inch
DOT....5-10 52-56
LPs: 10/12-inch
DOT (Except 102)....10-25 55-67
DOT (102 "Authentic Ragtime")....20-30 52
(10-inch LP.)
HAMILTON....10-15 64
PARAMOUNT....5-10 74

MADDOX, Rose C&W '59
Singles: 7-inch
CAPITOL....5-10 58-63
UNI....3-6 67
EPs: 7-inch
CAPITOL....10-20 58-60
COLUMBIA....10-20 58
LPs: 10/12-inch
CAPITOL (T-1312 "The One Rose")....25-35 60
(Monaural.)
CAPITOL (ST-1312 "The One Rose")....30-40 60
(Stereo.)
CAPITOL (ST-1437 "Glory Bound Train")....30-40 60
(Stereo.)
CAPITOL (ST-1437 "Glory Bound Train")....35-55 60
(Stereo.)
CAPITOL (T-1548 "Big Bouquet of Roses")....30-40 60
(Monaural.)
CAPITOL (ST-1548 "Big Bouquet of Roses")....35-45 60
(Stereo.)
CAPITOL (T-1799 "Rose Maddox Sings Bluegrass")....30-40 62
(Monaural.)
CAPITOL (ST-1799 "Rose Maddox Sings Bluegrass")....35-45 62
(Stereo.)
CAPITOL (T-1993 "Alone with You")....15-25 63
(Monaural.)
CAPITOL (ST-1993 "Alone with You")....20-30 63
(Stereo.)
COLUMBIA (1159 "Precious Memories")....40-50 58
HARMONY....10-20 64
PICKWICK/HILLTOP....10-15 60s
STARDAY....10-20 70
VARRICK....6-12 83
Session: Emmylou Harris; Bill Monroe; Vern Williams; Merle Haggard and the Strangers.
Also see HAGGARD, Merle
Also see HARRIS, Emmylou
Also see MONROE, Bill
Also see OWENS, Buck, & Rose Maddox

MADDOX, Susan
Singles: 7-inch
ZANZI....4-8

MADDOX, Sylvia
Singles: 7-inch
DUKE....4-8 67

MADDOX, Walt
Singles: 7-inch
CALICO (118 "Would I")....10-20
WESTERN WORLD....5-10

MADDY BROTHERS
Singles: 7-inch
CELESTIAL (109 "Rockin' Party")....60-80 58
RA-RA (900 "Mixed Up")....15-25

MADE IN JAPAN BAND
Singles: 7-inch
CAPITOL....3-5 71

MADE IN U.S.A. R&B '77
Singles: 7-inch
DE-LITE....3-5 77

MADELAINE
LPs: 10/12-inch
CHI-SOUND....5-10 78

MADERA, Johnny: see MADARA, Johnny

MADHATTANS
Singles: 78 rpm
ATLANTIC....10-15 57
Singles: 7-inch
ATLANTIC....10-15 57

MADHATTERS
Singles: 7-inch
CARDINAL (72 "Game Is Done")....25-35 67
CARDINAL (77 "You May See Me Cry")....25-35 67
Member: Dale Menton.
Also see BEST THINGS
Also see GESTURES
Also see MASON, Tommy, & Madhatters
Also see MENTON, Dale

MADHOUSE
LPs: 10/12-inch
TODAY....8-12 72

MADHOUSE R&B/LP '87
Singles: 7-inch
PAISLEY PARK....3-4 87
Picture Sleeves
PAISLEY PARK....3-4 87
LPs: 10/12-inch
PAISLEY PARK....5-8 87
Also see PRINCE

MADIGAN, Betty P&R '54
Singles: 78 rpm
CORAL....3-6 57
JAY DEE....3-6 54
MGM (11000 series)....3-6 53-56
Singles: 7-inch
CORAL....4-8 57-59
JAY DEE....5-10 54
MGM (11000 series)....5-10 53-56
MGM (13000 series)....4-6 66-67
20TH FOX....4-6 64
U.A....4-8 60-61
EPs: 7-inch
JAY DEE....5-10 54
MGM....5-10 57
LPs: 10/12-inch
CORAL....10-20 62
MGM....10-20 57-69

MADISON, Al
Singles: 7-inch
GOLDEN CREST ("The Society") 10-20 61
(Selection number not known.)

MADISON, Glen
Singles: 7-inch
EBONY (105 "When You Dance")....50-75 64
Also see DELCOS

MADISON, Ronnie
(With the Valmars, Skip Esterly & Orchestra)
Singles: 78 rpm
CORAL....10-20 57
Singles: 7-inch
CORAL (61812 "True Love Gone")....20-30 57
STORM (987 "Linda")....50-100 59

MADISON AVENUE
Singles: 12-inch
A&M....4-6 84

MADISON BROTHERS
Singles: 7-inch
APT (25050 "Trusting in You")....50-100 60
CEDARGROVE (314 "Trusting in You")....150-250 60
SURE (1002 "Give Me Your Heart")....150-250 58
V-TONE (231 "Did We Go Steady Too Soon")....40-60

MADISON REVUE
Singles: 7-inch
MADISON (4130 "Another Man")....15-25 67

MADISON STREET
Singles: 7-inch
INFINITY....3-5 79
MILLENIUM....3-6 78
Also see RANDY & RAINBOWS
Also see TRIANGLE

MADISONS
Singles: 7-inch
JOMADA (601 "Only a Fool")....10-20 65
LAWN (240 "The Wind and the Rain")....20-30 64
LIMELIGHT (3018 "Because I Got You")....10-20 64
MGM (13312 "Cheryl Anne")....20-30 65
Also see MADISONS / Monterays
Also see SANTOS, Larry

MADISONS
LPs: 10/12-inch
SELECT....5-8 81

MADISONS / Monterays
Singles: 7-inch
TWIN-HIT (2685 "Valerie")............25-30 65
Also see MADISONS
Also see MONTERAYS

MADMEN OF NOTE
Singles: 7-inch
RA (104 "Peppermint Fink")........... 5-10

MADNESS LP '80
Singles: 12-inch
GEFFEN...................................... 4-6 83
STIFF... 8-12
(Promotional only.)
Singles: 7-inch
GEFFEN...................................... 3-4 83-84
SIRE.. 3-5 80-81
Picture Sleeves
GEFFEN...................................... 3-4 83-84
LPs: 10/12-inch
GEFFEN...................................... 5-8 83-84
SIRE.. 5-8 80-81

MADNESS, Bernie
Singles: 7-inch
BANG...................................... 10-15 66

MADONNA P&R/R&B/D&D/LP '83
Singles: 12-inch
MAVERICK (6074 "Fever")............15-20 92
(Two colored vinyl discs. Promotional issue only.)
MAVERICK (40585 "Erotica")........... 4-8 92
SIRE (20212 "Borderline")........... 5-10 84
SIRE (20239 "Like a Virgin")........ 5-10 84
SIRE (20304 "Material Girl")........ 5-10 85
SIRE (20335 "Angel")................... 5-10 85
SIRE (20369 "Dress You Up")........ 5-10 85
SIRE (20461 "Live to Tell")........... 5-10 86
SIRE (20597 "Open Your Heart")..... 5-10 87
SIRE (20633 "La Isla Bonita")........ 5-10 87
SIRE (20762 "Causing a Commotion")........................ 5-10 87
SIRE (21170 "Like a Prayer")......... 5-10 89
SIRE (21225 "Express Yourself")..... 5-10 89
SIRE (21427 "Keep It Together").... 5-10 90
SIRE (21513 "Vogue")................... 5-10 90
SIRE (21820 "Justify My Love")...... 5-10 91
SIRE (21813 "Rescue Me")............. 5-10 91
SIRE (23867 "Holiday")................. 5-10 83
SIRE (26553 "True Blue")............... 5-10 86
SIRE (29715 "Physical Attraction").. 5-10 83
Singles: 7-inch
GEFFEN...................................... 3-5 85
SIRE (Black vinyl)........................ 3-6 83-92
SIRE (28591 "True Blue"))............. 5-8 86
(Colored vinyl.)
Picture Sleeves
GEFFEN...................................... 3-5 85
SIRE (Except 29354)..................... 3-8 83-90
SIRE (29354 "Borderline")............ 5-10 84
(Poster sleeve.)
LPs: 10/12-inch
Sire (PRO-A7311 "Bedtime Stories")................................45-55 ??
(Double colored vinyl LP set. Promotional issue only.)
SIRE (23867 "Madonna")................ 5-8 83
SIRE (25157 "Like a Virgin").......... 5-8 83
(Black vinyl.)
SIRE (1-25157 "Like a Virgin").....75-125 83
(Colored vinyl. Promotional issue only.)
SIRE (25442 "True Blue")............... 5-8 86
SIRE (25611 "Who's That Girl")...... 5-8 87
SIRE (25535 "You Can Dance")........ 5-8 87
SIRE (25844 "Like a Prayer")......... 5-8 89
SIRE (26209 "I'm Breathless")........ 5-8 90
Also see BERLIN / Madonna

MADRI HI FIVE
Singles: 7-inch
VEE JAY (523 "Putti Putti")...........10-20 63

MADRIGAL
Singles: 7-inch
PUBLIC.. 3-5
SSS INT'L.................................... 3-5

MADRIS, Bobby
Singles: 7-inch
PROFILE...................................... 3-4 86

MADURA LP '71
LPs: 10/12-inch
COLUMBIA................................10-15 71-73

MADURI, Carl
Singles: 7-inch
CAMEO...................................... 4-8 61
MERCURY.................................. 5-10 57
ROULETTE................................. 4-8 66
WARWICK.................................. 4-8 61

MAE, April, & Blue Skies: see APRIL MAE & Blue Skies

MAE, Daisy: see DAISY MAE & Her Hepcats

MAE, Maria: see MARIA MAE

MAEDER, Gene
Singles: 7-inch
VANDA (702 "Gremlin in the Kremlin")................................. 8-12

MAELEN, Jimmy
Singles: 7-inch
PAVILLION................................... 3-4 80

MAESEN, Liv
Singles: 7-inch
CADET.. 3-6

MAESTRO, Johnny P&R '61
(With the Crests; with Coeds; with Del Satins; Johnny Mastro)
Singles: 7-inch
APT (25075 "She's All Mine Alone")..15-25 65
BUDDAH...................................5-10 71-72
CAMEO....................................10-20 63-64
COED (545 "Model Girl")...............15-25 61
COED (549 "What a Surprise")......15-25 61
COED (552 "Mr Happiness")..........15-25 61
COED (557 "I.O.U.")......................25-35 61
COED (562 "Besame Baby")........75-100 61
COLLECTABLES............................ 3-4 80s
PARKWAY (118 "Is It You")...........10-20 67
PARKWAY (987 "Heartburn")........10-15 66
PARKWAY (987 "Heartburn")........30-40 66
(Single sided disc. Promotional issue only.)
SCEPTER (12112 "I'm Stepping Out of the Picture")..50-100 65
U.A. (474 "Before I Loved Her").....20-30 62
LPs: 10/12-inch
BUDDAH (5091 "The Johnny Maestro Story")......................................25-35 71
(Price includes inserts.)
HARVEY (1000 "Biggest Hits")......10-20 81
(Colored vinyl.)
Also see ARDELLS
Also see BROOKLYN BRIDGE
Also see CRESTS
Also see DEL SATINS
Also see JOEL & DYMENSIONS
Also see MASTERS, Johnny
Also see PACK

MAESTRO, Johnny, & Tymes
Singles: 7-inch
POPULAR REQUEST...................... 3-6
Also see MAESTRO, Johnny
Also see TYMES

MAFFERS
Singles: 7-inch
VOLT... 3-5 74

MAFFITT & DAVIES
Singles: 7-inch
CAPITOL.................................... 4-8 68
LPs: 10/12-inch
CAPITOL..................................10-15 68

MAG. SANCTUARY BAND
Singles: 7-inch
VERITAS..................................12-18
Also see FABULOUS FLIPPERS

MAGAZINE
LPs: 10/12-inch
VIRGIN.....................................5-10 80

MAGAZINE
Singles: 7-inch
I.R.S. 3-4 81-82
LPs: 10/12-inch
I.R.S. 5-8 81-82
Member: Howard Devoto.
Also see DEVOTO, Howard

MAGAZINE 60 P&R '86
Singles: 7-inch
BAJA.. 3-4 86

MAGEE, Dale
Singles: 7-inch
SPI (10830 "Long Live the King")..... 4-8 79

MAGEE, Sterling
Singles: 7-inch
TANGERINE................................ 4-8 67

MAGENTA
LPs: 10/12-inch
MAGENTA.................................10-12 76

MAGESTRO, Miss Toni
Singles: 7-inch
USA (1223 "My Boyfriend Charlie").......................................20-30 67

MAGGARD, Cledus C&W/P&R '75
(With the Citizen's Band)
Singles: 7-inch
MERCURY................................ 3-5 75-79
LPs: 10/12-inch
MERCURY..................................6-12 76

MAGI
Singles: 7-inch
WAND (197 "Rockin' Crickets").......8-12 65

MAGI
LPs: 10/12-inch
UNCLE DIRTY'S (6102 "Win Or Lose")...................................250-350 72
Members: Tom Stevens; Larry Stutzman.

MAGI
Singles: 7-inch
CLARIDGE (431 Overnight Sensation")..................................15-25 77
FARR (71271 "Rock & Roll Lady").10-20 71
MONSTER (0001 "I Think I Love You")......................................10-20 60s

MAGIC
Singles: 7-inch
ARMADILLO (22 "One Minus Two")......................................10-20 69
ARMADILLO (23 "California")........10-20 70
MONSTER (0001 "I Think I Love You")..15-25
LPs: 10/12-inch
ARMADILLO (8031 "Enclosed").200-400 70
RARE EARTH (527 "Magic").........10-15 71
Members: Nick King; Duane King; Joey Myrcia; Gary Harger.

MAGIC
Singles: 7-inch
CARDINAL...................................3-6 72
Members: Susan Deicicchi; Ron Montagna; Jack Burke; Jim Deicicchi.

MAGIC, Awood
Singles: 7-inch
MINIT.......................................4-8 61

MAGIC BAND
Singles: 7-inch
GNP...3-5

MAGIC BOTTLE
Singles: 7-inch
TRIPP......................................5-10 69

MAGIC CHRISTIANS
Singles: 7-inch
COMMONWEALTH UNITED...........4-8 70
Member: Trevor Burton.
Also see MOVE

MAGIC CIRCLE
Singles: 7-inch
MIRA..5-10 66

MAGIC CIRCLE
Singles: 7-inch
20TH FOX.................................3-5 73

MAGIC FERN
Singles: 7-inch
JERDEN (813 "Maggie")..............15-20 66
PICADILLY (235 "Maggie")...........10-15 67
PICADILLY (240 "Nellie")............10-15 67
LPs: 10/12-inch
PANORAMA (108 "Magic Fern") 100-150 80

MAGIC FLEET
Singles: 7-inch
HOT BISCUIT..............................4-8 68

MAGIC GRASS
Singles: 7-inch
DECCA......................................3-6 69

MAGIC KNIGHTS
Singles: 7-inch
CEE-JAY (577 "Searching for Tomorrow")...................................20-30 60

MAGIC LADY P&R '82
Singles: 12-inch
A&M...4-6 82
Singles: 7-inch
A&M...3-4 82
MOTOWN..................................3-4 88
LPs: 10/12-inch
A&M...5-8 82
ARISTA.....................................5-8 80
MOTOWN..................................5-8 88
Members: Linda Stokes; Jackie Ball; Kimberly Ball; Jackie Steele.

MAGIC LANTERN: see HAYMARKET SQUARE

MAGIC LANTERNS P&R '68
Singles: 7-inch
ATLANTIC.................................5-10 68-70
BIG TREE..................................3-5 71
CHARISMA.................................3-5 72
EPIC...4-8 66
Picture Sleeves
EPIC (10062 "Excuse Me Baby")...10-15 66
LPs: 10/12-inch
ATLANTIC.................................12-15 69
Members: Jim Bilsbury; Bev Beveridge; Mike "Ozzy" Osborne; Peter Garner; Harry Paul Ward; Albert Hammond.

MAGIC MUSHROOM
Singles: 7-inch
W.B. (5846 "I'm Gone")................15-25 66
Also see SONS

MAGIC MUSHROOMS P&R '66
Singles: 7-inch
A&M (815 "Never More")..............10-15 66
EAST COAST (1001 "Let the Rain Be Me")..10-15 68
PHILIPS (40483 "Look in My Face")..10-15 67
Members: Chris Gaylord; Michael Allen.
Also see LYRICS

MAGIC ORGAN LP '72
(Jerry Smith)
Singles: 7-inch
RANWOOD..................................3-5 72-77
LPs: 10/12-inch
RANWOOD..................................4-8 72-83
SUNNYVALE................................4-6 79
Also see SMITH, Jerry

MAGIC PLANTS
Singles: 7-inch
VERVE (10377 "I'm a Nothing").....20-30 66
Member: Tom Finn.
Also see LEFT BANKE

MAGIC REIGN
Singles: 7-inch
JAMIE.......................................5-8 68-69

MAGIC RING
Singles: 7-inch
MUSIC FACTORY.........................5-8 68
SMASH.......................................5-8 67
TANTRA (3105 "Do I Love You")...10-20 60s

MAGIC SAM
(Sam Maghett)
Singles: 78 rpm
COBRA....................................15-25 57
Singles: 7-inch
BRIGHT STAR (1037 "I'll Pay You Back")..5-10 69
CHIEF (7013 "Mr. Charlie")...........15-25 60
CHIEF (7033 "You Don't Have to Work")..15-25 60
CHIEF (7017 "Square Dance Rock")..15-25 61
CHIEF (7026 "Every Night About This Time")..15-25 61
CHIEF (7033 "Blue Light Boogie") 15-25 61
COBRA (5013 "All Your Love")......20-30 57
COBRA (5021 "Everything Gonna Be Alright")......................................20-30 57
COBRA (5025 "All Night Long").....20-30 58
COBRA (5029 "Easy, Baby")..........20-30 58
CRASH (425 "Out of Bad Luck")......8-12 66
MINIT...5-8 60s

MAGIC SAM BLUES BAND
LPs: 10/12-inch
DELMARK..................................10-15 68-69
INTERMEDIA...............................5-8

MAGIC SAND
LPs: 10/12-inch
UNI...10-12 71

MAGIC SHIP
Singles: 7-inch
B.T. PUPPY (548 "Green Plant")...10-20 68
P.I.P. (8936 "We Gotta Live On")....8-12 73
Members: Tom Nikosey; Cosmo Riozzi; Phil Polimeni; Mike Garrigan; Rob Buckman.
Also see MAJIC SHIP

MAGIC SLIM & TEARDROPS
Singles: 7-inch
JA-WES (0105 "Love My Baby").......25-50 68
MEAN MISTREATER.......................8-12
EPs: 7-inch
ROOSTER BLUES.............................5-8 81
LPs: 10/12-inch
ALLIGATOR....................................5-8 82

MAGIC STRAY
Singles: 7-inch
TRY (630 "Give Me Your Love")....20-30

MAGIC SWIRLING SHIP
Singles: 7-inch
CADET (5642 "Love in Your Eyes")..15-25 68

MAGIC TONES
Singles: 78 rpm
KING....................................100-150 53
Singles: 7-inch
KING (4665 "When I Kneel Down to Pray")...................................300-500 53
KING (4681 "How Can You Treat Me This Way")....................................300-500 53

MAGIC TONES
Singles: 7-inch
HOWFUM (3686 "Tears in My Eyes").................................2000-3000 57
(Identification number shown since no selection number is used.)

MAGIC TONES / Mustangs
Singles: 7-inch
STOOP SOUNDS (502 "Tears in My Eyes"/"Over the Rainbow")........100-150 96
(Limited edition. Estimates range from less than 10 to a few dozen made.)
Also see MAGIC TONES
Also see MUSTANGS

MAGIC TONES
(Magictones)
Singles: 7-inch
MAH'S (1037 "It's Better to Love") 10-15 68
WESTBOUND (152 "How Can I Forget You")......................................10-20 60s
WESTBOUND (180 "I've Changed")..10-20 65
WHEELSVILLE (106 "Got to Get a Little Closer")..15-25 66
WHEELSVILLE (114 "How Can I Forget You")..75-125 66
Also see UNDISPUTED TRUTH

MAGIC TONES
Singles: 7-inch
RAM-BROCK..................................4-8

MAGIC TOUCH R&B '71
Singles: 7-inch
BLACK FALCON (19102 "Step Into My World")..4-6 71

MAGIC TOUCH
(Vito & Salutations)
Singles: 7-inch
ROULETTE..................................5-10 73
Also see VITO & SALUTATIONS

MAGIC TRIPLETS
Singles: 7-inch
DECCA.......................................8-10 69
KEF..8-10 71
Also see ENERGIZERS

MAGICAL CONNECTION
Singles: 7-inch
SOLAR SUN..................................3-5 72

MAGICIANS
Singles: 7-inch
COLUMBIA (43435 "An Invitation to Cry")..5-10 65
COLUMBIA (43608 "About My Love")..5-10 66
COLUMBIA (43725 "And I'll Tell the World")..5-10 65
COLUMBIA (44061 "Double Good Feeling")..5-10 67
Picture Sleeves
COLUMBIA (43435 "An Invitation to Cry")..10-20 65
Members: Mike Appell; Garry Bonner; Everett Jacobs; Alan Gordon; John Townley; Jake Jacobs.
Also see BONNER, Garry
Also see JAKE & Family Jewels
Also see TEX & CHEX

MAGICIANS
Singles: 7-inch
VILLA (703 "Love, Let's Try Again")......................................25-50 66
VILLA (704 "Why Do I Do These Foolish Things")..................................100-150 66
VILLA (706 "Why Must You Cry")..50-75 66
(Has "Villa Records" on two lines at top.)
VILLA (706-A "Why Must You Cry")..15-25 66
(Has "Villa Records" on one line at top.)

MAGICIANS
Singles: 7-inch
LONDON.....................................5-10 66

MAGICS
Singles: 7-inch
DEBRA (1003 "Chapel Bells")........50-75 63
(First issued as by the Palisades. Some copies have "Magics" label applied on top of "Palisades" one.)
Also see GENOVA, Tommy
Also see LANZO, Mike, & Blue Counts
Also see PALISADES
Also see PRECISIONS

MAGICS
Singles: 7-inch
BELL (606 "Zombie Walk")..............5-10 64

MAGICTONES: see MAGIC TONES

MAGISTRATES P&R '68
Singles: 7-inch
MGM..4-8 68-69
Member: Jean Hillary.
Also see DOVELLS

MAGLIA, Brent
Singles: 7-inch
FANTASY....................................3-5 78

MAGMA
LPs: 10/12-inch
A&M...8-12 73-74
TOMATO......................................6-10 78

MAGNA CARTA
Singles: 7-inch
DUNHILL......................................3-5 70
LPs: 10/12-inch
ARIOLA AMERICA (50014 "Puttin' It Back")..8-12
DUNHILL (50091 "Sessions")........10-15 70

MAGNATONES
Singles: 7-inch
CEDARGROVE (313 "I Need You")..30-40 60
TIME (108 "I Need You")...............8-12

MAGNET
Singles: 7-inch
DATE..3-6 70

MAGNET
LPs: 10/12-inch
A&M..5-10 79

MAGNETICS
Singles: 7-inch
ALLRITE (620 "Where Are You")....25-35 62
BONNIE (107374 "Lady in Green").......................................500-1000
(We're not sure if this is the selection number or identification number.)
J.V. (2501 "Oh Love").................15-25

MAGNETICS
LPs: 10/12-inch
ROLLIN' ROCK.............................5-10 82
Members: Tom Svornich; Freda Johnson; Jeff Poskin; Steve Grindle; Tom Berghan.

MAGNETICS
Singles: 7-inch
RA-SEL.......................................8-12
SABLE...8-12

MAGNETS
Singles: 7-inch
GROOVE (0058 "You Just Say the Word")..25-35 65
RCA (7391 "When the School Bells Ring")..15-20 58

MAGNETS
Singles: 7-inch
KEYS (3 "Swingin' Organ")............10-15 59

MAGNETS
Singles: 7-inch
LONDON.....................................5-10 63

MAGNIFICENT FOUR
Singles: 7-inch
BLAST (210 "The Closer You Are")..25-35 63
COLLECTABLES............................3-4 80s
WHALE (506 "The Closer You Are")..50-75 61

MAGNIFICENT MALOCHI
Singles: 7-inch
BRUNSWICK.................................4-8 68

MAGNIFICENT MEN P&R/LP '67
Singles: 7-inch
CAPITOL 4-8 66-68
MERCURY 3-6 69
LPs: 10/12-inch
CAPITOL 10-20 67-68
MERCURY 8-12 70
Members: Dave Bupp; Buddy King; Tom Pane; Bob Angelucci; Terry Crousore; Tommy Hoover; Jimmy Seville; Billy Richter.
Also see DEL-CHORDS

MAGNIFICENT MONTA-GUE
Singles: 7-inch
ERA 8-12 58

MAGNIFICENT SIX
Singles: 7-inch
L BROWN (01659 "Forever More") 25-50 60s
(Identification number shown since no selection number is used.)

MAGNIFICENT SEVEN
Singles: 7-inch
THELMA (12282 "The Groove") 50-75 63
(Previously issued as *Let's Do It*, by Don Davis & His Groovers.)
Also see DAVIS, Don, & His Groovers

MAGNIFICENT 7
(Magnificent VII)
Singles: 7-inch
DIAL (4074 "Ooh Baby Baby") 10-20 68
DIMENSION 10-15 65
EASTERN (611 "Since You Been Gone") 20-30 66
LEMCO (882 "Stubborn Kind of Fellow") 10-20 65

MAGNIFICENT 7
LPs: 10/12-inch
POWER 5-10

MAGNIFICENTS R&B '56
Singles: 78 rpm
VEE JAY 25-50 56-58
Singles: 7-inch
CHECKER (1016 "Do You Mind") 5-10 62
COLLECTABLES 3-4 80s
KANSOMA (03 "Do You Mind") 5-10 62
VEE JAY (183 "Up on the Mountain") 30-60 56
VEE JAY (208 "Caddy Bo") 40-75 56
VEE JAY (235 "Off the Mountain") 30-60 57
VEE JAY (281 "Don't Leave Me") 50-75 58
VEE JAY (367 "Up on the Mountain") 10-15 60
Also see EL DORADOS

MAGNIFICENTS
Singles: 7-inch
DEE GEE (3008 "My Heart Is Calling") 30-40 65
KANSOMA (3 "Do You Mind") 20-30 60s

MAGNIFICENTS
Singles: 7-inch
BIRTH 4-6 69
Members: Richard Bogan; Helen Wrice; Howard West; Tony Rogers; Ron Morgan. Richard Osborne; Jake Kowal.
Also see HOT PROPERTY

MAGNOLIAS
Singles: 7-inch
MASTERCRAFT 10-15 63

MAGNUM
LPs: 10/12-inch
JET 5-8 78-82

MAGNUM FORCE R&B '85
Singles: 7-inch
PAULA 3-4 85
LPs: 10/12-inch
WIZARD 5-8 78

MaGOO, Mr: see BACKUS, Jim

MAGPIES
Singles: 7-inch
ABC 4-8 67

MAHAFFAY, Chuck, & Individuals
LP: 10/12-inch
21 RECORDS 10-15 64
Also see INDIVIDUALS

MAHAL, TAJ: see TAJ MAHAL

MAHALIC, Johnny
(Johnny Mihalic)
Singles: 7-inch
SELECT (725 "Cotton Fields") 5-10 63
Also see GILREATH, James
Also see NITE-LITERS

MAHAN, Benny
Singles: 7-inch
MONUMENT 3-5 70
SCRATCH (5582 "She Knows How") 10-20

MAHAR, Jamie
Singles: 7-inch
W.B. 4-8 64

MAHARAJAHS
Singles: 7-inch
FLIP (332 "Why Don't You Answer") 15-25 58
FLIP (335 "Oh Shirley") 35-50 58

MAHARIS, George P&R/LP '62
Singles: 7-inch
EPIC 4-6 62-66
Picture Sleeves
EPIC 4-6 62-64
LPs: 10/12-inch
EPIC 10-15 62-66

MAHARREY, Moe
Singles: 7-inch
MARLO (1527 "Giddy-Upa-Ding Dong") 8-12 62

MAHOGANY
Singles: 7-inch
EPIC 3-5 70
LPs: 10/12-inch
EPIC 10-12 70

MAHOGANY D&D '83
Singles: 12-inch
WEST END 4-6 82
Singles: 7-inch
WEST END 3-4 82

MAHOGANY RUSH LP '74
Singles: 7-inch
COLUMBIA 3-5 76-82
20TH FOX 3-5 74-75
LPs: 10/12-inch
COLUMBIA 8-12 76-82
20TH FOX 10-12 73-75
Member: Frank Marino.
Also see MARINO, Frank, & Mahogany Rush

MAHONEY, John Culliton
Singles: 7-inch
AMHERST 3-5 74

MAHONEY, Skip, & Casuals R&B '74
Singles: 7-inch
ABET 4-8 76-77
D.C. INT'L 4-6 74
Members: Skip Mahoney; Tracy Reid; Julius Jerome; Elwood Morgan.
Also see SKIP & CASUALS

MAI TAI R&B '85
Singles: 12-inch
MERCURY 4-6 87
Singles: 7-inch
CRITIQUE 3-4 85-86
MERCURY 3-4 87
Picture Sleeves
CRITIQUE 3-4 86
LPs: 10/12-inch
MERCURY 5-8 87
Members: Carol DeWindt; Jettie Well; Mildred Douglas.

MAIDEN, Sidney
(With the Ramblers)
Singles: 78 rpm
FLASH 15-25 55
IMPERIAL 20-30 52
Singles: 7-inch
FLASH (101 "Hurray, Hurray Baby") 30-50 55
IMPERIAL (5189 "Honey Bee Blues") 50-75 52
LPs: 10/12-inch
PRESTIGE BLUESVILLE 15-20 63

MAIDEN, Sidney / Al Simmons
Singles: 78 rpm
DIG (138 "Hand Me Down Baby") 15-25 56
Singles: 7-inch
DIG (138 "Hand Me Down Baby") 25-50 56
Also see MAIDEN, Sidney
Also see SIMMONS, Al, & Slim Green

MAILER MACKENZIE BAND
Singles: 7-inch
AMPEX 3-5 71
LPs: 10/12-inch
AMPEX 8-10 71

MAIN ATTRACTION
Singles: 7-inch
TOWER 4-8 68-69
LPs: 10/12-inch
TOWER 10-20 68
Also see ALLAN, Davie / Eternity's Children / Main Attraction / Sunrays

MAIN ATTRACTION R&B '86
Singles: 7-inch
RCA 3-4 86
LPs: 10/12-inch
RCA 5-8 86

MAIN CHANGE
Singles: 7-inch
NEBULA (Sunshine Is Her Way) 50-75 71
(Selection number not known.)

MAIN EVENTS
Singles: 7-inch
U.A. 3-5 71

MAIN INGREDIENT P&R/R&B/LP '70
(Featuring Cuba Gooding)
Singles: 7-inch
RCA 3-5 69-81
ZAKIA 3-4 86
Picture Sleeves
RCA 3-6 70-81
LPs: 10/12-inch
COLLECTABLES 5-8 88
RCA 8-12 70-81
Members: Cuba Gooding; Don McPhearson; Luther Simmons; Tony Sylvester.
Also see GOODING, Cuba
Also see POETS
Also see SYLVESTER, Tony, & New Ingredient

MAIN SQUEEZE
Singles: 7-inch
ROULETTE 3-5 72

MAINEGRA, Richard
Singles: 7-inch
COLUMBIA 3-5 75

MAINES BROTHERS BAND C&W '83
Singles: 7-inch
MERCURY 3-4 83-86
Members: Lloyd Maines; Donnie Maines; Kenny Maines; Steve Maines; Jerry Brownlow; Gary Banks; Richard Bowden.

MAINHORSE
LPs: 10/12-inch
VISA/IMPORT 8-10 71

MAINIERI, Mike
(Mike Mainieri Quartet)
Singles: 7-inch
ARISTA 3-5 78
SOLID STATE 4-6 68
LPs: 10/12-inch
W.B. 5-10 81

MAINSTREETERS R&B '73
Singles: 7-inch
EVENT 3-5 73

MAITLAND, Dexter
Singles: 7-inch
U.A. 3-6 69
Picture Sleeves
U.A. 3-6 69

MAJENICS
Singles: 7-inch
CONROY 4-8 68
Members: Pat Sabino; Sharon Daddio; Chip Murano; Paul Vanacore; Joe Mineri; Randy Buccelli.

MAJESTIC
Singles: 7-inch
EQUATOR (1401 "Send My Baby Back to Me") 40-50

MAJESTIC ARROWS
Singles: 7-inch
BANDIT 8-12

MAJESTICS
Singles: 78 rpm
MARLIN (802 "Nitey Nite") 100-200 56
Singles: 7-inch
MARLIN (802 "Nitey Nite") 300-400 56
Member: Sam Moore.
Also see CULMER, Little Iris
Also see SAM & DAVE

MAJESTICS
(Johnny Mitchell & Majestics)
Singles: 7-inch
CHEX (1000 "Give Me a Cigarette") 50-75 62
CHEX (1000 "So I Can Forget") 25-35 62
(Same number used twice.)
CHEX (1004 "Unhappy & Blue") 30-40 62
CHEX (1006 "Lonely Heart") 15-25 62
CHEX (1009 "Baby") 15-20 63
V.I.P. (25028 "Say You") 400-600 65
(Promotional issue only.)
Also see MITCHELL, Johnny

MAJESTICS
(With the Nightwinds; Majestic's)
Singles: 7-inch
CONTOUR (501 "Hard Times") 40-60 60
EIGHT BALL 10-20 59
FARO 10-20 59
NRC (502 "Please Don't Say No") 200-300 58
SIOUX (91459 "Lone Stranger") 30-40 59
20TH FOX (171 "Lone Stranger") 10-20 59

MAJESTICS
(With Al Rogers & His Combo)
Singles: 7-inch
KNIGHT (105 "Pennies for a Beggar") 100-150 60

MAJESTICS
Singles: 7-inch
JORDAN (123 "Angel of Love") 50-100 61
(First issue.)
LINDA (111 "Strange World") 30-50 63
LINDA (121 "Girl of My Dreams") 50-75 63
NU-TONE (123 "Angel of Love") 30-50 61
(First issue.)
PIXIE (6901 "Angel of Love") 20-30 61

MAJESTICS
Singles: 7-inch
CHANSON (1007 "Safari") 10-15 62
CHANSON (1008 "Blue Flame") 10-15 62
CHESS (1802 "Oasis") 10-15 61

MAJESTICS
Singles: 7-inch
BOSS (1001 "Let's Make It") 10-20 60s
DUNES (2014 "Boss Walk") 10-20 62
SAM (112 "Jaguar") 20-30 62
SAM (117 "Riptide") 20-30 62
SAM (123 "XL-3") 20-30 62
Also see PHANTOMS

MAJESTICS
Singles: 7-inch
SALVATION (11 "Movin' On") 8-12 62

MAJESTICS
Singles: 7-inch
JCP (1018 "Round & Round") 10-20 64

MAJESTICS
Singles: 7-inch
MGM 4-8 66

MAJESTICS
Singles: 7-inch
JCP (1018 "Round & Round") 10-20 64

MAJESTICS
Singles: 7-inch
MALA 5-10 60s

MAJESTY R&B '85
Singles: 7-inch
GOLDEN BOY 3-4 85

MAJIC SHIP
Singles: 7-inch
B.T. PUPPY (548 "Green Plant") 5-10 68
CRAZY HORSE (1311 Hummin' ") 10-20 69
CRAZY HORSE (1317 "On the Edge") 10-20 69
CRAZY HORSE (1322 "Night Time Music") 10-20 70
MAGIC-L (519 "Hummin' ") 20-30 66
LPs: 10/12-inch
BEL AMI (711 "Majic Ship") 300-500 67
Members: Tom Nikosey; Cosmo Riozzi; Phil Polimeni; Mike Garrigan; Rob Buckman.
Also see MAGIC SHIP

MAJIC STRAY
Singles: 7-inch
TRY 4-8 69

MAJIK
Singles: 12-inch
GOLD COAST 4-6 82
Singles: 7-inch
STORMY 3-5 80
LPs: 10/12-inch
STORMY 5-8 80

MAJOR & LIEUTENANTS
Singles: 7-inch
NIGHT OWL (6812 "The Thing") 10-20 68

MAJOR ARCANA
LP: 10/12-inch
A MAJOR 10-15 76
Members: Jim Spencer; Jay Borkenhagen; Sigmund Snopek; Tom Ruppenthal.
Also see BAROQUES
Also see BLOOMSBURY PEOPLE

MAJOR IV
Singles: 7-inch
VENTURE 4-8

MAJOR HOOPLE'S BOARDING HOUSE
Singles: 7-inch
CHELSEA 3-5 73

MAJOR LANCE: see LANCE, Major

MAJOR THINKERS
LPs: 10/12-inch
PORTRAIT 5-8 83

MAJORETTES
Singles: 7-inch
TROY (1000 "White Levis") 15-25 63
TROY (1004 "Let's Do the Kangaroo") 10-15 63
Picture Sleeves
TROY (1000 "White Levis") 25-35 63
Member: Becky Page; Shiela Page; Joanna Page; Suzy Page.

MAJORITY
Singles: 7-inch
LONDON 4-8 65

MAJORLETTES
Singles: 7-inch
MERCURY 3-5 70

MAJORS
Singles: 78 rpm
DERBY (763 "At Last") 200-300 51
DERBY (779 "Laughing on the Outside") 200-300 51
Singles: 7-inch
DERBY (763 "At Last") 500-1000 51
DERBY (779 "Laughing on the Outside") 500-1000 51
Member: Bernard Beckum.

MAJORS
Singles: 7-inch
FELSTED (8501 "Rockin' the Boogie") 15-25 57
FELSTED (8576 "Les Qua") 30-50 59
FELSTED (8707 "Les Qua") 20-30 64
FELSTED (8707 "I Found My Love") 15-25 64

MAJORS P&R/R&B '62
Singles: 7-inch
IMPERIAL 10-20 62-64
LPs: 10/12-inch
IMPERIAL (9222 "Meet the Majors") 50-75 63
(Monaural.)
IMPERIAL (12222 "Meet the Majors") 50-100 63
(Stereo.)
Members: Ricky Cordo; Eugene Glass; Idella Morris; Frank Troutt; Ronald Gathers.

MAJORS
(With the Osie Johnson Orchestra)
Singles: 78 rpm
ORIGINAL (1003 "Big Eyes") 100-150 54
Singles: 7-inch
ORIGINAL (1003 "Big Eyes") 300-500 54
(Colored vinyl.)

MAJORS
Singles: 7-inch
VENTURE (606 "Down in the Ghetto") 25-40

MAJORS
Singles: 7-inch
BIG THREE (403 "Lost in the City") 40-50
MAGNET 10-20

MAJORS, Farrah Fawcett
Singles: 7-inch
NBR 3-5 77
Picture Sleeves
NBR 5-8 77

MAJORS, Lee
Singles: 7-inch
SCOTTI BROS 3-5 82

MAKEBA, Miriam LP '63
Singles: 7-inch
KAPP 4-8 62
MERCURY 4-6 66
RCA 4-8 64
REPRISE 4-6 67-68
LPs: 10/12-inch
KAPP 10-20 62
MERCURY 10-15 66
PETERS INT'L 5-8 81
RCA 10-20 60-68
REPRISE 10-15 67
Also see BELAFONTE, Harry, & Miriam Makeba
Also see MANHATTAN BROTHERS & Miriam Makeba

MAKEM, Tommy: see CLANCY BROTHERS & Tommy Makem

MALABOUS, Ron: see MALABOUS RON

MALABOUS RON
Singles: 7-inch
TOMI 8-12 60s

MALACHI
LPs: 10/12-inch
VERVE (5024 "Holy Music") 20-30 67
(Monaural.)
VERVE (6-5024 "Holy Music") 30-40 67
(Stereo.)

MALCHAK, Tim C&W '86
Singles: 7-inch
ALPINE 3-4 86-88
UNIVERSAL 3-4 89

MALCHAK & RUCKER C&W '84
Singles: 7-inch
ALPINE 3-4 85-86
REVOLVER 3-4 84-85
Members: Tim Malchak; Dwight Rucker.
Also see MALCHAK, Tim

MALCOLM X R&B '84
Singles: 7-inch
TOMMY BOY 3-4 83-84
LPs: 10/12-inch
DOUGLAS 8-15 68-71

MALCOLM & CHRIS
LPs: 10/12-inch
BLUES TIME 10-12 70

MALCONTENTS
Singles: 7-inch
GEMS (18348 "Motivated Action") 8-12

MALDONEERS
(With the Deltairs)
Singles: 7-inch
VINTAGE 4-6 73
Member: Johnny Maldon.
Also see DELTAIRS

MALDOON
(Clive Maldoon)
LPs: 10/12-inch
W.B. 8-10 73
Also see CURTISS, Dave, & Clive Maldoon

MALEMEN
Singles: 7-inch
P.H. (3455 "My Little Girl") 15-25

MALEMEN
Singles: 12-inch
MERCURY 4-6 83-84
Singles: 7-inch
MERCURY 3-4 83-84
LPs: 10/12-inch
MERCURY 5-8 83

MALENA, Don C&W '87
Singles: 7-inch
MAXIMA 3-4 87-88

MALIBOOZ
LPs: 10/12-inch
RHINO 5-8 81

MALIBUS
Singles: 7-inch
DUKE (457 "I Just Can't Stand It") 10-20
SURE SHOT 8-15 65-68

MALIBUS
Singles: 7-inch
MALIBU (1 "Cry") 15-25 66
PLANET (58 "Cry") 10-15 67

MALIBUS
Singles: 7-inch
QUILL (104 "Runaway")....10-20 66

MALIBUS
(Malibu's)
Singles: 7-inch
WHITE WHALE....4-6 69

MALIBUS
Singles: 7-inch
ORLYN....8-12

MALIBU-BUS
(Malibu-Bu's)
Singles: 7-inch
CRH (101 "Caravan")....10-20 62

MALICE LP '87
LPs: 10/12-inch
ATLANTIC....5-8 87
ENIGMA....5-8

MALLARD
Singles: 7-inch
VIRGIN....3-5 77
LPs: 10/12-inch
VIRGIN....8-10 77
Also see CAPTAIN BEEFHEART

MALLARD, Earl, & His Web Feet of Rhythm / Maurice Douglas & His Dirty Hot Dogs / Seymour Tiptop's Mighty Weird Trio / Crab & Creech
Singles: 7-inch
1-SHOT (180 "Wax Donuts")....5-10 78
(Has one track by each group.)

MALLARD, Sax
Singles: 78 rpm
CHECKER (750 "Slow Caboose") 25-50 52
CHECKER (755 "I'm Yours")....25-50 52
MERCURY....10-15 52
Singles: 7-inch
MERCURY (70002 "The Bunny Hop")....15-25 52
Also see CORONETS

MALLETT, Dave
LPs: 10/12-inch
NEWORLD....5-10 78-79

MALLETT, Saundra, & Vandellas
Singles: 7-inch
TAMLA (54067 "Camel Walk")...400-600 62
(Reissued as by LaBrenda Ben.)
Also see BEN, LaBrenda
Also see ELGINS
Also see MARTHA & VANDELLAS

MALLORY, Lee
Singles: 7-inch
VALIANT....5-10 66-67

MALLORY, Willie
Singles: 78 rpm
LANOR....4-6

MALMKVIST, Siw P&R '64
(With Umberto Marcato)
Singles: 7-inch
JUBILEE....4-6 64
KAPP....4-8 61

MALMSTEEN, Yngwie J. LP '85
(Yngwie J. Malmsteen's Rising Force)
LPs: 10/12-inch
MERCURY....5-8 86
POLYDOR....5-8 85-88
Also see ALCATRAZZ
Also see DIO, Ronnie
Also see HEAR 'N AID

MALO P&R/LP '72
Singles: 7-inch
TRAQ....3-5 81
W.B....3-5 72-73
LPs: 10/12-inch
W.B....8-12 72-74
Also see AZTECA
Also see SANTANA, Jorge

MALONE, Cindy
Singles: 7-inch
CAPITOL....4-8 63-66

MALONE, Joan
Singles: 7-inch
CUCA (1236 "Admit It")....5-10 65

MALONE, J.J.
Singles: 7-inch
GALAXY....8-10 60s

MALONE, Ronnie
Singles: 7-inch
FLAGSHIP (914 "My Snow Man")..10-20 57
JUDD (1004 "Lightning Bug"....10-20 58

MALONE, Tommie
(Blind Tom Malone)
Singles: 78 rpm
DECCA....10-20 55
Singles: 7-inch
DECCA....15-25 55
EBONY (1055 "Cow Cow Shake") .20-30 60

MALONE, Tommy
Singles: 7-inch
STERLING (901 "It's Been So Long Baby")....100-200 55
(Red vinyl.)

MALOY, Vince
Singles: 78 rpm
ANGLE TONE....15-25 57
Singles: 7-inch
ANGLE TONE (520 "Flying Love")....15-25 57
END....10-15 58
FELSTED....10-15 59
1223 (475 "I've Been 'Round Your Door Before")....75-100

MALTAIS, Gene
Singles: 78 rpm
DECCA (30387 "Crazy Baby")...100-150 57
Singles: 7-inch
DECCA (30387 "Crazy Baby")...100-200 57
LILAC (3159 "The Raging Sea")....200-300 57
MASSABESIC....5-8 75
REGAL (7502 "Lovemakin' ")....100-150 58

MALTBY, Richard, & Orchestra P&R '54
Singles: 78 rpm
VIK....3-5 56
"X"....3-5 54-55
Singles: 7-inch
COLUMBIA....4-8 59
ROULETTE....4-8 60-61
VIK....5-10 56
"X"....5-10 54-55
Picture Sleeves
VIK....10-15 56
EPs: 7-inch
COLUMBIA....5-10 59
VIK....5-10 56
"X"....8-15 54-55
LPs: 10/12-inch
CAMDEN....10-20 60-62
COLUMBIA....10-20 59
HARMONY....10-20 61
ROULETTE....10-20 60-62
VIK (1051 "Hue-Fi Moods")....20-30 56
VIK (1068 "Manhattan Bandstand")....20-30 56
"X" (1038 "Make Mine Maltby")....20-30 56

MALTEES FOUR
Singles: 7-inch
PACIFIC CHALLENGER (111 "You")....10-15 66

MALVIN, Artie
Singles: 7-inch
BELL....4-8

MALVIN, Artie / Brigadiers
Singles: 78 rpm
PROM....5-10 54
Singles: 7-inch
PROM....10-15 54
(Colored vinyl.)

MAMA & Soul Babies
Singles: 7-inch
LAURIE....4-8 69

MAMA CASS: see ELLIOT, Cass

MAMA CATS
Singles: 7-inch
HIDEOUT (1225 "Miss You")....10-20 66

MAMA LION
Singles: 7-inch
FAMILY PRODUCTIONS....3-5 72-73
LPs: 10/12-inch
FAMILY PRODUCTIONS (Except 2702)....10-15 73
FAMILY PRODUCTIONS (2702 "Mama Lion")....15-20 72

MAMA'S BOYS LP '84
Singles: 7-inch
JIVE....3-4 84-87
LPs: 10/12-inch
JIVE....5-8 84-87

MAMA'S PRIDE
Singles: 7-inch
ATCO....3-5 78-81
LPs: 10/12-inch
ATCO....5-10 81

MAMAS & PAPAS P&R/LP '66
Singles: 7-inch
ABC....3-5 70
DUNHILL....4-8 65-72
MCA....3-5 80-82
Picture Sleeves
DUNHILL (4020 "California Dreamin' ")....50-100 65
(Promotional issue only.)
DUNHILL (4083 "Creeque Alley")....25-35 67
(Promotional issue only.)
DUNHILL (4113 "Dancing Bear")....4-8 67
EPs: 7-inch
ABC....8-15 71
(Promotional issues only.)
DUNHILL....15-20 65
LPs: 10/12-inch
ABC....6-10 76
DUNHILL....10-20 66-73
MCA....5-8 80-82
PICKWICK....6-10 72
Members: John Phillips "Mama" Cass Elliot; Denny Doherty; Michelle Phillips.
Also see BIG THREE
Also see DOHERTY, Denny
Also see ELLIOT, Cass
Also see PHILLIPS, John
Also see PHILLIPS, Michelle

MAMAS & PAPAS / Association / Fifth Dimension
LPs: 10/12-inch
TEE VEE/W.B. SPECIAL PRODUCTIONS....10-20 79
Also see ASSOCIATION
Also see FIFTH DIMENSION

MAMAS & PAPAS / Barry McGuire
EPs: 7-inch
DUNHILL (50005 "This Precious Time")....10-15 66
Also see MAMAS & PAPAS
Also see McGUIRE, Barry

MAMMATAPEE
Singles: 7-inch
WHITFIELD....3-5 80
LPs: 10/12-inch
WHITFIELD....5-8 80-81

MAMMOUTH
Singles: 7-inch
TIRINO....50-100 73

MAM'SELLES
Singles: 78 rpm
VIK....5-10 57
Singles: 7-inch
ABC....4-6 68
BISON....4-8
DIAMOND....4-8 64
VIK....5-10 57

MAN
Singles: 7-inch
COLUMBIA....3-6 69
LPs: 10/12-inch
COLUMBIA....10-12 69
Member: Richard Supa.
Also see SAN FRANCISCO ALL STARS
Also see SUPA, Richard

MAN
Singles: 7-inch
MCA....3-5 76
RCA....3-5 72
U.A....3-5 73-75
LPs: 10/12-inch
MCA....8-10 76
U.A....10-15 73-75
Also see MANPOWER

MAN & WIFE
Singles: 7-inch
EPIC....3-5 70

MAN MACHINE
Singles
KINGSPOT (113 "All Alone in the Zone")....4-8 84
(Football-shaped picture disc.)
Member: Freddie Solomon.

MAN PARRISH: see PARRISH, Man

MAN YOUNG: see YOUNG, Man

MANASSAS LP '72
LPs: 10/12-inch
ATLANTIC....8-12 72-73
Also see STILLS, Stephen

MANCHA, Steve R&B '66
(Clyde Wilson)
Singles: 7-inch
GROOVESVILLE (1001 "You're Still in My Heart")....10-20 65
GROOVESVILLE (1002 "I Don't Want to Lose You")....8-12 66
GROOVESVILLE (1004 "Friday Night")....50-75 66
GROOVESVILLE (1005 "Don't Make Me a Story Teller")....8-12 67
GROOVESVILLE (1007 "Sweet Baby")....10-20 67
WHEELSVILLE (102 "Did My Baby Call")....50-100 65
Also see BARNES, J.J., & Steve Mancha
Also see 100 PROOF Aged in Soul
Also see TWO FRIENDS

MANCHESTER, Melissa LP '73
Singles: 12-inch
ARISTA....4-6 82
CASABLANCA....4-6 84
MCA....4-6 85
Singles: 7-inch
ARISTA....3-5 75-84
BELL....3-5 74
CASABLANCA....3-4 84
MB....4-8 67
MCA....3-4 85
LPs: 10/12-inch
ARISTA....8-10 75-83
BELL....10-12 73-74
CASABLANCA....5-8 84
MCA....5-8 79-85
MFSL....25-50 79
Also see NATIONAL LAMPOON

MANCHESTER, Melissa, & Peabo Bryson P&R '81
Singles: 7-inch
ARISTA....3-5 81
Also see BRYSON, Peabo
Also see MANCHESTER, Melissa

MANCHESTERS
Singles: 7-inch
PEAK (7043 "I Wanna Hold Your Hand")....8-12 64
Picture Sleeves
PEAK (7043 "I Wanna Hold Your Hand")....15-25 64
LPs: 10/12-inch
DIPLOMAT (2307 "Beatlerama")....10-20 64
(Shows title only. No artist credited.)
DIPLOMAT (2307 "Beatlerama")....10-20 64
(Shown as by the Manchesters.)
GUEST STAR (2307 "Beatlerama")10-20 64
(Shows title only. No artists credited.)

MANCHESTERS
Singles: 7-inch
VEE JAY (700 "I Don't Come from England")....10-20 65
Member: David Gates.
Also see GATES, David

MANCHILD
Singles: 7-inch
CAPITOL....3-5 72
LPs: 10/12-inch
CAPITOL....10-15 72

MANCHILD R&B/LP '77
Singles: 7-inch
CHI-SOUND....3-5 77
LPs: 10/12-inch
CHI-SOUND....8-10 77
Members: Kenny Edmonds; Robert Parson; Chuck Bush; Daryl Simmons; Reggie Griffin.
Also see DEELE
Also see GRIFFIN, Reggie, & Technofunk
Also see REDD HOTT

MANCHILD
LPs: 10/12-inch
AZRA/DIPIAZZA (1001 "Manchild")....10-15 84
(Picture disc.)

MANCINI, Henry LP '59
(Henry Mancini's Orchestra & Chorus)
Singles: 7-inch
LIBERTY (1400 series)....3-4 82
LIBERTY (55000 series)....4-8 58-59
RCA (Except 8184)....3-8 59-85
RCA (8184 "Banzai Pipeline")....8-10 63
U.A....3-5 78
W.B....3-5 79-83
Picture Sleeves
RCA (Except 8184)....5-15 59-77
RCA (8184 "Banzai Pipeline")....10-15 63
W.B....3-5 79
EPs: 7-inch
RCA....5-15 60-62
LPs: 10/12-inch
AVCO EMBASSY....10-20 70
CAMDEN....5-15 66-74
LIBERTY (3000 series)....15-25 57-59
LIBERTY (51000 series)....4-8 82
MCA....6-12 75-76
PARAMOUNT....10-15 70
RCA (0013 thru 0098)....5-10 72-73
RCA (0270 "Country Gentleman")....5-8 74
RCA (0672 thru 1928)....5-10 74-76
RCA (1956 "Music from Peter Gunn")....15-25 59
RCA (2040 "More Music from Peter Gunn")....15-25 59
RCA (2101 "The Mancini Touch")..15-25 59
RCA (2147 "The Blues and the Beat")....15-25 60
RCA (2198 "Music from Mr. Lucky")....15-25 60
RCA (2360 "Mr. Lucky Goes Latin")....15-25 61
RCA (2362 "Just You and Me Together Love")....4-8 77
RCA (2258 "Combo")....15-20 62
RCA (2600 series)....10-20 63-64
RCA (2800 & 2900 series)....8-15 64-65
RCA (3000 series)....4-8 78
RCA (3356 "The Latin Sound of Henry Mancini")....10-20 65
RCA (3347 "Best of Henry Mancini, Volume 3")....5-8 79
RCA (3500 series)....6-12 66
RCA (3612 "Merry Mancini Christmas")....10-15 66
RCA (3667 "Pure Gold")....4-8 80
RCA (3668 "Mancini Country")....4-8 80
RCA (3694 thru 3713)....10-20 66-67
RCA (3756 "Warm Shade of Ivory")..4-8 80
RCA (3822 "Best of Henry Mancini") .4-8 80
RCA (3877 "Music of Hawaii")....4-8 81
RCA (3887 "Encore")....8-15 67
RCA (3943 "The Mancini Sound")....4-8 68
RCA (3954 "Country Gentleman")....4-8 67
RCA (3997 thru 4689)....5-15 68-72
RCA (5000 series)....4-8 85
RCA (6000 series)....8-15 66-72
SUNSET....5-10 66
U.A....10-12 70
W.B....10-20 59-73
For a complete listing of soundtracks by this artist, consult *The Official Price Guide to Movie/TV Soundtracks and Original Cast Albums.*
Also see ANN-MARGRET
Also see HIRT, Al / Henry Mancini / Perez Prado
Also see MATHIS, Johnny, & Henry Mancini
Also see PRIDE, Charley

MANCINI, Henry / Al Hirt / Robert Russell Bennett / Melachrino Strings
EPs: 7-inch
RCA (33-151 "Headline Hits")....8-12 61
(Promotional issue, made for Nestle's.)
Also see HIRT, Al
Also see MELACHRINO, George, & His Orchestra

MANCINI, Henry, & Doc Severinsen LP '73
LPs: 10/12-inch
RCA....5-8 72-80
Also see MANCINI, Henry
Also see SEVERINSEN, Doc

MANCINI, Nan, & Do-Its
LPs: 10/12-inch
WINDSONG (3498 "It's a Man's World")....8-12

MANDALA
LPs: 10/12-inch
ATLANTIC (8184 "Soul Crusade") 20-25 68

MANDEL, Harvey LP '69
Singles: 7-inch
PHILIPS....4-8 68
LPs: 10/12-inch
JANUS....8-12 70-74
OVATION....10-15 71
PHILIPS....10-15 68-69
Also see CANNED HEAT

MANDELL, Howie LP '86
LPs: 10/12-inch
W.B....5-8 86

MANDELL, Mike R&B '81
Singles: 7-inch
VANGUARD....3-5 81

MANDELLS
Singles: 7-inch
CHESS (1794 "Darling")....75-100 61
SMART (323 "Darling")....300-400 61
(First issue.)
SMART (325 "Because I Love You")....100-150 61
TRANS WORLD SOUND (222 "I Miss You Baby")....25-50 60s
TRANS WORLD SOUND (701 "There Will Be Tears")....15-20 60s
YORK (202 "It's No Good")....150-250 63

MAN-DELLS
Singles: 7-inch
DANDY (5308 "Bonnie")....50-100

MANDELS
Singles: 7-inch
LILLY (502 "My Kissin' Cousin")....30-40 61

MANDERINS
Singles: 7-inch
BAND BOX (236 "Going Away")....15-25 60

MANDO & CHILI PEPPERS
EPs: 7-inch
GOLDEN CREST (3023 "On the Road with Rock & Roll")....300-400 57
LPs: 10/12-inch
GOLDEN CREST (3023 "On the Road with Rock & Roll")....500-750 57
Members: Armando Mandarez; Jesse Perales; Rudy Martinez; Joe Elizando; Jesse Garcia.
Also see BOSSMEN

MANDOLPH, Bobby
Singles: 78 rpm
SPECIALTY....5-10 56
Singles: 7-inch
SPECIALTY....10-20 56
VAULT....5-15 68-69

MANDOLPH, Margaret
Singles: 7-inch
PLANETARY (102 "Silly Little Girl")....10-20 65
PLANETARY (106 "Something Beautiful")....50-75 65

MANDRAKE
Singles: 7-inch
COLUMBIA....5-10 60-61
Member: Vic Rogers.

MANDRAKE MEMORIAL
Singles: 7-inch
POPPY....5-10 69-70
LPs: 10/12-inch
POPPY (40002 "Mandrake Memorial")....15-25 68
POPPY (40003 "Medium")....15-25 69
POPPY (40006 "Puzzle")....20-30 70
Members: Randy Monaco; Michael Kac.

MANDRAKES
Singles: 7-inch
NOLTA....5-10 61

MANDRE R&B/LP '77
(Andre Lewis)
Singles: 7-inch
MOTOWN....3-5 77-79
LPs: 10/12-inch
MOTOWN....5-10 77-79
Also see MAXAYN

MANDRELL, Barbara C&W '69
Singles: 7-inch
ABC....3-5 78-79
ABC/DOT....3-6 75-78
COLUMBIA....4-8 69-75
EMI....3-4 87-88
KFC (003 "Sweet Weekend Encounter")....8-12 79
(Coincides with "National Winners Kentucky Fried Chicken Song Writing Contest." Promotional issue only.)
MCA (Black vinyl)....3-5 79-86
MCA (8950 "3 Out of 3 Ain't Bad") 40-60 79
(Picture disc. Promotional issue only.)
MCA (52737 "Fast Lanes and Country Roads")....15-20 85
(Colored vinyl. Promotional issue only.)
MCA (52802 "When You Get to the Heart")....15-20 86
(Colored vinyl. Promotional issue only.)
MOSRITE (190 "Queen for a Day")....30-50 66
Picture Sleeves
MCA....3-5 79-85

LPs: 10/12-inch
ABC 8-10 78-79
ABC/DOT 8-12 76-77
COLUMBIA 6-15 71-81
COLUMBIA SPECIAL PRODUCTS .. 5-8 82
EMI 5-8 88
MCA 5-10 79-86
SONGBIRD 5-8 82
TIME-LIFE 5-8 81
Session: Waylon Jennings; Randy Wright.
Also see ALLEN, Deborah
Also see FRICKE, Janie
Also see HOUSTON, David, & Barbara Mandrell
Also see JENNINGS, Waylon
Also see McCOY, Charlie
Also see WRIGHT, Randy

MANDRELL, Barbara, & Lee Greenwood *C&W/LP '84*
Singles: 7-inch
MCA 3-4 84
LPs: 10/12-inch
MCA 5-8 84
Also see GREENWOOD, Lee

MANDRELL, Barbara, & Oak Ridge Boys *C&W '86*
Singles: 7-inch
MCA 3-4 86
Also see MANDRELL, Barbara
Also see OAK RIDGE BOYS

MANDRELL, Louise *C&W '78*
Singles: 7-inch
EPIC 3-5 78-80
RCA 3-4 82-88
LPs: 10/12-inch
RCA 5-10 83-88

MANDRELL, Louise, & R.C. Bannon *C&W '79*
Singles: 7-inch
EPIC 3-5 79-82
LPs: 10/12-inch
EPIC 5-10 79-80
RCA 5-10 82-83
Also see BANNON, R.C.

MANDRELL, Louise, & Eric Carmen *C&W '88*
Singles: 7-inch
RCA 3-4 88
Also see CARMEN, Eric
Also see MANDRELL, Louise

MANDRILL *P&R/LP '71*
Singles: 7-inch
ARISTA 3-5 77-80
LIBERTY 3-4 83
MONTAGE 3-4 82
POLYDOR 3-5 71-74
U.A. 3-5 75-76
LPs: 10/12-inch
ARISTA 8-10 77-80
LIBERTY 5-8 83
POLYDOR 10-12 71-75
U.A. 8-10 75
Members: Louis Wilson; Richard Wilson; Carlos Wilson; Claude Cave; Omar Mesa; Charlie Pardo; Fudgie Kae.
Also see MASSER, Michael, & Mandrill
Also see SURFACE

MANFRED MANN: see MANN, Manfred

MANGANO, Silvana *P&R '53*
Singles: 78 rpm
MGM 3-6 53
Singles: 7-inch
MGM 5-10 53

MANGIONE, Chuck *P&R/LP '71*
(Chuck Mangione Quintet)
Singles: 7-inch
A&M 3-5 75-80
COLUMBIA 3-4 82-84
MERCURY 3-5 71-77
Picture Sleeves
A&M 3-5 78-80
LPs: 10/12-inch
A&M 5-10 75-81
COLUMBIA 5-8 82-84
JAZZLAND (84 "Recuerdo") 40-50 62
(Monaural.)
JAZZLAND (984 "Recuerdo") 50-60 62
(Stereo.)
MFSL 25-50 82
MERCURY 6-12 71-78
MILESTONE 5-8 77
Also see POTTER, Don

MANGIONE BROTHERS SEXTET
Singles: 7-inch
RIVERSIDE (446 "Struttin' with Sandra") 5-10 60
LPs: 10/12-inch
RIVERSIDE (335 "Jazz Brothers") 50-75 60
RIVERSIDE (371 "Jazz Brothers") 40-60 61
Members: Chuck Mangione; Gap Mangione.
Also see MANGIONE, Chuck

MANHATTAN BROTHERS & MIRIAM MAKEBA *P&R '56*
Singles: 78 rpm
LONDON 3-6 56
Singles: 7-inch
LONDON 5-10 56
Also see MAKEBA, Miriam

MANHATTAN RHYTHM KINGS
LPs: 10/12-inch
INNER CITY 5-8 81

MANHATTAN STRINGS
(With Bob Summers)
LPs: 10/12-inch
TOWER 5-10 67

MANHATTAN TRANSFER *P&R/LP '75*
Singles: 7-inch
ATLANTIC (3277 "Clap Your Hands") 5-10 75
ATLANTIC (3292 "Operator") 3-5 75
ATLANTIC (3349 "Helpless") 4-6 76
ATLANTIC (3374 "Chanson D'Amour") 4-6 76
ATLANTIC (3491 "It's Not the Spotlight") 3-5 78
ATLANTIC (3636 "Birdland") 3-5 79
ATLANTIC (3649 "Twilight Zone") 3-5 80
ATLANTIC (3772 "Trickle Trickle") ... 8-12 80
ATLANTIC (3855 "Smile Again") 3-5 81
ATLANTIC (3816 "Boy from New York City") 3-5 81
ATLANTIC (4034 "Route 66") 3-5 82
ATLANTIC (89094 "So You Say") 3-5 88
ATLANTIC (89156 "Soul Food to Go") 3-5 87
ATLANTIC (89533 "Ray's Rockhouse") 3-5 85
ATLANTIC (89594 "Baby Come Back to Me") 8-12 85
ATLANTIC (89695 "Mystery") 3-5 84
ATLANTIC (89720 "American Pop") 3-5 85
ATLANTIC (89786 "Spice of Life") 3-5 83
CAPITOL (2968 "Care for Me") 5-10 70
CAPITOL (3108 "Java Jive") 5-10 71
STOOP SOUNDS (102 "Gloria") 100-150 96
(Limited edition. Estimates range from less than 10 to a few dozen made.)
Picture Sleeves
ATLANTIC (89786 "Spice of Life") 3-6 83
LPs: 10/12-inch
ATLANTIC (16036 "Mecca for Moderns") 8-12 81
ATLANTIC (18133 "The Manhattan Transfer") 8-12 75
ATLANTIC (18183 "Coming Out") 8-12 76
ATLANTIC (19163 "Pastiche") 8-12 78
ATLANTIC (19319 "The Best of Manhattan Transfer") 8-12 81
ATLANTIC (19258 "Extensions") 8-12 79
ATLANTIC (80104 "Bodies and Souls") 8-12 83
ATLANTIC (81233 "Bop Doo-Wopp") 10-15 84
ATLANTIC (81266 "Vocalese") 8-12 85
ATLANTIC (81723 "Live") 8-12 87
ATLANTIC (81803 "Brasil") 8-12 87
COLLECTABLES 6-8 88
MFSL (022 "Live") 35-50 78
MFSL (199 "Extensions") 20-25 90s
Members: Tim Hauser; Alan Paul; Gary Chester; Garnett Brown; Ken Buttrey; Cheryl Bentyne; Janis Siegel; Don Roberts.
Also see CRITERIONS
Also see PISTILLI, Gene, & Manhattan Transfer
Also see YOUNG GENERATION

MANHATTANS
("Vocal By Herman Carter")
Singles: 78 rpm
PINEY (107 "Go Baby Go") 10-15 55
Singles: 7-inch
PINEY (107 "Go Baby Go") 40-60 55

MANHATTANS
Singles: 7-inch
WARNER RECORDS (1015 "How Do You Say I'm Sorry") 100-200 58

MANHATTANS
Singles: 7-inch
DOOTO (445 "My Big Dream") 40-50 59
Member: Eli Price.
Also see PRICE, Eli, & Manhattans

MANHATTANS
Singles: 7-inch
BOSS (404 "Far East Rock") 15-25 59

MANHATTANS
Singles: 7-inch
COLPIX (115 "Big Wheel Express") 10-15 59
Member: Jim Ford.
Also see FORD, Jim

MANHATTANS
Singles: 7-inch
KING (5228 "Ebb Tide") 8-10 59

MANHATTANS
Singles: 7-inch
GOLDEN WORLD (14 "Just a Little Loving") 15-25 64

MANHATTANS *P&R/R&B '65*
Singles: 12-inch
COLUMBIA 4-6 84-85
Singles: 7-inch
AVANTI (1601 "What Should I Do") 15-25 63
CAPITOL (4591 "I Ain't Down Yet") 10-20 62
CAPITOL (4730 "Sing all the Day") 10-20 62
CARNIVAL (504 "For the Very First Time") 10-20 64
CARNIVAL (506 "Call Somebody Please") 30-50 64
(Identification number is "CA-1010." Credits "A Joe Evans Production.")
CARNIVAL (506 "Call Somebody Please") 25-45 64
(Identification number is "CA-1010x. Credits "A Joe Evans-Bob McGhee Production.")
CARNIVAL (507 thru 542) 8-15 65-69
COLUMBIA 3-6 73-87
DELUXE 4-8 69-73
Picture Sleeves
COLUMBIA 3-4 85
LPs: 10/12-inch
CARNIVAL (201 "Dedicated to You") 100-150 66
CARNIVAL (202 "For You and Yours") 100-150 66
COLUMBIA 8-12 73-85
DELUXE 10-15 70-72
SOLID SMOKE 5-8 81
UPFRONT (120 "Doing Their Thing") 10-15
Members: George Smith; Ken Kelly; Sonny Bivens; Winfred Scott; Richard Taylor; Gerald Alston; Regina Bell.
Also see ALSTON, Gerald
Also see ROYAL FLUSH

MANHATTANS
Singles: 7-inch
STARFIRE 8-12

MANHATTENS
Singles: 7-inch
BIG MACK (823 "Why Should I Cry") 100-200 63

MANIFEST DESTINY
Singles: 7-inch
CHAMP (3404 "Sill Me") 10-20 66
CHAMP (3405 "I Hear Bells") 10-20 66

MANILLA MACHINE
Singles: 7-inch
ROULETTE 4-8 71
Also see MACHINE

MANILOW, Barry *P&R/LP '74*
Singles: 12-inch
ARISTA 5-10 78-87
Singles: 7-inch
ARISTA (Black vinyl) 3-5 74-90
ARISTA (ASPD 1 "One Voice") 25-35 83
(Profile-shaped picture disc, made for Fox Photo. Promotional issue only.)
BELL 3-5 73-74
FLASHBACK 3-4 76
RCA 3-4 86
Promotional Singles
ARISTA (11 "It's Just Another New Year's Eve") 4-8 77
ARISTA (9318 "Paradise Cafe") 3-5 84
(Clear vinyl.)
Picture Sleeves
ARISTA (Except 11) 3-5 78-88
ARISTA (11 "It's Just Another New Year's Eve") 4-8 77
(Promotional issue only.)
ARISTA (9318 "Paradise Cafe") 3-5 84
LPs: 10/12-inch
ARISTA (Except A2L-8601) 5-10 74-90
ARISTA (A2L-8601 "Greatest Hits") 10-20 78
(Two picture discs.)
BELL (1129 "Barry Manilow") 15-25 74
BELL (1314 "Barry Manilow II") 10-15
MFSL (097 "I" 25-35 82
RCA 5-8 86
Also see FEATHERBED
Also see LADY FLASH

MANILOW, Barry / Atlanta Rhythm Section
Singles: 7-inch
WHAT'S IT ALL ABOUT 3-5 79
Also see ATLANTA RHYTHM SECTION

MANILOW, Barry / Firefall
Singles: 7-inch
WHAT'S IT ALL ABOUT 3-5 79
Also see FIREFALL

MANILOW, Barry / Kid Creole & Coconuts *P&R '88*
Singles: 7-inch
ARISTA 3-4 88
Also see KID CREOLE & COCONUTS
Also see MANILOW, Barry

MANIN BROTHERS
Singles: 7-inch
APT 10-20 59

MANIS, Georgie
Singles: 7-inch
GIZMO 5-8 61

MANKIN, Bill
Singles: 7-inch
RCA 4-6 68

MANLEY, Lorenzo
Singles: 7-inch
ORIGINAL SOUND 4-6 66

MANN, Allen, & Mustangs
Singles: 7-inch
MUSTANG 5-10 65

MANN, Barbara
Singles: 7-inch
BUZZ 5-8 60
COUNT 5-8

MANN, Barry *P&R '61*
Singles: 7-inch
ABC 3-5 73
ABC-PAR 10-20 60-62
ARISTA 3-5 76
CAPITOL 4-8 66-68
CASABLANCA 3-4 80
COLPIX 5-10 63
JDS 15-25 59
MCA 3-4 80s
NEW DESIGN 3-5 71-72
RCA 3-5 74-76
RED BIRD 8-12 64
ROULETTE 3-5 70s
SCEPTER 3-5 70
U.A. 3-5 77-78
W.B. 3-5 79
LPs: 10/12-inch
ABC-PAR (ABC-399 "Who Put the Bomp in the Bomp Bomp Bomp") 50-80 62
(Monaural.)
ABC-PAR (ABCS-399 "Who Put the Bomp in the Bomp Bomp Bomp") 75-100 62
(Stereo.)
CASABLANCA 5-8 80
NEW DESIGN 10-12 71
RCA (0860 "Survivor") 8-12 75
RCA (1162 "Interview") 12-15 75
(Promotional issue only.)
U.A. 8-10 77
Also see HALOS

MANN, Billy
Singles: 78 rpm
DIG 10-20 56
Singles: 7-inch
DIG (111 "Lost Angel") 15-25 56
DIG (120 "Just Like Before") 15-25 56

MANN, Bobby
(Bobby Bloom)
Singles: 7-inch
KAMA SUTRA 5-10 66
Also see BLOOM, Bobby

MANN, Carl *P&R/R&B '59*
Singles: 7-inch
ABC/DOT 3-5 76
JAXON (502 "Gonna Rock and Roll Tonight") 200-300 57
PHILLIPS INT'L 10-20 59-61
SUN 3-5 70s
LPs: 10/12-inch
GRT/SUNNYVALE 6-10 77
PHILLIPS INT'L (1960 "Like Mann") 400-500 60

MANN, Charles *R&B '73*
Singles: 7-inch
ABC 3-5 73
LANOR (529 "Hey Little Girl") 5-15
LANOR (540 "Dreams to Remember") 5-15
LANOR (543 "Red Red Wine") 5-15
LANOR (543 "Red Red Wine") 5-15
Note: Confusion reigns here. We've seen these Lanor titles sold for from $4 to $20 for NM. Plus, there are others we haven't listed. Opinions vary widely for years of release. Finally, are Lanor & ABC by the same Mann?)

MANN, Frankie
Singles: 7-inch
APT 5-10 59

MANN, Gloria *P&R '55*
(With the Carter Rays; with Don Costa's Orchestra)
Singles: 78 rpm
ABC-PAR 5-10 57
DECCA 3-6 56
DERBY 4-8 56
JUBILEE 4-8 54
SLS 10-15 54
SOUND 5-10 54-55
Singles: 7-inch
ABC-PAR 5-10 57
DECCA 5-10 56
DERBY 5-10 56
JUBILEE 8-12 54
SLS (102 "Goodnight Sweetheart") 30-40 54
SOUND 10-20 54-55
Also see CARTER RAYS
Also see COSTA, Don, Orchestra
Also see MELLO-TONES / Gloria Mann

MANN, Herbie *LP '62*
Singles: 12-inch
ATLANTIC 4-6 83
Singles: 7-inch
A&M 3-5 68
ATLANTIC 3-8 60-83
BETHLEHEM 4-8 59-62
COLUMBIA 3-5 70
EMBRYO 3-5 71
PRESTIGE 4-6 66
Picture Sleeves
ATLANTIC 3-5 79
LPs: 10/12-inch
A&M 8-12 68
ATLANTIC (300 series) 8-12 72
ATLANTIC (1300 & 1400 series) ... 10-20 60-66
ATLANTIC (1500 thru 1600 series) .. 8-12 69-76
ATLANTIC (8000 series) 8-15 67
ATLANTIC (18000 and 19000 series) 5-10 77-83
BETHLEHEM (24 "Flamingo") 50-100 55
BETHLEHEM (40 "Herbie Mann") 50-100 56
BETHLEHEM (63 "Love and the Weather") 50-100 56
BETHLEHEM (1018 "East Coast Jazz") 75-100 54
(10-inch LPs.)
BETHLEHEM (6001 "The Bethlehem Years") 5-8 76
BETHLEHEM (6067 "The Epitome of Jazz") 25-35 63
COLUMBIA 8-18 65-81
EMBRYO 8-12 70-71
EPIC (3395 "Salute to the Flute") ... 60-80 57
EPIC (3499 "Herbie Mann") 50-70 58
FINNADAR 5-10 76
INTERLUDE 20-35 59
JAZZLAND (5 "Californians") 35-55 60
MILESTONE 8-12 73
MODE (114 "Flute Fraternity") 40-60 57
NEW JAZZ (8211 "Just Wailin' ") ... 50-60 58
PREMIER 20-30 63
PRESTIGE (7101 "Flute Souffle") 75-100 57
PRESTIGE (7124 "Flute Flight") .. 75-100 57
PRESTIGE (7136 "Mann in the Morning") 75-100 58
PRESTIGE (7432 "Best of Herbie Mann") 20-30 65
RIVERSIDE (03 "Blues for Tomorrow") 5-8 82
RIVERSIDE (234 "Sultry Serenade") 50-75 57
RIVERSIDE (245 "Great Ideas") 50-75 57
RIVERSIDE (3000 series) 8-12 69
ROULETTE 10-15 67
SAVOY (1100 series) 5-8 76
SAVOY (12107 "Mann Alone") 30-40 57
SAVOY (12108 "Yardbird Suite") ... 35-50 57
SOLID STATE 8-12 68
SURREY 10-15 65
U.A. (4000 & 5000 series) 20-40 59
U.A. (5300 series) 8-10 72
U.A. (14000 & 15000 series) 20-40 62-63
VSP 8-15 66
VERVE 20-40 57-61
(Reads "Verve Records, Inc." at bottom of label.)
VERVE 15-25 63
(Reads "MGM Records - A Division of Metro-Goldwyn-Mayer, Inc." at bottom of label.)
VERVE 5-10 69-73
(Reads "Manufactured By MGM Record Corp.," or mentions either Polydor or Polygram at bottom of label.)
Session: King Curtis; Little Milton.
Also see AYERS, Roy
Also see KING CURTIS
Also see LITTLE MILTON
Also see JONES, Tamiko, & Herbie Mann

MANN, Herbie, & Cissy Houston *R&B '76*
Singles: 7-inch
ATLANTIC 3-5 76
Also see HOUSTON, Cissy

MANN, Herbie / Maynard Ferguson
LPs: 10/12-inch
ROULETTE 8-12 71
Also see FERGUSON, Herbie
Also see MANN, Herbie

MANN, Jerry
Singles: 7-inch
HANOVER 5-10 60

MANN, Joey, & Statesmen
Singles: 7-inch
CLEVETOWN 4-8 66

MANN, Johnny
(With the Tornados; with Bill Eisenhauer & Orchestra)
Singles: 7-inch
DONNIE (27746 "Breaker of Dreams") 100-200 58
(Identification number shown since no selection number is used.)
SHREVE (1214 "Sorry") 15-25 58
SWAN (4018 "Chick-A-Lou") 15-25 58
TIARA (6118 "Too Young to Cry") 25-50 58

MANN, Johnny, Singers *LP '63*
Singles: 7-inch
DECCA 3-5 66
EPIC 3-5 72
EUREKA 4-8 60
LIBERTY 4-6 62-68
LPs: 10/12-inch
EPIC 5-10 72
LIBERTY 10-20 59-69
LIGHT 5-10 76
SUNSET 5-10 66-70
U.A. 6-12 71-72
Also see McDANIELS, Gene
Also see VEE, Bobby
Also see ZENTNER, Si

MANN, Levi
Singles: 78 rpm
ALADDIN 8-12 56
Singles: 7-inch
ALADDIN (3356 "Behind the Cotton Curtain") 15-25 56

MANN, Lorene *C&W '67*
Singles: 7-inch
RCA 4-8 67-69
LPs: 10/12-inch
RCA 10-15 69
Also see CAMPBELL, Archie, & Lorene Mann
Also see TUBB, Justin, & Lorene Mann

MANN, Manfred *P&R/LP '64*
(Manfred Mann's Earth Band)
Singles: 7-inch
ARISTA 3-4 84-85
ASCOT (Except 2157 & 2165) 6-12 64-68
ASCOT (2157 "Do Wah Diddy Diddy") 4-8 64
ASCOT (2165 "Sha La La") 4-8 64
MERCURY 3-6 66-69
POLYDOR 3-5 71-74
PRESTIGE 8-10 64
U.A. 4-8 66
W.B. 3-5 76-81
Picture Sleeves
ASCOT 10-20 64-65
MERCURY 8-15 68
W.B. 3-5 76

EPs: 7-inch
U.A. (10030 "Manfred Mann") ... 10-20 64
(Promotional issue only. Not issued with cover.)
LPs: 10/12-inch
ARISTA ... 5-8 83
ASCOT (13015 "Manfred Mann") ... 25-35 64
(Monaural.)
ASCOT (13018 "Five Faces of Manfred Mann") ... 25-35 65
(Monaural.)
ASCOT (13024 "Mann Made") ... 25-35 66
(Monaural.)
ASCOT (16015 "Manfred Mann") ... 35-45 64
(Stereo.)
ASCOT (16018 "Five Faces of Manfred Mann") ... 35-45 65
(Stereo.)
ASCOT (16024 "Mann Made") ... 35-45 66
(Stereo.)
CAPITOL ... 5-8 80
EMI AMERICA ... 10-12 77
JANUS ... 12-15 74
MERCURY ... 15-20 68
POLYDOR ... 10-15 70-74
U.A. ... 20-35 66-68
W.B. ... 5-8 74-81
Members: Manfred Mann; Mike D'Abo; Paul Jones; Tom McGuinness; Mick Rogers; Mick Vickers; Chris Slade; Colin Pattenden; Mike Hugg; Steve York; Mick Rogers.
Also see BELL, Madeline
Also see D'ABO, Mike
Also see FIRM
Also see McGUINNESS FLINT
Also see THOMPSON, Chris, & Night

MANN, Pete
Singles: 7-inch
POPLAR ... 5-10 59

MANN, Reverend Columbus
(With His Pentecostal Choir)
Singles: 7-inch
CYE (1001 "Soon Very Soon") ... 15-25 60s
TAMLA (54047 "Jesus Loves") ... 25-35 62
LPs: 10/12-inch
TAMLA (227 "They Shall Be Mine") ... 300-400 61
WINGATE (701 "He Satisfies Me") ... 200-300 60s

MANN, Scotty, & Masters
Singles: 78 rpm
PEACOCK ... 5-10 56
Singles: 7-inch
PEACOCK (1665 "Just a Little Bit of Loving") ... 10-20 56
Members: Scotty Mansfield; Frank Newman; Fred Council; Pavel Bess.
Also see CLEFS

MANN, Shadow
Singles: 7-inch
TOMORROW ... 5-10 74
LPs: 10/12-inch
TOMORROW (69001 "Come Live with Me") ... 40-60 74

MANN, Steve
LPs: 10/12-inch
CUSTOM FIDELITY ... 10-12

MANN, Tony
Singles: 7-inch
DECCA (32720 "Alabama Song") ... 10-15 70

MANNA
LPs: 10/12-inch
COLUMBIA ... 8-10 72

MANNA, Charlie LP '61
Singles: 7-inch
DECCA ... 4-6 61
JUBILEE ... 4-6 65
Picture Sleeves
DECCA ... 4-8 61
LPs: 10/12-inch
DECCA ... 10-20 61-62
VERVE ... 10-15 66

MANNEQUIN
LPs: 10/12-inch
RECORD ... 5-8 82

MANNERS, Zeke, & His Band C&W '46
(With the Singing Lariateers)
Singles: 78 rpm
VICTOR ... 4-8 46
Also see BRITT, Elton

MANNHEIM STEAMROLLER LP '84
LPs: 10/12-inch
AMERICAN GRAMAPHONE ... 5-8 75-90
Also see McCALL, C.W.
Also see WILLIAMS, Mason, & Mannheim Steamroller

MANNING, Bob
Singles: 78 rpm
CAPITOL ... 4-6 53-55
RCA ... 4-6 56
Singles: 7-inch
CAPITOL ... 5-10 53-55
RCA ... 5-10 56

MANNING, Linda C&W '68
Singles: 7-inch
BULLETIN ... 4-8 61
DOKE ... 5-10 60
GAYLORD ... 4-8 62
MERCURY ... 4-6 68
RICE ... 4-8 64-67

MANNING, Louise
Singles: 7-inch
TIARA ... 5-10 59

MANNING, Rhonda C&W '87
Singles: 7-inch
RAM ... 3-4 88
SOUNDWAVES ... 3-4 87

MANNING, Terry
LPs: 10/12-inch
ENTERPRISE ... 10-12
Also see DICKINSON, James Luther

MANNO, Tommy
Singles: 7-inch
ATLANTIC ... 4-8 62
FLIPPIN' ... 10-15 62

MANONE, Wingy, & Orchestra P&R '35
Singles: 78 rpm
BLUEBIRD ... 3-8 36-38
COLUMBIA ... 3-5 54
DECCA ... 4-8 57
VOCALION ... 3-8
Singles: 7-inch
COLUMBIA ... 5-10 54
DECCA ... 8-12 57
IMPERIAL ... 4-6 62
KEM ... 4-6 61
EPs: 7-inch
COLUMBIA ... 5-10 54
VIK ... 5-10 56
LPs: 10/12-inch
IMPERIAL ... 8-15 62
MCA ... 5-10 83
PRESTIGE ... 5-10 70
RCA ... 5-10 69
SAVOY ... 5-10 73
STORYVILLE ... 5-10 83
VIK ... 10-20 56

MANOR, A.J., & Jets
Singles: 7-inch
TWIRL (105 "I Know the Blues Are Blues") ... 10-20 60s

MANPOWER
LPs: 10/12-inch
PHILIPS ... 10-15 69
Also see MAN

MANSEL, Red
Singles: 78 rpm
ALLSTAR ... 40-60 57
Singles: 7-inch
ALLSTAR (7160 "Johnny on the Spot") ... 40-60 57

MANSFIELD, Darrell, Band
LPs: 10/12-inch
POLYDOR ... 5-8 80

MANSFIELD, Jayne
Singles: 78 rpm
HEAR ("Tab Hunter") ... 20-30 56
(Seven-inch, cardboard disc, originally attached to back cover of *Hear* magazine. Double this price for magazine with record intact. Front cover has a similar disc by Tab Hunter.)
Singles: 7-inch
ORIGINAL SOUND ... 4-8 64
Picture Sleeves
ORIGINAL SOUND ... 10-20 64
LPs: 10/12-inch
MGM (4202 "Shakespeare, Tchaikovsky and Me") ... 25-50 64
20TH FOX (3049 "Jayne Mansfield Busts Up Las Vegas") ... 75-100
Also see HUNTER, Tab
Also see JENSEN, Kurt, & His Orchestra
Also see LIGHT, Enoch, & His Orchestra
Also see LOPEZ, Vincent, & His Orchestra
Also see REGENT CONCERT ORCHESTRA
Also see RENÉ, Henri, & His Orchestra
Also see WASHBURN, Frank, & His Orchestra

MANSFIELD, Keith
(Keith Mansfield Orchestra)
Singles: 7-inch
EPIC ... 4-6 69

MANSHIP, Jimmy & Judy
Singles: 7-inch
BLUE HEN ... 8-12 59

MANSHIP, Jimmy, & Allison Sisters / Bill Price
Singles: 7-inch
BLUE HEN (236 "Broken Heart") ... 10-15 59
Also see MANSHIP, Jimmy & Judy

MANSON, Charles
LPs: 10/12-inch
AWARENESS (1 "Charles Manson") ... 5-10 87
AWARENESS (2144 "The Love and Terror Cult") ... 200-300 60s
ESP DISK (2003 "The Love and Terror Cult") ... 100-200 70

MANTELLI, Steve C&W '82
Singles: 7-inch
PICAP ... 3-4 82-83

MANTOVANI P&R '35
(Mantovani & His Orchestra)
Singles: 78 rpm
COLUMBIA ... 3-8 36
LONDON (Except 1761) ... 3-5 51-65
LONDON (1761 "Let Me Be Loved") ... 4-6 57
Singles: 7-inch
LONDON (Except 1761) ... 3-8 51-65
LONDON (1761 "Let Me Be Loved") ... 4-8 57
Picture Sleeves
LONDON (Except 1761) ... 4-8 57-65
LONDON (1761 "Let Me Be Loved") ... 30-45 57
(*Let Me Be Loved* is the main theme from the film, *The James Dean Story*. Sleeve pictures Dean.)
EPs: 7-inch
LONDON ... 4-8 51-59
LPs: 10/12-inch
BAINBRIDGE ... 5-10 82
LONDON ... 8-18 51-72
Also see DEAN, James
Also see PRESLEY, Elvis
Also see WHITFIELD, David

MANTRA R&B '81
Singles: 7-inch
CASABLANCA ... 3-4 81
LPs: 10/12-inch
CASABLANCA ... 5-10 81

MANTRONIX D&D '85
(With Wondress)
Singles: 12-inch
SLEEPING BAG ... 4-6 85
Singles: 7-inch
SLEEPING BAG ... 3-4 85
LPs: 10/12-inch
CAPITOL ... 5-8 88-90
SLEEPING BAG ... 5-8 86

MANU DIBANGO: see DIBANGO, Manu

MANUEL & RENEGADES
Singles: 7-inch
PIPER (7000 "Surf Walk") ... 15-25 63
PIPER (7001 "Rev-Up") ... 15-25 63

MANUEL & VIOLA
Singles: 7-inch
VILLA ... 4-8

MANY OTHERS
Singles: 7-inch
ORCHID ... 10-15

MANZANERA, Phil LP '79
(Phil Manzanera Quiet Sun; with 801; Manzanera)
Singles: 12-inch
EDITIONS E.G. ... 5-8 82
Singles: 7-inch
POLYDOR ... 3-5 78
LPs: 10/12-inch
ANTILLES ... 8-10
ATCO ... 8-10
EDITIONS E.G. ... 5-8 82
POLYDOR ... 8-10 78
Also see 801
Also see NICO
Also see ROXY MUSIC

MANZAREK, Ray LP '75
Singles: 7-inch
MERCURY ... 4-6 73-74
LPs: 10/12-inch
A&M ... 5-10 84
MERCURY ... 8-12 74-75
Also see DOORS
Also see RICK & RAVENS

MAPLES
(With Von Freeman Combo)
Singles: 78 rpm
BLUE LAKE ... 100-200 54
Singles: 7-inch
BLUE LAKE (111 "I Must Forget You") ... 300-400 54
Members: Johnny Jones; Albert Hunter; Andrew Smith.
Also see CLOUDS
Also see FASCINATORS
Also see FIVE CHANCES

MARA, Tommy P&R '58
Singles: 78 rpm
MGM ... 4-6 55
Singles: 7-inch
B&F ... 5-10 60
FELSTED ... 5-10 58-59
MGM ... 5-10 55

MARA, Tony
Singles: 7-inch
ATCO (6172 "Ramblin'") ... 10-20 60

MARAINEY, Big Memphis
Singles: 78 rpm
SUN ... 200-300 53
Singles: 7-inch
SUN (184 "Call Me Anything, But Call Me") ... 550-650 53

MARATHONS P&R/R&B '61
Singles: 7-inch
ARGO (5389 "Peanut Butter") ... 5-10 61
ARVEE (5027 "Peanut Butter") ... 10-12 61
(Other Arvee releases by the Marathons are by a different group. See the following section.)
CHESS (1790 "Peanut Butter") ... 5-10 61
PLAZA ... 5-10 62
EPs: 7-inch
MARK 56 ("Laura Scudder's Magic Record") ... 4-8 69
(Laura Scudder's potato chip mail-order, coupon giveaway item. Has three tracks, including *Peanut Butter*, imbedded in a single band on each side. When needle begins tracking, it's unknown which song will play. Price includes paper picture sleeve.)
LPs: 10/12-inch
ARVEE (428 "Peanut Butter") ... 50-75 61
Members: James Johnson; Carl Fisher; Dick Owens; Dave Govan; Don Bradley.
Also see JAYHAWKS
Also see VIBRATIONS

MARATHONS
Singles: 7-inch
ARVEE (Except 5027) ... 5-10 61-62
(Arvee 5027 is by a different group and is listed in the preceeding section.)

MARATHONS
Singles: 7-inch
SABRINA (334 "Don't Know Why") ... 100-150 59

MARAUDERS
Singles: 7-inch
HAWK (4002 "Sand Flea") ... 20-30 62
Member: Steve Wildermuth.

MARAUDERS
Singles: 7-inch
KISKI (2067 "Slidin'") ... 10-20 63

MARAUDERS
Singles: 7-inch
COULEE (110 "I Can Tell") ... 25-35 64
(Colored vinyl.)
Members: Rick Przywojski; Rick Miller; Jim Young; Terry Gardner.
Also see SATISFACTIONS

MARAUDERS
Singles: 7-inch
ROCKLAND (2 "Bad Girl") ... 15-25 65

MARAUDERS
Singles: 7-inch
LEE (9449 "Nightmare") ... 15-25 65

MARAUDERS
Singles: 7-inch
ALMO (221 "Like You") ... 8-10 65
FR (6143 "Motorcycle Bug") ... 25-35

MARAUDERS
Singles: 7-inch
SKYVIEW (001 "Since I Met You") ... 10-15 66
Picture Sleeves
SKYVIEW (001 "Since I Met You") ... 10-20 66

MARAUDERS
Singles: 7-inch
LAURIE (3356 "Jugband Music") ... 10-15 66

MARAUDERS
Singles: 7-inch
JIVE TIME ... 8-12 70
STUDIO CITY ... 10-15 67

MARBLE COLLECTION
Singles: 7-inch
COTIQUE ... 5-10 68
MARBLE DISC ... 4-8 69
Members: Charles Byrd; Len Eldridge; Jim White; Bruce Webb; Dave Coviello.

MARBLE PHROGG
Singles: 7-inch
DERRICK (8568 "Fire") ... 40-60 68
LPs: 10/12-inch
DERRICK (8868 "Marble Phrogg") ... 800-1200 68

MARBLES
Singles: 78 rpm
LUCKY (002 "Golden Girl") ... 200-400 54
Singles: 7-inch
LUCKY (002 "Golden Girl") ... 1000-2000 54
Members: Johnny Torrence; Dee Hawkins; James Brown; Rudy Jackson.
Also see JEWELS

MARBLES
Singles: 7-inch
COTILLION ... 3-6 68-70
LPs: 10/12-inch
COTILLION ... 10-12 70

MARBLES, Race
Singles: 7-inch
TOWER ... 4-8 65

MARCEL
Singles: 7-inch
SRO ... 3-4 86

MARCEL, Eddie
Singles: 7-inch
GLAD-HAMP (2034 "I Go Crazy") ... 100-200 60s

MARCEL, Pete
Singles: 7-inch
FUTURA ... 4-8 61

MARCELL, Beverly
Singles: 7-inch
GONE ... 4-8 63

MARCELL, Professor, & Collegians
Singles: 7-inch
MAYHAMS ... 4-8 67

MARCELL, Vic
Singles: 7-inch
DONBUT (17349 "Come Back to These Arms") ... 50-75 64

MARCELLE, Lydia
Singles: 7-inch
MANHATTAN (805 "Come On and Get It") ... 10-20 67
MANHATTAN (809 "It's Not Like You") ... 10-20 67

MARCELS P&R/R&B '61
(With the Stu Phillips Orchestra; Marcelles)
Singles: 7-inch
COLPIX (186 "Blue Moon") ... 15-25 61
COLPIX (186 "Blue Moon") ... 20-30 61
(Mistakenly credits "Marcelles." Canadian.)
COLPIX (196 "Summertime") ... 10-20 61
COLPIX (606 "You Are My Sunshine") ... 10-20 61
COLPIX (612 "Heartaches") ... 15-25 61
COLPIX (617 "Merry Twistmas") ... 15-25 61
COLPIX (621 "My Melancholy Baby") ... 100-200 62
(Promotional issue only.)
COLPIX (624 "My Melancholy Baby") ... 15-25 62
COLPIX (629 "Footprints in the Sand") ... 25-50 62
COLPIX (651 "Friendly Loan") ... 25-35 62
COLPIX (665 "Alright, Okay, You Win") ... 15-25 62
COLPIX (683 "That Old Black Magic") ... 10-20 63
COLPIX (687 "I Want to Be the Leader") ... 20-30 63
COLPIX (694 "One Last Kiss") ... 50-75 63
888 (101 "Lonely Boy") ... 10-15 63
ERIC ... 3-4 70s
KYRA ("Comes Love") ... 100-150 64
(No selection number used.)
MONOGRAM (113 "Over the Rainbow") ... 15-20 75
(Colored vinyl.)
MONOGRAM (115 "Two People in the World") ... 5-8 75
QUEEN BEE (47001 "In the Still of the Night") ... 10-15 73
SIR RENDER (005 "A Fallen Tear") ... 5-8
(Colored vinyl.)
ST. CLAIR ... 5-10 75
Picture Sleeves
COLPIX (186 "Blue Moon") ... 50-75 61
COLPIX (612 "Heartaches") ... 50-75 61
COLPIX (617 "Merry Twistmas") ... 50-75 61
LPs: 10/12-inch
COLPIX (416 "Blue Moon") ... 75-125 61
(Gold label.)
COLPIX (416 "Blue Moon") ... 30-50 63
(Blue label.)
CRYSTAL BALL ... 8-10 80s
EMUS ... 8-10 79
MURRAY HILL ... 8-10
Members: Cornelius Harp; Fred Johnson; Ron Mundy; Gene Bricker; Richard Knauss; Walt Maddox; Al Johnson.
Also see FABULOUS MARCELS
Also see JETS
Also see JOHNNIE & JOE / Marcels
Also see REGAN, Tommy

MARCELS (on Jody): see JEFFRIES, Bob

MARCH, Little Peggy P&R/R&B/LP '63
(Peggy March)
Singles: 7-inch
OLDE WORLD ... 3-5 75
RCA ... 4-8 62-71
Picture Sleeves
RCA ... 10-20 63
EPs: 7-inch
RCA ... 15-25 63
LPs: 10/12-inch
RCA (Except 2732) ... 15-20 65-68
RCA (LPM-2732 "I Will Follow Him") ... 50-60 63
(Monaural.)
RCA (LSP-2732 "I Will Follow Him") ... 75-100 63
(Stereo.)
Also see MARCH, Peggy, & Gary Marshal

MARCH, Little Peggy, & Bennie Thomas
LPs: 10/12-inch
RCA ... 15-20 65
Also see THOMAS, Bennie

MARCH, Myrna
Singles: 7-inch
COLUMBIA ... 4-8 64
ROULETTE ... 4-8 63
WARWICK ... 4-8 60
LPs: 10/12-inch
KAPP ... 10-12 69

MARCH, Peggy, & Gary Marshal
Singles: 7-inch
RCA ... 4-8 66
Also see MARCH, Little Peggy
Also see MARSHAL, Gary

MARCH, Tony
Singles: 7-inch
CHECKER (827 "Stompen Rock") ... 15-25 58
CROSSWAY (447 "Beatle Mania Blues") ... 10-20 64
TAMMY (1003 "Show Down") ... 15-25 60
TAMMY (1007 "Boston Bake Bean Baby") ... 15-25 60

MARCH WIND
Singles: 7-inch
STAX ... 4-6 72

MARCHAN, Bobby P&R/R&B '60
(With the Tick Tocks; with Clowns; Bobby Marchon)
Singles: 78 rpm
ACE ... 10-20 56
ALADDIN ... 10-20 53
DOT ... 10-20 54
FIRE (1022 "There's Something on Your Mind") ... 300-400 60
GALE ... 10-20 57
Singles: 7-inch
ABC ... 3-5 73
ACE (523 "Chickie Wah Wah") ... 20-30 56
ACE (557 "Rockin' Behind the Iron Curtain") ... 15-25 59
ACE (3000 series) ... 4-8 74-75

ALADDIN (3189 "Just a Little Walk")....30-40 53
BOBBY ROBINSON....3-6 73
CAMEO....5-10 66-67
DIAL....4-10 64-74
DOT (1203 "Just a Little Ol' Wine")....20-30 54
FIRE....10-20 59-62
FLASHBACK....3-5 65
GALE....20-30 57
GAMBLE....5-10 68
MERCURY....3-5 77
RIVER CITY....10-20
SANSU....5-10 60s
SPHERE SOUND....5-10 65
VOLT....8-12 63

LPs: 10/12-inch

COLLECTABLES....5-8 88
SPHERE SOUND (7004 "There's Something on Your Mind")....100-200 64

Also see SMITH, Huey

MARCHAND, Donnie

Singles: 7-inch

MOHAWK....4-8 61
TRANS ATLAS....4-8 62

MARCHAND, Glen

Singles: 7-inch

DORE (763 "Your Ship of Fools")..25-50 65

MARCHAND, Yvette

Singles: 7-inch

BETHLEHEM....4-8 63

MARCI & MATES

Singles: 7-inch

BIG TOP....8-12 62-63

MARCIA & LYNCHMEN

Singles: 7-inch

SCOTTY (94456740 "Ain't Gonna Eat Out My Heart")....25-35 60s

Also see PLASTIC ICE CUBE

MARCIA LYNN C&W '87

(Marcia Lynn Dickinson)

Singles: 7-inch

EVERGREEN....3-4 87
SOUNDWAVES....3-4 87

MARCO

Singles: 7-inch

MOHAWK (135 "I'm So Lonely")....5-10 63

MARCO, Nick, & Venetians

Singles: 7-inch

DWAIN (813 "Little Boy Lost")....30-50 60

Members: Nick Marco; Joe Walsh; Dennis Conboy; Bob Fava.

Also see LEDO, Les

MARCUS

LPs: 10/12-inch

KINETIC....10-15 70

MARCUS, Denny

(Danny Marcus)

Singles: 7-inch

ASSOCIATED ARTISTS....4-8 65
MUSICOR....3-6 68

MARCUS, Jonathan

Singles: 7-inch

MGM....4-8 66

MARCUS, Steve

LPs: 10/12-inch

VORTEX....12-15 68

MARCUS HOOK ROLL BAND

Singles: 7-inch

EMI....3-5 73

MARCY BROTHERS C&W '88

Singles: 7-inch

ATLANTIC....3-4 91
W.B....3-4 88-90

Members: Kris Marcy; Kevin Marcy.

MARCY DEE

Singles: 7-inch

CLARK....5-10

MARCY JO & EDDIE RAMBEAU

Singles: 7-inch

SWAN (4136 "Those Golden Oldies")....10-15 63
SWAN (4145 "The Car Hop & the Hard Top")....15-25 63

Also see MARCY JOE

Also see RAMBEAU, Eddie

MARCY JOE P&R '61

(Marcy Jo)

Singles: 7-inch

ROBBEE (110 "Ronnie")....10-15 61
ROBBEE (115 "Since Gary Went Into the Navy")....10-15 61
ROBBEE (117 "Take a Word")....10-15 61
SWAN (4116 "First Kiss")....8-12 62
SWAN (4128 "Night")....8-12 62

Session: Lou Christie.

Also see CHRISTIE, Lou

MARDEN, Janie

Singles: 78 rpm

LONDON....3-6 56

Singles: 7-inch

LONDON....5-8 56
REPRISE....4-6 65

MARDI GRAS

Singles: 7-inch

BELL....3-5 70s
MAP CITY....3-5 70

MARDIN, Arif

Singles: 7-inch

ATLANTIC....3-5 70-72

LPs: 10/12-inch

ATLANTIC....10-12 69

MARDIS, Bobby R&B '86

Singles: 12-inch

PROFILE....4-6 86

Singles: 7-inch

PROFILE....3-4 86

MARDONES, Benny P&R/LP '80

Singles: 7-inch

POLYDOR....3-5 80-89
PRIVATE STOCK....3-5 78

EPs: 7-inch

PRIVATE STOCK (1000 "Thank God for Girls")....5-8 78

(Colored vinyl. Promotional issue only.)

LPs: 10/12-inch

POLYDOR....5-10 80
PRIVATE STOCK....5-10 78

MARENO, Lee

(Lee)

Singles: 7-inch

NEW ART (103 "Goddess of Love")....30-50 61
SCEPTER (1222 "Goddess of Love")....15-25 61

Also see RUNAROUNDS

MARESCA, Ernie P&R/R&B '62

Singles: 7-inch

LAURIE....5-10 66
RUST....8-12 64
SEVILLE....8-12 60-65

LPs: 10/12-inch

LAURIE (4006 "Original Songs of Ernie Maresca")....10-15 78
SEVILLE (77001 "Shout! Shout! [Knock Yourself Out])"....30-60 62

(Monaural.)

SEVILLE (87001 "Shout! Shout! [Knock Yourself Out])"....40-80 62

(Stereo.)

Also see CHICAGO, Artie
Also see DEL SATINS
Also see DESIRES
Also see FOREIGN INTRIGUE
Also see HUBCAPS

MARESCO, Tony: see DYNAMICS, Featuring Tony Maresco

MARGRET, Ann: see ANN-MARGRET

MARGARET & CAROL

Singles: 7-inch

CHECKER....4-8

MARGARET & CHARMETTES

Singles: 7-inch

MARKAY....10-20 62

Also see CHARMETTES

MARGIE & FORMATIONS

Singles: 7-inch

COED (601 "Sad Illusion")....20-30 65

MARGILATORS

Singles: 7-inch

BLUE MOON (409 "Wait for Me")..25-35 59
BLUE MOON (411 "Just Waiting for You")....15-25 59

MARGO & MARVETTES

Singles: 7-inch

AMERICAN ARTS....8-12 65

MARGO, MARGO, MEDRESS & SIEGEL

Singles: 7-inch

W.B....4-8 68

Members: Mitchell Margo; Philip Margo; Henry Medress; Jay Siegel.

Also see TOKENS

MARGO & NORRO: see SMITH, Margo, & Norro Wilson

MARGULIS, Charles

Singles: 7-inch

CARLTON....5-10 59

MARIA, Vonda

Singles: 7-inch

PHIL-L.A. of SOUL....4-6 68

MARIA ANN

Singles: 7-inch

WARWICK....5-8 61

MARIA MAE

(With the Chaperones; with Peptones; with Maybees)

Singles: 7-inch

JAMIE....4-8 64
PHANTOM....5-10 61
SAVOY....4-8 62

MARIACHI BRASS (Featuring Chet Baker) LP '66

LPs: 10/12-inch

WORLD PACIFIC....8-12 66

MARIAH

Singles: 7-inch

U.A....3-5 75

LPs: 10/12-inch

U.A....6-10 75

MARIANI

LPs: 10/12-inch

SONOBEAT (1004 "Perpetuum Mobile")....2500-3500 70s

(Promotional issue only.)

Member: Vince Mariani.

MARIANNE

Singles: 7-inch

A-BET (9432 "The Woman in Me")..5-10 68

MARIANO & UNBELIEVABLES

LPs: 10/12-inch

CAPITOL....12-18 67

MARIDIAN

Singles: 7-inch

MERCURY....4-6 69

MARIE, Ann: see ANN MARIE

MARIE, Deanna

Singles: 7-inch

NASCO....3-5 70

MARIE, Diane D&D '83

Singles: 12-inch

PRELUDE....4-6 83

MARIE, Donna: see DONNA MARIE

MARIE, Kelly

Singles: 12-inch

COAST to COAST....4-6 81

Singles: 7-inch

COAST to COAST....3-5 81

LPs: 10/12-inch

COAST to COAST....5-10 81

MARIE, Rose: see ROSE MARIE

MARIE, Susan: see SUSAN MARIE

MARIE, Teena R&B/LP '79

Singles: 12-inch

EPIC....4-6 83-85

Singles: 7-inch

EPIC....3-4 83-88
GORDY....3-5 79-81
MOTOWN....3-4

Picture Sleeves

EPIC....3-4 84-88

LPs: 10/12-inch

EPIC....5-8 83-90
GORDY....5-10 79-81

Also see KING DREAM CHORUS & Holiday Crew

MARIE: see OSMOND, Marie

MARIE & DECCORS

Singles: 7-inch

CUB (9115 "I'm the One")....10-20 62

MARIE & REX P&R '59

Singles: 7-inch

CARLTON (502 "I Can't Sit Down")....10-15 59

Members: Marie Knight; Rex Garvin.

Also see GARVIN, Rex, & Mighty Cravers

Also see KNIGHT, Marie

MARIE SISTERS

Singles: 7-inch

BRUNSWICK....8-10 59

MARIGOLDS R&B '55

Singles: 78 rpm

EXCELLO....10-20 55

Singles: 7-inch

EXCELLO (2057 "Rollin' Stone")....20-40 55
EXCELLO (2061 "Two Strangers")..20-40 55
EXCELLO (2078 "Foolish Me")....20-40 56
EXCELLO (2091 "It's You, Darling, It's You")....20-40 56

Members: Johnny Bragg; Henry Jones; Hal Hebb; Willie Wilson.

Also see BRAGG, Johnny

MARILLION LP '83

Singles: 7-inch

CAPITOL....3-4 83-87

Picture Sleeves

CAPITOL....3-4 85

LPs: 10/12-inch

CAPITOL....5-8 83-87

Members: Fish; Steve Hogarth; Steve Rothany; Mark Kelly; Pete Trewavas; Ian Mosely.

Also see GTR

MARIMBA CHIAPAS P&R '56

Singles: 78 rpm

CAPITOL....3-6 56

Singles: 7-inch

CAPITOL....5-8 56

MARINERS P&R '50

Singles: 78 rpm

CADENCE....4-8 55-56
COLUMBIA....4-8 50-55

Singles: 7-inch

CADENCE....5-15 55-56
COLUMBIA....5-15 50-55
TIARA....5-10 58

EPs: 7-inch

COLUMBIA....5-10 51-55

LPs: 10/12-inch

CADENCE (1008 "Spirituals")....30-40 56

(10-inch LP.)

COLUMBIA....15-25 51-55
EPIC....10-20 59
HARMONY....10-20 59

Also see GODFREY, Arthur

MARINI, Marino

Singles: 7-inch

LONDON....4-8 62

MARINO, Del

Singles: 7-inch

SCEPTER....4-8 61

MARINO, Frank LP '77

(With Mahogany Rush)

Singles: 7-inch

COLUMBIA....3-5 77-81

LPs: 10/12-inch

COLUMBIA....5-10 77-81

Also see MAHAGONY RUSH

MARINO, Joe

Singles: 7-inch

ELECTRO VOX....4-8 62

MARINO, Lita

Singles: 7-inch

W.B....4-8 62

MARINO, Ronnie

Singles: 7-inch

BRITE STAR....4-8 67

MARIO & FLIPS

Singles: 7-inch

CROSS COUNTRY (100 "Once in Awhile")....20-25 59
DECCA (31252 "Twistin' Train")....10-20 61

MARION

(Marion Carpenter)

Singles: 7-inch

SANDY (1021 "Happy Lonesome")....5-8 61
SANDY (1026 "Cutie")....5-8 61

MARION & HERBIE

Singles: 7-inch

ULTRA-SONIC....5-10 60

MARIONETTES

Singles: 7-inch

LONDON....5-10 65

MARIPAT C&W '89

(Maripat Davis)

Singles: 7-inch

OAK....3-4 89

MARIS, Tommy

Singles: 7-inch

CAMEO....4-8 66
SHOWCASE....4-8 65

MARJOE

Singles: 7-inch

CHELSEA....3-5 72-73

LPs: 10/12-inch

CHELSEA....8-10 72

MARK

Singles: 7-inch

SUPER K....4-8 69
TEAM....4-8 69

Also see 1910 FRUITGUM COMPANY

MARK, Jon

Singles: 7-inch

DECCA....5-10 66

LPs: 10/12-inch

COLUMBIA....8-10 75

Also see MARK - ALMOND BAND

Also see SWEET THURSDAY

MARK, Ronald

Singles: 7-inch

GATEWAY (102 "Moonlight Sky")....200-300 64

MARK - ALMOND BAND LP '71

Singles: 7-inch

ABC....3-5 75
BLUE THUMB....3-5 72
COLUMBIA....3-5 72-73

LPs: 10/12-inch

A&M....8-10 78
ABC....8-10 76
BLUE THUMB....8-12 70-73
COLUMBIA....8-10 72-73
MCA....5-8
PACIFIC ARTS....8-10 81

Members: Jon Mark; Johnny Almond.

Also see ALMOND, Marc

Also see MARK, Jon

Also see MAYALL, John

MARK & CLARK BAND

Singles: 7-inch

COLUMBIA....3-5 77

LPs: 10/12-inch

COLUMBIA....8-10 77

MARK & ESCORTS

Singles: 7-inch

GNP....5-8 65

MARK II P&R '60

Singles: 7-inch

WYE....5-10 60-61

Member: Winston Cogswell.

Also see POWERS, Wayne

MARK III

Singles: 7-inch

ABC-PAR (10280 "Valerie")....5-10 61
BRB (100 "Valerie")....10-15 61

(First issue.)

CENTURY....5-8 60s
FULLER....5-8 65

MARK III

Singles: 7-inch

NIGHT OWL (108 "Jaw Breaker") 10-20 68

MARK III TRIO

Singles: 7-inch

ATCO (6468 "The Sleeper")....5-10 67

IN (6308 "Good Grease")....10-20 66

(First issue.)

IN (6309 "The Sleeper")....10-20 66

(First issue.)

WINGATE (015 "Good Grease")....8-12 66

MARK IV P&R '58

Singles: 7-inch

COSMIC....10-15 58
MERCURY (71000 series)....5-10 59

MARK FOUR

Singles: 7-inch

PACIFIC CHALLENGER....5-10 65

MARK IV

Singles: 7-inch

GIANT STAR (404 "Hey Girl, Won't You Listen")....10-15 66
GIANT STAR (405 "Won't You Believe Me")....10-15 66

MARK IV

Singles: 7-inch

COLUMBIA....5-10 66

MARK IV

Singles: 7-inch

TEE PEE (59/60 "Rollin' Stone")....10-20 68

MARK FOUR

Singles: 7-inch

PACIFIC CHALLENGER....5-10 65

MARK IV R&B '72

Singles: 7-inch

MERCURY (73000 series)....3-5 72-73

LPs: 10/12-inch

MERCURY....10-12 73

Members: James Ponder; Larry Jones.

MARK IVs

Singles: 7-inch

BARRY (105 "Tide Has Turned")....15-25 62

MARK 4'S

Singles: 7-inch

BONUS (7041 "Bonneville")....15-25

MARK V

(Mark Five)

Singles: 7-inch

ABC-PAR (10433 "Night Rumble")..5-10 63
CARMEN (1 "Baby Patsy")....5-10 63
CHARAY (20 "The Phantom")....10-20 65
CHARAY (20 "Talk About Love")....10-20 65

(Same selection number used twice.)

COUNTERPART (813 Hey Conductor")....5-10 60s
HEARTBEAT (58 "Jacqueline")....5-10 63
MILO (110 "Cry Baby")....5-10 60
SUNNY (1 "Jacqueline")....5-10 63

Also see LARRY & Blue Notes

MARK V

Singles: 7-inch

BLAST (215 "I Want to Say")....10-20 64

MARK V

Singles: 7-inch

BOLO....5-10 64
JANI....5-10 65
NWI....5-10 66

MARK V

Singles: 7-inch

IMPRESSION....4-8 65

MARK V

Singles: 7-inch

COUNTERPART (2591 "Hey Conductor")....20-25
JCP (102 "Pay")....10-20 60s

MARK V COMBO

Singles: 7-inch

VARIETY....4-8 62-65

MARK OF KINGS

Singles: 7-inch

FLIP TOP....4-8

MARK VI

Singles: 7-inch

ZEST (100 "Cleo")....20-40

MARKEES

Singles: 7-inch

GONE (5028 "Along Came Love")....25-50 58

MARKEES

(Marquees)

Singles: 7-inch

GRAND (141 "The Bells")....50-100 61

(Yellow label. No company address shown.)

Also see MARQUEES

MARKEETS

(With the Leon Ross Band)

Singles: 7-inch

MELATONE (1005 "Baby Please")....300-500 57

MAR-KELLS

Singles: 7-inch

JCP (1036 "Call")....10-20 64
JCP (1041 "Don't You Realize")....10-20 65

MARKELS

(With Bob Bravin's Orchestra)

Singles: 7-inch

R&M (407 "The Letter of Love")....200-300 58

MARKER, Morty

Singles: 7-inch

BACK BEAT....5-10 64

MARKETTS P&R '62
(Mar-Kets)
Singles: 7-inch
LIBERTY ... 8-12 62
MERCURY ... 3-5 73
UNI ... 4-6 69
UNION ... 15-20 61-62
W.B. (Except 5391) ... 4-8 63-66
W.B. (5391 "Outer Limits") ... 5-10 63
W.B. (5391 "Out of Limits") ... 4-8 63
(Note title change.)
WORLD PACIFIC ... 4-8 67
LPs: 10/12-inch
DORE ... 5-8 82
LIBERTY (3226 "Surfer's Stomp") .. 25-30 62
(Monaural.)
LIBERTY (3226 "Surfing Scene") ... 20-25 62
(Monaural. Reissue.)
LIBERTY (7226 "Surfer's Stomp") .. 30-35 62
(Stereo.)
LIBERTY (7226 "Surfing Scene") ... 25-30 62
(Stereo. Reissue.)
MERCURY ... 10-15 73
PHONORAMA ... 5-8 84
SEMINOLE (501 M*A*S*H Theme") .. 3-5 76
W.B. (W-1509 "Take to Wheels") ... 20-25 63
(Monaural.)
W.B. (WS-1509 "Take to Wheels") ... 25-30 63
(Stereo.)
W.B. (W-1537 "Out of Limits") ... 20-25 64
(Monaural.)
W.B. (WS-1537 "Out of Limits") ... 25-30 64
(Stereo.)
W.B. (W-1642 "Batman Theme") ... 20-30 66
(Monaural.)
W.B. (WS-1642 "Batman Theme") ... 25-30 66
(Stereo.)
WORLD PACIFIC (1870 "Sun Power") ... 15-25 67
Members: Ben Benay; Mike Henderson; Ray Pohlman; Tommy Tedesco; Bill Pittman; Gene Pello; Tom Hensley; Richard Hobaica.
Also see NEW MARKETTS
Also see TEDESCO, Tommy

MARK-ETTS
Singles: 7-inch
BIG 20 ... 5-8

MARKEYS
Singles: 7-inch
RCA (7256 "Hot Rod") ... 10-20 58

MAR-KEYS P&R/R&B '61
Singles: 7-inch
SATELITE (107 "Last Night") ... 10-15 61
STAX ... 4-8 61-66
LPs: 10/12-inch
ATLANTIC ... 20-25 61-62
STAX ... 10-20 66-71
Members: Donald Dunn; Steve Cropper; Don Nix; Charles Axton; Wayne Jackson; Smoochie Smith; Terry Johnson; Andrew Love; Joe Arnold.
Also see MEMPHIS HORNS
Also see PACKERS
Also see TRIUMPHS

MAR-KEYS / Booker T. & MGs LP '67
LPs: 10/12-inch
STAX (720 "Back to Back") ... 12-18 67
Also see BOOKER T. & MGs
Also see MAR-KEYS

MARKEYS
Singles: 7-inch
TWENTIETH FOX (1210 "Eternal Love") ... 30-40 61

MARKHAM, Don, & Marksmen
Singles: 7-inch
DONNA ... 8-12 60-61

MARKHAM, Junior, & Tulsa Review
Singles: 7-inch
UPTOWN ... 4-6 69

MARKHAM, Mark
(With the Jesters)
Singles: 7-inch
POWER (4225 "Marlboro Country") ... 20-30 66
RCA (8992 "Marlboro Country") ... 10-15 66
LPs: 10/12-inch
ATHENS FIRE ... 15-25
Session: Mark Markham; Scott Austin.

MARKHAM, Pigmeat P&R/R&B/LP '68
Singles: 7-inch
ABC ... 3-5 74
CHESS ... 4-8 64-70
WIG ... 6-12
EPs: 7-inch
CHESS (5128 "Pigmeat Markham – *The Trial* Excerpts") ... 10-15 61
LPs: 10/12-inch
CHESS ... 10-20 61-69
JEWEL ... 5-10 72-73
Also see MABLEY, Moms, & Pigmeat Markham

MARKLEY, Bob
(Markley)
Singles: 7-inch
W.B. (5140 "Tiajuna Ball") ... 15-25 60
W.B. (5167 "It Should've Been Me") ... 15-25 60
LPs: 10/12-inch
FORWARD (1007 "A Group") ... 15-25 69
Also see WEST COAST POP ART EXPERIMENTAL BAND

MARKLEY BAND
Singles: 7-inch
ACCORD ... 3-4 81
TOWNHOUSE ... 3-4 82
LPs: 10/12-inch
ACCORD ... 5-8 81
TOWNHOUSE ... 5-8 82

MARKS, David: see DAVE & MARKSMEN

MARKS, Guy P&R '68
Singles: 7-inch
ABC ... 4-6 68
ARIOLA AMERICA ... 3-5 76
RADNOR ... 3-5 70
LPs: 10/12-inch
ABC ... 10-20 66-68

MARKS, J.
(J. Marks & Shipen Lebzelter)
LPs: 10/12-inch
COLUMBIA (7193 "Rock and Other Four-Letter Words") ... 15-25 68
COLUMBIA (30006 "First National Nothing") ... 10-15 70

MARKS, Lou
Singles: 7-inch
ABC ... 4-8 66

MARKS, Roosevelt
Singles: 7-inch
BOBBIN ... 5-10 59

MARKS, Steve / Jack Richards / Corwins
EPs: 7-inch
GILMAR (214 "Six Hits") ... 20-30 57
Also see CORWINS

MARKS, Zachary
Singles: 7-inch
REEL ... 5-10 60

MARKSMEN
Singles: 78 rpm
CORAL (61453 "Hot Rod") ... 8-12 55
Singles: 7-inch
CORAL (61453 "Hot Rod") ... 15-25 55

MARKSMEN
Singles: 7-inch
STARDAY (320 "Don't Gamble with My Heart") ... 200-300 57

MARKSMEN
Singles: 7-inch
BLUE HORIZON (6052 "Night Run") ... 30-50 61
Members: Nokie Edwards, Howie Johnson.
Also see VENTURES

MARKSMEN
Singles: 7-inch
WESTCO (10 "Down the Tubes") .. 10-20
(Black vinyl.)
WESTCO (10 "Down the Tubes") .. 20-40
(Colored vinyl.)

MARKSMEN
Singles: 7-inch
SARA (65128 "Black Pepper") ... 15-25 65
Members: Dick Neu; Ken Locke; Bob Allen Humpa; Ed Porcaro; Dan Vance; Jerry Bellamy.

MARKSMEN
Singles: 7-inch
DEARBORN ... 5-8 66

MARKTONES
Singles: 78 rpm
EMBER ... 15-25 57
Singles: 7-inch
EMBER (1022 "Hold Me Close") ... 15-25 57
EMBER (1030 "Yes, Siree") ... 15-25 57

MARLAND, Cletus
Singles: 7-inch
GENEVA (109 "Every Now and Then") ... 10-20

MARLBROUGH, Felton
Singles: 7-inch
LANOR ... 4-6

MARLENE, Gary
Singles: 7-inch
MAVERICK (591 "Look for a Star") .. 8-12 60

MARLENE & DEBANETTES
Singles: 7-inch
SUNBURST (1111 "Play Something Slow") ... 10-20
SUNBURST (9780 "Bad Love") ... 15-25 65

MARLETTES
(With the Imperial Orchestra)
Singles: 7-inch
HOWFUM ("Just the Way You Are") ... 2000-3000 58
(No selection number used.)

MARLEY, Bob, & Wailers LP '75
(Wailers)
Singles: 7-inch
COTILLION ... 3-5 81
ISLAND ... 3-5 76-84
SHELTER ... 3-5 71
TUFF GONG ... 4-6 74
Picture Sleeves
ISLAND ... 3-4 83
LPs: 10/12-inch
AUDIO FIDELITY (350 "Bob Marley") ... 10-15 83
(Picture disc.)
CALLA (1200 series) ... 10-15 76
CALLA (34000 series) ... 8-10 77
COTILLION ... 5-10 81
ISLAND (11 "Babylon By Bus") ... 10-12 78
ISLAND (9000 series except 9329) .. 8-12 75-80
ISLAND (9329 "Catch a Fire") ... 15-25 75
(Shaped cover.)
ISLAND (9329 "Catch a Fire") ... 8-10 75
(Standard cover.)
ISLAND (90000 series) ... 5-10 83-86
MFSL (221 "Exodus") ... 20-25 94
MFSL (236 "Catch a Fire") ... 20-25 95
Also see MELODY MAKERS
Also see TOSH, Peter

MARLEY, Lloyd
Singles: 7-inch
UNITED SOUTHERN ARTISTS ... 5-8 61

MARLEY, Rita
Singles: 7-inch
STUDIO ONE (5 "You Lied") ... 25-50

MARLEY, Ziggy, & Melody Makers: see MELODY MAKERS

MARLEY MARL LP '88
LPs: 10/12-inch
COLD CHILL ... 5-8 88

MARLIN & MERMAIDS
Singles: 7-inch
ABC-PAR ... 5-8 64

MARLINS
Singles: 7-inch
SANDY (1002 "Now I'm So Lonesome") ... 150-200 58

MARLINS
Singles: 7-inch
CAMEO (333 "Swim") ... 6-12 64

MARLINS
Singles: 7-inch
SCOTTY (818 "Let Down") ... 5-10 60s

MARLO, Bob
Singles: 7-inch
RONCO (104 "Straighten Up and Fly Right") ... 15-25

MARLO, Micki P&R '57
Singles: 78 rpm
ABC-PAR (Except 9841) ... 5-10 57
ABC-PAR (9841 "What You've Done to Me") ... 10-20 57
(With "Vocal assist by Paul Anka.")
ABC-PAR (9841 "What You've Done to Me") ... 5-10 57
(Has the singer humming the lines done by Paul Anka on first pressing.)
CAPITOL ... 4-8 54-56
Singles: 7-inch
ABC-PAR (Except 9841) ... 5-10 57
ABC-PAR (9841 "What You've Done to Me") ... 10-20 57
(With "Vocal assist by Paul Anka.")
ABC-PAR (9841 "What You've Done to Me") ... 5-10 57
(Has the singer humming the lines done by Paul Anka on first pressing.)
CAPITOL ... 5-10 54-56
LPs: 10/12-inch
ABC-PAR ... 15-25 60
Also see ANKA, Paul

MARLO, Russ
Singles: 7-inch
U.A. (112 "Tom Cattin' ") ... 30-40 58

MARLOW, Jerry, & Full House
Singles: 7-inch
TRUMP ... 5-10 61

MARLOW, Ricky
(Ric Marlow)
Singles: 7-inch
LIBERTY (55098 "Pretty Baby") ... 5-10 57
PAT (760 "She's Gone") ... 15-25

MARLOW, Ric
Singles: 7-inch
ZEPHYR (7 "That's What I'm Gonna Be") ... 75-125

MARLOWE, Marion P&R '54
(With Frank Parker)
Singles: 78 rpm
CADENCE ... 4-6 55-56
COLUMBIA ... 4-6 53-54
Singles: 7-inch
CADENCE ... 5-10 55-56
COLUMBIA ... 5-10 53-54
EPs: 7-inch
COLUMBIA ... 6-12 53-55
LPs: 10/12-inch
BARNABY ... 5-8 76
COLUMBIA ... 20-35 53-55
HARMONY ... 10-15 60

MARMALADE P&R/LP '70
Singles: 7-inch
ARIOLA AMERICA ... 3-5 76
EMI ... 3-5 74
EPIC ... 4-8 67-69
LONDON ... 3-6 70-72
LPs: 10/12-inch
EPIC ... 10-15 70
G&P ... 8-10 81
LONDON ... 10-15 70
Members: Dean Ford; Junior Campbell.
Also see BLUE
Also see CAMPBELL, Junior

MARNEY, Ben C&W '81
Singles: 7-inch
SOUTHERN BISCUIT ... 3-4 81

MARONI, Chuck
Singles: 7-inch
IMPERIAL ... 5-8 58

MAROONS
Singles: 7-inch
QUEEN (24012 "Someday I'll Be the One") ... 50-75 62

MARQUE V
Singles: 7-inch
W.B. ... 3-5 67

MARQUEE MONSTERS
Singles: 7-inch
OUR BAG (102 "Laws and Restrictions") ... 20-30

MARQUEES
Singles: 78 rpm
GRAND (141 "The Bells") ... 50-100 56
Singles: 7-inch
COLLECTABLES ... 3-4 80s
GRAND (141 "The Bells") ... 300-400 56
(Yellow label. Rigid disc. No company address shown. Reissued as by the Markees.)
Also see MARKEES

MARQUEES
Singles: 78 rpm
OKEH ... 75-100 57
Singles: 7-inch
OKEH (7096 "Hey Little School Girl") ... 75-100 57
Members: Marvin Gaye; Reese Palmer; Bob Hawkins; Chester Simmons; Nolan Ellison.
Also see GAYE, Marvin
Also see MOONGLOWS
Also see SPINNERS
Also see STEWART, Billy

MARQUEES
(With the Gene Joseph Trio)
Singles: 7-inch
DAYSEL (1001 "Close to Me") ... 300-400 58

MARQUEES
Singles: 7-inch
LEN (100 "Say Hey") ... 75-100 58

MARQUEES
(With the "Big Sound of Don Ralke")
Singles: 7-inch
W.B. (5072 "Who Will Be the First One") ... 20-40 59
W.B. (5127 "Sunset to Sunrise") ... 20-40 59
W.B. (5139 "Until the Day I Die") ... 50-75 60
Also see RALKE, Don

MARQUEES
(With the Rosco Weathers Orchestra)
Singles: 7-inch
JO ANN (128 "Stay with Me") ... 100-200 60
JO ANN (130 "I Need a Helping Hand") ... 75-125 61
Also see BROWN, Terry, & Marquees

MARQUIS
Singles: 78 rpm
RAINBOW ... 25-50 55
Singles: 7-inch
RAINBOW (358 "I Don't Want Your Love") ... 50-75 55

MARQUIS
(With the Sammy Lowe Orchestra)
Singles: 78 rpm
ONYX ... 200-300 56
Singles: 7-inch
ONYX (505 "Bohemian Daddy") ... 1000-2000 56
Also see BATEMAN, June
Also see LOWE, Sammy, Orchestra

MARQUIS
Singles: 7-inch
NOBLE (719 "Never Forget") . 1000-2000 59
(Repressed crediting the Tabs.)
Also see TABS

MARQUIS
Singles: 7-inch
CLASS (251 "Strange Is Love") ... 15-25 59
EARL ... 5-10

MARQUIS
Singles: 7-inch
TEEN GRAVE (201,159 "Broken Mirror") ... 20-30 66

MARQUIS
Singles: 7-inch
JCP (1024 "Walking a Stranger") ... 10-20 64

MARQUIS, Dick
Singles: 7-inch
DELTA ... 10-20 58

MARR, Hank
(Hank Marr Trio; Quartet)
Singles: 7-inch
FEDERAL ... 4-8 61-64
KING ... 3-6 68-69
WINGATE (012 "The Out Crowd") .. 8-12 66
LPs: 10/12-inch
KING ... 10-20 63-69

MARR, Hank / Sonny Stitt
Singles: 7-inch
WINGATE ... 5-10 66
Also see MARR, Hank
Also see STITT, Sonny

MARR, Leah C&W '88
Singles: 7-inch
OAK ... 3-4 88-89

MARRELL'S MARAUDERS
Singles: 7-inch
FAN JR (1003 "I Wanta Do It") ... 25-50 66
(Reissued twice as by Robin and the Three Hoods.)
Also see ROBIN & THREE HOODS

MARREN, Howard
Singles: 7-inch
FARGO ... 8-12 58

MARRINER, Neville LP '84
LPs: 10/12-inch
FANTASY ... 5-8 84

MARRIOTS
Singles: 7-inch
ABC ... 4-6 69

MARRIOTT, John C&W '89
Singles: 7-inch
PHOENIX ... 3-4 89

MARRIOTT, Steve
Singles: 7-inch
A&M ... 3-5 75
LP: 10/12-inch
A&M ... 8-12 76
Also see HUMBLE PIE
Also see SMALL FACES

MARRS, Troy
Singles: 7-inch
SURE SHOT ... 4-8 66

MARS, Marlina
Singles: 7-inch
CAPITOL ... 5-10 63
MGM ... 10-20 65-66
OKEH (7213 "It's Love That Really Counts") ... 15-25 64

MARS, Mitzi R&B '53
Singles: 78 rpm
CHECKER (773 "I'm Glad") ... 15-25 53
Singles: 7-inch
CHECKER (773 "I'm Glad") ... 20-40 53

MARS, Sylvia
LPs: 10/12-inch
LYRIC (124 "Blues Walk Right In") ... 40-60

MARS BONFIRE: see BONFIRE, Mars

MARSALIS, Branford LP '84
(Branford Marsalis Quartet Featuring Terence Blanchard)
LPs: 10/12-inch
COLUMBIA ... 5-8 84-90

MARSALIS, Wynton LP '82
LPs: 10/12-inch
COLUMBIA ... 5-8 82-91
WHO'S WHO in JAZZ ... 5-8 83

MARSDEN, Beryl
Singles: 7-inch
CAPITOL ... 5-8 65

MARSDEN, Gerry
Singles: 7-inch
COLUMBIA ... 5-8 67
Also see GERRY & PACEMAKERS

MARSH
Singles: 7-inch
DECCA ... 3-5 70

MARSH, Billy
Singles: 7-inch
ARROW (716 "Don't Tell Me") ... 4-8

MARSH, Dick: see MARSH, Richie

MARSH, Little Toni D&D '83
Singles: 12-inch
PRISM ... 4-6 83

MARSH, Richie
(Dick Marsh)
Singles: 7-inch
ACAMA ... 10-15 61
AVA ... 10-15 63
ROSCO ... 10-20 60
SHEPHERD ... 10-20 60s
Also see SAXON, Sky

MARSHAL, Gary
Singles: 7-inch
RCA ... 4-8 66-67
LPs: 10/12-inch
RCA ... 10-15 66
Also see MARCH, Peggy, & Gary Marshal

MARSHALL, Bob, & Crystals
Singles: 7-inch
DC (0433 "Ain't No Big Thing") ... 10-20 59
L-REV ... 4-8

MARSHALL, Carl "Soul Dog"
Singles: 7-inch
DOUBLE HIT ... 8-12

MARSHALL, Chuck, & Twist Stars
LPs: 10/12-inch
DECCA ... 15-20 62

MARSHALL, Dick, & Nighthawks
Singles: 7-inch
CUCA (6311 "Jitterbug Joe") ... 20-40 62

MARSHALL, Dodi
Singles: 7-inch
PULSE ... 4-8 65

MARSHALL, Eric, & Chymes
Singles: 7-inch
SIRE ... 10-15 68

Also see T.C. ATLANTIC

MARSHALL, Frankie

Singles: 78 rpm

ATCO 5-10 55-56
SPARK 5-10 55

Singles: 7-inch

ATCO 10-15 55-56
SPARK 10-15 55

MARSHALL, Jack

Singles: 7-inch

CAPITOL 5-10 60-64

LPs: 10/12-inch

CAPITOL (T-1939 "My Son the Surf Nut") 20-30 63
(Monaural.)
CAPITOL (ST-1939 "My Son the Surf Nut") 20-30 63
Stereo.)

MARSHALL, Lynn

Singles: 7-inch

CREST (1034 "Borrowed Love") 8-12 58
(Black vinyl.)
CREST (1034 "Borrowed Love") 15-20 58
(Colored vinyl.)

MARSHALL, Maria

Singles: 7-inch

KENT 5-10 60

LPs: 10/12-inch

CROWN (208 "Chubby Jackson Discovers Maria Marshall") 10-20 61
(Black vinyl.)
CROWN (208 "Chubby Jackson Discovers Maria Marshall") 20-35 61
(Colored vinyl.)
Also see JACKSON, Chubby

MARSHALL, Percy

Singles: 7-inch

MARSHALL (101 "Leaving Town") 15-25

MARSHALL, Roger C&W '88

Singles: 7-inch

AVM 3-4 88
MASTER 3-4 88

MARSHALL, Ron

Singles: 7-inch

MOHAWK 4-8 63

MARSHALL, Sammy

(With the Sun Rays; with Rays with Kris Arden & the Rays; Singing Sammy Marshall)

Singles: 7-inch

BLUE HILL 5-10 62
BROSH 4-8 63
CHEYENNE 4-8 63
CRESCENDO 5-10
JABAR 10-15
KEEPSAKE 4-8 63
MAYHAMS 4-8 64
PLEDGE 4-8 62
RANCHWOOD 4-8 62
ROXIE 5-10 61-62
SHOW 4-8 62
WORLD'S FAIR 4-8 64

MARSHALL, Sammy / Cara Stewart

EPs: 7-inch

AIR (5027 "I'll Always Love You") 4-6
Also see MARSHALL, Sammy

MARSHALL, Sonny, & Key Tones

Singles: 7-inch

BROSH BROS. (400 "Until Eternity") 15-25 60s

MARSHALL, Wayne

Singles: 7-inch

JOSIE 4-8 65

MARSHALL & WES

Singles: 7-inch

MILESTONE 5-10 60

MARSHALL & CHI-LITES

Singles: 7-inch

DAKAR 4-8
Member: Marshall Thompson.
Also see CHI-LITES

MARSHALL ARTS

Singles: 7-inch

KICKAPOO 4-8 66

MARSHALL BROTHERS

SAVOY 25-50 51

Singles: 7-inch

SAVOY (825 "Who'll Be the Fool from Now On") 350-450 51
SAVOY (833 "Why Make a Fool Out of Me") 350-450 52
Member: Maithe Marshall; Rich Cannon; Ray Johnson.
Also see COOK, Bill, & Marshalls
Also see RAVENS

MARSHALL - HAIN P&R '78

Singles: 7-inch

HARVEST 3-5 78

LPs: 10/12-inch

HARVEST 5-8 78
Members: Julian Marshall; Kit Hain.
Also see EYE to EYE

MARSHALL TUCKER BAND LP '73

Singles: 7-inch

CAPRICORN 3-5 73-78
MERCURY 3-4 87-88
W.B. 3-5 79-83

Picture Sleeves

W.B. 3-5 79

LPs: 10/12-inch

CAPRICORN 8-12 73-78
MERCURY 5-10 87
W.B. 5-10 79-83
Members: Doug Gray; Tom Caldwell; Troy Caldwell; Franklin Wilkie; Jack Eubanks; Paul Riddle.
Also see CLEMENTS, Vassar

MARSHALLS

Singles: 7-inch

ISABELLE 3-5 80

MARSHANS

Singles: 7-inch

ETIQUETTE 10-20 65
JOHNSON 10-20 66

MARSHMALLOW HIGHWAY

Singles: 7-inch

KAPP 4-8 68

MARSHMALLOW WAY

Singles: 7-inch

U.A. 5-8 69

LPs: 10/12-inch

U.A. 10-20 69
Member: Billy Carl.
Also see BILLY & ESSENTIALS

MARSHMELLO

Singles: 7-inch

DUNHILL 4-8 70

MARSHMELLOW STEAMSHOVEL

Singles: 7-inch

HEAD (1908 "Steamshovel") 10-20 64

MARSHMELLOW TUGBOAT

Singles: 7-inch

BLUE CORAL (5474 "Michelle, Be My Girl") 10-15 67

MARSHMELLOWS

Singles: 7-inch

COLUMBIA 4-8 67
VEEP 5-10 65

MARSHON, Chris

Singles: 7-inch

NIF 3-5 77
PHONO 3-5 77

MARTEL, Bill

Singles: 7-inch

IMPALA 5-10 59

MARTEL, Marty C&W '79

Singles: 7-inch

RIDGETOP 3-5 79

MARTEL, Rick

Singles: 7-inch

ARWIN 5-10 59

MARTELL, Linda C&W '69

(With the Anglos)

Singles: 7-inch

FIRE (512 "Little Tear") 10-15 62
PLANTATION 3-6 69-70

LPs: 10/12-inch

PLANTATION 6-12 70

MARTELLS

(Martels; Eulis Mason & Martells with Bellatones Orchestra)

Singles: 7-inch

BELLA (20 "Rockin' Santa Claus") 75-125 61
BELLA (45 "Forgotten Spring") 100-150 61
CESSNA (477 "Forgotten Spring") 150-200 61
NASCO (6026 "Where Did My Woman Go") 10-20 59
RELIC (517 "Forgotten Spring") 10-15 64

MARTELLS

Singles: 7-inch

A-LA-CARTE (283 "In the Morning") 10-20

MARTELS: see MARTELLS

MARTERIE, Ralph, & Orchestra P&R '51

Singles: 78 rpm

MERCURY 3-5 50-57

Singles: 7-inch

MERCURY 4-8 50-60
U.A. 3-6 61-62

EPs: 7-inch

MERCURY 5-10 50-59

LPs: 10/12-inch

MERCURY 8-18 50-60
U.A. 5-10 61-62
WING 5-10 56-60

MARTHA & BOB

Singles: 7-inch

GOLDEN CREST 5-10 60

MARTHA & MUFFINS LP '80

(M+M)

Singles: 12-inch

RCA 4-6 83-84

Singles: 7-inch

DINDISC/VIRGIN 3-5 80
RCA 3-4 83-84

LPs: 10/12-inch

CURRENT 5-8 84
RCA 5-8 83
VIRGIN 5-8 80

MARTHA & VANDELLAS P&R/R&B/LP '63

(Martha Reeves & the Vandellas)

Singles: 7-inch

GORDY (7011 "I'll Have to Let Him Go") 15-25 62
GORDY (7014 "Come and Get These Memories") 10-20 62
GORDY (7022 thru 7062) 6-12 63-67
(Black vinyl.)
GORDY (7062 "Love Bug Leave My Heart Alone") 8-15 67
(Colored vinyl. Promotional issue only.)
GORDY (7067 thru 7127) 4-8 67-72
(Black vinyl.)
GORDY (7113 "In and Out of My Life") 8-15 71
(Colored vinyl. Promotional issue only.)
MOTOWN 3-4
MOTOWN/TOPPS (7 "Dancing in the Street") 50-75 67
(Topps Chewing Gum promotional item. Single-sided, cardboard flexi, picture disc. Issued with generic paper sleeve.)
MOTOWN/TOPPS (14 "Heat Wave") 50-75 67
(Topps Chewing Gum promotional item. Single-sided, cardboard flexi, picture disc. Issued with generic paper sleeve.)
TAMLA/MOTOWN 4-8

Picture Sleeves

GORDY (7033 "Dancing in the Street") 20-30 64

EPs: 7-inch

GORDY (60920 "Watchout") 15-25 67
MOTOWN (2009 "Martha & the Vandellas") 15-25
MOTOWN (2017 "Hittin' ") 15-25

LPs: 10/12-inch

ERA 5-10 79
GORDY (902 "Come and Get These Memories") 100-200 63
(Monaural.)
GORDY (S-902 "Come and Get These Memories") 200-300 63
(Stereo.)
GORDY (907 "Heat Wave") 50-75 63
(Monaural.)
GORDY (S-907 "Heat Wave") 60-80 63
(Stereo.)
GORDY (915 "Dance Party") 50-75 65
(Monaural.)
GORDY (S-915 "Dance Party") 60-80 65
(Stereo.)
GORDY (917 "Greatest Hits") 20-30 66
GORDY (920 "Watchout") 20-30 67
GORDY (925 "Live") 15-25 66
GORDY (926 thru 958) 15-20 68-72
MOTOWN (Except 100 & 200 series) 12-15 74
MOTOWN (100 & 200 series) 5-8 81-82
PICKWICK 5-8
Members: Martha Reeves; Rosalind Ashford; Annette Beard; Betty Kelly; Lois Reeves; Sandra Tilley.
Also see ALAN, Lee, & Vandellas
Also see BEN, LaBrenda
Also see BROWN, James / Martha & Vandellas
Also see DEL-PHIS
Also see GAYE, Marvin
Also see HONDELLS / Del Shannon / Martha & Vandellas
Also see HOOKER, John Lee
Also see MALLETT, Sandra, & Vandellas
Also see QUIET ELEGANCE
Also see REEVES, Martha
Also see VELVELETTES
Also see VELLS

MARTIANS

Singles: 7-inch

ADMIRAL (110 "Martian's Rock") 5-10 64

MARTIKA P&R '88

(Martika Marrero)

Singles: 7-inch

COLUMBIA 3-4 88-91

Picture Sleeves

COLUMBIA 3-4 88

LPs: 10/12-inch

COLUMBIA 5-8 89

MARTIN, Al

(Alan Martin; Al Martin Six)

Singles: 7-inch

ARROW 5-10 57
BELL 5-10 64

MARTIN, Angel

Singles: 7-inch

RITZ 4-8 63

MARTIN, Angela

Singles: 7-inch

ABC-PAR 4-8 65
ATCO 4-8 64-65
PORTRAIT 5-10 61

MARTIN, Aston, & Moon Discs

Singles: 7-inch

DEL RIO (2301 "Fallout") 20-30 61

MARTIN, Barry

Singles: 7-inch

FREEDOM (44019 "Minnie the Moocher") 5-10 59
RCA (7834 "Got a Whole Lot of Loving to Do") 10-15 61
RCA (7864 "Little Lonely One") 10-15 61

MARTIN, Benny C&W '63

Singles: 7-inch

ASTRO (109 "Darling Goodbye") 100-150 60
DECCA 8-12 59
GULF REEF 10-15 62
HI 4-8 63
RCA (7100 "Do Me a Favor") 8-12 58
STARDAY 5-10 63

LPs: 10/12-inch

CMH 5-10
FLYING FISH 8-10
GUEST STAR 10-15 60s
MARATHON 8-10
(Canadian.)
WING 8-10 60s
Also see RENO, Don, & Benny Martin

MARTIN, Benny, & Bobby Sykes

LPs: 10/12-inch

PICKWICK/HILLTOP 10-15 65
Also see MARTIN, Benny
Also see SYKES, Bobby

MARTIN, Bet E.

Singles: 7-inch

BRUNSWICK (55107 "Pretty Lies") 5-10 58
EPIC (9333 "Maybe You'll Be There") 20-30 59
EPIC (9362 "I Know a Girl") 10-15 60
EPIC (9414 "I Can't Find My Keys") 10-15 60
ERA 4-8 66
FORD (107 "Mrs. Santa Claus") 5-10 61

MARTIN, Betty C&W '78

Singles: 7-inch

DOOR KNOB 3-5 78

MARTIN, Billy

(With the Corvairs; Bill Martin)

Singles: 7-inch

LUCKY (0009 "If It's Lovin' That You Want") 25-50 60
MONITOR (1402 "I Found My Baby") 25-50 60s
TRIBUTE (115 "Come On") 10-15 62

MARTIN, Bobbi P&R '64

Singles: 7-inch

BUDDAH 3-5 71-72
CORAL 4-8 61-67
GREEN MENU 3-5 75
MGM 3-5 73
MAYPOLE 5-10 60
U.A. 4-6 68-70

Picture Sleeves

CORAL (62452 "I Love You So") 6-10 65

EPs: 7-inch

CORAL 8-12 65

LPs: 10/12-inch

BUDDAH 5-10 71
CORAL 10-20 65
SUNSET 5-10 71
U.A. 8-12 68-70
VOCALION 5-10 70

MARTIN, Bobby

(Bob Martin)

Singles: 7-inch

BEL-KAY ("Jo Jo Rock & Roll") 50-100 58
(Selection number not known.)
MAR-TONE (0001 "The World I Left Behind") 5-10 62
RUBY (390 "Sleepy Time Blues") 150-250 57
TIDE (0015 "My Heart Is Thumpy") 10-15 61
TODD (1013 "Hunk of Dynamite") 10-20 59
TREND 4-8 66

MARTIN, Buzz

Singles: 7-inch

RIPCORD (005 "Used Log Truck") 4-8 70

MARTIN, Chuck

Singles: 78 rpm

NASCO (6004 "Emma Lee") 20-30 57

Singles: 7-inch

JIN (128 "As Long As I Have You") 15-25
NASCO (6004 "Emma Lee") 20-30 57

MARTIN, Cliff, & Cliff Dwellers

Singles: 7-inch

CREST (500 "Full Time Job") 5-8

MARTIN, Danny

Singles: 7-inch

RIOT 15-20 57

Singles: 7-inch

RIOT (431 "Rockin' Memphis Mama") 25-30 57

MARTIN, David

Singles: 7-inch

DJM 3-4 79

MARTIN, Dean P&R '49

Singles: 78 rpm

APOLLO (1088 "Oh Marie") 100-150 47
APOLLO (1116 "Santa Lucia") 100-150 48
CAPITOL (545 thru 2001) 15-25 49-52
CAPITOL (2037 "Hey, Brother, Pour the Wine") 20-30 54
(Seven-inch 78 rpm. Promotional issue only.)
CAPITOL (2071 thru 3841) 10-20 52-57
CAPITOL (15000 series) 20-40 48-49
DIAMOND (2035 "Which Way Did My Heart Go") 100-150 46
DIAMOND (2036 "I Got the Sun in the Morning") 100-150 46
EMBASSY (124 "One Foot in Heaven") 500-1000 49

Singles: 7-inch

CAPITOL (401 "Dean Martin Sings") 75-100 53
(Boxed, four-disc set.)
CAPITOL (247 "Silver Bells") 10-15 66
(Promotional issue only.)
CAPITOL (691 thru 981) 25-35 49-50
CAPITOL (987 "Sleep Warm") 50-100 59
(Promotional issue only.)
CAPITOL (1002 thru 1458) 20-30 50-51
CAPITOL (1609 "I Met a Girl") 50-100 60
(Promotional issue only.)
CAPITOL (1703 thru 3238) 15-25 51-55
CAPITOL (3295 thru 4570) 10-20 55-61
CAPITOL (6000 series) 4-6 64
CAPITOL (44153 "That's Amore") 3-4 88
MCA (52662 "L.A. Is My Home") 15-25 85
REPRISE (190 thru 193) 6-12 64
(Compact 33 singles. Promotional issues only.)
REPRISE (200 "Sophia") 150-200 65
(Promotional issue only.)
REPRISE (0252 thru 1178) 4-8 64-73
REPRISE (20,000 series) 5-10 62-63
REPRISE (40,015 "Gigi") 15-25 62
(Stereo 33 single.)
REPRISE (40,016 "C'est Si Bon") 15-25 62
(Stereo 33 single.)
REPRISE (40,017 "Mimi") 15-25 62
(Stereo 33 single.)
REPRISE (40,018 "The River Seine") 15-25 62
(Stereo 33 single.)
REPRISE (40,019 "Mam'Selle") 15-25 62
(Stereo 33 single.)
TEXAS DESERT CIRCUS WEEK (2160 "It's 1200 Miles from Texas to Palm Springs") 50-100 58
(Single-sided promotional disc. Made especially for play in Palm Springs, promoting a circus. Incorrect title is shown on label—should read *It's 1200 Miles from Palm Springs to Texas.*)
W.B. (29584 "My First Country Song") 3-4 83
(With Conway Twitty.)
W.B. (29480 "Drinking Champagne") 3-4 83

Picture Sleeves

CAPITOL (987 "Sleep Warm") 100-200 59
CAPITOL (1609 "I Met a Girl") 50-100 60
(Promotional issue only. Sleeve reads: "From the Soundtrack of the Motion Picture *Bells are Ringing.*")
CAPITOL (4028 "Volare") 15-25 58
CAPITOL (4222 "On an Evening in Roma") 15-25 59
REPRISE (20,116 "Who's Got the Action") 15-20 62

EPs: 7-inch

CAPITOL (EAP-401 "Dean Martin Sings") 25-50 53
(Price is for either of two volumes.)
CAPITOL (EBF-401 "Dean Martin Sings") 75-125 53
(Boxed, two-disc set.)
CAPITOL (481 "Sunny Italy") 25-50 53
CAPITOL (576 "Swingin' Down Yonder") 20-40 59
(Price is for any of three volumes.)
CAPITOL (701 "Memories Are Made of This") 25-50 55
CAPITOL (702 "Artists & Models") 25-50 55
CAPITOL (806 "Hollywood Or Bust") 25-50 57
CAPITOL (840 "Ten Thousand Bedrooms") 25-50 57
CAPITOL (849 "Pretty Baby") 20-40 58
(Price is for any of three volumes.)
CAPITOL (939 "Return to Me") 20-40 58
CAPITOL (1027 "Volare") 20-40 58
CAPITOL (1285 "Winter Romance") 20-40 59
(Price is for any of three volumes.)
CAPITOL (1580 "Dean Martin") 20-30 61
(Compact Double 33.)
CAPITOL (EAP-1659 "Dino - Italian Love Songs") 15-25 61
CAPITOL (SU-1659 "Dino - Italian Love Songs") 15-25 61
(Juke box issue only. Includes title strips.)
CAPITOL (DU-2601 "The Best of Dean Martin") 15-25 61
(Juke box issue only. Includes title strips.)
CAPITOL (9123 "Dean Martin") 25-50 54
18 TOP HITS (27 "Dean Martin") 20-40 55
(Price for either 45 and 78 rpm EPs.)
LLOYDS (705 "Dean Martin") 25-50 54
(Mail-order offer.)
REPRISE 10-20 62-73
(Juke box 33 compact issues. Include title strips.)

LPs: 10/12-inch

CAPITOL (140 "The Best of Dean Martin, Vol. 2") 8-15 69
CAPITOL (378 "Dean Martin's Greatest") 8-15 69
CAPITOL (H-401 "Dean Martin Sings") 50-100 53
(10-inch LP.)
CAPITOL (T-401 "Dean Martin Sings") 25-50 55
(Red cover.)
CAPITOL (TT-401 "Dean Martin Sings") 10-20 59
(Pink cover.)
CAPITOL (523 "Return to Me"/"You're Nobody Till Somebody Loves You") 8-12 70
(Two discs.)
CAPITOL (524 "You're Nobody Till Somebody Loves You") 8-12 70
CAPITOL (576 "Swingin' Down Yonder") 30-40 55
CAPITOL (849 "Pretty Baby") 25-35 57
CAPITOL (T-1047 "This Is Dean Martin") 25-35 58
(Monaural.)
CAPITOL (DT-1047 "This Is Dean Martin") 8-12 63
(Stereo. Reprocessed.)
CAPITOL (1150 "Sleep Warm") 25-35 59
CAPITOL (1285 "A Winter Romance") 25-35 59

CAPITOL (1435 "Bells Are Ringing") 15-25 60
(Soundtrack.)
CAPITOL (1442 "This Time I'm Swingin' ") 15-25 60
CAPITOL (1659 "Italian Love Songs") 15-25 62
CAPITOL (1702 "Cha Cha De Amor") 15-25 62
CAPITOL (2212 "Hey Brother, Pour the Wine") 15-25 64
CAPITOL (2297 "Dean Martin Sings – Sinatra Conducts") 10-15 65
(Repackage of *Swingin' Down Yonder*.)
CAPITOL (2333 "Dean Martin Southern Style") 10-15 65
(Repackage of *Sleep Warm*.)
CAPITOL (2343 "Holiday Cheer") ..10-15 65
(Repackage of *A Winter Romance*.)
CAPITOL (2601 "Best of Dean Martin") 10-15 66
CAPITOL (2815 "Dean Martin Deluxe Set") 20-25 67
(Boxed, three-disc set.)
CAPITOL (2941 "Dean Martin Favorites") 8-12 68
CAPITOL (91285 "Winter Romance") 10-20 65
(Capitol Record Club series.)
COSMIC (450 "Dean Martin") 15-20
LONGINES (5234 "Memories Are Made of This") 25-50 73
(Boxed, five-disc set. Includes booklet.)
LONGINES (5235 "That's Amore").. 8-15 73
PAIR (1029 "Dreams & Memories") 8-10 83
(Two discs.)
PICKWICK 6-12 70s
REPRISE (2053 thru 2267) 8-15 72-78
REPRISE (5228 "Songbook") 10-15 70
(Two discs.)
REPRISE (6021 thru 6123) 15-25 62-64
REPRISE (6130 thru 6428) 10-20 64-70
REPRISE (93929 "On the Sunny Side") 10-20 68
(Capitol Record Club series.)
S.M.I. 10-20
SEARS 15-25 60s
TALKING BOOK (58007 "Look: December 26, 1967") 15-25 67
(Reading of a Dean interview/story in *Look*. Produced by the American Foundation for the Blind. Plays at 16 2/3 rpm.)
TEE VEE 10-20 78
TOWER (5006 "The Lush Years") 20-30 65
TOWER (5018 "Relaxin' ") 20-30 66
TOWER (5036 "Happy in Love") 20-30 66
TOWER (5059 "Like Never Before") 20-30 67
WALDORF (27 "Dean Martin Sings") 50-75 53
(10-inch LP.)
W.B. 5-8 83

Promotional LPs

("Dean Martin Testimonial Dinner") 200-300 59
(Presented by the Friars Club, and sold as a "Collectors Item" for $25 at the dinner. Three LPs in triple pocket jacket. No label name nor selection number used. With guest appearances by Jimmy Durante, Joey Bishop, Tony Martin, George Burns, Dinah Shore, Mort Sahl, Judy Garland; Sammy Cahn, Danny Thomas, Sammy Davis Jr., Bob Hope, Frank Sinatra and others.)
REPRISE ("Dean Martin as Matt Helm in the Silencers – Special Open-End Interview Record") 50-75 66
(Includes one-page script.)
REPRISE (246 "Dean Martin Radio Sampler") 35-50 66
Also see BURNS, George
Also see DURANTE, Jimmy
Also see GARLAND, Judy
Also see GILKYSON, Terry
Also see GOLDDIGGERS
Also see HOPE, Bob
Also see LEE, Peggy, & Dean Martin
Also see MARTIN, Tony
Also see SAHL, Mort
Also see SHORE, Dinah
Also see SINATRA, Frank, Sammy Davis Jr. & Dean Martin
Also see SINATRA, Nancy
Also see THOMAS, Danny
Also see TWITTY, Conway

MARTIN, Dean / Glen Campbell
LPs: 10/12-inch
ZENITH/CAPITOL 10-20 72
(Issued with paper cover. Special products.)
Also see CAMPBELL, Glen

MARTIN, Dean / Jeff Clark / Arlene James
EPs: 45/78 rpm
POPULAR (1035 "Oh Marie") 10-15 54
(78 rpm. Not issued with special cover.)
VICTORY (1031 "Walking My Baby Back Home") 10-15 54
(78 rpm. Not issued with special cover.)
POPULAR (1035 "Oh Marie") 10-20 54
(45 rpm. Not issued with special cover.)
VICTORY (1031 "Walking My Baby Back Home") 20-40 54
(45 rpm. Colored vinyl. Not issued with special cover.)

MARTIN, Dean, & Nat "King" Cole
Singles: 78 rpm
CAPITOL 4-6 54
Singles: 7-inch
CAPITOL 5-10 54
Also see COLE, Nat "King"

MARTIN, Dean / Bob Eberly / Gordon MacRae
LPs: 10/12-inch
BRIGADE (1310 "Dino, Gordon & Bob Sing") 20-40 50s
Also see DORSEY, Jimmy, Orchestra & Chorus
Also see MacRAE, Gordon

MARTIN, Dean / Jane Froman
Singles: 78 rpm
CAPITOL 5-10 53
Singles: 7-inch
CAPITOL (20030 "Who's Your Little Who Zis") 10-20 53
(Promotional issue only.)
Also see FROMAN, Jane

MARTIN, Dean / Jackie Gleason
LPs: 10/12-inch
CAPITOL SPECIAL MARKETS 8-10
Also see GLEASON, Jackie

MARTIN, Dean / Rock Hudson
Singles: 7-inch
NATIONAL FEATURES (2785 "Showdown") 20-30 73
(Interviews with *Showdown* film stars. Promotional issue only. Includes script.)
Also see HUDSON, Rock

MARTIN, Dean / Red Ingle & Natural Seven
Singles: 78 rpm
CAPITOL (726 "Vieni Su") 8-15 49
(Promotional issue only.)

MARTIN, Dean, & Jerry Lewis *P&R '48*
Singles: 78 rpm
CAPITOL (15000 series) 5-10 48
NATIONAL MASK & PUPPET CORP. ("Puppet Show") 10-20 50s
(Promotional issue only.)
EPs: 7-inch
CAPITOL (533 "Living It Up") 100-150 54
CAPITOL (752 "Pardners") 100-150 56
LPs: 10/12-inch
MEMORABILIA (714 "Dean Martin & Jerry Lewis - First Show") 10-15 74
RADIOLA (1102 "Dean Martin & Jerry Lewis on the Radio") 10-15
Also see LEWIS, Jerry

MARTIN, Dean / Nicolini Lucchesi
LPs: 10/12-inch
AUDITION (5936 "Dean Martin Sings, Niccolini Lucchesi Plays") 25-50 56

MARTIN, Dean / Johnny Mathis / St. James Pop Orchestra
EPs: 7-inch
JIMMY McHUGH (400 "Music by Jimmy McHugh") 30-40 10-15 81
(Promotional issue only.)
Also see MATHIS, Johnny

MARTIN, Dean, & Ricky Nelson
Singles: 7-inch
W.B. (2262 "My Rifle, My Pony and Me") 400-500 59
(Promotional issue only.)
Also see NELSON, Rick

MARTIN, Dean, & Nuggets
Singles: 78 rpm
CAPITOL 5-10 55
Singles: 7-inch
CAPITOL (3468 "I'm Gonna Steal You Away") 10-20 55
Also see NUGGETS

MARTIN, Dean, & Helen O'Connell
Singles: 78 rpm
CAPITOL 4-6 51
Singles: 7-inch
CAPITOL 5-10 51
Also see O'CONNELL, Helen

MARTIN, Dean / Patti Page
LPs: 10/12-inch
DECCA (79224 "Christmas Seals for 1962") 30-40 62
(Public service program for TB. Dean's show on one side, Patti's on flip.)
DECCA (79235 "Christmas Seals for 1962") 20-30 62
(Public service program for TB. Dean's and Patti's shows on one side, flip has Si Zenter and Vaughn Monroe.)
Also see MONROE, Vaughn
Also see PAGE, Patti
Also see ZENTER, Si

MARTIN, Dean, & Line Renaud
Singles: 78 rpm
CAPITOL 4-6 55
Singles: 7-inch
CAPITOL 5-10 55

MARTIN, Dean / Nelson Riddle
EPs: 7-inch
CAPITOL (1063 "Rio Bravo") 250-350 59
(Promotional only. Has special paper sleeve.)
Also see RIDDLE, Nelson

MARTIN, Dean, & Margaret Whiting
Singles: 78 rpm
CAPITOL 4-6 50
Singles: 7-inch
CAPITOL 5-10 50
Also see MARTIN, Dean
Also see WHITING, Margaret

MARTIN, Deana
Singles: 7-inch
REPRISE 4-6 66

MARTIN, Derek *P&R/R&B '65*
Singles: 7-inch
BUTTERCUP 5-10 70s
CRACKERJACK (4013 "Daddy Rollin' Stone") 10-20 63
ROULETTE (4631 "You Know") 8-10 65
ROULETTE (4647 "I Won't Cry Anymore") 8-10 65
ROULETTE (4670 "Don't Resist") 8-10 66
SUE (118 "Cha Cha Skate") 8-10 65
SUE (143 "Count to Ten") 10-20 66
VOLT 5-10 68
Also see FIVE PEARLS

MARTIN, Dewey, & Medicine Ball
Singles: 7-inch
RCA 5-8 71
UNI 5-8 70
LPs: 10/12-inch
UNI 10-15 70
Also see BUFFALO SPRINGFIELD
Also see SIR WALTER RALEIGH

MARTIN, Dick, & Swinging Strings
Singles: 7-inch
FILM CITY (2065 "Come Home") 150-200 59

MARTIN, Dino, Jr.
Singles: 7-inch
REPRISE 3-6 72
Also see DINO, DESI & BILLY

MARTIN, Dolores, & Striders
(Delores Martin)
Singles: 78 rpm
MYSTERY 10-20

MARTIN, Dude
Singles: 78 rpm
MERCURY 8-10 50
Singles: 7-inch
MERCURY 10-20 50
Also see THOMPSON, Sue

MARTIN, Eric *LP '83*
(Eric Martin Band)
Singles: 7-inch
CAPITOL 3-4 85
ELEKTRA 3-4 83
Picture Sleeves
CAPTIOL 3-4 85
LPs: 10/12-inch
ELEKTRA 5-8 83
Also see MR. BIG

MARTIN, Fred, & Matadors
Singles: 7-inch
SAXONY (1003 "Sharin' Sharon") .25-35 62
Also see LISS, Tommy, & Matadors
Also see WILLIS, Rollie, & Contenders

MARTIN, Freddy, & Orchestra *P&R '33*
Singles: 78 rpm
BLUEBIRD 3-6 38-42
BRUNSWICK 3-6 33-36
RCA 3-5 46-56
VICTOR 3-6 42-45
Singles: 7-inch
CAPITOL 4-6 63
DECCA 4-6 67-68
KAPP 4-6 61
RCA 5-8 50-56
EPs: 7-inch
CAMDEN 5-10 54-56
RCA 5-10 50-54
LPs: 10/12-inch
CAMDEN 10-20 54-56
CAPITOL 5-15 59-79
DECCA 5-10 67
KAPP 5-15 61-66
MCA 4-8 73-75
RCA 8-20 51-72
Also see GRIFFIN, Merv

MARTIN, Gail
Singles: 7-inch
REPRISE 4-8 68

MARTIN, Gene
Singles: 7-inch
LOOK 5-10 59

MARTIN, George, & Orchestra *P&R/LP '64*
Singles: 7-inch
U.A. (745 "Ringo's Theme") 15-20 64
U.A. (750 "A Hard Day's Night") 75-125 64
U.A. (800 series) 4-8 65
U.A. (50148 "Love in the Open Air") 20-25 67
Picture Sleeves
U.A. (745 "Ringo's Theme") 75-100 64
U.A. (750 "A Hard Day's Night") 1000-1200 64
Promotional Singles
U.A. (745 "Ringo's Theme") 20-30 64
(White label.)
LPs: 10/12-inch
U.A. (3377 "Off the Beatle Track") 30-40 64
(Monaural.)
U.A. (3383 "A Hard Day's Night") ...20-30 64
(Monaural.)
U.A. (3420 "George Martin") 15-25 65
(Monaural.)
U.A. (3448 "Help") 20-30 65
(Monaural.)
U.A. (3539 "The Beatle Girls") 25-35 66
(Monaural.)
Note: Promotional copies of 3383, 3448 & 3539 can be worth twice the above price ranges. We have yet to verify promo copies of the stereo versions, though, if any exist, at least the same increase would apply.
U.A. (6377 "Off the Beatle Track") 30-40 64
(Stereo.)
U.A. (6383 "A Hard Day's Night") ...20-30 64
(Stereo.)
U.A. (6420 "George Martin") 15-25 65
(Stereo.)
U.A. (6448 "Help") 20-30 65
(Stereo.)
U.A. (6539 "The Beatle Girls") 25-35 66
(Stereo.)
U.A. (6647 "London by George") 10-15 68
(Stereo.)
Also see BEATLES
Also see GERRY & PACEMAKERS

MARTIN, Grady
(With His Slew Foot Five; with Winging Strings)
Singles: 78 rpm
DECCA 3-6 53-55
Singles: 7-inch
DECCA 5-12 53-66
EPs: 7-inch
DECCA 6-18 55-64
MCA 3-5 73-78
LPs: 10/12-inch
DECCA 15-35 55-67
Also see CROSBY, Bing
Also see FOLEY, Red
Also see IVES, Burl, with Grady Martin & His Slew Foot Five
Also see TUBB, Ernest

MARTIN, Gypsy *C&W '81*
Singles: 7-inch
OMNI 3-4 81

MARTIN, J.D. *C&W '86*
Singles: 7-inch
CAPITOL 3-4 86

MARTIN, Jay
Singles: 7-inch
TOWER (403 "By Yourself") 20-30 67

MARTIN, Jack
Singles: 7-inch
CHART (3101 "Rocket Baby") 40-60

MARTIN, Janis *P&R '56*
Singles: 78 rpm
RCA (Except 6652) 10-20 56-57
RCA (6652 "My Boy Elvis") 15-25 56
Singles: 7-inch
BIG DUTCH 3-5 77
PALETTE (5071 "Teen Street") 5-10 61
RCA (6400 & 6500 series) 15-25 56
RCA (6652 "My Boy Elvis") 25-35 56
RCA (6700 thru 7300 series) 10-20 56-58
Promotional Singles
BIG DUTCH 4-6 77
PALETTE (5071 "Teen Street") 10-20 61
RCA (6400 & 6500 series) 20-40 56
RCA (6652 "My Boy Elvis") 35-45 56
RCA (6700 thru 7300 series) 20-40 56-58
EPs: 7-inch
RCA (4093 "Just Squeeze Me") ...75-100 58

MARTIN, Janis / Otto Bash
EPs: 7-inch
RCA (38 "Dealer's Prevue") 50-75 56
(Promotional issue only.)
Also see BASH, Otto

MARTIN, Janis / Hank Snow
EPs: 7-inch
RCA (76 "Love Me to Pieces") 25-50 56
(Promotional issue only.)
Also see MARTIN, Janis
Also see SNOW, Hank

MARTIN, Jean
Singles: 78 rpm
UNIQUE 4-8 56
Singles: 7-inch
CHART (1008 "Rock-A-Knock") 20-30
UNIQUE 5-10 56

MARTIN, Jerry
Singles: 7-inch
FREDIO (5901 "Janet") 150-250

MARTIN, Jerry *C&W '91*
Singles: 7-inch
DESERT STORM 3-5 91

MARTIN, Jesse
Singles: 7-inch
IMPALA 4-8 63

MARTIN, Jimmie
Singles: 7-inch
D (1219 "Signifyin' Monkey") 20-30 61

MARTIN, Jimmy *C&W '58*
(With the Sunny Mountain Boys; with J.D. Crowe)
Singles: 7-inch
DECCA (Except 30703) 3-8 59-72
DECCA (30703 "Rock Hearts") 10-15 58
EPs: 7-inch
DECCA 5-15 59-64
LPs: 10/12-inch
ANTHOLOGY of COUNTRY MUSIC 10-20
DECCA 10-30 60-72
GUSTO 5-10
MCA 5-10 72-81
Also see MONROE, Bill
Also see NITTY GRITTY DIRT BAND & Jimmy Martin
Also see OSBORNE BROTHERS

MARTIN, Jimmy, Combo
Singles: 7-inch
JAXON (501 "Rock the Bop") 200-300 57

MARTIN, Joey *C&W '78*
Singles: 7-inch
NICKELODEON 3-5 78

MARTIN, Kenny *R&B '58*
Singles: 7-inch
BIG TOP (3053 "Lovin' Man") 10-20 60
FEDERAL (12310 "I'm the Jivin' Mr. Lee") 50-75 57
FEDERAL (12330 "I'm Sorry") 25-50 58
FEDERAL (12350 "Now I Know") 25-50 59
FEDERAL (12354 "My Wish") 15-25 59
FEDERAL (12362 "Ask Me") 100-200 59
FEDERAL (12379 "Last Words of the Jivin' Mr. Lee") 15-25 60
PJ 5-10 66

MARTIN, Kenny Lee
Singles: 7-inch
DECCA 15-25 59
MGM 10-20 59

MARTIN, Lance
Singles: 7-inch
MALA 4-8 63

MARTIN, Larry
Singles: 7-inch
DeWITT (110 "A Man") 5-10 63

MARTIN, Lela
(With the Soul Providers)
Singles: 7-inch
MELA-TONE (401 "You Can't Have Your Cake") 25-35 63
STIGERS 5-10 60s

MARTIN, Lori
Singles: 7-inch
DEL-FI 4-8 63

MARTIN, Mandi
Singles: 7-inch
COLUMBIA 4-8 65

MARTIN, Marilyn *P&R/LP '86*
Singles: 7-inch
ATLANTIC 3-4 86-88
Picture Sleeves
ATLANTIC 3-4 86-88
LPs: 10/12-inch
ATLANTIC 5-8 86-88
Also see COLLINS, Phil, & Marilyn Martin

MARTIN, Martin
Singles: 7-inch
MGM 4-8 67

MARTIN, Marty
Singles: 7-inch
ANVIL 4-8 63

MARTIN, Mary
Singles: 7-inch
BUENA VISTA 5-10 58

MARTIN, Mickey
Singles: 7-inch
TALLY HO 4-8 61

MARTIN, Mike *C&W '85*
Singles: 7-inch
COMPLEAT 3-4 85
Also see DELRAY, Martin

MARTIN, Millicent
Singles: 7-inch
ABC-PAR 5-8 64

MARTIN, Moon *P&R/LP '79*
(John Martin)
Singles: 7-inch
CAPITOL 3-5 78-79
LPs: 10/12-inch
CAPITOL 5-10 78-82
Member: Jude Cole.
Also see COLE, Jude

MARTIN, Nancy *R&B '82*
Singles: 7-inch
ATLANTIC 3-4 82

MARTIN, Paul *R&B '65*
Singles: 7-inch
ASCOT 8-12 65
IMPEX 5-10 66

MARTIN, Pepe, & Features
Singles: 7-inch
TOP CATT 4-8 68

MARTIN, Ray, Orchestra *LP '61*
Singles: 7-inch
RCA 3-6 61-62
U.A. 4-8 58
Picture Sleeves
RCA 4-8 61
U.A. 5-10 58
LPs: 10/12-inch
CAMDEN 5-10 67-70
LONDON 8-12 63
MONUMENT 5-10 67
RCA 10-15 61

MARTIN, Red
Singles: 7-inch
SAGE (371 "Keep a Movin' ") 15-25 64

MARTIN, Ricci
Singles: 7-inch
CAPITOL 3-5 76

MARTIN, Rodge
Singles: 7-inch
BRAGG (227 "When She Touches Me") ... 5-10 60s
DOT (16394 "I'm Standing By") ... 8-12 62
DOT (16776 "I'm Standing By") ... 4-8 65
NEWARK ... 8-12 60s

MARTIN, Ronnie
Singles: 7-inch
BILLIE FRAN (4 "Storm of Love") ... 8-12 60s
CALDWELL ... 4-8

MARTIN, Rudy
Singles: 7-inch
CRYSTALETTE ... 5-8 62

MARTIN, Shane
Singles: 7-inch
COLUMBIA ... 10-20 68
EPIC ... 5-15 68-69

MARTIN, Sonny
Singles: 7-inch
EXCELLO ... 4-8 61
FELSTED ... 5-10 58

MARTIN, Steve
Singles: 7-inch
EMGE (1010 "Adorable One") ... 20-30
MAGNASOUND ... 4-8 63
Also see FIVE DISCS

MARTIN, Steve
Singles: 7-inch
ROULETTE ... 3-5 71
Also see LEFT BANKE

MARTIN, Steve P&R/LP '77
(With Toot Uncommons)
Singles: 7-inch
W.B. ... 3-5 77-79
Picture Sleeves
W.B. ... 3-5 77-78
LPs: 10/12-inch
W.B. ... 5-10 77-81

MARTIN, Tony P&R '38
Singles: 78 rpm
BRUNSWICK ... 4-8 38
DECCA ... 3-6 39-42
MERCURY ... 3-6 46-50s
RCA ... 3-6 47-57
Singles: 7-inch
CHART ... 3-5 70
DOT ... 4-6 61-66
DUNHILL ... 3-6 67
MERCURY ... 5-10 50s
MOTOWN ... 5-10 64-66
NAN ... 4-6 64
PARK AVENUE ... 4-6 63
RCA ... 5-10 50-60
EPs: 7-inch
DECCA ... 5-10 51-56
MERCURY ... 5-10 54-56
RCA ... 5-10 51-57
LPs: 10/12-inch
CAMDEN ... 10-20 59-60
CHART ... 5-10 70
CHARTER ... 10-15 63
CORAL ... 5-8 73
DECCA ... 15-25 51-56
DOT ... 10-15 61-62
MERCURY ... 10-20 54-61
RCA ... 15-25 51-60
20TH FOX ... 10-15 64
WING ... 10-15 59-60
Also see BABBIT, Harry / Tony Martin
Also see MARTIN, Dean
Also see SHORE, Dinah, Tony Martin, Betty Hutton & Phil Harris

MARTIN, Trade P&R '62
Singles: 7-inch
COED (570 "That Stranger Used to Be My Girl") ... 10-15 62
COED (575 "Strategy") ... 10-15 63
COED (590 "Send for Me") ... 10-15 63
COED (594 "Joanne") ... 30-50 64
GEE (1053 "La Mer") ... 10-15 59
RCA ... 4-8 66-67
ROULETTE (4258 "Pomp & Circumstance") ... 8-10 60
STALLION ... 4-6
TOOT ... 4-6 68
LPs: 10/12-inch
BUDDAH ... 10-15 72
Session: Tantones.
Also see GORGONI, Martin, & Taylor
Also see PIXIES THREE

MARTIN, Trudy
Singles: 7-inch
ADKORP ... 3-5 71-74

MARTIN, Vicky
Singles: 7-inch
BAND BOX (272 "Roller Coaster") ... 10-20

MARTIN, Vince P&R '56
(With the Tarriers; with Fred Neil)
Singles: 78 rpm
GLORY ... 5-10 56
Singles: 7-inch
ABC-PAR ... 5-10 59
GLORY ... 10-15 56
ELEKTRA ... 4-8 64
LPs: 10/12-inch
CAPITOL ... 5-10 73
ELEKTRA ... 10-20 64
Also see NEIL, Fred
Also see TARRIERS

MARTIN, Vinnie Jay
Singles: 7-inch
REPRISE ... 4-6 68
V.J.M. RUSS ... 4-8 65

MARTIN & FINLEY
Singles: 7-inch
MOTOWN ... 3-5 74
LPs: 10/12-inch
MOTOWN ... 8-12 74
Member: Tony Martin.
Also see BEVERLY HILLS BLUES BAND

MARTIN CIRCUS
Singles: 7-inch
ROULETTE ... 4-8 71
LPs: 10/12-inch
PRELUDE ... 8-10 79

MARTIN SISTERS
Singles: 7-inch
BARRY ... 4-8 66
DUB ... 8-10 57

MARTINDALE, Wink P&R/C&W '59
Singles: 7-inch
ABC/DOT ... 3-5 76
DOT ... 5-10 58-66
RANWOOD ... 3-5 73
Picture Sleeves
DOT ... 10-20 59-60
LPs: 10/12-inch
DOT ... 15-25 59-66
HAMILTON ... 10-20 64

MARTINDALE, Wink, & Robin Ward
Singles: 7-inch
DOT ... 4-8 63-64
LPs: 10/12-inch
DOT ... 15-25 64
Also see MARTINDALE, Wink
Also see WARD, Robin

MARTINE, Layng P&R '71
(Layng Martine Jr.)
Singles: 7-inch
BARNABY ... 3-5 71
DATE ... 5-10 66
GENERAL INT'L ... 4-8 66
PLAYBOY ... 3-5 76
Also see MORRISON, Professor

MARTINELS
Singles: 7-inch
SUCCESS (110 "Baby Think It Over") ... 20-25 63

MARTINEQUES
Singles: 7-inch
DANCELAND (777 "Tonight Is Just Another Night") ... 25-40 61
DANCELAND (779 "Broken Hearted Me") ... 25-40 62
DANCELAND (1002 "I Need Love") ... 20-30 62
ME-O ... 8-12 65

MARTINEZ, Frank, & Pharomen
Singles: 7-inch
SOMA (1419 "Jeanette") ... 40-60 60s

MARTINEZ, Hirth
LPs: 10/12-inch
W.B. (3031 "Big Bright Street") ... 5-10 77

MARTINEZ, Nancy P&R '86
Singles: 12-inch
ATLANTIC ... 4-6 86
Singles: 7-inch
ATLANTIC ... 3-4 86-87
LPs: 10/12-inch
ATLANTIC ... 5-8 86

MARTINEZ, Tony "Pepino"
LPs: 10/12-inch
DEL-FI ... 15-25 59

MARTINEZ, Val
Singles: 78 rpm
KING ... 4-8 53-54
Singles: 7-inch
GROOVE ... 4-8 62
KING ... 5-10 53-54
RCA ... 4-8 62-63

MARTINEZ-CHEDA PACHANGA BAND
Singles: 7-inch
DANCIN' (1001 "Tequila with a Twist") ... 10-15 62

MARTINI, Bernardo
Singles: 7-inch
PHILIPS (40090 "Silver Dust") ... 10-20 63

MARTINI, Dave
Singles: 7-inch
STONEWAY (1099 "Goofus") ... 5-10 73

MARTINI RANCE
Singles: 7-inch
SIRE ... 3-4
Picture Sleeves
SIRE ... 3-5

MARTINIQUES
Singles: 7-inch
DANCELAND (777 "Tonight Is Just Another Night") ... 50-100 62
DANCELAND (779 "Broken Hearted Me") ... 50-100 62
DANCELAND (1002 "I Need Love") ... 25-50 62
ROULETTE (4423 "Tonight Is Just Another Night") ... 15-25 62

MARTINIS
Singles: 7-inch
BAR (101 "Hung Over") ... 15-25 67
USA (893 "Holiday Cheer") ... 5-10 67

MARTINO, Al P&R '52
Singles: 78 rpm
BBS ... 5-10 52
CAPITOL ... 3-5 52-57
Singles: 7-inch
BBS (101 "Here in My Heart") ... 10-15 52
(Black vinyl.)
BBS (101 "Here in My Heart") ... 15-25 52
(Colored vinyl.)
CAPITOL (Except F-2122 thru F-4593) ... 3-8 62-81
CAPITOL (F-2122 thru F-4593) ... 5-15 52-61
JUBILEE (6000 series) ... 10-15 53
(Colored vinyl.)
MAZE (7025 "There's No Tomorrow") ... 5-10 62
20TH FOX ... 5-10 59-64
Picture Sleeves
CAPITOL ... 5-10 63-66
MAZE (7025 "There's No Tomorrow") ... 8-12 62
EPs: 7-inch
CAPITOL ... 10-15 63-64
(Juke box issues & Compact 33s.)
LPs: 10/12-inch
CAPITOL ... 5-20 62-80
GUEST STAR ... 5-10 64
MONTGOMERY WARD ... 10-15 60s
MOVIETONE ... 5-10 67
SPRINGBOARD ... 5-8 78
20TH FOX ... 10-20 59-65

MARTINO, Johnny
Singles: 7-inch
CHAM ... 10-15 58

MARTINSON, Vick, & 3 Bears
Singles: 7-inch
CUCA (1083 "Boo on You") ... 20-30 62

MARTY
Singles: 78 rpm
NOVELTY ... 10-15 56
Singles: 7-inch
NOVELTY (101 "Marty on Planet Mars") ... 20-30 56

MARTY
Singles: 7-inch
DI VENUS ... 8-12 67
Also see REGENTS

MARTY, Ellen
Singles: 7-inch
MARTY ... 4-8 64

MARTY & CHEETAS
Singles: 7-inch
COLUMBIA ... 5-8 66

MARTY & MELLOW YELLOW BUNCH
(With H.B. Barnum)
Singles: 7-inch
MEGA PHONE (101 "Two Bananas in Love") ... 5-10
Also see BARNUM, H.B.

MARTY & MERITS
Singles: 7-inch
KENILWORTH (9000 "Big Split Twist") ... 8-10 60s
KENILWORTH (9001 "Twist Twist Senora") ... 8-10 60s

MARTY & MONKS
Singles: 7-inch
ASSOCIATED ARTISTS ... 5-10 65

MARTY & SYMBOLS: see BASEMAN, M.R., & Symbols

MARTY'S MISFITS
Singles: 7-inch
TAPA ... 4-8 65

MARTYN, John
Singles: 7-inch
ISLAND ... 3-5 72
LPs: 10/12-inch
DUKE (90021 "Well Kept Secret") ... 5-8 82
ISLAND ... 8-10 73

MARTYN, John, & Beverly
Singles: 7-inch
W.B. ... 3-5 70
LPs: 10/12-inch
W.B. ... 10-12 70
Also see MARTYN, John

MARTZ, Jasun, & Neoteric Orchestra
LPs: 10/12-inch
ALL EARS ... 8-10 78

MARV & HARV
Singles: 7-inch
FILM (1020 "Sing Little Bird, Sing") 5-10 61

MARVA & SAVOYS
Singles: 7-inch
COED ... 5-10 63

MARVEL, Tina
Singles: 7-inch
LU-PINE (121 "Promises You Made to Me") ... 20-30 64

MARVELEERS
Singles: 78 rpm
DERBY ... 20-30 53
Singles: 7-inch
DERBY (829 "For the Longest Time") ... 50-75 53
DERBY (842 "All My Heart") ... 50-75 53
DERBY (844 "Love Me, Want Me") ... 50-75 53

MARVELETTES P&R/R&B '61
Singles: 7-inch
COLLECTABLES ... 3-4
MOTOWN ... 3-4
MOTOWN/TOPPS (12 "Please Mr. Postman") ... 50-75 67
(Topps Chewing Gum promotional item. Single-sided, cardboard flexi, picture disc. Issued with generic paper sleeve.)
TAMLA (54046 thru 54088) ... 6-12 61-63
TAMLA (54091 "He's a Good Guy [Yes He Is]") ... 6-12 64
(With subtitle.)
TAMLA (54091 "Yes He Is") ... 40-60 64
(No subtitle. Single-sided. Promotional issue only.)
TAMLA (54097 thru 54198) ... 5-10 64-71
(Black vinyl.)
TAMLA ... 8-12 69
(Colored vinyl. Promotional issues only.)
Picture Sleeves
TAMLA (54046 "Please Mr. Postman") ... 20-30 61
TAMLA (54054 "Twistin' Postman") ... 20-30 62
TAMLA (54097 "You're My Remedy") ... 15-25 64
EPs: 7-inch
MOTOWN (2003 "Marvelettes") ... 15-25 60s
TAMLA (60253 "Greatest Hits") ... 15-25 66
TAMLA (60274 "Marvelettes") ... 15-25 67
LPs: 10/12-inch
MOTOWN (Except 100 series) ... 10-15 75
MOTOWN (100 series) ... 5-8 82
TAMLA (228 "Please Mr. Postman") ... 150-250 61
TAMLA (229 "Marvelettes Sing Smash Hits of '62") ... 500-750 62
TAMLA (229 The Marvelettes Sing") ... 75-125 62
(Reissue with shorter title)
TAMLA (231 "Playboy") ... 50-100 62
TAMLA (237 "Marvelous Marveletes") ... 50-100 63
TAMLA (243 "On Stage") ... 50-75 63
TAMLA (253 "Greatest Hits") ... 15-20 66
TAMLA (274 "The Marvelettes") ... 15-20 67
TAMLA (286 thru 305) ... 10-20 68-70
Members: Gladys Horton; Kathy Anderson; Georgeanna Tillman; Wanda Young; Juanita Cowart; Ann Bogan.
Also see DARNELLS
Also see THEM / Marvelettes
Also see WESTON, Kim / Marvelettes

MARVELETTES / Mary Wells / Miracles / Marvin Gaye
Singles: 7-inch
TAMLA/MOTOWN ("Album Excerpts") ... 30-40 63
(Though from Tamla/Motown, no label name is shown, nor is there a title. Promotional issue only.)
Also see GAYE, Marvin
Also see MARVELETTES
Also see MIRACLES
Also see WELLS, Mary

MARVELIERS
Singles: 7-inch
COUGAR (1868 "Down") ... 100-200 60

MARVELIERS
Singles: 7-inch
JOANY (4439 "The Spider") ... 10-20

MARVELL, James C&W '81
Singles: 7-inch
CAVALEER ... 3-4 81
Also see COUNTRY CAVALEERS
Also see MERCY

MARVELLO, Bruce, & Red Coats
Singles: 7-inch
NIKKO (610 "Teen-Age Broken Hearts") ... 250-350 58

MARVELLOS
(Mar-Vellos; with "Jimmy Johnson Rhythm Acc.")
Singles: 78 rpm
THERON ... 100-200 55
Singles: 7-inch
CHA CHA (756 "Come Back My Love") ... 25-40 63
MARVELLO (5005 "Red Hot Mama") ... 150-250 62
MARVELLO (5005 "Cloud Nine") ... 100-150 62
STEPHANY (1818 "Come Back My Love") ... 100-150 58
THERON (117 "You're the Dream") ... 350-500 55

MARVELLOS
Singles: 7-inch
EXODUS (6214 "She Told Me Lies") ... 150-250 62
EXODUS (6216 "I Ask of You") ... 100-150 62
REPRISE (20088 "She Told Me Lies") ... 25-35 62

MARVELLOS
Singles: 7-inch
LOMA ... 4-8 66
MODERN ... 4-8 68
W.B. ... 4-8 67

MARVELLS
(With the Scott Johnson Orchestra)
Singles: 7-inch
MAGNET (1005 "Did She Leave You") ... 250-500 59

MARVELLS
Singles: 7-inch
FINER ARTS (2019 "The Miracle of Life") ... 10-20

MARVELOWS P&R/R&B '65
(Mighty Marvelows)
Singles: 7-inch
ABC ... 4-8 66-69
ABC-PAR ... 8-10 64-66
LPs: 10/12-inch
ABC ... 15-20 68
Members: Melvin Mason; Frank Paden; Johnny Paden; Jesse Smith; Sonny Stevenson; Andrew Thomas.
Also see NATURALS

MARVELS
Singles: 78 rpm
ABC-PAR ... 100-150 56
Singles: 7-inch
ABC-PAR (9771 "I Won't Have You Breaking My Heart") ... 200-300 56
Members: Richard Blandon; Jake Miller; Cleveland Still; Cordell Brown; Tom Gardner.
Also see DUBS
Also see HARRY M. & MARVELS

MARVELS
(Marvells)
Singles: 7-inch
LAURIE (3016 "So Young So Sweet") ... 50-75 58
WINN (1916 "For Sentimental Reasons") ... 150-200 61
(Artist credit not printed on label.)
WINN (1916 "For Sentimental Reasons") ... 100-150 61
(Artist credit printed on label.)
Also see SENATORS

MARVELS
Singles: 7-inch
MUNRAB (1008 "Just Another Fool") ... 1000-2000 59

MAR-VELS
(Mar-vells)
Singles: 7-inch
ANGIE (779 "Go on and Have Yourself a Ball") ... 10-20 63
BUTANE (779 "Go on and Have Yourself a Ball") ... 10-20 63
FOUR SONS ... 5-10 63
JASON SCOTT ... 4-8
LOVE (5011 "Cherry Lips") ... 75-100 58
(White label. Promotional issue only.)
LOVE (5011 "Cherry Lips") ... 50-75 58
(Red label.)
TAMMY (1016 "Somewhere in Life") ... 150-250 61
TAMMY (1019 "My Guardian Angel") ... 150-250 62
VEL (100 "Somewhere Love Is Waiting") ... 100-200

MARVELS
Singles: 7-inch
PYRAMID (6211 "Guiding Angel") ... 200-300 62
(The only copy of this we've seen is a promotional issue only that combines two "A-sides." So far, we do not know the flip of this, nor do we know the exact titles and numbers of the two commercial issues being promoted.)
Also see SEDAKA, Neil / Marvels

MAR-VELS
Singles: 7-inch
IN (102 "Endless Nights") ... 25-35 64

MAR-VELS
Singles: 7-inch
MELBOURNE (1538 "Someone Else") ... 15-25 66

MARVELS FIVE
Singles: 7-inch
UPTOWN ... 4-8 66

MARVELTONES
Singles: 78 rpm
REGENT (194 "So") ... 20-40 52
Singles: 7-inch
REGENT (194 "So") ... 50-75 52

MAR-VILLES
Singles: 7-inch
INFINITY (027 "The Drag") ... 10-20 62
(First issued by Eddie Ford. Reissued as by Rick & Rick-A-Shays.)
Also see FORD, Eddie
Also see RICK & Rick-A-Shays

MARVIN, Ken
Singles: 78 rpm
CAPITOL ... 4-8 50
MERCURY ... 10-15 51
RCA ... 3-6 54
Singles: 7-inch
CAPITOI (4000 series) ... 6-12 50
INTRO ... 5-8
RCA ... 5-10 54

MARVIN, Lee / Lee Marvin & Clint Eastwood
Singles: 7-inch
PARAMOUNT (10 "Wand'rin' Star") ... 4-8 69
Also see EASTWOOD, Clint

MARVIN, Long Tall
Singles: 7-inch
BOOGIE BOY ... 4-6

MARVIN, Paul
Singles: 7-inch
RON ... 5-10 59

MARVIN & CHIRPS
("Vocal by Marvin Williams")
Singles: 78 rpm
TIP TOP ... 75-125 58
Singles: 7-inch
TIP TOP (202 "I'll Miss You This Xmas") ... 100-200 58
Member: Marvin Williams.

MARVIN & FARRAR
LPs: 10/12-inch
EMI AMERICA ... 8-10
Members: Hank Marvin; John Farrar.
Also see MARVIN, WELCH & FARRAR
Also see SHADOWS

MARVIN & JOE
Singles: 7-inch
DORE (615 "The Picture Was Crying") ... 8-10 61

MARVIN & JOHNNY R&B '53
Singles: 78 rpm
ALADDIN ... 10-20 56
MODERN ... 15-30 54-56
RAYS ... 10-20 54
SPECIALTY ... 15-25 53-55
Singles: 7-inch
ALADDIN ... 15-25 56
ERIC ... 3-4 70s
FELSTED ... 4-8 63
FIREFLY ... 10-15 60
JAMIE ... 5-10 61
KENT (303 "Cherry Pie") ... 10-20 58
LIBERTY ... 3-5 80
MODERN ... 20-40 54-56
RAYS ... 15-25 54
SPECIALTY (Except 479) ... 25-50 53-55
SPECIALTY (479 "Baby Doll") ... 35-50 53
(Black vinyl.)
SPECIALTY (479 "Baby Doll") ... 50-80 53
(Colored vinyl.)
SWINGIN ... 8-12 61
LPs: 10/12-inch
CROWN (5381 "Marvin and Johnny") ... 35-55 63
UNITED (7796 "R&B Hits of the '50s") ... 10-15
Members: Marvin Phillips; Johnny Dean.
Also see ISLEY BROTHERS / Marvin & Johnny
Also see JESSE & MARVIN
Also see PHILLIPS, Marvin

MARVIN, WELCH & FARRAR
LPs: 10/12-inch
CAPITOL ... 10-12 71
SIRE ... 8-10 73
Members: Hank Marvin; John Farrar.
Also see MARVIN & FARRAR

MARVIN'S CIRCUS
Singles: 7-inch
MGM ... 4-8 67-68

MARX
(The Marx with Norman Baker Orchestra)
Singles: 7-inch
CHANTÉ (1002 "One Minute More") ... 50-100 59
DAHLIA (1002 "One Minute More") ... 150-250 59

MARX, Dick
Singles: 7-inch
OMEGA DISK ... 4-8 59

MARX, Groucho LP '72
Singles: 78 rpm
DECCA ... 4-8 51
YOUNG PEOPLE'S RECORDS ... 3-6 54
Singles: 7-inch
A&M ... 3-5 73
DECCA ... 10-20 51
YOUNG PEOPLE'S RECORDS ... 5-10 54
LPs: 10/12-inch
A&M (3515 "An Evening with Groucho") ... 5-10 72
A&M (PR-3515 "An Evening with Groucho") ... 15-20 78
(Picture disc. Includes booklet. Limited numbered edition.)
DECCA (5405 "Horray for Captain Spaulding") ... 100-150 52
(10-inch LP.)
Also see KAYE, Danny, Jimmy Durante, Jane Wyman & Groucho Marx
Also see MARX BROTHERS

MARX, Harpo
EPs: 7-inch
RCA (329 "Harp by Harpo") ... 15-25 50
LPs: 10/12-inch
MERCURY (20232 "Harpo in Hi-Fi") ... 25-45 57
(Monaural.)
MERCURY (20363 "Harpo at Work") ... 25-35 58
(Monaural.)
MERCURY (60232 "Harpo in Hi-Fi") ... 40-60 57
(Stereo.)
MERCURY (60363 "Harpo at Work") ... 30-50 58
(Stereo.)
RCA (27 "Harp by Harpo") ... 50-75 50
(10-inch LP.)
RCA (2720 "Harp by Harpo") ... 15-25 63
WING (12164 "Harpo") ... 20-40 59
Also see MARX BROTHERS

MARX, Melinda
Singles: 7-inch
VEE JAY ... 4-8 64

MARX, Richard P&R/LP '87
Singles: 7-inch
EMI ... 3-4 88-90
EMI/MANHATTAN ... 3-4 88
MANHATTAN ... 3-4 87
Picture Sleeves
EMI ... 3-4 89
EMI/MANHATTAN ... 3-4 88
MANHATTAN ... 3-4 87
LPs: 10/12-inch
CAPITOL ... 5-8 91-92
EMI ... 5-8 89
EMI/MANHATTAN ... 5-8 88
MANHATTAN ... 5-10 87
Also see SCHMIT, Timothy B.
Also see WAYBILL, Fee

MARX BROTHERS LP '69
LPs: 10/12-inch
DECCA (9169 "Marx Brothers") ... 8-12 69
(With Gary Owens.)
Also see MARX, Groucho
Also see MARX, Harpo

MARY & DESIRABLES
Singles: 7-inch
CHECKER ... 5-10 65

MARY B.
Singles: 7-inch
FLING ... 4-8 62

MARY BUTTERWORTH
Singles: 7-inch
CUSTOM FIDELITY ("Phase II") ... 10-20 69
(Selection number not known.)
LPs: 10/12-inch
CUSTOM FIDELITY (2092 "Mary Butterworth") ... 175-275 69
Members: Mike Hunt; Mike Ayling; Mike Eachus; Jim Giordano.

MARY Ds
Singles: 7-inch
ECHO ... 5-10 61
PRESIDENT ... 5-10 60

MARY ELLEN
(With Maxwell Davis Orchestra)
Singles: 7-inch
GRAMO (5504 "This Love of Mine") ... 20-30 60s
Also see DAVIS, Maxwell

MARY JANE GIRLS R&B/D&D/LP '83
Singles: 12-inch
GORDY ... 4-6 83-85
MOTOWN ... 4-6 85-87
Singles: 7-inch
GORDY ... 3-4 83-87
MOTOWN ... 3-4 85-87
Picture Sleeves
GORDY ... 3-4 85
MOTOWN ... 3-4 86
LPs: 10/12-inch
GORDY ... 5-8 83-87
Members: Joane "Jo Jo" McDuffie; Candice "Candy" Ghant; Kim "Maxi" Wuletich; Yvette "Corvette" Marine.

MARY SUE: see JALOPY FIVE

MARYLANDERS
Singles: 78 rpm
JUBILEE ... 50-100 52-53
Singles: 7-inch
JUBILEE (5079 "I'm a Sentimental Fool") ... 200-300 52
JUBILEE (5091 "Make Me Thrill Again") ... 200-300 52
JUBILEE (5114 "Fried Chicken") ... 100-150 53
(Black vinyl.)
JUBILEE (5114 "Fried Chicken") ... 200-300 53
(Colored vinyl.)

MARZ
LPs: 10/12-inch
LIBERTY ... 5-8 82

MAS, Carolyn P&R/LP '79
Singles: 7-inch
MERCURY ... 3-5 79
LPs: 10/12-inch
MERCURY ... 5-10 79

MASAKO
(Darlene Yoshimoto)
Singles: 7-inch
MAHALO ... 4-6 63
LPs: 10/12-inch
MAHALO ... 8-12 63

MASCARA D&D '84
Singles: 12-inch
OH MY ... 4-6 84

MASLON, Jimmie Lee
LPs: 10/12-inch
ROLLIN' ROCK ... 10-15 80s

MASCOTS
Singles: 7-inch
MGM ... 8-10 59

MASCOTS
Singles: 7-inch
KING (5377 "Story of My Heart") ... 50-100 60
KING (5435 "Lonely Rain") ... 40-60 60
Also see FERGUSON, H-Bomb / Escos / Mascots

MASCOTS
(With Vinny Catalano & Orchestra)
Singles: 7-inch
BLAST (206 "Once Upon a Love") ... 20-30 62
(Red label.)
BLAST (206 "Once Upon a Love") ... 15-20 63
(White label.)
MERMAID (107 "Bluebirds Over the Mountain") ... 50-100 64

MASEKELA, Hugh P&R/LP '67
(With the Union of South Africa)
Singles: 12-inch
JIVE AFRIKA ... 4-6 84
Singles: 7-inch
BLUE THUMB ... 3-5 74
CASABLANCA ... 3-5 75-77
CHISA ... 3-6 67-71
JIVE AFRIKA ... 3-4 84
MGM ... 3-6 66-68
MERCURY ... 3-8 63-68
UNI ... 3-6 67-69
LPs: 10/12-inch
BLUE THUMB ... 5-10 72-74
CASABLANCA ... 5-10 75-77
CHISA ... 8-15 67-71
IMPULSE ... 5-10 78
MGM ... 8-15 66-68
MERCURY ... 8-18 63-67
UNI ... 8-12 67-69
UPFRONT ... 5-8 77
VERVE ... 8-15 68
WING ... 6-12 68
Also see ALPERT, Herb, & Hugh Masekela

MASERANG
(With Charades)
Singles: 7-inch
EAGLE AMERICAN ... 3-5 78

MASH
Singles: 7-inch
COLUMBIA (45130 "Suicide Is Painless") ... 5-10 70

MASHBURN, Billy
("A Spectorious Production")
Singles: 7-inch
ATLANTIC (2208 "Don't It Sound Good") ... 8-12 63

MASHBURN, Jack, & Blue Notes
Singles: 7-inch
SPARKLE (101 "Blue Note Rock") ... 8-12

MASHER, Hugh
Singles: 7-inch
LAURIE ... 4-8 62

MASHERS
Singles: 7-inch
HAMILTON ... 4-8 63

MASHMAKHAN P&R '70
Singles: 7-inch
EPIC ... 3-6 70
JAMIE ... 4-8 69
LPs: 10/12-inch
EPIC ... 10-12 70-71
Members: Puerre Senecal; Jerry Mercer; Ray Blake; Brian Edwards.
Also see APRIL WINE

MASK, James
Singles: 7-inch
ARBEL (500 "I Miss My Teen Angel") ... 10-20
BANDERA (1306 "Save Your Love") ... 35-45 60

MASKED DEMONS
Singles: 7-inch
R.R.E. (1016 "Hi Surfin'") ... 20-30 63

MASKED MARAUDERS LP '70
Singles: 7-inch
DEITY ... 5-8 69
LPs: 10/12-inch
DEITY (6378 "Masked Marauders") ... 15-20 69
Also see CLEANLINESS & Godliness Skiffle Band

MASKED MARVELS
LPs: 10/12-inch
BETHLEHEM ... 15-25 62

MASKMAN & AGENTS R&B '68
Singles: 7-inch
DYNAMO ... 4-8 68-69
GAMMA ... 4-8 68
HITBOUND ... 3-5
LOOP ... 10-15 72
MUSICOR ... 3-5 70
VIGOR (707 "Stand Up") ... 5-10
LPs: 10/12-inch
DYNAMO ... 10-15 69
MUSICOR ... 10-15 70
Members: Harmon Bethea; Paul Williams; John Hood; Ty Gray.
Also see BETHEA, Harmon

MASON
LPs: 10/12-inch
ELEVENTH HOUR (1001 "Harbour") ... 50-75 71
Members: Jim Gaylon; Steve Arcese; Marg Hampton.

MASON R&B '87
Singles: 7-inch
ELEKTRA ... 3-4 87

MASON, Ann: see LITTLE MAC & Boss Sounds

MASON, Barbara P&R/R&B/LP '65
(With the Futures)
Singles: 12-inch
WEST END ... 4-8 83-84
Singles: 7-inch
ARCTIC ... 4-8 64-68
BUDDAH ... 3-5 71-75
CHARGER ... 4-8 65
NATIONAL GENERAL ... 3-5 70
PHONORAMA ... 3-5 84
PRELUDE ... 3-5 78
WMOT ... 3-5 80-81
WEST END ... 3-5 83-84
LPs: 10/12-inch
ARCTIC ... 15-25 65-68
BUDDAH ... 8-12 72-75
GNC ... 10-15 70
NATIONAL GENERAL ... 10-15 70
PHONORAMA ... 5-8 84
PRELUDE ... 8-10 78
WMOT ... 8-10 81
W.B. ... 8-12 77
WIND ... 8-10 81
Also see FUTURES
Also see HIGGINS, Monk

MASON, Barbara, & Larks
Singles: 7-inch
CRUSADER (111 "Dedicated to You") ... 8-12 64
Also see LARKS

MASON, Barbara, & Bunny Sigler
Singles: 7-inch
W.B. ... 3-5 77
Also see MASON, Barbara
Also see SIGLER, Bunny

MASON, Bonnie Jo
(Cher)
Singles: 7-inch
ANNETTE (1000 "Ringo, I Love You") ... 500-1000 64
Also see CHER

MASON, Clint
Singles: 7-inch
S.P.Q.R. ... 4-8 63

MASON, Dave P&R/LP '70
Singles: 7-inch
ABC ... 3-5 74
BLUE THUMB ... 3-5 70-78
COLUMBIA ... 3-5 73-81
MARBLE ... 3-4 83
LPs: 10/12-inch
ABC ... 8-10 75
BLUE THUMB (19 "Alone Together") ... 10-12 70
(Black vinyl.)
BLUE THUMB (19 "Alone Together") ... 20-30 70
(Multi-colored vinyl.)
BLUE THUMB (34 thru 54) ... 10-15 72-73
BLUE THUMB (800 series) ... 8-10 75
BLUE THUMB (6000 series) ... 8-10 74-78
COLUMBIA (Black vinyl) ... 8-10 73-81
COLUMBIA (Colored vinyl) ... 10-15 73-81
(Promotional only.)
ISLAND ... 5-8 83
Also see MERRYWEATHER, Neil
Also see TRAFFIC

MASON, Dave / Les Dudek / Southside Johnny & Asbury Jukes / Walter Egan
EPs: 7-inch
COLUMBIA (AE7-1119 "June Is CBS Records Month at Tower Records") ... 8-12 77
(Columbia/Epic promotional issue only.)
Also see DUDEK, Les
Also see EGAN, Walter
Also see SOUTHSIDE JOHNNY & ASBURY JUKES

MASON, Dave, & Cass Elliot LP '71
Singles: 7-inch
DUNHILL ... 3-5 70-71
LPs: 10/12-inch
BLUE THUMB ... 12-15 71
Also see ELLIOT, Cass
Also see MASON, Dave

MASON, Ed
Singles: 7-inch
MILKY WAY ... 10-20 66

MASON, Eulis: see MARTELLS

MASON, Harvey R&B '76
Singles: 7-inch
ARISTA ... 3-5 76-81
LPs: 10/12-inch
ARISTA ... 5-10 78-81

MASON, Jackie LP '62
Singles: 7-inch
VERVE ... 3-6 62
EPs: 7-inch
VERVE (5076 "The Greatest Comedian in the World, Only Nobody Knows It") ... 5-10 62
(Promotional issue only.)
LPs: 10/12-inch
VERVE ... 8-18 62-64
W.B. ... 5-8 87

MASON, Jerry
Singles: 7-inch
CHESS ... 5-10 60
KAPP ... 5-10 59
SWAN ... 4-8 62
VANCO ... 5-10 68

MASON, Little Billy
Singles: 78 rpm
APEX ... 5-10 56-57
(Canadian.)
RAMA ... 5-10 56-57
Singles: 7-inch
APEX ... 10-15 56-57
(Canadian.)
RAMA ... 10-15 56-57
Also see DAVIS, Bob

MASON, Lynn
Singles: 7-inch
BEST ... 5-10 59

MASON, Mitzi
Singles: 7-inch
EMBER ... 5-10 60

MASON, Nick LP '81
(Nick Mason's Fictitious Sports)
Singles: 12-inch
COLUMBIA ... 4-6 85
Singles: 7-inch
COLUMBIA ... 3-5 81-85
LPs: 10/12-inch
COLUMBIA ... 5-8 81-85
Also see PINK FLOYD

MASON, Nick, & Rick Fenn LP '85
Singles: 7-inch
COLUMBIA ... 3-4 85
LPs: 10/12-inch
COLUMBIA ... 5-8 85
Also see MASON, Nick

MASON, Peter
Singles: 7-inch
LAWN ... 5-10 60

MASON, Ronnie
Singles: 7-inch
CRYSTALETTE (719 "Kinda Like Love") ... 15-25 58

MASON, Russ
Singles: 12-inch
CBS ASSOCIATED ... 4-6 84

MASON, Sandy C&W '67
Singles: 7-inch
HICKORY ... 4-6 67
JMI ... 4-6
MGM ... 4-8 65-66
ROULETTE ... 4-8 63

MASON, Sharon
Singles: 7-inch
DORE ... 5-10 59

MASON, Steve
Singles: 7-inch
MASON ... 5-10

MASON, Tommy, & Madhatters
Singles: 7-inch
CARDINAL (72 "The Game Is Done") ... 15-25 67
Also see MADHATTERS

MASON, Vaughan P&R/R&B '80
(With the Crew)
Singles: 12-inch
BRUNSWICK ... 4-6 80-81
LPs: 10/12-inch
BRUNSWICK ... 5-8 80
Also see AM-FM

MASON, Vaughan, & Butch Dayo R&B '81
Singles: 12-inch
SALSOUL ... 4-6 83
Singles: 7-inch
SALSOUL ... 3-4 82-83
LPs: 10/12-inch
SALSOUL ... 5-8 83
Also see MASON, Vaughan

MASON DIXON C&W '83
Singles: 7-inch
CAPITOL ... 3-4 88-89
PREMIER ... 3-4 86-87
TEXAS ... 3-5 83-86
Members: Frank Gilligan; Jerry Dengler; Rick Henderson.

MASON & DIXON
Singles: 7-inch
TOWER ... 3-6 69
LPs: 10/12-inch
TOWER ... 10-12 69

MASON DIXON DANCE BAND R&B '79
Singles: 7-inch
ALEXANDER STREET ... 3-5 79

MASON PROFFIT LP '71
Singles: 7-inch
AMPEX ... 3-5 71
HAPPY TIGER ... 4-6 70
LPs: 10/12-inch
AMPEX ... 8-10 71
HAPPY TIGER ... 8-12 70-71
W.B. ... 8-10 72-73
Members: John Talbot; Terry Talbot.
Also see SOUNDS UNLIMITED
Also see TALBOT BROTHERS

MASONICS
Singles: 7-inch
INTERPHON ... 4-8 64

MASQUE
Singles: 7-inch
BELL ... 4-8 66

MASQUERADERS P&R/R&B '68

Singles: 7-inch

ABC....4-8 75-76
AGP (108 "I'm Just an Average Guy")....5-10 69
BANG (4806 "Desire")....4-6 80
BELL (733 "I Ain't Got to Love Nobody Else")....8-12 68
L.A. BEAT (6605 "A Family")....25-50 60s
WAND (1168 "Let's Face Facts")....15-25 67
WAND (1172 "Sweet Lovin' Woman")....25-35 67

LPs: 10/12-inch

ABC....10-15 75
Members: Lee Hatim; Robert Wrightsil; David Sanders; Harold Thomas; Sam Hutchins.

MASQUERADERS

Singles: 7-inch

HI....4-6 75
HOT BUTTERED SOUL....4-6 75-76
MK (101 "Man's Temptation")....10-15 60s
STAIRWAY....10-20 60s
TOWER....5-10 66

MASQUERADERS

Singles: 7-inch

LABEAT....8-12
SOULTOWN....8-12

MASS

Singles: 7-inch

RCA....3-4 86

LPs: 10/12-inch

RCA....5-10 85

MASQUERADES

Singles: 7-inch

FORMAL (1011 "These Red Roses")....400-600 60
(Blue label.)
FORMAL (1012 "These Red Roses")....100-150 60
(Green label. Note number change.)

MASQUERADES

Singles: 7-inch

BOYD (1027 "The Whip")....250-350 64

MASS MEDIA

Singles: 7-inch

SENECA....4-8 71

MASS PRODUCTION P&R/R&B/LP '77

Singles: 7-inch

COTILLION....3-5 76-83

LPs: 10/12-inch

COTILLION....5-8 76-83
Members: Larry Marshall; Tiny Kelly; Ricardo Williams; Greg McCoy; James Drumgole; Lecoy Bryant; Kevin Douglas; Tyrone Williams; Emmanuel Redding; Samuel Williams.

MASSACHUSETTS DELEGATION

Singles: 7-inch

ORACLE....4-8 68

MASSE, Paul

LPs: 10/12-inch

LIBERTY....5-10 8-12

MASSENGALE, Joey

Singles: 7-inch

JAA DEE (500 "Ma'm Selle")....50-75

MASSER, Michael, & Mandrill R&B '77

Singles: 7-inch

ARISTA....3-5 77

Picture Sleeves

ARISTA....3-5 77
Also see MANDRILL

MASSEY, Barbara

Singles: 7-inch

IMPERIAL (5786 "You Call Me Angel")....15-25 61

MASSEY, Bill

Singles: 7-inch

GUYDEN....5-10 62
LANIER (002 "Ghost Town")....15-25 57

MASSEY, Edith

Singles: 7-inch

EGG (001P "Punks Get Off the Grass")....15-20 84
(Picture disc.)

MASSEY, Jimmy

Singles: 7-inch

ROBBEE (113 "Moon Rock")....10-20 61

MASSEY, Wayne P&R '80

Singles: 7-inch

MCA....3-4 83
MERCURY....3-4 89
POLYDOR....3-5 80
Also see McCLAIN, Charly, & Wayne Massey

MASSI, Jimmy
(Jimmy Massey)

Singles: 7-inch

ROBBEE....5-10 60-61

MASSI, Nick

Singles: 7-inch

ONE WAY....4-6
Also see 4 SEASONS
Also see HOLLYWOOD PLAYBOYS
Also see NICKIE & NITELITES
Also see VICTORIANS

MASSIAH, Maurice D&D '83

Singles: 12-inch

RFC/QUALITY....4-6 83

MASSIEL

Singles: 7-inch

BELL....4-6 68

MASTER, Freddy: see MASTER FREDDY

MASTER, Ronnie, & Rainbows

Singles: 7-inch

LANDA (669 "I Don't Know")....20-30 61

MASTER FOUR

Singles: 7-inch

TAY-STER (012 "It's Not the End")....25-50 67

MASTER FREDDY & PLEDGES

Singles: 7-inch

KAREN....10-20 60

MASTER KEYS

Singles: 78 rpm

JUBILEE (5004 "I Got the Blues in the Morning")....15-25 49
20TH CENTURY....15-25 49

MASTER OF CEREMONY Featuring Don Barron R&B '87

Singles: 7-inch

4TH & BROADWAY....3-4 87-88

LPs: 10/12-inch

4TH & BROADWAY....3-4 88

MASTER PLAN

Singles: 7-inch

CRUSH....3-4 88

MASTERDON COMMITTEE R&B '86

Singles: 12-inch

PROFILE....4-6 86-87

Singles: 7-inch

PROFILE....3-4 86-87

LPs: 10/12-inch

PROFILE....5-8 86

MASTERETTES

Singles: 7-inch

LESAGE (716 "Follow the Leader")....50-75 61
Members: Brenda Reid; Sylvia Wilbur; Carol Johnson; Lillian Walker.
Also see EXCITERS

MASTERKEYS

Singles: 78 rpm

ABBEY (2017 "Mr. Blues")....30-40
SPORT (109 "If You Haven't Got Love")....15-25 67

MASTERMIND

LPs: 10/12-inch

PRELUDE....8-10 77

MASTERPIECE R&B '80

Singles: 7-inch

WHITFIELD....3-5 80

LPs: 10/12-inch

WHITFIELD....5-10 80

MASTERS

Singles: 7-inch

END (1100 "A Man Is Not Supposed to Cry")....150-200 61
LEN (103 "Til I Return")....50-100 58
LE SAGE (713 "I'm Searching")....250-500 61
Member: Herb Rooney.
Also see BRENDA & HERB

MASTERS
(Featuring Willie Morris)

Singles: 7-inch

BINGO (1008 "A Lovely Way to Spend an Evening")....50-75 60

MASTERS

Singles: 7-inch

EMMY (10082 "Breaktime")....35-50 62

MASTERS, A.J. C&W '85

Singles: 7-inch

BERMUDA DUNES....3-4 85-87

MASTERS, Johnny
(Johnny Maestro)

Singles: 7-inch

COED (527 "Say It Isn't So")....15-20 60
Also see MAESTRO, Johnny

MASTERS, Ken

Singles: 7-inch

DECCA (31084 "Too Late")....10-15 60

MASTERS, Rex / Four Jacks / Art Rouse / Clarence Cunningham

EPs: 7-inch

BIG 4....5-10 57

MASTERS, Sammy P&R '60

Singles: 78 rpm

DECCA....8-12 57
4 STAR....25-50 57

Singles: 7-inch

DECCA....8-12 57
DOT....5-10 60-66
4 STAR (1695 "Pink Cadillac")....30-50 57
4 STAR (1697 "Whop-T-Bop")....30-50 57
GALAHAD....4-8 62-72
KAPP....4-8 64
LODE....5-10 60-61
TJB BRANDES....5-10
W.B.....5-10 60

EPs: 7-inch

4 STAR (26 "Sammy Masters")....50-75 57
(Promotional issue only. Not issued with cover.)

MASTERS CHILDREN
(Master's Children)

Singles: 7-inch

T-A....3-5 70

MASTERS OF AIRWAVES

LPs: 10/12-inch

EPIC....8-10 74

MASTERS OF DECEIT

LPs: 10/12-inch

VANGUARD (6522 "Electric Jazz Band")....20-30 69
Member: Tom Hensley.

MASTERS OF HOUSTON

Singles: 7-inch

OVIDE....10-15

MASTERS OF SOUL

Singles: 7-inch

CAPITOL....5-10 68-69
DUKE....4-8 70-71
OVIDE (247 "I Need You")....10-20 60s
OVIDE (251 "The Vow")....10-20 60s
OVIDE (253 "Sad Face")....10-20 60s

MASTERS OF STONEHOUSE

Singles: 7-inch

DISCOTEQUE (2 "If You Treat Me Bad Again")....8-12

MASTER-TONES

Singles: 78 rpm

BRUCE....100-200 54

Singles: 7-inch

BRUCE (111 "What'll You Do")....350-450 54
(Black vinyl. With "45 R.P.M." above the top horizontal line. Reads: "N.Y. 19, N.Y.")
BRUCE (111 "What'll You Do")....200-250 50s
(Colored vinyl. With "45 R.P.M." between the parallel horizontal lines. Reads: "N.Y. 19, N.Y.")
BRUCE (111 "What'll You Do")....25-50 62
(Black vinyl. With "45 R.P.M." between the parallel horizontal lines. No postal zone shown for N.Y. address.)

MASTRIO, Johnny
(Johnny Mastrio Quartet; Quintet)

Singles: 7-inch

FRANKIE (1 "I Wish")....15-20 57
Also see CLASSMATES
Also see DE LISA, Pete

MASTRO, Johnny: see MAESTRO, Johnny

MATA, Billy C&W '88

Singles: 7-inch

BGM....3-4 88

MATADORS

Singles: 7-inch

SUE (700 "Vengeance")....75-125 58
SUE (701 "Be Good to Me")....45-55 58

MATADORS

Singles: 7-inch

CHAVIS (1034 "Carmen, I Wish You Were Here")....10-20 62
DUCHESS (1005 "If I Had Another Chance")....15-25 61
KEITH (6502 "If You Left Me Today")....20-30 62
KEITH (6504 "My Foolish Heart")....15-25 63

MATADORS

Singles: 7-inch

COLPIX (698 "Perfidia")....10-20 63
COLPIX (718 "I've Gotta Drive")....40-50 63
(*I Gotta Drive* is actually by Jan Berry, Dean Torrance & Jill Gibson.)
COLPIX (741 "C'mon, Let Yourself Go")....10-20 64
Members: Tony Minichiello; Vic Diaz; Manuel Sanchez.
Also see GIBSON, Jill
Also see JAN & DEAN

MATADORS
("Featuring John Lopacinski")

Singles: 7-inch

LEE (5466 "Should I Ever Love Again")....50-100 65

MATADORS

Singles: 7-inch

FEATURE (109 "You're a Better Man Than I")....15-25 66
Members: Ronnie Thone; Roman Brotz; Greg Busch; Lee McGlade; Tommy Raml.

MATADORS

Singles: 7-inch

CHART MAKER ("Let Me Dream")....100-200 66
FORBES (230 "Let Me Dream")....20-30 67

MATCH

Singles: 7-inch

RCA....3-5 70

LPs: 10/12-inch

RCA....8-12 69

MATCH BOX

Singles: 7-inch

SIRE....3-5 80

LPs: 10/12-inch

SIRE....5-10 80

MATCHBOX

Singles: 7-inch

BARNABY....3-5 72
MCA....3-4 81

MATCHES

Singles: 7-inch

JAGUAR (712 "Gonna Build Myself a Castle")....15-25 66

MATCHETT, Donnie

Singles: 7-inch

SCOTTY (945 "Come on Baby")....8-12

MATCHING MOLE

LPs: 10/12-inch

COLUMBIA....10-15 73

MATCHMAKERS

Singles: 7-inch

ROULETTE....3-4 85

Picture Sleeves

ROULETTE....3-4 85

MATEO, Gia

Singles: 7-inch

RCA (9138 "If You Can't Say Anything Nice")....15-25 67

MATERIAL

Singles: 12-inch

ELEKTRA....4-6 82

Singles: 7-inch

ELEKTRA....3-4 82-83

LPs: 10/12-inch

ELEKTRA....5-8 82-83

MATERIAL ISSUE LP '91

LPs: 10/12-inch

MERCURY....5-8 91

MATERLYN & CUPONS

Singles: 7-inch

IMPACT (29 "I'll Be Your Love Tonight")....10-20 64

MATERO, Ricky

Singles: 7-inch

HILLSIDE....4-8 62

MATERO, Rocky

Singles: 7-inch

ATCO....5-10 60

MATHENY, Linda

Singles: 7-inch

GALLO....4-8 63

MATHERS, Jerry "Beaver"

Singles: 7-inch

ATLANTIC....5-10 62

MATHEWS, Bill, & Balladeers
(With the Balladiers)

Singles: 78 rpm

ARLINGTON....15-25 49
MERCURY....20-30 48

MATHEWS, Dino

Singles: 7-inch

DOT (16365 "The Girl That I Love")....30-40 62

MATHEWS, Randy

Singles: 7-inch

MYRRH....3-5 75

MATHEWS, Ronnie

Singles: 7-inch

DAYHILL (2004 "Lonesome Teenager")....15-20

MATHEWS, Tobin P&R '60
(Tobin Mathews & Co.; Tobin Matthews)

Singles: 7-inch

CHIEF....8-12 60-61
COLUMBIA....4-8 63
U.S.A. (718 "Think It Over")....10-20 61

MATHEWS BROTHERS

Singles: 7-inch

ABC-PAR....15-20 63

MATHIESON, Muir

Singles: 78 rpm

COLUMBIA....4-6 56

Singles: 7-inch

COLUMBIA....5-10 56

MATHIEU, Mireille LP '69

LPs: 10/12-inch

CAPITOL....8-12 69

MATHIS, Bobby, & Sevilles

Singles: 7-inch

SIOUX (51860 "Girl in the Drugstore")....100-150 60

MATHIS, Country Johnny C&W '63

Singles: 7-inch

D....5-10 59-60
LITTLE DARLIN'....4-6 66
U.A.....4-8 61-65

LPs: 10/12-inch

HILLTOP....15-25 65
LITTLE DARLIN'....10-20 67-70
PICKWICK....6-12 70s
Also see JIMMY & JOHNNY

MATHIS, Joel C&W '74

Singles: 7-inch

CHART....3-5 74
SOUNDWAVES....3-5 78

MATHIS, Johnny P&R/R&B/LP '57
(With Ray Conniff)

Singles: 78 rpm

COLUMBIA....15-30 57-58

Singles: 7-inch

AURAVISION (6726 "Starbright")....8-12 64
(Cardboard flexi-disc, one of six by six different artists. Columbia Record Club "Enrollment Premium." Set came in a special paper sleeve.)
COLUMBIA (Except 40000 series)....3-5 74-85
COLUMBIA (40784 thru 42916)....5-15 58-63
COLUMBIA (44266 thru 46048)....3-8 67-74
MERCURY....4-8 63-66

Picture Sleeves

COLUMBIA (40993 "Chances Are")....10-20 57
COLUMBIA (41060 thru 42799)....5-10 58-63
MERCURY....4-8 63-66

EPs: 7-inch

COLUMBIA (Except 8800 series)....10-20 57-59
COLUMBIA (8871 thru 8873)....15-25 56

LPs: 10/12-inch

COLUMBIA (Except 887)....5-15 57-87
COLUMBIA (887 "Johnny Mathis")....35-50 56
COLUMBIA HOUSE (6030 "Johnny Mathis")....15-25 73
(Boxed 6-disc set. Record club offer.)
COLUMBIA SPECIAL PRODUCTS....5-8
CONCERT....8-12
(TV mail-order offer.)
HARMONY....5-10
MFSL (171 "Heavenly")....20-30 85
MERCURY....8-15 64-67
Also see CONNIFF, Ray
Also see FAITH, Percy, Orchestra / Johnny Mathis
Also see KNIGHT, Gladys, & Johnny Mathis
Also see NELSON, Willie / Nat "King" Cole / Johnny Mathis / Shirley Bassey

MATHIS, Johnny / Tony Bennett / North Carolina Ramblers / Ray Conniff & Jerry Vale

Singles

AURAVISION ("Most Beautiful Girl")....8-12 63
(Square cardboard picture disc. Sampler with highlights from each artist's new album.)
Also see BENNETT, Tony
Also see CONNIFF, Ray
Also see VALE, Jerry

MATHIS, Johnny, & Henry Mancini LP '87

LPs: 10/12-inch

COLUMBIA....5-8 87
Also see MANCINI, Henry

MATHIS, Johnny, & Dionne Warwick P&R '82

Singles: 7-inch

ARISTA....3-5 82
Also see WARWICK, Dionne

MATHIS, Johnny, & Deniece Williams P&R/R&B/LP '78

Singles: 7-inch

COLUMBIA....3-5 78-84

LPs: 10/12-inch

COLUMBIA (35435 "That's What Friends Are For")....30-50 78
(Picture disc. Promotional issue only.)
COLUMBIA (35435 "That's What Friends Are For")....5-10 78
(Standard vinyl disc.)
Also see MATHIS, Johnny
Also see WILLIAMS, Deniece

MATHIS, Kathy R&B '87

Singles: 7-inch

TABU....3-4 87

MATHIS, Lucille
(Lucille Matthis)

Singles: 7-inch

A-BET (9427 "I'm Not Your Regular Woman")....10-15 68

MATHIS & HILLYER

Singles: 7-inch

96X....3-6

MATHIS BROTHERS

Singles: 7-inch

HICKORY (1414 "When I Stop Dreaming")....10-20 60s

MATLOCK, Ronn R&B '79

Singles: 7-inch

COTILLION....3-5 79

MATRIX

LPs: 10/12-inch

PABLO....8-10
RARE EARTH....10-12 72
W.B.....8-10 78-79

MATRIX IX

LPs: 10/12-inch

RCA....8-10 77

MATT, Bill

Singles: 7-inch

LANOR....4-8 64

MATT & BRIAN
(Matt & Brian Band)

Singles: 7-inch

MARMATT....4-6 85-87
Members: Matt McGasko; Brian Marusak.
Also see MUSEUM

MATT & ROBERT

Singles: 7-inch

UNI....3-6 69

MATTEA, Kathy C&W '83
(With Tim O'Brien)

Singles: 7-inch

MERCURY....3-4 83-92

LPs: 10/12-inch
MERCURY 5-8 83-92
Also see GIBBS, Terri

MATTHEW, Otis
Singles: 7-inch
EXOTIC (8004 "Style of My Own") 15-25

MATTHEWS, Carl
Singles: 78 rpm
APOLLO 5-10 54
Singles: 7-inch
APOLLO 10-20 54

MATTHEWS, Dave
LPs: 10/12-inch
PEOPLE 10-15 71

MATTHEWS, David LP '77
LPs: 10/12-inch
CTI 5-10 77
Also see WASHINGTON, Grover, Jr.

MATTHEWS, Fat Man
Singles: 78 rpm
BAYOU 50-75 52
IMPERIAL 25-40 52
Singles: 7-inch
BAYOU (016 "I'm Thankful") 75-125 52
IMPERIAL (5235 "Down the Line") 50-80 52

MATTHEWS, Fat Man, & Four Kittens
Singles: 78 rpm
IMPERIAL 250-500 52
Singles: 7-inch
IMPERIAL (5211 "When Boy Meets Girl") 1000-1500 52
Also see MATHEWS, Fat Man

MATTHEWS, Hank
Singles: 7-inch
HOLLY 15-25

MATTHEWS, Ian LP '72
Singles: 7-inch
DECCA 3-5 70-71
COLUMBIA 3-5 76-77
ELEKTRA 3-5 73
MUSHROOM 3-5 78-79
VERTIGO 3-5 71-72
LPs: 10/12-inch
CAPITOL 8-10 71
COLUMBIA 8-10 77
DECCA 8-12 71
ELEKTRA 8-10 73-74
MUSHROOM (Except 5012) 8-10 78
MUSHROOM (5012 "Stealin' Home") 10-20 78
(Picture disc. Promotional issue only.)
MUSHROOM (5012 "Stealin' Home") 8-10 78
(Standard vinyl disc.)
VERTIGO 10-12 71-72
Also see FAIRPORT CONVENTION
Also see HI FI Featuring David Surkamp & Ian Matthews
Also see MATTHEWS' SOUTHERN COMFORT

MATTHEWS, Joannie Mae
(Johnnie Mae Mathews)
Singles: 7-inch
ART 8-12
BLUE ROCK 10-15 65
NORTHERN (3736 "Ooh Wee") 15-25 60
NORTHERN (3742 "So Lonely") 15-25 60
NORTHERN (10039 "It's Good") 15-25 60s
REEL (112 "My Little Angel") 20-30
SPOKANE 10-15 64
SUE 10-15 62

MATTHEWS, Joe
Singles: 7-inch
KOOL KAT (1001 "Ain't Nothing You Can Do") 100-200 59
THELMA (104 "She's My Beauty Queen") 100-200 64
THELMA (107 "Sorry Ain't Good Enough") 25-50 64

MATTHEWS, Little Arthur
Singles: 78 rpm
DIG 15-25 56
FEDERAL 15-25 55
Singles: 7-inch
DIG (117 "Bad Bad Buldog") 20-30 56
FEDERAL (12232 "I'm Gonna Whale on You") 20-30 55

MATTHEWS, Milt R&B '78
Singles: 7-inch
H&L 3-5 78

MATTHEWS, Randy
Singles: 7-inch
MYRRH 3-5 76
LPs: 10/12-inch
MYRRH 5-8 76
NEW PAX 5-8

MATTHEWS, Renee
Singles: 7-inch
SQUARE 4-8 61

MATTHEWS, Shirley
(With the Big Town Girls)
Singles: 7-inch
AMY 4-8 64-65
ATLANTIC 4-8 63-64
TAMARAC (602 "Big Town Boy") 15-25 63
Also see 4 SEASONS

MATTHEWS, Tobin: see MATHEWS, Tobin

MATTHEWS FAMILY
Singles: 7-inch
CAMTONE 5-10 59
OKEH 4-8 60

MATTHEWS' SOUTHERN COMFORT P&R/LP '71
(Featuring Ian Matthews)
Singles: 7-inch
DECCA 3-5 71
LPs: 10/12-inch
DECCA 10-15 70-71
MCA 5-10 78
Also see MATTHEWS, Ian
Also see SOUTHERN COMFORT

MATTHIS, Lucille: see MATHIS, Lucille

MATTICE, Bob, & Phaetons
Singles: 7-inch
CUCA (1016 "What's All This") 35-55 61
CUCA (1034 "Safari") 15-25 61
Members: Tom Loos; Tom Reischl; Ralph Barfell; Jim Kelly; Jerry Kowall.

MATTISON, Ti
Singles: 7-inch
ENJOY 4-8 63

MATTSON, Bart
Singles: 7-inch
TAMPA 10-15 58

MATTSON, Marilyn
Singles: 7-inch
ALLIED (102 "He Means So Much to Me") 15-20

MATTY, Jay
Singles: 7-inch
ERA 5-8 59
LUTE 5-8 61

MATUMBI
LPs: 10/12-inch
EMI AMERICA 5-8 80

MATYS BROS. P&R '63
Singles: 78 rpm
CORAL (61941 "Crazy Street") 20-40 57
DECCA 4-8 56
ESSEX 4-8 54
Singles: 7-inch
BEE-BEE 5-10
CORAL (61941 "Crazy Street") 25-50 57
DECCA 8-10 56
ESSEX 8-10 54
FAYETTE 4-6 64
SELECT 4-6 62
SOUND 8-10 54

MAUCK, Carl, & Oilers
Singles: 7-inch
BELLAIRE (PD4 ("Oiler Cannonball") 10-15 80
(Picture disc.)

MAUDS P&R '68
Singles: 7-inch
DUNWICH 5-10 67
MERCURY 4-8 67-69
RCA 3-6 70
LPs: 10/12-inch
MERCURY 15-25 67

MAULDIN, Dickie
Singles: 7-inch
TAGG 5-10 59

MAUNDY QUINTET
Singles: 7-inch
PARIS TOWER (103 "2's Better Than 3") 20-30 67
Member: Bernie Leadon.
Also see LEADON, Bernie

MAUPIN, Ramon
Singles: 7-inch
FERNWOOD (101 "No Chance") 50-100 58
FERNWOOD (105 "Rockin' Rufus") 100-150 58
MEMPHIS (101 "Hey Rena") 50-75 61

MAURIAT, Paul LP '67
Singles: 7-inch
PHILIPS 3-5 67-71
Picture Sleeves
PHILIPS 3-5 68
LPs: 10/12-inch
PHILIPS 8-18 67-71

MAURICE & MAC
Singles: 7-inch
BROWN SUGAR (0103 "Use That Good Thing") 4-8 72
CHECKER 10-15 67-69
Members: Maurice McAlister; Green McLauren.
Also see RADIANTS

MAURICE & RADIANTS: see RADIANTS

MAURO, Vince
Singles: 7-inch
POP-SIDE 5-10

MAUVE
Singles: 7-inch
CORI (31006 "You've Got Me Cryin' ") 15-25 66

MAVERICKS
Singles: 7-inch
SOMA (1406 "Tell Me How") 25-35 64
(Colored vinyl.)
SOMA (1408 "Cold Cold Darling") 10-20 64
Also see TIBOR BROTHERS

MAVERICKS
Singles: 7-inch
20TH FOX 5-10 65

MAVERICKS
Singles: 7-inch
CUCA (69103 "Patty Joanne, Christine") 10-15 69

MAVERICKS C&W '92
Singles: 7-inch
MCA 3-4 92-95
LPs: 10/12-inch
MCA 5-15 92-95

MAVRICKS
(Gary Paxton)
Singles: 7-inch
CAPITOL (4507 "Angel with a Heartache") 10-20 61
CAPITOL (4560 "Going to the River") 10-20 61
Note: If the Mavricks' 1958 recording of *You're Ruining My Gladness* is on record, we would like to know its label name and number.)
Also see PAXTON, Gary

MAV-RICKS
Singles: 7-inch
MAV-RICK 10-20

MAX, Mini: see MINI MAX

MAX DEMIAN: see DEMIAN, Max

MAX PLANCK / Kil-D-Kor
Singles: 7-inch
SANATY 3-4 86
Members: Rod Freeman; Eddie Forcier; Spike; Shane Peck; Brian Coloff; Brian Rand; Jeff Wilhelm; Don Martin.

MAX Q LP '89
LPs: 10/12-inch
ATLANTIC 5-8 89

MAX WEBSTER
LPs: 10/12-inch
CAPITOL 8-10 78-79
MERCURY 8-10 76-80

MAXAYN R&B '73
Singles: 7-inch
CAPRICORN 3-5 72-74
LPs: 10/12-inch
CAPRICORN 8-10 72-74
Members: Maxayn Lewis; Andre Lewis; Emilio Thomas; Marlo Henderson.
Also see IKETTES
Also see MANDRE

MAXEY, Hogman
LPs: 10/12-inch
ARHOOLIE 8-10

MAXEY, Mark
Singles: 7-inch
OUTSIDE ("Oral's Last Words") 4-6 80s
(No selection number used.)

MAXIM TRIO R&B '49
(Maxin Trio)
Singles: 78 rpm
DOWNBEAT (171 "Confession Blues") 40-60 49
Members: Ray Charles; Gosady McKee; Milton Garred.
Also see CHARLES, Ray

MAXIMAS
Singles: 7-inch
CREST (666 "Gladly") 10-15 70s

MAXIMILLIAN
(Max Crook)
Singles: 7-inch
BIG TOP 5-10 62
CUB 5-10 59
TWIRL 5-10 60
Also see SHANNON, Del

MAXIMILLIAN
LPs: 10/12-inch
ABC (696 "Maximillian") 20-40 69

MAXIMUS & His Projectors
Singles: 7-inch
MBM 4-8

MAXOPHONE
LPs: 10/12-inch
PAUSA 8-10 75

MAXUS
Singles: 7-inch
W.B. 3-4 82
LPs: 10/12-inch
W.B. 5-8 82

MAXWELL, Bobby, & Exploits
Singles: 7-inch
FARGO (1009 "Stay with Me") 50-75 59
FARGO (1010 "You're Laughing") 40-60 59

MAXWELL, Claude
Singles: 7-inch
W.B. 4-8 61

MAXWELL, Delores
Singles: 7-inch
BUMBLE BEE (506 "My Man") 30-40 60

MAXWELL, Diane P&R '59
Singles: 7-inch
CAPITOL 5-10 61
CHALLENGE 10-15 58-59
LPs: 10/12-inch
CHALLENGE (607 "Almost Seventeen") 30-40 59
(Monaural.)
CHALLENGE (2501 "Almost Seventeen") 40-60 59
(Stereo.)
Also see FULLER, Jerry, & Diane Maxwell

MAXWELL, Holly
Singles: 7-inch
CONSTELLATION 10-20 65
CURTOM 5-10 69
STAR 8-12 66

MAXWELL, Len
Singles: 7-inch
20TH FOX 4-8 64

MAXWELL, Martha
Singles: 7-inch
JO LAR 4-8 62
REED 4-8 63

MAXWELL, Robert P&R/LP '64
(Bobby Maxwell)
Singles: 78 rpm
MGM 3-5 57
MERCURY 3-5 52
TEMPO 3-5 51-52
Singles: 7-inch
DECCA 3-5 64
MGM 4-6 57
MERCURY 5-10 52
TEMPO 5-10 51-52
EPs: 7-inch
MGM 4-8 57
MERCURY 5-10 52
TEMPO 5-10 51-52
LPs: 10/12-inch
COMMAND 5-10 60s
DECCA 5-10 64
MGM 10-15 57
TEMPO 10-20 52

MAY, Billy, & His Orchestra P&R '52
Singles: 78 rpm
CAPITOL 3-5 50-56
Singles: 7-inch
CAPITOL 5-10 50-56
EPs: 7-inch
CAPITOL 5-10 50-56
LPs: 10/12-inch
CAPITOL 8-18 50-56

MAY, Brian LP '83
(Brian May & Friends)
Singles: 7-inch
CAPITOL 3-4 83
LPs: 10/12-inch
CAPITOL 5-8 83
Also see QUEEN
Also see REO SPEEDWAGON
Also see VAN HALEN

MAY, Don
Singles: 7-inch
BANDBOX 4-8 62

MAY, Gloria
Singles: 7-inch
CHESS 5-10 59

MAY, Patricia
Singles: 7-inch
PARKWAY 4-8 62

MAY, Ralph C&W '81
(With the Ohio River Band)
Singles: 7-inch
AMI 3-4 82
EVERGREEN 3-4 87
PRIMERO 3-4 82
SOUNDWAVES 3-5 81

MAY, Shirlee: see SHIRLEY MAY

MAY BLITZ
LPs: 10/12-inch
PARAMOUNT 10-12 70

MAYALL, John LP '68
(With the Blues Breakers Featuring Eric Clapton)
Singles: 7-inch
ABC 3-5 76
IMMEDIATE 4-8 67
LONDON 5-10 66-68
POLYDOR 3-8 69-74
LPs: 10/12-inch
ABC 8-12 76-78
BLUE THUMB 8-12 74
DJM 8-12 79
ISLAND 5-8 90
LONDON 10-15 67-78
MCA 5-8
MFSL (183 "Bluesbreakers Featuring Eric Clapton") 25-35 85
MFSL (246 "Blues Alone") 20-25 95
POLYDOR 10-12 69-74
Session: Jon Mark; Johnny Almond.
Also see BRUCE, Jack
Also see CLAPTON, Eric
Also see FLEETWOOD MAC
Also see GROUNDHOGS
Also see MARK - ALMOND BAND
Also see HARTLEY, Keef, Band
Also see TAYLOR, Mick

MAYANA D&D '83
Singles: 12-inch
ATLANTIC 4-6 83
Singles: 7-inch
ATLANTIC 3-4 83

MAYBE MENTAL
LPs: 10/12-inch
PLACEBO 6-10 84-86

MAYDAY
LPs: 10/12-inch
A&M 5-8 81-82

MAYE, Arthur Lee
(With the Crowns; Lee Maye; "Lee Maye of the Milwaukee Braves")
Singles: 78 rpm
DIG 25-75 56-57
FLIP 50-100 58
MODERN 50-100 54
RPM 50-75 55
SPECIALTY 20-30 56
Singles: 7-inch
ABC 5-8 68
ANTRELL (102 "Moonlight") 15-25 85
(Yellow label. Green vinyl.)
ANTRELL (102 "Moonlight") 3-5 85
(Gold label.)
CASH (1063 "Will You Be Mine") 100-150 58
CASH (1065 "All I Want Is Someone to Love") 100-150 58
DIG (124 "This Is the Night for Love") 150-250 56
DIG (133 "A Fool's Prayer") 100-150 57
(Original 45s of Dig 146 and 151 were not issued, though unauthorized discs do exist.)
FLIP (330 "Cause You're Mine Alone") 40-60 58
IMPERIAL (5790 "Will You be Mine") 35-50 61
JAMIE (1276 "How's the World Treating You") 10-15 64
JAMIE (1284 "Only a Game") 10-15 64
JAMIE (1287 "Even a Nobody") 10-15 65
KENT (406 "Love Me Always") 10-15 64
LENOX (5566 "Half Way") 10-15 63
MODERN (944 "Set My Heart Free") 200-300 54
RPM (424 "Truly") 100-200 55
RPM (429 "Love Me Always") 100-125 55
RPM (438 "Please Don't Leave Me") 75-125 55
SPECIALTY (573 "Gloria") 50-75 56
(With saw-tooth horizontal lines.)
SPECIALTY (573 "Gloria") 25-35 50s
(Without saw-tooth horizontal lines.)
TOWER (243 "At the Party") 8-10 66
Also see ANTRELL, Dave
Also see BERRY, Richard
Also see COUNTRY BOYS & CITY GIRLS
Also see LYNN, Barbara, & Lee Maye
Also see RAMS

MAYE, Lee: see MAYE, Arthur Lee

MAYE, Marilyn
Singles: 7-inch
RCA 3-6 67-68
LPs: 10/12-inch
RCA 10-15 66-67

MAYER, Nathaniel P&R/R&B '62
(With the Fabulous Twilights; with Fortune Braves; Nathaniel "Nay Dog" Mayer & Filthy McNasty Group Plus Free Style)
Singles: 7-inch
FORTUNE (449 "Village of Love") 15-25 62
FORTUNE (487 "Hurting Love") 30-40 62
FORTUNE (500 series) 10-20 62-69
LOVE DOG (101 "Raise the Curtain High") 4-6 80
LPs: 10/12-inch
FORTUNE (8014 "Goin' Back to the Village of Love") 100-200 64

MAYES, Jimmy, & Soul Breed
Singles: 7-inch
PORT 4-8 66

MAYES, Zilla
Singles: 7-inch
CHECKER (973 "A Prayer for Jackie") 15-25 61

MAYFIELD, Charles, & Casuals
Singles: 7-inch
GAME (392 "Throw It Out of Your Mind") 25-35

MAYFIELD, Curtis P&R/R&B/LP '70
Singles: 7-inch
ARISTA 3-4 89
BOARDWALK 3-5 81-82
CRC 3-4 85
CURTOM 3-5 70-80
RSO 3-5 80
Picture Sleeves
ARISTA 3-4 89
CURTOM 3-5 71-78
LPs: 10/12-inch
ABC 10-20 73
BOARDWALK 5-10 81-82
CURTOM 8-12 70-78
RSO 5-10 79-80
Also see IMPRESSIONS
Also see REED, Jimmy

MAYFIELD, Curtis, & Linda Clifford R&B '79
Singles: 7-inch
CURTOM 3-5 79-80
LPs: 10/12-inch
RSO 5-10 80
Also see CLIFFORD, Linda
Also see MAYFIELD, Curtis

MAYFIELD, Joe
Singles: 7-inch
EXCELLO 8-12 64
ROCKET 5-10

MAYFIELD, Percy P&R/R&B '50

Singles: 78 rpm

CHESS (1599 "Double Dealing")....25-50 55
KING (4480 "Two Years of Torture")....15-25 51
RECORDED in HOLLYWOOD ("Two Years of Torture")....25-35 51
(First issue. Selection number not known.)
SPECIALTY....10-30 50-57

Singles: 7-inch

ATLANTIC....3-5 74
BRUNSWICK....5-10 68
CHESS (1599 "Double Dealing")..50-100 55
IMPERIAL (5577 "One Love")........15-25 59
KING (4480 "Two Years of Torture")....50-100 51
RCA....4-6 70
SPECIALTY (375 "Please Send Me Someone to Love")....40-60 50
SPECIALTY (390 "Lost Love")......40-60 51
SPECIALTY (400 "Nightless Lover")....40-60 51
SPECIALTY (408 "My Blues")........40-60 51
SPECIALTY (416 "Cry Baby")........40-60 52
SPECIALTY (425 "Big Question")..40-60 52
SPECIALTY (432 "Louisiana")........40-60 52
SPECIALTY (439 "My Heart")........40-60 53
SPECIALTY (451 "I Dare You, Baby")....40-60 54
SPECIALTY (460 "Lonely One")....40-60 54
(Black vinyl.)
SPECIALTY (460 "Lonely One") 100-200 54
(Colored vinyl.)
SPECIALTY (473 "How Deep Is the Well")....40-60 54
(Black vinyl.)
SPECIALTY (473 "How Deep Is the Well")....100-200 54
(Colored vinyl.)
SPECIALTY (485 "I Need You So Bad")....40-60 54
SPECIALTY (499 "You Don't Exist No More....40-60 55
SPECIALTY (537 "You Were Lyin' to Me")....25-50 55
SPECIALTY (607 "Please Believe Me")....20-30 57
SPECIALTY (690 "What Must I Do")....15-25 60
TANGERINE....5-15 62-67

LPs: 10/12-inch

BRUNSWICK....10-20 69
RCA....10-15 70-71
SPECIALTY....8-12 70
TANGERINE....15-25 66-67

MAYMIE & ROBERT

(With Abie Baker Orchestra)

Singles: 7-inch

GLORY (260 "Parting Tears")........10-20 57
Also see BAKER, Abie

MAYNIE & HOWIE

Singles: 7-inch

SHO-MI (13083 "Library Rock") .100-200 58
Members: Maynard Horlick; Howard Sandler.
Also see HORLICK, Maynard, & Hep Teens

MAYO, Andy

Singles: 7-inch

TITAN....4-8 62

MAYO, Frankie, & Falcons

Singles: 78 rpm

RCA (7076 "Jigsaw Puzzle")..........10-20 57

Singles: 7-inch

RCA (7076 "Jigsaw Puzzle")..........10-20 57

MAYO, Mary

Singles: 7-inch

COLUMBIA....5-10 58

MAYO, Toni

Singles: 78 rpm

PLAZA....5-10 49

MAYPOLE

LPs: 10/12-inch

COLOSSUS (1007 "Maypole")........30-50 71

MAYS, Bredice

Singles: 7-inch

TWIN (33 "Miami Boogie")............50-75

MAYS, Carl

Singles: 7-inch

AZTEC (101 "Report Card Time")..20-30 64

MAYS, Jean

Singles: 7-inch

DIAMOND....4-8 64

MAYS, Willie

Singles: 7-inch

DUKE (350 "My Sad Heart")...........5-10 62
MATTEL ("Willie Mays")..............5-15 71
(Selection number not known. Picture disc. This is only known picture disc in the "Instant Replay Series." Only playable on special Mattel phonograph because of its small size without a play hole.)
Also see BASEBALL ("HOW TO" SERIES)

MAYS, Willie, & Treniers

("Willie Mays of the New York Giants"; with Quincy Jones & Orchestra)

Singles: 78 rpm

EPIC (9066 "Say Hey")..............10-15 54

Singles: 7-inch

EPIC (9066 "Say Hey")..............25-50 54
Also see JONES, Quincy
Also see MAYS, Willie
Also see TRENIERS

MAYS, Zilla

(With the Four Students)

Singles: 78 rpm

GROOVE....8-15 55
MERCURY....8-15 54

Singles: 7-inch

GROOVE....10-20 55
MERCURY....10-20 54
Also see FOUR STUDENTS

MAZARATI R&B/LP '86

Singles: 12-inch

PAISLEY PARK....4-6 86

Singles: 7-inch

PAISLEY PARK....3-4 86

LPs: 10/12-inch

PAISLEY PARK....5-8 86
Members: Casey Terry; Brown Mark.
Also see BROWNMARK

MAZE

Singles: 7-inch

CALLA....4-8 67

MAZE

LPs: 10/12-inch

MTA (5012 "Armageddon")..........40-60 69

MAZE P&R/R&B/LP '77

(Featuring Frankie Beverly)

Singles: 12-inch

CAPITOL....4-6 84

Singles: 7-inch

CAPITOL....3-5 77-86

Picture Sleeves

CAPITOL....3-5 81-85

LPs: 10/12-inch

CAPITOL....5-10 78-86
W.B....5-8 89
Also see BEVERLY, Frankie

MAZZA, Mary

Singles: 7-inch

ALPINE (55 "Cha Cha Italiano")....75-125 60

MBULU, Letta R&B/LP '77

Singles: 7-inch

A&M....3-5 77

LPs: 10/12-inch

A&M....5-10 77

McADAMS, Johnny

Singles: 7-inch

SPADE (1929 "Nine O'Clock")......10-20

McALISTER, Maurice

Singles: 7-inch

CHESS....4-8 68
Also see RADIANTS

McALISTER, Mike

Singles: 7-inch

HOB NOB....10-15

McALLISTER, Billie

LPs: 10/12-inch

KENT....10-15 73

McALLISTER, Red

Singles: 78 rpm

KING (4598 "Eggs & Grits")..........25-50 52

Singles: 7-inch

KING (4598 "Eggs & Grits")..........50-100 52

McALLISTERS

Singles: 7-inch

VIV (7 "But I Was Cool")............10-15 63

McANALLY, Mac P&R '77

Singles: 7-inch

ARIOLA....3-5 78
ARIOLA AMERICA....3-5 77
MCA....3-4 92
W.B....3-4 90

LPs: 10/12-inch

ARIOLA AMERICA....5-10 78

McAULEY SCHENKER GROUP

(MSG)

LPs: 10/12-inch

CAPITOL....5-8 87-89
Members: Robin McAuley; Michael Schenker.
Also see FAR CORPORATION
Also see SCHENKER, Michael, Group

McAULIFFE, Leon C&W '49

(With His Western Swing Band: with His Cimmaron Boys; Leon McAuliffe)

Singles: 78 rpm

COLUMBIA....5-10 49-54

Singles: 7-inch

CAPITOL....4-8 64-65
CIMARRON....5-10 59-62
COLUMBIA....10-15 52-54

EPs: 7-inch

CAPITOL....8-12 60s
DOT....8-12 58

LPs: 10/12-inch

ABC-PAR (ABC-394 "Cozy Inn")....25-35 61
(Monaural.)
ABC-PAR (ABCS-394 "Cozy Inn") 35-45 61
(Stereo.)
CAPITOL (2016 "Dancin'est Band Around")....20-30 64
CAPITOL (2148 "Everybody Dance, Everybody Swing")....20-30 64
CIMARRON (2002 "Swingin' Western Strings")....35-55 60
COLUMBIA....5-8 84
DELTA....5-10 82
DOT (3139 "Take Off")..............25-50 58
DOT (3689 "Golden Country Hits").15-20 66
PINE MOUNTAIN....6-12
SESAC (225 "Just a Minute")........50-75 59
SESAC (1601 "Points West")........50-75 59
STARDAY (171 "Mister Western Swing")....20-40 62
STARDAY (280 "Swinging West")....20-40
STARDAY (309 "Swingin' Western Strings")....20-40 64
STONEWAY....10-20
Member: Sam D. Bass.
Also see BASS, Sam D.
Also see WILLS, Bob

McBEE, Jerry C&W '80

Singles: 7-inch

DIMENSION....3-5 80

McBEE, Ronnie

Singles: 7-inch

SPANGLE....5-10 58

McBOOKER, Connie

(Connie Mac Booker; Connie Mack Booker with His Orchestra)

Singles: 78 rpm

EDDIE'S....15-25 49
FREEDOM....15-25 49
RPM....20-30 53

Singles: 7-inch

RPM (401 "Love Me Pretty Baby")....100-200 54
Also see KING, B.B.
Also see WILLIAMS, L.C.

McBRIDE, Barbara / Woody Carr

Singles: 7-inch

MARI....5-10

McBRIDE, Bob

Singles: 7-inch

EVOLUTION....3-5 72
MCA....3-5 78

LPs: 10/12-inch

EVOLUTION....8-10 72
MCA....5-10 78
Also see LIGHTHOUSE

McBRIDE, Dale C&W '71

Singles: 7-inch

CON BRIO....3-5 76-79
FAME....10-15 59
REPRISE....4-8 64
TEAR DROP....5-10 64
THUNDERBIRD....4-6 71

LPs: 10/12-inch

CON BRIO....8-10 77

McBRIDE, Jimmy

Singles: 7-inch

MADISON....10-15 58

McBRIDE, Lee

Singles: 7-inch

MARLO (1502 "Confusin' ")..........25-35 50s

McBRIDE & RIDE LP '91

Singles: 7-inch

MCA....3-4 91-92

LPs: 10/12-inch

MCA....5-8 91-92
Members: Terry McBride; Billy Thomas; Ray Herndon; Kenny Vaughn; Keith Edwards.

McCABE, Chuck

Singles: 7-inch

GRT (044 "Live at the Pet Rock Show")....3-5 75

McCABE, Tim

Singles: 7-inch

ATLANTIS....3-5

McCAFFERTY, Dan

Singles: 7-inch

A&M....3-5 75

LPs: 10/12-inch

A&M....8-10 75-76
Also see NAZARETH

McCAIN, Benny, & Ohio Untouchables

Singles: 7-inch

LU PINE....8-12 62
Also see OHIO UNTOUCHABLES

McCAIN, James: see WILLIAMS, Joe / James McCain

McCAIN, Jerry

(With His Upsetters; Jerry "Boogie" McCain)

Singles: 78 rpm

TRUMPET....40-60 54

Singles: 7-inch

CONTINENTAL....5-10 65
EXCELLO (2068 "Courtin' in a Cadillac")....40-60 56
EXCELLO (2079 "You Don't Love Me No More")....40-60 57
EXCELLO (2081 "Run, Uncle John, Run")....40-60 57
EXCELLO (2103 "My Next Door Neighbor")....50-100 58
EXCELLO (2111 "Bad Credit")........25-50 58
EXCELLO (2127 "Groom Without a Bride")....25-50 59
JEWEL....5-10 65-67
OKEH (7150 "Twist '62")............10-15 62
OKEH (7157 "Run Back Home")....10-15 62
OKEH (7158 "Popcorn")..............10-15 62
REX (1014 "She's Tough")..........15-25 60
RIC (153 "Here's Where You Get It")....5-10 65
TRUMPET (217 "Wine-O-Wine")....100-200 54
TRUMPET (231 "Stay Out of Automobiles")....100-200 54

LPs: 10/12-inch

ICHIBAN....5-10
Also see DIDDLEY, Bo

McCALL, Al R&B '83

Singles: 7-inch

PROFILE....3-4 83

McCALL, C.W. C&W/P&R '74

Singles: 7-inch

MGM....3-5 74-75
POLYDOR....3-5 76-79

LPs: 10/12-inch

MGM....5-10 75
POLYDOR....5-8 76-79
Session: Fort Calhoun Nuclear Power Plant Band, later known as Mannheim Steamroller.
Also see MANNHEIM STEAMROLLER

McCALL, Cash R&B '66

Singles: 7-inch

CHECKER....4-8 67
COLUMBIA....3-5 76-77
EXECUTIVE....4-6 60s
M-PAC....4-8 64
PAULA....3-5 75
RONN....3-5 75
THOMAS....4-8 66

McCALL, Darrell C&W '63

(With the Milestones)

Singles: 7-inch

ATLANTIC....3-4 74
CAPITOL....6-12 61
COLUMBIA....3-5 76-78
INDIGO....3-4 84
PHILIPS....4-8 61-63
RCA....3-5 80
WAYSIDE....3-6 68-70

LPs: 10/12-inch

COLUMBIA....10-15 77
WAYSIDE....10-15 70
Also see POTTER, Curtis, & Darrell McCall
Also see HANSON, Connie, & Friend

McCALL, Darrell, & Willie Nelson C&W '77

Singles: 7-inch

COLUMBIA....3-5 77
Also see NELSON, Willie

McCALL, Little Johnny

Singles: 7-inch

DONNA (1334 "My Love I Can't Hide")....75-125 60
WOW (1060 "My Love I Can't Hide")....200-400 60
(First issue.)

McCALL, Toussaint P&R/R&B '67

Singles: 7-inch

COLLECTABLES....3-4 80s
RONN....4-8 67-68

LPs: 10/12-inch

RONN....10-12 67
Also see NEVILLE, Aaron / Toussaint McCall

McCALLUM, David LP '66

Singles: 7-inch

CAPITOL....4-8 66

Picture Sleeves

CAPITOL....5-10 66

LPs: 10/12-inch

CAPITOL....10-15 66

McCANN, Denise

Singles: 7-inch

BUTTERFLY....3-5 78-79

LPs: 10/12-inch

BUTTERFLY....5-8 78-79

McCANN, Les LP '69

Singles: 7-inch

ATLANTIC....3-5 69-75
LIMELIGHT....4-6 65
PACIFIC JAZZ....4-8 60-65
WORLD PACIFIC....3-6 60s

LPs: 10/12-inch

ATLANTIC....5-10 69-75
LIMELIGHT....15-25 65
PACIFIC JAZZ (2 thru 91)........15-30 60-65
PACIFIC JAZZ (893 "Les McCann")....5-10 78
Also see FLACK, Roberta
Also see HOLMES, Richard "Groove," & Les McCann
Also see JAZZ CRUSADERS
Also see RAWLS, Lou, & Les McCann Ltd.

McCANN, Les, & Eddie Harris LP '69

Singles: 7-inch

ATLANTIC....3-5 69-70

LPs: 10/12-inch

ATLANTIC....5-10 69-71
Also see HARRIS, Eddie
Also see McCANN, Les

McCANN, Peter P&R/LP '77

Singles: 7-inch

COLUMBIA....3-5 79
20TH FOX....3-5 77

LPs: 10/12-inch

20TH FOX....8-10 77

McCANNON, George

(George McCannon III)

Singles: 7-inch

BELL....4-6 68
FUN 45....4-8 65
MERCURY....4-8 62-63
PARKWAY....4-8 63
TOWER....4-8 66

McCARTERS C&W '88

(Jennifer McCarter & the McCarters)

Singles: 7-inch

W.B....3-4 88-90
Members: Jennifer McCarter; Lisa McCarter; Teresa McCarter.

McCARTHY, Bobby Jay

Singles: 7-inch

1-2-3....3-6 69

McCARTNEY, Paul LP '70

(Wings; with Wings; with Linda McCartney)

Singles: 12-inch

CAPITOL (15212 "Spies Like Us") 10-20 85
CAPITOL (15235 "Press")............6-12 86
CAPITOL (15499 "Oui Est Le Soleil")....8-12 89
COLUMBIA (03019 "Take It Away")....8-12 82
COLUMBIA (05077 "No More Lonely Nights")....8-12 84
("Playout version.")
COLUMBIA (05077 "No More Lonely Nights")....20-30 84
("Special Dance Mix.")
COLUMBIA (10940 "Goodnight Tonight")....70-90 79
COLUMBIA (39927 "No More Lonely Nights")....15-20 84
(Picture disc.)

Promotional 12-inch Singles

CAPITOL (8574 "Maybe I'm Amazed")....60-80 77
CAPITOL (9556 "Spies Like Us")....20-30 85
CAPITOL (9763 "Press")............15-20 86
CAPITOL (9797 "Angry")............20-25 86
CAPITOL (9861 "Stranglehold")......20-25 86
CAPITOL (9928 "Pretty Little Head")....40-50 86
COLUMBIA (775 "Coming Up")......50-60 80
(Red label.)
COLUMBIA (775 "Coming Up")......40-50 80
(White label.)
COLUMBIA (1940 "No More Lonely Nights")....15-20 84
COLUMBIA (10940 "Goodnight Tonight")....15-25 79

Singles: 7-inch

APPLE (1829 "Another Day")..........8-12 71
APPLE (1837 "Uncle Albert Admiral Halsey")....10-20 71
(With sliced apple on flip side.)
APPLE (1837 "Uncle Albert Admiral Halsey")....40-50 71
(With unsliced apple on flip side.)
APPLE (1847 "Give Ireland Back to the Irish")....10-20 72
APPLE (1851 "Mary Had a Little Lamb")....8-10 72
APPLE (1857 "Hi Hi Hi")..............8-10 72
APPLE (1861 "My Love")..............5-8 73
APPLE (1863 "Live and Let Die")......5-8 73
APPLE (1869 "Helen Wheels")........5-8 73
APPLE (1871 "Jet"/"Mamunia") . 100-125 74
(Label has 2:49 on A-side.)
APPLE (1871 "Jet"/"Mamunia")........8-10 74
(Label has 4:08 on A-side.)
APPLE (1871 "Jet"/"Let Me Roll It")...5-8 74
APPLE (1873 "Band on the Run")......5-8 74
APPLE (1875 "Junior's Farm")........5-8 74
CAPITOL (1829 "Another Day")......10-15 76
CAPITOL (1837 "Uncle Albert Admiral Halsey")....10-15 76
CAPITOL (1847 "Give Ireland Back to the Irish")....15-20 76
CAPITOL (1851 "Mary Had a Little Lamb")....10-15 76
CAPITOL (1857 "Hi Hi Hi")..........10-15 76
CAPITOL (1861 "My Love")..........15-20 76
CAPITOL (1863 "Live and Let Die")....10-15 76
CAPITOL (1869 "Helen Wheels")....10-15 76
CAPITOL (1871 "Jet")................10-15 76
CAPITOL (1873 "Band on the Run")....10-15 76
CAPITOL (1875 "Junior's Farm")....10-15 76
CAPITOL (4091 "Listen to What the Man Said")....3-5 75
CAPITOL (4145 "Letting Go")........3-5 75
CAPITOL (4175 "Venus & Mars Rock Show")....3-5 75
CAPITOL (4256 "Silly Love Songs")...3-5 76
(Capitol custom label.)
CAPITOL (4256 "Silly Love Songs")...5-8 76
(Black label.)
CAPITOL (4293 "Let 'Em In")..........3-5 76
(Capitol custom label.)
CAPITOL (4293 "Let 'Em In")..........5-8 76
(Black label.)
CAPITOL (4385 Maybe I'm Amazed")....3-5 77
(Capitol custom label.)
CAPITOL (4385 Maybe I'm Amazed")....15-20 77
(Black label.)
CAPITOL (4504 "Mull of Kintyre")....100-125 77
(Purple label.)
CAPITOL (4504 "Mull of Kintyre")....3-5 77
(Black label.)
CAPITOL (4559 "With a Little Luck")....3-5 78
CAPITOL (4594 "I've Had Enough")..3-5 78
CAPITOL (4625 "London Town")......3-5 78
CAPITOL (5537 "Spies Like Us")......5-8 85
CAPITOL (5597 "Press")..............3-5 86
CAPITOL (5636 "Stranglehold")......3-5 86
CAPITOL (5672 "Only Love Remains")....3-5 87
CAPITOL (17318 "Off the Ground")....4-6 94
CAPITOL (17318 "Off the Ground")....4-6 93
(Black vinyl or colored vinyl.)
CAPITOL (17319 "Biker Like an Icon")....4-6 93
(Black vinyl.)
CAPITOL (17319 "Biker Like an Icon")....3-4 93

(Colored vinyl.)
CAPITOL (17489 "C'mon People").... 4-6 94
(Colored vinyl.)
CAPITOL (17643 "Wonderful Christmastime")............................ 4-6 94
(Colored vinyl.)
CAPITOL (44637 "My Brave Face") 5-10 89
CAPITOL (56785 "Biker Like an Icon") 4-6 93
COLUMBIA (02171 "Silly Love Songs") 15-25 81
COLUMBIA (03018 "Take It Away") .. 3-4 82
COLUMBIA (03235 "Tug of War")... 8-10 82
COLUMBIA (04127 "Wonderful Christmastime")..............................20-30 83
COLUMBIA (04296 "So Bad").......... 3-4 83
COLUMBIA (04581 "No More Lonely Nights") 3-4 84
COLUMBIA (10939 "Goodnight Tonight") 3-4 79
COLUMBIA (11020 "Getting Closer") 4-6 79
COLUMBIA (11070 "Arrow Through Me") 4-6 79
COLUMBIA (11162 "Wonderful Christmastime")............................ 5-10 79
COLUMBIA (11263 "Coming Up") 3-4 80
(Listed here as a single even though there are two tracks on the B-side.)
COLUMBIA (11335 "Waterfalls") 4-6 80
COLUMBIA (33000 series).............. 5-10 80
(Red label, "Hall of Fame" series.)
COLUMBIA (33000 series)............25-35 85
(Gray label, "Hall of Fame" series.)

Picture Sleeves

APPLE (1847 "Give Ireland Back to the Irish") 20-30 72
APPLE (1851 "Mary Had a Little Lamb") 25-35 72
("Little Woman Love" printed under photo, on reverse side of sleeve.)
APPLE (1851 "Mary Had a Little Lamb") 15-25 72
("Little Woman Love" not printed under photo, on reverse side of sleeve.)
CAPITOL (4091 "Listen to What the Man Said") 8-12 75
CAPITOL (4504 "Mull of Kintyre")... 8-12 77
CAPITOL (5537 "Spies Like Us") 3-5 85
CAPITOL (5597 "Press")................... 3-5 86
CAPITOL (5636 "Stranglehold")......... 3-5 86
CAPITOL (5672 "Only Love Remains") 3-5 87
CAPITOL (44637 "My Brave Face").. 3-5 89
COLUMBIA (03018 "Take It Away") 5-8 82
(Reads "Not for Sale" on back side. Promotional issue only.)
COLUMBIA (03018 "Take It Away").. 3-4 82
COLUMBIA (04296 "So Bad").......... 3-5 83
COLUMBIA (04296 "So Bad")......... 5-10 83
(Reads "Not for Sale" on back side. Promotional issue only.)
COLUMBIA (04581 "No More Lonely Nights") 4-6 84
(Title has white print.)
COLUMBIA (04581 "No More Lonely Nights") 20-30 84
(Title has gray print.)
COLUMBIA (11020 "Getting Closer")..20-30 79
COLUMBIA (11162 "Wonderful Christmastime")..............................10-15 79
COLUMBIA (11263 "Coming Up")..... 4-6 80
COLUMBIA (11335 "Waterfalls") 15-20 80

Promotional Singles

APPLE (1829 "Another Day")............60-75 71
APPLE (1837 "Uncle Albert Admiral Halsey") 60-75 71
APPLE (1851 "Mary Had a Little Lamb") 300-350 72
APPLE (1861 "My Love")...........150-200 73
APPLE (1871 "Jet")......................40-50 74
APPLE (1873 "Band on the Run") ..25-35 74
APPLE (1875 "Junior's Farm").......40-50 74
APPLE (1875 "Sally G")..................60-80 74
APPLE (6786 "Helen Wheels") 40-50 73
APPLE (6787 "Country Dreamer") 300-350 73
CAPITOL (4145 "Letting Go") 25-30 75
CAPITOL (4175 "Venus & Mars Rock Show")..25-30 75
CAPITOL (4256 "Silly Love Songs.")..20-25 76
CAPITOL (4293 "Let 'Em In").........20-25 76
CAPITOL (4594 "I've Had Enough")..20-25 78
(Add $20 if accompanied by special promotional flyer.)
CAPITOL (4625 "London Town")....20-30 78
CAPITOL (5597 "Press")................10-15 86
CAPITOL (5636 "Stranglehold").....10-15 86
CAPITOL (5672 "Only Love Remains")..10-15 87
CAPITOL (8138 "Listen to What the Man Said")..20-30 75
CAPITOL (8570/1 "Maybe I'm Amazed")..20-30 77
CAPITOL (8746/7 "Mull of Kintyre")..20-30 77
CAPITOL (8812 "With a Little Luck")..20-25 78
CAPITOL (9765 "Press")...........200-250 86
CAPITOL (9952 "Spies Like Us") ...15-20 85
CAPITOL (44367 "My Brave Face")..10-15 89
CAPITOL (79700 "This One") 300-350 89
COLUMBIA (1204 "Coming Up")....... 5-8 80
(Single-sided disc.)
COLUMBIA (03018 "Take It Away").. 8-10 82
COLUMBIA (03235 "Tug of War") 15-20 82
COLUMBIA (04296 "So Bad").......10-15 83
COLUMBIA (04581 "No More Lonely Nights")..8-10 84
COLUMBIA (10939 "Goodnight Tonight") 10-15 79
COLUMBIA (11020 "Getting Closer")..10-15 79
COLUMBIA (11070 "Arrow Through Me")..10-15 79
COLUMBIA (11162 "Wonderful Christmastime")..............................10-15 79
COLUMBIA (11263 "Coming Up") 10-15 80
COLUMBIA (11335 "Waterfalls") ...10-15 80
MIRAMAX (4202 "Rock Show")..500-600 75
(Contains three radio spots. Issued to radio stations only.)

LPs: 10/12-inch

APPLE (3363 "McCartney") 60-75 70
(Label with Capitol logo shows Paul's full name beneath LP title.)
APPLE (3363 "McCartney")...........20-30 70
(Label shows Paul's full name beneath LP title. No Capitol logo.)
APPLE (3363 "McCartney") 20-25 70
(Label doesn't show Paul's name beneath LP title.)
APPLE (3375 "Ram")....................40-50 71
(With Capitol logo.)
APPLE (3375 "Ram")....................20-30 71
(No Capitol logo. No "All Rights Reserved, etc." perimeter print.)
APPLE (3375 "Ram")..................75-100 75
(With "All Rights Reserved, etc." perimeter print.)
APPLE (3386 "Wild Life") 10-15 71
APPLE (3409 "Red Rose Speedway")..15-20 73
APPLE (3415 "Band on the Run")..15-20 73
(Price includes bonus poster.)
CAPITOL (3363 "McCartney").......15-25 70s
CAPITOL (3375 "Ram")................20-30 70s
CAPITOL (3386 "Wildlife")............20-30 70s
CAPITOL (3409 "Red Rose Speedway")..20-30 70s
CAPITOL (3415 "Band on the Run")..20-30 76
(Price includes bonus poster.)
CAPITOL (11419 "Venus & Mars")..10-15 75
(Price includes bonus posters and stickers.)
CAPITOL (11525 "Wings at the Speed of Sound")..8-10 76
CAPITOL (11593 "Wings Over America")..15-25 76
CAPITOL (11777 "London Town") 10-15 78
(Price includes bonus poster.)
CAPITOL (11901 "Band on the Run")..40-50 78
(Picture disc.)
CAPITOL (11905 "Wings Greatest")..10-15 78
(Price includes bonus poster.)
CAPITOL (12475 "Press to Play")....8-12 87
CAPITOL (48287 "All the Best!")....10-20 87
CAPITOL (91653 "Flowers in the Dirt")..10-20 89
CAPITOL (94778 "Tripping the Live Fantastic")..50-60 90
CAPITOL (595379 "Tripping the Live Fantastic: Highlights")..............................10-15 90
COLUMBIA (36057 "Back to the Egg")..5-10 79
(Photo label.)
COLUMBIA (36057 "Back to the Egg")..30-40 84
(Red label.)
COLUMBIA (36478 "McCartney") ..15-20 80
COLUMBIA (36479 "Ram")............15-20 80
COLUMBIA (36480 "Wild Life") 15-20 80
COLUMBIA (36481 "Red Rose Speedway")..15-20 80
COLUMBIA (JC-36482 "Band on the Run")..10-15 80
(Photo label.)
COLUMBIA (36482 "Band on the Run")..30-40 80
(Red label. With "JC" or "PC" prefix.)
COLUMBIA (HC-36482 "Band on the Run")..60-70 80
(Red label. Half-speed mastered.)
COLUMBIA (FC-36511 "McCartney II")..............................10-15 80
(Issued with bonus single [1204] *Coming Up*, which represents $5 to $8 of the price range. Photo label.)
COLUMBIA (FC-36511 "McCartney II")..............................15-25 80
(Red label.)
COLUMBIA (PC-36511 "McCartney II")..............................75-100 80
(Red label.)
COLUMBIA (36801 "Venus & Mars")..10-20 80
(Price includes bonus posters.)
COLUMBIA (36987 "The McCartney Interview")..8-12 80
COLUMBIA (37409 "Wings at the Speed of Sound")..15-20 81
COLUMBIA (TC-37462 "Tug of War")..5-10 82
(With Stevie Wonder on *Ebony and Ivory*)
COLUMBIA (PC-37462 "Tug of War")..20-30 84
(Photo label.)
COLUMBIA (PC-37462 "Tug of War")..75-100 84
(Red label.)
COLUMBIA (37990 "Wings Over America")..40-50 82
COLUMBIA (39149 "Pipes of Peace")..8-12 83
(With Michael Jackson on *Say Say Say*)
COLUMBIA (39613 "Give My Regards to Broad Street")..10-15 84
COLUMBIA (46482 "Band on the Run")..10-15 80
(Half-speed mastered.)
LIBERTY (50100 Live and Let Die")....5-8 84
(With McCartney on title track only.)
LONDON (76007 "Family Way")....80-90 67
(Soundtrack. Monaural.)
LONDON (82007 "Family Way")..90-120 67
(Soundtrack. Stereo.)
U.A. (100 "Live and Let Die") 15-20 73
(Copies with cut corners are valued at about one-half of the above price range. McCartney is heard on title track only.)

Promotional LPs

APPLE (3375 "Ram")............3000-3500 71
(Monaural.)
APPLE (6210 "Brung to Ewe By")..350-450 71
CAPITOL (2955 "Band on the Run Radio Interview")..............................1000-1200 73
CAPITOL (11525 "Wings at the Speed of Sound")..200-250 76
COLUMBIA (821 "The McCartney Interview")..30-40 80
COLUMBIA (36057 "Back to the Egg")..25-35 79
COLUMBIA (36511 "McCartney II")..20-30 80
W.B. ("The Family Way") 350-450 67
(10-inch LP. Ad spots for radio stations.)
Also see BAND AID
Also see BEATLES
Also see BRASS RING
Also see COUNTRY HAMS
Also see GREASE BAND
Also see HARPER, Roy
Also see LAINE, Denny
Also see LOMAX, Jackie
Also see COSTELLO, Elvis
Also see NEWMAN, Thunderclap
Also see PERKINS, Carl
Also see SUN FERRY AID
Also see SUZY & Red Stripes
Also see THORNTON, FRADKIN & UNGER
Also see THRILLINGTON
Also see TUDOR MINSTRELS

McCARTNEY, Paul, & Michael Jackson *P&R/R&B '82*

Singles: 12-inch

COLUMBIA (1758 "Say Say Say") .10-15 83
COLUMBIA (04169 "Say Say Say")..5-10 83

Promotional 12-inch Singles

COLUMBIA (04169 "Say Say Say")..12-18 83

Singles: 7-inch

COLUMBIA (04168 "Say Say Say")...3-4 83
EPIC (03288 "The Girl Is Mine") 3-4 82
EPIC (03372 "The Girl Is Mine") 8-12 82
(Single-sided pressing with small, LP size, hole.)

Picture Sleeves

COLUMBIA (04168 "Say Say Say")...3-4 83

Promotional Picture Sleeves

COLUMBIA (04168 "Say Say Say")..5-10 83
EPIC (03288 "The Girl Is Mine") 5-10 82

Promotional Singles

COLUMBIA (04168 "Say Say Say").8-12 83
EPIC (03288 "The Girl Is Mine") 8-12 82
(Identification number shown as 169138.)
EPIC (03288 "The Girl Is Mine") 20-30 82
(Identification number shown as 169202. Reads "New Edited Version.")
Also see JACKSON, Michael

McCARTNEY, Paul / Rochestra / Who / Rockpile

Singles: 12-inch

ATLANTIC (388 "Every Night") ..150-250 81
(Promotional issue only.)
Also see ROCKPILE
Also see WHO

McCARTNEY, Paul, & Stevie Wonder *P&R/R&B '82*

Singles: 12-inch

COLUMBIA (02878 "Ebony & Ivory")..8-12 82

Promotional 12-inch Singles

COLUMBIA (1444 "Ebony & Ivory")..20-30 82

Singles: 7-inch

COLUMBIA (02860 "Ebony & Ivory")..20-30 82
COLUMBIA (02860 "Ebony & Ivory")..3-4 82
(Ampersand [&] in title is replaced by "and.")

Promotional Singles

COLUMBIA (02860 "Ebony & Ivory")..15-25 82

Picture Sleeves

COLUMBIA (02860 "Ebony & Ivory")..8-10 82

Promotional Picture Sleeves

COLUMBIA (02860 "Ebony & Ivory")..5-10 82
Also see McCARTNEY, Paul
Also see WONDER, Stevie

McCARTY, John

Singles: 7-inch

RECORD SHOP ("Lobos #1")...........4-6 83

McCASLIN, Mary

LPs: 10/12-inch

MERCURY (3772 "Sunny California")..8-12 79

McCASLIN, Mary, & Jim Ringer

LPs: 10/12-inch

PHILO 6-10 78
Also see McCASLIN, Mary

McCLAIN, Alton, & Destiny
(With the Channels) *P&R/R&B/LP '79*

Singles: 7-inch

FORWARD (100 "Come Back Baby")..5-10
POLYDOR..3-6 79-81

LPs: 10/12-inch

POLYDOR..5-10 79-81
Also see ALTON & JOHNNY

McCLAIN, Charly *C&W '76*

Singles: 7-inch

EPIC..3-5 76-88
MERCURY..3-4 88-89

Picture Sleeves

EPIC..3-5

LP: 10/12-inch

CBS (91536 "On Tour") 75-125 84
(Promotional only picture disc.)
EPIC..5-10 77-88
MERCURY..5-8 88
Also see GILLEY, Mickey, & Charly McClain
Also see RODRIGUEZ, Johnny, & Charly McClain

McCLAIN, Charly, & Wayne Massey *C&W '86*

Singles: 7-inch

EPIC..3-4 85-86
Also see MASSEY, Wayne
Also see McCLAIN, Charly

McCLAIN, Janice *R&B '80*

Singles: 12-inch

MCA..4-6 86

Singles: 7-inch

MCA..3-4 86
RFC..3-4 80

LPs: 10/12-inch

MCA..5-8 86

McCLAM, Pro, & Orchestra

Singles: 78 rpm

VEE JAY 10-20 53-54

Singles: 7-inch

VEE JAY (102 "Boot-Um")............20-30 53
(Black vinyl.)
VEE JAY (102 "Boot-Um")............40-60 53
(Colored vinyl.)
VEE JAY (112 "Cinemascope Baby")..20-30 54
(Black vinyl.)
VEE JAY (112 "Cinemascope Baby")..40-60 54
(Colored vinyl.)

McCLANAHAN, Mac

Singles: 7-inch

TIGER (104 "That Nonsense Stuff")..8-10 61

McCLAREN, Ted

Singles: 7-inch

UFO ("Gemini Jump")..................10-20 64
(Selection number not known.)

McCLARY, Butch
(Don Curtis)

Singles: 7-inch

KLIFF (103 "Rockin' Rockin Hall")..50-100 58
Also see CURTIS, Don

McCLARY, Thomas *R&B '84*

Singles: 7-inch

MOTOWN..3-4 84-85

LPs: 10/12-inch

MOTOWN..5-8 85
Also see COMMODORES

McCLAY, Ernest
(With His Trio)

Singles: 78 rpm

MURRAY (506 "Big Timing Woman")..50-100 48

McCLAY, Yul, & Mondellos

Singles: 7-inch

RHYTHM (105 "Over the Rainbow")..............................200-300 57
Also see MONDELLOS

McCLEESE, James

Singles: 7-inch

MARCO (106 "A Million Tears").....20-30
Also see SOUL, Jimmy

McCLELAND, Tommy: see EMCEES

McCLENDON, Charlie, & Magnificents
(With the Magnificents)

Singles: 7-inch

COLLOSSUS (101 "We're Gonna Hate Ourselves"..............................10-15 69
L-REV 5-10 60s

McCLENNEY, Lloyd

Singles: 7-inch

SEVILLE..4-8 63

McCLINE, Charles

Singles: 7-inch

LARRY-O (103 "You Conquered Me")..20-30 64
(First issued as by Willie Logan & the Plaids.)
Also see LOGAN, Willie & Plaids

McCLINTON, Delbert *LP '79*
(With the Ron-Dels; Del McClinton)

Singles: 7-inch

ABC..3-5 75-77
BOBILL (101 "I Know She Knows")..8-10 67
BROWNFIELD 8-12 65
CAPITOL..3-5 80-81
CAPRICORN..3-5 78
JUBILEE (9012 "I Know She Knows")..8-12 65
LE CAM (717 "Hey Baby")..................3-5 79
LE CAM (1220 "Mr. Pitiful")..............3-5 79
LONDON (9544 "Angel Eyes").......15-25 62
PARAMOUNT (0016 "Fannie Mae")..5-10 69
SOFT (1041 "100 Pounds of Honey")..4-6 70

LPs: 10/12-inch

ABC..10-20 75-77
ACCORD..8-12 81
CAPITOL..8-12 80-81
CAPRICORN..10-15 78-79
INTERMEDIA..5-10 84
MCA..5-10 81
POLYDOR..10-20 79
Also see CHANNEL, Bruce
Also see CLINTON, Mac, & Straitjackets
Also see DELBERT & GLEN
Also see RONDELLS

McCLINTON, O.B. *C&W '72*
(With Peggy Jo Adams)

Singles: 7-inch

ENTERPRISE..3-5 72-75
EPIC..3-5 78-87
MERCURY..3-5 76
MOON SHINE..3-4 84
SUNBIRD..3-5 80

LPs: 10/12-inch

ENTERPRISE..8-10 72-74

McCLOUD, Coyote, & Clara Peller

Singles: 7-inch

AWESOME..3-4 84

Picture Sleeves

AWESOME..3-5 84

McCLURE, Bobby *P&R/R&B '66*

Singles: 7-inch

CHECKER..5-10 66-67
EDGE (005 "You Never Miss Your Water")..5-10
Also see BASS, Fontella, & Bobby McClure

McCOLLOUGH, Charles
(With the Silks; Charles McCullough)

Singles: 7-inch

DOOTO (462 "My Girl")...............15-25 61
DOOTO (465 "You're Not Too Young")..15-25 61
DOOTO (467 "I Cried All Night")....10-20 62

McCOLLOUGH, Lloyd

Singles: 7-inch

REPUBLIC ("Gonna Love My Baby")..25-50 50s

McCOLLOUGH, Rod

Singles: 7-inch

DOMINO..5-10 60

McCOLLUM, Hazel: see EL DORADOS

McCOLLUM, Tyrone, & Inclines

Singles: 7-inch

ATCO..3-5 69

McCONNELL, C. Lynda *D&D '84*

Singles: 12-inch

ATLANTIC..4-6 84

Singles: 7-inch

ATLANTIC..3-4 84

McCONNELL, Shannon

Singles: 7-inch

LOST GOLD (1016 "Too Much Too Soon")..3-4 91
(Red vinyl.)

Picture Sleeves

LOST GOLD (1016 "Too Much Too Soon")..3-4 91

McCONNVILLE, Jimmy, & Shamrocks

Singles: 7-inch

FARRALL (691 "Scorpion")...........10-20 60

McCOO, Marilyn *R&B '83*

Singles: 7-inch

RCA..3-4 83

LPs: 10/12-inch

RCA..5-8 83

McCOO, Marilyn, & Billy Davis Jr. *P&R/R&B/LP '76*

Singles: 12-inch

COLUMBIA..4-6 79

Singles: 7-inch

ABC..3-5 76-78
COLUMBIA..3-5 78

LPs: 10/12-inch

ABC..8-10 76-77
COLUMBIA..5-10 78
Also see FIFTH DIMENSION
Also see McCOO, Marilyn

McCOOK, Johnny

Singles: 7-inch

GONE..4-8 63

McCOOK, Tommy, & Super-Sonics

Singles: 7-inch

YEW (1005 "Liquidator")..................8-12

McCORD, Cali *C&W '87*

Singles: 7-inch

GAZELLE..3-4 87-88

McCORISON, Dan *C&W '77*

Singles: 7-inch

MCA..3-5 77

LPs: 10/12-inch

MCA..5-10 77

McCORMICK, Ann
Singles: 78 rpm
MERCURY 4-6 55
Singles: 7-inch
MERCURY 5-10 55

McCORMICK, Bambi
LPs: 10/12-inch
METROMEDIA 5-10 68

McCORMICK, Gayle P&R/LP '71
Singles: 7-inch
DECCA 3-5 72
DUNHILL 3-5 71-72
MCA 3-5 73
LPs: 10/12-inch
DECCA 10-12 72
DUNHILL 10-12 71
FANTASY 8-10 74
Also see SMITH

McCORMICK, George
Singles: 78 rpm
MGM 5-10 57
Singles: 7-inch
MGM 5-10 57

McCORMICK, George / Rusty Adams
LPs: 10/12-inch
SOMERSET 5-10 60s
Also see ADAMS, Rusty
Also see McCORMICK, George

McCORMICK, Patty
Singles: 7-inch
RIC 4-8 65

McCORMICK BROTHERS
Singles: 7-inch
HICKORY (1000 series) 10-20 57
HICKORY (1103 thru 1203) 8-12 59-63
HICKORY (1245 "Are You Feeling Blue") 4-8 64

McCOY, Carl
(Carl McVoy)
Singles: 7-inch
HI 4-8 62
Also see McVOY, Carl

McCOY, Charlie P&R '61/C&W '72
Singles: 7-inch
CADENCE 4-8 61-62
MONUMENT 3-6 68-83
EPs: 7-inch
MONUMENT (0001 "Charlie McCoy") 5-10
(Promotional issue only.)
LPs: 10/12-inch
EPIC 5-8 82
MONUMENT 5-10 69-78
Session: Barefoot Jerry.
Also see AREA CODE 615
Also see BAREFOOT JERRY
Also see BOYS from INDIANA
Also see DYLAN, Bob
Also see FOWLER, Wally
Also see GAS LANTERN
Also see LEE, Bobby
Also see MANDRELL, Barbara
Also see McDOWELL, Ronnie
Also see NASHVILLE SUPERPICKERS
Also see TUBB, Ernest

McCOY, Charlie, & Laney Smallwood C&W '81
(Charlie McCoy & Laney Hicks)
Singles: 7-inch
MONUMENT 3-5 74
Also see McCOY, Charlie
Also see SMALLWOOD, Laney

McCOY, Freddie P&R '67
Singles: 7-inch
PRESTIGE 4-6 67

McCOY, George & Ethel
LPs: 10/12-inch
ADELPHI 8-10

McCOY, Joe
Singles: 7-inch
TIARA 10-20 58

McCOY, Neal C&W '88
(Neal McGoy)
Singles: 7-inch
ATLANTIC 3-4 90-91
16TH AVE. 3-4 88

McCOY, Patty, & Renegades
Singles: 7-inch
COUNSEL 8-12 62

McCOY, Ray
Singles: 7-inch
FABLE (615 "Rockin' Baby") 75-100 58

McCOY, Robert
(With His Five Sins)
Singles: 7-inch
SOUL-O 4-8 64
VULKAN 5-10 58-63

McCOY, Rose Marie
Singles: 78 rpm
CAT 10-20 55
Singles: 7-inch
CAT (111 "Dippin' in My Business") 20-30 55

McCOY, Roy
LPs: 10/12-inch
FUNKY 8-10

McCOY, Rube
Singles: 7-inch
TESTAMENT 4-8 65
Also see WILLIAMS, Joe Big

McCOY, Van R&B '74
(With the Soul City Symphony; Van McCoy Strings)
Singles: 12-inch
MCA 4-8 79
Singles: 7-inch
AMHERST 3-5 70s
AVCO 3-5 74-75
CGC 3-5 70
COLUMBIA 4-8 65-66
EPIC 3-6 69
H&L 3-5 76
LIBERTY 4-8 62
MCA 3-5 78-79
ROCK 'N (101 "Mr. D.J.") 10-20 61
ROCK 'N (1012 "Girls Are Sentimental") 10-15 61
SHARE 3-5 69
SILVER BLUE 3-5 73
LPs: 10/12-inch
AVCO 8-10 74-75
BUDDAH 8-10 72-75
COLUMBIA 12-18 66
H&L 8-10 76
MCA 8-10 77-79
Also see SHELDON, Sandi
Also see TWYLIGHTS

McCOY BOYS
Singles: 7-inch
VERVE 10-15 60
Members: Gil Garfield; Perry Botkin Jr; Ray Campi.
Also see CAMPI, Ray
Also see DE VORZON, Barry, & Perry Botkin Jr.
Also see GOOD GUYS
Also see WOODS, Billy

McCOYS
Singles: 7-inch
RCA 10-15 58

McCOYS P&R/LP '65
Singles: 7-inch
BANG 8-12 65-67
MERCURY 8-15 68
SOLID GOLD 3-4 73
LPs: 10/12-inch
BANG (212 "Hang on Sloopy") 25-35 65
(Monaural.)
BANG (S-212 "Hang on Sloopy") 35-45 65
(Stereo.)
BANG (213 "You Make Me Feel So Good") 25-35 66
(Monaural.)
BANG (S-213 "You Make Me Feel So Good") 35-45 66
(Stereo.)
MERCURY (61163 "Infinite McCoys") 20-25 68
MERCURY (61207 "Human Ball") 20-25 69
Members: Rick Derringer; Randy Zehringer; Randy Hobbs; Ron Brandon.
Also see DERRINGER, Rick
Also see STRANGELOVES

McCRACKEN, Hugh
(With the Funatics)
Singles: 7-inch
CONGRESS 10-20 65-66
Also see POWERS of BLUE

McCRACKLIN, Jimmy P&R/R&B '58
(With His Blues Blasters; Jimmie McCracklin)
Singles: 78 rpm
ALADDIN 20-30 51
CAVATONE 25-50 47
COURTNEY 25-50 45
DOWN TOWN 20-30 48
EXCELSIOR 25-50 45
GLOBE 25-50 45
HOLLYWOOD 15-25 55
IRMA 15-30 56-57
MODERN 20-30 49
PEACOCK 15-25 52-54
RPM 20-30 50
SWING TIME 15-25 51-52
TRILON 25-50 49
Singles: 7-inch
ART-TONE 10-20 61-62
CHECKER 20-30 58
CHESS 10-15 62
GEDINSON'S 10-15 61
HI (2023 "Things I Meant to Say") 10-20 60
HOLLYWOOD (1054 "It's All Right") 25-35 55
IMPERIAL 6-12 62-67
IRMA (102 "You're the One") 20-40 56
IRMA (103 "Take a Chance") 20-40 56
IRMA (107 "I'm the One") 20-40 57
IRMA (109 "Love for You") 20-40 57
KENT 8-12 62
LIBERTY 4-6 70
MERCURY (71412 "The Wobble") 15-25 59
MERCURY (71516 "Let's Do It") 15-25 59
MERCURY (71613 "By Myself") 15-25 60
MERCURY (71666 "No One to Love Me") 15-25 60
MERCURY (71747 "The Bridge") 15-25 61
MERCURY (71766 "No One to Love Me") 10-20 61
MINIT 5-10 67-70
MODERN (926 "Blues Blasters Boogie") 20-40 54
MODERN (934 "Darlin' Share Your Love") 20-40 54
MODERN (951 "Forgive Me Baby") 20-40 54
MODERN (967 "Gonna Tell Your Mother") 20-40 55
OAK CITY 4-6
PEACOCK (1605 "She's Gone") 30-40 52
PEACOCK (1615 "Share and Share Alike") 30-50 53
PEACOCK (1634 "The End") 30-50 53
PEACOCK (1639 "The Cheater") 30-50 53
PEACOCK (1683 "The Swinging Thing") 20-30 58
PREMIUM (101 "You're the One") 15-25
PREMIUM (102 "I Don't Care") 15-25
SWING TIME (291 "House Rockin' Blues") 30-50 51
LPs: 10/12-inch
CHESS (1464 "Jimmy McCracklin Sings") 40-60 62
CROWN 15-20 61
IMPERIAL 20-35 63-66
MINIT 12-18 67-69
STAX 8-12 72-81
Also see BROWN, Charles, & Jimmy McCracklin

McCRACKLIN, Jimmy / T-Bone Walker / Charles Brown
LPs: 10/12-inch
IMPERIAL (9257 "Best of the Blues, Vol. 1") 15-25 64
Also see BROWN, Charles
Also see WALKER, T-Bone

McCREA, Darlene
Singles: 7-inch
JUBILEE 4-8 66
ROULETTE 5-10 59
TOWER 4-8 64

McCRAE, George P&R/R&B/LP '74
Singles: 7-inch
GOLD MOUNTAIN 3-4 84
SOUL CITY 4-8
T.K. 4-6 74-79
LPs: 10/12-inch
CAT 8-10 76
GOLD MOUNTAIN 5-8 84
TK 8-10 74-77

McCRAE, George & Gwen P&R/R&B '75
Singles: 7-inch
CAT 3-5 76
Also see GEORGE & GWEN
Also see McCRAE, George
Also see McCRAE, Gwen

McCRAE, Gwen R&B '70
Singles: 7-inch
ATLANTIC 3-4 81-83
BLACK JACK 3-4 84
CAT 3-5 74-75
COLUMBIA 4-6 72
LPs: 10/12-inch
ATLANTIC 5-8 81-83
CAT 8-10 74-76
Also see McCRAE, George & Gwen

McCRARYS P&R/R&B/LP '78
Singles: 7-inch
CAPITOL 3-4 80-82
PORTRAIT 3-5 78-79
LPs: 10/12-inch
CAPITOL 5-8 80
PORTRAIT 5-10 78
Members: Sam McCrary; Linda McCrary; Al McCrary; Charity McCrary.

McCREA, Jody
Singles: 7-inch
CANJO (106 "Chicken Surfer") 10-15 64

McCREARY, Mary
Singles: 7-inch
SHELTER 3-5 74-75
LPs: 10/12-inch
MCA 8-10 73
SHELTER 8-10 77
Also see RUSSELL, Mary

McCREE, Earl-Jean: see EARL-JEAN

McCRILL, Chandos
Singles: 7-inch
STARDUST (655 "Money Lovin' Woman") 75-125

McCRORY, Jim
Singles: 7-inch
KEY (5803 "Parking Lot") 50-100 58
KEY (5805 "Rock Ya Baby") 50-100 58

McCROY, Susan
Singles: 7-inch
ARROW 15-25 57

McCUE, Sam
Singles: 7-inch
FLIGHT 5-10 64
Also see CROWFOOT
Also see LEGENDS

McCULLA, Paula C&W '88
Singles: 7-inch
RIVERMARK 3-4 88

McCULLERS, Mickey
(With the Miracles)
Singles: 7-inch
TAMLA (54064 "Same Old Story") 25-35 62
V.I.P. (25009 "Same Old Story") 25-35 64
Also see MIRACLES

McCULLOCH, Danny
Singles: 7-inch
CAPITOL 4-6 68-69
LPs: 10/12-inch
CAPITOL 10-15 69
Also see ANIMALS

McCULLOUGH, Cecil
Singles: 7-inch
MANCO (1011 "Pick 'Em Up and Shake 'Em Up") 50-100 61

McCULLOUGH, Gary C&W '87
Singles: 7-inch
SOUNDWAVES 3-4 87

McCULLOUGH, Ian LP '89
LPs: 10/12-inch
SIRE 5-8 89

McCULLOUGH, Jonnie
Singles: 7-inch
LOG CABIN (2971 "Who Shot Sam") 25-40

McCULLOUGH, Marvin
Singles: 7-inch
BOYD 4-8 61
CAPITOL 4-8 62-63

McCULLOUGH, Ullanda R&B '81
Singles: 7-inch
ATLANTIC 3-5 81

McCURN, George P&R '63
Singles: 7-inch
A&M 4-8 63-64
LIBERTY 4-8 62
REPRISE 4-6 66
LPs: 10/12-inch
A&M 15-25 63

McDANIEL, Big Speed
Singles: 78 rpm
SWING BEAT 10-20 49

McDANIEL, Donna P&R '77
Singles: 7-inch
MIDLAND INT'L 3-5 77

McDANIEL, Lenny: see McDANIELS, Lenny

McDANIEL, Mel C&W '76
(With Oklahoma Wind; Mel McDaniels)
Singles: 7-inch
CAPITOL 3-4 76-89
LPs: 10/12-inch
CAPITOL 5-8 78-84

McDANIEL, Willard
Singles: 78 rpm
SPECIALTY 10-20 51
Singles: 7-inch
SPECIALTY (415 "Blues on the Delta") 20-30 51
SPECIALTY (424 "Ciri-Bri-Bin Boogie") 20-30 51
LPs: 10/12-inch
CROWN (5024 "88 A La Carte") 50-75 57

McDANIELS, Gene P&R/R&B '61
(Eugene McDaniels)
Singles: 7-inch
COLUMBIA 4-8 66-67
LIBERTY 8-15 60-65
MGM 3-5 73
ODE '70 3-5 75
EPs: 7-inch
LIBERTY 10-20 60s
LPs: 10/12-inch
ATLANTIC 10-15 70-71
LIBERTY 15-25 60-67
ODE '70 8-12 75
SUNSET 10-15 66
U.A. 8-12 75
Also see MANN, Johnny, Singers
Also see SULTANS

McDANIELS, Jimmie
Singles: 7-inch
DOT 5-8 61

McDANIELS, Lenny, & Last Nikle
(Lenny McDaniel)
Singles: 7-inch
MAINSTREAM 4-6 69
SEVEN B 10-15
Also see LAST NIKLE

McDANIELS, Luke
(Jeff Daniels)
Singles: 78 rpm
KING 10-20 54
TRUMPET 15-25 52
Singles: 7-inch
KING 15-25 54
TRUMPET (184 "Tribute to Hank Williams") 25-50 52
TRUMPET (185 "Whoa, Boy") 25-50 52
Also see DANIELS, Jeff

McDANIELS, Mel: see McDANIEL, Mel

McDEVITT, Charles, Skiffle Group P&R '57
(Featuring Nancy Wiskey)
Singles: 7-inch
CHIC 5-10 57
KAPP 5-8 58
ORIOLE 5-10 57

McDONALD, Country Joe P&R '75
Singles: 7-inch
FANTASY 3-5 75-79
VANGUARD 3-6 71-74
LPs: 10/12-inch
FANTASY 5-10 75-79
MFSL 25-50 81
PICCADILLY 10-15 78
VANGUARD 8-12 69-76
Also see COUNTRY JOE & FISH

McDONALD, Jim
Singles: 7-inch
KCM (3700 "Let's Have a Ball") 50-100

McDONALD, Kathi LP '74
Singles: 7-inch
CAPITOL 3-6 74
LPs: 10/12-inch
CAPITOL 10-20 74
Also see BALDRY, Long John, & Kathi McDonald
Also see BELLINGHAM ACCENTS
Also see BIG BROTHER & Holding Company
Also see UNUSUALS

McDONALD, Ken
Singles: 78 rpm
DELUXE 15-25 57
Singles: 7-inch
ABC-PAR 10-15 59
DELUXE 15-25 57
PREP (128 "One Love Alone") 20-30 58

McDONALD, Marie
Singles: 78 rpm
RCA 5-8 57
Singles: 7-inch
RCA 5-10 57
LPs: 10/12-inch
RCA (1585 "The Body Sings") 20-30 57

McDONALD, Michael P&R/R&B/LP '82
Singles: 7-inch
MCA 3-4 86
W.B. 3-4 82-85
Picture Sleeves
MCA 3-4 86
W.B. 3-4 82-85
LPs: 10/12-inch
MCA 5-8 86
MFSL (149 "If That's What It Takes") 20-30 85
REPRISE 5-8 90
W.B. 5-8 82-85
Also see CROSS, Christopher
Also see DAL BELLO, Lisa
Also see DOOBIE BROTHERS
Also see HOLLAND, Amy
Also see LABELLE, Patti, & Michael McDonald
Also see LARSON, Nicolette
Also see MEMPHIS HORNS
Also see PACK, David
Also see STEELY DAN
Also see WINANS
Also see WOOD, Lauren

McDONALD, Michael, & James Ingram P&R/R&B '83
Singles: 7-inch
QWEST 3-4 83
Also see INGRAM, James
Also see McDONALD, Michael

McDONALD, Mike
Singles: 7-inch
RCA 3-6 71

McDONALD, Rusty
Singles: 78 rpm
INTRO 25-50 52
Singles: 7-inch
INTRO (6035 "Baby Sittin' Boogie") 50-75 52

McDONALD, Skeets C&W '52
Singles: 78 rpm
CAPITOL (Except 3461) 5-15 51-57
CAPITOL (3461 "You Oughta See Grandma Rock") 15-25 56
FORTUNE 10-20 50
Singles: 7-inch
CAPITOL (Except 3461) 8-15 51-59
CAPITOL (3461 "You Oughta See Grandma Rock") 50-75 56
COLUMBIA 3-8 60-67
EPs: 7-inch
CAPITOL 15-25 54-58
LPs: 10/12-inch
CAPITOL (1040 "Goin' Steady with the Blues") 50-100 58
COLUMBIA 15-25 64
FORTUNE (3001 "Tattooed Lady Plus Other Songs") 30-50 69
HILLYBILLY HEAVEN 5-10
SEARS (116 "Skeets") 15-20 60s

McDONALD & GILES
LPs: 10/12-inch
COTILLION 10-12 71
Members: Ian McDonald; Peter Giles; Mike Giles; Steve Winwood.
Also see GILES, GILES & FRIPP
Also see WINWOOD, Steve

McDONOUGH, Megan
Singles: 7-inch
WOODEN NICKEL 3-5 71
LPs: 10/12-inch
WOODEN NICKEL 8-10 72

McDOUGALL, Robbie
Singles: 7-inch
RCA 3-5 72
LPs: 10/12-inch
RCA 8-10 72

McDOWELL, Bobby
Singles: 7-inch
ABC-PAR 4-8 63

McDOWELL, Carrie R&B '87
Singles: 7-inch
MOTOWN 3-4 87

McDOWELL, Chester
Singles: 7-inch
DUKE 5-10 59-60

McDOWELL, Mississippi Fred
LPs: 10/12-inch
ARHOOLIE 10-15 70s
CAPITOL 10-15 69
EVEREST 10-15 71
LABOR 10-15
SIRE 10-15 70
TESTAMENT 15-25 64

McDOWELL, Mississippi Fred / Guitar Junior
LPs: 10/12-inch
CAPITOL (403 "I Don't Play No Rock & Roll") 75-125 73
(Picture disc. Promotional issue only.)
Also see GUITAR JR.

McDOWELL, Roger
Singles: 7-inch
COMPASS 4-8 77

McDOWELL, Ronnie P&R/C&W '77
Singles: 7-inch
EPIC 3-5 79-85
GRT 3-5 77
MCA/CURB 3-4 86
SCORPION (Except 0533) 3-6 77-79
SCORPION (0533 "Only the Lonely") 4-8 77
LPs: 10/12-inch
DICK CLARK (79 "Elvis") 8-12 79
(TV soundtrack.)
EPIC 5-10 79-85
MCA/CURB 5-8 86
SCORPION (0010 "Live at the Fox") 10-15 78
SCORPION (8021 "The King Is Gone") 10-20 77
(Includes copy of front page of newspaper with news that 'The King' is gone.)
SCORPION (8028 "I Love You, I Love You, I Love You") 10-15 78
STRAWBERRY 8-10 70s
Session: Jordanaires; Conway Twitty; Kathy Westmoreland; Charlie McCoy; David Briggs; Chip Young; Dale Sellers; Bobby Ogden; Mike Leech.
Also see BRIGGS, David
Also see JORDANAIRES
Also see TWITTY, Conway

McDOWELL, Ronnie, & Jerry Lee Lewis C&W '89
Singles: 7-inch
CURB 3-5 88
Also see LEWIS, Jerry Lee
Also see McDOWELL, Ronnie

McDUFF, Brother Jack LP '63
Singles: 7-inch
ATLANTIC 4-8 67
CADET 3-6 68
BLUE NOTE 3-6 69
PRESTIGE 5-10 62
LPs: 10/12-inch
BLUE NOTE 8-12 69
PRESTIGE (7000 series) 25-50 60-64
(Yellow label.)
PRESTIGE (7000 series) 15-25 64-68
(Blue label.)
Also see BENSON, George

McDUFF, Brother Jack, & Gene Ammons
LPs: 10/12-inch
PRESTIGE (7228 "Brother Jack McDuff Meets the Boss") 50-75 61
(Yellow label.)
Also see AMMONS, Gene

McDUFF, Brother Jack, & Willis Jackson LP '66
LPs: 10/12-inch
PRESTIGE 15-25 66
Also see JACKSON, Willis

McDUFF, Brother Jack, Quintet, & David Newman
Singles: 7-inch
ATLANTIC (2488 "But It's Alright") 4-6 68
LPs: 10/12-inch
ATLANTIC (1498 "Double Barrelled Soul") 10-12 68
Also see McDUFF, Brother Jack
Also see NEWMAN, David "Fathead"

McDUFF, Freddy
Singles: 7-inch
SHORE BIRD 15-25

McEACHERN, Murray
Singles: 7-inch
SIGNATURE 4-8 60

McELROY, Sollie
Singles: 7-inch
JA-WES (101 "Angel Girl") 25-50 60s
Also see CHANTEURS
Also see FLAMINGOS
Also see MOROCCOS
Also see NOBLES

McENTIRE, Pake C&W '86
Singles: 7-inch
RCA 3-4 86-88
Also see McENTIRE, Reba

McENTIRE, Reba C&W '76
Singles: 7-inch
MCA 3-5 84-92
MERCURY 5-15 76-83
Picture Sleeves
MCA 3-5
LPs: 10/12-inch
MCA 5-8 84-90
MERCURY (1177 "Reba McEntire") 50-100 77
MERCURY (4047 "Unlimited") 15-25 82
MERCURY (5002 "Reba McEntire") 25-50 77
MERCURY (5017 "Out of a Dream") 25-50 79
MERCURY (5029 "Feel the Fire") 20-30 80
MERCURY (6003 "Heart to Heart") 20-30 81
MERCURY (57062 thru 76157) 10-15 81-82
MERCURY (812781 "Behind the Scene") 10-15 83
Session: Chris Austin; Pake McEntire.
Also see AUSTIN, Chris
Also see McENTIRE, Pake
Also see WARD, Jacky, & Reba McEntire
Also see WHITLEY, Keith

McEUEN, John C&W '85
Singles: 7-inch
W.B. 3-4 85

McFADDEN, Bob P&R '59
(With Dor)
Singles: 7-inch
BRUNSWICK 10-15 59
CORAL 8-12 60
U.S. RUBBER CO. ("Noah's Ark and What's a Nauga?") 5-10
(Promotional only issue. Square cardboard picture disc. Made for U.S. Naugahyde & Naugaweave Co.)
Picture Sleeves
BRUNSWICK (55140 "The Mummy") 15-25 59
LPs: 10/12-inch
BRUNSWICK (54056 "Songs Our Mummy Taught Us") 75-125 59
(Monaural.)
BRUNSWICK (7-54056 "Songs Our Mummy Taught Us") 100-150 59
(Stereo.)
Members: Bob McFadden; Rod McKuen.
Also see DOR & CONFEDERATES
Also see McKUEN, Rod

McFADDEN, Ruth
(With the Supremes; with Royaltones)
Singles: 78 rpm
OLD TOWN 20-40 56
Singles: 7-inch
APT 5-10 61
CAPITOL 5-10 62
OLD TOWN (1017 "Darling, Listen to the Words of This Song") 30-50 56
(The "Supremes" credited here are reportedly the Solitaires. Old Town also had another Supremes group on their label in 1956.)
OLD TOWN (1020 "Two in Love") 50-100 56
OLD TOWN (1030 "School Boy") 100-200 56
RECONA 5-10 64
SURE SHOT 5-10 65
TIARA 10-20 58
Also see ROYALTONES
Also see SOLITAIRES

McFADDEN & WHITEHEAD P&R/R&B/LP '79
Singles: 12-inch
PHILADELPHIA INT'L 4-8 79
SUTRA 4-6
Singles: 7-inch
CAPITOL 3-4 82-83
PHILADELPHIA INT'L 3-5 79
SUTRA 3-4
TSOP 3-4 80
LPs: 10/12-inch
CAPITOL 5-8 83
PHILADELPHIA INT'L 5-8 79
TSOP 5-8 80
Members: Gene McFadden; John Whitehead.
Also see WHITEHEAD, John

McFALL, Orphelia
Singles: 7-inch
SATURN 4-8 63

McFARLAND, Gary LP '69
Singles: 7-inch
SKYE 4-8 69
LPs: 10/12-inch
SKYE 10-15 69

McFARLAND, Jimmie
(Jimmy McFarland)
Singles: 7-inch
RPR (108 "Little Lover") 5-10 60s
VENUS 4-8 66

McFARLIN, Ronnie
Singles: 7-inch
CORBY (227 "Forty Days") 8-12

McFERRIN, Bobby LP '87
Singles: 7-inch
EMI 3-4 88-90
Picture Sleeves
EMI 3-4 88
LPs: 10/12-inch
BLUE NOTE 5-10 87
EMI 5-8 88-90

McFLY, Marty, & Starlighters
(Mark Campbell)
Singles: 7-inch
MCA 3-4 85
Picture Sleeves
MCA 3-5 85
LPs: 10/12-inch
MCA 5-10 85

McGEAR, Mike
Singles: 7-inch
W.B. 3-5 74
LPs: 10/12-inch
W.B. 10-12 74
Also see SCAFFOLD

McGEE, Al
Singles: 7-inch
DONNA 8-12 61

McGEE, Eddie
Singles: 7-inch
HI 5-10 70

McGEE, Howard
Singles: 7-inch
ARGO (4522 "House Warmin' ") 8-12 62
WINLEY (245 "Into Somethin' ") 10-20 60
WINLEY (264 "House Warmin' ") 10-20 62
(First issue.)

McGEE, Jerry
(Gerry Mc Gee)
Singles: 7-inch
A&M 4-8 65
REPRISE 5-10 62-63
Also see VENTURES

McGEE, Parker P&R '77
Singles: 7-inch
BIG TREE 3-5 77
LPs: 10/12-inch
BIG TREE 5-10 76

McGEE, Sam
LPs: 10/12-inch
ARHOOLIE (5012 "Grand Dad of the Country Guitar Pickers") 8-12

McGHEE, Brownie R&B '48
(With His Jook Block Busters; with His Sugar Men)
Singles: 78 rpm
ALERT 10-20 46-47
DERBY 10-20 52
DISC 10-20 47
DOT 50-75 53
ENCORE 10-20 53
HARLEM 20-30 52
LONDON 10-20 51
PAR 10-20 52
RED ROBIN 50-75 52-53
SAVOY 15-30 44-57
SITTIN' IN WITH 10-20 48
Singles: 7-inch
DOT (1184 "Cheatin' & Lying") 150-200 53
HARLEM (2323 "Christina") 30-50 52
HARLEM (2329 "Bluebird") 30-50 52
JACKSON (2304 "Mean Old Frisco") 100-150 52
(Red vinyl.)
JAX (304 "I Feel So Good") 75-100 52
(Red vinyl.)
JAX (307 "Meet You in the Morning") 75-100 52
(Red vinyl.)
JAX (310 "Stranger's Blues") 75-100 52
(Red vinyl.)
JAX (312 "I'm 10,000 Years Old") 75-100 52
(Red vinyl.)
JAX (322 "New Bad Blood") 75-100 52
(Red vinyl.)
RED ROBIN (111 "Don't Dog Your Woman") 100-200 53
SAVOY (778 "True Blues") 35-55 51
SAVOY (835 "Diamond Ring") 20-40 52
SAVOY (844 "Bottom Blues") 20-40 52
SAVOY (872 "Bad Nerves") 20-40 52
SAVOY (899 "Sweet Baby Blues") 20-40 53
SAVOY (1177 "I'd Love to See You") 15-25 55
SAVOY (1185 "Love's a Disease") 15-25 56
SAVOY (1564 "Be My Friend") 15-25 59
LPs: 10/12-inch
BLUESVILLE (1042 "Brownie's Blues") 30-50 60s
FOLKWAYS (Except 20, 30 & 2000 series) 8-10
FOLKWAYS (20, 30 & 2000 series) 20-40 54-55
STORYVILLE 5-8
VANGUARD 8-12 60s
Session: Sonny Terry; Mickey Baker.
Also see BAKER, Mickey
Also see COLLINS, Big Tom
Also see DUPREE, Champion Jack
Also see SPIDER SAM
Also see WILLIAMS, Blind Boy

McGHEE, Brownie, & Sonny Terry LP '73
(Sonny Terry & Brownie McGhee)
Singles: 78 rpm
SAVOY 10-20 44-48
Singles: 7-inch
PRESTIGE BLUESVILLE 5-10 60-62
LPs: 10/12-inch
A&M 8-10 73
BLUESWAY 10-12 69-73
EVEREST 10-12 69
FANTASY (3000 series) 15-25 61-62
(Black vinyl.)
FANTASY (3000 series) 25-50 61-62
(Colored vinyl.)
FANTASY (8000 series) 15-20 62
(Black vinyl.)
FANTASY (8000 series) 25-40 62
(Colored vinyl.)
FANTASY (24000 series) 8-10 72-81
FOLKWAYS (2000 & 3000 series) 15-30 55-61
FOLKWAYS (31000 series) 8-10
FONTANA 10-15 69
MFSL (233 "Sonny & Browny") 20-25 94
MAINSTREAM (6000 series) 15-20 65
MAINSTREAM (300 series) 8-10 71
MUSE 5-8 81
OLYMPIC 8-10 73
PRESTIGE (1000 series) 25-30 60
PRESTIGE (7000 series) 8-10 69-70
PRESTIGE BLUESVILLE 20-40 60-62
PRESTIGE FOLKLORE 12-15
ROULETTE 25-35 59
SAVOY (1100 series) 5-8 84
SAVOY (12000 series) 8-10 73
SAVOY (14000 series) 25-30 58
SHARP (2003 "Down Home Blues") 25-50 59
SMASH 15-20 65
VERVE 20-25 61
VERVE/FOLKWAYS 15-20 65
WORLD PACIFIC 25-30 60
Also see BROONZY, Big Bill
Also see GADDY, Bob
Also see HOPKINS, Lightnin' / Brownie McGhee & Sonny Terry
Also see McGHEE, Brownie
Also see TERRY, Sonny
Also see WILLIS, Ralph

McGHEE, Paul, & Rock-E-Teers
Singles: 7-inch
FLAME 5-10 59

McGHEE, Stick P&R/R&B '49
(With His Buddies; with Ramblers; Sticks McGhee)
Singles: 78 rpm
ATLANTIC 25-75 49-52
DECCA (48104 "Drinkin' Wine Spo-Dee-O-Dee") 15-25 47
ESSEX 10-15 52
HARLEM (1018 "Blues Mixture") 15-25 47
KING 20-30 53-55
LONDON 25-75 51
SAVOY 10-15 55
Singles: 7-inch
ATLANTIC (955 "Wee Wee Hours") 50-75 52
ATLANTIC (991 "New Found Love") 40-60 52
ATLANTIC CLASSICS (873 "Drinkin' Wine Spo-Dee-O-Dee") 10-20 71
("Classics Revisited" reissue series. Original Atlantic 45s of this number—from 1949—do not exist.)
GUSTO 3-4
HERALD 5-10 60
KING (4610 "Little Things We Used to Do") 50-75 53
KING (4628 "Blues in My Heart") 50-75 53
KING (4672 "Dealin' from the Bottom") 50-75 53
KING (4700 "I'm Doin' All the Time") 50-75 53
KING (4783 "Double Crossin' Liquor") 50-100 55
KING (4800 "Get Your Mind Out of the Gutter") 50-75 55
LONDON (978 "You Gotta Have Something on the Ball") 100-200 51
SAVOY 15-25 55

McGHEE, Sticks / John Lee Hooker
LPs: 10/12-inch
AUDIO LAB (1520 "Highway of Blues") 100-125 59
Also see DUPREE, Champion Jack
Also see HOOKER, John Lee
Also see McGHEE, Stick

McGHEE, Tommy
Singles: 78 rpm
EXCELLO 15-25 54
Singles: 7-inch
EXCELLO (2027 "Late Every Evening") 30-40 54

McGILL
Singles: 78 rpm
CAMEO 8-12 57
Singles: 7-inch
CAMEO 8-12 57

McGILL, Connie, & Visions
(With Roland Parker & Strollers)
Singles: 7-inch
TOY (107 "A Million Years") 20-30 63
TRIODE (115 "Peace of Mind") 25-50 63

McGILL, Jerry, & Top Coats
Singles: 7-inch
SUN 10-20 59

McGILL, Rollee R&B '55
(With the Rhythm Rockers; with Whippoorwills; Rollie McGill)
Singles: 78 rpm
MERCURY 10-15 55-56
PINEY 15-25 55
Singles: 7-inch
KAISER (1039 "People Are Talking") 4-8 77
LANDA (702 "Come Home") 8-10 64
MERCURY (70582 "There Goes That Train") 15-25 55
MERCURY (70652 "Rhythm Rockin' Blues") 15-25 55
MERCURY (70725 "There's Madness in My Heart") 15-25 55
MERCURY (70807 "Oncoming Train") 15-25 56
MERCURY (70914 "Come on In") 15-25 56
PINEY (104 "There Goes That Train") 40-60 55
(First issue.)

McGILL, Tony C&W '87
Singles: 7-inch
KILLER 3-4 87

McGILPIN, Bob P&R '78
Singles: 7-inch
BUTTERFLY 3-5 77-78
LPs: 10/12-inch
BUTTERFLY (Black vinyl) 5-10 78-79
BUTTERFLY (Colored vinyl) 12-18 78
CASABLANCA 5-8 80

McGINNIS, Marilyn, & Magic Circle
Singles: 7-inch
DUNHILL 3-5 68

McGLYNN, Pat
Singles: 7-inch
DECCA 3-5 77

McGONNIGLE, Mel
Singles: 7-inch
ROCKET (101 "Rattle Shakin' Mama") 150-200 59

McGOVERN, Maureen P&R/LP '73
Singles: 7-inch
CASABLANCA 3-5 70s
EPIC 3-5 78
MAIDEN VOYAGE 3-5 70s
20TH FOX 3-5 73-75
W.B. 3-5 79-80
WOODEN NICKEL 3-5 73
LPs: 10/12-inch
20TH FOX 8-12 73-75
W.B. 5-10 79

McGOWAN, Donnie
Singles: 7-inch
TANGERINE 4-8 64

McGOWAN, Ron
Singles: 7-inch
DORIAN 5-10 60

McGOY, Neal: see McCOY, Neal

McGRATH, Bat
LPs: 10/12-inch
EPIC 10-12 69

McGRATH, Suni
LPs: 10/12-inch
ADELPHI 10-12 70-71

McGRAW BROTHERS
Singles: 7-inch
CHELTENHAM 4-8 64

McGRIFF, Edna
(With Buddy Lucas & His Band of Tomorrow)
Singles: 78 rpm
BELL (4 "The Fool") 10-20 57
JOSIE (764 "Ooh Little Daddy") 10-20 54
JUBILEE 10-15 51-53
Singles: 7-inch
BELL 10-20 57
CAPITOL 4-8 64-65
JOSIE (764 "Ooh Little Daddy") 20-30 54
JUBILEE (5062 "Note Droppin' Papa") 20-30 51
JUBILEE (5073 "Heavenly Father") 20-30 52
JUBILEE (5087 "It's Raining") 20-30 52
JUBILEE (5089 "In a Chapel by the Side of the Road") 20-30 52
JUBILEE (5099 "Good") 20-30 52
JUBILEE (5109 "Edna's Blues") 20-30 53
(Black vinyl.)
JUBILEE (5109 "Edna's Blues") 50-75 53
(Colored vinyl.)
WILLOW 5-10 61
Picture Sleeves
BELL (4 "The Fool") 10-15 57
Also see BUDDY & EDNA
Also see LUCAS, Buddy

McGRIFF, Edna, & Sonny Til
Singles: 78 rpm
JUBILEE 10-20 52
Singles: 7-inch
JUBILEE (5090 "Once in a While") 20-30 52
Also see McGRIFF, Edna
Also see TIL, Sonny

McGRIFF, Jimmy P&R/R&B/LP '62
(Jimmy McGriff Trio)
Singles: 7-inch
BLUE NOTE 3-5 71
CAPITOL 3-5 70-71
COLLECTABLES 3-4 80s
GROOVE MERCHANT 3-5 75
JELL (100 series) 5-10 62
JELL (500 series) 4-8 65
LRC 3-5 78
MILESTONE 3-4 83
SOLID STATE 4-6 66-70
SUE 5-10 62-64
U.A. 3-5 71-78
EPs: 7-inch
SOLID STATE 8-12 66
LPs: 10/12-inch
BLUE NOTE 8-12 70-71
COLLECTABLES 6-8 88
51 WEST 5-8 80s
GROOVE MERCHANT 8-12 71-76
LRC 8-10 77-78
MILESTONE 5-8 81-83
SOLID STATE 10-15 66-70
SOUL SUGAR 10-12 70
SUE 20-30 62-65
U.A. 8-12 71
VEEP 10-15 68
Also see ADAMS, Faye / Jimmy McGriff
Also see HOLMES, Richard "Groove"
Also see PARKER, Little Junior, & Jimmy

McGriff

McGUFFEY LANE *P&R '81*
Singles: 7-inch
ATCO 3-4 81-82
ATLANTIC AMERICA 3-4 84
LPs: 10/12-inch
ATCO 5-10 82
Members: Robert McNelley; Steve Douglass.

McGUINN, Roger *LP '73*
Singles: 7-inch
COLUMBIA 3-5 73-77
LPs: 10/12-inch
ARISTA 5-8 90
COLUMBIA (Except "Airplay Anthology") 8-12 73-77
COLUMBIA ("Airplay Anthology") 20-30 77
(Promotional issue only.)
Members: Jim (Roger) McGuinn; Chris Hillman; Gene Clark.
Also see HILLMAN, Chris
Also see McGUINN, Roger
Also see MITCHELL, Chad, Trio

McGUINN, CLARK & HILLMAN *P&R/LP '79*
(Roger McGuinn & Chris Hillman featuring Gene Clark)
Singles: 7-inch
CAPITOL 3-5 79
LPs: 10/12-inch
CAPITOL 5-8 79-82
Members: Roger McGuinn; Gene Clark; Chris Hillman.
Also see BYRDS
Also see HILLMAN, Chris, & Roger McGuinn

McGUINNESS, Wayne
Singles: 78 rpm
METEOR 50-75 56
Singles: 7-inch
METEOR (5035 "Rock, Roll and Rhythm") 100-150 56

McGUINNESS FLINT *P&R/LP '71*
Singles: 7-inch
CAPITOL 3-5 70-71
LPs: 10/12-inch
CAPITOL 10-12 70-71
Members: Tom McGuinness; Hughie Flint.
Also see GALLAGHER & LYLE
Also see MANN, Manfred

McGUIRE, Barry *P&R/LP '65*
(With the Horizon Singers)
Singles: 7-inch
ABC 3-5 70
DUNHILL 4-8 65-66
HORIZON 4-8 63
ODE '70 3-5 70
MCA 3-5
MIRA 4-6 66
MOSAIC 4-8 61-62
MYRRH 3-5 73
ROULETTE 3-5
Picture Sleeves
DUNHILL 5-10 65
LPs: 10/12-inch
BIRDWING 5-8 80
DUNHILL 20-30 65
HORIZON 15-25 63
MYRRH 5-8 73-75
ODE '70 8-10 70
SPARROW 5-8 79
SURREY 12-15 65
Also see MAMAS & PAPAS / Barry McGuire
Also see NEW CHRISTY MINSTRELS

McGUIRE, Barry, & Barry Kane
Singles: 7-inch
HORIZON 4-8 62
LPs: 10/12-inch
HORIZON 15-25 62
SURREY 12-18 66

McGUIRE, Doug *C&W '80*
Singles: 7-inch
MULTI-MEDIA 3-5 80

McGUIRE, Lowell
Singles: 7-inch
NASCO (6007 "Spellbound") 10-15 58

McGUIRE, Phyllis *P&R '64*
Singles: 7-inch
REPRISE 4-6 64-65
ORPHEUM 4-6 68
LPs: 10/12-inch
ABC-PAR 10-20 66
Also see McGUIRE SISTERS

McGUIRE SISTERS *P&R '54*
(With Lawrence Welk)
Singles: 78 rpm
CORAL 4-8 54-58
Singles: 7-inch
ABC-PAR 4-6 66
CORAL (Except 61000 & 98000 series) 4-8 58-65
CORAL (61000 series) 5-10 54-58
CORAL (98000 series) 10-15 60
(Stereo.)
MCA 3-4 70s
REPRISE 4-6 63-65
Picture Sleeves
CORAL 5-15 56-61
EPs: 7-inch
CORAL 10-15 55-60
LPs: 10/12-inch
ABC-PAR 10-20 66
CORAL (6 "Best of the McGuire Sisters") 15-25 65
CORAL (56123 "By Request") 25-50 55
CORAL (57000 series) 15-25 56-65
MCA 5-8 78
VOCALION 10-20 60-67
Members: Phyllis McGuire; Dorothy McGuire; Christine McGuire.
Also see DESMOND, Johnny, Eileen Barton & McGuire Sisters
Also see McGUIRE, Phyllis
Also see WELK, Lawrence, & His Orchestra

McGUIRE SISTERS / Lancers / Dorothy Collins / Teresa Brewer
EPs: 7-inch
CORAL (98015 "Christmas Alphabet") 15-25 50s
(Promotional issue only.)
Also see BREWER, Teresa
Also see COLLINS, Dorothy
Also see LANCERS
Also see McGUIRE SISTERS

McGWIRE, Mo
Singles: 7-inch
WOODEN NICKEL 3-5 74

McHOUSTON, Big Red
("Vocal by Larry Dale"; Mickey Baker)
Singles: 78 rpm
GROOVE (0020 "I'm Tired") 15-25 54
Singles: 7-inch
GROOVE (0020 "I'm Tired") 30-40 54
Also see BAKER, Mickey
Also see DALE, Larry

McHUGH, Jimmy
Singles: 7-inch
DEE CAL 5-10 61
HUNCH 5-10 65
SUCCESS 5-10 63

McHUGH, Richie
Singles: 7-inch
RAEWOOD (587 "Joann") 50-75 63

McIAN, Peter *P&R '80*
Singles: 7-inch
COLUMBIA/ARC 3-5 80
LPs: 10/12-inch
COLUMBIA/ARC 5-8 80

McILVAINE, Red
Singles: 7-inch
PEGRED 4-6

McILWAINE, Ellen
Singles: 7-inch
POLYDOR 3-5 73
LPs: 10/12-inch
KOT'AI 8-10 75
POLYDOR 8-12 73

McINTYRE, Chester
(Chet McIntyre)
Singles: 7-inch
RENNER 5-10 62
SARG (180 "Gonna Rock My Baby") 40-60 61

McKAY, Allison
Singles: 7-inch
FOXFIDEL 5-10 60

McKAY, Rufus
(With the Red Tops)
Singles: 7-inch
ACE (602 "Bo-Weevil Junction") 8-12 60
SKY (703 "Swanee River Rock") 15-25 60
Also see RED TOPS

McKAY, Scotty
Singles: 7-inch
ACE 8-12 60-62
CAPRI 5-10 63
CHARAY (1004 "High on Life") 10-20 70
CLARIDGE 10-20 66
DESK 5-10 63
EVENT 5-10 59
FALCON 10-15 68
HBR 10-15 67
LAWN 10-15 60
MASTERS MAGIC 4-8 72
PARKWAY 10-15 59
PHILIPS 5-10 63
POMPEII 10-15 69
STARLING 8-12 63
SWAN 10-15 60
UNI 5-10 70
LPs: 10/12-inch
ACE (1017 "Tonight in Person") 40-50 61
MASTERS MAGIC 10-20 72
Also see LIPSCOMB, Max K.

McKEAG, Bob, & Fun
Singles: 7-inch
BUDDAH 3-5 77

McKEE, Lonette *R&B '74*
Singles: 7-inch
SUSSEX 3-5 74
W.B. 3-5 79

McKEE, Maria *LP '89*
Singles: 7-inch
GEFFEN 3-4 89
LPs: 10/12-inch
GEFFEN 5-8 89

McKEE, Rick
Singles: 7-inch
LE CAM 4-8 61

McKEE, Ron, & Rivieres
Singles: 7-inch
LINCOLN 4-8 64

McKENDREE, Fran
Singles: 7-inch
ARISTA 3-5 77
Picture Sleeves
ARISTA 3-5 77

McKENDREE SPRING *LP '70*
Singles: 7-inch
DECCA 3-6 69-72
MCA 3-5 73
PYE 3-5 76
LPs: 10/12-inch
DECCA 10-15 69-72
MCA 8-10 73
PYE 8-10 75-76

McKENNA, Mae
LPs: 10/12-inch
PYE 8-10 77

McKENNON, Kenny
Singles: 7-inch
FABLE (564 "Call Your Daddy, Baby") 40-60 57

McKENZIE, Bob & Doug *P&R/LP '82*
Singles: 7-inch
MERCURY 3-5 82
Picture Sleeves
MERCURY 3-5 82
LPs: 10/12-inch
MERCURY 5-10 81
Session: Geddy Lee.
Also see RUSH

McKENZIE, Don
Singles: 7-inch
MIRACLE (10 "Whose Heart") 50-75 61
RIDGE (6602 "Beauty") 50-75
Also see SUPREMES

McKENZIE, Lil, & Four Students
Singles: 78 rpm
GROOVE (0113 "Run Along") 15-25 55
Singles: 7-inch
GROOVE (0113 "Run Along") 30-40 55
Also see FOUR STUDENTS

McKENZIE, Scott *P&R/LP '67*
(McKenzie's Musicians)
Singles: 7-inch
CAPITOL 4-8 65-67
EPIC 3-6 67-72
ODE (Except 103) 4-8 67-71
ODE (103 "San Francisco [Wear Some Flowers in Your Hair]") 8-10 67
ODE (103 "San Francisco [Be Sure to Wear Flowers in Your Hair]") 4-8 67
(Note slight change in title.)
LPs: 10/12-inch
ODE (44000 series) 15-25 67
ODE (34000 series) 8-10 77
ODE (77000 series) 10-15 70
Also see JOURNEYMEN

McKINLEY, David Pete
(Pete McKinley)
Singles: 78 rpm
FIDELITY (3008 "Black Snake Blues") 25-35 52
GOTHAM (505 "Shreveport Blues") 25-35 52

McKINLEY, L.C.
Singles: 78 rpm
STATES (135 "Companion Blues") 10-20 53
VEE JAY 10-15 55
Singles: 7-inch
BEA & BABY (102 "Nit Wit") 15-25 59
STATES (135 "Companion Blues") 40-60 53
VEE JAY (133 "Strange Girl") 30-40 55
VEE JAY (159 "I'm So Satisfied") 30-40 55

McKINLEY, Pete: see McKINLEY, David Pete

McKINLEY, Travis
Singles: 7-inch
SOULTOWN 5-10

McKINLEY, Wilson
Singles: 7-inch
ELIJAH ("On Stage") 75-125
(Selection number not known.)
ELIJAH ("Heaven's Gonna Be a Blast") 75-125
(Selection number not known.)
ELIJAH ("The Spirit") 75-125
(Selection number not known.)

McKINLEYS
Singles: 7-inch
SWAN 8-12 64

McKINNEY, John, & Premiers
Singles: 7-inch
MAD (1009 "Angels in the Sky") 300-500 58

McKINNEY, Mary
Singles: 7-inch
DOT 5-10 59
SPOT 5-10 59

McKINNEY, Nathan
(With Valleyites)
Singles: 7-inch
DESERT BONE (40 "Very Special Lady") 5-10
RAYCO (526 "Weep No More") 25-35 64
RAYCO (532 "I'm Gonna Cry") 10-20 65

McKINNIES, Maurice, & Champions
Singles: 7-inch
BLACK & PROUD 4-8 69

McKINNON, Don
Singles: 7-inch
ANTENNA (6442 "Fat Fat Fat") 50-100 59
BELTONE (1013 "Should I Kiss You") 10-15 61

McKINNON, Harold, & Rimshots
Singles: 7-inch
CARTER ("Little Jump Joint") 25-50
(Selection number not known.)

McKNIGHT
Singles: 7-inch
CUSTOM (127 "You're Doin' Me Wrong") 25-35

McKNIGHT, June
Singles: 7-inch
JEANNIE 4-8 62

McKOWN, Gene
Singles: 7-inch
AGGIE (1001 "Rockabilly Rhythm") 100-200
AGGIE (1003 "Little Mary") 100-200
RICH (106 "I'm Out on the Town") 10-15 60s

McKUEN, Rod *P&R '62*
(With the Keytones; with Horizon Singers)
Singles: 7-inch
A&M 4-8 63
BUDDAH 3-5 73-74
DECCA 5-10 59
HORIZON 4-8 63
JUBILEE 4-8 62
KAPP 4-8 61
LIBERTY 8-12 56
RCA 4-8 66-67
SPIRAL 4-8 61-62
STANYAN 3-5 74
VISTA 3-5 71
W.B. 3-6 68-72
Picture Sleeves
VISTA 3-5 71
W.B. 3-5 71
LPs: 10/12-inch
DECCA (4900 series) 10-15 68
DECCA (8800 series) 20-30 59
DECCA (75000 series) 10-12 69
CAPITOL 15-20 64
HARMONY 8-10 71
HI FI 20-30 58-59
EPIC (600 & 3800 series) 15-20 62
EPIC (26000 series) 10-12 68
EVEREST 10-12 68
HORIZON 15-25 63
IN 15-20 64
JUBILEE 20-25 62
KAPP (1200 & 3200 series) 15-25 61
KAPP (1500 & 3500 series) 10-20 67
LIBERTY (Except 3011) 10-15 67
LIBERTY (3011 "Songs for a Lazy Afternoon") 25-40 56
PICKWICK 5-10 70s
RCA 10-20 65-69
STANYAN 10-15 66-72
SUNSET 8-10 70
TRADITION 10-12 68
VISTA 8-10 71
W.B. 8-15 67-76
Also see DALEY, Jimmy, & Ding-A-Lings
Also see DOR & CONFEDERATES
Also see McFADDEN, Bob
Also see SAN SEBASTIAN STRINGS

McKUHEN, Lanier *C&W '87*
Singles: 7-inch
SOUNDWAVES 3-4 87

McLACHLAN, Sarah *LP '89*
LPs: 10/12-inch
ARISTA 5-8 89

McLAGAN, Ian *LP '80*
Singles: 7-inch
MERCURY 3-5 79
LPs: 10/12-inch
MERCURY 5-10 79
Also see FACES
Also see SMALL FACES

McLAIN, Denny
LPs: 10/12-inch
CAPITOL 10-20 69

McLAIN, Tommy *P&R '66*
Singles: 7-inch
COLLECTABLES 3-4 80s
JIN (Except 197) 5-8 66-69
JIN (197 "Sweet Dreams") 10-20 66
MSL 5-8 66
STARFLITE 3-5 79
LPs: 10/12-inch
STARFLITE 10-15 79
Also see FENDER, Freddy, & Tommy McLain

McLANE, Jimmy
Singles: 7-inch
SWAY 4-8 61

McLAREN, Malcolm *D&D '83*
(With the World's Famous Supreme Band; with World's Famous Supreme Team)
Singles: 12-inch
ISLAND 4-6 82-85
Singles: 7-inch
ISLAND 3-4 82-85
LPs: 10/12-inch
ISLAND 5-8 83-85
Also see WORLD'S FAMOUS SUPREME TEAM

McLAUCHLAN, Murray
LPs: 10/12-inch
EPIC 8-10 71-74
ISLAND 5-8 76-77

McLAUGHLIN, John *LP '72*
(Mahavishnu Orchestra & John McLaughlin; Mahavishnu John McLaughlin; with One Truth Band)
LPs: 10/12-inch
COLUMBIA 5-10 72-83
DOUGLAS 8-12 72
POLYDOR 8-15 69-72
W.B. 5-8 81
Also see SANTANA, Carlos, & Mahavishnu John McLaughlin

McLAUGHLIN, Pat *LP '88*
LPs: 10/12-inch
CAPITOL 5-8 88

McLAURIN, Bette *P&R '52*
(With the Four Fellows; with Striders; Betty McLaurin)
Singles: 78 rpm
CENTRAL 10-15 54
CORAL 10-15 53
DERBY (700 series) 10-15 50-52
DERBY (804 "My Heart Belongs to Only You") 20-40 52
GLORY 10-15 55
JUBILEE 10-15 55
Singles: 7-inch
ALMONT (309 "You're the Greatest") 50-100 58
CAPITOL (4320 "Remember") 15-25 59
CENTRAL (1004 "It's Easy to Remember") 20-30 54
CORAL (61129 "If You Believed in Me") 15-25 53
DERBY (790 "I May Hate Myself in the Morning") 20-30 51
DERBY (804 "My Heart Belongs to Only You") 50-75 52
GLORY (233 "Grow Old Along with Me") 25-50 55
GLORY (237 "Just Come a Little Bit Closer") 25-50 55
GLORY (241 "I'm Past Sixteen") 25-50 55
JUBILEE (5139 "Please Don't Leave Me") 15-25 55
JUBILEE (5155 "Ever So Lonely") 15-25 55
JUBILEE (5179 "How Can I") 15-25 55
O GEE (100 "The Masquerade Is Over") 15-25 59
PULSE 5-10 65
Also see FOUR FELLOWS
Also see STRIDERS

McLAURIN, Sonny
Singles: 7-inch
FAYETTE 4-8 64

McLAWLER, Sarah
Singles: 78 rpm
BRUNSWICK 5-10 53
KING 25-40 52
VEE JAY 10-15 56
Singles: 7-inch
BRUNSWICK (84018 "Your Fool Again") 10-15 53
KING (4561 "Romance in the Dark") 50-100 52
VEE JAY 15-25 56

McLEAN, Chuck
Singles: 7-inch
BACK BEAT 4-6 69

McLEAN, Don *P&R/LP '71*
Singles: 7-inch
ARISTA 3-5 78
CAPITOL 3-4 87-88
EMI AMERICA (Except 9100) 3-4 87
EMI AMERICA (9100 "American Pie") 4-8 92
(Full length [8:30] version.)
LIBERTY 3-5
MEDIARTS 3-6 70
MILLENNIUM 3-5 81-83
RCA 3-4 83
U.A. 3-5 71-75
Picture Sleeves
U.A. 3-5 71-73
LPs: 10/12-inch
ARISTA (4149 "Prime Time") 5-10 77
(Black vinyl.)
ARISTA (4149 "Prime Time") 10-15 77
(Colored vinyl. Promotional issue only.)
CASABLANCA 8-10 79
GOLD CASTLE ("For the Memories") 20-30 89
(Selection number not known.)
LIBERTY 5-8 82-83
MEDIARTS (41-4 "Tapestry") 15-20 70
MILLENNIUM 5-8 81
RCA (3933 "Special Radio Series") 10-15 81
(Promotional issue only.)
U.A. 10-15 71-74
Promotional LPs

McLEAN, Penny *P&R/R&B '76*
Singles: 7-inch
ATCO 3-5 75-76
Also see SILVER CONVENTION

McLEAN, Phil *P&R '61*
Singles: 7-inch
VERSATILE 4-8 61-62

McLIN, Claude
(Claude McLin Combo)
Singles: 7-inch
ALLEGRO 4-8 62
DOOTO 4-8 64

McLOLLIE, Oscar
(With the Honey Jumpers; with Bobby Smith Combo; Oscar Lollie)
Singles: 78 rpm
CLASS....10-15 57
MERCURY....10-15 51-56
MODERN....10-20 52-55
WING....10-15 56
Singles: 7-inch
CLASS (206 "Say")....15-20 57
CLASS (216 "King of the Fools")....15-20 57
CLASS (238 "Rock-a-Cha")....15-20 58
CLASS (243 "Convicted")....15-20 58
CLASS (265 "Honey Jump")....10-20 60
CLASS (501 "Honey Jump")....15-25 56
CLASS (503 "Rain")....15-25 56
JET (517 "You Belong to Me")....10-20 61
MERCURY (70964 "The Penalty")...20-30 56
MODERN (902 "Honey Jump")....30-40 52
MODERN (915 "Be Cool, My Heart")....25-35 52
MODERN (920 "Falling in Love with You")....25-35 54
MODERN (928 "Mama Don't Like")....25-40 54
MODERN (938 "Hot Banana")....25-40 54
MODERN (940 "Love Me Tonight")....25-40 54
MODERN (943 "Dig That Crazy Santa Claus")....25-40 54
MODERN (950 "Hey Lolly Lolly")....25-40 55
MODERN (955 "Eternal Love")....25-40 55
MODERN (970 "Convicted")....25-50 55
SAHARA (100 "Tonight You Belong to Me")....10-15 63
SHOW TIME (600 "Ignore Me")....10-20 59
WING (90083 "God's Green Earth")....15-25 56
LPs: 10/12-inch
CROWN (5016 "Oscar McLollie & His Honey Jumpers")....150-250 56

McLOLLIE, Oscar, & Jeanette Baker P&R '58
Singles: 7-inch
CLASS (228 "Hey Girl - Hey Boy")....15-20 58
HI OLDIES....3-6
Also see BAKER, Jeanette

McLOLLIE, Oscar, & Nancy Lamarr
Singles: 7-inch
SAHARA....5-10 63
Also see McLOLLIE, Oscar

McLOONIE, Annie
LPs: 10/12-inch
RCA....5-10 76

McLUHAN
LPs: 10/12-inch
BRUNSWICK....10-15 72

McLUHAN, Marshall
LPs: 10/12-inch
COLUMBIA....15-25 67
Also see McLUHAN

McLYTE LP '89
LPs: 10/12-inch
FIRST PRIORITY....5-8 89

McMAHON, Ed
Singles: 7-inch
CAMEO....4-8 67
LPs: 10/12-inch
CAMEO (2009 "I'm Ed McMahon")....15-25 67

McMAHON, Gerard P&R '83
Singles: 7-inch
FULL MOON....3-4 83
LPs: 10/12-inch
FULL MOON....5-8 83

McMAKEN, Bill
Singles: 7-inch
REDWING (14204 "Call My Name")....15-25

McMANUS, Ross
Singles: 7-inch
IMPERIAL....5-8 64

McMILLAN, Cab, & His Fadaways
Singles: 78 rpm
MACY'S....15-25 50

McMILLAN, Jimmy C&W '80
Singles: 7-inch
BLUM....3-5 80-81

McMILLAN, Terry C&W '82
Singles: 7-inch
RCA....3-4 82

McMULLAN, Jim
Singles: 7-inch
SHAD....5-10 59

McMURRY, Beverly
Singles: 7-inch
ASSOCIATED ARTISTS....4-8 64

McMURTRY, James LP '89
LPs: 10/12-inch
COLUMBIA....5-8 89

McNAB, Cecil
Singles: 7-inch
KING (5516 "Clock Tickin' Rhythm")....100-200 58

McNAIR, Barbara
Singles: 7-inch
AUDIO FIDELITY....4-8 69
CORAL (61972 "He's Got the Whole World in His Hands")....15-25 58
CORAL (62071 "Going Steady with the Moon")....10-20 59
CORAL (62116 "Lover's Prayer")....10-20 59
KC (109 "Cross Over the Bridge")....20-40 63
MOTOWN (Except 1112)....10-20 65-69
MOTOWN (1112 "Steal Away Tonight")....100-200 67
SIGNATURE....5-15 60
W.B. (5633 "Wanted")....15-25 65
LPs: 10/12-inch
AUDIO FIDELITY (6222 "More Today Than Yesterday")....10-15 69
CORAL....15-25 59
MOTOWN (644 "Where I Am")....25-50 66
MOTOWN (680 "The Real Barbara McNair")....20-30 69
SIGNATURE (1042 "Love Talk")....20-30 60
W.B. (1541 "I Enjoy Being a Girl")....15-25 64
W.B. (1570 "Living End")....15-25 64

McNAIR, Harley
Singles: 7-inch
TOWER....4-8 68

McNAIR, Patricia
Singles: 7-inch
CREST....4-8 69

McNALLY, Larry John P&R '81
Singles: 7-inch
ARC....3-4 81

McNALLY, Mac
LPs: 10/12-inch
ARIOLA AMERICA....8-10 77

McNAMARA, Robin P&R '70
Singles: 7-inch
STEED....3-5 69-71
LPs: 10/12-inch
STEED....10-15 70

McNASTY, Filthy
Singles: 7-inch
X-RATED....5-10

McNAUGHTON, Byron, & His All-News Orchestra
Singles: 7-inch
JAMIE (1427 "Right from the Shark's Jaws")....4-8 75

McNEAL, Landy: see McNEIL, Landy

McNEAL, Larry
Singles: 7-inch
COLUMBIA....4-8 69

McNEELY, Big Jay R&B '49
(With His Blue Jays; with Little Sonny Warner)
Singles: 78 rpm
ALADDIN....20-30 49-54
BAYOU....20-30 53
FEDERAL....10-20 52-54
EXCLUSIVE....15-25 46
IMPERIAL....10-20 51-52
SAVOY....10-20 48-54
VEE JAY....10-20 55-56
Singles: 7-inch
ALADDIN (3242 "Real Crazy Cool")....15-25 54
BAYOU (014 "Hometown Jamboree")....40-60 53
BAYOU (018 "Catastrophe")....40-60 53
FEDERAL (12102 "The Goof")....20-30 52
FEDERAL (12111 "Earthquake")....20-30 52
FEDERAL (12141 "Nervous, Man Nervous")....20-30 53
FEDERAL (12151 "3-D")....20-30 53
FEDERAL (12168 "Mule Walk")....20-30 54
FEDERAL (12179 "Hot Cinders")....20-30 54
FEDERAL (12186 "Let's Work")....20-30 54
FEDERAL (12191 "Beachcomber")....20-30 54
IMPERIAL (5219 "Deacon's Express")....25-35 53
SAVOY (798 "The Deacon's Hop")..25-50 51
SAVOY (1143 "The Deacon's Hop")....15-25 54
SWINGIN'....10-15 59-61
VEE JAY (142 "Big Jay's Hop")....25-35 55
VEE JAY (212 "Jay's Rock")....25-35 56
W.B....4-8 63
EPs: 7-inch
FEDERAL (246 "Go! Go! Go! with Big Jay McNeely")....100-200 53
FEDERAL (301 Big Jay McNeely, Vol. 2")....100-150 54
FEDERAL (332 Wild Man of the Saxophone")....100-150 54
FEDERAL (373 Just Crazy")....75-100 55
LPs: 10/12-inch
COLLECTABLES....5-8 88
FEDERAL (96 "Big Jay McNeely")....600-800 54
(10-inch LP.)
FEDERAL (530 "Big Jay in 3-D")....300-500 57
KING (650 "Big Jay in 3-D")....50-100 59
SAVOY (15045 "Rhythm & Blues Concert")....250-350 55
(10-inch LP.)
W.B. (W-1523 "Big Jay McNeely")....25-35 63
(Monaural.)
W.B. (WS-1523 "Big Jay McNeely")....30-40 63
(Stereo.)
Session: Platters.
Also see DELEGATES / Big Jay McNeely
Also see OTIS, Johnny
Also see PLATTERS
Also see THREE DOTS and a DASH
Also see WARNER, Sonny

McNEELY, Big Jay / Paul Williams
Singles: 78 rpm
SAVOY....10-15 49-55
Singles: 7-inch
SAVOY (1100 series)....15-25 55
Also see McNEELY, Big Jay
Also see WILLIAMS, Paul

McNEIL, Aaron
(With the Tornados)
Singles: 7-inch
CJ (615 "Carolyn")....10-15 60s
CAPITOL (5105 "Crying on My Shoulder")....15-25 64
CAPITOL (5268 "Draculena")....15-25 65
TOWER....5-10 66-67
UPTOWN....5-10 66

McNEIL, Landy
(With the Corsairs; Landy McNeal)
Singles: 7-inch
KAPP (600 "Move It")....5-10 64
TUFF (402 "The Change in You")....8-12 66
Also see CORSAIRS

McNEIR, Ronnie R&B '75
Singles: 7-inch
CAPITOL....3-4 84
DETO (2878 "Sitting in My Class")....75-125
PRODIGAL....3-5 75
LPs: 10/12-inch
CAPITOL....5-8 84

McNICHOL, Kristy & Jimmy P&R/LP '78
Singles: 7-inch
RCA....3-5 78
Picture Sleeves
RCA....3-5 78
LPs: 10/12-inch
RCA....5-10 78

McNUTT, Marshall, & His Orchestra
Singles: 7-inch
ENITH....4-8 64

M'COOL, Shamus P&R '81
Singles: 7-inch
PERSPECTIVE....3-4 81

McPHAIL, Jimmy
Singles: 78 rpm
RCA....10-15 51
Singles: 7-inch
GAYE....10-15
RCA....15-25 51

McPHAIL, Prentiss
Singles: 7-inch
ARA (205 "It's Uncle Willie Time")....10-20 64
BANG....5-10 65

McPHATTER, Clyde P&R/R&B '56
(With Cookie & the Cues)
Singles: 78 rpm
ATLANTIC (1081 thru 1185)....20-30 56-57
ATLANTIC (1199 "A Lover's Question")....40-60 58
Singles: 7-inch
AMY....5-15 65-67
ATLANTIC (1000 series)....15-25 56-58
ATLANTIC (2000 series)....10-20 58-60
DECCA....4-8 70
DERAM....4-8 68-69
MGM (12000 series)....10-15 59-60
(Monaural.)
MGM (50134 "Let's Try Again")....20-40 60
(Stereo.)
MERCURY....6-12 60-65
Picture Sleeves
MGM....15-20 60
MERCURY....10-15 60-65
EPs: 7-inch
ATLANTIC (584 "Clyde McPhatter")....100-200 58
ATLANTIC (605 "Rock with Clyde McPhatter")....100-200 58
ATLANTIC (618 "Clyde McPhatter")....50-100 59
MERCURY ("Golden Blues Hits")..10-15 62
(Has paper sleeve. Number not known. Promotional issue only.)
LPs: 10/12-inch
ALLEGIANCE....5-8 80s
ATLANTIC (8024 "Love Ballads")....100-200 59
(Black label.)
ATLANTIC (8024 "Love Ballads")..25-50 59
(Red label.)
ATLANTIC (8031 "Clyde")....75-125 59
ATLANTIC (8077 "Best of Clyde McPhatter")....25-40 63
DECCA....15-25 70
MGM (E-3775 "Let's Start Over Again")....30-40 59
(Monaural.)
MGM (SE-3775 "Let's Start Over Again")....40-50 59
(Stereo.)
MGM (E-3866 "Greatest Hits")....30-40 60
(Monaural.)
MGM (SE-3866 "Greatest Hits")....40-50 60
(Stereo.)
MERCURY....20-35 60-64
WING....20-30 62
Session: King Curtis.
Also see BROWN, Ruth, & Clyde McPhatter
Also see DOMINOES
Also see DRIFTERS
Also see KING CURTIS
Also see LITTLE ESTHER & Clyde McPhatter
Also see WARD, Billy, & Dominoes

McPHATTER, Clyde / Little Richard / Jerry Butler
LPs: 10/12-inch
PICKWICK (3233 "Rhythm & Blues and Greens")....15-20 70s
Also see BUTLER, Jerry
Also see LITTLE RICHARD
Also see McPHATTER, Clyde

McPHERSON, Wyatt ("Earp") P&R/R&B '61
Singles: 7-inch
SAVOY....4-8 61

McPHERSON, Wyatt "Earp," & Paul Williams
Singles: 7-inch
BATTLE....4-8 63
Also see McPHERSON, Wyatt "Earp"
Also see WILLIAMS, Paul

McPHERSON, Wyley C&W '82
Singles: 7-inch
I.E....3-4 82

McQUAID, Betty
Singles: 7-inch
GO (5013 "Tongue Tied")....40-60

McQUAID, Jimmy, & Unique Echos
Singles: 7-inch
SWAN....5-8 67

McQUAIG, Scott C&W '89
Singles: 7-inch
UNIVERSAL....3-4 89

McQUINN, Kevin
Singles: 7-inch
DIAMOND....4-8 61-62
VIVID....4-8 63

McRAE, Carmen P&R '56
Singles: 78 rpm
DECCA....3-6 55-57
VENUS....4-8 54
Singles: 7-inch
COLUMBIA....4-6 62
DECCA....5-10 55-57
KAPP....4-8 63
VENUS....5-10 54
Picture Sleeves
COLUMBIA....4-8 62
EPs: 7-inch
DECCA....5-10 55
LPs: 10/12-inch
BETHLEHEM (1023 "Carmen McRae")....75-125 54
(10-inch LP.)
COLUMBIA....15-25 61-65
DECCA (8100 thru 8800 series)....40-60 55-58
(Black and silver label.)
DECCA (8100 thru 8800 series)....15-25 64
(Black label with horizonal rainbow stripe.)
FOCUS....15-25 65
KAPP....20-40 58-59
MAINSTREAM....10-20 65-67
TIME....15-25 63
Also see CONNOR, Chris / Julie London / Carmen McRae
Also see DAVIS, Sammy, Jr., & Carmen McRae
Also see SIMONE, Nina, Chris Connor & Carmen McRae

McRAE, Teddy
Singles: 7-inch
AMP 3....8-12

McREYNOLDS, Galen, Quintet
Singles: 7-inch
NOLTA....4-8 61
Members: Hal Champ; Galen McReynolds; Jimmy Buettner; Keith Purvis; Al Turay.

McRILL, Chandos
Singles: 78 rpm
STARDUST....20-30 56
Singles: 7-inch
STARDUST (655 "Money Lovin' Woman")....100-125 56

McSHANN, Jay P&R '41
(With His Orchestra; Combo; Trio; Quartet; Sextet; Kansas City Stompers; Jazz Men)
Singles: 78 rpm
ALADDIN....10-15 50
CAPITOL....10-20 44-45
DECCA....10-15 41-43
DOWN BEAT....10-15 48-49
MERCURY....10-15 45-46
MODERN....10-15 50
PHILO/ALADDIN....10-20 45
PREMIER....10-15 45
SWING TIME....10-15 48-52
VEE JAY....5-10 55-56
Singles: 7-inch
SWING TIME (314 "Jeromimo")....20-25 52
VEE JAY....10-20 55-56
EPs: 7-inch
DECCA (742 "Kansas City Memories")....50-100 54
LPs: 10/12-inch
CAPITOL....15-20 67
DECCA (5503 "Kansas City Memories")....200-300 54
(10-inch LP. With Charlie Parker, Al Hibbler, Walter Brown, & Paul Paul Quinichette.)
DECCA (9000 series)....10-15 68
Also see ADAMS, Faye / Jay McShann
Also see BROWN, Walter
Also see HIBBLER, Al
Also see WATERFORD, Crown Prince
Also see WITHERSPOON, Jimmy

McSHANN, Jay, With Johnny Moore's Three Blazers
Singles: 78 rpm
MODERN....10-15 50
Also see MOORE, Johnny

McSHANN, Jay, & Priscilla Bowman
Singles: 78 rpm
VEE JAY....5-10 55
Singles: 7-inch
VEE JAY....10-15 55
Also see BOWMAN, Priscilla
Also see McSHANN, Jay

McSHY D LP '87
LPs: 10/12-inch
LUKE SKYWALKER....5-8 87

McTELL, Blind Willie
(Blind Willie)
Singles: 78 rpm
REGAL (3260 "River Jordon")....50-75 50
REGAL (3272 "It's My Desire")....50-75 50
REGAL (3277 "Love Changing Blues")....50-75 50
LPs: 10/12-inch
ATLANTIC....8-12 72
BIOGRAPH....10-15 69-73
MELODEON (7323 "1940")....15-25 66
PRESTIGE....8-12 70
PRESTIGE BLUESVILLE (1040 "Last Session")....25-35 62
Also see BARRELHOUSE SAMMY
Also see PIG 'N WHISTLE BAND

McTELL, Blind Willie, & Memphis Minnie
LPs: 10/12-inch
BIOGRAPH....10-15 70
Also see MEMPHIS MINNIE
Also see McTELL, Blind Willie

McTELL, Ralph
Singles: 7-inch
PARAMOUNT....3-5 73
LPs: 10/12-inch
CAPITOL....10-12 69
20TH FOX....6-10 75
W.B....8-10 72

McVEA, Jack P&R/R&B '47
(With His All-Stars)
Singles: 78 rpm
APOLLO....10-15 45
BLACK & WHITE....10-20 45-47
EXCLUSIVE....10-15 47
COMBO....8-12 56
COMET (100 "B.B. Boogie")....10-15 48
MELODISC....10-20 45
Singles: 7-inch
COMBO (Except 55)....10-20 56
COMBO (55 "Let's Ride, Ride, Ride")....15-25 55
TAG....10-15 56
Also see BROWN, Clarence "Gatemouth"
Also see PHILLIPS, Gene
Also see SAVOYS / Jack McVea
Also see SHARPS / Jack McVea

McVICKER, Dana C&W '87
Singles: 7-inch
CAPITOL....3-4 88
EMI AMERICA....3-4 87

McVIE, Christine LP '76
Singles: 7-inch
W.B....3-4 84
Picture Sleeves
W.B....3-4 84
LPs: 10/12-inch
SIRE....8-10 76
W.B....5-8 84
Also see BURNETTE, Billy, & Christine McVie
Also see CHICKEN SHACK
Also see FLEETWOOD MAC
Also see PERFECT, Christine
Also see NEWMAN, Randy

McVOY, Carl
Singles: 7-inch
HI....10-15 58
PHILLIPS INT'L....10-15 58
TRI....5-10 61
Also see McCOY, Carl

McWILLIAMS, David
Singles: 7-inch
KAPP....5-8 68

McWILLIAMS, Paulette R&B '77
Singles: 7-inch
FANTASY....3-5 77
Also see AMERICAN BREED
Also see RUFUS

ME & DEM GUYS
(Me & Them Guys)
Singles: 7-inch
CORAL GABLES (2082 "Black Cloud")....25-35 66
(First issue.)
DEARBORN (550 "Black Cloud")....10-15 66
PALMER....5-10 60s
PYRENEES (16 "Simple Thoughts of Love")....10-15 60s
PYRENEES (41 "She Cried")....10-15 60s

ME & GUYS
Singles: 7-inch
PLA ME (101 "I Can't Take It")....15-25 66

ME & HIM DUO
Singles: 7-inch
PAZA (867 "On the Money")....10-20 66

ME & THE REST
Singles: 7-inch
BRASS CITY (2027 "Mark Time")..15-25 67

ME & THEM
Singles: 7-inch
GRE-TLE.......... 4-8
U.S. SONGS.......... 4-8 64

ME & YOU
Singles: 7-inch
PARKWAY.......... 8-15 66

MEAD, Montie
(Monty Mead)
Singles: 7-inch
FORTUNE.......... 5-10 60s
KING.......... 4-8 64

MEAD, Sister Janet P&R '74
Singles: 7-inch
A&M.......... 3-5 74

MEADE, Donna C&W '88
Singles: 7-inch
MERCURY.......... 3-4 88-89

MEADE, Freddie, & Calenders
Singles: 7-inch
20TH FOX (287 "Just Give Her My Love").......... 20-30 61

MEADE, Jimmy
Singles: 7-inch
TOP HAT.......... 4-8 64

MEADER, Vaughn LP '62
LPs: 10/12-inch
CADENCE.......... 10-20 62-63
KAMA-SUTRA.......... 8-15 60s

MEADOW
Singles: 7-inch
PARAMOUNT.......... 4-6 73
LPs: 10/12-inch
PARAMOUNT.......... 10-15 73
Member: Laura Branigan.
Also see BRANIGAN, Laura

MEADOWBROOKS
Singles: 7-inch
CATAMOUNT (106 "Time After Time").......... 10-15 65
CATAMOUNT (108 "Lover's Quarrel").......... 10-15 65

MEADOWLARKS
Singles: 78 rpm
IMPERIAL (5146 "Brother Bill").......... 15-25 51

MEADOWLARKS
Singles: 7-inch
AMAZON (101 "Goodnight My Love").......... 5-8 90s
(Colored vinyl. Promotional issue only.)

MEADOWLARKS / Neighbors
EPs: 7-inch
IRENE (503 "Christmas Songs")..... 5-10

MEADOWLARKS (With Don Julian): see JULIAN, Don, & Meadowlarks

MEADOWLARKS (Larks & Don Julian): see LARKS

MEADOWS
LPs: 10/12-inch
RADIO.......... 5-8 81

MEADOWS, Dave, & Neanderthals
Singles: 7-inch
MAGNUM (41160 "Angel").......... 10-20 60s

MEADOWS, Jayne & Audrey
Singles: 7-inch
RCA.......... 4-8 55-56
Picture Sleeves
RCA.......... 10-20 55
Also see ALLEN, Steve, & Jayne Meadows

MEADOWS, Larry
Singles: 7-inch
REGENCY (25 "Don't Hide Your Love").......... 20-40 62
REGENCY (27 "Pretending").......... 15-25 63
STRAT O LITE (969 "Phyllis").... 100-200 59

MEADOWS BROTHERS R&B '77
Singles: 7-inch
KAYVETTE.......... 3-4 87

MEAGAN D&D '84
Singles: 7-inch
NEXT PLATINUM.......... 4-6 84

MEAN MACHINE R&B '81
Singles: 7-inch
SUGAR HILL.......... 3-4 81

MEANS, Keith, & Knighters
Singles: 7-inch
RENA.......... 5-10 61

MEANTIME
Singles: 7-inch
ATCO.......... 8-12 67
Member: Ellie Greenwich.
Also see GREENWICH, Ellie

MEARS, Ray
Singles: 7-inch
FEDORA.......... 4-8 62

MEAT DEPARTMENT
Singles: 7-inch
POLAR BEAR.......... 10-15 60s

MEAT LOAF LP '77
(With Ellen Foley; Marvin Lee Aday)
Singles: 12-inch
EPIC (477 "Meat Loaf").......... 5-8 77
(Promotional issue only.)
Singles: 7-inch
EPIC.......... 3-5 77-83
RCA.......... 3-4 85
RSO.......... 3-5 74
Picture Sleeves
RCA.......... 3-5 85
LPs: 10/12-inch
CLEVELAND INT'L.......... 5-8 81-83
EPIC (30000 series, except 34974 & 36007).......... 5-10 77-80
EPIC (34974 "Bat Out of Hell").......... 5-10 77
EPIC (E99-34974 "Bat Out of Hell").......... 20-25 77
(Picture disc. With bats on front cover.)
EPIC (E99-34974 "Bat Out of Hell").......... 25-35 77
(Picture disc. Without bats on front cover. Promotional issue only.)
EPIC (34974 "Bat Out of Hell")...... 25-35 77
(Picture disc. Canadian.)
EPIC (36007 "Dead Ringer").......... 25-35 81
(Picture disc. Promotional issue only.)
EPIC (40000 series).......... 12-15 80
(Half-speed mastered.)
Also see FOLEY, Ellen
Also see POPCORN BLIZZARD
Also see STONEY & MEAT LOAF

MEAT PUPPETS
LPs: 10/12-inch
SST.......... 5-8 81-87
Members: Curt Kirkwood; Cris Kirkwood; Derrick Bostrom.

MEAUX, Huey
Singles: 7-inch
JIN (104 "73 Special").......... 15-25 59

MECHANICAL SWITCH
Singles: 7-inch
ONE WAY (906 "Everything Is Red").......... 20-40 60s
Picture Sleeves
ONE WAY (906 "Everything Is Red").......... 30-60 60s

MECHANICS
Singles: 7-inch
NORMAN (501 "Fastest Thing on Wheels").......... 15-25 61

MECKI MARK MEN
Singles: 7-inch
LIMELIGHT.......... 4-6 68-69
LPs: 10/12-inch
LIMELIGHT.......... 10-20 68-69

MECO P&R/R&B/LP '77
(Meco Monardo)
Singles: 12-inch
ARISTA.......... 4-6 83
Singles: 7-inch
ARISTA.......... 3-4 82-83
MILLENNIUM.......... 3-5 77-78
RSO.......... 3-5 80
LPs: 10/12-inch
ARISTA.......... 5-8 82-84
CASABLANCA.......... 5-10 79-80
MILLENNIUM.......... 5-10 77-78
RSO.......... 5-8 80
Also see STAR WARS INTERGALACTIC DROID CHOIR & CHORALE

MEDALLIONAIRES
Singles: 7-inch
MERCURY (71309 "Magic Moonlight").......... 150-200 58

MEDALLIONS
Singles: 78 rpm
ESSEX (901 "I Know").......... 50-100 55
Singles: 7-inch
ESSEX (901 "I Know").......... 200-300 55

MEDALLIONS
Singles: 7-inch
CARD (1 "Since You've Gone Away").......... 40-60 60
SINGULAR (1002 "Broken Heart").......... 40-60 57
SULTAN (1004 "Love That Girl") .50-100 59

MEDALLIONS
Singles: 7-inch
MINIT.......... 5-10 62
SARG (191 "I Love You True")...... 20-30 61
SARG (194 "Lovin' Time").......... 20-30 61

MEDALLIONS
Singles: 7-inch
LENOX (5556 "Why Do You Look at Me").......... 20-30 63

MEDALLIONS
Singles: 7-inch
WARPED (1001 "Leave Me Alone").......... 20-30 60s

MEDALLIONS
Singles: 7-inch
MEDALLION (010 "Hot Ice").......... 8-12

MEDALLIONS (with Vernon Green): see GREEN, Vernon, & Medallions

MEDEIROS, Glenn P&R/LP '87
Singles: 7-inch
AMHERST.......... 3-4 87-88
Picture Sleeves
AMHERST.......... 3-4 87-88
LPs: 10/12-inch
AMHERST.......... 5-8 87
MCA.......... 5-8 90
Also see PARKER, Ray, Jr.

MEDEIROS, Glenn, & Bobby Brown
Singles: 7-inch
MCA.......... 3-4 90
Picture Sleeves
MCA.......... 3-4 90
Also see BROWN, Bobby

MEDEIROS, Glenn, & Stylistics P&R '90
Singles: 7-inch
MCA.......... 3-4 90
Also see MEDEIROS, Glenn
Also see STYLISTICS

MEDICINE HEAD
Singles: 7-inch
ELEKTRA.......... 3-5 71
POLYDOR.......... 3-5 70
LPs: 10/12-inch
POLYDOR.......... 8-12 73

MEDICINE MEN
Singles: 7-inch
DUEL (510 "Fever").......... 10-20 62
LAUREL.......... 5-10 61

MEDINA, Renee
Singles: 7-inch
CHALLENGE.......... 4-8 64

MEDITATIONS
Singles: 7-inch
WORLD PACIFIC (77876 "Trancendental Meditation").......... 5-10 67

MEDIUM
LPs: 10/12-inch
GAMMA.......... 10-20

MEDLEY, Bill P&R/R&B/LP '68
Singles: 7-inch
A&M.......... 3-5 71-73
CURB.......... 3-5 89
ELEKTRA.......... 3-4 90
LIBERTY.......... 3-5 81
MGM.......... 4-8 68
PARAMOUNT.......... 3-5 71
PLANET.......... 3-4 82-83
RCA.......... 3-4 83-85
REPRISE.......... 4-8 65
SCOTTI BROTHERS.......... 3-4 88
U.A.......... 3-5 78-80
VERVE.......... 4-8 67
Picture Sleeves
SCOTTI BROTHERS.......... 3-4 88
LPs: 10/12-inch
A&M.......... 8-12 71-73
LIBERTY.......... 5-10 81
MCA/CURB.......... 5-10 88
MGM.......... 10-20 68-70
PLANET.......... 8-10 82
RCA.......... 5-8 83-85
U.A.......... 5-10 78-85
Also see CLOUDS
Also see KNIGHT, Gladys, & Bill Medley
Also see RIGHTEOUS BROTHERS
Also see SONNY & CHER / Bill Medley / Lettermen / Blendells

MEDLEY, Bill, & Jennifer Warnes P&R '87
Singles: 7-inch
RCA.......... 3-4 87
Picture Sleeves
RCA.......... 3-4 87
Also see MEDLEY, Bill
Also see WARNES, Jennifer

MEDLIN, Joe P&R '59
Singles: 7-inch
BRUNSWICK.......... 4-8 61
MERCURY.......... 4-8 59-60

MEDLOCKE, Rick, & Blackfoot
Singles: 7-inch
ATLANTIC.......... 3-4 87
Also see BLACKFOOT

MEDUSA
LPs: 10/12-inch
COLUMBIA.......... 5-10 79

MEDWICK, Joe
Singles: 7-inch
ALL BOY (8504 "You Ain't Treatin' Her Right").......... 5-10 62
DUKE (189 "You Still Send Me").... 10-20 58
DUKE (311 "Searchin' in Vain").......... 8-12 60
MONUMENT.......... 4-8 65

MEE & EWE
Singles: 7-inch
LOOK.......... 4-6 71
POMPEII.......... 4-6 69

MEEFORD, Ray
Singles: 7-inch
ACCENTS.......... 5-8

MEEHAN, Don
Singles: 7-inch
GRASS ROOTS.......... 4-8

MEEN
Singles: 7-inch
VARMINT (103 "Greenfields").......... 8-12

MEEP MEEP & ROADRUNNERS
Singles: 7-inch
BOMMERANG.......... 4-8 65

MEGADETH LP '86
EPs: 7-inch
MEGAFORCE.......... 5-10 89
LPs: 10/12-inch
CAPITOL.......... 5-8 86-90
Members: Dave Mustaine; Dave Ellefson; Gar Samuelson.

MEGATONES
Singles: 7-inch
AZRA (119 "Don't Drop the Bomb on My Boyfriend").......... 5-10 83
(Rectangular picture disc.)
AZRA (119 "Don't Drop the Bomb on My Boyfriend").......... 5-10 83
(Octogon or hexagon picture disc.)
AZRA (DTR 119 "Don't Drop the Bomb on My Boyfriend").......... 5-10 83
(8-inch picture disc.)

MEGATONS P&R '62
Singles: 7-inch
CHECKER.......... 5-10 62
DODGE.......... 10-15 62
FOREST.......... 4-8 63
JELL.......... 4-8 62
Member: Billy Lee Riley.
Also see RILEY, Billy Lee

MEGATONS
Singles: 7-inch
LAURIE.......... 10-20 65
Member: Eugene Thomas.

MEGATRONS P&R '59
Singles: 7-inch
ACOUSTICON (101 "Velvet Waters").......... 30-40 59
(First issue.)
AUDICON (101 "Velvet Waters")... 10-20 59
AUDICON (104 "Whispering Winds").......... 10-20 60
AUDICON (107 "Ranchero").......... 10-20 60
AUDICON (110 "By the Waters of Minnetonka").......... 10-20 61
LAURIE (3291 "Velvet Waters")...... 6-12 63
LAURIE (3310 "Detroit Sound")...... 6-12 65

MEI, Hao, & Rickshaw 5
Singles: 7-inch
ENCORE.......... 5-8 64

MEISBURG & WALTERS
Singles: 7-inch
PARCHMENT.......... 3-5 75-76
Picture Sleeves
PARCHMENT.......... 3-5 76
LPs: 10/12-inch
PARCHMENT.......... 8-12 75-76
Members: Steven Meisburg; John Walters.

MEISNER, Randy P&R/LP '80
Singles: 7-inch
ASYLUM.......... 3-5 78
EPIC.......... 3-5 80-82
LPs: 10/12-inch
ASYLUM.......... 8-10 78
EPIC.......... 5-10 80-82
Also see BLACK TIE
Also see EAGLES
Also see NELSON, Rick
Also see POCO

MEL & JERRY
Singles: 7-inch
W.B.......... 4-8 61

MEL & KIM P&R/R&B '87
Singles: 7-inch
ATLANTIC.......... 3-4 87
Picture Sleeves
ATLANTIC.......... 3-4 87
Members: Mel Appleby; Kim Appleby.

MEL & TIM P&R/R&B '69
Singles: 7-inch
BAMBOO.......... 4-6 69-70
COLLECTABLES.......... 3-4 80s
ERIC.......... 3-4 70s
STAX.......... 3-5 72-74
LPs: 10/12-inch
BAMBOO.......... 10-15 70
STAX.......... 8-12 72-74
Members: Mel Harden; Tim McPherson.

MELA, Denny
Singles: 7-inch
PARKWAY.......... 5-10 59

MELACHRINO, George, & His Orchestra LP '55
(Melachrino Strings & Orchestra)
Singles: 78 rpm
RCA.......... 3-5 50-57
Singles: 7-inch
RCA.......... 4-8 50-59
EPs: 7-inch
RCA.......... 5-10 50-59
LPs: 10/12-inch
RCA.......... 10-20 50-61
Also see MANCINI, Henry / Al Hirt / Robert Russell Bennett / Melachrino Strings

MELANIE LP '69
(With the Edwin Hawkins Singers)
Singles: 7-inch
ABC/MCA.......... 3-5 75
AMHERST.......... 3-4 85
ATLANTIC.......... 3-5 77
BLANCHE.......... 3-4 82
BUDDAH.......... 3-8 69-73
CASABLANCA.......... 3-5 74
COLUMBIA (44349 "God's Only Daughter").......... 10-15 67
COLUMBIA (44524 "Garden in the City").......... 8-12 68
ERIC.......... 3-4 78
FLASHBACK.......... 3-4 70s
GOLDIES.......... 3-4 70s
GORDIAN.......... 5-10 85
MIDSONG INT'L.......... 3-5 78-79
NEIGHBORHOOD.......... 3-5 71-75
PORTRAIT.......... 3-4 81
RADIO ACTIVE GOLD.......... 3-4 80s
STORK.......... 5-10 70
(Promotional issue only.)
TOMATO.......... 3-5 78-79
WHAT'S IT ALL ABOUT.......... 4-6 70s
(Promotional issue only.)
WORLD UNITED.......... 3-5 78
Picture Sleeves
BUDDAH.......... 3-4 70-72
NEIGHBORHOOD.......... 3-4 72-73
EPs: 7-inch
BUDDAH.......... 5-8 70
(Juke box issue.)
LPs: 10/12-inch
ABC.......... 8-10 75
ACCORD.......... 5-8 81-82
AMHERST.......... 8-10 85
ARISTA.......... 5-10 75-77
ATLANTIC.......... 8-10 76
BELL.......... 8-10 71
BLANCHE.......... 5-8 82
BUDDAH.......... 10-15 69-77
51 WEST.......... 5-8 79
KOALA.......... 5-10 79
MCA/MIDSONG.......... 5-10 77-78
NEIGHBORHOOD.......... 8-10 71-75
PAIR.......... 5-10 88
PICKWICK.......... 8-10 71
TELLENHOUSE.......... 15-25 78
TOMATO.......... 5-10 79
Also see HAWKINS, Edwin, Singers
Also see MOMMY

MELBA & KASHIF: see MOORE, Melba, & Kashif

MELBOURNE, Gloria
Singles: 7-inch
A&M (740 "Don't Let Him").......... 5-8 65

MELCHER, Terry
Singles: 7-inch
RCA/EQUINOX.......... 4-8 75
LPs: 10/12-inch
REPRISE.......... 10-15 74
Also see BEVERLY HILLS BLUES BAND
Also see DAY, Terry

MELCHER, Terry, & Bruce Johnston
Singles: 7-inch
RCA/EQUINOX.......... 4-8 75
Also see BRUCE & TERRY
Also see JOHNSTON, Bruce
Also see MELCHER, Terry

MELCHIOR, Dean
Singles: 7-inch
MEL (1000 "Baby Sister").......... 6-12 50s

MELI, Debbie
Singles: 7-inch
RCA.......... 10-15 66

MELINDA & MISFITS
Singles: 7-inch
U-NEK (711 "Don't Take Your Love Away").......... 15-25 60s

MELINDA SUE
Singles: 7-inch
B&O.......... 3-6 69

MELIS, Jose
Singles: 78 rpm
MERCURY/SAV-WAY (5038 Stardust").......... 100-150 47
(Picture disc. Promotional issue only.)

MELISSA
Singles: 7-inch
DECCA.......... 3-5 71
LPs: 10/12-inch
DECCA.......... 10-12 71

MELL, Bobby
Singles: 7-inch
DORE.......... 4-8 61-62

MELLAA R&B '83
Singles: 7-inch
LARC.......... 3-4 83

MELLARDS: see GREEN, Fred, & Mellards

MELLE MEL & DUKE BOOTEE R&B '82
Singles: 12-inch
SUGAR HILL.......... 4-6 82
Also see BOOTEE, Duke
Also see GRANDMASTER FLASH & Furious Five

MELLENCAMP, John Cougar P&R/LP '79
(John Cougar; Johnny Cougar; John Mellencamp)
Singles: 12-inch
MAIN MAN (4001 "Kid Inside").. 100-125 83
(Picture disc. Has four tracks. Promotional issue only.)
MAIN MAN (4001 "Kid Inside").... 75-100 83
(Picture disc. Has two tracks. Promotional issue only. Autographed.)
MAIN MAN (4001 "Kid Inside").......... 60-80 83
(Picture disc. Has two tracks. Promotional issue only. Not Autographed.)
Singles: 7-inch
MERCURY.......... 3-4 87-90
RIVA (Except 211 & 215).......... 3-5 79-85
RIVA (211 "Hand to Hold on To").......... 3-4 82

RIVA (211 "Hand to Hold on To")...20-25 82
(Promotional only picture disc.)
RIVA (215 "Pink Houses")......5-10 83
(Colored vinyl.)
Picture Sleeves
MERCURY......3-4 87-90
RIVA......4-8 79-86
EPs: 7-inch
GULCHER ("U.S. Male")......50-75 75
(Selection number not known.)
LPs: 10/12-inch
MCA (2225 "Chestnut Street Incident")......15-20 77
MAIN MAN ("Chestnut Street Incident")......30-40 76
MAIN MAN (601 "Kid Inside")......5-10 83
MERCURY (Except 349)......5-8 87-90
MERCURY (349 "Let It All Hang") 25-35 87
(Interview LP. Promotional issue only.)
MFSL (222 "Lonesome Jubilee")....20-25 94
RIVA......5-10 79-85
Members: John Cougar Mellencamp; Larry Crane; David Parman; Terrence Sala; Wayne Hall; Tom Wince; Michael Wanchic; Doc Rosser; Ken Aronoff; George Perry; Toby Myers; John Cascalle.
Also see LITTLE RICHARD & John Cougar Mellencamp

MELLO, Dennie
Singles: 7-inch
BLUE BELL (500 "Wailin' Guitar") 10-15 60

MELLO DROPS
Singles: 78 rpm
IMPERIAL......200-300 54
Singles: 7-inch
IMPERIAL (5324 "When I Grow to Old to Dream")......500-1000 54

MELLO KINGS
Singles: 78 rpm
IMPERIAL (5105 "Shirley")......40-60 50

MELLO-CHORDS
Singles: 7-inch
LYCO (1001 "Golden Vanity")......20-40 61

MELLODEERS: see MELODEERS

MELLO-FELLOWS
Singles: 78 rpm
LAMP (8006 "Iddy Biddy Baby").....10-15 54
Singles: 7-inch
LAMP (8006 "Iddy Biddy Baby").....25-30 54

MELLOHARPS
(Mello-harps)
Singles: 78 rpm
DO-RE-MI (203 "Love Is a Vow")......200-400 56
TIN PAN ALLEY......100-200 55-56
Singles: 7-inch
CASINO (104 "No Good")......50-100 58
DO-RE-MI (203 "Love Is a Vow")......2000-3000 56
TIN PAN ALLEY (145 "I Love Only You")......200-400 55
TIN PAN ALLEY (157 "What Good Are My Dreams")......300-500 56
Also see WILTSHIRE, Teacho, & Melloharps

MELLO-KINGS *P&R '57*
(Mellokings; Mellotones)
Singles: 78 rpm
HERALD (502 "Tonite Tonite")...150-250 57
(Credits "The Mellotones.")
HERALD (502 "Tonite Tonite").....75-125 57
(Credits "The Mello-Kings.")
Singles: 7-inch
COLLECTABLES......3-4 80s
FLASHBACK......3-5 65
HERALD (502 "Tonite Tonite")...300-500 57
(Credits "The Mellotones.")
HERALD (502 "Tonite Tonite")......15-25 57
(Credits "The Mello-Kings." Has logo in script print inside the flag.)
HERALD (502 "Tonite Tonite")......10-15
(Credits "The Mello-Kings." Has logo in block print inside the flag.)
HERALD (507 thru 567)......10-20 57-61
LESCAY......10-15 62
EPs: 7-inch
HERALD (451 "The Fabulous Mello-Kings")......200-250 60
LPs: 10/12-inch
COLLECTABLES......6-8 84
HERALD (1013 "Tonight Tonight")......350-500 60
RELIC......5-10 80s
Members: Larry Esposita; Bob Scholl; Jerry Scholl; Eddie Quinn; Neil Areana.
Also see ROAD

MELLO-LARKS
Singles: 7-inch
EPIC......5-10 54-56
LPs: 10/12-inch
CAMDEN (530 Just for a Lark")....20-40 59
EPIC (1106 "The Mello-Larks & Jamie")......20-40 55
(10-inch LP.)
Members: Tom Hamm; Adele Castle; Bob Wolter; Joseph Eich.

MELLO-LARKS & DELORES HAWKINS
LPs: 10/12-inch
EPIC (1122 "Broadway Success Story")......20-40 55
Also see HAWKINS, Dolores
Also see MELLO-LARKS

MELLO-MAIDS
Singles: 78 rpm
BATON......10-20 56-57
Singles: 7-inch
BATON......10-25 56-57

MELLOMEN
Singles: 7-inch
FULTON (113 "Daddy's Lullaby")...10-15
(Colored vinyl.)

MELLO-MOODS *R&B '52*
(Mellow Moods; Mello Moods; Mellomoods; with Teacho Wiltshire & Band; with Schubert Swanston Trio)
Singles: 78 rpm
PRESTIGE (799 "Call on Me")...100-200 53
PRESTIGE (856 "I'm Lost")......100-200 53
RED ROBIN (104 "I Couldn't Sleep a Wink Last Night")......200-400 52
ROBIN (105 "Where Are You")..100-300 52
Singles: 7-inch
HAMILTON (143 "I'm Lost")......10-15
PRESTIGE (799 "Call on Me")......1000-2000 53
PRESTIGE (856 "I'm Lost")...1000-2000 53
ROBIN (105 "Where Are You")......2000-3000 51
Members: Ray "Buddy" Wooten; Bobby Williams; Monte Owens; Bobby Baylor; Jimmy Bethea.
Also see PERSONALITIES
Also see SOLITAIRES

MELLOMOODS
Singles: 7-inch
RECORDED in HOLLYWOOD (399 "Song of Love")......200-350 54
Member: Al Frazier.
Also see HIGGINS, Chuck, & Mellomoods
Also see KEY, Troyce
Also see RIVINGTONS
Also see SHARPS

MELLON, LeGrand
Singles: 7-inch
COLUMBIA......4-8 66

MELLOTONES (On Herald): see MELLO-KINGS

MELLO-TONES
Singles: 78 rpm
COLUMBIA......25-40 50-51
OKEH......20-30 51
Singles: 7-inch
COLUMBIA (39051 "What Are They Doing in Heaven")......150-250 50
COLUMBIA (39215 "Flying Saucers")......150-250 51
OKEH (6828 "Rough and Rocky Road")......100-200 51

MELLO-TONES
(With Reginald Ashby Orchestra)
Singles: 78 rpm
DECCA......50-100 54
Singles: 7-inch
DECCA (48319 "I'm Just Another One in Love with You")......250-300 54
Also see BENITEZ, Marga, & Mello-Tones
Also see MELLO-TONES / Gloria Mann

MELLO-TONES / Gloria Mann
EPs: 7-inch
DECCA (2399 "Rhythm and Blues Bit")......50-75 56
Also see MANN, Gloria
Also see MELLO-TONES

MELLO-TONES *P&R '57*
(With Hank Ivory's Orchestra)
Singles: 78 rpm
FASCINATION......50-75 57
GEE......20-30 57
Singles: 7-inch
FASCINATION (1001 "Rosie Lee")......150-250 57
GEE (1037 "Rosie Lee")......25-50 57
GEE (1040 "Ca-Sandra")......25-50 57

MELLOTONES
Singles: 7-inch
MINARET (105 "He's a Friend").....10-20 62
TURRET (102 "Everything's Gonna Be Alright")......25-50 60s

MELLOW BRICK RODE
Singles: 7-inch
U.A. (50333 "Don't Put All Your Eggs in One Basket")......5-10 68
Members: Jerry Hudson; Phil Hudson; Joseph Hesse; Jim Hesse; Ralph Parker; Nick Distefano.
Also see ROAD

MELLOW DROPS
Singles: 78 rpm
IMPERIAL......50-75 54
Singles: 7-inch
IMPERIAL (5324 "When I Grow Too Old to Dream")......100-125 54

MELLOW FELLOWS
Singles: 7-inch
DOT (17135 "My Baby Needs Me")......8-12 68
DOT (17240 "Me Tarzan, You Jane")......8-12 69

MELLOW KEYS
Singles: 78 rpm
GEE (1014 "Listen, Baby")......15-25 56
Singles: 7-inch
GEE (1014 "Listen, Baby")......30-50 56

MELLOW JACKS
Singles: 7-inch
ASCOT (2115 "Gina Baby")......15-25 62
MARQUEE (83695 "Gina Baby")...30-50 62
(Identification number shown since no selection number is used.)

MELLOW LARKS
(With Clue J. & His Blues Blasters)
Singles: 7-inch
WORLDISC (104 "I'll Be True").100-200 58

MELLOW MAN ACE
LPs: 10/12-inch
CAPITOL......5-8 90

MELLOW MOODS
Singles: 7-inch
WE MAKE ROCK & ROLL RECORDS......4-8 68

MELLOW TONES
Singles: 78 rpm
HORIZON......10-20

MELLOWLARKS
Singles: 78 rpm
ARGO (5285 "Farewell to You").....10-15 57
Singles: 7-inch
ARGO (5285 "Farewell to You").....10-15 57

MELLOWS
("Featuring Lillian Leach;" "Featuring Lillian Lee;" with Sammy Lowe & His Orchestra)
Singles: 78 rpm
CANDLELIGHT......40-60 56
CELESTE......50-100 56
JAY DEE......20-35 55
Singles: 7-inch
CANDLELIGHT (1011 "Moon of Silver")......100-150 56
CELESTE (3004 "I'm Yours").....500-750 56
DAVIS......5-10
JAY DEE (793 "How Sentimental Can I Be")......50-100 54
JAY DEE (797 "Smoke from Your Cigarette")......50-100 55
(Yellow label.)
JAY DEE (797 "Smoke from Your Cigarette")......25-50 50s
(Orange label.)
JAY DEE (801 "I Was a Fool to Let You Go")......50-100 55
JAY DEE (807 "Yesterday's Memories")......50-100 55
LPs: 10/12-inch
RELIC......8-10
Members: Lillian Leach; Harry Johnson; John Wilson; Carl Spencer; Arthur Crier.
Also see LEACH, Lillian
Also see PRE-HISTORICS

MELO GENTS
Singles: 7-inch
W.B. (5056 "Baby Be Mine")......30-40 59

MELOAIRES
Singles: 7-inch
NASCO (6019 "You Know Baby")..20-30 58

MELODEARS
Singles: 7-inch
GONE (5033 "Summer Romance")......15-20 58
GONE (5040 "It's Love Because") 15-20 59

MELODEERS *P&R '60*
(Mellodeers)
Singles: 7-inch
SHELLEY (127 "The Letter")......10-20 61
SHELLEY (161 "Born to Be Mine") 15-25 62
STUDIO (9908 "Rudolph the Red Nosed Reindeer")......10-20 60
Picture Sleeves
STUDIO (9908 "Rudolph the Red Nosed Reindeer")......20-40 60
(Sleeve credits "Mellodeers.")
STUDIO (9909 "Happy Teenage Times")......15-25 60

MELODIANS
Singles: 12-inch
REAL AUTHENTIC SOUND......4-6 84
LPs: 10/12-inch
REAL AUTHENTIC SOUND......5-8 84

MEL-O-DOTS
Singles: 78 rpm
APOLLO......300-400 52
Singles: 7-inch
APOLLO (1192 "One More Time")......750-1000 52

MELO-DS
(Melo-D's with Chuck Hamilton)
Singles: 7-inch
MEL-O-D (201 "A Thousand Stars")......50-75

MELODY CHASERS
Singles: 7-inch
HICKMAN......5-10

MELODY MAKERS
(With Larry Clinton & Orchestra)
Singles: 78 rpm
HOLLIS (1001 "Carolina Moon")..50-100 57
Singles: 7-inch
HOLLIS (1001 "Carolina Moon")..75-125 57

MELODY MAIDS
Singles: 7-inch
LANIER (001 "Harry, Will You Marry Me")......10-20 58

MELODY MAKERS *P&R/LP '88*
(Ziggy Marley & Melody Makers)
Singles: 12-inch
EMI AMERICA......4-6 84-85
Singles: 7-inch
EMI AMERICA......3-4 84-85
VIRGIN......3-4 88
Picture Sleeves
VIRGIN......3-4 88
LPs: 10/12-inch
EMI AMERICA......5-8 84-85
VIRGIN......5-8 88-91
Members: David "Ziggy" Marley; Steve Marley; Cedella Marley; Sharon Marley. All are the children of Bob Marley.
Also see MARLEY, Bob

MELODY MASTERS
Singles: 78 rpm
APOLLO......15-25 46

MELOTONES
Singles: 7-inch
LEE TONE (700 "Prayer of Love")......250-350 52

MEL-O-TONES
Singles: 7-inch
KEY (5804 "Little Bit More")......15-25 60s

MELSON, Joe
Singles: 7-inch
HICKORY (1121 "Oh Yeah")......20-30 61
HICKORY (1128 "Shook Up")......20-30 61
HICKORY (1143 "Hey Mr. Cupid") 15-25 61
HICKORY (1155 "Wake Up Little Susie")......15-25 61
HICKORY (1175 "Love Is a Dangerous Thing")......25-50 63

MELSON, Lee "Red," & Missouri Nighthawks
EPs: 7-inch
RIDGECREST (1007 "Carmen Sue Rock"/"I'm Being Haunted"/"Rockin' Through the Tunnel of Love")......50-100 59

MELTING POT
Singles: 7-inch
AMPEX......3-5 71
LPs: 10/12-inch
AMPEX......8-12 71

MELTON, Barry
LPs: 10/12-inch
MUSIC IS MEDICINE (9007 "We Are Like the Ocean")......8-12 77
MUSIC IS MEDICINE (9014 "Level with Me")......8-12 78
VANGUARD (6551 "Bright Sun Is Shinning")......10-20 70
Also see COUNTRY JOE & FISH

MELTON, Levy, & Dey Brothers
Singles: 7-inch
COLUMBIA......3-5 75
MERCURY......4-8 68-69

MELTON, Ray
Singles: 7-inch
HOPE (1001 "Only Once")......15-25 60
IMAGE (1005 "Boppin' Guitar")...100-150 60

MEL-TONES
Singles: 7-inch
NEW (7780 "I'll Go")......8-10 60

MELTZER, David & Tina
LPs: 10/12-inch
VANGUARD (6519 "Poet Song")...20-30 69
Also see SERPENT POWER

MELVETTES
(With Curtis Freeman & Orchestra)
Singles: 7-inch
TELA-STAR (110 "Take One Step")......150-200 50s

MELVIN, George, & Poets
Singles: 7-inch
POETS......3-5 77

MELVIN, Harold *R&B '65*
(With the Bluenotes)
Singles: 12-inch
PHILADELPHIA INT'L......4-8 80
SOURCE......4-8 79-80
Singles: 7-inch
ABC......3-5 76-78
ARCTIC......5-10 67
LANDA (703 "You May Not Love Me")......25-35 64
MCA......3-5 81
PHILADELPHIA INT'L......3-5 72-79
PHIL-L.A. of SOUL......3-5 71
PHILLY WORLD......3-4 84-85
SOURCE......3-5 79-80
Picture Sleeves
PHILADELPHIA INT'L......3-5 72-75
LPs: 10/12-inch
ABC......8-10 77
MCA......5-8 81
PHILADELPHIA INT'L......8-12 72-76
PHILLY WORLD......5-8 84-85
SOURCE......5-10 80
Also see BLUENOTES
Also see PAIGE, Sharon
Also see PENDERGRASS, Teddy

MELVIN, Kim
Singles: 7-inch
HI......4-6 69-72

MELVIN & LEE
Singles: 7-inch
PANCHO......4-8 63

MELVINS: see NIRVANA / The Melvins

MEMBERS
Singles: 7-inch
LABEL......5-10

MEMORIES
Singles: 7-inch
WAY=LIN (101 "Love Bells")......200-300 59

MEMORIES
Singles: 7-inch
OLD SOUND......5-10 62

MEMORIES
Singles: 7-inch
TIMES SQUARE (11 "Darling, You're My Angel")......20-30 64

MEMORIES
Singles: 7-inch
FLASHBACK (2001 "Dedication Time")......20-30 63

MEMORIES
Singles: 7-inch
K.O. (107852 "Mercy Mercy")......10-20 66
Members: Tom Noffke; Chuck Posniak; Bob Fusfeld; Dennis Becker; Charles Reitzner; George Baer; Kip Kruse; Frank Criclear.

MEMORY
Singles: 7-inch
AVENUE D (0005 "Street Corner Serenade")......20-30 81
(Red vinyl. Reportedly 50 made.)
AVENUE D (0006 "Under the Boardwalk")......25-35 81
(Red vinyl. Reportedly 50 made.)
Members: Jaime DeJesus; Louis Benito; Herb Olson; Otis Harper; Leslie Uhl; Bobby Hepburn.

MEMOS
Singles: 7-inch
MEMO (5001 "I'm Going Home")...25-35 59
MEMO (34891 "My Type of Girl")..15-25 59
Members: Henry Austin; James Brown; Eugene Williams; Vernon Britton.
Also see HURRICANES

MEMPHIANS
Singles: 7-inch
PAWN......10-15

MEMPHIS *C&W '84*
Singles: 7-inch
MPI......3-4 84
Member: Woody Wright.

MEMPHIS BELLES
Singles: 7-inch
PHILLIPS INT'L......5-10 59

MEMPHIS EDDIE: see PEE, Eddie

MEMPHIS HORNS *R&B '76*
Singles: 7-inch
COTILLION......4-6 69
RCA......3-5 76-78
LPs: 10/12-inch
RCA......5-10 77-78
Members: Wayne Jackson; Andrew Love; Jimmy Brown; Andy Love; Floyd Newman; Don Chandler; Charlie Freeman; Tommy McClure; Sammy Creason.
Also see CRAY, Robert, Band, with the Memphis Horns
Also see MAR-KEYS
Also see McDONALD, Michael
Also see MOORE, Jackie
Also see POINTER SISTERS

MEMPHIS JIMMY
(James Clarke)
Singles: 78 rpm
BLUEBIRD......10-20 46
RCA......10-20 46-47
Also see CLARKE, James "Beale Street"

MEMPHIS MEN
Singles: 7-inch
MIRAMAR......5-8 65

MEMPHIS MILL
Singles: 7-inch
W.B. SOUND......3-5 77

MEMPHIS MINNIE
(With Her Combo; Memphis with Little Joe & His Band; with Kansas Joe; Lizzie Douglas)
Singles: 78 rpm
CHECKER (771 "Broken Heart")..75-125 52
COLUMBIA......15-25 44-49
J.O.B. (1101 "Kissing in the Dark")......75-125 54
OKEH......15-25 44-45
REGAL (3259 "Why Did I Make You Cry")......15-25 50
Singles: 7-inch
CHECKER (771 "Broken Heart")......300-400 52
J.O.B. (1101 "Kissing in the Dark")......300-400 54
LPs: 10/12-inch
BLUES CLASSICS......8-10
Also see LOUIS, Joe Hill
Also see McTELL, Blind Willie, & Memphis Minnie

MEMPHIS NOMADS
Singles: 7-inch
STAX (243 "Don't Pass Your Judgment")......15-25 68
(March of Dimes charity record.)

MEMPHIS ROCKABILLY BAND
Singles: 7-inch
HEARTBREAK HITS......4-6
MRB......4-6
Picture Sleeves
HEARTBREAK HITS......4-6
LPs: 10/12-inch
BLIND PIG......5-8 86

MEMPHIS SLIM *R&B '48*
(With His House Rockers; Peter Chatman)

Singles: 78 rpm

BLUEBIRD....25-50 40-41
CHESS (1491 "Walking Alone")....25-50 52
FEDERAL (12007 "Life Is Like That")....20-40 49
FEDERAL (12015 "Pacemaker Boogie")....20-40 49
FEDERAL (12021 "Midnight Jump")....20-40 49
HY-TONE (10 "Mistake in Life")....20-40 46
HY-TONE (17 "Slim's Boogie")....20-40 46
HY-TONE (19 "Cheatin' Around")....20-40 46
MASTER (1010 "Believe I'll Settle Down")....20-40 48
MASTER (1020 "Restless Nights")....20-40 49
MASTER (1030 "Love at Sight")....20-40 49
KING (4284 "Cheatin' Around")....20-40 49
KING (4312 "A Letter Home")....20-40 49
KING (4324 "Little Mary")....20-40 49
KING (4327 "Grinder Man Blues")....20-40 49
MELODY LANE....20-40 46
MERCURY....10-20 51-52
MIRACLE (102 "Kilroy's Been Here")....20-40 47
MIRACLE (103 "Rockin' the House")....20-40 47
MIRACLE (110 "Pacemaker Boogie")....20-40 47
MIRACLE (111 "Harlem Bound")....20-40 47
MIRACLE (125 "Midnight Jump")....20-40 48
MIRACLE (132 "Frisco Baby")....20-40 49
MIRACLE (136 "Help Me Some")....20-40 49
MIRACLE (145 "Nobody Loves Me")....20-40 49
MIRACLE (153 "Throw This Dog a Bone")....20-40 49
MONEY....15-25 54
OLD SWINGMASTER (1010 "Believe I'll Settle Down")....20-40 48
PEACOCK (1517 "The Girl I Love")....20-40 49
PREMIUM (850 "Flock Rocker")....20-30 50
PREMIUM (860 "Slim's Blues")....20-30 50
PREMIUM (867 "Really Got the Blues")....20-30 50
PREMIUM (873 "Trouble Trouble") 20-30 51
PREMIUM (878 "My Baby Left Me")....20-30 51
PREMIUM (903 "I'm Crying")....20-30 52
UNITED....15-25 52-54

Singles: 7-inch

JOSIE....5-8 67
KING (6300 series)....3-5 70
MERCURY (8251 "Train Time")....20-40 51
MERCURY (8266 "No Mail Blues") 20-40 51
MERCURY (8281 "The Question") 20-40 51
MERCURY (70063 "The Train Is Comin' ")....20-40 51
MONEY (212 "My Country Gal")....20-40 54
PEACOCK (1602 "Sittin' & Thinkin' ")....20-40 52
STRAND (25041 "Lonesome")....15-25 61
UNITED (138 "Back Alley")....35-50 52
UNITED (156 "The Comeback")....35-50 53
(Black vinyl.)
UNITED (156 "The Comeback")....50-100 53
(Red vinyl.)
UNITED (166 "Call Before You Go Home")....35-50 53
(Black vinyl.)
UNITED (166 "Call Before You Go Home")....50-100 53
(Red vinyl.)
UNITED (176 "Sassy Mae")....35-50 54
(Black vinyl.)
UNITED (176 "Sassy Mae")....50-100 54
(Red vinyl.)
UNITED (182 "I Love My Baby")....35-50 54
UNITED (186 "Memphis Slim U.S.A.")....35-50 54
UNITED (189 "She's Alright")....35-50 55
UNITED (201 "Got to Find My Baby")....35-50 56
VEE JAY (271 "Stroll On Little Girl")....10-15 58
VEE JAY (294 "What's the Matter")....10-15 58
VEE JAY (330 "Steppin' Out")....10-15 59
VEE JAY (343 "The Comeback")....10-15 60

LPs: 10/12-inch

BATTLE (6118 "Alone with My Friends")....20-30 63
BARNABY (31291 "Bad Luck and Troubles")....8-12 72
BLACK LION....8-10 74
BUDDAH (7505 "Mother Earth")....10-20 69
CANDID (8024 "Memphis Slim U.S.A.")....35-45 62
(Monaural.)
CANDID (9024 "Memphis Slim U.S.A.")....40-50 62
(Stereo.)
CHESS (1455 "Memphis Slim")....50-75 61
CHESS (1510 "Real Folk Blues")....20-35 66
EVEREST....10-15 68-74
FANTASY....10-12 72
FOLKWAYS....8-10 74
GNP (10002 "The Blues Is Everywhere")....8-12 74
JAZZMAN....5-8 82
JEWEL....8-12 71
JUBILEE (8003 "Legend of the Blues")....15-20 67
KING (885 "Memphis Slim")....40-60 64
KING (1082 "Messin' Around with the Blues")....10-15 70
MUSE....6-12 81
PEARL (10 "Memphis Slim, U.S.A.")....5-10 78
PRESTIGE BLUESVILLE (1018 "Just Blues")....20-40 61
PRESTIGE BLUESVILLE (1031 "No Strain")....20-40 61
PRESTIGE BLUESVILLE (1053 "All Kinds of Blues")....20-40 63
PRESTIGE BLUESVILLE (1075 "Steady Rollin' Blues")....20-40 64
SCEPTER (535 "Self-Portrait")....15-25 66
SPIN-O-RAMA (149 "Lonesome Blues")....10-20 60s
STORYVILLE....5-8 84
STRAND (1046 "World's Foremost Blues Singer")....25-40 61
TRIP....8-10 70s
U.A. (3137 "Broken Soul Blues")....30-40 61
(Monaural.)
U.A. (6137 "Broken Soul Blues")....40-50 61
(Stereo.)
VEE JAY (1012 "Memphis Slim at the Gate of Horn")....60-80 59
W.B. (1899 "Blue Memphis")....10-15 71
W.B. (2646 "South Side Reunion")....10-15 72
Session: Alex Atkins; Ernest Cotton; Willie Dixon; Ernest Crawford; Tim Overton; Betty Overton; Leon Hooper; Vagabonds; Floyd Hunt;Neil Green; Henry Taylor; Otho Allen.
Also see DIXON, Willie, & Memphis Slim
Also see HOOKER, Earl
Also see HOOKER, John Lee
Also see HUNTER, Ivory Joe / Memphis Slim
Also see JONES, Curtis
Also see WILLIAMSON, Sonny Boy

MEMPHIS SLIM & LOWELL FULSOM

LPs: 10/12-inch

INNER CITY....5-8
Also see FULSON, Lowell

MEMPHIS SLIM & CURTIS JONES

LPs: 10/12-inch

CANDID (8023 "Tribute to Big Bill Broonzy")....35-45 61
(Monaural.)
CANDID (9023 "Tribute to Big Bill Broonzy")....40-50 62
(Stereo.)
Also see JONES, Curtis

MEMPHIS SLIM & MATT MURPHY

LPs: 10/12-inch

ANTONE'S....5-10 87

MEMPHIS SLIM & ROOSEVELT SYKES

LPs: 10/12-inch

OLYMPIC....8-12 75
Also see SYKES, Roosevelt

MEMPHIS SLIM & VAGABONDS / Reverend Bounce

Singles: 78 rpm

PREMIUM....15-25 50
Also see MEMPHIS SLIM

MEMPHIS SOUL BAND

LPs: 10/12-inch

MINIT....10-15 70

MEMPHIS WILLIE B: see BORUM, Memphis Willie

MEN AT WORK *P&R/LP '82*

Singles: 12-inch

COLUMBIA....4-6 82-83

Singles: 7-inch

COLUMBIA....3-4 82-85

Picture Sleeves

COLUMBIA (Except 1633)....3-4 83-85
COLUMBIA (1633 "Overkill")....5-10 83
(Promotional issue only.)

LPs: 10/12-inch

COLUMBIA (1650 "Cargo World Premier Weekend")....10-15 83
(Promotional issue only.)
COLUMBIA (37978 "Business As Usual")....5-10 82
(With "ARC" or "FC" prefix.)
COLUMBIA (PAL-37978 "Business As Usual")....35-45 83
(Picture disc. Promotional issue only.)
COLUMBIA (38167 "Business As Usual")....5-8 82
COLUMBIA (38660 "Cargo")....5-8 83
COLUMBIA (40078 "Two Hearts")....5-8 85
COLUMBIA (47978 "Business As Usual")....10-15 85
(Half-speed mastered.)
COLUMBIA (48660 "Cargo")....10-15 85
Members: Colin Hay; Ron Strykert; Jerry Speiser; John Rees; Greg Ham.
Also see HAY, Colin James

MEN IN SPACE

Singles: 7-inch

ERA (3203 "Apollo 8")....10-15 69

MEN OF CHANCE

Singles: 7-inch

GATEWAY CUSTOM (105 "Count Down")....10-20 64

MEN WITHOUT HATS *P&R/D&D/LP '83*

Singles: 12-inch

BACKSTREET....4-6 83
MCA....4-6 83-84

Singles: 7-inch

BACKSTREET....3-4 83
MCA....3-4 83-84
MERCURY....3-4 87

Picture Sleeves

BACKSTREET....3-4 83
MCA....3-4 83
MERCURY....3-4 87

LPs: 10/12-inch

BACKSTREET....5-8 83
MCA....5-8 84
MERCURY....5-8 87

MENAGE *D&D '83*

Singles: 12-inch

PROFILE....4-6 83-85

Singles: 7-inch

PROFILE....3-4 83-85

LPs: 10/12-inch

PROFILE....5-8 83

MENAGERIE

Singles: 7-inch

VISION....4-8

MENDELBAUM

Singles: 7-inch

SMACK (6963 "Try So Hard")....10-20 69

MENDELL, Johnny

Singles: 7-inch

JAMIE....4-8 61-62

MENDELSOHN, Danny

Singles: 7-inch

X (0050 "Good Boogie Woogie")....10-20 60s

MENDES, Sergio *P&R/LP '66*
(With Brasil '66; Brasil '77; Trio)

Singles: 12-inch

A&M....4-6 82

Singles: 7-inch

A&M (807 thru 1257)....3-6 66-71
A&M (1279 thru 2700 series)....3-5 71-85
ATLANTIC....4-6 67-68
BELL....3-5 73
ELEKTRA....3-5 75-80

Picture Sleeves

A&M....3-6 68-69

LPs: 10/12-inch

A&M (Except 4100 series)....5-12 69-84
A&M (4100 series)....10-15 66-69
ATLANTIC....15-25 65-68
BELL....8-10 73-74
CAPITOL (T-2294 "In a Brazilian Bag")....40-50 65
(Monaural.)
CAPITOL (ST-2294 "In a Brazilian Bag")....50-60 65
(Stereo.)
ELEKTRA....8-10 75-79
EVEREST....8-10 74
MFSL....15-25 84
PHILIPS....10-12 68
TOWER (T-5052 "In a Brazilian Bag")....30-40 65
(Monaural.)
TOWER (ST-5052 "In a Brazilian Bag")....40-50 65
(Stereo.)
Also see ADDERLEY, Julian "Cannonball," & Sergio Mendes
Also see HALL, Lani

MENDOLA, Dom, & Lovers
(With the Mickey Moroni Orchestra)

Singles: 7-inch

MC (003 "You Are Welcome to My Heart")....25-50

MENERALS

Singles: 7-inch

HEAT WAVE (001 "Hot Night Down in Texas")....15-25 60s

MENG, Jimmy

Singles: 7-inch

JAY EM (1000 "True & Faithful")....15-25 61
LIBERTY (55346 "True & Faithful") 8-12 61

MENN

Singles: 7-inch

TWO & TWO (1 "One-Way Deal")....15-25 60s

MENSY, Tim *C&W '89*

Singles: 7-inch

COLUMBIA....3-4 89-90

MENTAL AS ANYTHING

Singles: 7-inch

A&M....3-4 82

LPs: 10/12-inch

A&M....5-8 82

MENTON, Dale
(With Batch; Dale Menten)

Singles: 7-inch

GROOVE SHOP....4-8 60s
MCA....3-5 70s
MISCIDE (7216 "Too Much A Lady")....25-35 60s

LPs: 10/12-inch

MCA/TALLY....8-10 75
Also see BEST THINGS
Also see GESTURES
Also see MADHATTERS

MENUDO *R&B/LP '84*

Singles: 7-inch

RCA....3-4 84-85

LPs: 10/12-inch

RCA....5-8 84-85
Also see KING DREAM CHORUS & Holiday Crew

MERC & MONK *R&B '85*

Singles: 7-inch

MANHATTAN....3-5 85
Members: Eric Mercury; Thelonious Monk.
Also see MERCURY, Eric
Also see MONK, Thelonious

MERCED BLUE NOTES

Singles: 7-inch

ACCENT (1069 "Rufus")....15-25 61
GALAXY (738 "Rufus Jr.")....10-20 65
GALAXY (744 "Mama Rufus")....10-20 65
MAMMOTH (5331 "Rufus Jr.")....15-25 60s
SOUL (35007 "Do the Pig")....200-300 64
TRI-PHI (1011 "Midnight Session") 15-25 62
TRI-PHI (1023 "Whole Lotta Nothing")....15-25 64

MERCEEDEES

Singles: 7-inch

GOLD SEAL....8-10
Member: Marietta Roberson.
Also see INDIVIDUALS

MERCER, Barbara

Singles: 7-inch

GOLDEN WORLD....10-20 65

MERCER, Big Jay

Singles: 7-inch

OAK (1522 "Bermudas")....10-20

MERCER, Jerry
(Jerry Mercer Orchestra)

Singles: 78 rpm

MERCURY....5-10 56

Singles: 7-inch

MERCURY....10-20 56

MERCER, Johnny *P&R '38*

Singles: 78 rpm

CAPITOL....4-8 42-52
DECCA....4-8 38

Singles: 7-inch

CAPITOL....5-10 50-52

EPs: 7-inch

CAPITOL (210 "Music of Kern")....10-20 50

LPs: 10/12-inch

CAPITOL (210 "Music of Kern")....40-50 50
(10-inch LP.)
CAPITOL (214 "Mercer Sings")....40-50 50
(10-inch LP.)
CAPITOL (907 "Ac-Cent-Tchu-Ate the Positive")....25-40 57
JUPITER (1001 "Just for Fun")....25-45 56
Also see CROSBY, Bing, & Johnny Mercer
Also see DARIN, Bobby, & Johnny Mercer

MERCER, Johnny, Jo Stafford & Pied Pipers

Singles: 78 rpm

CAPITOL....4-8 45
Also see PIED PIPERS
Also see STAFFORD, Jo

MERCER, Mabel

Singles: 7-inch

ATLAS (1207 "Sweet Little Angel")....10-20 60
(For records that actually play Mabel Mercer.)
ATLAS (1207 "Sweet Little Angel")....200-300 60
(For records that play a different song, by an unidentified R&B group.)

EPs: 7-inch

ATLANTIC (501 "Mabel Mercer Sings, Vol. 1")....10-20 55
ATLANTIC (522 "Mabel Mercer Sings, Vol. 2")....10-20 55
ATLANTIC (541/542/543 "Mabel Mercer Sings Cole Porter")....10-20 55
(Price is for any of three volumes.)

LPs: 10/12-inch

ATLANTIC (402 "Songs by Mabel Mercer, Vol. 1")....30-40 52
ATLANTIC (403 "Songs by Mabel Mercer, Vol. 2")....30-40 53
ATLANTIC (602 "The Art of Mabel Mercer")....30-40 57
ATLANTIC (1213 "Mabel Mercer Sings Cole Porter")....20-35 54
ATLANTIC (1244 "Midnight")....20-35 56
ATLANTIC (1300 series)....15-30 59-60

MERCER, Tommy

Singles: 7-inch

VOLCANO (1 "Volcano Rock")....200-300 59

MERCER, Wally

Singles: 78 rpm

DOT....15-25 52
MERTON....15-25 47
TRUMPET....15-25 54

Singles: 7-inch

DOT (1099 "Rock Around the Clock")....25-50 52
DOT (1120 "Looped")....25-50 52
RING (1502 "Hey, Miss Lula")....25-50 57
TRUMPET (227 "Too Old to Get Married")....25-50 54

MERCER, Will

Singles: 7-inch

SUN....5-10 59

MERCHANTS OF DREAM

Singles: 7-inch

A&M....5-10 68

LPs: 10/12-inch

A&M (4199 "Strange Night Voyage")....15-25 68
CAPITOL (102 "Soul Knight")....15-25 68
Also see DREAM MERCHANTS

MERCURY, Eric

LPs: 10/12-inch

AVCO EMBASSY....10-15 69
CAPITOL....5-10 81
ENTERPRISE....8-12 72-73
SACK (1 "Lonely Girl")....300-500
Also see FLACK, Roberta, & Eric Mercury
Also see MERC & MONK

MERCURY, Freddie *P&R/D&D '84*

Singles: 12-inch

COLUMBIA....4-6 84

Singles: 7-inch

COLUMBIA....3-5 84-85
EMI (6151 "Great Pretender")....30-40 87
(Antique radio-shaped picture disc.)

Picture Sleeves

COLUMBIA....4-8 84-85

LPs: 10/12-inch

COLUMBIA....5-8 85
Also see LUREX, Larry
Also see QUEEN

MERCURY, Freddie / Giorgio Moroder

Singles: 12-inch

COLUMBIA....4-6 84
Also see MERCURY, Freddie
Also see MORODER, Giorgio

MERCURY ALL-STARS

Singles: 78 rpm

MERCURY....4-8 54

Singles: 7-inch

MERCURY (70385 "I Got Rhythm")....8-12 54
Members: Chubby Jackson; Mike Simpson; Dick Marks; Red Saunders.
Also see JACKSON, Chubby
Also see SAUNDERS, Red

MERCURYS

Singles: 7-inch

MADISON (119 "Someone Touched Me")....50-75 59

MERCY *P&R/LP '69*

Singles: 7-inch

SUNDI....4-8 69
W.B....4-8 69

LPs: 10/12-inch

SUNDI....15-20 68
W.B....10-15 69
Members: James Marvell; Ronnie Coudill; Roger Fuentes; Buddy Good; Debbie Lewis; Brenda McNish.
Also see COUNTRY CAVALEERS
Also see MARVELL, James

MERCY BABY
(J. Mercy Baby)

Singles: 78 rpm

ACE....10-20 57
RIC....10-20 57

Singles: 7-inch

ACE....10-20 57
MERCY BABY....10-20 58
RIC....10-20 57

MERCY BOYS

Singles: 7-inch

MERRILIN (5300 "Spoonful")....15-25 65
PANORAMA....8-12 66

MERCY DEE *R&B '49*
(Mercy Dee Walton)

Singles: 78 rpm

BAYOU (003 "Please Understand")....25-50 50
BAYOU (013 "Danger Zone")....25-50 50
COLONY (102 "Happy Bachelor")....20-40 50
COLONY (107 "Old Fashioned Ways")....20-40 50
COLONY (111 "Honey Baby")....20-40 50
FLAIR....15-25 55
IMPERIAL (5104 "Honey Baby")....20-40 50
IMPERIAL (5110 "Big Foot Country")....20-40 50
IMPERIAL (5118 "Bought Love")....20-40 50
IMPERIAL (5127 "Danger Zone")....20-40 50
RHYTHM....50-75 54
SPECIALTY....15-25 53
SPIRE (001 "Lonesome Cabin Blues")....25-50 49
SPIRE (002 "Evil & Hanky")....25-50 49

Singles: 7-inch

BAYOU (013 "Danger Zone")....75-125 50
FLAIR (1073 "Romp & Stomp Blues")....40-60 55
FLAIR (1077 "True Love")....40-60 55
FLAIR (1078 "Have You Ever")....40-60 55
RHYTHM (1774 "Trailing My Baby")....150-200 54
SPECIALTY (Except 466)....20-40 53-54
SPECIALTY (458 "One Room Country Shack")....25-50 53
SPECIALTY (466 "Rent Man Blues")....25-50 53
(Black vinyl.)
SPECIALTY (466 "Rent Man Blues")....100-200 53
(Red vinyl.)
SPECIALTY (481 "Get to Gettin' ") 25-50 53

LPs: 10/12-inch

ARHOOLIE (1007 "Mercy Dee")....40-60 61
PRESTIGE BLUESVILLE (1039 "Pity and a Shame")....50-75 62
Also see THOMAS, Marcellus, & His Rhythm Rockets

MERCYFUL FATE

Singles: 12-inch

MEGAFORCE (369 "Melissa")....15-20 87
(Picture disc.)

Singles: 7-inch

WESSELS ("Black Masses")....5-10 80s
(Picture disc. No selection number used.)

MER-DA

LPs: 10/12-inch

JANUS....8-10 72

MEREDITH, Buddy *C&W '62*

Singles: 7-inch

NASHVILLE....4-8 62

LPs: 10/12-inch

DAVIS UNLIMITED....6-12
STARDAY....15-25 63

MEREDITH, Marv
Singles: 7-inch
STRAND 5-10 60

MERGE R&B '82
Singles: 7-inch
RCA 3-4 87

MERIAN, Leon
Singles: 7-inch
20TH FOX 5-10 59

'MERICAN XPRESS
Singles: 7-inch
VAULT 4-8 69

MERIDIANS
(With R. Lopez & Orchestra)
Singles: 7-inch
PARNASO (107 "Have You Forgotten") 1000-2000 60s
PARNASO (120 "Blame My Heart") 100-200 60s

MERITS
Singles: 7-inch
BANDSTAND USA (1002 "Arabian Jerk") 5-10
PARKWOOD (1005 "Dark Cloud") 4-8

MERKIN
LPs: 10/12-inch
WINDI (1005 "Music from Merkin") 250-350 72
Members: Ralph Hemingway; Robert Bouney; Rocky Baum; Kent Balog; Gary Balog; Richard Leavitt.

MERLIN, Jack
(With the Valiants)
Singles: 7-inch
CAMEO 8-12 64
DOT (16332 "Girl of My Dreams") 15-25 62
HICKORY 4-8 65-66
NEW PHOENIX 8-12 60s

MER-LYN
Singles: 7-inch
ABC-PAR 4-8 65

MERMAIDS: see MURMAIDS

MERMAN, Ethel P&R '32
Singles: 78 rpm
BRUNSWICK 4-8 33-35
DECCA 4-6 46-54
VICTOR 4-10 32-43
EPs: 7-inch
DECCA (2277 "Memories") 15-25 55
LPs: 10/12-inch
DECCA (153 "Autobiography") 25-35 58
DECCA (5053 "Songs She Made Famous") 40-60 49
(10-inch LP.)
DECCA (9028 "Memories") 30-45 55
VIK (1004 "On Stage") 25-35 55
For a complete listing of soundtracks by this artist, consult *The Official Price Guide to Movie/TV Soundtracks and Original Cast Albums.*

MERMAN, Ethel, & Dick Haymes P&R '51
Singles: 78 rpm
DECCA 3-5 51
Singles: 7-inch
DECCA 5-10 51
Also see HAYMES, Dick
Also see MERMAN, Ethel

MERRELL & EXILES
(Merrell & Xiles)
Singles: 7-inch
GLENN (426 "Tomorrow's Girl") 30-40 67
GOLDEN CROWN (102 "That's All I Want from You") 20-30 65
INTERLUDE (317 "Sorry for Yourself") 15-25 65
LPs: 10/12-inch
AMERICAN SOUND (1000 "The Early Years: 1964-1967") 20-40 94
Members: Merrell Fankhauser; Dan Parrish; Bill Dodd; Dick Lee.
Also see FANKHAUSER, Merrell

MERRIL, Lee
Singles: 7-inch
BOOM 4-8 66
Picture Sleeves
BOOM 10-15 66

MERRILL, Bobby "Mr. Blues"
Singles: 7-inch
BARGAIN (5002 "I Ain't Mad at You") 30-40 61

MERRILL, Buddy
Singles: 78 rpm
CORAL 4-6 56
Singles: 7-inch
ACCENT 4-8 64-68
CORAL 5-10 56
DOT 4-8 62
LPs: 10/12-inch
ACCENT 10-15 70-71

MERRILL, Helen
Singles: 78 rpm
MERCURY 5-10 57
Singles: 7-inch
MERCURY 5-10 57

MERRILL & JESSICA C&W '87
Singles: 7-inch
EMI AMERICA 3-4 87
Members: Merrill Osmond; Jessica Boucher.
Also see OSMONDS

MERRILL BROTHERS
Singles: 7-inch
GM (102 "Mercy Blues") 20-40

MERRI-MEN
Singles: 7-inch
APT (25051 "Big Daddy") 10-20 60
Also see HALEY, Bill

MERRIT, Lane
Singles: 7-inch
ECLIPSE 4-8 62-63
ORBIT 4-8 62
LPs: 10/12-inch
ECLIPSE 15-20 63

MERRITT, Daddy, Quintet
(Melvin Merritt)
Singles: 78 rpm
MONOGRAM 10-20 50

MERRITT, Jerry
(With the Crowns; with Royal Crowns; with John Ballard)
Singles: 7-inch
AMERICAN 4-8 65
LAVENDER 5-10 61-62
SCORPIO 4-6 68
SMART 4-8 67
TELL INT'L (300 series) 5-10 67-68
TELL INT'L (400 series) 3-4 85
Picture Sleeves
LAVENDER 10-15 62
Also see CARTER, Dean
Also see VINCENT, Gene

MERRITT, Little Jimmie
(With Cuba Sanchez Orchestra)
Singles: 7-inch
KRC (5004 "Fancy Free") 30-50 59

MERRY DRAGONS
Singles: 7-inch
ABC 4-8 66

MERRY ELVES
Singles: 7-inch
ARGUS 5-10 64
Members (Elves): Milton; Sleepy; Ringo.

MERRY MACS
LPs: 10/12-inch
ERA 10-20 56
HALO 10-15

MERRY MERMAIDS
Singles: 7-inch
RIVOLI 4-8 63

MERRY-GO-ROUND P&R/LP '67
Singles: 7-inch
A&M 5-10 67-69
LPs: 10/12-inch
A&M (4132 "Merry-Go-Round") 20-30 67
RHINO 5-8 85
Members: Emitt Rhodes; Joel Larson; Gary Kato; Bill Reinhart.
Also see GRASS ROOTS
Also see LEAVES
Also see RHODES, Emitt

MERRY-GO-ROUND
Singles: 7-inch
PICADILLY 5-10 60s

MERRYLANDERS
Singles: 7-inch
MERGER (100 "Rattlesnake") 10-20 60

MERRYWEATHER: see MERRYWEATHER, Neil

MERRYWEATHER, Neil LP '69
(With Friends; Merryweather)
Singles: 7-inch
CAPITOL 3-6 69
LPs: 10/12-inch
CAPITOL 10-20 69
MERCURY 10-15 74-75
Also see GOLDBERG, Barry / Harvey Mandell / Charlie Musselwhite / Neil Merryweather
Also see HEAVY CRUISER
Also see MASON, Dave
Also see MILLER, Steve

MERRYWEATHER, Neil, & John Richardson
LPs: 10/12-inch
KENT 10-15 72

MERRYWEATHER & CAREY
LPs: 10/12-inch
RCA 8-12 71
Members: Neil Merryweather; Lynn Carey.
Also see MERRYWEATHER, Neil

MERSEY, Robert
(Spencer Ross)
Singles: 7-inch
CAPITOL 4-8 63
CYCLONE 4-8 60s
Also see ROSS, Spencer

MERSEY BEATS OF LIVERPOOL
(Merseybeats)
LPs: 10/12-inch
ARC INT'L (834 "England's Best Sellers") 25-35 64
Also see MERSEYBEATS

MERSEY LADS
Singles: 7-inch
MGM 8-12 66

MERSEY MEN
Singles: 7-inch
WILD WOODS (2001 "I Can Tell") 20-30 60s

MERSEY SOUNDS
Singles: 7-inch
MONTEL 5-8 66

MERSEYBEATS
Singles: 7-inch
FONTANA 5-10 64-65
LPs: 10/12-inch
ARC INT'L (834 "England's Best Sellers") 25-35 64
Members: Bill Kinsley; John Banks; Tony Crane; Aaron Williams; Peter Clarke; John Gustafson.
Also see LIVERPOOL EXPRESS
Also see MERSEY BEATS of LIVERPOOL
Also see ROCKIN' HORSE

MERSEYBOYS
LPs: 10/12-inch
VEE JAY (1101 "15 Greatest Songs of the Beatles") 35-45 64
(Monaural.)
VEE JAY (1101 "15 Greatest Songs of the Beatles") 40-60 64
(Stereo.)
VEE JAY (1101 "15 Greatest Songs of the Beatles") 50-75 64
(White label. Promotional issue only.)

MERSEYBOYS
Singles: 7-inch
PANORAMA 5-10 60s

MERSEYS
Singles: 7-inch
MERCURY 5-10 66

MERSINARY
Singles
IRON WORKS ("Dead Is Dead") 8-12 89
(Feet-shaped and rectangular picture discs. 500 made of each shape. No selection number used.)
LPs: 10/12-inch
AZRA (27 "Choose Death") 10-15 88
(Picture disc. 500 made.)

MESA P&R '77
Singles: 7-inch
ARIOLA AMERICA 3-5 77

MES'AY R&B '87
Singles: 7-inch
SUPERSTAR I. 3-4 87

MESHEL, Billy
Singles: 7-inch
OLD TOWN 4-8 65

MESMERIZING EYE
LPs: 10/12-inch
SMASH 15-25 67

MESSENGERS
Singles: 7-inch
BEAM 5-10 64
ERA 4-8 65
MGM 4-8 64-65

MESSENGERS P&R '71
Singles: 7-inch
HOME MADE (01 "Right On") 15-25 69
RARE EARTH 3-6 71
SOUL 4-8 67
LPs: 10/12-inch
RARE EARTH (509 "Messengers") 8-12 69
(With standard cover.)
RARE EARTH (509 "Messengers") 20-25 69
(With rounded-top cover. Promotional issue.)
Members: Greg Jennings [Jeresek]; Jesse Roe; Peter Barans; Jeff Taylor; Augie Jurishica; Rob Leslie; Michael Morgan; Mike Demling; John Hoier; Bob Cavallo.
Also see MICHAEL & MESSENGERS
Also see MOVIES

MESSENGERS
Singles: 7-inch
SOMA (1427 "My Baby") 30-50 65
Members: Greg Jeresek; Greg Bambenek; Roy Burger; Chip Andrus; Mike Murphy.

MESSER, Richard, & Question Marks
Singles: 7-inch
CINCY (104 "Sad Sack") 15-20

MESSINA, Jim LP '79
(With the Jesters; Jimmy Messina)
Singles: 7-inch
AUDIO FIDELITY 15-25 64
COLUMBIA 3-5 79-80
VIV 10-15
W.B. 3-5 81-83
LPs: 10/12-inch
AUDIO FIDELITY (7037 "The Dragsters") 45-55 64
COLUMBIA 5-8 79
THIMBLE 10-12 73
W.B. 5-8 81-83
Also see BUFFALO SPRINGFIELD
Also see JESTERS
Also see LOGGINS & MESSINA
Also see POCO
Also see ULTIMATES
Also see YOUNG, Neil, & Jim Messina

MESSINA, Jim, & Pauline Wilson
Singles: 7-inch
W.B. 3-5 81
Also see MESSINA, Jim

MESSNER, Bud, & His Sky Line Boys C&W '50
Singles: 78 rpm
ABBEY 10-20 50

METAL CHURCH LP '86
LPs: 10/12-inch
ELEKTRA 5-8 86-89

METALLICA LP '84
Singles: 7-inch
ELEKTRA (Except 69357) 3-4 88-89
ELEKTRA (69357 "Eye of the Beholder") 5-10 88
Picture Sleeves
ELEKTRA (Except 69357) 3-5 88-89
ELEKTRA (69357 "Eye of the Beholder") 10-15 88
LPs: 10/12-inch
ELEKTRA (Except 60757) 5-10 84-89
ELEKTRA (60757 "Garage Days Revisited") 25-50 87
MEGAFORCE 12-25 84-86
Members: James Hetfield; Kirk Hammett; Lars Ulrich; Cliff Burton; Jason Newsted.

METALLICS
Singles: 7-inch
BARONET (2 "Need Your Love") 25-50 62
(No ribbon shown on label.)
BARONET (2 "Need Your Love") 10-20 62
(Ribbon shown on label.)
BARONET (14 "Drop By") 25-50 62
(No ribbon shown on label.)
BARONET (14 "Drop By") 10-20 62
(Ribbon shown on label.)
BARONET (16 "Let Me Love You") 25-50 62
BARONET (18 "It Hurts Me") 25-50 62

METAMORPHOSIS
LPs: 10/12-inch
LONDON 8-12 71

METAPHORS
Singles: 7-inch
RAD 4-8 60s

METELICA
Singles: 7-inch
CORN (3 "Train") 3-5 73

METEORS
Singles: 7-inch
AXE (1302 "El Paso Guitar") 15-25 58
AXE (1313 "The Death of Geronimo") 15-25 58

METEORS
Singles: 7-inch
BELTONE (2041 "Let's Start Anew") 100-200 63

METEORS
LPs: 10/12-inch
PVC 5-10 79

METERS P&R/R&B/LP '69
Singles: 7-inch
JOSIE 3-6 69-71
REPRISE 3-5 74-76
SANSU 4-6
W.B. 3-5 77
LPs: 10/12-inch
ISLAND 8-10 75
JOSIE 10-12 69-70
REPRISE 8-10 72-75
VIRGO 8-10 75
W.B. 8-10 77
Also see NEVILLE BROTHERS

METHENY, Pat LP '78
(With Lyle Mays)
Singles: 7-inch
ECM 3-4 79-84
LPs: 10/12-inch
ECM 5-10 76-84
EMI AMERICA 5-8 85
GEFFEN 5-8 87-90
W.B. 5-8 83
Also see BOWIE, David, & Pat Metheny Group

METHUSELAH
LPs: 10/12-inch
ELEKTRA 10-15 69

METIS, Frank
Singles: 7-inch
MAYFLOWER 5-10 60

METOYER, Herb
LPs: 10/12-inch
VERVE/FOLKWAYS 12-15 65

METRICS
Singles: 7-inch
CHADWICK (101 "I Found You") 50-100 64

METRO
LPs: 10/12-inch
SIRE 5-10 77

METRO-CHORDS
Singles: 7-inch
ADMIRAL (300 "It's a Shame") 150-250 61

METRO-LINERS
Singles: 7-inch
CATAMOUNT 3-5 76

METRONOMES
Singles: 78 rpm
SPECIALTY 200-300 53
Singles: 7-inch
SPECIALTY (472 "She's Gone") 1000-2000 53

METRONOMES
(With the Dave McRae Orchestra.)
Singles: 78 rpm
CADENCE (1310 "I Love My Girl") 50-75 57
CADENCE (1339 "How Much I Love You") 75-125 57
Singles: 7-inch
CADENCE (1310 "I Love My Girl") 50-75 57
CADENCE (1339 "How Much I Love You") 75-125 57
Member: Harold Wright.
Also see DIAMONDS
Also see REGALS

METRONOMES
EPs: 7-inch
WYNNE (101 "The Metronomes") 20-40 60
LPs: 10/12-inch
WYNNE (106 "And Now...the Metronomes") 50-100 60

METRONOMES
Singles: 7-inch
CHALLENGE (9157 "Tears Tears Tears") 10-15 62
MAUREEN (1000 "My Dearest Darling") 30-50 62
RIVERSIDE (4523 "Back Door Blues") 5-10 62
Also see ELLIS, Shirley

METRONOMES & LEON
Singles: 7-inch
CARNIVAL 5-8 66

METROPOLITAN BLUES ALLSTARS
LPs: 10/12-inch
JUNE APPAL 5-10

METROPOLITANS
Singles: 7-inch
JUNIOR (395 "So Much in Love") 20-30 58

METROS
Singles: 7-inch
JUST (1502 "All of My Life") 350-450 59

METROS P&R/R&B '67
Singles: 7-inch
1-2-3 4-6 69
RCA (8994 "Sweetest One") 4-8 66
RCA (9159 "Since I Found My Baby") 15-25 67
RCA (9333 "Let's Groove") 10-15 67
LPs: 10/12-inch
RCA (3776 "Sweetest One") 15-25 67

METROTONES
Singles: 78 rpm
COLUMBIA 5-10 55
Singles: 7-inch
COLUMBIA 10-15 55
EPs: 7-inch
COLUMBIA (2026/2027 "Tops in Rock & Roll") 15-25 55
(Price is for either of two volumes.)
LPs: 10/12-inch
COLUMBIA (6341 "Tops in Rock & Roll") 30-40 55
(10-inch LP.)

METROTONES
(With the Little Walkin' Willie Quartet)
Singles: 7-inch
RESERVE (116 "Please Come Back") 150-250 57
Members: Sonny Turner; Melvin Smith; James Frierson; Leonard Veal; Leuvenia Eaton.
Also see HESITATIONS
Also see PLATTERS

MEYERS, Augie C&W '88
(Augie)
Singles: 7-inch
ATLANTIC AMERICA 3-4 88
AXBAR 3-4 83
PARAMOUNT 3-4 73
TEXAS RE-CORD CO 3-5 75-79
SUPER BEET (Except 102) 3-4 87
SUPER BEET (102 "Velma from Selma") 5-10 87
SUPER BEET (102 "Mathilda") 3-4 87
(Both of above are numbered 102.)
Selma.)
VOL 4-8 68
LPs: 10/12-inch
ATLANTIC AMERICA 5-8 88
PARAMOUNT 15-20 73
POLYDOR 10-20 71
SUPER BEET 5-8 87
TEXAS RE-CORD CO 10-15 75-77
Also see AMIGOS DE MUSICA
Also see COPELAND, Johnny
Also see EZBA, Danny
Also see KEVIN & AUGIE
Also see KEVIN & BLACKTEARS
Also see LEWIS, Jerry Lee
Also see LONG, Joey
Also see LORD AUGUST & VISIONS
Also see MEYERS, Bernie
Also see MORGAN, Claude
Also see NELSON, Willie
Also see RAT RACE KID
Also see VINCENT, Gene

MEYERS, Bernie
(Augie Meyers)
Singles: 7-inch
JET STREAM (1 "As the World Turns Around") 10-20 62
Also see MEYERS, Augie

MEYERS, Brad, & Citations
Singles: 7-inch
SARA (101 "Just for You") 15-25 64
Also see CITATIONS

MEYERS, Dave, & Disciples
Singles: 7-inch
HARMONY PARK 8-12

MEYERS, Jimmy
Singles: 7-inch
FORTUNE....20-40 52-57

MEYERS, Johnny
Singles: 7-inch
INSTANT....5-10 62
PEACOCK....4-8 67

MEYERS, Louie, & Aces
Singles: 78 rpm
ABCO (104 "Just Wailin' ")....20-40 56
Singles: 7-inch
ABCO (104 "Just Wailin' ")....50-75 56

MEYERS, Michael C&W '82
Singles: 7-inch
MBP....3-4 82

MIAMI R&B '74
Singles: 7-inch
DRIVE....3-5 74-76
LPs: 10/12-inch
DRIVE....5-10 76
Member: Robert Moore.

MIAMI DISCO BAND R&B '79
Singles: 7-inch
SALSOUL....3-5 79
Member: Beverly Barkley.

MIAMI SOUND MACHINE P&R/R&B/D&D/LP '85
(Gloria Estefan & Miami Sound Machine)
Singles: 12-inch
EPIC....4-6 84-88
Singles: 7-inch
EPIC....3-4 84-88
Picture Sleeves
EPIC....3-4 85-88
LPs: 10/12-inch
EPIC....5-8 84-88
Members: Marcos Avila; Kiki Garcia; Gloria Estefan; Emilio Estefan Jr.
Also see ESTEFAN, Gloria

MIAMIANS
Singles: 7-inch
AMP 3 (1005 "Call Me a Coward")..10-20 58

MICE
Singles: 7-inch
VOXX....3-4 85

MICHAEL, Al, & Medallions
Singles: 7-inch
BRAGG (222 "I Wanna Talk to You")....15-25

MICHAEL, George
Singles: 7-inch
WFIL (84514 "Fantastic Philadelphia Flyers")....4-6 70s

MICHAEL, George P&R '86
Singles: 12-inch
COLUMBIA....4-6 86-87
Singles: 7-inch
COLUMBIA....3-4 86-90
Picture Sleeves
COLUMBIA....3-4 86-89
LPs: 10/12-inch
COLUMBIA....5-8 86-90
Also see ESTUS, Deon, & George Michael
Also see FRANKLIN, Aretha, & George Michael
Also see JOHN, Elton
Also see WHAM!

MICHAEL, Teddy Lee
Singles: 7-inch
FLEETWOOD (7001 "My Love Is Yours")....10-20 58

MICHAEL & CONTINENTALS
Singles: 7-inch
AUDIO FIDELITY....10-15 68

MICHAEL & MESSENGERS
Singles: 7-inch
U.S.A. (866 "Midnight Hour"/"Hard Hard Year")....10-15 67
U.S.A. (866 "Midnight Hour"/"Up Till News")....8-12 67
(Note different flip.)
U.S.A. (874 "Lies")....5-10 67
U.S.A. (889 "Run and Hide")....5-10 67
U.S.A. (897 "I Need Her Here")....5-10 68
Members: Jack DeCarolis; Ron Gagnon; Tom Fini; Paul Cosenza; Ken Menehan; Jerry Goodman.
Also see FLOCK
Also see MESSENGERS

MICHAEL & RAYMOND
Singles: 7-inch
RCA (9244 "Walking the Dog")....15-25 67

MICHAELANGELO
LPs: 10/12-inch
COLUMBIA....10-15 71

MICHAEL-ANN
Singles: 7-inch
KIP....4-8 63

MICHAELS, Andy
Singles: 7-inch
EL VEE....3-5 78

MICHAELS, Anne
Singles: 7-inch
AMBER....5-8 61

MICHAELS, Ben
Singles: 7-inch
CLINTON....4-8 63
Picture Sleeves
CLINTON....5-10 63

MICHAELS, Danny, & Rebel Playboys
Singles: 7-inch
CHAMBERS....8-12 64

MICHAELS, Dick
Singles: 7-inch
BANYAN....4-8 66
EXPLOSIVE....5-10 61

MICHAELS, Frankie
Singles: 7-inch
CARDINAL....3-5

MICHAELS, Jerri
Singles: 7-inch
CAMEO....4-8 66

MICHAELS, Jill
Singles: 7-inch
SCOTTI BROS....3-4 86
LPs: 10/12-inch
SCOTTI BROS....5-8 86
Also see SCHNEIDER, John, & Jill Michaels

MICHAELS, Joey
Singles: 7-inch
ARCADE (150 "16 Cats")....25-35 58

MICHAELS, Johnny "Mad Man"
Singles: 7-inch
MICHAELS (1194 "Czarnina Kid")..15-25 54
RAYNARD (8838 "Qwiazdop")....15-25 55

MICHAELS, Jorden
LPs: 10/12-inch
ERIKA (008 "Phases")....8-12 83
(Picture disc. Promotional issue only.)

MICHAELS, Kelly
Singles: 7-inch
CARLA....8-12

MICHAELS, Larry, & Monarchs
Singles: 7-inch
JAY EMM (424 "It's Been a Year Now")....8-12 62

MICHAELS, Lee LP '69
Singles: 7-inch
A&M....4-6 67-71
COLUMBIA....3-5 73
Picture Sleeves
A&M....4-6 70-71
LPs: 10/12-inch
A&M (Except 3158 & 4140)....10-15 67-73
A&M (3158 "Lee Michaels")....5-8 82
A&M (4140 "Carnival of Life")....15-25 67
COLUMBIA....10-12 73-75
Promotional LPs
COLUMBIA ("In Hawaii")....35-45 75

MICHAELS, Linda
LPs: 10/12-inch
VAULT....10-15 69

MICHAELS, Mickey
Singles: 7-inch
FELSTED....5-10 58

MICHAELS, Patty
Singles: 7-inch
COLUMBIA....5-10 65
EPIC....4-8 67

MICHAELS, Ronnie
Singles: 7-inch
MALA....4-8 65

MICHAELS, Tony
(Tony Micale)
Singles: 7-inch
DEBBIE....4-8
GOLDEN WORLD (41 "I Love the Life I Live")....10-20 66
Also see REFLECTIONS

MICHEL, Tiffany
Singles: 7-inch
MGM....5-10 66

MICHELE
LPs: 10/12-inch
ABC....10-12 69

MICHELE LEE: see LEE, Michele

MICHEL'LE P&R '89
Singles: 7-inch
RUTHLESS....3-4 89-90
LPs: 10/12-inch
RUTHLESS....5-8 89

MICHELLE & VALANETTES
Singles: 7-inch
SANTA....5-10 64

MICHELLE LYNN: see LYNN, Michelle

MICHELS, Ginny
Singles: 7-inch
MALA....4-8 62

MICK, Fred
Singles: 7-inch
HILLTOP (1876 "Daddy-O Goose")....20-30 62

MICK & SHAMBLES
Singles: 7-inch
VERVE/FOLKWAYS (5010 "Lonely Nights Again")....8-12 66

MICKEY & BONNIE
Singles: 7-inch
JERDEN....5-10 63

MICKEY & KITTY
Singles: 7-inch
ATLANTIC (2024 "Ooh-Sha-La-La")....8-15 59
ATLANTIC (2036 "First Love")....8-15 59
ATLANTIC (2046 "Buttercup")....8-15 59
Members: Mickey Baker; Kitty Noble.
Also see BAKER, Mickey

MICKEY & SYLVIA R&B '56
Singles: 78 rpm
CAT (102 "Fine Love")....10-20 54
GROOVE (0164 "No Good Lover")....20-30 56
GROOVE (0175 "Love Is Strange")....25-50 56
RAINBOW....10-20 55
VIK....10-20 57
Singles: 7-inch
ALL PLATINUM (2307 "Because You")....4-6 68
ALL PLATINUM (2310 "Anytime")....4-6 69
CAT (102 "Fine Love")....25-35 54
GROOVE (0164 "No Good Lover")....20-30 56
GROOVE (0175 "Love Is Strange")....20-30 56
KING (6006 "Love Is Strange")....5-10 65
RCA (0080 "Love Is Strange")....3-5 73
RCA (7403 "To the Valley")....10-15 58
RCA (47-7774 "Sweeter As the Day Goes By")....10-15 60
RCA (61-7774 "Sweeter As the Day Goes By")....20-30 60
(Stereo.)
RCA (47-7811 "What Would I Do")....10-15 60
RCA (61-7811 "What Would I Do")....20-40 60
(Stereo.)
RCA (37-7877 "Love Lesson")....20-40 61
(Compact 33 Single.)
RCA (47-7877 "Love Lesson")....8-12 61
RCA (8517 "Let's Shake Some More")....8-10 65
RCA (8582 "From the Beginning of Time")....8-10 65
RAINBOW (316 "I'm So Glad")....20-30 55
RAINBOW (318 "Rise Sally Rise")..15-25 55
RAINBOW (330 "Where Is My Honey")....15-25 55
STANG (5004 "Rocky Raccoon")....4-8 69
STANG (5047 "Baby, You're So Fine")....4-8 73
VIK (0252 "Love Is Strange")....10-20 57
VIK (0267 "There Ought to Be a Law")....10-20 57
VIK (0280 "Love Will Make You Fail in School")....10-20 57
VIK (0290 "Love Is a Treasure")....10-20 57
VIK (0297 "There'll Be No Backing Out")....10-20 57
VIK (0324 "Bewildered")....10-20 58
VIK (0334 "True True Love")....10-20 58
WILLOW (23000 "Baby, You're So Fine")....10-15 61
WILLOW (23002 "Darling")....10-15 61
WILLOW (23004 "Since I Fell for You")....10-15 62
WILLOW (23006 "Love Is Strange")....10-20 61
EPs: 7-inch
GROOVE (18 "Love Is Strange")..50-100 57
VIK (262 "Mickey & Sylvia")....40-60 57
LPs: 10/12-inch
CAMDEN (863 "Love Is Strange")..35-50 65
RCA (0327 "Do It Again")....15-20 73
VIK (1102 "New Sounds")....150-250 57
Members: Mickey Baker; Sylvia Vanderpool.
Session: King Curtis.
Also see BAKER, Mickey
Also see KING CURTIS
Also see LITTLE SYLVIA
Also see MICKEY & KITTY
Also see SYLVIA

MICKLE, Elmon
(With His Rhythm Aces)
Singles: 7-inch
E.M. (132 "Short 'N' Fat")....50-75 59
E.M. (132 "Jackson Blues")....40-60 59
ELKO (003 "Flatfoot Sam")....40-60 59
J. GEMS (1908 "Independent Walk")....25-35 59
Also see DRIFTIN' SLIM
Also see HARMONICA HARRY
Also see MODEL T. SLIM

MICO WAVE R&B '87
Singles: 7-inch
COLUMBIA....3-4 87-88

MICROBE / Microbop Ensemble
Singles: 7-inch
JAMIE....3-6 69

MID AMERICANS
Singles: 7-inch
PABLO (7014 "Lonely Surfer")....25-35 62
(First issue.)
TEARDROP (3103 "Lonely Surfer")....15-25 62

MID AMERICANS / Bonnie & Treasures
Singles: 7-inch
PABLO (7014 "Lonely Surfer")....20-25 60s
Also see BONNIE & TREASURES
Also see MID AMERICANS

MIDAS TOUCH
Singles: 7-inch
DECCA....3-6 69
LPs: 10/12-inch
DECCA....10-15 69-70

MIDAS TOUCH
Singles: 7-inch
PALISADES....3-5 79

MIDDLE EARTH
Singles: 7-inch
MUTUAL....8-10 64

MIDDLE OF THE ROAD
Singles: 7-inch
RCA....3-5 71-72
LPs: 10/12-inch
RCA....8-12 72

MIDDLETON, Eddie C&W '77
Singles: 7-inch
EPIC....3-5 77
LPs: 10/12-inch
EPIC....6-12 77

MIDDLETON, Gene
Singles: 7-inch
D&B....4-8 67

MIDDLETON, Rex
(Red Middleton's Hi-Fi's; with the Art Foxall Combo)
Singles: 7-inch
CAM (100-14 "Wow")....500-1000
(Identification number shown since no selection number is used.)

MIDDLETON, Tom
Singles: 7-inch
COLUMBIA....3-5 76

MIDDLETON, Tony
(With the Willows; with Dave Rhodes Orchestra & Chorus)
Singles: 7-inch
A&M (1084 "Angelea")....10-20 69
ABC-PAR (10695 "You Spoiled My Reputation")....20-30 65
ALFA (113 "My Home Town")....10-20 62
ALTO (2001 "I Need You")....10-20 60
BIG TOP (3037 "Unchained Melody")....10-20 60
ELDORADO (508 "First Taste of Love")....20-25 57
GONE (5015 ("Let's Fall in Love") 50-75 58
MGM (13493 "To the Ends of the Earth")....25-35 66
MALA (544 "Out of This World")....10-20 66
MR. G....5-10 68
PHILIPS (40184 "Too Hot to Handle")....8-12 64
ROULETTE (4345 "I'm Gonna Try Love")....10-20 61
SAXONY (104 "I'm on My Way")..35-45 58
TRIUMPH (600 "Count Your Blessings")....20-30 59
TRIUMPH (605 "The Universe")....20-30 59
U.A. (410 "Drifting")....10-15 62
Also see FIVE WILLOWS
Also see WILLOWS

MIDKNIGHTS
Singles: 7-inch
STYLE (2001 "Pain")....15-25 66

MID-KNIGHTERS
Singles: 7-inch
KEY (1003 "Baby My Heart")....15-25 61
PARAGON (814 "Charlena")....20-25 62
Members: Jimmy Rosetti; Keith Dreher; Charlie Lewondowski; Bill Hakow; Mel Lundie; Johnny Verbraken.

MIDLER, Bette P&R/LP '72
Singles: 12-inch
ATLANTIC....4-6
Singles: 7-inch
ATLANTIC....3-5 72-90
Picture Sleeves
ATLANTIC....3-5 72-89
LPs: 10/12-inch
ATLANTIC....5-10 72-90
Also see REDD, Sharon, Ula Hedwig & Charlotte Crossley
Also see U.S.A. for AFRICA

MIDNIGHT ANGELS
Singles: 7-inch
APEX (77073 "I'm Sufferin' ")....15-25 67
Picture Sleeves
APEX (77073 "I'm Sufferin' ")....25-35 67

MIDNIGHT BLUE
Singles: 7-inch
MOTOWN....3-5 81

MIDNIGHT FLYER
Singles: 7-inch
SWAN SONG....3-5 81
LPs: 10/12-inch
SWAN SONG....5-8 81

MIDNIGHT MAIL
Singles: 7-inch
AUDIO ARTS (60003 "I Can't Get It")....10-20 60s
Member: Jim Webb.
Also see WEBB, Jimmy

MIDNIGHT OIL LP '84
Singles: 12-inch
COLUMBIA....4-6 84
Singles: 7-inch
COLUMBIA....3-4 82-89
Picture Sleeves
COLUMBIA....3-5 82-88
LPs: 10/12-inch
COLUMBIA (Black vinyl)....5-8 84-90
COLUMBIA (45398 "Blue Sky Mining")....10-12 90
(Colored vinyl.)

MIDNIGHT REBELS
Singles: 7-inch
ATLANTIC....4-6 68

MIDNIGHT RHYTHM
Singles: 7-inch
ATLANTIC....3-5 79
LPs: 10/12-inch
ATLANTIC....5-10 79

MIDNIGHT RIDERS
Singles: 7-inch
IMPERIAL....8-12 61

MIDNIGHT SHIFT
Singles: 7-inch
MSI (1001 "Every Day Without You")....25-50

MIDNIGHT SONS
Singles: 7-inch
JERDEN....5-10
KG....10-15

MIDNIGHT STAR R&B '80
Singles: 12-inch
SOLAR....4-6 82-86
Singles: 7-inch
SOLAR....3-4 80-88
Picture Sleeves
SOLAR....3-4 86
LPs: 10/12-inch
SOLAR....5-8 82-88
Members: Cino-Vincent Calloway; Reggie Calloway; Jeff Cooper; Kenneth Gant; Melvin Gantry; William Simmons; Boas Watson.
Also see CALLOWAY

MIDNIGHT STRING QUARTET LP '66
LPs: 10/12-inch
VIVA....5-10 66-68

MIDNIGHT SUN
Singles: 7-inch
SONIC (5476 "I'll Find a Way")....10-20 68

MIDNIGHT SUN
LPs: 10/12-inch
KAPP....8-10 72

MIDNIGHTERS R&B '54
("The Midnighters, Formerly the Royals.")
Singles: 78 rpm
FEDERAL....25-75 54-57
Singles: 7-inch
FEDERAL (12169 "Work with Me Annie")....50-100 54
(Silver top label.)
FEDERAL (12169 "Work with Me Annie")....25-50 55
(Green label.)
FEDERAL (12177 "Give It Up")....50-75 54
FEDERAL (12185 "Sexy Ways")....50-75 54
FEDERAL (12195 "Annie Had a Baby")....50-75 54
FEDERAL (12200 "Annie's Aunt Fannie")....50-75 54
FEDERAL (12202 "Tell Them")....50-75 54
FEDERAL (12205 "Moonrise")....50-75 54
FEDERAL (12210 "Ashamed of Myself")....50-75 55
FEDERAL (12220 "Switchie, Witchie, Titchie")....50-75 55
FEDERAL (12224 "Henry's Got Flat Feet")....50-75 55
FEDERAL (12227 "It's Love Baby")....50-75 55
FEDERAL (12230 "Give It Up")....10-20 55
FEDERAL (12240 "That House on the Hill")....50-75 55
FEDERAL (12243 "Don't Change Your Pretty Ways")....50-75 55
FEDERAL (12251 "Partners for Life")....50-75 56
FEDERAL (12260 "Rock Granny Roll")....50-75 56
FEDERAL (12270 "Tore Up Over You")....30-60 56
FEDERAL (12285 "Come on and Get It")....30-60 56
FEDERAL (12288 "Let Me Hold Your Hand")....30-60 56
FEDERAL (12293 "In the Doorway Crying")....30-60 57
FEDERAL (12299 "Oh So Happy") 25-50 57
FEDERAL (12305 "Let 'Em Roll")..25-50 57
FEDERAL (12317 "Stay By My Side")....25-50 58
FEDERAL (12339 "Baby Please") 25-50 58
Members: Henry Booth; Hank Ballard; Sonny Woods; Charles Sutton; Lawson Smith; Alonzo Tucker.
Also see BALLARD, Hank, & Midnighters
Also see BOOTH, Henry
Also see JOHN, Little Willie / 5 Royales / Earl (Connelly) King / Midnighters
Also see ROYALS

MIDNIGHTERS
Singles: 7-inch
LUCKY STAR (100 "Rock These Blues Away")....15-25 59
20TH FOX....5-10 60

MIDNIGHTERS
Singles: 7-inch
CAPITOL (4981 "The Big Surfer") 10-15 63
Member: Dave Aerni.

MIDNIGHTERS
Singles: 7-inch
BARRY (3028 "Slow Walk")....15-25 60s
(Canadian.)

RCA (3308 "Goofy Foot")..............10-20 63
(Canadian.)
Also see RONNIE & COMETS

MIDNIGHTERS, Thee: see THEE MIDNIGHTERS

MIDNIGHTS
Singles: 7-inch
MUSIC CITY (746 "Annie Pulled a Hum-Bug")............................35-50 54
MUSIC CITY (762 "She Left Me")...50-100 54
(Colored vinyl.)

MIDNITE AUTO PARTS
Singles: 7-inch
MIDNITE (30144 "White Silver Sands")................................ 4-8 73

MID SOUTH SINGERS
Singles: 7-inch
DUKE (202 "See About Me").........35-45 58

MIDTOWN REPERTORY
Singles: 7-inch
KARATE.. 4-8 67

MIDWAY R&B/D&D '84
Singles: 12-inch
PERSONAL... 4-6 84
Singles: 7-inch
PERSONAL... 3-4 84

MIDWEST
Singles: 7-inch
METROBEAT.................................. 8-12 60s
Also see HOLIEN, Danny
Also see SHADES

MIFFLIN TRIPLETS
Singles: 7-inch
EMBER (1045 "I Do")...................75-125 58

MIGHTY ACCENTS
Singles: 7-inch
RODALA (69 "Sabre Stomp").........15-25 63
Member: Ray Salaz.

MIGHTY AVENGERS
Singles: 7-inch
PRESS.. 5-8 65

MIGHTY BABY
Singles: 7-inch
PHILIPS... 3-5
LPs: 10/12-inch
HEAD (025 "Mighty Baby")............35-50 69
Members: Reg King; Alan Bam King; Mike Evans; Martin Stone; Pete Watson; Roger Powell; Ian Whiteman.
Also see ACE

MIGHTY CLOUDS OF JOY R&B/LP '74
Singles: 12-inch
EPIC.. 4-6 79
Singles: 7-inch
ABC.. 3-5 76-77
DUNHILL.. 3-5 74-75
EPIC.. 3-5 79-80
MYRRH.. 3-4 82
PEACOCK.. 3-6 61-73
LPs: 10/12-inch
ABC.. 5-8 75-76
DUNHILL.. 5-8 74
EPIC.. 5-8 79
MYRRH.. 5-8 81-83
PEACOCK.. 5-10 65-73
PRIORITY... 5-8 82
Member: Bunker Hill.
Also see HILL, Bunker.
Also see ROGER

MIGHTY CRAVERS
Singles: 7-inch
KEYNOTE.. 5-10 63
MASTERCRAFT....................................... 5-10 62
Also see CRAVERS
Also see GARVIN, Rex, & Mighty Cravers

MIGHTY DIAMONDS
LPs: 10/12-inch
ALLIGATOR... 5-8 82
MANGO... 5-8
SHANACHIE... 5-8 83
VIRGIN.. 8-10

MIGHTY DUKES
Singles: 78 rpm
DUKE (104 "No Other Love").......50-100 52
Member: Billy Dawn Smith.
Also see DAWN, Billy, Quartet
Also see DUKES

MIGHTY FIRE R&B '80
Singles: 7-inch
ELEKTRA.. 3-4 81-82
ZEPHYR.. 3-5 80
LPs: 10/12-inch
ELEKTRA.. 5-8 81-82

MIGHTY FIVE
Singles: 7-inch
FLEETWOOD (1000 "Daddy Guitar").. 8-12

MIGHTY FLEA R&B '68
Singles: 7-inch
ELDO.. 4-8 67

MIGHTY FLYERS
LPs: 10/12-inch
RADIO ACTIVE MATERIAL........... 8-10 81
TAKOMA.. 5-8 80s

MIGHTY GROOVEMAKERS
Singles: 7-inch
PEANUT COUNTRY.....................15-25 60s

MIGHTY HANNIBAL R&B '66
(James T. Shaw)
Singles: 7-inch
DECCA...8-12 65
JOSIE...8-12 66-67
LOMA..8-12 68
SHURFINE...8-12 66
Also see HANNIBAL
Also see KING HANNIBAL

MIGHTY HIGH
LPs: 10/12-inch
MCA...5-10 79

MIGHTY JUPITERS
Singles: 7-inch
WARNER RECORDS (1020 "Your Love")..................................100-150 59

MIGHTY LEMON DROPS LP '90
LPs: 10/12-inch
SIRE..5-10 86-90
Members: Paul Marsh; David Newton; Tony Linehan; Keith Rowley.

MIGHTY MANFRED & WONDERDOGS
Singles: 7-inch
PARIS TOWER.................................15-25 68

MIGHTY MARVELOWS: see MARVELOWS

MIGHTY MOFOS
Singles: 12-inch
MIDNIGHT... 5-8

MIGHTY POPE R&B '77
Singles: 7-inch
PRIVATE STOCK.................................. 3-5 77

MIGHTY SAM
Singles: 7-inch
AMY (957 "Sweet Dreams")............5-10 66
AMY (963 "Fannie Mae")................5-10 66
AMY (973 "I'm a Man")...................5-10 66
AMY (984 "Talk to Me, Talk to Me")..5-10 67
AMY (990 "In the Same Old Way")..5-10 67
AMY (11001 "When She Touches Me")..5-10 67
AMY (11022 "I Just Came to Get My Baby")..5-10 68
AMY (11044 "I Who Have Nothing")...5-10 68
ATLANTIC (2711 "Evil Woman")...... 4-8 70
MALACO (1011 "Mr. & Mrs. Untrue").. 4-8 71
ORLEANS (42784 "Dancin' to the Music of Love")... 4-6 83

MIGHTY SPARROW
LPs: 10/12-inch
W.B...8-10 74

MIGHTY TROJANS: see TROJANS

MIGHTY VIKINGS
Singles: 7-inch
WINCOX (7 "Your Love Is Mine") ..40-60

MIGIL 5
Singles: 7-inch
CAMEO.. 5-8 64
HICKORY.. 5-8 65
MERCURY... 5-8 64

MIJAL & WHITE
Singles: 7-inch
ZATOP (2208 "I've Been You").......8-12

MIKE & BELAIRS
Singles: 7-inch
HOLIDAY (1002 "Jungle Trot").........8-12

MIKE & BILL R&B '75
Singles: 7-inch
ARISTA.. 3-5 75
Members: Mike Felder; Bill Daniels.

MIKE & CENSATIONS
Singles: 7-inch
HIGHLAND..8-10 67
REVUE.. 4-8 69

MIKE & DEAN
(Mike Love & Dean Torrence)
Singles: 7-inch
BUDWEISER (8246 "Budweiser Fight Song/Be True to Your Bud").....................35-45 83
(Add $8 to $12 if accompanied by two Mike & Dean posters and a story insert. Promotional issue only.)
HITBOUND..10-20 82
PREMORE (23/24 "Da Doo Ron Ron"/"Baby Talk")...20-30 83
Picture Sleeves
PREMORE (23/24 "Da Doo Ron Ron"/"Baby Talk")...20-30 83
LPs: 10/12-inch
PREMORE (983 "Rock'n Roll Again")..30-50 83
(Also has tracks by the Association, Rip Chords, and Paul Revere & Raiders.)
PREMORE (3009 "Rock'n Roll City")..30-50 83
(Also has tracks by other artists.)
Members: Mike Love; Dean Torrence.
Also see ASSOCIATION
Also see JAN & DEAN
Also see LOVE, Mike
Also see REVERE, Paul, & Raiders
Also see RIPCHORDS

MIKE & DEL RAYS
Singles: 7-inch
JOX...5-10 64

MIKE & JAYS
Singles: 7-inch
DOYL (1001 "Dingle Dangle Doll")..40-60 60
(Reissued as by Ron Bennet.)
Also see BENNET, Ron

MIKE & JIM
Singles: 78 rpm
JOSIE (825 "Dungaree Cutie").......20-30 57
Singles: 7-inch
JOSIE (825 "Dungaree Cutie").......20-30 57

MIKE & JOKERS
Singles: 7-inch
CHASE (6000 "There's Got to Be a Girl")...20-30
CHASE (6001 "Bound for Love") ...15-25

MIKE & LULU
Singles: 7-inch
TOP RANK..5-10 60

MIKE + MECHANICS P&R/LP '85
Singles: 7-inch
ATLANTIC...3-4 85-89
Picture Sleeves
ATLANTIC...3-4 85-89
LPs: 10/12-inch
ATLANTIC...5-8 85-90
Members: Mike Rutherford; Paul Carrack; Paul Young; Peter Van Hooke; Adrian Lee.
Also see CARRACK, Paul
Also see RUTHERFORD, Mike
Also see SAD CAFE
Also see YOUNG, Paul

MIKE & MODIFIERS
Singles: 7-inch
GORDY (7006 "I Found Myself a Brand New Baby")...................................40-60 62
Member: Mike Valvano.

MIKE & RAVENS
Singles: 7-inch
EMPIRE..10-15 62

MIKE & UTOPIANS
(Mike Lasman)
Singles: 7-inch
CEE=JAY (574 "Erlene/I Wish").150-250 60
CEE=JAY (574 "Erlene/I Found a Penny")..100-250 60

MIKE, JOHN & BILL
Singles: 7-inch
OMNIBUS (239 "How Can You Kiss Me")..30-50 65
Members: Mike Nesmith; John London; Bill Sleeper.
Also see LEWIS & CLARKE
Also see NESMITH, Mike

MIKE'S MESSENGERS
Singles: 7-inch
EL-EZ-DE...10-20

MIKI
(Miki Dallon)
Singles: 7-inch
GNP (428 "When I Was 15") 8-12 69
Also see DALLON, Miki

MIKIE & ARDONS
Singles: 7-inch
GALLANT...5-10 66
MAM'SELLE.......................................8-12 62
Session: Joe Bill Loudermilk.

MIKKELSEN, Don
(With the Birds; with Edell & the T-Birds)
Singles: 7-inch
DECK (600 "Chapel of Love")........40-60 59
IMPACT (15 "Now You're Gone")...15-25 61

MIKKI R&B '82
Singles: 7-inch
EMERALD INT'L...................................3-4 82-83
POP ART...3-4 84

MILAM, George, & Buzz Elliot
Singles: 7-inch
LAVENDER...4-8

MILAN
(Leather Boy Milan; World of Milan)
Singles: 7-inch
ABC-PAR (10718 "Cry, Lonely Boy")..10-15 65
BRUNSWICK (55292 "Follow the Sun")..10-15 66
BRUNSWICK (55298 "One Track Mind")..15-25 66
END (1123 "Innocence")..................5-10 62
20TH FOX (487 "I Am What I Am")..10-15 64
20TH FOX (552 "Angel's Lullaby") .10-15 65
Also see LEATHER BOY

MILAN, Mickey
(With the Montclairs)
Singles: 7-inch
PHILLIPS INT'L...................................4-6 58

MILANO, Bobby
Singles: 78 rpm
CAPITOL...5-10 55
Singles: 7-inch
CAPITOL...10-15 55
CHALLENGE (59005 "Life Begins At Four O'Clock")...40-60 58
TIME (1019 "Ruby")..........................10-15 60
W.B. (5027 "Water Under the Bridge")...5-10 59

MILBURN, Amos R&B '48
(With the Aladdin Chickenshackers)
Singles: 78 rpm
ALADDIN..10-40 45-56
Singles: 7-inch
ALADDIN (3014 "Chicken Shack Boogie")...75-125 50
ALADDIN (3018 "Bewildered").....50-100 50
ALADDIN (3023 "Hold Me Baby")...50-100 49
ALADDIN (3026 "In the Middle of the Night")...50-100 49
ALADDIN (3032 "Roomin' House Blues")...50-100 49
ALADDIN (3037 "Let's Make Christmas Merry, Baby")...50-100 49
ALADDIN (3038 "Real Pretty Mama Blues")...50-100 49
ALADDIN (3068 "Bad Bad Whiskey")..50-75 50
ALADDIN (3080 "Let's Rock Awhile")...50-75 51
ALADDIN (3090 "Everybody Clap Hands")..50-75 51
ALADDIN (3093 "Ain't Nothing Shaking")...50-75 51
ALADDIN (3105 "Boogie Woogie")..50-75 51
ALADDIN (3124 "Drinkin' and Thinkin'")..40-60 52
ALADDIN (3125 "Flying Home") 40-60 52
ALADDIN (3133 "Roll Mr. Jelly").....40-60 52
ALADDIN (3150 "Greyhound").......40-60 52
ALADDIN (3159 "Rock, Rock, Rock")..40-60 52
ALADDIN (3164 "Let Me Go Home, Whiskey")..30-50 53
ALADDIN (3168 "Please, Mr. Johnson")..30-50 53
ALADDIN (3197 "One Scotch, One Bourbon, One Beer")..........................30-50 53
ALADDIN (3218 "Good Good Whiskey")..25-45 53
ALADDIN (3226 "Rocky Mountain")..25-45 54
ALADDIN (3240 "Milk & Water")....25-45 54
ALADDIN (3248 "Glory of Love")....25-45 54
ALADDIN (3253 "Vicious Vicious Vodka")..25-45 54
ALADDIN (3269 "One Two Three Everybody")..25-45 54
ALADDIN (3293 "My Happiness Depends on You")..............................25-45 55
ALADDIN (3306 "House Party").....25-45 55
ALADDIN (3320 "I Need Someone")..20-40 56
ALADDIN (3332 "Chicken Shack")..20-40 56
IMPERIAL...5-10 62
KING (5000 series)...........................5-10 60-61
KING (6000 series)...........................4-8 67
MOTOWN (1038 "My Baby Gave Me Another Chance")..15-25 63
MOTOWN (1046 "My Daily Prayer")..15-25 63
LPs: 10/12-inch
ALADDIN (704 "Rockin' the Boogie")...................................500-1000 55
(Black vinyl. 10-inch LP.)
ALADDIN (704 "Rockin' the Boogie")...................................2500-3500 55
(Red vinyl. 10-inch LP.)
ALADDIN (810 "Rockin' the Boogie")...300-500 56
IMPERIAL (9176 "Million Sellers")..100-200 62
MOSAIC (155 "Complete Aladdin Recordings of Amos Milburn")........................140-150 90s
(Boxed 10-disc audiophile set. 3500 made.)
MOTOWN (608 "The Blues Boss")..500-750 63
SCORE (4012 "Let's Have a Party")...100-200 57
Also see BROWN, Charles, & Amos Milburn

MILBURN, Amos / Wynonie Harris / Velma Nelson / Crown Prince Waterford
LPs: 10/12-inch
ALADDIN (703 "Party After Hours")...................................500-1000 56
(Black vinyl. 10-inch LP.)
ALADDIN (703 "Party After Hours")...................................2000-3000 56
(Colored vinyl. 10-inch LP.)
Also see HARRIS, Wynonie
Also see MILBURN, Amos
Also see WATERFORD, Crown Prince

MILBURN, Amos, Jr.
Singles: 7-inch
BROWNFIELD......................................5-10 65
HOLLYWOOD.......................................4-8 68
LE CAM...5-10 62
SHALIMAR..8-12 63
Session: Ron-Dels.
Also see RON-DELS

MILBURN, Robert, & His Blue Notes
Singles: 7-inch
SUN LAND (107 "Money Hustlin' Woman")..3-4 92
(Black vinyl.)
SUN LAND (107 "Money Hustlin' Woman")..5-6 92
(Colored vinyl.)

MILE, Chuck, & Styles
Singles: 7-inch
DORE (630 "Be Mine Or Be a Fool")...20-30 62

MILE ENDS
Singles: 7-inch
5TH ESTATE (8447 "Bottle Up and Go")..15-25 60s

MILEM, Percy
Singles: 7-inch
GOLDWAX..4-8 67

MILES, Barry
(With Silverlight & Co.)
LPs: 10/12-inch
GRYPHON...5-10 77-78
LONDON...8-12 74-75
POPPY...8-10

MILES, Buddy P&R/LP '69
(Buddy Miles Express; with Freedom Express)
Singles: 7-inch
CASABLANCA....................................3-5 75-76
COLUMBIA...3-5 73-74
MERCURY...3-6 68-72
Picture Sleeves
MERCURY...3-6
LPs: 10/12-inch
CASABLANCA....................................8-10 75
COLUMBIA...8-12 73-74
MERCURY...10-15 68-72
Also see CALIFORNIA RAISINS
Also see ELECTRIC FLAG
Also see FIDELITYS
Also see HENDRIX, Jimi
Also see KARP, Charlie
Also see SANTANA, Carlos, & Buddy Miles

MILES, Dick C&W '68
Singles: 7-inch
CAPITOL...4-6 68
LPs: 10/12-inch
CAPITOL...10-15 68

MILES, Garry P&R '60
(With the Statues; Gary Miles; Buzz Cason)
Singles: 7-inch
LIBERTY (54000 series)....................5-8 68
LIBERTY (55000 series)....................10-15 60-64
Picture Sleeves
LIBERTY (55261 "Look for a Star")...10-20 60
EPs: 7-inch
LIBERTY (1005 "Look for a Star")..50-75 60
Also see CASON, Buzz
Also see STATUES

MILES, Jackie
LPs: 10/12-inch
IMPERIAL..15-25 61

MILES, John P&R/LP '76
Singles: 12-inch
LONDON..5-8 77-80
Singles: 7-inch
ARISTA..3-5 78
LONDON..3-5 76-77
WEA...3-4 85
LPs: 10/12-inch
ARISTA..5-10 78
CAPITOL..5-10 83
LONDON..5-10 76-80
VALENTINO..5-8 85
WEA...5-8 85
Also see PARSONS, Alan, Project

MILES, Lenny P&R '60
Singles: 7-inch
GROOVE..8-12 62
RCA...8-12 62
SCEPTER...8-12 60-61

MILES, Lizzy
LPs: 10/12-inch
COOK (1183 "Hot Songs")................30-60

MILES, Luke "Long Gone"
(Long Gone Miles & Boys from 25th St.)
Singles: 7-inch
SMASH..10-15 62
TWO KINGS...8-12 65
WORLD PACIFIC.................................8-12 64
LPs: 10/12-inch
WORLD PACIFIC.................................15-25 64

MILES, Mary Ann
(With the Zeke Strong Band)
Singles: 7-inch
CELESTE (201 "I'll Be Gone")..........6-12 65
CELESTE (801 "Without Someone to Love")..6-12 64
Also see AGEE, Ray, & Mary Ann Miles

MILEY, Lonnie
Singles: 7-inch
KIX (102 "Rockum Beat")..................8-12

MILITELLO, Bobby
Singles: 7-inch
GORDY..3-4 82-83
LPs: 10/12-inch
GORDY..5-8 82-83

MILITELLO, Bobby, & Jean Carn
Singles: 7-inch
GORDY..3-4 83
Also see CARNE, Jean

MILK
Singles: 7-inch
BUDDAH..4-8 68
Member: Johnny Cymbal.
Also see CYMBAL, Johnny

MILK, Christopher
LPs: 10/12-inch
REPRISE...8-10 72

MILKWOOD
LPs: 10/12-inch
A&M ...12-18 69

MILKWOOD
LPs: 10/12-inch
PARAMOUNT (6046 "How's the Weather")...25-35 73
Also see AUKEMA, Niki
Also see CARS

MILKWOOD TAPESTRY
LPs: 10/12-inch
METROMEDIA (1007 "Milkwood Tapestry")...20-25 69

MILKY WAY
Singles: 7-inch
CAPITOL...4-6 69

MILKY WAYS
Singles: 7-inch
LIBERTY...10-15 60

MILLAN, Al, & United States Robots
LPs: 10/12-inch
ELLIE MAE...5-8 83
SQUARE DEAL...5-8 83

MILLARD & DYCE
LPs: 10/12-inch
KAYMAR (265 "Millard & Dyce")...25-50 73

MILLBURNERS
LPs: 10/12-inch
BATTLE...15-25 63

MILLENNIUM
Singles: 7-inch
COLUMBIA...5-8 68-69
Picture Sleeves
COLUMBIA...10-15 68
LPs: 10/12-inch
COLUMBIA...15-20 68
Members: Curt Boetcher; Michael Fennelly; Sandy Salisbury.
Also see BOETCHER, Curt
Also see FENNELLY, Michael
Also see SALISBURY, Sandy

MILLER, Adam
LPs: 10/12-inch
CHELSEA...8-12 72

MILLER, Arlie, & Bullets
Singles: 7-inch
LUCKY (6197 "Lou Ann")...300-400 60
Also see CARTER, Dean
Also see CHESSMAN, Judy
Also see NEAVILLE, Arlie

MILLER, Arvada
Singles: 78 rpm
CORMAC...10-15

MILLER, Bert
Singles: 7-inch
LA LOUISIANNE...4-8 65

MILLER, Big
(With the Five Pennies; Clarence Miller)
Singles: 78 rpm
SAVOY...5-10 56
Singles: 7-inch
COLUMBIA...5-10 62
SAVOY (1181 "Try to Understand")...10-20 56
LPs: 10/12-inch
COLUMBIA...20-25 61-62
U.A. (3047 "Did You Ever Hear the Blues")...30-35 58
(Monaural.)
U.A. (6047 "Did You Ever Hear the Blues")...40-60 58
(Stereo.)
Also see FIVE PENNIES

MILLER, Bingo, & Velvetones
Singles: 7-inch
YOUNG ARTISTS (103 "Martha Sue")...50-100 58

MILLER, Bob
Singles: 7-inch
JUBILEE...5-10 58

MILLER, Bob
Singles: 7-inch
SCOTTY...4-8 71

MILLER, Bobby
Singles: 7-inch
CONSTELLATION (111 "The Big Question ")...10-20 64
CONSTELLATION (134 "I'm for the Girls")...15-25 64

MILLER, Brad
LP: 10/12-inch
MFLS (004 "Power & Majesty")...25-50 78

MILLER, Buddy
Singles: 7-inch
BAND BOX (311 "Teen Twist")...10-15 62
BAND BOX (322 "Little Bo Peep")...10-15 62
BAND BOX (335 "Walking Slowly from You")...10-15 62
EKO (401 "Honey Baby")...50-75 58
FELSTED (8557 "Buddy Boy")...25-35 59
GEM (102 "Little Bo Peep")...40-60 59
SECURITY (108 "Rock & Roll Irene")...30-40 58
SECURITY (110 "I Found My Love")...30-40 58
VEM (2226 "Teen Twist")...15-25 60
VEM (2228 "Little Bo Peep")...15-25 60
Picture Sleeves
BAND BOX (335 "Walking Slowly from You")...25-35 62
Also see TWITTY, Conway

MILLER, Carl
Singles: 7-inch
LU (503 "Rhythm Guitar")...150-250 58

MILLER, Carl C&W '83
Singles: 7-inch
COUNTRY BACH...3-4 83

MILLER, Chuck P&R '55
Singles: 78 rpm
CAPITOL...5-10 54-55
MERCURY...5-15 55-58
Singles: 7-inch
CAPITOL (2700 "After All")...10-15 54
CAPITOL (2841 "Hopahula Boogie")...10-15 54
CAPITOL (3187 "No Baby Like You")...10-15 55
MERCURY (70627 "The House of Blue Lights")...10-20 55
MERCURY (70697 "Hawk-Eye")...10-20 55
MERCURY (70767 "Boogie Blues")...10-20 55
MERCURY (70842 "Bright Red Convertible")...10-20 56
MERCURY (70942 "Cool It Baby")...10-20 56
MERCURY (71001 "Auctioneer")...10-20 56
MERCURY (71308 "Down the Road Apiece")...10-20 58
LPs: 10/12-inch
MERCURY (20195 "After Hours")...50-75 56
(10-inch LP.)

MILLER, Clint P&R '58
Singles: 7-inch
ABC-PAR (9878 "Bertha Lou")...15-25 58
BIG TOP (3013 "Lonely Traveler")...8-12 59
HEADLINE (1010 ("Do You Remember")...8-12 60
HEADLINE (1011 ("Till the End of the World Rolls 'Round")...8-12 61
HEADLINE (1013 ("Girl with the Ribbon in Her Hair")...8-12 61
LENOX (5557 "Forget-Me-Nots")...5-10 62

MILLER, Dale
LPs: 10/12-inch
KICKING MULE...5-10
(10-inch LP.)

MILLER, Dale / John James / Sam Mitchell / Ton Van Bergeyk
LPs: 10/12-inch
KICKING MULE...5-10
(10-inch LP.)
Also see MILLER, Dale
Also see MITCHELL, Sam
Also see VAN BERGEYK, Tom

MILLER, Dave
Singles: 7-inch
INDIO...5-10 61

MILLER, Dick
Singles: 7-inch
AGGIE...8-10
MERCURY...8-10 60
TOPPA...8-10 60
Also see WRANGLERS

MILLER, Dick, & Rhythmasters
(With the Saddle-ites)
Singles: 7-inch
GOLD STAR (105 "It")...15-25 60s
PAGEANT (717 "A Tear, a Heartbreak, a Love")...15-25 60s

MILLER, Don
Singles: 7-inch
KANGAROO...5-10 61
MELKER...5-10 59

MILLER, Ed, & Louisiana Playboys
Singles: 7-inch
PLAYBOYS (100 "I Had Someone Else")...5-10

MILLER, Eddie "Piano"
Singles: 78 rpm
RAINBOW...6-12 51
Singles: 7-inch
RAINBOW (138 "Eddie's Piano Boogie")...15-25 51
RAINBOW (209 "Put Your Arms Around Me")...8-12
RAINBOW (40044 "Honky Tonk Boogie")...10-15

MILLER, Ellen Lee C&W '89
Singles: 7-inch
GOLDEN TRUMPET...3-4 89

MILLER, Frankie
Singles: 7-inch
U.A....4-6 62

MILLER, Frankie C&W '59
Singles: 78 rpm
COLUMBIA...3-6 54-56
Singles: 7-inch
COLUMBIA...5-15 54-56
STARDAY...5-10 59-67
EPs: 7-inch
STARDAY...8-12 60
LPs: 10/12-inch
AUDIO LAB (1562 "Fine Country Singing")...40-50 63
STARDAY (134 "Country Music's New Star")...40-50 61
STARDAY (199 "Country Style")...40-50 62
STARDAY (338 "Blackland Farmer")...40-50 65

MILLER, Frankie P&R/LP '77
Singles: 7-inch
CAPITOL...3-4 82
CHRYSALIS...3-5 75-79
Picture Sleeves
CAPITOL...3-4 82
LPs: 10/12-inch
CAPITOL...5-10 82
CHRYSALIS...8-12 73-80

MILLER, Gene
(Gene "Bowlegs" Miller)
Singles: 7-inch
HI...4-8 67-69

MILLER, Glenn, & His Orchestra P&R '35
(New Glenn Miller Orchestra with Ray McKinley; with Buddy DeFranco)
Singles: 78 rpm
BLUEBIRD...5-10 38-44
BRUNSWICK...5-10 37-38
COLUMBIA...5-10 35
DECCA...15-25 37
RCA...4-8 47-58
VICTOR...5-10 42-46
Singles: 7-inch
DECCA (25000 series)...5-10 50s
EPIC...3-6 65-69
RCA...4-10 50-67
EPs: 7-inch
EPIC...5-15 54-56
RCA (Except 6700 series)...5-15 50-61
RCA (6700 "Anthology Limited Edition, Vol. 1")...25-50 56
RCA (6701 "Anthology Limited Edition, Vol. 2")...25-50 56
RCA (6702 "Army Air Force Band")...20-30 56
LPs: 10/12-inch
BRIGHT ORANGE...5-8 73
CAMDEN...5-10 63-74
COLUMBIA...5-8 82
EPIC (1000 & 3000 series)...20-40 54-56
EPIC (16000 series)...12-25 60
EPIC (24000 & 26000 series)...10-20 65-66
EVEREST (Except 4004)...5-8 82
EVEREST (4004 "Glenn Miller")...20-30 82
(Boxed, five-disc set.)
GREAT AMERICAN...5-10 77
HARMONY...5-10 70
KORY...5-8 77
MOVIETONE...8-15 67
RCA (16 thru 30)...25-50
(10-inch LPs.)
RCA (0600 thru 3800 series)...5-10 74-81
(With "ANL," "AYL" or "CPL" prefix.)
RCA (LPT-3000 series)...25-50 52-54
(10-inch LP.)
RCA (1000 thru 1500 series)...20-40 54-57
(Black label.)
RCA (1100 thru 1500 series)...5-10 68-69
(Orange label.)
RCA (1600 thru 3900 series)...10-25 58-68
(Black label. With "LPM" or "LSP" prefix.)
RCA (1900 thru 4100 series)...5-10 68-69
(Orange or gold label.)
RCA (5000 series)...5-10 75-80
RCA (6000 series)...5-15 69-73
RCA (6100 series)...15-30 59-63
RCA (6700 "Anthology–Limited Edition, Vol. 1")...75-100 56
(Five-LP set with booklet and special gold or silver case.)
RCA (6700 "Anthology–Limited Edition, Vol. 1")...50-75 62
(Reissue, has '60s RCA labels.)
RCA (6701 "Anthology–Limited Edition, Vol. 2")...75-100 56
(Five-LP set with booklet and special gold or silver case.)
RCA (6701 "Anthology–Limited Edition, Vol. 2")...50-75 62
(Reissue, has '60s RCA labels.)
RCA (6702 "Army Air Force Band")...50-75 56
SPRINGBOARD...4-8 77
20TH FOX (100 series)...20-30 59
20TH FOX (900 series)...5-10 73
20TH FOX (3000 series)...15-25 59
20TH FOX (3100 series)...10-15 65
20TH FOX (4100 series)...10-15 65
20TH FOX (72000 series)...6-12 73
Also see HELLER, Jackie / Glenn Miller

MILLER, Hal
(With the Rays)
Singles: 7-inch
AMY (900 "Love Another Girl")...20-30 64
AMY (909 "On My Own Two Feet")...75-100 64
AMY (920 "Blessing in Disguise")...50-75 64
TOPIX (6003 "An Angel Cried")...15-25 61
(With the 4 Seasons.)
Also see 4 SEASONS
Also see RAYS

MILLER, Jamene
LPs: 10/12-inch
U.A....10-15 71

MILLER, Jimmy
Singles: 7-inch
MAY...4-8 63

MILLER, Jody P&R '64/C&W '65
Singles: 7-inch
CAPITOL...5-10 63-70
EPIC...3-6 70-79
Picture Sleeves
CAPITOL...5-10 65
LPs: 10/12-inch
CAPITOL (1913 "Wednesday's Child Is Full of Woe")...15-25 63
CAPITOL (2349 thru 2996)...10-20 65-69
CAPITOL (11000 series)...5-10 73
EPIC...5-10 70-77
PICKWICK/HILLTOP...10-15 66
SEARS...8-12

MILLER, Jody, & Johnny Paycheck C&W '72
EPIC...3-5 72
Also see MILLER, Jody
Also see PAYCHECK, Johnny

MILLER, John
LPs: 10/12-inch
BLUE GOOSE...10-12 72-74

MILLER, Kenny
Singles: 7-inch
IMPERIAL...4-8 61
20TH FOX...4-8 63
VIKING...4-8 61

MILLER, Lesley
Singles: 7-inch
MGM...3-6 67-69
RCA...4-8 64-66

MILLER, Lisa
Singles: 7-inch
CANTERBURY (519 "Lonliest Christmas Tree")...10-20 67
TRIDENT (223 "Does She Know")...20-30 60s
Also see LITTLE LISA

MILLER, Marcus R&B '83
Singles: 12-inch
W.B....4-6 83-84
Singles: 7-inch
W.B....3-4 83-84

MILLER, Mary
Singles: 7-inch
FIRST...4-8 61
REPRISE...4-8 62-63
TOWER...4-8 64-65

MILLER, Mary K. C&W '77
(Mary Miller)
Singles: 7-inch
INERGI...3-5 77-80
RCA...3-5 79
LPs: 10/12-inch
INERGI...5-10 78

MILLER, Maurice
Singles: 7-inch
JERRY-O (801 "Fly Me to the Moon")...20-30

MILLER, Mickey
LPs: 10/12-inch
FOLKWAYS...15-20 59

MILLER, Mike, & Jack Casey
Singles: 78 rpm
CAMEO...8-12 57
Singles: 7-inch
CAMEO...8-12 57

MILLER, Mrs. Elva P&R/LP '66
(Mrs. Miller)
Singles: 7-inch
AMARET...4-8 69-70
CAPITOL...5-10 66
LPs: 10/12-inch
AMARET...10-20 69
CAPITOL...20-35 66-67

MILLER, Mr.
Singles: 7-inch
SWAN...4-8 66

MILLER, Mitch P&R '50
(Mitch Miller's Orchestra & Chorus; Mitch Miller & Sing-Along Gang)
Singles: 78 rpm
COLUMBIA...3-6 50-57
Singles: 7-inch
("Christmas Carol Medley")...5-8 50s
(Rectangular picture disc. Three other Christmas titles were made. Same value for each. No label name or selection numbers used.)
COLUMBIA...4-10 50-65
DECCA...3-6 65-66
DIAMOND...3-6 68
GOLD-MOR...3-5 73
U.A....3-6 68
Picture Sleeves
COLUMBIA...5-8 59-63
EPs: 7-inch
COLUMBIA...5-10 55-61
LPs: 10/12-inch
ATLANTIC...5-8 70
COLUMBIA (Except 2780/6380)...5-20 56-82
COLUMBIA (2780 "Major Dundee")...35-45 65
(Soundtrack. Monaural.)
COLUMBIA (6380 "Major Dundee")...45-55 65
(Soundtrack. Stereo.)
DECCA...5-12 66
HARMONY...5-12 65-71
Also see LAINE, Frankie
Also see SANDPIPERS with Mitch Miller & Orchestra / Mitch Miller & Orchestra

MILLER, Ned C&W/P&R '62
Singles: 78 rpm
DOT (Except 15601)...10-20 57
DOT (15601 "From a Jack to a King")...15-25 57
Singles: 7-inch
CAPITOL (2000 series)...3-6 68
CAPITOL (4600 series)...5-8 61
CAPITOL (5400 thru 5800 series)...3-8 65-67
DOT (Except 15601)...10-20 57
DOT (15601 "From a Jack to a King")...15-25 57
FABOR (114 thru 139)...4-8 62-65
FABOR (143 "Old Mother Nature")...10-20 57
JACKPOT (48020 "Ring the Bell for Johnny")...8-12 59
REPUBLIC...4-6 69-70
LPs: 10/12-inch
CAPITOL...10-15 65-67
FABOR (1001 "From a Jack to a King")...15-25 63
(Black vinyl.)
FABOR (1001 "From a Jack to a King")...50-100 63
(Colored vinyl.)
PLANTATION...5-8 81
REPUBLIC...8-10 70

MILLER, Olivette
Singles: 7-inch
PROTONE...5-8 59-61

MILLER, Red, Trio R&B '48
Singles: 78 rpm
BULLET...15-25 48
SWING BEAT...10-20 49
Singles: 7-inch
PRIZE (801 "Mary Jo")...20-30 50s
Also see GLENN, Lloyd

MILLER, Rex
Singles: 7-inch
ABNAK...10-20 65
NORMAN...4-8 63

MILLER, Roger C&W '60
Singles: 7-inch
BUENA VISTA...3-5 70
COLUMBIA...3-5 73-74
DECCA...5-10 59
ELEKTRA...3-4 81
MCA...3-4 85-86
MERCURY...3-5 70-72
MUSICOR (1102 "You're Forgettin' Me")...4-8 65
RCA (7000 series)...8-15 60-63
RCA (8000 series)...4-6 62-65
SMASH...3-8 64-76
STARDAY (356 "You're Forgettin' Me")...10-15 58
STARDAY (718 "Playboy")...4-8 65
STARDAY (7029 "Under Your Spell Again")...4-8 65
20TH CENTURY...3-5 79
WINDSONG...3-5 77
Picture Sleeves
BUENA VISTA...4-6 70
SMASH...5-10 64-68
LPs: 10/12-inch
CAMDEN...8-10 64-65
COLUMBIA...5-10 73
EVEREST...5-8 75
HILLTOP...8-12 60s
MCA...5-8 86
MERCURY...5-10 72
NASHVILLE...8-12
PICKWICK...5-10 70s
SMASH (Except 7000 series)...10-20 64-70
SMASH (7000 series)...5-8 82
STARDAY...10-20 65
20TH FOX...5-8 79
WINDSONG...5-8 77
WING...6-12 69
Also see LEWIS, Jerry Lee / Roger Miller / Roy Orbison
Also see NELSON, Willie, & Roger Miller
Also see TUBB, Justin / Roger Miller
Also see YOUNG, Donny, & Roger Miller

MILLER, Roger, & Willie Nelson C&W '82
(With Ray Price)
Singles: 7-inch
COLUMBIA...3-5 82
LPs: 10/12-inch
COLUMBIA...5-8 82
Also see MILLER, Roger
Also see NELSON, Willie
Also see PRICE, Ray

MILLER, Scott
Singles: 7-inch
GREY CLIFF (722 "I Got School")...40-60 59

MILLER, Stephen
LPs: 10/12-inch
PHILIPS...8-12 70

MILLER, Steve P&R/LP '68
(Steve Miller Band)
Singles: 12-inch
CAPITOL (Except 9992)...4-8 81-85
CAPITOL (9992 "I Wanna Be Loved")...5-10 86
(Colored vinyl. Promotional issue only.)
Singles: 7-inch
CAPITOL (2156 "Sittin' in Circles")...5-10 68
CAPITOL (2287 "Living in the USA")...5-10 68
CAPITOL (2447 thru 3344)...4-8 69-72
CAPITOL (3732 thru 4496)...3-5 73-77
CAPITOL (5000 series)...3-4 81-87
CAPITOL (44000 series)...3-4 88
Picture Sleeves
CAPITOL (2156 "Sittin' In Circles")...8-12 67
CAPITOL...3-4 80-88
LPs: 10/12-inch
CAPITOL (184 thru 748)...10-15 69-71
CAPITOL (2900 series)...15-20 68
CAPITOL (11000 thru 16000)...5-10 72-86
CAPITOL (11872 "Greatest Hits")...20-30 78
(Colored vinyl. Promotional issue only.)

CAPITOL (11903 "Book of Dreams")...15-20 78
(Picture disc.)
CAPITOL (48000 series)...5-8 88
MFSL (021 "Fly Like an Eagle")...50-75 78
MERCURY...5-10 81
Also see BERRY, Chuck
Also see DAVIS, Tim
Also see FRUMIOUS BANDERSNATCH
Also see GOLDBERG - MILLER BLUES BAND
Also see MERRYWEATHER, Neil
Also see SCAGGS, Boz
Also see SIDRAN, Ben

MILLER, Steve, Band / Band / Quicksilver Messenger Service
LPs: 10/12-inch
CAPITOL (288 "Steve Miller Band / The Band / Quicksilver Messenger Service")...35-45 69
(Three-disc set, with one by each group.)
Also see BAND
Also see MILLER, Steve
Also see QUICKSILVER

MILLER, Tal
Singles: 7-inch
GOLDBAND...10-20 58
HOLLYWOOD...10-20 59

MILLER, Terry
Singles: 7-inch
CAVALIER (877 "Teenage Lingo Jive")...15-25 59
E.D.S. (32062 "My Doll")...40-60
LUTE...5-10 60
REVEILLE...5-10 61

MILLER, Walter
(With the Barons; with Yellow Jackets)
Singles: 78 rpm
GOLDBAND...20-30 57
METEOR (5037 "My Last Mile")...15-25 56
Singles: 7-inch
GOLDBAND (1033 "I Was Wrong")...20-30 57
GOLDBAND (1039 "Wanna Rock & Roll")...25-35 57
METEOR (5037 "My Last Mile")...35-55 56

MILLER, Warren
Singles: 7-inch
U.A. (104 "Everybody's Got a Baby But Me")...50-100 58
Picture Sleeves
U.A. (104 "Everybody's Got a Baby But Me")...100-200 58

MILLER BROTHERS
Singles: 78 rpm
DECCA...5-10 55
MERCURY...5-10 58
Singles: 7-inch
COED...4-8 63
DECCA...5-10 55
MERCURY...5-10 58
STRAND...5-10 59

MILLER SISTERS
Singles: 78 rpm
FLIP (504 "Someday You Will Pay")...50-100 55
SUN (230 "There's No Right Way to Do Me Wrong")...25-50 55
SUN (255 "Ten Cats Down")...25-50 55
SUN (504 "Someday You Will Pay")...50-75 55
Singles: 7-inch
FLIP (504 "Someday You Will Pay")...150-250 55
(First issue.)
SUN (230 "There's No Right Way to Do Me Wrong")...50-100 55
SUN (255 "Ten Cats Down")...50-100 55
SUN (504 "Someday You Will Pay")...75-125 55
Member: Elsie Jo Miller; Mildred Wages.

MILLER SISTERS
Singles: 78 rpm
EMBER (1004 "Guess Who")...10-15 56
HERALD (455 "Until You're Mine")...10-15 55
HULL (718 "Do You Wanna Go")...10-15 56
ONYX (507 "Sugar Daddy")...25-50 57
Singles: 7-inch
ACME (717 "You Made Me a Promise")...20-30 57
EMBER (1004 "Guess Who")...15-25 56
GMC...4-8 67
GLODIS...5-10 61
HERALD (455 "Until You're Mine")...15-20 55
HERALD (527 "Until You're Mine")...8-12 58
HULL (718 "Do You Wanna Go")...15-25 56
HULL (752 "I Cried All Night")...10-15 62
MILLER...15-20 60
ONYX (507 "Sugar Daddy")...25-50 57
RAYNA...10-15 62
RIVERSIDE (4535 "Tell Him")...10-20 62
ROULETTE...4-8 63
STARDUST...4-8 64
YORKTOWN...4-8 65
Also see JEANNIE & Miller Sisters

MILLER SISTERS / Leo Price
Singles: 7-inch
HULL (736 "Just Wait and See")...10-20 60
Also see MILLER SISTERS

MILLET, Lil, & Creoles
Singles: 78 rpm
SPECIALTY (565 "Rich Woman")...10-20 55
Singles: 7-inch
SPECIALTY (565 "Rich Woman")...20-30 55

MILLET, Lou
Singles: 78 rpm
ACE...50-75 53
REPUBLIC...75-125 56
Singles: 7-inch
ACE (506 "Just You and Me")...150-250 53
REPUBLIC (7130 "Shorty the Barber")...200-300 56

MILLI VANILLI P&R/LP '89
Singles: 7-inch
ARISTA...3-4 89-90
Picture Sleeves
ARISTA...3-4 89
LPs: 10/12-inch
ARISTA...5-8 89-90
Members: Rob Pilatus; Fabrice Morvan.

MILLIKIN, Curley
Singles: 7-inch
TALOS (401 "Rock & Roll Country Boy")...50-75 59

MILLINDER, Lucky, & His Orchestra P&R/R&B '42
Singles: 78 rpm
DECCA...5-15 41-48
KING...10-30 51-57
RCA...10-20 49-51
Singles: 7-inch
KING (4449 "Chew Tobacco Rag")...25-45 51
KING (4453 "I'm Waiting for You")...25-45 51
KING (4476 "The Grape Vine")...25-45 51
KING (4496 "The Right Kind of Lovin'")...25-45 51
(Black vinyl.)
KING (4496 "The Right Kind of Lovin'")...50-100 51
(Colored vinyl.)
KING (4545 "When I Have You")...50-75 52
KING (4557 "Lord Knows I Tried")...50-75 52
KING (4571 "Please Be Careful")...50-75 52
KING (4803 "Goody Good Love")...15-25 55
KING (5200 series)...5-10 59
RCA (0054 "D Natural Blues")...30-50 51
(Colored vinyl.)
TODD...5-10 59
WARWICK...5-10 60
EPs: 7-inch
KING (268 "Lucky Millinder")...25-50 54
KING (336 "Lucky Millinder, Vol. 2")...25-50 54
Also see HARRIS, Wynonie
Also see STIDHAM, Arbee

MILLINDER, Lucky, & Admirals
Singles: 78 rpm
KING...25-35 55
Singles: 7-inch
KING (4792 "It's a Sad Sad Feeling")...40-60 55
Also see ADMIRALS
Also see MILLINDER, Lucky

MILLINGTON
Singles: 7-inch
U.A....3-6 77-78
LPs: 10/12-inch
U.A....8-12 77
Members: Jean Millington; June Millington.
Also see FANNY

MILLIONAIRES
Singles: 78 rpm
DAVIS (441 "Somebody's Lyin' ")...10-20 55
Singles: 7-inch
DAVIS (441 "Somebody's Lyin' ")...30-40 55
Members: Ollie Jones; Napoleon Allen; Abe DeCosta; James DeLoache.
Also see BLENDERS

MILLIONAIRES
Singles: 7-inch
SHAR...10-15 59

MILLIONAIRES
Singles: 7-inch
CUCA (6463 "I Got a Woman")...10-20 64
SOUNDS of WISCONSIN (6814 "Packer Backer")...8-12 68

MILLIONAIRES
Singles: 7-inch
BIG BUNNY...4-8 66
BUNNY...4-8 65
SPECIALTY...4-8 65-66

MILLIONAIRES
Singles: 7-inch
PHILIPS...4-8 67

MILLIONS LIKE US P&R/LP '87
Singles: 7-inch
VIRGIN...3-4 87
Picture Sleeves
VIRGIN...3-4 87
LPs: 10/12-inch
VIRGIN...5-8 87

MILLS, Alan
Singles: 7-inch
AMERICAN AUDIOGRAPHICS (Old MacDonald Had a Farm")...3-6 79
(Square cardboard picture disc. Selection number not known.)
LPs: 10/12-inch
FOLKWAYS...10-15

MILLS, Chuck
Singles: 7-inch
BAND BOX (221 "She's Mine")...50-80 60
BAND BOX (227 "Ding Dong")...15-25 60
TOPPA...4-8 67
Also see DAVIS, Gene / Chuck & Gene

MILLS, Denise, & Satinettes
Singles: 7-inch
CALJO (501 "Meet Me in the Moonlight")...25-50

MILLS, Everett
Singles: 7-inch
PROTONE (113 "Close Your Eyes")...15-25
PROTONE (114 "My Vision")...20-30

MILLS, Frank P&R '72
Singles: 7-inch
POLYDOR...3-4 78-79
SUNFLOWER...3-4 72
LPs: 10/12-inch
CAPITOL...5-8 85
POLYDOR...5-8 79
Also see BELLS

MILLS, Gary P&R '60
Singles: 7-inch
IMPERIAL...8-12 60
LONDON...5-10 62
TOP RANK...8-12 60

MILLS, Gene
Singles: 7-inch
JIN (284 "Rocking Rolling Ocean")...15-25

MILLS, Hank
Singles: 7-inch
BLAZE (103 "Mean Mean Mama")...25-35 59

MILLS, Hayley P&R '61
Singles: 7-inch
BUENA VISTA...8-15 61-62
MAINSTREAM...4-8 66
Picture Sleeves
BUENA VISTA (385 "Let's Get Together")...10-20 61
BUENA VISTA (395 "Johnny Jingo")...10-20 62
BUENA VISTA (401 "Side by Side")...10-20 62
BUENA VISTA (408 "Castaway")...10-20 62
LPs: 10/12-inch
BUENA VISTA (3311 "Let's Get Together")...20-25 62
(Monaural.)
BUENA VISTA (STER-3311 "Let's Get Together")...25-35 62
(Stereo.)
MAINSTREAM (6090 "Gypsy Girl")...15-25 66
(Soundtrack.)
Also see ANNETTE / Hayley Mills
Also see WAYFARERS

MILLS, Hayley, & Jimmie Bean
EPs: 7-inch
DISNEYLAND (93 "Pollyanna Songs")...15-25 60

MILLS, Hayley, & Maurice Chevalier
Singles: 7-inch
BUENA VISTA (409 "Enjoy It")...8-12 62

MILLS, Hayley, & Eddie Hodges
Singles: 7-inch
BUENA VISTA (420 "Flittering")...8-12 63
Picture Sleeves
BUENA VISTA (420 "Flittering")...10-20 64
Also see HODGES, Eddie

MILLS, Hayley, & Burl Ives
(With Eddie Hodges & Deborah Walley)
Singles: 7-inch
BUENA VISTA (4023 "Summer Magic")...5-8 63
(Alcoa Wrap promotional issue.)
Picture Sleeves
BUENA VISTA (4023 "Summer Magic")...10-15 63
(Alcoa Wrap promotional issue.)
EPs: 7-inch
ALCOA WRAP (701 "Music from *Summer Magic*")...15-25 63
(Promotional issue only.)
Also see HODGES, Eddie
Also see IVES, Burl
Also see MILLS, Hayley

MILLS, James, with Bailey's Nervous Kats
Singles: 7-inch
CAMELIA (100 "Cobra")...20-40 63
(First issue.)
MAGNET (106 "Cobra")...10-20 63
MAGNET (235 "Drummer Boy Blues ")...10-20 60s

MILLS, Margie
(With the Executives)
Singles: 7-inch
GROOVE...5-10 65
RCA (8673 "Goodbye, Boys, Goodbye")...8-12 66
RCA (8802 "You'll Know I'm Around ")...5-8 66
VEE JAY (549 "Knock on Any Door")...8-10 63

MILLS, Stephanie P&R/R&B/LP '79
Singles: 12-inch
CASABLANCA...4-6 82-85
MCA...4-6 85-86
20TH FOX...4-8 79-81
Singles: 7-inch
ABC...3-5 74
CASABLANCA...3-4 82-86
MCA...3-4 85-89
MOTOWN...3-5 75
PARAMOUNT...3-5 74
20TH FOX...3-5 79-81
Picture Sleeves
MCA...3-4 87
20TH FOX...3-5 80
LPs: 10/12-inch
ABC...8-10 75
CASABLANCA...5-8 82-85
MCA...5-8 86-89
MOTOWN (800 series)...8-10 75
MOTOWN (6000 series)...5-8 82
20TH FOX...5-10 79-81
Also see KING DREAM CHORUS & Holiday Crew

MILLS, Stephanie, & Teddy Pendergrass P&R/R&B '81
Singles: 7-inch
20TH FOX...3-5 81
Also see MILLS, Stephanie
Also see PENDERGRASS, Teddy

MILLS, Steve
Singles: 7-inch
LEAF (852 "Nothing to Do with Love")...100-150 64

MILLS, T.W.: see MILS, Telli .W.

MILLS, Yvonne: see SENSATIONS

MILLS BROTHERS P&R '31
Singles: 78 rpm
BANNER...5-10 34
BRUNSWICK...5-10 31-47
CONQUEROR...5-10
DECCA (100 thru 4300 series)...5-10 34-42
DECCA (11000 thru 24000 series)...5-10 42-57
Singles: 7-inch
ABC...3-5 74
DECCA...8-15 50-61
DOT (250 "My Shy Violet")...5-10 68
(Colored vinyl.)
DOT (15000 series)...5-10 58-59
DOT (16000 series)...4-6 60s
DOT (17000 series)...3-6 68-69
MCA...3-5 73-74
PARAMOUNT...3-5 71-72
RANWOOD...3-5 73-76
EPs: 7-inch
DECCA...5-15 50-63
DOT...5-10 58-59
LPs: 10/12-inch
ABC...5-8 74
DECCA (100 series)...10-15 66
DECCA (4000 series)...10-20 61-67
DECCA (5000 series)...20-50 49-55
(10-inch LPs.)
DECCA (7000 series)...20-30 55
DECCA (8000 series)...15-30 55-59
DECCA (75000 series)...5-10 70
DOT...5-20 58-70
EVEREST...5-10 75-77
GNP...5-8 73
MCA...5-10 73
MFP/MCA...5-8 82
PARAMOUNT...5-10 72-74
PICKWICK...5-10 70s
RANWOOD...5-10 74-81
SONGBIRD...6-12 74
VOCALION...5-10 66-69
Members: Herb Mills; Harry Mills; Donald Mills; John Mills.
Also see CROSBY, Bing, & Mills Brothers
Also see FITZGERALD, Ella, & Mills Brothers

MILLS BROTHERS, & Louis Armstrong P&R '37
Singles: 78 rpm
DECCA...5-15 40
Singles: 7-inch
DECCA...4-6 61
Also see ARMSTRONG, Louis

MILLS BROTHERS & COUNT BASIE
LPs: 10/12-inch
ABC...5-8 74
DOT...8-12 68
Also see BASIE, Count
Also see MILLS BROTHERS

MILNER, Jeff, & Embers
(With Bugs Bower Orchestra)
Singles: 7-inch
DALE (113 "No Greater Love")...15-25 59
DALE (114 "Then")...20-30 59

MILNER, Jimmy
Singles: 7-inch
EMBER (1052 "A Place in Your Heart")...35-50 59
YORK (101 "A Place in Your Heart")...50-75 59

MILO, Mad: see MAD MILO

MILO, Skip
(With the Bel Aires—Dynamics)
Singles: 7-inch
A (107 "Smallest Heart")...10-15 60
ARC (4453 "What's Wrong with Me")...15-25 59

MILO & KINGS
Singles: 7-inch
CAB...5-10 62

MILS, Telli .W.
(T.W. Mills; Slim Willet)
Singles: 7-inch
CARLTON (470 "Sneaky Pete")...15-25 58
WINSTON (1017 "Ain't Goin' Home")...50-75 57
WINSTON (1021 "Sneaky Pete")...25-45 58
Note: "Telli W. Mils" is essentially "Slim Willet" spelled backwards.
Also see WILLETT, Slim

MILSAP, Ronnie R&B '65/C&W '73
Singles: 7-inch
BOBLO...3-5 77
CAPITOL...3-4 90s
CHIPS...5-10 70
FESTIVAL...3-5 77
RCA (Black vinyl)...3-5 74-92
RCA (Colored vinyl)...5-10 74-89
(Promotional only.)
SCEPTER...10-20 65-69
W.B. (5405 "It Went to Your Head")...5-10 63
W.B. (8000 series)...3-5 75-76
Picture Sleeves
RCA...3-5 79-85
LPs: 10/12-inch
BUCKBOARD...8-10 76
CRAZY CAJUN...8-10 75
51 WEST...5-8 80s
HSRD...8-10 82
RCA...5-10 74-92
TIME-LIFE...5-10 81
TRIP...8-10 76
W.B....8-10 71-75
Also see PRESLEY, Elvis

MILSAP, Ronnie, & Mike Reid C&W '88
Singles: 7-inch
RCA...3-4 88
Also see REID, Mike

MILSAP, Ronnie, & Kenny Rogers C&W '87
Singles: 7-inch
RCA...3-4 87
Also see MILSAP, Ronnie
Also see ROGERS, Kenny

MILTON, Bobby, & Debutones
Singles: 7-inch
ARROW (1009 "A Place in My Heart")...30-50 50s

MILTON, Buddy, & Twilighters
Singles: 78 rpm
RPM (418 "Please Understand")...50-75 54
RPM (419 "Oo Wah")...15-40 54
Singles: 7-inch
RPM (418 "Please Understand")...200-300 54
RPM (419 "Oo Wah")...100-200 54

MILTON, Fred
Singles: 7-inch
SKYWAY (129 "Barbie Barbie")...25-45 61

MILTON, Roy P&R/R&B '46
(With His Solid Senders; Roy Milton Sextet)
Singles: 78 rpm
DOOTONE...20-30 55-56
DELUXE...15-25 50s
HAMP-TONE...20-40 45
JUKE BOX...20-40 46
KING...10-15 56-57
ROY MILTON (111 "Groovin' with Joe")...20-40 46
ROY MILTON (207 "Them There Eyes")...20-40 46
SPECIALTY...15-25 47-55
Singles: 7-inch
CENCO...10-15 61
DOOTONE (363 "I Cant' Go On")...25-50 55
DOOTONE (369 "You Got Me Reeling and Rocking")...25-50 55
DOOTONE (377 "I Want to Go Home")...25-50 55
DOOTONE (398 "Baby I'm Gone")...25-50 56
KING (4900 & 5000 series)...10-20 56-58
KING (5663 R.M. Blues")...5-10 62
SPACE (310 "Always Want You Around")...8-12
SPECIALTY (414 "Short, Sweet and Snappy")...20-40 50
SPECIALTY (429 "So Tired")...40-60 51
SPECIALTY (436 "Flying Saucer")...30-50 52
SPECIALTY (438 "Night & Day")...30-50 52
SPECIALTY (446 "Believe Me Baby")...50-75 52
SPECIALTY (458 "Some Day")...30-50 53
(Black vinyl.)
SPECIALTY (458 "Some Day")...75-125 53
(Colored vinyl.)
SPECIALTY (464 "Let Me Give You All My Love")...30-50 54
(Black vinyl.)
SPECIALTY (464 "Let Me Give You All My Love")...75-125 54
(Colored vinyl.)
SPECIALTY (480 thru 545)...20-30 54-55
SPECIALTY (700 series)...4-6 69
WARWICK (549 "Early in the Morning")...10-20 60
WARWICK (682 "So Tired")...10-20 60
LPs: 10/12-inch
KENT (554 "Great Roy Milton")...40-60 63
Also see HIGGINS, Chuck, & Roy Milton
Also see HOWARD, Camille, Trio
Also see HUMES, Helen

MILTON, Roy, & Mickey Champion
Singles: 78 rpm
DOOTONE (378 "Bam a Lam")...20-30 55
Singles: 7-inch
DOOTONE (378 "Bam a Lam")...25-50 55
Also see CHAMPION, Micky

MILTON, Roy / Joe Liggins
Singles: 78 rpm
SPECIALTY....10-20 53
Singles: 7-inch
SPECIALTY....20-25 53
Also see LIGGINS, Joe
Also see MILTON, Roy

MILWAUKEE SLIM
Singles: 7-inch
BLUE TOWN.... 5-8
STAR TOWN.... 8-12

MIMMS, Garnet P&R/R&B/LP '63
(With the Enchanters; with Trucking Co.)
Singles: 7-inch
ARISTA.... 3-5 77
GSF.... 3-6 72
LIBERTY.... 3-4 81
U.A..... 8-15 63-66
VEEP.... 4-8 66
VERVE.... 5-10 68-70
Picture Sleeves
U.A..... 5-10 63
LPs: 10/12-inch
ARISTA (4153 "Garnett Mimms Has It All").... 8-12 78
GUEST STAR (1907 "Garnet Mimms")....20-25 64
U.A. (3305 "Cry Baby")....25-40 63
(Monaural.)
U.A. (3396 "As Long As I Have You")....25-40 64
(Monaural.)
U.A. (3498 "I'll Take Good Care of You")....35-50 66
(Monaural.)
U.A. (6305 "Cry Baby")....35-50 63
(Stereo.)
U.A. (6396 "As Long As I Have You")....35-50 64
(Stereo.)
U.A. (6498 "I'll Take Good Care of You")....35-50 66
(Stereo.)
Members: Garnet Mimms; Samuel Bell; Charles Boyer; Zola Pearnell.
Also see ENCHANTERS
Also see GAINORS

MIMMS, Garnet / Maurice Monk
LPs: 10/12-inch
GRAND PRIX (424 "Garnett Mimms & Maurice Monk")....15-20 63
Also see MIMMS, Garnet

MIMS, T.S., & Mystics
(With "Vocal by Sabu")
Singles: 7-inch
COIN (1500 "Love You Betty")....50-100 59

MINA P&R '61
(With Her Orchestra "I Solitari")
Singles: 7-inch
CHIRP.... 4-8
TIME.... 4-8 61

MINCY TWINS
Singles: 7-inch
GROOVE.... 4-8 64
PHILIPS.... 4-8 63

MIND EXPANDERS
LPs: 10/12-inch
DOT (3773 "What's Happening")..50-100 67
(Monaural.)
DOT (25773 "What's Happening")..30-40 67
(Stereo.)

MIND GARAGE
Singles: 7-inch
RCA.... 4-8 69
LPs: 10/12-inch
RCA....10-20 69-70

MIND READERS
Singles: 7-inch
VILLAGE SOUNDS.... 5-10

MIND'S EYE
Singles: 7-inch
JOX (58 "Help, I'm Lost")....15-25 67
Also see CHILDREN

MIND'S EYE
Singles: 7-inch
AMY (050 "Mystic Woman")....10-20 69

MINDBENDERS P&R/LP '66
Singles: 7-inch
FONTANA.... 5-10 65-67
LPs: 10/12-inch
FONTANA (27554 "A Groovy Kind of Love")....30-40 66
(Monaural. With *Ashes to Ashes*)
FONTANA (27554 "A Groovy Kind of Love")....20-30 66
(Monaural. Without *Ashes to Ashes*)
FONTANA (67554 "A Groovy Kind of Love")....30-40 66
(Stereo. With *Ashes to Ashes*)
FONTANA (67554 "A Groovy Kind of Love")....20-30 66
(Stereo. Without *Ashes to Ashes*)
Members: Eric Stewart; Bob Lang; Ric Rothwell.
Also see FONTANA, Wayne, & Mindbenders

MINEO, Sal P&R '57
Singles: 78 rpm
EPIC....15-25 57
Singles: 7-inch
DECCA.... 4-8 64
EPIC....10-20 57-59
FONTANA.... 4-8 65
Picture Sleeves
EPIC....15-25 57-59
EPs: 7-inch
EPIC (7187 "Sal Mineo")....25-45 57
EPIC (7194/7195 "Sal")....25-45 58
(Price is for either volume.)
EPIC (7194 "Sal")....20-30 58
EPIC (7204 "Souvenirs of Summertime")....20-30 58
LPs: 10/12-inch
EPIC (3405 "Sal")....50-100 58

MINETS
Singles: 7-inch
ROCK-IT....5-10

MINETS OF ENGLAND
Singles: 7-inch
DCP.... 5-8 65

MINETTE, Corina
Singles: 7-inch
ABC-PAR....5-10 60

MINI, Leo
Singles: 7-inch
NICE.... 3-5 77

MINI MAX
Singles: 7-inch
SOUL STAR....5-10

MINIATURE MEN P&R '62
Singles: 7-inch
DOLTON (57 "Baby Elephant Walk")....5-10 62
Also see LEVINE, Hank

MINIMI, Ross
Singles: 7-inch
GULFSTREAM (7269 "Oh Janet")....100-200

MINIMUM DAILY REQUIREMENTS
Singles: 7-inch
TOWER.... 4-8 67

MINISTRY D&D/LP '83
Singles: 12-inch
ARISTA.... 4-6 83
SIRE.... 4-6 86
WAX TRAX.... 4-6 85
Singles: 7-inch
ARISTA.... 3-4 83
SIRE.... 3-4 86-89
WAX TRAX.... 3-4 85
LPs: 10/12-inch
ARISTA.... 5-8 83
SIRE.... 5-8 86-89

MINK DE VILLE LP '77
Singles: 7-inch
ATLANTIC.... 3-4 81-84
CAPITOL.... 3-5 77-78
LPs: 10/12-inch
ATLANTIC.... 5-8 81-83
CAPITOL.... 5-8 77-82

MINNEAPOLIS GENIUS 94 EAST R&B '86
Singles: 7-inch
HOT PINK.... 3-4 86

MINNELLI, Liza LP '64
Singles: 7-inch
A&M.... 3-6 68-71
ABC.... 3-5 73
CADENCE....5-10 63
CAPITOL (4900 thru 5700 series)....5-10 63-65
COLUMBIA.... 3-5 72-75
U.A..... 3-5 77
LPs: 10/12-inch
A&M....10-15 68-73
ABC (752 "Cabaret")....10-15 72
(Soundtrack. With Joel Grey.)
ARISTA (4069 "Lucky Lady")....8-10 76
(Soundtrack.)
CADENCE (4012 "Best Foot Forward")....30-40 63
(Monaural. Original cast.)
CADENCE (24012 "Best Foot Forward")....40-60 63
(Stereo. Original cast.)
CAPITOL (T-2100 and T-2400 series)....10-20 64-66
(Monaural.)
CAPITOL (ST-2100 and ST-2400 series)....15-25 64-66
(Stereo.)
CAPITOL (2200 series).... 5-8 78
CAPITOL (11000 series)....5-10 72-78
COLUMBIA....8-15 72-77
DRG (6101 "The Act")....8-10 78
EPIC.... 5-8 89
MCA (752 "Cabaret").... 5-8
(Soundtrack. With Joel Grey.)
STET....8-10
TELARC....10-12 87
Also see GARLAND, Judy, & Liza Minnelli

MINNESODA
Singles: 7-inch
CAPITOL.... 3-5 72
LPs: 10/12-inch
CAPITOL....8-10 72

MINNESOTA MARV & VANGUARDS
Singles: 7-inch
CUCA (1023 "Nobody's Darling But Mine")....25-35 61
LINDY (1551 "Sweet Little Wife")...40-60 60s
Picture Sleeves
LINDY....40-60 60s
Also see BLIHOVDE, Marv
Also see DENNIS, Marv

MINNESOTA MARV & ED CREE
Singles: 7-inch
CUCA (1025 "White Lightning")....25-35 61
Also see DENNIS, Marv, & Ed Cree
Also see MINNESOTA MARV & VANGUARDS

MINNIE PEARL C&W '66
Singles: 78 rpm
RCA....5-10 54-56
Singles: 7-inch
RCA....8-15 54-56
STARDAY....4-6 66
LPs: 10/12-inch
NASHVILLE....10-15 60s
PICKWICK/HILLTOP....10-15 60s
STARDAY (224 thru 397)....15-25 63-66
SUNSET....10-15 67
Also see JONES, Grandpa / Minnie Pearl
Also see STEVENS, Ray

MINOGUE, Kylie P&R/LP '88
Singles: 7-inch
GEFFEN....3-4 88
Picture Sleeves
GEFFEN....3-4 88
LPs: 10/12-inch
GEFFEN....5-8 88

MINOR, Dorothy
Singles: 7-inch
TEX (104 "Bye Bye Baby")....25-35 58

MINOR CHORDS
Singles: 7-inch
FLICK (5 "Fire")....15-25 59
FLICK (6 "Don't Let Me Down")....25-35 59
FLICK (9 "Let Me")....25-35 59
LU PINE (112 "Many a Day")....50-75 62
Also see ELMO, Sunnie, & Minor Chords
Also see HENDERSON, C., & Minor Chords

MINOR DETAIL P&R/LP '83
Singles: 7-inch
POLYDOR....3-4 83-84
Picture Sleeves
POLYDOR....3-4 83
LPs: 10/12-inch
POLYDOR....5-8 83
Members: John Hughes; Willie Hughes.

MINORBOPS
Singles: 78 rpm
LAMP....150-200 57
Singles: 7-inch
LAMP (2012 "Need You Tonight")....150-200 57

MINORS
Singles: 78 rpm
CELESTE (3007 "Jerry")....300-400 57
Singles: 7-inch
CELESTE (3007 "Jerry")....300-400 57

MINSTRELS THREE
LPs: 10/12-inch
WING....12-15 63

MINT, Little Eddie
Singles: 7-inch
MEMO....10-15 59

MINT JULEP
Singles: 7-inch
TY (7772 "Riptide")....10-15

MINT JULEPS
Singles: 78 rpm
HERALD (481 "Bells of Love")....40-60 56
Singles: 7-inch
HERALD (481 "Bells of Love")...100-150 56
(Yellow label with script logo in flag. Has "45 rpm on both sides of hole.)
HERALD (481 "Bells of Love")....15-25 60s
(Has "45 rpm on left side only.)
Members: William Terrel; Charles Thomas; Al Clarke; George Poitier; Emra Clemmons.

MINT TATOO
Singles: 7-inch
DOT....5-8 69
LPs: 10/12-inch
DOT (25918 "Mint Tatoo")....15-25 69
Members: Bruce Stephens; Burns Kellogg.
Also see BLUE CHEER

MINTER, Pat C&W '89
Singles: 7-inch
KILLER....3-4 89
SHOWCASE....4-8 79

MINTS: see COPELAND, Ken / Mints

MINTZ, Junier
(Frank Zappa)
Singles: 7-inch
REPRISE/STRAIGHT (1027 "Tears Began to Fall")....20-30 71
Also see ZAPPA, Frank

MINUTE MEN
Singles: 7-inch
CAPITOL....4-8 61
ORIGINAL SOUND....4-8 64
RUST....4-8 64

MINUTE MEN
Singles: 7-inch
ARGO....5-10 64

MINUTE MEN
Singles: 7-inch
PARROT....4-8 67
Members: Don Wetzel; Terry Wetzel.

MINUTE MEN
Singles: 7-inch
HOUR GLASS....4-8 69

MINUTE MEN
LPs: 10/12-inch
SST....5-8 83

MINUTEMEN
Singles: 7-inch
MGM....5-8 63

MINUTEMEN
Singles: 7-inch
KELTONE INT'L....4-8

MINZ, Arty, & Ellie Shepherd
Singles: 7-inch
CUCA (6661 "Which One of Us Is to Blame")....10-20 66

MIRABAI LP '75
LPs: 10/12-inch
ATLANTIC....5-10 75

MIRACLE MEN
Singles: 7-inch
CORAL (62022 "The Gander")....8-12 58

MIRACLE WORKERS
Singles: 7-inch
GET HIP....3-4 89

MIRACLES
Singles: 78 rpm
CASH (1008 "You're an Angel")....50-75 55
Singles: 7-inch
CASH (1008 "You're an Angel") 100-150 55

MIRACLES
Singles: 78 rpm
BATON (210 "A Lovers' Chant")....50-75 55
Singles: 7-inch
BATON (210 "A Lovers' Chant")....100-125 55

MIRACLES P&R '59
(Smokey Robinson & Miracles; featuring Bill Smokey Robinson; featuring Billy Griffin)
Singles: 12-inch
COLUMBIA....4-6 77
Singles: 7-inch
CHESS (119 "Bad Girl")....3-5 84
CHESS (1734 "Bad Girl")....25-50 59
(Black label.)
CHESS (1734 "Bad Girl")....10-20 59
(Blue label.)
CHESS (1768 "All I Want")....25-35 60
COLUMBIA....3-5 77-78
END (1016 "Got a Job")....45-55 58
END (1029 "Money")....40-50 58
(No mention of Roulette Records.)
END (1029 "Money")....30-40 58
(Has "A Division of Roulette Records Inc".)
END (1084 "Money")....10-15 61
MOTOWN (G1 "Bad Girl")....500-1000 59
MOTOWN (400 & 500 series)....3-5 80s
MOTOWN (2207 "Bad Girl")....400-450 59
MOTOWN/TOPPS (11 "Shop Around")....50-75 67
(Topps Chewing Gum promotional item. Single-sided, cardboard flexi, picture disc. Issued with generic paper sleeve.)
ROULETTE....3-5 70s
STANDARD GROOVE (13090 "I Care About Detroit")....150-200 68
(Tamla logo at top, Artist credit at bottom. Promotional issue only.)
STANDARD GROOVE (13090 "I Care About Detroit")....100-150 68
(Artist credit at top. Promotional issue only.)
TAMLA (009 "The Christmas Song")....100-200 63
(Promotional issue only.)
TAMLA (54028 "The Feeling Is So Fine"/"You Can Depend on Me")....300-400 60
(With common version of *You Can Depend on Me.*)
TAMLA (54028 "The Feeling Is So Fine"/"You Can Depend on Me")....400-500 60
(With alternate take of *You Can Depend on Me*, Can be identified by the letter "A" following the identification number in the trail-off.)
TAMLA (54028 "Way Over There"/"Depend on Me")....100-200 60
(With alternate take of *Way Over There*, sans strings. Not available elsewhere.)
TAMLA (54028 "Way Over There"/"Depend on Me")....25-50 60
(With the hit version of *Way Over There*, the same as is heard on their Tamla LPs.)
TAMLA (54034 "Shop Around") .100-125 60
(Horizontal lines across top half of label. Has an alternate take of *Shop Around.* Has either "H55518 A-2" or "45-L1 37003" etched in the trail-off.)
TAMLA (54034 "Shop Around")....35-50 60
(No horizontal lines and Tamla globe logo at top. Has an alternate, slower take of *Shop Around.* Etched in trail-off is "H55518 A-2.")
TAMLA (54034 "Shop Around")....10-20 60
(Has the hit version of *Shop Around.* Etched in trail-off is "L1" or "ARP L-1.")
TAMLA (54036 "Ain't It Baby")....50-75 61
TAMLA (54044 "Mighty Good Lovin'")....25-50 61
TAMLA (54048 "You Gotta Pay Some Dues")....50-100 61
(Note title variation.)
TAMLA (54048 "Everybody's Gotta Pay Some Dues")....25-50 61
TAMLA (54053 "What's So Good About Goodbye")....15-25 62
(Black vinyl.)
TAMLA (54053 "What's So Good About Goodbye")....20-30 62
(Colored vinyl. Promotional issue only.)
TAMLA (54059 "I'll Try Something New")....10-20 62
TAMLA (54069 "Way Over There")....10-20 62
TAMLA (54073 thru 54184)....5-10 62-69
TAMLA (54189 "Point It Out")....4-8 69
(Black vinyl.)
TAMLA (54189 "Point It Out")....15-20 69
(Colored vinyl. Promotional issue only.)
TAMLA (54194 thru 54268)....3-5 70-76
Picture Sleeves
TAMLA (54044 "Mighty Good Lovin'")....75-125 61
TAMLA (54048 "Everybody's Gotta Pay Some Dues")....50-75 61
TAMLA (54059 "I'll Try Something New")....40-60 62
TAMLA (54098 "I Like It Like That")....15-25 62
TAMLA (54127 thru 54194)....10-20 65-70
EPs: 7-inch
TAMLA ("Greatest Hits from the Beginning")....30-50 66
(Selection number not known.)
TAMLA (60267 "Going to a Go Go")....30-50 66
(Juke box issue only. Includes title strips.)
LPs: 10/12-inch
COLUMBIA....8-10 77-78
IMPERIAL HOUSE....8-12 79
MOTOWN (Except 793 & 8238)....5-10 82-84
MOTOWN (793 "Anthology")....12-18 74
MOTOWN (8238 "Greatest Hits from the Beginning")....8-12
NATURAL RESOURCES....5-10 78
TAMLA (220 "Hi! We're the Miracles")....250-500 61
(White label.)
TAMLA (220 "Hi! We're the Miracles")....250-350 61
(Yellow label with globes.)
TAMLA (223 "Cookin' with the Miracles")....250-500 61
(White label.)
TAMLA (223 "Cookin' with the Miracles")....200-300 62
(Yellow label with globes.)
TAMLA (230 "I'll Try Something New")....250-500 62
(White label.)
TAMLA (230 "I'll Try Something New")....100-150 62
(Yellow label with globes.)
TAMLA (236 "Christmas with the Miracles")....150-200 62
TAMLA (238 "The Fabulous Miracles")....150-200 63
TAMLA (238 "You Really Got a Hold on Me")....75-125 63
(Reissue with new title.)
TAMLA (241 "On Stage")....50-100 63
TAMLA (245 "Mickey's Monkey")....50-75 63
(Monaural.)
TAMLA (245 "Mickey's Monkey").75-125 63
(Stereo.)
TAMLA (254 "Greatest Hits from the Beginning")....25-35 63
(Monaural.)
TAMLA (254 "Greatest Hits from the Beginning")....35-45 63
(Stereo.)
TAMLA (267 "Going to a Go Go")..40-50 65
(Tamla globe label.)
TAMLA (271 thru 297)....15-30 66-70
TAMLA (301 thru 344)....10-20 71-76
Members: William "Smokey" Robinson; Pete Moore; Bobby Rogers; Ron White; Claudette Rogers; Billy Griffin; Marv Tarplin.
Also see GRIFFIN, Billy
Also see MARVELETTES / Mary Wells / Miracles / Marvin Gaye
Also see McCULLERS, Mickey
Also see ROBINSON, Smokey
Also see RON & BILL

MIRAN, Wayne, & Rush Release R&B '75
Singles: 7-inch
ROULETTE....3-5 75

MIRANDA, Billy
Singles: 7-inch
CHECKER (957 "Go Ahead")....10-15 60
QUEENS (721 "You Could've Had a Good Time")....50-75

MIRANDA, Bob
(With the Happenings)
Singles: 7-inch
ALLEGIANCE (75708 "Oh Diane")...5-10 89
(Promotional issue only.)
B.T. PUPPY....4-8 68
L.A. ROCK....4-8 87
MIDLAND INT'L....3-5 77
Also see HAPPENINGS

MIRANDA, Carmen P&R '41
(With the Bando Da Lua)
Singles: 78 rpm
DECCA....5-15 39-53
MGM....10-20
Picture Sleeves
DECCA....20-30 39
EPs: 7-inch
DECCA (2066 "Carmen Miranda")....15-25 53

MIRANDA, Carmen, & Andrews Sisters P&R '50
Singles: 78 rpm
DECCA....4-8 50
Also see ANDREWS SISTERS
Also see MIRANDA, Carmen

MIRANDA, Ralph
(Ralph Miranda & Del Toro's)
Singles: 7-inch
ROGO (1025 "The Flame")........100-200 59
ROGO ("A Little Bit of Love").........25-50 61
(Selection number not known.)
ROGO ("Angel of My Dreams").......25-50 62
(Selection number not known.)

MIRETTES *P&R/R&B '68*
Singles: 7-inch
MIRWOOD.......................................4-8 66
REVUE..4-8 67-69
UNI...3-6 69
LPs: 10/12-inch
REVUE...12-18 68
UNI..10-15 69
Members: Vanetta Fields; Jessie Smith; Robbie Montgomery.
Also see IKETTES

MIRIJIAN, Craig
Singles: 7-inch
W.B. 3-5 80
LPs: 10/12-inch
W.B. 5-10 80

MIRROR, Danny
Singles: 7-inch
REDWOOD.......................................4-6 78

MI-SEX
Singles: 7-inch
EPIC...3-5 80
LPs: 10/12-inch
EPIC...5-10 80

MISFITS
("Misfits & Band")
Singles: 7-inch
ARIES (7-10-4 "Midnight Star")..100-200 61
HUSH (105 "Give Me Your Heart")..............................100-200 61

MISFITS
Singles: 7-inch
JOEY (117 "Chicago Confidential")...........................10-15 61

MISFITS
Singles: 7-inch
IMPERIAL......................................5-10 64
SOUND STAGE 7..............................4-8 65

MISHAPS
Singles: 7-inch
HEMPHILL ("Come On Up")..........35-55 60s
(Selection number not known.)

MISS ABRAMS: see ABRAMS, Miss

MISS COUNTRY SLIM: see COUNTRY SLIM

MISS L.L. & 3 Mice
Singles: 7-inch
SKYWAY...4-8 63

MISS LA VELL
Singles: 7-inch
DUKE...5-10 59-65

MISS NICOLLET
Singles: 7-inch
SHAR...5-10 60

MISS PEACHES
(Elsie Griner)
Singles: 78 rpm
GROOVE...10-20 54
RCA...10-15 56
Singles: 7-inch
GROOVE (0009 "Calling Moody Field, Part 1")..15-25 54
RCA...10-20 56

MISS RHAPSODY
(Viola Underhill)
Singles: 78 rpm
SAVOY...5-10 44

MISS SHARECROPPER
(Dolores Williams)
Singles: 78 rpm
NATIONAL.......................................15-25 47

MISS THANG *R&B '86*
Singles: 12-inch
TOMMY BOY 4-6 86

MISS TONI FISHER: see FISHER, Miss Toni

MISSA DISCO
LPs: 10/12-inch
ARIOLA AMERICA...........................5-8 79

MISSILES
Singles: 7-inch
LAWN...5-10 63

MISSING LINKS
Singles: 7-inch
ROSCOE (418 "I Cried Goodbye").15-25 65

MISSING LINKS
Singles: 7-inch
DISCOVERY (102265 "You've Got Your Posies On")..15-25 65
SOCK-IT (203 "Don't Hang Me Up")..15-25 65

MISSING LINKS
Singles: 7-inch
AMY (960 "I Told You I Loved You")..5-10 66
JOWAR (105 "I Told You I Loved You")..25-35 66
Members: George Mesecke; Al Vertucci; Joe Parisi; Larry Rubenstein; Dennis Raffelock.

MISSING LINKS
Singles: 7-inch
PYRO (53 "Midnight Hour")...........10-15 66

MISSING LINKS
Singles: 7-inch
PARIS TOWER (115 "Where Were You Last Night")..15-25 67
SIGNET (931 "You Hypnotize Me")..10-15 67

MISSING LYNX
Singles: 7-inch
DYNO-VOICE (227 "Behind Locked Doors")..10-20 66

MISSING LYNX
Singles: 7-inch
UNITED SOUNDS (100 "Hang Around")..10-20 67

MISSING PERSONS *P&R/LP '82*
Singles: 12-inch
CAPITOL...4-6 82-86
Singles: 7-inch
CAPITOL...3-4 82-86
Picture Sleeves
CAPITOL...3-5 82-84
EPs: 7-inch
KOMOS...5-8 80
LPs: 10/12-inch
CAPITOL...5-8 82-86
Members: Dale Bozzio; Terry Bozzio; Warren Cuccurullo.
Also see BECK, Jeff
Also see DURAN DURAN
Also see MOTHERS of INVENTION

MISSION *R&B '74*
Singles: 7-inch
PARAMOUNT....................................3-5 74

MISSION *R&B '87*
Singles: 7-inch
COLUMBIA.......................................3-4 87-88
Member: Wayne Hussey.
Also see DEAD OR ALIVE
Also see MISSION

MISSION BELLS
Singles: 7-inch
LONDON..4-8 65

MISSION OF BURMA
Singles: 7-inch
ACE of HEARTS...............................3-4 81

MISSION U.K. *LP '87*
LPs: 10/12-inch
MERCURY 5-8 87-90

MISSISSIPPI MUD MASHERS
Singles: 78 rpm
BLUEBIRD.......................................25-50 35-37

MISSISSIPPI SHEIKS
LPs: 10/12-inch
MAMLISH..10-12 72
Member: Walter Vinson.

MISSLES
(Cadillacs)
Singles: 7-inch
NOVEL (200 "Space Ship")...........15-20 60
Also see CADILLACS

MISSLES
Singles: 7-inch
RD GLOBE (004 "Swanee River Rock")..4-8

MISSOURI *LP '79*
Singles: 7-inch
PANAMA..3-5 78
POLYDOR..3-5 79
LPs: 10/12-inch
PANAMA..8-12 77
POLYDOR..5-10 79

MISTAKES
Singles: 7-inch
LO-FI (2312 "Chapel Bells")..........30-50 59
(Black vinyl.)
LO-FI (2312 "Chapel Bells")..........10-15
(Colored vinyl.)

MR. BASSMAN: see MARTY & SYMBOLS

MR. BEAR
(With His Bearcats; Teddy McRae)
Singles: 78 rpm
GROOVE 10-15 55
KING..10-15 55
Singles: 7-inch
GROOVE (0125 "How Come").......20-30 55
GROOVE (0138 "Peek-a-Boo")......20-30 55
GROOVE (0150 "Mr. Bear Comes to Town")..20-30 55
KING..20-30 55
Session: King Curtis; Mickey Baker; Sam Taylor; Sticks Evans; Teacho Wiltshire; Milt Hinton; Al Lucas.
Also see BAKER, Mickey
Also see KING CURTIS
Also see TAYLOR, Sam "The Man"
Also see WILTSHIRE, Teacho

MR. BIG *P&R '77*
Singles: 7-inch
ARISTA...3-4 77
ATLANTIC..3-4 91
LPs: 10/12-inch
ARISTA...5-10 76
ATLANTIC..5-8 89
Members: Eric Martin.
Also see MARTIN, Eric

MR. BLOE
Singles: 7-inch
DJM (70017 "Sinful")......................8-12 69

MR. BO
(Mr. Bo & His Blues Boys)
Singles: 7-inch
BIG D..5-8 66
GOLD TOP.......................................15-25
NORTHERN......................................5-10 60

MR. BOO-SARD
Singles: 7-inch
HOLLYWOOD....................................5-10 67

MR. CLEAN
Singles: 7-inch
ORIGINAL SOUND (40 "Mr. Clean")..25-50 63
Also see ZAPPA, Frank

MR. CLEAN & CLEANERS
Singles: 7-inch
AUDIO...5-10 60s
CAMELOT..5-10 60s

MR. ECTOMY
Singles: 7-inch
NDSD (006 "Brains")........................8-12 89
(Head-shaped picture disc.)

MR. FLOOD'S PARTY
LPs: 10/12-inch
COTILLION.......................................10-15 69

MR. G. & HIS G-ETTS
Singles: 7-inch
HOT FUDGE.....................................3-4 84
(Flexible picture disc.)
Members: Laimons Juris G; Jim Lacefield; Mark Mattson; Lolita Putmanis.

MR. GASSER & WEIRDOS
Singles: 7-inch
CAPITOL ("Doin' the Surfing"/ "Finksville")..................................5-10 64
(Bonus promotional single, packaged with an LP by the Super Stocks.)
LPs: 10/12-inch
CAPITOL (T-2010 "Hot Rod Hootenanny")....................................30-50 63
(Monaural.)
CAPITOL (ST-2010 "Hot Rod Hootenanny")....................................40-60 63
(Stereo.)
CAPITOL (T-2057 "Rods 'N' Ratfinks")..40-60 63
(Monaural.)
CAPITOL (ST-2057 "Rods 'N' Ratfinks")..50-70 63
(Stereo.)
CAPITOL (T-2114 "Surfink")..........40-60 63
(Monaural. With *Midnight Run*, a bonus single by the Super Stocks.)
CAPITOL (T-2114 "Surfink")..........35-55 63
(Monaural. Without bonus single.)
CAPITOL (ST-2114 "Surfink")........50-70 63
(Stereo. With *Midnight Run*, a bonus single by the Super Stocks.)
CAPITOL (ST-2114 "Surfink")........45-55 63
(Stereo. Without bonus single.)
Also see DALE, Dick / Jerry Cole / Super Stocks / Mr. Gasser & Weirdos
Also see SUPER STOCKS

MR. GLOB
Singles: 7-inch
JACKPOT (48003 "Happy Hugo")....8-12 58

MR. GOON BONES & MR. FORD *P&R '49*
Singles: 78 rpm
CRYSTALETTE..................................4-8 49-56
Singles: 7-inch
CRYSTALETTE..................................5-10 56
DOT..4-8 59

MR. GOOGLE EYES: see AUGUST, Joseph

MISTER HIPP
Singles: 7-inch
U.S.A. (867 "Sloopy and the Red Moron")..15-20 67
(Single-sided. Promotional issue only.)

MR. HONEY
Singles: 7-inch
ARTIST (102 "Build a Cave").........10-20

MR. JIM & RHYTHM MACHINE
Singles: 7-inch
DATE..4-6 68
WIZDOM..3-5 71

MR "K" & KAROL
Singles: 7-inch
BATTLE (8571 "Brave Bobby Campbell")....................................8-12

MR. LEE
(Mr. Lee & Cherokees)
Singles: 7-inch
ADDIT...10-20 60
IMPERIAL..10-15 63
SURE SHOT.....................................5-10 65
WINTER (501 "The Decision").......25-35 60

MR. LEE & EL CAMINOS
Singles: 7-inch
NOLTA..10-15 64

MR. LEE & FRANK ANDRADE 5
Singles: 7-inch
SKYLARK (503 "Hey Mrs. Jones") 20-30 64

MR. LUCKY & GAMBLERS
Singles: 7-inch
DOT (16930 "Take a Look at Me") 10-20 66
JERDEN (799 "Take a Look at Me")...15-25 66
(Some question the existence of this number. We cannot yet confirm its release.)
KASINO (1001 "New Orleans")......15-25 65
PANORAMA (37 "Take a Look at Me")..10-20 66
PANORAMA (52 "Alice Designs")..10-15 66
UNITED INT'L (1001 "Searching") 10-20 65
UNITED INT'L (4404 "Koko Joe") 10-20 66
Members: Willy Reiner; Alan Gunter; Jim Dunlap.

MR. MaGOO: see BACKUS, Jim

MR. MILLER: see MILLER, Mr.

MR. MISTER *P&R/LP '84*
Singles: 7-inch
RCA...3-4 84-87
Picture Sleeves
RCA...3-4 85-87
LPs: 10/12-inch
RCA...5-8 84-87
Members: Richard Page; Pat Mastelotto; Steve Farris; Steve George; Buzz Feiten.
Also see LARSEN - FEITEN BAND
Also see PAGES

MR. P.T. & PARTY TIMERS
Singles: 7-inch
FEDERAL...5-10 61

MR. PERCOLATOR
Singles: 7-inch
WAX WELL......................................4-8 68

MR. PERCY
Singles: 78 rpm
DOT (1205 "Full of Misery")..........15-25 54
Singles: 7-inch
DOT (1205 "Full of Misery")..........25-50 54

MR. PITIFUL
Singles: 7-inch
JOSIE...4-8 68

MR. SAD HEAD
Singles: 78 rpm
RCA...25-50 52-53
Singles: 7-inch
RCA (4938 "Butcher Boy")...........50-100 52
RCA (5089 "Hot Weather Blues") ..40-60 52
RCA (5230 "I'm High")..................40-60 53
RCA (5388 "Make Haste")..............40-60 53

MR. SAKS
Singles: 7-inch
LE CAMP..5-10 61

MR. SHORT STUFF
LPs: 10/12-inch
SPIVEY...15-20

MR. SHORT STUFF & BIG JOE WILLIAMAS
LPs: 10/12-inch
SPIVEY...15-20
Also see MR. SHORT STUFF
Also see WILLIAMS, Big Joe, & Short Stuff Macon

MR. SOUL BOBO: see BOBO, Mr. Soul

MR. STRINGBEAN
(With Joe Morris & His Orchestra)
Singles: 78 rpm
HERALD...15-25 53
Singles: 7-inch
HERALD (418 "Pass the Juice, Miss Lucy")..20-30 53
(Black vinyl.)
HEARLD (418 "Pass the Juice, Miss Lucy")..40-60 53
(Colored vinyl.)
Also see MORRIS, Joe, & His Orchestra

MR. SWING
(With Bobby Plater's Orchestra)
Singles: 78 rpm
BULLET (327 "Beer Bottle Boogie")..50-75 50

MR. T. *R&B '84*
(Lawrence Tero)
Singles: 12-inch
COLUMBIA (9C9-39911 "Mr. T's Commandments")..............................8-12 84
(Picture disc.)
Singles: 7-inch
COLUMBIA......................................3-4 84
MCA...3-4 84
Picture Sleeves
COLUMBIA......................................3-4 84
LPs: 10/12-inch
COLUMBIA......................................5-8 84
MCA...5-8 84

MR. TEARS
Singles: 7-inch
FOUR J (509 "Don't Lead Me On")..20-30 63

MR. TWELVE STRING
(Glen Campbell)
Singles: 7-inch
WORLD PACIFIC.............................5-10 65
Also see CAMPBELL, Glen

MR. UNDERTAKER: see FOUR DEUCES / Mr. Undertaker

MR. X
Singles: 7-inch
VITA (152 "Rock Doc")..................25-50 57

MR. ZULU & WARRIORS
Singles: 7-inch
SCORE (7-11 "Anna") 250-500
(Colored vinyl.)

MISTERS
Singles: 7-inch
CHANTE (1002 "Too Many Girls") 20-30 59
(First issue.)
DECCA (31026 "Too Many Girls") 10-15 59

MISTERS VIRTUE
Singles: 7-inch
VECTOR (4979 "Captured")..........20-30

MISTICS
Singles: 7-inch
CAPRI (631 "Memories")................25-35 63

MISTRESS *P&R/LP '79*
Singles: 7-inch
RSO...3-5 79
LPs: 10/12-inch
RSO...5-10 79

MISTY & Do-Drops
Singles: 7-inch
IMPERIAL..8-12 63

MISTY / Jimmy Ellis
EPs: 7-inch
SUN (1136 "D.O.A.")..........................3-6 77
(Jimmy Ellis is not credited, but is the singer on side 2 (*That's All Right* and *Blue Moon of Kentucky*). Not issued with a special cover.)
Also see ELLIS, Jimmy

MISTY BLUES
Singles: 7-inch
STATURE (5-7 "I Feel No Pain") ... 15-25 66

MISTY WIZARDS
Singles: 7-inch
REPRISE...4-8 67

MISUNDERSTOOD
Singles: 7-inch
BLUES SOUND (13 "You Don't Have to Go")...20-25 60s
Member: Glenn Campbell.
Also see GOLDTONES

MITCH & GAIL
Singles: 7-inch
REPRISE...5-8 66
Member: Mitchell Torok.
Also see TOROK, Mitchell

MITCH & ECHOS
Singles: 7-inch
BETHLEHEM....................................5-8 63

MITCH & MISTYS
Singles: 7-inch
CHARAY..5-10 66
MGH...4-8

MITCH & PACEMAKERS
Singles: 7-inch
ACCA (106 "Mitch's Boogie")..........8-12

MITCHAM, Ray
Singles: 7-inch
UNITED SOUTHERN ARTISTS......5-10 61-62

MITCHEL, Lonnie
Singles: 7-inch
IVORY...10-15 61

MITCHELL, Adam
LPs: 10/12-inch
W.B. 5-8 79

MITCHELL, Arnold
Singles: 7-inch
NEWTOWN......................................5-8 64

MITCHELL, Barry
Singles: 7-inch
PHILIPS..5-8 68

MITCHELL, Billy *R&B '69*
(Billy Mitchell Group)
Singles: 78 rpm
ATLANTIC.......................................50-75 51-52
Singles: 7-inch
ATLANTIC (933 "My Love, My Desire")......................................150-250 51
CALLA (165 "Oh Happy Day")........5-10 69
JUBILEE (5400 "Short Skirts")..........8-12 61
POPLAR (105 "Bottomless Pit") 20-30 57
U.A. (235 "Call to Me")....................8-12 60
WARWICK (501 "It Doesn't Matter to Me")..10-15 59
Also see CLOVERS
Also see MORRIS, Joe, & His Orchestra

MITCHELL, Billy
Singles: 7-inch
IMPERIAL (5520 "Satellite Beep Bop")..10-20 58

MITCHELL, Billy
(With Hattie Noel)
Singles: 7-inch
DOOTO..5-8 60s
EPs: 7-inch
DOOTONE (210 "Party Songs") 10-15 56
LPs: 10/12-inch
DOOTONE (212 "Songs for Fun")...20-30 56

MITCHELL, Blue
Singles: 7-inch
BLUENOTE 4-6
MAINSTREAM 4-6 73
LPs: 10/12-inch
MAINSTREAM 5-10 74
Members: Blue Mitchell; Junior Cook; Chick Corea; Gene Taylor; Aloysius Foster.

MITCHELL, Bobby
Singles: 78 rpm
DERBY 10-15 49
MERCURY 10-15 49

MITCHELL, Bobby R&B '56
(With the Toppers; with Basie-Ites)
Singles: 78 rpm
IMPERIAL 25-50 53-57
Singles: 7-inch
IMPERIAL (5236 "I'm Cryin' ") 250-500 53
IMPERIAL (5250 "One Friday Morning") 250-500 53
IMPERIAL (5270 "Baby's Gone") .75-125 54
IMPERIAL (5282 "Angel Child") ...75-125 54
IMPERIAL (5295 "The Wedding Bells Are Ringing") 100-200 54
IMPERIAL (5309 "I'm a Young Man") 75-125 54
IMPERIAL (5326 "I Wish I Knew") 50-75 55
IMPERIAL (5346 "I Cried") 25-50 55
IMPERIAL (5378 "Try Rock & Roll") 15-25 56
IMPERIAL (5412 "You're My Angel") 15-25 56
IMPERIAL (5378 "No No No") 15-25 57
IMPERIAL (5392 "I Try So Hard") .. 15-25 57
IMPERIAL (5412 "I've Got My Fingers Crossed") 15-25 57
IMPERIAL (5440 "You Always Hurt the One You Love") 15-25 57
IMPERIAL (5475 "I'm Gonna Be a Wheel Someday") 15-25 57
IMPERIAL (5511 "I Love to Hold You") 15-25 58
IMPERIAL (5558 "Hearts of Fire") 15-25 58
IMPERIAL (5923 "I Don't Want to Be a Wheel No More") 10-20 63
RON (337 "Send Me Your Picture") 10-20 61
RON (342 "There's Only One of You") 10-20 61
SHOW-BIZ (717 "Well, I Done Got Over It") 15-25 59
Also see MITCHUM, Billy

MITCHELL, Buddy Ray
Singles: 7-inch
LONDON 4-8 67

MITCHELL, Chad
Singles: 7-inch
AMY 3-6 68-69
W.B. 4-8 66-67
LPs: 10/12-inch
BELL 10-15 69
W.B. 10-20 66-67

MITCHELL, Chad, Trio P&R/LP '62
Singles: 7-inch
COLPIX 5-10 59-61
KAPP 5-10 61-63
MAY 4-8 62
MERCURY 4-8 63-64
Picture Sleeves
KAPP 10-15 61
MERCURY 8-12 63-65
LPs: 10/12-inch
COLPIX 20-30 60
KAPP 15-25 61-64
MERCURY 15-20 63-64
Members: Chad Mitchell; Joe Frazier; Mike Kobluk; Jim [Roger] McGuinn.
Also see McGUINN, Roger
Also see MITCHELL, Chad
Also see MITCHELL TRIO

MITCHELL, Chad, Trio, & Gatemen
LPs: 10/12-inch
COLPIX 20-25 64
Also see GATEMEN
Also see MITCHELL, Chad, Trio

MITCHELL, Charles, & His Orchestra C&W '44
Singles: 78 rpm
BLUEBIRD 4-8 44

MITCHELL, Charlie C&W '88
Singles: 7-inch
SOUNDWAVES 3-4 88

MITCHELL, Dave
Singles: 7-inch
CRYSTAL ("Under the Rug") 10-20 63
(Selection number not known.)
MET (2768 "The Trip") 10-20 65

MITCHELL, Duke
Singles: 7-inch
CRYSTALETTE (743 "The Lion") ... 10-20 61
(Reissued as *Surf Stomp*, by the Crestriders.)
VERVE 4-8 60
Also see CRESTRIDERS
Also see SPINNERS

MITCHELL, Eddie, Trio
Singles: 7-inch
MOVIN' 4-8 63

MITCHELL, Evan
Singles: 7-inch
MALA 4-8 64

MITCHELL, Freddie, & Orchestra R&B '49
(With Rip Harrigan)
Singles: 78 rpm
ABC-PAR 4-8 57
BRUNSWICK 4-8 53
CORAL 4-8 53
DERBY 4-8 49-52
MERCURY 4-8 52
Singles: 7-inch
ABC-PAR 10-15 57-61
BRUNSWICK (84023 "Mr. Freddie's Boogie") 10-20 53
CORAL (61740 "Snow Blues") 10-20 53
DERBY 5-15 49-52
MERCURY (8286 "Perfidia") 10-20 52
MERCURY (70018 "Later Gator") .. 10-20 52
ROCK 'N ROLL (609 "Preachin' ") . 10-20 56
EPs: 7-inch
DERBY (102 "Boogie Woogie") 15-25 50s
LPs: 10/12-inch
ALLEGRO/ROYAL (1600 "That Boogie Beat") 30-50 50s
TRIP 10-15 60s
"X" (1030 "Boogie Bash") 50-75 56
Session: King Curtis.
Also see KING CURTIS

MITCHELL, Gordon
Singles: 7-inch
RIC 4-8 64

MITCHELL, Grover
Singles: 7-inch
DECCA 4-8 64-66
HUNTER (799 "Time Brings About a Change") 15-25
JOSIE 4-8 66-67
TCF HALL 4-8 64
U.A. 4-6 69
VANGUARD 4-6
VEE JAY 5-10 62

MITCHELL, Guy P&R '50
(Al Cernick)
Singles: 78 rpm
COLUMBIA 5-15 50-57
KING (15125 "Cabaret") 10-15 51
Singles: 7-inch
CHALICE (711 "My Angel"/"Bit of Love") 15-25 63
CHALICE (711 "My Angel"/"Mr. Hobo") 15-25 63
(Note different flip.)
CHALICE (712 "Take Your Time") 15-25 63
CHALICE (713 "Your Imagination") 15-25 63
COLLECTABLES 3-4 80s
COLUMBIA 10-20 50-61
ERIC 3-4 83
GMI 4-6 74
JOY 4-8 62-63
KING (15125 "Cabaret") 20-30 51
(Previously issued as by Al Grant, Al Cernick's pseudonym before using Guy Mitchell.)
REPRISE 4-6 66
STARDAY 4-6 67-69
Picture Sleeves
COLUMBIA (40769 "Singing the Blues") 15-20 56
COLUMBIA (40820 "Knee Deep in the Blues") 15-20 57
COLUMBIA (40877 "Rock-a-Billy") 10-20 57
COLUMBIA (41476 "Heartaches By the Number") 10-15 60
COLUMBIA (41853 "Sunshine Guitar") 10-15 60
COLUMBIA (42231 "Soft Rain") 10-15 61
EPs: 7-inch
COLUMBIA 10-15 54-57
LPs: 10/12-inch
COLUMBIA (1211 "Guy in Love") .. 15-25 58
(Monaural.)
COLUMBIA (1226 "Greatest Hits"). 15-25 59
COLUMBIA (1552 "Sunshine Guitar") 15-25 60
(Monaural.)
COLUMBIA (6231 "Open Spaces") 25-50 53
(10-inch LP.)
COLUMBIA (8011 "Guy in Love") .. 20-30 58
(Stereo.)
COLUMBIA (8352 "Sunshine Guitar") 20-30 60
(Stereo.)
KING (644 "Sincerely Yours") 150-250 59
(Mitchell pictured but not identified on cover. Includes tracks recorded as Al Grant.)
NASHVILLE 5-10 70
STARDAY 10-15 68-69
Also see CAVALLARO, Carmen, Featuring Al Cernick
Also see CLOONEY, Rosemary, & Guy Mitchell
Also see GRANT, Al

MITCHELL, Guy, & Mindy Carson
Singles: 78 rpm
COLUMBIA 5-10 52-53
Singles: 7-inch
COLUMBIA 8-12 52-53
Also see CARSON, Mindy

MITCHELL, Guy / Eileen Rodgers
EPs: 7-inch
COLUMBIA 10-15 56
Also see RODGERS, Eileen
Also see MITCHELL, Guy

MITCHELL, Jimmy
Singles: 7-inch
MERCURY (71522 "At This Moment") 20-30 59

MITCHELL, Jimmy
Singles: 7-inch
KCPX ("President Board & Jimmy Smarter") 4-6 76
(Selection number not known.)

MITCHELL, Jock
(With the Fabulous Angels)
Singles: 7-inch
GOLDEN HIT (103 "Free at Last") 75-125 60s
IMPACT (1004 "Work with Me Annie") 10-20 66
MPACT (1023 "Not a Chance in a Million") 50-100 66

MITCHELL, Joe
Singles: 7-inch
DART 5-10 60

MITCHELL, Johnny
Singles: 7-inch
TEAR DROP (3085 "A Letter to the President") 25-75 62
Also see MAJESTICS

MITCHELL, Joni LP '68
Singles: 7-inch
ASYLUM 3-5 72-80
ELEKTRA 3-5 75
GEFFEN 3-4 82-91
REPRISE 3-6 68-72
Picture Sleeves
GEFFEN 3-4 82-85
LPs: 10/12-inch
ASYLUM 8-10 72-80
GEFFEN 5-8 82-91
REPRISE 10-20 68-71

MITCHELL, Joni, & L.A. Express
LPs: 10/12-inch
ASYLUM (202 "Miles of Aisles") 20-30 74
Also see L.A. EXPRESS
Also see MITCHELL, Joni

MITCHELL, Kim P&R/LP '85
Singles: 7-inch
BRONZE 3-4 85
LPs: 10/12-inch
BRONZE 5-8 85

MITCHELL, Lee
(With the Curley Money Combo)
Singles: 7-inch
PHILLIPS INT'L 10-15 59
ROLL 5-10 75
SHARP (8062 "Rootie Tootie Baby") 200-300 59
SURE SHOT 4-8 67
TRACKDOWN 8-12

MITCHELL, Marilyn
Singles: 7-inch
BUX 4-8 63

MITCHELL, Marlon "Madman," & Rocketeers
Singles: 7-inch
VENA (100 "Ice Cold Baby") 75-125 57

MITCHELL, Marty C&W '74
Singles: 7-inch
ATLANTIC 3-5 74
HITSVILLE 3-5 76
MC 3-5 78
LPs: 10/12-inch
MC 5-10 78

MITCHELL, McKinley R&B '62
(With the Honey Duo Twins; McKinley "Soul" Mitchell)
Singles: 7-inch
BIG BOY (85 "I Need to See You") 4-6 85
BIG 3 (6141 "Trouble Blues") 5-10 75
BLACK BEAUTY (301 "Party Across the Hall") 4-8 72
BOXER (204 "Rock Everybody Rock") 25-35 59
CHESS (2046 "Playboy") 5-10 67
CHIMNEYVILLE (10213 "Trouble Blues") 5-10 77
CHIMNEYVILLE (10219 "The End of the Rainbow") 4-8 77
CHIMNEYVILLE (10225 "The Town I Live In") 4-6 78
MALACO (2067 "Trouble Blues"/"Run to Love") 8-10 78
MALACO (2067 "Trouble Blues"/ "Poverty") 4-6 80
(Note different flip side.)
MALACO (2071 "A Slave for Your Love") 3-6 80
MIDAS (2029 "The Town I Live In") 20-30 61
(Identification number shown since no selection number is used.)
ONE-DERFUL (4804 "The Town I Live In") 10-15 62
ONE-DERFUL (4808 "All of a Sudden") 10-15 62
ONE-DERFUL (4810 "I'm So Glad") 10-15 62
ONE-DERFUL (4812 "Darling That's What You Said") 10-15 62
ONE-DERFUL (4817 "A Bit of Soul") 10-15 63
ONE-DERFUL (4822 "Tell It Like It Is") 10-15 63
ONE-DERFUL (4826 "You Know I've Tried") 10-15 64
ONE-DERFUL (4832 "Watch Over Me") 10-15 64
RETTAS (005 "Road of Love") 4-6 82
RETTAS (007 "Watch Over Me") 4-6 83
RETTAS (009 "I Don't Know Which Way to Turn") 4-6 83
SOUTHERN BISCUIT (104 "Fallin' for Your Love") 4-6 80
SANDMAN (702 "This Place Ain't Getting No Better") 5-10 71
SPOONFUL (777-26 "Good Time Baby") 4-8 74
SPOONFULL (777-20 "That Last Home Run") 5-10 74
(Label name misspelled. Identification number shown since no selection number is used.)
TODDLIN' TOWN (117 "The Town I Live In") 5-8 69
Also see BLAND, Billy

MITCHELL, Mitch L.
Singles: 7-inch
ABC 4-8 66

MITCHELL, Peter
Singles: 7-inch
JARVEY 5-8 61

MITCHELL, Philip R&B '75
(Prince Philip Mitchell)
Singles: 7-inch
ATLANTIC 3-5 78-79
EVENT 3-5 75
HI (Except 2240) 5-10 72-73
HI (2240 "Oh How I Love You") 10-15 73
ICHIBAN 3-5 86

MITCHELL, Price C&W '75
(With Rene Sloane)
Singles: 7-inch
GRT 3-5 75-76
SUNBIRD 3-5 80

MITCHELL, Price, & Jerri Kelly C&W '75
Singles: 7-inch
GRT 3-5 75
LPs: 10/12-inch
GRT 5-10 76
Also see KELLY, Jerri
Also see MITCHELL, Price

MITCHELL, Priscilla C&W '65
Singles: 7-inch
MERCURY 4-6 67-68
Also see DRUSKY, Roy, & Priscilla Mitchell

MITCHELL, Robbie
Singles: 7-inch
WATTS 4-8 68

MITCHELL, Ronnie
Singles: 7-inch
ATLANTIC 5-10 60
BLUE CAT 4-8 65
BRUNSWICK 4-8 67
COLUMBIA 4-8 62
SEVILLE 5-10 60-61

MITCHELL, Rose
Singles: 78 rpm
IMPERIAL 15-25 54
Singles: 7-inch
IMPERIAL (5243 "Slippin' In") 30-50 54
IMPERIAL (5260 "Live My Life") 30-50 54

MITCHELL, Rubin LP '67
Singles: 7-inch
CAPITOL 3-6 67-68
Picture Sleeves
CAPITOL 4-8 67
LPs: 10/12-inch
CAPITOL 10-15 67

MITCHELL, Sam
LPs: 10/12-inch
KICKING MULE 5-10
Also see MILLER, Dale / John James / Sam Mitchell / Ton Van Bergeyk

MITCHELL, "Skinny" Johnny
Singles: 7-inch
KCPX 4-8 76

MITCHELL, Stan
Singles: 7-inch
GONE (5106 "Devil in Disguise") ... 15-25 61

MITCHELL, Stanley
(With the Tornados)
Singles: 78 rpm
CHESS 50-100 57
Singles: 7-inch
CHESS (1649 "Would You, Could You") 50-100 57
DYNAMO (111 "Get It Baby") 50-75 67

MITCHELL, Steve
Singles: 7-inch
MAST 4-8 62

MITCHELL, Stu
Singles: 7-inch
KAPP 4-8 67
Also see ROBERTS, Doug, & Stu Mitchell

MITCHELL, Tommy
Singles: 78 rpm
MERCURY 15-25 56
Singles: 7-inch
MERCURY (70930 "Juke Box, Help Me Find My Baby") 25-35 56

MITCHELL, Tony
Singles: 7-inch
CANADIAN-AMERICAN 5-10 63-64

MITCHELL, Walter
Singles: 78 rpm
J.V.B. (75827 "Stop Messing Around") 100-150 48
Also see PICKENS, Slim, & Walter Mitchell

MITCHELL, Willie P&R/R&B '64
(With the Four Kings, "Vocal D. Bryant"; Willie Mitchell Orchestra; "Vocal by Billy Taylor")
Singles: 7-inch
HI 4-8 62-69
HOME of the BLUES 5-10 60-61
MOTOWN 3-5
SKIPPER (1001 "Wasting My Time") 15-25
STOMPER TIME (1160 "Walking at Your Will") 500-1000 58
Picture Sleeves
HI 5-10 68
EPs: 7-inch
HI (72 "Willie Mitchell") 10-15 60s
HI (32026 "It's Dance Time") 10-15 60s
(Stereo. Juke box issue only.)
LPs: 10/12-inch
BEARSVILLE 5-8 81
HI (12010 thru 12042) 10-20 63-68
(Monaural.)
HI (32010 thru 32058) 10-25 63-71
(Stereo.)
HI (8000 series) 5-8 77
MOTOWN 8-10 82
Also see BRYANT, Don
Also see KING, B.B.
Also see TAYLOR, Billy
Also see YURO, Timi

MITCHELL TRIO LP '64
Singles: 7-inch
MERCURY 4-8 65-66
REPRISE 4-8 67
Picture Sleeves
MERCURY 5-10 63-66
LPs: 10/12-inch
MERCURY (20944 "Slightly Irreverent Mitchell Trio") 15-20 64
(Monaural.)
MERCURY (20992 "Typical American Boys") 15-20 65
(Monaural.)
MERCURY (21049 "That's the Way It's Gonna Be") 15-20 65
(Monaural.)
MERCURY (21067 "Violets of Dawn") 15-20 65
(Monaural.)
MERCURY (60944 "Slightly Irreverent Mitchell Trio") 20-25 64
(Stereo.)
MERCURY (60992 "Typical American Boys") 20-25 65
MERCURY (61049 "That's the Way It's Gonna Be") 20-25 65
(Stereo.)
MERCURY (21067 "Violets of Dawn") 20-25 65
(Stereo.)
REPRISE (6354 "Alive") 15-20 67
Members: Chad Mitchell; Joe Frazier; Mike Kobluk; John Denver; David Boise; Michael Johnson.
Also see DENVER, John
Also see JOHNSON, Michael
Also see MITCHELL, Chad, Trio

MITCHUM, Billy
(Billy Mitchell)
Singles: 7-inch
IMPERIAL (5616 "Twelve and Three Quarters") 8-12 59
Also see MITCHELL, Bobby

MITCHUM, Jim
Singles: 7-inch
CANDIX (324 "Lonely Birthday") 30-50 61
20TH FOX (277 "Lonely Birthday") 15-25 60
Picture Sleeves
20TH FOX (277 "Lonely Birthday") 25-50 60

MITCHUM, Robert P&R '58
(With the Calypso Band)
Singles: 78 rpm
CAPITOL 5-15 57-58
Singles: 7-inch
CAPITOL (Except 3986) 5-10 57
CAPITOL (3986 "The Ballad of Thunder Road") 8-12 58
(Purple label.)
CAPITOL (3986 "The Ballad of Thunder Road") 4-8 62
(Orange/yellow label.)
CAPITOL STARLINE 4-8 60s
MONUMENT 4-6 67
EPs: 7-inch
CAPITOL (853 "Calypso Is Like So") 15-25 57
(Price is for any of three volumes.)
LPs: 10/12-inch
CAPITOL (853 "Calypso Is Like So") 25-50 57
MONUMENT (8086 "That Man") 15-20 67
(Monaural.)
MONUMENT (18086 "That Man") .. 20-25 67
(Stereo.)

MITLO SISTERS
Singles: 7-inch
KLIK (8405 "Let Me Tell You") 15-25 58
Also see DREAMTONES

MIXED EMOTIONS
Singles: 7-inch
KUSTOM KUT (1 "I'll Fade Away") 25-35 60s

MIXED UP ZOMBIES
Singles: 7-inch
REL 5-10 63

MIXERS
Singles: 7-inch
BOLD (101 "You Said You're Leaving Me")....550-700 58
BOLD (102 "Love and Kisses") ..500-650 59

MIXTURES
Singles: 7-inch
LINDA....10-15 62-64
LPs: 10/12-inch
LINDA (3301 "Stompin' at the Rainbow")....50-100 62

MIXTURES P&R '71
Singles: 7-inch
SIRE.... 3-5 71

MIZE, Billy C&W '66
Singles: 78 rpm
DECCA.... 5-10 56
Singles: 7-inch
COLUMBIA.... 4-8 66-68
DECCA (29812 "Who Will Buy the Wine")....10-15 56
IMPERIAL.... 4-6 69-70
U.A..... 4-6 70-74
ZODIAC.... 3-5 76-77
Picture Sleeves
COLUMBIA (43546 "Don't Let the Blues Make You Bad").... 8-12 66
LPs: 10/12-inch
IMPERIAL....10-15 69
U.A..... 8-12 71
ZODIAC.... 5-10 76
Session: Jordanaires.
Also see BILLY & CLIFF
Also see JORDANAIRES

MIZELL, Hank
Singles: 7-inch
AMAZON (711 "Jungle Rock") 35-45 63
EKO (506 "Jungle Rock")....200-300 58
(Some copies credit Jim Bobo.)
KING (101 "Jungle Rock")....15-25 76
KING (5236 "Jungle Rock")....75-125 59

MIZELL, Hank, & Jim Bobo
Singles: 7-inch
KING (5445 "What Is Life Without You")....10-20 61
Also see BOBO, Jim
Also see MIZELL, Hank

MIZZ
Singles: 7-inch
CASABLANCA.... 3-5 80
LPs: 10/12-inch
CASABLANCA.... 5-10 80

MIZZELL, Bobby
Singles: 7-inch
CENTURY LIMITED (604 "San Antonio Rose").... 4-8 69
KIM (307 "Knockout")....75-125 57
KIM (308 "Rocket in My Pocket") 4-8 86
(Colored vinyl.)
PHILIPS....10-15 62
REED (605 "Atomic Fallout") 25-35 59
20TH FOX (160 "Same Thing")....50-75 59
Also see ACORN, Bobby, & Leaves
Also see BERNARD, Rod
Also see JIVIN' GENE
Also see LEE, Dickie
Also see NEAL & NEWCOMERS
Also see PRESTON, Johnny
Also see WINTER, Johnny
Also see WOODARD, Jerry

MIZZELL, Bobby, & Glenn Layne
Singles: 7-inch
CENTURY LTD (604 "Sunset Blues")....15-25 60
Also see MIZZELL, Bobby

MO, Finney: see FINNEY – MO

MO & JO
Singles: 7-inch
LITA.... 5-10 61
Members: Gaynel Hodge; Bobby Gross.
Also see HODGE, Gaynel

MOAG, Rodney
Singles: 7-inch
CUCA (6714 "Fool Over You").... 8-12 67

MOANIN' GLORIES
Singles: 7-inch
YORKSHIRE (1001 "She Took the Rain Out of My Mind")....30-50 67

MOB P&R '71
Singles: 7-inch
COLOSSUS.... 3-5 71-72
DAYLIGHT (1000 "Open the Door to Your Heart").... 8-12 60s
MGM.... 4-6 72-73
MERCURY.... 4-8 68
PRIVATE STOCK.... 3-5 76-77
TWINIGHT (111 "Unbelievable") 8-12 60s
Picture Sleeves
COLOSSUS.... 3-6 71-72
LPs: 10/12-inch
COLOSSUS....10-15 71
MGM (4839 "The Mob")....10-15 72
PRIVATE STOCK.... 8-12 75
Members: Art Herrera; Al Herrera; James Holvay; Gary Beiser; Jimmy Ford; Mike Sistak; Tony Nedza; Bobby Raffino; .
Also see ARTIE & PHARAOHS
Also see KANE & ABEL
Also see LIVERS

MOBILE FOUR
Singles: 78 rpm
COLUMBIA....15-25 28

MOBILE STRUGGLERS
Singles: 78 rpm
AMERICAN MUSIC (104 "Memphis Blues")....25-35 49

MOBLEY, John
Singles: 7-inch
TOWN & COUNTRY (6601 "Tunnel of Love")....50-75

MOBLEY, Sylvia
Singles: 7-inch
SANTO (502 "All by Myself")....15-25 50s

MOBY DICK & WHALERS
Singles: 7-inch
FOREST (2009 "You've Got a Bull")....35-45 60s

MOBY GRAPE P&R/LP '67
Singles: 12-inch
SAN FRANCISCO SOUND....100-125 84
(Set of six picture discs.)
Singles: 7-inch
COLUMBIA....6-12 67-69
Picture Sleeves
COLUMBIA....20-25 67
LPs: 10/12-inch
COLUMBIA (2698 "Moby Grape") 35-45 67
(Monaural. Cover pictures Don Stevenson's middle finger over washboard. Price includes bonus poster, which represents about $5 to $10 of the value.)
COLUMBIA (2698 "Moby Grape") 10-20 67
(Monaural. Cover pictures Don Stevenson's hand closed. Price includes bonus poster.)
COLUMBIA (9498 "Moby Grape") 40-50 67
(Stereo. Cover pictures Don Stevenson's middle finger over washboard. Price includes bonus poster, which represents about $5 to $10 of the value.)
COLUMBIA (9498 "Moby Grape") 10-20 67
(Stereo. Cover pictures Don Stevenson's hand closed. Price includes bonus poster.)
COLUMBIA (9613 "Wow")....10-15 68
COLUMBIA (9696 "Moby Grape '69")....10-15 69
COLUMBIA (9912 "Truly Fine Citizen")....10-15 69
COLUMBIA (31098 "Great Grape")....10-15 72
ESCAPE (A1A "Live Grape")....8-10 78
HARMONY (30393 "Omaha")....10-12 71
REPRISE (6460 "20 Granite Creek")....10-12 71
SAN FRANCISCO SOUND....10-15 83
(Black vinyl.)
SAN FRANCISCO SOUND (04830 "Moby Grape '84")....20-25 83
(Picture disc.)
Promotional LPs
COLUMBIA (MGS-1 "Grape Jam")....15-25 68
(With Mike Bloomfield and Al Kooper.)
ESCAPE (95018 "Live Grape")....15-25 78
(Colored vinyl.)
Members: Don Stevenson; Jerry Miller; Peter Lewis; Skip Spence; Jeff Blackburn.
Also see BLACKBURN & SNOW
Also see BLOOMFIELD, Mike, & Al Kooper
Also see FRANKLIN, Aretha / Union Gap /Blood, Sweat & Tears / Moby Grape
Also see FRANTICS

MOCCASIN
LPs: 10/12-inch
MGM....10-15 71

MOCEDADES P&R/LP '74
Singles: 7-inch
TARA.... 3-5 74
LPs: 10/12-inch
TARA....5-10 74

MOCKERS
Singles: 7-inch
MONTE VISTA (65-1 "Children of the Sun")....20-30 65

MOCKINGBIRDS
Singles: 7-inch
ABC-PAR (10653 "That's How")....10-15 65
Members: Graham Gouldman; Kevin Godley.
Also see 10CC

MOD & ROCKERS
LPs: 10/12-inch
JUSTICE (153 "Now")....200-300 69

MOD IV
Singles: 7-inch
EMERALD (121 "What Can I Do") .10-20 60s

MOD FUN
Singles: 7-inch
MIDNIGHT.... 3-5
LPs: 10/12-inch
MIDNIGHT.... 5-8

MOD ROCKERS
Singles: 7-inch
DOT....5-10 66

MOD VI
Singles: 7-inch
EMERALD (127 "What Can I Do") .15-25 67

MOD SQUAD
Singles: 7-inch
TANGERINE.... 4-8 69

MODDS
Singles: 7-inch
AMERICAN NATIONAL (3041 "Leave My House")....25-35 66

MODEL 500 D&D '85
Singles: 12-inch
METROPLEX....4-6 85

MODEL T. SLIM
(Elmon Mickle)
Singles: 7-inch
AUDIO BLUES....5-10 60s
KENT (504 "Christine")....5-10 69
KIM (1001 "15 Years My Love Was in Vain")....8-12
MAGNUM (739 "Good Morning Little Schoolgirl")....10-15 66
WONDER (15001 "Shake Your Boogie")....20-30 66
Also see MICKLE, Elmon

MODELS
Singles: 7-inch
MGM....10-15 67

MODELS P&R/LP '86
Singles: 12-inch
GEFFEN....4-6 86
Singles: 7-inch
GEFFEN....3-4 86
Picture Sleeves
GEFFEN....3-4 86
LPs: 10/12-inch
GEFFEN....5-8 86
WINDSONG....5-8 80

MODERN DESIGN
Singles
K-DISC (005 "If It's Only Love")....4-8 80
(Shaped picture disc.)

MODERN ENGLISH P&R/D&D/LP '83
Singles: 12-inch
SIRE....4-6 82-86
Singles: 7-inch
4AD....3-5 80-84
4AD/SIRE....3-4 83-86
LIMP ("Drowning Man")....5-8 79
(Selection number not known.)
SIRE....3-4 86
LPs: 10/12-inch
4AD/SIRE....5-10 83-84
SIRE....5-8 86
TVT....5-8 90

MODERN FOLK QUARTET
Singles: 7-inch
ALOHA....3-5
LPs: 10/12-inch
HOMECOMING....5-10 87
W.B.....15-25 63-64
Members: Chip Douglas; Stan White; Henry Diltz.
Also see CRUZ, Ernie
Also see MONKEES
Also see TURTLES
Also see WILCOX THREE

MODERN INK SPOTS
Singles: 7-inch
RUST (5052 "Together")....500-1000 62
Also see INK SPOTS

MODERN LOVERS
LPs: 10/12-inch
BESERKLEY....10-20 76-77
BOMP....8-12 82
HOME of the HITS (1910 "Modern Lovers")....20-40 75
MOHAWK....10-15 81
ROUNDER....5-8 88
Members: Jonathan Richman; Jerry Harrison; David Robinson; Ernie Brooks.
Also see CARS
Also see HARRISON, Jerry
Also see KIHN, Greg, Band / Earthquake / Modern Lovers / Rubinoos
Also see RICHMAN, Jonathan
Also see TALKING HEADS

MODERN RED CAPS
Singles: 7-inch
PENNTOWNE (101 "Never Kiss a Good Man Good-By")....25-50 65
SWAN (4243 "Golden Teardrops").15-25 66
Also see GIBSON, Steve
Also see TINDLEY, George, & Modern Red Caps

MODERN ROCKETRY D&D '83
Singles: 12-inch
MEGATONE....4-6 83

MODERN ROMANCE
Singles: 7-inch
ATLANTIC....3-4 82

MODERN SOUL TRIO
Singles: 7-inch
YOUNGSTOWN....8-12

MODERN TIMES
Singles: 7-inch
GOLDEN WORLD (115 "Stompin Crazy Legg")....10-20 73
Member: Ed Wingate.

MODERNAIRES P&R '45
(With Paula Kelly)
Singles: 78 rpm
COLUMBIA....3-6 45-50
CORAL....3-5 51-56
Singles: 7-inch
CAPITOL....3-6 69
COLUMBIA (38000 series)....5-10 50
CORAL....5-10 51-56
MERCURY....4-8 59
U.A.....4-6 62
EPs: 7-inch
CORAL....5-10 51-55
LPs: 10/12-inch
COLUMBIA....10-25 50-66
CORAL....15-25 51-55
LIBERTY....5-10 84
MERCURY....8-12 60
ROSS....5-10 79
U.A.....10-20 61-62
WING....10-15 62
Members: Paula Kelly; John Drake; Allan Copeland; Francis Scott; Hal Dickenson.

MODERNISTICS
Singles: 7-inch
PIONEER (7315 "Who Can I Turn To")....25-50 65

MODINE, Jerry
Singles: 7-inch
MERCURY....5-10 63

MODS
Singles: 7-inch
KNIGHT (105 "Empty Heart") 20-30 66

MODS
Singles: 7-inch
CEE THREE (10001 "It's for You")....20-30 66

MODS
Singles: 7-inch
KOOL (1028 "My Baby's Gone") 20-30 66

MODS
Singles: 7-inch
PECK (331 "I Give You an Inch")...20-30 66

MODS
Singles: 7-inch
DEE DEE....8-12 60s
PLAINS....8-12 60s

MODUGNO, Domenico P&R/R&B/LP '58
Singles: 7-inch
DECCA....5-15 58-64
MCA....3-5 78
MGM....4-6 66
RCA....4-6 68-72
U.A. INT'L....4-6 67
EPs: 7-inch
DECCA....10-15 58
LPs: 10/12-inch
DECCA....15-25 58-61
RCA....10-15 66
U.A. INT'L....8-12 67

MODULATION CORPORATION
Singles: 7-inch
ATOM (1001 "Worms")....25-35 67

MODULATIONS R&B '74
Singles: 7-inch
BUDDAH....3-5 74-75
LP: 10/12-inch
BUDDAH....8-12 74

MOE, ADRIAN, & SCULPTORS
Singles: 7-inch
COLUMBIA....4-8 65
Picture Sleeves
COLUMBIA....5-10 65

MOE & JOE: see STAMPLEY, Joe

MOEBAKKEN, Dick C&W '78
Singles: 7-inch
ASI....3-5 78

MOFFATT, Hugh C&W '78
Singles: 7-inch
MERCURY....3-5 78

MOFFATT, Katy C&W '76
Singles: 7-inch
COLUMBIA....3-5 76
PERMIAN....3-4 83-84
LPs: 10/12-inch
COLUMBIA....5-10 76-78
Also see MURPHEY, Michael, & Katy Moffatt

MOFFATT, Tom
(With the Flames)
Singles: 7-inch
BERTRAM INT'L (204 "Beyond the Reef")....20-30 57
MAHALO....5-10 63

MOFFETT, Johnny
Singles: 7-inch
CANTERBURY (518 "I Found Joy")...4-8 68

MOGAMBOS
(Mogambo's)
Singles: 7-inch
SUNBEAM (107 "Wa'tch You Mean")....15-25 58
Note: We're not yet sure what the Bobby Darin connection is here, but we are told there is one.
Also see DARIN, Bobby

MOGAN DAVID & WINOS
Singles: 7-inch
KOSHER (1 "Nose Job")....4-8 70s
LPs: 10/12-inch
RHINO....5-8
Members: Ira Miller; Harold Bronson.
Also see CONCEPTION CORPORATION

MOGEN DAVID & GRAPES OF WRATH
Singles: 7-inch
CHA CHA (757 "Little Girl Gone").... 1500-2000 67

MOGULS
Singles: 7-inch
TORK (1095 "Another Day")....8-12

MOHAWK, Essar
LPs: 10/12-inch
PRIVATE STOCK (2024 "Essar") 5-10 76

MOHAWKS
Singles: 7-inch
COLPIX (117 "Night Run")....15-25 59
Member: Jim Ford.
Also see FORD, Jim

MOHAWKS
Singles: 7-inch
COLPIX (117 "Night Run")....15-25 59

MOHAWKS
Singles: 7-inch
VAL-UE (211 "I Got a Gal")....50-75 60

MOHAWKS
Singles: 7-inch
MARK (147 "Shaggin' ")....10-20 60

MOHAWKS
Singles: 7-inch
MUTUAL (504 "Shopliftin' Molly") ..25-50 64

MOHAWKS
Singles: 7-inch
COTILLION....4-8 68-69

MOIRS
LPs: 10/12-inch
ROCKET....5-8 78

MOJAVE PLAYBOYS
Singles: 7-inch
MEGATONE (707 "Saigon Boogie")....8-12

MOJO
(George Buford)
Singles: 7-inch
ADELL....15-25 64
FOLK ART (101 "Knockin' on My Door")....10-15 60s
LPs: 10/12-inch
FOLK ART (101 "Shades of Folk Blues")....20-30 60s
Also see BUFORD, Mojo
Also see LITTLE MOJO

MOJO MEN
Singles: 7-inch
TIDE (2000 "Surfin' Fat Man") 20-30 64
Members: Denny King; Vic Blunt; Paul Case; Bruce Pollard.
Also see CANADIAN BEADLES
Also see DARNELLS
Also see HAHN, Tommy, & Mojo Men

MOJO MEN P&R '65
(Mojo)
Singles: 7-inch
AUTUMN....8-12 65-66
GRT....4-8 69
REPRISE....5-10 66-68
LPs: 10/12-inch
GRT (10003 "Mojo Magic")....15-20 69
Members: Dennis DeCarr; Paul Curcio; Jim Alaimo; Don Metchick.

MOJOS
Singles: 7-inch
PARROT....4-6 64

MOJOS
Singles: 7-inch
MOJO ("Love Does Its Harm")....15-25 65
(No selection number used.)
MOJO (88 "What She's Done to Me")....10-20 60s
Picture Sleeves
MOJO ("Love Does Its Harm")....25-35 65
(No selection number used.)
Members: Matt Lewis; Jon Earl; Skip Brown; John Percival.

MOKLESTAD, Teresa
Singles: 7-inch
NETWORK....3-5 78
LPs: 10/12-inch
NETWORK (1002 "Understudy") 5-10 78

MOLES
Singles: 7-inch
PAGE ONE....5-8
LPs: 10/12-inch
NO LABEL CO. (1566 "Moles")...... 15-25

MOLES, Gene
(With the Softwinds; Gene "The Draggin' King" Moles)
Singles: 7-inch
CHALLENGE (59249 "Burning Rubber")....10-20 64
(Also issued as *Batmobile*, by the Bats.)
GARPAX (44190 "Kaha Huna") 15-25 63
MOSRITE (210 "Durango")....8-12 66
STARVIEW (1001 "Fingerlickin' ") 5-8 66
THREE STAR (4304 "Raunchy") ...10-15 63
Also see BATS

MOLINA, Little Ralphie
Singles: 7-inch
CLEF-TONE (154 "Rock & Roll Vowels")....20-40 58

MOLINE, Bobby
(Bob Moline)
Singles: 7-inch
CALENDAR....4-8 64
CAHLLENGE....4-8 65-66
IMPERIAL....4-8 64
PARK AVE....4-8 64

MOLITTERI, Pat
Singles: 7-inch
TEEN (414 "The USA")....20-30 61

MOLLAND, Joey
LPs: 10/12-inch
EARTHTONE (1002 "After the Pearl") ... 5-10 83
Also see BADFINGER
Also see NATURAL GAS

MOLLEEN, Ronnie
Singles: 7-inch
KING (5365 "Rockin' Up") ... 75-100 60

MOLLY & HEYMAKERS — C&W '90
Singles: 7-inch
REPRISE ... 3-4 90-91
Members: Molly Sheer; Andy Dee; Jeff Nelson; "Solid" Joe Lindzius.

MOLLY HATCHET — LP '78
Singles: 7-inch
EPIC ... 3-5 79-86
Picture Sleeves
EPIC ... 3-5 79
EPs: 7-inch
CSP ("Molly Hatchet") ... 4-8 81
(Promotional issue only. Made for Nestle's candy.)
LPs: 10/12-inch
EPIC (Except picture discs and 40137) ... 5-10 78-87
EPIC (694 "Flirtin' with Disaster") ... 40-50 79
(Picture disc. Has die-cut cover. Promotional issue only.)
EPIC (884 "Beatin the Odds") ... 30-40 80
(Picture disc. Promotional issue only. 1350 made.)
EPIC (1320 "Take No Prisoners") ... 20-25 81
(Picture disc. Promotional issue only.)
EPIC (35347 "Molly Hatchet") ... 40-50 78
(Picture disc. Promotional issue only.)
EPIC (36110 "Flirtin' with Disaster") ... 50-60 79
(Picture disc. Promotional issue only. 450 made.)
EPIC (40137 "Double Trouble Live") ... 10-15 79
EPIC (40137 "Double Trouble Live") ... 15-25 79
(White label. Promotional issue only.)
Members: Danny Joe Brown; Jimmy Farrar.
Also see BROWN, Danny Joe

MOLOCH
LPs: 10/12-inch
ENTERPRISE ... 10-15 69

MOLLY MAGUIRES
Singles: 7-inch
TRANSACTION (709 "First Spring Rain") ... 10-20 69
TRANSACTION (713 "Our Favorite Melodies") ... 10-20 70
Picture Sleeves
TRANSACTION (709 "First Spring Rain") ... 10-20 69
Members: Art Mcclure; Jim Davidson; Dirk Weber; Eric Hartwig; Tom Franzini; Steve Kunes; Neil Wang.

MOM & DADS — LP '71
Singles: 7-inch
GNP ... 3-5 71-80
LPs: 10/12-inch
GNP ... 5-10 71-87
Members: Harold Hendren; Doris Crow; Les Welch; Quentin Ratliff.

MOM'S APPLE PIE
LPs: 10/12-inch
BROWN BAG (14200 "Mom's Apple Pie") ... 10-20 72
(Cover pictures a vulva in pie.)
BROWN BAG (14200 "Mom's Apple Pie") ... 8-12 72
(Reworked cover—no longer showing vulva.)
BROWN BAG (073 "Mom's Apple Pie #2") ... 8-12 73

MOMENT OF TRUTH — R&B '74
Singles: 7-inch
ROULETTE ... 3-5 75
Members: Bill Jones; Michael Garrison; Norris Harris.
Also see CHAIN REACTION
Also see CHOCOLATE SYRUP

MOMENTOS
Singles: 7-inch
REPRISE ... 4-6 62

MOMENTS — P&R '63
Singles: 7-inch
ERA ... 5-10 63-64
HIT ... 5-10 63
WORLD ARTISTS ... 4-8 64
Also see SHACKLEFORDS

MOMENTS — P&R/R&B '68
Singles: 7-inch
STANG ... 3-6 68-78
SUGAR HILL ... 3-4 80-81
LPs: 10/12-inch
STANG ... 8-12 70-78
VICTORY ... 5-8 82
Also see O'JAYS / Moments
Also see RAY, GOODMAN & BROWN
Also see SYLVIA & MOMENTS

MOMENTS & WHATNAUTS — R&B '74
Singles: 7-inch
STANG ... 3-5 74
Also see MOMENTS
Also see WHATNAUTS

MOMMY
Singles: 7-inch
U.A. ... 4-8 67

Also see MELANIE

MONA LISA
Singles: 7-inch
DADE ... 4-8 66

MONACLES
Singles: 7-inch
VARIETY (301 "I Can't Win") ... 15-25 66
(Black vinyl.)
VARIETY (301 "I Can't Win") ... 15-25 66
(Colored vinyl.)
VARIETY (401 "Debbie") ... 10-15 66
VARIETY (501 "I Found a Way") ... 10-15 66
VARIETY (601 "Everybody Thinks I'm Lonely") ... 10-15 66

MONAGRAMS
Singles: 7-inch
CHARRINGTON (1000 "Go-Go Marlin") ... 20-30

MONAE, Tia — D&D '84
Singles: 12-inch
FIRST TAKE ... 4-6 84

MONAHAN, Stephen
Singles: 7-inch
JAMIE ... 4-6 70
KAPP ... 4-6 67
Picture Sleeves
KAPP ... 5-8 67
LPs: 10/12-inch
KAPP ... 10-15 67

MONARCHS
Singles: 78 rpm
WING ... 25-50 55
Singles: 7-inch
WING (90040 "Angels in the Sky") ... 50-75 55

MONARCHS
Singles: 78 rpm
MELBA ... 15-25 56
NEIL ... 25-50 56
Singles: 7-inch
MELBA (101 "Pretty Little Girl") ... 50-75 56
NEIL (101 "Pretty Little Girl") ... 100-150 56
NEIL (103 "Always Be Faithful") ... 75-125 56

MONARCHS
Singles: 7-inch
JUKE BOX (110 "Yes! Uh! Huh Or Even Maybe") ... 100-150 57

MONARCHS
(Monarch's)
Singles: 7-inch
LIBAN (1002 "Love You That's Why") ... 1000-2000 59

MONARCHS
Singles: 7-inch
REEGAL (512 "Over the Mountain") ... 100-200 62

MONARCHS
Singles: 7-inch
ZONE (1067 "Friday Night") ... 10-15 63

MONARCHS
(Monarchs IV)
Singles: 7-inch
ERWIN (1069 "Surge") ... 15-25 64

MONARCHS
Singles: 7-inch
YUCCA (172 "Forever Lost") ... 20-30 64

MONARCHS — P&R '64
Singles: 7-inch
MONUMENT ... 4-6 60s
SOUND STAGE 7 ... 8-12 64
Also see ORIGINAL GROUP

MONARCHS
Singles: 7-inch
KENTONE ("Last Night I Dreamed") ... 50-75

MONARCHS
Singles: 7-inch
ROMAN (4040 "Needles & Pins") ... 20-30

MON—CLAIRES
Singles: 7-inch
JOEY (6101 "Please Come Back") ... 175-225 62

MONDA, Dick
Singles: 7-inch
MOONGLOW ... 4-8 66
VERVE ... 3-5 69
Picture Sleeves
VERVE ... 3-6 69
LPs: 10/12-inch
VERVE ... 10-12 69

MONDAY, Carla — C&W '87
Singles: 7-inch
MCM ... 3-4 87

MONDAY, Danny
(Dan Monday)
Singles: 7-inch
MODERN (1025 "Baby Without You") ... 100-150 64
PREVIEW ... 4-8

MONDAY, Florian, & Mondos
Singles: 7-inch
REALM (006 "Mondo") ... 20-30 64
REALM (007 "Rip It, Rip It Up") ... 20-30 64

MONDAY, Julie — P&R '66
Singles: 7-inch
RAINBOW ... 4-8 66
SSS INT'L ... 3-6 68

MONDAY AFTER — R&B '76
Singles: 7-inch
BUDDAH ... 3-5 76

MONDAY BLUES
Singles: 7-inch
VAULT ... 4-6 70
LPs: 10/12-inch
VAULT ... 12-15 70

MONDAY RAIN
Singles: 7-inch
A&M ... 3-5 69

MONDELL, Len
Singles: 7-inch
SMASH ... 4-8 63

MONDELLOS
Singles: 7-inch
RHYTHM (106 "That's What I Call Love") ... 250-500 57
RHYTHM (109 "Hard to Please") ... 250-500 57
Also see ALICE JEAN & MONDELLOS
Also see LAMBERT, Rudy
Also see McCLAY, Yul, & Mondellos

MONDO
Singles: 7-inch
ARCY ... 10-15 60

MONDO, Joe, & His Combo
Singles: 7-inch
EPI (1003 "Last Summer Love") ... 25-50 63

MONDO ROCK — P&R '87
Singles: 7-inch
ATLANTIC ... 3-4 82
COLUMBIA ... 3-4 85-87
LPs: 10/12-inch
ATLANTIC ... 5-8 82
COLUMBIA ... 5-8 85

MONEGAR, Cal
Singles: 7-inch
VERA (757 "Meanwhile Back at the White House") ... 4-6 71

MONET — R&B '87
Singles: 7-inch
LIGOSA ... 3-4 87

MONET & NOLAN THOMAS — R&B '87
Singles: 7-inch
LIGOSA ... 3-4 87
Also see MONET
Also see THOMAS, Nolan

MONET, Helen
Singles: 7-inch
ELGRAN ... 3-6

MONEY, Curley
Singles: 7-inch
MONEY (101 "Honky Tonk Man") ... 50-75 57
MONEY (105 "Little Queenie") ... 25-50 57
MONEY (8812 "Gonna Rock") ... 25-50 58
RAMBLER (552 "Gonna Rock") ... 50-75 58
RAMBLER (554 "That's My Darlin' ") ... 8-10 59
RAMBLER (2331 "Rambler") ... 25-50 59
RAMBLER (2471 "Hurricane Baby") ... 50-75 59
RAMBLER (2509 "Lover's Blues") 25-50 59
RAMBLER (3407 "Bo Jangles Rock") ... 25-50 60
RAMBLER (5466 "Shortnin' Bread") ... 25-50 60

MONEY, Eddie — P&R/LP '78
Singles: 12-inch
COLUMBIA ... 5-10 84
Singles: 7-inch
CBS (165196 "Maybe I'm a Fool") ... 20-30 79
(Picture disc. Promotional issue only.)
COLUMBIA ... 3-6 78-89
POLYDOR ... 3-5 85
Picture Sleeves
COLUMBIA ... 3-5 82-88
LPs: 10/12-inch
COLUMBIA ... 6-12 77-89
POLYDOR ... 5-10 85

MONEY, Eddie, & Zane Buzby
Singles: 7-inch
COLUMBIA ... 3-6 79

MONEY, Eddie, & Valerie Carter — P&R '80
Singles: 7-inch
COLUMBIA ... 3-6 80
Also see CARTER, Valerie

MONEY, Eddie, & Ronnie Spector
Singles: 7-inch
COLUMBIA ... 3-6 86
Also see MONEY, Eddie
Also see SPECTOR, Ronnie

MONEY, Zoot
Singles: 7-inch
EPIC ... 4-8 66
LPs: 10/12-inch
CAPITOL ... 15-20 69
EPIC ... 15-20 66
Also see SCAFFOLD

MONFORTE, Pat "The Cat"
Singles: 7-inch
BRUNSWICK (55076 "Blow Pat Blow") ... 15-25 58

MONGO SANTAMARIA: see SANTAMARIA, Mongo

MONGRELS
Singles: 7-inch
FRANKLIN (632 "Do You Know Your Mother") ... 10-20
M&L (101 "My Woman") ... 20-30 68
NICO ... 10-20 60s
RCA ... 8-12 60s
Picture Sleeves
FRANKLIN (632 "Do You Know Your Mother") ... 25-35 60s

MONIQUES
Singles: 7-inch
BENN-X (15 "Love So Wonderful") ... 25-35 62
BENN-X (55 "Hey Girl") ... 20-30 62

MONIQUES
Singles: 7-inch
CENTAUR (104 "Halo") ... 15-25 63
CENTAUR (105 "Rock Pretty Baby") ... 15-25 63
Also see LEE, Veronica, & Moniques

MONITORS
Singles: 78 rpm
ALADDIN ... 25-50 55
Singles: 7-inch
ALADDIN (3309 "Tonight's the Night") ... 50-100 55

MONITORS
Singles: 78 rpm
SPECIALTY ... 25-50 57-58
Singles: 7-inch
SPECIALTY (595 "Our School Days") ... 50-100 57
SPECIALTY (622 "Closer to Heaven") ... 100-200 58
SPECIALTY (636 "Hop Scotch") ... 50-75 58

MONITORS
Singles: 7-inch
CIRCUS (219 "A Boy Friend's Prayer") ... 100-150 58

MONITORS — P&R/R&B '66
Singles: 7-inch
BUDDAH ... 3-5 72
MOTOWN ... 3-5
SOUL (35049 "Step by Step") ... 8-15 68
V.I.P. (25028 thru 25046) ... 10-20 65-68
V.I.P. (25049 "Step by Step") ... 20-40 68
LPs: 10/12-inch
SOUL (714 "Greetings") ... 50-75 69
Members: John Fagin; Richard Street; Warren Harris; Sandra Fagin.

MONITORS
Singles: 7-inch
KELLI GREEN ... 4-8

MONK, T.S. — R&B '80
(Thelonious Monk Jr.)
Singles: 7-inch
MIRAGE ... 3-4 80-82
LPs: 10/12-inch
MIRAGE ... 5-8 81-82

MONK, Thelonious — LP '63
Singles: 7-inch
COLUMBIA ... 3-6 63-69
PRESTIGE ... 3-8 60-69
EPs: 7-inch
PRESTIGE ... 20-40 52
LPs: 10/12-inch
BLACK LION ... 5-10 74
BLUE NOTE (100 thru 500 series) ... 6-12 73-76
BLUE NOTE (1510 "Genius of Modern Music, Vol. 1") ... 50-75 56
(Label has Lexington Ave. street address for Blue Note Records.)
BLUE NOTE (1510 "Genius of Modern Music, Vol. 1") ... 40-50 58
(Label reads, "Blue Note Records Inc. New York, U.S.A.")
BLUE NOTE (1510 "Genius of Modern Music, Vol. 1") ... 15-25 60s
(Label reads "Blue Note Records - a Division of Liberty Records Inc.")
BLUE NOTE (1511 "Genius of Modern Music, Vol. 2") ... 50-75 56
(Label has Lexington Ave. street address for Blue Note Records.)
BLUE NOTE (1511 "Genius of Modern Music, Vol. 2") ... 40-50 58
(Label reads, "Blue Note Records Inc. New York, U.S.A.")
BLUE NOTE (1511 "Genius of Modern Music, Vol. 2") ... 15-25 60s
(Label reads "Blue Note Records - a Division of Liberty Records Inc.")
BLUE NOTE (5002 "Thelonious Monk") ... 200-400 52
(10-inch LP.)
BLUE NOTE (5009 "Thelonious Monk") ... 200-400 52
(10-inch LP.)
COLUMBIA (1900 thru 2600 series) ... 12-25 63-67
(Monaural.)
COLUMBIA (8700 thru 9800 series) ... 15-30 63-69
(Stereo.)
COLUMBIA (32000 thru 38000 series) ... 5-15 74-83
EVEREST ... 5-10 78
MILESTONE ... 5-15 75-84
PAUSA ... 5-10 83
PRESTIGE (142 "Thelonious Monk Trio") ... 100-200 52
(10-inch LP.)
PRESTIGE (180 "Thelonious Monk with Frank Foster") ... 100-200 54
(10-inch LP.)
PRESTIGE (189 "Thelonious Monk with Art Blakey") ... 100-200 54
(10-inch LP.)
PRESTIGE (7053 thru 7245) ... 30-60 56-62
(Yellow labels.)
PRESTIGE (7000 thru 7600 series) ... 15-25 65-69
(Blue labels.)
PRESTIGE (24000 series) ... 8-12 72
RIVERSIDE (12-201 thru 12-323) ... 30-60 55-60
RIVERSIDE (400 series) ... 15-30 62-67
RIVERSIDE (1100 series) ... 25-50 58-60
RIVERSIDE (3000 series) ... 10-20 68-69
RIVERSIDE (9400 series) ... 15-30 62-63
TOMATO ... 5-10 78
TRIP ... 5-10 73
Also see COLTRANE, John, & Thelonious Monk
Also see DAVIS, Miles, & Thelonious Monk
Also see MERC & MONK
Also see MULLIGAN, Gerry, & Thelonious Monk

MONK, Thelonious, & Sonny Rollins
EPs: 7-inch
PRESTIGE ... 20-40 52
LPs: 10/12-inch
PRESTIGE (166 "Thelonious Monk & Sonny Rollins") ... 150-250 52
(10-inch LP.)
PRESTIGE (200 series) ... 50-75 57-58
PRESTIGE (7000 series) ... 50-75 57-59
PRESTIGE (1100 series) ... 40-60 58

MONKEES — P&R/LP '66
Singles: 12-inch
ARISTA ... 8-12 86
(Promotional issue only.)
Singles: 7-inch
ARISTA (0201 "Daydream Believer") ... 5-10 76
ARISTA (9000 series) ... 3-6 76-86
COLGEMS ... 20-30 67
(Cardboard 5½-inch picture disc cutouts from cereal boxes. Four different graphic designs were used. Each lists four tracks, but only plays one. Song on any given disc is indicated by a number stamped into label area. A total of four different songs with four different pictures totals 16 variations.)
COLGEMS (1001 "I'm a Believer") ... 8-12 66
COLGEMS (1002 "Steppin' Stone") ... 8-12 66
COLGEMS (1004 "A Little Bit Me, a Little Bit You") ... 8-12 67
COLGEMS (1007 "Pleasant Valley Sunday") ... 8-12 67
COLGEMS (1012 "Daydream Believer") ... 8-12 67
COLGEMS (1019 "Valleri") ... 8-12 68
COLGEMS (1023 "D.W. Washburn") ... 8-12 68
COLGEMS (1031 "Porpoise Song") ... 15-25 68
COLGEMS (5000 "Tear Drop City") ... 20-30 69
COLGEMS (5004 "Listen to the Band") ... 15-25 69
COLGEMS (5005 "Good Clean Fun") ... 30-50 69
COLGEMS (5011 "Oh My My") ... 30-50 70
COLLECTABLES (0904300717 "18 Great Singles, Vol. 1") ... 30-40 94
(Colored vinyl.)
FLASHBACK ... 3-5 73
RHINO (Except 74411) ... 3-5 87
RHINO (74411 "Every Step of the Way") ... 15-20 87
(Picture disc.)
Picture Sleeves
ARISTA ... 3-5 86
COLGEMS (1001 "I'm a Believer") 10-15 66
COLGEMS (1002 "Steppin' Stone") ... 10-15 66
COLGEMS (1004 "A Little Bit Me, a Little Bit You") ... 10-15 67
COLGEMS (1007 "Pleasant Valley Sunday") ... 10-15 67
COLGEMS (1012 "Daydream Believer") ... 10-15 67
COLGEMS (1019 "Valleri") ... 10-15 68
COLGEMS (1023 "D.W. Washburn") ... 10-15 68
COLGEMS (1031 "Porpoise Song") ... 25-35 68
COLGEMS (5000 "Tear Drop City") ... 30-40 69
COLGEMS (5004 "Listen to the Band") ... 25-35 69
COLGEMS (5005 "Good Clean Fun") ... 40-60 69
COLGEMS (5011 "Oh My My") ... 40-60 70
RHINO ... 3-5 87
EPs: 7-inch
COLGEMS (Cardboard discs) ... 5-10 67
(Single-sided, four track discs, originally attached to cereal boxes. Not issued with covers, although discs were illustrated.)
COLGEMS (101 "The Monkees") ... 50-75 66
(Stereo 33 compact. Juke box issue.)
COLGEMS (102 "More of the Monkees") ... 50-75 67
(Stereo 33 compact. Juke box issue.)
LPs: 10/12-inch
ARISTA (4089 "Greatest Hits") ... 8-12 76
(Repackage of Bell 6081.)
ARISTA (8313 "Greatest Hits") ... 5-10 86
ARISTA (8432 "Then & Now") ... 8-12 86
BELL (6081 "Refocus") ... 40-50 73
(Cover pictures group in a camera lens.)
BELL (6081 "Refocus") ... 35-45 73
(Pictures group on stage, from TV show.)
COLGEMS (COM-101 "The Monkees") ... 40-50 66
(Monaural. With *Papa Gene's Blues.*)

COLGEMS (COS-101 "The Monkees")........40-50 66
(Stereo. With *Papa Gene's Blues*.)
COLGEMS (COM-101 "The Monkees")........20-30 66
(Monaural. Without *Papa Gene's Blues*.)
COLGEMS (COS-101 "The Monkees")........20-30 66
(Stereo. Without *Papa Gene's Blues*.)
COLGEMS (COM-102 "More of the Monkees")........20-30 67
(Monaural.)
COLGEMS (COS-102 "More of the Monkees")........20-30 67
(Stereo.)
COLGEMS (COM-103 "Headquarters")........20-30 67
(Monaural.)
COLGEMS (COS-103 "Headquarters")........20-30 67
(Stereo.)
COLGEMS (COM-104 "Pisces, Aquarius, Capricorn and Jones")........20-30 67
(Monaural.)
COLGEMS (COS-104 "Pisces, Aquarius, Capricorn and Jones")........20-30 67
(Stereo.)
COLGEMS (COM-109 "The Birds, The Bees, and the Monkees")........50-75 68
(Monaural.)
COLGEMS (COS-109 "The Birds, The Bees, and the Monkees")........20-30 68
(Stereo.)
COLGEMS (113 "Instant Replay")..25-35 69
COLGEMS (115 "The Monkees Greatest Hits")........30-50 69
COLGEMS (117 "The Monkees Present")........50-75 69
COLGEMS (119 "Changes")........75-100 70
COLGEMS (329 "Golden Hits")..100-125 71
(RCA Special Products issue.)
COLGEMS (1001 "A Barrel Full of Monkees")........50-75 71
COLGEMS (5008 "Head")........35-45 68
LAURIE HOUSE (8009 "The Monkees")........20-30 73
(Mail-order offer.)
PAIR (0188 "The Monkees")........15-25 82
RCA (329 "Golden Hits")........50-75 72
RCA (7868 "More of the Monkees")........8-10
RCA (7912 "Pisces, Aquarius, Capricorn and Jones")........8-10
RHINO (Except 701)........5-10 82-87
RHINO (701 "Monkee Business")...15-20 82
(Picture disc.)
SILHOUETTE (10012 "Tails of the Monkees")........10-15 83
(Picture disc.)
Members: Michael Nesmith; Davy Jones; Micky Dolenz; Peter Tork.
Also see DOLENZ, Micky
Also see DOLENZ, JONES & TORK
Also see JONES, Davy
Also see MODERN FOLK QUARTET
Also see NESMITH, Michael

MONKEES A-GO-GO
LPs: 10/12-inch
WYNCOTE (9203 "Monkees A-Go-Go")........15-20 66

MONKEY JOE & His Music Grinders
Singles: 78 rpm
OKEH........10-20 40s

MONN, Jeff
LPs: 10/12-inch
VANGUARD........10-15 68

MONN-KEYS
Singles: 7-inch
OMEGA (176 "Catch a Falling Star")........10-20 60s

MONO MEN: see MONOMEN

MONOCHROME SET
Singles: 7-inch
I.R.S. 3-5 79

MONOCLES
Singles: 7-inch
CHICORY (407 "Spider and the Fly")........20-30 67
DENCO........8-12 60s

MONOGRAMS
(With Count Fisher Trio)
Singles: 7-inch
MONOGRAM (106 "Tears in My Eyes")........5-10 75
RUST (5036 "Baby Blue Eyes")........20-30 61
SAFIRE (102 "Tears & Dreams")...10-20 60
SAGA (1000 "My Baby Dearest Darling")........40-60 57

MONOGRAMS
Singles: 7-inch
CARRINGTON........10-20

MONOMEN
(Mono Men)
Singles: 7-inch
DOG MEAT........3-4 93
ESTRUS........3-5 89
LANCE ROCK........3-4 92
LUCKY........3-4 92
MONO........3-4 92
REKKIDS........3-4 92
RISE........3-4 92
SCAT........3-4 92
SCREAMING APPLE........3-4 92
SUB POP........3-4 92
SYMPATHY........3-4 92
EPs: 7-inch
ESTRUS........4-8 91
GIFT of LIFE........4-8 91
REGAL SELECT........4-6 90
LPs: 10/12-inch
ESTRUS (123 "Wrecker")........8-10 92
(Black vinyl. Clothed girl cover.)
ESTRUS (123 "Wrecker")........10-20 92
(Colored vinyl. Nude girl cover. Approximately 1,500 made.)
POPLLAMA/ESTRUS........5-8 89
(Black vinyl.)
POPLLAMA/ESTRUS........8-12 89
(Colored vinyl.)
SCREAMING APPLE........5-8 92
Members: Dave Crider; Ledge Morrisette; Aaron Roeder; John Mortensen; Scott McCaughey; Diana Young.

MONOMONO
LPs: 10/12-inch
CAPITOL........8-10 74

MONOPOLY
Singles: 7-inch
POWER........4-8

MONORAILS
Singles: 7-inch
LUTE (6016 "Come to Me Darling")........200-250 61

MONORAYS
Singles: 7-inch
NASCO (6020 "It's Love Baby")......10-15 58

MONORAYS
(With Tony March & Orchestra)
Singles: 7-inch
RED ROCKET (476 "My Guardian Angel")........20-40 63
TAMMY (1005 "My Guardian Angel")........150-250 59
(Reads: "Tammy Records" at top.)
TAMMY (1005 "My Guardian Angel")........100-150 59
(Reads only "Tammy" at top. No mention of distribution by Jubilee.)
TAMMY (1005 "My Guardian Angel")........75-125 59
("Tammy" at top. Also indicates: "Nationally Distributed by Jubilee Records.")

MONORAYS
Singles: 7-inch
20TH FOX (594 "You're No Good")........30-40 65

MONOTONES P&R/R&B '58
Singles: 78 rpm
ARGO (5290 "Book of Love")....50-100 58
Singles: 7-inch
ARGO (Except 5339)........15-25 58-59
ARGO (5339 "Tell It to the Judge")........20-30 59
CHESS........3-5 73
COLLECTABLES........3-4 80s
ERIC........3-4 70s
HICKORY........5-10 64-65
HULL (735 "Reading the Book of Love")........50-60 60
HULL (743 "Daddy's Home But Momma's Gone")........15-20 61
MASCOT (124 "Book of Love")..250-500 57
ROULETTE........3-5 73
LPs: 10/12-inch
MURRAY HILL........5-8
Members: Warren Davis; Frank Smith; John Raynes; George Malone; Charles Patrick; James Patrick.

MONRO, Matt P&R/LP '61
Singles: 7-inch
CAPITOL........3-6 66-72
LIBERTY........3-8 62-66
U.A. 3-5 74
WARWICK........4-8 61
LPs: 10/12-inch
CAPITOL........8-15 67-70
LIBERTY........10-20 62-66
LONDON (1611 "Blue and Sentimental")........20-30 57
WARWICK (2045 "My Kind of Girl")........15-25 61
Also see BARRY, John

MONROE, Bill C&W '46
(With His Blue Grass Boys)
Singles: 78 rpm
BLUEBIRD........15-30 '30s
COLUMBIA........10-20 45-49
DECCA........10-15 50-57
Singles: 7-inch
DECCA (20000 series)........12-25 52-56
DECCA (30000 series)........8-15 56-64
DECCA (40000 series)........20-30 52
GLOBE (45 "Pelota")........10-15 81
(Picture disc. Has photo of Fernando Valenzuela of L.A. Dodgers.)
MCA........3-5 73
EPs: 7-inch
COLUMBIA........10-15 52-57
DECCA........5-15 56-65
LPs: 10/12-inch
ALBUM GLOBE........5-10 80s
CAMDEN........5-12 62-64
CORAL........5-8 80s
COUNTY........5-10
DECCA (Except 8731)........10-25 60-71
DECCA (8731 "Knee Deep in Bluegrass")........15-25 58
HARMONY........10-20 61-69
MCA........5-12 73-84
VOCALION........8-15 64-70
Members: Bill Monroe; Birch Monroe; Charles Monroe; Lester Flatt; Earl Scruggs; Chubby Wise; Cedric Rainwater; L.E. White; Waylon Jennings.
Also see CLEMENTS, Vassar
Also see FLATT, Lester, & Bill Monroe
Also see FLATT, Lester, Earl Scruggs & Bill Monroe
Also see JENNINGS, Waylon
Also see MARTIN, Jimmy
Also see MADDOX, Rose, & Bill Monroe
Also see WHITE, L.E., & Lola Jean Dillon

MONROE, Larry, & Don Keyes
Singles: 78 rpm
LIN........5-10 57
Singles: 7-inch
LIN........5-10 57

MONROE, Marilyn P&R '54
Singles: 78 rpm
RCA (5745 "River of No Return")........50-100 54
(Has picture of Marilyn on label. Promotional issue only.)
RCA (6033 "Heat Wave")........10-20 55
RCA/SIMON HOUSE (5745 "River of No Return")........100-200 54
(Has "Who Is She?" label. Promotional issue only.)
U.A. (161 "I Wanna Be Loved By You")........25-50 59
Singles: 7-inch
RCA (5745 "River of No Return")........50-100 54
(Has picture of Marilyn on label. Promotional issue only.)
RCA (6033 "Heat Wave")........15-25 55
20TH FOX (311 "River of No Return")........10-15 62
U.A. (161 "I Wanna Be Loved By You")........10-15 59
Picture Sleeves
RCA (5745 "River of No Return")........50-100 54
RCA (6033 "Heat Wave")........50-100 55
20TH FOX (311 "River of No Return")........50-75 62
EPs: 7-inch
MGM (208 "Gentlemen Prefer Blondes")........25-50 53
(Soundtrack. With Jane Russell.)
RCA (593 "There's No Business Like Show Business")........30-40 55
U.A. (1005 "Some Like It Hot")......25-35 59
(With "This Is Hot!" publicity insert for the film.)
U.A. (1005 "Some Like It Hot")......15-25 59
(Without film publicity insert.)
LPs: 10/12-inch
ASCOT (13500 "Some Like It Hot")........20-30 64
(Monaural. Soundtrack.)
ASCOT (16500 "Some Like It Hot")........30-40 64
(Stereo. Soundtrack. Also has selections from other films.)
AUDIO FIDELITY (50005 "The Ten")........25-35 84
(Picture disc.)
COLUMBIA (1527 "Let's Make Love")........30-50 60
(Monaural. Soundtrack.)
COLUMBIA (8327 "Let's Make Love")........40-60 60
(Stereo. Soundtrack.)
COLUMBIA/CSP (8327 "Let's Make Love")........8-12
(Soundtrack. With Yves Montand and Frankie Vaughan.)
MGM (208 "Gentlemen Prefer Blondes")........75-100 53
(10-inch LP.)
MGM (3231 "Gentlemen Prefer Blondes")........40-60 55
(Soundtrack. With Jane Russell. One side has music from *Till the Clouds Roll By*.)
MOVIETONE (72016 "Unforgettable")........15-25 67
SANDY HOOK (Except 2013)........5-10 79
SANDY HOOK (2013 "Rare Recordings 1948-'62")........30-40 84
STET (15005 "Never Before and Never Again")........8-12
(Soundtrack. With Jane Russell.)
20TH FOX (5000 "Marilyn")........75-125 62
(With bonus photo of Marilyn nude.)
20TH FOX (5000 "Marilyn")........50-75 62
(Without bonus photo.)
U.A. (272 "Some Like It Hot")........8-12 74
(Soundtrack.)
U.A. (4030 "Some Like It Hot")......35-55 59
(Monaural. Soundtrack.)
U.A. (5030 "Some Like It Hot")......50-75 59
(Stereo. Soundtrack.)
Also see RUSSELL, Jane

MONROE, Michael LP '89
LPs: 10/12-inch
MERCURY........5-8 89

MONROE, Smiley
Singles: 78 rpm
VITA (163 "Teenage Doll")........20-30 57
Singles: 7-inch
SAGE (403 "Pickin' Pete")........10-15 64
VITA (163 "Teenage Doll")........20-30 57

MONROE, Vaughn P&R '40
Singles: 78 rpm
BLUEBIRD........5-10 40-42
RCA........3-8 47-58
VICTOR........4-8 42-47
Singles: 7-inch
DOT........3-6 62-63
JUBILEE........4-6 61
MGM........4-6 60
RCA........5-8 50-59
ROD........3-5 68
U.A. 4-6 60
Picture Sleeves
RCA........10-15 57
EPs: 7-inch
CAMDEN........5-10 56
RCA........5-10 50-56
LPs: 10/12-inch
CAMDEN........15-25 56
DOT........10-20 62-64
HAMILTON........10-20 65
KAPP........10-20 65
RCA (11 thru 3066)........20-40 50-53
(10-inch LPs.)
RCA (1400 thru 1700 series)........15-25 56-58
(12-inch LPs.)
RCA (1100 series)........5-10 75
RCA (3800 series)........10-15 67
RCA (6000 series)........5-10 72
Also see MARTIN, Dean / Patti Page
Also see PRESLEY, Elvis / Vaughn Monroe / Gogi Grant / Robert Shaw

MONROE, Vince
Singles: 7-inch
EXCELLO........10-12 56

MONROE BROTHERS
Singles: 78 rpm
BLUEBIRD........20-30 '30s
Members: Bill Monroe; Birch Monroe; Charles Monroe.
Also see MONROE, Bill

MONROES P&R/LP '82
Singles: 7-inch
ALFA........3-5 82
LPs: 10/12-inch
ALFA (15015 "The Monroes")........5-10 82

MONSTERS
LPs: 10/12-inch
ROYAL ("Tribute to the Beatles")...35-50 60s
(Selection number not known.)

MONSTERS FOUR
Singles: 7-inch
VEE JAY........5-10 64

MONSTROSITIES
Singles: 7-inch
MONSTER........10-15 65

MONTAGE
Singles: 7-inch
LAURIE........4-8 68
LPs: 10/12-inch
LAURIE (2049 "Montage")........12-18 69
Members: Michael Brown; Vance Chapman; Mike Smyth; Lance Cornelius; Bob Steurer.
Also see LEFT BANKE

MONTAGUE
Singles: 7-inch
DUANE........5-8 68
MINIT........5-8 68

MONTAGUES
Singles: 7-inch
EARLY BIRD (1002 "School Rock")...4-6 95
(Colored vinyl.)

MONTAGUE, Roy
Singles: 7-inch
COLUMBIA........4-8 67
LEE........5-10 59-65

MONTAINE, Pat
Singles: 7-inch
COUNTERPOINT........5-10 59

MONTAINES
Singles: 7-inch
ROTATE........8-12

MONTALBAN, Ricardo
Singles: 7-inch
MMI........3-5 76
LPs: 10/12-inch
MMI........5-10 76

MONTALVO, Lenny, & Crystal Chords
(With Leroy Kirkland & Orchestra)
Singles: 7-inch
3D (373 "Be Mine Again")........100-200 58
Also see SOTOLONGO, Edward

MONTAN, Chris
Singles: 7-inch
20TH FOX........3-5 80
LPs: 10/12-inch
20TH FOX........5-10 80

MONTANA
Singles: 7-inch
ATLANTIC........3-5 78
LPs: 10/12-inch
ATLANTIC........5-10 78

MONTANA C&W '81
Singles: 7-inch
WATERHOUSE........3-5 81

MONTANA, Billy, & Long Shots C&W '87
Singles: 7-inch
W.B. 3-4 87-88

MONTANA ORCHESTRA LP '81
LPs: 10/12-inch
MJS........5-8 81

MONTANA SEXTET D&D '83
Singles: 12-inch
PHILLY SOUND........4-6 83

MONTANA SKYLINE C&W '81
Singles: 7-inch
SNOW........3-5 81

MONTANAS P&R '68
Singles: 7-inch
INDEPENDENCE........5-10 67-69
W.B. 4-8 66-68

MONTCLAIRS
("Featuring Eugene Arnold with Ted Walker & Orchestra"; with Douglas DuBois, Chico Chism & His Jettinaires)
Singles: 7-inch
HI-Q (5001 "Golden Angel")........200-300 57
(Has double horizontal lines. Indicates "Unbreakable 45 R.P.M.")
HI-Q (5001 "Golden Angel")........50-100 57
(Has single horizontal line. No mention of "Unbreakable 45 R.P.M.")
PREMIUM (404 "Give Me a Chance")........250-350 56
SONIC (104 "All I Want Is Love")........500-1000 56
Also see SMITH, Floyd, & Montclairs

MONTCLAIRS
Singles: 7-inch
TNT (154 "The Bells")........400-600 58

MONTCLAIRS
Singles: 7-inch
AUDICON (111 "Goodnight")........10-20 61

MONTCLAIRS
Singles: 7-inch
ABC-PAR (10463 "I Believe")........10-15 63

MONTCLAIRS
Singles: 7-inch
SUNBURST........4-8 65

MONTCLAIRS R&B '72
Singles: 7-inch
PAULA........3-6 71-74
LPs: 10/12-inch
PAULA........8-12 72
Members: Phil Perry; Kevin Samlin; George McLellan; David Frye; Scotty Williams.

MONTCLAIRS
Singles: 7-inch
UNITED INT'L (1007 "Lisa")........25-50 63
UNITED INT'L (1013 "Young Wings Can Fly")........25-50 64

MONTE, Del
Singles: 7-inch
1ST........5-10 61

MONTE, Lou P&R '54
Singles: 78 rpm
RCA (Except 6704)........3-5 53-56
RCA (6704 "Elvis Presley for President")........10-20 56
Singles: 7-inch
GWP........3-5 71-72
JAMIE........3-5 72
RCA (5382 thru 6600 series)........10-20 53-56
RCA (6700 thru 7600 series, except 6704)........5-15 56-60
RCA (6704 "Elvis Presley for President")........20-30 56
RCA (8700 thru 9000 series)........5-10 65-67
RAGALIA........3-6 69
REPRISE........5-10 62-65
ROULETTE........5-10 60-61
Picture Sleeves
REPRISE........8-12 62-63
EPs: 7-inch
RCA (Except 18)........10-20 57-59
RCA (18 "Elvis Presley for President")........25-35 56
(Promotional issue only. Not issued with cover.)
LPs: 10/12-inch
CAMDEN........15-20 58
DESIGN........10-15
HARMONY........10-15 68
RCA (1600 thru 1900 series)........20-35 57-59
RCA (3000 series)........10-20 66-67
ROULETTE........15-25 60
REPRISE........15-25 61-65
Also see PRESLEY, Elvis / Martha Carson / Lou Monte / Herb Jeffries

MONTE, Michael
Singles: 7-inch
CHRISTY (103 "Rock My Rockin' Chair")........25-50 58

MONTE, Vinnie
(With the Jay Birds; with Charles Calello & Orchestra)
Singles: 7-inch
DECANTER........5-10 59-60
FARGO........8-12 58
HARMON........4-8 62-63
JOSIE (793 "Your Cute Little Ways")........15-25 56
JUBILEE (5391 "Red Ink")........10-20 60
JUBILEE (5408 "Rocco's Theme")........10-20 61
JUBILEE (5419 "One of the Guys")........10-20 62
JUBILEE (5428 "Mashed Potato Girl")........15-25 62
RCA........5-10 65
TCF (7 "Hey, Look at the Winter Snow")........50-75 63

MONTEGOS
Singles: 7-inch
ABC........4-8 68

MONTELL, Freddie
Singles: 7-inch
ERMINE ... 5-10 59

MONTELLS
Singles: 7-inch
GOLDEN CREST (582 "A Ring a Ling") ... 15-25 63
GOLDEN CREST (585 "Gee Baby") ... 15-25 63
Member: Charles Dell.
Also see H.M. SUBJECTS

MONTELS
Singles: 7-inch
KINK (9365 "Rondevous [sic]") ... 100-200 61
UNIVERSAL (101 "Union Hall") ... 250-350 61
Also see FRANKIE & C-NOTES / Montels

MONTENEGRO, Hugo LP '66
(With Orchestra & Chorus)
Singles: 7-inch
RCA ... 3-5 64-75
TIME ... 4-6 61-63
20TH FOX ... 5-8 59
LPs: 10/12-inch
CAMDEN ... 10-20 62
GWP ... 5-10 70
MAINSTREAM ... 10-15 67-68
MOVIETONE ... 8-12 67
PICKWICK ... 5-10 70s
RCA (0025 thru 2300 series) ... 5-10 72-77
RCA (LOC-1113 "Hurry Sundown") ... 35-40 67
(Monaural. Soundtrack.)
RCA (LSO-1113 "Hurry Sundown") ... 40-50 67
(Stereo. Soundtrack.)
RCA (2900 series) ... 10-15 64
RCA (LPM-3475 "Man from U.N.C.L.E.") ... 25-35 65
(Monaural. Soundtrack.)
RCA (LSP-3475 "Man from U.N.C.L.E.") ... 30-40 65
(Stereo. Soundtrack.)
RCA (LPM-3574 "Man from U.N.C.L.E., Volume 2") ... 30-40 66
(Monaural. Soundtrack.)
RCA (LSP-3574 "Man from U.N.C.L.E., Volume 2") ... 35-45 66
(Stereo. Soundtrack.)
RCA (3500 thru 4600 series) ... 5-15 66-71
RCA (6000 series) ... 5-10 71
TIME ... 8-15 60-64
20TH FOX ... 5-15 59-68
Also see HIRT, Al, & Hugo Montenegro

MONTERAYS
Singles: 7-inch
BUFF ... 10-20 60s
SAHARA ... 10-20 60s
ULTIMA (704 "Deep Within My Heart") ... 15-25 64
Also see MADISONS / Monterays

MONTERAYS
Singles: 7-inch
PLANET (57 "You Never Cared") ... 25-35 63

MONTEREYS
Singles: 78 rpm
NESTOR (15 "Someone Like You") ... 100-200 56
TEENAGE (1001 "Someone Like You") ... 100-200 56
Singles: 7-inch
TEENAGE (1001 "Someone Like You") ... 300-400 56
Members: Dean Barlow; Bill Lindsay; Ed Jordan.
Also see BARLOW, Dean, & Montereys

MONTEREYS
Singles: 7-inch
ARWIN (130 "Goodbye My Love") ... 20-30 59
ASTRA (1018 "Face in the Crowd") ... 10-15 65
BLAST (219 "Face in the Crowd") ... 75-125 63
DOMINION (1019 "First Kiss") ... 50-100 64
EAST WEST (124 "I'll Love You Again") ... 10-20 59
GNP (314 "For Sentimental Reasons") ... 15-25 63
HILLSIDE (826 "Oh Cheryl") ... 30-50
IMPALA (213 "Without a Girl") ... 75-100 63
MAJOR (1009 "A Crowded Room") ... 75-125 59
PRINCE (5060 "Rita") ... 10-20 60
ROSE (109 "You're the Girl for Me") ... 100-200 58
SATURN (1002 "My Girl") ... 50-100 60
TRANS AMERICAN (1000 "Little Darlin' ") ... 300-500 60

MONTEREYS
Singles: 7-inch
CUCA (1002 "Rockin' Fool") ... 20-30 62
GOLD STAR (1001 "Whiplash") ... 20-30 62
Members: Kenny Loehrke; Wes Phillips; Orville Luebke; Rudd Hoger; Don Pinnow; Jimmy Thiele.

MONTEREYS
Singles: 7-inch
DEE-JAY (1013 "Party") ... 15-25 60s
T-HEE (700/1 "Bo-Did-It") ... 10-20 66

MONTEREYS & GRANDEURS
Singles: 7-inch
CARDINALE ... 8-12

MONTERO, Juan
Singles: 7-inch
EMBER (1088 "Freckles") ... 10-20 62

MONTEREYS QUARTET
Singles: 7-inch
J.C. (9317 "The Ballad of Take Me Back to Baltimore") ... 20-30 60

MONTEZ, Chris P&R/R&B '62
Singles: 7-inch
A&M ... 4-6 65-68
COLLECTABLES ... 3-4 80s
ERA ... 3-5 72
ERIC ... 3-4 70s
JAMIE ... 3-5 73
MONOGRAM ... 5-10 62-64
PARAMOUNT ... 3-5 71-73
LPs: 10/12-inch
A&M ... 10-20 66-67
MONOGRAM (100 "Let's Dance") ... 50-100 63
Members: Joel Hill; Carol Kaye; Julius Wechter; Pete Jolly; Tom Tedesco; Hal Blaine.
Also see BAJA MARIMBA BAND
Also see BLAINE, Hal
Also see CHRIS & KATHY
Also see HILL, Joel
Also see JOLLY, Pete
Also see TEDESCO, Tommy

MONTEZUMA'S REVENGE
LPs: 10/12-inch
FAN FARE ... 10-15 76

MONTGOMERY, Bob
Singles: 7-inch
BRUNSWICK (55157 "Because I Love You") ... 20-30 59
Also see BOB & CAROL
Also see HOLLY, Buddy

MONTGOMERY, Carol
Singles: 7-inch
SOUND STAGE 7 ... 4-8 63-64
Also see BOB & CAROL

MONTGOMERY, Christopher
Singles: 7-inch
DOLTON ... 10-20 63

MONTGOMERY, Gene
Singles: 7-inch
COLUMBIA ... 4-6 62
Picture Sleeves
COLUMBIA ... 4-8 62

MONTGOMERY, Gray
Singles: 7-inch
BEAGLE (101 "Right Now") ... 50-75

MONTGOMERY, Harold
Singles: 7-inch
WOLF TEX ... 5-10 61

MONTGOMERY, Jack
Singles: 7-inch
BARRACUDA (2-8030 "Don't Turn Your Back on Me") ... 25-50 60s
REVUE (11009 "Baby, Baby Take a Chance on Me") ... 10-15 60s
SCEPTER (12152 "Do You Believe It") ... 20-40 66

MONTGOMERY, James, Band
LPs: 10/12-inch
CAPRICORN ... 8-12 73-74
ISLAND ... 8-10 76

MONTGOMERY, Lee
Singles: 7-inch
LIBERTY ... 5-8 69

MONTGOMERY, Little Brother
(With His Vicksburgers; with His Bogalusa Boys; Quintet)
Singles: 78 rpm
CENTURY ... 10-20 47
EBONY ... 10-15 56
WINDIN' BALL ... 10-15 54
Singles: 7-inch
BLACKBIRD (705 "Pine Top Boogie Woogie") ... 10-20 61
EBONY ... 10-20 56-60
F.M. (1002 "Mini-Skirt Blues") ... 10-15 66
WINDIN' BALL ... 15-25 54
LPs: 10/12-inch
ADELPHI ... 10-12
PRESTIGE ... 5-8
PRESTIGE BLUESVILLE (1012 "Tasty Blues") ... 20-30 61
RCA ... 10-15 77
RIVERSIDE (9410 "Chicago, Living Legend") ... 20-30
Also see SUNNYLAND SLIM
Also see SYKES, Roosevelt, & Little Brother Montgomery

MONTGOMERY, Little Brother, & Mama Yancey
LPs: 10/12-inch
RIVERSIDE (403 "Southside Blues") ... 30-40 60
Also see MONTGOMERY, Little Brother
Also see YANCEY, Mama

MONTGOMERY, Marian
Singles: 7-inch
CAPITOL ... 4-6 63
LPs: 10/12-inch
CAPITOL ... 20-30 63

MONTGOMERY, Melba C&W '63
Singles: 7-inch
CAPITOL ... 3-5 69-76
COMPASS ... 3-4 86
ELEKTRA ... 3-5 73-75
KARI ... 3-5 80
MUSICOR ... 3-6 66-69
U.A. (500 thru 900 series) ... 4-8 63-66
U.A. (1000 & 1100 series) ... 3-5 77
Picture Sleeves
MUSICOR ... 4-8 66
LPs: 10/12-inch
CAPITOL ... 8-12 69-75
ELEKTRA ... 5-10 73-75
MUSICOR ... 10-20 66-68
UNART ... 8-12 67
U.A. (Except 600 series) ... 10-20 64
U.A. (600 series) ... 5-10 78
Also see JONES, George, Gene Pitney & Melba Montgomery
Also see JONES, George, & Melba Montgomery
Also see LOUVIN, Charlie, & Melba Montgomery
Also see PITNEY, Gene, & Melba Montgomery
Also see WEST, Dottie / Melba Montgomery

MONTGOMERY, Nancy C&W '81
Singles: 7-inch
OVATION ... 3-4 81

MONTGOMERY, Peanut, III
Singles: 7-inch
TOLLIE ... 4-8 64

MONTGOMERY, Robbie
Singles: 7-inch
TEENA ... 4-8 63

MONTGOMERY, Tammy P&R '63
(Tana Montgomery; Tammi Terrell)
Singles: 7-inch
CHECKER (1072 "If I Would Marry You") ... 25-35 64
(Maroon label.)
CHECKER (1072 "If I Would Marry You") ... 15-25 64
(Multi-color label.)
SCEPTER (1224 "If You See Bill") ... 30-50 61
TRY ME (28001 "I Cried") ... 20-30 63
WAND (123 "Voice of Experience") ... 20-30 62
Also see TERRELL, Tammi

MONTGOMERY, Tana: see MONTGOMERY, Tammy

MONTGOMERY, Wes LP '65
(Wes Montgomery Quartet)
Singles: 7-inch
A&M ... 3-5 67-70
PACIFIC JAZZ ... 4-8 60
RIVERSIDE ... 4-8 61-64
VERVE ... 4-6 65-68
EPs: 7-inch
A&M (126 "Greatest Hits") ... 5-10 70
(Juke box issue only. Includes title strips.)
A&M (3001 "A Day in the Life") ... 5-10 67
(Juke box issue only. Includes title strips.)
LPs: 10/12-inch
A&M ... 10-15 67-70
ACCORD ... 5-8 82
BLUE NOTE ... 6-12 75
MFSL (508 "Bumpin'") ... 15-20
MGM ... 10-15 70
MILESTONE ... 8-15 73-83
PACIFIC JAZZ (5 "Montgomeryland") ... 35-45 60
PACIFIC JAZZ (10000 & 20000 series) ... 10-20 66-68
RIVERSIDE (034 thru 089) ... 5-8 82-83
RIVERSIDE (300 & 400 series) ... 15-30 59-67
RIVERSIDE (3000 series) ... 10-15 68-69
VERVE ... 10-20 65-72
(Reads "MGM Records - A Division of Metro-Goldwyn-Mayer, Inc." at bottom of label.)
VERVE ... 5-10 73-84
(Reads "Manufactured By MGM Record Corp.," or mentions either Polydor or Polygram at bottom of label.)
Also see MONTGOMERY BROTHERS
Also see SMITH, Jimmy, & Wes Montgomery

MONTGOMERY BROTHERS
Singles: 7-inch
RIVERSIDE ... 5-10 61
EPs: 7-inch
RIVERSIDE (9362 "Groove Yard") ... 10-20 61
(Stereo. Juke box issue only.)
LPs: 10/12-inch
FANTASY (3308 "Montgomery Brothers") ... 30-40 60
(Monaural.)
FANTASY (3323 "In Candida") ... 30-40 61
(Monaural.)
FANTASY (8052 "Montgomery Brothers") ... 35-45 60
(Stereo.)
FANTASY (8066 "In Candida") ... 35-45 61
(Stereo.)
PACIFIC JAZZ (5 "Montgomeryland") ... 30-40 61
PACIFIC JAZZ (17 "Montgomery Brothers") ... 25-35 60
(Reissue of World Pacific 1240.)
RIVERSIDE (362 "Groove Yard") ... 25-35 61
(Monaural.)
RIVERSIDE (9362 "Groove Yard") ... 30-40 61
(Stereo.)
WORLD PACIFIC (1240 "Montgomery Brothers") ... 50-75 58
Members: Wes Montgomery; Buddy Montgomery; Monk Montgomery.
Also see MONTGOMERY, Wes
Also see SHEARING, George, & Montgomery Brothers

MONTGOMERYS, The
(Montgomery's)
Singles: 7-inch
AMY (883 "Promise of Love") ... 200-300 63

MONTI, Lou
(Lou Monti's Tu-Tones)
Singles: 7-inch
WEDGEWOOD ... 4-6

MONTI ROCK: see ROCK, Monti, III

MONTICELLOS
Singles: 7-inch
RED CAP (102 "Don't Hold Back") ... 25-50 67

MONTIONE, "Banana Joe"
Singles: 7-inch
WFIL (1 "Cakewalk to the Cup") ... 4-6 75

MONTRE-EL, Jackie R&B '68
Singles: 7-inch
ABC ... 5-10 68-69

MONTRELL, Roy
Singles: 78 rpm
SPECIALTY ... 10-20 56
Singles: 7-inch
MINIT ... 5-10 61
SPECIALTY ... 15-25 56

MONTROSE LP '74
Singles: 7-inch
W.B. ... 3-5 74-77
LPs: 10/12-inch
ENIGMA ... 5-8 87
W.B. ... 8-12 73-78
Members: Ronnie Montrose; Sammy Hagar.
Also see HAGAR, Sammy

MONTROSE
LPs: 10/12-inch
ENIGMA ... 5-8 87

MONTROSE, Ronnie LP '78
Singles: 7-inch
W.B. ... 3-5 78
LPs: 10/12-inch
W.B. ... 5-10 78
Also see GAMMA
Also see MONTROSE
Also see WINTER, Edgar

MONTY PYTHON LP '75
Singles: 7-inch
ARISTA ... 4-6 80
LPs: 10/12-inch
ARISTA (4039 "Matching Tie and Handkerchief") ... 10-20 75
ARISTA (4050 "Album of the Soundtrack of the Trailer of the Film of *Monty Python and the Holy Grail*") ... 10-20 75
ARISTA (4073 "Monty Python Live! at the City Center") ... 10-20 76
ARISTA (9536 "Monty Python's Contractual Obligation Album") ... 10-20 80
CHARISMA/BUDDAH (1049 "Another Monty Python Record") ... 15-25 72
CHARISMA/BUDDAH (1063 "Monty Python's Previous Record") ... 15-25 72
MCA (6121 "Meaning of Life") ... 8-12 83
W.B. (3396 "Life of Brian") ... 10-15 79
PYE (12116 "Monty Python's Flying Circus") ... 15-20 75
Members: John Cleese; Graham Chapman; Eric Idle; Michael Palin; Terry Jones; Terry Gilliam.
Also see RUTLES

MON-VALES
Singles: 7-inch
PEN JOY (501 "Carol-Ann") ... 100-200 58

MONYAKA D&D '83
Singles: 12-inch
EASY STREET ... 4-6 83

MONUMENTS
Singles: 7-inch
ALVERA (2 "I Need You") ... 20-30 66

MONZAS
Singles: 7-inch
A-LA-CARTE ... 8-12
MOON (5321 "Stubborn Kind of Fella") ... 20-25 60s
MOON (7330 "You Know You Turn Me On") ... 10-20 60s
PACIFIC (1002 "Instant Love") ... 30-50 60s
PACIFIC (1999 "Baby You Know") ... 15-20
PACIFIC (1120 "Hey! I Know You") ... 15-20
PACIFIC (7731 "In My Lonely Room") ... 20-25
WAND (1120 "Forever") ... 5-10 66
Members: Al Wilks; Bobby Cooper; Jimmy Lane; Jack Ferrell; Jerry McIntosh; Phil Mullins.

MONZELS
Singles: 7-inch
PRISM (1898 "Sharkskin") ... 15-25 64

MOOD
Singles: 7-inch
B&G (101 "In the Amber Fields") ... 20-30 60s

MOOD
LPs: 10/12-inch
RCA ... 5-8 83

MOOD, Barbara
Singles: 7-inch
GLORY ... 5-10 59

MOOD MAKERS
(With Rocky G. Bralter Orchestra)
Singles: 7-inch
BAMBI (8000 "Dolores") ... 50-100 61

MOODS
Singles: 7-inch
RENCO ... 4-6 62
SARG (162 "Little Alice") ... 40-60 59
SARG (176 "Easy Going") ... 20-30 59
SARG (179 "Let Me Have Your Love") ... 30-40 59
SARG (185 "Teenager's Past") ... 20-30 59

MOODS
Singles: 7-inch
KOOL ... 4-8 65
Also see EXCEPTIONS

MOODS
Singles: 7-inch
BANG ... 5-8 68
WAND ... 5-8 70

MOODY, Clyde C&W '48
(With Tommy Scott)
Singles: 78 rpm
DECCA (28785 "What a Life") ... 10-15 53
KING ... 10-15 48-50
Singles: 7-inch
DECCA (28785 "What a Life") ... 15-25 53
LPs: 10/12-inch
KING (891 "Best of Clyde Moody") ... 50-75 64
OLD HOMESTEAD ... 5-10
STARDAY ... 20-30 78

MOODY, Joan
Singles: 7-inch
TCF ... 4-8 66
20TH FOX ... 4-8 66

MOODY, Ron, & Centaurs
Singles: 7-inch
ABC ... 8-12
COLUMBIA ... 5-10 69
COLPAR (39 "If I Didn't Have a Dime") ... 10-20

MOODY & DELTAS
Singles: 7-inch
DAISY (504 "Monkey Climb") ... 15-25 64

MOODY BLUES P&R '65
Singles: 7-inch
DERAM ... 4-8 68-72
LONDON (200 series) ... 3-5 78
LONDON (1005 "This Is My House") ... 8-12 67
LONDON (9726 "Go Now") ... 5-10 65
LONDON (9764 "From the Bottom of My Heart") ... 10-15 65
LONDON (9799 "Ev'ry Day") ... 10-15 65
LONDON (9810 "Stop") ... 10-15 66
LONDON (20000 series) ... 8-12 66
POLYDOR (Black vinyl) ... 3-4 86-88
POLYDOR (7078 "The Other Side of Life") ... 4-6 86
(Colored vinyl.)
THRESHOLD (600 series) ... 3-4 81-85
THRESHOLD (67000 series) ... 3-6 70-72
Picture Sleeves
POLYDOR (7078 "The Other Side of Life") ... 4-6 86
POLYDOR (870990 "No More Lies") ... 3-4 88
POLYDOR (883906 "Your Wildest Dreams") ... 3-4 86
POLYDOR (885201 "The Other Side of Life") ... 3-4 86
POLYDOR (887600 "I Know You're Out There Somewhere") ... 3-4 88
THRESHOLD (602 "The Voice") ... 3-4 81
THRESHOLD (604 "Sitting at the Wheel") ... 3-4 81
THRESHOLD (67006 "The Story in Your Eyes") ... 3-5 71
LPs: 10/12-inch
DERAM (16012 "Days of Future Passed") ... 30-40 68
(Monaural.)
DERAM (18012 "Days of Future Passed") ... 10-20 68
(Stereo.)
DERAM (18017 "In Search of the Lost Chord") ... 10-20 68
(Gatefold cover.)
DERAM (18017 "In Search of the Lost Chord") ... 5-10
(Standard cover.)
DERAM (18025 "On the Threshold of a Dream") ... 10-20 69
(Gatefold cover.)
DERAM (18025 "On the Threshold of a Dream") ... 5-10 69
(Standard cover.)
DERAM (18051 "In the Beginning") ... 10-20 69
DERAM (820006 "Days of Future Passed") ... 5-10
LONDON (428 "Go Now") ... 20-25 65
(Stereo.)
LONDON (690/1 "Caught Live") ... 10-20 77
LONDON (708 "Octave") ... 8-10 78
(Black vinyl.)
LONDON (708 "Octave") ... 20-25 78
(Colored vinyl. Promotional issue only.)
LONDON (3428 "Go Now") ... 25-45 65
(Monaural.)
MFSL (042 "Days of Future Past") ... 50-70 80
MFSL (151 "Seventh Sojourn") ... 50-70 85
MFSL (215 "On the Threshold of a Dream") ... 20-25 94
MFSL (232 "Every Good Boy Deserves Favour") ... 20-25 95
POLYDOR (835765 "Sur la Mer") ... 5-10 88

POLYDOR (849433 "Keys of the Kingdom") 5-10 91
THRESHOLD (1 "To Our Children's Children's Children") 8-12 69
(Gatefold cover.)
THRESHOLD (1 "To Our Children's Children's Children") 5-10
(Standard cover.)
THRESHOLD (3 "A Question of Balance") 8-12 70
(Gatefold cover.)
THRESHOLD (3 "A Question of Balance") 5-10
(Standard cover.)
THRESHOLD (5 "Every Good Boy Deserves Favor") 8-10 71
(Gatefold cover.)
THRESHOLD (7 "Seventh Sojourn") 8-10 72
(Gatefold cover.)
THRESHOLD (12/13 "This Is the Moody Blues") 10-12 70
(Two LPs.)
THRESHOLD (2901 "Long Distance Voyager") 5-10 81
(Gatefold cover.)
THRESHOLD (2902 "The Present") 5-10 83
THRESHOLD (820155 "Voices in the Sky") 5-10 85
THRESHOLD (820517 "Prelude") 5-10 86
THRESHOLD (829179 "Other Side of Life") 5-10 86
THRESHOLD (840659 "Greatest Hits") 5-10 89
Members: Michael Pinder; Ray Thomas; Graeme Edge; Brian Hines (a.k.a. Denny Laine); Clint Warwick; John Lodge; Justin Hayward; Patrick Moraz; Rod Clarke.
Also see EDGE, Graeme
Also see HAYWARD, Justin, & John Lodge
Also see LODGE, John
Also see MORAZ, Patrick
Also see PINDER, Michael
Also see THOMAS, Ray

MOODY WALKERS
Singles: 7-inch
RAYNARD (10043 "We Never Loved Before") 15-25 65

MOOG MACHINE LP '69
LPs: 10/12-inch
COLUMBIA 5-10 69

MOOHAH
Singles: 78 rpm
STARMAKER 50-75 54
Singles: 7-inch
STARMAKER (501 "All Shook Out") 150-250 54

MOON
Singles: 7-inch
IMPERIAL (66285 "Mothers and Fathers") 15-25 68
IMPERIAL (66330 "Faces") 10-20 68
IMPERIAL (66415 "Pirate") 10-20 69
LPs: 10/12-inch
IMPERIAL (12381 "Without Faith") 20-30 68
IMPERIAL (12444 "The Moon") 20-30 69
Members: Matthew Moore; David Marks; Larry Brown; Dave Jackson.
Also see DAVE & MARKSMEN
Also see MOORE, Matthew

MOON, Chris, Group
Singles: 7-inch
KINETIC 3-5 70
LPs: 10/12-inch
BARNABY 8-10 70
KINETIC 10-15 70

MOON, Darryl
Singles: 7-inch
FAR GO (1001 "I Was Wrong") 25-35 60s

MOON, Joe
Singles: 7-inch
HILLCREST (120 "Live It Up") 200-300

MOON, Keith LP '75
Singles: 7-inch
MCA (40316 "Don't Worry Baby") 20-30
(Promotional issue.)
TRACK 3-5 75
LPs: 10/12-inch
MCA 8-10 75
Also see LORD SUTCH
Also see NELSON, Rick
Also see WHO

MOON, Mickey
Singles: 7-inch
CORAL (62088 "That's My Daisy") 10-20 59

MOON, Norman
Singles: 7-inch
SPANGLE 5-10 58

MOON, Roger
LPs: 10/12-inch
CAPITOL 10-12 75

MOON, Smiley, & Moontunes
Singles: 7-inch
STAR (601 "You Don't Understand") 50-75 60s

MOON, Sonny
Singles: 7-inch
W.B. (5018 "Countdown") 10-20 59

MOON MEN
Singles: 7-inch
SOUTHERN SOUND (114 "Other Side of the Moon") 15-25 64
Also see WRAY, Link

MOON PEOPLE
Singles: 7-inch
ROULETTE 4-6 69
SPEED 5-8 68

MOON RAKERS: see MOONRAKERS

MOON STARS BAND
Singles: 7-inch
GOOD SOUND 5-10 62

MOON STONES
Singles: 7-inch
DOLTON (70 "My True Love") 10-15 63
Session: Nokie Edwards.
Also see VENTURES

MOON SURFERS / Michael Dominico
Singles: 7-inch
GENIUS (2101 "Surfin' on the Moon") 20-30 60s

MOON'S TRAIN
Singles: 7-inch
MGM 4-8 67

MOONBEAMS
Singles: 7-inch
GREAT (100 "A Lover's Plea") 200-400 59

MOONBEAMS
Singles: 7-inch
CHECKER (912 "Cryin' the Blues") 20-30 59
(First issued on Sapphire as by the Moonbeems.)
Members: Simon Washington; John Meyers; Fontelle Land; Bill Turicot; Elaine Edwards.
Also see MOONBEEMS
Also see OTIS, Johnny

MOONBEEMS
(Moonbeams)
Singles: 7-inch
SAPPHIRE (1003 "Cryin' the Blues") 100-125 58
(Reissued on Checker as by the Moonbeams.)
SAPPHIRE (1053 "Teen Age Baby") 50-100 58
Also see MOONBEAMS

MOONBEEMS / Hawkettes
Singles: 7-inch
SAPPHIRE (2250 "Cryin' the Blues") 35-50 58
Also see HAWKETTES
Also see MOONBEEMS

MOON-DAWGS
Singles: 7-inch
BOFUZ (1115 "You're No Good") 25-35 60s
ROUND (69 "Keep on Pushing") 20-30 60s

MOONDOG
(With His Friends; with Louis T. Hardin)
EPs: 7-inch
BRUNSWICK (86000 "Improvisations at a Jazz Concert") 25-50 53
(Issued with a paper sleeve.)
EPIC (7015 "Moondog and His Friends") 15-25 54
MARS (A2 "Moondog on the Streets of New York") 20-30 55
MOONDOG (2 "Moondog and His Honking Geese") 25-50 50s
SMC (11 "Moondog in the Wide Open Spaces") 25-50 53
LPs: 10/12-inch
COLUMBIA 10-15 70-71
EPIC (1002 "Moondog and His Friends") 75-125 54
(10-inch LP.)
MUSICAL HERITAGE SOCITEY (3803 "Moondog") 15-25 78
PRESTIGE (7042 "Cariba") 30-60 56
PRESTIGE (7069 "More Moondog") 30-60 56
PRESTIGE (7099 "The Story of Moondog") 30-60 57

MOONEY, Art, & His Orchestra P&R '48
Singles: 78 rpm
MGM 3-5 48-57
VOGUE (Except R711 & R713) 25-40 46-48
(Picture discs.)
VOGUE (R711 "Seems Like Old Time"/"Warsaw Concerto") 300-400 46
(Picture disc.)
VOGUE (R711/R713 "Seems Like Old Time"/"I've Been Working on the Railroad") 60-80 46
(Picture disc.)
VOGUE (R713 "I've Been Working on the Railroad"/You're Nobody 'Til Somebody Loves You") 350-450 46
(Picture disc.)
VOGUE (R713/R732 "I've Been Working on the Railroad"/"I Don't Know Why") 60-80 46
(Picture disc.)
VOGUE (R-713-2/R-732-13 "I've Been Working on the Railroad"/"I Don't Know Why") 60-80 46
(Picture disc.)
VOGUE (R730 "Piper's Junction") 70-80 46
(Picture disc.)
VOGUE (R732 "In the Moonmist") 60-80 46
(Picture disc.)
VOGUE (R732-13/R732 "In the Moonmist") 70-90 46
(Picture disc.)
Singles: 7-inch
DECCA 3-6 61-62
KAPP 3-6 64-65
MGM (Except 12312) 4-8 50-64
MGM (12312 "Rebel Without a Cause"/"East of Eden") 10-15 56
RIVERSIDE 3-5 62
Picture Sleeves
MGM (12312 "Rebel Without a Cause"/"East of Eden") 20-40 56
(Billed as a "Tribute to James Dean.")
EPs: 7-inch
MGM (Except 1342) 5-10 55-56
MGM (1342 "Music from Movies Starring James Dean") 30-40 55-56
LPs: 10/12-inch
DECCA 10-15 62
DIPLOMAT 6-12 60s
KAPP 10-15 64
MGM 15-25 55-61
RCA 8-12 67
SPINORAMA 8-12 62
Also see AMES BROTHERS
Also see DEAN, James
Also see GORDON, Barry

MOONEY, Art / Frankie Carle
LPs: 10/12-inch
CORONET 5-10 60s
Also see MOONEY, Art, & His Orch.

MOONEY, Glenn
Singles: 7-inch
FRATERNITY 10-15 62

MOONEY, John
LPs: 10/12-inch
BLIND PIG 5-8 83

MOONEY, John, & Jim Thackery
LPs: 10/12-inch
SEYMORE 5-8
Also see THACKERY, Jim

MOONEY, Ralph
Singles: 7-inch
CHALLENGE 4-8 61
Also see BURTON, James, & Ralph Mooney

MOONGLOWS R&B '54
Singles: 78 rpm
CHAMPAGNE (7500 "I Just Can't Tell No Lie") 200-300 52
(Reportedly 2,500 made.)
CHANCE (1147 "Baby Please") 50-100 53
CHANCE (1150 "Just a Lonely Christmas") 50-100 53
CHANCE (1152 "Secret Love") 50-100 54
CHANCE (1156 "I Was Wrong") 50-100 54
CHANCE (1161 "219 Train") 50-100 54
CHESS (1500 & 1600 series) 25-50 54-57
QUALITY 25-50 56
(Canadian.)
Singles: 7-inch
BIG P 4-6 71
CHAMPAGNE (7500 "I Just Can't Tell No Lie") 1000-1500 52
(Reportedly 1,500 made.)
CHANCE (1147 "Baby Please") 1500-2000 53
(Red vinyl.)
CHANCE (1150 "Just a Lonely Christmas") 1500-2000 53
(Red vinyl.)
CHANCE (1152 "Secret Love") 750-1000 54
(Blue and silver label.)
CHANCE (1152 "Secret Love") 500-700 54
(Yellow and black label.)
CHANCE (1156 "I Was Wrong") 750-1000 54
(Yellow and black label.)
CHANCE (1156 "I Was Wrong") 550-650 54
(White and black label.)
CHANCE (1161 "219 Train") 800-1200 54
(White and black label.)
CHESS (1581 "Sincerely") 40-60 54
(Silver top label with chess pieces.)
CHESS (1581 "Sincerely") 8-10 60s
(Blue label.)
CHESS (1589 "Most of All") 40-60 54
(Silver top label with chess pieces.)
CHESS (1589 "Most of All") 8-10 60s
(Blue label.)
CHESS (1598 "Foolish Me") 40-60 55
(Silver top label with chess pieces.)
CHESS (1598 "Foolish Me") 8-10 60s
(Blue label.)
CHESS (1605 "Starlite") 40-60 55
(Silver top label with chess pieces.)
CHESS (1605 "Starlite") 8-10 60s
(Blue label.)
CHESS (1611 In My Diary") 30-50 55
(Silver top label with chess pieces.)
CHESS (1611 In My Diary") 8-10 60s
(Blue label.)
CHESS (1619 "We Go Together") 30-50 56
(Silver top label with chess pieces.)
CHESS (1619 "We Go Together") 8-10 60s
(Blue label.)
CHESS (1629 "See Saw") 25-50 56
(Silver top label with chess pieces.)
CHESS (1629 "See Saw") 8-10 60s
(Blue label.)
CHESS (1646 "Over and Over Again") 25-50 56
(Silver top label with chess pieces.)
CHESS (1646 "Over and Over Again") 8-10 60s
(Blue label.)
CHESS (1651 "I'm Afraid the Masquerade Is Over") 25-50 56
(Silver top label with chess pieces.)
CHESS (1651 "I'm Afraid the Masquerade Is Over") 8-10 60s
(Blue label.)
CHESS (1661 "Please Send Me Someone to Love") 25-50 57
(Silver top label with chess pieces.)
CHESS (1661 "Please Send Me Someone to Love") 8-10 60s
(Blue label.)
CHESS (1669 "The Beating of My Heart") 25-50 57
CHESS (1681 "Too Late") 15-25 58
CHESS (1689 "In the Middle of the Night") 15-25 58
CHESS (1701 "This Love") 15-25 58
CHESS (1717 "I'll Never Stop Wanting You") 15-25 59
CHESS (1770 "Junior") 10-20 60
CHESS (1781 "Mama") 15-25 61
CRIMSON (1003 "My Imagination") 15-20 64
LANA 4-6 64
QUALITY (1524 "See Saw") 40-60 56
(Canadian.)
RCA 4-6 72
TIMES SQUARE (30 "I've Got the Right") 10-15 64
VEE JAY (423 "Secret Love") 10-15 61
EPs: 7-inch
CHESS (5122 "Look! It's the Moonglows") 150-250 59
CHESS (5123 "Look! It's the Moonglows, Vol. 2") 100-200 59
LPs: 10/12-inch
CHESS (701 "The Moonglows") 10-15 76
CHESS (1471 "Best of Bobby Lester & the Moonglows") 10-15 70s
CHESS (1430 "Look, It's the Moonglows") 200-300 59
CHESS (8403 "Their Current Sides") 5-10 83
CONSTELLATION (2 "Collectors Showcase") 20-30 64
LOST-NITE 8-12 81
RCA 10-15 72
SUGARHILL/MCA 5-10 84
Members: Harvey Fuqua; Bobby Lester; Alex Graves; Prentiss Barnes; Marvin Gaye; Reese Palmer; James Knowland; Chester Simmons; George Thorpe; Dock Green; Berle Ashton.
Also see CROWNS
Also see DIDDLEY, Bo
Also see DRIFTERS
Also see FLAMINGOS / Moonglows
Also see GAYE, Marvin
Also see HARVEY & MOONGLOWS
Also see LESTER, Bobby
Also see MARQUEES

MOONGOONERS
Singles: 7-inch
CANDIX (335 "Moongoon Twist") 20-30 62
DONNA (1373 "Moongoon Twist") 10-20 62
ESSAR (1007 "Moongoon Twist") 25-50 62
Members: Scott Engel; John Stewart.
Also see ENGEL, Scott, & John Stewart

MOONLIGHTERS
Singles: 7-inch
JOSIE (843 "Broken Heart") 15-25 58
TARA (100 "Broken Heart") 40-50 58
TARA (102 "Rock-A-Bayou Baby") 40-50 58

MOONLIGHTERS
Singles: 7-inch
THUNDERBIRD 3-5
LPs: 10/12-inch
CENTURY 15-25

MOONLION P&R '76
Singles: 7-inch
P.I.P. 3-5 76

MOONQUAKE
Singles: 7-inch
FANTASY 3-5 74-75
LPs: 10/12-inch
FANTASY 8-10 74-75
Members: Walter Rossi; Jack Geisinger.
Also see LUKE & APOSTLES

MOONRAKERS
Singles: 7-inch
SHAMLEY (44012 "Love Train") 8-12 68
SHAMLEY (44015 "No Number to Call") 8-12 68
SHAMLEY (44021 "No Hidin' ") 8-12 68
TOWER (157 "I Was Wrong") 15-25 65
TOWER (180 "I'm Alright") 15-25 66
TOWER (222 "Trip and Fall") 15-25 66
TOWER (230 "Baby Please Don't Go") 15-25 66
LPs: 10/12-inch
SHAMLEY (704 "Together") 25-35 68
Members: Van Dorn; Randy Walrath; Joel Brandes; Dennis Flanagan.

MOONRIDER
LPs: 10/12-inch
ANCHOR 8-12 75

MOONRIDERS
Singles: 7-inch
CANDY 10-15 60

MOONS
Singles: 7-inch
DATE 4-8 67

MOONSHINE
Singles: 7-inch
U.A. 4-6 70
Also see JAY & AMERICANS

MOONSHINERS
Singles: 7-inch
SABINA 4-8 63
VILLAGE GATE 4-8 65
LPs: 10/12-inch
VILLAGE GATE 10-20 65

MOONSHYNE 29
Singles: 7-inch
A&M 3-5 70

MOOR, Det
Singles: 7-inch
GALLANT 4-6 62
LPs: 10/12-inch
GALLANT (4001 "Great Jazz from Great TV") 20-30 62

MOORE, Abe
Singles: 78 rpm
DIG (125 "Moore Boogie") 10-15 56
Singles: 7-inch
DIG (125 "Moore Boogie") 15-25 56

MOORE, Ada
LPs: 10/12-inch
DEBUT (15 "Jazz Workshop") 25-50 55
Also see RUSHING, Jimmy, Ada Moore & Buck Clayton

MOORE, Alexander
Singles: 78 rpm
RPM (326 "If I Lose You Woman") 25-50 51
LPs: 10/12-inch
ARHOOLIE 10-20

MOORE, Bernie
Singles: 7-inch
BURDETT 4-8 66
PLANET X (9622 "Rock Guitar Rock") 100-150 57

MOORE, Beth C&W '71
Singles: 7-inch
CAPITOL 3-5 71

MOORE, Betty
(With Ambassadors; with Esquires)
Singles: 7-inch
CUCA (1134 "Long Hot Summer") 15-25 63
CUCA (1467 "Long Hot Summer") 10-15 69
Also see ESQURES
Also see MOORER, Betty

MOORE, Bill R&B '48
Singles: 78 rpm
SAVOY 15-25 48
Also see WILLIAMS, Paul

MOORE, Billy Joe
Singles: 7-inch
RIC 4-8 65

MOORE, Bob P&R/R&B/LP '61
Singles: 7-inch
HICKORY 4-8 65-68
MONUMENT 5-10 59-64
Picture Sleeves
MONUMENT 5-10 62-63
LPs: 10/12-inch
HICKORY 10-15 66
MONUMENT 10-20 61-67
Also see ATKINS, Chet
Also see BOX, David
Also see DRAGON, Paul
Also see LEE, Bobby
Also see LEE, Brenda
Also see NASHVILLE ALL-STARS
Also see NELSON, Willie
Also see PRESLEY, Elvis
Also see STARR, Frank, & His Rock-Away Boys
Also see TIGRE, Terry

MOORE, Bob, & Temps
Singles: 7-inch
DAISY (502 "Trophy Run") 25-35 63
Member: Roy Buchanan.
Also see BUCHANAN, Roy

MOORE, Bobby P&R/R&B '66
(With the Rhythm Aces)
Singles: 12-inch
SCEPTER (12417 "Try to Hold On") .. 5-8 75
(Promotional issue only.)
Singles: 7-inch
CHECKER 5-10 66-68
SCEPTER 3-6 75
LPs: 10/12-inch
CHECKER (3000 "Searching for My Love") 20-25 66

MOORE, Bobby P&R/R&B '75
Singles: 7-inch
SCEPTER 3-5 75-76

MOORE, Buel, & Garnets
Singles: 7-inch
VITA (174 "Really Really Really") .. 40-60 58

MOORE, Cathy
Singles: 7-inch
MAJESTY 8-12 62

MOORE, Cecil
Singles: 7-inch
ATCO 4-8 64
LU TEX 3-6 78
SARG (150 "Walkin' Fever") 25-50 57

SARG (165 "Moonshine") ... 25-50 60
SARG (177 "G.I. Blues") ... 20-40 61
SARG (192 "My Money's Gone") ... 20-30 61
SARG (200 series, except 206) ... 5-10
SARG (206 "Rise and Shine") ... 15-25 62
TOTEM (103 "Stuff") ... 10-20 66

MOORE, Craig
EPs: 7-inch
RUMBLE ... 4-8 81
LPs: 10/12-inch
MCCM (8901 "Agonnagain" ... 25-30 89
(Two splash, multi-color vinyl discs.)
Also see GONN

MOORE, Daniel
LPs: 10/12-inch
DUNHILL ... 8-12 71

MOORE, Danny
Singles: 7-inch
ALLRITE (625 "Somebody New") ... 300-400
LPs: 10/12-inch
EVEREST (1211 "Folk Songs from Here and There") ... 10-20 63
(Monaural.)
EVEREST (5211 "Folk Songs from Here and There") ... 15-25 63
(Stereo.)

MOORE, David
Singles: 7-inch
LYNN (501 "Crazy Dream") ... 5-10 60

MOORE, Deacon John
Singles: 7-inch
BELL ... 8-10

MOORE, Debby
Singles: 7-inch
TOP RANK ... 5-10 60
LPs: 10/12-inch
TOP RANK (301 "Debby Moore") ... 15-25 59
(Monaural.)
TOP RANK (601 "Debby Moore") ... 20-30 59
(Stereo.)

MOORE, Donny Lee
Singles: 7-inch
GOLDEN CREST (512 "Fire") ... 20-40 59
GOLDEN CREST (527 "I'm Buggin' Out Little Baby") ... 50-75 59
SHELLEY (1000 "I'm Buggin' Out Little Baby") ... 60-80 59

MOORE, Dorothy *R&B '73*
(Dorothy Moore)
Singles: 12-inch
STREETKING ... 4-6 84
Singles: 7-inch
GSF ... 3-5 73
HANDSHAKE ... 3-4 82
MALACO ... 3-5 76-80
STREETKING ... 3-4 84
LPs: 10/12-inch
MALACO ... 5-8 76-78
Also see CHEE-CHEE & PEPPY
Also see POPPIES

MOORE, Dorothy, & Eddie Floyd *R&B '77*
Singles: 7-inch
MALACO ... 3-5 77
Also see FLOYD, Eddie
Also see MOORE, Dorothy

MOORE, Eddie
Singles: 7-inch
20TH FOX (101 "Phone Chick") ... 10-20 58
Also see LEWIS, Joe "Cannonball" / Eddie Moore

MOORE, Frank, Four
Singles: 7-inch
ALMO ... 4-8 64

MOORE, Gary *LP '83*
(Gary Moore Band)
Singles: 7-inch
JET ... 3-5 79
MIRAGE ... 3-4 83-86
VIRGIN ... 3-4 87-89
LPs: 10/12-inch
CHARISMA ... 5-8 90
JET ... 5-10 78
MIRAGE ... 5-8 83-86
PETERS INT'L (9004 "Grinding Stone") ... 12-15 73
(Red label.)
PETERS INT'L (9004 "Grinding Stone") ... 10-12 73
(Orange label.)
VIRGIN ... 5-8 87-89
Also see THIN LIZZY

MOORE, Gatemouth
Singles: 78 rpm
CHEZ PAREE ... 10-20 45
KING ... 10-20 47-48
NATIONAL ... 10-20 45-46
LPs: 10/12-inch
KING (684 "Gatemouth Moore Sings Blues") ... 750-1000 60

MOORE, Gene, & Chimes / Jake Porter with Gene Moore & Chimes
Singles: 78 rpm
COMBO (63 "Only a Dream") ... 75-125 55
Singles: 7-inch
COMBO (63 "Only a Dream") ... 200-300 55
Also see MOORE, Gene, & Metronomes
Also see PORTER, Jake

MOORE, Hank
Singles: 7-inch
5-4 (5425 "Reconsider, Baby") ... 15-25
5-4 (5426 "Sour Mash") ... 15-25

MOORE, Harv
Singles: 7-inch
AMERICAN ARTS (20 "Interview of the Fab Four") ... 30-40 64

MOORE, Henry
Singles: 7-inch
AFADA ... 10-15
KING ... 5-10 61
HERMITAGE ... 5-10 63
Also see BALLARD, Hank, & Midnighters

MOORE, Jackie *P&R/R&B '70*
(With the Memphis Horns; with Dixie Flyers)
Singles: 12-inch
COLUMBIA ... 4-8 79-84
Singles: 7-inch
ATLANTIC ... 4-6 70-73
CATAWBA ... 3-4 83
COLUMBIA ... 3-5 79-84
KAYVETTE ... 3-5 75-81
SHOUT ... 5-8 68
LPs: 10/12-inch
ATLANTIC ... 8-12 73
COLUMBIA ... 5-10 79
Also see LULU
Also see MEMPHIS HORNS

MOORE, James
Singles: 7-inch
SOFT (1014 "Cool") ... 8-12

MOORE, James, & Pretenders
Singles: 7-inch
TISHMAN (905 "To Be Loved") ... 50-100 64

MOORE, Jan
Singles: 7-inch
BOYD ... 5-10 61
WINSTON (1035 "Play It Cool") ... 50-75 59

MOORE, Jerry
Singles: 7-inch
COLUMBIA ... 4-6 67

MOORE, Jim, & Sidewinder *C&W '88*
Singles: 7-inch
WILLOW WIND ... 3-4 88

MOORE, Jimmy
Singles: 7-inch
LEGRAND ... 15-25 65

MOORE, Jimmy, & Peacocks
Singles: 7-inch
NOBLE (711 "Tender Love") ... 1000-2000 58
Also see KING BEES

MOORE; Johnny *R&B '46*
(With the Blazers; with Three Blazers; with New Blazers; with Twigs; with Rudy Toombs; with Eddie Williams; with Floyd Dixon; Johnny Moore's Orchestra with Mal Hogan & Twigs)
Singles: 78 rpm
ALADDIN ... 20-50 45-48
BLAZE ... 10-20 54
COMBO ... 10-20 55
EXCLUSIVE ... 20-40 46-48
HOLLYWOOD ... 10-20 55-56
MODERN ... 10-20 48-50
MODERN MUSIC ... 10-20 45-46
PHILO ... 10-20 46
RCA ... 15-25 50
SWING TIME ... 10-20 51
Singles: 7-inch
ALADDIN (112 "Drifting Blues") ... 100-150 51
BLAZE (101 "Miss Mosey") ... 25-50 54
BLAZE (108 "Pretty Please") ... 25-50 54
BRUNSWICK ... 4-6 71
COMBO (69 "Take Off My Wig") ... 25-50 55
(Vocal by Floyd Dixon.)
HOLLYWOOD (1031 "Why Johnny Why") ... 25-50 55
HOLLYWOOD (1045 "Christmas Eve Baby") ... 25-50 55
HOLLYWOOD (1056 "I Send My Love") ... 25-50 56
MODERN (800 & 900 series) ... 20-30 53
RCA (0009 "This Is One Time Baby") ... 50-100 50
(Colored vinyl.)
RCA (0018 "Bop-A-Bye Baby") ... 50-100 50
(Colored vinyl.)
RCA (0026 "Walkin' Blues") ... 50-100 50
(Colored vinyl.)
RCA (0031 "Shuffle Shuck") ... 50-100 50
(Colored vinyl.)
RCA (0043 "So Long") ... 50-100 50
(Colored vinyl.)
RCA (0073 "Misery Blues") ... 50-100 50
(Colored vinyl.)
RCA (0086 "Rain-Check") ... 50-100 50
(Colored vinyl.)
RCA (0095 "Jumping Jack") ... 50-100 50
(Colored vinyl.)
RENDEZVOUS (115 "Bullfrog") ... 10-15 60
SUE (726 "You're My Queen") ... 15-25 60
Members: Johnny Moore; Charles Brown; Eddie Williams.
Also see BELL, Hugh, & Twiggs
Also see BROWN, Charles
Also see COMPOSERS
Also see DIXON, Floyd, & Johnny Moore's Three Blazers
Also see FEATHERS
Also see McSHANN, Jay, & Johnny Moore's Three Blazers
Also see WILLIAMS, Eddie
Also see WOODS, Sonny

MOORE, Johnny, & Linda Hayes
Singles: 7-inch
HOLLYWOOD (1031 "Why, Johnny [Ace], Why") ... 30-50 55
Also see HAYES, Linda
Also see MOORE, Johnny

MOORE, Johnny
Singles: 7-inch
BLUE ROCK ... 5-10 68
DATE (1562 "Walk Like a Man") ... 15-25 67
WAND ... 8-12 67

MOORE, Johnny
Singles: 7-inch
BRIGHT STAR (145 "Sold on You") ... 8-12 66
BRIGHT STAR (148 "Your Love's Got Power") ... 8-12 66
CHI-CITY ... 8-12
MERCURY ... 8-12

MOORE, Joseph
Singles: 7-inch
MAR-V-LOUS ... 8-12

MOORE, Kenzie
Singles: 78 rpm
SPECIALTY ... 10-15 53-56
Singles: 7-inch
SPECIALTY (Black vinyl.) ... 15-20 53-56
SPECIALTY (Colored vinyl.) ... 20-30 53

MOORE, Larry
Singles: 7-inch
ORIGINAL SOUND ... 5-10 63

MOORE, Lattie *C&W '61*
Singles: 78 rpm
KING ... 10-20 56
SPEED (101 "Juke Joint Johnny") ... 50-100 52
Singles: 7-inch
ARC (8005 "Juke Joint Johnny") ... 100-200 57
KING (4955 "Lonesome Man Blues") ... 25-35 56
KING (5370 "Cajun Doll") ... 20-30 60
KING (5413 "Drunk Again") ... 5-10 61
KING (5723 "Just About Then") ... 5-10 63
SPEED (101 "Juke Joint Johnny") ... 300-400 52
STARDAY ... 10-20 58-59
LPs: 10/12-inch
AUDIO LAB (1555 "Best of Lattie Moore") ... 30-40 60
AUDIO LAB (1573 "Country Side") ... 25-35 62
DERBYTOWN (102 "Lattie Moore") ... 10-20 60s

MOORE, Lee
(With the Hank Trotter's Happy Rangers)
Singles: 78 rpm
CROSS COUNTRY (506 "The Cat Came Back") ... 25-50 55
Singles: 7-inch
CROSS COUNTRY (506 "The Cat Came Back") ... 50-100 55

MOORE, Lee *R&B '79*
Singles: 7-inch
SOURCE ... 3-5 79

MOORE, Little Bobby
Singles: 7-inch
KING ... 4-8 62

MOORE, Lucky
Singles: 7-inch
WAT-VEE (900 "Walking and Talking") ... 150-250 58

MOORE, Martha
Singles: 78 rpm
DELUXE ... 8-12 52
Singles: 7-inch
DELUXE ... 15-25 52

MOORE, Matthew
(Matthew Moore Plus Four)
Singles: 7-inch
CAPITOL ... 8-12 66-67
CARIBOU ... 3-5 78
GNP ... 4-8 65
WHITE WHALE (223 "Codyne") ... 20-30 65
LPs: 10/12-inch
CARIBOU ... 5-10 78
Members: Matthew Moore; David Marks.
Also see MOON

MOORE, Mel, & Marc Shaw
Singles: 7-inch
STERLING ... 4-8
Also see SHAW, Mark

MOORE, Melba *LP '71*
Singles: 12-inch
CAPITOL ... 4-6 83-86
EPIC ... 4-8 79-80
Singles: 7-inch
BUDDAH ... 3-5 75-78
CAPITOL ... 3-4 82-87
EMI AMERICA ... 3-4 81-82
EPIC ... 3-5 78-80
MERCURY ... 3-6 69-72
MUSICOR ... 4-8 66
Picture Sleeves
BUDDAH ... 3-5 76
LPs: 10/12-inch
ACCORD ... 5-10 81
BUDDAH ... 8-10 75-79
CAPITOL ... 5-8 83-86
EMI AMERICA ... 5-10 81
EPIC ... 5-10 78-80
MERCURY ... 10-15 70-72
Also see THOMAS, Lillo, & Melba Moore

MOORE, Melba, & Freddie Jackson *R&B '88*
Singles: 7-inch
CAPITOL ... 3-4 86-88
Also see JACKSON, Freddie

MOORE, Melba, & Kashif *R&B '86*
(Melba & Kashif)
Singles: 7-inch
CAPITOL ... 3-4 86
Also see KASHIF
Also see MOORE, Melba

MOORE, Melvin
Singles: 78 rpm
KING (4539 "Possessed") ... 25-50 52
Singles: 7-inch
KING (4539 "Possessed") ... 50-100 52

MOORE, Merrill
Singles: 78 rpm
CAPITOL ... 5-10 52-57
Singles: 7-inch
CAPITOL ... 5-15 52-57
EPs: 7-inch
CAPITOL (608 "Merrill Moore") ... 25-50 56

MOORE, Mike
Singles: 7-inch
CYCLONE (503 "The Chick") ... 10-15 60s

MOORE, Nunnie, & Peacocks
Singles: 7-inch
L&M (1002 "Bouquet of Roses") ... 500-1000 57

MOORE, Phil, & Phil Moore Four
Singles: 78 rpm
BLACK & WHITE ... 10-15 47
RCA ... 10-15 53
Singles: 7-inch
RCA ... 15-25 53
Members: Marty Wilson; Jimmy Lyons; Milt Hinton; Johnny Letman.

MOORE, Phil, & Chords
Singles: 7-inch
TIME (101 "Little Angel") ... 200-300 58

MOORE, Phil, III, & Afro-Latin Soultet
LPs: 10/12-inch
TOWER ... 10-20 67

MOORE, Ray: see MOORE, Rudy Ray

MOORE, Red
Singles: 7-inch
RED (840 "Crawdad Song") ... 250-350

MOORE, Rene
Singles: 7-inch
POLYDOR ... 3-4 88
LPs: 10/12-inch
POLYDOR ... 5-8 88

MOORE, Robert
Singles: 7-inch
DELUXE ... 4-8 69
HOLLYWOOD ... 4-8 68

MOORE, Ronnie
Singles: 7-inch
JARO ... 8-12 59
STOMPER TIME ... 15-25 58

MOORE, Rudy
Singles: 78 rpm
FEDERAL ... 5-10 56
Singles: 7-inch
FEDERAL ... 10-20 56

MOORE, Rudy Ray
(With the Raytones; with Raytones)
Singles: 7-inch
BALL (500 "Dear Ruth") ... 15-25
BALL (503 "My Baby") ... 15-25
BALL (504 "Your Tender Touch") ... 15-25
CASH (1059 "Until You're in My Arms") ... 50-75 58
CASH (1060 "I'm Ready") ... 50-75 58
COMEDIANS INC. (103 "You Could Be Ugly Too") ... 4-8
IMPERIAL ... 5-10 64
KENT ... 3-5 72
LEE (501 "Honey Hush") ... 15-25 58
Also see RAYTONES
Also see WHEATSTRAW, Peetie, & Rudy Ray Moore

MOORE, Sam
Singles: 7-inch
ATLANTIC ... 4-6 70-71
Also see SAM & DAVE

MOORE, Sandee
Singles: 7-inch
BRUNSWICK ... 8-12 58

MOORE, Scotty
(Scotty Moore Trio)
Singles: 7-inch
FERNWOOD (107 "Have Guitar Will Travel") ... 20-25 58
LPs: 10/12-inch
EPIC (24103 "The Guitar That Changed the World") ... 50-75 64
(Monaural.)
EPIC (24103 "The Guitar That Changed the World") ... 60-80 64
(White label. Promotional issue only.)
EPIC (26103 "The Guitar That Changed the World") ... 60-80 64
(Stereo.)
GUINNESS ... 20-30 77
Also see DONNER, Ral
Also see DRAGON, Paul
Also see LEE, Notorious Rockin'
Also see POINDEXTER, Doug, & Starlite Wranglers
Also see PRESLEY, Elvis
Also see SANFORD, Sandy
Also see TIGRE, Terry
Also see WHAT'S LEFT

MOORE, Shelly, & Eddie Harris
LPs: 10/12-inch
ARGO (4016 "For the First Time") ... 30-40 62
Also see HARRIS, Eddie

MOORE, Sparkle
Singles: 7-inch
FRATERNITY (751 "Skull and Cross Bones") ... 50-60 57
FRATERNITY (766 "Killer") ... 40-50 57

MOORE, Steve
Singles: 7-inch
SCOTT ... 4-8

MOORE, Tim *P&R '73*
Singles: 7-inch
ASYLUM ... 3-5 74-79
DUNHILL ... 3-5 73
Picture Sleeves
ASYLUM ... 3-5 75
LPs: 10/12-inch
ASYLUM ... 5-10 74-75
SMALL (0601 "Second Avenue") ... 10-15 74

MOORE, Turner
Singles: 7-inch
MEL-O-TONE (1500 "I'll Be Leavin' You") ... 75-125 57

MOORE, Vinnie *LP '88*
LPs: 10/12-inch
SQUAWK ... 5-8 88

MOORE, W.J., & Dynamic Upsetters
Singles: 7-inch
GUTTER ... 3-5 85

MOORE, Wendell
Singles: 7-inch
RIM ... 4-8 62

MOORE, Wild Bill
(With the Twistets)
Singles: 78 rpm
KING ... 10-15 50
OLD TOWN ... 10-15 56
SENSATION ... 20-30 49
Singles: 7-inch
OLD TOWN (1035 "The Wild One") ... 15-25 56
LPs: 10/12-inch
POPSIDE ... 15-20 62

MOORE, Woo Woo
Singles: 78 rpm
MERCURY (70204 "Something's Wrong") ... 10-15 53
Singles: 7-inch
MERCURY (70204 "Something's Wrong") ... 35-50 53

MOORE & MOORE
Singles: 7-inch
VALIANT ... 4-8 66
Session: Davie Allan.

MOOREHEAD, Dick, & Paramounts
Singles: 7-inch
CLOUD ... 4-8 66

MOORER, Betty
Singles: 7-inch
WAND (11202 "It's My Thing") ... 10-15 69
Also see ESQUIRES
Also see MOORE, Betty

MOORPARK INTERSECTION
Singles: 7-inch
CAPITOL ... 5-10 68

MOOSE & PELICANS
Singles: 7-inch
VANGUARD (35110 "We're Rockin' ") ... 5-10 71
VANGUARD (35129 "He's a Rebel") ... 12-15 71
Member: Darlene Love.
Also see LOVE, Darlene

MOOSE JOHN
(John Walker)
Singles: 78 rpm
ULTRA ... 10-20 56
Singles: 7-inch
ULTRA (102 "Wrong Doin' Woman") ... 20-30 56

MOOVERS
Singles: 7-inch
BRENT ... 4-8 67

MOP TOPS
Singles: 7-inch
TEEN (518 "Flipper") ... 10-20 63

MOQUETTES
Singles: 7-inch
MGM ... 5-10 64

MORAID, Buddy
Singles: 7-inch
RHAPSODY ... 10-15 59

MORALES, Ernie, & Lavenders
Singles: 7-inch
CRYSTAL BALL ... 4-8 77

MORALES, Michael P&R/LP '89
Singles: 7-inch
WING 3-4 89
Picture Sleeves
WING 3-4 89
LPs: 10/12-inch
WING 5-8 89

MORAN
Singles: 7-inch
EPIC 5-10 73

MORAZ, Patrick LP '76
LPs: 10/12-inch
ATLANTIC 8-12 76
CHRISIMA 5-8 78
IMPORT 8-10 77
PASSPORT 5-8
Also see MOODY BLUES
Also see REFUGEE
Also see YES

MORBID ANGEL
LPs: 10/12-inch
W.B. 8-10 90s

MORDOR
Singles
WORLD METAL (003 "Rock Warrior") 8-12 89
(Octagon picture disc. 500 made.)
WORLD METAL (003 "Rock Warrior") 15-20 89
(Square picture disc. 100 made.)

MORE
LPs: 10/12-inch
ATLANTIC 5-8 81-82

MORE, Chuck, & All-Stars
Singles: 7-inch
BOP CITY 5-10

MORE BEAUTIFUL DAZE
Singles: 7-inch
ALPHA 5-10 68

MOREIRA, Airto
(Airto)
Singles: 7-inch
BUDDAH 3-5 71
CTI 3-5 73
LPs: 10/12-inch
ARISTA 5-10 75-77
BUDDAH 8-12 70-76
CTI 8-10 72-73
SALVATION 8-10 74
W.B. 5-10 77
Also see DEODATO
Also see HART, Mickey, Airto & Flora Purim
Also see RHYTHM DEVILS

MORELAND, Little Richard: see MORELAND, Richie

MORELAND, Prentice
Singles: 7-inch
CHALLENGE 8-12 62-63
DONNA 10-15 60
EDSEL 10-20 59
Also see CHANTECLAIRS
Also see JACKS

MORELAND, Richie
(Little Richard Moreland & Pyramids; Richard Moreland)
Singles: 7-inch
CAPITOL 4-8 67
DART 4-8 61
IMPERIAL 4-8 65
PICTURE (7722 "Mailman Blues") 25-35

MORELAND, Tommy
Singles: 7-inch
COLUMBUS (1501 "Tennessee Blues") 20-30
SKOOP (1054 "Bang Bang") 25-35 60

MORENO, Buddy
Singles: 7-inch
NORMAN 4-8 62

MORE-TISHANS
Singles: 7-inch
PEAK (4453 "I've Got Nowhere to Run") 25-35 67

MORFORMEN
Singles: 7-inch
TEWA 4-8
Member: Daniel Gavurnik.

MORGAN
Singles: 7-inch
LAUREL 8-12 60

MORGAN
(Morgan Fisher)
LPs: 10/12-inch
IMPORT 8-10 76

MORGAN, Al C&W '49
Singles: 78 rpm
LONDON 4-8 49
UNIVERSAL 6-12 49

MORGAN, Billie C&W '59
Singles: 7-inch
STARDAY 5-10 59

MORGAN, Charlie
(Charlie Feathers)
Singles: 7-inch
WALMAY (100 "Dinky John") 150-250 60
Also see FEATHERS, Charlie

MORGAN, Chris, & Togas
Singles: 7-inch
CHALLENGE (59330 "There She Goes") 15-25 66
Also see TOGAS

MORGAN, Claude
Singles: 7-inch
SUPER BEET 3-4 87
Also see MEYERS, Augie

MORGAN, Dave
LPs: 10/12-inch
AMPEX 8-10

MORGAN, Denroy R&B '81
Singles: 12-inch
BECKET 4-6 81-82
Singles: 7-inch
BECKET 3-5 81

MORGAN, George C&W '49
(With Little Roy Wiggins)
Singles: 78 rpm
COLUMBIA 5-10 52-57
Singles: 7-inch
COLUMBIA 5-15 52-65
DECCA 3-5 71-73
4 STAR 3-5 75-79
MCA 3-5 73-74
STARDAY 4-8 67-68
STOP 3-6 69-70
EPs: 7-inch
COLUMBIA 5-15 52-58
LPs: 10/12-inch
COLUMBIA (Except 1044) 15-30 61-75
COLUMBIA (1044 "Morgan, By George") 30-40 57
4 STAR 6-12 75-77
HARMONY 8-15 67-69
MCA 5-10 74
NASHVILLE 6-12 69-71
POWER PAK 5-10 74
STARDAY (400 series) 10-20 67-69
STARDAY (900 series) 5-10 74
STOP 8-12 69
Also see MORGAN, Lorrie & George

MORGAN, George, & Marion Worth
LPs: 10/12-inch
COLUMBIA 20-30 64
Also see MORGAN, George
Also see WORTH, Marion

MORGAN, Henry
(Henrich von Morgan)
Singles: 7-inch
JUDSON 4-8
LPs: 10/12-inch
JUDSON (3016 "Best of Henry Morgan") 15-25

MORGAN, Jane P&R/LP '57
(With the Troubadors)
Singles: 78 rpm
KAPP 3-8 54-57
Singles: 7-inch
ABC 4-6 67-68
EPIC 4-6 65-68
COLPIX 4-8 63-65
KAPP 5-10 54-62
RCA 3-6 69-70
EPs: 7-inch
KAPP 5-10 55-59
Picture Sleeves
COLPIX 5-10 63
ELEKTRA 3-4 82
EPIC 4-8 65
KAPP 5-12 57-59
LPs: 10/12-inch
ABC 5-10 68
COLPIX 10-20 63-66
EPIC 10-15 65-67
KAPP 10-20 56-63
MCA 5-10 73
RCA (Except 1160) 8-12 69-70
RCA (1160 "Marry Me, Marry Me") 10-15 69
(Soundtrack.)
HARMONY 5-8 70
Also see WILLIAMS, Roger, & Jane Morgan

MORGAN, Janice
Singles: 7-inch
MARLEE (101 "Money Honey") 50-75 60

MORGAN, Jaye P. P&R '53
Singles: 78 rpm
DECCA 3-6 54-55
DERBY 3-6 53
RCA 3-6 54-56
Singles: 7-inch
ABC-PAR 4-6 65
BEVERLY HILLS 3-5 69-72
DECCA 5-10 54-55
DERBY 5-10 53
GIGOLO 3-5
MGM 4-8 59-63
RCA 5-10 54-56
EPs: 7-inch
DECCA 10-20 55
DERBY 10-20 53
LPs: 10/12-inch
BAINBRIDGE 5-10 82
BEVERLY HILLS 5-8 70
MGM 15-25 59-61
RCA (1155 "Jaye P. Morgan") 25-35 55
RCA (1682 "Just You, Just Me") 25-35 55
RONDO-LETTE (13 "Jaye P. Morgan Sings") 15-20 58
ROYALE (18122 "Jaye P. Morgan") 20-30 55
(10-inch LP. Side 2 has uncredited instrumentals.)
Also see ARNOLD, Eddy, & Jaye P. Morgan
Also see COMO, Perry, & Jaye P. Morgan
Also see HEXORCIST
Also see PRESLEY, Elvis / Jaye P. Morgan

MORGAN, Joe
Singles: 7-inch
FAME 8-12 59

MORGAN, Josh
Singles: 7-inch
FABLE 3-5 77

MORGAN, Lee P&R/R&B/LP '64
Singles: 7-inch
BLUE NOTE 4-6 64-69
BUZZ 3-5 79-80
VEE JAY 4-8 60
LPs: 10/12-inch
BLUE NOTE (200 series) 8-12 74
BLUE NOTE (900 & 1000 series) 5-10 79-81
BLUE NOTE (1500 series) 50-75 56-58
(Label gives New York street address for Blue Note Records.)
BLUE NOTE (1500 series) 25-50 58
(Label reads: "Blue Note Records Inc. - New York, USA.")
BLUE NOTE (1500 series) 15-25 66
(Label shows Blue Note Records as a division of either Liberty or United Artists.)
BLUE NOTE (4000 series) 30-40 61
(Label gives New York street address for Blue Note Records.)
BLUE NOTE (4000 series) 15-25 62
(Label reads: "Blue Note Records Inc. - New York, USA.")
BLUE NOTE (4000 series) 10-20 66
(Label shows Blue Note Records as a division of either Liberty or United Artists.)
BLUE NOTE (4100 thru 4200 series) 15-25 63
(Label reads: "Blue Note Records Inc. - New York, USA.")
BLUE NOTE (4100 thru 4200 series) 10-20 66-67
(Label shows Blue Note Records as a division of either Liberty or United Artists.)
BLUE NOTE (84000 series) 30-40 61
(Label gives New York street address for Blue Note Records.)
BLUE NOTE (84000 series) 20-30 62
(Label reads: "Blue Note Records Inc. - New York, USA.")
BLUE NOTE (84000 series) 10-20 66
(Label shows Blue Note Records as a division of either Liberty or United Artists.)
BLUE NOTE (84100 thru 84200 series) 15-30 63-69
(Label reads: "Blue Note Records Inc. - New York, USA.")
BLUE NOTE (84100 thru 84300 series) 10-20 66-70
(Label shows Blue Note Records as a division of either Liberty or United Artists.)
BLUE NOTE (89000 series) 10-15 71
GNP 6-12 73
JAZZLAND 15-25 62
MCA 5-8 74
PACIFIC JAZZ 5-8 81
PRESTIGE 5-8 81
SAVOY (12091 "Introducing Lee Morgan") 50-75 56
SUNSET 5-10 69
TRADITION 8-15 68
TRIP 6-10 73
VEE JAY 25-50 60-65

MORGAN, Lorrie C&W '79
Singles: 7-inch
ABC/HICKORY 3-6 79
MCA 3-5 79
RCA 3-4 88-91
LPs: 10/12-inch
RCA 5-8 88-90
Also see WHITLEY, Keith, & Lorrie Morgan

MORGAN, Lorrie & George C&W '79
Singles: 7-inch
FOUR STAR 3-5 79
Also see MORGAN, George
Also see MORGAN, Lorrie

MORGAN, Loumell
Singles: 78 rpm
ATLANTIC (953 "Charmaine") 50-75 51
Singles: 7-inch
ATLANTIC (953 "Charmaine") 100-200 51

MORGAN, Meli'sa R&B '85
Singles: 12-inch
CAPITOL 4-6 86
Singles: 7-inch
CAPITOL 3-4 86-88
Picture Sleeves
CAPITOL 3-4 86
LPs: 10/12-inch
CAPITOL 5-8 86-87
Also see KASHIF & Meli'sa Morgan

MORGAN, Michael
Singles: 7-inch
DECISION 3-5 78

MORGAN, Oliver
Singles: 7-inch
GNP 4-8 64

MORGAN, Rocket
Singles: 7-inch
ZYNN (502 "You're Humbuggin' Me") 100-200 58
ZYNN (507 "Tag Along") 200-300 59

MORGAN, Russ, & His Orchestra P&R '35
Singles: 78 rpm
BRUNSWICK 4-6 36-38
COLUMBIA 4-6 35
DECCA 3-5 38-56
Singles: 7-inch
DECCA 5-10 50-56
EVEREST 4-6 61
VEE JAY 4-6 64-65
EPs: 7-inch
DECCA 5-10 51-56
EPIC 5-10 53
LPs: 10/12-inch
CAPITOL 10-15 62
CIRCLE 5-10 81
DECCA 10-30 51-67
EVEREST 10-15 60-63
GNP 5-10 73
MCA 5-10 73
PICKWICK 5-10 65
SUNSET 8-12 66
VEE JAY 10-15 65

MORGAN, Tim
LPs:10/12-inch
FINK 10-20

MORGAN, Tony, & Muscle Power
Singles: 7-inch
CHESS 3-5 72

MORGAN, Vicki
Singles: 78 rpm
CHICAGO (111 "New Meat") 15-25 46

MORGAN BROTHERS P&R '59
Singles: 78 rpm
RCA 4-8 55
Singles: 7-inch
MGM 5-10 58-60
RCA (6000 series) 5-10 55
Members: Dick Morgan; Duke Morgan; Charley Morgan.

MORGAN TWINS
Singles: 7-inch
PEAK (1008 "Sittin' in the Drive-In") 10-20 59
RCA (7300 "TV Hop") 15-25 58
RCA (7373 "Let's Get Goin' ") 15-25 58

MORGANMASONDOWNS
LPs: 10/12-inch
ROULETTE 10-15 70

MORGAS & GHOULS
Singles: 7-inch
VIN (1013 "Lonely Boy") 15-20 59

MORGEN
(Steve Morgen)
Singles: 7-inch
PROBE (474 "Of Dreams") 8-12 69
LPs: 10/12-inch
PROBE (4507 "Morgen") 75-100 69

MORGON, Tim
LPs: 10/12-inch
FINK 15-25 63
ICE HOUSE 8-10 72

MORGUS
Singles: 7-inch
FULTON 5-10

MORI, Miki C&W '79
(Mickie Mori)
Singles: 7-inch
NSD 3-5 80
OAK 3-5 79-80
RED FEATHER 3-5 79
STARCOM 3-5 80-81

MORISETTE, Johnnie P&R/R&B '62
(Johnny Morisette)
Singles: 7-inch
BAYTONE (116 "Run") 15-25
CHECKER 5-10
ICEPAC (302 "My Change Done Come") 5-10 60s
SAR (104 "Never") 10-20 60
SAR (107 "Always on My Mind") 10-20 60
SAR (113 "Don't Cry Baby") 10-15 61
SAR (121 "Your Heart Will Sing") 10-15 61
SAR (133 "Wildest Girl in Town") 10-15 62
SAR (147 "Black Night") 10-15 63
SAR (151 "Never") 8-12 64
Also see COOKE, Sam / Johnny Morisette

MORLEY, Cozy P&R '57
Singles: 78 rpm
ABC-PAR 10-20 57
Singles: 7-inch
ABC-PAR 10-20 57

MORLOCKS
(Mor-Loks)
Singles: 7-inch
DECCA (31950 "What My Baby Wants") 10-15 66
LIVING LEGEND (100 "Elaine") 30-40 65
LPs: 10/12-inch
MIDNIGHT 5-8

MORLY GREY
LPs: 10/12-inch
STARSHINE (6900 "The Only Truth") 15-25 69

MORMON TABERNACLE CHOIR P&R/LP '59
Singles: 7-inch
COLUMBIA 3-5 59
Picture Sleeves
COLUMBIA 4-8 59
LPs: 10/12-inch
COLUMBIA 5-10 59-76
RCA 5-10 60

MORNING
Singles: 7-inch
VAULT 4-6 70
LPs: 10/12-inch
FANTASY 8-10 72
VAULT 10-12 70

MORNING AFTER
Singles: 7-inch
TAM (201, 369 "Things You Do") 15-25 60s

MORNING DEW
Singles: 7-inch
FAIRYLAND (1001 "No More") 25-50 67
FAIRYLAND (1003 "Be a Friend") 25-50 67

MORNING DEW
LPs: 10/12-inch
ROULETTE (R-41045 "Morning Dew") 75-125 70
(Monaural.)
ROULETTE (RS-41045 "Morning Dew") 100-150 70
(Stereo.)
Members: Malcolm Robinson; Tommy Smith; Ken Tebow; Blair Honeyman.

MORNING GLORIES
Singles: 7-inch
W.B. 4-8 67

MORNING GLORY
Singles: 7-inch
FONTANA 4-8 68
TOYA (100 "Happiness to the Homeland") 4-8
LPs: 10/12-inch
FONTANA 10-20 67

MORNING GLORY MAN
Singles: 7-inch
MR. G 4-8 67

MORNING MIST P&R '71
Singles: 7-inch
EVENT 3-5 71
Members: Terry Cashman; Tommy West.
Also see CASHMAN & WEST

MORNING, NOON & NIGHT R&B '77
Singles: 7-inch
ROADSHOW 3-5 77
LPs: 10/12-inch
ROADSHOW 8-10 77

MORNING RAIN
Singles: 7-inch
BUDDAH 4-8 71

MORNING REIGN
Singles: 7-inch
GARLAND 5-10 67
S 5-10 60s

MORNING SUN
Singles: 7-inch
CORBY 4-8 67
VMC 4-8 69

MORNING TYMES
Singles: 7-inch
MAAD (52268 "Every Day") 40-60 68

MORNINGLORY
LPs: 10/12-inch
TOYA (2001 "Growing") 15-25 72

MORNINGSIDE DRIVE
Singles: 7-inch
COPPERFIELD 3-5

MORNINGSTAR
Singles: 7-inch
COLUMBIA 3-5 77
KEF 3-5
LPs: 10/12-inch
COLUMBIA 8-10 77

MORNINGSTAR, Jackie
Singles: 7-inch
ORANGE (1018 "Rockin' in the Graveyard") 200-300 59
SANDY (1018 "Rockin' in the Graveyard") 150-250 59

MORNINGSTARR
Singles: 7-inch
LION (1003) 5-10 69
(Exact title not known.)
Picture Sleeves
LION (1003) 20-30 69

MOROCCOS
(With Al Smith & His Band; with the Lefty Bates Band)
Singles: 78 rpm
UNITED 50-100 55-56
Singles: 7-inch
B&F (193 "Somewhere Over the Rainbow") 15-25 60
(Mistakenly credits "*Sally* McElroy, Vocalist.")
B&F (1347 "What Is a Teen-Ager's Prayer") 15-25 60
UNITED (188 "Pardon My Tears") 150-250 55
UNITED (193 "Somewhere Over the Rainbow") 150-250 56
UNITED (204 "What Is a Teen-Ager's Prayer") 150-250 56
UNITED (207 "Sad, Sad Hours") 200-300 57
Member: Sollie McElroy.
Also see BATES, Lefty "Guitar"
Also see BROOKS, Lillian
Also see CHANTEURS
Also see McELROY, Sollie
Also see MORROCANS

Also see SMITH, Al

MORODER, Giorgio P&R '72
(Giorgio)
Singles: 12-inch
COLUMBIA....4-6 84
MCA....4-6 84
Singles: 7-inch
BACKSTREET....3-4
CASABLANCA....3-5 79-80
COLUMBIA....3-4 84
DUNHILL....3-5 72
EMI AMERICA....3-4 84
MCA....3-4 84
POLYDOR....3-5 80
VIRGIN....3-4
Picture Sleeves
COLUMBIA....3-4 84
LPs: 10/12-inch
CASABLANCA....5-10 77-79
DUNHILL....10-12 72
POLYDOR....5-10 80
Also see EINZELGANGER
Also see MERCURY, Freddie / Giorgio Moroder
Also see SUMMER, Donna

MORODER, Giorgio, & Phil Oakey D&D '84
Singles: 12-inch
VIRGIN....4-6 84
Also see HUMAN LEAGUE
Also see MORODER, Giorgio

MORRA, Tony
(With the Do-Wells; with Beltones; "Featuring Frankie Gray & His Orchestra")
Singles: 7-inch
ARCADE (152 "My Baby Scares Me")....25-50 58
DU-WELL (1005 "Looking for My Baby")....100-200 60

MORRELL, Don, & Meteors
EPs: 7-inch
SHADOW....8-10 83

MORRIE, Tiny
Singles: 7-inch
CHALLENGE....4-8 62-63
DOT....4-8 66
HURRICANE....10-15 59-64

MORRILL, Kent
Singles: 7-inch
BRC....4-8 71
CONGRESS....5-10 69
ETIQUETTE....10-15 63
LPs: 10/12-inch
CREAM....10-12
SUSPICIOUS....5-8 88
Also see WAILERS

MORRIS, Artie, & Combinations
Singles: 7-inch
COCO....20-30 59

MORRIS, Betty Jean
Singles: 78 rpm
CAPITOL....5-10 55
Singles: 7-inch
CAPITOL....8-12 55

MORRIS, Bob C&W '67
Singles: 7-inch
CAPITOL....4-6
CHALLENGE....4-6
MO-CATE....4-6
TOWER....4-6 67
Also see CHAMPS

MORRIS, Chick
Singles: 78 rpm
DELCRO....10-15
Singles: 7-inch
LEE (503 "Rattlesnake Daddy")...50-100 57

MORRIS, Christopher, Band
LPs: 10/12-inch
MCA....8-10 77

MORRIS, Count
Singles: 78 rpm
VEE JAY....5-10 55
Singles: 7-inch
VEE JAY....10-15 55

MORRIS, David, Jr. R&B '76
Singles: 7-inch
BUDDAH....3-5 76
PHILIPS....4-8 68

MORRIS, Elmore
(With the Spinners)
Singles: 7-inch
CRACKERJACK (4006 "It Seemed Like Heaven to Me")....15-25 61
LANDA (670 "Paradise Hill")....25-50 61
PEACOCK....8-12 60

MORRIS, Floyd
Singles: 7-inch
BBS (0578 "Bee Que")....10-15 68
BUNKY (7757 "Bee Que")....5-10 70s
DILLIE (102 "Dillie's Blues")....15-25 58
SELECT (737 "Pompton Turnpike")....10-20 64

MORRIS, Gary C&W '80
Singles: 7-inch
UNIVERSAL....3-4 89
W.B....3-5 80-88
LPs: 10/12-inch
W.B....5-8 82-88
Also see ANDERSON, Lynn, & Gary Morris
Also see GAYLE, Crystal, & Gary Morris

MORRIS, Gene
(With the Pages)
Singles: 7-inch
EDMORAL (1012 "Lovin' Honey")....150-250 57
VIK (0287 "Lovin' Honey")....50-75 57
WINSTON (1020 "I Need It")....20-30 58
WINSTON (1032 "I Crawfished")....20-30 59

MORRIS, Glen
Singles: 7-inch
LIBERTY BELL (9017 "I Got the Blues")....30-40 57

MORRIS, Joe, & His Orch R&B '53
(With Laurie Tate; Mr. Stringbean; Al Savage; "Joe Morris Blues Calvalcade Featuring Billy Mitchell with Joe Morris & His Orchestra")
Singles: 78 rpm
ATLANTIC (Except 950, 954 & 974)....10-20 47-57
ATLANTIC (950 "Verna Lee")....20-30 51
ATLANTIC (954 "Someday You'll Be Sorry")....20-30 52
ATLANTIC (974 "Bald Headed Woman")....20-30 52
DECCA....10-15 49-50
HERALD....10-20 53-54
MANOR....10-15 46-47
Singles: 7-inch
ATLANTIC (933 "Pack Up All Your Bags")....100-150 51
(Vocal by Billy Mitchell.)
ATLANTIC (950 "Verna Lee")....100-150 51
(Vocal by Billy Mitchell.)
ATLANTIC (954 "Someday You'll Be Sorry")....50-100 52
(Vocal by Billy Mitchell.)
ATLANTIC (974 "Bald Headed Woman")....50-100 52
(Vocal by Billy Mitchell.)
ATLANTIC (1100 series)....10-20 57
HERALD (Except 420)....15-30 53-54
HERALD (420 "Travelin' Man")....20-30 54
(Black vinyl.)
HERALD (420 "Travelin' Man")....40-60 54
(Colored vinyl.)
Also see ADAMS, Faye
Also see MR. STRINGBEAN
Also see MITCHELL, Billy
Also see SAVAGE, Al
Also see TATE, Laurie

MORRIS, Joe, & His Orchestra
(Featuring Billy Mitchell)
Singles: 78 rpm
ATLANTIC....10-20 51-52
Singles: 7-inch
ATLANTIC....20-40 51-52
Also see MITCHELL, Billy

MORRIS, Joe, & His Orchestra R&B '50
(Featuring Laurie Tate)
Singles: 78 rpm
ATLANTIC (914 "Anytime, Any Place, Anywhere")....25-50 50
ATLANTIC (923 "Don't Take Your Love Away from Me")....25-50 50
Also see TATE, Laurie

MORRIS, Joe "Guitar"
Singles: 7-inch
RON....5-10 61

MORRIS, Lamar C&W '66
Singles: 7-inch
MGM....4-6 66-73
Also see BAMA BAND
Also see WILLIAMS, Hank, Jr.
Also see YOUNG, Faron

MORRIS, Leo
(With Marcel & His Band)
Singles: 7-inch
IVORY....10-20 61

MORRIS, Marlowe, Quintet P&R '62
Singles: 7-inch
COLUMBIA....4-8 62

MORRIS, Rod
Singles: 78 rpm
CAPITOL....4-8 54
Singles: 7-inch
CAPITOL....5-10 54
LUDWIG....5-10 59

MORRIS, Rose, & Delighters
Singles: 7-inch
PUFF (1002 "I Love the Life I Live")....50-75 62

MORRIS, Russell
Singles: 7-inch
DIAMOND (263 "The Real Thing")...8-12 69
LPs: 10/12-inch
RCA....8-10 75

MORRISON, Bill
Singles: 7-inch
TNT (9029 "Baby Be Good")....25-35 60

MORRISON, Curley Jim: see MORRISON, Jim

MORRISON, David
Singles: 7-inch
VEE JAY....4-8 63

MORRISON, Dorothy P&R '69
Singles: 7-inch
BUDDAH....3-5 70
ELEKTRA....4-6 69
LPs: 10/12-inch
BUDDAH....10-15 70

Also see HAWKINS, Edwin, Singers

MORRISON, Jesse
Singles: 7-inch
ABET....4-8

MORRISON, Jim
(Curley Jim Morrison)
Singles: 7-inch
ARCTIC (2100 "Ready to Rock")....250-350 59
CURLEY-Q (5707 "My Old Standby")....50-75

MORRISON, Junie D&D '84
Singles: 12-inch
ISLAND....4-6 84
Singles: 7-inch
ISLAND....3-4 84
Also see JUNIE

MORRISON, Kent
Singles: 7-inch
MAYBARN....4-8 66

MORRISON, Professor P&R '68
(Professor Morrison's Lollipop)
Singles: 7-inch
WHITE WHALE....5-10 68-69
Also see MARTINE, Layng, Jr.

MORRISON, Van P&R/LP '67
Singles: 7-inch
BANG....4-8 67-68
MERCURY....3-4 85-90
SOLID GOLD....3-4 73
W.B....3-5 70-83
LPs: 10/12-inch
BANG (BLP-218 "Blowin' Your Mind")....20-25 67
(Monaural.)
BANG (BLPS-218 "Blowin' Your Mind")....25-30 67
(Stereo. White label. Has 45 rpm version of *Brown-Eyed Girl*, with "makin' love in the green grass behind the stadium" lyrics.)
BANG (BLPS-218 "Blowin' Your Mind")....25-30 67
(Stereo. White label. Has edited *Brown-Eyed Girl*, with "laughin' and a runnin' behind the stadium" lyrics.)
BANG (BLPS-218 "Blowin' Your Mind")....10-15 70
(Yellow label.)
BANG (222 "Best of Van Morrison")....15-20 70
BANG (400 "T.B. Sheets")....10-15 74
LONDON....10-15 74
MERCURY....5-10 85-90
W.B....8-15 68-83
Also see ELLIOTT, Ron
Also see JUSTICE V
Also see THEM

MORRISON, Van, & Chieftains LP '88
LPs: 10/12-inch
MERCURY....5-8 88
Also see CHIEFTAINS
Also see MORRISON, Van

MORRISON SISTERS
Singles: 78 rpm
DEED....5-10 56
Singles: 7-inch
DECCA (30683 "It's a Treat")....10-15 58
DEED (1016 "Rockin' Boogie Shuffle")....10-15 56

MORRISSEY LP '88
LPs: 10/12-inch
SIRE....5-8 88-91

MORRISSEY, Pat
(Pat Morrisey)
Singles: 78 rpm
DECCA....10-15 54-55
Singles: 7-inch
DECCA (28879 "Baby, It Must Be Love")....15-25 54
DECCA "29594 "House of Blue Night")....15-25 55
LPs: 10/12-inch
MERCURY (20197 "I Sing")....50-100 56

MORROCANS
(With Teddy Phillips Orchestra)
Singles: 7-inch
SALEM (1014 "Believe in Tomorrow")....200-300 57
Member: Sollie McElroy.
Also see MOROCCOS

MORROCO MUZIK MAKERS
Singles: 7-inch
MOTOWN (1047 "Back to School Again")....40-60 63

MORROW, Bruce
Singles: 7-inch
GLAD-HAMP (1015 "More Shimmy")....8-12 61

MORROW, Buddy, & Orchestra P&R '51
Singles: 78 rpm
MERCURY....3-5 54-57
RCA....3-5 50-57
Singles: 7-inch
EPIC....4-6 64
MERCURY....4-8 54-62
RCA....5-10 50-59
U.A....4-8 68
WING....4-8 55-56
EPs: 7-inch
MERCURY....5-15 54-61
RCA....5-15 52-61

LPs: 10/12-inch
EPIC (Except 24095 & 26095)....5-15 64-65
EPIC (24095 "Big Band Beatlemania")....15-25 64
(Monaural.)
EPIC (26095 "Big Band Beatlemania")....20-30 64
(Stereo.)
MERCURY....15-30 54-62
RCA (2000 & 2100 series)....10-20 59-60
RCA (2200 & series)....8-15 60
RCA (3100 & 3200 series)....25-50 52-54
(10-inch LPs.)
U.A....5-10 68
WING....10-20 56

MORSE, Ella Mae P&R/R&B '43
(With Freddie Slack; with Big Dave & His Orchestra)
Singles: 78 rpm
CAPITOL....5-15 43-57
Singles: 7-inch
CAPITOL (1600 thru 3400 series)....5-10 50-57
EPs: 7-inch
CAPITOL....10-20 54-57
LPs: 10/12-inch
CAPITOL (H-513 "Barrelhouse Boogie, and the Blues")....100-150 54
(10-inch LP.)
CAPITOL (T-513 "Barrelhouse Boogie, and the Blues")....50-75 55
CAPITOL (898 "Morse Code")....50-75 57
CAPITOL (1802 "Hits")....30-45 62

MORSE, Steve, Band LP '84
LPs: 10/12-inch
MCA....5-8 89
MUSICIAN/ELEKTRA....5-8 84
Also see DIXIE DREGS
Also see KANSAS

MORTALS
LPs: 10/12-inch
ESTRUS (124 "The Mortals")....5-10 92
Members: Steve Gatch; James Grapes; Denny Brown; Matt Becher; Michael Grimm.

MORTICIANS
Singles: 7-inch
MORTICIAN (101 "Little Latin Lupe Lu")....15-25 60s
PALMER (5027 "It's Gonna Take Awhile")....15-25 67
ROULETTE (4702 "Now That You've Left Me")....5-10 66

MORTIMER
Singles: 7-inch
PHILIPS (20 "Dedicated Music Man")....10-15 68
(Stereo. Promotional issue only.)
PHILIPS (40524 "Dedicated Music Man")....5-10 68
(Monaural.)
Picture Sleeves
PHILIPS (40524 "Dedicated Music Man")....15-25 68
LPs: 10/12-inch
PHILIPS (200267 "Mortimer")....15-25 68
(Monaural.)
PHILIPS (600267 "Mortimer")....15-25 68
(Stereo.)
Also see TEDDY BOYS

MORTIMER, Azie
(A.Z. Mortimer)
Singles: 7-inch
BIG TOP (3041 "Lips")....200-300 60s
(White label. Promotional issue only.)
Note: We have been given this price for a promo. It is not yet clear if there is a pink commercial issue. If so, we do not yet know if it has a value close to this range, or much less.
EPIC....5-10 63
OKEH....4-8 69
PALETTE....5-10 62
RCA....5-10 66
REGATTA....5-10 61
SWAN....5-10 63
TROY....5-10
U.A. (847 "The Other Half of Me") 15-25 65

MORTON, Ann J. C&W '76
Singles: 7-inch
PRAIRIE....3-5 76-81

MORTON, George
Singles: 7-inch
SWIRL....5-8

MORTON, Richard
Singles: 7-inch
MORTON (1 "Sad Sad Song")....50-75

MORY STORM BAND
LPs: 10/12-inch
SOUND MACHINE (49007 "Cry for the Dreamer")....35-55

MOSAIC TWEED
Singles: 7-inch
CAPITOL....4-6 69

MOSBY, Johnny & Jonie C&W '63
Singles: 7-inch
CAPITOL....3-6 67-73
CHALLENGE....8-12 60
COLUMBIA....4-8 62-66
STARDAY....4-6 65
TOPPA....5-10 61
Picture Sleeves
CAPITOL....3-5 70
LPs: 10/12-inch
CAPITOL....8-12 68-71
COLUMBIA....10-15 65
HARMONY....5-10 70

Also see JOHNNY & JONIE

MOSBY, Jonie C&W '73
Singles: 7-inch
CAPITOL....3-5 72-73
Also see MOSBY, Johnny & Jonie

MOSE JONES
LPs: 10/12-inch
MCA/SOUNDS of the SOUTH....10-12 73-74
RCA....5-10 78

MOSELEY, John
Singles: 7-inch
MOON PIE....3-5 77

MOSES, Johnny
Singles: 78 rpm
IMPERIAL....10-20 55
Singles: 7-inch
IMPERIAL (5329 "You're Torturing Me")....20-30 55

MOSES, Lee
Singles: 7-inch
FRONT PAGE....4-8 70
GATES....10-15 60s
MUSICOR....5-10 67

MOSES, Rick
Singles: 7-inch
20TH FOX....3-5 79

MOSES & JOSHUA
Singles: 7-inch
MALA....4-8 68

MOSES & TEN COMMANDMENTS
Singles: 7-inch
RAYNARD (1061 "Monkey Time") 15-25 67

MO-SHUNS
Singles: 7-inch
20TH FOX (6645 "What Can I Say")....25-50 65

MOSLEY, Bob
LPs: 10/12-inch
REPRISE....10-12 72

MOSLEY, Ernest
Singles: 7-inch
LA-CINDY (225 "Keep on Loving Me")....100-200

MOSLEY, Robert
Singles: 7-inch
CAPITOL....10-20 63
COED....5-10 60

MOSLEY, Tommy
Singles: 7-inch
ARVEE (5021 "Pretending")....5-10 60s
ERA (317 "Wishing Well")....20-30 67
UPTOWN (706 "For Her Love")....10-20 65

MOSQUITOS
LPs: 10/12-inch
VALHALLA....8-10 85
Members: Vance Brescia; Tony Millions; Iain Morrison; Steven Prisco; Mitch Towse.

MOSRITERS
Singles: 7-inch
CASTLE....4-8 66
NORALA....4-8 65

MOSS, Bill R&B '69
(With Celestials)
Singles: 7-inch
BELL....3-5 69
BILESSE....4-6

MOSS, Gene
Singles: 7-inch
RCA....8-10 64
LPs: 10/12-inch
RCA (LPM-2977 "Dracula's Greatest Hits")....20-35 64
(Monaural.)
RCA (LSP-2977 "Dracula's Greatest Hits")....30-45 64
(Stereo.)

MOSS, Keith
Singles: 7-inch
HARVEY (122 "Satisfaction Guaranteed")....100-200 63

MOSS, Lord Beverly, & Mossmen
Singles: 7-inch
TARGET (107/108 "Please, Please What's the Matter")....25-50 67
Members: Bob Timmers; Gary Laabs; Vic Wendt; Tom Gebheim.

MOSS, Roy
Singles: 78 rpm
MERCURY....50-75 56
Singles: 7-inch
FASCINATION (1002 "Wiggle Walkin' Baby")....100-200 58
MERCURY (70770 "You're My Big Baby Now")....100-200 56
MERCURY (70858 "Corinne Corinna")....100-200 56

MOST
Singles: 7-inch
COLUMBIA....4-8 66

MOST, Donny P&R '76
Singles: 7-inch
U.A....3-5 76-77
VENTURE....3-5 78
Picture Sleeves
U.A....3-5 76
LPs: 10/12-inch
U.A....8-12 76

MOST, Mickie
Singles: 7-inch
LAWN (263 "Sea Cruise")..............10-20 64

MOTE, Danny
Singles: 7-inch
OPAL (001 "Done You Wrong").....20-25 61
(First issue.)
VEE JAY (381 "Done You Wrong")..........10-15 61

MOTELS LP '79
Singles: 7-inch
CAPITOL..........3-6 79-85
Picture Sleeves
CAPITOL..........3-5 82-85
LPs: 10/12-inch
CAPITOL..........5-10 79-85
Members: Martha Davis; Martin Jourard; Jeff Jourard; Brian Glascock; Tim McGovern; Mike Goodroe.
Also see DAVIS, Martha

MOTEN, Bus, & His Men
Singles: 78 rpm
CAPITOL (831 "That Did It")..........10-15 50
Singles: 7-inch
CAPITOL (831 "That Did It")..........25-35 50

MOTHER BROWN
Singles: 7-inch
BAND BOX..........3-6 69

MOTHER EARTH LP '69
Singles: 7-inch
MERCURY..........4-8 68-69
REPRISE..........3-5 71
U.A...........5-10 68
LPs: 10/12-inch
MERCURY..........10-20 69-70
REPRISE..........10-15 71
Members: Tracy Nelson; John Andrews; Bob Arthur; George Rains. Session: Boz Scaggs.
Also see BORDERLINE
Also see NELSON, Tracy
Also see SCAGGS, Boz

MOTHER FREEDOM BAND
LPs: 10/12-inch
ALL PLATINUM..........5-10 77

MOTHER HEADS FAMILY REUNION
Singles: 7-inch
MARION..........5-10 67

MOTHER HUBBARD
Singles: 7-inch
COLUMBIA..........3-6 68
Picture Sleeves
COLUMBIA..........4-8 68

MOTHER MALLARD'S PORTABLE MASTERPIECE COMPANY
LPs: 10/12-inch
EARTHQUACK..........10-15 73

MOTHER LOVE
Singles: 7-inch
EPIC..........5-10 68
20TH FOX (6687 "Flim-Flam Man")..........10-20 67
LPs: 10/12-inch
EPIC..........10-15 70

MOTHER NIGHT
LPs: 10/12-inch
COLUMBIA..........8-12 72

MOTHER TRUCKER'S YELLOW DUCK
Singles: 7-inch
CAPITOL (2707 "Times Are Changing")..........15-25 69

MOTHER'S COOKIES
Singles: 7-inch
VALHALLA..........4-8 69

MOTHER'S FINEST P&R/LP '76
Singles: 12-inch
EPIC..........4-8 77-79
Singles: 7-inch
EPIC..........3-5 76-79
LPs: 10/12-inch
ATLANTIC..........5-10 81
EPIC..........5-10 76-79
RCA..........8-12 72
Members: Glenn Murdock; Joyce Kennedy; Gary Moore; Jerry Seay; Barry Borden; Michael Keek.
Also see KENNEDY, Joyce

MOTHER'S HEROS
Singles: 7-inch
THE LABEL..........4-8 67

MOTHER'S LITTLE HELPER
Singles: 7-inch
POPPY..........4-8 68

MOTHER'S ORPHANS
Singles: 7-inch
BACCHO..........15-20 60s

MOTHER'S WORRY
Singles: 7-inch
LOOK..........4-8 68
Members: Rick Purcell; John Zaffiro; Ernest Mathies; Keith Cravillion; Peter Alioto.

MOTHERFUCKER 666
Singles: 7-inch
GET HIP (166 "She's Outta the Scene")..........3-4 92
Picture Sleeves
GET HIP (166 "She's Outta the Scene")..........3-4 92
Members: Jeff Dahl; Mike Metoff; Alan Clark; Keith Telligman.

MOTHERLODE P&R/LP '69
Singles: 7-inch
BUDDAH..........4-6 69
EPs: 7-inch
BUDDAH (11 "When I Die")..........8-12 69
LPs: 10/12-inch
BUDDAH..........10-15 69-72

MOTHERLOVE
Singles: 7-inch
ELEKTRA..........3-5 79

MOTHERS OF INVENTION LP '67
(Mothers)
Singles: 7-inch
BIZARRE/REPRISE..........10-15 70
DISCREET..........6-10 73
VERVE (Except 10418)..........15-25 66-68
VERVE (10418 "How Could I Be Such a Fool")..........50-75 66
Promotional Singles
BIZARRE/REPRISE..........12-25 70
DISCREET..........8-10 73
VERVE (Except 10418)..........20-30 66-68
VERVE (10418 "How Could I Be Such a Fool")..........60-80 66
EPs: 7-inch
REPRISE (332 "Uncle Meat")..........35-45 69
(Promotional issue only.)
LPs: 10/12-inch
BIZARRE (2024 "Uncle Meat")..........35-45 69
(Blue label. With 12-page booklet.)
BIZARRE (2024 "Uncle Meat")..........20-30 69
(Blue label. Without booklet.)
BIZARRE (2024 "Uncle Meat")..........10-15 70s
(Brown label.)
BIZARRE (2028 "Weasles Ripped My Flesh")..........20-30 70
(Blue label.)
BIZARRE (2028 "Weasles Ripped My Flesh")..........5-10 70s
(Brown label.)
BIZARRE (2042 "The Mothers Live/Fillmore East")..........20-30 71
(Blue label.)
BIZARRE (2042 "The Mothers Live/Fillmore East")..........5-10 70s
(Brown label.)
BIZARRE (2075 "Just Another Band from L.A.")..........20-30 72
(Blue label.)
BIZARRE (2093 "Grand Wazoo")...20-30 72
(Blue label.)
BIZARRE (2093 "Grand Wazoo")..........5-10 70s
(Brown label.)
BIZARRE (6370 "Burnt Weeny Sandwich")..........30-40 69
(Blue label. With folder of bonus photos.)
BIZARRE (6370 "Burnt Weeny Sandwich")..........15-25 69
(Blue label. Without folder of photos.)
BIZARRE (6370 "Burnt Weeny Sandwich")..........5-10 70s
(Brown label.)
DISCREET (2149 "Over-Nite Sensation")..........15-25 73
DISCREET (MS4-2149 "Over-Nite Sensation")..........30-40 73
(Quadrophonic.)
MGM (112 "Mothers of Invention")..........30-40 70
MGM (4754 "Worst of the Mothers")..........25-35 71
REPRISE..........8-12 73-74
(Reissues of Bizarre catalog.)
VERVE (5005 "Freak Out!")..........75-125 66
(Monaural. With mail-order "Freak Out - Hot Spots" map/poster offer printed on inside of cover.)
VERVE (5005 "Freak Out!")..........50-100 67
(Monaural. Without mail-order map/poster offer printed on inside of cover.)
VERVE (V6-5005 "Freak Out!")...50-100 66
(Stereo. With mail-order "Freak Out - Hot Spots" map/poster offer printed on inside of cover.)
VERVE (V6-5005 "Freak Out!")....40-80 67
(Stereo. Without mail-order map/poster offer printed on inside of cover.)
VERVE (5013 "Absolutely Free")...60-80 67
(Monaural. Includes Libretto or Freak Map.)
VERVE (5013 "Absolutely Free")...50-75 67
(Monaural. Without Libretto or Freak Map.)
VERVE (V6-5013 "Absolutely Free")..........50-75 67
(Stereo. Includes Libretto or Freak Map.)
VERVE (V6-5013 "Absolutely Free")..........40-50 67
(Stereo. Without Libretto or Freak Map.)
VERVE (5045 "We're Only in It for the Money")..........50-75 67
(Monaural. With "Only Money" insert.)
VERVE (5045 "We're Only in It for the Money")..........30-50 67
(Monaural. Without "Only Money" insert.)
VERVE (V6-5045 "We're Only in It for the Money")..........50-75 67
(Stereo. With "Only Money" insert.)
VERVE (V6-5045 "We're Only in It for the Money")..........30-50 67
(Stereo. Without "Only Money" insert.)
VERVE (5068 "Mothermania")..........20-40 69
VERVE (5074 "XXXX of the Mothers")..........20-25 69
Notes: Price range of Verve LPs is for commercial copies on the blue & black labels as well as white MGM/Verve labels. Several reissues came out in the early '80s that are nearly identical to originals, except their cover stock is glossier than are '60s issues. Among the reissues we have verified are: *Freak Out, We're Only in It for the Money,* and *Absolutely Free.*)
W.B...........8-10 77
Promotional LPs
BIZARRE (2024 "Uncle Meat")..........40-60 69
BIZARRE (2028 "Weasles Ripped My Flesh")..........35-45 70
BIZARRE (2042 "The Mothers Live/Fillmore East")..........35-45 71
BIZARRE (2075 "Just Another Band from L.A.")..........30-40 72
BIZARRE (2093 "Grand Wazoo")..30-40 72
BIZARRE (6370 "Burnt Weeny Sandwich")..........30-30 69
VERVE (5005 "Freak Out!")..........100-200 66
VERVE (5013 "Absolutely Free").75-125 67
VERVE (5045 "We're Only in It for the Money")..........75-125 67
VERVE (5068 "Mothermania")..........50-100 69
VERVE (5074 "XXXX of the Mothers")..........50-100 69
Members: Frank Zappa; Jimmy Carl Black; Roy Estrada; Ray Collins; Elliot Ingber; Jim Pons; Lowell George.
Also see BLACK, Jimmy Carl
Also see CAPTAIN BEEFHEART
Also see DUKE, George
Also see FISCHER, Wild Man
Also see FLO & EDDIE
Also see GAMBLERS
Also see GERONIMO BLACK
Also see GEORGE, Lowell
Also see GRANDMOTHERS
Also see LEAVES
Also see LORD, Brian, & Midnighters
Also see MISSING PERSONS
Also see NED & NELDA
Also see PRESTON, Billy
Also see RUBEN & JETS
Also see SIMMONS, Jeff
Also see ZAPPA, Frank

MOTIFS
Singles: 7-inch
BATON..........5-10
SELSOM (107 "Molly")..........8-10 66
Picture Sleeves
SELSOM (107 "Molly")..........10-20 66

MOTIFS
Singles: 7-inch
LEJAC (3004 "Someday")..........25-35 60s

MOTION
Singles: 7-inch
MASCOT..........4-8 68

MOTIONS
Singles: 7-inch
LAURIE (3112 "Mr. Night")..........75-125 61
Also see EMOTIONS

MOTIONS
Singles: 7-inch
ABC-PAR..........5-10 64
CONGRESS..........5-10 65
MERCURY (Except 72297)..........5-10 64-65
MERCURY (72297 "Beatle Drums")..........10-20 64

MOTIONS
Singles: 7-inch
PHILIPS..........4-6 69
LPs: 10/12-inch
PHILIPS..........10-15 69

MOTIVATION R&B '83
Singles: 7-inch
DE-LITE..........3-4 83

MOTIVATIONS
Singles: 7-inch
PRIDE (301 "Motivate")..........10-20 63
Members: Greg Sevigny; Pete Johnson; Mike Wells.

MOTIVATIONS
Singles: 7-inch
DYNO VOICE..........4-8 66
EASTBOUND..........4-8

MOTIVE: MUSIC
Singles: 7-inch
SCEPTER..........4-8 68

MOTIVES
Singles: 7-inch
ATCO..........5-10 65

MOTLEY, Frank
(Jimmy Crawford Vocal; Frank Motley "Dual Trumpeter" and His Crew)
Singles: 78 rpm
DC (6004 "That Ain't Right")..........25-50 54
Singles: 7-inch
COOKIN'..........5-10 63
DC (0400 series)..........10-20 59-62
DC (6004 "That Ain't Right")..........50-100 54
(Also issued as by Jimmy Crawford with Frank Motley & His Crew.)
Also see CRAWFORD, Jimmy, with Frank Motley & His Crew
Also see ONTARIOS
Also see TRIBBLE, TNT, with Frank Motley & His Crew
Also see TWILIGHTERS

MOTLEY, Frank, & Curly Bridges
Singles: 7-inch
DC..........10-15 62
Also see MOTLEY, Frank

MOTLEY BLUES BAND
Singles: 7-inch
SCEPTER..........4-8 66

MOTLEY CRUE LP '83
Singles: 12-inch
WEA/ELEKTRA (60395 "Helter Skelter")..........50-60 84
(Picture disc. Includes poster.)
Singles: 7-inch
ELEKTRA..........3-4 83-88
Picture Sleeves
ELEKTRA..........3-4 84-89
LPs: 10/12-inch
ELEKTRA..........5-10 82-89
LEATHÜR ("Too Fast for Love")..........50-75 81
(Black lettering on cover.)
LEATHÜR ("Too Fast for Love")..........25-50 81
(White lettering on cover.)
Member: Vince Neil; Nikki Sixx; Mick Mars; Tommy Lee; John Corabi.
Also see JON & NIGHTRIDERS

MOTLEYS
Singles: 7-inch
VALIANT..........5-10 65-66

MOTORHEAD LP '82
Singles: 7-inch
MERCURY..........3-4 80-83
LPs: 10/12-inch
EMI AMERICA..........5-8 85
GWR/PROFILE..........5-8 86-87
MERCURY..........5-8 80-83
Members: Ian "Lemmy" Kilmister; Eddie Clarke; Phil Campbell; Pete Gill; Mick "Wurzel" Burston.
Also see FASTWAY
Also see GLITTER BAND
Also see HAWKWIND
Also see SAXON

MOTORMEN
Singles: 7-inch
MOMENTUM (661 "Rat Fink")..........15-25

MOTORS P&R/LP '80
Singles: 7-inch
VIRGIN..........3-5 77-80
Picture Sleeves
VIRGIN..........3-5 80
LPs: 10/12-inch
VIRGIN..........8-10 77-80
Also see TCHAIKOVSKY, Bram

MOTS MEN
Singles: 7-inch
LOREN (1005 "Comin' Or Goin' ")..15-25 66

MOTT LP '75
Singles: 7-inch
COLUMBIA..........3-5 75-76
LPs: 10/12-inch
COLUMBIA..........5-10 75-76
Also see MOTT the HOOPLE

MOTT, Charley, & Jokers
Singles: 7-inch
BRAVE..........4-8 68

MOTT THE HOOPLE LP '70
Singles: 7-inch
ATLANTIC..........4-6 70
COLUMBIA..........3-5 72-74
LPs: 10/12-inch
ATLANTIC..........12-18 70-74
COLUMBIA..........10-15 72-75
Member: Ian Hunter.
Also see BRITISH LIONS
Also see HUNTER, Ian
Also see MOTT

MOTTOLA, Tony LP '62
LPs: 10/12-inch
COMMAND..........10-15 62-65
PROJECT 3..........5-10 67-70

MOULD, Bob LP '89
LPs: 10/12-inch
VIRGIN..........5-8 88-90

MOULIN ROUGE
Singles: 7-inch
MCA..........3-5 79

MOULTRIE, Mary
(With Hutch's Trio)
Singles: 7-inch
AMERICANA (1002 "You Gotta Hum")..........10-15 60s
KING (6038 "Last Year, Senior Prom")..........10-15 66

MOULTRIE, Sam
Singles: 7-inch
WARREN (108 "I'll Always Love You")..........15-20

MT. AIRY
Singles: 7-inch
COLUMBIA..........3-5 73
THIMBLE..........3-5 73
LPs: 10/12-inch
THIMBLE..........8-12 73

MOUNT RUSHMORE
Singles: 7-inch
DOT..........5-10 68
LPs: 10/12-inch
DOT (25898 "High on Mount Rushmore")..........10-20 68
DOT (25934 "Mount Rushmore '69")..........10-20 69
Members: Mike Bolan; Glen Smith; Terry Kimball; Travis Fullerton.

MOUNTAIN P&R/LP '70
Singles: 7-inch
WINDFALL..........3-6 69-71
LPs: 10/12-inch
COLUMBIA..........10-15 73-74
SCOTTI BROTHERS..........5-8 85
WINDFALL..........10-15 69-72
Members: Leslie West; Corky Laing; Steve Knight; Felix Pappalardi; David Perry.
Also see LAING, Corky
Also see NATURAL GAS
Also see WEST, Leslie

MOUNTAIN BUS
LPs: 10/12-inch
GOOD (101 "Sundance")..........50-75 71
Members: Tom Jurkens; Bill Kees; Lee Sims; Ed Mooney.

MOURNING REIGN
Singles: 7-inch
CONTOUR (601 "Evil-Hearted You")..........15-25 67
LINK (1 "Satisfaction Guaranteed")..........20-30 66
LINK (2 "Evil-Hearted You")..........20-30 60s
Picture Sleeves
LINK (1 "Satisfaction Guaranteed")..........40-60 67

MOUSE
(With the Traps; Chris St. John)
Singles: 7-inch
BELL..........10-15 69
FRATERNITY..........10-20 65-68
SMUDGE (0703 "Bottom Line")..........10-15 81
Picture Sleeves
FRATERNITY (1005 "Sometimes You Just Can't Win")..........30-50 68
Members: Ronnie Weiss; Bugs Henderson; Dave Stanley; Ken Murray; Bobby Dale; Doug Rhone.
Also see POSITIVELY 13 O'CLOCK
Also see ST. JOHN Chris
Also see UNIQUES

MOUSE
Singles: 7-inch
CAPITOL..........5-10 69
Also see DUSTY CHAPS

MOUSE & BOYS
Singles: 7-inch
RUBIAT..........4-6 60s
SSS INT'L..........4-8 67

MOUSEKETEERS
Singles: 78 rpm
MICKEY MOUSE CLUB..........15-20 57
Singles: 7-inch
BUENA VISTA (346 "Hey Batter Batter")..........10-15 59
BUENA VISTA (569 "Disco Mouse")..3-4 77
DISNEYLAND..........15-25 61-75
Picture Sleeves
BUENA VISTA (569 "Disco Mouse")..3-4 77
LPs: 10/12-inch
DISNEYLAND (3918 "How to Be a Mouseketeer")..........20-30 62
Also see ANNETTE
Also see CRAWFORD, Johnny
Also see DODD, Jimmy
Also see GILLESPIE, Darlene

MOUSERS
Singles: 7-inch
APPLAUSE..........5-8 64

MOUSIE & TRAPS
Singles: 7-inch
TODDLIN' TOWN..........8-12 60s

MOUSKOURI, Nana LP '91
Singles: 7-inch
BELL..........3-5 72-74
CACHET..........3-5
CARRÉRE..........4-6
FONTANA..........4-8 62-71
MERCURY..........5-10 60
PRESIDENT..........5-10 61
RIVERSIDE..........4-8 62
Picture Sleeves
CACHET..........3-5
EPs: 7-inch
FONTANA
LPs: 10/12-inch
BELL..........5-10 73
FONTANA..........10-20 62-69
PHILIPS..........5-8 91
PICKWICK..........5-8 70s
RCA..........5-10
Also see BELAFONTE, Harry, & Nana Mouskouri
Also see HAYWARD, Justin

MOUTH & MacNEAL P&R/LP '72
Singles: 7-inch
PHILIPS..........3-5 72
Picture Sleeves
PHILIPS..........3-5 72
LPs: 10/12-inch
PHILIPS..........10-12 72-73
Members: Will Duyn; Maggie MacNeal.

MOUZON, Alphonse R&B/LP '82
(With Carol Dennis; Alphonze Mouzon)
Singles: 12-inch
PRIVATE I..........4-6 84
Singles: 7-inch
BLUE NOTE..........3-5 73-74
HIGHRISE..........3-4 82
PRIVATE I..........3-4 84
LPs: 10/12-inch
BLUE NOTE..........5-10 73-76
HIGHRISE..........5-8 82
PAUSA..........5-8 81
PRIVATE I..........5-8 84
Also see MOUZON'S ELECTRIC BAND

MOUZON, Alphonse, & Larry Coryell
LPs: 10/12-inch
ATLANTIC........................5-10 77
Also see CORYELL, Larry
Also see MOUZON, Alphonse

MOUZON'S ELECTRIC BAND
Singles: 12-inch
VANGUARD........................4-6 83
Singles: 7-inch
VANGUARD........................3-4 83
Also see MOUZON, Alphonse

MOVE P&R '72
Singles: 7-inch
A&M........................5-10 67-69
CAPITOL........................10-15 70
DERAM........................5-10 67
MGM........................8-10 71
U.A........................4-8 72-73
EPs: 7-inch
A&M ("Something Else")........75-125 68
(May have been released only in the U.K. If issued in the U.S., may have been a promo only. Verification needed. Selection number also needs to be verified from actual EP.)
LPs: 10/12-inch
A&M (3181 "Shazam")........5-8 82
A&M (3625 "Best of the Move")......15-25 74
A&M (4259 "Shazam")........20-25 69
CAPITOL........................15-25 71
PICKWICK........................10-15 70s
U.A........................10-15 73
Members: Jeff Lynne; Roy Wood; Bev Bevan; Denny Cordell; Richard Tandy; Carl Wayne; Rick Price; Trevor Burton; Ace Kefford.
Also see LYNNE, Jeff
Also see MAGIC CHRISTIANS
Also see WOOD, Roy

MOVEMENT
Singles: 7-inch
TINKER (3921 "Green Knight")......15-25 67

MOVEMENTS
Singles: 7-inch
PEANUT COUNTRY........................10-20

MOVERS
Singles: 7-inch
1-2-3 (1700 "Leave Me Loose")......15-25 68

MOVIES
Singles: 7-inch
A&M........................3-5 76
ARISTA........................3-5 76-77
LPs: 10/12-inch
A&M........................8-10 76
ARISTA........................8-10 76
Also see MESSENGERS

MOVIES R&B '86
Singles: 12-inch
CBS ASSOCIATED........................4-6 86
Singles: 7-inch
CBS ASSOCIATED........................3-4 86
RCA........................3-5 80-86
LPs: 10/12-inch
RCA........................5-10 80-81

MOVIN' MORFOMEN
Singles: 7-inch
DELTA (2242 "Run Girl Run")........15-25 67
NEL-RIC (301 "We Tried, Try It")...15-25 67

MOVING PARTS
Singles: 7-inch
BOBBY........................5-10 68

MOVING PICTURES P&R/LP '82
Singles: 7-inch
GEFFEN........................3-4 89
NETWORK........................3-5 82
Picture Sleeves
NETWORK........................3-5 82
LPs: 10/12-inch
NETWORK........................5-8 82
Members: Alex Smith; Garry Frost.
Also see 1927

MOVING SIDEWALKS
Singles: 7-inch
TANTARA (3101 "99th Floor")........25-35 67
TANTARA (3103 "I Want to Hold Your Hand")........25-35 68
TANTARA (3113 "Flashback")........20-30 69
WAND (1156 "99th Floor")........15-20 67
WAND (1167 "Need Me")........10-20 67
EPs: 7-inch
MUTT (1030 "The Moving Sidewalks")........75-125 60s
LPs: 10/12-inch
EVA (12002 "99th Floore")........8-12 82
TANTARA (6919 "Flash")........200-300 68
Members: Billy Gibbons; Tom Moore; Don Summers; Lanier Greig; Dan Mitchell.
Also see ZZ TOP

MOVING VIOLATIONS
Singles: 7-inch
ATLANTIC (3030 "Spinning Top")......4-6 74
GEM (101 "This Time")........35-55 60s
SSS INT'L (733 "You'd Better Move On")........10-20 68

MOWREY, Al
Singles: 7-inch
FINE........................8-12 59

MOXIES
Singles: 7-inch
MONZA........................4-8 65

MOXY
LPs: 10/12-inch
MERCURY........................8-10 76-78

MOY, June
(With the Feathers)
Singles: 78 rpm
SHOWTIME........................50-75 54
Singles: 7-inch
SHOWTIME (1103 "Castle of Dreams")........75-125 54
Also see FEATHERS

MOYA, Monte, & Surfers
LPs: 10/12-inch
EVEREST........................15-20 63

MOYET, Alison P&R/D&D/LP '85
Singles: 12-inch
COLUMBIA........................4-6 85
Singles: 7-inch
COLUMBIA........................3-4 85
Picture Sleeves
COLUMBIA........................3-4 85
LPs: 10/12-inch
COLUMBIA........................5-8 85-87
Also see YAZ

MOZART, Mickey, Quintet P&R '59
Singles: 7-inch
ROULETTE........................5-10 59-61

MR: see MISTER

MRS. MILLER: see MILLER, Mrs.

MTUME R&B '78
Singles: 12-inch
EPIC........................4-8 79-86
Singles: 7-inch
EPIC........................3-5 78-87
LPs: 10/12-inch
EPIC........................5-8 78-86
Members: James Mtume; Tawatha Agee.

MU
Singles: 7-inch
MANTRA (101 "Ballad of Brother Lew")........15-25 71
MU (101 "One More Day")........10-15 72
MU (103 "Too Naked for Demetrius")........10-15 73
LPs: 10/12-inch
APPALOOSA (071 "Last Album")....8-12 81
BLUE FORM (1 "Children of the Rainbow")........8-12 85
CASS (100 "Mu")........75-100 72
RTV (300 "Mu")........150-250 71
RECKLESS (7 "End of an Era")......10-15 88
U.A. (27909 "Mu")........30-40 74
Members: Merrell Fankhauser; Jeff Cotton; Randy Wimer; Jeff Parker; Mary Lee; Larry Willey.
Also see CAPTAIN BEEFHEART
Also see FANKHAUSER, Merrell

MUD
Singles: 7-inch
BELL........................3-5 74
P-NUT........................5-10 67

MUDCRUTCH
Singles: 7-inch
SHELTER (40357 "Depot Street")..10-20 75
Member: Tom Petty.
Also see PETTY, Tom, & Heartbreakers

MUDD
LPs: 10/12-inch
UNI........................10-15 70-71

MUDD FAMILY
Singles: 7-inch
SCEPTER........................4-8 66

MUDDY WATERS: see WATERS, Muddy

MUDLARKS
Singles: 7-inch
ROULETTE........................5-10 59

MUDSLINGER, Roger
Singles: 7-inch
RED BIRD (013 "Election Year 1964")........5-10 64

MUEHLEISEN, Maury
LPs: 10/12-inch
CAPITOL........................10-12 72

MUFFETS
Singles: 7-inch
CHELSEA LTD. (2002 "Make It Alright")........10-20
COUNTERPART ("Heather Girl")....10-20
(Selection number not known.)

MUFFINS
Singles: 7-inch
RCA (9211 "Subway Traveler")........5-10 67

MUFFINS, Thee: see THEE MUFFINS

MUGWUMPS
(Mugwump Establishment)
Singles: 7-inch
SIDEWALK (900 "Bald Headed Woman")........10-20 66
W.B........................5-10 64-67
LPs: 10/12-inch
W.B. (W-1697 "Mugwumps")........15-25 67
(Monaural.)
W.B. (WS-1697 "Mugwumps")........20-30 67
(Stereo.)
Members: Cass Elliot; Denny Doherty; James Hendricks; John Sebastian; Zal Yanovsky.
Also see ELLIOT, Cass
Also see DOHERTY, Denny
Also see HENDRICKS, James
Also see SEBASTIAN, John
Also see YANOVSKY, Zal

MUGS
Singles: 7-inch
JONNY-A........................4-8 67

MUHAMMAD, Idris P&R/R&B/LP '77
Singles: 12-inch
FANTASY........................4-6 83
Singles: 7-inch
FANTASY........................3-5 80-83
KUDU........................3-5 77-78
PRESTIGE........................3-5 72
LPs: 10/12-inch
FANTASY........................5-8 83
KUDU........................8-10 76-77
PRESTIGE........................8-10 72

MUHOBERAC, Larry
Singles: 7-inch
COVER (8201 "Tailspin")........10-15 63
Also see PRESLEY, Elvis

MULBERRY FRUIT BAND
Singles: 7-inch
BUDDAH........................4-8 67
Members: Peter Anders; Vinnie Poncia.
Also see ANDERS & PONCIA

MULCAYS
(With Fran McKenna; "Jimmy & Mildred;" with "Their Electric Harmonicas")
Singles: 78 rpm
CARDINAL........................5-10 52-55
Singles: 7-inch
CARDINAL........................8-12 52-55
CORAL (61607 "Perfidia")........8-12 51
ESSEX (400 "Harbor Lights")........5-10 55
ESSEX (402 "Sentimental Journey")........5-10 55
JUBILEE (5426 "Canadian Sunset")........5-10 62
TRANS-WORLD (719 "I Got the Blues")........8-12 57
LPs: 10/12-inch
JUBILEE (5017 "Magic Millions")...20-30 62

MULDAUR, Geoff
Singles: 7-inch
REPRISE........................3-5 76
LPs: 10/12-inch
PRESTIGE........................10-15 69
REPRISE........................8-12 75

MULDAUR, Geoff, & Bonnie Raitt
Singles: 7-inch
REPRISE........................3-5 76
Also see RAITT, Bonnie

MULDAUR, Geoff & Maria
Singles: 7-inch
REPRISE........................3-5 69
LPs: 10/12-inch
REPRISE........................10-15 69-72
Also see KWESKIN, Jim
Also see MULDAUR, Geoff
Also see MULDAUR, Maria

MULDAUR, Maria LP '73
Singles: 7-inch
REPRISE........................3-5 73-76
W.B........................3-5 78-79
LPs: 10/12-inch
MYRRH........................5-8 82
REPRISE........................8-12 73-76
TAKOMA........................5-8 80
W.B........................5-10 78-79

MULER
Singles: 7-inch
GAMMA RAY ("Share the Apple")......3-4 94
(Colored vinyl.)
Picture Sleeves
GAMMA RAY ("Share the Apple")......3-4 94
(Sleeve shows title as *Share an Apple*.)
Members: Dave Baumgartner; Kris Durso; Sean Leahy; Will Veeder.

MULESKINNERS
Singles: 7-inch
CUCA........................5-10 63
SARA........................8-12 63
SOMA........................8-12 64
TWIN TOWN........................8-12 65
WATER STREET........................5-10 70
Member: Jim Sundquist.
Also see FENDERMEN
Also see VASSER, Dave

MULL, Martin P&R '73
(Martin Mull Orchestra)
Singles: 7-inch
ABC........................3-5 77
CAPRICORN........................3-5 72-77
ELEKTRA........................3-5 79
LPs: 10/12-inch
ABC........................8-10 77-78
CAPRICORN........................8-12 73
ELEKTRA........................5-10 79
MCA........................5-8 80s

MULLANEY, Dave
Singles: 7-inch
LAURIE (3473 "An Extra Gas")......10-20 68

MULLEN, Bruce C&W '74
Singles: 7-inch
CHART........................3-5 74
Also see PETERSON, Oscar

MULLICAN, Moon C&W/P&R '47
(With the Showboys)
Singles: 78 rpm
KING........................15-25 46-56
Singles: 7-inch
CORAL 62042 "Moon's Rock")........20-30 58
DECCA (30962 "Cush Cush Ky-Yay")........10-20 59
HALL (1923 "I'll Pour the Wine")....10-20 60s
KING (830 "I'll Sail My Ship Alone")........25-40 49
KING (1000 series)........20-35 52-54
KING (4000 series)........15-25 55-56
KING (5000 series)........8-15 59-60
STARDAY........................5-10 60-61
EPs: 7-inch
KING (214 "King of the Hillbilly Piano Players")........20-30 50s
KING (227 "Piano Solos")........15-25 50s
KING (314 "Moon Mullican")........15-25 50s
STARDAY (154 "Moon Mullican")...20-30 60
LPs: 10/12-inch
AUDIO LAB........................50-75
CORAL (57235 "Moon Over Mullican")........150-250 58
KAPP........................20-30 69
KING (555 "All-Time Greatest Hits")........50-100 57
KING (628 "16 Favorite Tunes")....50-75 59
KING (681 "Many Moods")........50-75 60
KING (937 "24 Favorite Tunes")....40-60 65
NASHVILLE........................10-20 70
PHONORAMA........................5-8 83
PICKWICK/HILLTOP........................10-15 66
SPUR (3005 "Moon Mullican Sings & Plays")........100-150
STARDAY........................20-40 67
STERLING (601 "I'll Sail My Ship Alone")........50-75 50s
WESTERN........................5-8
Also see KERR, Anita

MULLICAN, Moon / Cowboy Copas / Red Sovine
LPs: 10/12-inch
DIPLOMAT........................5-10 60s

MULLICAN, Moon / Cotton Thompson
Singles: 78 rpm
KING........................10-20 48
Also see MULLICAN, Moon
Also see THOMPSON, Cotton

MULLIGAN, Gerry LP '59
(Gerry Mulligan Quartet; Jazz Combo)
Singles: 7-inch
PACIFIC JAZZ........................4-6 61
PHILIPS........................4-6 64
VERVE........................4-8 60
EPs: 7-inch
CAPITOL........................30-45 53
COLUMBIA........................10-20 59
EMARCY........................10-20 56
PACIFIC JAZZ........................25-50 53-57
PRESTIGE (1317 "Gerry Mulligan Blows")........50-100 52
PRESTIGE (1318 "Gerry Mulligan Blows")........50-100 52
U.A........................10-20 58
LPs: 10/12-inch
A&M........................8-12 72
ABC-PAR (225 "Jazz Concerto")..75-125 58
BLUE NOTE........................5-8 81
CTI........................8-12 75
CAPITOL (H-439 "Gerry Mulligan")........150-250 53
(10-inch LP.)
CAPITOL (691 "Modern Sounds")........100-150 56
(One side is by Shorty Rogers.)
CAPITOL (2000 series)........20-40 63
CAPITOL (11000 series)........8-12 72
CHIAROSCURO........................5-10 77
COLUMBIA (1307 thru 1932)......20-45 59-63
(Monaural.)
COLUMBIA (8116 thru 8732)........25-50 59-63
(Stereo.)
COLUMBIA (34000 series)........5-10 77
CROWN........................10-20 63-64
DRG........................5-8 80
EMARCY (1000 series)........5-8 81
EMARCY (36056 "Gerry Mulligan Sextet")........100-150 56
EMARCY (36101 "Mainstream")........100-150 57
GRP........................5-8 83
GENE NORMAN (3 "Gerry Mulligan Quartet")........150-250 52
(10-inch LP.)
GENE NORMAN (26 "Gerry Mulligan/Chet Baker/Buddy DeFranco")........50-100 57
GENE NORMAN (56 "Gerry Mulligan/Chet Baker/Buddy DeFranco")........20-40 61
INNER CITY........................5-8 80
KIMBERLY........................20-30 63
LIMELIGHT (82000 series)........12-25 65-66
(Monaural.)
LIMELIGHT (86000 series)........15-30 65-66
(Stereo.)
MERCURY (20453 "Profile")........40-60 59
ODYSSEY........................10-20 68
PACIFIC JAZZ (1 "Gerry Mulligan Quartet")........200-300 53
(10-inch LP.)
PACIFIC JAZZ (2 "Gerry Mulligan Quartet")........200-300 53
(10-inch LP.)
PACIFIC JAZZ (5 "Gerry Mulligan")........200-300 53
(10-inch LP.)
PACIFIC JAZZ (10 "Gerry Mulligan")........150-250 54
(10-inch LP.)
PACIFIC JAZZ (1201 "California Concert")........100-150 55
PACIFIC JAZZ (1207 "Original Quartet")........100-150 55
PACIFIC JAZZ (1210 "Paris Concert")........100-150 56
PACIFIC JAZZ (1228 "Mulligan at Storyville")........100-150 57
PACIFIC JAZZ (1237 "Songbook")........100-150 57
PACIFIC JAZZ (1241 "Reunion")........100-150 57
PACIFIC JAZZ (10000 & 20000 series)........10-20 66
PAUSA........................5-10 76
PHILIPS........................10-20 63-64
PRESTIGE (003 "Mulligan Plays Mulligan")........5-8 82
PRESTIGE (120 "Gerry Mulligan Blows")........200-300 52
(10-inch LP.)
PRESTIGE (141 "Mulligan Too Blows")........200-300 53
(10-inch LP.)
PRESTIGE (7006 "Gerry Plays Mulligan")........75-100 56
(Yellow label.)
PRESTIGE (7251 "Historically Speaking")........30-40 63
(Yellow label.)
SUNSET........................10-15 66
TRIP........................6-12 75-76
U.A. (4006 "I Want to Live")........30-40 58
(Monaural.)
U.A. (4006 "I Want to Live")........40-50 58
(Stereo.)
V.S.P........................10-20 66
VERVE........................25-50 58-60
(Reads "Verve Records, Inc." at bottom of label.)
VERVE........................10-25 61-72
(Reads "MGM Records - A Division Of Metro-Goldwyn-Mayer, Inc." at bottom of label.)
VERVE........................5-12 73-84
(Reads "Manufactured By MGM Record Corp.," or mentions either Polydor or Polygram at bottom of label.)
WHO'S WHO in JAZZ........................5-8 78
WING........................10-20 67
WORLD PACIFIC (1241 "Reunion")........50-100 58
WORLD PACIFIC (1253 "Annie Ross Sings with Mulligan")........50-100 59
Also see BRUBECK, Dave, & Gerry Mulligan
Also see GETZ, Stan, & Gerry Mulligan

MULLIGAN, Gerry, & Paul Desmond
(Gerry Mulligan / Paul Desmond)
LPs: 10/12-inch
FANTASY (220 "Gerry Mulligan/Paul Desmond")........100-150 56
(Colored vinyl.)
RCA (2642 "Two of a Mind")........40-60 62
VERVE (8246 "Gerry Mulligan/Paul Desmond")........50-100 58
(Reads "Verve Records, Inc." at bottom of label.)
VERVE (8246 "Gerry Mulligan/ Paul Desmond")........25-50 62
(Reads "MGM Records - A Division Of Metro-Goldwyn-Mayer, Inc." at bottom of label.)
Also see DESMOND, Paul

MULLIGAN, Gerry, & Johnny Hodges
LPs: 10/12-inch
VERVE........................30-40 60
(Reads "Verve Records, Inc." at bottom of label.)
VERVE........................15-25 62
(Reads "MGM Records - A Division of Metro-Goldwyn-Mayer, Inc." at bottom of label.)
Also see HODGES, Johnny

MULLIGAN, Gerry, & Thelonious Monk
LPs: 10/12-inch
MILESTONE........................8-12 82
RIVERSIDE (247 "Mulligan Meets Monk")........50-100 57
RIVERSIDE (1106 "Mulligan Meets Monk")........40-60 58
Also see MONK, Thelonious

MULLIGAN, Gerry, & Oscar Peterson
LPs: 10/12-inch
VERVE (8235 "Gerry & Oscar at Newport")........50-100 57
VERVE (8559 "Gerry & Oscar at Newport")........30-40 63
(Monaural.)
VERVE (68559 "Gerry & Oscar at Newport")........30-40 63
(Stereo.)
Also see PETERSON, Oscar

MULLIGAN, Gerry, & Ben Webster
LP: 10/12-inch
MFSL (234 "Gerry Mulligan Meets Ben Webster")........20-25 94
(Half-speed mastered.)
Also see MULLIGAN, Gerry

MULLIN, Terry
Singles: 7-inch
GASLIGHT (555 "The Hearse")........5-10

MULLINS, Dee C&W '68
Singles: 7-inch
MEL-O-DY........................10-15 64
PLANTATION........................3-5 69-71
SSS INT'L........................3-6 68
TRIUNE........................3-5 73
LPs: 10/12-inch
PLANTATION........................8-12 69

MULLINS, Hank "Soul Man"
Singles: 7-inch
AUDEL (362 "He Upset Your Dreams")........10-20

MULLINS, Lonnie
Singles: 7-inch
LOGAN..........5-10 59

MULLINS, Moon
(With the Night Raiders)
Singles: 7-inch
LANCE (005 "Gonna Dance Tonight")..........10-15 61
MART (113 "Bip Bap Boom").....200-300 58
Also see HAWKS, Mickey

MULLINS, Zeke
Singles: 7-inch
TIMBER..........5-10 64

MULRAYS
Singles: 7-inch
TRANS WORLD..........8-12 60s

MUL-TEE BAG
Singles: 7-inch
MERCURY..........4-8 68

MULTIPHONIC TRIBE
LPs: 10/12-inch
SUGAR HILL..........5-8 81

MULVANEY, Gary "Happo"
(With Baron Mack Ferguson & Orchestra)
Singles: 7-inch
TEEN-TIME (1001 "Every Little Thing I Do")..........100-200 61

MUMBLES
(Walter Horton)
Singles: 78 rpm
MODERN (809 "Little Boy Blue") .50-100 51
RPM (338 "Black Gal")..........100-125 51
Also see HORTON, Big Walter

MUMFORD, Gene
(With the Serenaders)
Singles: 7-inch
COLUMBIA (41233 "Please Give Me One More Chance")..........40-60 59
(Rerecorded—not reissue of Whiz track.)
LIBERTY (55241 "I'm Getting Sentimental Over You")..........10-20 60
LIBERTY (55274 "I Gotta Have My Baby Back")..........10-20 60
WHIZ (1500 "Please Give Me One More Chance")..........300-400 57
Also see LARKS
Also see WARD, Billy, & Dominoes

MUMFORD FAMILY BAND
Singles: 7-inch
GROOVE..........4-8 64

MUMMIES
LPs: 10/12-inch
ESTRUS (94015 "The Mummies").. 5-10 92

MUND HARMONICA TRIO
Singles: 7-inch
BRUNO..........4-8 60

MUNDY, Jim C&W '73
(With Terri Melton)
Singles: 7-inch
ABC..........3-5 73-75
ABC/DOT..........3-5 76
HILL COUNTRY..........3-5 77

MUNDY, Marilyn C&W '89
Singles: 7-inch
DOOR KNOB..........3-4 89-90

MUNDY, Nick R&B '84
Singles: 7-inch
COLUMBIA..........3-4 84

MUNGO JERRY P&R/LP '70
Singles: 7-inch
BELL..........3-6 71-73
FLASHBACK..........3-5 73
JANUS..........4-8 70-71
PYE..........3-6 72-75
LPs: 10/12-inch
JANUS (7000 "Mungo Jerry")..........10-15 70
PYE (504 "Mungo Jerry")..........8-12 70s
Members: Paul King; Colin Earl; Mike Cole; Ray Dorset.

MUNI, Scott
Singles: 7-inch
RCA (9291 "Letter to an Unborn Child")..........10-20 67

MUNICH MACHINE LP '78
Singles: 7-inch
CASABLANCA..........3-5 78
LPs: 10/12-inch
CASABLANCA..........5-10 78
Member: Chris Bennett.

MUNLEY, Terry
Singles: 7-inch
FLEETWOOD..........3-4 78

MUNRO, Sonny
Singles: 7-inch
EPIC (50174 "Open the Door to Your Heart")..........10-20 75

MUNSTERS
Singles: 7-inch
DECCA..........5-10 64
LPs: 10/12-inch
DECCA (4588 "The Munsters")......25-30 64
(Monaural.)
DECCA (7-4588 "The Munsters")...25-35 64
(Stereo.)
GOLDEN (139 "At Home")..........10-20 64

MUNX
Singles: 7-inch
JUBILEE..........4-8 68

MUPHETS
Singles: 7-inch
SOUND SPECTACTULAR (36001 "Why Can't You Go")..........10-15

MUPPETS
(Sesame Street Muppets)
Singles: 7-inch
ATLANTIC..........3-4 79-81
SESAME STREET..........3-4 78
Picture Sleeves
ATLANTIC..........3-4 79-81
SESAME STREET..........3-4 78
LPs: 10/12-inch
ARISTA..........5-8 77
ATLANTIC..........5-8 79-81
COLUMBIA..........5-10 70-72
SESAME STREET..........5-8 78
W.B...........5-10 71
Also see DENVER, John, & Muppets
Also see ERNIE / Sesame Street Kids
Also see HENSON, Jim
Also see KERMIT / Fozzie Bear

MURAD, Jerry: see HARMONICATS

MURALS
Singles: 7-inch
CLIMAX (110 "See You in September")..........25-50 59
Member: Billy Mure.
Also see MURE, Billy

MURDOCH, Bruce
LPs: 10/12-inch
STORMY FOREST..........10-15

MURDOCK, Judy
Singles: 7-inch
TOWER..........4-8 65

MURDOCK, Lydia R&B '83
Singles: 12-inch
TEEN..........4-6 83
Singles: 7-inch
TEEN..........3-4 83

MURDOCK, Shirley R&B '86
Singles: 12-inch
ELEKTRA..........4-6 86
Singles: 7-inch
ELEKTRA..........3-4 86-88
LPs: 10/12-inch
ELEKTRA..........5-8 87-88
Also see ZAPP

MURE, Billy P&R '59
(With the Wild-Cats; with Trumpeteers; with 7 Karats)
Singles: 78 rpm
RCA..........5-10 57-58
Singles: 7-inch
COLPIX..........5-8 61
DANCO..........4-8 65
EVEREST..........5-10 60
MGM..........4-8 60-66
PARIS..........5-10 60
RCA..........5-15 57-58
RIVERSIDE..........4-8 63
SRG..........5-8 61
SPLASH..........8-12 58
STRAND..........5-8 61
EPs: 7-inch
RCA..........10-15 58
LPs: 10/12-inch
EVEREST..........15-20 60-61
KAPP..........15-20 61
MGM..........15-20 59-66
RCA..........25-30 57-58
STRAND..........15-20 61
SUNSET..........10-12 67
U.A. (3031 "Bandstand Record Hop")..........30-40 59
Also see CHARLIE & BILLY
Also see DE MARCO, Ralph
Also see DESIRES
Also see DOVERS
Also see EMOTIONS
Also see HIGH, Scot, & Highlanders
Also see JORDAN, Lou
Also see LAWRENCE, Syd / Billy Mure
Also see MURALS
Also see PYRAMIDS
Also see SHANTONS
Also see SHAW, Ricky
Also see SUPERTONES
Also see TRUMPETEERS
Also see WILD-CATS

MURE, Billy & Benny
Singles: 7-inch
MGM..........4-8 64
Also see MURE, Billy

MURE, Gary
Singles: 7-inch
VERVE (10356 "Crack Up")..........10-15 65

MURE, Sal
Singles: 7-inch
U.A. (153 "Desire")..........20-30 59

MURFREESBORO
(With Jimmy Beck & Orchestra)
Singles: 7-inch
CHAMPION (1007 "Oh My Love")..........100-200 59

MURIETTA
LPs: 10/12-inch
CHERRY RED..........8-10 71

MURMAIDS P&R '63
(Mermaids)
Singles: 7-inch
CHATTAHOOCHEE (628 "Popsicles and Icicles")..........5-10 63
(Exists with three different flips: *Huntington, Flats, Comedy and Tragedy* and *Blue Dress.* We have yet to learn of a difference in value for any of the three releases.)
CHATTAHOOCHEE (636 "Heartbreak Ahead")..........5-10 64
CHATTAHOOCHEE (650 "Wild and Wonderful")..........5-10 65
CHATTAHOOCHEE (711 "Go Away")..........5-10 67
LIBERTY (56078 "Paper Sun")..........4-8 68
LPs: 10/12-inch
CHATTAHOOCHEE..........8-10 81
Members: Cathy Fischer; Terry Fischer; Sally Gordon.
Also see BRASHER, Cathy
Also see FISHER, Terry

MURPHEY, Chuck
Singles: 78 rpm
COLUMBIA..........10-15 54
Singles: 7-inch
COLUMBIA (21305 "Rhythm Hall")..........15-25 54

MURPHEY, Jim
Singles: 7-inch
RAMCO..........5-10 60

MURPHEY, Mark C&W '89
Singles: 7-inch
TRAVELER ENTERPRISES..........3-4 89

MURPHEY, Michael P&R/LP '72/C&W '76
(Michael Martin Murphey; with Ryan Murphey)
Singles: 7-inch
A&M..........3-5 72
CAPITOL..........3-5 74
EMI AMERICA..........3-4 84-85
EPIC..........3-5 74-79
LIBERTY..........3-4 82-84
W.B...........3-4 86-91
Picture Sleeves
A&M..........3-5 72
EPIC..........3-5 74
LPs: 10/12-inch
A&M..........8-10 72-73
EMI AMERICA..........5-8 84-85
EPIC..........8-12 74-78
LIBERTY..........5-8 82-83
W.B...........5-8 86-91
Also see DENVER, John
Also see LEE, Johnny, Michael Martin Murphey, & Charlie Daniels
Also see LEWIS & CLARKE
Also see TRINITY RIVER BOYS

MURPHEY, Michael Martin, & Holly Dunn C&W '87
Singles: 7-inch
W.B...........3-4 87
Also see DUNN, Holly

MURPHEY, Michael, & Katy Moffatt C&W '81
Singles: 7-inch
EPIC..........3-5 81
Also see MOFFATT, Katy
Also see MURPHEY, Michael

MURPHY, Chuck
Singles: 78 rpm
CORAL..........5-10 57
Singles: 7-inch
CORAL..........5-10 57

MURPHY, Don
Singles: 7-inch
COSMOPOLITAN (2264 "Mean Mama Blues")..........100-150

MURPHY, Donnie, & Ambassadors
Singles: 7-inch
REDBUG (0005 "My Love for You")..........40-60

MURPHY, Eddie R&B/LP '82
Singles: 12-inch
COLUMBIA..........4-6 83-85
Singles: 7-inch
COLUMBIA..........3-4 83-86
Picture Sleeves
COLUMBIA..........3-4 83-85
LPs: 10/12-inch
COLUMBIA (Except picture discs)..........5-8 82-86
COLUMBIA (1763 "Comedian")..........10-15 83
(Picture disc. Promotional issue only.)
COLUMBIA (9C9-39151 "Comedian")..........10-15 83
(Picture disc.)

MURPHY, Elliot
Singles: 7-inch
COLUMBIA..........3-5 77
RCA..........3-5 75
LPs: 10/12-inch
POLYDOR..........8-12 73
RCA..........5-10 75

MURPHY, Frank
Singles: 7-inch
FRANKIE..........4-8 63

MURPHY, Gwindon
Singles: 7-inch
CRAZY HORSE..........4-8 68

MURPHY, Guitar: see GUITAR MURPHY

MURPHY, J.F., & Salt
LPs: 10/12-inch
COLUMBIA..........8-12 73
ELEKTRA..........8-12 72

MURPHY, Jim, & Accents
Singles: 78 rpm
REV (3508 "I'm Gone Mama")..........20-30 57
Singles: 7-inch
REV (3508 "I'm Gone Mama")..........30-40 57

MURPHY, Jimmy C&W '86
Singles: 78 rpm
COLUMBIA..........25-50 56
RCA..........10-20 51-52
Singles: 7-inch
ARK..........8-12 63
COLUMBIA (21486 "Here Kitty Kitty")..........100-150 56
COLUMBIA (21534 "16 Tons Rock & Roll")..........100-150 56
COLUMBIA (21569 "Baboon Boogie")..........100-150 56
ENCORE..........3-4 86-87
RCA..........20-40 51-52
REM (340 "Half a Loaf")..........10-20
SUGAR HILL..........3-6 78
LPs: 10/12-inch
SUGAR HILL..........5-10 78

MURPHY, Joe
Singles: 7-inch
VIVID..........4-8 65

MURPHY, Keith, & Daze
Singles: 7-inch
KING (6171 "Dirty Ol Sam")..........75-100 68
Also see O'CONNER, Keith

MURPHY, Marvin
Singles: 7-inch
M.M. (103 "Crying for My Baby") .50-100 63

MURPHY, P.J.: see P.J. MURPHY

MURPHY, Peter LP '88
LPs: 10/12-inch
BEGGAR'S BANQUET..........5-8 88-90

MURPHY, Rock
Singles: 78 rpm
VERVE..........10-20 57
Singles: 7-inch
VERVE..........10-20 57
Also see NELSON, Ricky

MURPHY, Ron
Singles: 7-inch
ABC-PAR..........4-8 65
BEVMAR..........5-10 61
MGM..........5-10 60
20TH FOX..........4-8 63-64

MURPHY, Rose R&B '48
(With the Selah Jubilee Quartette; Rose Murphy Trio)
Singles: 78 rpm
DECCA..........5-10 55
MAJESTIC..........5-10 48
Singles: 7-inch
DECCA (29000 series)..........8-12 55
DECCA (32000 series)..........4-8 66
REGINA..........4-8 63
LPs: 10/12-inch
MUSE..........5-8
ROYALE (1835 "Rose Murphy")..........30-40 52
(10-inch LP.)
VERVE..........20-30 57
Also see BAILEY, Pearl / Rose Murphy / Ivie Anderson
Also see SELAH JUBILEE QUARTETTE

MURPHY, Rose, & Slam Stewart
Singles: 7-inch
DECCA..........3-5 61
LPs: 10/12-inch
U.A...........15-25 63
Also see MURPHY, Rose

MURPHY, Vern C&W '73
Singles: 7-inch
SUNSET..........3-5 73

MURPHY, Walter P&R/R&B/LP '76
(With the Big Apple Band)
Singles: 12-inch
PRIVATE STOCK..........4-8 77
Singles: 7-inch
MCA..........3-4 82
PRIVATE STOCK..........3-5 76-77
Picture Sleeves
MCA..........3-4 82
LPs: 10/12-inch
MCA..........5-8 82
PRIVATE STOCK..........5-10 76-77

MURPHY & MOB
Singles: 7-inch
TALISMAN (1823 "Born Loser")..........15-25 66

MURPHY'S R&B '82
Singles: 7-inch
GRT (130 "Dancin' ")..........4-6 77
THUNDERBIRD (514 "Great Pretender")..........10-20 60s
VENTURE..........3-5 82

MURRAY, Anne C&W/P&R/LP '70
(With Doug Mallory)
Singles: 7-inch
ARC..........5-10 69
(Canadian.)
CAPITOL..........3-5 70-86
Picture Sleeves
CAPITOL..........3-4 79-86
LPs: 10/12-inch
ARC (782 "What About Me")..........10-20 69
(Canadian.)
AURA..........5-8 83
CAPITOL (Except "Let's Keep It That Way" picture disc)..........5-10 70-87
CAPITOL ("Let's Keep It That Way")..........50-100 78
(Picture disc. Promotional issue only. One of a four-artist, four-LP set. 250 made.)
SESAME ST..........5-10 79
Also see CAMPBELL, Glen, & Anne Murray
Also see CAMPBELL, Glen / Anne Murray / Kenny Rogers / Crystal Gayle
Also see WINCHESTER, Jesse

MURRAY, Anne, & Dave Loggins C&W '84
Singles: 7-inch
CAPITOL..........3-4 84
Also see LOGGINS, Dave

MURRAY, Anne, & Kenny Rogers C&W '89
Singles: 7-inch
CAPITOL..........3-4 89
Also see MURRAY, Anne
Also see ROGERS, Kenny

MURRAY, Bill "Winehead Willie," & George "Sweet Lucy" Copeland
Singles: 7-inch
ANNA (1121 "Bigtime Spender")..........10-20 60

MURRAY, Clarence
Singles: 7-inch
SSS INT'L..........4-8 68
Also see MURRAY, Mickey & Clarence

MURRAY, Jack
Singles: 7-inch
GOLD ARROW..........4-8 63
LAURIE..........5-10 63

MURRAY, Joan
Singles: 7-inch
APPLAUSE..........5-8 61

MURRAY, Juggy
Singles: 7-inch
SUE..........4-8 66

MURRAY, Mickey P&R/R&B '67
Singles: 7-inch
SSS INT'L..........4-8 67-68
LPs: 10/12-inch
FEDERAL..........8-12 71
SSS INT'L..........10-15 67

MURRAY, Mickey & Clarence
Singles: 7-inch
SSS INT'L..........4-8 68
Also see MURRAY, Clarence
Also see MURRAY, Mickey

MURRAY, Mitch
Singles: 7-inch
HBR..........4-8 66
MGM..........4-8 66
Also see MURRAY'S MONKEY

MURRAY, Ray, & Dynamics
Singles: 7-inch
ARBO (222 "With All My Heart")..50-100 60

MURRAY, Ronnie
Singles: 7-inch
ALTO..........4-8 61
SOMBRERO..........4-8 62
SOMBRERO/ALTO..........4-8 63
VANDAN..........4-8 64

MURRAY, Scott
Singles: 7-inch
AUTUMN..........4-8 60s
STAR..........5-10 59

MURRAY, Virgil
(Virgil Murray's Tomorrow's Yesterday)
Singles: 7-inch
AIRTOWN (015 "I Still Care")..........5-8

MURRAY HILL MOB / Murray Hill Militia
Singles: 7-inch
STACY..........4-8 59-60

MURRAY the "K": see KAUFMAN, Murray

MURRAY'S MONKEY
(Mitch Murray)
Singles: 7-inch
HBR..........4-8 66
Also see MURRAY, Mitch

MURRELL, Johnny
Singles: 7-inch
B.I...........3-5 78

MUSCLE SHOALS HORNS R&B/LP '76
Singles: 7-inch
ARIOLA AMERICA..........3-5 77
BANG..........3-5 76
MONUMENT..........3-4 83
LPs: 10/12-inch
ARIOLA AMERICA..........8-12 77
BANG..........10-15 76
MONUMENT..........8-12 83

MUSCLEMEN
Singles: 7-inch
MUSICOR (1001 "Plunkin' ")..........10-20 61
Member: Al Kooper.
Also see KOOPER, Al

MUSE, Cynthia
Singles: 7-inch
DOT..4-8 62

MUSEUM
LPs: 10/12-inch
TKO..5-10 79
Also see MATT & BRIAN
Also see ORIGINAL MUSEUM

MUSHROOMS
Singles: 7-inch
HIDEOUT (1121 "Burned")..........15-25 60s

MUSIAL, Stan
EPs: 7-inch
RCA (141 "Stan's Hit Record").......10-15 61

MUSIC
LPs: 10/12-inch
ELEUTHERA..............................10-12 71

MUSIC ASYLUM
Singles: 7-inch
ASCOT......................................4-8 68
U.A. 3-5 70
LPs: 10/12-inch
U.A. 10-15 70

MUSIC BACHS
Singles: 7-inch
DATE..4-8 67-68

MUSIC CITY ALL STARS
Singles: 7-inch
MUSIC CITY..............................4-8 65

MUSIC CITY FIVE
Singles: 7-inch
GIANT 5-10 60s

MUSIC CITY FROGS
Singles: 7-inch
MUSIC CITY..............................5-8 64

MUSIC CITY SINGERS
Singles: 7-inch
HIT 4-8 62

MUSIC CITY SOUL BROTHERS
Singles: 7-inch
MUSIC CITY..............................4-8 64

MUSIC COMBINATION
Singles: 7-inch
AMERICAN MUSIC MAKERS.........4-8

MUSIC COMPANY
LPs: 10/12-inch
MIRWOOD (M-7002 "Rubber Soul Jazz")...............................15-20 66
(Monaural.)
MIRWOOD (MS-7002 "Rubber Soul Jazz")...............................20-25 66
(Stereo.)

MUSIC EMPORIUM
Singles: 7-inch
SENTINEL (501 "Nam Myo Ho Renge Kyo")....................................30-40 68
LPs: 10/12-inch
SENTINEL (100 "Music Emporium")..............................800-1200 68
SENTINEL (69001 "Music Emporium")..................................8-10 91
Members: Dave Padwin; Dora Wahl; Carolyn Lee; Casey Cosby.

MUSIC EXPLOSION P&R/LP '67
Singles: 7-inch
ATTACK (1404 "Little Black Egg") .10-20 66
LAURIE 5-10 67-69
LPs: 10/12-inch
LAURIE 20-30 67
Members: Jamie Lyons; Don Atkins; Bob Avery; Rick Nesta; Butch Stahl.
Also see BLOOM, Bobby
Also see KASENETZ-KATZ SINGING ORCHESTRAL CIRCUS

MUSIC EXPRESS
LPs: 10/12-inch
GRIT...5-10 79

MUSIC MACHINE P&R '66
Singles: 7-inch
BELL 5-10 69
ORIGINAL SOUND.......................5-10 66-67
W.B. 5-10 68
Picture Sleeves
ORIGINAL SOUND (82 "Hey Joe")....................................15-25 67
(Has die-cut center hole on both sides.)
LPs: 10/12-inch
ORIGINAL SOUND (5015 "Turn on the Music Machine")................................20-30 66
(Monaural.)
ORIGINAL SOUND (8875 "Turn on the Music Machine")................................75-100 66
(Stereo.)
Members: Sean Bonniwell; Mark Landon; Keith Olsen; Ron Edgar; Doug Rhodes.
Also see BONNIWELL'S MUSIC MACHINE

MUSIC MACHINE / Bubble Puppy
Singles: 7-inch
ORIGINAL SOUND.......................3-4 85
Also see BUBBLE PUPPY
Also see MUSIC MACHINE

MUSIC MAKERS
Singles: 7-inch
N.A.M. 4-8 64

MUSIC MAKERS P&R '67
Singles: 7-inch
GAMBLE 4-8 67-68
LPs: 10/12-inch
GAMBLE 12-18 68
Also see MFSB

MUSIC MASTERS
Singles: 7-inch
MARK 1.....................................5-10 60

MUSIC ROW C&W '81
Singles: 7-inch
DEBUT 3-5 81

MUSIC TRACK
Singles: 7-inch
INT'L ARTISTS (112 "Time Goes By")..10-20 66

MUSIC TYMES
Singles: 7-inch
COULEE....................................5-10 72

MUSICAL THEATRE
LPs: 10/12-inch
METROMEDIA............................10-15 69

MUSICAL TYMES
Singles: 7-inch
COULEE (10036 "Lonely Man").......5-10 70s

MUSICAL YOUTH P&R/R&B '82
Singles: 12-inch
MCA...4-6 82-84
Singles: 7-inch
MCA...3-4 82-84
Picture Sleeves
MCA...3-4 82-84
LPs: 10/12-inch
MCA...5-8 82-84

MUSICAL WADES
Singles: 7-inch
JANIE.......................................5-10 60

MUSICS
Singles: 7-inch
COLUMBIA.................................4-8 66

MUSIL, Jim, Combo
Singles: 7-inch
JAY EMM (423 "North Beach") 15-25 62

MUSIQUE P&R/R&B/LP '78
Singles: 12-inch
PRELUDE 5-10 78
Singles: 7-inch
PRELUDE 3-5 78-79
LPs: 10/12-inch
PRELUDE 5-10 78

MUSIQUE & LYRICS
Singles: 7-inch
VALIANT 4-8 66

MUSKATEERS
Singles: 78 rpm
ROXY......................................50-100 52
SWING TIME (331 "Deep in My Heart")..................................200-400 53
Singles: 7-inch
ROXY (801 "Goodbye My Love")....................................550-650 52
Members: Norman Thrasher; Noah Howell.
Also see ROYAL JOKERS

MUSKATEERS
Singles: 7-inch
DOT (15926 "Poor Boy No. 2") 8-12 59

MUSSELWHITE, Charles
(Charley Musselwhite; Charles Musselwhite Blues Band)
Singles: 7-inch
VANGUARD 4-6 69
LPs: 10/12-inch
PARAMOUNT...............................8-12 69
VANGUARD 8-12 69
Also see GOLDBERG, Barry / Harvey Mandell / Charlie Musselwhite / Neil Merryweather

MUSSIES
Singles: 7-inch
FENTON (2216 "Louie Go Home")...................................100-200 67

MUSSO, Vido
Singles: 78 rpm
CROWN 10-15 54
RPM 10-15 52-56
Singles: 7-inch
CROWN (110 "Musso's Boogie") ...15-25 54
CROWN (130 "Powerhouse Boogie")...................................15-25 54
RPM (387 "Vido's Boogie") 15-25 52
RPM (493 "Blues for Two") 15-25 56
LPs: 10/12-inch
CROWN (5029 "Teenage Dance Party")....................................30-50 57

MUSTACHE WAX
Singles: 7-inch
INNER 4-8 65

MUSTANG
Singles: 7-inch
ASCOT (2231 "Here, There and Everywhere")..............................15-25 67

MUSTANG, Harry, Singers
Singles: 7-inch
EPIC...4-8 64

MUSTANGS
Singles: 7-inch
VEST (51 "Over the Rainbow") 500-1000 63
Also see MAGIC TONES / Mustangs

MUSTANGS P&R '64
Singles: 7-inch
KEETCH....................................5-10 64
PROVIDENCE..............................8-12 63-64
SURE SHOT 5-10 64
LPs: 10/12-inch
PROVIDENCE (1 "Dartel Stomp") 35-45 64

MUSTANGS
Singles: 7-inch
CAPITOL...................................5-10 66
Also see TINA & MUSTANGS

MUSTANGS
Singles: 7-inch
JETSTAR (120 "How Funky Can You Get")......................................5-10 69
(Black vinyl.)
JETSTAR (120 "How Funky Can You Get")......................................10-20 69
(Colored vinyl. Promotional issue only.)
Also see PATTERSON, Bobby

MUSTANGS
Singles: 7-inch
SMEK (3051 "Jack the Ripper") 40-60 60s
Picture Sleeves
SMEK (3051 "Jack the Ripper") 50-75 60s
(Two different sleeves exist for this issue.)

MUSTANGS
Singles: 7-inch
DALE (101 "Don't Take Your Love").....................................25-45

MUSTARD MEN
Singles: 7-inch
RAYNARD (10036 "I Lost My Baby")......................................20-30 65
Members: Keith Papiham; Warren Wiegratz; Stan Kellicut; Jerry Wimmer; George Welik.
Also see FAMILY AT MAX
Also see PEASANTS

MUS-TWANGS
Singles: 7-inch
NERO (1-61 "Roch Lomond") 20-30 61
(First issue.)
NERO (1002 "Nova Blues") 15-25 62
NERO (1700 "Roch Lomond")..........10-20 61
SMASH (1700 "Roch Lomond") 10-20 61
SMASH (1709 "Frankie and Johnny")..................................10-15 61

MUTABARUKA
(With the High Times Players)
Singles: 12-inch
ALLIGATOR 4-6 83
Singles: 7-inch
ALLIGATOR 3-4 83
LPs: 10/12-inch
ALLIGATOR 5-8 83

MUTHA GOOSE
LPs: 10/12-inch
ALPHA OMEGA 5-8 79

MUTIMER, Steve, & Rhythm Kings
Singles: 7-inch
CUCA (1009 "Maj")......................15-25 60
INT'L ARTISTS (2121 "Stuck on Me")......................................15-25 60

MUTINY
LPs: 10/12-inch
COLUMBIA.................................5-10 79-80

MUTZIE
LPs: 10/12-inch
SUSSEX (7001 "Light of Your Shadow")..................................20-25 70
Members: "Mutzie" Lavenburg; Andy Lavenburg.

MYCHAEL
Singles: 7-inch
FREE FLIGHT..............................3-5 79

MYDDLE CLASS
Singles: 7-inch
BUDDAH (150 "I Happen to Love You")..5-10 69
TOMORROW (912 "Don't Look Back")......................................10-20 66
TOMORROW (7501 "Gates of Eden")......................................10-20 66
TOMORROW (7503 "I Happen to Love You")..15-25 66
Member: Dave Palmer.

MYER, Bob, & Rivieras
Singles: 7-inch
LAWN (238 "Behold")....................15-20 64

MYERS, Alicia R&B '82
Singles: 12-inch
MCA...4-6 81-85
Singles: 7-inch
MCA...3-4 81-85
LPs: 10/12-inch
MCA...5-8 84
Also see ONE WAY

MYERS, Dan
Singles
AZRA (1 "Peaceful Heart")...............4-8 83
(Dragonfly-shaped picture disc.)

MYERS, Dave
(With the Surftones; with Disciples; Dave Meyers' Effect)
Singles: 7-inch
HARMONY PARK 5-10 66
IMPACT (20 "Moment of Truth")....15-25 64
IMPACT (27 "Church Key")............15-25 64
WICKWIRE (13008 "Gear!")..........20-30 64
LPs: 10/12-inch
CAROLE (8002 "Greatest Racing Themes") 20-30 67
DEL-FI (LP-1239 "Hangin' 20")......25-30 63
(Monaural.)
DEL-FI (ST-1239 "Hangin' 20")......30-35 63
(Stereo.)
Members: Dave Myers; Johnny Curtis; Ed Quarry; Dennis Merritt; Seaton Blanco; Bob Colwell.

MYERS, Dave, & Surftones / Rhythm Kings
LPs: 10/12-inch
GNP 20-30 63
Also see MYERS, Dave
Also see RHYTHM KINGS

MYERS, Frank C&W '74
Singles: 7-inch
CAPRICE 3-5 74

MYERS, Gary
Singles: 7-inch
EDIT..15-25 63
Also see DARNELLS
Also see HAHN, Tommy, & Mojo Men
Also see PAUL & PACK / Mad Doctors
Also see PORTRAITS

MYERS, Jerry
Singles: 7-inch
VASSAR.....................................4-8 61

MYERS, Jim
Singles: 7-inch
FORTUNE...................................4-8 61

MYERS, Jim, & Tex Regan
Singles: 7-inch
FORTUNE.................................10-15 60
Also see MYERS, Jim

MYERS, Orella
Singles: 7-inch
ZERO.......................................5-10 60

MYERS, Sammie "Little John"
Singles: 7-inch
SOFT (1003 "Boss Bag")..................4-8 66
(Also issued as by Sammie John.)
Also see JOHN, Sammie

MYERS, Sam
(With the King Mose Royal Rockers. Sammy Myers)
Singles: 78 rpm
ACE.......................................20-30 57
Singles: 7-inch
ACE (Except 536).......................15-25
ACE (536 "My Love Is Here to Stay")......................................25-50 57
FURY (1035 "Sad, Sad, Lonesome Day")......................................20-40 60

MYLES, Alannah P&R/LP '90
Singles: 7-inch
ATLANTIC.................................3-4 89
LPs: 10/12-inch
ATLANTIC.................................5-8 89

MYLES, Big Boy
(With the Shaw-Wees)
Singles: 78 rpm
SPECIALTY 20-30 55-56
Singles: 7-inch
ACE (605 "New Orleans")..............10-20 60
ACE (637 "Oh Mary")...................10-20 61
SPECIALTY (564 "Who's Been Fooling You")......................................50-75 55
SPECIALTY (590 "Just to Hold My Hand")....................................50-75 56
V-TONE (232 "She's So Fine") 10-15 62
Also see SHA-WEEZ

MYLES, Billy P&R '57
Singles: 78 rpm
EMBER 15-25 57-58
Singles: 7-inch
COLLECTABLES 3-4 80s
DOT (15809 "King of Clowns").......10-20 58
EMBER (1026 "The Joker")............15-25 57
EMBER (1040 "Piece of Your Love")......................................10-20 58
EMBER (1046 "I'm Gonna Walk") ...10-20 58
KING (5395 "Dance Little Girl")........8-12 60

MYLES, Metrogene
Singles: 7-inch
HERALD.....................................5-10 64

MYLES & LENNY
LPs: 10/12-inch
COLUMBIA 8-10 75
Members: Myles Cohen; Lenny Solomon.

MYLESTONES
Singles: 7-inch
HAWK SOUND (102 "Sexy Lady").....3-5 70s

MYLON: see LE FEVRE, Mylon

MYRICK, Gary LP '83
(With the Figures)
Singles: 7-inch
EPIC...3-4 83-84
LPs: 10/12-inch
EPIC...5-8 83-84

MYROGENS
Singles: 7-inch
J.M. 5-10 59

MYRON, Mitch
Singles: 7-inch
BAY-TONE..................................8-12 62

MYRON & VAN DELLS
Singles: 7-inch
FLO-RUE (15 "Crazy Little Mama")....................................10-20 63

MYRTH
Singles: 7-inch
RCA 3-5 69
LPs: 10/12-inch
RCA 10-15 69

MYSNER, Billy
Singles: 7-inch
A'S 3-5

MYSTERIANS
Singles: 7-inch
JOREL (101 "The Fuzzy One").........5-10 64

MYSTERIES
Singles: 7-inch
JDL (3554 "Pink Panther")............10-20 65

MYSTERIES
Singles: 7-inch
MANHATTAN (815 "Please Agree") 15-25 68

MYSTERIONS
Singles: 7-inch
JOX (40 "Is It a Lie")....................25-35 65
Also see ? (Question Mark) & Mysterians

MYSTERIONS
Singles: 7-inch
BRS (1011 "Jerico Rock")..............10-15
FASCINATION (1004 "Transylvania")...............................15-25 59
FASCINATION (1009 "Down Hill").......................................10-20 60
WARWICK (521 "Transylvania") ...10-15 60
ZORDAN (101 "A-Bomb")..............10-20 60s

MYSTERY GIRL
Singles: 7-inch
COMO.......................................3-6 69

MYSTERY MEN
(With Joseph Ricci & Orchestra)
Singles: 7-inch
POW (1001 "Feel Like a Million")...................................50-100 63
(Reissued as by Tyrone & the Nu Ports)
Also see TYRONE & NU PORTS

MYSTERY MEN
Singles: 7-inch
CEVA (1020 "Pier X")...................10-20 60s
MONUMENT 5-10 64

MYSTERY TOUR
Singles: 7-inch
MGM.......................................10-15 69

MYSTERY TREND
Singles: 7-inch
VERVE (10499 "Johnny Was a Good Boy")......................................10-15 67
Members: Ron Nagel; Bob Cuff.
Also see SERPENT POWER

MYSTIC ASTROLOGIC CRYSTAL BAND
Singles: 7-inch
CAROLE (1004 "Flowers Never Cry") 10-20 67
LPs: 10/12-inch
CAROLE (8001 "Mystic Astrologic Crystal Band")....................................20-30 67
CAROLE (8003 "Clip on, Put on Book")......................................20-30 68
Members: Steve Hoffman; Ron Roman; John Leighton; John Moreland; Bob Phillips. Session: Phil Alagna; Gary Myers.

MYSTIC CRASH
Singles: 7-inch
ABC..5-8 67-68

MYSTIC FIVE
Singles: 7-inch
GO-GO (26000 "I'm Gonna Love You Too")......................................15-25 66

MYSTIC FIVE
Singles: 7-inch
MYSTIC (1 "It Doesn't Matter")......15-25 66

MYSTIC FIVE
(With the Explosions)
Singles: 7-inch
CUNITY (2730 "Don't Let Me Down")......................................5-10

MYSTIC KNIGHTS OF OINGO BOINGO
Singles: 7-inch
PELICAN (1001 "You Got Your Baby Back")......................................10-15 70s
(Add $5 to $10 if accompanied by an insert sheet of Patty Hearst cut-out paper dolls.)
Also see OINGO BOINGO

MYSTIC MERLIN R&B '81
Singles: 7-inch
CAPITOL.....................................3-5 80-82
LPs: 10/12-inch
CAPITOL...................................5-10 80-82
Members: Clyde Bullard; Jerry Anderson; Barry Strutt; Sly Randolph; Keith Gonzales; Freddie Jackson.
Also see JACKSON, Freddie

MYSTIC MOODS ORCHESTRA LP '66
Singles: 7-inch
PHILIPS 4-6 66-70
SOUNDBIRD................................3-5 75-78

W.B. 3-5 72-73

LPs: 10/12-inch

BAINBRIDGE 5-10 72
MFSL (001 "Emotions") 25-50 78
MFSL (002 "Cosmic Force") 25-50 78
MFSL (003 "Stormy Weekend") 25-50 78
PHILIPS 8-12 66-70
SOUNDBIRD 5-10 75-78
W.B. 5-10 72-73

MYSTIC NUMBER NATIONAL BANK

Singles: 7-inch

PROBE 3-6 69

LPs: 10/12-inch

PROBE 10-15 69

MYSTIC SIVA

LPs: 10/12-inch

VO (19713 "Mystic Siva") 550-650 71
(With gatefold cover.)
Members: Dave Mascarin; Al Tozzie; Mark Heckert; Art Trienel;

MYSTIC TIDE

Singles: 7-inch

ESQUIRE (719 "Mystic Eyes") 50-100 66
ESQUIRE (4677 "Stay Away") 50-100 65
SOLID SOUND (156 "Frustration") 50-100 66
SOLID SOUND (157 "Psychedelic Journey") 50-100 66
SOLID SOUND (158 "Running Through the Night") 50-100 67
SOLID SOUND (321 "Mystery Ship") 50-100 67
SOLID SOUND ("Mystic Eyes") 50-100 66
(Selection number not known.)

LPs: 10/12-inch

DISTORTIONS 8-10 91
Members: Joe Docko; James Thomas; Paul Picell; John Williams.

MYSTICS

Singles: 7-inch

CHATAM (350 "Teenage Sweetheart") 300-500 50s
(Reissued as by the Champs.)
Also see CHAMPS

MYSTICS P&R '59

Singles: 7-inch

AMBIENT SOUND ("Crazy for You") 8-12 82
(Selection number not known.)
COLLECTABLES 3-4 80s
LAURIE (3028 "Hushabye") 15-25 59
LAURIE (3028S "Hushabye") 40-60 59
(Stereo.)
LAURIE (3038 "Don't Take the Stars") 15-25 59
LAURIE (3047 "All Through the Night") 15-25 60
LAURIE (3058 "Blue Star") 15-25 60
LAURIE (3086 "Goodbye Mister Blues") 15-25 60
LAURIE (3104 "Sunday Kind of Love") 15-25 61

LPs: 10/12-inch

AMBIENT SOUND 10-15 82
COLLECTABLES 6-8 87
Members: Phil Cracolici; Albee Cracolici; Bob Ferrante; George Galfo.
Also see GARRETT, Scott
Also see RESOLUTIONS

MYSTICS / Passions

LPs: 10/12-inch

LAURIE 5-10 79
Also see MYSTICS
Also see PASSIONS

MYSTICS

Singles: 7-inch

KING (5678 "Mashed Potatoes with Me") 15-25 62
KING (5735 "Just for Your Love") 15-25 63

MYSTICS

Singles: 7-inch

CONSTELLATION 5-10 64
DOT 5-10 66
NOLTA (353 "Fox") 15-25 63

MYSTICS

Singles: 7-inch

TEAKO (370 "That's the Kind of Love") 25-50 64

MYSTICS

Singles: 7-inch

AFC 4-8 64
BEAR 15-25 65
CHARLIE 10-20 60s
METROMEDIA 8-12 69

Picture Sleeves

CHARLIE 20-25 60s

MYSTICS

Singles: 7-inch

BLACK CAT (501 "Snoopy") 20-30 66
Also see RATS

MYSTICS

Singles: 7-inch

METROMEDIA 4-8 69

MYSTICS

Singles: 7-inch

MARQUETTE (1001 "Jealous of You") 50-75 60s
STAFF (1001 "Peace of Mind") 15-25 60s

MYSTICS

Singles: 7-inch

SPECTRA (707 "Didn't We Have a Good Time") 20-25 60s

MYSTIFYING MONARCHS

Singles: 7-inch

CENTURY (27913 "Soldier of Fortune") 40-60 60s

MYSTIQUE R&B '77

Singles: 7-inch

CURTOM 3-5 77

LPs: 10/12-inch

CURTOM 5-10 77
Members: Ralph Johnson; Fred Lowrell; Larry Brownlee; Charles Fowler; Fred Simon.
Also see C.O.D.s
Also see IMPRESSIONS

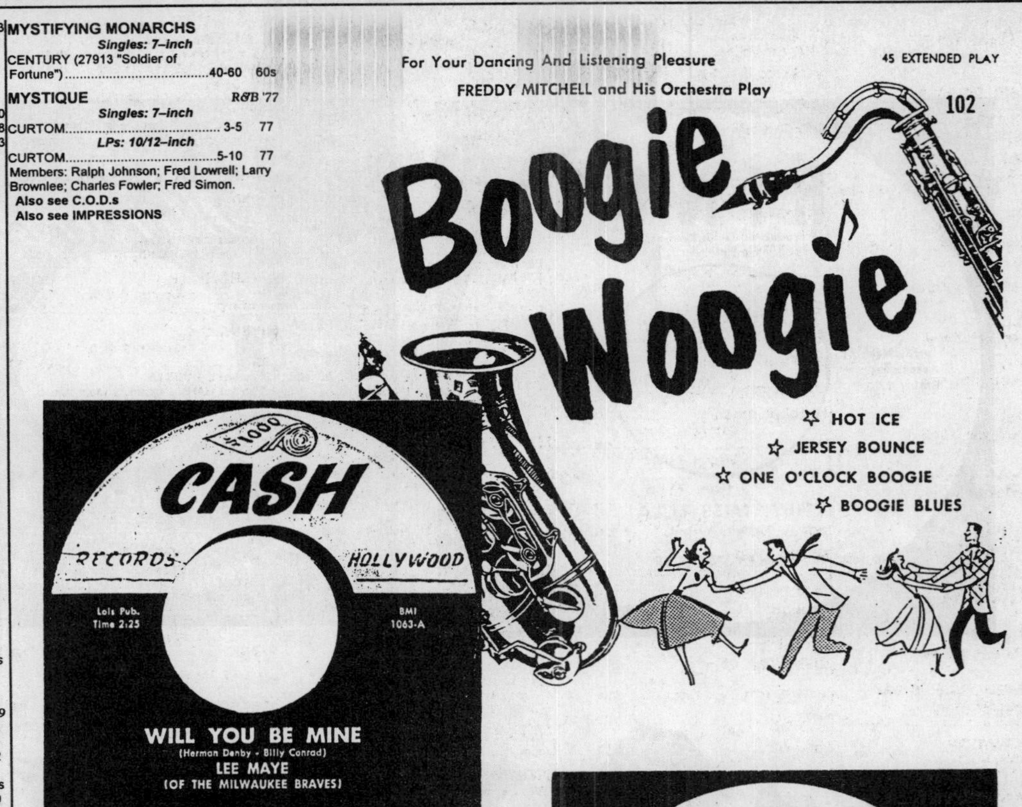

For Your Dancing And Listening Pleasure
45 EXTENDED PLAY
FREDDY MITCHELL and His Orchestra Play
102
Boogie Woogie
HOT ICE
JERSEY BOUNCE
ONE O'CLOCK BOOGIE
BOOGIE BLUES

CASH
RECORDS
HOLLYWOOD
Lois Pub.
Time 2:25
BMI
1063-A
WILL YOU BE MINE
(Herman Denby - Billy Conrad)
LEE MAYE
(OF THE MILWAUKEE BRAVES)

GROOVE
A PRODUCT OF RADIO CORPORATION OF AMERICA
MADE IN U.S.A.
4G-0020
(E4HW-4122)
45
RPM
I'M TIRED
(Mickey Baker)
Big Red McHouston
Vocal by Larry Dale

VITA
RECORDS
1486 No. Fair Oaks
Pasadena, Calif.
LES KANGAS
Music Pub. Co.
(BMI)
7902 Dewey
San Gabriel, Calif.
Time: 2:20
Vocal
"REALLY, REALLY BABY"
(Ric Masten-Don Stevens)
BUEL MOORE
and the GARNETS
45 V-174-XX

DISTRIBUTED NATIONALLY BY NATIONAL RECORDING CORP., 1224 FERNWOOD CIRCLE, N.E. ATLANTA 19, GA.
SHO-BIZ CORPORATION
Vence Pub.
— BMI
WELL, I DONE GOT OVER IT
(E. Jones)
BOBBY MITCHELL
S-717
© 1959
SUE, INC.
NEW YORK CITY
SAMPLE COPY
NOT FOR SALE
UNBREAKABLE
45 R.P.M.
RECORD NO.
726
(SR-970)
Lloyd-Logan Music
BMI
Time: 1:55
YOU'RE MY QUEEN
(Luther Dixon)
JOHNNY MOORE

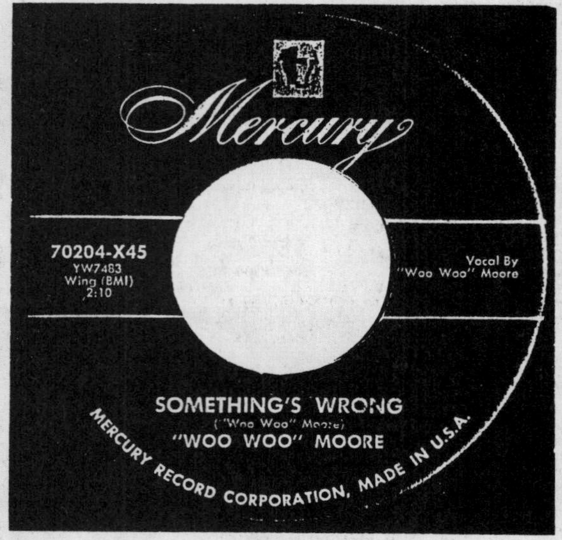

MCCM 8901 STEREO

AGONNAGAIN

CRAIG MOORE

N

N. GROUP
Singles: 7-inch
WES MAR (1021 "Keep on Running")...15-25 60s

NAIF GROUP
(North Atlantic Invasion Force)
Singles: 7-inch
CONGRESSIONAL (999 "Blue and Green Gown")...10-20 66
MAJESTIC (998 "Sweet Bird of Love")...10-20 67
MR. G. (808 "Black on White")...10-15 68
MR. G. (819 "Rainmaker")...5-10 68
STAFF (1006 "Love's No Game")...10-15 69
Members: George Morgio; Nick Tirozzi; Neil Mitchell; Jim Gaffney; Edward Dumbrowski.

N.C.C.U. R&B '77
Singles: 12-inch
U.A. ...4-8 77
Singles: 7-inch
U.A. ...3-5 77
LPs: 10/12-inch
U.A. ...5-10 77

NGC-4594
Singles: 7-inch
SMASH (2104 "Going Home")...10-20 67

N.J. ORANGE
Singles: 7-inch
VANGUARD...4-8 68

NRBQ LP '69
(New Rhythm & Blues Quintet)
Singles: 7-inch
BEARSVILLE...3-5 83
BUDDAH...3-5 74
COLUMBIA...4-8 69
KAMA SUTRA...4-6 73
MERCURY...4-6 78
RED ROOSTER...3-6 77
ROUNDER...3-5 80-83
VIRGIN...3-5 89-90
Picture Sleeves
RED ROOSTER...3-5 77
ROUNDER...3-5 80
EPs: 7-inch
ROUNDER...5-10 82
LPs: 10/12-inch
ANNUIT COEPTIS...10-15 76
BEARSVILLE...5-8 83
KAMA SUTRA...10-15 72-73
MERCURY...8-12 78
COLUMBIA...10-15 69
RED ROOSTER...8-10 77-83
ROUNDER...5-10 79-80
VIRGIN...5-8 89
Members: Frank Gadler; Terry Adams; G.T. Stanley; Jody St. Nicholas; Steve Ferguson; Don Adams; Al Anderson; Tom Staley; Joey Spampinato; Tommy Ardolino.
Also see ADAMS, Terry
Also see ANDERSON, Al
Also see DAVIS, Skeeter, & NRBQ
Also see INCREDIBLE CASUALS
Also see PERKINS, Carl, & NRBQ
Also see SEVEN of US

NU / IMIJ
Singles: 7-inch
AZRA (059 "Model T.A.")...6-12 82
(Picture disc.)

NV D&D '83
Singles: 12-inch
SIRE...4-6 83-84
Singles: 7-inch
SIRE...3-4 83-84

N.W.A. LP '89
(Niggas with Attitude)
LPs: 10/12-inch
N.W.A. ...5-8 89-90

NABAY
Singles: 7-inch
IMPACT (1032 "Believe It Or Not")...100-200 67

NABBIE, Jimmie
Singles: 7-inch
CARLTON (561 "Sweet Thing")...10-20 61
Also see BROWN DOTS
Also see FOUR TUNES

NABORS, Jim LP '66
(Jimmy Nabors)
Singles: 7-inch
COLUMBIA...3-6 65-74
RANWOOD...3-4 77
ROULETTE...8-12 58
LPs: 10/12-inch
COLUMBIA...5-15 65-75
HARMONY...5-10 71
RANWOOD...4-8 76-82
Also see STREISAND, Barbra / Doris Day / Jim Nabors / Andre Kostelanetz

NAGLE, Ron
LPs: 10/12-inch
W.B. ...10-20 70
Also see VALENTINO, Sal

NAIL, Linda C&W '78
Singles: 7-inch
GRAND PRIX...3-4 83
RIDGETOP...3-5 78-79
Also see WHITE, Danny, & Linda Nail

NAILL, Jerry C&W '80
Singles: 7-inch
EL DORADO...3-5 80

NAILS LP '86
Singles: 7-inch
RCA...3-4 86
LPs: 10/12-inch
RCA...5-8 86

NAIROBI & AWESOME FOURSOME R&B '82
Singles: 7-inch
STREETWISE...3-4 82

NAJEE R&B/LP '87
Singles: 7-inch
EMI...3-4 87-90
LPs: 10/12-inch
EMI...5-8 87-90
Also see THOMAS, Vaneese

NAKED, Buck, & Bare Bottom Boys
Singles: 7-inch
SCAM...3-5 92
Members: Buck Naked; Hector Naked; Stinky Le Pew.

NAKED EYES P&R/D&D/LP '83
Singles: 12-inch
EMI AMERICA...4-6 83-84
Singles: 7-inch
EMI AMERICA...3-4 83-84
Picture Sleeves
EMI AMERICA...3-4 83-84
LPs: 10/12-inch
EMI AMERICA...5-8 83-84
Members: Pete Byrne; Rob Fisher.
Also see CLIMIE FISHER

NAKED TRUTH
Singles: 7-inch
JUBILEE...4-8 68

NAN & JAN
Singles: 7-inch
DEBBY...8-12 64

NANCE, Ray
LPs: 10/12-inch
SOLID STATE...10-12 70

NANCY
(With St. Thomas Moore Folk Group)
Singles: 7-inch
MUSICOR...4-6 71

NANCY & MILLIONAIRES
Singles: 7-inch
FRANKIE...20-30 61
Member: Nancy Ann Zapp.
Also see NANCY ANN

NANCY ANN
(Nancy Ann Zapp)
Singles: 7-inch
FRANKIE...8-12 61
Also see NANCY & MILLIONAIRES

NANTOS, Nick, & Fireballers
LPs: 10/12-inch
STRAND...15-25 62
(May also be shown as Nick Nastos.)
SUMMIT...10-15 60s

NANTZ, Pete
Singles: 7-inch
CLIX (3873 "Flip, Flop and Fly")...15-25

NANTUCKET
Singles: 7-inch
EPIC...3-5 78
RCA...3-4 83
LPs: 10/12-inch
EPIC...5-10 78-80
RCA...5-8 83

NAPOLEON
Singles: 7-inch
A.P.I. ...4-8 65

NAPOLEON XIV P&R '66
(Jerry Samuels)
Singles: 7-inch
ERIC...3-5 76
W.B. (5800 series)...5-10 66
W.B. (7700 series)...4-6 73
LPs: 10/12-inch
RHINO...5-8 80s
W.B. (W-1661 "They're Coming to Take Me Away")...50-60 66
(Monaural.)
W.B. (W-1661 "They're Coming to Take Me Away")...75-100 66
(White label. Promotional issue only.)
W.B. (WS-1661 "They're Coming to Take Me Away")...75-100 66
(Stereo.)
Also see IMPOSSIBLES
Also see SAMUELS, Jerry

NAPOLEONIC WARS
Singles: 7-inch
HUNCH...4-8 66
20TH FOX...4-8 66

NAPOLI, Don
Singles: 7-inch
MOONGLOW...4-8 64

NARADA: see WALDEN, Narada Michael

NARDELLA, Steve
LPs: 10/12-inch
BLIND PIG...5-10 80

NARDON, Joe, & All Stars
Singles: 7-inch
MADISON...8-12 59
RED BIRD...5-10 67
TIMES SQUARE (123 "Wiggle")...8-12 60

NARIZ, Wazmo
LPs: 10/12-inch
I.R.S. ...5-10 80

NASEY, Ron Cameron: see NAZY, Ron Cameron

NASH, Bill C&W '81
Singles: 7-inch
LIBERTY...3-4 81-82

NASH, Cliff, & Rockaways
(Cliffie Nash.)
Singles: 7-inch
DO-RA-ME (5027 "No Time for Sisters")...40-60 61
DO-RA-ME (5028 "Jennie Lou")...50-75 61
KIM (1048 "This Little Boy's Gone Looking")...25-30
NASH (600 "Rampage")...20-30
NASH (601 "Cincinnati Rock")...25-50
NASH (602 "Band Stand")...40-60
Also see ROCKAWAYS

NASH, Gene
Singles: 78 rpm
JOSIE (826 "Beeline")...20-30 57
JUBILEE (5285 "Dandy Lion")...10-20 57
Singles: 7-inch
CAPITOL...5-10 59
JOSIE (826 "Beeline")...20-30 57
JUBILEE (5285 "Dandy Lion")...10-20 57

NASH, Graham P&R/LP '71
Singles: 7-inch
ATLANTIC (2000 series)...3-5 71-73
ATLANTIC (89000 series)...3-4 86
CAPITOL...3-5 79-80
Picture Sleeves
ATLANTIC...3-4 86
CAPITOL...3-5 79
LPs: 10/12-inch
ATLANTIC (7000 series)...8-12 71-73
ATLANTIC (81000 series)...5-8 86
CAPITOL...8-10 80
Also see CROSBY, David, & Graham Nash
Also see CROSBY, STILLS & NASH
Also see HOLLIES
Also see YOUNG, Neil, & Graham Nash

NASH, Johnny P&R '57
Singles: 12-inch
EPIC...5-8 79
Singles: 7-inch
ABC-PAR...8-15 57-61
ARGO...5-10 64-65
ATLANTIC...4-8 66
BABYLON...4-8 69
CADET (5528 "Teardrops in the Rain")...10-20 66
EPIC...3-6 72-80
GROOVE (18 "Helpless")...5-10 63
GROOVE (21 "Deep in the Heart of Harlem")...20-40 63
GROOVE (26 "It's No Good for Me")...5-10 63
GROOVE (30 "I'm Leaving")...5-10 64
JAD...4-8 68-70
JANUS...3-6 70
JODA...5-10 65-66
MGM...4-8 66-67
W.B. ...5-10 62-63
Picture Sleeves
ABC-PAR (9996 "As Time Goes By")...15-25 59
GROOVE (18 "Helpless")...10-15 63
EPs: 7-inch
ABC-PAR...10-20 58-61
LPs: 10/12-inch
ABC-PAR...20-30 58-61
ARGO...15-20 64
CADET...10-15 73
EPIC...10-15 72-74
JAD...12-25 68-69
Also see ANKA, Paul, George Hamilton IV & Johnny Nash

NASH, Johnny, & Kim Weston
Singles: 7-inch
BANYAN TREE (1001 "We Try Harder")...4-6 69
Also see NASH, Johnny
Also see WESTON, Kim

NASH, Linda C&W '73
Singles: 7-inch
ACE of HEARTS...3-5 73

NASH, Lloyd, & Cavaliers
Singles: 7-inch
GUM (1004 "The Right Time")...10-15 62
Also see CAVALIERS

NASH, Melvin
Singles: 7-inch
SHORE BIRD...10-15

NASH, Ted
Singles: 7-inch
REPEAT...4-8 64

NASH THE SLASH
Singles: 12-inch
PVC...4-6 83
Singles: 7-inch
PVC...3-4 83
LPs: 10/12-inch
PVC...5-8 83

NASHVILLE ALL-STARS
LPs: 10/12-inch
RCA (0126 "That Happy Nashville Sound")...8-12 67
RCA (LPM-2302 "After the Riot at Newport")...20-30 60
(Monaural.)
RCA (LSP-2302 "After the Riot at Newport")...25-35 60
(Stereo.)
Members: Chet Atkins; Boots Randolph; Hank Garland; Bob Moore; Floyd Cramer; Buddy Harman; Gary Burton; Brenton Banks.
Also see ATKINS, Chet
Also see CRAMER, Floyd
Also see MOORE, Bob
Also see RANDOLPH, Boots

NASHVILLE BRASS: see DAVIS, Danny

NASHVILLE NIGHTSHIFT C&W '85
Singles: 7-inch
NCA...3-5 85

NASHVILLE SUPERPICKERS C&W '81
Singles: 7-inch
SOUND FACTORY...3-5 81
Members: Charlie McCoy; Johnny Gimble; Phil Baugh; Hargus "Pig" Robbins; Buddy Emmons; Buddy Harman; Henry Strzelecki.
Also see BAUGH, Phil
Also see HAGGARD, Merle
Also see McCOY, Charlie
Also see PRICE, Ray

NASHVILLE TEENS P&R '64
Singles: 7-inch
LONDON (9689 "Tobacco Road")...10-20 64
(Blue label with silver print. Canadian.)
LONDON (9689 "Tobacco Road")...8-10 64
LONDON (9736 "Find My Way Back Home")...8-10 65
MGM...5-10 65-67
U.A. ...3-5 72
LPs: 10/12-inch
LONDON (407 "Tobacco Road")...40-50 64
(Stereo.)
LONDON (3407 "Tobacco Road")...50-60 64
(Monaural.)
Members: Arthur Sharp; John Allen; Roger Groom; Ray Phillips; Barry Jenkins.

NASTY SAVAGE
LPs: 10/12-inch
RESTLESS (72213 "Indulgence")...15-20 87
(Picture disc.)

NAT "THE COOL CAT"
Singles: 7-inch
TALOS ("Come By Here")...40-60
(Selection number not known.)

NATASHA D&D '83
Singles: 12-inch
EMERGENCY...4-6 83

NATHUNE, Joe
Singles: 7-inch
JAY TONE...4-8 61

NATIONAL GALLERY
LPs: 10/12-inch
PHILIPS (600266 "The National Gallery")...20-30 68

NATIONAL LAMPOON P&R/LP '72
Singles: 7-inch
BLUE THUMB...4-6 72-73
EPIC (193 "Have a Kung-Fu Christmas")...3-4 75
(Promotional issue only.)
LABEL 21...3-5 78-80
Picture Sleeves
EPIC (193 "Have a Kung-Fu Christmas")...4-6 75
(Promotional issue only.)
LABEL 21...3-5 78-80
EPs: 7-inch
EPIC (1095 "A History of the Beatles")...10-15 75
(Promotional issue only.)
LPs: 10/12-inch
BANANA...10-15 72-74
BLUE THUMB...10-15 72-74
EPIC...8-12 75-76
IMPORT...8-10 77
LABEL 21 (Except PIC-2001)...5-8 78-80
LABEL 21 (PIC-2001 "That's Not Funny, That's Sick")...20-30 80
(Picture disc.)
NATIONAL LAMPOON...15-20 74
PASSPORT...5-8 82
VISA...5-8 78
Members: John Belushi; Chevy Chase; Melissa Manchester; Tony Hendra; Jim Payne; John Lopresti.
Also see BELUSHI, John
Also see CHASE, Chevy
Also see GUEST, Chris
Also see MANCHESTER, Melissa

NATIVE
Singles: 7-inch
RCA...3-5 80
LPs: 10/12-inch
RCA...5-10 80

NATIVE R&B '84
Singles: 7-inch
JAMAICA...3-4 84

NATIVE BOYS
Singles: 78 rpm
COMBO...15-30 55-56
MODERN (939 "Native Girl")...50-75 54
Singles: 7-inch
COMBO (113 "Strange Love")...30-50 55
COMBO (115 "Tears")...40-60 56
COMBO (119 "Laughing Love")...40-60 56
COMBO (120 "Oh Let Me Dream")...35-45 56
MODERN (939 "Native Girl")...100-150 54

NATURA'ELLES
Singles: 7-inch
VENTURE...4-8 69

NATURAL BRIDGE BUNCH
Singles: 7-inch
ATCO...4-6 68

NATURAL FOUR R&B '69
Singles: 7-inch
ABC (11205 "Why Should We Stop Now")...4-6 69
ABC (11236 "Same Thing in Mind")...8-12 69
ABC (11253 "Hurt")...20-40 70
BOOLA BOOLA (2382 "I Thought You Were Mine")...40-60 69
BOOLA-BOOLA (6384 "Why Should We Stop Now")...40-60 69
(First issue. Note hypen added to label name.)
CHESS...5-10 72
CURTOM...4-8 73-76
PATH...8-12
LPs: 10/12-inch
CURTOM...8-12 74-75
Members: Chris James; Steve Striplin; Del Mos Whitley; Darryl Canady.

NATURAL GAS
Singles: 7-inch
FIREBIRD...3-5 70
LPs: 10/12-inch
FIREBIRD...10-12 70

NATURAL GAS
Singles: 7-inch
PRIVATE STOCK...3-5 76
LPs: 10/12-inch
PRIVATE STOCK...8-10 76
Members: Joey Molland; Jerry Shirley; Mark Clarke; Pete Wood; Felix Pappalardi.
Also see HUMBLE PIE
Also see MOLLAND, Joey
Also see MOUNTAIN

NATURAL GASS
LPs: 10/12-inch
SUPERSCOPE...10-15

NATURAL SOULS
Singles: 7-inch
SCORPI...4-8 67

NATURALS
Singles: 7-inch
MGM (11970 "Marty")...5-10 58
Picture Sleeves
MGM (11970 "Marty")...10-15 58

NATURALS
Singles: 7-inch
BEACON (462 "You Gave Me So Much")...25-35 58

NATURALS
Singles: 7-inch
ERA (1089 "The Mummy")...8-12 59

NATURALS
Singles: 7-inch
HUNT (325 "Blue Moon")...10-15 59
RED TOP (113 "Blue Moon")...20-25 58
Also see FOUR NATURALS

NATURALS
Singles: 7-inch
SMASH (1875 "Let Love Be True")...8-12 64
Members: Carlton Black; Charles Perry; Charles Woolridge; Arthur Cox; Andrew Thomas.
Also see DUVALS
Also see MARVELOWS

NATURALS
Singles: 7-inch
CHATTAHOOCHEE...5-10 64
LIBERTY...5-10 65
20TH FOX...5-10 64

NATURALS
Singles: 7-inch
JOWAR (120 "Internationally Me")...10-20 67
JOWAR (123 "Maiden in the East")...10-20 67

NATURALS R&B '72
Singles: 7-inch
CALLA...4-6 71
MOTOWN...4-6 72
Members: John Simon; William Thomas; Robert Fitzpatrick; Mike Williams.
Also see WALLACE BROTHERS

NATURE BOY & FRIENDS
Singles: 7-inch
BERTRAM INT'L (255 "Surfer John")...25-35 64

NATURE BOYS
Singles: 7-inch
UPTOWN...4-8 66

NATURE ZONE R&B '76
Singles: 7-inch
LONDON...3-5 76

NATURE'S DIVINE P&R/R&B/LP '79
Singles: 7-inch
INFINITY...3-5 79

LPs: 10/12-inch
INFINITY ... 5-10 79

NATURE'S GIFT R&B '74
Singles: 7-inch
ABC ... 3-5 74

NAUGHTON, David P&R '79
Singles: 7-inch
RSO ... 3-5 78-79
Picture Sleeves
RSO ... 3-5 79

NAUGHTY SWEETIES
LPs: 10/12-inch
RHINO/DAUNTLESS (906 "Live") ... 5-8 81
Members: Ian Jack; Simeon Pillich; Rollo Smith; Andy Doerschuk.

NAUTICALS
Singles: 7-inch
POLO (210 "Rockin' Chopin ") ... 10-15 61

NAVARRO
LPs: 10/12-inch
CAPITOL ... 5-10 77-78

NAVARRO, Danny, & Corvels
Singles: 7-inch
N.J.N. (175 "La Bomba") ... 50-75 64

NAVARRO, Tommy
LPs: 10/12-inch
URANIA (5900 "Twist Around") ... 25-50 61

NAVARROS
Singles: 7-inch
CORBY ... 5-10 60s

NAVASOTA
LPs: 10/12-inch
ABC ... 8-12 72

NAVIGATORS
Singles: 7-inch
MONUMENT ... 4-8 66

NAYLOR, Jerry P&R '70/C&W '75
Singles: 7-inch
COLUMBIA ... 3-6 68-71
HITSVILLE ... 3-5 76
MC/CURB ... 3-5 78
MGM ... 3-6 71-72
MELODYLAND ... 3-5 74-75
OAK ... 3-5 80
PACIFIC CHALLENGER ... 3-5 82
SKLYA ... 10-15 61-62
SMASH ... 5-10 65
TOWER ... 5-15 65-68
W.B./CURB ... 3-5 79
WEST ... 3-4 86
Session: Davie Allan.
Also see ALLAN, Davie
Also see CRICKETS
Also see HONDELLS

NAYLOR, Jerry, & Kelli Warren C&W '79
Singles: 7-inch
JEREMIAH ... 3-5 79
Also see NAYLOR, Jerry
Also see WARREN, Kelly

NAYOBE D&D '85
Singles: 12-inch
FEVER ... 4-6 85-86
Singles: 7-inch
FEVER ... 3-4 85-86

NAZARETH LP '73
Singles: 7-inch
A&M ... 3-5 73-80
MCA ... 3-4 83-84
W.B. ... 3-8 71
Picture Sleeves
A&M ... 3-5 75-80
LPs: 10/12-inch
A&M ... 5-10 73-82
MCA ... 5-8 83-84
W.B. ... 8-12 72
Members: Dan McCafferty; Pete Agnew; Darrell Sweet; Manny Charlton.
Also see McCAFFERTY, Dan

NAZTY R&B '76
Singles: 7-inch
MANKIND ... 3-5 76
LPs: 10/12-inch
MANKIND ... 5-10 76

NAZY, Ron Cameron
(Ron Cameron Nasey)
Singles: 7-inch
RENDEZVOUS (137 "The Panic") 10-20 60
TREY (150 "The Great Debate") ... 10-20 60

NAZZ
Singles: 7-inch
VERY RECORD (001 "Lay Down and Die, Goodbye") ... 750-1000 67
Members: Vince "Alice Cooper" Furnier; M. Bruce; G. Buxton; D. Dunaway; T. Speer.
Also see COOPER, Alice

NAZZ LP '68
Singles: 7-inch
S.G.C. (001 "Hello It's Me") ... 10-20 68
(Light yellow label. Periods after letters. No horizontal lines.)
SGC (001 "Hello It's Me") ... 8-12 69
(Dark yellow label. No periods in logo. With horizontal lines.)
SGC (001 "Hello It's Me") ... 4-8 70
(Green label with yellow top.)
SGC (006 "Not Wrong Long") ... 8-10 69
SGC (009 "Some People") ... 8-10 69
Picture Sleeves
S.G.C. (001 "Hello It's Me") ... 30-40 68
Promotional Singles
SGC (001 "Hello It's Me") ... 10-20 68
SGC (006 "Not Wrong Long") ... 10-15 69
SGC (009 "Some People") ... 10-15 69
SGC (009 "Kicks") ... 15-25 70
LPs: 10/12-inch
SGC (5001 "Nazz") ... 30-50 68
SGC (5002 "Nazz-Nazz") ... 40-60 69
(Black vinyl.)
SGC (5002 "Nazz-Nazz") ... 50-100 69
(Colored vinyl. Pink and orange label. SGC logo is blue. Identification number is 691531.)
SGC (5002 "Nazz-Nazz") ... 50-100 69
(Colored vinyl. White label. Promotional issue only.)
SGC (5002 "Nazz-Nazz") ... 75-100 69
(Colored vinyl. Mail-order edition. Red and orange label. SGC logo is purple. Identification number is 691531-MO.)
SGC (5004 "Nazz III") ... 30-50 71
(Black vinyl.)
SGC (5004 "Nazz III") ... 40-50 81
(Picture disc.)
Members: Todd Rundgren; Robert Antoni; Carson Van Osten; Tom Petersson; Rick Nielson.
Also see CHEAP TRICK
Also see RUNDGREN, Todd

N'COLE R&B '78
Singles: 7-inch
MILLENNIUM ... 3-5 78

NDUGU & Chocolate Jam Co. R&B '80
Singles: 7-inch
EPIC ... 3-5 80

NEACE, Zackie
Singles: 7-inch
LOG CABIN (794 "Tragedy of R.F.K.") ... 5-10 68

NEAL, Abbie, & Her Ranch Girls
Singles: 7-inch
ADMIRAL (15000 "Hillbilly Beat") ... 15-25

NEAL, Debi
EP: 10-inch
PLEADEIANS (9164 "Not This Girl") ... 30-35 81
(Picture disc. Promotional issue only. 250 numbered copies made.)

NEAL, Jerry
(Jerry Capehart)
Singles: 7-inch
DOT (15810 "I Hates Rabbits") ... 50-75 58
KW (501 "Oh Baby") ... 50-75 59
Session: Eddie Cochran.
Also see CAPEHART, Jerry
Also see COCHRAN, Eddie

NEAL, Pamela
LPs: 10/12-inch
FREE FLIGHT (11555 "Charlie Hustle") ... 25-30 79
(Picture disc. Promotional issue only.)
FREE FLIGHT (11555 "Charlie Hustle") ... 40-45 79
(Picture disc. Promotional issue only. Autographed by Pete Rose.)

NEAL, Raful
Singles: 7-inch
PEACOCK ... 10-20 60
WHIT ... 10-15 69
LPs: 10/12-inch
ICHIBAN ... 5-10

NEAL & NEWCOMBERS
Singles: 7-inch
HALL WAY ... 15-20 64
KIM (Colored vinyl) ... 4-6 86
Member: Bobby Mizzell.
Also see MIZZELL, Bobby

NEALE, Bill
Singles: 7-inch
FORR (444 "Strike Long Ball") ... 4-6

NEAT, Ron, & Janet Shay Trio
Singles: 7-inch
ALCAR (1501 "Ronnie") ... 5-10

NEAVILLE, Arlie
(The Rockin' "A"; with Lindsey Sisters)
Singles: 7-inch
FRATERNITY (900 "Alone on a Star") ... 5-10 62
FRATERNITY (1202 "Don't Throw Any Stones") ... 20-30 73
FRATERNITY (21122 "Gospel Music Man") ... 30-40 72
PING (8001 "Angel Love") ... 75-100 61
SHOUT N SHINE (143 "Sweet Side of Life") ... 3-5 75
SHOUT N SHINE (294 "It's Only Make Believe") ... 30-40 76
TELL INT'L (375 "Sunday Mornin' ") ... 10-20 69
TELL INT'L (378 "Drink My Wine") ... 30-40 70
LPs: 10/12-inch
FRATERNITY (1021 "The Birth of Christ") ... 50-75 73
FRATERNITY (1025 "The Gospel Music Man") ... 75-100 73
FRATERNITY (3121 "He Saved My Soul") ... 15-25 74
Also see BARNES, Dorothy
Also see CARTER, Dean
Also see CHESSMAN, Judy
Also see KINNEY, June
Also see MILLER, Arlie, & Bullets

NEBULAS
Singles: 7-inch
SURFSIDE (1010 "I Can Always Love") ... 5-8

NECESSARIES
Singles: 7-inch
IRS ... 3-5 79
Picture Sleeves
IRS ... 3-5 79

NECROPOLIS
LPs: 10/12-inch
BOMP ... 5-8 88

NED & GARY
Singles: 7-inch
LIBERTY (55160 "Lovin' ") ... 25-50 58

NED & NELDA
Singles: 7-inch
VIGAH (002 "Hey Nelda") ... 75-100 63
Members: Frank Zappa; Ray Collins.
Also see LORD, Brian, & Midnighters
Also see ZAPPA, Frank

NEDD, Ramona
Singles: 7-inch
LIN ... 8-12 57

NEDITCH, Stan, & Relations
Singles: 7-inch
REGENCY (8001 "Honestly") ... 250-500

NEE, Bernie
Singles: 78 rpm
COLUMBIA ... 8-12 57
Singles: 7-inch
COLUMBIA ... 8-12 57

NEEL, Joanna C&W '71
(Jo Anna Neel)
Singles: 7-inch
DECCA ... 3-5 71-72

NEELEY, Jimmy
Singles: 7-inch
TRU-SOUND ... 4-8 61

NEELEY, Ted
(Teddy Neeley Five)
Singles: 7-inch
CAPITOL ... 4-8 66-68
20TH FOX ... 3-5 77
LPs: 10/12-inch
CAPITOL ... 10-15 67
RCA ... 8-10 74

NEELY, Sam P&R/LP '72
Singles: 7-inch
A&M ... 3-5 74-75
CAPITOL ... 3-5 72-73
ELEKTRA ... 3-5 77
MCA ... 3-4 83-84
LPs: 10/12-inch
A&M ... 8-10 74
CAPITOL ... 8-12 72-73

NEEPS, Lou
Singles: 7-inch
MOONGLOW ... 4-8 64

NEEVETS
Singles: 7-inch
REON ... 5-10 64

NEGLIGEES
Singles: 7-inch
LANCER ... 5-10 65

NEIGHBORHOOD P&R '70
Singles: 7-inch
ACTA (813 "Maintain") ... 5-10 67
BIG TREE ... 4-8 70
BULLET (102269 "Why Can't You See") ... 15-25 69
LPs: 10/12-inch
BIG TREE ... 10-15 70

NEIGHBORHOOD BAKERY
Singles: 7-inch
CAPITOL ... 4-6 69

NEIGHB'RHOOD CHILDR'N
(Neighborhood)
Singles: 7-inch
ACTA (813 "Maintain") ... 10-20 67
ACTA (823 "Happy Child") ... 10-15 68
ACTA (828 "Behold the Lillies") ... 10-20 68
DOT (17238 "Women Think") ... 10-15 69
NAM (2014 "Dancing in the Street") ... 10-15 60s
LPs: 10/12-inch
ACTA (38005 "Neighb'rhood Childr'n") ... 60-90 68
Members: Rick Bolz; Dyan Hoffmann.

NEIGHBORS
Singles: 78 rpm
ABC-PAR ... 5-10 56
Singles: 7-inch
ABC-PAR ... 8-15 56

NEIGHBORS
Singles: 7-inch
MGM ... 4-8 62
VEE JAY ... 5-10 62

NEIGHBORS, Tex
Singles: 7-inch
EMERALD (2109 "Rock and Roll Dot") ... 100-200 58

NEIGHBORS COMPLAINT
LPs: 10/12-inch
COLLECTABLES (5012 "Remember Then") ... 5-10 84
(Black vinyl.)
COLLECTABLES (PDR 15 "Remember Then") ... 10-15 82
(Picture disc.)

NEIL, Fred
(Freddie Neil)
Singles: 7-inch
BRUNSWICK (55117 "Listen Kitten") ... 15-25 59
CAPITOL (2047 "Dolphins") ... 15-25 68
CAPITOL (2091 "Felicity") ... 15-25 68
CAPITOL (2256 "Everybody's Talkin' ") ... 15-25 68
CAPITOL (2604 "Everybody's Talkin' ") ... 10-20 69
EPIC (9334 "Love's Funny") ... 10-15 59
EPIC (9403 "You Don't Have to Be a Baby to Cry") ... 10-15 60
EPIC (9435 "Rainbow and the Rose") ... 10-15 59
LOOK (1002 "You Ain't Treatin' Me Right") ... 35-50 58
LPs: 10/12-inch
CAPITOL (294 "Everybody's Talkin' ") ... 20-30 69
CAPITOL (2665 "Fred Neil") ... 30-40 67
CAPITOL (2862 "Sessions") ... 30-40 68
Also see MARTIN, Vince

NEIL, Mary
Singles: 7-inch
AL-MAT ... 4-8 64

NEIL & JACK
Singles: 7-inch
DUEL (508 "You Are My Love at Last") ... 300-400 62
DUEL (517 "I'm Afraid") ... 300-400 62
Members: Neil Diamond; Jack Parker.
Also see DIAMOND, Neil

NEIL & Shocking Pinks see YOUNG, Neil

NEKTAR LP '74
Singles: 7-inch
PASSPORT ... 3-5 74-75
LPs: 10/12-inch
PASSPORT ... 8-12 74-76
POLYDOR ... 8-10 77
VISA ... 8-10 78

NELL, Lady: see LADY NELL

NELSON P&R/LP '90
Singles: 7-inch
DGC ... 3-4 90
LPs: 10/12-inch
DGC ... 5-8 90
Members: Gunnar Nelson; Matthew Nelson.

NELSON, Billy: see FIVE WINGS

NELSON, Bob
Singles: 78 rpm
SPOTLIGHT ... 5-10 46

NELSON, Bonnie C&W '86
Singles: 7-inch
DOOR KNOB ... 3-4 86-87

NELSON, Carrie
Singles: 7-inch
COED ... 5-10 60

NELSON, Chip
(Earl Nelson)
Singles: 7-inch
ASTRA (1011 "Honey for Sale") ... 5-10 65
EDSEL (783 "Honey for Sale") ... 20-30 60
Also see NELSON, Earl

NELSON, Clare
Singles: 7-inch
EPIC ... 10-15 58

NELSON, Clarence
Singles: 7-inch
MGM ... 4-8 67
PEN ... 5-10 64

NELSON, Darwin, & Blaze Makers
Singles: 7-inch
TEK ... 8-12 59

NELSON, Earl
(With the Pelicans)
Singles: 78 rpm
CLASS (209 "I Bow to You") ... 100-200 57
Singles: 7-inch
CLASS (209 "I Bow to You") ... 100-200 57
EBB ... 10-20 59
W.B. ... 3-5 74
Also see BOB & EARL
Also see DEE, Jay
Also see HOLLYWOOD FLAMES
Also see LEE, Jackie
Also see NELSON, Chip
Also see SATELLITES
Also see VOICES

NELSON, Grant
Singles: 7-inch
WAND ... 8-12 66

NELSON, Jay
Singles: 7-inch
DREW-BLAN ... 5-10 61
EXCELLO ... 5-10 59-60

NELSON, Jerry
Singles: 7-inch
DOT ... 4-8 66
RALLY ... 4-8 62
WORLD WIDE ... 4-8 65

NELSON, Jimmy R&B '51
(With the Peter Rabbit Trio)
Singles: 78 rpm
CHESS ... 15-25 53
OLLIET (100 "Baby Chile") ... 60-80 48
RPM ... 10-20 53
Singles: 7-inch
ALL BOY ... 5-10 62
CHESS (1587 "Free and Easy Mind") ... 25-50 53
CHESS (1800 series) ... 8-12 63
RPM (325 "T-99 Blues") ... 100-200 53
RPM (353 "Big Eyed, Brown Eyed Girl of Mine") ... 100-200 53
RPM (389 "Second Hand Fool") ... 50-75 53
RPM (385 "Meet Me with Your Black Dress On") ... 25-50 53
RPM (389 "Second Hand Fool") ... 25-50 53
RPM (397 "Mean Poor Girl") ... 25-50 53
Also see TURNER, Joe / Jimmy Nelson

NELSON, Jimmy
LPs: 10/12-inch
JURO ... 10-15 64

NELSON, Johnny
Singles: 7-inch
UP TOWN ... 5-10 59

NELSON, Karen, & Billy T. P&R '77
Singles: 7-inch
AMHERST ... 8-10 77
Members: Karen Nelson; Billy Tragesser.

NELSON, Lady, & Lords
Singles: 7-inch
DUNHILL ... 4-8 68
LPs: 10/12-inch
DUNHILL ... 10-15 68
Member: Porta Nelson.

NELSON, Larry
LPs: 10/12-inch
WORLD PACIFIC ... 12-18 65

NELSON, Lloyd
Singles: 7-inch
SYMBOL (903 "Blues After Midnight") ... 20-30 59

NELSON, Martha
Singles: 7-inch
RIC ... 5-10 60

NELSON, Nate
Singles: 7-inch
PRIGAN ... 5-10 61
Also see FLAMINGOS
Also see PLATTERS

NELSON, Peppermint
(Harrison Nelson)
Singles: 78 rpm
GOLD STAR ... 20-30 47
Also see PEPPERMINT HARRIS

NELSON, Phyllis R&B/D&D '85
Singles: 12-inch
CARRERE ... 4-6 85-86
Singles: 7-inch
CARRERE ... 3-4 85-86
Picture Sleeves
CARRERE ... 3-4 86
LPs: 10/12-inch
CARRERE ... 5-8 86

NELSON, Rick P&R/R&B/LP '57
(With the Stone Canyon Band; with Jordanaires; Ricky Nelson)
Singles: 12-inch
CAPITOL ... 5-10 82
Singles: 78 rpm
IMPERIAL ... 40-100 57-58
VERVE ... 40-60 57
Singles: 7-inch
DECCA ... 4-8 63-72
CAPITOL ... 4-8 82
EPIC ... 3-5 77-86
IMPERIAL (5463 "Be-Bop Baby") .. 30-40 57
(Maroon label.)
IMPERIAL (5463 "Be-Bop Baby") .. 10-20 58
(Black label.)
IMPERIAL (5483 "Stood Up") ... 25-35 57
(Maroon label.)
IMPERIAL (5483 "Stood Up") ... 10-20 58
(Black label.)
IMPERIAL (5503 "Believe What You Say") ... 15-25 58
IMPERIAL (5528 "Poor Little Fool") ... 15-25 58
IMPERIAL (5545 "Lonesome Town") ... 15-25 58
(Black vinyl.)
IMPERIAL (5545 "Lonesome Town") ... 150-200 58
(Colored vinyl.)
IMPERIAL (5565 "It's Late") ... 15-25 59
IMPERIAL (5595 "Just a Little Too Much") ... 10-20 59
IMPERIAL (5614 "Mighty Good") ... 10-20 59
IMPERIAL (5663 "Young Emotions") ... 10-20 60
IMPERIAL (5685 "I'm Not Afraid") . 10-20 60
IMPERIAL (5707 "You Are the Only One") ... 10-20 60
IMPERIAL (5741 "Travelin' Man") .. 10-15 61
(Black vinyl.)
IMPERIAL (5741 "Travelin' Man") ... 150-200 61
(Colored vinyl. Promotional issue only.)
IMPERIAL (5770 thru 5935) ... 10-15 61-63
IMPERIAL (5958 "Long Vacation") ... 8-12 63
(Black vinyl.)
IMPERIAL (5958 "Long Vacation") ... 50-100 63
(Colored vinyl.)

IMPERIAL (5985 "Time After Time")...10-12 63
IMPERIAL (66000 series)...8-15 63-64
LIBERTY...3-4 80s
MCA...3-5 73-86
VERVE (10047 "A Teenager's Romance")...25-35 57
VERVE (10070 "You're My One and Only Love")...25-35 57
(Flip is by Barney Kessell.)

Picture Sleeves

DECCA...8-18 63-70
EPIC...3-5 86
IMPERIAL (5483 "Stood Up")...20-30 57
IMPERIAL (5503 "Believe What You Say")...20-30 58
IMPERIAL (5545 "Lonesome Town")...15-25 58
IMPERIAL (5565 "It's Late")...15-25 59
IMPERIAL (5595 "Just a Little Too Much")...15-25 59
IMPERIAL (5614 "Mighty Good")...15-25 59
IMPERIAL (5663 "Young Emotions")...15-20 60
IMPERIAL (5685 "I'm Not Afraid")...15-20 60
IMPERIAL (5707 "You Are the Only One")...15-20 60
IMPERIAL (5741 "Travelin' Man")...10-20 61
IMPERIAL (5770 thru 5935)...10-20 61-63
MCA...3-5 86

EPs: 7-inch

DECCA (2760 "One Boy Too Late")...25-50 63
DECCA (4419 "For Your Sweet Love")...25-50 63
(Juke box issue only. Includes title strips.)
DECCA (4460 "Best Always")...25-50 65
(Juke box issue only. Includes title strips.)
IMPERIAL (153/154/155 "Ricky")...35-55 58
(Price is for any of three volumes.)
IMPERIAL (157/158 "Ricky Nelson")...35-55 58
(Price is for either of two volumes.)
IMPERIAL (159/160/161 "Ricky Sings Again")...35-55 58
(Price is for any of three volumes.)
IMPERIAL (162/163/164 "Songs By Ricky")...35-55 59
(Price is for any of three volumes.)
IMPERIAL (165 "Ricky Sings Spirituals")...50-75 60
VERVE (5048 "Ricky")...75-100 57
(Has one track by Barney Kessell.)

LPs: 10/12-inch

CAPITOL...5-8 81
DECCA (DL-4419 "For Your Sweet Love")...25-50 63
(Monaural.)
DECCA (DL7-4419 "For Your Sweet Love")...25-50 63
(Stereo.)
DECCA (DL-4479 "For You")...25-50 63
(Monaural.)
DECCA (DL7-4479 "For You")...25-50 63
(Stereo.)
DECCA (DL-4559 "The Very Thought of You")...25-50 64
(Monaural.)
DECCA (DL7-4559 "The Very Thought of You")...25-50 64
(Stereo.)
DECCA (DL-4608 "Spotlight on Rick")...25-50 64
(Monaural.)
DECCA (DL7-4608 "Spotlight on Rick")...25-50 64
(Stereo.)
DECCA (DL-4660 "Best Always")...25-50 65
(Monaural.)
DECCA (DL7-4660 "Best Always")...25-50 65
(Stereo.)
DECCA (DL-4678 "Love and Kisses")...25-50 65
(Monaural.)
DECCA (DL7-4678 "Love and Kisses")...25-50 65
(Stereo.)
DECCA (DL-4779 "Bright Lights and Country Music")...25-50 66
(Monaural.)
DECCA (DL7-4779 "Bright Lights and Country Music")...25-50 66
(Stereo.)
DECCA (DL-4827 "Country Fever")...25-50 67
(Monaural.)
DECCA (DL7-4827 "Country Fever")...25-50 67
(Stereo.)
DECCA (DL-4944 "Another Side of Rick")...25-50 67
(Monaural.)
DECCA (DL7-4944 "Another Side of Rick")...25-50 67
(Stereo.)
DECCA (75014 "Perspective")...15-25 68
DECCA (75162 "In Concert")...15-25 70
DECCA (75236 "Rick Sings Nelson")...15-25 70
DECCA (75297 "Rudy the Fifth")...15-25 71
DECCA (75391 "Garden Party")...15-25 72
EPIC...8-15 77-86
EPIC/NU-DISK...10-15 81
IMPERIAL (9048 "Ricky")...50-80 57
("Imperial" across top of label.)
IMPERIAL (9048 "Ricky")...15-25 64
("IR-Imperial" logo on left.)
IMPERIAL (9050 "Ricky Nelson")...45-65 58
("Imperial" across top of label.)
IMPERIAL (9050 "Ricky Nelson")...15-25 64
("IR-Imperial" logo on left.)
IMPERIAL (9061 "Ricky Sings Again")...25-50 59
(Monaural.)
IMPERIAL (9082 "Songs By Ricky")...25-50 59
(Monaural.)
IMPERIAL (9122 "More Songs By Ricky")...25-50 60
(Monaural.)
IMPERIAL (9152 "Rick Is 21")...20-40 61
(Monaural.)
IMPERIAL (9167 "Album Seven")...20-40 62
(Monaural.)
IMPERIAL (9218 "Best Sellers")...20-40 63
(Monaural.)
IMPERIAL (9223 "It's Up to You")...20-40 63
(Monaural.)
IMPERIAL (9232 "Million Sellers By Rick Nelson")...20-40 63
(Monaural.)
IMPERIAL (9244 "Long Vacation")...20-40 63
(Monaural.)
IMPERIAL (9251 "Rick Nelson Sings for You")...20-40 63
(Monaural.)
IMPERIAL (12059 "More Songs By Ricky")...40-60 60
(Stereo. Black vinyl.)
IMPERIAL (12059 "More Songs By Ricky")...300-400 60
(Stereo. Blue vinyl.)
IMPERIAL (12090 "Ricky Sings Again")...20-30 64
(Stereo.)
IMPERIAL (12071 "Rick Is 21")...20-40 61
(Stereo.)
IMPERIAL (12082 "Album Seven")...20-40 62
(Stereo.)
IMPERIAL (12218 "Best Sellers")...20-40 63
(Stereo.)
IMPERIAL (12223 "It's Up to You")...20-40 63
(Stereo.)
IMPERIAL (12232 "Million Sellers By Rick Nelson")...20-40 64
(Stereo.)
IMPERIAL (12244 "Long Vacation")...20-40 63
(Stereo.)
IMPERIAL (12251 "Rick Nelson Sings for You")...20-40 64
(Stereo.)
LIBERTY...5-10 81-83
MCA (Except 1517)...10-15 73-74
MCA (1517 "The Decca Years")...5-10 82
MCA/SILVER EAGLE...5-10 86
MGM (4256 "Teen Time"): see Various Artists section
RHINO (Except 259)...5-10 85
RHINO (259 "Greatest Hits")...8-12 85
(Picture disc.)
SESSIONS (1003 "Ricky Nelson Story")...15-30 79
(Three-disc, mail-order offer.)
SESSIONS (1003 "Ricky Nelson Story")...15-25 79
(Three-disc, mail-order offer.)
SUNSET...10-20 66-68
TIME-LIFE...10-15 86
U.A. (330 "Very Best of Rick Nelson")...10-15 75
U.A. (1004 "Ricky")...5-10 80
U.A. (9960 "Legendary Masters")...15-25 71
VERVE (2083 "Teen Time"): see Various Artists section
Session: James Burton; Joe Osborn; Jordanaires; Jerry Fuller; Randy Meisner; Al Kemp; Steve Duncan.
Also see APPLETREE THEATRE CO.
Also see BURTON, James
Also see DILLARDS
Also see FLEAS
Also see FULLER, Jerry
Also see GRAPPELLI, Stephane, & Barney Kessel
Also see JIM & JOE
Also see JORDANAIRES
Also see KESSEL, Barney / Grant Green / Oscar Moore / Mundell Lowe
Also see MARTIN, Dean, & Ricky Nelson
Also see MEISNER, Randy
Also see MOON, Keith
Also see MURPHY, Rock
Also see RIVERS, Johnny / Ricky Nelson / Randy Sparks
Also see THOMPSON, Claudia

NELSON, Rick, & Jack Lemmon

Singles: 7-inch

THEATRE PROMOTION RECORD (760 "Do You Know What It Means to Miss New Orleans")...150-200 60
(Promotional issue, made for theatre play.)
Also see LEMMON, Jack

NELSON, Rick / Joannie Sommers / Dona Jean Young

LPs: 10/12-inch

DECCA (DL-4836 "On the Flip Side")...20-30 66
(Monaural.)
DECCA (DL7-4836 "On the Flip Side")...25-35 66
(Stereo.)
Also see NELSON, Rick
Also see SOMMERS, Joannie

NELSON, Sandy — P&R/R&B '59

Singles: 7-inch

COLLECTABLES...3-4 80s
ERA...3-5 72
IMPERIAL...4-8 61-69
LIBERTY...3-4 80s
ORIGINAL SOUND...10-15 59
U.A....3-5 74
VEEBLETRONICS...3-5 81

EPs: 7-inch

IMPERIAL...10-20 65
(Stereo juke box "Little LPs.")

LPs: 10/12-inch

IMPERIAL (Except 9105/12044)...10-25 61-69
IMPERIAL (9105 "Teen Beat")...20-30 60
(Monaural.)
IMPERIAL (12044 "Teen Beat")...20-30 60
(Stereo.)
LIBERTY...5-10 82-83
SKYCLAD...5-8 89
SUNSET...10-20 66-70
U.A....8-12 75
Also see ALLEN, Richie
Also see BONFIRE, Mars
Also see GAMBLERS
Also see HOLLYWOOD ARGYLES
Also see TEDDY BEARS
Also see TYLER & FLIPS

NELSON, Teddy

Singles: 7-inch

JOHNNY DOLLAR...3-4

Picture Sleeves

JOHNNY DOLLAR...6-8

NELSON, Teri, Group

Singles: 7-inch

KAMA SUTRA...4-8 68
Also see KASENETZ-KATZ SINGING ORCHESTRAL CIRCUS

NELSON, Tommy

Singles: 7-inch

DIXIE (814 "Hobo Hop")...200-300 50s

NELSON, Tracy — LP '74

Singles: 7-inch

ATLANTIC...3-5 75
CAPITOL...3-5 77
MCA...3-5 75
MERCURY...5-10 69

LPs: 10/12-inch

ADELPHI...5-10 83
ATLANTIC...8-12 75
AUDIO DIRECTIONS...5-10 82
COLUMBIA...10-12 72
FLYING FISH...5-10 75-81
MCA...8-10 76-81
PRESTIGE (7303 "Deep Are the Roots")...15-20 65
PRESTIGE (7726 "Deep Are the Roots")...8-12 69
REPRISE...10-12 72
Also see MOTHER EARTH
Also see NELSON, Willie & Tracy

NELSON, Tyka — R&B '88

Singles: 7-inch

COOLTEMPO...3-4 88

NELSON, Vikki

(Vikki Nelson & Sounds)

Singles: 7-inch

MALA...8-12 61
PREMIUM (402 "By My Side")...35-45 57
VIK (0273 "Like a Baby")...15-25 57

NELSON, Willie — C&W '62

(Willy Nelson)

Singles: 78 rpm

SARG (260 "A Storm Has Just Begun")...100-200 55

Singles: 7-inch

AMERICAN GOLD...3-5 76
ATLANTIC...3-5 73-75
BETTY...10-15 64
BELLAIRE (107 "Night Life")...15-25 63
(Black vinyl.)
BELLAIRE (107 "Night Life")...40-50 63
(Colored vinyl.)
BELLAIRE (5000 series)...3-5 76
CAPITOL...3-5 78
COLUMBIA...3-5 75-91
D (1084 "Man With the Blues")...15-25 59
D (1131 "What a Way to Live")...15-25 60
DOUBLE BARREL...4-8
EVATONE/MUSIGRAM (92828 "Blue Christmas")...3-4 79
(Flexi-disc.)
LIBERTY (55155 "No Dough")...15-25 58
LIBERTY (55386 "Mr. Record Man")...10-15 61
LIBERTY (55439 thru 55638)...5-10 62-64
LIBERTY (56000 series)...4-6 69
LONE STAR...3-5 78
MONUMENT (800 series)...4-8 64
RCA (0100 thru 0800 series)...3-5 69-72
RCA (8500 thru 9900 series)...4-8 65-71
RCA (10000 thru 12000 0series)...3-5 75-81
SARG (260 "A Storm Has Just Begun")...200-300 55
SONGBIRD...3-5 80
U.A. (641 "Night Life")...5-10 63
U.A. (700 thru 1200 series)...3-5 76-78
WILLIE NELSON (628 "No Place for Me")...150-250 57
(Reportedly 3,000 made.)

Picture Sleeves

COLUMBIA...3-5 84
RCA (12000 series)...3-5 81

EPs: 7-inch

COLUMBIA (2687 "Red Headed Stranger")...8-12 75
(Promotional only issue.)

LPs: 10/12-inch

ACCORD...5-8 82-83
ALLEGIANCE...5-8 83
ATLANTIC...8-12 73-76
AUDIO FIDELITY (213 "Willie Nelson")...15-20
(Picture disc.)
AURA...5-8 82-83
BACK-TRAC...5-8
CBS (Except PAL-35305)...5-8 78-83
CBS (PAL-35305 "Stardust")...25-45 78
CAMDEN...8-12 70-74
CASINO...8-10 84
COLUMBIA (30000 series, except 38250 and picture discs)...5-15 75-91
COLUMBIA (38250 "Willie Nelson")...75-100 83
(Boxed, 10-disc set. Includes poster. Nine are black vinyl and one, *Always on My Mind*, is a picture disc.)
COLUMBIA (35305 "Stardust")...40-50 78
(Picture disc.)
COLUMBIA (35305 "Stardust")...25-35 78
(Picture disc.)
COLUMBIA (39943 "Always on My Mind")...15-25 83
(Picture disc.)
COLUMBIA (40000 series, except "HC," half-speed mastered series)...5-10 85-90
COLUMBIA (HC-40000 series)...20-35 82-83
(Half-speed mastered.)
DELTA...5-8 82
DOUBLE BARRELL...15-25
EXACT...5-8 83
HBO (171010 "Willie Nelson and Family")...30-40 83
(Picture disc. Promotional issue only.)
H.S.R.D....8-10 84
HEARTLAND...10-15 87
HOT SCHATZ...5-10 84
LIBERTY (3239 "And Then I Wrote")...25-35 62
(Monaural.)
LIBERTY (7239 "And Then I Wrote")...30-40 62
(Stereo.)
LIBERTY (10000 series)...5-10 80s
LONE STAR...8-12 78
MCA...5-10 80
MASTERS...5-10
OUT of TOWN DIST....5-10
PICKWICK...5-10 74-76
PICKWICK/CAMDEN...5-10 70s
PLANTATION...5-10 82
POTOMAC...10-15 82
PREMORE...5-10
RCA (1100 thru 3200 series)...5-10 75-79
RCA (LPM-3400 thru LPM-3900 series)...10-20 65-68
(Monaural.)
RCA (LSP-3400 thru LSP-4700 series)...10-25 65-72
(Stereo.)
RCA (3600 thru 4800 series)...4-8 80-83
(With "AYL1" prefix.)
RCA (7158 "Willie")...5-8 85
RCA/CANDELITE...8-10 80
SHOTGUN...20-30 77
SOLID GOLD...5-10
SONGBIRD...5-10 80
SUNSET...10-20 66
TAKOMA...5-8 83
TIME-LIFE (16000 series)...15-25 83
(Three-disc set.)
U.A....8-12 73-78
Session: Paul Buskirk; Herb Remington; Bob White; Clyde Brewer; Dick Shannon; Pete Wade; Ray Edenton; Jimmy Day; Hargus "Pig" Robbins; Bob Moore; Willie Ackerman; Billy Strange; Glen Campbell; Leon Russell; Red Callender; Muddy Berry; Harold Bradley; David Briggs; Anita Kerr Singers; Ernie Freeman; Cal Smith; Jerry Reed; Buddy Emmons; Velma Smith; Johnny Bush; Chet Atkins; Bill Pursell; Roy Huskey; Buddy Harman; Buddy Spicher.
Also see ATKINS, Chet
Also see BOWMAN, Don
Also see BRIGGS, David
Also see BRUCE, Ed
Also see BUSH, Johnny
Also see BUSKIRK, Paul, & His Little Men
Also see CAMPBELL, Glen
Also see CHARLES, Ray, & Willie Nelson
Also see COCHRAN, Hank, & Willie Nelson
Also see COE, David Allan, & Willie Nelson
Also see DARRELL, Johnny / George Jones / Willie Nelson
Also see DAVIS, Danny, Willie Nelson, & Nashville Brass
Also see EDDY, Duane
Also see GATLIN, Larry
Also see FREEMAN, Ernie
Also see HAGGARD, Merle, & Willie Nelson
Also see HARRIS, Emmylou
Also see IGLESIAS, Julio, & Willie Nelson
Also see JENNINGS, Waylon, & Willie Nelson
Also see KERR, Anita
Also see KRISTOFFERSON, Kris, Willie Nelson, Dolly Parton, & Brenda Lee
Also see LEE, Brenda, & Willie Nelson
Also see McCALL, Darrell, & Willie Nelson
Also see MILLER, Roger, & Willie Nelson
Also see MOORE, Bob
Also see MYERS, Augie
Also see PARTON, Dolly, & Willie Nelson
Also see PLACE, Mary Kay, & Willie Nelson
Also see PRICE, Ray, & Willie Nelson
Also see PURSELL, Bill
Also see ROSE, Pam, & Willie Nelson
Also see REED, Jerry
Also see SAHM, Doug
Also see SHAVER, Billy Joe
Also see SMITH, Cal
Also see SOME of CHET'S FRIENDS
Also see STEELE, Don / Willie Nelson
Also see STRANGE, Billy
Also see TUBB, Ernest

NELSON, Willie / Nat "King" Cole / Johnny Mathis / Shirley Bassey

EPs: 7-inch

JIMMY McHUGH (300 "Three Guys and a Gal")...8-12 81
(Promotional issue only. Includes Jimmy McHugh bio insert)
Also see BASSEY, Shirley
Also see COLE, Nat "King"
Also see MATHIS, Johnny

NELSON, Willie, & Shirley Collie — C&W '62

Singles: 7-inch

LIBERTY...5-10 62

NELSON, Willie, & Billy Dean

Singles: 7-inch

CAPITOL...3-4 90s
Also see DEAN, Billy

NELSON, Willie, & Kris Kristofferson — C&W/LP '84

LPs: 10/12-inch

COLUMBIA...5-8 84
Also see KRISTOFFERSON, Kris

NELSON, Willie, & Brenda Lee — C&W '83

Singles: 7-inch

MONUMENT...3-5 83
Also see LEE, Brenda

NELSON, Willie, & Johnny Lee

LPs: 10/12-inch

QUICKSILVER...5-8 84

NELSON, Willie / Johnny Lee / Mickey Gilley

LPs: 10/12-inch

PLANTATION...5-8 82
Also see GILLEY, Mickey
Also see LEE, Johnny

NELSON, Willie / Jerry Lee Lewis / Carl Perkins / David Allan Coe

LPs: 10/12-inch

PLANTATION...5-10 75
Also see COE, David Allan
Also see LEWIS, Jerry Lee
Also see PERKINS, Carl

NELSON, Willie & Tracy — C&W '74

Singles: 7-inch

ATLANTIC...3-5 74
Also see NELSON, Tracy

NELSON, Willie, & Webb Pierce — C&W '82

Singles: 7-inch

COLUMBIA...3-4 82

LPs: 10/12-inch

COLUMBIA...5-8 82
Also see PIERCE, Webb

NELSON, Willie, & Ray Price — C&W/LP '80

Singles: 7-inch

COLUMBIA...3-4 80

LPs: 10/12-inch

COLUMBIA...5-8 80
Also see PRICE, Ray

NELSON, Willie, & Leon Russell — C&W '79

Singles: 7-inch

COLUMBIA...3-5 79

LPs: 10/12-inch

COLUMBIA...5-10 79
Also see RUSSELL, Leon

NELSON, Willie, & Hank Wilson — C&W '84

Singles: 7-inch

PARADISE...3-4 84
Also see WILSON, Hank

NELSON, Willie / Faron Young

LPs: 10/12-inch

COLUMBIA...5-10
ROMULUS...5-10
Also see NELSON, Willie
Also see YOUNG, Faron

NELSON TRIO

Singles: 7-inch

GUARANTEED (203 "All in Good Time")...5-10 59

NEMETZ, Shelley

Singles: 7-inch

FANTASY...3-5 72

LPs: 10/12-inch

FANTASY...8-10 72

NEMO

Singles: 7-inch

OMEN...5-10 59

NENA — P&R/D&D '83

Singles: 12-inch

EPIC...4-6 83-84

Singles: 7-inch

EPIC...3-4 83-84

LPs: 10/12-inch

EPIC...5-8 84

NEOGY, Chitra

LPs: 10/12-inch

PULSAR...10-12 69

NEON
Singles: 7-inch
COLUMBIA 4-8 69
PARAMOUNT 3-5 73
LPs: 10/12-inch
PARAMOUNT 10-15 71

NEON BOYS
Singles: 7-inch
SHAKE 3-5 80
Members: Richard Hell; Tom Verlaine; Billy Ficca.
Also see HELL, Richard, & Voidoids
Also see VERLAINE, Tom

NEON LEON
Singles: 7-inch
BIG DEAL 4-8
Also see JAGGER, Mick

NEON PHILHARMONIC *P&R '69*
Singles: 7-inch
MCA 3-5 76
TRX 3-5 72
W.B. 4-6 69-71
LPs: 10/12-inch
W.B. 10-15 69

NEONS
Singles: 78 rpm
TETRA 25-35 56-57
Singles: 7-inch
CHALLENGE (9147 "Magic Moment") 75-125 62
CHALLENGE (59147 "Magic Moment") 25-50 63
GONE (5090 "Angel Face") 25-50 60
ROULETTE 3-5 70s
TETRA (4444 "Angel Face") 50-75 56
TETRA (4449 "Road to Romance") 50-75 57
VINTAGE 3-5 74
Members: Frank Vignari; Jeff Pearl; Norm Isacoff; Ron Derin.

NEONS
Singles: 7-inch
WALDON (1001 "My Lover") 500-750 61

NEOPHONIC STRING BAND
LPs: 10/12-inch
DIRECT to DISK (105 "Neophonic String Band") 10-20 79
Member: Jim Glaser.
Also see GLASER, Jim

NEPTUNES
Singles: 78 rpm
GLORY (269 "As Long As") 15-25 57
Singles: 7-inch
GLORY (269 "As Long As") 20-30 57

NEP-TUNES
Singles: 7-inch
THREE RIVERS (111 "Don't Condemn Me") 50-100 50s

NEP-TUNES
LPs: 10/12-inch
FAMILY (FLP-152 "Surfer's Holiday") 30-50 63
(Monaural.)
FAMILY (SFLP-152 "Surfer's Holiday") 50-75 63
(Stereo.)
Members: Al Torzelli; Steve Marcus; Ed Hawkins; Richard Schweitzer.

NEPTUNES
Singles: 7-inch
CHECKER (967 "So Little Time") ... 10-20 60
GEM 10-20
INSTANT (3255 "Make a Memory") 25-35 63
PAYSON (102 "If You Care") 20-40 58
RCA (7931 "This Is Love") 10-20 61
VICTORIA (102 "I Don't Cry Anymore") 15-20 64

NEPTUNES
Singles: 7-inch
MARLO (1534 "I Met You") 15-25 64

NEPTUNES
Singles: 7-inch
W.B. (5453 "Shame Girl") 5-10 64

NERO, Frances
Singles: 7-inch
SOUL (35020 "Keep on Lovin' Me") 10-20 66

NERO, Peter *LP '61*
(With Boston Pops Orchestra)
Singles: 7-inch
ARIOLA AMERICA 3-5 76
ARISTA 3-5 75
COLUMBIA 3-5 69-73
RCA 3-6 61-68
Picture Sleeves
RCA 3-5 62-63
LPs: 10/12-inch
ARISTA 5-10 75
CAMDEN 5-10 67-73
COLUMBIA 5-10 69-75
CONCORD JAZZ 5-8 78
HARMONY 5-10 71
PREMIER 10-15 63
RCA 5-15 61-76
Also see ANN-MARGRET
Also see BOSTON POPS ORCHESTRA
Also see CRAMER, Floyd / Peter Nero / Frankie Carle

NERVE
Singles: 7-inch
PAGE ONE (019 "Piece by Piece") ... 5-8

NERVES
EPs: 7-inch
NERVES 10-20 76

NERVOUS BREAKDOWNS
Singles: 7-inch
TAKE 6 (1001 "I Dig Your Mind") ... 15-25 67

NERVOUS EATERS
Singles: 7-inch
ELEKTRA 3-5 80
RAT 8-10 77
LPs: 10/12-inch
ELEKTRA 5-8 80
Members: Andy Paley; Jonathan Paley; Nicky Hopkins; Steve Cropper; Jeff Wilkinson; Steve Cataldo.
Also see CROPPER, Steve
Also see HOPKINS, Nicky
Also see PALEY BROTHERS

NERVOUS NORVUS *P&R '56*
(With Red Blanchard; Jimmy Drake)
Singles: 12-inch
BIG BEAT (12 "Transfusion") 10-15 85
(Includes picture cover.)
Singles: 78 rpm
DOT 10-25 56-57
QUALITY 20-30 56
Singles: 7-inch
BIG BEN (101 "Pure Gold") 10-15
DOT (15470 "Transfusion") 15-25 56
(Maroon label.)
DOT (15485 "Ape Call") 15-25 56
(Maroon label.)
DOT (15500 "The Fang") 15-25 56
(Maroon label.)
DOT (Black label) 10-15 57
(Black label.)
DOT (16765 "Transfusion") 4-8 65
EMBEE (117 "I Like Girls") 10-20 59
QUALITY ("Transfusion") 25-50 56
(Canadian. Selection number not known.)
QUALITY ("Ape Call") 25-50 56
(Canadian. Selection number not known.)
QUALITY (1548 "The Fang") 25-50 56
(Canadian.)
Also see BLANCHARD, Red
Also see FOUR JOKERS

NERVOUS REX
LPs: 10/12-inch
DREAMLAND 5-10 80

NERVOUS SYSTEM
Singles: 7-inch
JAMBEE 4-8

NESBITT, Jim *C&W '61*
(The "Lasses Sopper")
Singles: 7-inch
ACE 8-12 61
CHART 3-6 64-70
COUNTRY JUBILEE 8-12 61
DOT 5-10 61-63
RALLY 4-8 62
RUSH 5-10 62
SCORPIO 3-5 75
SMASH 4-8 62
LPs: 10/12-inch
CHART 8-15 64-71
SCORPION 6-10 76

NESMITH, Michael *P&R/LP '70*
(With the First National Band; with Second National Band)
Singles: 7-inch
EDAN (1001 "Just a Little Love") ... 50-75 65
ISLAND 5-8 77
OMNIBUS 15-25 63
PACIFIC ARTS 8-10 75-79
RCA 10-20 70-75
Picture Sleeves
RCA (0453 "Nevada Fighter") 15-25 71
LPs: 10/12-inch
PACIFIC ARTS ("Conversation with Michael Nesmith – Music Radio Special") ... 25-35 78
(Promotional issue only.)
PACIFIC ARTS (101 "The Prison") 25-50 78
(Boxed edition. With booklet.)
PACIFIC ARTS (101 "The Prison") 10-20 78
(Standard LP. With booklet.)
PACIFIC ARTS (106 thru 130) 10-20 78-79
PACIFIC ARTS (9486 "From a Radio Engine to the Photon Wing") 15-25 77
RCA 20-30 70-75
RHINO 8-10 89
Also see BLESSING, Michael
Also see CORVETTES
Also see EZBA, Denny
Also see MIKE, JOHN & BILL
Also see MONKEES
Also see RHODES, Red
Also see TRINITY RIVER BOYS
Also see WICHITA TRAIN WHISTLE

NESS, Lindy, & City Dudes
Singles: 78 rpm
VEGA 15-20 53

NESTRO, Frankie
Singles: 7-inch
FRAN-CO (1004 "My Love") 30-40 62

NETHERWORLD
LPs: 10/12-inch
REM (441 "Netherworld") 20-30 60s

NETTLES, Bill, & Dixie Blue Boys *C&W '49*
Singles: 78 rpm
BRUNSWICK 5-10 37
BULLET 8-12
MERCURY 5-10 49
VOCALION 10-15

NETTLES, Joe
Singles: 7-inch
CIRCLE (1174 "Oh Baby") 50-75

NETTLES, Roosevelt
Singles: 7-inch
BAMBOO (510 "Yes, Your Honor") 10-20 61
CAPITOL (5033 "Sorry for Me") 8-12 63
CHESS (1846 "Drifting Heart") 8-12 63
MASCOT (105 "Got You on My Mind") 15-25 57

NETTLES SISTERS
Singles: 78 rpm
RODEO 5-10 56
Singles: 7-inch
RODEO 8-12 56

NETTO, Loz *P&R '83*
Singles: 7-inch
21 .... 3-4 83
Picture Sleeves
21 .... 3-4 83
LPs: 10/12-inch
21 .... 5-8 82
Also see SNIFF 'N the TEARS

NETWORK
Singles: 7-inch
EPIC 3-5 78
LPs: 10/12-inch
EPIC 5-10 77-78
Also see BLODWYN PIG

NEU
LPs: 10/12-inch
BILLINGSGATE 10-12 73
CAPITOL 10-12 75

NEUMAN, Alfred E., & Furshlugginer Five
Singles: 7-inch
ABC-PAR (10013 "What-Me Worry") 15-25 59
MAD ("It's a Gas") 10-15 60s
(Square cardboard cutout picture disc with Mad Magazine. No selection number used.)
Picture Sleeves
ABC-PAR (10013 "What-Me Worry") 30-50 59

NEURON
LPs: 10/12-inch
ERECT 5-10 80

NEUROTIC SHEEP
Singles: 7-inch
BOFUZ (1117 "Season of the Witch") 25-35 60s
CAPITOL 10-20 60s

NEUTONES
Singles
ERIKA (11601 "Crazy Love") 8-12 84
(Shaped picture disc. One side is mirror-like.)

NEUTRONS
LPs: 10/12-inch
U.A. 8-12 74
Members: Caromay Dixon; Stu Gordon; Martin Wallace; Dave Charles; Phil Ryan.

NEVEGANS
(Nevegan's)
Singles: 7-inch
X-P-A-N-D-E-D (101 "Russian Roulette") 15-25 63
(Also issued as *Surf Bound* by the Teenbeats.)
Also see CHANTAYS
Also see TEENBEATS

NEVELS, Gail
Singles: 7-inch
DOTTY'S 8-12

NEVER NEVER BAND
Singles: 7-inch
BELL 3-5 73

NEVIL, Arlie: see NEAVILLE, Arlie

NEVIL, Robbie *P&R/R&B/LP '86*
Singles: 12-inch
MANHATTAN 4-6 86
Singles: 7-inch
EMI 3-4 88
MANHATTAN 3-4 86-87
Picture Sleeves
EMI 3-4 88
MANHATTAN 3-4 86-87
LPs: 10/12-inch
EMI 5-8 88
MANHATTAN 5-8 86

NEVILLE, Aaron *R&B '60*
(Arron Neville)
Singles: 7-inch
AIRECORDS (333 I've Done It Again") 15-25 63
BANDY (1501 "Let's Live") 5-10
BELL 5-10 68-69
HEAD 3-5
IMPERIAL (035 "Over You") 5-8 65
MERCURY 4-6 72-73
MINIT (612 "Over You") 10-20 60
MINIT (618 "Show Me the Way") ... 10-20 60
MINIT (624 "Reality") 10-20 61
MINIT (631 "Let's Live") 10-20 61
MINIT (639 "I'm Waitin' at the Station") 10-20 61
MINIT (657 "How Could I Help But Love You") 10-20 63
PAR-LO 5-10 66-67
POLYDOR 3-5 77
SAFARI (201 "Forever More") 5-10 67
WHO DAT? 4-6
LPs: 10/12-inch
COLLECTABLES 6-8 88
MINIT (40007 "Like It 'Tis") 15-25 67
(Monaural.)
MINIT (40007 "Like It 'Tis") 15-25 67
(Stereo.)
PAR-LO (1 "Tell It Like It Is") 20-30 67
(Monaural.)
PAR-LO (1 "Tell It Like It Is") 25-35 67
(Stereo.)
Also see NEVILLE BROTHERS
Also see RONSTADT, Linda, & Aaron Neville

NEVILLE, Aaron / Toussaint McCall
Singles: 7-inch
TRIP 3-5 70s
Also see McCALL, Toussaint
Also see NEVILLE, Aaron

NEVILLE, Art
Singles: 7-inch
CINDERELLA (1400 "My Dear, Dearest Darling"/"My Baby") 35-55 65
CINDERELLA (1401 "My Dear, Dearest Darling"/"Little Liza Jane") 25-50 65
(Note different flip side.)
INSTANT 8-15 61-66
SANSU 5-10 60s
SPECIALTY (656 "What's Going On") 15-25 59
Also see NEVILLE BROTHERS
Also see WILLIAMS, Larry

NEVILLE, Art / Aaron Neville
LPs: 10/12-inch
BANDY (70013 "The Best of Art & Aaron") 10-15 70s
Also see NEVILLE, Aaron
Also see NEVILLE, Art

NEVILLE, Cyril
Singles: 7-inch
JOSIE 3-6 69
Also see KILLER BEES & Cyril Neville
Also see NEVILLE BROTHERS

NEVILLE, Ivan *LP '88*
Singles: 7-inch
POLYDOR 3-4 88-89
LPs: 10/12-inch
POLYDOR 5-8 88

NEVILLE BROTHERS *LP '81*
Singles: 7-inch
A&M 3-5 81-90
CAPITOL 3-6 78
LPs: 10/12-inch
A&M 5-10 81-90
BLACK TOP 5-10 86
CAPITOL (11865 "Neville Brothers") 20-30 78
EMI AMERICA 5-8 87
RHINO 5-8 87
SPINDLE TOP 5-8 87
Members: Aaron Neville; Art Neville; Charles Neville; Cyril Neville.
Also see HAWKETTS
Also see METERS
Also see NEVILLE, Aaron
Also see NEVILLE, Art
Also see NEVILLE, Cyril
Also see SEATTLE HELPS the HUNGRY
Also see WILD TCHOUPITOULAS

NEW, Joyce & Linda
Singles: 7-inch
SPLIT (527 "I'm the Girl") 8-12

NEW, Paul, & Steel City
EPs: 7-inch
(371 "Minnesota") 4-6 70s
(No label name used. Bonus EP, packaged with *Catch This!* LP. Pittsburgh Steelers promotional issue.)
LPs: 10/12-inch
(371 "Catch This!") 15-25 70s
(No label name used. Includes bonus EP. Pittsburgh Steelers promotional issue.)

NEW ADVENTURES
LPs: 10/12-inch
POLYDOR 5-10 80

NEW APOCALYPSE
Singles: 7-inch
ID 4-8 68
MTA 4-6 70
LPs: 10/12-inch
MTA (5017 "Stainless Soul") 15-20 70

NEW ARRIVALS
Singles: 7-inch
MACY'S 5-10 60s
SOUTHBAY 5-10 60s
Also see PREPS

NEW BAG
Singles: 7-inch
DATE 4-8 66

NEW BIRTH *P&R/R&B/LP '71*
Singles: 7-inch
ARIOLA AMERICA 3-5 79
BUDDAH 3-5 75
RCA 3-5 71-75
W.B. 3-5 76-78
LPs: 10/12-inch
ARIOLA AMERICA 5-10 79
BUDDAH 8-12 75
COLLECTABLES 5-10 88
RCA (Except APD1-0285 & LSP-4000 series) 5-10 73-82
RCA (APD1-0285 "It's Been a Long Time") 15-25 74
(Quadrophonic.)
RCA (LSP-4000 series) 10-15 70-72
W.B. 8-12 76-77
Members: Harvey Fuqua; Tony Churchill; Alan Frye; Robert Jackson; Joe Porter; Leslie Wilson; Mel Wilson; Londee Loren; Bobby Downs; Ann Bogan; Austin Lander; James Baker; Leroy Taylor; Robin Russell; Ben Boytel; Roger Voice; James Hall.
Also see HARVEY
Also see LOVE, PEACE & HAPPINESS
Also see NITE-LITERS

NEW BLOCKBUSTERS
Singles: 78 rpm
ANTLER 15-20 55
Singles: 7-inch
ANTLER (4001 "Rock & Roll Guitar") 25-50 56
Also see BLOCKBUSTERS

NEW BLOODS
Singles: 7-inch
20TH FOX (554 "Self Service") 15-20 65

NEW BREED
Singles: 7-inch
DIPLOMACY (22 "Green Eyed Woman") 20-30 65
FRATERNITY (1003 "High Society Girl") 10-20 68
HBR 5-10 66
MERCURY 5-10 66
WORLD UNITED 5-10 66
LPs: 10/12-inch
CICADELIC 8-10 80s

NEW BREED
Singles: 7-inch
POLARIS (711 "Waiting My Time") 20-30 66

NEW BREED
Singles: 7-inch
BOYD 5-10 66
JAMIE 5-10 67

NEW BREED
Singles: 7-inch
PKC 5-10 69
Member: Alan Butler.

NEW BREED
Singles: 7-inch
NEW BREED (13635 "Don't Jive") 15-25 60s

NEW BREED
Singles: 7-inch
IN CROWD (001 "Sunny") 20-30 60s
IN CROWD (1234 "Big Time") 15-25 60s

NEW CACTUS BAND *LP '73*
Singles: 7-inch
ATCO 3-6 73
LPs: 10/12-inch
ATCO 8-12 73
Members: Mike Pinera; Duane Hitchings; Manuel Bertematti; Roland Robinson; Jerry Norris.
Also see CACTUS

NEW CENSATION *R&B '74*
Singles: 7-inch
PRIDE 3-5 74-75
LPs: 10/12-inch
PRIDE 8-12 74

NEW CENTURY SINGERS
Singles: 7-inch
SWAN 4-8 65

NEW CHOICE *R&B '87*
Singles: 7-inch
RCA 3-4 87

NEW CHRISTY MINSTRELS *P&R/LP '62*
Singles: 7-inch
COLUMBIA (42000 series) 4-8 62-63
COLUMBIA (43000 & 44000 series) .. 4-6 64-69
GREGAR 3-5 70-72
W.B. 3-5 79
Promotional Singles
COLUMBIA (Colored vinyl) 5-10 63-65
Picture Sleeves
COLUMBIA 4-8 62
LPs: 10/12-inch
COLUMBIA (1800 thru 2500 series) 10-20 62-66
(Monaural.)
COLUMBIA (8600 thru 9300 series) 10-30 62-66
(Stereo.)
COLUMBIA (9600 & 9700 series) .. 10-15 68
GREGAR 8-12 70
HARMONY 8-12 68-72
Members: Randy Sparks; Barry McGuire; Kenny Rogers; Mike Settle; Thelma Lou Camacho; Terry Williams; Mickey Jones; Jackie Miller; Gayle Caldwell; Gene Clark; Larry Ramos; Rex Kramer.
Also see ASSOCIATION
Also see CLARK, Dave, Five / New Christy Minstrels / Bobby Vinton / Jerry Vale
Also see CLARK, Dave, Five / Simon & Garfunkel / Yardbirds / New Christy Minstrels
Also see CLARK, Gene
Also see FIRST EDITION
Also see JACKIE & GAYLE
Also see KRAMER, Rex
Also see McGUIRE, Barry
Also see SPARKS, Randy

NEW COLONY SIX P&R '66
Singles: 7-inch
CENTAUR 4-8 66
MCA 3-6 74
MERCURY ("Attacking a Straw Man") 10-20 69
(Promotional issue only. Number not known.)
MERCURY (72737 thru 73004) 4-8 67-70
MERCURY (73063 "People & Me") . 8-15 70
MERCURY (73093 "Close Your Eyes Little Girl") 8-15 70
SENTAR 10-20 66-67
SUNLIGHT 3-5 71-72
TWILIGHT 3-5 73
Picture Sleeves
MERCURY 4-8 67-68
LPs: 10/12-inch
MERCURY 20-30 68-69
SENTAR (101 "Breakthrough") .. 150-250 66
SENTAR (3001 "Colonization") 50-75 67
Members: Ronnie Rice; Ray Graffia; Craig Kemp; Jerry Kollenberg; Pat McBride; Chick James; Billy Herman; Chuck Lobes; Wally Kemp.
Also see RICE, Ronnie

NEW CONCEPTS
Singles: 7-inch
PHILIPS 5-8 68-69

NEW CRUSADE
Singles: 7-inch
METROMEDIA 4-6 69

NEW DAWN
Singles: 7-inch
MAINSTREAM (664 "Slave of Desire") 10-20 66

NEW DAWN
Singles: 7-inch
IMPERIAL 4-8 69
RCA 4-8 68

NEW DAWN
Singles: 7-inch
GARLAND (2020 "Tears") 10-20 70
LPs: 10/12-inch
HOOT (4569 "A New Dawn") ... 750-1000 70

NEW DAY
Singles: 7-inch
KEF 4-8

NEW DIMENSIONS
LPs: 10/12-inch
SUTTON 25-40 63-64

NEW DIRECTION
LPs: 10/12-inch
NEPTUNE 10-12 70

NEW DYNAMICS
Singles: 7-inch
CUCA (1081 "Come Go with Me") 15-25 62
CUCA (1095 "Oh, I Like It Like That") 15-25 64
Member: Bobby Price.

NEW EDITION P&R/R&B/D&D/LP '83
Singles: 12-inch
MCA 4-6 84-86
STREETWISE 4-6 83
Singles: 7-inch
MCA (Black vinyl) 3-4 84-89
MCA (Colored vinyl) 4-6 85
STREETWISE 5-8 83
Picture Sleeves
MCA 3-5 84-89
LPs: 10/12-inch
MCA 5-8 84-89
STREETWISE 5-8 83
Members: Johnny Gill; Bobby Brown; Ricky Bell; Michael Bivins; Ronnie DeVoe.
Also see BELL BIV DeVOE
Also see BROWN, Bobby
Also see GILL, Johnny
Also see KING DREAM CHORUS & Holiday Crew

NEW ENGLAND P&R/LP '79
Singles: 7-inch
ELEKTRA 3-5 80-81
INFINITY (100103 "Don't Ever Want to Lose You") 3-5 79
(Black vinyl.)
INFINITY (100103 "Don't Ever Want to Lose You") 10-15 79
(Picture disc.)
LPs: 10/12-inch
ELEKTRA 5-10 80-81
INFINITY 5-10 79

NEW ENGLAND CONSERVATORY RAGTIME ENSEMBLE LP '73
Singles: 7-inch
ANGEL 3-4 80
LPs: 10/12-inch
ANGEL 5-8 73
GOLDEN CREST 5-10 75

NEW ERA
Singles: 7-inch
GREAT LAKES (2532 "We Ain't Got Time") 10-15 67

NEW ESTABLISHMENT P&R '69
Singles: 7-inch
COLGEMS 5-8 69
MERCURY 4-8 67

NEW EXPERIENCE
Singles: 12-inch
PHILLY WORLD 4-6 83

NEW F.B.I. BAND
Singles: 7-inch
WHITE WHALE 4-8 68

NEW FACES
Singles: 7-inch
DOT (16777 "You'll Be Too Late") .. 10-20 65
PARROT 5-8 68

NEW FORMULA
Singles: 7-inch
ROULETTE (7023 "Burning in the Background of My Mind") 10-15 68

NEW FOUNDATIONS
Singles: 7-inch
ATLANTIC 3-5 75

NEW FOURTH REICH
Singles: 7-inch
PLANET (68 "That Girl") 15-25 67

NEW FRONTIERS: see FRONTIERS

NEW FUGITIVES
Singles: 7-inch
GLO (5241 "That's Queer") 20-25 66

NEW GENERATION
Singles: 7-inch
IMPERIAL 4-8 68
KAPP 4-8 65

NEW GRASS REVIVAL C&W '86
Singles: 7-inch
CAPITOL 3-4 87-89
EMI AMERICA 3-4 86
LPs: 10/12-inch
FLYING FISH 5-10 80s
STARDAY 5-10 73
Members: John Cowan; Sam Bush; Bela Fleck.

NEW GUYS ON THE BLOCK R&B '83
Singles: 7-inch
SUGAR HILL 3-4 83

NEW HAPPINESS
Singles: 7-inch
COLUMBIA 4-8 66-68
Member: Smooth Lundull.

NEW HARLEQUINS
Singles: 7-inch
PACIFIC CHALLENGER (124 "Zelda Klotz") 20-30 60s

NEW HAWKS
Singles: 7-inch
BLACK ROSE (3002 "Walk Don't Run-Pipeline [Medley]") 10-20 60s

NEW HEAVENLY BLUE
Singles: 7-inch
RCA 3-5 71
LPs: 10/12-inch
ATLANTIC 8-10 72
RCA 8-12 70

NEW HOLIDAYS
Singles: 7-inch
WESTBOUND (157 "My Baby Ain't No Play Thing") 20-30

NEW HOLLYWOOD ARGYLES
(With Pepper Hellard)
Singles: 7-inch
KAMMY 5-10 66
RCA 4-8 75
Also see HOLLYWOOD ARGYLES

NEW HOPE P&R '70
Singles: 7-inch
JAMIE 4-8 69-71
LPs: 10/12-inch
JAMIE (3034 "The New Hope") 20-30 69
Members: Kit Stewart; Carl Von Hausman; John Bradley; Ron Shane.
Also see KIT KATS

NEW HORIZONS R&B '83
Singles: 7-inch
COLUMBIA 3-4 83
LPs: 10/12-inch
COLUMBIA 5-8 83
Members: Mark Thomas; Art Thomas; Varges Thomas.

NEW HUDSON EXIT
Singles: 7-inch
DATE 4-8 67

NEW INVICTAS
Singles: 7-inch
HALE (500 "Deeply in Love") 250-300 62

NEW JERSEY MASS CHOIR R&B/D&D '85
Singles: 12-inch
SAVOY 4-6 85
Also see FOREIGNER

NEW KIDS ON THE BLOCK R&B '86
Singles: 12-inch
COLUMBIA 4-6 86
Singles: 7-inch
COLUMBIA 3-4 86-90
Picture Sleeves
COLUMBIA 3-4 88
LPs: 10/12-inch
COLUMBIA 5-8 86-90
Members: Jordan Knight; Jon Knight; Joe McIntyre; Danny Wood; Donny Wahlberg.
Also see PAGE, Tommy

NEW KINGSTON TRIO
Singles: 7-inch
CAPITOL 3-6 71
Also see KINGSTON TRIO

NEW LEGION ROCK SPECTACULAR
Singles: 7-inch
SPECTACULAR 4-8 75
LPs: 10/12-inch
SPECTACULAR (7777 "Wild") 30-40 75
Also see BOOZE BROTHERS REVUE

NEW LIFE
Singles: 7-inch
AMARET 4-6 69-70
EPIC 4-6 69
LPs: 10/12-inch
AMARET 8-12 70

NEW LIME
Singles: 7-inch
COLUMBIA (44017 "That Girl") 10-20 67
COLUMBIA (44597 "Donna") 8-12 68
COUNTERPART (2495 "Walkin' the Dog") 10-20 60s
FRATERNITY (947 "And She Cried") 5-10 65
MINARET (150 "Sonny") 5-10 69

NEW LONDON RHYTHM & BLUES BAND
LPs: 10/12-inch
VOCALION 10-12 69

NEW LUVS
Singles: 7-inch
BARCLAY ("It's All Over") 20-30 60s
(Selection number not known.)

NEW MARKETTS R&B '76
(Danny Welton & New Marketts)
Singles: 7-inch
CALLIOPE 3-6 77
FARR 3-6 76-77
SEMINOLE 3-6 76
LPs: 10/12-inch
CALLIOPE 8-12 77
Also see MARKETTS
Also see WELTON, Danny

NEW MASON DIXONS
Singles: 7-inch
CENTENNIAL 8-12 60s

NEW MISS ALICE STONE LADIES SOCIETY ORCHESTRA
Singles: 7-inch
HARMONY CLUB 3-5 74
Picture Sleeves
HARMONY CLUB 3-5 74

NEW MIX
LPs: 10/12-inch
U.A. 10-20 68

NEW MUSIK
Singles: 7-inch
EPIC 3-5 80
LPs: 10/12-inch
EPIC 5-10 80

NEW ORDER
(Featuring Roger Joyce)
Singles: 7-inch
W.B. (5816 "You've Got Me High") 15-25 66
W.B. (5870 "Sailing Ship") 5-10 67

NEW ORDER R&B/D&D '83
Singles: 12-inch
FACTUS 4-6 83
QWEST 4-6 85
STREETWISE 4-6 83
Singles: 7-inch
QWEST 3-4 85-89
STREETWISE 3-4 83
Picture Sleeves
QWEST 3-4 87-89
LPs: 10/12-inch
QWEST (Except 25621) 5-8 85-89
QWEST (25621 "Substance") 8-12 87
Members: Bernard Sumner; Peter Hook; Gillian Gilbert; Stephen Morris.
Also see ELECTRONIC
Also see JOY DIVISION

NEW ORLEANS SLIM / Les Mozart
Singles: 78 rpm
OCTIVE 15-25 51
Also see AMOS, Ira

NEW PHOENIX
Singles: 7-inch
WORLD PACIFIC 8-10 66
Also see HARD TIMES
Also see T.I.M.E.

NEW PLAY
(Featuring Ruth Copeland)
Singles: 7-inch
INVICTUS 4-6 69
Also see COPELAND, Ruth

NEW POTATOES
Singles: 7-inch
CAPITOL 3-5 73

NEW RAGING STORM
Singles: 7-inch
TEE PEE (15 "Cry Girl") 10-20 67
Members: Ron Besaw; Dick Schelk; Rollie Ritchie; Roger Loos; Bob Anderson; Denny Noie.
Also see BESAW, Ron, & Mojo Men

NEW RENAISSANCE SOCIETY
LPs: 10/12-inch
HBR 10-20 66

NEW RIDERS OF THE PURPLE SAGE LP '71
Singles: 7-inch
COLUMBIA 3-5 71-74
MCA 3-5 76-77
LPs: 10/12-inch
A&M 5-8 81
BUDDAH 8-12 75
COLUMBIA 10-15 71-75
MCA 8-10 76-77
RELIX (Except 2025) 5-8 86-87
RELIX (2025 "Vintage") 5-8 87
(Black vinyl.)
RELIX (2025 "Vintage") 30-50 87
(Picture disc.)
Members: Skip Battin; David Turbert. Also, assorted Grateful Dead members guested on Columbia and Relix issues.
Also see BATTIN, Skip
Also see GRATEFUL DEAD
Also see KEITH & DONNA
Also see KINGFISH

NEW RIVER BAND
Singles: 7-inch
NEW RIVER BAND (001 "All He Was Saying") 8-10 80

NEW ROADRUNNERS
Singles: 7-inch
A-OK (1036 "Tired of Living") 10-15 67

NEW ROTARY CONNECTION
LPs: 10/12-inch
CHESS 8-12 71
Also see ROTARY CONNECTION

NEW SCENE
Singles: 7-inch
ERA 4-8 67

NEW SEEKERS P&R '70
Singles: 7-inch
ELEKTRA 3-5 70-72
MGM/VERVE 3-5 72-73
Picture Sleeves
MGM/VERVE 3-5 72-73
EPs: 7-inch
COCA-COLA 5-10 69
(Promotional issue only.)
LPs: 10/12-inch
ELEKTRA 10-12 71-72
MGM/VERVE 8-10 73
Member: Keith Potger.
Also see SEEKERS

NEW SILHOUETTES
Singles: 7-inch
JAMIE (1333 "We Belong Together") 15-25 67

NEW SOCIETY
Singles: 7-inch
GRAMOPHONE 4-8 65
RCA 4-8 66-67
LPs: 10/12-inch
RCA 10-15 66

NEW SOCIETY BAND
LPs: 10/12-inch
ELECTRIC LEMON 10-12 71

NEW SOULS
Singles: 7-inch
WINLEY 5-10 67

NEW STRING-A-LONGS
Singles: 7-inch
J-OHN 4-8 66
Also see STRING-A-LONGS

NEW SURVIVORS
Singles: 7-inch
SCEPTER (12227 "Pickle Protest") ... 4-8 68

NEW TESTAMENT
Singles: 7-inch
FUN CITY 4-8 67

NEW THINGS
Singles: 7-inch
ACCENT (1228 "Dumbo") 20-30 67

NEW TOKENS
(Tokens)
Singles: 7-inch
DOWNTOWN 4-8 85
Also see TOKENS

NEW TONES
Singles: 7-inch
DOT 4-8 64

NEW TRADITION
Singles: 7-inch
CAPITOL 4-6 69
U.A. 4-8 69

NEW TRAVELERS
Singles: 7-inch
YELLOW SAND 5-10 64

NEW TWEEDY BROTHERS
Singles: 7-inch
DOT (16910 "Good Time Car") 15-25 66
LPs: 10/12-inch
RIDON (234 "The New Tweedy Brothers") 1000-1500 66
(With hex cover.)

NEW US
Singles: 7-inch
JA BAR 10-20 60s

NEW VAUDEVILLE BAND P&R/LP '66
Singles: 7-inch
FONTANA 3-6 66-68
LPs: 10/12-inch
FONTANA 10-15 67

NEW VENTURES: see VENTURES

NEW WANDERERS
Singles: 7-inch
READY (1001 "Let Me Render My Service") 40-50
READY (1006 "This Man in Love") 40-50

NEW WAVE
Singles: 7-inch
CANTERBURY 4-8 67
LPs: 10/12-inch
CANTERBURY 10-20 67

NEW WORLD
Singles: 7-inch
RAK 3-5 72-73

NEW WORLD CONGESTION
Singles: 7-inch
ATCO 8-12 69
COULEE 10-15 68
Picture Sleeves
COULEE 20-30 68

NEW WORLD CONGREGATION
Singles: 7-inch
ATCO (6667 "My World Is Empty Without Your") 5-10 68
COULEE (123 "My World Is Empty Without You") 10-15 68
(First issue.)

NEW WORLD SOUL CHOIR
Singles: 7-inch
UNI 3-5 70

NEW YORK CITI PEECH BOYS R&B/D&D '83
Singles: 12-inch
GARAGE 4-6 83-84
ISLAND 4-6 83-84
Singles: 7-inch
ISLAND 3-4 83-84
LPs: 10/12-inch
ISLAND 5-8 84
Also see PEECH BOYS

NEW YORK CITY P&R/R&B/LP '73
Singles: 7-inch
CHELSEA 3-5 73-75
LPs: 10/12-inch
CHELSEA 10-15 73-77
Also see CADILLACS
Also see FIVE SATINS

NEW YORK CITY BAND
Singles: 7-inch
AMERICAN INT'L 3-5 79

NEW YORK COMMUNITY CHOIR R&B '77
Singles: 7-inch
RCA 3-5 77

NEW YORK DOLLS LP '73
Singles: 7-inch
MERCURY 3-5 73-76
Picture Sleeves
MERCURY 4-8 73
LPs: 10/12-inch
MERCURY (675 "New York Dolls") 20-25 73
MERCURY (1001 "Too Much, Too Soon") 15-20 74
REACH OUT INT'L 5-10 81
Members: David Johansen; Jerry Nolan; Arthur Kane; Johnny Thudners; Sylvain Sylvain.
Also see JOHANSEN, David
Also see SYLVAIN, Sylvain
Also see W.A.S.P.

NEW YORK FLYERS
Singles: 7-inch
EVA-TONE 3-5 82

NEW YORK PORT AUTHORITY
LPs: 10/12-inch
INVICTUS 8-10 77

NEW YORK ROCK & ROLL ENSEMBLE
(New York Rock Ensemble)
Singles: 7-inch
ATCO 4-8 67-69
LPs: 10/12-inch
ATCO 10-15 68-70
COLUMBIA 8-12 70-72

NEW YORK ROCK EXCHANGE
Singles: 7-inch
U.A. 4-8 68

NEW YORK SOUNDS
Singles: 7-inch
RED BIRD (10,060 "Drag Street") 8-12 66

NEW YORK THREE
Singles: 7-inch
AESOP'S 4-8 66

NEW YORK THRUWAY
Singles: 7-inch
MGM 4-8 69

NEW YORKERS P&R '61
Singles: 7-inch
WALL (547 "Miss Fine") 15-25 61
WALL (548 "Tears in My Eyes") 15-25 61
Members: Fred Parris; Richard Freeman; Wesley Forbes; Louis Peebles; Silvester Hopkins.
Also see FIVE SATINS

NEW YORKERS
Singles: 7-inch
PARK AVE (100 "I Know Why") 50-75 61

NEW YORKERS
Singles: 7-inch
TAC-FUL (101 "You Shold Have Told Me") 25-50 64
TAC-FUL (102 "There's Going to Be a Wedding") 12-25 65

NEW YORKERS
Singles: 7-inch
DECCA 5-10 69
JERDEN 8-12 68-69
SCEPTER 5-10 67
Members: Bill Hudson; Brett Hudson; Mark Hudson.
Also see HUDSON BROTHERS

NEW YORKERS
(With Horace Ott & Orchestra)
Singles: 7-inch
W.B. (7318 "Lonely") 5-10 69

NEW YORKERS 5
(With Jessie Powell & His Band; New Yorker's 5)
Singles: 78 rpm
DANICE 50-100 55
Singles: 7-inch
DANICE (801 "Gloria My Darling") 150-250 55
Members: J.R. Bailey; Shelly Dupont; Fred Barksdale; Rocky Smith.
Also see BAILEY, J.R.
Also see POWELL, Jesse

NEW YOUNG HEARTS *R&B '70*
Singles: 7-inch
ZEA (50001 "The Young Hearts Get Lonely Too") 4-6 70
Also see YOUNG HEARTS

NEWBAG, Johnny
Singles: 7-inch
ATLANTIC 5-10 66
PORT 10-20 65

NEWBEATS *P&R/LP '64*
Singles: 7-inch
ABC 3-5 74
HICKORY 4-8 64-72
PLAYBOY 3-5 74
EPs: 7-inch
HICKORY (120-005 "Bread and Butter") 20-30 65
(Compact 33. Promotional issue only.)
LPs: 10/12-inch
HICKORY (LP-120 "Bread and Butter") 25-45 65
(Monaural.)
HICKORY (LPS-120 "Bread and Butter") 75-125 65
(Stereo.)
HICKORY (LP-122 "Big Beat Sound") 25-45 65
(Monaural.)
HICKORY (LPS-122 "Big Beat Sound") 50-75 65
(Stereo.)
HICKORY (LP-128 "Run Baby Run") 25-45 65
(Monaural.)
HICKORY (LPS-128 "Run Baby Run") 50-75 65
(Stereo.)
Members: Larry Henley; Dean Mathis; Mark Mathis.
Also see DEAN & MARC
Also see HENLEY, Larry

NEWBERRY, Booker, III *R&B/D&D '83*
Singles: 12-inch
BOARDWALK 4-6 83
Singles: 7-inch
BOARDWALK 3-4 83
OMNI 3-4 86

NEWBERRY 4
Singles: 7-inch
MOOK (196 "That's Why

NEWBORN
LPs: 10/12-inch
TOMORROW (132 "Newborn") 5-10 77

NEWBORN, Calvin
Singles: 7-inch
ASTRO (765 "Buckwheat Cakes") 5-10

NEWBURY, Mickey *P&R/LP '71*
Singles: 7-inch
ABC/HICKORY 3-5 77-79
AIRBORNE 3-4 88
ELEKTRA 3-5 71-73
HICKORY (1312 thru 1463) 4-8 65-67
HICKORY (1600 series) 3-4 80
MCA 3-5 79
MERCURY 3-6 69-70
RCA 3-6 68-70
Picture Sleeves
RCA 3-6 68
LPs: 10/12-inch
ABC/HICKORY 5-10 77-79
MCA 5-8 79
ELEKTRA 8-10 71-75
MERCURY (4024 "After All These Years") 5-8 81
MERCURY (61236 "Looks Like Rain") 10-12 69
RCA 8-12 68-72

NEWBURY PARK
Singles: 7-inch
CREAM 3-5 71
LPs: 10/12-inch
CREAM 8-12 71

NEWBY, Diana
Singles: 7-inch
KAPP 4-8 65

NEWBY & JOHNSON
Singles: 7-inch
MERCURY 4-6 70

NEWCITY ROCKERS *P&R '87*
Singles: 7-inch
CRITIQUE 3-4 87
Picture Sleeves
CRITIQUE 3-4 87

NEWCLEUS *R&B '83*
Singles: 12-inch
SUNNYVIEW 4-6 83-86
Singles: 7-inch
SUNNYVIEW 3-4 83-86
LPs: 10/12-inch
SUNNYVIEW 5-8 84-86

NEWCOMERS
Singles: 7-inch
GIGOLO 5-10 65

NEWCOMERS *P&R/R&B '71*
Singles: 7-inch
STAX 3-5 71
TRUTH 3-5 74-75
VOLT 4-8 69
Members: Terry Bartlett; Bert Brown; William Sumlin.
Also see BAR-KAYS
Also see KWICK

NEWDAY
Singles: 7-inch
ON TOP 10-20

NEWELL, Skip, & Mustangs
Singles: 7-inch
TREND (4107 "Roadrunner") 15-25 63
Also see RIGHTEOUS BROTHERS

NEWHART, Bob *LP '60*
LPs: 10/12-inch
HARMONY 10-15 69
W.B. (1300 thru 1500 series) 20-30 60-65
W.B. (1600 thru 1700 series) 15-25 66-67

NEWKIRK, Bob
Singles: 7-inch
CLINTON 4-8 61-62
PHILIPS 4-6 62-69

NEWLEY, Anthony *P&R '60*
Singles: 7-inch
KAPP 4-6 69
LONDON 4-8 58-63
MGM 3-5 71-74
RCA 4-8 66-67
U.A. 3-5 76-77
W.B. 4-6 68
LPs: 10/12-inch
BELL 8-10 71
LONDON 10-20 62-66
MGM 8-12 71-73
RCA 10-20 64-69
U.A. 5-10 77

NEWLYWEDS
Singles: 7-inch
HOMOGENIZED SOUL (601 "Love Walked Out") 1500-2500 61

NEWLOOK
Singles: 7-inch
TRX 4-8 68

NEWMAN, Carl
Singles: 7-inch
JET (802 "Until I'm with You") 25-50
MAR-VEL (2350 "Rockin' and Boppin' ") 150-200 62
TRIO (849 "Tom-Tom") 15-25 60
(Also issued as by the Rockin' Rebels.)
Also see ROCKING REBELS

NEWMAN, David "Fathead"
Singles: 7-inch
ATLANTIC (2554 "Yesterday") 4-6 68
ATLANTIC (5002 "Hard Times") 8-12 59
LPs: 10/12-inch
ATLANTIC (1304 "Ray Charles Presents David 'Fathead' Newman") 40-60 59
ATLANTIC (1366 "Straight Ahead") 30-50 60
ATLANTIC (1399 "Fathead Comes On") 25-40 61
ATLANTIC (1505 "Bigger and Better") 10-15 68
RIVERSIDE (327 "Sounds of the Wide Open Spaces") 25-50 60
(Monaural.)
RIVERSIDE (1178 "Sounds of the Wide Open Spaces") 35-55 60
(Stereo.)
Also see McDUFF, Brother Jack, Quintet, & David Newman

NEWMAN, Floyd
Singles: 7-inch
STAX (143 "Frog Stomp") 10-20 64

NEWMAN, Herb, & Co.
Singles: 7-inch
HAPPY TIGER 4-6 69

NEWMAN, Jeanne
Singles: 7-inch
PHILLIPS INT'L 5-10 61

NEWMAN, Jimmy *C&W '54*
(Jimmy C. Newman; with Cajun Country)
Singles: 78 rpm
DOT 5-15 54-57
Singles: 7-inch
DECCA 3-8 60-71
DOT (Except 15766) 5-15 54-57
DOT (15766 "Carry On") 50-75 58
LA LOUISANNE 4-6 73
MGM 5-10 58-60
MONUMENT 3-5 72
PLANTATION 3-5 76-80
SHANNON 3-5 73
EPs: 7-inch
DECCA 5-10 64
LPs: 10/12-inch
CROWN 8-12 60s
DECCA 10-25 62-70
DELTA 5-8 82
DOT (3000 series) 30-40 60s
DOT (25000 series) 20-25 60s
LA LOUISANNE 5-10 73
MGM 25-35 59-62
PICKWICK/HILLTOP 8-12
PLANTATION 5-10 77-81
SWALLOW 5-8

NEWMAN, Jimmy C., Danny Davis & Nashville Brass
Singles: 7-inch
RCA 3-4 80
Also see DAVIS, Danny
Also see NEWMAN, Jimmy C.

NEWMAN, Randy *LP '71*
Singles: 78 rpm
REPRISE (0284 "I Think It's Gonna Rain Today") 8-10 78
(Promotional issue only.)
Singles: 7-inch
CHELSEA 3-5 74
DOT 4-8 62
REPRISE (Except 0771) 3-6 68-88
REPRISE (0771 "Last Night I Had a Dream") 10-20 68
W.B. 3-5 77-85
Picture Sleeves
REPRISE 3-4 88
W.B. 3-5 78
LPs: 10/12-inch
EPIC (147 "Peyton Place") 20-30 65
(TV Soundtrack.)
REPRISE (Except 6286) 5-10 70-88
REPRISE (6286 "Randy Newman") 15-20 68
(Cover pictures Randy in sweater and coat.)
REPRISE (6286 "Randy Newman") 10-15 68
(Cover picture is a close-up of Randy.)
W.B. 5-10 77-85
Also see BISHOP, Stephen
Also see EAGLES
Also see ELLIOTT, Ron
Also see McVIE, Christine
Also see RONSTADT, Linda
Also see SEGER, Bob

NEWMAN, Randy, & Paul Simon / Randy Newman *P&R '83*
Singles: 7-inch
W.B. 3-5 83
Picture Sleeves
W.B. 3-5 83
Also see NEWMAN, Randy
Also see SIMON, Paul

NEWMAN, Ted *P&R '57*
Singles: 78 rpm
REV 20-30 57
Singles: 7-inch
RCA (7251 "Hey Little Freshman") 10-20 58
REV (3505 "Plaything") 10-20 57
REV (3511 "I Double Dare You") 10-20 57

NEWMAN, Terri Sue *C&W '79*
Singles: 7-inch
TEXAS SOUL 3-5 79

NEWMAN, Thunderclap *P&R '69*
Singles: 7-inch
MCA 3-4 80s
TRACK (2000 series) 4-8 69-70
TRACK (60000 series) 3-5 75
LPs: 10/12-inch
ATLANTIC/TRACK 10-20 70
MCA/TRACK 5-10 73
Members: Andy Newman; Jimmy McCulloch; Speedy Keen.
Also see KEEN, Speedy
Also see McCARTNEY, Paul

NEWMAN, Tony
Singles: 7-inch
PARROT 4-8 68

NEWMAN, Wayne
Singles: 7-inch
NEW RANK 4-8

NEWMARKS
Singles: 7-inch
CHATTAHOOCHEE (627 "Why") 50-100 63

NEWMOANHEY
Singles: 7-inch
FOGGY MOUNTAIN 3-5 70
LPs: 10/12-inch
CAPITOL 10-15 70

NEWPORT NOMADS
Singles: 7-inch
PRINCE (6304 "Blue Mallard") 20-30 62

NEWPORTERS
Singles: 7-inch
SCOTCHTOWN (500 "Adventures in Paradise") 30-40 63
Members: Scott Engel; John Stewart.
Also see ENGEL, Scott, & John Stewart

NEWPORTS
Singles: 7-inch
MAP (2527 "Dream") 100-200 58
(Identification number shown since no selection number is used.)

NEWPORTS
Singles: 7-inch
AVENUE D (0018 "I Dreamt I Dwelt in Heaven") 4-6 93
(Black vinyl.)
AVENUE D (0018 "I Dreamt I Dwelt in Heaven") 10-15 93
(Pink swirl vinyl. Reportedly 100 made.)
AVENUE D (0020 "My Movie Queen") 4-6 94
(Black vinyl.)
AVENUE D (0020 "My Movie Queen") 8-12 94
(Gray vinyl.)
CRYSTAL BALL (134 "Denise") 5-8 80
GUYDEN (2067 "If I Could Tonight") 15-25 62
GUYDEN (2116 "Tears") 15-25 64
KANE (007 "If I Could Tonight") 50-75 62
(First issue.)

NEWPORTS
Singles: 7-inch
KENT (380 "The Wonder of You") 20-30 62

NEWPORTS
Singles: 7-inch
PARROT 8-12 66

NEWPORTS
Singles: 7-inch
LAURIE (3327 "The Trouble Is You") 10-20 66

NEWPORTS
Singles: 7-inch
IMAGE 5-10 78
Members: LiCalsi; Pace; Ed Engel.

NEWPORTS (With Sax Kari Show): see KARI, Sax

NEWS
Singles: 7-inch
COLOSSUS 3-5 70s
LPs: 10/12-inch
NEWS 10-15 74
Members: Michelle Montayne; Jeff Fortgang; Vic Machcinski.

NEWSHOUNDS
Singles: 7-inch
RAGUN (001 "Press Conference") 4-8 81
(Red vinyl.)

NEWSOM, Chubby *R&B '49*
(With Her Hip Shakers; with Lee Allen)
Singles: 78 rpm
DELUXE 15-25 49
MILTONE 15-25 49
Singles: 7-inch
WINLEY (216 "Toodle Luddle Baby") 25-40 57
Also see ALLEN, Lee
Also see GAYTEN, Paul

NEWSOME, Bobby *R&B '72*
Singles: 7-inch
SPRING 4-6 72

NEWSOME, Frankie *R&B '69*
Singles: 7-inch
GWP (515 "My Lucky Day") 4-6 69
U.S.A. (911 "Taunting Love") 5-10 68
W.B. (8056 "We're on Our Way") 4-6 74
Also see PARKER, Willie

NEWSOME, Jimmy
Singles: 78 rpm
MGM (11849 "Do That Thing") 15-25 54
MGM (55005 "Long Gone Lonesome Blues") 10-15 55
Singles: 7-inch
MGM (11849 "Do That Thing") 25-35 54
MGM (55005 "Long Gone Lonesome Blues") 15-25 55

NEWTON, Bobby
Singles: 7-inch
MERCURY 4-6 69
Also see BLOUNT, Tina, & Bobby Newton

NEWTON, Holder
(With the Apes; with Pygmies)
Singles: 7-inch
CAPITOL 5-10 61

NEWTON, Jim
Singles: 7-inch
KENOVA 4-8 64

NEWTON, Johnny, & Tags
Singles: 7-inch
BELL 10-15 59

NEWTON, Juice *P&R '78/C&W '79*
Singles: 7-inch
CAPITOL 3-5 78-84
RCA 3-4 84-89
Picture Sleeves
CAPITOL 3-5 81-83
RCA 3-4 84
LPs: 10/12-inch
CAPITOL 5-10 78-84
RCA 5-8 84-87
Also see RABBITT, Eddie, & Juice Newton

NEWTON, Juice, & Silver Spur *C&W '76*
Singles: 7-inch
CAPITOL 3-5 77
RCA 3-5 75-76
LPs: 10/12-inch
CAPITOL (11000 series) 8-10 77
CAPITOL (16000 series) 5-8 81
RCA (1000 series) 8-12 75
RCA (4000 series) 5-8 81
Also see NEWTON, Juice

NEWTON, Ronnie
Singles: 7-inch
ARMONEER (1003 "Workingman Blues") 200-300

NEWTON, Ted
Singles: 7-inch
SALEM (530 "Tennessee Rhythm") 50-100

NEWTON, Wayne *P&R/LP '63*
Singles: 7-inch
ARIES II 3-5 79-80
CAPITOL (Except 5338) 4-8 63-71
CAPITOL (5338 "Comin' on Too Strong") 10-20 64
(With Bruce Johnston & Terry Melcher.)
CHALLENGE 4-8 64
CHELSEA 3-5 72-76
GEORGE (7777 "Little White Cloud That Cried") 10-15 62
MGM 3-6 68
20TH FOX 3-5 78
W.B. 3-5 70-77
Picture Sleeves
CAPITOL 4-8 65-66
LPs: 10/12-inch
AIRES II 5-8 79-80
CAMDEN 5-10 74
CAPITOL (573 "Wayne Newton") 15-25 70
(Three-disc set.)
CAPITOL (600 series) 5-10 71
CAPITOL (T-1973 thru T-2847) 10-20 63-68
(Monaural.)
CAPITOL (ST-1973 thru ST-2847) 15-25 63-68
(Stereo.)
CAPITOL (SM-2300 series) 5-8 75
CAPITOL (SPC-3400 series) 5-8
CAPITOL (11000 series) 5-8 79
CAPITOL (16000 series) 5-8 80
CHELSEA 10-15 72-75
MGM 6-12 68-72
MUSICOR 5-8 79
SILVER EAGLE 8-10
20TH FOX 5-8 78
Also see BRUCE & TERRY

NEWTON, Wayne, & Tammy Wynette *C&W '89*
Singles: 7-inch
CURB 3-4 89
Also see NEWTON, Wayne
Also see WYNETTE, Tammy

NEWTON, Wood *C&W '78*
Singles: 7-inch
ELEKTRA 3-5 78-79

NEWTON BROTHERS
(Featuring Wayne)
Singles: 7-inch
CAPITOL (4236 "The Real Thing") 60-80 59
GEORGE (7778 "Little Juke box") 15-20 61
GEORGE (7780 "I Still ILove You") 10-15 61
LAMA (7794 "I Was Born When You Kissed Me") 25-50 63
Members: Wayne Newton; Jerry Newton.
Also see NEWTON RASCALS

NEWTON RASCALS
Singles: 7-inch
RANGER (401 "If the Easter Bunny Knew the Fun He'd Have on Xmas") 15-25 58
(Issued with a paper insert picturing 12-year-old Wayne and 14-year-old Jerry as "The Rascals in Rhythm." Value of insert is about the same as for disc.)
Members: Wayne Newton; Jerry Newton.
Also see NEWTON, Wayne
Also see NEWTON BROTHERS

NEWTON-JOHN, Olivia *P&R/LP '71*
Singles: 12-inch
MCA (Except 1150) 4-6 81-84
MCA (1150 "Twist of Fate") 5-10 83
(Promotional issue only.)
Singles: 7-inch
GEFFEN 3-4 89
KIRSHNER (5005 "Goin' Back") 10-15 70
MCA (Except 40043) 3-5 73-88
MCA (40043 "Take Me Home Country Roads") 5-10 73
RSO 3-5 78
UNI (55281 "If Not for You") 5-10 71
UNI (55304 "Banks of the Ohio") 4-8 71
UNI (55317 "What Is Life") 4-8 72
UNI (55348 "Just a Little Too Much") 8-12 72
Promotional Singles
MCA (1810 "Deeper Than the Night") 30-40 79
(Picture disc. Promotional issue only.)
WHAT'S IT ALL ABOUT 25-50 74
Picture Sleeves
MCA (Except 40418) 3-5 75-88
MCA (40418 "Please Mr. Please") 6-10 75

EPs: 7-inch
MCA 12-15 73
(Promotional issues only.)
LPs: 10/12-inch
GEFFEN.................... 5-8 89
MCA (389 "Let Me Be There")........10-12 73
MCA (411 "If You Love Me, Let Me Know") 12-15 74
(With *I Love You, I Honestly Love You.* Note longer title.)
MCA (411 "If You Love Me, Let Me Know") 8-10 74
(With *I Honestly Love You.* Note shorter title.)
MCA (2000 & 3000 series).............. 8-10 75-78
MCA (5000 & 6000 series).............. 5-8 80-83
MCA (37000 series).................... 5-8 80-83
MFSL (040 "Totally Hot")..............25-50 80
UNI (73117 "If Not for You")...........50-75 71
(Cover depicts a field scene.)
UNI (73117 "If Not for You")...........20-30 71
(Field scene removed from cover.)
Also see DENVER, John, & Olivia Newton-John
Also see FOSTER, David, & Olivia Newton-John
Also see TOMORROW
Also see WILSON, Carl

NEWTON-JOHN, Olivia, & Electric Light Orchestra *P&R/LP '80*
Singles: 7-inch
MCA (41285 "Xanadu").................... 3-5 80
Picture Sleeves
MCA (41285 "Xanadu").................... 3-5 80
LPs: 10/12-inch
MCA (6100 "Xanadu").................... 8-10 80
MCA (10384 "Xanadu")............750-1000 80
(Picture disc. Promotional issue only. Also has Cliff Richard, Gene Kelly, and the Tubes.)
Also see ELECTRIC LIGHT ORCHESTRA
Also see RICHARD, Cliff
Also see TUBES

NEWTON-JOHN, Olivia, & Andy Gibb *P&R '80*
Singles: 12-inch
POLYDOR (104 "Rest Your Love on Me") 10-15 79
Singles: 7-inch
RSO 3-5 80
Also see GIBB, Andy

NEWTON-JOHN, Olivia, & Cliff Richard *P&R '80*
Singles: 7-inch
MCA (51007 "Suddenly").................... 4-6 80
(Custom MCA/Xanadu label. Has artist credit at top, title at bottom.)
MCA (51007 "Suddenly").................... 3-5 80
(Standard MCA label. Has artist credit at bottom, title at top.)
Picture Sleeves
MCA (51007 "Suddenly").................... 3-5 80
Also see RICHARD, Cliff

NEWTON-JOHN, Olivia, & John Travolta *P&R '78*
Singles: 7-inch
RSO 3-5 78
Picture Sleeves
RSO 3-5 78
Also see NEWTON-JOHN, Olivia
Also see TRAVOLTA, John

NEWTONES
Singles: 7-inch
BATON (260 "Remember the Night")....................200-300 58
RELIC (1009 "Remember the Night")....................15-25 65
RELIC (1010 "Come On")..............10-15 65

NEXT EXIT
Singles: 7-inch
SPIRIT.................... 4-8 60s

NEXT FIVE
Singles: 7-inch
DESTINATION (637 "He Stole My Love") 10-20 67
WAND (1170 "Talk to Me Girl")........10-20 68
Members: Steve Thomas; Eric Olson; Mark Buscaglia; Gordon Wayne; Tom Stewart; John Peter; Gary Cooper; John Crook.
Also see TOY FACTORY

NEXT MORNING
LPs: 10/12-inch
CALLAS (2002 "Next Morning") ...50-100 71

NEXT MOVEMENT *R&B '84*
Singles: 7-inch
NUANCE.................... 3-4 84

NEYERLIN, James, & Millionaires
EPs: 7-inch
SUN BURST....................10-12

NEYMAN, June *C&W '78*
Singles: 7-inch
STARSHIP 3-5 78-79

NIC NACKS
Singles: 7-inch
OVATION.................... 4-8 63

NIC NACS
Singles: 78 rpm
RPM (313 "Found Me a Sugar Daddy")....................75-125 50
RPM (316 "Found Me a Sugar Daddy")....................50-100 51
RPM (342 "Found Me a Sugar Daddy")....................40-60 51
Also see ROBINS

NICE *LP '70*
Singles: 7-inch
IMMEDIATE 4-8 68
MERCURY 3-5 70-71
LPs: 10/12-inch
CHARISMA 8-12
COLUMBIA....................8-12
IMMEDIATE 10-15 68-71
MERCURY 10-12 70-72
SIRE....................10-12 75
Members: Keith Emerson; Lee Jackson; Brian Davison; Joe Harriot; Davy O'List.
Also see EMERSON, Keith, & Nice

NICHOLAS, Paul *P&R '77*
Singles: 7-inch
COLUMBIA.................... 3-5 74
RSO 3-5 76-78
LPs: 10/12-inch
RSO 5-10 77

NICHOLLS, Dave, & Coins
Singles: 7-inch
SPARTON (1062 "Bells Will Ring")....................100-200 61
(Canadian.)

NICHOLS, Ann
(With the Bluebirds; with Sentimentals)
Singles: 78 rpm
SITTIN' IN WITH (552 "Let Me Know")....................25-50 50
SITTIN' IN WITH (561 "Those Magic Words")....................25-50 50
Singles: 7-inch
TUXEDO (926 "Lover, I'm Waiting for You")....................25-50 58
Also see CARTER, James, & Sentimentals

NICHOLS, Billy
Singles: 7-inch
SUE.................... 4-8 68

NICHOLS, Joe Paul
(With Four Pennies)
Singles: 7-inch
CIMARRON.................... 4-8 63
CUSTOM.................... 4-8

NICHOLS, Little Al
Singles: 7-inch
STATUE (7004 "You Ought to Be Ashamed") 20-30 70s

NICHOLS, Mann
Singles: 78 rpm
FBC (125 "Walking Talking Blues")....................100-200 49
IMPERIAL (5162 "Get Going").....50-100 49
IMPERIAL (5173 "Worried Life Blues")....................50-100 49

NICHOLS, Mike, & Elaine May *LP '59*
Singles: 7-inch
MERCURY 3-6
LPs: 10/12-inch
MERCURY 15-30 59-72

NICHOLS, Nichelle
Singles: 7-inch
R-WAY 5-8
EPs: 7-inch
AMERICANA (1 "Dark Side of the Moon")....................25-35
(Double EP set.)
LPs: 10/12-inch
EPIC (26351 "Down to Earth") 40-50 68
R-WAY 10-15

NICHOLS, Rick
Singles: 7-inch
SOUND (231 "Infatuation") 5-10
Also see RICKY & LEXINGTONS

NICHOLS, Roger, Trio
(With the Small Circle of Friends)
Singles: 7-inch
A&M 4-6 66-69
LPs: 10/12-inch
A&M 10-15 68
Also see SMALL CIRCLE of FRIENDS

NICHOLSON, J.D.
(With His Jivin' 5)
Singles: 78 rpm
ELKO....................25-35 51
Singles: 7-inch
IMCO (110 "Annie Jo")..............15-25 63

NICK, Ford
Singles: 7-inch
GLENN (3600 "Gamblin' Man")........8-12

NICK & DINO
Singles: 7-inch
IMPACT (1016 "Wish I Was a Kid Again")....................15-25 66

NICK & ELVIS
Singles: 12-inch
COLUMBIA.................... 4-8 84
Members: Nick Lowe; Elvis Costello.
Also see COSTELLO, Elvis
Also see LOWE, Nick

NICK & JAGUARS
Singles: 7-inch
TAMLA (5501 "Cool & Crazy")...200-250 60

NICK & NACKS
Singles: 7-inch
BARRY (108 "The Night") 300-400 64

NICK & STING-RAYS
Singles: 7-inch
MILL-MONT (1628 "You Are So Beautiful")....................200-300 60s

NICKEL
LPs: 10/12-inch
MUSICOR 10-15 71

NICKEL BAG
LPs: 10/12-inch
KAMA SUTRA....................10-15 68

NICKEL REVOLUTION
Singles: 7-inch
PHILIPS (40569 "Oscar Crunch")...25-35 69

NICKELL, Betty
Singles: 7-inch
ABBEY (102 "Hot Dog")..............50-100 58

NICKELS, Joey
Singles: 7-inch
RCA 3-5 74

NICKERSON, Cleve
Singles: 7-inch
SAVOY (1626 "Big Bob")..............10-20 62

NICKIE & NACKS
Singles: 7-inch
CRYSTAL BALL (103 "Linda") 4-8 77

NICKIE & NITELITES
Singles: 7-inch
BRUNSWICK (55155 "Tell Me You Care") 35-45 59
Member: Nick Massi.
Also see MASSI, Nick

NICKIE LEE: see LEE, Nickie

NICKS, Lefty
Singles: 7-inch
NICKTONE (6020 "Model A Ford Blues")....................50-100 58

NICKS, Stevie *LP '81*
Singles: 12-inch
MODERN 4-8 81-86
Singles: 7-inch
MODERN 3-5 81-89
Picture Sleeves
MODERN 3-5 82-89
LPs: 10/12-inch
MFSL (121 "Bella Donna")..........25-35 84
MODERN 5-10 81-89
Also see BUCKINGHAM NICKS
Also see EGAN, Walter
Also see FLEETWOOD MAC
Also see LOGGINS, Kenny, & Stevie Nicks
Also see STEWART, John
Also see STEWART, Sandy

NICKS, Stevie, & Don Henley *P&R '81*
Singles: 7-inch
MODERN 3-5 81
Also see HENLEY, Don

NICKS, Stevie, & Tom Petty & Heartbreakers *P&R '81*
Singles: 7-inch
MODERN 3-5 81-86
Also see PETTY, Tom, & Heartbreakers

NICKS, Stevie, & Sandy Stewart
Singles: 7-inch
MODERN 3-4 83
Also see NICKS, Stevie
Also see STEWART, Sandy

NICKY & NOBLES
Singles: 7-inch
END (1021 "Schoolhouse Rock")....25-35 58
END (1098 "School Day Crush")....10-15 61
GONE (5039 "School Bells")..........40-50 58
(Black label.)
GONE (5039 "School Bells")..........10-15 61
(Multi-color label.)
ROULETTE....................3-5 70s
TIMES SQUARE (37 "School Bells")....................8-12 64
Also see NOBLES

NICKY C. & CHATEAUX
Singles: 7-inch
BAY SOUND (67012 "Try Some Soul")....................50-75 69

NICO
LPs: 10/12-inch
ELEKTRA (74029 "Marble Index") .15-20 68
ISLAND 8-10 75
REPRISE 10-15 70
VERVE (5032 "Chelsea Girl")........25-40 67
(Monaural.)
VERVE (V6-5032 "Chelsea Girl")...35-45 67
(Stereo.)
Also see AYERS, Kevin
Also see MANZANERA, Phil
Also see VELVET UNDERGROUND & NICO

NICOL, Jimmy
(With the Shubdubs; Sound of Jimmy Nicol)
Singles: 7-inch
MAR MAR (313 "Night Train")....100-150 64
(Nicol played drums for the Beatles in 1964, sitting in briefly for a ailing Ringo Starr. Label indicates his involvement with the Beatles.)
PARROT 10-20 65
Also see BEATLES

NICOL & MARSH
LPs: 10/12-inch
CAPRICORN....................8-12 74
Members: Ken Nicol; Peter Marsh.

NICOLE *R&B '85*
Singles: 12-inch
PORTRAIT....................4-6 85-86
Singles: 7-inch
EPIC....................3-4 88
PORTRAIT....................3-4 85-86
LPs: 10/12-inch
PORTRAIT....................5-8 86

NICOLLET, Miss
(Nicollet)
Singles: 7-inch
DECCA....................4-8 62
SHAR 5-10 60

NICOTINE SPYRAL SURFERS
Singles: 7-inch
DIONYSUS 3-4 91
Picture Sleeves
DIONYSUS 3-4 91

NIELSEN, Merlin
Singles: 7-inch
CUCA (6834 "How Long Must I Wait")....................10-15 68

NIELSEN, Ralph, & Chancellors
Singles: 7-inch
CRYPT 3-6
SURF (5302 "Scream")..............100-200 66
Picture Sleeves
CRYPT 4-8

NIELSEN, Shaun *C&W '80*
(Sherrill Nielsen)
Singles: 7-inch
AUDIOGRAPH 3-5 70s
ADONDA....................3-5 80
RCA 3-5 78
SCORPION 3-5 77
LPs: 10/12-inch
AUDIOGRAPH 5-10
MCA 5-10 81
Also see PRESLEY, Elvis

NIELSEN, Spade, & Gamblers
Singles: 7-inch
RCA 4-8 66

NIELSEN - PEARSON *P&R '80*
Singles: 7-inch
CAPITOL....................3-5 80-83
EPIC....................3-5 78
LPs: 10/12-inch
CAPITOL....................5-10 80-81
EPIC....................5-10 78
Members: Reid Nielsen; Mark Pearson.

NEILSEN WHITE BAND *C&W '86*
Singles: 7-inch
VISION....................3-4 86-87
Members: Gary Nielsen; Jack White; Tom Eckhoff.
Also see DILLMAN BAND
Also see TRASHMEN

NIGH TRANES
Singles: 7-inch
CUCA (1012 "Hangover") 15-25 60
Members: Ken Adamany; Jerry Chase; Bob Shebesta; Ron Boyer; Denny Gerg; Frank Ellefson.

NIGHT *P&R/LP '79*
Singles: 7-inch
PLANET....................3-5 79-81
Picture Sleeves
PLANET....................3-5 80-81
LPs: 10/12-inch
PLANET....................5-10 79-80
Members: Chris Thompson; Nicky Hopkins; Derek Austin; Bill Payne; Michael McDonald; Vince Melamed; Steve Porcaro; James Johnson.
Also see THOMPSON, Chris, & Night

NIGHT, Johnny
Singles: 7-inch
APRIL (223 "Secret Place") 15-25 59

NIGHT, Rocky
Singles: 7-inch
PEARL (708 "Teenage Bop").....100-200 57

NIGHT BEATS
Singles: 7-inch
SOUND (100 "Exotic")....................5-10 60
Also see EL RAY & NIGHT BEATS
Also see NOBLEMEN
Also see ROLLETTES ORCHESTRA

NIGHT BEATS
Singles: 7-inch
CUCA (1001 "Johnny B. Goode") ..10-20 59
Picture Sleeves
CUCA (1001 "Johnny B. Goode") ..15-25 59
Member: Dick Lodholz; Jim Drwek; Paul Pritzl; Dick Sternberg; Ken Heldt..

NIGHT BEATS
Singles: 7-inch
NEWLAND (4005 "Night Beat") 8-12

NIGHT CAPS
Singles: 7-inch
CHESS (1694 "Haunted Sax").......15-25 58
BRYTE (307 "Wildcat")..............10-20 62

NIGHT CAPS
Singles: 7-inch
ARC (1181 "Keep on Runnin' ") 20-30 60s

NIGHT CRAWLERS
Singles: 7-inch
MAAD (1566 "You Say")..............10-20 66

NIGHT CRAWLERS
Singles: 7-inch
SHADOW (101 "Let's Move") 20-30 66

NIGHT DREAMERS
Singles: 7-inch
FROGDEATH....................10-15 66

NIGHT HAWKS
Singles: 7-inch
STARS (550 "You're My Baby").....20-30 57

NIGHT HAWKS
Singles: 7-inch
DEL-FI (4122 "Big Top")..............10-20 59

NIGHT HAWKS
Singles: 7-inch
ALON (9001 "Rockin' Hawk").........10-20 62

NIGHT HAWKS
Singles: 7-inch
PACIFIC (352 "Bunny Ride") 8-12

NIGHT OWLS
LPs: 10/12-inch
NRC (15 "Loop the Hoop")............10-15 58

NIGHT OWLS
Singles: 7-inch
CLIMAX (103 "Stompin' ")..............10-15 59

NIGHT OWLS
Singles: 7-inch
VALMOR (14 "Be My Guest")..........5-10 62
VALMOR (14 "Be My Guest")..........10-15 62
(Single-sided. Promotional issue only.)
LPs: 10/12-inch
VALMOR (79 "Twistin' the Oldies") 25-40 62

NIGHT OWLS
Singles: 7-inch
CUCA (1075 "Waitin' by the School") 15-25 62
(5206 "The Country Inn") 15-25 60s
(No label name used.)
Also see ALLEN, Dick, & Fairlanes

NIGHT OWLS
Singles: 7-inch
BETHLEHEM (3087 "Bells Ring")..15-20 64

NIGHT OWLS
Singles: 7-inch
MICHELLE (916 "Muddy") 10-20 64

NIGHT PASTOR & SEVEN FRIENDS
LP: 10/12-inch
CLAREMONT (672 "Music to Lure Pigeons By")....................15-20 67
Member: Dick Ruedebush.

NIGHT PATROL
Singles: 7-inch
SPOTLITE....................15-25 60s

NIGHT PEOPLE
Singles: 7-inch
BERMA 5-10 61
OUTLAW 5-10 60s
SEAFAIR (103 "Istanbul")..............15-25 61
Picture Sleeves
SEAFAIR (103 "Istanbul")..............20-30 61

NIGHT RAIDERS: see HAWKS, Mickey

NIGHT RANGER *LP '82*
Singles: 7-inch
BOARDWALK....................3-4 83
MCA/CAMEL....................3-4 83-88
Picture Sleeves
MCA/CAMEL....................3-4 84-88
LPs: 10/12-inch
BOARDWALK....................5-10 82
MCA/CAMEL....................5-10 83-88
Member: Jack Blades.
Also see DAMN YANKEES
Also see FAAN BAND

NIGHT RIDERS
Singles: 7-inch
BOBLO (110 "Don't Say") 8-12

NIGHT SHADOWS
(Little Phil & Nightshadows)
Singles: 7-inch
BAJA (4504 "Turned On")..............15-25 67
BANNED (679 "Hot Dog Man").......20-30 66
DOT (16912 "So Much")..............15-25 66
GAYE (3031 "60 Second Swinger")....................20-30 66
NA-R-CO (100 "Station Break").......8-12 60s
NATIONAL (187 "Garbage Man")..10-15 60s
Picture Sleeves
GAYE (3031 "60 Second Swinger") 40-60 66
LPs: 10/12-inch
HOTTRAX (1414 "The Square Root of Two")....................30-40 79
HOTTRAX (1430 "Live at the Spot")....................15-20 81
HOTTRAX (1450 "Invasion of the Acid Eaters")....................10-20 82
ROTT ("Rock Anomaly")..............8-12 88
(Selection number not known.)
SPECTRUM ("The Square Root of Two")....................750-1000 68
(Selection number not known.)
Members: Little Phil Ross; Ronnie Farmer; Charles Spinks; Bobbie Newell.

NIGHT WATCH
Singles: 7-inch
ABC (10862 "Cloud Time")..............10-20 66

NIGHT WINDS
Singles: 7-inch
MGM....................4-8 62

NIGHTBEATS
Singles: 7-inch
ZOOM (002 "Lonesome Road Rock")....................100-125 58
ZOOM (004 "Cryin' All Night") 100-125 58
Members: Peter Ronstadt; Nate Foster; Bert Roberts; Lance Hoops; Don Grossberndt.

NIGHTBIRDS
Singles: 7-inch
TODD...5-10 59

NIGHTCAPS
Singles: 7-inch
MUSICOR (1057 "Nightcap Rock")...10-15 64
VANDAN (3223 "Thunderbird")...10-15 61
VANDAN (3587 "24 Hours")...10-15 61
VANDAN (4280 "Next Time You See Me")...4-8 66
VANDAN (4733 "Wine Wine Wine #2")...4-8 66
VANDAN (7066 "Darlin' ")...10-20 61
VANDAN (7491 "Wine Wine Wine")...10-15 60
(Reissued in 1963 and again in 1966, using the same selection number.)
LPs: 10/12-inch
BARON (Black vinyl)...10-12 80
BARON (Colored vinyl)...15-20 80
VANDAN (8124 "Wine Wine Wine")...100-125 61

NIGHTCAPS
Singles: 7-inch
AMBER...5-10

NIGHTCRAWLERS *P&R '67*
Singles: 7-inch
KAPP (110 "Little Black Egg")...8-12 67
KAPP (709 "Little Black Egg")...5-10 65
KAPP (746 "Basket of Flowers")...5-10 66
KAPP (826 "My Butterfly")...8-12 67
LEE (101 "Cry")...20-30 64
LEE (1012 "Little Black Egg")...10-20 65
MARLIN (1904 "Basket of Flowers")...10-15 66
SCOTT (28 "I Don't Remember")...8-12 66
LPs: 10/12-inch
KAPP (1520 "Little Black Egg")...25-40 67
(Monaural.)
KAPP (3520 "Little Black Egg")...30-50 67
(Stereo.)
Members: Chuck Conlon; Rob Rouse; Sylvan Wells; Tom Ruger; Pete Thomason.
Also see CONLON & CRAWLERS

NIGHTHAWK *R&B '82*
Singles: 7-inch
QUALITY...3-5 82

NIGHTHAWK, Robert *R&B '49*
(With His Nighthawks Band; Nighthawks; Robert McCollum)
Singles: 78 rpm
ARISTOCRAT (413 "Six Three O")...50-75 48
ARISTOCRAT (2301 "Black Angel Blues")...50-75 48
CHESS (1484 "My Sweet Lovin' Woman")...50-75 48
STATES...50-75 53
UNITED (102 "Kansas City Blues")...50-75 51
UNITED (105 "Feel So Sad")...50-75 51
Singles: 7-inch
STATES (131 "The Moon Is Rising")...200-300 53
LPs: 10/12-inch
ROUNDER...5-8
Also see TAYLOR, Hound Dog / Robert Nighthawk / John Littlejohn / Earl Hooker
Also see TAYLOR, Koko

NIGHTHAWKS
Singles: 7-inch
HAMILTON (50006 "All Your Love")...25-35 58

NIGHTHAWKS *LP '80*
LPs: 10/12-inch
ADELPHI...6-12 76-82
ALADDIN (101 "Rock & Roll")...50-75 75
CHESAPEAKE (Black vinyl)...5-10 83
CHESAPEAKE (Colored vinyl)...10-15 83
VARRICK...5-10 83
MERCURY...5-10 80
Members: Mark Wenner; Jim Thackery.
Also see ASSASINS
Also see MOONEY, John, & Jim Thackery
Also see WENNER, Mark, & Switchblade

NIGHTHOPPERS
Singles: 7-inch
AMERICAN INT'L...5-10 59

NIGHTINGALE, Maxine *P&R/R&B/LP '76*
Singles: 7-inch
A&M...3-5 81
HIGHRISE...3-5 82
RCA...3-5 80
U.A....3-5 76
WINDSONG...3-5 79
Picture Sleeves
WINDSONG...3-5 79
LPs: 10/12-inch
HIGHRISE...5-10 82
U.A....5-10 76-79
WINDSONG...5-10 80

NIGHTINGALE, Maxine, & Jimmy Ruffin *R&B '82*
Singles: 7-inch
HIGHRISE...3-5 82
Also see NIGHTINGALE, Maxine
Also see RUFFIN, Jimmy

NIGHTINGALE, Ollie *R&B '71*
Singles: 7-inch
MEMPHIS...3-5 71
PATHFINDER...3-5 78
PRIDE...3-5 72-73
LPs: 10/12-inch
PRIDE...8-12 73
Also see OLLIE & NIGHTINGALES

NIGHTINGALES
Singles: 7-inch
RAY STAR (784 "Love in Return")...15-25 62
TAMPA...10-15 59

NIGHTLIFE UNLIMITED
Singles: 12-inch
CASABLANCA...4-8 79

NIGHTLY RAID
Singles: 7-inch
RESOUND...3-5

NIGHTMARES
Singles: 7-inch
AMERICAN INT'L...5-10 59

NIGHTMARES
Singles: 7-inch
SCEPTER...4-8 65

NIGHTNOISE
LPs: 10/12-inch
WINDHAM HILL...5-8 88

NIGHTRANES
Singles: 7-inch
CUCA (0444 "Rockin' Abe")...15-25 60
Member: Ben Sidran.
Also see SIDRAN, Ben

NIGHTRIDERS
Singles: 78 rpm
SOUND (128 "Never")...15-25 56
Singles: 7-inch
SOUND (128 "Never")...30-40 56

NIGHTRIDERS
Singles: 7-inch
HUNCH...8-12 63
SUE (713 "Pretty Plaid Skirt")...10-20 58
SUE (719 "Lookin' for My Baby")...10-20 59
SUE (731 "Talk to Me Baby")...10-20 60
Also see SMITH, Mel, & Night Riders

NIGHT-RIDERS
Singles: 7-inch
DORE (613 "Big Game Hunter")...8-10 61

NIGHTROCKERS
Singles: 7-inch
ARCO (105 "Junction #1")...15-25 66
Picture Sleeves
ARCO (105 "Junction #1")...25-35 66

NIGHTS
LPs: 10/12-inch
ABC...8-10 77

NIGHTSTREETS *C&W '80*
(Streets)
Singles: 7-inch
EPIC...3-5 80-81
Also see STREETS

NIGHTWALKERS
Singles: 7-inch
JCP (1058 "It'll Only Hurt for a Little While")...20-30 65

NIGHTWALKERS
Singles: 7-inch
VISCOUNTS (4503 "In Our Time") 10-20 60s

NIKITA THE "K"
Singles: 7-inch
W.B. (7005 "Go Go Radio Moscow")...5-10 67

NIKKI & CORVETTES
Singles: 7-inch
BOMP...3-5 80
Picture Sleeves
BOMP...3-5 80
EPs: 7-inch
BOMP...5-10 80
LPs: 10/12-inch
BOMP...5-10 80

NILE, Willie *LP '80*
Singles: 7-inch
ARISTA...3-5 80-81
LPs: 10/12-inch
ARISTA...5-10 80-81

NILES, John Jacob
EPs: 7-inch
CAMDEN...10-20 54
LPs: 10/12-inch
CAMDEN...20-35 54-56
TRADITION...15-20 63

NILES, Johnny
Singles: 7-inch
MERCURY...4-8 63

NILES, Melva
Singles: 7-inch
FRATERNITY...5-10 59

NILLES, Lynn *C&W '77*
Singles: 7-inch
GRT...3-5 77

NILSSON, Harry *P&R/LP '69*
(With the New Salvation Singers; Nilsson)
Singles: 7-inch
POLYDOR...3-4 85
RCA...3-6 67-77
TOWER (100 series)...5-8 64-65
TOWER (500 series)...4-6 69
Picture Sleeves
RCA...3-6 74-77
EPs: 7-inch
RCA (248 "Excerpts from *The Point*)...8-10 71
(Promotional issue only.)
LPs: 10/12-inch
51 WEST...5-8 80s
MUSICOR...8-10 77
PICKWICK...5-10 70s
POLYDOR...5-8 85
RCA (0097 thru 0817, except "APD1" series)...8-12 73-75
RCA ("APD1" series)...10-20 74-75
(Quadrophonic.)
RCA (1003 "The Point")...10-12 71
(With Davy Jones and Mickey Dolenz.)
RCA (1031 thru 3811)...5-10 76-80
RCA (3874 "Pandemonium Shadow Show")...15-20 67
RCA (3956 "Aerial Ballet")...10-20 68
RCA (4197 thru 4717)...8-12 69-72
RAPPLE...8-12 74
SPRINGBOARD...5-10 78
TOWER (5095 "Spotlight")...10-15 69
Promotional LPs
RCA (567 "Scatalogue")...30-40 60s
RCA ("Pandemonium Shadow Show - Boxed Set")...50-75 67
(Includes photos and inserts.)
Also see BO PETE
Also see CHER & NILSSON
Also see DOLENZ, Mickey
Also see FOTO-FI FOUR
Also see JONES, Davy
Also see RIC-A-SHAYS
Also see STARR, Ringo, & Harry Nilsson

NILSSON TWINS
Singles: 78 rpm
CAPITOL...5-10 56
CORAL...5-10 54
Singles: 7-inch
CAPITOL...8-12 56
CORAL...8-12 54

NIMBLE, Jack B.
(With the Quicks)
Singles: 7-inch
DEL-RIO (2303 "Like Keyed")...10-20 61
DEL-RIO (2305 "Nut Rocker")...15-25 62
DOT (16319 "Nut Rocker")...8-10 62

NIMOY, Leonard *LP '67*
Singles: 7-inch
DOT...8-12 67-69
LPs: 10/12-inch
CAEDMON...10-15 70s
DOT...25-50 67-69
JRT ("The Mysterious Golem")...20-40 82
PARAMOUNT...20-40 74
PICKWICK...15-25 60s
SEARS...15-25 60s

NINAPINTA
Singles: 7-inch
DECCA...4-6 66

NINE BELOW ZERO
LPs: 10/12-inch
A&M...5-10 81

NINE INCH NAILS *LP '90*
LPs: 10/12-inch
TVT...5-8 90

9W NORTH
Singles: 7-inch
KIM (104 "Eileen")...75-100 65
(500 made.)

9TH CREATION *R&B '77*
Singles: 7-inch
HILLTAK...3-5 79-80
PRELUDE...3-5 77
LPs: 10/12-inch
PRELUDE...8-10 77
RITE TRACK...10-12

9TH STREET MARKET
Singles: 7-inch
FENTON (2136 "I'm a Baby")...100-150 67

95 SOUTH
Singles: 7-inch
ICHIBAN...3-4 93

95TH CONGRESS
Singles: 7-inch
SUSSEX...3-5 71

98 PER CENT AMERICAN MOM & Apple Pie 1929 Crash Band
LPs: 10/12-inch
LHI...10-15 67

9.9 *P&R/R&B/D&D/LP '85*
Singles: 12-inch
RCA...4-6 85-86
Singles: 7-inch
RCA...3-4 85-86
LPs: 10/12-inch
RCA...5-10 85

999 *LP '80*
Singles: 7-inch
POLYDOR...3-5 81
LPs: 10/12-inch
PVC...5-10 79
POLYDOR...5-10 80-81

1910 FRUITGUM CO. *P&R/LP '68*
Singles: 7-inch
ATTACK...4-8 70
BUDDAH...4-8 67-69
SUPER K...4-8 70
LPs: 10/12-inch
BUDDAH...15-25 68-70
Also see J.C.W. RATFINKS
Also see KASENETZ - KATZ SINGING ORCHESTRAL CIRCUS

1910 FRUITGUM COMPANY / Lemon Pipers
LPs: 10/12-inch
BUDDAH...15-20 68-70
Also see LEMON PIPERS
Also see 1910 FRUITGUM COMPANY

1927 *P&R '89*
Singles: 7-inch
ATLANTIC...3-4 89
Picture Sleeves
ATLANTIC...3-4 89
LPs: 10/12-inch
ATLANTIC...5-8 89
Members: Garry Frost; Eric Weideman; Bill Frost; Charles Cole.
Also see MOVING PICTURES

1929 DEPRESSION
Singles: 7-inch
PROVIDENCE...10-15 60s
Also see CORRENTE, Sal

1959
Singles: 7-inch
BLUE ORCHID...4-6 83
LPs: 10/12-inch
BLUE ORCHID...8-10 83
Members: Jim Foley; David Clawson; Steve Danko; Harlan Ice; Jack Johnson; Johnny Coons; Dave McIntosh; Donna Ice; Janet Nicholas; Bob Smiley; Bill Jean.
Also see FOLEY, Jim
Also see RONNY & JOHNNY
Also see STONE COUNTRY BAND

NINETEEN EIGHTY-FOUR
Singles: 7-inch
KAPP (2003 "Amber Waves")...5-10 69

1984
Singles: 7-inch
U.A....3-5 71

1984 LOVE MACHINE
Singles: 7-inch
ATHENA...5-10 69
MELON...10-20 60s

1994
Singles: 7-inch
A&M...3-5 79
LPs: 10/12-inch
A&M...5-10 78-79

NINJA
Singles
IRON WORKS (1015 "Eye on You")...8-12 86
(Square, logo-picture disc.)
IRON WORKS (1015 "Eye on You")...10-15 86
(Weapon-shaped picture disc.)
IRON WORKS (1015 "Eye on You")...15-25 86
(Two rectangular picture discs.)

NINO & EBB TIDES *P&R '61*
(Nino & Ebb-Tides)
Singles: 7-inch
MADISON (162 "Those Oldies But Goodies")...25-50 61
MADISON (166 "Juke Box Saturday Night")...20-40 61
MALA (480 "Linda Lou")...15-25 64
MARCO (105 "Someday")...50-100 61
MR. PEACOCK (102 "Wished I Was Home")...15-25 61
MR. PEACOCK (117 "Lovin' Time")...15-25 62
MR. PEEKE (123 "Tonight")...15-25 63
RECORTE (405 "Puppy Love")...25-50 58
RECORTE (408 "The Real Meaning of Christmas")...100-125 58
RECORTE (409 "I'm Confessin' ") 25-50 58
RECORTE (413 "I Love Girls")...25-50 58
Member: Nino Aiello.
Also see COLEMAN, Lenny
Also see EBB TIDES
Also see EBBS
Also see WINCHELL, Danny

NINO & EBB TIDES / Miss Frankie Nolan
Singles: 7-inch
MADISON (151 "A Week from Sunday")...10-20 61
Also see NINO & Ebb Tides
Also see NOLAN, Miss Frankie

NINTH STREET BRIDGE
Singles: 7-inch
CECILE (1968 "Wild Illusions")...20-30 68

NINTH STREET BRIDGE
Singles: 7-inch
FENTON (2136 "I'm a Baby")...125-150 60s

NIP & TUCK
Singles: 7-inch
DITTO...5-10 59

NIPTONES
Singles: 7-inch
LORRAINE...10-15 65

NIRVANA
Singles: 7-inch
BELL...4-8 68-69
LPs: 10/12-inch
BELL...15-25 68-69
METROMEDIA...10-20 70

NIRVANA *LP '91*
Singles: 12-inch
DGC (21673 "Smells Like Teen Spirit")...5-10 91
DGC (21707 "Come As You Are")...5-10 92
DGC (21818 "Lithium")...5-10 92
Singles: 7-inch
DGC (19050 "Smells Like Teen Spirit")...4-8 91
DGC (19120 "Come As You Are")...4-8 92
SUB POP (23 "Love Buzz")...50-100 88
(1,000 made.)
SUB POP (73 "Sliver")...15-25 90
(Colored vinyl.)
EPs: 7-inch
TUPELO (8 "Blew")...20-30 89
LPs: 10/12-inch
DGC (24425 "Nevermind")...10-15 91
DGC (24540 "Incesticide")...8-12 92
DGC (24607 "In Utero")...8-12 93
DGC (24727 "Unplugged")...8-12 94
DGC (25105 "From the Muddy Banks of the Wishkah")...8-12 96
DGC/SUB POP (24607 "In Utero")...20-30 93
(Clear vinyl, limited edition.)
MCA (24727 "Unplugged")...8-10 90s
MFSL (258 "Nevermind")...20-25 96
SUB POP (34 "Bleach")...35-50 89
(Colored vinyl.)
SUB POP (34 "Bleach")...15-25 89
(Black vinyl. Includes poster.)
Members: Kurt Cobain; Krist "Chris" Novoselic; Jason Everman; Chad Channing; Dave Grohl; Dave Foster.
Also see LANEGAN, Mark
Also see FOO FIGHTERS

NIRVANA / The Fluid
Singles: 7-inch
SUB POP (97 "Molly's Lips")...10-20 91
(Black vinyl. 3,500 made.)
SUB POP (97 "Molly's Lips")...10-20 91
(Colored vinyl. 4,000 made.)
Picture Sleeves
SUB POP (97 "Molly's Lips")...10-20 91

NIRVANA / Jesus Lizard
Singles: 7-inch
TOUCH & GO (83 "Puss")...5-10 93

NIRVANA / The Melvins
Singles: 7-inch
COMMUNION (25 "Here She Comes Now")...10-15 91
(Black vinyl.)
COMMUNION (25 "Here She Comes Now")...10-15 91
(Colored vinyl.)
Also see NIRVANA

NIRVANA BANANA
Singles: 7-inch
ATLANTIC...4-8 67

NISKER, Scoop
LPs: 10/12-inch
SCOOP NISKER...10-20 70

NITE & LITERS
Singles: 7-inch
VERVE (10256 "Jealous Hearts")...10-15 62

NITE, Norm N., & Fabulous Fortunes
Singles: 7-inch
GLOBE...4-6 71

NITE CAPS
Singles: 7-inch
BRYTE (307 "Wildcat")...10-15 62

NITE CITY
Singles: 7-inch
20TH FOX...3-5 77
LPs: 10/12-inch
20TH FOX...8-10 77

NITE DREAMERS
Singles: 7-inch
ALWIN...5-10 68

NITE HAWKS
Singles: 7-inch
BROOKE (112 "Hawk's Hop")...10-20 59

NITE LITES
Singles: 7-inch
SOUTHERN SOUND (106 "Bust Out")...10-20 61

NITE NIKS
Singles: 7-inch
LAWN (207 "Shawnee")...10-20 62

NITE OWLS
Singles: 78 rpm
COLUMBIA...5-10 48

NITE OWLS
Singles: 7-inch
REMBRANDT...8-12 60s
TAKE 3 (777 "Hip Monkey")...10-20 63
TOP DOG...8-12 66

NITE PEOPLE
Singles: 7-inch
AMSTERDAM (85008 "Hot Smoke and Sassafrass")...15-25 70

NITE RIDERS
Singles: 78 rpm
APOLLO (460 "Say Hey")...10-20 54
MGM...15-25 57
Singles: 7-inch
APOLLO (460 "Say Hey")...25-35 54
CHERRY (7886 "Aleph Beth")...15-25

MGM (12487 "Sittin' Sippin' Coffee")....15-25 57
Member: James "Doc" Starks.
Also see STARKS, Doc, & Nite Riders

NITE RIDERS
Singles: 7-inch
("Tornado") 15-25 60s
(No label name or number shown.)

NITE RIDERS
Singles: 7-inch
RIFF (101 "In My Dream") 50-100

NITE ROCKERS
Singles: 7-inch
RCA (7323 "Oh Baby")....10-20 58
SUPER (003 "Little Mama")....50-100

NITE ROCKERS
Singles: 7-inch
FORTUNE 8-12 62

NITE SOUNDS
Singles: 7-inch
FORTUNE (548 "I Love You with Tender Passion")....25-35 62
FORTUNE (552 "Harem Girl") 10-20 63
Member: Butch Vaden.
Also see DAVIS, Melvin
Also see VADEN, Butch

NITE TRAIN
Singles: 7-inch
ROULETTE 10-20 70

NITE WALKERS
Singles: 7-inch
RUSSELL (43107 "High Class")....20-30 66

NITEBEATS
Singles: 7-inch
PEACH (718 "Teen-Age Lover") 10-20 59

NITEBEATS
Singles: 7-inch
TIDE....10-15 63

NITE-CAPPERS
Singles: 7-inch
PAL (1150 "Out of Sight") 15-25 60s
PAL (9158 "Everything") 15-25 60s

NITECAPS
Singles: 78 rpm
GROOVE....30-60 55
Singles: 7-inch
GROOVE (0134 "A Kiss and a Vow")....100-150 55
GROOVE (0147 "Tough Mama")100-150 56
GROOVE (0158 "Bamboo Rock & Roll")....100-150 56
GROOVE (0176 "Let Me Know Tonight") 100-150 56
Also see DILLARD, Varetta

NITE-CAPS
Singles: 7-inch
FAN JR.... 5-10 61

NITECAPS
LPs: 10/12-inch
FORUM CIRCLE 10-15
SIRE.... 5-10 83

NITEFLYTE P&R/R&B '79
Singles: 7-inch
ARIOLA AMERICA 3-5 79-81
LPs: 10/12-inch
ARIOLA AMERICA 5-10 79-81
Also see JOHNSON, Howard

NITE-LITERS
Singles: 7-inch
SUDDEN (101 "Fat Sally")....20-30 60

NITE-LITERS
Singles: 7-inch
STATUE (601 "Jericho Road") 8-12 70s
STATUE (608 "What's Happening") 8-12 70s
VEE EIGHT (8 "Nervous") 10-15 62
VERVE (10256 "Nervous")....5-10 62
LPs: 10/12-inch
STATUE (6254 "The Nite-Liters")....15-25 76
Members: Johnny Mihalic; Jerry Hood; Thomas Kelly; Jimmy Ellis; Roy Cayson; Charles Watts.
Also see MAHALIC, Johnny

NITE-LITERS P&R/R&B/LP '71
Singles: 7-inch
RCA.... 3-5 71-72
LPs: 10/12-inch
RCA.... 8-12 71-72
Members: Harvey Fuqua; Tony Churchill; Austin Lander; James Baker; Robert Jackson; Leroy Taylor; Robin Russell; Ben Boytel; Roger Voice; James Hall.
Also see NEW BIRTH

NITE-LITES
(With the Rock-A-Fellas)
Singles: 7-inch
SEQUOIA (502 "Lovers Twist")....75-125

NITE-NIKS
Singles: 7-inch
LAWN (207 "Horn Shakin' ") 10-15 63

NITERIDERS
Singles: 7-inch
STAR-BRIGHT (3055 "Just "Call on Me")....15-20 65

NITESOUNDS
Singles: 7-inch
SEAFAIR 5-8 65

NITEWALKERS
Singles: 7-inch
NITE (115 "Corner of the World")...20-30 60s

NITRO LP '89
LPs: 10/12-inch
RHINO.... 5-8 89

NITRO EXPRESS
Singles: 7-inch
BUFFALO.... 4-6

NITTY GRITTY DIRT BAND P&R/LP '67
(Dirt Band)
Singles: 78 rpm
LIBERTY (2889 "Mr. Bojangles") ...20-30 70
(Promotional issue only.)
U.A. (69 "All the Good Times") 20-30 71
(Promotional issue only. Includes script and booklet.)
Singles: 7-inch
LIBERTY (1000 series) 3-5 81-84
LIBERTY (50000 series) 4-8 67-70
U.A. 3-5 71-80
W.B. 3-4 84-86
Picture Sleeves
LIBERTY (1000 series) 3-5 81-84
LIBERTY (50000 series) 8-12 67
U.A. 3-5 71-80
EPs: 7-inch
LIBERTY (37 "Special Radio Interview")....10-15 70
(Promotional issue only. Has paper cover.)
U.A. (69 "All the Good Times") 20-30 71
(Promotional issue only. Includes script and booklet.)
LPs: 10/12-inch
LIBERTY (1100 series) 5-10 81
LIBERTY (3501 "Nitty Gritty Dirt Band")....15-20 67
(Monaural.)
LIBERTY (7501 "Nitty Gritty Dirt Band")....15-25 67
(Stereo.)
LIBERTY (7501 thru 7611)....10-20 67-69
LIBERTY (7642 "Uncle Charlie") 100-125 70
(Gatefold promotional edition. Includes two bonus singles, photos and booklet.)
LIBERTY (LST-7642 "Uncle Charlie")....10-20 70
LIBERTY (LATO-7642 "Uncle Charlie")....5-8
LIBERTY (51146 "Let's Go") 5-8 83
U.A. (117 "Interview") 15-25 75
(Promotional issue only.)
U.A. (UA-LA184 "Stars and Stripes Forever")....10-20 74
U.A. (LWB-184 "Stars and Stripes Forever")....8-10
U.A. (469 "Dream")....8-12 75
U.A. (469 "Dream - Programmers Guide")....15-25 75
(Promotional issue only.)
U.A. (UA-LA670 "Dirt, Silver and Gold")....15-20 76
U.A. (LKCL-670 "Dirt, Silver and Gold")....10-12
U.A.(854 thru 1042) 5-10 78-80
U.A. (5500 series)....8-12 71
U.A. (9801 "Will the Circle Be Unbroken")....30-40 72
(Three-disc set.)
UNIVERSAL (12500 "Will the Circle Be Unbroken, Vol. 2")....10-15 89
W.B. 5-10 84-86
Session: Nicolette Larson; Al Garth; Merle Bregante.
Also see CLEMENTS, Vassar
Also see DENVER, John, & Nitty Gritty Dirt Band
Also see LARSON, Nicolette
Also see SKAGGS, Ricky

NITTY GRITTY DIRT BAND & ROY ACUFF C&W '71
Singles: 7-inch
U.A. 3-5 71
Also see ACUFF, Roy

NITTY GRITTY DIRT BAND, ROSANNE CASH & JOHN HIATT C&W '90
Singles: 7-inch
MCA.... 3-4 90
Also see CASH, Rosanne

NITTY GRITTY DIRT BAND & JIMMY MARTIN C&W '73
Singles: 7-inch
U.A. 3-5 73
Also see MARTIN, Jimmy

NITTY GRITTY DIRT BAND & LINDA RONSTADT
Singles: 7-inch
U.A. 3-5 79
Also see NITTY GRITTY DIRT BAND
Also see RONSTADT, Linda

NITZINGER LP '72
(John Nitzinger)
Singles: 7-inch
CAPITOL.... 4-6 72-73
20TH FOX 3-5 76
LPs: 10/12-inch
CAPITOL....10-15 72-73
20TH FOX....8-10 76
Members: John Nitzinger; Bugs Henderson.
Also see HENDERSON, Bugs

NITZSCHE, Jack P&R '63
Singles: 7-inch
FANTASY.... 3-5 76
MCA.... 3-5 78
REPRISE 4-8 63-65
Picture Sleeves
REPRISE (20,202 "Lonely Surfer") 15-25 63
LPs: 10/12-inch
MCA....8-10 78
REPRISE (2000 series) 8-12 73
REPRISE (6100 series) 15-25 63-64
REPRISE (6200 series) 10-20 66
Also see ALLEY CATS
Also see HALE & HUSHABYES
Also see SINNERS
Also see VERONICA

NIVENS, Pamela R&B '83
Singles: 7-inch
SUN VALLEY 3-5 83

NIX, Billy
Singles: 7-inch
GLENN (Except 1804)....10-20 59-60
GLENN (1804 "Get with the Beat")....50-75 60
MAR-VEL....10-15 63

NIX, Don P&R/LP '71
Singles: 7-inch
CREAM 3-5 76
ELEKTRA....3-5 71
LPs: 10/12-inch
CREAM 5-10 79
ELEKTRA....8-12 71
ENTERPRISE 8-10 73
Also see ALABAMA STATE TROUPERS

NIX, Donnie
Singles: 7-inch
WILROD (1001 "Ain't About to Go Home")....25-35

NIX, Ford, & Moonshiners
Singles: 7-inch
CLIX (621 "Nine Times Out of Ten")....100-200

NIX, Hoyle
Singles: 7-inch
BO-KAY (110 "I Don't Love Nobody")....15-25 60

NIX, Tom C&W '81
Singles: 7-inch
RMA....3-4 80-81

NIX, Willie
(With His Combo; the Memphis Blues Boy)
Singles: 78 rpm
CHANCE (1163 "Nervous Wreck")....100-200 53
CHECKER (756 "Truckin' Little Woman")....100-200 52
RPM (327 "Lonesome Bedroom Blues")....100-200 51
SABRE (104 "Just Can't Stay")....75-125 53
SUN (179 "Baker Shop Boogie")....400-500 53
Singles: 7-inch
CHANCE (1163 "Nervous Wreck")....300-500 53
SABRE (104 "All By Yourself") ..250-400 53

NIXON, Elmore
(With Henry Hayes; with His Hadacol Boys)
Singles: 78 rpm
IMPERIAL 15-25 55
LUCKY 15-25 49
MERCURY 15-25 51
PEACOCK....15-25 50
POST 15-25 55
SAVOY....15-25 52-54
SITTIN' IN WITH 15-25 50-51
Singles: 7-inch
IMPERIAL (5388 "You Left Me")....20-40 55
MERCURY (70061 "Playboy Blues")....30-50 51
POST (2008 "Don't Do It")....20-40 55
SAVOY....20-40 52-54
Also see HAYES, Henry

NIXON, Juanita
Singles: 7-inch
HAWK (150 "I Met My Sugar in a Candy Store")....10-15
KING....5-10 60

NIXON, Julie
Singles: 7-inch
COLUMBIA (45628 "Scuffle") 5-10

NIXON, Mel
Singles: 7-inch
JANUS 8-12

NIXON, Mojo, & Skid Roper LP '87
Singles: 7-inch
ENIGMA....3-5 87-89
LPs: 10/12-inch
ENIGMA....5-8 87-89

NIXON, Nick C&W '74
Singles: 7-inch
MCA....3-5 79
MERCURY 3-5 74-78
LPs: 10/12-inch
MERCURY 5-10 77
Session: Randy Wright.
Also see WRIGHT, Randy

NIXON, Richard
Singles: 7-inch
CBS/AURAVISION ("Nixon's the One")....10-20 68
(Picture disc postcard.)
LPs: 10/12-inch
CAPITOL (11350 "Resignation of a President")....10-15 74
Also see KENNEDY, John Fitzgerald / Richard M. Nixon

NIXON, Roy, & Down Beats
Singles: 7-inch
DEE-CEE ("Hard-Rockin' Daddy")....75-125
(Selection number not known.)
Members: Roy Nickson; Mel Thomas; Barry Steinberg; Brian Steinberg.

NO DEPOSIT, NO RETURN
Singles: 7-inch
PHILIPS 4-8 67

NO DICE
Singles: 12-inch
EMI (2727 "Come Dancing")....3-6
(Picture disc.)
Singles: 7-inch
CAPITOL....3-5 78
LPs: 10/12-inch
CAPITOL....5-10 78-79

NO HARD FEELINGS
Singles: 7-inch
FRATERNITY....3-6

NO NAME BAND
Singles: 7-inch
SCORPIO (472 "Israeli Stomp") 10-20 63

NO NAMES
Singles: 7-inch
GUYDEN (2114 "Love")....15-25 64

NO NAMES
Singles: 7-inch
TEE PEE (51/52 "Take It from Me")....10-20 68

NO SLACK
LPs: 10/12-inch
MERCURY....5-10 78

NO STRINGS ATTACHED
Singles: 7-inch
ACCENT 4-8 68

NOACK, Eddie C&W '58
Singles: 78 rpm
MERCURY 10-20 55
STARDAY....10-25 54-57
TNT....15-25 54
Singles: 7-inch
ALLSTAR....3-4
D (1019 "Have Blues, Will Travel") 10-20 58
D (1037 "Walk 'Em Off")....30-50 59
D (1060 "A Thinking Man's Woman")....10-20 59
D (1094 "Relief Is Just a Swallow Away")....10-20 59
D (1100 series)....5-10 59-61
D (1200 series)....3-8 61-72
K-ARK....4-6 69
MERCURY....15-25 55
STARDAY....15-25 54-57
TNT (110 "Too Hot to Handle")....20-30 54
TNT (1010 "Too Hot to Handle")....20-30 54
WIDE WORLD 3-5 70
LPs: 10/12-inch
WIDE WORLD 10-20 70

NOAH
Singles: 7-inch
DUNHILL....3-5 72
LPs: 10/12-inch
DUNHILL....8-12 72

NOAH'S ARC
Singles: 7-inch
MEDICAL (6081 "NASA, Fly Me to the Moon")....3-5
(Includes insert flyer.)
Members: Charley Bogdonoff; Pam Fox; Chris Vadala; Bubba Clark; Buddy Charlton; Tommy Hannum; John Robinson; Danny Gatton; Gant Kushner; Paul Allen; Steve Wolf; John Murphy; Thad Culbreath; Roy Reed; Marie Keitt; Debbie St. Ours.
Also see GATTON, Danny

NOAH'S ARK
Singles: 7-inch
DECCA....5-10 67
Members: Ron Elliott; Buddy Richardson.

NOAH'S ARK
Singles: 7-inch
ROULETTE....4-8 66
Member: Ron Dante.
Also see DANTE, Ron

NOAH'S ARK
Singles: 7-inch
LIBERTY 4-6 70
Member: Rodney Justo.

NOAH'S DOVE
Singles: 7-inch
PICCADILLY 5-10 67

NOAKES, Rab
LPs: 10/12-inch
W.B.....8-10 74

NOBELLS
Singles: 7-inch
MAR (101 "Cryin' Over You")....100-150 62

NOBELMEN
Singles: 7-inch
BEE (1826 "Vibration") 15-25 67

NOBELS
Singles: 7-inch
CUCA (6375 "Tossing & Turning") 10-20 63

NOBLE, Beverly
Singles: 7-inch
RALLY (502 "Better Off Without You")....8-12 65
SPARROW 5-10

NOBLE, Eddy
Singles: 7-inch
TOP HAT (1002 "There Go Frankie")....15-25

NOBLE, Gail
Singles: 7-inch
DFD 4-8 64

NOBLE, Johnny
Singles: 7-inch
VEEP 4-8 66

NOBLE, Kitty
Singles: 78 rpm
HERALD....10-15 54
Singles: 7-inch
HERALD (422 "Can't See Nobody But You")....15-25 54
MAY....5-10 62

NOBLE, Nick P&R '55
Singles: 78 rpm
MERCURY 5-15 56-57
WING....5-10 55-56
Singles: 7-inch
CAPITOL....3-5 73
CHESS....5-10 63-64
CHURCHILL....3-5 77-80
COLUMBIA 4-6 69
CORAL....8-12 59-66
DATE 4-6 67-68
EPIC 3-5 77
FRATERNITY....10-20 58
GONE (5039 "School Day Crush")....20-30 58
LIBERTY....4-8 62-63
MERCURY 10-20 56-57
TMS....3-5 79
20TH FOX....4-8 65
WING....10-15 55-56
LPs: 10/12-inch
COLUMBIA 8-12 69
LIBERTY....10-15 63
WING....15-25 60

NOBLE, Nick, & Lew Douglass C&W '79
Singles: 7-inch
TMS....3-5 79
Also see NOBLE, Nick

NOBLE, Nita
Singles: 7-inch
ACE 4-6

NOBLE KNIGHTS
Singles: 7-inch
COTILLION 3-5 69
Session: King Curtis.
Also see KING CURTIS

NOBLEMEN
Singles: 7-inch
PROFILE (4012 "Dirty Robber")....20-40 60
USA (1002 "Thunder Wagon")....30-45 59
(USA logo has no periods on this label.)
U.S.A. (1213 "Thunder Wagon")....20-30 63
U.S.A. (1222 "Dirty Robber") 15-25 63
Members: Brand Shank; Chuck Lalicata; Bob Stange; Jerry Sworske; Bruce Rudan; Raymond Ojeda.
Also see NIGHT BEATS

NOBLEMEN
Singles: 7-inch
GOLDEN GATE 8-12 60

NOBLEMEN
Singles: 7-inch
EPIC 4-8 64

NOBLEMEN
Singles: 7-inch
PRISM (1930 "She Still Thinks I Love Her")....10-20 65

NOBLEMEN
Singles: 7-inch
IGL (130 "Things Aren't the Same")....20-40 67
CJL (101 "Stop Your Running Around")....10-15 67

NOBLEMEN
Singles: 7-inch
PARIS TOWER (110 "Two-Faced Woman")....20-30 67

NOBLEMEN
Singles: 7-inch
CLARITY (103 "Everytime") 30-50

NOBLEMEN / Toni Majestro
Singles: 7-inch
U.S.A. (1215 "Sleep Beauty Sleep")....20-30 63
(Not the same group of Noblemen as heard on other U.S.A. issues.)

NOBLEMEN 4
Singles: 7-inch
RECAP (291 "What's Your Name")....50-75 60s
RECAP (292 "I Can Hear Raindrops")....50-75 60s

NOBLES
Singles: 78 rpm
SAPPHIRE....25-50 56

Singles: 7-inch
SAPPHIRE (151 "Do You Love Me")..........75-125 56

NOBLES
Singles: 7-inch
KLIK (305 "Poor Rock 'N Roll") ..100-200 57
LOST-NITE..........4-6 70s
TIMES SQUARE (1 "Poor Rock 'N Roll")..........10-20 60
(Colored vinyl.)
TIMES SQUARE (12 "Crime Don't Pay")..........10-20 63
(Colored vinyl.)
TIMES SQUARE (33 "Why Be a Fool")..........10-15 64
Members: Dick Bernardo; Pat Cosenza; Sal Tramauche; Joey Kakulis.
Also see NICKY & NOBLES

NOBLES
Singles: 7-inch
ABC-PAR (9984 "Standing Alone")..........15-25 58
ABC-PAR (10012 "Just for Me")..........15-25 58

NOBLES
Singles: 7-inch
STACY (926 "You Ain't Right")..........25-35 62
Member: Sollie McElroy.
Also see McELROY, Sollie

NOBLES
Singles: 7-inch
SELBON (1005 "Black Widow")..........20-30 63

NOBLES
Singles: 7-inch
U.S.A. (788 "Marlene")..........15-25 64
Also see CHICK & NOBELS

NOBLES
Singles: 7-inch
MARQUIS (4991 "Something Else")..........20-30 66

NOBLES, Cliff P&R/R&B/LP '68
(Cliff Nobels & Co.)
Singles: 7-inch
ATLANTIC (2352 "My Love Is Getting Stonger")..........45-65 66
ATLANTIC (2380 "Everybody Is Weak for Sombody")..........10-15 67
PHIL L.A. of SOUL..........4-8 68-69
JAMIE..........3-6 72
ROULETTE..........3-6 73
LPs: 10/12-inch
MOON SHOT (601 "Pony the Horse")..........15-25 60s
PHIL L.A. of SOUL (4001 "The Horse")..........15-25 68
Also see MFSB

NOBLETONES
Singles: 7-inch
C&M (182 "I Love You")..........30-60 58
C&M (182 "Who Cares About Love")..........25-50 58
(Same number used twice.)
C&M (188 "I'm Crying")..........25-50 58
RELIC..........4-8
TIMES SQUARE (17 "I Love You")..........10-15 63
(Colored vinyl.)
TIMES SQUARE (18 "Who Cares About Love")..........10-15 63
VINTAGE..........3-5 73
Member: Dottie Watkins.

NOBODYS
Singles: 7-inch
SAMAR..........4-8 67

NOBODY'S CHILDREN
Singles: 7-inch
BULLET..........5-10 68
U.A. (50090 "Junco Partner")..........15-25 67

NOBODY'S CHILDREN
Singles: 7-inch
GPC (1944 "Good Times")..........10-20 67

NOBODY'S CHILDREN
Singles: 7-inch
DELTA (2207 "St. James Infirmary")..........20-30 60s

NOC-A-BOUTS
Singles: 7-inch
COSMIC (706 "Session")..........10-20 58

NOCERA R&B '86
Singles: 7-inch
SLEEPING BAG..........3-4 86-87

NOCTURNAL DAYDREAM
Singles: 7-inch
COCONUT GROOVE (2039 "Had a Dream Last Night")..........30-50 60s

NOCTURNALS
Singles: 7-inch
BAT (101 "Twister's Stomp")..........15-25 62
REVIVE (101 "Twister's Stomp")..........10-15 63
REVIVE (104/5 "Stag Line")..........10-20 64
Member: Mike Metko; Tom Waldrup; Jack Griffin; Bill Caldwell; Stan Seymore.
Also see VANCE, Chico

NOCTURNALS
Singles: 7-inch
EMBASSY..........4-8 67

NOCTURNES
Singles: 7-inch
KAREN (1009 "Sh-Boom")..........10-20 60

NOCTURNES
("Featuring Dana Powers")
Singles: 7-inch
CARLSON INT'L (4105 "My Christmas Star")..........50-100 64

NOCTURNES
Singles: 7-inch
CUCA (6373 "Cyclone")..........10-20 63
CUCA (64103 "Little One")..........10-20 64
SOMA (1108 "Hot Night")..........15-25 59
Picture Sleeves
CUCA (64103 "Little One")..........15-25 64

NOCTURNS
Singles: 7-inch
FONTANA..........5-10 65
LTD..........5-10 66

NODAENS
Singles: 7-inch
GOLD (1001 "Beach Girl")..........50-75 60s
Member: Dave Nowlen.
Also see SURVIVORS

NOE, Dale
Singles: 78 rpm
SMART..........10-20 52
Singles: 7-inch
SMART (1016 "Hound Dog Boogie")..........20-40 52

NOEL
Singles: 7-inch
TOWER..........4-6 69

NOEL C&W '82
(Noel Haughey)
Singles: 7-inch
DEEP SOUTH..........3-4 82
MADD CASH..........3-4 85

NOEL P&R '87
(Noel Pagan)
Singles: 7-inch
4TH & BROADWAY..........3-4 87-88
VIRGIN..........3-4 79
Picture Sleeves
4TH & BROADWAY..........3-4 87-88
VIRGIN..........3-4 79
LPs: 10/12-inch
4TH & BROADWAY..........5-8 88

NOEL, Dick
Singles: 7-inch
CUCA (1301 "Little Lost Angel")..........10-15 65
FRATERNITY..........5-10 57
LIBERTY (55254 "Sugar Beat")..........10-15 60

NOEL, Didi
Singles: 7-inch
BLUE CAT..........5-10 66

NOEL, Nancy
Singles: 7-inch
FIREBIRD..........3-5 80

NOEL, Norm
Singles: 7-inch
NOMAR..........5-10 60

NOEL, Sid
Singles: 78 rpm
ALADDIN (3331 "Flying Saucer")..........10-20 56
Singles: 7-inch
ALADDIN (3331 "Flying Saucer")..........20-30 56

NOGUEZ, Jacky, & His Orchestra P&R '59
Singles: 7-inch
JAMIE..........4-8 59-60
Picture Sleeves
JAMIE..........8-10 60
LPs: 10/12-inch
JAMIE..........10-20 60

NOIE, Denny
(With 4th of Never; with Catalinas)
Singles: 7-inch
KNIGHT (100 "Dee Dee")..........15-25 65
TENER (150 "Dee Dee")..........10-15 67
Also see CATALINAS

NOISEMAKERS
Singles: 7-inch
ASTRA (102 "Zoobie")..........10-15 61
(Black vinyl.)
ASTRA (102 "Zoobie")..........15-25 61
(Colored vinyl.)
SWIRL INT'L (2 "Zoobie")..........15-20 61

NOISES & SOUNDS
Singles: 7-inch
PICCADILLY..........5-10 66

NOLAN: see PORTER, Nolan

NOLAN, Frankie
(Miss Frankie Nolan)
Singles: 7-inch
ABC-PAR (10231 "I Still Care")..........25-35 61
(With Frankie Valli.)
Also see NINO & Ebb Tides / Miss Frankie Nolan
Also see VALLI, Frankie

NOLAN, Kenny P&R '76
Singles: 7-inch
CASABLANCA..........3-5 79-80
DOT..........4-8 68
FORWARD..........4-8 69
HIGHLAND..........4-8 68
LION..........3-5 72
MGM..........3-5 71
POLYDOR..........3-5 78
20TH FOX..........3-5 76-77
LPs: 10/12-inch
CASABLANCA..........5-10 79
MCA..........5-10 82
POLYDOR..........5-10 78
20TH FOX..........5-10 77

NOLAND, Terry
Singles: 7-inch
BRUNSWICK (55010 "Hypnotized")..........20-30 57
Singles: 7-inch
APT..........10-15 62
BRUNSWICK (55010 "Hypnotized")..........25-50 57
BRUNSWICK (55036 "Patty Baby")..........15-25 57
BRUNSWICK (55054 "Look at Me")..........20-30 58
BRUNSWICK (55069 "Everyone But Me")..........20-30 58
BRUNSWICK (55092 "There Was a Fungus Among Us")..........20-30 58
BRUNSWICK (55122 "Guess I'm Gonna Fall")..........10-20 59
CORAL (62274 "There Was a Fungus Among Us")..........10-15 61
LPs: 10/12-inch
BRUNSWICK (54041 "Terry Noland")..........200-250 58
Also see FREED, Alan

NOLANS
LPs: 10/12-inch
EPIC..........5-10 82

NOLEN, Bob
Singles: 7-inch
FARO..........5-10 59

NOLEN, Jimmy
Singles: 78 rpm
ELKO..........20-40 55
FEDERAL..........10-15 55
IMPERIAL..........10-15 55
Singles: 7-inch
ELKO (254 "Slow Freight Back Home")..........50-75 55
FEDERAL..........15-25 55
IMPERIAL..........15-25 55

NOLEN, Lloyd
Singles: 7-inch
KING..........4-8 62

NOLEN & CROSSLEY
GORDY..........3-5 81-82
LPs: 10/12-inch
GORDY..........5-10 81-82
Members: Curtis Nolen; Ray Crossley.

NOMADS
Singles: 7-inch
SOMA (1112 "Ryders in the Sky")..........15-25 59
SOMA (1415 "Ryders in the Sky")..........10-15 64

NOMADS
Singles: 7-inch
BALBOA..........10-15 59
JOSIE..........10-20 59-63
NORTHERN (503 "Heart Attack")..........150-200 59

NOMADS
Singles: 7-inch
ABC-PAR..........5-10 61
GENIE..........5-10 61
PHAROS..........5-10 64
RUST..........5-10 61

NOMADS
Singles: 7-inch
KEL (1000 "You Come Around")..........15-25 65
Members: Jack Litjens; Mike Yanke; Joe Litjens; Larry Wolfe.

NOMADS
Singles: 7-inch
SOFT (958 "I Saw You Go")..........10-20 65
SPOTLIGHT (5019 "Be Nice")..........20-25 66
Picture Sleeves
SPOTLIGHT (5019 "Be Nice")..........25-35 66
Also see YELLOW PAYGES

NO-MADS
Singles: 7-inch
BATTLE of the BANDS (201,353 "Liverpool Lover")..........15-25 66

NOMADS
Singles: 7-inch
STARK (009 "Not for Me")..........20-30 66
TORNADO (159 "Thoughts of a Madman")..........25-35 67

NOMADS
Singles: 7-inch
MO-GROOV..........5-10 67
Members: Sonny Threatt; Phyllis Brown; Andy McKinney; Hugg Martin; Carroll Cox; Darrel McClinton.
Also see SONNY & PHYLLIS
Also see TANGENTS

NOMADS
Singles: 7-inch
DAMON (1 "Cry Baby")..........15-25 67
(Canadian.)
DAMON (2 "Dizzy Miss Lizzy")..........15-25 67
(Canadian.)
DAMON (3 "Come on Now")..........15-25 67
(Canadian.)
DAMON (4 "Hey Joe")..........15-25 67
(Canadian.)
DAMON (101 "I Walk Alone")..........15-25 67
(Canadian.)
MAINSTREAM..........10-20 60s
(Canadian.)
ORBIT (1121 "Three O'Clock")..........15-25 68
LP: 10/12-inch
POINT (333 "Hits of the Nomads")..........30-50 60s
Also see SMOKE

NOMADS
Singles: 7-inch
DISCOTEK..........10-15 60s
PRELUDE (1112 "Last Summer Day")..........20-30 60s
SAMTER..........10-15 60s

NOMADS
Singles: 7-inch
DERBY..........8-12
J&S..........8-12

NON CONFORMISTS
Singles: 7-inch
SCEPTER (12184 "Two-Legged Big-Eyed Canary")..........15-25 67

NO-NA-MEES
Singles: 7-inch
ERA (3165 "Gotta Hold On")..........10-20 66

NOON EXPRESS
Singles: 7-inch
EMBASSY (1970 "Flashback")..........15-25 67

NOONAN, Steve
LPs: 10/12-inch
ELEKTRA..........10-15 68

NOONE, Peter
Singles: 7-inch
BELL..........4-6 71-72
CASABLANCA..........4-6 73-75
PHILIPS..........4-6 73
LPs: 10/12-inch
JOHNSON..........5-10 82
Also see FANKHAUSER, Merrell
Also see HERMAN'S HERMITS

NORDINE, Ken
Singles: 7-inch
DOT..........8-12 58-59
LPs: 10/12-inch
BLUE THUMB..........8-12 72
DECCA (8550 "Concert in the Sky")..........40-50 57
DOT (3075 thru 3301)..........30-50 57-60
(Monaural.)
DOT (25115 thru 25301)..........30-50 58-60
(Stereo.)
DOT (25880 "Best of Word Jazz") 10-20 67
HAMILTON (102 "Voice of Love") 20-30 59
(Monaural.)
HAMILTON (12102 "Voice of Love")..........30-40 59
(Stereo.)
SNAIL..........8-10
PHILIPS..........15-25 67
Also see VAUGHN, Billy

NOREEN & DONNA
Singles: 7-inch
CARLTON..........5-10 60

NORELKOS
Singles: 7-inch
KINGSWOOD (102 "Tell Me Baby")..........300-500 61

NORELL, Jerry
Singles: 7-inch
AMY..........5-10 61
BRUNSWICK..........10-15 59
HAMILTON..........10-20 59
KAMA..........4-8 62
Also see JAY, Morty

NORFLEET BROTHERS
Singles: 7-inch
RUSH..........8-12 61
EPs: 7-inch
JERICO..........15-25 61

NORFLEET COUSINS
Singles: 7-inch
GEMINI STAR..........4-8 68
Also see NORFLEET BROTHERS

NORLEEN, Mari
Singles: 7-inch
BIG M..........4-8 62

NORM & TOBY
Singles: 7-inch
ENCORE..........4-8 62

NORMA D&D '83
(Norma Lewis)
Singles: 12-inch
ERC..........4-6 83

NORMA & LINDA
Singles: 7-inch
FABOR (4039 "Stop Right Here Where You Are")..........10-20 58
RADIO..........10-20 58

NORMA JEAN C&W '64
(Norma Jean Beasler-Taylor)
Singles: 7-inch
COLUMBIA..........5-10 58-62
RCA..........3-8 63-72
RIVERSIDE..........4-8 63
LPs: 10/12-inch
CAMDEN..........8-15 68-71
HARMONY..........10-15 66
RCA (2961 thru 3977)..........20-30 64-67
RCA (4060 thru 4695)..........12-25 68-72
Also see BARE, Bobby, Liz Anderson & Norma Jean
Also see GRAY, Claude, & Norma Jean
Also see SOME of CHET'S FRIENDS
Also see WAGONER, Porter

NORMA JEAN R&B/LP '78
(Norma Jean Wright)
Singles: 12-inch
BEARSVILLE (Black vinyl.)..........4-8 79-80
BEARSVILLE (Colored vinyl.)..........10-15 79-80
Singles: 7-inch
BEARSVILLE..........3-5 78-80
LPs: 10/12-inch
BEARSVILLE..........5-10 78
Also see CHIC

NORMAL
Singles: 7-inch
SIRE..........3-5 79

NORMAN, Don
Singles: 7-inch
MGM..........4-8 66

NORMAN, Gene, & Rockin' Rockets
Singles: 7-inch
SNAG (101 "Snaggle Tooth Ann")..........350-450 59

NORMAN, Gene, Group
Singles: 7-inch
GNP..........4-8 66
LPs: 10/12-inch
GNP (2015 "Dylan Jazz")..........10-15 66

NORMAN, Jim C&W '78
Singles: 7-inch
REPUBLIC..........3-5 78

NORMAN, Jimmy P&R/R&B '62
(With the Hollywood Teeners; with Viceroys; with H.B. Barnum; Jimmy Norman / Willie "The Moon Man" Echols)
Singles: 7-inch
DOT (16016 "Green Stamps")..........15-20 59
FUN (101 "A Boy and a Girl")..........10-20 61
FUN (102 "My Thanks")..........10-20 61
GOOD SOUND (105 "Here Comes the Night")..........15-20 61
GOOD SOUND (120 "True Love") 15-20 61
JOSAN (711 "Green Stamps")..........30-40 59
(First issue.)
JOSIE (994 "Gangster of Love")..........5-10 68
LITTLE STAR (113 "I Don't Love You No More")..........8-12 62
LITTLE STAR (121 "I Know I'm in Love")..........8-12 62
MERCURY (72658 "It's Beautiful")..........5-10 67
MERCURY (72727 "I'm Leaving") .20-30 67
MUN RAB (102 "Thank Him")..........10-20 59
POLO (211 "Dotted Line")..........5-10 64
RAY STAR (781 "I'll Never Be Free")..........10-15 61
RAY STAR (783 "One of These Days")..........10-15 62
SAMAR (116 "Can You Blame Me")..........4-8 66
LPs: 10/12-inch
BADCAT..........5-10
Also see BARNUM, H.B.
Also see BERRY, Dorothy, & Jimmy Norman
Also see CHARGERS
Also see COASTERS
Also see DUDLEY
Also see DYNA-SORES
Also see HARLEM RIVER DRIVE

NORMAN, Jimmy, & O'Jays
Singles: 7-inch
LITTLE STAR (126 "Love Is Wonderful")..........10-20 63
Also see NORMAN, Jimmy
Also see O'JAYS

NORMAN, Joey
Singles: 7-inch
WARRIOR..........5-10 60

NORMAN, Larry
Singles: 7-inch
CAPITOL..........4-8 70
MGM..........3-5 72-73
PHYDEAUX..........3-5 81
RCA..........3-5 73
SOLID ROCK..........3-5 76
VERVE..........3-5 72
Picture Sleeves
PHYDEAUX..........3-5 81
LPs: 10/12-inch
CAPITOL (446 "Upon This Rock")..........15-25 70
HEART WARMING..........5-8 70s
IMPAC..........8-12
MGM..........10-20 73
MYRRH..........5-8 80s
ONE WAY..........10-20 70-71
SOLID ROCK..........8-10 78
STREET LEVEL..........8-12
SUNRISE..........8-10
VERVE..........10-15 72
Also see FLIES
Also see PEOPLE

NORMAN, Neil
Singles: 7-inch
GNP (486 "Wild Boys")..........8-12 74
GNP (510 "Phaser Laser")..........4-6
GNP (813 "Star Wars")..........4-8 75

NORMAN, Patricia
(With "Music By Moakin")
Singles: 78 rpm
BRUNSWICK..........4-8
VOCALION (4547 "Pluckin' on a Golden Harp")..........4-8
(With "Pluck, pluck, pluckin' " lyrics.)
VOCALION (4547 "Pluckin' on a Golden Harp")..........15-25
(With "F*#ck, f*#ck, f*#ckin' " lyrics.)

NORMAN, Ray
Singles: 7-inch
NASCO....10-20 58

NORMAN, Val
Singles: 7-inch
VALOR (2005 "The Ballad of Barbara Graham")....10-15 59

NORMAN, Zack
Singles: 7-inch
POPLAR (111 "Hey Doll")....100-200 62

NORMANAIRES
Singles: 78 rpm
MGM (11622 "My Greatest Sin")....20-30 53
Singles: 7-inch
MGM (11622 "My Greatest Sin")....40-60 53

NORNETTS
Singles: 7-inch
WAND....4-8 64

NORRIS, Bob
(Bobby Norris)
Singles: 7-inch
CAPITOL (3945 "I Went Rockin' ") 20-30 58
CASCADE (5907 "Party Time")..100-150 59
NAME (1 "Yellow Pages")....10-15 60

NORRIS, Bobbe
Singles: 7-inch
COLUMBIA....4-6 66
Picture Sleeves
COLUMBIA....4-6 66
LPs: 10/12-inch
COLUMBIA....10-15 66

NORRIS, Charles
Singles: 78 rpm
ATLANTIC (994 "Messin' Up")....20-30 52
Singles: 7-inch
ATLANTIC (994 "Messin' Up")....30-50 52

NORRIS, Dennis
Singles: 7-inch
JEWEL....4-8 64

NORRIS, Joe
Singles: 7-inch
SOMA (1001 "Rock Out of This World")....200-300 58

NORRIS, Kathi
Singles: 7-inch
STUDIO CITY (1038 "Wise Men Say")....8-12 61

NORRIS the TROUBADOUR
(With the 3 Blue Chips)
Singles: 7-inch
CO-ED....10-20 58-59
MAYHAMS....5-10 61-65
MAYHAMS COLLEGIATE....4-8 68

NORSEMEN
Singles: 7-inch
M&M....10-15 60s
Members: Jim Walden; Bob Liles; Gary Grimes; Chris Riley.
Also see JEKYLL & HYDES
Also see VANDALS

NORTH, Angelmaye
Singles: 7-inch
HIGH COUNTRY....4-8 77
Picture Sleeves
HIGH COUNTRY....4-8 77

NORTH, Freddie P&R/R&B '71
Singles: 7-inch
A-BET....5-10 67-69
CAPITOL (4832 "Just to Please You")....10-15 62
CAPITOL (4873 "Just to Please You")....8-12 62
RIC (119 "The Hurt")....20-30 64
MANKIND....3-6 71-76
PHILLIPS INT'L (3574 "Don't Make Me Cry")....10-20 61
UNIVERSITY (605 "How to Cry")....10-20 60
LPs: 10/12-inch
A-BET....10-15
MANKIND....8-12 71-75
PHONORAMA....5-8 84

NORTH, Ian
LPs: 10/12-inch
CACHALOT....10-12 81

NORTH, Jay
Singles: 7-inch
KEM (2557 "Little Boy Blues")....5-10 60
LPs: 10/12-inch
COLPIX (204 "Dennis the Mennace")....25-35 60
KEM (27 "Look Who's Singing")....20-30 60

NORTH, Nicki
Singles: 7-inch
CANADIAN AMERICAN....4-8 62

NORTH ATLANTIC INVASION FORCE: see: NAIF

NORTHCOTT, Tom P&R '68
Singles: 7-inch
UNI....3-5 71
W.B.....4-8 67-69
LPs: 10/12-inch
UNI....8-12 71

NORTHERN LIGHT P&R '75
Singles: 7-inch
COLUMBIA....3-5 75
GLACIER....3-5 75-77

NORTHERN LIGHTS: see COLE, Fred E

NORTHWEST COMPANY
Singles: 7-inch
GRENADIER (1 "Hard to Cry")....20-30 60s

NORTON, Gene
Singles: 7-inch
BRAND X....5-10 61

NORTON, Hal
Singles: 7-inch
TREND (003 "Hocus Pocus")....30-50 58

NORTON BUFFALO: see BUFFALO, Norton

NORTONES
Singles: 7-inch
STACK....5-10 60
W.B.....10-15 59

NOR-TRONS
Singles: 7-inch
CUCA (1104 "Hey There")....15-25 62

NORVELLS
Singles: 7-inch
CHECKER (1037 "As I Walk Alone")....10-20 63

NORVUS, Nervous: see NERVOUS NORVUS

NORWOOD R&B '87
Singles: 7-inch
MAGNOLIA....3-4 87

NORWOOD, Dorothy R&B '73
(With the Norwood Singers)
Singles: 7-inch
GRC....3-5 72-75
JEWEL....3-5 78
SAVOY....4-8 63-69
LPs: 10/12-inch
JEWEL....5-10 78
SAVOY....8-18 63-83

NOTABLES
Singles: 7-inch
BIG TOP (3141 "Surfside")....5-10 63
(Issued first on Capitol by Digger Revell & Denvermen. Reissued a couple of weeks later on Big Top.)
Also see REVELL, Digger, & Denvermen

NOTATIONS
Singles: 7-inch
CLARITY (106 "On the Other Side of the World")....100-150
JASON SCOTT....4-8
WONDER (100 "What a Night for Love")....150-250 58

NOTATIONS R&B '70
Singles: 7-inch
C.R.A.....3-5 73
GEMIGO....3-5 75-76
MERCURY....3-5 77
SUE....4-8 69
TAD....5-8 68
TWINIGHT....3-5 70
LPs: 10/12-inch
GEMIGO....8-12 76
Members: Clifford Curry; Bobby Thomas; Lasalle Matthews; Jimmy Stroud; Walter Jones.
Also see CURRY, Clifford

NOTATIONS
Singles: 7-inch
BEVERLY (1555 "Miserlou")....25-35 60s
CAMELOT (101 "Ram Charger")....20-25 60s

NOTEABLES
Singles: 7-inch
RIBBON (6908 "Tonto")....15-20 60

NOTEABLES
Singles: 7-inch
SOUND CITY....4-8 69

NOTEMAKERS
Singles: 7-inch
SOTOPLAY (007 "Do I Have a Chance")....300-450 58
(Previously issued on Sotoplay's 006, credited to the Webs.)
Also see WEBS

NOTES
Singles: 78 rpm
CAPITOL....50-100 56
MGM....50-75 56
Singles: 7-inch
CAPITOL (3332 "Don't Leave Me Now")....150-250 56
MGM (12338 "Trust in Me")....100-150 56

NOTES
Singles: 7-inch
SARG (177 "Little Girl")....30-40 61
Member: Charlie England.

NOTES FROM THE UNDERGROUND
Singles: 7-inch
VANGUARD (35073 "Down in the Basement")....5-10 68
LPs: 10/12-inch
VANGUARD (6502 "Notes from the Underground")....50-100 68
WING (16337 "Psychedelic Visions")....75-100 67

NOTE-TORIALS
Singles: 7-inch
IMPALA (201 "My Valerie")....500-1000 59
(First issue.)
SUNBEAM (119 "My Valerie")....100-200 59

NOTORIOUS NOBLEMEN
Singles: 7-inch
BEDELL (80405 "If I Needed Someone")....40-60 67
IGL (130 "Night Rider")....40-60 67

NOTTING HILLBILLIES LP '90
LPs: 10/12-inch
W.B.....5-8 90

NOVA
LPs: 10/12-inch
ARISTA....5-10 77-78

NOVA, Aldo P&R/LP '82
Singles: 12-inch
PORTRAIT....5-8 82
(Black vinyl.)
PORTRAIT (1427 "Fantasy")....15-20 82
(Picture disc. Promotional issue only.)
Singles: 7-inch
PORTRAIT....3-4 82
Picture Sleeves
PORTRAIT....3-4 82
LPs: 10/12-inch
PORTRAIT....5-10 82-83
Also see CHEAP TRICK / Aldo Nova / Saxon

NOVA, Ars: see ARS NOVA

NOVA LOCAL
Singles: 7-inch
DECCA (32138 "Games")....10-20 67
DECCA (32194 "Other Girls....10-20 67
LPs: 10/12-inch
DECCA (74977 "Nova 1")....30-50 68
Members: Joe Mendyk; Randy Winburn; Ken Schinhan; Jim Opton; Bill Levasseur.
Also see BETTER DAYS

NOVAC
LPs: 10/12-inch
EMBRYO....8-10

NOVAS P&R '65
Singles: 7-inch
MEAN MOUNTAIN (1427 "The Crusher")....4-8 70s
(Canadian.)
PARROT (45005 "The Crusher")....30-50 64
TWIN TOWN (713 "Novas Coaster")....25-35 65

NOVAS
Singles: 7-inch
S.T.A.R. (001 "And It's Now")....25-35 66

NOVAS IX
Singles: 7-inch
ABC....4-8 68
HERITAGE (8876 "Pain")....8-12 68

NOVA-TONES
Singles: 7-inch
ROSCO (417 "Walk on the Surfside")....20-30 63

NOVELLE, Jay D&D '84
Singles: 12-inch
EMERGENCY....4-6 84

NOVELLS
LPs: 10/12-inch
MOTHERS (73 "A Happening")....30-40 68
Members: Bob Archer; Ed Benson; Chip Moore; Terry Tibbets.

NOVEMBER GROUP
Singles: 12-inch
A&M....4-6 85

NOVO COMBO LP '81
Singles: 7-inch
POLYDOR....3-5 82
LPs: 10/12-inch
POLYDOR....5-10 81-82
Member: Mike Shrieve.
Also see SANTANA

NOVY, Len
LPs: 10/12-inch
ATCO....8-12 69

NOVY, Len & Judy
LPs: 10/12-inch
PRESTIGE....10-20 65
Also see NOVY, Len

NO-YZ
LPs: 10/12-inch
AZRA (112 "Sheer Electronic Den")....15-20 83
(Promotional only picture disc. 500 made.)

NOW
Singles: 7-inch
COTILLION....3-6 68

NOW
Singles: 7-inch
MIDSONG INT'L....3-5 79
LPs: 10/12-inch
MIDSONG INT'L....5-10 79

NOW GENERATION
LPs: 10/12-inch
SOMERSET....10-15 68

NOWHEREFAST
LPs: 10/12-inch
SCOTTI BROS....5-10 82

NOWLIN, Ernie
Singles: 7-inch
MISSOURI (640 "Tally Ho")....40-60

NU BEATS
Singles: 7-inch
SOMA (1159 "Carlotta")....25-35 61

NU KATS
LPs: 10/12-inch
RHINO....8-10 80

NU LUVS
(Nu Luv's; Nu-Luvs)
Singles: 7-inch
CLOCK (2003 "Baby You Belong to Me")....25-50 65
MERCURY (72569 "Take My Advice")....5-10 66

NU ROMANCE CREW R&B '87
Singles: 7-inch
EMI AMERICA....3-4 87

NU SHOOZ P&R/R&B/LP '86
Singles: 7-inch
ATLANTIC....3-4 86-88
Picture Sleeves
ATLANTIC....3-4 86-88
LPs: 10/12-inch
ATLANTIC....5-8 86-88
Members: Valerie Day; John Smith.

NU SOUNDS & GARY RAY
Singles: 7-inch
LINCOLN....8-12 67

NU TORNADOS P&R '58
Singles: 7-inch
CARLTON (492 "Philadelphia U.S.A.")....10-15 58
CARLTON (497 "Let's Have a Party")....6-12 58
FELSTED (8577 "Cry, Baby, Cry")....6-12 59
Members: Ed Dono; Phil Dale; Tom Dell; Louie Mann; Mike Perna.

NUANCE R&B/D&D '84
(Featuring Vikki Love)
Singles: 12-inch
4TH & BROADWAY....4-6 84-85
Singles: 7-inch
4TH & BROADWAY....3-4 84-85

NUBIN, Katie Bell
LPs: 10/12-inch
VERVE....10-20 61

NUCHEZS
Singles: 7-inch
REMBRANDT (5001 "Open Up Your Mind")....25-35 66
Member: Rick Erickson.
Also see LEMON DROPS

NUCLEAR ASSAULT LP '88
LPs: 10/12-inch
I.R.S.....5-8 88
IN-EFFECT....5-8 89
UNDER ONE FLAG (21 "Survive") 15-20 88
(Picture disc.)

NUCLEAR VALDEZ LP '90
LPs: 10/12-inch
EPIC....5-8 90

NUCLEAR VISION
Singles: 7-inch
LAURIE (3518 "Night Time Child")....8-12 69
SKEE (7771 "Night Time Child")....15-25 69

NUCLEUS
LPs: 10/12-inch
MAINSTREAM (6120 "Nucleus")....40-60 68
Members: Hugh Leggat; Danny Taylor; Bob Horne; John Richardson.
Also see FOOT IN COLD WATER

NUCLEUS
LPs: 10/12-inch
CAPITOL....5-10 79
SIRE....8-10 75

NUDE ANTS
LPs: 10/12-inch
NEW DEAL....5-10 82

NU-DEMENSIONS
Singles: 7-inch
BURDETTE....5-10 67

NUGENT, Ted LP '75
(With the Amboy Dukes; with Brian Howe)
Singles: 7-inch
ATLANTIC....3-5 84-88
DISCREET....3-5 74
EPIC....3-5 76-80
Picture Sleeves
ATLANTIC....3-5 84
LPs: 10/12-inch
ATLANTIC....5-10 82-88
DISCREET....8-10 74
EPIC (Except 607)....8-15 75-81
EPIC (607 "State of Shock")....25-50 79
(Picture disc.)
MAINSTREAM (10-01 "Ted Nugent and the Amboy Dukes")....5-10 82
MAINSTREAM (421 "Ted Nugent and the Amboy Dukes")....8-12
POLYDOR (4035 "Survival of the Fittest")....10-20 71
Also see AMBOY DUKES
Also see BAD COMPANY
Also see DAMN YANKEES
Also see HEAR 'N AID

NUGGETS
Singles: 78 rpm
CAPITOL....5-10 54-56
Singles: 7-inch
CAPITOL....10-20 54-56
Member: Ollie Jones.
Also see CUES
Also see MARTIN, Dean, & Nuggets
Also see SINATRA, Frank

NUGGETS
Singles: 7-inch
RCA (7930 "Before We Say Goodnight")....15-25 61
RCA (8031 "Just a Friend")....8-12 62
Member: Val Poliuto.
Also see CALVANES
Also see HITMAKERS
Also see JAGUARS

NUGGETS
Singles: 7-inch
VINTAGE (1003 "Whisper")....20-25 73
(Colored vinyl.)

NUGGETS R&B '79
Singles: 7-inch
MERCURY....3-4 79
LPs: 10/12-inch
MERCURY....5-10 79

NULL, Cecil
Singles: 7-inch
REVOLVO....8-12 59
Also see CECIL & EMMITT

NULL, Cecil / Rusty Adams
Singles: 7-inch
BRIAR (153 "Wildwood Flower")....5-10
Also see ADAMS, Cecil
Also see NULL, Cecil

NULL, Jimmy, & Inversions
Singles: 7-inch
U.S.A.....5-10 67

NULL SET
Singles: 7-inch
DATE....4-8 66

NU-LUVS: see NU LUVS

NUMA BAND
LPs: 10/12-inch
OVATION....5-10 80

NUMAN, Gary LP '79
(With the Tubeway Army)
Singles: 7-inch
ATCO....3-5 79-81
LPs: 10/12-inch
ATCO....5-10 79-81

NUMBERS
Singles: 7-inch
BONNEVILLE (101 "My Pillow")..75-125 62
DORE (641 "My Pillow")....15-25 62
Also see APOLLO, Johnny

NUMBERS
LPs: 10/12-inch
VOXX....5-8

NUMONICS R&B '84
Singles: 7-inch
HODISK....4-8 84

NUNLEY, BILL C&W '88
(Country Bill Nunley)
Singles: 7-inch
CANNERY....3-4 88

NUNN, Bobby
(With the Robbins)
Singles: 78 rpm
MODERN (807 "Rockin' ")....75-125 51
Also see BYRD, Bobby
Also see COASTERS
Also see FOUR BLUEBIRDS / Johnny Otis & His Orchestra
Also see LITTLE ESTHER & Bobby Nunn
Also see ROBINS

NUNN, Bobby R&B/LP '82
(Bobby Nunn Jr.)
Singles: 7-inch
MOTOWN....3-4 82-84
LPs: 10/12-inch
MOTOWN....5-10 82-84

NUNN, Earl, & His Alabama Ramblers C&W '49
(With Billy Lee)
Singles: 78 rpm
SPECIALTY....5-10 49

NUNNERY, Stu
LPs: 10/12-inch
EVOLUTION....8-10 73

NUNS
LPs: 10/12-inch
BOMP....5-8 81

NURSE, Allan
(Allan Nurse's Blues Band)
Singles: 78 rpm
EBONY....15-25 44
SOUTHERN....15-25 45

NURSERY SCHOOL D&D '83
Singles: 12-inch
EPIC....4-6 83

NUTMEGS R&B '55
Singles: 78 rpm
HERALD....25-50 55-57
Singles: 7-inch
COLLECTABLES....3-4 80s
FLASHBACK....4-8 65
HERALD (452 "Story Untold")....25-50 55
HERALD (459 "Ship of Love")....25-50 55

HERALD (466 "Whispering Sorrows") 25-50 55
HERALD (475 "Key to the Kingdom") 50-75 56
HERALD (492 "A Love So True")...20-40 56
HERALD (538 "My Story") 25-35 59
HERALD (574 "Rip Van Winkle")...10-20 62
LANA....4-8 64
RELIC (528 "Down in Mexico") 5-10 65
RELIC (531 "Let Me Tell You")....5-10 65
RELIC (1006 "Shifting Sands")....5-10 65
TEL (1014 "A Dream of Love")...100-200 60
TIMES SQUARE (6 "Let Me Tell You") 50-75 63
(Colored vinyl.)
TIMES SQUARE (14 "The Way Love Should Be") 25-50 63
TIMES SQUARE (27 "Down in Mexico") 20-30 64
TIMES SQUARE (103 "You're Crying") 20-30 64

EPs: 7-inch

HERALD (452 "The Nutmegs") ..150-250 60

LPs: 10/12-inch

COLLECTABLES....5-10 84
LOST NITE....8-10
RELIC....8-12 70s
Members: Leroy Griffin; Jimmy Tyson; Leroy McNeil; James "Sonny" Griffin; Bill Emery; Ed Martin; Sonny Washburn; Harold Jones.
Also see BALLADS
Also see LYRES
Also see RAJAHS

NUTMEGS / Admirations

Singles: 7-inch

TIMES SQUARE (19 "Down to Earth") 25-50 64
Also see ADMIRATIONS

NUTMEGS / Volumes

Singles: 7-inch

RELIC (535 "Why Must We Go to School") 5-10 65
TIMES SQUARE (22 "Why Must We Go to School") 50-100 63
Also see NUTMEGS
Also see VOLUMES

NUTMEGS

Singles: 7-inch

BABY GRAND....4-8 73
NIGHTRAIN....4-8 73

LPs: 10/12-inch

QUICKSILVER (1001 "Shoo-Wop-A-Doo-Wop") 10-15 79
(Reissue of Strawberry LP.)
STRAWBERRY (6003 "Street Corner Soul") 40-60
YVONNE (609 "Live") 50-100 71
Member: Harry Jaynes.

NUTONES

(Nu-Tones)

Singles: 78 rpm

COMBO (127 "At Midnite") 50-100 56
HOLLYWOOD STAR (797 "Goddess of Love") 500-750 54
(45 rpm not yet known to exist.)
HOLLYWOOD STAR (798 "Annie Kicked the Bucket"/"Believe") 500-750 54
HOLLYWOOD STAR (798 "You're No Barking Dog"/"Believe") 100-200 55

Singles: 7-inch

COMBO (127 "At Midnite") 100-125 56
HOLLYWOOD STAR (798 "Annie Kicked the Bucket") 3000-4000 54
HOLLYWOOD STAR (798 "You're No Barking Dog") 300-500 55
(Same number used twice.)
SPIN-TIME (1001 "Teen-Age Heart") 100-200 59
20TH CENTURY ("Jump, Figaro, Jump") 15-25 50s
(Selection number not known.)

NU-TRENDS

Singles: 7-inch

LAWN (216 "Together") 1000-2000 63

NU-TRONS

Singles: 7-inch

ELDEE (85 "Beat") 10-20 63
FEDERAL (12495 "Tension") 5-10 63

NUTTER, Mayf C&W '70

Singles: 7-inch

CAPITOL....3-5 71-73
GNP....3-5 76-77
REPRISE....3-5 70

LPs: 10/12-inch

CAPITOL....6-12 73
CRESCENDO....5-10 77

NUTTY NED & MARVIN

Singles: 7-inch

ARCH (1812 "The Big Trial") 10-15

NUTTY NOVELTIES

LPs: 10/12-inch

DYNA (105 "Nutty Novelties") 20-30 61

NUTTY SQUIRRELS P&R/R&B '59

Singles: 7-inch

COLUMBIA....5-10 60
HANOVER....5-10 59-60
RCA....4-8 64

Picture Sleeves

COLUMBIA....10-15 60
HANOVER....10-15 59

EPs: 7-inch

HANOVER (301 "Nutty Squirrels") 15-25 60

LPs: 10/12-inch

COLUMBIA....20-25 61
HANOVER (8014 "Nutty Squirrels") 25-35 60

MGM....15-25 64
Also see BURLAND, Sascha, & Skip Jack Choir

NUTZ

LPs: 10/12-inch

A&M....8-12 74-76

NUU KATS

LPs: 10/12-inch

RHINO....5-8 80

NYE, Lonnie

Singles: 7-inch

LO-LON....5-10 60

NYE, Louis

(With the Status Seekers)

Singles: 7-inch

U.A....4-8 61
WIG....5-10 59

LPs: 10/12-inch

RIVERSIDE....15-25 60
U.A....15-25 61
Also see ALLEN, Steve

NYLONS

(Rumblers)

Singles: 7-inch

DOWNEY (109 "Maid-in-Japan") ...10-20 63
Also see RUMBLERS

NYLONS LP '86

Singles: 7-inch

OPEN AIR....3-5 82-87

Picture Sleeves

OPEN AIR....3-5 87

LPs: 10/12-inch

OPEN AIR....5-10 85-87
WINDHAM HILL....5-8 89
Members: Claude Morrison; Marc Connors; Paul Cooper; Arnold Robinson.

NYRO, Laura LP '68

Singles: 7-inch

COLUMBIA....3-6 68-71
VERVE/FOLKWAYS....4-8 66-67
VERVE/FORECAST....4-6 68-69

Picture Sleeves

COLUMBIA....4-8 68

LPs: 10/12-inch

COLUMBIA....5-15 68-84
VERVE/FOLKWAYS....10-20 67
VERVE/FORECAST....10-15 69
Also see LABELLE, Patti

NYTRO R&B '77

Singles: 12-inch

WHITFIELD....4-8 79

Singles: 7-inch

WHITFIELD....3-5 76-79

LPs: 10/12-inch

WHITFIELD....5-10 77-79

O

O

Singles: 7-inch

FEATHERROCK....3-5 70

O., Kenny: see KENNY O.

O. Rodney, & Joe Cooley

Singles: 12-inch

NASTYMIX....4-6 92

O ROMEO D&D '83

Singles: 12-inch

BOB CAT....4-6 83
OH MY....4-6 84
Members: Lorilee Svedberg; Dora Suppes; Terry Weinberg.

O.C. & ALL STARS

Singles: 7-inch

SAVOY (1533 "Stone Down") 15-25 58

O.C. & HOLIDAYS

Singles: 7-inch

W.B. (1019 "The Tuttle") 10-20 58

O.C. the MINUTE MAN

Singles: 7-inch

SOUL POTION....8-12

O.D. CORRAL

LPs: 10/12-inch

WILD WEST....10-15 75

O.K.s

Singles: 78 rpm

SUMMER....15-25 57

Singles: 7-inch

SUMMER (290 "Don't Leave Me Now") 15-25 57

O.M.D. see ORCHESTRAL MANOEUVERS in the DARK

O.R.S.

LPs: 10/12-inch

SALSOUL....5-10 79

OAK P&R '79

Singles: 7-inch

MERCURY....3-5 79-80
Also see PINETTE, Rick, & Oak

OAK RIDGE BOYS C&W '76

(Oak Ridge Quartet; Oaks)

Singles: 7-inch

ABC....3-5 78-79
ABC/DOT....3-5 77
CADENCE....6-12 59
COLUMBIA....3-5 73-79
HEARTWARMING....3-5 71
IMPACT....3-5 71
MCA....3-5 79-90
(Black vinyl.)
MCA (51247 "Sail Away") 25-50 79
(Picture disc. Promotional issue only. Made for Western Merchandiser's 11th Annual Convention.)
RCA....3-4 90-91
W.B....3-8 63

Picture Sleeves

MCA....3-5

LPs: 10/12-inch

ABC....5-10 78-79
ABC/DOT....8-10 77
ACCORD....5-10 81-82
CADENCE (3019 "The Oak Ridge Quartet") 35-55 58
CANAAN....8-15 66
COLUMBIA....5-10 74-83
EXACT....5-10 83
51 WEST....5-8
HEARTWARMING....5-8 71-74
INTERMEDIA....5-8
LIBERTY....5-8
MCA....5-10 80-86
NASHVILLE....8-10 70
OUT of TOWN DIST....5-10 82
PHONORAMA....5-8 83
PICKWICK....5-8 70s
POWER PAK....5-10 70s
PRIORITY....5-10 82
SKYLITE....10-20 64-66
STARDAY....10-20 65
U.A....10-20 66
VISTA....5-8
W.B....10-20 63
Members: William Lee Golden; Duane Allen; Rich Sterban; Joe Bonsall; Steve Sanders; Willie Wynn.
Also see BONSALL, Joe
Also see CASH, Johnny, Carter Family & Oak Ridge Boys
Also see GOLDEN, William Lee
Also see JONES, George
Also see LEE, Brenda, & Oak Ridge Boys
Also see MANDRELL, Barbara, & Oak Ridge Boys
Also see STEVENS, Even
Also see SUMNER, J.D., & Stamps
Also see SWEETWATER
Also see TENNESSEANS

OAKES, Bob, & Sultans

Singles: 78 rpm

REGENT....10-20 56

Singles: 7-inch

REGENT (7502 "Church Bells May Ring") 20-30 56

OAKEY, Philip: see MORODER, Giorgio, & Philip Oakey

OAKLAND, Ben

Singles: 7-inch

NAN....4-8 64

OAKTOWN'S 3-5-7 LP '89

LPs: 10/12-inch

CAPITOL....5-8 89
Also see HAMMER, M.C.

OAS, Holly D&D '84

Singles: 12-inch

DND....4-6 84

OATES, Titus: see TITUS OATES

O'BANION, John P&R/LP '81

Singles: 7-inch

ELEKTRA....3-5 81

LPs: 10/12-inch

ELEKTRA....5-10 81

O'BANION, Sammy, & Features

Singles: 7-inch

DELPHI (0012 "Mistaken Identity") 10-20

OBERLE, Scott

Singles: 7-inch

ATCO....8-12 64

OBJECTIVES

Singles: 7-inch

JEWEL (751 "Oh My Love") 15-25 65

OBOE

Singles: 7-inch

SAVOY....5-10 63

O'BRIEN, Betty

Singles: 7-inch

ABC-PAR....4-8 63
LIBERTY (55365 "She'll Be Gone") 10-20 62

O'BRIEN, Hugh

EPs: 7-inch

ABC-PAR....10-20 57

LPs: 10/12-inch

ABC-PAR (203 "Wyatt Earp Sings") 40-60 57

O'BRIEN, Johnny, & Steremonics

Singles: 7-inch

A&M....4-6 68

O'BRIEN, Rhys

Singles: 7-inch

LAURIE (3514 "Baby Shake Your Whoop Whoop") 10-15 70s
MGM....4-8 68

O'BRIEN, Richard

Singles: 7-inch

W.B....3-5 81

Picture Sleeves

W.B....3-5 81

O'BRIEN, Richie

Singles: 7-inch

MAY....4-8 63

O'BRIEN, Stacy

Singles: 7-inch

20TH FOX....3-5 76

O'BRIEN, Timmy

(With the Premiers)

Singles: 7-inch

LOOP (113 "Pitter Patter") 50-75
RASON (1001 "I've Been a Good Boy") 10-15 59

O'BRYAN P&R/R&B/LP '82

(O'Bryan Burnette)

Singles: 12-inch

CAPITOL....4-6 82-86

Singles: 7-inch

CAPITOL....3-4 82-87

LPs: 10/12-inch

CAPITOL....5-8 82-86

OBSESSIONS

Singles: 7-inch

ACCENT (1182 "Love Always") .100-150 65

OBVIOUS

Singles: 7-inch

CHALLENGE (59372 "Fate") 10-20 67

OBVIOUS

Singles: 7-inch

I WANNA (34108 "Two Thumbs Down") 3-4 93
(Red vinyl.)

Picture Sleeves

I WANNA (34108 "Two Thumbs Down") 3-4 93

EPs: 7-inch

I WANNA....4-6 93
Members: John Dubuc; Gregg Johnson; Tommy Gun.

OCAPELLOS

("Ocapello's"; with Hayes Thompson Orchestra)

Singles: 7-inch

CHECKER....5-10 66
GENERAL (107 "The Stars") 100-200 66
(Has a drawing of a general, saluting.)
GENERAL (107 "The Stars") 75-125 66
(No drawing of a general.)

OCASEK, Ric P&R/D&D/LP '83

Singles: 12-inch

GEFFEN....4-6 83

Singles: 7-inch

GEFFEN....3-4 83-86

Picture Sleeves

GEFFEN....3-4 83-86

LPs: 10/12-inch

GEFFEN....5-8 83-86
Also see CARS

OCCASIONALS

Singles: 7-inch

KNIGHT....5-8 64
PREMIER....5-8 64
WHIRL....5-8 64

OCCASIONS

Singles: 7-inch

BIG JIM (920 "There's No You") 10-20
BIG JIM (3273 "Baby Don't Go") 10-20

OCEAN P&R/LP '71

Singles: 7-inch

KAMA SUTRA....3-5 71-72
YORKVILLE ("Put Your Hand in the Hand") 8-12 71
(Canadian.)

LPs: 10/12-inch

KAMA SUTRA....8-12 71-72
Members: Janice Morgan; Greg Brown; David Tamblyn; Charles Slater.

OCEAN, Billy P&R/R&B '76

Singles: 12-inch

EPIC....4-8 80-82
JIVE....4-6 84-86

Singles: 7-inch

ARIOLA AMERICA....3-5 76
EPIC....3-5 77-82
JIVE....3-4 84-89

Picture Sleeves

JIVE....3-4 84-89

LPs: 10/12-inch

EPIC....5-10 81-82
JIVE....5-8 84-89

OCEAN BLUE LP '90

LPs: 10/12-inch

SIRE....5-8 90

OCHS, Phil LP '66

(With the Pan African Ngembo Rumba Band)

Singles: 7-inch

A&M....5-10 67-73
SPARKLE (9966 "Bwatue") 3-5 91
(Canadian. 1,000 numbered copies made.)

Picture Sleeves

SPARKLE (9966 "Bwatue") 3-5 91
(Canadian. 1,000 numbered copies made.)

LPs: 10/12-inch

A&M....10-20 67-76
ELEKTRA....15-25 64-66

O'CONNELL, Helen P&R '51

Singles: 78 rpm

CAPITOL....3-5 51-54
KAPP....3-5 55
VIK....3-5 57

Singles: 7-inch

CAMEO....4-6 63
CAPITOL....5-10 51-54
KAPP....5-8 55
VIK....5-8 57

EPs: 7-inch

CAPITOL....8-12 54
VIK....8-12 57

LPs: 10/12-inch

CAMDEN....10-20 59-62
CAMEO....10-15 63
LONGINES....5-10 70s
MARK 56....5-10 77
RCA....5-10 72
VIK (1093 "Helen O'Connell") 25-35 57
W.B....10-20 61
Also see MARTIN, Dean, & Helen O'Connell

O'CONNOR, Carroll LP '72

LPs: 10/12-inch

A&M....8-12 72
AUDIO FIDELITY....5-10 76
CAL STATE (6280 "Carnival of the Animals") 10-20 65

O'CONNOR, Carroll, & Jean Stapleton P&R '71

("As the Bunkers"; with Rob Reiner, Sally Struthers and Mike Evans)

Singles: 7-inch

ATLANTIC....3-5 71

Picture Sleeves

ATLANTIC....3-5 71

LPs: 10/12-inch

ATLANTIC....8-10 71
Also see O'CONNOR, Carroll

O'CONNER, Keith

(Keith Murphy)

Singles: 7-inch

STACY (958 "Cindy Lou") 10-20 63
Also see MURPHY, Keith, & Daze
Also see TORKAYS

O'CONNOR

LPs: 10/12-inch

BEARSVILLE....5-10 81

O'CONNOR, Sinead LP '88

Singles: 7-inch

CHRYSALIS....3-4 86
ENSIGN....3-4 90

LPs: 10/12-inch

CHRYSALIS....5-8 86
ENSIGN....5-8 90
Members: Sinead O'Connor; Andy Rourke; Mike Joyce.
Also see SMITHS

OCTAVES

Singles: 7-inch

VAL (1001 "You're Too Young") ...50-100 58

OCTAVIA R&B '86

Singles: 7-inch

POW WOW....3-4 86

OCTET: see RASPUTIN & MONKS / Octet

OCTOBER, Johnny

(Johnny Ottobre)

Singles: 7-inch

CAPITOL....5-10 59-60
ANOTHER FIRST....8-12 59

Picture Sleeves

CAPITOL (4267 "Growin' Prettier") 15-25 59
Also see FOUR DATES

OCTOBER COUNTRY

Singles: 7-inch

EPIC....5-10 67-69

LPs: 10/12-inch

EPIC (26381 "October Country") ...10-20 68

OCTOBERS

Singles: 7-inch

CHAIRMAN....8-12 63

OCTOPUS

Singles: 7-inch

BUDDAH....3-5 73

ODA

LPs: 10/12-inch

LOUD (80011 "Oda") 50-100 73
Members: Randy Oda; Kevin Oda.

O'DAY, Alan P&R/LP '77

Singles: 7-inch

PACIFIC....3-5 77-85
VIVA....3-5 71

LPs: 10/12-inch

PACIFIC....5-10 77

O'DAY, Anita P&R '47

Singles: 78 rpm

CLEF....5-10 53
CORAL....5-10 52
LONDON....5-10 51
SIGNATURE....5-10 47
MERCURY....5-10 52-53
VERVE....5-10 56-57

Singles: 7-inch

CLEF....5-15 53
CLOVER....4-6 66
COLUMBIA....3-5 76

CORAL 5-15 52
EMILY 3-5 79
LONDON 5-15 51
MERCURY 5-15 52-53
VERVE 5-15 56-62
EPs: 7-inch
CLEF 25-50 53
NORGRAN 20-40 54
LPs: 10/12-inch
ADVANCE (8 "Specials") 150-200 51
(10-inch LP.)
AMERICAN RECORDING SOCIETY (426 "For Oscar") 50-75 57
CLEF (130 "Anita O'Day") 100-150 53
COLUMBIA 8-10 74
CORAL (56073 "Singin' and Swingin' ") 100-150 53
DOBRE 5-10 78
EMILY 5-10 79-82
FLYING DUTCHMAN 5-10 74
GNP 5-10 79
MPS 5-10 73
NORGRAN (30 "Anita O'Day") 75-100 54
(10-inch LP.)
NORGRAN (1049 "Anita O'Day Sings Jazz") 50-75 55
NORGRAN (1057 "An Evening with Anita O'Day") 50-75 56
PAUSA 5-10 81
SIGNATURE 5-10 75
VERVE (2000 series) 30-60 56
(Has "Verve Records Inc." at bottom of label.)
VERVE (2100 series) 25-50 58-61
(Has "Verve Records Inc." at bottom of label.)
VERVE (6000 series) 25-50 59-60
(Has "Verve Records Inc." at bottom of label.)
VERVE (8200 thru 8500 series) 15-30 59-64
(Has "Verve Records Inc." at bottom of label.)
VERVE (2000 series) 30-60 56
(Has "Verve Records Inc." at bottom of label.)
VERVE 12-25 61-72
(Has "MGM Records - A Division Of Metro-Goldwyn-Mayer, Inc." at bottom of label.)
VERVE 5-10 79-82
(Has "Manufactured By MGM Record Corp." or mentions either Polydor or Polygram at bottom of label.)

O'DAY, Anita, & Cal Tjader
LPs: 10/12-inch
VERVE 15-25 62
(Has "MGM Records - A Division Of Metro-Goldwyn-Mayer, Inc." at bottom of label.)
Also see O'DAY, Anita
Also see TJADER, Cal

O'DAY, Pat
Singles: 78 rpm
MGM 3-5 53-56
RCA 5-10 57
Singles: 7-inch
ARGO 4-8 59
MGM 5-10 53-56
RCA 5-10 57
SEVILLE 4-8 59-60
LPs: 10/12-inch
GOLDEN CREST 15-25 56

O'DAY, Tommy C&W '78
Singles: 7-inch
NU-TRAYL 3-5 78-79

ODDBALLS
Singles: 7-inch
COLUMBIA 4-8 65
ROCKET 10-15 64

ODDIS, Ray
Singles: 7-inch
V.I.P. (25012 "Happy Ghoul Tide") 10-15 65

ODDS & ENDS
Singles: 7-inch
SOUTHBAY (102 "Cause You Don't Love Me") 15-25 66

ODDS & ENDS
Singles: 7-inch
RED BIRD (10083 "Before You Go") 5-10 66

ODDS & ENDS R&B '70
Singles: 7-inch
TODAY 4-6 71-72

ODEGARD, Kevin
Singles: 7-inch
MILL CITY 3-5 73
LPs: 10/12-inch
ASI 8-10 76
WOOFF 10-12 71

O'DELL, Brooks P&R/R&B '63
Singles: 7-inch
BELL (618 "Slow Motion") 10-20 65
GOLD (214 "Watch Your Step") 10-15 63
MANKIND (12010 "Got to Travel On") 4-6

O'DELL, Doye C&W '48
(With the Cass County Boys)
Singles: 78 rpm
EXCLUSIVE 5-10 48
Singles: 7-inch
INTRO (6047 "Diesel Smoke") 15-25 52
SAGE (297 "Everybody Likes a Little Lovin'") 30-40
LPs: 10/12-inch
CROWN 10-20 60s
ERA (20004 "Doye O'Dell") 20-30 60s
(Colored vinyl.)
LONGHORN 5-10 83
SAGE 10-20
SUNSET 6-12

O'DELL, Kenny P&R '67
Singles: 7-inch
ABC 3-5 73
CAPRICORN 3-5 73-79
KAPP 3-5 72
MAR-KAY 5-10 65
VEGAS 4-8 67-68
WHITE WHALE 4-6 69
LPs: 10/12-inch
CAPRICORN 5-10 74-78
VEGAS 15-25 68

ODESSA C&W '89
Singles: 7-inch
SING ME 3-4 89

ODETTA LP '63
(Odetta & Larry; Odetta Holmes)
Singles: 7-inch
DUNHILL 4-6 69
POLYDOR 3-5 70
RCA 4-8 63
RIVERSIDE 4-8 62
VANGUARD 5-10 59
VERVE/FOLKWAYS 4-6 66
VERVE/FORECAST 4-6 68
EPs: 7-inch
FANTASY (4017/4018 "Odetta & Larry") 15-20 54
(Price is for either of two volumes.)
LPs: 10/12-inch
EVEREST 5-10 73
FANTASY (15 "Odetta & Larry") 40-60 54
(10-inch LP.)
FANTASY (3252 "Odetta") 35-50 58
(Colored vinyl.)
POLYDOR 5-10 70
RCA 10-25 62-66
RIVERSIDE (400 series) 15-25 62
RIVERSIDE (3000 series) 10-20 68
RIVERSIDE (9400 series) 20-30 62
TRADITION (1010 "Odetta Sings Ballads and Blues") 25-35 57
TRADITION (1025 "At the Gate of Horn") 20-30 58
TRADITION (1052 "Best of Odetta") 10-15 67
(Monaural.)
TRADITION (2052 "Best of Odetta") 10-20 67
(Stereo.)
U.A. 5-10 76
VANGUARD 10-20 59-87
VERVE/FOLKWAYS 10-15 67

ODOM, Andrew
Singles: 7-inch
NATION 10-15
LPs: 10/12-inch
BLUESWAY 10-20

ODOM, Donna C&W '68
Singles: 7-inch
DECCA 3-6 68

ODOM, Joe
Singles: 78 rpm
CAPITOL 5-10 56
Singles: 7-inch
CAPITOL 5-15 56
1-2-3 3-6 69-70

ODOM, King
(King Odom Four; Quartette; with Dick Jacobs Orchestra)
Singles: 78 rpm
ABBEY (15064 "Lucky") 150-250 52
(Serial number shown since no selection number is used.)
DERBY 10-20 50-51
MUSICRAFT 10-20 49-49
PERSPECTIVE 10-20 52
Singles: 7-inch
ABBEY (15064 "Lucky") 500-750 52
(Serial number shown since no selection number is used.)
Members: Dave Odom; David Bowers; Isaiah Bing; Cleveland Bing.
Also see JACOBS, Dick, & His Orchestra
Also see LARKS
Also see RAVENS

ODOM, Noel, & Group
Singles: 7-inch
UPTOWN 4-8 69
Also see JACOBS, Dick, & His Orchestra

O'DOSKI, Gail C&W '87
Singles: 7-inch
DOOR KNOB 3-4 87-88

ODYSSEY
Singles: 7-inch
IMPERIAL 5-10 68
WHITE WHALE (263 "Little Girl Little Boy") 10-20 68

ODYSSEY P&R/R&B/LP '77
Singles: 12-inch
RCA 4-8 77-82
Singles: 7-inch
MOWEST 3-5 72
RCA 3-5 77-82
LPs: 10/12-inch
MOWEST 10-12 72
RCA 8-10 77-82
Members: Lillian Lopez; Louise Lopez.

OEDIPUS & MOTHERS
Singles: 7-inch
BEACON (1001 "How It Used to Be") 20-30 67

OERTLING, Jim
(With the Bayou Boys)
Singles: 7-inch
DEE-JAY JAMBOREE (107 "Old Moss Back") ??
(Since we have no information about this release, it is listed with neither price nor year. Original? Reissue? Readers: what say you?)
HAMMOND (267 "Old Moss Back") 250-350 59

OFARIM, Esther & Abraham P&R '68
(Esther Ofarim; with Abi Ofarim)
Singles: 7-inch
PHILIPS 4-6 64-68
LPs: 10/12-inch
CAPITOL 5-10 68
PHILIPS 5-15 63-70

OFF BEATS
Singles: 7-inch
WAM (2005 "Red Ants") 10-15 63

OFF BEATS
Singles: 7-inch
GUYDEN 10-15 64

OFF BEATS
Singles: 7-inch
TOWER 4-8 66

OFF BROADWAY USA P&R/LP '80
Singles: 7-inch
ATLANTIC 3-5 80
LPs: 10/12-inch
ATLANTIC 5-10 80

OFF KEYS
Singles: 7-inch
ROWE (003 "Our Wedding Day") 75-125 62
TECHNICHORD (1001 "Our Wedding Day") 25-50 62
Also see EVANS, Jerry, & Off Keys

OFF SET
Singles: 7-inch
BRENT (7051 "Just a Little Smile") 15-25 65
JUBILEE 5-10 66

OFFBEATS
Singles: 78 rpm
SALEM 5-10 57
Singles: 7-inch
SALEM 10-15 57

OFFBEATS
Singles: 7-inch
APACHE 10-15 61
CHEROKEE 10-15 61

OFFBEATS
Singles: 7-inch
TROPICAL (109 "Double Trouble") 15-25 64

OFF-BEATS
Singles: 7-inch
MERRITT (0001 "Mister Machine") 15-25 63
MERRITT (0002 "Grind") 15-25 63
Also see CAHILL, Graig, & Off-Beats

OFFENBACH
Singles: 7-inch
PAULA 4-6 68

OFFITT, Lillian P&R/R&B '57
Singles: 78 rpm
EXCELLO 10-20 57
Singles: 7-inch
CHIEF (7012 "The Man Won't Work") 20-30 60
EXCELLO 10-20 57

OGDEN, Bobby: see FONDA, Peter

OGDEN, Maurice
Singles: 7-inch
CHALLENGE (59233 "The Flag") 8-15 63

OGNIR & Nite People
Singles: 7-inch
SAMRON (102 "I Found a New Love") 15-25 65
W.B. (5682 "I Found a New Love") 10-20 65

OH ROMEO: see O ROMEO

O'GWYNN, James C&W '58
Singles: 7-inch
D 10-15 58
MERCURY 6-12 59-62
LPs: 10/12-inch
MERCURY 20-30 62
PLANTATION 5-10 76-78
WING 10-20 64

O'HARA, Faith
Singles: 7-inch
TITAN 5-10 60

O'HARA'S PLAYBOYS
LPs: 10/12-inch
FONTANA 10-15 67

O'HEARN, Patrick
LPs: 10/12-inch
PRIVATE 5-8 88

O'HEGARTY
Singles: 7-inch
VERVE/FOLKWAYS 4-8 66

O'HENRY, Lenny P&R/R&B '64
(With Short Stories)
Singles: 7-inch
ABC-PAR 10-15 61
ATCO 5-10 64-67
SMASH 5-10 63

O'HENRY & BARBARA
Singles: 7-inch
FERNWOOD 5-10 59

OHIO EXPRESS P&R '67
(Ohio Ltd.)
Singles: 7-inch
ATTACK 3-6 70
BUDDAH 4-6 68-73
CAMEO 5-8 67
ERIC 3-5 78
SUPER K 4-6 69-70
LPs: 10/12-inch
BUDDAH 10-20 68-70
CAMEO (20,000 "Beg, Borrow and Steal") 20-30 68
Also see KASENETZ-KATZ SINGING ORCHESTRAL CIRCUS
Also see RARE BREED
Also see REUNION
Also see 10CC

OHIO KNOX
Singles: 7-inch
REPRISE 3-5 71
LPs: 10/12-inch
REPRISE 10-15 71
Member: Peter Gallway.
Also see GALLWAY, Peter

OHIO LTD: see OHIO EXPRESS

OHIO PLAYERS R&B '68
Singles: 7-inch
AIR CITY 3-4 84
ARISTA 3-5 79
BOARDWALK 3-5 81
CAPITOL 4-6 69
COMPASS 4-8 68
MERCURY 3-5 74-78
TRC 4-6 70
TANGERINE 4-8 67
TRACK 3-4 88
WESTBOUND 3-5 71-76
LPs: 10/12-inch
ACCORD 5-10 81
ARISTA 5-10 79
BOARDWALK 5-10 81
CAPITOL (192 "Observations in Time") 10-20 69
CAPITOL (11291 "Ohio Players") 8-12 74
MERCURY 8-12 74-78
SPRINGBOARD 8-10 70s
TRIP 8-10 72
U.A. 8-10 75
WESTBOUND 8-12 72-75
Members: Joe Harris; Marshall Jones; Clarence Satchell; Jimmy Williams; Marvin Pierce; Billy Beck; Ralph Middlebrook; Leroy Bonner.
Also see JUNIE
Also see OHIO UNTOUCHABLES
Also see UNDISPUTED TRUTH
Also see SHADOW

OHIO UNTOUCHABLES
Singles: 7-inch
LU PINE (109 "She's My Heart's Desire") 10-20 62
LU PINE (110 "Forgive Me Darling") 10-20 62
LU PINE (116 "I'm Tired") 10-20 64
LU PINE (1009 "She's My Heart's Desire") 20-30 62
(First issue.)
LU PINE (1010 "Forgive Me Darling") 20-30 62
(First issue.)
LU PINE (1011 "I'm Tired") 20-30 64
(First issue.)
Also see FABULOUS PEPS
Also see FALCONS
Also see McCAIN, Benny, & Ohio Untouchables
Also see OHIO PLAYERS
Also see WARD, Robert, & Ohio Untouchables

OILY RAGS
LPs: 10/12-inch
FLYING DUTCHMAN 8-10 74

OINGO BOINGO LP '80
Singles: 12-inch
A&M 4-8 81
MCA 4-6 85-86
Singles: 7-inch
A&M 3-5 81-83
MCA 3-4 85-86
Picture Sleeves
MCA 3-4 85-86
LPs: 10/12-inch
A&M 5-10 81-89
I.R.S. 5-10 80
MCA 5-8 85-90
Members: Danny Elfman; Steve Bartek; John Hernandez; Dale Turner; Kerry Hatch; Richard Gibbs.
Also see ELFMAN, Danny
Also see MYSTIC KNIGHTS of the Oingo Boingo

O'JAHS
Singles: 7-inch
SOUND STAGE 7 4-8 67

O'JAYS P&R/R&B '63
Singles: 12-inch
PHILADELPHIA INT'L 4-8 83
Singles: 7-inch
ALL PLATINUM 3-5 74
APOLLO (759 "Miracles") 20-30 61
ASTROSCOPE 3-6 74
BELL 3-6 67-73
EPIC 3-4 83
IMPERIAL (5942 "How Does It Feel") 10-15 63
IMPERIAL (5976 "Lonely Drifter") 5-10 63
IMPERIAL (66007 thru 66131) 5-10 64-65
IMPERIAL (66145 "I'll Never Let You Go") 30-50 65
IMPERIAL (66162 "I'll Never Forget You") 25-35 66
IMPERIAL (66177 thru 66200) 5-10 66
LIBERTY 3-5 81
LITTLE STAR (124 "How Does It Feel") 15-25 63
LITTLE STAR (125 "Dream Girl") 15-25 63
LITTLE STAR (1401 "Just to Be with You") 15-25 63
MANHATTAN 3-4 89-90
MINIT 5-10 67
NEPTUNE 4-6 69-70
PHILADELPHIA INT'L 3-6 72-87
SARU 3-6 71
TSOP 3-5 80-81
LPs: 10/12-inch
BELL (6014 "Back on Top") 10-20 68
BELL (6082 "The O'Jays") 8-12 73
EMI 5-8 89-90
EPIC 5-8 83
IMPERIAL (9290 "Coming Through") 30-35 65
(Monaural.)
IMPERIAL (12290 "Coming Through") 35-40 65
(Stereo.)
KORY 8-10 77
MINIT (24008 "Soul Sounds") 20-30 67
(Stereo.)
MINIT (40008 "Soul Sounds") 15-25 67
(Monaural.)
PHILADELPHIA INT'L 5-10 72-86
SUNSET 10-15 68
TSOP 5-10 80
TRIP 8-10 73
U.A. 8-12 72
Members: Bob Massey; Eddie LeVert; Walt Williams; Bill Powell; Bill Isles; Sam Strain.
Also see CHIPS
Also see LITTLE ANTHONY & IMPERIALS
Also see MASCOTS
Also see NORMAN, Jimmy, & O'Jays
Also see PHILADELPHIA INTERNATIONAL ALL STARS

O'JAYS / Moments
LPs: 10/12-inch
STANG 8-12 74
Also see MOMENTS
Also see O'JAYS

O'KANES C&W '86
Singles: 7-inch
COLUMBIA 3-4 86-88
Members: Jamie O'Hara; Kieran Kane.
Also see KANE, Kieran

O'KAYSIONS P&R/R&B/LP '68
Singles: 7-inch
ABC 5-8 68
COTILLION 3-5 70
NORTH STATE (1001 "Girl Watcher") 20-30 68
ROULETTE 3-5 70s
SPARTON (1676 "Girl Watcher") 5-8 68
(Canadian.)
Picture Sleeves
NORTH STATE (1001 "Girl Watcher") 25-45 68
EPs: 7-inch
ABC (664 "Girl Watcher") 15-25 68
(Juke box issue.)
LPs: 10/12-inch
ABC (664 "Girl Watcher") 15-25 68
Members: Donnie Weaver; Jim Spidel; Jim Hennant; Ron Turner; Bruce Joyner.

O'KEEFE, Danny P&R/C&W/LP '72
Singles: 7-inch
ATLANTIC 3-5 75
JERDEN 4-8 66
SIGNPOST 3-5 72
W.B. 3-5 77-78
Picture Sleeves
W.B. 3-5 77-78
LPs: 10/12-inch
ATLANTIC 8-12 73-75
COTILLION 10-15 70
FIRST AMERICAN 8-10 70s
PANORAMA (105 "Introducing Danny O'Keefe") 20-30 66
SIGNPOST 10-12 72
W.B. 5-10 77-79
Also see CALLIOPE
Also see SEATTLE HELPS the HUNGRY

O'KEEFE, Johnny
Singles: 7-inch
BRUNSWICK (55067 "Real Wild Child") 50-75 58
LIBERTY 10-15 60-61
MR. PEACOCK 5-10 62
SIMS 4-6 68
Picture Sleeves
LIBERTY (55228 "She's My Baby") 20-30 60

OKEEFE, Johnny
Singles: 7-inch
RA-O 4-8

O'KEEFE, Larry
Singles: 7-inch
FREEDOM ... 5-10 59
LIBERTY ... 5-10 59

O'KEITH, Bryan
Singles: 7-inch
OHN-J ... 4-8 65

OKIE DOKE BAND
EPs: 7-inch
KING NOODLE ... 5-8 81
Members: Marc Bristol; Dan Kersten; Quentin Rhoton.
Also see BRISTOL, Marc

OL' PAINT
LPs: 10/12-inch
GWP ... 8-10

OLA & JANGLERS P&R '69
Singles: 7-inch
GNP ... 4-8 68-69
LONDON ... 4-8 67
LPs: 10/12-inch
GNP ... 15-20 69
Member: Ola Hakansson.

O'LAY, Ruth
Singles: 7-inch
ABC ... 4-8 66
LPs: 10/12-inch
ABC ... 10-20 67
EMARCY ... 20-40 58
EVEREST ... 15-30 63
MERCURY ... 20-40 59
U.A. ... 20-40 60

OLD AND IN THE WAY LP '75
LPs: 10/12-inch
ROUND (103 "Old and in the Way") ... 20-25 75
SUGAR HILL ... 5-8 85
Members: Peter Rowan; Jerry Garcia; Vassar Clements; David Grisman.
Also see GARCIA, Jerry
Also see ROWANS

OLD AND IN THE WAY / Keith & Donna / Robert Hunter / Phil Lesh & Ned Lagin
Singles: 7-inch
ROUND (02 & 03 "Sampler for Dead Heads") ... 40-60 75
(Promotional, fan club two-disc set. Price also includes a letter from Anton Round, a letter about members of the Grateful Dead, several miniature LP covers, and a mailer advertising posters.)
ROUND (02 & 03 "Sampler for Dead Heads") ... 20-30 75
(Price is for both discs, without inserts. Divide in half for either one of the two records.)
Also see GRATEFUL DEAD
Also see HUNTER, Robert
Also see KEITH & DONNA
Also see LESH, Phil, & Ned Lagin
Also see OLD and in the WAY

OLDE TYME RELIGION
Singles: 7-inch
W.B. ... 3-5 71

OLDFIELD, Mike LP '73
(With Sally Oldfield)
Singles: 7-inch
EPIC ... 3-5 81-82
VIRGIN ... 3-5 73-82
Picture Sleeves
VIRGIN ... 3-6 74
EPs: 7-inch
VIRGIN (199 "Tubular Bells") ... 5-10 74
(Promotional issue only.)
LPs: 10/12-inch
EPIC (44116) ... 5-10 81-82
EPIC (44116 "Tubular Bells") ... 20-40 73
(Half-speed mastered.)
VIRGIN (Except 2001) ... 5-15 73-88
VIRGIN (2001 "Tubular Bells") ... 10-12 73
(Picture disc.)
Also see SALLYANGIE

OLDFIELD, Sally
LPs: 10/12-inch
CHRYSALIS ... 5-10 79
Also see OLDFIELD, Mike
Also see SALLYANGIE

OLDHAM, Andrew, Orchestra
Singles: 7-inch
PARROT (9745 "I Get Around") ... 10-15 65
LPs: 10/12-inch
LONDON (457 "Rolling Stones Songbook") ... 30-45 65
(Stereo.)
LONDON (3457 "Rolling Stones Songbook") ... 35-50 65
(Monaural.)
PARROT (61003 "East Meets West") ... 25-35 65
(Monaural.)
PARROT (71003 "East Meets West") ... 30-40 65
(Stereo.)

OLDHAM, Spooner
Singles: 7-inch
ATLANTIC ... 4-6 68
LPs: 10/12-inch
ATTARACK ... 8-12 71

OLDSMOBUICKS
LPs: 10/12-inch
TONEMASTER (101 "Rockin' 'N' Boppin' ") ... 10-15 89
TONEMASTER (102 "Oldsmobuicks") ... 8-10 90
Members: Brian Dardeen; Rob Santos; Stan Kozlowski; Haney Kozlowski.

OLE JOSE & Golden Leaves
Singles: 7-inch
CHALLENGE ... 4-6 68

OLE MISS DOWN BEATS
Singles: 7-inch
ARDENT (103 "Mister Crump") ... 10-20 61

OLE MOON DADDY
Singles: 7-inch
RALLY ... 4-8 67

OLE SONNY BOY
Singles: 78 rpm
EXCELLO ... 15-25 56
Singles: 7-inch
EXCELLO (2086 "Blues and Misery") ... 25-40 56

OLENN, Johnny
(With the Blockbusters)
Singles: 7-inch
ANTLER (1101 "My Sweetie Pie") 20-30 59
ANTLER (1105 "Born Reckless") ... 20-30 59
ANTLER (4012 "My Sweetie Pie") 20-30 58
ANTLER (4018 "The Magic Touch") ... 20-30 59
PERSONALITY (1002 "Teenie") ... 30-40 59
TNT ... 10-20 58
LPs: 10/12-inch
LIBERTY (3029 "Just Rollin' ") ... 100-200 58
Also see BLOCKBUSTERS

OLIVE BRANCH
LPs: 10/12-inch
LONDON ... 8-12 71

OLIVER P&R/LP '69
(Bill Oliver Swofford)
Singles: 7-inch
CREWE ... 3-5 69-70
JUBILEE ... 4-6 69
LIBERTY ... 3-5
PARAMOUNT ... 3-5 73
PEOPLE SONG ... 3-5 82
U.A. ... 3-5 70-71
Picture Sleeves
CREWE ... 4-6 69
LPs: 10/12-inch
CREWE ... 10-15 69-70
U.A. ... 8-12 71
Also see BILLY & SUE
Also see GOOD EARTH TRIO
Also see VIRGINIANS

OLIVER
LPs: 10/12-inch
MCA ... 5-10 82

OLIVER, Big Danny
Singles: 7-inch
KAPP (944 "Sapphire") ... 10-20
TREND (012 "Sapphire") ... 40-60 58
TREND (016 "Blues for the 49") ... 20-40 58

OLIVER, Bobby
Singles: 7-inch
LUCKY FOUR ... 10-20 61

OLIVER, Dale
Singles: 7-inch
SANGELO (105 "Long Gone Daddy") ... 50-75 58

OLIVER, David R&B/LP '78
Singles: 7-inch
MERCURY ... 3-5 78-80
LPs: 10/12-inch
MERCURY ... 5-10 78-79

OLIVER, Debbie
Singles: 7-inch
CURRENT (225 "Yes I'm Ready") ... 5-8 75

OLIVER, Jimmy
(With the Rockers)
Singles: 7-inch
PORT ... 10-15 60
LPs: 10/12-inch
SUE ... 15-25 65

OLIVER, Johnny
(With Johnny Brantley Orchestra & Chorus)
Singles: 78 rpm
MGM (12319 "I Need You So") ... 10-15 56
Singles: 7-inch
JOSIE (860 "Sweet Sugar") ... 8-12 59
LIBERTY (55349 "Mail Man, Where's My Check") ... 5-10 61
LIBERTY (55463 "As Long As Time Goes On") ... 5-10 62
MGM (12319 "I Need You So") ... 25-35 56
MERCURY (71570 "That's All I'm Living For") ... 8-12 60
MERCURY (71662 "I Gave Him Back His Ring") ... 8-12 60
MIRA (981 "Walk a Chalk Line") ... 10-15
(Identification number shown since no selection number is used.)

OLIVER, O. Jay
(With the Crackerjacks; with Groove Riders)
Singles: 7-inch
COED ... 10-20 58

OLIVER, Tommy
Singles: 7-inch
W.B. (5011 "Rendezvous Rock") ... 15-25 58

OLIVER & ROCKETTES
Singles: 7-inch
MERCURY ... 3-5 76

OLIVER & TWISTERS
Singles: 7-inch
COLPIX (615 "Mother Goose Twist") ... 5-10 61
Picture Sleeves
COLPIX (615 "Mother Goose Twist") ... 10-15 61
LPs: 10/12-inch
COLPIX (423 "Look Who's Twistin' ") ... 25-35 61

OLIVERS
Singles: 7-inch
PHALANX (1022 "Bleeker Street") ... 40-60 66
RCA (9113 "Bleeker Street") ... 10-20 67

OLIVOR, Jane P&R/LP '77
Singles: 7-inch
COLUMBIA ... 3-5 77-85
LPs: 10/12-inch
COLUMBIA ... 5-10 77-85

OLLER, Shadie
Singles: 7-inch
SUMMIT (114 "Come to Me Baby") ... 200-250 59

OLLIE & JERRY P&R/R&B/D&D '84
Singles: 12-inch
POLYDOR ... 4-6 84-85
Singles: 7-inch
POLYDOR ... 3-4 84-85
Members: Ollie Brown; Jerry Knight.
Also see KNIGHT, Jerry

OLLIE & NIGHTINGALES P&R/R&B '68
Singles: 7-inch
STAX ... 4-8 68-69
LPs: 10/12-inch
STAX ... 10-15 69
Members: Ollie Nightingale; Quincy Billops, Jr.; Nelson Lesure; Bill Davis; Rochester Neal; Sir Mack Rice.
Also see MAD LADS
Also see NIGHTINGALE, Ollie
Also see OVATIONS
Also see RICE, Mack

OLLIE BABA
LPs: 10/12-inch
POLYDOR ... 5-10 78

OLNESS, Gunner
Singles: 7-inch
GO ... 8-12 66
LPs:10/12-inch
GO ... 15-25 67
Also see GAMINS

OLSEN, Dorothy
Singles: 78 rpm
RCA ... 4-8 56
Singles: 7-inch
RCA ... 5-10 56

OLSON, Rocky P&R '59
Singles: 7-inch
CHESS ... 10-15 59

OLSSON, Nigel P&R '75
Singles: 7-inch
BANG ... 3-5 78-79
COLUMBIA ... 3-5 78
ROCKET ... 3-5 75
UNI ... 3-5 71-72
LPs: 10/12-inch
BANG ... 5-10 79-80
COLUMBIA ... 5-10 78
ROCKET ... 8-12 73-75
UNI ... 8-12 71
Also see JOHN, Elton

OLVERA, Frankie
Singles: 7-inch
LOLA (104 "Huggie's Bunnies") ... 8-12 64

OLYMPIANS
Singles: 7-inch
TEMPE ... 5-10 60s

OLYMPIC RUNNERS R&B '74
Singles: 7-inch
LONDON ... 3-5 74-77
POLYDOR ... 3-5 79
LPs: 10/12-inch
LONDON ... 8-10 74-77
POLYDOR ... 5-10 79
Members: Pete Wingfield; DeLisle Harper; George Chandler; Joe Jammer. Glen LeFleur.
Also see WINGFIELD, Pete

OLYMPICS P&R/R&B '58
Singles: 78 rpm
DEMON (1508 "Western Movies") 50-75 58
Singles: 7-inch
ABC ... 3-5 73
ARVEE (562 "Hully Gully") ... 10-20 59
ARVEE (595 "Big Boy Pete") ... 10-20 60
ARVEE (5006 "Shimmy Like Kate") ... 10-20 60
ARVEE (5020 "Dance By the Light of the Moon") ... 10-20 61
ARVEE (5023 "Little Pedro") ... 10-20 61
ARVEE (5031 "Stay Where You Are") ... 30-50 61
ARVEE (5044 "The Stomp") ... 10-15 61
ARVEE (5051 "Twist") ... 10-15 62
ARVEE (5056 "The Scotch") ... 10-15 62
ARVEE (5073 "What'd I Say") ... 10-15 63
ARVEE (6501 "Big Boy Pete '65") 10-15 63
COLLECTABLES ... 3-4 80s
DEMON (1508 "Western Movies") 15-25 58
DEMON (1512 "Dance with the Teacher") ... 15-25 58
DEMON (1514 "Your Love") ... 15-25 59
DUO DISC (104 "The Boogler") ... 5-10 64
DUO DISC (105 "Return of Big Boy Pete") ... 5-10 64
ERIC ... 3-5 70s
JUBILEE (5674 "Cartoon Song") ... 5-10 69
LIBERTY ... 5-10 63
LOMA (2010 "I'm Comin' Home") ... 5-10 65
LOMA (2013 "Good Lovin' ") ... 10-15 65
LOMA (2017 "Baby I'm Yours") ... 10-15 65
MGM (14505 "The Apartment") ... 3-6 73
MIRWOOD (5504 "We Go Together") ... 5-10 66
MIRWOOD (5513 "Mine Exclusively") ... 5-10 66
MIRWOOD (5523 "Western Movies") ... 5-10 66
MIRWOOD (5525 "The Duck") ... 5-10 66
MIRWOOD (5529 "The Same Old Thing") ... 5-10 66
MIRWOOD (5533 "Big Boy Pete") ... 5-10 67
PARKWAY (6003 "Good Things") ... 5-10 68
TITAN (1718 "The Chicken") ... 15-25 61
TITAN (1801 "Western Movies") ... 10-15 60s
TRI DISC (106 "The Bounce") ... 10-15 62
TRI DISC (107 "Dancin' Holiday") .. 10-15 63
TRI DISC (110 "Bounce Again") ... 10-15 63
TRI DISC (112 "Broken Hip") ... 10-15 63
W.B. (7639 "Please Please Please") .. 3-5 70
ZEE (101 "The Slop") ... 15-25 58
ZEE (103 "Western Movies") ... 20-30 58
EPs: 7-inch
ARVEE (423 "Doin' the Hully Gully") ... 50-100 60
LPs: 10/12-inch
ARVEE (423 "Doin' the Hully Gully") ... 100-200 60
ARVEE (424 "Dance by the Light of the Moon") ... 100-125 61
ARVEE (429 "Party Time") ... 100-125 61
EVEREST ... 5-10 81
MIRWOOD (M-7003 "Something Old, Something New") ... 20-30 66
(Monaural.)
MIRWOOD (MS-7003 "Something Old, Something New") ... 25-35 66
(Stereo.)
POST ... 8-10 70s
RHINO ... 5-8 80s
TRI-DISC (1001 "Do the Bounce") 40-60 63
Members: Walter Ward; Eddie Lewis; Melvin King; Charles Figer; Julius McMichaels.
Also see PARAGONS
Also see REYNOLDS, Jody / Olympics
Also see WARD, Walter, & Challengers

O'MALLEY, Lenore P&R '80
Singles: 7-inch
POLYDOR ... 3-5 80

OMAR & HOWLERS LP '87
Singles: 7-inch
COLUMBIA ("Border Girl") ... 8-12 87
(Picture disc. Promotional issue only. No selection number used.)
LPs: 10/12-inch
COLUMBIA ... 5-8 87

OMAR & Village Idiots
Singles: 7-inch
PACIFIC CHALLENGER ... 5-10 60s

O'MARY, Slim
Singles: 7-inch
H&K (20 "Sink Or Swim") ... 30-50

OMEGA
LPs: 10/12-inch
FANTASY ... 5-10 78

OMEGAS
Singles: 7-inch
DECCA ... 10-15 59-60
GROOVE ... 5-10 61

OMEGAS
Singles: 7-inch
U.A. (50247 "I Can't Believe") ... 15-25 68

OMEN
Singles: 7-inch
ASCOT ... 4-8 67

OMENS
Singles: 7-inch
CODY (007 "Searching") ... 25-35 66

OMNIBUS
Singles: 7-inch
U.A. ... 3-5 70
LPs: 10/12-inch
U.A. ... 10-15 70

ON the SEVENTH DAY
Singles: 7-inch
MERCURY ... 3-5 70
LPs: 10/12-inch
MERCURY ... 8-10 70

ONBEATS
Singles: 7-inch
GRANITE ... 5-10 60

ONCOMERS
Singles: 7-inch
GATEWAY (103 "Every Day Now") ... 20-30 60s

ONE
Singles: 7-inch
COLUMBIA (44256 "Hey Taxi") ... 10-20 67
KAPP ... 8-12 67
LPs: 10/12-inch
GRUNT ... 10-15 72
STARBORNE ... 8-12 78
VILLAGE ... 20-30 77
Also see BLUE BEATS

ONE, Bobby
Singles: 7-inch
DECCA (30515 "Tell Me Again") ... 10-20 57
NRC (021 "Hummingbird") ... 15-25 59

ONE EYED JACKS
(One-Eyed Jacks)
Singles: 7-inch
LAKESIDE ... 4-8
ROULETTE ... 5-10 68-69
TY TEX ... 5-10
WHITE CLIFFS (265 "Love") ... 20-30 67
Members: Bill Schneider; Barry Fasman; Buddy Carr; George Gedzun; Mike Murphy.
Also see FAT WATER

ONE G PLUS THREE
Singles: 7-inch
GORDO ... 4-8 70
PARAMOUNT ... 3-5 70

ONE HUNDRED PERCENT WHOLE WHEAT
Singles: 7-inch
A.V.I. ... 3-5 77-79
LPs: 10/12-inch
A.V.I. ... 5-10 77-78

ONE OF HOURS
Singles: 7-inch
CHETWYD (45001 "It's Best") ... 50-100 66
CHETWYD (45005 "Psychedelic Illusion") ... 50-100 67

100 PROOF Aged in Soul P&R/R&B '69
Singles: 7-inch
HOT WAX ... 3-6 69-72
LPs: 10/12-inch
HOT WAX ... 10-15 70-73
Members: Steve Mancha; Joe Stubbs; Eddie Anderson.
Also see FALCONS
Also see MANCHA, Steve
Also see ORIGINALS
Also see STUBBS, Joe

101 NORTH
Singles: 7-inch
CAPITOL ... 3-4 88
LPs: 10/12-inch
CAPITOL ... 5-8 88

101 STRINGS LP '59
Singles: 7-inch
SOMERSET ... 3-5 59
LPs: 10/12-inch
ALSHIRE ... 5-10 60s
SOMERSET ... 5-10 59-61
STEREO FIDELITY ... 5-10 59-61

125TH ST. CANDY STORE
Singles: 7-inch
UP TITE ... 4-8 68-69

ONE IN A MILLION
Singles: 7-inch
POPPY ... 4-6 68

ONE ON ONE R&B '84
Singles: 7-inch
KEE WEE ... 3-4 84

1 PLUS 1
Singles: 7-inch
M.O.C. ... 4-8 66
Members: Don Bryant; Miriam Bittinum.
Also see BRYANT, Don

ONE STRING SAM
Singles: 78 rpm
J.V.B. (40 "My Baby Ooo") ... 100-200 56
Singles: 7-inch
J.V.B. (40 "My Baby Ooo") ... 400-500 56

ONE 2 MANY P&R '89
Singles: 7-inch
A&M ... 3-4 89
Picture Sleeves
A&M ... 3-4 89

ONE TO ONE P&R '86
Singles: 7-inch
W.B. ... 3-4 86
Picture Sleeves
W.B. ... 3-4 86
LPs: 10/12-inch
W.B. ... 5-8 86
Members: Louise Reny; Leslie Howe.

ONE WAY LP '79
(Featuring Al Hudson)
Singles: 12-inch
MCA ... 4-6 82-86
Singles: 7-inch
MCA ... 3-5 79-87
Picture Sleeves
MCA ... 3-5 86-87
LPs: 10/12-inch
MCA ... 5-10 79-86
Members: Alica Meyers; Cortez Harris; Dave Robertson; Kevin McCord; Gregory Green; Jonathan Meadows; Candice Edwards.
Also see HUDSON, Al
Also see MYERS, Alica

ONE WAY STREET
Singles: 7-inch
PAULA (281 "Tears in My Eyes") ... 10-15 66

ONE WAY STREET
Singles: 7-inch
SUNRISE (103 "We All Love Peanut Butter") ... 25-35 66

ONE WAY STREET
Singles: 7-inch
APOLLO (100 "Yard Dog") ... 10-15 67

SMASH (2155 "Girls Girls Girls") ...10-20 68
SMASH (2187 "What's Your Name")........................10-20 68

ONE WAY STREET
Singles: 7-inch
BOTIQUE 5-8 68

ONE WAY STREET
Singles: 7-inch
DEEK (101 "I Know I Love")..........15-25 67
DEEK (103 "Joy and Sorrow")........15-25 68

O'NEAL, Alexander R&B/D&D/LP '85
Singles: 12-inch
TABU........................ 4-6 85-86
Singles: 7-inch
TABU........................ 3-4 85-90
Picture Sleeves
TABU........................ 3-4 85-88
LPs: 10/12-inch
TABU........................ 5-8 85-90

O'NEAL, Alexander, & Cherrelle R&B '86
Singles: 7-inch
TABU........................ 3-4 86-88
Also see CHERRELLE
Also see O'NEAL, Alexander

O'NEAL, Austin C&W '83
Singles: 7-inch
PROJECT ONE........................ 3-4 83

O'NEAL, Coleman C&W '63
Singles: 7-inch
CHANCELLOR........................ 4-8 62-63

O'NEAL, Fluke
Singles: 7-inch
TE MA........................ 3-5 78

O'NEAL, Gradie: see O'NEIL, Grady

O'NEAL, Jackie, & Rebel Rockers
Singles: 7-inch
CAPA (111 "I Cry") 10-20 62

O'NEAL, Johnny
Singles: 78 rpm
KING 75-125 52
Singles: 7-inch
KING (4599 "So Many Hard Times") 250-350 52

O'NEAL, Lance
(With the Dave Kennedy & Ambassadors)
Singles: 7-inch
NORKO (1113 "I'm Twistin' Alone")........................15-25 60s
Also see KENNEDY, Dave

O'NEAL, Tom
Singles: 7-inch
PETAL (1001 "St. Louis Blues").....10-20 62

ONE-DERFUL BAND
Singles: 7-inch
ONE-DERFUL........................ 4-8 68

O'NEIL, Coleman
Singles: 7-inch
CHANCELLOR 4-8 62
SIMS 4-8 63

O'NEIL, Danny
Singles: 7-inch
PD........................ 4-6 68

O'NEIL, Grady
(Grady O'Neal)
Singles: 7-inch
BELLA (2205 "Baby Oh Baby") ..200-300 59
JAN ELL 4-6 60-62

O'NEIL, Jackie
Singles: 7-inch
CAPA (111 "You Broke My Heart")........................10-20

O'NEIL, Johnny
(O'Neill, Johnny)
Singles: 78 rpm
RCA........................ 5-10 57
Singles: 7-inch
IMPERIAL........................ 5-10 59
RCA........................ 8-12 57-58

O'NEIL, Leo
Singles: 7-inch
TRIBE........................ 8-12 67

O'NEILL, Jim
(Jimmy O'Neill)
Singles: 7-inch
DEL-FI........................ 5-10 60
TORCHLITE 5-10 62

O'NEILL, Johnny: see O'NEIL, Johnny

ONES, The
LPs: 10/12-inch
ASHWOOD HOUSE (1105 "The Ones")........................300-500 66
CONTRAPOINT (9010 "Maybe It's Both of Us")........................30-50 60s

ONES, The
Singles: 7-inch
FENTON (2514 "You Haven't Seen My Love")........................40-60 67
MOTOWN (1117 "You Haven't Seen My Love")........................ 8-15 67
(Black vinyl.)
MOTOWN (1117 "You Haven't Seen My Love")........................15-25 67
(Colored vinyl. Promotional issue only.)
MOTOWN (1130 "Don't Let Me Lose This Dream") 8-15 68
(Black vinyl.)
MOTOWN (1130 "Don't Let Me Lose This Dream") 15-25 68
(Colored vinyl. Promotional issue only.)
SPIRIT (0001 "You Haven't Seen My Love") 25-50 69
Also see HERNANDEZ, Danny, & Ones

ONES, The
Singles: 7-inch
BLUE RIBBON 5-10 70s

ONGG
Singles: 7-inch
COLUMBIA........................ 3-5 80

ONION
Singles: 7-inch
EPIC........................ 4-6 69

ONION RINGS
Singles: 7-inch
BLUE ONION (102 "She's Gonna Cry")........................20-30 67

ONLY ONES
Singles: 7-inch
PANIK 5-10 66
SIGHT 20-25 65
Also see GLIEDEN, Mike

ONLY ONES
Singles: 7-inch
EPIC........................ 3-5 79
LPs: 10/12-inch
EPIC........................5-10 79

ONLY ONZ
Singles: 7-inch
TIME (1076 "On the Road Again") 25-35 63

ONO, Yoko LP '71
(With the Plastic Ono Band)
Singles: 12-inch
POLYDOR........................5-10 85-86
Singles: 7-inch
APPLE........................ 4-8 71-73
GEFFEN........................ 3-5 81
POLYDOR........................ 3-5 82-86
Promotional Singles
APPLE (OYB-1 "Open Your Box")........................600-800 70
APPLE (1853 "Now Or Never")......25-30 72
APPLE (1867 "Woman Power").......20-25 73
GEFFEN........................ 5-8 81
POLYDOR........................ 4-6 82-86
Picture Sleeves
APPLE (1853 "Now Or Never")........8-12 72
GEFFEN........................ 3-4 81
LPs: 10/12-inch
APPLE........................15-20 71-73
GEFFEN........................5-10 81
POLYDOR........................5-10 82-86
Promotional LPs
GEFFEN (934 "Walking on Thin Ice")........................20-25 81
GEFFEN (975 "No No No")..........25-30 81
Also see LENNON, John

ONTARIO, Art
Singles: 7-inch
DIXIE (2019 "It Must Be Me").....150-200 59

ONTARIOS
(With Frank Motley & His Crew)
Singles: 78 rpm
BIG TOWN........................50-100 54
Singles: 7-inch
BIG TOWN (121 "Memories of You")........................400-500 54
Also see MOTLEY, Frank

ONYX
Singles: 7-inch
BURDETTE........................ 4-8 68
GREAT NORTHWEST 4-8 60s

OOGUM B. & TRICKS
Singles: 7-inch
PENTAGRAM (101 "You Are My Woman")........................25-30 69

OP BIRDS
Singles: 7-inch
EPIC........................ 4-8 63
Also see KELLY, Jimmy, & Op Birds

OPALS
Singles: 78 rpm
APOLLO........................25-50 54
Singles: 7-inch
APOLLO (462 "My Heart's Desire")........................100-150 54
(Flat label color.)
APOLLO (462 "My Heart's Desire")........................20-30 58
(Glossy label color.)
Members: Earl Wade; John Hopson; Ted Williams; Marty Brown.
Also see CADILLACS
Also see CRYSTALS

OPALS
Singles: 7-inch
BELTONE (2025 "Love") 20-25 62

OPALS
Singles: 7-inch
OKEH (7184 "Losers Weepers") 10-20 63
OKEH (7188 "Does It Matter").......10-20 64
OKEH (7202 "You Can't Hurt Me No More")........................10-20 64
OKEH (7224 "I'm So Afraid") 10-20 65

OPALS
Singles: 7-inch
LAURIE (3288 "Just Like a Little Bitty Baby")........................8-10 65

OPALS & BELAIRS 4
Singles: 7-inch
SALEM (006 "I Want You More")...15-25 60s

OPEN ROAD
Singles: 7-inch
LAURIE 3-5 71

OPEN SLOWLY
Singles: 7-inch
ROULETTE 4-8 68

OPEN WINDOW
LPs: 10/12-inch
VANGUARD 10-15 69

OPPER, Wolf
Singles: 7-inch
ACADEMY (1437 "Stompin to the Beat")........................100-200 59

OPPOSITE SIX
Singles: 7-inch
DOT (16700 "All Night Long") 8-10 65
SOUTH SHORE (720 "Down the Tubes")........................15-25 60s
SOUTH SHORE (721 "Church Key")........................15-25 60s

OPS 'N POPS
Singles: 7-inch
COLUMBIA........................4-8 67

OPTOMISTS
Singles: 7-inch
MERCURY 5-8 62

OPUS P&R/LP '86
Singles: 7-inch
POLYDOR........................3-4 86
LPs: 10/12-inch
POLYDOR........................5-8 86

OPUS 1
Singles: 7-inch
MUSTANG (3017 "Dodge in My Mind")........................15-20 66

OPUS IV
Singles: 7-inch
MGM 4-8 67

OPUS SEVEN R&B '79
Singles: 7-inch
SOURCE........................3-5 79
LPs: 10/12-inch
SOURCE........................5-10 79

OPUS 10 R&B '85
Singles: 7-inch
PANDISC 3-4 85

O'QUINN, Gene
Singles: 78 rpm
CAPITOL........................5-10 53-54
INTRO........................5-8 55
Singles: 7-inch
CAPITOL........................5-10 53-54
INTRO........................5-10 55

OR, John
(With Mick Jagger)
LPs: 10/12-inch
ATCO........................15-25 71
Also see JAGGER, Mick

ORACLE
Singles: 7-inch
VERVE/FORECAST........................4-8 67

ORANG UTAN
LPs: 10/12-inch
BELL (6054 "Orang Utan")............20-25 71

ORANGE, Allen
Singles: 7-inch
MINIT 5-10 60-62
SOUND STAGE 7 ....4-8 66

ORANGE COLORED SKY
Singles: 7-inch
UNI........................5-10 68-69
LPs: 10/12-inch
UNI (73031 "Orange Colored Sky")........................10-20 68
Member: Ernie Hernandez.
Also see YOUNGER BROTHERS

ORANGE GROOVE
LPs: 10/12-inch
SOMERSET 10-15 69

ORANGE WEDGE
Singles: 7-inch
BLUE FLAT (95097 "From the Womb to the Tomb")........................50-75 68

ORANGE WEDGE
LPs: 10/12-inch
("No One Left But Me") 200-300 70s
(Label and number not known.)
("Wedge")........................200-300 70s
(Label and number not known.)

ORANGUTANG
EPs: 7-inch
DEMIGOD (25061 "Bigger Chunk") 5-10 94
(Gold vinyl.)

ORBISON, Don
Singles: 7-inch
LAVENDER 4-8

ORBISON, Roy P&R '56
(With the Teen Kings; with Candy Men; with Roses; with Friends)
Singles: 78 rpm
QUALITY........................20-40 56
SUN (242 "Ooby Dooby") 30-50 56
SUN (251 "Rockhouse")...............30-50 56
SUN (265 "Sweet & Easy to Love")........................40-60 56
SUN (284 "Chicken Hearted")........50-75 58
Singles: 12-inch
VIRGIN (2667 "She's a Mystery to Me")........................10-15 89
(Includes cover.)
Singles: 7-inch
ASYLUM 3-5 78-79
COLLECTABLES 3-4 85
MGM 4-8 65-73
MGM CELEBRITY SCENE (CSN9-5 "Roy Orbison")........................50-75 66
(Boxed set of five singles with bio insert and juke box title strips.)
MERCURY 4-8 74
MONUMENT (409 "Paper Boy") 20-30 59
MONUMENT (412 "Uptown")..........15-25 59
MONUMENT (421 thru 467)..........10-20 60-62
MONUMENT (800 & 900 series)......8-15 63-66
MONUMENT (500 series)..............5-8 63
MONUMENT (8600 series)..............3-5 76
MONUMENT (8900 series)..............3-5 72
MONUMENT (45000 series)............3-5 76-77
QUALITY (1499 "Ooby Dooby")...50-100 56
(Canadian.)
QUALITY (1559 "Rockhouse").....50-100 56
(Canadian.)
RCA (7381 "Sweet & Innocent").......20-30 58
RCA (7447 "Jolie")........................20-30 59
SSS/SUN 3-5 70s
SUN (242 "Ooby Dooby") 40-60 56
SUN (251 "Rockhouse")...............40-60 56
SUN (265 "Sweet & Easy to Love") 25-50 56
SUN (284 "Chicken Hearted").........25-50 58
SUN (353 "Sweet & Easy to Love")15-25 61
(Yellow label.)
SUN (353 "Sweet & Easy to Love")........................25-50 61
(White label. Promotional issue only.)
VIRGIN........................3-5 87-89
Picture Sleeves
MGM 8-15 65-67
MONUMENT (400 series)..........15-25 60-62
MONUMENT (800 series)..........10-20 63-64
VIRGIN........................3-6 89
EPs: 7-inch
MGM (4379 "Classic Roy Orbison")........................30-50 66
(Juke box issue only.)
MONUMENT (2 "Crying") 20-30 62
(Compact 33, "Special Promotional Six-Pac." Not issued with special cover.)
MONUMENT (3 "Roy Orbison") 20-30 62
(Compact 33, "Special Promotional Six-Pac." Not issued with special cover.)
STARS INC. (101 "Roy Orbison and the Teen Kings")........................300-400 59
(Promotional issue, distributed to fan club members.)
LPs: 10/12-inch
ACCORD........................5-8 81
ASYLUM 5-8 78-79
BUCKBOARD........................8-10
CANDLELITE MUSIC..................10-15 70s
DESIGN 10-15 60s
MGM (E-4308 thru E-4514) 15-20 65-67
(Monaural.)
MGM (SE-4308 thru SE-4514).......20-30 65-67
(Stereo.)
MGM (4636 thru 4934)..............10-20 69-73
MGM/CAPITOL (90454 "There Is Only One Roy Orbison")........................10-20 65
(Label reads "Mfd. by Capitol Records." Record club issue.)
MERCURY........................8-12 75
MONUMENT (4002 "Lonely and Blue")........................100-200 61
(Monaural.)
MONUMENT (4007 "Crying".........50-100 62
(Monaural.)
MONUMENT (4009 "Greatest Hits")........................30-40 62
(Monaural.)
MONUMENT (6600 series).............8-10
MONUMENT (7600 "Regeneration")........................8-10 76
MONUMENT (8000 "Greatest Hits")........................25-30 63
(Monaural.)
MONUMENT (8003 "In Dreams")...30-40 63
(Monaural.)
MONUMENT (8023 "Early Orbison")........................30-40 64
(Monaural.)
MONUMENT (8024 "More Greatest Hits")........................20-25 64
(Monaural.)
MONUMENT (8035 "Orbisongs")...25-30 65
(Monaural.)
MONUMENT (8045 "Very Best")....30-40 66
(Blue cover. Monaural.)
MONUMENT (8045 "Very Best")...20-30 66
(Purple cover. Monaural.)
MONUMENT (14002 "Lonely and Blue")........................200-300 61
(Stereo.)
MONUMENT (14007 "Crying")...150-250 62
(Stereo.)
MONUMENT (14009 "Greatest Hits")........................40-50 62
(Stereo.)
MONUMENT (18000 "Greatest Hits")........................35-40 63
(Stereo.)
MONUMENT (18003 "In Dreams")........................40-50 63
(Stereo.)
MONUMENT (18024 "More Greatest Hits")........................25-30 64
(Stereo.)
MONUMENT (18035 "Orbisongs")........................35-40 65
(Stereo.)
MONUMENT (18023 "Early Orbison")........................30-40 64
(Stereo.)
MONUMENT (18045 "Very Best")...30-40 66
(Blue cover. Stereo.)
MONUMENT (18045 "Very Best")..20-30 66
(Purple cover. Stereo.)
MONUMENT (31484 "All-Time Greatest Hits")........................8-12 82
MONUMENT (38384 "All-Time Greatest Hits")........................6-10 82
RHINO 5-8 88
SPECTRUM 15-20 60s
SSS/SUN 5-10 69
SUN (1260 "Rock House").........200-300 61
SUNNYVALE........................8-10 77
TIME-LIFE........................10-15 86
TRIP........................8-10 74
VIRGIN........................6-12 87-89
Session: Bobby Goldsboro; Bruce Springsteen.
Also see CANDYMEN
Also see COOK, Ken
Also see DRIFTERS / Lesley Gore / Roy Orbison / Los Bravos
Also see GOLDSBORO, Bobby
Also see HIGGINS, Bertie, & Roy Orbison
Also see JAN & DEAN / Roy Orbison / 4 Seasons / Shirelles
Also see LEWIS, Jerry Lee / Roger Miller / Roy Orbison
Also see PERKINS, Carl, Jerry Lee Lewis, Roy Orbison & Johnny Cash
Also see SPRINGSTEEN, Bruce
Also see TEEN KINGS
Also see TRAVELING WILBURYS
Also see TUCKER, Rick
Also see WILSON, Peanuts

ORBISON, Roy / Bobby Bare / Joey Powers
LPs: 10/12-inch
CAMDEN........................15-25 64
Also see BARE, Bobby
Also see POWERS, Joey

ORBISON, Roy, & Emmylou Harris / Craig Hundley C&W/P&R '80
Singles: 7-inch
W.B. 3-5 80
Also see HARRIS, Emmylou

ORBISON, Roy, & k.d. Lang C&W '87
Singles: 7-inch
VIRGIN........................3-4 87
Also see LANG, k.d.
Also see ORBISON, Roy

ORBIT R&B '82
(Featuring Carol Hall)
Singles: 12-inch
QUALITY/RFC 4-6 82-84
Singles: 7-inch
QUALITY/RFC 3-4 82-84

ORBIT ROCKERS
Singles: 7-inch
WILLIAMETTE 10-15 59

ORBITEERS
Singles: 7-inch
FILM (716 "Landslide") 10-20 61

ORBITS
Singles: 78 rpm
ARGO (5286 "Mr. Hard Luck").......20-30 57
FLAIR-X (5000 "Message of Love")........................15-25 56
Singles: 7-inch
ARGO (5286 "Mr. Hard Luck")........25-50 57
DOOTO (601 "Tell Me Baby")..........10-20 60s
FLAIR-X (5000 "Message of Love")........................25-35 56
FRIDDELL........................30-40
NU-KAT (116 "Knock Her Down")...15-25 59

ORBITS
(Tommy Lee & Orbits)
Singles: 7-inch
GAITY (181 "Jingle Rock")...........25-35 61
SPACE (1116 "Queen Bee")......300-350 60

ORBITS
Singles: 7-inch
CUCA (1006 "Orbit Rock")..........10-20 66
(This is a different band than the Cuca one that follows.)
Member: Jerry Raimer; Bill Alexander; Bob Hoffer.

ORBITS
Singles: 7-inch
BIG SOUND (304 "Fuzzy")..........10-20 66
CUCA (6744 "Don't") 10-20 67
Member: Ron Hanson.

ORBITS
Singles: 7-inch
SSS INT'L 5-10 70s

ORBITS
(With the Rockin' Royals)
Singles: 7-inch
DON-J (48798 "I'm Home")........250-350

ORBITT III
LPs: 10/12-inch
BEVERLY HILLS........................8-12 73

ORCHESTRAL MANOEUVERS IN THE DARK LP '82
(OMD)
Singles: 12-inch
A&M....4-6 84-86
Singles: 7-inch
A&M....3-4 84-88
EPIC....3-5 82-83
Picture Sleeves
A&M....3-4 85-88
LPs: 10/12-inch
A&M....5-8 84-88
EPIC....5-10 82-83

ORCHID SPANGIAFORA
LPs: 10/12-inch
TWIN/TONE....5-8

ORCHIDS
Singles: 78 rpm
KING (4661 "Oh Why")....50-100 53
KING (4663 "I've Been a Fool from the Start")....50-100 53
PARROT (815 "Newly Wed")....50-100 55
PARROT (819 "You Said You Loved Me")....50-75 55
Singles: 7-inch
KING (4661 "Oh Why")....250-300 53
KING (4663 "I've Been a Fool from the Start")....250-300 53
LOST-NITE....4-8
PARROT (815 "Newly Wed")....250-300 55
PARROT (819 "You Said You Loved Me")....150-200 55
Members: Gilbert Warren; Buford Wright; Robert Nesbary.

ORCHIDS
Singles: 7-inch
HARLOW....10-15 62
ROULETTE....5-10 62-65
WALL....5-10 61
LPs: 10/12-inch
ROULETTE....20-30 62

ORCHIDS
Singles: 7-inch
COLUMBIA....5-10 63-64

ORCHIDS
Singles: 7-inch
MCA....3-5 80
LPs: 10/12-inch
MCA....5-10 80

ORDELLS
Singles: 7-inch
DIONN....4-8 67

ORDGE, Jimmy Arthur C&W '81
Singles: 7-inch
DORE....3-4 81

ORE'S HALYCON DAYS
LPs: 10/12-inch
AKASHIC (10-2-49-79 "Ore's Halycon Days")....8-12 79
(Picture disc.)

OREGON
LPs: 10/12-inch
ELEKTRA....5-10 78-80
VANGUARD....5-10 72-80

ORENDER, DeWayne C&W '76
Singles: 7-inch
NU-TRAYL....3-5 78
RCA....3-5 76-77
VOLUNTEER....3-5 78

ORGAN GRINDERS
Singles: 7-inch
SMASH....5-10 69
LPs: 10/12-inch
MERCURY (61282 "Out of the Egg")....15-25 70

ORIENT EXPRESS
LPs: 10/12-inch
MAINSTREAM (6117 "The Orient Express")....50-75 69
Members: Liz Damon; Guy Duris.
Also see DAMON, Liz

ORIENTALS
Singles: 7-inch
KAYO (346 "Please Come Back Home")....30-50 58
KAYO (927 "Get Yourself to School")....15-25 60s
NEW DAWN (413 "Misty Summer Night")....20-30 60s

ORIENTS
Singles: 7-inch
LAURIE (3232 "Queen of Angels")....15-20 64

ORIGINAL ANIMALS: see ANIMALS

ORIGINAL CADILLACS
Singles: 7-inch
JOSIE (821 "Hurry Home")....20-30 57
Members: Earl Carroll; Earl Wade; Charles Brooks; Bobby Phillips; Junior Glanton; Roland Martinez.
Also see CADILLACS
Also see CARROLL, Earl, & Original Cadillacs
Also see OPALS

ORIGINAL CAST
Singles: 7-inch
DOT....4-6 68

ORIGINAL CAST
(Featuring Kacey Cisyk)
Singles: 7-inch
ARISTA....3-5 77

ORIGINAL CASTE P&R '69
(Featuring Dixie Lee Innes)
Singles: 7-inch
DOT....4-8 68
T-A....4-8 69-70
Picture Sleeves
T-A....4-8 69
LPs: 10/12-inch
T-A....10-20 70
Also see INNES, Dixie Lee

ORIGINAL CASUALS P&R/R&B '58
(Featuring Gary Mears)
Singles: 7-inch
BACK BEAT (503 "So Tough")....10-20 58
BACK BEAT (510 "Ju-Judy")....10-20 58
BACK BEAT (514 "Three Kisses Past Midnight")....15-25 57
EPs: 7-inch
BACK BEAT (40 "Three Kisses Past Midnight")....50-100 58
Members: Gary Mears; Paul Kearney; Jay Adams.
Also see CASUALS

ORIGINAL CHARMERS
Singles: 7-inch
ANGLE TONE (550 "For Sentimental Reasons")....100-200 60

ORIGINAL CHARMERS
Singles: 7-inch
BLUE SKY....3-5 72

ORIGINAL CHECKERS
(Checkers)
Singles: 7-inch
KING....8-12 61
Also see CHECKERS

ORIGINAL CONCEPT R&B '86
Singles: 7-inch
DEF JAM....3-4 86

ORIGINAL CRESTS: see CRESTS

ORIGINAL DELL VIKINGS: see Del-Vikings

ORIGINAL DRIFTERS
Singles: 7-inch
SOUNDS SOUTH....3-5 78
Member: Bill Pinkney.
Also see PINKNEY, Bill

ORIGINAL DUKES
Singles: 7-inch
DOWN HOME (106 "Ain't About to Lose My Cool")....20-30 60s

ORIGINAL EMOTIONS
Singles: 7-inch
JOHNSON....3-5
Also see EMOTIONS

ORIGINAL FOUR ACES
Singles: 78 rpm
BIG TOWN....20-30 54
Singles: 7-inch
BIG TOWN (112 "I Can See an Angel")....50-75 54
BIG TOWN (118 "I Can See an Angel")....50-75 54
Also see FOUR ACES

ORIGINAL GROUP
(Monarchs)
Singles: 7-inch
SMASH (2219 "Look Homeward Angel")....4-6 69
Picture Sleeves
SMASH (2219 "Look Homeward Angel")....10-12 69
Also see MONARCHS

ORIGINAL HAUNTED
(Featuring Bob Burgess)
Singles: 7-inch
JET (4002 "Mona")....20-30 67
(Canadian.)
Also see HAUNTED

ORIGINAL HUSTLERS
Singles: 7-inch
LA BELLE (64121 "Cueball")....10-20 64
Also see HUSTLERS

ORIGINAL JUBALAIRES
Singles: 78 rpm
CROWN....50-75 54
Singles: 7-inch
CROWN (111 "Waiting All My Life for You")....75-125 54
CROWN (118 "You Won't Let Me Go")....50-100 54
Also see JUBALAIRES

ORIGINAL LAST POETS LP '71
LPs: 10/12-inch
JUGGERNAUT....10-15 71

ORIGINAL LIVERPOOL BEAT
LPs: 10/12-inch
20TH FOX (3144 "Original Liverpool Beat")....10-20 64
(Listed by title since there is no artist credited.)

ORIGINAL MIRRORS
LPs: 10/12-inch
ARISTA....5-10 80

ORIGINAL MUSEUM
Singles: 7-inch
TOM BOY....4-6 81
Also see MUSEUM

ORIGINAL MUSTANGS
Singles: 7-inch
HI-Q (5040 "Jump Lula")....10-20 61

ORIGINAL PLAYBOYS
Singles: 7-inch
LEISURE TIME (0001 "I'll Always Be By Your Side")....100-200

ORIGINAL PROPHETS
Singles: 7-inch
CIA (4509 "Ain't That Lovin' You Baby")....15-25 66

ORIGINAL PYRAMIDS
Singles: 7-inch
SHELL (304 "Ankle Bracelet")....15-25 61
Also see PYRAMIDS

ORIGINAL RED CAPS: see GIBSON, Steve

ORIGINAL RED TOPS
Singles: 7-inch
SKY (703 "Swanee River Rock")....8-12

ORIGINAL ROCKETS
Singles: 7-inch
RENDEZVOUS (164 "Garbage Can")....10-20 62

ORIGINAL ROYAL KINGS
Singles: 7-inch
CANDLELITE....5-10 63

ORIGINAL SINNERS
Singles: 7-inch
DISCOTECH (1001 "You'll Never Know")....15-25 66

ORIGINAL SMOKEHOUSE BAND
Singles: 7-inch
GLOW STAR (901 "Don't Let Your Mind Go Astray")....20-30 60s

ORIGINAL SOUNDTRACKS
Singles: 7-inch
LAWN....10-15 63

ORIGINAL STARFIRES: see STARFIRES

ORIGINAL SURFARIS: see SURFARIS

ORIGINAL SYMPTOMS
Singles: 7-inch
AMBITION....3-5 80
Picture Sleeves
AMBITION....3-5 81
Members: D. Clinton Thompson; Jim Wunderle; Lou Whitney; Maralie; Ron Gremp.

ORIGINAL TATOOS
LPs: 10/12-inch
MPS....8-10 72

ORIGINAL TEXAS PLAYBOYS: see TEXAS PLAYBOYS

ORIGINAL TWISTERS
LPs: 10/12-inch
WING....15-25 62

ORIGINALES
Singles: 7-inch
POOR BOY (110 Lend Me Your Ear")....50-100 60
Members: Tom Smalley; Ron Bonham; Sonny Johnson; Sam Dargo; Jan Conway.

ORIGINALS
Singles: 7-inch
JACKPOT (48007 "The Whip")....15-25 58
JACKPOT (48012 "Anna")....15-25 58
Also see RIO, Chuck

ORIGINALS
Singles: 7-inch
BRUNSWICK (55171 "A Kiss from Your Lips")....15-25 60

ORIGINALS
Singles: 7-inch
ORIGINAL SOUND....15-25 60

ORIGINALS
Singles: 7-inch
DIAMOND (102 "At Times Like This")....20-30 61
DIAMOND (116 "Summer School")....20-30 62

ORIGINALS
Singles: 7-inch
VAN (02165 "Blast Off!")....10-20 65
VAN (03065 "Night Flight")....10-20 65

ORIGINALS
Singles: 7-inch
RAYNARD (10039 "Now's the Time")....4-8 65
Members: Dan Helland; Jim Morrison; Pete Polzak; Jim Jandrain; Tim Polzak.

ORIGINALS
Singles: 7-inch
SARA....5-10 65
Members: Tom Spacek; Jim Nelner; Arthur Shore; Stanley Palkowitz; Bob Radusta; Steve Miscovey; David Bruce.

ORIGINALS
Singles: 7-inch
CHAMP....5-10 66

ORIGINALS P&R/R&B '69
Singles: 7-inch
FANTASY....3-5 78
MOTOWN (1 "Young Train")....100-200 73
(Promotional issue only.)
MOTOWN (1300 series)....4-6 75
PHASE II....3-5 81
SOUL (35029 thru 35061)....6-12 67-69
SOUL (35066 thru 35119)....4-8 69-76
(Black vinyl.)
SOUL (Colored vinyl)....8-15
(Promotional issue only.)
LPs: 10/12-inch
FANTASY....5-10 78-79
MOTOWN....5-10 74-80
SOUL (716 "Baby I'm for Real")....20-40 69
SOUL (724 "Portrait")....15-20 70
SOUL (729 "Naturally Together")....15-20 70
SOUL (734 thru 746)....8-15 73-76
Members: Ty Hunter; Henry Dixon; Joe Stubbs; Walt Gaines; C.P. Spencer; Freddie Gorman.
Also see CONTOURS
Also see FIVE STARS
Also see GORMAN, Freddie
Also see HUNTER, Ty
Also see STUBBS, Joe
Also see VOICE MASTERS

ORIGINALS & JERMAINE JACKSON
Singles: 12-inch
MOTOWN....4-8 76
Also see JACKSON, Jermaine
Also see ORIGINALS

O-R-I-G-I-N-A-L-S
LPs: 10/12-inch
STASH....5-10 80

ORIGINELLS 4
Singles: 7-inch
APT....10-15 65

ORIOLES P&R/R&B '48
(With the Sid Bass Orchestra; Sonny Til & Orioles; Sonny Til's Orioles)
Singles: 78 rpm
IT'S a NATURAL (5000 "It's Too Soon to Know")....50-150 48
JUBILEE (5000 "It's too Soon to Know")....25-75 48
JUBILEE (5001 "Dare to Dream")....25-75 48
JUBILEE (5001 "Lonely Christmas")....25-75 48
JUBILEE (5002 "Please Give My Heart a Break")....25-75 49
JUBILEE (5005 "Tell Me So")....25-75 49
JUBILEE (5008 "I Challenge Your Kiss")....25-75 49
JUBILEE (5009 "A Kiss and a Rose")....25-75 49
JUBILEE (5016 "So Much")....25-75 49
JUBILEE (5017 "What Are You Doing New Year's Eve")....25-75 49
JUBILEE (5018 "Would You Still Be the One in My Heart")....25-75 50
JUBILEE (5025 "At Night")....25-75 50
JUBILEE (5026 "Moonlight")....25-75 50
JUBILEE (5028 "You're Gone")....25-75 50
JUBILEE (5031 "I'd Rather Have You Under the Moon")....20-60 50
JUBILEE (5037 "I Need You So")....20-60 50
JUBILEE (5040 "I Cross My Fingers")....20-60 50
JUBILEE (5045 "Oh Holy Night")....20-60 50
JUBILEE (5051 "I Miss You So")....20-60 51
JUBILEE (5055 "Pal of Mine")....20-60 51
JUBILEE (5057 "Would I Love You")....20-60 51
JUBILEE (5061 "I'm Just a Fool in Love")....20-60 51
At least 10 of the above 78rpm singles were reissued around 1951 on 45s. It's likely that others in the 5001-5061 series appeared on early '50s Jubilee 45s, but those listed below are the only ones we have verified.
JUBILEE (5061 thru 5231)....15-45 51-56
QUALITY....20-30 53
(Canadian.)
VEE JAY....15-35 56-57
Singles: 7-inch
ABNER (1016 "Sugar Girl")....25-50 58
CHARLIE PARKER....8-15 62-63
COLLECTABLES....3-4 80s
JUBILEE (5000 "It's Too Soon to Know")....3000-5000 51
JUBILEE (5005 "Tell Me So") 2000-3000 51
JUBILEE (5016 "So Much")....1000-2000 51
JUBILEE (5017 "What Are You Doing New Year's Eve")....500-1000 51
JUBILEE (5025 "At Night")....500-1000 51
JUBILEE (5040 "I Cross My Fingers")....500-750 51
JUBILEE (5045 "Oh Holy Night")....500-750 51
JUBILEE (5051 "I Miss You So")....500-750 51
(Black vinyl.)
JUBILEE (5051 "I Miss You So")....1000-2000 51
(Red vinyl.)
JUBILEE (5061 "I'm Just a Fool in Love")....550-650 51
JUBILEE (5065 "Baby, Please Don't Go")....400-500 51
(Black vinyl.)
JUBILEE (5065 "Baby, Please Don't Go")....1000-2000 51
(Red vinyl.)
JUBILEE (5071 "When You're Not Around")....300-500 51
JUBILEE (5074 "Trust in Me")....550-650 52
JUBILEE (5082 "It's Over Because We're Through")....550-650 52
JUBILEE (5084 "Barfly")....300-500 52
JUBILEE (5092 "Don't Cry Baby")....300-500 52
(Black vinyl.)
JUBILEE (5092 "Don't Cry Baby")....1000-1500 52
(Red vinyl.)
JUBILEE (5102 "You Belong to Me")....300-500 52
JUBILEE (5107 "I Miss You So")....300-500 53
(Reissued in 1963, using the same catalog number, but credited to Sonny Til & Orioles. Black vinyl.)
JUBILEE (5107 "I Miss You So")....1000-1500 53
(Red vinyl.)
JUBILEE (5108 "Teardrops on My Pillow")....300-500 53
(Black vinyl.)
JUBILEE (5108 "Teardrops on My Pillow")....1000-1500 53
(Red vinyl.)
JUBILEE (5115 "Bad Little Girl")....300-500 53
JUBILEE (5120 "I Cover the Waterfront")....300-500 53
(Black vinyl.)
JUBILEE (5120 "I Cover the Waterfront")....1000-1500 53
(Red vinyl.)
JUBILEE (5122 "Crying in the Chapel")....50-100 53
JUBILEE (5127 "In the Mission of St. Augustine")....50-100 53
JUBILEE (5134 "There's No One But You")....50-100 54
JUBILEE (5137 "Secret Love")....50-100 54
JUBILEE (5143 "Maybe You'll Be There")....75-125 54
JUBILEE (5154 "In the Chapel in the Moonlight")....50-75 54
JUBILEE (5161 "If You Believe")....50-75 54
JUBILEE (5172 "Runaround")....50-75 54
JUBILEE (5177 "I Love You Mostly")....25-50 55
JUBILEE (5189 "I Need You Baby")....25-50 55
JUBILEE (5221 "Please Sing My Blues Tonight")....25-50 55
JUBILEE (5231 "Angel")....30-60 56
JUBILEE (5363 "Tell Me So")....10-20 59
JUBILEE (5384 "Come On Home")....10-20 60
JUBILEE (5394 "Night & Day")....50-75 60
JUBILEE (6001 "Crying in the Chapel")....10-15 59
(Jubilee 5066 & 5076 are credited to Sonny Til.)
QUALITY (1139 "Crying in the Chapel")....50-75 53
(Canadian.)
ROULETTE....3-5 70s
VEE JAY (196 "Happy Till the Letter")....25-50 56
VEE JAY (228 "For All We Know")....25-50 56
VEE JAY (244 "Sugar Girl")....25-50 57
VIRGO....3-5 70s
Picture Sleeves
JUBILEE (5017 "What Are You Doing New Year's Eve")....300-500 54
(Sleeve for 78 rpm.)
JUBILEE (5017 "What Are You Doing New Year's Eve")....550-650 54
(Sleeve for 45 rpm.)
JUBILEE (5045 "Oh Holy Night")....550-650 54
(Both Jubilee sleeves were issued in late 1954 and sold with 1954 pressings, actually second pressings of both. These were blue script Jubilee labels with the line under the logo.)
LANA....3-6 63
EPs: 7-inch
JUBILEE (5000 "The Orioles Sing")....1000-2000 53
LPs: 10/12-inch
BIG A RECORDS (2001 "Greatest All Time Hits")....20-30 69
CHARLIE PARKER (816 "Modern Sounds")....50-100 62
COLLECTABLES....5-10 84
MURRAY HILL....30-40 80s
(Boxed, five-disc set. Number not known.)
MURRAY HILL (61277 "The Orioles Featuring Sonny Til")....30-40 80s
(Boxed, five-disc set.)
ROULETTE....5-10
Members: Sonny Til; Alex Sharp; George Nelson; John Reed; Tom Gaither; Charles Harris; Greg Carroll; Billy Adams; Jerry Holman; Al Russell; Jerry Rodriguez; Bill Taylor.
Also see CADILLACS / Orioles
Also see REGALS
Also see TIL, Sonny

ORION C&W '79
(Jimmy Ellis)
Singles: 7-inch
KRISTAL....3-5 85
ORCHID....3-5 89
SUN....3-8 79-84
(Most, if not all, on colored vinyl – usually gold.)
Promotional Singles
SUN (1142 "Ebony Eyes"/"Honey")....10-20 79
(With unprinted white label. Includes flyer explaining blank label idea.)
EPs: 7-inch
ORION ("Merry Christmas")....10-15 80s
(Fan club issue.)

SUN (1152 "A Stranger in My Place")....15-25 80
(Promotional issue only. Price includes explanatory flyer. Not issued with cover.)
LPs: 10/12-inch
ARON....10-15 89
(Canadian.)
SUFFOLK MARKETING....10-15 81
(TV mail-order LP.)
SUN (Except 1012)....10-20 79-81
(Most Sun LPs are colored vinyl)
SUN (1012 "Orion Reborn")....20-30 78
(White cover. Often referred to as with the "Coffin Cover.")
SUN (1012 "Orion Reborn")....10-15 78
(Blue cover.)
Also see ELLIS, Jimmy
Also see LEWIS, Jerry Lee, & Friends

ORION
LPs: 10/12-inch
LONDON....8-10 75

ORION, P.J., & Magnates
LPs: 10/12-inch
MAGNATE (122459 "P.J. Orion and the Magnates")....75-125 60s

ORION the HUNTER P&R/LP '84
Singles: 7-inch
PORTRAIT....3-5 84-85
LPs: 10/12-inch
PORTRAIT (39239 "Orion the Hunter")....20-40 84
Member: Barry Goudreau.
Also see BOSTON

ORK, Jay Hodge
Singles: 7-inch
CORNUTO (1000 "Goatsville")....10-20
(Colored vinyl.)

ORLANDO, Tony
Singles: 7-inch
MILO (101 "Ding Dong")....30-50 59
Also see SIMON, Paul

ORLANDO, Tony P&R '61
Singles: 12-inch
CASABLANCA....5-10 79
Singles: 7-inch
ATCO....4-8 65
CAMEO....4-8 67
CASABLANCA....3-5 79-80
EPIC (9000 series)....5-10 61-64
Promotional Singles
EPIC (55299 "Happy Times Are Here to Stay")....8-12 61
LPs: 10/12-inch
EPIC (611 "Bless You")....35-40 61
(Stereo.)
EPIC (3808 "Bless You")....35-40 61
(Monaural.)
EPIC (33785 "Before Dawn")....10-12 75
CASABLANCA....5-10 79-80
Picture Sleeves
EPIC....8-10 61-62
Also see DACHE, Bertell
Also see JERRY & JEFF
Also see SHIELDS, Billy
Also see WIND

ORLANDO, Tony, & Dawn P&R/LP '70
Singles: 7-inch
ARISTA....3-5 75
BELL....3-5 71-74
ELEKTRA....3-5 75-78
LPs: 10/12-inch
ARISTA....8-10 75-76
ASYLUM....8-10 75
BELL (6000 series)....10-12 70-71
BELL (1000 series)....8-10 73-75
ELEKTRA....8-10 75-78
KORY....8-10 74-77
Also see DAWN
Also see ORLANDO, Tony

ORLANDOS
Singles: 7-inch
CINDY (3006 "Old MacDonald")....200-300 57
(Cindy logo is in block print with a shadow behind the letters.)
CINDY(3006 "Old MacDonald")....50-100 57
(Cindy logo is in a rectangular box at the top of the label.)

ORLEANS P&R/LP '75
Singles: 7-inch
ABC....3-5 73
ASYLUM....3-5 75-77
INFINITY....3-5 79
MCA....3-4 86
LPs: 10/12-inch
ABC....10-12 73-78
ASYLUM....8-10 75-76
INFINITY....5-10 79
RADIO....5-8 82
Member: John Hall.
Also see HALL, John

ORLIE & SAINTS
Singles: 7-inch
BAND BOX (253 "Detroit Twist and Freeze")....10-15 61
BAND BOX (253-H "Baltimore Twist and Freeze")....10-15 61
BAND BOX (264 "Annette")....10-20 61

ORLONS P&R/R&B/LP '62
Singles: 7-inch
ABC....4-8 67
ABKCO....3-5
CALLA (113 "Spinnin' Top")....8-12 66
CAMEO (198 "I'll Be True")....30-50 61
CAMEO (211 "Mr. Twenty-One")....30-50 62
CAMEO (218 thru 372)....8-15 62-65
CAMEO (384 "Envy")....30-40 65
JUKE BOX (509 "I'll Be True")....8-10
Picture Sleeves
CAMEO....8-15 62-64
LPs: 10/12-inch
CAMEO (1020 "Wah Watusi")....30-60 62
CAMEO (1033 "All the Hits")....25-50 62
CAMEO (1041 "South Street")....25-50 63
CAMEO (1054 "Not Me")....25-50 63
CAMEO (1061 "Biggest Hits")....25-50 63
CAMEO (1073 "Memory Lane")....25-50 63
Members: Shirley Brickley; Rosetta Hightower; Steve Caldwell; Marlena Davis.
Also see ZIP & ZIPPERS

ORLONS / Dovells
LPs: 10/12-inch
CAMEO (1067 "Golden Hits")....25-50 63
Also see DOVELLS
Also see ORLONS

ORMANDY
Singles: 7-inch
DECCA (32741 "Good Day")....10-15 70
KASABA (100 "Good Day")....10-20 70
STARSHINE (7203 "The Banker")....8-12 70s
Member: Alto Reed.
Also see SEGER, Bob

ORMSBY, Bobby
Singles: 7-inch
PLATINUM SOUND....3-4 85

ORO, Emmy, & Her Rhythm Escorts
Singles: 7-inch
CHELSEA (1001 "Is It a Sin")....25-40 61

ORPHAN
Singles: 7-inch
LONDON....3-5 72-74
LPs: 10/12-inch
LONDON....8-12 72-74

ORPHAN EGG
LPs: 10/12-inch
CAROLE (8004 "Orphan Egg")....15-25 68

ORPHANS
Singles: 7-inch
EPIC....4-8 68

ORPHENS
Singles: 7-inch
RED BIRD....5-10 65

ORPHEUS LP '68
Singles: 7-inch
MGM....4-6 68-69
Picture Sleeves
MGM....4-6 69
LPs: 10/12-inch
BELL....10-12 71
MGM....10-15 68-69

ORQUESTRA SOUL
(Orquesta Soul)
LPs: 10/12-inch
DOT....10-15 67
MERCURY....10-15 67

ORR, Benjamin P&R/LP '86
Singles: 7-inch
ELEKTRA....3-4 86
Picture Sleeves
ELEKTRA....3-4 86
LPs: 10/12-inch
ELEKTRA....5-8 86
Also see CARS

ORR, Chet, & Rumbles
Singles: 7-inch
STUDIO CITY (1012 "Be Satisfied")....40-60 60s
Members: Chet Orr; Dennis Konkel; Dave Lindemann; John Rookey; Don Fenn; John Grindal.

ORR, J.D.
Singles: 7-inch
SUMMIT (105 "Hula-Hoop Boogie")....200-300 58

ORRALL, Robert Ellis P&R/LP '83
(With Carlene Carter)
Singles: 7-inch
RCA....3-5 81-91
LPs: 10/12-inch
RCA....5-10 81-91
Also see CARTER, Carlene

ORRELL, David
Singles: 7-inch
FELSTED (8515 "Be My Baby")....50-75 58

ORRISON, Bob
Singles: 7-inch
LIBERTY....8-10 60

ORSI, Phil
(With the Little Kings)
Singles: 7-inch
LUCKY (1009 "Oh My Darling")....300-500 63
LUCKY (1015 "Don't You Just Know It")....25-50 64
SONIC....3-6 77
U.S.A....10-15 66
WISE WORLD (62770 "Oh My Darling")....100-200 63

ORTEGA, Frankie
Singles: 7-inch
JUBILEE (1106 "77 Sunset Strip")....15-25 59

ORTEGA, Gilbert C&W '78
Singles: 7-inch
LRJ....3-5 78
ORTEGA....3-5 78

ORTEGA, Paulito
Singles: 7-inch
RCA....3-5 67

ORVILLE & IVY C&W '67
Singles: 7-inch
IMPERIAL....4-6 67
Members: W.W. "Speedy" West; Jimmy Bryant.

ORVIS, John, & Smoke: see SMOKE

O'RYAN, Jack, & Al Tercek
Singles: 78 rpm
NOCTURNE (8 "Political Circus")....20-30 56
Singles: 7-inch
NOCTURNE (8 "Political Circus")....25-50 56

OSAMU
LPs: 10/12-inch
A&M....5-8 88
ISLAND....8-10 77

OSANNA
LPs: 10/12-inch
PETERS INT'L....10-12 73-74

OSBORN, Bill
Singles: 7-inch
CAMELOT....5-10

OSBORN, Bobby
Singles: 7-inch
KNICKERBOCKER....5-10

OSBORN, Richetta
Singles: 7-inch
BLUE RIVER....4-8 67

OSBORNE, Arthur
Singles: 7-inch
BRUNSWICK (55068 "Hey Ruby")....50-75 58

OSBORNE, B., & Tracers
Singles: 7-inch
RIC (165 "My Baby Gives Me Lovin'")....10-20

OSBORNE, Billy
Singles: 7-inch
CYCLONE (1000 "My Baby Blues")....25-35

OSBORNE, Chuck
Singles: 7-inch
ABC-PAR....4-8 63

OSBORNE, Jeffrey P&R/R&B/LP '82
Singles: 12-inch
A&M....4-6 82-86
Singles: 7-inch
A&M....3-5 82-88
ARISTA....3-4 90
Picture Sleeves
A&M....3-5 82-88
LPs: 10/12-inch
A&M....5-10 82-88
ARISTA....5-8 90
Also see KENNEDY, Joyce, & Jeffrey Osborne
Also see L.T.D.
Also see WARWICK, Dionne, & Jeffrey Osborne

OSBORNE, Jerry
Singles: 7-inch
JELLYROLL (10676 "The Country Side of '76")....4-6 76
(With Bruce Hamilton. 500 made.)
RECORD DIGEST (25794 "The Graceland Tour")....5-10 79
(Elvis break-in soundsheet, given as a bonus to *Presleyana* book buyers. 500 made)
Also see JAY, Jerry
Also see PRESLEY, Elvis
Also see SLINKY, Ratmore

OSBORNE, Jimmie C&W '48
Singles: 78 rpm
KING....5-10 48-55
Singles: 7-inch
KING....10-20 52-55
EPs: 7-inch
AUDIO LAB (3 "Jimmie Osborne")....10-15 59
LPs: 10/12-inch
AUDIO LAB (1527 "Songs He Wrote")....25-35 59
KING....15-25 61-65

OSBORNE, Johnny, & Mello Jacks
Singles: 78 rpm
TUNE (1002 "Sax Maniac")....5-10 54
Singles: 7-inch
TUNE (1002 "Sax Maniac")....15-25 54

OSBORNE, Kell
(With the Chicks; Kell Osborne's Band)
Singles: 7-inch
CLASS (302 "Do You Mind")....10-15 62
GLOWHILL (702 "That's What's Happening")....8-12 60s
LOMA (2023 "You Can't Outsmart a Woman")....8-10 65
REVIS (1010 "Somethin' for the Books")....8-12 60s
TITANIC (5008 "Quicksand")....50-100 63
TREY (3006 "Bells of St. Mary's")....15-25 60
Also see KELL & CHERRY

OSBORNE, Mary
Singles: 7-inch
WARWICK (531 "I Love Paris")....5-10 60
LPs: 10/12-inch
WARWICK (2004 "A Girl and Her Guitar")....15-25 60

OSBORNE, Tony
Singles: 7-inch
DERAM (85030 "Sun Spot")....8-12 68
KING (5525 "Swinging Gypsies")....10-20 61

OSBORNE & GILES R&B '85
Singles: 7-inch
RED LABEL....3-4 85
LPs: 10/12-inch
RED LABEL....5-8 85
Members: Billy Osborne; Attala Giles.

OSBORNE BROTHERS C&W '58
(With Red Allen)
Singles: 7-inch
CMH....3-5 80
DECCA....3-8 63-72
MCA....3-5 73-75
MGM (100 series)....3-5 64
MGM (12000 & 13000 series)....4-10 59-63
EPs: 7-inch
MGM....10-15 59
LPs: 10/12-inch
CMH....5-10 76-82
CORAL....5-10 73
DECCA....10-20 65-72
MCA....5-10 73-75
MGM (100 series)....5-10 70
MGM (3700 series)....25-35 59
MGM (4000 series)....15-25 62-63
PICKWICK....5-10 70s
ROUNDER....5-8 80s
SUGAR HILL....5-8 84
Members: Bobby Osborne; Sonny Osborne; Benny Birchfield. Session: Ronnie Reno; Jimmy Martin.
Also see MARTIN, Jimmy
Also see RENO, Ronnie

OSBORNE BROTHERS & Mac Wiseman C&W '79
(With Red Allen)
Singles: 7-inch
CMH....3-5 79
Also see OSBORNE BROTHERS
Also see WISEMAN, Mac

OSBOURNE, Ozzy LP '81
Singles: 12-inch
EPIC (37640 "Mr. Crowley Live")....30-40 82
(Picture disc.)
JETT (6400 "Mr. Crowley Live")....20-30 81
(Picture disc. Promotional issue only.)
JET (7670 "Diary of a Madman")....30-40 81
(Picture disc. Promotional issue only.)
JET (7670 "Diary of a Madman")....45-55 81
(Picture disc. Promotional issue only. Has KMET logo on one side.)
Singles: 7-inch
CBS ASSOCIATED....3-4 83-86
JET....3-5 82
Picture Sleeves
CBS ASSOCIATED....3-4 86
JET....3-5 82
LPs: 10/12-inch
CBS ASSOCIATED (Black vinyl)....5-8 83-90
CBS ASSOCIATED (40543 "Ultimate Live Ozzy")....25-35 86
(Picture disc. Promotional issue only.)
JET (Black vinyl)....5-10 81-82
JET (1327 "Diary of a Madman")....45-50 81
(Promotional only picture disc.)
Also see BLACK SABBATH
Also see FORD, Lita, & Ozzy Osbourne
Also see QUIET RIOT

OSBOURNE, Ozzy, & Randy Rhoads LP '87
LPs: 10/12-inch
CBS ASSOC....5-8 87

OSBURN, Bob
Singles: 7-inch
LE CAM....4-8 64

OSCAR
LPs: 10/12-inch
BASF/BUK....10-12 74
DJM....8-10 76

OSCAR & MAJESTICS
Singles: 7-inch
U.S.A. (851 "I Can't Explain")....15-25 66
Members: Oscar Hamod; Sam Hamod; Robert Wheeler; John Toda; Vince Jimkimzak.
Also see HAMOD, Oscar, & Majestics

OSCAR & ROMEO
Singles: 7-inch
MERCURY (71768 "Come On Home")....5-10 60
MERCURY (71954 "Phil's March")....5-10 62

OSCAR 5
Singles: 7-inch
D&C (171 "I Won't Be Your Fool")....15-25 67

O'SHEA, Cathy C&W '78
Singles: 7-inch
MCA....3-5 78

O'SHEA, Paul, with Four Jacks & a Jill
LPs: 10/12-inch
RIVERSIDE....25-35 60

O'SHEA, Shad C&W '76
(With the 18 Wheelers)
Singles: 7-inch
NORMAN....4-8 63
PRIVATE STOCK....3-5 76
SOUND STAGE 7....4-8 64-65
Also see BONEPARTE, Gonzalez

OSHINS, Milt
Singles: 78 rpm
PELVIS (169 "All About Elvis")....20-30 56
Singles: 7-inch
PELVIS (169 "All About Elvis")....30-50 56
(Some pressings have no artist credited.)

OSHUN
Singles: 7-inch
MERCURY (72685 "Battle of Life")....10-20 67

OSIBISA LP '71
Singles: 7-inch
DECCA....3-5 72
ISLAND....3-5 76-77
MCA....3-4
W.B....3-5 73-74
LPs: 10/12-inch
BUDDAH....8-10 73
DECCA....10-12 71-72
ISLAND....8-10 77
MCA....5-8
W.B....8-10 73-74

OSIRIS R&B '79
Singles: 7-inch
INFINITY....3-5 79
W.B....3-5 79
LPs: 10/12-inch
INFINITY....5-10 79
W.B....5-10 79
Members: Osiris Marsh.

OSKAR, Lee P&R/R&B/LP '76
Singles: 7-inch
ELEKTRA....3-5 78-81
U.A....3-5 76
LPs: 10/12-inch
ELEKTRA....5-10 78-79
U.A....8-10 76
Also see WAR

OSLIN, K.T. C&W '81
(Kay T. Oslin)
Singles: 7-inch
ELEKTRA....5-10 81
RCA....3-4 86-91
LPs: 10/12-inch
RCA....5-8 87-91

OSMOND, Donny P&R/LP '71
Singles: 7-inch
CAPITOL....3-4 89
MGM....3-5 71-75
POLYDOR....3-5 76-78
Picture Sleeves
CAPITOL....3-4 89
MGM....3-5 71-75
LPs: 10/12-inch
CAPITOL....5-8 89-90
MGM....8-10 71-74
POLYDOR....5-10 76-77
Also see OSMONDS

OSMOND, Donny & Marie P&R/C&W/LP '74
Singles: 7-inch
MGM....3-5 74-75
POLYDOR....3-5 76-78
LPs: 10/12-inch
MGM....8-10 74-75
POLYDOR....5-10 76-78
Also see D&M
Also see OSMOND, Donny
Also see OSMOND, Marie

OSMOND, Jimmy P&R/LP '72
(Little Jimmy Osmond)
Singles: 7-inch
MGM....3-5 70-75
MERCURY....3-5 78
LPs: 10/12-inch
MGM....8-10 72
Also see OSMONDS

OSMOND, Marie C&W/P&R/LP '73
(Marie)
Singles: 7-inch
CURB....3-4 90
CURB/CAPITOL....3-5 85-89
ELEKTRA/CURB....3-5 82-84
MGM....3-5 73-75
POLYDOR....3-5 76-78
RCA/CURB....3-5 84
Picture Sleeves
MGM....3-5 73-75
POLYDOR....3-5 77
RCA....3-5 84
LPs: 10/12-inch
CURB/CAPITOL....5-8 85-88
MGM....8-12 73-75
POLYDOR....5-8 77
Also see OSMOND, Donny & Marie
Also see OSMONDS

OSMOND, Marie, & Paul Davis C&W '86
Singles: 7-inch
CAPITOL....3-4 86-88
Also see DAVIS, Paul

OSMOND, Marie, & Osmond Brothers
LPs: 10/12-inch
UNITED (12924 "Our Best to You")....5-10 85
(Special products promotional issue, made for Case International.)
Also see OSMONDS

OSMOND, Marie, & Dan Seals C&W '85
Singles: 7-inch
CURB/CAPITOL....3-4 85

Also see OSMOND, Marie
Also see SEALS, Dan

OSMONDS *P&R/R&B/LP '71*
(Osmond Brothers)
Singles: 7–inch
BARNABY ... 4-6 68-69
CURB/EMI ... 3-4 85-86
EMI AMERICA ... 3-4 85-86
ELEKTRA/CURB ... 3-5 82-83
MGM (13126 thru 14159) ... 4-6 63-70
MGM (14193 thru 14831) ... 3-5 70-75
MERCURY ... 3-5 79
POLYDOR ... 3-5 76-77
UNI (55015 "I Can't Stop") ... 4-8 67
UNI (55276 "I Can't Stop") ... 3-5 71
W.B./CURB ... 3-5 83-85
Picture Sleeves
MGM ... 3-5 73-74
LPs: 10/12–inch
EMI AMERICA ... 5-8 86
ELEKTRA ... 5-10 82
MGM (7 "Preview—the Osmond Brothers") ... 15-20 70s
(Promotional issue only.)
MGM (4100 & 4200 series) ... 25-35 63-65
MGM (4724 thru 5012) ... 8-12 70-75
MERCURY ... 5-10 79
METRO ... 10-20 65
POLYDOR ... 5-10 76-77
W.B./CURB ... 5-8 83-85
Members: Donny Osmond; Alan Osmond; Merrill Osmond; Wayne Osmond; Jimmy Osmond; Marie Osmond.
Also see CURB, Mike
Also see MERRILL & JESSICA
Also see OSMOND, Donny
Also see OSMOND, Jimmy
Also see OSMOND, Marie

OSMONDS, Steve Lawrence & Eydie Gorme *P&R '72*
Singles: 7–inch
MGM ... 3-5 72
Also see LAWRENCE, Steve, & Eydie Gorme
Also see OSMONDS

OSMOSIS
Singles: 7–inch
RCA ... 3-5 70
LPs: 10/12–inch
RCA ... 10-15 70

OSMUS, Gib
Singles: 7–inch
CUCA (67115 "Bad Love") ... 10-15 67

OSPREYS
Singles: 7–inch
EAST WEST (110 "It's Good to Me") ... 15-25 58

OSTER, Al
Singles: 7–inch
TUNDRA (101 "Midnight Sun Rock") ... 200-300
LPs: 10/12–inch
ALKON (1001 "Alaska Purchase Centennial: Ballads of the North") ... 150-200 67
ALKON (1002 "Northland Ballads") ... 150-200 60s
ALKON (1003 "Alaska, Star 49") ... 150-200 60s
DOMINION (1321 "Echo of the Yukon") ... 150-200
FRONTIER (1006 "Yukon Ballads") ... 100-150
KLONDIKE (1 "Yukon Gold") ... 150-200

O'SULLIVAN, Gilbert *P&R/LP '72*
Singles: 7–inch
EPIC ... 3-5 77-81
MAM ... 3-8 71-76
Picture Sleeves
MAM ... 3-5 72
LPs: 10/12–inch
EPIC ... 5-10 81
MAM ... 10-15 72-73

OSWALD, Lee Harvey, vs Carlos Bringuier
(With narrator, Dr. Billy James Hargis)
LPs: 10/12–inch
EYEWITNESS (1002 "Lee Harvey Oswald Speaks") ... 35-55 64
(From a 1963 radio interview in New Orleans.)
KEY (880 "The President's Assassin Speaks") ... 35-55 64
(Debate between Oswald and Bringuier, taped three months before the assassination.)

OTHER BROTHERS
Singles: 7–inch
AMY ... 5-10 68
MODERN ... 8-12 67

OTHER FIVE
Singles: 7–inch
GREGMARK ... 5-10 61

OTHER FOUR
Singles: 7–inch
DECCA ... 4-8 66
MUSETTE ... 4-8 65

OTHER HALF
LPs: 10/12–inch
RESURRECTION (1266 "The Other Half") ... 8-10 84
7/2 (1 "The Other Half") ... 1000-1500 66
Members: Andrea Inganni; Bob Collett.

OTHER HALF
Singles: 7–inch
ACTA ... 10-20 67-68
GNP ... 10-15 68
LPs: 10/12–inch
ACTA (38004 "Other Half") ... 50-100 68
Members: Randy Holden; Jeff Nowlen; Craig Tawater; Mike Port.
Also see HOLDEN, Randy
Also see SONS of ADAM

OTHER HALF
Singles: 7–inch
ATCO ... 4-8 67-68

OTHER ONES
Singles: 7–inch
ABC-PAR ... 8-12 66
KNOLL ... 10-20 60s

OTHER ONES *P&R/LP '87*
Singles: 7–inch
VIRGIN ... 3-4 87
Picture Sleeves
VIRGIN ... 3-4 87
LPs: 10/12–inch
VIRGIN ... 5-8 87
Members: Alf Klimek; Johnny Klimek; Steven Gottwald; Andreas Schwartz-Ruszczynski.

OTHER SIDE
Singles: 7–inch
BRENT ... 8-12 66
Also see WILDFLOWER / Harbinger Complex / Euphoria / Other Side

OTHER SIDE
Singles: 7–inch
CENTER (1208 "I'm Not Hurt") ... 5-8
DE LITE ... 3-5 78
LPs: 10/12–inch
DE LITE ... 5-10 78

OTHER TIKIS
Singles: 7–inch
AUTUMN ... 5-10 65
Also see HARPERS BIZARRE
Also see TIKIS

OTHER TWO
Singles: 7–inch
JERDEN ... 5-8 65
PANORAMA ... 5-8 66
RCA ... 5-8 65

OTHER VOICES
Singles: 7–inch
ATLANTIC ... 4-8 68

OTHERS
Singles: 7–inch
FONTANA (1944 "Oh Yeah") ... 10-20 64

OTHERS
Singles: 7–inch
JUBILEE (5550 "My Friend the Wizard") ... 5-10 66
RCA (8669 "I Can't Stand This Love, Goodbye") ... 15-25 65
RCA (8776 "Lonely Street") ... 5-10 66

OTHERS
Singles: 7–inch
MERCURY (72602 "Revenge") ... 15-25 66

OTIS, Clyde
EPs: 7–inch
KAPP (755 "The Stroll") ... 10-15 58
MERCURY (71776 "Jungle Drums") ... 5-10 61

OTIS, Johnny *R&B '50*
(Johnny Otis Show; Quintette; with Peacocks; with Debbie Lindsay; with Barbara Morrison)
Singles: 78 rpm
CAPITOL ... 10-25 57
DIG ... 10-25 55-57
EXCELSIOR ... 15-25 45-47
MERCURY ... 10-25 51-53
PEACOCK (Except 1625) ... 10-25 52
PEACOCK (1625 "Young Girl") ... 20-40 52
REGENT ... 10-25 50-51
SAVOY ... 10-20 50-54
Singles: 7–inch
CAPITOL (3799-3802 "The Johnny Otis Show") ... 400-600 57
(Four discs with special four-pocket cover.)
CAPITOL (3799 thru 3802) ... 15-25 57
(Price for four records without cover.)
CAPITOL (3852 "Good Golly") ... 15-25 57
CAPITOL (3966 "Willie and the Hand Jive"/"Ring-A-Ling") ... 15-25 58
CAPITOL (3966 "Willie and the Hand Jive"/"Willie and the Hand Jive") ... 20-40 58
(Blue label. Promotional issue only.)
CAPITOL (4060 "Crazy Country Hop") ... 15-25 58
CAPITOL (4168 "Castin' My Spell") ... 15-25 59
(Monaural.)
CAPITOL (S-4168 "Castin' My Spell") ... 25-50 59
(Stereo.)
CAPITOL (4226 thru 4326) ... 10-20 59-60
DIG (119 "Let the Sunshine in My Life") ... 25-50 56
DIG (122 "Midnight Creeper") ... 25-50 56
DIG (131 "Tough Enough") ... 25-50 57
DIG (132 "My Eyes Are Full of Tears") ... 25-50 57
DIG (134 "Wa-Wa") ... 25-50 57
DIG (139 "The Night Is Young") ... 25-50 57
ELDO (105 "The New Bo Diddley") ... 10-20 60
ELDO (153 "Long Distance") ... 5-10 67
EPIC ... 3-5 70
HAWK SOUND ... 3-5 75
IT WILL STAND ... 3-5 82
JAZZ WORLD ... 3-5 78
KENT ... 4-6 69
KING ... 8-12 61-63
MERCURY (8263 "Oopy Doo") ... 50-75 51
MERCURY (8273 "Goomp Blues") ... 50-75 51
MERCURY (8289 "Call Operator 210") ... 50-75 52
MERCURY (8295 "Gypsy Blues") ... 50-75 52
MERCURY (70038 "Why Don't You Believe Me") ... 50-75 52
MERCURY (70050 "The Love Bug Boogie") ... 30-50 52
OKEH ... 4-6 69
PEACOCK (1625 "Young Girl") ... 50-75 52
PEACOCK (1636 "Shake It") ... 25-50 52
PEACOCK (1648 "Sittin' Here Drinkin' ") ... 25-50 52
PEACOCK (1675 "Butterball") ... 25-50 52
RED HOT ... 15-25
REGENT (1036 "Hangover Blues") ... 20-40 51
SAVOY ... 20-40 50-54
EPs: 7–inch
CAPITOL (940 "Johnny Otis Show") ... 75-100 58
CAPITOL (1134 "Johnny Otis") ... 50-75 59
RITZ-EE (5214 Blackouts of 1959) ... 40-60 59
(Has one Otis track, *Backstage at the Blackouts*. Promotional issue only. Not issued with cover.)
LPs: 10/12–inch
ALLIGATOR (4726 "The New Johnny Otis Show") ... 5-10 82
BLUES SPECTRUM ... 10-15
CAPITOL (940 "Johnny Otis Show") ... 150-250 58
DIG (104 "Rock & Roll Hit Parade") ... 500-750 57
(Gold cover. Counterfeits of Dig 104 exist, some of which have a yellow cover. Others have a gold cover. Regardless, the discs of originals are noticeably thicker than is used on the fakes.)
EPIC ... 10-15 70-71
JAZZ WORLD ... 5-10 78
KENT ... 10-20 70
RED HOT ... 5-10
SAVOY ... 5-10 78-80
Performed below are some of the artists who performed with the Johnny Otis Show, or with whom he or his orchestra appears.
Also see ACE, Johnny
Also see ADAMS, Marie
Also see ALLEN, Tony
Also see AUGUST, Joseph
Also see FOUR BLUEBIRDS / Johnny Otis Orchestra
Also see FREEMAN, Ernie
Also see GLADIATORS
Also see HODGE, Gaynel
Also see JACQUET, Illinois
Also see McNEELY, Big Jay
Also see MOONBEAMS
Also see OTISETTES
Also see PAYNE, Jackie
Also see RUSHING, Jimmy
Also see SCOTT, Marilyn
Also see WALKER, Mel
Also see WATSON, Johnny
Also see WILSON, Faye
Also see WILLIAMS, Mel

OTIS, Johnny, & Preston Love
Singles: 7–inch
KENT ... 3-5 70
Also see LOVE, Preston

OTIS, Johnny, Orchestra, with Little Esther & Mel Walker *R&B '50*
Singles: 78 rpm
REGENT ... 20-40 51
SAVOY ... 20-40 50-51
Singles: 7–inch
REGENT (1036 "I Dream") ... 50-75 51
SAVOY (750 "Cupid's Boogie") ... 50-75 50
SAVOY (775 "Love Will Break Your Heart") ... 50-75 51
Also see LITTLE ESTHER & Mel Walker

OTIS, Johnny, Quintette, with Little Esther & Robins *R&B '50*
Singles: 78 rpm
SAVOY ... 40-60 50
Singles: 7–inch
SAVOY (731 "Double Crossing Blues") ... 75-100 50
Also see LITTLE ESTHER
Also see OTIS, Johnny
Also see ROBINS

OTIS, Laura, & Satinettes
Singles: 7–inch
MEXIE (102 "I'm Gonna Make You Love Me") ... 100-200 62
(Reportedly, appproximately 100 made.)
Session: Johnny Otis (Laura's father).
Also see OTIS, Johnny

OTIS, Ray
EPs: 7–inch
BOBCAT (373317 "Young Raisin Rum ") ... 4-6 91
(Colored vinyl. Not issued with cover.)

OTIS, Shuggie *LP '70*
Singles: 7–inch
EPIC ... 3-5 70-75
LPs: 10/12–inch
EPIC ... 10-15 70-75
Also see KOOPER, Al, & Shuggie Otis

OTIS, Shuggie, & Preston Love
Singles: 7–inch
KENT ... 3-5 70
Also see OTIS, Johnny, & Preston Love
Also see OTIS, Shuggie

OTIS & CARLA *P&R/R&B/LP '67*
Singles: 7–inch
ATCO ... 4-6 69
STAX ... 5-10 67-68
LPs: 10/12–inch
STAX (716 "King & Queen") ... 10-20 67
Members: Otis Redding; Carla Thomas.
Also see REDDING, Otis
Also see THOMAS, Carla

OTISETTES
("Featured with the Johnny Otis Show")
Singles: 7–inch
EPIC (10879 "Sitting Alone") ... 4-6 72
Also see OTIS, Johnny

OTT, Paul *C&W '79*
Singles: 7–inch
ELEKTRA ... 3-5 79
MONUMENT ... 3-5 75
SHOW BIZ ... 3-5 72
THUNDER INT'L (1022 "Kitty Kat") ... 50-75 60

OTTEY, Kenny
Singles: 7–inch
RCA ... 10-15 58

OTTO & ELEVATORS
Singles: 7–inch
VERA ... 3-5 76
Member: Gary Tanin.

OTTY, John
LPs: 10/12–inch
MUMM ... 8-12

OUR DAUGHTER'S WEDDING
Singles: 7–inch
EMI AMERICA ... 3-5 82
LPs: 10/12–inch
EMI AMERICA ... 5-10 82

OUR GANG
Singles: 7–inch
BR'ER BIRD (001 "Summertime Summertime") ... 100-150 66
Members: Jan Berry; Dean Torrance.
Also see JAN & DEAN

OUR GANG
Singles: 7–inch
WARRIOR (166 "Careless Love") ... 15-25 66

OUR GENERATION
Singles: 7–inch
FENTON (970 "Baby Boy") ... 100-150 60s

OUR PATCH OF BLUE
Singles: 7–inch
W.B. ... 10-20 69

OUT CROWD
Singles: 7–inch
OMEN ... 5-10 66

OUTCASTS
Singles: 7–inch
STUDIO CITY (1040 "You Do Me Wrong") ... 15-25 62

OUTCASTS
Singles: 7–inch
VETTE (425 "Under Tow") ... 20-30 63

OUTCASTS
Singles: 7–inch
KARATE (531 "I Found Out About You") ... 10-20 65
SOLA (12 "People") ... 15-25 66

OUTCASTS
Singles: 7–inch
ASKEL (102 "I'm in Pittsburgh") ... 40-60 65
ASKEL (104 "I'll Set You Free") ... 10-20 66
ASKEL (107 "Route 66") ... 15-25 66
GALLANT (101 "1523 "Blair") ... 20-30 67

OUTCASTS
Singles: 7–inch
DOT ... 5-10 66

OUTCASTS
Singles: 7–inch
SHORE BIRD (1005 "I Wanted You") ... 10-15 67

OUTCASTS
Singles: 7–inch
CAMEO (477 "Today's the Day") ... 10-20 67
DECCA (32036 "Set Me Free") ... 8-12 66
LPs: 10/12–inch
CICADELIC ... 8-10 84

OUTCASTS
Singles: 7–inch
PLATO (80285 "Loving You Sometimes") ... 8-12 68

OUTCASTS
Singles: 7–inch
PRINCE (1265 "Run Away") ... 8-12

OUTCASTS
Singles: 7–inch
SPINNER (114 "Auctioneer Song") ... 8-12

OUTCRY
Singles: 7–inch
RILEYS ... 5-10

OUTER LIMITS
Singles: 7–inch
DERAM (7508 "Help Me Please") ... 15-25 67

OUTER LIMITS
Singles: 7–inch
GOLDUST (5014 "Don't Need You No More") ... 15-25 67

OUTER MONGOLIAN HEARD
Singles: 7–inch
DAISY (4846 "Hey Joe") ... 20-30 67

OUTFIELD *LP '85*
Singles: 7–inch
COLUMBIA ... 3-4 85-87
Picture Sleeves
COLUMBIA ... 3-4 86-87
LPs: 10/12–inch
COLUMBIA ... 5-8 85-87
Members: Tony Lewis; Alan Jackman; John Spinks.

OUTLAW BAND
Singles: 7–inch
CMH ... 3-4 84
Member: Bobby Clark.
Also see CLARK, Bobby

OUTLAW BLUES BAND
LPs: 10/12–inch
BLUESWAY ... 10-20 68-69

OUTLAWS
Singles: 7–inch
DOT (16512 "Hold Up") ... 10-20 63

OUTLAWS
Singles: 7–inch
CRUSADE (92765 "Chains") ... 10-20 65
SMASH ... 5-10 66

OUTLAWS *LP '76*
Singles: 7–inch
ARISTA ... 3-5 75-83
LPs: 10/12–inch
ARISTA ... 5-10 75-83
DIRECT DISC (16617 "Outlaws") ... 15-25 80s
(Half-speed mastered.)
PASHA ... 5-8 86
PEAR ... 8-12 84
Members: Hughie Thomasson; Henry Paul; David Dix; Billy Jones; Fred Salem; Rick Cua; David Dix; Harvey Dalton Arnold; Frank O'Keefe; Monte Yoho; Chuck Glass; Steve Grisham.
Also see CUA Rick
Also see PAUL, Henry, Band
Also see SALEM, Freddy, & Wildcats

OUTLAWS
Singles: 7–inch
PASHA ... 3-4 86
LPs: 10/12–inch
PASHA ... 5-8 86

OUTLAWS
Singles: 7–inch
BLACKNIGHT (902 "Midnight Hour") ... 25-50
(As by the Outlaws.)
BLACKNIGHT (902 "Midnight Hour") ... 15-25
(As by Kit & Outlaws.)
Also see KIT & OUTLAWS

OUTLER, Jimmy
Singles: 7–inch
DUKE ... 4-8 66

OUTNUMBERED
LPs: 10/12–inch
HOMESTEAD ... 5-10 85-86
Members: Jon Ginoli; Paul Budin; Tim McKeage; Ken Golub.

OUTPUT *R&B '84*
Singles: 12–inch
CBS ASSOCIATED ... 4-6 83
Singles: 7–inch
CBS ASSOCIATED ... 3-5 83
TUFF CITY ... 3-4 84

OUTRAGE
Singles: 7–inch
KAMA SUTRA ... 4-8 68-69
LPs: 10/12–inch
KAMA SUTRA ... 10-15 69

OUTSIDE IN
Singles: 7–inch
RIGHT RPM (6612 "You Ain't Gonna Bring Me to My Knees") ... 20-30 66

OUTSIDERS
Singles: 7–inch
EASTMAN ... 10-20 62

OUTSIDERS *P&R/LP '66*
Singles: 7–inch
BELL ... 4-6 70
CAPITOL ... 5-10 66-68
KAPP ... 4-6 70
Picture Sleeves
CAPITOL ... 8-12 66-67
LPs: 10/12–inch
CAPITOL ... 20-30 66-67
Members: Sonny Geraci; Bill Bruno; Tom King; Rickey Baker; Merdin Madsen.
Also see CLIMAX
Also see GERACI, Sonny
Also see STARFIRES

OUTSIDERS
Singles: 7–inch
ELLEN ... 10-15
KARATE ... 10-15 64

OUTSIDERS
Singles: 7–inch
CHA CHA ("Go Go Ferrari") ... 20-30 60s

KNIGHT (103 "She's Comin' on Strong")....10-20

OUTTA PLACE
LPs: 10/12-inch
MIDNIGHT.... 5-8

OVATIONS
Singles: 7-inch
ANDIE (5017 "My Lullabye")....15-25 60
BARRY (101 "The Day We Fell in Love")....20-25 61
EPIC (9470 "Oh What a Day")....25-30 61
Also see IDEALS

OVATIONS
Singles: 7-inch
CAPITOL (5082 "I Don't Wanna Cry")....10-20 63

OVATIONS
Singles: 7-inch
JOSIE (916 "Who Needs Love")....10-20 64
LPs: 10/12-inch
CRYSTAL BALL.... 5-10 87
Members: Sammy Cantos; Greg Malmeth; Gary Willet; Ronnie Brecheter; Tony Clementa; Frank Cox; Nick Kassy.
Also see KANNON, Sandy
Also see LITTLE ROMEO & CASANOVAS

OVATIONS P&R/R&B '65
(Ovation)
Singles: 7-inch
CHESS (2166 "Pure Natural").... 4-6 75
GOLDWAX (110 "Pretty Little Angel").... 8-12 64
GOLDWAX (113 "It's Wonderful to Be in Love").... 8-12 65
GOLDWAX (117 "I'm Living Good").... 8-12 65
GOLDWAX (300 "Don't Cry").... 8-12 66
GOLDWAX (306 "Qualifications").... 8-12 66
GOLDWAX (314 "They Say").... 8-12 66
GOLDWAX (332 "I've Gotta Go").... 8-12 67
GOLDWAX (342 "I'm Living Good").... 5-10 69
MGM.... 4-8 73
SOUNDS OF MEMPHIS.... 4-8 72-73
LPs: 10/12-inch
MGM....10-15 73
SOUNDS of MEMPHIS....10-20 72
Members: George Jackson; Louis Williams; Bill Davis; Rochester Neal; Quincy Billops Jr.
Also see JACKSON, George
Also see OLLIE & NIGHTINGALES

OVATIONS
Singles: 7-inch
HAWK (153 "I Still Love You")....75-125 63

OVELLA & OVERTURES
Singles: 7-inch
COLUMBIA.... 4-8 66

OVEN
("Featuring Frank Thomas")
Singles: 7-inch
CANYON (22 "Sailboat").... 3-5

OVERBEA, Danny R&B '53
Singles: 78 rpm
CHECKER....25-50 53-55
Singles: 7-inch
APEX (7751 "Don't Laugh At Me") 10-20 59
CHECKER (774 "40 Cups of Coffee")....50-100 53
(Black vinyl.)
CHECKER (774 "40 Cups of Coffee")....150-200 53
(Colored vinyl.)
CHECKER (768 "Train Train Train")....75-125 53
CHECKER (784 "Sorrento")....75-125 54
CHECKER (788 "Stomp and Whistle")....75-125 54
CHECKER (796 "Roamin' Man")..75-125 54
CHECKER (808 "A Toast to Lovers")....75-125 55
CHECKER (816 "Hey, Pancho")..50-100 55
FEDERAL (12434 "Book of Tears")....10-20 61
SHEP (101 "Like Crazy")....10-20 60

OVERCOAT
LPs: 10/12-inch
DIONYSUS.... 5-10 91
Members: Timothy Gassen; Debra Dickey; Mike Panico; Greg Rupp; Ernie Mendoza.

OVERKILL
Singles: 7-inch
SST.... 3-4 86
LPs: 10/12-inch
SST.... 5-8 86

OVERKILL
LPs: 10/12-inch
ATLANTIC.... 5-8 86

OVERKILL LP '87
LPs: 10/12-inch
MEGAFORCE.... 5-8 87-89

OVERLAND STAGE
(Overland Stage Company)
Singles: 7-inch
EPIC.... 3-5 72
FRANKLIN (630 "Airplane")....25-35 68
LPs: 10/12-inch
EPIC....10-15 72

OVERLANDERS P&R '64
Singles: 7-inch
HICKORY....10-15 64-66
MERCURY.... 5-10 63

OVERMAN, Rune
Singles: 7-inch
PARKWAY.... 4-8 63
STACY.... 4-8 63

OVERTON, C.B. R&B '78
Singles: 7-inch
SHOCK.... 3-5 78

OVERTONES
Singles: 7-inch
SLATE (3068 "I Wonder, I Wonder")....20-30 61

OVERTONES / Bob Fitzgerald
Singles: 7-inch
SLATE (4013 "This Old Love of Mine")....10-20 62
Also see OVERTONES

OVERTONES
Singles: 7-inch
AJAX (173 "Please Let Me Know")..25-50 66
AJAX (174 "From My Heart")....25-50 66
AJAX (175 "Home Type Girl")....25-50 67
AJAX (176 "I've Been There Before")....25-50 67

OVERTONES
LPs: 10/12-inch
TWIN/TONE.... 5-8 88

OVERSTREET, Paul C&W '82
Singles: 7-inch
MTM.... 3-4 88
RCA.... 3-4 82-91
LPs: 10/12-inch
BMG.... 5-8 91
Also see TUCKER, Tanya, Paul Davis & Paul Overstreet

OVERSTREET, Tommy C&W '69
(With the Nashville Express)
Singles: 7-inch
ABC.... 3-5 78-79
ABC/DOT.... 3-5 74-78
AMI.... 3-4 83
DOT.... 3-6 69-74
ELEKTRA.... 3-5 79-80
GERVASI.... 3-4 84
SILVER DOLLAR.... 3-4 86
TINA.... 3-5 79
LPs: 10/12-inch
ABC....5-10 78
ABC/DOT....6-12 75-77
AUDIOGRAPH ALIVE.... 5-8 82
CMH....5-10 80
DEJA VU.... 5-8 84
DOT....8-15 71-74
ELEKTRA....5-15 79-80
MCA.... 5-8 80s
PINNACLE....5-10 78

OWEN-B P&R '70
Singles: 7-inch
JANUS.... 3-5 70
LPs: 10/12-inch
MUS-I-COL (101209 "Owen-B")....40-60 70

OWEN, Doug
Singles: 7-inch
MCA.... 3-5 79

OWEN, Jeannie
Singles: 7-inch
TOP PIC.... 3-5
Picture Sleeves
TOP PIC.... 4-6

OWEN, Jim C&W '78
(With the Drifting Cowboys)
Singles: 7-inch
EPIC.... 3-5 78
SUN.... 3-4 80-82
LPs: 10/12-inch
EPIC (34852 "A Song for Us All")...10-15 77
(With Hank Williams poster.)
EPIC (34852 "A Song for Us All")....8-10 77
(Without Hank Williams poster.)
EVET....10-15
GOLD....10-15
SUN....10-15 82
Also see see DRIFTING COWBOYS

OWEN, Kenny: see OWENS, Kenny

OWEN, Mack
Singles: 7-inch
SUN....5-10 60

OWEN, Reg, & His Orchestra P&R '58
Singles: 7-inch
PALETTE.... 4-6 58-62
EPs: 7-inch
RCA....5-10 50s
LPs: 10/12-inch
PALETTE....15-25 59-60

OWEN, Rudy, & Ravens
Singles: 7-inch
STARTIME (3287 "Pretty Linda")...15-20 58

OWEN BROTHERS C&W '82
Singles: 7-inch
AUDIOGRAPH.... 3-4 82-83

OWENS, A.L. "Doodle" C&W '78
Singles: 7-inch
RAINDROP.... 3-5 78

OWENS, Bonnie C&W '63
(With the Strangers)
Singles: 7-inch
CAPITOL.... 4-6 65-69
TALLY....5-10 63-64
LPs: 10/12-inch
CAPITOL (195 thru 557)....10-20 69-70
CAPITOL (2403 thru 2861....15-30 65-68
Also see HAGGARD, Merle, & Bonnie Owens

OWENS, Buck C&W '59
(With the Buckaroos)
Singles: 78 rpm
CAPITOL....25-50 57
Singles: 7-inch
CAPITOL (2000 thru 4000 series)....3-8 67-75
(Orange label.)
CAPITOL (3824 "Come Back")....15-25 57
(Purple label.)
CAPITOL (3957 "Sweet Thing")....15-25 58
(Purple label.)
CAPITOL (4000 series)....8-15 59-63
(Purple or orange/yellow label.)
CAPITOL (5000 series)....3-6 63-67
CHESTERFIELD (44223 "Leavin' Dirty Tracks")....15-25 60s
HILLTOP (6027 "Hot Dog")....25-50 60s
NEW STAR (6418 "Hot Dog")....100-150 58
(Rerecorded version of "Corky Jones" track.)
PEP (105 "Down on the Corner of Love")....25-50 56
PEP (106 "Right After the Dance")....25-50 56
PEP (109 "There Goes My Love") 25-50 57
STARDAY (588 "Down on the Corner of Love")....10-20 61
STARDAY (5000 series)....4-8 64
W.B. (Except 8316)....3-6 76-80
W.B. (8316 "World Famous Holiday Inn")....5-10 77
W.B. (8316 "World Famous Paradise Inn")....3-5 77
(Note title change.)
Picture Sleeves
CAPITOL....10-25 66-69
EPs: 7-inch
CAPITOL....15-30 61-65
LPs: 10/12-inch
BUCKBOARD....5-10
CAPITOL (131 thru 550 series)....10-20 69-70
CAPITOL (574 "Buck Owens")....20-30 70
(Three-disc set.)
CAPITOL (628 thru 860)....10-15 70-72
CAPITOL (T-1482 thru T-1989)....30-40 61-63
(Monaural.)
CAPITOL (ST-1482 thru ST-1989).35-50 61-63
(Stereo.)
CAPITOL (DT-1400 series)....10-20 69
CAPITOL (2100 thru 2700 series) 12-25 64-67
CAPITOL (2800 thru 2900 series) 10-20 68
CAPITOL (2980 "Buck Owens Minute Masters")....30-40 66
(Promotional issue only.)
CAPITOL (11000 series)....5-8 72-78
COUNTRY FIDELITY....?? 83
GUEST STAR....8-12 60s
HALL of MUSIC....8-12
LA BREA (8017 "Buck Owens")....100-200 61
OUT of TOWN DIST....5-8 82
PICKWICK/HILLTOP....5-10 78
SPRINGBOARD....5-10
STARDAY (172 "Fabulous Country Music Sound of Buck Owens")....15-25 62
STARDAY (300 series)....15-20 64-65
STARDAY (400 series)....10-15 75
STARPAK....5-8 79
SUNRISE MEDIA....?? 81
TIME-LIFE....5-10 82
TRIP....5-8 76
W.B....5-10 76-77
Also see COLLINS, Tommy
Also see JONES, Corky
Also see JONES, George / Buck Owens / David Houston / Tommy Hill.
Also see WEBBER, Rollie
Also see YOAKAM, Dwight, & Buck Owens

OWENS, Buck, & Buddy Alan C&W '68
(Buck & Buddy; with the Buckaroos)
Singles: 7-inch
CAPITOL....4-6 68
Also see ALAN, Buddy

OWENS, Buck / Tennessee Ernie Ford
LPs: 10/12-inch
CAPITOL (6720 "Music Hall")....8-12
Also see FORD, Tennessee Ernie

OWENS, Buck, & Emmylou Harris
Singles: 7-inch
W.B....3-4 79
Also see HARRIS, Emmylou

OWENS, Buck, & Rose Maddox C&W '63
Singles: 7-inch
CAPITOL....5-8 63
Also see MADDOX, Rose

OWENS, Buck, & Susan Raye C&W/LP '70
Singles: 7-inch
CAPITOL....3-5 70-73
LPs: 10/12-inch
CAPITOL....5-10 70-73
Also see RAYE, Susan

OWENS, Buck, & Ringo Starr C&W '89
Singles: 7-inch
CAPITOL (79805 "Gonna Have Love")....5-8 89
(Commercial issue.)
CAPITOL (79805 "Gonna Have Love")....8-10 89
(Promotional issue.)
Also see STARR, Ringo

OWENS, Buck / Faron Young / Ferlin Husky
LPs: 10/12-inch
PICKWICK/HILLTOP....8-12 65
Also see HUSKY, Ferlin
Also see OWENS, Buck
Also see YOUNG, Faron

OWENS, Charlie
(With the Sensational Ink Spots)
Singles: 7-inch
KENT (355 "Diane")....15-25 61
Also see INK SPOTS

OWENS, Clyde
Singles: 7-inch
LINCO (1313 "Swing It Katy")....10-20 59
SPARTAN (200 "Right & Ready")..50-75 58

OWENS, Danny
Singles: 7-inch
IMPERIAL....5-10 60
MGM....5-10 59
MANHATTAN (804 "I Can't Be a Fool for You")....15-25 67

OWENS, Don
Singles: 7-inch
SOUND STAGE 7 (2503 "Your Fool")....5-10 63
Also see HIGHTOWER, Willie

OWENS, Donnie P&R '58
(Donny Owens)
Singles: 7-inch
ARA....4-8
GUYDEN....10-15 58-59
TREY....5-10 60
Also see EDDY, Duane

OWENS, Doodle
Singles: 7-inch
BACK BEAT....5-10 59

OWENS, Dusty
Singles: 78 rpm
COLUMBIA....5-10 54
Singles: 7-inch
ADMIRAL (1004 "Hey Honey")....20-30 57
COLUMBIA....10-15 54

OWENS, Freddy
Singles: 7-inch
BETHLEHEM....4-8 62
WALL....4-8 61

OWENS, Garland
Singles: 7-inch
LEGRAND....15-20 62
LE MONDE....8-12 60s

OWENS, Gary
(With the Mike Curb Congregation)
Singles: 7-inch
LION....4-8 72
PRIDE....3-5 72
W.B....8-10 61
Also see CURB, Mike
Also see HEXORCIST
Also see PRESLEY, Elvis / Gary Owens
Also see RAMJET, Rodger, & American Eagles

OWENS, Glen
Singles: 7-inch
ROCKET....10-15

OWENS, Gwen R&B '69
Singles: 7-inch
BIG TREE....3-5 79
JOSIE....4-6 69

OWENS, Hughie, & Blue Notes
(With Joe Tanner & Orchestra)
Singles: 7-inch
RENOWN (108 "Time Will Tell")...50-75 59
RENOWN (109 "That's What You Mean to Me")....50-75 59

OWENS, Kelly
Singles: 78 rpm
FLAIR-X....5-10 56
RAINBOW....10-15 54
Singles: 7-inch
ARROW (725 "Tweety")....15-25 58
FLAIR-X (5004 "The Sweeper")....10-20 56
RAINBOW (248 "Sweeper Shuffle")....15-25 54
U.A. (181 "Charlie's Dance")....15-25 59

OWENS, Kenny
(Kenny Owen)
Singles: 7-inch
POPLAR (106 "I Got the Bug")....75-125 57
RUTH (442 "Frog Man Hop")....20-30 58

OWENS, Kenny, & Travelers
LPs: 10/12-inch
ORK....10-20 70
Member: Larry Donn.
Also see DONN, Larry

OWENS, Marie C&W '74
Singles: 7-inch
CAPRICE (1000 "I Haven't the Heart")....3-5 72
(Black vinyl.)
CAPRICE (1000 "I Haven't the Heart")....4-8 72
(Colored vinyl. Promotional issue only.)
4 STAR....3-5 75
MCA....3-5 74
MMI....3-5 77
SING ME....3-5 77

OWENS, Nell
Singles: 7-inch
MUSIC CITY....3-5 78

OWENS, Smokey
Singles: 7-inch
DIMENSION....4-8 64

OWENS, Tony R&B '71
Singles: 7-inch
COTILLION....4-6 71
SANSU....10-20
SOUL SOUND....10-20 67
SOULIN'....5-10 67

OWENS BROTHERS
Singles: 78 rpm
ABC-PAR (9775 "Night Train")....15-25 57
Singles: 7-inch
ABC-PAR (9775 "Night Train")....20-30 57
(Previously issued as by the Four Chaps.)
Members: John Owens; Bob Owens; Bill Owens; D.J. Owens.
Also see FOUR CHAPS

O'WILLIAMS, Larry
Singles: 7-inch
ARHOOLIE....4-8 67

OWL
Singles: 7-inch
AXIS LTD. ("Spirits")....25-35
(Colored vinyl.)

OX
Singles: 7-inch
POLYDOR....3-5 71

OX TONES
Singles: 7-inch
PHONOGRAPH (1024 "Mickey")...30-50 58

OX-BOW INCIDENT
Singles: 7-inch
SMASH....4-8 68

OXEN FREEZ & Buffalo Hunters
Singles: 7-inch
AMOS....3-5 70

OXFORD, Vernon C&W '75
Singles: 7-inch
RCA....3-6 67-77
LPs: 10/12-inch
RCA (3704 "Woman, Let Me Sing You a Song")....20-30 67
RICH-R-TONE....10-20 60s
ROUNDER....10-15 78-80s
RUTA BAGA....10-15

OXFORD CIRCLE
Singles: 7-inch
WORLD UNITED (002 "Mind Destruction")....35-45
Members: Paul Whaley; Gary Yoder.
Also see BLUE CHEER

OXFORD CIRCUS
Singles: 7-inch
ZIG ZAG (101 "Tracy")....20-25 67

OXFORD WATCHBAND
Singles: 7-inch
HAND....5-10 69

OXFORDS, Los: see LOS OXFORDS

OXFORDS
Singles: 7-inch
GOLDEN CREST (569 "Toy Balloons")....10-20 63
MALA (550 "Time & Place")....5-10 67
NATIONAL (15881 "It's You")....8-12
PAULA (331 "Come on Back to Beer")....5-10 69
UNION JACK....8-12
LPs: 10/12-inch
UNION JAC (6497 "Flying Up")....20-30 68
Members: Jill DeMarco; Jay Petrech.

OXO P&R/LP '83
Singles: 7-inch
GEFFEN....3-4 83
LPs: 10/12-inch
GEFFEN....5-8 83
Also see FOXY

OXPETALS
Singles: 7-inch
MERCURY....3-5 70
LPs: 10/12-inch
MERCURY....10-12 70

OZ
Singles: 7-inch
GOODSPHERE....5-10 70s

OZ & ENDS
Singles: 7-inch
PACEMAKER (753 "Look Away")..15-25 66

OZ & SPERLINGS
Singles: 7-inch
VILLA (701 "Mo Jo Hanna")....10-20 60s

OZ BAND
Singles: 7-inch
CUB....8-12 68

OZ KNOZZ
LPs: 10/12-inch
OZONE (1000 "Ruff Mix")....350-500 75
Members: Richard Heath; Duane Massey; Monty Haul; Newton Bildo.

OZARK MOUNTAIN DAREDEVILS
P&R/LP '74

Singles: 7-inch

A&M 3-5 74-78
COLUMBIA 3-5 80

Picture Sleeves

A&M 3-5 75-76

LPs: 10/12-inch

A&M 8-12 73-78
COLUMBIA 5-10 80

Also see LEE, Larry
Also see LEWIE & 7 DAYS

OZARKS

Singles: 7-inch

CALIFORNIA (304 "The Saints") 15-25 63
Reissued as *The Saints Go Surfin' In*, and shown as by the Woodys.)
Also see WOODYS

OZELLS

Singles: 7-inch

CUB 8-10 63

OZO
P&R '76

Singles: 7-inch

DJM 3-5 76

LPs: 10/12-inch

DJM 5-10 76

OZONE
R&B '80

Singles: 7-inch

MOTOWN 3-5 80-83

LPs: 10/12-inch

MOTOWN 5-10 80-83

Members: Jimmy Stewart; Charles Glenn; Benny Wallace; Thomas Bumpass; Ray Woodward; William White; Greg Hargrove; Paul Hines.

OZUNA, Sunny: see SUNGLOWS

OZZ

Singles: 7-inch

EPIC 3-5 80

LPs: 10/12-inch

EPIC 5-10 80

P

P CREW R&B '83
Singles: 7-inch
PRELUDE.......3-4 83

P.C. LTD.
Singles: 7-inch
FONTANA.......4-6 69

P.D.U.S.M.
Singles: 7-inch
JUBILEE.......4-8 67

PFC
Singles: 7-inch
EPIC.......3-4 85

P.F.M. LP '73
(Premiata Forneria Marconi)
Singles: 7-inch
ASYLUM.......3-5 76-77
MANTICORE.......3-5 73-75
LPs: 10/12-inch
ASYLUM.......5-10 76-77
MANTICORE.......8-12 73-74
PETERS INT'L.......5-10 76

P. FUNK ALL-STARS R&B '82
Singles: 12-inch
UNCLE JAM.......4-6 84
Singles: 7-inch
CBS ASSOCIATED.......3-4 83
HUMP.......3-5 82
UNCLE JAM.......3-4 84
LPs: 10/12-inch
CBS ASSOCIATED.......5-8 84
UNCLE JAM.......5-8 84
Also see PARLIAMENT

PG&E: see PACIFIC GAS & ELECTRIC

PH.D
LPs: 10/12-inch
ATLANTIC.......5-8 81-83

PH PHACTOR
Singles: 7-inch
PICCADILLY (241 "Minglewood Blues").......10-15 67
LPs: 10/12-inch
PICCADILLY ("Merryjuana").......50-100 82
(Selection number not known.)

P.J.
(Patti Jerome)
Singles: 7-inch
TAMLA (54215 "T.L.C.").......10-20 71
V.I.P. (25062 "The Best Years of My Life").......15-25 70
Also see JEROME, Patti

P.J. & BOBBY
Singles: 78 rpm
BUTTERFLY (Black vinyl).......3-5 78
BUTTERFLY (Colored vinyl).......5-10 78
(Promotional issues only.)
LPs: 10/12-inch
BUTTERFLY.......5-10 78

P.J. & GALAXIES
Singles: 7-inch
P.M. (47 "Tally Ho!").......10-20 63
Member: Paul Johnson.
Also see JOHNSON, Paul

P.J. & HEADLINERS
Singles: 7-inch
ASTOR.......8-12 60

P.J. MURPHY
LP: 10/12-inch
LEAF (6475 "P.J. Murphy").......15-25 64
Members: Kathy McBroon; Gary Sagamiller; Ron Hileman; Jim Kasdorf; Andy Duvall.

P.J.s
Singles: 7-inch
MAP CITY.......4-6
ROULETTE.......3-5 73

P.K. LIMITED
Singles: 7-inch
COLGEMS.......4-8 69-70

P.M.
Singles: 7-inch
W.B.......3-4
Picture Sleeves
W.B.......3-4

P.P.F.
(Past Present Future)
Singles: 7-inch
MECCA.......4-8
Member: Charles Sherrill.
Also see SHERRILL, Charles

P.S.C.P.
Singles: 7-inch
VANCO.......5-10

P.T.s
Singles: 7-inch
OUTSTANDING (1 "Dragon Walk").......10-15 60s

PAAR, Jack
(With Jack Haskell)
Singles: 78 rpm
COLUMBIA.......5-10 56
Singles: 7-inch
COLUMBIA.......8-12 56
RCA.......5-10 58
Picture Sleeves
COLUMBIA.......10-15 56
RCA.......5-10 58

RAMROD
LP: 10/12-inch
RAMROD.......8-12

PABLO CRUISE LP '75
Singles: 7-inch
A&M.......3-5 75-84
Picture Sleeves
A&M.......3-5 77-84
LPs: 10/12-inch
A&M.......5-10 75-84
MFSL (029 "A Place in the Sun").......25-35 79
(Half-speed mastered.)
NAUTILUS.......10-20 81
Members: Dave Jenkins; Steven Price; Cory Lerios; Bud Cockrell.
Also see IT'S a BEAUTIFUL DAY
Also see SOUTHERN PACIFIC
Also see STONEGROUND

PAC MAN
LPs: 10/12-inch
KID STUFF (6012 "Sing Along with Mr. & Mrs. Pac Man").......10-15 80
(Picture disc.)

PACE
Singles: 7-inch
REPRISE.......4-8 68

PACE, Brent
Singles: 7-inch
ACME (101 "Take Back a Fool").......25-50 65
(Has a large "A" in the middle of "Acme.")
Also see JOHNSON, Joe D.

PACE, Glen, & Gliders
Singles: 7-inch
ABC-PAR (10091 "Next Year").......10-15 60
SATELLITE ("My Night Off").......15-25
(Selection number not known.)

PACE SETTERS
Singles: 7-inch
AURORA (1971 "Setting the Pace").......15-25 65

PACERS
(Pacers with Bobby Crawford)
Singles: 7-inch
RAZORBACK (103 "Front Street") 10-20 59
RAZORBACK (108 "Confound It") 10-20 61
RAZORBACK (112 "Don't Get Around Much").......10-20 62
RAZORBACK (115 "West Memphis").......10-20 63
RAZORBACK (118 thru 139).......5-15 64-68
LPs: 10/12-inch
RAZORBACK (121 "You Asked for It").......30-50 65
Members: Joe Cyr; Jim Aldridge; Fred Douglas; Bob Dalton; Bobby Crafford; Jerry Little.
Also see BURGESS, Sonny
Also see CRAFFORD, Bobby

PACERS
Singles: 7-inch
GUYDEN (2064 "How Sweet").......1000-2000 61
JASON SCOTT.......4-8

PACERS
Singles: 7-inch
UNITED SOUTHERN ARTISTS (112 "New Wildwood Flower").......10-15 61

PACERS
Singles: 7-inch
ALLEY (1013 "Skeeter Dope").......10-20 63
GEMINI (6301 "Settin' the Pace").......10-20 63

PACERS
Singles: 7-inch
CORAL.......4-8 64

PACERS
Singles: 7-inch
BIL-JON (101 "Bernie").......8-12
JANIE (9643/4 "Pace-In").......8-12

PACESETTERS
Singles: 7-inch
AURORA (1971 "Ooh-Poo-Pah-Doo").......10-20 61
CORREC-TONE.......5-10 63
MINIT.......8-12 60s
WINK.......10-15 62

PACE-SETTERS
Singles: 7-inch
AVA (161 "Mustang").......20-30 64

PACETTES
Singles: 7-inch
REGINA.......10-15 64

PACHUCO
LPs: 10/12-inch
EAGLE.......8-10 74

PACIFIC DRIFT
LPs: 10/12-inch
DERAM.......8-10 70

PACIFIC GAS & ELECTRIC LP '69
(PG&E; Pacific Gas & Electric Blues Band)
Singles: 7-inch
BRIGHT ORANGE.......5-10 68
COLUMBIA.......3-6 69-72
POWER.......5-10 69
LPs: 10/12-inch
ABC.......8-10 70s
BRIGHT ORANGE (701 "Get It On").......40-80 68
COLUMBIA.......8-12 69-73
KENT (547 "Get It On").......10-20 68
POWER.......10-15 69
Members: Charlie Allen; Frank Cook; Brent Block; Tom Marshall; Glenn Schwartz.
Also see ALLEN, Charlie
Also see SEEGER, Pete, & Pacific Gas & Electric

PACIFIC OCEAN
Singles: 7-inch
VMC.......4-8 68-69
LPs: 10/12-inch
VMC.......10-15 69

PACIFIC STEEL CO. C&W '80
(Featuring Jay Dee Maness)
Singles: 7-inch
PACIFIC ARTS.......3-5 80
LPs: 10/12-inch
PACIFIC ARTS.......5-10 79
Also see BYRDS

PACK
Singles: 7-inch
SOUND TEX (650529 "Time").......20-30 65

PACK
Singles: 7-inch
CAPITOL (2174 "Next to Your Fire").......5-10 68
WINGATE (007 "The Colour of Our Love").......10-15 65
Also see FABULOUS PACK
Also see KNIGHT, Terry, & Pack

PACK
Singles: 7-inch
ZANZIBAR.......8-12 82
Members: Johnny Maestro; Bobby Sedito; Sandy (Santo) Farina.
Also see MAESTRO, Johnny
Also see SANTO & JOHNNY

PACK
(Formerly Link Wray's Raymen)
Singles: 7-inch
SLASH (5859 "Rawhide").......4-6 79
SLASH (5860 "Cadillac Joe").......4-6 79
Picture Sleeves
SLASH (5859 "Rawhide").......5-10 79
SLASH (5860 "Cadillac Joe").......5-10 79
Also see WRAY, Link

PACK, Bob C&W '88
Singles: 7-inch
OAK.......3-4 88

PACK, Charlie
Singles: 7-inch
TRC (2819 "Fluffy Dog").......25-35

PACK, David P&R '86
Singles: 7-inch
W.B.......3-4 86
LPs: 10/12-inch
W.B.......5-8 86
Also see AMBROSIA
Also see McDONALD, Michael
Also see PARSONS, Alan, Project
Also see TREFETHEN

PACK, Ray C&W '89
Singles: 7-inch
HAPPY MAN.......3-4 89

PACKARDS
(With Paul Boyers Band)
Singles: 78 rpm
PARADISE.......25-50 56
PLA-BAC.......200-300 56
Singles: 7-inch
PARADISE (105 "Dream of Love").......200-400 56
PLA-BAC (106 "Ladise").......1000-2000 56

PACKARDS
LPs: 10/12-inch
SURFSIDE.......8-10 80

PACKERS P&R/R&B '65
Singles: 7-inch
HBR.......4-8 66
IMPERIAL.......4-6 69
PURE SOUL MUSIC.......4-8 65
SOUL BABY.......4-8 60s
TAG LTD.......4-8 67
TANGERINE.......4-8 68
LPs: 10/12-inch
IMPERIAL.......10-15 68
PURE SOUL MUSIC.......15-20 66
Member: Charles Axton.
Also see MAR-KEYS

PAC-KEYS
Singles: 7-inch
HOLLYWOOD.......5-10 66-67

PACO & CITATIONS
Singles: 7-inch
SARA (5036 "Cheryl, Mona, Marie").......15-25 60s
Members: Leroy "Paco" Beribeau; Jim Delongchamp; Dick Bjorkman.

PADDY, KLAUS & GIBSON
Singles: 7-inch
CHESS.......10-15 66

PADGETT, Linda
Singles: 7-inch
DOT.......4-8 61
TOPPA.......5-10 61

PADUA, Tony
Singles: 7-inch
CHRISTY.......10-15 59

PAEGENS
Singles: 7-inch
RAMPRO (122 "Good Day Sunshine").......10-20 67
Picture Sleeves
RAMPRO (122 "Good Day Sunshine").......20-30 67
Member: Bun E. Carlos.
Also see CHEAP TRICK

PAGAN, Bruni R&B '79
Singles: 7-inch
ELEKTRA.......3-5 79

PAGAN, Ralfi R&B '71
Singles: 7-inch
FANIA.......3-5 71
Also see SYLVIA & Ralfi Pagan

PAGANS
Singles: 7-inch
MUSIC CITY (832 "Lover's Plea").......150-200 60

PAGANS
Singles: 7-inch
STUDIO CITY (1034 "Stop Shakin' Your Head").......50-75 65

PAGE, Aaron
Singles: 7-inch
ROBEN.......4-8 63

PAGE, Allen
Singles: 7-inch
MOON.......15-30 59

PAGE, Bobby
Singles: 78 rpm
VITO ("Carioca").......10-15 54
Singles: 7-inch
RAM (1338 "Hippy Ti-Yo").......20-30 50s
VITO ("Carioca").......10-20 54
(No selection number used.)

PAGE, Charles
Singles: 7-inch
GOLDBAND.......6-12 61-64
TIC TOC (501 "Sweet Little Girl").......5-10 62

PAGE, Chris
Singles: 7-inch
PAGEANT.......4-8 63

PAGE, Duke
Singles: 7-inch
JUKE BOX.......4-8

PAGE, Gene LP '75
Singles: 7-inch
ARISTA.......3-5 78-80
ATLANTIC.......3-5 74-75
LPs: 10/12-inch
ARISTA.......5-10 78-80
ATLANTIC.......8-12 74-75

PAGE, Hal: see PAIGE, Hal

PAGE, Hot Lips
(Oran Page)
Singles: 78 rpm
APOLLO.......5-10 46
BLUEBIRD.......10-20 38
COLUMBIA.......4-8 47-50
COMMODORE.......5-10 44-45
CONTINENTAL.......5-10 44
HARMONY.......4-8 47
HUB.......5-10 45
SAVOY.......5-10 44-45
V-DISC.......8-12 44
Singles: 7-inch
KING (1404 "The Cadillac Song").......50-75 53
KING (4584 "Last Call for Alcohol").......100-200 52
KING (4594 "Ruby").......50-100 53
KING (4616 "What Shall I Do").......50-100 53
KING (15000 series).......15-25 52
RCA (50-0120 "Let Me In").......50-75 51
RCA (50-0129 "I Want to Ride Like the Cowboys Do").......50-75 51
EPs: 7-inch
BRUNSWICK (97102 "Jazztime U.S.A.").......15-25 54
REMINGTON (82 "Rhythm Blues") 15-25 50s
LPs: 10/12-inch
BRUNSWICK (54002 "Jazztime U.S.A.").......35-50 54
Also see ABERNATHY, Marion
Also see BOSTIC, Earl
Also see DOGGETT, Bill
Also see LITTLE SYLVIA

PAGE, Hot Lips, & Cozy Cole
LPs: 10/12-inch
CONTINENTAL.......20-30 62
Also see COLE, Cozy

PAGE, Hot Lips, & Randy Hall
(With the Tin Flutes)
Singles: 78 rpm
KING.......10-15 52
Singles: 7-inch
KING.......15-20 52
Also see PAGE, Hot Lips

PAGE, Howard, & Pearls
Singles: 7-inch
ASTOR (1005 "I Just Can't Stand It").......10-20

PAGE, Ian
LPs: 10/12-inch
COLUMBIA.......8-12 73

PAGE, Jerry
Singles: 7-inch
SONIC.......8-12 60s
Also see JERRY & CASUALS

PAGE, Jim
LPs:10/12-inch
WHID-ISLE.......10-20

PAGE, Jimmy LP '82
Singles: 7-inch
GEFFEN.......3-4 88
Picture Sleeves
GEFFEN.......4-6 88
(Promotional issue only.)
LPs: 10/12-inch
GEFFEN.......5-8 88
SPRINGBOARD (4038 "Early Works").......5-10 70s
SWAN SONG.......5-10 82
Also see CARTOONE
Also see CLAPTON, Eric, Jeff Beck & Jimmy Page
Also see COVERDALE & PAGE
Also see FIRM
Also see HERMAN'S HERMITS
Also see HONEYDRIPPERS
Also see LED ZEPPELIN
Also see LORD SUTCH
Also see SPANN, Otis
Also see STEWART, Al
Also see WILLIE & Poor Boys
Also see YARDBIRDS

PAGE, Jimmy, & Robert Plant
LPs: 10/12-inch
W.B. (62706 "No Quarter").......10-15 94
Also see PLANT, Robert

PAGE, Jimmy, and Sonny Boy Williamson
LPs: 10/12-inch
SPRINGBOARD.......10-20 72
Also see WILLIAMSON, Sonny Boy, & Yardbirds

PAGE, Joey
Singles: 7-inch
ROULETTE.......4-8 61

PAGE, Larry
(Larry Page Orchestra)
Singles: 7-inch
CALLA.......4-6 68
LPs: 10/12-inch
RHINO (257 "Kinky Music").......8-12 84
(Picture disc with Kinks photo. Has instrumental versions of Kinks' songs.)

PAGE, Lawanda
Singles: 7-inch
MOTOWN.......3-5 82
LPs: 10/12-inch
MOTOWN.......5-10 82

PAGE, Mayalta
Singles: 7-inch
ETIQUETTE.......5-8 64

PAGE, Mike
Singles: 7-inch
ROYCE (0005 "Long Black Shiny Car").......15-25 59

PAGE, Patti
(With Al Clauser & the Oklahomans)
Singles: 78 rpm
OKLA (66 "My Sweet Papa").......5-10 40s
(Listed primarily to distinguish this singer from the following Patti Page.)

PAGE, Patti P&R '48
(With the George Barnes Trio; with Jack Rael Quartet/Orchestra)
Singles: 78 rpm
MERCURY (A-95 thru A-1025).......5-15 50-52
(Boxed set of singles.)
MERCURY (505 "Confess").......5-10 50
MERCURY (5061 thru 5899).......5-10 47-52
MERCURY (70025 thru 71101).......5-10 52-57
MERCURY (71177 thru 71331).......10-20 57-58
PLAYCRAFT.......5-10 53-55
Singles: 7-inch
AVCO.......3-5 74-75
COLUMBIA.......4-6 62-70
EPIC.......3-5 73-74
LANGWORTH.......10-20 49
(Eight-inch, 33 1/3 rpm transcriptions.)
MERCURY (A-95 thru A-1025).......10-20 50-52
(Boxed set of singles.)
MERCURY (505 "Confess").......10-15 50
MERCURY (5344 thru 5899).......10-15 50-52
MERCURY (7000 series).......5-15 61
(Compact 33 stereo.)
MERCURY (10000 series).......5-10 58-60
(Stereo.)
MERCURY (30000 series).......5-10 58
MERCURY (70025 thru 72123).......5-15 52-62
MERCURY (73000 series).......3-5 70-72
PLANTATION.......3-5 81-83
(Black vinyl.)
PLANTATION.......4-8 81-83
(Colored vinyl.)
PLAYCRAFT.......5-10 53-55
Picture Sleeves
MERCURY.......10-20 54-63

EPs: 7-inch
MERCURY ... 8-18 52-61
PLAYCRAFT ... 5-10 59
LPs: 10/12-inch
ACCORD ... 5-10 82
AHED ... 5-8 76
BRYLEN ... 5-8 82
CANDLELITE ... 8-12 73
COLUMBIA (Except "CL" & "CS" series) ... 8-15 70-77
COLUMBIA (CL-2049 thru CL-2761) ... 10-20 63-68
(Monaural.)
COLUMBIA (CS-8849 thru CS-9999) ... 15-25 63-69
(Stereo.)
EMARCY (2-100 "The East Side The West Side") ... 50-80 58
(Two LPs.)
EMARCY (36074 "In the Land of Hi Fi") ... 40-60 56
(No Mercury logo on cover or label.)
EMARCY (36074 "In the Land of Hi Fi") ... 30-40 58
(Mercury logo on cover and label.)
EMARCY (80000 "In the Land of Hi Fi") ... 35-45 58
(Stereo.)
EMARCY (36116 "West Side") ... 20-30 58
(Monaural.)
EMARCY (36136 "East Side") ... 20-30 58
(Monaural.)
EMARCY (60113 "East Side") ... 20-30 59
(Stereo.)
EMARCY (60114 "West Side") ... 20-30 59
(Stereo.)
EVEREST ... 5-8 83
EXACT ... 5-8 80
51 WEST ... 5-8 79
GOOD MUSIC ... 5-8 85
HARMONY ... 5-10 69-70
HARTLAND ... 5-8 86
HINDSIGHT ... 5-8 86
IMPACT ... 5-8 79
MERCURY (100 series) ... 8-12 69
MERCURY (20076 thru 20226) ... 20-40 55-56
MERCURY (20318 thru 20952) ... 15-30 57-64
(Monaural.)
MERCURY (25059 thru 25210) ... 20-40 50-54
(10-inch LPs.)
MERCURY (60049 thru 60011) ... 20-40 57-58
(Stereo.)
MERCURY (60025 thru 60952) ... 20-35 58-64
(Stereo.)
MERCURY (61344 "I'd Rather Be Sorry") ... 10-20 71
PAIR ... 5-8 87
PICKWICK ... 5-8 72
PILLSBURY (001 "Big Records") ... 15-25 57
(Special products issue made for Pillsbury.)
PLANTATION ... 5-10 81-82
PLAYCRAFT (1300 "Patti Page") ... 15-25 58
SUFFOLK ... 5-8 88
WING (2-100 series) ... 5-12 72
WING (12121 thru 12174) ... 10-20 58-59
(Monaural.)
WING (12250 thru 12295) ... 5-12 65
(Monaural.)
WING (16000 series) ... 5-15 61-68
(Stereo.)
Also see MARTIN, Dean / Patti Page

PAGE, Patti, & Rex Allen
Singles: 78 rpm
MERCURY ... 5-10 50
EPs: 7-inch
MERCURY ... 5-15 53
Also see ALLEN, Rex

PAGE, Patti, & Vic Damone
Singles: 78 rpm
MERCURY ... 5-10 48
Also see DAMONE, Vic

PAGE, Patti, & Rusty Draper
EPs: 7-inch
MERCURY ... 5-15 53
PLAYCRAFT ... 5-10 59
Also see DRAPER, Rusty

PAGE, Patti, & Tom T. Hall *C&W '72*
Singles: 7-inch
MERCURY ... 3-5 72
Also see HALL, Tom T.
Also see PAGE, Patti

PAGE, Priscilla
Singles: 7-inch
ROSE (500 "My Letter") ... 25-35

PAGE, Rickie
Singles: 7-inch
EPIC ... 4-8 65

PAGE, Ricky
Singles: 7-inch
DOT ... 4-8 61
LANDA ... 5-10 61
RENDEZVOUS ... 8-12 60
SPAR ... 4-6 68

PAGE, Tommy *P&R/LP '89*
Singles: 7-inch
SIRE ... 3-4 89-90
Picture Sleeves
SIRE ... 3-4 89
LPs: 10/12-inch
SIRE ... 5-8 89-90
Also see NEW KIDS on the BLOCK

PAGE BOYS
Singles: 7-inch
ABC-PAR ... 4-8 62
CAMELOT ... 5-10 65
DECCA ... 4-8 63
HAMILTON ... 5-10 59
PREP ... 10-20 57

PAGE BOYS
Singles: 7-inch
RUFF ... 15-20 67

PAGEANTS
Singles: 7-inch
GOLDISC (3013 "Happy Together") ... 400-600 60
Also see DEE, Tony

PAGEANTS
Singles: 7-inch
BEACON (559 "It's Been So Long") ... 15-25 64
PAXLEY ... 10-20 61
Members: Roy Bronson; Barbara Reeves; Mel Riley.

PAGEANTS
Singles: 7-inch
GROOVE ... 4-8 65
RCA ... 4-8 65

PAGEBOYS
Singles: 7-inch
SEVILLE ... 10-15 64

PAGE-BOYS
Singles: 7-inch
WHIRL ... 10-12

PAGENTS
Singles: 7-inch
BAMBOO ... 5-10 64
ERA ... 8-12 63-64
IKE (631 "Big Daddy") ... 15-25 63

PAGES
Singles: 7-inch
DON TAN (0001 "Wind") ... 35-55 59
(Reportedly, the first issue.)
EAGLE (1006 "Wind") ... 30-40 59

PAGES
Singles: 7-inch
U.A. (667 "Sugar on the Road") ... 10-20 63

PAGES *P&R '79*
Singles: 7-inch
CAPITOL ... 3-5 81
EPIC ... 3-5 79-80
LPs: 10/12-inch
CAPITOL ... 5-10 81
EPIC ... 5-10 78-79
Members: Richard Page; Steve George; Russell Battelene; Jerry Manfredi; Peter Leinheiser.
Also see MR. MISTER

PAGLIARO
Singles: 7-inch
PYE ... 3-5 72

PAICE, ASHTON & LORD
LPs: 10/12-inch
W.B. ... 8-10 77
Members: Ian Paice; Tony Ashton; Jon Lord.
Also see ASHTON, Tony, & Jon Lord
Also see DEEP PURPLE

PAIGE, Dick
Singles: 7-inch
DEE JAY ... 4-6 64

PAIGE, Hal
(With the Whalers)
Singles: 78 rpm
ATLANTIC ... 50-75 52-53
FURY ... 50-75 57
Singles: 7-inch
ATLANTIC (996 "Drive It Home") ... 100-125 52
ATLANTIC (1032 "Big Foot May") ... 100-125 53
CHECKER ... 10-15 58
FURY (1002 "Don't Have to Cry No More") ... 50-75 57
FURY (1024 "After Hours Blues") ... 10-15 59
J&S (1601 "Thunder Bird") ... 15-25 57
Session: Mickey Baker.
Also see BAKER, Mickey

PAIGE, Joey
Singles: 7-inch
MIRA ... 4-8 65
PHILIPS ... 4-8 67
TOLLIE ... 5-10 64-65
VEE JAY ... 10-20 65
W.B. ... 10-20 63
Also see DICKEY DOO & DONT'S

PAIGE, Kevin *P&R/LP '89*
Singles: 7-inch
CHRYSALIS ... 3-4 89
Picture Sleeves
CHRYSALIS ... 3-4 89
LPs: 10/12-inch
CHRYSALIS ... 5-8 89

PAIGE, Joy
Singles: 7-inch
MONITOR ... 4-8 62

PAIGE, Kiki
Singles: 7-inch
GNP ... 4-8 62

PAIGE, Randy
Singles: 7-inch
BOYD ... 5-10 61
RCA ... 5-10 60

PAIGE, Ray
Singles: 7-inch
RCA ... 10-20 66

PAIGE, Sharon *P&R '75*
(With Harold Melvin & the Bluenotes)
Singles: 7-inch
PHILADELPHIA INT'L ... 3-5 75
SOURCE ... 3-5 80
Also see MELVIN, Harold

PAIGE, Wesley
Singles: 7-inch
ROJAC ... 5-8 69
635 ... 10-20 60s

PAINE, Jackie
Singles: 7-inch
JETSTREAM ... 4-8 66

PAINTED FACES
Singles: 7-inch
MANHATTAN (808 "Anxious Color") ... 15-25 67
MANHATTAN (811 "I Think I'm Going Mad") ... 15-25 67
MANHATTAN (814 "In the Heat of the Night") ... 15-25 68

PAINTED GARDEN
Singles: 7-inch
STEADY ... 4-6 69

PAINTED SHIP
Singles: 7-inch
LONDON (17351 "Frustration") ... 10-20 67
(Canadian.)
LONDON (17354 "Audience Reflections") ... 10-20 67
(Canadian.)
MERCURY (72663 "Frustration") ... 10-20 67

PAINTER *P&R '73*
Singles: 7-inch
ELEKTRA ... 3-5 73
LPs: 10/12-inch
ELEKTRA ... 8-12 73

PAIR EXTRAORDINAIRE
(The Pair)
Singles: 7-inch
LIBERTY ... 4-8 64-66
LPs: 10/12-inch
LIBERTY ... 10-20 66

PAIR OF KINGS
Singles: 7-inch
RCA ... 10-15 59
WARWICK ... 10-15 61
Member: Jerry Vance.

PAISLEYS
Singles: 7-inch
PEACE (70 "Wind") ... 10-20
LPs: 10/12-inch
AUDIO CITY (70 "Cosmic Mind at Play") ... 150-200 70

PAJAMA PARTY *P&R '89*
Singles: 7-inch
ATLANTIC ... 3-4 89
LPs: 10/12-inch
ATLANTIC ... 5-8 89

PAKALAMEREDITH
Singles: 7-inch
ELEKTRA ... 3-5 77
LPs: 10/12-inch
ELEKTRA ... 5-10 77

PAL, Ricki
(With Adam Ross Orchestra)
Singles: 7-inch
ARWIN ... 8-12 58

PAL & PROPHETS
Singles: 7-inch
JAMIE ... 4-6 69
PHIL-L.A. of SOUL ... 4-6 69
SCEPTER ... 4-8 64
Member: Pal Rakes.
Also see RAKES, Pal, & Prophets

PALACE, Eddie
Singles: 7-inch
JUKE BOX (109 "Kangaroo") ... 15-25 57

PALACE GUARD
Singles: 7-inch
ORANGE-EMPIRE (331 "All Night Long") ... 10-15 65
ORANGE-EMPIRE (332 "A Girl You Can Depend On") ... 10-15 66
ORANGE-EMPIRE (400 "Falling Sugar") ... 10-15 65
PARKWAY ... 8-12 66
VERVE ... 5-10 66
Members: Don Grady; Emitt Rhodes; Don Beaudine; Dick Beaudine; Mike Conley.
Also see GRADY, Don
Also see RHODES, Emitt

PALACE GUARDS
Singles: 7-inch
WHITE CLIFFS (269 "Gas Station Boogaloo") ... 20-25 67

PALADIN
Singles: 7-inch
EPIC ... 3-5 72
LPs: 10/12-inch
EPIC ... 10-15 72

PALADINS
LPs: 10/12-inch
ALLIGATOR ... 5-8 88

PALEY BROTHERS
Singles: 7-inch
SIRE ... 3-5 77-78
LPs: 10/12-inch
SIRE ... 5-10 77
Members: Andy Paley; Jonathan Paley.
Also see BEATLES COSTELLO
Also see NERVOUS EATERS
Also see RAMONES
Also see SMITH, Patti

PALIS ROYALS
Singles: 7-inch
NANCY (1001 "You Are My Sunshine") ... 8-12 60
RIDER (107 "Twistin' Freeze Boogie") ... 8-12 60
Also see STARR, Jimmy

PALISADES
Singles: 7-inch
CALICO (113 "Close Your Eyes") ... 15-25 60
DORE (609 "Oh My Love") ... 10-15 61
LEADER (806 "Dear Joan") ... 25-50 60
MEDIEVAL (205 "This Is the Night") ... 10-15 64

PALISADES
Singles: 7-inch
DEBRA (1003 "Chapel Bells") ... 150-250 63
(Reissued as by the Magics.)
Also see MAGICS

PALISADES
Singles: 7-inch
CHAIRMAN (4401 "Make the Night a Little Longer") ... 25-35 63
Session: Carole King.
Also see KING, Carole

PALLAS, Laura *D&D '84*
Singles: 12-inch
TVI ... 4-6 84

PALLBEARERS
Singles: 7-inch
FONTANA ... 4-8 67-68

PALM, Horace M., with Lefty Bates Orchestra
Singles: 7-inch
APEX (952 "Why Can't You Love Me") ... 10-15 59
Also see BATES, Lefty "Guitar"

PALM, Tommy
Singles: 7-inch
BOP (101 "Stroll with Me Baby") ... 35-50 57

PALM BEACH BAND BOYS *LP '67*
Singles: 7-inch
RCA ... 3-6 66-67
LPs: 10/12-inch
RCA ... 5-10 66-67

PALMER, Blues Boy: see PARKER, Bill

PALMER, Bruce
LPs: 10/12-inch
VERVE/FORECAST ... 10-15 70
Also see BUFFALO SPRINGFIELD

PALMER, Cal "Caldonia"
Singles: 78 rpm
EBONY ... 10-20 49
Also see PALMORE, Lil, & Her Caldonia Boys

PALMER, Clarence, & Jive Bombers: see JIVE BOMBERS

PALMER, Don, Quintet
Singles: 7-inch
ABNER ... 8-12 59

PALMER, Earl
(With the Jayhawks; with His Ten Piece Rockin' Band)
Singles: 78 rpm
ALADDIN ... 10-15 57
Singles: 7-inch
ALADDIN ... 10-15 57
CAPITOL ... 10-15 58
LIBERTY ... 4-8 61
ROULETTE ... 4-8 62
LPs: 10/12-inch
LIBERTY ... 20-30 61-62
Also see JAYHAWKS
Also see WILLIAMS, Larry
Also see WOODS, Donald

PALMER, Gladys *R&B '47*
Singles: 78 rpm
MIRACLE ... 10-20 47

PALMER, Jerry
Singles: 7-inch
CARLTON ... 10-15 63
CHATTAHOOCHEE ... 4-8 65
GAIETY ... 4-8 65-66
ROULETTE ... 4-8 62

PALMER, Odie
Singles: 7-inch
LITTLE GEM ... 3-5 77

PALMER, Patti
Singles: 7-inch
HANOVER ... 5-10 59

PALMER, Peter
Singles: 7-inch
USA (800 "Son of Honky Tonk") ... 5-10 64

PALMER, Rick
Singles: 7-inch
CARLTON (491 "You Threw a Dart") ... 20-30 58
Also see RICK & LEGENDS

PALMER, Robert *LP '75*
Singles: 12-inch
ISLAND ... 4-6 83-86
Singles: 7-inch
EMI/MANHATTAN ... 3-4 88
ISLAND ... 3-5 75-86
Picture Sleeves
EMI/MANHATTAN ... 3-4 88
ISLAND ... 3-5 83-88
LPs: 10/12-inch
EMI ... 5-8 88-90
ISLAND (Except 819) ... 5-10 75-86
ISLAND (819 "Secrets") ... 35-40 79
(Picture disc. Promotional issue only.)
Also see BOWN, Alan
Also see POWER STATION
Also see VINEGAR JOE

PALMER, Sal
(Butch Palmer)
Singles: 7-inch
VASSAR ... 4-8 62

PALMIERI, Eddie: see HARLEM RIVER DRIVE

PALMORE, Lil, & Her Caldonia Boys
Singles: 78 rpm
EBONY (1004 "I Believe I'll Go Back Home") ... 25-35 48
SITTIN' IN WITH (540 "I Believe I'll Go Back Home") ... 15-20 49
Also see PALMER, Cal "Caldonia"

PALMS
Singles: 78 rpm
UNITED (208 "Edna") ... 50-100 57
Singles: 7-inch
UNITED (208 "Edna") ... 150-250 57
Also see WILKINS, Artie, & Palms

PALS
(With Andy Gibson & His Orchestra)
Singles: 7-inch
GUYDEN (2019 "Summer Is Here") ... 10-20 59
TURF (1000 "Summer Is Here") ... 20-30 58

PALUMBO, John
LPs: 10/12-inch
LIFESONG ... 8-10 78

PAM & JANE
Singles: 7-inch
PETAL ... 4-8 64

PAMPLEMOUSSE, LE: see LE PAMPLEMOUSSE

PAMS
Singles: 7-inch
M.P. ... 4-8 67

PAN
Singles: 7-inch
COLUMBIA ... 4-6 73
LPs: 10/12-inch
COLUMBIA ... 8-12 73
Members: Keith Barbour; Ron Elliott; Don Francisco; Val Garay.
Also see BARBOUR, Keith
Also see ELLIOTT, Ron
Also see FREE BEER
Also see HIGHWAY ROBBERY

PAN, Peter: see PETER PAN

PANAMA
LPs: 10/12-inch
PETERS INT'L ... 5-10 78

PANAMA LIMITED JUG BAND
LPs: 10/12-inch
HARVEST ... 8-12 69

PANDA
Singles: 7-inch
GENERAL ... 5-10

PANDAS
Singles: 7-inch
SWINGTIME (1001 "Walk") ... 15-25 67

PANDEMONIUM SHADOW SHOW
Singles: 7-inch
TEEN TOWN (177 "Sunshine Summer Day") ... 5-10 70
Members: Kerry Narf; Janet Wagner.

PANDORAS
Singles: 7-inch
IMPERIAL ... 5-10 64
LIBERTY ... 5-8 67
OLIVER ... 5-10 66

PANDORAS
Singles: 7-inch
VOXX ... 3-4 82-85
Picture Sleeves
VOXX ... 3-4 82
LPs: 10/12-inch
RHINO ... 5-8 86
VOXX ... 8-10 82
Members: Paula Pierce; Melanie Vammen; Julie Patchouli; Karen Fields.

PANE, Davey
Singles: 7-inch
UNI ... 4-6 69

PANIC BUTTON *R&B '69*
Singles: 7-inch
CHALOM ... 4-8 68
GAMBLE ... 4-6 69

PANIC INC.
Singles: 7-inch
YARDBIRD ... 4-8

PANICKS
Singles: 7-inch
KYRA (1001 "Bad Doreen") 20-30 64

PANICKS
Singles: 7-inch
DUPREE (102 "Work") 15-25 66
DUPREE (200 "You're My Baby") .. 10-15 67

PANICS
Singles: 7-inch
ABC-PAR 8-12 59

PANICS
Singles: 7-inch
CHANCELLOR 5-10 62
PHILIPS 5-10 64
SWAN 5-10 66
LPs: 10/12-inch
CHANCELLOR 20-30 62
PHILIPS 15-25 64
Member: Sonny Richards.
Also see RICHARDS, Sonny, & Panics

PANICS
Singles: 7-inch
BOBBY (2004 "Love Riot") 10-20 66

PANICS
Singles: 7-inch
HICKMAN (2 "Panic") 8-12
LYNN (120 "Maypo") 8-12
SPORT (123 "Running Guitar") 8-12

PANIKS
Singles: 7-inch
20TH FOX 4-8 66

PANTHERS
Singles: 7-inch
D&C (12 "Bridgestone") 10-20 65
(Canadian.)
Picture Sleeves
D&C (12 "Bridgestone") 20-30 65
(Canadian.)

PAONE, Nicola P&R '59
Singles: 7-inch
ABC-PAR 3-6 59
CADENCE 3-6 59
EPs: 7-inch
CADENCE 5-10 59
LPs: 10/12-inch
ABC-PAR 10-20 59-60
ROULETTE 10-15 65

PAPA DON ASSOCIATION
Singles: 7-inch
AMY 4-8 68

PAPA DOO RON RON
Singles: 7-inch
RCA 8-12 75
LPs: 10/12-inch
TELARC 5-10 85
Also see JAN & DEAN

PAPA GEORGE: see LIGHTFOOT, Papa George

PAPA JOE'S MUSIC BOX C&W '69
Singles: 7-inch
ABC 3-6 69
Member: Jerry Smith.
Also see SMITH, Jerry

PAPA NEBO
LPs: 10/12-inch
ATLANTIC 8-12 70

PAPA'S RESULTS
Singles: 7-inch
MASTERTRACK 3-5 76
ATCO 3-5 76
Members: Grady Harrell; Rocquel Harrell.
Also see HARRELL, Grady

PAPER DOLLS
Singles: 7-inch
MGM 5-10 67
UNI 4-8 69
W.B. 4-8 68

PAPER DOLLS
Singles: 7-inch
TEKND TUNES 5-8 80

PAPER GARDEN
LPs: 10/12-inch
MUSICOR ("Paper Garden Presents") 20-30 69
(Selection number not known.)

PAPER LACE P&R/LP '74
Singles: 7-inch
BANG 3-5 72
MERCURY 3-5 74-75
LPs: 10/12-inch
MERCURY 8-10 74

PAPER TRAIN
Singles: 7-inch
CAPITOL 4-8 69

PAPPALA BROTHERS
Singles: 7-inch
PICTURE GRAM (5688 "Hawaiian Sunset") 10-20 74
(Picture disc. Made in Japan especially for distribution in Hawaii.)

PAPPALARDI, Felix
Singles: 7-inch
A&M 3-6 76-79
COLUMBIA (43773 "Love Someday") 10-20 66
LPs: 10/12-inch
A&M 5-10 76-79

PAPPAS, Peter
Singles: 7-inch
RU VAL 5-10

PARACHUTE CLUB D&D '83
Singles: 12-inch
RCA 4-6 83
Singles: 7-inch
RCA 3-4 83
LPs: 10/12-inch
RCA 5-8 83

PARADE P&R '67
Singles: 7-inch
A&M 4-8 67-69
Members: Jerry Riopelle; Murray MacLeod; Smokey Roberds.
Also see RIOPELLE, Jerry

PARADISE, Earl
Singles: 7-inch
ATCO 4-8 64

PARADISE EXPRESS P&R '79
Singles: 12-inch
FANTASY 4-8 78-81
Singles: 7-inch
FANTASY 3-5 78-81
LPs: 10/12-inch
FANTASY 5-10 78

PARADONS P&R/R&B '60
(With the Rockets Combo)
Singles: 7-inch
COLLECTABLES 3-4 80s
ERA 3-5 72
MILESTONE (2003 "Diamonds and Pearls") 15-20 60
(Maroon label.)
MILESTONE (2003 "Diamonds and Pearls") 10-15 60
(Red label.)
MILESTONE (2003 "Diamonds and Pearls") 5-10 60
(Green label.)
MILESTONE (2005 "Bells Ring") ... 15-20 60
MILESTONE (2015 "I Had a Dream") 25-35 62
TUFFEST (102 "This Is Love") ... 250-350 61
(Reissued as by the Trend-Tones.)
W.B. (5186 "Take All of Me") 10-15 61
Members: Bill Myers; Chuck Weldon; Wes Tyler; Bill Powers.
Also see TREND-TONES

PARADOX
Singles: 7-inch
MAGNA-GLIDE 3-5 77

PARAGONS P&R '61
("Featuring Mack Starr")
Singles: 78 rpm
WINLEY (215 "Florence") 40-60 57
WINLEY (220 "Let's Start All Over Again") 50-75 57
Singles: 7-inch
ABC 3-5 73
BUDDAH 3-5 75
COLLECTABLES 3-4 80s
LOST-NITE 4-8
MUSIC CLEF (3001 "Time After Time") 15-25 63
MUSICRAFT (1102 "Wedding Bells") 20-30 60
(Maroon label.)
MUSICRAFT (1102 "Wedding Bells") 15-25 60
(Red label.)
TAP (500 "If") 40-60 61
TAP (503 "Begin the Beguine") 25-50 61
TAP (504 "If You Love Me") 25-50 61
TIMES SQUARE (9 "So You Will Know") 15-25 63
VIRGO 3-5 72-73
WINLEY (215 "Florence") 50-100 57
(Has "Winley" in 3/8-inch letters.)
WINLEY (215 "Florence") 25-50 61
(Has "Winley" in 1/4-inch sans serif letters.)
WINLEY (215 "Florence") 15-25 61
(Has "Winley" in 1/4-inch serif letters.)
WINLEY (215 "Florence") 10-20 61
(Has "Winley" in 5/8-inch letters.)
WINLEY (220 "Let's Start All Over Again") 50-100 57
(Has "Winley" in 3/8-inch letters.)
WINLEY (220 "Let's Start All Over Again") 20-30 61
(Has "Winley" in 1/4-inch letters.)
WINLEY (223 "Two Hearts Are Better Than One") 50-100 58
(Has title in all upper case letters.)
WINLEY (223 "Two Hearts Are Better Than One") 20-30 61
(Has title in upper and lower case letters.)
WINLEY (227 "Twilight"/"The Wows of Love") 1000-1500 58
(Note spelling error on "Vows.")
WINLEY (227 "Twilight"/"The Vows of Love") 20-30 61
(Title error corrected.)
WINLEY (228 "So You Will Know") 25-50 59
(Has "Winley" in 3/8-inch letters.)
WINLEY (228 "So You Will Know") 20-30 61
(Has "Winley" in 1/4-inch letters.)
WINLEY (236 "Darling, I Love You") 25-50 59
WINLEY (240 "So You Will Know") 20-30 60
WINLEY (250 "Just a Memorie") 100-200 61
(Note spelling error on "Memory.")
WINLEY (250 "Just a Memory") 20-30 61
(Title error corrected.")
LPs: 10/12-inch
COLLECTABLES 6-8 86
LOST-NITE 8-12 81
RARE BIRD (8002 "Simply the Paragons") 35-50
Members: Julius McMichaels; Mack Starr; Al Brown; Don Travis; Ben Frazier; Bill Witt; Rick Jackson. Session: Dave "Baby" Cortez.
Also see COLLINS, Tommy, & Paragons
Also see CORTEZ, Dave "Baby"
Also see HARPTONES / Paragons
Also see JESTERS / Paragons
Also see OLYMPICS
Also see STARR, Mack

PARAGONS
LPs: 10/12-inch
MONTAGE 5-8

PARAGONS
Singles: 7-inch
LAFAYETTE ("Scramble") 10-20 61
(Selection number not known.)

PARAGONS / Samohi Serenaders
Singles: 7-inch
CENTURY CUSTOM (19317 "Surf Drums") 20-30 60s
Members: Mike Faulkner; Forrest Peque.

PARAKEETS
Singles: 7-inch
BIG TOP 5-10 62
JUBILEE 10-15 61

PARAKEETS
Singles: 7-inch
BARON 3-6 73
Also see PARAKEETS / Frank Motley

PARAKEETS / Frank Motley
Singles: 78 rpm
GEM (218 "Give Me Time") 100-150 54
Singles: 7-inch
GEM (218 "Give Me Time") 250-350 54
Also see PARAKEETS

PARAKEETS QUINTET
Singles: 78 rpm
ATLAS (1068 "I Have a Love") 50-75 56
ATLAS (1069 "My Heart Tells Me") 25-50 56
Singles: 7-inch
ATLAS (1068 "I Have a Love") .. 100-125 56
ATLAS (1069 "My Heart Tells Me") 75-100 56
Also see DONNA, Vic

PARALLELS
Singles: 7-inch
TWILIGHT (404 "Sax-A-Nova") 5-10 63
TWILIGHT (405 "Surf-A-Nova") 20-25 63
(Reissued on Twilight 406, as by the Tri-Tones.)
Also see TRI-TONES

PARAMONTS
Singles: 7-inch
CENTAUR (103 "When I Dream") 50-75 63
EMBER (1099 "In a Dream") 60-80 63

PARAMOR, Norrie, & His Orchestra LP '56
Singles: 78 rpm
ESSEX 3-6 53
Singles: 7-inch
ESSEX 5-10 53
EPs: 7-inch
CAPITOL 8-15 56
LPs: 10/12-inch
CAPITOL 10-25 55-66
ESSEX 10-20 54
HAYNES & BARRA 5-10 79

PARAMOUNTS
Singles: 7-inch
COMBO (156 "Take My Heart") . 100-200 59

PARAMOUNTS
(With Stan Vincent Orchestra)
Singles: 7-inch
FLEETWOOD (1014 "I Know You'll Be My Love") 75-125 60
Also see VINCENT, Stan

PARAMOUNTS
Singles: 7-inch
AVENUE D (0007 "Tell Me Why") . 20-30 82
(Blue vinyl. Reportedly 100 made.)
CARLTON (524 "Trying") 30-40 60
LAURIE (3201 "Just to be with You") 20-30 63
EPs: 7-inch
AVENUE D (0101 "We Belong Together") 8-12 85
Members: Willy Mendez; Kenny Demmo; Guy Tann; Joe Regusa; Larry Gilliam; Kevin Prothro; Steve Alous.
Also see DE MARCO, Ralph

PARAMOUNTS
Singles: 7-inch
DOT (16175 "Congratulations") 15-25 61
DOT (16201 "When You Dance") 15-25 61
Member: Robert Knight.
Also see KNIGHT, Robert

PARAMOUNTS
Singles: 7-inch
LIVERPOOL SOUND (903 "Poison Ivy") 20-30 64
Also see PROCOL HARUM

PARAMOUNTS
Singles: 7-inch
ELO 10-15 60s
MAGNUM (722 "Under Your Spell") 15-25 64
MERCURY 5-10 65

PARAMOUNTS
Singles: 7-inch
SARA (6567 "Shake a Tail Feather") 10-20 65
Member: Greg Berndt.

PARAMOURS
Singles: 7-inch
MOONGLOW (214 "There She Goes") 25-50 62
(Black vinyl.)
MOONGLOW (214 "There She Goes") 50-100 62
(Colored vinyl.)
SMASH (1701 "That's the Way We Love") 10-20 61
SMASH (1718 "Cutie Cutie") 10-20 61
Members: Bill Medley; Bobby Hatfield.
Also see RIGHTEOUS BROTHERS

PARASITES OF THE WESTERN WORLD
LPs: 10/12-inch
MATCHBOX 5-10 80
Members: Terry Censky; Mick Cascadden; Mike Audry; Hunt Sales.

PARCHMAN, Kenny
Singles: 7-inch
LU (504 "Satellite Hop") 250-450 58

PARDI, Dick
Singles: 7-inch
FRANKIE 4-8 63-64

PAREE, Paul
Singles: 7-inch
ZENITH 5-10 59

PARETTI SISTERS
Singles: 7-inch
AL-BRITE 5-10 60

PARFAYS
Singles: 7-inch
FONTANA (1526 "You've Got a Good Thing Goin' ") 15-25 65

PARHAM, Baby "Pee Wee"
Singles: 78 rpm
FLAIR 10-15 54
Singles: 7-inch
FLAIR (1036 "People Are Wondering") 25-50 54

PARIS
Singles: 7-inch
DOC (102 "Sleepless Nights") 100-125 60s
UNI 10-20

PARIS LP '76
Singles: 7-inch
CAPITOL 3-5 76
LPs: 10/12-inch
CAPITOL 8-12 76
Members: Bob Welch; Glen Cornick; Bernie Marsden; Thom Mooney.
Also see WELCH, Bob

PARIS LP '90
LPs: 10/12-inch
TOMMY BOY 5-8 90

PARIS, Bobby
(With the Centuries)
Singles: 7-inch
CAMEO (396 "Night Owl") 20-30 66
CAPITOL (5929 "I Walked Away") 25-35 67
CHATTAHOOCHEE (631 "Little Miss Dreamer") 10-20 63
INT'L GUILD (13007 "How Did Your Vacation Go") 50-100 60
JAIRICK (204 "Are You the One") 50-100 63
MAGENTA (03 "Dark Continent") .. 10-20 61
TETRAGRAMMATON 5-10 68-69

PARIS, Freddie
Singles: 7-inch
RCA (9358 "Little Things Can Make a Woman Cry") 4-8 67
RCA (9571 "There She Goes") 10-15 68
LPs: 10/12-inch
RCA (4064 "Lovin' Mood") 10-15 68
This artist is not Fred Parris, who performed with the Five Satins.

PARIS, Jack C&W '76
Singles: 7-inch
50 STATES 3-5 77-78
2-J 3-5 76

PARIS, Jackie
Singles: 78 rpm
MERCURY 4-8 56
Singles: 7-inch
MERCURY 5-10 56

PARIS, Laurie
Singles: 7-inch
ABC-PAR (10441 "Stay") 10-15 63

PARIS, Mica P&R/LP '89
Singles: 7-inch
ISLAND 3-4 89
Picture Sleeves
ISLAND 3-4 89
LPs: 10/12-inch
ISLAND 5-8 89

PARIS, Michael
Singles: 7-inch
DIMO 4-6 68

PARIS, Richie
Singles: 7-inch
TIP TOP (403 "I'm Gonna Get My Own Love") 10-20 61

PARIS & PERSIANS
Singles: 7-inch
AKU 10-20 61

PARIS BROTHERS
Singles: 7-inch
BRUNSWICK (55132 "This Is It") .. 20-30 59
CORAL (62220 "Funny Feeling") 10-20 60

PARIS CONNECTION
Singles: 7-inch
CASABLANCA 3-5 78
LPs: 10/12-inch
CASABLANCA 5-10 78

PARIS PILOT
LPs: 10/12-inch
HIP (With brown label logo) 10-15
HIP (With blue label logo) 8-10

PARIS SISTERS P&R '61
Singles: 78 rpm
CAVALIER 10-15
DECCA 10-15 54-56
IMPERIAL 10-15 57-58
Singles: 7-inch
ABC 3-5 73
CAPITOL 4-8 68
CAVALIER (828 "Bully, Bully Man") 15-25 53
CAVALIER (829 "Christmas in My Home Town") 15-25 53
COLLECTABLES 3-4 80s
DECCA (29000 series) 15-25 54-56
DECCA (30554 "Don't Tell Anybody") 10-20 58
ERIC 3-4 70s
GNP 5-8 68
GREGMARK (2 "Be My Boy") 15-25 61
GREGMARK (6 "I Love How You Love Me") 15-25 61
GREGMARK (10 "He Knows I Love Him Too Much") 15-25 61
GREGMARK (12 "Let Me Be the One") 15-25 62
GREGMARK (13 "Yes I Love You") 15-25 62
IMPERIAL (5465 "Old Enough to Cry") 10-20 57
IMPERIAL (5487 "Someday") 10-20 58
MGM 5-10 64
MERCURY 5-10 64-65
REPRISE 5-10 66-67
Picture Sleeves
MGM 10-20 64
MERCURY 8-10 64
LPs: 10/12-inch
REPRISE (R-6259 "Everything Under the Sun") 15-20 67
(Monaural.)
REPRISE (RS-6259 "Everything Under the Sun") 20-25 67
(Stereo.)
SIDEWALK 12-18
UNIFILMS 10-15
Members: Priscilla Paris; Sherrell Paris; Albeth Paris. Session: Davie Allan.
Also see ALLAN, Davie
Also see PRISCILLA

PARISH, Dean: see PARRISH, Dean

PARISH HALL
LPs: 10/12-inch
FANTASY 8-12 70

PARISIAN SEXTET
Singles: 7-inch
CHALLENGE (9151 "Baby Elephant Walk") 8-12 62

PARISIANS
Singles: 7-inch
ARGYLE 5-10 61
BULLSEYE 5-10 59
FELSTED 5-10 61
Member: Jimmy Wisner.
Also see WISNER, Jimmy

PARISIANS
Singles: 7-inch
POVA 10-15 62

PARK, Jan, Band
Singles: 7-inch
COLUMBIA 3-5 79
LPs: 10/12-inch
COLUMBIA 5-10 78

PARKAYS P&R '61
Singles: 7-inch
ABC-PAR 5-10 61
FONTANA 4-8 65

PARKE, Bernie, & Little Green Men
Singles: 7-inch
DYNASTY 10-15 59

PARKER, Alan
Singles: 7-inch
DECCA (32998 "Fanny Mae") 5-10 72

PARKER, Bill / Blues Boy Palmer
Singles: 7-inch
HOLLYWOOD (1090 "Busted") 8-12 59
Also see SHOWBOATS

PARKER, Billy *C&W '76*
(With "Friend"; with "Friends")
Singles: 7-inch
CANYON CREEK ... 3-4 88-89
OAK ... 3-4 81
SUNSHINE COUNTRY ... 3-5 76-79
SOUNDWAVES ... 3-4 81-83
LPs: 10/12-inch
RCA ... 8-15
SOUNDWAVES ... 10-20 82
SUNSHINE COUNTRY ... 5-10 76-77

PARKER, Billy, & Cal Smith *C&W '82*
Singles: 7-inch
SOUNDWAVES ... 3-4 82
Also see PARKER, Billy
Also see SMITH, Cal

PARKER, Bobby *P&R '61*
AMANDA (1001 "Foolish Love") ... 50-75 60
VEE JAY (279 "You Got What It Takes") ... 20-30 58
V-TONE (223 "Watch Your Step") . 15-20 61
(Hit version. Has "45-V-Tone 223A" etched in the vinyl trail-off.)
V-TONE (223 "Watch Your Step") .. 8-12 61
(Alternative take. Has "223AAX" in trail-off.)

PARKER, Bobby / Larry Green
Singles: 7-inch
LU-GREEN (101 "Watch Your Step"/"Sittin' Here") ... 10-15 60s
Also see GREEN, Larry
Also see PARKER, Bobby

PARKER, Brenda
Singles: 7-inch
FALCON ... 4-6 71

PARKER, Dave
Singles: 7-inch
MALA ... 4-8 62

PARKER, Deanie
Singles: 7-inch
VOLT ... 5-10 63

PARKER, Eddie
Singles: 7-inch
ASHFORD (1 "I Love You Baby") .. 15-25
MIKO ... 10-20
TRIPLE B ... 10-20

PARKER, Elbie
Singles: 7-inch
VEEP (1246 "Lucky Guy") ... 25-50 66

PARKER, Fess *P&R '55*
(With Buddy Ebsen)
Singles: 78 rpm
COLUMBIA ... 4-8 55
DISNEYLAND ... 5-10 57
Singles: 7-inch
BUENA VISTA ... 4-8 63
CASCADE (5910 "Eyes of an Angel") ... 8-12 59
COLUMBIA ... 10-15 55
DISNEYLAND ... 5-10 57
GUSTO ... 4-8 63
RCA ... 4-8 64-69
Picture Sleeves
BUENA VISTA ... 5-10 63
DISNEYLAND ... 10-20 57
RCA ... 4-8 64
EPs: 7-inch
COLUMBIA (2031 "Indian Fighter") ... 20-25 55
COLUMBIA (2032 "Davy Crockett Goes to Congress") ... 20-25 55
COLUMBIA (2033 "At the Alamo") 20-25 55
LPs: 10/12-inch
COLUMBIA (666 "Davy Crockett") ... 50-75 55
DISNEYLAND (1200 series) ... 10-20 64-65
DISNEYLAND (1300 series) ... 5-10 70
DISNEYLAND (1900 series) ... 10-20 63
DISNEYLAND (3007 "Yarns and Songs") ... 25-35 55
DISNEYLAND (3900 series) ... 10-20 64
HARMONY ... 10-20 60
RCA ... 10-20 64

PARKER, Fess, & Buddy Ebsen / Gene Autry
Singles: 7-inch
COLUMBIA/CHRYSLER (3 "Story of Davy Crockett") ... 5-10 55
(Promotional issue, made by Columbia for Chrysler. Plays at 16 2/3 rpm.)
Picture Sleeves
COLUMBIA/CHRYSLER (3 "Story of Davy Crockett") ... 10-15 55
(Promotional issue, made by Columbia for Chrysler.)
Also see AUTRY, Gene
Also see EBSEN, Buddy
Also see PARKER, Fess

PARKER, Gary Dale *C&W '90*
Singles: 7-inch
615 ... 3-4 90

PARKER, Gigi
(With the Lovelies)
Singles: 7-inch
CORAL (62314 "Lonely Girl Blue") ... 20-30 62
MGM ... 10-15 64

PARKER, Graham *P&R/LP '77*
(With Rumour; with Shot)
Singles: 7-inch
ARISTA ... 3-5 79-83
ELEKTRA ... 3-4 85
MERCURY ... 3-5 76-77
Picture Sleeves
ARISTA ... 3-5 80-83
ELEKTRA ... 3-4 85
MERCURY ... 3-5 77
EPs: 7-inch
MERCURY (74000 "Hold Back the Night") ... 5-8 77
(Colored vinyl.)
LPs: 10/12-inch
ARISTA ... 5-10 78-83
ELEKTRA ... 5-8 85
MERCURY ... 5-10 77-78
RCA ... 5-8 88-89
Promotional LPs
ARISTA (41 "Mercury Poisoning") .. 25-35 78
ARISTA (63 "Live Sparks") ... 25-35 79
Also see RUMOUR
Also see SPRINGSTEEN, Bruce

PARKER, Jack "The Bear"
(Featuring H-Bomb Ferguson; Featuring Emmet Davis)
Singles: 78 rpm
DERBY ... 20-30 50
PRESTIGE ... 10-15 50s
7-11 (2100 "Cheap Old Wine Whiskey") ... 50-75 53
7-11 (2101 "One More Kiss") ... 35-60 53
Singles: 7-inch
7-11 (2100 "Cheap Old Wine Whiskey") ... 100-150 53
7-11 (2101 "One More Kiss") ... 50-75 53
Also see DAVIS, Emmett
Also see FERGUSON, H-Bomb

PARKER, Jack, & Etta Jones
Singles: 78 rpm
DECCA ... 8-12 54
Singles: 7-inch
DECCA ... 10-20 54
Also see JONES, Etta

PARKER, Jesse
Singles: 7-inch
GILDA ... 4-8

PARKER, Jimmy
Singles: 7-inch
COMET (2156 "It's Wrong") ... 8-10 60s
HERALD ... 5-10 64
20TH FOX ... 5-10 66

PARKER, Johnny
(Johnny "Bird" Parker & the Fabulous Circons)
Singles: 78 rpm
CORAL ... 10-20 54
Singles: 7-inch
BRUNSWICK (55043 "I Must Be in Love") ... 30-50 58
CORAL (61290 "Hurts Me to My Heart") ... 15-25 54
WELLS ... 8-12 62

PARKER, Junior: see PARKER, Little Junior

PARKER, Lee
Singles: 7-inch
BIRTHSTONE (21622 "Mary-Lou") ... 100-150
CASCADE (5265 "Boy Meets Girl") ... 10-15 59
GOLDEN CREST (561 "Girl of My Dreams") ... 10-20 60
KING ... 5-10 59

PARKER, Leroy
Singles: 7-inch
CHALLENGE (9167 "Cross My Heart") ... 75-125 62

PARKER, Little Junior *R&B '57*
(With His Blue Flames; with Blue Blowers; with Bill Johnson's Blue Flames; Junior Parker)
Singles: 78 rpm
DUKE ... 15-30 54-57
MODERN (864 "Bad Women, Bad Whiskey") ... 25-50 52
Singles: 7-inch
ABC ... 3-5 73
BLUE ROCK ... 4-8 68-69
CAPITOL ... 3-6 70-71
DUKE (120 "Dirty Friend Blues") ... 25-50 54
DUKE (127 "Pretty Baby Blues") ... 25-50 54
DUKE (137 "Backtrackin' ") ... 25-50 55
DUKE (147 "Driving Me") ... 20-40 55
DUKE (157 "Mother-in-Law Blues") ... 20-40 56
DUKE (164 "My Dolly Bee") ... 20-40 56
DUKE (168 "Pretty Baby") ... 15-25 57
DUKE (177 "Peaches") ... 15-25 57
DUKE (184 "Wondering") ... 15-25 58
DUKE (193 "Barefoot Rock") ... 15-25 58
DUKE (300 series) ... 10-20 59-66
DUKE (400 series) ... 5-10 67
GM ... 4-8
MCA ... 3-4
MERCURY ... 5-10 66-68
MINIT ... 4-8 69
LPs: 10/12-inch
ABC ... 8-10 76
BLUE ROCK ... 10-15 69
BLUESWAY ... 8-12 73
CAPITOL ... 10-15 70
DUKE (76 "Driving Wheel") ... 60-100 62
(Cover pictures a Cadillac.)
DUKE (76 "Driving Wheel") ... 35-55 62
(Cover pictures a Wagon Wheel.)
DUKE (83 "Best of Junior Parker") .. 8-12 74
GROOVE MERCHANT ... 10-15
MCA ... 5-8
MERCURY ... 12-20 67
MINIT ... 10-15 69
Also see BLAND, Bobby / Little Junior Parker
Also see LITTLE JUNIOR'S BLUE FLAMES

PARKER, Little Junior, & Jimmy McGriff
LPs: 10/12-inch
CAPITOL ... 10-15 71
U.A. ... 10-15 71
Also see McGRIFF, Jimmy
Also see PARKER, Little Junior

PARKER, Little Willie
(With the Lorenzo Smith Orchestra)
Singles: 7-inch
MAR-VEL (2700 "Lookin' in from the Outside") ... 25-75 64
Also see SMITH, Lorenzo

PARKER, Lori *C&W '76*
Singles: 7-inch
CON BRIO ... 3-5 76-77
CORAL ... 5-10 60-61
Picture Sleeves
CORAL ... 8-15 60

PARKER, Milton
Singles: 7-inch
CLOSET (3101 "Women Like It Harder") ... 4-8

PARKER, Monister
Singles: 78 rpm
NUCRAFT (100 "Black Snake Blues") ... 75-100 52

PARKER, Neil
Singles: 7-inch
PAULA ... 3-5 70

PARKER, Pat, & Way-Mates
Singles: 7-inch
SKYLAND (1000 "Boy Watcher") ... 10-15 60s
Picture Sleeves
SKYLAND (1000 "Boy Watcher") ... 15-25 60s

PARKER, Paul
Singles: 7-inch
GLENN ... 5-10 64

PARKER, Paul *D&D '83*
Singles: 12-inch
MEGATONE ... 4-6 83

PARKER, Paulette
Singles: 7-inch
DUKE ... 3-6 69

PARKER, Penny
(With the Lew Douglas Orchestra & Chorus)
Singles: 7-inch
GUARANTEED (212 "Heartache Weather") ... 10-20 60

PARKER, Ray, Jr. *P&R/LP '80*
(With Raydio; with Helen Terry)
Singles: 12-inch
ARISTA ... 4-6 84-85
Singles: 7-inch
ARISTA (Except 1035) ... 3-5 80-85
ARISTA (1035 "Christmas Time Is Here") ... 3-5 82
(Promotional issue only.)
ATLANTIC ... 3-4 86
FLASHBACK ... 3-4 82
GEFFEN ... 3-4 87
Picture Sleeves
ARISTA (Except 1035) ... 3-4 80-85
ARISTA (1035 "Christmas Time Is Here") ... 3-5 82
(Promotional issue only.)
ATLANTIC ... 3-4 86
GEFFEN ... 3-4 87
LPs: 10/12-inch
ARISTA ... 5-8 80-85
GEFFEN ... 5-8 87
Members: J.D. Nicholas; Arnell Carmichael; Jack Ashford; Ollie Brown.
Also see MEDEIROS, Glenn
Also see RAYDIO

PARKER, Ray, Jr., & Natalie Cole *R&B '87*
Singles: 7-inch
GEFFEN ... 3-4 87
Also see COLE, Natalie
Also see PARKER, Ray, Jr.

PARKER, Richard
Singles: 7-inch
COMMONWEALTH (3013 "You're All I Need") ... 5-10 70
PHILIPS ... 8-12 63
RIGHT ON ... 8-12

PARKER, Robert *P&R/R&B '66*
Singles: 7-inch
HEAD ... 3-5 72
IMPERIAL (5842 "Mash Potatoes All Night Long") ... 10-15 62
ISLAND ... 3-5 75-76
NOLA ... 4-8 66-67
RON ... 5-10 59-60
SILVER FOX ... 4-6 69
LPs: 10/12-inch
NOLA (1001 "Barefootin' ") ... 20-30 66
(Monaural.)
NOLA (S-1001 "Barefootin' ") ... 30-40 66
(Stereo.)
Also see BO, Eddie

PARKER, Ronald
Singles: 7-inch
RICH-R-TONE (8010 "The Walking Blues") ... 50-75

PARKER, Sonny
(With His All Stars)
Singles: 78 rpm
ALADDIN ... 10-15 50
BRUNSWICK ... 15-25 53
COLUMBIA ... 10-15 49
PEACOCK ... 15-25 51
Singles: 7-inch
BRUNSWICK (84025 "Jealous Blues") ... 25-50 53
PEACOCK (1596 "Money Ain't Everything") ... 40-60 51
PEACOCK (1620 "Disgusted Blues") ... 40-60 51

PARKER, Terrie, & Plushpups
Singles: 7-inch
QUEEN (24011 "A Dream in the Night") ... 25-35 61

PARKER, Wayne / Dal-Tones
EPs: 7-inch
VELVET VOICE (58 "Ginger") ... 200-300
(We've have yet to learn if the tracks on the other side are by the same artists, or others. May not have been issued with cover.)

PARKER, Willie
(With the Sensational Souls; Frankie Newsome)
Singles: 7-inch
B and B (7401 "Why Not Tonight"). 10-15
M-PAC (7233 "I've Got to Fight It") .. 8-12 66
M-PAC (7236 "You Got Your Finger in My Eye") ... 15-25 67
Also see NEWSOME, Frankie

PARKER, Willis
Singles: 78 rpm
SITTIN' IN WITH (589 "733 Blues") ... 15-25 51

PARKER, Winfield *R&B '71*
Singles: 7-inch
ARCTIC ... 4-6 69
GSP ... 3-5 72
RU-JAC (24 "Fallen Star") ... 4-8 68
SPRING ... 3-5 71

PARKETTES
Singles: 7-inch
LUDIX ... 5-10 63

PARKING METER *D&D '84*
Singles: 12-inch
ATLANTIC ... 4-6 84
Singles: 7-inch
ATLANTIC ... 3-5 84

PARKS, Andy
LPs: 10/12-inch
CAPITOL ... 15-20 67

PARKS, Gino
(With the Hi Fidelities; with Love-Tones; Gino Purifoy)
Singles: 7-inch
CRAZY HORSE (1303 "Nerves of Steel") ... 15-25 68
FORTUNE (528 "Last Night I Cried") ... 50-75 57
GOLDEN WORLD (32 "My Sophisticated Lady") ... 10-15 66
MIRACLE (3 "Don't Say Bye Bye") ... 200-400 60
TAMLA (54042 "That's No Lie") ... 25-50 61
TAMLA (54066 "For This I Thank You") ... 25-50 62
Also see HI-FIDELITIES
Also see PURIFOY, Gino
Also see WILLIAMS, Andre, & Gino Parks

PARKS, Michael *LP '69*
Singles: 7-inch
MGM ... 3-5 70
LPs: 10/12-inch
MGM ... 10-15 69-70
VERVE ... 8-12 71

PARKS, P.J. *C&W '81*
Singles: 7-inch
KIK ... 3-5 81

PARKS, Ray
Singles: 78 rpm
CAPITOL ... 40-60 57
Singles: 7-inch
CAPITOL (3580 "You're Gonna Have to Bawl") ... 40-60 57
DIADON (60 "Rock Around the Barn") ... 20-40 58

PARKS, Sonny
Singles: 7-inch
ANOTHER FEATURE PRESENTATION (103 "Raindrops on a River") ... 10-20 60s
W.B. (5358 "New Boy in Town") ... 5-10 63

PARKS, Van Dyke
Singles: 7-inch
MGM (13441 ("Number One") ... 10-20 65
MGM (13570 "Come to the Sunshine") ... 5-10 66
W.B. (1727 "Song Cycle") ... 4-6 68
W.B. (2589 "Discover America") ... 3-5 72
W.B. (2878 "Clang of Yankee Reaper") ... 3-5 75
LPs: 10/12-inch
W.B. ... 10-20 67-75
Also see BEAU BRUMMELS
Also see BROWN, George Washington
Also see BYRDS
Also see COLLINS, Judy
Also see COODER, Ry
Also see DALTON, Kathy
Also see HARPERS BIZARRE
Also see RAITT, Bonnie
Also see STARR, Ringo

PARKTOWNS
Singles: 7-inch
CRIMSON (1006 " You Hurt Me Inside") ... 50-75 67
IMPALA (214 "You Hurt Me Inside") ... 100-150 63
(First issue.)
THOR (3258 "You Hurt Me Inside") ... 75-125 63

PARLAMENTS
Singles: 7-inch
U.S.A. (719 "My Only Love") ... 100-150 61

PARLAY BROTHERS
(With the Avantis)
Singles: 7-inch
VALJAY (2725 "My Girl") ... 20-30 65

PARLET *R&B '78*
("Parlet Featuring Jeanette Washington")
Singles: 7-inch
CASABLANCA ... 3-5 78-80
LPs: 10/12-inch
CASABLANCA ... 5-10 79
Members: Mahalia Franklin; Shirley Hayden.

PARLETTES
Singles: 7-inch
JUBILEE (5467 "Tonight I Met an Angel") ... 15-25 64

PARLEYS
Singles: 7-inch
COUNSEL (4901 "Big Ben") ... 10-20 64

PARLIAMENT *R&B '71*
(Parliament Thang)
Singles: 12-inch
CASABLANCA ... 5-10 78
Singles: 7-inch
CASABLANCA ... 3-6 74-81
INVICTUS ... 5-10 70-71
SOULTOWN ... 3-5
Picture Sleeves
CASABLANCA (950 "Aqua Boogie") .. 4-6 79
LPs: 10/12-inch
CASABLANCA (Except NBPIX-7125) ... 8-12 74-80
CASABLANCA (NBPIX-7125 "Motor Booty Affair") ... 10-15 79
(Picture disc.)
INVICTUS (7302 "Osmium") ... 50-75 70
Members: George Clinton; Raymond Davis; Calvin Simon; Clarence Haskins; Grady Thomas; Glen Collins; Pedro Bell; Mahalia Franklin; Shirley Hayden; Debbie Wright; Lynn Marby; William "Bootsy" Collins; Dawn Silva; Ron Banks; Larry Demps; Junie Morrison; Donny Sterling; Fred Wesley; Gary Shider; Eddie Hazell; Michael Brecker; Randy Brecker; Peter Chase; Jerome Bailey; Tiki Fulwood; Grady Thomas; Michael Hampton; Willie Nelson; Maceo Parker; Gary Cooper; Cordell Mosson.
Also see BOOTSY'S RUBBER BAND
Also see BRIDES of FUNKENSTEIN
Also see HAZEL, Eddie
Also see MACEO & MACKS
Also see P. FUNK ALL STARS
Also see PARLIAMENTS
Also see PARLET
Also see WORRELL, Bernie
Also see WESLEY, Fred

PARLIAMENT PLAYERS
Singles: 7-inch
MURBO ... 4-8 66

PARLIAMENT THANG see PARLIAMENT

PARLIAMENTS
Singles: 7-inch
APT (25036 "Party Boys") ... 10-20 59
FLIPP (100 "Lonely Island") ... 100-150 60
(Yellow label. First issue.)
FLIPP (100 "Lonely Island") ... 100-150 60
(Red label. Slightly longer version.)
LEN (101 "Don't Need You Anymore") ... 100-200 58
SYMBOL (917 "I'll Get You Yet") ... 15-25 63

PARLIAMENTS *P&R/R&B '67*
Singles: 7-inch
ATCO (6675 "A New Day Begins") .. 8-12 69
GOLDEN WORLD (46 "Heart Trouble") ... 25-50 67
REVILOT (207 "Testify") ... 10-20 67
REVILOT (211 "All Your Goodies Are Gone") ... 10-20 67
REVILOT (214 "The Goose") ... 10-20 68
REVILOT (217 "Sentimental Lady") ... 10-20 68
(Same number may have been used twice. We have verified *What You Been Growing*, but have yet to verify *Sentimental Lady* as #217.)
REVILOT (217 "What You Been Growing") ... 10-20 68
Members: George Clinton; Ray Davis; Calvin Simon; Clarence Haskins; Grady Thomas; Bernie Worrell; Bootsy Collins; Frank Waddy; Maceo Parker; Fred Wesley.
Also see CLINTON, George, Band
Also see FUNKADELIC
Also see PARLIAMENT

PARLIAMENTS
Singles: 7-inch
LEN (101 "Don't Need You Anymore") ... 25-35 58

PARLIAMENTS
Singles: 7-inch
CABELL ... 8-12
SOUL TOWN ... 8-12

PARMAN, Cliff
Singles: 7-inch
LENOX 4-8 63
PANORAMA 4-8 60s

PARNELL, Guy, & Nite Beats
Singles: 7-inch
VEE JAY 4-8 62

PARNELL, Lee Roy C&W '90
Singles: 7-inch
ARISTA 3-4 90-91
LPs: 10/12-inch
ARISTA 5-8 90

PARR, John P&R/LP '84
Singles: 12-inch
ATLANTIC 4-6 86
Singles: 7-inch
ATLANTIC 3-4 84-86
Picture Sleeves
ATLANTIC 3-4 85-86
LPs: 10/12-inch
ATLANTIC 5-8 84-86

PARR, Johnny
Singles: 7-inch
LAWN 4-8 63

PARRIS, Fred P&R '82
(With the Satins; with Five Satins; with "Scarlets Originally the Five Satins"; with Passionettes; with Black Satin; with Restless Hearts; Fred Paris)
Singles: 7-inch
ATCO 5-10 66
BIRTH 4-8
BUDDAH 3-5 75
CANDLELITE 5-10 63
CHECKER 5-10 65
ELEKTRA (47411 "Memories of Days Gone By") 5-10 82
GREEN SEA 5-10 66
KLIK (7905 "She's Gone") 100-150 58
MAMA SADIE (1001 "In the Still of the Night") 5-10 67
RCA (9232 "It's Okay to Cry") 5-10 67
(A Freddie Paris also recorded for RCA at this time. Note slightly different spelling.)
LPs: 10/12-inch
BUDDAH 30-50 75
ELEKTRA 10-15 82
Also see CHEROKEES
Also see FIVE SATINS
Also see PARIS, Freddie

PARRIS, Johnny, Co.
Singles: 7-inch
DUNHILL 4-8 67

PARRISH
Singles: 7-inch
UPTITE 4-6 69

PARRISH, Darrell, & Wildcats
Singles: 7-inch
WAYNE-WAY (119 "Rockin' Pneumonia") 10-20 63

PARRISH, Dean P&R '66
(Dean Parish)
Singles: 7-inch
BOOM 10-20 66
LAURIE 5-10 67
MUSICOR 5-10 65

PARRISH, Gene, & Orchestra
Singles: 78 rpm
RCA (4240 "Dream Blues") 8-12 51
Singles: 7-inch
RCA (4240 "Dream Blues") 20-30 51

PARRISH, Jimmy, & Nita Lynn
Singles: 7-inch
ALLSTAR 5-10 60

PARRISH, Man R&B '83
Singles: 7-inch
IMPORTE 3-4 83
SUGAR SCOOP 3-4 85
LPs: 10/12-inch
IMPORTE 5-8 83

PARRISH, Maxfield
LPs: 10/12-inch
CURNON 8-12 72

PARRISH, Paul
Singles: 12-inch
ABC (1013 "Song for a Young Girl") 5-10 79
(Picture disc. Promotional issue only.)
Singles: 7-inch
MUSIC FACTORY 4-8 68
W.B. 3-5 72
LPs: 10/12-inch
ABC 8-12 77
MUSIC FACTORY 10-15 68
W.B. 8-12 71

PARRISH & GURVITZ
Singles: 7-inch
DECCA 4-6 72
LPs: 10/12-inch
DECCA 10-15 72
Members: Paul Parrish; Adrian Gurvitz.
Also see GURVITZ, Adrian
Also see PARRISH, Paul

PARRISH & WILDE
Singles: 7-inch
INVADER (407 "Don't Fight It") 15-25 65

PARRISH BROTHERS
LPs:10/12-inch
CUCA 8-12 74

PARRISH TWINS
Singles: 7-inch
VISTONE (2016 "All Alone") 15-25 61
(Black vinyl.)
VISTONE (2016 "All Alone") 25-50 61
(Colored vinyl.)

PARROTS
Singles: 78 rpm
CHECKER 100-200 54
Singles: 7-inch
CHECKER (772 "Please Don't Leave Me") 300-400 54

PARROTS
Singles: 7-inch
MALA 5-10 67

PARRY, Kent, & Rogues
Singles: 7-inch
ALTON (600 "Stop, Then Rock") 20-30 59

PARSON, Gene
Singles: 7-inch
SOUTHFIELD (4501 "Night Club Rock & Roll") 250-350 59
SOUTHFIELD (4502 "I Found Out What Love Can Do"/"Please Don't Wait Til Tomorrow") 10-20 59
SOUTHFIELD (4503 "Please Be Mine"/"Wreck of Ol' No. 9") 10-20 59

PARSONS, Al
Singles: 78 rpm
SARG (140 "Wait for Me Baby") 20-25 56
Singles: 7-inch
SARG (140 "Wait for Me Baby") 40-50 56

PARSONS, Alan, Project P&R/LP '76
(Alan Parsons)
Singles: 12-inch
ARISTA (66 "Damned If I Do") 5-10 79
(Promotional issue only.)
ARISTA (9348 "Days Are Numbers") 4-8 85
(Promotional issue only.)
Singles: 7-inch
ARISTA 3-5 77-89
20TH FOX 3-5 76
Picture Sleeves
ARISTA 3-5 84-87
LPs: 10/12-inch
ARISTA (111 "No Gambler") 15-20 80
ARISTA (68 "Complete Audio Guide") 50-75 82
(Boxed, five-disc set.)
ARISTA (140 "Complete Audio Guide") 75-100 82
(Boxed, eight-disc set.)
ARISTA (4000 series) 5-10 78
(Black vinyl.)
ARISTA (4180 Pyramid") 15-20 78
(Colored vinyl. Promotional issue only.)
ARISTA (7002 I Robot") 5-10 77
ARISTA (8000 series, except 8263) 5-8 83-89
ARISTA (8263 "Vulture Culture") 5-8 85
ARISTA (PD-8263 "Vulture Culture") 30-40 85
(Picture disc. Promotional issue only.)
ARISTA (9000 series) 5-10 79-82
MERCURY (832 820 "Tales of Mystery and Imagination") 8-12 87
(Remastered limited edition with booklet.)
MFSL (084 "I Robot") 30-50 82
MFSL (UHQR 084 "I Robot") 75-100 82
(Boxed set.)
MFSL (175 "Best of the Alan Parsons Project) 25-35 85
MFSL (204 "Tales of Mystery and Imagination") 20-25 94
20TH FOX (508 "Tales of Mystery and Imagination") 15-25 76
(Includes eight-page booklet.)
20TH FOX (508 "Tales of Mystery and Imagination") 8-12 76
20TH FOX (539 "Tales of Mystery and Imagination") 5-10 77
Members: Alan Parsons; David Paton; Stuart Tosh; Eric Woolfson; Lenny Zakatek; Ian Bairnson; B.J. Cole; Stuart Elliott; Colin Blunstone; Allan Clarke; Andrew Powell; John Miles; Gary Brooker; Christopher Rainbow; Duncan Mackay; Richard Cottle; Laurie Cottle; Geoff Barradale.
Also see AMBROSIA
Also see BLUNSTONE, Colin
Also see BROOKER, Gary
Also see BROWN, Arthur
Also see CLARKE, Alan
Also see COCKNEY REBEL
Also see HOLLIES
Also see KEATS
Also see LYALL, William
Also see MILES, John
Also see PACK, David
Also see PILOT
Also see POWELL, Andrew
Also see RAINBOW, Christopher
Also see TREFETHEN
Also see VITAMIN Z
Also see ZAKATEK, Lenny

PARSONS, Bill P&R '58
(Bobby Bare)
Singles: 7-inch
ABC 3-5 73
COLLECTABLES 3-4 80s
FRATERNITY (835 "The All American Boy") 10-20 58
(Fraternity 838, by the real Bill Parsons—not Bobby Bare—is listed in the following section.)
Also see BARE, Bobby

PARSONS, Bill
Singles: 7-inch
FRATERNITY (838 "Educated Rock & Roll") 10-15 59
(Fraternity 835, credited to Bill Parsons [Bobby Bare], is listed in the preceding section.)
STARDAY (526 "Hot Rod Volkswagen") 25-35 60
STARDAY (544 "A-Waitin' ") 5-10 61

PARSONS, Gram LP '74
(With the Fallen Angels)
Singles: 7-inch
REPRISE 3-5 73
SIERRA 3-5 79
EPs: 7-inch
SIERRA 8-10 82
(Promotional issue only.)
LPs: 10/12-inch
REPRISE 8-12 73
SHILOH 10-15 73
SIERRA 5-10 79-82
Also see BYRDS
Also see FLYING BURRITO BROTHERS
Also see GUILBEAU & PARSONS
Also see HARRIS, Emmylou
Also see INTERNATIONAL SUBMARINE BAND

PARSONS, Jerry
Singles: 7-inch
AMP (791 "Don't Need No Job") 200-300 59

PARSONS, Rob C&W '82
Singles: 7-inch
MCA 3-4 82

PARTLAND BROTHERS P&R/LP '87
Singles: 7-inch
MANHATTAN 3-4 87
Picture Sleeves
MANHATTAN 3-4 87
LPs: 10/12-inch
MANHATTAN 5-8 87

PARTNERS
Singles: 7-inch
ALITHIA 3-5 73

PARTNERS
LPs: 10/12-inch
MARLIN 5-10 79

PARTNERS IN KRYME P&R '90
Singles: 7-inch
SBK 3-4 90

PARTNERSHIP
Singles: 7-inch
CUB 5-10 68
MGM 5-10 67
RCA 10-20 67

PARTNERSHIP
Singles: 7-inch
POCO 5-8
Members: Frank Pizani; John Allyn.
Also see PIZANI, Frank

PARTON, David
Singles: 7-inch
PRIVATE STOCK 3-5 77

PARTON, Dolly C&W '67
Singles: 12-inch
RCA (Black vinyl) 4-8 78-83
RCA (Colored vinyl) 8-12 78
Singles: 7-inch
COLUMBIA 3-4 90s
GOLDBAND (1086 "Puppy Love") 20-40 59
MERCURY (71982 "It's Sure Gonna Hurt") 15-25 62
MONUMENT (800 thru 1000 series) 5-10 65-68
RCA (0132 thru 0950) 3-6 69-76
RCA (5000 series) 3-4 86
RCA (9500 thru 9900 series) 4-6 68-71
RCA (10031 thru 11240) 3-5 74-78
RCA (11296 "Heartbreaker") 5-10 78
(Label mistakenly reads: "From the *Sure Thing* album.)
RCA (11296 "Heartbreaker") 3-5 78
(Label reads: "From the *Heartbreaker* album.)
RCA (11420 thru 14297) 3-5 78-86
RCA GOLD STANDARD 3-4 80
Promotional Singles
RCA (Colored vinyl) 4-8 77-85
Picture Sleeves
RCA 3-8 69-85
LPs: 10/12-inch
ALSHIRE 8-12 69-71
CAMDEN 5-10 72-78
COLUMBIA 5-8 87
MONUMENT (7600 series) 5-10 78
MONUMENT (8085 "Hello, I'm Dolly") 15-20 67
MONUMENT (18000 series) 12-20 67
MONUMENT (18100 series) 8-15 70
MONUMENT (31000 series) 8-15 72
MONUMENT (33000 series) 8-10 75
RCA (812 "HBO Presents") 15-20 83
(Picture disc. Promotional issue only.)
RCA (0033 thru 5000 series) 5-12 73-87
(With "AFL1," "AHL1," "APD1," "APL1," or "AYL1" prefix.)
RCA (2314 "Personal Music Dialogue") 10-20 77
(Interview. Promotional issue only.)
RCA (CPL1-3413 "Great Balls of Fire") 15-20 79
(Picture disc. Promotional issue only.)
RCA (LPM-3949 "Just Because I'm a Woman") 15-25 68
(Monaural.)
RCA (LSP-3949 "Just Because I'm a Woman") 15-20 68
(Stereo.)
RCA (LSP-4188 "My Blue Ridge Mountain Boy") 15-20 69
RCA (LSP-4099 "In the Good Old Days") 15-20 69
RCA (LSP-4288 "Fairest of Them All") 10-20 70
RCA (LSP-4387 "A Real Live Dolly") 20-30 70
RCA (LSP-4398 "Golden Streets of Glory") 30-50 71
RCA (4422 "Greatest Hits") 25-50 82
(Without *Islands in the Stream*)
RCA (4422 "Greatest Hits") 5-8 82
(With *Islands in the Stream*.)
RCA (LSP-4449 "Best of Dolly Parton") 10-20 70
RCA (LSP-4507 "Joshua") 10-20 71
RCA (LSP-4603 "Coat of Many Colors") 10-20 71
RCA (LSP-4686 "Touch Your Woman") 10-20 72
RCA (LSP-4752 "Dolly Parton Sings [Porter Wagoner]") 10-20 72
RCA ("HBO Presents Dolly") 15-25 83
(Picture disc. Promotional issue only.)
SOMERSET 10-20 63-68
STEREO-FIDELITY 10-20 63-68
TIME-LIFE 5-8 81
Session: Jordanaires; Ricky Skaggs; Porter Wagoner.
Also see ELLIOTT, Ron
Also see HARRIS, Emmylou
Also see JORDANAIRES
Also see KRISTOFFERSON, Kris, Willie Nelson, Dolly Parton, & Brenda Lee
Also see PHILLIPS, Bill
Also see ROGERS, Kenny, & Dolly Parton
Also see SOME OF CHET'S FRIENDS
Also see WAGONER, Porter, & Dolly Parton

PARTON, Dolly / George Jones
LPs: 10/12-inch
STARDAY (429 "Dolly Parton and George Jones") 30-40 68
Also see JONES, George

PARTON, Dolly, & Ricky Van Shelton C&W '91
Singles: 7-inch
COLUMBIA 3-4 91
Also see VAN SHELTON, Ricky

PARTON, Dolly, & Willie Nelson C&W '82
Singles: 7-inch
MONUMENT 3-4 82
Also see NELSON, Willie

PARTON, Dolly, Linda Ronstadt, & Emmylou Harris LP '87
LPs: 10/12-inch
W.B. 5-8 87
Also see HARRIS, Emmylou
Also see RONSTADT, Linda

PARTON, Dolly, & Ricky Van Shelton C&W '91
Singles: 7-inch
RCA 3-4 91
Also see SHELTON, Ricky Van

PARTON, Dolly / Kitty Wells
LPs: 10/12-inch
EXACT 5-8 80
Also see PARTON, Dolly
Also see WELLS, Kitty

PARTON, Randy C&W '81
Singles: 7-inch
RCA 3-4 81-83

PARTON, Stella C&W '75
Singles: 7-inch
AIRBORNE 3-4 89
COUNTRY SOUL 4-6 75
ELEKTRA 3-5 77-79
LUV 3-4 87
SOUL, COUNTRY & BLUES 3-5 75
TOWN HOUSE 3-4 82
LPs: 10/12-inch
ACCORD 5-8 82
COUNTRY SOUL 10-15 75
ELEKTRA 5-10 77-79
TOWN HOUSE 5-8 82
Also see TAYLOR, Carmol, & Stella Parton

PARTRIDGE FAMILY P&R/LP '70
("Starring Shirley Jones," "Featuring David Cassidy")
Singles: 7-inch
BELL 3-8 70-73
FLASHBACK 3-5 70s
Picture Sleeves
BELL (910 "I Think I Love You") 5-10 70
BELL (963 "Doesn't Somebody Want to Be Wanted") 5-10 70
LPs: 10/12-inch
BELL (1107 "Their Greatest Hits") 12-25 72
BELL (1111 "Notebook") 12-25 72
BELL (1122 "Crossword Puzzle") 12-25 73
BELL (1137 "Bulletin Board") 12-25 73
BELL (1319 "The World of the Partridge Family") 12-25 74
BELL (6050 "The Partridge Family Album") 20-30 70
(With bonus photo.)
BELL (6050 "The Partridge Family Album") 10-20 70
(Without bonus photo.)
BELL (6059 "Up to Date") 20-30 71
(With booklet cover.)
BELL (6059 "Up to Date") 10-20 71
(Standard cover.)
BELL (6064 "The Partridge Family Sound Magazine") 12-25 71
BELL (6066 "Christmas Card") 12-25 71
BELL (6072 "The Partridge Family Shopping Bag") 20-30 72
(With shopping bag.)
BELL (6072 "The Partridge Family Shopping Bag") 10-20 72
(Without shopping bag.)
Also see BONADUCE, Danny
Also see CASSIDY, David

PARTY LP '90
LPs: 10/12-inch
HOLLYWOOD 5-8 90

PARTY BROTHERS
Singles: 7-inch
REVUE 4-8 69

PARTY FAVORS
Singles: 7-inch
RSVP 5-10 65

PASADENAS LP '89
Singles: 7-inch
COLUMBIA 3-4 89
LPs: 10/12-inch
COLUMBIA 5-8 89

PASCAL, Nik: see RAICEVIC, Nik Pascal

PASH, Richard, & Back Door Society
Singles: 7-inch
SHOREMEN (1900 "I'm the Kind") 15-25 67

PASQUALE, Jessie
Singles: 7-inch
COMBO (148 "Pepperoni") 15-25 58

PASQUALE & LUNARTIKS
Singles: 7-inch
DINO (229 "La Pizza with Sazziza") 8-12
Member: Jessie Pasquale.
Also see PASQUALE, Jessie

PASS, Tony
Singles: 7-inch
ATCO 5-10 66

PASSENGERS
Singles: 7-inch
MALA 8-12 62
MUSE 10-20 60
Members: Johnny Seastrand; Jerry Greenberg;Charles Williams; Howie Liebewicz; Larry Mendelson; Johnny Fisco; Al Flamer.
Also see ACADEMICS
Also see GREEN, Jerry
Also see KING ARTHUR & KNIGHTS

PASSERALLO, Dave, & 4 Escorts
Singles: 7-inch
BI-MI (102 "By the Fire") 50-100 61

PASSING CLOUDS
LPs: 10/12-inch
PETE 8-12 69

PASSING FANCY
LPs: 10/12-inch
BOO 10-15

PASSION
Singles: 7-inch
TARGET 5-10 70
TEEN TOWN 5-10 71
Also see TONY'S TYGERS

PASSIONS P&R '59
Singles: 7-inch
ABC-PAR (10436 "The Empty Seat") 20-30 63
AUDICON (102 "Just to Be with You") 20-40 59
AUDICON (105 "I Only Want You") 20-40 59
AUDICON (106 "Gloria") 20-40 60
AUDICON (108 "Beautiful Dreamer") 20-40 60
AUDICON (112 "Made for Lovers") 20-40 61
COLLECTABLES 3-4 80s
CRYSTAL BALL 4-8 90
DIAMOND (146 "16 Candles") 30-50 63
DORE (505 "Tango of Love") 15-25 58
JASON SCOTT 4-8
JUBILEE (5406 "Lonely Road") 10-15 61
LAURIE 3-5 70s
OCTAVIA (8005 "Aphrodite") 500-750 62
LPs: 10/12-inch
CLIFTON 5-10
Members: Jim Gallagher; Tony Armato; Al Galione; Vince Acerno; Louis Rotondo.
Also see ALADDIN, Johnny
Also see HART, Rocky
Also see MYSTICS / Passions
Also see RESOLUTIONS
Also see SABER, Johnny, & Passions

PASSIONS
Singles: 7-inch
CAPITOL (3963 "Jackie Brown") 10-15 58
ERA (1063 "Jackie Brown") 15-25 58

PASSIONS
Singles: 7-inch
BACK BEAT (573 "Baby I Do") 5-10 66
TOPAZ 5-8 60s
TOWER 4-8 68-69

PASSIONS
Singles: 7-inch
PIC 1 (117 "Lively One") 20-30 65

PASSIONS
Singles: 7-inch
FANTASTIC (79 "Reason Why") ... 8-10 65
UNIQUE (79 "Reason Why") ... 8-10 65

PASSIONS
Singles: 7-inch
GSF ... 3-5 72

PASSIONS
Singles: 7-inch
EVITRUE (27916 "You Better Make a Move") ... 25-75

PASSPORT *LP '75*
Singles: 7-inch
ATCO ... 3-5 76
ATLANTIC ... 3-5 78
LPs: 10/12-inch
ATCO ... 8-12 74-77
ATLANTIC ... 5-10 78-82
REPRISE ... 8-12 72

PASTELL, James *C&W '77*
Singles: 7-inch
PAULA ... 3-5 77

PASTEL SIX *P&R '62*
Singles: 7-inch
CHATTAHOOCHEE (696 "I Can't Dance") ... 8-12 65
DOWNEY (101 "Twitchin' ") ... 10-20 62
DOWNEY (101 "Open House at the Cinder") ... 10-20 62
DOWNEY (102 "Brahm's Nightmare") ... 10-20 62
ERA ... 3-5 72
ZEN (102 "Cinnamon Cinder") ... 15-25 62
ZENITH (105 "A Sing-Along Song") ... 10-20 63
LPs: 10/12-inch
ZEN (1001 "Cinnamon Cinder") ... 50-100 62
Member: Sonny Patterson.
Also see INVICTAS
Also see PATTERSON, Sonny, & Invictas

PASTELS
("Fred Buckley, Vocalist")
Singles: 78 rpm
UNITED (196 "If You Put Your Arms Around Me") ... 75-100 55
UNITED (196 "Put Your Arms Around Me") ... 25-50 55
Singles: 7-inch
UNITED (196 "If You Put Your Arms Around Me") ... 200-300 55
UNITED (196 "Put Your Arms Around Me") ... 75-125 55
Member: Fred Buckley.

PASTELS *P&R/R&B '58*
Singles: 78 rpm
ARGO (5287 "Been So Long") ... 35-50 58
Singles: 7-inch
ARGO (5287 "Been So Long") ... 15-25 58
ARGO (5297 "You Don't Love Me Anymore") ... 15-25 58
ARGO (5314 "So Far Away") ... 10-20 58
CADET ... 3-5 70s
CHESS ... 3-5 73
MASCOT (123 "Been So Long") ... 150-250 57
Members: Big Dee Irwin; Richard Travis; Tony Thomas; J.B. Wellington.
Also see ERVIN, Dee
Also see IRWIN, Big Dee

PASTELS
Singles: 7-inch
LIMELIGHT (3007 "King of Fools") ... 20-30 63

PASTELS
Singles: 7-inch
ARK ... 8-12 60s
PASTEL (506 "Sleep Tight") ... 15-25 64
PUSH (110 "Weird Sounds") ... 15-25 60s

PASTELS
Singles: 7-inch
PHALANX (1006 "Cause I Love You") ... 10-20 66

PASTELS
Singles: 7-inch
CENTURY (22103 "Why Don't You Love Me") ... 10-20 65
CENTURY (23507 "Mirage") ... 15-25 66

PASTERNAK PROGRESS
Singles: 7-inch
ORIGINAL SOUND ... 4-8 67

PASTORIUS, Jaco *LP '81*
LPs: 10/12-inch
W.B. ... 5-8 81-83
Also see WEATHER REPORT

PASTORS
Singles: 7-inch
ALITHIA ... 3-5 72
GWP ... 3-6 69
LPs: 10/12-inch
ALITHIA ... 8-12 73

PASTRAMI MALTED
Singles: 7-inch
METROMEDIA (101 "Wiwwian Wevy") ... 15-25 69

PASTRANA, Joey
Singles: 7-inch
COTIQUE ... 4-8

PAT, Betty
Singles: 7-inch
VITA ... 5-10 58

PAT & AL
Singles: 7-inch
DELTAR ... 4-8 65

PAT & ANDRE
Singles: 7-inch
W.B. ... 4-8 66

PAT & BLENDERS
Singles: 7-inch
FAST EDDIE (102 "Just Because") ... 20-30
GAMBLE ... 3-5 72
T.S.O.P. ... 3-5 74

PAT & CALIFORNIANS
Singles: 7-inch
DOWNEY ... 10-20 64

PAT & EMPIRES
Singles: 7-inch
PARIS (548 "Autumn Leaves") ... 8-12 60

PAT & PAM
Singles: 7-inch
DAY DREAMING ... 8-12
OUR OWN ... 10-15

PAT & SATELLITES *P&R '59*
Singles: 7-inch
ATCO ... 10-15 59
Members: Pat Otts; King Curtis; Wayne Lips.
Also see KING CURTIS

PAT & WILDCATS
Singles: 7-inch
CRUSADER (100 "The Giggler") ... 8-12 64
Member: Pat Vegas
Also see VEGAS, Pat

PAT THE CAT & HIS KITTENS FEATURING VIC FONTAINE
Singles: 78 rpm
BSD (1009 "Little Rock Special") ... 50-100 52
Singles: 7-inch
BSD (1009 "Little Rock Special") ... 150-250 52

PATACHEK, John
Singles: 7-inch
PAGE (4101 "Bartender") ... 10-15 70s

PATCH, Billy, & Pirates
Singles: 7-inch
JOY (244 "Splittin' ") ... 10-20 60

PATCHWORK
LPs: 10/12-inch
RCA ... 8-12 72

PATE, Gus, & Jokers
Singles: 7-inch
SUMMIT (111 "Man Alive") ... 10-20 59

PATE, Johnny *P&R/R&B '58*
(Johnny Pate Trio: Johnnie Pate)
Singles: 78 rpm
FEDERAL ... 5-10 57
GIG ... 5-10 56
Singles: 7-inch
ARGO ... 5-10 64
DRAKE ... 8-12 61
FEDERAL ... 10-20 57-59
GIG ... 15-25 56
LPs: 10/12-inch
GIG ... 40-50 56
KING (561 "Jazz Goes Ivy League") ... 30-50 58
(Monaural.)
KING (KSD-561 "Jazz Goes Ivy League") ... 50-75 59
(Stereo.)
KING (584 "Swingin' Flute") ... 30-50 58
KING (611 "A Date with Johnny Pate") ... 30-50 58
SALEM ... 25-35 58
STEPHENY (4002 "Johnny Pate at the Blue Note") ... 45-55 57
Also see CANDLES
Also see DAYLIGHTERS
Also see UNIQUES

PATE, Ray
Singles: 7-inch
GULFSTREAM (6654 "My Shadow") ... 200-300

PATE, Wally
(With Fred Norman & Orchestra)
Singles: 7-inch
CARLTON (499 "Washboard Song") ... 8-12 59

PATENTS
Singles: 7-inch
HART-VAN (0127 "Blue Surf") ... 15-25 63

PATERNO, Pat
Singles: 7-inch
YALE ... 5-10 60

PATEY BROTHERS
Singles: 7-inch
RON-MAR (1004 "Jeanie") ... 50-75 59

PATHFINDERS
Singles: 7-inch
ABC-PAR ... 5-10 61
CAPEHART ... 5-10 61

PATIENCE *R&B '80*
Singles: 7-inch
COLUMBIA ... 3-5 80

PATIENCE & PRUDENCE *P&R '56*
Singles: 78 rpm
LIBERTY ... 10-15 56-57
Singles: 7-inch
CHATTAHOOCHEE ... 5-8 64-65
LIBERTY ... 10-20 56-57
U.A. ... 3-5 70s
Picture Sleeves
LIBERTY (55084 "You Tattletale") ... 20-30 57
Also see CLIFFORD, Mike, with Patience & Prudence

PATRICK
Singles: 7-inch
RSVP ... 4-8 65-66
Picture Sleeves
RSVP (1119 "Don't Let This Room Become Your World") ... 5-10 66

PATRICK, Butch
Singles: 7-inch
METROMEDIA ... 4-6 69

PATRICK, Gladys
(With the Charioteers; Gladys "Glad Rag" Patrick)
Singles: 78 rpm
MGM (55015 "Somebody Please") ... 25-50 56
Singles: 7-inch
ATLANTIC ... 4-6 69
CENTRAL ... 5-10 60s
MGM (55015 "Somebody Please") ... 50-100 56
O-GEE ... 5-10 59
Also see CHARIOTEERS

PATRICK, Joey
Singles: 7-inch
RADAR ... 4-8 62

PATRICK, Keith *R&B '86*
Singles: 7-inch
OMNI ... 3-4 86

PATRICK, Milt
Singles: 7-inch
CAPITOL ... 4-8 61
DEMON ... 5-10 59
EVEREST ... 4-8 62
TERRI ANN ... 4-8 62

PATRICK & PAUL
Singles: 7-inch
UNI ... 4-8 67

PATRIDGE, Prince: see PRINCE PATRIDGE

PATRIOTS
Singles: 7-inch
EVEREST ... 5-8 60
Also see BRENNAN, Walter

PATRIOTS
(With the New Dimensions)
Singles: 7-inch
MELIC ... 4-8 63

PATRIOTS
Singles: 7-inch
CHART ... 4-8 66
LOOK ... 5-10 67
MAINSTREAM (631 "I'll Be There") ... 10-20 65
MURBO (1025 "What a Drag It Is") ... 10-15 68
WHITE CLIFFS (238 "Eagle Feathers") ... 10-15 67

PATRIS *D&D '85*
Singles: 12-inch
EMERGENCY ... 4-6 85

PATRIZIA & JIMMY
Singles: 7-inch
ALA (1174 "Trust Your Child") ... 4-6 70s
Member: James Robins.
Also see ROBINS, Jimmy

PATT, Frank, Orchestra
Singles: 78 rpm
FLASH ... 10-20 57
Singles: 7-inch
FLASH (117 "You Going to Pay for It, Baby") ... 10-20 57
Also see HONEYBOY

PATT, Gerry, & His Pals
Singles: 7-inch
ASCOT ... 4-8 65

PATTEN, Alexander: see PATTON, Alexander

PATTERNS
Singles: 7-inch
ABC-PAR ... 5-10 61
CHATTAHOOCHEE ... 4-8 64

PATTERSON, Bobby *R&B '69*
(With the Mustangs)
Singles: 7-inch
ABNAK ... 8-12 65-66
ALL PLATINUM ... 3-5 77
GRANITE ... 3-5 76
JETSTAR (Black vinyl) ... 5-10 66-69
JETSTAR (109 "Let The Talk") ... 10-20 68
(Colored vinyl. Promotional issue only.)
JETSTAR (111 "Funky No More") ... 10-20 68
(Colored vinyl. Promotional issue only.)
JETSTAR (113 "Sweet Taste of Love") ... 10-20 69
(Colored vinyl. Promotional issue only.)
PAULA ... 6-12 72-73
PROUD ... 5-10
Also see MUSTANGS

PATTERSON, Brenda
Singles: 7-inch
EPIC ... 3-5 70
PLAYBOY ... 3-5 73
LPs: 10/12-inch
DISCREET ... 8-12 74
EPIC ... 10-15 70
PLAYBOY ... 8-12 73
Also see COON ELDER BAND
Also see DICKINSON, James Luther

PATTERSON, Don
Singles: 78 rpm
PRESTIGE (717 "Oh Happy Day") ... 4-6 50
Singles: 7-inch
PRESTIGE (717 "Oh Happy Day") ... 5-10 50
WINSTON (1051 "Gena") ... 5-10 61

PATTERSON, Kellee *P&R/R&B '77*
Singles: 7-inch
SHADYBROOK ... 3-5 75-77
LPs: 10/12-inch
SHADYBROOK ... 5-10 76-79
Shadybrook may also be shown as Shady Brook (two words).

PATTERSON, Mike
(Mike Patterson & Fugitives)
Singles: 7-inch
IMPERIAL ... 5-10 64-65
Also see RHYTHM ROCKERS

PATTERSON, Millie
Singles: 7-inch
HIGHLAND ... 4-8 61

PATTERSON, Pat
Singles: 78 rpm
STARDAY (142 "Mr. Hillbilly") ... 20-30 54
Singles: 7-inch
STARDAY (142 "Mr. Hillbilly") ... 25-50 54

PATTERSON, Sonny, & Invictas
Singles: 7-inch
VAULT (101 "Gone So Long") ... 10-20
(Reissue of Jack Bee 1003, a '59 release credited to the Invictas. Also on Vault 903, a '63 issue. We do yet know when Vault 101 came out, since all other Vault numbers seem to be in the 900 series.)
Also see INVICTAS
Also see PASTEL SIX

PATTERSON SINGERS
Singles: 78 rpm
KING ... 10-20 54
Singles: 7-inch
KING (4693 "All Day & All Night") ... 20-40 54
KING (4705 "He Answered My Prayer") ... 20-40 54

PATTI
Singles: 7-inch
METROMEDIA ... 3-5 70

PATTI & EMBLEMS: see PATTY & EMBLEMS

PATTI & LOVELITES
Singles: 7-inch
COTILLION ... 3-5 72-73

PATTI & MICKEY
Singles: 7-inch
IMPACT (1027 "My Guy/My Girl") ... 10-20 67
Members: Patti Jerome; Mickey Denton.
Also see DENTON, Mickey
Also see JEROME, Patti

PATTI & XLs
Singles: 7-inch
DOT ... 4-8 66

PATTI ANNE
Singles: 7-inch
ALADDIN ... 30-50 55

PATTI ANNE & FLAMES
Singles: 7-inch
ALADDIN (3162 "Midnight") ... 75-100 52
Member: Patti Anne Mesner.
Also see PATTI ANNE
Also see FLAMES

PATTI JO
Singles: 7-inch
SCEPTER ... 3-5 72
SOLLY ... 4-8 66

PATTI'S GROOVE
Singles: 7-inch
COLUMBIA ... 8-10 66

PATTI-CAKES
Singles: 7-inch
REVUE ... 4-8 68

PATTO
(Mike Patto)
LPs: 10/12-inch
ISLAND ... 8-12 72
VERTIGO ... 8-12 71-72
Also see BOXER

PATTON, Alexander
(Alexander Patten)
Singles: 7-inch
CAPITOL (5677 "No More Dreams") ... 15-25 66
DUO DISC ... 5-10 65

PATTON, Charlie
LP: 10/12-inch
YAZOO ... 15-25

PATTON, David
Singles: 7-inch
WOODEN NICKEL ... 3-5 73

PATTON, Freddie
Singles: 7-inch
CUCA (1147 "Have Mercy") ... 15-25 63

PATTON, Jimmy
Singles: 78 rpm
SIMS ... 10-20 55
Singles: 7-inch
HILLIGAN (001 "Okie's in the Pokie") ... 300-500 61
SAGE (261 "Yea, I'm Movin' ") ... 75-125 58
SAGE (282 "Ocean Full of Tears") ... 25-35 59
SIMS (103 "Guilty") ... 20-30 55
SIMS (104 "Teenage Heart") ... 20-30 55
SIMS (105 "Ocean of Tears") ... 20-30 55
SIMS (117 "Okie's in the Pokie") ... 100-200 61
SIMS (256 "Can't Shake the Blues") ... 5-10 65
LPs: 10/12-inch
MOON (101 "Make Room for the Blues") ... 25-30
SIMS (127 "Blue Darlin' ") ... 30-40 65
SOURDOUGH (127 "Blue Darlin' ") ... 35-50 65

PATTON, Pat
Singles: 78 rpm
KING ... 5-10 56
Singles: 7-inch
KING ... 8-12 56

PATTON, Robbie *P&R/LP '81*
Singles: 7-inch
ATLANTIC ... 3-4 83-85
BACKSTREET ... 3-5 79
LIBERTY ... 3-5 81
LPs: 10/12-inch
ATLANTIC ... 5-8 85
LIBERTY ... 5-10 81

PATTON, Robert G.
(With the Blue Belles)
Singles: 7-inch
NEWTIME ... 5-10 62
Also see BLUE BELLES

PATTON, Rosalind
Singles: 78 rpm
GROOVE ... 5-10 54
Singles: 7-inch
GROOVE ... 8-12 54

PATTON, William
Singles: 7-inch
KING (6116 "It Hurts Me") ... 8-12 67

PATTY & PETER
Singles: 7-inch
COLUMBIA ... 4-8 61
SANDS ... 4-8 62

PATTY & EMBLEMS *P&R/R&B '64*
(Patti & Emblems)
Singles: 7-inch
COLLECTABLES ... 3-4 80s
CONGRESS ... 10-20 66
HERALD ... 10-20 64
KAPP ... 10-20 66-68
LOST-NITE ... 3-5
SPHERE SOUND ... 10-20 64

PATTY ANNE
Singles: 78 rpm
ALADDIN ... 10-20 53
Singles: 7-inch
ALADDIN ... 25-35 53

PATTY CAKES
Singles: 7-inch
TUFF ... 8-12 64

PATTY FLABBIE'S COUGHED ENGINE
Singles: 7-inch
DIAMOND (252 "Billy's Got a Goat") ... 10-20 68

PAUL
(Ray Hildebrand)
Singles: 7-inch
DOT ... 4-8 66
LE CAM ... 5-10 60s
PHILIPS ... 4-8 64
TOWER ... 4-8 67
Also see HILDEBRAND, Ray
Also see PAUL & PAULA

PAUL / Ron-Dels
Singles: 7-inch
CHARAY (94 "Lollipops & Teardrops") ... 5-10 66
Also see PAUL
Also see RON-DELS

PAUL
Singles: 7-inch
JOSIE ... 4-8 65

PAUL, Barry
Singles: 7-inch
ZIRKON ... 5-10 60

PAUL, Billy *LP '70*
Singles: 12-inch
PHILADELPHIA INT'L ... 4-8 79
Singles: 7-inch
FINCH ... 8-12 60
JUBILEE (5081 "That's Why I Dream") ... 10-20 52
JUBILEE (5086 "You Didn't Know") ... 10-20 52
NEPTUNE ... 3-6 70
PHILADELPHIA INT'L ... 3-5 71-81
LPs: 10/12-inch
GAMBLE ... 10-20 67
NEPTUNE ... 10-15 70

PHILADELPHIA INT'L ... 5-10 71-80
Also see PHILADELPHIA INTERNATIONAL ALL STARS

PAUL, Buddy *C&W '60*
Singles: 7-inch
MURCO ... 5-8 60

PAUL, Bunny *P&R '53*
Singles: 78 rpm
BRUNSWICK ... 8-12 57
CAPITOL ... 8-12 55
DOT ... 8-12 53
GORDY ... 12-15 63
POINT ... 10-20 56
Singles: 7-inch
BRUNSWICK ... 10-20 57
CAPITOL ... 10-20 55
DOT ... 10-20 53
GORDY (7017 "I'm Hooked") ... 15-25 63
POINT (5 "Sweet Talk") ... 25-50 56
ROULETTE (4186 "Such a Night") ... 10-20 59

PAUL, Bunny, & Harptones
(Bunny Paul)
Singles: 78 rpm
ESSEX (352 "Such a Night") ... 20-30 54
ESSEX (352 "Lovey Dovey") ... 20-30 54
ESSEX (364 "I'll Never Tell") ... 30-50 54
Singles: 7-inch
ESSEX (352 "Such a Night") ... 50-100 54
ESSEX (352 "Lovey Dovey") ... 50-100 54
ESSEX (364 "I'll Never Tell") ... 100-200 54
Also see HALEY, Bill
Also see HARPTONES
Also see PAUL, Bunny

PAUL, Clarence
(With the Members; Clarence Pauling)
Singles: 7-inch
FEDERAL (12402 "Baby Don't You Leave Poor Me") ... 20-40 61
HANOVER (4519 "I Need Your Loving") ... 25-50 59
LONDON (218 "I'm in Love Again") ... 4-6 75
PRIDE (3 "Operation Breadbasket") ... 10-20 60
ROULETTE (4196 "Falling in Love Again") ... 20-30 59
Also see FIVE ROYALES
Also see WONDER, Stevie, & Clarence Paul

PAUL, Darlene
Singles: 7-inch
CAPITOL ... 4-6 64

PAUL, Dennis
(With Wes Dakus' Rebels)
Singles: 7-inch
KAPP ... 4-8 67
Also see DAKUS, Wes

PAUL, Glen
Singles: 7-inch
ATHENS (702 "I'm Learning to Live") ... 10-20 57
MERCURY ... 5-10 58

PAUL, Henry, Band *LP '79*
Singles: 7-inch
ATLANTIC ... 3-5 79-81
LPs: 10/12-inch
ATLANTIC ... 5-10 79-81
Also see OUTLAWS

PAUL, Jad
LPs:10/12-inch
LIBERTY ... 15-25 60s

PAUL, Jerry
Singles: 7-inch
GREAT ... 5-10 59
HOLIDAY ... 10-15 60

PAUL, Jessie
Singles: 7-inch
WORLD PACIFIC ... 4-8 64

PAUL, John, & Liberators
Singles: 7-inch
CUCA (66104 "Midnite Hour") ... 10-20 66
NIGHT OWL (6732 "Around & Around") ... 10-20 67

PAUL, Johnnie, Combo
Singles: 7-inch
EBONY (1075 "My Rock & Roll Man") ... 10-20 63

PAUL, Jon
Singles: 7-inch
ENVY ... 4-8 68

PAUL, Joyce *C&W '68*
Singles: 7-inch
DOT ... 4-8 61
IMPERIAL ... 4-8 64
U.A. ... 4-6 65-68

PAUL, Lafawn
(With the Whipporwills)
Singles: 78 rpm
ABBOTT ... 5-10 55
Singles: 7-inch
ABBOTT ... 10-15 55
VANDAN ... 8-12 64

PAUL, Larry
Singles: 7-inch
MALA ... 10-20 59-62

PAUL, Les *P&R '48*
(Les Paul Trio)
Singles: 78 rpm
CAPITOL ... 5-10 50-53
DECCA ... 5-10 54
Singles: 7-inch
CAPITOL ... 5-15 50-53
DECCA ... 5-15 54
EPs: 7-inch
DECCA ... 10-20 50-53
LPs: 10/12-inch
CAPITOL (200 series) ... 5-10 77
CAPITOL (16000 series) ... 5-8
DECCA (5018 "Hawaiian Paradise") ... 50-100 49
(10-inch LP.)
DECCA (5376 "Galloping Guitars") ... 50-75 52
(10-inch LP.)
DECCA (8589 "More of Les") ... 30-50 57
GLENDALE ... 5-8 78
LONDON ... 6-12 68-79
VOCALION ... 6-12 68
Also see ANDREWS SISTERS
Also see ATKINS, Chet, & Les Paul

PAUL, Les, & Mary Ford *P&R '50*
(Mary Ford with Les Paul; Mary Ford)
Singles: 78 rpm
CAPITOL ... 5-15 50-57
Singles: 7-inch
CALENDAR ... 3-5
CAPITOL ... 5-15 50-57
COLUMBIA ... 4-10 58-64
Picture Sleeves
COLUMBIA ... 4-8 58-64
EPs: 7-inch
CAPITOL ... 10-20 50-57
LPs: 10/12-inch
CAPITOL (SM-200 series) ... 5-8 78
CAPITOL (H-226 thru H-577) ... 25-50 50-55
(10-inch LPs.)
CAPITOL (T-226 thru T-802) ... 20-40 55-57
CAPITOL (T-1400 & T-1500 series) ... 15-25 60-61
(Monaural.)
CAPITOL (ST-1400 & ST-1500 series) ... 20-30 60-61
(Stereo.)
CAPITOL (11000 series) ... 5-10 74
COLUMBIA ... 10-20 61-63
HARMONY ... 8-12 61-65
Also see PAUL, Les

PAUL, Louis
LPs: 10/12-inch
ENTERPRISE ... 8-10 71

PAUL, Marvin
Singles: 7-inch
VAN ... 40-50

PAUL, Michael
Singles: 7-inch
RCA ... 4-8 67

PAUL, Pope: see POPE PAUL

PAUL & DALE
Singles: 7-inch
MERCURY ... 4-8 64

PAUL & DISCIPLES
Singles: 7-inch
AMERICAN INT'L ... 3-5 71

PAUL & FOURMOST
Singles: 7-inch
SHELLEY (170 "Cut Out") ... 10-20 63

PAUL & JOJO
Singles: 7-inch
BELL ... 3-5 73

PAUL & LYNN
Singles: 7-inch
ROULETTE ... 5-10 60

PAUL & PACK / Mad Doctors
Singles: 7-inch
TOWER (304 "Paper Clown") ... 8-12 67
(Promotional issue only.)
Members: Paul Stefan; Gary Myers; Phil Alagna; Pat Cibbarrich; John Rondell.
Also see MYERS, Gary
Also see STEFAN, Paul

PAUL & PAULA *P&R/R&B '62*
Singles: 7-inch
LE CAM (300 series) ... 3-5 74-82
LE CAM (99 "Beginning of Love") ... 8-12 63
PHILIPS (40000 series) ... 4-8 62-66
PHILIPS (44000 series) ... 3-5 70s
SOFT (106 "Hey Paula '69") ... 8-12 69
UNI ... 4-8 68
U.A. ... 3-5 70
Picture Sleeves
PHILIPS ... 8-12 63-64
LPs: 10/12-inch
PHILIPS (200078 "For Young Lovers") ... 25-40 63
(Monaural.)
PHILIPS (200089 "We Go Together") ... 25-40 63
(Monaural.)
PHILIPS (200101 "Holiday for Teens") ... 25-40 63
(Monaural.)
PHILIPS (600078 "For Young Lovers") ... 25-50 63
(Stereo.)
PHILIPS (600089 "We Go Together") ... 25-50 63
(Stereo.)
PHILIPS (600101 "Holiday for Teens") ... 25-50 63
(Stereo.)
Members: Ray Hildebrand; Jill Jackson.
Also see CHANNEL, Bruce / Paul & Paula
Also see JACKSON, Jill
Also see JILL & RAY
Also see PAUL

PAUL & PAULA
Singles: 7-inch
KARAT ... 5-8 67
Members: Sonny Threatt; Phyllis Brown-Threatt.
Also see SONNY & PHYLLIS

PAUL & VANITA
Singles: 7-inch
JOX ... 4-8 65

PAUL & VICTORS / Kim Fowley
Singles: 7-inch
CORBY (216 "Big Sur") ... 15-25 65
Also see FOWLEY, Kim

PAUL'S HIGH SCHOOL BAND
Singles: 7-inch
ROULETTE (4298 "Recess") ... 10-15 60
Member: Paul Vance.
Also see VANCE, Paul

PAULA, Marlena
Singles: 78 rpm
REGENT (7506 "I Wanna Spend Christmas with Elvis") ... 15-25 56
Singles: 7-inch
REGENT (7506 "I Wanna Spend Christmas with Elvis") ... 25-35 56

PAULEY, Everett
Singles: 7-inch
EVERETT PAULEY (11429 "Little Girl") ... 300-500

PAULEY, Joel
Singles: 7-inch
SAR ... 5-10 60

PAULETTE
(With the Larry Bee Combo)
Singles: 7-inch
ACCENT ... 4-8 63
ADANTI ... 4-8 65

PAULETTE & CUPIDS
Singles: 7-inch
PRISM ... 4-8 65

PAULETTE SISTERS *P&R '55*
Singles: 78 rpm
CAPITOL ... 4-8 55
Singles: 7-inch
ADMIRIAL ... 5-8
CAPITOL ... 5-10 55
CONTEMPO ... 4-8 63
DECCA ... 4-6 60s
RIBBON ... 4-8 60
20TH FOX ... 4-8 61

PAULINE & BOBBY
Singles: 7-inch
EXPO ... 5-10 68
LP: 10/12-inch
EXPO ... 15-25 68
Members:Pauline Shivers Banks; Bobby Jones.
Also see BIRDLEGS & PAULINE and Their Versatility Birds
Also see JONES, Bobby

PAULING, Ed, & Exciters
Singles: 7-inch
SAVOY (1625 "Soul House") ... 10-15 65

PAULSEN, Pat *LP '68*
Singles: 7-inch
MERCURY (105 "Open End Interview") ... 5-10 68
(Promotional issue only.)
LPs: 10/12-inch
MERCURY ... 8-15 68-70
Also see HEXORCIST

PAULSON, Butch
Singles: 7-inch
VIRGELLE (708 "Man from Mars") ... 100-150
VIRGELLE (718 "Candy Lou") ... 35-50

PAUPERS
Singles: 78 rpm
MELFORD (258 "Blue Sunday Morning") ... 40-60 49

PAUPERS *LP '67*
Singles: 7-inch
VERVE ("If I Called You By Some Name") ... 20-30 66
(Canadian. Selection number not known.)
VERVE/FOLKWAYS ... 8-15 66-67
VERVE/FORECAST ... 5-10 67-68
Picture Sleeves
VERVE/FOLKWAYS ... 10-20 67
LPs: 10/12-inch
VERVE/FORECAST ... 15-25 67-68

PAVAROTTI, Luciano *LP '79*
Singles: 7-inch
LONDON ... 3-4 79-84
LPs: 10/12-inch
LONDON ... 5-8 76-84

PAVLOV'S DOG *LP '75*
Singles: 7-inch
COLUMBIA ... 3-5 76
LPs: 10/12-inch
ABC ... 10-15 75
COLUMBIA ... 8-12 75-76
Members: David Surkamp; Mike Abebe; Murray Krugman; Sandy Pearlman; Mike Safron; Richard Stockton; David Hamilton; Doug Rayburn; Steve Scorfina; Bill Bruford.
Also see HI FI Featuring David Surkamp & Ian Matthews
Also see YES

PAVONE, Rita *P&R/LP '64*
Singles: 7-inch
RCA ... 4-8 63-66
Picture Sleeves
RCA ... 4-8 64-65
LPs: 10/12-inch
RCA ... 10-20 64-67

PAWNBROKERS
Singles: 7-inch
BIG SOUND (103 "Smell of Incense") ... 40-60 60s
IGL ... 10-20 68

PAWNEE DRIVE
Singles: 7-inch
FORWARD (103 "Ride") ... 8-12

PAWNS
(Featuring Ron Nowlan)
Singles: 7-inch
BAY-STATE (1267 "Summer") ... 25-50

PAXTON, Casey
Singles: 7-inch
CLARIDGE ... 4-8 66

PAXTON, Gary *C&W '76*
(With the Road Runners; with Nashville Mavericks; with the Bakersfield Sound; Gary S. Paxton; Gary Sanford Paxton)
Singles: 7-inch
BAKERSFIELD CENTENNIAL (1001 "Bakersfield") ... 15-25 69
("Collector's Edition" promo. Indicates being given "Compliments of Bakersfield Business.")
CAPITOL ... 4-8 65-67
FELSTED ... 5-10 63
GARPAX ... 5-10 63-64
LIBERTY ... 5-10 62-63
LONDON ... 5-10 64
LUTE ... 5-10 60
MGM ... 4-6 71
RCA ... 3-5 73-76
W.I.N. (28-45 "The Racedrivers Song") ... 3-5 80
Picture Sleeves
W.I.N. (28-45 "The Race Drivers Song") ... 3-5 80
(Promotional item made for NAPA Auto Parts. Note, sleeve shows title as "Race Driver," whereas disc label reads "Racedriver.")
LPs: 10/12-inch
GASLIGHT ... 10-15
NEW PAX ... 5-10 76-80
PARAGON ... 5-10 79
PAX ... 5-10 78-79
Also see BERRY, Richard
Also see CASSIDY, Ted
Also see GARY, Clyde, & His Orchestra
Also see GARY & CLYDE
Also see FIVE SUPERIORS
Also see HOLLYWOOD ARGYLES
Also see INNOCENTS
Also see MAVRICKS
Also see ROAD RUNNERS
Also see SALLES, Jessie, & Crypt-Kickers / Gary Paxton
Also see SKIP & FLIP
Also see YORK, Dave, & Beachcombers

PAXON, Peggy
Singles: 7-inch
PAULA ... 4-8 60s

PAXON, Sandy
LPs: 10/12-inch
ELEKTRA ... 15-25 58

PAXTON, Tom *LP '69*
Singles: 7-inch
ASYLUM ... 3-5 70
ELEKTRA ... 4-8 69
REPRISE ... 3-5 71
LPs: 10/12-inch
ANCHOR ... 8-12
ELEKTRA ... 10-15 64-71
FLYING FISH ... 5-8
PRIVATE STOCK ... 8-10 75
REPRISE ... 10-15 71-73

PAYCHECK, Johnny *C&W '65*
(With Chamissa)
Singles: 7-inch
ABC ... 3-5 74
AMI ... 3-5 84-85
CERTRON ... 4-6 70
CUTLASS ... 3-5 72
DAMASCUS ... 3-4 89
DESPERADO ... 3-4 88
EPIC ... 3-5 71-82
HILLTOP ... 8-15 64-66
LITTLE DARLIN' (008 thru 0072) ... 5-10 66-69
LITTLE DARLIN' (7000 series) ... 3-5 78-79
MERCURY ... 3-5 86-87
LPs: 10/12-inch
ACCORD ... 5-10 82
ALLEGIANCE ... 5-10 83
CERTRON ... 8-15 70
EPIC ... 5-10 71-83
EXCELSIOR ... 5-8 80
GUSTO ... 5-10 83
IMPERIAL ... 5-10 80
LAKESHORE ... 5-8
LITTLE DARLIN' (0571 thru 0792) ... 5-10 79-80
LITTLE DARLIN' (4001 "Johnny Paycheck at Carnegie Hall") ... 20-30 66
(Monaural.)
LITTLE DARLIN' (4001 "Johnny Paycheck in Concert") ... 10-15 66
(Repackage of *At Carnegie Hall.* Monaural.)
LITTLE DARLIN' (8001 "Johnny Paycheck at Carnegie Hall") ... 20-30 66
(Stereo.)
LITTLE DARLIN' (8001 "Johnny Paycheck in Concert") ... 15-20 66
(Repackage of *At Carnegie Hall.* Stereo.)
LITTLE DARLIN' (4003 thru 4006) . 10-20 66-67
(Monaural.)
LITTLE DARLIN' (8003 thru 8023) . 10-20 66-69
(Stereo.)
LITTLE DARLIN' (10000 series) ... 8-12 79
MERCURY ... 5-8 86
PICKWICK/HILLTOP ... 5-10 72
POWER PAK ... 5-8
Session: Jordanaires.
Also see HAGGARD, Merle, & Johnny Paycheck
Also see JENNINGS, Waylon / Johnny Paycheck
Also see JONES, George, & Johnny Paycheck
Also see JORDANAIRES
Also see MILLER, Jody, & Johnny Paycheck
Also see TUBB, Ernest
Also see YOUNG, Donny

PAYCHECK & HAGGARD *C&W '81*
Singles: 7-inch
EPIC ... 3-4 81
Members: Johnny Paycheck; Merle Haggard.
Also see HAGGARD, Merle
Also see PAYCHECK, Johnny

PAYMARKS
(Raymarks)
Singles: 7-inch
JERDEN ... 8-10 66
Also see RAYMARKS

PAYMENTS
Singles: 7-inch
LANDA (686 "Brand New Automobile") ... 5-10 62
(Flip, *Cantina*, was first issued as flip of Landa 676, as by the Tronics.)
Also see TRONICS

PAYNE, Benny
LPs: 10/12-inch
KAPP (1004 "Sunny Side Up") ... 20-30 55

PAYNE, Cavril
Singles: 7-inch
PULSE ... 4-8 65

PAYNE, Cecil, Orchestra *R&B '50*
Singles: 78 rpm
DECCA ... 5-10 50

PAYNE, Chuck
Singles: 7-inch
ATLAS (1057 "Escape") ... 10-15

PAYNE, Curtis
Singles: 7-inch
FIDELITY ... 8-12 59

PAYNE, Dennis *C&W '88*
Singles: 7-inch
TRUE ... 3-4 88

PAYNE, Dennis, & Renegades
Singles: 7-inch
GARPAX (4545 "California Girl") ... 5-10 81
RED MAN (1492 "Token") ... 50-100 69
LPs: 10/12-inch
RED MAN (1492 "We're Indian") ... 100-200 69
(LP and Red Man single, *Token*, have the same selection number.)

PAYNE, Diane
Singles: 7-inch
ROULETTE ... 5-8 60

PAYNE, Freda *R&B '69*
Singles: 12-inch
CAPITOL ... 4-8 79
Singles: 7-inch
ABC ... 3-5 75
ABC-PAR ... 5-10 62-63
CAPITOL ... 3-5 77-78
DUNHILL ... 3-5 74
IMPULSE ... 5-10 63
INVICTUS ... 3-8 69-73
MGM ... 10-20 66
RIPETE ... 3-6
SUTRA ... 3-5 82
Picture Sleeves
CAPITOL ... 3-5 77-78
INVICTUS ... 4-8 71-73
LPs: 10/12-inch
ABC ... 8-10 75
CAPITOL ... 5-10 78-79
DUNHILL ... 8-10 74
IMPULSE ... 15-25 64
INVICTUS ... 10-15 70-72
MGM ... 10-20 66-70
U.S.A. ... 10-15 71

PAYNE, Jackie
Singles: 7-inch
MIDSONG ... 4-8 80
Also see OTIS, Johnny

PAYNE, Jimmy *C&W '69*
Singles: 7-inch
EPIC ... 4-6 66-69
RIK ... 4-8
VEE JAY ... 4-8 63
LPs: 10/12-inch
EPIC ... 10-20 68

PAYNE, Jody, & Willie Nelson Family Band C&W '81
Singles: 7-inch
KARI..3-5 81
Also see NELSON, Willie

PAYNE, Johnny
Singles: 7-inch
BRENT..4-8 62

PAYNE, Leon C&W '49
Singles: 78 rpm
CAPITOL..5-10 49
DECCA..5-10 54
STARDAY..5-10 55-56
Singles: 7-inch
DECCA..10-20 54
STARDAY..10-20 55-56
LPs: 10/12-inch
STARDAY (231 "Living Legend of Country Music")..25-50 63
STARDAY (236 "Americana")........20-40 63
Also see ROGERS, Rock

PAYNE, Louis, Orchestra
("Vocal By Bonnie Buckner & Danny [Run Joe] Taylor;" Lou Payne)
Singles: 78 rpm
SAXONY..8-12 55
Singles: 7-inch
FEDERAL (12387 "Hand Out")........10-15 60
SAXONY (102 "That's Alright with Me")..20-30 55
Also see TAYLOR, Danny "Run Joe"

PAYNE, Raven
Singles: 7-inch
TOP SECRET..3-5 81

PAYNE, Scherrie D&D '84
(With Phillip Ingram)
Singles: 12-inch
MEGATONE..4-6 84
Singles: 7-inch
ALTAIR..3-5
INVICTUS..3-5 72
MOTOWN..3-5 80
SUPERSTAR INT'L..3-5
Also see DECO
Also see GLASS HOUSE
Also see SCHERRIE & SUSAYE
Also see SUPREMES

PAYNE, Tommy
Singles: 7-inch
FELSTED (8531 "I Go Ape")........15-25 58
XYZ (601 "Shy Boy")........10-15 59
XYZ (603 "Cruisin' Around")........15-25 59

PAYOLAS
Singles: 12-inch
I.R.S..4-6 81-86
Singles: 7-inch
I.R.S..3-5 81-86
LPs: 10/12-inch
I.R.S..5-10 81-86
Member: Paul Hyde.
Also see HYDE, Paul, & Payolas

PAYTON, Lawrence R&B '74
Singles: 7-inch
DUNHILL..3-5 73-74
Also see FOUR TOPS

PAYTON, Paul
(With Al Anderson)
Singles: 7-inch
PRESENCE..3-5 85
Also see ANDERSON, Al
Also see FABULOUS DUDES

PAYTON, Tommy
Singles: 7-inch
STAFF..8-12

PAZANT BROTHERS
Singles: 7-inch
RCA..4-6 69

PEABODY
Singles: 7-inch
BUSY B (7 "Forever Eyes")........10-15 68

PEACE, Elroy Shadow
Singles: 7-inch
KEEN..10-15 59
Also see SHADOWS

PEACE, Joe
LPs: 10/12-inch
RITE (29917 "Finding Peace")........100-200 72

PEACE, Mike
(With Filet of Sound)
Singles: 7-inch
MAGIC TOUCH..10-15 69
WAVEMAKERS..3-4 84
Also see FILET of SOUND

PEACE & LOVE
Singles: 7-inch
EX-PLO (011 "Girl I Have News for You")..10-20 60s

PEACE & QUIET
LPs: 10/12-inch
KINETIC..10-15 71

PEACHEROOS
Singles: 78 rpm
EXCELLO..100-150 54
Singles: 7-inch
EXCELLO (2044 "Be Bop Baby")..300-400 54
(Bootlegs we've seen spell the group name with one "o" – "Peacheros.")

PEACHES
Singles: 7-inch
BUMP'S (1503 "I'm Living in a Dream")..10-15 63
CONSTELLATION..5-10 66

PEACHES & HERB P&R/R&B '66
Singles: 7-inch
COLUMBIA..3-5 71-74
DATE..4-6 66-70
MCA..3-5 77
MERCURY..3-5 73
Picture Sleeves
DATE..4-8 67-68
LPs: 10/12-inch
DATE..10-20 67-68
EPIC..8-10 79
MCA..8-10 77
Members: Francine Barker; Herb Fame.
Also see BAKER, Francine "Peaches"
Also see SWEET THINGS

PEACHES & HERB LP '78
Singles: 12-inch
POLYDOR..4-8 78-79
Singles: 7-inch
COLUMBIA..3-5 83
POLYDOR..3-5 78-83
LPs: 10/12-inch
POLYDOR..5-10 78-81
Members: Linda Green; Herb Fame.

PEACOCKS
Singles: 7-inch
4 STAR (1718 "My New Hi-Fi")........50-75 58

PEAK, Bobby, & Imperials
Singles: 7-inch
TAMMY (2000 "Night Rock")........8-12 60s

PEAK, Buford
Singles: 7-inch
FERNWOOD (102 "Knock Down Drag Out")..100-200 58

PEANUT BUTTER CONSPIRACY P&R/LP '67
Singles: 7-inch
CHALLENGE..5-8 69
COLUMBIA..8-10 67
VAULT..10-15 66
LPs: 10/12-inch
CHALLENGE (200 "For Children of All Ages")..20-25 69
COLUMBIA (2654 "Peanut Butter Conspiracy Is Spreading")..20-25 67
(Monaural.)
COLUMBIA (2790 "The Great Conspiracy")..20-30 68
(Monaural.)
COLUMBIA (9454 "Peanut Butter Conspiracy Is Spreading")..25-30 68
(Stereo.)
COLUMBIA (9590 "The Great Conspiracy")..20-25 68
(Stereo.)
COLUMBIA (38000 series)........8-10 82
Members: Sandi Robison; Alan Brackett; Lance Fent; Bill Wolf; Jim Voight; John Merrill.

PEANUT BUTTER CONSPIRACY / Ashes / Chambers Brothers
LPs: 10/12-inch
VAULT (113 "West Coast Love-In")..30-50 68
Also see ASHES
Also see CHAMBERS BROTHERS

PEANUT GALLERY: see CIRCA 58 / Peanut Gallery

PEANUTS
Singles: 7-inch
SMASH..4-8 65
LPs: 10/12-inch
LONDON..10-15 65

PEANUTS
Singles: 7-inch
PIC-1 (113 "Sylvia")........10-20 65

PEARCE, Kevin C&W '84
Singles: 7-inch
EVERGREEN..3-4 87-88
ORLANDO..3-4 84-86

PEARL
LPs: 10/12-inch
LONDON..8-10 77

PEARL, Jess
Singles: 7-inch
LIKE YOUNG..4-8 65

PEARL, Leslie P&R '82
(L.D. Pearl)
Singles: 7-inch
LONDON..4-8 76
RCA..3-5 82

PEARL, Minnie: see MINNIE PEARL

PEARL & DELTARS
Singles: 7-inch
FURY..10-15 61

PEARL HARBOR LP '80
(With the Explosions)
Singles: 7-inch
W.B..3-5 80-81
LPs: 10/12-inch
W.B..5-10 80-81

PEARL JAM LP '92
Singles: 7-inch
EPIC (5610 "Angel")........5-10 94
(Promotional issue only.)
Picture Sleeves
EPIC (5610 "Angel")........10-15 94
(Promotional issue only.)
LPs: 10/12-inch
EPIC..5-10 91-95
Members: Eddie Vedder; Mike McCready; Jeff Ament; Stone Gossard; Dave Krusen.
Also see GREEN RIVER

PEARL MIXED COMPANY
Singles: 7-inch
PEARLTONE..5-10 69

PEARLESCENTS
Singles: 7-inch
JOC (101 "Ronnie's Night House")..10-20 63

PEARLETTES P&R '62
Singles: 7-inch
CRAIG (502 "He's Gone")........10-15 61
GO (712 "Can I Get Him")........25-35 61
(First issue.)
VEE JAY (422 "Can I Get Him")........10-15 61
VEE JAY (435 "Duchess of Earl")........10-15 62

PEARLS
Singles: 78 rpm
ATCO..10-20 55-56
ONYX (503 "Let's You and I Go Steady")..15-25 56
ONYX (506 "Tree in the Meadow")........50-75 56
ONYX (510 "Your Cheatin' Heart")..30-50 57
ONYX (511 "Ice Cream Baby")........40-60 57
ONYX (516 "The Wheel of Love")..75-100 57
Singles: 7-inch
ATCO (6057 "Shadows of Love")........15-25 55
ATCO (6066 "Bells of Love")........20-30 56
ON THE SQUARE (320 "Band of Angels")..15-25 59
ONYX (503 "Let's You and I Go Steady")..35-50 56
ONYX (506 "Tree in the Meadow")..75-125 56
ONYX (510 "Your Cheatin' Heart")..30-50 57
ONYX (511 "Ice Cream Baby")........35-50 57
ONYX (516 "The Wheel of Love")..75-125 57
Members: Howard Guyton; Dave "Baby" Cortez; Bob Spencer; Robert Gu; Earl Carroll.
Also see CADILLACS
Also see CORTEZ, Dave "Baby"
Also see FIVE PEARLS
Also see GUY, Bobby

PEARLS
Singles: 7-inch
AMBER (2003 "I Cried")........200-250 61
(Identification number, "M-114," is stamped in vinyl trail off.)
AMBER (2003 "I Cried")........25-50 60s
(No identification number in vinyl trail off.)

PEARLS
Singles: 7-inch
W.B. (5300 "Happy Over You")........10-15 62

PEARLS
Singles: 7-inch
BELL..3-5 73

PEARLS
Singles: 7-inch
LAMP (653 "Shooting Star")........20-30

PEARLS BEFORE SWINE LP '69
Singles: 7-inch
ESP (4554 "Morning Song")........20-30 67
ESP (4576 "I Saw the World")........20-30 68
REPRISE (0873 "These Things Too")..5-10 69
W.B./REPRISE (0949 "Rocket Man")..4-8 70
LPs: 10/12-inch
ADELPHI..8-12 80
ESP (1054 "One Nation Underground")..30-50 67
ESP (1075 "Balaklava")........20-40 68
W.B./REPRISE..10-20 69-71
Members: Tom Rapp; Richard Alderson; Bob Elizabeth; Warren Smith; Charlie McCoy; Lane Lender; Wayne Harley.
Also see RAPP, Tom

PEARLY, Don
Singles: 7-inch
CORVETTE (1004 "Drag Race")........15-25 57

PEARLY GATE
Singles: 7-inch
DECCA..4-8 69-70
Also see DANTE, Ron

PEARSON, Duke LP '69
Singles: 7-inch
BLUE NOTE..4-8 60-66
LPs: 10/12-inch
ATLANTIC..10-20 66
BLUE NOTE..25-40 59-61
(Label gives New York street address for Blue Note Records.)
BLUE NOTE..20-30 63-64
(Label reads "Blue Note Records Inc. - New York, USA.")
BLUE NOTE..10-20 66-74
(Label shows Blue Note Records as a division of either Liberty or United Artists.)
PRESTIGE..10-15 70

PEARSON, Jesse
Singles: 7-inch
DECCA..4-8 60
KAYO..5-10 59
RCA..4-8 63

PEARSON, Mr. Danny R&B '78
Singles: 7-inch
UNLIMITED GOLD..3-5 78
LPs: 10/12-inch
UNLIMITED GOLD..5-10 79

PEARSON, Randy
Singles: 7-inch
A&M..3-5 73
POLYDOR..3-5 72

PEARSON, Ronnie
Singles: 7-inch
HERALD (500 "Hot Shot")........50-100 57
HERALD (514 "She Bops a Lot")..50-100 58
MART..5-10

PEASANTS
Singles: 7-inch
RAYNARD (6289 "Big Boss Man")..10-20 70s
Also see MUSTARD MEN

PEASTON, David LP '89
LPs: 10/12-inch
GEFFEN..5-8 89

PEBBLES
Singles: 78 rpm
MIDDLETONE..75-100 55
Singles: 7-inch
MIDDLETONE (002 "Let Me Hear It Again")..200-300 55

PEBBLES
Singles: 7-inch
DOT..8-12 65

PEBBLES
Singles: 7-inch
EIFFEL (1005 "Oh, What a Beautiful Dream")..25-50

PEBBLES R&B '87
Singles: 7-inch
MCA..3-4 87-90
Picture Sleeves
MCA..3-4 87-88
LPs: 10/12-inch
MCA..5-8 87-90

PEBBLES & BAMM BAMM
Singles: 7-inch
HBR..5-10 65
Picture Sleeves
HBR..10-15 65

PEBBLES & FIREBALLS
Singles: 7-inch
SUPREME..5-10 60s
Also see FIREBALLS

PEBBLES & SHELLS
Singles: 7-inch
KAPP..4-8 67

PECK, Bill
Singles: 7-inch
LIN..10-15 55
Singles: 7-inch
LIN..15-20 55

PEDDLER
LPs: 10/12-inch
CHI-SOUND..8-10 76

PEDDLERS
Singles: 7-inch
EPIC..4-8 69
LPs: 10/12-inch
EPIC..10-15 69-70

PEDERSEN, Herb C&W '77
Singles: 7-inch
EPIC..3-5 76-77
LPs: 10/12-inch
EPIC (34933 "Sandman")........5-10 77
Also see DESERT ROSE BAND
Also see HARRIS, Emmylou
Also see HILLMAN, Chris

PEDERSON, Pete
Singles: 7-inch
JOSIE..5-10 59

PEDESTRIANS
Singles: 7-inch
ATCO (6567 "Think Twice")........5-10 67
BUYIT (2556 "Think Twice")........15-25 67
FENTON (2102 "Think Twice")........15-25 66
FENTON (2116 "It's Too Late")........15-25 66
FENTON (2226 "You Aren't Going to Say You Know")..10-20 67
Member: Tony Cooper.

PEDESTRIANS / Association / Five Americans / Soulblenders
EPs: 7-inch
WLAV (6873 "Think Twice")........10-20 60s
(Promotional issue only.)
Also see ASSOCIATION
Also see FIVE AMERICANS
Also see PEDESTRIANS
Also see SOULBLENDERS

PEDICIN, Mike P&R '56
(Michael Pedicin, Jr; Mike Pedicin Quintet; Quartet)
Singles: 78 rpm
CAMEO (125 "Shake a Hand")........10-20 57
MALVERN (100 "Dickie-Doo")........15-25 57
RCA..5-10 55-56
Singles: 12-inch
PHILADELPHIA INT'L..4-8 79-82
Singles: 7-inch
ABC-PAR..5-10 62
APOLLO (534 "Hey Pop, Give Me the Keys")..25-35 59
CAMEO (125 "Shake a Hand")........10-20 57
FEDERAL..8-12 61
MALVERN (100 "Dickie-Doo")........15-20 57
PHILADELPHIA INT'L..3-5 79-82
RCA (6150 "The Hot Barcarolle")........10-15 55
RCA (6369 "Large, Large House")........10-15 56
20TH CENTURY (5019 "Is That What You Call Love")..5-10 60s
EPs: 7-inch
RCA..15-25 56
("General Electric Flash Blub Limited Edition.")
LPs: 10/12-inch
APOLLO (484 "Musical Medicine")..75-125 59
PHILADELPHIA INT'L..5-10 79

PEDIGO, Tommy
Singles: 7-inch
OLO (103 "Red Headed Woman")..200-300 50s

PEDIGO BROTHERS & TENNESSEE RHYTHM BOYS
Singles: 7-inch
ATWELL (100 "She's Gone")........100-200 50s
Member: Tommy Pedigo.
Also see PEDIGO, Tommy

PEDRICK, Bobby P&R '58
(Bobby Pedrick Jr.)
Singles: 7-inch
BIG TOP..8-12 58-60
DUEL..5-10 62-63
MGM..4-8 65
SHELL..15-20 60
VERVE (10402 "Maybe")........40-50 66
Also see BOBBY & CONSOLES
Also see JOHN, Robert

PEE, Eddie
(Memphis Eddie; Memphis Eddie P. & His Trio)
Singles: 78 rpm
FOTO..15-25 48
GLOBE..10-15 45
RPM..10-15 50

PEE WEE & PROPHETS
Singles: 7-inch
CENTENNIAL (1863 "Tell Me")........50-75

PEEBLES, Ann R&B '69
Singles: 7-inch
HI..3-6 69-80
MOTOWN..3-4 82
LPs: 10/12-inch
HI..8-12 69-75
MOTOWN..5-8 82

PEEBLES, Robert
Singles: 7-inch
JAX (1001 "This Little Light of Mine")..100-125 59

PEECH BOYS R&B '82
Singles: 7-inch
WEST END..3-4 82
Also see NEW YORK CITI PEECH BOYS

PEEK
Singles: 12-inch
SUTRA..4-6

PEEK, Billy
(With the Love-Ins)
Singles: 7-inch
DARSA..8-10 63
MARLO (1521 "Twistin' Johnny B. Goode")..10-20 61
ROYAL CREST..8-10 62

PEEK, Dan P&R '79
Singles: 7-inch
LAMB & LION..4-6 79
SONGBIRD..3-5 79
LPs: 10/12-inch
LAMB & LION..6-12 79
SONGBIRD..5-10 79
Also see AMERICA

PEEK, Everett C&W '77
Singles: 7-inch
COMMERCIAL..3-5 77

PEEK, John, & His Orchestra
(Featuring Arlene Harris)
Singles: 78 rpm
CHESS..15-25 51

PEEK, Paul P&R '61
Singles: 7-inch
COLUMBIA..4-8 66
FAIRLANE..10-15 61
MERCURY..4-8 62-63
NRC..10-20 58-60
1-2-3..4-6 69

PEEL, Dave C&W '69
Singles: 7-inch
CHART..3-5 69-71
LPs: 10/12-inch
CHART..6-12 71
Also see EATON, Connie, & Dave Peel

PEEL, David, & Lower East Side LP '69
Singles: 7-inch
APPLE (6498 "F Is Not a Dirty Word")..100-125 72
(Promotional issue only.)
APPLE (6545 "Hippie from New York City")..100-125 72
(Promotional issue only.)
ORANGE..4-6 77
ORANGE PEEL (70078PD "Interview")..15-20 80

(Picture disc. With John Lennon.)
LPs: 10/12-inch
APPLE (3391 "The Pope Smokes Dope")....50-75 72
ELEKTRA (74032 "Have a Marijuana")....15-25 68
ELEKTRA (74069 "American Revolution")....15-25 70
ORANGE....8-12 77

PEEL, David, & Lower East Side / John Lennon & Yoko Ono
Singles: 7-inch
ORANGE (8374 "Amerika")....3-5 90
(Promotional bonus with book purchase.)
ORANGE (789001 "Ballad of New York City")....3-5 87
Picture Sleeves
ORANGE (8374 "Amerika")....3-5 90
(Promotional bonus with book purchase.)
Also see LENNON, John
Also see PEEL, David, & Lower East Side

PEELE, Steve, Five
Singles: 7-inch
F.G.I. (1000 "Frankie's Got It")....15-25

PEELS P&R '66
Singles: 7-inch
KARATE....4-8 66
LPs: 10/12-inch
KARATE (5402 "Juanita Banana") 55-65 66
(Monaural.)
KARATE (5402 "Juanita Banana") 65-75 66
(Stereo.)

PEELS, Leon
(With the Hi Tensions)
Singles: 7-inch
WHIRLY BIRD (2002 "A Casual Kiss")....15-25 64
WHIRLY BIRD (2008 "A Magic Island")....50-75 64
Also see BLUE JAYS
Also see HI TENSIONS

PEEP SHOW
LPs: 10/12-inch
PICKWICK....5-10 71

PEEPLE
Singles: 7-inch
WORLD ARTISTS....5-8 63

PEEPLES P&R '88
Singles: 7-inch
MERCURY....3-4 88
Picture Sleeves
MERCURY....3-4 88

PEEPLES, Nia R&B/LP '88
Singles: 7-inch
MERCURY....3-4 88
LPs: 10/12-inch
MERCURY....5-8 88

PEEPS
Singles: 7-inch
PHILIPS....4-8 65

PEERCE, Jan P&R '48
Singles: 78 rpm
RCA....3-6 48-51
BLUEBIRD....4-6 60
RCA....5-10 51
U.A....4-6 63
EPs: 7-inch
RCA....5-10 51
LPs: 10/12-inch
RCA (Except 2900 series)....10-20 51
RCA (2900 series)....5-10 78
U.A....5-15 63-65
VANGUARD....5-15 63-67

PEERMONTS
Singles: 7-inch
MURCO....4-8 67

PEERS
Singles: 7-inch
LEJAC (3005 "Once Upon a Time")....20-25 68

PEETIE WHEATSTRAW'S BUDDY
(Ray Harmon)
Singles: 78 rpm
DECCA....15-25 49
HY TONE....15-25 47

PEEVEY, Gayla
Singles: 78 rpm
COLUMBIA....5-10 50s
Singles: 7-inch
COLUMBIA (186 "I Want a Hippopotamus for Christmas")....8-12 50s
Picture Sleeves
COLUMBIA (186 "I Want a Hippopotamus for Christmas")....10-15 50s
(With die-cut center hole.)

PEEWEE: see PEE WEE

PEEWEES
Singles: 7-inch
JOSIE....5-10 58

PEFFERLY, Boot Hog
Singles: 7-inch
SOUND STAGE 7....4-8 63

PEGASUS
Singles: 7-inch
BURDETTE....3-5 71

PEGGY & BOB
Singles: 7-inch
HOWARD (802 "What You Do to Me")....25-35

PEGGY LEE: see LEE, Peggy

PEGGY SUE C&W '69
Singles: 7-inch
DECCA....3-6 69-71
DOOR KNOB....3-5 77-80
LPs: 10/12-inch
DECCA....8-12 69-70
DOOR KNOB....5-10 77

PEGGY SUE & Sonny Wright C&W '79
Singles: 7-inch
DOOR KNOB....3-5 79
LPs: 10/12-inch
COUNTRY INT'L....5-10 83
Also see PEGGY SUE
Also see WRIGHT, Sonny

PEIL, Danny
(With the Tigers; with Apollos; with Sound Majority)
Singles: 7-inch
CURTIS ("Four Days to St. Paul") 10-20 60s
(No selection number used.)
RAYNARD (602 "Jingle Jump")....10-15 65
Picture Sleeve
RAYNARD (602 "Jingle Jump")....15-20 65
Members: Denny McCarthy; Bobby Ray; Roland Stone Oeller; Duane Lundy; Pete Miller.
Also see CORPORATION
Also see STEFAN, Paul
Also see TIGERS

PEJOE, Morris
Singles: 78 rpm
ABCO....15-25 56
CHECKER....100-150 54
VEE JAY....15-25 55
Singles: 7-inch
ABCO (106 "Screaming and Crying")....25-50 56
ATOMIC-H....10-20 60
CHECKER (766 "Tired of Crying Over You")....300-400 54
(Black vinyl.)
CHECKER (766 "Tired of Crying Over You")....1500-2000 54
(Red vinyl.)
CHECKER (781 "Can't Get Along")....200-300 54
(Black vinyl.)
CHECKER (781 "Can't Get Along")....500-750 54
(Red vinyl.)
VEE JAY (148 "You Gonna Need Me")....25-50 55

PELICANS
Singles: 78 rpm
IMPERIAL (5307 "Chimes")....250-500 54
PARROT (793 "Aurelia")....250-500 54
Singles: 7-inch
IMPERIAL (5307 "Chimes")....1000-2000 54
LOST-NITE....4-8
PARROT (793 "Aurelia")....2000-4000 54
(Black vinyl.)
PARROT (793 "Aurelia")....3000-5000 54
(Red vinyl.)
Also see KIDDS

PELL, Dave
Singles: 7-inch
LIBERTY....3-5 70

PELL BROTHERS
Singles: 7-inch
JAY (259 "Let's Rock Tonight")....20-30 59

PEMBERTON, Jimmy
Singles: 7-inch
END (1052 "Rags to Riches")....8-12 59
MARK-X (8002 "Rags to Riches")....5-10 60
ORCHID (5002 "Ko-Ko-Mo Girl")....5-10

PEN ETTS
Singles: 7-inch
BECCO (1001 "If I Never See You Again")....40-60
Member: G. Penney.

PENDARVIS, Tracy
(With the Blue Notes; with Swampers)
Singles: 7-inch
DES CANT....8-12 62
SCOTT (1202 "One of These Days")....20-30 58
SCOTT (1203 "All You Gotta Do") 25-50 58
SUN....10-20 60-61

PENDERGAST
Singles: 7-inch
CHARAY (88 "Wow")....8-12 69

PENDERGRASS, Teddy P&R/R&B/LP '77
Singles: 12-inch
PHILADELPHIA INT'L....4-8 78-82
Singles: 7-inch
ASYLUM....3-4 84-88
ELEKTRA....3-4 88-90
PHILADELPHIA INT'L....3-5 77-84
Picture Sleeves
ELEKTRA....3-4 89
LPs: 10/12-inch
ASYLUM....5-8 84-86
ELEKTRA....5-8 88-90
EPIC....5-10 83
PHILADELPHIA INT'L (30000 series, except JZ-30595)....5-10 77-84
PHILADELPHIA INT'L (JZ-30595 "Life Is a Song")....15-25 78
(Picture disc. Promotional issue only.)
PHILADELPHIA INT'L (40000 series)....10-15 82
(Half-speed mastered.)
Also see MELVIN, Harold
Also see MILLS, Stephanie, & Teddy Pendergrass
Also see PHILADELPHIA INTERNATIONAL ALL STARS

PENDERGRASS, Teddy, & Whitney Houston P&R '84
Singles: 7-inch
ASYLUM....3-4 84
Picture Sleeves
ASYLUM....3-4 84
Also see HOUSTON, Whitney
Also see PENDERGRASS, Teddy

PENDLETONS
Singles: 7-inch
BLACK JACK....5-10 59

PENDLETONS
Singles: 7-inch
DOT (16511 "Blue Surf")....20-35 63
RENDEZVOUS (194 "Waddle")....15-25 63
Member: Richie Burns.
Also see HONDELLS

PENDRAGON
Singles: 7-inch
TOWER....4-6 69

PENDULUM
Singles: 7-inch
KAMA SUTRA....4-8 68-69
LPs: 10/12-inch
PERCEPTION....8-12 72

PENDULUM P&R '80
Singles: 7-inch
VENTURE....3-5 80
LPs: 10/12-inch
VENTURE....5-10 81

PENDULUMS
Singles: 7-inch
AURORA (160 "Love Is Summertime")....10-20 66

PENETRATION
LPs: 10/12-inch
HIGHER KEY....10-15 74

PENETRATIONS
Singles: 7-inch
ICON (1002 "Bring 'Em In")....20-25
(Black vinyl.)
ICON (1002 "Bring 'Em Back Alive")....20-25
(Black vinyl. Note title variation.)
ICON (1002 "Bring 'Em In")....35-50
(Colored vinyl.)

PENETRATIONS
Singles: 7-inch
CROYDEN (583 "Sweeter Than Wine")....20-30

PENETRATIONS
Singles: 7-inch
HIGHLAND....8-12
TERI-DE....8-12

PENETRATORS
Singles: 7-inch
SKYLARK (100 "Caravan")....10-20 60
SKYLARK (111 "One Love")....10-20 60
(First issued as by the Dissonaires.)
Also see DISSONAIRES

PENETRATORS
Singles: 7-inch
FENTON (992 "What Won't Go Wrong")....20-30 65

PENGUINS P&R/R&B '54
("Featuring Cleve Duncan"; Penquins)
Singles: 78 rpm
ATLANTIC....10-20 57
DOOTO....20-30 57
DOOTONE....20-30 54-55
MERCURY....15-25 55-57
WING....10-20 56
Singles: 7-inch
ATLANTIC (1132 "Pledge of Love")....10-20 57
DOOTO (348 "Earth Angel")....8-10 62
(Reissue of DooTONE 348.)
DOOTO (428 "That's How Much I Need You")....25-30 57
DOOTO (432 "Let Me Make Up Your Mind")....25-30 58
DOOTO (435 "Do Not Pretend")....25-30 58
(Dootone 345 is found in the following section: PENGUINS / Dootsie Williams Orchestra.)
DOOTONE (348 "Earth Angel")....75-125 54
(Red label.)
DOOTONE (348 "Earth Angel")....40-60 54
(Maroon label.)
DOOTONE (348 "Earth Angel")....35-45 54
(Blue label.)
DOOTONE (348 "Earth Angel")....20-30 54
(Black label.)
DOOTONE (353 "Love Will Make Your Mind Go Wild")....40-50 54
(Red label.)
DOOTONE (353 "Love Will Make Your Mind Go Wild")....30-40 54
(Maroon label.)
DOOTONE (353 "Love Will Make Your Mind Go Wild")....20-30 54
(Blue label.)
DOOTONE (353 "Love Will Make Your Mind Go Wild")....15-20 54
(Black label.)
DOOTONE (362 "Kiss a Fool Goodbye")....20-40 55
GLENVILLE....4-6
MERCURY (70610 "Be Mine Or Be a Fool")....20-30 55
MERCURY (70654 "It Only Happens with You")....20-25 55
MERCURY (70703 "Devil That I See")....20-30 55
MERCURY (70762 "Christmas Prayer")....40-50 55
MERCURY (70799 "My Troubles Are Not at an End")....25-35 56
(Maroon label.)
MERCURY (70799 "My Troubles Are Not at an End")....15-20 56
(Black label.)
MERCURY (70943 "Earth Angel")....20-25 56
MERCURY (71033 "Will You Be Mine")....15-25 57
ORIGINAL SOUND (27 "Memories of El Monte")....30-50 63
ORIGINAL SOUND (54 "Heavenly Angel")....15-25 65
POWER....4-8
SUN STATE (001 "Believe Me")....25-50 62
WING (90076 "Peace of Mind")....15-25 56
Picture Sleeves
POWER....5-10
EPs: 7-inch
DOOTO (241/243/244 "Cool, Cool Penguins")....40-60 59
(Price is for any of three volumes.)
DOOTONE (101 "The Penguins")....100-150 55
LPs: 10/12-inch
COLLECTABLES....5-8 80s
DOOTO (242 "Cool, Cool Penguins")....150-250 59
(Yellow label with red lettering. Full-color cover.)
DOOTO (242 "Cool, Cool Penguins")....10-15 60s
(Multi-color label.)
Members: Cleve Duncan; Curtis Williams; Dexter Tisby; Bruce Tate; Randy Jones; Ted Harper; Walter Saulsberry.
Also see DUNCAN, Cleve
Also see GUNTER, Cornell
Also see JULIAN, Don, & Meadowlarks
Also see VICEROYS

PENGUINS / Dootsie Williams Orchestra
Singles: 78 rpm
DOOTONE....25-40 54
Singles: 7-inch
DOOTONE (345 "No There Ain't No News Today")....75-100 54
Also see WILLIAMS, Dootsie, Orchestra

PENGUINS / Meadowlarks / Medallions / Dootones
LPs: 10/12-inch
DOOTONE (204 "Best in Rhythm & Blues")....150-250 57
(Flat maroon label.)
DOOTONE (204 "Best in Rhythm & Blues")....10-20 60s
(Glossy label.)
Note: All colored vinyl pressings of this LP are bootlegs.
Also see DOOTONES

PENGUINS / Meadowlarks / Medallions / Calvanes
LPs: 10/12-inch
DOOTONE (224 "The Best Vocal Groups in Rock 'N' Roll")....125-175 50s
(Orange & blue labels on thick vinyl.)
Also see CALVANES
Also see GREEN, Vernon, & Medallions
Also see JULIAN, Don, & Meadowlarks
Also see PENGUINS

PENIGAR, Eddie
(Eddie "Sugarman" Penigar & His Band)
Singles: 78 rpm
RCA (20-2700 and 22-0000 series)....15-25 47-49
Singles: 7-inch
RCA (0020 "Easy Baby")....25-50 50
(Colored vinyl.)

PENIX, William
Singles: 7-inch
DAFFAN (116 "Dig That Crazy Driver")....50-100 59

PENLAND, Marcus, & Pendants
Singles: 7-inch
PROBE....4-6 69

PENN, Bobby C&W '71
Singles: 7-inch
50 STATES....3-5 71-76
LPs: 10/12-inch
50 STATES....5-10 70s

PENN, Dan
Singles: 7-inch
ATLANTIC....4-6 69
BELL....3-5 73
EARTH....5-10 59
FAME....4-8 64
MGM....4-8 66
LPs: 10/12-inch
BELL....8-12 73

PENN, Little "Lambsie"
Singles: 78 rpm
ATCO (6082 "I Want to Spend Xmas with Elvis")....10-20 56
Singles: 7-inch
ATCO (6082 "I Want to Spend Xmas with Elvis")....20-25 56
ATCO (6082 "I Want to Spend Xmas with Elvis")....30-50 56
(Promotional issue only. Reads "Test Pressing" at left.)

PENN, Michael LP '89
Singles: 7-inch
RCA....3-4 89-90
Picture Sleeves
RCA....3-4 89
LPs: 10/12-inch
RCA....5-8 89

PENN, Tony
Singles: 7-inch
P.R.I....8-12 59-60

PENN, William
(With the Quakers; William Penn Fyve)
Singles: 7-inch
DUANE (104 "Coming Up My Way")....25-35 60s
HUSH (230 "Little Girl")....20-40 60s
MELRON (5024 "Philly")....25-50 67
MELRON (5024 "Sweet Caroline")....25-50 67
(Selection number 5024 used twice.)
THUNDERBIRD (502 "Blow My Mind")....20-30 66
TWILIGHT (410 "Ghost of the Monks")....15-25 67
UPTOWN (745 "Chrome Dome Wheeler Dealer")....20-30 67

PENN BOYS
Singles: 7-inch
BOBBY (502 "Have a Party")....15-25 59

PENNA, Dennis
(With the Freebees; Denny Penna; D.R. Penna Mississippi Jook Band)
Singles: 7-inch
DE-MAT....10-15 62
MUSITRON (105 "Battle of the Duals")....30-40 59-60
P&M....10-15

PENNANTS
Singles: 7-inch
WORLD (102 "Don't Go")....100-200 61

PENNDULUMS
("Members of U of Penn. Glee Club")
Singles: 7-inch
MAY (109 "Time Marches On")....150-250 61

PENNER, Dick
Singles: 78 rpm
SUN (282 "Your Honey Love")....25-50 57
Singles: 7-inch
SUN (282 "Your Honey Love")....25-50 57

PENNIE, Sue
Singles: 7-inch
DUMAR....10-20

PENNINGTON, J.P. C&W '91
Singles: 7-inch
MCA....3-4 91
Also see EXILE

PENNINGTON, Ray C&W '66
Singles: 7-inch
CAPITOL....4-8 66-68
KING....5-10 63
LEE (502 "Boogie Woogie Country Girl")....50-75 56
LEE (504 "My Steady Baby")....50-75 58
MONUMENT....3-6 69-71
RUBY (290 "Fancy Free")....30-50 57
LPs: 10/12-inch
MONUMENT....10-15 69-71
Also see BLUESTONE
Also see PERRY, Brenda Kaye, & Ray Pennington
Also see SWING SHIFT BAND

PENNIES
Singles: 7-inch
INTERNATIONAL....5-10 63

PENNSYLVANIA PLAYERS
Singles: 7-inch
ORON (101 "Washington Uptight")..8-12
Also see GOODMAN, Dickie

PENNY, Dayward
Singles: 7-inch
BIG HOWDY (8102 "Come Back Baby")....10-20 58
RUBY (330 "Bee Bop Song")....20-30 57

PENNY, Hank C&W '46
Singles: 78 rpm
DECCA....5-10 55
KING....5-10 46-52
RCA....5-10 50-53
Singles: 7-inch
DECCA....10-15 55
KING....10-20 52
RCA....10-20 50-53
LPs: 10/12-inch
AUDIO LAB (1508 "Hank Penny")..20-40 58
RAMBLER....8-12
Session: Noel Boggs; Boudleaux Bryant; Sheldon Bennett; Eddie Duncan.
Also see THOMPSON, Sue

PENNY, Joe C&W '64
Singles: 7-inch
DEL MAR....5-10 65
FEDERAL (12322 "Bip a Little, Bop a Lot")....100-200 58
SIMS....10-15 64

PENNY, Paul
Singles: 7-inch
JAM ... 4-8 60s
TILT ... 4-8 61

PENNY, Vince
Singles: 7-inch
SPACE ... 5-10 60

PENNY & EKOS
Singles: 7-inch
ARGO (5295 "Gimme What You Got") ... 25-50 58

PENNY & JEAN
Singles: 7-inch
RCA ... 5-10 61
LPs: 10/12-inch
RCA ... 15-25 61
Also see LIMELITERS

PENNY & PACEMAKERS
Singles: 7-inch
TEMPO (125936 "I Can't Stay") ... 25-30

PENNY ARCADE
Singles: 7-inch
SMASH ... 4-8 68
U.A. ... 5-10 68
Also see ANDERS & PONCIA

PENNY CANDY: see CANDY, Penny

PENNY CANDY MACHINE
Singles: 7-inch
STROBE ... 4-6 69

PENNY LANE: see LANE, Penny

PENNY SISTERS
Singles: 7-inch
B.T. PUPPY ... 4-8 64

PENNYWHISTLERS
Singles: 7-inch
FOLKWAYS ... 4-6 64
LPs: 10/12-inch
NONESUCH (2000 series) ... 10-15 66
NONESUCH (72000 series) ... 5-8
VERVE/FOLKWAYS ... 6-12 66

PENSE, Janie
Singles: 7-inch
ABC-PAR (10490 "Big You, Little Me") ... 10-15 64

PENSE, Lydia, & New Invaders
Singles: 7-inch
INVADER ("Forgive You, Then Forget You") ... 10-20
(Selection number not known.)
Also see COLD BLOOD

PENTAGONS *P&R '61*
Singles: 7-inch
DONNA (1337 "To Be Loved") ... 15-25 61
DONNA (1344 "For a Love That Is Mine") ... 15-25 61
ERIC ... 3-4 70s
FLEET INT'L (100 "To Be Loved") ... 100-150 60
JAMIE (1201 "I Wonder") ... 20-30 61
JAMIE (1210 "I'm in Love") ... 10-15 61
ORIGINAL SOUND (4560 "To Be Loved") ... 5-10
SPECIALTY (644 "It's Spring Again") ... 20-30 58
SUTTER (100 "Forever Yours") ... 50-100 61

PENTAGONS / Earl Phillips
Singles: 7-inch
OLDIES 45 ... 4-8 64
Also see PENTAGONS
Also see PHILLIPS, Earl

PENTAGONS
Singles: 7-inch
AUDIO DYNAMICS (153 "About the Girl I Love") ... 15-20 67

PENTANGLE *LP '68*
Singles: 7-inch
REPRISE ... 4-8 68-69
TRANSATLANTIC ... 4-6
LPs: 10/12-inch
REPRISE ... 10-20 68-72
Members: Jacqui McShee; Bert Jansch; Danny Thompson; John Renbourn; Terry Cox.
Also see JANSCH, Bert
Also see RENBOURN, John

PENTHOUSE FIVE
Singles: 7-inch
SOLAR (4211 "Bad Girl") ... 15-25 66

PENTWATER
LPs: 10/12-inch
BEEF ... 5-10 79

PEOPLE *P&R/LP '68*
Singles: 7-inch
CAPITOL ... 5-10 67-69
PARAMOUNT ... 4-8 69-70
POLYDOR ... 3-5 71
ZEBRA (102 "Come Back Beatles") 5-10 78
(Includes a note suggesting the Beatles reunite.)
LPs: 10/12-inch
CAPITOL ... 20-30 68-69
PARAMOUNT ... 10-20 69-70
Members: Larry Norman; Robb Levin; Tom Tucker; John Tristao; Gene Mason; Geoff Levin.
Also see NORMAN, Larry

PEOPLE
Singles: 7-inch
TEE PEE (69/70 "I Can't Stand It") .. 8-12 68
Members: Frank Ellefson; Michael Maltby; Bob Vandersteen; Roger Jerry; Mike Larsheid; John McVane.

PEOPLE OF THE SUNSET STRIP
Singles: 7-inch
ATCO ... 4-8 67

PEOPLE'S CHOICE
Singles: 7-inch
PALMER (5009 "Hot Wire") ... 100-200 66

PEOPLE'S CHOICE *P&R/R&B '71*
Singles: 7-inch
CASABLANCA ... 3-5 80
PALMER (5020 "Easy to Be True") ... 100-200 67
PHIL-L.A. of SOUL ... 4-8 71-73
PHILADELPHIA INT'L ... 4-8 71
PHILIPS ... 5-10 69
TSOP ... 3-5 74-77
LPs: 10/12-inch
CASABLANCA ... 5-10 80
DECCA ... 10-15 69
PHILADELPHIA INT'L ... 5-10 78
TSOP ... 8-10 75-76
Members: Roger Andrews; Guy Fiske; David Thompson; Bob Eli; Frankie Brunson.
Also see BRUNSON, Frankie
Also see FASHIONS
Also see MFSB

PEOPLE'S GAS
Singles: 7-inch
DESTINATION ... 4-8 67

PEPE & ASTROS
Singles: 7-inch
SWAMI (554 "Judy My Love") ... 50-100 61

PEPE & LOS PETS
Singles: 7-inch
ARWIN ... 4-6 64
Also see PETS

PEPETTES ALL GIRL TRIO
Singles: 7-inch
FENTON (995 "Peppett Rock") ... 20-30 65

PEPPEL, Harry
Singles: 7-inch
ARC ... 8-10 59

PEPPER
LPs: 10/12-inch
RCA ... 8-10 77

PEPPER, Bob
Singles: 7-inch
BADERA ... 5-10

PEPPER, Brenda *C&W '75*
Singles: 7-inch
PLAYBOY ... 3-5 75

PEPPER, Cynthia
Singles: 7-inch
FELSTED ... 4-8 62

PEPPER, Jim
LPs: 10/12-inch
EMBRYO ... 20-30

PEPPER & RED HOTS
(With Lew Douglas & Orchestra)
Singles: 7-inch
WHITE STAR (1104 "Rock & Roll on Forever") ... 100-200 59
Also see DOUGLAS, Lew

PEPPER & SHAKERS
Singles: 7-inch
CHETWYD (45002 "Need Your Love") ... 100-150 66
CORAL (62523 "I Always Love You") ... 10-15 67

PEPPER & SPOOKY
Singles: 78 rpm
CORAL ... 5-10 56
Singles: 7-inch
CORAL ... 10-15 56

PEPPER POTS
Singles: 7-inch
CRYSTAL ... 8-12 59-60
PANLIN ... 8-12 60
PERSONALITY ... 8-12 59
RELLA ... 8-12 62

PEPPER TREE
LPs: 10/12-inch
CAPITOL ... 10-15 71

PEPPERMINT, Danny, & Jumping Jacks *P&R '61*
Singles: 7-inch
CARLTON ... 5-10 61
LPs: 10/12-inch
CARLTON (LP-20001 "Danny Peppermint") ... 25-35 62
(Monaural.)
CARLTON (STLP-20001 "Danny Peppermint") ... 35-50 62
(Stereo.)
Member: Danny Lamego.
Also see LAMEGO, Danny, & Jumpin' Jacks

PEPPERMINT HARRIS *R&B '50*
(With the Cross Town Blues Band; Harrison Nelson)
Singles: 78 rpm
ALADDIN ... 20-40 51-52
CASH ... 50-75 54
COMBO ... 15-30 56
MODERN ... 20-40 51
MONEY ... 20-40 54
SITTIN' IN WITH ... 25-50 50-51
"X" ... 20-40 55
Singles: 7-inch
ALADDIN (3097 "I Got Loaded") ... 100-150 51
(Black vinyl.)
ALADDIN (3097 "I Got Loaded") ... 250-500 51
(Colored vinyl.)
ALADDIN (3107 "Have Another Drink and Talk to Me") ... 75-125 51
ALADDIN (3108 "P. H. Blues") ... 75-125 51
ALADDIN (3130 "Right Back On") ... 75-125 52
ALADDIN (3141 "There's a Dead Cat on the Line") ... 75-125 52
ALADDIN (3154 "I Sure Do Miss My Baby") ... 75-125 51
ALADDIN (3177 "Wasted Love") .. 75-125 51
ALADDIN (3183 "Don't Leave Me All Alone") ... 75-125 53
ALADDIN (3206 "I Never Get Enough of You") ... 75-125 51
CASH (1003 "Cadillac Funeral") 100-150 54
(First issue.)
COMBO (114 "Love at First Sight") ... 50-100 56
DART (103 "Messin' Around with the Blues") ... 15-25 59
DUKE (319 "Ain't No Business") ... 15-25 60
JEWEL ... 5-10 65-68
LUNAR ... 3-5
MAISON DE SOUL ... 5-10
MODERN (936 "Black Cat Bone") ... 50-100 51
MONEY (214 "Cadillac Funeral") .50-100 54
SITTIN' IN WITH (543 "Rainin' in My Heart") ... 100-125 51
"X" (0142 "I Need Your Lovin' ") 100-150 55
LPs: 10/12-inch
TIME (5 "Peppermint Harris") ... 50-100 62
Session: Laurels.
Also see LAURELS
Also see NELSON, Peppermint
Also see REED, Jimmy / Peppermint Harris

PEPPERMINT RAINBOW *P&R/LP '69*
Singles: 7-inch
DECCA ... 4-6 68-69
Picture Sleeves
DECCA ... 5-10 69
LPs: 10/12-inch
DECCA ... 15-20 69

PEPPERMINT RIDGE
Singles: 7-inch
BLUE EAGLE (135 "Live On") ... 20-30 60s
BLUE EAGLE (137 "Can't You Hear Me") ... 20-30 60s
Members: Ken Vandeyacht; Larry DeGroot; Bruce Taggart.

PEPPERMINT STIKS
Singles: 7-inch
SO-CHAR (101 "El Twisto") ... 8-12 62

PEPPERMINT TROLLEY CO. *P&R '68*
Singles: 7-inch
ACTA ... 8-12 67-68
VALIANT (752 "Lollipop Train") ... 10-15 66
LPs: 10/12-inch
ACTA (38007 "Peppermint Trolley Co.") ... 15-25 68

PEPPERMINTS
Singles: 78 rpm
MERCURY (70681 "Shuf-A-Lin") ... 10-15 55
Singles: 7-inch
MERCURY (70681 "Shuf-A-Lin") ... 15-25 55

PEPPERMINTS
(With the House of Beauty Orchestra)
Singles: 7-inch
HOUSE of BEAUTY ("Believe Me") ... 40-60 59
PEPPERMINT (1001 "Cherryl Ann") ... 40-60 65
RSVP (1112 "Peppermint Jerk") ... 60-75 65
Also see BARONS
Also see BLUE, Kattie, & Peppermints

PEPPERNOTES
Singles: 7-inch
TEARDROP (3145 "The Little Spark") ... 8-12

PEPPERS
Singles: 78 rpm
CHESS ... 50-100 54
Singles: 7-inch
CHESS (1577 "Rocking Chair Baby") ... 250-350 54

PEPPERS
Singles: 7-inch
JANE (105 "Blossoms") ... 10-20 58

PEPPERS
Singles: 7-inch
ENSIGN (1706 "One More Chance") ... 30-50 61
PRESS (2809 "It Wouldn't Be the Same") ... 10-15 63
Members: Willie Davis; Aaron Collins; George Hollis; Tom Miller; Robbie Robinson; Beverley Harris.
Also see CADETS
Also see FLARES

PEPPERS
Singles: 7-inch
HOLLY (105 "Soul and Inspiration") ... 15-25 60s
(May predate Righteous Brothers version.)
Also see RIGHTEOUS BROTHERS

PEPPERS *P&R/R&B '74*
Singles: 7-inch
BIG TREE ... 3-5 75
EVENT ... 3-5 74-75
LPs: 10/12-inch
EVENT ... 8-12 74

PEPPY, Ginger
Singles: 7-inch
JOSIE ... 5-10 60

PEPS
Singles: 7-inch
D-TOWN (1049 "Detroit Michigan") ... 20-40 65
Members: Joe Harris; Richard Street;.
Also see FABULOUS PEPS
Also see LITTLE JOE & MORROCOS
Also see STORM, Tom, & Peps
Also see TEMPTATIONS
Also see UNDISPUTED TRUTH

PEPSI & SHIRLIE *P&R '87*
Singles: 7-inch
POLYDOR ... 3-4 87-88
Picture Sleeves
POLYDOR ... 3-4 87-88
LPs: 10/12-inch
POLYDOR ... 5-8 88
Members: Pepsi DeMacque; Shirlie Holliman.
Also see WHAM!

PEPSI-TONES
Singles: 7-inch
PEPSI (15890 "Keep on Walking") 15-25 60s

PERCELLS *P&R '63*
Singles: 7-inch
ABC-PAR ... 5-10 63-64

PERCOLATOR, Mr: see MR. PERCOLATOR

PERCY, Donna
Singles: 7-inch
MGM ... 5-10 58

PERCY & ROCKIN' ACES
Singles: 7-inch
LIUVIA (5051 "Don't Cry in Vain") 50-75 61

PERCY & THEM *R&B '74*
Singles: 7-inch
PLAYBOY ... 3-5 73
ROULETTE ... 5-8 75

PERDEW, Wayne
Singles: 78 rpm
ZIPP (103 "Up Beam Baby") ... 10-20 56
Singles: 7-inch
ZIPP (103 "Up Beam Baby") ... 40-50 56

PERE UBU
Singles: 7-inch
HEARTHAN ... 15-25

PERENNIALS
Singles: 7-inch
BALL (1016 "My Big Mistake") ... 250-350 63

PEREZ, Lou
Singles: 7-inch
SABINA (514 "Mama, Mama") ... 5-8 63
SABINA (518 "Tengo Que Caminar") ... 5-8 63

PEREZ, Manny
(With the Emeralds)
Singles: 7-inch
MAGNET ... 5-10 61
VISTONE ... 6-12 59

PEREZ, Tony *C&W '89*
Singles: 7-inch
REPRISE ... 3-4 89

PEREZ BROS.
(With the Gents)
Singles: 7-inch
WOLFIE ... 5-10 63

PERFECT, Christine
(Christine McVie)
Singles: 7-inch
BLUE HORIZON ... 3-6 70s
EPIC ... 4-8 69
LPs: 10/12-inch
SIRE (6000 series) ... 5-8 77
SIRE (7000 series) ... 8-10 76
Also see McVIE, Christine

PERFECT GENTLEMEN *LP '90*
Singles: 7-inch
COLUMBIA ... 3-4 90

PERFECT STRANGERS
Singles: 7-inch
CAPITOL ... 4-8 66

PERFECTIONS
Singles: 7-inch
JUBILEE ... 4-6 69

PERFECTIONS
Singles: 7-inch
LOST NITE (111 "My Baby") ... 25-50 60s
(Colored vinyl.)
SVR (1005 "I Love You My Love") ... 75-150

PERFECTIONS
Singles: 7-inch
AGC ... 8-12
BIG B ... 8-12
DRUMHEAD (100 "Don't Take Your Love Away from Me") ... 10-20

PERFIDIANS
Singles: 7-inch
HUSKY (1 "La Paz") ... 15-25 62
(Black vinyl.)
HUSKY (1 "La Paz") ... 40-60 62
(Colored vinyl.)

PERFORMERS
("With Orchestra")
Singles: 78 rpm
ALLSTAR ... 50-100 56
TIP TOP ... 75-100 57
Singles: 7-inch
ALLSTAR (714 "I'll Make You Understand") ... 250-350 56
TIP TOP (402 "I'll Make You Understand") ... 75-100 57
(Black vinyl.)
TIP TOP (402 "I'll Make You Understand") ... 15-25 61
(Colored vinyl.)

PERFORMERS
Singles: 7-inch
ABC-PAR ... 4-8 66
MIRWOOD ... 4-8 68

PERICOLI, Emilio *P&R '62*
Singles: 7-inch
VESUVIUS ... 4-6 62
W.B. ... 4-6 62-63
Picture Sleeves
W.B. ... 5-10 62
LPs: 10/12-inch
W.B. ... 10-20 63-66
VESUVIUS ... 10-20 62

PERIDOTS
Singles: 7-inch
DEAUVILLE ... 5-10 61
TWIST ... 5-10 61

PERIGENTS
Singles: 7-inch
MALTESE ... 10-20 65

PERIGEO
LPs: 10/12-inch
RCA ... 8-12 75-76

PERILS
Singles: 7-inch
VELVA (7484 "Hate") ... 15-25 66

PERISCOPES
Singles: 7-inch
DESERT WELLS (2274 "Beavershot") ... 15-25 65

PERKINS, Al *R&B '69*
Singles: 7-inch
ATCO ... 4-6 69-70
HI ... 3-5 72
SALEM ... 5-10 61
U.S.A. ... 4-8 64-65
Also see DAYLIGHTERS
Also see EVERETT, Betty

PERKINS, Anthony: see PERKINS, Tony

PERKINS, Carl *C&W/P&R/R&B '56*
(The "Rockin' Guitar Man"; with the C.P. Express)
Singles: 78 rpm
FLIP (501 "Movie Magg") ... 200-300 55
QUALITY (Except 1571) ... 25-75 56-57
(Canadian.)
QUALITY (1571 "Gone Gone Gone") ... 50-100 56
(Canadian.)
SUN (224 "Gone Gone Gone") ... 50-100 56
SUN (234 thru 287) ... 25-75 56-57
Singles: 7-inch
AMERICA/SMASH ... 3-5 86-87
BANTAM ... 4-6
COLUMBIA (3-41000 & 3-42000 series) ... 25-50 60-62
(Compact 33 Singles.)
COLUMBIA (4-41000 thru 4-43000 series) ... 10-25 58-64
COLUMBIA (4-44000 & 4-45000 series) ... 5-10 64-72
DECCA ... 5-10 63-64
DOLLIE ... 15-25 67
FLIP (501 "Movie Magg") ... 300-500 55
JET ... 3-5 79
MERCURY ... 4-6 73-77
MUSIC MILL ... 4-6 76
QUALITY (1473 "Blue Suede Shoes") ... 40-60 56
(Canadian.)
QUALITY (1571 "Gone Gone Gone") ... 100-200 56
(Canadian.)
QUALITY (1557 "Dixie Fried") ... 50-75 56
(Canadian.)
QUALITY (1570 "Boppin' the Blues") ... 50-75 56
(Canadian.)
QUALITY (1579 "Matchbox") ... 40-60 57
(Canadian.)
QUALITY (1654 "Forever Yours") .. 40-60 57
(Canadian.)
QUALITY (1701 "Glad All Over") ... 40-60 57
(Canadian.)
SSS/SUN ... 3-5 70s
SUEDE ... 3-5 81
SUN (224 "Gone Gone Gone") .. 100-150 56
SUN (234 "Blue Suede Shoes") ... 35-50 56
SUN (243 "Boppin' the Blues") ... 35-50 56
SUN (249 "Dixie Fried") ... 40-60 56
SUN (261 "Matchbox") ... 35-50 57
SUN (274 "Forever Yours") ... 35-50 57
SUN (287 "Glad All Over") ... 35-50 57
(Counterfeits exist of most early Sun releases.)
UNIVERSAL ... 3-4 89

Picture Sleeves
AMERICA/SMASH........................... 3-5 86
COLUMBIA (41131 "Pink Pedal Pushers") 25-45 58
COLUMBIA (42405 "Hollywood City") 20-30 62
COLUMBIA (42514 "Hambone") 40-60 62
EPs: 7-inch
COLUMBIA (12341 "Whole Lotta Shakin' ") 200-300 58
SUN (115 "Blue Suede Shoes") .100-200 58
LPs: 10/12-inch
ACCORD.. 5-10 82
ALBUM GLOBE..................................... 8-12
ALLEGIANCE....................................... 5-10 84
COLUMBIA (1234 "Whole Lotta Shakin' ") 100-200 58
(Red label.)
COLUMBIA (1234 "Whole Lotta Shakin' ")............................150-250 58
(White label. Promotional issue only.)
COLUMBIA (9833 "Greatest Hits").10-20 69
COLUMBIA (10117 "Greatest Hits") 8-10 74
DESIGN..10-20 60s
DOLLIE..10-20 67
GRT/SUNNYVALE 8-12 77
HARMONY 8-12 72
HILLTOP 5-10
JET... 8-12 78
KOALA 5-10 80
MERCURY 8-12 73
PICKWICK/HILLTOP........................... 5-10
ROUNDER 5-10 89
SSS/SUN... 5-10 69-84
SUEDE 8-10 81
SUN (1225 "Dance Album") 500-750 57
SUN (1225 "Teen Beat") 200-250 61
(Repackage of *Dance Album*.)
TRIP 8-10 74
UNIVERSAL 5-10 89
TRIP 8-12 74
Also see McCARTNEY, Paul
Also see NELSON, Willie / Jerry Lee Lewis / Carl Perkins / David Allan Coe
Also see STATLER BROTHERS
Also see YOUNG, Faron / Carl Perkins / Claude King

PERKINS, Carl / Sonny Burgess
LPs: 10/12-inch
SSS/SUN.. 5-10
Also see BURGESS, Sonny

PERKINS, Carl, Jerry Lee Lewis, Roy Orbison & Johnny Cash LP '86
LPs: 10/12-inch
AMERICA ("Class of '55") 20-30 86
(Mail-order edition. Has souvenir booklet and audio cassette with interviews of the singers.)
AMERICA/SMASH (830002 "Class of '55").. 5-10 86
AMERICA/SMASH (830002 "Class of '55")...30-40 86
(Picture disc. Promotional issue only.)
Also see CASH, Johnny, Carl Perkins & Jerry Lee Lewis
Also see LEWIS, Jerry Lee, Carl Perkins & Charlie Rich
Also see ORBISON, Roy

PERKINS, Carl, & NRBQ
Singles: 7-inch
COLUMBIA... 3-5 70
LPs: 10/12-inch
COLUMBIA...10-15 70
Also see NRBQ
Also see PERKINS, Carl

PERKINS, Dal C&W '68
Singles: 7-inch
COLUMBIA 4-6 68
VIV (102 "Shy")..............................10-20 57

PERKINS, George P&R/R&B '70
(With the Silver Stars)
Singles: 7-inch
SILVER FOX 4-8 69
SOUL POWER 3-6 72
LPs: 10/12-inch
CRYIN' in the STREETS................... 8-12 77

PERKINS, Harold, & Don Clairs
Singles: 7-inch
AMP 3 (1001 "I Lost My Job")........20-30 58

PERKINS, Howard: see BOGGS, Lucky / Howard Perkins

PERKINS, Ike
Singles: 7-inch
CJ (101 "These Kissable Lips")....... 8-12

PERKINS, Jerry, & His Blues Blasters
Singles: 78 rpm
W&W (204 "Katherine Blues") 40-60 50

PERKINS, Jesse, & Bad Boys
Singles: 7-inch
SAVOY... 5-10 60
Also see JESSE & BUZZY

PERKINS, Joe P&R '63
("Featuring the Memphis Sound")
Singles: 7-inch
BERRY 5-10 60s
BLUFF CITY 4-6 74
MUSICOR (1064 "Natalie Would").. 5-10 65
PLUSH (100 "Wrapped Up in Your Love")
SOUND STAGE 7 (2511 "Little Eeefin' Annie").. 8-12 63

PERKINS, Joe, & Rookies
Singles: 78 rpm
KING 30-75 56-57

Singles: 7-inch
KING (5005 "Time Alone Will Tell") 40-50 56
KING (5030 "How Much Love Can One Heart Hold") 50-75 57
(Blue label.)
KING (5030 "How Much Love Can One Heart Hold") 75-100 57
(White bio label. Promotional issue only.)

PERKINS, Laura Lee
Singles: 7-inch
IMPERIAL (5493 "Kiss Me Baby") .20-35 58
IMPERIAL (5507 "Don't Wait Up") 20-35 58

PERKINS, Reggie
Singles: 7-inch
GEM (1201 "Saturday Night Party")...75-100 59
RAY NOTE (9 "High School Caesar")..20-30 59

PERKINS, Roy
Singles: 78 rpm
MELADEE (112 "You're Gone") .200-300 56
Singles: 7-inch
MELADEE (112 "You're Gone") 500-1000 56
MERCURY (71278 "Drop Top") 20-30 58

PERKINS, Sandra
Singles: 7-inch
CADENCE 4-8 62

PERKINS, Tony P&R '57
(Anthony Perkins)
Singles: 78 rpm
RCA...10-15 57-58
Singles: 7-inch
EPIC (9181 "Friendly Persuasion")....................................8-12 57
RCA (7020 "Moonlight Swim") 10-15 57
RCA (7078 "When School Starts Again")..10-15 57
RCA (7155 "Indian Giver")...........10-15 58
Picture Sleeves
RCA (7155 "Indian Giver")............20-30 58
LPs: 10/12-inch
EPIC (3394 "Tony Perkins")..........25-35 57
RCA (1679 "From My Heart")..........30-40 58
RCA (LPM-1853 "On a Rainy Afternoon")....................................30-40 58
RCA (LSP-1853 "On a Rainy Afternoon")....................................40-60 58

PERKINS, Tony / James Dean
Singles: 78 rpm
RAINBO (5-21-57 "Hear Hollywood")..................................40-60 57
(Cardboard picture disc.)
Also see DEAN, James
Also see PERKINS, Tony

PERKINS, Virgil
Singles: 78 rpm
RBF..5-10 55
Singles: 7-inch
RBF..8-12 55

PERKINS, Walter
Singles: 7-inch
PLA-ME..75-100

PERKINS, Walter, & MJT Plus 3: see MJT PLUS 3

PERLITCH, Michael
LPs: 10/12-inch
ATLANTIC 8-12 72

PERMANENT WAVE
EPs: 7-inch
BOMP..5-10 79

PERMANENTS
Singles: 7-inch
CHAIRMAN 8-10 63

PERNA, Lenny
Singles: 7-inch
CHANCELLOR (1013 "Love Is a Wonderful Thing")..10-20 58

PERPETUAL MOTION
Singles: 7-inch
DIAL (4078 "Neckin' Don't Make It")..5-10 68
ROCK 'N' JAZZ (9188 "Sally Brown")..10-20 67

PERPETUAL MOTION WORK SHOP
Singles: 7-inch
RALLY.. 4-8 60s

PERRAULT, Larry & Darryl
Singles: 7-inch
TANGERINE 4-8 65

PERRI, Renee
Singles: 7-inch
SOULVILLE..................................... 4-6 69

PERRIMAN, Paul
Singles: 7-inch
FIRE...5-10 60

PERRIN, Sue
Singles: 7-inch
GOLDEN WORLD 10-20 62-63
J.W. (1001 "Can't Let Go")............50-75 60s

PERRINE, Pep
LPs: 10/12-inch
HIDEOUT (1003 "Live and in Person")......................................75-100 60s

PERRY
EPs: 7-inch
ADVANCE 10-12 70

PERRY, Al
Singles: 7-inch
LOVE 4-8 67
TOWER...4-8 66

PERRY, Barbara
Singles: 7-inch
FERNWOOD.....................................5-10 61

PERRY, Berlin, & Gleams
Singles: 7-inch
RIBBON (6902 "Put That Tear Back")...100-200 59

PERRY, Billy, & Rammit
Singles: 7-inch
FANTASY...3-5 76
RON 3-5 70s

PERRY, Brenda Kaye C&W '78
Singles: 7-inch
MRC..3-5 77-79
Also see WALKER, Billy, & Brenda Kaye Perry

PERRY, Brenda Kaye, & Ray Pennington
Singles: 7-inch
MRC..3-5 78
Also see PENNINGTON, Ray
Also see PERRY, Brenda Kaye

PERRY, Charles
Singles: 7-inch
MGM 8-12
MAGNUM...12-18
MELIC (4119 "I'll Walk Through the Darkness")..10-15
MELIC (4138 "It Doesn't Matter Anymore")..10-15

PERRY, Clarence, & Mercy Blues
Singles: 7-inch
EPIC..3-5 76

PERRY, Frank
Singles: 7-inch
BELLE...5-10 59
EPIC..5-10 61
JULIE 5-10 60s

PERRY, Frank, & Dorothy Porter
Singles: 7-inch
EPIC..5-10 61
Also see PERRY, Frank

PERRY, Greg R&B '74
Singles: 12-inch
ALFA...4-6 82
Singles: 7-inch
ALFA...3-4 82
CASABLANCA 3-5 74-75
CHESS...4-8 68
RCA 3-5 77
LPs: 10/12-inch
CASABLANCA 8-12 75

PERRY, Ike, & His Lyrics
Singles: 7-inch
ANN (101 "Lovin' Poppa")...............50-75
AZELEA (101 "Don't Let It Get You Down")")..25-50 64
BRIDGE (110 "Star Steps to Heaven")......................................150-250 58
COURIER (828 "Don't Let It Get You Down")...50-75 64
COWTOWN (801 "I Got You Covered")..50-75 60
MAMA (1 "In My Letter to You")...75-125 63
MAMA (3614 "Don't Let It Get You Down")..50-100 63
(Identification number shown since no selection number is used.)
NAURLENE (100 "Don't Let It Get You Down")...10-20 65

PERRY, Jeff R&B '75
Singles: 7-inch
ARISTA 3-5 75-76
EPIC...3-5 77
Also see 3 of a Kind

PERRY, Jesse
Singles: 78 rpm
MODERN 15-25 45

PERRY, Jim, & Hesitations
Singles: 7-inch
BAND BOX (310 "Surfside Twist") 15-25 62

PERRY, JoAnne
Singles: 7-inch
GLAD 8-12 61
20TH FOX 5-10 59

PERRY, Joe
Singles: 7-inch
SUE..4-8 62

PERRY, Joe, Project LP '80
Singles: 7-inch
COLUMBIA..3-5 80-81
LPs: 10/12-inch
COLUMBIA..5-10 80-81
MCA 4-8 83
Members: Joe Perry; Ralph Morman; Ronnie Stewart; David Hull.
Also see AEROSMITH

PERRY, Johnny
Singles: 7-inch
BRONZE 4-6 69

PERRY, Johnny, Orchestra
(Featuring Ida Haymes)
Singles: 78 rpm
ATLAS (1038 "I Left My Baby")........10-15 54
JUBILEE..10-15 53
Singles: 7-inch
ATLAS (1038 "I Left My Baby")........15-25 54
JUBILEE (5125 "Terrible Feeling").15-25 53
MILO (101 "Milk Shake") 10-20 63

PERRY, June
Singles: 78 rpm
MERCURY 5-10 57
Singles: 7-inch
MERCURY 8-12 57

PERRY, King
(With the Pied Pipers; King Perry Quinitet)
Singles: 78 rpm
DELUXE...10-20 47
EXCELSIOR..10-20 45
LUCKY 10-15 54
MELODISC 10-20 45
SPECIALTY..10-20 50
Singles: 7-inch
DOT 15-25 52
LUCKY 10-20 54
RPM 20-30 53
TRILYTE 15-25

PERRY, Linda R&B '73
Singles: 7-inch
MAINSTREAM 3-5 73

PERRY, Lou
Singles: 7-inch
BELLA (2207 "Cupid's Arrow").......50-75 59
CORDAK..4-8 66

PERRY, Oscar
Singles: 7-inch
BACK BEAT 5-10 69
FERON 5-10
PERI-TON...8-12
PERI-TONE...8-12
(Two spellings exist of same label name.)

PERRY, Paul
Singles: 7-inch
NU SOUND (1008 "Got a Girl Named Dee")...150-250 61

PERRY, Rosetta
Singles: 78 rpm
BLUES BOYS KINGDOM..............15-25 57
Singles: 7-inch
BLUES BOYS KINGDOM (107 "Farewell Blues")..25-35 57

PERRY, Roxy D&D '83
Singles: 12-inch
PERSONAL..4-6 83

PERRY, Steve P&R '82
Singles: 7-inch
COLUMBIA 3-4 84-85
Picture Sleeves
COLUMBIA 3-4 84
LPs: 10/12-inch
COLUMBIA 5-8 84-85
Also see JOURNEY
Also see LOGGINS, Kenny, & Steve Perry
Also see U.S.A. for AFRICA

PERRY, Tony
Singles: 7-inch
EMBER (1015 "I'm Your Forever").30-40 57

PERRY & PETE
Singles: 7-inch
BRENT (7036 "Rockin' Wobble")...10-20 62

PERRY & HARMONICS
Singles: 7-inch
MERCURY 4-8 65
LPs: 10/12-inch
MERCURY 10-20 65

PERRY & SANLIN R&B '80
Singles: 7-inch
CAPITOL..3-5 80
LPs: 10/12-inch
CAPITOL..5-10 80

PERRY - KINGSLEY ELECTRONIC MUSIC
LPs: 10/12-inch
VANGUARD 10-15 67-69

PERRY MATES: see PERRYMATES

PERRY SISTERS
Singles: 7-inch
DECCA..5-10 59-60

PERRYMAN, Paul
Singles: 7-inch
DUKE (100 series)............................15-25 58
DUKE (300 series)..............................8-12 59

PERRYMATES
(Perry Mates)
Singles: 7-inch
LANAR (103 "Little Darlin' ") 25-50
MARKETTE (1050 "Hang Your Head")...25-35 60s

PERRYWELL, Charles, & Fairlanes
Singles: 7-inch
TIC-TOC (104 "You're Lonesome")..100-125

PERSIA
Singles: 7-inch
CASABLANCA 3-5 80
LPs: 10/12-inch
CASABLANCA 5-10 79

PERSIAN MARKET
Singles: 7-inch
LIGHTNING (103 "Flash in the Pan")..15-25 67

PERSIANETTES
Singles: 7-inch
OLYMPIA 10-15 63
Also see CARR, Timmy, & Persianettes
Also see TIMMY & PERSIANETTES

PERSIANS
Singles: 7-inch
GOLD EAGLE (1813 "Love Me Tonight")...15-25 62
GOLDISC (1 "Teardrops Are Falling")...40-60 63
GOLDISC (17 "When You Said Let's Get Married")..15-25 63
MUSIC WORLD (102 "Let's Get Married")..10-20 63
PAGEANT (601 "Steady Kind") 10-20 63
RSVP (114 "Tears of Love") 40-50 62
RTO (100 "Sunday Kind of Love") 10-20 62
SIR RAH (501 "Don't Let Me Down")...25-50 63

PERSIANS / Clifton Chenier
Singles: 7-inch
MASTERPIECE (1111 "Tears of Love")...5-10
(Colored vinyl.)
Also see CHENIER, Clifton
Also see PERSIANS

PERSIANS R&B '68
Singles: 7-inch
ABC 4-8 68
CAPITOL..3-5 71-72
GRAPEVINE 3-5 70
GWP 3-6 69-70
Members: James Gill; Freddie Lewis; James Harlee; Jim Brown.

PERSON, Houston R&B '75
Singles: 78 rpm
PRESTIGE...3-6 52
Singles: 7-inch
EASTBOUND...3-5
PRESTIGE..5-10 52
WESTBOUND...3-5 75-76

PERSONALITIES
(Featuring Ralph Molina; with Teacho Wiltshire Orchestra)
Singles: 78 rpm
SAFARI 100-200 57
Singles: 7-inch
SAFARI (1002 "Woe Woe Baby")..100-200 57
(Giraffe is pictured on label.)
SAFARI (1002 "Woe Woe Baby")..25-45
(No giraffe on label.)
Also see MELLO-MOODS

PERSPECTIVES
Singles: 7-inch
TRANS-WORLD (1101 "Git-Git Guitar")...10-20

PERSUADERS
Singles: 7-inch
CARLTON..5-10 62

PERSUADERS
Singles: 7-inch
WINLEY (235 "Tears")..................75-100 59

PERSUADERS
(Featuring Chuck "Tequila" Rio)
Singles: 7-inch
SATURN (404 "Surfing Strip").......15-25 63
SATURN (405 "Gremmie Bread")...15-25 63
LPs: 10/12-inch
SATURN (5000 "Surfer's Nightmare")....................................100-125 63
(Monaural.)
SATURN (S-5000 "Surfer's Nightmare")....................................125-150 63
(Stereo.)
Also see RIO, Chuck "Tequila"

PERSUADERS
Singles: 7-inch
ORIGINAL SOUND (39 "Grunion Run")...25-35 63
(Reissued as by the Hollywood Persuaders.)
Also see HOLLYWOOD PERSUADERS

PERSUADERS P&R/R&B '71
Singles: 7-inch
ATCO 4-8 71-75
CALLA...3-5 77
WIN OR LOSE 3-5 71-72
LPs: 10/12-inch
ATCO 8-12 73-74
CALLA..8-10 77
WIN OR LOSE 10-15 72
Members: Doug Scott; James Barnes; Charles Stodghill; Willie Holland; Thomas Hill; Richard Gant; Willie Coleman.

PERSUADERS
Singles: 7-inch
BUM BUM 5-10 60s

PERSUASIONS
Singles: 7-inch
CROWN POINT (1 "The Magic of Love")..25-50 64

PERSUASIONS LP '71
Singles: 7-inch
A&M 4-6 74-75
CAPITOL 5-10 71-72
CATAMOUNT (Black vinyl) 3-6 70s
CATAMOUNT (Colored vinyl).........10-15 70s

ELEKTRA ... 5-10
ERICA ... 10-20
KING TUT ... 5-10
MCA ... 3-5 73
PAY-4-PLAY ... 5-10
(Colored vinyl.)
REPRISE ... 10-15 70
TOWER ... 5-10 65-66
LPs: 10/12-inch
A&M ... 10-15 74
CAPITOL ... 15-25 71-72
CATAMOUNT ... 8-10 70s
ELEKTRA ... 10-12 77
FLYING FISH ... 5-10 79
MCA ... 8-12 73
ROUNDER ... 5-8 80s
STRAIGHT ... 25-35 70
Members: Jerry Lawson; Jimmy Hayes; Jayotis Washington; Joe Russell; Herb Rhoad.
Also see DONNA & PERSUASIONS

PERY MATES
Singles: 7-inch
CA-JO (210 "It Was You") ... 50-75 59

PET SHOP BOYS P&R/R&B/LP '86
Singles: 12-inch
EMI ... 4-6 86-87
Singles: 7-inch
EMI ... 3-4 86-90
Picture Sleeves
EMI ... 3-4 86-89
LPs: 10/12-inch
EMI (Except 90263) ... 5-10 86-90
EMI (90263 "Actually") ... 10-15 88
(With bonus 12-inch single, *Always on My Mind*)
Members: Neil Tennant; Chris Lowe.
Also see ELECTRONIC

PET SHOP BOYS & Dusty Springfield
Singles: 7-inch
EMI ... 3-4 87
Also see PET SHOP BOYS
Also see SPRINGFIELD, Dusty

PETAL PUSHERS
LPs: 10/12-inch
CHESS ... 8-10 68

PETALS
Singles: 7-inch
MERCURY ... 3-5 67

PETARDS
LPs: 10/12-inch
LIBERTY ... 5-8 82
Members: Klaus Ebert; Arno Dittrich; Horst Ebert.

PETE & ERNIE
Singles: 7-inch
KING ... 4-8 61-62

PETE & JIMMY
Singles: 7-inch
CASTLE (504 "So Wild") ... 100-200 58

PETE & VINNIE
Singles: 7-inch
BIG TOP (3155 "Hand Clappin' Time") ... 10-15 63
Members: Pete Anders; Vinnie Poncia.
Also see ANDERS & PONCIA

PETER & GORDON P&R/LP '64
Singles: 7-inch
CAPITOL ... 5-10 64-69
Picture Sleeves
CAPITOL ... 8-15 64-67
LPs: 10/12-inch
CAPITOL (T-2115 thru T-2882) ... 15-25 64-68
(Monaural.)
CAPITOL (ST-2115 thru ST-2882) ... 20-30 64-68
(Stereo.)
CAPITOL (SM-2549 "Best of Peter & Gordon") ... 5-10 77
CAPITOL (SN-16084 "Best of Peter & Gordon") ... 5-8 80
Members: Peter Asher; Gordon Waller.
Also see WALLER, Gordon

PETER & GORDON / Lettermen
Singles: 7-inch
CAPITOL CREATIVE PRODUCTS ... 5-10 66
(Fritos Company promotional issue.)
Also see LETTERMEN
Also see PETER & GORDON

PETER & INFINITS
Singles: 7-inch
RUVAL ... 4-8 66

PETER & PROPHETS
Singles: 7-inch
FENTON (2050 "Johnny of Dreams") ... 20-30 66

PETER & RABBITS
Singles: 7-inch
BELL ... 4-8 67

PETER & WOLVES
Singles: 7-inch
P.W. (500 "Hey Mama") ... 8-12

PETER DARING
LP: 10/12-inch
MOON (001 "Peter Daring") ... 5-10 81
Members: Scott Doornenbal; Buddy Travis; Don Cairns; Nelson Leonard.

PETER G. & PATTY
Singles: 7-inch
SHIRLEY ... 10-15

PETER PAN & GOOD FAIRIES
Singles: 7-inch
CHALLENGE ... 4-6 67

PETER PAN & WENDY
Singles: 7-inch
EPIC ... 4-6 69

PETER, PAUL & MARY P&R/LP '62
Singles: 7-inch
"EUGENE McCARTHY for PRESIDENT" ... 10-20 68
(Promotional issue only. No label name used.)
W.B. (5000 series) ... 4-8 62-66
W.B. (7000 series) ... 3-6 67-70
Picture Sleeves
W.B. ... 4-8 62-64
EPs: 7-inch
W.B. ... 5-10 63-64
(Juke box issues only.)
LPs: 10/12-inch
GOLD C. ... 5-8 87
W.B. (1449 thru 1648) ... 20-30 62-66
(Gold or gray labels.)
W.B. (1700 thru 2552) ... 8-15 67-70
W.B. (3000 series) ... 5-10 77-78
Members: Peter Yarrow; Paul Stookey; Mary Travers.
Also see STOOKEY, Paul
Also see TRAVERS, Mary
Also see YARROW, Peter

PETER PIANO: see PIANO, Peter

PETER'S PIPERS
Singles: 7-inch
PHILIPS ... 4-8 68

PETERIK, Jim
Singles: 7-inch
EPIC ... 3-5 76
LPs: 10/12-inch
EPIC ... 8-10 76
Also see IDES of MARCH
Also see SURVIVOR

PETERS, Ben C&W '69
Singles: 7-inch
CAPITOL ... 3-5 73
LIBERTY ... 3-6 69

PETERS, Bernadette P&R/LP '80
Singles: 7-inch
ABC-PAR ... 4-8 65
COLUMBIA ... 4-8 67
MCA ... 3-5 78-81
U.A. ... 5-10 62
Picture Sleeves
MCA ... 3-5 80-81
LPs: 10/12-inch
MCA ... 5-10 80-81

PETERS, Brock
(Broc Peters)
Singles: 78 rpm
BIG ... 5-10 55
Singles: 7-inch
BIG ... 8-12 55
LPs: 10/12-inch
U.A. (3041 "Sing'a Man") ... 15-25 59
(Monaural.)
U.A. (3062 "Brock Peters at the Village Gate") ... 15-25 60
(Monaural.)
U.A. (6041 "Sing'a Man") ... 20-30 59
(Stereo.)
U.A. (6062 "Brock Peters at the Village Gate") ... 20-30 60
(Stereo.)

PETERS, Debbie C&W '80
Singles: 7-inch
OAK ... 3-5 80

PETERS, Doug C&W '88
Singles: 7-inch
COMSTOCK ... 3-4 88

PETERS, Jimmy C&W '77
Singles: 7-inch
MERCURY ... 3-5 77-78
SUNBIRD ... 3-5 80

PETERS, Jimmy, & Linda K. Lance C&W '79
(Jimmie Peters & Linda K. Lance)
Singles: 7-inch
VISTA ... 3-5 79
Also see LANCE, Linda K.
Also see PETERS, Jimmy

PETERS, Gregg, Band
Singles: 7-inch
REELIN & ROCKIN' (1046 "The King on 45") ... 4-6 82
(Black vinyl.)
REELIN & ROCKIN' (1046 "The King on 45") ... 4-8 82
(Colored vinyl.)
LPs: 10/12-inch
REELIN & ROCKIN' (1003 "The King on Long Play") ... 8-12 81
(Clear vinyl.)

PETERS, Nancy
(With the Band of Harold "Beans" Bowles)
Singles: 7-inch
KUDO (664 "Cry Baby Heart") ... 50-75 58
Also see JOHNSON, Marv

PETERS, Pete
Singles: 7-inch
DIXIE (836 "Rockin' N My Sweet Baby's Arms") ... 200-300 50s

PETERS, Peter Scott
Singles: 7-inch
LUTE ... 4-8 61

PETERS, Reverend
Singles: 7-inch
W.B. ... 5-10 59

PETERS & LEE C&W '74
Singles: 7-inch
PHILIPS ... 3-6 65-74
LPs: 10/12-inch
PHILIPS ... 8-12 65-66
Members: Lennie Peters; Dianne Lee.

PETERSEN, Paul P&R '62
Singles: 7-inch
ABC ... 3-5 74
COLPIX (Except 720) ... 5-15 62-65
COLPIX (720 "She Rides with Me") ... 25-35 64
ERIC ... 3-4 70s
MCA ... 3-4
MOTOWN ... 10-20 67-68
Picture Sleeves
COLPIX (632 "Keep Your Love Locked") ... 10-20 61
COLPIX (663 "My Dad") ... 10-20 62
LPs: 10/12-inch
COLPIX (CP-429 "Lollipops and Roses") ... 25-35 62
(Monaural.)
COLPIX (SCP-429 "Lollipops and Roses") ... 35-45 62
(Stereo.)
COLPIX (CP-442 "My Dad") ... 30-40 63
(Monaural.)
COLPIX (SCP-442 "My Dad") ... 35-45 63
(Stereo.)
Session: Beach Boys; Honeys; Billy Strange; Hal Blaine; Tommy Tedesco; Plas Johnson; Steve Douglas; David Gates; Richie Frost.
Also see BEACH BOYS
Also see DARREN, James / Shelly Fabares / Paul Petersen
Also see DOUGLAS, Steve
Also see GATES, David
Also see HONEYS
Also see JOHNSON, Plas
Also see STRANGE, Billy

PETERSEN, Paul, & Shelly Fabares
Singles: 7-inch
COLPIX (631 "What Did They Do Before Rock & Roll") ... 5-10 62
Also see FABARES, Shelly
Also see PETERSEN, Paul

PETERSEN, Ron, & Accents
Singles: 7-inch
JERDEN (728 "Linda Lu") ... 15-25 64

PETERSON, Beth
Singles: 7-inch
SOUND STUDIOS ... 3-5 77
LPs: 10/12-inch
SOUND STUDIOS ... 8-10 77

PETERSON, Bobby P&R '59
(Bobby Peterson Quintet)
Singles: 7-inch
ATLANTIC (2152 "Every Now and Then") ... 5-10 62
GRAND (164 "It's Been So Long Baby") ... 8-12 63
V-TONE (205 "The Hunch") ... 8-12 59
V-TONE (210 "Rockin' Charlie") ... 8-12 59
V-TONE (214 "Irresistable You") ... 8-12 60
Members: Bobby Peterson; James Thomas; Joe Pyatt; Chico Green; David Butler.

PETERSON, Colleen C&W '76
Singles: 7-inch
CAPITOL ... 3-5 76
LPs: 10/12-inch
CAPITOL ... 5-10 76-78

PETERSON, Earl
(Michigan's Singing Cowboy)
Singles: 78 rpm
COLUMBIA ... 10-20 55
SUN (197 "Boogie Blues") ... 200-300 54
Singles: 7-inch
COLUMBIA (21364 "Boogie Blues") ... 30-40 55
COLUMBIA (21406 "You're Going to Break") ... 15-25 56
COLUMBIA (21540 "You Gotta Be My Baby") ... 20-30 56
SUN (197 "Boogie Blues") ... 400-500 54

PETERSON, Jackie, & Paramounts
(With Dominic Apolito & Orchestra)
Singles: 7-inch
WARWICK (127 "Funny Man") ... 10-20

PETERSON, Gil
Singles: 7-inch
KARIE ... 4-8 62

PETERSON, Jimmy
Singles: 7-inch
CHESS ... 4-8 64
FEDERAL ... 4-8 61-62

PETERSON, Joanne
Singles: 7-inch
SIOUX ... 4-8 64

PETERSON, Kris
Singles: 7-inch
BLUE ROCK ... 4-8 65
PELIKIN (101 "I Believe in You") ... 20-40 60s
STORMY FOREST ... 5-10

PETERSON, Leon
Singles: 7-inch
HOB (117 "This Creation") ... 20-40 61

PETERSON, Lucky, Blues Band R&B '71
Singles: 7-inch
TODAY ... 3-5 71
LPs: 10/12-inch
TODAY ... 10-15 71

PETERSON, Merv
Singles: 7-inch
VAGUEST IDEA ... 4-8 60s
Also see DRIFTERS

PETERSON, Oscar LP '63
(Oscar Peterson Trio; with Milt Jackson)
Singles: 78 rpm
CLEF ... 4-6 53-56
MERCURY ... 4-8 51-52
NORGRAN ... 4-6 55
VERVE ... 4-8 57
Singles: 7-inch
CLEF ... 5-15 53-56
LIMELIGHT ... 4-8 65-66
MERCURY (8900 series) ... 5-15 51-52
MERCURY (72000 series) ... 4-8 64
MERCURY (89000 series) ... 5-15 52-53
NORGRAN ... 5-15 55
PRESTIGE ... 4-6 69
VERVE ... 5-10 57-64
EPs: 7-inch
CLEF ... 25-50 52-55
RCA (3006 "This Is Oscar Peterson") ... 75-125 51
LPs: 10/12-inch
BASF ... 8-12 74-76
CLEF (106 "Piano Solos") ... 100-200 52
(10-inch LP.)
CLEF (107 "At Carnegie Hall") ... 100-200 52
(10-inch LP.)
CLEF (110 "Collates") ... 100-200 52
(10-inch LP.)
CLEF (116 "Oscar Peterson Quartet") ... 100-200 52
(10-inch LP.)
CLEF (119 "Oscar Peterson Plays Pretty") ... 100-200 52
(10-inch LP.)
CLEF (127 "Collates, No. 2") ... 100-150 53
(10-inch LP.)
CLEF (145 "Oscar Peterson Sings") ... 100-150 54
(10-inch LP.)
CLEF (155 "Oscar Peterson Plays Pretty, No. 2") ... 100-150 54
(10-inch LP.)
CLEF (168 "Oscar Peterson Quartet, No. 2") ... 100-150 55
(10-inch LP.)
CLEF (600 series) ... 50-100 53-56
EMARCY ... 8-12 76
LIMELIGHT (1000 series) ... 5-8 82
LIMELIGHT (82000 & 86000 series) ... 10-20 65-67
MFSL (243 "Very Tall") ... 20-25 95
(Half-speed mastered.)
MGM (100 series) ... 8-12 70
MPS ... 8-12 72-76
MERCURY (20975 "Trio+One") ... 20-30 64
(Monaural.)
MERCURY (60975 "Trio+One") ... 25-35 64
(Stereo.)
METRO ... 10-15 65
PABLO ... 6-12 75-83
PAUSA ... 5-10 79-81
PRESTIGE ... 8-15 69-74
RCA (3006 "This Is Oscar Peterson") ... 200-250 51
(10-inch LP.)
TRIP ... 5-8 75-76
VSP ... 10-20 66-67
VERVE ... 35-75 56-60
(Reads "Verve Records, Inc." at bottom of label.)
VERVE ... 10-25 61-72
(Reads "MGM Records - A Division of Metro-Goldwyn-Mayer, Inc." at bottom of label.)
VERVE ... 5-15 73-83
(Reads "Manufactured By MGM Record Corp.," or mentions either Polydor or Polygram at bottom of label.)
WING ... 8-12 67
Members (Oscar Peterson Trio): Oscar Peterson; Ray Brown; Herb Ellis.
Also see ARMSTRONG, Louis, & Oscar Peterson
Also see BASIE, Count, & Oscar Peterson
Also see FITZGERALD, Ella, & Oscar Peterson
Also see GETZ, Stan, & Oscar Peterson
Also see HUBBARD, Freddie, & Oscar Peterson
Also see MULLIGAN, Gerry, & Oscar Peterson
Also see RIDDLE, Nelson
Also see YOUNG, Lester, & Oscar Peterson

PETERSON, Pigmeat
Singles: 78 rpm
FEDERAL ... 25-40 52
Singles: 7-inch
FEDERAL (12081 "Everybody Loves a Fat Man") ... 50-75 52

PETERSON, Ray P&R '59
Singles: 7-inch
CLOUD 9 ... 3-5 75
DECCA ... 3-5 71
DUNES ... 5-10 60-63
MGM ... 4-8 64-66
POLYDOR ... 3-5 70s
RCA (47-7000 series) ... 10-15 58-60
RCA (47-8000 series) ... 4-8 64
RCA (61-7578 "My Blue Angel") ... 15-25 60
(Stereo.)
RCA (61-7745 "Tell Laura I Love Her") ... 15-25 60
(Stereo.)
RCA (61-7779 "Teenage Heartache") ... 15-25 60
(Stereo.)
REPRISE ... 4-6 69
UNI ... 3-5 70
Picture Sleeves
DUNES (2002 "Corrina Corrina") ... 8-12 60
MGM (13269 "Oh No") ... 5-10 64
MGM (13336 "House Without Windows") ... 5-10 64
RCA (7635 "Goodnight My Love") ... 8-12 59
EPs: 7-inch
RCA (4367 "Tell Laura I Love Her") ... 40-60 60
LPs: 10/12-inch
CAMDEN ... 10-20 66
DECCA ... 8-12 71
MGM ... 20-30 64-65
RCA (LPM-2297 "Tell Laura I Love Her") ... 40-60 60
(Monaural.)
RCA (LSP-2297 "Tell Laura I Love Her") ... 60-80 60
(Stereo.)
UNI ... 10-15 70

PETERSON, Willie
Singles: 7-inch
SOMA ... 4-8 60s

PETIT, Mike, & Stags
Singles: 7-inch
ANTHEM (601227 "It's a Reamer") ... 10-20 60

PETITE R&B '86
Singles: 7-inch
YORK'S ... 3-4 86

PETITE TEENS
Singles: 7-inch
BRUNSWICK ... 10-15 59

PETITES
Singles: 7-inch
ASCOT ... 5-10 64
COLUMBIA (41662 "Get Your Daddy's Car Tonight") ... 10-20 60
CUB ... 5-10 68
ELMOR (304 "The Beating of My Heart") ... 50-100 62
SPINNING (6003 "Marguerite") ... 10-20 58
SPINNING (6005 "Sweetie Pie") ... 10-20 58

PETITES
Singles: 7-inch
TROY (1001 "Baby Blue Mustang") ... 15-25 63

PETRA
Singles: 7-inch
A&M ... 3-4 84
LPs: 10/12-inch
A&M ... 5-8 84-85
MYRRH ... 5-8 80s

PETRI, Barry
(Barry Petricoin)
Singles: 7-inch
SWAN (4111 "Pretty Little Angel") 40-50 62
Also see PETRICOIN, Barry, & Belairs
Also see PETRICOIN, Barry, & Pretenders

PETRICOIN, Barry, & Belairs
Singles: 7-inch
AL-STAN (103 "Pretty Little Angel") ... 75-125 58

PETRICOIN, Barry, & Pretenders
(With the Belairs)
Singles: 7-inch
AL-STAN (1004 "Pretty Little Angel") ... 3-5 95
(Colored vinyl.)
Picture Sleeves
AL-STAN (1004 "Pretty Little Angel") ... 3-5 95
Also see PETRI, Barry
Also see PETRICOIN, Barry, & Belairs
Also see PRETENDERS

PETRIFIED FOREST
Singles: 7-inch
FONTANA ... 8-12 67

PETS P&R '58
Singles: 78 rpm
ARWIN ... 10-15 58
Singles: 7-inch
ARWIN ... 10-15 58
Member: Seph Acre.
Also see ACRE, Seph, & Pets
Also see PEPE & Los Pets
Also see WARREN, Jerry

PETS
Singles: 7-inch
MGM ... 4-8 65

PETS
LPs: 10/12-inch
ARISTA ... 5-10 78

PETTI, Mary
Singles: 7-inch
RCA ... 4-8 61-62

PETTICOAT & VINE
Singles: 7-inch
DECCA ... 4-8 70

PETTICOATS
Singles: 7-inch
UNIQUE (344 "Motorboat Song")...10-15 50s
UNIQUE (363 "High Heels")..........10-15 60s

PETTICOATS
Singles: 7-inch
CHALLENGE (9211 "Surfin' Sally") 10-20 63

PETTIS, Ray
Singles: 7-inch
DEE DEE (3903 "Hello There Pretty Baby")..........................10-20
DEE DEE (73173 "Together Forever")..........................10-20

PETTUS, Giorge R&B '87
Singles: 7-inch
MCA 3-4 86-88
Picture Sleeves
MCA 3-4 86

PETTY, Al
(With Patti Lewis)
Singles: 7-inch
4-STAR (1761 "My Lips Won't Talk")..........................10-20 60

PETTY, Eddie "Prince"
Singles: 7-inch
GUEST (1004 "I Simply Crack Up")..........................20-30

PETTY, Frank, Trio
Singles: 78 rpm
MGM 3-5 50-57
Singles: 7-inch
MGM 4-8 50-57
EPs: 7-inch
MGM 5-10 50-57
LPs: 10/12-inch
MGM 10-20 50-57

PETTY, Norman, Trio P&R '54
(Vi Petty)
Singles: 78 rpm
ABC-PAR 5-10 57
COLUMBIA (Except 41039)........... 5-10 57
COLUMBIA (41039 "Moondreams")..........................50-75 57
(With Buddy Holly on guitar.)
NOR VA JAK 15-20 57
"X" 4-8 54-55
Singles: 7-inch
ABC-PAR 8-12 57
COLUMBIA (Except 41039)........... 8-12 57
COLUMBIA (41039 "Moondreams")..........................50-75 57
(With Buddy Holly on guitar.)
FELSTED 5-10 62
JARO.......................... 8-12 60
NOR VA JAK (Except 1325)..........15-20 57-59
NOR VA JAK (1325 "True Love Ways")..........................50-75 60
NORMAN 8-12 60
PRISM (101 "The Plane Crash") 5-10
"X"..........................10-20 54-55
EPs: 7-inch
COLUMBIA (2139 "Four Hits").......15-25 58
COLUMBIA (10921 "Moondreams")..........................50-100 58
"X" (82 "In Full Fidelity")..........15-25 55
LPs: 10/12-inch
COLUMBIA (1092 "Moondreams")..........................50-100 58
TOP RANK (R-639 "Petty for Your Thoughts")..........................20-30 60
(Monaural.)
TOP RANK (RS-639 "Petty for Your Thoughts")..........................30-40 60
(Stereo.)
VIK (1073 "Corsage")..........................30-45 57
Members: Norman Petty; Vi Petty; Jack Petty.
Also see BOWMAN BROTHERS & Norman Petty Trio
Also see HOLLY, Buddy
Also see PICKS

PETTY, Tom, & Heartbreakers P&R/LP '77
Singles: 7-inch
BACKSTREET 3-5 79-83
(Black vinyl.)
BACKSTREET (52181 "Change of Heart").......................... 5-8 83
(Colored vinyl.)
MCA 3-5 85-93
SHELTER 3-5 77-78
Picture Sleeves
BACKSTREET.......................... 3-5 79-83
MCA 3-4 85-90
SHELTER 3-5 77-78
LPs: 10/12-inch
BACKSTREET.......................... 5-10 79-82
MCA 5-8 85-93
SHELTER 8-15 76-78
W.B. 5-12 94-96
Promotional LPs
SHELTER (12677 "Official Live 'Leg'")..........................15-25 76
SHELTER (52029 "You're Gonna Get It")..........................15-25 78
(Colored vinyl.)
Members: Tom Petty; Mike Campbell; Stan Lynch; Beaumont Tench; Ron Blair; Howie Epstein.
Also see DYLAN, Bob, & Heartbreakers / Michael Rubini
Also see MUDCRUTCH
Also see NICKS, Stevie, with Tom Petty & Heartbreakers

PETTY, Vi: see PETTY, Norman, Trio

PEWTER, Jim
(With the Saturday Revue)
Singles: 7-inch
CIRCUS..........................15-20 61
MGM.......................... 4-8 72-73
RCA.......................... 4-8 69
Session: Davie Allan.
Also see ALLAN, Davie
Also see ALLISON, Jerry, & Crickets
Also see CURTIS, Sonny
Also see JAMES, Deviny
Also see LEWIS & CLARKE
Also see PEWTER PALS
Also see TEMPO, Nino, & April Stevens

PEWTER PALS
Singles: 7-inch
MANHATTAN.......................... 4-8 67
Member: Jim Pewter.
Also see PEWTER, Jim

PEYTON, Dori
Singles: 7-inch
MARGO..........................10-15 64
OHIE..........................10-15 64

PEX'S BAD BOYS
Singles: 7-inch
SCEPTER 5-10 66-67

PEZBAND
Singles: 12-inch
PASSPORT.......................... 4-8 79
Singles: 7-inch
PASSPORT.......................... 3-5 77
LPs: 10/12-inch
PVC (Colored vinyl)..........................10-15
PASSPORT.......................... 5-10 77-79

PFEIFER, Diane C&W '80
Singles: 7-inch
CAPITOL.......................... 3-4 80-82
LPs: 10/12-inch
CAPITOL.......................... 5-10 80

PHAETONS
Singles: 7-inch
HI-Q (5012 "Fling")..........................10-15 59
VIN (1015 "I Love My Baby")..........40-50 59

PHAETONS
Singles: 7-inch
W.B. 4-8 67-68

PHAETONS / Premiers
Singles: 7-inch
SAHARA (103 "The Beatle Walk")...8-10 64

PHAFNER
Singles: 7-inch
DRAGON (1001 "Overdrive").......50-100 71
LPs: 10/12-inch
DRAGON ("Overdrive")..........2500-3500 71
Members: Greg Smith; Steve Smith; Dale Shultz; Tom Shultz; Steve Gustafson.

PHANTOM
Singles: 7-inch
CAPITOL (4055 "Whispering")..........5-10 58

PHANTOM
Singles: 7-inch
DOT (16056 "Love Me")..........75-100 60
Picture Sleeves
DOT (16056 "Love Me")..........100-150 60
Members: Marty Lott; H.H. Brooks; Bill Yates; Frank Holmes; Pete McCord.

PHANTOM
(Wayne Stierle)
Singles: 7-inch
PATTI.......................... 5-10 69
Also see STIERLE, Wayne

PHANTOM
Singles: 7-inch
CAPITOL (3857 "Calm Before the Storm").......................... 5-10 74
HIDEOUT (1080 "Calm Before the Storm")..........................10-15 73
LPs: 10/12-inch
CAPITOL (11313 "Divine Comedy")..........................40-60 74
GHOST ("The Lost Album")..........8-10 90

PHANTOM
LPs: 10/12-inch
ELECTRIC LEMON..........................10-15

PHANTOM FIVE
Singles: 7-inch
SKULL (817002 "Graveyard")..........40-60 60s
(Identification number used since no selection number is shown.)

PHANTOM LIMBS
LPs: 10/12-inch
ROMANCE.......................... 5-8 83-86
Members: Jim Parks; Jeff Keenan; Peter "Splat" Catalanotte.

PHANTOM, ROCKER & SLICK LP '85
Singles: 7-inch
EMI AMERICA.......................... 3-5 85-86
LPs: 10/12-inch
EMI AMERICA.......................... 5-10 85-86
Members: Jim Phantom; Lee Rocker; Earl Slick.
Also see SILVER CONDOR
Also see STRAY CATS

PHANTOM SURFERS
Singles: 7-inch
ESTRUS (4 "Bikini Drag").......... 3-4 92
(Includes insert.)
Picture Sleeves
ESTRUS (4 "Bikini Drag").......... 3-4 92
LPs: 10/12-inch
ESTRUS (125 "The Phantom Surfers Play")..........................5-10 92
Members: Johnny "Big Hand" Bartlett; Mel "Frostbite" Bergman; Maz "Tender Pants" Kattuah; Michael "Daddy Love" Lucas; Trent "Big Drag" Ruane.

PHANTOM'S DIVINE
Singles: 7-inch
CAPITOL ("Calm Before the Storm")..........................10-15

PHANTOMS
Singles: 78 rpm
BATON..........................10-15 57
Singles: 7-inch
BATON..........................10-15 57

PHANTOMS
Singles: 7-inch
CANTON (1786 "Birdland")..........10-15 60
ORIGINAL SOUND (11 "Night Theme")..........................8-12 60
PICO (2803 "Birdland")..........10-15
Also see HOUSTON, Joe / Phantoms

PHANTOMS
Singles: 7-inch
PALETTE (5014 "Phantom Guitar")..........................10-20 61

PHANTOMS
(Majestics)
Singles: 7-inch
SAM (123 "XL-3")..........................20-25 62
Also see MAJESTICS

PHANTOMS
Singles: 7-inch
FORD (137 "The Cruel Sea")..........8-12 63

PHANTOMS
Singles: 7-inch
GRAVES ("Hallucinogenic Odyssey")..........................40-60 60s
(Selection number not known.)
IRC (6937 "My Generation")..........20-30 66

PHANTOMS
Singles: 7-inch
RICKYTICK (102 "The Grinder")......8-12

PHANTOMS BAND
Singles: 7-inch
ELDO (102 "Phantom Freight")......10-15 60
Also see SAFARIS

PHANTONES
(Phantones & Combo)
Singles: 7-inch
BALE (105 "Waiting for Your Love")..........................50-75 59
CODE (707 "This Is Love")..........100-150 58

PHARAOHS
("Featuring Rickey")
Singles: 7-inch
CLASS (202 "Teenagers Love Song")..........................150-250 56

PHARAOHS
Singles: 7-inch
FASCINATION (001 "Walking Sad")..........................300-500 57

PHARAOHS
Singles: 7-inch
FLIP (352 "I'll Never Love Again") 25-35 60
Also see BERRY, Richard
Also see RICKY & PHARAOHS

PHARAOHS
Singles: 7-inch
PYRAMID ("Jacknife")..........................15-25 62
(Selection number not known.)

PHARAOHS
Singles: 7-inch
CHATTAHOOCHEE (660 "The Friendly Martian")..........................10-15 65
IONA (1002 "Green Werewolf")......10-15 60s

PHARAOHS
Singles: 7-inch
CAPITOL..........................3-5 71
LPs: 10/12-inch
SCARAB..........................8-12 72

PHARAOS
Singles: 7-inch
DONNA (1327 "The Tender Touch")..........................15-25 60

PHAROS
Singles: 7-inch
DEL-FI (4208 "Pintor")..........5-10 63

PHAROTONES
Singles: 7-inch
TIMELY (1002 "Give Me a Chance")..........1000-2000 58
Also see FIVE SATINS / Pharotones

PHARR, Gene, & Friends
Singles: 7-inch
SANDOLLAR..........................3-5 80

PHASE THREE
Singles: 7-inch
KARMIL..........................3-5

PHAST PHREDDIE & Thee Precisions
LPs: 10/12-inch
BOMP..........................8-10 82

PHATONS
Singles: 7-inch
UNIQUE..........................3-5 66

PHEASANTS
(With Bobby Eli & Orchestra)
Singles: 7-inch
THRONE (802 "Out of the Mist") ...15-25 63

PHELPS, James P&R/R&B '65
(With the Du-Ettes; Jimmy Phelps)
Singles: 7-inch
ARGO (5499 "Love Is a Five-Letter Word")..........................8-12 65
ARGO (5509 "Wasting Time")..........8-12 65
CADET (5534 "Action")..........5-10 66
FONTANA..........................5-10 66-67
MECCA (5 "Blue Point Drive")........20-30 60
PARAMOUNT..........................5-10 71-72
Also see SOUL STIRRERS

PHELPS, Johnny
Singles: 7-inch
SKI (5505 "Tom Kat")..........75-125

PHENOMENONS
Singles: 7-inch
A.V.I...........................3-5 78

PHEREMONES
Singles: 7-inch
EC (4520 "Feminine Deoderant Spray")..........................3-5 82
EC (4530 "Yuppie Drone")..........3-5 85

PHIFER, Bob
Singles: 7-inch
PLAY..........................4-8 61

PHIL & BEA BOPP
Singles: 7-inch
AMC..........................25-35 60s
Member: Phillip Walker; Ivor Beatrice.
Also see WALKER, Phillip

PHIL & CATALINAS
(With the Neutrons)
Singles: 7-inch
OLIMPIC (4479 "June 30th")........50-100 60
(Identification number shown since no selection number is used.)
Member: Phil Gary.
Also see GARY, Phil

PHIL & DEL
Singles: 7-inch
LINDA..........................10-15 62
RAMPART..........................5-10 67
Also see PHIL & HARV

PHIL & FLAKES
Singles: 7-inch
IO (1010 "Chrome Reversed Rails")..........................25-30 63
(Because complete selection number is "Fink 1010," label name is sometimes shown as "Fink.")
Member: Phil Pearlman.

PHIL & FRANTICS
Singles: 7-inch
ARA (1968 "Til You Get What You Want")..........................15-25 65
LA MAR (100 "She's My Gal")..........10-15 64
RABBITT (1219 "I Must Run")........20-30 66
RAMCO (1970 "I Must Run")..........10-20 66
SOUNDS LTD..........................25-30 60s
LPs: 10/12-inch
VOXX..........................5-8
Member: Phil Kelsey.

PHIL & HARV
Singles: 7-inch
RAMPART..........................5-10 61
Also see PHIL & DEL

PHIL & MARIE
Singles: 7-inch
SWAY..........................5-10 61

PHILADELPHIA
LPs: 10/12-inch
RCA..........................8-12 74

PHILADELPHIA INTERNATIONAL ALL STARS P&R/R&B '77
Singles: 7-inch
PHILADELPHIA INT'L..........................3-5 77
Members: Archie Bell; the O'Jays; Billy Paul; Teddy Pendergrass; Lou Rawls; Dee Dee Sharpe.
Also see BELL, Archie
Also see MFSB
Also see O'JAYS
Also see PAUL, Billy
Also see PENDERGRASS, Teddy
Also see RAWLS, Lou
Also see SHARPE, Dee Dee

PHILADELPHIA STORY R&B '77
Singles: 7-inch
H&L..........................3-5 77

PHILADELPHIA STUDENTS
Singles: 7-inch
CLIFTON..........................4-8 92

PHILADELPHIANS
Singles: 78 rpm
CAMPUS..........................15-25 55
Singles: 7-inch
CAMPUS (101 "Dear")..........25-50 55
CAMPUS (103 "Church Bells")........25-50 55

PHILADELPHIANS
Singles: 7-inch
CAMEO (218 "The Vow")..........15-25 62

PHILHARMONICS
Singles: 7-inch
FUTURE (2200 "Why Don't You Write Me")..........................30-40 58

PHILHARMONICS
Singles: 7-inch
DEL-FI..........................8-12 61

PHILHARMONICS P&R/R&B '77
Singles: 7-inch
CAPRICORN..........................3-5 77
LPs: 10/12-inch
CAPRICORN..........................5-10 77

PHILAMORE LINCOLN
LPs: 10/12-inch
EPIC..........................10-15 68

PHILIP & STEPHAN
Singles: 7-inch
INTERPHON (7711 "Meet Me Tonight Little Girl")..........................8-12 64
Members: Philip Sloan; Stephan Barri.
Also see FANTASTIC BAGGYS

PHILIPS, Terry
Singles: 7-inch
CORAL..........................4-8 61
U.A. (351 "My Foolish Ways") 40-60 61

PHILISTEENS
LPs: 10/12-inch
RADIO FREE AMERICA..........................5-8 82

PHILLEY STOMPERS
Singles: 7-inch
PAJ ("Two Step Stomp")..........75-125 60s

PHILLINGANES, Greg R&B '81
Singles: 12-inch
PLANET..........................4-6 85
Singles: 7-inch
PLANET..........................3-4 81-85
LPs: 10/12-inch
PLANET..........................5-8 81-85
Also see KING DREAM CHORUS & Holiday Crew

PHILLIP & GARY
Singles: 7-inch
DOT..........................4-8 66

PHILLIP & LEE
Singles: 7-inch
BOMAR (5005 "She Belongs to Me")..........................8-12 65

PHILLIP & LLOYD
LPs: 10/12-inch
SCEPTER..........................8-12 75
Members: Phillip James; Lloyd Campbell.

PHILLIP & VANESSA
LPs: 10/12-inch
ANCHOR..........................5-10 75

PHILLIPAIRS: see MOROCCANS / PHILLIPAIRS

PHILLIPS, Anthony LP '77
Singles: 7-inch
PASSPORT..........................3-5 77-78
LPs: 10/12-inch
PASSPORT (Except 9828)..........5-10 77-78
PASSPORT (9828 "Wise After the Event")..........................15-20 78
(Picture disc.)
Also see GENESIS

PHILLIPS, Bill C&W '64
(With Dolly Parton)
Singles: 7-inch
DECCA (Except 31901)..........................3-8 64-71
DECCA (31901 "Put It Off Until Tomorrow")..........................8-10 66
SOUNDWAVES..........................3-5 78-79
U.A...........................3-5 72-73
LPs: 10/12-inch
DECCA (Except 4792)..........................15-25 67-70
DECCA (DL-4792 "Put It Off Until Tomorrow")..........................15-20 66
(Monaural.)
DECCA (DL7-4792 "Put It Off Until Tomorrow")..........................20-25 66
(Stereo.)
HARMONY..........................12-18 64
GUINNESS..........................5-10
SEA SHELL..........................8-10
Also see PARTON, Dolly
Also see TILLIS, Mel, & Bill Phillips
Also see WELLS, Kitty / Bill Phillips / Bobby Wright / Johnny Wright

PHILLIPS, Bob
(Bobby Phillips)
Singles: 7-inch
BATON..........................5-10 58
COBAL..........................5-10 59

PHILLIPS, Carl
Singles: 7-inch
BOBBIN (110 "Wigwam Willie") 250-500 59
K-ARK (607 "Salty Dog Blues")......15-25

PHILLIPS, Charlie C&W '62
Singles: 7-inch
COLUMBIA..........................4-8 62-63
CORAL (61970 "Be My Bride")......30-40 58
Also see HOLLY, Buddy

PHILLIPS, D.D: see PHILLIPS, Miss D.D.

PHILLIPS, Dave
Singles: 7-inch
CHRISTY..........................4-8

PHILLIPS, Doug, & New Concepts
Singles: 7-inch
ATCO 4-6 69
Also see COTTONWOOD
Also see DARTELLS

PHILLIPS, Earl, Orchestra
Singles: 78 rpm
VEE JAY (158 "Oop De Oop") 10-20 55
Singles: 7-inch
VEE JAY (158 "Oop De Oop") 20-30 55
Also see PENTAGONS / Earl Phillips

PHILLIPS, Esther: see LITTLE ESTHER

PHILLIPS, Esther, & Joe Beck
LPs: 10/12-inch
KUDU 8-10 76
Also see BECK, Joe
Also see LITTLE ESTHER

PHILLIPS, Gene
(With His Rhythm Aces; with Jack McVea & His Orchestra)
Singles: 78 rpm
EXCLUSIVE 15-25 50
IMPERIAL 10-20 51
MODERN 15-25 47-49
RPM 15-25 50
LPs: 10/12-inch
CROWN 20-30 63
Also see McVEA, Jack

PHILLIPS, Joe
Singles: 7-inch
OMEN 4-8 65-66

PHILLIPS, John P&R/C&W/LP '70
Singles: 7-inch
ATCO 3-5 74
COLUMBIA 3-5 73
DUNHILL 3-5 70
LPs: 10/12-inch
DUNHILL 10-15 70
Also see JOURNEYMEN
Also see MAMAS & PAPAS

PHILLIPS, Kip
Singles: 7-inch
7 ARTS 4-8 61

PHILLIPS, Larose
Singles: 7-inch
GOLDISC 10-20 63

PHILLIPS, Little Esther: see LITTLE ESTHER

PHILLIPS, Marvin
(With the Men from Mars)
Singles: 78 rpm
MODERN 15-25 56
PARROT 50-75 54
SPECIALTY 25-50 52
SWING TIME 20-30 54
Singles: 7-inch
MODERN (982 "Yes I Do") 25-50 56
PARROT (786 "Salty Dog") 100-150 54
PARROT (795 "Anne Marie") 75-125 54
SPECIALTY (445 "Wine Boogie") 50-75 52
SPECIALTY (479 "Baby Doll") 50-75 52
(Black vinyl.)
SPECIALTY (479 "Baby Doll") 75-100 52
(Colored vinyl.)
SPECIALTY (488 "Jo Jo") 50-75 52
SPECIALTY (498 "School of Love") 50-75 52
SPECIALTY (530 "Day in Day Out") 50-75 52
SPECIALTY (554 "Ding Dong Daddy") 50-75 52
SWING TIME (339 "Salty Dog") 40-60 54
SWINGIN' 10-15 59
Also see JESSE & MARVIN
Also see LONG TALL MARVIN
Also see MARVIN & JOHNNY

PHILLIPS, Michelle
Singles: 7-inch
A&M 3-5 75-78
Picture Sleeves
A&M (1824 "No Love Today") 4-6 76
LPs: 10/12-inch
A&M 8-10 77
Also see MAMAS & PAPAS

PHILLIPS, Miss D.D.
Singles: 7-inch
EVOLUTION 3-6 69

PHILLIPS, Phil P&R/R&B '59
(With the Twilights)
Singles: 78 rpm
MERCURY (71465 "Sea of Love") 40-60 59
(Canadian.)
Singles: 7-inch
CLIQUE 4-8 66
KHOURY'S (711 "Sea of Love") 300-500 59
LANOR (It's All Right") 15-25 59
(Selection number not known.)
MERCURY (10021 "Verdi Mae") 20-30 59
(Stereo.)
MERCURY (71000 series) 10-20 59-61
MERCURY CELEBRITY SERIES 3-5
Also see K-DOE, Ernie / Phil Phillips

PHILLIPS, Phil
Singles: 7-inch
HARD BOILED (101 "Pyramid Game") 3-5

PHILLIPS, Ray
Singles: 7-inch
BOYD 4-8 61
DECCA 5-10 59

PHILLIPS, Reuben, & His Orchestra
Singles: 7-inch
ABCO 4-8 61
ASCOT 4-8 62
LPs: 10/12-inch
ASCOT 15-25 62

PHILLIPS, Richard: see JALOPY FIVE

PHILLIPS, Sammy
Singles: 7-inch
INFINITE 4-8 65-66

PHILLIPS, Sandra
Singles: 7-inch
BROADWAY 15-30 65-66
OKEH 5-10 68

PHILLIPS, Shawn LP '72
Singles: 7-inch
A&M 5-10 70-75
ASCOT (2152 "Cloudy Summer Afternoon") 15-25 64
LPs: 10/12-inch
A&M 10-20 70-77
RCA (3028 "Transcendence") 8-12 78
RCA (3873 "Transcendence") 8-12 78

PHILLIPS, Stu C&W '66
Singles: 7-inch
PARAGON 3-5 76
RCA 3-5 66-68
LPs: 10/12-inch
BANFF 15-30
PARAGON 5-10 76
RCA 15-30 66-68
RODEO 30-50

PHILLIPS, Stu, & His Orchestra
Singles: 7-inch
CAPITOL 3-5 73
COLPIX 10-20 62
COLUMBIA 4-8 62
MCA 3-5 78
SMASH 8-12 66
LPs: 10/12-inch
CAPITOL 15-20 65
Also see HOLLYRIDGE STRINGS

PHILLIPS, Susan
Singles: 7-inch
ALL PLATINUM 3-5 71
LPs: 10/12-inch
ALL PLATINUM 8-12 71

PHILLIPS, T.
Singles: 7-inch
FIREFLY 5-10 60

PHILLIPS, Teddy
Singles: 78 rpm
BALLY 5-10 57
KING 8-12 54
Singles: 7-inch
ALADDIN (3467 "Don't Do Anything") 10-15 60
BALLY 10-15 57
CRYSTALETTE (740 "Crazy Fever Blues") 15-25 60
(First issue.)
DOT (1690 "Crazy Fever Blues") 8-12 60
THANKS (251 "31 Steps") 60-75
KING (1333 "Please Unlock the Door") 15-25 54
EPs: 7-inch
DECCA (715 "Concert in the Sky") . 15-25 50s
Also see LOVETT, Coleen, & Ted Phillips

PHILLIPS, Terry
Singles: 7-inch
JARO 8-12 59

PHILLIPS, Travis, & Wonder Boys
Singles: 7-inch
ABC-PAR 4-8 65
JOX 4-8 65

PHILLIPS, Wade
Singles: 7-inch
JARO 5-10 60

PHILLIPS, Walt, & Barry Young
Singles: 7-inch
DELTONE (5023 "Surfin' Annie") ... 15-25 63

PHILLIPS, Warren, & Rockets
LPs: 10/12-inch
LONDON 5-10 79
PARROT 15-20 70
Also see SAVOY BROWN

PHILLIPS, Wes R&B/D&D '84
Singles: 12-inch
QUALITY 4-6 84
Singles: 7-inch
QUALITY 3-4 84

PHILLIPS - MACLEOD
Singles: 7-inch
POLYDOR 3-5 79-80
LPs: 10/12-inch
POLYDOR 5-10 80

PHILLIPSON, Larry Lee
(With the Larry Lee Trio)
Singles: 7-inch
CINCH (3858 "Bitter Feelings") .. 100-200 64
CUCA (6541 "Bitter Feelings") 40-60 65
CUCA (6565 "Milwaukee Road") 15-25 65
DEMO (1029 "Bitter Feelings") 50-75 64
PHILLIPSON 10-20
RAYNARD (770 "Milwaukee") 10-20 65
RAYNARD (1053 "Baby Sitter's Christmas") 10-20 66
TARGET (1010 "Barney") 5-10 69

PHILLY CREAM P&R/R&B '79
Singles: 12-inch
WMOT 4-8 79
Singles: 7-inch
FANTASY 3-5 79
WMOT 3-5 79
LPs: 10/12-inch
WMOT 5-10 79

PHILLY DEVOTIONS P&R/R&B '75
Singles: 7-inch
BRY-WEK (1038 "I'll Never Color You a Rainbow") 5-10 73
DON DE (127 "I Just Can't Say Goodbye") 4-8 74
COLUMBIA 3-5 75-76

PHILLY ROLLERS
LPs: 10/12-inch
SPRINGBOARD 8-10 77

PHILMON, Hiram
Singles: 7-inch
PHILMON 5-10 60

PHILOSOPHERS
LPs: 10/12-inch
PHILO (1001 "After Sundown") .. 100-150 69
(Front cover is identical to *White Light*, by White Light.)

PHILWIT & PEGASUS
LPs: 10/12-inch
CHAPTER 1 .... 8-12 70
Members: Roger Greenaway; Peter Lee Sterling; John Carter; Guy Fletcher; Chas Mills.
Also see DAVID & JONATHAN
Also see IVY LEAGUE

PHINEAS & LEMON FOGG
Singles: 7-inch
SCEPTER 4-8 68

PHIPPS, Charlie
Singles: 7-inch
CAPITOL 4-8 60
TOPPER 5-10 59

PHLEGETON
Singles: 7-inch
PRE-HEAT (200 "You're No Good") 10-15

PHLUPH
Singles: 7-inch
VERVE 8-15 67-68
LPs: 10/12-inch
VERVE (5054 "Phluph") 15-25 68
Members: Benson Blake; Joel Maisano; John Pell; Lee Dudley.

PHOENIX
Singles: 7-inch
ABC 3-5 70-72
LPs: 10/12-inch
ABC 8-12 72
CHARISMA 5-10 79

PHOENIX
LPs: 10/12-inch
COLUMBIA 8-12 76
Members: Russ Ballard; Rod Argent; Ray Minhinnit; Ron Cunningham; John Verity; Robert Henrit; Bruce Turgen; Jim Rodford.
Also see ARGENT

PHOENIX-70
Singles: 7-inch
L.H.I. 4-6 69

PHOENIX PYRE
Singles: 7-inch
C.A.V.U. (23665 "One Life Span") 10-20 68

PHONES
Singles: 7-inch
PHONES 3-5 81

PHONETICS
Singles: 7-inch
TRUDEL (1005 "Pretty Girl") 25-35
TRUDEL (1008 "Just a Boy's Dream") 100-200
TRUDEL (1012 "What Good Am I Without You") 50-75
Member: Willie Hutch.
Also see HUTCH, Willie

PHOTOGLO, Jim P&R/LP '80
(Photoglo)
Singles: 7-inch
CASABLANCA 3-5 83
20TH FOX 3-5 80-81
LPs: 10/12-inch
CASABLANCA 5-10 83
20TH FOX 5-10 80-81

PHOTOS
Singles: 12-inch
A&M 4-6 83
LPs: 10/12-inch
EPIC 5-10 80
Members: Wendy Wu; Dave Sparrow; Steve Eagles; Ollie Harrison.

PHREEK
Singles: 7-inch
ATLANTIC 3-5 79
LPs: 10/12-inch
ATLANTIC 5-10 78
Member: Michael Adams.

PHYREWORK
Singles: 7-inch
MERCURY 3-5 78
LPs: 10/12-inch
MERCURY 5-10 78

PIAF, Edith P&R '50
(With Theo Sarapo)
Singles: 78 rpm
CAPITOL 4-8 56-58
COLUMBIA 4-8 50-52
Singles: 7-inch
CAPITOL 5-15 56-61
CAPITOL STARLINE 4-6 60s
COLUMBIA 5-15 50-52
EPs: 7-inch
ANGEL 5-15 55-56
COLUMBIA 5-15 50-52
DECCA 5-15 54
LPs: 10/12-inch
ANGEL 25-40 55-56
CAPITOL (10210 "Piaf") 15-25 59
CAPITOL (10283 "Piaf of Paris") ... 10-20 61
CAPITOL (10295 "Potpourri Par Piaf") 10-20 62
CAPITOL (10348 "Piaf & Sarapo") 10-20 63
CAPITOL STARLINE 5-10 60s
CAPITOL (16000 series) 5-10 81-82
COLUMBIA (898 "La Vie En Rose") 20-40 56
COLUMBIA (6223 "Encore Parisiennes") 25-50 52
(10-inch LP.)
COLUMBIA (9500 series) 25-50 51-52
(10-inch LPs.)
COLUMBIA (37000 series) 5-10 81
DECCA (6004 "Chansons des Cafes de Paris") 25-50 54
(10-inch LP.)
DISCOS 20-30 56
PHILIPS 10-20 64-67
RCA 10-15 64
VOX (3050 "Edith Piaf Sings") 25-50 53
(10-inch LP.)
VOX (3060 "Edith Piaf Favorites") . 25-50 53
(10-inch LP.)

PIANO, Peter, & His Band
Singles: 7-inch
LUTE (6013 "Sabre Dance Rock") . 10-15 61

PIANO RED R&B '50
(Willie Perryman)
Singles: 78 rpm
CHECKER 20-40 58
GROOVE 15-30 54-57
RCA 20-50 50-57
Singles: 7-inch
CHECKER (911 "Get Up Mare") 15-25 58
GROOVE (0023 "Decatur Street Blues") 25-50 54
GROOVE (0101 "Pay It No Mind") 25-50 55
GROOVE (0118 "Six O'Clock Boogie") 25-50 55
GROOVE (0126 "Red's Blues") 25-50 55
GROOVE (0136 "She Knocks Me Out") 25-50 56
GROOVE (0145 "I'm Nobody's Fool") 25-50 56
GROOVE (0169 "You Were Mine for Awhile") 25-50 56
JAX (1000 "I Feel Good") 8-12 59
RCA (0099 "Rockin' with Red") 50-75 50
(Colored vinyl.)
RCA (0106 "The Wrong YoYo") 25-50 50
RCA (0118 "Jumpin' the Boogie") .. 25-50 51
RCA (0130 "Baby What's Wrong") 25-50 51
RCA (4265 "Let's Have a Good Time") 25-50 51
RCA (4380 "Hey Good Lookin' ") 25-50 51
RCA (4524 "Bouncin' with Red") 25-50 52
RCA (4766 "Sales Tax Boogie") 25-50 52
RCA (4957 "Voo Doopee Doo") 25-50 52
RCA (5101 "I'm Gonna Rock Some More") 20-35 52
RCA (5224 "I'm Gonna Tell Everybody") 20-35 53
RCA (5337 "Your Mouth's Got a Hole") 20-35 52
RCA (5544 "Right and Ready") 20-35 52
RCA (6000 & 7000 series) 15-25 57-58
EPs: 7-inch
GROOVE (3 "Jump Man, Jump") ... 40-60 56
GROOVE (10026/27/28 "Piano Red in Concert") 35-50 56
(Price is for any of three volumes.)
RCA (587 "Rockin' with Red") 50-100 54
RCA (5091 "Rockin' with Red") 40-60 59
(Black label.)
RCA (5091 "Rockin' with Red") 50-100 59
(Maroon label.)
LPs: 10/12-inch
ARHOOLIE 8-10
BLACK LION 8-10 76
GROOVE (1001 "Jump Man, Jump") 500-750 56
GROOVE (1002 "Piano Red in Concert") 200-400 56
KING (1117 "Underground Atlanta") 10-20 70
RCA 8-10 74
Also see DOCTOR FEELGOOD
Also see SHIRLEY, Danny, & Piano Red

PIANO RED / June Valli
EPs: 7-inch
RCA (92 "Dealer's Prevue") 15-25 56
(Promotional issue only.)
Also see PIANO RED
Also see VALLI, June

PIANO SLIM
(Willard Burton)
Singles: 7-inch
C&P (103 "Lot of Shakin' Lot of Jivin' ") 100-200 59
DART (148 "Squeezing") 10-20 63
JET STREAM (705 "Stagecoach to Boothill") 10-20 62
MYRIL (405 "Heartbeat of Love") ... 10-20 61
Also see BURTON, Willard

PIC & BILL
Singles: 7-inch
BLUE ROCK 10-15 69
CHARAY (60 "Over the Mountain") 10-20 67
CHARAY (67 "It's Not You") 10-20 67
CHARAY (73 "This Is It") 15-25 67
SMASH 5-10 67-68
LPs: 10/12-inch
LE CAM 8-10

PICARDI, Lou
Singles: 78 rpm
ROULETTE 10-15 57
Singles: 7-inch
ROULETTE 10-15 57

PICARDY
Singles: 7-inch
DUNHILL 4-8 68

PICASSO, Artie
Singles: 7-inch
HANOVER 4-8 59

PICHON, Walter "Fats"
Singles: 78 rpm
DELUXE 5-10 47
RAYNAC 5-10 45
Singles: 7-inch
DECCA 8-12 56
EPs: 7-inch
DECCA 10-20 56
LPs: 10/12-inch
DECCA 20-35 56

PICK, Al
Singles: 7-inch
PINK 5-10 60

PICKARD, George
Singles: 7-inch
BAR-TONE 5-10 77

PICKENS
LPs: 10/12-inch
ARIOLA AMERICA 5-10 78

PICKENS, Lee, Group
LPs: 10/12-inch
CAPITOL 8-10 73

PICKENS, Slim
(Eddie Burns)
Singles: 78 rpm
HOLIDAY (202 "Papa's Boogie") . 50-100 48
Also see BURNS, Eddie

PICKENS, Slim / Walter Mitchell
LPs: 10/12-inch
NIGHTHAWK 5-8 82
Also see PICKENS, Slim
Also see MITCHELL, Walter

PICKETT, Bobby P&R/R&B/LP '62
(Bobby [Boris] Pickett & Crypt-Kickers; Featuring Bobby Paine)
Singles: 12-inch
EASY STREET 4-8 84
Singles: 7-inch
ANTHEM 3-5
ATMOSPHERE 5-10 65
CAPITOL 5-10 63-64
EASY STREET 3-5 84
GARPAX (1 "Monster Mash") 10-15 62
(With distribution picked up by London, this was quickly reissued as Garpax 44167.)
GARPAX (724 "I'm Down to My Last Heartbreak") 5-10
GARPAX (44000 series) 5-10 62-64
LONDON 3-5 70s
METROMEDIA (0089 "Me and My Mummy") 4-8 68
METROMEDIA (9989 "Me and My Mummy") 3-6 73
PARROT 4-8 70-73
RCA 5-10 64
WHITE WHALE 4-8 70
Picture Sleeves
GARPAX (44167 "Monster Mash") 10-20 62
GARPAX (44171 "Monster's Holiday") 10-20 62
GARPAX (44175 "Graduation Day") 10-20 63
LPs: 10/12-inch
GARPAX (GP-67001 "Monster Mash") 30-50 62
(Monaural.)
GARPAX (SGP-67001 "Monster Mash") 50-75 62
(Stereo.)
PARROT 10-20 73
Session: Leon Russell; David Gates; Larry Nectal; Jesse Sailes; Chuck Hamilton.
Also see CORDIALS
Also see FERRARA, Peter, & Bobby Pickett
Also see GATES, David
Also see PICKETT & PAYNE
Also see RUSSELL, Leon
Also see STOMPERS

PICKETT, Courtland
Singles: 7-inch
ELEKTRA 3-5 73
LPs: 10/12-inch
ELEKTRA 8-12 73

PICKETT, Dan
Singles: 78 rpm
GOTHAM (201 "Baby, Laughing Rag") 25-50 48
GOTHAM (242 "Baby, How Long") 25-50 48
GOTHAM (510 "Ride to a Funeral in a V-8") 25-50 48

GOTHAM (512 "Baby, Something's Gone Wrong") ... 25-50 48
GOTHAM (516 "Lemon Man") ... 25-50 48

PICKETT, Kari
Singles: 7-inch
PAULA ... 3-5 78

PICKETT, Lee
Singles: 7-inch
JOLT (331 "Fatty Patty") ... 150-250 58

PICKETT, Leonard
Singles: 7-inch
CUCA (1526 "Ballad of Sittin' Bull") 5-10 70s

PICKETT, Travis
(Travis Pickett & Punk-A-Billies)
Singles: 7-inch
SRO ... 3-5 79

PICKETT, Wilson *P&R/R&B '63*
(With Elwood Blues Revue)
Singles: 7-inch
ATLANTIC (2200 thru 2400 series) . 6-12 64-67
ATLANTIC (2500 thru 2900 series) ... 4-8 68-72
ATLANTIC (8000 series) ... 3-4 88
BIG TREE ... 3-5 78
CORREC-TONE (501 "Let Me Be Your Boy") ... 40-60 62
CUB (9113 "Let Me Be Your Boy") ... 25-35 62
DOUBLE-L ... 8-12 63
EMI AMERICA ... 3-5 79-81
MOTOWN ... 3-4 87
RCA ... 3-5 73-74
ROWE/AMI ... 5-10 66
("Play Me" Sales Stimulator promotional issue.)
VERVE ... 10-20 65
WICKED ... 4-8 75-76
Picture Sleeves
ATLANTIC ... 3-4 88
EPs: 7-inch
ATLANTIC (SD-8250 "Right On") ... 10-15 70
(Stereo. Juke box issue only. With paper envelope-sleeve.)
LPs: 10/12-inch
ALA ... 8-10
ATLANTIC (Except 8100 series) ... 10-15 69-73
ATLANTIC (8100 series) ... 12-25 65-68
BIG TREE ... 5-10 78
BROOKVILLE ... 8-12 77
DOUBLE-L (DL-8300 "It's Too Late") ... 25-35 63
(Monaural.)
DOUBLE-L (SDL-8300 "It's Too Late") ... 30-40 63
(Stereo.)
EMI AMERICA ... 5-10 79-81
RCA ... 8-12 73-77
WAND ... 10-15 68
WICKED ... 8-12 76
Also see FALCONS

PICKETT, Wilson / Sam & Dave
LPs: 10/12-inch
ATLANTIC (ST-136 "Excerpts from *Hey Jude*") ... 15-25 69
(Promotional issue for in-store use.)
Also see PICKETT, Wilson
Also see SAM & DAVE

PICKETT & PAYNE
Singles: 7-inch
METROMEDIA (0089 "It's Not the Same Without You") ... 5-8 68
METROMEDIA (9989 "It's Not the Same Without You") ... 4-6 73
Members: Bobby Pickett; Joan Payne.
Also see PICKETT, Bobby

PICKETTYWITCH *P&R '70*
Singles: 7-inch
JANUS ... 3-5 70
PYE ... 3-5 71
LPs: 10/12-inch
JANUS ... 8-12 70
Member: Polly Brown.
Also see BROWN, Polly

PICKLEDISH, Thorndike: see THORNDIKE PICKLEDISH

PICKS
Singles: 7-inch
COLUMBIA (41039 "Moondreams") ... 50-75 57
(White label, promotional issue. Copies credited to the **Picks** may exist only on promo copies.)
COLUMBIA (41096 "Moondreams") ... 25-50 58
(Previously issued as by the Norman Petty Trio.)
Members: John Pickering; Bill Pickering; Bob Lapham.
Also see HOLLY, Buddy
Also see PETTY, Norman, Trio
Also see TUCKER, Rick

PICKWICKS
Singles: 7-inch
W.B. ... 4-8 64

PICO PETE
Singles: 7-inch
GROOMS ... 5-10 62
JET (100 "Hot Dog") ... 75-100 57

PICONE, Vito
(Vito)
Singles: 7-inch
ADMIRAL ... 10-20 63
I.P.G. ... 5-10 63
Also see CORDEL, Pat
Also see ELEGANTS

PICTORIAN SKIFFULS
Singles: 7-inch
SKIFFUL (15587 "In Awhile") ... 15-25 65

PICTURE
Singles: 7-inch
NASCO (002 "Reach Out") ... 5-10 68
WRN (101 "Dance of Love") ... 5-10 69
Members: Mick Milewski; Jim Milewski; Phil Shields; Wayne Babich; Mike Beaster; Lon Omitt; Bob McKenna; Michael Hollihan; Wayne LaPene; Bill Aiken.
Also see RICOCHETTES

PICTURE PERFECT *R&B '87*
Singles: 7-inch
ATLANTIC ... 3-4 87

PIDGEON
Singles: 7-inch
DECCA ... 3-6 69
LPs: 10/12-inch
DECCA ... 10-15 69

PIECES OF a DREAM *R&B/LP '81*
Singles: 12-inch
ELEKTRA ... 4-6 84
Singles: 7-inch
ELEKTRA ... 3-5 81-84
MANHATTAN ... 3-4 88
LPs: 10/12-inch
ELEKTRA ... 5-10 81-84
MANHATTAN ... 5-8 86

PIECES OF EIGHT *P&R '67*
Singles: 7-inch
A&M ... 5-10 67-68
ACTION ... 5-10 60s
MALA ... 5-10 68
Also see SWINGIN' MEDALLIONS

PIED PIPERS *P&R '44*
(With Paul Weston's Orchestra)
Singles: 78 rpm
CAPITOL ... 5-10 44-55
RCA ... 4-8 48
Singles: 7-inch
CAPITOL ... 8-12 49-55
RCA ... 5-10 48
EPs: 7-inch
CAPITOL ... 10-20 50-55
LPs: 10/12-inch
CAPITOL (H-212 "Harvest Moon") ... 30-50 50
(10-inch LP.)
GOLDEN TONE ... 5-10
Members: Jo Stafford; Chuck Lowry; Hal Hopper; Clark Yocum; June Hutton; Sue Allen.
Also see MERCER, Johnny, Jo Stafford & Pied Pipers
Also see PERRY, King
Also see SINATRA, Frank, & Pied Pipers
Also see STAFFORD, Jo

PIED PIPERS
Singles: 7-inch
HAMLIN TOWN (2510 "Stay in My Life") ... 15-25 60s

PIER, Babe
Singles: 7-inch
CROSBY ... 4-8 62

PIERCE, Alan, & Tone Kings
Singles: 7-inch
CHALLENGE (59093 "Swamp Water") ... 8-12 60
TOM TOM (101 "Swamp Water") ... 15-25 60
(First issue.)

PIERCE, Bobby, Combo
Singles: 7-inch
STAR-LIGHT (1021 "I Cried Over You") ... 10-20 60

PIERCE, Don
Singles: 7-inch
MAJESTY (1041 "Spook-A-Delic") ... 8-12 70

PIERCE, Henry, & Five Notes
Singles: 7-inch
SPECIALTY (461 "Thrill Me Baby") ... 250-500 52
(Black vinyl.)
SPECIALTY (461 "Thrill Me Baby") ... 1000-2000 52
(Colored vinyl.)

PIERCE, Webb *C&W '52*
Singles: 78 rpm
DECCA ... 5-15 51-52
4 STAR ... 10-20 51-52
Singles: 7-inch
DECCA (28091 thru 29804) ... 10-20 52-56
DECCA (30045 "Teenage Boogie") ... 25-35 56
DECCA (31000 thru 33000 series) ... 5-10 59-73
DECCA (46000 series) ... 10-20 51-52
KING ... 5-10 60
MCA ... 3-5 73-74
PLANTATION ... 3-5 75-77
SOUNDWAVES ... 3-4 83
EPs: 7-inch
DECCA ... 10-20 53-65
LPs: 10/12-inch
BULLDOG ... 5-10
CASTLE ... 5-10
CORAL ... 5-10 73
DECCA (181 "Webb Pierce Story") ... 15-25 64
(Includes booklet.)
DECCA (DL-4015 "Webb with a Beat") ... 20-30 60
(Monaural.)
DECCA (DL7-4015 "Webb with a Beat") ... 20-40 60
(Stereo.)
DECCA (DL-4079 thru 4964) ... 10-25 60-67
DECCA (DL7-4079 thru 4964) ... 15-30 60-67
DECCA (5536 "Wondering Boy") ... 40-60 53
(10-inch LP.)
DECCA (8129 "Webb Pierce") ... 20-40 55
DECCA (8295 "Wondering Boy") ... 20-40 56
DECCA (8728 "Just Imagination") 20-40 57
DECCA (DL-8889 "Bound for the Kingdom") ... 20-40 59
(Monaural.)
DECCA (DL7-8889 "Bound for the Kingdom") ... 25-50 59
(Stereo.)
DECCA (DL-8899 "Webb!") ... 20-30 59
(Monaural.)
DECCA (DL7-8899 "Webb!") ... 25-35 59
(Stereo.)
DECCA (74000 & 75000 series) ... 8-12 68-73
KING (648 "The One and Only Webb Pierce") ... 20-40 59
KOALA ... 5-8 80
MCA ... 5-12 73-78
MUSIC MASTERS ... 5-10
PICCADILLY ... 5-8 80
PICKWICK/HILLTOP ... 10-15 65
PLANTATION ... 5-8 76-77
SEARS ... 8-12 60s
SESAC ... 30-50 59
SKYLITE ... 5-8 77
VOCALION ... 5-15 66-70
Also see NELSON, Willie, & Webb Pierce
Also see SOVINE, Red, & Webb Pierce
Also see WELLS, Kitty, & Webb Pierce

PIERCE, Webb / Patsy Cline / T. Texas Tyler
LPs: 10/12-inch
DESIGN (901 "Three of a Kind") ... 8-12 63
Also see CLINE, Patsy
Also see TYLER, T. Texas

PIERCE, Webb / Loretta Lynn
LPs: 10/12-inch
PHILCO/MCA ... 15-25 69
Also see LYNN, Loretta

PIERCE, Webb / Wynn Stewart
LPs: 10/12-inch
DESIGN ... 8-12 62
Also see STEWART, Wynn

PIERCE, Webb, & Mel Tillis *C&W '63*
Singles: 7-inch
DECCA ... 4-6 62
Also see TILLIS, Mel

PIERCE, Webb, & Wilburn Brothers *C&W '54*
Singles: 78 rpm
DECCA ... 5-10 54
Singles: 7-inch
DECCA ... 10-15 54
Also see PIERCE, Webb
Also see WILBURN BROTHERS

PIERCE ARROW
Singles: 7-inch
COLUMBIA ... 3-5 77-78
LPs: 10/12-inch
COLUMBIA ... 8-12 77-78
Members: David Batteaux; David Buskin.
Also see BATTEAUX

PIERCE ARROW / Lake / Crawler / Ram Jam
EPs: 7-inch
COLUMBIA/EPIC (1150 "For Students Only") ... 10-15 70s
Also see BACK STREET CRAWLER
Also see LAKE
Also see PIERCE ARROW
Also see RAM JAM

PIERMEN
Singles: 7-inch
JESSE (1000 "Piermen Stomp") ... 15-25 62

PIERRE & ANNE-LYSE
Singles: 7-inch
VEE JAY ... 4-8 65

PIERRE & SLOPERS
Singles: 7-inch
KAPP ... 4-8 64

PIERSOL, Jeannie
Singles: 7-inch
CADET CONCEPT ... 4-6 68

PIERSON, Con
(With the Ekhoes)
Singles: 7-inch
FORD ... 10-15 60s
LE MANS ... 10-20 60s

PIERSON LAKE
Singles: 7-inch
CENTURY ... 8-12 69
SOUND ... 3-5 73
Also see EMBERMEN FIVE

PIG IRON
Singles: 7-inch
COLUMBIA ... 3-5 70-71
LPs: 10/12-inch
COLUMBIA ... 10-15 70

PIG 'N WHISTLE BAND
Singles: 78 rpm
REGAL (3277 "Love Changing Blues") ... 50-100 50
Member: Willie McTell.
Also see McTELL, Blind Willie

PIGEONS
LPs: 10/12-inch
WAND (687 "While the World Was Eating Vanilla Fudge") ... 15-25 68
Members: Tim Bogert; Vince Martell; Mark Stein; Joe Brenan.
Also see VANILLA FUDGE

PIGLETS
Singles: 7-inch
BELL ... 3-5 71
UK ... 3-5 72
Member: Jonathan King.
Also see KING, Jonathan

PIGMEES
Singles: 7-inch
MERCURY ... 4-8 65

PIKE, Jim
(With the Damons)
Singles: 7-inch
CAPITOL ... 3-5 70
W.B. ... 5-10 59
Also see LETTERMEN

PIKE, Travis
(Travis Pike's Tea Party)
Singles: 7-inch
ALMA (201,680 "If I Didn't Love You Girl") ... 15-25 67

PIKES, Charles, & Scholars
Singles: 7-inch
GRA-KEM (101 "What Do You Do") .. 4-8
Session: Ron-Dels.
Also see RON-DELS

PILGRIM HARMONEERS
Singles: 78 rpm
J&S (1754 "Wooden Church") ... 10-20 56
Singles: 7-inch
J&S (1754 "Wooden Church") ... 25-35 56

PILGRIMAGE
Singles: 7-inch
MERCURY ... 8-12 66-67

PILITTERE, Terry
Singles: 7-inch
NU SOUND LTD. ... 4-8 67

PILLAR, Dick
Singles: 7-inch
STELJO ... 5-10 64

PILLOW, Ray *C&W '65*
Singles: 7-inch
ABC ... 4-6 68
ABC/DOT ... 3-5 74-75
CAPITOL ... 4-8 65-67
FIRST GENERATION ... 3-4 81
HILLTOP ... 3-5 78
MCA ... 3-5 79
MEGA ... 3-5 72-74
PLANTATION ... 3-6 69
LPs: 10/12-inch
ABC ... 8-12 69
ABC/DOT ... 6-12 74
ALLIGEANCE ... 5-8 84
AUDIOGRAPH ALIVE ... 5-8 82
CAPITOL ... 10-20 65-67
FIRST GENERATION ... 5-10 81
MEGA ... 6-10 72
PICKWICK/HILLTOP ... 8-10 70s
PLANTATION ... 5-10 70
Also see SHEPARD, Jean, & Ray Pillow

PILOT
Singles: 7-inch
RCA ... 4-6 72
LPs: 10/12-inch
RCA (4730 "Pilot") ... 10-15 72
RCA (4825 "Point of View") ... 15-20 73
Members: Bruce Stephens; Leigh Stephens; Martin Quittenton; Mickey Waller; Neville Whitehead.
Also see BLUE CHEER

PILOT *P&R/LP '75*
Singles: 7-inch
ARISTA ... 3-5 77
CAPITOL ... 3-5 77
EMI ... 3-5 74-76
LPs: 10/12-inch
ARISTA ... 8-10 77
EMI ... 8-10 74-76
Members: David Paton; Ian Bairnson; Stuart Tosh; William Lyall.
Also see LYALL, William
Also see PARSONS, Alan, Project
Also see 10CC

PILTDOWN FIVE
Singles: 7-inch
PARLIAMENT (102 "'32 Ford") ... 25-35 63

PILTDOWN MEN *P&R '60*
Singles: 7-inch
CAPITOL ... 8-12 60-62
Members: Lincoln Mayorga; Bob Bain; Earl Palmer; Jack Kel.
Also see BAIN, Bob

PINA, Johnny
Singles: 7-inch
DIMENSION ... 4-8 64

PINAFORES
Singles: 7-inch
CAPITOL ... 4-8 62

PINARD, Henry, & Three Ds
Singles: 7-inch
LOWELL ... 4-8
Also see THREE Ds

PINCH
Singles: 7-inch
SWAMI ... 3-4 83
EPs: 7-inch
SWAMI ... 5-8 82
Members: George Signore; Gary Shaffer; Jan Paine; Tom Mozine; Roger Vincent.

PINCKNEY, Al
Singles: 7-inch
PA-GO-GO ... 4-8 66

PINCKNEY, Bill: see PINKNEY, Bill

PINDER, Michael *LP '76*
LPs: 10/12-inch
THRESHOLD (18 "The Promise") ... 8-12 76
Also see MOODY BLUES

PINE, Diane
Singles: 7-inch
TAKE ... 4-8 64

PINE, Richard
Singles: 7-inch
CRYSTALETTE ... 4-8 62

PINEAPPLE HEARD
Singles: 7-inch
DIAMOND (231 "Valerie") ... 15-25 68

PINERA, Mike *P&R '80*
Singles: 7-inch
CAPRICORN ... 3-5 78
SPECTOR ... 3-5 80
SRI ... 3-5 79
LPs: 10/12-inch
SRI ... 5-10 79
Also see BLUES IMAGE
Also see CACTUS
Also see FANZ
Also see IRON BUTTERFLY
Also see RAMATAM
Also see THEE IMAGE

PINETOP SLIM
Singles: 78 rpm
COLONIAL (106 "Applejack Boogie") ... 50-75 49

PINETOPPERS *C&W '50*
(With the Beaver Valley Sweethearts)
Singles: 78 rpm
CORAL ... 4-6 50-54
DECCA ... 3-5 54-56
Singles: 7-inch
CORAL ... 8-12 50-54
DECCA ... 5-10 54-56
PEER SOUTHERN ... 4-6 67
EPs: 7-inch
CORAL ... 5-10 50-56
LPs: 10/12-inch
CORAL ... 10-20 50-56
Members: Roy Horton; Vaughn Horton. Ray Smith; Trudy Martin; Gloria Martin; John Bowers; Rusty Keefer.

PINETTE, Rick, & Oak *P&R '80*
Singles: 7-inch
MERCURY ... 3-5 80
LPs: 10/12-inch
MERCURY ... 5-10 80
Also see OAK

PING PONGS
Singles: 7-inch
CUB (9062 "Big Ben") ... 15-25 60
G-NOTE (100 "You & Only You") 75-125 61
MUSICANZA ... 5-10
U.A. (236 "Summer Reverie") ... 15-20 60

PINK CHAMPAGNE
Singles: 7-inch
CAPQUARIUS (5674 "He's Back [Ali] Gonna Do It Again") ... 5-10

PINK CLOUD
Singles: 7-inch
TOWER ... 5-10 67

PINK FAIRIES
LPs: 10/12-inch
POLYDOR ... 8-12 73

PINK FLOYD *LP '67*
Singles: 12-inch
COLUMBIA (1635 "Selections/Final Cut") ... 15-20 83
(Promotional issue only.)
COLUMBIA (2878 "On the Turning Away") ... 8-12 87
(Promotional issue only.)
Singles: 7-inch
CAPITOL ... 5-15 71-78
COLUMBIA (Black vinyl) ... 3-8 75-94
COLUMBIA (Colored vinyl) ... 5-10 87
(Promotional issue only.)
HARVEST ... 5-15 73-74
TOWER (333 "Arnold Layne") ... 35-55 67
TOWER (356 "See Emily Play") ... 35-55 67
TOWER (378 "The Gnome") ... 35-55 67
TOWER (426 "It Would be So Nice") ... 35-55 68
TOWER (440 "Let There Be More Light") ... 35-55 68
Picture Sleeves
TOWER ... 100-200 67
(We are not yet certain which of the Tower 45s came with sleeves.)
COLUMBIA ... 3-8 80-87
EPs: 7-inch
HARVEST (6746/7 "Pink Floyd, from *Dark Side of the Moon*) ... 75-125 73
(Promotional issue only. Issued with paper sleeve.)
LPs: 10/12-inch
CAPITOL (Except 11902) ... 5-8 78-83

CAPITOL (11902 "Dark Side of the Moon")...30-40 78
(Picture disc.)
COLUMBIA (Except Half-Speed Mastered, Quadraphonic, & Colored vinyl)...6-10 75-88
COLUMBIA (HC-43453 "Wish You Were Here")...25-50 80
(Half-speed mastered.)
COLUMBIA (PCQ-43453 "Wish You Were Here")...40-60 75
(Quadraphonic.)
COLUMBIA (HC-47680 "Collection of Great Dance Songs")...20-40 80s
(Half-speed mastered.)
COLUMBIA (H2C-46183 "The Wall")...150-200 80s
(Half-speed mastered.)
COLUMBIA (64200 "Division Bell")...8-12 94
(Colored vinyl.)
HARVEST (STBB-388 "Ummagumma")...25-35 69
HARVEST (SMAS-382 "Atom Heart Mother")...15-20 70
HARVEST (759 "Relics")...10-15 71
HARVEST (832 "Meddle")...10-15 71
HARVEST (11078 "Obscured By Clouds")...10-15 72
HARVEST (11163 "The Dark Side of the Moon")...8-12 73
HARVEST (11198 "More")...10-15 73
(Soundtrack.)
HARVEST (11000 series)...10-15 72-73
HARVEST (11257 "A Nice Pair")...10-15 73
HARVEST (16234 "Relics")...5-10 82
MFSL (017 "Dark Side of the Moon")...60-80 78
MFSL/UHQR (017 "Dark Side of the Moon")...100-150 78
(Boxed set.)
MFSL (190 "Meddle")...40-60 79
MFSL (202 "Atom Heart Mother")...20-25 94
(Half-speed mastered.)
TOWER (T-5093 "Piper at the Gates of Dawn")...100-125 67
(Monaural.)
TOWER (ST-5093 "Piper at the Gates of Dawn")...50-75 67
(Orange label. Stereo.)
TOWER (5093 "Piper at the Gates of Dawn")...40-50 67
(Striped label.)
TOWER (5131 "A Saucerful of Secrets")...50-100 68
(Orange label.)
TOWER (5131 "A Saucerful of Secrets")...50-100 68
(Striped label.)
TOWER (5169 "More")...25-40 69
(Soundtrack.)

Promotional LPs

CAPITOL (8116 "Tour '75")...30-50 75
COLUMBIA (1 "Animals")...75-100 77
(With inserts.)
COLUMBIA (1636 "Final Cut")...15-20 83
(Tracks not banded for airplay.)
COLUMBIA (1636 "Final Cut")...30-40 83
(Tracks are banded for easy airplay.)
COLUMBIA (33453 "Wish You Were Here")...50-75 75
COLUMBIA (34474 "Animals")...40-60 77
(Quadraphonic.)
COLUMBIA (36183 "The Wall")...50-75 79
Members: David Gilmour; Roger Waters; Rick Wright; Nick Mason; Syd Barrett.
Also see BARRETT, Syd
Also see GILMOUR, David
Also see MASON, Nick
Also see WATERS, Roger
Also see WRIGHT, Richard

PINK LADY *P&R '79*

Singles: 7-inch

ELEKTRA...3-5 79

Picture Sleeves

ELEKTRA...3-5 79

LPs: 10/12-inch

ELEKTRA...5-10 79
Members: Mie; Kei.

PINK SLIP DADDY

EPs: 7-inch

APEX (58 "LSD")...8-10 88
(Limited edition, 10-inch, colored vinyl EP.)

LPs: 10/12-inch

APEX...5-10
Members: Mick Cancer; Ben Vaughn; Palmyra Delran; Barb Dwyer.

PINK TOOLS

Singles: 7-inch

D-TOWN...3-4 85

PINKARD & BOWDEN *C&W '84*

Singles: 7-inch

W.B....3-4 84-89
Members: Sandy Pinkard; Richard Bowden.
Also see SHILOH

PINKERTON COLOURS

Singles: 7-inch

FORTE (304 "Strange Things")...8-12

PINKERTON, Willie, & Spacemen

Singles: 7-inch

MARKEY...5-10 62

PINKERTONS

Singles: 7-inch

W.B....4-8 68

PINKERTON'S ASSORTED COLOURS

Singles: 7-inch

PARROT (40001 "Will Ya")...10-20 66

PINKIES

Singles: 7-inch

PHILIPS...3-5 75

PINKINY CANANDY

LPs: 10/12-inch

UNI...10-15 69

PINKNEY, Bill

(With the Original Drifters; with Turks; with Originals; Bill Pinckney)

Singles: 7-inch

FONTANA...5-10 64
GAME (393 "Ol' Man River")...125-150 64
(Logo at left.)
GAME (394 "Ol' Man River")...75-125 64
(Logo on top.)
PHILLIPS INT'L (3524 "After the Hop")...20-30 58
VEEP...5-10 67
Also see DRIFTERS
Also see FLYERS
Also see ORIGINAL DRIFTERS

PINKOOSHINS

Singles: 7-inch

MERCURY...3-5 71

PINKY, Bill: see PINKNEY, Bill

PINKY LEE: see LEE, Pinky

PINNA, Johnny

Singles: 7-inch

DIMENSION...5-10 64

PINNOCHIO & PUPPETS

Singles: 7-inch

MERCURY (72659 "Fusion")...10-20 67

PIN-UPS

Singles: 7-inch

STORK...10-15 64

PINUPS

Singles: 7-inch

COLUMBIA...3-4 82

Picture Sleeves

COLUMBIA...3-5 82

LPs: 10/12-inch

COLUMBIA...5-10 82

PIPE DREAM

Singles: 7-inch

RCA...4-6 69

LPs: 10/12-inch

RCA...10-15 69

PIPEDREAM

LPs: 10/12-inch

ABC...5-10 78

PIPEDREAM *D&D '84*

Singles: 12-inch

ZOO YORK...4-6 84

PIPER

Singles: 7-inch

A&M...3-5 77

LPs: 10/12-inch

A&M (3194 "Piper")...5-8 82
A&M (3195 "Can't Wait")...5-8 82
A&M (4564 "Can't Wait")...10-15 76
A&M (4615 "Piper")...10-15 76
Members: Billy Squire.
Also see SQUIER, Billy

PIPER, Jimmie

Singles: 7-inch

ROYCE (0001 "Bonfire")...20-30 59
ROYCE (0008 "Wasted Life")...40-60 60

PIPER, Wardell *R&B '79*

Singles: 7-inch

MIDSONG INT'L...3-5 79-80
Also see FIRST CHOICE

PIPES

Singles: 78 rpm

DOOTONE...50-75 56

Singles: 7-inch

DOOTO (388 "Be Fair")...15-25 60s
DOOTO (401 "You Are an Angel")...15-25 60s
DOOTONE (388 "Be Fair")...200-300 56
DOOTONE (401 "You Are an Angel")...200-300 56

PIPES

Singles: 7-inch

JACY (001 "So Long")...500-750 58

PIPES

Singles: 7-inch

CARLTON (575 "Teamwork")...5-10 62

Picture Sleeves

CARLTON (575 "Teamwork")...10-20 62

PIPKIN, Chester

Singles: 7-inch

AZUZA (1003 "Slow Jerk")...10-20 60s

PIPKIN, Jessie

Singles: 7-inch

NOBLE...10-15

PIPKIN, Jimmy, & Gallahads

(Jim Pipkin)

Singles: 7-inch

CAMELOT (128 "I'm Just a Lonely Guy")...10-20 60s
(Since we've yet to learn exact year of release -- especially with regard to Gallahads Del-Fi and Donna issues -- price is subject to change.)
DONNA (1361 "This Letter to You")...50-75 60
Also see GALLAHADS

PIPKINS *P&R/LP '70*

Singles: 7-inch

CAPITOL (2819 "Gimme Dat Ding")...5-8 70
CAPITOL (2874 "Sugar 'n Spice")...5-8 70

LPs: 10/12-inch

CAPITOL (483 "Gimme Dat Ding") 10-15 70
Members: Tony Burrows; Roger Greenaway.
Also see AFRICA
Also see ALLEY CATS
Also see BURROWS, Tony
Also see SQUIRES
Also see UNTOUCHABLES
Also see WHITE PLAINS

PIPS: see KNIGHT, Gladys

PIRANHAS

LPs: 10/12-inch

CUSTOM FIDELITY...15-20

PIRATES

(Temptations)

Singles: 7-inch

MEL-O-DY (105 "Mind Over Matter")...50-75 62
Also see TEMPTATIONS

PIRATES

Singles: 7-inch

BACK STAGE (5001 "Naughty Girl")...25-35 65
(May have been promo only.)
DEAUX (1150 "Big Boy Pete")...10-20 60s

PIRATES

Singles: 7-inch

W.B....3-5 78

LPs: 10/12-inch

PACIFIC ARTS...5-10 80
W.B....5-10 78-79
Also see KIDD, Johnny, & Pirates

PIRATES OF THE MISSISSIPPI *C&W '90*

Singles: 7-inch

CAPITOL...3-4 90-91

LPs: 10/12-inch

CAPITOL...5-8 91
Members: Bill McCorvey; Rich Alves; Pat Severs; Dean Townson; Jimmy Lowe.

PIRO, Killer Joe

Singles: 7-inch

ATLANTIC (2279 "Killer Joe")...8-12 65

PIROUETTES

Singles: 7-inch

DIAMOND...10-15 64

PISANO & RUFF

Singles: 7-inch

A&M...3-5 70

LPs: 10/12-inch

A&M...8-12 70

PISCES

Singles: 7-inch

EPIC...3-6 69

PISCOPO, Joe *D&D/LP '85*

Singles: 12-inch

COLUMBIA...4-6 85

Singles: 7-inch

COLUMBIA...3-5 85

Picture Sleeves

COLUMBIA...3-5 85

LPs: 10/12-inch

COLUMBIA...5-10 85

PISTILLI, Gene

Singles: 7-inch

CAPITOL...3-5 69
Also see CASHMAN, PISTILLI & WEST

PISTILLI, Gene, & Manhattan Transfer

Singles: 7-inch

CAPITOL...3-6 70-71

LPs: 10/12-inch

CAPITOL (778 "Jukin'")...8-12 71
CAPITOL (11405 "Jukin'")...6-10 75
CAPITOL (16223 "Jukin'")...5-8 80
MUSIC for PLEASURE...5-10
Also see MANHATTAN TRANSFER

PISTILLI, Gene, & Michael Small

(With Sporting Club Band)

Singles: 7-inch

BUDDAH...4-6 71
Also see PISTILLI, Gene

PISTONS

LPs: 10/12-inch

TWIN/TONE...5-8 85

PIT MEN

Singles: 7-inch

PIT (402 "Surf Bored")...20-30 60s

PITCH PIKES

Singles: 78 rpm

MERCURY...15-20 57

Singles: 7-inch

MERCURY (71099 "Zing Zing")...15-20 57
(Maroon label.)
MERCURY (71099 "Zing Zing")...10-15 57
(Black label.)
MERCURY (71147 "Come Back to Me")...8-12 57
(Maroon label.)

PITCHE BLENDE

Singles: 7-inch

VALLEY (1102 "My World Has Stopped")...40-60 60s

PITLIK'S CONSTRUCTION CO.

Singles: 7-inch

MISTER ED (7502 "Your Nose Is Gonna Grow")...10-20 65
Members: Bob Moes;. Hohn Pitlik; Jim Roehling; Mike Vlahakis.

PITMAN, Donnell *R&B '86*

(With the Chi-Lites)

Singles: 7-inch

AFTER FIVE...3-4 86
Also see CHI-LITES

PITMEN

Singles: 7-inch

EARTH (401 "Susie Q")...15-20

PITNEY, Gene *P&R '61*

Singles: 7-inch

COLLECTABLES...3-4 80s
EPIC...3-5 77
ERIC...3-4 70s
FESTIVAL (25002 "Please Come Back Baby")...20-30 61
MUSICOR (1002 "Love My Life Away")...10-20 60
MUSICOR (1011 "Every Breath I Take")...20-30 61
MUSICOR (1009 thru 1093)...8-15 60-65
MUSICOR (1100 thru 1400 series)...4-8 65-72

Picture Sleeves

MUSICOR (1000 series)...10-20 60-65
MUSICOR (1100 thru 1400 series)...8-15 66-69

EPs: 7-inch

MUSICOR (500 "Looking Through the Eyes of Love")...15-20 65
(Issued without cover. Promotional issue only.)

LPs: 10/12-inch

COLUMBIA HOUSE...10-15 75
(Columbia Record Club issue.)
EVEREST...5-8 81
KOALA...5-10 79
MUSIC DISC...10-15 69
MUSICOR (1000 series)...8-10
MUSICOR (2001 thru 2008)...20-35 62-64
(Monaural.)
MUSICOR (2015 thru 2134)...15-25 64-67
(Monaural.)
MUSICOR (3001 thru 3008)...20-40 62-64
(Stereo.)
MUSICOR (3015 thru 3134)...15-25 64-67
(Stereo.)
MUSICOR (3148 thru 3193)...10-20 67-71
MUSICOR (3200 series)...8-12 71-73
MUSICOR (5025 "This Is Gene Pitney")...15-25 68
(Columbia Record Club issue.)
MUSICOR (5600 series)...8-10 78
PHOENIX 20...6-12
RHINO...5-8 85
SPRINGBOARD...5-10 76
TRIP...5-10 76
51 WEST...5-10 79
Also see BRYAN, Billy
Also see JAMIE & JANE
Also see JONES, George, & Gene Pitney
Also see ROE, Tommy / Bobby Rydell / Gene Pitney

PITNEY, Gene, & Melba Montgomery *C&W '66*

Singles: 7-inch

MUSICOR...4-8 65

LPs: 10/12-inch

BUCKBOARD...8-10 76
MUSICOR...15-20 66
Also see MONTGOMERY, Melba

PITNEY, Gene / Newcastle Trio

LPs: 10/12-inch

DESIGN...8-12 60s
Also see PITNEY, Gene

PITRELLO, Carne

(Lynn Pratt.)

Singles: 7-inch

HORNET (1004 "The Saints")...30-40
Also see PRATT, Lynn

PITS

EPs: 7-inch

BOMP...8-10 75

PITT, Eugene

(With the Jyve Fyve; with Teacho Wiltshire & Orchestra)

Singles: 7-inch

AVCO...3-5 71-72
BELTONE (2027 "She's My Girl")...10-15 62
VEEP (1229 "Why Why Why")...5-10 66
Also see JIVE FIVE
Also see WILTSHIRE, Teacho

PITT, Joel

Singles: 7-inch

INNER GLOW...4-8 63

PITTMAN, Al

Singles: 7-inch

CLOWN (3008 "Woman, You Talk to Much")...8-12 59
Also see INK SPOTS

PITTMAN, Barbara

Singles: 78 rpm

SUN (253 "I Need a Man")...25-50 56

Singles: 7-inch

PHILLIPS INT'L (3518 "Two Young Fools in Love")...20-40 58
PHILLIPS INT'L (3527 "Cold Cold Heart")...20-40 59
PHILLIPS INT'L (3553 "Handsome Man")...10-15 60
SUN (253 "I Need a Man")...50-100 56

PITTMAN, Jackie, & Fugitives

Singles: 7-inch

PIXIE (6355 "Do the Jerk")...20-30 65

PITTS, Beverly, & Cheaters

Singles: 7-inch

RAYNARD (10055 "Satisfaction")...4-8 66
Also see CHEATERS

PITTS, Clyde

Singles: 7-inch

CHALLENGE...4-8 62
COLUMBIA...4-8 66
EVEREST...4-8 62
4 STAR...5-10 61
MONUMENT...4-6 68
TOPPA...5-10 60

PITTS, Gloria Jean

Singles: 78 rpm

IMPERIAL...15-25 56

Singles: 7-inch

IMPERIAL (5406 "I Don't Stand No Quittin'")...30-40 56

PITTS, Jerry

Singles: 7-inch

CROC-A-GATOR (101 "Elvis Medley")...15-25 69
TOMBIGBEE...5-10 69

PITTS, Nolan

Singles: 7-inch

MINIT (603 "What Is Life")...8-12 59

PITTSBURGH PHIL

Singles: 7-inch

BOB CAT...4-6

PIXIES

Singles: 7-inch

BALBOA (007 "Santa's Too Fat for the Hula Hoop")...10-15 58

PIXIES

Singles: 7-inch

AMC (102 "Cry Like a Baby")...15-20 62
DON-DEE (102 "Cry Like a Baby")...10-15 63

PIXIES

Singles: 7-inch

AUTUMN...5-10 65

PIXIES *LP '89*

LPs: 10/12-inch

ELEKTRA...5-8 89-90

PIXIES THREE *P&R '63*

Singles: 7-inch

MERCURY...8-12 63-64

Picture Sleeves

MERCURY (72130 "Birthday Party")...10-20 63
MERCURY (72208 "Cold, Cold Winter")...15-20 63
MERCURY (72288 "It's Summertime")...10-20 64

LPs: 10/12-inch

MERCURY (20912 "Party")...50-75 64
(Monaural.)
MERCURY (60912 "Party")...75-100 64
(Stereo.)
Members: Debra Swisher; Midge Bollinger; Kaye McCool; Bonnie Long. Session: Leon Huff; Trade Martin; Vinnie Bell.
Also see MARTIN, Trade
Also see SWISHER, Debra

PIZANI, Frank *P&R '57*

Singles: 78 rpm

BALLY...5-10 57

Singles: 7-inch

AFTON (616 "It's No Fun")...15-25 59
BALLY...5-10 57
WARWICK...5-10 59
Also see HIGHLIGHTS
Also see PARTNERSHIP

PIZARRO, Eddie

Singles: 7-inch

LON-DEE...4-8 63

PLACE, Mary Kay *C&W/P&R '76*

("Mary Kay Place as Loretta Haggers")

Singles: 7-inch

COLUMBIA...3-5 76-78

LPs: 10/12-inch

COLUMBIA...5-10 76-77
Session: Willie Nelson.

PLACE, Mary Kay, & Willie Nelson *C&W '77*

Singles: 7-inch

COLUMBIA...3-5 77
Also see NELSON, Willie
Also see PLACE, Mary Kay

PLAGUE

Singles: 7-inch

CRUSADER...5-10 66

PLAGUE

Singles: 7-inch

BIRCHMONT ("Love and Obey")...20-30 67
(Canadian. Selection number not known.)
REO (8962 "The Face of Time")...20-30 67
(Canadian.)
REO (8981 "Love and Obey")...15-25 67
(Canadian.)

LP: 10/12-inch

BIRCHMONT...25-50 67
(Canadian.)

PLAGUE
Singles: 7-inch
WRIGHT (6863 "Mr. White Collar Man") 15-25 68

PLAGUE
Singles: 7-inch
EPIDEMIC (2164 "Go Away") 15-25 66

PLAGUES
Singles: 7-inch
FENTON (2070 "I've Been Through It Before") 40-60 66
QUARANTINED (2020 "Why Can't You Be True") 10-20 66
QUARANTINED (41369 "That'll Never Do") 10-20 66

PLAGUES
Singles: 7-inch
RON (1000 "To Wander") 10-15 66

PLAGUES
Singles: 7-inch
SMITTY'S (1293 "Somebody Help Me") 50-100 60s

PLAIDS
Singles: 78 rpm
DARL 10-15 56
Singles: 7-inch
DARL (1001 "Keeper of My Heart") 20-30 56
DARL (1003 "Halfway to Heaven") 20-30 56

PLAIDS
Singles: 7-inch
ERA (3002 "Around the Corner") 15-25 59
LIBERTY (55167 "Hungry for Your Love") 30-50 58
(White label. Promotional issue only.)
LIBERTY (55167 "Hungry for Your Love") 200-300 58
(Green label.)
NASCO (6011 "My Pretty Baby") 10-20 58

PLAIN BROWN WRAPPER
Singles: 7-inch
MONSTER (0002 "Junior Saw It Happen") 25-35 69
SPIRIT (0010 "Stretch Out Your Hand") 15-25 70s
THIS IS MUSIC (2114 "And Now You Dream") 30-40 60s
Member: Gary Story.
Also see ZOOKIE & POTENTATES

PLAIN JANE
Singles: 7-inch
HOBBIT 5-10 69
LPs: 10/12-inch
HOBBIT (5000 "Plain Jane") 15-25 69
Members: Barry Ray; Jerry Schoenfeld; David Schoenfeld; Don Gleicher.

PLAINSONG
LPs: 10/12-inch
ELEKTRA 8-12 72
Also see BONZO DOG BAND

PLAN 9
Singles: 7-inch
MIDNIGHT 3-5
VOXX 3-5 81
LPs: 10/12-inch
MIDNIGHT 5-10

PLANE
Singles: 12-inch
GERIM 4-6 83

PLANET P P&R/LP '83
(Planet P Project)
Singles: 7-inch
GEFFEN 3-4 83
MCA (52515 "What I See") 3-5 84
(Colored vinyl.)
Picture Sleeves
GEFFEN 3-4 83
LPs: 10/12-inch
GEFFEN 5-8 83
Member: Tony Carey.
Also see CAREY, Tony

PLANET PATROL R&B '82
Singles: 12-inch
TOMMY BOY 4-6 83-84
Singles: 7-inch
TOMMY BOY 3-4 82-84
LPs: 10/12-inch
TOMMY BOY 5-8 84

PLANET, Richard
Singles: 7-inch
CAPITOL 3-5 73

PLANETS
("Featuring Bill Steward")
Singles: 7-inch
ERA (1038 "Never Again") 30-60 57
ERA (1049 "Be Sure") 30-60 57
NU-CLEAR (7422 "I Need You So") 25-50
Member: Bill Steward.

PLANETS
Singles: 7-inch
ALJON (1244 "Once in a Lifetime") 150-250 62

PLANETS
Singles: 7-inch
ROULETTE 8-12 64

PLANETS
Singles: 7-inch
MOTOWN 3-5 80
LPs: 10/12-inch
MOTOWN 5-10 80

PLANETS
Singles: 7-inch
CLASS-E (101 "Rocket Ride") 8-12

PLANETTS
Singles: 7-inch
GOLDISC 10-20 63

PLANNED OBSOLESCENCE
Singles: 7-inch
JETSET (2 "Exit Sticky Icky") 25-50
JETSET (4296 "Still in Love with You Baby") 25-50

PLANOTONES with Prof. LaPiano / Delghts
Singles: 7-inch
A&M (2040 "Rock & Roll Is Here to Stay") 8-10 78
Also see VANCE, Kenny

PLANT, Robert P&R/LP '82
Singles: 12-inch
ESPARANZA 5-8 85
Singles: 7-inch
ATLANTIC 3-5 83
ESPARANZA 3-4 83-89
SWAN SONG 3-5 82
Picture Sleeves
ATLANTIC 3-5 83
ESPARANZA 3-4 83-88
SWAN SONG 3-5 82
LPs: 10/12-inch
ESPARANZA (Except 2244) 5-8 83-90
ESPARANZA (2244 "Non-Stop, Go!") 30-50 88
(Interview on 2 LPs. Promotional issue only.)
SWAN SONG 5-10 82
Also see BAND of JOY
Also see HONEYDRIPPERS
Also see LED ZEPPELIN
Also see LISTEN
Also see PAGE, Jimmy, & Robert Plant

PLANT LIFE
Singles: 7-inch
DATE 4-8 67

PLANT & SEE
Singles: 7-inch
WHITE WHALE (309 "Henrietta") 8-12 69
LPs: 10/12-inch
WHITE WHALE (7120 "Plant and See") 15-25 69

PLANTS
("With Orchestra")
Singles: 7-inch
J&S (248 "I Searched the Seven Seas") 500-750 56
J&S (1602 "Dear, I Swear") 750-1000 57
(Label has company address under logo.)
J&S (1602 "Dear, I Swear") 40-60 57
(No company address on label.)
J&S (1617 "From Me") 500-1000 58

PLASMATICS LP '81
(Featuring Wendy O. Williams)
LPs: 10/12-inch
CAPITOL 5-8 82
PVC 5-8 84
STIFF AMERICA 8-10 80-81
Also see BEAUVOIR, Jean
Also see WILLIAMS, Wendy O.

PLASTER CASTER BLUES BAND
Singles: 7-inch
BLUESTIME 4-6 69

PLASTER CASTERS
LPs: 10/12-inch
BLUESTIME 10-12
CAPITOL 5-10 82

PLASTIC BERTRAND: see BERTRAND, Plastic

PLASTIC BLUES BAND
Singles: 7-inch
BUSY B 4-6 68-70

PLASTIC COW LP '69
Singles: 7-inch
DOT 4-6 69
LPs: 10/12-inch
DOT 10-15 69

PLASTIC ICE CUBE
Singles: 7-inch
WARICK (6750 "Won't Turn Back") 25-35 67
Also see FORREST, Andrea
Also see MARCIA & LYNCHMEN

PLASTIC IDOLS
Singles: 7-inch
VISION (25 "Einstein Experience") 3-6 80
Picture Sleeves
VISION (25 "Einstein Experience") 3-6 80
Members: Trazz; Loner; Hobbs; Bailey.

PLASTIC LAUGHTER
Singles: 7-inch
HEAVY (705 "I Don't Live Today") 75-100 67

PLASTIC ONO BAND: see LENNON, John

PLASTIC PENNY
Singles: 7-inch
BELL 4-8 68
PAGE ONE 4-8 68

PLASTIC PEOPLE
Singles: 7-inch
KAPP 5-10 66-67

PLASTIC PEOPLE
Singles: 7-inch
RCA 3-5 71

PLATINUM BLONDE P&R '86
Singles: 7-inch
EPIC 3-4 86-87
LPs: 10/12-inch
EPIC 5-8 86-87
Members: Mark Holmes; Ken MacLean.

PLATINUM HOOK
Singles: 7-inch
MOTOWN 3-5 78-80
RCA 3-4 83
LPs: 10/12-inch
MOTOWN 5-10 78-80
RCA 5-8 83

PLATINUMS
Singles: 7-inch
J&M 3-5 79

PLATO
Singles: 7-inch
CAMEO 5-10 64
PARKWAY 4-8 65

PLATO & PHILOSOPHERS
Singles: 7-inch
FAIRYLAND (1002 "Thirteen O'Clock Flight to Psychedelphia") 300-400 66
G.A.R. (104 "I Don't Mind") 20-30 67
I.T. (2313 "I Don't Mind") 20-30 67
Members: Ken "Plato" Tebow; Barry Orschein; Mike Imbler; Ben White; Mark Valentine.

PLATT, Eddie, & Orchestra P&R/R&B '58
Singles: 78 rpm
ABC-PAR 5-10 58
Singles: 7-inch
ABC-PAR 10-20 58
GONE 10-20 58
Also see FOUR WINDS

PLATTERMEN
Singles: 7-inch
GOAL (1 "Your Maw Said You Cried") 10-20

PLATTERS P&R/R&B '55
(Featuring Tony Williams)
Singles: 78 rpm
FEDERAL (12153 "Give Thanks") 50-75 53
FEDERAL (12164 "I Need You All the Time") 50-75 54
FEDERAL (12181 "Roses of Picardy") 30-50 54
FEDERAL (12188 thru 12204) 30-50 54-55
FEDERAL (12244 "Only You") 30-75 55
FEDERAL (12250 "Tell the World") 20-40 55
FEDERAL (12271 "I Need You All the Time") 20-40 56
MERCURY (Except 71289) 10-25 55-58
MERCURY (71289 "Twilight Time") 50-100 58
Singles: 7-inch
ANTLER 3-5 82
COLLECTABLES 3-4
FEDERAL (12153 "Give Thanks") 150-250 53
FEDERAL (12164 "I Need You All the Time") 200-300 54
FEDERAL (12181 "Roses of Picardy") 150-250 54
FEDERAL (12188 "Tell The World") 150-250 54
FEDERAL (12198 "Voo-Vee-Ah-Bee") 150-250 54
FEDERAL (12204 "Take Me Back") 150-250 54
FEDERAL (12244 "Only You") 200-300 55
FEDERAL (12250 "Tell The World") 100-150 55
FEDERAL (12271 "I Need You All the Time") 50-100 56
GUSTO 3-4 80s
MERCURY (10001 "Smoke Gets in Your Eyes") 25-50 58
(Stereo.)
MERCURY (10018 "Where") 25-50 59
(Stereo.)
MERCURY (10038 "Red Sails in the Sunset") 25-50 60
(Stereo.)
MERCURY (70633 "Only You") 25-50 55
(Pink label.)
MERCURY (70633 "Only You") 15-25 55
(Black label.)
MERCURY (70753 "The Great Pretender") 20-30 55
(Maroon label.)
MERCURY (70753 "The Great Pretender") 10-20 56
(Black label.)
MERCURY (70819 "The Magic Touch") 20-30 56
(Maroon label.)
MERCURY (70819 "The Magic Touch") 10-20 56
(Black label.)
MERCURY (70893 "My Prayer") 20-30 56
(Maroon label.)
MERCURY (70893 "My Prayer") 10-20 56
(Black label.)
MERCURY (70948 "You'll Never Never Know") 15-25 56
MERCURY (71011 "One in a Million") 20-30 56
(Maroon label.)
MERCURY (71011 "One in a Million") 10-20 56
(Black label.)
MERCURY (71032 "I'm Sorry") 20-30 56
(Maroon label.)
MERCURY (71032 "I'm Sorry") 10-20 56
(Black label.)
MERCURY (71093 "My Dream") 20-30 56
(Maroon label.)
MERCURY (71093 "My Dream") 10-20 56
(Black label.)
MERCURY (71184 "Only Because") 10-20 57
MERCURY (71246 "Helpless") 10-20 57
MERCURY (71289 "Twilight Time") 10-20 58
MERCURY (71320 "You're Making a Mistake") 10-20 58
MERCURY (71353 "I Wish") 10-20 58
MERCURY (71383 "Smoke Gets in Your Eyes") 10-20 58
MERCURY (71427 "Enchanted") 10-20 59
MERCURY (71467 "Remember When") 10-20 59
MERCURY (71502 "Wish It Were Me") 10-20 59
MERCURY (71538 "My Secret") 10-20 59
MERCURY (71563 "Harbor Lights") 10-20 60
MERCURY (71624 "Ebb Tide") 10-15 60
MERCURY (71656 "Red Sails in the Sunset") 10-15 60
MERCURY (71697 "To Each His Own") 10-15 60
MERCURY (71749 "If I Didn't Care") 10-15 60
MERCURY (71791 "Trees") 8-12 61
MERCURY (71847 "I'll Never Smile Again") 8-12 61
MERCURY (71904 "You'll Never Know") 8-12 61
MERCURY (71921 thru 72359) 8-15 62-64
MERCURY (30,000 series) 5-8 60s
(Celebrity Series reissues.)
MUSICOR 5-10 66-71
OWL 3-5 73
POWER (7012 "Only You") 5-10 60s
Picture Sleeves
MERCURY 15-25 60-64
POWER (7012 "Only You") 5-10 60s
EPs: 7-inch
FEDERAL (378 The Platters Sing for Only You") 300-400 56
KING (378 "The Platters") 100-200 56
KING (651 "The Platters") 100-200 56
(All copies of Federal 651 are bootlegs. Originals are only on King.)
MERCURY 25-75 56-61
LPs: 10/12-inch
CANDLELITE ("The Platters") 30-40 70s
(Boxed, four-disc set.)
EVEREST 5-10 81
FEDERAL (549 "The Platters") 500-1000 57
51 WEST 5-10 80s
GUEST STAR 10-15 60s
KING (651 "The Platters") 200-400 59
KING (5002 "10 Hits") 8-12 59
MERCURY (4000 series) 5-8 82
MERCURY (8000 series) 5-8
MERCURY (20146 "The Platters") 50-100 56
MERCURY (20216 "The Platters, Vol. 2") 50-100 56
MERCURY (20298 "The Flying Platters") 50-75 57
MERCURY (20410 thru 20983) 15-30 59-65
(Monaural.)
MERCURY (60043 thru 60983) 20-50 59-65
(Stereo.)
MUSIC DISC 10-12 69
MUSICO (1002 "Only You") 8-10 70
MUSICOR (2000 & 3000 series) 15-20 66-69
MUSICOR (4600 series) 10-15 77
PHOENIX 20 (615 "The Platters") 5-8 80s
PICKWICK 8-10 70s
RHINO 8-10 80s
SPRINGBOARD 8-10 76
TRIP 8-10 76
WING 12-25 62-67
Members: Tony Williams; David Lynch; Herb Reed; Linda Hayes; Sandra Dawn; Nate Nelson; Sonny Turner; Zola Taylor; Paul Robi; Alex Hodge.
Also see GUNTER, Cornel
Also see HAYES, Linda, & Platters
Also see LITTLE ANTHONY & IMPERIALS / Platters
Also see McNEELY, Big Jay
Also see METROTONES
Also see NELSON, Nate
Also see PLATTERS '65
Also see RAM, Buck
Also see TAYLOR, Zola
Also see TURNER, Sonny, & Sound Ltd.
Also see WILLIAMS, Tony

PLATTERS / Exotic Guitars
LPs: 10/12-inch
GUEST STAR 10-15 64
Also see EXOTIC GUITARS

PLATTERS / Inez & Charlie Foxx / Jive Five / Tommy Hunt
LPs: 10/12-inch
MUSICOR 10-20 67
Also see FOXX, Inez
Also see HUNT, Tommy
Also see JIVE FIVE

PLATTERS '65
Singles: 7-inch
ENTREE 4-8 65
Also see PLATTERS

PLATYPUS
Singles: 12-inch
CASABLANCA 4-8 79-80
Singles: 7-inch
CASABLANCA 3-5 79-80
LPs: 10/12-inch
CASABLANCA 5-10 79-80

PLAYBOY PETE
Singles: 7-inch
ZANDAN 4-8 63

PLAYBOYS
Singles: 78 rpm
CAT 15-25 54-55
Singles: 7-inch
CAT (108 "Tell Me") 25-35 54
CAT (115 "Good Golly, Miss Molly") 25-35 55
Members: Charlie White.
Also see RAVENS

PLAYBOYS
Singles: 78 rpm
TETRA (4447 "One Question") 50-100 57
Singles: 7-inch
TETRA (4447 "One Question") 75-100 57

PLAYBOYS
Singles: 78 rpm
MERCURY 10-15 57
Singles: 7-inch
MERCURY 10-15 57

PLAYBOYS P&R '58
Singles: 7-inch
CAMEO (142 "Over the Weekend") 15-25 58
MARTINIQUE (101 "Over the Weekend") 25-50 58
MARTINIQUE (400 "Please Forgive Me") 25-50 59

PLAYBOYS
Singles: 7-inch
SOUVENIR (1001 "Believe It Or Not") 50-100 59

PLAYBOYS
Singles: 7-inch
CRYSTALETTE (720 "Whatizit") 10-15 59

PLAYBOYS
Singles: 7-inch
ABC-PAR (10070 "Memories") 10-20 59
DOLTON (8 "Icy Fingers") 10-15 59
IMPERIAL (5586 "Crazy Daisy") 10-20 59
RIK (572 "Jungle Fever") 10-20 59

PLAYBOYS
(Playboys / Cousins)
Singles: 7-inch
CHANCELLOR 10-15 61-62

PLAYBOYS
Singles: 7-inch
COTTON (1008 "Girl of My Dreams") 15-25 62

PLAYBOYS
Singles: 7-inch
HEARTBEAT (60 "Harlem Nocturne") 10-15 63

PLAYBOYS
Singles: 7-inch
CUCA (6371 "Look at Me") 15-25 63
Members: Jim Peterman; Rick Kludt; Rick Bruhn; Paul Zoerb; Bill Patterson; Wayne Champion; Kevin Peterman; Nels Christiansen; Steve Sperry; Mike Warner.

PLAYBOYS
Singles: 7-inch
LEGATO (101 "Mope De Mope") 10-20 63

PLAYBOYS
Singles: 7-inch
ACE 4-8 64

PLAYBOYS
Singles: 7-inch
CATALINA 10-20 64
JEWEL 5-10 64
TITAN 5-10 65

PLAYBOYS
Singles: 7-inch
EVE ("Motorpsycho") 10-20
(Selection number not known.)

PLAYBOYS OF EDINBURG
Singles: 7-inch
CAPITOL 8-12 70
COLUMBIA 10-15 66-67
1-2-3 4-8 69
PHARAOH (141 "Wish You Had a Heart") 15-25 65
PHARAOH (142 "Look at Me Girl") 15-25 66
UNI 5-10 71
Members: Michael Williams; Jim Williams; Val Curl; Jerry McCord.

PLAYER P&R/R&B/LP '77
Singles: 7-inch
CASABLANCA 3-5 80
RCA 3-5 82
RSO 3-5 77-78

LPs: 10/12-inch
CASABLANCA ... 5-10 80
RCA ... 5-10 81
RSO ... 5-10 77-78
Member: J.C. Crowley.
Also see CROWLEY, J.C.
Also see BANDANA

PLAYERS
Singles: 7-inch
TARX (1007 "You Need a Love") ... 100-200 63

PLAYERS
Singles: 7-inch
ARTEMIS ... 10-15 60s
COLUMBIA (44239 "Giving Up Your Love") ... 10-20 67
(Also issued as by Twentie Grans.)
Member: Herman Griffin.
Also see GRIFFIN, Herman
Also see TWENTIE GRANS

PLAYERS R&B '66
Singles: 7-inch
MINIT ... 4-8 66-67
LPs: 10/12-inch
MINIT ... 10-20 68

PLAYERS ASSOCIATION R&B '80
Singles: 12-inch
VANGUARD ... 4-8 79-80
Singles: 7-inch
VANGUARD ... 3-5 77-80
LPs: 10/12-inch
VANGUARD ... 5-10 77-80

PLAYFUL PUPS
Singles: 7-inch
INTREPID ... 4-6 69

PLAYGIRLS
Singles: 7-inch
RCA (7546 "Hey Sport") ... 10-20 59
RCA (7719 "Gee But I'm Lonesome") ... 10-20 60
Also see BLOSSOMS

PLAYGROUND
Singles: 7-inch
PEE GEE ... 5-8

PLAYGUE
Singles: 7-inch
REBIC (19653 "I Gotta Be Goin' ") ... 40-50 65

PLAYHOUSE
Singles: 7-inch
STEED ... 4-6 69

PLAYMAKERS
Singles: 7-inch
TAP (501 "Bubble Gum") ... 100-200 61

PLAYMATES
Singles: 78 rpm
SAVOY ... 8-12 57
Singles: 7-inch
SAVOY ... 8-12 57
Also see THREE PLAYMATES

PLAYMATES P&R '58
Singles: 78 rpm
ROULETTE ... 15-25 57-58
Singles: 7-inch
ABC-PAR ... 5-10 63-64
BELL ... 3-5 71
COLPIX ... 5-10 64-65
CONGRESS ... 5-10 65
ROULETTE ... 10-25 57-63
LPs: 10/12-inch
FORUM ... 15-25 60
ROULETTE ... 20-40 57-61
Members: Donny Conn; Morey Carr; Chic Hetti.

PLAYTHINGS
Singles: 7-inch
LIBERTY ... 5-10 58

PLEASANT, Tommy
Singles: 7-inch
TRAVEL ... 4-8

PLEASANTRIES
Singles: 7-inch
RADIO SUN ... 3-4 94
Picture Sleeves
RADIO SUN ... 3-4 94
Members: Jim Fitzgerald; Andrew Fitzgerald; Chris Gray; John Greene; Greg Clarke; Frank Scott.

PLEASE, Bobby
Singles: 7-inch
ERA ... 5-10 61
JAMIE ... 8-12 59

PLEASE BE MINE (Title): see RHYTHM JESTERS

PLEASURE
(Featuring Billy Elder)
Singles: 7-inch
REVUE ... 4-8 69
TOWER ... 4-8 69

PLEASURE R&B/LP '76
Singles: 12-inch
FANTASY ... 4-8 76-80
Singles: 7-inch
FANTASY ... 3-5 76-80
RCA ... 3-4 82-83
LPs: 10/12-inch
FANTASY ... 5-10 76-80
RCA ... 5-8 82
Members: Sherman Davis; Nate McClain; Marlon McClain; Michael Hepburn; Donald Hepburn; Bruce Carter; Bruce Smith; Dennis Springer.

PLEASURE, King: see KING PLEASURE

PLEASURE & BEAST D&D '84
Singles: 12-inch
AIRWAVE ... 4-6 84

PLEASURE FAIR
Singles: 7-inch
UNI ... 4-8 67-68
LPs: 10/12-inch
UNI (3009 "Pleasure Fair") ... 15-20 67
Members: Robb Royer; Michele Cochrane; Tim Hallinan; Steve Cohn.
Also see BREAD

PLEASURE SEEKERS
Singles: 7-inch
CAPITOL (2050 "If You Climb the Tiger's Back") ... 10-15 67
HIDEOUT (1006 "Never Thought You'd Leave Me") ... 50-75 66
MERCURY (72800 "Good Kind of Hurt") ... 10-20 68
Also see QUATRO, Suzi

PLEASURES
Singles: 7-inch
CATCH (100 "Music City") ... 20-30 63
RSVP ... 10-20 64-65

PLEBIAN REBELLION
Singles: 7-inch
COLUMBIA (44231 "Good Sweet Love") ... 15-25 67

PLEBS
Singles: 7-inch
MGM ... 4-8 65

PLEDGES
Singles: 78 rpm
REV (3517 "Betty Jean") ... 10-20 57
Singles: 7-inch
REV (3517 "Betty Jean") ... 15-25 57
Members: Gary Paxton; Clyde Batton.
Also see SKIP & FLIP

PLEDGES
Singles: 7-inch
HAMILTON ... 8-12 59

PLEIS, Jack, & His Orchestra P&R '56
Singles: 7-inch
ATCO ... 4-6 65
COLUMBIA ... 4-6 61
DECCA ... 5-10 53-60
LONDON ... 5-10 50-51
RANWOOD ... 3-5 76
EPs: 7-inch
DECCA ... 5-10 55-57
LPs: 10/12-inch
CAMEO ... 10-20 63
COLUMBIA ... 10-15 61
DECCA ... 10-20 55-57
RANWOOD ... 5-8 76
Also see CORNELL, Don, & Teresa Brewer
Also see CARLE, Bobby, & Blendaires

PLEIS, Jack, & Owen Bradley
EPs: 7-inch
DECCA (2593 "Bandstand Hop") ... 10-15 58
LPs: 10/12-inch
DECCA (8724 "Bandstand Hop") ... 20-30 58
Also see BRADLEY, Owen
Also see PLEIS, Jack, & His Orchestra

PLIMSOULS LP '81
Singles: 12-inch
BEAT (1001 "Zero Hour") ... 15-25 80
BOMP ... 5-8 80
Singles: 7-inch
BOMP ... 3-5 80
GEFFEN ... 3-4 83
SHAKY CITY ... 3-5
Picture Sleeves
BOMP ... 3-5 80
GEFFEN ... 3-4 83
SHAKY CITY ... 3-5
LPs: 10/12-inch
GEFFEN ... 5-8 83
PLANET ... 5-10 81

PLOWMAN, Linda C&W '71
Singles: 7-inch
COLUMBIA ... 3-5 73
JANUS ... 3-5 71

PLUGZ
Singles: 7-inch
FATIMA ... 3-5 80
PLUG ... 4-6 79
LPs: 10/12-inch
PLUG ... 15-25 79
Members: Tito Larriva; Chalo Quintana.
Also see CRUZADOS

PLUM BEACH INCIDENT
Singles: 7-inch
ORPHEUM ... 4-8 68

PLUM NELLY
LPs: 10/12-inch
CAPITOL (692 "Deceptive Lines") ... 15-25 71

PLUM RUN
Singles: 7-inch
AVCO EMBASSY ... 4-6 69

PLUMMER, Dave, & Plungers
Singles: 7-inch
MAYBROOK (320 "Surfin' Monster") ... 25-35 60s

PLUNDERERS
Singles: 7-inch
ROULETTE ... 4-8 66

PLUNKERS
Singles: 7-inch
HBR (479 "Night Time Love") ... 5-10 66

PLURALS
(Plural's)
Singles: 7-inch
BERGEN (186 "Donna My Dear") ... 15-25 58
WANGER (186 "Donna My Dear") ... 50-75 58
(Has "Wanger" in sans serif typeface, and songwriters names in parenthesis.)
WANGER (186 "Donna My Dear") ... 25-50 58
(Has "Wanger" in serif typeface. Songwriters names are not in parenthesis.)
WANGER (188 "Goodnight") ... 25-50 58

PLUS
LPs: 10/12-inch
PROBE ... 10-15 69

PLUSH R&B '82
Singles: 7-inch
RCA ... 3-5 82
LPs: 10/12-inch
RCA ... 5-10 82

PLUSHTONES
Singles: 7-inch
PLUSH ... 10-20 60

PLYMOUTH ROCK
Singles: 7-inch
PLYMOUTH ROCK (206321 "Comin' Down") ... 20-30
TIGER ("Comin' Down") ... 25-35
(Selection number not known.)

PLYMOUTH ROCKERS
Singles: 7-inch
VALIANT (729 "Roll Over Stephen Foster") ... 10-15 65
VALIANT (737 "Don't Say Why") ... 10-15 66
W.B. (5475 "Around & Around") ... 5-10 64

PLYNTH
Singles: 7-inch
CASTLE (111 "Beyond the Clouds") ... 10-20

P-NUT BUTTER
Singles: 7-inch
FAT ORANGE ... 5-10
MASCOT ... 4-8 67
P-NUT ... 5-10 66
TOWER ... 5-10 66
Picture Sleeves
FAT ORANGE ... 10-15
P-NUT ... 15-20 66

P-NUT GALLERY P&R '71
(Circa '58 & Peanut Gallery)
Singles: 7-inch
BUDDAH ... 3-5 71

PO' BOYS
Singles: 7-inch
DECCA (32281 "White Rabbit") ... 4-8 68
Also see ANDERSON, Bill

POACHER C&W '78
Singles: 7-inch
REPUBLIC ... 3-5 78
Member: Tim Flaherty.

POCKETS R&B/LP '77
Singles: 7-inch
ARC ... 4-6 79
COLUMBIA ... 4-6 77-78
LPs: 10/12-inch
ARC ... 5-10 79
COLUMBIA ... 5-10 77-78
Members: Al McKinney; Larry Jacobs; Gary Grainger; Kevin Barnes; Charles Williams; George Gray; Irving Madison; Jacob Sheffer.

POCO LP '69
Singles: 7-inch
ABC ... 3-5 75-79
ATLANTIC ... 3-4 82-84
EPIC ... 3-6 69-75
MCA ... 3-5 79-82
RCA ... 3-4 89
Picture Sleeves
EPIC ... 3-6 70-72
MCA ... 3-5 80
RCA ... 3-4 89
LPs: 10/12-inch
ABC ... 8-12 75-78
ATLANTIC ... 5-8 82-84
EPIC (26460 "Pickin' Up the Pieces") ... 10-15 69
EPIC (26522 "Poco") ... 10-15 70
EPIC (30209 "Deliverin' ") ... 8-12 71
EPIC (EQ-30209 "Deliverin' ") ... 15-25 71
(Quadrophonic.)
EPIC (30753 "From the Inside") ... 5-10 71
EPIC (31601 "A Good Feelin' to Know") ... 5-10 72
EPIC (32354 "Crazy Eyes") ... 5-10 73
EPIC (EQ-32354 "Crazy Eyes") ... 10-15 73
(Quadrophonic.)
EPIC (32895 "Seven") ... 5-10 74
EPIC (33192 "Cantamos") ... 5-10 74
(Quadrophonic.)
EPIC (PEQ-33192 "Cantamos") ... 10-15 74
EPIC (33537 thru 36210) ... 5-10 75-81
MCA ... 5-10 80-82
MFSL (020 "Legend") ... 25-50 78
RCA ... 5-8 89
Members: Richie Furay; Jim Messina; Rusty Young; Timothy Schmit; Paul Cotton.
Also see BOENZEE CRYQUE
Also see BUFFALO SPRINGFIELD
Also see COTTON, Paul
Also see EAGLES
Also see FURRAY, Richie
Also see GLAD
Also see ILLINOIS SPEED PRESS
Also see MEISNER, Randy
Also see MESSINA, Jim
Also see SCHMIT, Timothy B.

PODIPTO
Singles: 7-inch
GRT ... 4-6 70
LPs: 10/12-inch
GRT ... 8-12 71
MINNESOTA GREEN ... 10-20
Member: Jack Sunrud.

PODOLOR, Dickie
(Richard Podolor)
Singles: 7-inch
RADIO (112 "Samoa") ... 15-25 59
RADIO (116 "She's My Baby") ... 15-25 59
Also see ALLEN, Richie
Also see REVELLS
Also see SURFARIS

POE
Singles: 7-inch
UNI ... 3-5 71
LPs: 10/12-inch
UNI ... 8-12 71

POE, Bobby
Singles: 7-inch
WHITE ROCK (1112 "Rock and Roll Boogie") ... 100-200 58

POET
(The Poet)
Singles: 7-inch
PULL (305 "Vowels of Love") ... 200-250 58
(First issued as by the Poets.)
Also see POETS

POET & ONE MAN BAND
LPs: 10/12-inch
PARAMOUNT ... 10-15 69

POETS
Singles: 7-inch
SHADE (1001 "Never Let You Go") ... 1000-2000 60

POETS
Singles: 7-inch
FLASH (129 "Vowels of Love") ... 150-250 58
(Black label.)
FLASH (129 "Vowels of Love") ... 50-75 58
(Maroon label. Reissued as by the Poet.)
Also see POET

POETS
Singles: 7-inch
IMPERIAL (5664 "I'm in Love") ... 10-15 60
SPOT (107 "I'm in Love") ... 20-30 60
(First issue.)

POETS
(James Brown & His Band)
Singles: 7-inch
TRY ME (28006 "Devil's Den") ... 10-15 63
Also see BROWN, James

POETS P&R/R&B '66
Singles: 7-inch
CHAIRMAN (4408 "Number One") ... 8-12 63
J-2 (1302 "Wrapped Around Your Finger") ... 75-125
SYMBOL (214 "She Blew a Good Thing") ... 8-12 66
SYMBOL (216 "So Young") ... 8-12 66
VEEP (1286 "The Hustler") ... 10-20 68

POETS
Singles: 7-inch
DYNO VOX ... 5-10 64

POETS
Singles: 7-inch
RED BIRD (046 "Merry Christmas Baby") ... 5-10 65
Members: Don McPherson; Luther Simmons; Tony Sylvester.
Also see MAIN INGREDIENT

POETS
Singles: 7-inch
AMG ... 3-5 75

POGUES LP '88
LPs: 10/12-inch
ISLAND ... 5-8 88-90

POHL, Barry, & Concessions
Singles: 7-inch
SIRE ... 4-8 68

POINDEXTER, Buster, & His Banshees of Blue P&R '87
Singles: 7-inch
RCA ... 3-4 87
Picture Sleeves
RCA ... 3-4 87
LPs: 10/12-inch
RCA ... 5-8 87
Members: David Johansen.
Also see JOHANSEN, David

POINDEXTER, Doug, & Starlite Wranglers
Singles: 78 rpm
SUN ... 200-250 54
Singles: 7-inch
SUN (202 "Now She Cares No More for Me") ... 350-400 54
Members: Doug Poindexter; Bill Black; Scotty Moore.
Also see BLACK, Bill
Also see MOORE, Scotty

POINDEXTER BROTHERS
Singles: 7-inch
VERVE ... 10-20 66

POINT BLANK LP '76
Singles: 7-inch
ARISTA ... 3-6 76-77
MCA ... 3-5 79-81
LPs: 10/12-inch
ARISTA ... 5-10 76-77
MCA ... 5-8 79-82
Members: Bubba Keith; John O'Daniel.

POINTER, Anita R&B '87
Singles: 7-inch
RCA ... 3-4 87-88
Also see CONLEY, Earl Thomas, & Anita Pointer
Also see POINTER SISTERS

POINTER, Bonnie P&R/R&B/LP '78
Singles: 12-inch
MOTOWN ... 4-8 78-81
PRIVATE I ... 4-6 84-85
Singles: 7-inch
MOTOWN (Except 1451) ... 3-5 78-81
MOTOWN (1451 "Free Me from My Freedom") ... 3-4 78
(Black vinyl.)
MOTOWN (1451 "Free Me from My Freedom") ... 4-8 78
(Colored vinyl.)
PRIVATE I ... 3-4 84-85
Picture Sleeves
MOTOWN (1451 "Free Me from My Freedom") ... 3-5 78
LPs: 10/12-inch
MOTOWN ... 5-10 78-79
PRIVATE I ... 5-8 84
Also see POINTER SISTERS

POINTER, June R&B '83
Singles: 12-inch
PLANET ... 4-6 83-84
Singles: 7-inch
PLANET ... 3-4 83-84
LPs: 10/12-inch
PLANET ... 5-8 83

POINTER, Noel LP '77
Singles: 12-inch
U.A. ... 4-6 77
Singles: 7-inch
BLUE NOTE ... 3-5 77
LIBERTY ... 3-5 81
U.A. ... 3-5 78-80
LPs: 10/12-inch
BLUE NOTE ... 5-10 77
LIBERTY ... 5-8 81
U.A. ... 5-8 78-80

POINTER SISTERS P&R/R&B/LP '73
Singles: 12-inch
PLANET ... 4-8 78-85
RCA ... 4-6 85-86
Singles: 7-inch
ABC ... 3-6 75-78
ATLANTIC (2845 "Don't Try to Take the Fifth") ... 10-20 72
ATLANTIC (2893 "Destination, No More Heartaches") ... 10-20 72
BLUE THUMB ... 3-6 73-78
MCA ... 3-4 87
PLANET ... 3-5 78-85
RCA ... 3-4 85-88
Picture Sleeves
MCA ... 3-4 87
PLANET ... 3-5 78-85
RCA ... 3-4 85-86
LPs: 10/12-inch
BLUE THUMB ... 8-12 73-77
MCA ... 5-10 81
PLANET ... 5-10 78-84
RCA ... 5-8 85-88
Members: Bonnie Pointer; Anita Pointer; Ruth Pointer; June Pointer.
Also see HOODOO RHYTHM DEVILS
Also see MEMPHIS HORNS
Also see POINTER, Anita, & Earl Thomas Conley
Also see POINTER, Bonnie
Also see POINTER, June

POISON R&B '75
Singles: 12-inch
ROULETTE ... 4-8 76
Singles: 7-inch
ROULETTE ... 3-5 75-76
LPs: 10/12-inch
ROULETTE ... 5-10 76

POISON LP '86
Singles: 7-inch
CAPITOL ... 3-4 87
ENIGMA ... 3-4 86-88
Picture Sleeves
CAPITOL ... 3-4 87
ENIGMA ... 3-4 87-88
LPs: 10/12-inch
CAPITOL ... 5-8 86-90
ENIGMA ... 5-8 86-88
Members: Bret Michaels; Rikki Rocket; C.C. DeVille; Bobby Dall; Richie Kotzen; Blues Saraceno.

POISON DOLLYS
LPs: 10/12-inch
PVC ... 5-8 86

POISON IDEA/Caveman Shoestore
Singles: 7-inch
EVA-TONE/TIMKERR ... 3-4 92

POLARAS
Singles: 7-inch
PHAROS 8-12 64

POLE, Keith R&B '85
Singles: 7-inch
SUPERTRONICS 3-4 85

POLICE P&R/LP '79
Singles: 12-inch
A&M (4401 "Don't Stand So Close to Me") 200-250 81
(Picture disc. Promotional issue only. 25 made.)
A&M (17122 "Message in a Bottle") 5-8 79
(Promotional issue only.)
Singles: 7-inch
A&M (Except 25000, and picture discs) 3-5 79-84
A&M (25000 "De Do Do Do, De Da Da Da") 10-20 80
(Spanish/Japanese language version.)
A&M ("Roxanne") 250-500 79
(Rose-shaped picture disc. Production pressing.)
A&M (2096 "Roxanne") 35-40 79
(Badge-shaped picture disc. Promotional issue only. Includes custom folder.)
A&M (4401 "Don't Stand So Close to Me") 25-30 81
(Star-shaped picture disc.)
A&M (4401 "Don't Stand So Close to Me") 30-35 81
(Star-shaped picture disc. Promotional issue only. Identified by promo sticker on cover.)
SIRE 3-4 86
Picture Sleeves
A&M (Except 25000) 3-5 80-86
A&M (25000 "De Do Do Do, De Da Da Da") 4-6 80
LPs: 10/12-inch
A&M (Except 3713 & 3735) 5-15 79-86
A&M (3713 "Reggatta de Blanc") 10-20 79
(Two 10-inch LPs. Includes poster. Promotional issue only.)
A&M (3735 "Synchronicity") 75-100 83
(Black and white cover.)
A&M (3735 "Synchronicity") 40-50 83
(Gold, gray and brown cover.)
NAUTILUS (40 "Ghost in the Machine") 40-50 80s
NAUTILUS (19 Zenyata Mondata") 25-35 81
Members: Gordon "Sting" Sumner; Andy Summers; Stewart Copeland.
Also see COPELAND, Stewart
Also see FRIPP, Robert, & Andy Summers
Also see STING

POLITICIANS R&B '72
Singles: 7-inch
HOT WAX 3-5 72
LPs: 10/12-inch
HOT WAX 8-12 72
Members: McKinley Jackson.

POLK, Frank
Singles: 7-inch
CAPITOL 4-8 64-65

POLK, Prentiss
Singles: 7-inch
COLUMBIA 4-8 61

POLKA DOT SLIM
Singles: 7-inch
INSTANT 8-12 63

POLKA DOTS
Singles: 7-inch
MODERN (945 "Ting-A-Ling") 10-15 54
Singles: 7-inch
MODERN (945 "Ting-A-Ling") 15-20 54

POLKA DOTS
Singles: 7-inch
ROLLS 5-10 60

POLLARD, Chuck C&W '78
Singles: 7-inch
MCA 3-5 78

POLLARD, Donnie, & Marauders
Singles: 7-inch
MI-JA (1001 "Hang Loose") 15-25 58

POLLARD, Little Willie
Singles: 7-inch
ARC (7462 " '67' Blues") 8-10 67
W.B.P. (001 "Blues on My Mind") .. 10-15 60s

POLLARD, Ray
Singles: 7-inch
DECCA (32111 "Lie, Lips, Lie") 8-12 67
DECCA (32189 "Wanderlust") 8-12 67
SHRINE (103 "No More Like Me") 150-250 65
U.A. (856 "My Girl and I") 15-25 65
U.A. (916 "Let Him Go") 25-35 65
U.A. (50012 "It's a Sad Thing") 30-50 65
Also see WANDERERS

POLLUTION
Singles: 7-inch
CAPITOL 3-6 69
PROPHESY 3-5 71-72
LPs: 10/12-inch
CAPITOL 10-15 69
PROPHESY 8-12 71-72

POLLYWOGS
Singles: 7-inch
CUB 5-10 59

POLNAREFF, Michel P&R/LP '76
Singles: 12-inch
ATLANTIC 4-8 76
Singles: 7-inch
ATLANTIC 3-5 76
4 CORNERS (141 "Time Will Tell") .8-12 67
KAPP 4-8 65-66
LPs: 10/12-inch
ATLANTIC 8-10 75
4 CORNERS 10-15 67

POLYANNAS
Singles: 7-inch
KINGS-X 5-10 59

POLYPHONIC SIZE
LPs: 10/12-inch
ENIGMA 5-8

POLYPHONICS
Singles: 7-inch
SEECO 5-10 60

POLYROCK
Singles: 7-inch
RCA 3-5 80
LPs: 10/12-inch
PVC 5-8 83
RCA 5-10 80
Promotional LPs
RCA ("Special Radio Series") 10-15 81

POLYUNSATURATES
Singles: 7-inch
MADTAD 4-8 72

POMERANZ, David
Singles: 7-inch
ARISTA 3-5 75
DECCA 3-5 72
LPs: 10/12-inch
ARISTA 5-10 75
DECCA 8-12 72

POMPA, Joe
Singles: 7-inch
TERON (406 "Untrue") 10-20 60s

POMPEII 99
Singles: 7-inch
NOSTRADAMUS (1002 "The Nothing Song") 3-6 82
(Picture disc.)

POMSL, Pat C&W '79
Singles: 7-inch
ASI 3-5 79

POMUS, Doc
Singles: 78 rpm
APOLLO 15-25 45
CHESS 10-15 50
SAVOY 10-15 48
SELMER 10-15 48
Also see SMITH, Tab

PONCE, Pablo, Four
(Kit Kats)
Singles: 7-inch
GUYDEN 8-10 66
Also see KIT KATS

PONCE, Poncie
Singles: 7-inch
W.B. 4-8 61
Picture Sleeves
W.B. 10-15 61

PONDEROSA TWINS + ONE P&R/R&B '71
Singles: 7-inch
ASTROSCOPE 3-5 72
HOROSCOPE 3-5 71
LPs: 10/12-inch
HOROSCOPE 8-12 71
Members: Alfred Pelham; Alvin Pelham; Keith Gardner; Kirk Gardner; Ricky Spencer.

PONDIROSAS
Singles: 7-inch
CO & CE 5-10 66

PONIES
Singles: 7-inch
OKEH 5-10 60

PONI-TAILS P&R/R&B '58
Singles: 78 rpm
ABC-PAR 20-40 57
MARC 10-20 57
POINT 10-20 57
Singles: 7-inch
ABC 3-5 73
ABC-PAR 10-20 57-60
MCA 3-4
MARC 10-20 57
POINT 10-20 57
Members: Toni Cistone; LaVern Novak; Pat McCabe.
Also see ELEGANTS / Poni-Tails

PONSAR, Serge D&D '83
Singles: 12-inch
W.B. 4-6 83
Singles: 7-inch
W.B. 3-4 83

PONSI SISTERS
Singles: 7-inch
BINGO 5-10 59

PONTY, Jean-Luc LP '75
Singles: 7-inch
ATLANTIC 3-5 76-85
LPs: 10/12-inch
ATLANTIC 5-10 75-85
BLUE NOTE 5-10 76-81
MPS 5-10 72-73
PACIFIC JAZZ 8-18 68-78
PAUSA 5-10 80
PRESTIGE 8-15 70
WORLD PACIFIC 15-25 69

PONY
Singles: 7-inch
20TH FOX 3-5 74
LPs: 10/12-inch
20TH FOX 8-12 74

PONY EXPRESS
Singles: 7-inch
REPRISE 4-8 67

POOCH
Singles: 7-inch
FLIPSIDE 3-4 91
Picture Sleeves
FLIPSIDE 3-4 91
Members: Pat DiPuccio; Tono DeBruno; James Monroe; Greg Oakland; J.T. Worth.

POOH & HEFFALUMPHS
Singles: 7-inch
LAURIE 5-10 66

POOKAH
LPs: 10/12-inch
U.A. 8-12 70

POOLE, Brian P&R '64
(With the Tremeloes)
Singles: 7-inch
DATE 5-10 66
LONDON 5-10 63
MONUMENT 5-10 64-65
LPs: 10/12-inch
AUDIO FIDELITY 15-25 66-67
Also see TREMELOES

POOLE, Cheryl C&W '68
Singles: 7-inch
PAULA 4-6 68-70

POOLE, Johnny
Singles: 7-inch
WIDE (430 "Barefoot Baby") 75-100

POOLE, LeRoy
Singles: 7-inch
BAMBOO 4-8 63

POOL-PAH
LPs: 10/12-inch
GREENE BOTTLE 8-10 73

POOR
Singles: 7-inch
DECCA 5-10 68
LOMA 8-12 66
YORK (402 "Love Is Real") 15-25 67
YORK (404 "My Mind Goes High") 15-25 67

POOR BOY
(James Oden)
Singles: 78 rpm
BLACK & WHITE 20-40 47
Also see ST. LOUIS JIMMY

POOR BOY & ORPHANS
Singles: 7-inch
BUTCH'S THANG 5-8

POOR BOY'S PRIDE
Singles: 7-inch
FENTON (3060 "I'm Here") 15-25 68
SWADE ("The Place") 10-15 67
(Selection number not known.)

POOR BOYS
Singles: 7-inch
APOLLO 10-15 61
SOMA (1116 "Driftin' ") 10-15 59
Also see KING RICHARD & Poor Boys

POOR BOYS
Singles: 7-inch
RARE EARTH 3-5 70
LPs: 10/12-inch
RARE EARTH 8-12 70

POOR BOYS
Singles: 7-inch
GENERAL AMERICAN (005 "Over the Hill") 10-20 60s

POOR LITTLE RICH KIDS
Singles: 7-inch
H.I.P. 4-8 66

POOR RIGHTEOUS TEACHERS LP '90
LPs: 10/12-inch
PROFILE 5-8 90

POOR SOULS
Singles: 7-inch
IT WILL STAND 3-5 81

POORE, Bobby
Singles: 7-inch
BETA 15-25 58-59

POORE BOYES
Singles: 7-inch
PATTY (1375 "Give") 20-25 60s
SUMMER (181 "It's Love") 20-25 67
UPTOWN (735 "It's Love") 20-25 67

POOTHER UNLIMITED
Singles: 7-inch
CADET (5653 "Tastee Freeze") 15-25 68

POOVEY, Joe
(Groovy Joe Poovey)
Singles: 7-inch
DIXIE (733 "Move Around") 150-250 58
DIXIE (2018 "Ten Long Fingers") 200-300 59
SIMS 4-8 62-64

POP
Singles: 7-inch
ARISTA 3-5 79
LPs: 10/12-inch
ARISTA 5-10 79
RHINO 5-8 81

POP, Iggy LP '73
(Iggy & Stooges)
Singles: 12-inch
A&M 4-8 86
Singles: 7-inch
A&M 3-4 86
RCA 3-5 77
SIAMESE 3-6 77
Picture Sleeves
A&M 3-4 86
EPs: 7-inch
BOMP 5-10 78
LPs: 10/12-inch
A&M 5-8 86
ANIMAL 5-10 82
ARISTA 8-12 79-81
BOMP (1018 "Kill City") 10-15 78
(Black vinyl.)
BOMP (1018 "Kill City") 20-30 78
(Colored vinyl.)
COLUMBIA 10-20 73
ENIGMA 5-8 84
IMPORT 8-10 77
INVASION 8-10 83
RCA 5-10 77-78
VIRGIN 5-8 90
Also see BOWIE, David / Iggy Pop
Also see IGUANAS
Also see STOOGES

POP, Iggy, & James Williamson
EPs: 7-inch
BOMP 5-10 78
LPs: 10/12-inch
BOMP 5-10 78
Also see POP, Iggy

POP ART
Singles: 7-inch
EPIC 5-10 66

POP CORN & MOHAWKS
Singles: 7-inch
MOTOWN (1002 "Shimmy Gully") 40-60 60
MOTOWN (1019 "Real Good Lovin' ") 30-40 61
NORTHERN (3732 "Pretty Girl") 40-60 60s
Member: Richard Wylie.
Also see WYLIE, Richard

POP EXPLOSION
Singles: 7-inch
WE MAKE ROCK & ROLL RECORDS 4-8 68

POP TARTS
Singles: 7-inch
FUNTONE USA 5-10 88
Members: Fenton Pop Tart; Randy Pop Tart; C.P. Roth; Alan Bezoz; Gabriel Rotello; Simon Girl.

POP TOPS P&R/R&B '68
(Los Pop Tops)
Singles: 7-inch
ABC 3-5 71
CALLA 4-8 68

POP UPS
Singles: 7-inch
HBR 4-8 66

POP WILL EAT ITSELF LP '89
LPs: 10/12-inch
RCA 5-8 89

POP WORKSHOP
Singles: 7-inch
PAGE ONE 4-8 68

POPCORN & MOHAWKS: see POP CORN & MOHAWKS

POPCORN BLIZZARD
Singles: 7-inch
DE-LITE (Good, Good Day") 10-20 69
(Having two groups with such a distinctive name, we have them listed together. However, while we have confirmed Meat Loaf's involvement with the Magenda issue, we are not yet certain about this release. Readers?)
MAGENDA (7411 "Once Upon a Time") 20-30 67
Member: Marvin Lee Aday.
Also see MEAT LOAF

POPCORN REBELLION
Singles: 7-inch
DATE 4-8 68
RCA 4-8 69
SMASH 4-8 69

POPCORNS
Singles: 7-inch
DECCA 5-8 62
VEE JAY 8-12 63

POPE, Raymond, & Love Tones
(With the Andrew McPherson's Band)
Singles: 7-inch
SQUALOR (1313 "I Love Nadine") 100-150 62

POPE JOHN XXIII LP '63
LPs: 10/12-inch
MERCURY 5-10 63

POPE JOHN PAUL II LP '79
LPs: 10/12-inch
BETHLEHEM 5-8 79
INFINITY 5-8 79
VOX CHRISTIANA 5-8 79

POPE PAUL VI
LPs: 10/12-inch
AMY 5-10 65
AUDIO FIDELITY 5-10 65
MGM 5-10 65
20TH FOX 5-10 64

POPPA HOP
(Poppy Hop)
Singles: 7-inch
IVORY (127 "I'm a Stranger") 30-40 60
IVORY (134 "Merry Christmas Darling") 30-40 60
Also see WILSON, Hop, & His Two Buddies

POPPEES
Singles: 7-inch
BOMP 3-5 75
EPs: 7-inch
BOMP 8-10 75

POPPIES P&R '66
Singles: 7-inch
EPIC (9893 "Lullaby of Love") 4-8 66
EPIC (10019 "He's Ready") 4-8 66
EPIC (10059 "Do It with Soul") 5-10 66
EPIC (10086 "There's a Pain in My Heart") 10-20 66
TUFF (372 "Johnny Don't Cry") 10-15 63
Picture Sleeves
EPIC (10019 "He's Ready") 5-10 66
LPs: 10/12-inch
EPIC (24200 "Lullaby of Love") 20-30 66
(Monaural.)
EPIC (26200 "Lullaby of Love") 25-35 66
(Stereo.)
Members: Dorothy Moore; Rosemary Taylor; Pet McCune.
Also see MOORE, Dorothy

POPPIT BROTHERS: see YESTERDAY'S NEWS / Poppit Brothers

POPPY FAMILY P&R/LP '70
(Featuring Susan Jacks)
Singles: 7-inch
LONDON 3-5 70-72
LPs: 10/12-inch
LONDON 10-15 70-71
Members: Susan Jacks; Terry Jacks.
Also see JACKS, Susan
Also see JACKS, Terry

POPPY HOP: see POPPA HOP

POPSICLES
Singles: 7-inch
KNIGHT (2002 "Thumb Print") 20-25 58

POPSICLES
Singles: 7-inch
GNP 5-10 65

POPULAR DEMAND
Singles: 7-inch
CRUNCH (001 "400 Mile Gas Line") .. 4-8 79

POPULAR FIVE
Singles: 7-inch
MINIT 8-12 68
MISTER CHAND 4-8 70
RAE COX (1001 "Sh-boom") 20-30 67
Member: Warren Wilson.

POPULAIRES
Singles: 7-inch
MARVELLO (5001 "I Lost My Heart") 100-150 57

POPULIST, Walter
Singles: 7-inch
FLAME 5-10 60

PORCELAIN BEARMEAT
LPs: 10/12-inch
DILL PICKLE 15-20 71

PORGIE, Georgie: see GEORGIE PORGIE

PORGY & MONARCHS
Singles: 7-inch
MALA (462 "Stay") 10-15 63
MUSICOR (1179 "That Girl") 15-25 66
MUSICOR (1221 "My Heart Cries for You") 20-30 66
SYLVES 5-10 68
VERVE 5-10 68

PORK CHOPS
Singles: 78 rpm
HERALD 10-15 56
Singles: 7-inch
HERALD 10-15 56

PORRAZZO
LPs: 10/12-inch
POLYDOR 5-8 80

PORTER, Bruce
Singles: 7-inch
LEE (100 "Rattlesnake") 25-40 58

PORTER, Bruce
LPs: 10/12-inch
JOSHUA TREE 5-8 84

PORTER, David R&B/LP '70
Singles: 7-inch
ENTERPRISE 3-5 70-72
STAX 10-15 64

LPs: 10/12-inch
ENTERPRISE........8-12 70-72
Also see HAYES, Isaac, & David Porter

PORTER, Fran
Singles: 7-inch
AMERICAN ARTISTS........3-5 68

PORTER, Frank
NEW LIFE........5-10
Session: Duane Eddy.
Also see EDDY, Duane

PORTER, Gordon
Singles: 7-inch
PALMETTO (102 "Yes I'm Crying")... 4-8

PORTER, Jake
(With the Combo-Nettes)
Singles: 78 rpm
COMBO........10-15 53-54
Singles: 7-inch
COMBO........15-20 53-54
KEM........4-8 61
Also see DUCHESS / Jake Porter
Also see MOORE, Gene, & Chimes / Jake Porter with Gene Moore & Chimes

PORTER, Jake, & Buzzards
Singles: 78 rpm
COMBO (91 "The Bop")........15-25 55
Singles: 7-inch
COMBO (91 "The Bop")........30-40 55

PORTER, Jake, & Ebbonaires
Singles: 78 rpm
COMBO........20-40 55-56
Singles: 7-inch
COMBO (110 "Doodle Doo Doo")..50-75 55
COMBO (111 "You")........40-60 55
COMBO (126 "Rosetta")........40-60 56

PORTER, Jake, & Laurels / Jake Porter
Singles: 78 rpm
COMBO (66 "Fine Fine Baby")..100-150 55
Singles: 7-inch
COMBO (66 "Fine Fine Baby")..200-250 55
Also see LAURELS
Also see PORTER, Jake

PORTER, Jerry
LPs: 10/12-inch
MIRROR........8-10

PORTER, Johnny
(Johnny Schoolboy Porter & His Schoolboys; with Chanceteers)
Singles: 78 rpm
CHANCE........15-25 51-53
Singles: 7-inch
CHANCE (1101 "Schoolboy's Boogie")........30-40 51
CHANCE (1103 "Tennessee Waltz")........30-40 51
CHANCE (1104 "Walk Heavy")......30-40 51
CHANCE (1105 "Kayron")........30-40 52
CHANCE (1111 "Stairway to the Stairs")........30-40 52
CHANCE (1114 "Soft Shoulder")....30-40 52
CHANCE (1117 "Fire Dome")........30-40 52
CHANCE (1119 "Break Through")...30-40 52
CHANCE (1132 "Small Squall")......30-40 53
Also see CHANCETEERS

PORTER, Lulu
Singles: 7-inch
MOONGLOW........4-8 65
MUSIC MAN........4-8 66
PEP........4-8 65

PORTER, Nolan *P&R/R&B '71*
(N.F. Porter; Nolan)
Singles: 7-inch
ABC........3-5 73
LIZARD........3-5 71
LPs: 10/12-inch
LIZARD........8-12 71

PORTER, Ralph
Singles: 7-inch
MERIDAN ("Hey Mr. Porter")......50-100
(Selection number not known.)

PORTER, Robie
Singles: 7-inch
MGM........4-6 67
LPs: 10/12-inch
MGM........10-15 67

PORTER, Roy
(Roy Porter Quintet)
Singles: 7-inch
KING........4-8 61
PICO........5-10 60

PORTER, Royce
Singles: 7-inch
D (1026 "Lookin' ")........50-75 58
LOOK (1001 "Yes I Do")........150-200 57
MERCURY (71314 "Good Time")...50-75 58

PORTER, Schoolboy: see PORTER, Johnny

PORTNOY, Gary *P&R '83*
Singles: 7-inch
APPLAUSE........3-4 83
EARTHTONE........3-4 84
Picture Sleeves
EARTHTONE........3-5 84

PORTO, Billy
Singles: 78 rpm
MERCURY........5-10 57
Singles: 7-inch
MERCURY........5-10 57

PORTRAIT OF FUN
Singles: 7-inch
HOLIDAY INN........4-6 68

PORTRAIT OF SOUND
Singles: 7-inch
STORM........4-6 69

PORTRAITS
Singles: 7-inch
CAPITOL (4181 "Close to You")....20-30 59
Also see HOLLYWOOD SAXONS
Also see TUXEDOS

PORTRAITS
Singles: 7-inch
RCA........5-10 61

PORTRAITS
Singles: 7-inch
TRI-DISC........5-10 63

PORTRAITS
Singles: 7-inch
NIKE ("It Had to Be You")........30-50 67
(No selection number used. 100 made.)
Members: Emil Rakovich; Peter Lewna; Bill Watson; Greg Stupek; Michael Szymborski.

PORTRAITS
(Jerry & Portraits)
Singles: 7-inch
SIDEWALK........10-20 67
Members: Jerry Tawney; Phil Anthony; Gary Myers; John Rondell.
Also see DARNELLS
Also see MYERS, Gary
Also see TAWNEY, Jerry

PORTRAITS
Singles: 7-inch
LIZ........8-12 60s

PORTRAITS
Singles: 7-inch
ARIOLA ("Hazards in the Home")..... 4-8 80
Also see FIXX

PORTSMOUTH SINFONIA
Singles: 7-inch
COLUMBIA........3-5 75

PORTUGESE JOE
Singles: 7-inch
SURF (5018 "Teenage Riot")........15-25 58

POSA, Peter
Singles: 7-inch
INTERPHON........4-8 64

POSEY, Clarence / Henry Smith
Singles: 78 rpm
FORTUNE (802 "Rockin' Chair Boogie")........50-75 52
Also see SMITH, Henry

POSEY, Sandy *P&R/LP '66/C&W '71*
Singles: 7-inch
AUDIOGRAPH........3-4 83
COLUMBIA........3-5 71-73
MGM........4-6 66-67
MONUMENT........3-5 76
POLYDOR........3-4 83
W.B........3-5 76-79
Picture Sleeves
MGM........4-8 66-67
LPs: 10/12-inch
COLUMBIA........5-10 72
51 WEST........5-8 83
GUSTO........5-8 80s
MGM........8-15 66-70

POSEY, Sandy / Skeeter Davis
LPs: 10/12-inch
GUSTO........5-8
Also see DAVIS, Skeeter
Also see POSEY, Sandy

POSITIVE FORCE
LPs: 10/12-inch
SUGAR HILL........5-8 81

POSITIVE NOISE
LPs: 10/12-inch
SIRE........5-8 82

POSITIVE SOURCE
LPs: 10/12-inch
WEST END........5-8

POSITIVELY THIRTEEN O'CLOCK
Singles: 7-inch
HBR (500 "Psychotic Reaction")....25-35 66
Also see MOUSE
Also see RABBIT, Jimmy

POSSESSIONS
Singles: 7-inch
BRITTON (1003 "No More Love")....5-10 64
(Black vinyl.)
BRITTON (1003 "No More Love")..10-20 64
(Colored vinyl.)
PARKWAY........8-12 64
Also see VITO & SALUTATIONS

POSSUM
Singles: 7-inch
HIGHLAND........10-15 66

POSSUM
Singles: 7-inch
CAPITOL........3-5 70
LPs: 10/12-inch
CAPITOL........8-12 70

POSSUM RIVER
LPs: 10/12-inch
OVATION........8-12 71

POSSUMS
Singles: 7-inch
JM (3824 "She's Loving Me")........15-25 66

POST, Bill & Doree
Singles: 7-inch
CREST........4-8 59-62
U.A........4-8 62
VALIANT........4-8 63
Also see ENDSLEY, Melvin / Doree Post

POST, Howie, & Swifties
Singles: 7-inch
DUEL........4-8 63

POST, Mike *P&R/LP '75*
(Mike Post Coalition)
Singles: 7-inch
BELL........3-5 71
ELEKTRA........3-4 81-82
EPIC........3-5 77
MGM........3-5 75
MUSIC FACTORY........4-6 68
POLYDOR........3-4 87
REPRISE........4-6 65-66
W.B........3-6 69
Picture Sleeves
ELEKTRA........3-5 81-82
LPs: 10/12-inch
ELEKTRA........5-8 82
RCA........5-8 83
MGM........5-10 75
POLYDOR........5-8 87
W.B........8-12 69
Also see CARLTON, Larry

POST, Preston
Singles: 7-inch
SMASH........4-8 63

POSTALETTES
Singles: 7-inch
DORE........4-8 63

POT OF FLOWERS
LPs: 10/12-inch
MAINSTREAM (56100 "With Love")........25-35 67
(Monaural.)
MAINSTREAM (6100 "With Love")........30-40 67
(Stereo.)

POTATOLAND
LPs: 10/12-inch
RHINO........5-8 81

POTLIQUOR *P&R/LP '72*
Singles: 7-inch
CAPITOL........3-5 79
JANUS........3-5 72
LPs: 10/12-inch
CAPITOL........5-10 79
JANUS........10-15 70-73

POTTER, Bobby
Singles: 7-inch
BANA........10-20 57

POTTER, Curtis
Singles: 7-inch
DOT........3-5 71
FOX (409 "Real Glad Daddy") ...150-250 58
HILLSIDE........3-5 80
WINSTON........10-15 59
LPs: 10/12-inch
DOT........10-20 71
HILLSIDE........5-10 80
Also see THOMPSON, Hank

POTTER, Curtis, & Darrell McCall *C&W '80*
(With "Friend")
Singles: 7-inch
HILLSIDE........3-5 80
Also see McCALL, Darrell
Also see POTTER, Curtis
Also see SANDERS, Ray / Curtis Potter / Darrell McCall

POTTER, Danny
Singles: 7-inch
W.B./SPECTOR........3-5 76

POTTER, Don
Singles: 7-inch
COLUMBIA........3-5 74
LPs: 10/12-inch
MIRROR........8-10
Also see MANGIONE, Chuck

POTTER - ST. CLOUD
LPs: 10/12-inch
MEDIARTS........10-15
Members: D.F. Potter; Endle St. Cloud.

POULSEN, Skip, & Beach Continentals
Singles: 7-inch
DEAUVILLE (1006 "A Pretzel Ain't Nothin' But a Twist")........8-12 62

POULTON, Dick, Trio
Singles: 7-inch
VIN (1016 "Susie")........10-20 59

POUND
LPs: 10/12-inch
A.M.S. (74840 "Odd Man Out")....35-55 74
Members: Dave Bither; Dave Franson; Greg Shannon; Pam Petros.

POURCEL, Franck *P&R/R&B '59*
(Franck Pourcel's French Fiddles)
Singles: 7-inch
BLUE........3-5 69
CAPITOL........4-8 59-64
IMPERIAL........3-6 66-68
PARAMOUNT........3-5 71-73
EPs: 7-inch
CAPITOL........5-10 59
LPs: 10/12-inch
ATCO........5-10 69
CAPITOL........5-20 56-79
IMPERIAL........5-15 66-68
PARAMOUNT........5-8 70-73
WESTMINSTER........10-25 54-55

POUSETTE-DART BAND *LP '77*
Singles: 7-inch
CAPITOL........3-5 76-79
LPs: 10/12-inch
CAPITOL........5-10 76-80
Member: Jon Pousette-Dart.

POUSSEZ
Singles: 12-inch
VANGUARD........4-8 79-80
Singles: 7-inch
VANGUARD........3-5 79-80
LPs: 10/12-inch
VANGUARD........5-10 79-80

POWDER BLUES
Singles: 12-inch
RCA (0365 "Uncut")........8-12 79
Singles: 7-inch
BLUE WAVE........3-5 84
LIBERTY........3-5 81-82
RCA........3-5 79-83
Picture Sleeves
LIBERTY (1423 "Thirsty Ears")........3-5 81
LPs: 10/12-inch
LIBERTY........5-10 80-83
Members: Tom Lavin; Jack Lavin; Willie MacCalder; Duris Maxwell; David Woodward. Session: Wayne Kozak; Gord Bertram; Mark Hasselbach.

POWDER PUFFS
(Angels)
Singles: 7-inch
IMPERIAL (66014 "My Boyfriend's Woody")........15-25 64
Also see ANGELS

POWDRILL, Pat
Singles: 7-inch
DOWNEY (139 "Do It")........20-30 65
REPRISE........5-10 63-64

POWE, Joseph S.: see SONGCRAFTERS

POWELL, Adam Clayton *LP '67*
LPs: 10/12-inch
JUBILEE........10-15 67

POWELL, Andrew
LPs: 10/12-inch
ATLANTIC (12481 "Ladyhawke").....8-10 85
(Soundtrack.)
EMI........5-8 83
Members: Andrew Powell; David Paton; Ian Bairnson; Stuart Elliot.
Also see KEATS
Also see PARSONS, Alan, Project

POWELL, Austin
(With the James Quintet; Austin Powell Quintet)
Singles: 78 rpm
ATLANTIC........50-75 52
DECCA........10-20 51
Singles: 7-inch
ATLANTIC (968 "Wrong Again")........100-200 52
DECCA (48206 "All This Can't Be True")........50-75 51
Also see CATS & FIDDLE
Also see JAMES QUINTET

POWELL, Bobby *P&R/R&B '65*
Singles: 7-inch
EXCELLO........5-10 73
HEP' ME (151 "A Fool for You")......5-10
HEP' ME (155 "The Glory of Love").5-10
HEP' ME (155 "Glory of Love [Short Version]"/"Glory of Love [Long Version]")....10-15
(Labeled "For Juke Box Only.")
JEWEL........5-10 67
WHIT........6-12 65-71
LPs: 10/12-inch
EXCELLO........10-15 73

POWELL, Chris, & Five Blue Flames
(With "Vocal Chorus by Johnny Echo, Sax Solo by Vance Wilson")
Singles: 78 rpm
COLUMBIA (Except 39407)........25-50 49-51
COLUMBIA (39407 "My Love Has Gone")........100-200 51
GRAND........15-25 53-54
GROOVE........10-20 55-56
OKEH (Except 6818)........50-75 51-52
OKEH (6818 "The Masquerade Is Over")........100-150 51
Singles: 7-inch
COLUMBIA (39272 "Country Girl Blues")........50-100 51
COLUMBIA (39407 "My Love Has Gone")........300-500 51
GRAND........25-50 53-54
GROOVE........20-30 55-56
OKEH (6818 "The Masquerade Is Over")........200-300 51
OKEH (6850 "Twilight")........100-150 51
OKEH (6875 "Ida Red")........100-150 52
OKEH (6900 "Blue Boy")........100-150 52
Member: Joe Van Loan.
Also see VAN LOAN, Joe

POWELL, Cozy *P&R '74*
Singles: 7-inch
CHRYSALIS........3-5 74
Also see BECK, Jeff
Also see BEDLAM
Also see EMERSON, LAKE & POWELL

POWELL, Dick
Singles: 7-inch
RPC........4-8 61

POWELL, Doug
Singles: 7-inch
JUDI (051 "Crazy Georgia Shake")........15-25 60
KETO (102 "Love We Feel")........10-20 61
MERCURY (71949 "Fort Lauderdale")........40-60 62
TIP TOP (713 "The Lord Made a Woman")........100-150 58

POWELL, Freddy
Singles: 7-inch
SHERATON........4-8 62

POWELL, George, & Troopers
Singles: 7-inch
LUMMTONE (101 "My Choice for a Mate")........150-250 59

POWELL, James
Singles: 7-inch
CHRISTY........5-10 61

POWELL, Jane *P&R '56*
Singles: 78 rpm
MGM........4-6 51
VERVE........4-6 56
Singles: 7-inch
RANWOOD........3-5 68
MGM........5-10 51
VERVE........4-8 56
LPs: 10/12-inch
COLUMBIA........15-30 55-57
LION........10-20 59
MGM........20-40 55
VERVE........20-35 56
Also see ASTAIRE, Fred, & Jane Powell

POWELL, Jerry
Singles: 7-inch
AUDIO MOBILE (800 "Look At Them Jaguars")........10-20 60s

POWELL, Jesse
(With the Caddys; Jessie Powell)
Singles: 78 rpm
FEDERAL (12056 "Walkin' Blues")........25-50 51
(With Fluffy Hunter.)
FEDERAL (12060 "My Natch Man")........25-50 51
(With Fluffy Hunter.)
FEDERAL (12159 "Rear Bumper")........15-25 53
FEDERAL (12171 "Hot Box")........15-25 53
JOSIE........5-10 55-58
Singles: 7-inch
FEDERAL (12056 "Walkin' Blues")........50-100 51
(With Fluffy Hunter.)
FEDERAL (12060 "My Natch Man")........50-100 51
(With Fluffy Hunter.)
FEDERAL (12159 "Rear Bumper")........40-60 53
FEDERAL (12171 "Hot Box")........40-60 53
FLING........10-20 60
JOSIE........10-20 55-58
KAPP........5-10 62
RONNEX........5-10 60s
TRU-SOUND........5-10 61
LPs: 10/12-inch
JUBILEE (1113 "Blow Man Blow") 40-60 60
KAPP........20-30 62
TRU-SOUND........20-30 62
(Titles and numbers needed for all of these LPs.)
Also see CADILLACS
Also see EXECUTIVE FOUR
Also see GUY, Bobby
Also see NEW YORKERS 5

POWELL, Jimmy
LPs: 10/12-inch
DECCA........8-12 70

POWELL, Keith, & Valets
Singles: 7-inch
STELLAR (1503 "Tore Up")........20-30 60s

POWELL, Pati, & Bob Gallion *C&W '73*
Singles: 7-inch
METRO COUNTRY........3-5 73
Also see GALLION, Bob

POWELL, Patty
Singles: 7-inch
SHOWBOAT (1507 "Special")........5-10 60

POWELL, Roger
Singles: 7-inch
BEARSVILLE (0323 "Pipeline '78")....4-8 78

POWELL, Sandy
Singles: 7-inch
HERALD (557 "Bon Bon")........100-125 61
IMPALA (211 "Bon Bon")........250-500 61
SINGULAR (714 "My Jimmie")......15-25 58
Also see STREET, Mel, & Sandy Powell

POWELL, Sue *C&W '81*
Singles: 7-inch
RCA........3-4 81
Also see DAVE & SUGAR

POWELL, Tiny
Singles: 7-inch
OCAMPO........4-8 65
WAX........4-8 64

POWELL SISTERS
Singles: 7-inch
KAYDEE.......... 5-10 61

POWELL TWINS
Singles: 7-inch
ACCENT (1063 "Tropical Moon")...10-15 60s

POWER
Singles: 7-inch
MGM.......... 4-8 67

POWER, Duffy
Singles: 7-inch
EPIC.......... 3-5 70
LPs: 10/12-inch
GSF.......... 8-12 70s

POWER, Jamie
Singles: 7-inch
JAMIE.......... 4-8 66

POWER, Johnny
Singles: 7-inch
TRIODEX.......... 5-10 60

POWER, Mike
Singles: 7-inch
ZELMAN (5301 "I Left My Love in Paris")..........300-500

POWER FORMULA
Singles: 7-inch
SHOWTOWN.......... 3-6 69

POWER PLANT
Singles: 7-inch
DIAMOND.......... 4-8 67

POWER STATION P&R/D&D/LP '85
Singles: 12-inch
CAPITOL.......... 4-6 85
Singles: 7-inch
CAPITOL.......... 3-4 85
Picture Sleeves
CAPITOL.......... 3-4 85
LPs: 10/12-inch
CAPITOL.......... 5-8 85
Members: Andy Taylor; John Taylor; Robert Palmer; Tommy Thompson.
Also see DURAN DURAN
Also see PALMER, Robert
Also see TAYLOR, Andy
Also see TAYLOR, John

POWERFUL PEOPLE
Singles: 12-inch
EPIC.......... 4-8 77
Singles: 7-inch
EPIC.......... 3-5 77

POWERHOUSE
LPs: 10/12-inch
ALADDIN.......... 20-30 75
POWERHOUSE.......... 5-10 83-87
Member: Tom Principato.
Also see PRINCIPATO, Tom

POWERPLAY
LPs: 10/12-inch
EPIC.......... 5-8 82

POWERS, Donna
Singles: 7-inch
MIDCO.......... 4-8 61

POWERS, Eddie
Singles: 7-inch
RONN.......... 4-8 67
SIMS.......... 4-8 64

POWERS, Freddy, & Powerhouse IV
LPs: 10/12-inch
W.B.......... 15-25 63

POWERS, Jackie
Singles: 7-inch
MOPIC.......... 4-8 62

POWERS, Jett
(James Smith)
Singles: 7-inch
BETA (1008 "Loud Perfume")....150-200 60
DESIGN (811 "Go Girl Go").......200-300 57
Session: Bumps Blackwell.
Also see PROBY, P.J.

POWERS, Joey P&R '63
(Joey Powers' Flower)
Singles: 7-inch
AMY.......... 5-10 63-67
MGM.......... 5-10 65
RCA (8000 series).......... 4-8 62
RCA (9700 series).......... 3-6 69
LPs: 10/12-inch
AMY.......... 15-25 64
Also see ORBISON, Roy / Bobby Bare / Joey Powers

POWERS, Johnny
(With His Rockets; with Stan Getz & Tom Cats)
Singles: 78 rpm
FORTUNE.......... 50-75 56
Singles: 7-inch
FORTUNE (199 "Honey Let's Go [To a Rock and Roll Show]")..........100-200 56
FOX (916 "Rock Rock/Long Blonde Hair, Red Rose Lips")..........300-400 57
HI-Q (5044 "Rock the Universe") .75-100 58
OLYMPIC.......... 3-5 76-78
SUN (327 "Be Mine All Mine")........30-50 59
SUN (600 series).......... 3-6 75
TEE PEE (398 "Seventeen")..........10-20 61
TRIODEX (103 "A Teenager's Prayer")..........10-15 60
Also see JUSTIS, Bill
Also see RICH, Charlie

POWERS, Roni
Singles: 7-inch
LT PRODUCTIONS (1022 "An Angel Up in Heaven")..........100-150 61

POWERS, Tina
Singles: 7-inch
PARKWAY.......... 4-8 62

POWERS, Tom P&R '77
Singles: 7-inch
BIG TREE.......... 3-5 77

POWERS, Wayne
(Wayne Cogswell)
Singles: 7-inch
PHILLIPS INT'L (3523 "My Love Song")..........25-35 58

POWERS' FLOWER
Singles: 7-inch
W.B.......... 4-8 69

POWERS OF BLUE
Singles: 7-inch
MTA.......... 5-10 66-67
LPs: 10/12-inch
MTA (5002 "Flip Out")..........20-30 67
Member: Hugh McCracken.
Also see McCRACKEN, Hugh

POWERSOURCE P&R '87
Singles: 7-inch
POWERVISION.......... 3-4 87

POYNTER, Joyce
Singles: 7-inch
GOLDEN ROD (301 "Chili Dippin' Baby")..........50-75 57

POZO - SECO SINGERS P&R/LP '66
(Susan Taylor & the Pozo Seco Singers; Pozo Seco; Pozo-Seco Singers Featuring Don Williams)
Singles: 7-inch
CERTRON.......... 3-5 70
COLUMBIA.......... 4-8 65-70
EDMARK (10017 "Down the Road I Go"/"Time")..........10-20 65
LPs: 10/12-inch
CERTRON.......... 10-15 70
COLUMBIA.......... 10-20 66-68
EXCELSIOR.......... 5-10 80
Members: Don Williams; Susan Taylor; Lofton Kline.
Also see WILLIAMS, Don

PRADO, Perez, & His Orchestra P&R '53
Singles: 78 rpm
RCA.......... 4-6 50-58
Singles: 7-inch
RCA.......... 5-15 50-64
U.A.......... 3-6 64
Picture Sleeves
RCA.......... 8-10 59
EPs: 7-inch
BELL (2 "Perez Prado").......... 5-10
RCA.......... 8-15 54-61
LPs: 10/12-inch
CAMDEN.......... 10-15 60
RCA.......... 5-10 76
(With "ANL1" prefix.)
RCA.......... 10-30 54-72
(With "LPM," "LSP" or "VPS" prefix.)
SPIN-O-RAMA.......... 8-12 62
SPRINGBOARD.......... 5-10 77
U.A.......... 10-15 65-68
Also see CLOONEY, Rosemary, & Perez Prado
Also see HIRT, Al / Henry Mancini / Perez Prado
Also see KITT, Eartha, & Perez Prado

PRAEGER, Billy
Singles: 7-inch
CRYSTAL (106 "Everybody's Rockin' ")..........75-125 59

PRAIRIE MADNESS
Singles: 7-inch
COLUMBIA.......... 3-5 72
LPs: 10/12-inch
COLUMBIA.......... 8-12 72

PRANCERS
Singles: 7-inch
GUARANTEED.......... 5-10 59

PRATT, Andy P&R/LP '73
Singles: 7-inch
COLUMBIA.......... 3-5 73
NEMPEROR.......... 3-5 76-77
LPs: 10/12-inch
COLUMBIA.......... 8-12 73
NEMPEROR.......... 5-10 76-79
POLYDOR.......... 10-15 70
Also see SPRINGSTEEN, Bruce / Andy Pratt

PRATT, Dave, & Sex Machine Band
Singles: 7-inch
98 KUPD.......... 3-5 84-86
LPs: 10/12-inch
98 KUPD.......... 5-10 85

PRATT, Lynn
Singles: 7-inch
HORNET (1000 "Tom Cat Boogie")..........150-250
HORNET (1001 "Troubles")..........150-250
HORNET (1002 "Come Here Mama")..........150-250
HORNET (1003 "Red Headed Woman")..........150-250
Also see PITRELLO, Carne

PRATT - McCLAIN P&R/LP '76
Singles: 7-inch
REPRISE.......... 3-5 76-77
LPs: 10/12-inch
DUNHILL.......... 8-12 73
REPRISE.......... 8-10 76
Members: Truett Pratt; Jerry McClain.

PRAYE, Johnny
Singles: 7-inch
SIDEWALK.......... 4-8 67

PREACHER JACK
LPs: 10/12-inch
ROUNDER.......... 5-10 80

PREACHERS
Singles: 7-inch
CHALLENGE.......... 5-10 60s
MOONGLOW.......... 5-10 65
PEP.......... 5-10 65

PRECIOUS FEW
Singles: 7-inch
NASCO (001 "The Carnival")..........5-10 60s
SALEM (501 "The Train Kept A-Rollin' ")..........20-30 66

PRECISIONS
(With Herchel Dwellingham & Orchestra)
Singles: 7-inch
WILD (903 "The Love")..........25-50

PRECISIONS
Singles: 7-inch
DREW (1002 "Why Girl")..........10-15 60s
DREW (1003 "If This Is Love")......10-15 60s
DREW (1004 "Instant Heartbreak")..........10-15 60s
DREW (1004 "Instant Heartbreak")..........10-15 68
DREW (1005 "A Place")..........10-15 60s
GOLDEN CREST (571 "Someone to Watch Over Me")..........10-15 62
HIGHLAND (300 "Eight Reasons Why I Love You")..........200-400 62
RAYNA (1001 "White Christmas")..........50-100
STRAND (25038 "Dream On").....50-100 61

PRECISIONS
Singles: 7-inch
DEBRA (1001 "Sweet Dreams").....30-50 63
Also see MAGICS

PRECISIONS P&R/R&B '67
Singles: 7-inch
ATCO.......... 4-8 69
D-TOWN (1033 "My Lover Come Back")..........100-150 65
D-TOWN (1055 "Mexican Love Song")..........10-20 65
DREW (1001 "Such Misery")........15-25 66
DREW (1003 "If This Is Love")........10-20 66
HEN-MAR.......... 3-5 73

PREDIKTORS
Singles: 7-inch
IMPERIAL.......... 5-10 64

PREFAB SPROUT LP '85
Singles: 7-inch
EPIC.......... 5-8 85
LPs: 10/12-inch
EPIC.......... 10-15 85

PRE-HISTORICS
Singles: 7-inch
EDSEL (779 "Alley Oop Cha-Cha-Cha")..........15-25 60
Members: Arthur Crier; Carl Spencer.
Also see FIVE CHIMES
Also see HALOS
Also see MELLOWS

PREHLE, Michelle
Singles: 7-inch
MAGIC CARPET (506 "Letter to Elvis")..........8-12 79

PRELUDE P&R '74
Singles: 7-inch
ISLAND.......... 3-5 74
PYE.......... 3-5 75
LPs: 10/12-inch
ISLAND.......... 8-10 74
PYE.......... 8-10 75

PRELUDES
Singles: 78 rpm
EMPIRE.......... 35-55 56
Singles: 7-inch
EMPIRE (103 "Don't Fall in Love Too Soon")..........50-100 56

PRELUDES
Singles: 7-inch
CUB (9005 "Kingdom of Love").....50-75 58

PRELUDES
Singles: 7-inch
ARLISS (1004 "Lorraine")..........50-75 61
OCTAVIA (8008 "A Place for You")..........30-50 62

PRELUDES FIVE P&R '61
(Preludes)
Singles: 7-inch
PIK (231 "Starlight")..........20-30 61

PREMEERS
Singles: 7-inch
HERALD (577 "Diary of Our Love")..........20-30 63

PREMIATA FORNERIA MARCONI: see P.F.M.

PREMIERE, Ronnie
(Ronnie Premier & the Royal Lancers)
Singles: 7-inch
LAURIE (1020 "Angel in My Eyes")..........10-20 61
SARA (1020 "Angel in My Eyes")...30-50 60

PREMIERES
Singles: 7-inch
SCEPTER.......... 3-5 71

PREMIERS
Singles: 78 rpm
DIG (106 "New Moon")..........20-40 56
DIG (113 "My Darling")..........50-75 56
FORTUNE (527 "When You Are in Love")..........15-25 56
RCA (6958 "Run Along Baby").......20-30 57
Singles: 7-inch
BEST (1004 "False Love")..........50-100 62
CINDY (3008 "Life Is Grand")......50-100 58
DIG (106 "New Moon")..........75-125 56
DIG (113 "My Darling")..........150-200 56
ECHO (6013 "Until")..........200-300
FORTUNE (527 "When You Are in Love")..........50-100 56
GONE (5009 "Is It a Dream")......350-500 57
GONE (5009 "Is It a Dream")......100-150 57
(Due to a production error, *Let Me Share Your Dream* [Delta 5010] appears on this side instead of *Is it a Dream.*)
RCA (6958 "Run Along Baby").....50-100 57
Also see DELTAS
Also see STEVENS, Julie

PREMIERS
Singles: 7-inch
BOND (5803 "Hop & Skip")..........10-20 58

PREMIERS
(Premieres)
Singles: 7-inch
NU-PHI (367 "Cruisin' ")..........20-30 59
NU-PHI (701 "Firewater")..........20-30 60
Also see WALTERS, Bucky & Jukes

PREMIERS
Singles: 7-inch
ALERT (706 "Jolene")..........50-100 58
FURY (1029 "I Pray")..........25-35 60
RUST (5032 "Falling Star")..........50-100 60
Members: Roger Koob; Billy Koob; Gus Delcos; Frank Polimus; Vinny Klump; Barbara Klump; Tim Vail; Joe Vece.
Also see FORMATION
Also see KOOB, Roger
Also see ROGER & TRAVELERS

PREMIERS
(With John Medora & Orchestra)
Singles: 7-inch
MINK (021 "Tonight")..........50-100 59
PARKWAY (807 "Tonight")..........15-25 61

PREMIERS
Singles: 7-inch
DICE (115 "Crazy Bells")..........15-25 61

PREMIERS
Singles: 7-inch
DORE (547 "True Deep Love")......15-25 60
DORE (603 "Evening Star")..........15-25 61
DORE (614 "What Makes Little Girls Cry")..........15-25 61

PREMIERS P&R '64
Singles: 7-inch
FARO.......... 6-12 64-67
FINE.......... 4-8 60s
LEO.......... 5-10 64
W.B.......... 4-8 64
LPs: 10/12-inch
RAMPART ("Farmer John")..........25-35 64
(Selection number not known.)
W.B. (1565 "Farmer John")..........15-25 64

PREMIERS
Singles: 7-inch
KING (6061 "I'm Better Off Now")..10-20 66
STAX (177 "Make It Me")..........15-25 65

PREMIERS
Singles: 7-inch
ODEX (1711 "Speaking of You")....25-50 60s

PREMIERS & INVICTAS
Singles: 7-inch
F-M (677 "Magic of Love")........100-150 59

PREMONITIONS
Singles: 7-inch
JADE (711 "Baby Baby")..........30-40 67

PRENTISS, Lee D&D '83
Singles: 12-inch
MSB.......... 4-6 83

PREPARATIONS R&B '68
Singles: 7-inch
HEART and SOUL.......... 4-8 68

PREPS
Singles: 7-inch
ANOTHER LOSER (176 "Pam Pam")..........5-10 64
DOT (16663 "Night Theme")..........5-10 64
SOUTHBAY.......... 5-10
WARPED (5000 "Night Theme")....15-25 64
(First issue.)

PREPS
Singles: 7-inch
COAST ("Moon Racers")..........30-40 60s
(Selection number not known.)
Also see NEW ARRIVALS

PRESCOTT, Ralph
Singles: 7-inch
LANOR (564 "Hot Hot Lips")........75-125 59

PRESENT, The
Singles: 7-inch
PHILIPS (40466 "I Know")..........15-25 67

PRESIDENTS
Singles: 7-inch
MERCURY.......... 10-15 62
W.B.......... 5-10 61

PRESIDENTS P&R/R&B '70
Singles: 7-inch
DELUXE.......... 4-8 69
HOLLYWOOD.......... 4-8 68
SUSSEX.......... 3-6 70-71
LPs: 10/12-inch
SUSSEX.......... 15-25 70
Members: Tony Boyd; Archie Powell; Bill Shorter.

PRESIDENTS BANNED
Singles: 7-inch
YORK TOWN (1000 "Gotcha Babe")..........20-30 60s

PRESLEY, Elvis C&W '55
(With Scotty & Bill; with Jordanaires; with Imperials; with J.D. Sumner & Stamps; with Mello Men; with Amigos; with Jubilee Four & Carol Lombard Trio)
Singles: 12-inch
RCA (0517 "Little Sister")..........125-150 83
(Promotional issue only.)
Singles: 78 rpm
(Commercial and Promotional)
RCA (6357 "Mystery Train").......100-150 55
RCA (6380 "That's All Right")....100-150 55
RCA (6381 "Good Rockin' Tonight")..........100-150 55
RCA (6382 "Milkcow Blues Boogie")..........100-150 55
RCA (6383 "Baby, Let's Play House")..........100-150 55
RCA (6420 "Heartbreak Hotel")....75-100 56
(Black label.)
RCA (6420 "Heartbreak Hotel") .400-500
(White label. Promotional issue only.)
RCA (6540 "I Want You, I Need You, I Love You")..........75-100 56
(Black label.)
RCA (6540 "I Want You, I Need You, I Love You")..........400-500
(White label. Promotional issue only.)
RCA (6604 "Don't Be Cruel")......75-100 56
(Black label.)
RCA (6604 "Don't Be Cruel")......400-500
(White label. Promotional issue only.)
RCA (6636 "Blue Suede Shoes").75-100 56
RCA (6637 "I Got a Woman")......75-100 56
RCA (6638 "I'm Gonna Sit Right Down and Cry")..........75-100 56
RCA (6639 "Tryin' to Get to You")..........75-100 56
RCA (6640 "Blue Moon")..........75-100 56
RCA (6641 "Money Honey")..........75-100 56
RCA (6642 "Lawdy, Miss Clawdy")..........75-100 56
RCA (6643 "Love Me Tender")....50-100 56
(Black label.)
RCA (6643 "Love Me Tender")...400-500
(White label. Promotional issue only.)
RCA (6800 "Too Much")..........75-125 57
(Black label.)
RCA (6800 "Too Much")..........400-500
(White label. Promotional issue only.)
RCA (6870 "All Shook Up")........75-125 57
(Black label.)
RCA (6870 "All Shook Up")........400-500
(White label. Promotional issue only.)
RCA (7000 "Teddy Bear")..........75-125 57
(Black label.)
RCA (7000 "Teddy Bear")..........400-500
(White label. Promotional issue only.)
RCA (7035 "Jailhouse Rock")......75-125 57
(Black label.)
RCA (7035 "Jailhouse Rock")....400-500
(White label. Promotional issue only.)
RCA (7150 "Don't")..........75-150 58
RCA (7240 "Wear My Ring Around Your Neck")..........200-300 58
RCA (7280 "Hard Headed Woman")..........200-300 58
RCA (7410 "One Night")..........500-750 58
ROYAL ("Elvis Presley Show")..200-300 56
(Single-sided disc, issued to radio stations to promote Elvis in concert. Includes an excerpt of *Heartbreak Hotel.*)
SUN (209 "That's All Right")..1000-1500 54
SUN (210 "Good Rockin' Tonight")..........1000-1500 54
(Credits "Elvis Presley, Scotty and Bill")
Tonight")..........800-1200 54
(Credits "Elvis Presley")
SUN (215 "Milkcow Blues Boogie")..........1500-2000 55
SUN (217 "Baby Let's Play House")..........800-1200 55
SUN (223 "Mystery Train")........700-1000 55
Notes: All Elvis RCA and Sun 78s were simultaneously issued on 45 rpm singles. For 78 rpm plastic soundsheets and flexi-discs, see a separate section that follows. RCA and Sun 78s can be found with many label variations. Sun promotional singles were marked with the word "sample" rubber stamped on the label. White label promotional 78s are still listed; however, their authenticity has been challenged by some experts.
Singles: 7-inch
(Commercial)
COLLECTABLES (Black vinyl)..........3-5 86-87

COLLECTABLES (Gold vinyl).......... 3-5 92
MEMPHIS FLASH (92444 "Beginnings – Elvis Style")......................10-20 78
RCA (0088 "Raised on Rock")........... 5-8 73
RCA (0130 "How Great Thou Art") .20-25 69
RCA (0196 "Take Good Care of Her") 4-6 74
RCA (0280 "If You Talk in Your Sleep")..................................10-15 74
(Has full title on one line.)
RCA (0280 "If You Talk in Your Sleep") 4-6 74
(Two lines are used for title.)
RCA (0572 "Merry Christmas Baby") 15-20 71
RCA (0619 "Until It's Time for You to Go") 4-6 72
RCA (0651 "He Touched Me") ...125-150 72
(Has the *He Touched Me* side pressed at about 35 rpm instead of 45. These copies – the result of a production error – are commercial issues. Flip, *Bosom of Abraham*, plays at 45 rpm.)
RCA (0651 "He Touched Me") 4-6 72
RCA (0672 "An American Trilogy") 10-20 72
RCA (0769 "Burning Love") 150-200 72
(Gray label.)
RCA (0769 "Burning Love") 4-6 72
(Orange label.)
RCA (0815 "Separate Ways")........... 4-6 71
RCA (0910 "Fool") 4-6 73
RCA (1017 "It's Only Love")............. 4-6 71
RCA (2458 "My Boy"/"Loving Arms")....................................650-750 74
(Add $150 to $200 if accompanied by insert, which reads: "Elvis Presley" and "My Boy." Produced in the U.S. for European distribution.)
RCA (6357 "Mystery Train")..........40-50 55
RCA (6380 "That's All Right")..........40-50 55
RCA (6381 "Good Rockin' Tonight")..40-50 55
RCA (6382 "Milkcow Blues Boogie")..40-50 55
RCA (6383 "Baby Let's Play House")..40-50 55
RCA (6420 "Heartbreak Hotel")......40-50 56
(Turquoise label.)
RCA (6420 "Heartbreak Hotel")......20-30 56
(Black label.)
RCA (6540 "I Want You, I Need You, I Love You")..20-30 56
RCA (6604 "Don't Be Cruel")..........20-30 56
RCA (6636 "Blue Suede Shoes") ...60-90 56
RCA (6637 "I Got a Woman") 40-50 56
RCA (6638 "I'm Gonna Sit Right Down and Cry")..40-50 56
RCA (6639 "Tryin' to Get to You")..40-50 56
RCA (6640 "Blue Moon") 40-50 56
RCA (6641 "Money Honey")............40-50 56
RCA (6642 "Lawdy, Miss Clawdy")..40-50 56
(Dog is pictured on label.)
RCA (6642 "Lawdy, Miss Clawdy")................................200-225 56
(Dog is not shown on label.)
RCA (6643 "Love Me Tender").......20-30 56
RCA (6800 "Too Much")..................20-30 57
(Dog is pictured on label.)
RCA (6800 "Too Much")............200-225 57
(Dog is not shown on label.)
RCA (6870 "All Shook Up")............20-30 57
RCA (7000 "Teddy Bear")...............20-30 57
RCA (7035 "Jailhouse Rock")..........20-30 57
(Black label, black vinyl.)
RCA (7035 "Jailhouse Rock"). 1500-2500 57
(Gold label, gold vinyl.)
Note: All RCA singles from 6357 through 7035 can be found on various black labels, both with or without a horizontal silver line. Some folks may add a $5 to $10 premium for copies with a line; however, first issues came without the line.)
RCA (7150 "Don't")........................10-15 58
RCA (7240 "Wear My Ring Around Your Neck")..10-15 58
RCA (7280 "Hard Headed Woman")..10-15 58
RCA (7410 "One Night")..................10-15 58
RCA (7506 "I Need Your Love Tonight")..10-15 59
RCA (7600 "A Big Hunk O' Love")..10-15 59
RCA (47-7740 "Stuck on You") 8-12 60
RCA (61-7740 "Stuck on You") ..400-500 60
(Living Stereo.)
RCA (47-7777 "It's Now Or Never")....................................750-1000 60
(Due to mixing error, piano track is omitted.)
RCA (47-7777 "It's Now Or Never")... 8-10 60
RCA (61-7777 "It's Now Or Never")..500-700 60
(Living Stereo.)
RCA (47-7810 "Are You Lonesome To-night").. 8-10 60
RCA (61-7810 "Are You Lonesome To-night")..600-800 60
(Living Stereo.)
RCA (37-7850 "Surrender")........500-700 61
(Compact 33 Single.)
RCA (47-7850 "Surrender")........ 8-10 61
RCA (61-7850 "Surrender")......750-1000 61
(Living Stereo.)
RCA (68-7850 "Surrender")....1000-1500 61
(Stereo Compact 33 Single.)
RCA (37-7880 "I Feel So Bad")....................................1000-1500 61
(Compact 33 Single.)
RCA (47-7880 "I Feel So Bad") 8-10 61
RCA (37-7908 "His Latest Flame")................................4000-6000 61
(Compact 33 Single.)
RCA (47-7908 "His Latest Flame").. 8-10 61
RCA (37-7968 "Can't Help Falling in Love")................................5000-8000 61
(Compact 33 Single.)
RCA (47-7968 "Can't Help Falling in Love") 8-10 61
RCA (37-7992 "Good Luck Charm")................................8000-12000 62
(Compact 33 Single.)
RCA (47-7992 "Good Luck Charm") 8-10 62
RCA (8041 "She's Not You")...........8-10 62
RCA (8100 "Return to Sender")........8-10 62
RCA (8134 "One Broken Heart for Sale") 8-10 63
RCA (8188 "Devil in Disguise") ..200-300 63
(Flip side title is incorrectly shown as *Please Don't Drag That String ALONG.*)
RCA (8188 "Devil in Disguise")........6-10 63
(Flip side title correctly shown as *Please Don't Drag That String AROUND.*)
RCA (8243 "Bossa Nova Baby") 6-10 63
RCA (8307 "Kissin' Cousins")...........6-10 64
RCA (8360 "Viva Las Vegas") 6-10 64
RCA (8400 "Such a Night") 6-10 64
RCA (8440 "Ask Me") 6-10 64
RCA (8500 "Do the Clam")................6-10 65
RCA (8585 "Easy Question") 6-10 65
RCA (8657 "I'm Yours") 6-10 65
RCA (8740 "Tell Me Why") 6-10 65
RCA (8780 "Frankie and Johnny")....6-10 66
RCA (8870 "Love Letters")................6-10 66
RCA (8941 "Spinout") 6-10 66
RCA (8950 "If Everyday Was Like Christmas")..6-10 66
RCA (9056 "Indescribably Blue")......6-10 67
RCA (9115 "Long Legged Girl") 6-10 67
RCA (9287 "Judy")..............................6-10 67
RCA (9341 "Big Boss Man")...............6-10 67
RCA (9425 "Guitar Man")...................6-10 68
RCA (9465 "U.S. Male")......................6-10 68
RCA (9547 "Your Time Hasn't Come Yet Baby")..6-10 68
RCA (9600 "You'll Never Walk Alone")..6-10 68
RCA (9610 "Almost in Love")..............6-10 68
Note: Commercial issues of all RCA singles from 6357 through 9600 are on black labels.
RCA (9670 "If I Can Dream")............ 4-6 68
RCA (9731 "Memories")................... 4-6 69
RCA (9741 "In the Ghetto")............... 4-6 69
RCA (9747 "Clean Up Your Own Back Yard") 4-6 69
RCA (9764 "Suspicious Minds") 4-6 69
RCA (9768 "Don't Cry Daddy") 4-6 69
RCA (9791 "Kentucky Rain")............... 4-6 70
RCA (9835 "The Wonder of You")..... 4-6 70
RCA (9873 "I've Lost You") 4-6 70
RCA (9916 "You Don't Have to Say You Love Me") 4-6 70
RCA (9960 "I Really Don't Want to Know")... 4-6 70
RCA (9980 "Rags to Riches")............ 4-6 71
RCA (9985 "Life")................................ 4-6 71
RCA (9998 "I'm Leavin' ") 4-6 71
Note: RCA numbers in the 10000 to 14000 series with a "GB" prefix are Gold Standards and are listed in a separate Gold Standard Singles section.
RCA (10074 "Promised Land")......... 4-6 74
(Orange label.)
RCA (10074 "Promised Land").......10-20 74
(Gray label.)
RCA (10191 "My Boy") 10-15 75
(Orange label.)
RCA (10191 "My Boy") 15-25 75
(Tan or brown label.)
RCA (10278 "T-r-o-u-b-l-e") 20-25 75
(Orange label.)
RCA (10278 "T-r-o-u-b-l-e") 8-10 75
(Tan label.)
RCA (10278 "T-r-o-u-b-l-e") 200-300 75
(Gray label.)
RCA (10401 "Bringing It Back")..200-300 75
(Orange label.)
RCA (10401 "Bringing It Back")........8-10 75
(Tan label.)
RCA (10601 "For the Heart")......... 4-6 76
(Tan label.)
RCA (10601 "For the Heart")........90-100 76
(Black label.)
RCA (10857 "Moody Blue").............. 3-5 76
(Black vinyl. Colored vinyl 45s of *Moody Blue*, were experimental and are listed in the Promotional Singles section that follows.)
RCA (10998 "Way Down")................. 3-5 77
RCA (11099 thru 11113)................... 3-4 77
(Discs in this series were originally packaged in either 11301 and/or 11340, both of which are boxed sets of singles with sleeves.)
RCA (11165 "My Way")..................... 3-5 77
(Flip side shown as *America.*)
RCA (11165 "My Way") 20-25 77
(Fith flip side shown as *America the Beautiful.*)
RCA (11212 " Unchained Melody") ... 3-5 78
RCA (11301 "15 Golden Records")..65-75 77
(Boxed set of 15 Elvis singles with picture sleeves.)
RCA (11320 "Teddy Bear") 3-5 78
RCA (11340 "20 Golden Hits").......65-75 77
(Boxed set of 10 Elvis singles with picture sleeves.)
RCA (11533 "Are You Sincere")........ 3-5 79
RCA (11679 "I Got a Feelin' in My Body")..12-18 79
(With production and backing credits shown on label.)
RCA (11679 ("I Got a Feelin' in My Body")... 3-5 79
(With backing credits removed, leaving only production credits.)
RCA (12158 "Guitar Man")................ 3-5 81
RCA (12205 "Lovin' Arms")................ 3-5 81
RCA (13058 "You'll Never Walk Alone")... 3-5 82
RCA (13351 "The Elvis Medley") 3-5 82
RCA (13500 "I Was the One") 3-5 83
RCA (13547 "Little Sister")..................3-5 83
RCA (13875 "Baby, Let's Play House")..15-25 84
(Gold vinyl.)
RCA (13885 thru 13890)......................3-4 84
(Gold vinyl. Discs in this series were originally packaged in 13897, *Golden Singles, Vol. I.* May include juke box title strips.)
RCA (13891 thru 13896).......................3-4 84
(Gold vinyl. Discs in this series were originally packaged in 13898, *Golden Singles, Vol. II.* May include juke box title strips.)
RCA (13897 "Golden Singles, Vol. I")..20-30 84
(Package of six gold vinyl singles with sleeves.)
RCA (13898 "Golden Singles, Vol. II")..20-30 84
(Package of six gold vinyl singles with sleeves.)
RCA (13929 "Blue Suede Shoes") .10-15 84
(Blue vinyl. Incorrectly shows *Blue Suede Shoes* as stereo and *Promised Land* as mono.)
RCA (13929 "Blue Suede Shoes") ...8-12 84
(Blue vinyl. Correctly shows *Blue Suede Shoes* as mono and *Promised Land* as stereo.)
RCA (14090 "Always on My Mind")..10-15 85
(Purple vinyl.)
RCA (14237 "Merry Christmas Baby")..10-15 85
(Black vinyl.)
RCA (14237 "Merry Christmas Baby")..15-20 85
(Green vinyl.)
RCA (62402 "Don't Be Cruel") 10-15 92
(Colored vinyl.)
RCA (62403 "Blue Christmas") 10-15 92
(Colored vinyl.)
RCA (62449 "Heartbreak Hotel")....10-15 92
(Colored vinyl.)
Note: RCA numbers in the 10000-14000 series with a "GB" prefix are Gold Standard Series and are listed in a separate Gold Standard Singles section. Regular series issues are in the preceding section.
SPOKEN WORD (100 "1955 Texarkana Interview")..8-12 78
SUN (209 "That's All Right") 800-1200 54
SUN (210 "Good Rockin' Tonight")................................800-1200 54
SUN (215 "Milkcow Blue Boogie")................................1200-1800 55
SUN (217 "Baby Let's Play House")................................800-1200 55
SUN (223 "Mystery Train")........500-900 55
TRIBUTE (501 "A Tribute to Elvis Presley")..50-100 56
(Has Elvis plus guest appearances by Edward R. Murrow, Steve Allen, Ed Sullivan, Danny Kaye, Jimmy Durante, Gabriel Heater, Sid Ceaser, Liberace, Mantovani, Jack Benny, Gene Vincent, Gloria DeHaven, Nat King Cole, Nelson Eddy, and Jane Russell.)
Note: Plastic soundsheets or flexi-discs are listed in a separate section that follows.

Picture Sleeves
(Commercial and Promotional)

LAUREL (41 623 "Treat Me Nice")................................5000-10000 57
(Pictures Elvis but credits Vince Everett. Black and white sleeve made as a prop for the *Jailhouse Rock* film. The printed sheets have no reverse side, but are applied to a randomly selected EP. No Laurel records of this title exist. Unlike 41 624 and 41 625, there is no question about the authenticity of this sleeve.)
LAUREL (41 624 "Jailhouse Rock")..75-100 57
LAUREL (41 625 "Young and Beautiful")..75-100 57
(Above two picture Elvis but credit Vince Everett. Black-and-white, cardboard, EP-like cover. May have been made as a film prop. While many researchers question the authenticity – and therefore the actual date of production – of these, these prices have been paid. No Laurel records of these titles exist.).
PECA ("Could I Fall in Love")................................4000-8000 66
(Pictures Elvis but credits Guy Lambert with George and His G-Men. A full color sleeve made as a prop for the *Double Trouble* film. No Peca records of this title exist.)
RCA (76 "Don't"/"Wear My Ring Around Your Neck")................................1000-2000 60
(Promotional issue only.)
RCA (0088 "Raised on Rock") 25-30 73
RCA (118 "King of the Whole Wide World")..200-250 62
(Promotional issue only.)
RCA (0130 "How Great Thou Art")..150-200 69
RCA (162 "How Great Thou Art")..150-200 67
(Promotional issue only.)
RCA (0196 " Take Good Care of Her")..10-15 74
RCA (0280 "If You Talk in Your Sleep")..20-25 74
RCA (0572 "Merry Christmas Baby")..40-50 71
RCA (0619 "Until It's Time for You to Go")..20-25 71
RCA (0651 "He Touched Me") ...100-150 71
RCA (0672 "An American Trilogy")..50-75 72
RCA (0769 "Burning Love") 10-15 72
RCA (0815 "Separate Ways").........10-15 71
RCA (0910 "Fool")..........................10-15 73
RCA (1017 "It's Only Love")..............8-12 71
RCA (6357 "Mystery Train")... 1000-2000 55
(Cartoon "This Is His Life" series. Previously thought to have come with *I Want You, I Need You, I Love You*, but recent evidence points strongly to it being *Mystery Train* – though no title is shown or referred to on the sleeve. Promotional issue only.)
RCA (6604 "Don't Be Cruel") 75-85 55
(Shows *Don't Be Cruel c/w Hound Dog.*)
RCA (6604 "Hound Dog") 65-75 56
(Shows *Hound Dog c/w Don't Be Cruel.*)
RCA (6643 "Love Me Tender") ..100-150 56
(Black and white sleeve.)
RCA (6643 "Love Me Tender") 75-100 56
(Black and green sleeve.)
RCA (6643 "Love Me Tender") 50-75 56
(Black and dark pink sleeve.)
RCA (6643 "Love Me Tender") 40-60 56
(Black and light pink sleeve.)
RCA (6800 "Too Much") 50-100 57
RCA (6870 "All Shook Up")...........50-100 57
RCA (7000 "Teddy Bear")...............50-100 57
RCA (7035 "Jailhouse Rock") 50-100 57
(Sleeve only.)
RCA/MGM "Jailhouse Rock"). 1000-1500 57
(MGM *Jailhouse Rock* film preview invitation ticket. A promotional item for the media, the ticket came wrapped around a commercial single and sleeve. Deduct about 50% if ticket stub is detached. Counterfeits exist.)
RCA (7150 "Don't")........................50-60 58
RCA (7240 "Wear My Ring Around Your Neck")..50-60 58
RCA (7280 "Hard Headed Woman")..40-50 58
RCA (7410 "One Night") 40-50 58
RCA (7506 "I Need Your Love Tonight")................................300-500 59
(Has advertising for the *Elvis Sails* EP on reverse.)
RCA (7506 "I Need Your Love Tonight")..35-45 59
(Lists Elvis EPs and 45s on reverse.)
RCA (7600 "A Big Hunk O' Love") .35-45 59
RCA (7740 "Stuck on You")...............30-35 60
(Die-cut sleeve which displays record label.)
RCA (7777 "It's Now Or Never") 20-30 60
RCA (7810 "Are You Lonesome To-night")..20-30 60
RCA (37-7850 "Surrender") 800-1000 61
(Compact 33 Single sleeve. Copies without some ring wear are very scarce.)
RCA (47-7850 "Surrender") 20-30 61
RCA (37-7880 "I Feel So Bad")................................1500-2000 61
(Compact 33 Single sleeve.)
RCA (47-7880 "I Feel So Bad")......20-30 61
RCA (37-7908 "His Latest Flame")................................4000-6000 61
(Compact 33 Single sleeve.)
RCA (47-7908 "His Latest Flame").15-25 61
RCA (37-7968 "Can't Help Falling in Love")................................5000-8000 61
(Compact 33 Single sleeve.)
RCA (47-7968 "Can't Help Falling in Love")..20-30 61
RCA (37-7992 "Good Luck Charm")................................8000-12000 62
(Compact 33 Single sleeve.)
RCA (47-7992 "Good Luck Charm")..20-30 62
RCA (8041 "She's Not You")...........20-30 62
RCA (8100 "Return to Sender").........20-30 62
RCA (8134 "One Broken Heart for Sale")..25-35 63
RCA (8188 "Devil in Disguise")......20-30 63
RCA (8243 "Bossa Nova Baby")......20-30 63
(Reads: "Coming Soon! *Fun in Acapulco* LP Album.")
RCA (8243 "Bossa Nova Baby")................................200-300 63
(No mention of *Fun in Acapulco* Album.")
RCA (8307 "Kissin' Cousins")...........20-30 64
RCA (8360 "Viva Las Vegas")..........30-40 64
(Reads "Coming Soon" regarding the *Viva Las Vegas* EP.)
RCA (8360 "Viva Las Vegas")........60-90 64
(Reads "Ask For" regarding the *Viva Las Vegas* EP.)
RCA (8400 "Such a Night")............20-30 64
RCA (8440 "Ask Me") 20-30 64
(Reads: "Coming Soon! *Roustabout* LP Album.")
RCA (8440 "Ask Me") 30-40 64
(Reads: "Ask For *Roustabout* LP Album.")
RCA (8500 "Do the Clam")...............20-35 65
RCA (8585 "Easy Question") 20-25 65
(Reads "Coming Soon! Special *Tickle Me* EP.")
RCA (8585 "Easy Question") 30-35 65
(Reads "Ask For Special *Tickle Me* EP.")
RCA (8657 "I'm Yours") 20-30 65
RCA (8740 "Tell Me Why") 20-30 65
RCA (8780 "Frankie & Johnny").......20-30 66
RCA (8870 "Love Letters")...............20-30 66
(Reads "Coming Soon – *Paradise Hawaiian Style.*")
RCA (8870 "Love Letters")..............50-75 66
(Reads "Ask For – *Paradise Hawaiian Style.*")
RCA (8941 "Spinout")......................20-30 66
(Reads "Watch For Elvis' *Spinout* LP.")
RCA (8941 "Spinout")......................30-40 66
(Reads "Ask For Elvis' *Spinout* LP.")
RCA (8950 "If Everyday Was Like Christmas")..25-35 66
RCA (9056 "Indescribably Blue") ...20-30 67
RCA (9115 "Long Legged Girl")........20-30 67
(Reads "Coming Soon – *Double Trouble* LP Album.")
RCA (9115 "Long Legged Girl") 30-40 67
(Reads "Ask For – *Double Trouble* LP Album.")
RCA (9287 "Judy")..........................20-30 67
RCA (9341 "Big Boss Man") 20-30 67
RCA (9425 "Guitar Man")..................20-25 68
(Reads "Coming Soon, *Elvis' Gold Records, Volume 4.*")
RCA (9425 "Guitar Man") 25-30 68
(Reads "Ask For *Elvis' Gold Records, Volume 4.*")
RCA (9465 "U.S. Male") 15-20 68
RCA (9547 "Your Time Hasn't Come Yet Baby")..20-30 68
(Reads "Coming Soon – *Speedway* LP.")
RCA (9547 "Your Time Hasn't Come Yet Baby")..30-40 68
(Reads "Ask For – *Speedway* LP.")
RCA (9600 "You'll Never Walk Alone")..75-125 68
RCA (9610 "Almost in Love")...........20-30 68
RCA (9670 "If I Can Dream")...........15-20 68
RCA (9731 "Memories") 20-25 69
RCA (9741 "In the Ghetto")..............15-20 69
(Reads "Coming Soon *From Elvis in Memphis* LP Album.")
RCA (9741 "In the Ghetto")............20-25 69
(Reads "Ask For *From Elvis in Memphis* LP Album.")
RCA (9747 "Clean Up Your Own Back Yard")..15-15 69
RCA (9764 "Suspicious Minds").....10-15 69
RCA (9768 "Don't Cry Daddy")........10-20 69
RCA (9791 "Kentucky Rain") 10-20 70
RCA (9835 "The Wonder of You") .10-20 70
RCA (9873 "I've Lost You")..............10-15 70
RCA (9916 "You Don't Have to Say You Love Me")..10-20 70
RCA (9960 "I Really Don't Want to Know")..10-20 70
(Reads "Coming Soon – New Album.")
RCA (9960 "I Really Don't Want to Know")..20-25 70
(Reads "Now Available – New Album.")
RCA (9980 "Rags to Riches") 35-40 71
RCA (9985 "Life")............................20-30 71
RCA (9998 "I'm Leavin' ")................15-20 71
RCA (10074 "Promised Land") 10-15 74
RCA (10191 "My Boy")....................40-50 75
RCA (10278 "T-r-o-u-b-l-e")............10-15 75
RCA (10401 "Bringing It Back") 20-25 75
RCA (10601 "For the Heart") 10-12 76
RCA (10857 "Moody Blue")..............10-20 76
RCA (10998 "Way Down")...............10-15 77
RCA (11099 thru 11113)....................3-4 77
(Sleeves in this series were originally packaged in either RCA 11301 and/or 11340, both boxed sets of singles with sleeves.)
RCA (11165 "My Way")....................10-15 77
(Flip side title shown as *America.*)
RCA (11165 "My Way")....................30-40 77
(Flip side title shown as *America the Beautiful*)
RCA (11212 "Unchained Melody")..10-15 78
RCA (11320 "Teddy Bear")................8-10 78
RCA (11533 "Are You Sincere")........8-10 79
RCA (11679 "I Got a Feelin' in My Body")..8-10 79
RCA (12158 "Guitar Man")................6-10 81
RCA (13058 "You'll Never Walk Alone")..10-15 82
RCA (13302 "The Impossible Dream")..75-100 82
(Promotional issue only.)
RCA (13351 "The Elvis Medley") ...10-15 82
RCA (13500 "I Was the One")..........5-10 83
RCA (13547 "Little Sister").............5-10 83
RCA (13875 "Baby, Let's Play House")..15-25 84
RCA (13885 thru 13896).....................3-4 84
(Sleeves in this series were originally packaged in RCA 13897 and 13898, *Golden Singles.*)
RCA (13929 "Blue Suede Shoes") .10-15 84
RCA (14090 "Always on My Mind")...5-10 85
RCA (14237 "Merry Christmas Baby")..10-15 85
Notes: There may be slight price differences for assorted variations in colors and paper stock used. Often, the difference is simply which one is needed to complete a run. Regardless, sleeve variations within the price range given do not require separate listings. If the value varies beyond the given range, a separate listing will be added. Sleeves for the RCA "447" Gold Standard Series are listed in a separate section following the Gold Standard Singles. A slight premium—perhaps $3 to $5—may be placed on RCA's "Living Stereo" paper sleeves. These were used for many different RCA stereo singles and were not exclusively an Elvis item.

Gold Standard Singles with "447" prefix
(Commercial)

RCA (0600 thru 0639)..................10-20 59-64
(Black label, dog on top.)
RCA (0600 thru 0639).....................6-12 65-66
(Black label, dog on side.)
RCA (0600 thru 0639)..................30-40 68-69
(Orange label.)
RCA (0600 thru 0639)..................10-15 70-74
(Red label.)
RCA (0600 thru 0639)........................3-5 77
(Black label, dog near top.)
RCA (0640 thru 0642)....................20-25 64
(Black label, dog on top.)
RCA (0640 thru 0642).....................8-12 65-66
(Black label, dog on side.)
RCA (0640 thru 0642)..................30-40 68-69
(Orange label.)
RCA (0640 thru 0642)..................10-15 70-74
(Red label.)
RCA (0643 "Crying in the Chapel") ..6-10 65
(Black label, dog on side.)
RCA (0643 "Crying in the Chapel") 5-8 70s
(Red label.)
RCA (0643 "Crying in the Chapel") 4-6 77
(Black label, dog near top.)
RCA (0644 thru 0646)....................25-35 65
(Black label, dog on top.)
RCA (0644 thru 0646)......................8-12 65
(Black label, dog on side.)

RCA (0644 thru 0646)....................30-40 68-69
(Orange label.)
RCA (0644 thru 0646).................... 5-10 70-74
(Red label.)
RCA (0644 thru 0646)....................... 4-6 77
(Black label, dog near top.)
RCA (0647 thru 0650)..................... 6-10 65
(Black label, dog on side.)
RCA (0647 thru 0650)..................... 8-12 70-74
(Red label.)
RCA (0647 thru 0650)....................... 3-5 77
(Black label, dog near top.)
RCA (0651 & 0652)........................20-25 66
(Black label, dog on side.)
RCA (0651 & 0652)........................10-15 70s
(Red label.)
RCA (0653 thru 0658).................... 8-12 66-68
(Black label, dog on side.)
RCA (0653 thru 0658).................... 5-10 70-74
(Red label.)
RCA (0653 thru 0658)....................... 4-6 77
(Black label, dog near top.)
RCA (0659 "Indescribably Blue")....10-15 70
(Red label.)
RCA (0660 "Long Legged Girl") 25-50 70
(Red label.)
RCA (0661 "Judy")........................10-20 70
(Red label.)
RCA (0662 "Big Boss Man")..........10-15 70
(Red label.)
RCA (0663 thru 0685)..................10-15 70-73
(Red label.)
RCA (0663 thru 0685)....................... 3-5 77
(Black label, dog near top.)
RCA (0720 "Blue Christmas") 10-20 64
(Black label, dog on top.)

Gold Standard Singles with "GB" prefix
(Commercial)

RCA (10156 thru 10489).................. 5-10 75-76
(Red label.)
RCA (10156 thru 10489).................. 3-5 77
(Black label, dog near top.)
RCA (11326 thru 13275)................... 3-5 77
(Black label, dog near top.)
Gold Standard *promotional* singles are in numerical sequence in the section for Promotional Singles.

Gold Standard Picture Sleeves

RCA (0601 "That's All Right")......250-300 64
RCA (0602 "Good Rockin' Tonight")..............................250-300 64
RCA (0605 "Heartbreak Hotel")..250-300 64
RCA (0608 "Don't Be Cruel")......250-300 64
RCA (0618 "All Shook Up")..........250-300 64
RCA (0639 "Kiss Me Quick")..........50-75 64
RCA (0643 "Crying in the Chapel")......................................20-30 65
RCA (0647 "Blue Christmas") 30-35 65
(Pictures Elvis on a Christmas card among wrapped gifts.)
RCA (0647 "Blue Christmas") 8-10 77
(Pictures Elvis in a circle among colored ornaments.)
RCA (0650 "Puppet on a String") ...40-50 65
RCA (0651 "Joshua Fit the Battle").....................................200-250 66
RCA (0652 "Milky White Way")...200-250 66
RCA (0651 & 0652 "Special Easter Programming Kit")..................900-1200 66
(Picture sleeve-mailer. Contained both 1966 Easter singles, *Joshua Fit the Battle* and *Milky White Way* in their sleeves and an Easter greeting card from Elvis. Price is for the complete kit.)
RCA (0651 & 0652 "Special Easter Programming Kit")....................800-1000 66
(Picture sleeve-mailer only.)
RCA (0720 "Blue Christmas") 45-55 64

Promotional Singles

CREATIVE RADIO ("Elvis 10th Anniversary"/"The Elvis Hour")...........................15-20 87
(Demonstration disc, promoting the syndicated 10th anniversary radio special.)
CREATIVE RADIO ("Memories of Elvis"/"The Elvis Hour")....................................15-20 87
(Demonstration disc, promoting the syndicated 10th anniversary radio special.)
For *Elvis 50th Birthday Special*, see PRESLEY, Elvis / Buddy Holly.
For *The Elvis Hour*, see PRESLEY, Elvis / Gary Owens.
CREATIVE RADIO ("Nearer My God to Thee")..10-20 89
(Promotional souvenir only. Issued as a bonus single with the LP, *Between Takes with Elvis*.)
CREATIVE RADIO ("Mystery Train").. 5-10 92
(Single-sided demonstration disc, taken from the syndicated 15th anniversary radio special.)
PARAMOUNT PICTURES ("Easy Come, Easy Go")...800-1000 67
(Issued only to select theatres, designed for lobby play.)
PARAMOUNT PICTURES (1800 "Blue Hawaii")....................................500-750 61
(Single-sided pressing. Issued only to select theatres, designed for lobby play. Has excerpts of songs from the film.)
PARAMOUNT PICTURES (2017 "Girls! Girls! Girls!")....................................800-1000 64
(Issued only to select theatres, designed for lobby play.)
PARAMOUNT PICTURES (2413 "Roustabout")........................2000-3000 64
(Issued only to select theatres, designed for lobby play. Track is an alternate take.)
RCA (15 "Old Shep")......................700-800 56
RCA (76 "Don't"/"Wear My Ring Around Your Neck")......................................800-1000 60
(Issued with special sleeve, listed in the Picture Sleeves section.)
RCA (0088 "Raised on Rock")........20-25 73
(Yellow label.)
RCA (118 "King of the Whole Wide World")....................................200-250 62
(Issued with a special sleeve, which is listed in the Picture Sleeves section. Includes "Deejay Notes from RCA Victor" one-page insert.)
RCA (0130 "How Great Thou Art")...75-125 69
(Yellow label.)
RCA (139 "Roustabout") 225-275 64
RCA (162 "How Great Thou Art")...150-200 67
(Issued with a special sleeve, listed in the Picture Sleeves section.)
RCA (0196 "Take Good Care of Her")...20-25 74
(Yellow label.)
RCA (0280 "If You Talk in Your Sleep")..15-20 74
(Yellow label.)
RCA (0572 "Merry Christmas Baby")..25-30 71
(Yellow label.)
RCA (0601 "That's All Right").......75-125 64
(White label.)
RCA (0602 "Good Rockin' Tonight")......................................75-125 64
(White label.)
RCA (0605 "Heartbreak Hotel")....75-125 64
(White label.)
RCA (0608 "Don't Be Cruel") 75-125 64
(White label.)
RCA (0618 "All Shook Up")..........75-125 64
(White label.)
RCA (0619 "Until It's Time for You to Go")..25-30 72
(Yellow label.)
RCA (0639 "Kiss Me Quick")..........40-50 64
(White label.)
RCA (0643 "Crying in the Chapel")..25-30 65
(White label.)
RCA (0647 "Blue Christmas") 35-40 65
(White label.)
RCA (0650 "Puppet on a String") ...30-35 65
(White label.)
RCA (0651 "Joshua Fit the Battle")...75-125 66
(White label.)
RCA (0652 "Milky White Way")....75-125 66
(White label. See Gold Standard Picture Sleeves section for special mailing sleeve used with 0651 & 0652.)
RCA (0651 "He Touched Me") ...100-150 72
(Yellow label.)
RCA (0672 "An American Trilogy")..20-25 72
(Yellow label.)
RCA (0720 "Blue Christmas") 35-40 64
(White label.)
RCA (0769 "Burning Love") 15-20 72
(Yellow label.)
RCA (0808 "Blue Christmas")................................2000-3000 57
(Identification number shown since no selection number is used.)
RCA (0815 "Separate Ways") 20-25 72
(Yellow label.)
RCA (0910 "Fool") 10-15 73
(Yellow label.)
RCA (6357 "Mystery Train").......300-400 55
(White "Record Prevue" label. Add $50 to $100 if accompanied by *Dee Jay Digest* Vol 2, No. 50, dated Dec. 2, 1955 – a four-page RCA record newsletter)
RCA (8360 "Viva Las Vegas")........45-50 64
(White label.)
RCA (8400 "Such a Night") 5000-7500 64
(White label.)
RCA (8440 "Ask Me") 40-50 64
(White label.)
RCA (8500 "Do the Clam")..............40-45 65
(White label.)
RCA (8585 "Easy Question") 40-45 65
(White label.)
RCA (8657 "I'm Yours") 40-45 65
(White label.)
RCA (8740 "Tell Me Why")..............40-45 65
(White label.)
RCA (8780 "Frankie & Johnny")......40-45 66
(White label.)
RCA (8870 "Love Letters")..............40-45 66
(White label.)
RCA (8941 "Spinout")......................40-45 66
(White label.)
RCA (8950 "If Everyday Was Like Christmas")...40-45 66
(White label.)
RCA (9056 "Indescribably Blue")....35-40 67
(White label.)
RCA (9115 "Long Legged Girl") 35-40 67
(White label.)
RCA (9287 "Judy")............................35-40 67
(White label.)
RCA (9341 "Big Boss Man")............35-40 67
(White label.)
RCA (9425 "Guitar Man")................20-30 68
(Yellow label.)
RCA (9465 "U.S. Male")...................25-35 68
(Yellow label.)
RCA (9547 "Your Time Hasn't Come Yet Baby")..30-35 68
(Yellow label.)
RCA (9600 "You'll Never Walk Alone")..25-35 68
(Yellow label.)
RCA (9610 "Almost in Love") 30-35 68
(Yellow label.)
RCA (9670 "If I Can Dream") 25-35 68
(Yellow label.)
RCA (9731 "Memories")..................20-30 69
(Yellow label.)
RCA (9741 "In the Ghetto")..............20-30 69
(Yellow label.)
RCA (9747 "Clean Up Your Own Back Yard")...10-15 69
(Yellow label.)
RCA (9764 "Suspicious Minds") 20-30 69
(Yellow label.)
RCA (9768 "Don't Cry Daddy").......20-30 69
(Yellow label.)
RCA (9791 "Kentucky Rain") 20-30 70
(Yellow label.)
RCA (9835 "The Wonder of You") 25-35 70
(Yellow label.)
RCA (9873 "I've Lost You")............20-25 70
(Yellow label.)
RCA (9916 "You Don't Have to Say You Love Me")...20-25 70
(Yellow label.)
RCA (9960 "I Really Don't Want to Know")..20-25 70
(Yellow label.)
RCA (9980 "Rags to Riches") 25-30 71
(Yellow label.)
RCA (9985 "Life")...........................25-30 71
(Yellow label.)
RCA (9998 "I'm Leavin' ") 20-25 71
(Yellow label.)
RCA (10074 "Promised Land").........8-10 74
(Yellow label.)
RCA (10191 "My Boy") 25-30 75
(Yellow label.)
RCA (10278 "T-r-o-u-b-l-e") 30-35 75
(Yellow label.)
RCA (10401 "Bringing It Back") 8-10 75
(Yellow label.)
RCA (10601 "Hurt") 20-25 76
(Yellow label.)
RCA (10857 "Moody Blue")............15-20 76
(Yellow label. Black vinyl.)
RCA (10857 "Moody Blue").... 2000-3000 77
(Experimental colored vinyl pressings. Not intended for distribution.)
RCA (10951 "Let Me Be There")....................................100-150 77
RCA (10998 "Way Down") 150-175 77
(White label.)
RCA (10998 "Way Down")..............15-20 77
(Yellow label.)
RCA (11165 "My Way")......................6-10 77
(Yellow label.)
RCA (11212 "Unchained Melody") .10-15 78
(Yellow label.)
RCA (11320 "Teddy Bear") 6-10 78
(Yellow label.)
RCA (11533 "Are You Sincere").....10-12 79
(Yellow label.)
RCA (11679 "I Got a Feelin' in My Body")...10-12 79
(Yellow label.)
RCA (12158 "Guitar Man")..............10-15 81
(Yellow label. Black vinyl.)
RCA (12158 "Guitar Man")........150-200 81
(Yellow label. Red vinyl.)
RCA (12205 "Lovin' Arms")............10-15 81
(Yellow label. Black vinyl.)
RCA (12205 "Lovin' Arms")........250-300 81
(Yellow label. Green vinyl.)
RCA (13058 "You'll Never Walk Alone")..10-15 82
(Yellow label.)
RCA (13302 "The Impossible Dream")..75-100 82
RCA (13351 "Elvis Medley")...........10-15 82
(Yellow label. Black vinyl.)
RCA (13351 "Elvis Medley") 100-200 82
(Gold label. Gold vinyl.)
RCA (13500 "I Was the One")........10-15 83
(Yellow label. Black vinyl.)
RCA (13500 "I Was the One")....100-200 83
(Yellow label. Colored vinyl.)
RCA (13547 "Little Sister")............10-15 83
(Yellow label. Black vinyl.)
RCA (13547 "Little Sister").........200-250 83
(Blue label. Blue vinyl.)
RCA (13875 "Baby, Let's Play House")....................................350-400 84
(Gold label on *Baby Let's Play House* and white label on *Hound Dog*. Gold vinyl.)
RCA (13875 "Baby, Let's Play House")..75-100 84
(Gold label on both sides. Neither side indicates mono or stereo. Gold vinyl.)
RCA (13875 "Baby, Let's Play House")...20-40 84
(Gold label on both sides. Both sides shown as "Stereo." Gold vinyl.)
RCA (13929 "Blue Suede Shoes)...15-25 84
(Gold label. Blue vinyl.)
RCA (14090 "Always on My Mind") 15-20 85
(Gold label. Purple vinyl.)
RCA (14237 "Merry Christmas Baby")..6-10 85
Note: Elvis 50th Anniversary singles—RCA 13875 through 14237—used the same gold label for both commercial and promotional issues. Promo singles have "Not For Sale" printed on the label.
RCA (4-834-115 "I'll Be Back")...................................5000-8000 66
(White label. Single-sided disc. Reads "For Special Academy Consideration Only." Made for submission to the Academy of Motion Picture Arts and Sciences.)
ROYAL CARIBBEAN CRUISE LINES (12690 "Follow That Dream - Take 2") 10-15 90
(Souvenir disc for Elvis cruise passengers.)
UNITED STATES AIR FORCE (125 "It's Now Or Never"): see PRESLEY, Elvis / Jaye P. Morgan.
UNITED STATES AIR FORCE (159 "Surrender"): see PRESLEY, Elvis / Lawrence Welk.
WHAT'S IT ALL ABOUT (78 "Life"): see PRESLEY, Elvis / Helen Reddy
WHAT'S IT ALL ABOUT (1840 "Elvis Presley") 70-75 80
WHAT'S IT ALL ABOUT (3025 "Elvis Presley")...50-60 82
Note: Plastic soundsheets and flexi-discs are listed in a separate section that follows. Promotional 78s are included with Singles: 78 rpm, at the beginning of the Presley section.

Plastic Soundsheets/Flexi-discs

EVA-TONE (38713 "Elvis Speaks! The Truth About Me")...................................30-40
(Eva-Tone number is not on label but is etched in the trail-off.)
EVA-TONE (52578 "The King Is Dead Long Live the King")..........................50-100 78
EVA-TONE (831942 "50,000,000 Elvis Fans Weren't Wrong!")............................5-10 83
EVA-TONE (726771 "The Elvis Presley Story")..8-15 77
EVA-TONE (1037710 "Elvis Live")...25-30 78
(Price for magazine, titled *Collector's Issue*, with bound-in soundsheet.)
EVA-TONE (1037710 "Elvis Live") 10-15 78
(Price for soundsheet only.)
EVA-TONE (1227785 "Thompson Vocal Eliminator").....................................15-20 78
(Has segments of songs by three artists including Elvis.)
EVA-TONE (10287733 "Elvis: Six Hour Special")...15-20 77
EVA-TONE/RCA ("Love Me Tender")..25-35 74
(Price for April 1974 issue of *Teen Magazine* with bound-in soundsheet.)
EVA-TONE/RCA ("Love Me Tender")..15-25 74
(Price for soundsheet only.)
LYNCHBURG AUDIO ("The Truth About Me")..125-150 56
(Lynchburg Audio number is not on label but is etched in the trail-off.)
RAINBO ("Elvis Speaks, in Person")....................................300-400 56
(Price for magazine, *Elvis Answers Back*, with 78rpm flexi-disc still attached to front cover.)
RAINBO ("Elvis Speaks, in Person")....................................100-150 56
(Price for flexi-disc only.)
RAINBO ("The Truth About Me")..300-400 56
(Price for magazine, *Elvis Answers Back*, with 78rpm paper flexi-disc still attached to front cover.)
RAINBO ("The Truth About Me")..100-150 56
(Price for flexi-disc only.)
RAINBO ("Elvis Show") 150-250 56
(Promotional issue for a June 3, 1956 concert.)
Note: All soundsheets and flexi-discs were used for some type of promotional purpose.

EPs: 7-inch
(Commercial and Promotional)

MEMPHIS FLASH (92444 "Elvis – My Life")...50-75 78
(Two seven-inch picture discs in gatefold, die-cut cover. Spoken word content from interviews, etc. "Collector Series" number on front cover. Reportedly 3,000 made
RCA (2 "Dealers' Prevue"): see Various Artists section
RCA (15 Extended Plays): see Various Artists section
(For just the Elvis EP from this set, see RCA 9089.)
RCA (19 "The Sound of Leadership"): see Various Artists section
(For just the Elvis EP from this set, see RCA 9113.)
RCA (22 "Elvis Presley")........ 2000-2500 56
(May have "Elvis" in either light or dark pink letters on front cover. Two-EP bonus promotional item. Discs are numbered 9121 & 9122.)
RCA (23 "Elvis Presley")........ 3500-4500 56
(Three-EP bonus promotional item. Includes "How to Use and Enjoy Your RCA Victor Elvis Presley Autograph Automatic 45 Victrola Portable Phonograph," which represents $75 to $100 of the value. Discs are numbered 9123, 9124 & 9125.)
RCA (26 "Great Country/Western Hits"): see Various Artists section
(For just the Elvis EP from this set, see RCA 9141.)
RCA (27 "Save-On Records"): see Various Artists section
RCA (37 "Perfect for Parties"): see Various Artists section
RCA (39 "Dealers' Prevue"): see Various Artists section
RCA (61 Extended Play Sampler): see Various Artists section
RCA (121 "RCA Family Record Center"): see Various Artists section
RCA (128 "Elvis by Request")......75-100 61
RCA (747 "Elvis Presley")..........100-125 56
(Black label, dog on top. Has song title strip across the top of front cover.)
RCA (747 "Elvis Presley")..........250-300 56
(Black label, without dog.)
RCA (747 "Elvis Presley")............60-100 65
(Black label, dog on side.)
RCA (747 "Elvis Presley")..........100-150 69
(Orange label.)
RCA (747 "Blue Suede Shoes")...............................1000-1800 56
(Temporary paper sleeve for 1956 issue of EPA-747. Price is for sleeve only.)
RCA (821 "Heartbreak Hotel") ...100-125 56
(Black label, dog on top. Has song title strip across the top of front cover.)
RCA (821 "Heartbreak Hotel") ...250-300 56
(Black label, without dog.)
RCA (821 "Heartbreak Hotel") 60-80 65
(Black label, dog on side.)
RCA (821 "Heartbreak Hotel") ... 100-150 69
(Orange label.)
RCA (830 "Elvis Presley")......... 100-125 56
(Black label, dog on top. Has song title strip across the top of front cover.)
RCA (830 "Elvis Presley").........250-300 56
(Black label, without dog.)
RCA (830 "Elvis Presley")............75-100 65
(Black label, dog on side.)
RCA (830 "Elvis Presley")......... 100-150 69
(Orange label.)
RCA (940 "The Real Elvis") 100-125 56
(Black label, dog on top. Has song title strip across the top of front cover.)
RCA (940 "The Real Elvis").......250-300 56
(Black label, without dog. Reissued as Gold Standard 5120.)
RCA (965 "Any Way You Want Me")..100-125 56
(Black label, dog on top. Has song title strip across the top of front cover.)
RCA (965 "Any Way You Want Me")...250-300 56
(Black label, without dog.)
RCA (965 "Any Way You Want Me")...60-80 65
(Black label, dog on side.)
RCA (965 "Any Way You Want Me")...100-150 69
(Orange label.)
RCA (992 "Elvis, Vol. 1") 75-100 56
(Black label, dog on top. Has song title strip across the top of front cover.)
RCA (992 "Elvis, Vol. 1") 225-275 56
(Black label, without dog.)
RCA (992 "Elvis, Vol. 1") 75-100 65
(Black label, dog on side.)
RCA (992 "Elvis, Vol. 1") 100-150 69
(Orange label.)
RCA (993 "Elvis, Vol. 2")..............75-100 56
(Black label, dog on top. Has song title strip across the top of front cover.)
RCA (993 "Elvis, Vol. 2") 225-275 56
(Black label, without dog.)
RCA (993 "Elvis, Vol. 2") 75-100 65
(Black label, dog on side.)
RCA (993 "Elvis, Vol. 2") 100-150 69
(Orange label.)
RCA (994 "Strictly Elvis") 100-125 56
(Black label, dog on top. Has song title strip across the top of front cover.)
RCA (994 "Strictly Elvis") 250-300 56
(Black label, without dog.)
RCA (994 "Strictly Elvis") 60-80 65
(Black label, dog on side.)
RCA (994 "Strictly Elvis") 100-150 69
(Orange label.)
RCA (1254 "Elvis Presley")........550-650 56
(Black label, without dog. Two EP set.)
RCA (1254 "Elvis Presley")........325-425 56
(Black label, dog on top. Two EP set.)
RCA (1254 "Most Talked-About New Personality")......................3500-5000 56
(Two EPs, also numbered 0793 & 0794, in a single pocket paper sleeve. Promotional issue only. Includes a copy of *Dee-Jay Digest*, which represents $50 to $75 of the value.)
RCA (1254 "Most Talked-About New Personality")......................1000-2000 56
(Price for the two EPs without the sleeve. Either disc would be worth about half the amount shown for both. Discs, numbered 0793 & 0794, are untitled. Promotional issue only.)
RCA (1-1515 "Loving You, Vol. 1")..75-100 57
(Black label, dog on top. Has song title strip across the top of front cover.)
RCA (1-1515 "Loving You, Vol. 1")...60-80 65
(Black label, dog on side.)
RCA (1-1515 "Loving You, Vol. 1")..100-150 69
(Orange label.)
RCA (2-1515 "Loving You, Vol. 2")..75-100 57
(Black label, dog on top. Has song title strip across the top of front cover.)
RCA (2-1515 "Loving You, Vol. 2")...60-80 65
(Black label, dog on side.)
RCA (2-1515 "Loving You, Vol. 2")..100-150 69
(Orange label.)
RCA (2006 "Aloha from Hawaii Via Satellite") 150-200 74
(Includes sheet of 10 title strips. Made for juke box operators only.)
RCA (4006 "Love Me Tender") 75-100 56
(Black label, dog on top. Has song title strip across the top of front cover.)
RCA (4006 "Love Me Tender") .. 225-275 56
(Black label, without dog. Has song title strip across the top of front cover.)
RCA (4006 "Love Me Tender") 60-80 65
(Black label, dog on side.)
RCA (4006 "Love Me Tender") .. 100-150 69
(Orange label.)
RCA (4041 "Just for You") 100-125 57
(Black label, dog on top. Has EP title strip across the top of front cover.)
RCA (4041 "Just for You")..........250-300 57
(Black label, without dog. Has EP title strip across the top of front cover.)
RCA (4041 "Just for You")..............60-80 65
(Black label, dog on side.)
RCA (4041 "Just for You")...........100-150 69
(Orange label.)
RCA (4054 "Peace in the Valley")...50-100 57
(Black label, dog on top. Has EP title strip across the top of front cover. Reissued as Gold Standard 5121.)

RCA (4108 "Elvis Sings Christmas Songs")....................................75-100 57
(Black label, dog on top. Has EP title strip across the top of front cover.)
RCA (4108 "Elvis Sings Christmas Songs")....................................60-80 65
(Black label, dog on side.)
RCA (4108 "Elvis Sings Christmas Songs")....................................150-200 69
(Orange label.)
RCA (4114 "Jailhouse Rock")........75-100 57
(Black label, dog on top.)
RCA (4114 "Jailhouse Rock").........60-80 65
(Black label, dog on side.)
RCA (4114 "Jailhouse Rock")......100-150 69
(Orange label.)
RCA (4319 "King Creole")............75-100 58
(Reissued as Gold Standard 5122.)
RCA (4321 "King Creole, Vol. 2")....................................75-100 58
(Black label, dog on top.)
RCA (4321 "King Creole, Vol. 2")....................................75-100 65
(Black label, dog on side.)
RCA (4321 "King Creole, Vol. 2")....................................100-150 69
(Orange label.)
RCA (4325 "Elvis Sails")............100-150 58
(Reissued as Gold Standard 5157.)
RCA (4340 "Christmas with Elvis")....................................200-250 58
(Black label, dog on top.)
RCA (4340 "Christmas with Elvis")....................................100-150 65
(Black label, dog on side.)
RCA (4340 "Christmas with Elvis")....................................150-200 69
(Orange label.)
RCA (4368 "Follow That Dream")...60-90 62
(Black label, dog on top. Playing times are incorrectly listed for three of the four tracks: *Follow That Dream* shown as 1:35, should be 1:38; *Angel* shown as 2:35, should be 2:40; and *I'm Not the Marrying Kind* shown as 1:49, should be 2:00.)
RCA (4368 "Follow That Dream")....................................50-100 62
(Black label, dog on top. All playing times are correctly shown.)
RCA (4368 "Follow That Dream")....................................150-225 62
(Special paper sleeve, issued to radio stations and juke box operators. Promotional issue only. Price is for sleeve only.)
RCA (4368 "Follow That Dream")...60-80 65
(Black label, dog on side.)
RCA (4368 "Follow That Dream")....................................100-150 69
(Orange label.)
RCA (4371 "Kid Galahad")............60-80 62
(Black label, dog on top.)
RCA (4371 "Kid Galahad")............50-70 65
(Black label, dog on side.)
RCA (4371 "Kid Galahad")..........100-150 69
(Orange label.)
RCA (4382 "Viva Las Vegas")......75-100 64
(Black label, dog on top.)
RCA (4382 "Viva Las Vegas")........60-80 65
(Black label, dog on side.)
RCA (4382 "Viva Las Vegas")....100-150 69
(Orange label.)
RCA (4383 "Tickle Me")..............75-100 65
(Black label, dog on side. Mentions "Special Elvis Anniversary LP Album" at bottom on front cover.)
RCA (4383 "Tickle Me")............100-125 65
(Black label, dog on side. No mention of "Special Elvis Anniversary LP Album.)
RCA (4383 "Tickle Me")............150-200 69
(Orange label.)
RCA (4387 "Easy Come, Easy Go")....................................60-80 67
(Black label, dog on side.)
RCA (4387 "Easy Come, Easy Go")....................................150-170 67
(White label. Promotional Issue Only.)
RCA (5088 "A Touch of Gold, Vol. I")....................................450-550 59
(Maroon label.)
RCA (5088 "A Touch of Gold, Vol. I")....................................100-125 59
(Black label, dog on top. Add $15 to $25 if accompanied by "I am a loyal Elvis fan" insert card.)
RCA (5088 "A Touch of Gold, Vol. I")....................................60-80 65
(Black label, dog on side.)
RCA (5088 "A Touch of Gold, Vol. I")....................................100-200 69
(Orange label.)
RCA (5101 "A Touch of Gold, Vol. II")....................................450-550 59
(Maroon label.)
RCA (5101 "A Touch of Gold, Vol. II")....................................75-100 59
(Black label, dog on top. Add $15 to $25 if accompanied by "I am a loyal Elvis fan" insert card.)
RCA (5101 "A Touch of Gold, Vol. II")....................................60-80 65
(Black label, dog on side.)
RCA (5101 "A Touch of Gold, Vol. II")....................................100-200 69
(Orange label.)
RCA (5120 "The Real Elvis") 700-800 59
(Maroon label. Reissue of 940.)
RCA (5120 "The Real Elvis") 100-125 59
(Black label, dog on top.)
RCA (5120 "The Real Elvis") 75-100 65
(Black label, dog on side.)
RCA (5120 "The Real Elvis") 100-150 69
(Orange label.)
RCA (5121 "Peace in the Valley")....................................500-750 59
(Maroon label. Reissue of 4054.)
RCA (5121 "Peace in the Valley")....................................60-80 59
(Black label, dog on top.)
RCA (5121 "Peace in the Valley")....................................50-70 65
(Black label, dog on side.)
RCA (5121 "Peace in the Valley")....................................100-150 69
(Orange label.)
RCA (5122 "King Creole")......5000-7500 59
(Maroon label. Listed based on one — and only one — person's report of it. Many collectors have doubts about the existence of a maroon label of this EP. We can't confirm it; however, if one should turn up, price range is a reality..)
RCA (5122 "King Creole")..............60-80 59
(Black label, dog on top.)
RCA (5122 "King Creole")..............60-80 65
(Black label, dog on side.)
RCA (5122 "King Creole")..........100-150 69
(Orange label.)
RCA (5141 "A Touch of Gold, Vol. 3")....................................425-500 60
(Maroon label.)
RCA (5141 "A Touch of Gold, Vol. 3")....................................75-100 60
(Black label, dog on top.)
RCA (5141 "A Touch of Gold, Vol. 3")....................................60-80 65
(Black label, dog on side.)
RCA (5141 "A Touch of Gold, Vol. 3")....................................100-200 69
(Orange label.)
RCA (5157 "Elvis Sails")..............75-100 65
(Black label, dog on top. Reissue of 4325.)
RCA (5157 "Elvis Sails")................50-70 65
(Black label, dog on side.)
RCA (5157 "Elvis Sails")............150-200 69
(Orange label.)
RCA (8705 "TV Guide Presents Elvis")....................................1000-1500 56
(Price for disc only. Insert sheets are priced separately below. No sleeve or special cover exists for this disc. Promotional issue only.)
RCA (8705 "TV Guide Presents Elvis")....................................50-100 56
(Price for "Elvis Exclusively" gray insert.)
RCA (8705 "TV Guide Presents Elvis")....................................100-200 56
(Price for *Elvis Exclusively* pink insert, with suggested continuity.)
RCA (9089 "SPD-15 Elvis EP")...400-500 56
(Black label. Just the Elvis disc from SPD-15.)
RCA (9089 "SPD-15 Elvis EP")...400-500 56
(Gray label. The Elvis disc from SPD-15. Gray label pressings were for juke box operators.)
RCA (9113 "SPD-19 Elvis EP")...300-400 56
(The Elvis disc from SPD-19, *The Sound of Leadership*.)
RCA (9141 "SPD-26 Elvis EP")..200-250 56
(Black label. The Elvis disc from SPD-15, *Great Country/Western Hits*.)
RCA (64476 "Heartbreak Hotel")....... 4-8 96
(Issued with paper sleeve.)
SHOW-LAND (1001 "The Beginning of Elvis")....................................60-80 79
TUPPERWARE (11973 "Tupperware's Hit Parade"): see Various Artists section
Notes: Unless listed and priced separately, all EP values include both disc and cover with approximately half of the total attached to each. Some of the rarer pieces that are often traded individually (disc or sleeve), as well as those sleeves that have an exceptionally higher value than their disc, are listed separately in this section. All EPs in the 5000 series are Gold Standard Series issues although none are identified as such on the labels, only on the covers. Remember, if you don't find the EP in this section it may contain two, three or four artists, and will be listed following the Presley LP section.

LPs: 10/12-inch
(Commercial and Promotional)

ABC RADIO (1003 "Elvis Memories")....................................425-525 78
(Boxed, three-disc set. Add $25 to $50 if accompanied by a 16-page programmer's booklet and four pages of added information. Issued only to radio stations. Add $40 to $50 if accompanied by a 7-inch reel tape, with spots and promo announcements. Program Highlights issue on Michelob 810.)
ASSOCIATED BROADCASTERS (1001 "Legend of a King") 125-150 80
(White label. Advance pressing.)
ASSOCIATED BROADCASTERS (1001 "Legend of a King") 50-75 80
(Picture disc. First pressings are numbered from 3000 through 6000. Number appears under "Side One" on the disc itself. Cover is standard, die-cut, picture disc cover. Has several spelling errors on back cover, including "idle" for idol and "Jordinaires" instead of Jordanaires.)
ASSOCIATED BROADCASTERS (1001 "Legend of a King") 30-50 80
(Picture disc. Second pressings are numbered from 6001 through 9000. Most of the spelling errors were corrected on this cover.)
ASSOCIATED BROADCASTERS (1001 "Legend of a King") 25-30 80
(Picture disc. Third pressings are numbered from 00001 through 02999 and 09001 through 15000. Cover errors have all been corrected.)
ASSOCIATED BROADCASTERS (1001 "Legend of a King") 15-20 84
(Picture disc. Fourth pressings are also numbered from 3000 through 6000, but were packaged in a clear plastic sleeve instead of a conventional cover.)
ASSOCIATED BROADCASTERS (1001 "Legend of a King") 8-15 85
(Picture disc. Discs are not numbered. Packaged in a plastic sleeve.)
ASSOCIATED BROADCASTERS ("Legend of a King")....................................200-250 85
(Three hour, three-disc set. Not boxed. Price includes six pages of cue sheets. Available to radio stations only.)
ASSOCIATED BROADCASTERS ("Legend of a King")....................................300-350 85
(Same as above, but packaged in a specially printed box.)
ASSOCIATED BROADCASTERS ("Legend of a King")....................................300-350 86
(Boxed, three-disc set, same as above except time on segment 1-B is increased from 14:25 to 15:15 in order to include a Johnny Bernero interview.)
ASSOCIATED PRESS (1977 "The World in Sound")....................................80-100 78
(News highlights of 1977, including coverage of Elvis' death.)
BOXCAR ("Having Fun with Elvis on Stage")....................................150-200 74
(No selection number used. Sold in conjunction with Elvis' concert appearances. Reissued as RCA CPM1-0818.)
CAEDMON (1572 "On the Record")....................................60-80 78
(Various news items and artists featured.)
CAMDEN (2304 "Flaming Star") 30-40 69
(First issued as RCA PRS-279, reissued in 1975 as Pickwick 2304.)
CAMDEN (2408 "Let's Be Friends")....................................25-35 70
(Reissued in 1975 as Pickwick 2408.)
CAMDEN (2428 "Elvis' Christmas Album")....................................30-40 70
(Eight songs on this LP were first issued on RCA LOC-1035. Reissued in 1975 as Pickwick 2428.)
CAMDEN (2440 "Almost in Love")....................................30-40 70
(With *Stay Away Joe*.)
CAMDEN (2440 "Almost in Love")....................................20-30 73
(*Stay Away* replaces *Stay Away Joe*.)
Note: Reissued in 1975 as Pickwick 2440.
CAMDEN (2472 "You'll Never Walk Alone")....................................30-40 71
(Reissued in 1975 as Pickwick 2472.)
CAMDEN (2518 "C'mon Everybody")....................................15-25 71
(Reissued in 1975 as Pickwick 2518.)
CAMDEN (2533 "I Got Lucky") 25-30 71
(Reissued in 1975 as Pickwick 2533.)
CAMDEN (2567 "Elvis Sings Hits from His Movies")....................................15-20 72
(Reissued in 1975 as Pickwick 2567.)
CAMDEN (2595 "Burning Love")....20-30 72
(Add $40 to $45 if accompanied by the bonus 8" x 10" Elvis photo. Reissued in 1975 as Pickwick 2595.)
CAMDEN (2611 "Separate Ways")....................................30-35 73
(Reissued in 1975 as Pickwick 2611.)
CREATIVE RADIO (E1 "Elvis Exclusive Interview")....................................175-200 88
(Price for *complete* 1956 Little Rock concert copies. Only the first 100 copies were pressed with the full concert. The only way to visually identify these is to check the disc. On the full concert pressings, the grooves take up nearly the entire disc.)
CREATIVE RADIO (E1 "Elvis Exclusive Interview")....................................20-30 88
(Has edited concert songs. On this pressing the grooves occupy only about two-thirds of the disc.)
CREATIVE RADIO ("Between Takes with Elvis")....................................150-250 89
(Three-disc set. Promotional issue only. Though not packaged inside covers—shrink wrapped at the factory—each LP set came with the bonus single, *Nearer My God to Thee/You Gave Me a Molehill*.)
CURRENT AUDIO MAGAZINE (1 "Elvis: Press Conference"): see Various Artists section
EMR ENTERPRISES (8 "The Age of Rock")....................................100-125 69
(Promotional issue only.)
ELEKTRA (60107 "Diner")............10-20 82
(Soundtrack.)
FRANKLIN MINT (4 "The Official Grammy Award Winners") 150-200 85
(Boxed set of four colored vinyl discs. One in a series of 14 boxed sets, but only this one (titled *The Great Singers*) has Elvis. Includes booklet.)
GOLDEN EDITIONS LIMITED (1 "The First Year")....................................8-15 79
(Print in upper corners on front cover is in white. Label is black. Add $5 to $8 if accompanied by a 12-page booklet and one-page copy of the 1954 Elvis/Scotty Moore contract.)
GOLDEN EDITIONS LIMITED (101 "The First Year")....................................15-25 79
(Print in upper corners on front cover is in gold. Label is white. Add $5 to $8 if accompanied by a 12-page booklet and one-page copy of the 1954 Elvis/Scotty Moore contract. Most of the material on this LP was previously issued on HALW 00001.)
GREAT NORTHWEST (4005 "The Elvis Tapes")....................................10-15 77
(Repackaged on Starday 995.)
GREAT NORTHWEST (4006 "The King Speaks")....................................8-10 77
(First issued as Green Valley 2001.)
GREEN VALLEY (2001 "Elvis 1961 Press Conference")....................................30-50 77
(Cover is thin, soft stock and does not have black bar on spine. Label does not show selection number.)
GREEN VALLEY (2001 "Elvis 1961 Press Conference")....................................12-15 77
(Cover is standard stock and has black bar on spine. Label has the selection number. Repackaged as one half of Green Valley 2001/2003.)
Note: Repackaged as Great Northwest 4006.
GREEN VALLEY (2001/2003 "Elvis Speaks to You")....................................25-30 78
(GV-2001 was first issued as a single LP.)
HALW (00001 "The First Years") ...25-30 78
(Repackaged in 1979 on Golden Editions 1.)
INTERNATIONAL HOTEL PRESENTS ELVIS 1969..........................2000-2500 69
(Custom gift box prepared by Col. Parker and RCA for International Hotel guests. Originally contained: RCA LPM-4088 & LSP-4155, three 8" x 10" Elvis photos, RCA Elvis catalog, calendar and a nine-page letter. Price is for complete set but box itself represents 90-95% of value.)
INTERNATIONAL HOTEL PRESENTS ELVIS 1970..........................2000-2500 70
(Custom gift box prepared by Col. Parker and RCA for International Hotel guests. Originally contained: RCA LSP-6020 & 45-9791, one 8" x 10" Elvis photo, photo album, RCA Elvis catalog, calendar, menu and letter. Price is for complete set but box itself represents 90-95% of value.)
K-TEL (9900 "Elvis Love Songs") ..15-20 81
LOUISIANA HAYRIDE (3061 "The Beginning Years")....................................400-500 84
(White label advance pressing from RCA, Indianapolis, where this LP was manufactured.)
LOUISIANA HAYRIDE (3061 "The Beginning Years")....................................20-25 84
(Price includes 20-page *D.J. Fontana Remembers Elvis* booklet, a four sheet copy of Elvis' Hayride contract and a 10" x 10" *Presleyana, Second Edition* flyer, all of which represent about $5 to $10 of the value.)
Note: Selections from this LP are also on the Music Works 3601 & 3602.
LOUISIANA HAYRIDE (8454 "The Louisiana Hayride")....................................500-700 76
(Yellow label. A program of various artists including Elvis. Issued to radio stations only.)
LOUISIANA HAYRIDE (8454 "The Louisiana Hayride")....................................300-350 81
(Gold label. A program of various artists including Elvis.)
MFSL (059 "From Elvis in Memphis")....................................50-80 82
(First issued as RCA LSP-4155.)
MARVENCO (101 "1954-1955, The Beginning")....................................10-15 88
(Tracks first issued on Golden Editions 101.)
MICHELOB (810 "Highlights of Elvis Memories") 100-200 78
(A Michelob in-house promotional issue only.) *Elvis Memories* was first issued on ABC Radio 1003.
MUSIC WORKS (3601 "The First Live Recordings")....................................15-20 84
(First issued on Louisiana Hayride 3061.)
MUSIC WORKS (3602 "Hillbilly Cat")....................................15-20 84
(First issued on Louisiana Hayride 3061.)
MUTUAL BROADCAST SYSTEM (4082 "The Frantic Fifties")..........................250-300 59
(Various news items and artists featured. Promotional issue only.)
OAK (1003 "Vintage 1955")...........60-80 91
PAIR (1010 "Double Dynamite")....20-25 82
(First issued as Pickwick 5001.)
PAIR (1037 "Remembering Elvis")....................................30-40 83
PICKWICK (2304 "Flaming Star")....8-10 75
(First issued as RCA PRS-279.)
PICKWICK (2408 "Let's Be Friends")....................................8-10 75
(Black vinyl.)
Note: First issued as Camden 2408.
PICKWICK (2408 "Let's Be Friends")....................................750-1000 70s
(Colored vinyl. Experimental pressing only. There is no colored vinyl commercial or promotional edition of this issue.)
PICKWICK (2428 "Elvis' Christmas Album")....................................8-10 75
(First issued as Camden 2428.)
PICKWICK (2428 "Elvis' Christmas Album")....................................20-40 86
(Has RCA Special Products on label and cover.)
PICKWICK (2440 "Almost in Love")....................................8-10 75
(First issued as Camden 2440.)
PICKWICK (2472 "You'll Never Walk Alone")....................................8-10 75
(First issued as Camden 2472.)
PICKWICK (2518 "C'mon Everybody")....................................8-10 75
(First issued as Camden 2518.)
PICKWICK (2533 "I Got Lucky")......8-10 75
(First issued as Camden 2533.)
PICKWICK (2567 "Elvis Sings Hits from His Movies")....................................8-10 75
(First issued as Camden 2567.)
PICKWICK (2595 "Burning Love")...8-12 75
(First issued as Camden 2595.)
PICKWICK (2611 "Separate Ways")....................................8-10 75
(First issued as Camden 2611.)
PICKWICK (5001 "Double Dynamite")....................................25-30 75
(Repackaged in 1982 as Pair 1010.)
PICKWICK (7007 "Frankie & Johnny")....................................10-15 75
(First issued as RCA 3553.)
PICKWICK (7064 "Mahalo from Elvis")....................................15-25 78
PREMORE (589 "Early Elvis").......20-40 89
(Mail-order album from the Solo Cup Company.)
RCA (EPC-1 "Special Christmas Program" Reel Tape) 350-400 67
(Price includes programming inserts, which represent $25-35 of the value.)
Note: Never issued commercially on disc, all 10-inch red vinyl LPs of this material are bootlegs.
RCA (TB-1 "Collectors Edition"). 100-150 76
(Boxed, five-disc set.)
RCA (0001 "Robert W. Samoff"): see Various Artists section
RCA (4 Untitled RCA Sampler): see Various Artists section
RCA (10 Untitled RCA Sampler): see Various Artists section
RCA (010 "Elvis! His Greatest Hits")....................................400-500 79
(White box edition. Boxed, eight-disc set, sold mail-order by *Reader's Digest*.)
RCA (010 "His Greatest Hits") 50-80 83
(Yellow box edition. Boxed, seven-disc set, sold mail-order by *Reader's Digest*. See RCA 181 for the bonus LP offered with this set.)
RCA (27 "August 1959 Sampler"): see Various Artists section
RCA RBA-040: see READER'S DIGEST 040
RCA (54 "October Christmas Sampler"): see Various Artists section
RCA (0056 "Elvis") 45-55 73
(Mustard color label. Cover shows "Brookville Records" in upper right. A mail-order LP offer.)
RCA (0056 "Elvis") 25-35 73
(Blue label. Cover doesn't show "Brookville Records." Mail-order LP offer. Repackaged in 1978 and titled *Elvis Commemorative Album*.)
RCA (0056 "Elvis Commemorative Album")....................................80-100 78
(Price includes a "Registered Certificate of Ownership." A mail-order LP offer. First titled *Elvis*, using the same selection number.)
RCA (59-7 "February Sampler"): see Various Artists section
RCA (66 "Christmas Programming from RCA"): see Various Artists section
RCA (072 "Great Hits of 1956-'57")....................................20-30 87
(Offered as a bonus LP from *Reader's Digest*, with the purchase of one of their non-Elvis boxed sets.)
RCA (96 "October 1960 Popular Stereo Sampler"): see Various Artists section
RCA (0108 "E-Z Country No. 2"): see Various Artists section
RCA (141 "October '61 Pop Sampler"): see Various Artists section
RCA (0168 "Elvis in Hollywood") 50-75 76
(Add $10 to $15 is accompanied by a 20-page photo booklet.)
RCA (181 "Elvis Sings Inspirational Favorites") 15-20 83
(Special Products, Reader's Digest mail-order bonus LP for buyers of the 1983 edition of RCA 010. Price includes 24-page Reader's Digest Music catalog.)
RCA (191 "Elvis, the Legend Lives On")....................................50-75 86
(Boxed, seven-disc set, sold mail-order by Reader's Digest. Includes booklet.)
RCA (0197 "E-Z Pop No. 6"): see Various Artists section
RCA (0199 "E-Z Country No. 3"): see Various Artists section
RCA (219 "September '63 Pop Sampler"): see Various Artists section
RCA (242 "Elvis Sings Country Favorites")....................................50-75 84
(Bonus LP from Reader's Digest, given with the purchase of their seven-disc boxed set, *The Great Country Entertainers*, which has no Elvis tracks.)
RCA (247 "December '63 Pop Sampler"): see Various Artists section
RCA (0263 "Elvis Presley Story") ..50-75 77
(Special Products five-disc boxed set. A Candelite Music mail-order offer.)
RCA (0264 "Songs of Inspiration") .15-20 77
(Special Products issue. A Candelite Music mail-order bonus LP for buyers of RCA 0263.)
RCA (272 "April '64 Pop Sampler"): see Various Artists section
RCA (279 "Singer Presents Elvis")....................................100-125 68
(Reissued in 1969 as Camden 2304 and in 1975 as Pickwick 2304.)
RCA (0283 "Elvis, Including Fool")....................................50-60 73
RCA (331 "April '65 Pop Sampler"): see Various Artists section
RCA (0341 "Legendary Performer, Vol. 1")....................................25-30 74
(With die-cut cover. Add $5 to $10 if accompanied by *The Early Years* booklet.)
RCA (0341 "Legendary Performer, Vol. 1")....................................12-25 83
(With standard cover—not die-cut.)
RCA (0341 "Legendary Performer, Vol. 1") 1000-2000 78
(Picture discs of the 0341 material but with pictures from any of about six different LP covers pressed on the disc. RCA in-house, experimental items.)
RCA (347 "August '65 Pop Sampler"): see Various Artists section
RCA (0347 "Memories of Elvis").....50-90
(Special Products five-disc boxed set. A Candelite Music mail-order offer. Add $8 to $10 if accompanied by a 16-page booklet and an Elvis print. Not all sets came with the print and booklet.)

RCA (0348 "Greatest Show on Earth")..........15-20 78
(Special Products issue. A Candelite Music mail-order bonus LP for buyers of RCA 0347.)
RCA (0388 "Raised on Rock")........30-40 73
(Orange label.)
RCA (0388 "Raised on Rock")......... 8-15 77
(Black label.)
RCA (403 "April '66 Pop Sampler"): see Various Artists section
RCA (0401 RCA Radio Victrola Division Spots")..........1000-1500 56
(Single-sided disc with four 50-second radio commercials for RCA's Victrolas, as well as for the SPD-22 and SPD-23 EPs that were offered as a bonus. Elvis is the announcer on all of the spots, which include excerpts of some of his songs. Issued only to radio stations scheduling the spots.)
RCA (0412 "The Legendary Recordings")..........100-125 79
(Special Products six-disc boxed set. A Candelite Music mail-order offer.)
RCA (0413 "Greatest Moments in Music")..........15-20 80
(Special Products issue. A Candelite Music mail-order bonus LP for buyers of RCA 0412.)
RCA (0437 "Rock 'N Roll Forever")..........15-20 81
(Candelite Music mail-order LP offer.)
RCA (461 "Special Palm Sunday Programming")..........600-800 67
(With programming packet. Promotional issue only.)
RCA (461 "Special Palm Sunday Programming")..........550-650 67
(Without programming packet. Promotional issue only.)
RCA (0461 "The Legendary Magic")..........15-20 80
(Candelite Music mail-order LP offer.)
RCA (CPL1-0475 "Good Times")...45-65 74
VICTOR (AFL1-0475 "Good Times")..........8-15 77
RCA (571 " Elvis As Recorded at Madison Square Garden")..........300-400 72
(Two-disc, double pocket issue. Promotional issue only. Commercially issued as RCA LSP-4776.)
RCA (APD1-0606 "On Stage in Memphis")..........200-300 74
(Quadradisc. Orange label.)
RCA (CPL1-0606 "On Stage in Memphis")..........25-30 74
(Orange label.)
RCA (DJL1-0606 "On Stage in Memphis")..........300-400 74
(Banded edition. Promotional issue only.)
RCA (CPL1-0606 "On Stage in Memphis")..........20-30 76
(Tan label.)
RCA (AFL1-0606 "On Stage in Memphis")..........8-15 77
RCA (0632 "The Elvis Presley Collection")..........75-100 84
(Special Products three-disc boxed set, produced for Candelite Music. Includes booklet. A mail-order LP offer.)
RCA (DPL1-0647 "Elvis Country")..25-35 84
(Special Products issue for ERA Records.)
RCA (DPK1-0679 "Savage Young Elvis")..........20-30 84
(Cassette tape of a package that was never available on LP. Price is for tape still attached to 12" x 12" photo card.)
RCA (0704 "Elvis, HBO Special") ..60-75 84
(Includes color poster. Special Products issue for HBO cable TV subscribers. This material was first issued as RCA LPM-4088.)
RCA (0710 "50 Years-50 Hits")......30-40 85
(Three-disc set. Offered by TV mail-order and through the RCA Record Club.)
RCA (0728 "Elvis, His Songs of Faith and Inspiration")..........50-80 86
(Two-disc, mail-order offer.)
RCA (CPM1-0818 "Having Fun with Elvis on Stage")..........30-40 74
(Orange label.)
RCA (CPM1-0818 "Having Fun with Elvis on Stage")..........20-25 76
(Tan label.)
RCA (AFM1-0818 "Having Fun with Elvis on Stage")..........25-35 77
(Black label.)
Note: First issued on Boxcar without a selection number.
RCA (0835 "Elvis Presley Interview Record – An Audio Self-Portrait")..........80-100 84
(Promotional issue only.)
RCA (APL1-0873 "Promised Land")..........50-60 75
(Orange label.)
RCA (APL1-0873 "Promised Land")..........15-20 76
(Tan label.)
RCA (AFL1-0873 "Promised Land")..........10-20 77
RCA (APD1-0873 "Promised Land")..........200-250 75
(Quadradisc. Orange label.)
RCA (APD1-0873 "Promised Land")..........100-150 77
(Quadradisc. Black label.)
RCA (ANL1-0971 "Pure Gold").......10-15 75
(Orange label.)
RCA (ANL1-0971 "Pure Gold")........ 8-12 76
(Yellow label.)
RCA (ANL1-0971 "Pure Gold")........ 6-10 77
(Black label.)
Reissued in 1980 as AYL1-3732.
RCA (1001 "The Sun Collection")...20-30 75
(Label does not have "Starcall" on it. Back cover pictures other LPs.)
RCA (1001 "The Sun Collection") ..10-20 75
(Label has "Starcall" on it. Back cover with liner notes.)
Note: This English import was distributed throughout the U.S. Repackaged in 1976 as RCA 1675.
RCA (LOC-1035 "Elvis' Christmas Album")..........6000-8000 57
(Experimental pressing only.)
RCA (LOC-1035 "Elvis' Christmas Album")..........550-650 57
(Black vinyl. With gold foil, gift-giving sticker.)
RCA (LOC-1035 "Elvis' Christmas Album")..........400-525 57
(Black vinyl. Without gold foil, gift-giving sticker.)
Note: Repackaged in 1958 as RCA 1951, in 1970 as Camden 2428 and in 1985 as RCA 5486. May be found with either gold or silver print on the spine.
RCA (APL1-1039 "Today")..........60-75 75
(Orange label.)
RCA (APL1-1039 "Today")..........20-30 76
(Tan label.)
RCA (AFL1-1039 "Today")..........8-15 77
RCA (APD1-1039 "Today")........200-250 75
(Quadradisc. Orange label.)
RCA (APD1-1039 "Today")........125-150 77
(Quadradisc. Black label.)
RCA (LPM-1254 "Elvis Presley")..........300-350 56
(Monaural. Black label, "Long Play" at bottom. Cover has selection number in upper right corner.)
RCA (LPM-1254 "Elvis Presley")..........100-150 63
(Black label, "Mono" at bottom. Cover has selection number on left.)
RCA (LPM-1254 "Elvis Presley")....50-75 64
(Black label, "Monaural" at bottom. Cover has selection number on left.)
RCA (LSP-1254e "Elvis Presley")..........200-300 62
(Stereo. Black label, all print on label is silver.)
RCA (LSP-1254e "Elvis Presley") ..25-50 64
(Black label, RCA logo is white, other label print is silver.)
RCA (LSP-1254e "Elvis Presley") ..30-50 68
(Orange label.)
RCA (LSP-1254e "Elvis Presley") ..15-25 76
(Tan label.)
RCA (LSP-1254e "Elvis Presley") ..10-18 77
(Black label, dog near top.)
RCA (AFL1-1254e "Elvis Presley") ..8-15 77
Note: Digitally remastered in 1984 on RCA 5198.
RCA (ANL1-1319 "His Hand in Mine")..........10-20 76
(First issued as LPM/LSP-2328.)
RCA (1349 "Legendary Performer, Vol. 2")..........55-65 76
(Does not have the false starts and outtakes on *Such a Night* and *Cane and a High Starched Collar*. Mistakenly has only the complete take of both songs. Add $5 to $10 if accompanied by *The Early Years Continued* booklet.)
RCA (1349 "Legendary Performer, Vol. 2")..........25-30 76
(With die-cut cover. Add $5 to $10 if accompanied by *The Early Years Continued* booklet.)
RCA (1349 "Legendary Performer, Vol. 2")..........15-25 83
(With standard cover—not die-cut.)
RCA (LPM-1382 "Elvis")..........600-800 56
(Monaural. Black label, "Long Play" at bottom. Cover has selection number in upper right corner. Mistakenly pressed with an alternative take of *Old Shep*, not available on any other authorized U.S. vinyl release. Any copy with a "15S," "17S" or "19S" matrix on side 2 (following identification number stamped in the vinyl trail-off – matrix on side 1 is irrelevant) is likely to have the alternative; however, playing the track is the way to be certain. Alternative is different throughout, instrumentally and vocally – especially Elvis' phrasing – but here are two lyric variations. Words in all upper case are exclusive to the alternative take (which can be heard on the 1992 CD boxed set *Elvis – The King of Rock 'N' Roll, The Complete '50s Masters*): 1) "As the years fast did roll, Old Shep he grew old AND his eyes were fast growing dim." 2) "He came to my side and he looked up at me, and HE laid his old head on my knee.")
RCA (LPM-1382 "Elvis")..........300-400 56
(Black label, selections numbered as "Band 1" through "Band 6.")
RCA (LPM-1382 "Elvis")..........250-300 56
(Black label, "Long Play" at bottom. Cover has selection number in upper right corner.)
RCA (LPM-1382 "Elvis")..........75-100 63
(Black label, "Mono" at bottom. Cover has selection number on left.)
RCA (LPM-1382 "Elvis")..........50-75 64
(Black label, "Monaural" at bottom. Cover has selection number on left.)
RCA (LSP-1382e "Elvis")..........150-200 62
(Stereo. Black label, all print on label is silver.)
RCA (LSP-1382e "Elvis")..........50-65 64
(Black label, RCA logo is white, other print on label is silver.)
RCA (LSP-1382e "Elvis")..........25-35 68
(Orange label. Rigid vinyl.)
RCA (LSP-1382e "Elvis")..........15-25 71
(Orange label. Flexible vinyl.)
RCA (LSP-1382e "Elvis")..........10-20 76
(Tan label.)
RCA (AFL1-1382e "Elvis")..........8-15 77
Note: Digitally remastered in 1984 on RCA 5199.
RCA (APL1-1506 "From Elvis Presley Boulevard")..........30-40 76
RCA (AFL1-1506 "From Elvis Presley Boulevard")..........10-18 77
RCA (LPM-1515 "Loving You")..250-300 57
(Monaural. Black label, "Long Play" at bottom. Cover has selection number in upper right corner.)
RCA (LPM-1515 "Loving You")..100-125 63
(Black label, "Mono" at bottom. Cover has selection number on left.)
RCA (LPM-1515 "Loving You")..........4000-6000 60s
(Picture disc, but with the cover of a European *G.I. Blues* album being the picture imbeded in the vinyl. Experimental disc—only one copy made. Has just five *Loving You* tracks, the others being randomly selected instrumentals which have nothing at all to do with Elvis.)
RCA (LPM-1515 "Loving You")......40-60 64
(Black label, "Monaural" at bottom. Cover has selection number on left.)
RCA (LSP-1515e "Loving You").100-200 62
(Stereo. Black label, all print on label is silver.)
RCA (LSP-1515e "Loving You")......40-60 64
(Black label, RCA logo is white, other label print is silver.)
RCA (LSP-1515e "Loving You").....35-40 68
(Orange label. Rigid vinyl.)
RCA (LSP-1515e "Loving You").....15-25 71
(Orange label. Flexible vinyl.)
RCA (LSP-1515e "Loving You").....15-25 76
(Tan label.)
RCA (AFL1-1515e "Loving You").....8-15 77
RCA (APM1-1675 "The Sun Sessions")..........20-25 76
RCA (AFM1-1675 "The Sun Sessions")..........10-20 77
Note: First issued as RCA HY-1001 and reissued in 1981 as RCA AYM1-3893.
RCA (LPM-1707 "Elvis' Golden Records")..........200-250 58
(Monaural. Black label, "Long Play" at bottom. Cover has selection number in upper right corner and LP title in light blue letters.)
RCA (LPM-1707 "Elvis' Golden Records")..........60-80 63
(Black label, "Mono" at bottom. Cover has selection number on left and LP title in white letters.)
RCA (LPM-1707 "Elvis' Golden Records")..........25-40 64
(Black label, "Monaural" at bottom. Cover has selection number on left.)
RCA (LSP-1707e "Elvis' Golden Records")..........200-300 62
(Stereo. Black label, all print on label is silver.)
RCA (LSP-1707e "Elvis' Golden Records")..........25-50 64
(Black label, RCA logo is white, other label print is silver.)
RCA (LSP-1707e "Elvis' Golden Records")..........30-40 68
(Orange label. Rigid vinyl.)
RCA (LSP-1707e "Elvis' Golden Records")..........15-25 71
(Orange label. Flexible vinyl.)
RCA (LSP-1707e "Elvis' Golden Records")..........10-20 76
(Tan label.)
RCA (AFL1-1707e "Elvis' Golden Records")..........8-15 77
RCA (AQL1-1707e "Elvis' Golden Records")..........8-15 79
Note: Digitally remastered in 1984 on RCA 5196.
RCA (1785 "WRCA Plays the Hits"): see Various Artists section
RCA (LPM-1884 "King Creole") .150-200 58
(Monaural. Black label, "Long Play" at bottom. Cover has selection number in upper right corner. Add $200-250 if accompanied by an 8" x 10" black and white photo of Elvis in uniform, which reportedly did not come packaged inside this LP, but was given to buyers by dealers at time of purchase.)
RCA (LPM-1884 "King Creole") 75-90 63
(Black label, "Mono" at bottom. Cover has selection number on left.)
RCA (LPM-1884 "King Creole") 60-75 64
(Black label, "Monaural" at bottom. Cover has selection number on left.)
RCA (LSP-1884e "King Creole") 125-200 62
(Stereo. Black label, all print on label is silver.)
RCA (LSP-1884e "King Creole")....50-75 62
(Black label, RCA logo is white, other label print is silver.)
RCA (LSP-1884e "King Creole")....35-40 68
(Orange label. Rigid vinyl.)
RCA (LSP-1884e "King Creole")....15-25 71
(Orange label. Flexible vinyl.)
RCA (LSP-1884e "King Creole")....20-30 76
(Tan label.)
RCA (AFL1-1884e "King Creole") ..10-18 77
Note: Reissued in 1980 as RCA AYL1-3733.
RCA (ANL1-1936 "Wonderful World of Christmas")..........8-12 77
(First issued as RCA LSP-4579.)
RCA (LPM-1951 "Elvis' Christmas Album")..........150-200 58
(Monaural. Black label, "Long Play" at bottom. Cover has selection number in upper right corner.)
RCA (LPM-1951 "Elvis' Christmas Album")..........60-80 63
(Black label, "Mono" at bottom. Cover has selection number on left.)
RCA (LPM-1951 "Elvis' Christmas Album")..........35-50 64
(Black label, "Monaural" at bottom. Cover has selection number on left.)
RCA (LSP-1951e "Elvis' Christmas Album")..........35-50 64
(Stereo. Black label, RCA logo is white, other label print is silver.)
RCA (LSP-1951e "Elvis' Christmas Album")..........60-75 68
(Orange label.
Note: Repackage of RCA LOC-1035. Repackaged again in 1970 as Camden 2428 and then again in 1985 as RCA AFM1-5486.
RCA (1981 "Felton Jarvis Talks About Elvis")..........270-350 81
(Price includes three script sheets. Add $25 to $50 if accompanied by silver and black *Guitar Man* engraved Elvis belt buckle.)
RCA (LPM-1990 "For LP Fans Only")..........250-300 59
(Monaural. Black label, "Long Play" at bottom. Cover has selection number in upper right corner.)
RCA (LPM-1990 "For LP Fans Only")..........75-100 63
(Black label, "Mono" at bottom. Cover has selection number on left.)
RCA (LPM-1990 "For LP Fans Only")..........50-75 65
(Black label, "Monaural" at bottom. Cover has selection number on left.)
RCA (LSP-1990 "For LP Fans Only")..........250-350 65
(Black label. Cover has same Elvis photo on front and back.)
RCA (LSP-1990e "For LP Fans Only")..........35-60 65
(Stereo. Black label, RCA logo is white, other label print is silver.)
RCA (LSP-1990e "For LP Fans Only")..........30-40 68
(Orange label.)
RCA (LSP-1990e "For LP Fans Only")..........25-35 76
(Tan label.)
RCA (LSP-1990e "For LP Fans Only")..........10-18 76
(Black label, dog near top.)
RCA (AFL1-1990e "For LP Fans Only")..........8-15 77
RCA (LPM-2011 "A Date with Elvis")..........500-700 59
(Monaural. Black label, "Long Play" at bottom. Has gatefold cover and 1960 calendar. With "New Golden Age of Sound" wrap-around banner.)
RCA (LPM-2011 "A Date with Elvis")..........300-400 59
(Black label, "Long Play" at bottom. Has gatefold cover and 1960 calendar, but *does not* have "New Golden Age of Sound" banner.)
RCA (LPM-2011 "A Date with Elvis")..........100-150 65
(Black label, "Mono" at bottom. Cover has selection number on left.)
RCA (LPM-2011 "A Date with Elvis")..........45-65 65
(Black label, "Monaural" at bottom. Cover has selection number on left.)
RCA (LSP-2011e "A Date with Elvis")..........35-55 65
(Stereo. Black label, RCA logo is white, other label print is silver.)
RCA (LSP-2011e "A Date with Elvis")..........25-35 68
(Orange label. Rigid vinyl.)
RCA (LSP-2011e "A Date with Elvis")..........20-30 71
(Orange label. Flexible vinyl.)
RCA (LSP-2011e "A Date with Elvis")..........10-20 76
(Tan label.)
RCA (LSP-2011e "A Date with Elvis")..........10-15 77
(Black label, dog near top.)
RCA (AFL1-2011e "A Date with Elvis")..........10-15 77
RCA (LPM-2075 "Elvis' Golden Records, Vol. 2")..........150-200 59
(Monaural. Black label, "Long Play" at bottom. Cover has selection number in upper right corner.)
RCA (LPM-2075 "Elvis' Golden Records, Vol. 2")..........70-90 63
(Black label, "Mono" at bottom. Cover has selection number on left.)
RCA (LPM-2075 "Elvis' Golden Records, Vol. 2")..........35-55 64
(Black label, "Monaural" at bottom. Cover has selection number on left.)
RCA (LSP-2075e "Elvis' Golden Records, Vol. 2")..........100-200 62
(Stereo. Black label, all print on label is silver.)
RCA (LSP-2075e "Elvis' Golden Records, Vol. 2")..........25-50 64
(Black label, RCA logo is white, other label print is silver.)
RCA (LSP-2075e "Elvis' Golden Records, Vol. 2")..........30-40 68
(Orange label. Rigid vinyl.)
RCA (LSP-2075e "Elvis' Golden Records, Vol. 2")..........15-25 71
(Orange label. Flexible vinyl.)
RCA (LSP-2075e "Elvis' Golden Records, Vol. 2")..........10-20 76
(Tan label.)
RCA (LSP-2075e "Elvis' Golden Records, Vol. 2")..........10-18 76
(Black label, dog near top.)
RCA (AFL1-2075e "Elvis' Golden Records, Vol. 2")..........8-15 77
Note: May also be shown as *50,000,000 Elvis Presley Fans Can't Be Wrong*. Digitally remastered in 1984 on RCA 5197.
RCA (2227 "Great Performances")..........30-40 90
RCA (LPM-2231 "Elvis Is Back")..........200-225 60
(Monaural. Black label, "Long Play" at bottom. No song titles printed on cover. Does not have yellow sticker on cover showing song titles, nor are contents printed on cover.)
RCA (LPM-2231 "Elvis Is Back")..........150-175 60
(Monaural. Black label, "Long Play" at bottom. No song titles printed on cover. Has yellow sticker, listing titles, on cover.)
RCA (LPM-2231 "Elvis Is Back") ...50-75 63
(Black label, "Mono" at bottom. Cover has selection number on left.)
RCA (LPM-2231 "Elvis Is Back") ...50-75 64
(Black label, "Monaural" at bottom. Cover has selection number on left.)
RCA (LSP-2231 "Elvis Is Back")..........250-300 60
(Stereo. Black label, "Living Stereo" at bottom. No song titles printed on cover. May or may not have yellow sticker on cover showing song titles.)
RCA (LSP-2231 "Elvis Is Back")....50-80 64
(Black label, RCA logo is white, other label print is silver.)
RCA (LSP-2231 "Elvis Is Back")....40-50 68
(Orange label.)
RCA (LSP-2231 "Elvis Is Back")....20-30 76
(Tan label.)
RCA (LSP-2231 "Elvis Is Back")....10-20 76
(Black label, dog near top.)
RCA (AFL1-2231 "Elvis Is Back") 8-15 77
RCA (LPM-2256 "G.I. Blues")......80-100 60
(Monaural. Black label, "Long Play" at bottom. Add $15 to $25 if accompanied by "Elvis Is Back" inner sleeve. Add $400 to $450 if cover has a heart-shaped announcement for *Wooden Heart.)*
RCA (LPM-2256 "G.I. Blues")......90-110 63
(Black label, "Mono" at bottom.)
RCA (LPM-2256 "G.I. Blues")........45-60 64
(Black label, "Monaural" at bottom.)
RCA (LSP-2256 "G.I. Blues")......100-125 60
(Stereo. Black label, "Living Stereo" at bottom. Add $15 to $25 if accompanied by "Elvis Is Back" inner sleeve. Add $400 to $450 if cover has a heart-shaped announcement for *Wooden Heart.)*
RCA (LSP-2256 "G.I. Blues")........40-60 64
(Black label, RCA logo is white, other label print is silver.)
RCA (LSP-2256 "G.I. Blues")........35-40 68
(Orange label. Rigid vinyl.)
RCA (LSP-2256 "G.I. Blues")........15-25 71
(Orange label. Flexible vinyl.)
RCA (LSP-2256 "G.I. Blues")........25-30 76
(Tan label.)
RCA (LSP-2256 "G.I. Blues")........10-18 76
(Black label, dog near top.)
RCA (AFL1-2256 "G.I. Blues")........8-15 77
(Reissued in 1980 as RCA AYL1-3735.)
Note: For *G.I. Blues* picture disc, see *Loving You* (RCA LPM-1515).
RCA (APL1-2274 "Welcome to My World")..........15-20 77
RCA (AFL1-2274 "Welcome to My World")..........8-15 77
RCA (AQL1-2274 "Welcome to My World")..........6-12 79
RCA (LPM-2328 "His Hand in Mine")..........100-125 60
(Monaural. Black label, "Long Play" at bottom.)
RCA (LPM-2328 "His Hand in Mine")..........60-80 63
(Black label, "Mono" at bottom.)
RCA (LPM-2328 "His Hand in Mine")..........25-50 64
(Black label, "Monaural" at bottom.)
RCA (LSP-2328 "His Hand in Mine")..........150-200 60
(Stereo. Black label, "Living Stereo" at bottom.)
RCA (LSP-2328 "His Hand in Mine")..........600-700 64
(Stereo. Black label. Has "Stereo" at bottom. All print on label – including RCA logo – is silver.)
RCA (LSP-2328 "His Hand in Mine")..........75-125 64
(Black label, RCA logo is white, other label print is silver.)
RCA (LSP-2328 "His Hand in Mine")..........45-55 68
(Orange label. Rigid vinyl.)
RCA (LSP-2328 "His Hand in Mine")..........10-20 76
(Orange label. Flexible vinyl.)
RCA (LSP-2328 "His Hand in Mine")..........15-25 76
(Tan label.)
Note: Repackaged in 1976 as RCA ANL1-1319 and in 1981 as RCA AYM1-3935.
RCA (2347 "Elvis-Greatest Hits, Vol. One")..........20-25 81
(Has embossed letters on front cover.)
RCA (2347 "Elvis-Greatest Hits, Vol. One")..........15-20 83
(Standard flat cover print – not embossed.)
RCA (LPM-2370 "Something for Everybody")..........125-150 61
(Monaural. Black label, "Long Play" at bottom. Back cover promotes Compact 33s.)
RCA (LPM-2370 "Something for Everybody")..........70-90 63
(Black label, "Mono" at bottom.)
RCA (LPM-2370 "Something for Everybody")..........40-60 64
(Black label, "Monaural" at bottom.)
RCA (LSP-2370 "Something for Everybody")..........150-200 61
(Stereo. Black label, "Living Stereo" at bottom. Back cover promotes Compact 33s.)
RCA (LSP-2370 "Something for Everybody")..........80-100 64
(Stereo. Black label, "Stereo" at bottom. All print on label is silver.)
RCA (LSP-2370 "Something for Everybody")..........40-60 64

(Black label, RCA logo is white, other label print is silver.)
RCA (LSP-2370 "Something for Everybody") 35-40 68
(Orange label. Rigid vinyl.)
RCA (LSP-2370 "Something for Everybody") 10-20 68
(Orange label. Flexible vinyl.)
RCA (LSP-2370 "Something for Everybody") 15-25 71
(Tan label.)
RCA (LSP-2370 "Something for Everybody")....................................10-18 76
(Black label, dog near top.)
RCA (AFL1-2370 "Something for Everybody") 8-15 77
Note: Reissued in 1981 as RCA AYM1-4116.
RCA (LPM-2426 "Blue Hawaii") ...75-100 61
(Monaural. Black label, "Long Play" at bottom. Has red sticker announcing the inclusion of *Rock-A-Hula Baby* and *Can't Help Falling in Love*. Sticker is permanently affixed to cover.)
RCA (LPM-2426 "Blue Hawaii") 50-65 63
(Monaural. Black label, "Long Play" at bottom. Does not have red sticker announcing the inclusion of *Rock-A-Hula Baby* and *Can't Help Falling in Love*.)
RCA (LPM-2426 "Blue Hawaii") 50-65 63
(Black label, "Mono" at bottom.)
RCA (LPM-2426 "Blue Hawaii") 40-60 64
(Black label, "Monaural" at bottom.)
RCA (LSP-2426 "Blue Hawaii")..140-160 61
(Stereo. Black label, "Living Stereo" at bottom. Has red sticker announcing the inclusion of *Rock-A-Hula Baby* and *Can't Help Falling in Love*. Sticker is permanently affixed to cover)
RCA (LSP-2426 "Blue Hawaii")......60-85 63
(Stereo. Black label, "Living Stereo" at bottom. Does not have red sticker announcing the inclusion of *Rock-A-Hula Baby* and *Can't Help Falling in Love*.)
RCA (LSP-2426 "Blue Hawaii")......40-60 64
(Black label, RCA logo is white, other label print is silver.)
RCA (LSP-2426 "Blue Hawaii")......35-40 68
(Orange label. Rigid vinyl.)
RCA (LSP-2426 "Blue Hawaii")......15-25 71
(Orange label. Flexible vinyl.)
RCA (LSP-2426 "Blue Hawaii")......10-20 76
(Tan label.)
RCA (LSP-2426 "Blue Hawaii")......10-15 76
(Black label, dog near top.)
RCA (LSP-2426 "Blue Hawaii")...............................8000-1000 77
(Blue vinyl. Experimental pressing only.)
RCA (AFL1-2426 "Blue Hawaii") 8-15 77
(Reissued in 1981 as RCA AYL1-3683.)
RCA (AFL1-2428 "Moody Blue")...................................1000-1200 77
(Colored vinyl – any color *other than blue or black*. Experimental production discs for RCA in-house use only.)
RCA (AFL1-2428 "Moody Blue") 10-18 77
(Blue vinyl.)
RCA (AFL1-2428 "Moody Blue")....................................150-200 77
(Black vinyl.)
RCA (AQL1-2428 "Moody Blue")....20-25 79
RCA (LPM-2523 "Pot Luck") 80-100 62
(Monaural. Black label, "Long Play" at bottom.)
RCA (LPM-2523 "Pot Luck") 100-125 64
(Black label, "Monaural" at bottom.)
RCA (LSP-2523 "Pot Luck")......100-150 62
(Stereo. Black label, "Living Stereo" at bottom.)
RCA (LSP-2523 "Pot Luck")...........50-75 64
(Black label, RCA logo is white, other label print is silver.)
RCA (LSP-2523 "Pot Luck")...........35-40 68
(Orange label.)
RCA (LSP-2523 "Pot Luck")...........20-25 76
(Tan label.)
RCA (LSP-2523 "Pot Luck")...........10-18 76
(Black label, dog near top.)
RCA (AFL1-2523 "Pot Luck")......... 8-15 77
RCA (APL1-2558 "Harum Scarum").................................... 8-15 77
(First issued as RCA LPM/LSP-3468. Reissued in 1980 as RCA AYL1-3734.)
RCA (APL1-2560 "Spinout")........... 8-15 77
(First issued as RCA LPM/LSP-3702. Reissued in 1980 as RCA AYL1-3684.)
RCA (APL1-2564 "Double Trouble") 8-15 77
(First issued as RCA LPM/LSP-3787.)
RCA (APL1-2565 "Clambake")......... 8-15 77
(First issued as RCA LPM/LSP-3893.)
RCA (APL1-2568 "It Happened at the World's Fair") 8-15 77
(First issued as RCA LPM/LSP-2697.)
RCA (APL2-2587 "Elvis in Concert")....................................20-30 77
RCA (CPL2-2587 "Elvis in Concert")....................................40-50 82
RCA (LPM-2621 "Girls! Girls! Girls!").......................................75-100 62
(Monaural. Black label, "Long Play" at bottom. Add $125 to $150 if accompanied by 11" x 11" 1963 calendar.)
RCA (LPM-2621 "Girls! Girls! Girls!")......................................60-80 63
(Black label, "Mono" at bottom.)
RCA (LPM-2621 "Girls! Girls! Girls!")......................................25-45 64
(Black label, "Monaural" at bottom.)
RCA (LSP-2621 "Girls! Girls! Girls!")....................................125-150 62
(Stereo. Black label, "Living Stereo" at bottom. Add $125 to $150 if accompanied by 11" x 11" 1963 calendar.)
RCA (LSP-2621 "Girls! Girls! Girls!")......................................50-75 64
(Black label, RCA logo is white, other label print is silver.)
RCA (LSP-2621 "Girls! Girls! Girls!")......................................35-45 68
(Orange label. Rigid vinyl.)
RCA (LSP-2621 "Girls! Girls! Girls!")......................................15-25 71
(Orange label. Flexible vinyl.)
RCA (LSP-2621 "Girls! Girls! Girls!")......................................25-30 76
(Tan label.)
RCA (LSP-2621 "Girls! Girls! Girls!")......................................10-18 76
(Black label, dog near top.)
RCA (AFL1-2621 "Girls! Girls! Girls!")..8-15 77
RCA (CPD2-2642 "Aloha from Hawaii")......................................30-40 75
(Orange label.)
RCA (CPD2-2642 "Aloha from Hawaii")......................................55-85 77
(Black label.)
Note: First issued as RCA VPSX-6089.
RCA (LPM-2697 "It Happened at the World's Fair")...................................100-150 63
(Monaural. Black label, "Long Play" at bottom. Add $200 to $250 if accompanied by 8" x 10" bonus color photo.)
RCA (LSP-2697 "It Happened at the World's Fair")...................................100-200 63
(Stereo. Black label, "Living Stereo" at bottom. Add $200 to $250 if accompanied by an 8" x 10" bonus color photo.)
RCA (LSP-2697 "It Happened at the World's Fair")......................................60-80 64
(Black label, RCA logo is white, other label print is silver. Reissued in 1977 as RCA APL1-2568.)
RCA (LPM-2756 "Fun in Acapulco")......................................70-90 63
(Monaural. Black label, "Mono" at bottom.)
RCA (LPM-2756 "Fun in Acapulco")......................................45-65 64
(Black label, "Monaural" at bottom.)
RCA (LSP-2756 "Fun in Acapulco")....................................90-110 63
(Stereo. Black label, all print on label is silver.)
RCA (LSP-2756 "Fun in Acapulco")......................................45-65 64
(Black label, RCA logo is white, other label print is silver.)
RCA (LSP-2756 "Fun in Acapulco")......................................35-40 68
(Orange label.)
RCA (LSP-2756 "Fun in Acapulco")......................................20-30 76
(Tan label.)
RCA (LSP-2756 "Fun in Acapulco")......................................10-18 76
(Black label, dog near top.)
RCA (AFL1-2756 "Fun in Acapulco")..8-15 77
RCA (LPM-2765 "Elvis' Golden Records, Vol. 3")......................................80-100 63
(Monaural. Black label, "Mono" at bottom.)
RCA (LPM-2765 "Elvis' Golden Records, Vol. 3")......................................55-70 64
(Black label, "Monaural" at bottom.)
RCA (LSP-2765 "Elvis' Golden Records, Vol. 3")....................................125-150 63
(Stereo. Black label, all print on label is silver.)
RCA (LSP-2765 "Elvis' Golden Records, Vol. 3")......................................25-50 64
(Black label, RCA logo is white, other label print is silver.)
RCA (LSP-2765 "Elvis' Golden Records, Vol. 3")......................................30-40 68
(Orange label.)
RCA (LSP-2765 "Elvis' Golden Records, Vol. 3")......................................10-20 76
(Tan label.)
RCA (LSP-2765 "Elvis' Golden Records, Vol. 3")......................................10-18 76
(Black label, dog near top.)
RCA (AFL1-2765 "Elvis' Golden Records, Vol. 3")..8-10 77
RCA (AFL1-2772 "He Walks Beside Me")......................................15-25 77
RCA (LPM-2894 "Kissin' Cousins")....................................150-200 64
(Monaural. Black label, "Mono" at bottom. *Does not* picture film cast in lower right corner photo on cover.)
RCA (LPM-2894 "Kissin' Cousins")......................................60-80 64
(Black label, "Mono" at bottom. Pictures film cast in lower right corner photo on cover.)
RCA (LPM-2894 "Kissin' Cousins")....................................150-200 64
(Monaural. Black label, "Monaural" at bottom. *Does not* picture film cast in lower right corner photo on cover.)
RCA (LPM-2894 "Kissin' Cousins")......................................85-125 64
(Black label, "Monaural" at bottom.)
RCA (LSP-2894 "Kissin' Cousins")....................................175-200 64
(Stereo. Black label, all print on label is silver. *Does not* picture film cast in lower right corner photo on cover.)
RCA (LSP-2894 "Kissin' Cousins")....................................100-125 64
(Black label, all print on label is silver. Pictures film cast in lower right corner photo on cover.)
RCA (LSP-2894 "Kissin' Cousins")......................................40-60 64
(Black label, RCA logo is white, other label print is silver.)
RCA (LSP-2894 "Kissin' Cousins")......................................35-40 68
(Orange label. Rigid vinyl.)
RCA (LSP-2894 "Kissin' Cousins")......................................15-25 71
(Orange label. Flexible vinyl.)
RCA (LSP-2894 "Kissin' Cousins")......................................20-30 76
(Tan label.)
RCA (LSP-2894 "Kissin' Cousins")......................................10-18 77
(Black label, dog near top.)
RCA (LSP-2894 "Kissin' Cousins")..................................1000-1500 77
(Blue vinyl. Experimental pressing only.)
RCA (AFL1-2894 "Kissin' Cousins")..8-15 77
Note: Reissued in 1981 as RCA AYM1-4115.
RCA (CPL1-2901 "Elvis Sings for Children")......................................15-25 78
(Includes "Special Memories" greeting card.)
RCA (CPL1-2901 "Elvis Sings for Children")..8-12 78
(Without "Special Memories" greeting card.)
RCA (LPM-2999 "Roustabout")....80-100 64
(Monaural. Black label, "Mono" at bottom.)
RCA (LPM-2999 "Roustabout")......60-75 65
(Black label, "Monaural" at bottom.)
RCA (LSP-2999 "Roustabout")...600-700 64
(Stereo. Black label. All print on label – including RCA logo – is silver.)
RCA (LSP-2999 "Roustabout")......40-60 64
(Black label, RCA logo is white, other label print is silver.)
RCA (LSP-2999 "Roustabout").......35-40 68
(Orange label. Rigid vinyl.)
RCA (LSP-2999 "Roustabout").......15-25 68
(Orange label. Flexible vinyl.)
RCA (LSP-2999 "Roustabout").......15-25 76
(Tan label.)
RCA (LSP-2999 "Roustabout").......10-18 77
(Black label. Dog near top.)
RCA (AFL1-2999 "Roustabout").......8-15 77
RCA (3078 "Legendary Performer, Vol. 3")......................................20-30 78
(Picture disc. Add $3 to $5 if accompanied by *Yesterdays* booklet. May be found with the actual disc pressed on either blue or black vinyl. Also issued on standard black vinyl as CPL1-3082.)
RCA (3082 "Legendary Performer, Vol. 3")......................................20-30 78
(Add $3 to $5 if accompanied by *Yesterdays* booklet. Also issued on a picture disc, as RCA 3078.)
RCA (3279 "Our Memories of Elvis") 15-25 79
(Add $30 to $40 if with "Are You Sincere" shrink sticker.)
RCA (LPM-3338 "Girl Happy") 50-60 65
(Monaural.)
RCA (LSP-3338 "Girl Happy")........50-60 65
(Stereo. Black label.)
RCA (LSP-3338 "Girl Happy")........35-40 68
(Orange label. Rigid vinyl.)
RCA (LSP-3338 "Girl Happy")........15-25 71
(Orange label. Flexible vinyl.)
RCA (LSP-3338 "Girl Happy")........25-30 76
(Tan label.)
RCA (LSP-3338 "Girl Happy")........10-18 76
(Black label, dog near top.)
RCA (AFL1-3338 "Girl Happy")........8-10 77
RCA (3448 "Our Memories of Elvis Vol. 2")......................................15-25 79
(Add $40 to $50 if with "There's a Honky Tonk Angel" shrink sticker. A sampling of these tracks is on RCA 3455, *Pure Elvis*.)
RCA (LPM-3450 "Elvis for Everyone")......................................50-70 65
(Monaural.)
RCA (LSP-3450 "Elvis for Everyone")......................................50-70 65
(Stereo. Black label.)
RCA (LSP-3450 "Elvis for Everyone")......................................30-40 68
(Orange label. Rigid vinyl.)
RCA (LSP-3450 "Elvis for Everyone")......................................20-25 71
(Orange label. Flexible vinyl.)
RCA (LSP-3450 "Elvis for Everyone")......................................10-20 76
(Tan label.)
RCA (LSP-3450 "Elvis for Everyone")......................................10-18 76
(Black label, dog near top.)
RCA (AFL1-3450 "Elvis for Everyone")..8-15 77
(Reissued in 1982 as RCA AYL1-4232.)
RCA (3455 "Pure Elvis")..........500-600 79
(Cover reads "Pure Elvis," but label shows "Our Memories of Elvis - Vol. 2." Promotional issue only.)
RCA (LPM-3468 "Harum Scarum")......................................40-60 65
(Monaural. Add $50 to $75 if accompanied by bonus 12" x 12" photo, and $20 to $25 if with sticker announcing the bonus photo.)
RCA (LSP-3468 "Harum Scarum")......................................45-65 65
(Stereo. Add $50 to $75 if accompanied by bonus 12" x 12" photo, and $20 to $25 if with sticker announcing the bonus photo.)
Note: Reissued in 1977 as APL1-2558 and in 1980 as AYL1-3734.
RCA (LPM-3553 "Frankie & Johnny")......................................40-60 66
(Monaural. Add $60 to $75 if accompanied by bonus 12" x 12" photo, and $20 to $25 if with sticker announcing the bonus photo.)
RCA (LSP-3553 "Frankie & Johnny")......................................45-65 66
(Stereo. Add $60 to $75 if accompanied by bonus 12" x 12" photo, and $20 to $25 if with sticker announcing the bonus photo.)
Note: Reissued in 1977 as RCA APL1-2559. A repackage appeared in 1976 as Pickwick 7007.
RCA (LPM-3643 "Paradise Hawaiian Style")......................................40-60 66
(Monaural.)
RCA (LSP-3643 "Paradise Hawaiian Style")......................................40-60 66
(Stereo. Black label. Rigid vinyl.)
RCA (LSP-3643 "Paradise Hawaiian Style")......................................70-85 66
(Stereo. Black label. Flexible vinyl, similar to '70s Dynaflex issues.)
RCA (LSP-3643 "Paradise Hawaiian Style")......................................35-40 68
(Orange label. Rigid vinyl.)
RCA (LSP-3643 "Paradise Hawaiian Style")......................................15-25 71
(Orange label. Flexible vinyl.)
RCA (LSP-3643 "Paradise Hawaiian Style")......................................10-15 76
(Tan label.)
RCA (LSP-3643 "Paradise Hawaiian Style")......................................10-15 76
(Black label, dog near top.)
RCA (AFL1-3643 "Paradise Hawaiian Style")..8-15 77
RCA (AYL1-3683 "Blue Hawaii")......5-10 80
(First issued as RCA LPM/LSP-2426.)
RCA (AYL1-3684 "Spinout") 5-10 80
(First issued as RCA LPM/LSP-3702, reissued in 1977 as RCA APL1-2560.)
RCA (CPL8-3699 "Elvis Aron Presley")......................................80-100 80
(Boxed, eight-disc set. Add $10 to $15 if accompanied by 20-page booklet, and $3 to $5 if with "25th Anniversary" shrink sticker.)
RCA (CPL8-3699 "Elvis Aron Presley")....................................200-275 80
(REVIEWER SERIES edition. Silver sticker on back also identifies the Reviewer Series copy as "NS-3699." Add $10 to $15 if accompanied by 20-page booklet, and $3 to $5 if with "25th Anniversary" shrink sticker.)
RCA (CPK8-3699 "Elvis Aron Presley")......................................80-100 80
(Boxed, four-cassette tape set. Add $10 to $15 if accompanied by 20-page booklet, and $3 to $5 if with "25th Anniversary" shrink sticker. Add $20 to $30 if accompanied by eight 12" x 12" Elvis photos.)
RCA (CPS8-3699 "Elvis Aron Presley")......................................90-125 80
(Boxed, four 8-track tape set. Add $10 to $15 if accompanied by 20-page booklet, and $3 to $5 if with "25th Anniversary" shrink sticker. Add $20 to $30 if accompanied by eight 12" x 12" Elvis photos.)
Note: *Excerpts* of songs in this set appear on RCA 3729. *Selections* from this LP are on RCA 3781.
RCA (LPM-3702 "Spinout")...........40-60 66
(Monaural. Add $40 to $60 if accompanied by bonus 12" x 12" photo.)
RCA (LSP-3702 "Spinout") 45-65 66
(Stereo. Add $40 to $60 if accompanied by bonus 12" x 12" photo.)
Note: Reissued in 1977 as APL1-2560.
RCA (3729 "Elvis Aron Presley Excerpts")....................................100-125 80
(Has 37 excerpts from RCA 3699. Promotional issue only.)
RCA (AYL1-3732 "Pure Gold") 5-10 80
(First issued as RCA ANL1-0971.)
RCA (AYL1-3733 "King Creole")......5-10 80
(First issued as RCA LSP-1884.)
RCA (AYL1-3734 "Harum Scarum").5-10 80
(First issued as RCA LPM/LSP-3468.)
RCA (AYL1-3735 "G.I. Blues")........5-10 80
(First issued as RCA LPM/LSP-2256.)
RCA (LPM-3758 "How Great Thou Art")......................................40-60 67
(Monaural.)
RCA (LSP-3758 "How Great Thou Art")......................................40-60 67
(Stereo. Black label.)
RCA (LSP-3758 "How Great Thou Art")......................................60-80 68
(Orange label. Rigid vinyl. Cover also shows mono number.)
RCA (LSP-3758 "How Great Thou Art")......................................30-40 68
(Orange label. Rigid vinyl. No mention of mono number.)
RCA (LSP-3758 "How Great Thou Art")......................................20-30 71
(Orange label. Flexible vinyl.)
RCA (LSP-3758 "How Great Thou Art")......................................20-25 76
(Tan label.)
RCA (LSP-3758 "How Great Thou Art")......................................10-18 76
(Black label, dog near top.)
RCA (AFL1-3758 "How Great Thou Art")..8-15 77
RCA (3781 "Elvis Aron Presley Selections")....................................100-125 80
(Has 12 selections from RCA 3699. Promotional issue only.)
RCA (LPM-3787 "Double Trouble")......................................40-60 67
(Monaural. Front cover reads "Special Bonus Full Color Photo." Add $40 to $50 if accompanied by bonus 7" x 9" photo.)
RCA (LPM-3787 "Double Trouble")......................................50-75 68
("Special Bonus Full Color Photo" is replaced by "Trouble Double.")
RCA (LSP-3787 "Double Trouble")......................................45-65 67
(Stereo. Front cover reads "Special Bonus Full Color Photo." Add $40 to $50 if accompanied by bonus 7" x 9" photo. Black label.)
RCA (LSP-3787 "Double Trouble")......................................50-75 68
("Special Bonus Full Color Photo" is replaced by "Trouble Double.")
RCA (LSP-3787 "Double Trouble")......................................35-40 68
(Orange label.)
RCA (LSP-3787 "Double Trouble")......................................10-20 76
(Tan label.)
Note: Reissued in 1977 as RCA APL1-2564.
RCA (AYL1-3892 "Elvis in Person")..8-10 81
(First issued as RCA LSP-4428.)
RCA (LPM-3893 "Clambake")....200-250 67
(Monaural. Add $40 to $50 if accompanied by bonus 12" x 12" photo.)
RCA (LSP-3893 "Clambake") 40-60 67
(Stereo. Add $40 to $50 if accompanied by bonus 12" x 12" photo.)
Note: Reissued in 1977 as RCA APL1-2565.
RCA (AYM1-3893 "Sun Sessions")..5-10 81
(First issued as RCA APM1-1675.)
RCA (AYM1-3894 "Elvis TV Special")..5-10 81
(First issued RCA LPM-4088.)
RCA (3917 "Guitar Man") 25-35 81
(Includes a "This Is Elvis" flyer. Producer Felton Jarvis talks about Elvis as well as the making of this LP on RCA 1981.)
RCA (LPM-3921 "Elvis' Gold Records, Vol. 4")..................................1500-2000 68
(Monaural.)
RCA (LSP-3921 "Elvis' Gold Records, Vol. 4")......................................30-50 68
(Stereo. Black label.)
RCA (LSP-3921 "Elvis' Gold Records, Vol. 4")......................................30-40 68
(Orange label. Rigid vinyl.)
RCA (LSP-3921 "Elvis' Gold Records, Vol. 4")......................................20-30 71
(Orange label. Flexible vinyl.)
RCA (LSP-3921 "Elvis' Gold Records, Vol. 4")......................................20-30 76
(Tan label.)
RCA (LSP-3921 "Elvis' Gold Records, Vol. 4")......................................10-18 76
(Black label, dog near top.)
RCA (AFL1-3921 "Elvis' Gold Records, Vol. 4")..8-15 77
RCA (AYM1-3935 "His Hand in Mine")..5-10 81
(First issued as RCA LPM/LSP-2328.)
RCA (AYL1-3956 "That's The Way It Is")..5-10 81
(First issued as RCA LSP-4460.)
RCA (LPM-3989 "Speedway") 1500-2000 68
(Monaural. Add $25 to $50 if accompanied by bonus 8" x 10" photo, and $20 to $25 if with shrink sticker announcing bonus photo.)
RCA (LSP-3989 "Speedway")........40-60 68
(Stereo. Black label. Add $25 to $50 if accompanied by bonus 8" x 10" photo, and $20 to $25 if with shrink sticker announcing bonus photo.)
RCA (LSP-3989 "Speedway")........35-40 68
(Orange label. Rigid vinyl.)
RCA (LSP-3989 "Speedway")........15-25 71
(Orange label. Rigid vinyl.)
RCA (LSP-3989 "Speedway")........10-20 76
(Tan label.)
RCA (LSP-3989 "Speedway")........10-28 76
(Black label, dog near top.)
RCA (AFL1-3989 "Speedway") 8-15 77
RCA (4031 "This Is Elvis")............15-25 80
(Add $10 to $15 if with "Contains Previously Unreleased Material" shrink sticker.)
RCA (LPM-4088 "Elvis TV Special")......................................40-50 68
(Orange label. Rigid disc.)
RCA (LPM-4088 "Elvis TV Special")......................................25-35 71
(Orange label. Flexible disc.)
RCA (LPM-4088 "Elvis TV Special")......................................15-25 76
(Tan label. Add $40 to $50 if with "Memories of Elvis" TV show shrink sticker.)
RCA (LPM-4088 "Elvis TV Special")......................................12-22 76
(Black label. Add $40 to $50 if with "Memories of Elvis" TV show shrink sticker.)
RCA (AFM1-4088 "Elvis TV Special")..8-15 77
Note: Reissued in 1981 as RCA AYM1-3894. Repackaged for HBO as RCA 0704.
RCA (AYL1-4114 "That's The Way It Is")..5-10 81
(First issued as RCA LSP-4445.)
RCA (AYM1-4115 "Kissin' Cousins")..5-10 81
(First issued as RCA LPM/LSP-2894.)
RCA (AYM1-4116 "Something for Everybody")..5-10 81
(First issued as RCA LPM/LSP-2370.)
RCA (LSP-4155 "From Elvis in Memphis")......................................40-50 69
(Orange label. Rigid disc. Add $30 to $40 if accompanied by 8" x 10" Elvis photo, and $5 to $10 if with shrink sticker announcing photo.)
RCA (LSP-4155 "From Elvis in Memphis")......................................30-45 72
(Orange label. Flexible disc.)
RCA (LSP-4155 "From Elvis in Memphis")......................................25-30 69
(Tan label.)
RCA (LSP-4155 "From Elvis in Memphis")......................................10-18 69
(Black label.)
RCA (AFL1-4155 "From Elvis in Memphis")..8-15 77
Note: A half-speed mastered issue of this LP was released in 1982 as MFSL 059.
RCA (AYL1-4232 "Elvis for Everyone")..5-10 82
(First issued as RCA LPM/LSP-3450.)
RCA (LSP-4362 "On Stage") 35-45 70
(Orange label. Rigid disc.)
RCA (LSP-4362 "On Stage") 20-30 72
(Orange label. Flexible disc.)

RCA (LSP-4362 "On Stage")..........25-35 76
(Tan label.)
RCA (LSP-4362 "On Stage")..........25-35 76
(Black label.)
RCA (AFL1-4362 "On Stage")........10-12 77
RCA (AQL1-4362 "On Stage") 5-10 83
RCA (4395 "Memories of Christmas") 10-15 82
(Add $5 to $8 if accompanied by 7" x 9" greeting card with Elvis' photo, and $3 to $5 if with shrink sticker announcing bonus card.
RCA (LSP-4428 "Elvis in Person") .45-55 70
(Orange label. Rigid vinyl.)
RCA (LSP-4428 "Elvis in Person") .40-50 71
(Orange label. Flexible vinyl.)
RCA (LSP-4428 "Elvis in Person") .20-25 76
(Tan label.)
RCA (LSP-4428 "Elvis in Person") .10-18 76
(Black label.)
RCA (AFL1-4428 "Elvis in Person") 8-15 77
Note: First released as half of RCA LSP-6020, then reissued in 1981 as RCA AYL1-3892.
RCA (LSP-4429 "Elvis Back in Memphis")....................................30-40 70
(Orange label. Rigid vinyl.)
RCA (LSP-4429 "Elvis Back in Memphis")....................................25-35 71
(Orange label. Flexible vinyl.)
RCA (LSP-4429 "Elvis Back in Memphis")....................................20-25 76
(Tan label.)
RCA (LSP-4429 "Elvis Back in Memphis")....................................10-18 76
(Black label.)
RCA (AFL1-4429 "Elvis Back in Memphis").................................. 8-12 77
Note: First issued as half of RCA LSP-6020.
RCA (LSP-4445 "That's the Way It Is") 50-100 70
(Orange label. Rigid vinyl.)
RCA (LSP-4445 "That's the Way It Is") 15-25 71
(Orange label. Flexible vinyl.)
RCA (LSP-4445 "That's the Way It Is") 15-25 76
(Tan label.)
RCA (LSP-4445 "That's the Way It Is") 10-18 77
(Black label.)
RCA (AFL1-4445 "That's the Way It Is") 8-10 77
Note: Reissued in 1981 as RCA AYL1-4114.
RCA (LSP-4460 "Elvis Country")....30-40 71
(Orange label. Rigid vinyl. Add $10 to $15 if accompanied by 7" x 9" Elvis photo, and $15 to $20 if with shrink sticker announcing bonus photo.)
RCA (LSP-4460 "Elvis Country")....15-25 71
(Orange label. Flexible vinyl. Add $10 to $15 if accompanied by 7" x 9" Elvis photo, and $15 to $20 if with shrink sticker announcing bonus photo.)
RCA (LSP-4460 "Elvis Country")....20-30 76
(Tan label. Black vinyl.)
RCA (LSP-4460 "Elvis Country")..............................1000-2000 77
(Tan label. Green vinyl. Experimental pressing only.)
RCA (LSP-4460 "Elvis Country")....10-20 76
(Black label.)
RCA (AFL1-4460 "Elvis Country")... 8-12 77
Note: Reissued in 1981 as RCA AYL1-3956.
RCA (LSP-4530 "Love Letters") 35-45 71
(Orange label. Full title, *Love Letters From Elvis*, on TWO lines on front cover.)
RCA (LSP-4530 "Love Letters") 20-35 71
(Orange label. Full title, *Love Letters From Elvis*, on THREE lines on front cover.)
RCA (LSP-4530 "Love Letters") 25-35 76
(Tan label.)
RCA (LSP-4530 "Love Letters") 20-30 76
(Black label.)
RCA (AFL1-4530 "Love Letters") ...15-25 77
Note: Reissued in 1981 as RCA AYL1-3956.
RCA (AHL1-4530 "Elvis Medley") ..10-15 82
RCA (LSP-4579 "Wonderful World of Christmas") 20-30 71
(Orange label. Add $20 to $25 if accompanied by a 5" x 7" Elvis postcard, and $15 to $20 if with shrink sticker announcing bonus photo. Reissued in 1977 as RCA ANL1-1936.)
RCA (LSP-4671 "Elvis Now") 80-100 72
(Has white titles/times sticker on front cover. Promotional issue only.)
RCA (LSP-4671 "Elvis Now") 25-35 72
(Orange label.)
RCA (LSP-4671 "Elvis Now") 20-30 76
(Tan label.)
RCA (LSP-4671 "Elvis Now") 10-18 76
(Black label.)
RCA (AFL1-4671 "Elvis Now") 8-15 77
RCA (LSP-4690 "He Touched Me") 80-100 72
(Has white titles/times sticker on front cover. Promotional issue only.)
RCA (LSP-4690 "He Touched Me") 30-40 72
(Orange label.)
RCA (LSP-4690 "He Touched Me") 10-20 76
(Tan label.)
RCA (LSP-4690 "He Touched Me") 10-18 76
(Black label.)
RCA (AFL1-4690 "He Touched Me") 8-15 77
RCA (4678 "I Was the One")........... 8-10 83
RCA (LSP-4776 " Elvis As Recorded at Madison Square Garden") 80-100 72
(Orange label. Has white programming stickers applied to front cover. Promotional issue only. Counterfeit stickers exist but can be identified by the misspelling of the title *Love Me*, which reads: "Live Me."For double disc promotional issue, see RCA 571.)
RCA (LSP-4776 " Elvis As Recorded at Madison Square Garden") 20-30 72
(Orange label.)
RCA (LSP-4776 " Elvis As Recorded at Madison Square Garden") 10-20 76
(Tan label.)
RCA (LSP-4776 " Elvis As Recorded at Madison Square Garden") 10-18 76
(Black label.)
RCA (AQL1-4776 " Elvis As Recorded at Madison Square Garden") 8-10 77
RCA (4848 "Legendary Performer, Vol. 4")..25-35 83
(Embossed cover. Price includes a 12-page *Memories of the King* booklet.)
RCA (4848 "Legendary Performer, Vol. 4")..15-25 86
(Standard flat print – not embossed – on cover.)
RCA (4941 "Elvis' Gold Records, Vol. 5")..5-10 84
RCA (5172 "Golden Celebration") 75-100 84
(Boxed, six-disc set. Price includes custom inner sleeves and an envelope containing an 8" x 10" Elvis photo and a 50th Anniversary flyer.)
RCA (5172 "Golden Celebration") ..25-35 84
(Special "Advance Cassette" boxed set sampler.)
RCA (5182 "Rocker") 20-25 84
RCA (5196 "Elvis' Golden Records") 15-20 84
(Digitally remastered, quality mono pressing. Price includes gold "The Definitive Rock Classic" banner. First issued as RCA LPM-1707.)
RCA (5197 "Elvis' Gold Records, Vol. 2")..15-20 84
(Digitally remastered, quality mono pressing. Price includes gold "The Definitive Rock Classic" banner. First issued as RCA LPM-2075.)
RCA (5198 "Elvis Presley")............15-20 84
(Digitally remastered, quality mono pressing. Price includes gold "The Definitive Rock Classic" banner. First issued as RCA LPM-1254.)
RCA (5199 "Elvis") 15-20 84
(Digitally remastered, quality mono pressing. Price includes gold "The Definitive Rock Classic" banner. First issued as RCA LPM-1382.)
RCA (5353 "Valentine Gift for You")..18-22 85
(Red vinyl. Add $4 to $5 if with shrink sticker announcing red vinyl.)
RCA (5353 "Valentine Gift for You")..5-10 85
(Black vinyl.)
RCA (5418 "Reconsider Baby")......18-22 85
(Blue vinyl. Add $4 to $5 if with shrink sticker announcing blue vinyl and "New Versions.")
RCA (5430 "Always on My Mind") ..18-22 85
(Purple vinyl. Add $4 to $5 if with shrink sticker announcing purple vinyl and contents.)
RCA (5486 "Elvis' Christmas Album") 18-22 85
(Green vinyl. Add $4 to $5 if with shrink sticker announcing green vinyl.)
RCA (5486 "Elvis' Christmas Album") 12-20 85
(Black vinyl. Thus far, all black vinyl copies discovered are packaged with stickers reading "pressed on green vinyl.")
RCA (5600 "Return of the Rocker")..10-20 86
RCA (5697 "Special Christmas Programming")......................1000-1500 67
(Identification number shown since no selection number is used. Promotional issue only.)
RCA (LSP-6020 "From Memphis to Vegas") 100-150 69
(Orange label. Rigid vinyl. Incorrectly shows writers of *Words* as Tommy Boyce & Bobby Hart. Also shows writer of *Suspicious Minds* as Frances Zambon. Add $40 to $50 if accompanied by two 8" x 10" black and white Elvis photos.)
RCA (LSP-6020 "From Memphis to Vegas") 80-120 69
(Orange label. Rigid vinyl. Correctly shows writers of *Words* as Barry, Robin & Maurice Gibb, and writer of *Suspicious Minds* as Mark James. Add $40 to $50 if accompanied by two 8" x 10" Elvis photos.)
RCA (LSP-6020 "From Memphis to Vegas") 25-50 69
(Orange label. Flexible vinyl.)
RCA (LSP-6020 "From Memphis to Vegas") 30-40 76
(Tan label.)
RCA (LSP-6020 "From Memphis to Vegas") 15-25 77
(Black label.)
Note: Each of the two LPs in this set was reissued individually, *Elvis in Person at the International Hotel* as LSP-4428 and *Elvis Back in Memphis* as LSP-4429, both in 1970.
RCA (VPSX-6089 "Aloha from Hawaii")................................3000-5000 73
(Has "Chicken of the Sea" sticker on cover. Quadradisc and contents stickers also are on cover. Includes programming insert card, which is valued at $100 to $200. Promotional in-house issue by the Van Camps Company.)
RCA (VPSX-6089 "Aloha from Hawaii")................................1000-2000 73
(Has white titles/times sticker on front cover. Promotional issue only.)
RCA (VPSX-6089 "Aloha from Hawaii").......................................75-100 73
(Has Quadradisc and contents stickers on cover. Red/orange label.)
RCA (VPSX-6089 "Aloha from Hawaii") 30-40 74
(Has Quadradisc/RCA logo in lower right corner of front cover. Titles are printed on back cover. Orange label.)
RCA (VPSX-6089 "Aloha from Hawaii") 25-30 76
(Tan label.)
Note: Issued through the RCA Record Club as RCA 213736 and later (1977) as RCA CPD2-2642.
RCA (6221 "Memphis Record")......25-35 87
(Includes a bonus color 15" x 22" poster and *Elvis Talks* LP flyer.)
RCA (6313 "Elvis Talks!").............20-30 87
(Mail-order offer.)
RCA (6382 "Number One Hits") 20-30 87
(Includes a bonus color 15" x 22" poster and *Elvis Talks* LP flyer.)
RCA (6383 "Top Ten Hits")............25-35 87
(Includes a bonus color 15" x 22" poster and *Elvis Talks* LP flyer.)
RCA (LPM-6401 "Worldwide 50 Gold Hits, Vol. 1")..70-90 70
(Orange label. Rigid vinyl. Boxed, four-disc set. Add $30 to $40 if accompanied by a 16-page Elvis photo booklet.)
RCA (LPM-6401 "Worldwide 50 Gold Hits, Vol. 1")..70-90 70
(Orange label. Flexible vinyl. Boxed, four-disc set. Add $30 to $40 if accompanied by a 16-page Elvis photo booklet.)
RCA (LPM-6401 "Worldwide 50 Gold Hits, Vol. 1")..30-40 76
(Tan label.)
RCA (LPM-6401 "Worldwide 50 Gold Hits, Vol. 1")..20-35 77
(Black label.)
Note: Two discs in this set were repackaged for the RCA Record Club in 1974 as RCA 213690. The remaining two came out in 1978 as RCA 214657.
RCA (LPM-6402 "Worldwide 50 Gold Hits, Vol. 2")..60-75 71
(Orange label. Boxed, four-disc set. Add $25 to $50 if accompanied by an Elvis print, and an envelope with piece of material.)
RCA (LPM-6402 "Worldwide 50 Gold Hits, Vol. 2")..30-40 76
(Tan label. With bonus items shown as included.)
RCA (LPM-6402 "Worldwide 50 Gold Hits, Vol. 2")..25-35 76
(Tan label. No bonus items shown as being included.)
RCA (LPM-6402 "Worldwide 50 Gold Hits, Vol. 2")..20-25 77
(Black label.)
Note: Two discs in this set were repackaged for the RCA Record Club in 1978 as RCA 214567.
RCA (6414 "The Complete Sun Sessions")..20-30 87
(Includes a bonus color 15" x 22" poster and *Elvis Talks* LP flyer.)
RCA (6738 "Essential Elvis") 15-25 88
RCA (6985 "The Alternate Aloha") .15-20 88
RCA (7031 "Elvis Forever") 30-45 74
(TV mail-order offer.)
RCA (9681 "E-Z Pop No. 5): see Various Artists section
RCA (7065 "Canadian Tribute") 15-20 78
(Price includes photo inner-sleeve. Canadian issues of this have the same number, but are clearly marked on back cover as Canadian.)
RCA (8468 "Elvis in Nashville") 20-40 88
RCA (8533 "Heartbreak Hotel"): see Various Artists section
RCA (9586 "Elvis Gospel") 20-40 89
RCA (9589 "Stereo '57, Essential Elvis, Vol. 2")..15-25 89
RCA (213690 "Worldwide Gold Award Hits, Parts 1&2")...............................100-150 74
(Orange label. RCA Record Club issue only.)
RCA (213690 "Worldwide Gold Award Hits, Parts 1&2")...30-40 76
(Tan label. RCA Record Club issue only.)
RCA (213690 "Worldwide Gold Award Hits, Parts 1&2")...15-25 77
(Black label. RCA Record Club issue only. The two discs in this set were first issued as half of RCA LPM-6401.)
RCA (213736 "Aloha from Hawaii") 50-75 73
(Orange label.)
RCA (213736 "Aloha from Hawaii") 40-60 76
(Tan label.)
RCA (214657 "Worldwide Gold Award Hits, Parts 3&4")...15-20 78
(RCA Record Club issue only. The two discs in this set were first issued as half of RCA LPM-6401.)
RCA (233299 "Country Classics") ..30-40 80
(RCA Record Club issue only.)
RCA (234340 "From Elvis with Love") 30-40 78
(RCA Record Club issue only.)
RCA (244047 "Legendary Concert Performances") 30-40 78
(RCA Record Club issue only.)
RCA (244069 "Country Memories")..30-40 78
(RCA Record Club issue only.)
SILHOUETTE (10001/10002 "Personally Elvis") 30-40 79
STARDAY (995 "Interviews with Elvis") 40-60 78
(Previously issued on Great Northwest 4005.)
SUN (1001 "The Sun Years").........15-25 77
(Light yellow label, "Memphis" at bottom. Light yellow cover with light brown printing.)
SUN (1001 "The Sun Years").........10-15 77
(Darker yellow label, four target circles. Dark yellow cover with dark brown printing.)
SUN (1001 "The Sun Years")...........8-12 77
(White cover with brown printing.)
TM ("The Presley Years") 100-200 81
(Boxed, 12-disc syndicated radio show. Includes script and cue sheets.)
TIME-LIFE (106 "Elvis Presley: 1954-1961") 25-30 86
(Boxed, three-disc set. Part of the *Rock 'N' Roll Era* series of sets available from Time-Life by mail-order. Includes brochure.)
UNITED STATIONS ("Elvis Presley Birthday Tribute")..................................125-150 89
(Four hour radio show. Includes four pages of cue sheets. Promotional issue only.)
WATERMARK ("The Elvis Presley Story, 1975")..800-900 75
(13-disc set. White label, pink letters. Includes a 48-page operations manual. Promotional issue only. Not issued with a special cover or package.)
WATERMARK ("The Elvis Presley Story, 1977")..700-800 77
(13-disc set. White label, pink letters. Includes a 48-page operations manual, which represents about $100 of the value. Promotional issue only. Not issued with a special cover or package.)
WESTWOOD ONE ("A Golden Celebration")..............................200-250 84
(Boxed, three-disc set. Price includes instructions and cue sheets, which represent $5-10 of the value. Issued to radio stations only.)
WORLD of ELVIS PRESLEY.......50-100 83
(One hour weekly radio show, numbered as program 1 through program 30. The show ceased operation after 30 programs. Each disc is accompanied by a single cue sheet. Price is for any one of the discs, although Program #3 is by far the rarest of them all.)
Session: Chet Atkins; Bill Black; Hal Blaine; Blossoms; David Briggs; James Burton; Floyd Cramer; D.J. Fontana; Glen Hardin; Jordanaires; Jerry Kennedy; Anita Kerr; Ronnie Milsap; Bob Moore; Scotty Moore; Larry Muhoberac; Shaun Neilsen; Boots Randolph; Jerry Reed; J.D. Sumner & Stamps; Sweet Inspirations; Kathy Westmoreland; John Wilkinson; Bobby Wood.
Also see ALLEN, Steve
Also see ATKINS, Chet
Also see AUDREY
Also see BLACK, Bill
Also see BLAINE, Hal
Also see BLOSSOMS
Also see BRIGGS, David
Also see BURTON, James
Also see COLE, Nat "King"
Also see CRAMER, Floyd
Also see CRICKETS
Also see DONNER, Ral
Also see DURANTE, Jimmy
Also see FONTANA, D.J., Band
Also see FOWLER, Wally
Also see HARRIS, Emmylou
Also see JARVIS, Felton
Also see JORDANAIRES
Also see KENNEDY, Jerry
Also see KERR, Anita
Also see LIBERACE
Also see MANTOVANI
Also see MILSAP, Ronnie
Also see MOORE, Bob
Also see MOORE, Scotty
Also see MUHOBERAC, Larry
Also see NIELSEN, Shaun
Also see OSBORNE, Jerry
Also see RANDOLPH, Boots
Also see REED, Jerry
Also see ROMANS, Charlie
Also see RUSSELL, Jane
Also see SINATRA, Nancy
Also see SUMNER, J.D., & Stamps
Also see SWEET INSPIRATIONS
Also see VINCENT, Gene
Also see WESTMORELAND, Kathy
Also see WILKINSON, John
Also see WOOD, Bobby

● Prefix letters or numbers are used on some LP listings in order to more quickly identify the variations available.

● A few items that have no label name are listed by title, such as the International Hotel boxed sets.

● LPs with a sticker applied over the selection number, showing a new number, are valued approximately the same as those without the sticker.

● Most various artists albums are now found in the chapter for such compilations. Those few still in the Elvis Presley section are oddities that are either not yet included in the Various Artists section or are more at home here.

● If you don't find a record in the preceding sections, it may contain two, three or four artists, and is listed in a section that follows.

● As imposing as our Presley section here may seem, it is but a drop in the bucket. For a far more in-depth study of Elvis Presley collectibles – including records, compact discs and memorabilia – get Jerry Osborne's *Presleyana IV – The Elvis Presley Record Price Guide*.

PRESLEY, Elvis / Beatles

Singles: 7–inch

OSBORNE ENTERPRISES ("The 1967 Elvis Medley") 10-15 88
(Flip side is titled ***The #1 Hits Medley, 1956-69***. Includes insert. 400 made.)
OSBORNE ENTERPRISES ("The 1967 Elvis Medley") 15-25 89
(Flip side is titled ***The #1 Hits Medley, 1956-70***. 100 made.)

LPs: 10/12–inch

UNITED DISTRIBUTORS (2382 "Lightning Strikes Twice")..............................25-50 81
(Promotional issue only. Has five songs by each artist.)
Also see BEATLES

PRESLEY, Elvis / Martha Carson / Lou Monte / Herb Jeffries

EPs: 7–inch

RCA (2 "Dealer's Prevue")..... 2000-3000 57
(Issued with paper envelope/sleeve, which represents about 2/3 of the value. Promotional issue only.)
Also see CARSON, Martha
Also see MONTE, Lou

PRESLEY, Elvis / Jean Chapel

EPs: 7–inch

RCA (7 "Love Me Tender") 150-200 56
(Not issued with a special sleeve or cover. Promotional issue only.)
Also see CHAPEL, Jean

PRESLEY, Elvis / Buddy Holly

Singles: 7–inch

CREATIVE RADIO ("Elvis 50th Birthday Special") 10-20 85
(Demonstration disc. A promotional issue.)
Also see HOLLY, Buddy

PRESLEY, Elvis / Fear

LPs: 10/12–inch

DISCONET (309 "The Original Elvis Presley Medley"/"Fear Medley")..................25-50 80
(Promotional issue only.)

PRESLEY, Elvis / David Keith

Singles: 7–inch

RCA (8760 "Heartbreak Hotel") ... 50-100 88
(White label. Promotional issue only.)
RCA (8760 "Heartbreak Hotel") 4-6 88
(Red label. Printing on both sides of label.)
RCA (8760 "Heartbreak Hotel") 4-8 88
(Red label. Printing on Elvis side only.)
RCA (8760 "Heartbreak Hotel") 4-8 88
(Red label. Printing on David Keith side only.)

Picture Sleeves

POPULAR LIBRARY/FAWCETT ("Heartbreak Hotel")..300-400 88
(Produced by the publisher of the book that inspired the screenplay. Promotional issue only.)
RCA (8760 "Heartbreak Hotel") 20-40
(Pictures, but doesn't identify, RCA's Butch Waugh. Promotional issue only.)
RCA (8760 "Heartbreak Hotel") 4-8 88
(Pictures Elvis and others in a Cadillac.)
Also see KEITH, David

PRESLEY, Elvis / Vaughn Monroe / Gogi Grant / Robert Shaw

EPs: 7–inch

RCA (3736 "Pop Transcribed 30 Sec. Spot")..500-700 58
(Not issued with a special sleeve or cover. Promotional issue only.)
Also see GRANT, Gogi
Also see MONROE, Vaughn

PRESLEY, Elvis / Jaye P. Morgan

Singles: 7–inch

UNITED STATES AIR FORCE (125 "It's Now Or Never") 300-400 61
(Add $100 to $125 if accompanied by printed, cardboard mailing box. Issued only to radio stations.)

EPs: 7–inch

RCA (992 & 689 "Elvis/Jaye P. Morgan")..............................8000-12000 56
(Two-disc set, coupling EPA-992 by Presley and EPA-689 by Jaye P. Morgan in a promotional package. Gatefold cover. Since the discs are standard pressings, nearly all of the value is represented by the custom cover.)
Also see MORGAN, Jaye P.

PRESLEY, Elvis / Gary Owens

Singles: 7–inch

CREATIVE RADIO ("Elvis Hour") ..20-30 86
(Demonstration disc. A promotional issue.)
Also see OWENS, Gary

PRESLEY, Elvis / Helen Reddy

Singles: 7–inch

WHAT'S IT ALL ABOUT (78 "Life")..45-55 77
(Issued only to radio stations.)
Also see REDDY, Helen

PRESLEY, Elvis / Dinah Shore

EPs: 7–inch

RCA (56 "Too Much") 150-200 57
(Not issued with a special sleeve or cover. Promotional issue only.)
Also see SHORE, Dinah

PRESLEY, Elvis / Frank Sinatra / Nat King Cole

EPs: 7–inch

CREATIVE RADIO ("Elvis Remembered")..............................40-45 79
(Promotional demonstration disc.)
Also see COLE, Nat "King"
Also see SINATRA, Frank

PRESLEY, Elvis / Hank Snow / Eddy Arnold / Jim Reeves
EPs: 7-inch
RCA (12 "Old Shep") ... 2000-3000 56
(Issued with a paper, "WOHO Featuring RCA Victor" sleeve. Deduct $1,500 to $2,000 if sleeve is missing. Promotional only.)
Also see ARNOLD, Eddy
Also see REEVES, Jim
Also see SNOW, Hank

PRESLEY, Elvis / Lawrence Welk
Singles: 7-inch
UNITED STATES AIR FORCE (159 "Surrender") ... 300-400 61
(Add $100 to $125 if accompanied by printed, cardboard mailing box. Issued only to radio stations.)
Also see WELK, Lawrence

PRESLEY, Elvis / Hank Williams
LPs: 10/12-inch
SUNRISE MEDIA (3011 "History of Country Music") ... 15-25 81
(Has four songs by each artist.)
Also see PRESLEY, Elvis
Also see WILLIAMS, Hank

PRESLEY, Elvis
(Michael Conley)
Singles: 7-inch
ELVIS CLASSIC (5478 "Tell Me Pretty Baby") ... 4-8 78
(Despite being labeled as a 1954 recording by Elvis Presley, this track is simply a 1978 recording by Michael Conley, performing in an Elvis style. It is listed separately to eliminate confusion.)
Picture Sleeves
ELVIS CLASSIC (5478 "Tell Me Pretty Baby") ... 8-10 78
(Sleeve pictures an artist's sketch of Elvis Presley.)

PRESLEY, Gaylon
Singles: 7-inch
UNITED SOUTHERN ARTISTS ... 5-10 61

PRESLEY, Grandpa Jesse
Singles: 7-inch
LEGACY PARK ... 4-6 78

PRESLEY, Uncle Vester
Singles: 7-inch
VES-PRES (1 "Message to Elvis Fans and My Friends") ... 4-6 79
Picture Sleeves
VES-PRES (1 "Message to Elvis Fans and My Friends") ... 4-6 79

PRESSURE *R&B '80*
Singles: 7-inch
LAX ... 3-5 79-80
MCA ... 3-5 80
LPs: 10/12-inch
LAX ... 5-10 79
Also see LAWS, Ronnie

PRESSURE DROP *R&B '82*
Singles: 12-inch
TOMMY BOY ... 4-6 82
Singles: 7-inch
TOMMY BOY ... 3-5 82

PRESSURE POINT
Singles: 7-inch
ELROD ... 3-4 81
Member: Lionel Crawford.

PRESTATIONS
Singles: 7-inch
TIMKEN ("Magic Twangin' ") ... 8-12
(Selection number not known.)

PRESTON
(Preston Carnes)
Singles: 7-inch
SOUND PATTERN (110 "This World Is Closing in on Me") ... 10-20 68
(Colored vinyl.)
Also see CARPENTER, Chris
Also see LENNY & THUNDERTONES

PRESTON, Billy *LP '65*
Singles: 12-inch
MEGATONE ... 4-6 84
MONTAGE ... 4-6 84
Singles: 7-inch
APPLE/AMERICOM (1808/433 "That's the Way God Planned It") ... 300-400 69
(Four-inch flexi, "pocket disc.")
APPLE ... 6-12 69-72
APPLE (1808/6555 "That's the Way God Planned It") ... 50-60 69
CAPITOL ... 4-8 66-69
CONTRACT ... 8-12 61
DERBY ... 8-12 63
MOTOWN ... 3-5 79-82
VEE JAY ... 5-10 65
Picture Sleeves
A&M ... 4-8 72-75
APPLE (1808 "That's the Way God Planned It") ... 5-10 69
APPLE (1817 "All That I've Got") ... 10-15 70
LPs: 10/12-inch
A&M ... 8-12 71-82
APPLE (3359 "That's the Way God Planned It") ... 40-50 69
(With portrait cover photo.)
APPLE (3359 "That's the Way God Planned It") ... 15-25 69
(Full figure cover photo.)
APPLE (3370 "Encouraging Words") ... 10-20 70
BUDDAH ... 10-15 69
CAPITOL (T-2532 "Wildest Organ") ... 10-15 66
CAPITOL (ST-2532 "Wildest Organ") ... 10-20 66
CAPITOL (SM-2532 "Wildest Organ") ... 5-8 75
DERBY (701 "16-Year-Old Soul") ... 50-75 63
EXODUS ... 15-20 65
GNP ... 10-15 73
MOTOWN ... 5-10 79-82
MYRRH ... 5-10 78
PEACOCK ... 8-12 73
PICKWICK ... 5-8 70s
SPRINGBOARD ... 5-10 78
TRIP ... 8-12 73
VEE JAY ... 15-25 65-66
Also see BEATLES
Also see MOTHERS of INVENTION
Also see VANDROSS, Luther

PRESTON, Billy, & Syreeta *R&B '80*
Singles: 7-inch
MOTOWN ... 3-5 79-81
TAMLA ... 3-5 80
LPs: 10/12-inch
MOTOWN ... 5-10 79-81
Also see PRESTON, Billy
Also see SYREETA

PRESTON, Bob
Singles: 7-inch
IMPACT ... 4-6

PRESTON, Don, & South
LPs: 10/12-inch
A&M ... 10-15 69
SHELTER ... 8-12 74
Also see RUSSELL, Leon

PRESTON, Earl
(Earl Preston's Realms)
LPs: 10/12-inch
CAPITOL ... 20-30 66

PRESTON, Eddie *C&W '89*
Singles: 7-inch
PLATINUM ... 3-4 89

PRESTON, Gene
Singles: 7-inch
DOT ... 4-8 64

PRESTON, Jimmy *R&B '49*
Singles: 78 rpm
DERBY ... 10-20 50
GOTHAM ... 15-25 49-50
Also see WILLIAMS, Cootie / Jimmy Preston

PRESTON, Johnny *P&R '59*
Singles: 7-inch
ABC ... 3-6 68-73
HALL/HALL WAY ... 4-8 64-66
IMPERIAL ... 4-8 63
MERCURY (10027 "Cradle of Love") ... 15-25 60
(Stereo [reprocessed].)
MERCURY (10036 "Feel So Fine") ... 20-30 60
(Stereo.)
MERCURY (71000 series) ... 8-12 59-62
(Monaural.)
TCF ... 4-8 65
Picture Sleeves
MERCURY ... 10-15 60-62
EPs: 7-inch
MERCURY (3397 "Johnny Preston") ... 30-50 60
LPs: 10/12-inch
MERCURY (20592 "Running Bear") ... 50-70 60
(Monaural.)
MERCURY (20609 "Come Rock with Me") ... 50-70 60
(Monaural.)
MERCURY (60250 "Running Bear") ... 60-90 60
(Stereo. Black label)
MERCURY (60250 "Running Bear") ... 8-12 81
(Chicago "Skyline" label)
MERCURY (60609 "Come Rock with Me") ... 60-90 60
(Stereo.)
WING (12246 "Running Bear") ... 20-30 63
(Monaural.)
WING (16246 "Running Bear") ... 25-35 63
(Stereo.)
Also see MIZZELL, Bobby

PRESTON, Kathy
Singles: 7-inch
EXCHANGE ... 4-8 66

PRESTON, Mike *P&R '58*
Singles: 7-inch
LONDON ... 5-8 58-63

PRESTON, Robert
Singles: 7-inch
CAPITOL CUSTOM ... 8-10 62

PRESTON, Terry
(Ferlin Husky)
Singles: 78 rpm
CAPITOL ... 8-15 52-53
Singles: 7-inch
CAPITOL ... 10-20 52-53
Also see HUSKY, Ferlin

PRESTON, Vic
Singles: 7-inch
ELITE (1 "Hot Rod") ... 15-25

PRESTON & PACEMAKERS
Singles: 7-inch
NEW SONG (128 "Stop & Go") ... 10-20 60

PRESTOS
Singles: 78 rpm
MERCURY ... 25-50 55
MERCURY (70747 "Till We Meet Again") ... 60-80 55
Also see EMPIRES
Also see WHIRLERS

PRESTWOOD, Hugh
Singles: 7-inch
MACH ... 4-6 72

PRE-TEENS
(With the Shytan Five)
Singles: 78 rpm
J&S ... 200-300 56
Singles: 7-inch
J&S (1756 "What Makes Me Love You Like I Do") ... 500-1000 56

PRETENDERS
("Featuring Jimmy Jones with Rhythm Accompaniment")
Singles: 78 rpm
WHIRLIN' DISC ... 50-75 56
RAMA ... 20-40 56
Singles: 7-inch
ABC-PAR (10094 "Blue & Lonely") ... 100-200 60
APT (25026 "Blue & Lonely") ... 250-500 59
CENTRAL (2605 "Blue & Lonely") ... 1000-2000 58
WHIRLIN' DISC (106 "Close Your Eyes") ... 200-300 56
RAMA (198 "Possessive Love") 100-150 56
Members: Jimmy Jones; Bobby Moore; Bill Walker; Mel Walton; Kerry Saxton; Irving Lee Gail.
Also see JONES, Jimmy, & Pretenders
Also see SAVOYS
Also see VOCALTONES

PRETENDERS
Singles: 7-inch
BETHLEHEM (3050 "The Day You Are Mine") ... 100-150 62

PRETENDERS
Singles: 7-inch
POWER-MARTIN (1001 "I'm So Happy") ... 75-125 61

PRETENDERS
Singles: 7-inch
AGAR (7169 "Surfer's Dream") ... 25-35 63

PRETENDERS
Singles: 7-inch
CHATTAHOOCHEE ... 5-10 65

PRETENDERS *P&R/LP '80*
Singles: 12-inch
SIRE ... 4-6 84
Singles: 7-inch
SIRE ... 3-5 79-90
Picture Sleeves
SIRE ... 3-5 80-87
LPs: 10/12-inch
NAUTILUS (38 "Pretenders") ... 25-35 80s
SIRE ... 5-10 80-90
Members: Chrissie Hynde; Robbie MacIntosh; Pete Farndon; Martin Chambers; Malcomb Foster.
Also see UB40

PRETENDERS
Singles: 7-inch
AL-STAN (1005 "Ding Dong Bells") ... 3-5 95
(Colored vinyl.)
Picture Sleeves
AL-STAN (1005 "Ding Dong Bells") ... 3-5 95
Members: Skip Pietrobone; Kenny Shott; Dan Wisniewski; Sam Talarico; Mick Diana.
Also see PETRICOIN, Barry, & Pretenders

PRETENDERS / Maurice Simon
Singles: 7-inch
CARNIVAL ... 4-8

PRETTY BOY
(Don Covay; with Johnny Fuller's Band)
Singles: 78 rpm
ATLANTIC (1147 "Bip Bop Bip") ... 50-75 57
BIG ... 50-75 57
RHYTHM (1768 "I'm Bad") ... 30-50 54
Singles: 7-inch
ATLANTIC (1147 "Bip Bop Bip") ... 50-75 57
BIG (617 "Switchin' in the Kitchen") ... 50-75 57
Session: King Curtis.
Also see COVAY, Don
Also see FULLER, Johnny
Also see KING CURTIS

PRETTY BOY FLOYD *LP '90*
LPs: 10/12-inch
MCA ... 5-8 90

PRETTY MAIDS *LP '87*
LPs: 10/12-inch
EPIC ... 5-10 87

PRETTY PEOPLE
LPs: 10/12-inch
CRESTVIEW ... 10-15 60s

PRETTY POISON *R&B/D&D '84*
Singles: 12-inch
MONTAGE ... 4-6 84
SVENGALI ... 4-6 84
Singles: 7-inch
MONTAGE ... 3-4 84
SVENGALI ... 3-4 84
VIRGIN ... 3-4 87-88
Picture Sleeves
VIRGIN ... 3-4 87-88
LPs: 10/12-inch
VIRGIN ... 5-10 88

PRETTY PURDIE: see PURDIE, Pretty

PRETTY THINGS *LP '75*
Singles: 7-inch
FONTANA ... 5-10 64-66
LAURIE ... 4-8 68
SWAN SONG ... 3-5 75-76
LPs: 10/12-inch
FONTANA (27544 "Pretty Things") ... 35-55 66
(Monaural.)
FONTANA (67544 "Pretty Things") ... 35-55 66
(Stereo.)
MOTOWN ... 10-15 76
RARE EARTH (506 "S.F. Sorrow") ... 15-25 69
(With standard square cover.)
RARE EARTH (506 "S.F. Sorrow") ... 20-40 69
(With rounded-top cover. Promotional issue.)
RARE EARTH (515 "Parachute") ... 15-20 70
RARE EARTH (549 "Rare Earth") ... 8-12 76
(Reissue of material from 506 & 515.)
SIRE ... 8-10 76
SWAN SONG ... 8-10 75-76
W.B. ... 8-10 73-80
Also see GREEN, Jack

PRETTY TONY *R&B '84*
(Tony Butler)
Singles: 7-inch
MUSIC ... 3-4 84

PREVIEWS
Singles: 7-inch
VEEP ... 4-8 65

PREVIN, Andre *P&R/LP '59*
(With the David Rose Orchestra)
Singles: 78 rpm
MODERN ... 3-5 51
Singles: 7-inch
COLUMBIA ... 3-6 60-64
DECCA ... 3-6 61
MGM ... 4-8 59
MODERN ... 10-20 51
RCA (214 "Andre Previn") ... 10-20 49
(Boxed, three-disc set.)
RCA (9000 series) ... 3-5 67
EPs: 7-inch
MGM ... 5-10 59
LPs: 10/12-inch
ALLEGIANCE ... 5-8 84
ANGEL ... 5-8 80-81
CAMDEN ... 5-10 64
COLUMBIA ... 10-20 60-65
CONTEMPORARY ... 15-30 57-60
CORONET ... 5-10 60s
DECCA (4000 series) ... 8-15 61-63
(Decca LP numbers in this series preceded by a "7" or a "DL-7" are stereo issues.)
DECCA (8000 series) ... 20-40 55-56
EVEREST ... 5-10 70
GUEST STAR ... 5-15 60s
HARMONY ... 5-10 67
MFSL ... 20-40 82
MGM ... 10-15 59-64
METRO JAZZ ... 10-20 59
MONARCH (203 "All Star Jazz") ... 60-80 54
(10-inch LP.)
MONARCH (204 "Andre Previn Plays Duke") ... 60-80 54
(10-inch LP.)
ODYSSEY ... 8-12 68
RCA (1000 series) ... 5-10 75
(With an "ARL1" prefix.)
RCA (1000 series) ... 20-45 54
(With an "LPM" prefix.)
RCA (1356 "Three Little Words") ... 40-60 56
RCA (2900 series) ... 6-12 67
RCA (3002 ("Andre Previn Plays Harry Warren") ... 75-100 51
(10-inch LP.)
RCA (3400 thru 3800 series) ... 10-20 65-67
U.A. (5200 series) ... 5-10 71
VERVE ... 15-25 63
For a complete listing of soundtracks by this artist, consult *The Official Price Guide to Movie/TV Soundtracks and Original Cast Albums*.
Also see ANDREWS, Julie, & Andre Previn / Vic Damone / Jack Jones / Marian Anderson
Also see ASTAIRE, Fred, & Red Skelton / Helen Kane
Also see CARROLL, Diahann, & Andre Previn
Also see DAY, Doris, & Andre Previn
Also see LAINE, Frankie, & Andre Previn
Also see ROSE, David
Also see SHORE, Dinah, & Andre Previn

PREYER, Ron *R&B '78*
Singles: 7-inch
SHOCK ... 3-5 78

PREZ, Kenneth
Singles: 7-inch
BISCAYNE ... 4-8 65-66

PRIBATA IDAHO
Singles: 7-inch
MUNSTER (7028 "Day After Day") ... 3-4 92
Picture Sleeves
MUNSTER (7028 "Day After Day") ... 3-4 92
(Cardboard, EP-like sleeve.)

PRICE, Alan *P&R '66*
(Alan Price Set)
Singles: 7-inch
COTILLION ... 4-8 69
EPIC ... 3-4 84
JET ... 3-5 77-79
PARROT ... 5-10 66-68
W.B. ... 3-5 72
LPs: 10/12-inch
ACCORD ... 5-10 82
JET ... 8-12 77-80
PARROT ... 15-25 68
TOWNHOUSE ... 5-10 81
W.B. ... 8-12 73
Also see ANIMALS
Also see FAME & PRICE

PRICE, Banny
Singles: 7-inch
JEWEL ... 4-8 64-65

PRICE, Big Walter
LPs: 10/12-inch
LUNAR (20017 "Boogie") ... 8-10 80
(10-inch LP.)
Also see BIG WALTER

PRICE, Bobby, & Dynamics
Singles: 7-inch
CUCA (1095 "Oh, I Like It Like That") ... 15-25 62
Also see DYNAMICS

PRICE, Chuck *C&W '74*
Singles: 7-inch
PLAYBOY ... 3-5 74-77

PRICE, David *C&W '64*
Singles: 7-inch
EPIC ... 4-8 62
GAYLORD ... 4-8 63
RICE ... 3-8 64-77
ROULETTE ... 4-8 65-66
Also see STEGALL, Red

PRICE, Del
Singles: 7-inch
ASCOT ... 4-8 63

PRICE, Denise *C&W '82*
Singles: 7-inch
DIMENSION ... 3-4 82

PRICE, Eli, & Manhattans
Singles: 7-inch
DOOTO (445 "My Big Dream") ... 35-45 59
(Yellow label. Reissued on a multi-color label as by the Manhattans.)
Also see MANHATTANS

PRICE, Hank, III
Singles: 7-inch
STRUT ... 10-15

PRICE, Herb, & Darts
(With Jay Peabody & Orchestra)
Singles: 7-inch
TEMPUS (1506 "Gone Too Long") ... 50-75 58

PRICE, Jesse
Singles: 78 rpm
CAPITOL ... 8-12 48

PRICE, Jim
LPs: 10/12-inch
A&M ... 8-12 71

PRICE, John
Singles: 7-inch
BIG TOP ... 4-8 62

PRICE, Kenny *C&W '66*
Singles: 7-inch
BOONE ... 4-8 66-69
DIMENSION ... 3-4 80
MRC ... 3-5 77-79
RCA ... 3-6 69-76
LPs: 10/12-inch
BOONE ... 10-20 67
DIMENSION ... 5-10 80
PHONORAMA ... 5-8 82
RCA ... 10-15 69-71
Also see SOME of CHET'S FRIENDS

PRICE, Leo
Singles: 7-inch
HULL ... 5-10 60
SPRING ... 4-8 67
UP & DOWN (712 "Quick Down") ... 20-30 65

PRICE, Lloyd *R&B '52*
(Lloyd Price Orchestra; with the Dukes)
Singles: 78 rpm
ABC-PAR ... 20-40 57
KRC (587 "Just Because") ... 30-50 57
SPECIALTY ... 10-15 55-56
Singles: 7-inch
ABC ... 3-6 67-73
ABC-PAR (Monaural) ... 10-20 57-60
ABC-PAR (S-9972 "Stagger Lee") ... 20-40 59
(Stereo.)
ABC-PAR (S-9997 "Where Were You") ... 20-30 59
(Stereo.)
COLLECTABLES ... 3-4 80s
DOUBLE-L ... 5-10 63-66
GSF ... 3-5 72-73
JAD ... 4-8 68
KRC (Except 587) ... 10-20 57-59
KRC (587 "Just Because") ... 40-50 57
LPG ... 3-5 76
LUDIX ... 5-10 63
MCA ... 3-4 70s
MONUMENT ... 4-8 64-65
PARAMOUNT ... 3-5 72
REPRISE ... 4-8 66
ROULETTE ... 3-5 70s
SCEPTER ... 3-5 71
SPECIALTY (SPBX series) ... 15-20 86
(Boxed sets of six colored vinyl 45s.)

SPECIALTY (428 "Lawdy, Miss Clawdy")....30-40 52
(Black vinyl.)
SPECIALTY (428 "Lawdy, Miss Clawdy")....50-100 52
(Colored vinyl.)
SPECIALTY (440 "Ooh Ooh Ooh")....30-40 52
SPECIALTY (452 "Ain't It a Shame")....30-40 53
(Black vinyl.)
SPECIALTY (452 "Ain't It a Shame")....50-75 53
(Colored vinyl.)
SPECIALTY (457 "What's the Matter Now")....30-40 53
(Black vinyl.)
SPECIALTY (457 "What's the Matter Now")....50-75 53
(Colored vinyl.)
SPECIALTY (463 "Where You At")....30-40 53
(Black vinyl.)
SPECIALTY (463 "Where You At")....50-75 53
(Colored vinyl.)
SPECIALTY (471 "I Wish Your Picture Was You")....30-40 54
SPECIALTY (483 "Let Me Come Home, Baby")....30-40 54
(Black vinyl.)
SPECIALTY (483 "Let Me Come Home, Baby")....50-75 54
(Colored vinyl.)
SPECIALTY (494 "Walkin' the Track")....30-40 54
SPECIALTY (535 "Oo Ee Baby")....15-25 55
SPECIALTY (540 "Trying to Find Someone to Love")....15-25 55
SPECIALTY (571 "Woe Ho Ho")....15-25 56
SPECIALTY (578 "Country Boy Rock")....15-25 56
SPECIALTY (582 "Forgive Me Clawdy")....15-25 56
SPECIALTY (602 "Baby Please Come Home")....15-25 57
SPECIALTY (661 "Lawdy, Miss Clawdy")....10-15 59
TURNTABLE.... 4-6 69

Picture Sleeves

DOUBLE-L (729 "Billie Baby")....10-15 64

EPs: 7-inch

ABC-PAR (14 "Rockin' on 5th Ave.")....25-50 59
(Promotional issue, made for Luden's Inc., maker of 5th Ave. candy bars.)
ABC-PAR (277 "The Exciting Lloyd Price")....25-50 59
ABC-PAR (315 "Mr. Personality Sings the Blues")....25-50 60
ABC-PAR (324 "Four Songs from Mr. Personality's Big 15 Hits")....25-50 60

LPs: 10/12-inch

ABC.... 8-10 72-76
ABC-PAR (ABC-277 "The Exciting Lloyd Price")....25-45 59
(Monaural.)
ABC-PAR (ABCS-277 "The Exciting Lloyd Price")....30-50 59
(Stereo.)
ABC-PAR (ABC-297 "Mr. Personality")....25-45 59
(Monaural.)
ABC-PAR (ABCS-297 "Mr. Personality")....30-50 59
(Stereo.)
ABC-PAR (ABC-315 "Mr. Personality Sings the Blues")....25-45 60
(Monaural.)
ABC-PAR (ABCS-315 "Mr. Personality Sings the Blues")....30-50 60
(Stereo.)
ABC-PAR (ABC-324 "Mr. Personality's Big 15")....25-45 60
(Monaural.)
ABC-PAR (ABCS-324 "Mr. Personality's Big 15")....30-50 60
ABC-PAR (ABC-346 "The Fantastic Lloyd Price")....25-45 60
(Monaural.)
ABC-PAR (ABCS-346 "The Fantastic Lloyd Price")....30-50 60
(Stereo.)
ABC-PAR (ABC-366 "Lloyd Price Sings the Million Sellers")....25-45 61
(Monaural.)
ABC-PAR (ABCS-366 "Lloyd Price Sings the Million Sellers")....25-45 61
(Stereo.)
ABC-PAR (ABC-382 "Cookin'")....25-45 61
(Monaural.)
ABC-PAR (ABCS-382 "Cookin'")....30-50 61
(Stereo.)
ABC-PAR (ABCX-763 "16 Greatest Hits")....10-15 72
DOUBLE-L....20-30 63
GRAND PRIX....10-15 60s
GUEST STAR....10-15 64
JAD....10-15 69
MCA.... 5-10 82
MONUMENT....10-20 65
OLDE WORLD.... 8-10 78
PICKWICK....10-15 67
SPECIALTY (2105 "Lloyd Price")....40-50 59
TSG (802 "Golden Dozen").... 8-12 76
TRIP.... 8-10 76
TURNTABLE....10-15 69
UPFRONT.... 8-12 70s
ANKA, Paul / Lloyd Price
Also see COOKE, Sam / Lloyd Price / Larry Williams / Little Richard
Also see DOMINO, Fats
Also see DUKES
Also see KING BEES

PRICE, Mel

(With His Santa Fe Rangers)

Singles: 7-inch

DIXIE (887 "Jailed")....25-50
DIXIE (2016 "Little Dog Blues")....75-125 59

PRICE, Priscilla — R&B '73

Singles: 7-inch

BASF.... 3-5 73
GENEVA (504 "Funny").... 4-6 70s

PRICE, Ray — C&W '52

(With the Cherokee Cowboys)

Singles: 78 rpm

BULLET (701 "Jealous Lies")....75-125 52
COLUMBIA....5-15 52-57

Singles: 7-inch

ABC.... 3-5 75
ABC/DOT.... 3-5 75-77
COLUMBIA (10000 series).... 3-4 74-77
COLUMBIA (20000 & 21000 series)....10-20 52-56
COLUMBIA (40000 thru 43000 series)....5-15 57-66
COLUMBIA (44042 "Danny Boy").... 4-8 67
(Black vinyl.)
COLUMBIA (44042 "Danny Boy")....8-10 67
(Green vinyl. Promotional issue only.)
COLUMBIA (44100 thru 45000 series)....3-6 67-73
COLUMBIA HALL of FAME.... 3-4
GOLDIES 45.... 3-4
DIMENSION.... 3-4 81-82
MONUMENT.... 3-5 78-79
MYRRH.... 3-4 74-75
STEP ONE.... 3-4 85-86
W.B..... 3-4 82-83
WORD.... 3-4 78

Picture Sleeves

COLUMBIA (44042 "Danny Boy")....8-12 67
(Promotional issue only.)

EPs: 7-inch

COLUMBIA (1700 thru 2800 series)....15-25 53-57
COLUMBIA (8556 "Ray Price")....10-20 50s
COLUMBIA (10000 thru 14000 series)....10-20 57-60
(White label. Promotional issue only.)

LPs: 10/12-inch

ABC/DOT....6-12 75-77
ARTCO....20-40
(Titel and selection number not known.)
CBS....5-10
COLUMBIA (28 "The World of Ray Price")....8-12 70
COLUMBIA (157 "The Same Old Me")....10-15 66
(Record club exclusive.)
COLUMBIA (1015 "Heart Songs")....30-40 57
COLUMBIA (1148 "Talk to Your Heart")....25-35 58
COLUMBIA (1400 thru 2600 series)....10-25 60-67
(Monaural)
COLUMBIA (8200 thru 9400 series, except 9422)....15-30 60-67
(Stereo)
COLUMBIA (9422 "Heart Songs")....25-35 67
(Stereo.)
COLUMBIA (9700 thru 9900 series)....8-12 68-70
COLUMBIA (10000 series)....5-10 73-79
COLUMBIA (30000 thru 37000 series)....5-10 70-81
COLUMBIA SPECIAL PRODUCTS 5-10
COLUMBIA STAR SERIES....5-15
DIMENSION.... 5-8 81
51 WEST.... 5-8 84
HARMONY....8-15 66-71
MONUMENT....5-10 79
MYRRH.... 5-8 74
PAIR....8-10 82
RADIANT.... 5-8 81
SEASHELL....5-10
STEP ONE....5-10 86
SUNRISE MEDIA.... 5-8 81
VIVA....5-10
W.B..... 5-8 83
WORD.... 5-8 77
Session: Johnny Bush; Willie Nelson; Johnny Gimble.
Also see ANDERSON, Lynn / Ray Price
Also see BUSH, Johnny
Also see MILLER, Roger, & Willie Nelson
Also see NASHVILLE SUPERPICKERS
Also see NELSON, Willie, & Ray Price
Also see ROBBINS, Marty / Johnny Cash / Ray Price

PRICE, Ray / Lefty Frizzell / Carl Smith

LPs: 10/12-inch

COLUMBIA (1257 "Greatest Western Hits")....20-30 59
(Monaural.)
COLUMBIA (8776 "Greatest Western Hits")....15-25 63
(Stereo.)
Also see FRIZZELL, Lefty
Also see SMITH, Carl

PRICE, Ray / Johnny Horton / Carl Smith / George Morgan

EPs: 7-inch

COLUMBIA (2157 "4 Big Hits")....20-25 60
Also see HORTON, Johnny
Also see SMITH, Carl

PRICE, Red

Singles: 7-inch

ROLLS....5-10 60

PRICE, Robert, & Exotics

Singles: 7-inch

MERCURY....5-10 63-64

PRICE, Ron

Singles: 7-inch

BANG....5-8 74

PRICE, Ronnie, & Velvets

Singles: 7-inch

CAROUSEL (1001 "White Bucks")....20-30

PRICE, Ruth

(With the Johnny Smith Quartet; with Shelly Manne & His Men)

Singles: 7-inch

CONTEMPORARY....4-6 61

LPs: 10/12-inch

AVA (54 "Live and Beautiful")....30-40 63
(Monaural.)
AVA (S-54 "Live and Beautiful")....35-45 63
(Stereo.)
CONTEMPORARY (3590 "At the Manne Hole")....35-45 61
(Monaural.)
CONTEMPORARY (7590 "At the Manne Hole")....40-50 61
(Stereo.)
KAPP (1006 "My Name Is Ruth Price")....50-60 58
ROOST (2217 "Sing!")....50-75 58

PRICE, Sam & His Texas Bluesicians

Singles: 78 rpm

SAVOY....5-10 56

Singles: 7-inch

SAVOY....8-12 56-59

PRICE, Shel

Singles: 7-inch

JOX....4-8 65

PRICE, Sheridan

LPs: 10/12-inch

GEMINI....10-15

PRICE, Toni — C&W '86

Singles: 7-inch

LUV....3-4 86
MASTER....3-4 86
PRAIRIE DUST....3-4 87

PRICE, Vincent

LPs: 10/12-inch

CAPITOL (342 "Witchcraft Magic")....20-30 69

PRICE, Vito

Singles: 7-inch

ARGO....10-15 58

PRIDE

LPs: 10/12-inch

WARNER (1848 "Pride")....15-25 70

PRIDE, Adrian

(Bernie Schwartz)

Singles: 7-inch

CALLIOPE....15-25
W.B.....8-12 65-66
Also see ATELLO, Don

PRIDE, Charley — C&W '66

(With the Pridesmen; with Henry Mancini; Country Charley Pride)

Singles: 7-inch

RCA (0073 thru 0942 series)....4-8 69-73
RCA (8700 & 8800 series)....5-10 66
RCA (9000 thru 9996)....4-8 66-71
RCA (10030 thru 11655)....3-6 74-79
RCA 11736 "Dallas Cowboys")....3-5 79
(Black label.)
RCA 11736 "Dallas Cowboys")....8-12 79
(Gray and blue label. Special Dallas Cowboys Edition.)
RCA (11751 thru 14296)....3-5 79-86
RCA GOLD STANDARD....3-5
16TH AVE.....3-4 87-89

Picture Sleeves

RCA....4-6 71-74

EPs: 7-inch

RCA....5-10 60s
(Juke box issues.)

LPs: 10/12-inch

CAMDEN....5-10 72
RCA (Except LPM/LSP 3700 thru 4800 series)....5-10 74-86
RCA (3700 thru 4800 series)....10-20 66-73
(With "LPM" or "LSP" prefix.)
RCA SPECIAL PRODUCTS (0208 "Charley's Favorites")....8-12
READER'S DIGEST/RCA ("Charley Pride")....30-40
(Boxed 6-LP set with booklet. Mail order offer.)
TELEHOUSE....5-10
Also see ANDERSON, Lynn / Charley Pride
Also see DAVE & SUGAR
Also see MANCINI, Henry
Also see SOME of CHET'S FRIENDS
Also see TEXAS VOCAL COMPANY

PRIDE, Lou

Singles: 7-inch

ALBATROSS....10-20
SUEMI....10-20

PRIDE & JOY

Singles: 7-inch

ACTA....8-12 67
DUNWICH....8-12 67

PRIESMAN, Magel

Singles: 7-inch

SUN (294 "I Feel So Blue")....15-20 58

PRIEST, Maxi — P&R/LP '88

Singles: 7-inch

VIRGIN....3-4 88

Picture Sleeves

VIRGIN....3-4 88

LPs: 10/12-inch

CHARISMA....5-8 90
VIRGIN....5-8 88

PRIMA, Louis — P&R '35

Singles: 78 rpm

BRUNSWICK....5-10 35
COLUMBIA....4-6 52-53
DECCA....4-8 54
HIT....5-10 44-45
MAJESTIC....4-8 45
MERCURY....4-8 50
RCA....4-8 47
ROBIN HOOD....4-8 50
SAVOY....4-8 53
VOCALION....5-10 37

Singles: 7-inch

ABC....3-6 68-74
BUENA VISTA....3-6 66-74
CAPITOL....4-8 62
COLUMBIA....5-10 52-53
DECCA....5-10 54
DOT....4-8 59-62
HBR....4-6 66
KAMA SUTRA....4-6 66
MERCURY....5-10 50
PRIMA....4-8 63-64
ROBIN HOOD....5-10 50
SAVOY....5-10 53
U.A.....3-6 67

EPs: 7-inch

CAPITOL....5-15 56
JUBILEE....5-15 55
VARSITY....5-15 54

LPs: 10/12-inch

BUENA VISTA....8-18 65-74
CAPITOL....10-20 56-62
DE-LITE....5-10 68
DOT....10-15 60
HBR....5-12 66
HAMILTON....5-10 65
MERCURY (25142 "For the People")....30-40 53
(10-inch LP.)
PRIMA....5-8 72-76
RONDO/RONDOLETTE....10-20 59
U.A.....5-10 67

PRIMA, Louis, & Keely Smith — P&R/R&B/LP '58

(With Sam Butera & the Witnesses)

Singles: 78 rpm

ROBIN HOOD....5-10 50

Singles: 7-inch

CAPITOL....4-8 58-59
DOT....4-8 59-61

Picture Sleeves

CAPITOL (4063 "That Old Black Magic")....5-10 58
(Sleeve has a die-cut center hole)
DOT....5-10 59

EPs: 7-inch

CAPITOL....8-12 58
DOT (103 "The Frantic 40's")....10-20 60
(Promotional issue, made for the Desert Inn as a giveaway.)
DOT (1093 "Louis & Keely")....5-10 60

LPs: 10/12-inch

CAPITOL (With "SM" prefix.)....5-8 75
CAPITOL (With "T" or "ST" prefix.)....20-35 58-61
COLUMBIA (1206 "Breaking It Up")....20-30 58
CORONET....10-15 60s
DESIGN....10-15 60s
DOT....15-25 59-60
Also see SMITH, Keely

PRIMA, Louis, & Keely Smith / Louis Prima & Sam Butera

Singles: 7-inch

CAPITOL (719 "Album Highlights")....10-15 57
(Promotional issue only.)
Also see BUTERA, Sam
Also see PRIMA, Louis
Also see PRIMA, Louis, & Keely Smith

PRIMATES

Singles: 7-inch

MARKO (923 "Knock on My Door")....15-25 65
MARKO (924 "Don't Press Your Luck")....20-30 66

PRIMATES

Singles: 7-inch

LEAF (667 "Girl Don't Tell Me")....15-25 66
Members: Mike Eubank; Tom Schilder; Clark Wessel; Gary Hildebrand; John Doll.

PRIMATES

LPs: 10/12-inch

VOXX....5-8

PRIMATIVES — LP '88

LPs: 10/12-inch

RCA....5-8 88-89

PRIME CUT

Singles: 7-inch

SHADY BROOK....3-5 74

PRIME MATES

Singles: 7-inch

SANSU (465 "Hot Tamales")....8-12 60s

PRIME MINISTERS

Singles: 7-inch

RCA....5-8 68

Member: Ronnie Barron.
Also see BARRON, Ronnie

PRIME MOVER

Singles: 7-inch

SOCKO (2002 "When You Made Love to Me")....10-15 68

PRIME TIME — R&B '84

Singles: 7-inch

TOTAL EXP.....3-4 84

PRIMETTES

(Supremes)

Singles: 7-inch

LUPINE (120 "Tears of Sorrow")....200-300 64
(Lu-pine [hyphenated] 120 is also a Joe Stubbs single.)
Also see STUBBS, Joe
Also see SUPREMES

PRIMEVAL UNKNOWN

Singles: 7-inch

SKYCLAD....5-8 89
Members: John Block; Orin Portnoy; Mike Jones; Jim Buscorino.

PRIMITIVE MAN

Singles: 7-inch

PARROT....3-5 71

PRIMITIVES

Singles: 7-inch

PICKWICK CITY (1001 "The Ostrich")....100-125 64
Members: Lou Reed; John Cale; Tony Conrad; Walter DeMaria.
Also see CALE, John
Also see REED, Lou

PRIMO, Tony

Singles: 7-inch

NOMAR....5-10 60

PRIMO PEOPLE

LPs: 10/12-inch

CAPITOL....8-10 71

PRIMROSE CIRCUS

Singles: 7-inch

MIRA....5-10 67

PRINCE — P&R/R&B/LP '78

(With the Revolution; "Artist Formerly Known As Prince")

Singles: 12-inch

BELLMARK (71003 "Beautiful Experience")....15-20
(Includes 10" x 10" booklet.)
HOT PINK (3223 "Just Another Sucker")....20-25 86
(Promotional issue only.)
PAISLEY PARK (1082 "Let's Pretend We're Married")....30-50 84
(Promotional issue only. With title sleeve.)
PAISLEY PARK (2300 "America") 15-20 85
(Promotional issue only. With title sleeve.)
PAISLEY PARK (2313 "Raspberry Beret")....15-20 85
(Promotional issue only. With title sleeve.)
PAISLEY PARK (2331 "Pop Life") 15-20 85
(Promotional issue only. With title sleeve.)
PAISLEY PARK (2448 "Kiss" [Edit])....8-12 86
(Promotional issue only.)
PAISLEY PARK (2458 "Kiss" [Extended])....8-12 86
(Promotional issue only.)
PAISLEY PARK (2476 "Mountains")....8-10 86
(Promotional issue only.)
PAISLEY PARK (2687 "Sign O' the Times")....8-10 87
(Promotional issue only.)
PAISLEY PARK (2758 "If I Was Your Girlfriend")....8-10 87
(Promotional issue only.)
PAISLEY PARK (2770 "I Could Never Take the Place of Your Man")....8-10 87
(Promotional issue only.)
PAISLEY PARK (2771 "U Got the Look")....8-10 87
(Promotional issue only.)
PAISLEY PARK (3704 "Scandalous Sex Suite")....8-10 89
PAISLEY PARK (4345 "Thieves in the Temple")....10-15 90
(Promotional issue only. With picture cover.)
PAISLEY PARK (4515 "New Power Generation")....8-10 90
(Promotional issue only.)
PAISLEY PARK (4578 "New Power Generation" [Remix])....8-10 90
(Promotional issue only.)
PAISLEY PARK (4977 "Gett Off") 10-15 91
(Promotional issue only.)
PAISLEY PARK (4977 "Gett Off")....250-300 91
(Special birthday issue, with artwork by Prince. Promotional issue only.)
PAISLEY PARK (5141 "Insatiable")....15-25 91
(Promotional issue only. With picture cover.)
PAISLEY PARK (5148 "Diamonds & Pearls")....8-12 91
(Promotional issue only.)
PAISLEY PARK (5298 "Money Don't Matter")....15-25 91
(Promotional issue only. With picture cover.)
PAISLEY PARK (5570 "Sexy M-F")....10-15 91
PAISLEY PARK (5770 "My Name Is Prince")....15-25 92
(Promotional issue only. With picture cover.)

PAISLEY PARK (20170 "Let's Pretend We're Married") ... 5-10 84
(With picture cover.)
PAISLEY PARK (20355 "Raspberry Beret") ... 5-8 85
(With picture cover.)
PAISLEY PARK (20357 "Pop Life") ... 5-8 85
(With picture cover.)
PAISLEY PARK (20389 "America") ... 5-8 85
(With picture cover.)
PAISLEY PARK (20516 "Anotherloverholenyohead") ... 5-8 85
(With picture cover.)
PAISLEY PARK (20728 "I Could Never Take the Place of Your Man") ... 8-10 87
(With picture cover.)
PAISLEY PARK (20930 "Alphabet St.") ... 5-8 88
(With picture cover.)
PAISLEY PARK (21074 "I Wish U Heaven") ... 5-8 88
(With picture cover.)
PAISLEY PARK (21422 "Scandalous Sex Suite") ... 5-8 89
(With picture cover.)
PAISLEY PARK (21598 "Thieves in the Temple") ... 5-8 90
(With picture cover.)
PAISLEY PARK (21783 "New Power Generation") ... 4-6 90
(With picture cover.)
PAISLEY PARK (40138 "Gett Off") ... 4-6 91
(With picture cover.)
PAISLEY PARK (40197 "Cream") ... 4-6 88
(With picture cover.)
PAISLEY PARK (41833 "Space") ... 4-6 94
(With picture cover.)
W.B. (741 "Just As Long As We're Together") ... 75-100 78
(Promotional issue only.)
W.B. (832 "I Wanna Be Your Lover") ... 50-75 79
(Promotional issue only.)
W.B. (848 "Why You Wanna Treat Me So Bad") ... 75-100 80
(Promotional issue only.)
W.B. (870 "Still Waiting") ... 75-100 79
(Promotional issue only.)
W.B. (904 "Uptown") ... 40-60 80
(Promotional issue only.)
W.B. (915 "Head") ... 50-75 80
(Promotional issue only. Single-sided.)
W.B. (916 "When You Were Mine") ... 50-75 80
(Promotional issue only.)
W.B. (937 "Head") ... 50-75 80
(Promotional issue only. Double-sided.)
W.B. (980 "Controversy") ... 30-50 81
(Promotional issue only. With title sleeve.)
W.B. (1004 "Let's Work") ... 50-75 81
(Promotional issue only.)
W.B. (1035 "Do Me Baby") ... 50-75 81
(Promotional issue only.)
W.B. (1070 "1999") ... 30-50 82
(Promotional issue only. With title sleeve.)
W.B. (1082 "Let's Pretend We're Married") ... 30-50 84
(Promotional issue only. With title sleeve.)
W.B. (2001 "Little Red Corvette") ... 30-50 83
(Promotional issue only. With title sleeve.)
W.B. (2080 "Delirious") ... 30-50 83
(Promotional issue only. With title sleeve.)
W.B. (2042 "1999") ... 30-50 82
(Promotional issue only. With title sleeve.)
W.B. (2139 "When Doves Cry") ... 15-25 84
(Black vinyl. Promotional issue only. With title sleeve.)
W.B. (2139 "When Doves Cry") ... 20-30 84
(Colored vinyl. Promotional issue only. With title sleeve.)
W.B. (2173 "Let's Go Crazy" [Edit]) ... 15-25 84
(Promotional issue only. With title sleeve.)
W.B. (2182 "Let's Go Crazy" [Dance Mix]) ... 15-25 84
(Promotional issue only. With title sleeve.)
W.B. (2192 "Purple Rain") ... 20-30 84
(Purple vinyl. Promotional issue only. With title sleeve.)
W.B. (2233 "I Would Die 4 U") ... 15-25 84
(Promotional issue only.)
W.B. (2263 "Take Me with U") ... 15-20 85
(Promotional issue only. With title sleeve.)
W.B. (3579 "Batdance") ... 5-8 89
(Promotional issue only.)
W.B. (3702 "Batdance") ... 8-12 89
(Promotional issue only.)
W.B. (3705 "Partyman") ... 8-12 89
(Promotional issue only.)
W.B. (20228 "When Doves Cry") ... 8-10 84
(With picture cover.)
W.B. (20246 "Let's Go Crazy") ... 5-8 84
(With picture cover.)
W.B. (20267 "Purple Rain") ... 5-8 85
(With picture cover.)
W.B. (20291 "I Would Die 4 U") ... 25-35 84
W.B. (21257 "Batdance") ... 4-6 89
Note: Designate promotional copies – as indicated by a gold sticker – of any 12-inch singles *not* listed separately, are roughly in the same price as commercial issues. Also, some may have picture covers or title sleeves, even though not shown here as with them.

Singles: 7-inch

PAISLEY PARK ... 4-8 85-93
W.B. (8619 "Soft and Wet") ... 15-25 78
W.B. (8713 "Just As Long As We're Together") ... 10-20 78
W.B. (20129 "Little Red Corvette") ... 20-25 83
(Picture disc.)
W.B. (22757 "Arms of Orion") ... 4-6 89
W.B. (22814 "Partyman") ... 3-6 89
W.B. (22824 "Scandalous") ... 3-6 89
W.B. (22924 "Batdance") ... 3-6 89
W.B. (29079 "Take Me with U") ... 4-6 85
W.B. (29121 "I Would Die 4 U") ... 4-6 84
W.B. (29174 "Purple Rain") ... 4-6 84
(Black vinyl.)
W.B. (29174 "Purple Rain") ... 8-10 84
(Purple vinyl.)
W.B. (29216 "Let's Go Crazy") ... 4-6 84
W.B. (29286 "When Doves Cry") ... 4-6 84
(Black vinyl.)
W.B. (29286 "When Doves Cry") ... 5-10 84
(Colored vinyl.)
W.B. (29503 "Delirious") ... 4-6 83
W.B. (29548 "Let's Pretend We're Married") ... 4-6 84
W.B. (29746 "Little Red Corvette") ... 5-10 83
(Black vinyl.)
W.B. (29746 "Little Red Corvette") 10-15 83
(Picture disc.)
W.B. (29896 "1999") ... 10-15 82
W.B. (49050 "I Wanna Be Your Lover") ... 10-20 79
W.B. (49178 "Why You Wanna Treat Me So Bad") ... 10-15 80
W.B. (49226 "Still Waiting") ... 20-30 80
W.B. (49559 "Uptown") ... 10-15 80
W.B. (49638 "Dirty Mind") ... 10-15 81
W.B. (49808 "Controversy") ... 10-15 81
W.B. (50002 "Let's Work") ... 10-15 81
W.B. BACK to BACK HITS ... 3-4

Promotional Singles

PAISLEY PARK (Except 2939 & 29052) ... 4-8 85-93
PAISLEY PARK (2939 "Hot Thing") ... 15-25 87
PAISLEY PARK (29052 "Paisley Park") ... 15-25 85
W.B. (8619 "Soft and Wet") ... 15-25 78
W.B. (8713 "Just As Long As We're Together") ... 10-20 78
W.B. (22757 "Arms of Orion") ... 4-6 89
W.B. (22814 "Partyman") ... 3-6 89
W.B. (22824 "Scandalous") ... 3-6 89
W.B. (22924 "Batdance") ... 3-6 89
W.B. (29079 "Take Me with U") ... 4-6 85
W.B. (29121 "I Would Die 4 U") ... 4-6 84
W.B. (29174 "Purple Rain") ... 4-6 84
(Black vinyl.)
W.B. (29174 "Purple Rain") ... 8-12 84
(Purple vinyl.)
W.B. (29216 "Let's Go Crazy") ... 4-6 84
W.B. (29286 "When Doves Cry") ... 4-8 84
(Black vinyl.)
W.B. (29286 "When Doves Cry") ... 8-10 84
(Colored vinyl.)
W.B. (29503 "Delirious") ... 4-6 83
W.B. (29548 "Let's Pretend We're Married") ... 4-8 84
W.B. (29746 "Little Red Corvette") ... 5-10 83
W.B. (29896 "1999") ... 10-15 82
W.B. (49050 "I Wanna Be Your Lover") ... 10-20 79
W.B. (49178 "Why You Wanna Treat Me So Bad") ... 10-15 80
W.B. (49226 "Still Waiting") ... 15-25 80
W.B. (49559 "Uptown") ... 10-15 80
W.B. (49638 "Dirty Mind") ... 10-15 81
W.B. (49808 "Controversy") ... 10-15 81

Picture Sleeves

PAISLEY PARK ... 4-8 85-89
W.B. (22757 "Arms of Orion") ... 4-6 89
W.B. (22814 "Partyman") ... 3-6 89
W.B. (22824 "Scandalous") ... 3-6 89
W.B. (22924 "Batdance") ... 3-6 89
W.B. (29079 "Take Me with U") ... 4-6 85
W.B. (29121 "I Would Die 4 U") ... 4-6 84
W.B. (29174 "Purple Rain") ... 4-6 84
W.B. (29216 "Let's Go Crazy") ... 4-6 84
W.B. (29286 "When Doves Cry") ... 4-6 84
W.B. (29503 "Delirious") ... 15-25 83
(Poster sleeve.)
W.B. (29548 "Let's Pretend We're Married") ... 4-8 84
W.B. (29896 "1999"/"1999") ... 15-20 82
(Promotional issue only.)
W.B. (29896 "1999"/"How Come U Don't Call Me Anymore") ... 10-15 82
W.B. (49178 "Why You Wanna Treat Me So Bad") ... 15-25 80
W.B. (49559 "Uptown") ... 10-15 80

LPs: 10/12-inch

HOT PINK (3223 "Minneapolis Genuis 94 East") ... 10-15 85
PAISLEY PARK (726 "Interruptus Collectus") ... 8-12 93
(Two discs.)
PAISLEY PARK (25286 "Around the World in a Day") ... 5-10 85
PAISLEY PARK (25395 "Parade") ... 5-10 86
PAISLEY PARK (25577 "Sign O' the Times") ... 8-12 87
(Two discs.)
PAISLEY PARK (25720 "Lovesexy") ... 5-8 88
(Tracks not banded.)
PAISLEY PARK (25720 "Lovesexy") ... 10-15 88
(Tracks are banded for easy selection.)
PAISLEY PARK (27493 "Graffiti Bridge") ... 5-10 88
W.B. (2896 "Yulesville") ... 40-60 78
(Colored vinyl. Promotional issue only.)
W.B. (3150 "For You") ... 10-15 78
W.B. (3328 "Winter Warnerland") ... 30-50 79
(Two colored vinyl discs; one red, one green. Promotional issue only.)
W.B. (3366 "Prince") ... 10-15 79
W.B. (3478 "Dirty Mind") ... 5-10 80
W.B. (3601 "Controversy") ... 10-15 81
(Includes poster.)
W.B. (3601 "Controversy") ... 5-10 81
(Without poster.)
W.B. (23720 "1999") ... 10-15 82
(Two discs.)
W.B. (25110 "Purple Rain") ... 8-10 84
(Black vinyl. Includes poster.)
W.B. (25110 "Purple Rain") ... 10-15 84
(Purple vinyl. Includes poster.)
W.B. (25110 "Purple Rain") ... 25-35 84
(Purple vinyl. Includes poster. With gold sticker. Promotional issue only.)
W.B. (25677 "Black Album") .. 3000-4000 87
(Blank cover. Reportedly contains four different mixes of *Batdance*.)
W.B. (25936 "Batman") ... 5-10 89
Note: Designate promotional copies – as indicated by a gold sticker – of any albums *not* listed separately, are in the $10 to $20 range.
Session: Lisa Coleman; Levi Seacer; Tony M.; Tommy Barbarella; Kirk Johnson; Damon Dickson; Sonny Thompson; Michael B.; Rosie Gaines; Dez Dickerson.
Also see BROWNMARK
Also see CYMONE, Andre
Also see LEWIS CONNECTION
Also see MADHOUSE
Also see REVOLVER
Also see SHEILA E.

PRINCE & SHEENA EASTON — *P&R '87*

Singles: 7-inch

PAISLEY PARK ... 3-5 87
W.B. ... 3-4 89

Picture Sleeves

W.B. ... 3-5 89
Also see EASTON, Sheena
Also see PRINCE

PRINCE, Al, & His Orchestra

Singles: 78 rpm

SWING TIME (319 "Don't Love a Married Woman") ... 20-40 52

Singles: 7-inch

RONN (39 "New Orleans") ... 5-10

PRINCE, Billy

Singles: 7-inch

VERVE ... 4-8 66

PRINCE, Bob

Singles: 7-inch

LA JOY ... 5-10 60

PRINCE, Bobby

Singles: 78 rpm

CHANCE ... 25-75 52-54
EXCELLO ... 15-25 54
MGM ... 10-15 54

Singles: 7-inch

CHANCE (1128 "Tell Me, Why? Why? Why?") ... 250-350 52
CHANCE (1158 "Better Think It Over") ... 250-350 54
EXCELLO (2039 "Too Many Keys") ... 25-50 54
MGM ... 15-25 54

PRINCE, Bobby Jack

Singles: 7-inch

CORVETTE ... 5-10 59

PRINCE, Dolph

Singles: 78 rpm

KING ... 5-10 57

Singles: 7-inch

KING ... 5-10 57
STRAND ... 5-10 59
TIVOLI ... 4-8 65

PRINCE, Dorothy

Singles: 7-inch

M-PAC (7202 "I Lost a Love") ... 10-20 63
M-PAC (7206 "Seek and You'll Find") ... 10-20 63
M-PAC (7208 "I Lost a Love") ... 8-15 63

PRINCE, Ed

Singles: 7-inch

BIG MAC ... 4-8 63

PRINCE, Jack

Singles: 78 rpm

SPADE (1934 "Rock Um Beat") ... 10-15 56

Singles: 7-inch

SPADE (1934 "Rock Um Beat") ... 20-40 56

PRINCE, James

Singles: 7-inch

Z ... 4-8 63

PRINCE, Patridge: see PRINCE PATRIDGE

PRINCE, Peppy

(With His Sugar Men)

Singles: 78 rpm

MERCURY ... 5-10 51
SELECTIVE ... 5-10 50

Singles: 7-inch

DOOTONE ... 10-20 56
HOLLYWOOD ... 15-25 54
MILLION ... 10-20 54

LPs: 10/12-inch

DOOTO ... 30-40 56

PRINCE, Rod

Singles: 7-inch

COMET ... 15-20

PRINCE, Wes, & His Rhythm Princes

Singles: 78 rpm

EXCELSIOR ... 15-25 46

PRINCE & PAUPERS

Singles: 7-inch

JRJ (2115 "Shoulder of a Giant") ... 60-80 65
Also see HELDER, Eddie

PRINCE & PAUPERS

Singles: 7-inch

CLARITY ("Don't Wake Up") ... 10-15 66

PRINCE & PRINCESS

Singles: 7-inch

BELL ... 4-8 65

PRINCE ARTHUR

Singles: 7-inch

ABC-PAR (10417 "Walkin' Uptown") ... 8-12 63

PRINCE BUSTER — *P&R/R&B '67*

(With the Sea Busters; Buster Campbell)

Singles: 7-inch

AMY ... 5-10 64
ATLANTIC ... 5-10 64
PHILIPS ... 4-8 67
RCA ... 4-8 67
STELLAR ... 5-10 64

LPs: 10/12-inch

RCA ... 10-20 67

PRINCE CHARLES

Singles: 7-inch

CLASS (301 "Good Luck Charm") 10-15 62
JET STREAM (715 "Sick") ... 10-15 63
JIN (127 "Cheryl Ann") ... 10-20 60

PRINCE CHARLES & CRUSADERS

Singles: 7-inch

GARLAND ... 4-8

PRINCE CONLEY: see CONLEY, Prince

PRINCE COOPER: see COOPER, Prince

PRINCE GABE

Singles: 7-inch

SIX-O-SIX ... 4-8 62

PRINCE GEORGE

Singles: 7-inch

EPIC ... 4-8 63

PRINCE HAROLD — *R&B '66*

Singles: 7-inch

MERCURY ... 4-8 66
SPRING ... 4-8 67
VERVE ... 4-8 67

PRINCE JESSE

Singles: 7-inch

GOLDEN CREST (554 "Sarah Lee") ... 10-15 60

PRINCE JOSEPH'S PREMIERS

Singles: 7-inch

CLOCK ... 5-10 61

PRINCE LA LA — *R&B '61*

Singles: 7-inch

AFO ... 5-10 61-62

PRINCE OF AMERICA

Singles: 7-inch

MEGA ... 3-5 71

PRINCE PATRIDGE

Singles: 78 rpm

CREST ... 10-15 55

Singles: 7-inch

CREST (1006 "How Come My Dog Don't Bark") ... 25-35 55
CREST (1114 "How Come My Dog Don't Bark") ... 10-15 62

PRINCE PAUL & SWINGIN' IMPERIALS

Singles: 7-inch

PARKER (9298 "In the Beginning") ... 125-150

PRINCE PHILLIP

Singles: 7-inch

SMASH (2152 "Keep on Talking") 15-25 68

PRINCE ROYALS

Singles: 7-inch

TUNE-KEL (609 "Circle of Life") ... 5-10 68

PRINCESS — *R&B/D&D '85*

Singles: 12-inch

NEXT PLATINUM ... 4-6 85-86
POLYDOR ... 4-6 86

Singles: 7-inch

POLYDOR ... 3-4 86-87

PRINCESS BUSTER & JAMAICANS

Singles: 7-inch

KING ... 4-8 67

PRINCETON, Gene

Singles: 7-inch

VANDAN ... 5-10 60

PRINCETON FIVE

Singles: 7-inch

PRINCETON (711 "Summertime Blues") ... 15-25 64

PRINCETON TRIO

LPs: 10/12-inch

CROWN ... 10-15 63

PRINCETONS

Singles: 7-inch

WRITERS ... 4-8 64

PRINCETONS

Singles: 7-inch

COLPIX (793 "Georgianna") ... 10-15 65
PHILIPS (40379 "You're My Love") ... 15-25 66
PRINCETON (1465 "Georgianna") ... 20-30 65
WAND ... 8-12 65

PRINCETONS FIVE

Singles: 7-inch

BECE (1001 "Goin' Nowhere") ... 10-20 61
BECE (1203 "Deadman") ... 10-20 61

PRINCIPAL EDWARDS MAGIC THEATRE

LPs: 10/12-inch

ELEKTRA ... 10-15 70

PRINCIPATO, Tom

LPs: 10/12-inch

POWERHOUSE ... 5-8 88
Also see ASSASSINS
Also see POWERHOUSE

PRINCIPLE, Jamie — *D&D '85*

Singles: 12-inch

PERSONA ... 4-6 85

PRINGLE, Peter

LPs: 10/12-inch

REPRISE ... 5-8 76

PRINE, John — *LP '72*

Singles: 7-inch

ASYLUM ... 3-5 78
ATLANTIC ... 3-5 71-75
OH BOY (Colored vinyl) ... 3-5 81-86

LPs: 10/12-inch

ASYLUM ... 5-10 78-80
ATLANTIC ... 8-12 71-76
OH BOY ... 5-8 84-86

PRINE, John / Daryl Hall & John Oates / Barnaby Bye / Delbert & Glen

EPs: 7-inch

ATLANTIC (195 "Something for Nothing") ... 5-8 73
Also see BARNABY BYE
Also see DELBERT & GLEN
Also see HALL, Daryl, & John Oates
Also see PRINE, John

PRINZ, Rosemary "Penny"

Singles: 7-inch

PHAROS ... 4-8 64

PRINZE, Freddie

EPs: 7-inch

COLUMBIA (1092 "Freddie Prinze") ... 4-8 75
(Promotional issue only. With paper sleeve.)

LPs: 10/12-inch

COLUMBIA ... 10-15 75

PRIOR, Maddy, & June Tabor

LPs: 10/12-inch

CHRYSALIS ... 8-10 76
Also see STEELEYE SPAN

PRISCILLA

(Priscilla Paris)

Singles: 7-inch

YORK ... 5-10 67

LPs: 10/12-inch

HAPPY TIGER ... 8-12
YORK (4005 "Priscilla Sings Herself") ... 20-30 67
Session: Davie Allan.
Also see ALLAN, Davie
Also see PARIS SISTERS

PRISCO, Tommy

Singles: 7-inch

EPIC (9302 "Till There Was You") 8-12 59
EPIC (9315 "Stingaree") ... 10-20 59

Picture Sleeves

EPIC ... 20-25 59
(We're not certain which of the two Epic singles had a sleeve. Though unlikely, perhaps both?)

PRISM — *P&R/LP '77*

Singles: 7-inch

ARIOLA AMERICA ... 3-5 77-79
CAPITOL ... 3-5 82

Picture Sleeves

CAPITOL ... 3-5 82

LPs: 10/12-inch

ARIOLA AMERICA (Except 50034) ... 10-15 77-79
ARIOLA AMERICA (50034 "Live Tonite") ... 15-25 78
(Promotional issue only.)
CAPITOL ... 5-10 80-82
Also see JACOBS, Dale, & Cobra

PRISONAIRES

("Confined to Tennessee State Prison Nashville, Tennessee")

Singles: 78 rpm

SUN (186 "Just Walkin' in the Rain") ... 100-150 53
SUN (189 "Softly & Tenderly") ... 100-150 53
SUN (191 "I Know") ... 75-125 53
SUN (207 "What'll You Do Next") ... 300-500 54

Singles: 7-inch

SUN (186 "Just Walkin' in the Rain") ... 300-500 53
(Black vinyl.)
SUN (186 "Just Walkin' in the Rain") ... 2500-3500 53
(Red vinyl.)
SUN (189 "Softly & Tenderly") ... 300-500 53
SUN (191 "I Know") ... 200-400 53
SUN (207 "What'll You Do Next") ... 3000-5000 54
Members: Johnny Bragg; John Drew; Marcell Andess; William Stewart.
Also see BRAGG, Johnny

PRISONER

Singles: 7-inch

W.B. ... 3-5 78

PRISTER, Jerome "Secret Weapon" — *R&B '88*

Singles: 7-inch

TUFF CITY ... 3-4 88

PRISTINES
Singles: 7-inch
DATE.. 4-8 67

PRITCHARD, Loyal
Singles: 7-inch
MOONBOW 5-10

PRITCHETT, Dub
Singles: 7-inch
DONA (1003 "I Don't Know How to Cook")..15-25
DONA (1001 "I Ain't Gonna Do It")..40-60

PRITCHETT, Jimmy
Singles: 7-inch
CRYSTAL (503 "That's the Way I Feel") 100-200 58

PRIVATE, Gary
Singles: 12-inch
ATLANTIC 4-6 83

PRIVATE EYE
Singles: 7-inch
FANTASY...................................... 3-4 83
LPs: 10/12-inch
CAPITOL....................................... 5-10 79
FANTASY...................................... 5-8 83

PRIVATE LIGHTNING
LPs: 10/12-inch
A&M 5-10 80

PRIVATE LINES
LPs: 10/12-inch
PASSPORT.................................... 5-10 80

PRIVATE PARTY
Singles
MASQUE (8911 "Living on the Edge")..15-20 89
(Guitar pick-shaped picture disc. 100 made.)

PRIVATE PROPERTY OF DIGIL
Singles: 7-inch
TARGET (110 "To My Friends").....30-50 67
TEE PEE (23 "Sunshine Flames") 30-50 67
TEE PEE (115 "Destination Nowhere") 30-50 67
TEE PEE (35/36 "Jewelry Lady") ...30-50 67
Members: Doug Yankus; Chuck Posniak; Dan Jacklyn; Steve Gertch; Gary Schibilski; Dave Faas.

PRIVATES & COLONELS
Singles: 7-inch
ABC-PAR 8-12 59

PRIVATES FIRST CLASS
Singles: 7-inch
JAMCO (103 "Instant Chops")......... 5-10 63

PRIVILEGE
LPs: 10/12-inch
T-NECK...10-15 69

PRIZES
Singles: 7-inch
PARKWAY 4-8 64

PRO, Noe, & Semitones
Singles: 7-inch
MERCURY 4-8 64

PROBABLE CAUSE
Singles: 7-inch
GRT (17 "Tailspin").......................10-20 70

PROBY, P.J. P&R '64
Singles: 7-inch
IMPERIAL...................................... 5-10 64
LIBERTY 8-15 61-68
LONDON 5-10 64
SURFSIDE 8-12 65
Picture Sleeves
LIBERTY 10-20 67
LPs: 10/12-inch
LIBERTY 15-30 65-68
Also see FOCUS & P.J. Proby
Also see POWERS, Jett

PROCESS & DOO RAGS R&B '85
Singles: 7-inch
COLUMBIA..................................... 3-4 85-87

PROCESSION
Singles: 7-inch
SMASH.. 3-6 69
LPs: 10/12-inch
SMASH..10-15 69

PROCLAIMERS LP '89
Singles: 7-inch
CHRYSALIS 3-5 89
EMI (17493 "I'm Gonna Be")............ 4-8 93
(Colored vinyl. Promotional issue, "For Jukeboxes Only")
EMI (24846 "I'm Gonna Be")............ 3-5 93
LPs: 10/12-inch
CHRYSALIS 5-8 89
Members: Craig Reid; Charlie Reid.

PROCOL HARUM P&R/R&B/LP '67
Singles: 7-inch
A&M 4-8 67-72
CHRYSALIS 3-6 73-77
DERAM 5-10 67
Picture Sleeves
A&M 4-8 72-73
CHRYSALIS 4-8 73
LPs: 10/12-inch
A&M (Except 4294 & 8053)............ 8-12 68-73
A&M (4294 "Broken Barricades") ...12-15 71
(With die-cut gatefold cover.)
A&M (4294 "Broken Barricades") ...10-12 72
(With standard cover.)
A&M (8053 "Procol Harum Lives") .30-40 70s
(Promotional issue only.)
CHRYSALIS 8-10 73-77
DERAM (16008 "Procol Harum") ...50-75 67
(Monaural. With bonus poster, which represents $15 to $20 of the value.)
DERAM (18008 "Procol Harum") ...50-75 67
(Stereo. Includes bonus poster which represents $15 to $20 of the value.)
Members: Gary Brooker; Bobby Harrison; Matthew Fisher; Dave Knights; Ray Royer; Robin Trower; Diz Derrick.
Also see BROOKER, Gary
Also see FISHER, Matthew
Also see PARAMOUNTS
Also see TROWER, Robin

PROCTOR, Billy
(With the Love System)
Singles: 7-inch
EPIC... 3-5 75
SOUL (35099 "What Is Black") 10-15 72

PROCTOR, Paul C&W '86
Singles: 7-inch
AURORA....................................... 3-4 86-87
19TH AVE. 3-4 87-88

PROCTOR, Phil, & Peter Bergman
LPs: 10/12-inch
COLUMBIA.....................................5-10 73
Also see FIRESIGN THEATRE

PROCTOR AMUSEMENT CO.
Singles: 7-inch
LAURIE (3396 "Call Out My Name")...8-12 67

PRODIGAL
Singles: 7-inch
MERCURY (72688 "You've Got Me")..10-20 67

PRODIGY
Singles: 7-inch
PRODIGY......................................10-15 73
Also see FLAMIN' OHS

PRODIGALS
Singles: 7-inch
ABNER (1011 "Judy")....................10-20 58
ABNER (1015 "Won't You Believe")......................................50-75 58
COLLECTABLES............................ 3-4 80s
FALCON (1011 "Judy")..................30-40 58
TOLLIE (9019 "Judy")...................10-20 64

PRODIGALS
Singles: 7-inch
ACADIAN 4-8

PRODUCERS P&R/LP '81
Singles: 7-inch
PORTRAIT..................................... 3-5 81-82
LPs: 10/12-inch
PORTRAIT.....................................5-10 81-82

PROFESSIONALS
Singles: 7-inch
GROOVE CITY (101 "That's Why I Love You")..150-250 60s

PROFESSOR
Singles: 7-inch
MAYHAMS 4-8 65

PROFESSOR & EFFICIENCY EXPERTS
Singles: 7-inch
STANSON...................................... 3-5 75

PROFESSOR ANONYMOUS
LPs: 10/12-inch
QUARK 5-10

PROFESSOR BUG
Singles: 7-inch
BEETLE (1600 "Beatlemania Beetle")..15-20 64

PROFESSOR FUNK & HIS EIGHTH STREET FUNK BAND R&B '73
Singles: 7-inch
ROXBURY...................................... 3-5 73

PROFESSOR GRIFF & LAST ASIATIC DISCIPLES LP '90
LPs: 10/12-inch
SKYYWALKER............................... 5-8 90

PROFESSOR HAMILTON & SCHOOL BOYS
(Robert Hamilton)
Singles: 7-inch
CONTOUR (0001 "Juanita of Mexico")..25-50 61

PROFESSOR JIM DANDIE: see DANDIE, Professor Jim

PROFESSOR LONGHAIR
(With the Clippers; with His Blues Scholars; with His Shuffling Hungarians; with His New Orleans Boys)
Singles: 78 rpm
ATLANTIC (897 "Mardi Gras in New Orleans")......................................75-125 50
ATLANTIC (906 "Walk Your Blues Away")..75-125 50
ATLANTIC (1020 "In the Night")...30-50 53
STAR TALENT (808 "Mardi Gras in New Orleans")....................................150-200 49
STAR TALENT (809 "She Ain't Got No Hair")...150-200 49
Singles: 7-inch
ATLANTIC (1020 "In the Night")...100-200 53
EBB (106 "Misery").........................50-100 57
EBB (101 "Cry Pretty Baby")........50-100 57
EBB (121 "Looka No Hair")...........50-100 57
RIP (155 "I Believe I'm Gonna Leave")..30-40 62
RON (326 "Cuttin' Out")..................10-15 58
(Yellow label.)
RON (329 "Goin' to the Mardi Gras")...10-15 59
(Yellow label.)
RON (Red label)..............................5-10
WATCH (1900 series).......................8-12 65
WATCH (6000 series).....................15-20 63
EPs: 7-inch
MERCURY 75-100
(1970s promotional EP, issued without special cover. Has two Professor Longhair tracks and two by other artists.)
LPs: 10/12-inch
ALLIGATOR.....................................5-8 80
ATLANTIC.......................................10-15 72-82
HARVEST 8-12 78
J.S.P. 8-12
NIGHTHAWK....................................5-10 82
MARDI GRAS...................................8-12
Also see BOYD, Robert
Also see BYRD, Roy

PROF. MARCELL & COLLEGIANS
Singles: 7-inch
MAYHAMS 8-12 60s

PROFESSOR MORRISON: see MORRISON, Professor

PROFESSORS
Singles: 7-inch
FAMAS (59002 "Look at Her") ...100-200 59

PROFFITT, Randy, & Beachcombers
(With the Jordanaires)
Singles: 7-inch
Bett-Coe (103 "Check That Baby Out One Time")..25-35 62
Also see JORDANAIRES

PROFILE
Singles: 7-inch
MERCURY 4-8 66

PROFILES
Singles: 7-inch
GOLDIE (1103 "Take a Giant Step")..20-30 62

PROFILES
Singles: 7-inch
GAIT (1444 "Never")................100-200 65

PROFILES R&B '68
Singles: 7-inch
BAMBOO 4-8 69
DUO...4-8 68

PROFITS
Singles: 7-inch
SIRE...4-8

PROFONIX, The
Singles: 7-inch
DAVEY-PAUL (4023 "Ain't No Sun")...10-20

PROGRESSIVE FOUR
Singles: 78 rpm
D.C. 10-20 47-48
SAVOY..10-15 49
Member: Harmon Bethea.
Also see BETHEA, Harmon
Also see PROGRESSIVEAIRES

PROGRESSIVEAIRES
Singles: 78 rpm
D.C. 10-15 53
Member: Harmon Bethea.
Also see BETHEA, Harmon

PROGRESSIVES
Singles: 7-inch
DOT 10-15 63

PROJECT FUTURE R&B '83
Singles: 12-inch
CAPITOL...4-6 83
Singles: 7-inch
CAPITOL...3-4 83

PROJECT X
Singles: 7-inch
VANGUARD 4-8 65

PROJECTION COMPANY
LPs: 10/12-inch
CUSTOM (1113 "Give Me Some Lovin' ")...15-20 60s

PROMENADE ORCHESTRA & CHORUS
EPs: 7-inch
PROMENADE (16 "Top 12 Hits")...10-15 61
(Two-discs with sleeve.)
PROMENADE (32 "El Rancho Rock + 5")...8-12 61

PROMINENTS
Singles: 7-inch
LUMMTONE (116 "Just a Little") ...10-20 65

PROMISES
Singles: 7-inch
ASCOT..5-10 65

PRONTO, Dennie, & Colonials
Singles: 7-inch
DEBLYN (7337 "It's No Secret") 40-60
(Also shows the number: "45-1." It's not clear which is the preferred selection number.)

PROOF
Singles: 7-inch
BJO..3-5 82
LPs: 10/12-inch
NEMPEROR...5-10 80

PROOF OF THE PUDDIN'
Singles: 7-inch
RCA 4-8 67

PROPAGANDA
LPs: 10/12-inch
EPIC..8-10 80

PROPOSITION
Singles: 7-inch
DOT 3-6 68

PROPHECY R&B '75
Singles: 7-inch
AIRBORNE 3-5 70s
ALL PLATINUM.....................................3-5 74
MAINSTREAM 3-5 75
Picture Sleeves
AIRBORNE 3-5 70s
Member: Nick Rozakis.

PROPHET LP '88
LPs: 10/12-inch
MEGAFORCE 5-8 88

PROPHET, Billy
Singles: 7-inch
MERRIMAC (1001 "Puppet on a String")..10-20 62
SUE (133 "What Can I Do")...........40-60 65

PROPHET, Jeremy
Singles: 7-inch
PHILIPS 4-8 67

PROPHET, Johnny
Singles: 7-inch
CATHAY (105 "Find a Penny") 10-20 60
J&P (150 "More")...............................8-12 60s
J.J. (2267 "I Didn't Mean to Love You")..10-15
LPs: 10/12-inch
J&H 15-20 67

PROPHET, Orval
Singles: 7-inch
CARLTON 4-8 63

PROPHET, Ronnie C&W '75
Singles: 7-inch
RCA 3-5 75-77
LPs: 10/12-inch
ART 10-20
AUDIOGRAPH ALIVE 5-8 82
GLOBE..10-20
PROPHET..10-20
RCA 5-10 76
TEE VEE 5-10
(Mail order offer.)
TRANS WORLD...................................10-20
VERA CRUZ 8-10

PROPHETEERS
Singles: 7-inch
CHOICE 8-12 60

PROPHETS
Singles: 78 rpm
ATCO (6078 "Stormy") 10-15 56
Singles: 7-inch
ATCO (6078 "Stormy") 20-30 56

PROPHETS
Singles: 7-inch
RAMCO (3712 "Japanese Twist") ..10-20 62

PROPHETS
Singles: 7-inch
JAIRICK (201 "Sha-La-La")........100-200 63

PROPHETS
Singles: 7-inch
TWIN-SPIN (3000 "Yes I Know") ...15-25 66

PROPHETS
Singles: 7-inch
CHESS..5-10 67
SHELL (105 "I Still Love You") 10-20 60s
STEPHAYNE (335 "My Kind of Girl")...10-20 66

PROPHETS
Singles: 7-inch
BSP 3-5 79
DELPHI ("Don't You Think It's Time")...15-25 67
(Selection number not known.)
DELPHI (007 "Talk Don't Bother Me")...15-25 67
ERIC 3-4 70s
JUBILEE (5565 "Talk Don't Bother Me")...15-25 66
JUBILEE (5596 "Don't You Think It's Time")...15-25 67
JUBILEE..10-15 66-67
RIPETE 3-4 83
SMASH (2161 "I Got the Fever") 5-10 68
Members: Tommy Witcher; Pete Pendleton; Barbara Pendleton; Fred Williamson; Jim Campbell; Billy Scott; Walter Stanley.
Also see GEORGIA PROPHETS
Also see SCOTT, Billy
Also see THREE PROPHETS

PROPHETS
Singles: 12-inch
EPIC 4-6 83
Singles: 7-inch
EPIC 3-5 83

PROPHETS, Thee: see THEE PROPHETS

PROPHETS OF PEACE
Singles: 7-inch
MAXX..4-8 60s

PROS & CONS
Singles: 7-inch
DECCA 4-8 65

PROTHEROE, Brian P&R '75
Singles: 7-inch
CHRYSALIS...3-5 75
LPs: 10/12-inch
CHRYSALIS...8-12 75-76

PROUD AS PUNCH
Singles: 7-inch
STAX (0081 "So Easy to See")........8-12 71

PROUD CITY SINGERS
Singles: 7-inch
MALTESE (103 "Beautiful Sound")...10-20 65

PROVERBIAL KNEE HIGHS
Singles: 7-inch
BEACHCOMBER (11 "Watch Out")..10-20 60s

PROVIDENCE
Singles: 7-inch
THRESHOLD 3-5 73
LPs: 10/12-inch
THRESHOLD 8-12 73

PROVINE, Dorothy LP '61
Singles: 7-inch
W.B. 3-6 61
LPs: 10/12-inch
W.B. 15-25 60-61

PROVINE, Dorothy, & Joe "Fingers" Carr
LPs: 10/12-inch
W.B. 15-25 60-62
Also see CARR, Joe "Fingers"
Also see PROVINE, Dorothy

PROVISOR, Denny
Singles: 7-inch
20TH FOX (506 "Mickey Mouse") 5-10 64
VALIANT (717 "Little Girl Lost").......8-12 65
VALIANT (728 "She's Not Mine Anymore")..8-12 65
Also see GRASS ROOTS
Also see HOOK

PROW, Jimmy Lee
Singles: 78 rpm
KING 10-15 56
Singles: 7-inch
KING 15-25 56

PROWLERS
Singles: 7-inch
ARAGON (302 "Rock Me Baby") ...50-75

PROYSOCK, Red: see PRYSOCK, Red

PRUDE, Terrell
Singles: 7-inch
TANGERINE 8-10 66

PRUETT, Jeanne C&W '71
(Jean Pruett)
Singles: 7-inch
AUDIOGRAPH 3-4 83
DECCA 3-6 68-72
IBC...3-5 79-80
MCA..3-5 73-77
MSR..3-4 87
MERCURY 3-5 78
PAID 3-4 81
RCA 4-6 63-64
LPs: 10/12-inch
ALLEGIANCE..5-8 84
AUDIOGRAPH 5-8 83
DECCA 8-12 72
IBC...5-10 79
MCA..5-10 73-75
OUT of TOWN DIST 5-10 82

PRUETT, Jeanne, & Marty Robbins C&W '83
Singles: 7-inch
AUDIOGRAPH 3-4 83
Also see PRUETT, Jeanne
Also see ROBBINS, Marty

PRUITT, Billy
Singles: 7-inch
KAYO (501 "Special Love Affair")....8-12 60

PRUITT, Lewis C&W '59
Singles: 7-inch
DECCA (Except 31201)......................5-10 60
DECCA (31201 "Crazy Bullfrog") ...30-50 61
GREAT..4-8 68
MUSIC TOWN 3-6 69
PEACH (703 "Pretty Baby")............50-75 59
PEACH (710 "This Little Girl") 50-75 59
PEACH (725 "Timbrook")................10-15 59
VEE JAY 5-10 63-64
Also see SMITH, Carl

PRUITT, Ralph
Singles: 7-inch
B.B. (226 "Louise") 100-200
LARK (1506 "Hey Mr. Porter") ...300-400

MERIDIAN (1507 "Hey Mr. Porter")....................200-300 58

PRYOR, Cactus, & His Pricklypears C&W '50

Singles: 78 rpm

FOUR STAR.................................... 5-8 50

PRYOR, Richard LP '74

Singles: 7-inch

LAFF 3-5 80
W.B. 4-6 76-79

LPs: 10/12-inch

DOVE..............................10-15 68
LAFF 5-10 71-81
PARTEE 5-10 74
REPRISE.................................... 6-12 68-77
TIGER LILY................................ 5-10 77
W.B. 5-10 76-85

PRYOR, Snooky

Singles: 78 rpm

J.O.B. (101 "Boogy Fool")..........50-100 50
J.O.B. (115 "I'm Getting Tired")....50-100 52
PARROT (807 "Crosstown Blues")......................50-100 53
VEE JAY (215 "Someone to Love Me")......................20-40 56

Singles: 7-inch

J.O.B. (1014 "Cryin' Shame")......150-250 53
J.O.B. (1126 "Uncle Sam, Don't Take My Man")..........................150-250 63
PARROT (807 "Crosstown Blues")......................200-300 53
(Black vinyl.)
PARROT (807 "Crosstown Blues")......................550-650 53
(Red vinyl.)
VEE JAY (215 "Someone to Love Me")......................50-75 56

LPs: 10/12-inch

BLUESWAY 8-12 73
TODAY (1012 "And the Country Blues")..............................35-45
Session: Sunnyland Slim; Eddie Taylor.
Also see SNOOKY & MOODY
Also see SUNNYLAND SLIM
Also see TAYLOR, Eddie
Also see YOUNG, Johnny

PRYSOCK, Arthur R&B '52

Singles: 78 rpm

DECCA.................................... 4-8 52-54
MERCURY 4-8 54-55
PEACOCK................................ 5-10 57

Singles: 7-inch

BETHLEHEM................................ 3-5 72
DECCA (25000 series).................. 4-8 65
DECCA (27000 thru 29000 series).. 5-10 52-54
DECCA (31000 series).................. 4-8 64-65
GUSTO 3-5 79
KING 3-6 69-71
MCA 3-5 78
MGM 3-5 70
MERCURY 5-10 54-55
OLD TOWN (100 series)................ 3-5 73-76
OLD TOWN (1000 series)................ 4-8 59-60
(Light blue label.)
OLD TOWN (1000 series)................ 3-5 76-77
(Dark blue or black label.)
OLD TOWN (1100 series)................ 4-6 61-66
PEACOCK.................................... 5-10 57
VERVE 3-6 66-69

EPs: 7-inch

OLD TOWN (9 "Double Header").... 8-10 65

LPs: 10/12-inch

DECCA..................................15-20 64-65
KING 8-12 69-71
MCA 5-10 78
OLD TOWN (100 series)..............20-30 60-62
OLD TOWN (2000 series)..............15-25 62-65
OLD TOWN (12000 series).............. 5-10 73-77
POLYDOR.................................... 5-10 77
VERVE......................................10-20 66-69
Also see ECKSTINE, Billy / Arthur Prysock
Also see JOHNSON, Buddy

PRYSOCK, Arthur, & Count Basie LP '66

Singles: 7-inch

VERVE 3-6 66

LPs: 10/12-inch

VERVE......................................15-20 66
Also see BASIE, Count

PRYSOCK, Arthur / Leroy Bivins

LPs: 10/12-inch

GUEST STAR.............................. 5-10 64
Also see PRYSOCK, Arthur

PRYSOCK, Red

(With the His House Rockers; Reo Prysock; Red Proysock)

Singles: 78 rpm

MERCURY 5-15 54-57
RED ROBIN (107 "Wiggles")........25-50 53
RED ROBIN (117 "Hard Rock")........15-25 53
RED ROBIN (139 "Hammer")........15-25 53
WING (90070 "Fruit Boots")............ 8-12 56

Singles: 7-inch

CHESS 3-6 68
GATEWAY 4-8 64
KING 4-8 62
MERCURY 5-10 54-61
RED ROBIN (107 "Wiggles")........75-100 53
RED ROBIN (117 "Hard Rock")........50-75 53
RED ROBIN (139 "Hammer")........50-75 53
WING (90070 "Fruit Boots")........15-25 56

EPs: 7-inch

MERCURY 40-60 56

LPs: 10/12-inch

MERCURY (20088 "Rock 'N Roll")..............................75-100 56
MERCURY (20307 "The Beat")......50-75 56
MERCURY (20512 "Swing Softly")..............................20-30 61
(Monaural.)
MERCURY (60188 "Swing Softly")..............................25-35 61
(Stereo.)
WING (12007 "Fruit Boots")..........35-50 57
Also see AUSTIN, Sil, & Red Prysock
Also see GRIMES, Tiny

PSEUDO ECHO P&R/LP '87

Singles: 7-inch

RCA.. 3-4 87

LPs: 10/12-inch

RCA.. 5-8 87

PSYCHEDELIC FURS LP '80

Singles: 12-inch

COLUMBIA.................................... 4-6 84-86

Singles: 7-inch

A&M 3-4 86
COLUMBIA...................................... 3-5 80-89

Picture Sleeves

A&M 3-4 86
COLUMBIA...................................... 3-5 80-87

LPs: 10/12-inch

COLUMBIA...................................... 5-10 80-89
Members: Tim Butler; Richard Butler; John Ashton; Mars Williams; Paul Garisto; Marty Williamson.

PSYCHOBUD

LPs: 10/12-inch

ENIGMA.. 5-8 85

PSYCHOPATHS

Singles: 7-inch

DAVID LLOYD (201,438 "Till the Stroke of Dawn")....................................10-15 67

PSYCHOS

Singles: 7-inch

FERNWOOD....................................5-10 60

PSYCHOTICS

Singles: 7-inch

ACID (24975 "If You Don't Believe Me, Don't")....................................40-60 60

PSYCHOTICS

Singles: 7-inch

UPTOWN (7666 "I'm Determined")..............................40-60 67

Picture Sleeves

UPTOWN (7666 "I'm Determined")..............................50-75 67

PUBLIC ENEMY R&B/LP '88

Singles: 7-inch

DEF JAM.. 3-4 88-90

LPs: 10/12-inch

DEF JAM.. 5-8 88-90

PUBLIC EYE

Singles: 7-inch

EVA-TONE.. 3-4 84
(Promotional issue only.)
Members: Joe Whiting; Mark Doyle.
Also see WHITING, Joe, & Bandit Band

PUBLIC FOOT THE ROMAN

LPs: 10/12-inch

SOVEREIGN......................................8-12 73

PUBLIC IMAGE LTD. LP '80

Singles: 12-inch

VIRGIN.. 4-6 87

LPs: 10/12-inch

ELEKTRA.. 5-8 86
ISLAND 8-10 80
VIRGIN.. 5-8 87-89
W.B. 8-10 81
Also see JAH WOBBLE
Also see SEX PISTOLS

PUBLIO & VALIANTS

Singles: 7-inch

MENARD (6252 "Image of Love")....................................500-750

PUCCINI

Singles: 7-inch

EDGE.. 3-5 74-75

PUCKETT, Dennis

(Dennis "The Rocket" Puckett)

Singles: 7-inch

MERALD (2018 "Rockin' Teens")..............................150-200 58
MERALD (2551 "Jungle Jive")..........5-10
(Suggested price indicates this must be a recent issue, probably of 1958 tracks.)

PUCKETT, Gary P&R '67

(With the Union Gap; Union Gap Featuring Gary Puckett)

Singles: 7-inch

COLUMBIA.. 4-8 67-72
COLUMBIA HALL of FAME 3-4 70s
GUSTO 3-4 81-83

Picture Sleeves

COLUMBIA..5-10 67-70

LPs: 10/12-inch

BACK-TRAC...................................... 5-8 85
CSP..8-10 72
COLUMBIA (Except 10171)..........10-20 68-71
COLUMBIA (10171 "Young Girl")......5-10
COLUMBIA HOUSE (6272/3 "Fillin' the Gap")..20-30 75
(Three-discs; one double and one single LP set.)
51 WEST...5-10 82
GUSTO 5-8 83
HARMONY 8-12 71
Members: Gary Puckett; Paul Wheatbread; Gary Withem; Kerry Chater; Dwight Bement.
Also see CHATER, Kerry
Also see FRANKLIN, Aretha / Union Gap / Blood, Sweat & Tears / Moby Grape

PUCKETT, Jerry C&W '83

Singles: 7-inch

ATLANTIC AMERICA..........................3-4 83
123..5-10 69
Also see CAMPBELL, Glen
Also see CHAMPS

PUDDIN' HEADS

Singles: 7-inch

CATCH (111 "Now You Say We're Through")....................................15-25 64

PUDDING

Singles: 7-inch

PRESS...4-8 68

PUDDLE

Singles: 7-inch

CANDY FLOSS 8-12 60s

PUDDLE JUMPERS

Singles: 7-inch

FEDERAL (12336 "Snake Charmer")......................................15-25 58
FEDERAL (12343 "Headin' South")..15-25 58
Also see GRAY, Johnny

PUFF

LPs: 10/12-inch

MGM..10-15 69

PUGH

LPs: 10/12-inch

VAULT..10-15 70

PUGSLEY MUNION

Singles: 7-inch

J&S (2 "Just Like You")..................15-25 69

LPs: 10/12-inch

J&S (001 "Just Like You")................60-80 69
Member: John Schuller.

PULLEN, Dwight

Singles: 7-inch

CARLTON (455 "Sunglasses After Dark")......................................100-200 61
SAGE (279 "By You, by the Bayou")..15-25 59

PULLEN, Whitey

Singles: 7-inch

SAGE (238 "You'll Get Yours") 50-75 59
SAGE (274 "Walk My Way Back Home")..50-75 59
SAGE (294 "Let's All Go Wild Tonight")..50-75 59
SAGE (313 "Tuscaloosa Lucy") 50-75 60
SAGE (372 "Crazy in Love")..........20-30 63
SAGE & SAND 10-15 64

PULLENS, Vern

Singles: 78 rpm

SPADE..50-100 56

Singles: 7-inch

SPADE (1927 "Bop Crazy Baby")..150-250 56
SPADE (1930 "It Took One Moment")..50-75 57
SPADE (11975 "Rock on Mabel") 5-10 75

PULLINS, Leroy C&W/P&R '66

Singles: 7-inch

KAPP 4-8 66

LPs: 10/12-inch

KAPP (3488 "I'm a Nut")..................20-30 66
KAPP (3557 "Funny Bones and Hearts")..15-25 68

PULLUM, Joe

Singles: 78 rpm

SWING TIME (267 "My Woman, Part 1")..20-30 48

PULSE

Singles: 7-inch

ATCO (6530 "Burritt Bradley") 10-15 67
POISON RING (711 "Another Woman")..5-10 69

LPs: 10/12-inch

POISON RING (2237 "Pulse") 15-25 69
Members: Carl Donnell; Peter Neri; Paul Rosano; Jeff Potter; Rich Bednarzyck; Benet Segal.
Also see BRAM RIGG SET
Also see SHAGS

PULSE

(Featuring Carlo Mastrangelo)

LPs: 10/12-inch

THIMBLE..10-20 72
Members: Carlo Mastrangelo; Kenny Sambolin; Richie Goggin; Chris Gentile.
Also see CARLO

PULSE R&B '82

Singles: 7-inch

SILVER CLOUD 3-5 82

PULTE, Jim

LPs: 10/12-inch

U.A. 8-12 72

PUMA, Larry

(With the Triotones)

Singles: 7-inch

INTRASTATE (43 "Valerie Jo")........35-45 59

PUMP, Randy, & Gas-O-Lettes

Singles: 7-inch

A&M 3-5 79

PUMP BOYS & DINETTES C&W 83

Singles: 7-inch

CBS..3-4 83

PUMPKIN

Singles: 78 rpm

BRUNSWICK......................................10-15 57

Singles: 7-inch

BRUNSWICK......................................10-15 57

PUMPKIN & PROFILE ALL-STARS R&B '84

Singles: 12-inch

PROFILE..4-6 84

Singles: 7-inch

PROFILE..3-4 84
Also see FRESH 3 MCs

PUNCH

Singles: 7-inch

A&M 3-5 70-71
BELL 3-5 72
RAFTIS 3-6

LPs: 10/12-inch

A&M 8-12 71

PUPPET

Singles: 7-inch

GRAMMY..4-8 68

PUPPET, Polly

Singles: 7-inch

CHALLENGE..5-10 61

PUPPET CHILDREN

Singles: 7-inch

INDEPENDENCE......................................4-8 68

PUPPETS

Singles: 7-inch

RED ROOSTER..4-8 60s

PUPPETS D&D '84

Singles: 12-inch

QUALITY/RFC..4-6 84

Singles: 7-inch

QUALITY/RFC..3-4 84

PUPPIES

Singles: 7-inch

STIFF 3-4 81

Picture Sleeves

STIFF 3-4 81

PURCELL, Sonny

Singles: 7-inch

ORGO 5-10 59

PURDIE, Pretty P&R/R&B '67

(Bernard Purdie)

Singles: 7-inch

COLUMBIA 4-6 69
DATE 4-8 67-68

LPs: 10/12-inch

DATE 10-20 67
FLYING DUTCHMAN 8-12 73
PRESTIGE 8-12 71

PURDY, Steve, & Studs

Singles: 7-inch

VESTA ("I Cried")..........................100-150 62
(Selection number not known. 500 copies made.)
VESTA (200 "The Weed") 100-150 62
(1000 copies made.)

PURE

Singles: 7-inch

M-A-P-L (39445 "Greedy")....................3-4 92
(Green vinyl. Identification number shown since no selection number is used.)

Picture Sleeves

M-A-P-L (39445 "Greedy")....................3-4 92

PURE ENERGY R&B '80

Singles: 12-inch

PRISM..4-6 80-84

Singles: 7-inch

PRISM..3-5 80-84

PURE FOOD & DRUG ACT

EPIC..4-8 72

LPs: 10/12-inch

EPIC..10-15 72

PURE GOLD

Singles: 7-inch

GREEN DOLPHIN......................................8-12

PURE JADE GREEN

Singles: 7-inch

CRAZY HORSE 3-5 70

PURE LOVE & PLEASURE LP '70

Singles: 7-inch

DUNHILL..3-5 70

LPs: 10/12-inch

DUNHILL..10-15 70

PURE PRAIRIE LEAGUE P&R/LP '75

Singles: 7-inch

RCA 3-5 72-79
CASABLANCA 3-5 80-81
EPIC..3-5 77

LPs: 10/12-inch

CASABLANCA 5-10 80-81
RCA 6-12 72-80
Members/Session: John Call; George Powell; Billy Hinds; David Sanborn; Mick Ronson; Michael O'Connor; Johnny Gimble; Don Felder; Vince Gill; Chet Atkins; Larry Goshorn.
Also see AMERICAN FLYER
Also see ATKINS, Chet
Also see FELDER, Don
Also see GILL, Vince
Also see RONSON, Mick
Also see SANBORN, David

PURE VELVET

Singles: 7-inch

OSIRIS..3-5 75

PURIFY, James & Bobby P&R/R&B '66

Singles: 7-inch

BELL 4-8 66-69
CASABLANCA 3-5 74-75
MERCURY 3-5 76-77
SPHERE SOUND..4-8 66

LPs: 10/12-inch

BELL 10-20 66-67
MERCURY 8-12 77
Members: James Purify; Bobby Dickey.

PURIM, Flora LP '75

LPs: 10/12-inch

MILESTONE 5-10 74-77
W.B. 5-10 77-78
Also see HART, Mickey, Airto & Flora Purim

PURPLE CUCUMBER

Singles: 7-inch

SMASH 4-8 68

PURPLE GANG

Singles: 7-inch

JERDEN (794 "Answer the Phone").5-10 66
MGM (13607 "Bring Your Own Self Down")..10-15 66

LPs: 10/12-inch

SIRE 10-15 69

PURPLE IMAGE

LPs: 10/12-inch

MAP CITY 10-15 71

PURPLE MUNDI

Singles: 7-inch

CAL..8-12

PURPLE PEOPLE

Singles: 7-inch

PURPLE (1001 "I Wanna Do It")........8-12 70s
TARGET (102 "Rock & Roll Music")..8-12 70s
Member: Doug McDade.

PURPLE PERSIANS

Singles: 7-inch

GALACTIC (1001 "I Heard the Word")..10-15 67

PURPLE ROSE OF CAIRO

LPs: 10/12-inch

MCA..5-8 80s

PURPLE REIGN P&R '75

Singles: 7-inch

GO-RILLA 4-8 75
HILLSIDE (1006 "Wish You Didn't Have to Go")..15-25
PRIVATE STOCK 3-5 75

PURPLE SUN

Singles: 7-inch

RAMPART STREET..10-20 60s

PURPLE UNDERGROUND

Singles: 7-inch

BOSS (010 "Count Back") 20-30

PURRELL, Eddie

Singles: 7-inch

HIT SOUND (222 "Had to Be a Lover")..5-10 68
VOLT (145 "My Pride Won't Let Me")..5-10 67

PURSELL, Bill P&R/R&B/LP '63

Singles: 7-inch

COLUMBIA 3-6 62-66
DOT 3-5 69
EPIC..3-5 67
SPAR 10-15 60s

LPs: 10/12-inch

COLUMBIA 8-15 63-65
Also see NELSON, Willie
Also see ROBBINS, Marty

PURSUIT OF HAPPINESS LP '88

LPs: 10/12-inch

CHRYSALIS..5-8 88

PUSEY, Joseph

LPs: 10/12-inch

CEREBELLA 8-10 77

PUSH

LPs: 10/12-inch

MOON..10-15

PUSH BUTTON & DIALTONES

(Denny Ezba & Goldens)

Singles: 7-inch

REMUS 5-10 66
Also see EZBA, Denny

PUSHCART

Singles: 7-inch

TOP DOG (109 "I've Got a Ticket to the World")..10-20 60s

PUSHE' D&D '84

Singles: 12-inch

PARTYTYME..4-6 84

PUSSYCATS

(Pussy Cats)

Singles: 7-inch

COLUMBIA 8-12 65-66
KEETCH 10-15 64
KEYMAN (6000 "Anniversary of Love")..50-100 63

PUSSYFOOT

Singles: 7-inch

LONDON 4-8 66

PUTMAN, Curly C&W '60
Singles: 7-inch
ABC ... 4-6 67
CHEROKEE ... 5-10 60
LPs: 10/12-inch
ABC ... 10-20 67

PUZZLE
Singles: 7-inch
ABC ... 4-8 69
LPs: 10/12-inch
ABC (671 "Puzzle") ... 15-20 69

PUZZLE
Singles: 7-inch
MOTOWN ... 3-5 73-74
LPs: 10/12-inch
MOTOWN ... 8-12 73-74

PUZZLES
Singles: 7-inch
FAT BACK ... 10-15 68
Also see FOUR PUZZLES

PYGMIES
Singles: 7-inch
LIBERTY ... 4-8 63

PYLE, Artimus, Band
LPs: 10/12-inch
MCA ... 5-8 82-83
Also see LYNYRD SKYNYRD

PYLE, Chuck C&W '85
Singles: 7-inch
URBAN SOUND ... 3-4 85-86

PYLE, Jack
LPs: 10/12-inch
CAMEO ... 10-20 63

PYNK PEACH MOB
Singles: 7-inch
NIGHT OWL (1558 "No Tears") ... 10-15 71
(Selection number not known.)

PYRAMID
Singles: 7-inch
PYRAMID (101 "Told You Lately I Love You") ... 10-20 70s
Also see RUDY, Roger, & Pyramid

PYRAMID
Singles: 7-inch
BANG ... 3-5 74-75
LPs: 10/12-inch
BANG ... 5-10 74
Member: Steve Sanders.
Also see SANDERS, Steve

PYRAMIDERS
Singles: 7-inch
SCOTT (1205 "Don't Ever Leave Me") ... 500-750 58

PYRAMIDS
(With Fletcher Smith's Band)
Singles: 78 rpm
C NOTE (108 "Someday") ... 500-750 55
FEDERAL (12233 "Deep in My Heart for You") ... 100-200 55
(Green label.)
FEDERAL (12233 "Deep in My Heart for You") ... 100-200 55
(White bio label. Promotional issue only.)
HOLLYWOOD (1047 "Someday") ... 250-350 55
Singles: 7-inch
C NOTE (108 "Someday") ... 2000-3000 55
FEDERAL (12233 "Deep in My Heart for You") ... 300-500 55
(Green label.)
FEDERAL (12233 "Deep in My Heart for You") ... 450-650 55
(White bio label. Promotional issue only.)
HOLLYWOOD (1047 "Someday") ... 1000-2000 55
Members: Sidney Correia; Joe Dandy; Melvin White; Kenneth Perdue; Lionel Cobbs; Tom Williams.
Also see TEMPO-MENTALS

PYRAMIDS
Singles: 78 rpm
DAVIS ... 15-25 56
Singles: 7-inch
DAVIS (453 "At Any Cost") ... 40-60 56
DAVIS (457 "Why Did You Go") ... 40-60 56
Members: Roland Douglas; Joe Stallings; Richard Foster; Hubie Saulsberry.
Also see WHITAKER, Ruby, & Pyramids

PYRAMIDS
Singles: 7-inch
RCA ... 8-10 59

PYRAMIDS
(With Billy Mure Orchestra)
Singles: 7-inch
COLLECTABLES ... 3-4 80s
SHELL (711 "Ankle Bracelet") ... 40-60 59
(Gray label. Pictures two sea shells.)
SHELL (711 "Ankle Bracelet") ... 15-25 64
(White label. No sea shells shown.)
Also see MURE, Billy
Also see ORIGINAL PYRAMIDS

PYRAMIDS
Singles: 7-inch
CUB (9112 "I'm the Playboy") ... 10-15 62
SONBERT ("I'm the Playboy") ... 30-40 62
(No selection number used.)
VEE JAY (489 "What Is Love") ... 10-20 63
Also see SATINTONES

PYRAMIDS P&R/LP '64
Singles: 7-inch
BEST (1 "Pyramid's Stomp") ... 15-25 63
BEST (102 "Penetration") ... 20-30 63
BEST (13001 "Pyramid's Stomp") ... 8-12 63
BEST (13002 "Penetration") ... 8-12 63
CEDWICKE (13005 "Midnight Run") ... 20-30 64
CEDWICKE (13006 "Contact") ... 20-30 64
SUNDAZED ... 5-10 90s
(Colored vinyl.)
Picture Sleeves
BEST (13002 "Penetration") ... 20-30 63
LPs: 10/12-inch
BEST (16501 "Penetration") ... 75-125 64
(Monaural.)
BEST (36501 "Penetration") ... 100-200 64
(Stereo.)
WHAT ... 5-8 83

PYRYMYD
LPs: 10/12-inch
CAPITOL ... 5-8 80

PYTHON LEE JACKSON P&R/LP '72
(With Rod Stewart)
Singles: 7-inch
EUROGRAM (5001 "In a Broken Dream") ... 10-15
GNP ... 4-6 72
LPs: 10/12-inch
GNP ... 10-15 72
Also see SMALL FACES
Also see STEWART, Rod

PYWACKETT
Singles: 7-inch
BELL (445 "Turn on to Life") ... 5-10 74

PYZOW, Nick
Singles: 7-inch
ASFAB ... 3-4 86
Picture Sleeves
ASFAB ... 3-4 86

Q

Q P&R/LP '77
Singles: 7-inch
EPIC ... 3-5 77
Picture Sleeves
EPIC ... 3-5 77
LPs: 10/12-inch
EPIC ... 8-10 77
Members: Robert Peckman; Don Garvin.
Also see JAGGERZ

Q, Stacey: see STACEY Q

Q FEEL P&R '89
Singles: 12-inch
JIVE (12004 "Dancing in Heaven") ... 5-10 82
Singles: 7-inch
JIVE (1220 "Dancing in Heaven") ... 3-4 89
JIVE (2001 "Dancing in Heaven") ... 4-8 82
Picture Sleeves
JIVE (1220 "Dancing in Heaven") ... 3-4 89

QUAD, Bill, & Ravens
Singles: 7-inch
FLING ... 10-20 59
SAHARA ... 5-10 65

QUADDELLS
Singles: 7-inch
VIDA ("Meatball") ... 10-15 62
(Selection number not known.)

QUADRANGLE
Singles: 7-inch
PHILIPS (40408 "She's Too Familiar Now") ... 15-25 66

QUADRANT SIX R&B/D&D '83
Singles: 12-inch
ATLANTIC ... 4-6 83
Singles: 7-inch
ATLANTIC ... 3-4 83

QUADRAPHONICS
Singles: 7-inch
INNOVATION II ... 3-5

QUADRELLS
Singles: 78 rpm
WHIRLIN' DISC ... 20-30 56
Singles: 7-inch
WHIRLIN' DISC (103 "Come to Me") ... 75-100 56
Also see KOPE, Billy, & Quadrells

QUADROPHONICS R&B '74
Singles: 7-inch
W.B. ... 3-5 74

QUADS
Singles: 7-inch
VAULT (907 "Surfin' Hearse") ... 15-20 63

QUADS / Grand Prix / Customs
LPs: 10/12-inch
VAULT (104 "Hot Rod City") ... 25-35 63
Also see CUSTOMS
Also see GRAND PRIX
Also see QUADS

QUAIL, Rex
Singles: 7-inch
APACHE (1836 "Good Rockin' Tonight") ... 50-75 60

QUAILS
Singles: 78 rpm
DELUXE ... 20-40 54
Singles: 7-inch
DELUXE (6085 "The Things She Used to Do") ... 45-55 55
Also see ROBINSON, Bill, & Quails

QUAILS
Singles: 7-inch
HARVEY (116 "My Love") ... 20-40 61
HARVEY (120 "I Thought") ... 20-40 63
Also see FIVE QUAILS

QUAITE, Christine P&R '64
Singles: 7-inch
WORLD ARTISTS ... 5-8 64

QUAKER CITY BOYS P&R '58
Singles: 7-inch
SWAN ... 8-15 58-59

QUALITY CONTROL
Singles: 7-inch
SURE SHOT (5040 "Grapevine") ... 8-12

QUALLS, Sidney Joe R&B '74
(Sidney Qualls)
Singles: 7-inch
DAKAR ... 3-5 74

QUANDO QUANDO D&D '83
Singles: 12-inch
FACTORY ... 4-6 83

QUARRY
Singles: 7-inch
BERKSHIRE HAMONY ... 4-8 60s

QUARRYMEN
Singles: 7-inch
SARA (6624 "Don't Try Your Luck") ... 10-20 66

QUARTER NOTES P&R '59
(Quarter-Notes)
Singles: 78 rpm
DOT (15685 "Like You Bug Me") ... 15-25 57
Singles: 7-inch
BISON (757 "Frantic Flip") ... 15-20 60
DOT (15685 "Like You Bug Me") ... 20-30 57
GLENN (2550 "The Shock") ... 10-20 62
(First issued as *Guitar Bass Boogie*, by Gary Vallet. Has sound effects added.)
GUYDEN (2083 "Pretty Pretty Eyes") ... 10-15 63
IMPERIAL (5647 "Frantic Flip") ... 10-15 60
LITTLE STAR (112 "Baby") ... 1000-2000 62
RCA (7327 "Punkanilla") ... 10-20 58
WIZZ (715 "Record Hop Blues") ... 15-25 59
Also see VALLET, Gary

QUARTERFLASH P&R/LP '81
Singles: 12-inch
GEFFEN ... 4-6 81-82
Singles: 7-inch
GEFFEN ... 3-5 81-85
W.B. ... 3-5 82
Picture Sleeves
GEFFEN ... 3-5 82-85
LPs: 10/12-inch
GEFFEN ... 5-10 81-85
Also see SEAFOOD MAMA

QUARTERMAN, Joe R&B '72
(With Free Soul)
Singles: 7-inch
GSF ... 3-5 72-74
MERCURY ... 3-5 74

QUARTERMASS
LPs: 10/12-inch
HARVEST ... 15-20 70

QUARTERNOTES
Singles: 7-inch
BOOM ... 5-10 66

QUARTETTE TRÉS BIEN
Singles: 7-inch
NORMAN ... 20-25 60s
LPs: 10/12-inch
DECCA ... 10-15 67

QUARTZ R&B '78
Singles: 7-inch
MARLIN ... 3-5 78
POLYDOR ... 3-5 79
LPs: 10/12-inch
MARLIN ... 5-10 78
POLYDOR ... 5-10 79

QUASEE, Nicole
Singles: 7-inch
DCP ... 4-8 65

QUATEMAN, Bill P&R '73
Singles: 7-inch
COLUMBIA ... 3-5 72-73
RCA ... 3-5 77-78
LPs: 10/12-inch
COLUMBIA ... 8-10 73
RCA ... 5-10 77-78

QUATRAIN
LPs: 10/12-inch
TETRAGRAMMATON ... 10-15 69

QUATRO, Michael
(Mike Quatro; Michael Quatro Jam Band)
Singles: 7-inch
SRI ... 3-5 80
SPECTOR ... 3-5 81
U.A. ... 3-5 75
LPs: 10/12-inch
EVOLUTION ... 10-15 72-73
PRODIGAL ... 5-10
SPECTOR ... 5-10 81
U.A. ... 8-12 75-76

QUATRO, Suzi P&R/LP '74
(Susie Quatro)
Singles: 7-inch
ARISTA ... 3-5 75
BELL ... 3-5 73-74
BIG TREE ... 3-5 76
DREAMLAND ... 3-5 80-81
RAK ... 5-10 72-74
RSO ... 3-5 79
Picture Sleeves
DREAMLAND ... 3-5 80
LPs: 10/12-inch
ARISTA ... 8-10 75
BELL ... 10-12 74
DREAMLAND ... 5-10 80
RSO ... 5-10 79
Also see PLEASURE SEEKERS

QUATRO, Suzi, & Chris Norman P&R '79
Singles: 7-inch
RSO ... 3-5 79
Also see QUATRO, Suzi
Also see SMOKIE

QUATTLEBAUM, Doug
Singles: 78 rpm
GOTHAM ... 25-50 53
Singles: 7-inch
GOTHAM (519 "Don't Be Funny, Baby") ... 50-75 53
LPs: 10/12-inch
PRESTIGE BLUESVILLE ... 25-35 62

QUAZAR R&B/LP '78
Singles: 7-inch
ARISTA ... 3-5 78
LPs: 10/12-inch
ARISTA ... 5-10 78

QUE, Johnnie
Singles: 7-inch
RHINO ... 3-5 81
Picture Sleeves
RHINO ... 3-5 81

QUEEN LP '73
Singles: 12-inch
CAPITOL ... 4-8 84-86
ELEKTRA (11401 "Fat Bottom Girls and Bicycle Race") ... 12-18
(Promotional issue.)
Singles: 7-inch
CAPITOL ... 3-5 84-89
ELEKTRA ... 3-6 74-82
HOLLYWOOD ... 3-4 92
Picture Sleeves
CAPITOL ... 3-5 84-89
ELEKTRA (Except 45478) ... 4-8 77-82
ELEKTRA (45478 "It's Late") ... 10-20 78
LPs: 10/12-inch
CAPITOL ... 5-10 84-89
ELEKTRA (Except 5064) ... 6-12 73-82
ELEKTRA (5064 "Queen") ... 10-15 73
(With gold foil title stamped on cover.)
ELEKTRA (5064 "Queen") ... 5-10 73
(With title printed on cover.)
ELEKTRA (5064 "Queen") ... 20-30 73
(Quadrophonic.)
MFSL (067 "A Night at the Opera") ... 35-50 82
MFSL (211 "The Game") ... 20-25 94
WARNER SPECIAL PRODUCTS ... 5-10 84
Promotional LPs
ELEKTRA (1026 "Sheer Heart Attack") ... 10-15 74
ELEKTRA (75082 "Queen II") ... 40-50 74
Members: Freddie Mercury; John Deacon; Brian May; Roger Taylor.
Also see MAY, Brian
Also see MERCURY, Freddie
Also see SMILE
Also see TAYLOR, Roger

QUEEN & DAVID BOWIE P&R '81
Singles: 7-inch
ELEKTRA ... 3-5 81
Picture Sleeves
ELEKTRA ... 3-5 81
Also see BOWIE, David
Also see QUEEN

QUEEN ANNES
Singles: 7-inch
TRIANGLE (9272 "I Thought of You") ... 3-4 84
Picture Sleeves
TRIANGLE (9272 "I Thought of You") ... 3-4 84

QUEEN ANNE'S LACE
Singles: 7-inch
MONA LEE ... 4-8 68
LPs: 10/12-inch
CORAL ... 10-15 69

QUEEN BITCH
LPs: 10/12-inch
BLUE VALENTINE (3001"Queen Bitch") ... 10-15 83
(Picture disc.)

QUEEN CITY KIDS
LPs: 10/12-inch
EPIC ... 5-10 82

QUEEN CITY SHOW BAND
Singles: 7-inch
POW ... 4-8 66

QUEEN IDA
LPs: 10/12-inch
GNP ... 5-10 90s

QUEEN LATIFAH LP '89
LPs: 10/12-inch
TOMMY BOY ... 5-8 89

QUEEN'S NECTARINE MACHINE
LPs: 10/12-inch
ABC (666 "Mystical Powers") ... 15-25 69

QUEENSRYCHE LP '83
Singles: 7-inch
EMI ... 3-4 83-86
LPs: 10/12-inch
CAPITOL (30711 "Promised Land") 8-10 90s
EMI (Except 01435) ... 5-8 83-90
EMI (01436 "Operation Mind Crime") ... 20-25 88
EMI (SPRO-01436 "Operation Mind Crime") ... 70-80 88
(Promotional only picture disc. 500 made.)
EMI (04194 "Speak the Word") ... 10-20 88
(Promotional only interview.)
EMI (19006 "Queensryche") ... 20-30
(Promotional issue only. Issued in metal film can with photo.)
Members: Geoff Tate; Chris DeGarmo; Michael Wilton; Eddie Jackson; Scott Rokenfield.

QUENTINS
Singles: 7-inch
ANDIE ... 10-20 59

QUESENBERRY BROTHERS
Singles: 7-inch
ECHO ... 3-5
Picture Sleeves
ECHO ... 5-10

QUEST
Singles: 7-inch
GRAMAPHONE (1270 "The Last Days") ... 20-30 70

QUESTELL, Connie
Singles: 7-inch
DECCA (31783 "Straighten Up") ... 20-30 65
DECCA (31855 "Give Up Girl") ... 20-30 65

? & THE MYSTERIANS P&R/LP '66
(Question Mark & the Mysterians)
Singles: 7-inch
ABKCO ... 3-5 80s
CAMEO (428 "96 Tears") ... 5-10 66
CAMEO (441 "I Need Somebody") ... 5-10 66
CAMEO (467 "Can't Get Enough of You Baby") ... 5-10 67
CAMEO (479 "Girl") ... 5-10 67
CAMEO (496 "Do Something to Me") ... 5-10 67
CAPITOL (2162 "Make You Mine") ... 6-12 68
CHICORY (410 "Talk Is Cheap") ... 10-20 67
LUV (159 "Hot 'N' Groovin' ") ... 5-8 72
MILLION SELLER ... 3-4
PA-GO-GO (102 "96 Tears") ... 75-125 66
PEACOCK ("Time Is on My Side") ... 5-10
(Selection number not known.)
SUPER K (102 "Hang In") ... 5-10 69
TANGERINE (392 "Ain't It a Shame") ... 5-10
LPs: 10/12-inch
CAMEO (2004 "96 Tears") ... 50-100 66
CAMEO (2006 "Action") ... 50-100 67
Members: Rudy Martinez; Robert Martinez; Frank Rodriguez; Larry Borjas; Bob Balderamma; Frank Lugo.
Also see MYSTERIONS
Also see SEMI COLONS

QUESTION MARKS: see HOLLYWOOD FLAMES / Question Marks

QUESTION MARKS
Singles: 7-inch
FIRST (102 "Ballad of a Boy and a Girl") ... 20-30 59

QUESTS
(Quest's)
Singles: 7-inch
FENTON (2032 "Psychic") ... 50-75 66
FENTON (2086 "Shadows in the Night") ... 40-60 66
FENTON (2174 "Shadows in the Night") ... 15-25 67

QUICA, Leo
Singles: 7-inch
LIBERTY ... 5-10 58

QUICK R&B '81
Singles: 12-inch
EPIC ... 4-6 82
PAVILLION ... 4-6 81
Singles: 7-inch
EPIC (37000 series) ... 3-5 82
PAVILLION ... 3-5 81
LPs: 10/12-inch
EPIC ... 5-10 82

QUICK
Singles: 7-inch
EPIC (10516 "Ain't Nothin' Gonna Stop Me") ... 10-15 69
Member: Eric Carmen.
Also see CARMEN, Eric

QUICK
LPs: 10/12-inch
MERCURY ... 10-15 76

QUICK, Al
Singles: 7-inch
QUICK ... 4-8 63

QUICKBREATH
Singles: 7-inch
PROD. UNLIMITED........................ 8-12 60s
SHOW-PRO.................................. 8-12 60s

QUICKEST WAY OUT R&B '75
Singles: 7-inch
W.B. 3-5 75-76

QUICKLY, Tommy
Singles: 7-inch
LIBERTY 4-8 64

QUICKSAND
Singles: 7-inch
MERCURY 3-5 70

QUICKSILVER LP '68
(Quicksilver Messinger Service)
Singles: 7-inch
CAPITOL.................................... 4-8 68-76
LPs: 10/12-inch
CAPITOL (120 "Happy Trails").......20-30 69
CAPITOL (288 "Quicksilver Messenger Service")..............................30-50 69
CAPITOL (391 thru 819)...............10-25 69-71
CAPITOL (2904 "Quicksilver Messenger Service")..............................20-30 68
CAPITOL (11000 series)................10-15 72-75
CAPITOL (16000 series)................ 5-10 80
Members: John Cipollina; Dave Freiberg.
Also see BROGUES
Also see COPPERHEAD
Also see FANKHAUSER, Merrell
Also see HOPKINS, Nicky
Also see JEFFERSON AIRPLANE
Also see MILLER, Steve / Band / Quicksilver Messinger Service
Also see SAN FRANCISCO ALL STARS
Also see VALENTI, Dino

QUID
Singles: 7-inch
EAGLE (1169 "Merseyside")..........10-20 60s

QUIET ELEGANCE R&B '73
Singles: 7-inch
HI 3-5 72-77
Members: Frankie Gearing; Mildred Vaney; Lois Reeves.
Also see GLORIES
Also see MARTHA & VANDELLAS

QUIET RIOT P&R/LP '83
Singles: 12-inch
PASHA...................................... 4-6 83-85
Singles: 7-inch
CBS... 3-4 83
PASHA...................................... 3-4 83-86
Picture Sleeves
CBS... 3-4 83
PASHA...................................... 3-4 83-86
LPs: 10/12-inch
MOONSTONE............................. 5-10 93
PASHA (Except 8Z8-39203).......... 5-10 83-88
PASHA (8Z8-39203 "Metal Health") 8-12 83
(Picture disc.)
RHINO...................................... 5-8 93
Members: Kevin DuBrow; Rudy Sarzo; Frankie Banali; Randy Rhoads; Chuck Wright; Paul Shortino; Sean McNabb; Kenny Hillery; Carlos Cavazo.
Also see HEAR 'N AID
Also see OSBOURNE, Ozzy

QUIET SUN
LPs: 10/12-inch
ANTILLES 8-10 75

QUIJANO, Joe
Singles: 7-inch
COLUMBIA.................................. 4-8 63

QUILL
LPs: 10/12-inch
COTILLION 8-10 70

QUILLS
Singles: 7-inch
CASINO (106 "Whose Love, But Yours")...................................500-750 59

QUINAIMES BAND
LPs: 10/12-inch
ELEKTRA.................................10-15 71

QUINCY
LPs: 10/12-inch
COLUMBIA................................. 5-10 80

QUINELLA R&B '81
Singles: 7-inch
BECKET..................................... 3-5 81

QUINN, Aileen, & Orphans
Singles: 7-inch
COLUMBIA................................. 3-4 82
Picture Sleeves
COLUMBIA................................. 3-4 82
LPs: 10/12-inch
COLUMBIA................................. 5-10 82

QUINN, Andy
Singles: 7-inch
DECCA...................................... 5-10 58-59

QUINN, Anthony
(With the Harold Spina Singers)
Singles: 7-inch
CAPITOL.................................... 4-6 67
Picture Sleeves
CAPITOL.................................... 5-10 67

QUINN, Bottie
Singles: 7-inch
REED (1016 "Teenage Bop").........20-30 57

QUINN, Buddy
Singles: 7-inch
COULEE (126 "I Need an Angel") 10-15 68
Picture Sleeves
COULEE (126 "I Need an Angel") 15-20 68

QUINN, Carmel LP '55
Singles: 78 rpm
COLUMBIA................................. 3-5 55-56
Singles: 7-inch
COLUMBIA.................................5-10 55-56
DOT..4-6 64
HEADLINE 4-8 59-62
EPs: 7-inch
COLUMBIA.................................8-12 55
LPs: 10/12-inch
CAMDEN....................................10-15 65
COLUMBIA.................................15-25 55-56
DOT..10-15 65
HEADLINE 10-20 59-62
Also see GODFREY, Arthur /Carmel Quinn / Frank Parker / Janette Davis

QUINN, Carole
Singles: 7-inch
MGM 5-10 64-65

QUINN, Donnie
LPs: 10/12-inch
BIG K 10-20

QUINNS
Singles: 7-inch
CYCLONE (111 "Oh Starlight")..100-150 57
(No address shown on label.)
CYCLONE (111 "Oh Starlight")......50-75 57
(Company address shown under label name.)
LOST-NITE.................................4-8

QUINSTRELLS
Singles: 7-inch
MOXIE (105 "I Got a Girl").............20-30 65
Also see DEARLY BELOVED

QUINTEROS, Eddie
Singles: 7-inch
BRENT (7009 "Come Dance with Me")..15-25 60
BRENT (7012 "Lookin' for My Baby")......................................20-30 60
BRENT (7014 "Lindy Lou") 40-50 60
ED-DAR.....................................5-10 62
M&K 10-15 60s

QUINTESCENTS
Singles: 7-inch
VIBRA 8-12 60s

QUINTESSENCE
LPs: 10/12-inch
ISLAND 10-15 71

QUINTET
LPs: 10/12-inch
U.A. 10-15 71-72

QUINTETTE PLUS
Singles: 7-inch
SVR (1004 "Work Song")...............20-30 65
SVR (4392 "Grits 'N' Grease")........10-20 60s

QUINTO, Gina
Singles: 7-inch
M.V.R. 4-8 62
Also see QUINTO SISTERS

QUINTO SISTERS
Singles: 7-inch
COLUMBIA................................. 4-8 64
LPs: 10/12-inch
COLUMBIA.................................10-20 64
Also see QUINTO, Gina

QUINTONES
Singles: 78 rpm
GEE (1009 "I'm Willing")...............20-40 56
Singles: 7-inch
GEE (1009 "I'm Willing")...............50-75 56

QUINTONES
Singles: 7-inch
CHESS (1685 "I Try So Hard").......25-35 58
PARK (112 "More Than a Notion")...................................200-300 57
Also see WITHERSPOON, Jimmy, & Quintones

QUIN-TONES P&R/R&B '58
Singles: 7-inch
COLLECTABLES........................... 3-4 80s
HUNT (321 "Down the Aisle of Love")......................................20-30 58
HUNT (322 "What Am I to Do").......25-50 58
RED TOP (108 "Down the Aisle of Love")......................................50-75 58
(Blue label)
RED TOP (108 "Down the Aisle of Love")......................................20-30 59
(Red label)
RED TOP (116 "Oh Heavenly Father")....................................50-75 59
Members: Roberta Haymon; Phylis Carr; Carolyn Holmes; Ronnie Scott; Jeannie Crist; Ken Sexton.

QUINTONES
Singles: 7-inch
LEE (1113 "Liverlips")...................15-25 61
Also see FOSTER, Pat, & Quintones

QUINTONES
Singles: 7-inch
PHILLIPS INT'L (3586 "Times Sho' Gettin' Ruff")......................................10-15 62

QUINTONES
Singles: 7-inch
JORDAN (1601 "Just a Little Loving") 200-300

QUINTRELS
Singles: 7-inch
MOXIE.......................................5-8
Also see BELOVED ONES
Also see INTRUDERS

QUIRE
LPs: 10/12-inch
GRYPHON 8-10 76

QUIVER
LPs: 10/12-inch
W.B. 10-15 71-72

QUIST, Jack C&W '82
Singles: 7-inch
GRUDGE 3-4 89
MEMORY MACHINE.....................3-4 82

QUOTATIONS
Singles: 7-inch
VERVE (10245 "Imagination") 15-25 61
VERVE (10252 "This Love of Mine")......................................20-30 62
VERVE (10261 "See You in September")................................20-30 62

QUOTATIONS
Singles: 7-inch
ADMIRAL (300 "It's a Shame") ..150-200 61
ADMIRAL (753 "In the Night")....250-350 64

QUOTATIONS
Singles: 7-inch
DI VENUS 8-12 68
DOWNSTAIRS.............................5-10 70
IMPERIAL 8-12 68-69
Member: Linda Evans.
Also see EVANS, Linda

QWORYMEN & Perfect Stranger
Singles: 7-inch
RHINO/ERIKA (107 "Beatlerap")......8-12 82
(Square picture disc with front cover artwork.)
RHINO/ERIKA (107 "Beatlerap")......5-10 82
(Square picture disc with back cover artwork.)

Q-ZEEN
Singles: 7-inch
YOLO (15 "Writing Your Name")......8-12 60s

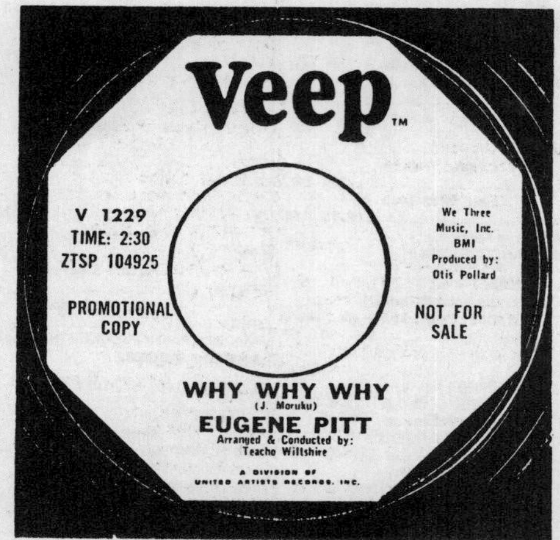

R

R JOHN
Singles: 7-inch
USD (1041 "Soul Man") 10-20 66

R. ROGUES
Singles: 7-inch
WASP (102 "The Sound") 25-35 60s

R.A.F.
Singles: 12-inch
CARRERE 4-6
LPs: 10/12-inch
A&M 5-10 80-81

R.C. & TAMBORINES
Singles: 7-inch
IKON 4-8

RCA CAMDEN ROCKERS
LPs: 10/12-inch
CAMDEN 10-20 59-60

RCR P&R/R&B '80
Singles: 7-inch
RADIO 3-5 80
Members: Donna Rhodes; Charles Chalmers; Sandy Rhodes.

R DELLS
(R-Dells)
Singles: 7-inch
DADE (1806 "You Say") 40-60 60

R DELLS
(R-Dells)
Singles: 7-inch
ADMIRAL (4014 "Drag Race") 20-30 60s
GONE (5128 "That's What I Want") 15-25 62

R.D.M. BAND
(Rovescio Della Medaglia)
Singles: 7-inch
VIRTUE 3-6 69
LPs: 10/12-inch
PETERS INT'L 8-12 74

R.E.M. P&R '83
Singles: 7-inch
EVA-TONE (105900 "Dark Globe") . 5-10 90
(Promotional issue, *Sassy* magazine insert. Add $3 to $5 if accompanied by the appropriate issue of *Sassy*.)
HIBTONE (Radio Free Europe") 50-75 81
I.R.S. 3-8 82-87
MCA 3-5 85
W.B. 3-6 88-93
Picture Sleeves
I.R.S. 4-8 82-88
W.B. 3-4 89
EPs: 7-inch
I.R.S. 5-10 82
LPs: 10/12-inch
I.R.S. 5-10 82-88
MFSL (231 "Murmur") 20-25 94
(Half-speed mastered.)
W.B. 5-8 88-93
Members: J. Michael Stipe; Bill Berry; Peter Buck; Mike Mills.
Also see CYNICS
Also see GOLDEN PALOMINOS
Also see HINDU LOVE GODS

REO SPEEDWAGON LP '74
Singles: 7-inch
EPIC (Except 10000 & 11000 series) 3-5 75-90
EPIC (10000 & 11000 series) 3-5 72-74
Picture Sleeves
EPIC 3-5 80-88
EPs: 7-inch
CSP 4-8 81
(Nestles candy promotional issue.)
LPs: 10/12-inch
EPIC (Except 40000 series) 6-12 71-90
EPIC (40000 series) 12-15 81-82
(Half-speed mastered.)
Promotional LPs
EPIC (643 "Nine Lives") 15-20 80s
EPIC (36844 "Hi Infidelity") 50-75 81
(Picture disc, made for Western Merchanders. All copies mistakenly have music by unknown artists. 100 made.)
Members: Kevin Cronin; Neal Doughty; Al Gratzer; Bruce Hall; Terry Luttrell.
Also see MAY, Brian
Also see SUBURBAN 9 to 5

RG'S ALL NITE FUNK BAND
Singles: 7-inch
HOTRAX 3-5 80-81

R.J. & RIOTS
Singles: 7-inch
J (101 "Little Honda") 20-30 60s

R.J.'S LATEST ARRIVAL R&B '81
(Ralph James)
Singles: 7-inch
ARIOLA AMERICA 3-5 79
ATLANTIC 3-4 85
BUDDAH 3-5 81
LARC 3-4 83
EMI MANHATTAN 3-4 88
MANHATTAN 3-4 87
QUALITY/RFC 3-4
SUTRA 3-5 81
ZOO YORK 3-5 82
LPs: 10/12-inch
ARIOLA AMERICA 5-10 79
ATLANTIC 5-8 85

RPM
Singles: 7-inch
W.B. 3-4 84-85
LPs: 10/12-inch
EMI AMERICA 5-10 82
W.B. 5-8 84

RPMs
Singles: 78 rpm
AMBASSADOR 5-10 54
Singles: 7-inch
AMBASSADOR 8-12 54
MALA 4-8 65
PORT 4-8 63

R.P.S.
LPs: 10/12-inch
MARS 30-40

R.T. POTLICKERS
Singles: 7-inch
HOOKS 4-8

RA CAN ROW
LPs: 10/12-inch
EYE (8108 "Acid Rock for the Eighties") 10-15 82
(Includes "My Summer Vacation" postcard and insert brochure.)
Members: Don Schott; Steve Sailer; Rick Biszantz; Paul Haneberg.

RABB, Johnny
Singles: 7-inch
BLOTTO 5-8 82
Picture Sleeves
BLOTTO 5-8 82

RABBIT
LPs: 10/12-inch
CAPRICORN 5-10 77
ISLAND 8-12 73-74
Also see KOSSOFF / Kirke / Tetsu / Rabbit

RABBIT, Jimmy
(With the Karats; Jimmy Rabbitt)
Singles: 7-inch
ATCO 3-5 72
JOSIE (947 "My Girl") 8-12 65
KNIGHT (1049 "Pushover") 20-30 65
KNIGHT (1052 "My Girl") 20-30 65
SOUTHERN SOUND (200 "Pushover") 15-25 65
Also see POSITIVELY 13 O'CLOCK

RABBIT 1
LPs: 10/12-inch
BELL 10-15 71

RABBITT, Eddie C&W '74
Singles: 7-inch
DATE 4-8 68
ELEKTRA (Except 378) 3-5 74-83
ELEKTRA (378 "Song of Ireland") 5-10 78
(Colored vinyl—green of course. With green insert. Promotional issue only.)
RCA 3-4 85-89
20TH FOX 5-10 64
UNIVERSAL 3-4 89
W.B. 3-5 83-85
Picture Sleeves
ELEKTRA 3-5 81
LPs: 10/12-inch
ELEKTRA 5-10 75-82
RCA 5-8 86
W.B. 5-8 84-85
Also see FRICKE, Janie

RABBITT, Eddie, & Crystal Gayle C&W/P&R '82
Singles: 7-inch
ELEKTRA 3-5 82
Also see GAYLE, Crystal

RABBITT, Eddie, & Juice Newton C&W '86
Singles: 7-inch
RCA 3-4 86
Also see NEWTON, Juice
Also see RABBITT, Eddie

RABBITT, Jimmy, & Renegade C&W '76
Singles: 7-inch
CAPITOL 3-5 76
Session: Waylon Jennings.
Also see JENNINGS, Waylon

RABBLE
Singles: 7-inch
AQUARIUS (5012 "Time Is on My Side") 15-25 60s
RCA (3409 "I'm a Laboundy Barn") 10-20 60s
TRANSWORLD (1675 "Golden Girl") 15-25 67
TRANSWORLD (1683 "Please Set Me Free") 15-25 67
TRANSWORLD (1692 "Rising of the Sun") 15-25 67
TRANSWORLD (1703 "Miss Money Green") 15-25 68
LPs: 10/12-inch
ROULETTE (42010 "The Rabble") 25-50
TRANSWORLD (6700 "The Rabble Rabble") 100-150 67
All Rabble releases listed above are Canadian.
TRANSWORLD (6707 "Give Us Back Elaine") 100-150 68
All Rabble releases listed above are Canadian.

RABIN, Mike
(With the Demons; with Toggery Five)
Singles: 7-inch
TOWER 5-10 64

RABIN, Trevor LP '78
Singles: 7-inch
CHRYSALIS 3-5 78-80
LPs: 10/12-inch
CHRYSALIS 5-10 78-80
ELEKTRA 5-8 89

RABKIN, Eddie
Singles: 7-inch
COLUMBIA 3-6 67

RABON, Michael
(With the Five Americans; with Choctaw)
Singles: 7-inch
ABNAK (134 "Virginia Girl") 4-8 69
(Colored vinyl.)
UNI 3-5 70-71
LPs: 10/12-inch
UNI 8-12 71
Also see FIVE AMERICANS
Also see GLADSTONE

RACE R&B '83
Singles: 12-inch
BLACK SUIT 5-10 82
Singles: 7-inch
OCEAN FRONT 3-4 83

RACE MARBLES
Singles: 7-inch
CAPITOL (72312 "Like a Dribbling Fram") 10-20 60s
TOWER (194 "Like a Dribbling Fram") 15-25 66

RACER X
LPs: 10/12-inch
SHRAPNEL 5-8 86
Members: Jeff Martin; Paul Gilbert.

RACERS
Singles: 7-inch
RSVP (1115 "Skate Board") 15-25 65

RACEY
Singles: 7-inch
INFINITY 3-5 79

RACHABANE, Barney
Singles: 12-inch
JIVE 4-6 86

RACHEAL & STRAWBERRY SHEPHARDS
Singles: 7-inch
UNI 3-5 70

RACHEL & ORIGINALS
Singles: 7-inch
NITE STAR (010 "I'll Always Remember") 150-200 62
Member: Rachel Legerretta.

RACHEL & REVOLVERS
Singles: 7-inch
DOT (16392 "The Revo-Lution") 250-300 62
DOT (16392 "The Revo-Lution") 200-250 62
(White label. Promotional issue only.)

RACHELL, Yank
Singles: 78 rpm
RCA 10-15 48

RACHELLS
Singles: 7-inch
DYNAMIC 8-12

RACING CARS LP '77
Singles: 7-inch
CHRYSALIS 3-5 77-78
LPs: 10/12-inch
CHRYSALIS 5-10 77-78

RACKET SQUAD
(Fenways)
Singles: 7-inch
JUBILEE (5591 "Higher than High") 15-25 67
JUBILEE (5601 "Romeo & Juliet") .10-15 67
JUBILEE (5613 "Loser") 10-15 68
JUBILEE (5623 "Higher Than High") 10-15 68
JUBILEE (5628 "That's How Much I Love My Baby") 10-15 68
JUBILEE (5638 "Loser") 10-15 68
JUBILEE (5657 "I'll Never Forget You Love") 10-15 69
JUBILEE (5682 "In Your Arms") 10-20 69
LPs: 10/12-inch
JUBILEE (8015 "Racket Squad") ..25-50 68
JUBILEE (8026 "Corners of Your Mind") 25-50 69
Member: Joey Covington.
Also see FENWAYS
Also see JEFFERSON AIRPLANE
Also see VIBRA-SONICS

RADAR, Don
(Don Rader)
Singles: 7-inch
STRATE 8 (1507 "Rock and Roll Grandpa") 75-100 59
STRATE 8 (1508 "She Sure Can Rock Me") 75-100 60

RADARS
Singles: 78 rpm
ABBEY (3025 "You Belong to Me") 50-100 51
PRESTIGE (478 "I Want a Little Girl") 50-100 52

RADARS
Singles: 7-inch
YEW (1004 "Soul Serenade") 8-12 60s

RADCLIFFE, Jimmy
(With Steve Karmen's Band)
Singles: 7-inch
AURORA (154 "My Ship Is Comin' In") 15-25 65
MUSICOR 10-20 62-64
RCA 5-10 69
SHOUT 8-12 66
U.A. 5-10 68

RADCLIFFE, P. Sterling, with His Sterling Sounds
Singles: 7-inch
VIA 4-6 77

RADER, Quantrell
Singles: 7-inch
RCA 8-15 63-64

RADER, Quantrell & Kathy
Singles: 7-inch
RCA 5-10 64
Also see RADER, Quantrell

RADHA KRISHNA TEMPLE
Singles: 7-inch
APPLE 5-10 69-70
(Commercial issues.)
APPLE 25-35 70
(Promotional issues.)
Picture Sleeves
APPLE 8-12 70
LPs: 10/12-inch
APPLE (3376 "Radha Krishna Temple") 15-20 71

RADIANCE R&B/D&D '85
(With Andrea Stone)
Singles: 12-inch
ARE 'N BE 4-6 83
Singles: 7-inch
W.B. 3-4 85

RADIANCE
Singles: 12-inch
QWEST 4-6 85

RADIANTS
(With Art Gordon & Music Maestro Orchestra)
Singles: 7-inch
WIZZ (713 "Ra Cha Cha") 200-300 58

RADIANTS P&R '62
(Maurice McAlister & Radiants; Maurice & Radiants)
Singles: 7-inch
CHESS 5-10 62-69
ERIC 3-4 70s
TWINIGHT 3-5 71
Members: Maurice McAlister; Wallace Sampson; Jerome Brooks; Elzie Butler; Green McLauren; Frank McCollum; Leonard Caston, Jr; James Jameson; Mitchell Bullock; Victor Caston.
Also see CASTON & MAJORS
Also see GREATER HARVEST BAPTIST CHURCH CHOIR
Also see MAURICE & MAC
Also see McALISTER, Maurice

RADIANTS
Singles: 7-inch
SOMA (1422 "Special Girl") 25-35 60s

RADIATORS LP '87
Singles: 7-inch
EPIC 3-4 87-89
LPs: 10/12-inch
EPIC 5-8 87-89
Members: Dave Malone; Frank Bua; Reggie Scanlan; Ed Volker; Camile Baudoin; Glenn Sears.

RADICE, Mark R&B '76
Singles: 7-inch
U.A. 3-5 76
LPs: 10/12-inch
ROADSHOW 8-12 77

RADIO HEART
(Featuring Gary Numan)
Singles: 7-inch
CRITIQUE 3-4 87
LPs: 10/12-inch
CRITIQUE (Black vinyl) 5-8 87
CRITIQUE (Picture discs) 8-12 87

RADIO HEARTS
Singles: 7-inch
GREENLINE 3-5 80

RADLEY, Raunch
(Hank Davis)
LPs: 10/12-inch
DUCKTAIL (502 "Alive Since '55") .10-15 79
REDITA 10-15
Also see DAVIS, Hank

RADNER, Gilda LP '79
Singles: 7-inch
W.B. 3-5 79-80
LPs: 10/12-inch
W.B. 5-10 79

RADO, Janice
(Jan Rado)
Singles: 7-inch
BELL 3-5 73
EDSEL 5-10 60

RAE, Della
Singles: 7-inch
GROOVE 4-8 64-65
RCA 4-8 65-67

RAE, Donny, & Defiants
Singles: 7-inch
ARLEN 10-15 64

RAE, Fonda R&B '82
(Fonda Raye)
Singles: 12-inch
POSSE 4-6 83
VANGUARD 4-6 82
Singles: 7-inch
VANGUARD 3-4 82
Also see WISH

RAE, Lana C&W '72
Singles: 7-inch
DECCA 3-5 72

RAE, Lenny
Singles: 7-inch
ASSOCIATED ARTISTS 4-8 65

RAE, Linda
Singles: 7-inch
MIKE (4002 "Tweenager") 15-25 66
MIKE (4010 "The Time to Love Is Now") 25-50 66

RAE, Nora
Singles: 7-inch
OUR (305 "Real Cool Kitty") 50-100 58

RAE, Penny
Singles: 7-inch
INFINITY 4-8 62

RAE, Robbie D&D '83
Singles: 12-inch
QUALITY 4-6 83
Singles: 7-inch
QUALITY 3-4 83

RAE, Ronnie, & Dynamics
Singles: 7-inch
R-J-R (702 "Breaktime") 10-20 64

RAEBURN, Boyd
EPs: 7-inch
COLUMBIA 10-15 56
LPs: 10/12-inch
COLUMBIA 20-25 56-57

RAEKWON
LPs: 10/12-inch
RCA 8-10 90s

RAELETTES P&R/R&B '67
(Raeletts; Raelets)
Singles: 7-inch
TRC 3-5 70
TANGERINE 3-6 67-73
LPs: 10/12-inch
TRC 8-12 71-72
TANGERINE 8-12 72
Members: Clydie King; Mable John; Merry Clayton; Margie Hendrix; Earl Jean McCree; Pat Lyles; Minnie Ripperton; Alexandra Brown; Gwendolyn Berry; Mabel John; Susaye Green; Vernita Amoss; Estella Yarbrough; Odia Coates.
Also see CHARLES, Ray
Also see CLAYTON, Merry
Also see EARL-JEAN
Also see COATES, Odia
Also see HENDRIX, Margie
Also see JOHN, Mable
Also see KING, Clydie
Also see RIPERTON, Minnie
Also see TURNER, Ike & Tina

RAES P&R '78
Singles: 7-inch
A&M 3-5 78
LPs: 10/12-inch
A&M 5-10 79
Members: Robbie Rae; Cherrill Rae.

RAETZLOFF, Ed
LPs: 10/12-inch
NEW PAX 5-10 80

RAFEY, Susan
Singles: 7-inch
JUBILEE 4-8 64-65
VERVE 4-8 65-67
LPs: 10/12-inch
VERVE 15-20 65

RAFFERTY, Gerry P&R/LP '78
Singles: 12-inch
U.A. (171 "Baker Street") 5-10 78
Singles: 7-inch
BLUE THUMB 3-5 72
LIBERTY 3-4 82
SIGNPOST 3-5 72
U.A. 3-5 77-80
Picture Sleeves
U.A. 3-5 77-78
LPs: 10/12-inch
BLUE THUMB 8-10 73-78
LIBERTY 5-8 82
MFSL 25-50 81
U.A. 8-10 78-80
VISA 5-10 78
Also see HUMBLEBUMS
Also see STEALERS WHEEL

RAFFERTY, Jim
Singles: 7-inch
LONDON 3-5 78
LPs: 10/12-inch
LONDON 5-10 78

RAFTSMEN
Singles: 7-inch
20TH FOX 4-8 67
RAG DOLLS P&R '64
Singles: 7-inch
MALA 8-12 65
Member: Jean Thomas.
Also see ANGIE & CHICKLETTES
RAG DOLLS / Caliente Combo
Singles: 7-inch
PARKWAY 5-10 64
Also see RAG DOLLS
RAGA & TALAS
Singles: 7-inch
WORLD PACIFIC 4-8 66
RAGAMUFFINS
Singles: 7-inch
TOLLIE 10-20 64
RAGE
LPs: 10/12-inch
CARRERE/MIRAGE 5-10 81
LIBERTY 5-8
RAGE, Alfred
Singles: 7-inch
SUITE 4-8 62
RAGE AGAINST THE MACHINE
Singles: 7-inch
EPIC 3-4 92
Picture Sleeves
EPIC 3-4 92
RAGGAMUFFINS
Singles: 7-inch
SEVILLE (141 "Four Days of Rain") 10-20 67
RAGING SLAB LP '89
LPs: 10/12-inch
RCA 5-8 89
RAGIN' STORMS
Singles: 7-inch
JAMIE 5-10 61
RAGING STORMS
Singles: 7-inch
FLAMES (1019 "High Octane") 25-35 60s
TRAN ATLAS 10-15 62
WARWICK 10-15 62
RAGLAND, Lou
(With the Bandmasters)
Singles: 7-inch
AMY (988 "Travel Alone") 100-200 67
WAY OUT (2605 "Never Let Me Go") 150-250 64
RAGNATION
Singles: 7-inch
BELL 3-5 71
RAGON, Don
Singles: 7-inch
WINDOW (1009 "Jungle Rock") 10-20 59
RAGS & RICHES
Singles: 12-inch
POLYDOR 4-6 85
Singles: 7-inch
POLYDOR 3-4 85
LPs: 10/12-inch
CASABLANCA 5-8 83
POLYDOR 5-8 85
RAGS OF RICHES
Singles: 7-inch
WEBCO (105 "Up on the Roof") 10-20 69
RAHEEM
LPs: 10/12-inch
A&M 5-8 88
RAIA, Frank, & Rhythmaires
Singles: 7-inch
INKREDIBLE (4479 "Mess Up") 8-12
RAICEVIK, Nik Pascal
(Nik Pascal)
LPs: 10/12-inch
NARCO (102 "Beyond the End") 20-30 71
NARCO (123 "Zero Gravity") 10-20 75
NARCO (321 "Magnetic Web") 10-20 73
NARCO (666 "Sixth Ear") 15-25 72
RAIDERS
Singles: 7-inch
ANDEX (4015 "Hocus Pocus") 75-100 59
ATCO (6125 "Castle of Love") 50-75 58
BRUNSWICK (55090 "Walking Through the Jungle") 15-25 58
RAIDERS
Singles: 7-inch
LIBERTY 4-8 61-62
LPs: 10/12-inch
LIBERTY 15-25 62
Member: Tommy Allsup.
Also see ALLSUP, Tommy
RAIDERS
Singles: 7-inch
VAN (00262 "Stick Shift") 25-50 62
VAN (00663 "On a Straight Away") 15-25 63
VAN (00763 "Supercharged") 15-25 63
VAN (01064 "Raisin' Cain") 15-25 64
VEE JAY (504 "Stick Shift") 8-10 63
RAIDERS
Singles: 7-inch
KORY (1256 "Take It Slow") 10-20 66
RAIDERS
Singles: 7-inch
SPRING DALE (102 "Raider's Rhythm") 40-50 64
RAIDERS & Paul Revere: see REVERE, Paul, & Raiders
RAIK'S PROGRESS
Singles: 7-inch
LIBERTY (55930 "Why Did You Rob Us, Tank") 15-25 66
RAIL LP '84
Singles: 7-inch
EMI AMERICA 3-4 84
LPs: 10/12-inch
DYNASTY 5-10 80
EMI AMERICA 5-8 84
PASSPORT 5-8 83
RAIL & CO.
(Rail)
Singles: 7-inch
SEA-WEST (119 "Rockin' You") 5-10 77
RAILHEAD
Singles: 12-inch
WAX-TRAX 5-8 87
Singles: 7-inch
WAX-TRAX 3-4 87
RAILWAY CHILDREN
LPs: 10/12-inch
VIRGIN 5-8 87
RAIN
Singles: 7-inch
A.P.I. (336 "E.S.P.") 20-30 66
A.P.I. (337 "Here You Cry") 20-30 67
LONDON (107 "E.S.P.") 15-25 66
LONDON (111 "Here You Cry") 20-30 67
RAIN
Singles: 7-inch
BELL 3-5 72
MGM (13622 "Take It Away") 10-20 66
PARAMOUNT (0087 "Show Me the Road Home") 10-15 71
LPs: 10/12-inch
WHAZOO (3046 "Live Xmas Night") 100-150 68
Also see DARTELLS
RAIN
Singles: 7-inch
H&L (4675 "Get on Your Job") 4-6 76
RAIN & TEARS
Singles: 7-inch
PHILIPS 4-8 68
RAIN DROPS
(With Ernie Freeman Orchestra)
Singles: 7-inch
SPIN IT (104 "Heaven in Love") 100-150 56
SPIN IT (106 "Little One") 100-150 56
Member: Henry Houston.
Also see FREEMAN, Ernie
RAIN PARADE
Singles: 7-inch
LLAMA 3-5 82
LPs: 10/12-inch
LLAMA 8-10 82
Members: Steven Roback; Matt Piucci; Will Glenn; Michael Murphy; Ed Kalwa.
Also see BANGLES
Also see DREAM SYNDICATE
RAINBEAUS
Singles: 7-inch
WORLD PACIFIC (810 "Maybe It's Wrong") 15-25 60
RAINBO
Singles: 7-inch
ROULETTE (7030 "John, You Went Too Far This Time") 10-20 69
Member: Cissy Spacek.
RAINBOW
LPs: 10/12-inch
GNP (2049 "After the Storm") 15-20 69
RAINBOW LP '77
Singles: 12-inch
MERCURY (195 "Stone Cold") 5-10 82
(Colored vinyl.)
Singles: 7-inch
MERCURY 3-4 82-83
POLYDOR 3-5 79
Picture Sleeves
MERCURY 3-4 82-83
LPs: 10/12-inch
MERCURY 5-10 82-86
OYSTER 8-12 77
POLYDOR 5-10 78-81
Members: Ritchie Blackmore; Roger Glover; Cozy Powell; Ronnie James Dio; Joe Turner; Tony Carey.
Also see ALCATRAZZ
Also see BLACKMORE'S RAINBOW
Also see CAREY, Tony
Also see GLOVER, Roger
RAINBOW
LPs: 10/12-inch
QUARK 5-10
RAINBOW, Christopher
LPs: 10/12-inch
EMI 8-10 79
POLYDOR 8-12 75-77
Also see PARSONS, Alan, Project
RAINBOW, Little Mary
Singles: 7-inch
PICADILLY 5-8 60s
RAINBOW BAND
LPs: 10/12-inch
ELEKTRA 8-12 71
RAINBOW CANYON
LPs: 10/12-inch
CAPITOL 8-10 74
RAINBOW PRESS
Singles: 7-inch
MR. G (817 "There's a War On") 8-12 68
MR. G (821 "Last Platoon") 8-12 69
LPs: 10/12-inch
MR. G (9003 "There's a War On") .. 20-30 69
MR. G (9004 "Sunday Funnies") 20-30 69
Members: Joe Groff; Dave Troup; Larry Milton; Charles Osborn; Marc Ellis. Bill Vergin.
RAINBOW PROMISE
LPs: 10/12-inch
NEW WINE (1 "Rainbow Promise") 200-300 70
RAINBOW RHYTHMAIRES: see CENTER, Sandy
RAINBOW SHIP
Singles: 7-inch
DUNHILL 4-6 69
RAINBOWS
("Featuring Sonny Spencer")
Singles: 78 rpm
PILGRIM (703 "Mary Lee") 10-20 56
PILGRIM (711 "Shirley") 50-100 56
RAMA (209 "They Say") 100-150 56
RED ROBIN (134 "Mary Lee") 200-300 54
Singles: 7-inch
ARGYLE (1012 "Shirley") 15-25 62
FIRE (1012 "Mary Lee") 10-20 60
PILGRIM (703 "Mary Lee") 25-35 56
PILGRIM (711 "Shirley") 150-200 56
RAMA (209 "They Say") 400-500 56
RED ROBIN (134 "Mary Lee") 400-600 54
Red Robin 141, Originals of *Stay/Shirley*, do not exist – only bootlegs.
Members: Sonny Spencer; Ron Miles; Don Covay; John Berry; Henry Womble; Don Watts; Frank Hardy; Jim Knowland; Chester Simmons.
Also see COVAY, Don
Also see SPENCER, Sonny
RAINBOWS
Singles: 7-inch
MGM (13058 "Ole Man's Twist") 20-25 62
RAINBOWS
Singles: 7-inch
DAVE (908 "I Know") 15-25 63
DAVE (909 "It Wouldn't Be Right") 20-30 63
GRAMO (5508 "Till Tomorrow") 10-20
Members: Duval Potter; Joe Walls; Layton McDonald; Victor English; Alvin Saunders.
RAINBOWS
Singles: 7-inch
DOT (16612 "My Ringo") 10-15 64
DOT (16920 "Down the Block") 5-10 66
RAINBOWS
Singles: 7-inch
EPIC (9900 "Ju Ju Hand" 4-8 66
JAMIE 4-8 67
RAINBOWS
Singles: 7-inch
CAPITOL 4-8 67-68
INSTANT 4-8 68
RAINBOWS
Singles: 12-inch
FOX-MOOR (1000 "Fourever Seasons") 8-10 81
Also see RANDY & RAINBOWS
RAINBOWS
Singles: 7-inch
BARON 3-5
RAINBOWS' END
Singles: 7-inch
KEF 4-6
RAINDROPS
(With the Foxes of Marrow Orchestra)
Singles: 7-inch
VEGA (105 "Dim Those Lights") 100-200 58
RAINDROPS
Singles: 7-inch
STARDAY (368 "I Don't Want a Sweetheart") 20-30 58
STARDAY (374 "Raiddrops") 20-30 58
RAINDROPS
Singles: 7-inch
CAPITOL (4136 "Rain") 20-30 59
HAMILTON (50021 "Oh Why") 15-25 59
RAINDROPS
Singles: 7-inch
CORSAIR (104 "Maybe") 50-100 60
DORE (561 "Maybe") 20-30 60
RAINDROPS
Singles: 7-inch
IMPERIAL (5785 "[I Remember] In the Still of the Night") 20-30 61
Also see JUMPIN' TONES
RAINDROPS P&R/R&B '63
Singles: 7-inch
JUBILEE (5444 "What a Guy") 15-25 63
JUBILEE (5455 "The Kind of Boy You Can't Forget") 15-25 63
JUBILEE (5466 "That Boy John") 15-25 63
JUBILEE (5469 "Book of Love") 15-25 64
JUBILEE (5475 "Let's Go Together") 15-25 64
JUBILEE (5487 "One More Tear") . 15-25 64
JUBILEE (5497 "Don't Let Go") 15-25 65
VIRGO 4-6 73
LPs: 10/12-inch
JUBILEE (J-5023 "Raindrops") 40-60 63
(Monaural.)
JUBILEE (SJ-5023 "Raindrops") 50-80 63
(Stereo.)
MURRAY HILL 8-10 80s
Members: Jeff Barry; Ellie Greenwich. (The third person pictured on the Roulette LP cover, Ellie's sister, Laura, is not heard on their records.)
Also see BARRY, Jeff
Also see GREENWICH, Ellie
RAINDROPS
Singles: 7-inch
AVENUE D (0016 "Jingle Bell Stomp") 4-6 89
(Black vinyl.)
AVENUE D (0016 "Jingle Bell Stomp") 10-15 89
(Yellow vinyl. Reportedly 100 made.)
RAINER, Chris
Singles: 7-inch
REDHEAD 10-15
RAINES, Jerry
Singles: 7-inch
DREW-BLAN (1001 "Dangerous Redhead") 30-50 61
DREW-BLAN (1003 "Barefoot Rock") 30-50 61
MERCURY (71585 "Dangerous Redhead") 15-25 60
RAINES, Leon C&W '83
Singles: 7-inch
AMERICAN SPOTLIGHT 3-4 83-84
ATLANTIC AMERICA 3-4 84-85
SOUTHERN TRACKS 3-4 87
RAINES, Rita P&R '56
Singles: 78 rpm
DEED 5-10 56
JAMIE 5-10 57
Singles: 7-inch
DEED 8-12 56
JAMIE 8-12 57
RAINEY, Big Memphis Ma: see MARAINEY, Big Memphis
RAINEY, Ma P&R '25
(Gertrude Rainey)
Singles: 78 rpm
PARAMOUNT (12000 series) .. 500-1000 24-38
LPs: 10/12-inch
BIOGRAPH 8-12 67-69
MILESTONE 8-12 67-74
RAINFORD, Tina C&W '77
Singles: 7-inch
EPIC 3-5 77
LPs: 10/12-inch
EPIC 5-10 77
RAINMAKERS
Sngles: 7-inch
DISCOTHEQUE 10-15 60s
LEE (9178 "Do You Feel It") 15-25 60s
PHALANX (1029 "Tell Her No") 15-25 67
RAINMAKERS LP '86
Sngles: 7-inch
ERA 5-10 65
RAINMAKERS
Singles: 7-inch
MERCURY 3-4 86
LPs: 10/12-inch
MERCURY 5-8 86-87
RAINSFORD, Billy
Singles: 7-inch
HERMITAGE (803 "Starry Eyes") 50-100
RAINSFORD, Willie C&W '77
Singles: 7-inch
LOUISIANA HAYRIDE 3-5 77
RAINTREE MINORITY
(Raintree)
Singles: 7-inch
AMARET (102 "You're Just What I Was Looking for Today") 5-10 69
AMARET (127 "Keep the Candle Burning") 5-10 70
RAINVILLE, Doris
Singles: 7-inch
BLUE RIVER 4-8 63
RAINWATER, Jack C&W '77
Singles: 7-inch
LAURIE 3-5 77
RAINWATER, Marvin C&W/P&R '57
Singles: 78 rpm
CORAL 5-10 56
MGM (Except 12240 & 12370) 5-15 55-57
MGM (12240 "Hot and Cold") 10-15 56
MGM (12370 "Get off the Stool") 10-15 56
Singles: 7-inch
BRAVE 4-6 63-67
CORAL 8-12 56
HILLTOP 5-10 70s
MGM (12000 & 12100 series) 10-20 55
MGM (12240 "Hot and Cold") 30-40 56
MGM (12313 "Why Did You Have to Go and Love Me") 10-20 56
MGM (12370 "Get off the Stool") 30-40 56
MGM (12412 thru 12938) 5-10 57-60
NU TRAYL 3-5 76
U.A. 4-6 65-66
W.B. 3-5 69-70
WARWICK 5-10 61
EPs: 7-inch
MGM (1464/1465/1466 "Songs by Marvin Rainwater") 15-25 57
(Price is for any of three volumes.)
LPs: 10/12-inch
CROWN 5-10 60s
GUEST STAR 5-10
MARK IV 8-12
MGM (3534 "Songs by Marvin Rainwater") 50-100 57
MGM (3721 "With a Heart With a Beat") 50-100 58
MGM (4046 "Gonna Find Me a Bluebird") 50-100 62
MOUNT VERNON 8-10
SPINORAMA 8-10 60s
Also see DEAN, Jimmy / Marvin Rainwater
Also see FRANCIS, Connie, & Marvin Rainwater
RAINY DAY
Singles: 7-inch
SUNBURST 3-5 73
RAINY DAY FRIENDS
Singles: 7-inch
WORLD PACIFIC 4-8 67
RAINY DAY PEOPLE
Singles: 7-inch
HBR (512 "Junior Executive") 15-25 67
RAINY DAYS
Singles: 7-inch
PANIK (7542 "Turn on Your Lovelight") 15-25 66
PANIK (7566 "I Can Only Give You Everything") 15-25 66
RAINY DAZE P&R '67
Singles: 7-inch
CHICORY (404 "That Acapulco Gold") 10-15 67
UNI 5-10 67
WHITE WHALE 5-10 68
LPs: 10/12-inch
UNI (73002 "That Acapulco Gold") 15-25 67
Members: Tim Gilbert; Bob Heckendorf; Mac Ferris; Kip Gilbert; Sam Fuller.
Also see GILBERT, Tim
RAIZY DAZE / King Toke
Singles: 7-inch
I.P. (100 "That Acapulco Gold") 25-35 66
Also see RAINY DAZE
RAISE THE DRAGON
Singles: 7-inch
I.R.S. 3-4 84
LPs: 10/12-inch
I.R.S. 5-8 84
RAISER, Freddie
Singles: 78 rpm
MGM 5-10 55
Singles: 7-inch
MGM (12269 "Rock & Roll Rhinelander") 10-20 55
RAISINS
Singles: 7-inch
DE-LITE 3-6 69
RAITT, Bonnie LP '72
Singles: 7-inch
CAPITOL 3-4 89-91
W.B. 3-4 72-86
Picture Sleeves
W.B. 4-8 72-79
LPs: 10/12-inch
CAPITOL 5-8 89-91
W.B. 6-12 71-86
Session: Van Dyke Parks.
Also see MULDAUR, Geoff, & Bonnie Raitt
Also see PARKS, Van Dyke
RAITT, Bonnie / Gilley's "Urban Cowboy" Band
Singles: 7-inch
FULL MOON/ASYLUM 3-5 80
Picture Sleeves
FULL MOON/ASYLUM 3-5 80
Also see RAITT, Bonnie
RAJAHS
(Nutmegs)
Singles: 7-inch
KLIK (7805 "I Fell in Love") 250-350 57
Also see NUTMEGS
RAKE R&B '83
Singles: 7-inch
PROFILE 3-4 83
RAKES, Pal C&W '77
(With the Prophets)
Singles: 7-inch
ATLANTIC 3-4 89
ATLANTIC AMERICA 3-4 88
VERVE 4-8 68
W.B. 3-5 77-79
Also see PAL & PROPHETS

RALEIGH, Kevin P&R '89
Singles: 7-inch
ATLANTIC......3-4 89
Picture Sleeves
ATLANTIC......3-4 89
Also see STANLEY, Michael

RALEIGH, Sir Walter
(With the Coupons)
Singles: 7-inch
TOWER......4-8 65-66

RALKE, Don P&R '59
("Big Sound of Don Ralke")
Singles: 78 rpm
CROWN......3-6 55
Singles: 7-inch
CROWN......5-15 55
DRUM BOY......4-6 66
REAL......5-15 56
W.B. 5-10 59-64
LPs: 10/12-inch
CROWN......10-20 55
W.B. 10-20 59-60
Also see BECKER, Gloria
Also see BYRNES, Edward
Also see CHAPMAN, Grady
Also see COOKE, Sam
Also see DEUCES WILD
Also see DICK & DEEDEE
Also see JAN & ARNIE
Also see MARQUEES
Also see THREE DIMENSIONS

RALKE-TALKIES
Singles: 7-inch
W.B. 4-6 63
Also see RALKE, Don

RALLO, Tony, & Midnite Band
LPs: 10/12-inch
CASABLANCA......5-10 79

RALLY PACKS
Singles: 7-inch
IMPERIAL (66036 "Move Out Little Mustang")......40-50 64
Members: Phil Sloan; Steve Barri. Session: Jan Berry; Dean Torrence.
Also see FANTASTIC BAGGYS
Also see JAN & DEAN

RALPH, Sheryl Lee D&D '84
Singles: 12-inch
NYM......4-6 84-85
Singles: 7-inch
NYM......3-4 84-85
Also see HARNEY, Ben, & Sheryl Lee Ralph

RALPH & MAGNETICS
Singles: 7-inch
EMASE......3-5 73

RALPH & PATTIE
Singles: 7-inch
TRIBUTE......4-8 63

RAM
LPs: 10/12-inch
POLYDOR......10-15 72

RAM, Buck
(Buck Ram Platters; Buck Ram All Stars)
Singles: 78 rpm
SAVOY......10-15 44
Singles: 7-inch
AVALANCHE......3-5 73
PERSONALITY......10-15
EPs: 7-inch
CAMDEN......10-20 57
LPs: 10/12-inch
MERCURY......20-30 59
Also see PLATTERS

RAM IN MEXICO
Singles: 7-inch
ENSIGN (5001 "Twilight Time")...... 5-10

RAM JAM P&R/LP '77
Singles: 12-inch
EPIC......5-10 77
Singles: 7-inch
EPIC......3-5 77-78
LPs: 10/12-inch
EPIC......8-12 77-78
Also see AUGUST
Also see LEMON PIPERS
Also see PIERCE ARROW / Lake / Crawler / Ram Jam
Also see WILSON, Dennis / Ram Jam / Joan Baez

RAM JAM HOLDER: see HOLDER, Ram Jam

RAM ROCK
Singles: 7-inch
HAMMER HEAD......5-10 70s
(No selection number used.)

RAMA D&D '84
Singles: 12-inch
SUGARSCOOP......4-6 84

RAMADAS
Singles: 7-inch
NEW WORLD......4-8 64
PHILIPS......5-10 63

RAMAL, Bill
Singles: 7-inch
HARVARD (811 "Rock Lamonde")..10-15 59
Also see BELLINO
Also see CAPP, Bill
Also see GOODMAN, Dickie
Also see LEGENDS
Also see SHIEKS
Also see VIRGINIANS

RAMATAM LP '72
Singles: 7-inch
ATLANTIC......3-5 72-73
LPs: 10/12-inch
ATLANTIC......10-15 72-73
Also see PINERA, Mike

RAMBEAU, Eddie P&R/LP '65
Singles: 7-inch
BELL......4-6 69
DYNA VOICE......4-8 65-66
SWAN......5-10 61-62
20TH FOX......4-8 64
VIRGO......3-5 73
LPs: 10/12-inch
DYNO VOICE......15-25 65
Also see MARCY JO & EDDIE RAMBEAU

RAMBEAU, Teddy
Singles: 7-inch
TOPS......5-10 59

RAMBLERS
Singles: 7-inch
JAX (319 "Search My Heart")......250-350 52
(Red vinyl.)

RAMBLERS
Singles: 78 rpm
MGM (11850 "Vadunt-Un-Va Song")......75-125 54
MGM (55006 "Bad Girl")......50-75 55
Singles: 7-inch
MGM (11850 "Vadunt-Un-Va Song")......200-250 54
MGM (55006 "Bad Girl")......100-125 55

RAMBLERS
Singles: 78 rpm
FEDERAL......50-75 56
Singles: 7-inch
FEDERAL (12286 "Heaven and Earth")......150-250 56

RAMBLERS P&R '60
Singles: 7-inch
ADDIT (1257 "Rambling")......10-20 60
Members: Chuck Kenney; Michael Burke; Michael Anthony; Kip Martin.

RAMBLERS
Singles: 7-inch
FUTURE......4-8 63
IMPACT......5-10 61

RAMBLERS P&R '64
Singles: 7-inch
ALMONT (311 "Father Sebastian")......15-25 64
ALMONT (313 "School Girl")......15-25 64
ALMONT (315 "Silly Little Boy")......15-25 64
SIDEWINDERS......10-20 64
Members: John Herbert; Sal Nastasi.

RAMBLERS
Singles: 7-inch
CORA (101 "Bye Bye Bye")......200-400 64

RAMBLERS THREE
LPs: 10/12-inch
MGM......10-20 62

RAMBLES, Renee, & Rhinestone
Singles: 7-inch
RCA......3-5 72

RAMBLETTES
Singles: 7-inch
DECCA......4-8 65
4 CORNERS......4-8 64
KAPP......4-8 64

RAMBLIN' EVERETT
Singles: 78 rpm
FABLE (546 "Cincinnati Woman")..25-50 56
Singles: 7-inch
FABLE (546 "Cincinnati Woman")......50-100 56

RAMBLIN' REBELS
Singles: 7-inch
DESS (7008 "Impact")......10-20 61

RAMBLIN' WILLIE & EUPHONICS
Singles: 7-inch
DORE......3-5

RAMBLING ROGUE C&W '45
(Fred Rose)
Singles: 78 rpm
BRUNSWICK......10-20 20s
OKEH......5-10 45

RAMBO, Dack & Dirk
Singles: 7-inch
ZING (1001 "Why Did You Leave, Genevieve")......10-20 60s

RAMBO, Ted, & Shades
Singles: 7-inch
PEAK (1201 "Sorority Girl")......150-250 57

RAMBOW, Philip
Singles: 7-inch
CAPITOL......3-5 80

RAMIN, Sid, & Orchestra LP '63
LPs: 10/12-inch
RCA......10-15 63
Also see HO-HOs

RAMISTELLA, Johnny
(Johnny Rivers)
Singles: 7-inch
SUEDE (1401 "Little Girl")......100-200 58
Also see RIVERS, Johnny

RAMJET, Rodger, & American Eagles
(Gary Owens)
LPs: 10/12-inch
CAMDEN......15-25 66
Also see OWENS, Gary

RAMM
Singles: 7-inch
SHOWTIME......3-5 77

RAMONES LP '76
Singles: 7-inch
RSO......3-6 81
SIRE......5-10 76-80
Picture Sleeves
SIRE......8-15 77-79
EPs: 7-inch
SIRE (805 "Rock 'N Roll High School")......12-18 79
(Promotional issue only.)
LPs: 10/12-inch
MCA (11273 "Adios Amigos")......8-10 90s
SIRE (Except 3571, 6063 & 7528)......5-8 76-89
SIRE (3571 "Pleasant Dreams")......5-8
SIRE (6063 "Road to Ruin")......10-20 78
(Black vinyl.)
SIRE (6063 "Road to Ruin")......25-35 78
(Yellow vinyl.)
SIRE (7528 "Leave Home")......15-25 77
(Has *Carbona Not Glue*, which is not on reissues.)
Also see PALEY BROTHERS

RAMONOS
Singles: 7-inch
HI......4-8 61

RAMOS, Juan
Singles: 7-inch
TEARDROP......3-5 77

RAMOS, Rudy
LPs: 10/12-inch
FANTASY......8-12 72

RAMP
LPs: 10/12-inch
BLUE THUMB......5-10 77

RAMPAGES
Singles: 7-inch
WEDGE......10-15 64

RAMPART RAMBLERS
Singles: 7-inch
SOULIN'......4-8 67

RAMPARTS
Singles: 7-inch
LIDO (617 "Freeze")......10-20 58

RAMROCKS
Singles: 7-inch
ANTLER (4010 "Hot Rock")......8-12 59
DISC JOCKEY (42 "Hot Rock")......10-20 58
FELSTED......5-10 60
PERSONALITY......5-10 59
PRESS......8-12 62-64
Also see FLARES / Ramrocks

RAMRODS
Singles: 7-inch
AD (70 "Morado")......10-20 59
Members: Mike Farrell; Pete Steele; Chip Specht; Butch Cavanaugh; Zonnie Frichi; Denny Lee Sesso.

RAMRODS P&R '61
Singles: 7-inch
AMY (813 "Riders in the Sky")......15-25 60
AMY (817 "Take Me Back to My Boots & Saddle")......10-20 61
AMY (846 "War Cry")......10-20 61
BARCLAY (13127 "War Party")......8-12 60s
QUALITY (1256 "Riders in the Sky")......15-25 60
(Canadian.)
QUEEN (24014 "Slee-Zee")......8-12 62
Members: Vincent Bell; Eugene Morrow; Richard Lane; Claire Lane.
Also see BELL, Vincent
Also see RANGERS

RAMRODS R&B '72
Singles: 7-inch
R&H (1001 "Night Ride")......15-25 63
RAMPAGE (1000 "Soultrain")......4-6 72
(First issued as *Hot Potato*, by the Rinky Dinks.)
Member: King Curtis.
Also see KING CURTIS
Also see RINKY DINKS

RAMRODS
Singles: 7-inch
PLYMOUTH (2965 "Flowers in My Mind")......10-15 67
Also see ROCKIN' RAMRODS

RAMRODS
Singles: 7-inch
FENTON (2014 "You Know I Love You")......15-25 66

RAMS
(Flairs)
Singles: 78 rpm
FLAIR (1066 "Sweet Thing")......30-50 55
Singles: 7-inch
FLAIR (1066 "Sweet Thing")......100-150 55
Also see FLAIRS
Also see MAYE, Arthur Lee

RAMSAY, Stu
Singles: 7-inch
MERCURY......4-8 63
Also see CHICAGO SLIM & Stu Ramsay

RAMSES
LPs: 10/12-inch
ANNUIT COEPTIS (1002 "La Leyla")......10-15 76

RAMSEY, Bill
Singles: 7-inch
DECCA......4-8 60

RAMSEY, Gloria
(With the Sound Dealers Orchestra)
Singles: 7-inch
HAP (1894 "My Love")......400-600 60
Session: Impressions.
Also see IMPRESSIONS

RAMSEY, Robert
Singles: 7-inch
KENT......3-5 71

RAMSEY, Willis Alan
LPs: 10/12-inch
SHELTER (8900 series)......8-12 72
SHELTER (52000 series)......5-8 76

RAMSEY SISTERS
Singles: 7-inch
SMASH......4-8 64

RANADO, Chuck, & Electronaires
Singles: 7-inch
COUNT (507 "My Baby's Gone")......50-100 59
Also see ELECTRONAIRES

RANCE, Jimmy
Singles: 7-inch
NRC......5-10 59

RANCHEROS
Singles: 7-inch
DOT (16572 "Linda's Tune")......10-15 63
LONNIE (5005 "Linda's Tune")......25-35 63

RAND, Bobby
Singles: 78 rpm
DOT......10-20 57
Singles: 7-inch
DOT (15580 "Don't Make My Poor Heart Weep")......10-20 57

RAND, D.C., & Jokers
Singles: 7-inch
CANDY (003 "Shake It Up")......75-125 59

RAND, Doug, & Purple Blues
Singles: 7-inch
LANCE......10-15 60s

RAND, Jay
Singles: 7-inch
CHALLENGE (59023 "Blue Dawn") 8-12 58

RAND, Jimmy
Singles: 7-inch
20TH FOX......5-10 60

RAND, Johnny
Singles: 7-inch
HERALD......4-8 61

RAND, Lee
Singles: 7-inch
DIAMOND......4-8 64

RAND, Rosalie
Singles: 78 rpm
KING......5-10 55
Singles: 7-inch
KING......8-12 55

RAND, Rose Marie
Singles: 78 rpm
VIK (0206 "Lies Lies Lies")......10-15 56
Singles: 7-inch
VIK (0206 "Lies Lies Lies")......15-25 56

RAND, Tony
Singles: 7-inch
COLUMBIA (40925 "Seven Come Eleven")......20-40 57

RANDAL, Johnny
Singles: 7-inch
COLONIAL (606 "Do Right")......10-20 64

RANDAL, Paul
Singles: 7-inch
ROULETTE......4-8 61

RANDALL, Billy
Singles: 7-inch
SAVOY......10-20 59

RANDALL, Buddy: see RANDELL, Buddy

RANDALL, Eddie, & Downbeats
Singles: 7-inch
QT (1629 "Downbeat Rock")......10-20 60

RANDALL, Elliott
Singles: 7-inch
KIRSHNER......3-6 77
Also see RANDALL'S ISLAND

RANDALL, Frankie
Singles: 7-inch
MERCURY......3-5 68
RCA......3-6 64-68
LPs: 10/12-inch
RCA......8-15 64-68

RANDALL, Jay
Singles: 7-inch
KHOURYS (713 "Never Have I")......20-30 59

RANDALL, Ricky
Singles: 7-inch
PEACOCK......4-8 65

RANDALL, Rory
Singles: 7-inch
LUCK......5-10 59

RANDALL, Terry
Singles: 7-inch
VALIANT......4-8 66

RANDALL, Todd
(With the Blue Notes)
Singles: 78 rpm
JOSIE (814 "Letters")......30-50 57
Singles: 7-inch
GLORY......5-10 59
JOSIE (814 "Letters")......30-50 57
Also see BLUE NOTES

RANDALL, Tony
Singles: 7-inch
IMPERIAL......4-8 61
MERCURY......3-6 67
LPs: 10/12-inch
IMPERIAL......20-30 61
MERCURY......10-20 67

RANDALL'S ISLAND
Singles: 7-inch
POLYDOR......3-5 71-72
LPs: 10/12-inch
KIRSHNER......8-10 77
POLYDOR......10-15 71-72
Member: Elliott Randall.
Also see RANDALL, Elliott

RANDAZZO, Jimmy
Singles: 7-inch
WINGATE (9 "Hungry for Love")......150-250 60s

RANDAZZO, Teddy P&R '58
(With All 6)
Singles: 7-inch
ABC-PAR......4-8 59-62
COLPIX......4-8 62-63
DCP......4-8 64-66
MGM......4-8 66
VERVE/FOLKWAYS......4-8 67
VIK......5-10 58
LPs: 10/12-inch
ABC-PAR......20-30 61-62
MGM......15-20 66
VIK (1121 "I'm Confessing")......30-50 58
Also see CHUCKLES
Also see THREE CHUCKLES

RANDELL, Buddy
(With the Knickerbockers; Buddy Randall)
Singles: 7-inch
CHALLENGE (59268 "All I Need Is You")......30-50 64
UNI......3-5 70
LPs: 10/12-inch
CHALLENGE (621 "Jerk & Twine Time")......25-35 65
Also see BLOWTORCH
Also see KNICKERBOCKERS
Also see ROCKIN' SAINTS
Also see ROYAL TEENS
Also see STEEL WOOL

RANDELL, Denny
Singles: 7-inch
ASCOT......5-10 63
CAMEO......4-8 63
JAMIE......4-8 63

RANDELL, Jackie
Singles: 7-inch
JUBILEE......5-10 60

RANDELL, Jay, & Epics
Singles: 7-inch
LANOR (548 "Oh Darling")......10-15 59
LANOR (552 "Stand by Me")......10-15 59

RANDELL, Johnny
Singles: 7-inch
COLONIAL (606 "Do Right")......10-20 64
COLONIAL ("How About That")......10-20 65
(Selection number not known.)

RANDELL, Lynne
Singles: 7-inch
EPIC (10147 "Stranger in My Arms")......10-20 67
Picture Sleeves
EPIC (10147 "Stranger in My Arms")......20-30 67

RANDELL, Rick
Singles: 7-inch
APT......5-10 60
DECCA......4-8 64
MGM......4-8 66
U.A. 4-8 62

RAN-DELLS P&R/R&B '63
Singles: 7-inch
RSVP (1104 "Beyond the Stars")......10-15 64
CHAIRMAN (4403 "Martian Hop")......10-15 63
CHAIRMAN (4407 "Come on and Love Me Too")......10-15 63
Picture Sleeves
CHAIRMAN (4403 "Martian Hop") 30-40 63
Members: Steve Rappaport; John Sprit.

RANDLE, Bobby
Singles: 7-inch
SHAD......8-10 58

RANDLE, Del
Singles: 7-inch
SHAKARI......5-10 64
Members: Garnell Cooper & Kinfolks; Booker T. & MGs.
Also see BOOKER T. & MGs

RANDLE, Dodie
Singles: 78 rpm
DECCA.......... 5-10 57
Singles: 7-inch
DECCA.......... 5-10 57

RANDLE, Johnny
Singles: 7-inch
CRICKET (2207 "By My Side") 10-20 60s

RANDLE, Rick
Singles: 7-inch
APT.......... 5-10 60

RANDLES, Robert
LPs: 10/12-inch
PRS (1005 "Portfolio of Film Music")..........30-40
(Picture disc. 400 made.)
PRS (1005 "Portfolio of Film Music")..........50-75
(Picture disc. Includes special plastic cover.)

RANDOLF & STILES
Singles: 7-inch
CAMEO (253 "Crossroads").......... 5-10 63

RANDOLPH, Barbara
Singles: 7-inch
SOUL..........10-20 67-68

RANDOLPH, Boots *P&R/R&B/LP '63*
(With Richie Cole; Homer Randolph)
Singles: 7-inch
LOGO.......... 4-8
MONUMENT.......... 3-8 61-83
PAJ (7041 "Yakety Sax").......... 4-8
PALO ALTO.......... 3-4
RCA (7611 "Sweet Talk").......... 8-12 59
RCA (7721 "Red Light").......... 8-12 60
RCA (7835 "Big Daddy")..........15-20 61
(With "37" prefix. Compact 33 Single.)
RCA (7835 "Big Daddy").......... 8-10 61
(With "47" prefix.)
Picture Sleeves
MONUMENT (852 "Mickey's Tune") 8-12 64
EPs: 7-inch
MONUMENT (002 "Boots Randolph")..........10-20 63
(Promotional issue only.)
MONUMENT (361 "Boots & Stockings").......... 5-10 69
(Promotional issue only.)
MONUMENT (514 "More Yakety Sax").......... 5-10 60s
(Promotional issue only.)
LPs: 10/12-inch
CAMDEN..........10-20 64
GUEST STAR.......... 5-10 64
MONUMENT (Except 8000 & 18000 series).......... 6-12 71-82
MONUMENT (8000 & 18000 series)..........10-20 63-71
PALO ALTO.......... 5-8
RCA (LPM-2165 "Yakety Sax")......20-30 60
(Monaural.)
RCA (LSP-2165 "Yakety Sax")......30-40 60
(Stereo.)
TEXIZE (1 "Nashville Sound")........10-15 68
(Promotional issue only.)
Also see ANN-MARGRET
Also see ATKINS, Chet, Floyd Cramer & Boots Randolph
Also see FRANCIS, Connie
Also see HIRT, Al, & Boots Randolph
Also see KNIGHTSBRIDGE STRINGS
Also see LEE, Brenda
Also see NASHVILLE ALL-STARS
Also see PRESLEY, Elvis
Also see RANDOLPH, Randy
Also see TILLOTSON, Johnny
Also see VELVETS

RANDOLPH, Boots / Bill Haley
Singles: 7-inch
LOGO (7005 "Yakety Sax").......... 8-12 61
Also see HALEY, Bill
Also see RANDOLPH, Boots

RANDOLPH, Cookie "Chainsaw"
Singles: 7-inch
93-KDKB.......... 3-4 86

RANDOLPH, Dean
Singles: 7-inch
APT.......... 5-8 65
CHANCELLOR.......... 5-10 63

RANDOLPH, Jimmy
Singles: 7-inch
ARLISS (1003 "Gonna Sit & Cry")..... 5-8 61

RANDOLPH, Randy
(Homer Randolph)
Singles: 7-inch
RCA (7395 "Yakety Sax")..........10-20 59
RCA (7515 "Blue Guitar")..........10-15 59
Also see RANDOLPH, Boots

RANDOM
Singles: 7-inch
RANDOM (1031 "Blue Eyed Believer")..........10-20 60s

RANDOM, Bob
Singles: 7-inch
DRAGONET (009 "An Open Letter to My Father")..........10-20 66

RANDOM BLUES BAND
Singles: 7-inch
SCEPTER.......... 3-6 66

RANDY
(With Skunks; Randy Klein)
Singles: 7-inch
TEEN TOWN (104 "By the Time I Get to Phoenix")..........8-12 68
Also see SKUNKS

RANDY, Dean
Singles: 7-inch
FARGO..........5-10 61

RANDY & CANDYMEN
Singles: 7-inch
BIG SOUND (6427 "Little Sister") ..15-25 64
Members: Randy Rybicki; Eddie Farah; Jim Hanna; Jim Jandrain; Andy Pigeon.

RANDY & HOLIDAYS
Singles: 7-inch
HICKORY..........8-12 67

RANDY & RADIANTS
Singles: 7-inch
SUN..........5-10 65-66

RANDY & RAINBOWS *P&R/R&B '63*
Singles: 7-inch
AMBIENT SOUND ("C'mon Let's Go")..........8-12 82
(Selection number not known.)
AMBIENT SOUND (02872 "Try the Impossible")..........8-12 82
B.T. PUPPY (535 "I'll Be Seeing You")..........5-10 67
CRYSTAL BALL (161 "It's Christmas Once Again")..........3-5 93
LAURIE..........3-5 70s
MIKE (4001 "Lovely Lies")..........5-10 66
MIKE (4004 "Quarter to Three")......5-10 66
MIKE (4008 "Can It Be")..........5-10 66
RUST (5059 "Denise")..........20-30 63
(Blue label.)
RUST (5059 "Denise")..........8-12 63
(Rust and white label.)
RUST (5073 "Why Do Kids Grow Up")..........10-15 63
RUST (5080 "Dry Your Eyes")......10-15 64
RUST (5091 "Little Star")..........10-15 64
STOOP SOUNDS (100 "In Your Letter")..........100-150 96
(Limited edition. Estimates range from less than 10 to a few dozen made.)
LPs: 10/12-inch
AMBIENT SOUND..........8-10 82
AMBIENT SOUND/ROUNDER........8-10 84
MAGIC CARPET..........8-10 79
Members: Dominick "Randy" Safuto; Frank Safuto; Mike Zero; Sal Zero; Ken Arcipowski.
Also see DIALTONES
Also see MADISON STREET
Also see RAINBOWS
Also see TRIANGLE

RANDY & RALPH
Singles: 7-inch
U.A...........5-10 58

RANDY & REST
Singles: 7-inch
JADE..........10-15 67
SSS INT'L (720 "The Vacuum")......15-25 68

RANDY & ROCKETS
Singles: 7-inch
AZALEA..........5-10 61
JIN..........5-10 62
VIKING..........8-12 59
Member: Gene Sledge.

RANDY PIE
Singles: 7-inch
POLYDOR..........3-5 77
LPs: 10/12-inch
POLYDOR..........8-12 75-77

RANDYANDY
Singles: 12-inch
A&M..........4-6 83
Singles: 7-inch
A&M..........3-4 83
LPs: 10/12-inch
A&M..........5-8 83

RANEY, Barbara
Singles: 7-inch
SHINE..........3-4 83
Also see CADILLAC SALLY
Also see DEEPWATER REUNION

RANEY, Dall, & Umbrellas
(Znydall Raney)
Singles: 7-inch
HOLLYWOOD (1105 "Fastback") ..15-25 61
Also see RANEY, Zyndall

RANEY, Sue
Singles: 7-inch
CAPITOL..........6-12 58-60
IMPERIAL..........4-6 66-68
KC..........4-8 62
EPs: 7-inch
CAPITOL (964 "When Your Lover Has Gone")..........10-15 58
LPs: 10/12-inch
CAPITOL (1335 "Songs for a Raney Day")..........15-25 60
CAPITOL (2032 "All by Myself")......10-20 64

RANEY, Wayne *C&W '45*
Singles: 78 rpm
KING..........8-12 48-51
Singles: 7-inch
KING..........8-15 51
LPs: 10/12-inch
KING..........20-30
NASHVILLE..........10-15
RIMROCK..........5-10

STARDAY..........15-20

RANEY, Zyndall
Singles: 7-inch
RIMROCK..........4-8 60s
Also see RANEY, Dall, & Umbrellas

RANGERS
Singles: 7-inch
FTP (404 "Four on the Floor")........20-30 61
(Though not credited, the B-side is by the Ramrods.)

RANGERS
Singles: 7-inch
CHALLENGE (59229 "Snow Skiing")..........10-15 63
CHALLENGE (59239 "Reputation")..........10-15 64
Members: Steve O'Reilly; Rick Henn; Ed Medora; Vince Hozier; Marty DiGiovanni.
Also see HENN, Rick
Also see RENEGADE V
Also see SNOW MEN

RANGLIN, Ernest
Singles: 7-inch
STUDIO (1 "Surfing")..........20-25
LPs: 10/12-inch
STEADY..........8-12 70

RANGOONS
Singles: 7-inch
LAURIE (3096 "Moon Guitar") 10-20 61

RANJI
Singles: 7-inch
ANTHEM..........3-5 71-72
Picture Sleeves
ANTHEM..........3-5 72

RANK, Ken / Jades
Singles: 7-inch
FENTON (2194 "Twin City Saucer")..........25-30 68
Also see JADES

RANK & FILE *LP '83*
Singles: 7-inch
SLASH..........3-4 83-84
LPs: 10/12-inch
SLASH..........5-8 83-84
Also see SEATRAIN

RANKIN, Billy *P&R/LP '84*
Singles: 7-inch
A&M..........3-4 84
LPs: 10/12-inch
A&M..........5-8 84

RANKIN, Kenny *LP '72*
(Ken Rankin)
Singles: 7-inch
ABC-PAR..........6-12 61
COLUMBIA..........4-8 63-65
DECCA..........10-15 58-60
LITTLE DAVID..........3-5 73-77
MERCURY..........4-6 68-69
Picture Sleeves
COLUMBIA..........8-12 63
MERCURY..........5-8 68
LPs: 10/12-inch
ATLANTIC..........5-10 80
LITTLE DAVID..........8-10 72-77
MERCURY..........10-15 67-69
Also see KENNY & YVONNE
Also see RANKINS, Kenneth, & Spars

RANKING ROGER *LP '88*
LPs: 10/12-inch
I.R.S...........5-8 88

RANKINS, Kenneth, & Spars
Singles: 78 rpm
GROOVE (0148 "Say a Prayer")....10-15 56
Singles: 7-inch
GROOVE (0148 "Say a Prayer")....25-50 56
Member: Kenny Rankin.
Also see RANKIN, Kenny

RANNELS
Singles: 7-inch
BOSS (2122 "Blue Island")......100-200 63

RANNO, Richie
LPs: 10/12-inch
VIOLATION..........5-8 84
Members: Peter Scance; Joe Dube; Brenden Harkin.
Also see HELLCATS
Also see STARZ

RANSOM, Joel, Four
Singles: 7-inch
3-H'S..........5-10 64

RAPER BROTHERS
Singles: 7-inch
STARLIGHT (1004 "Rock Hop Bop")..........75-150 58

RAPHAEL, Johnny
Singles: 7-inch
MERCURY..........5-10 60

RAPID TRANSIT
Singles: 7-inch
CLIFTON..........4-8

RAPIDTONES
Singles: 78 rpm
RAPID..........50-75 56
Singles: 7-inch
RAPID (1002 "Sunday Kind of Love")..........150-200 56
Also see HARPTONES

RAP-O-MATIC LTD.
Singles: 12-inch
PROFILE..........4-6 86

RAPP, Captain: see CAPTAIN RAPP

RAPP, Tom
Singles: 7-inch
BLUE THUMB..........3-6 72
REPRISE..........3-6 72
LPs: 10/12-inch
BLUE THUMB..........8-12 72-73
REPRISE..........8-12 72
Also see PEARLS BEFORE SWINE

RAPPER, Little Ray
LPs: 10/12-inch
FIRST AMERICAN..........5-8

RAPPIN' DUKE *R&B '86*
Singles: 12-inch
TOMMY BOY..........4-6 86

RARE BIRD *LP '70*
Singles: 7-inch
ABC..........3-5 72
POLYDOR..........3-5 73-74
PROBE..........3-5 70
LPs: 10/12-inch
ABC..........8-10 72
POLYDOR..........8-10 73-74
PROBE..........10-12 70

RARE BREAD
Singles: 7-inch
MGM..........3-6 70

RARE BREED
Singles: 7-inch
ATTACK (1401 "Beg, Borrow and Steal")..........20-30 66
(Reissued, with a different flip side, and shown as by the Ohio Express.)
ATTACK (1403 "Come and Take a Ride in My Boat")..........10-20 66
Also see OHIO EXPRESS

RARE EARTH *LP '69*
Singles: 7-inch
MOTOWN..........3-5 81
PRODIGAL..........3-4 78
RARE EARTH (Black vinyl)..........3-6 69-76
RARE EARTH (Colored vinyl)..........4-8 72
(Promotional issue only.)
VERVE..........4-8 68
Picture Sleeves
RARE EARTH..........4-6 71-73
LPs: 10/12-inch
MOTOWN..........5-8 81
PRODIGAL..........5-8 77-78
RARE EARTH (Except 507)..........8-12 70-76
RARE EARTH (507 "Get Ready")......8-12 69
(With standard, square cover.)
RARE EARTH (507 "Get Ready")..30-40 69
(With rounded-top cover. Promotional issue.)
VERVE..........10-20 68
Members: Peter Hoorelbeke; Gil Bridges; Ray Monette; Pete Rivera; Mark Olson; Michael Urso; Edward Guzman; John Persh; Ken James.
Also see HUB
Also see SUNLINERS

RARE ESSENCE *R&B '82*
Singles: 12-inch
FANTASY..........4-8 82
Singles: 7-inch
ATCO..........3-4 90

RARE GEMS
LPs: 10/12-inch
CALIFORNIA GOLD..........5-10 79

RARE GEMS ODYSSEY
Singles: 7-inch
CASABLANCA..........3-5 78
LPs: 10/12-inch
CASABLANCA..........8-10 77

RARE SILK
LPs: 10/12-inch
POLYDOR..........5-10 83

RARE SOUND
Singles: 7-inch
IN SOUND..........4-8 68

RASCALS *P&R '65*
(Young Rascals)
Singles: 7-inch
ATLANTIC (Except 2428)..........4-8 65-70
ATLANTIC (2428 "Groovin" [in Italian])..........10-20 67
(Backed with *Groovin'* in Spanish.)
ATLANTIC OLDIES..........3-4 70s
COLUMBIA..........3-5 71-72
Picture Sleeves
ATLANTIC..........5-10 66-70
EPs: 7-inch
ATLANTIC (190 "Time Peace") 10-15 68
(Promotional issue only.)
LPs: 10/12-inch
ATLANTIC (137 "Freedom Suite") .20-30 69
(Promotional issue only.)
ATLANTIC (901 "Freedom Suite") .20-30 69
(Without cut corner or BB holes.)
ATLANTIC (901 "Freedom Suite") .10-20 69
(With cut corner or BB holes.)
ATLANTIC (8123 thru 8148)..........15-25 66-67
ATLANTIC (8169 thru 8276)..........10-15 68-71
COLUMBIA..........8-12 71-72
PAIR..........8-10 86
RHINO..........5-8 87
W.F.O. (1000 "The Rascals")..........8-12 72
Members: Felix Cavaliere; Ed Brigati; Dino Danelli; Gene Cornish; David Brigati.
Also see BRIGATI

Also see BULLDOG
Also see CAVALIERE, Felix
Also see CORNISH, Gene
Also see DEE, Joey
Also see FOTOMAKER
Also see SWEET INSPIRATIONS

(YOUNG) RASCALS / Buggs / Four Seasons / Johnny Rivers
LPs: 10/12-inch
CORONET (283 "The Young Rascals")..........20-30 66
Also see BUGGS
Also see 4 SEASONS
Also see RIVERS, Johnny

(YOUNG) RASCALS / Isley Brothers
LPs: 10/12-inch
DESIGN (253 "Young Rascals and the Isley Brothers")..........15-25 60s
Also see ISLEY BROTHERS
Also see RASCALS

RASE, Bill
Singles: 78 rpm
KLIK (1005 "How Could I Know")......4-8 55
Singles: 7-inch
KLIK (1005 "How Could I Know")....10-15 55

RASMUSSEN
LPs: 10/12-inch
REPRISE..........8-12 71

RASMUSSEN, Gary
Singles: 7-inch
CUCA (69129 "Closet Full of Clothes")..........4-8 69

RASPBERRIES *P&R/LP '72*
Singles: 7-inch
CAPITOL..........4-8 72-74
Picture Sleeves
CAPITOL..........6-10 73
LPs: 10/12-inch
CAPITOL (11036 thru 11329)..........20-30 72-74
CAPITOL (11524 "Raspberries' Best")..........8-12 76
CAPITOL (16095 "Raspberries' Best")..........5-10 80
Members: Eric Carmen; Wally Bryson; Jim Bonfanti; John Aleksic; Dave Smalley.
Also see CHOIR
Also see FOTOMAKER
Also see TATTOO
Also see YELLOW HAIR

RASPBERRY, Larry, & Highsteppers
Singles: 7-inch
MERCURY..........3-5 79
LPs: 10/12-inch
BACKROOM..........8-10 75
ENTERPRISE..........8-10 74
Also see ALAMO
Also see GENTRYS

RASPBERRY PANTIES
Singles: 7-inch
ROD..........4-6 70

RASPBERRY PIRATES
Singles: 7-inch
ATCO..........4-8 68

RASPUT & SEPOY MUTINY
LPs: 10/12-inch
DESIGN (280 "Flower Power Sitar")..........10-20 67

RASPUTIN & MONKS / Octet
LPs: 10/12-inch
TRANS RADIO (200836 "Sum of My Soul")..........250-350 66
(One side of the LP by each group.)
Member: Bob "Rasputin" Raymond.

RASPUTIN'S STASH
Singles: 7-inch
COTILLION..........3-5 71
LPs: 10/12-inch
COTILLION..........10-15 71
GEMIGO..........8-10 74

RASTUS
Singles: 7-inch
GRT..........3-5 71
NEIGHBORHOOD..........3-5 72
LPs: 10/12-inch
GRT..........10-15 71
NEIGHBORHOOD..........8-12 72

RAT, Billy, & Finks
Singles: 7-inch
IGL (122 "Little Queenie")..........25-35 67
Also see SHOOP, Wally, & Zombies

RAT CHEESE
Singles: 7-inch
CAPITOL..........3-5 72

RAT PACK
Singles: 7-inch
DCP..........8-12 65

RAT PACK
Singles: 7-inch
RAYNARD (8796 "I Need You")......10-20 70s

RAT RACE KID
Singles: 7-inch
KEVIN KAT..........3-5 80-82
TEXAS RE-CORD..........3-5 80-81
LPs: 10/12-inch
KEVIN KAT..........5-10 82
Also see MEYERS, Augie

RATCHELL LP '72

Singles: 7-inch

DECCA....................................3-5 72

LPs: 10/12-inch

DECCA....................................10-15 71-72

RATFINKS, J.C.W.: see J.C.W. RATFINKS

RATH, Mome

Singles: 7-inch

RCA....................................3-5 71

RATIONALS P&R '66

Singles: 7-inch

A² (101 "Look What You're Doin' ").15-25 65
A² (103 "Feelin' Lost")..........10-20 66
A² (103/4 "Feelin' Lost"/"Respect")..10-20 66
A² (104 "Respect"/"Leavin' Here")..10-20 66
A² (107 "I Need You")..........10-20 68
A² (402 "I Need You")..........10-20 68
(Different song than on #107.)
CAMEO (437 "Respect")..........10-15 66
CAMEO (455 "Hold on Baby")........10-15 67
CAMEO (481 "Leavin' Here")........10-15 67
(Re-recorded version.)
CAPITOL (2124 "I Need You")........8-12 68
CREWE (340 "Guitar Army")........5-10 69
DANBY'S (125850 "Turn On")........30-40 66
(Promotional issue made for Danby's clothier. Identification number shown since no selection number is used.)
GENESIS (1 "Guitar Army")........8-12 69

LPs: 10/12-inch

ALIVE/TOTAL ENERGY..........5-10 95
(10-inch LP.)
CREWE (1334 "Rationals")..........25-35 69
Also see SRC / Rationals

RATLIFF, Bozo

Singles: 7-inch

SPACE (100 "Let Me In")..........200-300 58

RATLIFF, J.T.

Singles: 7-inch

PETAL....................................5-10 62

RATMORE SLINKY: see SLINKY, Ratmore

RATNER, Marc

Singles: 7-inch

RSO....................................3-5 79

RATS

Singles: 7-inch

LAURIE....................................4-8 64

RATS

Singles: 7-inch

BLACK CAT (502 "Rat's Revenge")..........50-100 66
Also see MYSTICS

RATT P&R/LP '84

Singles: 7-inch

ATLANTIC..............................3-4 84-89
TIME COAST..............................3-5 83-84

Picture Sleeves

ATLANTIC..............................3-4 84-88

LPs: 10/12-inch

ATLANTIC..............................5-8 84-90
TIME COAST..............................5-10 83-84
Members: Stephen Pearcy; Warren D. Martin; Robbin Crosby; Juan Crocier; Bobby Blotzer.

RATT, Biggie

Singles: 7-inch

APT....................................4-8 69

RATTERREE, Jimmy

Singles: 7-inch

DORE....................................5-10 59

RATTLES P&R '70

Singles: 7-inch

LONDON....................................3-5
MERCURY....................................5-10 66
PROBE....................................4-6 70

LPs: 10/12-inch

MERCURY (21127 "Greatest Hits")..........30-40 67
(Monaural.)
MERCURY (61127 "Greatest Hits")..........40-60 67
(Stereo.)
Also see SEARCHERS / Rattles

RATTLESNAKE ANNIE C&W '87

Singles: 7-inch

COLUMBIA..............................3-4 87-88

LPs: 10/12-inch

COLUMBIA..............................5-8 87

RATTRAY, Duke

Singles: 7-inch

GALLIO....................................4-8 65

RAUNCHETTES

LPs: 10/12-inch

BOMP....................................5-8 87

RAUSCH, Leon C&W '76

Singles: 7-inch

DERRICK..............................3-5 76-79
SOUTHLAND (7482 "Deep in the Heart of Texas")..........3-5 86
(Gold vinyl.)

LPs: 10/12-inch

DERRICK..............................5-10 76
DISCUS..............................10-20
SOUTHLAND (7311 "The Rausch Touch")..........8-10 85
(Gold vinyl.)
SOUTHLAND (7481 "Deep in the Heart of Texas")..........8-10 86
(Gold vinyl.)
Session: Eldon Shamblin; Waldo Weathers; Tom Morrell; Mark Harrell; Bob Meyers; Bob Boatright; Larry Reed; Dave Stanley; Ken Murray; John Anderson.
Also see ORIGINAL TEXAS PLAYBOYS

RAVA, Enrico

LPs: 10/12-inch

ELM....................................8-10 77

RAVAN, Genya P&R/LP '78

Singles: 7-inch

COLUMBIA..............................3-5 71-72
DE LITE..............................3-5 75
DUNHILL..............................3-8 73
20TH FOX..............................3-5 78-79

LPs: 10/12-inch

COLUMBIA..............................8-12 72
DUNHILL..............................8-15 73
20TH FOX..............................5-10 78-79
Also see GOLDIE & GINGERBREADS
Also see TEN WHEEL DRIVE

RAVEL, Chink

LPs: 10/12-inch

PIT BULL (9302 "Genesis Fall from Innocence")..........5-8 81
(Picture disc.)

RAVEL, Joe

Singles: 7-inch

COUNSEL (120 "Bye Bye Love")...40-60 63
GOAL (701 "The House of the Cool")..........50-75 64

RAVELL, Jackie, & Bandits

Singles: 7-inch

JORDAN....................................5-10 60

RAVELLES

Singles: 7-inch

MOBIE (3430 "Pshchedelic Movement")..........15-25 68
Members: John Richtig; Tom Lucas; Raymond Broullire; Rand Alquist; Carmella Altobelli.

RAVELS

Singles: 7-inch

DIAMOND (143 "Gonna Have Some Fun")..........8-12 63
Also see SHERIFF & RAVELS

RAVEN

Singles: 7-inch

RUST....................................5-10 63

RAVEN

Singles: 7-inch

COLUMBIA..............................4-6 69-70

LPs: 10/12-inch

COLUMBIA..............................10-20 69
DISCOVERY (36133 "Live at the Inferno")..........35-50 60s

RAVEN LP '85

Singles: 7-inch

RAMPART..............................3-5

LPs: 10/12-inch

ATLANTIC..............................5-8 85-86

RAVEN, Eddy C&W '74

(Eddie Raven)

Singles: 7-inch

ABC....................................3-5 74-75
ABC/DOT..............................3-5 75-76
CAPITOL..............................3-4 89-90
COSMOS..............................8-12 62
DIMENSION..............................3-5 79-81
ELEKTRA..............................3-4 81-82
LA LOUISIANNE (77 "Pictures")....10-20
MONUMENT..............................3-5 78
RCA....................................3-4 84-88
UNIVERSAL..............................3-4 89

LPs: 10/12-inch

ABC/DOT..............................5-10 75-76
DIMENSION..............................5-8 80
ELEKTRA..............................5-8 81
LA LOUISIANNE..............................10-15
RCA....................................5-8 84-88

RAVEN, Marcia D&D '83

Singles: 12-inch

PROFILE..............................4-6 83

Singles: 7-inch

PROFILE..............................3-5 83

RAVEN BROTHERS

Singles: 7-inch

SMASH..............................4-6 69

RAVENAIRS

Singles: 7-inch

ALGONQUIN (718 "Together Forever")..........75-125 58
(First issued as by the Rivieras.)

RAVENETTES

Singles: 7-inch

MOON (103 "Too Young to Know")..........25-35 59

RAVENETTES

Singles: 7-inch

JOSIE (967 "Talk About Soul")........8-10 66

RAVENS P&R '47

("Featuring Jimmy Ricks")

Singles: 78 rpm

ARGO..............................50-75 56-57
CHECKER..............................15-25 57
COLUMBIA..............................200-400 50-51
HUB (3032 "Out of a Dream")......50-100 46
HUB (3033 "Bye Bye Baby Blues")..........50-100 46
KING..............................50-100 48-49
JUBILEE..............................15-25 55-56
MERCURY..............................25-50 51-55
OKEH (6825 "Whiffenpoof Song")..........200-300 51
OKEH (6843 "That Old Gang of Mine")..........200-300 51
OKEH (6888 "Mam'selle")..........100-150 52
NATIONAL..............................200-300 47-51
RENDITION (5001 "Write Me a Letter")..........50-100 51

Singles: 7-inch

ARGO (5255 "Kneel and Pray")......50-75 56
ARGO (5261 "A Simple Prayer")..75-125 56
(Rigid disc.)
ARGO (5261 "A Simple Prayer")....50-75 56
(Flexible disc.)
ARGO (5276 "That'll Be the Day") 30-50 57
ARGO (5284 "Here Is My Heart")...30-50 57
CHECKER (871 "That'll Be the Day")..........15-25 57
COLUMBIA (1-903 "Time Takes Care of Everything")..........1000-2000 50
(Compact 33 Single.)
COLUMBIA (6-903 "Time Takes Care of Everything")..........1000-2000 50
COLUMBIA (1-925 "I'm So Crazy for Love")..........1000-2000 50
(Compact 33 Single.)
COLUMBIA (6-925 "My Baby's Gone")..........1000-2000 50
COLUMBIA (39112 "You Don't Have to Drop a Heart to Break It")..........1000-2000 51
COLUMBIA (39194 "You're Always in My Dreams")..........1000-2000 51
COLUMBIA (39408 "You Foolish Thing")..........1000-2000 51
JUBILEE (5184 "Bye Bye Baby Blues")..........25-50 55
JUBILEE (5203 "Green Eyes")........25-50 55
JUBILEE (5217 "On Chapel Hill")..25-50 55
JUBILEE (5237 "I'll Always Be in Love with You")..........25-50 55
MEDIA ("Sixty Minute Man")..........3-5 93
(Colored vinyl.)
MERCURY (5764 "There's No Use Pretending")..........150-250 51
MERCURY (5800 "Begin the Beguine")..........100-200 52
MERCURY (5853 "Why Did You Leave")..........100-200 52
MERCURY (8291 "Write Me One Sweet Letter")..........100-150 52
MERCURY (8296 "Too Soon")...100-150 52
MERCURY (70060 "Don't Mention My Name")..........100-200 52
MERCURY (70119 "Come a Little Bit Closer")..........100-150 53
MERCURY (70213 "Who'll Be the Fool")..........100-150 53
MERCURY (70240 "Without a Song")..........100-150 53
MERCURY (70307 "September Song")..........100-150 54
MERCURY (70330 "Lonesome Road")..........100-150 54
MERCURY (70413 "Love Is No Dream")..........200-300 54
(Pink label.)
MERCURY (70413 "Love Is No Dream")..........100-150 54
(Black label.)
MERCURY (70505 "White Christmas")..........200-300 54
(Pink label.)
MERCURY (70505 "White Christmas")..........75-125 54
(Black label.)
MERCURY (70554 "Write Me a Letter")..........200-300 55
(Pink label.)
MERCURY (70554 "Write Me a Letter")..........75-125 55
(Black label.)
NATIONAL (9111 "Count Every Star")..........2000-3000 50
OKEH (6825 "Whiffenpoof Song")..........1000-2000 51
OKEH (6843 "That Old Gang of Mine")..........1000-2000 51
OKEH (6888 "Mam'selle")..........400-600 52
SAVOY (1540 "White Christmas") 20-30 58
TOP RANK (2003 "Into the Shadows")..........15-25 59
TOP RANK (2016 "Solitude")..........15-25 59
VIRGO..............................3-5 72

Picture Sleeves

MEDIA ("Sixty Minute Man")..........3-4 93

EPs: 7-inch

KING (310 "The Ravens Featuring Jimmy Ricks")..........500-750 54
RENDITION (104 "Four Great Voices")..........500-750 52

LPs: 10/12-inch

HARLEM HITPARADE..........10-20 75
REGENT (6062 "Write Me a Letter")..........100-150 57
(Green label.)
REGENT (6062 "Write Me a Letter")..........50-100 50s
(Red label.)
SAVOY..............................10-15 78
Members: Warren Suttles; Ollie Jones; Joe Van Loan; Jimmy Ricks; Leonard Puzey; Maithe Marshall; Joe Medlin; Louis Heyward; James Stewart; Louis Frazier; Tom Evans; James Van Loan; David Bowers; Paul Van Loan; Rich Cannon; Bob Kornegay; Willis Sanders; Willie Ray.
Also see BELLS
Also see COBB, Arnett
Also see CUES
Also see DREAMERS
Also see KING ODOM
Also see KINGS
Also see MARSHALL BROTHERS
Also see PLAYBOYS
Also see RICKS, Jimmy
Also see VAN LOAN, Joe

RAVENS & DINAH WASHINGTON

Singles: 78 rpm

MERCURY..............................20-30 51

Singles: 7-inch

MERCURY (8257 "Hey Good Lookin' ")..........50-75 51
Also see WASHINGTON, Dinah

RAVENS / Three Clouds

Singles: 78 rpm

KING (4260 "Out of a Dream")......25-50 48
KING (4272 "Honey")..........25-50 49
KING (4293 "My Sugar Is So Refined")..........25-50 49
Also see RAVENS

RAVENS

Singles: 7-inch

SARA (6383 "The Shuck")..........15-25 63
Members: Mark Strauss; Mike McCabe; Merlin Wield; Dennis Thompson; Don Wendt.

RAVENS

Singles: 7-inch

HAVEN (197 "Sleepless Nights")...15-25 65

RAVENSCROFT, Thurl

(With the Jeff Alexander Quartet; with Sky Boys; with Ranger Chorus; Thurl Ravenscroft Singers)

Singles: 7-inch

AARDELL..............................10-15
FABOR..............................10-15
O-1 (1 "Cool Cool Bottle")..........10-15
BUENA VISTA (364 "Ten Who Dared")..........8-12 60

LPs: 10/12-inch

DOT (3430 "Great Hits")..........15-25 62
(Monaural.)
DOT (25430 "Great Hits")..........20-30 62
(Stereo.)
Also see ANDREWS SISTERS & THURL RAVENSCROFT
Also see DE CASTRO SISTERS

RAVE-ONS

Singles: 7-inch

RE-CAR (9016 "Baby Don't Love Me")..........20-30 65
TWIN TOWN (702 "Everybody Tells Me")..........20-30 66
TWIN TOWN (710 "Whenever")....20-30 66
Also see JOKERS WILD
Also see SOUTH 40

RAVES

Singles: 78 rpm

LIBERTY..............................8-12 56

Singles: 7-inch

LIBERTY..............................10-20 56

RAVES

Singles: 7-inch

SWADE (104 "Tell Me One More Time")..........40-50 59

RAVES

Singles: 7-inch

SMASH..............................8-12 67-68

RAVET, Kerney

Singles: 7-inch

MERCURY (71431 "Tyrone")........20-30 59

RAVIN' BLUE

Singles: 7-inch

MONUMENT (968 "Love")..........15-25 66
MONUMENT (1034 "Colors")..........5-10 67

RAVIN' IMAGE

Singles: 7-inch

CAPITOL..............................4-6 69

RAVING MADD

Singles: 7-inch

GOLSTAR..............................4-8 67

RAVON

Singles: 7-inch

RECORDO..............................5-10 61

RAVONS

(Rav-ons)

Singles: 7-inch

AARROW (734 "Teenage Hop")......25-50 58
DAVIS (464 "Don't Ever Break Your Baby's Heart")..........20-40 59

RAVONS

Singles: 7-inch

BANGAR (621 "Hey Little Girl")......20-30 63
Also see FIVE KEEYS

RAVONS

("Vocal by Jenny Johnson")

Singles: 7-inch

YUCCA (145 "Everybody's Laughing at Me")..........400-600 62
(Identification number is "D-10" and is on left side of label.)
YUCCA (145 "Everybody's Laughing at Me")..........50-75 62
(Identification number is "LH-14201" and is on right side of label.)
Member: Jenny Johnson.

RAVONS

Singles: 7-inch

GMA (13 "I Want You to Be")........15-25

RAVYNS

Singles: 7-inch

FULL MOON/ASYLUM..........3-4 82

RAVYNS / Don Felder

Singles: 7-inch

ELEKTRA/ASYLUM..............................3-4 82

Picture Sleeves

ELEKTRA/ASYLUM..............................3-4 82
Also see FELDER, Don

RAW

Singles: 7-inch

CORAL..............................3-5 71

LPs: 10/12-inch

CORAL (57515 "Raw Holly")..........20-30 71

RAW EDGE

Singles: 7-inch

SIDEWALK..............................4-8 68

RAW MEAT

Singles: 7-inch

BLUE HOUR..............................4-8 70s
CAPITOL..............................3-5 70
MUSICOR..............................4-8 68
Members: Gene Peranich; Don Gruender; Mike Jablonski.

RAW SILK R&B '82

Singles: 12-inch

WEST END..............................4-6 83

Singles: 7-inch

WEST END..............................3-5 82-83

RAW SPITT

Singles: 7-inch

U.A. (50813 "Song to Sing")..........8-12 71

LPs: 10/12-inch

U.A. (6795 "Maybe You Ain't Black")..........15-25 71

RAWLS, Lou LP '63

Singles: 12-inch

PHILADELPHIA INT'L..............................4-8 79

Singles: 7-inch

ARISTA..............................3-5 75
BELL..............................3-5 74
CANDIX..............................8-12 60-61
CAPITOL..............................4-8 61-70
EPIC..............................3-4 82-85
GAMBLE..............................3-4 87
MGM..............................3-5 71-73
PHILADELPHIA INT'L..............................3-5 76-81
SHAR-DEE..............................8-12 60

Picture Sleeves

CAPITOL..............................4-8 67

EPs: 7-inch

CAPITOL..............................5-10 60s
(Includes Juke box issues and 33 Compacts.)

LPs: 10/12-inch

ALLEGIANCE..............................5-8 84
BELL..............................8-10 74
CAPITOL (Except 1700 thru 2900 series)..........5-12 69-77
CAPITOL (1700 thru 2900 series)..12-25 63-68
EPIC..............................5-8 82-83
MGM..............................8-10 71-73
PHILADELPHIA INT'L..............................5-10 76-80
PICKWICK..............................5-10 69
POLYDOR..............................8-10 76
Also see COOKE, Sam
Also see PHILADELPHIA INTERNATIONAL ALL STARS
Also see SEEKERS / Lou Rawls
Also see VEGA, Tata

RAWLS, Lou, & Les McCann Ltd.

Singles: 7-inch

CAPITOL..............................4-6 62

LPs: 10/12-inch

CAPITOL..............................5-8 75
(With "SM" prefix.)
CAPITOL..............................20-30 62
(With "T" or "ST" prefix.)
Also see McCANN, Les
Also see RAWLS, Lou

RAY, Ada

Singles: 7-inch

ZELLS..............................4-8 62

RAY, Alder

Singles: 7-inch

LIBERTY..............................8-12 64
MINIT..............................4-8 66
REVUE..............................4-8 68

RAY, Anita

(With the Nature Boys; Annita Ray)

Singles: 7-inch

AVA..............................4-8 64
DREAM (1300 "Elvis Presley Blues")..........10-20 58
JAMIE..............................8-12 59

RAY, Baby: see BABY RAY

RAY, Billy

Singles: 7-inch

OKEH..............................25-50
TITAN..............................5-10 60

RAY, Bob

LPs: 10/12-inch

SOUL CITY..............................10-15 69

RAY, Bobby, & Cadillacs

Singles: 7-inch

CAPITOL..............................10-15 63
Also see CADILLACS

RAY, Bobby, & Gents

Singles: 7-inch

CRUSADER..............................4-8 64

RAY, Burch, & Walkers

Singles: 7-inch

LAVENDER..............................20-25 60s
RUFF (1017 "Love Question")......25-35 60s
SULLY (915 "Love Question")......25-35 60s

YELLOWSTONE ... 4-8 60s

RAY, Chuck
Singles: 7-inch
BUDDAH ... 8-12
GEMINI (101 "Reconsider") ... 3-5 75

RAY, Corki
Singles: 7-inch
BRENT ... 4-8 63

RAY, Danny
Singles: 7-inch
VIN (1025 "Love Me") ... 75-100 60

RAY, Dave
LPs: 10/12-inch
ELEKTRA ... 10-20 65-66

RAY, David
Singles: 7-inch
KLIFF (101 "Lonesome Baby Blues") ... 150-250 58
KLIFF (102 "Jitterbuggin' Baby") ... 200-300 58

RAY, Diane P&R '63
Singles: 7-inch
MERCURY ... 4-8 63-64
Picture Sleeves
MERCURY ... 10-15 63
LPs: 10/12-inch
MERCURY (20903 "The Exciting Years") ... 30-60 64
MERCURY (60903 "The Exciting Years") ... 50-100 64

RAY, Don
Singles: 7-inch
ARWIN (1004 "Roly Poly") ... 10-15 59
RCA (9170 "I Feel Love Coming on") ... 25-50 67
RCA (9438 "Born a Loser") ... 25-50 68
RODEO (129 "Those Rock & Roll Blues") ... 150-250 58
RODEO (130 "Doncha' Baby My Baby") ... 100-200 58

RAY, Don P&R/LP '78
Singles: 7-inch
POLYDOR ... 3-5 78
LPs: 10/12-inch
POLYDOR ... 5-10 78

RAY, Don, & Hornets
Singles: 7-inch
HORNET ... 5-10 60s

RAY, Donald, & Solid Sound
Singles: 7-inch
BEE & TEE (68005 "I Think About Love") ... 25-35

RAY, Eddie
Singles: 7-inch
GREAT ... 4-8 68

RAY, Enos, & Royal J's
Singles: 7-inch
HEART (889 "Moon Talk") ... 5-10 61

RAY, Frankie, & Bel Airs
(Franklin Ray)
Singles: 7-inch
CUCA (1192 "Broken Heart") ... 5-10 64
CUCA (6474 "Country Boy with a Big Guitar") ... 5-10 64

RAY, Harry R&B '82
Singles: 7-inch
SUGAR HILL ... 3-4 82-83
LPs: 10/12-inch
SUGAR HILL ... 5-8 83
Also see RAY, GOODMAN & BROWN

RAY, Gerald
Singles: 7-inch
REED (15 "Fussin' ") ... 5-10

RAY, James P&R '61
(With the Hutch Davie Orchestra)
Singles: 7-inch
CAPRICE ... 10-20 61-62
CONGRESS ... 10-20 63-64
DYNAMIC ... 10-20 62
LPs: 10/12-inch
CAPRICE (LP-1002 "James Ray") ... 40-60 62
(Monaural.)
CAPRICE (SLP-1002 "James Ray") ... 75-100 62
(Stereo.)
Also see DAVIE, Hutch
Also see GRANT, Janie

RAY, Jerr
Singles: 7-inch
GAN ... 4-8 65

RAY, Johnnie P&R '51
(With the Four Lads; with Maurice King & His Wolverines)
Singles: 78 rpm
COLUMBIA ... 5-10 52-58
OKEH ... 8-12 52
Singles: 7-inch
CADENCE ... 5-10 60
COLUMBIA ... 8-15 52-60
DECCA ... 4-6 63-64
GROOVE ... 4-8 64
LIBERTY ... 4-8 62
OKEH (6809 "Wiskey and Gin") ... 15-25 51
OKEH (6840 "Cry") ... 10-20 51
OKEH RHYTHM & BLUES (6840 "Cry") ... 15-25 51
U.A. ... 4-8 61
Picture Sleeves
COLUMBIA ... 10-20 57
EPs: 7-inch
COLUMBIA ... 10-20 52-59
EPIC ... 10-20 52-54
LPs: 10/12-inch
COLUMBIA (961 "The Big Beat") ... 30-50 57
COLUMBIA (1093 thru 1227) ... 20-40 57-59
COLUMBIA (1385 "On the Trail") ... 15-25 59
(Monaural.)
COLUMBIA (2510 "I Cry for You") ... 30-50 56
(10 Inch LP.)
COLUMBIA (6199 "Johnnie Ray") ... 35-55 51
(10 Inch LP.)
COLUMBIA (8180 "On the Trail") ... 20-30 59
(Stereo.)
EPIC (1120 "Johnnie Ray") ... 30-50 55
(10-inch LP.)
HARMONY ... 5-10 71
SUNSET ... 10-15 66
Also see DAY, Doris, & Johnnie Ray
Also see FOUR LADS
Also see KING, Maurice

RAY, Johnnie, & Timi Yuro
Singles: 7-inch
LIBERTY ... 5-8 61
Also see RAY, Johnnie
Also see YURO, Timi

RAY, Kai
Singles: 7-inch
BRITE STAR ... 5-10

RAY, Laverne
(With the Raytones)
Singles: 78 rpm
JUBILEE ... 10-20 49
OKEH (7091 "I'm in Love Again") ... 15-25 57
Singles: 7-inch
OKEH (7091 "I'm in Love Again") ... 15-25 57

RAY, Leda
Singles: 7-inch
ALLIED ARTISTS ... 3-5 77

RAY, Link: see WRAY, Link

RAY, Little Robey
Singles: 7-inch
INDIGO ... 5-10 60

RAY, Lonnie
Singles: 7-inch
FAME ... 4-8 65

RAY, Marla
Singles: 7-inch
CHANCELLOR ... 5-10 60

RAY, Merle, & Southern Rockets
Singles: 7-inch
BANDERA (1309 "I Won't Be Back Tonight") ... 10-15 62
BANDERA (1314 "Spanish Beat") ... 10-15 62

RAY, Nancy
Singles: 7-inch
COLPIX (634 "Growing Up Too Fast") ... 5-10 62

RAY, Neil
Singles: 7-inch
PLANTATION (2 "Big Fanny") ... 5-10 70s

RAY, Nelson
Singles: 7-inch
PHILLIPS INT'L ... 5-10 60

RAY, Ricardo P&R '68
Singles: 7-inch
ALEGRE ... 4-6 68

RAY, Ritchie
Singles: 7-inch
IMPERIAL ... 5-10 63

RAY, Rockin' Richie
Singles: 7-inch
RHINO ... 3-4 85

RAY, Ronnie
Singles: 7-inch
CIRCLE DOT (1002 "Mean Mama Blues") ... 200-300

RAY, Shirley
Singles: 7-inch
EPIC ... 4-8 63-64

RAY, Spider
Singles: 7-inch
BOSS ... 4-8 61

RAY, Tony
Singles: 7-inch
DOT ... 3-6 69

RAY, Wade
Singles: 78 rpm
FABOR (115 "Burning Desire") ... 5-10 54
Singles: 7-inch
FABOR (115 "Burning Desire") ... 10-20 54
RCA ... 10-20 50s
TOPPA (1058 "It's My Way") ... 15-25 57
TOPPA (1079 "Have Yourself a Party") ... 10-20 62

RAY & BOB P&R '62
Singles: 7-inch
LEDO ... 8-10 62
Members: Ray Swayne; Bob Appleberry.

RAY & DARCHAES
Singles: 7-inch
ALJON (1249 "Carol") ... 100-125 62
BUZZY (202 "Darling Forever") ... 100-125 62
Member: Ray Dahrouge.

RAY & DAVE
Singles: 7-inch
MICA ... 8-12

RAY & FURIES
Singles: 7-inch
COED (558 "Rapid Jenny") ... 10-20 61

RAY & GINO
Singles: 7-inch
PARAMOUNT ... 3-6

RAY & LAMAR
Singles: 7-inch
CAPA ... 5-10 62
VIN ... 10-15 60

RAY & LINDY
Singles: 7-inch
ATCO ... 5-10 59
ROCKET ... 10-15 57
U.A. ... 5-10 59

RAY & STRAYS
(Ray Stankes & His Orchestra)
Singles: 7-inch
LARRIC (101 "How Will I Know My Love") ... 50-75 62
Member: Ray Stankes.

RAY, GERALD & NANCY
Singles: 7-inch
ATCO ... 4-6 68

RAY, GOODMAN & BROWN R&B '79
Singles: 7-inch
EMI AMERICA ... 3-4 87
PANORAMIC ... 3-4 84
POLYDOR ... 3-5 80-81
LPs: 10/12-inch
POLYDOR ... 5-10 80-81
Members: Harry Ray; Al Goodman; Bill Brown.
Also see MOMENTS
Also see RAY, Harry

RAY BEATS
Singles: 7-inch
Z (8 "Calhoun Surf") ... 10-20 60s

RAY MEN
Singles: 7-inch
DIAMOND ... 5-10 65
Also see WRAY, Link

RAY DOTS
Singles: 78 rpm
VIBRO ... 100-200 56
Singles: 7-inch
VIBRO (1651 "I Need Someone") ... 500-750 56

RAYBEATS
LPs: 10/12-inch
PVC ... 5-10 81

RAYBURN, Rick
Singles: 7-inch
EVANA (0002 "You're Number One") ... 50-100

RAYBURN, Margie P&R '57
Singles: 78 rpm
ALMA ... 4-8 54
LIBERTY ... 5-10 56-57
S&G ... 4-8 54
Singles: 7-inch
ALMA ... 5-10 54
CAPITOL ... 4-6 65
CHALLENGE ... 4-8 61
DOT ... 4-8 62-66
LIBERTY ... 5-10 56-62
S&G ... 5-10 54
Picture Sleeves
LIBERTY ... 10-15 57
LPs: 10/12-inch
LIBERTY (3126 "Margie") ... 20-25 59
(Monaural.)
LIBERTY (7126 "Margie") ... 25-35 59
(Stereo.)

RAY-DARS
Singles: 7-inch
SOUTHERN ... 4-8

RAYDIO R&B '77
(Featuring Ray Parker Jr.)
Singles: 7-inch
ARISTA ... 3-5 78-79
Picture Sleeves
ARISTA ... 3-5 78-79
LPs: 10/12-inch
ARISTA ... 5-10 78-79
Also see KNIGHT, Jerry
Also see PARKER, Ray, Jr.

RAYDONS
Singles: 7-inch
TRIPLE-X (105 "Visibility Zero") ... 10-20 60

RAYE, Anthony
Singles: 7-inch
IMPACT (1009 "On the Edge of Sorrow") ... 20-30 66
IMPACT (1030 "Hold on to What You Got") ... 50-100 67

RAYE, Billy
Singles: 7-inch
CUCA (1026 "Melody of Love") ... 10-15 61

RAYE, Cal
Singles: 7-inch
PHAROAH ... 5-10
SUPER (101 "My Tears Start to Fall") ... 15-25

RAYE, Colin C&W/LP '91
Singles: 7-inch
EPIC ... 3-4 91-92
LPs: 10/12-inch
EPIC ... 5-8 91
Also see WRAYS

RAYE, Dina
Singles: 7-inch
CAMEO ... 4-8 61

RAYE, Fonda: see RAE, Fonda

RAYE, Jackie
ARCADE (114 "Crazy Cool") ... 10-20 53
Singles: 7-inch
ARCADE (114 "Crazy Cool") ... 20-30 53

RAYE, Jan, Quartet
("Featuring Lilyann")
Singles: 78 rpm
BATON (221 "You Fool") ... 10-15 56
Singles: 7-inch
BATON (221 "You Fool") ... 20-30 56

RAYE, Jay
Singles: 7-inch
EPIC (9241 "Steel Guitar Rock") ... 15-25 57

RAYE, Jean
Singles: 7-inch
WHIP (275 "Open Your Eyes") ... 10-20 62

RAYE, Jerry
(With Fenwyck; with New Trend)
Singles: 7-inch
DE VILLE ("I Cry") ... 8-12 69
(Selection number not known.)
DE VILLE (202 "Pray for Me") ... 10-15 68
(Red vinyl.)
DE VILLE (207 "State of Mind") ... 10-15 68
(Blue vinyl.)
PERSPECTIVE (6005 "The Simple Things of Life") ... 10-15 60s
LPs: 10/12-inch
DE VILLE (101 "The Many Sides of Jerry Raye Featuring Fenwyck") ... 450-650 67
(Red vinyl.)
Members: Jerry Raye; Pat Robinson; Pat Maroshek; Keith Knighter.
Also see FENWYCK
Also see RAYE, Jerry

RAYE, Jimmie
Singles: 7-inch
TUFF (401 "I Tried") ... 5-10 64

RAYE, Patsy
(With the Beatniks)
Singles: 7-inch
ROULETTE ... 5-10 59-61
Also see BEATNIKS

RAYE, Susan C&W/LP '70
Singles: 7-inch
CAPITOL ... 3-6 69-76
U.A. ... 3-5 76-77
WESTEXAS ... 3-4 85-86
Picture Sleeves
CAPITOL ... 3-5 71
LPs: 10/12-inch
CAPITOL ... 10-20 70-76
U.A. ... 5-10 77
Also see OWENS, Buck, & Susan Raye

RAYE, Tommy
Singles: 7-inch
PEN (351 "You Don't Love Me") ... 5-10

RAYE, RICK & RITA
Singles: 7-inch
SOUND STAGE 7 ... 4-8 65

RAYLENE & BLUE ANGELS
(With Dairylanders)
Singles: 7-inch
CUCA (1141 "Sentenced") ... 25-35 63
CUCA (6633 "Shakin' All Over") ... 25-35 66
Members: RAYLENE LOOS; ROGER LOOS; TOM LOOS; TOM REISCHL.
Also see RICKY & RAYLENE

RAYLOV, Bobby
Singles: 7-inch
LOVINN (200 "If We Can't Be Lovers") ... 20-30

RAYMARKS
Singles: 7-inch
JERDEN (752 "Louise") ... 10-15 66
PANORAMA (6 "Backfire") ... 10-15 64
Also see PAYMARKS

RAYMOND, Lee
Singles: 78 rpm
DECCA ... 4-8 55
Singles: 7-inch
DECCA ... 5-10 55

RAYMOND, Shirley
Singles: 7-inch
AT LAST ... 4-8 62

RAY-NEARS
Singles: 7-inch
FAM (501 "Hoochie") ... 10-20 63
FAM (503 "Surfin' Fever") ... 10-20 63

RAYNOR, Wilguis J.C.
(J.C. Raynor)
Singles: 7-inch
DECCA ... 4-6 64
RTF ... 4-8 77
Picture Sleeves
RTF ... 4-8 77

RAYONS
Singles: 7-inch
DECCA (32521 "Do You Love Me") ... 20-30 69
FORTE ... 10-20 60s

RAY-O-VACS R&B '49
Singles: 78 rpm
ATCO ... 10-20 57
COLEMAN ... 8-12 49
DECCA ... 5-10 50-53
JOSIE ... 10-15 54
JUBILEE ... 10-15 52
KAISER ... 10-15 56
Singles: 7-inch
ATCO ... 10-20 57
DECCA ... 10-20 50-53
JOSIE ... 15-25 54
JUBILEE ... 15-22 52
KAISER ... 15-25 56
SHARP ... 15-25 60
Members: Lester Harris; Herb Milliner.

RAYS P&R/R&B '57
Singles: 78 rpm
CAMEO (117 "Silhouettes") ... 20-40 57
CAMEO (128 "Triangle") ... 20-40 58
CHESS ... 10-30 55-57
XYZ (100 "My Steady Girl") ... 15-25 57
XYZ (102 "Silhouettes") ... 30-50 57
Singles: 7-inch
ABKCO ... 3-4 80s
ARGO (1074 "How Long Must I Wait") ... 15-25 57
CAMEO (117 "Silhouettes") ... 15-25 57
CAMEO (128 "Triangle") ... 15-25 58
CAMEO (133 "Rags to Riches") ... 15-25 58
CHESS (1613 "Tippity Top") ... 15-20 55
CHESS (1678 "Second Fiddle") ... 15-25 57
PERRI (1004 "Are You Happy Now") ... 15-25 62
(With Frankie Valli.)
XYZ (100 "My Steady Girl") ... 35-45 57
XYZ (102 "Silhouettes") ... 75-125 57
(Gray label.)
XYZ (102 "Silhouettes") ... 30-50 57
(Blue label.)
XYZ (106 "Souvenirs of Summertime") ... 30-40 58
XYZ (600 "Why Do You Look the Other Way") ... 30-40 59
XYZ (605 "Mediterranean Moon") ... 25-30 59
XYZ (607 "Magic Moon") ... 25-30 60
(Blue label.)
XYZ (607 "Magic Moon") ... 10-15 60
(Red label.)
XYZ (608 "Old Devil Moon") ... 10-15 60
XYZ (2001 "Souvenirs of Summertime") ... 25-35 58
(First issued in 1958 on XYZ 106.)
EPs: 7-inch
CHESS (5120 "The Rays") ... 150-250 58
Members: Harold "Hal" Miller; Walter Ford; David Jones; Harry James.
Also see MILLER, Hal

RAYS R&B '88
Singles: 7-inch
EMI MANHATTAN ... 3-4 87

RAYTONES: see MOORE, Ray

RAY-VONS
Singles: 7-inch
LAURIE (3248 "Judy") ... 100-200 64

RAZ, Rivka
Singles: 7-inch
BUDDAH ... 3-5 72

RAZE
Singles: 7-inch
COLUMBIA ... 3-4 88

RAZMATAZ
LPs: 10/12-inch
U.A. ... 8-10 72

RAZOR'S EDGE P&R '66
Singles: 7-inch
POW ... 10-15 66-67
POWER (4932 "Get Yourself Together") ... 15-25 67
Members: Bill Ande; Tom Condra; Dave Hieronymous; Jim Tolliver.
Also see AMERICAN BEATLES

RAZOR'S EDGE
Singles: 7-inch
KINGSTON (196716 "Gotta Find Her") ... 10-20 67
Member: Pat Farrell.
Also see FARRELL, Pat, & Believers
Also see TRIUMPHS

RAZORBACK C&W '87
Singles: 7-inch
COMPLEAT ... 3-4 87
ICR ... 3-4 87
MERCURY ... 3-4 88
Also see GRAYGHOST

RAZZ
EPs: 7-inch
LIMP ... 10-15

RAZZY & NEIGHBORHOOD KIDS
Singles: 7-inch
AQUARIAN (601 "I Hate Hate") ... 5-10
Member: Razzy Bailey.
Also see BAILEY, RAZZY R-DELLS: see R DELLS

REA, Chris P&R/LP '78
Singles: 7-inch
COLUMBIA ... 3-5 82

GEFFEN ... 3-4 89-90
MOTOWN ... 3-4 87
RCA ... 3-4 84
U.A. ... 3-5 78-79

Picture Sleeves

GEFFEN ... 3-4 89
MOTOWN ... 3-4 87
U.A. ... 3-5 78

LPs: 10/12-inch

COLUMBIA ... 5-8 80-82
GEFFEN ... 5-8 89-90
RCA ... 5-8 84
U.A. ... 5-8 78

Also see WILLIE & Poor Boys

REACTIONS

Singles: 7-inch

CLOUD (10498 "Just a Little Love") ... 10-15 65
COOL SOUND (701 "Just a Little Love") ... 20-30 64
MUTUAL (509 "Our Wonderful Love") ... 10-20 65
ROCK (5810 "In My Grave") ... 30-40 60s
TASSEL ... 10-20

REACTORS

Singles: 7-inch

CAMEO ... 5-8 67

READ, Bernadine

(With the Don Costa Orchestra)

Singles: 78 rpm

ABC-PAR ... 4-8 56

Singles: 7-inch

ABC-PAR ... 5-10 56

Also see COSTA, Don, Orchestra

READ, John Dawson P&R '75

Singles: 7-inch

CHRYSALIS ... 3-5 75

LPs: 10/12-inch

CHRYSALIS ... 5-10 75-76

READ, Otis

Singles: 7-inch

NANC ... 15-25 61

READY, Lynn

Singles: 7-inch

COWTOWN (809 "Jeremiah Peabody's Poly Unsaturated Quick Dissolving, Fast Acting, Pleasant Tasting Green & Purple Pills") ... 6-12 61
SPIN ... 5-10 60

READY FOR THE WORLD R&B '84

Singles: 12-inch

MCA ... 4-6 84-86

Singles: 7-inch

BLUE LAKE ... 4-6 84
MCA ... 3-4 84-87

Picture Sleeves

MCA ... 3-4 85-86

LPs: 10/12-inch

MCA ... 5-8 86-88

READYMEN

Singles: 7-inch

BANGAR (00655 "Surfer's Bues") 30-50 65

Picture Sleeves

BANGAR (00655 "Surfer's Bues") 50-75 65

REAGAN, Jimmy, & Rhythm Rockers

Singles: 7-inch

G&G (128 "Lonely Lonely Heart") ... 75-100 59
MONA-LEE (128 "Lonely Lonely Heart") ... 30-50 58

REAGAN, Joe

LPs: 10/12-inch

WYNCOTE (9047 "Tribute to Jim Reeves") ... 8-12 63

REAGAN, Ronald

Singles: 7-inch

EV (92166 "Year of Decision") ... 5-10
(Flexi-disc. Promotional issue only.)
LIVING AMERICAN STORIES (1831 "The Declaration of Independence") ... 15-25 56
(Colored vinyl.)

Picture Sleeves

EV (92166 "Year of Decision–To All Californians") ... 5-10
(Promotional issue only.)

EPs: 7-inch

"X" ... 10-15 56

LPs: 10/12-inch

BLUEBIRD ... 10-20 59
DECCA ... 10-15 67
KEY ... 15-20 64
KID STUFF (6005 "Space Shuttle, Columbia") ... 15-20 80
(With Astronauts. Picture disc. Reissued as *Space Shuttle: a True Space Adventure*. See Picture Disc Chapter for that listing.)
MCA/DECCA (DL7-4943 "Freedom's Finest Hour") ... 35-45 81
(Picture disc.)
X ... 25-35 56

Also see GOLDWATER, Barry

REAL GEORGE

Singles: 7-inch

GLOVER (1001 "Flip, Flop-Flop") ... 25-50

REAL IMPOSSIBLES

Singles: 12-inch

ATOMIC GIRAFFE ... 5-8 84

Members: Marc Platt; Wally Giffen; Harlan Steinberger; Probyn Gregory.

REAL KIDS

EPs: 7-inch

BOMP ... 5-8

REAL LIFE P&R '83

Singles: 12-inch

CURB/MCA ... 4-6 83-86

Singles: 7-inch

CURB/MCA ... 3-4 83-86

Picture Sleeves

CURB/MCA ... 3-4 84

LPs: 10/12-inch

CURB/MCA ... 5-8 83-89

REAL LIST

Singles: 7-inch

C.P. (102 "Pick Up the Marbles") ... 25-45

REAL ORIGINAL BEATLES

Singles: 7-inch

DOT ... 10-20 64

REAL PROS

Singles: 7-inch

CINEMA ... 3-5 75-78

REAL ROXANNE R&B '85

(With Hitman Howie Tee)

Singles: 12-inch

SELECT ... 4-6 85-86

REAL THING P&R/R&B '76

Singles: 12-inch

BELIEVE in a DREAM ... 4-6 81
EPIC ... 4-8 79

Singles: 7-inch

BELIEVE in a DREAM ... 3-5 81
EPIC ... 3-5 79
U.A. ... 3-5 76-77
WHIZ ... 4-6 69

LPs: 10/12-inch

U.A. ... 5-10 76

REAL to REEL R&B/D&D '84

Singles: 12-inch

ARISTA ... 4-6 83-84

Singles: 7-inch

ARISTA ... 3-4 83-84

LPs: 10/12-inch

ARISTA ... 5-8 83

REALISTICS

Singles: 7-inch

DE-LITE ... 3-6 73
LOMA ... 4-8 67-68

REALMS

Singles: 7-inch

MELODY (105 "All I Want") ... 10-20 67

REAM, Randy

Singles: 7-inch

SRO ... 3-5 80

LPs: 10/12-inch

SRO ... 5-10 80

REAR EXIT

Singles: 7-inch

MTA (132 "Excitation") ... 20-30 60s

REAR EXIT

Singles: 7-inch

NIGHT OWL (1527 "Thinking of You") ... 10-20 70

Members: Ken Burhop; Gary Leistikow; John Frederickson; Bill Preuss; Peter Bloom; Scott Yeager.

REARDON, Eddie

Singles: 7-inch

BRUNSWICK (55062 "Who Is Eddie") ... 15-25 58
(With the Three Friends.)

Also see FONTAINE, Eddie
Also see THREE FRIENDS

REASONABLE FACSIMILE

Singles: 7-inch

VERVE/FOLKWAYS ... 4-8 66

REASONS

Singles: 7-inch

U.A. ... 4-8 65-66

Picture Sleeves

U.A. ... 8-10 66

REASONS for BEING

Singles: 7-inch

FONTANA ... 4-8 66

REASONS WHY

Singles: 7-inch

SOUND TRACK (2000 "Melinda") ... 25-35 66

Also see LAVENDER HILL EXPRESS

REASONS WHY

Singles: 7-inch

AMY ... 10-15 66-67
CHA CHA (780 "The Game of War") ... 30-40 60s
KM (727 "All I Really Need Is Love") ... 20-30 67

REAVES, Paulette R&B '77

Singles: 7-inch

BLUE CANDLE ... 3-5 77-78

REAVES, Pearl, & Concords

Singles: 78 rpm

HARLEM ... 40-60 55

Singles: 7-inch

HARLEM (2332 "You Can't Stay Here") ... 100-150 55

Also see CONCORDS

REB & ROGUES

Singles: 7-inch

LOMA ... 4-8 65

REBB, Johnny, & Rebels

Singles: 7-inch

BULLSEYE (1027 "Rock On") ... 400-500 59

REBECCA

Singles: 7-inch

W.B. ... 5-8 62

REBECCA & Sunny Brook Farmers

LPs: 10/12-inch

MUSICOR (3176 "Rebecca and the Sunny Brook Farmers") ... 15-25 69

Members: Kiki; Ilene Novog; Ilene Rapaport; Cliff Mandell; Mark Kapner.

Also see COUNTRY JOE & FISH

REBECCA LYNN: see LYNN, Rebecca

REBEL, Johnny

Singles: 7-inch

PEPPER ... 10-20 60s
REBEL ... 10-20 67-68

REBEL, Tony

LPs: 10/12-inch

EPIC ... 8-10 90s

REBEL & JAGUARS

Singles: 7-inch

CENTURY CUSTOM (20748 "Take Off") ... 8-12

REBEL DAVIS: see DAVIS, Rebel

REBEL HEELS

Singles: 7-inch

ATLANTIC ... 3-4 88

Picture Sleeves

ATLANTIC ... 3-4 88

REBEL ROUSERS

Singles: 7-inch

HELENE (3 "War Paint") ... 10-15 60
HITT (102 "Peter Gunn Twist") ... 8-12 62
LOUIS (1006 "Swanee Twist") ... 8-12 62
MEMPHIS (107 "Thunder") ... 10-15 64
MEMPHIS (113 "Zombie Walk") ... 10-15 64

REBELS

Singles: 7-inch

DORE (510 "Marathon Walk") ... 15-25 58

REBELS

Singles: 7-inch

KINGS-X (3362 "In the Park") .. 500-1000 59

REBELS

Singles: 7-inch

PEACOCK (1909 "Just Give Me Your Hand") ... 10-15 61

REBELS P&R '62

Singles: 7-inch

MAR-LEE (0094 "Wild Weekend") 20-40 60
QUALITY (1024 "Wild Weekend") 25-50 60
(Canadian.)

Members: Tom Gorman, Paul Balon, Mickey Kipler, Jim Kipler.

Also see BUFFALO REBELS
Also see ROCKIN' REBELS

REBELS

Singles: 7-inch

GASLIGHT (558 "Run Little Sheba") ... 300-500 60s
(Previously issued as by the Twisters.)

Also see SMITH, Bob
Also see TWISTERS

REBELS

Singles: 7-inch

REBEL (1070 "The Rebel Beat") ... 10-20 60s
(Reissued as by John & Ed Strickand.)

Also see STRICKLAND, Jon & Ed

REBENNACK, Mac

(With the Soul Orchestra)

Singles: 7-inch

AFO (309 "The Point") ... 15-25 62
ACE (611 "Good Times") ... 15-25 61
REX (1008 "Storm Warning") ... 30-50 59

Also see ANDERSON, Elton
Also see DR. JOHN

REBIRTH

LPs: 10/12-inch

AVANT GARDE ... 8-12 71

REBNER, Paul

Singles: 7-inch

MILESTONE ... 4-8 62

REBOUNDS

Singles: 7-inch

TOWER ... 4-8 66

REBS

Singles: 7-inch

CAPITOL (4040 "Bunky") ... 10-15 58

REBS

LPs: 10/12-inch

FREDLO (6830 "A.D. Break Through") ... 400-600 68
(Reportedly 200 to 250 copies made.)

RECALLS

Singles: 7-inch

ARROW (2002 "No Reason") ... 50-75

RECITATIONS

Singles: 7-inch

DOUBLE SHOT (136 "The Great Night Hunter") ... 4-8 69

RECORD, Donnie C&W '83

Singles: 7-inch

BRIARROSE ... 3-4 83

RECORD, Eugene R&B '77

Singles: 12-inch

W.B. ... 4-8 79

Singles: 7-inch

W.B. ... 3-5 77-79

LPs: 10/12-inch

W.B. ... 5-10 77-79

Also see CHANTEURS
Also see CHI-LITES

RECORDS P&R/LP '79

Singles: 7-inch

VIRGIN ... 3-5 79-81

Picture Sleeves

VIRGIN ... 3-5 79-81

EPs: 7-inch

VIRGIN ... 3-6 79
(Issued as a bonus with Virgin LP 13130, *The Records*.)

LPs: 10/12-inch

VIRGIN ... 8-10 79-82

RECTOR, Hank

Singles: 7-inch

STARLITE (713 "I'm Gonna Let You Go") ... 20-30

RED, L.A.

Singles: 7-inch

ATLAS ... 5-10 60

RED & BLUE

Singles: 7-inch

HERALD (525 "Rockin' Red Riding Hood") ... 25-35 58

RED & FLAMES

Singles: 7-inch

RMP (1027 "Little Cinderella") ... 10-20 64

Also see GARRISON, Red, & Zodiacs

RED APPLE & TURNOVERS

Singles: 7-inch

VIVID (1001 "Tin Lizzy") ... 10-15

RED ARROW & BRAVES

Singles: 7-inch

KINZUA ... 4-8 63

RED BEANS & RICE

(Featuring "Spareribs" Ray Draber)

Singles: 7-inch

EPIC ... 4-6 69

LPs: 10/12-inch

EPIC ... 10-15 69

RED BEARD & PIRATES

Singles: 7-inch

GAYE (3043 "Go on, Leave") ... 8-12

RED BOW, Buddy

Singles: 7-inch

TATANKA ... 3-5 83
(Price includes bonus booklet.)

RED COATS

Singles: 7-inch

DEL-CO (4002 "I Never Knew") ... 25-30 59
(Reissued as by the Colts.)

Member: Joe Grundy.

Also see COLTS

RED COATS

Singles: 7-inch

KITE (2003 "Perkin' ") ... 10-20 61

Also see ALAIMO, Steve

RED COATS

Singles: 7-inch

LAURIE ... 4-8 65
VALIANT ... 5-10 64

RED CRAYOLA

LPs: 10/12-inch

INT'L ARTISTS (2 "Parable of Arable Land") ... 60-100 67
(Does NOT have "Masterfonics" stamped in the vinyl trail-off.)
INT'L ARTISTS (7 "God Bless the Red Crayola") ... 30-45 68
(Does NOT have "Masterfonics" stamped in the vinyl trail-off.)
INT'L ARTISTS ... 10-20 79
(Reissues. With "Masterfonics" stamped in the vinyl trail-off.)

Members: Mayo Thompson; Steve Cunningham; Rick Barthelme; Danny Schact; Bonnie Emerson.

Also see THOMPSON, Mayo

RED DOGS

Singles: 7-inch

ATCO ... 5-10 67
VERITAS (460 "Fixit") ... 5-10

RED FLAG LP '89

LPs: 10/12-inch

ENIGMA ... 5-8 89

RED HOOK

LPs: 10/12-inch

BLUE LION ... 10-15
RED HOOK ... 10-15

RED HOT CHILI PEPPERS LP '87

Singles: 12-inch

EMI AMERICA ... 4-6 85

Singles: 7-inch

EMI AMERICA ... 3-4 84-85
EMI RECORDS GROUP ... 4-6
("For Juke boxes Only!" series.)
W.B. ... 3-4 91

LPs: 10/12-inch

CAPITOL (29665 "Out in L.A.") ... 8-10 90s
EMI AMERICA ... 5-8 84-85
EMI MANHATTAN ... 5-8 87
W.B. (Except 5170) ... 5-8 91
W.B. (5170 "Blood Sugar Sex Magic") ... 15-25 91
(Double LP "Radio Ready" [censored] issue. Promotional issue only.)

Members: Anthony Kiedis; Jack Irons; Hillel Slovak; Mike Balzary; John Frusciante; Chad Smith.

Also see WILSON, Nancy / Red Hot Chili Peppers

RED LIPSTIQUE

Singles: 12-inch

MAGNET (221 "Drac's Back") ... 4-6

RED RIDER

(Johnny Angelos)

Singles: 7-inch

SCEPTER ... 4-8 75

Also see AMBOY DUKES
Also see DAVIS, Jesse Ed
Also see TORPEDOS

RED RIDER P&R/LP '80

Singles: 7-inch

CAPITOL ... 3-5 80-86

Picture Sleeves

CAPITOL ... 3-5 80-84

LPs: 10/12-inch

CAPITOL ... 5-10 80-86

Members: Tom Cochrane; Rob Baker; Peter Boynton; Ken Greer; Jeff Jones.

Also see COCHRANE, Tom

RED RIVER DAVE P&R '60

(Dave McEnery)

Singles: 7-inch

COPYRIGHT ... 4-8 61
SAVOY ... 4-8 60-65

EPs: 7-inch

TNT (1 "James Dean Album") ... 50-75 56
VARSITY ... 5-10

LPs: 10/12-inch

BLUEBONNET ... 8-12 60s
CONTINENTAL ... 10-20 62
PLACE ... 10-15 60s
SUTTON ... 5-10

RED ROCKERS P&R/D&D/LP '83

Singles: 12-inch

COLUMBIA ... 4-6 83-85

Singles: 7-inch

COLUMBIA ... 3-4 83-85

LPs: 10/12-inch

COLUMBIA ... 5-8 83

RED RYDERS

Singles: 7-inch

MERCURY ... 4-8 64

LPs: 10/12-inch

MERCURY ... 10-20 65

RED 7 LP '85

Singles: 7-inch

MCA ... 3-4 87

Picture Sleeves

MCA ... 3-4 87

LPs: 10/12-inch

MCA ... 5-8 85-87

RED SIREN LP '89

LPs: 10/12-inch

MERCURY ... 5-8 89

RED TAM

Singles: 7-inch

DADE ... 5-8 68

RED TOPPERS

Singles: 7-inch

DAN (3214 "I Never Had a Girl Like You") ... 15-25

RED TOPS

Singles: 7-inch

GLODUS (1650 "Mustard") ... 10-15 60s

RED TOPS

(Original Red Tops Featuring Rufus McKay)

Singles: 7-inch

SKY (703 "Swanee River Rock") ... 15-25 60

Also see McKAY, Rufus

RED, WHITE & BLUE (GRASS) C&W '73

Singles: 7-inch

GRC ... 3-5 73

Members: Grant Boatwright; Ginger Boatwright.

RED, WILDER, BLUE

Singles: 7-inch

PENTAGRAM ... 3-5 71-72

LPs: 10/12-inch

PENTAGRAM ... 8-12 71

RED WILLOW BAND C&W '79

Singles: 7-inch

LOST ... 3-5 79

REDBONE P&R/LP '70

Singles: 7-inch

EPIC ... 3-5 71-74
RCA ... 3-5 78

LPs: 10/12-inch

ACCORD ... 5-10 82
EPIC ... 8-15 70-75
RCA ... 5-10 77

Members: Pat Vegas; Lolly Vegas; Tony Bellamy.

Also see VEGAS, Pat & Lolly

REDBONE, Leon LP '76

Singles: 78 rpm

W.B. ... 5-10 78
(Promotional only.)

Singles: 7-inch

EMERALD CITY ... 3-8 81
W.B. ... 5-12 77-78

LPs: 10/12-inch

ACCORD ... 10-15 82
EMERALD CITY ... 10-15 81

W.B. ... 15-30 77-78

REDCAPS
Singles: 7-inch
HUNT (326 "Cheryl Lee") ... 20-30 59

REDCOATS
Singles: 7-inch
MAE (1002 "Cobra") ... 20-30

REDD R&B '87
Singles: 7-inch
RCA ... 3-4 87

REDD, Alton, & His Down Blues Band
Singles: 78 rpm
BEL-TONE ... 15-25 46
BLACK & WHITE ... 15-25 45-46

REDD, Barbara
Singles: 7-inch
S.P.Q.R. (3311 "I'll Be Alone") ... 10-20 63

REDD, Gene
(With the Globe Trotters)
Singles: 7-inch
KING ... 5-10 59-60

REDD, Johnny
Singles: 7-inch
CORALLEN (11 "I Flipped My Top") ... 50-100 60
CORALLEN (106 "Rockin' Peg") ... 50-100 60

REDD, Sharon R&B '81
Singles: 12-inch
PRELUDE ... 4-6 81-83
Singles: 7-inch
COLUMBIA ... 3-5 78
PRELUDE ... 3-5 81-83
VEEP ... 4-8 67
LPs: 10/12-inch
COLUMBIA ... 5-10 78
PRELUDE ... 5-8 82

REDD, Sharon, Ula Hedwig & Charlotte Crossley
Singles: 7-inch
COLUMBIA ... 3-5 77-78
Also see MIDLER, Bette
Also see REDD, Sharon

REDD, Vi
(Vi Redd Sextet)
LPs: 10/12-inch
ATCO ... 20-30 63
SOLID STATE ... 10-15 69
U.A. ... 25-35 62

REDD HOLT UNLIMITED
Singles: 7-inch
PAULA ... 3-5 75

REDD HOT R&B '81
(Redd Hott)
Singles: 7-inch
VENTURE ... 3-5 81-82
Members: Kevin "Flash" Ferrell; Robert Parson; Daryl Simmons; Greg Russell; De Morris Smith.
Also see MANCHILD

REDD KROSS
LPs: 10/12-inch
BIT ... 5-8 87
POSH BOY ... 5-10 85-86

REDDING, Dexter
Singles: 7-inch
CAPRICORN ... 3-5 74
Also see REDDINGS

REDDING, Edward
Singles: 7-inch
APEX ... 5-10 59
CHESS ... 5-10 59
DEMPSEY ... 5-10 60

REDDING, Gene P&R/R&B '74
Singles: 7-inch
HAVEN ... 3-5 74

REDDING, Leroy
Singles: 7-inch
BABY ... 8-10

REDDING, Noel, Band
LPs: 10/12-inch
RCA ... 8-12 75
Also see HENDRIX, Jimi
Also see ROAD

REDDING, Otis P&R/R&B '63
(With the Pinetoppers; with Pinetones; with Shooters)
Singles: 7-inch
ATCO ... 5-10 68-71
BETHLEHEM (3083 "Shout Bamalama") ... 10-15 64
CONFEDERATE (135 "Shout Bamalama") ... 20-40 62
FINER ARTS (2016 "She's All Right") ... 30-50 61
(Previously issued as by the Shooters.)
KING (6149 "Shout Bamalama") ... 5-10 68
ORBIT (135 "Shout Bamalama") ... 50-75 61
STONE (209 "You Left the Water Running") ... 4-8 76
VOLT (103 thru 121) ... 10-20 62-64
VOLT (124 thru 163) ... 10-15 65-68
EPs: 7-inch
VOLT (70413 "The Soul Album") ... 20-30 66
(Juke box issue only. Includes title strips.)
LPs: 10/12-inch
ATCO (33-161 "Pain in My Heart") ... 50-70 64
(Monaural.)
ATCO (SD-33-161 "Pain in My Heart") ... 60-80 64
(Stereo.)
ATCO (200 series) ... 10-15 68-69
ATCO (300 series) ... 8-12 70
ATCO (801 "The Best of Otis Redding") ... 10-20 72
(Reissues available with same selection number.)
ATLANTIC ... 5-10 82
VOLT (Except 411) ... 20-35 65-68
VOLT (411 "Soul Ballads") ... 35-55 65
(Monaural.)
VOLT (411 "Soul Ballads") ... 40-60 65
(Stereo.)
Members: Steve Cropper; Booker T. Jones; Isaac Hayes; Donald "Duck" Dunn; Lewis Steinberg; Al Jackson Jr. Session: Wayne Cochran; Johnny Jenkins; William Bell; Tommie Lee Williams; Veltones; Drapels.
Also see BAR-KAYS
Also see BOOKER T. & MGs
Also see COCHRAN, Wayne
Also see CROPPER, Steve
Also see HAYES, Isaac
Also see JENKINS, Johnny
Also see SHOOTERS

REDDING, Otis / Little Joe Curtis
LPs: 10/12-inch
ALSHIRE ... 8-12 68
SOMERSET ... 8-12 68

REDDING, Otis / Jimi Hendrix LP '70
LPs: 10/12-inch
REPRISE (2029 "Otis Redding/The Jimi Hendrix Experience") ... 10-15 70
(Disc reads: "Historic Performances Recorded At The Monterey International Pop Festival.")
REPRISE (2029 "Otis Redding/The Jimi Hendrix Experience") ... 15-25 70
(White label. Promotional issue only.)
REPRISE (93371 "Otis Redding/The Jimi Hendrix Experience") ... 15-20 70
(Different front cover than 2029. Disc reads: "Music from the Monterey Pop Soundtrack.")
Also see HENDRIX, Jimi

REDDING, Otis / King Curtis
LPs: 10/12-inch
ATCO (265/266 "Promotional LP for Record Department-in-Store Play") ... 15-20 68
(Promotional issue only.)
Also see KING CURTIS

REDDING, Otis / Carla Thomas / Sam & Dave / Eddie Floyd
LPs: 10/12-inch
STAX (722 "Stax/Volt Revue, Vol. 2") ... 15-25 67
Also see FLOYD, Eddie
Also see OTIS & CARLA
Also see REDDING, Otis
Also see SAM & DAVE
Also see THOMAS, Carla

REDDINGS P&R/R&B/LP '80
Singles: 12-inch
BELIEVE in a DREAM ... 4-8 83
Singles: 7-inch
BELIEVE in a DREAM ... 3-5 80-83
POLYDOR ... 3-4 85-88
LPs: 10/12-inch
BELIEVE in a DREAM ... 5-10 80-83
POLYDOR ... 5-8 85
Members: Otis Redding III; Dexter Redding; Mark Locket.
Also see REDDING, Dexter

REDDLEMEN
Singles: 7-inch
CUSTOM (131 "I Can't Go On This Way") ... 20-30 66

REDDS & BOYS R&B '85
Singles: 7-inch
4TH & BROADWAY ... 3-5 85

REDDY, Bobby
Singles: 7-inch
TEE-CUE ... 8-12 59

REDDY, Helen P&R/LP '71
Singles: 12-inch
CAPITOL ... 4-6 79
Singles: 7-inch
CAPITOL ... 3-5 71-81
FONTANA ... 3-6 68
MCA ... 3-5 81-83
LPs: 10/12-inch
CAPITOL ... 5-10 71-81
MCA ... 5-8 81-83
Also see PRESLEY, Elvis / Helen Reddy

REDELL, Teddy
Singles: 7-inch
ATCO (6162 "Judy") ... 25-45 60
HI ... 10-20 60
RIMROCK (215 "I See the Moon") 10-20 63
VADEN (110 "Knocking on the Backside") ... 75-125 60
VADEN (115 "Corinna Corinna") ... 75-125 60
VADEN (116 "Judy") ... 75-125 60
VADEN (117 "Pipeliner") ... 75-125 61

REDEYE P&R/LP '70
Singles: 7-inch
PENTAGRAM ... 3-5 70-71
LPs: 10/12-inch
PENTAGRAM ... 10-15 70-71
Members: Doug "Red" Mark; David Hodkins; Bobby Bereman; Bill Kman.
Also see SUNSHINE COMPANY

REDJACKETS
Singles: 7-inch
SMASH ... 4-8 62

REDJACKS P&R '58
Singles: 7-inch
APT (25006 "Big Brown Eyes") ... 20-30 58
OKLAHOMA (5005 "Big Brown Eyes") ... 75-125 58

RED-LITE DISTRICT
Singles: 7-inch
SCEPTER ... 4-8 69

REDMAN
LPs: 10/12-inch
POLYDOR ... 8-10 90s

REDMAN, Nicki
Singles: 7-inch
CAMP (1278 "Cop's Rock") ... 10-15 63

REDMAN, Terry
Singles: 7-inch
CUB (9042 "The Dreamer") ... 10-20 59
HURON (22005 "Stomp") ... 10-20 61
MGM (12735 "Come on Back") ... 25-35 58

REDMOND, Frankie
Singles: 7-inch
IMPERIAL (5718 "Anytime Anywhere") ... 8-12 61
IMPERIAL (8718 "Make Believe World") ... 8-12 60s

REDMOND, Robb C&W '77
Singles: 7-inch
NBC ... 3-5 77

REDMOND, Roy
Singles: 7-inch
LOMA ... 4-8 67-68

REDNOW, Eivets P&R '68
(Stevie Wonder)
Singles: 7-inch
GORDY (7076 "Alfie") ... 10-20 68
LPs: 10/12-inch
GORDY (932 "Eivets Rednow") ... 25-35 68
Also see WONDER, Stevie

REDS
Singles: 7-inch
A&M ... 3-5 79
LPs: 10/12-inch
A&M ... 5-10 79
STONY PLAIN ... 5-8 81

REDWAY, Michael P&R '73
(Mike Redway)
Singles: 7-inch
LONDON ... 4-8 64
PHILIPS ... 3-5 73

REDWING
Singles: 7-inch
FANTASY ... 4-8 71-73
LPs: 10/12-inch
ATCO ... 5-10 77
FANTASY ... 10-15 70-74
Members: Tom Phillips; George Hullin; Ron Flogel.
Also see GLAD

REDWOODS
(Jeff Barry)
Singles: 7-inch
EPIC (9447 "Shake Shake Sherry") ... 20-30 61
(Also issued as by the Flairs.)
EPIC (9473 "Never Take It Away") ... 20-30 61
EPIC (9505 "Where You Used to Be") ... 30-40 62
Also see BARRY, Jeff
Also see FLAIRS

REE, Mamie
Singles: 78 rpm
COMBO (93 "You Lied") ... 20-30 55
Singles: 7-inch
COMBO (93 "You Lied") ... 40-60 55

REECE, Ben C&W '75
Singles: 7-inch
POLYDOR ... 3-5 76
20TH CENTURY ... 3-5 75-76

REED, A.C.
Singles: 7-inch
AGE (29103 "Come On Home") ... 10-20 61
AGE (29112 "Mean Cop") ... 10-20 62
COOL (5001 "Ma Baby Is Fine") ... 15-25
ICE CUBE (5926 "I Am Fed Up with This Music") ... 4-8 81
(Labeled "X-Rated Blues.")
NIKE ... 5-10
LPs: 10/12-inch
ICE CUBE (Take These Blues and Shove 'Em") ... 8-10 81
Also see HOOKER, Earl, & A.C. Reed

REED, Al
Singles: 7-inch
AXE ... 5-10 67
DOT (15720 "I Love Her So") ... 25-35 58
INSTANT (3238 "Ring the Ding Dong Bells") ... 8-10 61
TNT (150 "I Love Her So") ... 40-50 58

REED, Bob
(With Lucky Ivory)
Singles: 7-inch
DENA ... 5-10 61
MAR-VEL (333 "Choctaw Boogie") ... 50-75 56
MELATONE ... 10-15
Also see TAYLOR, Ted

REED, Bobby
Singles: 7-inch
BRUNSWICK (55282 "You Are") ... 10-20 65
CLAY TOWN (17700 "You Are") ... 50-75 65
(First issue.)
CYCLONE (501 "High School USA") ... 10-20 60s
DOT ... 10-15 60
LOMA ... 5-10 68

REED, Bobby C&W '83
Singles: 7-inch
CBO ... 3-4 83

REED, Chuck
Singles: 78 rpm
DECCA ... 10-15 57
MERCURY ... 10-15 54-55
Singles: 7-inch
CHOCTAW (101 "Just Plain Hurt") ... 40-60 62
DECCA ... 15-20 57
HIT (101 "Just Plain Hurt") ... 40-60 61
JAMIE (1194 "So Long") ... 8-12 61
MERCURY ... 15-25 54-55
MINARET (107 "Mark My Word") ... 5-10 63
MINARET (110 "Lots of Happiness") ... 5-10 64
MINARET (119 "Conscience") ... 5-10 65
ROULETTE (4058 "No School Tomorrow") ... 15-25 58
U.A. ... 4-8 66

REED, Clarence: see REID, Clarence

REED, Clyde
Singles: 7-inch
TAMPER ("Tippin") ... 8-12
(Selection number not known.)

REED, Dan, Network P&R/LP '88
Singles: 7-inch
MERCURY ... 3-4 88-89
Picture Sleeves
MERCURY ... 3-4 88
LPs: 10/12-inch
MERCURY ... 5-8 88-89

REED, Dean P&R '59
Singles: 7-inch
CAPITOL (4121 "Annabelle") ... 10-20 59
CAPITOL (4198 "I Kissed a Queen") ... 10-20 59
CAPITOL (4273 "Our Summer Romance") ... 10-20 59
CAPITOL (4438 "Pistolero") ... 25-35 60
CAPITOL (4608 "Female Hercules") ... 10-15 61
IMPERIAL (5733 "Once Again") ... 8-12 61

REED, Denny P&R '60
Singles: 7-inch
ASPIRE ... 3-5 77
DOT ... 5-10 62
MCI (1024 "A Teenager Feels It Too") ... 30-40 60
(First issue.)
TREY (3007 "A Teenager Feels It Too") ... 10-20 60
TREY (3014 "Lonely Little Bluebird") ... 10-15 61
TOWER ... 4-8 65
U.A. ... 8-12 61

REED, Don
Singles: 7-inch
A&R ... 5-10 61
DOT ... 10-15 59

REED, Earl
Singles: 78 rpm
TRUMPET ... 10-20 51

REED, Earl, & His Rhythm Rockers
(Featuring Johnny Scoggins)
Singles: 7-inch
CHEROKEE (778 "Drink Wine") ... 300-500 58
CHEROKEE (779 "Flat Foot Sam") ... 200-300 58

REED, Gable
Singles: 7-inch
MINARET (151 "Who's Been Warming My Oven") ... 5-8 69

REED, Gerri
Singles: 7-inch
SPAN ... 4-8 63

REED, James
Singles: 78 rpm
BIG TOWN ... 50-75 54
FLAIR ... 50-75 54
MONEY ... 50-75 54
RHYTHM (1775 "Tin Pan Alley") ... 300-400 54
Singles: 7-inch
BIG TOWN (117 "Things Ain't What They Used to Be") ... 75-100 54
FLAIR (1034 "My Mama Told Me") ... 100-150 54
FLAIR (1042 "Dr. Brown") ... 100-150 54
MONEY (201 "Oh People") ... 100-150 54

REED, Jerry P&R '62/C&W '67
(With the Hully Girlies; with Seidina; with Friends)
Singles: 78 rpm
CAPITOL ... 5-15 55-56
Singles: 7-inch
CAPITOL ... 10-20 55-56
COLUMBIA ... 5-10 61-63
NRC ... 5-10 59
RCA (Except 8500 thru 9700) ... 3-5 69-85
RCA (8500 thru 9700) ... 4-8 65-69
Picture Sleeves
COLUMBIA ... 8-10 61
RCA ... 3-4 72-85
LPs: 10/12-inch
CAMDEN ... 5-10 72-74
HARMONY ... 8-12 71
PICKWICK/HILLTOP ... 5-10
RCA (Except "LPM" & "LSP" series) ... 5-10 73-83
RCA ("LPM" & "LSP" series) ... 8-18 67-73
Also see HART, Freddie / Sammi Smith / Jerry Reed
Also see JENNINGS, Waylon, & Jerry Reed
Also see JUSTIS, Bill / Jerry Reed
Also see NELSON, Willie
Also see PRESLEY, Elvis
Also see SOME of CHET'S FRIENDS

REED, Jerry, & Chet Atkins
LPs: 10/12-inch
RCA ... 10-20 72
Also see ATKINS, Chet
Also see REED, Jerry

REED, Jimmie, Jr.
Singles: 7-inch
MERCURY (72668 "I Ain't Going Nowhere") ... 10-20 67

REED, Jimmy R&B '55
("With His Trio")
Singles: 78 rpm
CHANCE (1142 "High and Lonesome") ... 75-125 53
VEE JAY (100 thru 253) ... 20-40 53-57
VEE JAY (270 thru 298) ... 30-50 53-57
VEE JAY (304 "I Told You Baby") ... 50-100 59
VEE JAY (314 "Take Out Some Insurance") ... 75-125 59
VEE JAY (326 "I Wanna Be Loved") ... 100-150 59
VEE JAY (333 "Baby What You Want Me to Do") ... 150-200 59
Singles: 7-inch
ABC ... 3-5 73
ABC-PAR (10887 "Got Nowhere to Go") ... 4-8 66
BLUESWAY ... 4-8 67
CANYON ... 3-6 70
CHANCE (1142 "High and Lonesome") ... 300-400 53
(Reissue of Vee Jay 100.)
COLLECTABLES ... 3-4 80s
EXODUS (2005 "Knockin' at Your Door") ... 5-10 66
EXODUS (2008 "Cousin Peaches") . 5-10 66
MAGIC ... 8-12
OLDIES 45 ... 4-8 64
RRG ... 4-8
TRIP ... 3-5 70s
VEE JAY (100 "High and Lonesome") ... 100-200 53
(Black vinyl.)
VEE JAY (100 "High and Lonesome") ... 250-350 53
(Red vinyl.)
VEE JAY (105 "I Found My Baby") ... 100-150 53
(Black vinyl.)
VEE JAY (105 "I Found My Baby") ... 200-300 53
(Red vinyl.)
VEE JAY (119 "You Don't Have to Go") ... 50-75 54
(Black vinyl.)
VEE JAY (119 "You Don't Have to Go") ... 200-300 54
(Red vinyl.)
VEE JAY (132 "Pretty Thing") ... 40-60 55
VEE JAY (153 "She Don't Want Me No More") ... 25-50 55
VEE JAY (168 "Ain't That Lovin' You Baby") ... 20-40 56
VEE JAY (186 "Can't Stand to See You Go") ... 20-40 56
VEE JAY (203 "I Love You Baby") . 20-40 56
VEE JAY (226 "You've Got Me Dizzy") ... 20-40 56
VEE JAY (237 "Little Rain") ... 20-30 57
VEE JAY (248 "The Sun Is Shining") ... 20-30 57
VEE JAY (253 "Honest I Do") ... 15-25 57
VEE JAY (270 "You're Something Else") ... 15-25 58
VEE JAY (275 "Go on to School") . 15-25 58
VEE JAY (287 "Down in Virginia") . 15-25 58
VEE JAY (298 "I'm Gonna Get My Baby") ... 15-25 58
VEE JAY (304 "I Told You Baby") .. 15-25 59
VEE JAY (314 "Take Out Some Insurance") ... 15-25 59
VEE JAY (326 "I Wanna Be Loved") ... 15-25 59
VEE JAY (333 "Baby What You Want Me to Do") ... 15-25 59
VEE JAY (347 "Found Love") ... 15-25 60
VEE JAY (357 "Hush Hush") ... 15-25 60
VEE JAY (373 "Close Together") ... 15-25 61
VEE JAY (380 "Big Boss Man") ... 15-25 61
VEE JAY (398 "Bright Lights, Big City") ... 15-25 61
VEE JAY (425 "What's Wrong Baby") ... 10-20 61
VEE JAY (449 "Tell Me You Love Me") ... 10-20 62
VEE JAY (459 "Too Much") ... 10-20 62
VEE JAY (473 "Let's Get Together") ... 10-20 62
VEE JAY (509 "Shame Shame Shame") ... 10-20 63
VEE JAY (552 "Mary Mary") ... 10-20 63
VEE JAY (570 "St. Louis Blues") ... 10-20 63

VEE JAY (584 "Wee Wee Baby") ..10-20 64
VEE JAY (593 "Help Yourself")......10-20 64
VEE JAY (616 "Down in Mississippi")..........10-20 64
VEE JAY (622 "I'm Going Upside Your Head")..........10-20 64
VEE JAY (642 "I Wanna Be Loved")..........10-20 65
VEE JAY (702 "Left Handed Woman")..........10-20 65
VEE JAY (709 "When Girls Do It") .10-20 65
EPs: 7-inch
VEE JAY (1050 "Just Jimmy Reed")..........15-25 62
(Stereo. Juke box issue only. Includes title strips.)
LPs: 10/12-inch
ANTILLES..........10-20
BLUES on BLUES..........8-10
BLUESWAY..........10-30 67-73
BUDDAH..........10-15 69
EVEREST..........5-10 69
EXODUS..........10-15 66
GNP..........8-10 74
KENT..........8-12 69-71
RRG..........10-20
ROKER..........5-10
SUNSET..........10-15 68
TRADITION..........8-12
TRIP..........8-15 71-78
UPFRONT..........8-12
VEE JAY (1004 "I'm Jimmy Reed")..........75-125 58
(Maroon label.)
VEE JAY (1004 "I'm Jimmy Reed")..........50-75 59
(Black label.)
VEE JAY (1008 "Rockin' with Reed")..........60-100 59
(Maroon label.)
VEE JAY (1008 "Rockin' with Reed")..........40-60 59
(Black label.)
VEE JAY (1022 "Found Love").......25-50 60
VEE JAY (1025 "Now Appearing")..........25-50 60
VEE JAY (1035 "At Carnegie Hall")..........25-40 61
VEE JAY (1039 thru 1095)..........20-40 62-64
VEE JAY (8501 "The Legend, the Man")..........20-30 65
VERSATILE..........8-10 78
Also see DIXON, Willie
Also see MAYFIELD, Curtis
Also see TAYLOR, Eddie
Also see UPCHURCH, Phil

REED, Jimmy / Peppermint Harris
EPs: 7-inch
LUNAR (2009 "Tells It Like It Is") 5-10 81
Also see PEPPPERMINT HARRIS
Also see REED, Jimmy

REED, Larry, & Shados
Singles: 7-inch
ARLEN (515 "Little Miss Surfer")....15-25 63

REED, Lou LP '72
(With the Velvet Underground)
Singles: 12-inch
RCA..........4-8 84
Singles: 7-inch
ARISTA..........3-5 76
RCA..........3-5 73-86
LPs: 10/12-inch
ARISTA..........5-10 76-80
PRIDE..........8-12 73
RCA ("AFL1" series)..........5-10 80-83
RCA ("ANL1" series)..........5-10 77
RCA ("APL1" series)..........6-12 73-77
RCA ("AYL1" series)..........5-8 80-83
RCA ("CPL1" series)..........8-12 74
RCA ("LSP" series)..........8-12 72
SIRE..........5-8 89-90
Also see BEACH NUTS
Also see DION
Also see JADES
Also see PRIMITIVES
Also see VELVET UNDERGROUND

REED, Lou, & John Cale LP '90
LPs: 10/12-inch
SIRE..........5-8 90
Also see CALE, John
Also see REED, Lou

REED, Louis
Singles: 7-inch
LABEL..........4-8 61

REED, Lulu
(With the Teeners; Lula Reed)
Singles: 78 rpm
KING..........15-25 53-56
Singles: 7-inch
ARGO..........10-20 59-60
FEDERAL (12407 "I'm a Woman").15-25 61
FEDERAL (12416 "I Got a Notion")..........15-25 61
FEDERAL (12426 "Know What You're Doing")..........15-25 61
FEDERAL (12440 "Ain't No Cotton' Pickin' Chicken")..........15-25 61
GUSTO..........3-4 80s
KING (4590 "Heavenly Road").......25-50 53
KING (4630 "My Poor Heart")..........25-50 53
KING (4649 "Don't Make Me Love You")..........25-50 53
KING (4688 "Your Key Don't Fir No More")..........25-50 53
KING (4703 "Troubles on Your Mind")..........25-50 54
KING (4712 "I Ain't No Watch Dog")..........25-50 54
KING (4718 "I'm Beggin' & Pleadin' ")..........25-50 54
KING (4714 "Just Whisper")..........25-50 54
KING (4726 "Wonderful Love")......25-50 54
KING (4737 "What Could I Do But Believe in Jesus")..........20-40 54
KING (4748 "Sick & Tired")..........25-50 54
KING (4767 "Rock Love")..........25-50 55
KING (4796 "Without Love")..........25-50 55
KING (4811 "I'm Giving All My Love")..........25-50 55
KING (4969 "Three Men")..........25-50 56
KING (4996 "Waste No More Tears")..........25-50 56
TANGERINE..........5-10 62-67
LPs: 10/12-inch
KING (604 "Blue and Moody")....500-750 59
Session: Sonny Thompson; Isaac Cole; Bill Johnson.
Also see KING, Freddy, & Lulu Reed
Also see THOMPSON, Sonny

REED, Madam Louise
Singles: 7-inch
VEE JAY..........5-10 61

REED, Norman
Singles: 7-inch
AWARD..........5-10 59

REED, Ramona
Singles: 7-inch
CHALLENGE..........4-8 66

REED, Scott
Singles: 7-inch
AWARD..........5-10 59

REED, Tawny
Singles: 7-inch
CONGRESS..........5-10 66
RED BIRD (044 "Needle in a Haystack")..........20-30 65

REED, Tommy
(With the Runaways)
Singles: 7-inch
KIP..........5-10 61
TOKEN (103 "Swamp Rider")........10-20 63

REED, Ursula
(With the Solitaires)
Singles: 78 rpm
OLD TOWN..........100-150 54
Singles: 7-inch
OLD TOWN (1001 "You're Laughing Cause I'm Crying")..........250-350 54
Also see SOLITAIRES

REED, Vivian R&B '68
Singles: 7-inch
ATCO..........3-5 73
EPIC..........5-10 68-69
H&L..........4-6 76
U.A...........3-5 78-79
LPs: 10/12-inch
EPIC..........10-15 69
U.A...........5-10 78

REEDER, Bill
Singles: 7-inch
FERNWOOD (121 "You're My Baby")..........50-75 60
HI (2037 "Till I Waltz Again with You")..........50-75 61
HI (2041 "Judy")..........10-15 62
VOLL (100 "Till I Waltz Again with You")..........100-200 61

REEDER, Eskew
(S.Q. Reeder; Esquerita)
Singles: 7-inch
CROSSTONE (1007 "You Better Believe It")..........50-75 60s
EVEREST..........10-20 63
INSTANT..........8-12 63-64
MINIT..........10-20 62
OKEH..........8-12 66
Also see ESQUERITA
Also see RIO ROCKERS

REEDS, Ensenada, Orchestra
Singles: 7-inch
M&P (001 "Summertime")..........30-40

REEFERS
Singles: 7-inch
MEGA..........3-5 75

REEGAN, Vala, & Valrons
Singles: 7-inch
ATCO (6412 "Fireman")..........20-30 66

REE-GENTS
Singles: 7-inch
CONBIE (1000 "Downshiftin' ")....15-20 658

REEKERS
Singles: 7-inch
RU-JAC (13 "Grindin' ")..........20-30 64
Also see HANGMEN

REELS
LPs: 10/12-inch
POLYDOR..........5-10 80

REES, Jerry, & Monarcks
Singles: 7-inch
SOMA (1184 "Streak of Lightning")..........20-25 60s
Picture Sleeves
SOMA (1184 "Streak of Lightning")..........25-50 60s

REESE, Bill
(Bill Reese Quintet & Coronets; with His Rhythm Kings, vocal by Tommy Malone)
Singles: 78 rpm
PENNANT..........40-60 55
STERLING..........100-150 55
Singles: 7-inch
PENNANT (334 "Whiskey, Ol' Whiskey")..........100-150 55
STERLING (903 "Don't Deprive Me")..........300-400 55

REESE, Danny
Singles: 7-inch
CHARTWHEEL (101 "Country Mama Boogie")..........10-15 77

REESE, Della P&R '57
(With the Meditation Singers; with Sid Bass Orchestra)
Singles: 78 rpm
JUBILEE..........10-20 57
Singles: 7-inch
ABC..........3-6 67-73
ABC-PAR..........4-6 65-66
AVCO EMBASSY..........3-6 69-72
CHI-SOUND..........3-5 77
JUBILEE (5000 series)..........10-15 57-59
(Monaural.)
JUBILEE (9007 "Stormy Weather")..........15-25 58
(Stereo.)
LMI..........3-5 73
RCA..........8-12 59-64
VIRGO..........3-5 72
Picture Sleeves
AVCO EMBASSY..........4-8 69-72
RCA..........10-15 60-63
EPs: 7-inch
RCA..........10-20 61
LPs: 10/12-inch
ABC..........5-10 76
ABC-PAR..........15-20 65-67
APPLAUSE..........5-8 83
DESIGN..........5-10
JUBILEE (1000 & 5000 series)..........20-30 57-63
JUBILEE (6000 series)..........10-15 69
LMI..........5-10 73
PICKWICK..........5-8 78
RCA (2000 thru 4600 series)..........10-25 60-72
SUNSET..........5-10 71
Also see ANN-MARGRET / Kitty Kalen / Della Reese
Also see ARMSTRONG, Louis / Della Reese / Wild Bill Davidson
Also see LIMELITERS / Della Reese /Mario Lanza / Norman Luboff Choir

REESE, Dela, & Kirk Stuart
Singles: 7-inch
JUBILEE..........5-10 59
Also see REESE, Dela
Also see STUART, Kirk

REESE, Jackson
Singles: 7-inch
PARKWAY..........4-8 67

REESE, Lloyd
Singles: 7-inch
CORAL..........5-10 60

REESE, Reatha
Singles: 7-inch
DOT (16630 "Only Lies")..........100-200 64

REESE, Slim
Singles: 78 rpm
SITTIN' in WITH (581 "Got the World in a Jug")..........20-50 51

REEVES, Barbara, & Pageants
Singles: 7-inch
BEACON (559 "It's Been So Long")..........15-25 64

REEVES, Danny
Singles: 7-inch
D (1206 "Bell Hop Blues")..........200-300 61

REEVES, Del C&W '61
(With the Goodtime Charlies)
Singles: 7-inch
CHART..........3-5 70
COLUMBIA..........4-6 64
DECCA..........4-8 61-62
KOALA..........3-5 80-82
LAS VEGAS..........10-15 59
PEACH..........10-15 60
PLAYBACK..........3-4 86
REPRISE..........4-8 63
U.A...........3-6 66-78
Picture Sleeves
KOALA..........3-4 80
U.A...........3-6 67
LPs: 10/12-inch
KOALA..........5-8 79-80
STARDAY..........5-8
SUNSET..........5-10 69-70
U.A. (200 thru 600 series)..........5-10 73-76
U.A. (3000 & 6000 series)..........10-20 65-71

REEVES, Del, & Penny DeHaven C&W '72
Singles: 7-inch
U.A...........3-5 72
Also see DeHAVEN, Penny

REEVES, Del, & Bobby Goldsboro C&W '68
Singles: 7-inch
U.A...........3-6 65-71
LPs: 10/12-inch
U.A...........10-20 68
Also see GOLDSBORO, Bobby

REEVES, Del / Red Sovine
LPs: 10/12-inch
EXACT..........5-8 80
Also see SOVINE, Red

REEVES, Del, & Billie Jo Spears C&W '76
Singles: 7-inch
U.A...........3-5 76
LPs: 10/12-inch
LIBERTY..........5-8 82
U.A...........5-10 76
Also see REEVES, Del
Also see SPEARS, Billie Jo

REEVES, Dianne R&B/LP '88
Singles: 7-inch
BLUE NOTE..........3-4 87
LPs: 10/12-inch
BLUE NOTE..........5-8 88
EMI..........5-8 90

REEVES, Eddie
Singles: 7-inch
ASCOT (2155 "Heartbreakin")........15-25 64
KAPP (2164 "Tulsa Turnaround")........4-8 72
WARWICK (667 "Cry Baby")........10-15 61
Picture Sleeves
WARWICK (667 "Cry Baby")........15-25 61

REEVES, Glenn
Singles: 78 rpm
ATCO..........20-30 57
RCA..........5-10 56
Singles: 7-inch
ATCO (6080 "Rockin' Country Style")..........30-50 57
DECCA (30589 "Rock-A-Boogie Lou")..........20-30 58
DECCA (30780 "Tarzan")..........20-30 58
RCA..........10-15 56
REPUBLIC..........5-10 58
TNT (120 "I'm Johnny on the Spot")..........50-75 58
TNT (129 "I Ain't Got Room to Rock")..........50-75 58

REEVES, Harriet
Singles: 7-inch
EON (103 "Just Friends")..........10-15

REEVES, Jack
Singles: 7-inch
ADKORP..........3-5 72-73

REEVES, Jim C&W '53
(With His Circle O Ranch Boys)
Singles: 78 rpm
ABBOTT (Black plastic)..........15-25 53-55
ABBOTT (Colored plastic)..........25-50 53-55
MACY'S (115 "Teardrops of Regret")..........150-250 50
MACY'S (132 "I've Never Been So Blue")..........150-250 51
QUALITY (1177 "Bimbo")..........15-25 53
(Canadian.)
RCA..........10-20 55-57
Singles: 7-inch
ABBOTT (100 series, except 116) 10-25 53-55
(Black vinyl.)
ABBOTT (115 "Wagon Load of Love")..........15-25 53
(Black vinyl.)
ABBOTT (115 "Wagon Load of Love")..........35-50 53
(Colored vinyl.)
ABBOTT (116 "Mexican Joe")........15-25 53
(Black vinyl.)
ABBOTT (116 "Mexican Joe")........35-50 53
(Colored vinyl.)
ABBOTT (137 "Butterfly Love")......15-25 53
(Black vinyl.)
ABBOTT (137 "Butterfly Love")......35-50 53
(Colored vinyl.)
ABBOTT (143 "El Rancho Del Rio")..........15-25 53
(Black vinyl.)
ABBOTT (143 "El Rancho Del Rio")..........35-50 53
(Colored vinyl.)
ABBOTT (148 "Bimbo")..........15-25 53
(Black vinyl.)
ABBOTT (148 "Bimbo")..........35-50 53
(Colored vinyl.)
ABBOTT (160 thru 186)..........10-20 54-55
ABBOTT (3000 series)..........10-20 55
ABBOTT (4000 series)..........4-8
QUALITY (1177 "Bimbo")..........35-50 53
(Canadian.)
RCA (0135 thru 0963)..........3-8 69-74
RCA (6200 thru 7557)..........10-20 55-59
RCA (7643 "He'll Have to Go")..........8-12 59
RCA (7643 "He'll Have to Go") ..150-250 59
(Single-sided. Promotional issue only.)
RCA (7756 thru 9969)..........4-10 60-71
RCA (10133 thru 13693)..........3-6 75-84
Picture Sleeves
RCA (7756 "I'm Gettin Better")......10-15 60
RCA (7800 "Am I Losing You")......10-15 60
RCA (8080 "I'm Gonna Change Everything")..........8-12 62
RCA (8127 "Is This Me")..........8-12 63
RCA (8193 "Guilty")..........8-12 63
RCA (8252 "Señor Santa Claus")...15-20 63
RCA (8625 "Is It Really Over")..........5-10 65
EPs: 7-inch
RCA (133 "Tall Tales & Short Tempers")..........20-30 61
(Compact 33 Double.)
RCA (757 "Singing Down the Lane")..........20-30 56
RCA (1256 "Singing Down the Lane")..........50-100 56
(Two discs.)
RCA (1410 "Bimbo")..........15-25 57
RCA (1576 "Jim Reeves")..........15-25 57
RCA (2487 "A Touch of Velvet")......10-20 62
(Stereo. Juke box issue only. Includes title strips.)
RCA (4062 "Four Walls")..........15-25 57
RCA (4357 "He'll Have to Go")......15-25 57
RCA (5124 "Jim Reeves Hits")......10-20 59
RCA (5145 "Am I Losing You")......10-20 60
LPs: 10/12-inch
ABBOTT (5001 "Jim Reeves Sings")..........800-1200 56
CMF (008 "Live at the Opry")..........5-10
CAMDEN (Except 583 thru 686)......5-15 64-73
CAMDEN (583 thru 686)..........10-20 60-63
CANDLELIGHT ("Jim Reeves")......15-25 83
(Boxed five-disc set. Selection number not known.)
GUEST STAR..........10-15 64
HISTORY of COUNTRY MUSIC......6-10 72
PAIR..........6-12 82
PICKWICK..........5-10 72
PICKWICK/HILLTOP..........5-10 74
RCA (0039 thru 5044)..........5-10 73-84
(With "AHL," "ANL," "APL," "AYL" or "CPL" prefix.)
RCA (0126 "The Jim Reeves Collection")..........10-15 75
(Special Products issue, Two LPs.)
RCA (0246 "Take My Hand, Precious Lord")..........10-15
(Special Products issue. Two LPs.)
RCA (0587 "Golden Collection")......30-35
(Special Products issue, five-disc set.)
RCA (LPM-1256 "Singing Down the Lane")..........100-200 56
RCA (LPM-1410 "Bimbo")..........40-60 57
RCA (LPM-1576 "Jim Reeves")......30-50 57
RCA (LPM-1685 "Girls I Have Known")..........25-50 58
RCA (LPM-1950 "God Be with You")..........20-40 58
(Monaural.)
RCA (LSP-1950 "God Be with You")..........20-40 58
(Stereo.)
RCA (LPM-2001 thru LPM-2339)....15-25 59-61
(Monaural.)
RCA (LSP-2001 thru LSP-2339)....20-30 59-61
(Stereo.)
RCA (LPM-2487 thru LPM-3903)....10-20 62-67
RCA (LSP-2487 thru LSP-3903)....10-25 62-67
RCA (LPM-3987 "A Touch of Sadness")..........25-35 68
(Monaural.)
RCA (LSP-3987 "A Touch of Sadness")..........10-15 68
(Stereo.)
RCA (LSP-4062 thru LSP-4749)......8-15 68-72
RADIANT..........5-10
READER'S DIGEST/RCA (210 "Unforgettable Jim Reeves")..........25-35 76
(Boxed, six-disc set.)
TAMPA/RCA SPECIAL PRODUCTS (0126 "Jim Reeves")..........8-10 75
Also see BLUE BOYS
Also see CRAMER, Floyd
Also see JORDANAIRES
Also see KERR, Anita
Also see PRESLEY, Elvis / Hank Snow / Eddy Arnold / Hank Snow
Also see WRIGHT, Ginny

REEVES, Jim, & Deborah Allen C&W '79
Singles: 7-inch
RCA..........3-5 79-80
Also see ALLEN, Deborah

REEVES, Jim, & Patsy Cline C&W '81
(Patsy Cline & Jim Reeves)
Singles: 7-inch
MCA..........3-5 82
RCA..........3-5 81
LPs: 10/12-inch
MCA..........5-10 82
RCA..........5-10 81
Also see CLINE, Patsy

REEVES, Jim / Alvadean Coker
Singles: 78 rpm
ABBOTT..........10-20 54
Singles: 7-inch
ABBOTT..........15-25 54
Also see COKER, Al

REEVES, Jim / Hugi & Lugi Chorus
Singles: 7-inch
U.S.A.F. (89 "In a Mansion Stands My Love")..........20-30 60s
(Promotional issue only.)

REEVES, Jim, & Dottie West
Singles: 7-inch
RCA..........4-6 64
Also see REEVES, Jim
Also see WEST, Dottie

REEVES, Jimmy, Jr.
LPs: 10/12-inch
CHECKER..........8-10 71

REEVES, John Rex C&W '81
Singles: 7-inch
SOC-A-GEE..........3-5 81

REEVES, Martha P&R/R&B '74
Singles: 12-inch
FANTASY..........4-8 78-79
Singles: 7-inch
ARISTA..........3-5 75-77
FANTASY..........3-4 78-80
MCA..........3-4 74-75
LPs: 10/12-inch
ARISTA..........8-10 76
FANTASY..........5-8 78-80

MCA ... 8-12 74
PHONORAMA ... 5-8 83
Also see MARTHA & VANDELLAS

REEVES, Steve
Singles: 7-inch
COOL (104 "Come Along with Me") ... 25-50 58

REFLECTIONS
(With the Pete Bennett Orchestra)
Singles: 7-inch
CROSSROADS (401 "Maybe Tomorrow") ... 50-100 61
CROSSROADS (402 "Rocket to the Moon") ... 50-100 62

REFLECTIONS P&R '64
Singles: 7-inch
ABC-PAR (10794 "Like Adam and Eve") ... 15-25 66
ABC-PAR (10822 "You're Gonna Find Out You Need Me") ... 20-30 66
ERIC ... 3-4 70s
FLAX ... 4-8
GOLDEN WORLD ... 10-15 64-65
KAY•KO (1003 "Helpless") ... 100-150 63
MALONE ... 10-15 60s
TIGRE (602 "In the Still of the Night") ... 20-30 62
LPs: 10/12-inch
GOLDEN WORLD (300 "[Just Like] Romeo & Juliet") ... 50-75 64
Members: Tony Micale; John Dean; Phil Castrodale; Dan Bennie; Ray Steinberg.
Also see HIGH & The MIGHTY
Also see LARADOS
Also see MICHAELS, Tony

REFLECTIONS P&R/R&B '75
Singles: 7-inch
CAPITOL (4078 "3 Steps from True Love") ... 10-15 75
CAPITOL (4137 "Love On Delivery") ... 10-15 75
CAPITOL (4222 "Day After Day") ... 5-10 76
CAPITOL (4358 "Gift Wrap My Love") ... 5-10 76
Members: Herman Edwards; Josh Pridgen; Edmund "Butch" Simmons; John Simmons.

REFLECTIONS
Singles: 7-inch
SONIC ... 8-12 60s

RE-FLEX P&R/D&D/LP '83
Singles: 12-inch
CAPITOL ... 4-6 83-84
Singles: 7-inch
CAPITOL ... 3-4 83-84
Picture Sleeves
CAPITOL ... 3-4 83-84
LPs: 10/12-inch
CAPITOL ... 5-8 83

REFUGEE
LPs: 10/12-inch
CHARISMA ... 8-12 74
Member: Patrick Moraz.

REGAL, Mike
Singles: 7-inch
KAPP (506 "Too Young") ... 30-40 63

REGAL DEWY R&B '77
Singles: 12-inch
MILLENNIUM ... 8-10 77
Singles: 7-inch
MILLENNIUM ... 3-5 77

REGAL FUNKHARMONIC ORCHESTRA
LPs: 10/12-inch
MOTOWN ... 5-8 82

REGAL-AIRS
Singles: 7-inch
STAR-X (504 "It") ... 10-20 57

REGALS
Singles: 78 rpm
ALADDIN ... 15-25 54
ATLANTIC ... 10-20 55
MGM ... 10-15 54
Singles: 7-inch
ALADDIN (3266 "Run Pretty Baby") ... 75-100 54
ATLANTIC (1062 "I'm So Lonely") ... 25-50 55
MGM (11869 "When You're Home") ... 15-25 54
Members: Harold Wright; Billy Adams; Jerry Holman; Al Russell.
Also see DIAMONDS
Also see METRONOMES
Also see ORIOLES

REGALS
Singles: 7-inch
LAST CHANCE ... 5-10 61
LAVENDER ... 10-15 60
U.A. ... 10-15 61

REGAN, Bob
Singles: 7-inch
CHALLENGE ... 4-8 64

REGAN, Bob, & Lucille Starr C&W '70
Singles: 7-inch
DOT ... 3-5 69
LP: 10/12-inch
A&M ... 8-12
Also see BOB & LUCILLE
Also see CANADIAN SWEETHEARTS
Also see REGAN, Bob

REGAN, Denise
Singles: 7-inch
DEE GEE ... 4-8 65

REGAN, Eddie
Singles: 7-inch
ABC-PAR (10795 "Playin' Hide and Seek") ... 20-30 66

REGAN, Joan P&R '53
Singles: 78 rpm
LONDON ... 3-5 53-55
Singles: 7-inch
COLUMBIA ... 4-6 66
LONDON ... 5-10 53-55
Picture Sleeves
COLUMBIA ... 4-8 66

REGAN, Russ
Singles: 7-inch
ABC-PAR (9949 "I Never Know") ... 10-15 58
CAPITOL ... 5-10 59
Also see BAGGYS
Also see DANCER, PRANCER & NERVOUS
Also see SUMMERS, Little Davey

REGAN, Tex, & Jim Myers
Singles: 7-inch
FORTUNE ... 8-10 60

REGAN, Tommy
Singles: 7-inch
COLPIX (725 "I'll Never Stop Loving You") ... 60-80 64
WORLD ARTISTS ... 5-10 65
Also see MARCELS

REGENT CONCERT ORCHESTRA
LPs: 10/12-inch
REGENT (6091 "Amor") ... 25-50 58
(Cover pictures Jayne Mansfield, although she is not heard on the disc.)
Also see MANSFIELD, Jayne

REGENTS
Singles: 7-inch
KAYO (101 "No Hard Feelings") ... 20-25 60
PEORIA (8 "Summertime Blues") ... 8-12 60s
Also see FIVE SPENDERS

REGENTS P&R/R&B '61
Singles: 7-inch
ABC ... 3-5 73
APEX (76753 "Barbara Ann") ... 15-25 61
(Canadian.)
COUSINS (1002 "Barbara-Ann") ... 200-250 61
GEE (1065 "Barbara Ann") ... 20-25 61
GEE (1071 "Runaround") ... 20-30 61
GEE (1073 "Don't Be a Fool") ... 15-25 61
GEE (1075 "Lonesome Boy ") ... 15-25 62
ROULETTE ... 3-5 70s
LPs: 10/12-inch
CAPITOL (KAO-2153 "Live at the AM-PM Discotheque") ... 35-45 64
(Monaural.)
CAPITOL (SKAO-2153 "Live at the AM-PM Discotheque") ... 45-55 64
(Stereo.)
EMUS ... 5-10 79
GEE (GLP-706 ("Barbara-Ann") ... 75-100 61
(Monaural.)
GEE (SGLP-706 ("Barbara-Ann") ... 100-125 61
(Stereo.)
MURRAY HILL ... 5-8 85
Members: Guy Villari; Sal Cuomo; Chuck Fassert; Don Jacobucci; Tony Gravagna.
Also see CARDBOARD ZEPPELIN
Also see DEE, Sonny
Also see DESIRES
Also see HARPER, Chuck
Also see LYNDON, Frank
Also see MARTY
Also see RUNAROUNDS
Also see TREMONTS
Also see VILLARI, Guy

REGENTS
Singles: 7-inch
REPRISE (0430 "When I Die, Don't You Cry") ... 15-25 65
Member: Michael McDonald.
Also see McDONALD, Michael

REGENTS
Singles: 7-inch
BLUE CAT ... 5-10 65
DOT ... 4-8 66
PENTHOUSE ... 4-8 66

REGGAES
LPs: 10/12-inch
SPARERIB ... 8-12 72

REGGIE & REMARKABLES
Singles: 7-inch
U.A. ... 5-10 63

REGINA
Singles: 7-inch
COLUMBIA ... 4-8 65

REGINA P&R/R&B/LP '86
(Regina Richards)
Singles: 7-inch
ATLANTIC ... 3-4 86-88
Picture Sleeves
ATLANTIC ... 3-4 86-88
LPs: 10/12-inch
ATLANTIC ... 5-8 86

REGULARS: see GALAXIES / Regulars

REHABILITATION CRUISE
Singles: 7-inch
RONDON (21119 "Mini Skirts") ... 10-15 60s

REID, Clarence P&R/R&B '69
(With the Delmiras; Clarence Reed)
Singles: 7-inch
ALSTON ... 4-8 68-74
DEEP CITY ... 10-20 60s
DIAL ... 8-12 64
PHIL-L.A. of SOUL ... 5-10 67
REID (2744 "I Refuse to Give Up") ... 20-30 60s
SELMA ... 10-20 63
TAY-STER ... 5-10 67
WAND (1106 "Somebody Will") ... 10-20 65
WAND (1121 "I'm Your Yes Man") ... 20-30 65
LPs: 10/12-inch
ATCO (307 "Dancin' with Nobody But You Babe") ... 15-25 69

REID, Eddie
Singles: 7-inch
TWIRL (2010 "One Summer Love") ... 10-20 60s

REID, Irene
Singles: 7-inch
MGM ... 4-8 63
OLD TOWN (2004 "Just Loving You") ... 5-8 67
VERVE ... 5-8 63-66
LPs: 10/12-inch
MGM (4159 "It's Only the Beginning") ... 10-15 63
VERVE (5003 "It's Too Late") ... 10-15 66

REID, Jon
Singles: 7-inch
MGM ... 4-8 65

REID, Matthew
Singles: 7-inch
ABC-PAR (10259 "Jane") ... 15-25 61
ABC-PAR (10305 "Through My Tears") ... 15-25 62
DECCA ... 5-10 64
PHILIPS ... 4-6 69
SCEPTER (1238 "Faded Roses") ... 15-25 62
TOPIX (6006 "Cry Myself to Sleep") ... 30-40 63
Also see VALLI, Frankie

REID, Mike C&W '90
Singles: 7-inch
COLUMBIA ... 3-4 90
Also see MILSAP, Ronnie, & Mike Reid

REID, Terry LP '68
Singles: 7-inch
ATLANTIC ... 3-5 73
CAPITOL ... 3-5 78
EPIC ... 4-6 69
LPs: 10/12-inch
ATLANTIC ... 8-12 73
CAPITOL ... 5-10 78
EPIC ... 10-15 68-69

REIDEL, Jay
Singles: 7-inch
FORD ... 4-8 62

REIDY, Bob, Blues Band
(Bob Reidy Chicago Blues Band)
LPs: 10/12-inch
FLYING FISH ... 5-10 75
ROUNDER ... 5-10 73

REILLY, Betty
LPs: 10/12-inch
GOLDEN TONE ... 8-12

REILLY, Mike P&R '71
Singles: 7-inch
PARAMOUNT ... 3-5 70-71

REILLY, Suzy
Singles: 7-inch
AMERICAN INT'L ... 5-10 59

REILLY & MALONEY
LPs: 10/12-inch
FRECKLE ... 5-8 85-87
Members: Ginny Reilly; Dave Maloney.
Also see SEATTLE HELPS the HUNGRY

REINDEER
Singles: 7-inch
FELSTED ... 5-10 60

REINER, Carl, & Mel Brooks LP '73
LPs: 10/12-inch
CAPITOL (1600 series) ... 15-25 61
CAPITOL (2900 series) ... 10-15 68
W.B. (2741 "2000 & Thirteen") ... 5-10 73
W.B. (2744 "2000 Years with Carl Reiner & Mel Brooks") ... 15-25 73
(Three-disc set.)
WORLD PACIFIC (1401 "2000 Years with Carl Reiner & Mel Brooks") ... 25-35 60

REINKE, Gary
Singles: 7-inch
SARA (1541 "The War Is Over and Done") ... 10-15 70s

REIPLINGER, Rap
LPs: 10/12-inch
MOUNTAIN APPLE ... 5-10 78

REIRRUC, Det: see DET REIRRUC

REIS, Faye
Singles: 7-inch
CANDIX ... 4-8 61

REISMAN, Joe, & His Orchestra P&R '56
Singles: 78 rpm
RCA ... 4-8 55-57
Singles: 7-inch
LANDA ... 5-10 61
RCA ... 10-20 55-59
ROULETTE ... 5-10 59-60
EPs: 7-inch
RCA ... 5-10 56
LPs: 10/12-inch
CAMDEN ... 5-10 72
RCA ... 15-30 56
ROULETTE ... 10-20 59-60
Also see DE CASTRO SISTERS
Also see VALLI, June

REITZ, Ken
Singles: 7-inch
SARA (65112 "Willing Consent") ... 10-20 65

REIVERS
Singles: 7-inch
WHITE WHALE ... 3-5 70

REJECTS
Singles: 7-inch
AUDIO ART (5813 "The Reject") ... 25-35 65
STARLITE (6440 "Yogi") ... 8-12

REJECTS
Singles: 7-inch
BIG SOUND (305 "Hey Girl") ... 30-50 66

REJECTS
Singles: 7-inch
CABELL (107 "All My Life") ... 8-12

REJOICE P&R '68
Singles: 7-inch
DUNHILL ... 4-6 68-69
LPs: 10/12-inch
DUNHILL ... 10-15 69
Members: Tom Brown; Nancy Brown.

REKNOWN
Singles: 7-inch
G.A.R. (108 "You and Me") ... 10-15 67

REL YEAS
Singles: 7-inch
KAYE (101 "Good Good Lovin' ") ... 50-100
WILDCAT (0044 "Round Rock Boogie") ... 20-40 60
WILDCAT (0056 "Country Boy") ... 20-40 61

RELATION
LPs: 10/12-inch
R&A ... 5-10 81

RELATIONS
Singles: 7-inch
KAPE (504 "Until We Two Are One") ... 10-20 63
KAPE (703 "What Did I Do Wrong") ... 10-15 63
MICHELE ... 5-10 63
REENA ... 4-8 68
UTOPIA ... 10-15 60s
ZELL'S ... 5-10 60s

RELATIONS
Singles: 7-inch
DAVY JONES PRESENTS (664 "Back to the Beach") ... 15-20 67
DEMAND (501 "Back to the Beach") ... 25-35 67
Picture Sleeves
DAVY JONES PRESENTS (664 "Back to the Beach") ... 20-30 67

REL-ATI-ONS
Singles: 7-inch
COMMUNITY (2000 "Soul Train Funky-Monkey") ... 4-8

RELATIVES
Singles: 7-inch
ALMONT (303 "I'm Just Looking for Love") ... 25-35 63
ALMONT (306 "I'm Just Looking for Love") ... 20-30 64
MUSICOR ... 4-8 65
WOW ... 4-8 68

RELAXATIONS
Singles: 7-inch
BLUE MOON ... 4-6

RELF, Bobby
(With the Laurels; with Ernie Freeman Combo; Bob Relf)
Singles: 78 rpm
CASH (1019 "Our Love") ... 15-25 55
DOT (15510 "I'm Not Afraid") ... 10-20 56
FLAIR (1063 "Yours Alone") ... 50-75 55
Singles: 7-inch
CASH (1019 "Our Love") ... 35-50 55
DEE DEE (103 "I'm a Big Wheel") ... 10-20 59
DOT (15510 "I'm Not Afraid") ... 15-20 56
FLAIR (1063 "Yours Alone") ... 100-125 55
FONTANA (1679 "Yesterday") ... 4-8 69
TRANS-AMERICAN (0010 "Girl, You're My Kind of Wonderful") ... 10-15 68
Also see ANGELLE, Bobby
Also see BOB & EARL
Also see FREEMAN, Ernie
Also see LAURELS
Also see VALENTINO, Bobby

RELF, Keith
Singles: 7-inch
EPIC (10044 "Mr. Zero") ... 10-20 66
(Black vinyl.)
EPIC (10044 "Mr. Zero") ... 50-75 66
(Colored vinyl. Promotional issue only.)
EPIC (10110 "Shapes in My Mind") ... 10-20 66
(Black vinyl.)
EPIC (10110 "Shapes in My Mind") ... 50-75 66
(Colored vinyl.)
MCCM (002 "Together Now") ... 3-5 89
(Black vinyl.)
MCCM (002 "Together Now") ... 4-8 89
(Colored vinyl. Promotional issue only.)
Picture Sleeves
EPIC (10110 "Shapes in My Mind") ... 40-50 67
MCCM (002 "Together Now") ... 3-5 89
Also see RENAISSANCE
Also see YARDBIRDS

RELIABLES
Singles: 7-inch
ANDERSON (22532 "Dreams That We Once Knew") ... 50-75 60s

RELLA, Cindy
Singles: 7-inch
CARLTON ... 4-8 62-64
DRUM BOY ... 8-10 64

REMAINING FEW
Singles: 7-inch
ASKEL (112 "Painted Air") ... 15-25 67

REMAINDERS
(With J. Parker & Accents)
Singles: 7-inch
VICO ("Over the Rainbow") ... 50-100
(No selection number used.)

REMAINS
Singles: 7-inch
EPIC (9783 "Why Do I Cry") ... 40-80 65
EPIC (9842 "I Can't Get Away") ... 40-80 65
EPIC (10001 "Diddy Wah Diddy") ... 40-80 66
(Black vinyl.)
EPIC (10001 "Diddy Wah Diddy") ... 50-100 66
(Colored vinyl.)
EPIC (10060 "Don't Look Back") ... 40-80 66
SPOONFED ... 4-8 78
(Colored vinyl.)
Picture Sleeves
EPIC (10001 "Diddy Wah Diddy") ... 40-50 66
LPs: 10/12-inch
EPIC (24214 "The Remains") ... 150-250 66
(Monaural.)
EPIC (26214 "The Remains") ... 200-300 66
(Stereo.)
SPOONFED (3205 "The Remains") ... 8-12 78
(Black vinyl.)
SPOONFED (3205 "The Remains") ... 15-25 78
(Colored vinyl.)
Also see SMART, N.D., & Kangaroo

REMARKABLE MARQUIS
Singles: 7-inch
DAWN ... 10-20 60s

REMARKABLES
Singles: 7-inch
CHASE (1600 "Write Me") ... 150-250 64

REMARKABLES
Singles: 7-inch
AUDIO ART ... 5-10 66

REMBRANDTS LP '91
LPs: 10/12-inch
ATCO ... 5-8 90

REMICKS
Singles: 7-inch
EVE LTD. (1001 "This Little Girl of Mine") ... 10-20 60s

REMINGTON, Herb
Singles: 7-inch
D (1186 "Soft Shoe Slide") ... 10-20 60
U.A. (482 "Swinging Cow Bells") ... 10-20 62

REMINGTON, Rita C&W '73
(With the Smokey Valley Symphony)
Singles: 12-inch
PLANTATION (171 "To Each His Own") ... 4-8 78
(Promotional issue only.)
Singles: 7-inch
PLANTATION ... 3-5 73-82
LPs: 10/12-inch
PICKWICK ... 5-10 80
PLANTATION ... 5-10 77-78

REMINGTONS C&W '91
Singles: 7-inch
BNA ... 3-4 91-92
Members: James Griffin; Rick Yancey; Richard Mainegra.
Also see CYMARRON
Also see GRIFFIN, James

REMINISCENTS
(With the Goldtones)
Singles: 7-inch
CLEOPATRA (104 "For Your Love") ... 150-250 63
DAY (1000 "Zoom Zoom Zoom") ... 50-100 63
MARCEL (1000 "Cards of Love") ... 100-200 62

REMUS, Eugene
(With the Rayber Voices)
Singles: 7-inch
MOTOWN (1001 "You Never Miss a Good Thing"/"Hold Me Tight") ... 300-400 61
MOTOWN (1001 "You Never Miss a Good Thing"/"Gotta Have Your Lovin' ") ... 250-350 61
Also see HOLLAND, Eddie

RENAE, Eddie
Singles: 7-inch
PINE ... 15-20

RENAIRE, Ronny
Singles: 7-inch
UTOPIA....4-8 61

RENAISSANCE
Singles: 7-inch
GNP....4-8 68
KAPP....3-6 69
PARKWAY....4-8 67
TODDLIN' TOWN....4-8 60s

RENAISSANCE LP '73
Singles: 7-inch
I.R.S.....3-4 82
SIRE (Except 1022)....3-5 76-78
SIRE (1022 "Northern Lights")....12-18 78
(Picture disc. Promotional issue only.)
LPs: 10/12-inch
CAPITOL....8-12 72-78
ELEKTRA (74068 "Renaissance")....15-25 69
I.R.S.....5-8 81-83
MFSL (099 "Scheherazade and Other Stories")....25-40 82
SIRE....8-10 74-79
SINGCORD....8-10 76-77
SOVEREIGN....8-12 73
Members: John Tout; Mike Dunford; Jim McCarty; Annie Haslam; Keith Relf; Jon Camp; Terry Sullivan; Louis Cennamo; Jane Relf.
Also see ARMAGEDDON
Also see HASLAM, Annie
Also see RELF, Keith

RENAISSANCE LP '71
Singles: 7-inch
RANWOOD....3-5 71
LPs: 10/12-inch
RANWOOD....5-10 70

RENAISSANCE
Singles: 7-inch
PAGE....4-8 70s

RENAISSANCE FAIR
Singles: 7-inch
ASTRAL PROJECTION (170 "She's a Woman")....15-25 60s

RENAISSANCE OF RHYTHM
Singles: 7-inch
RMP (212 "There Is No Time")....8-12

RENAISSANCE SOCIETY
LPs: 10/12-inch
HBR....10-20 60s

RENALDO & LOAF: see: RESIDENTS

RENARD, Jacques, & Orchestra P&R '30
Singles: 78 rpm
BRUNSWICK....3-8 30-45

RENAULTS
Singles: 7-inch
CHICORY (1600 "10 Questions")....20-25 63
WAND....5-10 61-62
W.B. (5094 "Stella")....15-20 59

RENAULTS
Singles: 7-inch
BRYTE (306 "Rockin' with Joe")....35-50 62

RENAY, Diane P&R/LP '64
Singles: 7-inch
ATCO....5-10 62-63
D MAN (101 "Can't Help Lovin' ")....15-25
DICE (8018 "Navy Blue")....15-20 87
ERIC....3-4 70s
FONTANA....8-15 69
MGM (13335 "I Had a Dream")....10-20 64
NEW VOICE....5-10 65
REX (293 "Maybe")....15-25
20TH FOX....8-15 64
U.A. (50048 "Please Gypsy")....10-15 66
LPs: 10/12-inch
20TH FOX (TF-3133 "Navy Blue")....25-40 64
(Monaural.)
20TH FOX (TFS-3133 "Navy Blue")....30-50 64
(Stereo.)

RENBOURN, John
LPs: 10/12-inch
REPRISE....10-15 70-73
Also see PENTANGLE

RENDELLS
Singles: 7-inch
CARMAX (101 "Hot Licks")....10-20 63

RENDER, Denny
Singles: 7-inch
TAV (901017 "Lonely Woman")....10-20 60s

RENDER, Rudy R&B '49
Singles: 78 rpm
LONDON....4-6 49-51
Singles: 7-inch
DOT....4-8 60-61
EDISON INT'L....4-8 59
LONDON....5-10 51

RENDEZVOUS
Singles: 7-inch
REPRISE (20089 "Congratulations Baby")....25-50 62
RUST (5041 "It Breaks My Heart")....25-35 63

RENDEZVOUS STOMPERS
Singles: 7-inch
DORE (626 "Gremmies Unite")....15-25 62

RENDITIONS
Singles: 7-inch
KISKI....8-12 64

RENE, Delia R&B '81
Singles: 7-inch
AIRWAVE....3-5 81

RENE, Googie R&B '60
Singles: 78 rpm
CLASS....8-15 57-58
Singles: 7-inch
CLASS....5-15 57-66
KAPP....4-6 62
NEW BAG....3-5 67
REED....5-10 60
RENDEZVOUS....8-12 60
Picture Sleeves
RENDEZVOUS....10-20 60
LPs: 10/12-inch
CLASS....15-30 59-63
Also see GOOGIE & McCRARY

RENÉ, Henri, & His Orchestra P&R '40
Singles: 78 rpm
RCA....3-5 48-56
STANDARD....3-5 52-53
VICTOR....3-6 40-47
Singles: 7-inch
DECCA....3-6 62
IMPERIAL....4-8 59
RCA....4-8 51-56
STANDARD....4-8 52-53
Picture Sleeves
RCA....5-10 55
EPs: 7-inch
CAMDEN....5-10 54-57
RCA....5-10 53-56
LPs: 10/12-inch
CAMDEN....10-20 54-57
KAPP....5-10 67
RCA (Except 1046 & 3000 series)....10-20 56-61
RCA (1046 "Music for Bachelors")....30-50 54
(Cover pictures Jayne Mansfield, although she is not heard on the disc.)
RCA (3049 "Serenede to Love")....15-25 53
(10-inch LP.)
RCA (3076 "Listen to René")....15-25 53
(10-inch LP.)
Also see BELL SISTERS
Also see MANSFIELD, Jayne

RENE, Ricky
(With Fabulous Desires)
Singles: 7-inch
ERA (3138 "Ouch")....8-12 64

RENE, Wendy
Singles: 7-inch
STAX....4-8 64

RENE & ANGELA R&B '80
Singles: 12-inch
MERCURY....4-6 85-86
Singles: 7-inch
CAPITOL....3-5 80-83
MERCURY....3-4 85-86
Picture Sleeves
MERCURY....3-4 85-86
LPs: 10/12-inch
CAPITOL....5-10 80-83
MERCURY....5-8 85-86

RENE & RAY P&R '62
Singles: 7-inch
DONNA (1360 "Queen of My Heart")....10-15 62
DONNA (1368 "Too Late")....10-15 62

RENE & RENE P&R '64
Singles: 7-inch
ABC....3-5 73
ABC-PAR....4-8 65
ARU....4-8 64
CERTRON....3-5 71
COBRA....4-8 65
COLUMBIA....4-8 64
EPIC....3-6 69
FALCON....4-8 68
JOX....8-10 64-66
WHITE WHALE....3-6 68-69
Picture Sleeves
COLUMBIA....8-12 64
LPs: 10/12-inch
CERTRON....8-10 70
EPIC....10-15 69
WHITE WHALE....10-15 68
Members: Rene Ornelas; J. Ramirez.

RENEE, Bette, & Thrillettes
Singles: 7-inch
LAWN....8-12 64

RENEE, Perri
Singles: 7-inch
SOULVILLE....4-8 68

RENEE, Rhea
Singles: 7-inch
SARA....4-8 61

RENEE & RHINESTONE RAMBLES
Singles: 7-inch
RCA (10846 "Backstage with Renee")....4-6 78
Also see CHRISTIE, Lou

RENEGADE
Singles: 7-inch
ALLIED ARTISTS....3-4 86
LPs: 10/12-inch
ALLIED ARTISTS....5-8 86
Member: Luis Cardenas.
Also see CARDENAS, Luis

RENEGADE V
Singles: 7-inch
CONTE....5-10 63
Members: Steve O'Reilly; Rick Henn; Ed Medora; Vince Hozier; Marty DiGiovanni.
Also see HENN, Rick
Also see SNOW MEN
Also see SUNRAYS

RENEGADES
Singles: 7-inch
AMERICAN INT'L....10-20 59-62
Also see GAMBLERS

RENEGADES
Singles: 7-inch
DORSET (5007 "Stolen Angel")....30-40 61

RENEGADES
Singles: 7-inch
CITATION (5005 "Istanbul")....15-25 63
Members: Mickey Slutzky; Richard Schurk; Paul Rubitzky; Keith Dreher; Bob Barian; Kurt Kronhelm; Denny Sachse; Denny Scheuneman; Louie Friedman.
Also see WALKING STICKS

RENEGADES
Singles: 7-inch
POLARIS (501 "Waiting for You")....15-25 65

RENEGADES
Singles: 7-inch
CHARDO....10-20 60s
CONGRESS (241 "Cadillac")....15-25 65

RENEGADES
Singles: 7-inch
GARLAND....5-10
KARATE....10-15 66

RENEGADES
Singles: 7-inch
CAMBRIDGE (12110 "Raving Blue")....50-100
CAMBRIDGE ("She's Your Find")....50-75
(Selection number not known.)

RENEGADES IV
Singles: 7-inch
FENTON (945 "Greensleeves")....15-25 64

RENEGAIDS
Singles: 7-inch
GNP (193 "Surfin' Tragedy")....10-15 63
Member: Bob Vaught.
Also see VAUGHT, Bob

RENES
Singles: 7-inch
RIBA....10-15 65

RENFRO, Anthony R&B '76
(Anthony C. Renfro Orchestra)
Singles: 7-inch
RENFRO (43 "Gloria's Theme")....3-5 76
RENFRO (122 "This Is Our Moment of Love")....25-50

RENI, Chet, & Kings
Singles: 7-inch
GEORGIE (101 "What's Wrong with Me")....75-125 59

RENNER, Dianne
Singles: 7-inch
ACCENT (1088 "Quicksand")....30-50 63

RENNEY, Lee
Singles: 7-inch
BETHLEHEM....8-12 64

RENNIE, Mary Lue
LPs: 10/12-inch
R.S.V.P.....10-15 65

RENO, Al
Singles: 7-inch
KAPP (432 "Cheryl")....50-75 61
Also see CHESTERFIELDS
Also see SELECTIONS

RENO, Bobby
Singles: 7-inch
MORGIL....4-8 62

RENO, Don
(With His Tennessee Cut-Ups; with Don Wayne Reno)
LPs: 10/12-inch
CMH....5-10 78-79
DOT (3617 ""Mr. Five Strings")....15-20 65
(Monaural.)
DOT (25617 ""Mr. Five Strings")....20-25 65
(Stereo.)
KING (1065 "Fastest Five Strings Alive")....10-15 69
MONUMENT....10-20 66
SARDIS....5-10
WANGO....8-12 76

RENO, Don, & Benny Martin C&W '66
(With the Tennessee Cut-Ups)
Singles: 7-inch
MONUMENT....4-6 65
LPs: 10/12-inch
CABIN CREEK....5-8
Also see MARTIN, Benny
Also see RENO, Don

RENO, Frank
Singles: 7-inch
DIAMOND....4-8 62

RENO, Ginette
Singles: 7-inch
PARROT....3-5 71
LPs: 10/12-inch
PARROT....15-20 71

RENO, Jack C&W '67
Singles: 7-inch
DOT....3-6 68-70
JAB....4-6 67-68
TARGET....3-5 71-72
U.A.....3-5 73-74
LPs: 10/12-inch
ATCO....10-15 68
DERBYTOWN....5-10 78
DOT....10-15 68-69
TARGET....8-12 72

RENO, Mike, & Ann Wilson P&R '84
Singles: 7-inch
COLUMBIA....3-4 84
Picture Sleeves
COLUMBIA....3-4 84
Also see LOVERBOY
Also see WILSON, Ann

RENO, Nick
Singles: 7-inch
GES (0100 "I Had a Dream")....50-100 59

RENO, Ronnie C&W '83
Singles: 7-inch
EMH....3-4 83
LPs: 10/12-inch
MCA....5-10 75
Also see HAGGARD, Merle
Also see OSBORNE BROTHERS
Also see RENO BROTHERS

RENO, Tony, & Sherwoods
Singles: 7-inch
JOHNSON....8-12 63
Also see SHERWOODS

RENO BAND: see HALEY, Bill

RENO & SMILEY C&W '61
Singles: 78 rpm
KING....5-10 52-57
Singles: 7-inch
KING (Except 1235 thru 5169)....4-8 59-62
KING (1235 thru 5169)....5-15 53-58
EPs: 7-inch
KING....5-10 58-62
LPs: 10/12-inch
ATTEIRAM....5-10
DOT....10-20 63
GUSTO....5-8
KING (550 thru 693)....20-30 58-59
KING (701 thru 1091)....10-25 61-70
NASHVILLE....10-15 69
STARDAY....5-10 73-75
STARDAY/KING....5-8
Members: Don Reno; Red Smiley.
Also see CHICK & HOT RODS

RENO BROTHERS C&W '88
Singles: 7-inch
STEP ONE....3-4 88-89
Members: Ronnie Reno; Dale Reno; Don Reno.
Also see RENO, Ronnie

RENOLDS, Mike, & Infants of Soul
Singles: 7-inch
FROG DEATH (3 "When Will I Find Her")....15-25 64

RENOVATIONS
Singles: 7-inch
ANGEL TOWN....5-10 60s

RENOWNS
Singles: 7-inch
EVEREST (19396 "My Mind's Made Up")....30-40 61
Member: Marjorie Lake.

RENRUT, Icky
("Vocal by Jimmy Thomas"; Ike Turner)
Singles: 7-inch
STEVENS (104 "Jack Rabbit")....25-35 59
STEVENS (107 "Ho - - - Ho")....25-35 59
Also see THOMAS, Jimmy
Also see TURNER, Ike

RENTE, Damon
LPs: 10/12-inch
TBA....5-8 86

RENTTALB, Seluj
(Jules Blattner)
LP: 10/12-inch
MGM....10-15 72
Also see BLATTNER, Jules

RENWICK, Tim
LPs: 10/12-inch
CBS....5-10 80
Also see STEWART, Al
Also see BROOKER, Gary

REO, Dave
Singles: 7-inch
TERRILYN....5-10 59

REO, Diamond: see DIAMOND REO

REO, Steve
Singles: 7-inch
TWIN....5-10 59

REPAIRS
Singles: 7-inch
MOWEST....3-5 72
RARE EARTH....3-5 71
LPs: 10/12-inch
MOWEST....5-10 72
RARE EARTH....5-10 71

REPARATA P&R '65
(With the Delrons; Mary Aiese)
Singles: 7-inch
BIG TREE (114 "Just You")....4-8 71
KAPP (989 "Bowery")....5-10 69
KAPP (2010 "San Juan")....5-10 69
KAPP (2050 "Walking in the Rain")....5-10 70
LAURIE (3589 "Octopus' Garden")....4-6 72
MALA (573 "I Believe")....6-12 67
MALA (589 "Captain of Your Ship")....6-12 68
MALA (12000 "Saturday Night Didn't Happen")....6-12 68
MALA (12016 "Summer Laughter")....6-12 68
MALA (12026 "Weather Forecast")....6-12 68
NORTH AMERICAN MUSIC....4-6 74
POLYDOR (14271 "Shoes")....4-6 75
RCA (8721 "I Can Tell")....10-15 65
RCA (8820 "I'm Nobody's Baby Now")....10-15 66
RCA (8921 "Mama's Little Girl")....10-15 66
RCA (9123 "Boys & Girls")....10-15 67
RCA (9185 "I Can Hear the Bells")....10-15 67
WORLD ARTISTS (1036 "Whenever a Teenager Cries")....8-12 64
WORLD ARTISTS (1051 "Tommy")....8-12 65
WORLD ARTISTS (1062 "The Boy I Love")....8-12 65
WORLD ARTISTS (1075 "He's the Greatest")....8-12 65
LPs: 10/12-inch
AVCO EMBASSY (33008 "1970 Rock & Roll Revolution")....10-20 70
WORLD ARTISTS (3006 "Whenever a Teenager Cries")....40-60 65
Members: Mary Aiese; Sheila Reillie; Carol Drobnicki; Nanette Licari; Lorraine Mazzola; Cookie Sirico.
Also see DEL-RONS

REPLACEMENTS LP '86
Singles: 7-inch
SIRE....3-5 85-90
TWIN TONE....3-5 82-84
Picture Sleeves
SIRE....3-5 89
LPs: 10/12-inch
SIRE....5-10 85-90
TWIN/TONE....5-10 84
Promotional LPs
SIRE ("Interview with Paul Westerberg")....20-25 85
Members: Paul Westerberg; Tom Stinson; Chris Mars.

REPTILE RHYTHM BAND
Singles: 7-inch
REPTOID (3097 "Tight Butt")....3-5 82
Picture Sleeves
REPTOID (3097 "Tight Butt")....3-5 82

REPTILES
Singles: 7-inch
MBM (60724 "Ballad of Mrs. George Wallace")....10-20 60
RADIANT (1503 "Lizard Gizzard")....10-20 61

RERUN OF OLD MEMORIES
Singles: 7-inch
NASCO....3-5 70

RESEARCH
Singles: 7-inch
FLICK CITY (3005 "I Don't Walk There No More")....10-15 67
FLICK CITY (3007 "Can You Baby")....10-15 67
LPs: 10/12-inch
FLICK CITY (5001 "In Research")....35-55 67

RESIDENTS
Singles: 12-inch
RALPH (8006 "Diskomo")....6-12 80
(Black vinyl.)
RALPH (8006 "Diskomo")....10-15 80
(Colored vinyl.)
RALPH (8721 "Hit the Road Jack [Dance Mix]")....5-8 87
Singles: 7-inch
RALPH ("17 X 7")....80-120 87
(Boxed set. Includes *It's a Man's Man's, Man's World* picture disc.)
RALPH (1SP-1 "Earth vs. The Flying Saucers")....3-5 86
(Colored vinyl. Bonus single, packaged with collector's edition of *The Cryptic Guide to the Residents*.)
RALPH (0577 "Beatles Play the Residents / Residents Play the Beatles")....20-30 77
RALPH (0776 "Satisfaction")....20-30 76
RALPH (1272 "Santa Dog")....40-60 72
(Two-disc set titled *Santa Dog*.. Includes *Fire/Aircraft Damage* and *Lightning/Explosion*. Selection number represents release date: i.e. 12/72.)
RALPH (7803 "Satisfaction")....3-5
(Reissue.)
RALPH (7812 "Santa Dog '78")....5-10 78
(Selection number is transposed release date: i.e. 12/78.)
RALPH (8422 "It's a Man's Man's, Man's World")....3-5 87
(Black vinyl.)
RALPH (8422 "It's a Man's Man's, Man's World")....10-15 87
(Picture disc.)
RALPH (8621 "Kaw-Liga")....10-15 86
(Picture disc.)
RALPH (8622 "Kaw-Liga")....3-5 86
(Black vinyl.)
RALPH (8622 "Kaw-Liga")....5-10 86
(Black vinyl.)
RALPH (8721 "Hit the Road Jack")....3-5 87

RALPH (8721 "Hit the Road Jack")....................10-15 87
(Picture disc.)
RALPH/EVA-TONE ("Meet the Residents Sampler")....................10-20 74
(Five-inch, Eva-Tone soundsheet. Issued in a nine-inch, paper, gatefold jacket.)
REFLEX/EVA-TONE (10371900-1 "Diskomo Live")....................5-10 88
(Soundsheet. Promotional issue only.)

Picture Sleeves

RALPH (1272 "Santa Dog")..........50-100 72
RALPH (0577 "Beatles Play the Residents / Residents Play the Beatles")..........30-50 77
RALPH (7812 "Santa Dog '78")......10-15 78

EPs: 7-inch

RALPH (0377 "Babyfingers")..........50-75 79
RALPH (1177 "Duckstab")..............20-30 78
RALPH (1177 "Duckstab")..............10-15 70s
(EP "Combo Pack.")
RALPH (8007 "Buy Or Die #5")......15-25 80
(Promotional issue only.)
RALPH (8050 "Buy Or Die #6")......15-25 80
(Promotional issue only.)
RALPH (11271 "Buy Or Die #14")..15-25 87
(Promotional issue only.)
RALPH (11271 "Buy Or Die #14.5")....................15-25 87
(Promotional issue only.)
RALPH WEIRD (1 "Babyfingers")... 5-10
W.E.I.R.D. (1 "Babyfingers")........... 5-10

LPs: 10/12-inch

CRYPTIC (18335 "For Elsie")......... 8-12
(Colored vinyl. Single-sided pressing.)
EPISODE (21 "Census Taker")......15-25 85
(Black vinyl. Soundtrack.)
EPISODE (21 "Census Taker")......35-45 85
(Colored vinyl. Soundtrack.)
RALPH (001 "Mole Show")............15-25 83
RALPH (002A "Mole Show")...........20-30 83
(Picture disc.)
RALPH (0274 "Meet the Residents")....................100-150 74
RALPH (0278 "Duck Stab/Buster Glen")....................5-8 78
RALPH (0677 "Meet the Residents")....................10-15 77
RALPH (1075 "Third Reich & Roll")....................30-40 76
(Cover indicates "First Pressing, 1000 Copies." Selection number represents final recording date: i.e. 10/75.)
RALPH (1075 "Third Reich & Roll"). 5-10 77
(Second through fourth pressings—no mention of "first pressing.")
RALPH (1075 "Third Reich & Roll")....................15-25 70s
(Numbered, boxed set.)
RALPH (1174 "Not Available").......25-45 78
(Maroon label.)
RALPH (1174 "Not Available")......... 5-8 78
(Yellow label.)
RALPH (1276 "Fingerprince")........20-35 77
(Cover indicates "First Pressing.")
RALPH (1276 "Fingerprince")........10-15 77
(No mention of first pressing.)
RALPH (7707 "Meet the Residents")....................20-30 85
(Picture disc.)
RALPH (7707 "Special 13th Anniversary Edition")....................20-30 85
(Picture disc.)
RALPH (7901 "Please Don't Steal It")....................20-30 79
(Promotional issue only.)
RALPH (7906 "Eskimo")...............15-20 79
(Colored vinyl.)
RALPH (7906 "Eskimo")................. 5-8 79
(Black vinyl.)
RALPH (7906 "Eskimo")...............20-30 80
(Picture disc.)
RALPH (8052 "Commercial Album")....................8-15 80
RALPH (8152 "Mark of the Mole") 20-30 81
(Colored vinyl, signed collector's edition with lyrics.)
RALPH (8152 "Mark of the Mole")..10-15 81
(Black vinyl.)
RALPH (8202 "Tunes of Two Cities")....................8-12 82
RALPH (8252 "Intermission")......... 8-12 82
RALPH (8202 "George & James")..10-20 82
RALPH (8315 "Title in Limbo").....10-20 83
(As Renaldo & Loaf.)
RALPH (8452 "Whatever Happened to Vileness Fats")....................10-20 84
(Video soundtrack.)
RALPH (8552 "Big Bubble")..........10-15 85
(Colored vinyl.)
RALPH (8552 "Big Bubble")........... 5-10 86
(Black vinyl.)
RALPH (8602 "Eyeball Show")...... 5-10 86
RALPH (8652 "Stars and Hank Forever")....................5-10 86
RALPH (82761 "Fingerprince")........ 5-10
(Reissue.)
RALPH (87521 "Duck Stab/Buster Glen")....................5-8
(Reissue.)
RALPH (88521 "Meet the Residents")....................5-8
(Reissue.)
RYKO (0044 "God in 3 Persons")..... 5-10 88
(Clear vinyl.)
RYKO (0045 "God in 3 Persons Instrumental")....................5-10 88
(Clear vinyl. Soundtrack.)
UWEB (0011 "Stranger Than Supper")....................5-9 91
Members: Phil Lithman; Pamela Zeibak; Peggy Honeydew; Chris Cutler; Don Jackovich; Don Preston.
Also see SCHWUMP

RESISTANT MILITIA

EPs: 12-inch

AZRA (8891 "Living By Law")..........8-12 89
(Picture disc. Promotional issue only.)

RESNICK, Art
(Artie Resnick)

Singles: 7-inch

WHITE WHALE....................3-5 69

LPs: 10/12-inch

SYMPOSIUM....................10-15

RESOLUTION

Singles: 7-inch

GM (717 "The Old Man").................. 3-5

RESOLUTIONS

Singles: 7-inch

VALENTINE ("January 1, 1962")....35-55 60s
Member: Billy Vera (plus members from the Passions and Mystics).
Also see MYSTICS
Also see PASSIONS
Also see VERA, Billy

RESONETS

Singles: 7-inch

LINDA LEE (002 "Surf Carnival")...10-20 60s

RESONICS

Singles: 7-inch

LIL-LARRY (1005 "With Your Love to Guide Me")....................50-100 60s
LUCKY TOKEN (108 "I'm Really in Love")....................35-50 64
UNITY (101 "Split Personality")......10-15 63

RESTIVO, Johnny *P&R '59*

Singles: 7-inch

EPIC (9537 "My Reputation")..........10-15 62
RCA (47-7559 "The Shape I'm In")....................10-15 59
(Monaural.)
RCA (61-7559 "The Shape I'm In")....................25-50 59
(Stereo.)
RCA (7601 "Dear Someone")..........10-15 59
RCA (7636 "Come Closer")............10-15 59
RCA (7697 "High School Play").....10-15 60
RCA (7758 "I Can't Take It")..........10-15 60
RCA (7818 "Two Crazy Kids")........10-15 60
20TH FOX (260 "Sweet Lovin' ")....10-15 61
20TH FOX (279 "Doctor Love")......10-15 61

Picture Sleeves

RCA (7559 "The Shape I'm In").....20-30 59
RCA (7601 "Dear Someone")..........15-25 59
20TH FOX (279 "Doctor Love")......15-25 61

LPs: 10/12-inch

RCA (LPM-2149 "Oh Johnny")......40-60 59
(Monaural.)
RCA (LSP-2149 "Oh Johnny")......50-100 59
(Stereo.)
Session: King Curtis.
Also see KING CURTIS

RESTLESS FEELINS

Singles: 7-inch

U.A. (50053 "A Million Things")........8-12 66

RESTLESS HEART *C&W '85*

Singles: 7-inch

RCA (Except 28487).................. 3-4 85-91
RCA (28487 "Why Does It Have to Be")....................10-15 87
(Picture disc. Promotional issue only.)

Picture Sleeves

RCA....................3-4

LPs: 10/12-inch

RCA....................5-8 85-91

RESTRICTIONS

Singles: 7-inch

IGL (147 "She's Gone Away").......10-20 60s

RESTUM, Willie

Singles: 7-inch

COLUMBIA....................4-8 65

EPs: 7-inch

CAPITOL (688 "Honkin' ")..........10-20 55

LPs: 10/12-inch

GONE (5011 "At the Dream Lounge")....................75-100 60
ROULETTE (25152 "Dream Bar") 30-40 61

RESULTS

Singles: 7-inch

APT....................4-8 65
PHILIPS....................4-8 66
TOP CATT....................3-5 69

RETREDS

Singles: 7-inch

R&T (6601 "Black Mona Lisa")......10-20 66

RETURN to FOREVER *LP '73*

Singles: 7-inch

COLUMBIA....................3-5 77-79
POLYDOR....................3-5 75

LPs: 10/12-inch

COLUMBIA....................5-10 76-79
ECM....................8-10 75
POLYDOR....................8-12 73-75
Members: Chick Corea; Lenny White; Stanley Clarke; Al DiMeola.
Also see CLARKE, Stanely
Also see COREA, Chick
Also see DI MEOLA, Al
Also see WHITE, Lenny

REUBEN & CHAINS

Singles: 7-inch

PEACOCK....................10-15 65

REUNION *P&R '74*

Singles: 7-inch

MR. G....................4-8 68
RCA....................3-5 74-75
Also see OHIO EXPRESS

"REUNION"

Singles: 7-inch

CLUB ("Reunion")....................10-15 70
(Listed by title since no artist is credited. No selection number used.)

REUNION

Singles: 7-inch

BELL....................3-5 72

REUNION

Singles: 7-inch

RRR (1001 "Reunion Medley")...........4-6 86
(Colored vinyl. Promotional issue.)
Members: James Pike; Bob Engemann; Ric de Azevedo.
Also see LETTERMEN

REUNION

Singles: 7-inch

CLIFTON....................3-4 88

LPs: 10/12-inch

CLIFTON....................5-10 88

REUNION BAND & FRIENDS

LPs: 10/12-inch

LIVING LOVE....................8-10 77

REVALONS

Singles: 7-inch

COLLECTABLES....................3-4 80s
PET (802 "Dreams Are for Fools")....................75-125 58

REVANCHE

Singles: 7-inch

ATLANTIC....................3-5 79

LPs: 10/12-inch

ATLANTIC....................5-10 79

REVEL

LPs: 10/12-inch

STAR CITY....................5-10 79

REVELAIRES
(With the Ross Dristy Orchestra)

Singles: 78 rpm

BURGANDY....................100-200 54

Singles: 7-inch

BURGANDY (1001 "Only the Angels Know")....................300-400 54

REVELAIRES

Singles: 7-inch

CRYSTALETTE....................8-12 60

REVELAIRES

Singles: 7-inch

DECCA....................5-10 65

REVELAIRS

Singles: 78 rpm

DELUXE....................10-20 46

REVELATION *P&R/R&B '76*

Singles: 7-inch

COMBINE....................4-8 67
HANDSHAKE....................3-5 80-82
MERCURY....................3-5 70
MUSIC FACTORY....................4-8 68
RCA....................3-5 79
RSO....................3-5 76

LPs: 10/12-inch

HANDSHAKE....................5-10 82
MERCURY....................8-12 70
RCA....................5-10 79

REVELERS

Singles: 7-inch

PJ....................5-10 64

REVELIERS

Singles: 7-inch

G-CLEF (702 "Hangin' Five").........15-25 63
LAWN (237 "Part III")...................10-15 64
RED FOX (101 "Part III")..............15-20 64
(First issue.)

REVELIERS

Singles: 7-inch

SOMA....................10-20 62

REVELIERS 4

Singles: 7-inch

TROY (227 "It's Not Right")...........15-25 63

REVELL, Digger, & Denvermen

Singles: 7-inch

CAPITOL (4934 "Surfside")............5-10 63
(Reissued a couple of weeks later on Big Top, but credited to the Notables. By an Austrailian pop band, this is not *surf music.*)
Also see NOTABLES

REVELLE, John

Singles: 7-inch

CHARM....................4-6

REVELLES

Singles: 7-inch

FREEPORT....................5-10 65

REVELLES

Singles: 7-inch

JIM-KO (106 "Little Girl")..............20-30 60s

REVELLS

LPs: 10/12-inch

REPRISE (R-6160 "The Go Sound of the Slots")....................40-60 65
(Monaural.)
REPRISE (RS-6160 "The Go Sound of the Slots")....................40-60 65
(Stereo.)
Members: Chuck Girard; Joe Kelly; Richard Podolor; Richard Burns; Bill Cooper.
Also see GIRARD, Chuck
Also see PODOLOR, Dickie

RE'VELLS

Singles: 7-inch

ROMAN PRESS (201 "Let It Please Be You")....................50-75 63

RE-VELS

Singles: 7-inch

CHESS (1708 "False Alarm").....100-150 58

RE-VELS
(With Gene Kutch & the Butch Ballard Orchestra)

Singles: 78 rpm

SOUND....................15-25 56
TEEN (122 "So in Love")...............50-75 56

Singles: 7-inch

SOUND (129 "You Lied to Me").100-200 56
SOUND (135 "Dream My Darling Dream")....................100-200 56
TEEN (122 "So in Love")...........550-650 56

REVELS *P&R/R&B '59*

Singles: 7-inch

NORGOLDE (103 "Dead Mans' Stroll")....................30-50 59
NORGOLDE (103 "Midnight Stroll")....................10-15 59
NORGOLDE (104 "Foo Man Choo")....................10-20 59

REVELS
(With Barbara Adkins)

Singles: 7-inch

ANDIE....................5-10 60
CT (1 "Church Key")....................25-50 60
DOWNEY (123 "Intoxica")..............8-10 64
IMPACT (1 "Church Key")..............8-12 60
(Black vinyl.)
IMPACT (1 "Church Key")............20-30 60
(Colored vinyl.)
IMPACT (3 "Intoxica")....................8-12 61
(Black vinyl. Colored vinyl possible but not yet confirmed.)
IMPACT (7 "Rampage")....................8-12 62
(Black vinyl.)
IMPACT (7 "Rampage")..................15-25 62
(Colored vinyl.)
IMPACT (13 "Party Time")............10-15 63
(Black vinyl. Colored vinyl possible but not yet confirmed.)
IMPACT (22 "Revellion"/"Conga Twist")....................8-12 64
(Black vinyl.)
IMPACT (22 "Revellion"/"Conga Twist")....................15-25 64
(Colored vinyl.)
IMPACT (22 "Revellion"/"Monkey Bird")....................8-12 64
(Black vinyl.)
IMPACT (22 "Revellion"/"Monkey Bird")....................15-25 64
(Colored vinyl.)
LYNN (1302 "Six Pak")..................15-25 59
PALETTE....................10-15 61
SWINGIN' (620 "Six Pak")............10-20 60
WESTCO (3 "It's Party Time")..........5-10 63
(Black vinyl.)
WESTCO (3 "Party Time")............15-25 63
(Colored vinyl.)
WESTCO (4 "Soft Top")...............25-35 63

LPs: 10/12-inch

IMPACT (1 "On a Rampage")......75-125 64
SUNDAZED....................5-10 90s
(Colored vinyl.)
Members: Brian English; Dan Darnold Dave Davis; Jim McRae; Norman Knowles; Sam Eddy; Dean Sorenson; Paul Sorenson.
Also see APOLLO, Guiseppi
Also see EDDY, Sam, & Revels
Also see SENTINELS

REVELS

Singles: 7-inch

KAPP (621 "Downtown")................10-20 64

REVELS

Singles: 7-inch

JAMIE....................4-8 68

RE-VELS QUARTETTE

Singles: 78 rpm

ATLAS (1035 "My Lost Love")...100-200 54

Singles: 7-inch

ATLAS (1035 "My Lost Love")...200-300 54

REVENGE *LP '90*

LPs: 10/12-inch

CAPITOL....................5-8 90

REVENGERS

Singles: 7-inch

MGM....................5-8 66

LPs: 10/12-inch

METRO....................10-20 66

REVENS

Singles: 7-inch

NIGHT OWL (67116 "For You")......15-25 67

REVERBERI *LP '76*

Singles: 7-inch

U.A....................3-5 77

LPs: 10/12-inch

U.A....................5-10 76

REVERBS

Singles: 7-inch

REPRO (425 "Lie in the Shade of the Sun")....................10-20 60s

REVERE, Paul, & Raiders *P&R '61*
(Raiders; "Featuring Mark Lindsay")

Singles: 7-inch

("The Judge")....................20-30 69
(Promotional 33 rpm for Pontiac GTO. No label name or selection number used.)
APEX (106 "Beatnik Sticks")........50-100 60
(First issue.)
COLUMBIA (10126 "Your Love").......5-8 75
COLUMBIA (42814 "Louie Louie") 10-20 63
COLUMBIA (43008 "Louie – Go Home")....................10-20 64
COLUMBIA (43114 "Over You")....10-20 64
COLUMBIA (43273 "Oh Poo Pah Doo")....................10-20 65
COLUMBIA (43375 "Steppin' Out") .5-10 65
(Black vinyl – commercial or promo.)
COLUMBIA (43375 "Steppin' Out")....................25-35 65
(Colored vinyl. Promotional issue only.)
COLUMBIA (43461 "Just Like Me") .5-10 65
(Black vinyl – commercial or promo.)
COLUMBIA (43461 "Just Like Me")....................25-35 65
(Colored vinyl. Promotional issue only.)
COLUMBIA (43556 "Kicks")............5-10 66
(Black vinyl – commercial or promo.)
COLUMBIA (43556 "Kicks")..........25-35 66
(Colored vinyl. Promotional issue only.)
COLUMBIA (43678 "Hungry")..........5-10 66
(Black vinyl – commercial or promo.)
COLUMBIA (43678 "Hungry").......25-35 66
(Colored vinyl. Promotional issue only.)
COLUMBIA (43810 "The Great Airplane Strike")....................5-10 66
(Black vinyl – commercial or promo.)
COLUMBIA (43810 "The Great Airplane Strike")....................25-35 66
(Colored vinyl. Promotional issue only.)
COLUMBIA (43907 "Good Thing")...5-10 67
(Black vinyl – commercial or promo.)
COLUMBIA (43907 "Good Thing") 15-25 67
(Colored vinyl. Promotional issue only.)
COLUMBIA (44018 "Ups & Downs")..5-8 67
COLUMBIA (44094 "Him Or Me, What's It Gonna Be")....................5-8 67
COLUMBIA (44227 "I Had a Dream")....................5-8 67
COLUMBIA (44335 "Peace of Mind")....................5-8 67
COLUMBIA (44444 "Too Much Talk")....................5-8 68
COLUMBIA (44553 "Don't Take It So Hard")....................5-8 68
COLUMBIA (44655 "Cinderella Sunshine")....................5-8 68
COLUMBIA (44744 "Mr. Sun, Mr. Moon")....................5-8 69
COLUMBIA (44854 "Let Me")...........5-8 69
COLUMBIA (44970 "We Gotta All Get Together")....................5-8 69
COLUMBIA (45082 thru 45898)..........3-6 70-74
COLUMBIA (105499 "SS 396"/"Corvair Baby")....................10-20 66
(Promotional issue only.)
DRIVE (6248 "Ain't Nothin' Wrong")....................4-8 76
GARDENA (106 "Beatnik Sticks")..20-30 60
GARDENA (115 "Paul Revere's Ride")....................20-30 61
GARDENA (116 "Like Long Hair") 20-30 61
GARDENA (118 "Like, Charleston")....................15-25 61
GARDENA (123 "All Night Long")..15-25 62
GARDENA (127 "Like, Bluegrass")....................15-25 62
GARDENA (131 "Shake It Up")......15-25 62
GARDENA (137 "Tall Cool One")..15-25 62
JERDEN (807 "So Fine")................15-25 63
RAIDER AMERICA....................5-10 82
SANDE (101 "Louie Louie")...........25-35 63
TEEN SCOOP ("Interview")..........15-25 60s
(Square cardboard picture disc. Included in magazine.)
20TH FOX (2281 "The British Are Coming")....................3-6 76

Picture Sleeves

COLUMBIA (10126 "Your Love")....10-15 75
COLUMBIA (43678 "Hungry")..........5-10 66
COLUMBIA (43810 "The Great Airplane Strike")....................15-20 66
COLUMBIA (43907 "Good Thing")...5-10 67
COLUMBIA (44018 "Ups & Downs") 5-10 67
COLUMBIA (44094 "Him Or Me, What's It Gonna Be")....................5-10 67
COLUMBIA (44227 "I Had a Dream")....................5-10 67
COLUMBIA (44335 "Peace of Mind")....................5-10 67
COLUMBIA (44444 "Too Much Talk")....................5-10 68
COLUMBIA (44553 "Don't Take It So Hard")....................5-10 68
COLUMBIA (44655 "Cinderella Sunshine")....................5-10 68
COLUMBIA (44744 "Mr. Sun, Mr. Moon")....................5-10 69
COLUMBIA (45601 "Powder Blue Mercedes Queen")....................10-15 72

EPs: 7-inch

JERDEN (JRLS-7004 "In the Beginning")....................40-60 66
(Juke box issue only. Includes title strips.)

LPs: 10/12-inch

BACK-TRAC....................5-8 85
COLUMBIA (12 "Two All-Time Great Selling LPs")....................15-20 69
COLUMBIA (462 "Greatest Hits")..20-25 67
(Monaural.)
COLUMBIA (2307 "Here They Come")....................25-40 65
(Monaural.)
COLUMBIA (2451 "Just Like Us")..25-40 66
(Monaural.)

COLUMBIA (2508 "Midnight Ride")....25-40 66
(Monaural.)
COLUMBIA (2595 "Spirit of '67")....25-40 66
(Monaural.)
COLUMBIA (2662 "Greatest Hits").25-40 67
(Monaural.)
COLUMBIA (2721 "Revolution").....25-40 67
(Monaural.)
COLUMBIA (2755 "Christmas Present and Past")....40-60 67
(Monaural.)
COLUMBIA (2805 "Goin' to Memphis")....20-30 68
(Monaural.)
COLUMBIA (9107 "Here They Come")....25-40 65
(Stereo.)
COLUMBIA (9251 "Just Like Us")..25-40 66
(Stereo.)
COLUMBIA (9308 "Midnight Ride")....25-40 66
(Stereo.)
COLUMBIA (9395 "Spirit of '67")....25-40 66
(Stereo.)
COLUMBIA (9462 "Greatest Hits").25-40 67
(Stereo.)
COLUMBIA (9521 "Revolution").....25-40 67
(Stereo.)
COLUMBIA (9555 "Christmas Present and Past")....40-60 67
(Stereo.)
COLUMBIA (9605 "Goin' to Memphis")....20-25 68
(Stereo.)
COLUMBIA (9665 "Something Happening")....10-20 68
COLUMBIA (9753 "Hard 'N' Heavy")....10-20 69
(Black and white cover.)
COLUMBIA (9753 "Hard 'N' Heavy")....15-25 69
(Color cover.)
COLUMBIA (9905 "Alias Pink Puzz")....10-20 69
COLUMBIA (9905 "Alias Pink Puzz")....10-20 69
COLUMBIA (9964 "Collage")....10-20 70
COLUMBIA (30386 "Greatest Hits, Vol. 2")....10-20 71
COLUMBIA (30768 "Indian Reservation")....10-20 71
COLUMBIA (31196 "Country Wine")....30-50 71
COLUMBIA SPECIAL PRODUCTS (141714 "The Judge")....150-200 69
(Promotional issue only.)
HARMONY (30089 "Paul Revere & the Raiders Featuring Mark Lindsay")....10-15 70
HARMONY (30975 "Good Thing").10-15 71
HARMONY (31183 "Movin' On")....10-15 72
GARDENA (1000 "Like Long Hair")....250-300 61
JERDEN (7004 "In the Beginning")....75-125 66
PICKWICK (3176 "Paul Revere and the Raiders")....10-15 70s
RAIDER....10-15 82
SANDE (1001 "Paul Revere and the Raiders")....250-300 63
SEARS....40-50 60s
(Special Products Sears promotional issue.)
Members: Mark Lindsay; Freddy Weller; Paul Revere; Keith Allison; Joe Correro Jr; Carl Driggs; Omar Martinez; Doug Heath; Ron Foos; Danny Krause; Mike Smith; Drake Levin; Philip Volk; Mike Holiday.
Also see ALLISON, Keith
Also see BROTHERHOOD
Also see CYRKLE / Paul Revere & Raiders
Also see JOYRIDE
Also see LINDSAY, Mark
Also see MIKE & DEAN
Also see VALLEY, Jim
Also see WELLER, Freddy

REVERE, Paul, & Raiders / Simon & Garfunkel / Byrds / Aretha Franklin
EPs: 7-inch
COLUMBIA SPECIAL PRODUCTS (546 "The Moving Crowd")....25-30 66
(Promotional issue only. Made for National Shoes & Mary Jane Shoe Stores)
Also see BYRDS
Also see FRANKLIN, Aretha
Also see REVERE, Paul, & Raiders
Also see SIMON & GARFUNKEL

REVEREND BOUNCE: see MEMPHIS SLIM & VAGABONDS

REVERES
Singles: 7-inch
JUBILEE (5463 "Beyond the Sea").10-20 63

REVERES
Singles: 7-inch
VALIANT (6041 "Big T")....15-25 64

REVERES / Honeystrollers
Singles: 7-inch
GLORY....10-15 58

REVIERAS
(With Cliff Parman & Orchestra)
Singles: 7-inch
VICTORIA (103 "Walk Away")....15-25 64

REVIVAL
Singles: 7-inch
KAMA SUTRA....3-5 72
LPs: 10/12-inch
KAMA SUTRA....8-10 72

REVIVALS
Singles: 7-inch
AVENUE D (0014 "Too Young")....4-6 87
(Black vinyl.)
AVENUE D (0014 "Too Young")....10-20 87
(Red vinyl. Reportedly 100 made.)
AVENUE D (0017 "No No No")....5-8 91
(Black vinyl.)
AVENUE D (0017 "No No No")....5-10 91
(Maroon vinyl.)
Picture Sleeves
AVENUE D (0014 "Too Young")....5-8 87
Members: Cathy Santaniello; John Oswald; Joe Inzirello; Louie Caporusso; Vinny Scire.

REVLONS
Singles: 7-inch
CAPITOL (4739 "Dry Your Eyes").15-25 62
RAE COX (105 "I Promise Love")..10-20 61

REV-LONS
Singles: 7-inch
GARPAX (44168 "Boy Trouble")....10-20 62

REVLONS
Singles: 7-inch
PARKWAY....5-10 66
REPRISE....8-12 63-64
SHURFINE (006 "Sugaree")....15-25 60s
TOY....10-20 60s

REVOLTING 3
Singles: 7-inch
QUE PASA....8-10 60s

REVOLUTION
Singles: 7-inch
MERCURY (72549 "Shades of Blue")....5-10 66

REVOLUTION
Singles: 7-inch
BOSS CITY (150 "Wake Me, Shake Me")....10-20 68

REVOLUTION
Singles: 7-inch
REVOLUTION ("Revolt")....10-20 60s
(No selection number used.)

REVOLUTIONARY BLUES BAND
LPs: 10/12-inch
CORAL....10-15 69

REVOLVER
Singles: 7-inch
FUTURE (30488 "Little Miss Hip") 40-60 60s
Member: Dez Dickerson
Also see PRINCE

REVOLVERS
Singles: 7-inch
JL (101 "The Pounding of My Heart")....5-10 93
(Colored vinyl.)
TY TEX (127 "Like Me")....20-30 65
TY TEX (128 "Good Lovin' Women")....20-30 65
TY TEX (131 "I Like Lovin' You")...20-30 65

REVS
Singles: 7-inch
SPEEDWAY (2578 "Go Or Blow Twist")....10-20 62

REWIS, Susan
Singles: 7-inch
COLUMBIA....4-8 66

REX
Singles: 7-inch
COLUMBIA....3-5 77
LPs: 10/12-inch
COLUMBIA....8-10 77
Also see SMITH, Rex

REX, T.: see T REX

REX, Tim, & Oklahoma C&W '80
Singles: 7-inch
DEE JAY....3-5 80-81

REY, Ernest C&W '79
Singles: 7-inch
MCA....3-5 79

REY, Little Bobby
Singles: 78 rpm
FLAIR....5-10 55
Singles: 7-inch
FLAIR....10-15 55
INDIGO....10-15
ORIGINAL SOUND....5-10 59
(Black label, silver print.)
ORIGINAL SOUND....3-5 70s
(Black label, white print.)
Also see HOLLYWOOD ARGYLES

REY, Rayner
Singles: 7-inch
JERDEN (781 "Whiplash")....15-25 66

REYES, Ricky
Singles: 7-inch
FALCON....4-8 60s

REYNOLDS, Allen C&W '78
Singles: 7-inch
CAMEO....4-8 64
HALL WAY....4-8 62
RCA....4-8 61-63
TRIPLE I....3-5 78

REYNOLDS, Art, Singers
Singles: 7-inch
CAPITOL (2206 "I've Made Up My Mind")....4-6 68
LPs: 10/12-inch
CAPITOL (2534 "Tellin' It Like It Is")....15-25 66
CAPITOL (2811 "Long Dusty Road")....10-20 67
Member: Thelma Houston.
Also see HOUSTON, Thelma

REYNOLDS, Big Jack, & His Blues Men
Singles: 7-inch
HI-Q (5036 "You Won't Treat Me Right")....50-75 62
MAH'S (10 "You Don't Treat Me Right")....25-50 62
(Note title change.)

REYNOLDS, Bob, & B. Jays
Singles: 7-inch
SNAP....5-10 60s

REYNOLDS, Brad
Singles: 7-inch
ZERO....5-10 59

REYNOLDS, Buddy
Singles: 7-inch
ZERO....5-10 60

REYNOLDS, Burt C&W/P&R '80
Singles: 7-inch
MCA....3-5 80
MERCURY....3-5 73-74
Picture Sleeves
MCA....3-5 80
LPs: 10/12-inch
MERCURY....8-12 73

REYNOLDS, Debbie P&R '57
Singles: 78 rpm
CORAL....5-10 57
MGM....4-8 55-57
Singles: 7-inch
ABC....3-5 74
ABC-PAR....4-8 65
BEVERLY HILLS....3-5 72
CORAL....5-10 57-58
DOT....4-8 59-63
JANUS....3-5 70
MCA....3-4 80s
MGM (11000 & 12000 series)....5-10 55-59
MGM (13000 series)....4-8 63-66
PARAMOUNT....3-5 73
Picture Sleeves
DOT....5-10 60
MGM....8-15 58-66
EPs: 7-inch
CORAL....10-20 58
MGM....10-20 55
LPs: 10/12-inch
DOT (Except 25295)....15-20 59-63
DOT (25295 "Am I That Easy to Forget")....15-25 60
(Black vinyl.)
DOT (25295 "Am I That Easy to Forget")....50-75 60
(Colored vinyl.)
MGM....15-25 60-66
METRO....10-15 65
Also see CARPENTER, Carleton, & Debbie Reynolds
Also see FISHER, Eddie, & Debbie Reynolds

REYNOLDS, Eddie
Singles: 7-inch
DIXIE (838 "What Was It")....75-125 58
TIME....5-10 59

REYNOLDS, Jeannie R&B '75
Singles: 7-inch
CASABLANCA....3-5 75

REYNOLDS, Jo Ann
Singles: 7-inch
BANNER....4-8 66

REYNOLDS, Jody P&R/R&B '58
Singles: 78 rpm
DEMON (1507 "Endless Sleep")....50-75 58
Singles: 7-inch
ABC....3-5 73
BRENT....5-10 63
COLLECTABLES....3-4 80s
DEMON (1507 "Endless Sleep")....15-25 58
DEMON (1509 "Fire of Love")....10-20 58
DEMON (1511 "Elope with Me")....10-20 58
DEMON (1515 "Golden Idol")....20-30 59
DEMON (1519 "The Storm")....20-30 59
DEMON (1523 "Whipping Post")....10-20 59
DEMON (1524 "Stone Cold")....10-20 59
PULSAR....4-6 69
SMASH....5-10 63
TITAN....4-8 66
LPs: 10/12-inch
TRU-GEMS....8-12 78
Also see CASEY, Al
Also see CLARK, Sanford

REYNOLDS, Jody, & Bobbie Gentry
Singles: 7-inch
TITAN....4-8 67
Also see GENTRY, Bobbie

REYNOLDS, Jody / Olympics
Singles: 7-inch
DEMON....10-20 58
LIBERTY....4-8 63
TITAN....4-8 62
Picture Sleeves
DEMON (1801 "Endless Sleep")....15-25 58
Also see OLYMPICS

REYNOLDS, Jody, & Storms
Singles: 7-inch
INDIGO (127 "Thunder"/"Tarantula")....15-25 61
(Remake of both sides of Sundown 114, shown as by the Storms.)
Also see CASEY, Al
Also see REYNOLDS, Jody
Also see STORMS

REYNOLDS, Joey: see 4 Seasons

REYNOLDS, L.J. R&B '71
(With Chocolate Syrup)
Singles: 12-inch
CAPITOL....4-6 82
Singles: 7-inch
CAPITOL....3-5 81-82
FANTASY....3-4 85-87
LAW-TON....3-5 71-72
MAINSTREAM....4-6 69
MERCURY....3-4 84
LPs: 10/12-inch
CAPITOL....5-10 81-82
MERCURY....5-8 84
Also see CHOCOLATE SYRUP
Also see DRAMATICS

REYNOLDS, Larry
Singles: 7-inch
TRI-SPIN (1004 "Sweet Tooth")....10-20 68

REYNOLDS, Lawrence P&R '69
Singles: 7-inch
COLUMBIA....3-5 72
W.B....3-6 69-70
LPs: 10/12-inch
W.B....8-12 69

REYNOLDS, Ricky
(Eric Nathanson)
Singles: 7-inch
MOHAWK....5-10
Also see LONNIE & CAROLLONS
Also see ROME & PARIS
Also see VOCALAIRES

REYNOLDS, Sammy
Singles: 7-inch
DORE....4-8 62

REYNOLDS, Steve
Singles: 7-inch
LAURIE....4-8 62-63

REYNOLDS, Teddy
(With the Twisters)
Singles: 78 rpm
SITTIN' IN WITH (517 "Walkin' the Floor Baby")....15-25 49
SITTIN' IN WITH (558 "Why Baby Why")....15-25 50
SITTIN' IN WITH (586 "You Put a Voodoo Spell on Me")....15-25 51
SITTIN' IN WITH (594 "Strange Mysterious Woman")....15-25 51
SITTIN' IN WITH (613 "Waitin' at the Station")....15-25 51
Singles: 7-inch
KENT (371 "Do You Wanna Twist")...5-8 62
MERCURY (71281 "Puppy Dogs")....20-30 58
NEWMAN....5-8 66
LPs: 10/12-inch
CROWN (247 "The Twist")....25-50 62
Also see WILEY, Ed

REYNOLDS, Teddy, & Twisters / Joe Houston
EPs: 7-inch
GILMAR (94 "The Twist")....8-12 60s
Also see HOUSTON, Joe

REYNOLDS, Teddy / Lala Wilson
Singles: 7-inch
AURA....4-8 63
Also see REYNOLDS, Teddy

REYNOLDS, Terry
LPs: 10/12-inch
CROWN....10-20 60s

REYNOLDS, Timmy
Singles: 7-inch
OPERATORS....4-8 62

REYNOLDS, Tommy
Singles: 7-inch
LIBERTY....4-8 67

REYNOLDS, Wesley
(Wes Reynolds)
Singles: 7-inch
BISMARK (1005 "I Wonder")....10-15
ROSE (108 "Trip to the Moon")....75-100 57
ROSE (117 "Rag Mop")....60-80 57
VALOR ("Shut Down")....10-15
(Selection number not known.)

RHAMBO, Bo
Singles: 7-inch
IMPERIAL (5657 "Two for the Blues")....8-12 60

RHAPSODY
Singles: 7-inch
SUNSET BEACH....3-5 81
LPs: 10/12-inch
SUNSET BEACH....5-10 81

RHEAD BROTHERS
LPs: 10/12-inch
EMI....8-10 77

RHEIMS, Robert LP '59
(Robert Rheims Carrolers)
Singles: 7-inch
RHEIMS....3-5 59
EPs: 7-inch
RHEIMS....4-8 59
LPs: 10/12-inch
MISTLETOE....5-8 75
RHEIMS....5-15 58-63
U.A....5-8 72-74

RHINES, Bobby, & Rogues
Singles: 7-inch
APPLAUSE....5-10 61

RHINESTONES
Singles: 7-inch
20TH FOX....3-5 75
LPs: 10/12-inch
20TH FOX....8-10 75

RHINOCEROS LP '68
Singles: 7-inch
ELEKTRA....4-6 69-70
LPs: 10/12-inch
ELEKTRA....10-20 68-70
Members: Alan Gerber; Billy Mundi; Michael Fonfara; John Finley; Danny Weis; Jerry Penrod; Peter Hodgson.
Also see EARTH OPERA

RHINTONES
Singles: 7-inch
CHIP....5-10 59

RHOADS, Randy C&W '90
Singles: 7-inch
BLUE RIDGE....3-4 90

RHODES, Danny
Singles: 7-inch
CORAL....4-8 67

RHODES, Darrell
Singles: 7-inch
WINSTON (1026 "Four O'Clock Baby")....50-75 58
WINSTON (1029 "Lou Lou")....50-75 58
WINSTON (1041 "Runnin' and Chasin' ")....50-75 59

RHODES, Donna
Singles: 7-inch
HI....4-6 73

RHODES, Emitt LP '70
Singles: 7-inch
DUNHILL....3-5 70-73
LPs: 10/12-inch
A&M....10-15 70
DUNHILL....8-12 70-73
Also see MERRY-GO-ROUND
Also see PALACE GUARD

RHODES, Jimmy
Singles: 7-inch
CUPID (5005 "I Wanna Go")....25-50 58
JASON (111 "I Wanna Go")....25-50 59

RHODES, Red
Singles: 7-inch
BLUE RIVER....4-8
COUNTRYSIDE....3-5 73
LPs: 10/12-inch
COUNTRYSIDE....8-10 73
Also see NESMITH, Michael

RHODES, Sam
Singles: 7-inch
CAPITOL....4-6 68

RHODES, Slim
(Featuring Sandy Brooks; with Brad Suggs; with Dusty & Dot)
Singles: 78 rpm
GILT EDGE....15-25 53
SUN (216 "Uncertain Love")....25-75 55
SUN (225 "House of Sin")....25-75 55
SUN (238 "Gonna Romp and Stomp")....50-75 56
SUN (256 "Do What I Do")....15-25 56
Singles: 7-inch
SUN (216 "Uncertain Love")....75-100 55
SUN (225 "House of Sin")....75-100 55
SUN (238 "Gonna Romp and Stomp")....100-125 56
SUN (256 "Do What I Do")....40-60 56
Also see SUGGS, Brad

RHODES, Sonny
LPs: 10/12-inch
AVENT....5-10 77

RHODES, Todd R&B '48
Singles: 78 rpm
KING....10-15 48-54
MODERN....10-15 49
SENSATION (Except 6)....10-20 47-49
SENSATION (6 "Blues for the Red Boy")....25-35 47
VITACOUSTIC....10-20 47
Singles: 7-inch
KING (4469 "Gin Gin Gin")....50-75 51
KING (4486 "Good Man")....30-50 51
KING (4509 "Your Daddy's Doggin' Around")....30-50 51
(Black vinyl.)
KING (4509 "Your Daddy's Doggin' Around")....60-80 51
(Colored vinyl.)
KING (4528 "Rocket 69")....60-80 52
KING (4556 thru 4601)....15-25 52-53
(Lavern Baker is the vocalist on one side of each of the four King issues in the 4556-4601 series)
KING (4648 thru 4775)....10-20 53-54

EPs: 7-inch
KING 30-40 52-54
LPs: 10/12-inch
KING (88 "Todd Rhodes Plays the Hits") 75-100 53
KING (658 "Dance Music") 35-55 60
Also see ALLEN, Connee
Also see BAKER, Lavern
Also see BARTHOLOMEW, Dave

RHODES, Walter
Singles: 7-inch
MASCOT (129 "Uncle Sam") 20-30 60

RHODES KIDS
LPs: 10/12-inch
GRC 8-10 74

RHODES SISTERS
Singles: 7-inch
DIAL 4-8 65

RHOMBERG, Dude
Singles: 7-inch
COULEE (111 "Your Broken Heart's Starting to Show") 15-25 65

RHOTON, Howard
Singles: 7-inch
CANARY (1008 "I'll Skip School") ..20-30

RHYS, John, & Lively Set
Singles: 7-inch
IMPACT (1024 "Nothing But Love") 10-20 67

RHYTHM R&B '76
Singles: 7-inch
POLYDOR 3-5 76

RHYTHM, Johnny
(With the Audios)
Singles: 7-inch
MGM (13043 "This Is It") 30-40 61

RHYTHM ACES
Singles: 78 rpm
ACE 10-20 56
VEE JAY 50-75 54-55
Singles: 7-inch
ACE (518 "Look What You've Done") 20-25 56
VEE JAY (124 "I Wonder Why") 100-150 54
(Black vinyl.)
VEE JAY (124 "I Wonder Why") 300-400 54
(Colored vinyl.)
VEE JAY (138 "Whisper to Me") 100-150 55
(Black vinyl.)
VEE JAY (138 "Whisper to Me") 300-350 55
(Colored vinyl.)
VEE JAY (160 "That's My Sugar") 75-100 55

RHYTHM ACES
("Gil Haas, Vocalist")
Singles: 78 rpm
KAMPUS 5-10 55
Singles: 7-inch
KAMPUS (1001 "The Blues Are Here") 10-20 55
KAMPUS (1002 "Well, Waddaya Know") 10-20 55

RHYTHM ACES
Singles: 7-inch
MARK-X (8004 "Boppin' Sloppin' Baby") 15-25 60
Members: Lou Fallo; Herb Glazer; John D'Amaro; Steve Freeman; Vinnie Fiore.

RHYTHM ACES
Singles: 7-inch
ROULETTE (4268 "Mohawk Rock") 8-12 60
ROULETTE (4426 "Raunchy Twist") 5-10 62
SIOUX (82260 "Allan's Rock") 10-15 60
UNIVERSAL ARTISTS (3160 "Mohawk Rock") 20-30 60

RHYTHM ACES
Singles: 7-inch
STARLITE (61 "Wherever You May Go") 75-125
STARLITE (66 "Oh My Darling") ..75-125

RHYTHM CADETS
("Featuring George Singleton")
Singles: 7-inch
VESTA (501 "Dearest Doryce") 500-1000 57
Member: George Singleton.

RHYTHM CASTERS
Singles: 78 rpm
EXCELLO 50-100 57
Singles: 7-inch
EXCELLO (2115 "Oh My Darling") 150-200 57

RHYTHM CATS
Singles: 78 rpm
SPECIALTY 10-15 54
Singles: 7-inch
SPECIALTY (496 "Blue Saxophone") 10-20 54

RHYTHM CORPS LP '88
LPs: 10/12-inch
PASHA 5-8 88

RHYTHM DEVILS
LPs: 10/12-inch
PASSPORT 10-20 80
Members: Mickey Hart; Phil Lesh; Mike Hinton; Jordan Amarantha; Bill Kruetzmann; Jim Lovelace; Greg Errico; Airto Moreira.
Also see HART, Mickey

RHYTHM FIVE
Singles: 7-inch
TIFCO (829 "Baby Please Don't Go") 10-15 62

RHYTHM GENTS
Singles: 7-inch
MERRI (6008 "Linda") 15-25 64

RHYTHM HEIRS
Singles: 7-inch
YUCCA (105 "Cradle Rock") 10-15 59

RHYTHM HERITAGE P&R/R&B '75
Singles: 12-inch
ABC 4-8 78
Singles: 7-inch
ABC 3-5 75-78
LPs: 10/12-inch
ABC 5-10 76-77
Members: Steve Barri; Mike Omartian; Luther Waters.
Also see BARRI, Steve

RHYTHM JESTERS
Singles: 78 rpm
RAMA (213 "Rock to the Music") ...15-25 56
Singles: 7-inch
LECTRA (501 "Please Be Mine") ...20-30 62
(No group credited.)
LECTRA (501 "Please Be Mine") ...15-20 62
(Credits the Rhythm Jesters.)
RAMA (213 "Rock to the Music") ...50-75 56
Also see DAVIES, Bob

RHYTHM KINGS
Singles: 78 rpm
APOLLO (1171 "Merry Christmas One and All") 25-50 50
APOLLO (1181 "Why My Darling, Why") 25-50 51
IVORY (751 "Night After Night") 40-60 49
(Various artists EPs on Ivory are bootlegs.)
EPs: 7-inch
LLOYDS (707 "Rhythm Kings") ..200-300 54

RHYTHM KINGS
Singles: 7-inch
ACEMGA 3-5
BROOKE (118 "Boppin' Guitar") 10-20 60
CHALLENGE (9178 "Bordertown") 10-20 62
CUCA ("Maj") 10-20 60
(Selection number not known.)
GNP (196 "Exotic") 8-12 63
TOLLIE 5-10 64
VELPA 3-5
Members: Al Garcia; Fred Mendoza; Vince Bumatay; Art Rodriguez.
Also see CHARADES
Also see GARCIA, Al, & Rhythm Kings
Also see LINK - EDDY COMBO
Also see MYERS, Dave, & Surftones / Rhythm Kings

RHYTHM MAKERS R&B '76
Singles: 7-inch
VIGOR 3-5 76
LPs: 10/12-inch
VIGOR 8-10 76

RHYTHM MASTERS
Singles: 78 rpm
FLIP (314 "Baby We Two") 50-75 56
Singles: 7-inch
FLIP (314 "Baby We Two") 150-250 56

RHYTHM MASTERS
Singles: 7-inch
ACE 8-12 61
MOBILE FIDELITY 5-10 64

RHYTHM OUTLAWS
Singles: 7-inch
CO (430 "Steel Guitar Rag") 8-12
KALOX (1028 "Walking to Kansas City") 10-20 60

RHYTHM PLAYBOYS
Singles: 7-inch
SS (16210 "Rhythm Playboys Stomp") 8-12

RHYTHM RASCALS
(With Bebbie Boy Butch)
Singles: 7-inch
ROULETTE (4696 "Girl By My Side") 10-20 66
SONIC (117 "Girl By My Side") 50-100 66

RHYTHM RASCALS
Singles: 7-inch
JAR 10-20 60s

RHYTHM RIDERS
Singles: 7-inch
RYDER (1000 "Cajun Baby") 15-25 62
SOUTH SEA (112 "Knockout") 8-12 60s

RHYTHM ROCKERS
(Rythm Rockers)
Singles: 78 rpm
CROSS COUNTRY 75-100 56
SUN 50-75 56
Singles: 7-inch
CROSS COUNTRY (524-35 "Juke box, Help Me Find My Baby"") 150-250 56
(First issue.)
SUN (248 "Juke box, Help Me Find My Baby") 75-100 56
Members: Hardrock Gunter; Buddy Durham.
Also see GUNTER, Hardrock

RHYTHM ROCKERS
("Featuring Chet Atkins")
Singles: 78 rpm
RCA 6919 "Martinique") 8-10 57
Singles: 7-inch
RCA 6919 "Martinique") 10-15 57
Also see ATKINS, Chet

RHYTHM ROCKERS
Singles: 7-inch
OASIS (104 "Thinkin' About You") 50-75 59
SATIN (921 "Oh Boy") 50-75 60
SQUARE (505 "Oh, Oh Honey") 50-75 59
Picture Sleeves
SATIN (921 "Oh Boy") 75-100 60

RHYTHM ROCKERS
Singles: 7-inch
GOLDEN CREST (535 "Slide") 10-15 60
MADONNA (219 "Stinger") 8-12 60s

RHYTHM ROCKERS
(Mike Patterson & Rhythm Rockers)
Singles: 7-inch
CHALLENGE (9196 "Rendezvous Stomp") 10-15 63
WIPE OUT (1001 "Foot Crusing") ..15-25 63
LPs: 10/12-inch
CHALLENGE (617 "Soul Surfin' ") 40-60 63
Members: Mike Patterson; Mike Moran.
Also see PATTERSON, Mike

RHYTHM ROCKERS
Singles: 7-inch
FENTON (944 "Three Strikes") 15-25 64

RHYTHM ROCKETS
Singles: 7-inch
FARO 8-12 59

RHYTHM ROCKETS
Singles: 7-inch
MOONGLOW (2002 "Pachuko Hop") 5-10 63
(First issued as by Runaways.)
Also see LETTERMEN
Also see RUNAWAYS

RHYTHM ROCKETS
Singles: 7-inch
PRESTO (101 "School of Rock & Roll") 3-5 89
Picture Sleeves
PRESTO (101 "School of Rock & Roll") 4-6 89

RHYTHM ROUSERS
Singles: 7-inch
ROUSER (7423 "Just Because") 75-125

RHYTHM ROYALS
Singles: 7-inch
SAHARA 8-12 65
TEST 8-12 65
Members: Roger Sohrweide; Phil Cornelisen; Dennis Swaer; Mark Thompson; Roger Pagel; Dave Swaer.

RHYTHM ROYALS
Singles: 7-inch
WARMOUTH (0001 "Rockin' Christmas") 10-20 60

RHYTHM STARS
Singles: 7-inch
CLOCK (1007 "Lynn") 50-100 59
CORSICAN (0057 "My Girl Babe") 50-100 59

RHYTHM STEPPERS
Singles: 7-inch
SPINNING 10-15 59

RHYTHM SURFERS
Singles: 7-inch
DAYTONE (6301 "502") 25-35 63

RHYTHM TONES
Singles: 7-inch
VEST (828 "Something Wrong Upstairs") 75-125 59

RHYTHM WILLIE
(With His Gang)
Singles: 78 rpm
OKEH 10-20 40s
PREMIUM (866 "I Got Rhythm") 30-40 50

RHYTHMAIRES
Singles: 78 rpm
SWAN 15-25 46

RHYTHMAIRES
Singles: 7-inch
RHYTHM (113 "Screw Driver") 30-40 57

RHYTHMERES
Singles: 7-inch
BRUNSWICK (55083 "Elaine") 40-50 58

RHYTHMETTES
Singles: 78 rpm
BRUNSWICK 5-10 57
RCA 5-10 55-56
Singles: 7-inch
BRUNSWICK 5-10 57
CORAL 10-15 60
RCA 10-15 55-56

RHYZE R&B '80
Singles: 7-inch
SAM 3-5 80
20TH FOX 3-5 81
LPs: 10/12-inch
20TH FOX 5-10 81

RIA
(With the Reasons; with Revellons)
Singles: 7-inch
AMY (888 "Memories Linger") 15-25 64
(Black vinyl.)
AMY (888 "Memories Linger") 40-60 64
(Colored vinyl.)
RSVP (1110 "He's Not There") 15-20 65

RIALTOS
Singles: 7-inch
PIKE (5907 "Like Thunder") 15-25 61
Also see HOLLISTER, Bobby, & Rialtos

RIALTOS
Singles: 7-inch
CB (5009 "Let Me In") 200-300 62

RIATS
Singles: 7-inch
OMEGA (35449 "Riders in the Sky") 5-10

RIBBON OF BLUE
Singles: 7-inch
DOT 4-8 68

RIBBONS P&R '63
Singles: 7-inch
ERA 3-5 72
MARSH 10-15 63
PARKWAY 5-10 64

RIBEIRO, Alfonso R&B '85
Singles: 7-inch
PRISM 3-4 85

RIBITONES
LPs: 10/12-inch
CLIFTON 5-10 79

RICARDO, Ricky
Singles: 7-inch
WYE 10-15 61

RICARDOS
Singles: 7-inch
STAR-X (512 "Mary's Little Lamb") 100-150 58

RIC-A-SHAYS
Singles: 7-inch
LOLA (002 "Turn On") 10-20 65
Members: Ron Story; Harry Nilsson.
Also see NILSSON, Harry
Also see TRAVELERS

RICE, Bill C&W '71
(Billy Rice)
Singles: 7-inch
CAPITOL 3-5 71
DOT 4-8 61
EPIC 3-5 72
FERNWOOD 10-15 60
ONDA 5-10 59
POLYDOR 3-5 77-78
Also see JOHNSON, Lois, & Bill Rice

RICE, Bobby G. C&W '70
Singles: 7-inch
CHARTA 3-5 81
DOOR KNOB 3-4 85-88
GRT 3-5 74-77
METROMEDIA 3-5 72-73
REPUBLIC 3-5 78-79
ROYAL AMERICAN 3-5 70-72
SUNBIRD 3-5 80-81
SUNSET 3-5 79
LPs: 10/12-inch
AUDIOGRAPH ALIVE 5-8 82
GRT 6-12 74-76
METROMEDIA 6-12 73
ROYAL AMERICAN 6-12 72
SUNBIRD 5-10 80
Also see KEMP, Wayne, & Bobby G. Rice

RICE, Bobby G., & Perry LaPointe C&W '88
Singles: 7-inch
DOOR KNOB 3-4 88
Also see LaPOINTE, Perry
Also see RICE, Bobby G.

RICE, Denny
Singles: 7-inch
FRATERNITY 4-8 64

RICE, Dumpy
Singles: 7-inch
AIRTOWN (003 "Blooze") 5-10 66
AIRTOWN (2010 "Last Date-Blueberry Hill") 5-10 66
JUKE (2016 "Movin' ") 5-10
JUKE (2022 "Lullaby of Birdland") ...5-10

RICE, Eldon
Singles: 7-inch
EL RIO (413 "Don't Let Love Break Your Heart") 300-400

RICE, Jimmy
Singles: 7-inch
RED BIRD 10-15 65

RICE, Lorraine
Singles: 7-inch
BUTTERNUT 10-15 66
CUCA 10-15 66

RICE, Mack R&B '65
(Sir Mack Rice)
Singles: 7-inch
ATCO 3-6 69
BLUE ROCK 4-8 69
CAPITOL 15-20
LUPINE 4-8 63-64
MAX DAY 5-10
MERCURY (72541 "It's All Right") 20-30 66
STAX 3-6 67-78
TRUTH 3-6 78
Also see FALCONS
Also see FIVE SCALDERS
Also see OLLIE & NIGHTINGALES

RICE, Robin
Singles: 7-inch
CRACKERJACK 10-15 60s
METRO INT'L 4-8 63

RICE, Ronnie
(With the Gents; with Silvertones)
Singles: 7-inch
IRC 5-10 60s
LIMELIGHT 4-8 64
MGM 4-8 63-64
QUILL 5-10 60s
Also see NEW COLONY SIX

RICE, Sir Mack: see RICE, Mack

RICE, Stormy
Singles: 7-inch
ODE 5-10 68
Also see WOOLIES

RICE, Tony
(With the Overtones)
Singles: 7-inch
ACTION (100 "My Darling") 15-25 60
PRINCETON (101 "Summer's Love") 75-125 60
RAE COX (106 "Little School Girl") 15-25 61

RICE KRYSPIES
LPs: 10/12-inch
FANFARE 10-20
TORTILLA 10-20

RICE-MILTON, Terry
Singles: 7-inch
DATE 4-8 69
Also see CUPID'S INSPIRATION

RICH, Buddy LP '66
(Buddy Rich Band)
Singles: 78 rpm
CLEF 4-8 54
NORGRAN 4-8 55-56
Singles: 7-inch
ARGO 4-8 61
CLEF 5-10 54
EVEREST 3-5 71
GROOVE MERCHANT 3-5 74
MCA 3-4 81
NORGRAN 5-10 55-56
PACIFIC JAZZ 3-6 66-67
RCA 3-5 76
EPs: 7-inch
NORGRAN 20-40 54-56
LPs: 10/12-inch
ARGO (676 "Playtime") 35-45 61
CLEF (684 "Gene Krupa & Buddy Rich") 100-150 56
EMARCY 10-20 65-76
GREAT AMERICAN GRAMOPHONE 5-8 78
GROOVE MERCHANT 5-10 74-75
GRYPHON 5-10 79
LIBERTY 8-12 70
MCA 5-8 81
MERCURY (126 "Buddy Rich Story") 10-20 69
MERCURY (20448 "Rich vs. Roach") 50-75 59
(Monaural.)
MERCURY (20451 "Richcraft") 50-75 60
(Monaural.)
MERCURY (20461 "The Voice Is Rich") 40-60 60
(Monaural.)
MERCURY (60133 "Rich vs. Roach") 60-85 59
(Stereo.)
MERCURY (60136 "Richcraft") 60-85 60
(Stereo.)
MERCURY (60144 "The Voice Is Rich") 45-65 60
(Stereo.)
NORGRAN (26 "Swingin' ") 75-125 54
NORGRAN (1031 "Sing and Swing") 60-80 55
NORGRAN (1038 "Buddy Rich and Sweets Edison") 60-80 55
NORGRAN (1052 "Swingin' ") 60-80 55
NORGRAN (1078 "Wailing") 50-75 56
NORGRAN (1086 "One for Basie") 50-75 56
PACIFIC JAZZ (Except 10000 series) 8-18 66-70
PACIFIC JAZZ (10000 series) 5-8 81
PAUSA 5-8 80s
RCA 8-12 72-77
ROOST 10-20 66
TRIP 8-10 76
VSP 10-15 67
VERVE (2009 "Buddy Rich Sings Johnny Mercer") 50-75 57
VERVE (8129 "Buddy Rich and Sweets Edison") 50-75 57
VERVE (8142 "Swingin' ") 50-75 57
VERVE (8168 "Wailin' ") 50-75 57
VERVE (8176 "One for Basie") 50-75 57
VERVE (8285 "In Miami") 50-75 58
VERVE (8425 "Blue Caravan") 30-40 62
VERVE (8471 "Burnin' Beat") 30-40 62
(Monaural.)
VERVE (8484 "Drum Battle: Gene Krupa & Buddy Rich") 25-40 62
VERVE (68471 "Burnin' Beat") 35-45 62
(Stereo.)
VERVE (68778 "Super Rich") 10-15 69
VERVE (68824 "Monster") 10-15 73

WHO'S WHO in JAZZ ... 5-10 78
WING ... 8-12 69
WORLD PACIFIC ... 10-15 68
Also see DAVIS, Sammy, Jr., & Buddy Rich
Also see TORME, Mel
Also see YOUNG, Lester, Nat "King" Cole & Buddy Rich

RICH, Buddy, & Max Roach
LPs: 10/12-inch
MERCURY ... 5-10 81
Also see RICH, Buddy

RICH, Cathy
Singles: 7-inch
WORLD PACIFIC ... 5-8 70

RICH, Charlie *P&R '60/C&W '68*
Singles: 7-inch
COLUMBIA ... 3-4 82
EPIC ... 3-5 70-81
ELEKTRA ... 3-5 78-81
GROOVE ... 4-8 63-64
HI ... 4-8 66-67
MERCURY ... 3-5 73-74
MONUMENT ... 3-5
PHILLIPS INT'L ... 15-25 59-63
RCA (Except 8000 series) ... 3-5 74-77
RCA (8000 series) ... 4-8 64-65
SSS/SUN ... 3-5 70s
SMASH ... 4-8 65-66
U.A. ... 3-5 78-80
Picture Sleeves
GROOVE (0020 "She Loved Everybody But Me") ... 10-20 63
EPIC (AE7-1065 "Big Boss Man") ... 4-8 73
(Promotional bonus only)
MONUMENT ... 4-6
EPs: 7-inch
EPIC (1099 "Silver Linings") ... 8-12 76
(Promotional issue only.)
LPs: 10/12-inch
BUCKBOARD ... 8-10 70s
CAMDEN ... 8-10 70-74
CELEBRITY INT'L ... 5-8 91
EPIC (Except 139) ... 6-12 68-78
EPIC (139 "Everything You Wanted to Hear by Charlie Rich") ... 15-20 76
(Promotional issue only.)
ELEKTRA ... 5-10 80
51 WEST ... 5-10
GROOVE (G-1000 "Charlie Rich") ... 15-25 64
(Monaural.)
GROOVE (GS-1000 "Charlie Rich") ... 20-30 64
(Stereo.)
HARMONY ... 8-10 73
HI (Except 32037) ... 8-10 74-77
HI (32037 "Charlie Rich") ... 15-25 67
HILLTOP ... 8-10 70s
MERCURY ... 10-15 74
PHILLIPS INT'L (1970 "Lonely Weekends") ... 500-750 60
PHONORAMA ... 5-8 83
PICKWICK ... 5-10 70s
POWER PAK ... 8-10 74-75
RCA (Except 3000 series) ... 8-10 73-77
RCA (3000 series) ... 15-25 65-66
SSS/SUN ... 5-10 69-79
SMASH ... 15-25 65-66
SUNNYVALE ... 5-10 77
TIME-LIFE ... 5-10 81
TRIP ... 8-10 74
U.A. ... 5-10 78-79
WING ... 15-25 69
Session: Jordanaires; David Wills; Anita Kerr Singers.
Also see CASH, Johnny
Also see HARRIS, Ray
Also see JORDANAIRES
Also see KERR, Anita
Also see LEWIS, Jerry Lee, Carl Perkins & Charlie Rich
Also see POWERS, Johnny
Also see SHERIDAN, Bobby
Also see TUBB, Ernest
Also see WILLS, David

RICH, Charlie, & Janie Fricke *C&W '78*
Singles: 7-inch
EPIC ... 3-5 78
Also see FRICKE, Janie
Also see RICH, Charlie

RICH, Dave
Singles: 78 rpm
RCA ... 10-25 56-57
Singles: 7-inch
RCA (6595 "Ain't It Fine") ... 25-35 56
RCA (7045 "Chicken House") ... 15-25 57
RCA (7141 "School Blues") ... 15-25 57
RCA (7334 "Rosie Let's Get Cozy") ... 15-25 58
STOP ... 4-6 68-69
LPs: 10/12-inch
STOP (10007 "Soul Brother") ... 10-15 69

RICH, Debbie *C&W '88*
Singles: 7-inch
DOOR KNOB ... 3-4 88-89

RICH, Don
LPs: 10/12-inch
CAPITOL (643 "That Fiddlin' Man") ... 15-25 71
Also see BUCKAROOS

RICH & BAGS
Singles: 7-inch
DIRT BAG ... 10-15 60s

RICH & RAYS
Singles: 7-inch
RICHLY (101 "My Heart") ... 50-75

RICH KIDS
Singles: 7-inch
STEED ... 4-6 67-68

RICH MOUNTAIN TOWER
LPs: 10/12-inch
OVATION ... 8-12 71

RICHARD, Belton
Singles: 7-inch
CHAMO (102 "Snoozin") ... 10-15 60
SWALLOW ... 4-8

RICHARD, Cliff *P&R '59*
(With the Drifters; with Shadows)
Singles: 12-inch
EMI AMERICA ... 4-8 83
Singles: 7-inch
ABC-PAR ... 10-15 59-61
BIG TOP ... 4-8 62
CAPITOL ... 10-15 59
DOT ... 4-8 62
EMI AMERICA ... 3-5 79-84
EPIC ... 4-8 63-67
MONUMENT ... 3-5 70-72
ROCKET ... 3-5 76-79
SIRE ... 3-5 73
STRIPED HORSE ... 3-4 87
UNI ... 5-10 68-69
W.B. ... 4-6 69
Picture Sleeves
EMI AMERICA ... 3-5 80-81
EPIC ... 8-15 63-66
STRIPED HORSE ... 3-4 87
LPs: 10/12-inch
ABC-PAR (ABC-321 "Cliff Sings") ... 30-40 60
(Monaural.)
ABC-PAR (ABCS-321 "Cliff Sings") ... 40-60 60
(Stereo.)
ABC-PAR (ABC-391 "Listen to Cliff") ... 25-35 61
(Monaural.)
ABC-PAR (ABCS-391 "Listen to Cliff") ... 35-45 61
(Stereo.)
EMI AMERICA ... 5-10 79-83
EPIC ... 15-25 63-65
ROCKET ... 5-10 76-78
Also see NEWTON-JOHN, Olivia, & Electric Light Orchestra
Also see NEWTON-JOHN, Olivia, & Cliff Richard
Also see SHADOWS

RICHARD, Cliff, & Sarah Brightman
Singles: 7-inch
POLYDOR ... 3-4 86
Picture Sleeves
POLYDOR ... 3-4 86
Also see BRIGHTMAN, Sarah, & Hot Gossip
Also see RICHARD, Cliff

RICHARD, Little: see LITTLE RICHARD

RICHARD, Robert
Singles: 78 rpm
KING (4274 "Wigwam Woman") ... 75-125 48
Also see RICHARD BROTHERS

RICHARD, Robert / Joseph Von Battle
Singles: 78 rpm
JVB (75828 "Cadillac Woman") ... 100-150 48
Also see RICHARD, Robert

RICHARD & SHELLS
Singles: 7-inch
TURNTABLE (150/1 "Something Different") ... 10-20 65

RICHARD & YOUNG LIONS *P&R '66*
Singles: 7-inch
PHILIPS ... 4-8 66-67
Picture Sleeves
PHILIPS ... 10-20 66
Member: Richard Bloodworth.

RICHARD BROTHERS
Singles: 7-inch
STRATE 8 (1500 "Stolen Property") ... 30-40 59
Members: Robert Richard; Howard Richard.
Also see RICHARD, Robert

RICHARD SISTERS
Singles: 7-inch
LAURIE ... 4-8 61

RICHARDS, Ann
Singles: 7-inch
CAPITOL ... 5-10 58

RICHARDS, Barry
Singles: 7-inch
COLUMBIA ... 3-6 68
EMAR ... 4-8 67
EPIC ... 4-8 62
GROOVE ... 4-8 61
LINDA ... 4-8 64
UNI ... 4-8 67
Picture Sleeves
EPIC ... 4-8 62

RICHARDS, Cal
Singles: 7-inch
VI TOSE ... 10-15 65

RICHARDS, Dave
Singles: 7-inch
CELESTIAL ... 4-8 65

RICHARDS, Diane *R&B '83*
Singles: 7-inch
ZOO YORK ... 3-4 83

RICHARDS, Dick
(With Eddie Zack & Dude Ranchers)
Singles: 78 rpm
COLUMBIA ... 20-30 57
Singles: 7-inch
COLUMBIA (40957 "Blue-Jean Baby") ... 25-35 57
Also see ZACK, Eddie, & Cousin Richie

RICHARDS, Digby
Singles: 7-inch
RCA ... 3-5 74

RICHARDS, Donald
Singles: 7-inch
CHEX (1003 "I Cried for Your Love") ... 15-25 62

RICHARDS, Earl *C&W '69*
Singles: 7-inch
ACE of HEARTS ... 3-5 73-75
U.A. ... 3-6 69-70

RICHARDS, Emil
(With the Microtonal Blues Band)
LPs: 10/12-inch
IMPULSE ... 10-15 68-69
UNI ... 10-15 67-68

RICHARDS, Fred
Singles: 7-inch
FLIP ... 5-10 59

RICHARDS, Gil
Singles: 7-inch
ESSAR ... 4-8 63
SATURN ... 4-8 63

RICHARDS, Jay
Singles: 7-inch
GOLDBAND ... 5-10 60
HOLLYWOOD (1099 "Gosh Dog Baby") ... 15-25 59
HOLLYWOOD (1100 "Little Shyrel") ... 10-15 59

RICHARDS, Jimmy
Singles: 7-inch
A&M ... 4-8 68-69
COLUMBIA (41083 "Cool As a Moose") ... 15-25 58
LAVETTE ... 4-8 64

RICHARDS, Joey
Singles: 7-inch
ASTRA ... 4-8 63

RICHARDS, Keith *LP '88*
Singles: 7-inch
ROLLING STONES (316 "Before They Make Me Run") ... 5-10 78
ROLLING STONES (39311 "Run Rudolph, Run") ... 4-6 79
VIRGIN (99287 "Take It So Hard") ... 3-4 88
Picture Sleeves
ROLLING STONES (316 "Before They Make Me Run") ... 10-15 78
VIRGIN (99287 "Take It So Hard") ... 4-6 88
(Promotional issue only.)
ROLLING STONES (316 "Before They Make Me Run") ... 10-15 78
LPs: 10/12-inch
VIRGIN ... 5-8 88
Also see ROLLING STONES

RICHARDS, Lee
Singles: 7-inch
WANGER ... 4-8

RICHARDS, Lisa
Singles: 7-inch
SURE SHOT ... 4-8 65

RICHARDS, Mark
Singles: 7-inch
ABC-PAR ... 4-8 65

RICHARDS, Marty
Singles: 7-inch
ASCOT ... 4-8 64
MUSIC MAKERS ... 8-15 60s

RICHARDS, Norm
Singles: 7-inch
DEE GEE ... 5-10 66
IMPERIAL (5567 "Tease Me") ... 15-25 59

RICHARDS, Sonny, & Panics
Singles: 7-inch
CHANCELLOR ... 10-15 62
Also see PANICS

RICHARDS, Sue *C&W '71*
(Maggie Sue Wimberley)
Singles: 7-inch
ABC/DOT ... 3-5 75-76
DOT ... 3-5 73-74
EPIC ... 3-5 71-78
LPs: 10/12-inch
ABC/DOT ... 5-10 74-76
Also see HITCHCOCK, Stan, & Sue Richards
Also see WIMBERLY, Maggie Sue
Also see WYNETTE, Tammy

RICHARDS, Todd
Singles: 7-inch
ABC-PAR ... 5-10 60

RICHARDS, Tony
(With the Twilights)
Singles: 7-inch
CARLTON ... 5-10 62
COLPIX (178 "Please Believe Me") ... 50-70 60

RICHARDS, Trig
Singles: 7-inch
FALCON (205 "Hollywood Cat") ... 35-45

RICHARDS, Trudy
Singles: 78 rpm
CAPITOL ... 5-10 57
DERBY ... 4-8 53-54
JUBILEE ... 4-8 55
Singles: 7-inch
CAPITOL ... 5-10 57
DERBY ... 5-10 53-54
JUBILEE ... 5-10 55
EPs: 7-inch
CAPITOL ... 10-15 57
LPs: 10/12-inch
CAPITOL ... 15-25 57

RICHARDS, Turley *P&R '70*
(Richard Turley)
Singles: 7-inch
ATLANTIC ... 3-5 80
COLUMBIA ... 4-8 66-67
EPIC ... 3-5 76-78
KAPP ... 4-8 68
MGM ... 4-8 64
20TH FOX ... 4-8 65
W.B. ... 3-5 70
Picture Sleeves
COLUMBIA ... 4-8 66
LPs: 10/12-inch
ATLANTIC ... 5-10 80
EPIC ... 5-10 76
20TH FOX ... 10-20 65
W.B. ... 10-15 70-71
Also see TURLEY, Richard

RICHARDS, Val
Singles: 7-inch
SCENE (601 "My Oh My") ... 30-45

RICHARDS, Walt
LPs: 10/12-inch
ATON ... 8-12 75

RICHARDS, Zone
Singles: 7-inch
BIG TOP (3122 "Juarez") ... 10-20 62

RICHARDSON, Del
(With Herb Buchanan & Orchestra)
Singles: 7-inch
CORAL ... 5-10 63
MGM (13088 "Boys Night Out") ... 10-15 62
SMASH (1729 "Don't Cry Linda") ... 15-25 62
STELLAR (1010 "You Pass This Way Only Once") ... 15-25 62
STELLAR (1729 "Don't Cry Linda") ... 50-75 61
(First issue.)

RICHARDSON, Groundhog
LPs: 10/12-inch
TURBO ... 8-12 71

RICHARDSON, Henry
Singles: 7-inch
ELOIS ... 4-8 67

RICHARDSON, Jape
(With His Japettes)
Singles: 78 rpm
MERCURY ... 15-25 57
Singles: 7-inch
MERCURY (71219 "Beggar to a King") ... 20-40 57
MERCURY (71312 "Teenage Moon") ... 25-50 58
Also see BIG BOPPER

RICHARDSON, Jerry
Singles: 7-inch
CHESS ... 3-5 74

RICHARDSON, Jimmy
Singles: 7-inch
HOLLYWOOD ... 5-10 61
NASHVILLE ... 10-15 60

RICHARDSON, Lee
Singles: 78 rpm
DELUXE ... 4-8 55
Singles: 7-inch
DELUXE ... 5-10 55

RICHARDSON, Murle
Singles: 7-inch
CARON (6103 "Mean & Cruel") ... 50-100

RICHARDSON, Richie
Singles: 7-inch
GALAXY ... 5-10 60

RICHARDSON, Rudi
Singles: 78 rpm
SUN (271 "Fools Hall of Fame") ... 20-40 57
Singles: 7-inch
SUN (271 "Fools Hall of Fame") ... 20-40 57

RICHARDSON, Rudy, Trio
Singles: 78 rpm
MANOR ... 15-25 46

RICHARDSON, Skeet
Singles: 7-inch
VIBRATONE ("To My Baby") ... 300-500 63

RICHARDSON, Tender Joe
Singles: 7-inch
HOT BISCUIT ... 4-8 68
VEEP ... 4-8 67

RICHETTES
Singles: 7-inch
APT ... 10-20 62

RICHEY, George
Singles: 7-inch
ASCOT ... 4-8 64

RICHEY, Karl
LPs: 10/12-inch
STUDIO 10 ... 10-15 69

RICHIE
Singles: 7-inch
KIP (241 "Cherié") ... 15-25 61
Picture Sleeves
KIP (241 "Cherié") ... 25-50 61

RICHIE, Joe
Singles: 7-inch
BUDDY (122 "Across the Bay") ... 20-30 59

RICHIE, Lionel *P&R/R&B/LP '82*
Singles: 12-inch
MOTOWN (Except 139) ... 4-8 83-86
MOTOWN (139 "Hello") ... 8-12 84
(Picture disc. Promotional issue only.)
Singles: 7-inch
MOTOWN ... 3-4 82-92
Picture Sleeves
MOTOWN ... 3-4 83-87
LPs: 10/12-inch
MOTOWN ... 5-8 82-86
Also see COMMODORES
Also see ROSS, Diana, & Lionel Ritchie
Also see U.S.A. for AFRICA

RICHIE, Lionel, & Alabama *C&W '86*
Singles: 12-inch
MOTOWN (195 "Special Motown Service to Country Radio") ... 8-12 86
(Promotional issue only.)
Singles: 7-inch
MOTOWN ... 3-4 86
Also see ALABAMA
Also see RICHIE, Lionel

RICHIE & REBELS
Singles: 7-inch
BARCLAY (13348 "Rebel Rock") ... 15-25 60s

RICHIE & REKNOWNS
(Richie & Renowns)
Singles: 7-inch
STREKE (247 "Please Say You Want Me") ... 100-200 63

RICHIE & ROYALS
Singles: 7-inch
GOLDEN CREST (573 "Be My Girl") ... 20-30 62
RELLO (1 "Goody Goody") ... 20-30 61
RELLO (3 "Be My Girl") ... 100-200 62
(First issue.)

RICHIE & RUNAROUNDS
Singles: 7-inch
ASCOT (2136 "Lost in the Crowd") ... 10-20 63
Members: Lou Christie; Kripp Johnson.
Also see CHRISTIE, Lou
Also see JOHNSON, Kripp

RICHIE & SAXONS
Singles: 7-inch
TIP ... 10-20 65

RICHIE'S RENEGADES
Singles: 7-inch
POLARIS (65 "Baby It's Me") ... 10-20 64

RICHIE'S ROOM 222 GANG *R&B '71*
Singles: 7-inch
SCEPTER ... 3-5 71

RICHMAN, Jonathan
(With the Modern Lovers)
Singles: 7-inch
BESERKLEY ... 3-5 76
Picture Sleeves
BESERKLEY ... 3-5 76
LPs: 10/12-inch
BESERKLEY ... 15-25 76
SIRE ... 8-12 83
Also see MODERN LOVERS

RICHMAN, Jonathan / Earthquake
Singles: 7-inch
BESERKLEY ... 3-5 75
Picture Sleeves
BESERKLEY ... 3-5 75
Also see EARTHQUAKE
Also see RICHMAN, Jonathan

RICHMOND, Alex
LPs: 10/12-inch
CAPITOL ... 8-10 72

RICHMOND, Pat
Singles: 7-inch
VULCO (1500 "Don't Stop Rockin' ") ... 100-150 58

RICHMOND EXTENSION *R&B '74*
Singles: 7-inch
SILVER BLUE ... 3-5 74

RICHMOND GROUP / Earl Preston's Realms / Michael Allen Group
LPs: 10/12-inch
CAPITOL (T-2544 "Where It All Began") ... 20-25 66
(Monaural.)
CAPITOL (ST-2544 "Where It All Began") ... 25-30 66
(Stereo.)

RICHY, Paul
Singles: 7-inch
RICHWOOD (1000 "Framed") ... 10-15 59
SUN (338 "Legend of the Big Steeple") ... 15-25 60

RICK & Cast of Idoits: see DEES, Rick

RICK & DONNA
Singles: 7-inch
A&M 5-10 63
TOWER 4-8 65

RICK & EDDY
Singles: 7-inch
HIT-TEEN 5-10 61

RICK & FAIRLANES
Singles: 7-inch
TAP ("Liberty Bell Rock") 15-25 59
(Selection number not known.)

RICK & JERRY
Singles: 7-inch
LOLA 4-8 65

RICK & JOHNNY
Singles: 7-inch
ABC-PAR 4-8 62

RICK & KEENS P&R '61
Singles: 7-inch
AUSTIN (303 "Peanuts") 35-50 61
JAMIE (1219 "Your Turn to Cry") ... 10-15 62
LE CAM (721 "Peanuts") 25-35 61
LE CAM (133 "Darla") 15-25 61
SMASH (1705 "Peanuts") 10-15 61
TOLLIE (9016 "Darla") 10-15 64
TROY 20-30 63

RICK & LANCE
Singles: 7-inch
BIG TOP 4-8 62

RICK & LEGENDS
Singles: 7-inch
U.A. 5-10 66
Member: Rick Palmer.
Also see PALMER, Rick

RICK & MASTERS
Singles: 7-inch
CAMEO (226 "Here Comes Nancy") 30-50 62
CAMEO (247 "Let It Please Be You") 30-50 63
HARAL (778 "Bewitched, Bothered, Bewildered") 40-60 62
TABA (101 "Flame of Love") 150-250 62
Also see YOUNG, Bobby

RICK & RAIDERS
Singles: 7-inch
SONIC 8-12 60s

RICK & RANDELLS
Singles: 7-inch
ABC-PAR (10055 "Let It Be You") 20-30 59

RICK & RAVENS
(Featuring Ray Daniels)
Singles: 7-inch
AURA (4506 "Henritta") 40-50 64
AURA (4511 "Soul Train") 30-40 65
POSAE (101 "Big Bucket T") 40-50 60s
Member: Ray Daniels.
Also see MANZAREK, Ray

RICK & RICK-A-SHAYS
Singles: 7-inch
REPRISE (20,226 "The Drag") 10-15 63
(First issued by Eddie Ford. First reissue is by the Mar-Villes.)
Also see FORD, Eddie
Also see MAR-VILLES

RICK & RIOTS
Singles: 7-inch
SHAZZAM (111 "Traffic Jam") 10-20 65

RICK & ROCKERS
Singles: 7-inch
ARC (4445 "I'm Hurt") 10-20 58

RICK & RON
Singles: 7-inch
IBIS 4-8 65

RICK & RONNIE
Singles: 7-inch
SPRITE (5001 "Don't Do Me This Way") 15-25 66

RICK & SANDY
Singles: 7-inch
PRESS 4-8 66

RICK, ROBIN & HIM
Singles: 7-inch
V.I.P. (25035 "Three Choruses of Despair") 10-20 66

RICKELS, Rick
Singles: 7-inch
BISHOP (1001 "I'm Gone") 4-6

RICKETT, Nooney
(With Pure; with Nooney Rickett Four)
Singles: 7-inch
CAPITOL 3-6 69
DIMENSION 4-8 65
IT 3-5 66-67
MGM 3-5 60
20TH FOX 3-5 64

RICKIE & HALLMARKS
Singles: 7-inch
AMY (877 "Wherever You Are") 30-50 63
Member: Rick Lisi.

RICKIE & JENNELL
Singles: 78 rpm
FLAIR (1033 "Each Step") 10-20 54
Singles: 7-inch
FLAIR (1033 "Each Step") 25-40 54
Members: Richard Berry; Jennell Hawkins.
Also see BERRY, Richard
Also see HAWKINS, Jennell

RICKIE & VICKIE
Singles: 7-inch
ANGELTONE 4-8 64

RICKLES, Don LP '68
LPs: 10/12-inch
W.B. 8-12 68-69

RICKOCHETS
Singles: 7-inch
BON BON (1313 "Monkey Scratch") 10-20 63
Also see COYNE, Ricky, & His Guitar Rockers

RICKS, Jimmy
(With the Rickateers; with Raves; with Surburbans)
Singles: 78 rpm
JOSIE 10-20 56
MERCURY 20-30 54
PARIS 10-20 57
Singles: 7-inch
ARNOLD (1011 "Canadian Sunset") 8-12 63
ATCO (6220 "Daddy Rollin' Stone") 20-40 62
ATLANTIC (2246 "Romance in the Dark") 10-15 64
BATON (236 "I'm a Fool to Want You") 15-25 57
DECCA (30443 "Lazy Mule") 15-25 57
FELSTED (8582 "Here Come the Tears Again") 15-25 59
FESTIVAL (703 "Ol Man River") 50-75 66
FESTIVAL (25004 "Daddy Rollin' Stone") 15-25 62
FURY 10-15 62
JOSIE (796 "She's Fine, She's Mine") 20-30 56
JUBILEE (5559 "Lonely Man") 5-10 67
JUBILEE (5561 "Wigglin' and Gigglin' ") 5-10 67
JUBILEE (5619 "Snap Your Fingers") 5-10 68
MERCURY (8296 "Too Soon") 40-60 52
MERCURY (70119 "She's Got to Go") 40-60 53
MERCURY (70330 "Going Home") 40-60 54
PARIS (504 "Do You Promise") 15-25 57
SIGNATURE (12013 "At Sunrise") . 10-20 59
SIGNATURE (12040 "I Needed Your Love") 10-20 60
LPs: 10/12-inch
JUBILEE (8021 "Tell Her You Love Her") 10-20 69
MAINSTREAM (6050 "Vibrations") . 15-25 65
SIGNATURE (1032 "Jimmy Ricks") 150-250 60
Also see BAKER, LaVern, & Jimmy Ricks
Also see RAVENS
Also see SUBURBANS

RICKS, Ricky
Singles: 7-inch
SURE SHOT 4-8 66

RICKS, Steve C&W '86
Singles: 7-inch
SOUTHWIND 3-4 86

RICKS, Travis
Singles: 7-inch
ORDELL (502 "No Need to Cry") ... 10-15 63

RICKY & CONTINENTALS
Singles: 7-inch
UP-BEAT (3 "Pitter Patter") 8-12

RICKY, Ron, & Semi-Tones
Singles: 7-inch
SEMI-TONE (1 "There's a Girl in My Heart") 250-500

RICKY & HITCH-HIKERS
Singles: 7-inch
DORE (690 "Undertow") 10-20 63
(Reissued as by Billy Joe & Checkmates.)
Also see BILLY JOE & CHECKMATES

RICKY & LEXINGTONS
Singles: 7-inch
SATELITE 10-15 60s
Member: Rick Nichols.
Also see NICHOLS, Rick

RICKY & PHARAOHS
(Richard Berry)
Singles: 78 rpm
CLASS 75-125 57
Singles: 7-inch
CLASS (202 "Teenagers Love Song") 75-125 57
Also see BERRY, Richard

RICKY & RAYLENE
Singles: 7-inch
TEE PEE (17/18 "It Must Be Love") 10-20 67
Members: Ricky Leigh Smolinski; Raylene Loos; Roger Loos; Tom Loos.
Also see RAYLENE & BLUE ANGELS

RICKY & ROBBY
Singles: 7-inch
GOLDEN CREST 10-15 59

RICKY & SAINTS
Singles: 7-inch
7 TEEN 5-10 62

RICKY & STOMPERS
Singles: 7-inch
PRINCETON (102 "Wild One") 50-75 58

RICKY & VACELS
Singles: 7-inch
EXPRESS (711 "Lorraine") 20-30 62
FARGO (1050 "His Girl") 15-25 63
(Black vinyl.)
FARGO (1050 "His Girl") 30-50 63
(Blue vinyl.)
Also see SHAGGY BOYS
Also see VACELS

RICO, Fred
Singles: 7-inch
DEE LITE 5-10 60

RICO & RAVENS
Singles: 7-inch
AUTUMN (6 "Don't You Know") 8-12 65
COLLECTABLES 3-4 80s
RALLY (1601 "Don't You Know") 20-30 65

RICOCHETTES
Singles: 7-inch
DESTINATION (629 "I Don't Want You") 15-25 67
CONTINENTAL (500 "Find Another Boy") 10-20 66
MEAN MOUNTAIN 3-4 82
QUILL (102 "Losing You") 25-50 66
RAYNARD (10030 "I'll Be Back") 5-10 65
UNIVERSAL ("I'll Be Back") 15-25 60s
(Promotional issue only. No selection number used.)
Members: Ar Kriegel; Jerry Wollenzien; Herb Hohnke; John Galobich; Bob Heuhofer; Mick Milewski; Bruce Cole.
Picture Sleeves
MEAN MOUNTAIN 3-4 82
Also see HAPPY DAYS REVUE
Also see PICTURE
Also see STEVENS, Ar, & Rockin' Ricochettes

RIDDELL, Allan C&W '60
Singles: 7-inch
PLAID 5-10 60

RIDDLE, Dick
Singles: 7-inch
RIDDLE (501 "Cool Me Baby") 10-15 60

RIDDLE, Don
(Don Riddle 5)
Singles: 7-inch
GENERAL AMERICAN 5-10 65

RIDDLE, Jimmy
(Larry Evans)
Singles: 7-inch
MARINA (502 "Why") 10-20 66
TODD (1074 "Let's Go") 8-10 62
Also see EVANS, Larry

RIDDLE, Nelson, & His Orchestra P&R '54
Singles: 78 rpm
CAPITOL 3-5 53-57
Singles: 7-inch
CAPITOL 4-10 53-62
EPIC 3-6 67
LIBERTY 3-6 67
REPRISE 3-6 63-66
20TH FOX 3-6 66
VERVE 5-8 59
Picture Sleeves
CAPITOL 5-10 60
EPIC 4-8 67
EPs: 7-inch
CAPITOL 8-15 55-59
VERVE 6-12 59
LPs: 10/12-inch
ALSHIRE 5-10 70-71
AVON 5-8 70
CAPITOL 5-20 55-78
DAYBREAK 5-8 73
HARMONY 5-10 69
LIBERTY 5-10 67
MPS 5-10 73
PICKWICK 5-10 65
REPRISE 5-15 63-65
SOLID STATE 5-10 67
SUNSET 5-10 68
U.A. 5-10 68
VERVE 5-15 59
For a complete listing of soundtracks by this artist, consult *The Official Price Guide to Movie/TV Soundtracks and Original Cast Albums.*
Also see FITZGERALD, Ella
Also see MARTIN, Dean / Nelson Riddle
Also see PETERSON, Oscar
Also see RONSTADT, Linda

RIDDLE, Ricky, & His Band
Singles: 78 rpm
DECCA 15-25 56
MGM 10-20 54
TENNESSEE (758 "Cold Icy Feet") 25-35 51
Singles: 7-inch
DECCA (29813 "I'm a Whip-Crackin' Daddy") 15-25 56
MGM (11741 "Steamboat Boogie") 20-30 54

RIDDLE, Sam
Singles: 7-inch
TOWER 4-8 66

RIDDLERS
Singles: 7-inch
MIKE (4000 "Batman Theme") 10-20 66

RIDDLES
Singles: 7-inch
MERCURY 10-15 67

RIDE THE RIVER C&W '87
Singles: 7-inch
ADVANTAGE 3-4 87-88

RIDERS OF THE MARK
Singles: 7-inch
20TH FOX (6694 "The Electronic Insides and Metal Complexion That Make Up Herr Doktor Kreig") 15-25 67

RIDGELEY, Andrew LP '90
LPs: 10/12-inch
COLUMBIA 5-8 90
Also see WHAM!

RIDGLEY, Tommy
Singles: 78 rpm
DECCA 20-40 51
HERALD 10-20 56-57
IMPERIAL 20-40 50-53
Singles: 7-inch
ATLANTIC (1009 "Oh Lawdy") 35-45 53
ATLANTIC (1039 "Jam Up") 15-25 54
ATLANTIC (2000 series) 5-10 62
DECCA (48226 "Anything But Love") 40-60 51
HEP'ME 5-8
HERALD 10-20 56-59
IMPERIAL (5198 "I Live My Life") 50-100 52
IMPERIAL (5203 "Looped") 50-100 52
IMPERIAL (5214 "Monkey Man") 50-100 53
IMPERIAL (5223 "Good Times") .. 50-100 53
INTERNATIONAL CITY 5-10
JOHEN 5-10 64
MAISON DE SOUL 4-8
ORBIT 10-15
RIC 5-10 60-62
RONN 4-8 69
SANSU 5-10
WHITE CLIFFS 4-8 67
LPs: 10/12-inch
ROUNDER 5-8

RIDGWAY, Stan LP '86
Singles: 7-inch
I.R.S. 3-4 86
LPs: 10/12-inch
I.R.S. 5-8 86
Also see WALL of VOODOO

RIDLEY, Jimmy, & the Sentinels
Singles: 7-inch
HEM (101 "Rock-A-Bye Baby") 50-75 58

RIDLEY, Sharon
Singles: 7-inch
TABU 3-5 79

RIEGERT, Lou, & Troops
(Lou Waters, now of CNN)
Singles: 7-inch
SOMA 10-20 64

RIELS
Singles: 7-inch
LAURIE 5-10 64

RIENZI, Nino
Singles: 7-inch
TRANS ATLAS (699 "Persian King") 50-75

RIFF, Eddie
(Mickey Baker)
Singles: 7-inch
DOVER (102 "My Baby's Gone Away") 200-300 57
Also see BAKER, Mickey

RIFF RAFF
LPs: 10/12-inch
ATCO 5-10 81

RIFFS
Singles: 7-inch
JAMIE (1296 "Tell Her") 8-12 64
LUBEE (1296 "Tell Her") 15-25 64
OLD TOWN (1179 "Tell Tale Friends") 50-100 65
SUNNY (22 "Little Girl") 50-100 64
Also see CHIMES

RIFFS
Singles: 7-inch
CORI (31005 "Outside That Door") .. 5-10 66

RIFT, Zoogz: see ZOOGZ RIFT

RIG
LPs: 10/12-inch
CAPITOL (473 "Rig") 15-20 70

RIGBY, Eleanore
Singles: 7-inch
AMSTERDAM 4-6 69

RIGG, Bram, Set: see BRAM RIGG SET

RIGGS
LPs: 10/12-inch
FULL MOON/ASYLUM 5-8 82

RIGGS, Linda
Singles: 7-inch
KING 8-15 65
KNIGHT 4-8 64

RIGHT CHOICE R&B '88
Singles: 7-inch
MOTOWN 3-4 88

RIGHT KIND R&B '68
Singles: 7-inch
GALAXY 4-8 68

RIGHTEOUS BROTHERS P&R '63
Singles: 7-inch
HAVEN 3-5 74-76
MGM 3-5 78-79
MGM CELEBRITY SCENE (8 "Righteous Brothers") 40-50 66
(Boxed set of five singles with bio insert and juke box title strips.)
MGM GOLDEN CIRCLE 3-5
MOONGLOW (215 "Little Latin Lupe Lu") 10-15 63
MOONGLOW (223 "My Babe") 8-12 63
MOONGLOW (224 "Koko Jo") 8-12 63
MOONGLOW (231 "Try to Find Another Man") 8-12 64
MOONGLOW (234 "Bring Your Love to Me") 8-12 65
MOONGLOW (235 "This Little Girl of Mine") 8-12 65
MOONGLOW (238 "Bring Your Love to Me") 8-12 65
MOONGLOW (239 "You Can Have Her") 8-12 65
MOONGLOW (242 "Justine") 8-12 65
MOONGLOW (243 "For Your Love") 8-12 65
MOONGLOW (244 "Georgia on My Mind") 8-12 66
MOONGLOW (245 "Bring Your Love to Me") 8-12 65
PHILLES (124 "You've Lost That Lovin' Feelin' ") 8-12 64
PHILLES (127 "Just Once in My Life") 8-12 65
PHILLES (129 "Hung on You") 8-12 65
PHILLES (130 "Ebb Tide") 1000-1500 65
(Custom label. Has Phil Spector's picture on the label. Promotional issue only.)
PHILLES (130 "Ebb Tide") 5-10 65
(No picture on label.)
PHILLES (132 "White Cliffs of Dover") 8-12 66
POLYDOR 3-6
VERVE 5-10 65-70
VERVE SOUNDS of FAME 3-5 70s
Picture Sleeves
PHILLES (127 "Just Once in My Life") 10-15 65
PHILLES (129 "Hung on You") 10-15 65
PHILLES (130 "Ebb Tide") 10-15 65
PHILLES (132 "White Cliffs of Dover") 10-15 66
VERVE (10383 "Soul and Inspiration") 8-12 66
VERVE (10406 "He") 8-12 66
VERVE (10551 "Stranded in the Middle of Noplace") 8-12 67
EPs: 7-inch
MOONGLOW (71004 "Best of the Righteous Brothers") 10-20 66
(Juke box issue.)
LPs: 10/12-inch
HAVEN 10-15 74-75
MGM 10-15 70-73
MOONGLOW (1001 "Right Now") 20-30 63
MOONGLOW (1002 "Some Blue Eyed Soul") 20-30 64
MOONGLOW (1003 "This Is New") 20-30 65
MOONGLOW (1004 "Best of the Righteous Brothers") 20-30 66
PHILLES (4007 "You've Lost That Lovin' Feeling") 25-45 64
PHILLES (4008 "Just Once in My Life") 25-45 65
PHILLES (4009 "Back to Back") 25-45 65
RHINO 8-12 89
VERVE (5001 "Soul and Inspiration") 15-20 66
VERVE (5004 "Go Ahead and Cry") 15-20 66
VERVE (5010 "Sayin' Something") 15-20 67
VERVE (5020 "Greatest Hits") 15-20 67
VERVE (5031 "Souled Out") 15-20 66
VERVE (5058 "One for the Road") 15-20 68
VERVE (5076 "Re-Birth") 15-20 69
(With Jimmy Walker instead of Bill Medley.)
Members: Bill Medley; Bobby Hatfield.
Also see HATFIELD, Bobby
Also see MEDLEY, Bill
Also see NEWELL, Skip, & Mustangs
Also see PARAMOURS
Also see PEPPERS
Also see WALKER, Jimmy

RIGUEZ, Rod
Singles: 7-inch
IMPACT (1031 "You'd Like to Admit It") 15-25 67
SUSSEX 10-20 71-72

RIKI & RIKATONES
Singles: 7-inch
MANHATTAN (201 "TNT") 100-150

RILEY, Allan
Singles: 7-inch
PROSPECT 5-10 59

RILEY, Billy Lee P&R '72
(With His Little Green Men)
Singles: 78 rpm
SUN 25-75 56-57
Singles: 7-inch
ATLANTIC 4-8 68
BRUNSWICK (55085 "Rockin' on the Moon") 150-250 58
ENTRANCE 3-5 72

GNP ... 4-8 66
HIP ... 4-8 68
HOME of the BLUES (233 "Flip, Flop and Fly") ... 20-30 61
MERCURY ... 5-10 64-65
MOJO ... 4-8 67
SUN (245 "Rock with Me Baby") ... 50-100 56
SUN (260 "Flying Saucers Rock & Roll") ... 50-100 57
(Counterfeits exist of this release.)
SUN (277 "Red Hot") ... 35-55 57
SUN (289 "Wouldn't You Know") ... 15-25 58
SUN (313 "No Name Girl") ... 15-25 58
SUN (322 "Got the Water Boiling") ... 50-75 59
SSS/SUN ... 4-6 69-70

LPs: 10/12-inch

CROWN (5277 "Harmonica & the Blues") ... 50-100 63
GNP ... 15-20 66
MERCURY ... 15-25 64-65
MOJO (1933 "Southern Soul") ... 30-50 79
Also see ALTON & JIMMY
Also see DONN, Larry
Also see JANES, Roland
Also see LEE, Darron
Also see LIGHTNIN' LEON
Also see MEGATONS
Also see ROCKIN' STOCKINGS
Also see SANDY & SANDSTORMS
Also see WILEY, Skip

RILEY, Bob

Singles: 7-inch

CORAL (62125 "I Think It's a Shame") ... 10-20 59
DOT (15625 "Without Your Love") ... 15-25 57
MGM (12612 "Wanda Jean") ... 75-100 58
ST. CLAIR (1003 "Case O' the Blues") ... 5-10 66
TIBOR (4500 "Weekend Vacation") ... 8-12 61
YORK (805 "Big Dog") ... 75-125

EPs: 7-inch

CORAL (81186 "Bruce Morrow's Musical Museum") ... 25-50 59

RILEY, Cheryl Pepsii — P&R/LP '88

Singles: 7-inch

COLUMBIA ... 3-4 88

Singles: 7-inch

COLUMBIA ... 3-4 88

Picture Sleeves

COLUMBIA ... 3-4 88

LPs: 10/12-inch

COLUMBIA ... 5-8 88

RILEY, Dan — C&W '79

Singles: 7-inch

ARMADA ... 3-5 79

RILEY, Jeannie C. — C&W/P&R/LP '68

(With the Red River Symphony)

Singles: 7-inch

CAPITOL ... 3-6 69
CROSS COUNTRY ... 3-4 79
GARPAX ... 3-4 80
GOD'S COUNTRY ... 3-5 75
MCA ... 3-4 82
MGM ... 3-5 71-74
MERCURY ... 3-5 74
PLANTATION (Black vinyl) ... 3-4 68-72
PLANTATION (Colored vinyl) ... 4-8 68-72
W.B. ... 3-5 76

Picture Sleeves

PLANTATION ... 4-8 68-72

EPs: 7-inch

PLANTATION ... 5-10 68

LPs: 10/12-inch

ALBUM GLOBE ... 5-8 80s
CAPITOL ... 8-12 69
CROSS COUNTRY ... 5-10 79
HSRD/PLEASANT SOUNDS ... 5-8 82
HEARTWARMING ... 4-8 79
LITTLE DARLIN' ... 10-15 68
MGM ... 10-15 72-74
OUT of TOWN DIST. ... 5-8 82
PICKWICK ... 5-10 70s
PLANTATION ... 5-12 68-82
POWER PAK ... 5-8 80s
SONGBIRD ... 4-8 81-83
TRIP ... 8-12 74
Also see CASH, Johnny / Jerry Lee Lewis / Jeanie C. Riley
Also see CASH, Johnny / Jeanie C. Riley

RILEY, Larry — C&W '81

Singles: 7-inch

F&L ... 3-4 81

RILEY, Otis

(With the Losers)

Singles: 7-inch

KAPPA (208 "Rock & Roll Riley") ... 25-50
SPHINX (6107 "Goodbye Love") ... 15-25

RILEY, Pat

(With His Tin Pan Alley Trio & Orchestra)

Singles: 7-inch

REED (1201 "Little Bop-a-Little") ... 50-75 60
TIN PAN ALLEY (175 "Without You to Love") ... 100-200 57

RILEY, Ray Wong

Singles: 7-inch

SSS INT'L ... 4-6 68

RILEY, Russ, & Five Sounds

(With Al Browne's Orchestra)

Singles: 7-inch

ALJON (115 "Tonight Must Live On") ... 150-200 60

RILEY, Teddy, & Guy

Singles: 7-inch

MOTOWN ... 3-4 89
Also see GUY

Also see KIDS at WORK

RIMSHOTS — R&B '72

Singles: 7-inch

A-1 (4000 "Soul Train") ... 4-8 72
A-1 (4002 "Save That Thing") ... 8-12 72
ASTROSCOPE ... 3-5 74
HAPPY HEARTS ... 3-5
STANG ... 3-5 76-77

LPs: 10/12-inch

STANG ... 5-10 76

RINCON SURFSIDE BAND

Singles: 7-inch

DUNHILL (1 "Surfing Songbook") ... 10-20 65
(Promotional issue only. Excerpts from the LP *Surfing Songbook*.)

Picture Sleeves

DUNHILL (1 "Surfing Songbook") ... 20-30 65
(Promotional issue only.)

LPs: 10/12-inch

DUNHILL (50001 "Surfing Songbook") ... 40-60 65
Also see FANTASTIC BAGGYS

RING-A-DINGS

Singles: 7-inch

ABC ... 4-8 66
REPRISE ... 4-8 66
TITANIC ... 5-10 61

RINGER, Jim

LPs: 10/12-inch

PHILO ... 8-10 77

RINGLEADERS

Singles: 7-inch

M-PAC (7232 "Let's Start Over") ... 50-100 63

RINGO, Eddie

Singles: 7-inch

TWIN STAR (106 "Full Racing Cam") ... 20-30 60

RINGO, Jimmy

Singles: 7-inch

DOT (15787 "I Like This Kind of Music") ... 15-25 58

RINGO, Ron, & Originals

Singles: 7-inch

JUGGY (701 "Queen of the Jerk") ... 15-25 64

RINGOS

Singles: 7-inch

HI ... 5-10 63

RINGS — P&R/LP '81

Singles: 7-inch

MCA ... 3-5 81

LPs: 10/12-inch

MCA ... 5-10 81

RINKER, Al, & Ramblers

Singles: 7-inch

TROY (400 "Pierrot") ... 10-20 60s

RINKY-DINKS — P&R/R&B '58

(Featuring Bobby Darin)

Singles: 7-inch

ATCO (6121 "Early in the Morning") ... 25-50 58
(Previously issued as by the Ding Dongs. Later issued as by "Bobby Darin & the Rinky Dinks.")
Also see DARIN, Bobby

RINKY DINKS

Singles: 7-inch

CAPITOL ... 5-10 59

RINKY DINKS

Singles: 7-inch

ENJOY (1010 "Hot Potato") ... 10-15 62
(Reissued as *Soultrain*, by the Ramrods.)
Member: King Curtis.
Also see KING CURTIS
Also see RAMRODS

RINO, Ginette

Singles: 7-inch

CORAL ... 4-8 64

RIO

Singles: 7-inch

ZERO ... 3-5 76

RIO, Bobby

(With the Revelles; Bobby "King" Rio)

Singles: 7-inch

ABC-PAR ... 10-15 65
LENOX ... 10-15 63

RIO, Chico

Singles: 7-inch

CONGRESS ... 4-8 66

RIO, Chuck

(Chuck "Tequila" Rio & Originals; with individuals; with Kreshendos; Danny Flores)

Singles: 7-inch

CHALLENGE ... 10-20 58-60
FLAIR (103 "Big Boy") ... 15-25 62
JACKPOT (48016 "Margarita") ... 15-25 59
KENT ... 15-25 58
SATURN (402 "Kreschendo Stomp") ... 15-25 63
TEQUILA (103 "If You Were the Only Girl in the World") ... 50-100 60
Also see CHAMPS
Also see CONTENDERS
Also see CRESCHENDOES
Also see CRUCHENDOES
Also see FLORES, Danny
Also see ORIGINALS
Also see PERSUADERS
Also see ROSS, Johnny

RIO, Chuck, & Delaney

Singles: 7-inch

TOPPA ... 8-12 62
Members: Chuck Rio; Delaney Bramlett.
Also see BRAMLETT, Delaney
Also see RIO, Chuck

RIO, Jerry, & Stompmen

Singles: 7-inch

PNR (1 "The Empire Stomp") ... 10-20 62

RIO & Little Red Ryders

Singles: 7-inch

LANJO (7780 "You Better Believe It") ... 75-125 60

RIO GRANDE

LPs: 10/12-inch

RCA ... 10-15 71
Member: Ronnie Weiss.
Also see UNIQUES

RIO ROCKERS

Singles: 7-inch

CAPITOL (3884 "Mexican Rock & Roll") ... 25-50 58
Members: Don Cole; Paul Smith; Rusty Isabell; Sam Babcock; Eskew Reeder.
Also see COLE, Don
Also see ISABELL, Rusty
Also see REEDER, Eskew

RIO TRIO

Singles: 7-inch

LOTUS ... 5-10 62

RIOPELLE, Jerry

Singles: 7-inch

ABC ... 3-5 74
CAPITOL ... 3-5 71

LPs: 10/12-inch

ABC ... 10-15 74-75
CAPITOL (ST series) ... 10-20 71
CAPITOL (SM series) ... 5-10 77
LITTLE ESKIMO ... 5-10 77-79
Also see PARADE

RIOS, Augie — P&R '58

(With the Notations)

Singles: 7-inch

MGM ... 4-8 60-64
METRO ... 5-10 58-59
SHELLEY ... 10-20 63-64

RIOS, Miguel — LP '70

Singles: 7-inch

A&M ... 3-5 70

Picture Sleeves

A&M ... 3-5 70

LPs: 10/12-inch

A&M ... 10-15 70

RIOS, Waldo de los — P&R/LP '71

LPs: 10/12-inch

U.A. ... 5-10 71

RIOT — LP '81

Singles: 7-inch

MOTOWN ... 3-5 74

LPs: 10/12-inch

CBS ... 5-8 88
CAPITOL ... 5-8 80-82
ELEKTRA ... 5-8 81-82
FIRE-SIGN (87001 "Rock City") ... 15-25 78
MOTOWN ... 8-10 74
QUALITY/RFC ... 5-8 84

RIOT SQUAD

Singles: 7-inch

HBR ... 4-8 67
REPRISE ... 4-8 66
ROULETTE ... 4-8 65

RIP CHORDS — P&R '63

Singles: 7-inch

COLUMBIA (42687 "Here I Stand") ... 10-15 63
COLUMBIA (42812 "Gone") ... 10-15 63
(Black vinyl.)
COLUMBIA (42812 "Gone") ... 20-30 63
(Colored vinyl. Promotional issue only.)
COLUMBIA (42921 "Hey Little Cobra") ... 10-15 63
(Black vinyl.)
COLUMBIA (42921 "Hey Little Cobra") ... 20-30 63
(Colored vinyl. Promotional issue only.)
COLUMBIA (43035 "Three Window Coupe") ... 10-15 64
(Black vinyl.)
COLUMBIA (43035 "Three Window Coupe") ... 20-30 64
(Colored vinyl. Promotional issue only.)
COLUMBIA (43093 "One-Piece, Topless Bathing Suit") ... 10-15 64
COLUMBIA (43221 "Don't Be Scared") ... 10-15 64
COLUMBIA (3-42000 series) ... 10-20 63
(Compact 33 singles.)

Picture Sleeves

COLUMBIA (42687 "Here I Stand") ... 15-25 63
(Promotional issue only.)
COLUMBIA (42812 "Gone") ... 15-25 63

LPs: 10/12-inch

COLUMBIA (2151 "Hey Little Cobra") ... 25-35 64
(Monaural.)
COLUMBIA (2216 "Three Window Coupe") ... 30-40 64
(Monaural.)
COLUMBIA (8951 "Hey Little Cobra") ... 25-35 64
(Stereo.)
COLUMBIA (9016 "Three Window Coupe") ... 30-40 64
(Stereo.)
Members: Bruce Johnston; Terry Melcher; Phil Stewart; Ernie Bringas; Steve Barri; Phil Sloan; Glen Campbell; Hal Blaine; Tommy Tedesco.
Also see BRUCE & TERRY
Also see CAMPBELL, Glen
Also see FANTASTIC BAGGYS
Also see MIKE & DEAN
Also see ROGUES
Also see TEDESCO, Tommy

RIP TIDES

Singles: 7-inch

CHALLENGE ... 10-15 59-61

RIP TIDES

Singles: 7-inch

CAPITOL ... 3-5 79
EPIC ... 3-5 77

RIP-CHORDS

Singles: 78 rpm

ABCO ... 100-200 56

Singles: 7-inch

ABCO (105 "I Love You the Most") ... 250-500 56
(Black vinyl.)
ABCO (105 "I Love You the Most") ... 500-1000 56
(Red vinyl.)

RIP-CHORDS

Singles: 7-inch

M.M.I. (1236 "I Laughed So Hard") ... 150-250 58

RIPERTON, Minnie — LP '74

Singles: 12-inch

EPIC ... 4-8 77

Singles: 7-inch

CAPITOL ... 3-5 79-81
EPIC ... 3-5 74-77
GRT ... 3-5 72
JANUS ... 3-5 75-76

LPs: 10/12-inch

ACCORD ... 5-8 82
CAPITOL ... 5-10 79-81
EPIC ... 10-12 74-77
51 WEST ... 5-8 80s
GRT ... 10-15 70
JANUS ... 8-12 74
Also see DAVIS, Andrea
Also see JONES, Quincy
Also see RAELETTES
Also see ROTARY CONNECTION

RIPLEY COTTON CHOPPERS

Singles: 78 rpm

SUN (190 "Silver Bells") ... 1000-2000 53

RIPP TIDES

Singles: 7-inch

SURF WAX (105 "Wild Surf") ... 3-6 81

RIPPER

LPs: 10/12-inch

IRON WORKS (1007 "And the Dead Shall Rise") ... 10-15 87
(Picture disc.)

RIPPINGTONS Featuring Russ Freeman — LP '88

LPs: 10/12-inch

GRP ... 5-8 89
PASSPORT ... 5-8 88
Member: Steve Reid.

RIPPLE — P&R/R&B '73

Singles: 7-inch

GRC ... 3-5 73-75
SALSOUL ... 3-5 77-78

LPs: 10/12-inch

GRC ... 8-10 74
SALSOUL ... 5-8 77

RIPPLE BLAST SINGERS & BAND

LPs: 10/12-inch

POWER ... 10-15 64

RIPPLES

Singles: 7-inch

ABNAK ... 5-8 65
Member: Bobby Clark.
Also see CLARK, Bobby

RIPPLES

Singles: 7-inch

BOND (1479 "Please Let Me Love You") ... 300-500

RIPPLES & WAVES PLUS MICHAEL

(Jackson Five)

Singles: 7-inch

STEELTOWN (688 "Let Me Carry Your School Books") ... 25-50 69
(Mono. "Steeltown" is in all upper case letters on label.)
STEELTOWN (688 "Let Me Carry Your School Books") ... 50-75 69
(Stereo. "Steeltown" is in upper and lower case letters.)
Also see JACKSONS

RIPPY, Rodney Allen

LPs: 10/12-inch

BELL ... 8-12 74

RIPTIDES

Singles: 7-inch

SIDEWALK ... 8-12 66

RISE

Singles

AZRA (45-55 "Becky") ... 15-20 81
(Square picture disc with Asian girl photo.)
AZRA (45-55 "Becky") ... 10-15 81
(Square picture disc, shows Hollywood scene.)

RISE & SHINE

Singles: 7-inch

MONOLITH ... 5-10 72
Also see JOHNSON, Debb

RISERS

LPs: 10/12-inch

IMPERIAL (9269 "She's a Bad Motorcycle") ... 20-30 64
(Monaural.)
IMPERIAL (12269 "She's a Bad Motorcycle") ... 20-30 64
(Stereo.)

RISHARD, Rod — C&W '83

Singles: 7-inch

SOUNDWAVES ... 3-4 83-84

RISING SONS

Singles: 7-inch

AMY ... 5-10 65

RISING SONS

Singles: 7-inch

COLUMBIA (43534 "Candy Man") ... 15-25 66
Members: Taj Mahal; Ed Cassidy; Ry Cooder; Kevin Kelly; Gary Marker; Jesse Lee Kincade.
Also see COODER, Ry
Also see SPIRIT
Also see TAJ MAHAL

RISING STORM

LPs: 10/12-inch

ARF ARF (007 "Alive in Anover Again") ... 75-100 83
(Numbered edition of 1,000 copies.)
REMNANT (3571 "Calm Before . . .the Rising Storm") ... 800-1200 66
STANTON PARK (001 "Calm Before . . .the Rising Storm") ... 8-10 91
(Reissued using original cover art.)
Members: Tony Thompson; Todd Cohen; Bob Cohan; Tom Scheft; Charlie Rockwell; Rich Weinberg.

RISING SUNS

Singles: 7-inch

SULLY ... 5-10 65

RIS-KAYS

Singles: 7-inch

HI-G LO-C ... 4-6 64

RITA & TIERRAS

Singles: 7-inch

DORE (783 "Gone with the Wind Is My Love") ... 75-125 67

RITCHARD, Cyril — LP '61

LPs: 10/12-inch

RIVERSIDE ... 8-15 61-62

RITCHIE, John

Singles: 7-inch

20TH FOX (269 "Gone, Gone, Gone") ... 20-30 61

RITCHIE, Little Joe

LPs: 10/12-inch

BRUNSWICK ... 10-15 68

RITCHIE, Tony

Singles: 7-inch

GNP ... 4-8 68

RITCHIE FAMILY — P&R/R&B/LP '75

Singles: 12-inch

MARLIN ... 4-8 76
RCA ... 4-6 82

Singles: 7-inch

CASABLANCA ... 3-5 79-80
MARLIN ... 3-5 76-78
RCA ... 3-4 82-83
20TH FOX ... 3-5 75

LPs: 10/12-inch

CASABLANCA ... 5-10 79-80
MARLIN ... 5-10 76-78
RCA ... 5-8 82
20TH FOX ... 5-10 75

RITENOUR, Lee — LP '77

Singles: 7-inch

ELEKTRA ... 3-4 81-82
EPIC ... 3-5 76-80

Picture Sleeves

ELEKTRA ... 3-4 81

LPs: 10/12-inch

ELEKTRA ... 5-8 78-84
EPIC ... 5-10 76-80
GRP ... 5-8 85
JVC ... 5-10 78
MFSL (147 "Captain Fingers") ... 20-30 85
MUSICIAN ... 5-8 82
Also see ANGELO
Also see FOURPLAY
Also see GRUSIN, Dave, & Lee Ritenour

RITES

Singles: 7-inch

DECCA (32218 "Things") ... 10-20 67

RITES OF SPRING

Singles: 7-inch

PARKWAY (109 "Why") ... 15-25 66

RITTER, Dewey

Singles: 7-inch

SHOESTRING ... 8-12

RITTER, Tex — C&W/P&R '44

(With the Texans; with Plainsmen)

Singles: 78 rpm

CAPITOL ... 5-10 44-57
CHAMPION ... 10-20 30s

CONQUEROR....10-20 30s
DECCA....5-10 30s-41
U.A. ("High Noon Ballad—Do Not Forsake Me")....30-40 52
(Single-sided disc. Promotional issue only.)
Singles: 7-inch
CAPITOL (1100 thru 3900 series)..10-20 50-58
(Purple labels.)
CAPITOL (2000 thru 4000 series)..... 3-8 68-76
(Orange labels.)
CAPITOL (4000 thru 5900 series)... 5-15 58-67
CAPITOL (10485 "High Noon")......25-35 52
(Single-sided disc. Promotional issue only.)
Picture Sleeves
CAPITOL.... 5-10 68
EPs: 7-inch
CAPITOL (Except 431)....10-20 59-60
CAPITOL (431 "Tex Ritter Sings")....20-40 53
LPs: 10/12-inch
ALBUM GLOBE.... 5-8 80s
BUCKBOARD.... 5-8 80s
CAPITOL (213 thru 467).... 8-12 69-71
CAPITOL (971 "Songs from the Western Screen")....25-40 58
CAPITOL (1100 "Psalms")....20-30 59
CAPITOL (T-1292 "Blood on the Saddle")....15-25 60
(Monaural.)
CAPITOL (ST-1292 "Blood on the Saddle")....15-30 60
(Stereo.)
CAPITOL (SM-1292 "Blood on the Saddle").... 5-10 78
CAPITOL (1623 thru 2800)....10-20 61-68
CAPITOL (W-1562 "The Lincoln Hymns")....25-30 61
(Monaural.)
CAPITOL (SW-1562 "The Lincoln Hymns")....30-35 61
(Stereo.)
CAPITOL (4004 "Cowboy Favorites")....50-75 53
(10-inch LP.)
CORONET.... 8-12 60s
HILLTOP....10-15 60s
LA BREA (8036 "Jamboree")....30-40 62
PICKWICK/HILLTOP.... 6-12 66-68
PREMIER.... 5-10
SHASTA.... 8-12 60s
SPIN-O-RAMA.... 8-12 60s
Session: Rio Grande River Boys.
Also see KENTON, Stan, & Tex Ritter

RITTER, Tex / Merle Travis
Singles: 7-inch
CAPITOL (40143 "Fort Worth Jail"/"Sioux City Sue")....20-35 50s
(One 45 from *Cowboy Hit Parade*, Capitol album ADF-4000, a multi-disc set. At this time, we lack the titles and artists for the other records in what we presume to be a boxed set. Probably also issued on 78 rpm.)
Also see RITTER, Tex
Also see TRAVIS, Merle

RITTERBUSH, Bob
Singles: 78 rpm
DECCA (30285 "Raindrop")....10-15 57
Singles: 7-inch
DECCA (30285 "Raindrop")....10-15 57

RITUAL
Singles: 7-inch
HASTLE (1306 "Speed Freak")......25-35 69

RITUALS
Singles: 7-inch
ARWIN (120 "Girl in Zanzibar")....10-20 59
ARWIN (127 "This Is Paradise")....25-35 60
ARWIN (128 "Surfer's Rule")....10-20 60
Member: Arnie Ginsburg.
Also see JAN & ARNIE

RITZ
LPs: 10/12-inch
EPIC.... 5-10 79

RIVALS
Singles: 78 rpm
APOLLO (1166 "Don't Say You're Sorry")....25-50 50

RIVALS
Singles: 7-inch
DARRYL (722 "I Must See You Again")....25-50 57

RIVALS
Singles: 7-inch
JUNIOR (990 "Come with Me")..100-150 63
PUFF (1001 "Love Me")....30-35 62
PUFF (3912 "She's Mine")....20-25 62
TREYCO (401 "I'll Never Walk Alone")....20-30 63

RIVALS
(With T.J. Fowler's Band)
Singles: 7-inch
LU PINE (118 "It Gonna Work Out Fine")....15-25 64

RIVER CITY
(River City Street Band)
Singles: 7-inch
ENTERPRISE.... 3-5 72-73
LPs: 10/12-inch
ENTERPRISE.... 8-12 73

RIVER DEEP
Singles: 7-inch
BELL.... 4-6 69

RIVER ROVERS
Singles: 78 rpm
APOLLO....40-60 51
Singles: 7-inch
APOLLO (432 "Bald Headed Daddy")....100-200 51

RIVERA, Cholla, & Latin Soul Drives
Singles: 7-inch
COTIQUE.... 3-6 69

RIVERA, Hector *R&B '66*
Singles: 7-inch
BARRY....5-10 66
LPs: 10/12-inch
EPIC....10-20 61
WING....10-20 60

RIVERA, Johnny, & Tequila Brass
Singles: 7-inch
COTIQUE.... 3-6 68

RIVERA, Little Bobby, & Hemlocks
Singles: 78 rpm
FURY (1004 "Coralee")....75-125 57
Singles: 7-inch
FURY (1004 "Coralee")....75-125 57
(Red label.)
FURY (1004 "Coralee")....15-25 62
(Yellow label.)

RIVERA, Lucy
Singles: 7-inch
END (1041 "Make Me Queen")......10-15 59

RIVERA, Luis
Singles: 7-inch
FEDERAL.... 4-6 55
LPs: 10/12-inch
IMPERIAL....15-25 61
KING....20-30 59
Also see BAGBY, Doc / Luis Rivera

RIVERA, Ray
Singles: 7-inch
DECCA....5-10 60
MGM.... 4-8 60s
MERCURY.... 4-8 68
RCA.... 4-8 64
LPs: 10/12-inch
MERCURY....10-15 68

RIVERA, Scarlet
Singles: 7-inch
W.B.... 3-5 78
LPs: 10/12-inch
W.B....5-10 77-78
Also see DYLAN, Bob

RIVERBOAT SOUL BAND
Singles: 7-inch
MERCURY.... 4-8 68
LPs: 10/12-inch
MERCURY....10-15 68

RIVERMEN
Singles: 7-inch
LAKESIDE.... 4-8 65

RIVERS, Bob, Comedy Corp.
Singles: 7-inch
CRITIQUE.... 3-6 87
Picture Sleeves
CRITIQUE.... 4-8 87
LPs: 10/12-inch
CRITIQUE....5-10 87

RIVERS, Candy, & Falcons
Singles: 78 rpm
FLIP....50-75 54
Singles: 7-inch
FLIP (302 "You Are the Only One")....150-250 54
Also see FALCONS

RIVERS, Cliff
Singles: 7-inch
THANKS (1201 "True Lips")........75-125

RIVERS, Eddie *C&W '77*
(With the Carol Lee Singers)
Singles: 7-inch
CHARTA.... 3-5 77-89

RIVERS, Jack *C&W '48*
Singles: 78 rpm
CAPITOL.... 4-8 48

RIVERS, James
Singles: 7-inch
EIGHT BALL....5-10 67
KO4-8....8-12 65

RIVERS, Jimmy, Combo
Singles: 7-inch
BLUE EAGLE....5-10 60

RIVERS, Joan *LP '93*
LPs: 10/12-inch
BUDDAH....5-10 69
GEFFEN.... 5-8 83
W.B....10-15 65

RIVERS, Joey
Singles: 7-inch
PAT.... 4-8 63

RIVERS, Johnny *P&R/LP '64*
(Johnny Ramistella)
Singles: 7-inch
ATLANTIC.... 3-5 74
BIG TREE.... 3-5 77-78
CAPITOL....5-10 62-64
CHANCELLOR....8-12 61-62
CORAL....5-10 64
CUB (9047 "Everyday")....10-20 59
CUB (9058 "Answer Me, My Love")....10-15 60
DEE DEE (239 "Your First & Last Love")....15-25 59
EPIC.... 3-5 75-76
ERA....5-10 61
GONE (5026 "Baby Come Back")..20-30 58
GUYDEN (2003 "Hole in the Ground")....10-15 58
GUYDEN (2110 "Hole in the Ground")....4-8 64
IMPERIAL....4-8 64-70
MCA....3-4 84
MGM....5-8 64
RSO....3-5 80
RIVERAIRE (1001 "Don't Bug Me Baby")....10-20 59
ROULETTE (4565 "Baby Come Back")....8-12 64
ROWE/AMI....5-10 66
("Play Me" Sales Stimulator promotional issue.)
SOUL CITY (Except 008)....3-5 76-77
SOUL CITY (008 "Slow Dancing").....4-8 77
U.A. (Except 700 series)....3-5 71-73
U.A. (700 series)....4-8 64
Picture Sleeves
EPIC....3-5 75
IMPERIAL....5-10 64-69
U.A....3-5 71
LPs: 10/12-inch
ATLANTIC (7301 "Road")....8-10 74
BIG TREE....8-10 77
CAPITOL (T-2161 "Sensational Johnny Rivers")....35-50 64
(Monaural.)
CAPITOL (ST-2161 "Sensational Johnny Rivers")....50-75 64
(Stereo.)
CUSTOM....8-12 60s
EPIC....8-10 75
GUEST STAR....10-15 64
IMPERIAL....10-20 64-70
KOALA....5-10 79
LIBERTY....5-8 82
MCA....5-8 85
PICKWICK....8-10 70s
PRIORITY....5-8 83
RSO....5-10 80
SEARS (417 "Mr. Teenage")....20-30 60s
(Special Products issue for Sears stores)
SOUL CITY....8-10 77
SUNSET....8-12 67-69
U.A. (Except UAL, UAS & UXS series)....5-10 73-76
U.A. (UAL-3386 "Go Johnny Go")..20-25 64
(Monaural.)
U.A. (UAS-6386 "Go Johnny Go") 20-30 64
(Stereo.)
U.A. (UAS-5532 "Homegrown").....10-15 71
U.A. (UAS-5650 "L.A. Reggae")....10-15 72
U.A. (UXS-93 "Superpak")....12-15 72
Also see 4 SEASONS / Neil Sedaka / J Brothers / Johnny Rivers
Also see JONES, Tom / Freddie & Dreamers / Johnny Rivers
Also see RAMISTELLA, Johnny
Also see WILSON, Brian

RIVERS, Johnny / Steve Alaimo
LPs: 10/12-inch
CUSTOM....8-12 60s
Also see ALAIMO, Steve

RIVERS, Johnny / Jerry Cole
LPs: 10/12-inch
CROWN....10-20 64
Also see COLE, Jerry

RIVERS, Johnny / 4 Seasons / Jerry Butler / Jimmy Soul
LPs: 10/12-inch
GLADWYNNE (2004 "Shindig Hullabaloo Spectacular")....10-20 65
Also see BUTLER, Jerry
Also see 4 SEASONS
Also see SOUL, Jimmy

RIVERS, Johnny / Trini Lopez
LPs: 10/12-inch
CUSTOM....8-12 60s
Also see LOPEZ, Trini

RIVERS, Johnny / Ricky Nelson / Randy Sparks
LPs: 10/12-inch
MGM (E-4256 "Johnny Rivers, Ricky Nelson, Randy Sparks")....20-25 64
(Monaural.)
MGM (SE-4256 "Johnny Rivers, Ricky Nelson, Randy Sparks")....20-30 64
(Stereo.)
Also see NELSON, Ricky
Also see RASCALS / Buggs / Four Seasons / Johnny Rivers
Also see SIMON, Paul
Also see SPARKS, Randy

RIVERS, Johnny / Tremonts / Luke Gordon / Charlie Francis
LPs: 10/12-inch
CORONET (246 "Swingin' Shindig")....10-20 64
PREMIER (P-9037 "Swingin' Shindig")....10-20 64
(Monaural.)
PREMIER (PS-9037 "Swingin' Shindig")....15-25 64
(Stereo.)
Also see RIVERS, Johnny

RIVERS, Little Jimmy, & Tops
Singles: 7-inch
SWAN....10-15 61
Also see LITTLE JIMMY & TOPS

RIVERS, Mason
Singles: 7-inch
INDIE-GO (1 "Legend of Elvis Presley")....4-6 77

RIVERS, Norma
Singles: 7-inch
VASSAR....4-6

RIVERS, Tony, & Castaways
Singles: 7-inch
CONSTELLATION....8-12 64

RIVERS, Violet
Singles: 7-inch
DECCA....4-8 63

RIVIARES
Singles: 7-inch
ADEN (101 "The Bug")....15-25 64

RIVIERAS
Singles: 78 rpm
VICTORIA....5-10 52
Singles: 7-inch
VICTORIA....10-15 52

RIVIERAS
Singles: 7-inch
ALGONQUIN (718 "A Night to Remember")....150-250 58
(Reissued as by the Ravenairs.)

RIVIERAS *P&R '58*
Singles: 7-inch
COED (503 "Count Every Star").....25-35 58
(Red label.)
COED (503 "Count Every Star").....10-15 61
(Black label.)
COED (508 "Moonlight Serenade")....25-35 58
COED (513 "Our Love")....20-30 59
COED (522 "Since I Made You Cry")....20-30 59
COED (529 "Moonlight Cocktails").20-30 60
COED (538 "My Friend")....20-30 60
COED (542 "Easy to Remember") 20-30 60
COED (561 "Eldorado")....15-25 61
COED (592 "Moonlight Cocktails")...5-10 64
COLLECTABLES....3-4 80s
ERIC....3-4 70s
HOUSE of SOUNDS....4-8 60s
LOST-NITE....4-8 70s
LPs: 10/12-inch
POST....10-15 70s
Members: Ronald Cook; Homer Dunn; Andy Jones; Charles Allen.
Also see DUPREES / RIVIERAS
Also see FIVE BOB-O-LINKS

RIVIERAS *P&R/LP '64*
Singles: 7-inch
DELTA (3211 "California Sun")......10-20 63
(Canadian.)
LANA....4-6 60s
RIVIERA (1401 "California Sun"/"H.B. Goose Step")....5-10 63
RIVIERA (1401 "California Sun"/"Played On")....15-25 63
(1,000 made. Note different flip.)
RIVIERA (1402 "Little Donna")........8-10 64
RIVIERA (1403 "Rockin' Robin")......8-10 64
RIVIERA (1405 "Rip It Up"/"Whole Lotta Shakin'")....8-10 64
RIVIERA (1405 "Whole Lotta Shakin'"/"Lakeview Lane")....10-15 64
(Has a different take of *Lakeview Lane* than found on 1406.)
RIVIERA (1406 "Let's Go to Hawaii"/"Lakeview Lane")....8-10 65
RIVIERA (1407 "Somebody New")...8-10 65
(Credited to Rivieras, but actually by Bobby Whiteside.)
RIVIERA (1409 "Bug Juice")..........10-15 65
LPs: 10/12-inch
RIVIERA (701 "Campus Party")...50-100 64
USA (102 "Let's Have a Party")...50-100 64
Members: Marty Fortson; Paul Dennert; Otto Nuss; Doug Gean; Joe Pennell.
Also see WHITESIDE, Bobby

RIVIERAS
Singles: 7-inch
RILEY'S (369 "You Counter Feit Girl")....15-25 60s
Members: Joey King Fish; Jim Riley.

RIVILEERS
Singles: 78 rpm
BATON....30-50 53-57
Singles: 7-inch
BATON (200 "A Thousand Stars")....75-100 53
BATON (201 "Forever")....75-100 54
BATON (205 "Eternal")....75-100 54
BATON (207 "For Sentimental Reasons")....30-50 54
BATON (209 "Little Girl")....40-60 55
BATON (241 "A Thousand Stars") .20-30 57
DARK (241 "A Thousand Stars")...10-20 57
Members: Gene Pearson; Herb Crosby; Milt Edwards; Errol Lennard; Al Delaney; Pete LeMonier; Mel Dancey.
Also see EMBERS

RIVINGTONS *P&R '62*
Singles: 7-inch
A.R.E. AMERICAN (100 "All That Glitters")....15-25 64
BATON MASTER....5-10 67
COLUMBIA....5-10 66
J.D....3-5 76
LADERA....3-5
LIBERTY (55427 "Papa Oom Mow Mow")....10-20 62
LIBERTY (55513 "Kickapoo Joy Juice")....10-20 62
LIBERTY (55528 "Mama Oom Mow Mow")....10-20 62
LIBERTY (55553 "The Bird's the Word")....10-20 63
LIBERTY (55585 "The Shaky Bird")....10-20 63
LIBERTY (55610 "Cherry")....20-40 63
LIBERTY (55671 "Fairy Tales")....10-20 64
NEWMAN (605 "Just Got to Be Mine")....10-20
QUAN....5-10 67
RCA....5-10 69
REPRISE....5-10 64
VEE JAY....5-10 64-65
WAND....3-5 73
Picture Sleeves
LIBERTY (55553 "The Bird's the Word")....15-25 63
LPs: 10/12-inch
LIBERTY (3282 "Doin' the Bird")....50-60 63
(Monaural.)
LIBERTY (7282 "Doin' the Bird")....50-75 63
(Stereo.)
LIBERTY (10184 "Papa-Oom-Mow-Mow")....5-10 82
Members: Carl White; Al Frazier; Sonny Harris; Turner Wilson; Darryl White.
Also see CRENSHAWS
Also see EBBTIDES
Also see ELL, Carl, & Buddies
Also see HODGE, Gaynel
Also see LAMPLIGHTERS
Also see MELLOMOODS
Also see SHARPS
Also see TENDERFOOTS

RIVITS
LPs: 10/12-inch
ANTILLES....5-10 80

RIX, Jerry *R&B '77*
Singles: 7-inch
A.V.I....3-5 77

ROACH, Little Bobby, & Combo
Singles: 7-inch
FIRE (1013 "Mush")....10-20 60

ROACHES
Singles: 7-inch
GUYDEN....5-10 64

ROACHES
Singles: 7-inch
CROSSWAY....8-12 64

ROACHFORD *P&R/LP '89*
Singles: 7-inch
EPIC....3-4 89

ROAD *LP '70*
Singles: 7-inch
GOODTIME....4-6
KAMA SUTRA....4-6 68-71
RADIOACTIVE GOLD....3-5
LPs: 10/12-inch
KAMA SUTRA....10-15 69-71
Members: Jerry Hudson; Phil Hudson; Joseph Hesse; Jim Hesse; Ralph Parker; Nick Distefano; Don Jakubowski.
Also see HUDSON, Jerry
Also see MELLOW BRICK RODE

ROAD
Singles: 7-inch
NATURAL RESOURCES....3-5 72
LP: 10/12-inch
NATURAL RESOURCES....10-12 72
Members: Noel Redding; Rod Richards; Leslie Sampson.
Also see REDDING, Noel, Band

ROAD
Singles: 7-inch
BLUE ONION (106 "You Rub Me the Wrong Way")....15-25 69
LEMON LIME (101 "You Rub Me the Wrong Way")....10-20 69

ROAD APPLES *P&R '75*
Singles: 7-inch
MUMS....3-5 75
POLYDOR....3-5 75

ROAD DUCKS
Singles: 7-inch
EASTERN (Colored vinyl)....4-6

ROAD HOG & NEON CACTUS
Singles: 7-inch
EPIC (50305 "Presidential Debate")...4-6 76

ROAD HOME
LPs: 10/12-inch
DUNHILL....8-12 71

ROAD RUNNERS
(Roadrunners)
Singles: 7-inch
CHALLENGE (9197 "Dead Man")....8-10 63
FELSTED (8692 "Quasimoto")....15-25 63
FOOTNOTE (701 "El Skid")....20-30 60s
LONDON (5208 "Cute Little Colt") 15-25 64
MIRAMAR (116 "I'll Make It Up to You")....10-15 65
MOROCCO (001 "Goodbye")....10-15 66
REPRISE (0418 "I'll Make It Up to You")....10-15 65
LPs: 10/12-inch
LONDON (381 "New Mustang")....40-60 64
(Monaural.)
LONDON (3381 "New Mustang")...50-75 64
(Stereo.)
Members: John Youngblood; Dave Scheilbach; Jerry Schillinger; Charles Casper; Gary Usher.
Also see PAXTON, Gary
Also see USHER, Gary

ROAD RUNNERS
Singles: 7-inch
CHAN (111 "Little Pig")....25-35 64

COMMERCE (560 "Little Pig")......15-25 64

ROAD RUNNERS
Singles: 7-inch
MICHIGAN NICKEL (003 "Roadrunner Walk")......10-20 65

ROAD RUNNERS
Singles: 7-inch
CHAMP (3402 "It's So Hard")......10-20 65
RAYNARD (10031 "It's So Hard")..10-20 65
Members: Jimmy Dentici; Kenny Jablonski; Rudy Villasenor; Dave Frashenski; Mike Kowaleski; Richie Rendzik; Tom Fabre; Kenny Rogers; Doug Schanning.
Also see BOGIS CHIMES

ROAD SHOW
Singles: 7-inch
W.B. 4-6 69

ROADCREW
Singles: 7-inch
MERCURY 3-5 75

ROADMAP
LPs: 10/12-inch
CHERRY 8-10 78

ROADMASTER
Singles: 7-inch
MERCURY 3-5 79
VILLAGE 3-5 76
LPs: 10/12-inch
MERCURY 5-10 78-80
VILLAGE 5-10 76-78

ROADRUNNERS
Singles: 7-inch
COLOSSUS......4-6 69

ROAD-RUNNERS
Singles: 7-inch
("Makin Out")......8-12 60s
(No label name or selection number used.)

ROADRUNNERS
Singles: 7-inch
PENNY (1485 "Roadrunner")......8-12

ROAD'S END
Singles: 7-inch
BRAHMA (621661 "Why")......10-20 66

ROADSTERS
Singles: 7-inch
DONNA (1390 "Mag Rims")......15-20 63
20TH FOX (486 "Drag")......10-15 64

ROAMERS
Singles: 78 rpm
SAVOY......15-20 55
Singles: 7-inch
SAVOY (1147 "I'll Never Get Over You")......25-35 55
SAVOY (1156 "Never Let Me Go")......25-35 55
Also see DILLARD, Varetta
Also see HARRISON, Wilbert

ROAMERS
Singles: 7-inch
APPRO......5-8 64

ROAMERS / Jalopy Five see JALOPY FIVE

ROAMIN' TOGAS
Singles: 7-inch
LIGHTNING (101 "Bar the Door")...20-30 67

ROB BASE & D.J. EZ-Rock *P&R/R&B/LP '88*
(Rob Base)
Singles: 7-inch
PROFILE......3-4 88-89
Picture Sleeves
PROFILE......3-4 89
LPs: 10/12-inch
PROFILE......5-8 88

ROB ROYS
(Rob & Roy)
Singles: 7-inch
COLUMBIA......5-10 60-61

ROB ROYS
Singles: 7-inch
ACCENT (1213 "Do You Girl")......5-10 67
ACCENT (1216 "It's Wrong")......5-10 67

ROB ROYS (Featuring Norman Fox): see FOX, Norman

ROBB, Dee
(With the Robbins)
Singles: 7-inch
ARGO (5439 "The Prom")......5-10 63
SCORE (1006 "Say That Thing")......5-10 64
Also see ROBBS

ROBB, Johnny
Singles: 7-inch
FLAME......8-12 59

ROBBE, Warren
Singles: 7-inch
MYSTIC (811 "Single Man")......75-125

ROBBER, Robby, & Hi Jackers
LPs: 10/12-inch
PREMIER......10-20 60s
SPINORAMA......10-20 62
Members: Bob Gibson; Steve Barnes; Joey Grant.

ROBBIE & JOE
Singles: 7-inch
GREAT......4-8 62

ROBBIE & REVELATIONS
Singles: 7-inch
DECCA......5-10 65

ROBBIN, Bill
(With the Blue Jays)
Singles: 7-inch
PINK......10-15 60
Also see ROBIN, Bill, & Blue Jays

ROBBIN, Mark
Singles: 7-inch
GROOVE 4-8 65

ROBBINS
Singles: 7-inch
CASHMERE......5-10 59
REDHEAD......5-10 59

ROBBINS, Billy
Singles: 78 rpm
DIG......10-20 56
Singles: 7-inch
DIG (127 "Baby Please Come Home")......20-30 56

ROBBINS, Cheri
Singles: 7-inch
ACTION......4-8 61
Also see BRAGG, Doug, & Cheri Robbins

ROBBINS, Christopher
Singles: 7-inch
RCA......4-8 66-67

ROBBINS, Dennis *C&W '87*
Singles: 7-inch
MCA......3-4 87
Also see BILLY HILL

ROBBINS, Eddie
Singles: 7-inch
DAVID......10-20 61
POWER (214 "A Girl Like You")....50-75 57

ROBBINS, Hargus "Pig" *C&W '79*
Singles: 7-inch
ELEKTRA......3-5 79
Also see BANDY, Moe
Also see LEE, Bobby
Also see NASHVILLE SUPERPICKERS

ROBBINS, James / Roy Wright
Singles: 7-inch
MICA (2016 "I Can't Please You") .25-35 60s
Also see ROBINS, James

ROBBINS, Jenny *C&W '78*
Singles: 7-inch
EL DORADO......3-5 78

ROBBINS, Marty *C&W '52*
(With the Ray Conniff Orchestra & Chorus)
Singles: 78 rpm
COLUMBIA (20965 thru 21324)......15-25 52-54
COLUMBIA (21351 thru 21545)......20-30 54
COLUMBIA (21352 thru 21414)......10-20 54-55
COLUMBIA (40000 thru 41000 series)......20-50 56-58
Singles: 7-inch
COLUMBIA (02000 & 03000 series)..3-4 81-83
COLUMBIA (10305 thru 11425)......3-5 76-81
COLUMBIA (20965 thru 21324)......20-30 52-54
COLUMBIA (21351 "That's All Right")......30-50 54
COLUMBIA (21352 thru 21414)......15-25 54-55
COLUMBIA (21446 "Maybellene") 30-50 55
COLUMBIA (21461 "Pretty Mama")......30-50 55
COLUMBIA (21477 "Tennessee Toddy")......30-50 56
COLUMBIA (21508 "Singing the Blues")......25-35 56
COLUMBIA (21545 "Singing the Blues")......10-20 56
COLUMBIA (30589 "Big Iron")......20-40 60
(Compact 33 stereo.)
COLUMBIA (31749 "Little Rich Girl")......20-40 62
(Compact 33 stereo.)
COLUMBIA (31751 "Kinda Halfway Feel")......20-40 62
(Compact 33 stereo.)
COLUMBIA (33013 "El Paso")......20-40 61
(Compact 33 stereo.)
COLUMBIA (40679 "Long Tall Sally")......30-50 56
COLUMBIA (40706 "Respectfully Miss Brooks")......30-50 56
COLUMBIA (40815 thru 41408)......8-15 57-59
COLUMBIA (41511 thru 43770)......4-8 59-66
COLUMBIA (43845 thru 45775)......3-6 67-73
DECCA......4-6 72
MCA......3-5 73-75
PALAMINO......100-200 72
(Title and selection number not known.)
Picture Sleeves
COLUMBIA (40815 thru 41408)......10-30 57-59
COLUMBIA (41511 thru 43770)......5-15 59-66
EPs: 7-inch
COLUMBIA (1785 "Marty Robbins")......20-40 56
COLUMBIA (2116 "Singing the Blues")......20-40 56
COLUMBIA (2134 "A White Sport Coat")......20-30 57
COLUMBIA (2153 "Marty Robbins")......15-25 56
COLUMBIA (2808 "Marty Robbins")......20-30 57
COLUMBIA (2814 "Marty Robbins")......10-20 58
COLUMBIA (9020 "R.F.D.")......10-15 64
(Stereo juke box issue.)
COLUMBIA (9761/9762/9763 "The Song of Robbins")......10-20 57
(Price is for any of three volumes.)
COLUMBIA (10000 thru 14000 series)......10-20 57-60
LPs: 10/12-inch
ARTCO (110 "Best of Marty Robbins")......40-50 73
(Covers shows 110 but label has 644.)
CBS (19738 "Cause I Love You")......5-10 84
CANDLELITE......8-12 77
COLUMBIA (15 "Marty's Country")......10-15 69
COLUMBIA (31 "Open-End Columbia Artists Interviews")......35-50 60s
(Promotional issue only.)
COLUMBIA (32 "Columbia Artists Interviews with Frank Jones")......50-75
(Includes 42-page booklet. Promotional issue only.)
COLUMBIA (237 "Saddle Tramp")......25-35 66
(Columbia Record Club issue.)
COLUMBIA (445 "Bend in the River")......35-45 68
(Columbia Record Club issue.)
COLUMBIA (890 "Marty Robbins Gold")......8-10 75
COLUMBIA (976 "The Song of Robbins")......25-45 57
COLUMBIA (1087 "Song of the Islands")......25-45 57
COLUMBIA (1189 "Marty Robbins")......25-45 58
COLUMBIA (1256 "Return of the Gunfighter")......15-20 69
(Columbia "Country Star" series.)
COLUMBIA (1325 "Marty's Greatest Hits")......15-25 59
(Monaural.)
COLUMBIA (1349 "Gunfighter Ballads and Trail Songs")......15-25 59
(Monaural.)
COLUMBIA (1481 "More Gunfighter Ballads and Trail Songs")......15-25 60
(Monaural.)
COLUMBIA (1599 "Marty's Greatest Hits")......15-20 69
(Columbia "Country Star" series issue.)
COLUMBIA (1635 "More Greatest Hits")......15-25 61
(Monaural.)
COLUMBIA (1666 "Just a Little Sentimental")......15-25 61
(Monaural.)
COLUMBIA (1801 "Marty After Midnight")......40-50 62
(Monaural.)
COLUMBIA (1855 "Portrait of Marty")......25-35 62
(With bonus portrait of Marty. Monaural.)
COLUMBIA (1855 "Portrait of Marty")......15-25 62
(Without bonus portrait of Marty. Monaural.)
COLUMBIA (1918 "Devil Woman")......15-20 62
(Monaural.)
COLUMBIA (2016 "The Heart of Marty Robbins")......80-100 69
(Columbia "Country Star" series issue.)
COLUMBIA (2040 "Hawaii's Calling Me")......20-30 62
(Monaural.)
COLUMBIA (2072 "Return of the Gunfighter")......15-20 63
(Monaural.)
COLUMBIA (2167 "Island Woman")......25-35 64
(Monaural.)
COLUMBIA (2220 "R.F.D.")......25-35 64
(Monaural.)
COLUMBIA (2304 "Turn the Lights Down Low")......20-40 65
(Monaural.)
COLUMBIA (2448 "What God Has Done")......15-20 65
(Monaural.)
COLUMBIA (2527 "The Drifter")....10-20 66
(Monaural.)
COLUMBIA (2563 "What God Has Done")......15-20 69
(Columbia "Country Star" series issue.)
COLUMBIA (2601 "Rock'n Roll'n Robbins")......500-750 56
(10-inch LP.)
COLUMBIA (2645 "My Kind of Country")......15-20 67
(Monaural.)
COLUMBIA (2725 "Tonight Carmen")......10-20 67
(Monaural.)
COLUMBIA (2735 "Christmas with Marty Robbins")......20-30 67
(Monaural.)
COLUMBIA (2762 "More Gunfighter Ballads and Trail Songs")......15-20 69
(Columbia "Country Star" series issue.)
COLUMBIA (2817 "By The Time I Get to Phoenix")......20-30 68
(Monaural.)
COLUMBIA (3557 "The Drifter")....15-20 69
(Columbia "Country Star" series issue.)
COLUMBIA (3867 "My Kind of Country")......15-20 69
(Columbia "Country Star" series issue.)
COLUMBIA (5489 "Tonight Carmen")......15-20 69
(Columbia "Country Star" series issue.)
COLUMBIA (5498 "Christmas with Marty Robbins")......15-20 69
(Columbia "Country Star" series issue.)
COLUMBIA (5812 "Marty")......20-40 72
(Five-LP set. Columbia Special Products issue.)
COLUMBIA (6994 "I Walk Alone") 15-20 69
(Columbia "Country Star" series issue.)
COLUMBIA (CS-8158 "Gunfighter Ballads and Trail Songs")......15-25 59
(Stereo.)
COLUMBIA (PC-8158 "Gunfighter Ballads and Trail Songs")......5-10
COLUMBIA (CS-8272 "More Gunfighter Ballads and Trail Songs")......15-25 60
(Stereo.)
COLUMBIA (PC-8272 "More Gunfighter Ballads and Trail Songs")......5-10
COLUMBIA (CS-8435 "More Greatest Hits")......15-20 61
(Stereo.)
COLUMBIA (PC-8435 "More Greatest Hits")......5-10
COLUMBIA (8466 "Just a Little Sentimental")......15-25 61
(Stereo.)
COLUMBIA (8601 "Marty After Midnight")......25-35 62
(Stereo.)
COLUMBIA (8639 "Marty's Greatest Hits")......15-25 62
(Stereo.)
COLUMBIA (8655 "Portrait of Marty")......25-35 62
(With bonus portrait of Marty. Stereo.)
COLUMBIA (8655 "Portrait of Marty")......15-25 62
(Without bonus portrait. Stereo.)
COLUMBIA (8718 "Devil Woman")......15-20 62
(Stereo.)
COLUMBIA (8840 "Hawaii's Calling Me")......20-30 62
(Stereo.)
COLUMBIA (8872 "Return of the Gunfighter")......15-20 63
(Stereo.)
COLUMBIA (8976 "Island Woman")......35-40 64
(Stereo.)
COLUMBIA (CS-9020 "R.F.D.")......25-35 64
(Stereo.)
COLUMBIA (CSRP-9020 "R.F.D.") .8-10
(Columbia Special Products issue.)
COLUMBIA (9104 "Turn the Lights Down Low")......20-40 65
(Stereo.)
COLUMBIA (CS-9248 "What God Has Done")......15-20 65
(Stereo.)
COLUMBIA (ACS-9248 "What God Has Done")......5-10
(Columbia Special Products issue.)
COLUMBIA (9327 "The Drifter")....10-20 66
(Stereo.)
COLUMBIA (9421 "The Song of Robbins")......30-40 67
(Stereo.)
COLUMBIA (9445 "My Kind of Country")......15-25 67
(Stereo.)
COLUMBIA (9525 "Tonight Carmen")......10-20 67
(Stereo.)
COLUMBIA (9535 "Christmas with Marty Robbins")......10-20 67
(Stereo.)
COLUMBIA (9617 "By the Time I Get to Phoenix")......10-15 68
(Stereo.)
COLUMBIA (9725 "I Walk Alone") 10-15 68
COLUMBIA (9811 "It's a Sin")......20-30 69
COLUMBIA (9978 "My Woman, My Woman, My Wife")......8-12 70
COLUMBIA (10022 thru 10579)......8-10 73-75
(Columbia's Limited Edition series. All Have an "LE" prefix.)
COLUMBIA (10980 "Christmas with Marty Robbins")......15-20 70
(Columbia Special Products issue.)
COLUMBIA (11221 "By the Time I Get to Phoenix")......5-10 80s
(Columbia Special Products issue.)
COLUMBIA (11222 "Marty's Greatest Hits")......5-10 75
COLUMBIA (11311 "By the Time I Get to Phoenix")......5-10 70
(Columbia Special Products issue.)
COLUMBIA (11513 "By the Time I Get to Phoenix")......15-20 71
(Columbia Special Products issue.)
COLUMBIA (12416 "Marty Robbins' Own Favorites")......12-15 74
(Special Products issue for Vaseline Hair Tonic.)
COLUMBIA (13358 "Christmas with Marty Robbins")......5-10 72
(Columbia Special Products issue.)
COLUMBIA (14035 "Legendary Music Man")......8-12 77
(Columbia Special Products issue.)
COLUMBIA (14613 "Best of Marty Robbins")......5-10 78
(Columbia Special Products issue.)
COLUMBIA (15594 "Number One Cowboy")......5-10 81
(Columbia Special Products issue.)
COLUMBIA (15812 "Marty Robbins' Best")......5-10 82
(Columbia Special Products issue.)
COLUMBIA (16561 "Reflections")....5-10 82
(Columbia Special Products issue.)
COLUMBIA (16578 "Classics")......15-20 83
(Three-LP set. Columbia Special Products issue.)
COLUMBIA (16914 "Country Classics")......5-10 83
(Columbia Special Products issue.)
COLUMBIA (17120 "Sincerely")......5-10 83
(Columbia Special Products issue.)
COLUMBIA (17136 "Forever Yours")......5-10 83
(Columbia Special Products issue.)
COLUMBIA (17137 "That Country Feeling")......5-10 83
(Columbia Special Products issue.)
COLUMBIA (17138 "Banquet of Songs")......5-10 83
(Columbia Special Products issue.)
COLUMBIA (17159 "The Great Marty Robbins")......5-10 83
(Columbia Special Products issue.)
COLUMBIA (17206 "The Legendary Marty Robbins")......5-10 83
(Columbia Special Products issue.)
COLUMBIA (17209 "Country Cowboy")......5-10 83
(Columbia Special Products issue.)
COLUMBIA (17367 "Song of the Islands")......5-10 83
(Columbia Special Products issue.)
COLUMBIA (17730 "Great Love Songs")......5-10 80s
(Columbia Special Products issue.)
COLUMBIA (30000 thru 40000 series)......5-12 70-86
DECCA......8-12 72
GUSTO/COLUMBIA......8-10 81
HARMONY (Except 31258)......8-15 69-72
HARMONY (31258 "Song of the Islands")......20-25 72
K-TEL......8-10 77
MCA......6-12 73-74
ORBIT......8-10 84
PICKWICK......5-10 70s
READER'S DIGEST (054 "Greatest Hits")......20-30 83
(Boxed, five-disc set.)
SUNRISE MEDIA......5-10 81
TIME-LIFE......5-10 81
WORD......5-10
Session: Ray Conniff Singers; Jordanaires; David Briggs; Bobby Braddock; Grady Martin; Bob Bishop; Bill Pursell; Buddy Spicher; Arlene Harden; Bobby Sykes.
Also see BISHOP, Bob
Also see BRADDOCK, Bobby
Also see BRIGGS, David
Also see CONNIFF, Ray
Also see EMERSON, Lee, & Marty Robbins
Also see HARDEN, Arlene
Also see JORDANAIRES
Also see PRUETT, Jeanne, & Marty Robbins
Also see PURSELL, Bill
Also see SMITH, Carl / Lefty Frizzell / Marty Robbins
Also see TUBB, Ernest

ROBBINS, Marty / Johnny Cash / Ray Price
LPs: 10/12-inch
COLUMBIA 8-10 70
Also see CASH, Johnny
Also see PRICE, Ray

ROBBINS, Marty Jr: see ROBBINS, Ronny

ROBBINS, Mel
(Mel "Pigue" Robbins)
Singles: 7-inch
ARGO (5340 "Save It")......75-100 59
MR. PEACOCK (103 "Fidgety")......10-20 61
WILDCAT (1001 "Go Ahead On")...10-20 61
LPs: 10/12-inch
SMASH......15-25 62

ROBBINS, Myrna
Singles: 7-inch
CUCA (1068 "Silver Wings")......10-20 61

ROBBINS, Nicky
Singles: 7-inch
STRAND......4-8 61

ROBBINS, Randy
Singles: 78 rpm
FLASH (103 "Sticky Stuff")......10-15 56
Singles: 7-inch
FLASH (103 "Sticky Stuff")......15-25 56

ROBBINS, Robbie
Singles: 7-inch
HEP (2001 "Hurry")......40-60 60s

ROBBINS, Rockie *R&B '79*
Singles: 7-inch
A&M......3-5 79-81
MCA......3-4 85
Picture Sleeves
A&M......3-5 80
LPs: 10/12-inch
A&M......5-10 80-81
MCA......5-8 85

ROBBINS, Ronny *C&W '78*
(Marty Robbins Jr.)
Singles: 7-inch
ARTIC......3-5 78-79
COLUMBIA......3-4 84
TRC......3-5 79
LPs: 10/12-inch
COLUMBIA......10-20 70
THUNDER......5-10 81

ROBBINS, Roy, & Availables
Singles: 7-inch
ACTION......5-10 66

ROBBINS, Sylvia
Singles: 7-inch
JUBILEE (5386 "Come Home")......5-10 60
SUE (106 "Our Love")......5-10 65

ROBBINS, Terri
Singles: 7-inch
WORLD ... 4-8 61

ROBBINS, Tracie
Singles: 7-inch
BRUNSWICK (55331 "That's What You Are to Me") ... 10-20 67
DECCA (31810 "What Was She Doing") ... 10-20 65

ROBBINS & PAXTON
Singles: 7-inch
RORI (704 "Teen Angel") ... 10-15 62

ROBBS LP '68
Singles: 7-inch
ABC ... 4-6 70-71
ATLANTIC ... 5-10 68
DUNHILL ... 4-8 69-70
MERCURY ... 5-10 66-67
Picture Sleeves
ABC ... 4-8 70
MERCURY ... 8-12 67
LPs: 10/12-inch
ABC (719 "Cherokee") ... 10-20 71
MERCURY (21130 "The Robbs") ... 20-25 67
(Monaural.)
MERCURY (61130 "The Robbs") ... 20-30 67
(Stereo.)
Members: David Donaldson; Robert Donaldson; George Donaldson; Dick Gonia; Dennis Sachse; Teddy Peplinski; Craig Krampf.
Also see CHEROKEE
Also see ROBB, Dee
Also see ROBBY & ROBINS
Also see TONY'S TYGERS / Skunks / Robbs

ROBBY & ROBINS
Singles: 7-inch
TODD (1089 "Surfer's Life") ... 15-25 63
Also see ROBBS

ROBBY & TEENS: see LYNN, Robby, & Teens

ROBE R&B '87
Singles: 7-inch
2000 AD ... 3-4 87

ROBERDS, Smokey
Singles: 7-inch
EPIC (10322 "Love Is the People's Choice") ... 4-8 68
Session: David Gates.
Also see GATES, David

ROBERSON BRO'S
Singles: 7-inch
VERL ("Wishing") ... 50-100 62
(No selection number used. First issued as by Walt, Percy & the Tracers.)
Members: Walt Roberson; Percy Roberson.
Also see WALT, PERCY & TRACERS

ROBERT & JIMMY
Singles: 7-inch
K ... 8-12 59

ROBERT & JOHNNY P&R/R&B '58
Singles: 78 rpm
OLD TOWN ... 15-25 56-57
Singles: 7-inch
ATLANTIC OLDIES SERIES ... 3-5 70s
COLLECTABLES ... 3-4 80s
OLD TOWN ... 12-25 56-62
SUE (792 "A Perfect Wife") ... 15-20 62
Members: Robert Carr; Johnny Mitchell.

ROBERT & JOHNNY / Fiestas
Singles: 7-inch
ATCO ... 3-5 80s
Also see FIESTAS
Also see ROBERT & JOHNNY

ROBERT & RANDY
Singles: 7-inch
HOLIDAY INN ... 4-8 60s

ROBERTA
Singles: 7-inch
LU-CEE (103 "I'll Try") ... 100-200

ROBERTA LEE: see LEE, Roberta

ROBERTINO LP '62
Singles: 7-inch
KAPP ... 4-6 61
LPs: 10/12-inch
KAPP ... 10-20 61-62

ROBERTO
(Roberto Ketally)
Singles: 7-inch
CORAL ... 3-6
DEESON (103 "Rockin' with Roberto") ... 15-25 58

ROBERTS, Allen
Singles: 7-inch
CHEVELL ... 5-10 64
KNIGHT ... 8-12 59

ROBERTS, Andy
LPs: 10/12-inch
AMPEX ... 8-12 70-71
Also see LIVERPOOL SCENE
Also see SCAFFOLD

ROBERTS, Art
Singles: 7-inch
IMPERIAL ... 10-20 58

ROBERTS, Austin P&R '72
Singles: 7-inch
ARISTA ... 3-5 78
CHELSEA ... 3-5 72-75
COLLECTABLES ... 3-4 80s
GUSTO ... 3-4 80s
PHILIPS ... 4-6 68-71
PRIVATE STOCK ... 3-5 75-76
LPs: 10/12-inch
CHELSEA ... 8-12 72-73
PRIVATE STOCK ... 6-10 75

ROBERTS, Bill, & Internationals
Singles: 7-inch
GARRETT ... 8-12 67

ROBERTS, Bobby
(With the Ravons; Ravons with Bobby Roberts)
Singles: 7-inch
CAMEO ... 8-12 64
GMA ... 10-20 60s
HUT (4707 "Hop, Skip & Jump") ... 100-200 58
SKY (101 "Big Sandy") ... 250-350 58

ROBERTS, Bruce
Singles: 7-inch
ELEKTRA ... 3-5 78

ROBERTS, Buddy, & HiLiters
Singles: 7-inch
BONANZA (689 "Ding Dong") ... 15-25 60

ROBERTS, Chuck
Singles: 7-inch
CAPITOL ... 5-10 60
DOLTON ... 4-8 61

ROBERTS, Danny
Singles: 7-inch
HONEY BEE ... 3-5 77

ROBERTS, Dave
Singles: 7-inch
PL (14 "Wonderous") ... 150-250 58

ROBERTS, Dave, & Kingtones
Singles: 7-inch
EUCALYPTUS ... 10-20 76
Also see KINGTONES

ROBERTS, Dennis
Singles: 7-inch
JERDEN ... 4-8 65
YUCCA (133 "Come On") ... 10-20 61

ROBERTS, Derrik
Singles: 7-inch
ROULETTE (4656 "There Won't Be Any Snow, Christmas in the Jungle") ... 10-20 66

ROBERTS, Don "Red"
Singles: 78 rpm
RAMA (230 "Only One") ... 30-50 57
Singles: 7-inch
RAMA (230 "Only One") ... 30-50 57

ROBERTS, Doug, & Stu Mitchell
Singles: 7-inch
FRANKIE (106 "Wild Kitten") ... 5-10 60s
Also see FIREBALLS
Also see MITCHELL, Stu

ROBERTS, Frank
Singles: 7-inch
IMPERIAL ... 4-8 66-67

ROBERTS, Frank, & Band
(Featuring Dallas Schachere)
Singles: 7-inch
NOLTA ... 5-10 61

ROBERTS, Gip
Singles: 7-inch
J.V.B. (29 "No One Monkey Goin' Ruin My Show") ... 30-50 58

ROBERTS, Hoot
Singles: 7-inch
CHOCO ... 4-8 68

ROBERTS, Howard
LPs: 10/12-inch
ARISTA ... 5-8
CAPITOL ... 10-20 63-66
COLUMBIA ... 8-10
IMPULSE ... 8-10 71-75

ROBERTS, Jack
Singles: 7-inch
JERDEN ... 4-8 63
RENDEZVOUS ... 5-10 60

ROBERTS, Jesse
Singles: 7-inch
GLENN ... 3-5 73

ROBERTS, Jerry
Singles: 7-inch
ABC-PAR ... 5-10 60
APT (27070 "Little Bitty Lover") ... 20-30 61
JERDEN ... 5-10 63

ROBERTS, Jerry, & Toppers
Singles: 7-inch
GAITY (165 "Hopelessly") ... 40-60 59
KAY BEE (2037 "Rendevous") ... 20-40 60s

ROBERTS, Joey
(Joey Roberts Jr.)
Singles: 7-inch
CAMEO ... 4-8 66

ROBERTS, John P&R/R&B '67
Singles: 7-inch
DUKE ... 4-8 67-69

ROBERTS, Judy, Band
Singles: 7-inch
INNER CIRCLE ... 3-5 80
PAUSA ... 3-4
Picture Sleeves
INNER CIRCLE ... 3-5 80
PAUSA ... 4-8
LPs: 10/12-inch
INNER CIRCLE ... 5-10 80

ROBERTS, Kenny
Singles: 7-inch
DECCA (30073 "Broken Teen-Age Heart") ... 10-20 58
Also see DOWN HOMERS

ROBERTS, Lance
Singles: 7-inch
DECCA (30955 "Gonnna Have Myself a Ball") ... 15-25 59
SUN (348 "Time Is Right") ... 10-20 60

ROBERTS, Lea R&B '69
Singles: 7-inch
MINIT ... 4-8 69
U.A. ... 3-5 74-75

ROBERTS, Lee, & Echoes
Singles: 7-inch
SPOTLIGHT (101 "School Days") ... 75-125

ROBERTS, Lenny
Singles: 7-inch
CHARTMAKER ... 4-8 66

ROBERTS, Lou
Singles: 7-inch
GENIE (101 "Rattle Snake Shake") ... 200-300 65

ROBERTS, Lou, & Marks
Singles: 7-inch
MGM (13347 "Gettin' Ready") ... 15-25 65

ROBERTS, Lucy
Singles: 7-inch
VIK (0201 "Leap Year Red") ... 10-20 60s

ROBERTS, Lynn, & Phantoms
Singles: 7-inch
ORIOLE (101 "I'll Be Around") ... 500-750 54
(Black vinyl.)
ORIOLE (101 "I'll Be Around") ... 1000-1500 54
(Colored vinyl.)
ROULETTE ... 8-12 61

ROBERTS, Marty
Singles: 7-inch

ROBERTS, Marty
(With Saxons)
Singles: 7-inch
ARC (8003 "Your Feets Too Big") 40-60 57
FLAME ("Tangle-Weed") ... 10-20 60
(Selection number not known.)

ROBERTS, Nicky
Singles: 7-inch
ARMOUR (3355 "Simpatica") ... 5-10 60
CINEMA (103 "Simpatica") ... 4-8 62

ROBERTS, Pat C&W '72
Singles: 7-inch
DOT ... 3-5 72-74

ROBERTS, Pernell
LPs: 10/12-inch
RCA ... 15-25 63

ROBERTS, Pete
Singles: 7-inch
RENDEZVOUS (124 "Hold Me") ... 4-8 60
(First issued as by Larry Bright.)
Also see BRIGHT, Larry

ROBERTS, Peter
Singles: 7-inch
LIZA ... 5-10 62
Also see HO-HOs

ROBERTS, Renee
Singles: 7-inch
NEW PHOENIX ... 8-12 62
STACY ... 5-10 64

ROBERTS, Rick
Singles: 7-inch
A&M ... 3-5 73
Also see FIREFALL

ROBERTS, Rockin' Robin
Singles: 7-inch
ETIQUETTE ... 10-15 61

ROBERTS, Rocky
(With the Airedales)
Singles: 7-inch
BRUNSWICK ... 5-10 67-68
ROULETTE ... 5-10 63-65
LPs: 10/12-inch
BRUNSWICK ... 10-20 68

ROBERTS, Roy
Singles: 7-inch
NINANDY (1011 "The Legend of Otis Redding") ... 20-30 68

ROBERTS, Sherman: see SHERMAN & NOTATIONS

ROBERTS, Skippy
Singles: 7-inch
LARK ... 8-10 59

ROBERTS, Sonny & Echoes
Singles: 7-inch
IMPALA (1001 "I'll Never Let You Go") ... 300-350 58

ROBERTS, Stan
Singles: 7-inch
DEB-LYN ... 4-8

ROBERTS, Vivian
Singles: 7-inch
VAULT ... 10-20 65

ROBERTS, Wayne
(Neil Bogart)
Singles: 7-inch
20TH FOX ... 10-15 66
Also see CONCORDS
Also see SCOTT, Neal

ROBERTSON, Don P&R '56
Singles: 78 rpm
CAPITOL ... 3-5 56-57
Singles: 7-inch
CAPITOL ... 4-8 56-59
MONUMENT ... 3-5 66-76
RCA ... 3-8 61-68
LPs: 10/12-inch
RCA ... 10-15 65
Also see ECHOES

ROBERTSON, Dot, & Lou Dinning
Singles: 78 rpm
DOT ... 5-10 57
Singles: 7-inch
DOT ... 5-10 57

ROBERTSON, Doug
(With the Good Guys)
Singles: 7-inch
JERDEN ... 5-10 64
UPTOWN ... 4-8 65

ROBERTSON, Jack C&W '88
Singles: 7-inch
SOUNDWAVES ... 3-4 88

ROBERTSON, Jeannie
Singles: 7-inch
DERBY (1004 "Memories") ... 15-20 63

ROBERTSON, Jessie Mae: see ROBINSON, Jessie Mae

ROBERTSON, Lester, & Upsetters
Singles: 7-inch
MONTEL ... 8-12 59

ROBERTSON, Oscar
Singles: 7-inch
FOUNTAIN ... 4-8 66

ROBERTSON, Robbie LP '87
Singles: 7-inch
GEFFEN ... 3-4 87
Picture Sleeves
GEFFEN ... 3-4 87
LPs: 10/12-inch
GEFFEN ... 5-8 87
Also see BAND

ROBERTSON, Ruby
LPs: 10/12-inch
ASNES ... 10-15

ROBERTSON, Texas Jim C&W '46
(With the Panhandle Punchers)
Singles: 78 rpm
RCA ... 5-10 46-50
EPs: 7-inch
CAMDEN ... 8-12
LPs: 10/12-inch
DESIGN ... 10-20 60s
GRAND PRIX ... 10-20 60s
INT'L AWARD ... 10-20 60s
STRAND (1016 "Texas Jim Robertson [Tales and Songs of the Old West]") ... 25-35 61

ROBERTSON, Walter
(Walter Robinson)
Singles: 78 rpm
FLAIR ... 50-75 54
Singles: 7-inch
FLAIR (1053 "Sputterin' Blues") ... 150-200 54
Also see ROBINSON BROTHERS

ROBEY P&R/D&D '85
Singles: 12-inch
SILVER BLUE ... 4-6 84-85
Singles: 7-inch
SILVER BLUE ... 3-5 84-85

ROBEY, Loretta C&W '77
Singles: 7-inch
SOUNDWAVES ... 3-5 77

ROBIC, Ivo P&R '59
Singles: 7-inch
LAURIE ... 4-8 59-60
PHILIPS ... 3-6 62

ROBIN
(Robin Ward)
Singles: 7-inch
DOT (16519 "Top 40 Blues") ... 5-10 63
Also see WARD, Robin

ROBIN
(Robin Abnor)
Singles: 7-inch
ABNAK ... 3-6 69
Also see JON & ROBIN

ROBIN, Bill, & Blue Jays
Singles: 7-inch
MGM ... 8-12 61
Also see ROBBIN, Bill

ROBIN, Cheri, & Stingrays
Singles: 7-inch
RIVERS ... 4-6

ROBIN, Cock: see COCK ROBIN

ROBIN, Don
Singles: 7-inch
JERDEN ... 8-12 64

ROBIN, Richie
Singles: 7-inch
GOLDISC ... 5-10 60
GONE (5083 "Strange Dreams") ... 10-15 59

ROBIN, Rocky
Singles: 7-inch
RAM ... 4-8

ROBIN, Ruth
Singles: 7-inch
TITAN ... 4-8 62

ROBIN, Tina P&R '61
Singles: 78 rpm
CORAL ... 5-10 57
Singles: 7-inch
CORAL ... 6-12 57-59
MERCURY ... 5-8 61-63
Picture Sleeves
CORAL (61822 "My Mammy") ... 10-20 57

ROBIN & BATMEN
Singles: 7-inch
DJ (670 "The Riddler") ... 10-20 67
SARA ("6614 "Batskinner") ... 10-20 66

ROBIN & CRUISER C&W '87
Singles: 7-inch
16TH AVE. ... 3-4 87
Members: Robin Gordon; Cruiser Gordon.

ROBIN & THREE HOODS
Singles: 7-inch
FAN JR. (1003 "I Wanta Do It") ... 15-25 66
(First issued as by Marrell's Marauders.)
FAN JR. (5678 "We the Living") ... 10-20 66
FAN JR (5680 "I Wanna Do It") ... 10-15 66
(Reissue of #1003.)
HOLLYWOOD (1110 "I Wanna Do It") ... 5-10 66
Members: Dave Reed; Jim Schwartz; Bob Bernhagen; Bruce Benson; Mike Warner.
Also see MARRELL'S MARAUDERS

ROBIN & COOL CATS
Singles: 7-inch
PUSSY CAT (501 "Give Me Your Love") ... 400-600

ROBIN & JO
Singles: 7-inch
A&M ... 3-5

ROBIN HOOD & MERRI MEN
Singles: 7-inch
DELSEY (303 " We Had a Quarrel") ... 30-40 65
MOHAWK (130 "Ellen") ... 20-30 60

ROBIN HOOD BRIANS
Singles: 7-inch
FRATERNITY (1012 "Papaga-Yo") ... 15-25 69
RBE (101 "Only One Heart") ... 10-15 60s

ROBIN HOODS
Singles: 7-inch
MERCURY ... 4-8 65-66

ROBINS R&B '50
(Robbins; with Maggie Hathaway)
Singles: 78 rpm
ALADDIN (3031 "Don't Like the Way You're Doing") ... 200-300 49
ATCO ... 25-50 55
CROWN ... 50-75 54
QUALITY ... 30-50 54
(Canadian.)
RCA ... 50-75 53
RECORDED in HOLLYWOOD (112 "Bayou Baby Blues") ... 150-250 51
RECORDED in HOLLYWOOD (121 "Falling Star") ... 150-250 51
RECORDED in HOLLYWOOD (150 "School Girl Blues") ... 150-250 51
SAVOY (726 "If It's So Baby") ... 50-75 50
SAVOY (732 "Turkey Hop") ... 50-75 50
SAVOY (738 "Our Romance Is Gone") ... 50-75 50
SAVOY (752 "There's Rain in My Eyes") ... 50-75 50
SAVOY (762 "I'm Through") ... 50-75 50
SCORE (4010 "Around About Midnight") ... 50-75 49
SPARK ... 30-50 54-55
WHIPPET ... 30-50 56-57
Singles: 7-inch
ARVEE (5001 "Just Like That") ... 15-25 60
ARVEE (5013 "Oh No!") ... 15-25 60
ATCO (6059 "Smokey Joe's Cafe") ... 30-50 55
CROWN (106 "I Made a Vow") .. 150-250 54
CROWN (120 "Key to My Heart") ... 150-250 54
GONE (5101 "Baby Love") ... 15-25 61
KNIGHT (2001 "Quarter to Twelve") ... 25-50 58
KNIGHT (2008 "It's Never Too Late") ... 50-75 58
QUALITY (1269 "Riot in Cell Block No. 9") ... 200-300 54
(Canadian.)
RCA (5175 "A Fool Such As I") .. 300-500 53
RCA (5271 "All Night Baby") ... 200-400 53
RCA (5434 "How Would You Know") ... 200-400 53
RCA (5486 "My Baby Done Told Me") ... 200-300 53
RCA (5489 "Ten Days in Jail") ... 100-200 53
RCA (5564 "Don't Stop Now") ... 100-200 53
SPARK (103 "Riot in Cell Block No. 9") ... 200-300 54

(Red label with silver print. Copies with yellow and black labels are '70s counterfeits.)
SPARK (107 "Framed") ... 200-300 54
SPARK (110 "If Teardrops Were Kisses") ... 200-300 55
SPARK (113 "One Kiss") ... 200-300 55
SPARK (116 "I Must Be Dreaming") ... 100-200 55
SPARK (122 "Smokey Joe's Cafe") ... 200-300 55
WHIPPET (100 "Cherry Lips") ... 75-100 56
WHIPPET (200 "Cherry Lips") ... 50-75 56
WHIPPET (201 "Hurt Me") ... 50-75 56
WHIPPET (203 "Since I First Met You") ... 50-75 56
WHIPPET (206 "A Fool in Love") ... 50-75 57
WHIPPET (208 "Every Night") ... 50-75 57
WHIPPET (211 "In My Dreams") ... 50-75 57
WHIPPET (212 "You Wanted Fun") ... 50-75 58

LPs: 10/12-inch

GNP ... 8-10 75
WHIPPET (703 "Rock 'N' Roll with the Robins") ... 500-750 58
Members: Ty Terrell; Bobby Nunn; Carl Gardner; Bill Richards; Grady Chapman; H.B. Barnum; Roy Richards; Richard Berry.
Also see BARNUM, H.B.
Also see BERRY, Richard
Also see CHAPMAN, Grady
Also see COASTERS
Also see LITTLE RICHARD
Also see NIC NACS
Also see NUNN, Bobby
Also see OTIS, Johnny, Quintette, with Little Esther & Robins
Also see SUEDES

ROBINS / Mel Walker & Bluenotes

Singles: 78 rpm

REGENT (1016 "I'm Not Falling in Love with You") ... 25-50 50
Also see ROBINS
Also see WALKER, Mel

ROBINS

Singles: 7-inch

TEXAS FILM (1 "Zombie") ... 10-20 60

ROBINS

Singles: 7-inch

LAVENDER (001 "White Cliffs of Dover") ... 25-50 61
LAVENDER (002 "Magic of a Dream") ... 25-50 61

ROBINS

Singles: 7-inch

NEW HIT (3010 "Johnny") ... 10-15 63
SWEET TAFFY (400 "Johnny") ... 20-30 62

ROBINS

Singles: 7-inch

ARDENT ... 5-10 66
MUSICOR ... 5-10 64

ROBINS

Singles: 7-inch

PUSH (764 "Moving Out") ... 5-10 60s
Member: Andre Goodwin.

ROBINS, Chuck

Singles: 7-inch

JAMBETH ... 4-8 66

ROBINS, Jimmy — R&B '67

(James Robbins)

Singles: 7-inch

ALA (1173 "Repossesing My Love") ... 4-6
FEDERAL (12504 "I'll Be There") ... 8-12 63
JERHART (207 "I Can't Please You") ... 5-10 67
(Previously issued as by James Robbins, with Roy Wright on the flip.)
KENT ... 4-8 68
TANGERINE (995 "Lonely Street") ... 5-10 60s
20TH FOX (6661 "Shine It On") ... 5-10 66
Also see PATRIZIA & JIMMY
Also see ROBBINS, James / Roy Wright

ROBINSON, Al

Singles: 7-inch

IMPERIAL (5727 "Pain in My Heart") ... 8-12 61
IMPERIAL (5762 "Wake Up") ... 8-12 61
IMPERIAL (5824 "Oh Red") ... 8-12 62
(First issue.)
POST (10001 "Oh Red") ... 5-10 62
PULSAR ... 4-8 69

ROBINSON, Alvin — P&R/R&B '64

Singles: 7-inch

ATCO ... 5-8 68
BLUE CAT ... 8-12 65
JOE JONES ... 5-10 66
RED BIRD ... 5-10 64
TIGER ... 5-10 64

ROBINSON, Andy

(Andrew Robinson)

Singles: 7-inch

DIAMOND ... 3-6 69

LPs: 10/12-inch

PHILIPS ... 10-15 69

ROBINSON, Bert — R&B '87

Singles: 7-inch

CAPITOL ... 3-4 87
Also see BLU, Peggi, & Bert Robinson

ROBINSON, Betty Jean — C&W '74

(With the Nashville Grass)

Singles: 7-inch

4 STAR ... 3-5 75
MCA ... 3-5 74

LPs: 10/12-inch

CMH ... 5-10 81
4 STAR ... 5-10 78
Also see BELEW, Carl, & Betty Jean Robinson

ROBINSON, Bill, & Quails

Singles: 78 rpm

DELUXE ... 50-75 54-55

Singles: 7-inch

AMERICAN ... 5-10 63
DATE ... 3-5 68
DELUXE (6030 "Lonely Star") ... 100-150 54
DELUXE (6047 "I Know She's Gone") ... 150-200 55
DELUXE (6057 "Little Bit of Love") ... 100-150 54
DELUXE (6059 "Why Do I Wait") ... 100-150 55
DELUXE (6074 "Love of My Life") ... 75-100 55
Also see QUAILS

ROBINSON, Billy

Singles: 12-inch

COAST to COAST ... 4-8 83

Singles: 7-inch

COAST to COAST ... 3-5 83

ROBINSON, Billy, & Burners

Singles: 7-inch

CRAZY HORSE (1305 "I'm a Lonely Black Boy") ... 25-50 68

ROBINSON, Bobby

Singles: 7-inch

ABC-PAR ... 4-8 66
Also see ROCKINGHAM, David, Trio

ROBINSON, Bobby, & His Tymani Six

Singles: 78 rpm

ALADDIN ... 15-20 47

ROBINSON, Claude

Singles: 7-inch

STUDIO (1002 "Kisses") ... 100-150 59

ROBINSON, Cleveland

Singles: 7-inch

ASCOT ... 10-15 63

ROBINSON, Dick

Singles: 78 rpm

MCI (1006 "Boppin' Martian") ... 40-60 56

Singles: 7-inch

MCI (1006 "Boppin' Martian") ... 75-100 56

ROBINSON, Dutch — R&B '84

Singles: 7-inch

CBS ASSOCIATED ... 3-4 84-85

ROBINSON, Earl

LPs: 10/12-inch

FOLKWAYS ... 8-12 63

ROBINSON, Ed — R&B '70

Singles: 7-inch

COTILLION ... 3-5 70

ROBINSON, Fabor

Singles: 78 rpm

FABOR ... 10-15 56

Singles: 7-inch

FABOR (4010 "Stop the Clock") ... 15-25 56
FAVOR (4012 "Why Am I Falling") ... 15-25 56

ROBINSON, Faithe

Singles: 7-inch

DOLPHIN (792 "My Birthday Wish") ... 300-400 60

ROBINSON, Fat Man — R&B '49

Singles: 78 rpm

MOTIF ... 10-20 49

ROBINSON, Fenton

(With His Dukes; with His Castle Rockers; Fention Robinson)

Singles: 7-inch

DUKE (312 "School Boy") ... 10-20 59
DUKE (329 "Tennessee Woman") ... 10-20 61
GIANT ... 8-12
METEOR (5041 "Tennessee Woman") ... 150-250 57
PALOS (1200 "Somebody") ... 10-20
SOUND STAGE 7 (2654 "Leave You in the Arms of Your Other Man") ... 4-8 70
U.S.A. (842 "From My Heart") ... 5-10 66

LPs: 10/12-inch

ALLIGATOR ... 5-10 74-78
SEVENTY-7 ... 8-12 72

ROBINSON, Fenton / David Dean's Combo

Singles: 7-inch

DUKE ... 5-10 58
Also see DEAN, David
Also see ROBINSON, Fenton

ROBINSON, Floyd — P&R/R&B '59

Singles: 7-inch

DOT ... 5-10 61-62
GROOVE ... 4-8 64
JAMIE ... 5-10 61
RCA ... 10-20 59-60
U.A. ... 5-10 63-66

EPs: 7-inch

RCA (4350 "Makin' Love") ... 50-75 59

LPs: 10/12-inch

RCA (LPM-2162 "Floyd Robinson") ... 30-60 60
(Monaural.)
RCA (LSP-2162 "Floyd Robinson") ... 50-100 60
(Stereo.)

ROBINSON, Freddy — P&R/R&B/LP '70

Singles: 7-inch

CHECKER ... 10-15 66
LIBERTY ... 3-5 70
LIMELIGHT ... 10-15 58
MERCURY ... 10-15 58
PACIFIC JAZZ ... 3-5 69-70
QUEEN ... 8-12 61
WORLD PACIFIC ... 3-5 70

LPs: 10/12-inch

ENTERPRISE ... 8-12 71
PACIFIC JAZZ ... 10-15 69-70
Also see LITTLE WALTER
Also see HOWLING WOLF

ROBINSON, Harry, Crew

Singles: 7-inch

PHILIPS ... 4-8 64

ROBINSON, Hubert

(With His Yardbirds)

Singles: 78 rpm

EDDIE'S ... 15-25 49
JADE ... 10-20 51
MACY'S ... 15-25 50
Also see AMY, Curtis

ROBINSON, J.P. — R&B '69

Singles: 7-inch

ALSTON ... 3-6 68-69

ROBINSON, Jackie — R&B '76

Singles: 7-inch

ARIOLA AMERICAN ... 3-5 76

ROBINSON, James — R&B '87

Singles: 7-inch

TABU ... 3-4 87

ROBINSON, Jay, & Dynamics

Singles: 7-inch

MALA ... 4-8 67

ROBINSON, Jessie Mae

(With Little Fry & Monroe Tucker's Orchestra; Jessie Mae Robertson)

Singles: 78 rpm

DISCOVERY ... 10-20 46

Singles: 7-inch

BLAZE (111 "Rock 'Em & Roll 'Em") ... 15-25 50s
(Identification number shown since no selection number is used.)
MELIC ... 5-10 63
Also see TUCKER, Monroe

ROBINSON, Jim

Singles: 78 rpm

EPIC ... 100-150 57

Singles: 7-inch

BRILL (2 "Man From Texas") ... 75-125 50s
EPIC (9234 "Whole Lot of Lovin'") ... 100-150 57
(With Buddy Holly on guitar.)
Also see HOLLY, Buddy
Also see JACK & JIM

ROBINSON, Jimmy Lee

Singles: 7-inch

BANDERA (2506 "Chicago Jump") ... 25-50 60
BANDERA (2510 "Twist It Baby") ... 20-30 61
Also see JIMMY LEE
Also see LONESOME LEE

ROBINSON, Joey

Singles: 7-inch

MONT ... 10-15 62

ROBINSON, Johnny

Singles: 7-inch

EPIC ... 5-10 69-70
MERCURY ... 10-15 65
OKEH (7307 "Gone But Not Forgotten") ... 50-75 68
OKEH (7317 "Poor Man") ... 10-15 68
OKEH (7328 "Green Grass of Home") ... 8-12 68

LPs: 10/12-inch

EPIC ... 10-20 70

ROBINSON, L.C.

Singles: 7-inch

RHYTHM (1772 "If I Lose You Baby") ... 50-100 54

LPs: 10/12-inch

ARHOOLIE ... 8-10 72
BLUESWAY ... 8-10 74
Also see ROBINSON BROTHERS

ROBINSON, L.C. "Good Rockin'" / Lafayette "Thing" Thomas / Dave Alexander

LPs: 10/12-inch

WORLD PACIFIC ... 10-15 69
Also see ROBINSON, L.C.
Also see THOMAS, Lafayette

ROBINSON, Lucius "Mushouth"

Singles: 78 rpm

BLACK & WHITE ... 15-25 45

ROBINSON, Mark

(With Duane Eddy)

Singles: 7-inch

JAMIE (1103 "Pretty Jane") ... 10-20 58
TEE GEE ... 10-15 58
Also see EDDY, Duane

ROBINSON, Matt

Singles: 7-inch

COLUMBIA ... 3-5 72

ROBINSON, Nat

Singles: 7-inch

NU KAT ... 5-10 59

ROBINSON, Othello

Singles: 7-inch

BABY LUV (35 "So in Luv") ... 75-125 67
ERA (3179 "So in Luv") ... 50-75 67

ROBINSON, Robbie

Singles: 7-inch

CENCO ... 5-10 62
FLAIR ... 5-10 62

ROBINSON, Roscoe — P&R/R&B '66

(Rosco Robinson)

Singles: 7-inch

ATLANTIC ... 3-5 69
FAME ... 3-5 70
PAULA ... 3-5 70s
SOUND STAGE 7 ... 4-8 67-69
TUFF ... 4-6 70s
WAND ... 4-8 66-67
Also see SOUTHERN SONS QUARTET

ROBINSON, Rudy

Singles: 7-inch

WHEEL CITY (40 "Mustang") ... 15-25 65

ROBINSON, Sharon — C&W '87

Singles: 7-inch

NIGHTFALL ... 3-4 87

ROBINSON, Shawn

Singles: 7-inch

MINIT (32013 "My Dear Heart") ... 35-55 66

ROBINSON, Smokey — P&R/R&B/LP '73

(William Robinson)

Singles: 7-inch

TAMLA ... 3-5 73-86
MOTOWN ... 3-4 87-88

Picture Sleeves

MOTOWN ... 3-4 87

LPs: 10/12-inch

MOTOWN ... 5-10 82-90
TAMLA ... 5-12 73-86
Also see JAMES, Rick, & Smokey Robinson
Also see KENNY G. & Smokey Robinson
Also see MIRACLES
Also see ROSS, Diana, Stevie Wonder, Marvin Gaye & Smokey Robinson
Also see TEMPTATIONS
Also see U.S.A. for AFRICA
Also see VANITY / Smokey Robinson

ROBINSON, Smokey, & Barbara Mitchell — P&R/R&B '83

Singles: 7-inch

TAMLA ... 3-5 83
Also see HIGH INERGY
Also see ROBINSON, Smokey

ROBINSON, Stan — P&R '59

Singles: 7-inch

AMY ... 5-10 60-61
MONUMENT ... 5-10 59
TOTSY (601 "Start to Jump") ... 75-100 59

ROBINSON, Sugar "Chile" — R&B '49

Singles: 78 rpm

CAPITOL ... 20-30 49-50

Singles: 7-inch

CAPITOL (1259 "Christmas Boogie") ... 50-75 50

LPs: 10/12-inch

CAPITOL (589 "Boogie Woogie") ... 75-125 55

ROBINSON, Sugar "Chile" / Harry Belafonte

Singles: 78 rpm

CAPITOL (70037 "Numbers Boogie") ... 15-25 49
(Promotional issue only.)

Singles: 7-inch

CAPITOL (70037 "Numbers Boogie") ... 25-50 49
(Promotional issue only.)
Also see BELAFONTE, Harry
Also see ROBINSON, Sugar "Chile"

ROBINSON, Sugar Ray

LPs: 10/12-inch

CONTINENTAL ... 10-20 63

ROBINSON, Tom, Band — LP '78

Singles: 7-inch

HARVEST ... 3-5 78-79
I.R.S. ... 3-5 80

LPs: 10/12-inch

HARVEST ... 5-10 78-79
I.R.S. ... 5-8 80

ROBINSON, Vicki Sue — P&R/R&B/LP '76

Singles: 12-inch

PROFILE ... 8-12 83-84

Singles: 7-inch

PROFILE ... 3-4 83-84
RCA ... 3-5 76-77

LPs: 10/12-inch

PROFILE ... 5-8 83
RCA ... 5-10 76-81

ROBINSON, Wanda — LP '71

LPs: 10/12-inch

PERCEPTION ... 5-10 71

ROBINSON, Wayne

Singles: 7-inch

TIME ... 4-8 62

ROBINSON BROTHERS

Singles: 78 rpm

BLACK & WHITE (107 "I Got to Go") ... 40-60 45
BLACK & WHITE (108 "L.C. Boogie") ... 40-60 45
Members: L.C. Robinson; Walter Robinson.
Also see ROBINSON, L.C.
Also see ROBERTSON, Walter

ROBISON, Carson — C&W '45

(With His Pleasant Valley Boys; with His Old Timers)

Singles: 78 rpm

CLARION ... 5-15 40s
COLUMBIA ... 5-15 55
MGM ... 5-15 48
VICTOR ... 5-15 45

Singles: 7-inch

COLUMBIA ... 5-10 55

EPs: 7-inch

MGM ... 6-12 52-58
RCA ... 6-12 53

LPs: 10/12-inch

COLUMBIA (2551 "Square Dance") ... 10-20 55
(10-inch LP.)
COLUMBIA (6029 "Square Dance") ... 10-20 49
(10-inch LP.)
GLENDALE ... 8-10
MGM (13 "Call Your Own Square Dances") ... 10-20 52
(10-inch LP.)
MGM (557 "Square Dances") ... 10-20 52
(10-inch LP.)
MGM (3258 "Square Dances") ... 10-20 55
MGM (3594 "Life Gets Tee-Jus, Don't It") ... 15-20 58
METRO (504 "Square Dance Calls") ... 10-20 60s
RCA (3030 "Square Dances") ... 10-25 53
(10-inch LP.)
Also see DALHART, Vernon, & Carson Robison

ROBISON, Chris, & Rockaways

Singles: 7-inch

BUDDAH ... 4-8 74
Also see ROCKAWAYS

ROBOTNICK, Alexander — R&B '85

Singles: 7-inch

SIRE ... 3-5 85

ROBY, Dick

Singles: 7-inch

LION ... 10-15 60s
Member: ROBY, Dick
Also see CASTAWAYS

ROBY, L.C.

Singles: 7-inch

BLUE SOUL ... 4-6

ROBY, Weldon

Singles: 7-inch

ROY ... 4-8 64

ROC

Singles: 7-inch

INFINITY ... 3-5 79

ROCCA, John — R&B/D&D '84

Singles: 12-inch

STREETWISE ... 4-6 84

Singles: 7-inch

STREETWISE ... 3-4 84
Also see FREEEZ

ROCCO, Lenny

Singles: 7-inch

DELSEY (301"Sugar Girl") ... 200-300 61

ROCCO, Pat

Singles: 7-inch

TIDE ... 5-10 60

ROCCO, Tommy

Singles: 7-inch

E&M (3264 "Midnight Train") ... 10-20
RAZORBACK (102 "Back to School") ... 15-25 58

ROCHE, Maggie & Terre

LPs: 10/12-inch

COLUMBIA ... 10-15 75
Also see ROCHES

ROCHE, Nina

Singles: 7-inch

RAYCO ... 5-10 60

ROCHELL & CANDLES — P&R/R&B '61

Singles: 7-inch

CHALLENGE (9158 "Each Night") ... 40-50 62
CHALLENGE (9191 "Let's Run Away and Get Married") ... 15-25 62
COLLECTABLES ... 3-4 80s
SWINGIN' (623 "Once Upon a Time") ... 10-20 60
SWINGIN' (634 "So Far Away") ... 10-20 61
SWINGIN' (640 "Peg O' My Heart") ... 10-20 61
SWINGIN' (652 "Long Time Ago") ... 10-20 62
Members: Rochell Henderson; Johnny Wyatt; T. C. Henderson; Mel Sasso.
Also see WYATT, Johnny

ROCHELLE — D&D '85

Singles: 12-inch

W.B. ... 4-6 85

Singles: 7-inch

W.B. ... 3-4 85

ROCHES — LP '79

LPs: 10/12-inch

W.B. ... 5-10 79-82
Members: Maggie Roche; Terre Roche; Suzzy Roche.
Also see ROCHE, Maggie & Terre

ROCK, Bob E.
(With Tex Rubinowitz & Evan Johns)
Singles: 7-inch
RENEGADE 3-5 80s
Also see RUBINOWITZ, Tex

ROCK, Bobby
Singles: 7-inch
RHYTHMIC SOUND 3-5 74

ROCK, Jimmy
Singles: 7-inch
TODD 10-15 59

ROCK, Johnny, & Hollywod Rollers
Singles: 7-inch
RIBBON 5-10 70s

ROCK, Monti, III
(Sir Monti Rock III)
Singles: 7-inch
MERCURY 4-8 65
LPs: 10/12-inch
EVEREST 5-8 82
Also see DISCO-TEX & His Sex-O-Lettes

ROCK & HYDE *P&R/LP '87*
Singles: 7-inch
CAPITOL 3-4 87
Picture Sleeves
CAPITOL 3-4 87
LPs: 10/12-inch
CAPITOL 5-8 87

ROCK & ROLL DOUBLE BUBBLE TRADING CARD CO. OF PHILADELPHIA, 19141 *P&R '69*
Singles: 7-inch
BUDDAH 4-8 68

ROCK & ROLL & GIRLS, GIRLS, GIRLS
LPs: 10/12-inch
MODERN SOUND (515 "Rock & Roll and Girls, Girls, Girls") 10-20 63
(Listed by title since no artist is credited.)

ROCK & ROLL GYPSIES
Singles: 7-inch
ORIGINAL SOUND 4-8 67

ROCK & ROLL REVIVAL
LPs: 10/12-inch
DUNHILL 10-15 69
Member: Jerry Tawney.

ROCK & ROLL SCHOOLTEACHER
Singles: 7-inch
OKEH 5-10 59

ROCK & ROLL SOCIETY
Singles: 7-inch
DIAMOND 4-8 66

ROCK BREAKERS
Singles: 7-inch
MUSICOR 4-8 68

ROCK BROTHERS
Singles: 78 rpm
KING 8-12 55
Singles: 7-inch
KING 10-20 55

ROCK CANDY
Singles: 7-inch
MGM 3-5 70
LPs: 10/12-inch
MGM 10-15 70
Also see ROCKICKS

ROCK CANDY
Singles: 12-inch
PROFILE 4-6 82

ROCK CANDY MOUNTAIN
Singles: 7-inch
MOON 3-6 69

ROCK FLOWERS *P&R '72*
Singles: 7-inch
WHEEL 4-8 71-73
Picture Sleeves
WHEEL (282 "Number Wonderful") 20-40 71
Members: Ardie Tillman; Debbie Clinger; Rindy; Jacquie Wiseman.
LPs: 10/12-inch
WHEEL 10-15 71-72

ROCK FORMATION
Singles: 7-inch
RAF 3-5 70
Also see FORMATION

ROCK GARDEN
Singles: 7-inch
B.T. PUPPY 4-8 68

ROCK GARDEN
Singles: 7-inch
CAPITOL 5-10 70
Also see FREDRIC

ROCK GAZERS
Singles: 7-inch
PILGRIM 3-5 76

ROCK GENERATION
LPs: 10/12-inch
CAMDEN 8-10 73

ROCK GODDESS
Singles: 7-inch
A&M 3-5 84
LPs: 10/12-inch
A&M 5-10 84

ROCK ISLAND
Singles: 7-inch
PROJECT 3 .... 3-5 70
LPs: 10/12-inch
PROJECT 3 .... 8-10 70

ROCK MASTER SCOTT & DYNAMIC THREE *R&B '84*
Singles: 12-inch
REALITY 4-6 84-85
Singles: 7-inch
REALITY 3-4 84-85

ROCK 'N' ROLL: see ROCK & ROLL

ROCK ROSE
Singles: 7-inch
COLUMBIA 3-5 79
LPs: 10/12-inch
COLUMBIA 5-10 79

ROCK SHOP
Singles: 7-inch
ROWENA 15-20 60s

ROCK SQUAD *D&D '85*
Singles: 12-inch
TOMMY BOY 4-6 85

ROCK STEADY CREW *D&D '84*
Singles: 12-inch
ATLANTIC 4-6 83-84
Singles: 7-inch
ATLANTIC 3-4 83-84

ROCK STONE: see CWAZY WABBITS

ROCKA, Billy
Singles: 7-inch
BRUNSWICK 10-20 58

ROCKADILES
LPs: 10/12-inch
TROTTER 8-10 83

ROCK-A-BEATS
Singles: 7-inch
BENZ (4 "French Fries") 10-20 60s

ROCK-A-BOUTS
Singles: 7-inch
CHANCELLOR (1030 "She's a Fat Girl") 10-20 59
Also see STARGLOWS / Rock-A-Bouts / Cecil Young Quartet

ROCK-A-FELLAS
Singles: 7-inch
ABC-PAR (9923 "Red Lips") 10-20 58
COED (512 "Night Party") 15-25 59
DEVERE (313 "Don't Torment Me") 30-40 58
Also see BELL, Eddie

ROCKAFELLAS
(Rocka-Fellas)
Singles: 7-inch
SCA (18003 "Strike It Rich") 20-30 63
SOUTHERN SOUND (112 "Strike It Rich") 25-35 62

ROCK-A-FELLERS
Singles: 7-inch
CUCA (1039 "Reaction") 15-20 61
Members: Bob Merkt; Del Stralo; Miles Merkt; Ken Berdoll; Jim Sessody.

ROCK-A-FIRE EXPLOSION
Singles: 7-inch
CREATIVE 3-4 81

ROCKANDY
Singles: 7-inch
SUGAR SHACK 3-5 75

ROCK-A-NOVAS
Singles: 7-inch
HEP (650 "Howdy") 10-15

ROCKATEENERS
Singles: 7-inch
VISCOUNT ("Don't Mess Around") 8-12
(Selection number not known.)

ROCK-A-TEENS *P&R '59*
Singles: 7-inch
APEX (76591 "Woo-Hoo") 10-20 59
(Canadian.)
DORAN (3515 "Woo-Hoo") 40-60 59
ROULETTE (4192 "Woo-Hoo") 10-20 59
ROULETTE (4217 "Doggone It Baby") 15-20 60
LPs: 10/12-inch
MURRAY HILL 5-10 80s
ROULETTE (R-25109 "Woo-Hoo") 75-125 60
(Monaural.)
ROULETTE (SR-25109 "Woo-Hoo") 100-200 60
(Stereo.)

ROCKATEERS
Singles: 78 rpm
STARS, INC. 10-15 57
Singles: 7-inch
STARS, INC. (544 "Rock Bottom") 15-25 57

ROCKATONES
Singles: 7-inch
MELBOURNE 5-10 64

ROCK-A-TONES
Singles: 7-inch
JUDY-TONE (369 "Please Don't Talk About Me") 100-150
WHAMMY (7450 "One More Chance") 10-20 61

ROCKATONES
Singles: 7-inch
FONTAINE (1575 "Shandia") 8-12
(Canadian.)

ROCKATS
Singles: 12-inch
RCA 5-8 81
(Promotional only.)
Singles: 7-inch
KAT TALE (1 "Rockabilly Doll") 10-15 80
(Includes poster.)
RCA 3-5 83
Picture Sleeves
KAT TALE (1 "Rockabilly Doll") 5-10 80
LPs: 10/12-inch
ISLAND 5-10 81
RCA 5-8 83
Promotional LPs
ISLAND (9626 "Live at the Ritz") 20-25 81
(With gatefold cover. Songs shown only on label.)
Also see LEVI & ROCKATS

ROCKAWAYS
Singles: 7-inch
NASH (600 "Rampage") 20-40
Member: Cliff Nash.
Also see NASH, Cliff, & Rockaways

ROCKAWAYS
Singles: 7-inch
RED BIRD (005 "Top Down Time") 10-20 64
Members: Kenny Vance; Marty Sanders.
Also see VANCE, Kenny.
Also see ROBISON, Chris

ROCKBUSTERS
Singles: 7-inch
CADENCE 8-12 59

ROCKBUSTERS
Singles: 7-inch
M.C.R. 5-10 63

ROCKEN HORSE
Singles: 7-inch
ERECT 3-5 81
LPs: 10/12-inch
ERECT 5-10 81

ROCKER, Johnny
(With the Cheques)
Singles: 7-inch
FEDERAL (12425 "Queen") 10-15 61
LARK (4514 "Song of the Lonely Guitar") 150-250 61
(Colored vinyl.)

ROCKER'S REVENGE *R&B '82*
Singles: 12-inch
STREETWISE 4-6 83-84
Singles: 7-inch
STREETWISE 3-5 82-84

ROCKERS
(With Emmet Carter Combo)
Singles: 78 rpm
CARTER (3029 "Tell Me Why") 200-400 55
FEDERAL (12267 "What Am I to Do") 50-75 56
FEDERAL (12273 "Why Don't You Believe Me") 25-50 56
Singles: 7-inch
CARTER (3029 "Tell Me Why") 500-1000 55
FEDERAL (12267 "What Am I to Do") 150-250 56
(Green label.)
FEDERAL (12267 "What Am I to Do") 200-300 56
(White label with bio. Promotional issue only.)
FEDERAL (12273 "Why Don't You Believe Me") 100-150 56
Member: Art Larson.
Also see FANANDOS

ROCKERS
Singles: 7-inch
ROCK (101 "Mean Mean Woman") 35-50

ROCKET *R&B/D&D '83*
Singles: 12-inch 33/45
QUALITY/RFC 4-6 83
LPs: 10/12-inch
QUALITY/RFC 5-8 83

ROCKET, Robin
Singles: 7-inch
LODE 5-10 60
W.B. 5-10 60

ROCKET 88
Singles: 7-inch
ATLANTIC 3-5 81
LPs: 10/12-inch
ATLANTIC 8-12 81
Members: Charlie Watts; Hal Singer; Alexis; Korner; Colin Smith; Jack Bruce.
Also see BRUCE, Jack
Also see KORNER, Alexis
Also see ROLLING STONES

ROCKET 88's
Singles: 7-inch
PRO INDIE 3-5 85
LPs: 10/12-inch
PRO INDIE 5-10 85

ROCKET TONES
Singles: 7-inch
OPERATORS (2015 "Fireball") 20-30 62

ROCKETEERS
Singles: 78 rpm
HERALD 50-75 53
Singles: 7-inch
HERALD (415 "Foolish One") 200-300 53
(Black vinyl.)
HERALD (415 "Foolish One") 500-750 53
(Red vinyl.)

ROCKETEERS
Singles: 78 rpm
MODERN 10-20 56
Singles: 7-inch
MODERN (999 "Talk It Over Baby") 20-30 56

ROCKETEERS
Singles: 7-inch
GLAD HAMP (2017 "Drag Strip") 15-25 63
VAL-UE (1002 "Rippin' and Rockin' ") 10-20 60

ROCKETEERS
Singles: 7-inch
M.J.C. (501 "My Reckless Heart") 1000-2000 55
Also see CADETS
Also see CLASS-NOTES

ROCKETONES
Singles: 78 rpm
MELBA (113 "Mexico") 25-50 57
Singles: 7-inch
MELBA (113 "Mexico") 25-50 57
Members: Bill Witt; Arthur Blackman; Ron Johnson; Al Days; Harold Chapman.

ROCKET-TONES
Singles: 7-inch
3 SONS (928 "Too Many Loves") 75-125 62

ROCKETS
Singles: 78 rpm
MODERN 10-20 56
Singles: 7-inch
MODERN (992 "You Are the First One") 20-30 56
Also see BEASLEY, Jimmy
Also see JACKS

ROCKETS
Singles: 7-inch
COLUMBIA 8-12 59

ROCKETS
Singles: 7-inch
WHITE WHALE 4-8 68
LPs: 10/12-inch
WHITE WHALE 15-20 68
Members: Ralph Molina; Danny Whitten; Bob Notkoff; Billy Talbot; Leon Whitsell; George Whitsell.
Also see CRAZY HORSE

ROCKETS *P&R/LP '79*
Singles: 7-inch
RSO 3-5 79
TORTOISE INT'L 3-5 77-78
LPs: 10/12-inch
ELEKTRA 5-10 81
RSO 5-10 79-80
TORTOISE INT'L 8-12 77
Members: Jim McCarty; Dennis Robbins.
Also see DETROIT
Also see ROBBINS, Dennis
Also see RYDER, Mitch

ROCKETS
LPs: 10/12-inch
TOM 'N JERRY 5-10 78

ROCKETS
Singles: 7-inch
COOL (712 "Always Alone") 20-30 50s
COOL (9035 "Moovin' & Groovin' ") 15-25 58
Also see LEE, Lois

ROCKETS
Singles: 7-inch
REVIS (1224 "Tater Pie") 8-12
WIDE (935 "Johnny B. Goode") 8-12

ROCKETS, Stan, D.
Singles: 7-inch
CLIX (812 "Satan's Angels") 8-12

ROCKETTES
Singles: 78 rpm
PARROT (789 "I Can't Forget") 200-400 53
Singles: 7-inch
PARROT (789 "I Can't Forget") 750-1000 53

ROCK-FELLERS
Singles: 7-inch
VALOR (2004 "Ours") 25-50 59

ROCKFIELD CHORALE
Singles: 7-inch
GNP (810 "Jingle Jangle") 10-15

ROCKFORD, Gino
Singles: 7-inch
EDISON INT'L 5-10 59

ROCKICKS
LPs: 10/12-inch
RSO 8-10 77
Also see ROCK CANDY

ROCKIN' ACES
Singles: 7-inch
MERCURY (71619 "Thunder") 10-20 60

ROCKIN' BERRIES
Singles: 7-inch
REPRISE 5-10 64-66
Member: Geoff Turton.
Also see JEFFERSON

ROCKIN' BRADLEY
(With His Rockers)
Singles: 7-inch
FIRE (1007 "Lookout") 50-75 59
HULL (729 "She's Mine Not Yours") 100-200 58

ROCKIN' CAPRIS
Singles: 7-inch
BETHLEHEM (3084 "Lights Out") 4-8 69
CONCO (145 "Money") 8-12 62
CONFEDERATE (145 "Money") 8-12 62
Also see FUNKY FIVE

ROCKIN' CHAIRS
Singles: 7-inch
RECORTE (402 "Rockin' Chair Boogie") 75-100 58
RECORTE (404 "Come On Baby") 30-50 58
RECORTE (412 "Memories of Love") 30-50 59
Members: Lenny Dean; Bob Gerardi; Carmine Ray; Rick Baxter; Joe Cary.
Also see GERARDI, Bob, & Classic 4
Also see DEAN, Lenny, & Rockin' Chairs

ROCKIN' CONTINENTALS
Singles: 7-inch
CASINO (10 "Cobra 289") 20-30 63

ROCKIN' DENNY
(With the Real Gone Guys)
Singles: 7-inch
PRESTO (100 "Bop Boogie") 3-5 85
Picture Sleeves
PRESTO (100 "Bop Boogie") 4-6 85

ROCKIN' DEVILS
Singles: 7-inch
ORFEON (1699 "Wooly Bully") 15-25 60s
ORFEON (1752 "Gloria") 15-25 60s

ROCKIN' DUKES
Singles: 7-inch
OJ (1007 Angel and a Rose") 200-250 57

ROCKIN' DUKES
Singles: 7-inch
SHELLEY (128 "Cross Current") 15-25 61
(Also issued as by Sterly Singleton.)
Also see SINGLETON, Sterly

ROCKIN' FLAMES
Singles: 7-inch
JAN (14160 "Cricket") 8-12

ROCKIN' FOO
Singles: 7-inch
HOBBIT (42001 "Rochester River") 4-8 69
Picture Sleeves
HOBBIT (42001 "Rochester River") 8-10 69
LPs: 10/12-inch
HOBBIT (5001 "Rockin Foo") 15-25 69
UNI 8-12 71

ROCKIN' G's
Singles: 7-inch
TOWN (1967 "Lani") 10-15 60

ROCKIN' HI LOS
Singles: 7-inch
MARK (114 "Hey, Maryann") 200-300 57

ROCKIN' HORSE
Singles: 7-inch
RCA 3-5 74-76
LPs: 10/12-inch
RCA 8-12 75

ROCKIN' HORSE
Singles: 7-inch
VOXX 3-5
Member: Bill Kinsley.
Also see LIVERPOOL EXPRESS
Also see MERSEYBEATS

ROCKIN' HORSE PEOPLE
Singles: 7-inch
MERCURY 3-5 70

ROCKIN' HORSES
Singles: 78 rpm
GRAND (139 "House Rocker") 15-25 56
Singles: 7-inch
GRAND (139 "House Rocker") 30-50 56

ROCKIN' JESTERS
Singles: 7-inch
OKLAHOMA (5004 "I Was Too Blind") 75-100 58

ROCKIN' JIMMY & BROTHERS OF THE NIGHT
LPs: 10/12-inch
PILGRIM 5-10 82

ROCKIN' KIDS
Singles: 7-inch
DOT (15749 "Black Stockings") 15-25 58

ROCKIN' R's *P&R '59*
Singles: 7-inch
STEPHENY (1842 "Walking You to School") 15-25 60
TEMPUS (1507 "Heat") 15-20 59
TEMPUS (7541 "The Beat") 20-30 59
VEE JAY (334 "I'm Still in Love with You") 10-20 60
VEE JAY (346 "Hum Bug") 10-20 60
Also see VOLZ, Ron, & Rockin' R's

ROCKIN' RAMRODS
(Ramrods)
Singles: 7-inch
BON-BON (1315 "She Lied") 20-30 64
CLARIDGE (301 "Don't Fool with Fu Manchu") 5-10 65
CLARIDGE (317 "Play It")...............15-25 66
EXPLOSIVE (101 "Jungle Call") 15-25 63
PLYMOUTH (2961 "I Wanna Be Your Man") 15-25 64
PLYMOUTH (2963 "Bright Lit Blue Skies")..10-20 66
SOUTHERN SOUND (205 "Wild About You") 10-15 65
Picture Sleeves
PLYMOUTH (2961 "I Wanna Be Your Man") 20-30 64
Also see RAMRODS

ROCKIN' RAZORBLADES
LPs: 10/12-inch
NEBULA CIRCLE 15-20 83

ROCKIN' REBELLIONS
Singles: 7-inch
GOLD GROOVE (111 "Anyway the Wind Blows")..20-30 67

ROCKIN' REBELS P&R '62
Singles: 7-inch
ABC... 3-5 73
ERIC.. 3-4 70s
ITZY (8 "Wild Weekend")..............15-25 60s
REO 10-20 62-63
(Canadian.)
REO GOLDEN TREASURES 4-8 67
(Canadian.)
STORK (3 "Bongo Blue Beat").......10-15 64
SWAN (4125 "Wild Weekend")....... 8-12 62
SWAN (4140 "Rockin' Crickets")....10-15 63
(Previously issued as by the Hot Toddys.)
SWAN (4150 "Another Wild Weekend") 8-12 63
SWAN (4161 "Monday Morning").... 8-12 63
SWAN (4248 "Wild Weekend")......10-20 66
(Thought not credited, the flip of 4248, *Donkey Twine*, is by Kathy Lynn & Playboys.)
LPs: 10/12-inch
SWAN (509 "Wild Weekend").......50-100 63
Members: Tom Gorman; Paul Balon; Mickey Kipler; Jim Kipler.
Also see BUFFALO REBELS
Also see HOT TODDYS
Also see LYNN, Kathy
Also see REBELS

ROCKIN' ROADRUNNERS
Singles: 7-inch
LEE C (696 "Go Away") 15-25 66
LEE C (970 "King of the Jungle") ...10-15 66
TENER (1015 "Down")....................15-25 67

ROCKIN' RONALD & REBELS
Singles: 7-inch
END (1043 "Cuttin' Out")................15-25 59
Member: Ronnie Hawkins.
Also see HAWKINS, Ronnie

ROCKIN' SAINTS
Singles: 7-inch
DECCA (30990 "Alright Baby") 20-25 59
DECCA (31144 "Cheat on Me, Baby") 50-75 60
Member: Buddy Randell.
Also see RANDELL, Buddy

ROCKIN' SID
Singles: 7-inch
AVENUE (1926 "Misery")...........150-250 57

ROCKIN' SIDNEY: see ROCKIN' SYDNEY

ROCKIN' STOCKINGS
Singles: 7-inch
SUN (350 "Rockin' Lang Syne").....10-15 60
SUN (1960 "Rockin' Lang Syne") ...15-20 60
Member: Billy Lee Riley.
Also see RILEY, Billy Lee

ROCKIN' STRINGS
Singles: 7-inch
RCA.. 5-10 59
LPs: 10/12-inch
DECCA..10-20 60

ROCKIN' SYDNEY LP '85
(With His All Stars; Rockin' Sidney)
Singles: 7-inch
AVENUE... 5-10 60s
EPIC.. 3-5 84-85
JIN.. 8-12 59-63
MAISON DE SOUL (1024 "My Toot Toot") 3-5 85
LPs: 10/12-inch
EPIC.. 5-10 85
Member: Sidney Sidiem.
Also see COUNT ROCKIN' SYDNEY

ROCKIN' TONES / Jerry & Casuals: see JERRY & CASUALS / Rockin' Tones

ROCKIN' VICKERS
Singles: 7-inch
COLUMBIA.. 5-10 66

ROCKINENTALS
Singles: 7-inch
SIOUX (11762 "L'il Liza") 10-20 62
Also see FABULOUS CONTINENTALS

ROCKING BROTHERS
Singles: 78 rpm
ELKO (901 "Play Boy Hop")...........25-50 55
IMPERIAL (5333 "Rock It").............. 8-10 55
R&B (1309 "Rock It") 10-15 55
SAVOY (1144 "Play Boy Hop") 10-20 55
WHIPPET (207 "Yeah! Yeah!") 10-20 57
Singles: 7-inch
ELKO (901 "Play Boy Hop")........75-125 55
(First issue.)
IMPERIAL (5333 "Rock It") 10-20 55
R&B (1309 "Rock It") 15-25 55
SAVOY (1144 "Play Boy Hop") 20-40 55
WHIPPET (207 "Yeah! Yeah!").......10-20 57
Members: Jason; Wilbur.

ROCKING CAPRIS
Singles: 7-inch
BETHLEHEM..................................... 4-8 64
CONFEDERATE 4-8 62

ROCKING GHOSTS
Singles: 7-inch
MOD (1001 "Belinda")....................10-20 66

ROCKING MARTIN
Singles: 7-inch
STARDAY (658 "All Because of You") 250-500 58
(Promotional issue only. This same number is also used on a 1963 Cowboy Copas release.)
Also see COPAS, Cowboy

ROCKING REBELS
Singles: 7-inch
TRIO (849 "Tom-Tom")..................15-25 60
Also see NEWMAN, Carl

ROCKINGHAM, David, Trio P&R '63
Singles: 7-inch
DEE DEE..8-12 63
JOSIE... 4-8 63-64
Also see ROBINSON, Bobby

ROCKINHORSE C&W '86
Singles: 7-inch
LONG SHOT 3-4 86

ROCKIT, Billy
Singles: 7-inch
ROBIN RED (005 "Dancing Fool") ...5-10
(Black vinyl.)
ROBIN RED (005 "Dancing Fool") 10-15
(Colored vinyl.)

ROCKIT, Doctor: see DOCTOR ROCKIT

ROCKITE, Walter
Singles: 7-inch
WESTBOUND (5022 "Pet Rocks Are Coming") 3-6 75

ROCK-ITS
Singles: 7-inch
SPANGLE (2010 "It's L-o-v-e") 75-100 58
Also see WRIGHT, Dale

ROCKMASTERS
Singles: 7-inch
ONE-DERFUL 10-15 63
ROMULUS 15-20 63

ROCKMELONS
Singles: 7-inch
ATLANTIC.. 3-4 89
Picture Sleeves
ATLANTIC.. 3-4 89

ROCKMEN & TADS
Singles: 7-inch
MALAPI (10001 "Safari") 10-15 60s

ROCK'N RAVENS
Singles: 7-inch
RUMBLE 3-6 79

ROCK'N ROLLERS
Singles: 7-inch
VEN (100 "For You")...................100-200

ROCKPILE P&R/LP '80
Singles: 7-inch
COLUMBIA.. 3-5 80
EPs: 7-inch
COLUMBIA (1219 "Nick Lowe and Dave Edmunds") 3-5 80
(Bonus EP, issued with the LP *Seconds of Pleasure*.)
LPs: 10/12-inch
COLUMBIA (36886 "Seconds of Pleasure") 5-10 80
(Includes the bonus EP, 1219, *Nick Lowe & Dave Edmunds*.)
Members: Nick Lowe; Dave Edmunds; Terry Williams; Billy Bremmer.
Also see CARTER, Carlene
Also see LOWE, Nick, & Dave Edmunds
Also see McCARTNEY, Paul / Rochestra / Who / Rockpile

ROCKS
Singles: 7-inch
GOLD MASTER (1003 "Rock Pretty Baby")...15-25 60s

ROCKS
Singles: 7-inch
U.A. 3-5 75

ROCKSPURS
LPs: 10/12-inch
DJM...5-10 78-79

ROCKVILLE JUNCTION
Singles: 7-inch
20TH FOX 3-5 74
LPs: 10/12-inch
20TH FOX 8-12 74

ROCKWELL P&R/R&B/D&D/LP '84
Singles: 12-inch
MOTOWN 4-6 84-86
Singles: 7-inch
MOTOWN 3-4 84-86
LPs: 10/12-inch
MOTOWN 5-8 84-86
Also see JACKSON, Michael

ROCKWELL, Denny
Singles: 7-inch
TOWER...4-8 66

ROCKWELL, Gene
Singles: 7-inch
APT-TO (9560 "Somewhere, Somehow, Someday")..10-15
PUBLIC 4-6 69

ROCKY
Singles: 7-inch
PHILIPS 4-8 65

ROCKY & BORDER KINGS
Singles: 7-inch
EPIC (10901 "Michoacan") 5-10 72
Members: Kim Fowley; Sir Douglas Quintet.
Also see FOWLEY, Kim
Also see SIR DOUGLAS QUINTET

ROCKY & CHYANN
Singles: 7-inch
WINDSONG 3-5 77
LPs: 10/12-inch
WINDSONG 8-10 77

ROCKY & HAL
Singles: 7-inch
T..4-8 63

ROCKY & HIS FRIENDS
Singles: 7-inch
TOWER...5-10 65
Member: Rocky Rhoades.
Also see IMPERIALS
Also see ROCKY & RIDDLERS

ROCKY & MILLIONAIRES
Singles: 7-inch
ORCHESTRA (102 "Remember Me") 500-1000 63

ROCKY & RIDDLERS
Singles: 7-inch
PANORAMA (28 "Flash & Crash")...15-25 66
Member: Rocky Rhoades.
Also see IMPERIALS
Also see ROCKY & His Friends

ROCKY & ROCKY FELLOWS
Singles: 7-inch
GOLDWATER (424 "Paint the Town Red")..150-200

ROCKY & VAL
Singles: 7-inch
ABC..4-8 68

ROCKY FELLERS P&R '63
Singles: 7-inch
DONNA 5-10 63
PARKWAY...5-10 62
SCEPTER 8-15 62-63
W.B. 4-8 64-65
Picture Sleeves
SCEPTER (1254 "Like the Big Guys Do") 10-15 63
LPs: 10/12-inch
SCEPTER (SP-512 "Killer Joe") 25-35 63
(Monaural.)
SCEPTER (SPS-512 "Killer Joe")...30-40 63
(Stereo.)
Members: Eddie; Albert; Tony; Junior; Pop.

ROD R&B '80
Singles: 7-inch
PRELUDE 3-5 80

ROD & COBRAS
LPs: 10/12-inch
SOMERSET.....................................15-20 63

ROD & TERRY
Singles: 7-inch
CUCA (1206 "That's All Right") 75-100 65
Also see LAVENDERS

ROD TWISTERS
Singles: 7-inch
ZULU (100 "Speed Limit")...............25-30

RODANS
Singles: 7-inch
VEST (825 "Time Is Passing") 50-100 58

RODDENBERRY, Gene, & Inside Star Trek Orchestra
Singles: 7-inch
COLUMBIA...3-8 76

RODDIE, Vin
Singles: 7-inch
CROSSTOWN (1000 "Wheels") 10-15 62

RODEN, Jess, Band
Singles: 7-inch
SIRE...3-4 80
LPs: 10/12-inch
ISLAND 8-10 74-80

RODENTS
Singles: 7-inch
PEQUOD ("And Your Bird Can Sing")...50-100 66
Members: David Lindley; Mark Freedman.
Also see KALEIDOSCOPE

RODEO
Singles: 7-inch
ST. PETER..3-5

RODERICK, Judy
LPs: 10/12-inch
COLUMBIA 10-15 64
VANGUARD 10-15 65

RODGERS, Eileen P&R '56
Singles: 78 rpm
COLUMBIA 3-6 56-57
Singles: 7-inch
COLUMBIA 5-10 56-60
KAPP 4-6 61
EPs: 7-inch
COLUMBIA 5-10 58
LPs: 10/12-inch
COLUMBIA 15-25 58
Also see MITCHELL, Guy / Eileen Rodgers

RODGERS, Jesse: see ROGERS, Jesse

RODGERS, Jimmie C&W '55
Singles: 78 rpm
BLUEBIRD 40-80 30s
ELECTRADISK (1830 "Moonlight and Skies")....................................250-500 32
ELECTRADISK (1966 "Looking for a New Mama")...................................200-400 32
ELECTRADISK (1983 "Whisper Your Mother's Name") 200-400 33
ELECTRADISK (1999 "Whippin' That Old T.B.")...................................200-400 33
ELECTRADISK (2008 "Mother, the Queen of My Heart")...............................200-400 33
ELECTRADISK (2009 "You and My Old Guitar") 200-400 33
ELECTRADISK (2042 "Mississippi Moon")..200-400 33
ELECTRADISK (2060 "Waiting for a Train")..200-400 33
ELECTRADISK (2109 "In the Jailhouse Now") 200-400 33
ELECTRADISK (2155 "Jimmie Rodgers' Last Blue Yodel")..............................200-400 33
MONTGOMERY WARD..............50-100 30s
SUNRISE (3104 "Moonlight and Skies") 200-300 33
SUNRISE (3131 "Looking for a New Mama")...200-300 33
SUNRISE (3142 "Whisper Your Mother's Name")..200-300 33
SUNRISE (3157 "Whippin' That Old T.B.") 200-300 33
SUNRISE (3167 "Mother, the Queen of My Heart") 200-300 33
SUNRISE (3168 "Down the Old Road to Home") 200-300 33
SUNRISE (3169 "Why Should I Be Lonely")...200-300 33
SUNRISE (3170 "You and My Old Guitar") 200-300 34
SUNRISE (3171 "Let Me Be Your Side Track")..200-300 34
SUNRISE (3172 "Blue Yodel")...200-300 34
SUNRISE (3217 "Mississippi Moon") 200-300 34
SUNRISE (3244 "Waiting for a Train")..200-300 34
SUNRISE (3306 "In the Jailhouse Now") 200-300 34
SUNRISE (3362 "Jimmie Rodgers' Last Blue Yodel")...200-300 34
SUNRISE (3418 "Lullaby Yodel")...200-300 34
VICTOR (20864 thru 23574)...........25-75 27-30s
VICTOR (23580 thru 24456).........50-100 30s
VICTOR (4000 series) 15-25
VICTOR (5000 & 6000 series) 5-15 49-56
VICTOR (18-6000 "Cowhand's Last Ride")...................................1500-2500 33
(Picture disc.)
Note: Many of Jimmie Rodgers' releases in the early '30s were made by Victor/Bluebird specifically for sale in department store chains: Elektradisk (Woolworth's), Sunrise (W.T. Grant, Kress, McCrory), and Montgomery Ward, with its own label.
Albums: 78 rpm
RCA (244 "Yodelingly Yours")....100-150 52
(Includes three 78 rpm singles.)
RCA (282 "Yodelingly Yours, Vol. 2")..100-150 52
(Includes three 78 rpm singles.)
RCA (318 "Yodelingly Yours, Vol. 3")..100-150 52
(Includes three 78 rpm singles.)
RCA (3035 "Yodelingly Yours, Vol. 4")..100-150 52
(Includes three 78 rpm singles.)
Singles: 7-inch
RCA (0017 thru 6408)...................10-20 49-56
EPs: 7-inch
RCA (6 "Immortal Performances By Jimmie Rodgers")..................................35-50 50
RCA (10 "Jimmie Rodgers, Vol. 1")..35-50 51
RCA (21 "Jimmie Rodgers Memorial Album, Vol. 1")..35-50 52
RCA (22 "Jimmie Rodgers Memorial Album, Vol. 2")..35-50 52
RCA (409 "Jimmie Rodgers Memorial Album, Vol. 4")..35-50 52
RCA (410 "Jimmie Rodgers Memorial Album, Vol. 5")..35-50 52
RCA (411 "Jimmie Rodgers Memorial Album, Vol. 6")..35-50 52
RCA (793 "Never No Mo' Blues")...25-35 56
(Two EPs)
RCA (1232 "Never No Mo' Blues") 35-55 55
(Two EPs)
RCA (3073 "Travelin' Blues")........50-100 52
(2-EPs)
RCA (5097 "Legendary Jimmie Rodgers")...20-30 58
LPs: 10/12-inch
ANTHOLOGY of COUNTRY MUSIC (11 "Unissued Jimmie Rodgers").........15-25 83
PICKWICK 6-12 76
RCA (0075 "Legendary Jimmie Rodgers")..10-20 74
(Mail order offer.)
RCA (LPM-1232 ("Never No Mo' Blues")..20-30 55
RCA (AHM1--1232 ("Never No Mo' Blues")..5-10 70s
RCA (LPM-1640 "Train Whistle Blues")..20-30 57
RCA (AHM1--1640 "Train Whistle Blues")..5-10 70s
RCA (LPM-2112 "My Rough and Rowdy Ways")..15-25 60
RCA (ANL1-2112 "My Rough and Rowdy Ways")..5-10 75
RCA (LPM-2213 "Jimmie the Kid") 15-25 61
RCA (AHM1-2213 "Jimmie the Kid")..5-10 70s
RCA (2504 "A Legendary Performer")..6-12 78
RCA (AHM1-2531 "Country Music Hall of Fame")..5-10 70s
RCA (LPM-2531 "Country Music Hall of Fame")..15-25 62
RCA (LPM-2634 "The Short But Brilliant Life of Jimmie Rodgers")..15-25 55
RCA (AHM1-2634 "The Short But Brilliant Life of Jimmie Rodgers")..5-10 70s
RCA (LPM-2865 "My Time Ain't Long")..15-25 64
RCA (AHM1-2865 "My Time Ain't Long")..5-10 70s
RCA (3037 "Jimmie Rodgers Memorial Album, Vol. 1 – Yodelingly Yours")........ 150-250 52
(10-inch LP.)
RCA (3038 "Jimmie Rodgers Memorial Album, Vol. 2 – Yodelingly Yours")........ 150-250 52
(10-inch LP.)
RCA (3039 "Jimmie Rodgers Memorial Album, Vol. 3 – Yodelingly Yours")......150-250 52
(10-inch LP.)
RCA (3073 "Travelin' Blues")..... 150-250 53
(10-inch LP.)
RCA (LPM/LSP-3315 "Best of the Legendary Jimmie Rodgers")..........................10-15 65
RCA (AHL1-3315 "Best of the Legendary Jimmie Rodgers")..........................5-10 70s
RCA (6091 "This Is Jimmie Rodgers")..8-12 73

RODGERS, Jimmie
("With Michele") P&R/C&W/R&B/LP '57
Singles: 78 rpm
ROULETTE.......................................10-30 57
Singles: 7-inch
A&M...3-6 67-70
ABC 3-5 73
DOT 4-8 62-67
EPIC..3-5 71-72
RCA 3-5 73-75
ROULETTE (Monaural) 5-10 57-61
ROULETTE (SSR-4158 "Ring-a-Ling-a-Lario")...................................10-20 59
(Stereo.)
ROULETTE (SSR-4218 "T.L.C.")...10-20 60
(Stereo.)
ROULETTE (SSR-8001 "Bo Diddley")......................................15-25 59
(Stereo.)
ROULETTE (SSR-8007 "Froggy Went A-Courtin' ") 10-20 59
(Stereo.)
SCRIMSHAW......................................3-5 78
Picture Sleeves
DOT 4-8 62-64
ROULETTE.......................................10-15 58-61
EPs: 7-inch
ROULETTE.......................................10-20 57-60
LPs: 10/12-inch
A&M...8-15 67-70
DOT 10-20 62-67
FORUM..10-20 60
HAMILTON.......................................10-20 64-65
RCA 8-12 73-75
ROULETTE (25020 thru 25057) 20-30 57-59
ROULETTE (R-25071 thru R-25199)..10-20 59-63
(Monaural.)
ROULETTE (SR-25071 thru SR-25199)..15-25 59-63
(Stereo.)
ROULETTE (42000 series)..............5-10
SCRIMSHAW......................................5-10 78

RODGERS, Jimmie
Singles: 7-inch
ZIG-ZAG 4-8

RODGERS, Lori
Singles: 7-inch
YALE...4-8 60

RODGERS, Michael
Singles: 7-inch
WTG 3-4 88

RODGERS, Morris, & Continentals
Singles: 7-inch
DELTA (602 "Wonders of Love")..100-150 63
(Flip side is #601.)

RODGERS, Nile P&R/R&B/D&D '85
Singles: 12-inch
W.B. 4-6 85
Singles: 7-inch
W.B. 3-4 85
LPs: 10/12-inch
MIRAGE...5-10 84
W.B. 5-8 85
Also see CHIC
Also see HONEYDRIPPERS

RODGERS, Paul LP '83
Singles: 7-inch
ATLANTIC ... 3-5 83
Picture Sleeves
ATLANTIC ... 3-5 83
LPs: 10/12-inch
ATLANTIC ... 5-10 83
Also see BAD COMPANY
Also see FIRM
Also see FREE

RODGERS, Rod
Singles: 7-inch
FILM CITY ... 4-8 60s

RODMAN, Judy C&W '85
Singles: 7-inch
MTM ... 3-4 85-88

RODNEY & BLAZERS
Singles: 7-inch
DORE (572 "Teenage Cinderella") ... 20-30 60
DORE (588 "Tell Me Baby") ... 15-25 61
KAMPUS (100 "Teenage Cinderella") ... 35-50 60
(First issue.)
KAMPUS (880 "Warpaint") ... 20-30 60

RODNEY & BRUNETTES
Singles: 7-inch
BOMP ... 3-5 80

RODNEY-O - JOE COOLEY LP '89
LPs: 10/12-inch
ATLANTIC ... 5-8 90
EGYPT ... 5-8 89

RODRIGUEZ, Johnny C&W '72
Singles: 7-inch
CAPITOL ... 3-4 87-89
COLUMBIA ... 3-5 80
EPIC ... 3-5 79-86
MERCURY ... 3-6 72-79
Picture Sleeves
MERCURY ... 3-5 77
LPs: 10/12-inch
EPIC ... 5-10 80-85
K-TEL ... 5-10 77
MERCURY ... 5-12 73-79
Session: Waylon Jennings.
Also see HALL, Tom T.
Also see JENNINGS, Waylon
Also see TOMORROW'S WORLD

RODRIGUEZ, Johnny, & Charly McClain C&W '79
Singles: 7-inch
EPIC ... 3-5 79
Also see McCLAIN, Charly
Also see RODRIGUEZ, Johnny

RODS
LPs: 10/12-inch
ARISTA ... 5-10 81

RODWAY P&R '82
(Steve Rodway)
Singles: 7-inch
MILLENNIUM ... 3-5 82
LPs: 10/12-inch
MILLENNIUM ... 5-10 82

ROE, Marlys C&W '73
(With Talismen)
Singles: 7-inch
ABC ... 10-15 68
A-OK ... 8-12 67
GRC ... 3-5 73
Also see TALISMEN

ROE, Tommy P&R/R&B/LP '62
(With the Satins; with Flamingos; with Roemans)
Singles: 7-inch
ABC ... 4-8 66-71
ABC-PAR ... 5-10 62-66
AERTAUN (1108 "Wendy") ... 5-8 60s
CURB/MCA ... 3-5 85-86
JUDD (1018 "Caveman") ... 15-25 60
JUDD (1022 "Sheila") ... 25-45 62
MCA ... 3-4 70s
MGM/SOUTH ... 3-5 72-73
MARK IV (001 "Caveman") ... 25-50 60
MERCURY ... 3-5 86-87
MONUMENT ... 3-5 72-77
ROULETTE ... 3-5 70s
TRUMPET (1401 "Caveman") ... 50-75 60
W.B./CURB ... 3-5 78-80
Picture Sleeves
ABC ... 4-8 66-70
ABC-PAR (10362 "Susie Darlin' ") ... 8-12 62
LPs: 10/12-inch
ABC (594 thru 762) ... 10-15 67-72
ABC-PAR (ABC-423 thru ABC-574) ... 20-35 62-66
(Monaural.)
ABC-PAR (ABCS-423 thru ABCS-575) ... 25-40 62-66
(Stereo.)
ACCORD ... 5-10 82
GUSTO ... 5-10 80s
MCA ... 5-10 82
MONUMENT ... 8-12 76-77
Also see ROEMANS

ROE, Tommy / Bobby Rydell / Gene Pitney
LPs: 10/12-inch
INT'L AWARD ... 10-15 60s
Also see PITNEY, Gene

ROE, Tommy / Bobby Rydell / Ray Stevens
LPs: 10/12-inch
DESIGN (178 "Young Lovers") ... 15-20 63
Also see RYDELL, Bobby
Also see STEVENS, Ray

ROE, Tommy / Al Tornello
LPs: 10/12-inch
DIPLOMAT ... 10-20 60s

ROE, Tommy / Bobby Lee Trammell
LPs: 10/12-inch
CROWN ... 15-20 63
Also see ROE, Tommy
Also see TRAMMELL, Bobby Lee

ROECKER, Sherrill
Singles: 7-inch
SWAN ... 4-8 64

ROEMANS
Singles: 7-inch
ABC ... 5-10 66
ABC-PAR ... 10-15 64-66
Member: Bertie Higgins.
Also see HIGGINS, Bertie
Also see ROE, Tommy

ROGER P&R/R&B/LP '81
(Featuring Shirley Murdock; with Mighty Clouds of Joy; Roger Troutman)
Singles: 7-inch
REPRISE ... 3-4 87-88
W.B. ... 3-5 81-85
Picture Sleeves
REPRISE ... 3-4 87
LPs: 10/12-inch
REPRISE ... 5-8 87
W.B. ... 5-10 81-84
Also see MIGHTY CLOUDS OF JOY
Also see SCRITTI POLITTI & ROGER
Also see ZAPP

ROGER & GYPSIES
Singles: 7-inch
SEVEN B ... 10-15 66

ROGER & ROGER
LPs: 10/12-inch
DINGO ... 8-10 73

ROGER & TRAVELERS
Singles: 7-inch
CRYSTAL BALL ... 4-8 78
EMBER (1079 "You're Daddy's Little Girl") ... 100-150 61
(Multi-color label with "logs" logo.)
EMBER (1079 "You're Daddy's Little Girl") ... 50-75 62
(Black label with "flames" logo.)
Member: Roger Koob; Billy Koob; John Roddy; Joe Vece.
Also see KOOB, Roger
Also see PREMIERS

ROGERS, Buck
Singles: 7-inch
MONTEL ... 10-20 59-60

ROGERS, Buck, Movement: see BUCK ROGERS MOVEMENT

ROGERS, Carol
Singles: 7-inch
STEAK CITY (7401 "Ooo Blah-Dee") ... 4-6 74

ROGERS, D.J. P&R/R&B/LP '76
Singles: 12-inch
COLUMBIA ... 4-8 79
Singles: 7-inch
ARC ... 3-5 79-80
COLUMBIA ... 3-5 78-80
RCA ... 3-5 75-76
LPs: 10/12-inch
COLUMBIA ... 5-10 78-80
RCA ... 5-10 76-77
SHELTER ... 5-10 77
Also see RUSHEN, Patrice, & D.J. Rogers

ROGERS, Dan
Singles: 7-inch
ERA (3131 "Lost Without You") ... 25-50 64

ROGERS, Dann P&R '79
Singles: 7-inch
IA ... 3-5 79
MCA ... 3-4 87
LPs: 10/12-inch
IA ... 8-10 79
Also see CUMMINGS, Burton
Also see DELANEY & BONNIE

ROGERS, David C&W '68
Singles: 7-inch
ATLANTIC ... 3-5 73-74
COLUMBIA ... 3-6 68-72
HAL KAT ... 3-4 84
KARI ... 3-5 81
MUSIC MASTER ... 3-4 82-83
REPUBLIC ... 3-5 76-79
U.A. ... 3-5 75
LPs: 10/12-inch
ATLANTIC (7283 "Farewell to the Ryman") ... 10-20 73
ATLANTIC (7306 "Hey There Girl") ... 8-12 74
COLUMBIA ... 8-12 70-72
HAL KAT ... 5-10 84
REPUBLIC ... 5-10 76

ROGERS, Dick
Singles: 7-inch
DA MAR ... 4-8 62

ROGERS, Don, & Ann Tanner
Singles: 7-inch
ASI (15 "Hey Girl, Hey Boy") ... 20-30 59

ROGERS, Eric, & His Orch. LP '61
LPs: 10/12-inch
LONDON/PHASE 4 ... 5-15 61-66

ROGERS, Frantic Johnny
(Al Casey)
Singles: 7-inch
CINDY (3010 "Ramrod") ... 30-40 58
Also see CASEY, Al

ROGERS, Hebrew
Singles: 7-inch
ORIGINAL SOUND ... 3-5 70s

ROGERS, Jack
Singles: 7-inch
KEEN ... 5-10 59

ROGERS, James C&W '89
Singles: 7-inch
SOUNDWAVES ... 3-4 89

ROGERS, Jesse, & His 49ers
(Jesse Rodgers) C&W '49
Singles: 78 rpm
BLUEBIRD ... 10-25 35-49
COWBOY ... 8-10

ROGERS, Jesse
Singles: 7-inch
ARCADE (Except 169) ... 10-20 59-61
ARCADE (169 "Jump Cats, Jump") ... 50-100 62

ROGERS, Jimmy R&B '57
(With His Trio; with His Rocking Four)
Singles: 78 rpm
CHESS (1435 "That's All Right") ... 25-50 50
CHESS (1442 "Going Away Baby") ... 25-50 50
CHESS (1453 "The World Is in a Tangle") ... 25-50 51
CHESS (1476 "Chance to Love") ... 25-50 51
CHESS (1506 thru 1659) ... 15-30 52-57
Singles: 7-inch
CHESS (1506 "I Used to Have a Woman") ... 75-125 52
CHESS (1519 "The Last Time") ... 50-100 52
CHESS (1543 "Left Me with a Broken Heart") ... 50-75 53
CHESS (1574 "Chicago Bound") ... 50-75 54
CHESS (1616 "You're the One") ... 40-60 55
CHESS (1643 "Walking By Myself") ... 40-60 56
CHESS (1659 "One Kiss") ... 40-60 57
CHESS (1721 "My Last Meal") ... 20-30 59
LPs: 10/12-inch
CHESS (407 "Chicago Bound") ... 8-12 74
Also see SUNNYLAND SLIM
Also see WATERS, Muddy
Also see WILLIAMSON, Sonny Boy

ROGERS, Jimmy, & Freddy King
LPs: 10/12-inch
SHELTER (8921 "Gold Tailed Bird") ... 8-12 73
Also see KING, Freddy
Also see ROGERS, Jimmy

ROGERS, Joey
Singles: 7-inch
ABC-PAR ... 5-10 60

ROGERS, Johnny, & Time Travelers
Singles: 7-inch
FRATERNITY ... 3-5 85

ROGERS, Juanita, & Lynn Hollings
(With Mr. V's Five Joys)
Singles: 7-inch
PINK CLOUDS (333 "Teenager's Letter of Promises") ... 50-100 58

ROGERS, Julie P&R '64
Singles: 7-inch
MEGA ... 3-5 72
MERCURY ... 4-8 64-66
Picture Sleeves
MERCURY ... 5-10 65
LPs: 10/12-inch
MEGA ... 5-10 72
MERCURY ... 15-25 65

ROGERS, Junior, Combo
Singles: 7-inch
VANESSA ... 4-8 61

ROGERS, Ken
Singles: 7-inch
NATIONAL ... 4-8 67

ROGERS, Kenny C&W '75
(Kenneth Rogers; with Linda Davis)
Singles: 7-inch
CARLTON (454 "That Crazy Feeling") ... 25-50 58
CARLTON (468 "For You Alone") ... 25-50 58
EVA-TONE/READER'S DIGEST ("His Greatest Hits") ... 10-15 83
(Single-sided, square, cardboard soundsheet. Promotional issue only.)
JOLLY ROGERS ... 3-5 73-74
KEN-LEE (102 "Jole Blon") ... 50-100 50s
LIBERTY ... 3-4 80-86
MERCURY ... 5-10 66
RCA ... 3-4 84-89
REPRISE ... 3-4 89-91
U.A. ... 3-5 76-80
Picture Sleeves
LIBERTY ... 3-4 80-83
RCA ... 3-4 84-86
U.A. ... 3-5 79-80
LPs: 10/12-inch
BREAKAWAY ... 5-8 84
JOLLY ROGERS (5001 "Backroads") ... 100-200 75
(Promotional picture disc.)
LIBERTY (Except 8344) ... 5-10 80-85
LIBERTY (8344 "HBO Presents Kenny Rogers Greatest Hits") ... 15-20 83
(Promotional only picture disc.)
MFSL (044 "The Gambler") ... 25-35 80
MFSL (049 "Greatest Hits") ... 25-35 80
MASTERS ... 5-10
PICKWICK ... 5-10 79
QSP ... 5-10 84
RCA ... 5-8 84-87
REPRISE ... 5-8 89
U.A. (Except 934) ... 5-8 76-80
U.A. (934 "The Gambler") ... 5-10 78
(Black vinyl.)
U.A. (934 "The Gambler) ... 50-100 78
(Picture disc. Promotional issue only. One of a four-artist, four-LP set.)
Also see CAMPBELL, Glen / Anne Murray / Kenny Rogers / Crystal Gayle
Also see DAVIS, Linda
Also see DOYLE, Bobby
Also see MILSAP, Ronnie, & Kenny Rogers
Also see MURRAY, Anne, & Kenny Rogers
Also see U.S.A. for AFRICA

ROGERS, Kenny, & Kim Carnes C&W/P&R '80
Singles: 7-inch
U.A. ... 3-5 80
Picture Sleeves
U.A. ... 3-5 80
Also see CARNES, Kim

ROGERS, Kenny, Kim Carnes & James Ingram C&W/P&R/R&B '84
Singles: 7-inch
RCA ... 3-4 84
Picture Sleeves
RCA ... 3-4 84
Also see INGRAM, James
Also see ROGERS, Kenny, & Kim Carnes

ROGERS, Kenny, & Holly Dunn C&W '90
Singles: 7-inch
REPRISE ... 3-4 90
Also see DUNN, Holly

ROGERS, Kenny, & Sheena Easton C&W/P&R '83
Singles: 7-inch
LIBERTY ... 3-4 83
Picture Sleeves
LIBERTY ... 3-4 83
LPs: 10/12-inch
LIBERTY ... 5-10 84
Also see EASTON, Sheena

ROGERS, Kenny, & Dolly Parton P&R '83
Singles: 7-inch
RCA ... 3-4 83-85
REPRISE ... 3-4 90
Picture Sleeves
RCA ... 3-4 83
Also see PARTON, Dolly

ROGERS, Kenny, & Nickie Ryder C&W '86
Singles: 7-inch
RCA ... 3-4 86

ROGERS, Kenny, & First Edition P&R/C&W/LP '69
Singles: 7-inch
JOLLY ROGERS ... 3-5 72-73
REPRISE ... 4-8 68-72
LPs: 10/12-inch
JOLLY ROGERS ... 8-12 72-73
REPRISE ... 10-25 69-72
Members: Kenny Rogers; Mike Settle; Terry Williams; Mickey Jones; Kin Vassey; Mary Arnold.
Also see FIRST EDITION

ROGERS, Kenny, & Dottie West C&W '78
Singles: 7-inch
LIBERTY ... 3-5 81-84
U.A. ... 3-5 78-79
LPs: 10/12-inch
U.A. ... 5-10 78-80
LPs: 10/12-inch
Also see ROGERS, Kenny
Also see WEST, Dottie

ROGERS, Lee R&B '65
Singles: 7-inch
DIAMOND JIM (1006 "Sweetest Woman Ever Born") ... 5-10
DIAMOND JIM (1008 "Sex Appeal") ... 5-10
D-TOWN (1029 "Sad Affair") ... 10-20 64
D-TOWN (1035 "I Want You to Have Everything") ... 10-20 64
D-TOWN (1041 "Cream of the Crop") ... 10-20 64
D-TOWN (1050 "Boss Love") ... 10-20 64
D-TOWN (1062 "You Won't Have to Wait Til Christmas") ... 10-20 65
D-TOWN (1067 "I'm a Practical Guy") ... 10-20 65
INSTANT ... 3-5 72
LOADSTONE ... 3-5 72
MAH'S (9 "Walk on By") ... 15-25 62
PLATINUM SOUND ... 3-5 79
PREMIUM STUFF (4 "Jack the Playboy") ... 15-25 67
WHEELSVILLE ... 15-25 66

ROGERS, Lelan
Singles: 7-inch
LYNN (502 "Hold It") ... 20-30 60

ROGERS, Lori
Singles: 7-inch
OLD TOWN ... 4-8 61
SCEPTER ... 4-8 62

ROGERS, Menard
Singles: 7-inch
MARGARET ... 4-8 82

ROGERS, Milt
Singles: 7-inch
DOT (16296 "Let's Go Trippin' ") ... 10-20 61

ROGERS, Pauline
Singles: 78 rpm
FLAIR-X ... 10-20 56
Singles: 7-inch
FLAIR-X (5001 "I've Been Pretending") ... 20-30 56

ROGERS, Rock
(Leon Payne)
Singles: 78 rpm
STARDAY (245 "That Ain't It") ... 25-50 56
Singles: 7-inch
STARDAY (245 "That Ain't It") ... 75-100 56
Also see PAYNE, Leon

ROGERS, Rod
Singles: 7-inch
FILM CITY (3024 "Move Along Surfing Girl") ... 20-30 60s
LUTONE (900 "I've Been Missing Someone") ... 10-20 60s

ROGERS, Ronnie C&W '81
Singles: 7-inch
EPIC ... 3-4 83
LIFESONG ... 3-4 81-82
MTM ... 3-4 87-88

ROGERS, Roy P&R '38/C&W '46
(With Dale Evans; with Sons of the Pioneers)
Singles: 78 rpm
DECCA ... 10-20 40-44
GOLDEN ... 4-6 50s
RCA ... 5-15 50-57
VICTOR ... 8-15 45-48
VOCALION ... 20-30 38
Singles: 7-inch
CAPITOL ... 3-5 70-71
GOLDEN ... 5-8 50s
MCA ... 3-5 80
NEW DISC ... 8-12 56
RCA (Except 215) ... 5-15 51-52
RCA (215 "Souvenir Album") ... 20-40 49
(Boxed set of three colored vinyl 45s.)
20TH FOX ... 3-5 74-75
Picture Sleeves
GOLDEN ... 5-8 50s
EPs: 7-inch
BLUEBIRD ... 10-20 50s
RCA (Except 3041) ... 12-25 50-57
RCA (3041 "Souvenir Album") ... 25-50 52
LPs: 10/12-inch
BLUEBIRD ... 15-25 59
CAMDEN ... 10-20 60-75
CAPITOL ... 10-30 62-72
GHOST TOWN ... 10-20 70s
GOLDEN ... 15-30 62
NOSTALGIA MERCHANT ... 8-10
PICKWICK ... 5-10 70s
RADIOLA ... 8-10
RCA (1439 "Sweet Hour of Prayer") ... 20-30 57
RCA (3041 "Souvenir Album") ... 40-60 52
(10-inch LP.)
RCA (3168 "Hymns of Faith") ... 30-50 54
(10-inch LP.)
20TH FOX ... 5-10 75
WORD ... 4-8 73-77
Also see SONS of the PIONEERS

ROGERS, Roy, & Clint Black C&W '91
Singles: 7-inch
RCA ... 3-4 91
Also see BLACK, Clint

ROGERS, Roy, with Spade Cooley's Buckle Busters
Singles: 78 rpm
CORAL (8004 "Square Dances") ... 15-25 50
(Boxed, three-disc set.)
Singles: 7-inch
CORAL (8004 "Square Dances") ... 25-50 50
(Boxed, three-disc set.)
Also see COOLEY, Spade
Also see ROGERS, Roy

ROGERS, Shorty
(Mickey Shorty Rogers)
Singles: 7-inch
TAMPA (154 "Big Boy") ... 15-25 58
Also see BROWN, Boots
Also see COOL, Calvin

ROGERS, Smokey C&W '49
Singles: 78 rpm
CAPITOL ... 5-10 49
LPs: 10/12-inch
SHASTA ... 5-10

ROGERS, Timmie P&R '57
(Timmie "Oh Yeah" Rogers; with Excelsior Hep Cats; with Stomp Russell Trio; Timmy Rogers; Super Soul Brother Alias Clark Dark.)
Singles: 78 rpm
CAMEO ... 10-25 57-58
CAPITOL ... 5-10 53
EXCELSIOR ... 10-20 45
MAJESTIC ... 10-20 46
MERCURY ... 10-20 54

REGIS ... 10-20 45
VARSITY ... 10-20 50s

Singles: 7-inch

CADET ... 3-5 71
CAMEO ... 5-10 57-58
CAPITOL ... 5-10 53
EPIC ... 4-8 65-66
MERCURY (70451 "If I Give My Heart to You") ... 20-30 54
PARKWAY ... 5-10 60
PARTEE ... 3-5 73
PHILIPS ... 4-8 62
SIGNATURE ... 5-10 60

LPs: 10/12-inch

EPIC ... 15-20 65
PARTEE ... 10-15 73
PHILIPS ... 15-20 63

ROGERS, Vinnie

Singles: 7-inch

DUEL (512 "Flash Flood") ... 8-12 62

ROGERS, Weldon

Singles: 78 rpm

IMPERIAL ... 50-75 57

Singles: 7-inch

IMPERIAL (5451 "So Long, Good Luck and Goodbye"/"Tryin to Get to You") ... 50-75 57
(This track of *Trying to Get to You* was previously issued as by the Teen Kings on Je-wel.)
Also see TEEN KINGS

ROGERS, Weldon, & Wand Wolfe

Singles: 78 rpm

JE-WEL ... 50-100 56

Singles: 7-inch

JE-WEL (103 "Everybody Wants You") ... 200-300 56
(With Glen Campbell.)
Also see CAMPBELL, Glen
Also see ROGERS, Weldon

ROGERS & SCHWARTZ

Singles: 7-inch

MAELSTROM (1 "Election 1980") ... 4-6 80

ROGUES

Singles: 78 rpm

OLD TOWN ... 10-30 56-57

Singles: 7-inch

OLD TOWN (300 "If You Love Me") ... 20-30 56
OLD TOWN (304 "Puppy Love") ... 20-30 57
OLD TOWN (1056 "I've Been Dreaming") ... 15-20 58

ROGUES

Singles: 7-inch

GUYDEN (2007 "Lullaby") ... 8-10 59

ROGUES

Singles: 7-inch

BING (4900 "Barracuda") ... 20-30 64

ROGUES

Singles: 7-inch

COLUMBIA (43190 "Everyday") ... 10-20 64
COLUMBIA (43253 "Come on Let's Go") ... 10-20 65
Members: Bruce Johnston; Terry Melcher; Phil Stewart; Ernie Bringas.
Also see BRUCE & TERRY
Also see RIP CHORDS

ROGUES

Singles: 7-inch

STO-VA-CO (6406 "I'm Not That Way at All") ... 8-12 65

ROGUES

Singles: 7-inch

COMPASS (1857 "Don't Follow Me") ... 10-15 65

ROGUES

Singles: 7-inch

MBM (2002 "Put You Down") ... 15-25 65

ROGUES

Singles: 7-inch

RAZORBACK (127 "Wait & See") ... 5-10 65

ROGUES

Singles: 7-inch

ROGUE (130 "She's the One") ... 8-12 66

ROGUES

Singles: 7-inch

PEYTON (2081 "Oh No") ... 20-30 66
Also see SQUIRES

ROGUES

Singles: 7-inch

AUDITION (6110 "Train Kept A-Rollin'") ... 15-25 66

ROGUES

Singles: 7-inch

THUNDERBIRD (507 "Secondary Man") ... 5-10 66
THUNDERBIRD (511 "Should You Care") ... 5-10 66

ROGUES

Singles: 7-inch

ACTION (6400 "Anything You Say") ... 10-20 66

ROGUES

Singles: 7-inch

KAPAN (713 "It's Gonna Work Out Fine") ... 15-25 66
KAPAN (999 "Tell Me No Lies") ... 15-25 67

ROGUES

Singles: 7-inch

MIRAGE (601 "Something Beautiful Is Dying") ... 15-25 67

ROGUES

Singles: 7-inch

LA LOUISIANE (8094 "Tonight") ... 15-25 67

ROGUES

Singles: 7-inch

WELHAVEN (9582 "Sam") ... 40-60 67

ROGUES

Singles: 7-inch

NIGHT OWL (67102 "The Secret") ... 10-15 67
Members: John Castellano; Larry Krzeminski; Rick Rebstock; Casey Dutcavich; Ron Olenik.

ROGUES

Singles: 7-inch

TALENT ASSOCIATES ("Good Lovin'") ... 20-30 60s
("Talent Associates" name and address is on the label, but may not be a label name. However, there is no other indication of a label name. Sold at the group's concerts.)

ROGUES

Singles: 7-inch

BOSS CITY (160 "No Lies") ... 10-20 68
BOSS CITY (166 "Tobacco Road") ... 10-20 68

ROGUES

Singles: 7-inch

LYN LOU (1126 "How Many Times") ... 5-10 60s

ROGUES FIVE

Singles: 7-inch

PRIDE INC. (7339 "It's On Again") ... 10-15 60s
Member: Randy Ess.

ROHRS, Donnie *C&W '78*

Singles: 7-inch

AD-KORP ... 3-8 78
PACIFIC CHALLENGER ... 3-5 81

LPs: 10/12-inch

PACIFIC CHALLENGER ... 5-10 81

ROK

Singles: 7-inch

MARK VII (1012 "Transparent Day") ... 15-25 66

ROKES

Singles: 7-inch

RCA (9199 "Let's Live for Today") ... 5-10 67
RCA (9546 "When the Wind Arises") ... 5-10 67

LPs: 10/12-inch

RCA INT'L (185 "Che Mondo Strano") ... 30-50 67

ROLAND, Adrian *C&W '60*

Singles: 7-inch

ALLSTAR ... 5-10 60

ROLAND, Danny

Singles: 7-inch

BAYOU ... 5-10 61

ROLLE, Ralph *D&D '85*

Singles: 12-inch

STREETWISE ... 4-6 85

Singles: 7-inch

STREETWISE ... 3-4 85

ROLLER, Lonesome Long John / Ned Mullan

Singles: 7-inch

FLAGPOLE (28 "Blue Am I") ... 100-150
FLAGPOLE (301 "Long John's Flagpole Rock") ... 100-150

ROLLER COASTERS

Singles: 7-inch

DEL-FI ... 5-10 63
HOLIDAY INN ... 5-10 61-62

ROLLERS *P&R/R&B '61*

Singles: 7-inch

LIBERTY (55303 "Got My Eye on You") ... 10-15 61
LIBERTY (55320 "The Continental Walk") ... 10-15 61
LIBERTY (55357 "The Bounce") ... 10-15 61
Member: Al Wilson; Eddie Wilson; Don Sampson; Willie Willingham.
Also see WILSON, Al

ROLLERS

Singles: 7-inch

BELLE STAR ... 4-8 62

ROLLERS

Singles: 7-inch

ARISTA ... 3-5 79

LPs: 10/12-inch

ARISTA ... 5-10 79
Also see BAY CITY ROLLERS

ROLLETTES

Singles: 78 rpm

CLASS ... 10-15 56

Singles: 7-inch

CLASS (201 "Sad Fool") ... 20-30 56
CLASS (203 "More Than You Realize") ... 20-30 56

ROLLETTES

Singles: 7-inch

MELKER (103 "An Understanding") ... 1000-2000 60

ROLLETTES ORCHESTRA

Singles: 7-inch

CINCH (2025 "Venus Rock") ... 20-40 58
CINCH ("Satellite Boogie") ... 20-40 59
(Selection number not known.)
Member: Raymond Ojeda; Leroy Titzi; Floyd Jester; Ray Titzi; Gerry Bartelmas.
Also see NIGHT BEATS

ROLLIN, Dana *P&R '66*

Singles: 7-inch

TOWER ... 4-8 67

ROLLING CREW

("With Orchestra")

Singles: 78 rpm

ALADDIN (3301 "Crying Emma") ... 20-30 55

Singles: 7-inch

ALADDIN (3301 "Crying Emma") ... 50-100 55

ROLLING STONE QUINTET

Singles: 7-inch

CHOICE ... 5-10 60

ROLLING STONES *P&R/LP '64*

Singles: 12-inch

ATCO (4616 "Miss You") ... 10-20 79
ROLLING STONES (70 "Hot Stuff") ... 50-100 76
(Promotional issue only.)
ROLLING STONES (119 "Miss You") ... 25-50 78
(Promotional issue only.)
ROLLING STONES (253 "If I Was a Dancer") ... 25-50 79
(Promotional issue only.)
ROLLING STONES (367 "Emotional Rescue") ... 20-40 80
(Promotional issue only.)
ROLLING STONES (397 "Start Me Up") ... 20-40 81
(Promotional issue only. Price includes special cover.)
ROLLING STONES (574 "She Was Hot") ... 20-40 84
(Promotional issue only.)
ROLLING STONES (685 "Undercover of the Night") ... 25-40 83
(White label. Promotional issue only.)
ROLLING STONES (685 "Undercover of the Night") ... 20-40 83
(Yellow label. Promotional issue only.)
ROLLING STONES (692 "Too Much Blood") ... 20-40 85
(Promotional issue only. Price includes special cover.)
ROLLING STONES (2275 "Harlem Shuffle") ... 10-15 86
(Price includes special cover.)
ROLLING STONES (2275 "Harlem Shuffle") ... 10-20 86
(Promotional issue only. Price includes special cover.)
ROLLING STONES (2340 "One Hit") ... 10-15 86
(Price includes color cover.)
ROLLING STONES (2340 "One Hit") ... 20-30 86
(Price includes black and white cover. Promotional issue only.)
ROLLING STONES (4609 "Miss You") ... 10-15 78
(Price includes special cover.)
ROLLING STONES (4616 "Miss You"/"Hot Stuff") ... 15-25 78
ROLLING STONES (96902 "Too Much Blood") ... 10-15 85
(Price includes special cover.)
ROLLING STONES (96978 "Undercover of the Night") ... 10-15 83
(Price includes special cover.)

Singles: 7-inch

ABKCO (4701 "I Don't Know Why") ... 5-10 75
ABKCO (4702 "Out of Time") ... 5-10 75
COLUMBIA ... 3-5 90-91
LONDON (901 thru 910) ... 4-8 66-69
LONDON (9641 "Stoned") ... 3000-4000 64
LONDON (9657 "Not Fade Away") ... 10-20 64
(Purple and white label.)
LONDON (9657 "Not Fade Away") ... 8-10 65
(Blue and white swirl label.)
LONDON (9682 "Tell Me") ... 10-20 64
(Purple and white label.)
LONDON (9682 "Tell Me") ... 8-10 65
(Blue and white swirl label.)
LONDON (9687 "It's All Over Now") ... 10-20 64
(Purple and white label.)
LONDON (9687 "It's All Over Now") ... 8-10 65
(Blue and white swirl label.)
LONDON (9708 "Time Is on My Side") ... 10-20 64
(Purple and white label.)
LONDON (9708 "Time Is on My Side") ... 25-50 64
(Purple label with silver print. Canadian.)
LONDON (9708 "Time Is on My Side") ... 8-10 65
(Blue and white swirl label.)
LONDON (9725 "Heart of Stone") ... 10-20 65
(Purple and white label.)
LONDON (9725 "Heart of Stone") ... 25-50 65
(Purple label with silver print. Canadian.)
LONDON (9725 "Heart of Stone") ... 5-10 65
(Blue and white swirl label.)
LONDON (9741 "The Last Time") ... 10-12 65
(Purple and white label.)
LONDON (9741 "The Last Time") ... 5-10 65
(Blue and white swirl label.)
LONDON (9766 "Satisfaction") ... 5-10 65
LONDON (9766 "Satisfaction") ... 25-50 65
(Purple label with silver print. Canadian.)
LONDON (9792 "Get Off of My Cloud") ... 5-10 65
LONDON (9808 "As Tears Go By") ... 5-10 65
LONDON (9823 "19th Nervous Breakdown") ... 5-10 66
ROLLING STONES (Except 99724) ... 3-5 71-86
ROLLING STONES (99724 "Miss You"/"Too Tough") ... 10-15 78
VIRGIN (38448 "Love Is Strong") ... 3-4 94
WMEE 97FM (001 "The Stones on 97") ... 4-8
Note: The three Canadian purple label with silver print issues are the only ones we have confirmed so far with that label — the same as used by London in the '50s and early '60s. If any other early Stones singles came on this label, we would like to know of them.

Promotional Singles

ABKCO (4701 "I Don't Know Why") ... 8-12 75
ABKCO (4702 "Out of Time") ... 8-12 75
COLUMBIA ... 5-10 90
LONDON (901 thru 910) ... 20-30 66-69
LONDON (9641 "Stoned") ... 1000-2000 64
LONDON (9657 "Not Fade Away") ... 50-100 64
LONDON (9682 "Tell Me") ... 25-50 64
LONDON (9687 "It's All Over Now") ... 25-50 64
LONDON (9708 "Time Is on My Side") ... 25-50 64
LONDON (9725 "Heart of Stone") ... 25-50 65
LONDON (9741 "The Last Time") ... 25-50 65
LONDON (9766 "Satisfaction") ... 15-25 65
LONDON (9792 "Get Off of My Cloud") ... 15-25 65
LONDON (9808 "As Tears Go By") ... 15-25 65
LONDON (9823 "19th Nervous Breakdown") ... 15-25 66
ROLLING STONES (228 "Time Waits for No One") ... 15-25 76
ROLLING STONES (316 "Before They Make Me Run") ... 15-25 78
ROLLING STONES (05000 series) ... 5-15 86
ROLLING STONES (19000 thru 21301, except 19307) ... 5-15 71-82
ROLLING STONES (19307 "Miss You"/Far Away Eyes") ... 5-15 78
ROLLING STONES (19307 "Far Away Eyes"/ Far Away Eyes") ... 50-100 78
ROLLING STONES (90000 series, except 99724) ... 5-10 82-85
ROLLING STONES (99724 "Miss You"/"Miss You") ... 15-25 78

Picture Sleeves

LONDON (901 "Paint It Black") ... 15-25 66
LONDON (902 "Mother's Little Helper") ... 15-25 66
LONDON (903 "Have You Seen Your Mother Baby, Standing in the Shadows") ... 15-25 66
LONDON (904 "Ruby Tuesday") ... 15-25 67
LONDON (905 "Dandelion") ... 100-150 67
LONDON (906 "She's a Rainbow") ... 15-25 67
LONDON (908 "Jumpin' Jack Flash") ... 10-20 68
LONDON (909 "Street Fighting Man") ... 5000-10000 68
(Thus far, 12 copies are known to exist.)
LONDON (910 "Honky Tonk Women") ... 10-20 69
LONDON (9657 "Not Fade Away") ... 150-250 64
LONDON (9682 "Tell Me") ... 75-125 64
LONDON (9687 "It's All Over Now") ... 50-100 64
LONDON (9708 "Time Is on My Side") ... 50-100 64
LONDON (9725 "Heart of Stone") ... 550-650 65
LONDON (9741 "The Last Time") ... 25-50 65
LONDON (9766 "Satisfaction") ... 50-100 65
LONDON (9792 "Get Off of My Cloud") ... 25-35 65
LONDON (9808 "As Tears Go By") ... 25-35 65
LONDON (9823 "19th Nervous Breakdown") ... 25-45 66
ROLLING STONES (Except 228, 316 and 19309) ... 3-6 78-86
ROLLING STONES (228 "Time Waits for No One") ... 15-25 76
(Promotional issue only.)
ROLLING STONES (316 "Before They Make Me Run") ... 15-25 78
(Promotional issue only.)
ROLLING STONES (19309 "Beast of Burden") ... 1000-2000 78
ROLLING STONES ... 3-6 71-81
(For generic, die-cut paper sleeves with Rolling Stones tongue logo. Not for any specific release.)
VIRGIN (38448 "Love Is Strong") ... 3-4 94

EPs: 7-inch

ATLANTIC (900 "Exile on Main Street") ... 50-75 72
(Juke box issue only.)
ATLANTIC (5901 "Goats Head Soup") ... 50-75 73
(Juke box issue only.)
LONDON (34 "Rolling Stones Now") ... 100-200 64
(Juke box issue only.)
LONDON (37 "Out of Our Heads") ... 100-200 64
(Juke box issue only.)
LONDON (43 "December's Children") ... 100-200 64
(Juke box issue only.)
LONDON (54 "Their Satanic Majesties Request") ... 150-250 64
(Juke box issue only.)
ROLLING STONES (287 "The Rolling Stones") ... 50-100 77
(Promotional issue only.)

LPs: 10/12-inch

ABKCO (0268 "Greatest Hits") ... 20-25 70s
(TV mail-order offer.)
ABKCO (1077 "30 Greatest Hits") ... 20-25 77
(Canadian.)
ABKCO (1089 "Greatest Hits, Vol. II") ... 20-25 77
ABKCO (1218 "Singles Collection") ... 15-25 89
(Four-LP set.)
CAPITOL (61755 "Voodoo Lounge") ... 10-15 90s
CAPITOL (7527 "Stripped") ... 10-15 90s
CRAWDADDY ("Rolling Stones Tour Special") ... 150-200 76
(Promotional issue to college radio stations only.)
D.I.R. (312 "King Biscuit Flower Hour") ... 150-200 80
(Promotional issue only.)
D.I.R. (325 "King Biscuit Flower Hour") ... 150-200 80
(Promotional issue only.)
INS RADIO (1003 "It's Here Luv") ... 75-125 65
LONDON (1 "Big Hits") ... 25-50 66
(Monaural.)
LONDON (RSD1 "The Promotional Album") ... 800-1000
LONDON (2 "Their Satanic Majesties Request") ... 100-200 67
(Monaural. Has 3-D cover.)
LONDON (2 "Their Satanic Majesties Request") ... 25-50 67
(Stereo. Has 3-D cover.)
LONDON (2 "Their Satanic Majesties Request") ... 10-15 70
(Stereo. With standard cover.)
LONDON (3 "Through the Past Darkly") ... 8-10 69
LONDON (4 "Let It Bleed") ... 10-20 69
(With bonus poster.)
LONDON (4 "Let It Bleed") ... 8-10 69
(Without poster.)
LONDON (5 "Get Your Ya-Yas Out") ... 8-10 70
LONDON (375 "Rolling Stones") ... 30-50 64
(Stereo. Add $75 to $100 if accompanied by a 12" x 12" bonus, color photo. Cover has printed note about photo at lower left. With "Full Frequency Range Recording" label.)
LONDON (375 "Rolling Stones") ... 8-10 65
(No mention of photo on cover. Does not have "Full Frequency Range Recording" on label.)
LONDON (402 "12 x 5") ... 30-50 64
(Stereo. With "Full Frequency Range Recording" label.)
LONDON (402 "12 x 5") ... 8-10 65
(Does not have "Full Frequency Range Recording" on label.)
LONDON (420 "Rolling Stones Now") ... 30-50 65
(Stereo. With "Full Frequency Range Recording" label.)
LONDON (420 "Rolling Stones Now") ... 8-10 65
(Does not have "Full Frequency Range Recording" on label.)
LONDON (429 "Out of Our Heads") ... 30-50 65
(Stereo. With "Full Frequency Range Recording" label.)
LONDON (429 "Out of Our Heads") ... 8-10 65
(Does not have "Full Frequency Range Recording" on label.)
LONDON (451 "December's Children") ... 30-50 65
(Stereo. With "Full Frequency Range Recording" label.)
LONDON (451 "December's Children") ... 8-10 65
(Does not have "Full Frequency Range Recording" on label.)
LONDON (476 "Aftermath") ... 8-10 66
(Stereo.)
LONDON (493 "Got Live If You Want It") ... 8-10 66
(Stereo.)
LONDON (499 "Between the Buttons") ... 8-10 67
(Stereo.)
LONDON (509 "Flowers") ... 8-10 67
(Stereo.)
LONDON (539 "Beggars Banquet") ... 8-12 68
(All songs are shown as written by Jagger & Richard.)
LONDON (539 "Beggars Banquet") ... 8-10 60s
(*Prodigal Son* is shown as written by Rev. Wilkins.)
LONDON (606/7 "Hot Rocks") ... 10-12 71
LONDON (626/7 "More Hot Rocks") ... 10-12 72
LONDON (3375 "The Rolling Stones") ... 75-100 64
(Monaural. With "Full Frequency Range Recording" label. Add $75 to $100 if accompanied by a 12" x 12" bonus, color photo. Cover has printed note about photo at lower left.)
LONDON (3375 "The Rolling Stones") ... 30-40 65
(Does not have "Full Frequency Range Recording" on label.)
LONDON (3375 "The Rolling Stones") ... 500-1000 64
(White label, monaural. Promotional issue only.)

LONDON (3402 "12 x 5")..............50-75 64
(Monaural. With "Full Frequency Range Recording" label.)
LONDON (3402 "12 x 5")..............30-40 65
(Does not have "Full Frequency Range Recording" on label.)
LONDON (3420 "Rolling Stones Now")..............50-75 65
(Monaural. With "Full Frequency Range Recording" label.)
LONDON (3420 "Rolling Stones Now")..............30-40 65
(Does not have "Full Frequency Range Recording" on label.)
LONDON (3429 "Out of Our Heads")..............50-75 65
(Monaural. With "Full Frequency Range Recording" label.)
LONDON (3429 "Out of Our Heads")..............30-40 65
(Does not have "Full Frequency Range Recording" on label.)
LONDON (3451 "December's Children")..............50-75 65
(Monaural. With "Full Frequency Range Recording" label.)
LONDON (3451 "December's Children")..............30-40 65
(Does not have "Full Frequency Range Recording" on label.)
LONDON (3476 "Aftermath")..........20-30 66
(Monaural.)
LONDON (3493 "Got Live If You Want It")..............20-30 66
(Monaural.)
LONDON (3499 "Between the Buttons")..............20-30 67
(Monaural.)
LONDON (3509 "Flowers")............20-30 67
(Monaural.)
LONDON (9134 "Big Hits, High Tide & Green Grass")..............1000-1500 69
(Test picture disc. Some have photo of the group Ten Years After on one side. All have music from *Thru the Past Darkly*.)
LONDON/ABKCO (66671 "Hot Rocks")..............15-18 96
LONDON/ABKCO (62671 "Fazed Cookies")..............15-18 96
LONDON/ABKCO (70,000 series) 10-15 96
LONDON/ABKCO (80,000 series) 10-15 96
MFSL (1 "Rolling Stones")..........250-300 85
(11-LP boxed set, includes booklet, postcard and alignment tool.)
MFSL (060 "Sticky Fingers")..........30-50 82
MFSL (087 "Some Girls")..........30-50 82
MUTUAL BROADCASTING SYSTEM ("Rolling Stones: Past and Present")......800-1200 84
(Boxed, 12-disc set, issued only to radio stations. Price includes programming sheets.)
ROLLING STONES (2900 "Exile on Main St.")..............10-15 72
(Add $3 to $5 if accompanied by sheet of 12 bonus postcards.)
ROLLING STONES (9001 "Love You Live")..............10-15 77
ROLLING STONES (16015 "Emotional Rescue")..............5-10 80
ROLLING STONES (16028 "Sucking in the Seventies")..............5-10 81
ROLLING STONES (16052 "Tattoo You")..............5-10 81
ROLLING STONES (39108 "Some Girls")..............10-15 78
(With all girls' faces shown.)
ROLLING STONES (39108 "Some Girls")..............5-10 78
(Not all girls' faces shown. Cover is "Under Construction.")
ROLLING STONES (39113 "Still Life")..............5-10 82
ROLLING STONES (39114 "Still Life")..............40-50 82
(Picture disc.)
ROLLING STONES (40250 "Dirty Work")..............5-10 86
ROLLING STONES (45333 "Steel Wheels")..............5-10 89
ROLLING STONES (47456 "Flashpoint")..............8-10 91
ROLLING STONES (59100 "Sticky Fingers")..............8-10 71
(Yellow label.)
ROLLING STONES (59100 "Sticky Fingers")..............150-250 71
(White label. Promotional issue only.)
ROLLING STONES (59101 "Goats Head Soup")..............8-10 73
ROLLING STONES (79101 "It's Only Rock & Roll")..............8-10 74
ROLLING STONES (79102 "Made in the Shade")..............8-10 75
ROLLING STONES (79104 "Black and Blue")..............8-10 76
ROLLING STONES (90120 "Undercover")..............5-10 83
ROLLING STONES (90176 "Rewind")..............5-10 84
SILHOUETTE (10005 "Precious Moments")..............10-15 81
(Picture disc. Is this title correct?)
VIRGIN..............8-10 94
Members: Mick Jagger; Keith Richards; Bill Wyman; Brian Jones; Charlie Watts; Mick Taylor; Ron Wood.
Also see BEACH BOYS
Also see FAITHFUL, Marianne
Also see HOPKINS, Nicky
Also see JAGGER, Mick
Also see JAMESON, Bobby
Also see JONES, Brian
Also see RICHARDS, Keith
Also see ROCKET 88
Also see TAYLOR, Mick
Also see WILLIE & Poor Boys
Also see WOOD, Ron
Also see WYMAN, Bill

ROLLINS, Bird
Singles: 7-inch
HARVARD..............5-10 60
JOHNSON (105 "Pretty Little School Girl")..............25-35 57
SKYMAC..............4-8 64
VANGUARD (35003 "You Are My Angel")..............50-75 58

ROLLINS, Debbie
Singles: 7-inch
ASCOT..............4-8 64

ROMA, Anthony
(Tony Roma)
Singles: 7-inch
CAPITOL..............4-8 63
MGM (13056 "Heaven")..............5-10 62
PREP..............5-10 60s
SONIC..............5-10 60s

ROMA, Teena
Singles: 7-inch
ARTEEN..............8-12 61

ROMA, Tony: see ROMA, Anthony

ROMAINE, Dave
Singles: 7-inch
NEWPORT (102 "Night Train")........8-12

ROMAINES
Singles: 78 rpm
GROOVE..............15-25 54
Singles: 7-inch
GROOVE (35 "Your Kind of Love")..............35-50 54

ROMAN, Bud: see SMITH, Hank

ROMAN, Danny
Singles: 7-inch
AD LIB..............10-15 60
TAZ (1005 "Let's Cut Out")..........25-35 57

ROMAN, Diana
Singles: 7-inch
LAURIE..............4-8 62

ROMAN, Dick P&R '62
Singles: 78 rpm
ABC-PAR..............4-8 56
DOUBLE AA..............4-6 55-56
Singles: 7-inch
ABC-PAR..............5-10 56
CHARLIE PARKER..............4-8 62
CORAL..............4-6 60s
DOUBLE AA..............5-10 55-56
EPIC..............4-8 59-61
FORD..............4-8 60s
HARMON..............5-10 62-63
MGM..............4-6 60s
PRESIDENT..............4-6 60s
SEVILLE..............4-6 60s
SMASH..............4-8 63
LPs: 10/12-inch
HARMON..............15-25 62

ROMAN, Don
Singles: 7-inch
DAANI..............20-30 63
Also see ZAPPA, Frank

ROMAN, Lyn R&B '86
Singles: 7-inch
DOT..............4-6 68
ICHIBAN..............3-4 86

ROMAN, Murray
Singles: 7-inch
U.A...............3-6 72
LPs: 10/12-inch
EVEREST..............15-25 60
NERO..............20-30 60
TETRAGRAMMATON..............10-15 68-69
U.A. (5595 "Busted")..............15-20 72
(Promotional issue only. With bonus single and bio insert.)

ROMAN, Net
(Nap Roman)
Singles: 7-inch
SAHARA (102 "Tears from My Eyes")..............1000-1500 63
(Credits Net Roman.)
SAHARA (102 "Tears from My Eyes")..............500-1000 63
(Credits "Nap" Roman.)

ROMAN, Rich
Singles: 7-inch
C.G. (5003 "Truly, Baby")..............40-60
X..............10-15 60

ROMAN, Ron, & Proposition
Singles: 7-inch
DOT..............3-6 69

ROMAN, Scott
Singles: 7-inch
TERRACE..............4-8 62

ROMAN & LEE
Singles: 7-inch
BOBB-ETTE (358 "Carter's Creed").. 4-6 70s

ROMAN CHARIOT
Singles: 7-inch
SOFT..............4-8 67

ROMAN HOLLIDAY P&R/LP '83
Singles: 12-inch
JIVE..............4-6 83
Singles: 7-inch
JIVE..............3-4 83-85
LPs: 10/12-inch
JIVE..............5-10 83

ROMAN NUMERALS
Singles: 7-inch
COLUMBIA (44314 "The Come On")..............8-12 67
Picture Sleeves
COLUMBIA (44314 "The Come On")..............15-25 67

ROMAN REBELLION
Singles: 7-inch
MR. G..............5-10 68
RCA..............4-8 68

ROMANAIRES
Singles: 7-inch
D&J (100 "Is It Too Late")..............50-75 60s

ROMANCERS
Singles: 78 rpm
DOOTONE..............20-30 56
Singles: 7-inch
BAY TONE (101 "You Don't Understand")..............20-30 58
DOOTONE (381 "I Still Remember")..............50-75 56
(Red label.)
DOOTONE (381 "I Still Remember")..............40-60 56
(Maroon label.)
Members: Al Thomas; Bob Freeman; Woody Blake; Tyrone French; James Shelbourne.

ROMANCERS
Singles: 7-inch
BEACON (701 "No Greater Love").25-50 61
CELEBRITY (701 "No Greater Love")..............50-75 61
(First issue.)

ROMANCERS
Singles: 7-inch
LINDA (117 "Don't Let Her Go").....15-25 64
LINDA (119 "My Heart Cries")..........15-25 65
LINDA (120 "Do You Cry")..........15-25 65
LINDA (123 "She Gives Me Love")..............10-20 66
LINDA (124 "That's Why I Love You")..............10-20 66
MEDIEVAL (202 "It Only Happens with You")..............10-20 64
PALETTE (5067 "Moody")..........25-50 60
PALETTE (5075 "It Only Happens with You")..............25-50 61
PALETTE (5085 "That Lucky Old Sun")..............25-50 62
PALETTE (5095 "What About Love")..............25-50 62

ROMANCERS
("Featuring Wilbert Burlson")
Singles: 7-inch
MARQUEE (701 "Meet Me at the Altar")..............30-50 62
Member: Wilbert Burlson.

ROMANCERS
Singles: 7-inch
DEL-FI (4225 "Slauson Shuffle").....10-15 63

ROMANCERS
Singles: 7-inch
VINTAGE (1013 "Eternal Love")........5-8 73

ROMANO, Bob
Singles: 7-inch
20TH FOX..............4-8 66

ROMANO, Rock
Singles: 7-inch
COLUMBIA..............4-8 63

ROMANS
Singles: 78 rpm
HAVEN..............15-25 57
Singles: 7-inch
HAVEN..............15-25 57
Members: Tony Leone; Chick Leone; Joe Apuzzo; Chick Ciccolallo; Stan Dortch.
Also see FIVE SATINS

ROMANS
Singles: 7-inch
JUNO (014 "You Are My Only Love")..............500-750 58
M.M.I. (1238 "Wild Ideas")..........200-300 58

ROMANS
Singles: 7-inch
D.B. (41765 "The Drag")..............15-25 65
(Number is also release date, 4-17-65.)
PANIC (100 "Doin' the Drag")........10-15 66
(*Doin' the Drag* is a rerecording of *The Drag*.)
Members: Richard Reisinger; Tom Henry; Tom Flicker; Barry Leach.

ROMANS
Singles: 7-inch
MY (2905 "I'll Find a Way")..........10-20 66
MY (2908 "I Just Had to Fall")..........10-20 66
Picture Sleeves
MY (2905 "I'll Find a Way")..........20-30 66

ROMANS (With Little Caesar): see LITTLE CAESAR & ROMANS

ROMANS, Charlie
Singles: 7-inch
CANDELLIGHT ("Miss You in Memphis")..............4-6 85
(Colored vinyl.)
Members: Bobby Woods; Reggie Young; Gene Christman; Mike Leech; Bobby Emmons.

ROMANTIC, Ronny
Singles: 7-inch
ROYAL STANDARD..............4-8 68

ROMANTICS P&R/LP '80
Singles: 12-inch
NEMPEROR..............4-8 83-85
Singles: 7-inch
BOMP..............4-6 78
NEMPEROR..............3-5 80-85
SPIDER..............8-12 77
Picture Sleeves
BOMP..............4-6 78
NEMPEROR..............3-5 80-85
EPs: 7-inch
BOMP..............5-8 78
LPs: 10/12-inch
NEMPEROR..............5-10 80-85

ROME, Billy
Singles: 7-inch
SULTAN..............10-15 60-62
Also see CAMEOS Featuring Billy Rome

ROME, Johnny
Singles: 7-inch
PHILIPS (40443 "Baby Doll")........10-20 67

ROME, Richard
Singles: 7-inch
FAYETTE..............4-8 65

ROME, Vinnie
(With the Rainbows)
Singles: 7-inch
APT..............10-15 59
ROULETTE..............4-6 67

ROME & PARIS
Singles: 7-inch
ROULETTE..............5-10 66
20TH FOX..............5-10
Member: Eric Nathanson.
Also see REYNOLDS, Ricky

ROMEO
LPs: 10/12-inch
IRON WORKS (11309 "Rocks")........5-8 85
(Picture disc.)

ROMEO R&B '87
Singles: 7-inch
TRIPLE..............3-4 87

ROMEO, Al
Singles: 7-inch
LAURIE..............5-10 63

ROMEO & JULIET P&R '69
("Dialogue from film soundtrack")
Singles: 7-inch
CAPITOL..............3-6 69

ROMEO VOID LP '82
Singles: 12-inch
COLUMBIA..............4-6 82-84
415 (007 "Never Say Yes")..........5-10 81
Singles: 7-inch
COLUMBIA..............3-4 82-84
LPs: 10/12-inch
COLUMBIA..............5-8 82-84
415..............8-12 82
Members: Debora Iyall; Peter Woods; Benjamin Bossi; Larry Carter; Frank Zincavage.

ROMEO'S DAUGHTER P&R/LP '88
Singles: 7-inch
JIVE..............3-4 88
Picture Sleeves
JIVE..............3-4 88
LPs: 10/12-inch
JIVE..............5-8 88

ROMEOS
Singles: 78 rpm
APOLLO (461 "Love Me")..........100-150 54
APOLLO (466 "Rags")..............25-50 54
Singles: 7-inch
APOLLO (461 "Love Me")..........200-250 54
APOLLO (466 "Rags")..............75-100 54

ROMEOS
(With George Braxton Band; with Lucky Lee Band)
Singles: 78 rpm
ATCO (6107 "Moments to Remember")..............30-40 57
Singles: 7-inch
ATCO (6107 "Moments to Remember")..............30-40 57
FOX (748/9 "Gone Gone Get Away")..............100-150 57
(Cream color label.)
FOX (748/9 "Gone Gone Get Away")..............50-100 57
(Yellow label.)
FOX (845/6 "Moments to Remember")..............250-300 58
(Cream color label.)
FOX (845/6 "Moments to Remember")..............50-100 58
(Yellow label.)
Members: Lamont Dozier; Tyrone Hunter; Gene Dyer; Ken Johnson; Don Davenport; Leon Ware.
Also see DOZIER, Lamont
Also see HUNTER, Ty
Also see LARADO
Also see WARE, Leon

ROMEOS
Singles: 7-inch
AMY..............5-10 62
FELSTED..............10-15 63
LOMA..............4-8 66

ROMEOS P&R/R&B '67
Singles: 7-inch
MARK II..............4-8 67
LPs: 10/12-inch
MARK II..............15-20 67
Members: Kenny Gamble; Thom Bell; Roland Chambers; Winnie Walford; Karl Chambers; Leon Huff.
Also see GAMBLE, Kenny
Also see HUFF, Leon

ROMEOS
Singles: 7-inch
COLUMBIA (43000 series)..............4-8 64

ROMEOS
Singles: 7-inch
COLUMBIA (11000 series)..............3-5 80
Picture Sleeves
COLUMBIA (11000 series)..............3-5 80
LPs: 10/12-inch
COLUMBIA..............5-10 80

ROMER, Maxwell
Singles: 7-inch
FORD..............3-5

ROMERO, Chan
Singles: 7-inch
CHALLENGE (59285 "It's Not Fine")..............8-12 65
DEL-FI (4119 "Hippy Hippy Shake")..............50-75 59
DEL-FI (4126 "My Little Ruby")......40-60 59
PHILIPS (40391 "Humpty Bumpty") 5-10 66

ROMERO, Joe
Singles: 7-inch
DORE..............5-10 59

ROMERO, Rudy
Singles: 7-inch
TUMBLEWEED..............3-5 72
LPs: 10/12-inch
TUMBLEWEED (108 "To the World")..............15-20 72
(White vinyl. Gatefold cover.)
TUMBLEWEED (108 "To the World")..............10-12 72
(Black vinyl. Gatefold cover.)
TUMBLEWEED (108 "To the World")..............8-10 72
(Black vinyl. Standard cover.)

ROMMELS
Singles: 7-inch
TREND (4104 "Those Wedding Bells")..............200-300 60

ROMMY & CENTURIES
Singles: 7-inch
LUNA (3076 "Mister Mirror")..........15-25 62

RON & BILL
Singles: 7-inch
ARGO (5350 "It")..............35-45 59
TAMLA (54025 "It")..............50-75 60
Members: Ron White; Bill "Smokey" Robinson.
Also see MIRACLES

RON & CONTINENTALS
Singles: 7-inch
CUCA (1156 "Rolling Stone")..........15-25 63

RON & D.C. CREW P&R '87
Singles: 7-inch
PROFILE..............3-4 87

RON & EMBRACERS
Singles: 7-inch
SPECTRUM..............10-20

RON & JOE & CREW
Singles: 7-inch
STRAND..............10-15 59

RON & JON
Singles: 7-inch
SICK (50 "Hawaii Strikes Back")......25-35 59
Members: Ron Jacobs; Jon Demarco.
Also see CHILD'S GARDEN OF GRASS

RON & MOTIONS
Singles: 7-inch
REDBUG (6 "Last Night's Dream") 50-65

RON-ALS
Singles: 7-inch
STONE (13130 "Beach Rat")..........8-12
(Canadian.)

RON C LP '90
LPs: 10/12-inch
PROFILE..............5-8 90

RON RICKY: see RICKY, Ron

RONALD & RUBY P&R '58
Singles: 7-inch
RCA (7174 "Lollipop")..............10-15 58
Members: Lee Morris; Beverly Ross.
Also see ROSS, Beverly

RONCONE, Mike
Singles: 7-inch
CAPITOL..............5-10 61
TAMMY..............10-20 61

RONDELL, Chuck
Singles: 7-inch
HART VAN..............4-8 63

RONDELLS
Singles: 7-inch
PIKE ("Demo Derby")..............15-25 64
(No selection number used.)

RONDELLS
(Ron-Dells; Rondels)
Singles: 7-inch
ABC-PAR (10690 "Don't Say That You Love Me") 8-10 65
CARLTON (467 "Dreamy") 15-25 58
DOT (16593 "On the Run") 8-12 64
XPRESS 5-10 60s

RONDELLS
Singles: 7-inch
IGL 4-8 70s

RONDELS P&R '61
Singles: 7-inch
AMY (825 "Back Beat No. 1") 8-12 61
AMY (830 "My Prayer") 8-12 61
AMY (839 "Caldonia") 8-12 62
AMY (857 "Cover Charge") 8-12 62
NOTE (4001 "Come on Let's Go Sweetheart") 10-15 61
Members: Leonard Petze; James Petze; Ray Pizzi; Leonard Collins.

RON-DELS P&R '65
(Rondels; Ron-Dells)
Singles: 7-inch
ARLEN (723 "Slow Down") 15-25 63
BILLIE FRAN (101 "Matilda") 15-25 60s
BROWNFIELD (2 "Hey Baby '66") 10-15 66
BROWNFIELD (13 "100 Pounds of Honey") 10-15 66
BROWNFIELD (16 "Just When You Think You're Somebody") 10-20 65
BROWNFIELD (18 "If You Really Want Me to, I'll Go") 10-20 65
BROWNFIELD (23 "Lost My Love Today") 10-20 65
BROWNFIELD (33 "Cryin' Over You") 10-15 66
BROWNFIELD (303 "I Know She Knows") 10-20 64
BROWNFIELD (1037 "You Made Me Cry") 8-12 67
CHARAY (75 "100 Pounds of Honey") 4-6
DOT (17323 "Matilda") 4-6 70
LE CAM (130 "Matilda") 25-35 63
(First issue.)
LE CAM (130 "Matilda") 3-6 73
SHAH (980 "I Ain't Never") 15-25 63
SHALIMAR (104 "Matilda") 15-25 63
SMASH (1986 "If You Really Want Me to, I'll Go") 8-12 65
SMASH (2002 "She's My Girl") 8-12 65
SMASH (2014 "Lose Your Money") 8-12 65
Members: Delbert McClinton; Billy Sanders; Jerry Foster; Jimmy Rodgers; Ronnie Kelly; Mike Clark; Darrell Norris; Carl Tanner; Ray Torres. Session: Ray Hildebrand; Bruce Channel.
Also see CHANNEL, Bruce
Also see CURTIS, Mac
Also see DAWSON, Ronnie
Also see HILDEBRAND, Ray
Also see JESTER, Charlie
Also see JOHNNY & MARK V / Ron-Dels
Also see KELLY, Nat / Ron-Dels
Also see KELLY, Ronnie
Also see McCLINTON, Delbert
Also see MILBURN, Amos, Jr.
Also see PAUL / Ron-Dels
Also see PIKES, Charles, & Scholars
Also see UPTOWNERS / Ron-Dels
Also see WATSON, Phil / Ron-Dels

RONDINO, Joe, & Nite Beats
Singles: 7-inch
ARC 5-8 64

RONDO, Don P&R '56
Singles: 78 rpm
DECCA 3-5 55
JUBILEE 5-10 56-57
Singles: 7-inch
ATLANTIC 4-8 63
CARLTON 4-8 60-61
DECCA 5-10 55
JUBILEE 5-10 56-66
ROULETTE 4-8 59-60
TRIP 3-5
TUBA 4-6 65
U.A. 4-6 66-67
VIRGO 3-5 72
LPs: 10/12-inch
JUBILEE 10-20 57-58
VOCALION 5-10 70

RONE, Roger C&W '89
Singles: 7-inch
TRUE 3-4 89

RONETTES P&R/R&B '63
(Ronnettes; "Featuring Veronica")
Singles: 7-inch
A&M 5-10 69
BUDDAH 5-10 73-74
COLPIX (646 "I'm Gonna Quit While I'm Ahead") 40-60 62
MAY (114 "Silhouettes") 30-40 63
MAY (138 "The Memory") 30-40 63
PAVILLION 3-5 82
PHILLES 10-15 63-66
Promotional Singles
A&M 8-12 69
BUDDAH 10-15 73-74
COLPIX (646 "I'm Gonna Quit While I'm Ahead") 30-40 62
MAY (114 "Silhouettes") 30-40 63
MAY (138 "The Memory") 30-40 63
PAVILLION 4-8 82
PHILLES 10-20 63-66
Picture Sleeves
PHILLES (123 "Walking in the Rain") 25-35 64
PHILLES (126 "Born to Be Together") 25-35 65
PHILLES (128 "Is This What I Get for Loving You") 30-40 65
LPs: 10/12-inch
COLPIX (486 "The Ronettes, Featuring Veronica") 50-100 65
(Blue label. Monaural.)
COLPIX (486 "The Ronettes, Featuring Veronica") 75-150 65
(Gold label. Monaural.)
COLPIX (486 "The Ronettes, Featuring Veronica") 60-75 65
(Blue label. Stereo.)
COLPIX (486 "The Ronettes, Featuring Veronica") 100-200 65
(Gold label. Stereo.)
COLPIX (486 "The Ronettes, Featuring Veronica") 75-100 65
(White label. Promotional issue only.)
PHILLES (4006 "Presenting the Fabulous Ronettes") 100-200 64
(Blue label. Monaural.)
PHILLES (4006 "Presenting the Fabulous Ronettes") 75-150 64
(Yellow label. Monaural.)
PHILLES (4006 "Presenting the Fabulous Ronettes") 200-300 64
(Yellow label with red print. Stereo.)
PHILLES (4006 "Presenting the Fabulous Ronettes") 200-250 64
(Yellow label with black print. Stereo issue through Capitol Record Club.)
MURRAY HILL 5-10 86
Members: Veronica Bennett-Spector; Estelle Bennett; Nedra Talley-Ross.
Also see DEE, Joey
Also see LOVE, Darlene / Ronettes
Also see RONNIE & RELATIVES
Also see ROSS, Nedra
Also see SPECTOR, Ronnie

RONETTES / Crystals / Darlene Love
Singles: 7-inch
PAVILLION (1354 "Phil Spector's Christmas Medley") 3-5 81
(Promotional issue only.)

RONETTES / Crystals / Darlene Love / Bob B. Soxx & Blue Jeans
EPs: 7-inch
PHILLES ("Christmas EP") 20-40 63
LPs: 10/12-inch
APPLE (3400 "Phil Spector's Christmas Album") 20-30 72
PASSPORT (3604 "Phil Spector's Christmas Album") 5-8 85
PAVILLION 5-10 81
PHILLES (4005 "A Christmas Gift for You") 50-100 63
(Blue label.)
PHILLES (4005 "A Christmas Gift for You") 40-60 63
(Yellow and red label.)
W.B./SPECTOR 8-12
(Phil Spector is heard speaking on this LP. The Apple and Passport LPs are reissues of the Philles album.)
Also see BOB B. SOXX & Blue Jeans
Also see CRYSTALS
Also see HARVEY, Phil
Also see LOVE, Darlene
Also see RONETTES

RONICK, Holly C&W '89
Singles: 7-inch
HAPPY MAN 3-4 89

RONIN
LPs: 10/12-inch
MERCURY 5-10 80

RONNIE & BONNIE
Singles: 7-inch
ARWIN 4-8 64

RONNIE & COMETS
Singles: 7-inch
SOMA (1172 "Memories") 12-18 61
Also see MIDNIGHTERS

RONNIE & CRAYONS
Singles: 7-inch
COUNSEL (102 "Birchard's Bread") 10-15 64
(First issue.)
DOMAIN (1402 "Birchard's Bread") 8-10 64
Also see CRAYONS

RONNIE & DEADBEATS
LPs: 10/12-inch
CHECK 10-20

RONNIE & DELAIRES
Singles: 7-inch
CORAL (62404 "Drag") 20-25 64
Members: Ronny Linares; John Becker; Bob Osborne; Garry Jones.
Also see DEL-AIRES

RONNIE & DEVILLES
Singles: 7-inch
MGM 4-8 66

RONNIE & DIRT RIDERS
Singles: 7-inch
RCA 4-6 76
Member: Ron Dante.
Also see DANTE, Ron

RONNIE & HI-LITES P&R '62
Singles: 7-inch
ABC-PAR (10685 "High School Romance") 10-20 65
COLLECTABLES 3-4 80s
ERIC 3-4 70s
JOY (260 "I Wish That We Were Married") 15-25 62
JOY (265 "Send My Love") 15-25 62
RAVEN (8000 "Valerie") 10-15 63
(Black label.)
RAVEN (8000 "Valerie") 15-25 63
(White label. Promotional issue only.)
WIN (250 "A Slow Dance") 15-25 63
WIN (251 "The Fact of the Matter") 15-25 63
WIN (252 "High School Romance") 20-30 63

RONNIE & HOP KATS
Singles: 7-inch
COUGAR (101 "Persian Melon & Passion Pink") 10-20 60s

RONNIE & JOEY
Singles: 7-inch
LITTLE STAR 5-10 61

RONNIE & JOYCE
Singles: 7-inch
ALPHA 8-12

RONNIE & LYNDA
Singles: 7-inch
MALA 4-8 65

RONNIE & MANHATTANS
Singles: 7-inch
ENJOY 8-12 64

RONNIE & MARLENE
Singles: 7-inch
WESTPORT (144 "I Wanna Love You") 30-40 59

RONNIE & PEGGY
(Ronny & Peggy)
Singles: 7-inch
LIMELIGHT 4-8 64
SHAH 4-8 64

RONNIE & POMONA CASUALS
Singles: 7-inch
DONNA 5-10 64-65
LPs: 10/12-inch
DONNA (2112 "Everybody Jerk") 15-25 65

RONNIE & PREMIERS
Singles: 7-inch
HIGHLAND (1014 "Sharon") 15-25 61

RONNIE & RAMBLERS
Singles: 7-inch
R&R 5-8 60s

RONNIE & RED CAPS
Singles: 7-inch
REB ("Conquest") 8-12
(Selection number not known.)

RONNIE & RELATIVES
(Ronettes)
Singles: 7-inch
COLPIX (601 "I Want a Boy") 50-100 61
MAY (111 "My Guiding Angel") 100-150 62
Also see RONETTES

RONNIE & RENEGADES
Singles: 7-inch
SULTAN (1003 "Blue Guitar") 10-20 60

RONNIE & ROBYN
(Ronnie & Robin)
Singles: 7-inch
HBR (489 "Cradle of Love") 10-15 66
SIDRA (9007 "Sidra's Theme") 15-25 67
SIDRA (9011 "As Long As You Love Me") 15-25 67

RONNIE & ROCKIN' KINGS
Singles: 7-inch
RCA (7248 "Rock 'N Roll Sal") 40-60 58

RONNIE & ROY
Singles: 7-inch
CAPITOL (4192 "Big Fat Sally") 25-35 59
(Monaural.)
CAPITOL (4192 "Big Fat Sally") 35-55 59
(Stereo.)
CAPITOL (4246 "Get Up and Dance") 10-20 59

RONNIE & SCHOOLMATES
Singles: 7-inch
COED (604 "Just Born") 15-25 65
COLLECTABLES 3-4 80s

RONNIE & SENSASHUNS
Singles: 7-inch
WHAM (99041 "Laugh It Up Baby") 20-30 60s

RONNIE & UNCALLED FOUR
Singles: 7-inch
DONNA (1384 "Hot Toddy") 10-15 63

RONNY
Singles: 7-inch
LONDON 4-8 64

RONNY & DAYTONAS P&R/LP '64
Singles: 7-inch
BARRY (562 "G.T.O.") 5-10 67
(Canadian.)
BARRY (3272 "G.T.O.") 10-20 64
(Canadian.)
BARRY (3349 "Beach Boy") 5-10 64
(Canadian.)
MALA 6-12 64-66
RCA 5-10 66-68
SHOW-BIZ 8-12 68
Picture Sleeves
BARRY (562 "G.T.O.") 10-15 66
(Generic "Golden Treasures on Wax" sleeve, with title imprint at top. Canadian.)
RCA (8896 "Dianne, Dianne") 15-25 66
LPs: 10/12-inch
MALA (4001 "G.T.O.") 50-100 64
MALA (4002 "Sandy") 20-35 66
(Monaural.)
MALA (4002-S "Sandy") 75-100 66
(Stereo.)
Members: Ronny Dayton; John "Bucky" Wilkin; Buzz Cason.
Also see BUZZ & BUCKY
Also see CASON, Buzz

RONNY & JOHNNY
Singles: 7-inch
LUCKY (1001 "Massacre") 150-200 60
Members: Ronny Roach; Johnny Coons.
Also see FOLEY, Jim
Also see 1959

RONNY & PEGGY: see RONNIE & PEGGY

RONNY & SATELLITES
(With the Raiders; Ronny & Satelites)
Singles: 7-inch
DOLLY (22254 "Bunny Lee") 50-100 60
ROSE (1001 "Dream of You") 100-200 59

RONSON, Mick LP '74
LPs: 10/12-inch
RCA 8-12 74
Also see HUNTER, Ian, & Mick Ronson
Also see PURE PRAIRIE LEAGUE

RONSON, Rick
Singles: 7-inch
SEAN 4-8 64

RONSTADT, Linda P&R '68/C&W '74
(With the Stone Poneys; with Nelson Riddle Orchestra)
Singles: 7-inch
ASYLUM 3-5 73-85
CAPITOL (2004 "Different Drum") 5-10 67
CAPITOL (2110 "Up to My Neck in High Muddy Water") 10-15 68
CAPITOL (2195 "Some of Shelly's Blues") 5-10 68
CAPITOL (2438 "Dolphins") 5-10 69
CAPITOL (2767 "Lovesick Blues") 4-8 70
CAPITOL (2846 thru 4050) 3-6 70-75
CAPITOL (5838 "All the Beautiful Things") 8-12 67
CAPITOL (5910 "Evergreen") 5-10 67
ELEKTRA 3-5 75-78
SIDEWALK (937 "So Fine") 75-100 66
Picture Sleeves
ASYLUM 3-5 78-82
CAPITOL (2110 "Up to My Neck in High Muddy Water") 15-25 68
LPs: 10/12-inch
ASYLUM (Except 401 & 60489) 5-10 73-86
ASYLUM (401 "Living in the USA") 10-15 78
(Picture disc.)
ASYLUM (60489 "'Round Midnight") 10-15 86
CAPITOL (208 thru 635) 10-15 69-72
CAPITOL (2000 series) 12-18 68
CAPITOL (11000 series) 8-12 74-77
CAPITOL (16000 series) 5-10 80
ELEKTRA 5-10 80-87
MFSL (158 "What's New") 20-30 85
NAUTILUS (26 "Simple Dreams") 15-25 81
PICKWICK 8-10 70s
Session: Davie Allan; Nelson Riddle.
Also see ALLAN, Davie
Also see AXTON, Hoyt
Also see CASH, Johnny / Roy Clark / Linda Ronstadt
Also see CHRISTMAS SPIRIT
Also see CORVETTES
Also see EAGLES
Also see GLASS, Phillip
Also see NEWMAN, Randy
Also see NITTY GRITTY DIRT BAND & LINDA RONSTADT
Also see PARTON, Dolly, Linda Ronstadt, & Emmylou Harris
Also see RIDDLE, Nelson
Also see SHILOH
Also see STONE PONEYS
Also see THOMAS, David Clayton / Linda Ronstadt

RONSTADT, Linda, & Emmylou Harris
Singles: 7-inch
ASYLUM 3-5 75
Also see HARRIS, Emmylou

RONSTADT, Linda, & James Ingram P&R '86
Singles: 7-inch
MCA 3-4 86
Picture Sleeves
MCA 3-4 86
Also see INGRAM, James

RONSTADT, Linda, & Aaron Neville LP '89
LPs: 10/12-inch
ELEKTRA 5-8 89
Also see NEVILLE, Aaron

RONSTADT, Linda, & J.D. Souther C&W '82
Singles: 7-inch
ASYLUM 3-4 82
Also see RONSTADT, Linda
Also see SOUTHER, J.D.

ROOFTOP SINGERS P&R/C&W/R&B/LP '63
Singles: 7-inch
ATCO 4-6 67
VANGUARD 4-8 62-65
Picture Sleeves
VANGUARD 5-10 63
LPs: 10/12-inch
VANGUARD 10-20 63-65
Members: Erik Darling; Lynne Taylor; Bill Svanoe.
Also see TARRIERS

ROOKEYS
Singles: 7-inch
ABC-PAR 8-10 63

ROOKIES
Singles: 7-inch
DONNA 5-10 59

ROOKS
Singles: 7-inch
ETIQUETTE (14 "I'll Be the One") 5-10 65
JO-WAY (5000 "Ice & Fire") 5-10 67
MERCURY (72644 "Empty Heart") 10-15 67
MUSTANG (3008 "Gimme a Break") 15-25 65

ROOKS, Wayne
Singles: 7-inch
CAPITOL 4-8 62-63
JAMIE 5-10 59

ROOM FULL OF ROSES
LPs: 10/12-inch
BLUE FLAME 5-10 81

ROOMFUL OF BLUES
Singles: 7-inch
ROOMTONE (1001 "You Rascal, You") 10-20 75
ROOMTONE (1002 "Reelin' & Rockin' ") 5-10 82
LPs: 10/12-inch
ANTILLES (7071 "Let's Have a Party") 10-20 79
BLUE FLAME (1001 "Hot Little Mama") 15-25 81
ISLAND (9474 "Roomful of Blues") 15-25 77
VARRICK 5-10 84-87
Members: Duke Robillard; Al Copley; Preston Hubbard; John Rossi; Greg Piccolo; Richard Latailie; Doug James; Ronnie Earl; Jimmy Wimpfheimer; Porky Cohen; Danny Motta; Bob Enos; Rory MacLeod; Ron Levy; Curtis Salgado; Chris Vachon; Carl Querfurth; Matt McCabe; Ken Grace; Sugar Ray Norcia.
Also see JUNIOR & CLASSICS
Also see KING, Earl, & Roomful of Blues
Also see TURNER, Joe, & Roomful of Blues
Also see VINSON, Eddie "Cleanhead," & Roomful of Blues

ROOMATES P&R '61
Singles: 7-inch
ADDIT (2211 "Making Believe") 10-20 60
BAN (691 "A Place Called Love") 3-5 85
CAMEO (233 "A Sunday Kind of Love") 20-25 62
CANADIAN AMERICAN (166 "My Heart") 15-25 64
COLLECTABLES 3-4 80s
PHILIPS (40105 "Gee") 15-20 63
PHILIPS (40153 "The Nearness of You") 20-30 63
PHILIPS (40153 "The Nearness of You") 15-25 64
PROMO (2211 "Making Believe") 10-15 64
VALMOR (8 "Glory of Love") 10-15 61
VALMOR (10 "Band of Gold") 10-15 61
VALMOR (13 "My Foolish Heart") 10-20 61
LPs: 10/12-inch
RELIC 5-10 80s
Also see CATHY JEAN & ROOMATES

ROONEY, Mickey
Singles: 78 rpm
KING (1296 "Alimony Blues") 5-10 54
Singles: 7-inch
KING (1296 "Alimony Blues") 10-20 54

ROONEY, Mickey, Jr.
Singles: 7-inch
ORANGE-EMPIRE 3-5
Picture Sleeves
ORANGE-EMPIRE 5-10

ROONEY, Teddy
Singles: 7-inch
IMPERIAL (5644 "Bite Your Tongue") 20-30 60

ROOS, Robyne
Singles: 7-inch
SAX 5TH AVE 4-8 64

ROOSEVELT, Franklin D.
Singles: 78 rpm
COLUMBIA (36516 "President Roosevelt's War Message to Congress and the Nation, December 8, 1941") 5-15 42
NATIONAL VOICE LIBRARY ("Fireside Chats") 200-300 45
(Five cardboard picture discs with mailer envelope. No selection numbers used.)
NATIONAL VOICE LIBRARY ("Fireside Chat on Defense 12-29-40") 40-60 45
NATIONAL VOICE LIBRARY ("Report of Nazi Attack") 40-60 45
NATIONAL VOICE LIBRARY ("Declaration of War 12-8-41") 40-60 45

NATIONAL VOICE LIBRARY ("State of Union 1-6-42")....40-60 45
NATIONAL VOICE LIBRARY ("D-Day Proclamation 6-6-44")....40-60 45

ROOSTERS
Singles: 7-inch
EPIC.... 5-10 62
FELSTED.... 5-10 62
PHILIPS.... 5-8 68
SHAR-DEE....10-15 59

ROOSTERS
Singles: 7-inch
ENITH (125 "Ain't Gonna Cry Anymore").... 8-12 67
PROGRESSIVE SOUNDS (11032 "One of These Days")....25-30 66

ROOT BOY SLIM & SEX CHANGE BAND
(With the Rootettes)
Singles: 7-inch
ILLEGAL (9007 "World War III").... 3-6 79
Picture Sleeves
ILLEGAL (9007 "World War III").... 3-6 79
LPs: 10/12-inch
I.R.S..... 5-10
W.B..... 5-10 78

ROOTS
Singles: 7-inch
BROWNFIELD (22 "Lost One")....20-30 65
Also see WYLD

ROPE, Skip: see SKIPPY ROPE

ROPER, Skip
Singles: 7-inch
COLPIX.... 4-8 61

ROQ-IN ZOO
Singles: 12-inch
MOTOWN.... 4-6 86
Singles: 7-inch
MOTOWN.... 3-4 86

ROQUEMORE, Larry
Singles: 7-inch
GUYDEN.... 4-8 65
Also see LARRY & BLUE NOTES

RORY-O
Singles: 7-inch
CORAL.... 4-8 63

ROS, Edmundo, & His Orch. P&R '58
Singles: 78 rpm
LONDON.... 3-5 51-57
Singles: 7-inch
LONDON.... 4-8 51-63
EPs: 7-inch
CORAL.... 5-10 54
LONDON.... 5-10 52-59
LPs: 10/12-inch
CORAL.... 8-15 54
LONDON.... 5-15 52-78

ROSALETTS / Kin Folks
Singles: 7-inch
REVIS.... 5-10 62

ROSANOVA, Joe, & Vineyard
LPs: 10/12-inch
ASTRO SONIC (4000 "In Dedication to the Ones We Love")....50-75 67

ROSCO & BARBARA
Singles: 7-inch
OLD TOWN.... 5-10 65
Member: Roscoe Gordon.
Also see GORDON, Roscoe

ROSCOE & LITTLE GREEN MEN
Singles: 7-inch
FOUR WINDS....20-25 61
(Title and selection number not known.)
GOLDEN WING....10-20 62
PONTIAC (105 "Roll Over Beethoven")....40-60 59
RGM....40-60
(Title and selection number not known.)
RSVP....20-25 63
20TH FOX (166 "Weird")....10-15 59
Members: Roscoe Wharton; Denny Lee.
Also see GREEN, Johnny, & Greenmen
Also see GREEN MEN
Also see KIT KATS
Also see LAURENCE, T., & Sherwood Greens

ROSCOE & MABLE R&B '77
Singles: 7-inch
CHOCOLATE CITY.... 3-5 77

ROSE
LPs: 10/12-inch
MILLENNIUM.... 5-10 80

ROSE, Andy P&R '58
(With the Thorns)
Singles: 7-inch
AAMCO (103 "My Devotion")....20-30 58
CORAL.... 5-15 59-62
EMBER.... 4-8 64
GOLDEN CREST.... 4-8 64

ROSE, Biff LP '69
Singles: 7-inch
BUDDAH.... 3-5 71
TETRAGRAMMATON.... 3-5 68-70
LPs: 10/12-inch
BUDDAH.... 8-12 71
TETRAGRAMMATON....10-15 68-69
U.A..... 8-12 73

ROSE, C.G.
(Ron Dante)
Singles: 7-inch
MERCURY.... 5-10 68
Also see DANTE, Ron

ROSE, David, & His Orch. P&R '43
Singles: 78 rpm
MGM.... 3-5 50-57
VICTOR.... 4-6 43-44
Singles: 7-inch
CAPITOL.... 3-6 66-69
MGM.... 3-8 50-67
Picture Sleeves
MGM.... 4-8 56-62
EPs: 7-inch
KAPP.... 5-10 59
MGM.... 5-10 51-58
ROYALE.... 5-10 50s
LPs: 10/12-inch
CAPITOL.... 8-15 66-69
DINO.... 5-10 72
KAPP....10-20 59-61
LION....10-20 59
MCA.... 5-8 83
MGM.... 5-20 51-70
METRO.... 5-15 65-66
SPIN-O-RAMA.... 5-10 60s
Also see PREVIN, Andre

ROSE, Dusty
Singles: 7-inch
FABOR....10-20 64

ROSE, Edyth & Kathy
Singles: 7-inch
EVEREST.... 5-10 59

ROSE, Henri
Singles: 7-inch
DEL-FI.... 5-10 58

ROSE, Julian
Singles: 7-inch
DORE.... 4-8 60

ROSE, Pam C&W '77
Singles: 7-inch
CAPITOL.... 3-5 77
Also see CLAMITY JANE

ROSE, Pam, & Willie Nelson C&W '80
(Pam Rose with Friend)
Singles: 7-inch
EPIC.... 3-5 79-80
Also see NELSON, Willie
Also see ROSE, Pam

ROSE, Richard & Gary C&W '88
Singles: 7-inch
CAPITOL.... 3-4 88

ROSE, Stewart
Singles: 7-inch
FELSTED.... 4-8 61

ROSE, Tim
Singles: 7-inch
COLUMBIA.... 4-8 66-67
LPs: 10/12-inch
CAPITOL.... 8-12 70
COLUMBIA....10-15 68-69
PLAYBOY.... 8-12 72
Also see BIG THREE

ROSE BROTHERS R&B '86
Singles: 12-inch
MUSCLE SHOALS.... 4-6 86
Singles: 7-inch
MUSCLE SHOALS.... 3-4 86-88
LPs: 10/12-inch
MUSCLE SHOALS.... 5-8 86
Members: Bob Rose; Larry Rose; Kenny Rose; Greg Rose.

ROSE COLORED GLASS P&R '71
Singles: 7-inch
BANG.... 3-5 71

ROSE GARDEN P&R '67
Singles: 7-inch
ATCO.... 5-10 67-68
LPs: 10/12-inch
ATCO (255 "Rose Garden")....15-25 68
Members: Diana DiRose; James Groshong; John Noreen; Bill Fleming; Bruce Boudin.

ROSE MARIE
Singles: 78 rpm
MERCURY.... 5-10 57
Singles: 7-inch
MERCURY.... 5-10 57
RAYNARD.... 4-6 67
LPs: 10/12-inch
KAPP....10-20 64

ROSE MARIE & Bill Ivey
Singles: 7-inch
JAMECO.... 4-8 64

ROSE ROYCE P&R/R&B/LP '76
Singles: 12-inch
MONTAGE.... 4-8 84
Singles: 7-inch
C&R.... 3-4 84
MCA.... 3-5 76-77
OMNI.... 3-4 86-87
WHITFIELD.... 3-5 77-82
LPs: 10/12-inch
EPIC.... 5-8 82
MCA.... 5-10 76
WHITFIELD.... 5-10 77-81

ROSE TATTOO LP '80
Singles: 7-inch
MIRAGE.... 3-5 80-82
LPs: 10/12-inch
MIRAGE.... 5-10 80-82

ROSEBLOODS
EPs: 7-inch
GET HIP (115 "Angeline").... 4-6 89
(Issued with paper sleeve.)

ROSEBUD
Singles: 7-inch
REPRISE.... 3-5 71
LPs: 10/12-inch
REPRISE.... 8-12 71
Members: Jerry Yester; Judy Henske.
Also see HENSKE, Judy, & Jerry Yester

ROSEBUDS
Singles: 7-inch
GEE (1033 "Dearest Darling")....25-50 57
LANCER (102 "Kiss Me Goodnight")....40-60 59

ROSEBUDS
Singles: 7-inch
BOBWIN (148 "South Side High") 20-30 62

ROSEBUDS
Singles: 7-inch
TOWER.... 5-10 64

ROSELLA, Carmela
Singles: 7-inch
NANCY (1004 "Oh! It Was Elvis")..10-20 61

ROSELLI, Jimmy LP '65
Singles: 7-inch
RIC.... 4-8 65
U.A..... 4-6 65-69
LPs: 10/12-inch
RIC....10-15 65
U.A..... 5-12 65-72

ROSELLI, Mickey
Singles: 7-inch
ROULETTE.... 5-8 60

ROSEMARY & ROSEBUDS
Singles: 7-inch
LARKWOOD (1101 "What Do I Mean to You")....50-100 62

ROSEMARY JUNE: see JUNE, Rosemary

ROSENTHAL, Rochelle, & Kickball Queen
Singles: 7-inch
SUPER BOLT (33170 "Lottery")....20-30 60s

ROSES
Singles: 7-inch
DOT (15816 "Almost Paradise")....10-20 58
Also see DON & His Roses
Also see GUESS, Don

ROSETTES
Singles: 7-inch
HERALD....10-15 61

ROSIE P&R '60
(With the Originals; Rosie "Formerly with the Originals")
Singles: 7-inch
ABC.... 3-5 73
HIGHLAND....10-20 60-61
BRUNSWICK....10-20 61
LPs: 10/12-inch
BRUNSWICK (54102 "Lonley Blue Nights")....60-80 61
(Monaural.)
BRUNSWICK (754102 "Lonley Blue Nights")....70-100 61
(Stereo.)

ROSIE & RON
Singles: 7-inch
DONNA.... 5-10 61

ROSIE'S BABY DOLLS
Singles: 7-inch
FARGO.... 5-10 61

ROSKO
(With the Desires)
Singles: 7-inch
A&M (1640 "The Gift").... 3-6 74
DOMAIN (1021 "The B.M.T.")....10-20 65
FLYING DUTCHMAN.... 4-8 69
LANGDON (110 "Rosko the Preacher").... 8-12 63
W.B..... 4-8 68

ROSLYN
(Roslyn Valencia)
Singles: 7-inch
AISLE (003 "Fast Movin' Mama").... 3-4 92
(Black vinyl. 900 made.)
AISLE (003 "Fast Movin' Mama").... 4-8 92
(Blue vinyl. 100 made.)
Picture Sleeves
AISLE (003 "Fast Movin' Mama").... 3-4 92

ROSS
(Alan Ross)
LPs: 10/12-inch
RSO.... 8-12 74

ROSS, Adam
Singles: 7-inch
INVICTA.... 4-8 62

ROSS, Beverly
Singles: 7-inch
COLUMBIA.... 5-10 58
Also see RONALD & RUBY

ROSS, Bobby
Singles: 7-inch
BASE CAMP.... 3-5 80s

ROSS, Brian, & Playboys
Singles: 7-inch
PROTONE.... 4-8 64

ROSS, Charlie P&R '75
Singles: 7-inch
BIG TREE.... 3-5 75-76
TOWN HOUSE.... 3-4 82-83

ROSS, Danny
Singles: 7-inch
MINOR (107 "Look At You Go") 150-200 57
STONEWAY (1057 "St. Louis Blues")....10-15
STONEWAY (1072 "Carroll County Blues")....10-15

ROSS, Dee Dee
Singles: 7-inch
ADKORP.... 3-5 73

ROSS, Diana P&R/R&B/LP '70
Singles: 12-inch
MOTOWN.... 5-10 78-80
Singles: 7-inch
MCA.... 3-4 88
MOTOWN.... 3-6 70-89
(Black vinyl.)
MOTOWN.... 5-10 70-81
(Colored vinyl. Promotional only.)
RCA.... 3-5 81-87
Picture Sleeves
MOTOWN.... 3-6 70-80
RCA.... 3-5 82-87
EPs: 7-inch
MOTOWN (7588 "Sneak Preview from Lady Sings the Blues").... 8-12 72
(Promotional issue only.)
LPs: 10/12-inch
DORAL (104 "Diana Ross")....150-200 60s
(Promotional mail-order issue, from Doral cigarettes.)
KORY.... 8-10 77
MOTOWN (100 series).... 5-10 81-83
MOTOWN (711 thru 907).... 8-12 70-78
MOTOWN (923 "The Boss").... 5-10 79
(Black vinyl.)
MOTOWN (923 "The Boss")....10-20 79
(Colored vinyl. Promotional issue only.)
MOTOWN (951 thru 960).... 6-12 81
MOTOWN (5000 series).... 5-15 83
MOTOWN (6000 series).... 6-12 83-89
(Black vinyl.)
MOTOWN (6381 "Remixes")....10-12 90s
(Colored vinyl. Promotional issue only.)
PARAMOUNT (181/182 "Lady Sings the Blues")....35-50 72
(An "MRA Multiple Record Album, serving the requirements of both radio and TV stations," this LP has a 15-minute interview with Diana Ross. Includes scripts. Promotional issue only.)
RCA.... 5-10 81-87
Also see DENVER, John / Diana Ross
Also see GAYE, Marvin, & Diana Ross
Also see IGLESIAS, Julio, & Diana Ross
Also see SUPREMES
Also see TEMPTATIONS
Also see U.S.A. for AFRICA

ROSS, Diana, & Bill Cosby / Diana Ross & Jackson Five
EPs: 7-inch
MOTOWN.... 5-10 70
Also see COSBY, Bill
Also see JACKSONS

ROSS, Diana, & Michael Jackson P&R/R&B '78
Singles: 7-inch
MCA.... 3-5 78
Picture Sleeves
MCA.... 3-5 78
Also see JACKSON, Michael

ROSS, Diana, & Lionel Richie P&R/R&B '81
Singles: 7-inch
MOTOWN.... 3-5 81
POLYGRAM ("Dreaming of You")..10-15 81
(Promotional issue only. No number given.)
Also see RICHIE, Lionel

ROSS, Diana, Stevie Wonder, Marvin Gaye, Smokey Robinson P&R/R&B '79
Singles: 7-inch
MOTOWN (1455 "Pops, We Love You").... 3-5 79
(Black vinyl.)
MOTOWN (1455 "Pops, We Love You").... 5-10 79
(Heart shaped disc. Red vinyl.)
MOTOWN (1455 "Pops, We Love You")....10-20 79
(Green vinyl. Promotional issue only.)
LPs: 10/12-inch
MOTOWN.... 5-10 79
Also see DIAMOND, Neil / Diana Ross & Supremes
Also see GAYE, Marvin
Also see ROBINSON, Smokey
Also see ROSS, Diana
Also see WONDER, Stevie

ROSS, Dianna
Singles: 7-inch
CARSAN.... 4-8 64

ROSS, Dick, & Royal Counts
Singles: 7-inch
PLANET (46 "Fun House").... 8-12 62

ROSS, Doctor
(With His Jump & Jive Boys; with His Orbits; Charles Ross)
Singles: 78 rpm
CHESS (1504 "Country Clown")....100-200 52
SUN (193 "Come Back Baby")....100-200 54
SUN (212 "Boogie Disease")....100-200 54
Singles: 7-inch
D.I.R. (101 "Industrial Boogie")....25-50 58
FORTUNE (857 "Cat Squirrel")....15-20 59
HI-Q (5027 "Cannonball")....10-20 61
HI-Q (5033 "Call the Doctor")....10-20 61
SUN (193 "Come Back Baby")....300-400 54
SUN (212 "Boogie Disease")....300-400 54
LPs: 10/12-inch
FORTUNE (3011 "The Harmonica Boss")....15-25 71
TESTAMENT (2206 "Dr. Ross")....10-15

ROSS, Donna
Singles: 7-inch
DART.... 4-8 61

ROSS, Gene
Singles: 7-inch
HERALD.... 5-10 57
INDIE.... 4-8 60s
TIME.... 5-10 61

ROSS, Jack P&R '62
Singles: 7-inch
DOT.... 4-8 61-63
ROMAL.... 5-10 61
LPs: 10/12-inch
DOT (3429 "Cinderella")....15-25 62

ROSS, Jackie P&R/R&B '64
(Jacki Ross)
Singles: 7-inch
BRUNSWICK.... 4-8 67-68
CAPITOL.... 3-5 76
CHESS.... 5-10 64
FOUNTAIN.... 4-6 69
GSF.... 3-5 72-73
MERCURY.... 3-5 70-71
SAR (129 "Hard Times")....10-20 62
SCEPTER.... 3-5 72
U.S.A. (103 "Man Is Born").... 5-10 67
LPs: 10/12-inch
CHESS (1489 "Full Bloom")....15-25 64
Also see LITTLE MILTON & JACKIE ROSS

ROSS, Jeris C&W '72
Singles: 7-inch
ABC.... 3-5 73-75
ABC/DOT.... 3-5 75
CARTWHEEL.... 3-5 72
DOOR KNOB.... 3-5 79-80
GAZELLE.... 3-5 77
LPs: 10/12-inch
ABC/DOT.... 6-10 75

ROSS, Jerry
Singles: 7-inch
APEX (7763 "Out'er Drive")....10-20 61
MURCO (1016 "Ever'body's Tryin'")....100-150 59

ROSS, Jerry, Symposium
Singles: 7-inch
COLOSSUS.... 3-5 70-71

ROSS, Jimmy R&B '81
Singles: 7-inch
RFC.... 3-5 81

ROSS, Joe E.
Singles: 7-inch
IPG (1003 "Ohh Ooh!").... 5-10 62
ROULETTE (4584 "Are You Lonesome Tonight").... 4-8 64
Picture Sleeves
IPG (1003 "Ohh Ooh!")....10-15 62

ROSS, Johnny
("A&R Man Chuck Tequila Rio")
Singles: 7-inch
CORVETTE (1006 "My Dreams Have Gone")....1000-2000 58
Also see RIO, Chuck

ROSS, Lanny, with Stephen Kisley & His Orchestra & Amory Brothers
Singles: 78 rpm
MAJESTIC (1195 "The Wiffenpoof Song").... 8-12 47
(The Amory Brothers are believed to be the Ames Brothers.)
Also see AMES BROTHERS

ROSS, Lee
Singles: 78 rpm
DECCA.... 5-10 56
LIBERTY.... 5-10 57
Singles: 7-inch
CHANCELLOR.... 4-8 63
DECCA.... 8-12 56
ELBEE.... 4-8 60s
LIBERTY.... 8-12 57
RAY.... 5-10 58-59
SIMS.... 4-8 60s

ROSS, Nedra
Singles: 7-inch
NEW SONG.... 3-5 78
LPs: 10/12-inch
NEW SONG.... 8-10 77-78
Also see RONETTES

ROSS, Patty
Singles: 78 rpm
AARDEL (002 "Rock It Davy").... 5-10 56
Singles: 7-inch
AARDEL (002 "Rock It Davy")....20-30 56

ROSS, Roy
Singles: 78 rpm
ANCHOR 5-10 55
Singles: 7-inch
ANCHOR 10-15 55

ROSS, Scott
Singles: 7-inch
CAPITOL (2593 "My Little Annette") 10-15 69

ROSS, Sonny
Singles: 7-inch
EVENT 3-5 73

ROSS, Spencer P&R '60
(Robert Mersey)
Singles: 7-inch
BIGTOP 5-10 60
COLUMBIA 8-12 59-60
LPs: 10/12-inch
COLUMBIA 15-25 60
Also see MERSEY, Robert

ROSS, Spencer P&R '60
Singles: 7-inch
COLUMBIA 4-6 59-60
LPs: 10/12-inch
COLUMBIA 10-20 60

ROSS, Stan
Singles: 7-inch
DEL-FI 8-12 63
REPRISE 15-25 62
WORLD PACIFIC 15-25 60
LPs: 10/12-inch
DEL-FI (DF-1233 "My Son the Copy Cat") 20-30 63
(Monaural.)
DEL-FI (DFS-1233 "My Son the Copy Cat") 30-40 63
(Stereo.)
Also see ARBOGAST & ROSS
Also see HUSKIES

ROSS, Ted
(Teddy Ross)
Singles: 7-inch
ARWIN 5-10 59
DOLTON 4-8 61

ROSS BROTHERS
Singles: 7-inch
IMPERIAL 5-10 58

ROSSI, Frankie, & Dreams
Singles: 78 rpm
MARK (7001 "Dream Boy") 15-25 57
Singles: 7-inch
MARK (7001 "Dream Boy") 20-40 57

ROSSI, Johnny
Singles: 7-inch
DORE (913 "Cruisin' in Van Nuys") 5-10 74

ROSSI, Kenny
Singles: 7-inch
ADELPHIA 5-10 59
ARCTIC 4-8 66
GEE 5-10 60-61
MERCURY 4-8 63
ROULETTE 5-10 60-61

ROSSI, Nita
Singles: 7-inch
HICKORY 10-20

ROSSI, Steve
Singles: 7-inch
ABC-PAR 5-10 62

ROSSINE, Tony
(With the Chippers)
Singles: 7-inch
SUN 8-12 61-63

ROSSINGTON - COLLINS BAND P&R/LP '80
(Rossington Band)
Singles: 7-inch
MCA 3-5 80-88
LPs: 10/12-inch
MCA 5-10 80-88
Members: Gary Rossington; Al Collins.
Also see LYNYRD SKYNYRD

ROSY
LPs: 10/12-inch
RCA 8-10 77

ROTA, Nino P&R '72
Singles: 7-inch
PARAMOUNT 3-5 72
U.A. 3-5 72

ROTARY CONNECTION LP '68
Singles: 7-inch
CADET CONCEPT 4-8 68-70
LPs: 10/12-inch
CADET CONCEPT 15-25 68-70
Members: Minnie Riperton; Sidney Barnes.
Also see ALIOTTA, HAYNES & JEREMIAH
Also see BARNES, Sidney
Also see NEW ROTARY CONNECTION
Also see RIPPERTON, Minnie

ROTATIONS
Singles: 7-inch
ORIGINAL SOUND (41 "Crusher") 8-12 63
Members: Paul Buff; David Aerni.
Also see LORD, Brian, & Midnighters

ROTATIONS
Singles: 7-inch
FRANTIC (200 "D - 9") 100-150 65
FRANTIC (202 "Changed Man") 50-100 67
MALA (576 "Misty Roses") 15-25 67

ROTATORS
Singles: 7-inch
FELSTED 5-10 62

ROTH, Arlen
LPs: 10/12-inch
ROUNDER 5-10 80

ROTH, David Lee P&R/LP '85
Singles: 7-inch
W.B. 3-4 85-90
Picture Sleeves
W.B. 3-4 85-88
LPs: 10/12-inch
W.B. 5-10 85-90
Also see BEACH BOYS
Also see VAN HALEN

ROTH, Lillian
EPs: 7-inch
CROWN 8-12 57
LPs: 10/12-inch
EPIC (3206 "I'll Cry Tomorrow") 15-25 57
TOPS (1567 "Lillian Roth Sings") 10-20 50s

ROTH, Linda
Singles: 7-inch
BIG TOP 4-8 63
INTRASTATE 5-10 59

ROTHSCHILDS
Singles: 7-inch
COLUMBIA 4-8 60s
Member: Hal Linden.

ROTINJAIL, Blink
Singles: 7-inch
DITTO 5-10 60

ROTTEN KIDS
Singles: 7-inch
MERCURY 4-8 66

ROTTERS
Singles: 7-inch
ROTTEN (2 "Sit on My Face") 8-12 78

ROUBIAN, Bob
Singles: 78 rpm
CAPITOL 5-10 56
PREP 10-25 56-57
Singles: 7-inch
CAPITOL 5-10 56
PREP (101 "Rocket to the Moon") 15-25 56
PREP (109 "Cracker Stacker") 15-25 57

ROUGES
Singles: 7-inch
WAVERLEY (108 "The Next Guy") 20-30 66

ROUGH DIAMOND LP '77
Singles: 7-inch
ISLAND 3-5 77
LPs: 10/12-inch
ISLAND 8-10 77
Members: Byron Britton; Geoff Britton.
Also see URIAH HEEP

ROUGH RIDERS
Singles: 7-inch
HANOVER (4527 "Stampede") 8-12 59
Members: Dick Hyman, Milt DeLugg.
Also see HYMAN, Dick

ROUGH TRADE P&R '82
Singles: 7-inch
BOARDWALK 3-5 82
LPs: 10/12-inch
UMBRELLA 10-15 77

ROULETTE, Freddie
LPs: 10/12-inch
JANUS (3053 "Sweet, Funky Steel") 20-30 73
Also see HOOKER, Earl

ROULETTES
("Singing Roulettes")
Singles: 7-inch
SCEPTER (1204 "Hasten Jason") 500-750 59

ROULETTES
(With the Al Browne Band)
Singles: 7-inch
CHAMP (102 "I See a Star") 50-75 59
EBB (124 "You Don't Care Anymore") 25-35 57
Also see BROWNE, Al
Also see GALLANT, Billy

ROULETTES
Singles: 7-inch
ANGLE (1001 "Surfer's Charge") 8-12 63
(Also issued as *Invasion* by the Invaders.)
Also see INVADERS

ROULETTES
Singles: 7-inch
U.A. 5-10 64-66
Also see CURRY, Dalyce, & Roulettes

ROULETTES
LPs: 10/12-inch
TAKOMA 5-8 81

ROUND, Jonathon
LPs: 10/12-inch
WESTBOUND (2009 "Jonathon Round") 10-15 71
(With round cover.)
WESTBOUND (2009 "Jonathon Round") 8-10 71
(With square cover.)

ROUND ROBIN P&R '64
Singles: 7-inch
CAPITOL 4-8 67
DOMAIN 5-10 63-65
SHOT 4-8 66
LPs: 10/12-inch
CHALLENGE (620 "Land of 1000 Dances") 15-25 65
DOMAIN (101 "Greatest Dance Hits Slauson Style") 25-35 64

ROUND ROBINS / Joe Cenna
Singles: 7-inch
BELL 4-8 60s
Also see ROUND ROBIN

ROUND TRIP
LPs: 10/12-inch
MCA 5-10 81

ROUNDABOUTS
Singles: 7-inch
CAPITOL 5-10 66

ROUNDS, Harrel
Singles: 7-inch
STARGEM 3-5

ROUNDTREE R&B '78
Singles: 12-inch
ISLAND 4-8 78
Singles: 7-inch
ISLAND 3-5 78
Members: Diva Gray; Bernard Edwards; Luther Vandross; David Lasley.
Also see CHIC
Also see GRAY, Diva, & Oyster
Also see VANDROSS, Luther

ROUNDTREE, Richard R&B '76
Singles: 7-inch
ARTISTS of AMERICA 3-5 76
MGM 3-5 73
VERVE 3-5 72-73
LPs: 10/12-inch
MGM 8-12 72

ROUSSOS, Demis P&R/LP '78
Singles: 7-inch
BIG TREE 3-5 74-75
MGM 3-5 73
MERCURY 3-5 76-78
Picture Sleeves
MERCURY 3-5 78
LPs: 10/12-inch
BIG TREE 8-12 74-75
MGM 10-15 72
MERCURY 5-10 76-78
Also see APHRODITES CHILD

ROUSTABOUTS
Singles: 7-inch
ELKO 5-10

ROUTERS P&R '62
Singles: 7-inch
W.B. 8-12 62-64
LPs: 10/12-inch
MERCURY 10-15 73
W.B. (1490 "Let's Go") 20-30 63
W.B. (1524 "1963's Great Instrumental Hits") 20-30 63
W.B. (1559 "Charge!") 20-30 64
W.B. (1595 "Chuck Berry Songbook") 20-30 65
Members: Joe Saraceno; Rene Hall; Mike Gordon. Ed Kay.

ROUVAUN
(With Ernie Freeman's Orchestra)
Singles: 7-inch
KALAMO (201 "James Dean Theme") 10-20
Also see FREEMAN, Ernie

ROUX, Le: see LE ROUX

ROUZAN, Wanda
Singles: 7-inch
FRISCO 4-8 66
Also see ROUZAN SISTERS

ROUZAN SISTERS
Singles: 7-inch
FRISCO 4-8 65
Also see ROUZAN, Wanda

ROVER BOYS P&R '56
Singles: 78 rpm
ABC-PAR 5-10 56
CORAL 5-10 54
VIK 10-15 56-57
Singles: 7-inch
ABC 3-5 73
ABC-PAR 10-20 56
CORAL 10-20 54
DECCA 5-10 63
RCA 8-12 58-59
U.A. 5-10 61
VIK 10-20 56-57
Member: Billy Albert.

ROVERS
Singles: 78 rpm
MUSIC CITY 10-20 55
Singles: 7-inch
CAPITOL (3078 "Why Oh-h") 25-50 55
MUSIC CITY (750 "Why, Oh-h") 50-75 54
(Black vinyl.)
MUSIC CITY (750 "Why, Oh-h") 150-250 54
(Colored vinyl.)
MUSIC CITY (780 "Salute to Johnny Ace") 50-75 55
(Black vinyl.)
MUSIC CITY (780 "Salute to Johnny Ace") 150-250 55
(Colored vinyl.)
Also see 5 ROVERS
Also see GAYLARKS / Rovers

ROVERS
Singles: 7-inch
KAPP 5-8 59

ROVERS
Singles: 7-inch
CHATTAHOOCHEE 4-8 64

ROVERS
Singles: 7-inch
VINTAGE 4-8 74

ROVERS C&W '81
(Irish Rovers)
Singles: 7-inch
EPIC 3-5 81
LPs: 10/12-inch
CLEVELAND INT'L 5-10 81-82
Also see IRISH ROVERS

ROVIN' FLAMES
Singles: 7-inch
BOSS (002 "I Can't") 15-25 66
DECCA (32191 "How Many Times") 10-15 67
FULLER (2627 "Gloria") 25-35 65
TAMPA BAY (1111 "Seven Million People") 15-25 66

ROVIN' GAMBLERS
Singles: 7-inch
MAVERICK (614 "Do the Fly") 10-15 61

ROVIN' KIND
Singles: 7-inch
COUNTERPOINT (9006 "Everybody") 10-20 65
DUNWICH (146 "My Generation") 10-15 66
DUNWICH (154 "She") 10-15 67
ROULETTE (4687 "Night People") 8-12 66
SMASH (2102 "You Can't Sit Down") 5-10 67
Members: Paul Cotton; Kal David; Mike Anthony; Frank Bartoli; Fred Page.
Also see ILLINOIS SPEED PRESS

ROWAN, Chuck, & Cliques
Singles: 7-inch
OPEN 4-8 65

ROWAN & MARTIN
Singles: 7-inch
EPIC (10354 "Hang on the Bell, Nellie") 4-8 68
Members: Dan Rowan; Dick Martin.

ROWANS P&R '76
Singles: 7-inch
ASYLUM 3-5 75-76
COLUMBIA 3-5 72-73
LPs: 10/12-inch
ASYLUM 8-10 75-77
COLUMBIA 10-15 72
Members: Peter Rowan; Chris Rowan; Lorin Rowan.
Also see EARTH OPERA
Also see GARCIA, Jerry
Also see OLD and in the WAY

ROWE, Lloyd
Singles: 7-inch
GOATSVILLE (1000 "Jay Hodge Oak") 8-12
(Colored vinyl.)

ROWE, Lynn
Singles: 7-inch
HITT (181 "Red Rover") 50-75 58

ROWE, Normie
Singles: 7-inch
JUBILEE 4-8 65

ROWE, Stacey C&W '79
Singles: 7-inch
SABRE 3-5 79

ROWE, Steve
Singles: 7-inch
(21304 "Minor Chaos") 100-125 60s
(No label name used.)

ROWE, Tyron
Singles: 7-inch
FURY 10-15 62

ROWELL, Ernie C&W '71
Singles: 7-inch
GRASS 3-5 79-81
PRIZE 3-5 71
REVOLVER 3-4 87

ROWLAND, Dave C&W '82
Singles: 7-inch
ELEKTRA 3-4 82
LPs: 10/12-inch
ELEKTRA 5-10 82
Also see DAVE & SUGAR

ROWLAND, J.P.
Singles: 7-inch
IMPERIAL 5-10 60

ROWLAND, Roc
(With the Cineramas)
Singles: 7-inch
RHAPSODY (71987 "Playing for Keeps") 15-25 60
Also see CINERAMAS

ROWLAND, Steve
(With the Ring Leaders; with Family Dogg)
Singles: 78 rpm
LIBERTY 5-10 56
Singles: 7-inch
BELL 4-8 69
CROSS COUNTRY (1818 "Out Ridin'") 8-12 63
LIBERTY 8-12 56
VIRGO 10-20 59
Picture Sleeves
CROSS COUNTRY (1818 "Out Ridin'") 10-20 63
Also see FAMILY DOGG

ROWLAND, Will
Singles: 78 rpm
GOLD STAR (657 "Reefer Blues") 25-50 47
MODERN 15-25 46-47

ROWLES, John P&R/LP '71
Singles: 7-inch
KAPP 3-6 68-71
UNI 3-6 68
LPs: 10/12-inch
KAPP 10-15 69-71
MCA 5-8

ROWLY, Major
Singles: 7-inch
AMY 4-8 65

ROX
Singles: 7-inch
BOARDWALK 3-4 81
LPs: 10/12-inch
BOARDWALK 5-10 81

ROXANNE P&R '88
Singles: 7-inch
SCOTTI BROS 3-4 88
Members: Jamie Brown; John Butler; Dave Landry; Joe Infante.

ROXANNE with UTFO D&D '85
Singles: 12-inch
SELECT 4-6 85
Singles: 7-inch
SELECT 3-4 85
Also see UTFO

ROXETTE P&R/LP '89
Singles: 12-inch
CAPITOL (15018 "Hartland") 5-10 84
Singles: 7-inch
EMI (Except 04409) 3-4 89
EMI (04409 "Listen to Your Heart") 3-6 89
(Promotional issue only. Commercial single release on cassette only.)
LPs: 10/12-inch
EMI 5-8 89-91

ROXSTERS
Singles: 7-inch
ART (175 "Goodbye Baby") 300-450 58
Members: Butch Watts; Wesley Hardin; Don Ward; Dave Hieronymus; Keith MacKendrick.
Also see CHAMPS
Also see HARDIN, Wesley, & Roxsters
Also see THINK

ROXY
Singles: 7-inch
ELEKTRA 3-6 69
LPs: 10/12-inch
ELEKTRA 10-15 69
Member: Bob Segarini.

ROXY & DAYCHORDS
Singles: 7-inch
CANDLELITE 5-10 60s
CLIFTON (24 "Mary Lou") 4-6
DON-EL (116 "Mary Lou") 75-100 62
Also see DAYCHORDS

ROXY MUSIC LP '73
Singles: 12-inch
W.B. (2033 "Avalon") 5-8 82
Singles: 7-inch
ATCO 3-6 75-80
REPRISE 4-8 72
W.B. (Except 7779) 3-5 82-83
W.B. (7779 "Do the Strand") 4-8 73
Promotional Singles
ATCO 5-10 75-80
W.B. 3-5 82-83
Picture Sleeves
W.B. 3-5 82-83
LPs: 10/12-inch
ATCO (Except 106 & 8114) 8-15 74-83
ATCO (106 "Country Life") 20-35 75
(Cover pictures two women in their underwear.)
ATCO (106 "Country Life") 8-15 75
(The two women are not pictured on cover.)
ATCO (38114 "Manifesto") 25-30 75
(Picture disc. Promotional issue only.)
ATLANTIC 8-10 74
REPRISE (2114 "Roxy Music") 15-25 72
W.B. (Except 2696) 5-10 82-83
W.B. (2696 "For Your Pleasure") 15-25 73
Member: Bryan Ferry.
Also see CARRACK, Paul
Also see ENO, Brian
Also see FERRY, Bryan, & Roxy Music
Also see MANZANERA, Phil

ROY, Barbara D&D '84
Singles: 12-inch
ASCOT 4-6 84
Singles: 7-inch
RCA 3-4 86
Also see ECSTASY, PASSION & PAIN

ROY, Bobbie C&W '72
Singles: 7-inch
CAPITOL 3-5 72-73
LPs: 10/12-inch
CAPITOL 6-12 72

ROY, Bobby, & Chord-A-Roys
Singles: 7-inch
J.D.S. (5001 "Little Girl Lost") 25-35 59

ROY, Doty
Singles: 7-inch
TRIBE 4-8 65

ROY, George
Singles: 7-inch
DANCO 4-8 66

ROY, Lee
(Brother Lee Roy & His Band)
Singles: 78 rpm
EPIC 5-10 53-54
Singles: 7-inch
EPIC 10-15 53-54
SANWAYNE 5-8 62
EPs: 7-inch
EPIC (7027 "Teen-Age Party Dances") 15-25 54
EPIC (7037 "Sock Hop") 15-25 54
LPs: 10/12-inch
EPIC (1011 "Teenage Party Dances") 25-50 54
EPIC (1014 "Sock Hop") 25-50 54

ROY, Ricky
Singles: 7-inch
SPANN (416 "Screamin' Mimi") 15-25 59

ROY & GLORIA
Singles: 78 rpm
DELUXE 8-12 57
Singles: 7-inch
DELUXE 8-12 57

ROY C. R&B '65
(Roy Charles Hammond)
Singles: 7-inch
ALAGA 3-5 71
BLACK HAWK 4-8 65-66
MERCURY 3-5 73-77
SHOUT 4-6 66
UPTOWN 4-6 66
LPs: 10/12-inch
MERCURY 8-12 77
Also see GENIES

ROY - SARAH & TRAITS
Singles: 7-inch
LORI (9551 "You'll Never Make Me Blue") ...10-20 60s
(Same song as *Treat Me Right*, the title track of Roy Head's Scepter LP.)
Member: Roy Head.
Also see HEAD, Roy

ROYAL, Bill
Singles: 7-inch
ODESSA (504 "Caffine, Nicotine, Gasoline") 150-250

ROYAL, Billy Joe P&R/LP '65
Singles: 7-inch
ALL WOOD 5-10 62
ATLANTIC (2300 series) 4-8 66
ATLANTIC (87000 thru 89000 series) 3-4 85-91
ATLANTIC AMERICA 3-5 85-89
COLUMBIA (43305 "Down in the Boondocks") .. 4-8 65
(Black vinyl.)
COLUMBIA (43305 "Down in the Boondocks") ..10-20 65
(Colored vinyl. Promotional issue only.)
COLUMBIA (43390 "I Knew You When") 4-8 65
(Black vinyl.)
COLUMBIA (43390 "I Knew You When") 10-20 65
(Colored vinyl. Promotional issue only.)
COLUMBIA (43465 thru 45620) 4-8 65-72
FAIRLANE 8-12 61-62
KAT FAMILY 3-5 81
MGM/SOUTH 3-5 73
MERCURY 3-5 80
PLAYER'S 5-10 65
PRIVATE STOCK 3-5 78
SCEPTER 3-5 76
TOLLIE 5-10 64
Picture Sleeves
ATLANTIC AMERICA 3-6 80s
TOLLIE 8-12 64
LPs: 10/12-inch
ATLANTIC AMERICA 5-10 86-89
BACK-TRAC 5-8 85
BRYLEN 5-10
COLUMBIA (Except 45063) 15-25 65-69
COLUMBIA (45063 "Greatest Hits") 5-8 89
51 WEST 5-10 83
KAT FAMILY 5-10 81
MERCURY 5-10 80
Also see FARGO, Donna, & Billy Joe Royal
Also see SOUTH, Joe / Billy Joe Royal
Also see WINE, Toni, & Billy Joe Royal

ROYAL, Chuck
Singles: 7-inch
BELLA 10-20 59

ROYAL, Duke
Singles: 7-inch
DEBBIE 4-8 68

ROYAL, Ernie, & Mutineers
Singles: 7-inch
COLPIX 3-5 62
Picture Sleeves
COLPIX 4-8 62

ROYAL AIRCOACH
Singles: 7-inch
FLYING MACHINE (8868 "Wondering Why") 15-25 68

ROYAL BLUE
Singles: 7-inch
CAPITOL 3-6 69
LPs: 10/12-inch
CAPITOL 10-15 69

ROYAL BOYS
Singles: 7-inch
TROPELCO (1007 "Darling Angel") 2000-3000 60

ROYAL CANAL STREET BAND
Singles: 7-inch
ATCO 4-6 67

ROYAL CHESSMEN
Singles: 7-inch
NIGHT OWL (2016 "Can't You See") 10-20 67

ROYAL COACHMEN
Singles: 7-inch
CHALLENGE (59251 "Loophole") ..10-20 64
COACHMEN (200,915 "Bama-Lama") 40-60 60s
GE GE (102 "Tidal Wave") 15-25 60s

ROYAL COLLECTION
Singles: 7-inch
COTILLION 4-6 69

ROYAL COUNTS
Singles: 7-inch
CATAMOUNT 3-5 72
LPs: 10/12-inch
CATAMOUNT 8-12 72
Members: Mike Murphy; Herman Hammond; Bill Jones; Charlie Small; Ted West.

ROYAL DEBS
Singles: 7-inch
TIFCO (826 "I Do") 10-20 62

ROYAL DEMONS
Singles: 7-inch
RHYTHM (5004 "What's the Matter Baby") ...10-20 59

ROYAL DEMONS
Singles: 7-inch
PEK (8101 "Trembling Hand") 500-750 61

ROYAL DRIFTERS
Singles: 7-inch
TEEN (506 "Little Linda") 100-150 59
TEEN (508 "To Each His Own") 100-150 59

ROYAL FIVE
(Royal-Five)
Singles: 7-inch
ARCTIC (160 "Ain't No Big Thing") ..5-10 60s
P&L (317 "Over the Rainbow") ...500-750 66
TYLER (200 "Say It to My Face") 50-75 60s

ROYAL FLAIRS
Singles: 7-inch
MARINA (503 "Suicide") 50-75 65
SAM (119 "Dream Angel") 20-40 60s
Also see UNLIMITED

ROYAL FLUSH
Singles: 7-inch
DELUXE 4-8 73
Also see MANHATTANS

ROYAL GALAXIES
Singles: 7-inch
CAPITOL (4488 "Over and Done With") 15-25 60

ROYAL GROOVE
Singles: 7-inch
MONUMENT 3-6 69

ROYAL GUARDSMEN P&R '66
Singles: 7-inch
LAURIE (3359 "Baby Let's Wait") ..10-15 66
LAURIE (3366 "Squeaky Vs. the Black Knight") 30-50 66
(Re-recorded as *Snoopy Vs. the Red Baron*. Canadian. We have yet to verify a US issue of this title.)
LAURIE (3366 "Snoopy Vs. the Red Baron") .5-10 66
LAURIE (3379 "Return of the Red Baron") ..5-10 67
LAURIE (3391 "Airplane Song") 5-10 67
LAURIE (3397 "Wednesday") 5-10 67
LAURIE (3416 "Snoopy's Christmas") 5-10 67
LAURIE (3428 "I Say Love") 5-10 68
LAURIE (3451 "Snoopy for President") 5-10 68
LAURIE (3461 "Baby Let's Wait") 5-10 68
LAURIE (3494 "Mother, Where's Your Daughter") 5-10 69
LPs: 10/12-inch
AUDIO FIDELITY (1913 "Snoopy's Christmas") 10-15 83
(Picture disc.)
LAURIE (2038 "Snoopy Vs. the Red Baron") .15-20 67
LAURIE (2039 "Return of the Red Baron") ..15-20 67
LAURIE (2042 "Snoopy & His Friends, the Royal Guardsmen") 15-20 67
LAURIE (2046 "Snoopy for President") 15-20 68
Members: Chris Nunley; Barry Winslow; Bill Balough; Tom Richards.
Also see WINSLOW, Barry

ROYAL HALOS
Singles: 7-inch
ALADDIN (3460 "My Love Is True") 30-40 59

ROYAL HARMONY QUARTET R&B '42
Singles: 78 rpm
KEYNOTE 5-10 42
Members: Julius Ginyard; Ted Brooks; Bill Johnson; John Jennings; George McFadden.
Also see JUBALAIRES

ROYAL HAWK
(Roy Hawkins)
Singles: 78 rpm
FLAIR (1013 "The Royal Hawk") 20-40 53
Singles: 7-inch
FLAIR (1013 "The Royal Hawk") ..50-100 53
Also see HAWKINS, Roy

ROYAL HOLIDAYS
Singles: 7-inch
CARLTON (472 "I'm Sorry") 25-35 58
HERALD (536 "Rockin' at the Bandstand") ..75-125 59
PENTHOUSE (9357 "I'm Sorry") ..75-125 58

ROYAL HOST
Singles: 7-inch
AT (684 "Whatever Happened to Joey") 10-20 68
Also see LEE, Robin

ROYAL HOUSE R&B '88
Singles: 7-inch
IDLERS WAR 3-4 88

ROYAL JACKS
Singles: 7-inch
AMY (865 "Anticipation") 10-15 62
DANCO (503 "You'll Never Be Mine") 15-25 64
OPERATORS 10-15 61
STUDIO (9903 "Night After Night") 75-125 59
20TH FOX (100 "I'm in Love Again") 15-25 58

ROYAL JACKS
(With Vince Catalano & Orchestra)
Singles: 7-inch
STUDIO (9903 "Night After Night") 75-125 59

ROYAL JESTERS
("Vocal with orch. by Charlie & the Jives")
Singles: 7-inch
HARLEM (105 "My Angel of Love") 300-400 60
Also see CHARLIE & JIVES

ROYAL JESTERS
(With the Casuals)
Singles: 7-inch
COBRA (2222 "Love Me") 20-30 62
COBRA (7777 "I Want to Be Loved") 25-35 63
COBRA (611025 "Ask Me to Move a Mountain") 25-35 61
JESTER (102 "Wisdom of a Fool") 25-35 62
JESTER (103 "My Love, My Love") 20-30 62
JESTER (104 "We Go Together") 15-25 62
JESTER (106 "Let There Be You") 15-25 62
JOX (036 "Wishing Ring") 15-25 65

ROYAL JESTERS
Singles: 7-inch
BELL 3-5 71

ROYAL JOKERS P&R '55
Singles: 78 rpm
ATCO 10-20 55-56
HI-Q 15-25 57
Singles: 7-inch
ATCO (6052 "You Tickle Me Baby") 25-35 55
ATCO (6062 "Don't Leave Me, Fanny") 20-30 55
ATCO (6077 "She's Mine, All Mine") 25-35 55
FORTUNE (560 "You Tickle Me Baby") 15-20 63
FORTUNE (840 "Sweet Little Angel") 20-25 57
HI-Q (5004 "September in the Rain") 25-30 57
Also see MUSKATEERS

ROYAL JOKERS
LPs: 10/12-inch
DAWN (1119 "Rock & Roll Spectacular") 50-100 57

ROYAL JOKERS
Singles: 7-inch
MURCO (1015 "Beatnik") 15-25 58

ROYAL JOKERS
Singles: 7-inch
BIG TOP 8-12 60
KELDON (322 "Lovey Dovey") 10-15 60
METRO 5-10 60

ROYAL JOKERS
Singles: 7-inch
WINGATE (020 "From A to Z") 10-20 60s

ROYAL KHANS
Singles: 7-inch
LE CAM 5-10 61

ROYAL KINGS
(With the Cashmers)
Singles: 7-inch
FORLIN (502 "Keep It to Yourself") 100-150 61

ROYAL KINGS
Singles: 7-inch
CLIFTON (2005 "Doggin' Around") ..5-10 85
LPs: 10/12-inch
CLIFTON 8-12 85

ROYAL KNIGHTS
Singles: 7-inch
FIREBALL (104 "Knight-Mare") 10-20 64
SHADOW (108 "Midnight Drag") ...20-30 60s
SNAP (005 "I Don't Want to Go") ...25-35 60s

ROYAL KNIGHTS
Singles: 7-inch
NITE (1005 "I Wanna Know") 15-25 66
Picture Sleeves
NITE (1005 "I Wanna Know") 25-35 66

ROYAL KNIGHTS
Singles: 7-inch
SHADOW (108 "Midnight Drag") 8-12

ROYAL LANCERS
Singles: 7-inch
ABC-PAR (10751 "Baby, I Love You") 8-12 65
HI MAR (502 "This Time") 15-25 63
LAWN (205 "Oh Little Girl") 25-35 63
(Also issued as by the Lancers.)
LAWN (215 "Hey Little One") 25-35 63
Member: Keith "Corky" Weiss.
Also see LANCERS

ROYAL NOTES
Singles: 7-inch
DESTINY 8-12 61

ROYAL NOTES / Phil Johnson & Duvals
(With Floyd Williams & Orchestra)
Singles: 7-inch
KELIT (7034 "You Are My Love") 300-500 58
Also see JOHNSON, Phil, & Duvals

ROYAL PHILHARMONIC ORCHESTRA P&R/LP '81
(Conducted by Louis Clark)
Singles: 7-inch
RCA 3-4 81-83
LPs: 10/12-inch
RCA 5-8 81-83

ROYAL PLAY BOYS
Singles: 7-inch
IMPERIAL 5-10 61

ROYAL PLAYBOYS
LPs: 10/12-inch
WALDORF MUSIC HALL (136 "Spirituals and Jubilees") 50-75 53
(10-inch LP.)

ROYAL PLAYBOYS
Singles: 7-inch
DO DE (101 "Happy Hours") 15-25 64
DO DE (111 "Arabia") 50-100 64

ROYAL PREMIERS
Singles: 7-inch
M.B.S. (105 "I Can Make It") 10-20 65

ROYAL RAVENS
Singles: 7-inch
MAH'S (0015 "All Over You") 50-75 63

ROYAL REBELS
Singles: 7-inch
KISKI (2067 "Drive-in") 20-30

ROYAL REVERES
Singles: 7-inch
JUMP-UP (114 "Such a Fool") 50-75 60s

ROYAL RHYTHMS
Singles: 7-inch
ROYAL (5070 "Lovey Dovey") 50-80

ROYAL ROBINS
Singles: 7-inch
ABC-PAR (10504 "Turn Me Loose") 15-25 63
ABC-PAR (10542 "Something You've Got Baby") 15-25 64

ROYAL ROCKERS
Singles: 7-inch
DEE (1112 "Jet II") 10-20 60

ROYAL SHANDELS
Singles: 7-inch
MERCHANDISING DIRECTORS (7379 "Be Careful with Your Car Full") 5-10 66
(Promotional issue only.)
Member: Ron Oswalt.

ROYAL SCOTS DRAGOON GUARDS P&R/LP '72
Singles: 7-inch
RCA 3-5 72
LPs: 10/12-inch
RCA 5-10 72

ROYAL SONS QUINTET
(Five Royales)
Singles: 78 rpm
APOLLO (253 "Bedside of a Neighbor") 100-200 52
APOLLO (266 "Come Over Here") 50-100 52
Members: Johnny Tanner; Lowman Pauling; Clarence Pauling; William Samuels; Otto Jeffries; Clarence Pauling; Johnny Holmes.
Also see CASHMERES
Also see COSYTONES
Also see FIVE ROYALES
Also see KING & SHARPETTES

ROYAL SPADES
Singles: 7-inch
MARQUEE 10-20 62

ROYAL TEENS P&R/R&B '58
("Joey Villa & Royal Teens")
Singles: 78 rpm
ABC-PAR 20-50 57-58
POWER (215 "Short Shorts") 50-100 57
Singles: 7-inch
ABC 3-5 73
ABC-PAR (9882 "Short Shorts") 15-25 57
ABC-PAR (9918 "Big Name Button") 15-25 58
ABC-PAR (9945 "Hangin' Around") 15-25 58
ABC-PAR (9955 "My Kind of Dream") 15-25 58
ALLNEW (1415 "Royal Twist") 10-20 62
ASTRA (1012 "Mad Gass") 5-10 65
CAPITOL (4261 "Believe Me") 25-35 59
(Capitol dome logo at top.)
CAPITOL (4261 "Believe Me") 10-20 59
(Capitol dome logo at left side.)
CAPITOL (4335 "Was It a Dream") 20-30 60
CAPITOL (4402 "With You") 20-30 60
JUBILEE (5418 "Royal Twist") 5-10 62
MCA 3-4 80s
MIGHTY (111 "Leotards") 15-25 58
MIGHTY (112 "Cave Man") 20-30 59
MIGHTY (200 "My Memories of You") 20-30 58
MUSICOR (1398 "Smile a Little Smile for Me") 5-8 70
POWER (113 "Mad Gass") 20-30 59
POWER (215 "Short Shorts") 75-100 57
SPARTON (534 "Short Shorts") 25-50 58
(Canadian. Runs 2:39. That's 27 seconds longer than ABC-Paramount single, which fades out at 2:12.)
SWAN (4200 "I'll Love You") 50-75 65
(Previously issued on Bluejay as by the Bluetones.)
TCF (117 "Bad Girl") 5-10 65
LPs: 10/12-inch
DEMAND (010 "Believe Me") 10-20
MUSICOR (3186 "Newies But Oldies") 10-20 70
TRU-GEMS (101 "Music Gems") 8-12 74
Members: Bob Gaudio; Al Kooper; Buddy Randell; Joey Villa; Billy Crandall; Tom Austin; Tony Grochowski.
Also see BLUETONES
Also see DISENTRI, Turner
Also see 4 SEASONS
Also see KOOPER, Al
Also see RANDELL, Buddy
Also see VILLA, Joey

ROYAL TONES
Singles: 7-inch
EMPIRE (1001 "Creeping Thunder") 20-30 60
TITANIC (5014 "Black Lightnin' ") ..15-25 60s

ROYAL VIKINGS
Singles: 7-inch
METROPOLIS (7001 "Surfin' Mary") 15-25 63

ROYAL-AIRES
(With the Lee Clark Orchestra)
Singles: 7-inch
GALLO (108 "Baby Baby") 20-40 57

ROYALAIRES
Singles: 7-inch
QUEEN (30001 "Frying Chicken") .10-20 61

ROYALCASH R&B '83
Singles: 12-inch
SUTRA 4-6 83
Singles: 7-inch
SUTRA 3-5 83

ROYALE, Arturo
Singles: 7-inch
ORIGINAL SOUND 4-8 66

ROYALE COACHMEN
Singles: 7-inch
JOWAR 5-10 60s

ROYALE MONARCHS
Singles: 7-inch
DELL (101 "Sombrero Stomp") 15-25 62
DELL STAR (102 "Surf's Up") 15-25 62
DELL STAR (104 "Teen Scene") 15-25 64
Member: Roger Stafford.

ROYALETTES P&R/R&B '65
Singles: 7-inch
CHANCELLOR 8-12 62-63
MGM 8-12 64-66
ROULETTE 5-10 67
W.B. 5-10 64
LPs: 10/12-inch
MGM 15-25 65-66
Members: Anita Ross; Sheila Ross; Terry Jones; Ronnie Brown.

ROYALITES
Singles: 7-inch
MOJAK (5265 "Harlem Nocturne") 15-25 65

ROYALS
Singles: 78 rpm
OKEH (6832 "If You Love Me") . 100-200 51

Singles: 7-inch
OKEH (6832 "If You Love Me")..400-500 51
Also see WILLIS, Chuck

ROYALS R&B '53
Singles: 78 rpm
FEDERAL (12064 "Every Beat of My Heart")....100-200 52
FEDERAL (12077 "Starting from Tonight")....100-200 52
FEDERAL (12088 "Moonrise")....100-200 52
FEDERAL (12098 "A Love in My Heart")....50-100 52
FEDERAL (12113 "Are You Forgetting")....50-100 52
FEDERAL (12121 "The Shrine of St. Cecilia")....50-100 53
FEDERAL (12133 "Get It")....40-60 53
FEDERAL (12150 "Hey Miss Fine")....40-60 53
FEDERAL (12160 "That's It")....40-60 54
FEDERAL (12169 "Work with Me Annie")....40-60 54
Singles: 7-inch
FEDERAL (12064 "Every Beat of My Heart")....500-750 52
(Black vinyl.)
FEDERAL (12064 "Every Beat of My Heart")....2500-3500 52
(Blue vinyl.)
FEDERAL (12077 "Starting from Tonight")....1000-2000 52
FEDERAL (12088 "Moonrise")....1000-2000 52
FEDERAL (12098 "A Love in My Heart")....750-1000 52
FEDERAL (12113 "Are You Forgetting")....500-1000 52
FEDERAL (12121 "The Shrine of St. Cecilia")....500-1000 53
FEDERAL (12133 "Get It")....200-300 53
FEDERAL (12150 "Hey Miss Fine")....150-250 53
FEDERAL (12160 "That's It")....150-250 54
FEDERAL (12169 "Work with Me Annie")....150-250 54
FEDERAL (12177 "Give It Up")..150-250 54
(White label. Test pressing only. Commercial copies credit: "The Midnighters, Formally Known as the Royals.")
GUSTO.... 3-5 80s
Note: Federal titles reissued as by the Midnighters are in the Midnighters' section.
Members: Henry Booth; Hank Ballard; Charles Sutton; Lawson Smith; Alonzo Tucker; Sonny Woods.
Also see BALLARD, Hank
Also see BOOTH, Henry
Also see MIDNIGHTERS

ROYALS
Singles: 78 rpm
VENUS....50-100 54
Singles: 7-inch
VENUS (103 "Someday We'll Meet Again")....200-300 54
Also see SCOOTERS

ROYALS
Singles: 7-inch
PENGUIN (1008 "Thunder Wagon")....15-25 59

ROYALS
Singles: 7-inch
MONUMENTAL.... 4-8 64
VAGABOND (134 "Surfin' Lagoon")....10-20 62
VAGABOND (444 "Christmas Party")....10-20 63
(Black vinyl.)
VAGABOND (444 "Christmas Party")....30-50 63
(Colored vinyl.)

ROYALS
Singles: 7-inch
CORI (31002 "I'm All Alone")....10-20 65
CROYDON ("Slow Down Boy")....10-15 67
(No selection number used.)
ODYSSEY (711 "Comin' & Goin'")....25-35 60s

ROYALS
Singles: 7-inch
COPELAND (2130 "Say You Love Me")....25-35

ROYALTONES
Singles: 78 rpm
OLD TOWN (1018 "Crazy Love")...20-30 56
Singles: 7-inch
OLD TOWN (1018 "Crazy Love")...50-75 56
Also see McFADDEN, Ruth

ROYALTONES P&R '58
Singles: 7-inch
ABC.... 3-5 73
GOLDISC....10-15 60-61
JANUS GOLD.... 3-5
JUBILEE (Blue label)....10-15 58-59
JUBILEE (Black label).... 5-10 62
MALA.... 5-10 63-64
PENTHOUSE (777 "Clip Clop")....25-35 59
PORT (70037 "Poor Boy").... 8-12 64
ROULETTE.... 3-5 71
TWIRL.... 5-8 62
VIRGO.... 3-5 72

ROYALTONES
Singles: 7-inch
FEDERAL....10-15 60
Also see EL PAULING

ROYALTONES
(Royal-Tones)
Singles: 7-inch
ADMIRAL (110 "Royal Shuffle")....10-20 60s
ADMIRAL (4038 "Royal Flush")....10-20 60s

ROYALTY
Singles: 7-inch
W.B.... 3-4 88

ROYBAL, Lenny
Singles: 7-inch
CANTERBURY (509 "Don't").... 4-8 67
CORBY (224 "Little Daisy").... 4-8 60s

ROYCE
Singles: 7-inch
U.K.... 3-5 74

ROYCE, Benny, & Company
Singles: 7-inch
DELMAR....10-20

ROYE, Cené
Singles: 7-inch
CYCLONE (122 "I'd Do It All Over Again")....10-15 62

ROYE, Lee, & Emeralds
Singles: 7-inch
REDBUG (0003 "Hesitation")....15-20 60s

ROYER, Luke
Singles: 7-inch
BEE JAY (1375 "One's All the Law Will Allow")....25-35

ROYSTER, Jimmy
Singles: 7-inch
SKY (1 "They May Not Like Me")....150-250
(Colored vinyl.)

ROZAKIS, Michael & Yorgos
LPs: 10/12-inch
DANCE-A-THON/HOTTRAX.... 5-8 80

ROZIER, Alice
Singles: 7-inch
KING (5896 "My Candy Man")....5-10 64

ROZZI, Little Sammy, & Guys
Singles: 7-inch
PELHAM (722 "Christine")....200-300 61
(Reissued as by Little Sammy & the Tones.)
Also see LITTLE SAMMY & TONES

RUBBER BAND
Singles: 7-inch
ABC.... 4-8 66
COLUMBIA.... 4-8 66-67
REPRISE.... 4-8 67
LPs: 10/12-inch
GREENWOOD (1650 "The Band That Wouldn't Die")....15-20 85
Members: Johnny Wyker; Tippy Armstrong; Tommy Stuart; John Townsend; Lou Mullinix; Brook Clement; Bill Connell.
Also see ALLMAN JOYS
Also see SAILCAT
Also see SANFORD - TOWNSEND BAND

RUBBER BAND
Singles: 7-inch
COULEE (122 "My Baby Left Me")....10-15 68

RUBBER BAND LP '69
Singles: 7-inch
GRT.... 4-6 69
LPs: 10/12-inch
GRT....10-15 69

RUBBER CITY REBELS
Singles: 7-inch
CAPITOL.... 3-5 80
LPs: 10/12-inch
CAPITOL....5-10 80

RUBBER MAZE
Singles: 7-inch
RUFF (1098 "Mrs. Griffith")....15-25 68
TOWER (351 "Mrs. Griffith")....8-12 67

RUBBER MEMORY
LPs: 10/12-inch
RPC (69401 "Welcome")....200-250 66

RUBBER RODEO P&R '84
Singles: 7-inch
MERCURY.... 3-5 84-85
LPs: 10/12-inch
MERCURY....5-10 85

RU-BEE-ELS
Singles: 7-inch
FLIP (359 "I'll Try")....10-15 62

RUBEN & JETS
(Mothers of Invention)
Singles: 7-inch
VERVE (10632 "Any Way the Wind Blows")....20-30 68
VERVE (10632 "Deseri")....20-30 68
LPs: 10/12-inch
VERVE (5055 "Crusin' with Ruben and the Jets")....30-40 68
(Issued with three paper inserts, any of which can add $15 to $25 to the value.)
Also see MOTHERS OF INVENTION

RUBEN & JETS
Singles: 7-inch
MERCURY.... 3-5 73
LPs: 10/12-inch
MERCURY....10-12 73

Member: Ruben Guevara; Johnny Martinez; Tony Duran; Robert Zamora; Bob Roberts; Robert Camarena; Jim Sherwood.
Also see GUEVARA, Ruben

RUBETTES P&R '74
Singles: 7-inch
MCA....3-5 76
POLYDOR....3-5 74-75
LPs: 10/12-inch
MCA....6-10 76

RUBICON P&R/LP '78
Singles: 7-inch
20TH FOX....3-5 78-79
LPs: 10/12-inch
20TH FOX....5-10 78-79
Also see SLY & Family Stone

RUBIES
Singles: 7-inch
DISTRICT (301 "Loaded with Goodies")....20-30 61
START ("Loaded with Goodies")....10-15 61

RUBIES
Singles: 7-inch
EMPRESS (103 "He Was an Angel")....10-15 61
EMPRESS (103 "He Was an Angel")....15-25 61
(Single-sided. Promotional issue only.)
TNT (101 "Zing Went the Strings of My Heart")....10-15 60s
VEE JAY (596 "Spanish Boy")....8-12 64
Picture Sleeves
VEE JAY (596 "Spanish Boy")....15-25 64
(Promotional issue only.)

RUBIES
Singles: 7-inch
ENITH INT'L....8-12 63
Member: Gaynel Hodge.
Also see HODGE, Gaynel

RUBIN
Singles: 7-inch
KAPP (869 "You've Been Away")...25-50 68

RUBINOOS P&R '77
Singles: 12-inch
W.B....4-8 80-83
Singles: 7-inch
BESERKLEY....3-5 77-79
W.B....3-4 84
Picture Sleeves
BESERKLEY....3-5 77-79
LPs: 10/12-inch
BESERKLEY....5-10 77-79
Also see KIHN, Greg, Band / Earthquake / Modern Lovers / Rubinoos
Member: Jon Rubin.

RUBINOWITZ, Tex
Singles: 7-inch
RIPSAW....3-5 79-81
Picture Sleeves
RIPSAW....3-5 79-81
LPs: 10/12-inch
NCP....8-10
Also see ANGEL, Eddie
Also see HANCOCK, Billy
Also see HULL, Martha
Also see ROCK, Bob E.

RUBINS, Joey, Jr.
Singles: 7-inch
D-TOWN....3-5 82

RUBY
Singles: 7-inch
CHRYSALIS....3-5 74
LPs: 10/12-inch
CHRYSALIS....8-10 74

RUBY
Singles: 7-inch
GINSENG....3-5 75
PBR INT'L....3-5 76
LPs: 10/12-inch
PBR INT'L....8-12 76-78
Members: Tom Fogerty; Bobby Cochran; Anthony Davis; Randy Oda; Ed Bogas.
Also see FOGERTY, Tom

RUBY
Singles: 7-inch
ABC....10-20
GOLDEN TOKEN (100 "Feminine Ingenuity")....100-125

RUBY, Don
Singles: 7-inch
CUB (9012 "Rockin' Piano, Outta Tune Guitar")....50-75 58

RUBY & PARTY GANG R&B '71
Singles: 7-inch
GAMBLE....3-5 72
LAW-TON....3-5 71

RUBY & ROMANTICS P&R/R&B/LP '63
Singles: 7-inch
A&M....4-6 69
ABC....4-8 67-68
KAPP....5-10 62-67
MCA....3-4 70s
Picture Sleeves
KAPP....5-10 63-64
LPs: 10/12-inch
ABC....10-20 68
KAPP....15-25 63-67
MCA....5-10 80s
PICKWICK....8-10 70s
Members: Ruby Nash; Edward Roberts; Ronald Mosley; Leroy Fann; George Lee.

RUBY JEAN
Singles: 7-inch
MONSTER MASTERS....4-8 64

RUCKER, Ervin: see JACKSON, Mattie

RUDE BOYS
LPs: 10/12-inch
ATLANTIC....5-8 90

RUDD, Lawson
Singles: 7-inch
HARVEST (709 "Shake This Town")....50-75

RUDD, Norma
Singles: 7-inch
SURE SHOT....4-8 66

RUDOLPH, Billy
Singles: 7-inch
JOYETTE....5-10 60

RUDOLPH, Lorri
Singles: 7-inch
JET STREAM (817 "Keep Coming Back for More")....35-45
TRI PHI (1003 "Don't Let Them Tell Me")....10-20 61
Also see LOE & JOE

RUDOLPH, Randy
Singles: 7-inch
PREVIEW (1507 "Little Surfer Teen")....15-25 60s

RUDY
Singles: 7-inch
POLYDOR....3-5 79
LPs: 10/12-inch
POLYDOR....5-10 79

RUDY, Jan
Singles: 7-inch
ATLANTIC....3-5

RUDY, Roger, & Pyrmid
Singles: 7-inch
PYRAMID (102 "Travelin' Band")...10-15 60s
Also see PYRAMID

RUDY & JOHNNY
Singles: 7-inch
MERCURY....5-8 62

RUDY & PUBS
Singles: 7-inch
LMS ("Bridge to Seventeen")....4-6 92
(No selection number used.)

RUDY & TRADEWINDS
Singles: 7-inch
ANGLE TONE (543 "Careless Love")....50-75 62

RUDY & WHEELS
Singles: 7-inch
CURTIS (751 "It's Not for Me")..200-300 59

RUDY & VINCE
Singles: 7-inch
TEEN TIME....5-10 62

RUE R&B '87
Singles: 7-inch
ASIANA....3-4 87

RUE, Arnie C&W '79
Singles: 7-inch
NSD....3-5 79

RUE-TEENS
(Ru-Teens)
Singles: 7-inch
LOUIS....8-12 64
OLD TIMER....8-12 65

RUFF, Bill

RUFF, Bill
Singles: 78 rpm
GATEWAY....10-15 56
Singles: 7-inch
GATEWAY (1163 "Juke box Baby")....20-30 56

RUFF, Ray
(With the Checkmates; Ray Ruffin)
Singles: 7-inch
BOLO....10-20 63
LIN (5034 "Beatle Maniacs")....25-35 64
LIN (5035 "Angel Blue")....15-25 64
LIN (5036 "In Dreamland")....10-15 64
NORMAN....10-20 61-63

RUFF & REDDY
Singles: 7-inch
CAVALIER (876 "Henry Goes to the Moon")....10-15 58

RUFFIN, Bruce
Singles: 7-inch
BELL (265 "Mad About You")....5-8 72

RUFFIN, David P&R/R&B/LP '69
Singles: 7-inch
ANNA (1127 "I'm in Love")....35-55 60
CHECK MATE (1003 "You Can Get What I Got")....30-50 61
CHECK MATE (1010 "Mr. Bus Driver")....30-50 61
MOTOWN....3-6 69-76
W.B....3-5 79-80
LPs: 10/12-inch
MOTOWN (100 & 200 series)....5-10 82
MOTOWN (600 series)....10-15 69
MOTOWN (700 & 800 series)....8-10 73-76
W.B....8-10 77-80
Also see BUSH, Little David
Also see HALL, Daryl, John Oates, David Ruffin & Eddie Kendrick
Also see TEMPTATIONS
Also see VOICE MASTERS

RUFFIN, David, & Eddie Kendricks R&B '87
Singles: 7-inch
RCA....3-4 87-88
Also see KENDRICKS, Eddie

RUFFIN, David & Jimmy P&R/R&B '70
(Ruffin Brothers)
Singles: 7-inch
SOUL....3-6 70
LPs: 10/12-inch
MOTOWN....5-10 80
SOUL (728 "My Brother's Keeper") 10-20 70
Also see RUFFIN, David
Also see RUFFIN, Jimmy

RUFFIN, Jimmy P&R/R&B '66
Singles: 12-inch
EPIC....4-8 77
Singles: 7-inch
EPIC....3-4 77
MIRACLE (1 "Heart")....50-100 61
MOTOWN....3-5
RSO....3-5 80
SOUL (Except 35002 & 35022)....8-15 65-71
SOUL (35002 "Since I've Lost You")....15-25 64
SOUL (35022 "What Becomes of the Broken Hearted")....5-10 66
(Black vinyl.)
SOUL (35022 "What Becomes of the Broken Hearted")....15-25 66
(Colored vinyl. Promotional issue only.)
EPs: 7-inch
SOUL (69704 "Top Ten")....15-25 66
LPs: 10/12-inch
RSO....5-8 80
SOUL (704 "Sings Top Ten")....20-30 66
SOUL (708 "Ruff 'N Ready")....20-30 67
SOUL (727 "Groove Governor")....15-25 70
Also see FOUR HOLLIDAYS
Also see NIGHTINGALE, Maxine, & Jimmy Ruffin
Also see RUFFIN, David & Jimmy

RUFFIN, Kenneth
Singles: 7-inch
CARNIVAL (536 "I'll Keep Holding On")....20-30 68

RUFFIN, L.
Singles: 7-inch
CROSS....5-10 67

RUFFIN, Mr.: see RUFFIN, Riff

RUFFIN, Riff
(Mr. Ruffin)
Singles: 78 rpm
CASH....8-12 56
EBB....10-15 57
SPARK (115 "Touch of Heaven")....8-12 55
Singles: 7-inch
CASH....10-20 56
DUKE....4-8 66
EBB (103 "No More")....10-20 57
EBB (116 "Combination")....10-20 57
ENJOY....5-10 64-65
FIRE (1019 "All My Life")....10-15 60
FURY (1043 "Dig That Rock & Roll")....10-15 60
OLD TOWN....5-10 57
SPARK (115 "Touch of Heaven")..10-20 55

RUFFNECKS
Singles: 7-inch
LE CAM (962 "Tally Ho")....10-20 62

RUFFNER, Mason LP '87
LPs: 10/12-inch
CBS ASSOC....5-8 87

RUFUS
(Rufus Jagneaux)
Singles: 7-inch
JIN....5-10 68-69
Also see JAGNEAUX, Rufus

RUFUS R&B/LP '73
("Featuring Chaka Khan")
Singles: 12-inch
W.B....4-8 83-84
Singles: 7-inch
ABC....3-5 74-78
ATLANTIC....3-5 74
BEARSVILLE....3-5 75
EPIC....3-6 70-71
MCA (Except picture discs)....3-5 79-81
MCA (9162 "Party 'Til You're Broke")....20-25 81
(Dollar-shaped picture disc. Promotional issue only. Includes picture cover.)
MCA (9288 "Do You Love What You Feel")....15-25 81
(Strawberry-shaped picture disc. Promotional issue only. Includes strawberry scented picture cover. 1000 made.)
W.B....3-4 83-84
LPs: 10/12-inch
ABC (Except picture discs)....8-10 73-78
ABC (AA-1049 "Street Player")....25-30 78
(Picture disc. Promotional issue only.)
ABC (AA-1098 "Numbers")....20-25 79
(Picture disc. Promotional issue only. 100 made.)
ABC/COMMAND (40023 "Rufusized")....15-25 75
(Quadraphonic.)
ABC/COMMAND (40024 "Rags to Rufus")....15-25 75
(Quadraphonic.)

MCA 5-10 79-82
W.B. (23679 "Stompin' at the Savoy") 8-12 83
(Two discs.)
W.B. (23753 "Seal in Red") 5-10 83
Members: Paulette McWilliams; Chaka Khan.
Also see AMERICAN BREED
Also see KHAN, Chaka
Also see McWILLIAMS, Paulette

RUFUS & CARLA
(Carla & Rufus)
Singles: 7-inch
ATCO (6177 "Cause I Love You") .10-15 60
STAX 5-10 64-65
Members: Rufus Thomas; Carla Thomas.
Also see THOMAS, Carla
Also see THOMAS, Rufus

RUG RATS
LPs: 10/12-inch
A&M 5-8 84

RUGBYS P&R '69
Singles: 7-inch
AMAZON (Except 1) 5-10 69-70
AMAZON (1 "You, I") 5-8 69
(Black vinyl.)
AMAZON (1 "You, I") 10-15 69
(Colored vinyl. Promotional issue only.)
SMASH 5-10 65
TOP DOG (2315 "Endlessly") 10-15 66
LPs: 10/12-inch
AMAZON (1000 "Hot Cargo") 15-20 70
Members: Steve McNicol; Jim McNicol; Chris Hubbs; Ed Vernon; Mike Morner; Glen Howerton.

RUGOLO, Pete, & His Orchestra
Singles: 7-inch
MERCURY (71499 "Teen Age Rock") 5-10 59
LPs: 10/12-inch
W.B. (1371 "Behind Brigitte Bardot") 20-30 60
Also see BARDOT, Brigitte
Also see DIAMONDS, & Pete Rugolo

RUINS
Singles: 7-inch
MUTT (27319 "The End") 10-15 67

RUMBLERS P&R '63
Singles: 7-inch
DOT 5-10 63-64
DOWNEY 10-20 63-65
HIGHLAND (1026 "Intersection") ... 20-30 62
LPs: 10/12-inch
DOT (3509 "Boss") 20-25 63
(Monaural.)
DOT (25509 "Boss") 25-30 63
(Stereo.)
DOWNEY (DLP-1001 "Boss") 40-60 63
(Monaural.)
DOWNEY (DLPS-1001 "Boss") 50-75 63
(Stereo.)
Members: Adrian Lloyd; Johnny Kirkland; Bob Jones; Wayne Matteson; Mike Kelishes; Greg Crowner.
Also see ADRIAN & SUNSETS
Also see BEL CANTOS
Also see LITTLE JOHNNY & RUMBLERS
Also see NYLONS

RUMBLES LTD.
(Rumbles)
Singles: 7-inch
CAPITOL 5-10 70
DAD'S (101 "Everybody's Talkin' ") 30-40 65
DAD'S (103 "Wildest Christmas") ... 15-25 68
DAWN CORY (1003 "Wait It") 40-60 64
GNP 5-10 69
LEMON 8-12 69
MAGIC 4-6 80
MERCURY 8-15 66-68
RUMBLES 3-5 82
SIRE 10-15 69
Picture Sleeves
DAD'S (101 "Everybody's Talkin") .. 60-80 65
DAD'S (103 "Wildest Christmas") ... 25-35 68
LPs: 10/12-inch
MAGIC (28124 "How Can This Be") 10-20 80
RUMBLES 10-20 83
Members: Rich Clayton; Bud Phillips.
Also see CLAYTON, Rich, & Rumbles
Also see FABULOUS RUMBLES

RUMORS
Singles: 7-inch
GEMCOR (5002 "Hold Me Now") ... 15-25 66

RUMOUR LP '77
Singles: 7-inch
ARISTA 3-5 79
MERCURY 3-5 78
LPs: 10/12-inch
ARISTA 5-10 79
MERCURY 8-10 77
Also see PARKER, Graham
Also see SCHWARTZ, Brinsley

RUMPF, Inga
LPs: 10/12-inch
RCA 5-8 79

RUMPLESTILTSKIN
(Rumplestiltskin Kartoon)
Singles: 7-inch
JAMIE 4-6 68
LPs: 10/12-inch
BELL 10-15 70

RUN - D.M.C. R&B '83
Singles: 12-inch
PROFILE 4-6 83-86
QUALITY/RFC 4-6 83
Singles: 7-inch
PROFILE (Black vinyl) 3-4 83-90
PROFILE (Colored vinyl) 4-8 89
Picture Sleeves
PROFILE 3-4 86-88
LPs: 10/12-inch
PROFILE 5-8 84-90
Members: "Run" Joe Simmons; Daryll McDaniels; Jason Mizell.
Also see AEROSMITH
Also see KING DREAM CHORUS & Holiday Crew
Also see KRUSH GROVE ALL STARS

RUNABOUTS
(With Johnny Hammer)
Singles: 7-inch
HI JINX (9661 "Swampwater") 15-25 61
KEM (2766 "Lobo") 10-20 61

RUNABOUTS
Singles: 7-inch
COLUMBIA 5-10 61-62
JUBILEE 5-10 61

RUNABOUTS
Singles: 7-inch
GAMA (699 "Surfer's Fright") 15-25 63

RUNABOUTS
Singles: 7-inch
VOX ("The Chase") 20-30 65
(No selection number used.)

RUN-A-BOUTS
Singles: 7-inch
KAY-GEE (4817 "Hi Hat") 20-30 65

RUNAROUNDS
(Emotions)
Singles: 7-inch
PIO (107 "The Nearest Thing to Heaven") 100-150 61
Also see EMOTIONS

RUNAROUNDS
(Run-A-Rounds)
Singles: 7-inch
CAPITOL (5644 "Perfect Woman") 10-20 66
FELSTED (8704 "Carrie") 20-30 64
KC (116 "Unbelievable") 25-50 63
(Black vinyl.)
KC (116 "Unbelievable") 50-75 63
(Colored vinyl.)
MGM 10-15 67
TARHEEL (065 "Are You Looking for a Sweetheart") 15-25 63
Also see MARENO, Lee
Also see REGENTS

RUNAROUNDS / Regents
LPs: 10/12-inch
CRYSTAL BALL 8-10
Also see REGENTS

RUN-A-ROUNDS
Singles: 7-inch
MANEL (100 "I Can't Take You Back") 15-25 66

RUN-AROUNDS
Singles: 7-inch
HYLAND (3018 "Oh Why") 100-200

RUNAWAY PANCAKE
Singles: 7-inch
RAMA RAMA 4-8 69

RUNAWAYS
Singles: 7-inch
ALAMO 5-10 60s
HITT 8-12 64
MOONGLOW (202 "Pachuko Hop") 10-15 61
(Reissued as by the Rhythm Rockets.)
Also see RHYTHM ROCKETS

RUN-A-WAYS
Singles: 7-inch
ROYAL AUDIO (2090 "Night Creature") 10-20 63

RUNAWAYS
Singles: 7-inch
TEENSOUND (1924 "Teenage Style") 50-100 60s

RUNAWAYS LP '76
Singles: 7-inch
MERCURY 5-10 76-77
LPs: 10/12-inch
MERCURY (1090 "Runaways") 15-25 76-77
MERCURY (1126 "Queens of Noise") 15-25 77
MERCURY (3705 "Waiting for the Night") 15-25 77
RHINO (250 "Little Lost Girls") 5-10 82
RHINO (250 "Little Lost Girls") 25-30 82
(Picture disc.)
Members: Joan Jett; Cherie Currie; Lita Ford; Sandy West; Micki Steele; Jackie Fox; Vickie Blue.
Also see BANGLES
Also see FORD, Lita
Also see JETT, Joan

RUNDGREN, Todd LP '71
(Todd Rundgren's Utopia)
Singles: 7-inch
BEARSVILLE (Except 0003) 3-5 77-83
BEARSVILLE (0003 "I Saw the Light") 5-10 72
(Black vinyl.)
BEARSVILLE (0003 "I Saw the Light") 10-15 72
(Colored vinyl.)
LPs: 10/12-inch
BEARSVILLE (524 "Todd Rundgren Radio Show") 40-50 70s
(Promotional issue only.)
BEARSVILLE (597 "Radio Interview") 120-130 81
(Promotional issue only.)
BEARSVILLE (788 "Todd Rundgren Radio Sampler") 25-40 79
(Promotional issue only.)
BEARSVILLE (2066 "Something/Anything") 10-12 72
BEARSVILLE (2066 "Something/Anything") 150-200 72
(Colored vinyl. Price includes lyrics insert.
BEARSVILLE (2133 "A Wizard/A True Star") 5-10 73
BEARSVILLE (3522 "Healing") 8-10 81
(Price includes the bonus single, *Time Heals*.)
BEARSVILLE (6952 "Todd") 12-15 74
(Price includes bonus poster.)
BEARSVILLE (6957 "Initiation") 8-10 75
BEARSVILLE (6961 "Another Live") 10-12 75
BEARSVILLE (6963 "Faithful") 8-10 76
BEARSVILLE (6965 "Ra") 10-12 77
BEARSVILLE (6970 "Oops, Wrong Planet") 10-12 77
BEARSVILLE (6981 "Hermit of Mink Hollow") 5-8 78
BEARSVILLE (6986 "Back to the Bars") 8-10 78
BEARSVILLE (23732 "Ever Popular Tortured Artist Effect") 5-8 83
MFSL (225 "Something Anything") 30-35 94
RHINO (71109 "Back to the Bars") ... 8-12 90s
Also see NAZZ
Also see RUNT
Also see TYLER, Bonnie
Also see UTOPIA

RUNNER LP '79
Singles: 7-inch
ISLAND 3-5 79
LPs: 10/12-inch
ISLAND 5-10 79
Members: Steve Gould; Mickie Feat; David Dowle; Allan Merrill.
Also see LYALL, William

RUNNERS / Treetoppers
Singles: 7-inch
BELL 3-5

RUNT P&R '70
(Featuring Todd Rundgren)
Singles: 7-inch
AMPEX 5-10 70
BEARSVILLE 4-8 71
LPs: 10/12-inch
AMPEX (10105 "Runt") 100-150 70
(With *Say No More* and a full-length version of *Baby Let's Swing*.)
AMPEX (10105 "Runt") 50-100 70
(Does not have *Say No More*. Has *Baby Let's Swing* as part of a medley.)
AMPEX (10116 "The Ballad of Todd Rundgren") 50-100 71
W.B. 5-8 85-91
Also see RUNDGREN, Todd

RUPERT'S PEOPLE
Singles: 7-inch
BELL (687 "Reflections of Charlie Brown") 10-15 67

RURAL
LPs: 10/12-inch
MOLE 8-10 74

RUSH
Singles: 7-inch
DUCAL 4-8

RUSH LP '74
Singles: 7-inch
MERCURY 3-5 75-87
MOON (001 "Not Fade Away") 500-1000 73
Picture Sleeves
MERCURY 3-5 81-85
EPs: 7-inch
MERCURY 5-10 80
LPs: 10/12-inch
ATLANTIC 5-8 89
MERCURY (1000 thru 4000 series, except 1300) 5-8 74-82
MERCURY (1300 "Hemispheres") 35-45 78
(Picture disc.)
MERCURY (7000 series) 8-12 76-81
MERCURY (9000 series) 10-15 76-81
MERCURY (800000 series) 5-8 84-88
Members: Geddy Lee; Neil Peart; Alex Lifeson.
Also see McKENZIE, Bob & Doug

RUSH, Bobby R&B '71
Singles: 7-inch
ABC 3-6 68
CHECKER 4-8 67
GALAXY 48 71
ICHIBAN 3-4 93
JEWEL 4-8 60s-73
PHILADELPHIA INT'L 3-5 79
SALEM 8-12 69
SEDGRICK 8-12
TOP 3-5 70s
LPs: 10/12-inch
PHILADELPHIA INT'L 5-10 79

RUSH, Hazel
Singles: 7-inch
VEE-EIGHT (8000 "Salvation Is Free") 20-25 64

RUSH, Jennifer P&R '86
Singles: 7-inch
EPIC 3-4 86
LPs: 10/12-inch
EPIC 5-8 86-87

RUSH, Jennifer, & Elton John P&R '87
Singles: 7-inch
EPIC 3-4 87
Also see JOHN, Elton

RUSH, Merrilee P&R/LP '68
(With the Turnabouts)
Singles: 7-inch
AGP 3-6 69-70
BELL 4-8 68
GTP 4-8 68
MERRILIN 10-15 65-66
RU-RO 8-12 67
SCEPTER 3-5 71
SPHERE SOUND 3-5
U.A. 3-5 77-78
LPs: 10/12-inch
BELL 10-20 68
LIBERTY 5-8 82
U.A. 8-10 77
Also see SEATTLE HELPS the HUNGRY

RUSH, Neil, & Aztecs
Singles: 7-inch
TERRY (103 "Does It Really Mean That Much") 15-25 60

RUSH, Otis R&B '56
Singles: 78 rpm
COBRA 10-20 56-57
Singles: 7-inch
BLUES TOWN 15-25
CHESS (1751 "So Many Roads, So Many Trains") 25-35 60
CHESS (1775 "You Know My Love") 25-35 60
COBRA (5000 "I Can't Quit You Baby") 25-50 56
COBRA (5005 "Violent Love") 25-50 56
COBRA (5010 "Groaning the Blues") 25-50 57
COBRA (5015 "Love That Woman") 25-50 57
COBRA (5023 "Three Times a Fool") 25-50 58
COBRA (5027 "It Takes Time") 25-50 58
COBRA (5030 "Double Trouble") 25-50 59
COBRA (5032 "All Your Love") 25-50 59
COTILLION 4-8 69
DUKE (356 "Home Work") 5-10 62
LPs: 10/12-inch
BLUE HORIZON 10-15 68-70
BULLFROG 8-10 77
COTILLION 10-20 69
DELMARK 10-20 75-79
Session: Bob Neely; Lafayette Leake; Matt Murphy; Willie Dixon; Odie Payne; Ike Turner.
Also see DIXON, Willie
Also see KING, Albert, & Otis Rush
Also see TURNER, Ike

RUSH, Ray
Singles: 7-inch
GINA 5-10 63
PARKWAY 4-8 62

RUSH, Tom LP '66
Singles: 7-inch
COLUMBIA 3-5 72-74
ELEKTRA 4-6 66-70
PRESTIGE 4-8 64
LPs: 10/12-inch
COLUMBIA 6-12 70-76
ELEKTRA 8-15 65-70
FANTASY 5-10 72
LY CORNU 15-20
PRESTIGE 10-20 64-68

RUSH HOUR
(Ingredients)
Singles: 7-inch
PHILIPS 5-10 69
Also see INGREDIENTS

RUSH HOUR
LPs: 10/12-inch
JERU 5-10 80

RUSHEN, Patrice LP '77
Singles: 12-inch
ELEKTRA 4-8 79-84
Singles: 7-inch
ARISTA 3-4 87
ELEKTRA 3-5 80-84
PRESTIGE 3-5 76
Picture Sleeves
ELEKTRA 3-5 80-82
LPs: 10/12-inch
ARISTA 5-8 87
ELEKTRA 5-10 78-84
PRESTIGE 5-10 75-80

RUSHEN, Patrice, & D.J. Rogers R&B '80
Singles: 7-inch
ELEKTRA 3-5 80
Also see ROGERS, D.J.
Also see RUSHEN, Patrice

RUSHING, Jim C&W '80
Singles: 7-inch
OVATION 3-5 80

RUSHING, Jimmy
(Little Jimmy Rushing; "Mr. 5 x 5")
Singles: 78 rpm
COLUMBIA 15-25 46
EXCELSIOR 15-25 46
GOTHAM 20-30 53
KING 25-50 51-52
PARROT 100-150 53
Singles: 7-inch
BLUESWAY 4-8 67
COLPIX 4-8 63
COLUMBIA 10-20 58
GOTHAM (230 "Lotsa Poppa") 50-75 53
GOTHAM (247 "Hey Miss Bessie") 50-75 53
KING (4502 "I'm So Lonely") 75-100 51
KING (4564 "Go Get Some More") 75-100 51
KING (4588 "In the Moonlight") 75-100 52
KING (4606 "She's Mine, She's Yours") 75-100 52
PARROT (797 "Mr. Five By Five") 250-350 53
U.A. 10-15 62
EPs: 7-inch
COLUMBIA (11521 "Little Jimmy Rushing") 25-35 58
KING (305 "Jimmy Rushing") 30-40 54
LPs: 10/12-inch
BLUESWAY 10-20 67-73
CAMDEN 15-25 60
COLPIX 20-30 63
COLUMBIA 30-60 57-61
JAZZTONE 25-35
MJR 8-10
RCA 8-12 71
VANGUARD (2008 "If This Ain't the Blues") 40-60 58
VANGUARD (8011 "Jimmy Rushing Sings the Blues") 75-100 55
(10-inch LP.)
VANGUARD (8500 series) 30-45 55-58
Jimmy Rushing may be shown with such artists as Buddy Tate, Dave Brubeck, Coleman Hawkins, Count Basie, Buck Clayton, Frank Culley, and Zoot Sims.
Also see BRUBECK, Dave, Quartet
Also see CHARLES, Ray / Ivory Joe Hunter / Jimmy Rushing
Also see CULLEY, Frank
Also see OTIS, Johnny
LPs: 10/12-inch

RUSHING, Jimmy / Jack Dupree
LPs: 10/12-inch
AUDIO LAB (1512 "Two Shades of Blues") 40-50 59
Also see DUPREE, Champion Jack

RUSHING, Jimmy / Al Hibbler
LPs: 10/12-inch
GRAND PRIX (407 "Big Boy Blues") 15-25 60s
Also see RUSHING, Jimmy
Also see HIBBLER, Al

RUSHING, Jimmy, Ada Moore & Buck Clayton
LPs: 10/12-inch
COLUMBIA (778 "Cat Meets Chick") 50-75 55
Also see MOORE, Ada
Also see RUSHING, Jimmy

RUSK, Johnny
LPs: 10/12-inch
COMSTOCK 10-15 78

RUSKIN, Barbara
Singles: 7-inch
ABC-PAR 4-8 66
SCEPTER 4-8 66

RUSKIN, Richard
(Rick Ruskin)
LPs: 10/12-inch
TAKOMA 5-10 74-77

RUSS, Irvin
Singles: 7-inch
BONNIE BEE 8-12 63
FELCO (201 "Crazy Alligator") ... 250-350 59
Picture Sleeves
FELCO (201 "Crazy Alligator") ... 300-400 59

RUSS, Lonnie P&R '62
(Lonn Russ)
Singles: 7-inch
4J (501 "My Wife Can't Cook") 10-15 62
KERWOOD 8-12

RUSS & STING-RAYS
Singles: 7-inch
CAROL (102 "Do the Surf") 20-30 60s

RUSSEL, Ray
Singles: 7-inch
TOPPA 4-8 62

RUSSEL, Tony
Singles: 7-inch
GREEN IVY 4-8 63

RUSSELL, Al, Trio
(With the Do-Re-Me Trio)
Singles: 78 rpm
COLUMBIA 40-60 51
EXCELSIOR 5-15 50s
OKEH 25-50 51
QUEEN (4162 "Holiday Blues") 20-40 47
Singles: 7-inch
COLUMBIA (39385 "No More Dreams") 100-150 51
OKEH (6806 "How Can You Say You Love Me") 75-100 51

OKEH (6845 "I Love Each Move You Make") ... 75-100 51
Also see DO-RE-ME TRIO

RUSSELL, Andy
Singles: 7-inch
CAPITOL ... 4-6 67-68

RUSSELL, Barbara
Singles: 7-inch
U.A. ... 4-6 60

RUSSELL, Bobby C&W/P&R '68
(With the Beagles; with Tennessee Three; with Sadie Russell)
Singles: 7-inch
COLUMBIA ... 3-5 73-74
D ... 5-10 60
ELF ... 4-6 68-69
FELSTED ... 5-10 59
FILLY-COLT ... 3-5 78
IMAGE ... 4-8 61
MONUMENT ... 4-8 65-66
NATIONAL GENERAL ... 3-5 70
PRIVATE STOCK ... 3-5 75
RISING SONS ... 3-5 67
SPAR ... 10-15 64
U.A. ... 3-5 71-72
VISTA ... 3-6 69
LPs: 10/12-inch
BELL ... 8-12 69
ELF ... 10-15 68
U.A. ... 8-10 71

RUSSELL, Bonnie
Singles: 7-inch
HAMMOND (104 "Too High Class") ... 20-30 59

RUSSELL, Brenda P&R/R&B/LP '79
(With Joe Esposito)
Singles: 7-inch
A&M ... 3-4 79-88
HORIZON ... 3-5 79
Picture Sleeves
A&M ... 3-4 88
LPs: 10/12-inch
A&M ... 5-8 79-88
HORIZON ... 5-8 79
Also see ESPOSITO, Joe "Bean"
Also see RUSSELL, Brian & Brenda

RUSSELL, Brian & Brenda
Singles: 7-inch
ROCKET ... 3-5 76-77
Also see RUSSELL, Brenda

RUSSELL, C.J.
Singles: 7-inch
MERCURY (72139 "The Girl I Lost in the Rain") ... 5-10 63

RUSSELL, Clifford C&W '83
Singles: 7-inch
SUGARTREE ... 3-4 83

RUSSELL, Gene, Trio
Singles: 7-inch
DOT (16995 "Norwegian Wood") ... 10-20 67
KRIS (106 "Doin' the Snake Hips") ... 8-12 60s

RUSSELL, George
Singles: 7-inch
A-OK ("Cherokee Stomp") ... 10-20 65
(Selection number not known.)

RUSSELL, Harvey
(With the Rogues)
Singles: 7-inch
HANDS (1001 "Keep a Knockin' ") 15-25 60s
ROULETTE ... 4-8 66

RUSSELL, Jane
Singles: 78 rpm
CAPITOL ... 5-10 56
CORAL ... 5-10 53-54
MERCURY ... 5-10 54
Singles: 7-inch
CAPITOL ... 10-15 56
CORAL ... 10-15 53-54
MERCURY ... 10-15 54
Also see FOUR GIRLS
Also see MONROE, Marilyn
Also see PRESLEY, Elvis

RUSSELL, Jimmy
(Jimmy Russell Combo)
Singles: 7-inch
CUCA (1167 "Find Me a Job") ... 10-20 64
CUCA (1233 "Moo Moo") ... 10-20 65
ODESSA (2001 "Come Here My Love") ... 10-20 61
TYLJA (1111 "Nursery Rhyme Rock & Roll") ... 10-20 60s

RUSSELL, Jimmy C&W '76
Singles: 7-inch
CHARTA ... 3-5 76

RUSSELL, Johnny C&W '71
Singles: 7-inch
MERCURY ... 3-5 78-81
POLYDOR ... 3-5 78
RCA ... 3-5 71-77
LPs: 10/12-inch
RCA ... 10-15 71-77
Session: Jordanaires; Beverly Heckel; Janie Fricke
Also see FRICKE, Janie
Also see HECKEL, Beverly
Also see JORDANAIRES
Also see SOME of CHET'S FRIENDS

RUSSELL, Johnny, & Little David Wilkins C&W '87
Singles: 7-inch
16TH AVE. ... 3-4 87
Also see RUSSELL, Johnny
Also see WILKINS, Little David

RUSSELL, K.C.
Singles: 7-inch
UPTOWN ... 4-8 65

RUSSELL, Kurt
Singles: 7-inch
CAPITOL ... 4-6 70
LPs: 10/12-inch
CAPITOL ... 10-15 70

RUSSELL, Lee
(Leon Russell)
Singles: 7-inch
BATON ... 10-15 59
ROULETTE ... 10-20 58
Also see RUSSELL, Leon

RUSSELL, Leon LP '70
(With the Shelter People; with New Grass Revival)
Singles: 7-inch
A&M (734 "Cindy") ... 8-12 64
A&M (1200 series) ... 3-5 71
ABC ... 3-5 78
COLUMBIA ... 3-5 70s
DOT (16771 "It's Alright with Me") ... 5-10 65
MCA ... 3-4
PARADISE ... 3-6 76-81
SHELTER ... 3-6 70-76
Picture Sleeves
PARADISE (8667 "Elvis and Marilyn") ... 5-10 78
SHELTER (40210 "If I Were a Carpenter") ... 3-5 74
LPs: 10/12-inch
MCA ... 5-10 79
OLYMPIC ... 8-12 73
PARADISE ... 5-10 78-81
SHELTER (1000 & 2000 series) ... 10-20 70-75
SHELTER (8000 series, except 8917) ... 10-15 71-73
SHELTER (8917 "Leon Live") ... 12-20 73
SHELTER (52000 series) ... 8-10 76
Also see ASYLUM CHOIR
Also see BLACK GRASS
Also see CATALINAS
Also see CLAPTON, Eric
Also see COCKER, Joe
Also see CRIMSON TIDE
Also see DAVID & LEE
Also see HARRISON, George
Also see IN-GROUP
Also see JAN & DEAN
Also see KING, Freddie
Also see KNIGHTS
Also see LEGENDARY MASKED SURFERS
Also see NELSON, Willie, & Leon Russell
Also see PICKETT, Bobby
Also see PRESTON, Don, & South
Also see RUSSELL, Lee
Also see WILSON, Hank

RUSSELL, Leon & Mary P&R '76
Singles: 7-inch
PARADISE ... 3-5 76-77
LPs: 10/12-inch
PARADISE ... 8-10 76-77
Also see RUSSELL, Leon
Also see RUSSELL, Mary

RUSSELL, Lilly
Singles: 7-inch
S.P.Q.R. ... 4-8 63

RUSSELL, Luis R&B '46
Singles: 78 rpm
APOLLO ... 10-20 46-48

RUSSELL, Mary
LPs: 10/12-inch
PARADISE ... 5-10 79
Also see McCREARY, Mary
Also see RUSSELL, Leon & Mary

RUSSELL, Nathan
(With the Honeydreamers)
Singles: 78 rpm
BALLY (1035 "Similau") ... 10-15 57
Singles: 7-inch
BALLY (1035 "Similau") ... 15-25 57
HUX (601 "Cheer Up Baby") ... 10-20

RUSSELL, Randy
Singles: 7-inch
MONTEL ... 4-8 63

RUSSELL, Red Hot
Singles: 7-inch
PORTER ... 10-15 58

RUSSELL, Sam R&B '73
Singles: 7-inch
PLAYBOY ... 3-5 73

RUSSELL, Saxy
Singles: 7-inch
AGE (29107 "I'll Be Loving You") ... 20-30

RUSSELL, Shake, & Dana Cooper Band
Singles: 7-inch
SOUTH COAST ... 3-5 81
LPs: 10/12-inch
SOUTH COAST ... 5-10 81

RUSSELL, Sonny
Singles: 7-inch
BAND BOX (332 "50 Megatons") ... 75-125 63

RUSSELL, Ted
(With the Rhythm Rockers)
Singles: 7-inch
GLEE (0568 "Real Cool") ... 20-30 60
TEROCK ... 10-15 61

RUSSELL, Todd
Singles: 7-inch
PYRAMID ... 4-8

RUSSELL BROTHERS
Singles: 7-inch
KAPP ... 4-8 63
R.R.E. ... 4-8 63
SHELL ... 5-10 61

RUSSELLS
Singles: 7-inch
ABC-PAR ... 4-8 62

RUSSETT, Barry
Singles: 7-inch
VASSAR ... 5-10 60

RUSSIA
Singles: 7-inch
W.B. ... 3-5 80
LPs: 10/12-inch
W.B. ... 5-10 80

RUSSO, Charlie P&R '63
Singles: 7-inch
DIAMOND ... 4-8 63
LAURIE ... 4-6 67
PART ... 4-8 64

RUSSO, Lynda, & Altons
Singles: 7-inch
PARK AVE (712 "My Heart Won't Behave") ... 10-20

RUSSO, Mike
Singles: 7-inch
AMERICAN AUDIOGRAPHICS ("She Lets Me Watch Her Mom & Dad Fight") ... 10-15
(Square picture disc included with a Mad Magazine issue. No selection number used.)
CROSLEY (218 "I'm Gonna Knock on Your Door") ... 25-35 60
Also see DELLWOODS / Mike Russo / Jeanne Hayes

RUSSO BROTHERS
Singles: 7-inch
ERA ... 5-10 60
VANRUSS ... 5-10 61

RUST, Lee
Singles: 7-inch
ROFRAN (1003 "Scramble") ... 15-25

RUSTAD & WIERMAN
Singles: 7-inch
CUCA (1037 "Meanwhile Back at the Pad") ... 8-12 61

RUSTILS
Singles: 7-inch
YE OLD KING (1000 "Can't Get You Out of My Heart") ... 20-40 65
Also see FAINE JADE

RUSTIX LP '69
Singles: 7-inch
RARE EARTH ... 4-8 69
LPs: 10/12-inch
RARE EARTH (508 "Bedlam") ... 8-12 69
(Standard cover.)
RARE EARTH (508 "Bedlam") ... 20-40 69
(Rounded-top cover. Promotional issue.)

RUSTY & DOUG C&W '55
Singles: 78 rpm
HICKORY ... 5-15 55-57
Singles: 7-inch
HICKORY (1000 & 1100 series) ... 10-20 55-61
LPs: 10/12-inch
HICKORY (103 "Favorites") ... 30-50 60
Members: Rusty Kershaw; Doug Kershaw.
Also see KERSHAW, Doug

RUSTY & DUSTY
Singles: 7-inch
CAPRICE ... 5-10 60

RU-TEENS: see RUE-TEENS

RUTH, Babe: see BABE RUTH

RUTH, Babe, & Lou Gehrig: see BABE & LOU

RUTH & AL
Singles: 78 rpm
IMPERIAL ... 4-8 56
Singles: 7-inch
IMPERIAL ... 5-10 56

RUTH & SHERRY
Singles: 7-inch
SWAN ... 4-8 65

RUTHANNE & INVICTAS
Singles: 7-inch
MAVIS (220 "Little Angel") ... 8-12

RUTHERFORD, Don
Singles: 7-inch
FINER ARTS ... 4-8 65
RECITAL ... 5-10 64

RUTHERFORD, Mike LP '80
Singles: 7-inch
ATLANTIC ... 3-4 83
LPs: 10/12-inch
ATLANTIC ... 5-8 83
PASSPORT ... 5-10 80
Also see GENESIS
Also see MIKE + the MECHANICS

RUTLEDGE, Bob
Singles: 78 rpm
ZIPP (11216 "Go Slow Fatso") ... 25-50 56
Singles: 7-inch
ZIPP (11216 "Go Slow Fatso") ... 50-100 56

RUTLEDGE, James
LPs: 10/12-inch
CAPITOL ... 8-10 76
Also see BLOODROCK

RUTLES LP '78
Singles: 12-inch
W.B. (723 "The Rutles") ... 15-20 78
(Colored vinyl. Promotional issue only.)
Singles: 7-inch
PASSPORT ... 3-5 70s
W.B. ... 3-5 78
LPs: 10/12-inch
W.B. (3151 "Meet the Rutles") ... 10-15 78
(Add $4 to $6 if accompanied by bonus booklet.)
Members: Neil Innes; Rick Fataar; Eric Idle; John Hasley.
Also see BONZO DOG BAND
Also see FLAME
Also see MONTY PYTHON

RUTS
LPs: 10/12-inch
VIRGIN INT'L ... 5-10 80

RUUD, Nancy C&W '80
Singles: 7-inch
C&R ... 3-4 81
CALICO ... 3-4 80

RUZICKA, Bob
LPs: 10/12-inch
MCA ... 8-10 73
SIGNPOST ... 10-12 72

RYAN, Allen
(With Rikki Dawn & His Orchestra)
Singles: 7-inch
SONIC (1600 "You Left Me") ... 50-100

RYAN, Barry P&R '68
Singles: 7-inch
MGM ... 4-8 68
POLYDOR ... 3-6 70
PRIDE ... 3-5 71

RYAN, Buck
(Charlie Ryan)
Singles: 7-inch
GILT EDGE (5088 "West Virginia Express") ... 10-15 61
Also see RYAN, Charlie

RYAN, Cathy
(With the Admirals)
Singles: 78 rpm
KING ... 10-15 55-56
Singles: 7-inch
KING (4848 "Come Home") ... 15-25 55
KING (4890 "Only a Dream") ... 15-25 56
Also see ADMIRALS

RYAN, Charlie C&W/P&R '60
(With the Timberline Riders; with Livingston Brothers)
Singles: 78 rpm
SOUVENIR (101 "Hot Rod Lincoln") ... 10-20 55
Singles: 7-inch
4 STAR ... 8-15 60-63
SOUVENIR (101 "Hot Rod Lincoln") ... 20-40 55
Picture Sleeves
4 STAR (1745 "Side Car Cycle") ... 10-20 60
LPs: 10/12-inch
KING (751 "Hot Rod") ... 100-200 61
Also see RYAN, Buck

RYAN, Declan
Singles: 7-inch
LONDON ... 5-10 65

RYAN, Irene
Singles: 7-inch
NASHWOOD ... 3-5
Picture Sleeves
NASHWOOD ... 4-6

RYAN, Jamie C&W '67
(Jamey Ryan)
Singles: 7-inch
ATLANTIC ... 3-5 73
COLUMBIA ... 4-6 67
SHOW BIZ ... 3-5 69-72

RYAN, Paul & Barry
Singles: 7-inch
MGM ... 4-8 65-68
Also see RYAN, Barry

RYAN, Peter
Singles: 7-inch
AARDVARK ... 5-10 73

RYAN, Tim C&W '90
Singles: 7-inch
EPIC ... 3-4 90-91

RYAN, Wesley C&W '81
Singles: 7-inch
NSD ... 3-4 81

RYCHUS SYN
LPs: 10/12-inch
AZRA (38 "License to Kill") ... 8-12 89
(Picture disc.)

RYDELL, Bobby P&R/R&B '59
Singles: 7-inch
ABKCO ... 3-4 70s
CAMEO ("Steel Pier") ... 15-25 63
(No selection number used. Single-sided, promotional issue from the Steel Pier in Atlantic City.)
CAMEO (160 "Please Don't Be Mad") ... 25-50 59
CAMEO (164 "All I Want Is You") ... 10-20 59
CAMEO (167 thru 186) ... 5-15 59-61
CAMEO (190 thru 361) ... 4-8 61-65
CAMEO (1070 "Forget Him"/"A Message from Bobby") ... 10-15 63
(Packaged as a bonus single with *Top Hits of 1963*.)
CAPITOL ... 4-8 64-66
P.I.P. ... 3-5 76
PERCEPTION ... 3-5 74
RCA ... 3-5 70
REPRISE ... 4-6 68
TIME ... 5-8 59
VEKO (731 "Fatty Fatty") ... 25-50 58
VENISE (201 "Fatty Fatty") ... 15-25 62
Picture Sleeves
CAMEO ... 8-15 59-64
CAPITOL ... 5-10 64
EPs: 7-inch
CAPITOL ... 10-20 65
LPs: 10/12-inch
CAMEO (1006 "We Got Love") ... 50-80 59
CAMEO (1007 "Bobby Sings, Bobby Swings") ... 25-35 60
CAMEO (1009 "Bobby's Biggest Hits") ... 40-50 61
(Gatefold cover. With 12 x 12 photo insert.)
CAMEO (1009 "Bobby's Biggest Hits") ... 30-35 61
(Gatefold cover. Without 12 x 12 photo.)
CAMEO (1009 "Bobby's Biggest Hits") ... 15-25 62
(Standard cover. Some copies with 1009 on the cover may have Cameo 1008 on the disc.)
CAMEO (1010 "Bobby Rydell Salutes the Great Ones") ... 20-30 61
CAMEO (1011 "Rydell at the Copa") ... 20-30 61
(Monaural.)
CAMEO (SC-1011 "Rydell at the Copa") ... 25-35 61
(Stereo.)
CAMEO (1019 "All the Hits") ... 20-30 62
CAMEO (1028 "Bobby's Biggest Hits, Vol. 2") ... 25-35 62
CAMEO (1040 "All the Hits, Vol. 2") ... 20-30 62
(Monaural.)
CAMEO (SC-1040 "All the Hits, Vol. 2") ... 25-35 62
(Stereo.)
CAMEO (1043 "Bye Bye Birdie") ... 25-30 63
(Monaural.)
CAMEO (SC-1043 "Bye Bye Birdie") ... 30-35 63
(Stereo.)
CAMEO (1055 "Wild [Wood] Days") ... 20-30 63
(Monaural.)
CAMEO (1070 "Top Hits of 1963 Sung by Robby Rydell") ... 25-35 63
(Monaural. With bonus single *Forget Him/A Message from Bobby*.)
CAMEO (1070 "Top Hits of 1963 Sung by Robby Rydell") ... 15-25 63
(Monaural. Without bonus single.)
CAMEO (SC-1070 "Top Hits of 1963 Sung by Robby Rydell") ... 30-40 63
(Stereo. With bonus single *Forget Him/A Message from Bobby*.)
CAMEO (SC-1070 "Top Hits of 1963 Sung by Robby Rydell") ... 20-30 63
(Stereo. Without bonus single.)
CAMEO (1080 "Forget Him") ... 20-30 64
CAMEO (2001 "18 Golden Hits") ... 20-30 60s
CAMEO (4017 "An Era Reborn") ... 20-30 64
(Monaural.)
CAMEO (SC-4017 "An Era Reborn") ... 25-35 64
(Stereo.)
CAPITOL (2281 "Somebody Loves You") ... 15-25 65
DESIGN ... 10-20 60s
P.I.P. ... 8-12 76
SPINORAMA ... 10-20 60s
STRAND (1120 "Bobby Rydell Sings") ... 35-45 60
Also see CHECKER, Chubby, & Bobby Rydell
Also see CHRISTIE, Lou / Len Barry & Dovells / Bobby Rydell / Tokens
Also see ROE, Tommy / Bobby Rydell / Gene Pitney
Also see ROE, Tommy / Bobby Rydell / Ray Stevens

RYDELL, Bobby / Barry Norman / Steve Garrick
LPs: 10/12-inch
VENISE (7035 "Twistin' ") ... 15-20 62
Also see RYDELL, Bobby

RYDELL, Mark
Singles: 7-inch
PHILIPS ... 4-8 62

RYDELL, Rick
Singles: 7-inch
INPHASION (7200 "Eddie the Grease") ... 5-8 78

RYDER, John & Anne P&R '69
Singles: 7-inch
DECCA ... 4-6 69
LPs: 10/12-inch
DECCA ... 10-15 70

RYDER, Junior, & Peacocks
Singles: 78 rpm
DUKE (119 "Sad Story") ... 25-50 54
Singles: 7-inch
DUKE (119 "Sad Story") ... 75-100 54

RYDER, Mitch *P&R '65*
(With the Detroit Wheels)

Singles: 7–inch

ABC 3-5 73
AVCO EMBASSY 3-6 70
DOT 4-6 69
DYNO VOICE 4-8 67-68
ERIC 3-4
NEW VOICE (Except 820) 4-8 65-68
NEW VOICE (820 "Sock It to Me Baby") 5-10 67
(With "Feels like a punch" lyrics.)
NEW VOICE (820 "Sock It to Me Baby") 4-6 67
(With "Hits me like a punch" lyrics.)
RIVA 3-4 83
VIRGO 3-4 73

Picture Sleeves

NEW VOICE 4-8 67

LPs: 10/12–inch

CREWE 12-15
DOT 12-15 69
DYNO VOICE 10-20 67
NEW VOICE 20-30 66-68
RIVA 5-8 83
ROULETTE 5-10
SEEDS & STEMS 5-10 78-80
VIRGO 8-10 73

Members: Mitch Ryder; Joe Kubert; Jim McCallister; Jim McCarty; Johnny Badanjek.
Also see DETROIT
Also see LEE, Billy, & Rivieras
Also see ROCKETS

RYE

LPs: 10/12–inch

BEVERLY HILLS 8-12 71

RYLAND, Little Sir

Singles: 7–inch

USA (1214 "My Worried Lover") 15-25 60s

RYLE, Skipper

Singles: 7–inch

SAXONY (1004 "Wolf Gal") 5-10 63

RYLES, John Wesley *C&W/P&R '68*
(John Wesley Ryles I)

Singles: 7–inch

ABC 3-5 78-79
ABC/DOT 3-5 77
COLUMBIA 4-6 68-70
GRT 3-5 70
MCA 3-5 79-83
MUSIC MILL 3-5 75-76
PLANTATION 3-5 71-73
PRIMERO 3-5 82-83
RCA 3-5 74
16TH AVE. 3-4 84
W.B. 3-4 87-88

LPs: 10/12–inch

ABC 5-10 78
ABC/DOT 8-10 77
COLUMBIA 10-15 69
MCA 5-10 79-83
PLANTATION 5-10 77

RYSER, Jimmy *P&R '90*

Singles: 7–inch

ARISTA 3-4 90

RYTHEM ROCKERS

Singles: 7–inch

GAITY (6105 "Twang") 50-75 60s

RYTHEM ROYALS

Singles: 7–inch

TEST 10-20 60s

RZEPPA, Zip, & Stanley Cup Gang

Singles: 7–inch

CHAMPIONSHIP (312002 "Who Dey Bruins") 5-8 83

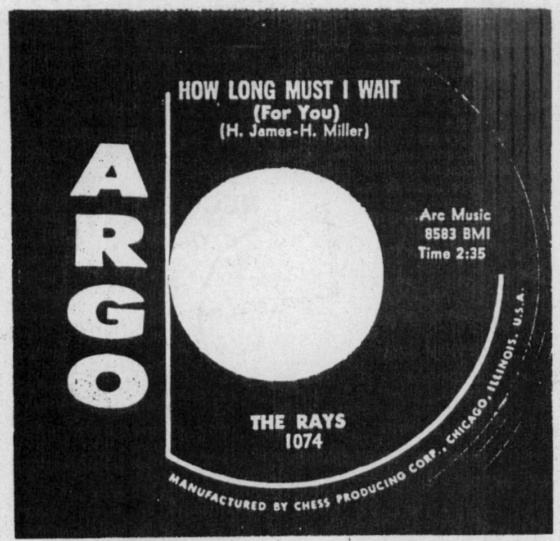
ARGO
HOW LONG MUST I WAIT
(For You)
(H. James-H. Miller)
Arc Music
8583 BMI
Time 2:35
THE RAYS
1074
MANUFACTURED BY CHESS PRODUCING CORP., CHICAGO, ILLINOIS, U.S.A.

PRIDE INC.
4232 E. Young Pl.
Tulsa, Okla.
Produced by
Bill Ess
Vocal by
Randy Ess
BMI
IT'S ON AGAIN
(R. Ess-I. J. Ganem)
THE ROGUES FIVE
660P-7339
T4KM-7339

Quality
1024X-S1
By Arr'mt. with
Swan Records
1024X
(BMI) 2:15
WILD WEEKEND
(Todaro - Shannon)
THE REBELS
MANUFACTURED BY QUALITY RECORDS LTD.

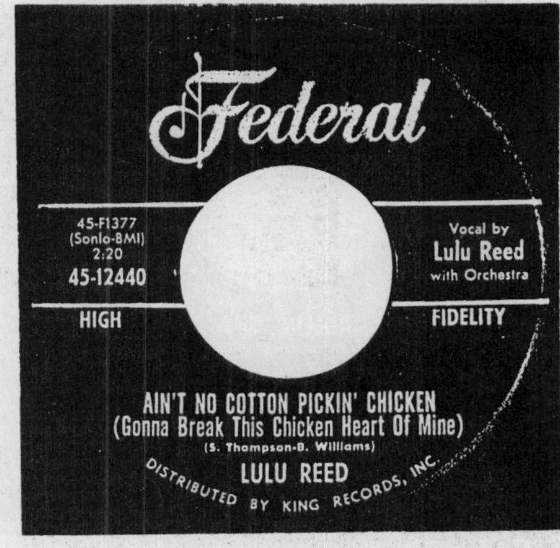
Federal
45-F1377
(Sonlo-BMI)
2:20
45-12440
Vocal by
Lulu Reed
with Orchestra
HIGH
FIDELITY
AIN'T NO COTTON PICKIN' CHICKEN
(Gonna Break This Chicken Heart Of Mine)
(S. Thompson-B. Williams)
LULU REED
DISTRIBUTED BY KING RECORDS, INC.

Aladdin
BEVERLY HILLS, CALIFORNIA
45-3301
(JO-2515)
Q
Vocal - 2:08
Gallo-Otis
Music Publ.
CRYIN' EMMA
(Cleo Page)
ROLLING CREW
With Orchestra

Baton
RECORDS, INC.
New York City
45 R.P.M.
RECORD NO.
221
(5404)
Romance Music
Time 2:30 (BMI)
YOU FOOL
(George Brown)
THE JAN RAYE QUARTET
Featuring
LILYANN

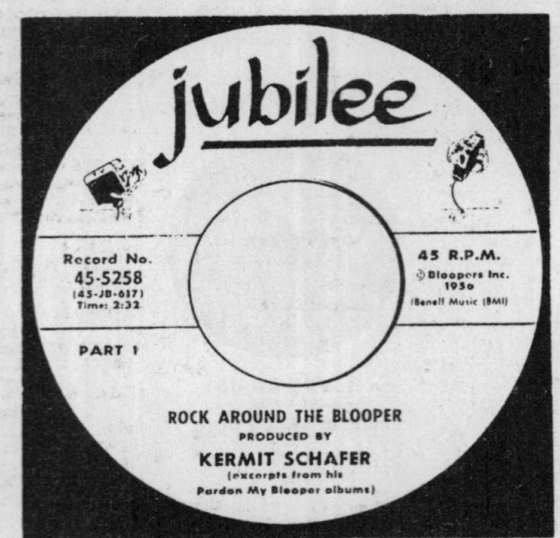
jubilee
Record No.
45-5258
(45-JB-617)
Time: 2:32
45 R.P.M.
Bloopers Inc.
1956
(Benell Music (BMI)
PART 1
ROCK AROUND THE BLOOPER
PRODUCED BY
KERMIT SCHAFER
(excerpts from his
Pardon My Blooper albums)

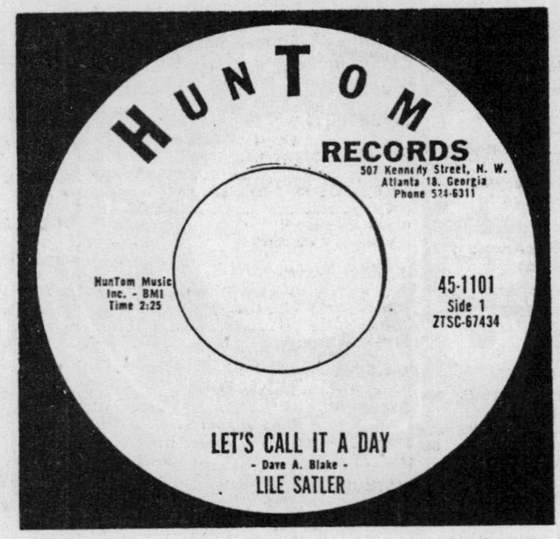
HunTom
RECORDS
507 Kennedy Street, N. W.
Atlanta 18, Georgia
Phone 524-6311
HunTom Music
Inc. - BMI
Time 2:25
45-1101
Side 1
ZTSC-67434
LET'S CALL IT A DAY
- Dave A. Blake -
LILE SATLER

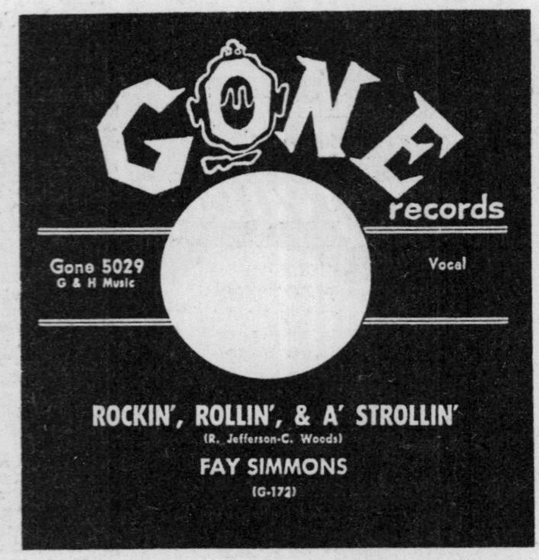
GONE
records
Gone 5029
G & H Music
Vocal
ROCKIN', ROLLIN', & A' STROLLIN'
(R. Jefferson-C. Woods)
FAY SIMMONS
(G-172)

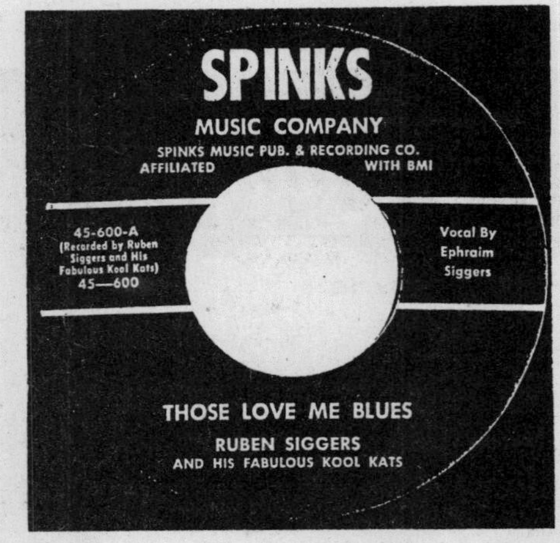
SPINKS
MUSIC COMPANY
SPINKS MUSIC PUB. & RECORDING CO.
AFFILIATED WITH BMI
45-600-A
(Recorded by Ruben Siggers and His Fabulous Kool Kats)
45—600
Vocal By
Ephraim
Siggers
THOSE LOVE ME BLUES
RUBEN SIGGERS
AND HIS FABULOUS KOOL KATS

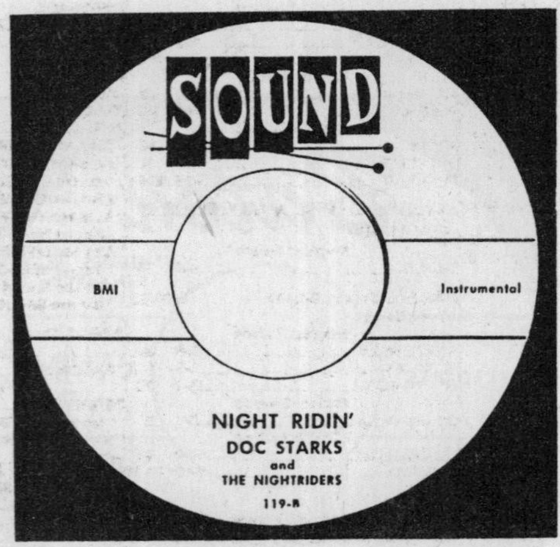
SOUND
BMI
Instrumental
NIGHT RIDIN'
DOC STARKS
and
THE NIGHTRIDERS
119-R

SEG-WAY
A Division of PONTIAC RECORDS, INC.
101F
(1308)
Ludix Publ. Co., Inc.
(BMI)
45 RPM
TELL IT LIKE IT IS
(Arnold-Thomas)
THE SOUL BROTHERS

S

S., Randy, & Westwood Paper
Singles: 7-inch
AMERICAN GRAMOPHONE (667 "Haight-Ashbury Blues") 5-10

S&H SCAMPS
Singles: 7-inch
GREGMARK (1 "Sassy") 10-20 61
GREGMARK (3 "Punjab") 10-20 61
Members: Lee Hazlewood, Lester Sills.
Also see HAZLEWOOD, Lee

S.C.R.A.
(Southern Contemporary Rock Assembly)
LPs: 10/12-inch
ATLANTIC 8-12 72

S EXPRESS: see S-EXPRESS

S.J. & CROSSROADS
Singles: 7-inch
Singles: 7-inch
DEUCE (101 "Darkest Hour") 15-25 60s
MARK VII (1019 "Play Your Game") 15-25 60s
SALMAR (100 "Darkest Hour") 15-25 66
SALMAR (101 "Ooh Poo Pah Doo") 15-25 66
SALMAR (103 "London Girl") 15-25 66
SALMAR (105 "In the Beginning") 15-25 68

S-K-O: see SCHUYLER, KNOBLOCH & OVERSTREET

S.N. & CTs
Singles: 7-inch
SUNBURST 4-6 67

S.O.S. BAND P&R/LP '80
Singles: 12-inch
TABU 4-6 80-89
Singles: 7-inch
TABU 3-5 80-89
Picture Sleeves
TABU 3-5 84-86
LPs: 10/12-inch
TABU 5-10 80-89
Member: Mary Davis; Willie Killebrew; Billy Ellis; Jason Bryant; John Simpson; Bruno Speight; James Earl Jones III; Jerome Thomas; Abdul Raoof; Pennye Ford.
Also see DAVIS, Mary

S.O.S. UNLIMITED
Singles: 7-inch
WHITTIER 4-8 68

S.O.U.L.
Singles: 7-inch
MUSICOR 3-5 71-74
LPs: 10/12-inch
MUSICOR 8-12 72

SPK
LPs: 10/12-inch
ELEKTRA 5-8 84

SRC LP '68
(Scott Richard Case)
Singles: 7-inch
A² (301 "I'm So Glad") 10-20 67
BIG CASINO (1001 "Born to Love") 5-10 71
CAPITOL 5-10 68-69
Picture Sleeves
BIG CASINO (1001 "Born to Love") 10-15 71
LPs: 10/12-inch
CAPITOL (134 "Milestones") 30-40 69
CAPITOL (273 "Travelers Tale") 15-25 69
CAPITOL (2991 "SRC") 40-60 68
Members: Scott Richardson; Steve Lyman; Glen Quackenbush; Gary Quackenbush; Robin Dale.
Also see BLUE SCEPTER
Also see FUGITIVES

SRC / Rationals
Singles: 7-inch
A² (402 "Get the Picture") 10-20 67
Also see RATIONALS
Also see SRC

SS FOOLS
Singles: 7-inch
COLUMBIA 3-5 76
LPs: 10/12-inch
COLUMBIA 6-12 76

SS-20
LPs: 10/12-inch
VOXX 5-10

S.S.O. P&R '76
Singles: 7-inch
SHADY BROOK 3-5 75-76

S.S.Q. D&D '84
Singles: 12-inch
ENIGMA 4-6 84
Singles: 7-inch
EMI 3-4 84
ENIGMA 3-4 84
LPs: 10/12-inch
EMI 5-8 84
ENIGMA 5-8 84

Also see ST. JAMES, Jon
Also see STACEY Q

SVT
LPs: 10/12-inch
415 RECORDS 5-10 80

SAAB, Cliff
Singles: 7-inch
ROULETTE 4-8 68

SAAD, Sue, & Next LP '80
Singles: 7-inch
PLANET 3-5 80
LPs: 10/12-inch
PLANET 5-10 80

SABER, Johnny
Singles: 7-inch
ADONIS (103 "Wish It Could Be Me") 150-250 59
HITSVILLE (1137 "The Note That I Wrote") 50-75
Session: Passions.
Also see PASSIONS

SABER, Sonny
Singles: 7-inch
ARCADE (151 "Little Daisy") 25-35 60
MALA 5-10 61
MYERS 8-12 60

SABERS
Singles: 78 rpm
BULLSEYE 40-60 55
Singles: 7-inch
BULLSEYE (101 "You Can Depend on Me") 100-200 55

SABERS
Singles: 78 rpm
CAL-WEST 100-150 55
Singles: 7-inch
CAL-WEST (847 "Cool, Cool Christmas") 250-350 55
Member: Billy Storm.
Also see STORM, Billy

SABLAN, Johnny
(With the Blends)
Singles: 7-inch
SKYLARK (105 "Big Fat Lie") 100-200 60

SABLES
Singles: 7-inch
RCA 4-8 65

SABRAS
Singles: 7-inch
TIKVA 10-15

SABRE
LPs: 10/12-inch
MASQUE (8703 "Hidden Visions") 10-15 88
(Picture disc. 500 made.)

SABRES
Singles: 78 rpm
RCA 8-12 57
Singles: 7-inch
RCA 8-12 57
EPs: 7-inch
RCA (979/980/981 "Ridin' High with the Sabres") 10-15 56
(Price is for either volume.)
RCA (1979/1980/1981 "Rockin' with the Sabres") 10-20 57
(Price is for either volume.)
RCA (4102 "Rockin' with the Sabres") 20-30 57
LPs: 10/12-inch
RCA (1376 "Ridin' High with the Sabres") 25-50 56
Members: Jerry Wright; Dick Henson; Fritz Weybright.

SABRES
Singles: 7-inch
LIBERTY (55128 "Lulu") 5-10 58

SABRES
Singles: 7-inch
DIAL 4-8 59
FOX 4-8 60
GALA (114 "Hot Rod Kelly") 100-150 60
KILMAC (1412 "Take Up the Slack, Daddy-O") 25-40 59

SABRES
Singles: 7-inch
SCOTTIE (1316 "Sabre Dance Rock") 10-20 60

SABRES
Singles: 7-inch
PRINCE (101 "Gonna Leave") 30-40 60s

SABOR, Johnny
Singles: 7-inch
HITSVILLE 5-10 61

SABU
(Paul Sabu)
Singles: 7-inch
MCA 3-4 80
OCEAN 3-5 79-80
LPs: 10/12-inch
MCA 5-10 80
OCEAN 5-10 79
Also see KIDD GLOVE

SABY & ORIENTALS
Singles: 7-inch
MEL-PAR (1114 "Little Girl") 50-100

SACCA, Jimmy
Singles: 78 rpm
DOT 5-10 54
Singles: 7-inch
DOT 8-12 54
Also see HILLTOPPERS

SACCHI, Robert
Singles: 12-inch
COMPLEAT 4-6 83

SACCO
(Lou Christie)
Singles: 12-inch
LIFESONG (81775 "People Theme") 8-10 78
Singles: 7-inch
LIFESONG (81775 "People Theme") 30-50 78
Also see CHRISTIE, Lou

SACIOUS, Seb
Singles: 7-inch
PULSATION (5767 "Pictures of Elvis") 5-10

SACRED MUSHROOM
Singles: 7-inch
MINARET (131 "Breakaway Girl") 10-15 67
LPs: 10/12-inch
PARALLAX (4001 "Sacred Mushroom") 50-100 69
Members: Larry Goshorn; Danny Goshorn; Joe Stewart; Rusty York.
Also see PURE PRAIRIE LEAGUE

SACRED REICH LP '90
LPs: 10/12-inch
ENIGMA 5-8 90
METAL BLADE (73411 "Surf Nicaragua") 10-15 89
(Picture disc.)

SAD CAFE P&R/LP '79
Singles: 7-inch
A&M 3-5 78-79
SWAN SONG 3-5 81
Picture Sleeves
SWAN SONG 3-5 81
LPs: 10/12-inch
A&M 5-10 78-79
ATLANTIC 5-8 85
SWAN SONG 5-10 81
Members: Paul Young; Doreen Chanter; Irene Chanter; John Stimpson; Vic Emerson; Ian Wilson; Ashley Mulford; Lenni Zaksen.
Also see MIKE + the MECHANICS
Also see YOUNG, Paul

SAD HEAD, Mr: see MR. SAD HEAD

SAD SACKS
Singles: 7-inch
IMPERIAL (5517 "Sack Dresses") 15-25 58

SADANE, Marc R&B '81
(Sadane)
Singles: 7-inch
W.B. 3-5 81-82
Picture Sleeves
W.B. 3-5 81
LPs: 10/12-inch
W.B. 5-10 81

SADD, Sue, & Next
Singles: 7-inch
W.B. 3-5 81

SADDLE-LITE DAN & ORBITS
Singles: 7-inch
SOMA (1103 "Don't Go Away") 75-125 60s

SADDLER, Reggie
(With the Dynamics; Reggie Saddler Combo; Reggie Saddler Revue; with Jammers)
Singles: 7-inch
AQUARIUS 4-8 69
DE-LITE 3-5 72-73
ECLIPSE 3-5 71
PANTHER 5-10 68
LPs: 10/12-inch
JUSTICE 75-100 66
Members: Reggie Saddler; Janice Saddler; Richie Shade
Also see JANICE

SADE R&B/D&D '84
Singles: 12-inch
PORTRAIT 4-6 84-86
Singles: 7-inch
EPIC 3-4 88
PORTRAIT 3-4 84-86
Picture Sleeves
EPIC 3-4 88
PORTRAIT 3-4 84-86
LPs: 10/12-inch
EPIC 5-8 88
PORTRAIT 5-8 85-86

SADINA
Singles: 7-inch
SMASH (1979 "Who Am I Kidding") 20-30 65
SMASH (2005 "It Comes and Goes") 10-20 66

SADISTIC MIKA BAND
Singles: 7-inch
HARVEST 4-8 65
LPs: 10/12-inch
HARVEST 8-12 74

SADLER, Barry P&R/C&W/LP '66
(S/SGT. Barry Sadler)
Singles: 7-inch
GAS 3-5 78
RCA 4-6 66-67
VETERAN 3-5 74
Picture Sleeves
RCA 5-10 66-67
LPs: 10/12-inch
RCA 10-20 66-67
VETERAN 8-12 74
Also see ANN-MARGRET

SADLER, Haskell, & His Orchestra
Singles: 78 rpm
FLASH (103 "Do Right Mind") 20-40 55
Singles: 7-inch
FLASH (103 "Do Right Mind") 50-75 55
MELODIA 10-20
Also see COOL PAPA

SADLER, Sammy C&W '89
Singles: 7-inch
EVERGREEN 3-4 89-90

SADLY MISTAKEN
Singles: 7-inch
CHALLENGE 4-8 66
MARC 4-8 66

SAEGER, Denny
Singles: 7-inch
CAPITOL 4-6 69

SAENZ, Mary
Singles: 7-inch
BIG BEN 4-8 65
DOT 4-8 64

SAFARIS P&R '60
(With Phantoms Band)
Singles: 7-inch
DEE JAY (203 "My Image of a Girl") 3-5 89
ELDO (101 "Image of a Girl") 15-25 60
ELDO (105 "Girl With a Story in Her Eyes") 15-25 60
ELDO (110 "Shadows") 15-25 60
ELDO (113 "Garden of Love") 15-25 60
OLD HIT 3-5
Members: Jimmy Stephens; Sheldon Breier; Marv Rosenberg.
Also see ANGELS
Also see PHANTOMS BAND
Also see STEVENS, Jimmy
Also see SUDDENS

SAFARIS
Singles: 7-inch
VALIANT (6036 "Kick Out") 10-20 63

SAFE AS MILK
Singles: 7-inch
ROULETTE 4-8 68

SAFETY IN NUMBERS
Singles: 7-inch
LITTLE ROUND 8-12

SAFETY LAST
LPs: 10/12-inch
TWIN TONE 8-10 81

SAFETY PATROL
Singles: 7-inch
COLOSSAL 4-8 69

SAFFAN, Mike, & Keepers
Singles: 7-inch
PLANET 3-5 81
LPs: 10/12-inch
PLANET 5-10 81

SA-FIRE P&R/LP '88
Singles: 7-inch
CUTTING 3-4 88-89
MERCURY 3-4 89
Picture Sleeves
CUTTING 3-4 88-89
MERCURY 3-4 89
LPs: 10/12-inch
CUTTING 5-8 88

SAFT
Singles: 7-inch
POLYDOR 3-5 72

SAGA P&R/LP '82
Singles: 7-inch
ATLANTIC 3-4 87
POLYDOR 3-5 79
PORTRAIT 3-4 82-85
Picture Sleeves
ATLANTIC 3-4 87
PORTRAIT 3-4 83
LPs: 10/12-inch
ATLANTIC 5-8 87
POLYDOR 5-10 79
PORTRAIT 5-10 82-85

SAGEBRUSH PHIL & WILD DOGS OF KENTUCKY
Singles: 7-inch
1-SHOT 4-8 75

SAGER, Carole Bayer P&R '77
(Carole Bayer)
Singles: 7-inch
BOARDWALK 3-5 81
ELEKTRA 3-5 77-78
METROMEDIA 3-5 72
Picture Sleeves
BOARDWALK 3-5 81
LPs: 10/12-inch
BOARDWALK 5-10 81
ELEKTRA 5-10 77-78

SAGES
Singles: 7-inch
RCA (8760 "In the Beginning") 10-20 66

SAGITTARIUS P&R '67
Singles: 7-inch
COLUMBIA 5-10 67-69
TOGETHER 5-10 68-69
LPs: 10/12-inch
BACK-TRAC 5-10 85
COLUMBIA (9644 "Present Tense") 20-30 68
TOGETHER (1002 "Blue Marble") 25-35 69
Members: Gary Usher; Glen Campbell; Bruce Johnston; Terry Melcher; Curt Boetcher; Mike Fennelly; Lee Mallory; Ron Edgar.
Also see BOETCHER, Curt
Also see BRUCE & TERRY
Also see CAMPBELL, Glen
Also see USHER, Gary

SAHANAJA, Darian
Singles: 7-inch
X (85 "Do You Have Any Regrets") 3-5 93
(Blue vinyl.)
Picture Sleeves
X (85 "Do You Have Any Regrets") 3-5 93
(Single-sided insert, applied to paper sleeve. Pictures Brian Wilson.)
Also see WILSON, Brian

SAHARA
LPs: 10/12-inch
PETERS INT'L 8-10 77

SAHARAS
Singles: 7-inch
FENTON (2016 "I'm Free") 15-25 66
UNITED 10-15 60s

SAHL, Mort LP '60
Singles: 7-inch
GNP 3-5 73
REPRISE 3-6 61
VERVE 4-8 60
LPs: 10/12-inch
GNP 5-10 73
MERCURY 8-12 67
REPRISE 10-20 61
VERVE 10-20 59-64
Also see MARTIN, Dean

SAHM, Doug LP '73
(With the Mex Trip; with Texas Tornados)
Singles: 7-inch
ABC/DOT 4-6 76
ATLANTIC 5-10 73
CASABLANCA (0828 "Roll with the Punches") 10-20 75
CHRYSALIS 3-5 81
COBRA (116 "Just a Moment") 40-50 61
CRAZY CAJUN 3-5 74
HARLEM (107 "Why, Why, Why") 20-35 60
HARLEM (108 "Baby, Tell Me") 20-30 60
(Black vinyl.)
HARLEM (108 "Baby, Tell Me") 40-60 60
(Colored vinyl. Promotional issue only.)
HARLEM (116 "Just a Moment") 40-50 61
PERSONALITY (260 "Baby, What's on Your Mind") 30-50 59
PERSONALITY (3504 "Baby What's on Your Mind") 20-30 62
PLAYBOY 3-5 76
RENNER (212 "Big Hat") 20-30 61
(Black vinyl.)
RENNER (212 "Big Hat") 50-75 61
(Colored vinyl. Promotional issue only.)
RENNER (215 "Baby, What's on Your Mind") 20-30 61
(Black vinyl.)
RENNER (215 "Baby, What's on Your Mind") 50-75 61
(Colored vinyl.
(Promotional issue only.)
RENNER (226 "Just Because") 20-30 62
RENNER (232 "Cry") 20-30 63
RENNER (240 "Lucky Me") 20-30 63
RENNER (247 "Mr. Kool") 20-30 64
SATIN (100 "Crazy Daisy") 30-50 59
SOFT (1031 "Cry") 20-30 65
SWINGIN' (625 "Why, Oh Why") 15-25 60
TEXAS RECORD (108 "Henrietta") 10-20 76
W.B. 3-5 74
WARRIOR (507 "Crazy Daisy") 40-60 58
Picture Sleeves
CHRYSALIS 3-5 81
LPs: 10/12-inch
ANTONE'S 5-8 88
ATLANTIC 8-12 73
HARLEM 8-10 79
MERCURY 10-20 73
TAKOMA 5-10 80
W.B. 10-20 74
Also see BROMBERG, David
Also see DR. JOHN
Also see DOUGLAS, Wayne
Also see DYLAN, Bob
Also see FENDER, Freddy, & Sir Douglas
Also see HIM
Also see LITTLE DOUG
Also see NELSON, Willie
Also see SALDAÑA, Sir Doug
Also see SIR DOUGLAS QUINTET

SAHM, Doug, & Augie Meyers
Singles: 7-inch
TEARDROP 3-4 83
Picture Sleeves
TEARDROP 3-5 83
Also see MEYERS, Augie
Also see SAHM, Doug

SAI WHATT??
Singles: 7-inch
STACHE 3-5 80

SAIGONS
Singles: 78 rpm
DOOTONE 50-100 55
Singles: 7-inch
DOOTONE (375 "You're Heavenly") 200-300 55

SAIGON SAUCERS
Singles: 7-inch
WADE 5-10 60s

SAILCAT P&R/LP '72
Singles: 7-inch
ELEKTRA 3-5 72-73
LPs: 10/12-inch
ELEKTRA 10-15 72
Members: Johnny Wyker; Court Pickett.
Also see RUBBER BAND

SAILES, Jesse, & Waves
Singles: 7-inch
FELSTED (8690 "Monkey Drums") 8-12 63
Also see SALLES, Jessie, & Crypt-Kickers

SAILOR
Singles: 7-inch
CARIBOU 3-5 80-81
EPIC 3-5 73-78
LPs: 10/12-inch
CARIBOU 5-10 80
Also see KAJANUS PICKET

SAILOR BOY
(Alex Spearman)
Singles: 78 rpm
DIG 20-40 56
Singles: 7-inch
DIG (126 "What Have I Done Wrong") 50-75 56

SAILOR BOY / Preston Love
Singles: 78 rpm
DIG (116 "Country Home") 20-40 56
Singles: 7-inch
DIG (116 "Country Home") 50-75 56
Also see LOVE, Preston
Also see SAILOR BOY

SAILS, Johnny
Singles: 7-inch
MAR-V-LUS 4-8 63

SAIN, Oliver R&B '75
Singles: 7-inch
ABET 3-5 71-77
BOBBIN 4-8 62
HCRC 3-5 82
VANESSA 5-10
LPs: 10/12-inch
ABET (400 series) 8-12 71-73
ABET (8700 series) 5-10 77
Also see DAVIS, Larry

SAINT, Billy
(With the Bill Osborne Combo)
Singles: 7-inch
A&M 4-6 63
DORE 4-8 62
DOT 4-8 62
JERDEN 4-8 63-64
SEAFAIR 5-10 60-61
Picture Sleeves
SEAFAIR 5-10 61

SAINT, Bobby
Singles: 7-inch
WREN 10-15 59

SAINT, Cathy
Singles: 7-inch
DAISY (501 "Big Bad World") 25-35 63

SAINT, Del, & Devils
Singles: 7-inch
CHECKER (897 "Rock Yea") 25-35 58

SAINT & STEPHANIE
Singles: 7-inch
ARISTA 3-5 79
LPs: 10/12-inch
ARISTA 5-10 79

SAINT CLAIR, Bobby
Singles: 7-inch
PHILIPS (40358 "Fool That I Am") 10-20 66

ST. CLAIR, Nicky, & Five Trojans
Singles: 7-inch
EDISON INT'L (410 "I Hear Those Bells") 50-100 59
Also see FIVE TROJANS

ST. CLAIR, Renee
(With Marty Lennard)
Singles: 7-inch
JUBILEE 4-8 67

ST. CLAIRE, Ace
Singles: 7-inch
SOUND STAGE 7 4-8 63
STACY 4-8 64

ST. CLAIRE, Sylvia
Singles: 7-inch
BRUNSWICK (55276 "Bring Back Yesterday") 25-35 65
BRUNSWICK (55279 "Just Love Me") 10-20 65

ST. CLOUD, Endle
Singles: 7-inch
INT'L ARTISTS (129 "Tell Me One More Time") 10-20 68
INT'L ARTISTS (139 "She Wears It Like a Badge") 10-20 70
LPs: 10/12-inch
INT'L ARTISTS (12 "Thank You All Very Much") 35-55 68

ST. GEORGE & TANA
LPs: 10/12-inch
KAPP 10-15 67

ST. JAMES, Bobby
Singles: 7-inch
WATTS (901 "I Was Taken for a Ride") 20-30 68

ST. JAMES, Holly
Singles: 7-inch
ABC (10996 "That's Not Love") 40-60 68
ABC (11042 "Magic Moments") 10-20 68

ST. JAMES, Jon R&B '84
Singles: 12-inch
EMI AMERICA 4-6 84
Singles: 7-inch
EMI AMERICA 3-4 84
LPs: 10/12-inch
EMI AMERICA 5-10 84
Also see SSQ

ST. JAMES, Rod
Singles: 7-inch
PAULA 3-5 72
LPs: 10/12-inch
PAULA 8-10 72

ST. JOHN, Barry
Singles: 7-inch
GRT 3-6 69

ST. JOHN, Bridget
LPs: 10/12-inch
DANDELION 10-12 70
ELEKTRA 8-10 71

ST. JOHN, Chris
Singles: 7-inch
FRATERNITY 8-12 67
Also see MOUSE

ST. JOHN, Dick
Singles: 7-inch
DOT 4-6 68
LIBERTY 5-10 61
PHILIPS 4-8 65
POM POM 10-15 61
ROMA 10-15 60
Also see DICK & DEEDEE

ST. JOHN, Dick & Sandy
Singles: 7-inch
CONGRESS 4-8 60s
OAK 3-5 72
Also see ST. JOHN, Dick

ST. JOHN, Rose, & Wonderettes
Singles: 7-inch
U.A. (997 "Mend My Broken Heart") 10-15 66
VEEP (1231 "I Know the Meaning") 10-20 66
Also see WONDERETTES

ST. JOHN, Tammy
Singles: 7-inch
CONGRESS 5-10 66

ST. JOHN, Tommy C&W '83
Singles: 7-inch
RCA 3-4 83

ST. JOHN & CARDINALS
Singles: 7-inch
SHURFINE (010 "Rampage") 15-25 60s

ST. JOHN'S FLEA CIRCUS
Singles: 7-inch
WR (4720 "Good Day") 20-30 60s

ST. LOUIS JIMMY
(James Oden)
Singles: 78 rpm
ARISTOCRAT (7001 "Florida Hurricane") 50-75 48
DUKE (110 "Drinkin' Woman") 40-60 53
HERALD (407 "Hard Luck Boogie") 40-60 52
HERALD (408 "Whiskey Drinkin' Woman") 25-50 52
J.O.B. (101 "Mother's Day") 20-40 49
MIRACLE (134 "Biscuit Roller") 20-40 48
OPERA (4 "Coming Up Fast") 20-40 53
PARROT (823 "Goin' Down Slow") 40-60 55
Singles: 7-inch
DUKE (110 "Drinkin' Woman") 75-125 53
HERALD (407 "Hard Luck Boogie") 150-200 52
HERALD (408 "Whiskey Drinkin' Woman") 150-200 52
PARROT (823 "Goin' Down Slow") 150-200 55
LPs: 10/12-inch
PRESTIGE/BLUESVILLE (1028 "Goin' Down Slow") 25-35 61
Also see POOR BOY

ST. LOUIS LEE
Singles: 7-inch
WRIGHT 5-10 72

ST. LOUIS UNION
Singles: 7-inch
PARROT 4-8 66

ST. MARIE, Susan C&W '73
Singles: 7-inch
CINNAMON 3-5 73
PINNACLE 3-5 77

ST. PARADISE
Singles: 7-inch
W.B. 3-5 79
LPs: 10/12-inch
W.B. 5-10 79

ST. PAUL R&B '87
(Paul Peterson)
Singles: 7-inch
ATLANTIC 3-4 87
MCA 3-4 87
Picture Sleeves
ATLANTIC 3-4 87
MCA 3-4 87
Also see FAMILY
Also see TIME

ST. PAUL, Elliot
Singles: 7-inch
MAGIC 3-5
Picture Sleeves
MAGIC 5-8

ST. PAUL, Fonda
Singles: 7-inch
B-W 3-5
Picture Sleeves
B-W 4-6

ST. PAUL DREAMCYCLE R&B SOUL BAND
Singles: 7-inch
MARGIE 5-10 60s

ST. PETERS, Crispian P&R '66
Singles: 7-inch
JAMIE 4-8 66-68
LPs: 10/12-inch
JAMIE (3027 "The Pied Piper") 20-30 66

ST. PIERRE, Alan
Singles: 7-inch
DMO 12-18 67
Also see UNBELIEVABLE UGLIES

ST. REGIS
Singles: 7-inch
CASABLANCA 3-5 84

ST. ROMAIN, Kirby P&R '63
Singles: 7-inch
DIMENSION 5-10 63
IMCO 4-8 64
INETTE 5-10 63-64
KARSONG 5-10 63
TEARDROP 5-10 64
Also see BUDDY & HEARTS
Also see SHUT DOWNS

ST. SHAW, Mike
(With Thee Neon; with Prophets; Mike St. Shaw Trio)
Singles: 7-inch
REPRISE (0273 "Take This Hammer") 5-8 64
REPRISE (0282 "Mike's Mid-Nite Special") 5-8 64
REPRISE (0325 "Send Me Some Lovin'") 8-10 64
LPs: 10/12-inch
REPRISE (6128 "Mike St. Shaw Trio") 10-20 64
Members: Mike St. Shaw; Ray Garcia; Harold Logan; Danny Taylor; Chuck Hatfield.
Also see ESQUIRES / Mike Shaw & Prophets / Thunder Frog Ensemble

SAINT STEVEN
Singles: 7-inch
PROBE (463 "Louisiana Home") 10-15 69
LPs: 10/12-inch
PROBE (4506 "Over the Hills") 40-60 69

SAINT TROPEZ LP '77
Singles: 12-inch
BUTTERFLY (Except 3100) 4-8 77-79
BUTTERFLY (3100 "Belle De Jour") 15-25 79
(Picture disc. Promotional issue only. 1000 made.)
DESTINY 4-6 82-83
Singles: 7-inch
BUTTERFLY 3-5 77-79
DESTINY 3-4 82-83
LPs: 10/12-inch
BUTTERFLY (Black vinyl) 5-10 77-79
BUTTERFLY (Colored vinyl) 10-15 77-79
DESTINY 5-10 82

SAINTE ANTHONY'S FYRE
Singles: 7-inch
ZONK (001 "Sainte Anthony's Fyre") 50-100 71

SAINTE-MARIE, Buffy LP '66
Singles: 7-inch
ABC 3-5 76
MCA 3-5 74-75
VANGUARD 3-8 65-72
LPs: 10/12-inch
ABC 5-10 76
MCA 5-10 74-75
VANGUARD 8-15 64-74

SAINTS
Singles: 7-inch
CUE (7934 "Will You") 15-25 57

SAINTS
Singles: 7-inch
PRESCOTT (1570 "Snap Dragon") 15-20 58

SAINTS
Singles: 7-inch
KENT 5-10 67
RAYDIN (101 "Girl Forgive Me") 20-25 67
REVUE (11069 "Mirror Mirror on the Wall") 4-8 70s

SAINTS
Singles: 7-inch
SIRE 3-5 77
LPs: 10/12-inch
SIRE 8-10 77-78

SAINTS
Singles: 7-inch
FORMAT (57 "Leaving You Baby") 10-15
SALEM (1012 "Rock & Roll Ruby") 50-75
Picture Sleeves
FORMAT (57 "Leaving You Baby") 10-15

SAINTS
LPs: 10/12-inch
CLIFTON 5-10
Members: Lola Foy; Tom Foy; Joe Orlando; Andy Kachianos; Kenny Galeano.

SAINTS
Singles: 7-inch
FLAG (115 "Saint's Rock") 5-10

SAINTS FIVE
Singles: 7-inch
PENTAGON (2001 "Mercy Mercy") 15-25 66
Members: Santo Cincotta; Kenny Rogers; Brad Mckay; Jim Nowicki; Stu Moebus; Gary Lane; Gordy Elliot; John Grignon; Mike Fitzpatrick; John Dombeck.

SAINTS & SINNERS
Singles: 7-inch
LLP 4-8 65

SAITH
Singles: 7-inch
GOLI (501 "Bad Days Walk") 20-30 60s

SAKAMOTO, Kyu P&R/R&B/LP '63
Singles: 7-inch
CAPITOL 4-6 63-64
EMI 3-4 75
LPs: 10/12-inch
CAPITOL 10-20 63

SAKKARIN
Singles: 7-inch
LONDON 3-5 71
Member: Jonathon King.
Also see KING, Jonathan

SAL, Freddy
Singles: 7-inch
JOX 4-8 65

SAL, Frankie
Singles: 7-inch
DECCA (30878 "Fabulous Cure") 6-12 59

SAL & CONTINENTALS
Singles: 7-inch
441 (34 "I'm Goin' Away") 15-25 64

SAL & STURGES
Singles: 7-inch
CONGRESS 4-8 65

SAL & WATCHERS
Singles: 7-inch
PIO 8-12

SALADIN
Singles: 7-inch
CARICATURE (101 "Honey Do") 50-75 62
CARICATURE (102 "Tough 'N Rough") 50-75 62
Picture Sleeves
CARICATURE (101 "Honey Do") 50-75 62

SALADOS
Singles: 7-inch
TSM (9623 "Spider Walk") 20-25 66

SALAS BROTHERS
(With the Jaguars)
Singles: 7-inch
FARO 5-10 64-66
Also see JAGUARS
Also see TIERRA

SALDAÑA, Sir Doug
(Doug Sahm)
Singles: 7-inch
KEVIN KAT (116 "Will You Love Me Mañana") 3-4 90
Also see SAHM, Doug

SALEM, Freddie, & Wildcats
LPs: 10/12-inch
EPIC 8-10 84
Also see OUTLAWS

SALEM MASS
LPs: 10/12-inch
SALEM MASS (101 "Witch Burning") 250-300 70s

SALEM WITCHCRAFT
Singles: 7-inch
CHAOS (7629 "Keep on Rollin'") 5-10

SALEMS
Singles: 7-inch
EPIC 8-12 61
MERCURY 8-12 61

SALES, Mac
Singles: 78 rpm
METEOR (5022 "Yakety Yak") 40-60 56
Singles: 7-inch
METEOR (5022 "Yakety Yak") 75-125 56

SALES, Soupy P&R/LP '65
Singles: 7-inch
ABC-PAR 5-10 65
CAPITOL 5-10 66
MOTOWN (1141 "Muck-Arty Park") 15-25 69
REPRISE 5-10 62
WIZDOM 3-5
Picture Sleeves
CAPITOL 10-15 66
LPs: 10/12-inch
ABC-PAR 15-25 64-65
MOTOWN (686 "A Bag of Soup") 25-35 69
REPRISE 20-30 61-62
Also see SALESMEN

SALES, Tony, & Tigers
Singles: 7-inch
ROULETTE 4-8 65

SALESMEN
Singles: 7-inch
N.Y. SKYLINE 4-8 65
Also see SALES, Soupy

SALIENS
Singles: 7-inch
LOOK 4-8 67

SALINAS
LPs: 10/12-inch
CADET 8-12 74

SALISBURY, Sandy
Singles: 7-inch
TOGETHER 10-20 68-69
Also see MILLENNIUM

SALISBURY TWINS
Singles: 7-inch
ABC-PAR 4-8 64

SALLEE, Vicki
Singles: 7-inch
DOT 8-15 64-65

SALLES, Jessie, & Crypt-Kickers / Gary Paxton
Singles: 7-inch
GARPAX (44169 "Gary's Theme") 8-12 62
Session: Gary Paxton.
Also see PAXTON, Gary
Also see SAILES, Jesse, & Waves

SALLOOM, Sinclair, & Mother Bear
LPs: 10/12-inch
CADET CONCEPT 10-15 68

SALLY, Carl
Singles: 7-inch
TERRY 5-10 59

SALLY & ROSES
Singles: 7-inch
COLUMBIA 8-12 63

SALLY & SALLYCATS
Singles: 7-inch
RENDEZVOUS 8-12 59

SALLYANGIE
LPs: 10/12-inch
W.B. 10-15 69
Members: Mike Oldfield; Sally Oldfield.
Also see OLDFIELD, Mike
Also see OLDFIELD, Sally

SALMA, Doug, & Highlanders
Singles: 7-inch
PHILIPS 5-10 63

SALMAS BROTHERS
Singles: 78 rpm
IMPERIAL 10-20 56
Singles: 7-inch
ERA (1029 "Go Let Her Go") 15-20 57
IMPERIAL (3001 "Spark of Love") 20-30 56
KEEN (2017 "Things I Love") 10-20 59
KEEN (2018 "Kissin' Bug") 10-20 59
KEEN (82116 "Lolita") 10-20 60

SALO, Georgie
Singles: 7-inch
HI-Q 4-8 60

SALOONATICS
Singles: 7-inch
BETHLEHEM 4-6 65
LPs: 10/12-inch
BETHLEHEM 5-15 65

SALSOUL ORCHESTRA P&R/R&B/LP '75
(Featuring Cognac)
Singles: 12-inch
SALSOUL 4-6 78-83
Singles: 7-inch
SALSOUL 3-5 75-83
LPs: 10/12-inch
SALSOUL 5-10 75-83
Member: Jocelyn Brown.
Also see BROWN, Jocelyn
Also see CHARO
Also see HOLLOWAY, Loleatta

SALT
Singles: 7-inch
COTILLION 4-8 68

SALT & PEPPER
Singles: 7-inch
EPIC 3-5 70-71
POMPEII 4-8 68-69

SALT-N-PEPA P&R/R&B/LP '87
Singles: 7-inch
NEXT PLATEAU 3-4 87-90
LPs: 10/12-inch
NEXT PLATEAU 5-8 87-90

SALT 'N PEPPER
Singles: 7-inch
FELSTED 4-8 61

SALT WATER TAFFY
Singles: 7-inch
BUDDAH 5-10 68-70
METROMEDIA 3-6 71
Member: Tommy West.
LPs: 10/12-inch
BUDDAH 10-20 68-70

SALTY DOG LP '90
LPs: 10/12-inch
GEFFEN 5-8 90

SALTY PEPPERS
Singles: 7-inch
CAPITOL 4-8 69
Members: Maurice White; Wade Flemons.
Also see EARTH, WIND & FIRE
Also see FLEMONS, Wade

SALUGA, Bill
Singles: 7-inch
A&M 3-5 79

SALUTATIONS
LPs: 10/12-inch
LIFESTREAM (1701 "From Doo Wopp to Disco") 8-12 80

SALVADOR, Pat
Singles: 7-inch
HOUMA (113 "Sleep Walk") 10-20 59

SALVADORE, Bobby
Singles: 7-inch
IPG (1012 "Stick 'Em Up Santa") 10-20 63

SALVADORS
Singles: 7-inch
WISE WORLD 8-12

SALVAGE P&R '71
Singles: 7-inch
ODAX 3-5 71

SALVATION
Singles: 7-inch
ABC 5-10 68
U.A. 4-6 70
LPs: 10/12-inch
ABC (623 "Salvation") 10-20 67
ABC (653 "Gypsy Carnival Caravan") 10-20 68
Members: Al Linde; Joe Tate; Rick Levin; Art McLean; Art Resnick.
Also see THIRD RAIL

SALVATORE, Bobby
Singles: 7-inch
IPG 4-8 63

SALVIN, Dick
Singles: 7-inch
GRAVEYARD 10-15

SALVO, Sammy P&R '58
Singles: 78 rpm
RCA 10-20 57
Singles: 7-inch
DOT 10-15 60
HICKORY 5-10 61-63
IMPERIAL 5-10 59-60
MARK V 10-20 58
RCA 10-20 57-59

SALYERS, Loretta
Singles: 7-inch
PARAMOUNT 3-5 73

SAM, Butch, & Station Band R&B '85
Singles: 7-inch
PRIVATE I 3-4 85

SAM & BILL P&R/R&B '65
Singles: 7-inch
DECCA (32143 "I Feel Like Cryin' ") 10-15 67
JODA (100 "For Your Love") 5-10 65
JODA (104 "Fly Me to the Moon") 5-10 65
Members: Sam Gary; Bill Johnson.
Also see SOUL BROTHERS

SAM & BOB & SOULMEN
LPs: 10/12-inch
SABO (1001 Mississippi Mud") .. 200-225 60s
(Approximately 400 made.)
Members: Sam Mosley; Bob Johnson.
Session: Doris Badie.

SAM & DAVE P&R/R&B/LP '66
Singles: 7-inch
ATLANTIC 3-8 68-71
ROULETTE 5-10 62-66
STAX 5-10 65-68
U.A. 3-5 74-75
LPs: 10/12-inch
ATLANTIC (8205 "I Thank You") 15-20 68
ATLANTIC (8218 "Best of Sam & Dave") 8-12 69
GUSTO 5-10
ROULETTE (25323 "Sam & Dave") 15-25 66
STAX (708 "Hold On I'm Coming") 20-30 66
STAX (712 "Double Dynamite") 20-30 66
STAX (725 "Soul Men") 20-30 67
U.A. 8-12 74-75
Members: Sam Moore; Dave Prater.
Also see MOORE, Sam
Also see PICKETT, Wilson / Sam & Dave
Also see REDDING, Otis / Carla Thomas / Sam & Dave / Eddie Floyd
Also see STARS on 45 (Featuring Sam & Dave)

SAM & IRIDESCENTS
Singles: 7-inch
CAPITOL 4-8 67

SAM & KITTY
Singles: 7-inch
FOUR BROTHERS (400 "Don't Hit on Me") 10-15 67
FOUR BROTHERS (452 "Love Is the Greatest") 8-10 66
Members: LeRoy Dandridge; Edith Brown
Also see BROWN, Edith

SAM & SALLY
Singles: 7-inch
EXCELLO (2238 "Hello Heartaches") 5-10 63

SAM & WESTSIDERS
Singles: 7-inch
INTEGRITY (692 "Little Girl") 100-200 64
Session: Marquerite Cockins.

SAM APPLE PIE
LPs: 10/12-inch
SIRE 10-15 70

SAM, ERV & TOM
Singles: 7-inch
DYNAMO 4-8 68

SAM THE BAND
LPs: 10/12-inch
CASABLANCA 5-10 79

SAM THE SHAM & PHARAOHS
(Sam the Sham Revue; Sam; Sam Samudio) P&R/R&B/LP '65
Singles: 7-inch
DINGO (001 "Haunted House") 20-30 64
FRETONE (048 "The Wookie") 3-5 77
MGM (13000 series, except 13972) 5-10 64-69
MGM (13972 "I Couldn't Spell !!*@!") 10-15 69
MGM (14000 series) 3-5 73
POLYDOR 3-4 80s
TUPELO (2982 "Betty & Dupree") 35-55 63
WARRIOR 20-30 60s
XL (905 "Signifyin' Monkey") 50-75 64
XL (906 "Wooly Bully") 75-125 65
Picture Sleeves
MGM 8-12 65-67
LPs: 10/12-inch
MGM 15-25 65-68
Also see SAMUDIO, Sam

SAME
Singles: 7-inch
BARRINGTON 4-8 67

SAMI JO: see COLE, Sami Jo

SAMMY
Singles: 7-inch
PASTEL 5-10 68
PHILIPS 3-6 73
LPs: 10/12-inch
PHILIPS 10-15 73

SAMMY & DEL-LARDS
Singles: 7-inch
STOP (101 "Sleepwalk") 15-25 61

SAMMY & DEL LARKS
Singles: 7-inch
EA-JAY (100 "I Never Will Forget") 100-200 61
Session: Teacho Wiltshire.
Also see SAMMY & DEL-LARDS
Also see WILTSHIRE, Teacho

SAMMY & EMERALDS
Singles: 7-inch
FIESTA (1001 "Am I Blue") 10-20 60s

SAMMY & FIVE NOTES
Singles: 7-inch
LUCKY FOUR 10-20 61-62

SAMMY & TEASERS
Singles: 7-inch
AIRPORT 4-6

SAMOHI SERENADERS: see PARAGONS / Samohi Serenaders

SAMONE, Stephany C&W '80
Singles: 7-inch
MDJ 3-5 80

SAMPLE, Joe LP '78
Singles: 7-inch
ABC 3-5 78-79
MCA 3-4 80-83
LPs: 10/12-inch
ABC 5-10 78-79
MCA 5-8 81-83
MFSL 25-50 78
W.B. 5-8 89
Also see CRUSADERS

SAMPLES, Junior C&W '67
Singles: 7-inch
CHART 4-6 67
LPs: 10/12-inch
CHART 10-15 67
MOUNTAIN DEW 8-10
PICKWICK (6113 "Moonshining") 5-10 70s

SAMPSON, Don Ray
Singles: 7-inch
E 4-8 66

SAMPSON, Jana
(With Randall Parr)
Singles: 7-inch
ROCK-IT (501 "From Lisa Marie") 4-8 79
(Black vinyl.)
ROCK-IT (501 "From Lisa Marie") 8-12 79
(Colored vinyl.)
ROCK-IT (2001 "From Lisa Marie") 20-30 79
(Colored viny. Santa-shaped disc.)
ROCK-IT (2001 "From Lisa Marie") 20-30 79
(Colored vinyl. Bell-shaped disc.)
Picture Sleeves
ROCK-IT (2001 "From Lisa Marie") 4-8 79

SAMPSON, Jean
Singles: 7-inch
COLUMBIA (41554 "Lucky in Love") 10-20 60
COLUMBIA (41728 "Summer Rain") 10-20 60
LIGHTHOUSE 4-6 77

SAMPSON, Linda
Singles: 7-inch
EPIC 5-10 59

SAMPSON, Phil
(Sam Chatman)
Singles: 7-inch
BEA & BABY 10-15 60
Also see SINGIN' SAM

SAMPSON & DELILAH
Singles: 7-inch
ABC 4-8 67
BLACK PRINCE 4-6 69

SAMPSON & GOLIATHS
Singles: 7-inch
FINESSE 10-15 59

SAMS, The
Singles: 7-inch
EBONY (4551 "Please Come on Back") 40-60 66
EBONY (4553 "My Guardian Angel") 40-60 67

SAMUDIO, Sam
Singles: 7-inch
ATLANTIC 3-5 70
LPs: 10/12-inch
ATLANTIC 10-15 71
Also see SAM the SHAM & PHARAOHS

SAMUELS, Bill R&B '46
(With the Cats 'N' Jammer Three; Cats 'N' Jammers)
Singles: 78 rpm
MERCURY 20-50 46-48
Singles: 7-inch
MERCURY (70205 "I Cover the Waterfront") 50-75 53

SAMUELS, Bill
Singles: 7-inch
NORTH STAR 8-12 60s
SOMA 8-12 61

SAMUELS, Clarence
Singles: 78 rpm
ARISTOCRAT (1001 "Boogie Woogie Blues") 20-30 48
DELUXE (3219 "Gimmie") 15-25 50
EXCELLO 10-20 56
FREEDOM (1533 "Lost My Head") 15-25 49
FREEDOM (1541 "She Walk, She Walk, She Walk") 15-25 49
FREEDOM (1544 "Hey Joe") 15-25 49
LAMP 15-25 54
SWING TIME (131 "Household Troubles") 15-25 48
SWING TIME (149 "Deep Sea Diver") 15-25 48
Singles: 7-inch
APT (25028 "We're Goin' to the Hop") 20-30 59
EXCELLO (2093 "Chicken Hearted Woman") 20-40 56
LAMP (8004 "Life Don't Mean a Thing") 25-50 54
LAMP (8005 "Cryin' 'Cause I'm Troubled") 25-50 54
SHARON ("Cryin' 'Cause I'm Troubled") 8-12 66
Also see CARTER, Goree / Clarence Samuels

SAMUELS, Gayle
Singles: 12-inch
PROFILE 4-6 84

SAMUELS, Jerry
Singles: 7-inch
J.E.P. 8-12 60s
Also see NAPOLEON XIV

SAN DIEGO
Singles: 7-inch
LE CAM 3-5
Members: Sonny Threatt; Phyllis Brown-Threatt.
Also see SONNY & PHYLLIS

SAN FERNANDO VALLEY MUSIC BAND C&W '79
Singles: 7-inch
C&S 3-5 79

SAN FRANCISCO ALL STARS
LPs: 10/12-inch
FLYING HORSES 5-10 80
Also see COPPERHEAD
Also see LEWIS, Huey, & News
Also see MAN
Also see QUICKSILVER MESSENGER SERVICE

SAN FRANCISCO COMMITTEE OF CORRESPONDENCE
Singles: 7-inch
CONGRESSIONAL 4-6 73

SAN FRANCISCO EARTHQUAKE
Singles: 7-inch
SMASH 5-10 67-68

SAN FRANCISCO SYMPHONY ORCHESTRA LP '73
LPs: 10/12-inch
DG 8-12 73

SAN MATEO SINGERS
Singles: 7-inch
POPPY 3-6 68

SAN REMO GOLDEN STRINGS P&R '65
Singles: 7-inch
GORDY 10-20 67
RIC-TIC 8-15 65-66
LPs: 10/12-inch
GORDY (923 "Hungry for Love") 25-35 67
GORDY (928 "Swing") 15-25 68
RIC-TIC (901 "Hungry for Love") .. 30-60 66

SAN SEBASTIAN STRINGS LP '67
(With the San Sebastian Strings)
Singles: 7-inch
W.B. 3-6 67-73
LPs: 10/12-inch
W.B. (Except 2754) 8-15 67-75
W.B. (2754 "Spring, Summer, Winter, Autumn") 15-20 73
(Four-disc set.)
Also see McKUEN, Rod

SANBORN, David R&B/LP '76
Singles: 12-inch
W.B. 4-8 81-85
Singles: 7-inch
REPRISE 3-4 88
W.B. 3-5 76-87
LPs: 10/12-inch
REPRISE 5-8 88
W.B. 5-10 76-87
Also see JAMES, Bob, & David Sanborn
Also see PURE PRAIRIE LEAGUE

SANCHEZ, Joe
Singles: 7-inch
IMPERIAL (66190 "Unlucky Me") 10-15 66

SANCTUARY
LPs: 10/12-inch
VERITAS 10-15

SAND
Singles: 7-inch
DICTO (1004 "Sleep") 10-15 60s

SAND
Singles: 7-inch
BARNABY 3-5 72-73
LPs: 10/12-inch
BARNABY 8-12 73

SANDABS
Singles: 7-inch
BAMBOO 8-12 62

SANDALS LP '67
Singles: 7-inch
WORLD PACIFIC (405 "Scrambler") 10-20 64
WORLD PACIFIC (415 "Theme from *Endless Summer*") 10-15 64
WORLD PACIFIC (421 "Always") .. 15-25 64
WORLD PACIFIC (77000 series) 8-12 65-67
LPs: 10/12-inch
WORLD PACIFIC (WP-1832 "Endless Summer") 20-25 66
(Monaural. Soundtrack)
WORLD PACIFIC (ST-1832 "Endless Summer") 25-30 66
(Stereo. Soundtrack)
WORLD PACIFIC (21884 "Last of the Ski Bums") 10-15
Members: John Blakely; Danny Brawner; John Gibson; Gaston Georis; Walter Georis.
Also see SANDELLS
Also see STONEGROUND

SANDALWOOD
Singles: 7-inch
BELL 3-5 73
LPs: 10/12-inch
BELL 8-12 73

SANDALWOOD CANDLE
Singles: 7-inch
440 PLUS 3-5 70

SANDELLS
Singles: 7-inch
AURA (4501 "School's Out!") 10-15 65
WORLD PACIFIC (405 "Out Front") 10-15 64
LPs: 10/12-inch
WORLD PACIFIC (WP-1818 "Scramblers") 25-35 64
(Monaural.)
WORLD PACIFIC (ST-1818 "Scramblers") 35-45 64
(Stereo.)
WORLD PACIFIC (1818 "Scramblers") 50-75 64
(Colored vinyl.)
Also see SANDALS

SANDER, Jimmy
Singles: 7-inch
VULCO 5-10 59

SANDERS C&W '88
Singles: 7-inch
AIRBORNE 3-4 88-89
Members: Dale Sanders; Vicki Sanders.
Also see VICKI DAWN

SANDERS, Andy
Singles: 7-inch
DOTTIE (1010 "Rock & Roll Baby") 20-30

SANDERS, Arlen
(With the Pacifics)
Singles: 7-inch
FARO (616 "Hopped-Up Mustang") 15-25 64

SANDERS, Ben C&W '88
(The 5th Avenue Country Boy)
Singles: 7-inch
LUV 3-4 88

SANDERS, Billy
Singles: 7-inch
ATLANTIC 5-10 59

SANDERS, Bobby
(With the Performers)
Singles: 7-inch
KAYBO (618 "I'm on My Way") .. 100-150 61
KENT (382 "You've Forgotten Me") 500-750 62
PICK-A-HIT 10-15 60s
SOUND-O-RAMA (117 "Cleopatra") 100-150 63
Also see BOBBY & VELVETS
Also see TRAVIS, McKinley

SANDERS, Curly
(With the Sanitones; Ray Sanders)
Singles: 78 rpm
JAMBOREE (590 "Brand New Rock & Roll") 50-75 56
Singles: 7-inch
CONCEPT (897 "Dynamite") 75-100 57
CONCEPT (898 "This Time") 25-50 57
JAMBOREE (590 "Brand New Rock & Roll") 75-100 56
Also see SANDERS, Ray

SANDERS, Debbie C&W '89
Singles: 7-inch
K-ARK 3-4 89

SANDERS, Ed, & Hemptones
(Ed Saunders)
LPs: 10/12-inch
REPRISE (2105 "Beer Cans on the Moon") 20-25 73
REPRISE (6374 "Sanders Truckstop") 20-25 69
Also see FUGS

SANDERS, Felicia P&R '55
Singles: 78 rpm
COLUMBIA 3-5 52-57
Singles: 7-inch
COLUMBIA 5-10 52-57
DECCA 4-8 59-61
MGM 4-8 65
TIME 4-8 60
EPs: 7-inch
COLUMBIA 8-12 55-56
LPs: 10/12-inch
COLUMBIA 15-25 55-57
DECCA 15-20 58
SPECIAL EDITIONS 5-10 67
TIME 10-15 60-64
Also see FAITH, Percy
Also see VALE, Jerry, Peggy King & Felicia Sanders

SANDERS, Fred, & Pearl House Rockers
Singles: 7-inch
SPIN (111 "I'm Just Another Fool in Love") 300-400 61

SANDERS, Gary
Singles: 7-inch
W.B. 5-10 64

SANDERS, Hank
Singles: 7-inch
CREST (1039 "How Much") 75-125 58

SANDERS, Honey
Singles: 7-inch
BRIGHTON 4-8 63

SANDERS, Jan
Singles: 7-inch
TODD 4-8 62

SANDERS, Mack C&W '78
Singles: 7-inch
PILOT 3-5 78

SANDERS, Pharoah LP '69
Singles: 7-inch
ARISTA 3-5 78
LPs: 10/12-inch
ARISTA 5-10 78
IMPULSE 10-15 69-74
INDIA NAVIGATION 5-10 77
NOVUS 5-10 81
THERESA 5-12 80-81
TRIP 8-12 71
Also see COLTRANE, Alice, & Pharoah Sanders

SANDERS, Ray C&W '60
Singles: 7-inch
GNP 4-6 67-68
HILLSIDE 3-4 80
IMPERIAL 4-6 69
LIBERTY 5-10 60-63
REPUBLIC 3-5 77-78
STADIUM 4-8 64
TOWER 4-8 65-66
U.A. 3-5 70-73
LPs: 10/12-inch
IMPERIAL 10-15 69

REPUBLIC 8-10 77
U.A. 8-12 72
Also see SANDERS, Curly

SANDERS, Ray / Curtis Potter / Darrell McCall
LPs: 10/12-inch
HILLSIDE 5-10 80
Also see POTTER, Curtis, & Darrell McCall

SANDERS, Sharon
Singles: 7-inch
MGM 4-6 70

SANDERS, Steve
Singles: 7-inch
MGM 4-8 66
LPs: 10/12-inch
CANAAN 4-8
MGM 10-15 66
Also see LITTLE STEVE & Sego Brothers
Also see PYRAMID

SANDERS, Willis
(With the Fabulous Embers; with Embers; with Duprees; with Art Harris & Orchestra; Will Sanders)
Singles: 7-inch
CORAL (62146 "Time Out for Tears") 20-30 59
JUNO (213 "Your Souvenir") 300-500 57
JUNO (215 "I'll Be with You") 300-500 57
JVPITER (213 "Your Souvenir") 550-650 57
(First issue. From Jupiter Record Co., though label mistakenly reads "Jvpiter.")
MILLIONAIRE (775 "Loveable You") 150-250 58
REGATTA (2000 "Summertime") 25-50 61
REGATTA (2003 "Living Truth") 25-50 61
UNART (2004 "Lovable You") 25-50 58
Also see EMBERS

SANDERSON, Bob, & Minors
Singles: 7-inch
20TH FOX (216 "My Hands") 8-12 60

SANDETTS
Singles: 7-inch
SMOKEY (109 "Without You") 100-150 60

SANDFORD, Chris
Singles: 7-inch
FONTANA 4-8 65

SANDFORD, Ralph
Singles: 7-inch
RIVIERA 10-20 59

SANDI & STYLERS
Singles: 7-inch
RACHEL 10-15 60s
LPs: 10/12-inch
NJ (1003 "Do Me") 15-25

SANDIFER, McKinley
Singles: 7-inch
DAWSON & SANDIFER (135 "Mosquito Bite") 10-20 65

SANDLER, Tony, & Ralph Young *LP '66*
(Sandler & Young)
Singles: 7-inch
CAPITOL 3-6 66-70
LPs: 10/12-inch
A.V.I. 5-10 79
CAPITOL 5-15 66-78
Also see CAMPBELL, Glen / Lettermen / Ella Fitzgerald / Sandler & Young

SANDLIN, Billy
Singles: 7-inch
GALA (115 "Teenager's Dream") 10-20 61
VIM (1006 "She's Mean") 15-25 59

SANDMEN
Singles: 78 rpm
OKEH 15-25 55
Singles: 7-inch
OKEH (7052 "When I Grow Too Old to Dream") 20-40 55
Member: Brook Benton.
Also see BENTON, Brook
Also see WILLIS, Chuck

SANDMEN
Singles: 7-inch
BLUE JAY (5002 "Searching for a New Love") 20-30 65

SANDMEN
Singles: 7-inch
NIGHT OWL 10-15 67

SANDMEN
Singles: 7-inch
STUDIO CITY 10-20 60s

SANDO
Singles: 7-inch
ALLSTAR 8-15 67

SANDO, Rene
Singles: 7-inch
GAPOCA (202 "The Winnie") 8-12
(Colored vinyl.)

SANDOVAL, Danny
Singles: 7-inch
CASHMERE (1641 "Angel City Jam") 8-12

SANDOVAL, Gil
Singles: 7-inch
WESTBEND 3-5

SANDOVAL, Jimmy, & Gauchos
Singles: 7-inch
DIPLOMACY 8-12 64
Also see DOVAL, Jim

SANDPAPERS
Singles: 7-inch
CHARGER (114 "Ain't Gonna Kiss Ya") 25-50 65

SANDPEBBLES *P&R/R&B '67*
Singles: 7-inch
ABC 3-5 73
CALLA 5-10 67-69
Members: Calvin White; Lonzine Wright; Andrea Bolden.
Also see C & SHELLS

SANDPIPERS *P&R/LP '66*
Singles: 7-inch
A&M 3-6 66-72
KISMET 15-25 66
TRU-GLOW-TOWN 5-10 66
EPs: 7-inch
THREE on ONE 5-10
LPs: 10/12-inch
A&M 8-15 66-73
Also see GRADS

SANDPIPERS
Singles: 7-inch
GIANT (705 "Lonely Too Long") 10-20 60s

SANDPIPERS with Mitch Miller & Orchestra / Mitch Miller & Orchestra
Singles: 7-inch
LITTLE GOLDEN 5-10
Also see MILLER, Mitch

SANDRA
Singles: 7-inch
RED BULLET 4-6

SANDRA & GAYLE
Singles: 7-inch
EPIC 4-8 65

SANDS
Singles: 7-inch
CAPRI (522 "Open Your Eyes") 15-25 67

SANDS
Singles: 7-inch
JCP (1042 "Little Things") 15-25 65

SANDS, Evie *P&R '69*
Singles: 7-inch
ABC-PAR 5-10 63-64
A&M 4-8 68-70
BLUE CAT 8-12 65
CAMEO 5-8 66-68
GOLD 5-8 64
HAVEN 3-5 75-76
RCA 3-5 79
LPs: 10/12-inch
A&M 10-15 69
HAVEN 8-10 74
RCA 5-10 79

SANDS, Frank
Singles: 7-inch
MARK (138 "Shamrock") 10-20 59
MGM (12626 "Tarrentella Rock") 10-20 58
MGM (12678 "Let's Go Rock n' Roll") 10-20 58

SANDS, Frankie
Singles: 7-inch
IMPERIAL 5-10 58
MASTERSOUND 4-8 61
PROTONE (121 "Shiga Diga Ding Boom") 10-15 60s

SANDS, Jeri Lynn
Singles: 7-inch
ARCADE (153 "Steady Freddy") 20-30 59
BIG TOP (3015 "If") 10-15 59

SANDS, Jodie *P&R '57*
Singles: 78 rpm
BERNLO 8-12 57
CHANCELLOR 5-10 57
TEEN 5-10 55
Singles: 7-inch
ABC 3-5 74
ABC-PAR 8-12 62-63
BERNLO 10-20 57
CHANCELLOR 10-20 57-59
PARIS 8-12 60-61
SIGNATURE 8-12 59
TEEN 10-20 55
THOR 10-15 59

SANDS, Lola
Singles: 7-inch
BISON 8-12

SANDS, Norman, & Valiants
Singles: 7-inch
WARWICK (598 "Rockin' with Joe") 10-20 60

SANDS, Pat, & Pebbles
Singles: 7-inch
SUSSEX 3-5 71

SANDS, Tommy *P&R/R&B/LP '57*
(With the Raiders)
Singles: 78 rpm
CAPITOL 10-25 57
RCA 8-12 54-56
Singles: 7-inch
ABC-PAR 4-8 63-64
CAPITOL ("Graduation Day") 15-25 57
(No selection number used, though *Steady Date* LP number [T-848] is shown. Promotional issue only.)
CAPITOL (3639 thru 4082) 10-15 57-58
CAPITOL (4160 thru 4580) 5-10 59-61
IMPERIAL 4-8 66-67
LIBERTY 4-8 65
RCA 10-20 54-56
SUPERSCOPE 3-6 69
Picture Sleeves
CAPITOL 10-20 58-59
EPs: 7-inch
CAPITOL (1-2-3 848 "Sing Boy Sing") 15-25 57
(Price is for any of three volumes.)
CAPITOL (898 "Teen-Age Crush") 20-30 57
CAPITOL (1-2-3 929 "Sing Boy Sing") 15-25 58
(Price is for any of three volumes.)
CAPITOL (1123 "This Thing Called Love") 15-20 59
LPs: 10/12-inch
BRUNSWICK 8-10 78
CAPITOL (848 "Steady Date") 35-50 57
CAPITOL (929 "Sing Boy Sing") 35-50 58
CAPITOL (1081 "Sands Storm") 30-50 58
CAPITOL (T-1123 "This Thing Called Love") 30-40 59
(Monaural.)
CAPITOL (ST-1123 "This Thing Called Love") 35-45 59
(Stereo.)
CAPITOL (T-1239 "When I'm Thinking of You") 30-40 59
(Monaural.)
CAPITOL (ST-1239 "When I'm Thinking of You") 35-45 59
(Stereo.)
CAPITOL (T-1364 "Sands at the Storm") 30-40 60
(Monaural.)
CAPITOL (ST-1364 "Sands at the Sands") 35-45 60
(Stereo.)
CAPITOL (T-1426 "Dream with Me") 30-40 60
(Monaural.)
CAPITOL (ST-1426 "Dream with Me") 35-45 60
(Stereo.)
Also see ANNETTE & Tommy Sands
Also see BLAINE, Hal
Also see VINCENT, Gene / Tommy Sands / Sonny James / Ferlin Husky

SANDS, Tony
Singles: 7-inch
LOST GOLD (1 "Star of Bethlehem") 3-4 89
(White vinyl.)
LOST GOLD (1011 "It's After Midnight") 3-4 90
Picture Sleeves
LOST GOLD (1 "Star of Bethlehem") 3-4 89
LOST GOLD (1011 "It's After Midnight") 3-4 90

SANDS OF TIME
Singles: 7-inch
W.B. 4-8 66

SANDS OF TIME
Singles: 7-inch
STERLING AWARD (1082 "Red Light") 15-25 66

SANDS OF TIME
Singles: 7-inch
STEARLY (8167 "Come Back Little Girl") 15-25 67

SANDS of TIME
(Tokens)
Singles: 7-inch
KIRSHNER 4-8 76
Also see TOKENS

SANDY
(Sandi)
Singles: 7-inch
CHARTER 5-10 64
Also see ACCENTS
Also see SANDY & CUPIDS

SANDY
Singles: 7-inch
OUR 4-8 67

SANDY, Frank, & Jackals
Singles: 7-inch
MARK (138 "Shamrock") 10-20 59
MGM (12626 "Tarrentella Rock 25-50 58
MGM (12678 "Let's Go Rock and Roll") 75-100 58

SANDY & BEACHCOMBERS
Singles: 7-inch
SPAR (760 "2 + 2") 15-20 65

SANDY & CUPIDS
Singles: 7-inch
CHARTER 5-10 63
Also see SANDY

SANDY & JOAN
Singles: 7-inch
SURE 5-10 60

SANDY & PEBBLES
Singles: 7-inch
MERCURY 4-8 67

SANDY & SANDSTORMS
Singles: 7-inch
ERA 5-10 63
Member: Billy Lee Riley.
Also see RILEY, Billy Lee

SANDY & SHERIDANS
Singles: 7-inch
DEVILLE (119 "Sir Michael") 8-12

SANDY & SOPHOMORES
Singles: 7-inch
COLUMBIA 4-8 64

SANDY & TROY
Singles: 7-inch
MONUMENT 4-8 65

SANDY THE SOUND MAN
Singles: 7-inch
BLUEBIRD (99 "Honey Dreamers") 5-10 58
Picture Sleeves
BLUEBIRD (99 "Honey Dreamers") 10-15 58

SANETTES
Singles: 7-inch
OHN-J 4-8 64

SANFORD, Arnold
(With Frankie & Playboys)
Singles: 7-inch
BOB GRADY 3-5 87
HAP 4-6 65
MILLION 3-5 72
SAN 3-5 84
STOP 4-8 67
TENNALAGA 4-8 63
Also see SANFORD, Sandy

SANFORD, Ralph
Singles: 7-inch
RIVIERA 4-6

SANFORD, Sandy
("Show Up" Sandy Sanford)
Singles: 7-inch
KILLER (143 "That's Why I Sing This Way") 4-6 91
Session: Scotty Moore; D.J. Fontana; Tommy Dee.
Also see DEE, Tommy
Also see FONTANA, D.J., Band
Also see MOORE, Scotty
Also see SANFORD, Arnold

SANFORD - TOWNSEND BAND *P&R/LP '77*
Singles: 7-inch
W.B. 3-5 77-79
LPs: 10/12-inch
W.B. 5-10 78-79
Members: Ed Sanford; John Townsend.
Also see RUBBER BAND

SANFORDS
Singles: 7-inch
KING 3-5 72

SANG, Samantha *P&R '77*
Singles: 7-inch
ATCO 4-6 69-72
PRIVATE STOCK 3-5 77-78
U.A. 3-5 79
LPs: 10/12-inch
PRIVATE STOCK 5-10 77-78
U.A. 5-10 79
Also see BEE GEES

SANGRE MEXICANA
Singles: 7-inch
LATIN SOUL (114 "Good Cause") 15-25 69

SANGRILADS
Singles: 7-inch
WHAP (318 "Think of What You're Saying") 10-15

SANITY ASSASSINS
EPs: 7-inch
DIONYSUS 3-5 91
(With paper sleeve. Colored vinyl.)

SAN-JO
Singles: 7-inch
ASTROSONIC 3-5 71

SANLAND BROTHERS
Singles: 7-inch
CAPITOL 4-6 69

SANO, Dick
Singles: 7-inch
MORGAN 10-15

SANO, Johnny
Singles: 7-inch
RANDA 5-10 61

SANO, Moto
Singles: 12-inch
EPIC 4-6 84

SANO & SAINTS FIVE
Singles: 7-inch
PENTAGON (2001 "Mercy Mercy") 10-15 60s

SANS, Billie *P&R '71*
Singles: 7-inch
INVICTUS 3-5 71

SANS, Peggy
Singles: 7-inch
TOLLIE 4-8 64

SANSHERS
Singles: 7-inch
KWEEK ("Gonna Git That Man") 15-25 64

SANSOM, Bobby
(With Light Years)
Singles: 7-inch
ACTA 4-8 67-68
METROMEDIA 3-6 69
SUBLIME 4-8 67

SANSON, Barbara
Singles: 7-inch
ARVIS 4-8 61

SANSONE, Peter
Singles: 7-inch
CORAL 5-10 60

SANSONE, Tony
Singles: 7-inch
DI VENUS 4-8 66

SANTA ESMERALDA *P&R/LP '77*
Singles: 12-inch
CASABLANCA 4-8 77-78
Singles: 7-inch
CASABLANCA 3-5 77-78
LPs: 10/12-inch
CASABLANCA 5-10 77-80
Member: Leroy Gomez.

SANTA FE
LPs: 10/12-inch
AMPEX 10-15 71
RTV 10-15 72

SANTAMARIA, Mongo *P&R/R&B/LP '63*
(With His Afro-Latin Group)
Singles: 12-inch
TAPPAN ZEE 4-8 79
Singles: 7-inch
ATLANTIC 3-6 69-72
BATTLE 4-8 63
COLLECTABLES 3-4 80s
COLUMBIA 4-6 64-69
FANTASY 4-8 61-62
RIVERSIDE 4-8 62-66
TAPPAN ZEE 3-5 79
TRIP 3-6
VAYA 3-5 73
LPs: 10/12-inch
ATLANTIC 8-12 70
BATTLE 15-25 63
COLUMBIA 5-15 65-79
FANTASY 10-25 59-62
MILESTONE 6-12 73-76
PRESTIGE 6-12 72
RIVERSIDE 10-20 62-66
VAYA 6-12 73-74

SANTANA *P&R/LP '69*
(Carlos Santana)
Singles: 12-inch
COLUMBIA 4-6 85
Singles: 7-inch
COLUMBIA 3-5 69-90
Picture Sleeves
COLUMBIA 3-5 70-85
LPs: 10/12-inch
COLUMBIA (Except quad and half-speed mastered) 5-15 69-90
COLUMBIA (CQ-30130 "Abraxas") 15-25 75
(Quadraphonic.)
COLUMBIA (CQ-32900 "Illuminations") 15-25 74
(Quadraphonic.)
COLUMBIA (HC-40130 "Abraxas") 40-60 81
(Half-speed mastered.)
Members: Devadip Carlos Santana; Armando Peraza; Graham Lear; David Margen; Richard Baker; Alex Ligertwood; Orestes Vilato; Raul Rekow.
Also see AZTECA
Also see BOOKER T. & MGs
Also see COLTRANE, Alice, & Carlos Santana
Also see ESCOVEDO, Coke
Also see FABULOUS THUNDERBIRDS
Also see FRANKLIN, Aretha
Also see HAGAR, SCHON, AARONSON, SHRIEVE
Also see HANCOCK, Herbie
Also see NOVO COMBO

SANTANA, Carlos, & Mahavishnu John McLaughlin *LP '73*
LPs: 10/12-inch
COLUMBIA (32034 "Love, Devotion, Surrender") 5-10 73
Also see McLAUGHLIN, John

SANTANA, Carlos, & Buddy Miles *P&R/LP '72*
Singles: 7-inch
COLUMBIA 3-5 72
LPs: 10/12-inch
COLUMBIA 6-12 72
Also see MILES, Buddy
Also see SANTANA

SANTANA, Jorge *R&B '79*
Singles: 7-inch
TOMATO 3-5 78-79
LPs: 10/12-inch
TOMATO 5-10 78
Also see MALO

SANTELLS
Singles: 7-inch
COURIER 8-12 64
KMC 4-8 67

SANTIAGO *R&B '76*
Singles: 7-inch
AMHERST 3-5 76

SANTO
(Santo Farina)
LPs: 10/12-inch
PAUSA 5-8
Also see SANTO & JOHNNY

SANTO, Joey
Singles: 7-inch
PALACE 5-10 60

SANTO & JOHNNY P&R/R&B '59
Singles: 7-inch
CANADIAN AMERICAN 5-12 59-66
ERIC 3-4 70s
IMPERIAL 4-8 67-68
PAUSA 3-5 76
U.A. 4-8 66
Picture Sleeves
CANADIAN AMERICAN 8-15 60-65
LPs: 10/12-inch
CANADIAN AMERICAN 20-40 59-64
IMPERIAL 10-20 67-69
Members: Santo Farina; Johnny Farina.
Also see PACK
Also see SANTO

SANTOS, Larry P&R '76
Singles: 7-inch
ATLANTIC (2250 "Someday") 10-20 64
CASABLANCA 3-5 76-77
EVOLUTION 5-15 69-71
LPs: 10/12-inch
CASABLANCA 8-10 77
EVOLUTION 10-20 69
Also see 4 SEASONS
Also see MADISONS
Also see TONES

SANTS
Singles: 7-inch
FORMAT (118 "High Tide") 15-20 66

SAPO
Singles: 7-inch
BELL 3-5 74
LPs: 10/12-inch
BELL 8-10 74

SAPODILLA PUNCH
LPs: 10/12-inch
PHILIPS 10-20 69

SAPORITA, Ray
Singles: 7-inch
FLO 5-10
I.P.G. (1006 "Hercules") 10-15 63
Picture Sleeves
I.P.G. (1006 "Hercules") 10-20 63

SAPPHIRE
Singles: 12-inch
BECKET 4-6 83

SAPPHIRE THINKERS
Singles: 7-inch
HOBBIT 5-10 69
LPs: 10/12-inch
HOBBIT (5003 "From Within") 15-25 69
Members: Peggy Richmond; Bill Richmond; Steve Richmond; Tim Lee.

SAPPHIRES
Singles: 7-inch
RCA 10-15 58

SAPPHIRES P&R/R&B '64
Singles: 7-inch
ABC 3-5 73
ABC-PAR 5-15 64-66
COLLECTABLES 3-4 80s
ERIC 3-4 70s
ITZY (5 "Who Do You Love") 20-30 63
SWAN 8-10 63-64
LPs: 10/12-inch
SWAN (513 "Who Do You Love") 50-100 64
Members: Carol Jackson; George Gainer; Joe Livingston.

SARA SUE
Singles: 7-inch
VANDAN 4-8 64

SARAH
LPs: 10/12-inch
CREAM 8-12 72

SARAH C&W '87
(Sarah Vogt)
Singles: 7-inch
HUB 3-4 87-88

SARATOGAS
Singles: 7-inch
IMPERIAL (5738 "I'll Be Loving You") 25-50 61

SARAYA P&R/LP '89
Singles: 7-inch
POLYDOR 3-4 89
Picture Sleeves
POLYDOR 3-4 89
LPs: 10/12-inch
POLYDOR 5-8 89

SARDAMS
Singles: 7-inch
JCP (1038 "Somethin' You Got") 10-20 64

SARDE, Cliff
Singles: 7-inch
ASLAN 3-5 81
LPs: 10/12-inch
MCA 5-10 87-88

SARDO, Frank
(Frankie Sardo)
Singles: 7-inch
ABC-PAR 8-12 59
LIDO 8-12 59
MGM 10-15 60
NEWTOWN 10-20 60
RAYNA 8-12 62
STUDIO (9910 "Just You Watch Me") 20-35 61
20TH FOX 8-12 60
Also see FRANKIE and JOHNNY

SARDO, Johnny
Singles: 7-inch
CHOCK FULL O' HITS (104 "Take a Ride with Me") 75-100 58
W.B. (5044 "Late to School") 15-25 59

SARDUCCI, Father Guido LP '80
Singles: 7-inch
A&M 3-5 74
W.B. 3-4 80
LPs: 10/12-inch
W.B. 5-10 80

SARGE, Mike
Singles: 78 rpm
MERCURY 5-10 56
Singles: 7-inch
MERCURY (70945 "Bobby Sox Baby") 10-15 56

SARGEANTS, Gary C&W '73
Singles: 7-inch
MERCURY 3-5 73-74
Also see HALL, Tom T.

SARGENT, Bobby
Singles: 7-inch
XL-FORTE 4-8 65

SARGENT, Chuck, & Ambassadors
Singles: 7-inch
CUCA (1079 "Don't You Ever Go") 50-75 62
Also see KENNEDY, Dave

SARGENT, Don
(With the Buddies)
Singles: 7-inch
CATALINA (4514 "Leadfoot") 10-15 59
GOLDEN MELODY 5-10 61
MECCA (101 "Rockin' Chair Roll") 25-50 53
RCA (7128 "Red Ruby Lips") 20-40 58
RCA (7241 "10 Minutes to Heaven") 20-40 58
WORLD PACIFIC 10-15 59

SARGENT, Lou
(Lou Sargent's Band)
Singles: 78 rpm
CHESS (1465 "Ridin' the Boogie") 15-25 51

SARI & SHALIMARS
Singles: 7-inch
VEEP 4-8 68

SARIDIS, Saverio P&R '62
Singles: 7-inch
U.A. 3-6 66
W.B. 4-8 61-62
Picture Sleeves
W.B. 4-8 61
LPs: 10/12-inch
W.B. 10-20 62

SARNE, Mike
Singles: 7-inch
CAMEO 5-10 62

SAROFEEN & SMOKE
LPs: 10/12-inch
GWP 10-15 71

SARSTEDT, Clive
Singles: 7-inch
RCA 3-5 70-71
LPs: 10/12-inch
RCA 8-12 70-71

SARSTEDT, Peter P&R '69
Singles: 7-inch
SIRE 3-5 78
U.A. 3-5 72
WORLD PACIFIC 4-6 69
LPs: 10/12-inch
U.A. 8-12 71
WORLD PACIFIC 10-15 69

SARSTEDT, Richard
LPs: 10/12-inch
EVOLUTION 8-12 71

SA-SHAYS
Singles: 7-inch
ALFI (1 "Boo Hoo Hoo") 10-20 61
ZEN (110 "Boo Hoo Hoo") 8-12 61

SASKIA & SERGE C&W '78
Singles: 7-inch
ABC/HICKORY 3-5 78

SASS R&B '77
Singles: 7-inch
20TH FOX 3-5 77

SASSAFRAS
Singles: 7-inch
CHRYSALIS 3-5 75
LPs: 10/12-inch
CHRYSALIS 8-10 75

SATAN, Jimmy
Singles: 7-inch
MALTESE (102 "Look at the Clock") 25-50 66

SATAN & ANGELS
LPs: 10/12-inch
PANTOMINE 5-10

SATAN & DISCIPLES
Singles: 7-inch
GOLDBAND (1188 "Mummies Curse") 15-25 69
LPs: 10/12-inch
GOLDBAND (7750 "Underground") 15-25 69

SATAN'S BREED
Singles: 7-inch
A-L-M (201,130 "Laugh Myself to the Grave") 15-25 66

SATANS
LPs: 10/12-inch
("Raisin' Hell") 50-100 62
(No label name is shown.)

SATANS
Singles: 7-inch
SATAN ("Say It Again") 10-20 63
(Selection number not known.)

SATANS
Singles: 7-inch
MANHATTAN (801 "Making Deals") 15-20 66

SATANS FOUR
Singles: 7-inch
B.T. PUPPY 8-12 65
Also see DEL SATINS

SATANS FOUR / Cinnamon Angels
LPs: 10/12-inch
B.T PUPPY (1010 "Mixed Soul") 10-15 70
Also see CINNAMON ANGELS
Also see SATANS FOUR

SATELLITE, Billy: see BILLY SATELLITE

SATELLITES
Singles: 7-inch
CLASS (234 "Heavenly Angel") 50-100 58
(First issue.)
MALYNN (234 "Heavenly Angel") 50-100 58
Members: David Ford; Earl Nelson; Curt Williams; Curley Dinkins.
Also see DAY, Bobby
Also see HOLLYWOOD FLAMES
Also see NELSON, Earl

SATELLITES
Singles: 7-inch
U.A. (141 "I Found a Girl") 25-35 58

SATELLITES
Singles: 7-inch
CHECKER (891 "Blast Off") 15-25 58
CHESS (1789 "Blast Off") 10-15 62
RONNIE (204 "Blast Off") 25-50 58
(First issue.)

SATELLITES
Singles: 7-inch
CUPID (Cupid 5004 "Linda Jean") 40-60 58
Member: Mickey Brazell.

SATELLITES
Singles: 7-inch
ABC-PAR (10038 "Linda Jean") 25-35 59
D-M-G (4001 "Each Night") 15-25 60
(With the High Seas.)
PALACE 10-15 60
3 SONS 5-10 63
Also see HIGH SEAS

SATELLITES
Singles: 7-inch
PARROT 10-15 67

SATIN, Ginny
Singles: 7-inch
PHILIPS 4-8 65

SATIN, Jimmy
Singles: 7-inch
ABC-PAR 4-8 65

SATIN, Lonnie: see SATTIN, Lonnie

SATIN, Richard
Singles: 7-inch
ENTRA 4-8 61

SATIN, Sonny
Singles: 7-inch
GNP 4-8 65

SATIN BELLS
Singles: 7-inch
SHAMLEY 4-8 68

SATIN SOUL
Singles: 7-inch
BRUNSWICK 3-5 74

SATINS
Singles: 7-inch
ALDON (8627 "Get Out of My Life") 10-20 60s

SATINTONES
Singles: 7-inch
MOTOWN (1000 "My Beloved") 200-300 60
(Without strings. ID number is MT-12345.)
MOTOWN (1000 "My Beloved") 200-300 60
(Strings added. ID number is 1000-G3.)
MOTOWN (1006 "Tomorrow and Always") 100-200 61
(Without strings.)
MOTOWN (1006 "Tomorrow and Always") 100-200 61
(Strings added.)
MOTOWN (1006 "Angel") 600-800 61
(Male lead vocal. Serial number is H-625.)
MOTOWN (1006 "Angel") 400-500 61
(Male/Female duet. Serial number is H-55596.)
MOTOWN (1010 "My Kind of Love") 75-125 61
MOTOWN (1020 "Zing Went the Strings of My Heart") 100-200 62
TAMLA (54026 "Going to the Hop") 300-500 60
Members: Chico Leverette; Freddie Gorman; Briant Holland; Sonny Sanders; Robert Bateman; James Ellis; Sonny Sanders; Vernon Williams; Sammy Mack; Robert Bateman; Joe Charles.
Also see FIVE MASTERS
Also see GORMAN, Freddie
Also see HOLLAND, Brian
Also see HOLLAND, Eddie
Also see LEVERETTE, Chico
Also see LOE & JOE
Also see PYRAMIDS

SATISFACTIONS
Singles: 7-inch
CHESAPEAKE (610 "We Will Walk Together") 30-50 62
IMPERIAL (66170 "Bring It All Down") 10-15 66
1-2-3 .... 5-8 69
SMASH (2059 "Give Me Your Love") 10-15 66
SMASH (2098 "Take It Or Leave It") 15-25 66

SATISFACTIONS
Singles: 7-inch
RADIANT (1515 "Satisfaction") 10-20 65

SATISFACTIONS
Singles: 7-inch
LEE (3735 "Bad Times") 45-65 66
LEE (3736 "Only Once") 40-50 66

SATISFACTIONS
TWIN TOWN (714 "Bad Times") 10-20 66
Also see MARAUDERS

SATISFACTIONS P&R/R&B '70
Singles: 7-inch
LIONEL (3201 "This Bitter Earth") 8-12 70
LIONEL (3205 "One Light, Two Lights") 10-15 71
Members: James Isom; Earl Jones; Lorenzo Hines; Fletcher Lee.

SATISFIED MINDS
Singles: 7-inch
PLATO (80284 "I Can't Take It") 15-25

SATISFIERS
Singles: 78 rpm
CORAL 6-12 56-57
Singles: 7-inch
CORAL 10-15 56-58
SO-LO (1002 "Let Me Know") 8-10 63
VEGAS (626 "Ghost of a Chance") 10-20 60

SATLER, Lile
Singles: 7-inch
HUNTOM (1101 "Let's Call It a Day") 15-25 67

SATO, Steve
Singles: 7-inch
U.W. RECORDS 4-8

SATORI
Singles: 7-inch
STEFFEK ("1,000 Micrograms") 20-30 67

SATRIANI, Joe LP '87
Singles: 12-inch
RELATIVITY (8193 "Always with Me") 4-8 87
(Clear vinyl. Promotional issue only.)
LPs: 10/12-inch
RELATIVITY (Black vinyl) 5-8 87-89
RELATIVITY (8110 "Not of This Earth") 10-15 88
(Colored vinyl.)

SATTEN, Steve
LPs: 10/12-inch
COLUMBIA 8-10 75

SATTERFIELD, Esther LP '76
Singles: 7-inch
A&M 3-5 76
LPs: 10/12-inch
A&M 5-10 76

SATTIN, Lonnie
(Lonnie Satin)
Singles: 7-inch
CAPITOL (3879 "My Heart's Your Home") 10-15 58
DECCA 5-10 61
SCEPTER 5-10 62-63
SUNBEAM 10-15 58
W.B. 8-12 59-60
LPs: 10/12-inch
SCEPTER 15-25 63

SATURDAY, Patty
Singles: 7-inch
SWAN 5-10 59

SATURDAY KNIGHTS
(Saturday Nights)
Singles: 7-inch
NOCTURNE (1030 "Sea Mist") 30-50 60s
SWAN (4075 "Ticonderoga") 10-15 61
Credited to Saturday Nights.)
SWAN (4075 "Ticonderoga") 5-10 61
Credited to Saturday Knights.)
SWAN (4081 "Texas Tommy") 5-10 61
Member: Van Trevor.
Also see SHELDON, Rick, & Saturday Knights
Also see TREVOR, Van

SATURDAY KNIGHTS
Singles: 7-inch
JET (101 "Dum Diddly Dum") 15-20 60s

SATURDAY MORNING CARTOON SHOW
Singles: 7-inch
ELF 4-6 68-69

SATURDAY NIGHT BAND R&B/LP '78
Singles: 7-inch
PRELUDE 3-5 78
LPs: 10/12-inch
PRELUDE 5-10 78

SATURDAY'S CHILDREN
Singles: 7-inch
ABC-PAR 4-8 63
DUNWICH 4-8 66-67
LPs: 10/12-inch
ABC-PAR 10-20 64

SATURDAY'S CROWD
Singles: 7-inch
BOTANIC 4-6 68

SATURDAY'S PHOTOGRAPH
Singles: 7-inch
COLUMBIA 4-6 69

SATYRICON
Singles: 7-inch
MGM 3-5 71

SAUCEDO, Rick
(With the Jordanaires)
Singles: 7-inch
ECLIPSE 4-6 77
FRATERNITY 4-6 78
Picture Sleeves
ECLIPSE 4-8 77
FRATERNITY 4-8 78
LPs: 10/12-inch
REALITY 10-20
Session: D.J. Fontana; Millie Kirkham; Jordanaires.
Also see FONTANA, D.J., Band
Also see JORDANAIRES

SAUCEMAN, Carl
Singles: 7-inch
N 8-12

SAUCERS
(Frank Jordan & the Saucers)
Singles: 7-inch
FELCO (104 "Why Do I Dream") 300-400 59
(Identification number is "ZTSC-10407.")
FELCO (104 "Why Do I Dream") 200-300 59
(Identification number is "TB-155.")
KICK (516 "Flossie Mae") 350-450 58
(Black label.)
KICK (516 "Flossie Mae") 150-200 58
(Yellow and red label.)
LYNNE (101 "Hello Darling") 200-300 64
LPs: 10/12-inch
GULF COAST 5-10 89
Members: Frank Jordan; Jim Beacham; Charles Beacham; Leonard Allen; Verdie Lee Thomas; James Stanley.

SAUCY SYLVIA
LPs: 10/12-inch
JUBILEE 10-15 67

SAUL, Hender
Singles: 7-inch
LIBERTY TONE (104 "Ain't Gonna Rock Tonight") 200-300

SAULS, Corkey C&W '79
Singles: 7-inch
SAND MOUNTAIN 3-5 79

SAULSBERRY, Rodney R&B '84
Singles: 7-inch
ALLEGIANCE 3-4 84-85
RYAN 3-4 88

SAUNDERS, Jimmy
Singles: 7-inch
COMPANION 5-10 60
Also see CAROL, Lily Ann, & Jimmy Saunders

SAUNDERS, Kathy
(Cathy Saunders)
Singles: 7-inch
EDIT 5-10 60-63
TIDE 4-8 61-67
Also see CANDLETTS

SAUNDERS, Little Butchie
(Little Butchie Saunders & His Buddies)
Singles: 78 rpm
HERALD 15-25 56
Singles: 7-inch
HERALD (485 "Lindy Lou") 25-45 56
HERALD (491 "Great Big Heart") 25-45 56
Also see ELCHORDS
Also see LITTLE BUTCH & VELLS

SAUNDERS, Merl LP '73
(Merle Saunders & Heavy Turbulence)
Singles: 7-inch
FANTASY 4-8 64-69
GALAXY 3-5 71
LPs: 10/12-inch
FANTASY 10-20 68-73
Session: Tom Fogerty.
Also see FOGERTY, Tom
Also see GARCIA, Jerry

SAUNDERS, Red
("Featuring Delores Hawkins")
Singles: 78 rpm
BLUE LAKE 5-10 54
OKEH (Except 6862) 5-10 46-55
OKEH (6862 "Hambone") 15-25 52
(With Dee Clark.)
SAVOY 10-15 45
SULTAN 10-15 46
SUPREME 5-10 49
Singles: 7-inch
BLUE LAKE (101 "Summertime") ... 15-25 54
(Colored vinyl.)
OKEH (6801 thru 6856) 10-15 51-52
OKEH (6862 "Hambone") 25-50 52
(With Dee Clark.)
OKEH (6884 thru 6953) 10-15 52-53
OKEH (7061 "Mistreatin' Woman Blues") 10-20 55
OKEH (7166 "Hambone") 8-12 63
Picture Sleeves
OKEH (7166 "Hambone") 10-15 63
Also see CLARK, Dee
Also see MERCURY ALL-STARS

SAUNDERS, Roger
LPs: 10/12-inch
W.B. 8-10 72

SAUNDERS, Slim
Singles: 78 rpm
CHESS 15-25 54
LAMP 10-20 55
Singles: 7-inch
CHESS (1563 "Let's Have Some Fun") 35-55 54
LAMP (2004 "No One Can Love You Like I Do") 15-25 55

SAUSAGE, Doc: see DOC SAUSAGE

SAUSSY, Tupper, & Wayward Bus
Singles: 7-inch
RCA 4-8 68

SAUTERELLES
Singles: 7-inch
LONDON 3-6 68

SAVAGE, Al
(With Joe Morris & His Orchestra)
Singles: 78 rpm
HERALD 4-8 55-56
Singles: 7-inch
HERALD (Black vinyl) 10-15 55-56
HERALD (Colored vinyl) 20-30 55
LIDO 5-10 59
Also see MORRIS, Joe

SAVAGE, Big Sam
Singles: 7-inch
DATE (1003 "Ohh-Gosh!") 10-15 59

SAVAGE, Bob
Singles: 7-inch
ABC-PAR 10-15 58

SAVAGE, Derek, & Foundation
Singles: 7-inch
DATE 4-8 67

SAVAGE, Duke, & Arribins
Singles: 7-inch
ARGO (5346 "Your Love") 20-30 59

SAVAGE, John
Singles: 7-inch
REAL FINE 4-8 62

SAVAGE, Jon
Singles: 7-inch
VEE JAY 5-10 64

SAVAGE, Lee
Singles: 7-inch
MERRI 5-10 60

SAVAGE, Robert
LPs: 10/12-inch
PARAMOUNT 8-10

SAVAGE GRACE *LP '70*
Singles: 7-inch
REPRISE 3-5 70-71
LPs: 10/12-inch
REPRISE 10-15 70-71

SAVAGE RESURRECTION
Singles: 7-inch
MERCURY (72778 "Thing in E") 5-10 68
LPs: 10/12-inch
MERCURY (61156 "Savage Resurrection") 15-25 68
Members: John Palmer; Bill Harper.

SAVAGE ROSE
Singles: 7-inch
GREGAR 3-5 70-71
Picture Sleeves
GREGAR 3-5 70
LPs: 10/12-inch
GREGAR 8-12 70-71
POLYDOR 10-15 69

SAVAGE SONS of YA HO WA: see YA HO WA 13

SAVAGES
Singles: 7-inch
RED FOX (111 "Cheating On Me") 10-20 65

SAVAGES
Singles: 7-inch
DUANE (1043 "No No No") 10-20 66
DUANE (1049 "Roses Are Red") 10-20 66
DUANE (1054 "The World Ain't Round, It's Square") 30-50 66
LPs: 10/12-inch
DUANE (1047 "Live and Wild") .. 300-400 66
(Counterfeits exist, using same label and number.)

SAVAGES
Singles: 7-inch
NATIONAL 5-10

SAVALAS, Telly *LP '75*
Singles: 7-inch
MCA 3-5 74-75
LPs: 10/12-inch
AUDIO FIDELITY 5-10 75
MCA 5-10 74-76

SAVANNAH *C&W '83*
Singles: 7-inch
MERCURY 3-4 83-84

SAVATAGE *LP '86*
Singles: 7-inch
ATLANTIC 3-4 86-90
LPs: 10/12-inch
ATLANTIC 5-8 86-90
Members: Jon Olivia; Criss Olivia; Steve Wacholz; Johnny Lee Middleton.

SAVETES
Singles: 7-inch
CHOICE 5-10 63

SAVINA
Singles: 7-inch
LOVE 4-8 60
RANDOM 4-8 60
Picture Sleeves
LOVE 4-8 60

SAVITT, Buddy
LPs: 10/12-inch
PARKWAY 15-20 63

SAVONICS
Singles: 7-inch
MTA 5-10 68

SAVOY, Ashton, Combo
Singles: 7-inch
HOLLYWOOD 15-25 58

SAVOY, Jules, & Chromatics
("Singing Discovery of Hesperia Inn, Hesperia, Calif.")
Singles: 7-inch
REAL (1320 "Would You") 500-750 59

SAVOY, Ronnie *P&R '61*
Singles: 7-inch
CANDELO 5-10 59
EPIC 4-8 63-64
GONE 5-10 59
MGM 10-20 60-61
PHILIPS 4-8 62-63
TUFF (416 "Pitfall") 20-30 65
WINGATE (001 "Loving You") 10-20 65

SAVOY BROWN *P&R/LP '69*
(Savoy Brown Blues Band)
Singles: 7-inch
LONDON 3-5 74-75
PARROT 3-6 69-73
TOWN HOUSE 3-5 81
LPs: 10/12-inch
LONDON (600 & 700 series) 8-10 74-77
LONDON (50000 "Best of Savoy Brown") 5-8 77
PARROT 10-15 68-73
TOWN HOUSE (Except 7562) 8-12 81
TOWN HOUSE (7562 "Prime Cuts") 10-15 81
(Promotional issue only.)
Also see ANDERSON, Miller
Also see CHICKEN SHACK
Also see FOGHAT
Also see PHILLIPS, Warren, & Rockets
Also see YOULDEN, Chris

SAVOYS
Singles: 78 rpm
COMBO 50-100 55
Singles: 7-inch
COMBO (75 "Darling Stay with Me") 200-300 55
(Purple label. Has "Combo Records, Hollywood, Calif." at top.)
COMBO (75 "Darling Stay with Me") 50-75 55
(Red label, or purple label with only "Combo" at top.)
COMBO (81 "Evil Ways") 100-150 55

SAVOYS / Jack McVea
Singles: 78 rpm
COMBO (90 "Chop Chop Boom") .. 20-30 55
Singles: 7-inch
COMBO (90 "Chop Chop Boom") .. 25-50 55
Also see McVEA, Jack
Also see SAVOYS

SAVOYS
Singles: 78 rpm
SAVOY (1188 "Say You're Mine") 15-25 56
Singles: 7-inch
SAVOY (1188 "Say You're Mine") 30-50 56
Members: Jimmy Jones; Bill Walker; Bobby Moore; Ken Saxton; Melvin Walton.
Also see JONES, Jimmy
Also see PRETENDERS

SAVOYS
(With the Bella Tones)
Singles: 7-inch
BELLA (18 "I Love My Baby") 15-25 59
BELLA (58 "Mortal Monster Man") 15-20 59
CHRISTY (130 "You're the Beating of My Heart") 75-125 60

SAVOYS
Singles: 7-inch
RAYNARD (10019 "Charlena") 10-20 65
Members: Mike Minikel; Ron Faith; Ron LaBode; Brad True; Bruce Cole.

SAVOYS
Singles: 7-inch
NRM (904 "Slappin' Rods and Leaky Oil") 20-30 66
PDQ ("Slappin' Rods and Leaky Oil") 50-75 60
(Selection number not known.)

SAVOYS
Singles: 7-inch
CATAMOUNT (101 "If You Were Gone from Me") 15-25 63
CATAMOUNT (105 "Gloria") 10-15 65

SAVOYS
Singles: 7-inch
SUMMIT (403 "Can It Be") 20-30 66

SAVOYS
Singles: 7-inch
STUDIO (1000 "Razorback") 8-12 60s
TESS (6 "Barracuda") 8-12 60s

SAWBUCK
Singles: 7-inch
FILLMORE 4-6 72
LPs: 10/12-inch
FILLMORE 10-15 72

SAWMILL CREEK BAND *C&W '81*
Singles: 7-inch
COWBOY 3-5 81-83
LPs: 10/12-inch
COWBOY 5-10 82-83
Member: Bruce "Bru Hau" Hauser.
Also see HAUSER, Bruce

SAWYER, Henry, & Jupiters
("Music by Mike Tam")
Singles: 7-inch
PLANET X (9621 "It Takes Two") 1500-2500 57

SAWYER, Ray *P&R/C&W '76*
Singles: 7-inch
CAPITOL 3-5 76-79
SANDY (1030 "Rockin' Satellite") .. 20-30 60
SANDY (1037 "I'm Gonna Leave") 10-20 61
LPs: 10/12-inch
CAPITOL 8-10 76
Also see DR. HOOK

SAWYER, Steve
Singles: 7-inch
CASABLANCA 3-5 76

SAWYER, Tommy, & Twains
Singles: 7-inch
DIAMOND 4-8 62

SAWYER BROWN *C&W '84*
Singles: 7-inch
CAPITOL 3-5 84-90
LPs: 10/12-inch
CAPITOL 5-10 85-90
Members: Mark Miller; Bob Randall; Jim Scholten; Gregg Hubbard; Joe Smyth.

SAWYER BROWN & "Cat" Joe Bonsall *C&W '86*
Singles: 7-inch
CAPITOL 3-4 86
Also see BONSALL, Joe
Also see SAWYER BROWN

SAWYER SISTERS
Singles: 7-inch
DYNASTY 10-15 59

SAX, Bobby
Singles: 7-inch
DE PLACE (2826 "Taste of Soul") ... 8-12 64
RU-JAC (0015 "Sout at Last") 15-25 59

SAXON *LP '83*
Singles: 7-inch
CARRERE 3-5 83-84
LPs: 10/12-inch
CAPITOL 5-10 83-87
Also see CHEAP TRICK / Aldo Nova / Saxon
Also see MOTORHEAD

SAXON, Eddie
(With the Paramounts)
Singles: 7-inch
EMPRESS (106 "Blues No More") 150-200 62
(Single-sided disc. Promotional issue only.)
EMPRESS (106 "Blues No More") 100-200 62
FORD (104 "What a Night") 10-20 61

SAXON, Ronnie
Singles: 7-inch
CORAL 5-10 61

SAXON, Sky
(Sky Saxon Blues Band)
Singles: 7-inch
CONQUEST (777 "They Say") 15-25 64
LPs: 10/12-inch
GNP (2040 "Full Spoon of Seedy Blues") 20-30 67
(Originals have the logo, "GNP Crescendo," on a horizontal line. Reissues have the name in a circular pattern.)
VOXX 5-10
Also see ALLRIGHT FAMILY BAND
Also see MARSH, Ritchie
Also see SEEDS
Also see YA HO WA 13

SAXONS
Singles: 7-inch
OUR ("Please Be My Love Tonight") 300-500 57

SAXONS
Singles: 7-inch
CONTENDER (1313 "Is It True") 50-100 58
TAMPA (139 "Tryin' ") 35-50 58
Also see HOLLYWOOD SAXONS

SAXONS
Singles: 7-inch
SHO-BIZ (1003 "Camel Walk") 15-25 59

SAXONS
EPs: 7-inch
MORDAN 15-25 64

SAXONS
Singles: 7-inch
MIRASONIC 5-10 65
LPs: 10/12-inch
MIRASONIC (A-1017 "Saxons") 30-40 66
(Monaural.)
MIRASONIC (AS-1017 "Saxons") .. 40-50 66
(Stereo.)

SAXONS
Singles: 7-inch
YORKSHIRE (101 "Everybody Puts Her Down") 5-10 64
YORKSHIRE (127 "Things Have Been Bad") 15-25 66

SAXTON, Anglo
Singles: 7-inch
LUCKY ELEVEN 4-8 60s

SAXTONS
Singles: 7-inch
REGINA 8-12 64

SAYER, Leo *P&R/LP '75*
Singles: 7-inch
W.B. 3-5 73-84
LPs: 10/12-inch
W.B. 6-10 75-84

SAYERS, Peter
Singles: 7-inch
MTA 3-5 70

SAYLES, Johnny
Singles: 7-inch
BRUNSWICK 8-12
CHESS (2033 "Lilly Mae") 10-15 67
CHESS/LAKESIDE (2012 "Teardrops") 10-20 67
CHI-TOWN 8-12
DAKAR 4-8 69
MAR-V-LUS 5-10 64
MINIT 10-15 66
ST. LAWRENCE 5-10 67
LPs: 10/12-inch
DAKAR 10-15 70

SAYLOR, Adam
Singles: 7-inch
ORIGINAL SOUND 4-8 65

SAYNT, Sylia
Singles: 7-inch
COLUMBIA 5-8 61

SCAFFOLD *P&R '68*
Singles: 7-inch
BELL 4-8 68
W.B. 3-5 74
LPs: 10/12-inch
BELL (6018 "Thank U Very Much") 25-30 68
Members: Mike McGear; Roger McGough; John Gorman; Mike Vickers; Lol Creme; Andy Roberts; Zoot Money.
Also see GODLEY, Kevin, & Lol Creme
Also see McGEAR, Mike
Also see MONEY, Zoot
Also see ROBERTS, Andy

SCAGGS, Boz *P&R/LP '71*
Singles: 7-inch
ATLANTIC 4-8 69
COLUMBIA 3-8 71-88
FULL MOON 3-5 81
Picture Sleeves
COLUMBIA 3-6 76-88
EPs: 7-inch
COLUMBIA 5-10 76
LPs: 10/12-inch
ATLANTIC (8239 "Boz Scaggs") 8-12 69
ATLANTIC (19166 "Boz Scaggs") 5-8 78
COLUMBIA (Except 40000 series) ... 6-10 71-80
COLUMBIA (40463 "Other Roads") ... 5-8 88
COLUMBIA (43920 "Silk Degrees") 15-20 80
(Half-speed mastered.)
Promotional LPs
COLUMBIA (A2S-71 "Boz Scaggs KSAN Live Concert") 200-300 74
(Promotional issue only. Two discs.)
COLUMBIA (203 "The Boz Scaggs Sampler") 10-20 76
Also see MILLER, Steve
Also see MOTHER EARTH

SCAGGS, Boz / Kris Kristofferson
EPs: 7-inch
PLAYBACK/COLUMBIA (1001 "Boz Scaggs [Live]") 20-40 74
Also see KRISTOFFERSON, Kris
Also see SCAGGS, Boz

SCAGWAY, Sue
Singles: 7-inch
ACCENT 3-5

SCALES, Alonzo
Singles: 78 rpm
ABBEY 25-45 50s
WING 25-45 55
Singles: 7-inch
WING (90020 "She's Gone") 50-75 55
WING (90049 "Hard Luck Child") ... 50-75 55

SCALES, Harvey *P&R/R&B '67*
(With the Seven Sounds)
Singles: 12-inch
KASHGOLD 4-6 90
Singles: 7-inch
CADET CONCEPT 4-8 71
CASABLANCA 3-5 79
CHESS 4-8 69-70
CUCA 5-15 63-67
EARTHTONE 3-4 86-91
KASHGOLD 3-4 90
MAGIC TOUCH 3-8 67-76
MERCURY 4-6 69
STAX 3-5 72
LPs: 10/12-inch
CASABLANCA 8-10 78-79
Members: Rudy Jacobs; Rollo Armstead; Ben Petrey; Monnie Smith; Al Vance; Vic Pitts; Roy Scott; Billy Stonewall; Melvin Taylor.
Also see HARVEY & Seven Sounds
Also see TWISTIN' HARVEY
Also see VANCE, Al

SCALES, James
Singles: 7-inch
VERRO 4-8 65

SCALE-TONES
Singles: 78 rpm
JAY DEE 40-60 56
Singles: 7-inch
JAY DEE (810 "Everlasting Love") 75-125 56
Members: Tom Gardner; Cleveland Still; James Montgomery; James Miller; Don Archer.
Also see DUBS
Also see 5 WINGS
Also see MARVELS

SCALLYWAGS
(Skallywags)
Singles: 7-inch
SOLA (5 "Surfin' Mickey") 20-30 63

SCALYWAGS
Singles: 7-inch
APT 4-8 65

SCAM CITY WATER BOYS
Singles: 7-inch
ABC 4-8 67

SCAMBOOZIE
Singles: 7-inch
REPRISE 3-5 72

SCAMPS
Singles: 78 rpm
MODERN 15-25 47

SCAMPS
Singles: 78 rpm
PEACOCK 15-25 55
Singles: 7-inch
PEACOCK (1655 "Yes, My Baby") 35-55 55

SCAMPS
Singles: 7-inch
ARLAN 5-10 59
SCOUT 5-10 61
LPs: 10/12-inch
PROJECT (8002 "Teen Dance") 15-25 62

SCANDAL
Singles: 7-inch
PEPPER 5-8 67

SCANDAL
(Featuring Lee Genesis)
Singles: 7-inch
SAM (5019 "I Wanna Do It") 3-4 81

SCANDAL *P&R '82*
(Featuring Patty Smyth)
Singles: 12-inch
COLUMBIA 4-6 82-85
Singles: 7-inch
COLUMBIA 3-5 82-85
Picture Sleeves
COLUMBIA 3-5 83-85
EPs: 7-inch
COLUMBIA (8C8-39905 "Warrior") 10-15 82
(Picture disc.)
LPs: 10/12-inch
COLUMBIA 5-10 82-85
Also see SMYTH, Patty

SCANDLIN, Billy, & Embers
Singles: 7-inch
VIKING 10-15 59

SCARABEES
Singles: 7-inch
20TH FOX 4-8 64

SCARBROUGH, Bud
Singles: 7-inch
TOPPA 4-8 62

SCARBURY, Joey *P&R '71*
Singles: 7-inch
BELL 3-5 71-73
BIG TREE 3-5 73

COLUMBIA....3-5 77-79
ELEKTRA....3-5 81
LIONEL....3-5 71
PLAYBOY....3-5 74
RCA....3-4 84
REENA....4-6 68
Picture Sleeves
ELEKTRA....3-5 81
LPs: 10/12-inch
ELEKTRA....5-10 81

SCARECROW
Singles: 7-inch
DATE....4-8 68

SCARFS
Singles: 7-inch
ARC (745 "The Jerk Is the Thing") .. 5-10 64

SCARLET & BLACK LP '88
Singles: 7-inch
VIRGIN....3-4 88
Picture Sleeves
VIRGIN....3-4 88
LPs: 10/12-inch
VIRGIN....5-8 88
Members: Robin Hild; Sue West.

SCARLET COMBO
Singles: 7-inch
ZIN-A-SPIN....5-10 61

SCARLET HENCHMEN
Singles: 7-inch
NIGHT OWL (6835 "Ring Dreams")....10-20 68
NIGHT OWL (6913 "Crystal Palace")....10-20 69
Picture Sleeves
NIGHT OWL....15-25 68-69
Members: Carl Trieloff; Jim Johnson; James Gardner; John Schaller.
Also see HENCHMEN

SCARLETS
Singles: 7-inch
DOT (16004 "Stampede")....10-15 59
PRINCE (1207 "Stampede")....25-35 59
(First issue.)

SCARLETS
Singles: 7-inch
FURY (1036 "Truly Yours")....15-25 60

SCARLETS
("With Rhythm Accompaniment")
Singles: 78 rpm
RED ROBIN....50-100 54
Singles: 7-inch
EVENT (4287 "Dear One")....30-40 58
LOST NITE....4-8
OLDIES....4-6
RED ROBIN (128 "Dear One")...300-500 54
RED ROBIN (133 "Darling, I'm Yours")....300-500 54
RED ROBIN (135 "True Love")..300-500 55
RED ROBIN (138 "Kiss Me")....350-550 55
Members: Fred Parris; Nat Mosley; Silvester Hopkins; Al Denby; Bill Powers.
LPs: 10/12-inch
LOST-NITE (143 "Greatest Hits").... 8-12 70s
(Red vinyl.)
Also see FIVE SATINS
Also see 4 SEASONS / Scarlets

SCATT BROTHERS
Singles: 7-inch
CASABLANCA....3-5 80

SCATTERBRAIN LP '90
LPs: 10/12-inch
IN-EFFECT....5-8 90

SCAVENGERS
Singles: 7-inch
FENTON (987 "Curfew")....20-30 64
MOBILE FIDELITY (1005 "The Angels Listened In")....50-75 63
MOBILE FIDELITY (1212 "Devil's Reef")....15-25 64
STARS of HOLLYWOOD (1210 "Shotgun"/"Cream Puff")....20-30 63
STARS of HOLLYWOOD (1211 "Shotgun"/"Zip Code")....15-25 63
(1210 and 1211 have the same B-side track, but with different titles.)
STARS of HOLLYWOOD (1212 "Devil's Reef")....15-25 63

SCAVENGERS
Singles: 7-inch
SUEMI (4552 "Bogus")....10-20 65

SCENE
Singles: 7-inch
B.T. PUPPY....4-8 67

SCEPTERS
Singles: 7-inch
("All Night Long ")....5-10 60s
(No label name or selection number used.)
M.O.C....4-8 65
Member: John Matsik.

SCHAEFER, Freddy
Singles: 7-inch
KING....5-10 62

SCHAEFER, Hal, & His Orchestra
Singles: 7-inch
U.A. (130 "March of the Vikings")...... 4-8 58
Picture Sleeves
U.A. (130 "March of the Vikings")...15-25 58

SCHAEFFER, Big Bill
Singles: 7-inch
FOUR WINDS....4-8 61

SCHAFER, Kermit LP '58
Singles: 78 rpm
JUBILEE....8-12 56
Singles: 7-inch
JUBILEE (5258 "Rock Around the Blooper")....15-25 56
LPs: 10/12-inch
AUDIO FIDELITY....8-12 69
JUBILEE....10-20 58-63
KAPP....8-12 68-70
KING....10-15 64
MCA....5-10 74-77
Kermit Schafer has also released numerous comedy albums of "Bloopers," which we have not attempted to list. Their value is minimal, usually under $10.

SCHAFF, Murray
(With the Aristocrats)
Singles: 78 rpm
JOSIE (788 "Unfinished Rock")......10-15 56
Singles: 7-inch
JOSIE (788 "Unfinished Rock")......25-35 56

SCHAFFER, Janne
LPs: 10/12-inch
COLUMBIA....8-10 76

SCHAFFER, Norm C&W '88
Singles: 7-inch
DSP....3-4 88

SCHARMEERS / Jive Chords
Singles: 7-inch
VINTAGE....3-6 74

SCHEEREN, Frank
(With Joe Hintz & Orchestra)
Singles: 7-inch
STYLE (101 "I Got Trouble")....50-75 61

SCHELL, Tristen
Singles: 7-inch
CORAL....4-6 67

SCHEMATICS
Singles: 7-inch
VVV (001 "South of the Surf")....10-20 60s

SCHENKER, Michael, Group LP '80
Singles: 7-inch
CHRYSALIS....3-5 80-83
LPs: 10/12-inch
CHRYSALIS....5-10 80-83
Also see ALCATRAZZ
Also see McAULEY SCHENKER GROUP
Also see UFO

SCHENZEL, Roger, & Flav-o-rites
(Robin Lee)
Singles: 7-inch
PFAU ("We Are Meant to Be")....25-35 57
(Selection number not known.)
Also see LEE, Robin

SCHEREE C&W '79
Singles: 7-inch
COMPASS....3-5 79

SCHERRIE & SUSAYE
Singles: 7-inch
MOTOWN....3-5 79
LPs: 10/12-inch
MOTOWN....5-10 79
Member: Scherrie Payne
Also see PAYNE, Scherrie

SCHICKEL, Steve
Singles: 78 rpm
MERCURY....5-10 56
Singles: 7-inch
MERCURY....10-20 56

SCHIFRIN, Lalo LP '62
Singles: 12-inch
CTI....5-10 76
TABU....4-8 78-79
Singles: 7-inch
A&M....3-5 75
CTI....3-5 76-77
DOT....3-5 67
MCA....3-5 77-83
MGM....4-6 63-70
PABLO....3-5 77
PARAMOUNT....4-6 69
TABU....3-5 78-79
TETRAGRAMMATON....4-6 69
20TH FOX....3-5 74-75
U.A....3-5 70
VERVE....4-6 63-71
W.B....3-6 68-69
LPs: 10/12-inch
AUDIO FIDELITY....5-15 62-68
CTI....5-10 76-77
COLPIX....10-20 64
DOT (25852 "There's a Whole Lalo Schifrin Goin' On")....10-15 68
MCA (5000 series)....5-10 81
MGM....5-15 63-70
ROULETTE....10-15 62
TABU....5-10 79
TICO....10-20 60
VERVE (Except 8624)....10-20 63-69
Rockin' Records has dropped the many soundtrack albums by this artist. Publication of *The Official Price Guide to Movie/TV Soundtracks and Original Cast Albums*, containing over 8,000 show tune releases, allows us eliminate many lengthy sections of soundtrack LPs from this book—space which can now be devoted to more appropriate listings.

SCHILLER, Lawrence
(With Dr. Sidney Cohen)
LPs: 10/12-inch
CAPITOL....15-20 66-67

SCHILLING, Johnny, & Sherwoods
Singles: 7-inch
C&A (507 "King of the World")...100-150 63
(May also be credited to Little John & the Sherwoods.)
Also see LITTLE JOHN & SHERWOODS

SCHILLING, Nina D&D '84
Singles: 12-inch
MOBY DICK....4-6 84

SCHILLING, Peter P&R/D&D/LP '83
Singles: 12-inch
ELEKTRA....4-6 83
Singles: 7-inch
ELEKTRA....3-4 83-89
Picture Sleeves
ELEKTRA....3-4 89
LPs: 10/12-inch
ELEKTRA....5-10 83

SCHILT, Norman
Singles: 7-inch
TEXAS TORNADO....3-5 78

SCHLITZ, Don C&W '78
Singles: 7-inch
CAPITOL....3-5 78-79

SCHLOSS
LPs: 10/12-inch
OASIS....8-10 75

SCHMALTZ
Singles: 7-inch
DANCE-A-THON....4-8 79
LPs: 10/12-inch
DANCE-A-THON/HOTTRAX....5-10 81

SCHMIDLING, Tyrone
Singles: 7-inch
ANDEX (4022 "You're Gone")....150-200 58

SCHMIDT, Joe: see SCMIDT, Joe

SCHMIT, Timothy B. P&R '82
Singles: 7-inch
FULL MOON....3-5 82
MCA....3-4 87
Picture Sleeves
FULL MOON....3-5 82
MCA....3-4 87
LPs: 10/12-inch
ASYLUM....5-10 84
MCA....5-8 87
Also see EAGLES
Also see MARX, Richard
Also see POCO

SCHMITZ SISTERS
Singles: 7-inch
DORSET....4-8

SCHMUCKER, Paul C&W '78
Singles: 7-inch
STAR-FOX....3-5 78-79

SCHNEIDER, Fred, & Shake Society D&D '84
Singles: 12-inch
W.B....4-6 84
Singles: 7-inch
W.B....3-4 84

SCHNEIDER, Helen
Singles: 7-inch
WINDSONG....3-5 78
Picture Sleeves
WINDSONG....3-5 78
LPs: 10/12-inch
WINDSONG....5-8 77

SCHNEIDER, John C&W/P&R/LP '81
Singles: 7-inch
MCA....3-4 84-87
SCOTTI BROS....3-5 81-83
Picture Sleeves
MCA....3-4 84-87
SCOTTI BROS....3-5 81-83
LPs: 10/12-inch
MCA....5-8 84-87
SCOTTI BROS....5-10 81-83
Session: Waylon Jennings.
Also see JENNINGS, Waylon

SCHNEIDER, John, & Jill Michaels
Singles: 7-inch
SCOTTI BROS....3-4 83
Also see MICHAELS, Jill
Also see SCHNEIDER, John

SCIUTO, Tony
Singles: 7-inch
EPIC....3-4 80
LPs: 10/12-inch
EPIC (36152 "Island Nights")....5-10 80

SCHOCK, Harriet
Singles: 7-inch
20TH FOX....3-5 75

SCHOFIELD, Michael
Singles: 7-inch
WILSTONE....8-12

SCHOLARS
Singles: 78 rpm
CUE....10-15 56
DOT....5-10 56
Singles: 7-inch
CUE (7927 "What Did I Do Wrong")....20-30 56
CUE (7931 "Spin the Wheel")....20-30 56
(First issue.)
DOT (15498 "Spin the Wheel")....10-15 56
DOT (15519 "If You Listen with Your Heart")....10-15 56
PIC (026 "Women Drivers")....10-15 50s

SCHOLARS
Singles: 78 rpm
IMPERIAL....15-25 57
Singles: 7-inch
IMPERIAL (5449 "Beloved")....20-30 57
IMPERIAL (5459 "Eternally Yours")....20-30 57

SCHOLARS
Singles: 7-inch
RUBY RAY (1 "I Need Your Lovin' ")....20-30 60s

SCHOLARS / Perenials
Singles: 7-inch
RUBY RAY (2 "Please Please")...75-125 60s

SCHOLL, Danny
Singles: 78 rpm
NATIONAL....5-10 50
Singles: 7-inch
FORD....4-8 64
NATIONAL (9110 "Open Parachute")....10-20 50
SCHOLL....4-8

SCHON, Neal, & Jan Hammer LP '81
LPs: 10/12-inch
COLUMBIA....5-10 81-83
Also see HAGAR, SCHON, AARONSON, SHRIEVE
Also see HAMMER, Jan
Also see JOURNEY

SCHOOL BELLES
Singles: 7-inch
CREST....8-12 62
DOT....8-12 58
HANOVER....5-10 59

SCHOOL GIRLS
Singles: 7-inch
EXPRESS (712 "Guess We're Not in Love")....20-30 62

SCHOOLBOY CLEVE
(School Boy Cleve; Cleve White)
Singles: 78 rpm
FEATURE (3013 "She's Gone")....20-40 54
Singles: 7-inch
CHERRIE....4-6 74
FEATURE (3013 "She's Gone")....50-75 54

SCHOOLBOYS P&R/R&B '57
Singles: 78 rpm
OKEH....15-30 56-57
Singles: 7-inch
JUANITA (103 "Angel of Love")....75-100 58
OKEH (7076 "Please Say You Want Me")....25-35 56
(Purple label.)
OKEH (7076 "Please Say You Want Me")....10-20 57
(Yellow label.)
OKEH (7085 "Mary")....25-35 57
OKEH (7090 "Carol")....15-25 57
(Purple label.)
OKEH (7090 "Carol")....25-35 57
(White label. Promotional issue only.)
OKEH (7090 "Carol")....10-20 57
(Yellow label.)
Members: Les Martin; Jim Edwards; Roger Hayes; Jim McKay; Renaldo Gamble.
EPs: 7-inch
MAGIC CARPET....5-10
Also see CADILLACS
Also see KODOKS

SCHOOLBOYS
LPs: 10/12-inch
PALACE (777 "Beatle Mash")....35-45 64
(Also issued as by the Liverpool Kids.)
Also see LIVERPOOL KIDS

SCHOOLEY D LP '88
LPs: 10/12-inch
JIVE....5-8 88

SCHOOLHOUSE FOUR PLUS 2
Singles: 7-inch
WORLD ARTISTS....4-8 64

SCHOONERS
Singles: 7-inch
EMBER (1041 "Schooner Blues")..20-40 58
PEEK-A-BOO (106 "No Letter Today")....20-40 58
Also see ARMEN, Smokey, & Schooners

SCHORY, Dick LP '59
(Dick Schory's Percussion Pops Orchestra)
LPs: 10/12-inch
RCA....5-15 59-63

SCHRAIER, Don
Singles: 7-inch
ORBIT (510 "Pigtail")....15-25 58

SCHROECK, Artie
Singles: 7-inch
ABC....4-8 67
COLUMBIA....4-8 66
VERVE....4-8 67
LPs: 10/12-inch
VERVE....10-20 67

SCHROEDER, David
Singles
CONDOR CLASSIX (021 "I'm Looking for a Sex Partner")....8-12 87
(Barroom-shaped picture disc. 500 made.)
CONDOR CLASSIX (021 "I'm Looking for a Sex Partner")....10-15 87
(Rectangular picture disc. 100 made.)

SCHROEDER, Don
Singles: 7-inch
PHILIPS....4-8 62
SOUND STAGE 7....4-8 63

SCHROEDER, Gene, Trio
Singles: 78 rpm
BLACK & WHITE....10-20 44
Members: Gene Schroeder; Bob Casey; Joe Grauso.

SCHROEDER, John
Singles: 7-inch
CAMEO....4-8 66

SCHULTZ, Dave
Singles: 7-inch
ALL-PRO....3-5
Picture Sleeves
ALL-PRO....4-6

SCHULZE, Klaus
LPs: 10/12-inch
ISLAND....8-10 77

SCHUMACHER, Christine, & Supremes
Singles: 7-inch
MOTOWN ("Mother You, Smother You")....200-250 68
(In a radio contest, Christine won the chance to record with the Supremes – thus this disc.)
Also see SUPREMES

SCHUMANN, Walter P&R '53
(Voices of Walter Schumann)
Singles: 78 rpm
CAPITOL....3-5 52
RCA....3-5 53-56
Singles: 7-inch
CAPITOL....4-6 52
RCA....4-6 53-56
EPs: 7-inch
CAPITOL....5-10 52
RCA....5-10 53-56
LPs: 10/12-inch
CAPITOL....5-15 52
RCA....5-15 53-56

SCHURB, Duane
Singles: 7-inch
ENTERPRISE (1226 "Roly Poly")..35-45 59

SCHUTT, Dawn C&W '89
Singles: 7-inch
MASTER....3-4 89

SCHUUR, Diane LP '88
(With Jose Feliciano)
Singles: 7-inch
GRP (3016 "American Wedding Song")....3-4 85
(With insert.)
LPs: 10/12-inch
GRP....5-8 88-90
Also see FELICIANO, Jose

SCHUYLER, Thom C&W '83
Singles: 7-inch
CAPITOL....3-4 83
LPs: 10/12-inch
CAPITOL....5-8 83
Also see SCHUYLER, KNOBLOCH & OVERSTREET

SCHUYLER, KNOBLOCH & OVERSTREET C&W '86
(S-K-O)
Singles: 7-inch
MTM....3-4 86-88

SCHUYLER, KNOBLOCH & BICKHARDT C&W '87
Singles: 7-inch
MTM....3-4 86-87
Also see BICKHARDT, Craig
Also see SCHUYLER, Thom

SCHUYLER BROTHERS
Singles: 7-inch
SUNBEAM (110 "The Snake")....10-20 58

SCHWARZ, Brinsley
Singles: 7-inch
CAPITOL....3-5 70
U.A....3-5 72
LPs: 10/12-inch
CAPITOL (500 & 700 series)....10-20 70-71
CAPITOL (11000 series)....10-15 78
LIBERTY....5-10 81
U.A....8-12 72
Also see GOMM, Ian
Also see LOWE, Nick
Also see RUMOUR

SCHWARTZ, Bernie
Singles: 7-inch
W.B....4-8 60s
Also see ATELLO, Don

SCHWARTZ, Eddie P&R '81
Singles: 7-inch
ATCO....3-5 81-82
LPs: 10/12-inch
ATCO....5-10 82

SCHWARTZ, Phil, & Harold Wagner
Singles: 7-inch
DOCTOR-MY-EYES ("Interview with Joe P.C.O.") ... 5-8 77

SCHWARTZ, Stephen Michael
LPs: 10/12-inch
RCA ... 8-12 74

SCHWARTZ, Tonto
Singles: 7-inch
WYNNE ... 5-10 59

SCHWUMP
(Residents)
Singles: 7-inch
RALPH (0766 "Aphids in the Hall") ... 20-30 76
Picture Sleeves
RALPH (0766 "Aphids in the Hall") ... 40-60 76
Also see RESIDENTS

SCIENTISTS OF SOUL
Singles: 7-inch
KASHE ... 4-8 69

SCI-FIs
Singles: 7-inch
ERA ... 5-10 64
Also see TOWERS

SCIUTO, Tony
LPs: 10/12-inch
EPIC ... 5-8 80

SCMIDT, Joe, Trio
Singles: 7-inch
REM ... 4-6
(Label credits Joe "Scmidt," but also shows the name as "Schmidt.")
Members: Joe Schmidt; Dick LeBeau; Bruce Maher.

SCOFIELD, John
LPs: 10/12-inch
CAPITOL (27327 "Hand Jive") ... 8-10 90s

SCOOBIE & DOOBIE
Singles: 7-inch
CLIMAX (101 "Side Saddle") ... 5-10 59

SCOOP
Singles: 7-inch
ESSAR (7602 "Patty") ... 5-8 76

SCOOTER
Singles: 12-inch
PRELUDE ... 4-6 82

SCOOTERS
("Featuring Alexander Ames")
Singles: 78 rpm
DAWN ... 100-200 57
Singles: 7-inch
DAWN (224 "Someday We'll Meet Again") ... 300-400 57
ERA (1065 "Everybody's Got a Girl") ... 25-35 58
ERA (1072 "Everybody's Got a Girl") ... 15-25 58
Member: Alexander Ames.
Also see ROYALS

SCOOTERS
LPs: 10/12-inch
EMI AMERICA ... 5-10 80-81

SCORPIO & ASCENDANTS
Singles: 7-inch
GAMBLE ... 4-6 69

SCORPIO TUBE
Singles: 7-inch
VITA (001 "Yellow Listen") ... 15-25 67

SCORPION
LPs: 10/12-inch
TOWER (5171 "Scorpion") ... 30-40 69

SCORPIONS LP '79
Singles: 7-inch
MERCURY ... 3-4 79-91
RCA ... 3-5 74-80
Picture Sleeves
MERCURY ... 3-4 84-88
LPs: 10/12-inch
MERCURY ... 5-8 79-90
RCA ... 5-10 74-84
Members: Klaus Meine; Francis Bucholz; Matt Jabs; Herman Rarebell; Uli Roth; Rudolf Schenker.

SCOT
Singles: 7-inch
KAMMY ... 4-6 67

SCOT, Patricia
Singles: 78 rpm
TIFFANY ... 4-6 54
Singles: 7-inch
TIFFANY ... 5-10 54

SCOTCHTONES
Singles: 7-inch
RUSTONE (1402 "Do You Have the Right") ... 250-500 60

SCOTLAND YARDLEYS
Singles: 7-inch
SMASH ... 4-8 66

SCOTSMEN
Singles: 7-inch
PANORAMA (22 "Tuff Enough") ... 10-20 65

SCOTSMEN
Singles: 7-inch
SCOTTY (65 "Beer Bust Blues") ... 50-75
SCOTTY (1803 "Beer Bust Blues") ... 15-25 60s

SCOTT, Al "Mr Soul"
Singles: 7-inch
GENUINE ... 8-12

SCOTT, Albert
Singles: 7-inch
ACE ... 8-12 57
VIN ... 8-12 58

SCOTT, Allan
LPs: 10/12-inch
TOWER ... 10-12 69

SCOTT, Beverley, Trio
Singles: 78 rpm
MURRAY (503 "Shakin' the Boogie") ... 50-100 48
Members: Beverley Scott; Louis Jackson; Ernest McCoy.

SCOTT, Billy P&R '58
Singles: 78 rpm
CAMEO ... 10-20 57
Singles: 7-inch
CAMEO ... 10-20 57-58
EVEREST ... 5-10 59

SCOTT, Billy
(With the Georgia Prophets; with Prophets)
Singles: 7-inch
CADDY ... 3-5 82
CAROLINA ... 3-5 89
LAMON ... 3-5 83-89
3-P ... 4-6 78
LPs: 10/12-inch
FLIP SIDE ... 5-10 83
LAMON ... 5-10 88-89
Also see GEORGIA PROPHETS
Also see PROPHETS
Also see THREE PROPHETS

SCOTT, Bob
Singles: 7-inch
MILO ... 10-15 59
REF (100 "Moon Up Above") ... 15-25 62
REF (107 "Fast Suds") ... 15-25 62

SCOTT, Bobby P&R '56
Singles: 78 rpm
ABC-PAR ... 5-10 56
Singles: 7-inch
ABC ... 3-5 73
ABC-PAR ... 10-15 56

SCOTT, Bobby
Singles: 7-inch
MERCURY ... 4-8 62-63
LPs: 10/12-inch
MERCURY ... 15-20 63

SCOTT, Bobby
Singles: 7-inch
COLUMBIA ... 3-5 69
VERVE (2007 "Danny Boy") ... 5-10
LPs: 10/12-inch
COLUMBIA ... 5-15

SCOTT, Calvin
Singles: 7-inch
ATCO (6696 "Sonny Boy") ... 5-10 69
ATCO (6729 "Cry Like a Baby") ... 5-10 69
STAX ... 4-8 71-72
LPs: 10/12-inch
STAX ... 8-12 72
Note: Though not yet confirmed, many feel this is the same singer as Calvin Leavy. Readers?
Also see LEAVY, Calvin

SCOTT, Cheyenne
Singles: 7-inch
ALTO ... 4-8 63

SCOTT, Christopher LP '69
(Sir Christopher Scott)
LPs: 10/12-inch
DECCA ... 5-10 69-70
MCA ... 5-10 73

SCOTT, Cindy
Singles: 7-inch
VEEP (1253 "I Love You Baby") ... 20-30 67
VEEP (1268 "Time Can Change a Love") ... 10-20 67

SCOTT, Clifford
(With the 6 Stars)
Singles: 7-inch
AURA (409 "Beach Bunny") ... 4-8 64
KING ... 4-8 62-64
OMEGA (501/2 "Beach Bunny") ... 5-10 64
LPs: 10/12-inch
WORLD PACIFIC (1811 "Clifford Scott Plays the Big Ones") ... 15-25 63
(Black vinyl.)
WORLD PACIFIC (1811 "Clifford Scott Plays the Big Ones") ... 30-40 63
(Colored vinyl.)
WORLD PACIFIC (1825 "Lavender Sax") ... 35-45 63
Also see DOGGETT, Bill

SCOTT, Colin
LPs: 10/12-inch
IMPORT ... 8-10

SCOTT, Dean
Singles: 7-inch
SCEPTER ... 4-8 66

SCOTT, Earl C&W '62
Singles: 7-inch
DECCA ... 4-6 65-68
KAPP ... 4-8 62
MERCURY ... 4-8 63-64

SCOTT, Esther Mae
LPs: 10/12-inch
BOMP ... 15-20

SCOTT, Francine
Singles: 7-inch
CHATTAHOOCHEE ... 4-8 64

SCOTT, Freddie P&R/R&B '63
(With the Symphonics; with Shytone 5 Orchestra; with Teddy McRae Orchestra)
Singles: 7-inch
ABC ... 3-5 74
BOW (307 "Tell Them for Me") ... 5-10
COLPIX ... 5-10 63-64
COLUMBIA ... 5-15 64-65
ELEPHANT V LTD. ... 4-6
ENRICA (1002 "A Blessing to You") ... 5-8
ERIC ... 3-5 68
J&S (1761 "Turn Lamps Down Low") ... 20-30 56
JOY ... 10-15 61-63
MAINSTREAM (5562 "You're So Hard to Forget") ... 3-6 74
P.I.P. ... 3-5 72
PROBE ... 4-6 70
SHOUT ... 4-8 66-71
SOLID GOLD ... 3-5 73
VANGUARD ... 3-5 71
LPs: 10/12-inch
COLPIX (CP-461 "Freddie Scott Sings") ... 40-80 64
(Gold label. Monaural.)
COLPIX (SCP-461 "Freddie Scott Sings") ... 50-100 64
(Gold label. Stereo.)
COLPIX (CP-461 "Freddie Scott Sings") ... 30-40 64
(Blue label.)
COLPIX (SCP-461 "Freddie Scott Sings") ... 35-50 64
(Blue label.)
COLUMBIA (2258 "Everything I Have Is Yours") ... 10-20 64
(Monaural.)
COLUMBIA (2660 "Lonely Man") ... 10-20 67
(Monaural.)
COLUMBIA (9058 "Everything I Have Is Yours") ... 10-20 64
(Stereo.)
COLUMBIA (9460 "Lonely Man") ... 10-20 67
(Stereo.)
PROBE (451 "I Shall Be Released") ... 10-15 70
SHOUT (501 "Are You Lonely for Me") ... 10-20 67
Also see CHIMES
Also see SYMPHONICS

SCOTT, Freddy, & Four Steps
Singles: 7-inch
MARLIN (16004 "Same Old Beat") ... 5-10 66

SCOTT, Gary
Singles: 7-inch
TITANIC (5010 "Beverly") ... 50-100 63

SCOTT, George
Singles: 7-inch
FAIRLANE ... 5-8 61
MARGO ... 5-8 61

SCOTT, Glen
Singles: 7-inch
RUBY (200 "Katy Bar the Door") ... 25-35 57
SHERMAN (930 "The Show Must Go On") ... 15-25

SCOTT, Gloria R&B '74
Singles: 7-inch
CASABLANCA ... 3-5 74-75

SCOTT, Gloria, & Tonettes
Singles: 7-inch
W.B. ... 5-10 64

SCOTT, Greg, & Embers
Singles: 7-inch
DELOSS (101 "Cheryl") ... 25-35 60s
RIVERA (4911 "Movin', Twistin' Around") ... 25-35 60s
SOMA (1162 "When I Say Goodbye") ... 40-60 60s
Also see SCOTT, Mumbles, & Esquires

SCOTT, Isaac
LPs: 10/12-inch
MUSIC IS MEDICINE ... 10-20

SCOTT, J., & Actions
Singles: 7-inch
MERCURY ... 4-8 66

SCOTT, Jack P&R/R&B '58
(With the Chantones)
Singles: 78 rpm
ABC-PAR ... 50-100 57
SPARTON ... 50-100 57
Singles: 7-inch
ABC (10843 "Before the Bird Flies") ... 5-10 66
ABC-PAR (9818 "Baby, She's Gone") ... 50-100 57
(Black label.)
ABC-PAR (9818 "Baby, She's Gone") ... 50-75 57
(White label. Promotional issue only.)
ABC-PAR (9860 "Two Timin' Woman") ... 50-100 57
(Black label.)
ABC-PAR (9860 "Two Timin' Woman") ... 50-75 57
(White label. Promotional issue only.)
CAPITOL (4554 "A Little Feeling") ... 15-25 61
CAPITOL (4597 "My Dream Come True") ... 15-25 61
CAPITOL (4637 "Steps 1 & 2") ... 15-25 61
CAPITOL (4689 "Cry Cry Cry") ... 15-25 62
CAPITOL (4738 "The Part Where I Cry") ... 15-25 62
CAPITOL (4796 "I Can't Hold Your Letters") ... 15-25 62
CAPITOL (4855 "If Only") ... 15-25 62
CAPITOL (4903 "Laugh and the World Laughs with You") ... 15-25 63
CAPITOL (4955 "All I See Is Blue") ... 15-25 63
CAPITOL (6077 "What in the World's Come over You") ... 4-8 65
(Starline Series.)
CARLTON (462 "My True Love") ... 15-25 58
CARLTON (483 "With Your Love") 15-25 58
CARLTON (493 "Goodbye Baby") 15-25 58
CARLTON (504 "I Never Felt Like This") ... 10-20 59
(Beige label.)
CARLTON (504 "I Never Felt Like This") ... 25-35 59
(Red label. Promotional issue only.)
CARLTON (514 "The Way I Walk") ... 10-20 59
CARLTON (519 "There Comes a Time") ... 10-20 59
(Monaural.)
CARLTON (ST-519 "There Comes a Time") ... 25-50 59
(Stereo.)
COLLECTABLES ... 3-4 80s
CURB (76820 "Cooper, Cagney & Gable") ... 3-5 90
DOT ... 3-5 73
ERIC ... 3-4 70s
GRT ... 3-5 70
GROOVE (0027 "There's Trouble Brewin' ") ... 10-15 63
GROOVE (0031 "I Knew You First") ... 5-10 64
GROOVE (0037 "Wiggle on Out") 10-15 64
GROOVE (0042 "Thou Shalt Not Steal") ... 10-15 64
GROOVE (0049 "Flakey John") ... 10-15 64
GUARANTEED (209 "What Am I Living For") ... 10-20 60
GUARANTEED (211 "Go Wild Little Sadie") ... 15-25 60
JUBILEE ... 5-10 67
RCA (8505 "I Don't Believe in Tea Leaves") ... 8-12 65
RCA (8685 "Looking for Linda") ... 8-12 65
RCA (8724 "Don't Hush the Laughter") ... 8-12 65
SPARTON (348 "Baby, She's Gone") ... 50-75 57
(Canadian.)
TOP RANK (2028 "What in the World's Come Over You") ... 15-25 60
TOP RANK (2041 "Burning Bridges") ... 15-25 60
(Monaural.)
TOP RANK (2041 "Burning Bridges") ... 35-55 60
(Stereo.)
TOP RANK (2055 "It Only Happened Yesterday") ... 15-25 60
TOP RANK (2075 "Patsy") ... 15-25 60
TOP RANK (2093 "Is There Something on Your Mind") ... 15-25 60
Picture Sleeves
CAPITOL (4554 "A Little Feeling") 25-35 61
CAPITOL (4597 "My Dream Come True") ... 25-35 61
CAPITOL (4637 "Steps 1 & 2") ... 25-35 61
CAPITOL (4689 "Cry Cry Cry") ... 25-35 62
CAPITOL (4738 "The Part Where I Cry") ... 25-35 62
CARLTON (483 "With Your Love") 25-35 58
CARLTON (493 "Goodbye Baby") 25-35 58
TOP RANK (2041 "Burning Bridges") ... 25-35 60
TOP RANK (2093 "Is There Something on Your Mind") ... 25-35 60
EPs: 7-inch
CARLTON (1070 "Jack Scott") ... 50-100 58
CARLTON (1071 "Presenting Jack Scott") ... 50-100 58
CARLTON (1072 "Jack Scott Sings") ... 50-100 59
TOP RANK (1001 "Jack Scott") ... 50-100 60
LPs: 10/12-inch
CAPITOL (2035 "Burning Bridges") ... 100-125 64
CAPITOL (8-2035 "Burning Bridges") ... 100-125 64
(Capitol Record Club issue.)
CARLTON (LP-107 "Jack Scott") ... 100-150 58
(Monaural.)
CARLTON (STLP-12 107 "Jack Scott") ... 150-200 58
(Stereo.)
CARLTON (LP-122 "What Am I Living For") ... 100-200 60
(Monaural.)
CARLTON (STLP-12 122 "What Am I Living For") ... 200-300 60
(Stereo.)
JADE ... 10-15
PONIE ... 8-10 74-77
SESAC (4201 "Soul Stirring") ... 75-100 59
TOP RANK (348 "The Spirit Moves Me") ... 75-125 60
TOP RANK (319 "I Remember Hank Williams") ... 75-125 60
(Monaural.)
TOP RANK (619 "I Remember Hank Williams") ... 100-150 60
(Stereo.)
TOP RANK (326 "What in the World's Come Over You") ... 75-125 61
(Monaural.)
TOP RANK (626 "What in the World's Come Over You") ... 100-150 61
(Stereo.)
Also see CHANTONES

SCOTT, Jay & Tommy
Singles: 7-inch
FIDELITY (4060 "Angela") ... 15-25 63

SCOTT, Jeffrey
Singles: 7-inch
SCOTTOWN (1001 "Sooner Football, 1975") ... 4-8 75

SCOTT, Jimmy
(Little Jimmy Scott)
Singles: 78 rpm
CORAL ... 5-10 52
KING ... 5-10 57
ROOST ... 5-10 50-51
SAVOY ... 5-10 55
Singles: 7-inch
ANTONIO ... 8-12
BRUNSWICK (84000 "Something of a Fool") ... 10-15 52
CORAL (60650 "Wheel of Fortune") ... 10-20 52
CORAL (60668 "They Saw You Cry") ... 10-20 52
CORAL (60825 "You Never Miss the Water") ... 10-15 52
EARWAX (776 "Love Language") ... 4-6
EASTBOUND ... 8-12
KING (5086 thru 5201) ... 10-15 57-59
KING (5800 series) ... 4-8 64
ROOST (600 series) ... 10-20 53-53
SAVOY (1100 series) ... 10-15 55-56
SAVOY (1500 series) ... 5-10 61
SHARP (100 "I'm Afraid the Masquerade Is Over") ... 10-20 60
SHARP (109 "An Evening in Paradise") ... 10-20 60
LPs: 10/12-inch
SAVOY (1100 series) ... 5-10
SAVOY (12027 "Very Truly Yours") ... 50-75 55
SAVOY (12150 "Fabulous Songs") ... 25-40 61
SAVOY (12300 "Soul of Little Jimmy Scott") ... 10-20 69
SAVOY (14003 "If You Only Knew") ... 20-30 58
TANGERINE ... 15-20 63

SCOTT, Joan
Singles: 78 rpm
IMPERIAL ... 50-100 54
Singles: 7-inch
IMPERIAL (5328 "My Wedding Day") ... 150-250 54

SCOTT, Joe
Singles: 7-inch
PEACOCK ... 5-10 62

SCOTT, Joel
Singles: 7-inch
PHILLES ... 10-15 62

SCOTT, John
Singles: 7-inch
ABC ... 4-8 68

SCOTT, Judy P&R '57
Singles: 78 rpm
DECCA ... 5-10 57
Singles: 7-inch
CAPITOL ... 4-8 60
DECCA ... 5-10 57-59
EMBER ... 4-8 64
TOP RANK ... 4-8 59

SCOTT, Ken
Singles: 7-inch
K.E.Y. ... 3-5 78

SCOTT, Kurtis
Singles: 7-inch
MARKY HO ... 3-6 75
SURE SHOT ... 4-8 66

SCOTT, Lang C&W '84
Singles: 7-inch
MCA ... 3-4 84

SCOTT, Lannie, Trio
(Lonnie Scott)
Singles: 78 rpm
SAVOY ... 10-20 46

SCOTT, Lee, & Windsors
Singles: 7-inch
BACK BEAT (506 "My Gloria") ... 4000-6000 58
(Possibly on promo only. Commercial copies not yet known to exist.)

SCOTT, Linda P&R/R&B '61
Singles: 7-inch
CANADIAN AMERICAN ... 10-20 61-62
CONGRESS ... 8-15 62-64
ERIC ... 3-4 70s
KAPP ... 5-10 64-66
RCA ... 4-8 68
EPs: 7-inch
CONGRESS (1005 "Starlight Starbright") ... 25-35 62
CONGRESS (3001 "Linda Scott") ... 25-35 62
(Promotional issue only. Issued with picture insert, but not with cover.)

LPs: 10/12-inch
CANADIAN AMERICAN (CALP-1005 "Starlight Starbright") ... 35-55 61
(Monaural.)
CANADIAN AMERICAN (SCALP-1005 "Starlight Starbright") ... 50-75 61
(Stereo.)
CANADIAN AMERICAN (CALP-1007 "Great Scott") ... 35-45 62
(Monaural.)
CANADIAN AMERICAN (SCALP-1007 "Great Scott") ... 40-50 62
(Stereo.)
CONGRESS (3001 "Linda") ... 25-35 62
KAPP (3424 "Hey Look at Me Now") ... 25-35 65

SCOTT, Linda Gaye
Singles: 7-inch
APOGEE ... 4-8 64

SCOTT, Little Jimmy: see SCOTT, Jimmy

SCOTT, Little Rena
Singles: 7-inch
BLACK ROCK ... 4-8

SCOTT, Lizabeth
LPs: 10/12-inch
VIK (1130 "Lizabeth") ... 20-30 57

SCOTT, Lori
Singles: 7-inch
ASCOT ... 4-8 63

SCOTT, Mabel R&B '48
Singles: 78 rpm
BRUNSWICK ... 5-10 52
CORAL ... 5-10 51-52
EXCELSIOR ... 8-12 47-48
EXCLUSIVE ... 8-12 48
FESTIVAL ... 5-10 55
HOLLYWOOD ... 5-10 54
HUB ... 10-15 46
KING ... 5-10 50-51
PARROT ... 15-25 53
Singles: 7-inch
BRUNSWICK (84001 "Wailin' Daddy") ... 15-25 52
CORAL ... 15-25 51-52
FESTIVAL ... 15-25 55
HOLLYWOOD ... 15-25 54
PARROT (780 "Mr. Fine") ... 20-30 53
(Black vinyl.)
PARROT (780 "Mr. Fine") ... 50-75 53
(Colored vinyl.)
PARROT (794 "Fool Burro") ... 20-30 53
Also see BROWN, Charles

SCOTT, Marilyn
(With Johnny Otis & His Orchestra)
Singles: 78 rpm
REGENT ... 15-25 51
Also see OTIS, Johnny

SCOTT, Marilyn P&R '77
Singles: 7-inch
BIG TREE ... 3-5 77
MERCURY ... 3-4 83-85
LPs: 10/12-inch
ATCO ... 5-10 79
MERCURY ... 5-8 83

SCOTT, Mark
(Mark Scott Teens)
Singles: 7-inch
CHALLENGE ... 4-8 62
DCP ... 4-8 64
T.S.M. ... 3-6 68

SCOTT, Mark, & Dicky Treadway
Singles: 7-inch
T.S.M. ... 3-6 68
Also see SCOTT, Mark

SCOTT, Maureen
Singles: 7-inch
VISTA ... 4-8 63

SCOTT, Mike
Singles: 7-inch
OMEGA ... 5-10 59

SCOTT, Millie R&B '86
(Mildred Scott)
Singles: 7-inch
4TH & BROADWAY ... 3-4 86-87

SCOTT, Moody
Singles: 7-inch
SOUND STAGE 7 (2647 "A Man in Need") ... 4-6 69

SCOTT, Mumbles, & Esquires
Singles: 7-inch
APPLAUSE (1005 "Searchin'") ... 40-60 64
Also see SCOTT, Greg, & Embers

SCOTT, Neal P&R '61
(With the Concords; Neil Scott; Neil Bogart)
Singles: 7-inch
CAMEO ... 5-10 67
CLOWN ... 10-15 60
COMET ... 10-15 62
HERALD ... 10-15 63
PORTRAIT ... 8-12 61-62
Also see BECK, BOGART & APPICE
Also see CONCORDS
Also see JERRY & JEFF
Also see ROBERTS, Wayne

SCOTT, Peggy
Singles: 7-inch
SSS INT'L ... 4-8 69

SCOTT, Peggy, & Jo Jo Benson P&R/R&B '68
Singles: 7-inch
ATCO ... 4-8 71
SSS INT'L ... 4-8 68-69
SUN ... 3-5 70s
LPs: 10/12-inch
AVI ... 5-10 84
SSS INT'L ... 10-15 69
Also see BENSON, Jo Jo
Also see SCOTT, Peggy

SCOTT, Ramblin' Tommy: see SCOTT, Tommy

SCOTT, Ray
(With the Demens; with Scottsmen)
Singles: 7-inch
ANTLER (1104 "Let's Be Friends") ... 30-40 59
DECCA (32068 "Right Now") ... 10-20 66
ERWIN (700 "Boppin' Wigwam Willie") ... 100-200 57
GOLDBAND ... 5-10 61
RAN DEE ... 5-10 62
SATELLITE (104 "You Drive Me Crazy") ... 250-350 59
STOMPER TIME (1161 "Boy Meets Girl") ... 25-50 61
TRIESS ... 10-15 60

SCOTT, Raymond
Singles: 7-inch
TOP RANK (2049 "Twilight Zone") ... 10-15 59

SCOTT, Rena R&B '79
Singles: 7-inch
BUDDAH ... 3-5 79
EPIC ... 3-5 72-74
SEDONA ... 3-4 88

SCOTT, Rhoda, Trio
Singles: 7-inch
SCOOP (1201 "Rhapsody in Blue") 5-10

SCOTT, Ricky
Singles: 7-inch
CUB ... 5-10 60
X-CLUSIVE (1001 "I Didn't Mean It") ... 50-75 60

SCOTT, Robby
Singles: 7-inch
SUNNYSIDE ... 5-10

SCOTT, Rock Master, & Dynamic 3
Singles: 12-inch
PROFILE ... 4-6 83

SCOTT, Rodney
Singles: 7-inch
CANON (225 "Granny Went Rockin' ") ... 100-150 61
CANON (231 "You're So Square") ... 100-150 61
MR. PEEKE (119 "You're So Square") ... 50-75 62
MR. PEEKE (126 "That's The Way It Goes") ... 15-25 63

SCOTT, Sam
Singles: 7-inch
OKEH ... 4-8 66

SCOTT, Sandy
Singles: 7-inch
CHOICE (5605 "Mister Big") ... 50-75 57
CHOICE (5606 "Shake It Up") ... 50-75 57
SAMSH (1927 "Bridle Path") ... 8-10 64

SCOTT, Sharon
Singles: 7-inch
RCA ... 5-10 66

SCOTT, Seaphus, & Five Masqueraders
(With the Billy Gale Orchestra)
Singles: 7-inch
JOYCE (303 "Summer Sunrise") ... 500-750 58

SCOTT, Sherman
(With the Vails)
Singles: 7-inch
FREEDOM ... 10-15 59
Also see VAILS

SCOTT, Sherree
Singles: 7-inch
ROBBINS (101 "Whole Lotta Shakin'") ... 100-150 59
ROCKET (1036 "Fascinating Baby") ... 150-200 59
(With photo insert.)
ROCKET (1036 "Fascinating Baby") ... 100-150 59
(Without photo insert.)

SCOTT, Shirley J.
Singles: 7-inch
STEPHANYE (333 "Goose Pimples") ... 20-30 60s

SCOTT, Simon
Singles: 7-inch
IMPERIAL ... 8-12 64-65

SCOTT, Steve
(Steven Scott)
Singles: 7-inch
JARO ... 4-8 59
20TH FOX ... 4-8 61

SCOTT, Sylvester
Singles: 78 rpm
JUKE BOX ... 15-25 46

SCOTT, Terry
Singles: 7-inch
VALIANT ... 4-8 62

SCOTT, Tina
Singles: 7-inch
DOT ... 4-8 59
MERCURY ... 4-8 59

SCOTT, Tom
Singles: 7-inch
HEP (2140 "Record Hop") ... 250-350 58

SCOTT, Tom R&B/LP '74
(With the L.A. Express; with California Dreamers)
Singles: 12-inch
SIRE ... 4-6 83
Singles: 7-inch
A&M ... 3-5 72
ATLANTIC ... 3-5 83
COLUMBIA ... 3-5 79
IMPULSE ... 4-6 68
ODE ... 3-5 74-79
SIRE ... 3-4 83
LPs: 10/12-inch
COLUMBIA ... 5-10 78-81
EPIC/ODE ... 5-8 84
IMPULSE ... 20-30 68
ODE ... 8-10 74-77
MUSICIAN ... 5-10 82
RCA ... 5-10 81
Also see CLAYTON, Merry
Also see HARRISON, George
Also see L.A. EXPRESS

SCOTT, Tommy
(Ramblin' Tommy Scott)
Singles: 78 rpm
FEDERAL (Except 10003) ... 10-15 51
FEDERAL (10003 "Rockin' and Rollin' ") ... 30-50 51
KING ... 15-25 52
Singles: 7-inch
FEDERAL (Except 10003) ... 15-25 51
FEDERAL (10003 "Rockin' and Rollin' ") ... 50-100 51
KING (1129 "What Do You Know") ... 30-50 52

SCOTT, Troy, & Sultans
Singles: 7-inch
COUNSEL ... 10-15 62

SCOTT, Walt
Singles: 7-inch
RUBY (240 "One Life to Live") ... 50-75 57

SCOTT, Walter
(With the Kapers)
Singles: 7-inch
EAGLE (1003 "On the Way Out") ... 15-25 58
IVANHOE (5018 "I Want to Thank You") ... 10-15 65
MUSICLAND U.S.A. ... 5-15 66-67
PZAZZ ... 4-8 69
VANESSA ... 3-6 74
WHITE WHALE ... 10-20 67
LPs: 10/12-inch
MUSICLAND U.S.A. ... 15-25 67
WHITE WHALE ... 15-20 70
Also see KUBAN, Bob

SCOTT & SHELLEY
Singles: 7-inch
COLUMBIA (43586 "Coolin' It") ... 10-20 66

SCOTT BROTHERS
Singles: 7-inch
COMET ... 8-12 63
FTP ... 5-10 61
FABOR ... 4-8 63
N.Y. SKYLINE ... 10-15 59-60
PARKWAY ... 10-15 62
PIK ... 5-10 60s
RIBBON ... 10-15 60
SCOLARON (100 "Teenage Lovers") ... 10-15 60s
SMASH ... 4-8 67
SKYLINE (502 "Part of You") ... 20-30
ZACHRON ... 5-10

SCOTT BROTHERS ORCHESTRA
Singles: 7-inch
TODDLIN' TOWN ... 8-12 60s

SCOTT-HERON, Gil R&B '78
(With Pretty Purdie & Playboys)
Singles: 7-inch
ARISTA ... 3-5 75-84
FLYING DUTCHMAN ... 3-5 71-74
LPs: 10/12-inch
ARISTA ... 6-12 75-84
FLYING DUTCHMAN (100 thru 0600 series) ... 8-15 71-74
FLYING DUTCHMAN (3800 series) ... 5-8 80

SCOTT-HERON, Gil, & Brian Jackson P&R/LP '75
Singles: 7-inch
ARISTA ... 3-5 75-80
LPs: 10/12-inch
ARISTA ... 6-12 75-80
STRATA-EAST ... 8-15 74
Also see SCOTT-HERON, Gil

SCOTTI, Michelle
Singles: 7-inch
ABC ... 4-8 66
PHILIPS ... 4-8 64-65

SCOTTI, Toni
Singles: 7-inch
20TH FOX ... 4-8 65
WORLD PACIFIC ... 4-8 66

SCOTTIES
Singles: 7-inch
SCOTTIE (1305 "Let Me Love You Tonight") ... 25-35 59

SCOTTY & BOBO WITH THE MASTERTONES
Singles: 7-inch
BAND BOX ... 5-10 60
Also see TAYLOR, Elaine, & Mastertones

SCOUNDRELS
Singles: 7-inch
ABC ... 4-8 66-67
VERVE ... 4-8 66

SCOUTS
Singles: 7-inch
HI-OLDIES (419 "Custer's Stomp") ... 10-15 60s
RENDEZVOUS ... 5-10 62

SCRAMBLERS
Singles: 7-inch
ARVEE ... 10-20 65
DEL-FI (4237 "Beatles Walk") ... 10-20 64
LPs: 10/12-inch
CROWN ... 15-25 64
WYNCOTE ... 15-25 64

SCRAPING FOETUS OFF THE WHEEL
LPs: 10/12-inch
PVC ... 5-10

SCRATCH BAND
LPs: 10/12-inch
BIG SOUND ... 5-10 77-86
RESCUE ... 5-10 79
Members: Christine Ohlman; Robert Orsi; Paul J. Ossola; Tom MacGregor; Mickey Curry; G.E. Smith.

SCRATCH BAND
LPs: 10/12-inch
MCA ... 5-10 82
Member: Danny Flowers.

SCRATCH BONGOWAX
Singles: 7-inch
DIONYSUS (74530 "Pallbearing") ... 3-4 91
(Green marble vinyl.)
Picture Sleeves
DIONYSUS (74530 "Pallbearing") ... 3-4 91
Members: Craig Weatherwax; Robert Armstrong; Jim McDowell; Susan Mathewson; Aaron Jenson.

SCREAMERS
Singles: 7-inch
KAY BANK (1519 "I Dig") ... 100-200
Also see VELAIRES

SCREAMIN' BLUE MESSIAHS LP '88
LPs: 10/12-inch
ELEKTRA ... 5-8 87

SCREAMIN' LORD JIM & PICADILLY SQUARES
Singles: 7-inch
CONTINENTAL LTD ... 10-12 60s

SCREAMIN' SIRENS
LPs: 10/12-inch
ENIGMA ... 8-10 84

SCREAMING GYPSY BANDITS
LPs: 10/12-inch
BRBQ (004 "The Dancer Inside You") ... 25-35 74
BRBQ (22185 "In the Eye") ... 40-50 73
Members: Tina Lane; Mark Bingham; Bruce Anderson; Bob Lucas.

SCREAMING TREES
LPs: 10/12-inch
SST ... 5-8 87
VELVETONE ... 5-10 86
Members: Mark Lanegan; Gary Lee Conner; Van Conner; Mark Pickerel.
Also see LANEGAN, Mark

SCREAMING WILDMAN
Singles: 7-inch
U.S.A. ... 5-8 67
Also see BONAFEDE, Carl

SCREAMS
Singles: 7-inch
INFINITY ... 3-5 79
LPs: 10/12-inch
INFINITY ... 5-10 79

SCREEAGH
Singles: 7-inch
ASTRA ... 10-15 63

SCREEN, Jeanie
Singles: 7-inch
JOSIE ... 4-8 65

SCREEN TEST
Singles: 7-inch
NORTHSIDE ... 3-5 82

SCREWBALLS
Singles: 7-inch
COLUMBIA ... 5-10 61

SCRITTI POLITTI D&D '84
Singles: 12-inch
W.B. ... 4-6 84-86
Singles: 7-inch
W.B. ... 3-4 84-88
Picture Sleeves
W.B. ... 3-4 85-88
LPs: 10/12-inch
W.B. ... 5-8 84-86

SCRITTI POLITTI & ROGER P&R '88
Singles: 7-inch
W.B. ... 3-4 88
Picture Sleeves
W.B. ... 3-4 88
Also see ROGER
Also see SCRITTI POLITTI

SCROUNGER
LPs: 10/12-inch
ANCHOR ... 8-10 77

SCRUBBALOE CAINE
LPs: 10/12-inch
RCA ... 8-12 73

SCRUFFS
LPs: 10/12-inch
POWER PLAY ... 8-10 77

SCRUFFY THE CAT LP '88
Singles: 12-inch
RELATIVITY ... 4-6 87
LPs: 10/12-inch
RELATIVITY ... 5-8 88

SCRUGG
Singles: 7-inch
PHILIPS ... 3-6 69

SCRUGGS, Earl C&W '70
(Earl Scruggs Revue)
Singles: 7-inch
COLUMBIA ... 3-5 70-83
LPs: 10/12-inch
COLUMBIA ... 5-10 73-83
Session: Waylon Jennings.
Also see FLATT, Lester, & Earl Scruggs
Also see HALL, Tom T., & Earl Scruggs
Also see JENNINGS, Waylon
Also see SKAGGS, Ricky

SCRUGGS, Faye: see ADAMS, Faye

SCUBA CROWNS
Singles: 7-inch
CHALLENGE ... 10-15 63

SCURVY KNAVES
Singles: 7-inch
TWELVE HANDS ("Gypsy Baby") ... 15-25 66
(Selection number not known.)

SCUZZIES
Singles: 7-inch
CRS ... 5-10 64

SEA, Johnny C&W '59
(Johnny Seay)
Singles: 7-inch
CAPITOL ... 4-8 61
COLUMBIA ... 3-5 67-69
NRC ... 5-10 59-60
PHILIPS ... 4-6 64-65
VIKING ... 3-5 70-71
W.B. ... 4-6 66-67
Picture Sleeves
COLUMBIA ... 3-5 68
LPs: 10/12-inch
GUEST STAR ... 8-12 66
PHILIPS ... 10-15 64-65
PICKWICK/HILLTOP ... 8-12 65
W.B. ... 10-20 66

SEA DOG
(Seadog)
Singles: 7-inch
HAPPY TIGER ... 3-5 71
SCEPTER ... 3-5 73
LPs: 10/12-inch
BUDDAH ... 8-12 72

SEA DOGS
Singles: 7-inch
TAPISTRY ... 3-6 70

SEA HAGS LP '89
LPs: 10/12-inch
CHRYSALIS ... 5-8 89

SEA LARKS
Singles: 7-inch
JOLT (333 "Christmas on the Prairie") ... 10-15 50s

SEA LEVEL LP '77
Singles: 7-inch
ARISTA ... 3-5 80
CAPRICORN ... 3-5 77-79
LPs: 10/12-inch
ARISTA ... 5-10 80
CAPRICORN ... 5-10 77-80
Also see ALLMAN BROTHERS BAND

SEA SHELLS
Singles: 7-inch
GOLIATH (1357 "Love Those Beach Boys") ... 15-25 64
JUBILEE (5587 "Hit the Surf") ... 8-12 67
VILLAGE (1000 "Quiet Home") ... 40-60

SEABURY, Levi
Singles: 7-inch
BLUES BOYS KINGDOM (101 "Boogie Beat") ... 100-125 57

SEACRIST, Eddie
Singles: 7-inch
K&C ... 10-15 59

SEA-DERS
Singles: 7-inch
SYMBOL (001 "Thanks a Lot") ... 15-25

SEADOG: see SEA DOG

SEAFOOD MAMA
(Quarterflash)
Singles: 7-inch
WHITEFIRE (808-24 "Harden My Heart") ... 15-25 80
(Identification number shown since no selection number is used.)
Picture Sleeves
WHITEFIRE ("Harden My Heart") ... 30-40 80
Also see QUARTERFLASH

SEAGRAMS
Singles: 7-inch
RIK ... 10-15 58

SEAGULL SIX
Singles: 78 rpm
SEAFAIR ... 5-10 56
Singles: 7-inch
SEAFAIR ... 10-15 56

SEAGULLS
Singles: 7-inch
DATE ... 4-8 66-67

SEAL P&R '91
(Sealhenry Samuel)
Singles: 7-inch
SIRE ... 3-4 91

SEAL, Jim C&W '80
Singles: 7-inch
NSD ... 3-4 80

SEALEY, Milt
(Milt Sealey Trio)
Singles: 7-inch
CLOUD ... 4-8 66
PHILIPS ... 3-6 67

SEALS, Dan P&R '80
(England Dan Seals)
Singles: 7-inch
ATLANTIC ... 3-5 80-82
CAPITOL ... 3-4 87-90
EMI AMERICA ... 3-4 84-87
LIBERTY ... 3-4 83-84
LPs: 10/12-inch
ATLANTIC ... 5-10 80-82
EMI AMERICA ... 5-8 84-87
LIBERTY ... 5-8 83
Also see ENGLAND DAN & John Ford Coley
Also see TOMORROW'S WORLD

SEALS, Dan, & Marie Osmond
Singles: 7-inch
CAPITOL ... 3-4 85
Also see OSMOND, Marie
Also see SEALS, Dan

SEALS, Jimmy
Singles: 7-inch
CARLTON (470 "Sneaky Pete") ... 20-30 58
CHALLENGE ... 10-20 62-65
WINSTON ... 10-20 58
Also see SEALS & CROFTS
Also see UNCLE SOUND

SEALS, Son, Blues Band
LPs: 10/12-inch
ALLIGATOR ... 6-12 73-83

SEALS, Troy C&W '73
Singles: 7-inch
ATLANTIC ... 3-5 73-74
CALLA ... 4-8 67
ELEKTRA ... 3-4 80
COLUMBIA ... 3-5 75-77
RISING SONS (715 "Mama, Hold My Hand") ... 15-25 69
LPs: 10/12-inch
ATLANTIC ... 8-12 73
COLUMBIA ... 5-10 76
Also see JO ANN & TROY

SEALS & CROFTS LP '70
Singles: 7-inch
T.A. ... 4-6 69-71
W.B. ... 3-5 71-80
Picture Sleeves
W.B. ... 3-5 77
LPs: 10/12-inch
T.A. ... 20-25 69-70
W.B. (Except 2809) ... 6-12 71-80
W.B. (2809 "Seals & Crofts I & II") ... 10-12 74
Members: Jimmy Seals; Dash Crofts. Session: Louie Shelton; Jack Lenz; Ed Green; Wilton Felder; Jim Horn.
Also see CHAMPS
Also see SEALS, Jimmy
Also see TROPHIES
Also see TUCKER, Tanya

SEAMEN
Singles: 7-inch
PHILIPS (40025 "Riptide") ... 10-20 62

SEAN & BRANDYWINES
Singles: 7-inch
DECCA (31910 "She Ain't No Good") ... 10-20 65

SEAN & SHEAS
Singles: 7-inch
YORKSHIRE ... 4-8 60s

SEANOR & KOSS
Singles: 7-inch
REPRISE ... 3-5 72
LPs: 10/12-inch
REPRISE ... 8-10 72

SEARCH
Singles: 7-inch
ERA (3181 "Everybody's Searchin' ") ... 4-8 67
IN SOUND ... 4-8 67

SEARCH PARTY
LPs: 10/12-inch
("Montgomery's Chapel") ... 3000-3500 69
(Approximately a dozen made. No label name or selection number used.)

SEARCHERS
Singles: 7-inch
CLASS (223 "Wow-Wow Baby") ... 10-20 58

SEARCHERS
(With the Kayos)
Singles: 7-inch
MAC (351 Yvonne") ... 400-600 61

SEARCHERS P&R/LP '64
Singles: 7-inch
ERIC ... 3-4
KAPP ... 5-10 64-67
LIBERTY (55646 "Sugar & Spice") ... 8-12 63
LIBERTY (55689 "Sugar & Spice") ... 5-10 63
MERCURY ... 5-10 63
RCA ... 4-6 71-72
SIRE ... 3-5 80-81
SOUND CLASSICS ... 3-5
Picture Sleeves
KAPP (577 "Needles and Pins") ... 10-20 64
KAPP (609 "Some Day We're Gonna Love Again") ... 10-20 64
LPs: 10/12-inch
KAPP ... 20-30 64-66
MERCURY (20914 "Hear! Hear!") 25-35 64
(Monaural. Red label.)
MERCURY (20914 "Hear! Hear!") 40-60 64
(White label. Promotional issue only.)
MERCURY (60914 "Hear! Hear!") 25-35 64
(Stereo. Red label.)
MERCURY (60914 "Hear! Hear!") 40-60 64
(White label. Promotional issue only.)
PYE ... 10-12 76
RHINO ... 5-8 85
SIRE ... 8-10 80-81

SEARCHERS / Rattles
LPs: 10/12-inch
MERCURY (20994 "The Searchers Meet the Rattles") ... 35-45 65
(Monaural. Red label.)
MERCURY (20994 "The Searchers Meet the Rattles") ... 50-75 65
(White label. Promotional issue only.)
MERCURY (60994 "The Searchers Meet the Rattles") ... 35-45 65
(Stereo. Red label.)
MERCURY (60994 "The Searchers Meet the Rattles") ... 50-75 65
(White label. Promotional issue only.)
Also see RATTLES
Also see SEARCHERS

SEARCHERS
Singles: 7-inch
WORLD PACIFIC ... 5-10 66

SEARS, Al
(With His Rock 'N' Rollers; Big Al Sears; Al Sears Orchestra)
Singles: 78 rpm
CORAL ... 10-15 55
GROOVE ... 10-15 55-56
HERALD ... 10-20 54
JUBILEE ... 10-15 57-58
KING ... 10-15 51
RCA ... 10-15 52
Singles: 7-inch
BLUE FLAME ("Montreal Express") ... 40-60
CORAL ... 10-20 55
DERRICK ... 10-20 58
GATOR ... 10-20 61
GROOVE ... 10-20 55-56
HERALD ... 15-25 54
JUBILEE ... 10-20 57-58
KING ... 10-20 51
PRESTIGE ... 10-15 61
RCA ... 15-25 52
Picture Sleeves
BLUE FLAME ("Montreal Express") ... 50-75
EPs: 7-inch
KING (270 "Al Sears' All Stars, Vol. 1") ... 20-40 54
KING (271 "Al Sears' All Stars, Vol. 2") ... 20-40 54
Also see DUNGAREE DARLINGS
Also see DUNGAREE DOLLS

SEARS, J.T., & Roebux
Singles: 7-inch
BOONE (1068 "Walking Down Main Street") ... 5-10 68

SEARS, J.T., & Roebux / Charmaines
Singles: 7-inch
SAXONY (2005 "Walking Down Main Street"/ "Where Is the Boy Tonight") ... 4-6 97
Also see CHARMAINES
Also see SEARS, J.T., & Roebux / Charmaines

SEASE, Marvin LP '87
LPs: 10/12-inch
LONDON ... 5-8 87

SEASHELLS
Singles: 7-inch
COLUMBIA ... 3-5 71-73

SEATON, Dick
Singles: 7-inch
K-ARK ("Jukebox Rock") ... 50-100
(Selection number not known.)

SEATON, Johnny
Singles: 7-inch
RENEGADE ... 3-4
Picture Sleeves
RENEGADE ... 3-4
LPs: 10/12-inch
RENEGADE ... 8-10
ROUNDER ... 8-10

SEATRAIN LP '69
Singles: 7-inch
A&M ... 4-8 68
CAPITOL ... 3-6 71-72
W.B. ... 3-5 73
LPs: 10/12-inch
A&M ... 10-15 69
CAPITOL (800 series) ... 8-12 71
CAPITOL (16000 series) ... 5-10 80
W.B. ... 8-10 73
Also see BLUES PROJECT
Also see RANK & FILE

SEATTLE HELPS THE HUNGRY
Singles: 7-inch
DJ (001 "Give Just a Little") ... 3-5 85
(On each side, the song is done by a different group of singers.)
Picture Sleeves
DJ (001 "Give Just a Little") ... 3-5 85
Members: (Side One): Cheri Adams; Christine Baespflug; Peter Barnes; Donna Beck; Dave Belzer; Stevie Bensusen; Anita Bishop; Duffy Bishop; Mark Bishop; Jody Breeding; Kathy Burke; Norma Conger; Chuck Conlon; Dan Dean; Danny Deardorff; Annie Rose De Armas; Marjorie de Muynck; Gary Draper; Chris Egerton; Tom Erak; Joe Ericksen; Ian Fisher; David Friend; Philip Georgas; George Gleason; Karen Goldfeder; Kibi Good; Jean Gratton; Jim Gratton; Kelly Harland; Kathy Herivel; Ricky Lynn Johnson; Gerard Jones; Maury King; Gigi Lob; Maureen Matthews; Nick Moore; Ned Neltner; Mike Neun; Faith O'Neil; Shauna Rogers-Gill; Valerie Rosa; Jim St. John; Sara St. John; Sally Schlosstien; Valerie Smith; Neal Speer; Shelley Stockstill; Teresa Vannoy; Donna Welling. (Side Two): Ami Adler; Wayne Cody; Ashley Eichrodt; Tamara Grothe; Michael Jackson; Paul Johns; Jeff King; Brenda Kutz; David Lanz; Carrie La Porte; Carolee Mayne; Bill McCarthy; Gary Minkler; Pamela Moore; R.P. McMurphy; Bruce Murdock; Charlie Murphy; Aaron Neville; Charles Neville; Tim Noah; Danny O'Keefe; Jim Page; David Perry; Dick Powell; Andrew Ratshin; Daryl Redeker; Renee Redeker; Wade Reeves; Ginny Reilly; Ashley Rey; Rainer Rey; Cindy Rinehart; Truck Rogers; Martin Ross; Merrilee Rush; Mark Sargent; Bill Scott; Marva Scott; Joe Shikany; Sam Smith; Lori Michutka-Speer; Rick Stone; Eric Tingstad; Michael Tomlinson; Gwenda; Tuthill; Walt Wagner; Nick Walker; Gloria Weems; Terry James Young; Jim Zorn.
Also see JR. CADILLAC
Also see NEVILLE BROTHERS
Also see O'KEEFE, Danny
Also see REILLY & MALONEY
Also see RUSH, Merrilee

SEAU, Shawkey, & Muffins see BROUGHTON, John, & Muffins

SEAWIND LP '77
Singles: 7-inch
A&M ... 3-5 80-82
CTI ... 3-5 77-78
HORIZON ... 3-5 79
LPs: 10/12-inch
A&M ... 5-10 80-82
CTI ... 5-10 77-78
HORIZON ... 5-10 79

SEAY, Eddie
Singles: 7-inch
IMPERIAL ... 4-8 66
P.P.I. ... 4-8 66

SEAY, Johnny: see SEA, Johnny

SEBASTIAN
Singles: 7-inch
COLT ... 4-8 63
DECCA ... 3-5 70
MR. MAESTRO (801 "Too Young") ... 30-50 59
LPs: 10/12-inch
MCA ... 10-15 70

SEBASTIAN
(Sonny DiNuzio)
Singles: 7-inch
SEGUE ... 4-8 60s
Also see FENWAYS

SEBASTIAN, Joel
Singles: 7-inch
MIRACLE (9 "Blue Cinderella") ... 30-50 61

SEBASTIAN, John P&R '69
Singles: 7-inch
KAMA SUTRA ... 4-6 68-70
MGM ... 4-6 68-70
REPRISE ... 3-5 70-77
Picture Sleeves
KAMA SUTRA ... 4-8 69
LPs: 10/12-inch
KAMA SUTRA ... 10-15 70
MGM ... 10-15 69-70
REPRISE ... 8-12 70-76
Also see LOVIN' SPOONFUL
Also see MUGWUMPS
Also see SIMPSONS

SEBASTIAN HARDIE
Singles: 7-inch
MERCURY ... 3-5 76
LPs: 10/12-inch
MERCURY ... 8-10 76

SEBESKY, Don, & Jazz-Rock Syndrome
Singles: 7-inch
VERVE ... 3-5 68
LPs: 10/12-inch
VERVE ... 10-15 68

SECO, Pozo, Singers: see POZO SECO SINGERS

2ND CENTURY
Singles: 7-inch
SSP ... 3-5 77
Also see CENTURYS

SECOND COMING
(2nd Coming)
Singles: 7-inch
MERCURY ... 4-8 70-71
STEADY ... 5-10 69
LPs: 10/12-inch
MERCURY ... 10-15 70
Also see BUDDY & CITATIONS

SECOND EDITION
Singles: 7-inch
SOLA (13 "Sasa Fras") ... 10-15 66

SECOND EDITION
Singles: 7-inch
SCOTTY (6730 "To Keep You") ... 10-20 67
(At least one source gives 944 as the selection number, and 1969 as the year. We don't yet know which is correct—or was it issued twice?)

SECOND HALF
Singles: 7-inch
IGL (131 "Forever in Your World") ... 15-25 67

SECOND HAND BITTER SWEET
Singles: 7-inch
CEI ... 10-15

SECOND HELPING
Singles: 7-inch
VIVA (603 "Hard Times") ... 5-10 66
VIVA (605 "On Friday") ... 5-10 67
VIVA (613 "Children of the Night") ... 5-10 67
Member: Kenny Loggins.

SECOND IMAGE
Singles: 12-inch
MCA ... 4-6 84
POLYDOR ... 4-6 84

SECOND NATURE
Singles: 7-inch
BANG ... 3-5 74

SECOND SEASON
Singles: 7-inch
JANUS ... 3-5 76

SECOND SET
Singles: 7-inch
RAVEN (2 "Picture Window") ... 10-20

SECOND SOCIETY
Singles: 7-inch
STAX ... 3-5 74

SECOND STORY
Singles: 7-inch
BUDDAH ... 4-6 69

SECOND SUMMERS
Singles: 7-inch
CONN (202,079 "Sad Vibrations") 25-35 68

SECOND THOUGHT
Singles: 7-inch
BRITE LEAF ... 5-10 68
GLORIA ... 10-20 66-67
Also see DEVILLES

SECOND TIME
Singles: 7-inch
TOWER ... 5-10 68
LPs: 10/12-inch
TOWER ... 15-20 68

SECOND VERSE R&B '74
Singles: 7-inch
IX CHAINS ... 3-5 74

SECRET AFFAIR
LPs: 10/12-inch
SIRE ... 5-10 80

SECRET AGENTS
Singles: 7-inch
ASCOT ... 4-8 63
JERDEN ... 4-8 66

SECRET OYSTER
LPs: 10/12-inch
PETER'S INT'L ... 10-15 73-75

SECRET TIES P&R '86
Singles: 7-inch
NIGHT WAVE ... 3-4 86

SECRET WEAPON R&B '82
Singles: 7-inch
PRELUDE ... 3-5 82-83

SECRETS
Singles: 78 rpm
DECCA ... 10-15 57
Singles: 7-inch
DECCA (30350 "See You Next Year") ... 10-20 57
(Previously issued as by the Five Secrets.)
Also see FIVE SECRETS

SECRETS
Singles: 7-inch
SWAN (4097 "Twin Exhaust") ... 10-15 62

SECRETS P&R '63
Singles: 7-inch
DCP (1139 "Shu Guy") ... 8-12 65
OMEN (15 "Here I Am") ... 8-12 66
PHILIPS (40146 "The Boy Next Door") ... 8-12 63
PHILIPS (40173 "Hey Big Boy") ... 8-12 63
PHILIPS (40196 "Here He Comes Now") ... 8-12 64
PHILIPS (40222 "He's the Boy") ... 8-12 64
Picture Sleeves
PHILIPS (40173 "Hey Big Boy") ... 10-20 64
Members: Jackie Allen; Pat Miller; Karen Gray; Carol Raymont.

SECRETS
Singles: 7-inch
RAYNARD (10047 "I Don't Know") ... 10-20 66
Members: Larry Fenlon; Pat Noel; Tom Bertrand; Bob Pitton; Dave Krieger.

SECRETS
Singles: 7-inch
RED BIRD (10076 "Every Day") ... 8-12 66

SECRETS
Singles: 7-inch
WAND ... 3-5 75

SECRETS
LPs: 10/12-inch
QUALITY/RFC ... 5-8 83

SECTION
Singles: 7-inch
CAPITOL ... 3-5 77
W.B. ... 3-5 72-73
LPs: 10/12-inch
CAPITOL ... 5-10 77
W.B. ... 8-12 72-73

SECTION 5
Singles: 7-inch
AUDIO DYNAMICS (105 "Pusher's Route") ... 15-25 67

SEDACCA, Chuck
Singles: 7-inch
SMASH ... 4-8 62

SEDAKA, Dara
Singles: 7-inch
RSO (892 "My Guy") ... 3-5 78
Picture Sleeves
RSO (892 "My Guy") ... 3-6 78
Also see SEDAKA, Neil & Dara

SEDAKA, Neil P&R '58
(With the Marvels)
Singles: 12-inch
CURB ... 4-8
ELEKTRA ... 4-8 70s
Singles: 7-inch
CURB ... 3-5
DECCA (30520 "Laura Lee") ... 50-75 57
(We have yet to confirm U.S. 78 rpms of this, or any of Neil's singles, though they may exist—especially the Decca and first RCAs.)
ELEKTRA ... 3-5 77-80
GUYDEN (2004 "Ring-a-Rockin' ") 35-50 58
KIRSHNER ... 3-5 72-80
LEGION (133 "Ring-a-Rockin' ") ... 50-75 58
MCA ... 3-5 75-84
MGM ... 3-5 73
RCA (96 "Special DJ Spots") ... 2-50 60
(Promotional issue only.)
RCA (7408 "The Diary") ... 10-20 58
(Black label.)
RCA (7408 "The Diary") ... 25-40 58
(White, photo label. Promotional issue only.)
RCA (7473 "I Go Ape") ... 15-25 59
RCA (47-7595 "Oh Carol") ... 10-15 59
(Monaural.)
RCA (61-7595 "Oh Carol") ... 25-50 59
(Stereo.)
RCA (47-7709 "Stairway to Heaven") ... 10-15 60
(Monaural.)
RCA (61-7709 "Stairway to Heaven") ... 25-50 60
(Stereo.)
RCA (47-7781 "Run Sampson Run") ... 10-15 60
(Monaural.)
RCA (61-7781 "Run Sampson Run") ... 25-50 60
(Stereo.)
RCA (37-7829 "Calendar Girl") ... 25-50 60
(Compact 33 Single.)
RCA (47-7829 "Calendar Girl") ... 10-15 60
(Monaural.)
RCA (61-7829 "Calendar Girl") ... 25-50 60
(Stereo.)
RCA (37-7874 "Little Devil") ... 25-50 61
(Compact 33 Single.)
RCA (47-7874 "Little Devil") ... 10-15 61
RCA (37-7922 "Sweet Little You") 15-25 61
(Compact 33 Single.)
RCA (47-7922 "Sweet Little You") 10-15 61
RCA (37-7957 "Happy Birthday Sweet Sixteen") ... 25-50 61
(Compact 33 Single.)
RCA (47-7957 "Happy Birthday Sweet Sixteen") ... 10-15 61

RCA (37-8007 "King of Clowns")....25-50 62
(Compact 33 Single.)
RCA (47-8007 "King of Clowns")....10-15 62
RCA (37-8007 "King of Clowns")....25-50 62
(Compact 33 Single.)
RCA (8046 thru 9004)..................... 8-15 62-66
RCA GOLD STANDARD................... 3-6 60s-80s
RSO 3-4
ROCKET 3-5 74-76
S.G.C. 5-8 68-69

Picture Sleeves

RCA...10-20 60-65
RSO 3-4

EPs: 7-inch

RCA (105 "Neil's Best")...............15-25 61
(Compact 33 Double.)
RCA (135 "Little Devil")................15-25 61
(Compact 33 Double.)
RCA (4334 "I Go Ape") 30-40 59
RCA (4353 "Oh Carol")....................25-35 59

LPs: 10/12-inch

ACCORD.. 5-10 81
CAMDEN... 8-12 60s
CROWN 10-20 60s
CURB 5-10
ELEKTRA....................................... 5-10 77-81
51 WEST... 5-8 80s
GUEST STAR.................................10-20 60s
INTERMEDIA 5-8 85
KIRSHNER....................................10-15 71-72
MCA 5-10 84
ORBIT (17196 "Bravo!") 5-10 83
PICKWICK 10-15 70s
POLYDOR....................................... 5-10
RCA (AFL1 & APL1 series)............. 8-10 75-78
RCA (ANL1 series)......................... 5-10 75-79
RCA (VPL1 series).......................... 8-12 76
RCA (LPM-2035 "Neil Sedaka")......35-45 59
(Monaural.)
RCA (2035 "Neil Sedaka") 50-100 59
(Stereo.)
RCA (LPM-2317 thru LPM-2627) ...20-30 61-62
(Monaural.)
RCA (LSP-2317 thru LSP-2627) 25-35 61-62
(Stereo.)
RCA (10181 "Smile")......................15-20 66
ROCKET 8-10 74-77
Session: King Curtis.
Also see ANKA, Paul / Sam Cooke / Neil Sedaka
Also see COOKE, Sam / Rod Lauren / Neil Sedaka / Browns
Also see 4 SEASONS / Neil Sedaka / J Brothers / Johnny Rivers
Also see JOHN, Elton
Also see KING CURTIS
Also see MARVELS
Also see SIMON, Paul
Also see 10CC
Also see WILLOWS

SEDAKA, Neil / Ann-Margret / Browns / Sam Cooke

EPs: 7-inch

RCA (33-149 "Headline Hits") 10-20 61
(Promotional issue, made for Nestle's.)
Also see ANN-MARGRET
Also see BROWNS
Also see COOKE, Sam

SEDAKA, Neil & Dara — P&R '80

Singles: 7-inch

ELEKTRA.. 3-5 80
MCA 3-4 84
Also see SEDAKA, Dara

SEDAKA, Neil / Marvels

Singles: 7-inch

PYRAMID (623 "Oh Delilah")........20-30 62
Also see MARVELS

SEDAKA, Neil, & Tokens

LPs: 10/12-inch

GUEST STAR.................................10-20 60s
VERNON 10-15 60s

SEDAKA, Neil, & Tokens / Coins

LPs: 10/12-inch

CROWN (366 "Neil Sedaka").........10-20 63

SEDAKA, Neil, & Tokens / Angels / Jimmy Gilmer & Fireballs

LPs: 10/12-inch

ALMOR (105 "Teen Bandstand")....15-25 60s
Also see ANGELS
Also see GILMER, Jimmy
Also see SEDAKA, Neil
Also see TOKENS

SEDARES, Bill

Singles: 7-inch

TEENAGE (602 "Crazy 'Bout the Teacher in Rom 202")..................................15-25

SEDATES

Singles: 7-inch

MRB (171 "Please Love Me Forever")....................................25-50 58
PORT (70004 "Please Love Me Forever")....................................20-30 58
TWENTIETH CENTURY (1212 "Please Love Me Forever")..............................20-30 61

SEDATES

Singles: 7-inch

TRANS ATLAS (692 "Girl of Mine") 150-250 62

SEDLAR, Jimmy

Singles: 7-inch

BIG M (1000 "Shorty's Got to Go")..25-50

EPs: 7-inch

RCA Victor (4075 "Teenagers Dance the Rockabilly")...................................50-75 57

SEDUCTION — P&R/LP '89

Singles: 7-inch

VENDETTA 3-4 89-90

LPs: 10/12-inch

A&M 5-8 89
VENDETTA 5-8 90
Members: April; Michelle; Idalis.

SEEDS — P&R '66

(Featuring Sky Saxon)

Singles: 7-inch

GNP (354 "Can't Seem to Make You Mine"/ "Daisy Mae") 5-10 65
GNP (354 "Can't Seem to Make You Mine"/"I Tell Myself") 4-8 67
GNP (364 "Your Pushing Too Hard"/"Out of the Question")..8-12 65
(Reissued on 372 as *Pushing too Hard*, with a different flip, *Try to Understand*.)
GNP (370 "The Other Place") 5-10 65
GNP (372 thru 422) 4-8 66-69
MGM 8-12 69-70

Picture Sleeves

GNP (354 "Can't Seem to Make You Mine"/"I Tell Myself")...................................10-20 67
GNP (383 "Mr. Farmer") 10-20 67
GNP (394 "A Thousand Shadows").......................................10-20 67

LPs: 10/12-inch

GNP (2023 thru 2043).......................20-30 66-67
(All Seeds LPs, except 2043, *Raw and Alive*, were reissued with original selection numbers. First issue, red label, 1960s LPs have the logo, "GNP/Crescendo," on a horizontal line. Reissues have the label name in a circular manner on the label.)
GNP (2100 series)...............................5-10 77
Also see FULLER, Bobby / Seeds
Also see SAXON, Sky

SEEDS OF EUPHORIA

Singles: 7-inch

TMP-TING (120 "Let's Send Batman to Viet Nam")...10-20 66

SEEDS OF LIFE

Singles: 7-inch

SEDGRICK... 3-5

SEEDS OF TIME

Singles: 7-inch

COAST (1971 "My Home Town")...10-15 71

SEEGER, Peggy

LPs:10/12-inch

PRESTIGE 20-30

SEEGER, Pete — LP '63

Singles: 7-inch

COLUMBIA.. 4-6 63-67
FOLKWAYS 5-10 59
PIONEER 4-8 60

LPs: 10/12-inch

ARAVEL 10-20 63-64
ARCHIVE of FOLK MUSIC 10-15 65
BROADSIDE 10-20 63
CAPITOL..10-20 64-67
COLUMBIA..10-20 63-72
DISC..10-20 64
FOLKWAYS 8-20 59-75
(Black vinyl.)
FOLKWAYS (7610 "Animal Folk Songs")..25-35
(Colored vinyl.)
HARMONY 5-10 68-70
ODYSSEY...8-12 68
OLYMPIC 5-10 73
PHILIPS 10-20 63
STINSON (57 "Pete Seeger Concert")..20-30 54
(10-inch LP.)
STINSON (90 "Pete") 5-10 70
TRADITION...5-10 73
VANGUARD 6-12 78
VERVE/FOLKWAYS 10-20 65
VOX...5-10 72
W.B. 5-10 79
Also see ALMANAC SINGERS
Also see BROONZY, Big Bill, & Pete Seeger
Also see SEEGERS
Also see WEAVERS

SEEGER, Pete, & Arlo Guthrie — LP '75

LPs: 10/12-inch

REPRISE...8-12 75
W.B. 5-10 81
Also see GUTHRIE, Arlo

SEEGER, Pete, with Pacific Gas & Electric

LPs: 10/12-inch

COLUMBIA (3540 "Tell Me That You Love Me, Junie Moon")......................................10-15 70
(Soundtrack.)
Also see PACIFIC GAS & ELECTRIC

SEEGERS

LPs: 10/12-inch

PRESTIGE 10-20 65
Members: Pete Seeger; Peggy Seeger; Mike Seeger; Barbara Seeger; Penny Seeger.
Also see SEEGER, Pete

SEEKERS — P&R/LP '65

Singles: 7-inch

ATMOS 5-8 65
CAPITOL 5-10 65-68
MARVEL 5-8 65

Picture Sleeves

CAPITOL (5430 "A World of Our Own")..8-10 65

LPs: 10/12-inch

CAPITOL (100 series).............................8-12 69
CAPITOL (2000 series)..........................10-20 65-67
CAPITOL (16000 series)..........................5-10 80
MARVEL 15-20 65
Members: Judy Durham; Keith Potger.
Also see JAMES, Sonny / Seekers
Also see NEW SEEKERS

SEEKERS / Lou Rawls

Singles: 7-inch

CAPITOL (50 "Island of Dreams")....5-10 67
(Promotional issue, made for Frito-Lay.)

Picture Sleeves

CAPITOL (50 "Island of Dreams")......4-8 67
(Paper sleeve with die-cut hole. Promotional issue, made for Frito-Lay.)
Also see SEEKERS
Also see RAWLS, Lou

SEELY, Jeannie — C&W/P&R '66

Singles: 7-inch

CHALLENGE...4-6 64-65
COLUMBIA..3-5 77-78
DECCA...3-5 69-73
MCA...3-5 73-75
MONUMENT 3-5 66-68

LPs: 10/12-inch

DECCA...6-12 69-70
HARMONY 5-10 72
MCA..5-8 73
MONUMENT 6-12 66-77
Also see COCHRAN, Hank
Also see GREENE, Jack, & Jeannie Seely

SEEMON & MARIJKE

LPs: 10/12-inch

A&M 8-12 71

SEES, B.H.

Singles: 7-inch

NEW-HITS 4-8

SEEVERS, Les — C&W '69

(With Oaks)

Singles: 7-inch

CHESTNUT..4-6
DECCA..3-6 69
EVENT 5-10

SEGAL, George — LP '67

(With the Imperial Jazzband)

Singles: 7-inch

FLYING DUTCHMAN 3-5 74
PHILIPS 4-6 67

LPs: 10/12-inch

PHILIPS 10-20 67
SIGNATURE 5-10 74

SEGALL, Ricky

(With the Segals)

LPs: 10/12-inch

BELL 8-10 73
CASABLANCA 5-8 83

SEGER, Bob — P&R '68

(With the Last Heard; with Silver Bullet Band; Bob Seger System)

Singles: 12-inch

CAPITOL (8433 "Travelin' Man") ...10-15 75
(Promotional issue.)
CAPITOL (9085 "Old Time Rock & Roll")..8-10 83
(Promotional issue.)

Singles: 7-inch

ABKCO...3-6 72-75
CAMEO (438 "East Side Story") 15-25 66
CAMEO (444 "Sock It to Me Santa")...20-30 66
CAMEO (465 "Persecution Smith")..15-25 66
CAMEO (473 "Vagrant Winter")......15-25 66
CAMEO (494 "Heavy Music") 10-20 67
CAPITOL (2297 thru 3187) 5-10 68-71
CAPITOL (4116 thru 5658).................3-6 71-86
HIDEOUT (1013 "East Side Story")...25-50 66
HIDEOUT (1014 "Persecution Smith")...25-50 66
MCA (53094 "Shakedown") 3-4 87
PALLADIUM 4-6 71-74
REPRISE 4-6 72

Promotional Singles

CAPITOL (4653 "We've Got Tonight") 4-8 78
(Colored vinyl.)
CAPITOL (9878 "Shame on the Moon")...4-6 82
(Edited version [4:22], not the promo that runs 4:55.)

Picture Sleeves

CAPITOL (4653 thru 4904)...................3-8 78-80
CAPITOL (4951 "Horizontal Bop")...30-50 80
CAPITOL (5042 thru 5623)......................3-6 81-80
MCA (53094 "Shakedown")......................3-5 87

LPs: 10/12-inch

CAPITOL (ST-172 "Ramblin' Gamblin' Man")...15-25 69
CAPITOL (SM-172 "Ramblin' Gamblin' Man")..8-10 75
CAPITOL (ST-236 "Noah")....................50-70 69
CAPITOL (SKAO-499 "Mongrel")......15-25 70
CAPITOL (SM-499 "Mongrel") 8-10 75
CAPITOL (ST-731 "Brand New Morning")......................................30-50 71
CAPITOL (8433 "Live Bullet, Consensus Cuts")...20-30 75
(Promotional issue only.)
CAPITOL (11000 series, except 11557 & 11904)...6-12 75-78
CAPITOL (ST-11557 "Night Moves")...5-10 78
CAPITOL (ST-11557 "Night Moves")...25-35 78
(Picture disc. Promotional issue only. 800 made.)
CAPITOL (SW-11904 "Stranger in Town")..5-10 78
CAPITOL (SEAX-11904 "Stranger in Town")..15-20 79
(Picture disc.)
CAPITOL (12000 series)....................6-10 80-86
CAPITOL (16000 series)......................5-8 80
CAPITOL (30334 "Greatest Hits")..10-15 90s
CAPITOL (91124 "Fire Inside").........8-10 91
INNER VIEW ("Demonstration Record: Bob Seger")...15-25 76
(Promotional issue only.)
MFSL (034 "Night Moves") 35-50 79
MFSL (127 "Against the Wind") 25-30 85
PALLADIUM (1006 "Smokin' O.P.'s")..15-25 72
PALLADIUM (2126 "Back in '72") ..50-75 73
REPRISE 10-15 72-74
Members: Alto Reed; Robyn Robbins; Drew Abbott; Chris Campbell; Charlie Martin.
Session: Glenn Frey; Don Henley; Timothy B. Schmit.
Also see BEACH BUMS
Also see BROWN, Doug
Also see BROWNSVILLE STATION
Also see FREY, Glenn
Also see NEWMAN, Randy
Also see ORMANDY

SEGMENTS OF TIME

Singles: 7-inch

SUSSEX...3-5 73

SEGO BROTHERS & NAOMI — C&W '64

Singles: 7-inch

SONGS of FREEDOM............................4-6 64

SEINER, Barbara — C&W '79

Singles: 7-inch

STARSHIP 3-5 79

SELAH JUBILEE QUARTETTE

LPs: 10/12-inch

REMINGTON (1023 "Spirituals") .50-100 51
(10-inch LP.)
Also see LARKS
Also see MURPHY, Rose

SELBY, Dayton

(Dayton Selby Trio; with Wilene Barton)

Singles: 7-inch

ABC-PAR 5-10 59

EPs: 7-inch

RCA Victor (4055 "Teenagers Dance the Tonky Honk")...20-30 57

SELDOM SCENE

Singles: 7-inch

SUGAR HILL...3-5 81

LPs: 10/12-inch

SUGAR HILL..5-10 81

SELECTIONS

(With the Electras)

Singles: 7-inch

ANTONE (101 "Guardian Angel")..150-250 58
MONA LEE (129 "Guardian Angel")..50-75 58
Member: Al Reno.
Also see RENO, Al

SELECTIVE SERVICE

Singles: 7-inch

MAIN LINE (1363 "Green Onions")..10-20 60s

SELECTIVES

Singles: 7-inch

UPTOWN...4-8 65

SELECTOR — LP '80

Singles: 7-inch

CHRYSALIS...3-5 79-81

LPs: 10/12-inch

CHRYSALIS..5-10 79-81

SELENA — P&R '95

Singles: 7-inch

EMI LATIN...3-4 95
FREDDIE (451 "No Puedo Estar Sin Ti")..50-100 79
(Reports indicate approximately 100 made.)
Members: Selena Quintanilla; Abraham Quintanilla; A.B. Quintanilla; Suzette Quintanilla; Rena Dearman; Rodney Pyeatt.

SELF, Alvie

Singles: 7-inch

ACCENT 3-4 81-86
DON RAY (5960 "Let's Go Wild")...75-125 60
FORD (1015 "Rain Dance") 50-75 60

SELF, Jimmy

Singles: 7-inch

CORAL (62009 "Oh Babe")............20-30 58

SELF, Mack

Singles: 7-inch

BLAKE 5-10 66
SABRE 3-4 76
SUN (273 "Easy to Love")....................10-20 57
ZONE (1062 "Mexican Limbo") 15-25 62
ZONE (1085)...5-10 65
(Title not known.)

SELF, Mack, & Charlie Feathers

Singles: 7-inch

PHILLIPS INT'L 10-15 59
Also see FEATHERS, Charlie
Also see SELF, Mack

SELF, Ronnie — P&R '58

Singles: 78 rpm

ABC-PAR 25-50 56
COLUMBIA 15-25 57

Singles: 7-inch

ABC-PAR (9714 "Pretty Bad Blues")...75-100 56
ABC-PAR (9768 "Sweet Love") 50-75 56
AMY (11009 "High on Self") 5-10 68
COLUMBIA (40989 "Ain't I'm a Dog")..25-35 57
COLUMBIA (41101 "Bop-A-Lena") 25-35 58
COLUMBIA (41166 "Big Blon Baby")...25-35 58
COLUMBIA (41241 "Petrified") 75-125 58
DECCA (30958 "Big Town") 15-25 59
DECCA (31131 "I've Been There") 10-20 60
DECCA (31351 "Instant Man") 10-20 62
DECCA (31431 "Oh Me, Oh My") ..10-20 62
KAPP (546 "Houdini")............................8-12 63

EPs: 7-inch

COLUMBIA (2149 "Ain't I'm a Dog") 175-225 57

SELF, Stewart

(With the Gents)

Singles: 7-inch

ERMINE (46 "Mary Ellen")..............25-50 63
ERMINE (49 "Lady Lonliness") 20-40 63
STARRETT (5709 "Mary Ellen") 100-200 63
(First issue.)

SELF, Ted — C&W '60

Singles: 7-inch

PLAID..5-10 60
SAVOY...5-10 60

SELF, Vicky

LP: 10/12-inch

COLUMN ONE...5-10 81

SELLARS, Marilyn — C&W/P&R '74

Singles: 7-inch

MEGA 3-5 74-77
ZODIAC 3-5 76-77

LPs: 10/12-inch

MEGA 5-10 74-77
ZODIAC 5-10 77

SELLERS, Johnny

(Brother John Sellers)

Singles: 78 rpm

CHANCE...25-50 52-53
CINCINNATI..15-25 45
DECCA 15-25 45
GOTHAM 15-25 48
KING 15-25 46-51
MIRACLE 15-25 47
RCA 15-25 47
SOUTHERN 15-25 45

Singles: 7-inch

CHANCE (1120 "Josie Jones") 50-100 52
CHANCE (1123 "Mighty Lonesome")....................................50-100 52
CHANCE (1138 "Mirror Blues")....50-100 53

LPs: 10/12-inch

LONDON (1705 "In London") 35-50 57
MONITOR (335 "Baptist Shouts") ..15-25 60
MONITOR (505 "Big Beat Up the River")..25-30 59
VANGUARD (7022 "Jack of Diamonds")...25-45 55
VANGUARD (8005 "Folk Songs and Blues")..25-45 54
VANGUARD (9036 "Blues and Folk Songs")..25-45 58
Session: Doc Bagby; Mickey Baker; Willie Dixon; Sonny Terry.
Also see BAGBY, Doc
Also see BAKER, Mickey
Also see DIXON, Willie
Also see TERRY, Sonny

SELLERS, Maxine

Singles: 7-inch

CHALLENGE..4-6 60s

SELLERS, Peter

Singles: 7-inch

CAPITOL...5-10 59

LPs: 10/12-inch

ANGEL (35884 "Best of Sellers") ...20-30 60
Also see HOLLIES / Peter Sellers

SELLERS, Peter, & Sophia Loren

LPs: 10/12-inch

ANGEL (35910 "Peter Sellers and Sophia Loren")..20-30 61
Also see SELLERS, Peter

SELLERS, Tom

Singles: 7-inch

DECCA (32356 "Tears") 15-25 68

SELPH, Jimmy

Singles: 7-inch

COIN (106 "Tom Cattin' Around") ..25-35 57

SELSIE, Sandy

Singles: 7-inch

COLUMBIA 4-8 62-63

SELTAEB

Singles: 7-inch

BANANA (1522 "I Want You") 8-12 70
BANANA (1550 "You're the Only Girl for Me")..8-12 71
Members: Jeff Roberts; Dick Lane; Bruce Bradley; Dick Middleton.

SELUJ RENTTALB: see RENTTALB, Seluj

SELVIDGE, Sid

LPs: 10/12-inch

ENTERPRISE 8-12 69

SEMBELLO, Michael — P&R/D&D/LP '83

Singles: 12-inch

CASABLANCA 4-6 83
W.B. 4-6 83-84

Singles: 7-inch
A&M ... 3-4 86
CASABLANCA ... 3-5 83
GEFFEN ... 3-4 85
W.B. ... 3-5 83-84
LPs: 10/12-inch
A&M ... 5-8 86
MCA ... 5-8 85
W.B. ... 5-10 83

SEMBELLO, Michael / Basil Poledouris
Singles: 7-inch
W.B. ... 3-4 82
Picture Sleeves
W.B. ... 3-4 82
Also see SEMBELLO, Michael

SEMI COLONS
Singles: 7-inch
CAMEO (468 "Beachcomber") ... 8-12 67
Also see ? & the MYSTERIANS

SEMINOLES
(Featuring Joey Finaro)
Singles: 7-inch
CHECK MATE (1012 "It Takes a Lot") ... 100-150 62
GO-GEE (287 "Open Your Eyes") ... 50-100 61
HI-LITE (109 "Meant to Be") ... 25-50 61
MID TOWN (101 "Forever") ... 150-250 62
(Reissued as by the Embers.)
Also see EMBERS

SENA, Tommy
(With the Val-Monts)
Singles: 7-inch
VALMONT (905 "Onions") ... 20-30 62
(Reads "Valmont Records" at top.)
VALMONT (905 "Onions") ... 10-20 62
(Reads only "Valmont" at top.)

SENATOR BOBBY P&R '67
Singles: 7-inch
RCA ... 10-20 67-68
Also see HARDLY WORTHIT PLAYERS

SENATOR BOLIVAR E. GASSAWAY: see GASSAWAY, Senator Bolivar E.

SENATOR McKINLEY: see HARDLY WORTHIT PLAYERS

SENATORS
Singles: 7-inch
ABNER (1031 "Julie") ... 40-60 59
GOLDEN CREST (514 "Poor Little Puppet") ... 100-150 58

SENATORS
(With John Dickerson & Orchestra)
Singles: 7-inch
BRISTOL (1916 "Scheming") ... 100-150 59
WINN (1917 "Wedding Bells") ... 150-250 62
(Artist credit handwritten—not printed—on label.)
WINN (1917 "Wedding Bells") ... 75-125 62
(Artist credit printed on label.)
Also see MARVELS

SENATORS
Singles: 7-inch
ABC-PAR (10178 "Sing-a-Long Song") ... 5-10 61

SENAY, Eddy R&B '72
Singles: 7-inch
SUSSEX ... 3-5 72-73
LPs: 10/12-inch
SUSSEX ... 8-12 72

SENDERS
Singles: 7-inch
ENTRA (711 "Pretty Little Girl") ... 150-250 61
(Black label.)
ENTRA (711 "Pretty Little Girl") ... 50-75 61
(Red label.)
KENT (320 "I Dream of You") ... 25-50 59
KENT (324 "One More Kiss") ... 50-100 59

SENDERS
Singles: 7-inch
IGL (149 "She Told Me") ... 10-15 67

SENECA, Joe
Singles: 7-inch
EVEREST ... 5-10 59-60

SENIORS
Singles: 78 rpm
EXCELLO (2130 "Why Did You Leave Me") ... 20-30 58
TETRA ... 50-75 56
Singles: 7-inch
EXCELLO (2130 "Why Did You Leave Me") ... 20-30 58
LOST-NITE ... 4-8
TETRA (4446 "Evening Shadows Falling") ... 100-150 56

SENIORS
Singles: 7-inch
DECCA ... 8-10 60-61
KENT (342 "Pitter Patter Heart") ... 8-12 60
TAMPA (163 "It's Been a Long Time") ... 20-30 59

SENIORS
(With Daniel Monroe Orchestra)
Singles: 7-inch
E S V (1016 "Rock & Rolly") ... 15-25 60

SENIORS
Singles: 7-inch
ABC-PAR (10736 "No Surfin' 'Round Here") ... 10-20 65

SENNE, Paul
Singles: 7-inch
DRAKE (732 "Bull Dog Tail Blues") ... 10-20 62
REO (1001 "Cool Man Rock") ... 15-25

SENNS, Charles
Singles: 7-inch
O.J. (1014 "Gee Whiz Liz") ... 150-200 58

SEÑOR SOUL R&B '69
Singles: 7-inch
DOUBLE SHOT ... 4-8 67-68
WHIZ ... 3-6 69-70
LPs: 10/12-inch
DOUBLE SHOT ... 10-15 68-69

SEÑOR WENCES: see WENCES, Señor

SENORS
Singles: 7-inch
SUE (756 "May I Have This Dance") ... 15-25 62

SENORS
Singles: 7-inch
CAMEO ... 4-8 63

SENSATION ALEX HARVEY BAND
Singles: 7-inch
ATLANTIC ... 3-5 74
VERTIGO ... 3-5 74-75

SENSATION-IVIES
Singles: 7-inch
WILLOW (23003 "Tell Me") ... 10-15 61

SENSATIONAL DELLOS
Singles: 7-inch
MIDA (106 "So Shy") ... 75-125 58
MIDA (109 "Lost Love") ... 75-125 58
Also see SHAW, John, & Dell-os

SENSATIONAL EPICS
Singles: 7-inch
CAMEO ... 4-8 67
CAPITOL ... 3-6 69
W.B. ... 4-8 68

SENSATIONAL JUBILETTES
Singles: 7-inch
MESSAGE (1234 "Jordan River") ... 25-45 60s

SENSATIONAL MANHATTANS
Singles: 7-inch
YOUR (1988 "I Guess That's Love") ... 50-75

SENSATIONAL SAINTS OF OHIO / Sensational Skylarks of Detroit
Singles: 7-inch
MESSAGE (1235 "Come On") ... 25-50 60s

SENSATIONAL SLEEPERS
Singles: 7-inch
MAAD (32468 "Hey Girl") ... 25-35 68

SENSATIONAL SPIRITONE SINGERS
Singles: 7-inch
RAE COX ... 4-8 64

SENSATIONALS
Singles: 7-inch
CANDIX ... 8-12 61

SENSATIONS R&B '56
(Yvonne Mills & Sensations; Yvonne Baker & Sensations)
Singles: 78 rpm
ATCO ... 15-25 55
Singles: 7-inch
ARGO (5391 "Music Music Music") ... 10-20 61
ARGO (5405 "Let Me In") ... 10-20 62
ARGO (5412 "That's My Desire") ... 10-20 62
ARGO (5420 "Party Across the Hall") ... 10-20 62
ATCO (6056 "Yes Sir, That's My Baby") ... 25-50 55
ATCO (6067 "Please Mr. Disc Jockey") ... 25-50 56
ATCO (6075 "My Heart Cries for You") ... 25-50 56
ATCO (6083 "Such a Love") ... 25-50 57
ATCO (6090 "My Debut to Love") ... 25-50 57
ATCO (6115 "Romance in the Dark") ... 25-50 58
CHESS ... 3-5 73
JUNIOR (1002 "We Were Meant to Be") ... 15-25 62
JUNIOR (1005 "You Made a Fool Out of Me") ... 15-25 63
JUNIOR (1006 "Baby") ... 15-25 63
JUNIOR (1010 "I Can't Change") ... 10-20 63
JUNIOR (1021 "We Were Meant to Be") ... 8-12 64
TOLLIE (9009 "You Made a Fool Out of Me") ... 10-15 64
LPs: 10/12-inch
ARGO (4022 "Let Me In") ... 150-250 63
Also see BAKER, Yvonne

SENSATIONS
Singles: 7-inch
RIVER (228 "The Price of Love") ... 35-50 62

SENSATIONS
Singles: 7-inch
DRAEGER (01 "Wild Cat 401") ... 10-20 63
Members: Ray Plauske; Harry Voss; Dave Villo; Jeff Gertanbach; Pete Ruffalo.

SENSATIONS
Singles: 7-inch
WAY OUT ... 8-12 66-69

SENSATIONS
Singles: 7-inch
KING CO ... 5-10 60s

SENSATIONS
Singles: 7-inch
LA LOUISIANNE (805 "Bo-Time") 20-40

SENSORS
Singles: 7-inch
TY TEX ... 8-12 65

SENTIMENTAL REASONS
Singles: 7-inch
DEBRA (1008 "Let It Please Be You") ... 20-25 96
(Colored vinyl.)

SENTIMENTALISTS
(Four Tunes)
Singles: 78 rpm
MANOR (1049 "I'd Rather Be Safe Than Sorry") ... 20-30 46
MANOR (8002 "Silent Night") ... 20-30 46
MANOR (8003 "White Christmas") 20-30 46
Also see FOUR TUNES

SENTIMENTALS
Singles: 78 rpm
CHECKER ... 20-30 57
Singles: 7-inch
CHECKER (875 "I Want to Love You") ... 20-40 57
KNAP TOWN (0010 "I Know You Too Well") ... 5-10 70
MINT (801 "I Want to Love You") ... 40-60 57
MINT (802 "Wedding Bells") ... 50-100 57
(Has straight horizontal lines.)
MINT (802 "Wedding Bells") ... 40-60 57
(Has waxy horizontal lines.)
MINT (803 "I'm Your Fool") ... 30-50 58
MINT (805 "You're Mine") ... 30-50 59
MINT (807 "I'll Miss These Things") ... 10-15 68
MINT (808 "I Want to Love You") ... 5-10 72
Also see CARTER, James

SENTIMENTALS
Singles: 7-inch
CORAL (62100 "We Three") ... 15-25 59
CORAL (62172 "Two Different Worlds") ... 15-25 60
VANITY (589 "Love Is a Gamble") ... 15-25 59

SENTIMENTS
Singles: 7-inch
NIECE ... 5-10 61

SENTINAL SIX: see SENTINALS

SENTINALS
(Sentinal Six; Sentinels)
Singles: 7-inch
ADMIRAL (900 "Roughshod") ... 15-25 61
DEL-FI (4197 "Big Surf") ... 10-15 63
ERA (3082 "Latin'ia") ... 10-15 62
ERA (3097 "Latin Soul") ... 10-15 63
POINT (5100 "The Bee") ... 20-30 60
(Reissued as by Kenny Hinkle.)
POINT (5101 "Bony Maronie") ... 20-30 61
(Reissued as by Kenny Karter.)
WCEB (23 "Latin'ia") ... 20-30 62
(First issue.)
WESTCO (12 "I've Been Blue") ... 10-20 63
WESTCO (14 "Tell Me") ... 10-20 63
LPs: 10/12-inch
DEL-FI (DFLP-1232 "Big Surf") ... 25-40 63
(Monaural.)
DEL-FI (DFST-1232 "Big Surf") ... 35-50 63
(Stereo.)
DEL-FI (DFLP-1241 "Surfer Girl") 25-40 63
(Monaural.)
DEL-FI (DFST-1241 "Surfer Girl") 35-50 63
(Stereo.)
SUTTON (SU-338 "Vegas Go Go") ... 20-25 64
(Monaural.)
SUTTON (SSU-338 "Vegas Go Go") ... 25-30 64
(Stereo.)
Members: Norman Knowles; Tommy Nunes; Lee Michales; Kenny Hinkle; Johnny Barbata; Merrell Fankhauser.
Also see BARBATA, Johnny
Also see FANKHAUSER, Merrell
Also see HINKLE, Kenny
Also see KARTER, Kenny

SEOL, Randy, & Goldtones: see GOLDTONES

SEOMPI
Singles: 7-inch
YIN YANG (101 "Summer's Comin' on Heavy") ... 30-50 60s

SEPIA TONES
Singles: 78 rpm
JUKE BOX ... 8-12 55
SPECIALTY ... 5-10 54
Singles: 7-inch
JUKE BOX ... 20-30 55
SPECIALTY (500 "Boogie No. 1") . 15-25 54

SEPIANAIRES
Singles: 78 rpm
SPINIT (0101 "All I Can Do Is Dream") ... 20-30 50

SEPTORS
Singles: 7-inch
DOME (4005 "Den of Thieves") ... 25-50

SEQUENCE R&B '80
Singles: 7-inch
SUGAR HILL ... 3-5 80-82
LPs: 10/12-inch
SUGAR HILL ... 5-10 81

SEQUINS
Singles: 78 rpm
RED ROBIN ... 100-125 56
Singles: 7-inch
RED ROBIN (140 "Why Can't You Treat Me Right") ... 200-300 56

SEQUINS
Singles: 7-inch
BOXER (203 "Lullaby of Birdland") ... 20-40 59
Also see JESSIE & SEQUINS

SEQUINS
Singles: 7-inch
A&M ... 4-8 65
ASCOT ... 8-10 63
CAMEO (161 "To Be Young") ... 10-15 59
TERRACE ... 10-15 62-63

SEQUINS R&B '70
Singles: 7-inch
GOLD STAR ... 3-5 70
Members: Linda Jackson; Ronnie Gonzalez; Dottie Hayes.

SEQUINS
Singles: 7-inch
CRAJON ... 3-5 71

SEQUINS
Singles: 7-inch
FANTASY ... 3-5 72

SEQUINS
Singles: 7-inch
DETROIT SOUND ... 8-12
RENFRO ... 8-12

SERATT, Howard
Singles: 78 rpm
SUN ... 100-150 54
Singles: 7-inch
SUN (198 "Troublesome Waters") ... 250-350 54

SERENADERS
Singles: 78 rpm
CORAL ... 40-60 52
DELUXE ... 50-75 53
J.V.B. ... 50-100 52
RED ROBIN ... 50-75 53
SWING TIME ... 200-300 54
Singles: 7-inch
CORAL (60720 "It's Funny") ... 100-200 52
CORAL (65093 "Misery") ... 100-200 52
DELUXE (6022 "Please, Please Forgive Me") ... 175-225 53
J.V.B. (2001 "Tomorrow Night") . 200-300 52
RED ROBIN (115 "Will She Know") ... 175-225 53
SWING TIME (347 "M-a-y-b-e-I-I") ... 800-1200 54

SERENADERS
Singles: 7-inch
CHOCK FULL O' HITS (101 "I Wrote a Letter") ... 200-300 57
CHOCK FULL O' HITS (103 "Give Me a Girl") ... 100-200 57
MGM (12623 "I Wrote a Letter") .. 50-100 58
MGM (12666 "Dance Darling Dance") ... 50-100 58
MOTOWN (1046 "I'll Cry Tomorrow") ... 750-1000 63
RAE COX (101 "Gotta Go to School") ... 25-50 59
RIVERSIDE (4549 "Adios My Love") ... 50-75 63
STARFIRE ... 3-6 80
V.I.P. (25002 "I'll Cry Tomorrow") ... 50-100 64
Members: Sidney Barnes; George Kerr; Timothy Wilson; Luke Gross.
Also see BARNES, Sidney
Also see KERR, George
Also see WILSON, Timothy

SERENADERS
(With Hal Gordon & Orchestra)
Singles: 7-inch
TEEN LIFE (9 "Love Me Now") .. 300-400 58
Member: Nick Forrest.

SERENADERS
Singles: 78 rpm
COLONY ... 10-15 50s
Singles: 7-inch
HANOVER ... 5-10 58

SERENADES
Singles: 78 rpm
CHIEF ... 100-150 57
Singles: 7-inch
CHIEF (7002 "A Sinner in Love") ... 200-250 57

SERENADETTS
Singles: 7-inch
ENRICA ... 5-10 61

SERENDERS
Singles: 7-inch
CLIFTON ... 4-8

SERENDIPITY SINGERS P&R/LP '64
Singles: 7-inch
PHILIPS ... 4-8 64-66
U.A. ... 3-5 67-69
Picture Sleeves
PHILIPS ... 4-8 64-66
LPs: 10/12-inch
PHILIPS ... 10-20 64-65
WING ... 8-12 68

SERETTA, Jimmy
Singles: 7-inch
BOYD ... 4-8 66

SERFMEN
Singles: 7-inch
NEMFRES (101 "Back Again") ... 15-20 65

SERFS
Singles: 7-inch
CAPITOL ... 4-6 69
LPs: 10/12-inch
CAPITOL ... 10-15 69

SERGE! R&B '83
Singles: 7-inch
W.B. ... 3-5 83

SERGENT, Shorty
Singles: 7-inch
JET (501 "Record Hop") ... 25-35 58

SERINO
Singles: 7-inch
PIONEER ... 4-8 61
ROULETTE ... 4-8 61

SERINO, Al
Singles: 7-inch
AL-FRED ... 4-6

SERIOUS BROTHERS
Singles: 7-inch
TUNETOWN (101 "It's Another Joyful Elvis Presley Christmas") ... 5-10 88
(Colored vinyl.)
Members: Greg Tamblyn; Richard Helm.

SERIOUS INTENTION D&D '84
Singles: 12-inch
EASY STREET ... 4-6 84

SERMON
Singles: 7-inch
KAMA SUTRA ... 4-6 70
Member: Kal Dee.
Also see FIRST, Carl, & Showmen
Also see SIR MEN

SERPENT POWER
LPs: 10/12-inch
VANGUARD (9252 "Serpent Power") ... 35-50 67
(Monaural.)
VANGUARD (79252 "Serpent Power") ... 30-40 67
(Stereo.)
Members: Tina Meltzer; David Meltzer; Denny Ellis; Clark Coolidge; Bob Cuff.
Also see MELTZER, David & Tina
Also see MYSTERY TREND

SERRATT, Kenny C&W '72
(Kenny Seratt)
Singles: 7-inch
HITSVILLE ... 3-5 76-77
MDJ ... 3-4 80-81
MGM ... 3-5 72-73
MELODYLAND ... 3-5 75

SERTIFIED SOUND
Singles: 7-inch
TEE PEE (25/26 "Love Is Strange") ... 10-15 67

SERVANT
LPs: 10/12-inch
TUNESMITH ... 8-10 79-80

SERVICEMEN
Singles: 7-inch
CHARTMAKER (408 "Connie") .. 100-200 66
PATHWAY (101 "My Turn") ... 20-30 67
PATHWAY (102 "Helping Hand") .. 20-30 67
WIND HIT (100 "Are You Angry") ... 250-500 65

SESAME STREET KIDS: see ERNIE

SESSIONS
Singles: 7-inch
FONTANA ... 4-8 65
GUYDEN ... 4-8 61

SESSIONS
Singles: 7-inch
ARCADE ... 3-5 76

SESSIONS
Singles: 7-inch
KEDLEN (2005 "Lonesome Surf") .. 15-25

SESSIONS, Don
Singles: 7-inch
VERTICO (1001 "You're a Cheater") ... 50-100

SESSIONS, Ronnie C&W '72
(Little Ronnie Sessions)
Singles: 7-inch
COMPLEAT ... 3-4 86
MCA ... 3-5 75-79
MGM ... 3-5 72-73
MOSRITE ... 4-8 66
PIKE ... 10-15 61
REPUBLIC ... 3-6 69
LPs: 10/12-inch
MCA ... 5-10 77

SETH, Larry
(Larry "Big El" Seth & TCB Orchestra)
Singles: 7-inch
CASTLE ... 3-5 78
LPs: 10/12-inch
CASTLE ... 10-20 78

SETTLE, Mike
(With the Settlers)
Singles: 7-inch
AMOS....3-5 70
FOLK SING....4-8 62-63
RCA....4-8 65
UNI....3-5 71-72
LPs: 10/12-inch
FOLK SING....15-25 62-63
REPRISE....15-20 65
Also see FIRST EDITION
Also see SUGAR BEARS

SETZER, Brian LP '86
Singles: 7-inch
EMI....3-4 86-88
LPs: 10/12-inch
EMI....5-8 86-88
Also see STRAY CATS

SEVELLE, Taja P&R/R&B '87
Singles: 7-inch
PAISLEY PARK....3-4 87
REPRISE....3-4 87-88
Picture Sleeves
REPRISE....3-4 87

SEVEN
Singles: 7-inch
THUNDERBIRD....4-6
LPs: 10/12-inch
THUNDERBIRD....10-15

SEVEN, Johnny, & Kilowatts
EPs: 7-inch
BLACK SMOKE (1002 "School Days")....5-10 83

SEVEN, Michael
Singles: 12-inch
ROMANCE....4-6 84

707 P&R '80
Singles: 7-inch
BOARDWALK....3-5 82
CASABLANCA....3-5 80
LPs: 10/12-inch
BOARDWALK....5-10 82
CASABLANCA....5-10 80

7A3
Singles: 7-inch
GEFFEN....3-4 88
LPs: 10/12-inch
GEFFEN....5-8 88

SEVEN BLENDS
LPs: 10/12-inch
ROULETTE (R-25172 "Twistin' at the Miami Beach Peppermint Lounge")....15-20 62
(Monaural.)
ROULETTE (SR-25172 "Twistin' at the Miami Beach Peppermint Lounge")....20-25 62
(Stereo.)

SEVEN DWARFS P&R '38
Singles: 78 rpm
VICTOR (25735 "Heigh-Ho")....10-20 38

7 DWARFS
Singles: 7-inch
IDEAL (1168 "Stop Girl")....15-25 67

VII EMOTIONS
Singles: 7-inch
K-P....8-12

SEVEN OF US
Singles: 7-inch
RED BIRD (069 "How Could You")....10-20 66
RED BIRD (080 "Jamboree")....10-20 66
Members: Frankie Gadler; Terry Adams; Jody Stampanato.
Also see NRBQ

SEVEN SEAS
Singles: 7-inch
GLADES....3-5 75

SEVEN SECONDS LP '89
LPs: 10/12-inch
RESTLESS....5-8 89

SEVEN SECRETS
Singles: 7-inch
AISLE (002 "On Sunday Afternoon")....5-10 92
(Black vinyl. 900 made.)
AISLE (002 "On Sunday Afternoon")....10-15 92
(Red vinyl. 100 made.)
Picture Sleeves
AISLE (002 "On Sunday Afternoon")....3-5 92
Members: Derrich Lewis; Edward Legree; William Sherrill Jr.; Roy Holden; Rod Bostic; Rod Holden; Ivory Williams.
Also see KARI, Sax & Rockin' Jukes / Seven Secrets / Tony & Rockin' Orbits

SEVEN SOULS
Singles: 7-inch
OKEH (7289 "I Still Love You")....25-45 67
VENTURE....5-10 68

SEVENS, Sammy
Singles: 7-inch
SWAN (4146 "Here Comes the Bride")....5-10 63
SWAN (4159 "Everybody Crossfire")....15-25 63

SEVENTEENS
Singles: 7-inch
GOLDEN CREST....8-12 58

17TH AVENUE EXIT
Singles: 7-inch
MODERN (1035 "A Man Can Cry")....8-12 67

7TH AVENUE AVIATORS
Singles: 7-inch
CONGRESS (255 "You Should 'O Held On")....75-125 65

SEVENTH CINDERS
Singles: 7-inch
GREEZIE (502 "One Day")....10-20 60s

SEVENTH COURT
Singles: 7-inch
PROPHONICS (2027 "One Eyed Witch")....10-20 60s

7TH DAY CREATION
Singles: 7-inch
COULEE (133 "She's My Reason")....5-10 70s

SEVENTH SONS
Singles: 7-inch
DYNAR....8-12 67
IGL....20-25 65
SOMA....20-25 65
STANAL....10-20 66
VTI....10-20 67

SEVENTH SONS
LPs: 10/12-inch
ESP....10-15

SEVENTH STRANGER
LPs: 10/12-inch
MASQUE (8807 "Money & Promises")....10-20 89
(Picture disc. Promotional issue only.)

SEVENTH WAVE
LPs: 10/12-inch
JANUS....8-10 74-75

7TH WONDER R&B '73
(Seventh Wonder)
Singles: 12-inch
CASABLANCA....4-6 80
PARACHUTE....4-8 79
Singles: 7-inch
ABET....3-5 73
CASABLANCA....3-5 80
CHOCOLATE CITY....3-5 80
PARACHUTE....3-5 78-79
LPs: 10/12-inch
CHOCOLATE CITY....5-10 80
PARACHUTE....5-10 78-79
Members: Allen Williams; Wilbert Cox; Deborah Matthews; William Butler; Lloyd Obie; Julius Chislom; Jerome Thorton; Marvin Patton; Johnnie Hammon.

SEVENTY SEVENS
LPs: 10/12-inch
EXIT....5-8 83

SEVERINSEN, Doc, Orchestra LP '66
(With the Dodge City Boys; Tonight Show Band with Doc Severinsen)
Singles: 7-inch
COMMAND....3-5 65-70
EPIC....4-6 59-76
FRONTLINE....3-4 80
RCA....3-4 72-73
Picture Sleeves
COMMAND....3-5 70
LPs: 10/12-inch
ABC....5-10 71-73
AMHERST....5-8 86
COMMAND....5-15 61-73
EPIC....5-8 76-81
EVEREST....5-8 78
JUNO....5-10 70-79
MCA....4-8 82
RCA....5-10 71
Also see MANCINI, Henry, & Doc Severinsen

SEVERSON, John
LPs: 10/12-inch
CAPITOL....15-20 63

SEVILLE, David P&R '56
(Ross Bagdasarian)
Singles: 78 rpm
LIBERTY....5-15 56-57
Singles: 7-inch
LIBERTY....8-15 56-61
Picture Sleeves
LIBERTY (55079 "Gotta Get to Your House")....10-20 57
EPs: 7-inch
LIBERTY (1003 "Witch Doctor")....35-50 57
(Issued with paper sleeve.)
LPs: 10/12-inch
LIBERTY (3073 "The Music of David Seville")....50-75 57
LIBERTY (3092 "Witch Doctor")....50-75 58
Also see ALFI & HARRY
Also see BAGDASARIAN, Ross
Also see CHIPMUNKS

SEVILLE, Joanna
Singles: 7-inch
ACE....4-8 62

SEVILLES P&R '61
Singles: 7-inch
CAL-GOLD (172 "Don't You Know I Care")....10-20 62
GALAXY....10-15 63-64
J.C. (116 "Charlena")....20-30 60
J.C. (118 "Louella")....20-25 61
J.C. (120 "Fat Sally")....10-15 61

SEVILLES
Singles: 7-inch
REN-CO (1056 "Burnell Blues")....10-20 62
Members: Joe Zampach; Jack Abuya; Virgil Herder; Jerry Crocker; Ronnie Lalich; Charlie Lewondowski; Mel Lewondowski.

SEVILLES
(With the Chick Morris Five)
Singles: 7-inch
VAGABOND....3-6
Also see MORRIS, Chick

SEWARD, Alec
LPs: 10/12-inch
BLUE LABOR....20-30
PRESTIGE/BLUESVILLE (1076 "Creepin' Blues")....20-40 65

SEWARD, Slim, & Fat Boy Hayes
(Alec Seward; Louis Hayes)
Singles: 78 rpm
MGM (10306 "Travelin' Boy's Blues")....15-25 47
MGM (10770 "Railroad Blues")....15-25 47
Also see BACK PORCH BOYS
Also see BLUES BOY
Also see BLUES KING
Also see JELLY BELLY & Slim Seward
Also see SEWARD, Alec

SEX CLARK FIVE
LPs: 10/12-inch
RECORDS to RUSSIA....5-10 87
Members: Jay Johnson; Rick Storey; Trick McKala; James Butler.

SEX PISTOLS LP '77
Singles: 7-inch
W.B. (8516 "Submission")....3-6 78
Picture Sleeves
W.B. (8516 "Submission")....3-6 78
LPs: 10/12-inch
W.B. (3147 "Never Mind the Bollocks, Here's the Sex Pistols")....15-20 77
(With cover sticker which reads: "Includes Submission.")
W.B. (3147 "Never Mind the Bollocks, Here's the Sex Pistols")....10-15 77
(Without "Submission" cover sticker.)
W.B. (72256 "Swindle Continues")....8-10 90s
W.B. (72511 "Live at Chelmsford Prison")....8-10 90s
Also see PUBLIC IMAGE LTD.
Also see SIOUXSIE & BANSHEES

S-EXPRESS P&R '88
Singles: 7-inch
CAPITOL....3-4 88
Picture Sleeves
CAPITOL....3-4 88

SEXTON, Ann R&B '73
Singles: 7-inch
DASH....3-5 77
IMPEL....5-10
MONUMENT....3-5 77
SEVENTY-SEVEN....5-10 72-74
SOUND STAGE....3-5 77

SEXTON, Charlie P&R/LP '85
Singles: 7-inch
MCA....3-4 85-89
Picture Sleeves
MCA....3-4 85-89
LPs: 10/12-inch
MCA....5-8 86-89
Also see ELY, Joe

SEXTON, Charlie, & Ron Wood
LPs: 10/12-inch
MCA....5-8 84
Also see SEXTON, Charlie
Also see WOOD, Ron

SEXTON, Mark C&W '79
Singles: 7-inch
SUN-DE-MAR....3-5 79

SEXTON, Orden
Singles: 7-inch
CAMELLIA (100 "Rock-A-Way")....100-150

SEXTON, Patsy
Singles: 7-inch
DELTA....3-5 78
LPs: 10/12-inch
DELTA....8-10 78

SEXUAL HARASSMENT
LPs: 10/12-inch
MONTAGE....5-8 84

SEXX
LPs: 10/12-inch
IRON WORKS (1011 "Think About It")....5-10 87
(Picture disc. 500 made.)
IRON WORKS (1011PRO "Think About It")....10-15 87
(Picture disc. Promotional issue only. 100 made.)

SEYMOUR, Cy
Singles: 7-inch
GOLDEN CREST (509 "Yankee Clipper")....10-20 58

SEYMOUR, Patti
Singles: 7-inch
SOLLY (929 "The Silencer")....10-20

SEYMOUR, Phil P&R/LP '81
Singles: 7-inch
BOARDWALK....3-5 81
LPs: 10/12-inch
BOARDWALK....5-10 81
Also see TEXTONES
Also see TWILLEY, Dwight, Band

SEYMOUR, Tony
Singles: 7-inch
CARIB....4-8 64

SHA NA NA LP '69
Singles: 7-inch
KAMA SUTRA....3-5 70-75
SUTRA....3-5 74
Picture Sleeves
KAMA SUTRA....3-5 71
LPs: 10/12-inch
ACCORD....5-10 81-83
BUDDAH....5-10 77
CSP....8-12 78
EMUS....5-10 78
K-TEL....5-10 81
KAMA SUTRA....10-15 69-76
NASHVILLE....5-10 80
Members: Lennie Baker; Jon "Bowzer" Bauman; Johnny Contardo; Denny Green; Henry Gross; Jocko Marcellino; Danny McBride; Scott Powell; David-Allan "Chico" Ryan; "Screamin' Scott Simon; Donny York.
Also see CONTARDO, Johnny
Also see EDDIE & EVERGREENS
Also see GROSS, Henry
Also see SIMON, Screamin' Scott
Also see TRAVOLTA, John / Sha Na Na

SHABBADOO
Singles: 7-inch
DORE....3-5

SHACK R&B '71
Singles: 7-inch
VOLT....5-10 71

SHACKLEFORDS P&R '63
Singles: 7-inch
CAPITOL....4-6 66
LHI....4-6 67-68
MERCURY....5-10 63
LPs: 10/12-inch
CAPITOL....10-20 66
MERCURY....15-25 63
Members: Lee Hazlewood; Marty Cooper; Al Stone; Garcia Nitzsche.
Also see HAZLEWOOD, Lee
Also see MOMENTS

SHAD, Bobby
LPs: 10/12-inch
MAINSTREAM....8-10 70

SHADDEN & King Lears
Singles: 7-inch
ARBET (1014 "All I Want Is You")....15-25 67

SHADDOWS
Singles: 7-inch
UNITED AUDIO (80245 "Stormy Weather")....50-100

SHADE, Tiffany
Singles: 7-inch
MAINSTREAM....4-8 68

SHADE, Will
LPs: 10/12-inch
ROUNDER....5-8 83

SHADEMEN
Singles: 7-inch
VERANN (501 "That's Tuff")....15-25 66

SHADES
Singles: 7-inch
ALADDIN (3453 "Dear Lori")....150-250 59
(Black label.)
ALADDIN (3453 "Dear Lori")....200-300 59
(White label. Promotional issue only.)

SHADES
Singles: 7-inch
MAYPOLE....10-15 61
SCOTTIE....10-15 59

SHADES
Singles: 7-inch
SMART (322 "Weird Walk")....10-15 61
STARLITE (054 "Weird Walk")....10-15 61

SHADES
Singles: 7-inch
ARDENT (104 "Shady Lady")....10-20 61

SHADES
Singles: 7-inch
JOEY (6206 "Skip It")....10-15 63

SHADES
Singles: 7-inch
TIMES SQUARE....10-15 63

SHADES
Singles: 7-inch
SIGN....4-8
SOMA (1437 "Please, Please, Please")....25-35 65
WELHAVEN (4957 "I Feel So Fine")....25-35 65
Also see MIDWEST
Also see HOLIEN, Danny

SHADES
Singles: 7-inch
CADET (5608 "Ballot Bachs")....10-20 66

SHADES
Singles: 7-inch
A-OK (1028 "Gingerbread Man")....15-25 67

SHADES
Singles: 7-inch
PRINCETON (7012 "When You Said Goodbye")....15-25 68

SHADES
Singles: 7-inch
RAPA ("Cry Over You")....15-25 60s
(No selection number used.)

SHADES
Singles: 7-inch
FRANCE....10-15 60s
METROPOLIS (7003 "Denny")....25-45

SHADES / Knott Sisters
(Shades Featuring the Knott Sisters)
Singles: 7-inch
BIG TOP (3003 "Sun Glasses")....5-10 58

SHADES OF BLACK LIGHTNING
Singles: 7-inch
TOWER....4-8 68

SHADES OF BLUE P&R/R&B '66
Singles: 7-inch
COLLECTABLES....3-4 80s
IMPACT....8-15 66-67
SHADES....5-10 68
LPs: 10/12-inch
IMPACT (101 "Happiness Is")....30-50 66
(Monaural.)
IMPACT (101 "Happiness Is")....50-75 66
(Stereo.)
Member: George Shuput.

SHADES OF BROWN
Singles: 7-inch
CADET....3-5 70

SHADES OF JOY
Singles: 7-inch
DOUGLAS....4-8 80s
FONTANA....4-8 69
LPs: 10/12-inch
FONTANA....10-15 69

SHADES OF LOVE R&B '82
Singles: 7-inch
VENTURE....3-5 82

SHADES OF NIGHT
Singles: 7-inch
ALAMO AUDIO (111 "Fluctuation")....15-25 67

SHADES OF RHYTHM
(Featuring Bob Williams)
Singles: 78 rpm
CADDY (102 "Gumbo")....10-20 56
Singles: 7-inch
CADDY (102 "Gumbo")....20-30 56

SHADES OF SOUL
Singles: 7-inch
SURE-FIRE....8-12

SHADOE & HIGHBROWS
Singles: 7-inch
GEM (102/1 "Tomboy")....8-12

SHADOS
Singles: 7-inch
ARLEN (515 "Little Miss Surfer")....10-20 63

SHADOW
Singles: 7-inch
CLEAN (60002 "I'm Drifting")....10-20 60s

SHADOW
Singles: 7-inch
NASCO....3-5 70

SHADOW
LPs: 10/12-inch
STAKERS....8-10 75

SHADOW R&B '79
Singles: 7-inch
ELEKTRA....3-5 79-81
LPs: 10/12-inch
ELEKTRA....5-10 79-81
Members: Jimmy Williams; Billy Beck; Chet Willis.
Also see OHIO PLAYERS

SHADOW CASTERS
Singles: 7-inch
J.R.P. (002 "Going to the Moon")....15-25 68
J.R.P. (003 "Cinnamon Snowflake")....15-25 68

SHADOWFAX LP '83
Singles: 7-inch
WINDHAM HILL....3-5 82
LPs: 10/12-inch
CAPITOL....5-8 88
PASSPORT....8-10 76
WINDHAM HILL....5-8 82-86

SHADOWS R&B '50
Singles: 78 rpm
LEE (200 "I've Been a Fool")....15-25 49
LEE (202 "I'd Rather Be Wrong Than Blue")....15-25 50
LEE (207 "Don't Blame My Dreams")....15-25 50
Members; Jasper Edwards; Ray Reed; Sam McClure; Scott King; Bobby Buster.

SHADOWS
Singles: 78 rpm
DECCA....30-50 53-54
HUB....15-25 53
SITTIN' IN WITH....15-25 50-52
Singles: 7-inch
DECCA (28765 "Stay")....100-200 53
DECCA (48307 "Tell Her")....150-250 54

DECCA (48322 "Big Mouth Mama") ... 150-250 54
Also see FOUR TUNES /Shadows

SHADOWS
Singles: 7-inch
DELTA (1509 "Bop-A-Lena") ... 50-100 57

SHADOWS
Singles: 7-inch
FRATERNITY (795 "You Make My Heart Sing Ah!") ... 20-30 58
Member: Elroy Peace.
Also see PEACE, Elroy Shadow

SHADOWS
Singles: 7-inch
DEL-FI (4109 "Under Stars of Love") ... 35-55 58

SHADOWS
Singles: 7-inch
DOTTIE (1006 "I Wonder Why") ... 10-15 61

SHADOWS
Singles: 7-inch
ABC-PAR ... 10-20 60
ATLANTIC ... 8-12 61-64
EPIC ... 5-8 65-66
LPs: 10/12-inch
ATLANTIC (8089 "Surfing with the Shadows") ... 30-40 63
(Monaural.)
ATLANTIC (SD-8089 "Surfing with the Shadows") ... 40-50 63
(Stereo.)
ATLANTIC (8097 "The Shadows Know") ... 25-30 64
(Monaural.)
ATLANTIC (SD-8097 "The Shadows Know") ... 30-40 64
(Stereo.)
Members: Jet Harris; Bruce Welch; Hank Marvin; Tony Meehan.
Also see FOUR JETS
Also see HARRIS, Jet, & Tony Meehan
Also see MARVIN & FARRAR
Also see RICHARD, Cliff
Also see WELCH, Bruce

SHADOWS
Singles: 7-inch
U.S.A. (106 "No Other Love") ... 20-30 60s
WOODRICH (18507 "If You Love Me") ... 10-20 60s

SHADOWS
Singles: 7-inch
JAM (109 "Shake Sherry") ... 15-25 60s

SHADOWS
Singles: 7-inch
DANNY BOY (7614 "Wind Down") ... 8-12

SHADOWS
Singles: 7-inch
DOLEJO (1001 "Shadow Break") ... 5-8

SHADOWS FIVE
Singles: 7-inch
PEACOCK (1912 "Twistin' Shadows") ... 8-12 62
SULLY ... 10-20 61
TECH (4836 "Gathers No Moss") ... 10-20 60s
Members: Leon Sanders; Rich Girssom; Gary Sullivan.
Also see CHAMPS

SHADOWS FOUR
Singles: 7-inch
D-M-E (200,964 "I'm Beggin' You") ... 15-25 65
FLEETWOOD (4553 "Heart of Wood") ... 20-30 65

SHADOWS FOUR
Singles: 7-inch
JCP (1037 "Leaving Today") ... 10-20 64

SHADOWS OF KNIGHT *P&R/LP '66*
Singles: 7-inch
ATCO ... 8-12 69
COLUMBIA/AURAVISION ("Shadows of Knight Sing Potato Chip") ... 50-75 66
(Square 5-inch cardboard picture disc. Included in boxes of Fairmont Potato Chips.)
DUNWICH (116 "Gloria") ... 10-20 66
(Label makes no reference to distribution by Atco.)
DUNWICH (116 "Gloria") ... 5-10 66
(Label reads "Distributed by Atco.")
DUNWICH (122 thru 167) ... 10-20 66-67
SUPER K ... 5-10 69
TEAM ... 5-10 68
Picture Sleeves
DUNWICH (122 "Oh Yeah") ... 15-20 66
DUNWICH (128 "Bad Little Woman") ... 20-30 66
LPs: 10/12-inch
DUNWICH (666 "Gloria") ... 50-100 66
DUNWICH (667 "Back Door Men") ... 50-100 66
SUNDAZED ... 5-10 90s
SUPER K (6002 "The Shadows of Knight") ... 15-25 69

SHADOWS OF TIME
Singles: 7-inch
SOL (201 "Search Your Soul") ... 10-20 67

SHADRACK
Singles: 7-inch
SONIC (202 "It Was Me") ... 10-20 60s
LPs: 10/12-inch
IGL (132 "Chameleon") ... 250-350 71

SHADRICK, Mike
Singles: 7-inch
BANGAR ... 8-12 60s

SHADY DAYS
Singles: 7-inch
RPR (104 "Little Girl") ... 15-25 69

SHADY DAZE
Singles: 7-inch
IT'S a GAS ("You Don't Know Like I Know") ... 15-25 60s
U.S.A. (883 "I'll Make You Pay") ... 15-25 67
Members: Gregg Owen; Breg Biela; Mark Drzewiecki.

SHAFER, Whitey *C&W '80*
Singles: 7-inch
ELEKTRA ... 3-4 80-81

SHAFFER, Beverly
Singles: 7-inch
ONE-DERFUL ... 4-8 65-66

SHAFTO, Bobby *P&R '64*
Singles: 7-inch
RUST ... 5-8 64-65

SHAG
Singles: 7-inch
CAPITOL (5995 "Stop & Listen") ... 15-25 67
Also see SHAGS

SHAGGS
LPs: 10/12-inch
MCM (6311 "Wink") ... 1000-2000 67
Members: Geoff Gillette; Franklin Krakowski; Rick Medich; Ted Poulos; Ray Wheatley.

SHAGGS
Singles: 7-inch
PALMER ... 5-10 60s
POWER (103 "Hummin' ") ... 10-15 60s
Members: Richie Chimelis; Craig Caraglior; Mike Latona; Cleve Johns; Denis O'Barry; Gregg Shaw; Don Ricketts.

SHAGGS
Singles: 7-inch
CAPITOL ... 4-8 69

SHAGGS
LPs: 10/12-inch
ROUNDER ... 8-12 82
THIRD WORLD (3001 "Philosophy of the World") ... 200-300 72
(Reportedly 2,000 made.)
Members: Betty Wiggin; Dorothy Wiggin; Helen Wiggin.

SHAGGY
LPs: 10/12-inch
CAPITOL (43502 "Bombastic") ... 8-10 90s

SHAGGY BOYS
Singles: 7-inch
RED BIRD (10074 "In the Morning") ... 8-12 66
U.A. ... 8-12 66-67
Also see RICKY & VACELS

SHAGNASTY, Boliver
Singles: 7-inch
FUN (10000 "Tapping That Thing") ... 10-15 60s
QUARTERCASH (70 "Tapping That Thing") ... 40-60 60s

SHAGS
(Shag)
Singles: 7-inch
RAYNARD (10034 "Dance Woman") ... 15-25 65
Members: John Sahli; Mike Lamers; Don Luther; Paul Greenwald.
Also see DUCKS
Also see SHAG

SHAGS
Singles: 7-inch
CONCERT (1-78-65 "Louis Louis") ... 40-60 65

SHAGS
Singles: 7-inch
CAMEO (470 "As Long As I Have You") ... 5-10 67
KAYDEN (407 "As Long As I Have You") ... 10-15 67
KAYDEN (408 "Breathe in My Ear") ... 10-15 67
LAURIE (3353 "I Call Your Name") ... 10-15 66
NUTTA (101 "Wait and See") ... 8-12 65
SAMMY (102 "By My Side") ... 8-12 65
TAURUS (1881 "Don't Press Your Luck") ... 20-30 66
Members: Carl Donnell; Tommy Roberts; Bill Hall; Johnny Stanton; Aaron Perkins; Lance Gardner.
Also see DELTONS
Also see PULSE

SHAGS
Singles: 7-inch
GOLDEN VOICE ... 5-10 67
JO-JO ... 5-10 60s

SHAGS
Singles: 7-inch
EAGLE (123 "Smiling Fenceposts") ... 25-35

SHAKATAK *D&D '84*
Singles: 12-inch
POLYDOR ... 4-6 82-84
Singles: 7-inch
POLYDOR ... 3-4 82-84
LPs: 10/12-inch
POLYDOR ... 5-8 82

SHAKE
Singles: 7-inch
WHITE WHALE ... 3-5 70

SHAKERS
Singles: 7-inch
ABC ... 4-8 67
AUDIO FIDELITY ... 5-10 66
LPs: 10/12-inch
AUDIO FIDELITY (2155 "The Shakers Break It All") ... 30-40 66
(Monaural.)
AUDIO FIDELITY (2155 "The Shakers Break It All") ... 35-45 66
(Stereo.)

SHAKES
Singles: 12-inch
SELECT ... 4-6 86

SHAKESPEARES
Singles: 7-inch
GLAD-HAMP (2037 "I Like You") ... 10-15 67

SHAKEY JAKE
(With the All Stars; James Harris)
Singles: 7-inch
ARTISTIC (1502 "Roll Your Moneymaker") ... 15-25 58
PRESTIGE BLUESVILLE (807 "My Foolish Heart") ... 10-15 60
LPs: 10/12-inch
PRESTIGE BLUESVILLE (1008 "Good Times") ... 30-40 60
PRESTIGE BLUESVILLE (1027 "Mouth Harp Blues") ... 30-40 61
WORLD PACIFIC ... 25-35 60s

SHAKEY LEGS
LPs: 10/12-inch
PARAMOUNT ... 8-12 71

SHAKEY VICK
LPs: 10/12-inch
JANUS ... 8-12 70

SHAKIN' PYRAMIDS
Singles: 7-inch
ROCK 'N' ROLL ... 3-5 83
LPs: 10/12-inch
ROCK 'N' ROLL ... 5-10 84

SHAKIN' STEVENS: see STEVENS, Shakin'

SHAKIN' STREET
LPs: 10/12-inch
COLUMBIA ... 5-10 80

SHALAMAR *P&R/R&B/LP '77*
Singles: 12-inch
COLUMBIA ... 4-6 84-85
SOLAR ... 4-6 79-85
Singles: 7-inch
COLUMBIA ... 3-4 84-85
ELEKTRA ... 3-4 85
MCA ... 3-4 84
SOLAR ... 3-5 78-87
SOUL TRAIN ... 3-5 77
Picture Sleeves
COLUMBIA ... 3-4 84
SOLAR ... 3-5 83
LPs: 10/12-inch
SOLAR ... 5-10 78-85
SOUL TRAIN ... 5-10 77
Members: Howard Hewett; Jody Watley; Jeffrey Daniel; Gerald Brown; Delisa Davis; Micki Free; Sidney Justin.
Also see HEWETT, Howard
Also see WATLEY, Jody

SHALIMARS
Singles: 7-inch
BRUNSWICK (55281 "Montezuma") ... 8-12 65
VERVE (10388 "Baby") ... 15-25 66

SHALLOWS
Singles: 7-inch
RAE COX (108 "Wrecking My Life") ... 15-25 61

SHALLOWS
Singles: 7-inch
FORLIN (503 "I Wonder") ... 35-55 62

SHALONS
Singles: 7-inch
RONNIE ... 10-15 60s

SHAM 69
LPs: 10/12-inch
POLYDOR ... 5-10 80
SIRE ... 5-10 79

SHAMANS
(With the William Powell Group)
Singles: 7-inch
KAYHAM (1 "Valley of Tears") ... 100-150 59
KAYHAM (3 "I'll Wait Forever") ... 100-150 59

SHAMBLES
Singles: 7-inch
ATCO ... 8-12 68

SHAMBLIN, Michael *C&W '86*
Singles: 7-inch
F&L ... 3-4 86

SHAME
Singles: 7-inch
POPPY (501 "Too Old to Go Away") ... 10-20 67

SHAMES
Singles: 7-inch
RFT (1001 "The Special Ones") ... 15-25 66

SHAM-ETTES
(Shamettes)
Singles: 7-inch
GOLD DUST ("Wasting Your Time") ... 75-125
(Selection number not known.)
MGM (13618 "Big Bad Wolf") ... 8-12 66
MGM (13798 "He'll Come Back") ... 8-12 67

SHAMROCKS
Singles: 7-inch
54 (5424 "Danny Boy") ... 100-125 59

SHAMROCKS
Singles: 7-inch
ANDIE (5021 "Scrappy") ... 8-12 61
(First issued as by the Check-Mates.)
Member: Jim Ford.
Also see CHECK-MATES
Also see FORD, Jim

SHAMROCKS
Singles: 7-inch
LIBERTY (55460 "Lonely Island") ... 10-20 62
Members: Dorsey and Johnny Burnette.
Also see BURNETTE, Johnny & Dorsey

SHANA *P&R '89*
(Shana Petrone)
Singles: 7-inch
VISION ... 3-4 89
LPs: 10/12-inch
VISION ... 5-8 89

SHAND, Terry
Singles: 78 rpm
IT'S a HIT ... 10-20

SHANDELLS
Singles: 7-inch
BANGAR (0659 "Gorilla") ... 100-125 64
STUDIO CITY (1037 "Here Comes the Pain") ... 25-35 66
Members: Jeff Gottheardt; Grant Gilbertson; Mick Zirngible; Jim Coggins.

SHAN-DELLS
Singles: 7-inch
BIRDGE SOCIETY (112 "Chimes") ... 50-100
BRIDGE SOCIETY (114 "I've Got to Love Her") ... 100-150

SHANDELLS / Fab Four
Singles: 7-inch
SIZZLE (5130 "Mary Mary") ... 25-35 60s

SHANDELS
Singles: 7-inch
MUSIC TOWN (113 "Stop Your Cryin' ") ... 15-25 66

SHANDELS
(Shandells; Shan Dells)
Singles: 7-inch
KING ... 4-8 62
LA SALLE ... 4-8 67

SHANDELS
Singles: 7-inch
CARDELL (510 "No Way Out") ... 8-12 66
SHOWCASE (407 "Please Stay") ... 10-15 66

SHANDELS
Singles: 7-inch
DSP (1004 "Rick's Tune") ... 8-12
FIVE (1009 "Team Beat") ... 8-12
SK (809 "Team Beat") ... 8-12

SHANE
Singles: 7-inch
BRENT ... 4-8 65
MAINSTREAM ... 10-15 66
TOP CATT ... 4-8 68
UNITY ... 5-10 62

SHANE, Hylton
Singles: 7-inch
LIBERTY ... 5-10 59

SHANE, Jackie
Singles: 7-inch
SUE ... 4-8 63

SHANE, Jerry
Singles: 7-inch
VALIANT ... 4-8 62

SHANE, Johnny
Singles: 7-inch
B.B.J. ... 4-8 64
IMPERIAL ... 4-8 64
WORLD ARTISTS ... 4-8 65

SHANE, Lonnie, & Faye Lane
Singles: 7-inch
DANRITE ... 3-5 70

SHANE, Michael *C&W '89*
Singles: 7-inch
REGAL ... 3-4 89

SHANE, Mike
Singles: 7-inch
DOT ... 4-6 68
SOUND STAGE 7 ... 4-6 67

SHANE CHAMPAGNE
Singles: 7-inch
PURE & EASY ... 3-5 79
Picture Sleeves
PURE & EASY ... 3-5 79
LPs: 10/12-inch
PURE & EASY ... 8-10 80

SHANES
Singles: 7-inch
CAPITOL ... 4-8 67

SHANGHAI
Singles: 7-inch
CHRYSALIS ... 3-5 82
LPs: 10/12-inch
CHRYSALIS ... 5-10 82

SHANGO *P&R '69*
Singles: 12-inch
CELLULOID ... 4-8 83
Singles: 7-inch
A&M ... 4-6 69
CELLULOID ... 3-4 83
GNP ... 3-6 69
LPs: 10/12-inch
A&M ... 10-15 69
DUNHILL ... 8-12 70
Also see BAMBAATAA, Afrika

SHANGRI-LAS *P&R/R&B '64*
(Shangra-Las)
Singles: 7-inch
COLLECTABLES ... 3-4 80s
ERIC ... 3-5 70s
LANA ... 4-8 60s
MERCURY (72645 "Sweet Sounds of Summer") ... 5-8 66
MERCURY (72670 "Take the Time") ... 5-8 67
RED BIRD (008 "Remember") ... 8-12 64
RED BIRD (014 "Leader of the Pack") ... 8-12 64
RED BIRD (018 "Give Him a Great Big Kiss") ... 8-12 64
RED BIRD (019 "Maybe") ... 8-12 64
RED BIRD (025 "Out in the Streets") ... 8-12 65
RED BIRD (030 "Give Us Your Blessing") ... 8-12 65
RED BIRD (036 "Right Now and Not Later") ... 8-12 65
RED BIRD (043 "I Can Never Go Home Anymore") ... 8-12 65
RED BIRD (048 "Long Live Our Love") ... 8-12 66
RED BIRD (053 "He Cried") ... 8-12 66
RED BIRD (068 "Past, Present and Future") ... 8-12 66
SSS INT'L ... 3-5 80s
SCEPTER (1291 "Wishing Well") ... 10-15 65
SMASH ... 10-20 63
SPOKANE (4006 "Wishing Well") ... 15-25 64
TRIP ... 3-5 70s
LPs: 10/12-inch
BACK-TRAC ... 5-10 85
COLLECTABLES (5011 "At Their Best") ... 5-10 82
(Black vinyl.)
COLLECTABLES (5011 "At Their Best") ... 10-15 82
(Picture disc.)
MERCURY (21099 "Golden Hits of the Shangri-las") ... 20-30 66
(Monaural.)
MERCURY (21099 "Golden Hits") ... 50-75 66
(Shown as monaural but plays in true stereo.)
MERCURY (61099 "Golden Hits") ... 25-35 66
(Stereo.)
POST ... 10-12
RED BIRD (101 "Leader of the Pack") ... 30-50 65
RED BIRD (104 "Shangri-Las '65") ... 60-100 65
RED BIRD (104 "I Can Never Go Home Anymore") ... 50-85 65
Members: Mary Weiss; Marge Ganser; Mary Ann Ganser.

SHANK, Bud *P&R/LP '66*
Singles: 78 rpm
GOOD TIME JAZZ ... 4-6 54
Singles: 7-inch
GOOD TIME JAZZ ... 5-10 54
PACIFIC JAZZ ... 3-8 61-70
WORLD PACIFIC ... 3-6 64-68
EPs: 7-inch
NOCTURNE (3/4 "The Bud Shank Quintet") ... 50-75 53
(Price is for either volume.)
PACIFIC JAZZ ... 20-30 54-58
LPs: 10/12-inch
CONCORD JAZZ ... 5-8 76
CROWN ... 10-20 63
KIMBERLY ... 10-20 63
NOCTURNE (2 "The Bud Shank Quintet") ... 150-200 53
(10-inch LP.)
PACIFIC JAZZ (14 "Bud Shank with Three Trombones") ... 75-125 54
(10-inch LP.)
PACIFIC JAZZ (20 "Bud Shank & Bob Brookmeyer") ... 75-125 55
(10-inch LP.)
PACIFIC JAZZ (4 thru 89) ... 15-25 60-65
(12-inch LPs.)
PACIFIC JAZZ (404 "Jazz Swings Broadway") ... 40-60 57
PACIFIC JAZZ (411 "The Swing's to TV") ... 40-60 57
PACIFIC JAZZ (1205 "Bud Shank & Shorty Rogers") ... 40-60 55
PACIFIC JAZZ (1213 "Strings and Trombones") ... 40-60 56
PACIFIC JAZZ (1215 "The Bud Shank Quartet") ... 40-60 56
PACIFIC JAZZ (1219 "Jazz at Cal-Tech") ... 40-60 56
PACIFIC JAZZ (1226 "Flute 'N Oboe") ... 40-60 57
PACIFIC JAZZ (1230 "The Bud Shank Quartet") ... 40-60 57

PACIFIC JAZZ (10000 & 20000 series) ... 5-15 66-81
SUNSET ... 8-12 66
WORLD PACIFIC (1000 thru 1200 series) ... 20-40 58-60
WORLD PACIFIC (1400 series) ... 15-30 61-63
WORLD PACIFIC (1800 series) ... 15-20 64-67
WORLD PACIFIC (21000 series) ... 10-20 66-68
Also see FOLKSWINGERS
Also see LONDON, Julie, & Bud Shank Quintet

SHANK & MAYDIEA
Singles: 7-inch
FLIP ... 4-8 62

SHANKAR, L.
LPs: 10/12-inch
ZAPPA ... 8-10

SHANKAR, Ravi LP '67
(With Yehudi Menuhin)
Singles: 7-inch
APPLE (1838 "Joi Bangla") ... 5-10 71
DARK HORSE ... 3-5 75
PACIFIC ... 4-8 60s
WORLD PACIFIC ... 4-8 59-68
Picture Sleeves
APPLE (1838 "Joi Bangla") ... 20-25 71
LPs: 10/12-inch
ANGEL ... 10-20 67
APPLE (3384 "Raga") ... 12-18 71
APPLE (3396 "In Concert 1972") ... 40-50 73
CAPITOL ... 10-20 67-72
COLUMBIA ... 10-20 66-68
DARK HORSE ... 8-12 74-76
FANTASY ... 5-10 73
PRESTIGE ... 10-20 68
SPARK ... 5-10 73
WORLD PACIFIC ... 10-20 59-69
Also see BEATLES
Also see HARRISON, George

SHANKLIN, Martha
Singles: 7-inch
YANKEE DOODLE ... 4-8 62

SHANKS, Junior
Singles: 7-inch
MADISON ... 10-15 58

SHANNON P&R '69
(Marty Wilde)
Singles: 7-inch
EPIC/MAGNET ... 3-5 75
HERITAGE ... 4-6 69
Also see WILDE, Marty

SHANNON P&R/R&B/D&D '83
(Brenda Shannon Greene)
Singles: 12-inch
EMERGENCY ... 4-6 83-84
MIRAGE ... 4-6 84-85
Singles: 7-inch
ATLANTIC ... 3-4 86
EMERGENCY ... 3-5 83-84
MIRAGE ... 3-5 84-85
Picture Sleeves
MIRAGE ... 3-5 84-85
LPs: 10/12-inch
MIRAGE ... 5-10 84-85

SHANNON, Bobby
(Bobby Gregory)
Singles: 7-inch
ADAIRE ("Your Last Goodbye Sounded Different") ... 40-50
(Selection number not known.)
Also see GREGORY, Bobby, & Cardinals

SHANNON, Bonnie C&W '80
Singles: 7-inch
DOOR KNOB ... 3-4 80

SHANNON, Del P&R/R&B '61
Singles: 7-inch
AMY ... 4-8 64-65
BERLEE ... 5-10 63-64
BIG TOP ... 10-20 61-63
COLLECTABLES ... 3-4 80s
DUNHILL ... 4-8 69
ERIC ... 3-5 70s
ISLAND ... 3-5 75
LANA ... 3-6 60s
LIBERTY ... 5-10 66-68
NETWORK ... 4-6 81-82
TERRIFIC ... 3-5
TRIP ... 3-6
TWIRL ... 4-6 60s
W.B. ... 3-5 85
Picture Sleeves
LIBERTY ... 8-12 68
LPs: 10/12-inch
AMY (8003 "Handy Man") ... 30-50 64
(Monaural.)
AMY (S-8003 "Handy Man") ... 40-60 64
(Stereo.)
AMY (8004 "Del Shannon Sings Hank Williams") ... 30-50 65
(Monaural.)
AMY (S-8004 "Del Shannon Sings Hank Williams") ... 40-60 65
(Stereo.)
AMY (8006 "1,661 Seconds") ... 30-50 65
(Monaural.)
AMY (S-8006 "1,661 Seconds") ... 40-60 65
(Stereo.)
BIG TOP (1303 "Runaway") ... 150-250 61
(Monaural.)
BIG TOP (1303 "Runaway") ... 550-650 61
(Stereo.)
BIG TOP (1308 "Little Town Flirt") ... 40-60 63
BUG ... 5-10 85
DOT (3834 "Best of Del Shannon") ... 25-45 67
(Monaural.)
DOT (25834 "Best of Del Shannon") ... 25-45 67
(Stereo.)
LIBERTY ... 20-30 66-68
NETWORK/ELEKTRA ... 8-10 81
PHOENIX 20 ... 8-10 80
PICKWICK ... 8-10 70s
POST ... 10-15
SIRE ... 10-15 75
SUNSET ... 10-15 70
U.A. ... 10-15 73
Also see HONDELLS / Del Shannon / Martha & Vandellas
Also see MAXIMILLIAN

SHANNON, Guy C&W '73
Singles: 7-inch
CINNAMON ... 3-5 73

SHANNON, Jackie
(Jackie Shannon & Cajuns; Jackie DeShannon)
Singles: 7-inch
DOT (15928 "Just Another Lie") ... 15-20 59
FRATERNITY (836 "Just Another Lie") ... 10-15 59
P.J. (101 "Trouble") ... 30-40 59
SAGE (290 "Just Another Lie") ... 20-30 59
SAND (330 "Trouble") ... 20-30 59
Also see DE SHANNON, Jackie

SHANNON, Mark
Singles: 7-inch
TOWER ... 4-8 66-67

SHANNON, Pat
(With the Anita Kerr Singers & Owen Bradley Orchestra)
Singles: 7-inch
DECCA (Except 30666) ... 8-12 58-60
DECCA (30666 "You're So Wild") ... 15-25 58
UNI ... 4-6 69
W.B. ... 4-8 68
LPs: 10/12-inch
UNI ... 10-15 69
Also see KERR, Anita
Also see BRADLEY, Owen

SHANNON, Ron, & Saharas
(Ronny Shannon)
Singles: 7-inch
STON-ROC ... 15-20 60s
UNITED ... 5-10 60s

SHANNONS
Singles: 7-inch
L&M ... 10-15 58
LIBERTY ... 4-8 68

SHANTE, Roxanne R&B/D&D '85
Singles: 12-inch
POP ART ... 4-6 85
Singles: 7-inch
POP ART ... 3-4 85
LPs: 10/12-inch
POP ART ... 5-8 85
Also see JAMES, Rick, & Roxanne Shante

SHANTELLE R&B '85
Singles: 7-inch
PANDISC ... 4-6 85

SHANTONES
Singles: 7-inch
TRILYTE (5001 "Come to Me") ... 1000-2000 56

SHAN-TONES
Singles: 7-inch
ANGELA (101 "Sheba") ... 10-20 60

SHANTONS
(With Billy Mure & His Orchestra)
Singles: 7-inch
JAY-MAR (165 "Triangle Love") 200-250 59
(Identification number shown since no selection number is used.)
JAY-MAR (182 "Christmas Song") ... 100-200 60
(Identification number shown since no selection number is used.)
JAY-MAR (241 "Lucille") ... 500-750 59
(Identification number shown since no selection number is used.)
Also see BROWN, Skip, & Shantons
Also see JACKSON, Skip
Also see MURE, Billy

SHAPARELLS
Singles: 7-inch
BENNETT ENTERPRISES (324 "Knock on Wood") ... 10-20 68

SHAPE OF THINGS
Singles: 7-inch
LAURIE ... 4-8 67

SHAPE OF THINGS
Singles: 7-inch
MEGA ... 3-5 71
Picture Sleeves
MEGA ... 3-5 71

SHAPIRO, Helen P&R '61
Singles: 7-inch
CAPITOL ... 8-10 61-62
EPIC ... 4-8 62-63
JANUS ... 3-5 70
MUSICOR ... 4-6 65
TOWER ... 4-6 67
Picture Sleeves
EPIC ... 4-8 62
LPs: 10/12-inch
EPIC ... 10-20 63

SHAPRELS
Singles: 7-inch
CHESS ... 4-8 67
FEATURE ... 5-10 66-67
P.K.C. ... 5-10 69
TEE PEE ... 5-10 67
Members: Jimmy Meier; Bob Sczweda; Tom Richards Bob Mehring; Don Hornjak.

SHAPRELS
Singles: 7-inch
BENNETT ... 5-10 60s

SHA-RAE, Billy R&B '71
(Sha-Rae)
Singles: 7-inch
BAY-UKE ... 5-10 61-62
HOUR GLASS ... 3-5
LAURIE ... 3-5
SPECTRUM ... 4-6 71
Also see HEBB, Bobby / Billy Sha-Rae

SHARADES
Singles: 7-inch
FASCINATTON (701 "Only a Tear") ... 10-20

SHARELL, Jerry
(With Mark III)
Singles: 7-inch
ALANNA (560 "Everybody Knows") ... 15-25 61
FUZZY (1-1 "Centerpiece") ... 15-25 66
(First issue.)
MAIN LINE (1365 "It'll Never Happen Again") ... 5-10 67
VERVE (10453 "Centerpiece") ... 5-10 66
Session: Valerie Simpson.
Also see SIMPSON, Valerie
Also see VELVETS

SHARKEY
LPs: 10/12-inch
FIREWORKS DISCORPORATION (1234 "Signposts") ... 10-15 75

SHARKEY TODD: see TODD, Sharkey

SHARKEY, Feargal P&R/LP '86
Singles: 12-inch
A&M/VIRGIN ... 4-6 86
Singles: 7-inch
A&M/VIRGIN ... 3-4 86-88
Picture Sleeves
A&M/VIRGIN ... 3-4 86-88
LPs: 10/12-inch
A&M/VIRGIN ... 5-8 86
Also see ASSEMBLY
Also see UNDERTONES

SHARKEY & BARRACUDAS
Singles: 7-inch
CLASS (701 "Cowabunga") ... 10-15 65

SHARKS
Singles: 7-inch
SAPIEN (1003 "Big Surf") ... 20-25 63
Also see VEGAS, Pat & Lolly

SHARKS LP '73
Singles: 7-inch
MCA ... 3-5 73-74
LPs: 10/12-inch
MCA ... 8-12 73-74

SHARKS
LPs: 10/12-inch
IRON WORKS (2001 "Alter Ego") ... 5-8 86
(Picture disc.)

SHARKS
Singles: 7-inch
BROADCAST ... 5-10
CLIFTON ... 4-8
Also see FIVE SHARKS

SHARLETS
Singles: 7-inch
EXPLOSIVE ... 5-10 66
Session: Davie Allan.
Also see ALLAN, Davie

SHARMEERS
Singles: 7-inch
RED TOP (109 "A School Girl in Love") ... 100-125 58

SHARMETTES
Singles: 7-inch
KING ... 6-12 62

SHARON
Singles: 7-inch
JANA (0001 "Black Cloud") ... 8-12 60s

SHARON & BITS O' HONEY
Singles: 7-inch
PENTHOUSE (1003 "Don't Push My Love Aside") ... 40-60

SHARON, Ralph
Singles: 7-inch
DUCHESS ... 4-8
Also see BENNETT, Tony

SHARON MARIE
Singles: 7-inch
CAPITOL (5064 "Runaround Lover") ... 50-75 63
CAPITOL (5195 "Thinkin' 'Bout You Baby") ... 50-75 64
Also see HONEYS

SHARP, Becky
Singles: 7-inch
ZODIAC ... 4-8 64

SHARP, Benny, & Sharpees
Singles: 7-inch
MIDAS (303 "Music") ... 5-8 69
Also see LITTLE MISS JESSIE / Benny Sharp & His Band
Also see SHARPEES

SHARP, Bobby
Singles: 7-inch
DESTINY (401 "I Love You My Baby") ... 20-25
EPIC (9849 "I Don't Want to See You Again") ... 5-8 65
WING (90056 "Flowers, Mr. Florist Please") ... 5-10 58

SHARP, Dee Dee P&R/R&B/LP '62
(Dee Dee Sharp Gamble)
Singles: 7-inch
ABKCO ... 3-5 83-84
ATCO ... 4-8 66-68
CAMEO ... 5-10 62-66
FAIRMOUNT ... 5-10 66
GAMBLE (219 "You're Gonna Miss Me") ... 8-12 68
PHILADELPHIA INT'L ... 3-5 77-81
TSOP ... 3-5 76
Picture Sleeves
CAMEO ... 5-10 62-65
LPs: 10/12-inch
CAMEO (C-1018 "It's Mashed Potato Time") ... 20-30 62
CAMEO (C-1022 "Songs of Faith") ... 20-30 62
(Monaural.)
CAMEO (SC-1022 "Songs of Faith") ... 30-40 62
(Stereo.)
CAMEO (C-1032 "All the Hits") ... 20-30 62
(Monaural.)
CAMEO (SC-1032 "All the Hits") ... 20-30 62
(Stereo.)
CAMEO (C-1050 "Do the Bird") ... 20-30 62
(Monaural.)
CAMEO (SC-1050 "Do the Bird") ... 20-30 62
(Stereo.)
CAMEO (C-1062 "Biggest Hits") ... 20-30 63
(Monaural.)
CAMEO (SC-1062 "Biggest Hits") ... 20-30 63
(Stereo.)
CAMEO (C-1074 "Down Memory Lane") ... 20-30 63
(Monaural.)
CAMEO (SC-1074 "Down Memory Lane") ... 20-30 63
(Stereo.)
CAMEO (C-2002 "18 Golden Hits") ... 20-30 60s
(Monaural.)
CAMEO (SC-2002 "18 Golden Hits") ... 20-30 60s
(Stereo.)
PHILADELPHIA INT'L ... 8-10 75-81
Also see CHECKER, Chubby, & Dee Dee Sharp
Also see KING, Ben E., & Dee Dee Sharp
Also see PHILADELPHIA INTERNATIONAL ALL STARS

SHARP, Rosemary C&W '87
Singles: 7-inch
CANYON CREEK ... 3-4 87-88

SHARP, Sidney
Singles: 7-inch
W.B. ... 4-8 61

SHARP, Terri
Singles: 7-inch
FONTANA ... 4-8 66
SHARTÉR ... 4-6 60s

SHARP, Billy
Singles: 7-inch
KUDO (668 "Stars in My Eyes") ... 200-300

SHARPE, Buddy
(With the Shakers)
Singles: 78 rpm
FEE BEE (230 "Linda Lee") ... 10-15 56
Singles: 7-inch
BISHOP ... 4-8
FEE BEE (230 "Linda Lee") ... 20-25 56
RAMBLE ("The Shake") ... 8-12 62
(Selection number not known.)
SPEAR (2 "Please Please Please") ... 50-75 50s
STAR (312 "Tooth Ache") ... 50-75 57

SHARPE, Cathy
Singles: 7-inch
GLOBAL (723 "North Pole Rock") 50-75 59

SHARPE, Henry
Singles: 7-inch
GLOBAL (717 "Shortnin' Rock & Roll") ... 100-200 59

SHARPE, Mike P&R '67
Singles: 7-inch
LIBERTY ... 4-8 66-69
LPs: 10/12-inch
LIBERTY ... 10-20 67-69
Also see CLASSICS IV

SHARPE, Ray P&R/R&B '59
(With the Blues Whalers; with Soul Set)
Singles: 7-inch
A&M ... 3-6 71
ATCO ... 4-8 66
DOT (15974 "That's the Way I Feel") ... 10-15 59
FLYING HIGH ... 3-5
GAREX ... 5-10 63
GREGMARK (14 "Linda Lu") ... 5-10 62
HAMILTON (50002 "Oh, My Baby's Gone") ... 10-20 58
JAMIE (1128 "Linda Lu"/"Monkey's Uncle") ... 10-20 59
JAMIE (1128 "Linda Lu"/"Red Sails In the Sunset") ... 8-12 59
JAMIE (1138 "T.A. Blues") ... 8-12 59
JAMIE (1149 "Bermuda") ... 8-12 60
JAMIE (1155 "Red Sails In the Sunset") ... 8-12 60
JAMIE (1164 "Kewpie Doll") ... 8-12 60
LHI ... 5-8 60s
MONUMENT ... 5-8 65
PARK AVE ... 5-8 60s
SOCK & SOUL ... 5-8 60s
TREY (3011 "Justine") ... 8-12 61
LPs: 10/12-inch
AWARD (711 "Welcome Back") ... 25-50
FLYING HIGH ... 5-10
Session: Duane Eddy; Al Casey; Jim Horn; King Curtis.
Also see CASEY, Al
Also see EDDY, Duane
Also see KING CURTIS

SHARPE, Ray
Singles: 7-inch
AVIS ... 3-5

SHARPE, Sunday C&W '74
Singles: 7-inch
PLAYBOY ... 3-5 76-77
U.A. ... 3-5 74-76
LPs: 10/12-inch
U.A. ... 6-12 74

SHARPE & KERLIN
Singles: 7-inch
CAPE ... 10-15

SHARPEES P&R '66
Singles: 7-inch
ONE-DERFUL (4835 "Do the 45") 10-15 65
ONE-DERFUL (4839 "Tired of Being Lonely") ... 10-15 65
ONE-DERFUL (4843 "I've Got a Secret") ... 10-15 66
ONE-DERFUL (4845 "The Sock") .. 10-15 66
Members: Herbert Reeves; Benny Sharp; Vernon Guy; Horise O'Toole; Stacy Johnson.
Also see GUY, Vernon
Also see JOHNSON, Stacy
Also see LITTLE HERBERT & ARABIANS
Also see SHARP, Benny, & Sharpees

SHARPLES, Bob P&R '56
(Bob Sharples' Living Strings)
Singles: 78 rpm
LONDON ... 3-5 56-57
Singles: 7-inch
LONDON ... 4-6 56-61
LPs: 10/12-inch
CAMDEN ... 5-10 60
LONDON ... 5-15 61-64
METRO ... 5-10 65

SHARPS
Singles: 78 rpm
ALADDIN ... 20-40 57
JAMIE ... 20-40 57
TWO MIKES (101 "Heaven Only Knows") ... 100-150 54
Singles: 7-inch
ALADDIN (3401 "What Will I Gain") ... 30-50 57
COMBO (146 "All My Love") ... 40-60 58
(First issue.)
DARROW (511 "Crusin' ") ... 20-30 60
DOT (15806 "All My Love") ... 10-20 58
JAMIE (1040 "Sweet Sweetheart") 25-35 57
JAMIE (1108 "Have Love Will Travel") ... 35-55 58
(With Duane Eddy.)
JAMIE (1114 "Here's My Heart") ... 30-50 58
LAMP (2007 "Our Love Is Here to Stay") ... 25-35 57
STAR-HI (10460 "Double Clutch") 20-30 60
WIN (702 "We Three") ... 40-60 58
Members: Carl White; Al Frazier; Sonny Harris; Turner Wilson.
Also see DON & DEWEY
Also see EDDY, Duane
Also see ELL, Carl, & Buddies
Also see HARRIS, Thurston
Also see KEY, Troyce
Also see MELLOMOODS
Also see RIVINGTONS

SHARPS
Singles: 7-inch
DARROW (511 "Crusin' ") ... 20-30 60
STAR-HI (10460 "Double Clutch") ... 20-30 60

SHARPS / Jack McVea
Singles: 7-inch
CHESS (1690 "Six Months, Three Weeks") ... 20-30 58
TAG (2200 "Six Months, Three Weeks") ... 75-100 58
Also see McVEA, Jack
Also see SHARPS

SHARPSTERS
Singles: 7-inch
BELLA ... 10-15 59

SHARPTONES
(With Steve Pulliam & Orchestra)
Singles: 78 rpm
POST ... 50-100 55
Singles: 7-inch
ACE (133 "I'll Always Remember") ... 100-150 58
KUDO (668 "Stars in My Eyes") ... 100-200 58
POST (2009 "Since I Fell for You") ... 200-300 55

SHARRON, Debbie
Singles: 7-inch
BAMBOO.. 4-8 61

SHARRON, Ralph
LPs: 10/12-inch
GORDY (903 "Modern Innovations on C&W")..50-100 63

SHARX
EPs: 7-inch
PACHUCCO (4952 "Don't Confess") 4-8
Members: J. Hollis Wood; Amie Rod; Jon Memolo.

SHATNER, William
Singles: 7-inch
DECCA..10-15 69
LPs: 10/12-inch
DECCA (75043 "The Transformed Man")..40-60 69
K-TEL (494 "Captain of the Starship") 40-60
(Two discs.)
LEMLI..10-15

SHATSWELL, Danny C&W '78
Singles: 7-inch
MERCURY 3-5 78

SHATTERED IMAGE
Singles
MASQUE (8910 "Eye to Eye") 8-12 89
(Band-shaped picture disc. 500 made.)
MASQUE (8910 "Eye to Eye") 15-20 89
(Rectangular picture disc. 50 made.)

SHATTOES
Singles: 7-inch
STUDIO CITY (1010 "Surf Fever")..100-200 64
(Reportedly 400 to 500 made.)
Also see CHATEAUX

SHAUL, Lawrence
Singles: 7-inch
REED (1049 "Hey Little Mama" 50-75 60

SHAVER, Billy Joe C&W '73
Singles: 7-inch
CAPRICORN.. 3-5 78
COLUMBIA.. 3-4 82
MONUMENT 3-5 73
LPs: 10/12-inch
CAPRICORN.. 5-10 76-77
COLUMBIA.. 5-10 81-82
MONUMENT 6-12 73-78
Also see CROWELL, Rodney
Also see HARRIS, Emmylou
Also see NELSON, Willie
Also see SKAGGS, Ricky

SHAVER, Elliot
(With the Blazers; Elliot Shavers)
Singles: 7-inch
BLAUN 5-10
ELLEN (502 "Shake 'Em Up")........10-15 62
(Black vinyl.)
ELLEN (502 "Shake 'Em Up")........20-30 62
(Colored vinyl.)
IMCO (101 "Lincoln Continental")....10-20 61
IMCO (102 "Scratch That Itch")......10-20 61
(First issue.)
KING (5546 "Scratch That Itch") 5-10 61
MAGNUM (718 "Fool, Fool, Fool").. 8-12 61
MAGNUM (738 "Soulin' Back") 8-12
RAJA.. 5-10 65
SWINGIN' (630 "Do You Think I Care").. 5-10 61
ZAN-DAN 5-10

SHAW, Allan
Singles: 7-inch
COS ("Stranded") 8-12
(Selection number not known.)

SHAW, Allen
LPs:10/12-inch
GRAND LIB. 5-10 73
SOUND 80.. 8-12

SHAW, Arlane
Singles: 7-inch
MIST (1016 "Lotta Lovin' ") 20-30 62

SHAW, Bennie
Singles: 7-inch
EXCELLO (2313 "What Price for Love") 4-8 71

SHAW, Brian C&W '73
Singles: 7-inch
RCA.. 3-5 73-74
REPUBLIC.. 3-5 76-77

SHAW, Carol
Singles: 7-inch
ATCO (6278 "Jimmy Boy") 10-15 63
TALENT..10-15 60s

SHAW, Eddie
Singles: 7-inch
CJ (647 "Ridin' High") 10-20 64
COLT (647 "Ridin' High") 10-20 64

SHAW, Georgie P&R '54
Singles: 78 rpm
DECCA (Except 28937) 3-6 53-56
DECCA (28937 "Honeycomb")........ 5-10 54
Singles: 7-inch
DECCA (Except 28937)................. 5-10 53-56
DECCA (28937 "Honeycomb")..........10-15 54
METRO 5-10 58
EPs: 7-inch
DECCA.. 5-10 56
LPs: 10/12-inch
DECCA..10-20 53-56
Also see KALLEN, Kitty, & Georgie Shaw

SHAW, Jim
Singles: 7-inch
C&W (115 "Rockin' Boppin' Teenager")..20-30

SHAW, Jimmy
Singles: 7-inch
IMPERIAL..10-15 59

SHAW, Joan
Singles: 78 rpm
ABC-PAR 4-6 56
Singles: 7-inch
ABC-PAR 5-10 56
COLPIX 4-8 62

SHAW, Joan, & Billy Ford
Singles: 78 rpm
ABBEY (3030 "Rock My Soul") 10-15 51
Singles: 7-inch
ABBEY (3030 "Rock My Soul") 20-30 51
Also see FORD, Billy
Also see SHAW, Joan

SHAW, John, & Dell-os
(John Shaw & Dell-o's; with Billy Cooke & Orchestra)
Singles: 7-inch
U-C (5002 "Why Did You Leave Me")..1500-2500 58
Also see SENSATIONAL DELLOS

SHAW, Johnny, & Jaywalkers
Singles: 7-inch
JUBILEE (5511 "Wild Surfer's Call")..10-20 65

SHAW, Mark
Singles: 7-inch
STERLING 5-8
Also see MOORE, Mel, & Marc Shaw

SHAW, Marlena P&R/R&B '67
Singles: 12-inch
COLUMBIA.. 4-8 79
SOUTH BAY.. 4-6 83
Singles: 7-inch
BLUE NOTE.. 3-5 72-76
CADET 4-6 66-69
COLUMBIA.. 3-5 77-79
SOUTH BAY.. 3-5 83
Picture Sleeves
CADET 4-8 67
LPs: 10/12-inch
BLUE NOTE.. 8-12 72-75
CADET 10-15 68-69
COLUMBIA.. 5-10 77-79

SHAW, Mike
Singles: 7-inch
GONE (5098 "Coal Mine") 10-20 60
PERFECT (111 "Long Gone Baby")..150-250 57

SHAW, Rick, & Mandarins
Singles: 7-inch
CAMPUS (105 "Martian Chant") 15-25 57
(Colored vinyl.)

SHAW, Ricky
(With Billy Mure & Orchestra)
Singles: 7-inch
CLOUD..10-15 65
PRESIDENT (822 "A Fool's Memory")..50-75 62
PRESIDENT (830 "Don't Waste Your Time")..15-25 63
Also see MURE, Billy

SHAW, Robert
LPs: 10/12-inch
ARHOOLIE..10-15 63
RCA.. 8-15 57-63

SHAW, Robert, Chorale LP '57
Singles: 78 rpm
RCA.. 3-5 50-58
Singles: 7-inch
RCA.. 4-8 50-62
EPs: 7-inch
RCA.. 5-10 54-56
LPs: 10/12-inch
ALMANAC 5-10 66
CAMDEN.. 5-10 64
RCA.. 5-15 50-70
VICTROLA 4-8 70

SHAW, Roland, Orchestra LP '65
Singles: 78 rpm
LONDON.. 3-5 56-57
Singles: 7-inch
LONDON.. 3-6 56-67
LPs: 10/12-inch
LONDON.. 5-10 64-78

SHAW, Ron C&W '77
(With the Desert Wind Band)
Singles: 7-inch
PACIFIC CHALLENGER 3-5 77-81

SHAW, Sandie P&R '64
Singles: 7-inch
MERCURY 4-8 64
RCA.. 3-6 68-70
REPRISE.. 4-8 64-67
LPs: 10/12-inch
REPRISE..15-20 65-66

SHAW, Sandy
Singles: 7-inch
MOONGLOW (5006 "Rock Is Here to Stay")..15-25 57

SHAW, Timmy P&R/R&B '64
Singles: 7-inch
JAMIE..5-15 61-62
SCEPTER 4-6 73
WAND..5-10 63-64

SHAW, Timmy, & Little Melvin
Singles: 7-inch
PREMIUM STUFF..10-20 60s
Also see LITTLE MELVIN
Also see SHAW, Timmy

SHAW, Tommy P&R/LP '84
Singles: 7-inch
A&M..3-4 84-85
ATLANTIC..3-4 88
Picture Sleeves
A&M..3-4 84-85
ATLANTIC..3-4 88
LPs: 10/12-inch
A&M..5-8 84-85
Also see STYX

SHAW, Victoria C&W '84
Singles: 7-inch
MPB..3-4 84

SHAW BROTHERS
Singles: 7-inch
BRANDYWINE (1004 "New Hampshire Naturally")..4-6
BRANDYWINE (1006 "Ballad of the Concord Coach")..4-6
RCA..3-5 74
Picture Sleeves
BRANDYWINE (1004 "New Hampshire Naturally")..8-10
BRANDYWINE (1006 "Ballad of the Concord Coach")..10-15
LPs: 10/12-inch
RCA..8-10 74

SHA-WEEZ
Singles: 78 rpm
ALADDIN..300-400 52
Singles: 7-inch
ALADDIN (3170 "No One to Love Me")..2000-3000 52
Members: Edgar Miles; Warren Miles; James Crawford; Irving Bannister.
Also see MYLES, Big Boy

SHAWN, Damon R&B '72
Singles: 7-inch
WESTBOUND..3-5 73

SHAWN, Dick, & Little People
Singles: 7-inch
20TH FOX..4-6 64-65
LPs: 10/12-inch
20TH FOX..10-15 64

SHAWN, Robbi
Singles: 7-inch
LINDE-JO..4-8 61
TOPPA..4-8 62

SHAWNEE
Singles: 7-inch
TEE PEE..3-5 71

SHAY, Dorothy C&W '47
Singles: 78 rpm
COLUMBIA..4-8 47

SHAY, Janet
(With the Four Jacks; with Don Neal & Playboys)
Singles: 78 rpm
LIN..10-15 54
Singles: 7-inch
ALCAR (1502 "Busy Bee")..............20-30 60
LIN..20-30 54
PELPAL..10-15
Also see FOUR JACKS

SHAY, Ricky, & Bullets
Singles: 7-inch
CHATTAHOOCHEE..4-8 65

SHAYDE
(Shaydes)
Singles: 7-inch
INTERNATIONAL ARTISTS (132 "Search the Sun")..15-25 68
INTERNATIONAL ARTISTS (137 "Third Number")..15-25 69

SHAYNE, Charity
Singles: 7-inch
AUTUMN..5-8 65

SHAYNE, Pepper
Singles: 7-inch
MOONLITE..3-5 71

SHAYNES
Singles: 7-inch
PEE VEE (140 "You Tell Me Girl")..20-30 66
PEE VEE (142 "From My Window")..25-45 66
PEE VEE (5000 "Valarie") 30-50 61

SHAYS
Singles: 7-inch
ASTRA..4-8 65

SH-BOOMS
(Chords)
Singles: 78 rpm
CAT..10-20 55
VIK..15-25 57
Singles: 7-inch
ATCO (6213 "Sh-Boom")..............10-20 61
ATLANTIC (2074 "Blue Moon")........15-25 60
CAT (117 "Could It Be")..................25-35 55
VIK (0295 "I Don't Want to Set the World on Fire")..20-30 57
Also see CHORDS

SHE
Singles: 7-inch
KENT..10-15 60s

SHEAN & JENKYNS
Singles: 7-inch
GNP (197 "Goofy Footer Ho-Dad")..10-20 63

SHEAR, Jules D&D '84
Singles: 12-inch
EMI AMERICA..4-6 84-85
Singles: 7-inch
EMI AMERICA..3-4 84-85
Picture Sleeves
EMI AMERICA..3-4 85
LPs: 10/12-inch
EMI AMERICA..5-8 83
Also see JULES & Polar Bears

SHEARING, George, Quintet LP '56
Singles: 78 rpm
CAPITOL..3-5 55-57
MGM..3-6 50-56
Singles: 7-inch
CAPITOL..4-8 55-67
LONDON..3-6 63
MGM..6-12 50-56
SHEBA..3-5 71
EPs: 7-inch
CAPITOL..5-15 55-60
MGM..5-15 51-55
LPs: 10/12-inch
ARCHIVE of FOLK MUSIC..............6-12 68
BASF..5-10 73
CAPITOL (Except 648 thru 1628).....5-20 62-77
CAPITOL (648 thru 1628)..............20-40 55-61
CONCORD JAZZ..5-8 80-82
CORONET..5-10 60s
DISCOVERY (3002 "George Shearing Quintet")..30-50 50
(10-inch LP.)
EVEREST..5-10 69
LION..10-20 59
MGM (90 "A Touch of Genius") 20-40 51
(10-inch LP.)
MGM (155 "I Hear Music")..............20-40 52
(10-inch LP.)
MGM (226 "When Lights Are Low")..20-40 53
(10-inch LP.)
MGM (252 "An Evening with George Shearing")..20-40 55
(10-inch LP.)
MGM (100 series)..5-10 70
MGM (3000 series)..15-25 55-60
MGM (4000 series)..10-20 62-63
MPS..5-10 74-75
METRO..10-15 65
MOSAIC (157 "Complete Capitol Live Recordings")..90-100 90s
(Boxed, seven-disc audiophile set. 7500 made.)
PAUSA..5-8 79-82
PICKWICK..5-8
SAVOY (12093 "Midnight on Cloud 69")..15-25 57
SAVOY (15003 "Piano Solo") 30-50 51
(10-inch LP.)
SHEBA..5-10 71-76
VSP..10-15 66-67
Also see COLE, Cozy
Also see COLE, Nat "King," & George Shearing
Also see COLE, Natalie
Also see LEE, Peggy, & George Shearing

SHEARING, George & Montgomery Brothers
Singles: 7-inch
JAZZLAND..3-6 62
LPs: 10/12-inch
JAZZLAND (55 "George Shearing & Montgomery Brothers)..............25- 40 61
(Cover pictures Shearing with the three brothers.)
JAZZLAND (55 "George Shearing & Montgomery Brothers)..................15- 25 62
(Cover pictures a woman.)
RIVERSIDE..5-10 82
Also see MONTGOMERY BROTHERS
Also see SHEARING, George, Quintet
Also see WILSON, Nancy, & George Shearing

SHEARS, Billy, & All Americans
Singles: 7-inch
SILVER FOX..5-10 60s

SHEATHER, Sonny
Singles: 7-inch
BEAVER (101 "Orbit with Me") 10-20 63
BEAVER (102 "Mississippi Ride") 8-12 63

SHED, Henry
Singles: 7-inch
LIBERTY..3-5 70

SHEEHAN, Steve
EPs: 7-inch
NO LABEL NAME (11550 "Recovery")..5-10 84
Also see DIGITAL SEX

SHEELY, Jerry, & Versatiles
Singles: 7-inch
STARR (220 "Love Only Me")....400-600 60s

SHEELY, Ted
Singles: 7-inch
J-V-B (5003 "Eagle Shuffle") 15-25 59

SHEEN, Bobby R&B '75
Singles: 7-inch
CAPITOL..10-20 66-69
CHELSEA..3-5 75
DIMENSION..8-12 65
LIBERTY..5-10 62
W.B. 10-15 72
Also see ALLEY CATS
Also see BOB B. SOXX & Blue Jeans

SHEENA & ROKKETS
Singles: 7-inch
A&M..3-5 81
LPs: 10/12-inch
A&M..5-10 81

SHEEP P&R '66
Singles: 7-inch
BOOM (6000 "Hide & Seek") 15-25 66
BOOM (6007 "Dynamite")..............15-25 66
Members: Bob Feldman; Jerry Goldstein; Richie Gottehrer. Session: Tom Kobus; Jack Raczka; John Shine; Richie Lauro.
Also see STRANGELOVES

SHEER, Anita
Singles: 7-inch
VERVE..4-8 66

SHEER COINCIDENCE
Singles: 7-inch
WRIGHT (6951 "I Didn't Lie") 10-20 69

SHEER ELEGANCE
Singles: 7-inch
ABC..3-5 76

SHEETS, Sonny
Singles: 7-inch
SATURN (1200 "Skippin' Class") 25-35

SHEFFIELD, Charles
(Mad Dog Sheffield)
Singles: 7-inch
EXCELLO..8-10 61
GOLDBAND (1045 "Mad Dog") 25-35 58
HOLLYWOOD (1079 "Mad Dog") 20-30 58

SHEFFIELDS
Singles: 7-inch
DESTINATION (613 "Please Come Back to Me")..8-12 66
DESTINATION (621 "Do You Still Love Me")..8-12 66
FENTON (980 "Nothing I Can Do")..20-30 65
FENTON (2118 "Fool Minus a Heart")..15-25 66

SHEIKS
Singles: 78 rpm
CAT (116 "Walk That Walk")..........10-20 55
EF-N-DE (1000 "Give Me Another Chance")..200-300 55
FEDERAL (12237 "So Fine")..........50-100 55
Singles: 7-inch
CAT (116 "Walk That Walk")..........25-50 55
EF-N-DE (1000 "Give Me Another Chance")..500-750 55
FEDERAL (12237 "So Fine").......200-300 55
Also see BELVIN, Jesse

SHEIKS
Singles: 7-inch
JAMIE (1147 "Candlelight Cafe")......5-10 59
Also see GILMORE, Geoff / Sheiks

SHEIKS
Singles: 7-inch
SULTAN (1001 "Ya-Habibi")...........10-20 59

SHEIKS
Singles: 7-inch
AMY (807 "Come On Back")...... 150-250 60

SHEIKS (on Legrand, MGM): see SHIEKS

SHEILA
LPs: 10/12-inch
PHILIPS..10-15 64

SHEILA R&B '80
(Sheila B. Devotion; Anny Chancel)
Singles: 7-inch
CARRERE..3-5 80-81
CASABLANCA..3-5 78
Picture Sleeves
CARRERE..3-5 80-81
Promotional Singles
CARRERE (37675 "Little Darlin' ") 4-6 81
(Price includes special sleeve.)
LPs: 10/12-inch
CARRERE..5-10 80
CASABLANCA..5-10 78

SHEILA E. P&R/R&B/D&D/LP '84
(Sheila Escovedo)
Singles: 12-inch
W.B. 4-6 84-85
Singles: 7-inch
PAISLEY PARK..3-4 85-87
W.B. 3-4 84-85
Picture Sleeves
PAISLEY PARK..3-4 85-87
W.B. 3-4 84
LPs: 10/12-inch
PAISLEY PARK..5-10 85-87
W.B. 5-10 84-91
Also see KRUSH GROOVE ALL-STARS
Also see PRINCE

SHEKERYK, Pete, & Delua-Tones
Singles: 7-inch
UKEY (101 "Believe in Me") 500-750

SHELBY, Ernie
Singles: 7-inch
CAPITOL ... 4-8 62

SHELBY, Jim
Singles: 7-inch
BARTON (409 "Long Gone Daddy") ... 50-75

SHELDON
(With the Overland Swingin' Top Brass)
Singles: 7-inch
CROW MUSIC ... 3-5

SHELDON, Doug
Singles: 7-inch
CONGRESS ... 4-8 66
MGM ... 4-8 64

SHELDON, Jack
(With the Grammophone Five Featuring the Lovables)
Singles: 7-inch
DONNA ... 5-8 61

SHELDON, Mike
Singles: 7-inch
20TH FOX ... 4-8 64

SHELDON, Rick, & Saturday Knights
Singles: 7-inch
MANSION ... 5-8 60s
Also see SATURDAY KNIGHTS

SHELDON, Sandi
Singles: 7-inch
OKEH (7277 "Baby You're Mine") ... 15-25 67
Session: Van McCoy.
Also see McCOY, Van

SHELDONS
Singles: 7-inch
PHILIPS ... 4-8 62

SHELK, Dena
Singles: 7-inch
SWEETHEART ... 4-8 61

SHELL, Larry
Singles: 7-inch
MINARET (158 "Maggie Brown") ... 4-6 70s

SHELL & CRUSH
Singles: 7-inch
CURB ... 3-5 83
LPs: 10/12-inch
CURB ... 5-10 83

SHELL BROTHERS
Singles: 7-inch
END ... 8-12 59

SHELLEY, Pete P&R '74
(Peter Shelley)
Singles: 12-inch
ARISTA ... 4-6 82-83
Singles: 7-inch
ARISTA ... 3-4 82-83
BELL (45,614 "Gee Baby") ... 4-6 74
LPs: 10/12-inch
ARISTA ... 5-8 82-83
Also see BUZZCOCKS

SHELLEY & KIM
Singles: 7-inch
COULEE (107 "We Love Them All") ... 8-10 64
Picture Sleeves
COULEE (107 "We Love Them All") ... 10-20 64
Members: Shelley Hutchins; Kim Slater.

SHELLS P&R '60
Singles: 78 rpm
CANDLELITE (436 "Baby Oh Baby") ... 10-15 72
(Colored vinyl.)
Singles: 7-inch
ABC ... 3-5 75
BOARDWALK ... 3-5 75
COLLECTABLES ... 3-4 80s
END (1022 "Pretty Little Girl") ... 50-100 58
END (1050 "Whispering Winds") ... 25-40 59
GONE (5103 "Pretty Little Girl") ... 10-20 61
JOHNSON (099 "My Cherie") ... 4-8 72
JOHNSON (104 "Baby, Oh Baby"/"Angel Eyes") ... 35-55 57
(Has selection number [104] centered between the horizontal lines.)
JOHNSON (104 "Baby, Oh Baby"/"What's in an Angel Eyes") ... 15-25 60
(Has two sets of parallel lines, one thinner than the other. These lines are both the same thickness on the '57 issue. Most 1957 issues have the shorter flip side title, whereas those with the longer title are 1960 issues.)
JOHNSON (106 "Pleading No More") ... 150-250 58
JOHNSON (107 "Explain It to Me") ... 20-30 61
JOHNSON (109 "Better Forget Him") ... 20-30 61
JOHNSON (110 "In the Dim of the Dark") ... 20-30 61
JOHNSON (112 "Sweetest One") ... 20-30 61
JOHNSON (119 "Deep in My Heart") ... 25-50 62
JOHNSON (120 "A Toast on Your Birthday") ... 20-25 62
JOHNSON (127 "On My Honor") ... 30-40 63
JOHNSON (332 "Explain It to Me") ... 15-25 61
JOSIE (912 "Deep in My Heart") ... 15-25 63
ROULETTE (4156 "She Wasn't Meant for Me") ... 15-25 59
SELSOM ... 10-15 65
SNOWFLAKE (1959 "If You Were Gone from Me"/"Misty") ... 10-20 64
(Blank, orange labels.)
SOUNDS from the SUBWAY ... 4-6 77
(Colored vinyl.)
LPs: 10/12-inch
CANDLELITE ... 10-15 70s
COLECTABLES ... 5-8 80s
GRECO ... 5-8
JUBILEE ... 10-20
SNOWFLAKE (1000 "Acappella Session with the Shells") ... 25-35
Members: Nathaniel Bouknight; Shade Alston; Bobby Nurse; Danny Small; Gus Geter; Roy Jones.
Also see DUBS / Shells
Also see FIVE SATINS / Youngtones / Youngstones / Shells
Also see LITTLE NAT & ETIQUETTES
Also see LITTLE NATE & CHRYSLERS

SHELLS
(With Bob Gross & Orchestra)
Singles: 7-inch
GENIE (100 "Dear One") ... 200-300 58

SHELLS
Singles: 7-inch
CONLO (879 "Whiplash") ... 15-25 60s

SHELTO, Steve D&D '83
Singles: 12-inch
SAM ... 4-6 83

SHELTON, Anne P&R '49
Singles: 78 rpm
COLUMBIA ... 4-6 56
Singles: 7-inch
COLUMBIA ... 5-10 56
EPIC ... 4-8 59

SHELTON, Bill
Singles: 7-inch
POPPY ... 5-10 59
SMASH ... 5-8 65

SHELTON, Curley
Singles: 7-inch
FALCON (609 "Have You Seen My Baby") ... 20-30

SHELTON, Gary
Singles: 7-inch
MERCURY (71310 "Kissin' at the Drive-In") ... 25-35 58

SHELTON, Gary
Singles: 7-inch
ALPINE (56 "Honey Bee") ... 15-25 60
MARK (145 "Goodbye Darlin' Goodbye") ... 150-250 60
Also see SHONDELL, Troy

SHELTON, Gary
Singles: 7-inch
REGIS (1001 "The Trance") ... 25-35

SHELTON, Gil
Singles: 7-inch
GILLY-BOY (100 "I'm Afraid to Love You") ... 10-15
(Colored vinyl.)
LUTE (6004 "Shirley My Love") ... 10-15 61

SHELTON, Johnny, & His Rockabillies
Singles: 7-inch
SENIC (806 "Groovy Joe's") ... 20-30

SHELTON, Ricky Van C&W '86
Singles: 7-inch
COLUMBIA ... 3-4 86-92
LPs: 10/12-inch
COLUMBIA ... 5-8 87-91
Also see JOEL, Billy / Ricky Van Shelton
Also see PARTON, Dolly, & Ricky Van Shelton

SHELTON, Roscoe R&B '65
Singles: 7-inch
BATTLE (45905 "Yesterday's Mistakes") ... 10-15 62
BATTLE (45913 "My Best Friend") ... 10-15 63
EXCELLO (2167 "Pleadin' for Love") ... 15-25 59
EXCELLO (2170 "It's My Fault") ... 15-25 60
EXCELLO (2176 "We've Been Wrong") ... 15-25 60
EXCELLO (2181 "Miss You") ... 15-25 60
EXCELLO (2192 "It's Too Late Baby") ... 15-25 61
EXCELLO (2198 "Baby, It's True Love") ... 15-25 61
EXCELLO (2198 "Baby, It's True Love") ... 15-25 61
SIMS (156 "Love Is the Key") ... 8-12 63
SIMS (190 "Master Mind") ... 8-12 64
SIMS (217 "Question") ... 8-12 65
SOUND PLUS (2106 "Running for My Life") ... 5-10
SOUND STAGE 7 ... 5-10 65-68
LPs: 10/12-inch
EXCELLO (8002 "Roscoe Shelton Sings") ... 50-75 61
SOUND STAGE 7 ... 15-25 66

SHELYNE, Carole
Singles: 7-inch
LIBERTY ... 4-8 65

SHEMWELL, Sylvia
Singles: 7-inch
PHILIPS ... 10-15 64
Also see SWEET INSPIRATIONS

SHENENDOAH C&W '87
Singles: 7-inch
COLUMBIA ... 3-4 87-91

SHENENDOAH 3
Singles: 7-inch
GOAL ... 4-8 62

SHENENDOAH TRIO
Singles: 7-inch
NEFI ... 5-10 63

SHEP
LPs: 10/12-inch
VANGUARD ... 10-15 69

SHEP, Shane: see SHEPPARD, Shane

SHEP & LIMELITES P&R/R&B '61
(Featuring James Sheppard)
Singles: 7-inch
ABC ... 3-5 73
HULL (Except 770) ... 15-20 61-65
HULL (770 "A Party for Two") ... 20-30 65
ROULETTE ... 3-5 73
LPs: 10/12-inch
HULL (1001 "Our Anniversary") 300-400 62
ROULETTE (25350 "Our Anniversary") ... 35-45 67
Also see ALSTON, Shirley
Also see HEARTBEATS
Also see HEARTBEATS / Shep & Limelites
Also see SHEPPARD, Shane

SHEPARD, Alan
Singles: 7-inch
REDSTONE ... 4-8 61

SHEPARD, Jean C&W/P&R '53
Singles: 78 rpm
CAPITOL ... 4-8 53-57
Singles: 7-inch
CAPITOL ... 5-10 53-61
(Purple labels.)
CAPITOL ... 3-8 61-72
(Orange, orange/yellow, or red labels.)
MERCURY ... 3-5 72
SCORPION ... 3-4 78
U.A. ... 3-5 73-77
EPs: 7-inch
CAPITOL ... 5-10 56-61
LPs: 10/12-inch
CAPITOL (100 thru 800 series) ... 10-20 69-71
CAPITOL (700 thru 1200 series) ... 15-25 56-59
(With a "T" prefix.)
CAPITOL (1500 thru 2900 series) 10-15 61-68
CAPITOL (11000 series) ... 5-10 72-79
FIRST GENERATION ... 5-10 81
MERCURY ... 5-10 71
PICKWICK/HILLTOP ... 5-12 67-68
POWER PAK ... 5-8 75-80s
U.A. ... 5-10 73-76
Session: Justin Tubb; Red Sovine.
Also see TUBB, Justin
Also see YOUNG, Faron / Jean Shepard

SHEPARD, Jean, & Ferlin Huskey C&W/P&R '53
Singles: 78 rpm
CAPITOL ... 3-5 53
Singles: 7-inch
CAPITOL ... 4-8 53
Also see HUSKY, Ferlin

SHEPARD, Jean, & Ray Pillow C&W '66
Singles: 7-inch
CAPITOL ... 4-6 66
LPs: 10/12-inch
CAPITOL ... 10-15 66
Also see PILLOW, Ray
Also see SHEPARD, Jean

SHEPARD, Joe
Singles: 7-inch
END (1024 "What's the Matter Baby") ... 20-40 58

SHEPARD, Jolly Boy
Singles: 7-inch
OKEH ... 5-10 60

SHEPARD, Kenny
Singles: 7-inch
MAXX (332 "What Difference Does It Make") ... 40-60

SHEPARD, Ollie
Singles: 78 rpm
GEE (1044 "My Baby Is Gone") ... 10-15 57
OKEH ... 10-20 40s
Singles: 7-inch
GEE (1044 "My Baby Is Gone") ... 10-15 57

SHEPARD, Red, & Flock
Singles: 7-inch
PHILIPS ... 4-8 66
Picture Sleeves
PHILIPS ... 5-10 66

SHEPARD SISTERS: see SHEPHERD SISTERS

SHEPARDS
Singles: 7-inch
ABC-PAR (10758 "Little Girl Lost") ... 10-20 66
PALMER (1018 "When Johnny Comes Marching Home") ... 8-12 60s

SHEPHARDS
Singles: 7-inch
IMPACT (1018 "Poor Man's Thing") ... 20-30

SHEPHERD
Singles: 7-inch
TANGENT ... 5-10 70s

SHEPHERD, Buddy
Singles: 7-inch
PLAY ME (3517 "I'm Hypnotized") 10-15 59
Picture Sleeves
PLAY ME (3517 "I'm Hypnotized") 20-30 59

SHEPHERD, Cybil
(With Stan Getz)
LPs: 10/12-inch
INNER CITY (1097 "Made About the Boy") ... 8-12 80
Also see GETZ, Stan

SHEPHERD, Johnnie
Singles: 7-inch
COLUMBIA ... 10-15 67
TILDEN (3001 "How Blue My Heart") ... 15-25 61

SHEPHERD, Wyatt "Big Boy"
Singles: 7-inch
U.A. (216 "You Don't Want Me No More") ... 35-55 60

SHEPHERD SISTERS P&R '57
(Sheppard Sisters; Shepard Sisters; Shephard Sisters)
Singles: 78 rpm
LANCE ... 5-10 57
MELBA ... 5-10 56
MERCURY ... 5-10 57
Singles: 7-inch
ABC ... 3-5 73
ATLANTIC ... 5-10 63
COLLECTABLES ... 3-4 80s
LANCE ... 5-10 57
MGM ... 4-8 59
MELBA ... 10-15 56
MERCURY ... 5-10 57
20TH FOX ... 4-8 64
U.A. ... 5-10 61
WARWICK ... 5-10 59-60
YORK ... 4-8 65
EPs: 7-inch
MERCURY (3369 "The Sheppard Sisters") ... 20-30 57
Members: Mary Lou Shepherd; Judy Shepherd; Martha Shepherd; Gayle Shepherd.

SHEPHERDS
Singles: 7-inch
MIRWOOD ... 4-8 67

SHEPPARD, Bill, Combo
Singles: 7-inch
ABNER ... 4-8 62

SHEPPARD, Buddy, & Holidays
Singles: 7-inch
SABINA (506 "My Love Is Real") ... 20-30 62
SABINA (510 "Now It's All Over") ... 25-35 63
Also see BELMONTS
Also see TONY & HOLIDAYS

SHEPPARD, Neil
Singles: 7-inch
ALMONT ... 8-10 64

SHEPPARD, Rick
Singles: 7-inch
BANG ... 4-8 65

SHEPPARD, Shane
(With the Limelites; Shane Shep)
Singles: 7-inch
APT (25046 "I'm So Lonely") ... 20-30 60
Also see SHEP & LIMELITES

SHEPPARD, T.G. C&W '74
Singles: 7-inch
COLUMBIA ... 3-4 85
HITSVILLE ... 3-5 76
MELODYLAND ... 3-5 74-75
W.B. ... 3-4 77-85
LPs: 10/12-inch
COLUMBIA ... 5-8 85
CURB ... 5-8 84
HITSVILLE ... 5-10 76
MELODYLAND ... 8-10 75-76
W.B. ... 5-8 78-83
Also see COLLINS, Judy, & T.G. Sheppard
Also see EASTWOOD, Clint, & T.G. Sheppard
Also see GATLIN, Larry

SHEPPARD, T.G., & Karen Brooks C&W '82
Singles: 7-inch
W.B. ... 3-4 82
Also see BROOKS, Karen

SHEPPARD, T.G., & Clint Eastwood C&W/P&R '84
Singles: 7-inch
W.B. ... 3-4 84
Also see EASTWOOD, Clint
Also see SHEPPARD, T.G.

SHEPPARD, Zeke
Singles: 7-inch
PRESIDENT (831 "Snow Surfin' ") 15-25 64

SHEPPARD SISTERS: see SHEPHERD SISTERS

SHEPPARDS
Singles: 78 rpm
THERON (112 "Love") ... 50-100 55
UNITED (198 "Sherry") ... 50-75 56
Singles: 7-inch
ABC (10758 "Let Yourself Go") ... 5-10 66
ABNER (7006 "Loving You") ... 8-12 62
APEX (7750 "Island of Love") ... 25-50 59
APEX (7752 "Just Like You") ... 20-30 59
APEX (7755 "Meant to Be") ... 20-30 60
APEX (7759 "Society Girl") ... 20-30 60
APEX (7760 "Just Like You") ... 15-25 60
APEX (7762 "Tragic") ... 20-30 60
CONSTELLATION (123 "Island of Love") ... 8-10 64
CONSTELLATION (176 "Island of Love") ... 5-8 66
KING TUT ... 3-5 78
MIRWOOD ... 10-20 66
OKEH (7173 "Pretend You're Still Mine") ... 10-20 63
OWL ... 3-5 74
PAM (1001 "Never Let Me Go") ... 15-25 61
SHARP ... 4-8 69
UNITED (198 "Sherry") ... 150-250 56
VEE JAY (406 "Every Now and Then") ... 10-20 61
VEE JAY (441 "Tragic") ... 15-25 62
WES ... 10-15 61
LPs: 10/12-inch
CONSTELLATION (4 "The Sheppards") ... 25-50 64
SOLID SMOKE ... 5-10 80
Members: Mill Edwards; Oscar Boyd; James Dennis Issac; George "Sonny" Parker; John Pruitt; Nate Tucker; Kent McGhee; Murrie Eskridge; Kermit Chandler.

SHEPPARDS
Singles: 7-inch
IMPACT (1018 "Poor Man's Thing") ... 15-25 66
Also see ESQUIRES

SHEPPARDS
Singles: 7-inch
BUNKY (7764 "Steal Away") ... 5-10 69

SHEPS
Singles: 7-inch
EARLY BIRD (5002 "I'm Destroyed") ... 4-6 96
(Colored vinyl.)

SHERBET P&R '76
(Sherbs)
Singles: 7-inch
ATCO ... 3-5 81
MCA ... 3-5 76-77
LPs: 10/12-inch
ATCO ... 5-10 80-82
MCA ... 5-10 76-77
Also see HIGHWAY

SHERBS: see SHERBET

SHERIDAN, Bobby
(Charlie Rich)
Singles: 7-inch
SUN (354 "Sad News") ... 10-20 61
Also see RICH, Charlie

SHERIDAN, Mike, & Nightriders
Singles: 7-inch
LIVERPOOL SOUND (902 "Please Mr. Postman") ... 60-80 64
Also see IDLE RACE

SHERIDAN, Tony & Beat Brothers: see BEATLES

SHERIFF P&R '83
Singles: 7-inch
CAPITOL ... 3-5 83
Picture Sleeves
CAPITOL ... 3-5 83
LPs: 10/12-inch
CAPITOL ... 5-8 83
OBSERVATORY ... 6-10 79
Members: Wolf Hassel; Arnold Lanni; Fred Curci; Steve DeMarchi.
Also see ALIAS
Also see FROZEN GHOST

SHERIFF & RAVELS
Singles: 7-inch
VEE JAY (306 "Shombalor") ... 30-40 58
Also see RAVELS

SHERIFF DAVE
Singles: 7-inch
MARSHALL (8735 "His Legend Lives On") ... 4-6

SHERIFF JOHN
Singles: 78 rpm
IMPERIAL ... 10-20 54
Singles: 7-inch
IMPERIAL (8270 "Birthday Cake Polka") ... 15-25 54

SHERLEY, Glen C&W '71
Singles: 7-inch
MEGA ... 3-5 71
LPs: 10/12-inch
MEGA ... 5-10 71

SHERLOCKS
Singles: 7-inch
DOT (16890 "Skin of My Teeth") ... 10-15 66
DOT (16953 "Too Good to Be True") ... 5-10 66

SHERMAN, Allan LP '62
(With Friends; with Boston Pops Orch.)
Singles: 7-inch
RCA ... 4-6 68
W.B. ... 5-10 63-66
Picture Sleeves
W.B. ... 8-15 63-64
LPs: 10/12-inch
JUBILEE ... 10-20 62
RCA (Except 310) ... 10-15 64
RCA (310 "Alan Sherman and You") ... 20-30 64

(Promotional issue only. Includes 25-page script, letter from Allan and a comments postcard.)
RHINO... 5-8 85-86
W.B. ... 15-25 62-65
Also see BOSTON POPS ORCHESTRA

SHERMAN, Bobby *P&R/LP '69*
Singles: 7-inch
CAMEO (403 "Happiness Is")... 4-8 66
CAMEO (403 "Happiness Is")... 8-12 66
(Single-sided. Promotional issue only.)
CONDOR... 4-8 69
DECCA... 8-15 64-65
DOT... 4-8 63
EPIC... 4-8 67
GRT... 3-5 76
JANUS... 3-5 75
METROMEDIA... 3-5 69-73
PARKWAY... 5-10 65
STARCREST... 5-10 62
Picture Sleeves
DECCA... 8-12 65
METROMEDIA... 3-5 69-72
EPs: 7-inch
METROMEDIA ("Bobby Sherman") 5-10 70
(Cardboard cutout picture discs from cereal boxes. Four different pictures made, each listing five songs. The song actually on the disc is stamped into the label area. 20 different picture/song variations exist.)
LPs: 10/12-inch
METROMEDIA... 5-10 69-73

SHERMAN, Eileen
Singles: 7-inch
OKEH... 4-8 60

SHERMAN, Garry
Singles: 7-inch
EPIC (9859 "Space Walk")... 10-20 65

SHERMAN, Joe, & His Orchestra *P&R '63*
(With the Arena Brass)
Singles: 78 rpm
KAPP... 3-5 56-57
Singles: 7-inch
EPIC... 3-5 65-66
KAPP... 4-6 56-61
WORLD ARTISTS... 3-6 63-65
LPs: 10/12-inch
COLUMBIA... 5-10 68
EPIC... 5-10 66
RCA... 5-10 67
WORLD ARTISTS... 5-12 63-64
Also see FOUR COINS
Also see VIDELS

SHERMAN & DARTS
Singles: 7-inch
FURY (1014 "Remember")... 50-75 58

SHERMAN & NOTATIONS
Singles: 7-inch
KIT (1012 "Conscience")... 150-250

SHERRICK *R&B '87*
Singles: 7-inch
W.B. ... 3-4 87

SHERRILL, Billy
(Bill Sherrell)
Singles: 7-inch
ABC-PAR... 10-15 63
EPIC... 3-4 78
MERCURY... 10-15 60
SEE (1005 "Hear Her Rave On")... 30-50
TYME (101 "Don't You Rock Me Daddy-O")... 75-125 57
TYME (102 "Cadillac Baby")... 75-125 58
TYME (103 "Rock On, Baby")... 75-125 58
TYME (104 "Kool Kat")... 150-250 58
TYME (106 "Rock & Roll Teenager")... 50-100 58
Also see VANDELLS

SHERRILL, Charles
Singles: 7-inch
UPTOWN... 4-8 67
Also see P.P.F.

SHERRY, Ruby
Singles: 7-inch
TAKE 6 (1002 "Feminine Ingenuity")... 75-125 60s

SHERRY & BILL
Singles: 7-inch
TANGERINE... 4-8 66

SHERRY & INVERTS
Singles: 7-inch
TOWER... 10-20 68

SHERRY SATINS
Singles: 7-inch
KARATE... 4-8 66

SHERRY SISTERS
Singles: 7-inch
EPIC... 4-8 64-66
JAMIE... 3-5 72
OKEH... 10-15 63
Also see SHERRYS

SHERRYS *P&R/R&B '62*
Singles: 7-inch
GUYDEN... 10-15 62-63
MERCURY... 5-10 64
ROBERTS... 5-10 60s
LPs: 10/12-inch
GUYDEN (503 "At the Hop")... 100-200 62
GUYDEN (503 "At the Hop")... 200-300 62
(White label. Promotional issue only.)
Also see SHERRY SISTERS

SHERVINGTON, Lou
Singles: 7-inch
KENCO... 4-8 61

SHERWIN, Ben
Singles: 7-inch
GOLD ARROW... 4-8 62
LIBERTY... 4-8 60

SHERWOOD
Singles: 7-inch
SMASH... 4-6 69

SHERWOOD, Lee
Singles: 7-inch
WMAQ-670 (7737 "Blizzard of '79").. 4-6 79

SHERWOOD, Roberta *P&R '56*
Singles: 78 rpm
DECCA... 3-5 56-57
Singles: 7-inch
DECCA... 4-8 56-64
DUNHILL... 3-6 68
HAPPY TIGER... 3-6 69
HARMON... 3-6 62-63
KING... 3-5 71-72
MCA... 3-5 73
OLEN... 4-6 65
EPs: 7-inch
DECCA... 5-10 56-59
LPs: 10/12-inch
ABC-PAR... 5-15 63-64
DECCA... 8-18 56-65
HARMONY... 5-15 63
KING... 5-8 70
VOCALION... 5-10 66-68

SHERWOOD, Wayne
Singles: 7-inch
AURORA... 4-8 61

SHERWOODS
Singles: 7-inch
JOHNSON... 8-12 61-63
MAGGIE (101/2 "Nanette")... 8-12 61
Member: Tony Reno.
Also see RENO, Tony, & Sherwoods

SHERWOODS
(Concords)
Singles: 7-inch
DOT (16540 "Cold and Frosty Morning")... 15-20 63
Also see CONCORDS

SHERWOODS
Singles: 7-inch
EASTWOOD... 10-15 60s
EXETER... 15-25 64
KAPP... 4-8 65
MAGGIE... 4-8
MAGNIFICO... 8-12 64
MERCURY... 8-12 63
V-TONE... 10-15 59

SHERWOODS
Singles: 7-inch
REN VELL... 4-8 68

SHERWOODS
Singles: 7-inch
CRIMSON (1004 "Moffitt's Mess")... 8-12
NOW SOUND 91002 "I Know You Cried")... 8-12

SHES
Singles: 7-inch
INTERNATIONAL ARTISTS... 5-10 66

SHEVELLES
Singles: 7-inch
WORLD ARTISTS... 5-10 64

SHEVETON, Tony
Singles: 7-inch
PARROT... 4-8 67

SHIBLEY, Arkie *C&W '50*
(With His Mountain Dew Boys)
Singles: 78 rpm
GILT-EDGE (#8)... 10-20 50
(Title not known.)
GILT-EDGE (5021 "Hot Rod Race")... 50-60 51
GILT-EDGE (5036 "Arkie Meets the Judge")... 50-60 51
GILT-EDGE (5078 "Arkie's Talking Blues")... 30-50 53
MAE-MAE (#77)... 35-50
(Title not known.)
Singles: 7-inch
4 STAR (1737 "Pickin' My Guitar")... 40-60 59
MOUNTAIN DEW (101 "Hot Rod Race")... 25-50 50s
(Reissue of Gilt Edge 5021. Exact year of issue not yet known.)

SHIEKS
(Sheiks)
Singles: 7-inch
MGM (12876 "Baghdad Rock")... 10-20 60
TRINE (1101 "Baghdad Rock")... 25-35 59
Member: Bill Ramal.
Also see RAMAL, Bill

SHIEKS
Singles: 7-inch
LEGRAND (1013 "What I'd Do for Your Love")... 25-35 62
LEGRAND (1016 "Twist That Twist")... 10-15 62

SHIELDS *P&R/R&B '58*
Singles: 7-inch
DOT (136 "You Cheated")... 5-10 66
(Black vinyl.)
DOT (136 "You Cheated")... 20-30 66
(Colored vinyl. Promotional issue only.)
DOT (15805 "You Cheated")... 20-30 58
DOT (15856 "I'm Sorry Now")... 30-40 58
DOT (15940 "Play the Game Fair")... 20-30 59
FALCON (100 "The Girl Around the Corner")... 50-75 60
TENDER (513 "You Cheated")... 50-75 58
(Label does NOT read "Dist. By Dot.")
TENDER (513 "You Cheated")... 20-40 58
(Label reads "Dist. By Dot.")
TENDER (518 "I'm Sorry Now")... 30-50 59
TENDER (521 "Play the Game Fair")... 30-50 59
TENDER (567 "You Cheated")... 10-15
TRANSCONTINENTAL (1013 "The Girl Around the Corner")... 100-200 60
(First issue.)
LPs: 10/12-inch
BRYLEN... 5-10
Members: Frankie Ervin; Charles Wright; Nathaniel Wilson; Jesse Belvin; Johnny "Guitar" Watson; Mel Williams. Session: Tony Allen
Also see ALLEN, Tony
Also see BELVIN, Jesse
Also see ERVIN, Frankie
Also see WATSON, Johnny
Also see WRIGHT, Charles

SHIELDS
Singles: 7-inch
CONTINENTAL (4072 "You Told a Lie")... 500-750 61

SHIELDS
Singles: 7-inch
ATCO... 3-5 77

SHIELDS, Billy
(Tony Orlando)
Singles: 7-inch
HARBOUR... 10-15 69
Also see ORLANDO, Tony

SHIELDS, Bobby
(With the Street Singers & Orchestra)
Singles: 78 rpm
DAWN... 15-25 55
MELBA... 15-25 56
Singles: 7-inch
DAWN (211 "I Was Dreaming")... 30-50 55
MELBA (105 "Land of Rock & Roll")... 30-50 56

SHIFTER, Hank
Singles: 7-inch
STEED... 4-8 67

SHIFTERS
Singles: 7-inch
SQUIRE... 8-12 60

SHILLINGS
Singles: 7-inch
FANTASY... 5-10 67
FONTANA... 5-10 66
THREE RIVERS... 5-10 66
VIRTUE... 4-8 69

SHILOH
Singles: 7-inch
AMOS... 4-8 71
LPs: 10/12-inch
AMOS (7015 "Shiloh")... 15-25 71
LAMB & LION... 5-8
Members: Al Perkins; Don Henley; Jim Ed Norman; Mike Bowden; Richard Bowden.
Also see FLYING BURRITO BROTHERS
Also see HENLEY, Don
Also see PINKARD & BOWDEN
Also see RONSTADT, Linda

SHILOH
Singles: 7-inch
SHANE... 3-5 77

SHILOS
Singles: 7-inch
NORFOLK (201,269 "Cause I Love You")... 10-20 66

SHIN, Gee Gee
(With the Boogie Kings)
Singles: 7-inch
LA LOUISIANNE... 5-10 60s
MONTEL... 4-8 65

SHINALL, Joe
Singles: 7-inch
ATTEIRAM... 3-5 74

SHIN-DIG SMITH & SOUL SHAKERS
Singles: 7-inch
PITTER - PAT (101 "Thourgh Fooling Around")... 5-10 60s

SHIN-DIGGERS
Singles: 7-inch
ABC-PAR... 4-8 64

SHINDIGS
(Bobby Fuller Four)
Singles: 7-inch
MUSTANG... 10-15 65
Also see FULLER, Bobby

SHINDOGS *P&R '66*
Singles: 7-inch
VIVA... 4-8 66
W.B. ... 4-8 65
Members: Delaney Bramlet; Bonnie Bramlett.
Also see DELANEY & BONNIE

SHINE
Singles: 7-inch
PULSAR... 3-6 69

SHINEHEAD *LP '88*
LPs: 10/12-inch
ELEKTRA... 5-8 88-90

SHINER, Murv *C&W '49*
(Merv Shiner)
Singles: 78 rpm
DECCA... 4-8 49-50
Singles: 7-inch
MGM... 4-6 67-69
LPs: 10/12-inch
CERTRON... 10-15 60s
LITTLE DARLIN'... 10-15 60s

SHINES, Johnny
Singles: 78 rpm
J.O.B. (116 "Ramblin' ")... 75-125 52
J.O.B. (1010 "Evening Sun")... 50-100 53
Singles: 7-inch
J.O.B. (1010 "Evening Sun")... 200-250 53
JOLIET (206 "Skull & Crossbone Blues")... 3-6
LPs: 10/12-inch
ADVENT... 8-10 74
BLUE HORIZON... 10-15
BLUE LABOR... 8-10 77
CHESS... 8-10
ROUNDER... 5-10 84

SHINES, Johnny, & Big Walter Horton
LPs: 10/12-inch
TESTAMENT... 10-20 60s
Also see HORTON, Big Walter
Also see SHINES, Johnny

SHINY BROTHERS
Singles: 7-inch
DOC (101 "The Brush")... 10-15 64

SHIP
Singles: 7-inch
ELEKTRA... 3-5 72
LPs: 10/12-inch
ELEKTRA... 8-12 72

SHIPLEY, Ellen
Singles: 7-inch
NEW YORK INT'L... 3-5 79
LPs: 10/12-inch
RCA... 5-10 80
Promotional LPs
RCA ("Special Radio Series")... 10-15 81

SHIPLEY, Reese
Singles: 78 rpm
VALLEY (106 "Catfish Boogie")... 10-20 53
Singles: 7-inch
VALLEY (106 "Catfish Boogie")... 25-35 53

SHIPMAN, Jerry
Singles: 7-inch
RIDGECREST (1206 "Rock & Roll Queen")... 30-40 59

SHIPPELL, Bob, & Royals
Singles: 7-inch
CHARM (9572 "The Chicken and the Bop")... 25-35 59

SHIRA
Singles: 7-inch
JAMIE (1413 "Frank's Ant Farm").. 10-15 69

SHIRLEE MAY
(Shirley Ellis)
Singles: 7-inch
MERCURY (71969 "Lonely Birthday")... 8-12 62
Also see ELLIS, Shirley

SHIRELLES *P&R '58*
Singles: 7-inch
COLLECTABLES... 3-4 80s
BLUE ROCK... 4-8 68
DECCA... 10-20 58-61
ERIC... 3-4 70s
GUSTO... 3-4
RCA... 5-10 71-73
SCEPTER (1203 "Dedicated to the One I Love")... 15-25 59
(White label.)
SCEPTER (1203 "Dedicated to the One I Love")... 10-15 59
(Red label.)
SCEPTER (1205 thru 1208)... 15-20 59-60
(White label.)
SCEPTER (1205 thru 1208)... 10-15 59-60
(Red label.)
SCEPTER (1211 "Tomorrow")... 20-25 60
SCEPTER (1211 "Will You Love Me Tomorrow")... 10-15 60
(Note longer title.)
SCEPTER (1217 thru 1292)... 8-12 61-64
SCEPTER (12000 series)... 4-8 65-67
TIARA (6112 "I Met Him On a Sunday")... 100-150 57
U.A. ... 3-5 70-71
Picture Sleeves
SCEPTER (1248 "Foolish Little Girl")... 10-20 63
SCEPTER (1255 "Don't Say Goodnight and Mean Goodbye")... 10-20 63
LPs: 10/12-inch
BACK-TRAC... 5-10 85
EVEREST... 5-10 81
GUSTO... 5-10 80s
PHOENIX... 5-10 81
PRICEWISE... 15-25 60s
RCA... 10-15 71-72
RHINO... 5-8 85
SCEPTER (M-501 "Tonight's the Night")... 60-80 61
(Monaural.)
SCEPTER (S-501 "Tonight's the Night")... 75-100 61
(Stereo.)
SCEPTER (M-502 "Shirelles Sing to Trumpets & Strings")... 25-50 61
(Monaural.)
SCEPTER (S-502 "Shirelles Sing to Trumpets & Strings")... 40-60 61
(Stereo.)
SCEPTER (M-504 "Baby It's You")... 25-50 62
(Monaural.)
SCEPTER (S-504 "Baby It's You")... 40-60 62
(Stereo.)
SCEPTER (M-507 "Greatest Hits") 25-50 63
(Monaural.)
SCEPTER (S-507 "Greatest Hits") 40-60 63
(Stereo.)
SCEPTER (M-511 "Foolish Little Girl")... 25-50 63
(Monaural.)
SCEPTER (S-511 "Foolish Little Girl")... 40-60 63
(Stereo.)
SCEPTER (M-514 "It's a Mad, Mad, Mad, Mad World")... 20-40 63
(Monaural.)
SCEPTER (S-514 "It's a Mad, Mad, Mad, Mad World")... 25-50 63
(Stereo.)
SCEPTER (M-516 "Golden Oldies")... 20-40 64
(Monaural.)
SCEPTER (S-516 "Golden Oldies")... 25-50 64
(Stereo.)
SCEPTER (560 "Greatest Hits, Vol. 2")... 20-40 67
SCEPTER (562 "Spontaneous Combustion")... 20-40 67
SCEPTER (599 "Remember When")... 15-20 72
SPRINGBOARD... 8-10 72
U.A. ... 10-15 71-75
Members: Shirley Jackson-Alston; Beverly Lee; Doris Coley-Jackson; Addie "Micki" Harris-McFadden.
Also see ALSTON, Shirley
Also see JAN & DEAN / Roy Orbison / 4 Seasons / Shirelles
Also see KING, Carole
Also see SHIRLEY & SHIRELLES
Also see VALLI

SHIRELLES & KING CURTIS
LPs: 10/12-inch
SCEPTER (M-505 "A Twist Party")... 25-50 62
(Monaural.)
SCEPTER (S-505 "A Twist Party") 40-60 62
(Stereo.)
SCEPTER (569 "Eternally Soul")... 25-35 68
Also see KING CURTIS

SHIRELLES / Don Julian & Larks
Singles: 7-inch
ORIGINAL SOUND (4514 "Soldier Boy"/"I Want You Back")... 4-6
Also see LARKS
Also see SHIRELLES

SHIRLEY
Singles: 7-inch
PAULA... 5-8 68
WHIZ... 3-6 69

SHIRLEY, Danny *C&W '84*
Singles: 7-inch
AMOR... 3-4 84-88
Also see CONFEDERATE RAILROAD

SHIRLEY, Danny, & Piano Red *C&W '85*
Singles: 7-inch
AMOR... 3-4 84-88
Also see PIANO RED
Also see SHIRLEY, Danny

SHIRLEY, Dell, & Joe Brown
(With the Playetts)
Singles: 7-inch
LOGAN (3118 "Cliff's Rocket")... 15-25 60

SHIRLEY, Donald *LP '55*
(Don Shirley Trio)
Singles: 7-inch
BARNABY... 3-4 76
CADENCE... 4-8 60-64
COLUMBIA... 3-6 68-69
EPs: 7-inch
CADENCE... 8-15 56-59
LPs: 10/12-inch
ATLANTIC... 5-12 72
AUDIO FIDELITY... 10-25 59
CADENCE... 20-40 55-63
COLUMBIA... 10-15 65-69

SHIRLEY, Shirley
Singles: 7-inch
TIME... 4-8 63

SHIRLEY & COMPANY *P&R/R&B/LP '75*
Singles: 7-inch
VIBRATION... 3-5 75-76
LPs: 10/12-inch
VIBRATION... 8-10 75
Members: Shirley Goodman; Kenny Jeremiah.
Also see SHIRLEY & LEE
Also see SOUL SURVIVORS

SHIRLEY & JESSIE
Singles: 7-inch
WAND (1116 "You Can't Fight Love") 10-15 66

SHIRLEY & JOHNNY
Singles: 7-inch
CAPITOL 4-8 64
WORLD PACIFIC 4-8 68

SHIRLEY & LEE P&R '52
Singles: 78 rpm
ALADDIN 10-30 52-57
Singles: 7-inch
ABC 3-4 73
ALADDIN (3153 "I'm Gone") 50-75 52
ALADDIN (3173 "Baby") 50-100
ALADDIN (3192 "Shirley's Back") ...30-50 53
ALADDIN (3205 "Two Happy People") 25-40 53
ALADDIN (3222 "Why Did I") 25-40 53
ALADDIN (3244 "Confessin' ") 25-40 54
ALADDIN (3258 "Comin' Over") 25-40 54
ALADDIN (3289 "Feel So Good") ...15-25 55
ALADDIN (3302 "Lee's Dream") 15-25 55
ALADDIN (3313 "That's What I'll Do") 20-30 55
ALADDIN (3325 "Let the Good Times Roll") 10-20 56
ALADDIN (3338 "I Feel Good") 10-20 56
ALADDIN (3362 "When I Saw You") 10-20 57
ALADDIN (3369 "I Want to Dance") 10-20 57
ALADDIN (3380 "Rock All Night") ..10-20 57
ALADDIN (3390 "Rockin' with the Clock") 10-20 57
ALADDIN (3405 "I'll Thrill You") 10-20 57
ALADDIN (3418 "Everybody's Rockin' ") 10-20 58
ALADDIN (3432 "All I Want to Do Is Cry") 10-20 58
ALADDIN (3455 "True Love") 10-20 59
IMPERIAL 5-10 62-63
LIBERTY 3-4 80s
U.A. 3-5 73
WARWICK 5-10 60-61
LPs: 10/12-inch
ALADDIN (807 "Let the Good Times Roll") 400-600 56
IMPERIAL (9179 "Let the Good Times Roll") 50-100 62
SCORE (4023 "Let the Good Times Roll") 100-150 57
U.A. (340 "Legendary Masters") 20-25 74
WARWICK (2028 "Let the Good Times Roll") 75-100 61
Members: Shirley Goodman; Leonard Lee.
Also see ADAMS, Faye / Little Esther / Shirley & Lee
Also see GENE & EUNICE / Shirley & Lee
Also see KING, Ben E.
Also see SHIRLEY & COMPANY

SHIRLEY & SHEP
Singles: 7-inch
WHIZ (608 "Snake in the Grass") 5-10 60s

SHIRLEY & SHIRELLES
(Featuring Shirley Alston)
Singles: 7-inch
BELL 8-12 69
Also see ALSTON, Shirley
Also see SHIRELLES

SHIRLEY & SQUIRRELY C&W/P&R '76
Singles: 7-inch
GRT 3-5 76
LPs: 10/12-inch
GRT 5-10 76
Also see SHIRLEY, SQUIRRELY & MELVIN

SHIRLEY & ZARNOFF
Singles: 7-inch
INSTANT 4-8 61

SHIRLEY ANN
Singles: 7-inch
20TH FOX 4-8 67

SHIRLEY JEAN
(With the Clay County Playboys)
Singles: 7-inch
LIFETIME (1026 "It Keeps Right On A-Hurtin' ") 5-10
MYRL (403 "Alone Am I") 5-10 61

SHIRLEY, SQUIRRELY & MELVIN
Singles: 7-inch
EXCELSIOR 3-4 81
Picture Sleeves
EXCELSIOR 3-5 81
LPs: 10/12-inch
EXCELSIOR 5-10 81
Also see SHIRLEY & SQUIRRELY

SHIRT TAIL RELATION
Singles: 7-inch
MOBIE 5-8 68

SHIRTAILS
Singles: 7-inch
DATE 10-20 66

SHIRTS
Singles: 7-inch
CAPITOL 3-5 79
LPs: 10/12-inch
CAPITOL 5-10 78-81

SHIVA'S HEADBAND
Singles: 7-inch
ARMADILLO 8-12 71-76
IGNITE (681 "Kaleidoscopic") 15-25 67
Picture Sleeves
ARMADILLO (3 "Country Boy") 15-25 70s
ARMADILLO (6-1 "Extension") 15-25 76
LPs: 10/12-inch
APE (1001 "Yesterdays") 10-15 78
ARMADILLO ("Coming to a Head") 75-125 70
(No selection number used.)
CAPITOL (538 "Take Me to the Mountains") 40-60 70
MOONTOWER 8-10 85
Members: Spencer Perskin; Shawn Siegel; Susan Perskin; Kenny Parker; Robert Gladwin; Richard Finnell; Bob Tonreid.

SHIVEL, Bunny
Singles: 7-inch
CAPITOL 4-8 66

SHIVERS
Singles: 7-inch
GENERAL MUSIC (3007 "Flyin' Blind") 10-20 60s
(Single-sided. Promotional issue only.)

SHIVERS
Singles: 7-inch
PRIVATE STOCK 3-5 77

SHIVERS, Pauline
Singles: 7-inch
O-PEX (111 "Won't You Come Back Home") 5-10
LP: 10/12-inch
OPEX 10-20 69-70
Also see BIRDLEGS & PAULINE and Their Versatility Birds

SHOBIZZ
Singles: 7-inch
CAPITOL 3-5 79
LPs: 10/12-inch
CAPITOL 5-10 79

SHOCK
Singles: 7-inch
DOWNTOWN 3-5 78
(Colored vinyl.)
Picture Sleeves
DOWNTOWN 3-5 78
EPs: 7-inch
IMPACT 8-10 78
(Colored vinyl. Issued with a paper sleeve.)
Members: Paul Lesperance; Steve Reiner; Kip Brown; Gaylord.
Also see LITTLE GIRLS
Also see SILVERHEAD

SHOCK R&B '81
Singles: 12-inch
FANTASY 4-6 81-83
Singles: 7-inch
FANTASY 3-4 81-83
NEBULA 3-5 79
LPs: 10/12-inch
FANTASY 5-10 81-82

SHOCK-A-RA
Singles: 7-inch
FUTURE 3-4 88

SHOCKED, Michelle P&R/LP '88
Singles: 7-inch
MERCURY 3-4 88-89
Picture Sleeves
MERCURY 3-4 88
LPs: 10/12-inch
MERCURY 5-8 88-89

SHOCKETTES
Singles: 7-inch
SYMBOL (914 "Hold Back the Tears") 20-30 61

SHOCKING BLUE P&R '69
Singles: 7-inch
BUDDAH 3-5 71
COLOSSUS 3-6 69-71
MGM 3-5 72-73
Picture Sleeves
COLOSSUS 4-6 69-70
LPs: 10/12-inch
COLOSSUS 10-20 70
Members: Robby Van Leevwen; Mariska Veres; Klassje Van Der Wal; Cornelis Van Der Beck.

SHOELACES
Singles: 7-inch
BRITE LEAF (4065 "Ball & Chain") ... 4-8 63

SHOES P&R/LP '79
Singles: 7-inch
BOMP 3-5 78
ELEKTRA 3-5 79
Picture Sleeves
BOMP 3-5 78
ELEKTRA 3-5 79
EPs: 7-inch
BOMP 5-10 78
LPs: 10/12-inch
BLACK VINYL 8-12 70s
ELEKTRA 5-10 77-82
PVC 5-10 78
Members: John Murphy; Jeff Murphy; Gary Klebe; Skip Meyer.

SHOESTRING
Singles: 7-inch
20TH FOX 4-8 68

SHOFFNER, Rufus
(With Joyce Songer)
Singles: 7-inch
AMERICAN ARTISTS (7317 "Orbit Twist") 300-500 62
HI-Q (17 "Every Little Raindrop") ...20-30 61

SHOHN, Admiral, Ice
Singles: 7-inch
ADMIRAL ICE 3-5 82

SHO-MEN
Singles: 7-inch
SAM (114 "Breakaway") 8-12

SHONA & Party Lights
Singles: 7-inch
CHICORY (1601 "Nice Guy") 10-15 63

SHONDELL, Troy P&R '61
(Troy Shondel; Troy Shundell; Gary Shelton)
Singles: 7-inch
AVM 3-4 88
BRITE STAR 3-5 73-74
COLLECTABLES 3-4 80s
COMMERCIAL 3-5 78
DECCA 4-8 64
EVEREST 4-8 62-64
GAYE (2010 "This Time") 20-25 61
GOLDCREAST (161 "This Time") 15-20 61
(Note misspelled label name.)
GOLDCREST (161 "This Time") 10-15 61
LIBERTY 5-10 61-62
LUCKY 3-5 75
MASTER 10-15 60s
RIC 4-8 65
STAR-FOX 3-5 79
SUNSHINE 3-5 76
TRX 4-8 67-69
TELESONIC 3-5 80-81
3 RIVERS 4-8 60s
WRITERS & ARTISTS (001 "This Time") 25-35 61
LPs: 10/12-inch
EVEREST (1206 "Many Sides") 25-35 63
STAR-FOX 5-10 79
SUNSET 10-15 67
Also see JIANTS
Also see SHELTON, Gary

SHONDELLS
("Vocal By Novella Simmons, Shirley Brooks and the Shondells")
Singles: 7-inch
KING (5597 "Don't Cry My Soldier Boy") 10-20 62
KING (5656 "Wonderful One") 10-20 62
KING (5705 "Special Delivery") 10-20 62
KING (5755 "Ooo Sometimes") 10-20 63

SHONDELLS
Singles: 7-inch
LA LOUISIANNE (8042) 25-50 63
(Title not known.)

SHONDELLS / Rod Bernard / Warren Storm / Skip Stewart
LPs: 10/12-inch
LA LOUISIANNE (109 "At the Saturday Hop") 50-75 64
Also see BERNARD, Rod
Also see SHONDELLS
Also see STEWART, Skip
Also see STORM, Warren

SHONDELLS
(Featuring Tommy James)
Singles: 7-inch
RED FOX (110 "Hanky Panky") 15-25 66
SELSOM (102 "Why Do Fools Fall in Love") 10-20 65
SNAP (101 "Pretty Little Red Bird") 25-45 63
SNAP (102 "Hanky Panky") 50-75 63
(No mention of distribution by Red Fox.)
SNAP (102 "Hanky Panky") 20-25 65
(Reads: "Distributed by Red Fox Records.")
Also see JAMES, Tommy

SHONDELLS
(With Andre Martel)
LPs: 10/12-inch
HELL-O 10-12 74

SHONDELS
Singles: 7-inch
CHALLENGE 4-8 65

SHO-NUFF R&B '78
Singles: 12-inch
MALACO 4-6 81-84
Singles: 7-inch
MALACO 3-4 81-84
STAX 3-5 78-79
LPs: 10/12-inch
STAX 5-10 78

SHOOK, Jerry
Singles: 7-inch
PHILIPS 4-8 64

SHOOP, Shelley
(With the Shakers.)
Singles: 7-inch
GROOVE 10-15 65

SHOOP, Wally
(With the Zombies; with Fubur)
Singles: 7-inch
AJS NEW HORIZON (1001 "Evening in the City") 40-60 71
STUDIO FIVE 5-8 60s
Also see BILLY RAT & FINKS

SHOOT
LPs: 10/12-inch
EMI 8-12 73

SHOOTERS
(Featuring Otis Redding)
Singles: 7-inch
TRANS WORLD (6908 "She's All Right") 50-100 60
(Reissued on Finer Arts as by Otis Redding & the Shooters.)
Also see REDDING, Otis

SHOOTERS C&W '87
Singles: 7-inch
EPIC 3-4 87-89
Members: Walter Alridge; Gary Baker. Mike Dillon; Barry Billings; Chalmers Davis.

SHOOTING STAR P&R/LP '80
Singles: 7-inch
EPIC 3-4 82
GEFFEN 3-4 85
VIRGIN 3-5 80
Picture Sleeves
GEFFEN 3-4 85
VIRGIN 3-5 80
LPs: 10/12-inch
ENIGMA 5-8 89
EPIC 5-8 81-83
VIRGIN 5-10 80-82
Members: Gary West; Van McLain; Ron Verlin; Keith Mitchell; Charles Waltz; Bob Guffy; Steve Thomas.

SHOOTING STARS
Singles: 7-inch
RANDOLPH (10001 "I Love Her Anyway") 15-25 66

SHOOTYZ GROOVE: see DOWNSET / Shootyz Groove

SHOPPE, The C&W '80
Singles: 7-inch
AMERICAN COUNTRY 3-4 84-85
MTM 3-5 88
NSD 3-4 81
RAINBOW SOUND 3-5 80

SHOR, Betty Ann
Singles: 7-inch
JUSTICE 5-10 59

SHORE, Dinah P&R '40
(With Dick Todd; with Woody Herman)
Singles: 78 rpm
BLUEBIRD 5-10 40-42
COLUMBIA 4-8 46
RCA 3-6 50-57
VICTOR 4-8 40-46
Singles: 7-inch
CAPITOL 4-8 60-62
CAPITOL CUSTOM (3793 "Purex Presents Dinah Shore") 5-10 61
(Single-sided promotional issue, made for Purex.)
DECCA 3-5 69
MERCURY 3-5 74
PROJECT 3 ....3-6 67-68
RCA 8-15 50-57
Picture Sleeves
CAPITOL CUSTOM (3793 "The Purex Dinah Shore Special") 5-10 61
(Promotional issue, made for Purex.)
RCA 10-20 53
EPs: 7-inch
CAMDEN 5-10 56
CAPITOL 4-8 59
CAPITOL CUSTOM ("Season's Greetings: Dinah Shore") 5-10 50s
COLUMBIA 4-8 59
RCA 5-15 51-57
LPs: 10/12-inch
BAINBRIDGE 5-8 82
CAMDEN 5-10 59-60
CAPITOL (1200 series) 10-20 59-60
CAPITOL (1354 "Dinah Sings Some Blues with Red Norvo") 20-30 60
CAPITOL (1600 & 1700 series) 10-20 62
COLUMBIA (6000 series) 20-40 50-51
(10-inch LPs.)
COLUMBIA (34000 series) 5-10 77
DECCA 5-10 69
HARMONY 5-10 59-60
NABISCO (001 "Nabisco Invitational") 30-40 83
(Picture disc. Promotional issue only.)
PROJECT 3 ....5-10 68
RCA (11 "Tangos") 25-35 51
RCA (1100 & 1200 series) 20-30 55-56
RCA (3000 series) 20-30 53-54
(10-inch LPs.)
REPRISE 10-15 65
S&H GREEN STAMPS (1 "Dinah") 10-20 62
(TV show preview LP. Promotional issue only.)
Also see CUGAT, Xavier, & Dinah Shore
Also see KINGSTON TRIO / Dinah Shore
Also see MARTIN, Dean

SHORE, Dinah, & Tony Martin
Singles: 78 rpm
RCA 5-10 51
Singles: 7-inch
RCA 10-15 51

SHORE, Dinah, Tony Martin, Betty Hutton & Phil Harris
Singles: 78 rpm
RCA 5-10 51
Singles: 7-inch
RCA 10-15 51
Also see HARRIS, Phil
Also see HUTTON, Betty
Also see MARTIN, Tony

SHORE, Dinah, & Andre Previn
LPs: 10/12-inch
CAPITOL 15-25 60
Also see PREVIN, Andre
Also see SHORE, Dinah

SHORE, Jerry
Singles: 7-inch
PHILIPS 3-6 68

SHORE, Roberta
Singles: 7-inch
BUENA VISTA 4-8 60s
DISNEYLAND 5-10 59
DOT 4-8 61-62
LPs: 10/12-inch
DISNEYLAND (3044 "Shaggy Dog") 30-40 57
Also see LUKE, Robin, & Roberta Shore

SHORE, Sammy
Singles: 78 rpm
VIK (187 "Seventeen Tons") 5-10 55
Singles: 7-inch
VIK (187 "Seventeen Tons") 10-15 55

SHOREMEN
Singles: 7-inch
WYNWOOD (1956 "She's Bad") 10-15 65

SHORR, Mickey, & Cutups P&R '62
Singles: 7-inch
TUBA (8001 "Ben Basey") 10-15 62
Also see SPENCER & SPENCER

SHORR'S STREAKERS
Singles: 7-inch
EASTBOUND (625 "Streakin' '74") 4-6 74

SHORROCK, Glenn P&R '83
Singles: 7-inch
CAPITOL 3-4 83
Picture Sleeves
CAPITOL 3-5 83
Also see LITTLE RIVER BAND

SHORT, Bill
(With the Shocks)
Singles: 7-inch
RESCUE 5-10
TOWN 5-10 60

SHORT, Bobby LP '72
LPs: 10/12-inch
ATLANTIC 10-25 59-72

SHORT, L.
Singles: 7-inch
RUST 5-10 61

SHORT CROSS
LPs: 10/12-inch
GRIZLY (16013 "Arising") 200-250 70
Members: Velpo Robertson; Gray McCalley; Burch Owens; Bird Sharp.

SHORT CUTS
Singles: 7-inch
CARLTON (513 "Don't Say He's Gone") 10-20 59
Members: Mary-Ellen Keegan; Margie Keegan.

SHORT KUTS
Singles: 7-inch
PEPPER 4-6 68-69

SHORT PEOPLE
Singles: 7-inch
GUSTO 3-5 78

SHORT STUFF
(Junior Brantley)
Singles: 7-inch
AGE of AQUARIUS 3-5 74
BIRDIE 3-5 70s
THIRD COAST 3-5 77
LPs: 10/12-inch
THIRD COAST 8-10 76-80
Also see JUNIOR & CLASSICS

SHORT TWINS
Singles: 7-inch
EAGLE 5-10 58
JEWEL 5-10 59
20TH FOX 5-10 61

SHORTALL, Gary
Singles: 7-inch
VISTA 5-10 61

SHORTER, Rick
Singles: 7-inch
COLUMBIA 4-6 67
MGM 4-6 67

SHORTER, Wayne LP '75
LPs: 10/12-inch
BLUE NOTE 20-30 62
(Label reads "Blue Note Records Inc. - New York, USA.")
BLUE NOTE 15-20 66
(Label shows Blue Note Records as a division of either Liberty or United Artists.)
COLUMBIA 5-10 75
VEE JAY (Maroon label) 30-40 60
VEE JAY (Black label) 20-30 61-62
Also see WEATHER REPORT

SHORTY
Singles: 7-inch
EPIC 3-5 70
SOUL 4-6 68
LPs: 10/12-inch
EPIC 10-15 70

SHORTY JOE
Singles: 78 rpm
GOLDEN WEST 10-15

SHOT GUNS
Singles: 7-inch
PROMPT (101 "Searching") 10-20 60s

SHOT IN THE DARK P&R '81
Singles: 7-inch
RSO 3-5 81
LPs: 10/12-inch
RSO 5-10 81
Members: Peter White; Bryan Savage; Krysia Kristianne; Robin Lamble; Adam Yurman.
Also see STEWART, Al

SHOTGUN R&B '77
Singles: 12-inch
MONTAGE 4-6 82
Singles: 7-inch
ABC 3-5 77-79
MCA 3-5 80
MONTAGE 3-5 82
LPs: 10/12-inch
ABC 5-10 77-79
MCA 5-10 79-80
MONTAGE 5-10 82
Members: Tyrone Steels; Richard Sebastion; Greg Ingram; Billy Talbert; Ernest Latimore; Larry Austin.
Also see SUN, Joe, & Shotgun

SHOTGUN EXPRESS
Singles: 7-inch
UPTOWN (747 "I Could Feel the Whole World") 10-20 67
Members: Rod Stewart; Peter Bardens; Beryl Marsden.
Also see BARDENS, Peter
Also see STEWART, Rod

SHOTGUN LTD.
LPs: 10/12-inch
PROPHESY 10-12 71

SHOTGUN MESSIAH LP '89
LPs: 10/12-inch
RELATIVITY 5-8 89

SHOTGUNS
LPs: 10/12-inch
WYNCOTE 10-20 60s

SHOW OF HANDS
LPs: 10/12-inch
ELEKTRA 10-15 69

SHOW STOPPERS P&R '68
(Showstoppers)
Singles: 7-inch
AMBER 5-10 63
COLLECTABLES 3-4 80s
COLUMBIA 10-15 66-67
HERITAGE 4-6 68
SHOWTIME 4-8 67
LPs: 10/12-inch
COLLECTABLES 5-10

SHOWBOATS
Singles: 7-inch
GOLDBAND 5-10 63
Members: Bill Parker; Chester Randle; Paul Lewis; D. Jones; Roosevelt Dickerson.

SHOWBOYS
Singles: 12-inch
PROFILE 4-6 86
Singles: 7-inch
PROFILE 3-4 86

SHOWCASES
Singles: 7-inch
GALAXY (732 "This Love Was Real") 500-1000 64

SHOWDOWN R&B '77
Singles: 7-inch
HONEY BEE 3-5 77
LPs: 10/12-inch
HONEY BEE 5-10 77

SHOWMEN P&R '61
Singles: 7-inch
AIRECORDS 10-20
AMY 5-10 68
BB (4015 "In Paradise") 10-15 67
IMPERIAL (66033 "It Will Stand") 8-12 64
IMPERIAL (66071 "Country Fool") .. 8-12 64
JOKERS THREE (100 "A Little Bit of Your Love") 50-75
LIBERTY 4-8 70-81
MINIT (632 "It Will Stand") 20-40 61
(Orange label.)
MINIT (632 "It Will Stand") 15-25 60s
(Black label.)
MINIT (643 "The Wrong Girl") 20-40 62
MINIT (647 "Comin' Home") 15-25 62
MINIT (654 "True Fine Mama") 15-25 62
MINIT (662 "39-21-46") 15-25 63
(Orange label.)
MINIT (662 "39-21-46") 8-12 60s
(Black label.)
SWAN (4213 "In Paradise") 15-25 65
SWAN (4241 "Please Try to Understand") 15-25 65
Member: General Johnson.
Also see JOHNSON, General
Also see THOMAS, Irma / Ernie K-Doe / Showmen / Benny Spellman.

SHOWMEN
Singles: 7-inch
SAM (114 "Slowly") 15-25 63

SHOWMEN
Singles: 7-inch
USA (795 "Ghost Train") 10-15 64

SHOWMEN
Singles: 7-inch
TEXAS RECORD CO 10-15 66

SHOWMEN
Singles: 7-inch
TWIN TOWN 10-20 60s

SHOWMEN & BOBBY LEE
Singles: 7-inch
COULEE (113 "Alright") 15-25 65
Members: Bobby Lee; Mike Gutch; Bob Smith; Terry Hoepner; Dave Preston.

SHOWTIME, INC.
Singles: 7-inch
BLACK CIRCLE (6006 "Take This Heart of Mine") 12-15

SHOWTIME PARTS I & II
Singles: 7-inch
CANDY FLOSS 20-25 68

SHRAYDER, Pete
Singles: 7-inch
ASCOT 4-8 63-64

SHRIEKBACK D&D/LP '83
Singles: 12-inch
ARISTA 4-6 84
W.B. 4-6 83
Singles: 7-inch
W.B. 3-4 83
LPs: 10/12-inch
ISLAND 5-8 87-88
W.B. 5-8 83
Members: Barry Andrews; David Allen.
Also see GANG of FOUR
Also see XTC

SHRIMPERS
(Tony Douglas Presents the Shrimpers)
Singles: 7-inch
PAULA (1236 "Rascal") 5-10 60s
Also see DOUGLAS, Tony

SHRUB
Singles: 7-inch
PARAMOUNT 3-5 71

SHRUM, Walter, & His Colorado Hillbillies C&W '45
Singles: 78 rpm
COAST 5-10 45

SHU SHU & JOCKEYS
Singles: 7-inch
KING OF MUSIC (11081 "Visit to Planet Earth") 4-8 76
(Includes photo insert.)

SHUGGY BO
Singles: 7-inch
MAGIC LAMP 4-8 64

SHUNDEL, Troy: see SHONDELL, Troy

SHUFFLERS
Singles: 78 rpm
OKEH 40-60 54
Singles: 7-inch
OKEH (7040 "Ain't That Nothin' Wrong with That") 75-125 54

SHUFFLERS
Singles: 7-inch
CRACKERJACK 8-12
J.A.G. 10-20
PENNINGTON (01 "Thick Syrup") 10-20 64

SHUFFLES
Singles: 7-inch
RAY-CO (508 "Do You Remember My Darling") 400-600 63

SHUFFLES
Singles: 7-inch
DATE (1670 "Madeleine") 3-6 71

SHURFINE SINGERS
Singles: 7-inch
JOSIE 4-8 66

SHURFIRE C&W '87
Singles: 7-inch
AIR 3-4 87-88

SHURTLEFF, Jeffrey
LPs: 10/12-inch
A&M 8-10 72

SHU-SHU & SPACE JOCKEYS
Singles: 7-inch
KING of MUSIC 8-12

SHUT DOWNS
Singles: 7-inch
DIMENSION (1016 "Four on the Floor") 10-20 63
KARSONG (101 "Four on the Floor") 20-40 63
Member: Kirby St. Romain.
Also see ST. ROMAIN, Kirby

SHUTTERS, Harold
Singles: 78 rpm
GOLDEN ROD 50-100 56
Singles: 7-inch
GOLDEN ROD (204 "Rock & Roll, Mister Moon") 200-300 56
GOLDEN ROD (300 "Bunny Honey") 200-300 56

SHY LP '87
Singles: 7-inch
RCA 3-4 87
LPs: 10/12-inch
RCA 5-8 87

SHY GUYS
Singles: 7-inch
TRUMP (816 "Girl with Flaxen Hair") 10-20 59

SHY GUYS
Singles: 7-inch
BURGER (504 "The Burger Song") 10-15 66
PALMER (5005 "We Gotta Go") 10-15 66
PANIK (5111 "We Gotta Go") 10-15 66

SHY GUYS
Singles: 7-inch
CANUSA 5-10 67

SHY GUYS
Singles: 7-inch
LITTLE FORT (9663 "Rockin' Pneumonia and the Booga Loo Flu") 20-30 67
SHAMLEY (44001 "Payin' My Dues") 10-15 68
UNI (55035 "Rockin' Pneumonia and the Booga Loo Flu") 10-15 67
Also see BERNADETTE, Sunny, & Her Fabulous Guys
Also see JOHNNY & SHY GUYS

SHY GUYS
Singles: 7-inch
MU ("Goodbye to You") 20-30 60s

SHY ONES
Singles: 7-inch
DISCA-TECH 8-12

SHY TALK
Singles: 7-inch
COLUMBIA 3-4 85
LPs: 10/12-inch
COLUMBIA 5-8 85

SHYTANS
Singles: 78 rpm
BRUCE 10-15 54
POWER 10-15 54
Singles: 7-inch
POWER (106 "BMT Special") 20-30 54
(First issue.)
BRUCE (106 "BMT Special") 15-20 54
BRUCE (110 "Skokian") 15-20 54

SHYTONE FIVE
Singles: 7-inch
J&S (1622 "Sack Rock") 8-12

SHYLO C&W '76
Singles: 7-inch
COLUMBIA 3-5 75-76
MERCURY 3-4 82
LPs: 10/12-inch
COLUMBIA 8-10 76-79

SHYRES
Singles: 7-inch
CORI (31001 "Where Is Love") 15-25 67

SHY-TONES
(With Sammy Fields Orchestra)
Singles: 7-inch
GOODSPIN (401 "Lover's Quarrel") 100-150 60
(Reissued as *Lovers Quarrel,* and credited to the Hi-Tones.)
Members: Sal Covais; Graham True; Bill Scarpa; Al Seavozzo; Fred Alverez.
Also see EMOTIONS
Also see HI-TONES
Also see TRENTONS

SHYTONES
Singles: 7-inch
SPOT (14 "White Bucks") 100-200 61
SPOT (15 "Annette") 100-200 61

SIBERRY, Jane LP '86
Singles: 7-inch
OPEN AIR 3-4 86
LPs: 10/12-inch
OPEN AIR 5-8 86

SIBERT, Jerry
Singles: 7-inch
CUSTOM SOUND (216 "Message from a King") 4-6

SICKNIKS
Singles: 7-inch
AMY 5-8 61
Picture Sleeves
AMY 10-15 61
LPs: 10/12-inch
AMY (2 "Sick #2") 20-30 61
Member: Will Jordan.

SIDE EFFECT R&B '76
Singles: 12-inch
FANTASY 4-6 78-81
Singles: 7-inch
ELEKTRA 3-4 80-82
FANTASY 3-5 75-81
LPs: 10/12-inch
ELEKTRA 5-8 80-82
FANTASY 5-8 75-81
Members: Miki Howard; Augie Johnson; Louis Patton; Sylvia Nabors; Gregory Matta; Helen Lowe; Sylvia St. James.
Also see HOWARD, Miki
Also see L.A. BOPPERS

SIDE OF THE ROAD GANG C&W '76
Singles: 7-inch
CAPITOL 3-5 76
LPs: 10/12-inch
CAPITOL 8-10 76

SIDE SHOW
Singles: 7-inch
ATLANTIC 3-5 70
GRT 4-6 69
LPs: 10/12-inch
ATLANTIC 10-15 70

SIDE THREE
Singles: 7-inch
MOHAWK 3-6 68

SIDEKICKS P&R '66
Singles: 7-inch
RCA 4-8 66-67
LPs: 10/12-inch
RCA 10-20 66

SI-DELLS
Singles: 7-inch
EAST COAST (101 "Watch Out Mother") 10-20 68

SIDEWALK SKIPPER BAND
Singles: 7-inch
CAPITOL 5-10 66-68
TEEN TOWN 5-10 69
Member: Brian Balestrieri; Dave McDowell; Rick Novac; Joe Balestrieri; Tom Youkam; Barry Biehoff; Tom Janovic.
Also see BALESTRIERI, Brian

SIDEWALK SOUNDS
Singles: 7-inch
SIDEWALK 10-20 60s
TOWER (352 "Billy Jack's Theme") 10-20 67
TOWER (480 "Let's Go") 10-20 69
Members: Mike Curb, Bob Summers.
Also see CURB, Mike
Also see SUMMERS, Bob

SIDEWALK SURFERS
Singles: 7-inch
JUBILEE (5496 "Skate Board") 10-20 65
Member: Bruce Johnston.
Also see JOHNSTON, Bruce

SIDEWINDERS
Singles: 7-inch
IMPERIAL 5-10 59

SIDEWINDERS
Singles: 7-inch
LOOK (5006 "Get Out of My Life") . 15-25 67

SIDEWINDERS
Singles: 7-inch
RCA 3-5 72
LPs: 10/12-inch
RCA 10-12 72

SIDEWINDERS LP '89
LPs: 10/12-inch
MAMMOTH 5-8 89

SIDNEY, Ann
Singles: 7-inch
CAPITOL 4-8 65

SIDNEY & CHIMPS
Singles: 7-inch
FARO 15-25 60s

SIDRAN, Ben
Singles: 7-inch
ARISTA 3-5 77-79
BLUE THUMB 3-5 73-74
CAPITOL 3-5 71
LPs: 10/12-inch
ANTILLES 5-8 80
ARISTA 5-10 79
BLUE THUMB 5-10 74
CAPITOL 8-12 71
GO JAZZ 5-8 90
HORIZON 5-10 79
Also see MILLER, Steve
Also see NIGHTRANES

SIDWELL, Sandra
Singles: 7-inch
SUTRA 3-4 81

SIEBEL, Paul
LPs: 10/12-inch
ELEKTRA 5-10 79

SIEFERT, Jerry
Singles: 7-inch
NOTE (10018 "Dirty White Bucks") 50-75 58

SIEGEL, Corky
LPs: 10/12-inch
DHARMA 5-10 74
Also see SIEGEL - SCHWALL BAND

SIEGEL, Dan
Singles: 7-inch
CRS ASSOC 3-4 88

SIEGEL - SCHWALL BAND
Singles: 7-inch
DEUTSCHE GRAMMOPHON 3-5 73
WOODEN NICKEL 3-5 72-74
LPs: 10/12-inch
VANGUARD 12-25 66-70
WOODEN NICKEL 15-30 72-74
Members: Corky Siegel; Jim Schwall.
Also see SIEGEL, Corky

SIEGLING & LARRABEE
LPs: 10/12-inch
LOOK 10-15 70

SIERRA
Singles: 7-inch
MERCURY 3-5 77
LPs: 10/12-inch
MERCURY 8-10 77

SIERRA C&W '83
Singles: 7-inch
AWESOME 3-4 84-85
CARDINAL 3-5 83
MUSICOM 3-5 83

SIERRA, Don
Singles: 7-inch
EVEREST 5-8 61

SIERRAS
(With Bob Cox Orchestra; Sierra's)
Singles: 7-inch
KNOX (102 "So Many Sleepless Nights") 50-100 62

SIERRAS
Singles: 7-inch
CHAM (101 "Then I'll Still Love You") 20-30 64
DOT (16569 "Then I'll Still Love You") 10-15 64
GOLDISC (4 "I Should Have Loved You") 20-30 63

SIERRAS
Singles: 7-inch
YARDBIRD 4-8 67

SIERRAS
Singles: 7-inch
MAIL CALL ("Stormy Weather") 100-150 63
(No selection number used.)

SIERRAS
Singles: 7-inch
BANGAR (644 "Party at Taco Towne") 40-60 60s

SIERRAS
Singles: 7-inch
DORIAN (1001 "Donkey Call") 5-10 60s

SIFFRE, Labi R&B '87
Singles: 7-inch
CHINA 3-4 87

SIGGERS, Ruben, & His Fabulous Kool Kats
("Vocal By Ephraim Siggers")
Singles: 7-inch
SPINKS (600 "Those Love Me Blues") 500-750 57
Members: Ruben Siggers; Ephraim Siggers.

SIGHT & SOUND
Singles: 7-inch
FONTANA 4-6 69

SIGHT UNSEEN
Singles: 7-inch
REAL 4-6 69

SIGLER, Bunny P&R/R&B '67
("Mr. Emotions")
Singles: 12-inch
SALSOUL 4-6 80
Singles: 7-inch
BEE (1114 "Laddy Daddy") 10-20 59
(Bee 1114 is also the number of a Don Ellis release.)
CRAIG 10-15 61
DECCA 10-25 65-67
GOLD MINE 3-6 78-79
NEPTUNE 5-10 60s
PARKWAY 5-10 67-69
PHILADELPHIA INT'L 5-15 71-76
SALSOUL 3-5 80
EPs: 7-inch
PARKWAY (6000 "Bunny Sigler") .. 10-15 67
CAMEO PARKWAY (6000 "Bunny Sigler") 5-10 68
LPs: 10/12-inch
GOLD MIND 5-10 78-79
PARKWAY (50,000 "Let the Good Times Roll") 10-20 67
SALSOUL 5-10 80
Also see ELLIS, Don, & Royal Dukes
Also see HOLLOWAY, Loleatta, & Bunny Sigler
Also see MASON, Barbara, & Bunny Sigler

SIGLEY, Ernie, & Denise Drysdale
Singles: 7-inch
INTERNATIONAL (875 "Hey Paula") 4-6 74

SIGNALS
Singles: 7-inch
LEONEAL (1483 "Show Me the Way") 50-75

SIGNALS
LPs: 10/12-inch
INVASION 8-10 83

SIGNATURES
Singles: 7-inch
NORMAN (210 "Julie Is Her Name") 200-250 57
WHIPPIT (210 "Julie Is Her Name") 25-35 57

SIGNIFICANT OTHER
Singles: 7-inch
CRITIQUE 10-20 60s

SIGUE SIGUE SPUTNIK LP '86
Singles: 12-inch
MANHATTAN 4-6 86
Singles: 7-inch
MANHATTAN 3-4 86
LPs: 10/12-inch
MANHATTAN 5-10 86
Member: Tony James.
Also see GENERATION X

SILAS, Alfie R&B '82
(Alfie)
Singles: 7-inch
MOTOWN ... 3-4 84-86
RCA ... 3-4 82-84
LPs: 10/12-inch
MOTOWN ... 5-8 85
RCA ... 5-8 82-84
Also see KING, Bobby

SILBERMAN, Benedict
Singles: 7-inch
PALETTE ... 4-8 59

SILENCERS P&R '80
Singles: 7-inch
PRECISION ... 3-5 80
LPs: 10/12-inch
PRECISION ... 5-10 80-81
Member: Frank Czuri.
Also see DIAMOND REO

SILENCERS P&R/LP '87
Singles: 7-inch
RCA ... 3-4 87
LPs: 10/12-inch
RCA ... 5-8 87-90

SILENT MAJORITY
Singles: 7-inch
HOT ICE ... 3-5
Members: Victor Drayton; Jerry Akines; Reginald Turner; Ernie Brooks; Johnny Bellman.
Also see FORMATIONS

SILENT UNDERDOG R&B '85
Singles: 12-inch
PROFILE ... 4-6 85

SILHOUETTES P&R/R&B '58
(With Dave McRae Orchestra)
Singles: 78 rpm
EMBER ... 50-75 57
JUNIOR ... 50-100 57
Singles: 7-inch
ABC ... 3-5 73
ACE (552 "I Sold My Heart to the Junkman") ... 12-15 58
COLLECTABLES ... 3-4 80s
EMBER (1029 "Get a Job") ... 20-30 57
(Red or orange label.)
EMBER (1029 "Get a Job") ... 10-20 60
(Black label.)
EMBER (1032 "Headin' for the Poorhouse") ... 15-25 58
EMBER (1037 "Bing Bong") ... 50-100 58
(Glossy red label.)
EMBER (1037 "Bing Bong") ... 15-25 58
(Flat red label.)
FLASHBACK ... 4-8 65
GOODWAY (101 "Not Me Baby") ... 100-200 68
GRAND (142 "I Wish I Could Be There") ... 150-250 61
IMPERIAL (5899 "The Push") ... 10-15 62
JUNIOR (391 "Get a Job") ... 250-500 57
(Brown label.)
JUNIOR (391 "Get a Job") ... 200-300 57
(Blue label.)
JUNIOR (396 "I Sold My Heart to the Junkman") ... 75-125 58
JUNIOR (400 "Evelyn") ... 1000-2000 59
JUNIOR (993 "Your Love") ... 50-75 63
LPs: 10/12-inch
GOODWAY (100 "Get a Job") ... 100-150 68
Also see HORTON, Bill, & Silhouettes
Also see KING, Ben E.

SILICON TEENS
LPs: 10/12-inch
SIRE ... 5-10 80

SILK LP '69
Singles: 7-inch
ABC ... 5-10 69
DECCA ... 4-6 71
LPs: 10/12-inch
ABC (694 "Smooth As Raw Silk") ... 15-25 69
Members: Michael Stanley Gee; Chris Jones; Randy Sabo; Courtney Johns.
Also see STANLEY, Michael, Band

SILK R&B '77
Singles: 12-inch
PHILADELPHIA INT'L ... 4-8 79-80
Singles: 7-inch
PHILADELPHIA INT'L ... 3-5 79-80
PRELUDE ... 3-5 77
PYE ... 3-5 76
LPs: 10/12-inch
ARISTA ... 5-10 77
PHILADELPHIA INT'L ... 5-10 79
Member: Debra Henry.
Also see BUTLER, Jerry, & Debra Henry

SILK, J.M. D&D '85
Singles: 12-inch
D.J. INT'L ... 4-6 85

SILK WINGED ALLIANCE
Singles: 7-inch
ACCENT (1277 "Hometown") ... 20-30 60s

SILKIE P&R '65
Singles: 7-inch
FONTANA ... 4-8 65-66
LPs: 10/12-inch
FONTANA (27548 "You've Got to Hide Your Love Away") ... 20-30 65
(Monaural.)
FONTANA (67548 "You've Got to Hide Your Love Away") ... 25-35 65
(Stereo.)
Also see BEATLES

SILKS: see McCOLLOUGH, Charles

SILKY & SAGE
Singles: 7-inch
DATE ... 3-5 69

SILKY & SHANTUNGS
Singles: 7-inch
MUSICOR ... 8-12 63

SILLER, Bob
LPs: 10/12-inch
DUNHILL ... 10-15 68

SILLS, Billy
Singles: 7-inch
CHAIRMAN ... 4-8 63
COLPIX ... 5-10 60
DECCA ... 10-15 58
MOTION ... 4-8 62

SILLY
Singles: 7-inch
MAYPOLE ... 5-10 60

SILLY SAVAGES
Singles: 7-inch
DORE ... 4-8 66

SILLY SURFERS
LPs: 10/12-inch
MERCURY (20977 "Sounds of the Silly Surfers") ... 20-30 65
MERCURY (60977 "Sounds of the Silly Surfers") ... 25-35 65

SILLY SURFERS / Weird-Ohs
LPs: 10/12-inch
HAIRY (101 "Sounds of the Silly Surfers") ... 75-125 65
(One side of LP is by each group.)
Members: Gary Usher; Chuck Girard; Richard Burns; Shary Richards.
Also see HONDELLS
Also see SILLY SURFERS
Also see WEIRD-OHS

SILO, Susan
Singles: 78 rpm
CANDLELIGHT ... 5-10 56
Singles: 7-inch
CANDLELIGHT (1005 "Dear Diary") ... 10-20 56

SILOS LP '90
LPs: 10/12-inch
RCA ... 5-8 90

SILVA, Bob, & Silva-Tones
Singles: 7-inch
DEBBIE (1409 "I'll Hold You in My Heart") ... 50-75 59
Also see SILVA-TONES

SILVA, Margie, & Bossa Novas
Singles: 7-inch
RENDEZVOUS ... 4-8 63

SILVA-TONES P&R '57
Singles: 78 rpm
ARGO ... 20-30 57
MONARCH ... 25-50 57
Singles: 7-inch
ARGO (5281 "That's All I Want from You") ... 20-30 57
(Silver and black label with "ship" logo.)
ARGO (5281 "Chi-Wa-Wa, That's All I Want from You") ... 15-25 57
(Black label, silver print. No "ship" logo. Note title variation.)
MONARCH (615 "That's All I Want from You") ... 30-50 57
(Yellow label.)
MONARCH (615 "That's All I Want from You") ... 20-30 57
(Black label.)
Also see SILVA, Bob, & Silva-Tones

SILVER P&R/LP '76
Singles: 7-inch
ARISTA ... 3-5 76-77
LPs: 10/12-inch
ARISTA ... 8-10 76
Members: John Batdorf; Brent Mydland.
Also see BATDORF, John
Also see GRATEFUL DEAD

SILVER, Horace, Quintet LP '65
Singles: 78 rpm
BLUE NOTE ... 4-8 54-57
Singles: 7-inch
BLUE NOTE (300 thru 1000 series) ... 3-5 73-77
BLUE NOTE (1600 & 1700 series) ... 5-10 54-61
BLUE NOTE (1800 & 1900 series) ... 4-8 61-69
LPs: 10/12-inch
BLUE NOTE (1518 "Horace Silver Quintet") ... 50-75 56
(Label gives New York street address for Blue Note Records.)
BLUE NOTE (1518 "Horace Silver Quintet") ... 25-50
(Label gives New York street address for Blue Note Records.)
BLUE NOTE (1520 "New Faces") ... 50-75 56
(Label gives New York street address for Blue Note Records.)
BLUE NOTE (1520 "New Faces") ... 25-50
(Label reads "Blue Note Records Inc. - New York, U.S.A.")
BLUE NOTE (1562 "Stylings") ... 50-75 57
(Label gives New York street address for Blue Note Records.)
BLUE NOTE (1562 "Stylings") ... 25-50
(Label reads "Blue Note Records Inc. - New York, U.S.A.")
BLUE NOTE (1562 "Stylings") ... 15-25
(Label shows Blue Note Records as a division of Liberty.)
BLUE NOTE (1589 "Further Explorations") ... 50-75 58
(Label gives New York street address for Blue Note Records.)
BLUE NOTE (1589 "Further Explorations") ... 25-50
(Label reads "Blue Note Records Inc. - New York, U.S.A.")
BLUE NOTE (1589 "Further Explorations") ... 15-25
(Label shows Blue Note Records as a division of Liberty.)
BLUE NOTE (4000 series) ... 30-50 59-60
(Label gives New York street address for Blue Note Records.)
BLUE NOTE (4000 series) ... 20-30 59-65
(Label reads "Blue Note Records Inc. - New York, U.S.A.")
BLUE NOTE (4000 series) ... 15-20 66-68
(Label shows Blue Note Records as a division of either
BLUE NOTE (5018 "New Faces") ... 100-150 53
(10-inch LP.)
BLUE NOTE (5034 "Horace Silver Trio") ... 100-150 54
(10-inch LP.)
BLUE NOTE (5058 "Horace Silver Quintet") ... 100-150 55
(10-inch LP.)
BLUE NOTE (5062 "Horace Silver Quintet") ... 100-150 55
(10-inch LP.)
BLUE NOTE (84000 series) ... 30-40 59-60
(Label gives New York street address for Blue Note Records.)
BLUE NOTE (84000 series) ... 20-30 59-65
(Label reads "Blue Note Records Inc. - New York, U.S.A.")
BLUE NOTE (84000 series) ... 10-20 66-80
(Label shows Blue Note Records as a division of either
EPIC (3326 "Silver's Blue") ... 75-125 57
EPIC (16006 "Silver's Blue") ... 60-80 58
Also see STITT, Sonny, Kai Winding & Horace Silver

SILVER, Horace, Quintet, & Stanley Turrentine
LPs: 10/12-inch
BLUE NOTE ... 10-15 68
Also see SILVER, Horace, Quintet
Also see TURRENTINE, Stanley

SILVER, J.
Singles: 7-inch
COLUMBIA ... 3-5 80

SILVER, Long John
Singles: 7-inch
STAR BRITE ... 5-10 59

SILVER, Karen
Singles: 7-inch
ARISTA ... 3-5 79
LPs: 10/12-inch
ARISTA ... 5-10 79

SILVER, Mike
LPs: 10/12-inch
MCA/ROCKET ... 8-10 73

SILVER, Rhonda
Singles: 7-inch
KING ... 4-8 64

SILVER, Steven
(Jimmy Ellis)
Singles: 7-inch
VULCAN (1060 "Down in Mississippi") ... 5-10 87
Also see ELLIS, Jimmy

SILVER APPLES LP '68
Singles: 7-inch
KAPP ... 4-8 68-69
LPs: 10/12-inch
KAPP ... 10-15 68-69

SILVER BELLES
Singles: 7-inch
ANDEX ... 5-10 59

SILVER BLUE
Singles: 12-inch
EPIC ... 4-8 78
Singles: 7-inch
EPIC ... 3-5 78
LPs: 10/12-inch
EPIC ... 5-10 78

SILVER BULLETS
Singles: 7-inch
TEEN TOWN (115 "Lone Ranger") ... 10-15 70
Also see TODAY'S TOMORROW

SILVER BYKE
Singles: 7-inch
BANG (557 "I've Got Time") ... 10-15 68

SILVER CITY BAND C&W '77
Singles: 7-inch
COLUMBIA ... 3-5 77-78

SILVER CONDOR P&R/LP '81
Singles: 7-inch
COLUMBIA ... 3-4 81
Picture Sleeves
COLUMBIA ... 3-5 81
LPs: 10/12-inch
COLUMBIA ... 5-10 81
Members: Joe Cerisano; Earl Slick; John Corey; Claude Pepper; Jay Davis.
Also see PHANTOM, ROCKER & SLICK

SILVER CONVENTION P&R/R&B/LP '75
Singles: 7-inch
MIDLAND INT'L ... 3-5 75-77
MIDSONG INT'L ... 3-5 77-78
Picture Sleeves
MIDLAND INT'L ... 3-5 76
LPs: 10/12-inch
MIDLAND INT'L ... 5-10 75-77
MIDSONG INT'L ... 5-10 77
Member: Penny McLean.
Also see McLEAN, Penny

SILVER CREEK C&W '81
Singles: 7-inch
CARDINAL ... 3-4 81
Also see IVIE, Roger, & Silvercreek

SILVER EAGLE
Singles: 7-inch
MGM ... 4-8 67

SILVER FLEET
(10CC)
Singles: 7-inch
UNI (55271 "Look Out World") ... 10-20 71
Also see 10CC

SILVER LAUGHTER
Singles: 7-inch
FANFARE ... 3-5 77

SILVER METRE
Singles: 7-inch
NATIONAL GENERAL ... 3-5 72
LPs: 10/12-inch
NATIONAL GENERAL ... 10-15 70

SILVER NOTES
Singles: 7-inch
SARA (6881 "The Girl I Love the Most") ... 10-15 68

SILVER PHOENIX BAND
Singles: 7-inch
BREWSTER ... 3-4 85

SILVER PLATINUM R&B '80
Singles: 7-inch
SRI ... 3-5 81
SPECTOR ... 3-5 81
LPs: 10/12-inch
SPECTOR ... 5-10 81

SILVER, PLATINUM & GOLD R&B '75
Singles: 7-inch
FARR ... 3-5 76-77
W.B. ... 3-5 74-75
LPs: 10/12-inch
NEPTUNE ... 5-10 82

SILVER SHADOW
LPs: 10/12-inch
MAJOR PACIFIC (1006 "Silver Shadow") ... 10-20 83
(Picture disc.)

SILVER SISTERS
Singles: 7-inch
CAN-DEE ... 5-10 59

SILVERA, Silvio
Singles: 7-inch
BARCLAY ... 4-6

SILVERADO P&R '81
Singles: 7-inch
PAVILLION ... 3-5 81
RCA ... 3-5 77
LPs: 10/12-inch
PAVILLION ... 5-10 81
RCA ... 5-10 77

SILVERBIRD
Singles: 7-inch
CAPITOL ... 3-5 71
COLUMBIA ... 3-5 72
LPs: 10/12-inch
CAPITOL ... 8-12 71
COLUMBIA ... 8-12 72

SILVERHEAD
Singles: 7-inch
MCA ... 3-5 73-74
LPs: 10/12-inch
MCA ... 8-10 73-74
SIGNPOST ... 8-10 72
Members: Clem Burke; Nigel Harrison.
Also see BLONDIE
Also see CHEQUERED PAST
Also see LITTLE GIRLS
Also see SHOCK

SILVERS, Herb
Singles: 7-inch
SUTTER (150 "Attracted to You") ... 15-25

SILVERS, Johnny
Singles: 7-inch
SIMS ... 10-15 60

SILVERSPOON, Dooley P&R/R&B '75
Singles: 7-inch
COTTON ... 3-5 74-75
Also see LITTLE DOOLEY & Fabulous Tears

SILVERSTEIN, Shel LP '73
Singles: 7-inch
COLUMBIA ... 3-6 71-75
ELEKTRA ... 8-12 60
RCA ... 4-6 69-70
LPs: 10/12-inch
ATLANTIC (8072 "Inside Folk Songs") ... 20-30 63
(Monaural.)
ATLANTIC (SD-8072 "Inside Folk Songs") ... 25-35 63
(Stereo.)
ATLANTIC (8200 series) ... 10-15 70
CBS (39611 "Where the Sidewalk Ends") ... 8-12 84
(Picture disc.)
CADET ... 15-25 65-66
COLUMBIA ... 5-12 72-84
CRESTVIEW ... 15-25 63
ELEKTRA (176 "Hairy Jazz") ... 30-40 59
(Monaural.)
ELEKTRA (7-176 "Hairy Jazz") ... 40-50 59
(Stereo.)
FLYING FISH ... 5-8 80
JANUS ... 8-12 73
PARACHUTE (Except 20512) ... 5-10 78
PARACHUTE (20512 "Selected Cuts from *Songs and Stories*") ... 15-20 78
(Promotional issue only.)
RCA ... 10-15 69

SILVERTONES
Singles: 7-inch
ELGIN (5 "My Only Love") ... 25-50 59
SILVER SLIPPER (1000 "Sentimental Memories") ... 10-15 60

SILVERTONES
Singles: 7-inch
TILT (777 "Jumpin' Jack") ... 10-20 60

SILVERTONES
Singles: 7-inch
USA (717 "Hong Kong") ... 10-15 62

SILVERTONES
Singles: 7-inch
GOLIATH (1355 "Get It") ... 10-20 63
SWEET (16 "Seven Piece Bathing Suit") ... 10-20 60s
VALIANT (6045 "Get It") ... 8-12 64

SILVERTONES
Singles: 7-inch
JOEY (302 "Thinking of You") ... 75-150 63

SILVETTI P&R/R&B '77
Singles: 7-inch
SALSOUL ... 3-5 77
LPs: 10/12-inch
SALSOUL ... 5-10 77

SIMEONE, Harry, Chorale P&R '58
Singles: 7-inch
COLUMBIA ... 3-5 66-67
KAPP ... 3-5 64-68
MERCURY ... 3-5 62-64
MISTLETOE ... 3-4 74
20TH FOX ... 3-5 58-79
Picture Sleeves
MERCURY ... 4-6 62
20TH FOX ... 4-8 58-63
Promotional Picture Sleeve
20TH FOX (121 "Little Drummer Boy") ... 5-10 58
(This "Prepare to Be Enchanted" sleeve was sent only to radio stations.)
LPs: 10/12-inch
DECCA ... 5-15 62-64
DIPLOMAT ... 5-10 60s
KAPP ... 5-10 65
MERCURY ... 5-15 63-64
MISTLETOE ... 4-8 73
MOVIETONE ... 5-10 67
20TH FOX ... 5-15 58-79
WING ... 5-10 69

SIMIELE, Ernie, & Eratics
Singles: 7-inch
KIND A ROUND (11765 "Special Girl") ... 550-650
(Also shows "RB 105." It's not clear which is the correct selection number.)

SIMMON, Little Mack see LITTLE MACK

SIMMON, Ray
Singles: 7-inch
END ... 8-10 60

SIMMONS, Al, & Slim Green
(With the Cats from Fresno)
Singles: 78 rpm
DIG ... 15-25 56
Singles: 7-inch
DIG (138 "Old Folks' Boogie") ... 40-50 56
DIG (142 "You Ain't Too Old") ... 30-40 56
Also see GREEN, Slim
Also see MAIDEN, Sidney / Al Simmons

SIMMONS, Aleese
Singles: 7-inch
ORPHEUS ... 3-4 88

SIMMONS, Chandra R&B '87
Singles: 7-inch
FRESH ... 3-4 87

SIMMONS, Fay
(With the Royals; with "Michelle on Organ"; Faye Simmons)
Singles: 78 rpm
PINEY ... 8-12 55
Singles: 7-inch
GONE (5029 "Rockin', Rollin' & A' Strollin' ") ... 15-25 58
JORDAN (120 "Secret Love") ... 10-20 60
JORDAN (122 "Shake It Up") ... 10-20 60
JORDAN (124 "He's Got the Whole World in His Hands") ... 10-20 61
PALM (300 "It's a Sin to Tell a Lie") ... 10-15 62
(First issue.)
PINEY (110 "I'll Always Call Your Name") ... 20-30 55

POP-SIDE (8 "Just to Hold My Hand") ... 8-12 62
PORT (5002 "I Can See Through You") ... 15-25 57
RUTHIE (1038 "Rain") ... 5-10 62
SENCA (126 "Lonely Girl") ... 10-20 61
V-TONE (237 "It's a Sin to Tell a Lie") ... 8-12 62

SIMMONS, Gene P&R/LP '64
(Jumpin' Gene Simmons; Morris Gene Simmons)
Singles: 7-inch
AGP ... 8-10 60s
CHECKER (948 "Goin' Back to Memphis") ... 20-30 60
EPIC ... 3-5 70
DELTUNE ... 3-5 77-78
HI ... 8-15 61-67
HURSHEY ... 3-5 73
MALA ... 5-10 68
SANDY ... 8-12 60s
STATUE (7005 "Call Sam [Phillips]") ... 20-25 66
SUN (299 "Drinkin' Wine") ... 25-50 58
TUPELO (2981 "Little Rag Doll") ... 100-200 60s
LPs: 10/12-inch
HI (2018 "Jumpin' Gene Simmons") ... 20-40 64
(Monaural.)
HI (32018 "Jumpin' Gene Simmons") ... 25-50 64
(Stereo.)

SIMMONS, Gene P&R/LP '78
Singles: 7-inch
CASABLANCA ... 3-4 78-79
LPs: 10/12-inch
CASABLANCA (7120 "Gene Simmons") ... 12-20 78
(With poster order form.)
CASABLANCA (7120 "Gene Simmons") ... 8-12 78
(Without poster order form.)
CASABLANCA (PIX-7120 "Gene Simmons") ... 50-60 79
(Picture disc.)
Also see CHRISTOPHER, Lyn
Also see KISS

SIMMONS, Jeff
LPs: 10/12-inch
REPRISE ... 8-12 70
STRAIGHT ... 10-15 69
Also see MOTHERS of INVENTION

SIMMONS, Jimmy
Singles: 7-inch
ATCO ... 10-20 58
7 STAR (901 "Everyday Lady") ... 4-6 79
7 STAR (0001 "You Gotta Love People") ... 6-10 74

SIMMONS, Lonnie, Quartet
Singles: 78 rpm
PARROT (790 "Black Orchid") ... 25-50 53
Singles: 7-inch
PARROT (790 "Black Orchid") ... 50-100 53
(Black vinyl.)
PARROT (790 "Black Orchid") ... 200-300 53
(Red vinyl.)

SIMMONS, Maurice: see SIMON, Maurice

SIMMONS, Morris
Singles: 7-inch
SANDY ... 4-8 60
STRAND ... 5-10 59

SIMMONS, Patrick P&R/R&B/D&D/LP '83
Singles: 12-inch
ELEKTRA ... 4-8 83
Singles: 7-inch
ELEKTRA ... 3-5 83
LPs: 10/12-inch
ELEKTRA ... 5-10 83
Also see DOOBIE BROTHERS
Also see EAGLES

SIMMONS, Simtec R&B '75
(With the Mechanical Monster; with Band; Simtec)
Singles: 7-inch
AVI (208 "Funny Thing") ... 3-6
INNOVATION II (8047 "Some Other Time") ... 3-6 75
MAURCI (105 "Tea Pot") ... 5-8 67
MAURCI (107 "Limber Up") ... 5-8 67
MAURCI (113 "Swingin' Loose") ... 5-8 67
Also see COMPUTER & LITTLE FOOLER

SIMMONS, Simtec, & Wylie Dixon
Singles: 7-inch
TODDLIN' TOWN (114 "Sockin' Soul Power") ... 4-8 69
Also see DIXON, Wyle, & Wheels
Also see SIMMONS, Simtec
Also see SIMTEC & WYLIE

SIMMONS TWINS
Singles: 7-inch
DWAIN (808 "How Are We Going to Go Steady") ... 10-20 59

SIMMS, Al, Sextet
Singles: 7-inch
AMERICAN INT'L ... 8-12 59

SIMMS, Carl
Singles: 7-inch
HOLLYWOOD ... 4-8 68

SIMMS, John & Arthur R&B '80
Singles: 7-inch
CASABLANCA ... 3-5 80
LPs: 10/12-inch
CASABLANCA ... 5-10 80

SIMMS, Johnny
Singles: 7-inch
ALITE ... 5-10

SIMMS, LuAnn
Singles: 78 rpm
JUBILEE ... 5-10 57
Singles: 7-inch
JUBILEE ... 5-10 57
VEE JAY ... 5-8 63

SIMMS BROTHERS
Singles: 7-inch
ELEKTRA ... 3-5 79-80
LPs: 10/12-inch
ELEKTRA ... 5-10 79-80

SIMMS TWINS: see SIMS TWINS

SIMON, Carly P&R/LP '71
Singles: 7-inch
ARISTA ... 3-4 86-90
COLUMBIA ... 3-5 73
ELEKTRA ... 3-5 71-79
EPIC ... 3-4 85-86
MIRAGE ... 3-5 82
W.B. ... 3-5 80-83
Picture Sleeves
ARISTA (Except 9525) ... 3-5 86-89
ARISTA (9525 "Coming Around Again") ... 4-8 86
(Pictures Meryl Streep and Jack Nicholson.)
ARISTA (9525 "Coming Around Again") ... 3-5 86
(Pictures Carly Simon.)
ELEKTRA ... 3-5 75-79
W.B. ... 3-5 80-83
LPs: 10/12-inch
ARISTA ... 5-8 86-90
ELEKTRA ... 5-10 71-79
EPIC ... 5-8 85-86
W.B. ... 5-10 80-83
Also see JAGGER, Mick
Also see SIMON SISTERS

SIMON, Carly, & James Taylor P&R '74
Singles: 7-inch
ELEKTRA ... 3-5 74-78
Also see SIMON, Carly
Also see TAYLOR, James

SIMON, Eddie
Singles: 7-inch
TORNADO ... 4-8 65

SIMON, Freddie, Quintet
Singles: 78 rpm
COMBO ... 5-10 53
RECORDED in HOLLYWOOD ... 5-10 52
Singles: 7-inch
COMBO ... 15-25 53
RECORDED in HOLLYWOOD ... 15-25 52
Also see SIMON, Maurice

SIMON, Jimmy
Singles: 7-inch
PHOENIX ... 4-8

SIMON, Joe R&B '65
(With the Checkmates; with Mainstreeters; with Johnny Heartsman's Band)
Singles: 7-inch
COMPLEAT ... 3-5 70s
DOT ... 5-10 64
GEE BEE (077 "Say") ... 15-25
HUSH (103 "It's a Miracle") ... 15-25 60
HUSH (104 "Call My Name") ... 15-25 61
HUSH (106 "Pledge of Love") ... 15-25 61
HUSH (107 "Troubles") ... 15-25 61
HUSH (108 "Land of Love") ... 15-25 62
IRRAL (778 "Only a Dream") ... 6-12 63
MONUMENT ... 3-6 70-72
POSSE ... 3-5 81-82
SOUND STAGE 7 ... 4-8 66-72
SPRING ... 3-6 69-75
VEE JAY ... 5-10 64-65
Picture Sleeves
GEE BEE (077 "Say") ... 15-25
SPRING ... 3-5 71-73
LPs: 10/12-inch
BUDDAH ... 10-15 69
POSSE ... 5-8 81-82
SOUND STAGE 7 ... 8-15 67-75
SPRING ... 8-12 71-78
Also see GOLDEN TONES
Also see HEARTSMAN, Johnny

SIMON, Lowrell
Singles: 12-inch
ZOO YORK ... 4-6 81
Singles: 7-inch
ZOO YORK ... 3-5 81
Also see LOST GENERATION
Also see LOWRELL

SIMON, Maurice
(With the Pie Men; with Freddie Simon;; Maurice Simmons)
Singles: 78 rpm
DOWN BEAT ... 10-20 49
HOLLYWOOD ... 10-15 53
Singles: 7-inch
CARNIVAL (525 "The Git-Go") ... 5-10 67
FLASH (113 "Flashy") ... 10-20 56
Also see SIMON, Freddie

SIMON, Micky
Singles: 78 rpm
DOWN BEAT ... 10-15 49

SIMON, Paul P&R/LP '72
(With Urubamba; with Los Incas)
Singles: 12-inch
W.B. (2503 "You Can Call Me Al") ... 4-8 86
(Promotional issue.)
W.B. (2652 "Boy in the Bubble") ... 4-8 86
(Promotional issue.)
Singles: 7-inch
COLUMBIA ... 3-5 72-77
W.B. ... 3-4 80-90
Picture Sleeves
COLUMBIA ... 3-8 73-77
W.B. ... 3-5 80-87
LPs: 10/12-inch
COLUMBIA (Except C5X & 43000 series) ... 6-12 72-77
COLUMBIA (C5X-37581 "Paul Simon's Collected Works") ... 30-40 81
(Boxed, five-disc set.)
COLUMBIA (43000 series) ... 15-20 81
(Half-speed mastered.)
DMG ("Songs of Paul Simon") see Various Artists Section
MCP (8027 "Paul Simon Plus"): see Various Artists Section
W.B. (140 ""Interview Show") ... 20-30 86
(Promotional issue only. Two LPs with interview and *Graceland* songs.)
W.B. (3472 "One-Trick Pony") ... 5-10 80
W.B. (23942 thru 26098) ... 5-10 80-90
Also see BOOKER T. & MGs
Also see CYRKLE
Also see DION
Also see DIXIE HUMMINGBIRDS
Also see 4 SEASONS
Also see FRANKLIN, Aretha
Also see GARFUNKEL, Art, James Taylor & Paul Simon
Also see GLASS, Philip
Also see GREGORY, Harrison
Also see KANE, Paul
Also see LANDIS, Jerry
Also see NEWMAN, Randy, & Paul Simon
Also see ORLANDO, Tony
Also see RIVERS, Johnny
Also see SEDAKA, Neil
Also see SIMON & GARFUNKEL
Also see TAYLOR, True
Also see TICO & TRIUMPHS
Also see U.S.A. for AFRICA
Also see URUBAMBA
Also see VALERY, Dana
Also see YES

SIMON, Paul, & Phoebe Snow P&R '75
(With the Jessy Dixon Singers)
Singles: 7-inch
COLUMBIA ... 3-5 75
Also see SNOW, Phoebe

SIMON, Roger
Singles: 7-inch
DOUBLE L ... 4-8 64

SIMON, Screamin' Scott
LPs: 10/12-inch
ROLLIN' ROCK ... 5-10 82
Also see SHA NA NA

SIMON & GARFUNKEL P&R '65
Singles: 7-inch
ABC-PAR (10788 "This Is My Story") ... 10-15 66
COLUMBIA (10000 series) ... 3-5 75
COLUMBIA (11000 series) ... 5-8 66
COLUMBIA (33000 series) ... 3-6 60s
COLUMBIA (43396 "The Sounds of Silence") ... 4-8 65
COLUMBIA (43396 "The Sounds of Silence") ... 30-40 65
(Colored vinyl. Promotional issue only.)
COLUMBIA (43511 "Homeward Bound") ... 4-8 66
COLUMBIA (43511 "Homeward Bound") ... 30-40 66
(Colored vinyl. Promotional issue only.)
COLUMBIA (43617 "I Am a Rock") ... 4-8 66
COLUMBIA (43617 "I Am a Rock") ... 30-40 66
(Colored vinyl. Promotional issue only.)
COLUMBIA (43728 thru 45663) ... 4-8 66-75
TEEN SCOOP/Columbia ("Exclusive Interview") ... 20-35 65
(Square cardboard picture disc issued in premier issue of *Teen Scoop* magazine. Includes magazine with disc intact.)
TEEN SCOOP/Columbia ("Exclusive Interview") ... 10-20 65
(Square cardboard picture disc issued in premier issue of *Teen Scoop* magazine. No selection number used.)
TEEN SCOOP (789 "Visits with Simon & Garfunkel") ... 10-20 66
(*Teen Scoop* magazine bonus soundsheet.)
W.B. ... 3-5 82
Picture Sleeves
COLUMBIA ... 5-10 66-75
EPs: 7-inch
COLUMBIA ... 10-20 68-69
(Juke box issues only.)
LPs: 10/12-inch
COLUMBIA (CL-2249 "Wednesday Morning 3 A.M.") ... 10-20 64
(Monaural.)
COLUMBIA (CL-2469 "Sounds of Silence") ... 10-20 66
(Monaural.)
COLUMBIA (CL-2563 "Parsley, Sage Rosemary and Thyme") ... 10-20 66
(Monaural.)
COLUMBIA (KCL-2729 "Bookends") ... 15-25 68
(Monaural. Includes poster.)
COLUMBIA (OS-3180 "The Graduate") ... 12-15 68
(Soundtrack.)
COLUMBIA (3654 "Concert in Central Park") ... 8-12 82
COLUMBIA (CS-9049 "Wednesday Morning 3 A.M.") ... 10-15 64
(Stereo.)
COLUMBIA (PC-9049 "Wednesday Morning 3 A.M.") ... 5-10
COLUMBIA (CS-9269 "Sounds of Silence") ... 10-15 66
(Stereo.)
COLUMBIA (CS-9363 "Parsley, Sage Rosemary and Thyme") ... 10-15 66
(Stereo.)
COLUMBIA (PC-9363 "Parsley, Sage Rosemary and Thyme") ... 5-10
COLUMBIA (KCS-9529 "Bookends") ... 10-15 68
(Stereo. Includes poster.)
COLUMBIA (PC-9529 "Bookends") 5-10
COLUMBIA (9914 "Bridge over Troubled Water") ... 10-15 70
COLUMBIA (30995 "Bridge over Troubled Water") ... 10-20 71
(Quadrophonic.)
COLUMBIA (31350 "Greatest Hits") ... 5-10 72
COLUMBIA (37587 "Simon & Garfunkel's Collected Works") ... 30-40 81
(Boxed, five-disc set.)
COLUMBIA (41350 "Greatest Hits") ... 10-15 81
(Half-speed mastered.)
COLUMBIA (49914 "Bridge over Troubled Water") ... 40-60 80
(Half-speed mastered.)
MFSL (173 "Bridge over Troubled Water") ... 20-30 85
OFFSHORE ... 10-15
PICKWICK (3059 "Hit Sound of Simon & Garfunkel") ... 50-75 66
SEARS (435 "Simon & Garfunkel") ... 20-30
W.B. ... 5-8 82
Members: Paul Simon; Art Garfunkel.
Also see CLARK, Dave, Five / Simon & Garfunkel / Yardbirds / New Christy Minstrels
Also see GARFUNKEL, Art
Also see REVERE, Paul, & Raiders / Simon & Garfunkel / Byrds / Aretha Franklin
Also see SIMON, Paul
Also see TOM & JERRY

SIMON & PIEMEN
Singles: 7-inch
CARNIVAL (525 "Git-Go") ... 8-12 66
CHARTBOUND (007 "Cut It Out") ... 15-25 60s

SIMON & VERITY C&W '85
Singles: 7-inch
EMI AMERICA ... 3-4 85

SIMON F: see F., SIMON

SIMON SAID R&B '75
Singles: 7-inch
ATCO ... 3-5 75-76
ROULETTE ... 3-5 75

SIMON SISTERS P&R '64
Singles: 7-inch
COLUMBIA (02600 series) ... 3-4 82
COLUMBIA (45000 series) ... 3-5 73
KAPP ... 4-8 64-65
LPs: 10/12-inch
COLUMBIA (21525 "Lobster Quadrille") ... 10-15 69
COLUMBIA (21539 "Simon Sisters Sing for Children") ... 10-12 73
COLUMBIA (24506 "Lobster Quadrille") ... 15-20 69
(Special childrens' book edition.)
COLUMBIA (37000 series) ... 5-10 82
KAPP ... 15-25 64
W.B. ... 5-10 80
Members: Carly Simon; Lucy Simon.
Also see DOOBIE BROTHERS / Kate Taylor & Simon-Taylor Family
Also see SIMON, Carly

SIMONE, Frank
Singles: 7-inch
ADONIS ... 5-10 59
QUICK ... 5-10 59

SIMONE, Nina P&R/R&B '59
Singles: 7-inch
BETHLEHEM ... 3-8 59-70
CTI ... 3-5 78
COLPIX ... 4-8 59-63
PHILIPS ... 4-6 64-66
RCA ... 3-6 67-71
TRIP ... 3-4 72
EPs: 7-inch
BETHLEHEM ... 5-10 59
LPs: 10/12-inch
ACCORD ... 5-10 80
BETHLEHEM ... 20-30 59
CTI ... 5-10 78-79
COLPIX ... 15-30 59-66
PHILIPS ... 10-20 64-69
QUINTESSENCE ... 5-10 80
RCA ... 8-15 67-76
STROUD ... 5-10 73
TRIP ... 5-10 72-77
UPFRONT ... 5-10 72
VERSATILE ... 5-10 78
Also see LYNNE, Gloria / Nina Simone / Billie Holiday

SIMONE, Nina, Chris Connor & Carmen McRae
LPs: 10/12-inch
BETHLEHEM ... 20-30 60
Also see CONNOR, Chris
Also see McRAE, Carmen
Also see SIMONE, Nina

SIMONS, Maurice
Singles: 78 rpm
FLASH ... 5-10 56
Singles: 7-inch
FLASH ... 10-20 56

SIMPLE MINDS LP '83
Singles: 12-inch
A&M ... 4-6 82-86
Singles: 7-inch
A&M ... 3-4 82-86
Picture Sleeves
A&M ... 3-5 84-86
LPs: 10/12-inch
A&M ... 5-10 82-91
PVC ... 8-10 79
VIRGIN ... 5-8 81
Members: John Giblin; Charles Burchill; Jim Kerr; Michael MacNeil; Mel Gaynor.

SIMPLY RED D&D '85
Singles: 12-inch
ELEKTRA ... 4-6 85-86
Singles: 7-inch
ELEKTRA ... 3-4 85-89
Picture Sleeves
ELEKTRA ... 3-4 86-89
LPs: 10/12-inch
ELEKTRA ... 5-8 85-89
Member: Mick Hucknall.

SIMPSON
LPs: 10/12-inch
COLUMBIA ... 6-12 71

SIMPSON, Big Daddy
Singles: 7-inch
M-PAC ... 4-8 65

SIMPSON, Bill
Singles: 7-inch
LIN (100 "Jelly Roll Man") ... 10-15
SUNN (1 "Elvis–the Music Machine") ... 4-6

SIMPSON, Carl
Singles: 7-inch
VALLI (304 "Baby Blues Rock") ... 40-60 60

SIMPSON, Donald, & Rockenettes
Singles: 7-inch
MAJOR (1002 "Woe-Oh Baby") 100-125 58

SIMPSON, Eddie
Singles: 7-inch
BACKBEAT (616 "Stoned Soul Sister") ... 5-10 69
DUKE (470 "Big Black Funky Slave") ... 5-10 71
MAMIE ... 5-10

SIMPSON, Jimmy
Singles: 78 rpm
HIDUS ... 10-15 55
Singles: 7-inch
HIDUS ... 15-25 55
JIFFY ... 10-20 50s

SIMPSON, John
LPs: 10/12-inch
PERCEPTION ... 8-10

SIMPSON, Paul D&D '83
(Paul Simpson Connection)
Singles: 12-inch
EASY STREET ... 4-6 85
STREETWISE ... 4-6 83
Singles: 7-inch
STREETWISE ... 3-4 83

SIMPSON, Red C&W '66
Singles: 7-inch
CAPITOL ... 3-6 66-73
K.E.Y. ... 3-5 79
W.B. ... 3-5 76
LPs: 10/12-inch
CAPITOL ... 10-15 66-73
51 WEST/SEA SHELL ... 5-8 82
PICKWICK ... 5-10 70s

SIMPSON, Valerie LP '71
Singles: 7-inch
TAMLA ... 3-5 71-72
LPs: 10/12-inch
TAMLA ... 8-10 71-77
Also see ASHFORD & SIMPSON
Also see SHARELL, Jerry

SIMPSON SISTERS
Singles: 7-inch
DCP ... 4-8 65

SIMPSONS LP '90
Singles: 7-inch
GEFFEN ... 3-4 91
LPs: 10/12-inch
GEFFEN (24308 "Sing the Blues") ... 5-8 90
Members: Dan Castellaneta; Julie Kavner; Nancy Cartwright; Yeardley Smith; Matt Groening. Session: Harry Shearer; Ron Taylor; Harry Shearer; Buster Poindexter; Joe Walsh; B.B. King; John Sebastian; D.J. Jazzy Jeff; Andrew Gold; Dr. John.
Also see D.J. JAZZY JEFF & Fresh Prince
Also see DR. JOHN
Also see GOLD, Andrew
Also see KING, B.B.
Also see SEBASTAIN, John

Also see WALSH, Joe

SIMS, Al

Singles: 7-inch

YUCCA (104 "Green Gatorater")....25-35 58

SIMS, Artie

Singles: 78 rpm

APOLLO....10-20 46

Singles: 7-inch

A-1....5-10 61
STAR DUST....5-10 60

SIMS, Bobby, & Simmers

Singles: 7-inch

WM & RC....4-8 66
Also see JALOPY FIVE

SIMS, Charles

Singles: 7-inch

ALADDIN....15-25 60

SIMS, Chuck

Singles: 7-inch

SPANGLE....15-25 58
TREND....10-15 58

SIMS, Frankie Lee

Singles: 78 rpm

ACE....10-15 57
BLUE BONNET (147 "Home Again, Blues")....100-150 48
BLUE BONNET (148 "Don't Forget Me, Baby")....100-150 48

Singles: 7-inch

ACE....10-15 57
SPECIALTY....15-25 53
VIN....10-15 58

LPs: 10/12-inch

SPECIALTY (2124 "Lucy Mae Blues")....20-30 65

SIMS, Gerald

Singles: 7-inch

OKEH (7183 "Cool Breeze")....10-20 63
OKEH (7199 "Little Echo")....10-20 64
Also see DAYLIGHTERS

SIMS, Jerry

Singles: 7-inch

RCA....5-8 59

SIMS, Joyce

Singles: 7-inch

SLEEPING BAG....3-4 86-88

SIMS, Lee

Singles: 78 rpm

BIG....5-10 57

Singles: 7-inch

BIG....5-10 57

SIMS, Lloyd

Singles: 7-inch

ATLANTIC (2078 "For Sentimental Reasons")....10-15 60

SIMS, Mack: see LITTLE MACK

SIMS, Marvin
(Marvin L. Sims)

Singles: 7-inch

KAREN (1547 "Sweet Thang")....5-10 69
MELLOW (1002 "What Can I Do")..8-12 66
MELLOW (1004 "Have You Seen My Baby")....8-12 67
MELLOW (1005 "Hurting Inside")....8-12 67
MERCURY (73288 "Dream a Dream")....4-6 72
MERCURY (73340 "You Gotta Go")..4-6 72
REVUE (11024 "Talkin' 'Bout Soul")....5-10 68
REVUE (11038 "Get Off My Back")..5-10 69
RIVERTOWN (498 "Love Is on the Way")....4-6 80
UNI (55217 "It's Your Love")....4-8 70

SIMS, Syl

Singles: 7-inch

N-JOY ("Landslide")....10-20 62
(Selection number not known.)

SIMS TWINS *P&R/R&B '61*
(Simms Twins)

Singles: 7-inch

ABKCO....3-5 70s
CROSSOVER....4-6 74
KENT....4-6 71
PARKWAY....5-10 68
SAR....10-15 61-62
SPECIALTY....4-6 72
Members: Bobby Sims; Kenneth Sims.

SIMTEC & WYLIE

Singles: 7-inch

MISTER CHAND....4-6 70-73
SHAMA (4003 "Do It Like Mama")....4-8 69
SHAMA (4004 "Put Another Plus to Your Heart")....4-8 70

LPs: 10/12-inch

MISTER CHAND (40001 "Gettin' Over the Hump")....8-12 71
Members: Simtec Simmons; Wylie Dixon.
Also see KRYSTAL GENERATION
Also see SIMMONS, Simtec, & Wylie Dixon
Also see SOUTHSIDE MOVEMENT

SIN

Singles: 7-inch

AZRA (1129 "On the Run")....8-12 83
(Snake-shaped picture disc with black rim. 500 made.)
AZRA (1129 "On the Run")....15-20 83
(Snake-shaped picture disc yellow or blue or red rim. 25 to 50 made of each variation.)

SIN CITY BAND

LPs: 10/12-inch

STRAIGHT FACE....5-10 80

SIN SAY SHUNS

Singles: 7-inch

AMERICAN (3367 "You Said to Me")....10-15 66
(Selection number not known.)
VENETT (106 "I'll Be There")....10-15 66
VENETT (108 "All My Lonely Waiting")....10-15 66

LPs: 10/12-inch

VENETT (940 "I'll Be There")....20-25 66
Members: Bill Edison; Tony Visco; Bob Cottle.

SINATRA, Frank *P&R '42*
(With Harry James & His Orchestra; with Axel Stordahl & His Orchestra; with Big Dave's Music; "Tommy Dorsey Orchestra Featuring Frank Sinatra")

Singles: 78 rpm

BLUEBIRD (10726 "East of the Sun")....50-75 42
BLUEBIRD (10771 "Whispering")..50-75 42
BLUEBIRD (11463 "Night & Day")..50-75 42
BLUEBIRD (11515 "The Song Is You")....50-75 42
BRUNSWICK (8443 "From the Bottom of My Heart")....600-750 39
(Credited to Harry James & His Orchestra.)
CAPITOL (1699 thru 3900)....5-15 53-58
COLUMBIA (5492 "Soliloquy")....15-25 46
(12-inch disc. At least one source says this selection number is 7492. We don't yet know who's right.)
COLUMBIA (35209 thru 41133)....5-15 39-58
COLUMBIA (50003 thru 50079)....4-8 50s
COLUMBIA (55037 "Ol Man River")....15-25 44
(12-inch disc.)
RCA (1522 thru 3500)....5-10 43-49
RCA (13247 "Oh Look at Me Now")....40-60 82
(Single-sided. Promotional issue only. 1000 numbered copies made.)
RCA (36396 "Without a Song")....15-25 42
(12-inch disc.)
VICTOR (26500 thru 27974)....5-10 40-43
(Some in this series may be shown as "RCA Victor.")

Albums: 78 rpm

COLUMBIA (112 "The Voice of Frank Sinatra")....25-50 46
(Four discs.)
COLUMBIA (117 "All Time Favorites by Harry James")....25-50 46
(Four discs. *Ciribiribin* is by Sinatra.)
COLUMBIA (117 "All Time Favorites by Harry James")....15-25 46
(Four discs. *Ciribiribin* is by Harry James.)
COLUMBIA (124 "Songs by Sinatra")....25-50 47
(Four discs.)
COLUMBIA (167 "Christmas Songs by Sinatra")....25-50 48
(Four discs.)
COLUMBIA (185 "Frankly Sentimental")....25-50 49
(Four discs.)
COLUMBIA (197 "Dedicated to You")....25-50 50
(Four discs.)
COLUMBIA (218 "Sing and Dance with Frank Sinatra")....25-50 50
(Four discs.)
COLUMBIA (455 "Young at Heart")....25-50 51
(Four discs.)
COLUMBIA (637 "Frank Sinatra Conducts the Music of Alec Wilder")....100-150 46
(Three 12-inch Masterworks discs.)
RCA (80 "Getting Sentimental")....20-40 40
(Four discs.)
RCA (150 "Starmaker")....20-40 41
(Four discs.)
RCA (163 "All Time Hits")....20-40 42
(Four discs.)
RCA (247 "And the Band Sang Too")....20-40 43
(Three discs)

Singles: 12-inch

QUEST (2216 "Mack the Knife")....10-20 84
(Promotional issue only.)
REPRISE (674 "Night & Day")....50-75 77
(Promotional issue only. Only 647 made.)
REPRISE (865 "New York, New York")....25-50 80
(Promotional issue only.)

Singles: 7-inch

CAPITOL ("No One Ever Tells You")....35-45 56
(No selection number used. Promotional issue only. Add $4 to $6 if accompanied by Capitol "Rush" paper sleeve.)
CAPITOL (596 "All the Way")....250-350 58
(Promotional issue only. 101 made.)
CAPITOL (1069 "Come Dance with Me")....50-75 59
(Five singles in a paper sleeve. For juke box use. With "XE" prefix.)
CAPITOL (1417 "Nice 'N' Easy")....50-75 60
(Five singles in a paper sleeve. For juke box use. With "XE" prefix.)
CAPITOL (1491 "Sinatra's Swingin' Session")....50-75 61
(Five singles in a paper sleeve. For juke box use. With "XE" prefix.)
CAPITOL (1594 "Come Swing with Me")....50-75 62
(Five singles in a paper sleeve. For juke box use. With "XE" prefix.)
CAPITOL (1676 "Point of No Return")....50-75 63
(Five singles in a paper sleeve. For juke box use. With "XE" prefix.)
CAPITOL (1699 "I've Got the World on a String")....20-30 51
CAPITOL (1729 "Sinatra Sings of Love and Things")....50-75 60s
(Five singles in a paper sleeve. For juke box use. With "XE" prefix.)
CAPITOL (1707/8 "Mistletoe & Holly")....75-100 60
(Promotional issue for Christmas Seals.)
CAPITOL (2450 "Lean Baby")....15-25 53
CAPITOL (2505 thru 4070)....10-20 53-58
CAPITOL (4103 "To Love and Be Loved")....8-12 58
CAPITOL (4103 "To Love and Be Loved")....150-250 58
(White label. Promotional issue only.)
CAPITOL (4155 "French Foreign Legion")....8-12 59
CAPITOL (4214 "High Hopes")....8-12 59
(Purple label.)
CAPITOL (4214 "High Hopes")....50-100 60
(Red label. Promotional issue only.)
CAPITOL (4284 thru 4815)....6-12 59-62
CAPITOL (6019 thru 6195)....4-6 62
(Starline reissue series.)
COLUMBIA (112 "The Voice of Frank Sinatra")....50-75 46
(Four discs.)
COLUMBIA (167 "Christmas Songs by Sinatra")....50-75 48
(Four discs.)
COLUMBIA (197 "Dedicated to You")....50-75 50
(Four discs.)
COLUMBIA (218 "Sing and Dance with Frank Sinatra")....50-75 50
(Four discs.)
COLUMBIA (673 "If I Ever Love Again")....40-60 67
(Promotional issue only.)
COLUMBIA (1-106 thru 1-936)....40-60 48-51
(Microgroove 33 singles.)
COLUMBIA (6-718 thru 6-936)....15-25 50-51
(45 rpm.)
COLUMBIA (3842 "I Guess I'll Have to Dream the Rest")....40-60 71
(Promotional issue only.)
COLUMBIA (12194 "All Or Nothing at All")....30-40 55
(Promotional issue only.)
COLUMBIA (33000 series)....3-8 60s
(Hall of Fame series. With "13" prefix.)
COLUMBIA (33011 thru 39213)....40-60 50s
(Microgroove 33 singles. With "3" prefix.)
COLUMBIA (36814 thru 41133)....15-30 50-58
(45 rpm. With "4" prefix.)
COLUMBIA (50003 thru 50079)....10-15 55-59
(Hall of Fame series. With "4" prefix.)
COLUMBIA (116427 "White Christmas")....40-60 63
(Promotional issue only.)
"HIGH HOPES with JACK KENNEDY"/"Jack Kennedy All the Way"....150-250 60
(Presidential campaign promotional issue only. No label name or artist shown. Reportedly 1,000 made.)
RCA (15 "Getting Sentimental")....35-50 50
(Boxed, four-disc set.)
RCA (20 "All Time Hits")....35-50 51
(Boxed, four-disc set.)
RCA GOLD STANDARD SERIES....4-8 60-70
(With "447" prefix.)
REPRISE ("A Special Message to You from Frank Sinatra")....750-1000 61
(Single-sided. Made as a Reprise sales and promotional tool. No selection number used. Two different pressings exist.)
REPRISE (45 "Frank Sinatra reads from Gunga Din")....450-650 66
(Promotional issue only.)
REPRISE (PRO-162 thru PRO-406)....25-50 63-69
(White label, promotional issues only.)
REPRISE (0243 thru 0380)....5-10 63-65
REPRISE (396 "Radio Spot for *Watertown*")....15-25 70
(Promotional issue only.)
REPRISE (0398 thru 1386)....3-8 65-77
REPRISE (20001 thru 20151)....4-8 61-63
REPRISE (20157 "California")....150-250 77
(Promotional issue only. Reportedly 1000 made.)
REPRISE (20184 "Come Blow Your Horn")....4-8 63
REPRISE (20184 "Come Blow Your Horn")....50-75 63
(White label. Promotional issue only.)
REPRISE (20209 thru 20235)....4-8 63
REPRISE (28000 & 29000 series)....3-4 82
REPRISE (40001 thru 40050)....8-10 60s
(33 rpm. Juke box issues.)
REPRISE (40063 thru 40092)....4-8
(33 rpm. Juke box issues.)
REPRISE (49000 series)....3-5 80-83
REPRISE/CAL NEVADA LODGE (101 "Ring-A-Ding-Ding")....50-75 63
(Promo souvenir, available from the lodge.)

Picture Sleeves

CAPITOL (596 "All the Way")....250-350 58
(Promotional issue only. 101 made.)
CAPITOL (4103 "To Love and Be Loved")....250-350 58
(Promotional issue only.)
CAPITOL (4214 "High Hopes")..250-350 60
(Promotional issue only.)
REPRISE (0429 "It Was a Very Good Year")....10-20 65
REPRISE (0531 "That's Life")....10-20 66
REPRISE (20010 "Granada")....10-20 61
REPRISE (20063 "Everybody's Twistin' ")....10-20 62
REPRISE (20157 "California")....300-400 77
(Promotional issue only. Reportedly 1000 made.)
REPRISE (20184 "Come Blow Your Horn")....100-150 63
(Promotional issue only.)
REPRISE (29903-7 "To Love a Child")....8-12 82
(Dedicated to Mrs. Nancy Reagan. With the Reprise Children's Chorus featuring Nikka Costa. Promotional issue only.)
REPRISE (49233 "New York, New York")....3-5 80
REPRISE/CAL NEVADA LODGE (101 "Ring-A-Ding-Ding")....100-150 63
(Promo souvenir, available from the lodge.)
SINATRA....3-4 75

EPs: 7-inch

CAPITOL (3 "Vocal Standards")....5-15 60s
(33 rpm.)
CAPITOL (100 "Special 1981 Birthday Tribute")....75-125 81
(33 rpm. Promotional issue only. Includes "Thank You" insert.)
CAPITOL 254: see Various Artists Chapter
CAPITOL (280 "Disc Jockey Interview Record for the film *High Society*")....125-175 56
(Promotional issue only.)
CAPITOL 304: see Various Artists Chapter
CAPITOL 426: see SINATRA, Frank / Roger Wagner / Hollywood Bowl Symphony
CAPITOL (434 "Selections from *Pal Joey*.)....125-175 57
(Promotional issue only.)
CAPITOL (488 thru 1594)....8-18 53-62
(Single-disc EPs, with "EAP" prefix.)
CAPITOL (488 thru 855)....12-25 53-57
(Two-disc EPs, with "EBF" prefix.)
CAPITOL (SU-581 "In the Wee Small Hours")....5-15 60s
(33 rpm.)
CAPITOL (DU-653 "Songs for Swingin' Lovers")....5-15 60s
(33 rpm.)
CAPITOL (DU-768 "This Is Sinatra")5-15 60s
(33 rpm.)
CAPITOL (SU-920 "Come Fly with Me")....5-15 60s
(33 rpm.)
CAPITOL (1069 "Come Dance with Me")....15-25 59
(Promotional issue only.)
CAPITOL (1549 "Selections from *Can-Can*")....300-500 60
(Promotional issue only.)
CAPITOL (1762 "The Great Years") 5-15 60s
(33 rpm.)
Capitol (1864 "Come Swing with Capitol - New Albums for August 1961")....30-50 61
(Promotional issue only.)
CAPITOL 4470: see Various Artists Chapter
CAPITOL (11583 "Frank Sinatra") 10-15 60s
(33 rpm.)
COLUMBIA (112 thru 455)....40-60 50-54
(Two discs.)
COLUMBIA (1524 thru 2641)....10-25 50-59
(Single-disc EPs.)
COLUMBIA (7431 thru 9533)....10-20 55-57
(Single-disc EPs.)
COLUMBIA (10321/10322 "Christmas Dreaming")....10-15 57
(Price is for either volume.)
COLUMBIA (28595 "Nancy")....75-100 58
(Promotional issue, made for B.T. Babbit and attached to their soap boxes. With custom cover.)
RCA (102 "Tommy Dorsey Originals")....10-20 60
(Compact 33 Double.)
RCA (3005 "This Is Tommy Dorsey")....25-50 50
(Two discs.)
RCA (3028 "Getting Sentimental") 25-50 50
(Two discs.)
RCA (3030 "All Time Hits")....25-50 51
(Two discs.)
RCA (3063 "Fabulous Frankie")....25-50 52
(Two discs.)
RCA (5007 thru 5147)....12-25 58-60
RCA (6038 "This Is Tommy Dorsey")....10-15 60s
(Juke box issue only.)
REPRISE....10-15 62-74
(Juke box issues.)

LPs: 10/12-inch

CAMDEN (650 thru 800)....5-15 61-73
CAMDEN (9027 I'm Getting Sentimental Over You")....8-12 72
CAPITOL ("Radio/TV Sampler") 200-250 58
(Number unknown. Yellow label. Promotional issue only.)
CAPITOL (200 & 300 series, except LS-308)....8-15 69
CAPITOL (LS-308 "Sinatra: The Works")....75-125 71
(Boxed, 10-disc set. Includes booklet. Add $75 to $100 if accompanied by the bonus LP, *Sinatra* CAPITOL (443: see Various Artists Chapter
CAPITOL (H-488 thru H-581)....30-50 54-55
(10-inch LPs.)
CAPITOL (488 thru 1164, except 735)....20-30 54-59
(With "T" or "W" prefix.)
CAPITOL (W-735 "Frank Sinatra Conducts Tone Poems of Color")....75-100 56
CAPITOL (581 thru 1676)....5-15 61-78
(With "DT," "DW," "SM," "STBB," "SW," or "W" prefix.)
CAPITOL (T-1221 thru T-1676)....10-20 59-62
(Monaural.)
CAPITOL (ST-1221 thru ST-1676)....10-20 59-62
(Stereo.)
CAPITOL (PRO-1624 "The Best of Sinatra")....75-100 61
(Promotional issue only. Issued with paper sleeve.)
CAPITOL (1729 "Love & Things")..10-20 62
CAPITOL (1762 "Sinatra: The Great Years")....20-30 62
(Three-disc set.)
CAPITOL (1825 thru 2700)....15-30 62-68
(With "T" or "W" prefix. Monaural.)
CAPITOL (1825 thru 2700)....10-20 62-68
(With "DT" or "DW" prefix. Reprocessed stereo.)
CAPITOL (2814 "Deluxe Set")....40-60 67
(Boxed, six-disc set.)
CAPITOL (2974 "Frank Sinatra Minute Masters")....100-150 65
CAPITOL (7630 "The Sinatra Touch")....50-75 68
(Boxed, six-disc set. Includes booklet.)
CAPITOL (11000 & 12000 series)....5-10 74-80
CAPITOL (16000 series)....5-8 80-82
CAPITOL (89611 "Duets")....8-10 90s
CAPITOL (90000 thru 94000 series)....20-40 64-74
(Capitol Record Club issues.)
COLUMBIA (6 "The Frank Sinatra Story")....15-25 58
COLUMBIA (S3S-42 "Essential Frank Sinatra")....20-30 67
(Boxed, three-disc set. Stereo.)
COLUMBIA (S3S-842 "Essential Frank Sinatra")....10-20
(Boxed, three-disc set. Reissue.)
COLUMBIA (S3S-842 "Essential Frank Sinatra")....10-20
(Boxed, three LP set. Reissue.)
COLUMBIA (606 "Frankie")....25-40 55
(Cover pictures Sinatra wearing a hat and alone.)
COLUMBIA (606 "Frankie")....15-25 50s
(Cover pictures Sinatra not wearing a hat and with two other people.)
COLUMBIA (743 "The Voice of Sinatra")....25-35 55
COLUMBIA (902 "That Old Feeling")....20-30 56
COLUMBIA (842 "Essential Frank Sinatra")....30-50 67
(Three-disc set. Includes booklet.)
COLUMBIA (953 "Adventures of the Heart")....15-25 57
COLUMBIA (1032 "Christmas Dreaming")....15-25 57
COLUMBIA (1130 thru 1359)....20-40 58-59
COLUMBIA (1448 "Reflections")....30-60 60
COLUMBIA (CL-2474 "Greatest Hits: The Early Years, Vol. 1")....10-15 66
(Monaural.)
COLUMBIA (2521 "Get Happy")....25-40 55
(10-inch LP.)
COLUMBIA (2539 "I've Got a Crush on You")....25-40 55
(10-inch LP.)
COLUMBIA (2542 "Christmas with Frank Sinatra")....25-40 55
(10-inch LP.)
COLUMBIA (CL-2572 "Greatest Hits: The Early Years, Vol. 2")....10-15 66
(Monaural.)
COLUMBIA (2475 "The Voice, Sampler")....10-15 86
(Samples tracks from C6X-40343.)
COLUMBIA (CL-2739 thru CL-2913)....10-15 66-69
(Monaural.)
COLUMBIA (4271 "Frank Sinatra Conducts the Music of Alec Wilder")....125-175 50
(Green Masterworks label.)
COLUMBIA (6001 "The Voice of Sinatra")....75-100 48
(10-inch LP.)
COLUMBIA (6059 "Frankly Sentimental")....50-75 49
(10-inch LP.)
COLUMBIA (6087 "Songs by Sinatra, Vol. 1")....50-75 50
(10-inch LP.)
COLUMBIA (6096 "Dedicated to You")....50-75 50
(10-inch LP.)
COLUMBIA (6143 "Sing and Dance with Frank Sinatra")....50-75 50
(10-inch LP.)
COLUMBIA (6290 "I've Got a Crush on You")....50-75 52
(10-inch LP.)
COLUMBIA (6339 "Young at Heart")....50-75 54
(10-inch LP.)
COLUMBIA (CS-9274 "Greatest Hits: The Early Years, Vol. 1")....8-15 66
(Stereo.)
COLUMBIA (CS-9372 "Greatest Hits: The Early Years, Vol. 2")....8-15 66
(Stereo.)
COLUMBIA (CS-9539 thru CS-9541)....8-15 66-67
(Stereo.)
COLUMBIA (10000 series)....5-10 73
COLUMBIA (30000 thru 45000 series, except 31358 & 40343)....5-12 73-87
COLUMBIA (31358 "In the Beginning")....8-12 72
(Two-disc set.)
COLUMBIA (40343 "The Voice")....30-50 86
(Boxed, six-disc set.)
EARTH NEWS....50-100 80
(Radio show on disc. Includes cue sheet/script.)
HARMONY....10-20 66-71
KATWHISKER ("Frank Sinatra: Biography in Song")....750-1000 75
(Boxed, eight-disc set. Includes cue sheets.

Promotional issue only. Reportedly only 25 made.)
MFSL (1 "Frank Sinatra")..........350-500 85
(Boxed, 16-disc set. Includes booklet and alignment tool. Numbered edition of 25,000 made.)
MFSL (086 "Nice 'N' Easy")............25-30 82
MFSL (130 "Swing Easy")..............25-30 85
MFSL (131 "In the Wee Small Hours")..........................25-30 85
MFSL (132 "Close to You")............25-30 85
MFSL (133 "A Swingin Affair").......25-30 85
MFSL (134 "Where You Are")..........25-30 85
MFSL (2-135 "A Jolly Christmas") 30-40 85
MFSL (136 "Come Fly with Me")....25-30 85
MFSL (137 "Only the Lonely")........25-30 85
MFSL (138 "Come Dance with Me")..........................25-30 85
MFSL (139 "Look at Your Heart")...25-30 85
MFSL (140 "No One Cares")...........25-30 85
MFSL (141 "Sinatra's Swingin") 25-30 85
MFSL (142 "All the Way")..............25-30 85
MFSL (143 "Come Swing with Me")25-30 85
MFSL (145 "Sinatra Swings").........25-30 85
MFSL (146 "Songs for Swingin' Lovers")..........................25-30 85
NARWOOD ("U.S. Army Reserve Presents William B. & Company")...........150-200 76
(Two-LP, public service radio show. Has Sinatra interview. Promotional issue only.)
ODYSSEY.................................10-20 68
PICKWICK...............................5-10 70s
RCA (10 "Getting Sentimental").....35-50 50
(10-inch LP.)
RCA (15 "All Time Hits")...............35-50 51
(10-inch LP.)
RCA (017 "I'll See You in My Dreams")..........................8-12 70s
RCA (050 "What'll I Do")................5-8
RCA (474 "The Radio Years").........5-10 74
RCA (0497 "What'll I Do")..............8-10 74
RCA (583 "This Love of Mine").......8-12
RCA (1569 "Frankie & Tommy")....20-40 57
RCA (1586 "Frank Sinatra with the Tommy Dorsey Orchestra")......................5-8 75
RCA (1632 "We Three")................20-40 57
RCA (3005 "This Is Tommy Dorsey")..............................25-50 50
(10-inch LP.)
RCA (3063 "Fabulous Frankie").....25-50 52
(10-inch LP.)
RCA (4334 "The Dorsey/Sinatra Sessions, Vols. 1 & 2").........................8-10 82
RCA (4335 "The Dorsey/Sinatra Sessions, Vols. 3 & 4").........................8-10 82
RCA (4336 "The Dorsey/Sinatra Sessions, Vols. 5 & 6").........................8-10 82
RCA (6003 "The Sentimental Gentleman")........................20-40 53
(10-inch LP.)
RCA (4700 series)........................5-8 83
RCA/PAIR.................................5-10 84
REPRISE (R-1001 thru R-1010).....10-15 61-63
(Monaural.)
REPRISE (R9-1001 thru R9-1010)..............................10-20 61-63
(Stereo.)
REPRISE (F-1001 thru F-1010)......5-10 60s
(Monaural reissues.)
REPRISE (FS-1001 thru FS-1010)..8-12 60s
(Stereo reissues.)
REPRISE (1011 thru 1015)............8-12 64-65
REPRISE (1016 "A Man and His Music")..............................10-15 66
(Two discs.)
REPRISE (1016 "A Man and His Music, Part II")..........................300-400 66
(Promotional issue, made for Budweiser Beer distributors. About 1,000 made.)
REPRISE (FS4-1029 thru FS4-2207)............................15-25 70s
(Quadraphonic.)
REPRISE (1018 thru 1034)............8-15 66-72
REPRISE (2013 thru 2022)...........20-40 62-64
REPRISE (2155 thru 2275)............5-15 73-78
REPRISE (2300 "Trilogy")............15-25 80
(Three-disc set.)
REPRISE (2305 "She Shot Me Down").............................5-8 81
REPRISE (5230 "Songbook, Vol. 1")...............................25-35 71
REPRISE (5267 "Songbook, Vol. 2")............................50-100 72
(Two-disc set.)
REPRISE (6000 series)...............15-25 61-72
SINATRA..................................5-10 75
Session: Nuggets.
Also see ALI, Muhammad, & Frank Sinatra
Also see ANTHONY, Ray
Also see BLOCH, Ray, & Orchestra
Also see CROSBY, Bing / Grace Kelly / Frank Sinatra / Celeste Holm
Also see CROSBY, Bing, & Frank Sinatra
Also see DAY, Doris & Frank Sinatra
Also see DORSEY, Tommy, Orchestra
Also see JAMES, Harry
Also see KINGSTON TRIO / Frank Sinatra
Also see NUGGETS
Also see PRESLEY, Elvis / Frank Sinatra / Nat King Cole
Also see VINCENT, Gene / Frank Sinatra / Sonny James / Ron Goodwin
Also see ZENTNER, Si

SINATRA, Frank, & Charioteers

Singles: 78 rpm

COLUMBIA................................5-15 45
Also see CHARIOTEERS

SINATRA, Frank, & Count Basie *LP '63*

EPs: 7-inch

REPRISE (1012 "It Might As Well Be Swing").................................8-12 63
(Promotional issue only.)

LPs: 10/12-inch

REPRISE..................................10-20 63-66
Also see BASIE, Count

SINATRA, Frank / Nat "King" Cole

EPs: 7-inch

CAPITOL (500 "Witchcraft").........35-55 58
(Promotional issue only.)
Also see COLE, Nat "King"

SINATRA, Frank, Bing Crosby & Russ Columbo

Singles: 7-inch

RCA (5 "Immortal Performances")........................50-75 50
(Boxed three disc set, one by each artist. Includes bio/booklet.)

LPs: 10/12-inch

RCA (5 "Immortal Performances")........................50-75 50
(10-inch LP.)

SINATRA, Frank, Bing Crosby & Dean Martin

Singles: 7-inch

REPRISE (20,217 "The Oldest Established [Permanent Floating Crap Game in New York])..........................15-25 62

Picture Sleeves

REPRISE (20,217 "The Oldest Established [Permanent Floating Crap Game in New York])........................100-125 62

SINATRA, Frank, Bing Crosby, & Fred Waring

LPs: 10/12-inch

REPRISE..................................10-15 64
Also see CROSBY, Bing
Also see CROSBY, Bing, & Grace Kelly / Bing Crosby & Frank Sinatra
Also see WARING, Fred

SINATRA, Frank, Sammy Davis Jr. & Dean Martin *P&R '62*

(Frankie, Dino & Sammy)

Singles: 7-inch

REPRISE (20,128 "Me and My Shadow"/ "Sam's Song")............................4-6 62

Picture Sleeves

REPRISE (20,128 "Me and My Shadow"/ "Sam's Song")..........................10-15 62

LPs: 10/12-inch

LATIMER (247-17 "Summit Meeting at the 500, Atlantic City, N.J.")...............250-350 64
(Private issue only, by the 500 Club. Three different paste-on covers exist for this LP.)

SINATRA, Frank, & Duke Ellington *LP '68*

Singles: 7-inch

REPRISE.....................................3-5 68

LPs: 10/12-inch

REPRISE.....................................8-15 68
Also see ELLINGTON, Duke

SINATRA, Frank, & Antonio Carlos Jobim *LP '67*

LPs: 10/12-inch

REPRISE.....................................8-15 67-71
Also see JOBIM, Antonio Carlos

SINATRA, Frank / Jonah Jones

Singles: 7-inch

CAPITOL (4214 "High Hopes")....50-100 60
(Promotional issue only.)

Picture Sleeves

CAPITOL (4214 "High Hopes")...300-400 60
(Promotional issue only.)

SINATRA, Frank, with Quincy Jones & His Orchestra *LP '84*

Singles: 12-inch

QWEST (2216 "Mack the Knife")...25-50 84

Singles: 7-inch

QWEST......................................3-5 84

LPs: 10/12-inch

QWEST......................................5-10 84
Also see JONES, Quincy

SINATRA, Frank, Dean Martin, Sammy Davis Jr., & Bing Crosby

LPs: 10/12-inch

REPRISE (5031 "Summit")......500-1000 64
(British issue only.)
Also see CROSBY, Bing
Also see DAVIS, Sammy, Jr.
Also see MARTIN, Dean

SINATRA, Frank, & Pied Pipers

Singles: 78 rpm

RCA...4-8 41
Also see PIED PIPERS

SINATRA, Frank, & Keely Smith *P&R '58*

Singles: 78 rpm

CAPITOL (3952 "Nothing in Common")..............................15-25 58
(This is the last commercially-issued Sinatra 78 rpm.)

Singles: 7-inch

CAPITOL (3952 "Nothing in Common")..............................5-10 58
Also see SMITH, Keely

SINATRA, Frank / Roger Wagner Chorale / Hollywood Bowl Symphony

EPs: 7-inch

CAPITOL (426 "Christmas Around the World")...........................75-100 57
(Promotional issue only.)

SINATRA, Frank & Nancy *P&R '67*

(Sinatra Family)

Singles: 7-inch

REPRISE....................................3-6 66-71

LPs: 10/12-inch

REPRISE....................................8-15 69
Members: Sinatra Family included Frank Sinatra, Frank Jr., Nancy and Tina.
Also see FLAIR & Flat Foots
Also see SINATRA, Nancy

SINATRA, Nancy *P&R '65*

Singles: 7-inch

ELEKTRA...................................3-5 80
PRIVATE STOCK...........................3-5 75-77
RCA...3-5 72-73
REPRISE....................................3-6 61-71

Picture Sleeves

REPRISE....................................4-8 62-67

EPs: 7-inch

REPRISE..................................10-12 66
(Juke box issue only.)

LPs: 10/12-inch

RCA...8-10 72
REPRISE..................................15-30 66-72
Also see BARRY, John
Also see MARTIN, Dean
Also see PRESLEY, Elvis
Also see SINATRA, Frank & Nancy
Also see TILLIS, Mel, & Nancy Sinatra

SINATRA, Nancy, & Lee Hazlewood *P&R/LP '68*

Singles: 7-inch

PRIVATE STOCK...........................3-5 76
RCA...3-5 72
REPRISE....................................4-8 67-68

LPs: 10/12-inch

RCA...8-10 72
REPRISE..................................10-15 68
Also see HAZLEWOOD, Lee
Also see SINATRA, Nancy

SINBAD, Paul

Singles: 7-inch

HYPE.......................................10-20 60s
KNOX..5-10 60s
LAP..5-10 65
POWERTREE ("I Was a Fool").....30-50

SINBAD, Sonny

Singles: 7-inch

CLASS.......................................5-10 60

SINCERELY YOURS

Singles: 7-inch

IMPACT (1020 "Little Girl")...........25-50 67

SINCERES

(With L. Bergo & Orchestra)

Singles: 7-inch

JORDAN (117 "You're Too Young").......................200-300 60
RICHIE (545 "Please Don't Cheat on Me")..........................750-1000 61
(No mention of Roulette distribution on label.)
RICHIE (545 "Please Don't Cheat on Me")..............................75-100 61
(Label indicates "Distributed by Roulette.)
SIGMA (1004 "Darling")...........200-400 60
Member: Jay Proctor.
Also see JAY & TECHNIQUES

SINCERES

Singles: 7-inch

COLUMBIA (43110 "Sincerely").......8-12 64
EPIC (9583 "Our Winter Love").....10-15 63
TAURUS (377 "Magic of Love").....15-25 66

SINCEROS

Singles: 7-inch

COLUMBIA..................................3-5 79-81

LPs: 10/12-inch

COLUMBIA..................................5-10 79-81

SINCEROS / Hounds / The Beat / Jules & Polar Bears

EPs: 7-inch

COLUMBIA (1187 "Now Wave Sampler")...............................5-10 79
(Promotional issue only.)
Also see BEAT, The
Also see HOUNDS
Also see JULES & Polar Bears

SINCLAIR, Gordon *P&R '74*

Singles: 7-inch

AVCO..3-5 74

SINCLAIR, John

(With His Blues Scholars; with Wayne Kramer)

LPs: 10/12-inch

ALIVE/TOTAL ENERGY...............5-10 95
(10-inch LP.)
Also see KRAMER, Wayne
Also see MC 5

SINCLAIR, Terry

Singles: 7-inch

D.P.G.......................................10-20 64

SINFIELD, Pete *LP '73*

Singles: 7-inch

MANTICORE................................3-5 73

LPs: 10/12-inch

MANTICORE................................8-10 73
Also see KING CRIMSON

SING-A-LONG WITH THE BEATLES

LPs: 10/12-inch

TOWER (5000 "Sing-A-Long with the Beatles")..........................50-100 65
(Instrumental tracks of Beatles tunes. Listed by title since no artist is credited.)

SINGER, Artie, & His Orchestra

Singles: 7-inch

CHECKER (888 "Café Concertina")..............................6-10 59

SINGER, Hal

(Hal "Cornbread" Singer)

Singles: 78 rpm

CORAL.......................................5-10 51
SAVOY.......................................5-10 48-56

Singles: 7-inch

CORAL (65070 "Buttermilk & Beans")..................................15-25 51
PRESTIGE..................................5-10 59
SAVOY......................................10-15 52-56
TIME...10-20 58

LPs: 10/12-inch

PRESTIGE.................................15-25 59

SINGER, Joey

Singles: 7-inch

ERA..5-10 59

SINGERS

Singles: 7-inch

DATE..4-8 66
GOLDEN EAGLE...........................4-8 60s
LOMA..4-8 64

SINGIN' SAM

(Sam Chatman)

Singles: 7-inch

MISS..10-15 60
Also see SAMPSON, Phil

SINGING BELLES *P&R '60*

Singles: 7-inch

MADISON...................................8-10 60

SINGING DOGS *P&R '55*

(Don Charles Presents the Singing Dogs)

Singles: 78 rpm

RCA..3-5 55

Singles: 7-inch

RCA..3-8 55-72

Picture Sleeves

RCA (6344 "Oh! Susanna")..........10-20 55
RCA (6432 "Hot Dog Rock & Roll") 10-20 56

SINGING LARKS

Singles: 7-inch

FINK..4-8 62

SINGING NUN *P&R/LP '63*

(Soeur Sourire; Janine Deckers)

Singles: 7-inch

PHILIPS....................................3-5 63-64

Picture Sleeves

PHILIPS....................................4-8 63-64

LPs: 10/12-inch

PHILIPS....................................5-15 63-69

SINGING REINDEER

Singles: 7-inch

CAPITOL...................................4-8 59-60

Picture Sleeves

CAPITOL..................................10-15 59

SINGING ROULETTES: see ROULETTES

SINGING SAM & SPARKS

Singles: 7-inch

DEE DEE (2223 "Messin' ")..........15-20 66

SINGING WANDERERS

Singles: 78 rpm

DECCA......................................25-50 54

Singles: 7-inch

DECCA (29230 "Say Hey, Willie Mays")................................50-75 54
DECCA (29298 "Three Roses")....75-125 54
Also see WANDERERS

SINGLE BULLET THEORY *P&R '83*

Singles: 7-inch

NEMPEROR................................3-4 83

Picture Sleeves

NEMPEROR................................3-4 83

LPs: 10/12-inch

NEMPEROR................................5-8 83

SINGLETON, Bebo

(With Jeff & Notes)

Singles: 7-inch

STENTOR (1001 "The Shrine of the Echoes")..........................300-500 60

SINGLETON, Charlie

(With the All Stars; Charlie "Hoss" Singleton)

Singles: 78 rpm

APOLLO....................................10-20 49
ATLAS......................................10-15 52-53
ATLANTIC.................................10-15 54
FAITH......................................10-15 50s
LEE..10-15 50s
RAINBOW..................................10-15 50
SATURN....................................10-20 52
STAR..10-15 50

Singles: 7-inch

ATLANTIC (1032 "Boardwalk").......15-25 54
ATLAS (1029 "Pony Express").......25-35 53
DECCA......................................15-25 51
SUNSET....................................10-20 54-55

LPs: 10/12-inch

CAMDEN (713 "Big Twist Hits")......10-20 62
Also see CHARLIE & ROSIE

SINGLETON, Charlie

Singles: 7-inch

ARISTA.....................................3-4 85

LPs: 10/12-inch

ARISTA.....................................5-8 85
Also see CAMEO
Also see COBHAM, Billy

SINGLETON, Charlie, & Modern Man

Singles: 7-inch

EPIC...3-4 87-88

SINGLETON, Eddie

(With the Chromatics)

Singles: 7-inch

AMSCO (3701 "Too Late")........100-200 57
GLOVER (211 "Let Me Know")......10-15 60
JOKER (1001 "It's Not My Fault")..10-15 62

SINGLETON, Eddie, & Chromatics / Augie Austin & Chromatics

Singles: 7-inch

BRUNSWICK (55080 "Too Late")..35-45 58
Also see AUSTIN, Augie
Also see CHROMATICS
Also see SINGLETON, Eddie

SINGLETON, Jimmy, & Royal Satins

(With the Hi-Fis)

Singles: 7-inch

DEVERE (006 "Sally")..........1000-2000 60
MARK (148 "Each Passing Day")...........................150-250 60
Also see Hi-Fis

SINGLETON, Margie *C&W '59*

Singles: 7-inch

ASHLEY.....................................4-8 67-68
MERCURY..................................4-8 61-64
STARDAY...................................5-10 59-60
U.A..4-6 65-66

LPs: 10/12-inch

ASHLEY....................................10-15 67
PICKWICK..................................5-10 68-70s
U.A...10-15 65
Also see ASHLEY, Leon, & Margie Singleton
Also see JONES, George, & Margie Singleton
Also see YOUNG, Faron, & Margie Singleton

SINGLETON, Rome

Singles: 7-inch

BUD..4-8

SINGLETON, Sterly

Singles: 7-inch

SHELLEY (128 "Cross Current")....15-25 61
(Also issued as by the Rockin' Dukes.)
Also see ROCKIN' DUKES

SINITTA *P&R '89*

Singles: 7-inch

ATLANTIC..................................3-4 88-89
OMNI..3-4 87

Picture Sleeves

ATLANTIC..................................3-4 88-89

SINK, Earl

Singles: 7-inch

CAPITOL (4885 "Be Good")..........15-25 63
W.B. (5197 "Look for Me")...........5-10 61

SINNAMON *D&D '83*

Singles: 12-inch

BECKET.....................................4-6 82-83
JIVE..4-6 84

Singles: 7-inch

BECKET.....................................3-4 82-83

SINNAMON, Shandi

LPs: 10/12-inch

ASYLUM....................................5-10 76

SINNERS

(With the Jack Nitzsche Orchestra)

Singles: 7-inch

EDEN (1 "Could This Be Love") 100-125 62
Also see NITZSCHE, Jack

SINNERS

Singles: 7-inch

MERCURY (72453 "Goin' Out of My Mind")..............................10-20 65
Session: Davie Allan.
Also see ALLAN, Davie

SINNERS

Singles: 7-inch

JERDEN.....................................5-10 65

SINNERS

LPs: 10/12-inch

PENTAGON (141 "Rocky Road")...........................50-100 65
(Canadian.)
Members: Darek Middleton; Myles Devine; Bob Burns; Larry Goguen; Roy Feener.

SINS OF SATAN

LPs: 10/12-inch

BUDDAH....................................5-10
U.A..8-12 77

SIN-SAY-SHUNS: see SIN SAY SHUNS

SINTRIFICAL FOURS

Singles: 7-inch

MR. G.......................................4-8 68

SIOUXSIE & BANSHEES *LP '84*

Singles: 12-inch

GEFFEN....................................4-6 84-86
PVC..4-8 80-82

Singles: 7-inch

GEFFEN....................................3-4 84-88
PVC..3-5 80-82
POLYDOR..................................3-5 79

Picture Sleeves

GEFFEN....................................3-4 88

LPs: 10/12-inch
GEFFEN..5-8 84-90
PVC..5-10 80-82
POLYDOR..8-10 79
Also see SEX PISTOLS

SIPE, P.W., & Country Folks
Singles: 7-inch
JCP (1052 "Meet Me Tonight Little Darling")..10-20 65

SIPES, Leonard, & Rhythm Oakies
Singles: 78 rpm
MORGAN (106 "Campus Boogie")..400-800
Member: Tommy Collins.
Also see COLLINS, Tommy

SIR ALBERT
Singles: 7-inch
ROZAN (1101 "For Your Love")....10-15 68

SIR ARTHUR
Singles: 7-inch
COLEMAN..4-8 60s
TOWER (216 "Louie Louie")..........5-10 66
Also see SIR RALEIGH
Also see SIR WALTER RALEIGH

SIR CHAUNCEY *P&R '60*
(Ernie Freeman)
Singles: 7-inch
PATTERN..10-15 60
W.B...4-8 60
Also see FREEMAN, Ernie

SIR DAVID & KNIGHTS
Singles: 7-inch
PA-GO-GO (103 "Shotgun")..........8-12 60s

SIR DOUGLAS QUINTET *P&R '65*
(Sir Douglas Band)
Singles: 7-inch
ATLANTIC..4-8 73
CASABLANCA (0828 "Roll with the Punches")..5-15 75
MERCURY..3-5 71
PACEMAKER (260 "Sugar Bee")...15-20 64
PHILIPS..3-5 70-71
SMASH..4-8 68-70
TRIBE..5-10 65
(No Indian on label.)
TRIBE..4-8 65-67
(Label pictures Indian.)
Picture Sleeves
PHILIPS..3-5 70-71
LPs: 10/12-inch
ACCORD..5-10 82
ATLANTIC..10-15 73
MERCURY..10-15 72
PHILIPS..15-25 70-71
SMASH..15-25 68-70
TAKOMA..5-10 80-83
TRIBE (47001 "Best of Sir Douglas Quintet")..40-60 66
Members: Doug Sahm; Augie Meyers; Jack Barber; Leon Baetty; John Perez; Frank Morin; Jim Stallings.
Also see AMIGOS DE MUSICA
Also see ATWOOD THE ELECTRIC ICEMAN
Also see CASCADES / Sir Douglas Quintet
Also see DEVONS
Also see GOLDIE, Don
Also see LIGHT, J.J.
Also see LONG, Joey
Also see MEYERS, Augie
Also see ROCKY & Border Kings
Also see SAHM, Doug

SIR FOX
Singles: 7-inch
FOXY..4-8 68

SIR FROG & TOADS
Singles: 7-inch
DOWNEY..10-20 65

SIR GUY & ROCKING CAVALIERS
Singles: 7-inch
DPG..4-8 69

SIR HENRY
(With His Butlers)
Singles: 7-inch
ABC..4-6 68
DECCA..4-8 64
MERCURY..5-10 60

SIR JOE & MAIDENS
Singles: 7-inch
LENOX (5563 "Jivin' Jean")..........10-15 63

SIR JOHN QUINTET
Singles: 7-inch
JOSIE..4-8 66

SIR LANCELOT
Singles: 78 rpm
APOLLO..4-8 49
FIESTA..5-10 57
Singles: 7-inch
FIESTA..5-10 57
EPs: 7-inch
MERCURY..8-12 52
LPs: 10/12-inch
MERCURY..15-25 52

SIR LAWRENCE & CRESCENTS
Singles: 7-inch
TWIN TOWN (723 "Flip Me Over")..50-75 60s

SIR LORD BALTIMORE *LP '71*
Singles: 7-inch
MERCURY..3-5 70-71
LPs: 10/12-inch
MERCURY..8-12 70-71

SIR MEN
Singles: 7-inch
THUNDERBIRD..4-6 69
Member: Kal Dee.
Also see FIRST, Carl, & Showmen
Also see SERMON

SIR MIX-A-LOT *P&R/LP '88*
Singles: 7-inch
NASTYMIX..3-4 88-90
Picture Sleeves
NASTYMIX..3-4 88
LPs: 10/12-inch
NASTYMIX..5-8 88-90

SIR MONTI ROCK III: see ROCK, Monti, III

SIR RALEIGH
(With the Cupons)
Singles: 7-inch
A&M..5-10 64
JERDEN..10-20 65
Also see ARTHUR
Also see SIR WALTER RALEIGH

SIR RICHARD
Singles: 7-inch
SAXONY (1012 "Here I Stand").......5-10 67

SIR RICHARD & LORD ALAN
Singles: 7-inch
CANNON..4-8 64

SIR ROBIN & MARK V BANDITS
Singles: 7-inch
LORI (9555 "I Don't Wish You No Bad Luck")..4-8

SIR VANCE
Singles: 7-inch
PETAL..4-8 63

SIR WALTER & DE JAYS
Singles: 7-inch
SOMA..8-12 62

SIR WALTER RALEIGH
(Dewey Martin)
Singles: 7-inch
TOWER..8-12 65
Also see MARTIN, Dewey, & Medicine Ball
Also see SIR ARTHUR
Also see SIR RALEIGH

SIR WHITE: see WHITE, Sir

SIR WINSTON & COMMONS
Singles: 7-inch
NAUSEATING BUTTERFLY (2207 "Not in the Spirit of India")..25-35 67
SOMA (1454 "Come Back Again")..50-75 66

SIREN
Singles: 7-inch
MIDSONG INT'L..3-5 79
LPs: 10/12-inch
ELEKTRA (74087 "Locomotion")...10-20 71
DANDELION..10-15 70

SIRENNE, Gianni *D&D '84*
Singles: 12-inch
ATLANTIC..4-6 84
Singles: 7-inch
ATLANTIC..3-4 84

SIRS
Singles: 7-inch
AMRECO..4-8 68-71
Picture Sleeves
AMRECO..5-10 68
Members: Randy Calcagno; Dick Yandell; Everett Simila; Arthur Salizar; Roger Stuart; Roy Ikada.

SIRS
Singles: 7-inch
CHARAY..8-12 64
SOFT..8-12 65

SISCO, Bobby
Singles: 78 rpm
CHESS (1650 "Go, Go, Go").....200-300 57
MAR-VEL (111 "Honky Tonkin' Rhythm")..50-100 56
Singles: 7-inch
BRAVE..5-10 64
CHESS (1650 "Go, Go, Go").....200-300 57
GLENN..5-10 60-61
MAR-VEL (111 "Honky Tonkin' Rhythm")..150-250 56
VEE JAY (544 "Are You the Type")..5-10 63

SISCO, Gene
(With Ramblin' Ramblers)
Singles: 7-inch
BAY SHORE (1 "Somebody to Love")..10-20 62
DESS (7001 "Grandma Rock & Roll")..75-100
DESS (7003 "Turning the Tables")..75-100

SISK, Shirley
Singles: 7-inch
SUN..5-10 61

SISNEROS, Gilbert, & Saints
("Gilbert Sisneros Meets the Saints")
Singles: 7-inch
DANT (101 "Little Girl of My Dreams")..100-200

SISTER & BROTHERS
Singles: 7-inch
CALLA..3-5 71
UNI..3-5 70

SISTER RACHEL
Singles: 7-inch
CHALLENGE..4-6 67

SISTER SLEDGE *P&R '75*
Singles: 12-inch
ATLANTIC..4-6 85
COTILLION..4-8 79-83
Singles: 7-inch
ATCO..3-5 73-75
ATLANTIC..3-4 85
COTILLION..3-5 76-83
Picture Sleeves
ATLANTIC..3-4 85
LPs: 10/12-inch
ATCO..8-10 75
ATLANTIC..5-8 85
COTILLION..5-10 76-83

SISTERS
Singles: 7-inch
DEL-FI..5-8 64

SISTERS LOVE
("Sisters' Love"; with Monk Higgins Orchestra)
Singles: 7-inch
A&M..4-8 69-71
MAN-CHILD (5001 "This Time Tomorrow")..4-8
MOWEST..3-6 73
Members: Merry Clayton; Vermetta Royster; Lillie Fort; Gwen Berry; Jeanie Long; Odia Coates.
Also see CLAYTON, Merry
Also see COATES, Odia

SISTERS OF MERCY *LP '88*
Singles: 12-inch
ELEKTRA..4-8 83-87
LPs: 10/12-inch
ELEKTRA..5-8 88-90
Members: Wayne Hussey; Andrew Eldritch; Doktor Avalanche; Patricia Morrison.
Also see DEAD OR ALIVE
Also see MISSION

SISTERS OF RIGHTEOUS
Singles: 7-inch
KING..6-12 69-70

SITES, Linda & Betty
Singles: 7-inch
JERDEN..4-6 63

SIX MILE CHASE
Singles: 7-inch
DOT..4-6 68

SIX PAK
("Lead Vocal by Stevie")
Singles: 7-inch
GORDO (701 "Tombstone Shadow")..15-25 60s
GORDO (704 "Weep No More")....15-25 60s

SIX PENTS
Singles: 7-inch
KIDD (1335 "She Lied")................20-35 60s

6 7/8
Singles: 7-inch
DOT..4-8 66

SIX SHOOTERS
Singles: 7-inch
CUCA (1011 "You Just Don't Know It")..15-25 60
Member: Vilas Craig.

SIX TEENS *P&R '56*
("Featuring 13-Year-Old Trudy Williams"; "Featuring Trudy & Louise")
Singles: 78 rpm
FLIP (315 thru 326)..........................15-25 56-57
FLIP (329 "My Secret")..................25-50 58
Singles: 7-inch
FLIP (315 "A Casual Look")..........20-25 56
FLIP (317 "Send Me Flowers")........20-25 56
FLIP (320 "My Special Guy")........20-25 56
FLIP (322 "Arrow of Love")..........20-25 56
FLIP (326 "My Surprise")..............20-25 57
FLIP (329 "My Secret")..................20-25 58
FLIP (333 "Danny")........................20-25 58
FLIP (338 "Baby-O")......................20-25 58
FLIP (346 "Why Do I Go to School")..25-30 59
FLIP (350 "So Happy")....................20-25 60
FLIP (351 "A Little Prayer")..........20-25 60
Members: Trudy Williams; Louise Williams; Ed Wells; Beverly Pecot; Kenneth Sinclair; Darryl Lewis.
Also see ELEMENTS
Also see ELGINS
Also see TRUDY & LOUISE

SIX TEENS / Brenda & Tabulations
Singles: 7-inch
COBRA..3-5
Also see BRENDA & TABULATIONS

SIX TEENS / Donald Woods / Richard Berry
LPs: 10/12-inch
FLIP (1001 "12 Flip Hits")..........100-125 59
Also see BERRY, Richard
Also see WOODS, Donald

SIX THE HARD WAY
Singles: 7-inch
CAPITOL..4-6 69
W.B...5-10 67

SIXPENCE
(Thee Sixpence)
Singles: 7-inch
ALL AMERICAN (313 "Fortune Teller")..20-30 66
ALL AMERICAN (333 "Hey Joe")...15-25 67
ALL AMERICAN (353 "Fortune Teller")..15-25 67
DOT (16959 "Fortune Teller")........10-20 66
Members: Randy Seol; Ed King; Lee Freeman; George Bunnel; Gary Loverto; Mark Weitz.
Also see STRAWBERRY ALARM CLOCK

SIXPENCE
Singles: 7-inch
IMPACT (1025 "You're the Love")..15-25 67

SIXPENTZ
Singles: 7-inch
BRENT (7062 "Please Come Home")..10-20 67
BRENT (7064 "Don't Say You're Sorry")..10-20 67
Also see FUN & GAMES

6680 LEXINGTON
Singles: 7-inch
MGM..3-5 71
LPs: 10/12-inch
MGM..10-15 71

60,000,000 BUFFALO
LPs: 10/12-inch
ATCO..8-10 72

SIZE SEVEN GROUP
Singles: 7-inch
MERCURY..4-8 65

SIZZLE
Singles: 12-inch
MERCURY..4-6 84
SUTRA..4-6 84

SKA KINGS *P&R '64*
Singles: 7-inch
ATLANTIC..4-8 64

SKAFISH
LPs: 10/12-inch
I.R.S...5-10 80

SKAGGS, Ricky *C&W '80*
(With Tony Rice; with Sharon White)
Singles: 7-inch
EPIC..3-5 81-90
ROUNDER..3-6 80
SUGAR HILL (3700 series)..............3-6 80
SUGAR HILL (04000 series)............3-5 83-84
LPs: 10/12-inch
EPIC..5-10 81-86
REBEL (1550 "That's It")..............10-15 75
ROUNDER..5-10 82
SUGAR HILL..5-10 79-80
WEL DUN..10-15 78
Also see BOONE CREEK
Also see CASH, Rosanne
Also see COUNTRY GENTLEMEN
Also see FRICKE, Janie
Also see HARRIS, Emmylou
Also see NITTY GRITTY DIRT BAND
Also see PARTON, Dolly
Also see SCRUGGS, Earl
Also see SHAVER, Billy Joe

SKAGGS, Ricky, & Keith Whitley
LPs: 10/12-inch
REBEL..10-15 71-72
Also see SKAGGS, Ricky
Also see WHITLEY, Keith

SKALLYWAGS: see SCALLYWAGS

SKAPEGOAT
Singles: 7-inch
ALCEE (1001 "Good Times, Bad Times")..15-25 60s

SKARLETTONES
Singles: 7-inch
EMBER (1053 "Do You Remember")..40-60 59

SKATALITES
LPs: 10/12-inch
ALLIGATOR..5-10

SKATT BROTHERS
Singles: 7-inch
CASABLANCE..3-5 80
LPs: 10/12-inch
CASABLANCA..5-10 79

SKAVENGERS
Singles: 7-inch
MAYN (200758 "Lend Me Your Love")..15-25 60s

SKEE BROTHERS
Singles: 7-inch
EPIC (9275 "Big Deal")..................50-75 58
OKEH (7108 "That's All She Wrote")..25-35 59
ROULETTE..10-15 59

SKEENE, Danny, & Ricquettes
Singles: 7-inch
VALEX (105 "Over the Rainbow")..50-100

SKEL, Bobby
(Bobby Skelton)
Singles: 7-inch
FAIRLANE..5-10 61
KING..4-8 64
SOFT..4-8 64-65
UNI..4-8 68-69

SKELLERN, Peter *P&R '72*
Singles: 7-inch
LONDON..3-5 72
PRIVATE STOCK..3-5 75
LPs: 10/12-inch
LONDON..5-10 76

SKELTON, Bobby: see SKEL, Bobby

SKELTON, Eddie
Singles: 7-inch
CHART (5077 "Colorado Queenie")..10-15
DIXIE (2011 "Gotta Keep Swinging")..200-250 58
STARDAY (294 "My Heart Gets Lonely")..100-150 57
STARDAY (315 "That's Love")......50-100 57

SKELTON, John, & Hot Goods
Singles: 7-inch
BIL-MAR..3-5 74

SKELTON, Red *P&R '69*
Singles: 78 rpm
MGM..4-6 56
Singles: 7-inch
CBS/AURAVISION ("Pledge of Allegiance")..10-15 69
(Promotional 5-inch cardboard picture disc. Made for Burger King.)
COLUMBIA..4-6 69
MGM..5-10 56
LPs: 10/12-inch
LIBERTY..10-15 65-66
Also see ASTAIRE, Fred, & Red Skelton / Helen Kane

SKEPTICS
Singles: 7-inch
KAMPUS (814 "Ride Child")..........15-25 60s
KAMPUS (815 "Certain Kind of Girl")..15-25 60s
SCRATCH (7823 "East Side Tenement House")..15-25 60s
SHO-BOAT (106 "Turn It On")........15-25 60s
SPRING ("I'm Lonely Again")........15-25 60s
(No selection number used.)
Also see WAUGH, Jerry, & Skeptics

SKETCHES
Singles: 7-inch
DENIM..8-12

SKHY, A.B: see A.B. SKHY

SKI, Gene, & Troubadours
Singles: 7-inch
SARA (6632 "Six Foot Down")..........8-12 66
TEE PEE (1004 "To Hell with Love")..8-12 69

SKI STOMPERS
Singles: 7-inch
MERCURY..4-8 63

SKID ROW *P&R/LP '89*
Singles: 7-inch
ATLANTIC..3-4 89
EPIC..3-5 71
Picture Sleeves
ATLANTIC..3-4 89
LPs: 10/12-inch
ATLANTIC..5-8 89-91
EPIC..10-15 71

SKIDMORE, Bill
(Bill Skidmore III)
Singles: 7-inch
CREST (1037 "Try")..10-15 58
(Black vinyl.)
CREST (1037 "Try")..15-25 58
(Colored vinyl.)
CREST (1040 "Dait Bait")..............10-15 58

SKIDMORE, Daniel E., III
Singles: 7-inch
PARKWAY..3-6 67

SKIFS, Bjorn
Singles: 7-inch
RCA..3-5 85
Also see BLUE SWEDE

SKI-KING & LIFE BUOYS
Singles: 7-inch
DIXIE (1109 "Bomp Bompa Du Bomp")..15-25

SKILES, Johnny
Singles: 7-inch
HONEY B (102 "After Tonight").....15-25 59
RUMAC (301 "Rockin' & Rollin' ")..30-50 59
RURAL RHYTHM (518 "Is My Baby Comin' Back")..100-150 59

SKIN
Singles: 7-inch
MELBA..4-8 60s

SKIN ALLEY
Singles: 7-inch
STAX..3-5 73-74
LPs: 10/12-inch
STAX..8-10 73-74

SKINNER, Jimmie *C&W '49*
(Jimmie Skinner / Jimmie Logsdon)
Singles: 78 rpm
CAPITOL..4-8 51-54
DECCA..4-8 53-55
MERCURY..4-8 57
RADIO ARTIST..5-10 49
Singles: 7-inch
CAPITOL..5-10 51-54
DECCA..5-10 53-55
MERCURY..4-8 57-63
STARDAY..5-10 58-64

DECCA.....4-8 53-55
MERCURY.....4-8 57
RADIO ARTIST.....5-10 49
Singles: 7-inch
CAPITOL.....5-10 51-54
DECCA.....5-10 53-55
MERCURY.....4-8 57-63
STARDAY.....5-10 58-64
EPs: 7-inch
MERCURY.....5-10 61
LPs: 10/12-inch
COUNTRY CORNER ("Jimmie Skinner").....100-150
(Selection number not known.)
DECCA (4132 "Country Singer").....35-45 61
MERCURY (20352 "Songs That Make the Juke Box Play").....30-50 57
MERCURY (20700 "Jimmie Skinner Sings Jimmie Rodgers").....15-25 62
(Monaural.)
MERCURY (60700 "Jimmie Skinner Sings Jimmie Rodgers").....25-35 62
(Stereo.)
QCA.....5-10 70s
RICH-R-TONE.....5-10
STARDAY (240 "Jimmie Skinner, the Kentucky Colonel").....30-40 63
STARDAY (988 "#1 Bluegrass").....5-10
VETCO.....10-15 76
WEL DUN.....10-15 78
WING.....10-15 64
Also see HALL, Connie

SKINNY DYNAMO: see DYNAMO, Skinny

SKINYARD
Singles: 10-inch
CRUZ (702 "1000 Smiling Knuckles").....3-5 91
Picture Sleeves
CRUZ (702 "1000 Smiling Knuckles").....3-5 91

SKIP
Singles: 7-inch
BOLO.....5-10 59

SKIP & CASUALS R&B '74
Singles: 7-inch
D.C. INT'L.....3-5 74
Members: Skip Mahoney; Tracy Reid; Julius Jerome; Elwood Morgan.
Also see MAHONEY, Skip, & Casuals

SKIP & CREATIONS
LPs: 10/12-inch
JUSTICE ("Mobam").....150-200 60s
(Selection number not known.)

SKIP & DUKES: ARNE, Skip, & Dukes

SKIP & ECHOTONES
Singles: 7-inch
DR (1001 "Born to Love").....25-50 59
WARWICK (634 "Born to Love").....10-20 61

SKIP & ERNEST
Singles: 7-inch
BUNKY.....4-8 60s

SKIP & FLIP P&R '59
(With Clyde Gary & His Orchestra)
Singles: 7-inch
BRENT (7002 "It Was I").....10-20 59
BRENT (7005 "Fancy Nancy").....10-20 59
BRENT (7010 "Cherry Pie").....10-20 60
BRENT (7013 "Teenage Honeymoon").....10-20 60
BRENT (7017 "Green Door").....10-20 61
COLLECTABLES.....3-4 80s
ERIC.....3-4 70s
TIME (1031 "Betty Jean").....10-15 61
Members: Clyde "Skip" Battin; Gary Paxton.
Also see BATTIN, Skip
Also see GARY, Clyde, & His Orchestra
Also see GARY & CLYDE
Also see PAXTON, Gary
Also see PLEDGES

SKIP & FLIPS
Singles: 7-inch
CALIFORNIA (2325 "Everyday I Have to Cry").....8-10 63

SKIP & GAIL
Singles: 7-inch
CUCA (6712 "Sweet Thang").....10-20 67

SKIP & HUSTLERS
Singles: 7-inch
INVICTA (9001 "In the Soup").....15-25 57

SKIP & JOHNNY
Singles: 7-inch
INVICTA.....4-8 62
LOTUS.....4-8 63

SKIP & LINDA C&W '82
Singles: 7-inch
MDJ.....3-4 82
Members: Skip Eaton; Linda Davis.

SKIPPER, Buddy
(With the Code Blues Band)
Singles: 7-inch
FURY.....8-12 61-62
GUTTER (Colored vinyl).....5-8 85
SMASH.....4-8 68

SKIPPER, Macy
Singles: 7-inch
LIGHT (2020 "Who Put the Squeeze on Eloise").....50-75
STAX (111 "Goofin' Off").....10-15 62

SKIPPER & WRECKING CREW
Singles: 7-inch
SAMAR.....4-8 66

SKIPPY & HI-LITES
Singles: 7-inch
ELMOR (1027 "Old Man River").....100-150 62
(First issue.)
STREAM-LITE (1027 "Old Man River").....50-100 62

SKIPPY & SHANTONS: see JACKSON, Skip

SKIPPY ROPE
Singles: 7-inch
OCTAVIA.....5-10 60s

SKIPWORTH & TURNER D&D '85
Singles: 12-inch
4TH & BROADWAY.....4-6 85
W.B......4-6 86
Singles: 7-inch
4TH & BROADWAY.....3-4 85
W.B......3-4 86
LPs: 10/12-inch
W.B......5-8 86
Members: Rodney Skipworth; Philip Turner.

SKO: see SCHUYLER, KNOBLOCH & OVERSTREET

SKOODLE DUM DOO & SHEFFIELD
(Seth Richard)
Singles: 78 rpm
MANOR (1056 "Broome Street Blues").....75-125 43
REGIS (107 "Tampa Blues").....75-125 43
Members: Seth Richard; Sheffield.

SKOOL BOYZ
Singles: 12-inch
COLUMBIA.....4-6 84-85
Singles: 7-inch
COLUMBIA.....3-4 84-85
DESTINY.....3-5 81-82
LPs: 10/12-inch
DESTINY.....5-10 81
Members: Stan Sheppard; Bill Sheppard; Chauncy Matthews.
Also see BY ALL MEANS
Also see LIVIN' PROOF
Also see TRIPLE "S" CONNECTION

SKRATCH D&D '85
Singles: 12-inch
PASSION.....4-6 85

SKULL CONTROL
Singles: 7-inch
ILOKI (103 "Building Models").....3-4 92
(Red vinyl. Includes bio insert.)
Picture Sleeves
ILOKI (103 "Building Models").....3-4 92
Members: Billy Bones; Kidd Spike; Keith Miller; Hermann Senac.

SKULL SNAPS
Singles: 7-inch
GRI.....3-6 75
LPs: 10/12-inch
GSF.....8-10 73

SKUNKS
Singles: 7-inch
ARVEE.....8-12 59

SKUNKS
Singles: 7-inch
MERCURY (72449 "Youthquake").....5-10 65

SKUNKS
Singles: 7-inch
QUILL (120 "Don't Ask Why").....10-20 66
QUILL (121 "Little Angel").....10-20 66
SHERRI (100 "Heart Teaser").....8-12 69
TEEN TOWN (103 "I Need No One").....10-15 67
TEEN TOWN (106 "Small Town Girl").....10-15 68
TEEN TOWN (110 "Doing Nothing").....10-15 69
U.S.A. (865 "Elvira").....8-12 67
WATER STREET.....4-8 60s
WHITE WHALE (322 "Doing Nothing").....8-12 69
WHITE WHALE (325 "Doing Nothing").....5-10 69
WORLD PACIFIC (77889 "I Need No One").....5-10 67
EPs: 7-inch
WRIT.....10-15 66
LPs: 10/12-inch
TEEN TOWN (101 "Getting Started").....25-50 68
Members: Larry Lynne Ostricki; Rick Allen Sutherland; Tony Kolp; Duane Lundy; Randy Klein; Paul Fredericks; Jack Tappy; Teddy Paplinski.
Also see BONNEVILLES
Also see LYNNE, Larry, Group
Also see RANDY
Also see TONY'S TYGERS / Skunks / Robbs
Also see UNBELIEVABLES

SKWARES
Singles: 7-inch
MERCURY.....3-4 88

SKY
Singles: 7-inch
ASCOT.....4-8 68
DYNO VOICE.....4-8 66

SKY LP '70
Singles: 7-inch
RCA.....3-5 71-72
LPs: 10/12-inch
RCA.....10-12 70-71

SKY LP '80
Singles: 7-inch
ARISTA.....3-5 81
LPs: 10/12-inch
ARISTA.....8-10 80
Member: Doug Fieger.
Also see KNACK

SKY, Patrick
Singles: 7-inch
CAPITOL.....3-5 70
VANGUARD.....4-8 66
LPs: 10/12-inch
ADELPHI.....8-12 73
VANGUARD.....10-15 65-66
VERVE/FORECAST.....10-15 68

SKYBAND
Singles: 7-inch
RCA.....3-5 74
LPs: 10/12-inch
RCA.....8-10 74

SKYBOYS
LPs: 10/12-inch
FIRST AMERICAN.....5-10 79

SKYHOOKS
Singles: 7-inch
MERCURY.....3-5 76

SKYLAR, Norm
Singles: 7-inch
CREST (1044 "Rock & Roll Blues").....100-150 58

SKYLAR, Rick
Singles: 7-inch
CARLTON.....4-8 63-64

SKYLARK P&R/LP '73
Singles: 7-inch
CAPITOL.....3-5 72-73
Picture Sleeves
CAPITOL.....3-5 73
LPs: 10/12-inch
CAPITOL.....8-10 72-74
Members: Donny Gerrard; Carl Graves; B.J. Cook; David Foster; Duris Maxwell; Norm McPherson; Steven Pugsley.
Also see GERRARD, Donny
Also see FOSTER, David
Also see GRAVES, Carl

SKYLARKS
Singles: 78 rpm
DECCA.....50-100 51
Singles: 7-inch
DECCA (48241 "Glory of Love").....250-350 51

SKYLARKS
Singles: 7-inch
VERVE.....10-15 57

SKYLARKS
Singles: 7-inch
HART (1502 "Drop In").....10-20 59

SKYLARKS
Singles: 7-inch
EVERLAST (5022 "Everybody's Got Somebody").....20-30 63

SKYLARKS
Singles: 7-inch
ADMIRAL (500 "How Many Times").....15-20 65

SKYLIGHTERS
Singles: 7-inch
PEN.....4-8 62

SKYLINE DRIVE
Singles: 7-inch
REVUE.....4-8 69

SKYLINERS P&R '59
(Jimmy Beaumont & Skyliners; with Lenny Martin Orchestra.)
Singles: 12-inch
TORTOISE INT'L (11345 "Love Bug").....8-10 78
(Promotional issue only.)
Singles: 7-inch
ATCO (6270 "Since I Fell for You").....25-35 63
CALICO (103 "Since I Don't Have You").....20-30 59
CALICO (106 "This I Swear").....20-30 59
CALICO (109 "It Happened Today").....20-30 59
CALICO (114 "How Much").....15-25 60
CALICO (117 "Pennies from Heaven").....15-25 60
CALICO (120 "Believe Me").....15-25 60
CAMEO (215 "Three Coins in the Fountain").....15-25 62
CAPITOL (3979 "I Could Have Loved You").....15-25 75
CLASSIC ARTISTS.....4-6 90
COAST.....5-8
COLPIX (188 "I'll Close My Eyes").....20-30 61
COLPIX (613 "Close Your Eyes").....20-30 61
JUBILEE.....8-12 65-66
ORIGINAL SOUND (35 "Since I Don't Have You").....8-10 63
ORIGINAL SOUND (36 "Pennies from Heaven").....8-10 63
ORIGINAL SOUND (37 "This I Swear").....8-10 63
ORIGINAL SOUND (4500 series).....3-4 84
TORTOISE INT'L.....4-8 77
VIRGO.....3-5 73
VISCOUNT (104 "Comes Love").....15-25 62
LPs: 10/12-inch
CALICO (3000 "Skyliners").....350-450 59
KAMA SUTRA (2026 "Once Upon a Time").....15-25 71
ORIGINAL SOUND (5010 "Since I Don't Have You").....15-25 63
(Monaural.)
ORIGINAL SOUND (8873 "Since I Don't Have You").....20-30 64
(Stereo.)
ORIGINAL SOUND (8873 "Greatest Hits").....5-10 87
(Reissued using same number, but with 20 tracks.)
RELIC (5051 "Pre Flight").....5-10 85
TORTOISE INT'L.....8-10 78
Members: Jimmy Beaumont; Janet Vogel; Wally Lester; Jack Taylor; Joe Verscharen.
Also see BEAUMONT, Jimmy
Also see DEANE, Janet

SKYLINERS / Preston Epps
Singles: 7-inch
OLDIES 45.....4-8 60s
Also see EPPS, Preston

SKYLINERS / Wade Flemons
Singles: 7-inch
OLDIES 45.....4-8 60s
Also see FLEMONS, Wade
Also see SKYLINERS

SKYLINERS
Singles: 7-inch
DOUBLE AA.....5-10 60s

SKYLINERS
("Featuring Lindsay Bray")
Singles: 7-inch
SUNCOAST (1002 "Rock-a-Baby Rock").....10-20

SKYLITE
Singles: 7-inch
RAMPART.....4-8 60s

SKYLITERS
Singles: 7-inch
SCOTTE (2666 "Tidal Wave").....15-25 63

SKYLITES
(With Mike Joseph & Orchestra)
Singles: 7-inch
TA-RAH (101 "My Only Girl").....50-75 61
TA-RAH (102 "King of Wealth").....40-60 61

SKYNYRD, Lynyrd: see LYNYRD SKYNYRD

SKYSCRAPERS
Singles: 78 rpm
MIRACLE (119 "Last Call").....10-20 47
MERCURY.....10-20 56
RAMA (16 "Lost in the Shuffle").....20-30 53
Singles: 7-inch
ALTON (256 "Flying Low").....10-20 59
MERCURY (70795 "I Thought You'd Care").....60-80 56
RAMA (16 "Lost in the Shuffle").....50-75 53
Also see GUY, Browley, & Skyscrapers

SKYY LP '79
Singles: 12-inch
CAPITOL.....4-6 86
SALSOUL.....4-8 79-85
Singles: 7-inch
CAPITOL.....3-4 86
SALSOUL.....3-5 79-85
Picture Sleeves
CAPITOL.....3-4 86
LPs: 10/12-inch
ATLANTIC.....5-8 89
CAPITOL.....5-8 86
SALSOUL.....5-10 79-83
Members: Denise Dunning; Bonnie Dunning; Delores Dunning; Solomon Roberts; Anibal Sierra; Larry Greenberg; Tommy McConnell; Gerald LaBou.

SLACK
Singles: 12-inch
STREETWISE.....4-6 83

SLACK, Freddie: see MORSE, Ella Mae

SLADE P&R/LP '72
Singles: 7-inch
CBS ASSOCIATED.....3-4 84-85
COTILLION.....3-5 71-72
POLYDOR.....3-5 72-73
REPRISE.....3-5 73
W.B......3-5 73-76
LPs: 10/12-inch
CBS ASSOCIATED.....5-8 84-85
COTILLION.....10-15 70
POLYDOR.....8-10 72-73
REPRISE.....10-12 73
W.B......8-10 74-76
Also see AMBROSE SLADE

SLADE, Carol
Singles: 7-inch
DOMAIN (1015 I Wanna Know Right Now").....8-12 63
HIGHLAND.....8-12 62

SLADE, Prentis
Singles: 7-inch
HAMILTON.....10-15 59
HICK.....10-15 60
KING.....5-10 61-62

SLADER, Frank, & Chaparral
Singles: 7-inch
CANDLELITE.....3-5 76

SLADES P&R '58
Singles: 7-inch
DOMINO (500 "You Cheated").....35-45 58
(Add $50 to $75 if accompanied by photo/bio insert.)
DOMINO (800 "You Gambled").....25-35 58
DOMINO (901 "Just You").....20-30 59
DOMINO (906 "It's Your Turn").....25-35 61
DOMINO (1000 "You Must Try").....20-30 61
LIBERTY (55118 "You Mean Everything to Me").....15-25 58
Picture Sleeves
DOMINO (901 "Just You").....40-60 59
Member: Don Burch.
Also see SPADES

SLANE, Keith
LPs: 10/12-inch
AURAL EXPLORER.....8-10 71

SLATER, David C&W '88
Singles: 7-inch
CAPITOL.....3-4 88-89

SLATER, Nelson
LPs: 10/12-inch
RCA.....8-10 76

SLATKIN, Felix, Orchestra P&R '60
Singles: 7-inch
LIBERTY.....5-10 60-62
LPs: 10/12-inch
ANGEL.....5-10 72
CAPITOL.....10-15 59
LIBERTY.....10-15 60-64
SUNSET.....5-10 66-68
U.A......5-10 71

SLAUGHTER P&R/LP '90
Singles: 7-inch
CHRYSALIS.....3-4 90
LPs: 10/12-inch
BITE BACK.....5-10 80
CHRYSALIS.....5-8 90
DJM.....5-10 80
Members: Mark Slaughter; Dana Strum; Mike Ross; Eddie Garrity; Howard; Bates; Phil Rowland.
Also see VINCENT, Vinnie, Invasion

SLAUGHTER, Chuck / Roxie Williams
(With Buddy Ray & the Shamrocks)
Singles: 7-inch
LUCKY 11 ("Lucky 11 Rock").....10-15 60s
(No selection number used.)

SLAVE P&R/LP '77
(Slave-Arrington)
Singles: 12-inch
COTILLION.....4-6 83
Singles: 7-inch
COTILLION.....3-5 77-84
ICHIBAN.....3-4 86-87
LPs: 10/12-inch
COTILLION.....5-10 77-84
ICHIBAN.....5-8 86
Members: Steve Arrington; Steve Washington; Floyd Miller; Charles Bradley; Tom Lockett, Jr.; Mark Adams; Mark Hicks; Danny Webster; Orion Wilhoite; Tim Dozier; Starleana Young.
Also see ARRINGTON, Steve
Also see AURRA
Also see DEJA

SLAVIN, Slick
Singles: 7-inch
COMMANDER (1003 "Hey, Mr. Krushchev").....8-12 61
DEL-FI (4157 "Albert the Astronaut").....5-10 61
GRAVEYARD (3000 "Dr. Finkenstein's Castle").....10-20
IMPERIAL (5540 "Speed Crazy").....20-30 58

SLAY, Emitt
(Emitt Slay Trio; Emitt Slay's Slayriders with Sweetie Dolores)
Singles: 78 rpm
SAVOY.....10-15 52-53
Singles: 7-inch
CHECKER (898 "Honey Bun").....25-50 58
J.V.B......8-12 59
SAVOY.....15-25 52-53

SLAY, Frank, & His Orchestra P&R '61
Singles: 7-inch
SCA.....4-8 63
SWAN.....8-10 61
Also see ANDREWS, Lee
Also see CANNON, Freddy
Also see LARSEN, Key
Also see LY-DELLS
Also see SLAY RIDERS

SLAY RIDERS
(Frank Slay & Orchestra)
Singles: 7-inch
ATCO.....5-10 63
Also see SLAY, Frank, & His Orchestra

SLAYER LP '86
Singles: 7-inch
METAL BLADE.....3-4 85
LPs: 10/12-inch
DEF AMERICAN.....5-8 90
DEF JAM.....5-8 86-88
ENIGMA (72015 "Live Undead").....15-25 85
(Picture disc.)
ENIGMA/METAL BLADE.....5-8 85
W.B. (45522 "Divine Intervention")..8-10 90s

SLEDGE, H.Y.: see H.Y. SLEDGE

SLEDGE, Nat
Singles: 7-inch
BLUEJAY (1000 "Cry'n Baby") ...100-150 61

SLEDGE, Percy P&R/LP '66
Singles: 7-inch
ATLANTIC 5-10 66-72
CAPRICORN 4-6 74-76
MONUMENT 3-5 83
RIPETE 3-4 89
EPs: 7-inch
ATLANTIC (8180 "Take Time to Know Her") 20-30 68
LPs: 10/12-inch
ATLANTIC (8125 "When a Man Loves a Woman") 15-20 66
ATLANTIC (8132 "Warm & Tender Soul") 15-20 66
ATLANTIC (8146 "The Percy Sledge Way") 12-18 67
ATLANTIC (8180 "Take Time to Know Her") 12-18 68
ATLANTIC (8210 "Best of Percy Sledge") 10-15 69
ATLANTIC (80212 "Percy Sledge") 5-10 87
CAPRICORN (0147 "I'll Be Your Everything") 8-10 74
MONUMENT (38532 "Percy") 5-10 83
Also see JACKSON, Chuck / Percy Sledge

SLEDGE, Sister: see SISTER SLEDGE

SLEDGEHAMMER
Singles: 7-inch
MAUDZ (005 "I'll Stop Pretending") 10-15 60s

SLEEPERS
Singles: 7-inch
MARVY ("I Want a Love") 15-25 66
(No selection number used.)

SLEEPLESS KNIGHTS
Singles: 7-inch
JERROC (1000 "You're Drivin' Me Crazy") 15-25 60s

SLEEPY HOLLOW
Singles: 7-inch
FAMILY PRODUCTIONS 3-5 73
LPs: 10/12-inch
FAMILY PRODUCTIONS 10-15 73

SLEEPY JOE'S WASHBOARD BAND
(Ralph Willis)
Singles: 78 rpm
SAVOY 10-20 47
Also see WILLIS, Ralph

SLEEPY KING: see KING, Sleepy

SLEEZE BEEZ LP '90
LPs: 10/12-inch
ATLANTIC 5-8 90

SLEWFOOT C&W '86
Singles: 7-inch
STEP ONE 3-4 86

SLICK
Singles: 12-inch
FANTASY 4-6 80
Singles: 7-inch
FANTASY 3-5 80
LPs: 10/12-inch
FANTASY 5-10 80
WMOT 5-10 79
Also see WELLS, Brandi

SLICK, Grace LP '68
(With the Great Society)
Singles: 7-inch
GRUNT 4-6 72-74
RCA 3-5 80-81
Picture Sleeves
RCA 3-5 80
LPs: 10/12-inch
COLUMBIA (CS-9624 "Conspicuous Only") 20-30 68
COLUMBIA (PC-9624 "Conspicuous Only") 5-10
COLUMBIA (CS-9702 "How It Was") 15-20 68
COLUMBIA (30459 "Collector's Item") 10-15 71
GRUNT 8-12 74
HARMONY 10-15 71
RCA 5-10 80-83
Promotional LPs
RCA ("Dreams Interview") 25-30 80
RCA (3922 "Wrecking Ball Interview") 20-30 81
RCA (3923 "Special Radio Series") 10-15 81
RCA (13708 "Interview LP") 5-10 80s
Also see CROSBY, David
Also see GREAT!! SOCIETY!!
Also see JEFFERSON AIRPLANE
Also see KANTNER, Paul, & Grace Slick

SLICK, Rory, & Roadsters
Singles: 7-inch
PRO-GRESS 5-10 69

SLICK RICK LP '89
LPs: 10/12-inch
DEF JAM 5-8 88

SLICK SLAVIN: see SLAVIN, Slick

SLICKAPHONICS
LPs: 10/12-inch
ENJA 5-8 83

SLICKEE BOYS
Singles: 7-inch
DACOIT 4-6
Picture Sleeves
DACOIT 5-10
LPs: 10/12-inch
DACOIT 8-12

SLIDERS
Singles: 7-inch
CHEVRON (012 "Love Is Like a Mountain") 50-75 60s
STRAND (25033 "Blue Nights") 10-15 61
Member: Dennis Quitmann.
Also see QUITMANN, Dennis

SLIDERS
Singles: 7-inch
CHOICE (40 "Sly Dog") 10-15 63

SLIGHTLY TWISTED DISAPPOINTER SISTERS
Singles: 7-inch
ROX (422 "No More Madonna") 3-5 85

SLIGO STUDIO BAND C&W '81
Singles: 7-inch
GBS 3-4 81

SLIK
Singles: 7-inch
ARISTA 3-5 76
POLYDOR 3-5 74
LPs: 10/12-inch
ARISTA 8-10 77

SLIM, Fender Guitar: see FENDER GUITAR SLIM

SLIM, Guitar: see GUITAR SLIM

SLIM, Jimmy: see JIMMY SLIM

SLIM, Lightnin': see LIGHTNIN' SLIM

SLIM, Memphis: see MEMPHIS SLIM

SLIM, Model T.: see MODEL T. SLIM

SLIM, Tarheel: see TARHEEL SLIM

SLIM & ANN: see TARHEEL SLIM & Little Ann

SLIM & TWILITES
Singles: 7-inch
DORE 5-10 62

SLIM from TIMES
(Slim Rose)
Singles: 10-inch
CANDLELITE (435 "Slim from Times") 8-12 62
(Colored vinyl.)
Singles: 7-inch
PATTI 3-6 72

SLIM HARPO: see HARPO, Slim

SLINGSHOT D&D '83
Singles: 12-inch
QUALITY/RFC 4-6 83
Singles: 7-inch
QUALITY/RFC 3-4 83

SLINKY, Ratmore
(Jerry Osborne)
Singles: 7-inch
JELLYROLL (69 "Plane Crazy") 4-6 75
(500 made.)
Also see OSBORNE, Jerry

SLIP & DELL
Singles: 7-inch
MODERN ARTIST (100 "Don't Take a Chance") 250-500

SLITS
LPs: 10/12-inch
ANTILLES 5-10 79

SLLEDNATS
(Standells)
Singles: 7-inch
TOWER (312 "Don't Tell Me What to Do") 15-20 67
Also see STANDELLS

SLO, Audry
Singles: 7-inch
SWAN (4262 "Gonna Find the Right Boy") 10-20 66

SLOAN
LPs: 10/12-inch
AUDIO 7 .... 8-10 71

SLOAN, Flip
(P.F. Sloan)
Singles: 7-inch
ALADDIN (3461 "All I Want Is Loving") 10-20 59
Also see SLOAN, P.F.

SLOAN, Jimmy
Singles: 7-inch
TOWNE HOUSE 4-8 63

SLOAN, P.F. P&R '65
(Phil Sloan; Phillip "Flip" Sloan)
Singles: 7-inch
ATCO 4-6 69
DUNHILL 4-8 65-67
MART (802 "She's My Girl") 50-75 60
MUMS 3-5 72
Picture Sleeves
DUNHILL (4064 "Sunflower") 5-8 67
LPs: 10/12-inch
ATCO 10-15 68
DUNHILL 10-20 65-66
MUMS 8-10 72
RHINO 5-8 86
Also see FANTASTIC BAGGYS
Also see GRASS ROOTS
Also see IMAGINATIONS
Also see INNER CIRCLE
Also see SLOAN, Flip
Also see STREET CLEANERS

SLOANE, Carol
Singles: 7-inch
COLUMBIA (43307 "Stay") 20-30 65

SLOBOS
Singles: 7-inch
NEBRA (113 "Famous Willie's Birthday") 4-6 84

SLOCUM, Wanda
Singles: 7-inch
TOPPA 5-8 63

SLONIKER, Mark
LPs: 10/12-inch
SANDSTONE 5-8 88

SLOOPYS
Singles: 7-inch
SIDEWALK 5-10 67

SLOW CHILDREN
Singles: 7-inch
ENSIGN 3-5 82
LPs: 10/12-inch
ENSIGN 5-10 82
Promotional LPs
RCA ("Special Radio Series") 10-15 81

SLUGS
Singles: 7-inch
RITDONG (101 "Running Around") 3-5 80s
(Identification number shown since no selection number is used.)
Picture Sleeves
RITDONG (101 "Running Around") 4-6 80s
Members: Steve Bosley; John Burton; Rick Baker; Simon Kendall; John Wally Watson.
Also see DOUG & SLUGS

SLY
(Sly Stone; Sly Stewart)
Singles: 7-inch
AUTUMN (14 "Buttermilk") 10-15 65
AUTUMN (26 "Temptation Walk") 10-15 65
Also see SLY & FAMILY STONE
Also see STONE, Sly
Also see STEWART, Sly

SLY & FAMILY STONE P&R/LP '68
Singles: 12-inch
EPIC 4-8 79
Singles: 7-inch
EPIC 3-6 67-75
W.B. 3-5 79-85
Picture Sleeves
EPIC 3-6 68-70
EPs: 7-inch
EPIC 15-20 60s
(Juke box only.)
LPs: 10/12-inch
EPIC (264 "Everything You Always Wanted to Hear") 10-20 76
(Promotional issue only.)
EPIC (26000 series) 10-15 67-69
EPIC (KE-30325 "Greatest Hits") 8-12 70
EPIC (PE-30325 "Greatest Hits") 5-10 70s
EPIC (EQ-30325 "Greatest Hits") 25-50 73
(Quadrophonic. Has some true stereo tracks that were rechanneled on earlier issues.)
EPIC (30335 thru 37071) 5-10 70-81
W.B. 5-10 79-83
Members: Sylvester "Sly Stone" Stewart; Rose Stone; Larry Graham; Fred Stone; Gregg Errico; Jerry Martini.
Also see BANKS, Rose
Also see GRAHAM, Larry
Also see RUBICON
Also see SLY
Also see STEWART, Sly
Also see STEWART BROTHERS
Also see STONE, Sly

SLY & ROBBIE
Singles: 7-inch
ISLAND 3-4 86-87
LPs: 10/12-inch
ISLAND 5-8 86-87
Members: Sly Dunbar; Robbie Shakespeare.

SLY BOOTS
Singles: 7-inch
FAITHFUL VIRTUE 3-6
Also see WENDROFF, Michael

SLY FOX
Singles: 78 rpm
SPARK (112 "Alley Music") 25-50 55
Singles: 7-inch
SPARK (112 "Alley Music") 50-100 55

SLY FOX P&R '85
Singles: 12-inch
CAPITOL 4-6 85-86
Singles: 7-inch
CAPITOL 3-4 85-86
Picture Sleeves
CAPITOL 3-4 86
LPs: 10/12-inch
CAPITOL 5-8 86
Members: Mike Camacho; Gary Cooper.

SLY, SLICK & WICKED
LPs: 10/12-inch
JU-PAR 8-10 77

SLYE, Carrie C&W '83
Singles: 7-inch
FRIDAY 3-4 83

SMACK
LPs: 10/12-inch
AUDIO HOUSE ("Smack") 1500-2000 67
(Reportedly 200 made.)

SMACK
Singles: 7-inch
GARLAND 3-6

SMACKS
Singles: 7-inch
ALEAR (109 "I've Been Foolin' Around") 15-25 66
ALEAR (116 "Reckless Ways") 15-25 66

SMALL, Danny
Singles: 78 rpm
DELUXE 5-10 52
Singles: 7-inch
DELUXE 10-15 52
U.A. 4-8 62
LPs: 10/12-inch
U.A. 15-20 62

SMALL, Drink
LPs: 10/12-inch
ICHIBAN 5-10

SMALL, Elliott
Singles: 7-inch
BANG 3-6 69

SMALL, Karen
Singles: 7-inch
VENUS 4-8 66

SMALL, Mary
Singles: 7-inch
CAPITOL 4-8 61
SEECO 4-8 61
VITALENT 4-8 66

SMALL, Millie P&R/LP '64
("The Blue Beat Girl")
Singles: 7-inch
ATCO 5-10 65
ATLANTIC 5-10 64
BRIT 5-10 65
SMASH 4-8 64
LPs: 10/12-inch
SMASH 15-25 64

SMALL, Neva
Singles: 7-inch
MGM 4-8 67

SMALL, Wee Willie
Singles: 7-inch
CO-STAR (101 "Tall People") 4-8 77

SMALL CIRCLE OF FRIENDS
Singles: 7-inch
A&M 3-6 67
Also see NICHOLS, Roger, Trio

SMALL FACES P&R '67
Singles: 7-inch
IMMEDIATE 5-10 67-68
PRESS 8-12 65-68
RCA 8-12 66
W.B. 4-8 70-75
Picture Sleeves
IMMEDIATE (5003 "Tin Soldier") 10-20 68
W.B. 5-10 73
LPs: 10/12-inch
ABKCO 8-12 73
ACCORD 5-10 82
ATLANTIC 8-10 77-78
COMPLEAT 5-8 86
IMMEDIATE (002 "There Are But Four Small Faces") 20-30 68
IMMEDIATE (008 "Ogden's Nut Gone Flake") 20-30 68
IMMEDIATE (4225 "Ogden's Nut Gone Flake") 10-15 73
MGM 10-15 74
PRIDE 10-15 72-73
SIRE 10-15
W.B. 10-15 70
Members: Steve Marriott; Ronnie Lane; Kenny Jones; Ian McLagen.
Also see FACES
Also see HUMBLE PIE
Also see LANE, Ronnie
Also see MARRIOTT, Steve
Also see McLAGAN, Ian
Also see PYTHON LEE JACKSON
Also see WHO

SMALL FRIES
Singles: 7-inch
MUTUAL (501 "Just Yesterday") 10-15 64

SMALL TALK
LPs: 10/12-inch
MCA 5-10 81

SMALL TOWN WORLD
Singles: 7-inch
CHECKER 4-8 68

SMALL WONDER
Singles: 7-inch
COLUMBIA 3-5 75-77
LPs: 10/12-inch
COLUMBIA 8-10 76-77

SMALL WORLD
Singles: 7-inch
MIRA 4-8 68

SMALLEY, Leroy
Singles: 7-inch
GOLDEN WORLD (107 "Girls Are Sentimental") 20-30 62

SMALLS, C., & Company
Singles: 7-inch
A&M 4-8 68

SMALLWOOD, Joan
Singles: 7-inch
WEDGE 4-8 64

SMALLWOOD, Laney C&W '78
(Laney Hicks)
Singles: 7-inch
MONUMENT 3-5 78-83
Also see McCOY, Charlie, & Laney Smallwood

SMART, Jimmy C&W '60
Singles: 7-inch
ALLSTAR 5-10 60
CHANCELLOR 4-8 62
JED 4-6 67
K-ARK (622 "Shorty") 5-10 61
PEACH 5-10 59-60
PLAID (1004 "Shorty") 10-15 61
PONZER 4-8 64
TULIP 4-8 63

SMART, N.D., & Kangaroo
Singles: 7-inch
MGM (13962 "Frog Giggin' ") 5-10 68
Also see KANGAROO
Also see REMAINS

SMART, Sue & Del
Singles: 7-inch
NEWHALL 4-8 66

SMART SET
Singles: 7-inch
W.B. 4-8 59

SMART TONES
Singles: 7-inch
HERALD (529 "Bob O Link") 50-75 58
(Yellow label.)
HERALD (529 "Bob O Link") 40-60 58
(Multi-color label.)

SMASH
LPs: 10/12-inch
SOURCE 5-10 79

SMASH PALACE
Singles: 7-inch
EPIC 3-4 86
LPs: 10/12-inch
CBS 5-8 85

SMASHERS
Singles: 7-inch
KAT FAMILY 3-4 81
LPs: 10/12-inch
KAT FAMILY 5-10 81

SMASHING PUMPKINS LP '91
Singles: 7-inch
VIRGIN ("Tonight Tonight") 10-15 95
(No selection number used.)
VIRGIN (38522 "Bullet with Butterfly Wings") 4-8 95
(Promotional issue only.)
Picture Sleeves
VIRGIN ("Tonight Tonight") 15-20 95
(No selection number used.)
VIRGIN (38522 "Bullet with Butterfly Wings") 4-8 95
(Promotional issue only.)
LPs: 10/12-inch
CAROLINE (1705 "Gish") 8-12 91
CAROLINE (1767 "Pisces Iscariot") 8-10 90s
(Colored vinyl.)
CAROLINE (61740 "Siamese Deam") 10-15 90s
Members: Darcy Wretzky; James Iah; Billy Corgon; Jimmy Chamberlain.

SMECK, Roy, & His Magic Ukulele
Singles: 7-inch
ABC-PAR 4-8 63

SMEDLEY, Ralph
Singles: 7-inch
GASP 4-8 62

SMILE
Singles: 7-inch
MERCURY (72977 "Step on Me") .. 30-40 69
LPs: 10/12-inch
PICKWICK (3288 "Smile") 25-35 73
Members: Brian May; Roger Taylor.
Also see QUEEN

SMILE
Singles: 7-inch
UNI 3-5 72

SMILER
Singles: 7-inch
ARIOLA AMERICA 3-5 77
Picture Sleeves
ARIOLA AMERICA 3-5 77

SMILEY, Austin
Singles: 7-inch
BRUNSWICK (55061 "Pretty Baby-O") 10-20 58

SMILEY, Red: see RENO & SMILEY

SMILEY MOON: see MOON, Smiley

SMITH P&R/LP '69
Singles: 7-inch
DUNHILL 4-6 69-70
GOLDIES 3-5 73

ROULETTE 3-5 70s
Picture Sleeves
DUNHILL 4-8 69
LPs: 10/12-inch
DUNHILL 10-15 69-70
Member: Gayle McCormick.
Also see McCORMICK, Gayle

SMITH, Al
("Al Smith & Band")
Singles: 78 rpm
CHANCE (1124 "Slow Mood") 50-100 53
METEOR 25-50 55
Singles: 7-inch
ABNER 5-10 59
CHANCE (1124 "Slow Mood") 150-200 53
FALCON 10-20 57
IRMA (105 "Leaving You Baby") ..75-125 57
METEOR (5013 "Beale Street Stomp") 100-150 55
METEOR (5026 "Chop Chop Boogie") 75-125 55
(Same track as *Beale Steet Stomp*.)
PRESTIGE 5-10 59-60
PRESTIGE BLUESVILLE 5-10 60
LPs: 10/12-inch
PRESTIGE BLUESVILLE (1013 "Midnight Special") 20-30 61
Also see FALCONS
Also see HENDERSON, Big Bertha, & Al Smith Orchestra
Also see MOROCCOS

SMITH, Al, & Savoys / Jack McVea with Al Smith & Savoys
Singles: 78 rpm
COMBO (90 "Chop Chop Boom") ..50-75 55
Singles: 7-inch
COMBO (90 "Chop Chop Boom") 75-100 55
Also see McVEA, Jack
Also see SAVOYS
Also see SMITH, Al

SMITH, Al
Singles: 7-inch
GOLDBAND 5-10 59

SMITH, Al
Singles: 7-inch
IRMA 15-25 57
PRESTIGE 10-15 59-60
PRESTIGE BLUESVILLE 8-12 60
LPs: 10/12-inch
PRESTIGE BLUESVILLE 20-30 61

SMITH, Alvin
(Al King)
Singles: 78 rpm
MUSIC CITY (743 "On My Way") ... 10-20 54
Singles: 7-inch
MUSIC CITY (743 "On My Way") ... 25-50 54
Also see KING, Al

SMITH, Andy Lee C&W '89
(With the Jordanaires)
Singles: 7-inch
615 ..... 3-4 89
Also see JORDANAIRES

SMITH, Arlene
Singles: 7-inch
BIG TOP (3073 "Love, Love Love") 20-30 61
SPECTORIOUS (150 "Good Girls") 15-25 60s
Also see CHANTELS

SMITH, Arthur C&W/P&R '48
(Arthur "Guitar Boogie" Smith; with Crossroads Quartet)
Singles: 78 rpm
MGM 5-10 48-57
SUPER DISC (1004 "Guitar Boogie") 20-30 48
Singles: 7-inch
MGM (10229 thru 12791) 5-15 49-60
STARDAY 4-8 63
EPs: 7-inch
DOT (600 "Original Guitar Boogie") 8-12 64
(Stereo. Juke box issue only.)
MGM 10-20 51-56
LPs: 10/12-inch
ABC-PAR 15-25 63
DOT 10-15 64-66
FOLKWAYS 10-15 64
HAMILTON 10-15 64
MGM (236 "Foolish Questions") 25-50 54
(10-inch LP.)
MGM (533 "Fingers on Fire") 25-50 51
(10-inch LP.)
MGM (3301 "Specials") 25-50 56
MONUMENT 6-12 70-75
NASHVILLE 8-12 68
STARDAY (186 thru 415) 15-30 62-68
Also see HAMILTON, George, IV / Arthur Smith

SMITH, Arthur, Trio
(With the Dixieliners)
Singles: 78 rpm
BLUEBIRD 15-30 30s
MONTGOMERY WARD 25-35 30s
LPs: 10/12-inch
COUNTY 5-10 80s
STARDAY (202 "Rare, Old Time Fiddle Tunes") 15-25 62
(Listed primarily to distinguish this singer from the preceding Arthur Smith, who also had releases on Starday.)

SMITH, Ben, Quartet
Singles: 78 rpm
ABBEY 10-15 50
COLEMAN 10-15 49
COLUMBIA 10-15 50
RAMA (17 "Big Fat Lips") 25-50 53
Singles: 7-inch
RAMA (17 "Big Fat Lips") 50-100 53

SMITH, Bernard, & Jokers Wild
Singles: 7-inch
GROOVE (504 "Gotta Be a Reason") 15-25

SMITH, Bessie P&R '23
Singles: 78 rpm
COLUMBIA (3000 & 4000 series) .. 25-50 23
COLUMBIA (13000 & 14000 series) 25-50 23-33
OKEH (8000 series) 20-30 31
Singles: 7-inch
OKEH (6893 "Gimmie a Pig Foot") 20-30 52
LPs: 10/12-inch
COLUMBIA 10-15 70-72

SMITH, Betty P&R '58
(Betty Smith Group)
Singles: 7-inch
ECHO (584 "Oh Yeah") 20-30
LONDON 5-10 58

SMITH, Bill
(Bill Smith Combo; with Jeanette)
Singles: 7-inch
CHESS (1773 "Heartbreak Hotel") 10-15 60
CHESS (1780 "Raunchy") 10-15 60
LE BILL (303 "Tough") 15-25 60
LE BILL (305 "Heartbreak Hotel") ... 15-25 60
LE BILL (306 "Snookie") 10-20 60

SMITH, Bill
Singles: 7-inch
TAL (301 "Wondering") 5-10

SMITH, Bill, & & Corvairs
("Featuring Little Joe & Joyce")
Singles: 7-inch
TWIN (19671 "I'm Gonna Marry You") 50-75 62
Members: Bill Smith; Little Joe Williams.
Also see CORVAIRS

SMITH, Billie, & Good Beats
Singles: 7-inch
RAE COX (1000 "The Whammer") .. 8-12 60s

SMITH, Blaine
Singles: 78 rpm
DOME 5-10 50

SMITH, Bob
(Bobby Smith)
Singles: 7-inch
BUZZ 15-25 59
FOX 10-20 60
R.R.E. 8-12 63
YONAH 10-20 63
Also see REBELS
Also see TWISTERS

SMITH, Bob
LPs: 10/12-inch
KENT (551 "The Visit") 50-75 70
(Add $10 to $15 if accompanied by bonus poster.)
Also see THORNDIKE PICKLEDISH

SMITH, Bobbie
(With the Dream Girls)
Singles: 7-inch
AMERICAN ARTS (2 "Miss Strongehearted") 15-25 64
BIG TOP (3085 "Mr. Fine") 10-15 61
BIG TOP (3100 "Dutchess of Earl") 15-20 62
BIG TOP (3111 "Here Comes Baby") 10-15 62
BIG TOP (3129 "Now He's Gone") 10-15 62
Also see DREAM GIRLS

SMITH, Bobby
(With the Shades, with Neat Beats)
Singles: 7-inch
CUCA (1071 "Be My Baby") 10-20 62
CUCA (1126 "Come Back, Laurie") 10-20 62

SMITH, Bobby
(With the Spinners)
Singles: 7-inch
TRI-PHI (1018 "She Don't Love Me") 15-25 62
Also see SPINNERS

SMITH, Bobby C&W '77
Singles: 7-inch
AUTUMN 3-5 77
LIBERTY 3-4 81-82

SMITH, Bobby
LPs: 10/12-inch
RIPSAW 5-8 87
Members: Danny Gatton; Johnny Castle; Mitch Collins.

SMITH, Bobby Lee
Singles: 7-inch
KING (5843 "I'm Gonna Put You Down") 5-10 64

SMITH, Bro P&R '76
Singles: 7-inch
BIG TREE 3-5 76
Picture Sleeves
BIG TREE 3-5 76

SMITH, Buster
(With His Heat Waves)
Singles: 78 rpm
BIG TOWN 10-15 55
METEOR 15-25 56
Singles: 7-inch
BIG TOWN 10-20 55
METEOR 25-35 56
LPs: 10/12-inch
ATLANTIC (1323 "The Legendary Buster Smith") 30-50 60

SMITH, Byther, & Nightriders
LPs: 10/12-inch
GRITS 8-10 83
RAZOR 5-8 88

SMITH, Cal C&W '67
Singles: 7-inch
DECCA 3-5 70-73
KAPP 3-6 66-70
PLAID 5-10 60
MCA 3-5 73-79
SOUNDWAVES 3-4 82
STEP ONE 3-4 86
LPs: 10/12-inch
CORAL 5-10 73
DECCA 8-12 72
KAPP 10-25 66-70
MCA 5-10 73-77
Also see NELSON, Willie
Also see PARKER, Billy, & Cal Smith
Also see TUBB, Ernest

SMITH, Carl C&W '51
(With the Tunesmiths)
Singles: 78 rpm
COLUMBIA 5-10 51-57
Singles: 7-inch
ABC/HICKORY 3-5 76-78
COLUMBIA (20000 & 21000 series) 8-15 51-56
COLUMBIA (40823 thru 42858) 4-10 57-63
COLUMBIA (42949 thru 45923) 3-8 64-73
HICKORY 3-5 74-76
Picture Sleeves
COLUMBIA 5-10 59
EPs: 7-inch
COLUMBIA (2801 thru 10223) 8-15 57-58
COLUMBIA (10964 "Taste of Country") 5-10 72
(Juke box issue.)
COLUMBIA (11721) 8-15 58
LPs: 10/12-inch
ABC/HICKORY 10-15 77-78
COLUMBIA (31 "Anniversary Album") 8-12 70
COLUMBIA (DS-341 thru DS-517) ... 5-15
(Record club issues.)
COLUMBIA (900 thru 1100 series) 25-50 57-58
COLUMBIA (1500 thru 2600 series) 10-20 60-69
COLUMBIA (2579 "Carl Smith") 50-75 56
(10-inch LP.)
COLUMBIA (8300 thru 9800 series) 10-20 60-72
COLUMBIA (9023 "Sentimental Songs") 50-75 54
(10-inch LP.)
COLUMBIA (9026 "Softly and Tenderly") 50-75 54
(10-inch LP.)
COLUMBIA (10000 series) 5-10 73
COLUMBIA (30000 series) 10-20 70-84
COLUMBIA SPECIAL PRODUCTS (8000 series) 10-15
COUNTRY CLASSICS 5-10
GUSTO 5-8 80
HICKORY 5-10 75
HARMONY 5-15 64-72
LAKE SHORE 5-10
Session: Lewis Pruitt.
Also see PRICE, Ray / Lefty Frizzell / Carl Smith
Also see PRICE, Ray / Johnny Horton / Carl Smith / George Morgan
Also see PRUITT, Lewis
Also see TUNESMITHS

SMITH, Carl / Lefty Frizzell / Marty Robbins
LPs: 10/12-inch
COLUMBIA (2544 "Carl, Lefty & Marty") 150-250 56
(10-inch LP.)
Also see FRIZZELL, Lefty
Also see ROBBINS, Marty
Also see SMITH, Carl

SMITH, Chester
Singles: 7-inch
DECCA (30603 "You Gotta Move") 25-50 58

SMITH, Chris
Singles: 7-inch
CMA 3-5 78

SMITH, Clemmon
Singles: 7-inch
BIG Q (1001 "I Want to Thank You") 10-15

SMITH, Columbus
Singles: 7-inch
COLUMBIA 4-6 66
Picture Sleeves
COLUMBIA 4-8 66

SMITH, Connie C&W '64
Singles: 7-inch
COLUMBIA 3-5 73-77
EPIC 3-4 85
MONUMENT 3-5 77-83
RCA 3-8 64-74
Picture Sleeves
RCA 4-6 67
LPs: 10/12-inch
CAMDEN 10-15 67-72
COLUMBIA 10-20 73-77
MONUMENT 5-8 77-78
RCA (0100 thru 1200 series) 5-10 73-75
RCA (3300 thru 4800 series) 10-20 65-73
Also see SOME OF CHET'S FRIENDS

SMITH, Connie, & Nat Stuckey C&W '70
Singles: 7-inch
RCA 3-5 70
Also see SMITH, Connie
Also see STUCKEY, Nat

SMITH, Cool Papa, & His Orchestra
Singles: 78 rpm
UPTOWN (202 "Christmas Blues") 75-125 49

SMITH, Dale
Singles: 7-inch
BOLO 4-8 61

SMITH, Darden C&W '88
Singles: 7-inch
EPIC 3-4 88

SMITH, David C&W '79
Singles: 7-inch
MDJ 3-5 79

SMITH, Dawson
Singles: 7-inch
ROADSHOW/SCEPTER 3-5 75

SMITH, Dennis C&W '80
Singles: 7-inch
ADONDA 3-4 80

SMITH, Dickie
(With Don Gardner & His Sonotones)
Singles: 78 rpm
BRUCE (103 "New Kind of Love") . 10-20 54
Singles: 7-inch
BRUCE (103 "New Kind of Love") . 30-50 54
Also see FIVE KEYS
Also see GARDNER, Don

SMITH, Doris
Singles: 7-inch
LIMELIGHT 4-8 64

SMITH, Dorothy
Singles: 7-inch
DONDEE 4-8 62

SMITH, Driftin': see DRIFTIN' SLIM

SMITH, Earl Dean
Singles: 7-inch
COLISEUM (201 "Unite Me") 15-25 63
LIBERTY 5-10 65

SMITH, Eddie
(With the Chief; with Hornets)
Singles: 78 rpm
KING 10-15 51-55
Singles: 7-inch
KING (1002 "Bow Wow Boogie") ... 15-25 51
KING (1019 "Annie's Rag") 15-25 51
KING (1204 "Hot Shot Rag") 15-25 53
KING (1479 "Jumping Jennie") 15-25 55
REL (601 "Uptum") 10-15 59
V-TONE (1002 "Bow Wow Boogie") 10-20

SMITH, Effie
(With the Squires)
Singles: 78 rpm
ALADDIN 10-20 46-53
G&G 10-20 45
GEM 10-20 45
MILTONE 10-20 47
VITA (117 "Guiding Angel") 15-25 55
VITA (124 "Champagne Mind with a Soda Water Income") 5-10 56
Singles: 7-inch
ALADDIN (3302 "Dial That Telephone") 25-35 53
ALADDIN (3303 "Standing in the Doorway") 25-35 53
DUO DISC 4-8 64-65
EEE CEE 5-10 68
SPOT 8-12 59
VITA (117 "Guiding Angel") 50-75 55
VITA (124 "Champagne Mind with a Soda Water Income") 15-25 56
LPs: 10/12-inch
JUBILEE 15-25 66
Also see CARPENTER, Ike
Also see SQUIRES

SMITH, Elson
Singles: 7-inch
EPIC 5-10 60
FRATERNITY 4-8 61

SMITH, Ernie
LPs: 10/12-inch
GENERATION 5-10 81
STEADY (137 "Greatest Reggae Hits") 10-20

SMITH, Eugene
Singles: 7-inch
BIG TREE 3-5 76

SMITH, Evelyn
Singles: 7-inch
MAGIC TOUCH (2006 "Don't Make Me No Promises") 10-20 67

SMITH, Floyd
(Floyd Smith's Combo)
Singles: 78 rpm
CHESS 5-15 50
HY-TONE 5-15 46
DECCA (48000 series) 5-15 50
Singles: 7-inch
DECCA (28000 series) 15-25 52

SMITH, Floyd
(With the Montclairs)
Singles: 7-inch
DAKAR (604 "Getting Nowhere Fast") 8-12 69
FORTUNE 10-15 60
Also see MONTCLAIRS

SMITH, Frankie P&R/LP '81
Singles: 12-inch
WMOT 4-6 81
Singles: 7-inch
WMOT 3-5 81
LPs: 10/12-inch
WMOT 5-10 81

SMITH, Fraser, & Dumb Blondes & Malibu Mudhens
Singles
CRUSHED TOY (KLOS "Cool Patrol") 20-30 82
(Picture disc. Promotional issue only.)

SMITH, Freddy
Singles: 7-inch
DYER 4-8 63

SMITH, G.E.
LPs: 10/12-inch
MIRAGE 8-12 81

SMITH, Gary
(Gary Smith's Blues Band)
EPs: 7-inch
MESSAROUND (001 "Gary Smith's Blues Band") 15-20 74
Members: Gary Smith; John Garcia; Steve Gomes; Johny Moon; Jim Gordon.
Session: Jack Gusto; Lynn; Gary Horsman; Louie; Marilyn; Green Street Winos.

SMITH, Gene
(Gene Smith's 4 Notes)
Singles: 78 rpm
BLUE KEY 25-50 52
Singles: 7-inch
BLUE KEY (1001 "I Didn't Mean to Be So Mean") 75-125 52
Members: Gene Smith; Ted Queen; Roy Magee; Earl Thomas.

SMITH, Gene
Singles: 7-inch
REM (440 "Rubber Legs") 75-100

SMITH, Geechie
(Vernon Smith)
Singles: 78 rpm
CAPITOL 5-10 46-47
KICKS (5 "Geneva Sue") 10-15 54
Singles: 7-inch
KICKS (5 "Geneva Sue") 20-30 54

SMITH, George
(George "Harmonica" Smith; Little George Smith)
Singles: 78 rpm
RPM 15-25 55-56
Singles: 7-inch
BARBARY COAST 5-10 59
RPM (434 "Telephone Blues") 40-60 55
RPM (456 "Love Life") 40-60 56
TURNTABLE (713 "I've Had It") ... 20-30 65
LPs: 10/12-inch
BLUESWAY 10-15 69
DERAM 8-12 71
WORLD PACIFIC 10-15 69
Also see ALLEN, George
Also see HARMONICA KING
Also see SPANN, Otis

SMITH, Grant, & Power
Singles: 7-inch
MGM 4-8 68

SMITH, Hagen
Singles: 7-inch
SWELL ("Among the Unloved") 20-40 65
(No selection number used.)

SMITH, Hank
(George Jones; with Nashville Playboys; Hank Smith / Bud Roman & Topppers / "Scat" Benny / Sue Richards / Bob Sandy)
Singles: 78 rpm
GILMAR 30-40 50s
EPs: 7-inch
HOLLYWOOD HIT CLUB (280 "Heartbreak Hotel") 30-50 56
TOPS (280 "Heartbreak Hotel") 30-40 56
Also see JONES, George

SMITH, Helene
Singles: 7-inch
DEEP CITY 10-20 68
PHIL-L.A. of SOUL 5-10 67-69

SMITH, Henry, & His Blue Flames
Singles: 78 rpm
DOT 25-40 54
Singles: 7-inch
DOT (1220 "Good Rocking Mama") 75-125 54
Also see POSEY, Clarence / Henry Smith

SMITH, Huey P&R '57
(With His Band; with Clowns; with Pitter Pats; Huey "Piano" Smith)
Singles: 78 rpm
ACE 10-25 56-58
SAVOY 20-30 54
Singles: 7-inch
ABC 3-5 73
ACE (521 thru 571) 15-25 56-59

ACE (584 thru 672) 8-15 60-65
COLLECTABLES 3-4 80s
CONSTELLATION 5-10 63
COTILLION 3-5 72
IMPERIAL (5721 "Someone to Love") 8-10 61
INSTANT 5-8 68-69
OLDIES 45 4-6 64
SAVOY (1113 "You Made Me Cry") 40-60 54
VIN (1024 "I Didn't Do It") 10-15 60

EPs: 7-inch

ACE (104 "Having Fun") 50-75 59

LPs: 10/12-inch

ACE (1004 "Having Fun") 100-150 59
ACE (1015 "For Dancing") 100-150 61
ACE (1027 "Twas the Night Before Christmas") 100-200 62
ACE (2021 "Rock & Roll Revival") 25-35 74
GRAND PRIX 10-20 60s
Session: Lee Allen.
Also see ALLEN, Lee
Also see CHIMES / Huey "Piano" Smith
Also see CRAWFORD, James
Also see FORD, Frankie
Also see GORDON, Junior
Also see HUEY & CURLEY
Also see HUEY & JERRY
Also see KING, Earl
Also see LITTLE SHELTON
Also see MARCHAN, Bobby
Also see SUPREMES

SMITH, Hurricane P&R '72

Singles: 7-inch

CAPITOL 3-5 72-73
EMI 3-5 74

LPs: 10/12-inch

CAPITOL 8-10 72

SMITH, J.L.

Singles: 7-inch

FRIENDLY FIVE 10-20

SMITH, Jack

Singles: 78 rpm

UNIQUE 3-5 56

Singles: 7-inch

UNIQUE 4-8 56

Picture Sleeves

UNIQUE 5-10 56

SMITH, Jack

EPs: 7-inch

BARON (504 "Mind Your Own Business") 10-15
(Colored vinyl.)

SMITH, Jack, & Rockabilly Planet

Singles: 12-inch

RUCKUS 8-10 84

SMITH, Jack C.

Singles: 7-inch

LIBERTY (55257 "Honeysuckle Rose") 15-25 60

SMITH, Janice

Singles: 78 rpm

BRUNSWICK 5-10 57

Singles: 7-inch

BRUNSWICK 5-10 57

SMITH, Jeff

Singles: 7-inch

RADIO (106 "Chemise") 10-20 57

SMITH, Jennie

Singles: 7-inch

CANADIAN AMERICAN 5-10 62-63
TOP RANK 5-10 60

EPs: 7-inch

RCA (1523 "Jennie") 10-15 57

LPs: 10/12-inch

CANADIAN AMERICAN 15-25 63
COLUMBIA (1242 Love Among the Young") 20-30 58
(Monaural.)
COLUMBIA (8028 Love Among the Young") 25-40 58
(Stereo.)
DOT 10-20 64
RCA (1523 "Jennie") 20-30 57

SMITH, Jerry C&W/P&R/LP '69
(With His Pianos)

Singles: 7-inch

ABC 3-5 69
AD 4-8 59-61
CHART 4-6 67
DECCA 3-5 70-72
RANWOOD 3-5 73-78
RICE 4-6 67
SOUND STAGE 7 4-8 65

LPs: 10/12-inch

ABC 5-10 69
DECCA 5-10 70-72
RANWOOD 5-8 73-75
Also see CORNBREAD & JERRY
Also see DIXIEBELLES
Also see MAGIC ORGAN
Also see PAPA JOE'S MUSIC BOX

SMITH, Jimmie
(Gene Autry)

Singles: 78 rpm

TIMELY TUNES (1554 "I'm a Truthful Fellow") 25-75
TIMELY TUNES (1555 "I'm Blue and Lonesome") 25-75
TIMELY TUNES (1556 "Bear Cat Mama from Homer Comer") 25-75
TIMELY TUNES (1557 "She's a Hum Dinger") 25-75
Also see AUTRY, Gene

SMITH, Jimmie
(Jimmy Smith)

Singles: 7-inch

FLIP 10-15 59
WONDER (110 "Pinch Me Quick") 100-200 59

SMITH, Jimmy P&R/LP '62

Singles: 7-inch

BLUE NOTE 4-8 56-63
MGM 3-4 78
MERCURY 3-4 77
PRIDE 3-5 74
VERVE 3-6 62-73

LPs: 10/12-inch

BLUE NOTE 40-80 56-60
(Label gives New York street address for Blue Note Records.)
BLUE NOTE 20-30 61-63
(Label reads "Blue Note Records Inc. - New York, USA.")
BLUE NOTE 10-20 66-73
(Label shows Blue Note Records as a division of either Liberty or United Artists.)
COBBLESTONE 6-12 72
ELEKTRA 5-10 82-83
GUEST STAR 8-12 64
INNER CITY 5-10 81
MGM 8-12 70
MERCURY 5-10 77-78
METRO 8-15 67
MOJO 5-10 75
PRIDE 5-10 74
SUNSET 5-10 70
VERVE 10-25 63-72
(Reads "MGM Records - A Division of Metro-Goldwyn-Mayer, Inc." at bottom of label.)
VERVE 5-10 73-84
(Reads "Manufactured By MGM Record Corp.," or mentions either Polydor or Polygram at bottom of label.)
Also see BURRELL, Kenny, & Jimmy Smith

SMITH, Jimmy, & Wes Montgomery LP '67

LPs: 10/12-inch

VERVE 10-20 66-69
Also see MONTGOMERY, Wes
Also see SMITH, Jimmy

SMITH, Jo Ann

Singles: 7-inch

CENTURA 4-8 63
COLUMBIA 4-8 65

SMITH, Jojo

Singles: 7-inch

STATURE 8-12 60s
Also see UNDERBEATS

SMITH, Kate P&R '27
(With Guy Lombardo's Orchestra)

Singles: 78 rpm

COLUMBIA 3-6 27-46
VICTOR 3-6 38-42
MGM 3-5 48

Singles: 7-inch

ATLANTIC 3-5 74
CRICKET 4-8
MGM 3-4 78
RCA 3-5 63-68
TOPS 4-6 60

Picture Sleeves

RCA 4-8 63-64

EPs: 7-inch

MGM 4-8 52-57
RCA 4-8 59

LPs: 10/12-inch

CAMDEN 4-8 70-73
CAPITOL 5-15 54-57
COLUMBIA (6000 series) 10-20 50
(10-inch LPs.)
HARMONY 5-12 57
KAPP 5-15 58
LION 5-12 57-60
MGM 5-15 52-66
METRO 5-10 67
RCA 5-15 63-80
RONDO 5-10 60s
TOPS 5-10
Also see LOMBARDO, Guy

SMITH, Keely LP '58

Singles: 78 rpm

CAPITOL 3-8 56-58

Singles: 7-inch

ATLANTIC 4-6 67
CAPITOL 5-15 56-58
DOLTON 3-5 64
DOT 5-10 59-62
RCA 3-6 66-71
REPRISE 4-8 63-66

Picture Sleeves

CAPITOL ("Capitol Introduces a New Capitol Artist") 4-8 56
(Generic Capitol "New Artist" sleeve. Includes Kelly Smith bio/picture insert.)
DOT 8-12 60

EPs: 7-inch

CAPITOL 10-15 58-59
DOT 8-12 60

LPs: 10/12-inch

CAPITOL 10-25 58-75
DOT 10-15 59-62
HARMONY 5-10 69
REPRISE 8-15 63-65
Also see PRIMA, Louis, & Keely Smith
Also see SINATRA, Frank, & Keely Smith

SMITH, Kenny

Singles: 7-inch

CHESS 4-8 65
FRATERNITY 4-8 63-67
GAR 10-20 60s
Also see JACKSON, Jeri, & Kenny Smith

SMITH, L.C.

Singles: 7-inch

WEDGE (1020 "Corrine, Corrina") 25-35

SMITH, Larry

Singles: 7-inch

DORE 4-8 64

SMITH, Leon
(With the Basics; with Ponsonby Sisters; with Orbit Rockers)

Singles: 7-inch

EPIC (9326 "Little '40 Ford") 25-35 59
LAVENDAR (1851 "Jailer, Bring Me Water") 15-20 65
WILLIAMETTE (101 "Little '40 Ford") 75-125 59
(First issue.)
WILLIAMETTE (105 & 106) 10-15 59
(Titles not known.)

SMITH, Leslie, & Merry Clayton

Singles: 7-inch

ELEKTRA 3-5 82
Also see CLAYTON, Merry

SMITH, Lester, Jr., & Upnilons
("Lester [Smith] Jr. & the Upnilons)

Singles: 7-inch

LUMMTONE (117-13 "Do the Movement") 10-20 64

SMITH, Little George: see SMITH, George

SMITH, Liza

Singles: 7-inch

BIG TOP 10-20 60

SMITH, Lloyd "Fat Man"
(With Caldonia's Boys Orchestra)

Singles: 78 rpm

PEACOCK 10-20 53

Singles: 7-inch

PEACOCK (1593 "Giddy-Up, Giddy-Up") 20-30 53
PEACOCK (1611 "My Clock Stopped") 20-30 53

SMITH, Logan C&W '74

Singles: 7-inch

BRAND X 3-5 74

SMITH, Lonnie LP '70

Singles: 7-inch

BLUE NOTE 3-6 69-70
GROOVE MERCHANT 3-5 75
LRC 3-5 78-79

LPs: 10/12-inch

BLUE NOTE 8-15 68-70
COLUMBIA 10-15 67
GROOVE MERCHANT 5-10 75-76
KUDU 5-10 71
LRC 5-10 78

SMITH, Lonnie Liston LP '75
(With the Cosmic Echoes)

Singles: 12-inch

COLUMBIA 4-8 79

Singles: 7-inch

COLUMBIA 3-5 78-80
DOCTOR JAZZ 3-4 83
FLYING DUTCHMAN 3-5 75-76
RCA 3-5 77

LPs: 10/12-inch

COLUMBIA 5-10 78-79
DOCTOR JAZZ 5-8 83
FLYING DUTCHMAN 6-12 73-76
RCA 5-10 76-77

SMITH, Lorenzo

Singles: 7-inch

C.J. 5-10 59
GLENN 5-10
MAR-VEL 8-12 62
Also see PARKER, Little Willie

SMITH, Lou C&W '60

Singles: 7-inch

KRC 8-12 59-60
SALVO 5-10 61
TOP RANK 5-10 60

SMITH, Lucy, Singers

Singles: 78 rpm

STATES 5-10 55

Singles: 7-inch

STATES 10-20 55

SMITH, Mack Allen

Singles: 7-inch

ACE (3011 "King of Rock & Roll") 15-25 60s
ACE (3014 "Baby, When I'm Gone") 15-25 60s
CYNTHIA (1961 "Lonely Weekends") 15-25
DELTA SOUNDS (1 "I See the Want in Your Eyes") 8-12 60s
JAB 5-10 67
MARITEEN (6602 "Big Silver Tears") 50-75 60s
STATUE (602 "Such a Night") 25-50 60s
STATUE (607 "Mean Ol' Frisco") 25-50 60s
VEE-EIGHT (1006 "I'm a Hobo Man") 500-750 64

SMITH, Margo C&W '75

Singles: 7-inch

AMI 3-4 82
BERMUDA DUNES 3-4 85
MOON SHINE 3-4 83-84
PLAYBACK 3-4 88
20TH CENTURY 3-6 75
W.B. 3-5 76-81

LPs: 10/12-inch

BERMUDA DUNES 10-15
CAMERON 5-8 81
20TH CENTURY 6-12 75
W.B. 5-10 75-80
Also see ALLEN, Rex, Jr., & Margo Smith

SMITH, Margo, & Tom Grant C&W '85

Singles: 7-inch

BERMUDA DUNES 3-4 85
Also see GRANT, Tom

SMITH, Margo, & Norro Wilson C&W '77
(Margo & Norro)

Singles: 7-inch

W.B. 3-5 77
Also see SMITH, Margo
Also see WILSON, Norro

SMITH, Martha

Singles: 7-inch

CAMEO 4-8 65

SMITH, Marvin

Singles: 7-inch

BRUNSWICK 4-8 66-67
MAYFIELD 3-5 71
Also see ARTISTICS
Also see FOUR EL DORADOS

SMITH, Maurice

LPs: 10/12-inch

MAINSTREAM 10-15 66

SMITH, Melvin
(With the Night Riders)

Singles: 7-inch

CAMEO 15-20 58
CHIME 8-12 62
GROOVE 10-20 54
METRO 10-15 59
RCA 15-25 52-54
SMASH 8-12 62
Also see NIGHTRIDERS

SMITH, Michael

LPs: 10/12-inch

STORYVILLE 8-10 72

SMITH, Mike, & Barbara Barrow

LPs: 10/12-inch

BELL 8-10 74

SMITH, Moses

Singles: 7-inch

DIONN (508 "Hey Love") 25-50 68

SMITH, Myrna

Singles: 7-inch

VERVE 4-8 67
Also see SWEET INSPIRATIONS

SMITH, O.C. P&R/LP '68
(With Joe Lipman & Orchestra; Ocie Smith)

Singles: 78 rpm

CADENCE 5-10 56-57
MGM 5-10 56

Singles: 7-inch

BIG TOP (3039 "Well, I'm Dancin'") 8-12 60
BROADWAY 10-20
CADENCE (1304 "Forbidden Fruit") 10-20 56
CADENCE (1312 "If You Don't Love Me") 10-20 57
CADENCE (1329 "Too Late") 10-20 57
CARIBOU 3-5 76-77
CITATION 10-15 59
COLUMBIA 3-8 66-74
FAMILY 3-5 80
GORDY 3-5 82
MGM (12321 "At Last My Baby's Comin' Home") 10-20 56
MOTOWN 3-5 82
RENDEZVOUS 3-4 86-87
SHADYBROOK 3-4 78
SOUL WEST 3-5 72
SOUTH BAY 3-4 82

Picture Sleeves

COLUMBIA 5-8 69

LPs: 10/12-inch

CARIBOU 5-10 79
COLUMBIA 8-12 67-74
HARMONY 8-10 71
MGM 8-10 72
MOTOWN 5-10 82
SOUTH BAY 5-8 82

SMITH, Patti LP '75
(Patti Smith Group)

Singles: 7-inch

ARISTA 3-5 76-79
MER (601 "Hey Joe") 50-75 74
SIRE 3-6 74-77

Picture Sleeves

ARISTA 4-8 78-79

LPs: 10/12-inch

ARISTA 6-12 75-88
Members: Patti Smith; Ivan Kral; Jay Dee Daugherty; Lenny Kaye; Allen Lanier; Richard Sohl; Andy Paley.
Also see KAYE, Lenny
Also see PALEY BROTHERS

SMITH, Penny

Singles: 78 rpm

KAHILL 5-10 55-56

Singles: 7-inch

KAHILL 8-15 55-56

SMITH, Phyllis

Singles: 7-inch

YEW (1003 "I Need Somebody to Love") 4-6

SMITH, R.C: see SMITH, Robert Curtis

SMITH, Ralph

Singles: 7-inch

COLLIER 5-10 61

SMITH, Ray P&R '60

Singles: 7-inch

ABC 3-5 73
ADAIRE (90 "It's Love") 10-20 61
CELEBRITY CIRCLE (6901 "I Walk the Line") 5-10 64
CINNAMON 3-5 73-74
COLLECTABLES 3-4 80s
CORONA 3-5 75-77
DIAMOND (193 "Everybody's Goin' Somewhere") 5-10 65
HEART (250 "Gone Baby, Gone") 150-200 50s
INFINITY (003 "After This Night Is Through") 10-20 61
INFINITY (007 "Let Yourself Go") 10-20 61
JUDD (1016 "Rockin' Little Angel") 15-25 59
JUDD (1017 "Put Your Arms Around Me Honey") 15-25 59
JUDD (1019 "Makes Me Feel Good") 15-25 60
JUDD (1021 "Blond Hair, Blue Eyes") 15-25 60
NATIONAL 10-20
SMASH (1787 "Those Four Precious Years") 5-8 62
SSS INT'L 3-5 70s
SSS/SUN 3-5 70s
SUN (298 "Right Behind You Baby") 20-30 58
SUN (308 "Why Why Why") 15-25 59
SUN (319 "Rockin' Bandit") 15-25 59
SUN (372 "Traveling Salesman") 15-25 62
SUN (375 "Candy Doll") 15-25 62
TOLLIE (9029 "Did We Have a Party") 8-10 64
VEE JAY (579 "Robbin' the Cradle") 5-10 64
W.B. (5371 "I'm Snowed") 5-10 63
WIX 3-5 78

LPs: 10/12-inch

BOOT 5-10 78
JUDD (701 "Travelin' with Ray") 200-300 60
T (56062 "Best of Ray Smith") 20-30
WIX 10-15
Also see DONNER, Ral / Ray Smith / Bobby Dale
Also see K-DOE, Ernie / Ray Smith

SMITH, Ray / Pat Cupp

LPs: 10/12-inch

CROWN (5364 "Ray Smith & Pat Cupp") 50-75 63
Also see CUPP, Pat
Also see SMITH, Ray

SMITH, Ray

Singles: 7-inch

NU-TONE (1182 "She's Mine") 4-8 64
TOPPA (1071 "Almost Alone") 5-10 62

LPs: 10/12-inch

COLUMBIA 15-25 63

SMITH, Red

Singles: 78 rpm

CORAL 10-15 54

Singles: 7-inch

CORAL 15-25 54

SMITH, Red Willie

Singles: 78 rpm

FOLKWAYS 10-15 50

SMITH, Rex P&R/LP '79

Singles: 7-inch

COLUMBIA 3-5 76-81

Picture Sleeves

COLUMBIA 3-5 79-80

LPs: 10/12-inch

COLUMBIA 5-10 76-81
Also see REX

SMITH, Rex, & Rachel Sweet

Singles: 7-inch

COLUMBIA 3-5 81

Picture Sleeves

COLUMBIA 3-5 81
Also see SMITH, Rex
Also see SWEET, Rachel

SMITH, Richard

Singles: 7-inch

HI-Q (5042 "Mama Cried") 5-10

SMITH, Richard Jon D&D '83

Singles: 12-inch

JIVE 4-6 83

Singles: 7-inch

JIVE 3-4 83

LPs: 10/12-inch

JIVE 5-8 83

SMITH, Rick C&W '76

Singles: 7-inch

CIN KAY 3-5 76

SMITH, Rick, Band

LPs: 10/12-inch

DEEP DISH RECORDS 5-10 81

SMITH, Robert

Singles: 7-inch

CAMELIA (100 "Traveling Sam") 25-35

SMITH, Robert Curtis
(R.C. Smith)

Singles: 7-inch

ARHOOLIE 5-10 61

LPs: 10/12-inch

PRESTIGE BLUESVILLE 20-30 63

SMITH, Robert T.
Singles: 7-inch
BOBBIN'...15-25 60

SMITH, Roger P&R '59
Singles: 7-inch
JEROME...4-8 61
W.B. ...5-10 59
Picture Sleeves
W.B. ...10-15 59
LPs: 10/12-inch
W.B. (1305 "Beach Romance")...30-40 59

SMITH, Ron Louis
LPs: 10/12-inch
SUNSHINE SOUND...5-8 79

SMITH, Ronnie
Singles: 7-inch
BRUNSWICK (55137 "Lookie Lookie Lookie")...30-50 59
HAMILTON...10-20 58
IMPERIAL...15-25 60

SMITH, Roy
Singles: 7-inch
ASCOT...5-8 68
LIBERTY...5-10
PRESTIGE (2301 "Love Me Long")...20-30
U.A. ...4-8 70
VANGUARD...10-15

SMITH, Russell C&W '84
Singles: 7-inch
CAPITOL...3-4 84
EPIC...3-4 88-89
LPs: 10/12-inch
CAPITOL...5-10 82
Also see AMAZING RHYTHM ACES

SMITH, Sammi C&W '68
Singles: 7-inch
COLUMBIA...3-8 67-69
CYCLONE...3-5 79
ELEKTRA...3-5 75-78
MEGA...3-5 70-76
SOUND FACTORY...3-4 80-82
STEP ONE...3-4 86
TRIP...3-4 74
ZODIAC...3-4 76
Picture Sleeves
MEGA...3-5 70
LPs: 10/12-inch
BARNABY...5-10
BUCKBOARD...5-10 70s
CYCLONE...5-8 79
ELEKTRA...5-10 76-78
HARMONY...5-10 71
MEGA...5-10 70-75
PICKWICK...5-10 70s
SOUND FACTORY...3-4 80-82
STEP ONE...3-4 85-86
TRIP...5-8 74
U.A. ...5-10 75
ZODIAC...5-8 76
Also see HART, Freddie / Sammi Smith / Jerry Reed
Also see NELSON, Willie
Also see STEVENS, Even, & Sammi Smith

SMITH, Sammy
Singles: 7-inch
MONA...15-25 59
WE-RE-BEL (102 "Satellite Rock")...100-200 58

SMITH, Shad
Singles: 7-inch
SMASH...4-8 62

SMITH, Shelby
Singles: 7-inch
REBEL (728 "Rockin' Mama")...25-35 62

SMITH, Shorty, & His Rhythm
(Arthur Smith)
Singles: 78 rpm
LENOX...15-25 48
Also see SONNY BOY & LONNIE
Also see SONNY BOY & SAM

SMITH, Shuggy
(Shuggy Ray Smith)
Singles: 7-inch
IMPERIAL...5-10 63
KAMMY...5-10 62
PZAZZ...4-8 68-69
TOWER...5-10 66

SMITH, Smiley
Singles: 7-inch
APOLLO...5-10 59

SMITH, Smokey
Singles: 7-inch
CARDINAL (501 "Bayou Boogie")..20-30

SMITH, Smoochie
Singles: 7-inch
CASTAWAYS (1000 "It's All Your Fault")...15-25

SMITH, Snuffy, & Hootin' Holler Twisters
Singles: 7-inch
TEMPWOOD...4-8 62

SMITH, Somethin,' & Redheads P&R '55
Singles: 78 rpm
EPIC...4-8 54-57
Singles: 7-inch
EPIC...5-10 54-59
MGM...4-8 61
Picture Sleeves
EPIC...10-15 58
EPs: 7-inch
EPIC...10-20 59
LPs: 10/12-inch
EPIC...15-25 59
MGM...10-20 61

SMITH, Spadachene
Singles: 7-inch
LYNNE...8-12 64

SMITH, Steve, & Naked
Singles: 7-inch
PAYOLA...5-10 80
Picture Sleeves
PAYOLA...5-10 80

SMITH, Steve, & Soule Champions
Singles: 7-inch
SOCK-IT...4-8 68

SMITH, Susan
Singles: 7-inch
DYNAMIC SOUND (502 "A Letter to Susan")...10-15 62
ROULETTE...5-8 66
SAL...5-10 63-64

SMITH, Sylvia
LPs: 10/12-inch
ABC...8-10 75

SMITH, Tab P&R '51
(With His Band; with His Orchestra; with Robie Kirk & the Ruppert-Aires)
Singles: 78 rpm
ARCO...5-10 48
ATLANTIC...10-15 52
CHESS...5-10 52
DECCA...5-10 44
HARLEM...5-10 46
HUB...5-10 45-46
KING...5-10 46
MANOR...5-10 44-48
QUEEN...5-10 46
REGIS...5-10 44
SOUTHERN...5-10 46
20TH CENTURY...5-10 45
UNITED...5-15 51-57
Singles: 7-inch
ARGO...10-20 58-59
ATLANTIC (961 "Echo Blues")...15-25 52
B&F...10-15 61
CHECKER...10-15 59
CHESS...20-40 52
EBONY (1008 "Romance Time")...50-100 58
KING (4000 series)...20-40 52
KING (5000 series)...10-15 60-61
UNITED (Black vinyl)...15-25 51-57
UNITED (Red vinyl)...25-50 51
EPs: 7-inch
KING (263 "Tab Smith")...15-25 54
LPs: 10/12-inch
CHECKER (2971 "Keeping Tab") 50-100 59
(Black vinyl.)
CHECKER (2971 "Keeping Tab")...200-400 59
(Multi-color vinyl. Promotional issue only.)
UNITED (001 "Music Styled by Tab Smith")...75-125 52
UNITED (003 "Red Hot and Cool Blue Moods")...75-125 53
Also see POMUS, Doc

SMITH, Thunder
(Wilson Smith)
Singles: 78 rpm
ALADDIN (165 "West Coast Blues")...50-100 46
ALADDIN (166 "L.A. Blues")...50-100 46
GOLD STAR (615 "Cruel Hearted Woman")...50-75 47
GOLD STAR (644 "Sante Fe Blues")...50-75 49
Also see HOPKINS, Lightnin,' & Thunder Smith
Also see STONEHAM, Luther
Also see THOMAS, Andrew

SMITH, Thunder, & Rockie
Singles: 78 rpm
DOWN TOWN (2011 "Thunder's Unfinished Boogie")...40-60 48
DOWN TOWN (2012 "New Worried Life Blues")...40-60 48
DOWN TOWN (2013 "West Coast Blues")...40-60 48
Members: Wilson Smith; Luther Stoneham.
Also see SMITH, Thunder

SMITH, Tommy
Singles: 7-inch
ABC...4-6 69
VANDAN...8-12 64

SMITH, Tony, & His Aristocrats
Singles: 78 rpm
MERCURY...5-10 56
Singles: 7-inch
MAD...10-15 58
MERCURY...10-15 56
Members: Tony Smith; Bill Casimir; Gene Gilmore.

SMITH, Truly
Singles: 7-inch
PARROT...3-6 67

SMITH, Verdelle P&R '66
Singles: 7-inch
CAPITOL...5-10 66-67
COLUMBIA...4-8 65
JANUS...3-5 75
Picture Sleeves
COLUMBIA...4-8 65
LPs: 10/12-inch
CAPITOL (2476 "In My Room") .150-250 66
JANUS...8-12 75

SMITH, Vince
Singles: 7-inch
FOUR WINDS...3-4 86-88
LPs: 10/12-inch
FOUR WINDS...5-10 87-88

SMITH, Warren P&R '57/C&W '60
Singles: 78 rpm
QUALITY...50-100 56
(Canadian.)
SUN...50-100 56-57
Singles: 7-inch
LIBERTY...6-12 60-64
MERCURY...4-8 68
QUALITY (1493 "Rock & Roll Ruby")...75-125 56
(Canadian.)
QUALITY (1558 "Ubangi Stomp")..50-75 56
(Canadian.)
SUN (239 "Rock 'M' Roll Ruby") 100-125 56
(With slight title misprint.)
SUN (239 "Rock 'N' Roll Ruby")...50-100 56
(Title is correct.)
SUN (250 "Ubangi Stomp")...50-75 56
SUN (268 "So Long I'm Gone")...15-25 57
SUN (286 "I've Got Love if You Want It")...15-25 58
SUN (314 "Sweet Sweet Girl")...15-25 59
SSS/SUN...3-5 80
W.B. (5125 "Dear Santa")...10-20 59
LPs: 10/12-inch
LIBERTY (3199 "First Country Collection")...35-45 61
(Monaural.)
LIBERTY (7199 "First Country Collection")...40-60 61
(Stereo.)

SMITH, Warren, & Shirley Collie C&W '61
Singles: 7-inch
LIBERTY...5-10 61
Also see COLLIE, Shirley
Also see SMITH, Warren

SMITH, Washington
Singles: 7-inch
OKEH...4-8 67

SMITH, Wendell
Singles: 7-inch
U.A. ...5-10 59

SMITH, Whispering
Singles: 7-inch
EXCELLO...4-8 63-64
LPs: 10/12-inch
EXCELLO...8-12

SMITH, Whistling Jack P&R '67
Singles: 7-inch
DERAM...4-6 67-69
LPs: 10/12-inch
DERAM...10-15 67

SMITH, Willie "Long Time"
Singles: 78 rpm
COLUMBIA...10-15 47-48
GENUINE...8-12

SMITH, Winfred
LPs:10/12-inch
RCA CUSTOM...10-20
TENNESSEE SQUIRE...8-12

SMITH, Youngblood
Singles: 7-inch
VERVE...8-12

SMITH, Yugene
Singles: 78 rpm
TRIODE...10-15 55
Singles: 7-inch
TRIODE (105 "No Dreams for Me")...15-25 55

SMITH BROTHERS
Singles: 7-inch
ORANGE...5-10 59
STARS UNLIMITED...5-10 66
T-NECK...10-20 70

SMITH CONNECTION
Singles: 7-inch
MUSIC MERCHANT...3-5 73
Members: Michael Smith; Louis Smith.
Also see LOVESMITH

SMITHER, Chris
LPs: 10/12-inch
POPPY...8-10 72

SMITHEREENS LP '86
Singles: 7-inch
CAPITOL/ENIGMA...3-4 88
ENIGMA...3-5 85-86
Picture Sleeves
CAPITOL/ENIGMA...3-4 88
ENIGMA...3-5 85-86
LPs: 10/12-inch
CAPITOL/ENIGMA...5-8 88-89
ENIGMA...5-10 85-89
Members: Pat Dinizio; Jim Babjak; Dennis Diken; Mike Mesaros.

SMITHS
Singles: 7-inch
COLUMBIA...5-10 68

SMITHS LP '84
Singles: 12-inch
SIRE...4-6 84-86
Singles: 7-inch
SIRE...3-4 84-88
LPs: 10/12-inch
SIRE...5-8 84-88
Members: Andy Rourke; Mike Joyce.
Also see O'CONNOR, Sinead

SMITHSONIAN INSTITUTE
Singles: 7-inch
TAMBOURINE...4-8 68

SMITTY & VISCOUNTS
Singles: 7-inch
LYNN...8-10 59

SMOGGS
Singles: 7-inch
EVENT...3-5

SMOKE
LPs: 10/12-inch
SIDEWALK (5912 "The Smoke")...30-40 68
Member: Michael Lloyd.
Also see CANNED HEAT

SMOKE
(John Orvis & Smoke)
Singles: 7-inch
UNI...5-10 69
LPs: 10/12-inch
UNI...15-25 69-70
Also see NOMADS

SMOKE
Singles: 7-inch
MO-SOUL (1971 "Oh Love")...5-8 71
SPEEDWAY...4-8 71

SMOKE CITY
Singles: 7-inch
EPIC...3-4 84-85

SMOKE RING P&R '69
Singles: 7-inch
BUDDAH...4-8 69
CERTRON...3-5 70
MALA...5-10 67

SMOKE RINGS
Singles: 7-inch
DOT (16975 "Love's the Thing")...10-15 66
PROSPECT (101 "Love's the Thing")...20-30 66
Also see LITTLE JOE & RAMRODS

SMOKE RISE
Singles: 7-inch
PARAMOUNT...4-6 71
LPs: 10/12-inch
PARAMOUNT (9000 "Survival of St. Joan")...10-20 71
(Includes 10-page booklet.)

SMOKESTACK
(Earls)
Singles: 7-inch
DAISY...4-8
DAKAR...4-8
Also see EARLS

SMOKESTACK LIGHTNIN' LP '69
Singles: 7-inch
BELL...4-6 68-70
WHITE WHALE...4-6 67
LPs: 10/12-inch
BELL...10-15 69

SMOKEY
(John Condon)
Singles: 7-inch
S&M (104 "Leather")...4-6
(White label.)
S&M (104 "Leather")...3-5
(Black label.)
S&M (105 "Topaz"/"Topanga")...4-8
(Colored vinyl.)
S&M (105 "Topaz"/"Butchie & Claudine")...3-5
(Colored vinyl.)
S&M (106 thru 108)...3-5
SMOKEY ("Leather")...4-8
SMOKEY ("Leather")...8-12
(Compact 33 single.)
Picture Sleeves
S&M...4-8

SMOKEY / Vince La Spada
Singles: 7-inch
CAMEO (254 "There's a Hole in My Cigarette")...8-12 63
Also see LA SPADA, Vince

SMOKEY & HIS SISTER
Singles: 7-inch
COLUMBIA...4-8 67
W.B. ...3-6 69
LPs: 10/12-inch
W.B. ...10-15 68

SMOKEY BABE
LPs: 10/12-inch
ARHOOLIE...5-8
FOLK-LYRIC...15-20 60s
PRESTIGE BLUESVILLE...15-25 63

SMOKEY JOE
(Smokey Joe Baugh)
Singles: 78 rpm
FLIP...40-75 55
SUN...30-60 55
Singles: 7-inch
FLIP (228 "The Signifying Monkey")...100-150 55
SUN (228 "The Signifying Monkey")...75-125 55
SUN (393 "The Signifying Monkey")...25-50 64
Also see EMERSON, Billy "The Kid" / Smokey Joe
Also see TAYLOR, Bill, & Smokey Joe

SMOKEY VINCE LA SPADA
Singles: 7-inch
CAMEO...4-8 63

SMOKIE P&R '75
(Smokey)
Singles: 7-inch
MCA...3-5 75
RSO...3-5 76-79
LPs: 10/12-inch
MCA...8-10 75
RSO...5-10 76-79
Members: Chris Norman; Terry Utley; Peter Spencer.
Also see QUATRO, Suzi, & Chris Norman

SMOKY & FABULOUS BLADES
Singles: 7-inch
DORE (723 "Jerk, Baby, Jerk")...25-35 65

SMOOTH TONES
Singles: 78 rpm
EMBER (1001 "Dear Diary")...15-25 56
Singles: 7-inch
COLLECTABLES...3-4 80s
EMBER (1001 "Dear Diary")...40-60 56
(Red label.)
EMBER (1001 "Dear Diary")...15-25 60
(Multi-color label.)

SMOOTHIES
Singles: 7-inch
DECCA...10-15 60
Members: John Phillips; Scott McKenzie.
Also see McKENZIE, Scott
Also see PHILLIPS, John

SMOOTHTONES
(With the Walt Harper's Orchestra)
Singles: 78 rpm
JEM...20-30 55
OKEH...20-30 57
Singles: 7-inch
JEM (412 "Bring Back Your Love")...50-75 55
OKEH (7078 "Little Cupid")...25-50 57

SMOTHERMAN, Michael
Singles: 7-inch
WINDSONG (2416 "Michael Smotherman")...5-10 75

SMOTHERS, Dick
Singles: 7-inch
MERCURY (72717 "Saturday Night at the World")...10-20 67
Picture Sleeves
MERCURY (72717 "Saturday Night at the World")...15-25 67
Also see SMOTHERS BROTHERS

SMOTHERS, Smokey
Singles: 7-inch
FEDERAL (12385 "Crying Tears").15-25 60
FEDERAL (12395 "I Ain't Gonna Be No Monkey Man No More")...15-25 60
FEDERAL (12405 "Come On, Rock Little Girl")...15-25 61
FEDERAL (12420 "Honey, I Ain't Teasin' ")...15-25 61
FEDERAL (12441 "Blind and Dumb Man")...15-25 61
FEDERAL (12466 "Twist with Me Annie")...10-20 60
FEDERAL (12488 "Give It Back")..10-20 63
FEDERAL (12503 "The Case Is Closed")...10-20 63
LPs: 10/12-inch
KING (779 "Backporch Blues")..500-800 62

SMOTHERS BROTHERS LP '62
Singles: 7-inch
MERCURY...5-10 62-65
SMOTHERS INCORPORATED ("The Christmas Bunny")...25-35 69
(No selection number used. Promotional issue only.)
Picture Sleeves
MERCURY (72483 "Three Song")..8-12 64
MERCURY (72519 "The Toy Song")...8-12 65
SMOTHERS INCORPORATED ("The Christmas Bunny")...25-50 69
(Promotional issue only.)
EPs: 7-inch
MERCURY (104 "Comedy Hour")..10-15 68
(Promotional issue only.)
MERCURY (628 "Two Sides")...10-20 62
LPs: 10/12-inch
MERCURY (20 "Best of the Smothers Brothers")...25-35 64
(Promotional issue only.)
MERCURY (25 "Brothers Smothers Month")...25-35 64
(Promotional issue only. Open-end interview.)
MERCURY (20000 series, except 20904)...10-20 61-68
(Monaural.)
MERCURY (20904 "It Must Have Been Something I Said")...15-20 64
(Commercial issue.)
MERCURY (20904 "It Must Have Been Something I Said")...20-30 60s
(White label. Promotional issue. Has some different material than on commercial copies.)
MERCURY (60000 series)...12-25 61-68
(Stereo.)
Members: Dick Smothers; Tom Smothers.

Also see SMOTHERS, Dick
Also see TOM & DICK
Also see WILLIAMS, Mason / Smothers Brothers

SMUBBS
Singles: 7-inch
ABC 4-8 66
MONUMENT 4-8 68-69
SPRING 4-8 68
LPs: 10/12-inch
MONUMENT 10-15 69

SMUGGLERS
Singles: 7-inch
NARDWUAR (2 "Up and Down") 3-5 90
LPs: 10/12-inch
NARDWUAR (3 "At Marineland") 8-10 90
POPLLAMA (22 "Atlanta Whiskey Flats") 5-10 92
(Label does not show artist or titles. That information plus group bio and photos are on an 8 x 10 insert sheet.)
Members: Grant Lawrence; Nicholas Thomas; David Carswell; K. Beezley; Bryce Dunn.

SMYTH, Patty P&R/LP '87
Singles: 7-inch
COLUMBIA 3-4 87
Picture Sleeves
COLUMBIA 3-4 87
LPs: 10/12-inch
COLUMBIA 5-8 87
Also see DION
Also see SCANDAL

SNAFU
LPs: 10/12-inch
CAPITOL 8-10 73-75

SNAIL P&R/LP '78
Singles: 7-inch
CREAM 3-5 78-79
LPs: 10/12-inch
CREAM 5-10 78-79

SNAILS
Singles: 7-inch
PERFECTIONS 8-12

SNAKEFINGER
Singles: 7-inch
RALPH 3-4 81
Picture Sleeves
RALPH 3-5 81
LPs: 10/12-inch
RALPH 5-10 81-82

SNAP! LP '90
Singles: 7-inch
ARISTA 3-4 90
LPs: 10/12-inch
ARISTA 5-8 90

SNAPPERS
Singles: 7-inch
IMPERIAL 4-8 69
20TH FOX 10-15 59

SNAPSHOTS
Singles: 7-inch
FEDERAL (12496 "I Need You") 15-20 63

SNATCH
EPs: 7-inch
BOMP 8-10 75

SNEAKER P&R/LP '81
Singles: 7-inch
HANDSHAKE 3-4 81-82
Picture Sleeves
HANDSHAKE 3-4 81
LPs: 10/12-inch
HANDSHAKE 5-10 81

SNEAKERS
Singles: 7-inch
DELTA (2141 "It's Just Not Funny Anymore") 15-25 60s

SNEAKERS
Singles: 7-inch
BEARSVILLE 3-5 80
LPs: 10/12-inch
CITY LIGHTS 5-10 80

SNEAKERS & LACE
Singles: 7-inch
P.I.P. 3-6 77
LPs: 10/12-inch
ARTH 5-10 78
P.I.P. 5-10 77

SNEAKY PETE & SNEAKERS
(Pete Kleinow)
Singles: 7-inch
ALWAYS in SOUNDS (200 "One Part of the Human Race") 15-25 67
LPs: 10/12-inch
SHILO (4086 "Sneaky Pete") 20-30 79
Also see see FLYING BURRITO BROTHERS

SNEED, Brady & Grady
Singles: 7-inch
DOLTON (38 "Little Bitty Heart") 8-12 61
Also see GRADY & BRADY
Also see SNEED, Grady

SNEED, Don, & Sneed Family
Singles: 7-inch
CASCADE 4-8 62
Also see SNEED FAMILY

SNEED, Grady
Singles: 7-inch
REPRISE 4-8 63
Also see SNEED, Brady & Grady

SNEED, Leslie
(With the Sneed Family)
Singles: 7-inch
CASCADE 5-10 60-62
Also see SNEED FAMILY

SNEED, Lois
Singles: 7-inch
CAPITOL 3-5 73

SNEED, Mary
Singles: 7-inch
CAPITOL 4-8 64

SNEED FAMILY
Singles: 7-inch
CASCADE 5-10 62
Members: Don Sneed; Leslie Sneed.
Also see SNEED, Don, & Sneed Family
Also see SNEED, Leslie

SNEEKERS
Singles: 7-inch
COLUMBIA 5-10 65
Picture Sleeves
COLUMBIA 10-15 65

SNEEZER, Ebe, & Epidemics
(Featuring John D. Loudermilk)
Singles: 7-inch
COLONIAL 10-15 57
Also see LOUDERMILK, John D.

SNEL, Billy
Singles: 7-inch
WILD (100 "One Too Many Heads") 50-75 60

SNELL, Annette
Singles: 7-inch
DIAL (Except 1023) 4-8 73-74
DIAL (1023 "You Oughta Be Here with Me") 10-15 73
EPIC 3-5 77

SNELL, Eddie
Singles: 7-inch
IMPACT 5-10 61
PROMOTIONAL 10-15

SNELL, Tony
LPs: 10/12-inch
ESP 10-12

SNIDER, Len
(With the Jokers)
Singles: 7-inch
ALL BOY (8507 "Everyone Knows") 10-20 62
ALL BOY (8514 "I'm So Lonely") 5-10 64
ALL BOY (8516 "Nobody Knows") 5-10 64

SNIDER, Tony
Singles: 7-inch
WESTWOOD 5-10 60

SNIFF 'N' THE TEARS P&R/LP '79
Singles: 7-inch
ATLANTIC 3-5 79-80
MCA 3-5 81
LPs: 10/12-inch
ATCO 5-10 79
ATLANTIC 5-10 79-80
MCA 5-10 81
Members: Paul Roberts; Mick Dyche; Luigi Salvoni; Alan Fealdman; Chris Birkin; Noz Netto.
Also see NETTO, Loz

SNOBS
Singles: 7-inch
LONDON 5-8 64

SNODGRASS, Elmer, & Musical Pioneers C&W '60
Singles: 7-inch
DECCA 4-8 60-61

SNO-FLAKES
Singles: 7-inch
HI NOTE 4-8 64

SNOOKY & MOODY
Singles: 78 rpm
MARVEL ("Stockyard Blues") 75-100 47
(Selection number not known.)
OLD SWINGMASTER (18 "Boogie") 40-60 48
OLD SWINGMASTER (22 "Stockyard Blues") 40-60 48
PLANET (101 "Boogie") 75-100 48
Members: James Edward Pryor; Floyd Jones.
Also see PRYOR, Snooky

SNOOPY & OTHERS
Singles: 7-inch
HICKORY (1432 "You Better Take Me Home") 10-15 67

SNOPEK III, Sigmund
Singles: 7-inch
COUTH YOUTH 3-4 83
MOUNTAIN RAILROAD 3-5 79-81
LP: 10/12-inch
CHAMELEON 5-8 87
COUTH YOUTH (1001 "Nobody to Dream") 10-15 75
AKASHIC (1002 "Trinity Seize, Sees, Seas") 10-15 74
MOUNTAIN RAILROAD 8-12 78-82
WATER STREET (1001 "Virginia Wolf") 10-15 72

SNOW
Singles: 7-inch
CASTLE (108 "Johnny B. Goode") 10-20
EPIC 5-10 68-69
LPs: 10/12-inch
EPIC 10-20 69

SNOW, B.F.
Singles: 7-inch
DEE BEE (20 "Elvis Is a Legend") 4-6 77

SNOW, Eddie
Singles: 78 rpm
SUN (226 "Ain't That Right") 40-60 55
Singles: 7-inch
SUN (226 "Ain't That Right") 75-100 55

SNOW, Glenn
Singles: 7-inch
KANGAROO 10-15 61-62

SNOW, Hank C&W '49
(The Singing Ranger & His Rainbow Ranch Boys; with Kelly Foxton)
Singles: 78 rpm
BLUEBIRD 15-30 40s
RCA 5-10 49-57
Singles: 7-inch
RCA (0100 & 0900 series) 3-5 69-74
(Orange labels.)
RCA (0300 & 0400 series) 8-12 50-51
(Green or gray labels.)
RCA (4346 thru 7748) 5-10 52-60
RCA (7803 thru 9907) 3-6 61-70
RCA (10000 & 11000 series) 3-5 74-80
Picture Sleeves
RCA 4-8 63
EPs: 7-inch
RCA (295 thru 1113) 12-25 54-56
RCA (1156 "Old Doc Brown") 35-45 55
RCA (1200 series) 20-30 55
RCA (1400 series) 15-25 57
RCA (3000 series) 30-50 52-54
RCA (4000 series) 15-20 58
RCA (5000 series) 12-25 58-60
LPs: 10/12-inch
CAMDEN 8-15 59-74
DETOUR 5-10
HANK SNOW SCHOOL of MUSIC (1149/50 "The Guitar") 250-300 58
(Special issue from the Hank Snow School of Music. Includes guitar instruction booklet.)
PICKWICK 5-10 75-76
RCA (0134 "Living Legend") 100-125 78
(RCA Special Products issue.)
RCA (0162 thru 0908) 5-10 73-75
RCA (1004 "I'm Movin' On") 15-20 82
(RCA Special Products issue.)
RCA (1052 thru 3511) 5-10 75-79
(With ""AHL1, "ANL1" or APL1" prefix.)
RCA (1113 "Just Keep-A-Movin' ") 25-35 55
(With "LPM" prefix.)
RCA (1156 "Old Doc Brown") 150-175 55
RCA (1233 thru 1861) 25-45 55-58
RCA (2043 thru 4708) 10-25 60-72
RCA (3026 "Country Classics") 75-150 52
(10-inch LP.)
RCA (3070 "Hank Snow Sings") 75-150 52
(10-inch LP.)
RCA 3131 "Hank Snow Salutes Jimmie Rodgers") 50-100 53
(10-inch LP.)
RCA (3192 "Tennessee Jamboree") 50-100 53
(10-inch LP.)
RCA (3220 "Country Western Caravan") 50-100 54
(10-inch LP.)
RCA (3267 "Country Guitar") 50-100 53
(10-inch LP.)
RCA (6014 "This Is My Story") 20-30 66
RCA SPECIAL PRODUCTS/KRAFT FOODS 10-20 64-67
(TV mail-order offer.)
RCA SPECIAL PRODUCTS/TEE VEE 10-15 74-78
READER'S DIGEST (216 "I'm Movin' On") 125-150
(Six-LP boxed set.)
Session: Jordanaires; Anita Kerr Singers; Jimmy Snow.
Also see JORDANAIRES
Also see KERR, Anita
Also see MARTIN, Janis / Hank Snow
Also see PRESLEY, Elvis / Hank Snow / Eddy Arnold / Hank Snow
Also see SOME of CHET'S FRIENDS

SNOW, Hank, & Chet Atkins
Singles: 78 rpm
RCA 4-8 55
Singles: 7-inch
RCA (5900 series) 5-10 55
LPs: 10/12-inch
RCA (2952 "Reminiscing") 20-30 64
RCA (4254 "By Special Request") 20-30 70
Also see ATKINS, Chet

SNOW, Hank, & Anita Carter C&W '51
(Anita Carter & Hank Snow; with the Rainbow Ranch Boys)
Singles: 78 rpm
RCA 4-8 51-56
Singles: 7-inch
RCA 8-12 51-56
LPs: 10/12-inch
RCA (2580 "Together Again") 15-25 62
Also see CARTER, Anita

SNOW, Hank / Hank Locklin / Porter Wagoner
LPs: 10/12-inch
RCA (2723 "Three Country Gentlemen") 15-25 63
Also see LOCKLIN, Hank
Also see SNOW, Hank
Also see WAGONER, Porter

SNOW, Hap, & Whirlwinds
Singles: 7-inch
FLEETWOOD (1005 "Banshee") 30-50

SNOW, Phoebe LP '74
Singles: 7-inch
COLUMBIA 3-5 76-78
MIRAGE 3-5 81
SHELTER 3-5 74-75
LPs: 10/12-inch
COLUMBIA 5-10 76-81
ELEKTRA 5-8 89
MCA 5-10 79
MIRAGE 5-10 81
SHELTER 8-10 74
Also see GOODMAN, Steve, & Phoebe Snow
Also see JEFFREYS, Garland, & Phoebe Snow
Also see SIMON, Paul, & Phoebe Snow

SNOW, Tom
Singles: 7-inch
CAPITOL 3-5 75-76
Picture Sleeves
CAPITOL 3-5 76
LPs: 10/12-inch
CAPITOL 8-10 75-76

SNOW, Valaida
Singles: 78 rpm
BEL-TONE 10-15 45
CHESS 25-50 53
DERBY 20-30 51
Singles: 7-inch
CHESS (1555 "I Ain't Gonna Tell") 50-100 53
DERBY (735 "Coconut Head") 50-100 51
(Colored vinyl.)

SNOW MEN
Singles: 7-inch
CHALLENGE 10-15 63
Members: Ed Medora; Vince Hozier; Marty DiGiovanni; Davey Holt.
Also see HOLT, Davey, & Hubcaps
Also see RANGERS
Also see SUNRAYS

SNOW WHITE: see WHITE, Snow

SNOWFLAKE
LPs: 10/12-inch
51 WEST 5-8 80s

SNOWMEN
(Concords)
Singles: 7-inch
HERALD (597 "Cold and Frosty Morning") 8-10 65
(Issued in 1963 on Herald 578, shown as by the Concords.)
Also see CONCORDS

SNUFF C&W '82
Singles: 7-inch
ELEKTRA 3-4 82
W.B./CURB 3-4 83
Member: Jim Bowling.

SNYDER, Jimmy C&W '70
Singles: 7-inch
E.I.O. 3-4 80
WAYSIDE 3-5 70

SNYDER, Rick C&W '88
Singles: 7-inch
CAPITOL 3-4 88

SNYDER, Terry, & All-Stars: see LIGHT, Enoch

SO P&R/LP '88
Singles: 7-inch
EMI 3-4 88
Picture Sleeves
EMI 3-4 88
LPs: 10/12-inch
EMI 5-8 88

SOBER, Errol P&R '79
Singles: 7-inch
ABC 3-5 74
ABNAK 3-5 70
BELL 3-5 72
CAPITOL 3-5 76
NUMBER ONE 3-4 79

SOCCER
LPs: 10/12-inch
TVI 5-10 80

SOCCIO, Gino P&R/LP '79
Singles: 12-inch
ATLANTIC 4-6 80-84
W.B./RFC 4-6 79-80
Singles: 7-inch
ATLANTIC 3-5 80-84
W.B./RFC 3-5 79-82
LPs: 10/12-inch
ATLANTIC 5-10 80-84
W.B./RFC 5-10 79-80

SOCIAL DEVIANTS
LPs: 10/12-inch
ALIVE/TOTAL ENERGY 5-10 95
(10-inch LP.)

SOCIAL DISTORTION LP '90
LPs: 10/12-inch
EPIC 5-8 90
RCA (43500 "Mommy's Little Monster") 8-10 90s
RCA (43501 "Prison Bound") 8-10 90s
RCA (43502 "Mainliner") 8-10 90s

SOCIAL OUTCASTS
Singles: 7-inch
SULTAN (1003 "Mad") 20-30

SOCIALAIRS
Singles: 7-inch
CRYSTALETTE 5-10 62

SOCIALITES
Singles: 7-inch
ARRAWAK 10-15 63
SCOTT 10-15
W.B. 5-10 64

SOCIETY
Singles: 7-inch
MARK VII (1005 "High & Mighty") 15-25 66
(One source shows this number as 105. We're not yet sure which is correct.)

SOCIETY
Singles: 7-inch
FEATURE (112 "For Me") 15-25 66
Members: Kevin Kohl; Roger Jerry; Mike Dennis; Kenny Rogers; John Blarjeske.

SOCIETY
Singles: 7-inch
A-B-E (1670 "It's Really Me") 8-12

SOCIETY GIRLS
Singles: 7-inch
VEE JAY (525 "S.P.C.L.G.") 8-10 63

SOCIETY HILL SEVEN
Singles: 7-inch
SWAN 4-8 64

SOCIETY OF SEVEN
LPs: 10/12-inch
SILVER SWORD 8-10
UNI 8-10 71
Members: Al Romero; Don Gay.

SOCIETY'S CHILDREN
Singles: 7-inch
ATCO (Except 6618) 5-10 67-68
ATCO (6618 "Tribute to the 4 Seasons") 10-20 69
CHA CHA 10-20 60s

SOCIETY'S PEOPLE
Singles: 7-inch
SMILE (432 "That's the Way of Our Day") 50-75 67

SOCRATES
LPs: 10/12-inch
PI 10-15 73

SOD
Singles: 7-inch
DECCA 3-5 71-72
LPs: 10/12-inch
DECCA 8-10 71-72

SODAMAN
LPs: 10/12-inch
VISUAL VINYL (1005 "Adventures of Sodaman") 30-40 83
(Picture disc. Canadian.)

SODER, Skip, Band
Singles: 7-inch
ARTEEN (1019 "Begin the Beguine") 10-20 62
CANDIX (336 "Beguine the Beguine") 8-12 62

SOEHNER, Barbara
Singles: 7-inch
ROARING 4-8 67

SOEUR SOURIRE: see SINGING NUN

SOFFICI, Piero P&R '61
Singles: 7-inch
JUBILEE 4-8 61
KIP 4-8 61

SOFFOS, Phil
Singles: 7-inch
MEM 5-10 61

SOFT BOYS
LPs: 10/12-inch
TWO CRABS 10-15
Member: Kimberley Rew.
Also see KATRINA & WAVES

SOFT CELL P&R/LP '82
Singles: 12-inch
SIRE 4-6 82
Singles: 7-inch
SIRE 3-5 82
Picture Sleeves
SIRE 3-5 82
LPs: 10/12-inch
ACCORD 5-10 82
SIRE 5-10 82-83
Members: Marc Almond; David Ball.
Also see ALMOND, Marc

SOFT MACHINE LP '68
Singles: 7-inch
PROBE 4-6 69
LPs: 10/12-inch
ACCORD 5-10 82
COLUMBIA 8-12 70-73
COMMAND (964 "Soft Machine") 15-20 73
(Two discs.)
PROBE (4500 "Soft Machine") 20-30 68
(With movable parts cover.)
PROBE (4500 "Soft Machine") 15-20 69
(With standard cover.)
PROBE (4505 "Soft Machine, Vol. 2") 15-25 69
RECKLESS 5-10 88

Also see WYATT, Robert

SOFT PILLOW
Singles: 7-inch
MUSICOR 3-6 69

SOFT SUMMER SOUL STRINGS
Singles: 7-inch
COLUMBIA.. 3-6 69

SOFT THUNDER
LPs: 10/12-inch
COLISEUM.. 5-10 80

SOFT TONES
Singles: 78 rpm
SAMPSON.. 15-25 55
Singles: 7-inch
SAMPSON (103 "My Mother's Eyes").. 75-100 55
(Rigid – or thicker – disc.)
SAMPSON (103 "My Mother's Eyes").. 25-50 55
(Flexible – or thinner – disc.)

SOFT TOUCH
Singles: 7-inch
POWWOW.. 3-4 87

SOFT WHITE UNDERBELLY
LPs: 10/12-inch
ELEKTRA ("Soft White Underbelly").. 35-45 69
(Selection number not known.)
Also see BLUE OYSTER CULT

SOFTLY, Mike
Singles: 7-inch
EPIC.. 3-5 70

SOF-TONES
Singles: 7-inch
CEEBEE (1062 "Oh Why") 4000-6000 57
Also see DELMIRAS / Sof-Tones

SOFTONES
(Soft Tones)
Singles: 7-inch
AVCO.. 4-6 73-75
H&L.. 3-5 77
Picture Sleeves
H&L.. 3-5 77

SOFTWINDS
Singles: 7-inch
HAC (105 "Cross My Heart")......... 15-20 61

SOHL, Don
(With the Roadrunners)
Singles: 7-inch
DREEM (728 "Voo-Doo")............ 50-100 59
DREEM (1005 "Knockout")........... 50-75 60
DREEM (1667 "Paper Doll")........... 40-60 61
DREEM (2349 "Twin City Bues").... 50-75 61
PALMS.. 25-50 60s
(Title and selection number not known.)

SOHO P&R/LP '90
Singles: 7-inch
ATCO.. 3-4 90
LPs: 10/12-inch
ATCO.. 5-8 90

SOIREE
LPs: 10/12-inch
ROADSHOW.. 8-10 79

SOL, Billy
Singles: 7-inch
DOMAR.. 4-8 66

SOLAR FLARE
Singles: 7-inch
RCA.. 3-5 78

SOLAR HEAT
Singles: 7-inch
ABC.. 3-5 79
LPs: 10/12-inch
ABC.. 5-10 79

SOLARIS R&B '80
Singles: 7-inch
DANA.. 3-5 80
LPs: 10/12-inch
DANA.. 5-10 80

SOLDIER BOYS
Singles: 7-inch
SCEPTER (1230 "I'm Your Soldier Boy").. 25-50 62
Session: Don Covay; Wally Roker.
Also see COVAY, Don

SOLE SURVIVORS
Singles: 7-inch
CORI (31008 "There Were Times").. 10-20 60s

SOLENOID
LPs: 10/12-inch
RUFERT.. 8-10 77

SOLID GOLD
Singles: 7-inch
PLAYBOY.. 3-5 75

SOLID GOLD
LPs: 10/12-inch
SOLID GOLD.. 8-10 77
Members: Gaynel Hodge; Jack Charles Wagner.
Also see CHARLES & KAYE
Also see HODGE, Gaynel

SOLID GOLD BAND C&W '81
Singles: 7-inch
NSD.. 3-4 81-82

SOLID GROUND
Singles: 7-inch
APRO (01 "Sad Now").................... 8-12 60s

SOLID SOUL
Singles: 7-inch
1-2-3.. 4-8 69

SOLIDEERS
Singles: 78 rpm
COLEMAN.. 10-15 49

SOLITAIRES
Singles: 78 rpm
OLD TOWN.. 50-100 55-57
Singles: 7-inch
ARGO (5316 "Walking Along") 10-20 58
MGM (13221 "Fool That I Am")...... 15-25 64
OLD TOWN (1000 "Blue Valentine").. 300-400 54
(Black vinyl.)
OLD TOWN (1000 "Blue Valentine").. 500-750 54
(Colored vinyl.)
OLD TOWN (1006/1007 "Please Remember My Heart").. 300-400 54
(Black vinyl.)
OLD TOWN (1006/1007 "Please Remember My Heart").. 500-750 54
(Colored vinyl.)
OLD TOWN (1006/1006 "Please Remember My Heart").. 100-200 54
(Note different flip side number.)
OLD TOWN (1008 "Chances I've Taken").. 200-400 54
OLD TOWN (1008 "Please Remember My Heart").. 15-25 60s
(Blue label.)
OLD TOWN (1010 "I Don't Stand a Ghost of a Chance").. 200-400 55
OLD TOWN (1012 "What Did She Say").. 150-300 55
(Logo in Old English typestyle.)
OLD TOWN (1012 "What Did She Say").. 50-100 56
(Logo in block typestyle.)
OLD TOWN (1014 ("Wedding")... 50-100 55
OLD TOWN (1015 ("Magic Rose").. 50-100 55
OLD TOWN (1019 ("Honeymoon").. 50-100 56
OLD TOWN (1026 "You've Sinned"/"You're Back With Me").. 150-300 56
OLD TOWN (1026 "You've Sinned"/"The Angels Sang").. 50-100 56
OLD TOWN (1032 "Give Me One More Chance").. 100-200 56
OLD TOWN (1034 "Walking Along").. 50-100 57
(Yellow label.)
OLD TOWN (1034 "Walking Along").. 15-25 60s
(Blue label.)
OLD TOWN (1044 "I Really Love You So").. 150-300 57
OLD TOWN (1049 "Walking and Talking").. 50-100 58
OLD TOWN (1059 "Please Remember My Heart").. 25-50 58
OLD TOWN (1066 "Embraceable You").. 25-50 59
OLD TOWN (1071 "Light a Candle in the Chapel").. 25-50 59
OLD TOWN (1096 "Lonesome Lover").. 25-50 60
OLD TOWN (1139 "The Time Is Here").. 15-25 63
LPs: 10/12-inch
MURRAY HILL.. 5-10 84
Members: Herman Curtis; Monte Owens; Bobby Williams; Bobby Baylor; Buzzy Willis; Pat Gaston; Milton Love; Reggie Barnes; Cecil Holmes; Fred Barksdale; Wally Roker.
Also see CADILLACS
Also see McFADDEN, Ruth
Also see REED, Ursula
Also see SOLITAIRES

SOLITARY CONFINEMENT
Singles: 7-inch
SOUND IMPRESSION.................... 8-12

SOLLEY, Jim
(With the Lubocs.)
Singles: 7-inch
DEB (8791 "Yes I Do")............... 15-20 59
LUBOC.. 8-12
NRC (511 "Yes I Do")................ 10-15 60
RCA.. 4-8
STESO.. 4-8

SOLO D&D '84
Singles: 12-inch
NEXT PLATINUM.. 4-6 84

SOLO, Sam E.
Singles: 7-inch
IMPERIAL.. 4-8 66

SOLO, Sandy
Singles: 7-inch
SEECO.. 6-12 59-60

SOLOMAN, King: see SOLOMON, King

SOLOMON, Ed
Singles: 7-inch
DIAMOND (160 "Beatle Flying Saucer").. 10-15 64

SOLOMON, King
(With the Lad Teens Band; King Soloman; Ellis Solomon)
Singles: 78 rpm
BIG TOWN (102 "Mean Trail")....... 20-30 53
Singles: 7-inch
ASHANTI (003 "I Got a Sweet Tooth").. 5-10 60s
BIG TOWN (102 "Mean Trail")....... 50-100 53
CADILLAC (503 "Louisiana Groove").. 5-10 60s
CAPITOL.. 4-6 69
CHECKER (980 "Non-Support Blues").. 10-20 61
DON-J.. 5-10 60s
FRANKLIN.. 5-10
HIGHLAND.. 4-8 69
KENT (446 "Mr. Bad Luck")............ 5-8 66
KENT (451 "S.K. Blues")............. 5-8 66
LE BAM (1201 "Something's Wrong with Me").. 15-25
MADER-D (302 "Little Dab Will Do It").. 10-15 60s
MAGNUM.. 3-6
RCA (8474 "I Believe").................. 4-6 64
RESIST.. 4-8 66
STANSON (003 "If I Were a Strong Man").. 5-8
TOMSEY.. 4-8 60s
WORLD'S.. 3-6
U.A. (967 "It's a Good Thing")......... 5-8 66
LPs: 10/12-inch
RCA (2837 "The Golden Voice of Gospel").. 10-15 64
RCA (2985 "You'll Never Walk Alone").. 10-15 65
RCA (3430 "Where He Leads Me").. 10-15 65

SOLOTONES
Singles: 78 rpm
EXCELLO (2060 "Pork & Beans").. 20-30 55
Singles: 7-inch
EXCELLO (2060 "Pork & Beans").. 50-100 55

SOLUTION
Singles: 7-inch
IGL.. 10-20 60s

SOLUTION
LPs: 10/12-inch
FIRST AMERICA.. 5-10 82
ROCKET.. 5-10 75

SOME, Belouis P&R '85
Singles: 12-inch
CAPITOL.. 4-6 85
Singles: 7-inch
CAPITOL.. 3-4 85
Picture Sleeves
CAPITOL.. 3-4 85
LPs: 10/12-inch
CAPITOL.. 5-10 85

SOME OF CHET'S FRIENDS C&W '67
Singles: 7-inch
RCA (0799 "Chet's Tune")............ 4-6 67
Picture Sleeves
RCA (0799 "Chet's Tune")............ 4-6 67
Members: Eddy Arnold; Bobby Bare; Don Bowman; Bud Brewer; Jim Ed Brown; Johnny Bush; Archie Campbell; Scotti Carson; Jessi Colter; Floyd Cramer; Pat Daisy; Danny Davis & Nashville Brass; Skeeter Davis; Jimmy Dean; Lester Flatt; Dallas Frazier; George Hamilton IV; Homer & Jethro; Waylon Jennings; Red Lane; Dickie Lee; Hank Locklin; John D. Loudermilk; Willie Nelson; Norma Jean; Dolly Parton; Kenny Price; Charley Pride; Jerry Reed; Johnny Russell; Connie Smith; Hank Snow; Nat Stuckey; Buck Trent; Porter Wagoner; Charlie Walker; Dottie West; Billy Edd Wheeler; Norro Wilson; Mac Wiseman.
Also see ARNOLD, Eddy
Also see BARE, Bobby
Also see BOWMAN, Don
Also see BROWN, Jim Ed
Also see BUSH, Johnny
Also see CAMPBELL, Archie
Also see COLTER, Jessi
Also see CRAMER, Floyd
Also see DAISY, Pat
Also see DAVIS, Danny
Also see DAVIS, Skeeter
Also see DEAN, Jimmy
Also see FLATT, Lester, & Earl Scruggs
Also see FRAZIER, Dallas
Also see HAMILTON, George, IV
Also see JENNINGS, Waylon
Also see LANE, Red
Also see LEE, Dickey
Also see LOCKLIN, Hank
Also see LOUDERMILK, John D.
Also see NELSON, Willie
Also see NORMA JEAN
Also see PARTON, Dolly
Also see PRICE, Kenny
Also see PRIDE, Charley
Also see REED, Jerry
Also see RUSSELL, Johnny
Also see SMITH, Connie
Also see SNOW, Hank
Also see STUCKEY, Nat
Also see WAGONER, Porter
Also see WALKER, Charlie
Also see WEST, Dottie
Also see WHEELER, Billy Edd
Also see WILSON, Norro
Also see WISEMAN, Mac

SOME OTHER ANIMAL
Singles: 7-inch
CYPHER (103 "All Alone on the Highway").. 10-15

SOMEBODY'S CHYLDREN
Singles: 7-inch
UPTOWN.. 4-8 66

Also see WHITCOMB, Ian

SOMERVILLE, David
Singles: 7-inch
PARAMOUNT.. 3-5 73
Picture Sleeves
PARAMOUNT.. 3-5 73
Also see DIAMONDS

SOMERVILLE, Jimmy LP '90
LPs: 10/12-inch
LONDON.. 5-8 90
Also see BRONSKI BEAT
Also see COMMUNARDS

SOMETHING WILD
Singles: 7-inch
PSYCHEDELIC (1691 "Trippin' Out").. 25-50 60s

SOMETHING YOUNG
Singles: 7-inch
FONTANA (1556 "Oh, Don't Come Crying").. 10-20 67

SOMMER, Bert P&R '70
Singles: 7-inch
BUDDAH.. 3-5 71
CAPITOL.. 3-5 77-78
ELEUTHERA.. 3-5 70
LPs: 10/12-inch
BUDDAH.. 8-12 71
CAPITOL.. 8-10 77
ELEUTHERA.. 10-15 70

SOMMERS, Elke
LPs: 10/12-inch
MGM (E-4321 "Love in Any Language").. 10-20 65
(Monaural.)
MGM (SE-4321 "Love in Any Language").. 15-25 65
(Stereo.)

SOMMERS, Gary
Singles: 7-inch
TOLLIE.. 4-8 64

SOMMERS, Joanie P&R '60
Singles: 7-inch
ABC.. 3-5 78
CAPITOL.. 4-6 67
COLUMBIA.. 4-8 66
HAPPY TIGER.. 3-5 70
W.B. (107 "Sommers' Hot, Sommers' Here").. 10-15 60
(Promotional issue only.)
W.B. (5000 series).. 4-8 60-65
W.B. (7000 series).. 3-5 68
LPs: 10/12-inch
COLUMBIA.. 10-20 66
DISCOVERY.. 5-10 83
W.B.. 15-25 59-62
Also see BYRNES, Edd "Kookie," with Joanie Sommers & Mary Kaye Trio
Also see NELSON, Rick / Joanie Sommers / Dona Jean Young

SOMMERS, Joanie, & Laurindo Almeida
LPs: 10/12-inch
W.B.. 15-25 64
Also see ALMEIDA, Laurindo
Also see SOMMERS, Joanie

SOMMERS, Richie
Singles: 7-inch
VALIANT.. 4-8 66

SOMMERS, Ronny
(Sonny Bono)
Singles: 7-inch
SAWMI (1001 "Don't Shake My Tree").. 25-35 61
(Label name misspelled. Should be "Swami.")
SWAMI (1001 "Don't Shake My Tree").. 15-25 61
(Label name spelled correctly.)
Also see SONNY

SON OF PETE
Singles: 7-inch
BESERKLEY.. 3-5 74

SONARS
Singles: 7-inch
VULCO.. 5-10 60
Picture Sleeves
VULCO.. 10-15 60

SONDRA & PENNY
Singles: 7-inch
ZUMA.. 5-10 60

SONG
Singles: 7-inch
MGM.. 3-5 70
LPs: 10/12-inch
MGM.. 10-15 70
Member: Curt Boetcher.
Also see BOETCHER, Curt

SONG SPINNERS
Singles: 7-inch
BIG.. 5-10 60s
POWER.. 5-10 60s

SONGCRAFTERS
(Joseph S. Powe's Songcrafters)
Singles: 7-inch
ANTON (106 "Please Tell Me").... 75-125 61

SONGSPINNERS
Singles: 7-inch
LEILA (1602 "Bobbie")............ 50-75 58

SONGWRITERS
Singles: 7-inch
ADAM'S RIB.. 3-5 77

SONIC PRISM
Singles: 7-inch
PAW PRINTZ (45127 "Situation") 10-20 60s

SONIC YOUTH LP '90
LPs: 10/12-inch
DGC.. 5-8 90
ENIGMA.. 5-10 80s
HOMESTEAD.. 5-10 80s
MFSL (257 "Goo").. 20-25 96
SST.. 5-10 80s
W.B. (71591 "Made in the USA")...... 8-12 90s
(Colored vinyl.)
Members: Thurston Moore; Kim Gordon; Lee Ranaldo; Steve Shelley.

SONIC'S RENDEZVOUS
Singles: 7-inch
ORCHIDE (1002 "City Slang")......... 5-10 78
Also see MC 5

SONICS
Singles: 7-inch
GAIETY (114 "Marlene")........ 1000-1500 59

SONICS
(With Bill Fontaine Orchestra)
Singles: 7-inch
NOCTURNE (110 "Triangle Love").. 50-75 59

SONICS
("Featuring Donald Sheffield")
Singles: 7-inch
AMCO (001 "It's You")............ 150-250 62
CANDLELITE (416 "Once in a Lifetime").. 10-15 63
CHECKER (922 "This Broken Heart").. 10-20 59
GROOVE (0112 "As I Live On") 100-150 59
HARVARD (801 "This Broken Heart").. 200-400 59
HARVARD (922 "This Broken Heart").. 25-50 59
JAMIE (1235 "Sugaree")............ 10-15 62
X-TRA (107 "Once In a Lifetime").. 500-1000 58
Members: Donald Sheffield; Kenny "Butch" Hamilton.
Also see 5 WINGS

SONICS
Singles: 7-inch
ARMONIA (102 "Funny")........... 100-150 62

SONICS
Singles: 7-inch
LITTLE MARK (1939 "Two Degrees North").. 10-20 62

SONICS
Singles: 7-inch
BYRON.. 5-10 64
Members: Myles Reese; Bobby White; Marty Markiewicz; Harry Jeroleman; Ginter Schatz; Bob Short.
Also see CHOSEN FEW

SONICS
Singles: 7-inch
BOMP.. 3-5 80
BURDETTE.. 4-8 75
ETIQUETTE (ET-11 "Psycho"/"The Witch").. 30-50 65
ETIQUETTE (11 "Keep a Knockin' ").. 20-30 64
ETIQUETTE (16 "Hustler")............ 20-30 65
ETIQUETTE (18 "Shot Down")...... 20-30 65
ETIQUETTE (23 "Louie Louie")...... 20-30 65
GREAT NORTHWEST MUSIC......... 3-5 79
JERDEN (809 "Love Lights")......... 8-12 66
JERDEN (810 "The Witch")........... 8-12 66
JERDEN (811 "Psycho")............... 8-12 66
JERDEN (909 "Love-Itis")............. 8-12 67
PICCADILLY (244 "Lost Love")...... 10-20 67
PICCADILLY (255 "Love-Itis")....... 15-25 67
UNI (55039 "Lost Love")............. 5-10 67
LPs: 10/12-inch
BOMP (4011 "Sinderella") 10-15 80
BUCKSHOT (001 "Explosives"). 150-175 73
ETIQUETTE (024 "Here Are the Sonics").. 100-150 66
ETIQUETTE (024 "Here Are the Sonics").. 5-10 84
(Reissues the 1984 date on back cover.)
ETIQUETTE (027 "The Sonics Boom").. 100-150 67
ETIQUETTE (1184 "Full Force")...... 8-12 85
FIRST (7719 "The Sonics")........... 10-15 78
FIRST AMERICAN (7719 "Unreleased").. 10-15 80
FIRST AMERICAN (7779 "Fire and Ice").. 10-15 83
JERDEN (7007 "Introducing the Sonics").. 100-150 67
Members: Gerry Roslie; Andy Parypa; Larry Parypa; Rob Lind; Bob Bennett; Jim Brady; Randy Haitt; Steve Mosier; Ron Foos.

SONICS / Wailers
Singles: 7-inch
ETIQUETTE (22 "Don't Believe in Christmas").. 10-15 65

SONICS / Wailers / Galaxies
LPs: 10/12-inch
ETIQUETTE (ETALB-025 "Merry Christmas").. 100-150 66
ETIQUETTE (025 "Merry Christmas").. 5-10 84
(Reissues the 1984 date on back cover.)

ETIQUETTE (028 "The Northwest Collection")....125-150
(Six-LP boxed set.)
Also see DEAL, Harry, & Galaxies
Also see SONICS
Also see WAILERS

SONICS
Singles: 7-inch
WHITE CLIFFS (230 "Crescent Walk")....10-15 66

SONICS
Singles: 7-inch
COURTIN' (5013 "Sherry")....5-10

SONICS
Singles: 7-inch
BLACK BEAUTY....5-10
GOODIE (206 "Guardian Angel")...10-20

SONICS / Flash Terry / Crowns / Vibes
LPs: 10/12-inch
WHEEL (8011 "Cruisin' the Drag").10-15 60s

SONNETS
Singles: 7-inch
GUYDEN (2112 "Forever for You"). 8-12 64
HERALD (477 "Why Should We Break Up")....35-50 56
LANE (501 "Angel of My Dreams")....100-125 58
Also see DEL VIKINGS / Sonnets

SONNETTES
Singles: 7-inch
'KO' KNOCKOUT (1 "I've Gotton [sic] Over You")....50-100 63
'KO' KNOCKOUT (2 "Hit and Run Lover")....50-100 63

SONNIER, Joel C&W '75
(Jo-el Sonnier)
Singles: 7-inch
MERCURY....3-5 75-76
RCA....3-4 87-90
LPs: 10/12-inch
ROUNDER....5-10 80

SONNIX
Singles: 7-inch
TOWER....4-8 68

SONNY P&R '65
(Sonny Bono)
Singles: 7-inch
ATCO....4-8 65-67
HIGHLAND....5-10 63
MCA....3-5 72-74
SPECIALTY....3-8 65-72
LPs: 10/12-inch
ATCO....12-20 67
Also see CHRISTY, Don
Also see SOMMERS, Ronny
Also see SONNY & CHER

SONNY & CHER P&R/LP '65
Singles: 7-inch
ATCO....4-8 65-70
KAPP....3-6 71-72
MCA....3-5 73-74
REPRISE....5-10 64-65
VAULT (916 "The Letter")....10-15 65
W.B.....3-5 77
Picture Sleeves
VAULT (916 "The Letter")....10-15 65
EPs: 7-inch
ATCO....8-12 65
(Juke box issues only.)
REPRISE....15-25 65
LPs: 10/12-inch
ATCO....12-20 65-72
KAPP....10-15 71-72
MCA....8-12 73-74
TVP....8-10 77
Members: Salvatore Bono; Cher LaPiere; Cher Bono.
Also see CAESAR & CLEO
Also see CHER
Also see HALE & HUSHABYES
Also see SONNY

SONNY & CHER / Bill Medley / Lettermen / Blendells
LPs: 10/12-inch
REPRISE (6177 "Baby Don't Go")....25-35 65
(Shown as by "Sonny & Cher and Friends.")
Also see BLENDELLS
Also see LETTERMEN
Also see MEDLEY, Bill
Also see SONNY & CHER

SONNY & DEMONS
LPs: 10/12-inch
U.A. (3316 "Drag Kings")....20-25 64
(Monaural.)
U.A. (6316 "Drag Kings")....25-30 64
(Stereo.)
Also see DRAG KINGS

SONNY & DIANE
Singles: 7-inch
EPIC (50280 "Love Trap")....10-15 76

SONNY & DUKES
Singles: 7-inch
REVERB....4-8 63

SONNY & EAGLES
Singles: 7-inch
GOLD EAGLE....4-8 61
LPs: 10/12-inch
U.A.....10-20 63

SONNY & JAYCEE
Singles: 7-inch
EMBER....5-8 58
Members: Sonny Terry; J.C. Burris.
Also see TERRY, Sonny

SONNY & PHYLLIS
(With the Danes; Sunny & Phyllis)
Singles: 7-inch
SOFT....8-10 67
UNI....4-8 68
Members: Sonny Threatt; Phyllis Brown-Threatt.
Also see BERRY STREET STATION
Also see BROWN, Phyllis
Also see GULF
Also see JESSIE & JESSICA
Also see JOHNNY & MARK V
Also see NOMADS
Also see PAUL & PAULA
Also see SAN DIEGO
Also see THREATT, Sonny

SONNY BOY & LONNIE
Singles: 78 rpm
CONTINENTAL....15-25 47
LPs: 10/12-inch
CONTINENTAL....30-35 61
Members: Arthur Smith; Lonnie Johnson.
Also see LIGHTNIN' GUITAR'S BAND
Also see SMITH, Shorty, & His Rhythm

SONNY BOY & SAM
Singles: 78 rpm
CONTINENTAL....15-25 47
Members: Arthur Smith; Sam Bradley.
Also see SMITH, Shorty, & His Rhythm
Also see SONNY BOY & LONNIE

SONNY TERRY: see TERRY, Sonny

SONNY V & VELVETS
Singles: 7-inch
ZENETTE (2010 "Baby")....200-300

SONODA, Harry
Singles: 7-inch
HANA HO....3-6 68
LPs: 10/12-inch
HANA HO....10-15 68

SONOMA
Singles: 7-inch
DUNHILL....3-5 73-75
LPs: 10/12-inch
DUNHILL....8-10 73

SONOTONES: see GARDNER, Don

SONS
Singles: 7-inch
COASTLINE (101 "I'm Gone")....30-40 66
Also see MAGIC MUSHROOM

SONS OF ADAM
Singles: 7-inch
ALAMO ("Take My Hand")....25-30 66
(First issue. Selection number not known.)
ALAMO (5473 "Feathered Fish")....20-30 66
DECCA (31887 "Take My Hand")....15-20 66
DECCA (31995 "You're a Better Man Than I")....15-25 66
PENTACLE (104 "Brown Eyed Woman")....10-20
EPs: 7-inch
MOXIE (1032 "Sons of Adam")....5-10 80
Members: Craig Tawater; Mike Port; Michael Stuart; Joe Cookin; Marcus David.
Also see OTHER HALF

SONS OF ADAM
Singles: 7-inch
PENTACLE (101 "Thinking Animal")....15-25 60s

SONS OF BARBEE DOLL
Singles: 7-inch
CODE (1 "Psychedelic Seat")....10-20

SONS OF BURGUNDY
Singles: 7-inch
CARLTON....5-10 59

SONS OF CAJUN
Singles: 7-inch
ATCO....4-8 67

SONS OF CHAMPLIN LP '69
(Sons)
Singles: 7-inch
ARIOLA AMERICA....4-6 75-77
CAPITOL....4-8 69-70
COLUMBIA....4-6 73
GOLDMINE....8-12
VERVE....5-10 67
LPs: 10/12-inch
ARIOLA AMERICA....8-10 75-77
CAPITOL (200 "Loosen Up Naturally")....20-30 69
CAPITOL (332 "Sons Minus Seeds and Stems")....15-20 69
MILL VALLEY ("Sons Minus Seeds and Stems")....20-30 94
(Reportedly 1000 made.)
SONS of CHAMPLIN ("Sons Minus Seeds and Stems")....300-400 69
(Reportedly 100 made.)
COLUMBIA....10-15 73
Members: Bill Champlin; Geoff Palmer; Bill Bowen; Al Strong; Jim Myers; Tim Caine.
Also see CHAMPLIN, Bill

SONS OF GINZA
Singles: 7-inch
ELF....3-6 68

SONS OF KEYSTONE KOPS
Singles: 7-inch
PUBLIC....3-6 69

SONS OF MAY
Singles: 7-inch
SONIC (2746 "Tossin' & Turnin' ")..10-20 67

SONS OF MISSISSIPPI
Singles: 7-inch
REBEL....8-12 67

SONS OF MOSES
Singles: 7-inch
CORAL....4-8 68

SONS OF MOURNING
Singles: 7-inch
MIDGARD (204 "Come on Everybody")....25-35 67

SONS OF SLUM
Singles: 7-inch
STAX....3-5 72

SONS OF PIONEERS P&R '34/C&W '45
Singles: 78 rpm
DECCA....5-10 34-44
RCA....4-8 45-56
Singles: 7-inch
BLUEBIRD (105 "Sugarfoot")....5-10 58
CORAL....5-10 54
DECCA (29000 series)....5-10 56
RCA (0100 thru 0400 series)....5-10 50-51
(Black vinyl.)
RCA (0100 thru 0400 series)....10-20 50-51
(Colored vinyl.)
RCA (2000 thru 6000 series)....5-10 50-56
RCA (8000 series)....4-6 60s
Picture Sleeves
BLUEBIRD (105 "Sugarfoot")....10-20 58
EPs: 7-inch
RCA (103 "Tumbling Tumbleweeds")....8-15 61
RCA (168 "Cowboy Classics")....25-40 52
(Boxed set of three colored discs.)
RCA (400 thru 1400 series)....5-15 55-57
RCA (3000 series)....15-25 52-53
RCA (4000 series)....8-12 58
RCA (5000 series)....5-10 59
LPs: 10/12-inch
AMERICAN FOLK MUSIC....6-12 81
CAMDEN....8-18 58-73
COLUMBIA....5-8 82
GRANITE....6-10 76
HARMONY....10-15 64
J.E.M.F.....8-10
LONG....10-15
MCA....4-8 83
PICKWICK....5-10 75
RCA (1092 "Cool Water")....5-10 76
RCA (1130 thru 2957, except 1431)....20-40 55-64
(With "LPM" or "LSP" prefix.)
RCA (1431 "How Great Thou Art") 30-40 57
RCA (2332 thru 2808)....5-10 77-78
RCA (3032 "Cowboy Classics")....30-50 52
(10-inch LP.)
RCA (3095 "Cowboy Hymns and Spirituals")....30-50 52
(10-inch LP.)
RCA (3162 "Western Classics")....30-50 53
(10-inch LP.)
RCA (3351 thru 4119)....10-20 65-68
(With "LPM" or "LSP" prefix.)
RCA (3468 "Best of the Sons of the Pioneers")....5-10 79
RCA (4000 series)....4-8 81
VOCALION....8-12 64
Members: Roy Rogers; Tim Spencer; Bob Nolan; Ken Curtis; Hugh Farr; Karl Farr; Lloyd Perryman; Shug Fisher; Tommy Doss; Pat Brady.
Also see ALLEN, Rex, Jr., & Sons of the Pioneers
Also see CURTIS, Ken / Rex Allen & Arizona Wranglers
Also see ROGERS, Roy

SONS OF WATTS
Singles: 7-inch
BLUE ROCK....4-6 69

SONTAG, Hedy
Singles: 7-inch
PHILIPS....4-8 64
VEE JAY....4-8 63

SONYA
(With the Sensations)
Singles: 7-inch
DOT....5-10 61-62
GEND (3239 "Oh Lonesome Heart")....15-25 63

SOOTHERS
Singles: 7-inch
PORT (70041 "Little White Cloud")....10-20 64
(Black vinyl.)
PORT (70041 "Little White Cloud")....20-30 64
(Colored vinyl.)
Members: Hank Jernigan; Fred Taylor; Nicky Clark; Bill Dempsey; Curt Cerebin.
Also see HARPTONES

SOOTHSAYERS
(Higher Elevation)
Singles: 7-inch
ACROPOLIS (6601 "Please Don't Be Mad")....15-25 66
ACROPOLIS (6612 "Do You Need Me")....15-25 66
Picture Sleeves
ACROPOLIS (6601 "Please Don't Be Mad")....25-35 66
ACROPOLIS (6612 "Do You Need Me")....25-35 66
Also see DIAMOND, Dave

SOOTZ, Manny, & Thieves
Singles: 78 rpm
PIRATE (841 "Cape Canaveral")....10-20 57
Singles: 7-inch
PIRATE (841 "Cape Canaveral")....20-30 57

SOPHISTICATED LADIES
Singles: 7-inch
MAYHEW....3-5 77

SOPHISTICATES
Singles: 7-inch
MUTT (27318 "I Need You")....15-25
SONNY....8-12
VIVA....10-15 60

SOPHOMORES
Singles: 7-inch
CHORD (1302 "Charades")....50-75 57
DAWN (216 "Every Night About This Time")....25-35 56
DAWN (218 "Linda")....25-35 56
DAWN (223 "Ocean Blue")....15-25 56
DAWN (225 "Is There Someone for Me")....15-25 57
DAWN (228 "If I Should Lose Your Love")....15-25 57
DAWN (237 "Each Time I Hold You")....15-25 57
EPIC (9259 "Charades")....10-20 57
LPs: 10/12-inch
SEECO (451 "The Sophomores")..50-75 58

SOPHOMORES
Singles: 7-inch
SOUND STAGE 7....4-8 64

SOPWITH CAMEL P&R '66
Singles: 7-inch
KAMA SUTRA....4-8 66-67
REPRISE....3-5 73
Picture Sleeves
KAMA SUTRA....4-8 67
LPs: 10/12-inch
KAMA SUTRA....15-20 67-73
REPRISE....15-20 73
Member: Peter Kraemer.

SORCE, Pete: see SOURCE, Pete

SORENSEN, Roy, Group
Singles: 7-inch
COLD WART (78 "If You Could Read Me")....40-50 60s

SORENSEN BROS.
Singles: 7-inch
MARLINDA (7507 "They've Landed")....35-50

SORROWS
Singles: 7-inch
W.B.....5-8 65
Member Don Fardon.
Also see DALLON, Mikki
Also see FARDON, Don

SORROWS
Singles: 7-inch
PAVILLION....3-5 80-86
LPs: 10/12-inch
PAVILLION....5-10 80-83

SOSEBEE, Tommy C&W '53
Singles: 78 rpm
CORAL....4-8 53
Singles: 7-inch
CORAL....5-10 53

SOT WEED FACTOR
Singles: 7-inch
ORIGINAL SOUND....4-8 67

SOTELO, Islea
Singles: 7-inch
MOTOWN....3-4 82

SOUCHEK & 5 YANKS
Singles: 7-inch
COULEE (124 "Laendler")....8-12 68

SOTOLONGO, Edward
(With Leroy Kirkland & Orchestra)
Singles: 7-inch
3D (374 "When in the World")....100-200 58
Session: Crystal Chords.
Also see MONTALVO, Lenny, & Crystal Chords

SOUDERS, Jackie
(Featuring Johnny Weber)
Singles: 7-inch
NOLTA....4-8 62
LPs: 10/12-inch
SEAFAIR....10-20 62

SOUL: see S.O.U.L.

SOUL, Billy
Singles: 7-inch
KING....10-15 64
MUSICOR....10-20 67

SOUL, David P&R/LP '77
Singles: 7-inch
MGM....4-6 66-67
PARAMOUNT....3-5 70
PRIVATE STOCK....3-5 77
LPs: 10/12-inch
PRIVATE STOCK....8-10 77

SOUL, Jimmy P&R '62
(With the Chants; James McCleese)
Singles: 7-inch
S.P.Q.R. (3300 "Twistin' Matilda")..8-12 62
S.P.Q.R. (3302 "When Matilda Comes Back")....8-12 62
S.P.Q.R. (3304 "Guess Things Happen That Way")....8-12 63
S.P.Q.R. (3305 "If You Wanna Be Happy")....8-12 63
S.P.Q.R. (3310 "Treat 'Em Tough").8-12 63
S.P.Q.R. (3312 "Everybody's Gone Ape")....8-12 63
S.P.Q.R. (3314 "Change Partners") 8-12 63
S.P.Q.R. (3315 "My Girl, She Sure Can Cook")....8-12 64
S.P.Q.R. (3318 "Take Me to Los Angeles")....8-12 64
S.P.Q.R. (3319 "Twistin' Matilda")..5-10 64
S.P.Q.R. (3321 "My Little Room")....8-12 64
20TH FOX (413 "Respectable")....5-10 63
Picture Sleeves
S.P.Q.R. (3302 "When Matilda Comes Back")....15-25 62
S.P.Q.R. (3305 "If You Wanna Be Happy")....15-25 63
LPs: 10/12-inch
S.P.Q.R. (2000 "Greatest Hits")....15-25
S.P.Q.R. (16001 "If You Wanna Be Happy")....50-100 63
Session: Bill Deal.
Also see BENTON, Brook / Chuck Jackson / Jimmy Soul
Also see DEAL, Bill
Also see McCLEESE, James
Also see RIVERS, Johnny / 4 Seasons / Jerry Butler / Jimmy Soul

SOUL, Jimmy / Belmonts / Connie Francis
LPs: 10/12-inch
SPINORAMA (125 "Jimmy Soul & the Belmonts")....20-25 63
Also see BELMONTS
Also see FRANCIS, Connie
Also see SOUL, Jimmy
Also see BELMONTS
Also see SOUL, Jimmy

SOUL, John Philip
Singles: 7-inch
PEPPER....4-8 68

SOUL, Johnny
Singles: 7-inch
FEDERAL....10-20 70
SSS INT'L....5-10 69

SOUL, Little Nicky
Singles: 7-inch
SHEE (101 "I Wanted to Tell You")....4-8 64

SOUL, Sharon
Singles: 7-inch
CORAL....10-20 66
WILD DEUCE (1001 "How Can I Get to You")....15-25 65

SOUL, Steve
Singles: 7-inch
FEDERAL (12551 "Soul President")....5-10 69
KING (12850 "James Brown Talks with the News")....4-8 70s

SOUL AGENTS
Singles: 7-inch
CAMEO (350 "Seventh Son")....10-15 65
INTERFON (7702 "Mean Woman Blues")....10-15 64

SOUL AGGREGATION
Singles: 7-inch
CAPITOL (5902 "I Can't Find Love")....8-12 67

SOUL AMBASSADORS
Singles: 7-inch
SOUND STAGE 7 (2614 "I've Got the Feeling")....5-10 68

SOUL ANGELS
Singles: 7-inch
JOSIE (1002 "It's All in Your Mind") 5-10 69

SOUL APPARATUS
Singles: 7-inch
BLACK & BLUE....5-10 69

SOUL ASYLUM LP '92
LPs: 10/12-inch
EPIC....8-10 90s
TWIN/TONE....8-10 88
W.B.....8-10 90s
Members: Dan Murphy; Grant Young; Dave Pirner; Karl Mueller.

SOUL BANDITS
Singles: 7-inch
RIGHT GROOVE....8-12

SOUL BELIEVERS
Singles: 7-inch
SMAK (778 "Charlene")....8-12 68

SOUL BENDERS
Singles: 7-inch
PHANTASM (2530 "Hey Joe")....10-15 67
PHANTASM (2568 "Seven and Seven Is")....10-15 67
Picture Sleeves
PHANTASM (2530 "Hey Joe")....30-40 67
Member: Aris Hampers.

SOUL BROTHERS
Singles: 7-inch
BLUE CAT (107 "Keep It Up")........10-20 65
BRUNSWICK (55397 "She Put a Hurtin' on Me") 5-10 69
D-TOWN (1069 "Heartaches")........ 5-10 60s
MERCURY (72575 "Good Lovin' Never Hurt") 8-12 66
MERCURY (72632 "My Only Reason for Living").. 8-12 66
MUSIC CITY (856 "Every Night I See Your Face") 10-15 64
SEG-WAY (101 "Tell It Like It Is") ..10-15
SOUL 4-8
WAND (125 "Notify Me")................10-20 62
Member: Sam Gary.
Also see SAM & BILL

SOUL BROTHERS INC.
(Soul Bros. Inc.)
Singles: 7-inch
GOLDEN EYE (1001 "Pyramid")...............................200-225
COMMONWEALTH
SALEM (500 "Teardrops")..............25-35
UNITED 5-10 70
S.B.I. 10-15
Member: George Brown.

SOUL BROTHERS SIX *P&R '67*
Singles: 7-inch
ATLANTIC (2406 "Some Kind of Wonderful")......................................25-35 67
ATLANTIC (2456 "You Better Check Yourself")......................................15-25 67
ATLANTIC (2535 "Your Love Is Such a Wonderful Love") 15-25 68
ATLANTIC (2592 "Somebody Else Is Loving My Baby")..15-25 69
ATLANTIC (2645 "Drive")...............15-25 69
GRT (116 "Can You Feel the Vibrations").................................... 5-10 76
(Canadian.)
FINE ("Stop Hurting Me")...........200-300 65
(Selection number not known.)
LYDELL (746 "Don't Neglect Your Baby")......................................100-150 66
PHIL-L.A. of SOUL (360 "You Gotta Come a Little Closer")................................ 5-10 73
PHIL-L.A. of SOUL (365 "Lost the Will to Live") 5-10 74
Members: John Ellison; Sam Armstrong; Charles Armstrong; Von Elle Benjamin; Lester Peleman; Moses Armstrong.
Also see ELLISON, John

SOUL CADETS
Singles: 7-inch
WORLD PACIFIC (77920 "Hey Little Girl") 5-10 69

SOUL CHILDREN *P&R/LP '69*
Singles: 12-inch
STAX... 4-8 78-79
Singles: 7-inch
EPIC... 3-6 75-76
STAX... 4-8 68-74
LPs: 10/12-inch
EPIC... 8-10 76
STAX... 8-12 69-79
Members: Anita Louis; Shelbra Bennett; John Colbert; Norman West.
Also see BLACKFOOT, J.D.

SOUL CITY
Singles: 7-inch
GOODTIME (801 "Everybody Dance")..10-20 66
MERCURY (72735 "I Shot for the Moon")..10-20 67

SOUL CLAN *P&R '68*
Singles: 7-inch
ATLANTIC (2530 "Soul Meeting") ... 8-12 68
Picture Sleeves
ATLANTIC (2530 "Soul Meeting") ..10-15 68
LPs: 10/12-inch
ATCO ("Soul Meeting").................15-25 68
(Selection number not known.)
Members: Solomon Burke; Arthur Conley; Don Covay; Ben E. King; Joe Tex.
Also see BURKE, Solomon
Also see CONLEY, Arthur
Also see COVAY, Don
Also see KING, Ben E.
Also see TEX, Joe

SOUL CLINIC
Singles: 7-inch
BAY SOUND (67006 "So Sharp") ... 8-12 68

SOUL CLUB
Singles: 7-inch
MCA 3-4 87

SOUL COMMANDERS
Singles: 7-inch
LIFETIME....................................... 5-10

SOUL COMMUNICATORS
Singles: 7-inch
FEE BEE 8-12

SOUL CONGRESS
Singles: 7-inch
BANG (563 "Playboy Shuffle")........ 5-10 68

SOUL CONTINENTALS
Singles: 7-inch
SOUND STAGE 7 (2609 "Bowlegs")...................................... 5-10 68

SOUL COP
Singles: 7-inch
NORFOLK INT'L.............................. 8-12 76

SOUL CRUSADERS
Singles: 7-inch
MORE SOUL.....................................5-10 70

SOUL DOG
Singles: 7-inch
AMHERST.. 3-5 76
LPs: 10/12-inch
AMHERST..8-12 77

SOUL DUO
Singles: 7-inch
JOSIE (1007 "This Is Your Day") 5-10 69

SOUL EAST
Singles: 7-inch
DELUXE (108 "Funky Lady") 5-10 69

SOUL EXCITEMENT
Singles: 7-inch
PINK DOLPHIN 8-12 69

SOUL EXCITERS
Singles: 7-inch
1-2-3 (1708 "Shoot the Monkey") 8-12 69

SOUL EXPRESS
Singles: 7-inch
EXPRESS (8843 "Jeanette")..........25-35 68

SOUL FINDERS
LPs: 10/12-inch
CAMDEN (2170 "Soul Music").......10-20 67
CAMDEN (2239 "Soul Man")..........10-20 68

SOUL FLUTES
Singles: 7-inch
A&M (952 "Try a Little Tenderness") . 4-8 68
A&M (999 "Day-O")........................... 4-8 68
LPs: 10/12-inch
A&M (3009 "Trust in Me") 10-15 68

SOUL 4
Singles: 7-inch
RINGO (4321 "Misery")..................10-15 65

SOUL GENTS
(Soul Generation)
Singles: 7-inch
EBONY SOUNDS..............................5-10 72-74
FROS RAY (Except 2707) 8-15 68-71
FROS-RAY (2707 "If I Should Win Your Love") 30-40 69
LPs: 10/12-inch
EBONY SOUNDS.............................10-15 72

SOUL IMPACTS
Singles: 7-inch
ECCO...10-15
S.I.M. (32669 "Here's Some Dances") 10-15 60s

SOUL INCORPORATED
Singles: 7-inch
JOLI (075 "It Really Doesn't Matter Now")..10-15 65
SOCK (1002 "Funky Lady") 8-10 68
Also see SULLIVAN, Niki

SOUL INCORPORATED
(Soul Inc.)
Singles: 7-inch
BOSS (9920 "60 Miles High") 15-25 67
COUNTERPOINT ("Love Me When I'm Down")..10-20 68
FRATERNITY (962 "Don't You Go") 8-12 66
LAURIE (3430 "Love Me When I'm Down") 5-10 68
RONDO..5-10 69
Members: Jimmy Orton; Wayne Young; Frank Bugbee; Jim Settle; Marvin Maxwell.
Also see ELYSIAN FIELD

SOUL INCORPORATED
(Soul Inc.)
Singles: 7-inch
EMBLEM (101 "What Goes Up Must Come Down") 300-400
LPs: 10/12-inch
EMBLEM (106 "Live! at the Cellar, Charlotte, N.C.")......................................250-350
Members: Eddie Zommerfeld; Freddie Pugh; Pete Tolio; Edgar Smith; Skip Davis; Robbie Robinson.

SOUL INJECTION
Singles: 7-inch
ACCENT...5-10 71

SOUL INVADERS
Singles: 7-inch
ABC..5-10

SOUL KINGS
Singles: 7-inch
INFINITY (029 "Pachuko Soul").....10-20 62

SOUL KINGS
Singles: 7-inch
GOLD MOUNTAIN 3-5

SOUL LOVERS
Singles: 7-inch
PACEMAKER.................................. 3-4 83

SOUL MACHINE
Singles: 7-inch
A&M (953 "Nature Boy") 5-10 68

SOUL MAJESTICS
Singles: 7-inch
AL-TOG...5-10

SOUL MATES
Singles: 7-inch
ERA (3109 "I Want a Boyfriend") ...10-15 63

SOUL MEN
Singles: 7-inch
LOLA (105 "Road House") 8-12 64

SOUL NOTES
Singles: 7-inch
WAY OUT (1001 "How Long Will It Last")..10-20 68
WAY OUT (1006 "I Got Everything I Need")...15-25 69

SOUL PARTNERS
Singles: 7-inch
BELL (758 "Walk On Judge")...........5-10 69
BELL (792 "Spread").........................5-10 69

SOUL PATROL
Singles: 7-inch
DISCOVERY 5-10
HIGHLAND.......................................5-10
SHAMLEY (44017 "Saigon Strut") ...5-10 69
STUD 5-10 60s

SOUL PLEASERS
Singles: 7-inch
LIVING LEGEND (102 "I Found a Love") 15-25 60s

SOUL POTION
Singles: 7-inch
SUNBURST......................................8-12 73
Also see VITO & SALUTATIONS

SOUL PROCEDURES
Singles: 7-inch
FIVE-O (506 "But What Is This Feeling") 50-100 69

SOUL PURPOSE
Singles: 7-inch
SMASH (2215 "Ticket for Tomorrow")...5-10 69

SOUL REPS
Singles: 7-inch
LIMELIGHT (3026 "Soul Food").......5-10 64

SOUL ROCKERS
Singles: 7-inch
BUDDAH 5-10 70
SUSSEX...5-10 70

SOUL RUNNERS
(Charles Wright & Watts 103rd Street Rhythm Band)
Singles: 7-inch
MO SOUL (101 "Spreadin' Honey")..30-40 66
Also see GADSON, James
Also see WRIGHT, Charles, & Watts 103rd Street Rhythm Band

SOUL SEARCHERS
Singles: 7-inch
POLYDOR.......................................4-6 75
SUSSEX..5-8 72-74
LPs: 10/12-inch
SUSSEX.......................................10-15 73-74
Members: Chuck Brown; John Ewell; Frank Wellman.
Also see BROWN, Chuck, & Soul Searchers

SOUL SEEKERS
Singles: 7-inch
REVELATION...................................10-15
WESTCHESTER (266 "Boom Boom")..10-20 67

SOUL SENSATIONS
Singles: 7-inch
MUSIC CITY.....................................8-12

SOUL SENSATIONS & COACHMAN REVIEWS BAND
Singles: 7-inch
AUDIOFONICS 8-12

SOUL SET
Singles: 7-inch
BB (4012 "Flunky-Flunky")...............5-10 67
BI-ME (7683 "Will You Ever Learn")..35-45
GOODTIME (1 "Call On Me") 10-20 66
JOHNSON (737 "Love, Love, Love")...5-10 67
JOHNSON (738 "For You Love") 5-10 67
LPs: 10/12-inch
JOHNSON (1001 "Soul Set").........15-25 67

SOUL SETTERS
Singles: 7-inch
ONACREST (503 "Out O' Sight")....15-25 66

SOUL SHAKERS
Singles: 7-inch
LOMA (2027 "Cool Letter") 10-20 66
LOMA (2047 "It's Love")..................20-30 66

SOUL SISTERS *P&R '64*
Singles: 7-inch
GUYDEN (2066 "Warm-Up") 10-20 62
KAYO (5101 "I Can't Let Him Go").10-20 63
SUE (005 "Good Time Tonight") 10-15 64
SUE (107 "Foolish Dreamer") 10-15 64
SUE (111 "Just a Moment Ago")....10-15 64
SUE (130 "The Right Time")...........10-15 65
SUE (140 "Give Me Some Satisfaction").................................10-15 66
SUE (799 "I Can't Stand It")...........10-15 63
VEEP (1291 "You Got 'Em Beat")....8-10 68
LPs: 10/12-inch
SUE (1022 "I Can't Stand It") 35-50 64
Members: Theresa Cleveland; Ann Gissendanner.

SOUL SOCIETY
Singles: 7-inch
DOT (17136 "Sidewinder")...............5-10 68
SHOWCO ("What Cha Gonna Do")..8-12 67
(Selection number not known.)
SHOWCO (001 "Knock on Wood") ..8-12 67
LPs: 10/12-inch
DOT (25842 "Satisfaction")............10-20 68

SOUL SOUNDS
LPs: 10/12-inch
SUNSET (5249 "Best of the Soul Hits")...10-15 69

SOUL SOUP
Singles: 7-inch
KAMA SUTRA (262 "Everybody Listen")...4-8 69

SOUL STEPPERS
Singles: 7-inch
KRIS (8085 "Steppin' Up")..............8-12

SOUL STIRRERS
Singles: 78 rpm
ALADDIN.......................................15-25 53
SPECIALTY (300 series) 10-20 50-51
Singles: 7-inch
CHECKER...4-8 65-71
SPECIALTY (800 series) 15-25 51-56
(Black vinyl.)
SPECIALTY (800 series) 25-45 50s
(Red vinyl.)
LPs: 10/12-inch
CHESS (10063 "Tribute to Sam Cooke")..8-12 71
SPECIALTY (Except 2106)..............6-12 69-75
SPECIALTY (2106 "Soul Stirrers")...15-25 59
Members: Sam Cooke; Johnnie Taylor; James Carr; James Phelps.
Also see CARR, James
Also see COOKE, Sam
Also see PHELPS, James
Also see TAYLOR, Johnnie

SOUL SUPERIORS
Singles: 7-inch
SOUL BEAT (107 "Trust in Me Baby")..10-20

SOUL STOPPERS
Singles: 7-inch
CAPP-MATT (601 "Let's Sit Down") 25-50 66
(Reportedly, 500 made.)
Members: Johnny Matthews; Lenny Goldberg.
Also see JOHNNY & EXPRESSIONS

SOUL STRINGS
LPs: 10/12-inch
SOLID STATE (18042 "Souls Strings and a Funky Horn")..................................8-12 68

SOUL SURFERS / Delicates
Singles: 7-inch
CHALLENGE (59267 "Home from Camp") 10-15 63
Also see DELICATES
Also see JAN & DEAN / Soul Surfers
Also see WALLACE, Jerry / Soul Surfers

SOUL SURVIVORS
Singles: 7-inch
DOT (16793 "Look at Me")............20-30 65
DOT (16830 "Snow Man")..............10-20 66
Members: Gene Chalk; Pat Shanahan; Allen Kemp; Bob Webber.
Also see NELSON, Rick
Also see SUGARLOAF

SOUL SURVIVORS *P&R/LP '67*
Singles: 7-inch
ATCO..5-10 68-69
CRIMSON 5-10 67-68
DECCA..5-10 67
PHILADELPHIA INT'L.......................3-5 76
TSOP...3-5 74-75
LPs: 10/12-inch
ATCO (277 "Take Another Look")...15-20 69
CRIMSON (502 "When the Whistle Blows")..20-25 67
TSOP..8-10 75
Members: Richard Ingui; Charles Ingui; Kenny Jeremiah; Chuck Trois; Paul Venturini.
Also see SHIRLEY & COMPANY

SOUL SYNDICATE
LPs: 10/12-inch
EPIPHANY.......................................5-10 80

SOUL THREE
Singles: 7-inch
OMEN (9 "These Things") 10-20 65

SOUL TORNADOES
Singles: 7-inch
BURT (4000 "Funky Thang") 8-12 69

SOUL TOWN SYMPHONY
LPs: 10/12-inch
ANVIL..5-10 70

SOUL TRAIN GANG *P&R '75*
Singles: 7-inch
SOUL TRAIN.....................................3-5 75-77
LPs: 10/12-inch
SOUL TRAIN....................................8-10 76

SOUL TRIPPERS
Singles: 7-inch
PROVIDENCE (415 "King Bee")....15-25 65

SOUL TWINS
Singles: 7-inch
BACK BEAT (599 "She's the One") .8-12 69

KAREN (1533 "Quick Change Artist")..25-35 67
KAREN (1535 "Just One Look")....10-20 67

SOUL TWISTERS
Singles: 7-inch
ROMAT (1002 "Swinging on a Grapevine") 15-25 60s

SOUL II SOUL *P&R/LP '89*
Singles: 7-inch
VIRGIN...3-4 89
Picture Sleeves
VIRGIN...3-4 89
LPs: 10/12-inch
VIRGIN...5-8 89-90

SOUL X-2
Singles: 7-inch
SOUND STAGE 7 (2612 "I'm Alright Now")..5-10 68

SOULATIONS
Singles: 7-inch
CEI (126 "Will You Be Mine") 250-500

SOULBENDERS
Singles: 7-inch
MALA (596 "7 and 7 Is")...................8-12 67
PHANTASM (2530 "Hey Joe").......15-25 67
PHANTASM (2568 "7 and 7 Is") ...15-25 67
Picture Sleeves
PHANTASM (2530 "Hey Joe")......20-30 67
Also see PEDESTRIANS / Association / Five Americans / Soulblenders

SOULE, George
Singles: 7-inch
LA LOUISIANNE 5-10 65
FAME..3-5 73
TETRAGRAMMTON 4-8 69

SOULE, George, & Ava Aldridge
Singles: 7-inch
MCA...3-5 78
Also see SOULE, George

SOULFOLKS
Singles: 7-inch
O'RETTA..4-6 71

SOULFUL BOWLFUL
Singles: 7-inch
20TH FOX (6688 "For All That I Am")..5-10 67

SOULFUL DYNAMICS
Singles: 7-inch
BUDDAH...4-6 70

SOULFUL ILLUSION
Singles: 7-inch
MERCURY (72754 "Searching for Love")..5-10 67
TUDOR 4-6 71

SOULFUL SEVEN
Singles: 7-inch
MGM..3-5 70

SOULFUL STRINGS *LP '67*
Singles: 7-inch
CADET..3-8 66-73
LPs: 10/12-inch
CADET...5-10 67-73

SOULFUL TWINS
Singles: 7-inch
SABLE 15-25

SOULJERS
Singles: 7-inch
RAMPART (648 "Chinese Checkers")..5-8 66
RAMPART (649 "Crazy Little Thing")..5-8 66
LPs: 10/12-inch
RAMPART (3302 "Move Over Ramsey")..20-30 66

SOUL-JERS
Singles: 7-inch
STEPPING STONES 8-12

SOULMAKERS
Singles: 7-inch
DARAN 8-12

SOULMASTERS
("Featuring John & Jerry")
Singles: 7-inch
BEACH...8-12
RAVEN...8-12
Members: John; Jerry.

SOULOSOPHY
Singles: 7-inch
ABC 4-8 69
EPIC...3-5 70-71

SOULS OF SLAIN
Singles: 7-inch
RICKSHAW (101 "7 and 7 Is").......15-25 60s

SOULSONIC FORCE
Singles: 7-inch
TOMMY BOY 3-4 83

SOULTONES
Singles: 7-inch
VALISE (1900 "You & Me Baby")....10-20

SOULVILLE ALL-STARS
Singles: 7-inch
SOULVILLE......................................8-12

SOUNCATIONS
Singles: 7-inch
HEAD (1001 "Exit") 8-12

SOUND APPARATUS
Singles: 7-inch
BLACK & BLUE (901 "Travel Agent Man") 15-20 69

SOUND BARRIER
Singles: 7-inch
ZOUNDS (1004 "My Baby's Gone")....................30-50 67
UNITED AUDIO (90411 "Greasy Heart")....................10-20 69
Picture Sleeves
UNITED AUDIO (90411 "Greasy Heart")....................20-30 69

SOUND BARRIER
LPs: 10/12-inch
MCA 5-8 83

SOUND BREAKERS
Singles: 7-inch
RADIANT....................5-10 61

SOUND CONTROL
Singles: 7-inch
CUCA (1506 "I'll Be Back Again") ... 5-10 70
Member: John Rogge.

SOUND DEPT.
Singles: 7-inch
CITE (68102 "Plain Girl") 15-25 68

SOUND DOCTOR
Singles: 12-inch
ZOO YORK 4-6 84
Singles: 7-inch
ZOO YORK 3-4 84

SOUND EXPERIENCE
Singles: 7-inch
SOULVILLE....................3-5 74
LP: 10/12-inch
BUDDAH 5-10 70s

SOUND EXTRACTION
Singles: 7-inch
J-THREE (509 "I Feel Like Crying")....................8-12

SOUND FOUNDATION
Singles: 7-inch
SMOBRO 4-6 69
LPs: 10/12-inch
SMOBRO 10-15 69

SOUND HEMISPHERE
Singles: 7-inch
AMERICAN....................4-8 75

SOUND IDEA
Singles: 7-inch
CORAL....................4-6 68

SOUND JUDGMENT
Singles: 7-inch
KAPP....................4-8 68

SOUND LABORATORY
Singles: 7-inch
SSS INT'L (764 "Sherry, Sherry")...... 5-8 69

SOUND MACHINE
Singles: 7-inch
CANTERBURY....................5-10 67
FLEETWOOD (4599 "Backroads of Your Mind")....................10-20 68

SOUND MASTERS: see SOUND-MASTERS

SOUND 9418
Singles: 7-inch
UK/BIG TREE....................3-5 76
Member: Jonathan King.
Also see KING, Jonathan

SOUND OF FEELING
Singles: 7-inch
LIMELIGHT 5-8 69
VERVE 5-8 68

SOUND OF SIX
Singles: 7-inch
LAURIE 3-6 69

SOUND OF SOUL
Singles: 7-inch
JOSIE....................5-10 66-67

SOUND OF SEVENTH SON
Singles: 7-inch
TOWER (169 "I'll Be on My Way").. 5-10 65

SOUND OFFS
Singles: 7-inch
ERA....................5-10 63
Also see TOWERS

SOUND SANDWICH
Singles: 7-inch
VIVA....................10-20 67-68

SOUND 70s
Singles: 7-inch
CAPITOL....................3-5 70

SOUND SEVENTY
Singles: 7-inch
MIJJI....................4-8 67

SOUND SIRCUS
Singles: 7-inch
MERCURY (72925 "Blue-Eyed Pussy Cat")....................5-8 69

SOUND SOLUTION
Singles: 7-inch
KAPP 4-6 69

SOUND SYMPOSIUM
Singles: 7-inch
DOT 4-6 69
LPs: 10/12-inch
DOT 8-10 69

SOUND SYSTEM
Singles: 7-inch
ROMAT (1001 "Take a Look at Yourself")....................15-25 67

SOUND VENDOR
Singles: 7-inch
LIQUID STEREO (25 "Mister Sun")....................10-15 69

SOUNDBREAKERS
Singles: 7-inch
SYMBOL 4-8 67

SOUNDGARDEN LP '90
Singles: 7-inch
A&M (17933 "Hands All Over") 4-6 89
(Promotional issue only.)
EPs: 7-inch
"SCREAMING LIFE"....................5-8 87
(Colored vinyl.)
LPs: 10/12-inch
A&M 5-8 89
SST (911 "Flower")....................10-15 89
(Colored vinyl.)
Members: Chris Cornell; Hiro Yamamoto; Matthew Cameron; Kim Thayil.

SOUND-MASTERS
Singles: 7-inch
JULET (102 "I Want You to Be My Baby")....................50-75

SOUNDS
Singles: 7-inch
MODERN (975 "So Unnecessary")....................30-40 55
MODERN (981 "Sweet Sixteen") ...30-40 55
(Red label.)
MODERN (981 "Sweet Sixteen") ...20-30 55
(Black label.)
Also see BYRD, Bobby
Also see DEL-VIKINGS / Sonnets

SOUNDS
Singles: 7-inch
HOP-TEL....................10-12 59
QUEEN 5-10

SOUNDS
Singles: 7-inch
SUNGLOW (126 "Little Joe")........20-30 67

SOUNDS FOUR
Singles: 7-inch
SAINTMO (203 "Hey Girl")...........30-40 68

SOUNDS, INC.
Singles: 7-inch
LIBERTY 10-20 64-65
U.A. 5-10 70-71

SOUNDS INCORPORATED
Singles: 7-inch
LIBERTY 5-8 64-65

SOUNDS LIKE US
Singles: 7-inch
FONTANA (1570 "Outside Chance")....................40-60 67
JILL ANN (101 "Outside Chance")....................40-60 66
SOMA (8108 "It Was a Very Good Year")....................20-25 67

SOUNDS NICE
Singles: 7-inch
RARE EARTH (5008 "Love at First Sight")....................5-8 69

SOUNDS OF DAWN
Singles: 7-inch
DOT 4-8 67
TWIN STACKS....................5-10 60s

SOUNDS OF GOLD
Singles: 7-inch
CATALANO....................5-10

SOUNDS OF HARLEY
Singles: 7-inch
MGM 5-10 71
Session: Davie Allan.
Also see ALLAN, Davie

SOUNDS OF MODIFICATION
Singles: 7-inch
JUBILEE....................4-6 68-69
LPs: 10/12-inch
JUBILEE....................10-15 68

SOUNDS OF OUR TIMES
Singles: 7-inch
CAPITOL....................4-8 68
LPs: 10/12-inch
CAPITOL....................8-12 67-69

SOUNDS OF SIX
Singles: 7-inch
FOX....................15-25 66

SOUNDS OF SUNSHINE P&R/LP '71
Singles: 7-inch
P.I.P. 3-5 76
RANWOOD 3-5 71-73
LPs: 10/12-inch
P.I.P. 5-10 76
RANWOOD 5-10 71-72

SOUNDS OF TIME
Singles: 7-inch
ENGLISH ("Tranquility")....................10-20 60s
(Selection number not known.)
Picture Sleeves
ENGLISH ("Tranquility")....................15-25 60s

SOUNDS ORCHESTRAL P&R/LP '65
Singles: 7-inch
JANUS 4-8 60s
PARKWAY....................5-8 62-67
LPs: 10/12-inch
PARKWAY....................10-15 62-67

SOUNDS UNLIMITED
Singles: 7-inch
ABC-PAR (10803 "Nobody But You")....................10-15 66

SOUNDS UNLIMITED
Singles: 7-inch
DUNWICH (157 "A Girl As Sweet As You")....................10-20 67
Also see MASON PROFIT

SOUNDS UNLIMITED
Singles: 7-inch
SOLAR (101 "Keep Your Hands Off")....................10-20 60s

SOUNDTRIP
Singles: 7-inch
PIECE (1011 "Someday")....................15-25 67

SOUP
Singles: 7-inch
TARGET (1005 "Big Boss Man")....10-20 69
LPs: 10/12-inch
ARF ARF (1 "Soup")....................75-100 70
BIG TREE 10-20 71
Members: Doug Yankus; Dave Faas; Rob Griffith; Roger Jerry.
Also see WHITE DUCK

SOUP DRAGONS LP '90
LPs: 10/12-inch
BIG LIFE 5-8 90
POLYDOR (522732 "Hydrophonic").5-10 90s
SIRE....................5-10 87

SOUP GREENS
Singles: 7-inch
GOLDEN RULE (5000 "Like a Rolling Stone")....................15-25 65

SOUPY SALES: see SALES, Soupy

SOUR TONES
Singles: 7-inch
TERRI ANN....................4-8 62

SOURCE
(Featuring Candi Staton)
Singles: 7-inch
SOURCE....................3-4 86
Also see STATON, Candi

SOURCE
Singles: 7-inch
AMERICAN INT'L....................3-5

SOURCE, Pete
(With the Driftwoods; with Good Intentions; Pete Sorce)
Singles: 7-inch
COUNT (1002 "I'm Too Young for Love")....................20-30 59
FAN JR. (5080 "I'm Too Young for Love")....................10-20 63
Also see BIG APPLE
Also see CATALINAS
Also see DRIFTWOODS
Also see GOOD INTENTIONS

SOURDOUGH
Singles: 7-inch
METROMEDIA....................3-5 73

SOURIRE, Soeur: see SINGING NUN

SOUTH
Singles: 7-inch
A&M....................4-8 68
SILVER FOX....................5-10 69
LPs: 10/12-inch
A&M....................10-15 69

SOUTH, Barbara
Singles: 7-inch
CAPITOL....................4-8 66

SOUTH, Joe P&R '58
(With the Believers)
Singles: 7-inch
A&M (922 "Yo Yo")....................4-8 68
ALL WOOD (402 "Just Remember You're Mine")....................10-20 62
APT (25084 "I've Got to Be Somebody")....................8-12 65
CAPITOL....................3-8 67-75
COLUMBIA (43893 "Backfield in Motion")....................8-12 67
COLUMBIA (44218 "Fool in Love")..8-12 67
FAIRLANE (21006 "You're the Reason")....................10-15 61
FAIRLANE (21010 "I'm Sorry for You")....................10-15 61
FAIRLANE (21015 "Slippin' Around")....................10-15 61
ISLAND 3-5 75
MGM (13145 "Same Old Song").......8-12 63
MGM (13196 "Concrete Jungle") 8-12 63
MGM (13276 "Little Queenie")..........8-12 64
NRC (002 "I'm Snowed")....................30-40 58
NRC (041 "Little Bluebird") 10-20 60
NRC (5000 "The Purple People Eater Meets the Witch Doctor")....................15-25 58
NRC (5001 "One Fool to Another")....................15-25 58
SOUTHERN TRACKS (2018 "River Dog") 3-5 90
LPs: 10/12-inch
ACCORD....................5-10 81
CAPITOL....................8-15 68-72
ISLAND....................8-12 75
MINE....................8-12 70
Also see CHIPS

SOUTH, Joe / Dells
LPs: 10/12-inch
APPLE (3377 "Come Together")....15-25 71
Also see DELLS

SOUTH, Joe / Billy Joe Royal
LPs: 10/12-inch
NASHVILLE (2092 "You're the Reason")....................5-10 70s
Also see ROYAL, Billy Joe
Also see SOUTH, Joe

SOUTH CENTRAL AVENUE MUNICIPAL BLUES BAND
LPs: 10/12-inch
BLUESWAY....................10-15 68

SOUTH 40
Singles: 7-inch
METROBEAT....................5-10 67-68
LPs: 10/12-inch
METROBEAT....................15-20 68
Also see CROW
Also see RAVE-ONS

SOUTH SHORE COMMISSION P&R '75
Singles: 7-inch
ATLANTIC....................5-10
WAND....................3-5 75-76
Members: Frank McCurry; Sheryl Henry.
Also see FIVE DU-TONES

SOUTH STREET MISSION BAND
Singles: 7-inch
CAMEO (415 "Theme from the Young Ones")....................4-8 66

SOUTH STREET SOUL GUITARS
Singles: 7-inch
SILVER FOX....................4-6 69

SOUTHBOUND FREEWAY
Singles: 7-inch
RED ROOSTER (67001 "Psychedelic Used Car Lot Blues")....................15-25 67
ROULETTE (4739 "Psychedelic Used Car Lot Blues")....................10-15 67
SWAN (4272 "Crazy Shadows") 8-12 67
TERA SHIRMA (67001 "Psychedelic Used Car Lot Blues")....................20-30 67
(First issue.)

SOUTHBOUND FREEWAY
Singles: 7-inch
ATCO (6690 "Roll with It")........5-10 69
QUALITY (1852 "Revelations")........5-10 69
(Canadian.)
QUALITY (1937 "Roll with It") 5-10 69
(Canadian.)

SOUTHCOASTERS
Singles: 7-inch
ALL BOY....................5-10 62

SOUTHCOTE P&R '74
Singles: 7-inch
BUDDAH....................3-6 74

SOUTHER, J.D. LP '76
(John David Souther)
Singles: 7-inch
ASYLUM....................3-5 74-76
COLUMBIA....................3-5 79
W.B. 3-4 85
LPs: 10/12-inch
ASYLUM....................8-10 72-76
COLUMBIA....................5-10 79
W.B. 5-8 85
Also see CINDERS
Also see JOHN DAVID & CINDERS
Also see LONGBRANCH PENNYWHISTLE
Also see RONSTADT, Linda, & J.D. Souther
Also see TAYLOR, James, & J.D. Souther
Also see TILLOTSON, Johnny, & J.D. Souther

SOUTHER - HILLMAN - FURAY BAND P&R/LP '74
Singles: 7-inch
ASYLUM....................3-5 74-75
LPs: 10/12-inch
ASYLUM....................8-10 74-75
Members: J. D. Souther; Chris Hillman; Richie Furay.
Also see FURAY, Richie
Also see HILLMAN, Chris
Also see SOUTHER, J.D.

SOUTHERN, Guy
Singles: 7-inch
YORK....................5-10 59

SOUTHERN, Jack
Singles: 7-inch
CHALLENGE....................4-8 65

SOUTHERN, Jeri P&R '51
Singles: 78 rpm
DECCA....................4-8 51-58
Singles: 7-inch
CAPITOL....................4-8 59
DECCA....................5-10 51-58
ROULETTE....................5-10 57-59
EPs: 7-inch
DECCA....................5-10 55-56
LPs: 10/12-inch
CAPITOL....................10-20 59
DECCA....................15-25 55-58
ROULETTE....................10-20 57-59

SOUTHERN, Johnny
Singles: 7-inch
GUYDEN....................5-10 61
LIBERTY....................5-10 62-63

SOUTHERN ASHE C&W '81
Singles: 7-inch
SOUNDWAVES....................3-4 81

SOUTHERN BELL SINGERS
Singles: 7-inch
VEE JAY....................5-10 63

SOUTHERN COMFORT LP '71
Singles: 7-inch
CAPITOL....................3-5 71-72
COTILLION....................4-6 69
LPs: 10/12-inch
BRYLEN....................5-8
CAPITOL....................10-12 71
COLUMBIA....................10-12 70
SIRE....................12-15 69
Also see MATTHEWS' SOUTHERN COMFORT

SOUTHERN COOKIN'
Singles: 7-inch
POLYDOR....................3-5 79
LPs: 10/12-inch
POLYDOR....................5-10 79

SOUTHERN DEATH CULT: see CULT

SOUTHERN FRIED
Singles: 7-inch
CREAM....................3-5 70s
LPs: 10/12-inch
MERCURY....................8-12 71

SOUTHERN HARMONAIRES
(Larks)
Singles: 78 rpm
APOLLO (200 series) 10-20 50
Singles: 7-inch
APOLLO (529 "I'm So Glad")........25-35 58
Also see LARKS

SOUTHERN MALE QUARTET
Singles: 78 rpm
BRUNSWICK....................10-30 39-40

SOUTHERN NEGRO QUARTETTE
(Southern Quartet)
Singles: 78 rpm
COLUMBIA....................25-50 21-24

SOUTHERN PACIFIC C&W '85
Singles: 7-inch
W.B. 3-4 85-90
Picture Sleeves
W.B. 3-4 88
Members: Tim Goodman; Stuart Cook; John McFee; Keith Knudsen; Kurt Howell; David Jenkins. Session: Emmylou Harris.
Also see CREEDENCE CLEARWATER REVIVAL
Also see DOOBIE BROTHERS
Also see HARRIS, Emmylou
Also see PABLO CRUISE

SOUTHERN PACIFIC & Carlene Carter C&W '89
Singles: 7-inch
W.B. 3-4 89
Also see CARTER, Carlene
Also see SOUTHERN PACIFIC

SOUTHERN REIGN C&W '86
Singles: 7-inch
REGAL....................3-4 86-87
STEP ONE....................3-4 87-88
Members: Jeff Crocker; Patsy McKeehan.

SOUTHERN SONS QUARTET
Singles: 78 rpm
TRUMPET (118 "Search Me Lord")....................30-50 50
TRUMPET (119 "Peace in the Valley")....................30-50 50
Members: Roscoe Robinson; David Smith; Earl Ratliff; Cliff Givens.
Also see ROBINSON, Roscoe

SOUTHERN TRAVELERS
Singles: 78 rpm
BIG TOWN....................15-25 54

SOUTHROAD CONNECTION
Singles: 12-inch
U.A. 4-8 79-80
Singles: 7-inch
LIBERTY....................3-5 80
MAHOGANY 3-5 78
U.A. 3-5 79-80
LPs: 10/12-inch
U.A. 5-10 80

SOUTHSIDE JOHNNY & ASBURY JUKES LP '76
(With the Jukes; Jukes; Southside Johnny)
Singles: 7-inch
ATLANTIC....................3-4 86
EPIC 3-5 77-78
MERCURY....................3-5 79
MIRAGE....................3-4 83-84
Picture Sleeves
ATLANTIC....................3-4 86
LPs: 10/12-inch
ATLANTIC....................5-8 86
CYPRESS....................5-8 88
EPIC 8-10 76-79
MERCURY....................5-10 79-81

MIRAGE 5-8 83-84
Also see FIVE SATINS
Also see MASON, Dave / Les Dudek / Southside Johnny & Asbury Jukes / Walter Egan

SOUTHSIDE MOVEMENT P&R '73
Singles: 7-inch
20TH FOX 3-5 74-75
WAND 3-5 73
LPs: 10/12-inch
20TH FOX 5-10 75
WAND 8-10 73
Also see SIMTEC & WYLIE

SOUTHWEST F.O.B. P&R '68
Singles: 7-inch
GPC 4-8 68
HIP 5-10 68-69
LPs: 10/12-inch
HIP (7001 "Smell of Incense") 25-35 69
Members: Dan Seals; John Ford Coley; Shane Keister.
Also see ENGLAND DAN & John Ford Coley
Also see THESE FEW

SOUTHWIND
Singles: 7-inch
BLUE THUMB 3-6 69-71
VENTURE 4-8 68
LPs: 10/12-inch
BLUE THUMB 10-15 69
VENTURE 10-15 68

SOUTHWINDS
Singles: 7-inch
FURY 8-12 58

SOUVENIR
Singles: 12-inch
MCA 4-6 84
Singles: 7-inch
MCA 3-4 84

SOUVENIRS
Singles: 78 rpm
DOOTO (412 "So Long Daddy") 50-75 57
Singles: 7-inch
DOOTO (412 "So Long Daddy") 50-100 57

SOUVENIRS
Singles: 7-inch
PRO 3-5 60s
REPRISE 3-5 62
LPs: 10/12-inch
REPRISE 15-25 62

SOUVENIRS
(With the Larry Lucie Orchestra)
Singles: 7-inch
INFERNO (2001 "I Could Have Danced All Night") 25-35 67

SOVEREIGN COLLECTION
Singles: 7-inch
CAPITOL (3094 "Hullabaloo of the Butterflies") 4-8 71

SOVINE, Red C&W '55
(With the Girls)
Singles: 78 rpm
DECCA (Except 30239) 5-10 54-57
DECCA (30239 "Juke Joint Johnny") 10-15 57
MGM 5-10 50-53
Singles: 7-inch
CHART 3-5 71-75
DECCA (Except 30239) 5-10 54-66
DECCA (30239 "Juke Joint Johnny") 20-30 57
GUSTO 3-5 77-80
MGM 8-15 50-53
RCA 4-8 62
RIC 4-6 64-65
STARDAY (Except 500 thru 800 series) 3-5 70-78
STARDAY (500 thru 800 series) 4-8 60-70
EPs: 7-inch
MGM 10-20 57
LPs: 10/12-inch
CMI 5-10 77
CHART 5-10 72-74
DECCA (4400 series) 15-25 64
DECCA (4700 series) 10-20 66
GUSTO/STARDAY 5-10 78
LAKE SHORE 8-12
MGM (3465 "Red Sovine") 30-40 57
METRO 10-15 67
NASHVILLE 6-12 70
POWER PAK 5-10 80s
RIC 10-15 65
SOMERSET 8-12 63
STARDAY (Except 100 series) 10-20 65-76
STARDAY (100 series) 15-25 61-62
STEREO FIDELITY 8-12 63
VOCALION 8-12 68
Also see BEAVERS, Clyde, & Red Sovine
Also see FELTS, Narvel / Red Sovine / Mel Tillis
Also see MULLICAN, Moon / Cowboy Copas / Red Sovine
Also see REEVES, Del / Red Sovine
Also see SHEPARD, Jean

SOVINE, Red, & Goldie Hill C&W '55
Singles: 78 rpm
DECCA 4-8 55
Singles: 7-inch
DECCA 5-10 55
Also see HILL, Goldie

SOVINE, Red, & Webb Pierce C&W '56
Singles: 78 rpm
DECCA 4-8 56
Singles: 7-inch
DECCA 8-12 56
Also see PIERCE, Webb
Also see SOVINE, Red

SOVINE, Roger C&W '68
Singles: 7-inch
IMPERIAL 4-6 68-69

SOWDER, Kenny
Singles: 7-inch
HOME of the BLUES (241 "Twisting Around the Mountains") 8-12 62

SOWELL, John
Singles: 7-inch
CITATION (1038 "So Help Me Hannah") 25-35 59

SOWELS, Scott
Singles
COLUMBIA ("April 14, 1981: America—Quest for the Stars") 10-15 83
(Shaped picture disc. 500 made.)

SOXX, Bob B.: see BOB B. SOXX & Blue Jeans

SPACE P&R '79
Singles: 12-inch
CASABLANCA 4-6 79-80
Singles: 7-inch
CASABLANCA 3-5 79-80
U.A. 3-5 77
LPs: 10/12-inch
CASABLANCA 5-10 78-79
U.A. 8-10 77
Also see BELL, Madeline

SPACE
Singles: 7-inch
CRAZY HORSE 4-8 68
LPs: 10/12-inch
HAND 10-15 69

SPACE
Singles: 7-inch
STAR (1976 "The Shark Hop") 8-12

SPACE, Sam, & Cadets
Singles: 7-inch
CABOT 5-10 59

SPACE ARK
LPs: 10/12-inch
COLOR WORLD 10-12

SPACE BAND
Singles: 7-inch
DUNWICH (159 "Winchester Cathedral") 4-8 67

SPACE MAN & SATELLITES
Singles: 7-inch
CHESS (1789 "Man in Orbit") 8-12 61

SPACE MEN
Singles: 7-inch
ERA 4-6 69

SPACE OPERA
Singles: 7-inch
EPIC 3-5 73
LPs: 10/12-inch
EPIC 8-10 73

SPACE PEOPLE
Singles: 7-inch
CAPITOL 3-5 82
LPs: 10/12-inch
CAPITOL 5-10 82

SPACE PROJECT
LPs: 10/12-inch
RCA 5-10 78

SPACEK, Sissy C&W '80
Singles: 7-inch
ATLANTIC AMERICA 3-4 83-84
MCA 3-5 80
Picture Sleeves
ATLANTIC AMERICA 3-4
MCA 3-5 80
LPs: 10/12-inch
ATLANTIC AMERICA 5-10 83

SPACEK, Sissy, & Beverly D'Angelo
Singles: 7-inch
MCA 3-5 80
Also see SPACEK, Sissy

SPACEMEN P&R '59
(Space Men)
Singles: 7-inch
ALTON 10-15 59-60
FELSTED 10-15 59
JAMECO 5-10 65
JUBILEE 10-15 59
MARKEY 5-10 62
LPs: 10/12-inch
ROULETTE 15-25 64-66

SPACEMEN
Singles: 7-inch
BIG SOUND (303 "Modman") 25-50 66
BIG SOUND (309 "Same Old Grind") 25-50 66
GEMINI (5566 "Spacewalk") 25-50 65
Picture Sleeves
BIG SOUND (309 "Same Old Grind") 40-60 66
Members: Gene Fondow; Bob Jilek; Tom Mcmahon; John Schuster; Loren Skaare.

SPACES
Singles: 7-inch
ARISTA 3-5 81
LPs: 10/12-inch
ARISTA 5-10 81

SPACEWALKERS
Singles: 7-inch
GAMBLE (229 "Apollo 9") 5-10 69
MOONGLOW (5001 "Gemini") 5-10 65
UFO (245 "Swamp Gas") 10-20 60s

SPADACHENE, Smith
Singles: 7-inch
L&Q (100 "Beatle Twist") 15-25 64

SPADE, Tony, & His Band
Singles: 7-inch
BACK BEAT (505 "What's Gwyne [sic] On") 50-100 57

SPADES
(Slades)
Singles: 7-inch
LIBERTY (55118 "You Mean Everything to Me") 50-75 58
Also see SLADES

SPADES
Singles: 7-inch
MAJOR (1007 "Close to You") 40-50 58

SPADES
(Thirteenth Floor Elevators)
Singles: 7-inch
ZERO (10001 "I Need a Girl") 100-200 65
ZERO (10002 "You're Gonna Miss Me") 200-300 65
(A different recording than later issued by the 13th Floor Elevators.)
Also see THIRTEENTH FLOOR ELEVATORS

SPAGHETTI HEAD
Singles: 7-inch
PRIVATE STOCK 3-5 75

SPAIN, Joanne
Singles: 7-inch
CASINO 3-5 77

SPAK, Emil, & Encores
Singles: 7-inch
WGW (3004 "Stuck Up") 70-90 63

SPANDAU BALLET P&R/D&D/LP '83
Singles: 12-inch
CHRYSALIS 4-6 84-85
Singles: 7-inch
CHRYSALIS 3-4 83-85
Picture Sleeves
CHRYSALIS 3-5 83-85
LPs: 10/12-inch
CHRYSALIS 5-8 83-85
MFSL (152 "True") 20-30 85
Also see BAND AID

SPANDELLS
Singles: 7-inch
DIMENSION 5-10 65

SPANGLER, Randy
Singles: 7-inch
MART (112 "Rock 'N Roll Baby") 100-200 58

SPANIELS P&R '57
(Spanials)
Singles: 78 rpm
CHANCE (1141 "Baby It's You") 50-100 53
VEE JAY (101 "Baby, It's You") 100-200 53
VEE JAY (103 "Bells Ring Out") 50-100 53
VEE JAY (107 "Goodnite Sweetheart, Goodnite") 75-100 54
(Mistakenly credits the "Spanials.")
VEE JAY (107 "Goodnite Sweetheart, Goodnite") 50-75 54
(Properly credits the "Spaniels.")
VEE JAY (116 thru 200 series) 25-75 54-58
Singles: 7-inch
BUDDAH (153 "Maybe") 5-8 69
CALLA (172 "Fairy Tales") 4-6 70
CANTERBURY (101 "Peace of Mind") 3-5 74
CHANCE (1141 "Baby It's You") 250-350 53
(Black vinyl.)
CHANCE (1141 "Baby It's You") 550-650 53
(Red vinyl.)
COLLECTABLES 3-4 80s
ERIC 3-5 70s
LOST-NITE 4-6
NORTH AMERICAN (101 "Fairy Tales") 5-8 70
(First issue.)
NORTH AMERICAN (102 "Stand in Line") 4-6 70
NORTH AMERICAN (3114 "Money Blues") 4-6 70s
OWL 3-5 73
TRIP 3-5
VEE JAY (101 "Baby It's You") 550-650 53
(Black vinyl. Maroon label.)
VEE JAY (101 "Baby It's You") 3000-5000 53
(Red vinyl.)
VEE JAY (101 "Baby It's You") 20-30 61
(Black label.)
VEE JAY (103 "Bells Ring Out") 100-200 53
(Black vinyl.)
VEE JAY (103 "Bells Ring Out") 500-750 53
(Red vinyl.)
VEE JAY (107 "Goodnite Sweetheart, Goodnite") 125-200 54
(Black vinyl. Credited to the Spanials.)
VEE JAY (107 "Goodnite Sweetheart, Goodnite") 100-150 54
(Black vinyl. Credited to Spaniels.)
VEE JAY (107 "Goodnite Sweetheart, Goodnite") 300-500 54
(Red vinyl. No "Trade Mark Reg." on label.)
VEE JAY (107 "Goodnite Sweetheart, Goodnite") 8-12 93
(Red vinyl, Vee Jay commemorative issue. Has "Trade Mark Reg." on label.)
VEE JAY (116 "Play It Cool") 50-75 54
(Black vinyl.)
VEE JAY (116 "Play It Cool") 500-750 54
(Red vinyl.)
VEE JAY (131 "Do-Wah") 40-60 55
(Black vinyl.)
VEE JAY (154 "You Painted Pictures") 40-50 55
VEE JAY (154 "Painted Picture") 30-40 55
(Shown as by the Spanials.)
VEE JAY (178 "False Love") 75-100 56
VEE JAY (189 "Dear Heart") 75-100 56
VEE JAY (202 "Since I Fell for You") 75-100 56
VEE JAY (229 thru 328) 30-45 56-58
VEE JAY (342 "People Will Say We're in Love") 50-75 59
VEE JAY (350 "I Know") 20-25 60
Picture Sleeves
VEE JAY (107 "Goodnite Sweetheart, Goodnite") 2-4 93
(Commemorative issue with this title although no specific artist or titles are shown.)
LPs: 10/12-inch
LOST-NITE (19 "The Spaniels") 8-12 81
LOST-NITE (137 "The Spaniels") 15-20 70s
VEE JAY (1002 "Goodnite, It's Time to Go") 200-300 59
(Maroon label.)
VEE JAY (1002 "Goodnite, It's Time to Go") 75-100 61
(Black label.)
VEE JAY (1024 "Spaniels") 200-250 60
UPFRONT 10-20
Members: Pookie Hudson; Jerry Gregory; Ernest Warren; Willie Jackson; Opal Courtney; James Cochran; Carl Rainge; Don Porter; Andy Magruder; Bill Carey.
Also see HUDSON, Pookie

SPANKY & OUR GANG P&R/LP '67
Singles: 7-inch
EPIC 3-5 75-76
MERCURY 4-8 67-69
Picture Sleeves
MERCURY 4-8 67-68
EPs: 7-inch
MERCURY (90 "Like to Get to Know You") 10-20 67
(Promotional issue only. Issued with paper sleeve.)
LPs: 10/12-inch
EPIC 8-10 75
MERCURY 10-20 67-71
RHINO 5-8 86
Members: Elaine "Spanky" McFarlane; Lefty Baker; Malcolm Hale; Nigel Pickering; John Seiter.

SPANN, Lucille
(With the Chicago Blues Band)
Singles: 7-inch
TORRID (5000 "Country Girl Returns") 5-8
LPs: 10/12-inch
BLUESWAY 8-10 74

SPANN, Otis
Singles: 7-inch
CHECKER (807 "It Must Have Been the Devil") 150-250 55
EXCELLO 5-10
LPs: 10/12-inch
ARCHIVE of FOLK MUSIC 10-15 68
BARNABY 10-12 70
BLUE HORIZON 10-12 70
BLUES TIME 10-12 70
BLUESWAY 10-15 67-73
CANDID (9001 "Otis Spann Is the Blues") 75-100 61
CRY 10-15
LONDON 10-15 68-69
PRESTIGE 8-10 69
VANGUARD 8-10 70
Also see CLAPTON, Eric
Also see COTTON, James
Also see DIDDLEY, Bo
Also see DIXON, Willie
Also see GUY, Buddy
Also see PAGE, Jimmy
Also see SMITH, George
Also see WATERS, Muddy
Also see WELLS, Junior
Also see WILLIAMSON, Sonny Boy

SPANN, Otis, & Fleetwood Mac
LPs: 10/12-inch
BLUE HORIZON 15-25 70
Also see FLEETWOOD MAC

SPANN, Otis, & Robert Lockwood Jr.
LPs: 10/12-inch
BARNABY 10-20 72
Also see LOCKWOOD, Robert, Jr.
Also see SPANN, Otis

SPARK PLUGS
LPs: 10/12-inch
SUTTON 10-15 60s

SPARKLERS
Singles: 7-inch
TAMPA (124 "Dreamy Eyes") 150-250 57

SPARKLERS FOUR
Singles: 7-inch
RUBU ("My Heart Still Remembers") 8-12 62
(No selection number used.)
Members: George Nauman; John Christmas; Jay Riness; Jim Passell.

SPARKLES
Singles: 7-inch
POPLAR (119 "We Got It") 10-15 63

SPARKLES
Singles: 7-inch
CARON (94 "The U.T.") 10-15 62
HICKORY (1364 "The Hip") 10-20 65
HICKORY (1390 "Something That You Said") 10-20 66
HICKORY (1406 "Jack and the Beanstalk") 10-20 66
HICKORY (1443 "No Friend of Mine") 10-20 67
HICKORY (1474 "Hipsville 29 BC") 10-20 67

SPARKLETONES
Singles: 7-inch
PAGEANT (604 "Just One Chance") 25-40 63

SPARKLETONES, with Joe Bennett: see BENNETT, Joe, & Sparkletones

SPARKLETTES
Singles: 7-inch
BELMONT (4007 "Doodling Around") 10-15 62
Also see HODGE, Gaynel

SPARKS
Singles: 78 rpm
HULL (723 "Danny Boy") 200-300 57
HULL (724 "Adreann") 50-100 57
Singles: 7-inch
HULL (723 "Danny Boy") 200-300 57
HULL (724 "Adreann") 50-100 57

SPARKS
Singles: 7-inch
ARWIN 10-15 58
CARLTON 10-15 59
DECCA 10-20 57-59
PETAL 5-10 64

SPARKS
Singles: 7-inch
CUB 4-8 67
DELLA 4-8 67

SPARKS LP '74
Singles: 12-inch
ATLANTIC 4-6 84
Singles: 7-inch
ATLANTIC 3-4 82-84
BEARSVILLE 3-5 72
COLUMBIA 3-5 78
ELEKTRA 3-5 79
FINE ARTS 3-4 88
ISLAND 3-5 73-76
RCA 3-5 81
Picture Sleeves
ATLANTIC 3-4 82-83
LPs: 10/12-inch
ATLANTIC 5-10 82-84
BEARSVILLE 12-15 72-73
COLUMBIA (Black vinyl) 8-10 77
COLUMBIA (Colored vinyl) 12-15 77
ELEKTRA 8-10 79
ISLAND 8-10 74-76
RCA 5-10 81
Members: Ron Mael; Russell Mael.
Also see HALFNELSON

SPARKS & JANE WIEDLIN P&R '83
Singles: 12-inch
ATLANTIC 4-6 83
Singles: 7-inch
ATLANTIC 3-4 83
Picture Sleeves
ATLANTIC 3-4 83
Also see SPARKS
Also see WIEDLIN, Jane

SPARKS
Singles: 7-inch
RPM 10-20

SPARKS, Ernie
Singles: 7-inch
LAKE (710 "Vacation Twist") 8-12 62

SPARKS, Melvin
Singles: 7-inch
WESTBOUND 3-5 75

SPARKS, Milton
(With Sammy Lowe & Orchestra)
Singles: 7-inch
HUNT (320 "A Certain Smile") 5-10 58
Also see DELROYS
Also see LOWE, Sammy, Orchestra

SPARKS, Randy
(Randy Sparks Three)
Singles: 7-inch
AIR 3-5
COLUMBIA 4-6 64
MGM 3-5 71
VERVE 4-8 59-61
Picture Sleeves
COLUMBIA 4-8 64
LPs: 10/12-inch
BUBBLE UP (25339 "Music to Drink Bubble Up By") 30-50 61
(Promotional issue only.)
DISNEYLAND 8-10 69
MGM 8-10 71

VERVE ... 20-25 60
Also see NEW CHRISTY MINSTRELS
Also see RIVERS, Johnny / Ricky Nelson / Randy Sparks

SPARKS OF RHYTHM
Singles: 78 rpm
APOLLO ... 25-50 55
Singles: 7-inch
APOLLO (479 "Don't Love You Anymore") ... 75-125 55
APOLLO (481 "Stars Are in the Sky") ... 100-150 55
APOLLO (541 "Handy Man") ... 20-40 60
Member: Jimmy Jones.
Also see JONES, Jimmy

SPARKTONES: see FIVE BLIND BOYS of MONTANA

SPARKY & FRIENDS
Singles: 7-inch
JUBILEE ... 4-6 67

SPARKY D D&D '85
Singles: 12-inch
NIA ... 4-6 85

SPARQUE D&D '84
Singles: 12-inch
WEST END ... 4-6 84

SPARROW
Singles: 7-inch
SPARK ... 3-5 72
LPs: 10/12-inch
SPARK ... 8-10 73
Member: W.D. Sparrow.

SPARROW, Johnny R&B '50
(With His Bows & Arrows)
Singles: 78 rpm
GOTHAM ... 10-15 53-54
MIRAGE ... 10-15 50
"X" ... 5-10 55
Singles: 7-inch
GOTHAM (7282 "Sparrow in the Barrel") ... 15-25 53
GOTHAM (7292 "Paradise Rock") 20-30 54
(Colored vinyl.)
"X" (0103 "Sparrow's Nest") ... 10-15 55

SPARROWS
(Jack London & the Sparrows)
Singles: 7-inch
CAPITOL (72203 "If You Don't Want My Love") ... 25-35 65
(Canadian.)
CAPITOL (72210 "Dream on Dreamer") ... 25-35 65
(Canadian.)
CAPITOL (72229 "Sparrows and Daisys") ... 25-35 65
(Canadian.)
CAPITOL (72257 "Hard Times with the Law") ... 25-35 65
(Canadian.)
COLUMBIA ... 10-15 66-67
LAURIE (3285 "If You Don't Want My Love") ... 10-15 66
Picture Sleeves
COLUMBIA ... 15-20 66
LPs: 10/12-inch
CAPITOL (6115 "Jack London & the Sparrows") ... 200-250 65
(Canadian.)
Members: Jack London; Jerry Edmonton; Dennis Edmonton; Nick St. Nicholas; Art Ayre; John Kay.
Also see BONFIRE, Mars
Also see STEPPENWOLF

SPARROWS
Singles: 78 rpm
DAVIS ... 50-75 56
JAY DEE ... 100-150 53
Singles: 7-inch
DAVIS (456 "Love Me Tender") . 150-200 56
JAY DEE (783 "Tell Me Baby") .. 250-300 53
JAY DEE (790 "I'll Be Loving You") ... 250-300 54
Also see BLENDERS / Sparrows

SPARROWS
LPs: 10/12-inch
ELKAY (3009 "Mersey Sound") ... 25-35 64

SPARTANS
(With Banjo Bill & His Rhythm Kings)
Singles: 7-inch
CAPRI (7201 "Faith, Hope and Charity") ... 250-500 54

SPARTANS
Singles: 7-inch
AUDIO INT'L ... 8-12 61

SPARTANS
Singles: 7-inch
PRINCESS (53 "Mr. Moto") ... 15-25 63

SPARTANS
Singles: 7-inch
WEB (1 "Can You Waddle") ... 10-20 63

SPARTANS
Singles: 7-inch
KELTONE ... 4-8 64

SPARTAS
Singles: 7-inch
HIT (154 "I'm Crying") ... 10-20 60s

SPATS P&R '64
Singles: 7-inch
ABC-PAR ... 5-10 64-66
ENITH ... 10-20 64
JANO ... 10-20 67
LPs: 10/12-inch
ABC-PAR ... 20-25 65
Member: Dick Johnson.

SPAULDING WOOD AFFAIR
Singles: 7-inch
KAPP ... 4-8 68

SPEAR, Roger Ruskin
Singles: 7-inch
U.A. ... 3-5 73
LPs: 10/12-inch
U.A. ... 8-10 73
Also see BONZO DOG BAND

SPEARMINTS
Singles: 7-inch
AUTUMN ... 4-8 65

SPEARS, Billie Jo C&W '68
Singles: 7-inch
CAPITOL ... 3-5 68-71
LIBERTY ... 3-4 81
PARLIAMENT ... 3-4 84
U.A. (Except 50000 series) ... 3-5 74-80
U.A. (50000 series) ... 3-6 66-67
LPs: 10/12-inch
CAPITOL ... 5-15 68-79
KOALA ... 5-10 80s
LIBERTY ... 5-8 81
PICKWICK/HILLTOP ... 5-8 70s
U.A. ... 5-10 75-80
Also see BUTLER, Larry, & Friends
Also see REEVES, Del, & Billie Jo Spears

SPEARS, Bobby
Singles: 7-inch
MANCO ... 4-8 63
Also see CASSADY, Linda

SPEARS, Calvin
Singles: 7-inch
VIN ... 10-15 60

SPEARS, Merle, & Treats
Singles: 7-inch
ATLANTIC ... 4-8 64

SPECIAL, Bob
Singles: 7-inch
SEECO ... 5-10 59

SPECIAL AKA D&D '84
Singles: 12-inch
CHRYSALIS ... 4-6 84
Singles: 7-inch
CHRYSALIS ... 3-4 84
LPs: 10/12-inch
CHRYSALIS ... 5-8 84
Also see SPECIALS

SPECIAL DELIVERY
Singles: 7-inch
VERVE ... 4-6 68

SPECIAL DELIVERY R&B '76
(Featuring Terry Huff)
Singles: 7-inch
MAINSTREAM ... 3-5 75-76
SHIELD ... 3-5 77-78
Also see BRUNSON, Tyrone "Tystick"
Also see HUFF, Terry

SPECIAL ED LP '89
LPs: 10/12-inch
PROFILE ... 5-8 89-90

SPECIAL FORCES
LPs: 10/12-inch
AZRA (050 "Tools of the Trade") ... 5-10 82
(Picture disc. Promotional issue only.)

SPECIAL REQUEST
Singles: 12-inch
TOMMY BOY ... 4-6 83

SPECIALS
Singles: 7-inch
MARC (103 "Kissin' Like Lovers") .. 15-25 63

SPECIALS
Singles: 7-inch
SATCH (512 "You Stood Me Up") ... 100-150 60s

SPECIALS LP '80
Singles: 12-inch
CHRYSALIS ... 4-6 81
Singles: 7-inch
CHRYSALIS ... 3-5 79-80
Picture Sleeves
CHRYSALIS ... 3-5 79
LPs: 10/12-inch
CHRYSALIS ... 5-10 80
Also see FUN BOY THREE
Also see SPECIAL AKA

SPECIMEN
Singles: 7-inch
SIRE ... 3-4 84
LPs: 10/12-inch
SIRE ... 5-8 84

SPECK & DOYLE – THE WRIGHT BROTHERS
Singles: 7-inch
SYRUP BUCKET (1000 "Big Noise, Bright Lights") ... 40-50
Members: Speck Wright; Doyle Wright.

SPECKULATIONS
Singles: 7-inch
SPECK (6129 "Hulu Hoop") ... 10-20 58

SPECTACLE
Singles: 7-inch
FISH ... 5-10 68
Also see CELLOPHANE SPECTACLE

SPECTOR, Phil
Singles: 7-inch
PHILLES ("Thanks for Giving Me the Right Time") ... 150-250 63
(No selection number used. Promotional issue only.)
Also see HARVEY, Phil
Also see SPECTORS THREE

SPECTOR, Ronnie P&R '71
(With the Ronettes; with E Street Band)
Singles: 12-inch
EPIC/CLEVELAND INT'L (350 "Say Goodbye to Hollywood") ... 8-12 77
(Promotional issue only.)
Singles: 7-inch
ALSTON ... 5-8 78
APPLE ... 5-10 70-71
BUDDAH ... 4-6 74
EPIC/CLEVELAND INT'L (50374 "Say Goodbye to Hollywood") ... 5-10 77
COLUMBIA ... 3-4 87
POLISH ... 3-5 80
TOM CAT (Black vinyl) ... 3-5 75-76
TOM CAT (Colored vinyl) ... 5-8 75
(Promotional issues only.)
W.B./SPECTOR ... 3-5 76
Picture Sleeves
APPLE ... 8-10 71
COLUMBIA ... 3-5 87
EPIC/CLEVELAND INT'L (50374 "Say Goodbye to Hollywood") ... 20-25 77
LPs: 10/12-inch
POLISH ... 8-12 80
Also see MONEY, Eddie, & Ronnie Spector
Also see RONETTES
Also see SPRINGSTEEN, Bruce
Also see VERONICA

SPECTORS THREE
Singles: 7-inch
TREY ... 10-20 59-60
Member: Phil Spector.
Also see SPECTOR, Phil
Also see TEDDY BEARS

SPECTRES
Singles: 7-inch
N-JOY ... 5-10 66
SALEM (004 "So Near to Me") ... 10-20 60s

SPECTRUM
Singles: 7-inch
DCR (10203 "For You") ... 10-20 60s
UDELL (61219 "Bald Headed Woman") ... 10-20 60s

SPECTRUMS
Singles: 7-inch
KNIGHT (4969 "Wine Wine Wine") ... 15-25 60s

SPEED, Bobby, & Amenders
Singles
AZRA (32 "Dianne") ... 8-12 88
(Shaped picture disc.)

SPEED LIMIT
Singles: 7-inch
WATTS ... 3-5 72
LPs: 10/12-inch
JT ... 5-10 81

SPEEDO & CADILLACS
(Cadillacs)
Singles: 7-inch
JOSIE (876 "It's Love") ... 20-25 60
Members: Earl Carroll; Roland Martinez; Kirk Davis; Ronnie Bright.
Also see CADILLACS

SPEEDO & IMPALAS
(Impalas)
Singles: 7-inch
CUB (9066 "All Alone") ... 15-25 60
Also see IMPALAS

SPEEDO & PEARLS
Singles: 7-inch
JOSIE (865 "Who Ya Gonna Kiss") ... 10-20 59
Member: Earl Carroll.
Also see CADILLACS
Also see SPEEDO & CADILLACS

SPEEDWAY BLVD
Singles: 7-inch
EPIC ... 3-5 80
LPs: 10/12-inch
EPIC ... 5-10 80
Members: Glen Dove; Gregg Hoffman; Jordan Rudes; Roy Herring, Jr; Dennis Feldman.

SPEEDY & ALKA-SELTZERS
Singles: 7-inch
FEATURE (501 "Donna") ... 15-25 66
TEE PEE (3302 "I Wonder What She's Doin' Tonight") ... 15-25 68
Members: Jerry Lariden; Bob Kenison; Bruce Benson; Jim Donovan; Jim Bisbee; Bob Bellard; Jim Lombard; Lance Massey.

SPEEDY & REVERBS
Singles: 7-inch
REVERB (51 "100 Proof") ... 15-25 60s

SPEEDY KEEN: see KEEN, Speedy

SPEEGLE, David C&W '89
(With Lonerider)
Singles: 7-inch
BITTER CREED ... 3-4 89

SPEEKS, Ronnie C&W '81
(With His Elrods)
Singles: 7-inch
DIMENSION ... 3-5 81
KING (5548 "What Is Your Technique") ... 75-100 61
PALETTE (5094 "Mister Glenn") ... 4-8 63

SPEIDELS
("Vocal by Bill Bagby"; Spidels)
Singles: 7-inch
CROSLEY (201 "Dear Joan") ... 50-75 58
(Has "Crosley" all in same size letters.)
CROSLEY (201 "Dear Joan") ... 25-35 58
(Has "Crosley" in letters of different sizes.)
MINARET (112 "I'll Catch a Rainbow") ... 20-30 63
(Credits: "Spidels.")
MINARET (112 "I'll Catch a Rainbow") ... 15-20 63
(Credits: "Speidels.")
MONTE CARLO (101 "Oh Baby") ... 150-200 60

SPEKTRUM
Singles: 7-inch
SOMETHIN' GROOVY (500 "I Was a Fool") ... 15-25 60s

SPEKTRUMS
Singles: 7-inch
IMPACT ... 5-10 61

SPELLBINDERS P&R '65
Singles: 7-inch
COLUMBIA ... 5-10 65-66
DATE ... 5-10 67
MIRAMAR (115) ... 10-15 65
(Exact title not known.)
LPs: 10/12-inch
COLUMBIA (2514 "Magic of the Spellbinders") ... 15-25 66
(Monaural.)
COLUMBIA (9314 "Magic of the Spellbinders") ... 15-25 66
(Stereo.)
Members: Bob Shivers; Jimmy Wright; Ben Grant; McArthur Munford; Elouise Pennington.

SPELLBOUND P&R '78
Singles: 7-inch
EMI AMERICA ... 3-5 78
LPs: 10/12-inch
EMI AMERICA ... 5-10 78

SPELLING ON THE STONE C&W '88
Singles: 7-inch
CURB/LS (10522 "Spelling on the Stone") ... 3-5 88
LS (53 "Spelling on the Stone") ... 5-10 88
LPs: 10/12-inch
CURB/LS (10608 "Spelling on the Stone") ... 5-10 88
Since no artist is credited on this release, it is listed here by title. The singer reportedly is Dan Willis.

SPELLMAN, Benny P&R '62
Singles: 7-inch
ACE (630 "Roll on Big Wheel") ... 10-20 61
ALON ... 4-8 66
ATLANTIC ... 5-10 65
MINIT (644 "Lipstick Traces") ... 10-20 62
SANSU ... 4-8 67
WATCH ... 5-10 64
LPs: 10/12-inch
BANDY (70018 "Benny Spellman") 10-15 70s
Also see K-DOE, Ernie
Also see THOMAS, Irma / Ernie K-Doe / Showmen / Benny Spellman

SPELLMAN, Jimmy
Singles: 78 rpm
DOT ... 15-25 57
VIV ... 10-20 56
Singles: 7-inch
DOT (15564 "Here I Am") ... 15-25 57
DOT (15607 "Doggonit") ... 15-25 57
VIK (0320 "Deep Love") ... 15-25 58
VIV (1000 "Give Me Some of Yours") ... 15-25 56
VIV (1002 "It's You, You, You") ... 15-25 56
VIV (1004 "No Escape") ... 15-25 56

SPENCE, Alexander "Skip"
LPs: 10/12-inch
COLUMBIA ... 10-15 69

SPENCE, Johnny
(With Taxi)
Singles: 7-inch
ALTAIR ... 3-6

SPENCE, Judson P&R/LP '88
Singles: 7-inch
ATLANTIC ... 3-4 88
Picture Sleeves
ATLANTIC ... 3-4 88
LPs: 10/12-inch
ATLANTIC ... 5-8 88

SPENCER
Singles: 7-inch
MIDTOWN ... 4-8 66

SPENCER, Bob
Singles: 7-inch
APOLLO ... 5-10 59
EPIC ... 8-12 55-56

SPENCER, Carl
(With the Mellows; with Sammy Lowe Orchestra)
Singles: 78 rpm
CANDLELIGHT ... 50-75 56
Singles: 7-inch
CANDLELIGHT (1012 "Farewell, Farewell") ... 100-150 56
RUST (5104 "Cover Girl") ... 25-50 66
SOUTHSIDE (1002 "Prayer") ... 50-100 59
WREN (306 "One Last Kiss") ... 10-20 60
Also see MELLOWS

SPENCER, Don
Singles: 7-inch
20TH FOX (440 "XL5") ... 10-20 63

SPENCER, Elvin
Singles: 7-inch
WINNER ... 8-12

SPENCER, James
Singles: 7-inch
MEMPHIS ... 5-10

SPENCER, Jeremy
(With the Children; Jeremy Spencer Group)
Singles: 7-inch
ATLANTIC ... 3-5 79
COLUMBIA ... 3-5 73
LPs: 10/12-inch
ATLANTIC ... 5-10 79
COLUMBIA ... 8-12 72
Also see FLEETWOOD MAC

SPENCER, Jim, & Son Rize
Singles: 7-inch
ARMADA ... 3-5 79
Also see SUNRISE

SPENCER, Richard, & Winstons
Singles: 7-inch
METROMEDIA ... 4-6 69
Also see WINSTONS

SPENCER, Sammy, & Tilts
Singles: 7-inch
TOWNHOUSE ... 5-10 59

SPENCER, Sonny P&R '59
Singles: 7-inch
MEMO (17984 "Gilee") ... 10-20 59
MUSIC HALL (24002 "Hold My Hand") ... 20-30
ONDA (111 "Bessie Lou") ... 15-25
Also see RAINBOWS

SPENCER, Teddy C&W '88
Singles: 7-inch
OAK ... 3-4 88

SPENCER, Tracie P&R/LP '88
Singles: 7-inch
CAPITOL ... 3-4 88-91
Picture Sleeves
CAPITOL ... 3-4 88-89
LPs: 10/12-inch
CAPITOL ... 5-8 88-91

SPENCER, Vicki
(Vicky Spencer)
Singles: 7-inch
BRUNSWICK ... 5-10 62
FRATERNITY ... 5-10 61

SPENCER & SPENCER P&R '59
Singles: 7-inch
ARGO (5331 "Russian Bandstand") ... 10-20 59
GONE (5053 "Stagger Lawrence") 15-25 59
Members: Dickie Goodman; Mickey Shorr.
Also see GOODMAN, Dickie
Also see SHORR, Mickey, & Cutups

SPERRY, Steve P&R '77
Singles: 7-inch
CUCA (1008 "Our Summer Love") 15-25 60
MERCURY ... 3-5 77
Also see LANGDON, Jim, Trio

SPHEERIS, Chris
LPs: 10/12-inch
COLUMBIA ... 5-8 88

SPHEERIS, Jimmie LP '75
Singles: 7-inch
COLUMBIA ... 3-5 72
EPIC ... 3-5 75
LPs: 10/12-inch
EPIC ... 8-10 75

SPIC & SPAN
Singles: 7-inch
LEN ... 10-15 61

SPICE
Singles: 7-inch
REDD HEDD (007 "Broken Down in Tiny Pieces") ... 10-20 78

SPICE
Singles: 12-inch
JIVE ... 4-6 83
Singles: 7-inch
JIVE ... 3-5 83

SPICE OF LIFE
Singles: 7-inch
POPPY ... 4-8 68

SPICE RACQ
Singles: 7-inch
LIBERTY ... 4-6 69

SPICES
Singles: 7-inch
CARLTON (480 "Tell Me Little Girl") ... 250-450 59

SPIDELLS
Singles: 7-inch
CORAL (62508 "Pushed Out of the Picture") ... 25-50 66

CORAL (62531 "Don't You Forget That You're My Baby")....................15-25 67
MONZA (1112 "Find Out What's Happening")....................10-20 64
MONZA (1123 "Hmmm, with Feeling")....................10-20 65

SPI-DELLS
Singles: 7-inch
SPI-DELLS/LITTLE TOWN............10-20 60s

SPIDELS
Singles: 7-inch
CHAVIS (1035 "You Know I Need You")....................10-20 62

SPIDELS (on Minaret): see SPEIDELS

SPIDER
Singles: 7-inch
CAPITOL.................................. 3-5 72
LPs: 10/12-inch
CAPITOL.................................. 8-12 72

SPIDER *P&R/LP '80*
Singles: 7-inch
DREAMLAND.............................. 3-5 80-81
Picture Sleeves
DREAMLAND.............................. 3-5 80
LPs: 10/12-inch
DREAMLAND.............................. 5-10 80-81
Member: Holly Knight.
Also see KNIGHT, Holly

SPIDER & MUSTANGS
Singles: 7-inch
SANDS (10662 "So Long Child")..... 8-12

SPIDER MAN
LPs: 10/12-inch
LIFESONG.............................. 8-12 76

SPIDER SAM
Singles: 78 rpm
ATLANTIC (980 "After Midnight")...25-35 50
Members: Van Walls; Brownie McGhee.
Also see McGHEE, Brownie
Also see WALLS, Van

SPIDER, SNAKE & EEL
Singles: 7-inch
L.A. BEAT (6054 "Only a Boy")......15-25 60s

SPIDER WEBB: see WEBB, Spider

SPIDERS *R&B '54*
Singles: 78 rpm
IMPERIAL..............................25-75 54-57
Singles: 7-inch
IMPERIAL (5265 "I Didn't Want to Do It")....................75-125 53
IMPERIAL (5280 "Tears Began to Flow")....................75-125 54
IMPERIAL (5291 "I'm Searching")....................75-125 54
IMPERIAL (5305 "Real Thing")....75-125 54
IMPERIAL (5318 "She Keeps Me Wondering")....................50-100 54
IMPERIAL (5331 "That's Enough")....................50-100 55
IMPERIAL (5344 "Am I the One")....................50-100 55
IMPERIAL (5354 "Bells in My Heart")....................75-100 55
(Red label.)
IMPERIAL (5354 "Bells in My Heart")....................25-50 57
(Black label.)
IMPERIAL (5366 "Is It True") 100-150 55
(Blue label.)
IMPERIAL (5366 "Is It True") 25-50 55
(Red label.)
IMPERIAL (5376 "Don't Pity Me") ..20-30 56
IMPERIAL (5393 "Dear Mary")........20-30 56
IMPERIAL (5405 "Goodbye")............20-30 56
IMPERIAL (5423 "Honey Bee")........20-30 56
IMPERIAL (5618 "I Didn't Want to Do It")....................20-30 59
IMPERIAL (5714 "You're the One")....................15-25 60
IMPERIAL (5739 "Witchcraft").......15-25 61
OWL.................................. 3-5 73
LPs: 10/12-inch
IMPERIAL (9142 "I Didn't Want to Do It")....................250-500 61
Member: Chuck Carbo.
Also see CARBO, Chuck

SPIDERS
Singles: 7-inch
MASCOT (112 "Why Don't You Love Me")....................750-1000 65
SANTA CRUZ (003 "Don't Blow Your Mind")....................350-400 66
Members: Vince "Alice Cooper" Furnier; John Speer; Glen Buxton; Dennis Dunaway; Mike Bruce.
Also see COOPER, Alice

SPIDERS
Singles: 7-inch
LAWN.................................. 8-10 64
Also see WRAY, Link

SPIDERS
Singles: 7-inch
PHILIPS.................................. 4-8 66

SPIDERS
Singles: 7-inch
BROKEN RECORDS........................ 3-5 81
Picture Sleeves
BROKEN RECORDS........................ 3-5 81
Members: Billy Bastiani; Fast Floyd; Franko St. Andrew; Linwood Land; Tali Jackson.
Also see FAST FLOYD & His Famous Firebirds

SPIDERS from MARS *LP '76*
Singles: 7-inch
PYE.................................. 3-5 76
LPs: 10/12-inch
PYE..................................8-10 76
Also see BOWIE, David

SPIEDELS
Singles: 7-inch
CROSLEY (201 "Dear John").........20-30
PROVIDENCE.............................. 4-8

SPIELERS
Singles: 7-inch
CALDWELL (401 "Yeah, Yeah, Yeah")....................15-25 59

SPIERS, Arvile
Singles: 7-inch
GO (105 "Western Swingsters Rock")....................8-12

SPIKE DRIVERS
Singles: 7-inch
OM 1000 (1676 "High Time")........20-30 66
REPRISE (0535 "High Time")........10-15 66
REPRISE (0558 "Strange Mysterious Sounds")....................10-15 67

SPIKE MICHAEL
Singles: 7-inch
CUCA (1151 "Billy Boy")................10-15 63

SPIN *P&R '76*
Singles: 7-inch
ARIOLA AMERICA........................ 3-5 76
LPs: 10/12-inch
ARIOLA AMERICA........................8-10 76

SPINAL TAP *LP '84*
Singles: 7-inch
ENIGMA (1144 "Christmas with the Devil")....................8-12 84
(Picture disc.)
POLYDOR.................................. 3-4 84
Picture Sleeves
ENIGMA (1143 "Christmas with the Devil")....................3-5 84
LPs: 10/12-inch
MCA (10514 "Break Like the Wind")....................10-12 92
(Picture disc.)
POLYDOR.................................. 5-8 84
Also see CREDIBILITY GAP
Also see HEAR 'N AID

SPINDIG
Singles: 7-inch
JERDE..................................5-10 60s

SPINDLE
Singles: 7-inch
JERDEN.................................. 4-8 69
PICCADILLY..............................5-10 68

SPINDLES
Singles: 7-inch
ABC-PAR (10802 "To Make You Mine")....................10-20 66
ABC-PAR (10850 "Ten Shades of Blue")....................15-25 66

SPINDRIFT
Singles: 7-inch
SCEPTER.................................. 4-8 66

SPINDRIFTS
(Featuring Freddy Cannon; with the Downbeats)
Singles: 7-inch
ABC-PAR (9904 "Cha Cha Doo")...25-35 58
HOT ("Cha Cha Doo")................50-100 58
(Selection number not known.)
Also see CANNON, Freddy

SPINNERS
Singles: 7-inch
RHYTHM (125 "Marvella").........500-750 58

SPINNERS
Singles: 7-inch
CAPITOL (3955 "Love's Prayer") ...20-30 58
END (1045 "Bird Watchin' ") 60-80 58
(Gray label.)
END (1045 "Bird Watchin' ") 25-35 59
(Multi-Color label.)
Member: Don Barksdale.

SPINNERS
Singles: 7-inch
CRYSTALETTE (736 "Boomerang")....................15-25 60
(Reissued as *Surf Stomp*, by the Crestriders and as *The Lion*, by Duke Mitchell.)
Also see CRESTRIDERS
Also see MITCHELL, Duke

SPINNERS
Singles: 7-inch
RCA.................................. 3-5 64
SMASH.................................. 3-5 63
W.B..................................4-6 60

SPINNERS
Singles: 7-inch
LAWSON (324 "Beetle Mania")......10-20 64

SPINNERS
LPs: 10/12-inch
TIME..................................15-30 63

SPINNERS *P&R '61*
(Spinners / Harvey)
Singles: 7-inch
ATLANTIC.................................. 3-6 72-85
MOTOWN (1067 thru 1136)..............8-15 64-68
MOTOWN (1155 "In My Diary")....................500-1000 69
MOTOWN (1235 "Bad Bad Weather")....................4-6 73
TRI-PHI (1001 "That's What Girls Are Made For")....................10-20 61
TRI-PHI (1004 "Love")..............15-20 61
TRI-PHI (1007 "What Did She Use")....................15-20 62
TRI-PHI (1010 "She Loves Me So")....................15-20 62
TRI-PHI (1013 "I've Been Hurt") 15-20 62
V.I.P. (25050 "In My Diary")..........10-20 69
V.I.P. (25054 "Message from a Black Man")....................10-20 70
V.I.P. (25057 "It's a Shame") 4-8 70
V.I.P. (25060 "We'll Have It Made") ...4-8 70
LPs: 10/12-inch
ATLANTIC..............................6-10 73-84
MOTOWN (Except 639)................5-10 73-82
MOTOWN (639 "Original Spinners")....................20-40 67
PICKWICK..............................8-10 76
V.I.P. (405 "Second Time Around")20-40 70
Members: Bobby Smith; Henry Fambrough; Pervis Jackson; Bill Henderson; G.C. Cameron; Philippe Wynne; Reese Palmer; Jim Knowland; Ed Edwards; Chester Simmons.
Also see ABBA / Spinners / Firefall / England Dan & John Ford Coley
Also see CAMERON, G.C.
Also see HARVEY
Also see LOE & JOE
Also see MARQUEES
Also see SMITH, Bobby
Also see WARWICK, Dionne, & Spinners
Also see WYNNE, Philippe

SPINNING WHEEL
Singles: 7-inch
CENTURY (36668 "Funky Alien") 5-8 60s

SPIRAL STARECASE *P&R/LP '69*
Singles: 7-inch
COLUMBIA..............................4-6 69-70
LPs: 10/12-inch
COLUMBIA (9852 "More Today Than Yesterday")....................15-20 69
COLUMBIA (10172 "More Today Than Yesterday")....................8-12
Members: Pat Upton; Dick Lopes; Vinny Parello; Bob Raymond; Harvey Kaplan.
Also see UPTON, Pat

SPIRALS
Singles: 7-inch
CAPITOL (4084 "The Rockin' Cow")....................15-20 58

SPIRALS
Singles: 7-inch
INDIGO (500 "Baby You Just Wait")....................500-700 60

SPIRALS
Singles: 7-inch
ADMIRAL (913 "Forever and a Day")....................500-1000 61
SMASH (1719 "Forever and a Day")....................50-100 61

SPIRALS
Singles: 7-inch
LUXOR (1012 "My Humble Prayer")....................400-600 62

SPIRES, Big Boy
(With His Trio; Arthur Spires)
Singles: 78 rpm
CHANCE..............................200-400 53
Singles: 7-inch
CHANCE (1137 "About to Lose My Mind")....................500-1000 53
(Colored vinyl. With John Lee Henley.)
Also see JOHN LEE

SPIRES OF OXFORD
Singles: 7-inch
MY (2923 "But You're Gone") 15-25 67

SPIRIT
Singles: 7-inch
ROULETTE..............................5-8 67

SPIRIT *LP '68*
Singles: 12-inch
MERCURY..............................4-6 84
Singles: 7-inch
EPIC..............................3-6 70-74
MERCURY..............................3-5 75-76
ODE..............................4-8 68-70
POTATO..............................3-5 78
RHINO..............................3-4 81
Picture Sleeves
EPIC..............................4-8 74
POTATO..............................3-4 78
LPs: 10/12-inch
EPIC..............................8-12 70-73
MERCURY (Except 818514)..........10-15 75-77
MERCURY (818514 "Spirit of '84") 5-8 84
ODE (44003 "Spirit")..................20-25 68
(Monaural.)
ODE (44004 "Spirit")..................15-20 68
(Stereo.)
ODE (44014 "The Family That Plays Together")....................10-20 68
ODE (44016 "Clear")..................10-15 69
POTATO..............................10-15
RHINO..............................5-8 81
Members: Jay Ferguson; Randy California; Mark Andes; Ed Cassidy; John Locke; John Arliss.
Also see FERGUSON, Jay
Also see FIREFALL
Also see HEART
Also see RISING SONS

Also see YELLOW BALLOON

SPIRIT in FLESH
LPs: 10/12-inch
METROMEDIA..............................10-12 71

SPIRIT OF ATLANTA
Singles: 7-inch
BUDDAH..............................3-4 73
LPs: 10/12-inch
BUDDAH..............................8-10 73

SPIRIT OF LOVE
LPs: 10/12-inch
DARK HORSE..............................8-10 77

SPIRIT OF MEMPHIS
Singles: 78 rpm
KING..............................10-20 49-53
PEACOCK..............................5-10 53-55
Singles: 7-inch
AUDIO LAB (22 "The 10 Commandments")....................20-40 59
KING (4538 "That Awful Day")......50-100 52
KING (4562 "Just to Behold His Face")....................50-100 52
KING (4575 "God's Amazing Grace")....................50-100 52
KING (4576 "Lord Jesus")............50-100 52
KING (4614 "There's No Sorrow")...50-75 53
PEACOCK (1700 series) 15-25 53-55

SPIRIT OF US
LPs: 10/12-inch
VIVA..............................8-10 70

SPIRITS
Singles: 7-inch
PERSONALITY..............................4-8 61
PLAZA..............................4-8 62
U.A..............................4-8 61

SPIRITS
Singles: 7-inch
TOOT..............................4-6 67
Also see UNDERTAKERS / Spirits

SPIRITS & WORM
Singles: 7-inch
A&M (1104 "Fanny Firecracker") 15-25 69
LPs: 10/12-inch
A&M (4229 "Spirits & Worm")....150-250 69

SPIRITS OF BLUE LIGHTNING
Singles: 7-inch
LAVENDER (2009 "Love Muscle") 10-20 60s

SPIRITS OF RHYTHM
Singles: 78 rpm
BLACK & WHITE (23 "She Ain't No Saint")....................15-25 45
Members: Georgie Vann; Leo Watson; Leonard Feather; Teddy Bunn; Ulysses Livingstone; Red Callender.

SPIRITUAL CONCEPT
LPs: 10/12-inch
PHILADELPHIA INT'L..............................8-10 73

SPIRITUAL HARMONIZERS
Singles: 7-inch
GLORY (4004 "Do You Know Him")....................15-25

SPIRITUAL TRAVELERS
Singles: 78 rpm
EXCEL (103 "Remember Me").......15-20 55
Singles: 7-inch
EXCEL (103 "Remember Me")........25-50 55

SPITFIRES
Singles: 7-inch
JARO..............................4-6 59

SPITZ, Michele *C&W '81*
Singles: 7-inch
50 STATES..............................3-4 81

SPIVEY, Joyce, & Melvettes
Singles: 7-inch
OLIMPIC..............................10-15 65

SPIVEY, Victoria
Singles: 7-inch
QUEEN VEE..............................3-5 62
Also see JOHNSON, Lonnie
Also see THREE KINGS & a Queen

SPIZZLES
Singles: 7-inch
A&M..............................3-4 81
LPs: 10/12-inch
A&M..............................5-8 81

SPLENDORS
Singles: 7-inch
TAURUS (101 "Golden Years")..100-150 60

SPLENDORS
Singles: 7-inch
JANO (004 "Puddin' Tan") 75-100 62
KARATE (520 "Please Don't Go")..50-75 66

SPLIFF
LPs: 10/12-inch
EPIC..............................5-8 83

SPLINTER *P&R/LP '74*
Singles: 7-inch
DARK HORSE..............................3-6 74-77
LPs: 10/12-inch
DARK HORSE..............................8-10 74-77
Members: Bill Elliott; Bob Purvis.
Also see ELLIOTT, Bill, & Elastic Oz Band
Also see HARRISON, George

SPLIT
Singles: 7-inch
SOLID (8417 "Blowin Smoke").........8-12 77

Also see BRIGMAN, George

SPLIT ENDS
Singles: 7-inch
CFP (4 "Rich with Nothin' ") 25-50 66
Also see BOOT

SPLIT ENZ *P&R/LP '80*
Singles: 7-inch
A&M (Except 2339 & AMS-8128).......3-5 80-84
A&M (2339 "One Step Ahead")..........4-6 82
("Laser Etched Single.")
A&M (AMS-8128 "Shark Attack") .75-100 82
(Laser etched, shaped picture disc. Promotional issue only.)
Picture Sleeves
A&M..............................3-5 80-82
EPs: 7-inch
A&M (4848 "I Don't Want to Dance")....................15-25 81
(Picture disc. Promotional issue only.)
LPs: 10/12-inch
A&M..............................5-10 80-84
CHRYSALIS..............................8-10 77
Members: Tim Finn; Neil Finn.
Also see CROWDED HOUSE
Also see FINN, Tim

SPLIT IMAGE
Singles: 12-inch
CAPITOL..............................4-6 84

SPLIT LEVEL
Singles: 7-inch
DOT..............................3-5 67-68
LPs: 10/12-inch
DOT..............................10-12 68

SPO-DE-ODEE
Singles: 7-inch
VERUS..............................4-6 60

SPOELSTRA, Mark
Singles: 7-inch
FANTASY..............................3-4 71

SPOKES
Singles: 7-inch
SCORPIO (401 "Mini-Bike") 20-25 60s

SPOKESMEN *P&R '65*
Singles: 7-inch
DECCA..............................4-8 65-66
WINCHESTER..............................4-8 67
LPs: 10/12-inch
DECCA..............................25-30 65
Members: Johnny Madara; David White.
Also see MADARA, Johnny

SPONGETONES
LPs: 10/12-inch
RIPETE..............................5-8 83

SPONGY & DOLLS
Singles: 7-inch
BRIDGEVIEW (7001 "It Looks Like Love")....................60-80 60s

SPONTANEOUS COMBUSTION
Singles: 7-inch
HARVEST..............................3-6 72-73
ROD..............................10-15 68
LPs: 10/12-inch
CAPITOL..............................10-12 72
FLYING DUTCHMAN..............................12-15 69
HARVEST..............................10-12 72

SPONTANES
Singles: 7-inch
BEAVER..............................4-6 60s
CASINO (4797 "Share My Name")....................15-20 60s
ECLIPSE..............................5-10 60s
U.A..............................3-5 68
LPs: 10/12-inch
HIT ATTRACTIONS (7999 "Solid Soul")....................100-150 60s
(Selection number not known.)

SPOOKY TOOTH *LP '69*
(Gary Wright's Spooky Tooth)
Singles: 7-inch
A&M..............................4-6 69
MALA..............................5-10 68
ISLAND..............................3-5 72
LPs: 10/12-inch
A&M..............................10-15 69-73
ACCORD..............................5-10 82
BELL..............................15-20 68
ISLAND..............................8-10 73-74
Members: Gary Wright; Mike Harrison; Luther Grosvenor.
Also see BOXER
Also see GROSVENOR, Luther
Also see HARRISON, Mike
Also see WRIGHT, Gary

SPOONBREAD
Singles: 7-inch
STANG..............................3-5 72

SPOONER & SPOONS
Singles: 7-inch
FAME..............................3-5 65

SPOONER'S CROWD
Singles: 7-inch
CADET..............................3-5 66

SPOONIE GEE
Singles: 12-inch 33/45
CBS ASSOCIATED..............................4-6 83
Singles: 7-inch
CBS ASSOCIATED..............................3-5 83
SUGAR HILL..............................3-5 81
TUFF CITY..............................3-5 83

SPOONS
Singles: 12-inch 33/45
A&M 4-6 83
Singles: 7-inch
A&M 3-4 82-83
LPs: 10/12-inch
A&M 5-8 82

SPORTIN' LIFE
Singles: 7-inch
RILSA 10-15 60s

SPORTS P&R/LP '79
Singles: 7-inch
ARISTA 3-5 79
Picture Sleeves
ARISTA 3-5 79
LPs: 10/12-inch
ARISTA 5-10 79-80

SPORTSMEN
(With Pep Boys: Manny, Moe & Jack; with Bob Bain's Music)
Singles: 78 rpm
KEY (503 "Hot Rod Hop") 10-15 55
KEY (513 "Me & My Shadow") 15-25 56
Singles: 7-inch
A (104 "Dreaming") 10-20 59
KEY (503 "Hot Rod Hop") 20-30 55
KEY (513 "Me & My Shadow") 25-50 56
RONROY 3-5 62

SPORTTONES
("With Rhythm Acc.")
Singles: 7-inch
MUNICH (101 "In My Dreams") 1000-1500 59

SPOTFINDERS
Singles: 7-inch
BLUES OUTLET 3-5 83

SPOTLIGHTERS
(With Bob Thompson & Band)
Singles: 78 rpm
IMPERIAL (5342 "It's Cold") 40-60 55
Singles: 7-inch
ALADDIN (3436 "Please Be My Girlfriend") 50-100 58
ALADDIN (3441 "This Is My Story") 25-50 58
IMPERIAL (5342 "It's Cold") 75-100 55
(Black vinyl.)
IMPERIAL (5342 "It's Cold") 150-200 55
(Colored vinyl.)
Also see THOMPSON, Bob, Orchestra

SPOTLIGHTERS
Singles: 7-inch
PLEASANT 3-5 64

SPOTLIGHTS
Singles: 7-inch
SMASH 3-5 66
U.A. 3-5 63

SPOTLITES
Singles: 7-inch
CATALINA 10-15 59

SPOTNICKS
Singles: 7-inch
ATCO 5-10 62
FELSTED (8649 "Old Spinning Wheel") 20-30 62
LAURIE 5-10 64-65

SPREADEAGLE
Singles: 7-inch
CHARISMA 3-4 72
LPs: 10/12-inch
CHARISMA 10-12 72

SPRIGGS, Walter
(Walter Spreegs)
Singles: 78 rpm
APOLLO 10-15 53
ATCO 10-20 56-57
BLUE LAKE 10-25 50s
Singles: 7-inch
APOLLO 15-30 53
ATCO 10-20 56-57
BLUE LAKE 35-50 50s
Also see FIVE ECHOES
Also see WILSON, Wally

SPRING
Singles: 7-inch
U.A. (50848 "Now That Everything's Been Said") 10-15 71
U.A. (50907 "Good Time") 25-30 72
LPs: 10/12-inch
U.A. 15-25 72
Members: Marilyn Wilson; Diane Rovell.
Also see AMERICAN SPRING
Also see HONEYS

SPRING
Singles: 7-inch
IX CHAINS 3-5 73

SPRING, McKendree: see McKENDREE SPRING

SPRING FEVER
Singles: 7-inch
SPLITSOUND 5-8 67
Also see GRODES

SPRING FEVER
Singles: 7-inch
CAPITOL 4-8 68

SPRINGER BROTHERS C&W '80
Singles: 7-inch
ELEKTRA 3-4 80

SPRINGERS
Singles: 7-inch
WAY OUT (2699 "I Know Why") 20-30 65

SPRINGFIELD, Bob
Singles: 7-inch
STRIKER 3-5

SPRINGFIELD, Bobby Lee C&W '83
Singles: 7-inch
EPIC 3-4 87
KAT FAMILY 3-4 83

SPRINGFIELD, Dusty P&R/LP '64
Singles: 7-inch
ATLANTIC 3-6 68-71
CASABLANCA 3-5 82
DUNHILL 3-5 73
PHILIPS 4-8 63-68
20TH FOX 3-5 80
U.A. 3-5 77-79
Picture Sleeves
PHILIPS 5-10 64-67
ATLANTIC 4-6 68
LPs: 10/12-inch
ATLANTIC 10-15 69-70
CASABLANCA 5-8 82
DUNHILL 8-10 73
PHILIPS 12-20 64-67
U.A. 5-10 78-79
WING 10-15 68
Also see HONDELLS / Dusty Springfield
Also see PET SHOP BOYS & Dusty Springfield
Also see SPRINGFIELDS

SPRINGFIELD, Rick P&R/LP '72
Singles: 12-inch
RCA 4-6 83-84
Singles: 7-inch
CAPITOL 3-6 72-73
CHELSEA 3-5 76-77
COLUMBIA 3-5 74
MERCURY 3-4 84-85
RCA 3-5 81-85
Picture Sleeves
CAPITOL 4-8 72
MERCURY 3-5 84
RCA 3-5 81-88
LPs: 10/12-inch
CAPITOL (11000 series) 15-20 72-73
CAPITOL (16000 series) 5-10 81
CHELSEA 8-12 76
COLUMBIA (KC-32000 series) 10-15 73
COLUMBIA (PC-32000 series) 5-8
MERCURY 5-8 84
RCA 5-10 80-88

SPRINGFIELD, Rick, & Randy Crawford P&R '84
Singles: 7-inch
RCA 3-5 84
Picture Sleeves
RCA 3-5 84
Also see CRAWFORD, Randy
Also see SPRINGFIELD, Rick

SPRINGFIELD REVIVAL
Singles: 7-inch
VERVE/GTO 3-5 72
LPs: 10/12-inch
MGM 8-10 73

SPRINGFIELD RIFLE
(Springfield Rifles)
Singles: 7-inch
ABC 4-8 66
BURDETTE 5-10 69
JERDEN 5-10 67
TOWER 5-10 68
LPs: 10/12-inch
BURDETTE (5159 "Springfield Rifle") 15-25 69
Members: Terry Afdem; Jeff Afdem; Harry Wilson; Bob Perry; Joe Cavender.
Also see DYNAMICS

SPRINGFIELDS C&W/P&R '62
Singles: 7-inch
PHILIPS 4-6 62-63
LPs: 10/12-inch
PHILIPS 15-25 62-63
Members: Dusty Springfield; Tom Springfield; Tim Field.
Also see SPRINGFIELD, Dusty

SPRINGS, Kenny, & Scat Cats
Singles: 7-inch
SPOT 10-15

SPRINGSTEEN, Bruce P&R/LP '75
(With the E Street Band)
Singles: 12-inch
COLUMBIA (1329 "Santa Claus Is Comin' to Town") 30-40 81
(White label. Promotional issue only.)
COLUMBIA (2007 "I'm on Fire") 20-25 85
(Red label. Black and white cover. Promotional issue only.)
COLUMBIA (2082 "Glory Days") 20-25 85
(Red label. Black and white cover. Promotional issue only.)
COLUMBIA (2174 "I'm Goin' Down") 20-25 85
(Red label. Black and white cover. Promotional issue only.)
COLUMBIA (2233 "My Hometown") 20-25 85
(Red label. Black and white cover. Promotional issue only.)
COLUMBIA (2543 "Bruce Springsteen & E Street Band Live, 1975-85") 20-25 86
(Eight track sampler. Promotional issue only.)
COLUMBIA (05028 "Dancing in the Dark") 5-8 84
COLUMBIA (05028 "Dancing in the Dark") 20-30 84
(With black and white cover. Promotional issue only.)
COLUMBIA (05028 "Dancing in the Dark") 15-25 84
(Promotional issue with color cover and gold promo stamp.)
COLUMBIA (05087 "Cover Me") 5-8 84
COLUMBIA (05147 "Born in the USA") 4-6 84
COLUMBIA (05147 "Born in the USA") 15-20 84
(White label. Promotional issue only.)
COLUMBIA (44445 "Chimes of Freedom") 5-8 88
Singles: 7-inch
COLUMBIA (03243 "Hungry Heart") 3-5 84
COLUMBIA (04463 "Dancing in the Dark") 3-5 84
COLUMBIA (04561 "Cover Me") 3-5 84
COLUMBIA (04680 "Born in the USA") 3-5 84
COLUMBIA (04772 "I'm on Fire") 3-5 85
COLUMBIA (04924 "Glory Days") 3-5 85
COLUMBIA (05606 "I'm Goin' Down") 3-5 85
COLUMBIA (05728 "My Hometown") 3-5 85
COLUMBIA (06432 "War") 3-4 86
COLUMBIA (06657 "Fire") 3-4 87
COLUMBIA (07595 "Brilliant Disguise") 3-4 87
COLUMBIA (07663 "Tunnel of Love") 3-4 87
COLUMBIA (07726 "One Step Up") 3-4 88
COLUMBIA (08400 series) 3-4 88
(Columbia Hall of Fame series.)
COLUMBIA (10209 "Born to Run") 10-15 75
COLUMBIA (10274 "Tenth Avenue Freeze-Out") 8-12 75
COLUMBIA (10763 "Prove It All Night") 8-12 78
COLUMBIA (10801 "Badlands") 3-6 78
COLUMBIA (11391 "Hungry Heart") 3-4 80
COLUMBIA (11431 "Fade Away"/ "To Be True") 15-25 81
COLUMBIA (11431 "Fade Away"/ "Be True") 3-4 81
COLUMBIA (33323 "Born to Run") 8-10 76
(Red label. Columbia Hall of Fame series.)
COLUMBIA (33323 "Born to Run") 3-4 84
(Gray label. Columbia Hall of Fame series.)
COLUMBIA (45805 "Blinded By the Light") 150-250 73
COLUMBIA (45864 "Spirit in the Night") 300-500 73
Promotional Singles: 7-inch
COLUMBIA (1329 "Santa Claus Is Comin' to Town") 10-15 81
COLUMBIA (2557 "War") 10-15 86
(Has 1:55 spoken intro on one side.)
COLUMBIA (04463 "Dancing in the Dark") 8-10 84
COLUMBIA (04561 "Cover Me") 6-10 84
COLUMBIA (04680 "Born in the USA") 6-10 84
COLUMBIA (04772 "I'm on Fire") 6-10 85
COLUMBIA (04924 "Glory Days") 6-10 85
COLUMBIA (05606 "I'm Goin' Down") 6-10 85
COLUMBIA (05728 "My Hometown") 6-10 85
COLUMBIA (06432 "War") 5-8 86
COLUMBIA (07595 "Brilliant Disguise") 5-8 87
COLUMBIA (07663 "Tunnel of Love") 5-8 87
COLUMBIA (07726 "One Step Up") 5-8 88
COLUMBIA (10209 "Born to Run") 30-35 75
(With large letters on label.)
COLUMBIA (10209 "Born to Run") 20-25 75
(With small letters on label.)
COLUMBIA (10274 "Tenth Avenue Freeze-Out") 15-20 75
COLUMBIA (10763 "Prove It All Night") 15-20 78
COLUMBIA (10801 "Badlands") 15-20 78
COLUMBIA (11391 "Hungry Heart") 15-20 80
COLUMBIA (11431 "Fade Away") 10-15 81
COLUMBIA (45805 "Blinded By the Light") 45-55 73
COLUMBIA (45864 "Spirit in the Night") 35-45 73
Picture Sleeves
COLUMBIA (1329 "Santa Claus Is Comin' to Town") 15-20 81
(Promotional issue only.)
COLUMBIA (2557 "War") 10-15 86
(Sleeve for spoken intro promo.)
COLUMBIA (04463 "Dancing in the Dark") 5-10 84
COLUMBIA (04561 "Cover Me") 5-10 84
COLUMBIA (04680 "Born in the USA") 5-10 84
COLUMBIA (04772 "I'm on Fire") 5-10 85
COLUMBIA (04924 "Glory Days") 5-10 85
COLUMBIA (05606 "I'm Goin' Down") 5-10 85
COLUMBIA (05728 "My Hometown") 5-10 85
COLUMBIA (06432 "War") 4-8 86
COLUMBIA (07595 "Brilliant Disguise") 4-8 87
COLUMBIA (07663 "Tunnel of Love") 4-8 87
COLUMBIA (07726 "One Step Up") 4-8 88
COLUMBIA (11391 "Hungry Heart") 4-8 80
COLUMBIA (11431 "Fade Away") 4-8 81
COLUMBIA (45805 "Blinded By the Light") 300-500 73
LPs: 10/12-inch
COLUMBIA (KC-31903 "Greetings from Asbury Park") 15-20 73
COLUMBIA (PC-31903 "Greetings from Asbury Park") 8-12 75
COLUMBIA (JC-31903 "Greetings from Asbury Park") 5-8 78
COLUMBIA (KC-32432 "The Wild Innocent and the E Street Shuffle") 15-18 73
COLUMBIA (PC-32432 "The Wild Innocent and the E Street Shuffle") 10-15 73
COLUMBIA (JC-32432 "The Wild Innocent and the E Street Shuffle") 5-8 78
COLUMBIA (PC-33795 "Born to Run") 25-30 75
(Credits show Jon Landau as "John.")
COLUMBIA (PC-33795 "Born to Run") 15-20 75
(Has "Jon" correction strip applied to cover.)
COLUMBIA (PC-33795 "Born to Run") 8-12 75
(Has "Jon" correction printed on cover.)
COLUMBIA (JC-33795 "Born to Run") 5-8 78
COLUMBIA (JC-35318 "Darkness on the Edge of Town") 5-8 78
COLUMBIA (36854 "The River") 10-15 80
COLUMBIA (38358 "Nebraska") 5-8 82
COLUMBIA (38653 "Born in the USA") 5-8 84
COLUMBIA (40558 "Bruce Springsteen & E Street Band Live, 1975-85") 30-40 86
(Includes 36-page booklet.)
COLUMBIA (40999 "Tunnel of Love") 5-8 87
COLUMBIA (HC-43795 "Born to Run") 25-35 80
(Half-speed mastered.)
COLUMBIA (HC-45318 "Darkness on the Edge of Town") 40-60 81
(Half-speed mastered.)
COLUMBIA (67060 "Greatest Hits") 10-15 95
COLUMBIA (67484 "The Ghost of Tom Joad") 8-10 96
Promotional LPs
COLUMBIA (978 "As Requested Around the World") 30-40 81
COLUMBIA (1957 "Born in the USA") 20-30 84
COLUMBIA (31903 "Greetings from Asbury Park") 35-45 73
(White label.)
COLUMBIA (32432 "The Wild Innocent and the E Street Shuffle") 35-45 73
(White label.)
COLUMBIA (33795 "Born to Run") 750-1000 75
(With "script" title cover.)
COLUMBIA (33795 "Born to Run") 40-50 75
(White label.)
COLUMBIA (JC-35318 "Darkness on the Edge of Town") 30-40 78
(White label.)
COLUMBIA (PAL-35318 "Darkness on the Edge of Town") 100-150 78
(Picture disc. 200 made. Add $15 to $25 if lyric sheet is included.)
COLUMBIA (36854 "The River") 25-35 80
(White label.)
COLUMBIA (38358 "Nebraska") 15-25 82
(White label.)
COLUMBIA (38653 "Born in the USA") 15-20 84
(White label.)
Also see ADDEO, Nicky
Also see BONDS, Gary "U.S."
Also see CLEMONS, Clarence
Also see LITTLE STEVEN
Also see ORBISON, Roy
Also see PARKER, Graham
Also see SPECTOR, Ronnie
Also see THOMPSON, Robbin, Band
Also see U.S.A. for AFRICA

SPRINGSTEEN, Bruce / Jackson Browne
Singles: 12-inch
ASYLUM (11442 "Medley") 40-50 70
(45 rpm. Has plain sleeve with info sticker.)
Also see BROWNE, Jackson

SPRINGSTEEN, Bruce / Andy Pratt
Singles: 7-inch
COLUMBIA/PLAYBACK (AS-45 "Blinded By the Light") 75-100 73
(Add $40 to $50 if accompanied by booklet.)
Picture Sleeves
COLUMBIA/PLAYBACK (AS-45 "Blinded By the Light") 5-10 73
Also see PRATT, Andy

SPRINGSTEEN, Bruce / Loudon Wainwright III / Taj Mahal / Albert Hammond
Singles: 7-inch
COLUMBIA/PLAYBACK (AS-52 "The Circus Song [Recorded Live]") 75-100 73
(Add $40 to $50 if accompanied by booklet.)
Picture Sleeves
COLUMBIA/PLAYBACK (AS-52 "The Circus Song") 5-10 73
Also see HAMMOND, Albert
Also see TAJ MAHAL
Also see WAINWRIGHT, Loudon, III

SPRINGSTEEN, Bruce / Johnny Winter / Hollies
Singles: 7-inch
COLUMBIA/PLAYBACK (AS-66 "Rosalita") 75-100 73
(Add $40 to $50 if accompanied by booklet.)
Picture Sleeves
COLUMBIA/PLAYBACK (AS-66 "Rosalita") 5-10 73
Also see HOLLIES
Also see SPRINGSTEEN, Bruce
Also see WINTER, Johnny

SPRINGSTONE, Bruce
Singles: 12-inch
COLD CUTS 4-6 85
Singles: 7-inch
CLEAN CUTS 3-4 85
Picture Sleeves
CLEAN CUTS 3-4 85

SPRINGWELL P&R '71
Singles: 7-inch
PARROT 3-5 71

SPRINGWHEEL
LPs: 10/12-inch
GREEN BOTTLE 8-10 73

SPRITES
Singles: 7-inch
PATIENCE (100 "My Picture") 15-25 62
Members: Bobby Hendricks; Bill Pinkney; Andrew Thrasher; Gerhart Thrasher.
Also see DRIFTERS

SPROUTS
Singles: 7-inch
MERCURY 3-5 60
RCA 8-10 57
SPANGLE 15-25 57

SPRYTES
Singles: 7-inch
MORTICIAN (104 "Land of 1,000 Dances") 10-20 66

SPUDD, Bud, & Sprouts
Singles: 7-inch
EM 4-8 62

SPUNK
Singles: 7-inch
GOLD COAST 3-5 81
LPs: 10/12-inch
GOLD COAST 5-10 81

SPUNKIES
Singles: 7-inch
LEE (1001 "Spunky") 10-20 59
LEE (1003 "Jamaican Jungle") 10-20 59

SPUR
LPs: 10/12-inch
CINEMA (1500 "Spur of the Moment") 20-40 60s

SPURILL, Wild Jimmy
(Jimmy "Wildman" Spruill)
Singles: 7-inch
CEE JAY (581 "Jumping In") 20-30 56
ENJOY (2006 "Cut & Dried") 8-12 64
EVERLAST (5004 "Jumping In") 10-15 57
EVERLAST (5017 "Scratch and Twist") 8-12 60
FIRE (1006 "Hard Grind") 15-25 59
VIM (521 "Scratchin' ") 5-10 64
Also see COOPER, Horace
Also see HARRISON, Jim & Bob
Also see WALKER, Charles, & Band

SPURLIN, Tommy
Singles: 7-inch
ART (131 "Heart Throb") 50-60 70s
(First issue of tracks made in the mid-'50s.)
PERFECT (109 "Hang Loose") 200-250 56

SPURLING, Charles
Singles: 7-inch
KING (6077 "You'd Be Surprised") 10-15 65

SPURLOCK, Virginia
Singles: 7-inch
EPIC 4-8 62

SPURRLOWS
Singles: 7-inch
YAS (106 "Summertime") 3-5

SPURZZ C&W '80
Singles: 7-inch
EPIC 3-5 80
Member: Tony Ingram.
Also see ATLANTA
Also see WELLER, Freddy

SPUTNIKS
Singles: 78 rpm
CLASS (217 "My Love Is Gone") 25-35 57
Singles: 7-inch
CLASS (217 "My Love Is Gone") 50-75 57
CLASS (222 "Wait a Little Longer") 30-50 57
PAM MAR (601 "My Love Is Gone") 250-500 57

SPY
LPs: 10/12-inch
KIRSHNER 5-10 80

SPYDELS
(Spydells)
Singles: 7-inch
ADDIT (1220 "We're in Love") 20-30 60
ASSAULT 10-15 60s
MZ (112 "No More Teasin' ") 20-30 61

SPYDER
Singles
AZRA (17 "No Reason for War") 5-10 87
(Diamond-shaped picture disc.)
AZRA (17 "No Reason for War") 8-12 87
(Rectangular picture disc.)

SPYDER C.
Singles: 12-inch
WEST END 4-8 80s

SPYDER-D
(Spyder-D & D.J. Divine
Singles: 12-inch
PROFILE 4-6 84-86
Singles: 7-inch
PROFILE 3-4 86

SPYDER'S GANG
Singles: 7-inch
SCEPTER 3-5 72

SPYDERS
Singles: 7-inch
MTA 4-8 67

SPYRES Featuring Mark Prewitt
Singles: 7-inch
VIX (1001 "Baby, Let Me Take You Home") 15-25 60s

SPYRO GYRA P&R/LP '78
Singles: 7-inch
AMHERST 3-5 78
INFINITY 3-5 79
MCA 3-5 80-85
Picture Sleeves
INFINITY 3-5 79
EPs: 7-inch
INFINITY (1011 "Live Spyro Gyra") 5-10 79
(Promotional issue only. With insert. Not issued with cover.)
LPs: 10/12-inch
AMHERST 5-10 78
GRP 5-8 90-91
INFINITY 5-10 79
MCA (5000 series) 5-10 80-86
MCA (6000 series) 8-10 84-89
MCA (9004 "Morning Dance") 40-60 79
(Picture disc. Promotional issue only.)
MCA (42000 series) 5-8 87
Members: Chet Catallo; Jay Beckenstein.

SPYS P&R/LP '82
Singles: 7-inch
EMI AMERICA 3-5 82
LPs: 10/12-inch
EMI AMERICA 5-10 82
Also see FOREIGNER

SQUALLS
Singles: 7-inch
I.R.S. 3-4 87
Picture Sleeves
I.R.S. 3-4 87

SQUARE ROOT OF TWO
Singles: 7-inch
BAJA (4504 "Turned On") 30-40

SQUARES
Singles: 7-inch
BRISTOL (10001 "Davey's Drag") 15-25 59
(First issue.)
TEL (1003 "Davey's Drag") 10-15 59
Member: Dave Sanderson.

SQUASH
LPs: 10/12-inch
STASIMA 5-10 81

SQUEAKY CLEAN
LPs: 10/12-inch
DRIP DRY 8-10 84

SQUEEZE LP '80
(U.K. Squeeze)
Singles: 7-inch
A&M 3-5 79-87
Picture Sleeves
A&M 3-5 80-87
LPs: 10/12-inch
A&M (Except 3413 & 4687) 5-10 79-89
A&M (3413 "Squeeze") 10-20 72
A&M (4687 "U.K. Squeeze") 10-15 78
I.R.S. 5-8 90
Members: Chris Difford; Glenn Tilbrook; Jools Holland; Gilson Lavis; Keith Wilkinson; Andy Metcalfe.
Also see CARRACK, Paul
Also see DIFFORD & TILBROOK
Also see HOLLAND, Jools, & Millionaires

SQUEEZER
LPs: 10/12-inch
NOW 10-12 74

SQUEEZY, John Cameron
Singles: 7-inch
PRINCESS (4022 "The Bearded Leader" [Fidel Castro]) 15-25 63

SQUIDDLY DIDDLY
LPs: 10/12-inch
HBR (2043 "Squiddly Diddly's Surfin' Surfari") 30-50 65

SQUIER, Billy LP '80
Singles: 7-inch
CAPITOL (Except 79694) 3-5 80-88
CAPITOL (79694 "Don't You Love Me") 5-10 89
(Promotional issue only. Commercial single release on cassette only.)
Picture Sleeves
CAPITOL 3-5 80-86
LPs: 10/12-inch
CAPITOL 5-10 80-91
Also see PIPER

SQUIRE, Chris LP '76
Singles: 7-inch
ATLANTIC 3-5 76
LPs: 10/12-inch
ATLANTIC 8-10 76
Also see YES

SQUIRES
Singles: 78 rpm
COMBO (35 "Let's Give Love a Try") 50-100 53
COMBO (42 "Oh Darling") 75-125 54
Singles: 7-inch
COMBO (35 "Let's Give Love a Try") 250-350 53
(Red label.)
COMBO (42 "Oh Darling") 350-450 54
(Red label.)
Members: Delmar Wilburn; Ethel Brown; Otis White; James Richardson; James Myles; Maudice Giles.

SQUIRES
Singles: 78 rpm
FLAIR (1030 "Sayonara") 8-12 54
Singles: 7-inch
FLAIR (1030 "Sayonara") 10-20 54

SQUIRES
Singles: 78 rpm
GUYDEN 8-12 55
Singles: 7-inch
GUYDEN (714 "Bobby Sox Jamboree") 15-25 55
Also see ESQUIRE BOYS

SQUIRES
(Blue Jays)
Singles: 78 rpm
ALADDIN (3360 "Dreamy Eyes") ... 40-60 57
KICKS (1 "A Dream Come True") 100-200 54
MAMBO (105 "Sindy") 35-50 55
VITA 20-40 55
Singles: 7-inch
ALADDIN (3360 "Dreamy Eyes") . 75-100 57
KICKS (1 "A Dream Come True") 500-1000 54
MAMBO (105 "Sindy") 150-250 55
(Maroon label.)
MAMBO (105 "Sindy") 100-150 55
(Black label.)
VITA (105 "Sindy") 50-100 55
VITA (113 "Sweet Girl") 50-100 55
VITA (116 "Heavenly Angel") 50-100 55
Members: Don Bowman; Dewey Terry; Leon Washington; Chester Pipkin; Bob Armstrong; Lee Goudeau.
Also see BLUE JAYS
Also see DON & DEWEY
Also see PIPKINS
Also see SMITH, Effie

SQUIRES
Singles: 7-inch
V (109 "The Sultan") 50-75 61
Also see YOUNG, Neil

SQUIRES
Singles: 7-inch
CHAN 10-15 61-62
MGM 5-10 61

SQUIRES
Singles: 7-inch
GEE (1082 "Don't Accuse Me") 25-50 62
HERALD (580 "Why Should I Suffer") 15-25 63

SQUIRES
Singles: 7-inch
COMMERCIAL 5-10 64
STARLITE (1 "Movin' ") 15-25 64

SQUIRES
Singles: 7-inch
CONGRESS (223 "Joyce") 40-60 64

SQUIRES
Singles: 7-inch
LEAF (6581 "Dear Jan") 10-15 65

SQUIRES
Singles: 7-inch
ATCO (6442 "Going All the Way") 15-25 66
Also see ROGUES

SQUIRES
Singles: 7-inch
NORTHWESTERN 10-20
PENGUIN (161 "Batmobile") 10-20 60s

S'QUIRES
Singles: 7-inch
BARRY (3312 "Green Surf") 8-12 60s
(Canadian.)
BARRY (3398 "Remember") 8-12 60s
(Canadian.)

SQUIRES
Singles: 7-inch
ROBWAY 4-8

SQUIRES, Dorothy
Singles: 7-inch
BELL 3-5 72

SQUIRRELS
Singles: 7-inch
CAMEO 4-8 63

SQUIRRELS
Singles: 7-inch
RCA 4-8 67

STABILIZERS P&R '87
Singles: 7-inch
COLUMBIA 3-4 87
Picture Sleeves
COLUMBIA 3-4 87

STACCATOS
Singles: 7-inch
CAPITOL 10-15 68
SYNCRO (661 "Gypsy Girl") 15-25 66
TOWER 10-20 67
Member: Les Emmerson.
Also see FIVE MAN ELECTRICAL BAND

STACCATOS
Singles: 7-inch
KANDY KANE (1004 "Moon Dawg") 20-30 60s

STACEY, Carl, Trio
Singles: 7-inch
CADEL (4501 "The Big Gass") 25-50
(Identification number shown since no selection number is used.)
Members: Carl Stacey; El Gassaway; Don Dunckon.

STACEY, Clint
Singles: 7-inch
JET 4-8 62

STACEY, Phil
Singles: 7-inch
20TH FOX 4-8 63
Picture Sleeves
20TH FOX 5-10 63

STACEY Q P&R/LP '86
(Stacey Swain)
Singles: 12-inch
ATLANTIC 4-6 86-87
Singles: 7-inch
ATLANTIC 3-4 86-88
ON the SPOT 3-4 87
Picture Sleeves
ATLANTIC 3-4 86-88
LPs: 10/12-inch
ATLANTIC 5-8 86-88
Also see SSQ

STACK, Billy C&W '78
Singles: 7-inch
CAPRICE 3-5 78-79

STACKHOUSE, Ruby
(Ruby Andrews)
Singles: 7-inch
KELLMAC 4-8 65
Also see ANDREWS, Ruby

STACKRIDGE LP '74
Singles: 7-inch
DECCA 3-5 71-72
MCA 3-5 73
ROCKET 3-5 76
SIRE 3-5 74-75
LPs: 10/12-inch
DECCA 10-12 71
MCA 8-10 73
ROCKET 5-10 76
SIRE 8-10 74-75
Members: Andrew Davis; Jim Warren; Mutter Slater.
Also see KORGIS

STACY, Brian
Singles: 7-inch
ATCO 4-8 66
DOT 4-8 66

STACY, Chuck
Singles: 7-inch
BRYTE 4-8 64

STACY, Clarence
Singles: 7-inch
CAROL (4114 "Jack the Ripper") ... 15-25 61
GLORY (301 "Forget Me") 10-20 60
SPARKLE (101 "Lonely Guy") 15-25 58

STACY, Clyde P&R '57
(With the Nitecaps)
Singles: 7-inch
ARGYLE (1001 "So Young") 15-25 59
BULLSEYE (1004 "Baby Shame") 15-25 58
BULLSEYE (1008 "Sure Do Love You Baby") 40-60 58
BULLSEYE (1014 "You Want Love") 10-20 58
CANDLELIGHT (1015 "Hoy Hoy") 30-40 57
G&H (101 "Baby Shame") 35-50 58
(First issue.)
LEN (1015 "You're Satisfied") 25-35 61

STACY, Homer
Singles: 7-inch
GALAHAD (545 "For Better Or Worse") 15-25 61

STACY'S FIFTH
Singles: 7-inch
JUBILEE 4-8 66

STAEHELY BROTHERS
LPs: 10/12-inch
EPIC 8-12 73

STAFF, Bobbi C&W '66
Singles: 7-inch
RCA 4-6 66

STAFFORD, Jim P&R '73
Singles: 7-inch
COLUMBIA 3-4 84
ELEKTRA 3-5 80-81
ISLAND 3-5 74
MGM 3-5 73-75
POLYDOR 3-5 75-78
TOWN HOUSE 3-5 82
W.B. 3-5 76-80
LPs: 10/12-inch
MGM 8-10 74-75
POLYDOR 5-10 76
Also see LOBO

STAFFORD, Jo P&R '44
Singles: 78 rpm
CAPITOL 3-8 43-50
COLUMBIA 3-5 50-57
COLUMBIA/SNOWY BLEACH (22270 "St. Louis Blues") 10-15 50s
(Promotional issue for Snowy Bleach and Glass Wax. No actual label name shown. Seven-inch 78 rpm.)
Singles: 7-inch
COLPIX 4-6 62
COLUMBIA 5-10 50-60
DECCA 4-6 68
DOT 4-6 65
REPRISE 4-6 63
EPs: 7-inch
CAPITOL 5-15 50-57
COLUMBIA 5-15 50-59
LPs: 10/12-inch
BAINBRIDGE 5-8 82
CAPITOL (H-75 thru H-435) 20-40 50-53
(10-inch LPs.)
CAPITOL (T-197 thru T-435) 15-25 55
CAPITOL (T-1653 thru T-2166) 10-20 62-64
(Monaural.)
CAPITOL (ST-1653 thru ST-2166) 12-25 62-64
(Stereo.)
CAPITOL (9014 "Songs of Faith") . 20-30 54
(10-inch LP.)
CAPITOL (11000 series) 5-8 79
COLUMBIA (584 thru 1339) 15-25 54-59
(Monaural.)
COLUMBIA (1561 "Jo Plus Jazz") 30-50 60
(Monaural.)
COLUMBIA (2500 series) 15-30 55
(10-inch LPs.)
COLUMBIA (6000 series) 20-35 50-54
(10-inch LPs.)
COLUMBIA (8080 "I'll Be Seeing You") 20-30 59
(Stereo.)
COLUMBIA (8139 "Ballad of the Blues") 20-30 59
(Stereo.)
COLUMBIA (8361 "Jo Plus Jazz") 40-60 60
(Stereo.)
COLUMBIA/SNOWY BLEACH (22500 "I Only Have Eyes for You") 15-25 50s
(Promotional issue for Snowy Bleach. No actual label name shown.)
DECCA 10-15 68
DOT 10-15 66
TRIBUTE 5-10 71
VOCALION 8-12 68-69
Also see EDWARDS, Jonathan & Darlene
Also see INGLE, Red, & Natural Seven
Also see LAINE, Frankie, & Jo Stafford
Also see MacRAE, Gordon, & Jo Stafford
Also see MERCER, Johnny, Jo Stafford & Pied Pipers
Also see PIED PIPERS
Also see WESTON, Paul

STAFFORD, Sonny
Singles: 7-inch
BLUE MOON (476 "Record Hop Blues") 50-75 61

STAFFORD, Terry P&R/LP '64
Singles: 7-inch
ATLANTIC 3-5 73-74
CASINO 3-5 77
COLLECTABLES 3-4 80s
CRUSADER 5-10 64
ERIC 3-5 70s
FIRSTLINE 3-5 81
LANA 3-6 60s
MGM 3-5 71
MELODYLAND 3-5 75
MERCURY 4-8 66
PLAYER 3-4 89
SIDEWALK 4-8 66-67
TERRIFIC 3-5
W.B. 3-6 69
LPs: 10/12-inch
ATLANTIC 8-12 73
CRUSADER (1001 "Suspicion!") ... 20-25 64
(Monaural)
CRUSADER (1001 "Suspicion!") ... 25-35 64
(Stereo)
Session: Davie Allan.
Also see ALLAN, Davie

STAFFS
Singles: 7-inch
PA-GO-GO (118 "Another Love") .. 15-25 66

STAGE DOLLS P&R/LP '89
Singles: 7-inch
CHRYSALIS 3-4 89
LPs: 10/12-inch
CHRYSALIS 5-8 89

STAGE HANDS
Singles: 7-inch
RIC (147-64 "Rocking Horse") 5-10 65

STAGE MEN
Singles: 7-inch
CUCA (6472 "Fallout") 35-50 64
Members: Wally Messner; Bob King; Ed Lenop; Eric Henry.

STAGEHANDS
Singles: 7-inch
T.A. (101 "You Started It") 25-50 64

STAGEMASTERS
Singles: 7-inch
HIT KINGDOM (1801 "Baby, I'm Here Just to Love You") 25-50 66
SLIDE (2101 "Baby, I'm Here Just to Love You") 15-25 66

STAGG, Tommy
Singles: 7-inch
BAMBI 10-15

STAGGS, Jimmy
Singles: 7-inch
SAGITARIO (9060 "Dear Elvis") 4-6 77

STAGS
Singles: 7-inch
M&S (502 "Sailor Boy") 150-250 58

STAINED GLASS
Singles: 7-inch
CAPITOL 5-10 68-69
RCA 5-10 66-67
LPs: 10/12-inch
CAPITOL 10-15 68

STAINLESS STEAL
LPs: 10/12-inch
W.B. 5-10 79

STAINS
Singles: 7-inch
LOTUS (1000 "Now and Then") 25-35 60s

STAIRCASES
Singles: 7-inch
SOUND CITY (001 "Lost in the World of a Dream") 15-25 60s

STAIRSTEPS
Singles: 7-inch
BUDDAH 3-5 71-72
DARK HORSE 3-5 75-76
Picture Sleeves
DARK HORSE 3-5 75
Also see FIVE STAIRSTEPS

STAIRWAY to STARS
Singles: 7-inch
BRITE STAR (17910 "Cry") 20-30 67

STAIRWAYS
Singles: 7-inch
RITCHIE 5-10 66

STALEY, George
Singles: 7-inch
KC 4-8 63

STALEY, Karen C&W '88
Singles: 7-inch
MCA 3-4 88-89

STALKS, Veniece
Singles: 7-inch
HI 3-8 65-75
Also see VENICE

STALLCUP, James, & Flairs
Singles: 7-inch
LE CAM 8-12 61

STALLINGS, James Michael
Singles: 7-inch
BEEGEE 3-5 73
Also see LIGHT, J.J.

STALLINGS, Jimmy
Singles: 7-inch
PAXLEY (101 "I Played the Fool") 200-300 61

STALLION P&R/LP '77
Singles: 7-inch
CASABLANCA 3-5 77-78
LPs: 10/12-inch
CASABLANCA 5-10 77-78

STALLONE, Frank P&R '80
Singles: 12-inch
RSO 4-6 83
Singles: 7-inch
POLYDOR 3-4 84-85
SCOTTI BROS 3-5 80
Picture Sleeves
POLYDOR 3-4 84
LPs: 10/12-inch
POLYDOR 5-8 84

STAMFORD BRIDGE
Singles: 7-inch
MONUMENT 4-8 70
Also see FLOWERPOT MEN

STAMPEDERS P&R/LP '71
Singles: 7-inch
BELL 3-5 71
CAPITOL 3-5 73
FLASHBACK 3-4 74
MGM 4-8 68
QUALITY 3-5 76
LPs: 10/12-inch
BELL 10-15 71
CAPITOL 8-12 73-74
PRIVATE STOCK/QUALITY 8-10 76
Also see WOLFMAN JACK

STAMPERS
Singles: 7-inch
DOT 5-8 61

STAMPLEY, Joe C&W '71
Singles: 7-inch
ABC 3-5 77
ABC/DOT 3-5 75-76
CHESS (1798 "Creation of Love") . 10-20 63
DOT 3-6 70-74
EPIC 3-5 75-86

EVERGREEN 3-4 88-89
IMPERIAL 10-15 59
PARAMOUNT 3-6 70
PAULA 3-5 74
LPs: 10/12-inch
ABC 5-10 77
ABC/DOT 8-12 74-76
ACCORD 5-10 82
DOT 8-12 73
EPIC 5-10 75-85
PHONORAMA 5-8 83
Also see BANDY, Moe, & Joe Stampley
Also see UNIQUES

STAN & DOUG
Singles: 7-inch
GOLDEN CREST 4-6
LPs: 10/12-inch
GOLDEN CREST 8-12
Members: Stan Boreson; Doug Setterberg.

STANBACK, Jean
Singles: 7-inch
PEACOCK (1958 "I Still Love You") 15-25 68

STANDARDS
Singles: 7-inch
AMOS 5-10 69
CHESS (1869 "Hello Love") 25-50 63
DEBRO (3178 "Tears Bring Heartaches") 100-200 63
GLENDEN (1315 "It Isn't Fair") 50-75 64
MAGNA (1314 "Hello Love") 100-150 63
MAGNA (1315 "It Isn't Fair") 75-100 63
MAGNA (1869 "Hello Love") 75-100 63
ROULETTE (4487 "Tears Bring Heartaches") 15-25 63

STANDELLS P&R/LP '66
Singles: 7-inch
COLLECTABLES 3-4 80s
LIBERTY 10-20 64
MGM 10-20 65
SUNSET 10-20 66
TOWER 10-20 66-68
VEE JAY 10-20 65
Picture Sleeves
TOWER 15-20 67
VEE JAY 15-25 65
LPs: 10/12-inch
LIBERTY (3384 "In Person at P.J.'s") 40-50 64
(Monaural.)
LIBERTY (7384 "In Person at P.J.'s") 50-60 64
(Stereo.)
RHINO 5-8
SUNSET (1136 "Live and Out of Sight") 15-25 66
(Monaural.)
SUNSET (5136 "Live and Out of Sight") 20-30 66
(Stereo.)
TOWER (T-5027 "Dirty Water") 40-50 66
(Monaural.)
TOWER (ST-5027 "Dirty Water") 50-60 66
(Stereo.)
TOWER (T-5044 "Why Pick On Me") 40-50 66
(Monaural.)
TOWER (ST-5044 "Why Pick On Me") 50-60 66
(Stereo.)
TOWER (T-5049 "Hot Ones") 40-50 66
(Monaural.)
TOWER (ST-5049 "Hot Ones") 50-60 66
(Stereo.)
TOWER (T-5098 "Try It") 40-50 66
TOWER (ST-5098 "Try It") 50-60 66
Members: Dick Dodd; Larry Tamblyn; Gary Lane; Tony Valentino; Dave Burke.
Also see DODD, Dick
Also see SLLEDNATS
Also see TAMBLYN, Larry

STANDLEY, Johnny P&R '52
Singles: 78 rpm
CAPITOL 4-8 52-56
Singles: 7-inch
CAPITOL 8-15 52-56
MAGNOLIA (1003 "Rock & Roll Must Go") 40-60 60
EPs: 7-inch
CAPITOL (697 "It's in the Book") 25-45 52

STANFORD, Dick, & Teenbeats
Singles: 7-inch
DODE (104 "Money Honey") 25-35

STANFORD, Ted
Singles: 7-inch
WYNNE 5-10 59

STANG, Larry
Singles: 7-inch
JERILYN (800 "Super Stang") 4-6 80s

STANGE, Howie
Singles: 7-inch
JENN (101 "Real Gone Daddy") 100-200 59

STANGIS, Linda
Singles: 7-inch
EDISON INT'L 10-15 59

STANKY BROWN GROUP LP '76
(Stanky Brown)
Singles: 7-inch
ARISTA 3-5 75
SIRE 3-5 76-78
LPs: 10/12-inch
SIRE 8-10 76-78
Members: Stanky; James Brown.

STANLEY, Chuck
Singles: 7-inch
DEF JAM 3-4 87

STANLEY, Dayle
LPs:10/12-inch
SQUIRE 15-20

STANLEY, Earl, & Stereos
Singles: 7-inch
PITASSY (210 "Midnight in New Orleans") 10-20 62

STANLEY, James Lee
Singles: 7-inch
WOODEN NICKEL 3-5 74
LPs: 10/12-inch
WOODEN NICKEL 8-10 73

STANLEY, Michael, Band LP '75
Singles: 7-inch
ARISTA 3-5 78-79
EMI AMERICA 3-5 80-83
EPIC 3-5 77
TUMBLEWEED 3-5 72-73
LPs: 10/12-inch
ARISTA 5-8 78-79
EMI AMERICA 5-8 80-83
EPIC 8-10 75-76
MCA 10-12 73
TUMBLEWEED 8-12 73
Also see CIRCUS
Also see RALEIGH, Kevin
Also see SILK
Also see TREE STUMPS

STANLEY, Pamala D&D '83
Singles: 12-inch
KOMANDER 4-6 83
MIRAGE 4-6 84-85
TSR 4-6 84
Singles: 7-inch
EMI AMERICA 3-5 79
MIRAGE 3-4 84-85
LPs: 10/12-inch
EMI AMERICA 5-10 79

STANLEY, Paul P&R/LP '78
Singles: 7-inch
CASABLANCA 3-5 78
LPs: 10/12-inch
CASABLANCA (7123 "Paul Stanley") 12-20 78
(With poster order form.)
CASABLANCA (7123 "Paul Stanley") 8-12 78
(Without poster order form.)
CASABLANCA (PIX-7123 "Paul Stanley") 50-60 79
(Picture disc.)
Also see KISS

STANLEY, Ray
Singles: 78 rpm
ARGO 10-15 57
CAPITOL 8-12 56
ZEPHYR (70011 "Pushin' ") 15-20 56
Singles: 7-inch
ARGO 10-15 57
CAPITOL 15-25 56
ZEPHYR (70011 "Pushin' ") 30-50 56
Also see COCHRAN, Eddie
Also see TERRIFICS

STANLEY, Sally
Singles: 7-inch
EXCELLO 4-8 63

STANLEY, Skip
Singles: 7-inch
SATELLITE 8-12

STANLEY & ROBERT
Singles: 7-inch
LANCE (126 "Big Guitar") 15-25 57

STANLEY BROTHERS C&W '60
Singles: 78 rpm
COLUMBIA 4-8 51-52
KING 4-8 58
MERCURY 4-8 53-55
RICH-R-TONE 5-10 47
Singles: 7-inch
COLUMBIA 5-10 52
KING 4-8 58-65
MERCURY 5-10 53-55
EPs: 7-inch
COLUMBIA 10-15 58
KING 5-10 61-62
STARDAY 8-12 59
LPs: 10/12-inch
CABIN CREEK (1 "Stanley Series, Vol. 1") 30-40
(Four individual LPs.)
CABIN CREEK (2 "Stanley Series, Vol. 2") 5-10
(Single LP.)
CABIN CREEK (203 "Bluegrass Gospel Favorites") 40-60 66
COLLECTOR'S CLASSICS 5-10
COOPER CREEK 5-10
COUNTY 6-12 73
GTO (103-108) 50-75 83
(Six individual LPs, pakaged as a set.)
GUSTO 5-10 80
GUSTO/KING 6-12 75-76
HARMONY 12-25 61-66
KING (645 thru 1013) 15-30 59-67
MELODEON 5-10
MERCURY (20349 "Country Pickin' and Singin' ") 30-50 58
MERCURY (20384 "Hard Times") 25-35 63
(Monaural.)
MERCURY (60384 "Hard Times") 30-40 63
(Stereo.)
NASHVILLE 8-12 70
OLD HOMESTEAD 5-10
POWER PAK 5-10 80s
REBEL 5-10
RIMROCK 5-10
ROUNDER 5-10
STARDAY (106 "Mountain Song") 25-35 59
STARDAY (122 "Sacred Songs") 25-35 60
STARDAY (201 "Mountain Music") 20-30 62
STARDAY (384 "Jacob's Vision") 15-25 66
STARDAY (834 "Folk Concert") 6-12 76
STARDAY (3003 "16 Hits") 5-10
STARDAY/KING 5-10
VINTAGE COLLECTOR'S CLUB (002 "Live at Antioch College") 50-75 61
WANGO 6-12 76
WING 15-20 66
Members: Ralph Stanley; Carter Stanley.

STANLEY STEAMER
LPs: 10/12-inch
JOLLY ROGER 8-10 73

STANSFIELD, Lisa P&R/LP '90
Singles: 7-inch
ARISTA 3-4 90
Picture Sleeves
ARISTA 3-4 90
LPs: 10/12-inch
ARISTA 5-8 90

STANTE, Toni
Singles: 7-inch
PARKWAY 4-8 65

STANTON, Gene, & Satellites
Singles: 78 rpm
A-A DOUBLE 5-10 55
Singles: 7-inch
A-A DOUBLE 10-15 55

STANTON, Johnny, & Feathers: see FEATHERS

STANTON, L., & Charlettes
Singles: 7-inch
SAPIEN (1004 "Love Notes") 10-20 60s

STANTON, Lee
Singles: 7-inch
CHATTAHOOCHEE 5-8 66

STANTON, Sandy
Singles: 78 rpm
FABLE (556 "Sadie Lou") 25-35 57
Singles: 7-inch
FABLE (556 "Sadie Lou") 25-35 57

STAPLE SINGERS P&R '67
(The Staples)
Singles: 78 rpm
UNITED 50-100 54
Singles: 7-inch
ABC 3-5 73
CURTOM 3-5 75-77
EPIC 3-6 64-71
PRIVATE I 3-4 84-86
RIVERSIDE 4-6 62-63
SHARP 4-8 60
STAX 3-6 68-74
20TH FOX 3-5 81
UNITED (165 "It Rained, Children") 200-300 54
VEE JAY 4-8 59-62
W.B. 3-5 76-80
LPs: 10/12-inch
BUDDAH 5-10 69
CREED 5-10 73
CURTOM 5-10 76
EPIC 8-12 65-71
EVEREST 8-12 68-69
FANTASY 5-10 73
51 WEST 5-8 80s
GOSPEL 5-15 59
HARMONY 5-10 72
MILESTONE 5-10 75
PRIVATE I 5-8 84-86
RIVERSIDE 10-15 62-65
STAX 5-10 68-81
20TH FOX 5-10 81
TRIP 5-10 71-77
VEE JAY 10-15 59-63
W.B. 5-10 76-78
Members: Mavis Staples; Roebuck Staples; Cleo Staples; Yvonne Staples.
Also see STAPLES, Mavis

STAPLES, Gordon, & Motown Strings
Singles: 7-inch
MOTOWN (1180 "Strung Out") 10-20 71
LPs: 10/12-inch
MOTOWN (722 "Strung Out") 15-25 71

STAPLES, Mavis P&R/LP '70
Singles: 7-inch
CURTOM 3-5 77
PHONO 3-4 84
VOLT 3-5 70-72
W.B. 3-4 79-86
LPs: 10/12-inch
VOLT 8-12 69-70
W.B. 5-10 79-86
Also see BELL, William, & Mavis Staples
Also see FLOYD, Eddie, & Mavis Staples
Also see STAPLE SINGERS

STAPLES, Roebuck
(Pop Staples)
Singles: 7-inch
STAX 3-5 70
VEE JAY 4-8 60
LPs: 10/12-inch
CAPITOL 8-10 90s
Also see KING, Albert
Also see STAPLE SINGERS

STAPLETON, Cyril, & His Orchestra P&R '56
Singles: 78 rpm
LONDON 3-5 51-63
MGM 3-5 55-56
Singles: 7-inch
DECCA 3-6 67
LONDON 4-8 51-63
MGM 4-8 55-56
STAGE 3-6 62
EPs: 7-inch
LONDON 4-8 55-57
MGM 4-8 55-56
LPs: 10/12-inch
IMPERIAL 5-10 61
LONDON 5-15 55-59
MGM 5-15 55-56
RICHMOND 5-15 59-61

STAPLETON, Eddie
Singles: 7-inch
FORTUNE 15-25 64

STAPLETON - MORLEY EXPRESSION
Singles: 7-inch
DUNHILL 4-6 67
LPs: 10/12-inch
DUNHILL 10-15 67
Members: Stapleton; Morley.

STAR, Bobby
Singles: 7-inch
CONTINENTAL ARTS 4-8 64
U.A. 4-8 66
Also see ALLEN, Tony

STAR, Chuck
Singles: 7-inch
ATLANTIC 4-8 63

STAR, Linda, & Starlets
Singles: 7-inch
JOEY 10-15 63

STAR, Little Brenda
Singles: 7-inch
VEGAS 4-8 64

STAR COMBO
Singles: 7-inch
SKIPPY (102 "Mr. Rock & Roll") 50-75 58

STAR-DRIFTERS
Singles: 7-inch
GOLDISC (3 "An Eye for an Eye") 10-15 63

STAR FIRES
(Starfires)
Singles: 7-inch
ATOMIC (1912 "Love Will Break Your Heart") 20-30 61
HARAL (777 "Each Night at Nine") 50-75 63
LAURIE 5-10 66
Also see STARFIRES

STAR STEPPERS
Singles: 7-inch
AMY (801 "You're Gone") 25-35 60

STAR TONES
Singles: 7-inch
BAND BOX (354 "The Chase") 10-20 64

STAR TREK
Singles: 7-inch
POWER (25 "Passage to Moauv") 10-20 75
POWER (26 "Crier In Emptiness") 10-20 75

STAR WARS INTERGALACTIC DROID CHOIR & CHORALE P&R '80
Singles: 7-inch
RSO 3-5 80
Picture Sleeves
RSO 3-5 80
Also see MECO

STARBOW
Singles: 12-inch
AVI 4-6

STARBOYS
Singles: 7-inch
CRIMINAL (822 "Pennies in a Jar") 10-20 75
EPs: 7-inch
DISH ("Hey Mama") 10-20 69
(Selection number not known.)
Members: John Sieger; Gregg Kishline; Frank Niccolai; Phil Clark; Ken Vanderpoel; Cy Costabile; Mike Sieger.
Also see STUDEBAKER BROTHERS

STARBREAKER
Singles: 7-inch
CHRYSALIS 3-5 77

STARBUCK P&R/LP '76
Singles: 7-inch
A.V.I. 3-4 84
ATCO 3-5 73
ELEKTRA 3-5 71
PRIVATE STOCK 3-5 76-77
U.A. 3-5 78-79
LPs: 10/12-inch
PHONORAMA 5-8 80s
PRIVATE STOCK 8-10 76
U.A. 8-10 78
Members: Bruce Blackman; James Cobb; Ken Crysler; Sloan Hayes; Dave Shaver; Bo Wagner.
Also see ETERNITY'S CHILDREN
Also see KORONA

STARBUCK & RAINMAKERS
Singles: 7-inch
VALIANT (744 "I Who Have Nothing") 10-20 66

STARCASTLE LP '76
Singles: 7-inch
EPIC 3-5 76-78
LPs: 10/12-inch
EPIC (Except PAL-34935) 5-10 76-79
EPIC (PAL-34935 "Citadel") 50-75 79
(Picture disc. Promotional issue only.)

STARCHER, Buddy C&W '49
Singles: 78 rpm
4 STAR 4-8 49-50s
Singles: 7-inch
BOONE 3-6 66
DECCA 3-6 66
4 STAR 5-10 50s
HEARTWARMING 3-5 67
STARDAY 4-8 59-66
EPs: 7-inch
4 STAR 5-10 50s
STARDAY 5-10 61
LPs: 10/12-inch
BLUEBONNET 10-20
DECCA 10-20 66
HEARTWARMING 5-10 68
STARDAY 10-20 62-66

STARDRIVE
(Robert Mason & Stardrive)
LPs: 10/12-inch
COLUMBIA 8-10 74
ELEKTRA 8-10 73

STARDUST, Alvin
Singles: 7-inch
BELL/MAGNET 3-5 73-74
U.A. 3-5 77

STARDUSTERS
Singles: 7-inch
BLUE RIBBON (101 "Cy Boogie") 8-12
JIM SIM 5-10 59
JO-RAY-ME (001 "Rockin' Boat") 10-20 62

STARETTES
Singles: 7-inch
JEWEL 4-8 66

STARETTS
Singles: 7-inch
VENETT 5-10 62

STARFIRE
LPs: 10/12-inch
CRIMSON 5-10 74
DYNAMIC ARTISTS 5-10 79
Member: Linda Carriere.
Also see DEBLANC
Also see DYNASTY

STARFIRE
Singles: 7-inch
SHERRY 3-6 70s

STARFIRES
Singles: 7-inch
BERNICE (201 "Yearning for Love") 100-125 59
BERNICE (202 "You Are Mine") 150-300 59
DECCA (30730 "Three Roses") 25-50 58
DECCA (30916 "Love Is Here to Stay") 25-50 58

STARFIRES
(Original Starfires)
Singles: 7-inch
APT (25030 "Fender Bender") 15-20 59
PACE (101 "Fender Bender") 25-35 59
(First issue.)
Member: Jim Ford.

STARFIRES
Singles: 7-inch
ATOMIC (1912 "Love Will Break Your Heart") 25-50 61
BARGAIN (5001 "Your the One") 40-60 61
BARGAIN (5003 "Love Will Break Your Heart") 40-60 61
(First issue.)
D&H (200 "These Foolish Things") 75-125 61

STARFIRES
Singles: 7-inch
PAMA (117 "Billy's Blues") 20-30 61
Members: Bill Bruno; Tom King; Rickey Baker; Merdin Madsen.
Also see OUTSIDERS

STARFIRES
Singles: 7-inch
ACCENT 5-10 64
COLLEGE 8-12 62
DUEL (518 "Fools Fall in Love") 15-25 62
TRIUMPH (61 "Fink") 10-25 60s
EPs: 7-inch
OHIO RECORDING SERVICE 10-15 64
LPs: 10/12-inch
OHIO RECORDING SERVICE 15-20 64

STARFIRES
Singles: 7-inch
ROUND (1016 "Space Needle") 10-15 62
Picture Sleeves
ROUND (1016 "Space Needle") 20-30 62

STARFIRES
Singles: 7-inch
SONIC (7163 "Re-Entry") 15-25 63
Members: Joe Santiloni; Henry Rice; Pete Tabili; Stan Wojtym; Ronnie Barret.

STARFIRES
Singles: 7-inch
ROMCO (104 "Something Else") ...10-15 63

STARFIRES
Singles: 7-inch
SARA (6363 "Nervous Breakdown")....15-25 63
Member: Tommy Lee Lindermann; Rick Sherman; Kip Maercklein; Bill Orr; Bill Kucharet; Mickey Abrams.

STARFIRES
Singles: 7-inch
LAURIE (3332 "You Done Me Wrong')....10-20 65

STARFIRES
Singles: 7-inch
G.I. (4001 "I Never Loved Her") 100-150 65
G.I. (4002 "Rockin' Dixie")....25-35 65
G.I. (4004 "Cry for Freedom")....25-35 65
YARDBIRD (4005 "Unchain My Heart")....10-20 66
YARDBIRD (4006 "The Hardest Way")....10-20 66
LPs: 10/12-inch
LA BREA (8018 "Teenbeat a Go Go")....15-25 64
Members: Chuck Butler; Dave Anderson; Jack Emerick; Freddy Gields; Sonny Lathrop.

STARFIRES
Singles: 7-inch
BIG SOUND (301 "Please Go Away")....25-35 65
Members: Forrest Jehn; Gary Van Sleet; Mike Reinecke; Wayne Leitermann; Dick Sternberg.

STARFIRES
Singles: 7-inch
(200, 597 "She's Long and Tall")....15-25 65
(No label name used.)

STARFOXX
Singles: 7-inch
DANCE-A-THON.... 4-6 79
LPs: 10/12-inch
DANCE-A-THON/HOTTRAX.... 5-8 79

STARGARD P&R/LP '78
Singles: 12-inch
W.B.... 4-8 79-81
Singles: 7-inch
MCA.... 3-5 77-78
W.B.... 3-5 79-81
LPs: 10/12-inch
MCA.... 5-10 78-82
W.B.... 5-10 79-81
Members: Debra Anderson; Janice Williams; Rochelle Runnells.

STARGAZE D&D '83
Singles: 12-inch
T.N.T.... 4-8 83

STARGAZERS
Singles: 7-inch
PALETTE.... 4-8 60

STARGLOWS
Singles: 7-inch
ATCO (6272 "Let's Be Lovers")....30-40 63
Member: Nate Nelson.
Also see FLAMINGOS

STARGLOWS / Rock-A-Bouts / Cecil Young Quartet
EPs: 7-inch
SPINNING (7 "Let's Be Lovers") 4-8
Also see ROCK-A-BOUTS
Also see YOUNG, Cecil

STARJETS
Singles: 7-inch
PORTRAIT.... 3-5 79
LPs: 10/12-inch
PORTRAIT.... 5-10 79

STARK, Donna C&W '80
Singles: 7-inch
RCI.... 3-5 80

STARK, Johnny
Singles: 7-inch
CRYSTALETTE....15-25 57-58
POP.... 8-12 59

STARK & McBRIEN P&R '75
Singles: 7-inch
RCA.... 3-5 74-76
LPs: 10/12-inch
RCA (1065 "Big Star").... 8-10 75
Members: Fred Stark; Rod McBrien.

STARK NAKED
(With the Car Thieves)
Singles: 7-inch
ATTRACK/MGM.... 4-8 60s
ORO.... 4-8 60s
RCA.... 3-5 71
SUNBURST.... 4-8 68
LPs: 10/12-inch
RCA....10-15 71

STARK REALITY
Singles: 7-inch
BIG YELLOW.... 4-6 69

STARKS, Doc, & Nite Riders
(With the Night Riders; with Nightriders)
Singles: 78 rpm
CAPITOL.... 8-12 55
Singles: 7-inch
BERNLO....15-25 57
CAPITOL (3236 "Night Ridin' ")....15-25 55
LINDA (109 "Rockin' to School")....50-75 58
MODERN SOUND (6908 "Rockin' to School")....50-75 58
SOUND (119 "Night Ridin' ")....35-50 55
(First issue.)
SOUND (128 "Never")....35-50 55
SWAN....10-20 58
TEEN....20-30 57
Also see NITE RIDERS

STARKS, Jan
Singles: 7-inch
PICO.... 4-8 61

STARLAND VOCAL BAND P&R/C&W/LP '76
Singles: 7-inch
WINDSONG.... 3-5 76-80
LPs: 10/12-inch
WINDSONG....8-10 76-80
Members: Bill Danoff; Taffy Danoff.
Also see BILL & TAFFY
Also see FAT CITY

STARLARKS
(Featuring Wes Forbes)
Singles: 7-inch
ANCHO (102 "My Dear")....100-200 57
COLLECTABLES.... 3-4 80s
ELM (001 "The Fountain of Love")....300-400 57
EMBER (1013 "The Fountain of Love")....50-100 57
Member: Wes Forbes.
Also see FIVE SATINS

STARLARKS
Singles: 7-inch
ASTRA (100 "Darling, Please Love Me")....50-75 64
(Reportedly 1,000 made.)

STARLETS
Singles: 7-inch
ASTRO (202 "P.S. I Love You")....20-30 60
ASTRO (204 "Romeo & Juliet")....15-20 60
Also see ANGELS

STARLETS P&R '61
Singles: 7-inch
LUTE (5909 "I'm So Young")....15-25 60
PAM (1003 "Better Tell Him No")...10-20 61
PAM (1004 "My Last Cry")....10-20 61
PEAK (5000 "Missing You")....150-250 57
Members: Maxine Edwards; Bernice Williams; Liz Walker; Mickey McKinney; Jane Hall.
Also see BLUE BELLES

STARLETS
Singles: 7-inch
TOWER (144 "You Don't Love Me")....5-10 65
Session: Davie Allan.
Also see ALLAN, Davie

STARLETS
Singles: 7-inch
CHESS....10-20 67-68

STARLETTES
Singles: 7-inch
CHECKER (895 "Please Ring My Phone")....50-75 58

STARLETTES
Singles: 7-inch
SIANA....5-10 64

STARLETTS
Singles: 7-inch
SCARLETT....5-10 63

STARLIGHTERS
Singles: 78 rpm
IRMA....50-100 56
Singles: 7-inch
IRMA (101 "Love Cry")....200-300 56
SUNCOAST (1001 "Until You Return")....1000-2000 58

STARLIGHTERS
Singles: 7-inch
INTRO....25-35 58

STARLIGHTERS
Singles: 7-inch
END (1031 "It's Twelve O'Clock")....150-200 59
END (1049 "I Cried")....50-100 59
END (1072 "A Story of Love")....100-150 60

STARLIGHTERS
Singles: 7-inch
NUGGETT (1002 "A Fool's Understanding")....50-100 59

STARLIGHTERS
Singles: 7-inch
WHEEL (1004 "Creepin' ")....10-20 60

STARLIGHTS
Singles: 7-inch
CLIMAX (107 "Starfire")....10-15 59

STARLINERS
Singles: 7-inch
NO-NEE (101 "Gotz")....20-30 60s
REED (1066 "Thunder")....8-12
ULTRACON (101 "Kooknik")....10-20 60s
VISCOUNT (101 "Watusi Time") ...10-15 61
LPs: 10/12-inch
LEJAC (1001 "Live at Papa Joe's")....1000-1500 60s

STARLINGS
Singles: 78 rpm
DAWN....100-200 55
JOSIE....100-150 54
Singles: 7-inch
DAWN (212 "I'm Just a Crying Fool")....300-400 55
DAWN (213 "I Gotta Go Now") ..200-300 55
JOSIE (760 "My Plea for Love")....250-300 54

STARLINGS
Singles: 7-inch
WORLD PACIFIC (809 "All I Want")....20-30 59

STARLITE, Steve, & Padre Pio Trio
EPs: 7-inch
SNORKO....3-5 83
(Issued with paper sleeve.)
LPs: 10/12-inch
SNORKO....8-10 83
Members: Stephen Pacelli; Gordon Patriarca; Jack Cook; Jimmy Johanson.

STARLITERS
Singles: 7-inch
DOT (16345 "Parkwood Twist")....5-10 62

STARLITERS
Singles: 7-inch
4 SONS (4107 "Don't Ever Leave Me")....100-200

STARLITERS with Jonesy's Combo
Singles: 78 rpm
COMBO (73 "Arline")....100-200 55
Singles: 7-inch
COMBO (73 "Arline")....350-500 55
(Red label.)
COMBO (73 "Arline")....75-100 56
(Purple label.)

STARLITES
(With Al Browne & Band)
Singles: 78 rpm
PEAK (5000 "Missing You")....100-150 57
Singles: 7-inch
PEAK (5000 "Missing You")....100-200 57
Also see BROWNE, Al
Also see DREAMS
Also see EDDIE & STARLITES
Also see ESQUIRE, Kenny, & Starlites

STARLITES
Singles: 7-inch
QUEEN (5000 "My Darling")....50-100 60

STARLITES
Singles: 7-inch
EVERLAST (5027 "Valarie")....15-25 64

STARLITES
Singles: 7-inch
FLASHBACK....5-10 65
FURY (1034 "Valerie")....50-75 60
FURY (1045 "Silver Lining")....25-50 60
SPHERE SOUND (705 "Seven Day Fool")....50-75 65
Also see JACKIE & STARLITES
Also see KODAKS / Starlites

STARLITES
Singles: 7-inch
RELIC GOLD....8-12 65

STARLITES
Singles: 7-inch
BARCLAY (15016 "Stagger Lee") ..15-25 66
BARCLAY (17134 "I Can't See You")....15-25 67
Also see BEATIN' PATH

STARLITES
Singles: 7-inch
STARLITE (6298 "Starlite Rock")....8-12 60s

STARLYN, Sherry
Singles: 7-inch
SUNBURST....10-15

STARNOTES
(With the Al Hogan Combo)
Singles: 7-inch
CAPER (101 "Say the Word")....20-30 62

STARO, Frankie
Singles: 7-inch
TEMPOTONE....4-8 62

STARPOINT LP '81
Singles: 12-inch
BOARDWALK....4-6 83
CHOCOLATE CITY....4-8 80-82
ELEKTRA....4-6 83-85
Singles: 7-inch
BOARDWALK....3-4 83
CHOCOLATE CITY....3-5 80-82
ELEKTRA....3-4 83-87
Picture Sleeves
ELEKTRA....3-4 85-87
LPs: 10/12-inch
CHOCOLATE CITY....5-10 80-82
ELEKTRA....5-8 83-87
Members: George Phillips; Greg Phillips; Ernest Phillips; Orlando Phillips; Renee Diggs; Kayode Adeyemo.
Also see DAWSON, Cliff, & Renee Diggs

STARR, A. / Glitters
Singles: 7-inch
BIG (23 "Mama Didn't Lie")....5-10

STARR, Andy
(Frank "Andy" Starr)
Singles: 78 rpm
ARCADE (115 "I Love You Baby")....50-75 53
KAPP....10-15 57
MGM (12263 "Rockin' Rollin' Stone")....50-75 56
Singles: 7-inch
ARCADE (115 "I Love You Baby")....150-250 53
KAPP (190 "Do It Right Now")....15-25 57
MGM (12263 "Rockin' Rollin' Stone")....100-200 56
MGM (12315 "She's a Going, Jessie")....100-200 56
MGM (12264 "Round and Round")....100-200 57
MGM (12421 "One More Time")....100-200 57
VALIANT (101 "Just A-Walking") ...50-75
Also see STARR, Frank, & His Rock-Away Boys

STARR, Berde
Singles: 7-inch
AZTEC (111 "What My Heart's Too Blind to See")....8-12

STARR, Betty Jo & Johnny
Singles: 7-inch
ALASKA (1279 "Eskimo Boogie") ..50-75
ALASKA (1410 "Son of a Sourdough")....15-25
Also see STARR, Johnny

STARR, Bill
(With the Rhythm Jesters; with Rock Brooks; with Students)
Singles: 7-inch
APPLAUSE (1235 "Love for a Year")....50-75 60
BANA (8-12 "The Wanderer")....15-25 60
SCHOCK (8-11 "Grizzly Bear")..400-500 58

STARR, Billy
Singles: 7-inch
TWI-LITE ("Every Little Wrong")....20-30

STARR, Bob
Singles: 7-inch
ACCENT....5-10 60
BEN-HUE (1001 "I Want to Rock & Roll")....25-50
ROCKIN (603 "One Tank of Gas")....4-8 74

STARR, Bobby
(Tony Allen)
Singles: 7-inch
RADIO (120 "Please Give Me a Chance")....75-125 59
Also see ALLEN, Tony

STARR, Brenda K. D&D '85
Singles: 12-inch
MIRAGE....4-6 85
Singles: 7-inch
MCA....3-4 87-88
MIRAGE....3-4 85
Picture Sleeves
MCA....3-4 87-88
LPs: 10/12-inch
MCA....5-8 88

STARR, Buddy, & Starliners
Singles: 7-inch
KANGAROO (26 "Hold It")....8-12

STARR, Cal
Singles: 7-inch
REGO (306 "Robbin the Cradle")....5-10 60
(Reissued in 1964 using the same number. Any label differences that would distinguish originals are not yet known to us.)
FRATERNITY....4-8 66-67

STARR, Charlie
LPs: 10/12-inch
PROPHESY....8-10 72

STARR, Edwin P&R '65
Singles: 12-inch
20TH FOX....4-8 77-80
Singles: 7-inch
A.S.R. (29116 "Hit Me with Your Love")....4-6 70s
CASABLANCA....3-4 84
GRANITE....3-5 75-76
GORDY (Black vinyl)....3-8 67-71
GORDY (Colored vinyl)....10-20 69-70
(Promotional issues only.)
MONTAGE....3-4 82
MOTOWN....3-5 73-74
RIC-TIC (103 "Agent Double-O Soul")....10-15 65
RIC-TIC (107 "Back Street")....10-15 65
RIC-TIC (109 "Stop Her on Sight [S.O.S.]")....10-15 66
RIC-TIC (109X "Scott's on Swingers [S.O.S.]")....40-50 66
(Promotional issue only.)
RIC-TIC (114 "Headline News")....10-15 66
RIC-TIC (118 "It's My Turn Now")...10-15 66
RIC-TIC (120 "You're My Mellow")....25-50 67
SOUL....3-5 72-73
20TH FOX....3-5 77-84
LPs: 10/12-inch
GORDY (931 "Soul Masters")....15-25 68
GORDY (940 "25 Miles")....15-25 69
GORDY (948 "War & Peace")....10-20 70
GORDY (956 "Involved")....10-15 71
GRANITE....8-10 75
MOTOWN....8-10 73-82
20TH FOX....8-10 77-81
Also see FUTURETONES
Also see HOLIDAYS

STARR, Edwin, & Blinky
Singles: 7-inch
GORDY....4-8 69
LPs: 10/12-inch
GORDY (945 "Just We Two")....10-20 69
Also see BLINKY
Also see STARR, Edwin

STARR, Frank, & His Rock-Away Boys
(Andy Starr)
Singles: 7-inch
HOLIDAY INN (104 "Knees Shaking")....50-75 62
HOLIDAY INN (108 "Little Bitty Feeling")....20-30 62
LIN (1009 "Dig Them Squeeky Shoes")....75-100 55
LIN (1013 "Tell Me Why")....25-35 55
LIN (5033 "Me and the Fool")....10-15 63
Session: Boots Randolph; Floyd Cramer; Bob Moore; Jordanaires; Murray Harman; Ray Edenton.
Also see CRAMER, Floyd
Also see JORDANAIRES
Also see MOORE, Bob
Also see RANDOLPH, Boots
Also see STARR, Andy

STARR, Frankie
Singles: 7-inch
SIMS (212 "Elevator Baby")....15-25 64
STAR-WIN (7003) "Elevator Boogie")....50-75 64
STAR-WIN (7008) "Elevator Baby")....50-75 64
(First issue.)

STARR, Freddie
Singles: 7-inch
THUNDERBIRD....3-5 75

STARR, Harry
Singles: 7-inch
END (1129 "Another Time, Another Place")....20-40 66

STARR, Jerry
Singles: 7-inch
PIC-ONE (104 "Teenage Tangle") 10-20 59
(First issue.)
ROCKO (521 "High Ride")....8-12
RON (321 "Teenage Tangle")....8-12 59
ZINN (1012 "Side Steppin")....8-12 59
ZINN (1015 "Love Dreams")....8-12 59

STARR, Jimmy
(With the Palis Royals)
Singles: 7-inch
DEBBIE....10-15 59
ESTATE....5-10 61
LAUREL....5-10 60
NASHVILLE....4-8 63
RIDER....5-10 61
Also see PALIS ROYALS

STARR, Johnny
Singles: 7-inch
EASTERN (1 "Don't Hold Back") ...10-20 60s
MALA (10219 "Do Re Mi Fa So La Ti Do")....10-20 68
OLYMPIA (7006 "Marizinia")....40-60
Also see STARR, Betty Jo & Johnny

STARR, Karen
Singles: 7-inch
RSVP....5-10 65

STARR, Kay P&R '48
(With the Crystalette All Stars)
Singles: 78 rpm
CAPITOL....5-10 48-57
CRYSTALETTE....10-15 50
JEWEL (1000 "I Ain't Gonna Cry")....20-40 45
MODERN....15-25 49
RCA....4-8 55-57
Singles: 7-inch
ABC....3-5 67-68
CAPITOL (811 thru 2887)....10-20 50-54
CAPITOL (4000 & 5000 series) 5-15 58-64
CRYSTALETTE (632 "Where Or When")....15-25 50
(Black vinyl.)
CRYSTALETTE (632 "Where Or When")....20-40 50
(Colored vinyl.)
DOT....4-6 68
GNP....3-5 74-75
HAPPY TIGER....3-5 70
RCA (0100 series)....3-5 73
RCA (6000 & 7000 series)....5-15 55-59
Picture Sleeves
CAPITOL....8-12 62
EPs: 7-inch
CAPITOL....10-20 50-61
RCA....10-15 55-58
LPs: 10/12-inch
ABC....5-15 68
ALLEGRO....5-10
CAMDEN....10-20 60-61
CAPITOL (With "DT" or "SM" prefix)....5-15 63-75
(Reissue series including reprocessed stereo.)
CAPITOL (H-211 "Songs by Kay Starr")....50-100 50
(10-inch LP.)
CAPITOL (T-211 "Songs by Kay Starr")....30-40 55
CAPITOL (H-363 "Kay Starr Style")....50-75 53
(10-inch LP.)
CAPITOL (T-363 "Kay Starr Style")....30-40 55
CAPITOL (H-415 "The Hits of Kay Starr")....50-75 53
(10-inch LP.)
CAPITOL (T-415 "The Hits of Kay Starr")....30-40 55
(10-inch LP.)
CAPITOL (T-580 "In a Blue Mood")....30-40 55

CAPITOL (1254 thru 1681) 25-40 59-62
(With "T" or "ST" prefix.)
CAPITOL (1795 thru 2100 series)..15-30 62-64
(With "T" or "ST" prefix.)
CAPITOL (11000 series)..............5-10 74-79
CORONET 10-20 63
CRYSTALETTE (4500 "Kay Starr Sings") 50-100 52
(10-inch LP.)
EVON...10-15 50s
GNP 5-10 74-75
GALAXY 5-10
LIBERTY (3280 "Swingin' with the Starr") 15-25 63
LIBERTY (9001 "Swingin' with the Starr") 35-45 56
RCA (1100 thru 1700 series)..........15-25 55-57
RONDO-LETTE (3 "Them There Eyes") 20-30 58
SUNSET.....................................8-12 60s
Also see WILLIAMS, Tex

STARR, Kay, & Count Basie
LPs: 10/12-inch
MCA 5-8 83
PARAMOUNT...............................10-15 69
Also see BASIE, Count

STARR, Kay, & Tennessee Ernie Ford
Singles: 78 rpm
CAPITOL....................................4-8 50-56
Singles: 7-inch
CAPITOL....................................10-20 50-56
EPs: 7-inch
CAPITOL....................................5-15 56
Also see FORD, Tennessee Ernie

STARR, Kay / Erroll Garner
LPs: 10/12-inch
CROWN (5003 "Singin' & Swingin' ") 30-40 57
MODERN (1203 "Singin' & Swingin' ") 50-75 56
Also see GARNER, Erroll
Also see STARR, Kay

STARR, Kenny
Singles: 7-inch
SAGE (278 "Rock Me")....................25-35 59

STARR, Kenny C&W '73
Singles: 7-inch
MCA 3-5 73-78
SRO 3-5 82
S.S. TITANIC...............................3-4 81
LPs: 10/12-inch
MCA 5-10 75
SRO 5-10 82
Also see LYNN, Loretta

STARR, Lucille P&R '64
Singles: 7-inch
A&M 4-8 66
ALMO 4-8 64-65
EPIC...4-8 67-69
LPs: 10/12-inch
A&M 20-30 66
EPIC...20-30 69
Also see BOB & LUCILLE
Also see CANADIAN SWEETHEARTS

STARR, Mack
(With the Mellows)
Singles: 7-inch
CHENE.......................................8-12 64
CUB (9117 "Drifting Apart")...........15-25 62
Also see PARAGONS

STARR, Martha
Singles: 7-inch
THELMA (111 "No Part Time Love for Me") 15-25 65
THELMA (112 "Love Is the Only Solution") 75-125 65
THELMA (113 "I Wanna Be Your Girl") 50-75 65

STARR, Maxine
Singles: 7-inch
NEW HITS...................................4-8 62

STARR, Penny C&W '67
(Penny DeHaven)
Singles: 7-inch
BAND BOX..................................4-8 66-67
Also see DeHAVEN, Penny

STARR, Randy P&R '57
Singles: 78 rpm
DALE...8-12 57
Singles: 7-inch
DALE...8-12 57-59
MAYFLOWER...............................5-10 59
Also see ISLANDERS

STARR, Randy, & Frank Metis
LPs: 10/12-inch
MAYFLOWER...............................15-25 59
Also see STARR, Randy

STARR, Ray
Singles: 7-inch
FEDERAL....................................10-15 60
KING..5-10 62
LEE (505 "Billy Jo")......................15-25 58
MUSIC TOWER 3-5 78

STARR, Ricki & His All Stars
Singles: 7-inch
RCA (7640 "Shooting Star")............5-10 59

STARR, Rickie
Singles: 7-inch
MAGIC CIRCLE.............................4-8 61

STARR, Ringo P&R/LP '70
Singles: 12-inch
ATLANTIC (93 "Drowning in the Sea of Love") 15-20 77
(Promotional issue only.)
Singles: 7-inch
APPLE (1831 "It Don't Come Easy") . 4-8 71
APPLE (1849 "Back Off Boogaloo") 40-60 72
(With a blue apple on the label.)
APPLE (1849 "Back Off Boogaloo")..4-6 73
(With a green apple on the label.)
APPLE (1865 "Photograph") 3-5 73
APPLE (1870 "You're Sixteen") 5-8 73
(With standard apple label.)
APPLE (1870 "You're Sixteen") 4-6 73
(With 5-point star label.)
APPLE (1872 "Oh My My")...............4-6 74
APPLE (1876 "Only You")................4-6 74
APPLE (1880 "No No Song")............4-6 75
APPLE (1882 "It's All Down to Goodnight Vienna") 4-6 75
APPLE (2969 "Beaucoups of Blues") 4-8 70
ATLANTIC (3361 "Dose of Rock 'N' Roll") 10-20 76
ATLANTIC (3371 "Hey Baby")..........10-20 76
ATLANTIC (3412 "Drowning in the Sea of Love") 75-100 77
ATLANTIC (3429 "Wings")................8-12 77
BOARDWALK (130 "Wrack My Brain") 3-5 81
BOARDWALK (134 "Private Property") 3-5 82
CAPITOL (Orange label)..................4-8 75
CAPITOL (Purple label)...................3-5 78
CAPITOL (Black label).....................3-4 83
PORTRAIT (70015 "Lipstick Traces") 5-10 78
PORTRAIT (70018 "Heart on My Sleeve") 4-8 78
Picture Sleeves
APPLE (1826 "Beaucoups of Blues") 25-35 70
(Selection number 2969 mistakenly shown as Apple 1826.)
APPLE (1831 "It Don't Come Easy") 10-15 71
APPLE (1849 "Back Off Boogaloo") 10-15 72
APPLE (1865 "Photograph") 8-12 73
APPLE (1870 "You're Sixteen")........8-12 73
APPLE (1876 "Only You")................5-10 74
APPLE (1882 "It's All Down to Goodnight Vienna") 8-10 75
APPLE (2969 "Beaucoups of Blues") 12-18 70
(Selection number correctly shown.)
BOARDWALK (130 "Wrack My Brain") 3-5 81
Promotional Singles
APPLE (1831 "It Don't Come Easy") 15-20 71
APPLE (1849 "Back Off Boogaloo") 35-45 72
(White label.)
APPLE (1865 "Photograph")............20-30 73
APPLE (1870 "You're Sixteen").......20-30 73
APPLE (1872 "Oh My My")..............20-30 74
APPLE (1876 "Only You")...............20-30 74
APPLE (1880 "No No Song")...........20-30 75
APPLE (1882 "It's All Down to Goodnight Vienna") 20-30 75
APPLE (1882 "Oo-Wee")................25-30 75
ATLANTIC (3361 "Dose of Rock 'N' Roll") 20-30 76
(White label.)
ATLANTIC (3361 "Dose of Rock 'N' Roll") 10-15 76
(Blue label.)
ATLANTIC (3371 "Hey Baby")..........20-30 76
(White label.)
ATLANTIC (3371 "Hey Baby")..........10-15 76
(Red-white and blue labels.)
ATLANTIC (3371 "Hey Baby")..........25-35 76
(Single-sided disc.)
ATLANTIC (3412 "Drowning in the Sea of Love") 10-20 77
ATLANTIC (3429 "Wings")..............20-25 77
(White label.)
ATLANTIC (3429 "Wings")..............10-12 77
(Red-white and blue labels.)
BOARDWALK (130 "Wrack My Brain") 8-12 81
BOARDWALK (134 "Private Property") 8-12 82
PORTRAIT (70015 "Lipstick Traces") 8-12 78
PORTRAIT (70018 "Heart on My Sleeve") 8-12 78
RIGHT STUFF (18179 "Wrack My Brain") 5-10 94
(Colored vinyl. Promotional issue, made "For Jukeboxes Only.")
LPs: 10/12-inch
APPLE (3365 "Sentimental Journey") 10-15 70
APPLE (3368 "Beaucoups of Blues") 10-15 70
APPLE (3417 "Goodnight Vienna") 10-15 75
APPLE (3422 "Blast from Your Past") 10-15 75
APPLE (3413 "Ringo")....................15-20 73
(Includes a 20-page booklet.)
APPLE (3413 "Ringo")....................10-15 73
(With 4:05 version of *Six O'Clock.*)
ATLANTIC (18193 "Ringo's Rotogravure") 8-12 76
ATLANTIC (19108 "Ringo the 4th") 8-12 77
BOARDWALK (33246 "Stop and Smell the Roses") 8-10 81
CAPITOL.....................................5-12 80-81
PORTRAIT (35378 "Bad Boy") 8-10 78
Promotional LPs
APPLE (3413 "Ringo")..................100-125 73
(With 5:26 version of *Six O'Clock.* Some copies list the track at 5:26 though it actually runs only 4:05.)
ATLANTIC (18193 "Ringo's Rotogravure") 10-20 76
(With programming sticker on front cover.)
ATLANTIC (19108 "Ringo the 4th") 10-20 77
(With programming sticker on front cover.)
PORTRAIT (35378 "Bad Boy")........25-30 78
(Labels reads "Advance Promotion.")
PORTRAIT (35378 "Bad Boy")........15-20 78
(Labels reads "Demonstration, Not For Sale.")
Session: Van Dyke Parks.
Also see BEATLES
Also see CLAPTON, Eric
Also see FRAMPTON, Peter
Also see JOHN, Elton
Also see LOMAX, Jackie
Also see NILSSON
Also see OWENS, Buck, & Ringo Starr
Also see PARKS, Van Dyke

STARR, Rita
Singles: 7-inch
HALA..3-5

STARR, Rocky
Singles: 78 rpm
CROWN 10-20 53
MERCURY 5-10 53
Singles: 7-inch
CROWN (3588 "Rock-a-Bye Boogie") 25-30 53
MERCURY (70192 "Rock-a-Bye Boogie") 10-20 53

STARR, Ruby
(With Grey Ghost)
Singles: 7-inch
CAPITOL.....................................3-5 76
EMOTION 5-10 70-71
Picture Sleeves
EMOTION 5-10 70
LPs: 10/12-inch
CAPITOL.....................................8-12 75-77
Also see BLACK OAK ARKANSAS
Also see JONES, Ruby

STARR, Sally
Singles: 7-inch
ARCADE (157 "Rocky the Rockin' Rabbit") 20-30 60
CLYMAX (103 "Rockin' in the Nursery") 30-40 59
EPs: 7-inch
CLYMAX (1001/2/3 "Our Gal Sal") 75-125 59
(Three discs in gatefold cover.)
LPs: 10/12-inch
ARCADE (1001 "Our Gal Sal")......40-60 60
CLYMAX (1001 "Our Gal Sal")...100-150 59

STARR, Suzy
Singles: 7-inch
MORGIL (102 "Lover's Quarrel")....50-75 61

STARR, Tommy
Singles: 7-inch
LOMA...4-8 68

STARR, Winnie
Singles: 7-inch
WINNIE HUNT (1206 "Baby by Rock") 25-35

STARR SISTERS
Singles: 7-inch
LUTE...5-10 60

STARRY EYED & LAUGHING
LPs: 10/12-inch
COLUMBIA..................................8-10 75

STARS
Singles: 7-inch
VEGA (001 "Let's Cuddle Again")..10-15 59
VEGA (002 "No Letter from You") 10-15 60

STARS ON P&R/LP '81
(Stars on 45; Stars on Long Play)
Singles: 12-inch
RADIO..5-8 81-82
Singles: 7-inch
RADIO..3-5 81-82
21..3-4 83
LPs: 10/12-inch
RADIO..5-10 81-82
21..5-8 83

STARS ON 45 FEATURING SAM & DAVE
Singles: 7-inch
21 (99636 "Sam & Dave Medley") 3-5 85
(First issue. Has titles listed in correct order.)

STARS ON 45 FEATURING NEW SAM & DAVE REVUE
Singles: 7-inch
21 (99636 "Sam & Dave Medley") 3-5 85
(Reissue. Has titles listed in wrong order.)
Also see SAM & DAVE
Also see STARS ON
Also see STARS on 45 Featuring Sam & Dave

STARSHINE D&D '83
Singles: 12-inch
PRELUDE 4-6 83
Singles: 7-inch
PRELUDE 3-4 83

STARSHIP
Singles: 7-inch
LION...4-8 72
Members: Mickey Dolenz; Michael Lloyd.
Also see DOLENZ, Mickey
Also see LLOYD, Michael

STARSHIP P&R/LP '85
(Jefferson Starship)
Singles: 12-inch
GRUNT (14226 "We Built This City") 5-10 85
Singles: 7-inch
GRUNT 3-4 85-87
RCA 3-4 87-89
Picture Sleeves
GRUNT 3-4 85-87
RCA 3-5 87-89
LPs: 10/12-inch
GRUNT 5-8 85-89
Also see JEFFERSON STARSHIP

STARSKI, Love Bug
ATLANTIC....................................3-4 85
EPIC...3-4 85
FEVER 3-4 87

STAR-TELS
Singles: 7-inch
LAMARR 8-12

STARTERS
Singles: 7-inch
STILLWIND (0103 "Tonight It's Gonna Be Kentucky") 8-12 83
(Picture disc.)

STARTIME KIDS
Singles: 7-inch
OKEH...5-10 59

STARTONES
(Carnations)
Singles: 78 rpm
RAINBOW...................................15-25 56
Singles: 7-inch
RAINBOW (341 "Forever My Love") 50-75 56
Also see CARNATIONS

STARTONES
Singles: 7-inch
BILLIE FRAN (001 "One Rose") 250-500 65

STAR-TREKS
Singles: 7-inch
VEEP (1254 "Gonna Need Magic") 20-30 67

STARWOOD
LPs: 10/12-inch
COLUMBIA..................................8-10 77
WINDSONG..................................8-10 76

STARZ P&R/LP '76
Singles: 7-inch
CAPITOL.....................................3-5 76-79
(Black vinyl.)
CAPITOL (4399 "Cherry Baby").......5-10 77
(Colored vinyl.)
CAPITOL (4434 "Sing It, Shout It")..5-10 78
(Colored vinyl.)
Picture Sleeves
CAPITOL.....................................3-5 76-79
LPs: 10/12-inch
CAPITOL.....................................8-10 76-78
(Black vinyl.)
CAPITOL (11617 "Violation").........15-20 77
(Colored vinyl.)
VIOLATION..................................5-8 83
Member: Richie Ranno; Joe Dube; Brendan Harkin.
Also see RANNO, Richie

STATE DEPT.
Singles: 7-inch
ABBOTT (37004 "Wild Honey").........4-8 72

STATE OF GRACE D&D '83
Singles: 12-inch
PROFILE.....................................4-6 83
Singles: 7-inch
PROFILE.....................................3-4 83

STATE OF MICKY & TOMMY
Singles: 7-inch
MERCURY (72712 "With Love from One to Five") 15-25 67

STATE OF MIND
Singles: 7-inch
CHAVIS (1038 "Move")..................10-20 66
CHAVIS (1041 "Goin' Away")...........8-12 67

STATENS
Singles: 7-inch
MARK-X (8011 "Summertime Is the Right Time for Love") 50-70 61
LPs: 10/12-inch
CRYSTAL BALL.............................8-10 82

STATES
Singles: 7-inch
CHRYSALIS..................................3-5 79
LPs: 10/12-inch
BOARDWALK................................5-10 81
CHRYSALIS..................................5-10 79

STATESIDERS
Singles: 7-inch
PROVIDENCE................................8-12

STATESMEN
Singles: 7-inch
BRADLEA (200 "Rampage")..............8-12 61
JAMIE 5-10

TEMA (137 "Stop and Get a Ticket") 5-10 68
Picture Sleeves
TEMA (137 "Stop and Get a Ticket") 10-15 68

STATESMEN
Singles: 7-inch
RAYNARD (014 "Teen Theme")....10-20 65

STATIC DISRUPTERS
Singles: 7-inch
WASP...3-5 82

STATICS
Singles: 7-inch
MANTIS (102 "Shanghaied") 25-50 61
Also see DEE, Lynn, & Statics

STATICS
Singles: 7-inch
VARDAN......................................8-12

STATICS & TINY TONY
Singles: 7-inch
CAMELOT (110 "Harlem Shuffle") 10-20 61
Also see TINY TONY & STATICS

STATLER, Darrell C&W '69
Singles: 7-inch
DOT 3-6 69

STATLER BROTHERS C&W/P&R '65
Singles: 7-inch
COLUMBIA 4-6 64-69
MERCURY 3-6 70-90
Picture Sleeves
MERCURY 3-4
LPs: 10/12-inch
CBS 5-10 82-85
COLUMBIA (CL-2000 series).........15-25 66-67
(Monaural.)
COLUMBIA (CS-9000 series) 12-25 66-69
(Stereo.)
COLUMBIA (PC-9000 series) 5-8 80s
COLUMBIA (31000 series) 8-10 70s
51 WEST 5-8 80s
HARMONY...................................6-12 71-73
MERCURY...................................5-10 71-90
PRIORITY....................................5-8 82
REALM..5-10
TIME-LIFE....................................5-8 81
Members: Harold Reid; Don Reid; Lew DeWitt; Phil Balsley; Jimmy Fortune. Session: Carl Perkins; Ernest Tubb.
Also see CASH, Johnny
Also see DeWITT, Lew
Also see PERKINS, Carl
Also see TUBB, Ernest

STATON, Candi P&R '69
Singles: 7-inch
FAME..3-6 69-73
L.A. 3-4 81
SUGAR HILL.................................3-4 82
UNITY (711 "Now That You Have the Upper Hand") 75-125
W.B. 3-5 74-80
LPs: 10/12-inch
FAME..8-12 70-72
SUGAR HILL.................................5-8 82
W.B. 8-10 74-80
Also see SOURCE, & Candi Staton

STATON, Dakota LP '58
Singles: 78 rpm
CAPITOL.....................................4-8 55-63
Singles: 7-inch
CAPITOL.....................................4-8 55-63
GROOVE MERCHANT 3-5 72
EPs: 7-inch
CAPITOL.....................................5-15 58-60
LPs: 10/12-inch
CAPITOL (800 thru 1600 series)....20-40 58-63
HALF MOON................................5-8 83
LONDON......................................10-15 67
U.A. 10-20 63-64
VERVE..8-12 71

STATON, Danny
Singles: 7-inch
ALMAR..8-10 60
FELSTED.....................................8-10 59

STATON, Johnny, & Feathers / Jaguars
Singles: 7-inch
CLASSIC ARTISTS..........................4-6 89
Also see FEATHERS
Also see JAGUARS

STATUES P&R '60
Singles: 7-inch
LIBERTY (55245 "Blue Velvet")....15-25 60
LIBERTY (55279 "Dream Girl")......15-25 60
LIBERTY (55292 "White Christmas") 10-20 60
LIBERTY (55363 "Love at First Sight") 10-20 61
Members: James "Buzz" Cason (a.k.a. Garry Miles); Richard Williams; Hugh Jarrett.
Also see CASON, Buzz
Also see MILES, Garry

STATUS CYMBAL
Singles: 7-inch
RCA 4-8 67-68
LPs: 10/12-inch
RCA 10-15 68

STATUS QUO P&R '68
Singles: 7-inch
A&M 3-5 73-74
CADET/CONCEPT..........................4-8 68-69
CAPITOL.....................................3-5 75-77
JANUS..3-5 72

PYE 3-5 75
RIVA 3-5 80
LPs: 10/12-inch
A&M 8-10 73-74
CADET CONCEPT 10-15 68
CAPITOL 8-10 74-79
JANUS 10-12 71
PYE 10-12 72
Also see BAND AID

STATUS QUO
Singles: 7-inch
GRANT (690 "They All Want Her Love") 15-25 60s

STATUS VI D&D '83
Singles: 12-inch
RADAR 4-6 83

STAVELY MAKEPEACE
Singles: 7-inch
LONDON 3-5

STAVIS, George
LPs: 10/12-inch
VANGUARD 8-10 69

STAYMER, Hans, Band
LPs: 10/12-inch
CSF 8-10 72

STAYTON, Jimmy
(James Stayton)
Singles: 7-inch
BLUE HEN (220 "Hot Hot Mama") 100-200 60
BLUE HEN (224 "You're Gonna Treat Me Right") 100-200 60
20TH FOX (310 "More Than You'll Ever Know") 40-60 62

STEADIES
Singles: 7-inch
JOSIE 5-10 58
TAD 5-10 59

STEADY B LP '87
LPs: 10/12-inch
JIVE 5-8 87-88

STEAGALL, Red C&W '72
(With the Coleman County Cowboys; Red Stegall)
Singles: 7-inch
ABC 3-5 78
ABC/DOT 3-5 76-77
CAPITOL 3-5 72-75
ELEKTRA 3-4 79-80
LPs: 10/12-inch
ABC/DOT 6-12 76
CAPITOL 10-20 72-74
HESSTON 5-8 83
MCA 5-10
Also see PRICE, David

STEALER
Singles: 7-inch
MCA 3-5 82
LPs: 10/12-inch
MCA 5-10 82

STEALERS WHEEL P&R/LP '73
Singles: 7-inch
A&M 3-5 73-78
Picture Sleeves
A&M 3-5 73
LPs: 10/12-inch
A&M 6-12 73-78
PICKWICK 5-8 80
Members: Gerry Rafferty; Joe Egan.
Also see RAFFERTY, Gerry

STEALIN' HORSES LP '88
Singles: 7-inch
ARISTA 3-4 88
LPs: 10/12-inch
ARISTA 5-8 88

STEAM P&R '69
Singles: 7-inch
FONTANA 3-6 69
MERCURY 3-5 70-76
Picture Sleeves
MERCURY (30160 "Na Na Hey Hey Kiss Him Goodbye") 10-15 76
(Promotional Chicago White Sox sleeve.)
LPs: 10/12-inch
MERCURY 12-18 69

STEAMHAMMER
Singles: 7-inch
EPIC 3-5 69-70
LPs: 10/12-inch
EPIC 15-20 69-70

STEARNS, June C&W '68
Singles: 7-inch
COLUMBIA 3-6 68-69
DECCA 3-5 70-71
LPs: 10/12-inch
COLUMBIA 10-15 69
Also see AGNES & ORVILLE
Also see DUNCAN, Johnny, & June Stearns

STEBBINS, Cathie
Singles: 7-inch
PRINCIPLE (4330 "Samantha's Song") 3-5 73
Picture Sleeves
PRINCIPLE (4330 "Samantha's Song") 3-5 73

STEEL
Singles: 7-inch
EPIC 3-5 71
LPs: 10/12-inch
EPIC 8-10 71

STEEL, Danny
Singles: 7-inch
SOLAR (1013 "Chinese Twist") 10-15 62

STEEL, Jake & Jeff
Singles: 7-inch
PEACH/MINT (6065 "Impeachment Story") 3-5 74

STEEL, Ric C&W '87
Singles: 7-inch
PANACHE 3-4 87-88

STEEL, Tracy
(With the Outlaws; Tracy Steele)
Singles: 7-inch
C-WAY (227 "Take Me with You") 50-75 60s
DELAWARE (1705 "Letter to Paul") 20-30 64

STEEL BREEZE
Singles: 7-inch
BRAND X 10-20 60s

STEEL BREEZE LP '82
Singles: 7-inch
RCA 3-4 82-83
LPs: 10/12-inch
RCA 5-8 82

STEEL GLASS
Singles: 7-inch
LAMARR (245 "I Told My Baby") 10-20 60s

STEEL IMAGE
Singles: 7-inch
FONTANA 3-5 69
LPs: 10/12-inch
FONTANA 10-15 70

STEEL PULSE LP '82
Singles: 7-inch
ELEKTRA 3-4 82-84
LPs: 10/12-inch
ELEKTRA 5-8 82-84
MCA 5-8 88
MANGO 5-8 80

STEEL RIVER
Singles: 7-inch
EVOLUTION 3-5 70-71
LPs: 10/12-inch
EVOLUTION 8-10 70-71

STEEL WOOL
Singles: 7-inch
WHITE WHALE 4-8 71
Member: Buddy Randell.
Also see RANDELL, Buddy

STEELE, Ben, & His Bare Hands D&D '83
Singles: 12-inch
VANITY 4-6 83

STEELE, Bette Anne
Singles: 78 rpm
ABC-PAR 8-12 56
Singles: 7-inch
ABC-PAR (9744 "Is This the Way") 15-25 56

STEELE, Billy
Singles: 7-inch
KING 5-10 59

STEELE, Don
("The Real Don Steele")
Singles: 7-inch
CAMEO (399 "Tina Del Gado Is Alive") 8-12 66
PATCHES (102 "Cecil, the Unwanted French Fry") 5-10 69

STEELE, Don / Willie Nelson
LPs: 10/12-inch
CATHOLIC COMMUNITY SERVICES (1986 "Renegade Heart") 5-10 86
(Promotional, C.C.S. benefit issue only. Has only one Nelson track, *Healing Hands of Time*.)
Also see STEELE, Don
Also see NELSON, Willie

STEELE, Jo Ann
Singles: 7-inch
COLUMBIA 4-8 68

STEELE, John, & Del-Mates
Singles: 7-inch
WAND 4-8 65

STEELE, Johnny
Singles: 7-inch
FAME 3-5 69

STEELE, Larry C&W '66
(With the Wranglers)
Singles: 7-inch
ASSULT 4-8 63
K-ARK 4-8 65-66

STEELE, Little Joe
Singles: 7-inch
ABC-PAR 4-8 64

STEELE, Maureen P&R '85
Singles: 7-inch
MOTOWN 3-4 85
Picture Sleeves
MOTOWN 3-4 85

STEELE, Nancy
Singles: 7-inch
CELEBRITY (7120 "Our Future") 8-12

STEELE, Ray
Singles: 7-inch
SUE 4-8 63

STEELE, Ron
LPs: 10/12-inch
OVATION 8-10 76

STEELE, Tommy
Singles: 7-inch
BUENA VISTA 4-6 67
LONDON 5-10 58-60
RCA 4-8 65
WAM (1 "Elevator Rock") 10-20 60s
Picture Sleeves
BUENA VISTA 5-10 67
LPs: 10/12-inch
LIBERTY 10-20 65

STEELE, Tracy: see STEEL, Tracy

STEELE, Wally
Singles: 7-inch
GO GO GTO 4-8 66

STEELERS P&R '69
Singles: 7-inch
DATE 4-8 69
EPIC 3-6 71
Members: Leonard Truss; Wes Wells; Wales Walace; Alonzo Wells; George Wells.

STEELERS
Singles: 7-inch
CRASH (428 "The Flame Remains") 10-20
GLOW STAR (815 "Walk Alone") 10-20

STEELEYE SPAN LP '75
Singles: 7-inch
CHRYSALIS 3-5 72-78
LPs: 10/12-inch
BIG TREE 12-15 71
CHRYSALIS 8-12 72-78
MFSL (027 "All Around My Hat") 30-50 79
TAKOMA 8-10 81
Also see PRIOR, Maddy, & June Taylor

STEELHEART
LPs: 10/12-inch
MCA 5-8 90

STEELY DAN P&R/LP '72
Singles: 7-inch
ABC 3-6 72-78
MCA 3-5 78-81
EPs: 7-inch
ABC ("Pretzel Logic") 10-20 74
(Quadraphonic. Juke box "Special Promotional Record." Includes title strips.)
ABC (779 "Countdown to Ecstasy") 5-10 73
(Juke box issue. Includes title strips.)
ABC (12003 "Steely Dan") 5-10 77
(Juke box issue. Includes title strips.)
LPs: 10/12-inch
ABC 6-12 72-78
ABC/COMMAND (40009 "Can't Buy a Thrill") 15-25 74
(Quadraphonic.)
ABC/COMMAND (40010 "Countdown to Ecstasy") 15-25 74
(Quadraphonic.)
ABC/COMMAND (40015 "Pretzel Logic") 15-25 74
(Quadraphonic.)
MCA 5-10 79-82
MFSL (007 "Katy Lied") 25-50 79
MFSL (033 "Aja") 40-60 79
Members: Donald Fagen; Walter Becker; Jim Hodder; Jeff Baxter. Session: Bernard Purdie; Chuck Rainey; Victor Feldman; Larry Carlton; Tom Scott.
Also see BEAD GAME
Also see FAGEN, Donald
Also see McDONALD, Michael
Also see ULTIMATE SPINACH

STEEPLE PEOPLE
Singles: 7-inch
B.T. PUPPY 4-8 67

STEEPLECHASE
Singles: 7-inch
POLYDOR 3-5 70
LPs: 10/12-inch
POLYDOR 10-12 70

STEFAN, Paul
(With Royal Lancers; with Apollos; Paul Steffen.)
Singles: 7-inch
CITATION (5003 "I Fought the Law") 15-25 62
(Black vinyl.)
CITATION (5003 "I Fought the Law") 20-30 62
(Colored vinyl.)
CITATION (5004 "Baby I Don't Care") 40-60 62
CITE (5006 "Good for a Laugh") 15-25 63
CITE (5007 "Hey Lonely One") 15-25 63
CITE (5008 "You") 15-25 64
DOT 8-12 64
Also see APOLLOS
Also see PAUL & PACK / Mad Doctors
Also see CRAIG, Vilas, & Royal Lancers / Badgers
Also see PEIL, Danny
Also see PREMIERE, Ronnie
Also see STONE, Roland
Also see VALIANTS

STEFF
Singles: 7-inch
EPIC 4-8 66

STEFFIN SISTERS C&W '89
Singles: 7-inch
WINWARD 3-4 89

STEGALL, Keith C&W '80
Singles: 7-inch
CAPITOL 3-5 80-81
EMI AMERICA 3-4 82
EPIC 3-4 84-86

STEGALL, Red: see STEAGALL, Red

STEIN, Frank N., & Tombstones
Singles: 7-inch
MARCO (003 "Mess Around") 25-35 62

STEIN, Frankie, & His Ghouls
Singles: 7-inch
POWER (338 "Goon River") 8-10 64
Picture Sleeves
POWER (338 "Goon River") 10-15 64
LPs: 10/12-inch
POWER 15-25 64-65

STEIN, Franklyn
Singles: 7-inch
COLPIX 5-10 62

STEIN, Lou P&R '57
Singles: 78 rpm
BRUNSWICK 3-5 52-53
EPIC 3-5 55-56
JUBILEE 3-5 54
MERCURY 3-5 55-58
RKO UNIQUE 3-5 57
Singles: 7-inch
BRUNSWICK 4-6 52-53
EPIC 4-6 55-56
JUBILEE 4-6 54
MERCURY 4-6 55-58
MURBO 3-5 69
RKO UNIQUE 4-6 57
EPs: 7-inch
EPIC 4-8 55-56
JUBILEE 4-8 54
LPs: 10/12-inch
CHIAROSCURO 4-8 76-81
CORAL 5-15 53
EPIC 5-15 55-56
EVEREST 5-12 60
JUBILEE 5-15 54
MERCURY 5-15 55-60
MUSICOR 5-10 67-68
OLD TOWN 5-15 61
WING 5-10 62
WORLD JAZZ 4-8 81
Also see COLLINS, Al "Jazzbo," & Lou Stein

STEINBERG, David LP '71
Singles: 7-inch
COLUMBIA 3-5 74
LPs: 10/12-inch
COLUMBIA 5-10 74-75
ELEKTRA 5-10 70
UNI 8-15 68

STEINBERG, Dianne
LPs: 10/12-inch
ABC 5-10 77
ATLANTIC 5-10 74

STEINBERG, Wilbur
Singles: 7-inch
HUT (4401 "Mop Bop Boogie") 150-250 58

STEINMAN, Jim P&R/LP '81
Singles: 7-inch
EPIC/CLEVELAND INT'L 3-6 81
Picture Sleeves
EPIC/CLEVELAND INT'L 4-8 81
LPs: 10/12-inch
EPIC/CLEVELAND INT'L 5-10 81

STEINWAYS
Singles: 7-inch
OLIVER (2002 "My Heart's Not in It Anymore") 15-25 66
OLIVER (2007 "Call Me") 15-25 66

STEMMONS EXPRESS
Singles: 7-inch
KARMA (201 "Woman, Love Thief") 25-50 69
WAND (1198 "Woman, Love Thief") 10-20 69

STENMARK - MUELLER C&W '87
Singles: 7-inch
ENVELOPE 3-4 87

STENNER, Stan
Singles: 7-inch
DYNASTY (630 "Teri") 8-12 59

STEPHAN & JANIS
Singles: 7-inch
COLUMBIA 4-8 66
Members: Stephan Palmier; Janis Palmier.

STEPHENS, Barbara
Singles: 7-inch
STAX 10-20 61

STEPHENS, Big Will
Singles: 7-inch
CORVET (1013 "Saturday Night") 40-50

STEPHENS, Bobby
Singles: 7-inch
KASH 4-8 64

STEPHENS, Julie: see STEVENS, Julie

STEPHENS, Leigh
Singles: 7-inch
PHILIPS 5-8 69
LPs: 10/12-inch
PHILIPS (600294 "Red Weather") 30-50 69
Also see BLUE CHEER

STEPHENS, Ott C&W '63
Singles: 7-inch
CHANCELLOR 4-8 63
CHART 4-6 65
REPRISE 4-6 64

STEPHENS, Patti
Singles: 7-inch
FARGO 3-5
Picture Sleeves
FARGO 4-6

STEPHENS, Steve
(With Stevedores)
Singles: 7-inch
REBEL (1314 "Weird Session") 10-20 59
UNITED SOUTHERN ARTISTS (103 "Pizza Pete") 20-30 61

STEPHENS, Steve
Singles: 7-inch
UNITED SOUTHERN ARTISTS (103 "Pizza Pete") 20-40 61

STEPHENS, Tennyson
(Tenison Stephens)
Singles: 7-inch
ARIES 4-6 69
CHESS 4-6 69
BACK BEAT 4-8 61
Also see HUGHES, Rheta, & Tennyson Stephens
Also see UPCHURCH, Phil, & Tennyson Stephens

STEPHENS, Tommy
Singles: 7-inch
ABC-PAR (9842 "Camel's Jump") 15-25 57

STEPHENSON, N.A.
Singles: 7-inch
WESTWOOD (201 "Boogie-Woogie Country Girl") 150-250 59

STEPHENSON, Van P&R '81
Singles: 7-inch
HANDSHAKE 3-5 81
MCA 3-4 84
Picture Sleeves
MCA 3-4 84
LPs: 10/12-inch
HANDSHAKE 5-10 81
MCA 5-8 84

STEPIN' FETCHIT
(Stepin' Fetchett)
Singles: 78 rpm
HOLLYWOOD 10-15 55
Singles: 7-inch
HOLLYWOOD (1037 "Davy Crockett Boogie") 15-25 55
VEE JAY (382 "Fairy Tales") 5-10 61
LPs: 10/12-inch
VEE JAY (1032 "Stepin' Fetchit") 25-35 61

STEPPENWOLF P&R/LP '68
Singles: 7-inch
ABC 3-5 70
DUNHILL 4-8 67-71
IMMEDIATE 4-8 67
MCA 3-4 80s
MUMS 3-5 74-75
ROULETTE 3-5 70s
Picture Sleeves
DUNHILL 4-8 71
MUMS 3-5 74
EPs: 7-inch
DUNHILL 5-10 68
(Juke box issues only.)
LPs: 10/12-inch
ABC 8-12 75-76
ALLEGIANCE 5-8
DUNHILL (Except 50053) 10-20 68-73
DUNHILL (50053 "At Your Birthday Party") 20-30 69
EPIC 8-12 75-76
MCA 5-10 79
MUMS 8-10 74
Members: John Kay; Goldy McJohn; Michael Monarch; Jerry Edmonton; Nick St. Nicholas.
Also see HARD TIMES
Also see KAY, John
Also see SPARROWS
Also see T.I.M.E.

STEP-PERS
Singles: 7-inch
BRIDGES 5-10 68

STEPPERS
Singles: 7-inch
AWARE 10-12

STEPPES
LPs: 10/12-inch
VOXX 5-8 87

STEPPING STONES
Singles: 7-inch
DIPLOMACY 10-15 60s
FLAIR 5-10 68
PHILIPS 5-10 63

STEPSON
Singles: 7-inch
ABC 3-5 74
LPs: 10/12-inch
ABC 8-10 74

STEPTOE
Singles: 12-inch
FANTASY 4-6 82

Singles: 7-inch
FANTASY ... 3-5 82

STEREO FUN INC. D&D '83
Singles: 12-inch
MOBY DICK ... 4-6 83

STEREO SHOESTRINGS
Singles: 7-inch
ENGLISH (1302 "Tell Her No") ... 50-75 68

STEREOPHONICS
Singles: 7-inch
APT (25003 "No More Heartaches") ... 15-20 58

STEREOS
Singles: 7-inch
MINK (22 "Memory Lane") ... 40-60 59
(*Memory Lane* was reissued later in 1959, showing the group as the Tams. the same track was again issued in 1963, shown as by the Tams and then by the Hippies.)
Also see HIPPIES / Reggie Harrison
Also see TAMS

STEREOS
Singles: 7-inch
AFS (306 "Hot Rod") ... 20-30 59

STEREOS P&R '61
Singles: 7-inch
CADET (5577 "Stereo Freeze") ... 5-8 67
CADET (5626 "I Can't Stop These Tears") ... 5-8 67
COLLECTABLES ... 3-5 86
CUB (Except 9106) ... 10-20 61
CUB (9106 "Do You Love Me") ... 10-15 62
(Black vinyl.)
CUB (9106 "Do You Love Me") ... 25-35 62
(Black vinyl.)
GIBRALTAR (105 "A Love for Only You") ... 20-40 59
(Dark blue label.)
GIBRALTAR (105 "A Love for Only You") ... 15-25 59
(Light blue label.)
WORLD ARTISTS (1012 "Good News") ... 10-15 63
Members: Bruce Robinson; Ronnie Collins; Sam Profit; George Otis; Nathaniel Hicks.

STEREOS
Singles: 7-inch
COLUMBIA (42626 "Echo in My Heart") ... 500-750 62
COLUMBIA (42626 "Echo in My Heart") ... 300-500 62
(Promotional issue.)
Also see BUCKEYES

STEREOS
Singles: 7-inch
ROBIN NEST (101 "My Heart") ... 25-50 62
ROBIN NEST (1588 "Don't Cry Darling") ... 15-25 62

STERIOS
Singles: 7-inch
IDEA ... 10-20

STERLING
Singles: 7-inch
MOTOWN ... 3-5 79
LPs: 10/12-inch
A&M ... 5-10 80

STERLING, Don
Singles: 7-inch
CORVETTE (1008 "Wonderful Someone") ... 25-35

STERLING, Michael
Singles: 7-inch
SUCCESS ... 3-4 83

STERLING, Spencer
Singles: 7-inch
BIG TOP (3104 "Jilted") ... 10-20 62
JAM ... 10-20 60s

STERLING BROTHERS
Singles: 7-inch
HERALD (579 "What Is This Called Love") ... 10-20 62

STERLING GUITARS
Singles: 7-inch
SAX 5TH AVE. (209 "Go Kart") ... 15-25 63

STERLINGS
Singles: 7-inch
DECCA ... 4-8 65
MERCURY ... 4-8 66

STERN, Nina
Singles: 7-inch
JERDEN ... 8-12 65

STETSAPHONIC
Singles: 7-inch
TOMMY BOY ... 3-4 87

STEVE
Singles: 7-inch
PRESIDENT ... 5-10 61

STEVE & ALBERT
Singles: 7-inch
BELL (853 "Follow the Bouncing Ball") ... 5-8 69
Member: Albert Hammond.
Also see HAMMOND, Albert

STEVE & DONNA
Singles: 7-inch
LIBERTY (55192 "All the Better to Love You") ... 8-12 59

STEVE & DYNAMICS
Singles: 7-inch
RAYCO (101 "Down Payment") ... 10-15 62
RAYCO (520 "I Wanna Love Somebody") ... 10-15 62
STERLING (101 "Down Payment") ... 15-25 62
(First issue.)

STEVE & EMPERORS
Singles: 7-inch
BEST (103 "The Breeze and I") ... 15-25 64
Also see EMPERORS

STEVE & EYDIE: see LAWRENCE, Steve, & Eydie Gorme

STEVE & HOLIDAYS
Singles: 7-inch
DANDY (101 "Unemployment") ... 8-12

STEVE & TEE
Singles: 7-inch
STUDIO ... 5-10 60

STEVE & YOUNGER SET
Singles: 7-inch
SOUND CORE (1001 "After Dark") ... 15-25 60s

STEVENS, April P&R '51
(April)
Singles: 78 rpm
RCA ... 5-10 51-52
SOCIETY (10 "Don't Do It") ... 10-15 50
Singles: 7-inch
A&M ... 3-5 72
ATCO ... 4-6 65
CONTRACT ... 4-8 61
IMPERIAL ... 4-8 59-65
KING ... 4-6 64
MGM ... 4-6 67
RCA ... 8-12 51-52
SOCIETY (10 "Don't Do It") ... 15-25 50
VERVE ... 3-5 71
EPs: 7-inch
KING ... 10-20 54
LPs: 10/12-inch
IMPERIAL ... 15-20 61-64
LIBERTY ... 5-8 83
Also see APRIL
Also see TEMPO, Nino, & April Stevens

STEVENS, April / Marg Phelan
LPs: 10/12-inch
AUDIO LAB ... 15-20 59
Also see STEVENS, April

STEVENS, Ar, & Rockin' Ricochettes
LP: 10/12-inch
OTTERTAIL ... 5-10 85
Also see RICOCHETTES

STEVENS, Bobby, & Checkmates Ltd.
LPs: 10/12-inch
RUSTIC ... 10-15 71
Also see CHECKMATES LTD.

STEVENS, Carol
EPs: 7-inch
ATLANTIC (598 "Satin Doll") ... 10-20 57

STEVENS, Cat P&R/LP '71
Singles: 12-inch
A&M ... 5-8 77
Singles: 7-inch
A&M ... 3-5 70-79
DERAM ... 4-6 66-72
Picture Sleeves
A&M ... 3-5 71-78
EPs: 7-inch
A&M ... 8-10 70
(Juke box issue only.)
LPs: 10/12-inch
A&M ... 5-10 69-84
DERAM ... 10-15 67-72
LONDON ... 5-10 78
MFSL (035 "Tea for the Tillerman") ... 60-80 79
MFSL (UHQR 035 "Tea for the Tillerman") ... 80-100 79
(Boxed set.)
MFSL (244 "Teaser & the Firecat") ... 20-25 95
MFSL (254 "Izitso") ... 20-25 96

STEVENS, Connie P&R '60
Singles: 7-inch
BELL ... 4-8 70-72
MGM ... 10-15 68
PARAMOUNT ("Why Can't He Care for Me") ... 35-50 58
(Promotional issue only. No actual label name or number is shown, but this may have been distributed by Paramount to promote the film, *Rock-A-Bye Baby*, in which Connie starred.)
W.B. (Except 5092) ... 5-10 59-66
W.B. (5092 "Apollo") ... 10-20 59
Picture Sleeves
W.B. (5159 "Too Young to Go Steady") ... 15-25 60
LPs: 10/12-inch
HARMONY ... 10-20 69
W.B. (1208 "Conchetta") ... 40-50 58
W.B. (1335 thru 1460) ... 20-40 59-62
Also see BYRNES, Edward

STEVENS, Debbie
(With the Deltones)
Singles: 7-inch
ABC-PAR ... 5-10 59
APT ... 10-20 59
ROULETTE ... 10-15 58

STEVENS, Dodie P&R '59
(Geraldine Stevens)
Singles: 7-inch
CRYSTALETTE (724 "Pink Shoe Laces") ... 10-20 59
CRYSTALETTE (728 "Yes-Sir-ee") ... 10-20 59
DOLTON ... 5-10 63
DOT ... 8-15 59-62
IMPERIAL ... 5-10 63
Picture Sleeves
CRYSTALETTE (724 "Pink Shoe Laces") ... 30-50 59
LPs: 10/12-inch
DOT ... 20-40 60-61
Session: Billy Vaughn Orchestra.
Also see STEVENS, Geraldine
Also see VAUGHN, Billy, Orchestra

STEVENS, Duke
Singles: 7-inch
OKEH ... 4-8 60

STEVENS, Even C&W '75
Singles: 7-inch
ELEKTRA ... 3-5 75-76
LPs: 10/12-inch
ELEKTRA ... 5-10 77

STEVENS, Even, & Sammi Smith C&W '75
Singles: 7-inch
ELEKTRA ... 3-5 75
Also see SMITH, Sammi

STEVENS, Even, & Sherry Grooms C&W '77
Singles: 7-inch
ELEKTRA ... 3-5 77
Also see GROOMS, Sherry
Also see STEVENS, Even

STEVENS, Eddie
Singles: 7-inch
CARLTON ... 4-8 61

STEVENS, Flip Flop
(With Famous Pop Tops Orchestra)
Singles: 7-inch
SHIPTOWN ... 5-8

STEVENS, Geoffrey
Singles: 7-inch
AVCO EMBASSY ... 4-6 69
DECCA ... 4-6 68
YORK ... 4-8 67

STEVENS, Geraldine C&W '69
Singles: 7-inch
WORLD PACIFIC ... 4-6 69
Also see STEVENS, Dodie

STEVENS, Hoyt
Singles: 7-inch
LOG CABIN (6171 " '55 Chevy") ... 150-200

STEVENS, Hunt
Singles: 7-inch
U.A. ... 5-10 58
Picture Sleeves
U.A. ... 10-15 58

STEVENS, Jeff, & Bullets C&W '86
Singles: 7-inch
ATLANTIC AMERICA ... 3-4 86-89

STEVENS, Jimmy
(Jimmy Stephens)
Singles: 7-inch
ELDO ... 4-8 61
VALIANT ... 4-8 63
VIAPHONIC ... 15-25
Also see SAFARIS

STEVENS, Jimmy
Singles: 7-inch
RSO ... 3-5 74

STEVENS, Johnny
Singles: 7-inch
FORD (123 "Oh Yeah") ... 15-25 63
PARKWAY (805 "Hm-Mm-Baby-Hm-Mm") ... 50-100 59

STEVENS, Julie
(With the Premiers; Julie Stephens)
Singles: 7-inch
DIG (115 "Blue Mood") ... 35-50 56
DIG (129 "Take My Heart") ... 35-50 57
DORE (547 "True Deep Love") ... 20-30 60
DORE (614 "What Makes Little Girls Cry") ... 15-25 61
DORE (603 "Evening Star") ... 10-15 61
ELDO (107 "Blue Mood") ... 15-25 60
SURE (104 "Don't Worry About Me") ... 10-15 60
Also see PREMIERS

STEVENS, Kenny
Singles: 7-inch
JONI ... 5-10 60
OLD TOWN ... 10-15 64

STEVENS, Larry
(With the Three Dolls)
Singles: 7-inch
EPIC ... 10-15 60
FINER ARTS ... 4-6 61

STEVENS, Lee J. C&W '89
Singles: 7-inch
REGAL ... 3-4 88-89

STEVENS, Leith
(Leith Stevens' All Stars)
Singles: 78 rpm
DECCA ... 5-10 54
Singles: 7-inch
DECCA (29067 "Blues for Brando") ... 8-12 54

STEVENS, Lisa, & Pure Energy
Singles: 12-inch
PRISM ... 4-6

STEVENS, Mark, & Charmers
Singles: 7-inch
ALLISON (921 "Magic Rose") ... 50-75 62

STEVENS, Matt
Singles: 7-inch
CAMEO ... 5-10 60

STEVENS, N., & Dee Vines
Singles: 7-inch
BRUNSWICK (55096 "More and More") ... 10-20 60s

STEVENS, Nancy
Singles: 7-inch
CHANCELLOR ... 5-8 61

STEVENS, Neil
(With the Temptations; with Dee-Vines)
Singles: 7-inch
BRUNSWICK (55095 "What Could Be Better") ... 15-25 58
GOLDISC ... 10-20 61
Also see TEMPTATIONS

STEVENS, Randy
Singles: 7-inch
LOMA (301 "All My Love") ... 50-75 59

STEVENS, Ray P&R '61/C&W '69
(With the Merry Melody Singers)
Singles: 7-inch
BARNABY ... 3-5 70-76
CAPITOL ... 8-12 58-59
MCA (Except 53661) ... 3-4 85-89
MCA (53661 "I Saw Elvis in a UFO") ... 5-10 89
MERCURY (66 "Butch Barbarian") ... 10-15 64
(Promotional issue only.)
MERCURY (71000 & 72000 series) ... 5-10 61-68
MERCURY (810000 series) ... 3-5 83
MONUMENT ... 4-8 65-69
NRC ... 10-20 59-60
PREP ... 10-20 57
PRIORITY ... 3-4 80s
RCA ... 3-5 81-82
W.B./AHAB ... 3-5 76-79
Picture Sleeves
BARNABY ... 4-6 70
MCA ... 3-5 86
MERCURY ... 10-20 61-64
W.B./AHAB ... 3-5 79
EPs: 7-inch
MERCURY (85 "Ray Stevens") ... 10-20 62
(Promotional issue only. Not issued with cover.)
LPs: 10/12-inch
BARNABY ... 8-10 70-78
MCA ... 5-8 85-89
MERCURY (20732 "1,837 Seconds of Humor") ... 50-75 62
MERCURY (20732 "Ahab the Arab") ... 20-25 62
(Reissue of *1,837 Seconds of Humor*.)
MERCURY (20828 "This Is Ray Stevens") ... 20-30 63
MERCURY (60732 "1,837 Seconds of Humor") ... 60-80 62
MERCURY (60732 "Ahab the Arab") ... 25-35 62
(Reissue of *1,837 Seconds of Humor*.)
MERCURY (60828 "This Is Ray Stevens") ... 25-35 63
MERCURY (61272 "The Best of Ray Stevens") ... 10-15 70
MERCURY (810000 series) ... 5-8 83
MONUMENT ... 10-15 66-69
PICKWICK ... 5-10
PRIORITY ... 5-8 82
RCA ... 5-10 80-82
W.B. ... 5-10 76-79
WING ... 10-15 68
Session: Minnie Pearl; Jerry Clower.
Also see ARCHIES
Also see 4 SEASONS / Ray Stevens
Also see HENHOUSE FIVE PLUS TOO
Also see KOCK ROBYNS
Also see MINNIE PEARL
Also see ROE, Tommy / Bobby Rydell / Ray Stevens
Also see VELVETS

STEVENS, Ray / Hal Winters
LPs: 10/12-inch
CROWN ... 12-18 63
Also see STEVENS, Ray

STEVENS, Ricky
Singles: 7-inch
CAPITOL ... 4-8 62

STEVENS, Rosie
Singles: 7-inch
SPINNING ... 10-15 59

STEVENS, Scott
Singles: 7-inch
ABC-PAR ... 5-10 59
APT ... 5-10 59-60

STEVENS, Shakin' P&R '84
Singles: 7-inch
EPIC ... 3-5 81-84
EPIC/NU-DISKS ... 3-5 81-84
LPs: 10/12-inch
EPIC ... 5-10 81-84

STEVENS, Stel
Singles: 7-inch
SURE ... 5-10 59
WINK ... 5-10 61

STEVENS, Steve LP '89
(Steve Stevens' Atomic Playboys)
LPs: 10/12-inch
W.B. ... 5-8 89

STEVENS, Stevie
Singles: 7-inch
TCF ... 4-8 65

STEVENS, Tari
(Terri Stevens)
Singles: 78 rpm
DOUBLE AA ... 5-10 55
RCA ... 5-10 55-57
Singles: 7-inch
DOUBLE AA (101 "Unsuspecting Heart") ... 10-20 55
DOUBLE AA (109 "Just Wonderful") ... 10-20 55
FAIRMONT (1001 "False Alarm") ... 20-30 66
FELSTED (8586 "Adonis") ... 8-12 59
RCA (6165 "Why Am I to Blame") ... 5-10 55
RCA (7014 "Pin-Up Girl") ... 10-15 57
RPC (506 "The Boy Next Door") ... 15-25 62
LPs: 10/12-inch
EVEREST ... 15-25 60

STEVENS, Tracy
Singles: 7-inch
LORD BINGO (106 "My Golden One") ... 15-25 63

STEVENSON, B.W. P&R/LP '73
Singles: 7-inch
MCA ... 3-5 80
PRIVATE STOCK ... 3-5 78
RCA ... 3-5 73
W.B. ... 3-5 77-78
LPs: 10/12-inch
MCA ... 5-10 80
RCA ... 5-10 72-77
W.B. ... 5-10 77

STEVENSON, Vern
Singles: 7-inch
JET ... 4-8 62

STEVIE B P&R/LP '88
Singles: 7-inch
LMR ... 3-4 87-90
LPs: 10/12-inch
LMR ... 5-8 87
Also see JAYA

STEWARD, Herb
Singles: 7-inch
AVA ... 4-8 63

STEWARD, Jimmy
Singles: 7-inch
CORAL ... 4-6 68

STEWART, Al LP '74
Singles: 7-inch
ARISTA ... 3-5 78-82
ENIGMA ... 3-4 88
JANUS ... 3-5 74-77
Picture Sleeves
JANUS ... 3-5 74
LPs: 10/12-inch
ARISTA (Except 40) ... 5-10 78-81
ARISTA (40 "Live Radio Concert") ... 25-35 80
(Promotional issue only.)
ENIGMA ... 5-8 88
EPIC ... 20-25 70
JANUS ... 10-15 74-77
MFSL (009 "Year of the Cat") ... 40-60 78
MFSL (082 "Time Passages") ... 25-35 82
Also see PAGE, Jimmy
Also see RENWICK, Tim
Also see SHOT in the DARK

STEWART, Amii P&R/LP '79
Singles: 12-inch
ARIOLA (Black vinyl) ... 4-8 79
ARIOLA (7736 "Knock on Wood"/"When You Are Beautiful") ... 8-12 79
(Picture disc.)
ARIOLA (7736 "Knock on Wood"/"Knock on Wood") ... 15-25 79
(Picture disc.)
ARIOLA (7736 "Knock on Wood"/"Light My Fire") ... 20-30 79
(Picture disc. Promotional issue only.)
EMERGENCY ... 4-6 85
Singles: 7-inch
ARIOLA ... 3-5 79
EMERGENCY ... 3-4 85
LPs: 10/12-inch
ARIOLA AMERICA ... 5-10 79
HANDSHAKE ... 5-8 81

STEWART, Amii, & Johnny Bristol P&R '80
Singles: 7-inch
HANDSHAKE ... 3-5 80
Also see BRISTOL, Johnny
Also see STEWART, Amii

STEWART, Andy P&R '61
Singles: 7-inch
CAPITOL ... 4-6 62
EPIC ... 4-6 64
WARWICK ... 4-8 61
LPs: 10/12-inch
CAPITOL ... 5-15 62-72

EPIC 5-15 64-68
GREEN LINNET 4-8 83
WARWICK 15-25 61

STEWART, Baron P&R '75
Singles: 7-inch
U.A. 3-5 75
LPs: 10/12-inch
U.A. 8-10 75

STEWART, Billy P&R '62
(With the Marquees)
Singles: 78 rpm
ARGO (5256 "Billy's Blues") 10-15 56
CHESS (1625 "Billy's Blues") 15-25 56
OKEH (7095 "Baby, You're My Only Love") 150-200 57
Singles: 7-inch
ARGO (5256 "Billy's Blues") 20-40 56
CHESS (Except 1625) 5-15 62-73
CHESS (1625 "Billy's Blues") 40-60 56
(Reissued three months later on Argo.)
ERIC 3-4 70s
OKEH (7095 "Baby, You're My Only Love") 150-200 57
U.A. 8-12 61
LPs: 10/12-inch
CADET 8-10 74
CHESS (1496 "I Do Love You") . 100-125 65
(Red cover. Black label.)
CHESS (1496 "I Do Love You") ... 50-100 65
(Blue cover. Blue label.)
CHESS (1499 "Unbelievable") 20-40 65
CHESS (1513 "Billy Stewart Teaches Old Standards New Tricks") 15-25 67
CHESS (1547 "Billy Stewart Remembered") 10-15 70
CHESS (50059 "Cross My Heart") 10-15
Also see MARQUEES
Also see STEWART, Billy

STEWART, Bob
Singles: 7-inch
HI-G LO-C 4-8 62

STEWART, Bobby D&D '83
Singles: 12-inch
SOS 5-8 82
W.B. 4-6 83
Singles: 7-inch
SOS 3-5 86
Also see FIVE DISCS

STEWART, Carla
Singles: 7-inch
SPIN 5-10 59-60

STEWART, Celestine, & Charmers
Singles: 78 rpm
HUB 15-25 46

STEWART, Danny
(Danny [Sly] Stewart)
Singles: 7-inch
LUKE (1008 "Long Time Alone") 500-750 61
(Reissued as by Sylvester Stewart.)
PHILLIPS INT'L (3561 "I'll Change My Ways") 20-30 60
Also see STEWART, Danny
Also see STEWART, Sly

STEWART, Darryl
Singles: 7-inch
WAND (11209 "Name It and Claim It") 15-25 69

STEWART, Dave, & Barbara Gaskin P&R '81
Singles: 7-inch
PLATINUM 3-5 81

STEWART, Franklin
Singles: 7-inch
JAXON (500 "That Long Black Train") 100-200 57
LU (501 "That Long Black Train") 500-750 57
(First issue.)

STEWART, Gary C&W '73
(With the Nashville Edition; with Dean Dillon)
Singles: 7-inch
CORY (101 "Walk On Boy") 10-20 64
DECCA 3-5 71
HIGHTONE 3-4 88-89
KAPP 3-6 68-70
MCA 3-5 75
RCA 3-5 73-83
RED ASH 3-4 84
Picture Sleeves
RCA 3-5 82
LPs: 10/12-inch
MCA 4-8 75
RCA 5-10 75-83
Also see CROWLEY, Rodney
Also see HARRIS, Emmylou

STEWART, Gene
Singles: 7-inch
KING 10-15 58

STEWART, Gwen
Singles: 7-inch
CALL ME 4-6

STEWART, James
(Harmonica Cat)
Singles: 7-inch
FOLK STAR (1192 "Sweet Woman") 35-45 54

STEWART, James
Singles: 7-inch
DECCA 4-6 65
Picture Sleeves
DECCA 8-10 65
Also see STEWART, Jimmy, & Henry Fonda

STEWART, James, & Curt Gowdy
Singles: 7-inch
FLEETWOOD (6 "Professional Baseball – The First 100 Years") 4-6 69
Picture Sleeves
FLEETWOOD (6 "Professional Baseball – The First 100 Years") 4-8 69
Also see STEWART, James

STEWART, Jermaine P&R/LP '85
Singles: 12-inch
ARISTA 4-6 84-86
Singles: 7-inch
ARISTA 3-4 84-88
Picture Sleeves
ARISTA 3-4 86-88
LPs: 10/12-inch
ARISTA 5-8 85-88
Also see CULTURE CLUB

STEWART, Jimmie
Singles: 7-inch
ACE 4-8 61

STEWART, Jimmy
Singles: 7-inch
CRYSTAL (Rock on the Moon") 150-250 58
(Selection number not known.)
EKO ("Rock on the Moon") 400-500 58
(Selection number not known.)
TRUMP (817 "Livin' Doll") 15-25 59

STEWART, Jimmy
(With the Sirs)
Singles: 7-inch
CHARAY 4-8 69
SHAMLEY 3-6 69
UNI 4-8 68

STEWART, Jimmy
LPs: 10/12-inch
CATALYST 5-10 77

STEWART, Jimmy, & Henry Fonda
Singles: 7-inch
NATIONAL GENERAL 3-5 70
Picture Sleeves
NATIONAL GENERAL 4-6 70
Also see STEWART, James

STEWART, John P&R/LP '69
Singles: 7-inch
ALLEGIANCE 3-4
CAPITOL 4-6 69
RCA 3-5 73-75
RSO 3-5 77-80
W.B. 3-5 71
Picture Sleeves
RCA 3-5 70s
LPs: 10/12-inch
ALLEGIANCE 5-8 80s
CAPITOL 10-15 69-70
RCA 5-10 73-75
RSO 5-10 77-80
SHIP 5-8 87
W.B. 8-12 71
Also see BUCKINGHAM, Lindsey
Also see KINGSTON TRIO
Also see NICKS, Stevie

STEWART, John, & Buffy Ford
LPs: 10/12-inch
CAPITOL 10-15 68

STEWART, John, & Nick Reynolds
LPs: 10/12-inch
TAKOMA 5-10
Also see KINGSTON TRIO
Also see STEWART, John

STEWART, John, & Scott Engel: see ENGEL, Scott, & John Stewart

STEWART, Johnny
Singles: 7-inch
SHELLEY 10-15 61
START (642 "C'mon and Monkey with Me") 5-10 63
VITA (169 "Rockin' Anna") 25-50 58

STEWART, Judy, & Her Beatle Buddies
Singles: 7-inch
DIPLOMAT 5-10 64

STEWART, Keith
LPs: 10/12-inch
STEADY 8-12 70

STEWART, Marlow
(With His Four Guitars; with Illusions)
Singles: 7-inch
SOUVENIR (102 "Riptide") 10-20 63
VP (201 "Earthquake") 10-20 60s
Picture Sleeves
SOUVENIR (102 "Riptide") 25-50 63
(One source shows this label as "Variety" instead of "Souvenir." We're not yet sure which is correct.)

STEWART, Mel
Singles: 12-inch
MERCURY 4-6 83
Singles: 7-inch
MERCURY 3-4 83

STEWART, Mike
Singles: 7-inch
DWAIN 4-8 60

STEWART, Poindexter
LPs: 10/12-inch
SST (229 "College Rock") 5-8 93
(10-inch LP.)
Members: Poindexter Stewart; Greg Ginn; Dale Nixon; David Raven.

STEWART, Rex, & Vernon Story
Singles: 78 rpm
DIAL 10-15

STEWART, Rod LP '69
(With Faces)
Singles: 12-inch
W.B. 5-10 78-82
Singles: 7-inch
GEFFEN 3-4 87
GNP 3-5 73
MERCURY 4-8 70-76
POLYDOR 3-4 92
PRESS (8722 "Good Morning Little Schoolgirl") 15-25 65
PRIVATE STOCK 3-5 76
W.B. 3-4 75-93
Picture Sleeves
GEFFEN 3-4 87
MERCURY 5-15 72-73
POLYDOR 3-4 92
W.B. 3-5 78-93
LPs: 10/12-inch
ACCORD 5-8 81
MERCURY (Except 61000 series) ... 8-12 71-76
MERCURY (61000 series) 10-20 69-70
MFSL (054 "Blondes Have More Fun") 25-50 81
PRIVATE STOCK 8-10 77
SPRINGBOARD 8-12 72
TRIP 8-10 77
W.B. (Except BSP-3276) 5-10 75-88
W.B. (BSP-3276 "Blondes Have More Fun") 10-15 79
(Picture disc.)
Also see ADAMS, Bryan, Sting, & Rod Stewart
Also see APPICE, Carmine
Also see BECK, Jeff, & Rod Stewart
Also see FACES
Also see G.T.O.
Also see PYTHON LEE JACKSON
Also see SHOTGUN EXPRESS

STEWART, Rod, & Ronald Isley P&R '90
Singles: 7-inch
W.B. 3-4 90
Also see ISLEY, Ron

STEWART, Rod, & Ronnie Wood
Singles: 7-inch
W.B. 3-4 93
Picture Sleeves
W.B. 3-4 93
Also see STEWART, Rod
Also see WOOD, Ron

STEWART, Sandy P&R '53
Singles: 78 rpm
EPIC 3-6 54
OKEH 3-6 53
20TH CENTURY 3-6 54
"X" 3-6 55
Singles: 7-inch
ATCO 4-8 59
COLPIX 4-8 62-63
DCP 3-6 64
EAST WEST 4-8 58
EPIC 5-10 54
OKEH 5-10 53
20TH CENTURY 5-10 54
U.A. 4-8 60-61
"X" 5-10 55
Picture Sleeves
COLPIX 5-10 62
LPs: 10/12-inch
COLPIX (441 "My Coloring Book") 15-20 63

STEWART, Sandy / Dave Garroway
Singles: 7-inch
DICK CHARLES ("May You Always") 8-12 63
(Promotional issue only. No selection number used.)

STEWART, Sandy
Singles: 7-inch
MODERN 3-4 83
LPs: 10/12-inch
MODERN 5-8 84
Also see NICKS, Stevie, & Sandy Stewart

STEWART, Skip
Singles: 7-inch
PAULA 4-8 65
TAMM 4-8 60s
Also see SHONDELLS / Rod Bernard / Warren Storm / Skip Stewart

STEWART, Slam
Singles: 78 rpm
CONTINENTAL 8-10

STEWART, Sly
Singles: 7-inch
AUTUMN (3 "I Just Learned to Swim") 10-20 64
Also see SLY
Also see SLY & FAMILY STONE
Also see STEWART, Danny
Also see STEWART BROTHERS
Also see STONE, Sly

STEWART, Sylvester
Singles: 7-inch
G&P (901 "Long Time Alone") 250-350 61
(First issued as by Danny [Sly] Stewart.)
Also see STEWART, Danny
Also see STEWART, Sly

STEWART, Ty, & Jokers
Singles: 7-inch
AMY 10-20 61

STEWART, Vernon C&W '63
Singles: 7-inch
CHART 4-8 63
PEACH (751 "Mean Mean Baby") 40-60 61

STEWART, Wynn C&W '56
(With the Tourists; Win Stewart)
Singles: 78 rpm
CAPITOL 5-10 56-57
INTRO (6088 "I've Waited a Lifetime") 15-20 54
Singles: 7-inch
ATLANTIC 3-4 74
CAPITOL (2000 series) 3-5 67-71
CAPITOL (3000 series) 8-15 56-57
CAPITOL (5000 series) 4-8 62-67
CHALLENGE 5-10 59-64
4 STAR 3-4 80
JACKPOT 10-15 59
PLAYBOY 3-5 75-76
PRETTY WORLD 3-4 85
RCA 3-5 72-73
WINS 3-5 78-79
Picture Sleeves
CAPITOL 4-8 67-69
LPs: 10/12-inch
CAPITOL 10-20 67-75
PICKWICK/HILLTOP 5-12 67
PLAYBOY 5-10 76
STARDAY 8-12 68
WRANGLER (1006 "Wynn Stewart") 15-25 62
Member: Bobby Austin.
Also see AUSTIN, Bobby
Also see PIERCE, Webb / Wynn Stewart

STEWART, Wynn, & Jan Howard C&W '60
Singles: 7-inch
CHALLENGE 5-10 60
LPs: 10/12-inch
CHALLENGE (611 "Sweethearts of Country Music") 25-35 60
STARDAY (421 "Their Hits") 15-20 68

STEWART BROTHERS
Singles: 7-inch
ENSIGN (4032 "The Rat") 75-125 59
KEEN (82113 "Sleep on the Porch") 15-25 60
Picture Sleeves
KEEN (82113 "Sleep on the Porch") 25-50 60
Member: Syl Stewart; Danny Stewart.
Also see STEWART, Danny
Also see STEWART, Sly

STEWART SISTERS
Singles: 7-inch
SPECIALTY 5-10 58

STICK LEGS
("Stick Leg's & the Butchering Persian's" [sic])
Singles: 7-inch
HARD-TIMES (3002 "The Wedding") 500-750 62

STICK SHIFTS
Singles: 7-inch
CHISWICK (118 "Paramatta Road") 8-12 60s

STICKS & BRICKS
Singles: 7-inch
JOSIE (839 "Kiss the Pretty Girl Twice") 15-25 57

STICKS & STONES
Singles: 7-inch
CORAL 4-8 67
MGM 5-10 65
POINT (6 "Desperately") 6-12 60s
SONIC 5-10 60s

STICKY FINGERS
Singles: 7-inch
PRELUDE 3-5 79
LPs: 10/12-inch
PRELUDE 5-10 79

STIDHAM, Arbee
Singles: 78 rpm
ABCO 20-30 56
CHECKER 25-50 52
RCA 10-20 47-52
SITTIN' IN WITH 15-25 51
STATES 10-20 57
Singles: 7-inch
ABCO (100 "I'll Always Remember") 40-60 56
ABCO (107 "When I Find My Baby") 40-60 56
BLUES CITY (1113 "Mighty Long Time") 20-30 50s
CHECKER (778 "Don't Set Your Cap for Me") 50-100 53
RCA (0003 "I Found Out for Myself") 50-75 49
(Colored vinyl.)
RCA (0024 "What the Blues Will Do") 50-75 49
(Colored vinyl.)
RCA (0037 "Send My Regrets") 50-75 49
(Colored vinyl.)
RCA (0083 "Let My Dreams Come True") 50-75 50
(Colored vinyl.)
RCA (0093 "Feel Like I'm Losing You") 50-75 50
(Colored vinyl.)
RCA (0101 "You'll Be Sorry") 50-75 49
(Colored vinyl.)
RCA (4951 "I Found Out for Myself") 50-75 52
STATES (164 "Look Me Straight in the Eyes") 20-30 57
LPs: 10/12-inch
FOLKWAYS (31033 "There's Always Tomorrow") 15-25
MAINSTREAM 8-10 72
PRESTIGE BLUESVILLE (1021 "Tired of Wandering") 50-100 61
Also see CHARLES, Ray / Arbee Stidham / Li'l Son Jackson / James Wayne.
Also see MILLINDER, Lucky

STIERLE, Wayne
Singles: 7-inch
CANDLELITE 4-6 70
LPs: 10/12-inch
CANDLELITE 10-25 70-73
(Black vinyl.)
CANDLELITE 25-35 70-73
(Colored vinyl.)
Also see PHANTOM

STIFF LITTLE FINGERS
Singles: 7-inch
CHRYSALIS 3-5 80-81
LPs: 10/12-inch
CHRYSALIS 5-10 80-81

STIGWOOD, Robert, Orchestra
Singles: 7-inch
ATLANTIC 4-6 68

STILL, Pat
Singles: 7-inch
RAMBLIN 4-8 66
ROULETTE 4-8 66

STILLINGER, Buzz
Singles: 7-inch
NANCY 4-8 61

STILLMAN-DAVIS BAND
Singles: 7-inch
COLLEGETOWN (3006 "Orange Bowl Reflections") 10-15 81
(Tiger paw-shaped picture disc. Tribute to Clemson University Tigers Orange Bowl appearance.)
Singles: 7-inch
SP (0102 "We Are Vandy") 8-12 82
(Picture disc.)
LPs: 10/12-inch
BULLDAWG (1001 "Bulldawg Boogie") 10-15 82
(Picture disc. Tribute to University of Georgia football team.)
COLLEGETOWN (3001 "Hoosier High NCAA Champs") 10-15 81
(Picture disc. Tribute to Indiana University basketball team.)
COLLEGETOWN (3002 "Orange Breakout") 10-15 81
(Picture disc. Tribute to Clemson University basketball team.)
COLLEGETOWN (3003 "Carolina Fever") 10-15 81
(Picture disc. Tribute to North Carolina Tar Heels football team.)
GAMECOCK ROCK (1001 "Gamecock Rock") 10-15 81
(Picture disc. Tribute to South Carolina football team.)
SPORT SONG (1002 "Gator Jaws") 10-15 82
(Picture disc. Tribute to University of Florida football team.)
SPORT SONG (1003 "Wolfpack Tracks") 10-15 83
(Picture disc. Tribute to North Carolina State University basketball.)
SPORT SONG (1004 "Hawkeye Boogie") 10-15 83
(Picture disc. Tribute to Iowa University Hawkeyes.)
SPORT SONG (6006 "Illinois Rose") 10-15 83
(Picture disc. Tribute to Illinois University football team.)

STILLROCK
Singles: 7-inch
ENTERPRISE 3-5 71
LPs: 10/12-inch
ENTERPRISE 10-15 71

STILLROVEN
Singles: 7-inch
AUGUST (101 "Little Picture Playhouse") 20-25 68
AUGUST (102 "Have You Seen Me") 20-25 68
AUGUST (102 "Come in the Morning") 80-120 68
(Same selection number used twice.)
FALCON (69 "Hey Joe") 30-50 67
FALCON (7296 "She's My Woman") 150-175 66
ROULETTE (4748 "Hey Joe") 20-25 67

STILLS, Stephen P&R/LP '70
(With Manassas; with Michael Finnigan)
Singles: 7-inch
ATLANTIC 3-5 70-84
COLUMBIA 3-5 75-78
Picture Sleeves
ATLANTIC 3-5 71-84
EPs: 7-inch
ATLANTIC (77206 "Stephen Stills Two") 6-12 71
LPs: 10/12-inch
ATLANTIC 5-10 70-84
COLUMBIA (Except PCQ-33575) 5-10 75-78
COLUMBIA (PCQ-33575 "Stills") 10-15 75
(Quadrophonic.)

Also see AU GO-GO SINGERS
Also see BLOOMFIELD, Mike, Al Kooper & Steve Stills
Also see BUFFALO SPRINGFIELD
Also see CROSBY, STILLS & NASH
Also see JEFFERSON AIRPLANE
Also see MANASSAS
Also see STILLS - YOUNG BAND

STILLS - YOUNG BAND LP '76
Singles: 7-inch
REPRISE ... 3-5 77
LPs: 10/12-inch
REPRISE ... 5-10 76
Members: Stephen Stills; Neil Young.
Also see STILLS, Stephen
Also see YOUNG, Neil

STILLWATER P&R '77
Singles: 7-inch
CAPRICORN ... 3-5 77-78
LPs: 10/12-inch
CAPRICORN ... 5-10 78-79
Member: Jimmy Hall.

STING P&R/D&D/LP '85
(Gordon Sumner)
Singles: 12-inch
A&M ... 4-6 85-87
Singles: 7-inch
A&M ... 3-4 85-90
ABC ... 3-5 78
Picture Sleeves
A&M ... 3-4 85-88
LPs: 10/12-inch
A&M ... 5-8 85-90
ABC ... 5-10 78
Also see ADAMS, Bryan, Sting, & Rod Stewart
Also see BAND AID
Also see POLICE

STING RAYS
Singles: 7-inch
COIN (1511 "Sting Ray Stomp") ... 15-25 60s
HITT (07 "Run on Home") ... 10-20 63
L&M (201 "Fast Track") ... 15-25 61
RAY (3473 "Mad Surfer") ... 10-20 64
ROSE (101 "Hot Sausage") ... 10-20 63

STING REYS
Singles: 7-inch
CRAZY TOWN (101 "When You Wish Upon a Star") ... 20-30 64

STINGERS
LPs: 10/12-inch
CROWN ... 15-25 63

STINGERS
Singles: 7-inch
STAX ... 3-5 69

STINGLEY, Roy
Singles: 7-inch
JERDEN ... 4-8 66

STINGRAY
LPs: 10/12-inch
CARRERE ... 5-10 80

STINGRAYS
Singles: 7-inch
SATURN ... 5-10 63

STINGRAYS
Singles: 7-inch
JOBEL (100 "Dynamite") ... 10-20 65
VAN (04567 "Girl, You Said Again") ... 50-75 60s
VERMILLION (107 "I Need Her") ... 10-15 65

STINGRAYS
Singles: 7-inch
WELLHAVEN (8852 "Shaggy Dog") ... 40-60 67

STING-RAYS OF NEWBURGH
Singles: 7-inch
COLUMBIA ... 10-20 67

STING-RAYS OF SPRINGFIELD
Singles: 7-inch
RAY (877 "Surfer's Walk") ... 20-30 67

STINIT, Dane
Singles: 7-inch
SUN ... 5-10 66-67

STINSON BROTHERS
(Ray Stinson)
Singles: 7-inch
CANADIAN AMERICAN ... 10-15 67
EVEREST ... 10-20 60s
RKO (1224 "Diggin' That Rock and Roll") ... 60-80 60s
RKO (1225 "Everyone's Got Rainbows in Their Eyes") ... 10-20 60s
SOMA (1153 "Joker") ... 10-20 60s
SOMA (1183 "Jenny Twist") ... 10-20 60s
LPs:10/12-inch
CANADIAN AMERICAN ... 8-12 67

STIRLING SILVER
Singles: 7-inch
COLUMBIA ... 3-5 76

STITCH in TIME
Singles: 7-inch
YORKVILLE ... 15-20 66

STITES, Gary P&R '59
Singles: 7-inch
CARLTON ... 10-15 59-60
EPIC ... 4-8 66
MADISON ... 10-15 60-61
MR. PEEKE ... 8-12 62
LPs: 10/12-inch
CARLTON (STLP-120 "Lonely for You") ... 40-50 60
(Monaural.)
CARLTON (STLP-120 "Lonely for You") ... 50-75 60
(Stereo.)

STITES, Gary, & Sammi Smith
Singles: 7-inch
JEANNIE ... 3-6
Also see SMITH, Sammi
Also see STITES, Gary

STITT, Sonny LP '67
Singles: 78 rpm
PRESTIGE ... 5-10 50s
ROYAL ROOST ... 5-10 54
Singles: 7-inch
ARGO ... 5-10 58-65
ATLANTIC ... 4-6 63
CADET ... 3-5 74
CATALYST ... 3-5 77
ENTERPRISE ... 3-5 69
IMPULSE ... 4-8 64
PRESTIGE ... 5-10 63-69
ROULETTE ... 4-6 65-67
ROYAL ROOST ... 5-10 54
WINGATE ... 8-15 65-66
WORLD PACIFIC ... 4-6 63
EPs: 7-inch
PRESTIGE ... 10-25 53
LPs: 10/12-inch
ARGO ... 20-50 58-65
ATLANTIC ... 15-30 62-64
CADET ... 10-25 65-74
CATALYST ... 5-10 76-77
CHESS ... 8-12 76
COLPIX ... 10-20 66
EVEREST ... 5-8 82
FLYING DUTCHMAN ... 5-10 75-76
IMPULSE ... 15-25 63-64
JAMAL ... 8-12 71
JAZZLAND ... 20-40 62
MUSE ... 5-10 73-82
PACIFIC JAZZ ... 20-30 63
PAULA ... 5-10 74
PRESTIGE (060 "Kaleidoscope") ... 5-10 83
PRESTIGE (103 "Sonny Stitt Plays") ... 100-200 51
(10-inch LP.)
PRESTIGE (111 "Mr. Saxophone") ... 100-200 51
(10-inch LP.)
PRESTIGE (126 "Favorites") ... 100-200 52
(10-inch LP.)
PRESTIGE (148 "Favorites") ... 100-200 53
(10-inch LP.)
PRESTIGE (7000 series) ... 25-75 56-64
(Yellow label.)
PRESTIGE (7000 series) ... 10-25 65-70
(Blue labels.)
PRESTIGE (10000 series) ... 8-12 71-74
PRESTIGE (20000 series) ... 8-15 74
ROOST (418 "At the Hi Hat") ... 150-250 52
(10-inch LP.)
ROOST (1200 series) ... 30-50 56
ROOST (2200 series) ... 15-35 57-66
ROULETTE ... 10-25 65-70
SAVOY (9006 "Be-Bop") ... 100-200 53
(10-inch LP.)
SOLID STATE ... 10-15 69
TRIP ... 8-12 73
UPFRONT ... 5-10 77
VERVE ... 40-80 57-59
(Reads "Verve Records, Inc." at bottom of label.)
VERVE ... 12-25 62-72
(Reads "MGM Records - A Division Of Metro-Goldwyn-Mayer, Inc." at bottom of label.)
VERVE ... 5-10 73-84
(Reads "Manufactured By MGM Record Corp." or mentions either Polydor or Polygram at bottom of label.)

STITT, Sonny, & Kai Winding
LPs: 10/12-inch
JAZZTONE (1231 "Early Modern") ... 70-100 56
JAZZTONE (1263 "Early Modern") ... 50-75 57

STITT, Sonny, Kai Winding & Horace Silver
LPs: 10/12-inch
ROOST (415 "From the Pen of Johnny Richards") ... 150-250 52
(10-inch LP.)
Also see AMMONS, Gene, & Sonny Stitt
Also see SILVER, Horace
Also see STITT, Sonny
Also see WINDING, Kai

STIX & STONES
Singles: 7-inch
BUMPSHOP (136 "Rouge Plant Blues") ... 5-10 74
CAPITOL (3865 "Rouge Plant Blues") ... 3-5 74

STIX & STONZ
Singles: 7-inch
COLUMBIA ... 4-6 69

STOBER, Orville
LPs: 10/12-inch
UNI ... 8-10 71

STOCKING HEADS
LPs: 10/12-inch
ROADSIDE (1 "Stocking Heads") ... 10-15 83
(Picture disc.)

STODDARD, Robert
Singles: 7-inch
ELEKTRA ... 3-5 80

STOECKLEIN, Val
Singles: 7-inch
DOT (17200 "Sounds of Yesterday") ... 10-15 69
DOT (17234 "All the Way Home") 10-15 69
LPs: 10/12-inch
DOT (25904 "Grey Life") ... 25-35 68
Also see BLUETHINGS

STOICS
Singles: 7-inch
BRAMS (101 "Hate") ... 40-60 67
Also see CHILDREN

STOKER, Billy
Singles: 7-inch
BETTY (1212 "Miami") ... 15-25 64
Also see CAMPBELL, Dick

STOKES
Singles: 7-inch
II BROS (1 "My Sandra's Jump") ... 10-20 62

STOKES
Singles: 7-inch
ALON (9019 "Whipped Cream") ... 6-12 65
ALON (9023 "Fat Cat") ... 6-12 65
ALON (9026 "Bump Bump") ... 6-12 65
ALON (9029 "One Mint Julep") ... 6-12 66
ALON (9032 "Crystal Ball") ... 6-12 66
Members: Allen Toussaint; Billy Fayard; Al Fayard.
Also see FAYARD, Al
Also see FAYARD, Bill
Also see TOUSSAINT, Allen
Also see YOUNG ONES

STOKES, Simon P&R '69
(With the Nighthawks; Simon T. Stokes)
Singles: 7-inch
CASABLANCA ... 3-5 74
ELEKTRA ... 4-8 69-70
IN SOUND ... 5-10 68
U.A. ... 3-5 77
LPs: 10/12-inch
MGM ... 10-15 70
SPINDIZZY ... 8-12 73
U.A. ... 5-10 77

STOKLEY, Jimmy, & Exiles
Singles: 7-inch
LTD ... 4-8 66

STOLLER, Mike, & Stoller System
Singles: 7-inch
AMY ... 5-10 68
Also see LEIBER & STOLLER
Also see LONDON, Bob

STOLOFF, Morris P&R '56
(Morris Stoloff Conducts the Columbia Studio Orchestra)
Singles: 78 rpm
DECCA ... 3-5 56
MERCURY ... 3-5 54
Singles: 7-inch
COLPIX ... 4-8 59
DECCA ... 5-10 56
MERCURY ... 5-10 54
REPRISE ... 3-6 65
LPs: 10/12-inch
DECCA ... 5-15 56
W.B. (1416 "Fanny") ... 25-35 61
(Soundtrack.)

STOMPERS
Singles: 7-inch
SOUVENIR (1003 "I Miss You So") ... 40-60 60

STOMPERS
Singles: 7-inch
GONE (5120 "Stompin' Round the Xmas Tree") ... 100-150 61

STOMPERS P&R '62
Singles: 7-inch
LANDA ... 10-20 61-62
MERCURY (72111 "Frump") ... 8-12 63
Members: Bobby Pickett; Leonard Capizzi; Bill Capizzi; Ron Deltorto; Lou Toscano; Don Squire.
Also see CORDIALS
Also see PICKETT, Bobby

STOMPERS
Singles: 7-inch
STOMP (5477 "I Still Love You") ... 25-35 65
STUDIO CITY (1028 "Hey Baby") ... 40-60 65

STOMPERS P&R '83
Singles: 7-inch
BOARDWALK ... 3-5 83
MERCURY (880000 series) ... 3-4 84
LPs: 10/12-inch
MERCURY ... 5-8 84
Members: Sal Baglio; Mark Cuccinello; David Friedman; Stephan Gilligan.

STOMPERS / Dick Dale
LPs: 10/12-inch
CLOISTER (6301 "Sounds of the Silver Surf") ... 50-75 63
Also see DALE, Dick

STONE
Singles: 7-inch
W.B. ... 3-5 70

STONE
Singles: 7-inch
WEST END ... 3-5 82

STONE, Albert
Singles: 7-inch
REPRISE ... 4-8 65

STONE, Beverly
Singles: 7-inch
RHAPSODY ... 10-15 59

STONE, Cherry
Singles: 7-inch
DIAL ... 4-8 66

STONE, Cliffie, & His Orchestra C&W '47
(With His Barn Dance Band; Cliffie Stone Singers; Cliffie Stone's Country Hombres)
Singles: 78 rpm
CAPITOL (Except 2910) ... 3-6 47-57
CAPITOL (2910 "Blue Moon of Kentucky") ... 4-8 54
Singles: 7-inch
CAPITOL (Except 2910) ... 4-10 50-69
CAPITOL (2910 "Blue Moon of Kentucky") ... 10-20 54
TOWER ... 3-6 67
LPs: 10/12-inch
CAPITOL (100 thru 300 series) ... 5-10 68-69
CAPITOL (1000 thru 1600 series) ... 20-40 58-62
CAPITOL (2100 series) ... 10-20 64
TOWER ... 10-15 67
Also see ADAMS, Kay
Also see CARSON, Cindy

STONE, Daniel A.
(With Jack Nitzsche Orchestra & Chorus)
Singles: 7-inch
CAPITOL (4590 "Little Miss Cool") ... 10-15 61
Also see NITZSCHE, Jack

STONE, Doug LP '90
LPs: 10/12-inch
EPIC ... 5-8 90

STONE, George
Singles: 7-inch
MUSICOR (1122 "My Beat") ... 8-12 65

STONE, Jeff
Singles: 7-inch
SARG (151 "Everybody Rock") ... 35-45 57

STONE, Jesse
Singles: 78 rpm
ATCO ... 8-12 54
ATLANTIC ... 10-15 54
RCA ... 10-20 47-49
Singles: 7-inch
ATCO ... 15-25 54
ATLANTIC ... 20-30 54
POPLAR (109 "The Stash") ... 15-25 59
RCA ... 25-35 49

STONE, Jesse, & Pebbles
Singles: 7-inch
BOMARC ... 4-8 61

STONE, Jimmy
Singles: 7-inch
CROSS COUNTRY (523 "Found") ... 100-200 56
GONE (5001 "Found") ... 100-150 57

STONE, John
(Johnny Stone)
Singles: 78 rpm
EBB ... 8-12 57
Singles: 7-inch
ACE ... 5-10 60
EBB ... 8-12 57
SPECIALTY ... 8-12 59

STONE, Judy
Singles: 7-inch
CAMEO ... 4-8 64

STONE, Kirby, Four P&R/LP '58
(Kirby Stone Quartet)
Singles: 78 rpm
COLUMBIA ... 4-8 57
Singles: 7-inch
COLUMBIA ... 5-15 57-65
MGM ... 4-8 67
W.B. ... 4-8 63-64
LPs: 10/12-inch
CADENCE ... 10-15
COLUMBIA ... 10-20 58-62
CORONET ... 8-12 60s
GOLDEN TONE ... 8-12
RONDO ... 8-12 60s
W.B. ... 10-15 63-64
Members: Kirby Stone; Edward Hall; Michael Gardner; Larry Foster.
Also see FOUR FRESHMEN / Kirby Stone Four / University Four
Also see U.S. DOUBLE QUARTET

STONE, Lawrence
Singles: 78 rpm
DIG (130 "Everytime") ... 15-20 57
Singles: 7-inch
DIG (130 "Everytime") ... 20-25 57

STONE, Lee
Singles: 7-inch
R.R.E. ... 4-8 63
ROYAL CREST ... 3-6 68
SANDURA ... 4-8 64

STONE, Lenny
Singles: 7-inch
TRIODEX ... 5-10 61

STONE, Miles
Singles: 7-inch
MONOGRAM ... 4-8 63

STONE, Rock, & Al Moore: see CWAZY WABBITS

STONE, Roland
Singles: 7-inch
ACE ... 10-15 60-62
SPINETT (1002 "Preacher's Daughter") ... 10-20
LPs: 10/12-inch
ACE ... 25-35 61

STONE, Roland
Singles: 7-inch
U.S.A. (1212 "Lost Love") ... 10-20 59
Also see APOLLOS
Also see STEFAN, Paul

STONE, Ronny
Singles: 7-inch
DU-WELL ... 4-8 61

STONE, Rosetta
Singles: 7-inch
PRIVATE STOCK ... 3-5 77
Member: Ian Mitchell.
Also see BAY CITY ROLLERS

STONE, Skip
Singles: 7-inch
ACADEMY ... 5-10 63

STONE, Sly LP '75
(Sylvester "Sly Stone" Stewart)
Singles: 12-inch
EPIC ... 4-8 80
Singles: 7-inch
A&M ... 3-4 86
EPIC ... 3-5 75-79
LPs: 10/12-inch
EPIC ... 5-10 79
Also see DAVIS, Martha, & Sly Stone
Also see JOHNSON, Jesse, & Sly Stone
Also see SLY & Family Stone
Also see STEWART, Sly

STONE AXE
Singles: 7-inch
RAMPART STREET ("Snakebite") ... 4-6
(Selection number not known.)
Members: Pete Bailey; Mike "Wolf" Long; Jerry Ontiverez.
Also see JOSEFUS

STONE BRIDGE
Singles: 7-inch
INTREPID ... 3-5 69

STONE CIRCUS
Singles: 7-inch
MAINSTREAM (694 "Mister Grey") ... 10-15 69
LPs: 10/12-inch
MAINSTREAM (6119 "Stone Circus") ... 50-75 69
Members: Ronnie Page; Jonathan Caine; Sonny Haines; Mike Burns; Dave Keeler.

STONE CITY BAND
Singles: 7-inch
GORDY ... 3-5 80-83
LPs: 10/12-inch
GORDY ... 5-10 80-83
Members: Tom McDermott; Oscar Alston; Lanise Hughes; Levi Ruffin Jr.; Erkskine Williams.
Also see JAMES, Rick

STONE COUNTRY
Singles: 7-inch
RCA ... 4-8 68

STONE COUNTRY BAND
(1959)
Singles: 7-inch
AMHERST ... 3-5
BLUE ORCHID ... 5-10 81
Also see 1959

STONE CRUSHERS
Singles: 7-inch
RCA ... 5-10 58

STONE FLOUR
Singles: 7-inch
TRANSACTION (712 "Till We Kissed") ... 5-10 69
Picture Sleeves
TRANSACTION (712 "Till We Kissed") ... 10-20 69

STONE FURY LP '84
Singles: 7-inch
MCA ... 3-4 84
LPs: 10/12-inch
MCA ... 5-8 84

STONE PILLOW
LPs: 10/12-inch
LONDON ... 10-15 69

STONE PONEYS P&R/LP '67
(Featuring Linda Ronstadt)
Singles: 7-inch
CAPITOL ... 5-10 67
Picture Sleeves
CAPITOL ... 5-10 67
LPs: 10/12-inch
CAPITOL (2600 & 2700 series) ... 15-25 67
Also see RONSTADT, Linda

STONE ROSES LP '90
LPs: 10/12-inch
SILVERTONE ... 5-8 90

STONE THE CROWS
LPs: 10/12-inch
POLYDOR ... 10-15 70-72
Member: Maggie Bell
Also see AVERAGE WHITE BAND
Also see BELL, Maggie

STONEBOLT P&R '78
Singles: 7-inch
PARACHUTE 3-5 78-79
RCA 3-5 80
LPs: 10/12-inch
PARACHUTE 5-10 78
RCA 5-10 80

STONED HINGE
Singles: 7-inch
CANDID (2805 "Janis") 15-25 60s

STONEGROUND
Singles: 7-inch
FLAT-OUT 3-5 76
W.B. 3-5 71-78
LPs: 10/12-inch
FLAT OUT 8-10 76
W.B. (1895 "Stoneground") 10-15 71
W.B. (1956 "Stoneground Family Album") 15-20 71
W.B. (2645 "Stoneground 3") 10-15 72
W.B. (3187 "Hearts of Stone") 8-10 78
Members: Sal Valentino; Tim Barnes; Pete Sears; Annie Sampson; Deirdre La Porte; Luther Bildt; Lynne Hughes; Steven Price; Cory Lerios.
Also see HUGHES, Lynne
Also see JEFFERSON STARSHIP
Also see PABLO CRUISE
Also see SANDALS
Also see VALENTINO, Sal

STONEHAM, Luther
Singles: 78 rpm
MERCURY 25-40 51
Also see SMITH, Thunder

STONEHENGE
Singles: 7-inch
BOZO ("King Snake") 20-30
(Selection number not known.)
RENEGADE 4-8 70

STONEHILL, Randy
LPs: 10/12-inch
MYRRH 5-8 83
ONE WAY 5-8 70
SOLID ROCK 5-8 80
SONRISE 5-8

STONEMANS C&W '66
(With the Tracy Schwartz Band; Stoneman Family)
Singles: 7-inch
MGM 4-6 66-68
STARDAY 4-8 62
LPs: 10/12-inch
CMH 5-12 76-82
FOLKWAYS 10-20
MGM 10-20 66-70
NASHVILLE 8-12 68
RCA 6-12 70-71
STARDAY (393 "White Lightning") 15-25 65
SUNSET 10-15 68
WORLD PACIFIC 15-20 64
Members: Pop Stoneman; Donna Stoneman; Scott Stoneman; Van Stoneman; Roni Stoneman.
Also see DEAN, Jimmy / Stoneman Family

STONEMEN
Singles: 7-inch
BIG TOPPER (1017 "No More") 10-15 66

STONES
Singles: 7-inch
SULLY 15-25 66
Also see TRACERS

STONES THROW
LPs: 10/12-inch
SIERRA 5-10 80

STONEY & MEAT LOAF P&R '71
Singles: 7-inch
RARE EARTH 3-5 71
LPs: 10/12-inch
PRODIGAL 5-10 78
RARE EARTH 10-15 71
Also see MEAT LOAF

STONY BROOK PEOPLE
Singles: 7-inch
COLUMBIA 4-8 69

STOOGES LP '69
(Featuring Iggy Pop)
Singles: 7-inch
ELEKTRA 5-10 69-70
LPs: 10/12-inch
BOMP (114 "Jesus Loves the Stooges") 8-12 78
(10-inch LP. With 3-D cover and 3-D glasses.)
ELEKTRA 15-25 69-70
Also see POP, Iggy

STOOKEY, Paul P&R/LP '71
Singles: 7-inch
ERIC 3-5 70s
W.B. 3-5 71-72
LPs: 10/12-inch
NEWPAX 5-8
W.B. 10-15 71
Also see PETER, PAUL & MARY

STOP, Dickie
Singles: 7-inch
B.E.A.T. 5-10 59

STOPPE
Singles: 7-inch
TEE PEE 3-5 71

STOPPERS
Singles: 7-inch
JUBILEE 4-8 66

STORCH, Jeremy
LPs: 10/12-inch
RCA 8-10 71

STORCH, Larry
Singles: 78 rpm
ROULETTE 8-12 57
Singles: 7-inch
ROULETTE 8-12 57

STOREY, Dean
Singles: 7-inch
SURF (1521 "Ring-a Ding Ding") 50-100 58
Members: Dick Sherman; Robert Sherman.

STOREY, Denny
Singles: 7-inch
SONIC 5-8 60s
Also see DEE JAY & RUNAWAYS
Also see CHEVELLES
Also see JERRY & CASUALS / Rockin' Tones

STOREY, Lewis C&W '86
Singles: 7-inch
EPIC 3-4 86

STOREY SISTERS P&R '58
Singles: 7-inch
BATON 10-20 58
CAMEO 10-20 58
MERCURY 10-15 59
Members: Lillian Storey; Ann Storey.

STORIE, James C&W '88
Singles: 7-inch
GMC 3-4 88

STORIES P&R/LP '72
(Ian Lloyd & Stories)
Singles: 7-inch
ERIC 3-5 70s
KAMA SUTRA (Except 545) 3-5 72-74
KAMA SUTRA (545 "I'm Coming Home") 5-8 72
(Cardboard cover.)
RADIOACTIVE GOLD 3-5 74
LPs: 10/12-inch
KAMA SUTRA 8-12 72-73
Members: Michael Brown; Ian Lloyd; Bryan Madey; Steve Love.
Also see BROWN, Michael
Also see LLOYD, Ian

STORM
Singles: 7-inch
PHI KAPPA 3-5 74
LPs: 10/12-inch
CAPITOL 5-8 83
MCA 5-10 77

STORM, Billy P&R '59
(With the Valiants)
Singles: 7-inch
ATLANTIC 10-15 60-61
BARBARY COAST (1001 "The Way to My Heart") 100-200 58
BUENA VISTA 8-12 63
COLUMBIA 10-20 59
EARLY BIRD (1001 "This Is the Nite") 4-6 95
(Colored vinyl.)
EARLY BIRD (1003 "Please Wait My Love") 4-6 95
(Colored vinyl.)
ENSIGN (4035 "We Knew") 15-25 59
GREGMARK 10-15 61
HBR (474 "Please Don't Mention Her Name") 10-15 66
INFINITY 10-15 62-63
LOMA 8-12 64-65
ODE 5-10 69
Picture Sleeves
HBR (474 "Please Don't Mention Her Name") 15-20 66
LPs: 10/12-inch
BUENA VISTA (3315 "Billy Storm") 20-30 63
FAMOUS (504 "This Is the Night") 100-200 69
Also see CHARADES
Also see CHAVELLES
Also see ELECTRAS
Also see SABERS
Also see VALIANTS

STORM, Danny
Singles: 7-inch
AD LIB 4-8 62

STORM, Gale P&R '55
(With Billy Vaughn's Orchestra)
Singles: 78 rpm
DOT 5-15 55-56
Singles: 7-inch
CONFIDEO 5-10
DOT (Maroon label) 12-25 55-56
DOT (Black label) 5-10 57-60
DOT (Orange label) 3-6 60s
Picture Sleeves
DOT 10-20 58
EPs: 7-inch
DOT 15-25 55-56
LPs: 10/12-inch
DOT 25-35 56-59
HAMILTON 10-15 66
MCA 5-10 82
Also see VAUGHN, Billy, Orchestra

STORM, Rocky
Singles: 7-inch
JOSIE 15-25 58
RENDEZVOUS 10-20 59

STORM, Rory, & Hurricanes / Faron's Flamingos
Singles: 7-inch
COLUMBIA (43018 "I Can Tell") 20-30 64

STORM, Tom, & Peps
Singles: 7-inch
GE GE ("That's the Way Love Is") 20-30 65
(No selection number used.)
Also see PEPS

STORM, Warren P&R '58
Singles: 78 rpm
NASCO (6015 "Prisoner's Song") 20-30 58
NASCO (6025 "Troubles Troubles") 25-45 59
Singles: 7-inch
ATCO 4-8 68
DOT (16272 "Gotta Go Back to School") 10-15 61
KINGFISH 4-8
NASCO (6015 "Prisoner's Song") 15-25 58
NASCO (6025 "Troubles Troubles") 15-25 59
NASCO (6028 "I've Got My Heart in My Hand") 15-25 59
ROCKO (512 "Oh Oh Baby") 15-20 59
SINCERE (102 "Love Me Cherry") 20-40 57
SINCERE (107 "Honky Tonk Song") 20-40 58
SOUTH STAR 3-4 83
STARFLITE 3-5 79
ZYNN 10-20
Also see SHONDELLS / Rod Bernard / Warren Storm / Skip Stewart

STORM, Wayne
Singles: 7-inch
ATLAS 4-8 62
CORAL 4-8 66

STORM TRIO
Singles: 7-inch
JUBILEE (5306 "My Wonderful Lover") 10-20 57

STORME, Rob, & Whispers
Singles: 7-inch
CAPITOL 5-10 65

STORMIN' NORMAN & SUZY
LPs: 10/12-inch
POLYDOR 5-10 78

STORMS
Singles: 7-inch
SUNDOWN (114 "Thunder"/ "Tarantula") 35-45 59
(Both sides were rerecorded in 1961 [Indigo 127] as by Jody Reynolds & the Storms.)
Members: Al Casey; Jody Reynolds; Plas Johnson; Billie Ray; Noel Stutte; Ray Martinez.
Also see CASEY, Al
Also see REYNOLDS, Jody, & Storms

STORMS
Singles: 7-inch
IMPALA (212 "Thunder") 10-20 60
(Despite identical title, this is a different band and music than the Storms on Sundown.)

STORMTROOPER
LPs: 10/12-inch
IRON WORKS (1005 "Armies of the Night") 10-15 86
(Picture disc.)

STORMY
Singles: 7-inch
TWINIGHT 8-12

STORMY & GABRIEL
Singles: 7-inch
ODE 3-5 68

STORMY HERMAN & HIS MIDNIGHT RAMBLERS
Singles: 7-inch
DOOTONE (358 "The Jitterbug") 25-35 55

STORMY WEATHER
Singles: 7-inch
AMERAMA 3-5 77
F.R.A. 5-10 77
Members: Henry Farag; Jim Ham; Jim Calinski; Dave Mitchell; Nick Pavlitza.

STORRS, David, & Chris "The Glove" Taylor
Singles: 12-inch
POLYDOR 4-6 85
Singles: 7-inch
POLYDOR 3-4 85

STORY, Allen
(Allen Bo Story)
Singles: 7-inch
ANNA (1118 "Blue Moon") 25-35 60
CHECK MATE (1014 "Why Oh Why") 15-25 62

STORY, Ben
Singles: 7-inch
AMAZON 8-12

STORY, Dwain
Singles: 7-inch
STALLION 4-8 65

STORY, Nat
Singles: 7-inch
QCE 8-15

STORY SPINNERS
Singles
QUICKSILVER (Tom Sawyer & the White Picket Fence") 10-15 85
(Bucket-shaped picture disc.)

STORY TELLERS
Singles: 7-inch
$TACK (500 "You Played Me a Fool") 100-200 59

STORY TELLERS
Singles: 7-inch
TRYSTERO (101 "Cry with Me") 20-30 67

STORYBOOK
Singles: 7-inch
SIDEWALK 5-8 68

STORYBOOK PEOPLE
Singles: 7-inch
DUNHILL 5-8 67-68

STORYTELLERS
Singles: 7-inch
CAPITOL (5042 "I Don't Want an Angel") 8-10 63
CLASSIC ARTISTS 4-6 89-90
DIMENSION (1014 "When Two People") 15-25 63
RAMARCA (501 "When Two People") 25-35 63
Members: Steve Barri; Carol Connors.
Also see BARRI, Steve
Also see CONNORS, Carol

STOTT, Lally P&R '71
Singles: 7-inch
PHILIPS 3-5 71

STOTTS, Ronnie
LPs: 10/12-inch
TMI 8-10 72

STOUT, Cliff
Singles: 7-inch
PAGE (1001 "Happy Birthday Elvis") 4-6

STOVAL SISTERS
LPs: 10/12-inch
REPRISE 8-10 71

STOVALL, Babe
LPs: 10/12-inch
VERVE 10-15

STOVALL, LaVern
Singles: 7-inch
FELSTED (8516 "Left Behind") 500-1000 58
KIP (400 "Your Love") 25-35 59

STOVALL, Vern C&W '67
(With Janet McBride)
Singles: 7-inch
LONGHORN 4-6 67
LPs: 10/12-inch
LONGHORN 15-25 67

STOVER, Mal
Singles: 7-inch
MINARET (114 "Memphis") 5-8 63

STOWAWAYS
LPs: 10/12-inch
JUSTICE (148 "Stowaways") 350-450 68

STRACHAN, Frank, D.M.
Singles: 7-inch
ATLANTEAN 3-6

STRAGGLERS
Singles: 7-inch
BRISTOL (6005 "Girl of My Dreams") 40-50

STRAIGHT
Singles: 7-inch
ATCO (7070 "Half Heaven, Half Heartache") 4-6 76
ENCORE (1001 "Save Your Breath") 8-12 75
SCEPTOR (12403 "Save Your Breath") 5-8 75

STRAIGHT A's
Singles: 7-inch
KAPP 3-5 69
LPs: 10/12-inch
KAPP 10-15 69

STRAIGHT LINES
LPs: 10/12-inch
EPIC 5-10 80-82

STRAIGHT UP
Singles: 7-inch
STRAIGHT UP 10-15 60s
Member: Tom Murray
Also see LITTER

STRAIT, George C&W '81
Singles: 7-inch
D 15-25 76
MCA 3-5 81-91
LPs: 10/12-inch
MCA 5-10 81-91

STRAITJACKETS
Singles: 7-inch
U.A. (453 "Gigolo") 15-25 62
Members: Delbert McClinton; Ronnie Kelly; Bob Jones; Billy Cox; Ray Torres.
Also see CHANNEL, Bruce
Also see CLINTON, Mac, & Straitjackets

STRAITON, Jim
Singles: 7-inch
CASCADE (363 "Guilty One") 5-10

STRAKER, Nick, Band
Singles: 7-inch
PRELUDE 3-5 82
LPs: 10/12-inch
PRELUDE 5-10 82

STRALEY, Teresa
Singles: 7-inch
ALFA 5-8 82

STRAND
LPs: 10/12-inch
ISLAND 5-8 80
Members: Damon Doiron; Bruce Connole; Alan Ross Willey.

STRAND, Tommy
(With the Upper Hand)
Singles: 7-inch
FAME 3-6 69
R 4-8 67

STRANDS
Singles: 7-inch
FIREFLY (331 "How Will I Know") 50-75 60
TRI-ODE (101 "Never") 25-50 62

STRANGE
(With "Narration by Edmond Good")
Singles: 7-inch
OUTER GALAXY (11229 "Jimi") 15-25 73
OUTER GALAXY (11229-A "Color My World") 15-25 73
OUTER GALAXY (11250-A "My Sweet Daddy's Home") 15-25 74
OUTER GALAXY (11250-2-A "I Dreamt I Love You") 20-40 74
OUTER GALAXY (305322 "Jimi") 15-25 73
OUTER GALAXY (321570 "Annihilation") 15-25 73
Note: On some releases, label name may be shown as "Outer Galaxie." As is shown, their numbering pattern is indeed strange.
LPs: 10/12-inch
OUTER GALAXY (1000 "Translucent World") 75-100 73
OUTER GALAXY (1001 "Raw Power") 75-100 76
Members: Terry Brooks; Don Haste; John Kotch; Donnie Capetta; Jim Chapman; Don Hall; Brian Leary.
Also see BROOKS, Terry, & Strange

STRANGE, Billy P&R/LP '64
(With the Telstars; with Transients)
Singles: 78 rpm
CAPITOL 5-10 54-55
DECCA 5-10 55
Singles: 7-inch
BUENA VISTA 4-8 62-63
CAPITOL 5-15 54-55
COLISEUM 4-8 63
DECCA 5-15 55
GNP 4-8 64-65
LIBERTY 4-8 61-62
TOWER 4-6 69
LPs: 10/12-inch
COLISEUM 10-20 62
GNP 5-15 63-75
HORIZON 10-15 63
SUNSET 8-10 68
SURREY 10-15 65
TRADITION 8-12 68
Also see AVALANCHES
Also see CAMPBELL, Glen, & Billy Strange
Also see CATALINAS
Also see CHALLENGERS & Billy Strange
Also see JOHNSON, Sweetpea
Also see NELSON, Willie
Also see PETERSEN, Paul
Also see TRANSIENTS

STRANGE, Giles
Singles: 7-inch
BOOM 4-8 66

STRANGE, Jean
Singles: 78 rpm
DOT 4-8 54-55
Singles: 7-inch
DOT 5-10 54-55

STRANGE, Tommy
Singles: 7-inch
ERA 4-8 66
RAMCO 4-8 67
ROCKO (504 "Nervous and Shakin' All Over") 50-75 59

STRANGE ADVANCE
Singles: 7-inch
CAPITOL 3-5 83
Picture Sleeves
CAPITOL 3-5 83
LPs: 10/12-inch
CAPITOL 5-8 83

STRANGE BEDFELLOWS
Singles: 7-inch
SSS INT'L 4-8 67

STRANGE BREW
LPs: 10/12-inch
JUKE 5-10 80
Also see CAMEL

STRANGE BROTHERS SHOW
Singles: 7-inch
SIRE 8-10 68
Also see BELMONTS

STRANGE CREEK SINGERS
LPs: 10/12-inch
ARHOOLIE 10-20 64

STRANGE FATE
Singles: 7-inch
CAR (2002 "Hold Me Baby") 15-25 67

STRANGEBREW
Singles: 7-inch
ABC.................................. 3-6 69

STRANGELOVES P&R/LP '65
Singles: 7-inch
BANG.................................. 8-12 65-67
SIRE.................................. 4-8 68
SWAN (4192 "I'm on Fire")..........10-20 64
LPs: 10/12-inch
BANG (BLP-211 "I Want Candy") ..35-55 65
(Monaural.)
BANG (BLPS-211 "I Want Candy")..............................55-65 65
(Stereo.)
Members: Bob Feldman; Jerry Goldstein; Richie Gottehrer. Session: Tom Kobus; Jack Raczka; John Shine; Richie Lauro; George Young; Joe Piazza; Ken Jones.
Also see HUMBLE MUD
Also see McCOYS
Also see SHEEP

STRANGER
LPs: 10/12-inch
EPIC.................................. 5-10 82

STRANGER TO STRANGER
LPs: 10/12-inch
SSTRANGE.......................... 5-10 89

STRANGERS
Singles: 78 rpm
KING 25-75 54-56
Singles: 7-inch
KING (4697 "My Friends")..........200-400 54
KING (4709 "Blue Flowers")........300-500 54
KING (4722 "Hoping You'll Understand")..................200-400 54
KING (4745 "Drop Down to My Place")..............................200-300 54
KING (4766 "How Long Must I Wait")..............................200-300 54
(Blue label.)
KING (4766 "How Long Must I Wait")..............................250-350 54
(White bio label. Promotional issue only.)
KING (4821 "Without a Friend") 200-300 55
(Does not have "High Fidelity" on label.)
KING (4821 "Without a Friend").....50-75 56
(With "High Fidelity" on label.)
Members: William Clarke; John Grant; Pringle Sims; Woodrow Jackson; Seifert Brizant; Al Brizant.

STRANGERS
Singles: 7-inch
CHRISTY (107 "We're in Love") 15-25 59
CHRISTY (108 "Song About Judy")................................10-15 59
KCM (3703 "Guns")..................10-15 59

STRANGERS P&R '59
Singles: 7-inch
TITAN (1701 "Caterpillar Crawl") ...10-20 59
TITAN (1702 "Hill Stomp")...........10-20 59
TITAN (1704 "Boogie Man")...........10-20 60
TITAN (1711 "Navajo")................10-20 60
Member: Joel Hill.
Also see HILL, Joel

STRANGERS
Singles: 7-inch
CHOICE (5 "Bret Maverick")..........10-15 60

STRANGERS
Singles: 7-inch
CHECKER (1010 "Darlin' ")............ 8-10 62
MASKE.................................10-20 60

STRANGERS
Singles: 7-inch
CUCA (1172 "Runaway") 40-60 64
LIBERTY 8-12 62-63
Member: Bill Velline; Dick Dunkirk; Bob Korum; Ken Harvey.
Also see DUNKIRK, Dick, & Strangers
Also see JOHNSON, Dave, & Shadows
Also see TORNADOES
Also see VEE, Bobby

STRANGERS
Singles: 7-inch
KCM ("Honky tonk Woman")..........15-25 60s
KL (115 "Land of Music")...............15-25 66
LINDA (118 "Tell Me")...................15-25 65
W.B. (5438 "Night Winds")............10-20 64

STRANGERS
Singles: 7-inch
CHATTAHOOCHEE 8-10 66
JUBILEE.............................. 8-10 65

STRANGERS
Singles: 7-inch
ORIEL (341 "What a Life")............10-20 60s

STRANGERS
Singles: 12-inch
SALSOUL................................ 4-6 83
Singles: 7-inch
SALSOUL................................ 3-5 83
LPs: 10/12-inch
SALSOUL.............................. 5-10 83

STRANGERS IN TOWN
Singles: 7-inch
DATE.................................. 5-8 66
TOY TIGER (1003 "You'll Never Know")..................................10-20 67

STRANGEWAYS
LPs: 10/12-inch
RCA (6569 "Native Sons") 5-10 87
Members: Terry Brock; Ian Stewart; David Stewart; Jim Drummond.

STRANGLERS LP '87
Singles: 12-inch
EPIC.................................. 4-6 83
Singles: 7-inch
A&M.................................. 3-5 77
EPs: 7-inch
A&M (1973 "Something Better Change")..............................10-15 77
LPs: 10/12-inch
A&M (Black vinyl) 5-10 77-78
A&M (Colored vinyl)......................10-15 78
(Promotional only.)
EPIC.................................. 5-8 83-87
I.R.S.................................. 5-10 80
STIFF 5-10 81

STRAPPS
LPs: 10/12-inch
HARVEST 8-10 77

STRASSMAN, Marcia
Singles: 7-inch
UNI.................................. 4-8 67
Picture Sleeves
UNI.................................. 5-10 67

STRATFORDS
(With the Ambassadors)
Singles: 7-inch
UNIVERSAL ARTISTS (1215 "Promise Her Anything")..............................100-150 61

STRATFORDS
Singles: 7-inch
O'DELL (100 "Never Leave Me") 8-12 64

STRATOCASTERS
Singles: 7-inch
VITTO (351 "Three Guitar Theme")..................................8-12

STRATO-JACS
Singles: 7-inch
PARROT 5-10 64

STRAT-O-LITES
Singles: 7-inch
TEL (1008 "Hot Foot")..................10-20 59

STRAUSS, Sharon
Singles: 7-inch
ABC-PAR 4-8 62
Picture Sleeves
ABC-PAR 5-10 62

STRAWBED
Singles: 7-inch
ACT II 3-5 73
Also see BUCKWEET

STRAWBERRY ALARM CLOCK P&R/LP '67
Singles: 7-inch
ALL AMERICAN (373 "Incense and Peppermints")..............................40-60 67
MCA.................................. 3-4 73-80s
UNI (Except 55218)....................5-15 67-70
UNI (55218 "California Day") 10-20 70
LPs: 10/12-inch
BACK-TRAC..........................5-10 85
UNI (73014 "Incense and Peppermints")..............................20-40 67
UNI (73025 "Wake Up, It's Tomorrow")..............................20-40 67
UNI (73035 "The World in a Seashell")..............................20-40 68
UNI (73054 "Good Morning Starshine")..............................20-40 69
UNI (73074 "The Best of the Strawberry Alarm Clock")..................................20-40 70
VOCALION (73915 "Changes")......15-20 71
Members: George Munford; Randy Seol; Ed King; Lee Freeman; George Bunnel; Gary Loverto; Mark Weitz; Jimmy Pitman; Gene Gunnels.
Also see GOLDTONES
Also see IRIDESCENTS
Also see LYNYRD SKYNYRD
Also see SIXPENCE
Also see WHO / Strawberry Alarm Clock

STRAWBERRY CHILDREN
Singles: 7-inch
SOUL CITY (758 "Love Years Coming")..............................10-20 67
Member: Jimmy Webb.

STRAWBERRY STREET SINGERS
Singles: 7-inch
RCA.................................. 3-6 69
LPs: 10/12-inch
RCA..................................10-15 69

STRAWBS LP '72
Singles: 7-inch
A&M.................................. 4-8 68-75
ARISTA 3-5 78
OYSTER 3-5 76-77
LPs: 10/12-inch
A&M..................................8-15 71-78
ARISTA 5-10 78
OYSTER 8-10 76-77
Also see DENNY, Sandy, & Strawbs
Also see HUDSON-FORD
Also see LAMBERT, Dave
Also see WAKEMAN, Rick

STRAY
LPs: 10/12-inch
MERCURY 10-15 71
TRANSATLANTIC 8-10

STRAY CATS P&R/LP '82
(With 14 Karat Soul)
Singles: 7-inch
EMI AMERICA (8122 "Stray Cat Strut")..................................4-6 82
EMI AMERICA (8132 "Rock This Town")..................................4-6 82
EMI AMERICA (8168 "Sexy + 17") 4-6 83
EMI AMERICA (8169-1/2 "Sexy + 17" & "Cruisin' ")..............................5-10 83
(Two singles in gatefold cover.)
EMI AMERICA (8185 "I Won't Stand In Your Way")..................................5-10 83
EMI AMERICA (8194 "Look at That Cadillac")..............................4-6 84
Picture Sleeves
EMI AMERICA..........................4-6 82-84
EPs: 7-inch
EMI AMERICA..........................5-10 83
LPs: 10/12-inch
EMI (91401 "Blast Off")................5-10 89
EMI AMERICA (17070 "Built for Speed")..................................5-10 82
EMI AMERICA (17102 "Rant'n Rave with the Stray Cats")..............................5-10 83
EMI AMERICA (17226 "Rock Therapy") 5-10 86
Members: Brian Setzer; Lee Rocker; Slim Jim Phantom; Brian McDonald; Gary Barnacle; Lee Allen.
Also see ALLEN, Lee
Also see PHANTOM, ROCKER & SLICK
Also see SETZER, Brian

STRAY DOG
LPs: 10/12-inch
MANTICORE..........................8-12 73-74

STREAK
Singles: 7-inch
A&M..................................3-5 72

STREAM OF CONSCIOUSNESS see VALDEZ, Sonny / Stream of Consciousness

STREAMERS
Singles: 7-inch
DOT..................................8-12 64
Session: Davie Allan.
Also see ALLAN, Davie

STREAMLINE EWING
Singles: 7-inch
EDSEL 5-10 60

STREAMLINE MAE
Singles: 78 rpm
OKEH..................................6-12 41

STREAMLINERS with JOANNE
Singles: 7-inch
U.A.................................. 4-8 65

STREAPLERS
Singles: 7-inch
CENTURY (0007 "Yes Tonight, Josephine")..............................15-20 60s

STREEK P&R '81
Singles: 7-inch
COLUMBIA............................3-5 81
LPs: 10/12-inch
COLUMBIA............................5-10 81

STREEP, Meryl, & George Winston
LPs: 10/12-inch
DANCING CAT........................5-8 85
Also see WINSTON, George

STREET
Singles: 7-inch
VERVE/FORECAST......................3-6 69
LPs: 10/12-inch
VERVE/FORECAST......................10-15 68

STREET, Hillard
Singles: 7-inch
REPRISE 4-8 62

STREET, Janey P&R/LP '84
Singles: 7-inch
ARISTA 3-4 84
Picture Sleeves
ARISTA 3-4 84
LPs: 10/12-inch
ARISTA 5-8 84-85

STREET, Mel C&W '72
(With Sandy Powell)
Singles: 7-inch
GRT 3-5 74-77
MERCURY 3-5 78
METROMEDIA COUNTRY................3-5 72-73
POLYDOR..............................3-5 77-78
ROYAL AMERICAN......................3-5 72
SUNBIRD 3-5 80-81
SUNSET..............................3-5 79
LPs: 10/12-inch
GRT 10-15 74-77
LAKESHORE 8-12
MERCURY 10-15 78
METROMEDIA COUNTRY................10-15 72-73
PHONORAMA 5-10 82
POLYDOR..............................10-15 77-78
SUNBIRD 10-15 80

STREET, Mike
Singles: 7-inch
TEMPUS 5-10 59

STREET, Richard, & Distants
Singles: 7-inch
HARMON (1002 "Answer Me")...100-200 62
Members: Richard Street; Eddie Kendricks; Paul Williams.
Also see DISTANTS
Also see TEMPTATIONS

STREET CHRISTIANS
Singles: 7-inch
P.I.P.................................. 3-5 73

STREET CLEANERS
Singles: 7-inch
AMY 10-20 64
Members: Phil Sloan; Steve Barri.
Also see FANTASTIC BAGGYS

STREET CORNER SOCIETY
Singles: 7-inch
JUBILEE..............................4-8 67

STREET CORNER SYMPHONY
Singles: 7-inch
BANG 3-5 75
LPs: 10/12-inch
ABC..................................5-10 77

STREET FARE
Singles: 7-inch
ATLANTIC 3-4 87

STREET NOISE
Singles: 7-inch
EVOLUTION 5-10 69
LPs: 10/12-inch
EVOLUTION 15-20 70

STREET PEOPLE P&R '70
Singles: 7-inch
MUSICOR 4-8 69-70
VIGOR 3-5 75-77
LPs: 10/12-inch
MUSICOR 15-20 70
PICKWICK 8-10 72
Also see HOLMES, Rupert

STREET PLAYERS
Singles: 7-inch
ARIOLA AMERICA......................3-5 79
LPs: 10/12-inch
ARIOLA AMERICA......................5-10 79

STREET SINGERS
Singles: 7-inch
TUXEDO (899 "Tonight Was Like a Dream")..............................100-125 56

STREETDANCER
LPs: 10/12-inch
DHARMA..............................5-10 77
FUTURE/DHARMA......................8-10 74

STREETER, Von
(With His Orchestra)
Singles: 78 rpm
CORAL..............................5-10
SAVOY..............................5-10 49
SCOOP 5-10 49

STREETFEET C&W '83
Singles: 7-inch
TRIPLE T 3-4 83

STREETHEART
LPs: 10/12-inch
ATLANTIC 5-10 79

STREETS P&R/LP '83
(Nightstreets)
Singles: 7-inch
ATLANTIC 3-4 83-84
EPIC..................................3-5 79-80
LPs: 10/12-inch
ATLANTIC 5-8 83-84
EPIC..................................5-10 79
Member: Steve Walsh; Rick Taylor; Rick Taylor; Joyce Hawthorne.
Also see KANSAS
Also see NIGHTSTREETS

STREETSINGERS
Singles: 7-inch
COMET 3-5

STREETWALKERS
LPs: 10/12-inch
MERCURY 8-12 76-77

STREISAND, Barbra LP '63
Singles: 12-inch
COLUMBIA (White label)..............15-25 79-85
(Promotional issues only.)
COLUMBIA (39909 "Emotion") 20-30 85
(Picture disc.)
COLUMBIA (99-1791 "The Way He Makes Me Feel")..............................30-40 85
(Picture disc. Promotional issue only.)
Singles: 7-inch
ARISTA (123 "More Than You Know")..................................4-6 75
COLUMBIA (02065 thru 05680)..........3-5 83-85
COLUMBIA (10450 thru 11364)..........3-6 76-80
COLUMBIA (3-42648 "My Coloring Book")..............................20-30 62
(Compact 33 Single.)
COLUMBIA (4-42648 "My Coloring Book")..............................8-12 62
COLUMBIA (42631 "Happy Days Are Here Again")..............................5-10 63
COLUMBIA (42965 thru 43469)..........4-6 64-65
COLUMBIA (43518 thru 46024)..........3-5 66-74
COLUMBIA (80826 "All I Ask of You")..................................4-8 88
Promotional Singles
COLUMBIA (02065 thru 05680) 4-8 83-85
COLUMBIA (10450 thru 11364) 4-8 76-80
COLUMBIA (4-42648 "My Coloring Book")..............................20-30 62
COLUMBIA (42631 "Happy Days Are Here Again")..............................15-25 63
COLUMBIA (42965 thru 43469).....10-20 64-65
(Black vinyl.)
COLUMBIA (42965 "People")........40-60 64
(Colored vinyl.)
COLUMBIA (43518 thru 46024).......6-12 66-74
COLUMBIA (79581 "People—Special Open-End Interview")..............................15-25 64
(Promotional issue only. Compact 33.)
COLUMBIA (80826 "All I Ask of You")..................................5-10 88
Picture Sleeves
COLUMBIA (Except 43896 & 79581)..................................3-5 73-85
COLUMBIA (43896 "Ave Maria").......4-8 66
COLUMBIA (79581 "People—Special Open-End Interview")..............................15-25 64
(Promotional issue only.)
EPs: 7-inch
CAPITOL (2636 "Complete Solo Tracks from the Capitol Original Broadway Cast Album *Funny Girl*")..............................15-25 64
LPs: 10/12-inch
ARISTA 8-10 75
CAPITOL (2059 "Funny Girl")........10-20 64
COLUMBIA (1779 "The Legend of Barbra Streisand")..............................35-45 83
(Promotional, one-hour interview program.)
COLUMBIA (CL-2007 thru CL-2682)..............................15-25 63-67
(Monaural. Black vinyl.)
COLUMBIA (2054 "The Second Barbra Streisand Album")....................100-200 63
(Colored vinyl. Promotional issue only.)
COLUMBIA (2478 "Color Me Barbra")..............................100-200 66
(Colored vinyl. Promotional issue only.)
COLUMBIA (3220 "Funny Girl")......10-15 68
COLUMBIA (CS-8807 thru CS-9557)..............................15-25 63-68
(Stereo. Black vinyl.)
COLUMBIA (8854 "The Second Barbra Streisand Album")....................100-200 63
(Colored vinyl. Promotional issue only.)
COLUMBIA (9278 "Color Me Barbra")..............................100-200 66
(Colored vinyl. Promotional issue only.)
COLUMBIA (9710 thru 9968).........10-15 68-70
COLUMBIA (PC-8000 & PC-9000 series) 5-8
COLUMBIA (JC-9000 series)...........5-8
COLUMBIA (30086 thru 39480).........5-15 70-84
With "FC," "JC," "KC," "M" or "PC" prefix.)
COLUMBIA (30378 thru 33815).......10-20 71-75
(Quadrophonic. With "PCQ" prefix.)
COLUMBIA (40092 thru 45369).......5-10 85-89
COLUMBIA (42801 thru 47678).......15-30 82
(Half-speed mastered. With "HC" prefix.)
20TH FOX..............................10-15 69
Also see ARLEN, Harold, with "Friend"
Also see BLOOD, SWEAT & TEARS

STREISAND, Barbra, & Kim Carnes P&R '84
Singles: 7-inch
COLUMBIA..............................3-4 84
Also see CARNES, Kim

STREISAND, Barbra / Marilyn Cooper
Singles: 7-inch
COLUMBIA..............................5-10
(Promotional issue only.)

STREISAND, Barbra / Doris Day / Jim Nabors / Andre Kostelanetz
LPs: 10/12-inch
COLUMBIA (1075 "Season's Greetings from Barbra Streisand & Friends")........15-25
(Special products issue for Maxwell House Coffee Co.)
Also see DAY, Doris
Also see KOSTELANETZ, Andre, & His Orchestra
Also see NABORS, Jim

STREISAND, Barbra, & Neil Diamond P&R/C&W '78
Singles: 7-inch
COLUMBIA..............................3-5 78
Also see DIAMOND, Neil

STREISAND, Barbra, & Barry Gibb P&R '80
Singles: 7-inch
COLUMBIA..............................3-4 80-81
Also see GIBB, Barry

STREISAND, Barbra, & Don Johnson P&R '88
Singles: 7-inch
COLUMBIA..............................3-4 88
Picture Sleeves
COLUMBIA..............................3-4 88
Also see JOHNSON, Don

STREISAND, Barbra, & Donna Summer P&R '79
Singles: 12-inch
COLUMBIA/CASABLANCA................8-10 79
(Promotional issue only. With special cover.)
Singles: 7-inch
COLUMBIA..............................3-5 79
Picture Sleeves
COLUMBIA..............................3-5 79
Also see STREISAND, Barbra
Also see SUMMER, Donna

STRENGTH, Bill
("Texas" Bill Strength)
Singles: 78 rpm
CAPITOL..............................8-10 52-54
Singles: 7-inch
CAPITOL (2294 "It Ain't Much, But It's Home")..............................10-20 52

CAPITOL (2701 "Six Fools") ... 10-20 54
GOLDEN RING (3024 "Tears in My Beers") ... 5-10 62
STARDAY (9272 "Hillbilly Hades") ... 10-20 60s
SUN (346 "I Guess I'd Better Go") 10-20 60

STRETCH
Singles: 7-inch
ANCHOR ... 3-5 75
LPs: 10/12-inch
ANCHOR ... 5-10 77
Member: Elmer Gantry.
Also see PARSONS, Alan, Project

STREYS
Singles: 7-inch
BWM (635 "She Cools My Mind") .. 20-30 60s

STRICKLAND, Jan
("With the Shadows Orchestra Conducted by Preston Standiford")
Singles: 78 rpm
HUB ... 100-125 55
"X" ... 10-15 54-55
Singles: 7-inch
HUB (556 "Love Me, Baby") ... 300-500 55
"X" (0080 "Come to Me My Little Darling") ... 25-50 54
"X" (0122 "Something to Remember You By") ... 25-50 55

STRICKLAND, Jimmy
Singles: 7-inch
ARLINGWOOD (8608 "Gonna Buy Me a Record That Cries") ... 5-10 64
DAVCO (104 "Touch of Heaven") ... 8-12 61
DAVCO (107 "Ring in My Pocket") ... 8-12 61
DOT (16956 "Don't Get Your Hopes Up") ... 5-10 66
SAM (109 "Funny Feeling") ... 8-12 62
WAYSIDE ... 5-10 68

STRICKLAND, Johnny
Singles: 7-inch
ROULETTE (Except 4119) ... 5-10 59-61
ROULETTE (4119 "She's Mine") ... 25-50 59

STRICKLAND, Jon & Ed
Singles: 7-inch
REBEL (2665 "The Rebel Beat") ... 8-12 60s
(First issued as by the Rebels.)
Also see REBELS

STRICKLAND, Steve
Singles: 7-inch
BASCO ... 3-5 78

STRICKLAND, Van
Singles: 7-inch
JUDSON ... 8-12 60
PALETTE ... 5-10 60

STRIDEL, Gene
Singles: 7-inch
ATLANTIC ... 4-6 68-69
COLUMBIA ... 4-8 64
VERVE ... 4-8 62
LPs: 10/12-inch
COLUMBIA ... 10-15 64

STRIDER
Singles: 7-inch
W.B. ... 3-5 73
LPs: 10/12-inch
W.B. ... 10-20 73

STRIDERS
Singles: 78 rpm
APOLLO ... 50-75 50
CAPITOL ... 20-40 48
DERBY ... 50-75 54
Singles: 7-inch
APOLLO (480 "Hesitating Fool") ... 150-250 55
DERBY (857 "Come Back to Me") ... 125-175 54
Also see CHURCHILL, Savannah
Also see MARTIN, Dolores, & Striders
Also see McLAURIN, Bette

STRIDERS
Singles: 7-inch
COLUMBIA (43738 "Sorrow") ... 10-20 66
COLUMBIA (43948 "Am I On Your Mind") ... 10-20 66
COLUMBIA (44143 "When You Walk in the Room") ... 10-15 67
DELTA (2137 "Give Me a Break") .. 15-25 66
LAVETTE (5007 "When You Walk in the Room") ... 15-25 66

STRIDES
Singles: 7-inch
M-S (202 "I Can Get Along") ... 20-30 67

STRIGO, Bobby
(With Blue Notes)
Singles: 7-inch
RENOWN ... 10-15 59

STRIKE
LPs: 10/12-inch
BUDDAH ... 10-15 69

STRIKE FORCE
EPs: 12-inch
MASQUE (8914 "Strike Force") ... 8-12 89
(Picture disc. Promotional issue only.)

STRIKER
Singles: 7-inch
ARISTA ... 3-5 78
LPs: 10/12-inch
ARISTA ... 5-10 78

STRIKERS *LP '81*
Singles: 7-inch
PRELUDE ... 3-5 81
LPs: 10/12-inch
PRELUDE ... 5-10 81

STRIKES
(With the Three Pelves)
Singles: 7-inch
IMPERIAL (5433 "If You Can't Rock Me") ... 25-50 57
IMPERIAL (5446 "Rockin' ") ... 25-50 57
LIN (5006 "If You Can't Rock Me") ... 50-75 57
Members: A.B. Cornelius; Ken Scott; Paul Kunz; Willie Jacobs; Walter; Parsons; Don Alexander.
Also see TERRY, Don

STRIMBLING BLIMBLES
Singles: 7-inch
MERCURY ... 3-5 69

STRING & BEANS
Singles: 7-inch
FAT CITY (6130 "Come Back to Me") ... 15-25 66

STRING CHEESE
LPs: 10/12-inch
WOODEN NICKEL ... 10-20 71
Member: John Maggi.
Also see TURNQUIST REMEDY

STRING DRIVEN THING
Singles: 7-inch
FAMOUS CHARISMA ... 3-5 73
20TH FOX ... 3-5 75
LPs: 10/12-inch
FAMOUS CHARISMA ... 8-10 72-73
20TH FOX ... 8-10 75

STRING KINGS
Singles: 7-inch
GAIETY (144 "Blood Shot") ... 400-500 64
Also see TRASHMEN

STRING-A-LONGS *P&R '61*
Singles: 7-inch
ATCO (6694 "Popi") ... 10-15 69
(Reportedly recorded by the Fireballs but credited to the String-A-Longs.)
DOT ... 5-10 62-65
WARWICK (603 "Wheels"/"Tell the World") ... 10-15 60
WARWICK (603 "Wheels"/"Am I Asking Too Much") ... 8-10 61
WARWICK (606 "Tell the World") 10-15 61
WARWICK (625 thru 675) ... 8-12 61-62
LPs: 10/12-inch
ATCO (241 "World Wide Hits") ... 15-25 68
(Reportedly recorded by the Fireballs but credited to the String-A-Longs.)
DOT ... 15-25 62-66
WARWICK (W-2036 "Pick-A-Hit") 40-50 61
(Monaural.)
WARWICK (WST-2036 "Pick-A-Hit") ... 50-75 61
(Stereo.)
Members: Keith McCormick; Jimmy Torres; Don Allen; Aubrey Lee de Cordova; Richard Stephens.
Also see BOYD, Mickey, & Plain Viewers
Also see FIREBALLS
Also see NEW STRING-A-LONGS

STRINGBEANS
Singles: 7-inch
GINA (7001 "Starbright") ... 250-500 63

STRINGMEN
Singles: 7-inch
EPIC ... 4-8 62

STRINGS OF FORTUNE
Singles: 7-inch
OHN-J ... 4-8 66-67
RCA ... 3-6 67

STRINGSHIFTERS
Singles: 7-inch
NU SOUND ... 4-8

STROBEL, Joey
(With the Runaways)
Singles: 7-inch
BEAR ... 8-12 66
REGALIA ... 10-15 60s
SAT. SAINT ... 8-12 60s

STRODE, Lance *C&W '89*
Singles: 7-inch
BOOTSTRAP ... 3-4 89

STROGIN, Henry
(With the Crowns; with Crown)
Singles: 7-inch
BALL (1015 "Why Do You Go Away") ... 40-60 63
DYNAMIC (1002 "Why Do You Go Away") ... 75-125 60
HANK (5001 "Misery") ... 15-25 63
HANK (5002 "Why Did You Go Away") ... 15-25 63

STROKE
Singles: 12-inch
OMNI ... 4-6 85

STROLL KINGS
Singles: 7-inch
CORAL ... 5-10 58

STROLLERS
Singles: 7-inch
ZEBRA (22 "You're the Only One for Me") ... 100-200 57

STROLLERS
Singles: 78 rpm
STATES ... 100-150 57
Singles: 7-inch
STATES (163 "In Your Dreams") ... 100-200 57

STROLLERS
Singles: 7-inch
WARNER RECORDS (1018 "Crowded Classroom") ... 10-20 58

STROLLERS
Singles: 7-inch
ALADDIN ... 10-20 58-59

STROLLERS
Singles: 7-inch
CUB (9060 "Favors") ... 15-25 60
DART (1017 "That Look in Your Eye") ... 15-25 60
20TH FOX (226 "One Summer Love") ... 20-30 60

STROLLERS *P&R '61*
Singles: 7-inch
CARLTON (546 "There's No One But You") ... 15-25 61

STROLLERS
Singles: 7-inch
JUBILEE ... 5-10 63

STROLLS
Singles: 7-inch
SKY ROCKET ... 5-10 60

STROMAN, Gene *C&W '87*
Singles: 7-inch
CAPITOL ... 3-4 87

STRONG, Barrett *P&R '60*
(With the Rayber Voices)
Singles: 78 rpm
ANNA (1111 "Money") ... 100-200 60
Singles: 7-inch
ANNA (1111 "Money") ... 15-25 60
ANNA (1116 "Yes No, Maybe So") ... 15-25 60
ATCO (6225 "Seven Sins") ... 25-35 62
CAPITOL ... 3-5 75
EPIC ... 3-5 73
MOTOWN ... 3-4
TAMLA (54022 "Let's Rock") ... 800-1200 60
TAMLA (54027 "Money") ... 35-55 60
(Horizontal lines on label.)
TAMLA (54027 "Money") ... 15-25 60
(Tamla globe logo on label.)
TAMLA (54029 "Yes No, Maybe So") ... 30-50 60
TAMLA (54033 "Whirlwind") ... 30-50 60
TAMLA (54035 "Money and Me") ... 30-50 61
TAMLA (54043 "Misery") ... 30-50 61
TOLLIE (9023 "I Better Run") ... 15-25 64
Picture Sleeves
EPIC ... 3-5 73
LPs: 10/12-inch
CAPITOL ... 8-10 74
Also see HOLLAND, Eddie

STRONG, Benny, & His Orchestra
Singles: 78 rpm
CAPITOL ... 4-6 50
DECCA ... 5-10 57
TOWER ... 4-6 47
Singles: 7-inch
CAPITOL ... 5-10 50
DECCA ... 5-10 57

STRONG, Elsie
Singles: 7-inch
FINALLY ... 10-20 60s
LEGRAND ... 10-20 60s

STRONG, Garrett G.
Singles: 7-inch
JAF ... 4-8 61

STRONG, Larry
Singles: 7-inch
REVOLVO ... 5-10 61

STRONG, Nolan
Singles: 7-inch
FORTUNE ... 8-12 66-69
Some Fortune releases before 1966 credit just Nolan Strong—without the Diablos—but they are still found in the Diablo's section.
Also see DIABLOS

STRONG, Zeke
(Zeke Strong Combo)
Singles: 7-inch
MISS ADY ... 10-15
FARO ... 5-10 64
PROGRESS (531 "All By Myself") 10-15 63
PROWLING (406 "Cry, You Cry Alone") ... 10-15 60s
PROWLING (2602 "North Beach") . 10-15 60s
Also see UNDERWOOD, Carl

STRONGBOW
LPs: 10/12-inch
SOUTHWIND ... 8-10 75

STRONGMEN
Singles: 7-inch
LINDA ... 5-10 60

STRUCK, Nolan
LPs: 10/12-inch
ICHIBAN ... 5-10

STRUMMER, Joe
Singles: 12-inch
MCA ... 4-6 86
VIRGIN ... 5-8 87
LPs: 10/12-inch
CBS ... 5-10 89
Also see CLASH

STRUNK, Jud *C&W/P&R/LP '73*
(With the Coplin Kitchen Band)
Singles: 7-inch
CAPITOL ... 3-5 74
COBURT ... 3-5 71
COLUMBIA ... 3-5 70
MCA ... 3-5 77
MGM ... 3-5 72-73
MELODYLAND ... 3-5 75-76
LPs: 10/12-inch
COLUMBIA ... 6-12 70
HARMONY ... 5-10 73
MCA ... 5-10 77
MGM ... 5-10 71-73

STRYPER *LP '85*
Singles: 7-inch
ENIGMA (Except 1135) ... 3-4 84-89
ENIGMA (1135 "Reason for the Season") ... 5-10 84
(Picture disc.)
Picture Sleeves
ENIGMA ... 3-4 87-88
LPs: 10/12-inch
ENIGMA (Except 73277) ... 5-8 84-90
ENIGMA (73277 "Stryper") ... 10-20 86
(Picture disc.)
Members: Michael Sweet; Oz Fox; Tim Gaines; Robert Sweet.

STUART, Alice
LPs: 10/12-inch
ARHOOLIE ... 10-15 64

STUART, Bobby
Singles: 7-inch
VALMOR ... 4-8 62

STUART, Chad
Singles: 7-inch
COLUMBIA ... 4-8 66
SIDEWALK ... 4-8 69
Also see CHAD & JEREMY

STUART, Chad & Jill
Singles: 7-inch
COLUMBIA ... 4-8 66
Picture Sleeves
COLUMBIA ... 5-10 66
Also see STUART, Chad

STUART, Debbie
Singles: 7-inch
PHILIPS ... 4-8 62-63

STUART, Gary
Singles: 7-inch
KRISTIN (14001 "Interview on Capitol Hill") ... 4-6 80

STUART, Glen
(Glen Stuart Orchestra)
Singles: 7-inch
ABEL ... 5-10 60
LAURIE (3255 "Just Loafin' ") ... 4-8 64
Also see CARLO
Also see COMO, Nicky

STUART, Jeb
(With the Reflextions; Soulful Jeb Stuart)
Singles: 7-inch
BINGO ... 15-25 60s
EUREKA ... 10-20 66
GREAT AMERICAN ... 5-10 69
KING ... 5-10 66
PHILIPS INT'L ... 10-20 61-62
PURE GOLD ... 10-20 65
SHAR (2 "What a Beautiful Face") ... 50-75 60

STUART, Kirk
(With the Honeydreamers)
Singles: 7-inch
JOSIE (832 "Gladly") ... 10-15 58
JUBILEE ... 8-12 59
Also see REESE, Dela, & Kirk Stuart

STUART, Lisa
Singles: 7-inch
CUB ... 5-10 59

STUART, Marty *C&W '85*
Singles: 7-inch
COLUMBIA ... 3-4 85-88
MCA ... 3-4 89-92
LPs: 10/12-inch
RIDGE RUNNER (00013 "Marty") ... 8-12 78
SUGAR HILL ... 5-10 80s
Session: Johnny Cash; Michael Coleman; Jerry Douglas; Lester Flatt; Carl Jackson; Earl Scruggs; Doc Watson; Merle Watson.
Also see CASH, Johnny
Also see FLATT, Lester, & Earl Scruggs
Also see JACKSON, Carl, Marty Stuart & Vicki Cook
Also see TRITT, Travis, & Marty Stuart
Also see WATSON, Doc

STUART, Mary
Singles: 7-inch
BELL ... 4-6 74
LP: 10/12-inch
BELL ... 8-12 73

STUART, Scotty
Singles: 7-inch
MMC ... 5-10 60
Also see HONEY & DEW DROPS

STUARTI, Enzo
Singles: 7-inch
JUBILEE ... 4-8 60s
LEGRAND (1023 "For All We Know") ... 40-60 61
ROULETTE ... 10-20 61-68
LP: 10/12-inch
DIPLOMAT ... 8-15 60s
EPIC ... 8-15 65
JUBILEE ... 8-15 60s
RAGU ... 10-20 60s
(Mail order offer.)

STUARTS
Singles: 7-inch
ASCOT (2209 "Just a Little Bit More") ... 8-12 66

STUBBLEFIELD, Bill
Singles: 78 rpm
IMPERIAL ... 5-10 57
LIN ... 10-20 57
Singles: 7-inch
IMPERIAL ... 5-10 57
LIN ... 10-20 57

STUBBS, Joe
Singles: 7-inch
LU-PINE (120 "Keep on Lovin' Me") ... 100-200 64
(Lupine [not hyphenated] 120 is also a Primettes single.)
Also see CONTOURS
Also see FALCONS
Also see 100 PROOF Aged in Soul
Also see ORIGINALS

STUBBY & BUCCANEERS *C&W '49*
Singles: 78 rpm
DECCA ... 4-8 49
Also see IVES, Burl, with Captain Stubby & Buccaneers

STUCKEY, Nat *C&W '66*
Singles: 7-inch
MCA ... 3-5 76-78
PAULA ... 4-6 66-68
RCA ... 3-6 68-75
LPs: 10/12-inch
CAMDEN ... 5-10 74
MCA ... 5-10 76
PAULA ... 10-20 66-67
RCA (Except "APD" series) ... 8-12 69-74
RCA (APD1-0080 "Nat Stuckey") ... 15-25 73
(Quadraphonic.)
Also see SMITH, Connie, & Nat Stuckey

STUDD PUMP
Singles: 7-inch
UNI (55285 "Spare the Children") ... 3-6 70

STUDEBAKER BROTHERS
Singles: 7-inch
LITTLE FORT (010 "Lie'n in the Grave") ... 15-25 60s
Member: Greg Kishline.
Also see STARBOYS

STUDEBAKER HAWK
Singles: 7-inch
POLYDOR ... 3-5 75

STUDEBAKER "7"
Singles: 7-inch
COOKHOUSE (7325 "In the Still of the Night") ... 25-50 70
COULEE (142 "One Fine Day") ... 25-50 72

STUDENT BODY
Singles: 7-inch
INTREPID ... 4-6 69
Picture Sleeves
INTREPID ... 4-6 69

STUDENT NURSES
Singles: 7-inch
RCA ... 10-20 64

STUDENTS
Singles: 7-inch
RED TOP (100 "My Heart Is an Open Door") ... 100-200 57
(Blue label.)
RED TOP (100 "My Heart Is an Open Door") ... 25-50 58
(Red label.)

STUDENTS *R&B '61*
(With Jimmy Coe & Orchestra)
Singles: 78 rpm
CHECKER (902 "I'm So Young") ... 50-75 58
Singles: 7-inch
ARGO (5386 "I'm So Young") ... 15-25 61
BRASS RING ... 4-6 71
CADET ... 5-10 65
CHECKER (902 "I'm So Young") ... 20-30 58
CHECKER (1004 "My Vow to You") ... 15-25 61
CHESS ... 3-5 73
COLLECTABLES ... 3-4 80s
NOTE (10012 "I'm So Young") ... 200-300 58
NOTE (10019 "My Vow to You") ... 200-300 58
Members: Leroy King; Emerson "Rocky" Brown; Rich Havens.
Also see BROWN, Rocky
Also see JEWELS

STUDIO A
Singles: 7-inch
KAPP ... 4-8 67

STUDIO '79
LPs: 10/12-inch
SPRINGBOARD INT'L ... 5-10 79

STUFF *LP '76*
Singles: 7-inch
W.B. ... 3-5 76-80

LPs: 10/12-inch
W.B. 5-10 76-80

STUFF
Singles: 7-inch
PREMIUM (1 "Why Are You Blowing My Mind") 20-30 60s

STUFF 'N' RAMJETT
Singles: 7-inch
CHELSEA 3-5 76

STUFFIN'
LPs: 10/12-inch
A&M 10-15 69

STUFFY & FROZEN PARACHUTE BAND
LPs: 10/12-inch
PARAMOUNT 8-10 73
Member: Stuffy Schmidt.

STUMBLEBUNNY
Singles: 7-inch
MERCURY 3-5 79

STUMP WIZARDS
Singles: 7-inch
GET HIP (111 "Firemine") 3-4 89
Picture Sleeves
GET HIP (111 "Firemine") 3-4 89
LPs: 10/12-inch
GET HIP (Naked 56 "Smokestack") 5-10 89
Members: Jack Chiara; Clude McGeary; Eric Vermillion.

STUMPO, Phil
Singles: 7-inch
B-W 4-8 62

STUMPS
Singles: 7-inch
BOYD (159 "My Generation") 15-25 67

STURGES, Jeff
Singles: 7-inch
MAM 3-5 71
LPs: 10/12-inch
MAM 10-15 71

STURGIS, Rodney
(With Louis Jordan's Elks Rendezvous Band)
Singles: 78 rpm
DECCA 10-15 38
Also see JORDAN, Louis

STURM, Sammy
Singles: 7-inch
MALA 4-8 61

STUTZ BEARCAT
Singles: 7-inch
KAPP 4-8 68
W.B. 4-8 66

STYLE COUNCIL *LP '83*
Singles: 7-inch
GEFFEN 3-4 84-85
POLYDOR 3-4 83-88
Picture Sleeves
GEFFEN 3-4 84
LPs: 10/12-inch
GEFFEN 5-8 84-85
POLYDOR 5-8 83-88
Also see BAND AID
Also see JAM

STYLE KINGS
Singles: 7-inch
SOTOPLAY (011 "Kissing Behind the Moon") 30-40 64
SOTOPLAY (014 "House Party") 15-25 64

STYLE SISTERS
(With the Camarata Orchestra)
Singles: 7-inch
COLISEUM (601 "Should I") 4-8 62
Picture Sleeves
COLISEUM (601 "Should I") 5-10 62
Members: Joan; Deanna; Deanda.

STYLERS
Singles: 78 rpm
KICKS 50-100 54
Singles: 7-inch
KICKS (2 "Gentle As a Teardrop") 200-300 54

STYLERS *P&R '56*
(Dick Thomas & Stylers)
Singles: 78 rpm
GOLDEN CREST 15-25 57
JUBILEE 10-15 55-57
Singles: 7-inch
GOLDEN CREST (1181 "You Tell Me") 15-25 57
GOLDEN CREST (1291 "Kiss and Run Lover") 15-25 57
GOLDEN CREST (1292 "Sweetheart of All My Dreams") 15-25 58
GORDY (7018 "Going Steady Anniversary") 25-35 63
JUBILEE 12-25 54-57

STYLES
Singles: 7-inch
JOSIE (920 "School Bells to Chapel Bells") 30-40 64
PARK AVE. (39635 "Scarlet Angel") 5-8 95
SERENE (1501 "Scarlet Angel") 100-150 61
TORCH (953 "Trying") 25-50

STYLES
Singles: 7-inch
MODERN 5-8 68
SWAN 5-8 66

STYLES, Donnie
Singles: 7-inch
TIME SQUARE 5-10 63

STYLETTES
Singles: 7-inch
CAMEO 8-12 64-65

STY-LETTS
Singles: 7-inch
PILLAR (515 "Hello My Darling") 20-30 62

STYLISTICS *P&R/LP '71*
Singles: 7-inch
AMHERST 3-4 85
AVCO 3-6 70-76
H&L 3-5 76-79
MERCURY 3-5 79
PHILADELPHIA INT'L 3-5 82
SEBRING (8370 "You're a Big Girl Now") 15-25 70
STREETWISE 3-4 84-86
TSOP 3-4 80-84
Picture Sleeves
AVCO 3-5 76
LPs: 10/12-inch
AVCO 5-10 71-75
H&L 5-10 76-79
MERCURY 5-10 78-79
PHILADELPHIA INT'L 5-10 82
STREETWISE 5-8 84-86
TSOP 5-10 80-81
Members: Russell Tompkins, Jr.; Airrion Love; Herb Murrell; James Dunn; James Smith.
Also see MEDEIROS, Glenn, & Stylistics

STYLISTS
Singles: 7-inch
JAY WING (5807 "Move It Over, Baby") 50-100 59
SAGE (317 "I've Been Waiting for You") 15-25 60

STYLISTS
(With Al Browne's Orchestra)
Singles: 7-inch
ROSE (16 "I Wonder") 30-50 60
Also see BROWNE, Al

STYLISTS
Singles: 7-inch
V.I.P. (25066 "What Is Love") 10-20 67

STYLLE BAND
Singles: 7-inch
GOLD STAR 8-12

STYNER, Ronnie
Singles: 7-inch
CAPA (101 "Love Me Faithfully") 10-20 62
CAPA (109 "Hey, Hey, Hey") 10-20 62

STYVERS, Laurie
LPs: 10/12-inch
W.B. 8-10 71

STYX
Singles: 7-inch
ABC 4-8 66

STYX
Singles: 7-inch
ONYX (2208 "Puppetmaster") 15-25 67
Also see ENGLE, Butch, & Styx

STYX *P&R '72*
Singles: 7-inch
A&M 3-5 76-84
PARAMOUNT 3-5 71-72
RCA 3-5 76
WOODEN NICKEL 3-5 72-78
Picture Sleeves
A&M 3-5 77-84
LPs: 10/12-inch
A&M (Except 4604 & PR-4724) 5-10 75-84
A&M (4604 "Crystal Ball") 20-30 76
A&M (PR-4724 "Pieces of Eight") 10-15 79
(Picture disc.)
MFSL (026 "Grand Illusion") 25-50 79
NAUTILUS (27 "Cornerstone") 20-30 81
RCA 5-10 72-82
WOODEN NICKEL 8-10 72-77
Promotional LPs
A&M (8431 "Styx Radio Special") 15-25 77
(Two-disc set.)
A&M (17053 "Styx Radio Special") 35-40 78
(Three-disc set.)
A&M (17222 "Radio Sampler") 10-20 83
JIM LADD HOSTS (26-5 "Innerview") 8-12 76
ROLLING STONE (82-46 "Continuous History of Rock & Roll") 10-15 81
Members: Dennis De Young; James Young; Tommy Shaw; John Panozzo; Chuck Panozzo.
Also see DE YOUNG, Dennis
Also see SHAW, Tommy

SUADES
Singles: 7-inch
SPINNING (6011 "Everybody's Trying to Be My Baby") 15-25 61

SUAVE *P&R/LP '88*
Singles: 7-inch
CAPITOL 3-4 88
Picture Sleeves
CAPITOL 3-4 88
LPs: 10/12-inch
CAPITOL 5-8 88

SUB ZERO BAND
Singles: 7-inch
LAVENDER 5-10

SUBJECT *D&D '85*
Singles: 12-inch
POW WOW WOW 4-6 85

SUBTERRANEAN MONASTERY
Singles: 7-inch
RCA (9512 "Curiosity") 5-8 68

SUBURBAN LAWNS
Singles: 7-inch
I.R.S. 3-5 81
SUBURBAN/INDUSTRIAL 3-5 79
LPs: 10/12-inch
I.R.S. 5-10 81

SUBURBAN NIGHTMARE
LPs: 10/12-inch
MIDNIGHT 5-10

SUBURBAN 9 to 5
Singles: 7-inch
GOLDEN VOICE (2630 "Sunshine Becomes You") 20-30 68
GOLDEN VOICE (5778 "I Wanna Be There") 20-30 68
LEDGER (18810 "Walk Away") 20-25 68
Member: Gary Richrath.
Also see REO SPEEDWAGON

SUBURBANS
Singles: 78 rpm
BATON 15-25 56-57
Singles: 7-inch
BATON (227 "I Remember") 20-40 56
BATON (240 "Leave My Gal Alone") 25-50 57
Also see COLE, Ann, & Suburbans
Also see RICKS, Jimmy, & Suburbans

SUBURBANS
Singles: 7-inch
FLAMINGO (539 "Love Me") 50-75 61
(Reissued as by the Five Classics, then again by the Suburbans on Gee.)
PORT (70011 "Alphabet of Love") 40-60 59
GEE (1076 "Love Me") 15-25 62
KIP (221 "Little Bird") 20-40 60
SHELLY (184 "Walk Beside Me") 50-75 63
Also see FIVE CLASSICS

SUBURBANS
Singles: 7-inch
VERMILLION (268 "Love That I Had") 10-15 65

SUBWAY RIDERS
Singles: 7-inch
MOONSHOT 10-20 67

SUBWAY SERENADERS
Singles: 7-inch
AVENUE D (0004 "White Christmas") 10-15 80
(Green vinyl. Reportedly 300 made.)
AVENUE D (0004 "White Christmas") 8-10 80
(Green vinyl. Reportedly 400 made.)
Members: Rich Peritora; Bob Emrick; John Blewitt; Chris Mahoney; Rick Nocolini.
Also see DECADES

SUDANO, Bruce
LPs: 10/12-inch
MILLENNIUM 5-8 81

SUDDENS
(Safaris)
Singles: 7-inch
SUDDEN (103 "Garden of Love") 40-60 61
Also see SAFARIS

SUDDERTH, Anna *C&W '80*
Singles: 7-inch
VERITE 3-5 80

SUDELLS
Singles: 7-inch
AMERICAN ARTS (12 "Suzuki") 10-20 65

SUE, Bobby: see BOBBY SUE

SUE, Karen: see KAREN SUE

SUE & DYNAMICS
Singles: 7-inch
FENTON (948 "Love in My Eyes") 15-25 64

SUE & SUNNY
Singles: 7-inch
DERAM 4-8 68
EPIC 4-6 69

SUE ANN
Singles: 7-inch
MCA 3-4 88
W.B. 3-5 81
Picture Sleeves
MCA 3-4 88
LPs: 10/12-inch
W.B. 5-10 81

SUEDES
Singles: 78 rpm
MONEY (204 "I Love You So") 40-60 54
Singles: 7-inch
MONEY (204 "I Love You So") 100-150 54
Member: Grady Chapman.
Also see ROBINS

SUEDES
Singles: 7-inch
DART 10-20 59

SUEDES
Singles: 7-inch
PSYCHEDELIC (113 "13 Stories High") 25-50 66

SUGAHH
Singles: 7-inch
MERCURY 3-5 84

SUGAR
Singles: 7-inch
CAROUSEL 5-8 72-73
ROCKY ROAD 3-5 72

SUGAR & HONEYCOMBS
Singles: 7-inch
DORE (699 "Out of Sight") 10-20 64

SUGAR & PEE WEE
Singles: 7-inch
ALADDIN (3416 "One, Two, Let's Rock") 10-15 58
Members: Umpeylia Balinton; Pee Wee Kingsley.
Also see DE SANTO, Sugar Pie

SUGAR & SPICE
Singles: 78 rpm
MERCURY 8-10 56
Singles: 7-inch
GROOVE 4-8 64
KAPP 3-6 68-69
LOMA 4-8 64
MERCURY 10-15 56

SUGAR & SPICE
Singles: 7-inch
FRANKLIN 8-12 60s
WHITE WHALE 8-12 69
Picture Sleeves
FRANKLIN 10-20 60s

SUGAR & SPICE
Singles: 7-inch
WEST END 3-5 79

SUGAR & SPICES
Singles: 7-inch
STACY 5-10 63
SWAN 5-10 65
TOLLIE 5-10 64
VEE JAY 5-10 64

SUGAR & SPICES
Singles: 7-inch
20TH FOX (618 "Duck Walk") 10-20 65
Members: Rene Hall, Bobby Womack.
Also see HALL, Rene
Also see WOMACK, Bobby

SUGAR & SWEET
Singles: 7-inch
FOREMOST 5-10 63
MORTON 10-20
PEP 5-10 66
S.S.J. 5-10 65

SUGAR & SWEET
Singles: 7-inch
FOREMOST 5-10 63
MORTON 10-20
PEP 5-10 66
S.S.J. 5-10 65

SUGAR BABES
Singles: 7-inch
MCA 3-4 87

SUGAR BEAR
LPs: 10/12-inch
SUGAR BEAR 5-10 78

SUGAR BEARS *P&R '72*
Singles: 7-inch
BIG TREE 4-6 72
LPs: 10/12-inch
BIG TREE 10-20 71
Members: Michael McGinnis; Kim Carnes; Baker Knight; Mike Settle; Mitch Murray.
Also see CARNES, Kim
Also see KNIGHT, Baker
Also see SETTLE, Mike

SUGAR BEATS
Singles: 7-inch
A&M 4-8 66
Members: Al Candaleria; Darron Stankey; Larry Knew.
Also see INNOCENTS

SUGAR BILLY
Singles: 7-inch
FAST TRACK 3-5 75
LPs: 10/12-inch
FAST TRACK 5-10 75

SUGAR BLUES
Singles: 7-inch
BELL 3-5 69

SUGAR BOY & HIS CANE CUTTERS
(James Crawford)
Singles: 78 rpm
CHECKER 25-50 53-54
Singles: 7-inch
CHECKER (783 "I Don't Know What I'll Do") 50-100 53
CHECKER (787 "Jock-O-Mo") 50-100 53
CHECKER (795 "No More Heartaches") 50-100 54
Also see CRAWFORD, James

SUGAR BOY & SUGAR LUMPS
Singles: 7-inch
PEACOCK 4-8 63

SUGAR BUNS
Singles: 7-inch
W.B. 5-10 59

SUGAR BUS
Singles: 7-inch
POLYDOR 3-5 72

SUGAR CAKES
Singles: 7-inch
W.B. 3-6 69

SUGAR CANES
Singles: 7-inch
FEDERAL 10-15 58
KING 10-15 58

SUGAR CANYON
Singles: 7-inch
BUDDAH 4-8 68

SUGAR CREEK
LPs: 10/12-inch
METROMEDIA (1020 "Please Tell a Friend") 40-60 69

SUGAR CUBES *LP '88*
Singles: 12-inch
ELEKTRA 4-6 88
Singles: 7-inch
ELEKTRA 3-4 88-89
Picture Sleeves
ELEKTRA 3-4 88-89
LPs: 10/12-inch
ELEKTRA 5-10 88-89
Members: Björk Gudmundsdottir; Bragi Olafsson; Einar Örn; Margret Ornolfsdottir; Sigtryggur Baldursson; Thor Eldon.

SUGAR DADDY
Singles: 12-inch
BC 4-6 81
Singles: 7-inch
BC 3-5 81

SUGAR LUMPS
Singles: 7-inch
UPTOWN 4-8 66-67

SUGAR PLUMS
Singles: 7-inch
PHI DAN 4-8 66

SUGAR RAY & BLUETONES
(Featuring Little Ronnie)
EPs: 7-inch
BARON 5-10 79
Member: Sugar Ray Norcia.
Also see ROOMFUL of BLUES

SUGAR RAY ROLL
Singles: 7-inch
BEAUTY (2140 "My Heart and I") 5-10

SUGAR SHACK
Singles: 7-inch
SMASH (2256 "I Want Candy") 5-10 69

SUGAR SHOPPE
Singles: 7-inch
CAPITOL 4-8 68
EPIC 4-8 69
LPs: 10/12-inch
CAPITOL 10-15 68

SUGAR TONES
(Sugartones; Enchanters)
Singles: 78 rpm
OKEH 50-100 51
ONYX (2007 "Anabelle") 40-60 51
ONYX (2008 "They Said It Couldn't Happen") 40-60 51
Singles: 7-inch
BENIDA (5021 "Scandal") 250-350 50s
CANNON (391 "How Can I Pretend") 35-50 60
CANNON (392 "Baby") 35-50 61
OKEH (6814 "You Fool Again") 200-300 51
OKEH (6837 "It's Over") 200-300 51
OKEH (6877 "Today Is Your Birthday") 200-300 52
OKEH (6992 "I Just Want to Dream") 200-300 52
Also see ENCHANTERS

SUGAR TOWNES
Singles: 7-inch
RCA 3-6 69

SUGARCANE & HIS VIOLIN
(Don Harris)
Singles: 7-inch
ELDO 10-15 61
Also see HARRIS, Don "Sugar Cane"

SUGARHILL
Singles: 7-inch
WASHINGTON (101 "That's Love") 5-10 70s

SUGARHILL FOUR
Singles: 7-inch
LIMELIGHT 4-8 64

SUGARHILL GANG *P&R '79*
Singles: 12-inch
SUGAR HILL (Except 542) 5-10 80-85
SUGAR HILL (542 "Rapper's Delight") 20-30 79
Singles: 7-inch
SUGAR HILL 3-5 79-85
LPs: 10/12-inch
SUGAR HILL 5-10 80-85
Also see FURIOUS FIVE & Sugarhill Gang

SUGARLOAF *P&R/LP '70*
(With Jerry Corbetta)
Singles: 7-inch
BRUT 3-5 73-74
CLARIDGE 3-5 74-76
LIBERTY 3-5 70-71
U.A. 3-5 71
Picture Sleeves
BRUT 4-6 73-74
LIBERTY 4-6 71

LPs: 10/12-inch

BRUT 8-10 73
CLARIDGE 8-10 75
LIBERTY 10-15 70-71

Members: Jerry Corbetta; Bob Webber.
Also see CORBETTA, Jerry

SUGARMAN

Singles: 78 rpm

SITTIN' IN WITH (609 "Which Woman Do I Love") 25-35 51

SUGARMINTS

Singles: 7-inch

BRUNSWICK (55042 "You'll Have Everything") 10-20 57

SUGARTONES: see SUGAR TONES

SUGGS, Brad

(With the Swingsters)

Singles: 78 rpm

METEOR 50-100 56

Singles: 7-inch

METEOR (5034 "Charcoal Suit") 200-250 56
PHILLIPS INT'L 8-12 59-61

Also see ANTHONY, Rayburn
Also see RHODES, Slim

SUICIDAL TENDENCIES LP '87

Singles: 7-inch

FRONTIER 3-4 84

LPs: 10/12-inch

CAROL 5-8 87
EPIC 5-8 88-90
JANA 8-10 86

Members: Mike Muir; Rocky George; Mike Clark; R.J. Herrera; Bob Heathcote; Robert Trujillo.

SUICIDE

LPs: 10/12-inch

RED STAR 5-10 80

SUICIDE COMMANDOS

LPs: 10/12-inch

BLANK 5-8 78
TWIN/TONE 5-8

SUITER, Jeri

Singles: 7-inch

LIMELIGHT 10-15

SUKMAN, Harry, & Orchestra

Singles: 7-inch

LIBERTY (55210 "Crimson Kimono") 3-5 59

Picture Sleeves

LIBERTY (55210 "Crimson Kimono") 10-20 59

LPs: 10/12-inch

LIBERTY 10-20 59-60

SULKE, Steff

Singles: 7-inch

DIAL 4-8 67-68

SULLENS, Roy

Singles: 7-inch

ACE 5-10 59

SULLIVAN, Artie

Singles: 7-inch

SWAN 4-8 63

SULLIVAN, Big Jim

Singles: 7-inch

MERCURY 4-8 68

LPs: 10/12-inch

EUPHORIA 8-10 71
MERCURY 15-20 67

SULLIVAN, Carolyn

Singles: 7-inch

PHILIPS 4-8 68

SULLIVAN, Gene C&W '57

Singles: 78 rpm

COLUMBIA 5-10 57

Singles: 7-inch

COLUMBIA 5-10 57

Also see WILEY & GENE

SULLIVAN, Jerry

Singles: 78 rpm

VEE (100 "Curly Headed Baby") 25-45 56

Singles: 7-inch

VEE (100 "Curly Headed Baby") 50-75 56

SULLIVAN, Niki

Singles: 7-inch

DOT (15751 "It's All Over") 40-60 58
JOLI (073 "Do the Dive") 40-50
JOLI (075 "It Really Doesn't Matter") 40-60

Also see CRICKETS
Also see HOLLYHAWKS
Also see SOUL INCORPORATED

SULLIVAN, Phil C&W '59

Singles: 7-inch

STARDAY 5-10 59

SULLIVAN, Tom

Singles: 7-inch

ABC 3-5 75-77
W.B. 3-5 78

SULLY, Peter

Singles: 7-inch

COTILLION 3-6 69

SULTANS

Singles: 78 rpm

JUBILEE (5054 "Lemon Squeezing Daddy") 50-75 51
JUBILEE (5077 "Don't Be Angry") 50-100 52

Singles: 7-inch

JUBILEE (5054 "Lemon Squeezing Daddy") 125-200 51
JUBILEE (5077 "Don't Be Angry") 200-300 52

SULTANS

Singles: 78 rpm

DUKE 25-75 54

Singles: 7-inch

DUKE (125 "Good Thing Baby") 75-100 54
DUKE (133 "I Cried My Heart Out") 75-100 54
DUKE (135 "What Makes Me Feel This Way") 50-100 54
DUKE (178 "If I Could Tell") 40-60 57

Members: Richard Beasley; Wesley Devereaux; Willie Barnes; Eugene McDaniels; James Farmer.
Also see ADMIRALS
Also see BARNES, Billy
Also see McDANIELS, Gene

SULTANS

Singles: 7-inch

DECADE (101 "I Always Will") 100-200
GUYDEN (2079 "Christina") 10-15 63
JAM (103 "Tossin' in My Sleep") 20-30 62
JAM (107 "Mary Mary") 20-30 63
JAM (113 "Poor Boy") 20-30 63
TILT (782 "It'll Be Easy") 50-100 61
(Yellow label.)
TILT (782 "It'll Be Easy") 30-50 61
(Black label.)

SULTANS

Singles: 7-inch

ASCOT 5-10 67

SULTANS

Singles: 7-inch

GLEN (0072 "Sultan's Groove") 10-15

SULTANS

Singles: 7-inch

COUNSEL 8-12

SULTANS, Les: LES SULTANS

SULTANS FIVE

Singles: 7-inch

ENTERPRISE THIRTEEN (1066 "You Know, You Know") 8-12 67
RAL (1754-03 "Tonight Is the Night") 10-20 64
RAL (7934 "Walk with Me") 10-20 64
RAYNARD (10052 "Tonight Is the Night") 10-20 65
RAYNARD (10053 "Daisy") 10-20 65

Picture Sleeves

RAYNARD (10053 "Daisy") 15-25 65

Members: Ray Plauske; Len Juliano; Ken Allen; Tim Michna; Vic Weinfurter Jr.; Tom Zager; Butch Kieffer.

SULTON, Kasim LP '82

Singles: 7-inch

EMI AMERICA 3-5 82

LPs: 10/12-inch

EMI AMERICA 5-10 82

SUM PEAR

LPs: 10/12-inch

EUPHORIA (1 "Sum Pear") 20-25 71

SUMAC, Yma

Singles: 7-inch

CAPITOL 8-15 51-56
CORAL (8058 "Presenting Yma Sumac") 40-50 54
(Boxed set of four discs.)

Picture Sleeves

CAPITOL (1819 "Birds") 20-35 51

EPs: 7-inch

CAPITOL (244 "Voice of the Xtabay") 50-75 52
(Double EP.)
CORAL (81050/51"Presenting Yma Sumac") 25-35 54
(Price is for either of two volumes.)
CAPITOL (1-299/2-299 "Legend of the Sun Virgin") 25-35 55
(Price is for either of two volumes.)
CAPITOL (FBF-299 "Legend of the Sun Virgin") 50-75 55
(Double EP.)
CAPITOL (FBF-423 "Inca Taqui") 50-75 53
(Double EP.)
CAPITOL (1-564/2-564 "Mambo") 25-35 54
(Price is for either of two volumes.)
CAPITOL (1-770/2-770/3-770 "The Legend of Jivaro") 10-20 56
(Price is for any of three volumes.)
CORAL (81050 "Presenting Yma Sumac") 35-45 54

LPs: 10/12-inch

CAPITOL (H-244 "Voice of the Xtabay") 50-75 52
(10-inch LP.)
CAPITOL (W-244 "Voice of the Xtabay") 35-45 55
CAPITOL (L-299 "Legend of the Sun Virgin") 50-75 52
(10-inch LP.)
CAPITOL (T-299 "Legend of the Sun Virgin") 35-45 55
CAPITOL (L-423 "Inca Taqui") 35-45 53
CAPITOL (H-564 "Mambo") 50-75 54
(10-inch LP.)
CAPITOL (T-564 "Mambo") 35-45 55
CAPITOL (T-770 "The Legend of Jivaro") 35-45 56
CAPITOL (T-1169 "Fuego Del Ande") 30-40 59
(Monaural.)
CAPITOL (T-1169 "Fuego Del Ande") 35-45 59
(Stereo.)
CAPITOL ("M" & "SM" series) 5-10 75-80
CORAL (56058 "Presenting Yma Sumac") 50-75 54
(10-inch LP.)
LONDON (608 "Miracles") 8-10 72

SUMMER, Donna P&R/LP '75

Singles: 12-inch

CASABLANCA 5-8 78-80
GEFFEN 4-8 80-87
MERCURY 4-8 83
OASIS 5-10 75-76

Singles: 7-inch

ATLANTIC 3-4 89
CASABLANCA 3-5 75-80
GEFFEN 3-4 80-87
MERCURY 3-4 83
OASIS 3-6 75-76

Picture Sleeves

ATLANTIC 3-4 89
GEFFEN 3-5 80-87
MERCURY 3-4 83
OASIS 3-6 76

LPs: 10/12-inch

ATLANTIC 5-8 89
CASABLANCA (Except NBPIX-7119 & 20110) 5-10 75-80
CASABLANCA (NBPIX-7119 "The Best of Live and More") 10-20 78
(Picture disc.)
CASABLANCA (20110 "Once Upon a Time") 12-15 77
(Promotional issue only.)
GEFFEN 5-10 80-87
MERCURY 5-10 83
OASIS 6-12 75-76

Also see BROOKLYN DREAMS
Also see MORODER, Giorgio
Also see STREISAND, Barbra, & Donna Summer

SUMMER, Henry Lee LP '88

Singles: 7-inch

CBS ASSOCIATED 3-4 88-89

Picture Sleeves

CBS ASSOCIATED 3-4 88

LPs: 10/12-inch

CBS ASSOCIATED 5-8 88-89

SUMMER, Johnny

Singles: 7-inch

JAB 3-5 67

SUMMER, Scott C&W '79

Singles: 7-inch

CON BRIO 3-5 79

SUMMER, FALL, WINTER, SPRING

Singles: 7-inch

U.A. 4-8 67

SUMMER SET

Singles: 7-inch

KEM 8-12 61

SUMMER SET

Singles: 7-inch

ROULETTE 10-15 67

SUMMER SNOW

Singles: 7-inch

CAPITOL (2031 "Flying on the Ground") 20-25 67

SUMMER WINDS

Singles: 7-inch

METROMEDIA 4-6 69

SUMMER WINE

Singles: 7-inch

DIRTY PIERRE (001 "Rock & Roll Man") 5-8
SIRE 3-5 73

SUMMER'S CHILDREN

Singles: 7-inch

APT 4-8 65
DATE 4-8 66

SUMMERHILL

Singles: 7-inch

TETRAGRAMMATON 3-6 69

LPs: 10/12-inch

TETRAGRAMMATON 10-12 69

SUMMERS, Andy, & Robert Fripp: see FRIPP, Robert, & Andy Summers

SUMMERS, Bill LP '81

(With Summers Heat)

Singles: 12-inch

MCA 4-6 81-84

Singles: 7-inch

MCA 3-5 81-84
PRESTIGE 3-5 77-80

LPs: 10/12-inch

MCA 5-10 81
PRESTIGE 5-10 77

Also see HANCOCK, Herbie

SUMMERS, Bob

(Sleepy Summers)

Singles: 7-inch

CAPITOL 6-12 59-60
CHALLENGE 5-8 62-65
CHEVRON (201 "Take the "A" Train") 8-12 62
CRUSADER 8-12 64
GOLD LEAF 10-15 61
LIBERTY 4-8 64
VOGUE INT'L 10-15

EPs: 7-inch

4 STAR 8-12

Member: Jerry Lefors.
Also see SIDEWALK SOUNDS

SUMMERS, Bobby

Singles: 7-inch

UNI 4-8 61

SUMMERS, Davey: see SUMMERS, Little Davey

SUMMERS, Diane, & Love Planet

Singles: 7-inch

ROULETTE 3-5 72

SUMMERS, Gene

(With the Tom Toms)

Singles: 78 rpm

JAN (100 "School of Rock 'N Roll") 200-300 58
(100 copies made for 78rpm juke boxs.)

Singles: 7-inch

ALTA 5-10
CAPRI (502 "Blue Diamond") 10-15
CAPRI (507 "Alabama Shake") 20-30
JAMIE 5-10 64
JAN (100 "School of Rock 'N Roll") 25-50 58
JAN (102 "Nervous") 20-30 58
JAN (106 "Twisteen") 25-35 58
JANE 15-25 58
MERCURY 4-8 66
TEARDROP (3405 "Goodbye Priscilla [Bye Bye Baby Blue]") 4-8 77

Promotional Singles

TEARDROP (3405 "Goodbye Priscilla [Bye Bye Blue Baby]") 8-12 77
(Single-sided disc. Label mistakenly shows subtitle as "Bye Bye Blue Baby.")

LPs: 10/12-inch

LAKE COUNTY 8-10 78

SUMMERS, John

Singles: 7-inch

CONGRESS 4-8 66

SUMMERS, Johnny

Singles: 7-inch

YORKTOWN (1007 "Prove It to Me") 200-400

SUMMERS, Little Davey

(With the Singing Ants; Russ Regan)

Singles: 7-inch

DORE 5-10 63
VIM 5-10 63
ZEN 5-10 62

Also see DANCER, PRANCER & NERVOUS
Also see REGAN, Russ

SUMMERS, Ronnie

Singles: 7-inch

BAMBOO 5-10 61
LOCKET 4-8 61
R.R.E. 4-8 63
RADIO (124 "Salt and Pepper") 15-25 59

SUMMERS, Sandi

Singles: 7-inch

CHARM 5-10 59

SUMMERS, Sleepy: see SUMMERS, Bob

SUMMERS, Steve

Singles: 7-inch

LEONE 5-10 60

SUMMERS, Susan

Singles: 7-inch

DIAMOND 4-8 61-62

SUMMER'S CHILDREN

Singles: 7-inch

DATE (158 "Milk & Honey") 8-12 66

SUMMERTIME TRIO

Singles: 7-inch

CUCA (6882 "Summertime") 8-12 68

SUMMIT, Clark

Singles: 7-inch

MAY (104 "Why Not") 10-20 61

SUMMITS

Singles: 7-inch

DC INTERNATIONAL 4-6
DECCA 5-10 61
HARMON 15-25 63
LA SALLE 10-20
RUST 8-12 63
TIMES SQUARE 10-20 61

SUMMITS

Singles: 7-inch

RAMPART (651 "Hey Joe") 10-20 66

SUMNER, J.D., & Stamps Quartet

Singles: 7-inch

HEART WARMING 3-4 72
QCA (461 "Elvis Has Left the Building") 3-5 77

Picture Sleeves

QCA (461 "Elvis Has Left the Building") 5-10 77

LPs: 10/12-inch

BLUE MARK (373 "Memories of Our Friend Elvis") 10-20 78
HEART WARMING 4-8 71-74
QCA (362 "Elvis' Favorite Gospel Songs") 8-10 77

Members: J.D. Sumner; Ed Enoch; Donnie Sumner; Richard Sturbin; Bill Baise; Kenny Parker; Nick Bruno; Phil Johnson.
Also see BAIZE, Bill
Also see FOWLER, Wally
Also see OAK RIDGE BOYS
Also see PRESLEY, Elvis

SUMPIN' ELSE

Singles: 7-inch

LIBERTY 10-15 66

SUN P&R '76

Singles: 7-inch

AIR CITY 3-4 84
CAPITOL 3-5 76-82

Picture Sleeves

CAPITOL 3-5 76-82

LPs: 10/12-inch

CAPITOL 5-10 77-82

Members: Nikki Buzz; Randy Fredrix; Clyde Isom; Tim Hollans.

SUN, Jimmy, & Radiants

Singles: 7-inch

CUCA (1046 "Cocaine Blues") 10-20 61
CUCA (6636 "Rockpile") 10-20 66

Member: Jimmy Sundquist; Don Phillips; Tom Gress; John Christanovich; Dave Vasser; Shorty DeLongchamp; Johnny Zolinski; Ray Peters; Cliff Johnson; Bob Edmondson.
Also see FENDERMEN

SUN, Joe C&W '78

Singles: 7-inch

A.M.I. 3-4 84-85
ELEKTRA 3-4 82-83
OVATION 3-5 78-80

LPs: 10/12-inch

ELEKTRA 5-8 82-83
OVATION 5-10 78-80

Also see ANDREWS, Sheila, & Joe Sun

SUN, Joe, & Shotgun C&W '82

Singles: 7-inch

ELEKTRA 3-4 82

Also see SHOTGUN
Also see SUN, Joe

SUN CHILD

Singles: 7-inch

MCA 3-5 74

LPs: 10/12-inch

MCA 8-10 74

SUN DOG

Singles: 7-inch

MUSICOR 4-6 72

Also see HAPPENINGS

SUN DRAGON

Singles: 7-inch

MUSIC FACTORY 4-8 68

SUN FERRY AID

Singles: 12-inch

PROFILE 10-15 87
(Commercial issues.)
PROFILE 30-40 87
(Promotional issues.)

Singles: 7-inch

PROFILE (5147 "Let It Be") 4-8 87

Picture Sleeves

PROFILE (5147 "Let It Be") 4-8 87

Also see BOY GEORGE
Also see BUSH, Kate
Also see KNOPFLER, Mark
Also see McCARTNEY, Paul

SUN LIGHTNING INCORPORATED

Singles: 7-inch

WHAP (319 "Quasar 45") 10-15 69

Member: Philip R. Armstrong.

SUNBEAMS

Singles: 78 rpm

HERALD (451 "Tell Me Why") 50-100 55

Singles: 7-inch

ACME (719 "Please Say You'll Be Mine") 150-250 57
COLLECTABLES 3-4 80s
HERALD (451 "Tell Me Why") 150-250 55

SUNBEAR

Singles: 7-inch

SOUL TRAIN 3-5 77

LPs: 10/12-inch

SOUL TRAIN 5-10 77

SUNBLIND LION

Singles: 7-inch

HOMEGROWN 4-6 70s
SUNBLIND 4-6 70s

LPs: 10/12-inch

HOMEGROWN 8-10 76-80

Also see LOVE SOCIETY

SUNDAE FLAVOR

Singles: 7-inch

CRAZY HORSE 4-6 69

SUNDAE SERVANTS

Singles: 7-inch

DAD'S 15-25 66

SUNDAE TRAIN

Singles: 7-inch

B.T. PUPPY 4-8 68
20TH FOX 4-8 67

SUNDANCE

Singles: 7-inch

KAPP 3-5 71
MERCURY 3-5 71

LPs: 10/12-inch

KAPP 8-12 71

SUNDANCE

Singles: 7-inch

20TH FOX 3-5 75

LPs: 10/12-inch

20TH FOX 8-10 75

Members: Tom Hyman; Steve Welkom.

SUNDANCE
(Featuring Kevin Stevenson)
Singles: 7-inch
FATIMA ... 3-4 87

SUNDANCERS
Singles: 7-inch
BREAK OUT (111 "Devil Surf") ... 25-35 60s

SUNDAY
Singles: 7-inch
CHESS ... 3-5 69

SUNDAY, Vicki
Singles: 7-inch
TCF ... 4-8 64

SUNDAY, Whitney: see WHITNEY SUNDAY

SUNDAY & MENN
Singles: 7-inch
SIDEWALK (922 "You Cheated") ... 10-15 67

SUNDAY DRIVE
Singles: 7-inch
AMG (543 "I Ride") ... 3-6

SUNDAY FUNNIES
Singles: 7-inch
CAPITOL ... 5-10 66
HIDEOUT ... 15-25 60s
MERCURY ... 5-10 66
RARE EARTH ... 4-8 71-72
VALHALLA (671 "A Pindaric Ode") ... 20-30 67
LPs: 10/12-inch
RARE EARTH ... 8-10 71-72
Members: Richard Fidge; Ron Aitken; Richard Mitchell; Richard Kosinski.

SUNDAY GROUP
Singles: 7-inch
DOWNEY ... 10-20 65

SUNDAY PEOPLE
Singles: 7-inch
JAMIE ... 4-8 72

SUNDAY SERVANTS
Singles: 7-inch
WORLD PACIFIC ... 10-20 66

SUNDAY SHARPE: see SHARPE, Sunday

SUNDAYS LP '90
LPs: 10/12-inch
DGC ... 5-8 90

SUNDAY'S CHILD
Singles: 7-inch
REPRISE ... 3-5 70
LPs: 10/12-inch
REPRISE ... 10-12 70

SUNDHOLM, Roy
LPs: 10/12-inch
ENSIGN ... 5-10 79

SUNDIALS
Singles: 7-inch
GUYDEN (2065 "Chapel of Love") ... 150-200 62

SUNDOG
Singles: 7-inch
AMERICAN (1591 "Eat at Home") ... 4-8 70
AMERICAN (5054 "Going Back to California") ... 4-8 70s

SUNDOWN
Singles: 7-inch
UA ... 4-8
Also see VELAIRES

SUNDOWN, Lonesome: see LONESOME SUNDOWN

SUNDOWN COMPANY P&R '76
Singles: 7-inch
POLYDOR ... 3-5 76

SUNDOWN PLAYBOYS
Singles: 7-inch
APPLE (1852 "Saturday Night Special") ... 10-20 72

SUNDOWNERS
Singles: 7-inch
CIRCLE C (711 "Rockin' Spot") ... 30-50 59
Member: Curley Coldiron.

SUNDOWNERS
Singles: 7-inch
WINK (1009 "Rumble") ... 10-20 61

SUNDOWNERS
Singles: 7-inch
FARGO (1051 "Someone to Care") ... 50-100 63
Session: Del Satins.
Also see DEL SATINS

SUNDOWNERS
Singles: 7-inch
COED (603 "Leave Me Never") ... 8-12 65
JAMIE (1271 "Come On In") ... 15-25 64

SUNDOWNERS
Singles: 7-inch
DECCA ... 4-8 67-69
LPs: 10/12-inch
DECCA ... 10-15 68

SUNDOWNERS
Singles: 7-inch
TRC ... 10-15 60s

SUNDOWNERS
Singles: 7-inch
SOUND ... 3-5 73

SUNFIRE
Singles: 12-inch
W.B. ... 4-6 82
Singles: 7-inch
W.B. ... 3-5 82
LPs: 10/12-inch
W.B. ... 5-10 82

SUNGLOWS P&R/LP '63
(Sunny & Sunglows; Sunny & Sunliners; Sunny Ozuna & Sunliners)
Singles: 7-inch
BLACK WHALE ... 5-10
DISCO GRANDE (1021 "Peanuts") ... 15-20 65
KEY LOC ... 4-8 66
LONDON ... 5-10
OKEH ... 5-10 61
RPR ... 4-6 69
SUNGLOW ... 6-12 62-66
TEAR DROP ... 4-8 63-64
LPs: 10/12-inch
KEY LOC ... 10-20 66
SIESTA (101 "Original Peanuts") ... 20-30 65
SUNGLOW (103 "Peanuts") ... 25-35 65
TEAR DROP (2000 "Talk to Me") ... 30-50 63
Also see LOS STARDUSTERS

SUNKEL, Bill
Singles: 7-inch
LAURIE ... 3-4 90

SUNLIGHT'S SEVEN
Singles: 7-inch
ENTRA ... 4-8 69
WINDI ... 4-8 60s
Member: G.C. Prophet.
Also see CREATION of SUNLIGHT

SUNLINERS
Singles: 7-inch
GOLDEN WORLD (31 "All Alone") 15-25 66
HERCULES (182 "Sweet Little Girl") ... 25-50 60s
HERCULES (183 "Hit It") ... 25-50 60s
HERCULES (184 "So in Love") ... 50-100 60s
MGM (13809 "Land of Nod") ... 10-20 67
Also see RARE EARTH

SUNNY & PHYLLIS: see SONNY & PHYLLIS

SUNNY & HIS GANG
Singles: 7-inch
PORT (70003 "Babette") ... 5-10 58

SUNNY & HORIZONS
Singles: 7-inch
LUXOR (1016 "Nature's Creation") ... 100-150 62
(Yellow label.)
LUXOR (1016 "Nature's Creation") ... 50-100 62
(Red label.)

SUNNY & SUNGLOWS or SUNLINERS: see SUNGLOWS

SUNNY & HIS GANG
Singles: 7-inch
PORT (70003 "I'm a Rollin' ") ... 10-15 58
Member: Sunny Skylar.

SUNNY BOYS
Singles: 7-inch
MR. MAESTRO (805 "For the Rest of My Life") ... 20-30 59
MR. MAESTRO (806 "Chapel Bells") ... 35-50 59
TAKE 3 (2001 "Chapel Bells") ... 40-60 59
(First issue.)

SUNNY DAZE
Singles: 7-inch
METROMEDIA ... 4-6 69

SUNNY FOUR
Singles: 7-inch
EPIC ... 4-6 69

SUNNY FUNNY CO.
Singles: 7-inch
STANAL (712 "Alone") ... 30-50 60s

SUNNY LADS
Singles: 7-inch
JAX (103 "That's My Desire") ... 20-30 59

SUNNY MONDAY
Singles: 7-inch
DECCA ... 4-8 69

SUNNYLAND SLIM
(With His Playboys; with His Sunny Boys; with His Sunnyland Boys; with Lefty Bates Combo; Albert Luandrew)
Singles: 78 rpm
APOLLO ... 20-30 50
BLUE LAKE ... 50-75 54
CLUB 51 (C-106 "Be Mine Alone") ... 25-50 55
COBRA (5006 "It's You, Baby") ... 20-30 56
HYTONE ... 20-30 49
MERCURY ... 20-30 49-51
REGAL ... 15-25 51
SUNNY (101 "Back to Korea Blues") ... 50-75 50
TEMPO TONE (1001 "Blue Baby") ... 75-100 48
J.O.B. ... 25-50 50-54
Singles: 7-inch
AIRWAY (4743 "See My Lawyer") 15-25
BLUE LAKE (105 "Going Back to Memphis") ... 100-200 54
(Black vinyl.)
BLUE LAKE (105 "Going Back to Memphis") ... 300-400 54
(Red vinyl.)
BLUE LAKE (107 "Shake It Baby") ... 100-200 54
(Black vinyl.)
BLUE LAKE (107 "Shake It Baby") ... 300-400 54
(Red vinyl.)
CLUB 51 (C-106 "Be Mine Alone") ... 75-125 55
COBRA (5006 "It's You, Baby") ... 75-125 56
J.O.B. (1101 "Woman Trouble") ... 75-125 54
J.O.B. (1105 "Shake It, Baby") ... 75-125 54
J.O.B. (1108 "That Woman") ... 75-125 55
MISS (117 "Worried About My Baby") ... 15-20 61
PRESTIGE BLUESVILLE (811 "Baby, How Long") ... 10-20 60
LPs: 10/12-inch
BLUE HORIZON ... 10-15
BLUESWAY ... 8-12 73
JEWEL ... 8-10 73
PRESTIGE ... 5-10 69
PRESTIGE BLUESVILLE ... 25-45 61
WORLD PACIFIC ... 20-30 69
Session: King Curtis.
Also see BABY FACE
Also see BRIM, John
Also see DELTA JOE
Also see DOCTOR CLAYTON'S BUDDY
Also see HORTON, Walter
Also see KING CURTIS
Also see LENOIR, J.B.
Also see LITTLE WALTER
Also see MONTGOMERY, Little Brother
Also see PRYOR, Snooky
Also see ROGERS, Jimmy
Also see TAYLOR, Eddie

SUNNYLAND SLIM & MUDDY WATERS
Singles: 78 rpm
ARISTOCRAT ... 25-50 47-48
TEMPO TONE (1002 "Blue Baby") ... 50-75 48
Also see WATERS, Muddy

SUNNYLAND TRIO
Singles: 78 rpm
J.O.B. ... 25-50 52
Members: Sunnyland Slim; Billy Howell; Robert Lockwood Jr.
Also see BABY FACE
Also see LOCKWOOD, Robert, Jr.
Also see SUNNYLAND SLIM

SUNNYSIDERS P&R '55
Singles: 78 rpm
KAPP ... 4-6 55-57
MARQUEE ... 4-6 55-56
Singles: 7-inch
KAPP ... 5-10 55-60
MARQUEE ... 5-10 55-56
NRC ... 4-8 60
ZENITH ... 4-8 60
EPs: 7-inch
KAPP ... 5-10 56
LPs: 10/12-inch
KAPP ... 10-20 56

SUNRAYS
Singles: 7-inch
SUN (293 "Lonely Hours") ... 25-35 58

SUNRAYS P&R '65
Singles: 7-inch
CAPITOL (72275 "I Live for the Sun") ... 15-25 65
(Canadian.)
TOWER (101 "Car Party") ... 8-12 64
TOWER (148 "I Live for the Sun") ... 8-12 65
TOWER (191 "Andrea") ... 8-12 66
TOWER (224 "Still") ... 8-12 66
TOWER (256 "Don't Take Yourself Too Seriously") ... 8-12 67
TOWER (290 "Hi, How Are You") ... 8-12 66
TOWER (340 "Loaded with Love ") . 8-12 67
W.B. (5253 "Talk to Him") ... 10-20 62
Picture Sleeves
TOWER (340 "Loaded with Love"). 15-25 67
LPs: 10/12-inch
TOWER (5017 "Andrea") ... 50-100 66
Members: Rick Henn; Bryon Case; Vince Hozier; Ed Medora; Marty DiGiovanni.
Also see ALLAN, Davie / Eternity's Children / Main Attraction / Sunrays
Also see HENN, Rick

SUNRAYS
Singles: 7-inch
(1162 "Rock & Roll Fever") ... 4-8 60s
(No label name used.)

SUNRISE
Singles: 7-inch
ZOROKOTHORA ... 4-8 70s
Also see SPENCER, Jim, & Son Rize

SUNRISE
LPs: 10/12-inch
CRUNCH ... 8-10 74
Also see CREACH, Papa John

SUNRISE HIGHWAY
Singles: 7-inch
DECCA ... 4-8 68

SUNRISERS
Singles: 7-inch
PATTY (101 "I Saw Her Yesterday") ... 15-25 66

SUNRIZE
Singles: 7-inch
BOARDWALK ... 3-4 82

SUNS: see CAMELOTS / Suns

SUNSET BLUES BAND
LPs: 10/12-inch
SUNSET ... 8-10 69
Also see CRAYTON, Pee Wee

SUNSET BOMBERS
Singles: 7-inch
ZOMBIE ... 3-5 78
Picture Sleeves
ZOMBIE ... 3-5 78
Member: Doug Fieger.
Also see KNACK

SUNSET SURF
LPs: 10/12-inch
CAPITOL ... 10-20 63

SUNSETS
(With the Eddie Wilcox Orchestra)
Singles: 7-inch
RAE COX (102 "How Will I Remember") ... 25-50 59
Also see WILCOX, Eddie, Orchestra

SUNSETS
Singles: 7-inch
CHALLENGE (9198 "Lonely Surfer Boy") ... 15-25 63
CHALLENGE (9208 "My Little Beach Bunny") ... 15-25 63
PETAL (1040 "Lydia") ... 50-100 63
LPs: 10/12-inch
PALACE ... 30-35 63
Members: Gary Usher; Richard Burns.

SUN-SETS
Singles: 7-inch
MOONGLOW ... 4-8 64

SUNSHINE
Singles: 7-inch
BUMPSHOP ("Sunshine") ... 25-35
CAPITOL ... 3-5 71
KIRSHNER ... 3-5 74
LPs: 10/12-inch
BACK BEAT ... 10-12 70

SUNSHINE BAND: see KC & Sunshine Band

SUNSHINE BOYS
Singles: 7-inch
SCOTTIE ... 5-10 59

SUNSHINE COMPANY P&R/LP '67
Singles: 7-inch
IMPERIAL ... 4-8 67-68
LPs: 10/12-inch
IMPERIAL ... 10-20 67-68
Members: Doug "Red" Mark; Maury Manseau; Larry Sims; Merle Bregante; Mary Nance.
Also see REDEYE

SUNSHINE RUBY C&W '53
Singles: 78 rpm
RCA ... 4-8 53
Singles: 7-inch
RCA ... 5-10 53
Session: Sonny James.
Also see JAMES, Sonny

SUNSHINE WARD
Singles: 7-inch
RCA ... 4-8 67

SUNSHIP
LPs: 10/12-inch
CAPITOL ... 8-10 74

SUNSHYNE
Singles: 7-inch
PN ... 4-8

SUNSTONE LOLLIPOP
Singles: 7-inch
KEL (8515 "People of Today") ... 10-20 68
KEL (8516 "Never Sad") ... 10-20 68
KEL (8518 "Mr. Keat") ... 10-20 68
Picture Sleeves
KEL ... 15-25 68
Members: Keith Diciani; David Diciani; Tom Hansen.

SUPA, Richard
Singles: 7-inch
ARISTA ... 3-5 75
EPIC ... 3-5 76
PARAMOUNT ... 3-5 72-73
POLYDOR/SILVER CLOUD ... 3-5 78-79
LPs: 10/12-inch
PARAMOUNT ... 8-10 72
Also see BELLINE, Danny
Also see MAN

SUPER CIRKUS
Singles: 7-inch
SUPER K ... 4-6 69

SUPER K GENERATION
Singles: 7-inch
LAURIE ... 4-8 67

SUPER GRIT COWBOY BAND C&W '81
Singles: 7-inch
HOODSWAMP ... 3-4 81-83
LPs: 10/12-inch
HOODSWAMP ... 5-10 81-83
Members: Curtis Wright; Bill Ellis.
Also see WRIGHT, Curtis

SUPER LOVER CEE & Casanova Rud
LPs: 10/12-inch
ELEKTRA ... 5-8 88

SUPER MAX
Singles: 7-inch
VOYAGE ... 3-5 79

SUPER NATURE D&D '85
Singles: 12-inch
POP ART ... 4-6 85

SUPER SONICS: see SUPER-SONICS

SUPER STOCKS
Singles: 7-inch
CAPITOL ... 5-10 64-68
LPs: 10/12-inch
CAPITOL (T-2060 "Thunder Road") ... 40-60 64
(Monaural.)
CAPITOL (ST-2060 "Thunder Road") ... 50-75 64
(Stereo.)
CAPITOL (T-2113 "Surf Route 101") ... 50-100 64
(Monaural.)
(Includes bonus single by Mr. Gasser & Weirdos. Deduct $5-$10 if this 45 is missing.)
CAPITOL (ST-2113 "Surf Route 101") ... 100-150 64
(Stereo.)
(Includes bonus single by Mr. Gasser & Weirdos. Deduct $5-$10 if this 45 is missing.)
CAPITOL (T-2113 "School Is a Drag") ... 40-60 64
(Monaural.)
CAPITOL (ST-2113 "School Is a Drag") ... 50-75 64
(Stereo.)
Members: Gary Usher; Jerry Cole.
Also see COLE, Jerry
Also see DALE, Dick / Jerry Cole / Super Stocks / Mr. Gasser & Weirdos
Also see GHOULS
Also see MR. GASSER & WEIRDOS
Also see USHER, Gary

SUPER STOCKS / Hot Rod Rog (Roger Christian) / (Steve) Shutdown Douglas
LPs: 10/12-inch
CAPITOL (T-1997 "Hot Rod Magazine Rally") ... 25-35 63
(Monaural. Special *Hot Rod Magazine* edition)
CAPITOL (T-1997 "Hot Rod Rally") 15-25 63
(Monaural.)
CAPITOL (ST-1997 "Hot Rod Rally") ... 20-30 63
(Stereo.)
Also see CHRISTIAN, Roger
Also see DOUGLAS, Steve
Also see SUPER STOCKS

SUPER STU
(With Dennis Allen & the Disco Turkeys)
Singles: 7-inch
BROWN DOG (9016 "The Great Debate") ... 5-10 76

SUPERBS P&R '64
Singles: 7-inch
ALTEEN (3004 "You Don't Care") .. 10-20
COLLECTABLES ... 3-4 80s
DT (107 "In and Out of Love") ... 10-20 60s
DORE ... 15-30 64-67
HERITAGE (103 "Rainbow of Love") ... 25-35 61

SUPERBS
Singles: 7-inch
SYMBOL 8 ... 3-6 69

SUPERCHARGE
Singles: 7-inch
VIRGIN ... 3-5 77
LPs: 10/12-inch
VIRGIN ... 5-10 77

SUPERFINE DANDELION
Singles: 7-inch
MAINSTREAM ... 5-10 67
LPs: 10/12-inch
MAINSTREAM (6102 "Superfine Dandelion") ... 15-25 67
Members: Mike McFadden; Mike Collins; Ed Black; Rick Anderson.
Also see GOOSE CREEK SYMPHONY

SUPERIOR ANGELS
Singles: 7-inch
SKYLARK (0023 "Crying in the Chapel") ... 15-25 64

SUPERIOR MOVEMENT
Singles: 7-inch
CHYCAGO INT'L ... 3-5 81-82
LPs: 10/12-inch
CHYCAGO INT'L ... 5-10 82

SUPERIORS
Singles: 78 rpm
ATCO (6106 "Lost Love") ... 25-50 57
Singles: 7-inch
ATCO (6106 "Lost Love") ... 50-100 57
MAIN LINE (104 "Lost Love") .. 500-1000 58
(Shows "1510 Fairmount Ave., Philadelphia, Pa" address on label.)
MAIN LINE (104 "Lost Love") ... 25-50 62
(Has only "Philadelphia, Pennsylvania" address on label.)
REAL FINE (837 "Eternal Dream") ... 200-300 61

SUPERIORS
(With the Modernistics)
Singles: 7-inch
FAL (301 "What Is Love") 50-100 61

SUPERIORS
Singles: 7-inch
FEDERAL (12436 "Dance of Love") 20-40 61

SUPERIORS
Singles: 7-inch
MGM 5-10 66
SUE 4-8 69
VERVE 10-20 65

SUPERLATIVES
Singles: 7-inch
DYNAMICS (1011 "Do What You Want to Do") 20-30
DYNAMICS (1012 "Won't You Please") 20-30
DYNAMICS (1016 "Lonely in a Crowd") 20-30
DYNAMICS (1017 "Don't Let True Love Die") 20-30
UPTITE 4-8 66
WALLY 5-10
WESTBOUND 4-6 69

SUPERLOVE
LPs: 10/12-inch
COSMOSTAR 5-10 78

SUPERMAN
LPs: 10/12-inch
REGGAE 8-10 70

SUPERMAX
Singles: 7-inch
ELEKTRA 3-5 79
LPs: 10/12-inch
ELEKTRA 5-10 79
VOYAGE/PARADISE 5-10 78

SUPER-PHONICS
Singles: 7-inch
LINDY (102 "Teenage Partner") 15-25 61
Members: Ronnie Hanson; Pete Larkin; George Eberdt; Al Banasik; Gary Wolfe.
Also see KENNEDY, Dave / Super-Phonics
Also see VINCENT, Gene / Super-Phonics

SUPERSAX *LP '73*
LPs: 10/12-inch
CAPITOL 5-10 73-74
MFSL (511 "Play Bird") 20-30 80s

SUPERSISTER
LPs: 10/12-inch
DWARF 20-25

SUPERSNAZZ / American Soul Spiders / Jackie & Cedrics / Beyonds
EPs: 7-inch
ESTRUS (727 "Tales from Estrus, Vol. II") 5-8 92
(Cover doubles as eight-page comic.)

SUPER-SONICS *P&R '53*
(With Third Dimension Sound)
Singles: 78 rpm
RAINBOW 10-20 53
Singles: 7-inch
RAINBOW (214 "New Guitar Boogie Shuffle") 10-25 53
(Black vinyl.)
RAINBOW (214 "New Guitar Boogie Shuffle") 25-35 53
(Colored vinyl.)
RAINBOW (214 "Guitar Boogie Shuffle") 15-25 55
(Note title change.)
RAINBOW (217 "Tabu") 15-25 55
RAINBOW (222 "New Cherokee Boogie") 15-25 55

SUPERTONES
Singles: 7-inch
EVEREST 10-15 60
Member: Billy Mure.
Also see MURE, Billy

SUPERTRAMP *LP '74*
Singles: 12-inch
A&M 4-6 82-85
Singles: 7-inch
A&M 3-5 71-85
Picture Sleeves
A&M 3-5 77-85
LPs: 10/12-inch
A&M (Except 3730 & 17236) 8-12 70-87
A&M (3730 "Breakfast in America") 400-600 79
(Picture disc. Promotional issue only.)
A&M (17236 "Supersampler") 10-15 83
(Promotional issue only.)
MFSL (005 "Crime of the Century") 50-70 78
MFSL/UHQR (005 "Crime of the Century") 75-125 78
(Boxed set.)
MFSL (045 "Breakfast in America") 40-60 80
Members: Rick Davies; Roger Hodgson; Doug Thomson; Bob Benberg; John Helliwell.
Also see HODGSON, Roger

SUPREMES
Singles: 78 rpm
OLD TOWN (1024 "Tonight"/"She Don't Want Me No More") 40-80 56
OLD TOWN (1024 "Tonight"/"My Babe") 30-50 56
(Note different flip.)
Singles: 7-inch
OLD TOWN (1024 "Tonight"/"She Don't Want Me No More") 100-150 56
OLD TOWN (1024 "Tonight"/"My Babe") 75-100 56
(Note different flip.)

SUPREMES
Singles: 78 rpm
KITTEN 100-150 56
Singles: 7-inch
KITTEN (6969 "Could This Be You") 300-400 56
Members: Ralph Murphy; Jace Murphy; Archie Moore; Bill Perry; Calude Brown; Lee Murphy; John Brown.

SUPREMES
(Featuring Huey Smith)
Singles: 78 rpm
ACE (534 "Just for You and I") 20-30 57
Singles: 7-inch
ACE (534 "Just for You and I") 50-75 57
Members: Forrest Porter; Jay Robinson; Ed Jackson; Bob Isbell; Ed Dumas; Eddie Jackson.
Also see FOUR PHAROAHS
Also see SMITH, Huey

SUPREMES
Singles: 7-inch
MARK (129 "Nobody Can Love You") 500-750 58

SUPREMES
Singles: 7-inch
MASCOT (126 "Little Sally Walker") 50-75 60

SUPREMES
Singles: 7-inch
APT (25055 "Another Chance to Love") 25-35 60

SUPREMES
(Supremes 4)
Singles: 7-inch
SARA (1032 "I Love You, Patricia") 1200-2000 61
(Credits "Supremes")
SARA (1032 "I Love You, Patricia") 1000-1800 61
(Credits "Supremes 4")
Members: Lovelace Redmond; Homer Walton; Carl Campbell; Phillips Green.

SUPREMES *P&R '62*
(Diana Ross & Supremes)
Singles: 12-inch
MOTOWN 8-10 79-81
Singles: 7-inch
AMERICAN INT'L PICTURES ("Dr. Goldfoot and the Bikini Machine") 30-40 66
(Single-sided disc, used to promote the film of the same name.)
GEORGE ALEXANDER INC. (1079 "The Only Time I'm Happy") 30-40 65
(Special premium record. Has a Supremes interview on the flip.)
COLGEMS ("Snatches from the Soundtrack: *The Happening*") 50-100 67
(No selection number used. Promotional issue only.)
EEOC ("Things Are Changing") 50-100 65
(Equal Employment Opportunity Center promotional issue.)
MOTOWN (400 series) 3-4
MOTOWN (1008 "I Want a Guy") 500-1000 61
MOTOWN (1027 "Your Heart Belongs to Me") 15-25 62
MOTOWN (1034 "Let Me Go the Right Way") 35-50 62
MOTOWN (1040 "My Heart Can't Take It No More") 25-45 63
MOTOWN (1044 "A Breath Taking, First Sight Soul Shaking, One Night Love Making, Next Day Heart Breaking Guy") 50-75 63
(Promotional issue only.)
MOTOWN (1044 "A Breath Taking Guy") 15-25 63
(Reissue, with much shorter title.)
MOTOWN (1051 "When the Lovelight Starts Shining Through His Eyes") 10-15 63
MOTOWN (1054 "Run Run Run") 15-25 64
MOTOWN (1060 thru 1080) 10-15 64-65
MOTOWN (1083 "I Hear a Symphony") 5-10 65
(Black vinyl.)
MOTOWN (1083 "I Hear a Symphony") 20-30 65
(Colored vinyl. Promotional issue only.)
MOTOWN (1085 "Children's Christmas Song") 15-25 65
(Colored vinyl. Promotional issue only.)
MOTOWN (1089 thru 1156) 5-10 66-69
MOTOWN (1488 "Medley of Hits") 3-5 80
MOTOWN (1523 "Medley of Hits") 3-5 81
MOTOWN/TOPPS (1 "Baby Love") 50-75 67
MOTOWN/TOPPS (2 "Stop in the Name of Love") 50-75 67
MOTOWN/TOPPS (3 "Where Did Our Love Go") 50-75 67
MOTOWN/TOPPS (15 "Come See About Me") 50-75 67
MOTOWN/TOPPS (16 "My World Is Empty Without You") 50-75 67
(Motown 1 through 16 are Topps Chewing Gum promotional, single-sided, cardboard, flexi, picture discs. Issued with generic sleeves.)
TAMLA (54038 "I Want a Guy") 75-125 61
TAMLA (54045 "Buttered Popcorn") 50-100 61
Picture Sleeves
EEOC ("Things Are Changing") 50-100 65
(Equal Employment Opportunity Center promotional issue.)
MOTOWN (1027 "Your Heart Belongs to Me") 50-100 62
MOTOWN (1060 "Where Did Our Love Go") 20-40 64
MOTOWN (1066 "Baby Love") 20-40 64
MOTOWN (1074 "Stop in the Name of Love") 20-40 64
MOTOWN (1075 "Back in My Arms Again") 20-40 65
MOTOWN (1080 "Nothing But Heartaches") 20-40 65
MOTOWN (1085 "Children's Christmas Song") 20-40 65
MOTOWN (1097 "You Can't Hurry Love") 15-25 66
MOTOWN (1101 "You Keep Me Hanging On") 15-25 66
EPs: 7-inch
MOTOWN (60621 "Where Did Our Love Go") 25-50 64
MOTOWN (60623 "A Little Bit of Liverpool") 25-50 64
MOTOWN (60627 "More Hits") 25-50 65
MOTOWN (60649 "A Go Go") 20-40 66
LPs: 10/12-inch
MOTOWN (100 & 200 series) 5-10 80-82
MOTOWN (606 "Meet the Supremes") 500-750 63
(Front cover pictures each member sitting on a chair.)
MOTOWN (606 "Meet the Supremes") 50-75 63
(Front cover pictures the head of each group member.)
MOTOWN (621 "Where Did Our Love Go") 20-40 64
MOTOWN (623 "A Little Bit of Liverpool") 20-30 64
MOTOWN (625 "Country Western and Pop") 20-30 65
MOTOWN (627 "More Hits") 15-25 65
MOTOWN (629 "We Remember Sam Cooke") 20-30 65
MOTOWN (636 "At the Copa") 20-30 65
MOTOWN (638 "Merry Christmas") 25-35 65
MOTOWN (643 thru 708) 15-25 66-70
MOTOWN (737 "Touch") 10-20 70s
MOTOWN (794 "Anthology") 15-20 74
(Three-disc set. Includes 12-page booklet.)
MOTOWN (900 series) 5-10 75
MOTOWN (5000 series, except 5381) 5-12 83-84
MOTOWN (5381 "25th Anniversary") 15-20 86
(Three-LP set. Includes 12-page booklet.)
NATURAL RESOURCES 5-10 78
Members: Diana Ross; Mary Wilson; Florence Ballard; Cindy Birdsong.
Also see BALLARD, Florence
Also see DIAMOND, Neil / Diana Ross & Supremes
Also see HORTON, Willie
Also see McKENZIE, Don
Also see PRIMETTES
Also see ROSS, Diana
Also see SCHUMACHER, Christine, & Supremes
Also see WILSON, Mary

SUPREMES & FOUR TOPS *P&R '70*
Singles: 7-inch
MOTOWN (400 series) 3-4
MOTOWN (1100 series) 4-8 70-71
EPs: 7-inch
MOTOWN (717 "Magnificent Seven") 5-15 70
(Juke box issue.)
LPs: 10/12-inch
MOTOWN (100 series) 5-10 82
MOTOWN (700 series) 10-15 70-71
Also see FOUR TOPS

SUPREMES & TEMPTATIONS *P&R/LP '68*
Singles: 7-inch
MOTOWN (400 series) 3-4
MOTOWN (1100 series) 4-8 68-69
Picture Sleeves
MOTOWN (1137 "I'm Gonna Make You Love Me") 10-20 68
LPs: 10/12-inch
MOTOWN (100 series) 5-10 82
MOTOWN (600 series) 10-15 68-69
Also see SUPREMES
Also see TEMPTATIONS

SUPREMES *P&R/LP '70*
Singles: 7-inch
MOTOWN (400 series) 3-4
MOTOWN (1162 thru 1415) 4-8 70-77
(Black vinyl.)
MOTOWN (1172 "Stoned Love") 10-15 70
(Colored vinyl. Promotional issue only.)
LPs: 10/12-inch
MOTOWN (102 "Touch") 15-20 71
(Open-end interview LP. Price includes script. Promotional issue only.)
MOTOWN (702 thru 904) 6-12 70-78
Members: Jean Terrell; Mary Wilson; Cindy Birdsong.
Also see PAYNE, Scherrie
Also see TERRELL, Jean

SUPREMES 4: see SUPREMES

SUR ROYAL DA COUNT & PARLIAMENTS
Singles: 7-inch
VILLA YORE (606 "Sgt. Ralph Yore, U.S.M.C.") 15-25 66

SURE CURE
Singles: 7-inch
PARKWAY 5-8 67

SURF, Adam, & Pebble Beach Band
Singles: 7-inch
PALADIN (3 "Fun, Fun, Fun") 10-20 64

SURF, Sammy
Singles: 7-inch
NU SOUND (1023 "Love That First Step") 5-10 62

SURF BOYS
Singles: 7-inch
KARATE 5-10 66
SCEPTER 10-20 66

SURF BREAKERS
Singles: 7-inch
MERCURY 10-20 63

SURF BUNNIES
Singles: 7-inch
DOT (16523 "Our Surfer Boys") 10-15 63
GOLIATH (1352 "Our Surfer Boys") 25-35 63
GOLIATH (1353 "Surf City High") 25-35 63
Members: Pat; Donna; Patty.

SURF DWELLERS
Singles: 7-inch
SWIFT (102 "Wave Breaker") 10-20 60s

SURF KINGS: see BEACH BOYS / Dick Dale / Surfaris / Surf Kings

SURF KNIGHTS
Singles: 7-inch
TIKI (1001 "Midnight Surf") 20-30 67

SURF M.C.'S
Singles: 7-inch
PROFILE 3-4 87
Picture Sleeves
PROFILE 3-4 87

SURF PUNKS
LPs: 10/12-inch
EPIC 5-10 80
DAY-GLO (457 "Locals Only") 10-15 82
Members: Dennis Dragon; Roy Ban.
Also see JOYOUS NOISE

SURF RAIDERS
Singles: 7-inch
AZRA (9677 "Monster Mash") 8-12 82
(Pumpkin-shaped picture disc.)
AZRA (060 "Surf Raiders Theme Song") 8-12 82
(Surfer-shaped or rectangular picture disc.)
BOBBETTE 3-6 83
SURF WAX 4-8 81-85
Picture Sleeves
SURF WAX 4-8 81
EPs: 7-inch
MOXIE (1039 "Surfin' 81") 8-10 81
SURF WAX SWEP (1002 "California Surf") 10-12 82
LPs: 10/12-inch
SURFWAX (1001 "Raiders of the Lost Surf") 10-12 82
(Promotional issue.)
SURFWAX (Black vinyl) 8-10 82-84
SURFWAX (Colored vinyl) 8-12 82-84

SURF RIDERS
Singles: 7-inch
NASCO (6008 "I'm Out") 50-75 58

SURF RIDERS
Singles: 7-inch
DECCA 5-10 63

SURF SONS
Singles: 7-inch
BEN 10-15 60s

SURF STOMPERS
(Bruce Johnston)
Singles: 7-inch
DEL-FI (4202 "The Original Surfer Stomp") 25-35 63
(Promotional issue only. Reissued commercially as by Bruce Johnston.)
DONNA (1354 "Do the Surfer Stomp") 30-40 62
(Promotional issue only. Reissued commercially as by Bruce Johnston.)
LPs: 10/12-inch
DEL-FI (DFLP-1236 "The Original Surfer Stomp") 30-40 63
(Monaural.)
DEL-FI (DFST-1236 "The Original Surfer Stomp") 40-50 63
(Stereo.)
Also see JOHNSTON, Bruce

SURF TEENS
LPs: 10/12-inch
SUTTON (SU-339 "Surf Mania") 25-35 63
(Monaural.)
SUTTON (SSU-339 "Surf Mania") 35-45 63
(Stereo.)

SURF TRIO
LPs: 10/12-inch
VOXX 5-8 87-88

SURFACE *P&R/LP '87*
Singles: 12-inch
COLUMBIA 4-6 86
SALSOUL 4-6 83
Singles: 7-inch
COLUMBIA 3-4 86-90
SALSOUL 3-4 83
LPs: 10/12-inch
COLUMBIA 5-8 86-90
Members: Bernard Jackson; David Townsend; Dave Conley.
Also see MANDRILL

SURFACE, Dennis, & Wind
Singles: 7-inch
RIBBON 5-10 70s

SURFARIS *P&R/LP '63*
Singles: 7-inch
ABC 3-4 74
CHANCELLOR 5-8 63
DFS (11 "Wipe Out") 500-1000 63
DECCA 5-10 63-66
DOT (Except 144 & 16479) 5-10 65-67
DOT (144 "Wipe Out") 4-6 66
(Black vinyl.)
DOT (144 "Wipe Out") 25-30 66
(Colored vinyl. Promotional issue only.)
DOT (16479 "Wipe Out") 4-8 63
KOINKIDINK (101 "Scatter Shield") 3-5 82
MCA 3-5 73
PRINCESS (50 "Wipe Out") 25-50 63
(Short version, same as Dot issue. Has "RE-1" etched in the vinyl trail-off.)
PRINCESS (50 "Wipe Out") 50-75 63
(Long version. Does not have "RE-1" etched in the vinyl trail-off.)
REGANO 5-10 63
UNIVERSAL (965 "Wipe Out") 20-40 63
Picture Sleeves
KOINKIDINK (101 "Scatter Shield") 3-5 82
EPs: 7-inch
DECCA (2765 "Wipe Out") 20-40 63
LPs: 10/12-inch
DECCA 25-45 63-65
DOT (3535 "Wipe Out") 30-45 63
(Front cover reads "The Original Hit Version, Wipe Out.")
DOT (3535 "Wipe Out") 25-35 63
(Front cover reads "Wipe Out and Surfer Joe and Other Popular selections By Other Instrumental Groups." The Surfaris are heard only on *Wipe Out* and *Surfer Joe*. Remaining tracks are by the Challengers.)
DIPLOMAT 15-25 60s
PICKWICK 10-15 78
SUNDAZED 5-10 90s
Members: Ron Wilson; Jim Fuller; Jim Pash; Pat Connolly; Bob Berryhill; Ken Forssi. Session: Richie Podolor; Chuck Girard; Gary Usher.
Also see DALE, Dick / Surfaris / Fireballs
Also see GIRARD, Chuck
Also see HONEYS
Also see PODOLOR, Dickie
Also see SURFARIS / Challengers
Also see USHER, Gary

SURFARIS
(Original Surfaris)
Singles: 7-inch
CHANCELLOR (1143 "Midnight Surf") 10-20 63
DEL-FI (4219 "Surfari") 10-20 63
FELSTED (Except 8688) 10-15 64
FELSTED (8688 "Psyche-Out") 10-20 64
REGANO (201 "Surfin' 63") 15-20 63
(First issued as *Steppin' Out*, credited to the Customs.)
SURFARI (301 "Gum Dipped Slicks") 20-30 64
LPs: 10/12-inch
DIPLOMAT 15-25 63
Members: Larry Weed; Doug Weisman; Mike Biondo; Jim Tran; Chuck Vehle.
Also see CUSTOMS
Also see DALE, Dick / Surfaris / Surf Kings (Beach Boys)
Also see ORIGINAL SURFARIS
Also see SURFARIS / Biscaynes

SURFARIS / Biscaynes
Singles: 7-inch
NORTHRIDGE (1001 "Moment of Truth") 15-25 63
REPRISE (20180 "Moment of Truth") 10-15 63
Also see SURFARIS (Original Surfaris)
Also see WALKER, Gary

SURFARIS / Challengers
Singles: 7-inch
DOT 5-10 65
Also see CHALLENGERS
Also see SURFARIS

SURFER GIRLS
Singles: 7-inch
COLUMBIA (43001 "Draggin' Wagon") 15-25 64

SURFERS
Singles: 7-inch
ORBIT (526 "Blue Hawaii") 5-10 58
(Monaural.)
ORBIT (526 "Blue Hawaii") 15-25 58
(Stereo.)
ORBIT (538 "Mambo Jambo") 5-10 58

SURFERS
Singles: 7-inch
DRA (318 "Widgit") 15-25 62

SURFERS
LPs: 10/12-inch
HI-FI (408 "The Surfers") 75-125 60s

SURFERS
Singles: 7-inch
(260 "Wherever There's a Will") 10-20 60s
(No label name used.)

SURFERS
LP: 10/12-inch
DAYBREAK (2001 "Live & Well at Hop Louie's Latitude 20°") 15-25 60s
STEREO SOUNDS (10 "Hawaii a Go Go") 15-25 60s
Members: Clayton Naluai; Alan Naluai; Buddy Naluai; Pat Sylva; Ray Pader; Joe Stevens.

SURFETTES
(Carol Connors)
Singles: 7-inch
MUSTANG (3001 "Sammy, the Sidewalk Surfer") 15-25 65
Also see CONNORS, Carol

SURFMEN
Singles: 7-inch
TITAN (1723 "Extacy") 15-25 62
TITAN (1723 "Paradise Cove") 10-20 62
(Same track as *Extacy.*)
TITAN (1727 "Malibu Run") 15-25 62
TITAN (1729 "The Breakers") 15-25 63
Members: Jim Masoner; Ron Griffith; Tim Fitzpatrick; Ed Chiaverini.
Also see EXPRESSOS
Also see LIVELY ONES

SURFRIDERS
Singles: 7-inch
BRASS (172 "Island in the Sun") 10-20 60s
CENTURY (1027 "Radiation") 10-20 60s

SURFRIDERS
LPs: 10/12-inch
VAULT (105 "Surfbeat, Vol. 2") 25-35 63
Also see CHALLENGERS

SURFS
(Les Surfs)
Singles: 7-inch
RCA 4-8 64

SURFSIDE FOUR
Singles: 7-inch
CLOISTER (6202 "Surfboard") 10-20 62
Picture Sleeves
CLOISTER (6202 "Surfboard") 30-40 62

SURFSIDE SIX
Singles: 7-inch
PALISADES (20 "South Bay") 15-25 60s

SURFSIDERS
Singles: 7-inch
20TH FOX (298 "My Friend the Sea") 5-10 62

SURFSIDERS
Singles: 7-inch
ASTRO (101 "Chug-a-Lug Charlie") 15-20 64

SURFSIDERS
LPs: 10/12-inch
DESIGN (208 "Beach Boys Songbook") 10-20 65

SURPRISE
Singles: 7-inch
KAPE 5-10

SURPRISE PACKAGE
Singles: 7-inch
COLUMBIA 8-12 66-68
LHI 5-10 68
LPs: 10/12-inch
LHI (12006 "Free Up") 15-25 68
Members: Mike Rogers; Fred Zenfeldt; Rob Lowery; Greg Beck.
Also see VICEROYS

SURREALISTIC PILLAR
Singles: 7-inch
TAMM (2027 "I Like Girls") 15-25 67

SURRENDER
LPs: 10/12-inch
CAPITOL 5-10 79

SURRETT, Alfonzo
Singles: 7-inch
MCA 3-5 80

SURREY, Ron
Singles: 7-inch
INSURANCE CITY 4-6 73

SURROUNDERS
Singles: 7-inch
SHIELD 4-8
Picture Sleeves
SHIELD 8-10

SURVIVOR *P&R/LP '80*
Singles: 12-inch
SCOTTI BROS 4-6 79-86
Singles: 7-inch
CASABLANCA 3-4 84
SCOTTI BROS 3-5 80-88
Picture Sleeves
SCOTTI BROS 3-5 82-87
LPs: 10/12-inch
SCOTTI BROS (Except 362) 5-10 79-88
SCOTTI BROS (362 "Rebel Girl") 10-12 80
(Promotional issue only.)
Members: Dave Bickler; Jim Peterik; Frank Sullivan; Dennis Johnson; Gary Smith; Jim Jameson.
Also see COBRA
Also see PETERIK, Jim

SURVIVORS
Singles: 7-inch
CAPITOL (5102 "Pamela Jean") 150-200 64
Members: Brian Wilson; Dave Nowlen; Bob Norberg; Rich Peterson.
Also see BEACH BOYS
Also see BOB & SHERRY
Also see NODAENS

SUSAN *LP '79*
Singles: 7-inch
RCA 3-5 79
SCEPTER 3-5 70
LPs: 10/12-inch
RCA 5-10 79

SUSAN & DYNAMICS
Singles: 7-inch
DOT 5-8 63

SUSAN MARIE
Singles: 7-inch
TEE PEE (61 "The Moon Won't Tell") 10-20 68

SUSIE
Singles: 7-inch
REQUEST 8-12 59

SUSIE & FOUR TRUMPETS
Singles: 7-inch
U.A. (471 "Starry Eyes") 50-100 62

SUSIE & NIGHT OWLS
Singles: 7-inch
BOLO 4-8 62

SUSIE D.
Singles: 7-inch
GUILLOTINE 4-8 66

SUTCH, Screaming Lord: see LORD SUTCH

SUTHERLAND BROTHERS *P&R/LP '73*
(With Quiver)
Singles: 7-inch
COLUMBIA 3-5 75-79
ISLAND 3-5 72-73
LPs: 10/12-inch
COLUMBIA 6-10 75-76
ISLAND 6-10 72-74
Members: Gavin Sutherland; Ian Sutherland.

SUTTER, Hub
Singles: 7-inch
COLUMBUS (103 "Gone Goslin") 40-60

SUTTON, Glenn *C&W/P&R '79*
Singles: 7-inch
ABC 3-5 73
EPIC 4-6 67
MGM 4-8 64-65
MERCURY 3-5 78-86
LPs: 10/12-inch
MERCURY 5-10 79
Also see KELLUM, Murray / Glenn Sutton

SUTTON, Gregg
LPs: 10/12-inch
COLUMBIA 5-10 79

SUTTON, Jess "88"
Singles: 78 rpm
TIFFANY 10-15 55
Singles: 7-inch
TIFFANY (1314 "I Ain't Got Nobody") 15-25 55

SUTTON, Little Emmett
Singles: 7-inch
FEDERAL 4-8 63-64

SUTTON, Mike & Brenda
Singles: 7-inch
SAM 3-5 81-82
Also see FINISHED TOUCH
Also see SUTTONS

SUTTON, Ronnie
Singles: 7-inch
MAR-VEL (5000 "Country Rock") 10-20 64

SUTTONS
Singles: 7-inch
ROCSHIRE 3-4 84
LPs: 10/12-inch
ROCSHIRE 5-8 84
Members: Mike Sutton; Brenda Sutton.
Also see SUTTON, Mike & Brenda

SUZANNE
(With Full House; with Band-Aides)
Singles: 7-inch
LIBERTY 5-10 61
TRUMP 5-10 61
Member: Suzanne Mullins.

SUZETTES
Singles: 7-inch
ATOMIC 4-8 67
MOONGLOW 8-12 63

SUZUKI, Pat
Singles: 78 rpm
VIK 5-10 57-58
Singles: 7-inch
RCA 8-12 59
VIK 5-10 57-58
LPs: 10/12-inch
CAPITOL 10-20 61
RCA 10-20 59-60
VIK (1127 "Many Sides") 15-25 58
VIK (1147 "Pat Suzuki") 15-25 58

SUZY
Singles: 7-inch
APT 4-8 65

SUZY
LPs: 10/12-inch
ATLANTIC 5-10 81

SUZY & COPYCATS
Singles: 7-inch
BRENT 10-15 61

SUZY & RED STRIPES *P&R '77*
(Linda McCartney & Wings)
Singles: 12-inch
CAPITOL (15244 "Seaside Woman") 10-20 86
EPIC (361 "Seaside Woman") 20-30 77
(Promotional issue only.)
Singles: 7-inch
CAPITOL (5608 "Seaside Woman") 3-6 86
(Remixed version.)
EPIC (50403 "Seaside Woman") 4-8 77
Promotional Singles
CAPITOL (5608 "Seaside Woman") 10-15 86
EPIC (50403 "Seaside Woman") 30-40 77
(Colored vinyl.)
EPIC (50403 "Seaside Woman") 35-45 77
(Black vinyl. White label, states "Advance Promotion")
EPIC (50403 "Seaside Woman") 40-50 77
(Black vinyl. White label, no mention of "Advance Promotion")
Also see McCARTNEY, Paul

SUZY Q
Singles: 7-inch
ATLANTIC 3-5 81

SVENSSON, Bo
LPs: 10/12-inch
GOLDEN BOY 5-8 88

SWADE, Del
Singles: 7-inch
PRODUCTION 15-25

SWAFFORD, Gary
Singles: 7-inch
CELESTIAL 4-8 65

SWAGGART, Jimmy
LPs: 10/12-inch
JIM (24-141 "25th Anniversary") 30-40 81
(Picture disc.)
L (3364 "Homeward Bound") 50-60
(Picture disc. Promotional issue only.)

SWAGS
Singles: 7-inch
DEL-FI (4143 "Rockin' Matilda") 10-15 60
WESTWIND (1003 "Rockin' Matilda") 10-20 60
Picture Sleeves
WESTWIND (1003 "Rockin' Matilda") 20-30 60
Members: Gailen Ludtke; Allen Barr; Wayne Morisett; Chet Dow; George Johnson; Bruce Reddick.

SWAIN, Doris
Singles: 7-inch
BELTONE 4-8 62

SWAIN, Jim, & Keynotes
Singles: 7-inch
HI-G LO-C 4-8 66

SWAIN, Vern
Singles: 7-inch
FINER ARTS 4-8 65

SWALLOW
Singles: 7-inch
W.B. 3-5 72
LPs: 10/12-inch
W.B. 8-10 72-73

SWALLOWS *R&B '51*
Singles: 78 rpm
AFTER HOURS (104 "My Baby") 100-200 54
KING (4458 "Will You Be Mine") 100-200 51
KING (4466 "Since You've Been Away") 150-250 51
KING (4501 "Eternally") 100-200 51
KING (4515 "Tell Me Why") 150-250 51
KING (4525 "Beside You") 50-100 52
KING (4533 "I Only Have Eyes for You") 50-100 52
KING (4579 "Where Do I Go from Here") 50-100 52
KING (4612 "Laugh") 50-100 53
KING (4632 "Nobody's Lovin' Me") 50-100 53
KING (4656 "Trust Me") 50-100 53
KING (4676 "I'll Be Waiting") 50-100 53
Singles: 7-inch
AFTER HOURS (104 "My Baby") 800-1200 54
GUSTO 3-5 80s
KING (4458 "Will You Be Mine") 1000-1500 51
KING (4501 "Eternally") 800-1200 51
(Black vinyl.)
KING (4501 "Eternally") 2000-3000 51
(Blue vinyl.)
KING (4501 "Eternally") 2000-3000 51
(Green vinyl.)
KING (4515 "Tell Me Why") 800-1200 51
(Black vinyl.)
KING (4515 "Tell Me Why") 2000-3000 51
(Blue vinyl.)
KING (4525 "Beside You") 500-750 52
KING (4533 "I Only Have Eyes for You") 500-1000 52
KING (4579 "Where Do I Go from Here") 500-1000 52
KING (4612 "Laugh") 500-1000 53
KING (4632 "Nobody's Lovin' Me") 450-700 53
KING (4656 "Trust Me") 450-700 53
KING (4676 "I'll Be Waiting") 450-700 53
Members: Junior Denby; Ed Rich; Earl Hurley; Fred Johnson; Norris Mack; Dee Bailey; Buddy Bailey; Irving Turner; Al France; Cal Kollette.
Also see DENBY, Junior

SWALLOWS *P&R '58*
Singles: 7-inch
FEDERAL (12319 "Angel Baby") 50-75 58
FEDERAL (12328 "We Want to Rock") 40-60 58
FEDERAL (12329 "Beside You") 50-75 58
FEDERAL (1233 "Itchy Twitchy Feeling") 50-75 58

SWALLOWS
(Guides)
Singles: 7-inch
GUYDEN (2023 "How Long Must a Fool Go On") 50-100 59
(By the Guides, but credited to the Swallows on some promotional copies.)
Also see GUIDES

SWALLOWS
Singles: 7-inch
STARBOUND (Colored vinyl) 4-6 86
Members: Leroy Miller; Al Smith; Rick Brown; Ed Rich; Ted Estep.

SWAMP DOGG
(With Riders of the New Funk)
Singles: 7-inch
ALA 3-4 82
ATOMIC ARTS 3-5 79
BRUT 3-5 73
CANYON 4-6 70
CREAM 3-5 73
ELEKTRA 3-5 72
ISLAND 3-5 73
MUSICOR 3-5 77
RARE BULLET 3-4 83-85
ROKER 4-6 71
STONEDOGG 3-5 73
SWAMP DOGG PRESENTS 3-5 72
WIZARD 3-5 77
LPs: 10/12-inch
ALA 5-10 82
CANYON 10-20 70
CREAM 6-10 72
ELEKTRA 8-12 71
ISLAND 6-10 73
MUSICOR 5-10 77
TAKOMA 5-10 81
WAR BRIDE 5-10 82
WIZARD 5-10 78
Member: Jerry Williams.
Also see WILLIAMS, Jerry

SWAMP PEOPLE
Singles: 7-inch
METROMEDIA 4-6 69

SWAMP RATS
Singles: 7-inch
CO & CE (245 "It's Not Easy") 10-20 67
ST. CLAIR (69 "Louie Louie") 25-50 66
ST. CLAIR (2222 "Psycho") 100-200 66
ST. CLAIR (3333 "Two Tymes Two") 25-50 66
ST. CLAIR (711,711 "It's Not Easy") 25-50 66
LPs: 10/12-inch
KEYSTONE (39 "Disco Sucks") 10-15 79
Members: Bob Hocko; Dick Newton; Denny Nicholson.
Also see FANTASTIC DEE-JAYS
Also see GALACTUS

SWAMP ZOMBIES
Singles: 7-inch
JA-JA 3-4 85
Picture Sleeves
JA-JA 3-5 85

SWAMPGAS
Singles: 7-inch
BUDDAH 3-5 72
LPs: 10/12-inch
BUDDAH 8-10 72

SWAMPSEEDS
Singles: 7-inch
EPIC 6-12 68-69

SWAMPWATER *C&W '71*
Singles: 7-inch
KING 3-5 70
RCA 3-5 71
LPs: 10/12-inch
KING 10-15 70
RCA 10-12 71
Member: Gib Guilbeau.
Also see BURRITO BROTHERS

SWAN, Billy *C&W/P&R/LP '74*
Singles: 7-inch
A&M 3-5 78-79
COLUMBIA 3-5 76-77
EPIC 3-4 81-83
MGM 5-10 68
MERCURY 3-4 86-87
MONUMENT 4-6 66-76
RISING SONS 4-6 67
LPs: 10/12-inch
A&M 5-10 78
COLUMBIA/MONUMENT 5-10 77
EPIC 5-10 81
MONUMENT 5-10 74-78
Also see BLACK TIE

SWAN, Jimmy
(With the Sons of the South; with Plummer Davis & Orchestra)
Singles: 78 rpm
MGM 10-20 56
PEACOCK 10-20 53
TRUMPET 10-20 52-53
Singles: 7-inch
CHECKER (946 "Little Fine Healthy Thing") 10-15 60
DECCA (31043 "Don't Conceal Your Wedding Ring") 10-20 60
JB (105 "Rattle Shakin' Daddy") 20-40 57
MGM (12348 "Country Cattin' ") 15-25 56
PEACOCK (1622 "Hey No Baby, Hey") 25-50 53
TRUMPET 15-25 52-53

SWAN, Mary
Singles: 7-inch
SWAN 5-10 59
UNART 5-10 59

SWAN SILVERTONES
Singles: 78 rpm
KING 10-20 51
SPECIALTY 5-10 52-54
VEE JAY 5-10 57-58
Singles: 7-inch
HOB 3-5 74
KING (4542 "Grant It Lord") 50-100 51
SPECIALTY 15-25 52-54
VEE JAY (100 & 200 series) 10-20 56
VEE JAY (800 & 900 series) 5-15 57-64
LPs: 10/12-inch
HOB 5-10 74
VEE JAY (5052 "The Best of the Swan Silvertones") 15-25 64
VEE JAY INT'L 5-10 74
Members: Claude Jeter; Paul Owens; Louis Johnson; Azell Monk; Lonwood Hargrove.

SWANEE & ROCK-A-BILLIES
Singles: 7-inch
HAPPY HEARTS (121 "I'll Prove It One Day") 8-12 61

SWANEE SPIRITUAL SINGERS
Singles: 7-inch
DUKE (200 "God Spoke to Me") 25-50 58

SWANETTES
Singles: 7-inch
BELTONE 5-10 61

SWANGER, Sandy
Singles: 7-inch
CONNIE 5-10 59

SWANKS
Singles: 7-inch
CHARM (6081 "Ghost Train") 5-10 65

SWANN, Bettye *P&R '67*
Singles: 7-inch
A-BET 3-6 72-74
ATLANTIC 3-6 72-76
BIG TREE 3-5 70s
CAPITOL 4-8 68-70
FAME 3-5 71
MONEY 5-10 65-67
Picture Sleeves
CAPITOL 4-8 69
LPs: 10/12-inch
A-BET 8-10 72
ATLANTIC 8-10 72-75
CAPITOL 10-12 69
MONEY 10-20 67
Also see DEES, Sam, & Bettye Swann

SWANN, Claudia
(With Buddy Griffin & His Orchestra)
Singles: 78 rpm
CHESS 8-12 55
Singles: 7-inch
CHESS (1586 "Please Come Back") 25-35 55

SWANS
Singles: 78 rpm
RAGE 50-100 54
Singles: 7-inch
RAGE (101 "Fools Fall in Love") 300-500 54
(Also issued as by Mel Williams & the Montclairs.)
Also see WILLIAMS, Mel

SWANS
(With Gene Nero Orchestra)
Singles: 78 rpm
BALLAD 100-200 54-55
FORTUNE 100-150 55
RAINBOW 100-200 53
Singles: 7-inch
BALLAD (1006 "Night Train") 300-400 54
BALLAD (1007 "Happy") 300-400 55
FORTUNE (822 "I'll Forever Love You") 500-1000 55
LOST-NITE 4-8
RAINBOW (233 "My True Love") 1000-2000 53
(Colored vinyl.)
STEAMBOAT (101 "Believe in Me") 200-300 50s
Also see LEWIS, Paul, & Swans

SWANS *P&R '64*
Singles: 7-inch
CAMEO (302 "The Boy with the Beatle Hair") 25-35 64
SWAN (4151 "He's Mine") 10-15 63
Also see ALICE WONDER LAND

SWANS
Singles: 7-inch
CRITERIA ("Mashed Potatoes")...... 5-10 60
(No selection number used.)

SWANSON, Bernice
Singles: 7-inch
CHESS....................10-20 65

SWANSON, Bob, & Bee Jays
Singles: 7-inch
R.S.P.................... 4-8 66-67

SWANSON, Bobby
(With the Sonics)
Singles: 7-inch
DONNA....................15-25 60-62
IGLOO (16 "Angel")..........50-75 61
IGLOO (1003 "Rockin' Little Eskimo")..........150-200 59

SWANSON, Brad, & His Whispering Organ Sound LP '69
LPs: 10/12-inch
THUNDERBIRD.............. 5-10 69

SWANSON, Earl
Singles: 7-inch
LEGRAND (1002 "Tiger Rock")......15-30 60

SWATLEY, Hank
Singles: 7-inch
AARON (101 "Oakie Boogie")........50-75

SWAYDES
Singles: 7-inch
ACCOLADE (1 "Remember Me")....25-35 65

SWAYDES
Singles: 7-inch
PARIS TOWER (108 "Anymore")...15-25 67
(Add $15 to $25 if accompanied by 5" x 8" photo insert.)
Members: Jack Chastain; Jim Adams; Pat Rooney; Billy Ayo; Barry Crook.

SWAYZE, Patrick P&R '87
(Featuring Wendy Fraser)
Singles: 7-inch
RCA.................... 3-4 87
Picture Sleeves
RCA.................... 3-5 87

SWAYZE, Patrick, & Wendy Fraser / Maurice Williams & Zodiacs
Singles: 7-inch
RCA.................... 3-5 88
Also see SWAYZE, Patrice
Also see WILLIAMS, Maurice

SWEAT, Isaac Payton C&W '78
Singles: 7-inch
BELLAIRE.................. 3-5 80
GUSTO.................... 3-5 78
LPs: 10/12-inch
BELLAIRE.................. 5-10 80
PAID..................... 5-8

SWEAT, Keith P&R/LP '88
(With Jacci McGhee)
Singles: 7-inch
ELEKTRA.................. 3-4 87
VINTERTAINMENT............ 3-4 88-90
Picture Sleeves
VINTERTAINMENT............ 3-4 88
LPs: 10/12-inch
VINTERTAINMENT............ 5-8 88-90
Also see ENTOUCH

SWEAT BAND LP '80
Singles: 7-inch
UNCLE JAM................ 3-5 80
LPs: 10/12-inch
UNCLE JAM................ 5-10 80
Also see BOOTSY'S RUBBER BAND

SWEATHOG P&R '71
Singles: 7-inch
COLUMBIA.................. 3-5 71
LPs: 10/12-inch
COLUMBIA.................. 8-10 71-72

SWEATHOG / Free Movement / Bob Dylan / Edgar Winter's White Trash
EPs: 7-inch
COLUMBIA/PLAYBACK (31 "Hallelujah")..............25-35 72
Also see DYLAN, Bob
Also see FREE MOVEMENT
Also see SWEATHOG
Also see WINTER, Edgar

SWEATT, Al
Singles: 7-inch
ALVERA (94 "Moochin' Smoochin' ")..................25-35

SWE-DANES
Singles: 7-inch
W.B. 5-10 60

SWEDEN HEVEN & HELL: see UMILANI, Piero

SWEDISH, Steve
Singles: 7-inch
WAN-KEE.................. 4-8

SWEENEY, Jimmy
(With the Varieteers; Jim Sweeney)
Singles: 78 rpm
HICKORY (1004 "Deep Blues")......50-75 53
TENNESSEE (#714)..........50-75 50
(Title not known.)
Singles: 7-inch
BUCKLEY (1101 "She Wears My Ring")................ 5-10 62
COLUMBIA.................. 5-10 58-59
DATE..................... 4-6 60s
HICKORY (1004 "Deep Blues")..100-150 53
HICKORY (1136 "She Wears My Ring")................10-15 53
Also see FIVE BARS
Also see VARIETEERS

SWEENY TODD P&R '76
Singles: 7-inch
LONDON.................... 4-8 76
LPs: 10/12-inch
LONDON (694 "If Wishes Were Horses")..............20-25 77
Members: Nick Gilder; James McCulloch; Bryan Guy Adams.
Also see ADAMS, Bryan
Also see GILDER, Nick

SWEET
Singles: 7-inch
SMASH.................... 8-15 67-68

SWEET P&R '71
Singles: 7-inch
BELL..................... 3-5 71-74
CAPITOL.................. 3-5 75-79
PARAMOUNT................. 5-10 71
LPs: 10/12-inch
BELL..................... 10-20 73
CAPITOL (Except 16000 series)......8-10 75-79
CAPITOL (16000 series)...... 5-8 80-82
KORY..................... 8-10 77
Promotional LPs
CAPITOL (8849 "Short and Sweet")..................20-30 78
CAPITOL (11129 "Cut Above the Rest")..................45-55 79
(Boxed set, containing the LP, 8-track and cassette issues of *Cut Above the Rest*, plus a group photo and biography.)
Members: Brian Connolly; Steve Priest; Andy Scott; Mick Tucker.

SWEET, Arlon
(Arlon Sweet & Bonnevilles)
Singles: 7-inch
TOPPA.................... 4-8 62

SWEET, Clifford
Singles: 7-inch
EXCELLO.................. 4-8 64

SWEET, Matthew LP '92
LPs: 10/12-inch
ZOO/BMG (1 "Girlfriend")...........8-10 91
(Colored vinyl. Promotional issue only.)

SWEET, Rachel C&W '76
Singles: 12-inch
STIFF/COLUMBIA............10-15 79
(Promotional issue only.)
Singles: 7-inch
COLUMBIA.................. 3-5 81-83
DERRICK.................. 3-5 76-78
PREMIER.................. 3-5 74
STIFF/COLUMBIA............ 3-5 79-80
LPs: 10/12-inch
ARC...................... 5-10 81
COLUMBIA.................. 5-10 81-82
STIFF/COLUMBIA............ 5-10 79-80
Also see SMITH, Rex, & Rachel Sweet

SWEET & SASSY
Singles: 7-inch
DEL PAT.................. 5-10 59

SWEET & HIRSCHI
Singles: 7-inch
BLUE RIBBON (101 "Go on Out to California Tonight").................. 4-8 72

SWEET APPLE
Singles: 7-inch
COLUMBIA.................. 3-5 70
LPs: 10/12-inch
COLUMBIA.................. 8-10 70

SWEET BIPPIES
Singles: 7-inch
A&M...................... 4-8 68

SWEET BREEZE
Singles: 7-inch
2001..................... 3-5 78

SWEET BROTHERS
Singles: 7-inch
RAE COX.................. 5-8 64

SWEET CHERRIES
Singles: 7-inch
T-NECK.................... 4-6 69

SWEET CREAM
Singles: 12-inch
SHADYBROOK................ 4-8 78
Singles: 7-inch
SHADYBROOK................ 3-5 78

SWEET DELIGHTS
Singles: 7-inch
ATCO..................... 4-8 68

SWEET DREAMS P&R '74
Singles: 7-inch
ABC...................... 3-5 74
Member: Polly Brown.
Also see BROWN, Polly

SWEET ECSTASY
Singles: 12-inch
QUALITY/RFC................ 4-6 83

SWEET F.A. LP '90
LPs: 10/12-inch
MCA...................... 5-8 90

SWEET G. D&D '83
Singles: 12-inch
FEVER.................... 4-6 83

SWEET HEARTS: see SWEETHEARTS

SWEET INSPIRATIONS P&R '67
Singles: 12-inch
RSO...................... 4-8 79
Singles: 7-inch
ATLANTIC.................. 3-8 67-71
CARIBOU.................. 3-5 77
RSO...................... 3-5 79
STAX..................... 3-5 73-74
LPs: 10/12-inch
ATLANTIC.................. 10-12 68-70
RSO...................... 5-10 79
STAX..................... 8-10 73
Members: Cissy Houston; Sylvia Shemwell; Myrna Smith; Estelle Brown.
Also see BROWN, Estelle
Also see FIT
Also see FRANKLIN, Aretha
Also see HOUSTON, Cissy
Also see PRESLEY, Elvis
Also see RASCALS
Also see SHEMWELL, Sylvia
Also see SMITH, Myrna

SWEET LIFE
Singles: 12-inch
WEST END.................. 4-6 83

SWEET LIGHTNIN'
Singles: 7-inch
RCA...................... 3-5 72
LPs: 10/12-inch
RCA...................... 8-10 72

SWEET LINDA DIVINE
Singles: 7-inch
COLUMBIA.................. 4-6 69

SWEET MAMA LOVE
Singles: 7-inch
AVCO EMBASSY.............. 3-5 71

SWEET MARIE
Singles: 7-inch
YARDBIRD.................. 3-5 72-73

SWEET MARQUEES
Singles: 7-inch
APACHE (1516 "You Lied").......125-175 61

SWEET MUSIC
Singles: 7-inch
WAND..................... 3-5 76

SWEET NUTHINS
Singles: 7-inch
SWAN..................... 5-10 64

SWEET OBSESSION
Singles: 7-inch
EPIC..................... 3-4 88
LPs: 10/12-inch
EPIC..................... 5-8 88

SWEET PAIN
Singles: 7-inch
MERCURY.................. 4-6 69
U.A...................... 3-5 71
LPs: 10/12-inch
MERCURY.................. 10-12 69
U.A...................... 8-10 71

SWEET PANTS
LPs: 10/12-inch
(1141 "Fat Peter Presents Sweet Pants")................150-200 69
(No label name used.)
Members: Mike Mulloney; Mike Carr; Tony Molla.

SWEET PIE & BILL MALONEY
LPs: 10/12-inch
RIG ESP.................. 15-25

SWEET POTATOES
Singles: 7-inch
SABRINA (511 "Mother Please")......5-10 63

SWEET PROMISE
Singles: 7-inch
ALA (102 "Funky Jungle")..........3-5 78

SWEET REVIVAL
Singles: 7-inch
SSS INT'L (Colored vinyl)..........5-10 70s

SWEET ROCK
Singles: 7-inch
MUSIC MERCHANT............ 3-5 72

SWEET SALVATION
Singles: 7-inch
ELEKTRA.................. 3-5 72
LPs: 10/12-inch
ELEKTRA.................. 8-10 72

SWEET SENSATION P&R/LP '75
Singles: 7-inch
PYE...................... 3-5 74-75
LPs: 10/12-inch
PYE...................... 5-10 75

SWEET SENSATION P&R '87
Singles: 7-inch
ATCO..................... 3-4 88-90
NEXT PLATEAU.............. 3-4 86-87
Picture Sleeves
ATCO..................... 3-4 88-89
LPs: 10/12-inch
ATCO..................... 5-8 88-90

SWEET SICK TEENS
Singles: 7-inch
RCA (37-7940 "The Pretzel").........30-40 62
(Compact 33 Single.)
RCA (47-7940 "The Pretzel")........20-25 62

SWEET SMOKE
Singles: 7-inch
AMY...................... 10-15 68-69
JAN-GI.................... 10-20 68

SWEET SOULS
Singles: 7-inch
RPR...................... 5-8 69
Members: Johnny Fortune; Glen Campbell.
Also see CAMPBELL, Glen
Also see FORTUNE, Johnny

SWEET STAVIN' CHAIN
LPs: 10/12-inch
COTILLION................. 8-10 70

SWEET TALKS
LPs: 10/12-inch
MERCURY.................. 5-10 79

SWEET TEE LP '89
Singles: 7-inch
PROFILE.................. 3-4 88
LPs: 10/12-inch
PROFILE.................. 5-8 88

SWEET TEENS
Singles: 78 rpm
FLIP (311 "Forever More")..........20-40 56
GEE (1030 "With This Ring").........25-50 57
Singles: 7-inch
FLIP (311 "Forever More")..........25-50 56
GEE (1030 "With This Ring").........25-50 57

SWEET THINGS
Singles: 7-inch
DATE (1504 "You're My Lovin' Baby")..................10-20 66
DATE (1522 "Baby's Blue")..........15-25 66
Picture Sleeves
DATE (1504 "You're My Lovin' Baby")..................15-25 66
Member: Francine Barker.
Also see PEACHES & HERB

SWEET THREE
Singles: 7-inch
CAMEO.................... 10-20 67
DECCA.................... 8-12 66

SWEET THUNDER LP '78
Singles: 7-inch
FANTASY.................. 3-5 78-79
WMOT..................... 3-5 79
LPs: 10/12-inch
WMOT..................... 5-10 78

SWEET THURSDAY
Singles: 7-inch
GREAT WESTERN GRAMAPHONE.................. 3-5 72
TETRAGRAMMATON............ 4-8 68
LPs: 10/12-inch
GREAT WESTERN GRAMAPHONE.................. 8-10 72
TETRAGRAMMATON............ 10-20 69
Member: Jon Mark.
Also see MARK, Jon

SWEET TOOTHE
LPs: 10/12-inch
DOMINION (7360 "Testing")......200-300 71
Member: Michael Hopkins.

SWEET TYMES
Singles: 7-inch
EPIC..................... 4-8 67
Also see WILLIAMS, George, & Tymes

SWEET WILLIAM
(With His Sugar Lads)
Singles: 7-inch
BB (1001 "Sugar Shake")...........8-12 65
JED...................... 4-8 66

SWEET WINE
Singles: 7-inch
ARCAIDE.................. 4-8 60s

SWEET YOUNGUNS
Singles: 7-inch
PULSAR.................... 4-8 69

SWEETARTS
Singles: 7-inch
SONOBEAT (101 "Without You")..15-25 67
VANDAN (8195 "So Many Times")..................10-20 66
Picture Sleeves
SONOBEAT (101 "Without You")..25-35 67

SWEETBOTTOM
Singles: 7-inch
ELEKTRA.................. 3-5 78-79
LPs: 10/12-inch
ELEKTRA.................. 5-10 78-79
SWEETBOTTOM............... 8-10 77
Members: Darryl Stuermer; Warren Wiegratz.

SWEETHEARTS
Singles: 7-inch
BRUNSWICK (55237 "In Between Kisses")..................10-20 62
BRUNSWICK (55240 "What Did I Do")..................10-20 63
BRUNSWICK (55255 "What Will Mother Say")..................10-20 63
BRUNSWICK (55265 "No No").......10-20 64
COMO..................... 5-10 68
D&H (500 "My Baby").............20-30 61
HARRIS (1001 "You'll Always Know")..................50-75
HI-III (116 "Puppy Love")..........20-30 63
HI-III (117 "Summer Days")........15-25 63
RAY STAR (778 "Sorry Daddy")....40-50 61
(Yellow label.)
RAY STAR (778 "Sorry Daddy")....20-30 61
(Blue label.)

SWEETHEARTS OF RODEO C&W '86
Singles: 7-inch
COLUMBIA.................. 3-4 86-91
Members: Janis Oliver; Kristine Oliver.

SWEETIES
Singles: 7-inch
END...................... 10-15 61

SWEETS
Singles: 7-inch
VALIANT.................. 5-10 65
Member: Felice Taylor.
Also see TAYLOR, Felice

SWEETS
Singles: 7-inch
SIDEWALK.................. 4-8 67

SWEETTARTS
Singles: 7-inch
VANDAN.................... 4-8 66

SWEETWATER LP '69
Singles: 7-inch
REPRISE.................. 3-6 68-71
LPs: 10/12-inch
REPRISE.................. 10-15 68-71

SWEETWATER C&W '81
Singles: 7-inch
FAUCET.................... 3-4 81
Member: Willie Wynn.
Also see OAK RIDGE BOYS
Also see TENNESSEANS

SWENSON, Inga
LPs: 10/12-inch
LIBERTY.................. 20-30 64

SWIFT, Allen
Singles: 7-inch
LEADER (815 "Are You Lonesome Tonight")..................10-15 61

SWIFT, Allen, Pat Bright & Herb Duncan
Singles: 7-inch
MAD ("Gall in the Family Fare")........4-8 73
(Plastic 33 rpm soundsheet.)
Also see SWIFT, Allen

SWIFT, Basil, & Seegrams
Singles: 7-inch
MERCURY (72386 "Farmer's Daughter")..................15-25 65
Also see HUTTON, Danny

SWIFT, Bill
Singles: 7-inch
MALA..................... 4-8 67

SWIFT, Joe
(With the Internationals)
Singles: 78 rpm
EXCLUSIVE................ 5-10 48
Singles: 7-inch
ONACREST.................. 4-8 66

SWIFT, Jonathan
Singles: 7-inch
DECCA.................... 4-6 70
LPs: 10/12-inch
DECCA.................... 8-10 70

SWIFT, Pepper
Singles: 7-inch
WHIRLAWAY................. 4-8 65

SWIFT, Tom
(With the Electric Grandmothers; with Electric Bag)
Singles: 7-inch
SOUND TEX................ 15-20 60s
LPs: 10/12-inch
CUSTOM (1115 "Are You Experienced")..................20-25 60s

SWIFT RAIN
LPs: 10/12-inch
HI........................ 8-10 71

SWIMMING POOL Q's
Singles: 7-inch
A&M...................... 3-5 82

SWINDELLS, Steve
LPs: 10/12-inch
ATCO..................... 5-10 80

SWINE, Seymour
(With the Squeelers)
Singles: 7-inch
BIG PIG.................. 3-6 85
SWINE ("Blue Christmas")..........4-8 85
(No selection number used.)

SWING
Singles: 7-inch
PLANET.................... 3-4 81
Picture Sleeves
PLANET.................... 3-4 81
LPs: 10/12-inch
PLANET.................... 5-10 81

SWING, Bill
Singles: 7-inch
BURTON ("Messed Up")..............25-50
(Selection number not known.)

SWING, Mr. see MR. SWING

SWING BROTHERS
(Eddie Burns)
Singles: 78 rpm
PALDA ("Papa's Boogie") 75-100 48
(Selection number not known.)
Also see BURNS, Eddie

SWING KINGS
Singles: 78 rpm
METEOR (5016 Mary Jane") 15-25 54
Singles: 7-inch
METEOR (5016 Mary Jane") 25-50 54
Member: Skeet Williams.

SWING OUT SISTER P&R/LP '87
Singles: 7-inch
FONTANA 3-4 89
MERCURY 3-4 87
Picture Sleeves
FONTANA 3-4 89
MERCURY 3-4 87
LPs: 10/12-inch
FONTANA 5-8 89
MERCURY 5-8 87
Members: Andy Connell; Corrine Drewery; Martin Jackson.

SWING SHIFT BAND C&W '88
Singles: 7-inch
STEP ONE 3-4 88

SWINGALONGS
Singles: 7-inch
CUCA 5-10 65

SWINGERS
Singles: 7-inch
WORLD PACIFIC 8-12 59

SWINGERS
Singles: 7-inch
J.C. PENNY (100 "Bay-Hay Bee Doll") 8-12 66
(Promotional issue only. Made for J.C. Penny Sportswear.)
Picture Sleeves
J.C. PENNY 8-12 66

SWINGERS
LPs: 10/12-inch
BACKSTREET 5-10 82

SWINGIN' APOLLOES
Singles: 7-inch
WHITE CLIFFS 4-8 67

SWINGIN' DEACON
Singles: 7-inch
EAGLE 4-8 68

SWINGIN' GRANNY
Singles: 7-inch
IRRAL 4-8 64

SWINGIN' MEDALLIONS P&R/LP '66
Singles: 7-inch
CAPITOL 4-8 68
COLLECTABLES 3-4 80s
DOT 5-10 65
4 SALE (002 "Double Shot") 20-30 66
1-2-3 .... 3-5 70
SMASH 4-8 66-67
LPs: 10/12-inch
SMASH (27083 "Double Shot") 25-35 66
(Monaural.)
SMASH (67083 "Double Shot") 25-35 66
(Stereo.)
Also see PIECES of EIGHT

SWINGIN' ROCKS
Singles: 7-inch
ESTA 5-10 59

SWINGIN' SENSATIONS
Singles: 7-inch
SOUND SENSATION (8616 "There Is a Girl") 15-25

SWINGIN' YO YOs
Singles: 7-inch
JUBILEE 4-8 67

SWINGIN' YO YOs
Singles: 7-inch
JUBILEE 4-8 67

SWINGING BLUE JEANS P&R/LP '64
Singles: 7-inch
CAPITOL (72143 "The Hippy Hippy Shake") 10-20 64
(Canadian.)
CAPITOL (72152 "Good Golly Miss Molly") 10-20 64
(Canadian.)
IMPERIAL 8-15 64-67
LPs: 10/12-inch
IMPERIAL (9261 "The Hippy Hippy Shake") 50-75 64
(Monaural.)
IMPERIAL (12261 "The Hippy Hippy Shake") 30-50 64
(Stereo.)
LIBERTY 5-10 82
Members: Ray Ennis; Ralph Ellis; Les Braid; Norman Kuhlke.

SWINGING EARLS
Singles: 7-inch
VEGA (1001 "Yum-Yum") 8-12 59

SWINGING EMBERS
Singles: 7-inch
ACE 10-15 61
Member: Jackie Hamilton Gore.
Also see EMBERS

SWINGING ERUDITES
Singles: 12-inch
AIRWAVE (9400 "Walk with an Erection") 5-8 87
(Promotional issue only.)
Singles: 7-inch
AIRWAVE 3-6 87
LPs: 10/12-inch
AIRWAVE ("Swinging Erudites") 8-10 87
(Selection number not known.)
ONE DIMENSIONAL (66666 "Pretentious Crapola") 8-10 89
Members: Johnny Angel; Susie Sasume; Meg A. Bux; Clive Duncan; Greg Urebassist; Terry Dactyl.

SWINGING HEARTS
Singles: 7-inch
DIAMOND (162 "Please Say It Isn't So") 10-15 64
(Black vinyl.)
DIAMOND (162 "Please Say It Isn't So") 25-35 64
(Colored vinyl. Promotional issue only.)
LUCKY FOUR (101 "Please Say It Isn't So") 30-40 61
LUCKY FOUR (1011 "Something Made Me Stop") 35-50 62
MAGIC TOUCH (2001 "You Speak of Love") 25-50 65
NRM (1002 "How Can I Love You") 200-300 63
620 (1002 "How Can I Love You") 100-200 63
(Black vinyl.)
620 (1002 "How Can I Love You") 200-300 63
(Colored vinyl.)
620 (1005 "Something Made Me Stop Shopping Around 50-100 63
620 (1009 "You Speak of Love") 75-125 64

SWINGING HEARTS
Singles: 7-inch
MAGIC TOUCH (2001 "You Speak of Love") 10-20 67

SWINGING LIVER
Singles: 7-inch
U.S.A. 5-8 65

SWINGING MACHINE
Singles: 7-inch
S.P.Q.R. (1101 "Do You Have to Ask") 15-25 66

SWINGING PHILLIES
Singles: 7-inch
DELUXE (6171 "L-o-v-e") 100-150 58
Members: Charles Cosome; Phillip Hurt; Richard Hill; Ronald Headin; Al Hirt.

SWINGING STINGRAYS
Singles: 7-inch
FUJIMO (6017 "Teen Queen") 10-20 63

SWINGING TIGERS
Singles: 7-inch
TAMLA (54024 "Snake Walk") ...100-200 60

SWINGING VYNE
Singles: 7-inch
EPIC 4-8 66

SWINGLE SINGERS LP '63
LPs: 10/12-inch
COLUMBIA 4-6 76
PHILIPS 5-10 63-72

SWINGSTERS
Singles: 7-inch
DIXIETONE (5856 "Southern Drums") 15-25 66
Member: J.D. Wyatt.
Also see WYATT, J.D. & Thunderbolts

SWINGTONES
Singles: 7-inch
ABC-PAR 8-10 58
RHYTHM 10-15 58

SWISHER, Debra
Singles: 7-inch
BOOM (60001 "You're So Good to Me") 5-10 66
Also see ANGELS
Also see PIXIES THREE

SWISS MOVEMENT
Singles: 7-inch
CASABLANCA 4-8 74
PERKY (101 "Spoonful") 20-30 68
RCA 3-5 73
LPs: 10/12-inch
RCA 8-12 73

SWITCH P&R/LP '78
Singles: 7-inch
Also see DE GORDY (Black vinyl) 3-4 78-82
GORDY (Colored vinyl) 4-8 78-82
(Promotional issues only.)
TOTAL EXPERIENCE 3-4 82-84
LPs: 10/12-inch
GORDY 5-10 78-81
TOTAL EXPERIENCE 5-8 82-84
Members: Philip Ingram; Bobby DeBarge; Tommy DeBarge; Greg Williams; Jody Sims; Eddie Fluellen.
BARGE
Also see DECO

SWITCHMEN
Singles: 7-inch
RAMPART 4-8 62

SWOFFORD, Bill Oliver: see OLIVER

SWOLLEN MONKEYS
LPs: 10/12-inch
CACHALOT 5-10 82

SWORDSMEN
Singles: 7-inch
SEMAC (2114 "Kathi, Please Don't Cry") 20-40 61

SWORDSMEN
Singles: 7-inch
NINANDY 4-8 68
RCA 3-5 69-71
LPs: 10/12-inch
RCA 10-15 69-71

SYBERT, Tony Lee
Singles: 7-inch
METROMEDIA 3-5 71

SYBIL P&R/LP '89
Singles: 7-inch
NEXT PLATEAU 3-4 87-89
LPs: 10/12-inch
NEXT PLATEAU 5-8 87-89

SYCAMORES
Singles: 78 rpm
GROOVE 50-75 55
Singles: 7-inch
GROOVE (0121 "I'll Be Waiting") 100-200 55

SYDELLS
Singles: 7-inch
BELTONE (2032 "In the Night") 10-15 63
(Black vinyl.)
BELTONE (2032 "In the Night") 15-25 63
(Black vinyl.)

SYKES, Bobby
Singles: 7-inch
COLUMBIA (41946 "Memphis Address") 15-25 62
DECCA (30573 "Touch of Loving") 25-50 58
JMI 8-12
Also see BISHOP, Bob
Also see MARTIN, Benny, & Bobby Sykes

SYKES, Keith LP '80
Singles: 7-inch
BACKSTREET 3-5 80
LPs: 10/12-inch
BACKSTREET 5-10 80
MIDLAND INT'L 8-10 77
VANGUARD 10-12 70-71

SYKES, Roosevelt
(With the Honeydrippers)
Singles: 78 rpm
BLACK & WHITE 15-25 45
BLUEBIRD 20-50 44-46
BULLET 15-25 49
HOUSE of SOUND 50-75 57
IMPERIAL 15-25 55
RCA 15-25 46-49
REGAL 15-25 50-51
UNITED 25-35 51
Singles: 7-inch
HOUSE of SOUND (505 "She's Jail Bait") 50-75 57
IMPERIAL (5367 "Crazy Fox") 25-35 55
PRESTIGE BLUESVILLE 5-10 60
RCA (0025 "I Know How You Feel") 50-75 49
(Colored vinyl.)
RCA (0040 "Southern Blues") 50-75 49
(Colored vinyl.)
UNITED (120 "Raining in My Heart") 25-35 52
UNITED (129 "Walking This Boogie") 25-35 52
UNITED (139 "Four O'Clock Blues") 25-35 53
(Black vinyl.)
UNITED (139 "Four O'Clock Blues") 50-75 53
(Colored vinyl.)
UNITED (152 "Come Back Baby") 25-35 53
LPs: 10/12-inch
BARCLAY 20-30
BLIND PIG 5-10 78
BLUE LABOR 20-30
BLUESVILLE 10-20
BLUESWAY 8-12 73
CROWN 15-25 62
DELMARK 8-15 66-73
INNER CITY 8-15
JEWEL 8-12 73
PRESTIGE 8-12 69
PRESTIGE BLUESVILLE 25-35 60-61
UNITED 8-12
Also see GILLUM, Jazz
Also see MEMPHIS SLIM & Roosevelt Sykes
Also see THREE KINGS & a Queen
Also see WASHBOARD SAM

SYKES, Roosevelt, & Little Brother Montgomery
LPs: 10/12-inch
FANTASY 8-12 73
Also see MONTGOMERY, Little Brother
Also see SYKES, Roosevelt

SYLTE SISTERS
Singles: 7-inch
COLISEUM 4-8 62-63

SYLVAIN, Sylvain LP '80
Singles: 7-inch
RCA 3-5 79
LPs: 10/12-inch
RCA 5-10 79
Also see NEW YORK DOLLS

SYLVAIN, Syl, & Teardrops
Singles: 7-inch
RCA 3-5 81
LPs: 10/12-inch
RCA 5-10 81
Promotional LPs
RCA ("Special Radio Series") 10-15 81

SYLVERS P&R '72
Singles: 12-inch
CASABLANCA 4-8 79
GEFFEN 4-6 84-85
SOLAR 4-6 81-82
Singles: 7-inch
CAPITOL 3-5 75-78
CASABLANCA 3-5 78-79
GEFFEN 3-4 84-85
MGM 3-5 72-74
PRIDE 3-5 72-73
SOLAR 3-4 81-82
VERVE 3-5 71
Picture Sleeves
GEFFEN 3-4 84-85
PRIDE 3-5 72-73
LPs: 10/12-inch
CAPITOL 5-10 75-78
CASABLANCA 5-10 78-79
CONCEPT 5-10 81
GEFFEN 5-8 84
MGM 8-10 72-74
PRIDE 8-10 72-73
SOLAR 5-10 81
Members: Foster Sylvers; Edmund Sylvers; Pay Sylvers; Angie Sylvers.
Also see LITTLE ANGELS
Also see SYLVERS, Edmund
Also see SYLVERS, Foster

SYLVERS, Edmund
Singles: 7-inch
CASABLANCA 3-5 80
LPs: 10/12-inch
CASABLANCA 5-10 80
Also see SYLVERS

SYLVERS, Foster P&R/LP '73
Singles: 7-inch
MGM 3-5 73
PRIDE 3-5 73
LPs: 10/12-inch
MGM 6-10 74
PRIDE 8-10 73
Also see SYLVERS

SYLVESTER P&R/LP '78
(Sylvester James)
Singles: 12-inch
FANTASY 4-8 78-79
MEGATONE 4-6 83-86
Singles: 7-inch
FANTASY (Black vinyl) 3-5 78-79
FANTASY (Colored vinyl) 4-8 78-79
(Promotional issues only.)
HONEY 3-5 80-81
MEGATONE 3-4 83-86
W.B. 3-4 87
LPs: 10/12-inch
FANTASY 5-10 78-81
HONEY 5-10 80-81
MEGATONE 5-8 83-86
W.B. 5-8 87

SYLVESTER, Max
Singles: 7-inch
BIG J 4-8 64

SYLVESTER, Terry
Singles: 7-inch
EPIC 4-6 74-78
Also see HOLLIES

SYLVESTER, Tony, & New Ingredient
Singles: 7-inch
MERCURY 3-5 76
Also see MAIN INGREDIENT

SYLVESTER & Hot Band
LPs: 10/12-inch
BLUE THUMB 8-10 73

SYLVIA P&R/LP '73
(Sylvia Vanderpool; Sylvia Robinson)
Singles: 12-inch
SUGARHILL 4-6 82
VIBRATION 4-8 77
Singles: 7-inch
ALL PLATINUM 3-5 74
STANG 3-5 70
SUGARHILL 3-5 81
VIBRATION 3-5 73-78
LPs: 10/12-inch
SUGARHILL 5-10 81
VIBRATION 6-10 73-78
Also see LITTLE SYLVIA
Also see MICKEY & SYLVIA
Also see SYLVIA & CHUCK JACKSON
Also see SYLVIA & MOMENTS
Also see SYLVIA & RALFI PAGAN
Also see TURNER, Ike & Tina

SYLVIA & CHUCK JACKSON
Singles: 7-inch
VIBRATION 3-6 77
Also see JACKSON, Chuck
Also see SYLVIA

SYLVIA & MOMENTS P&R/R&B '74
Singles: 7-inch
ALL PLATINUM 3-5 74
Also see MOMENTS

SYLVIA & RALFI PAGAN R&B '73
Singles: 7-inch
VIBRATION 3-5 73
Also see PAGAN, Ralfi
Also see SYLVIA

SYLVIA C&W '79
(Sylvia Kirby Allen)
Singles: 7-inch
RCA 3-5 79-87
RCA GOLD STANDARD 3-4 81
Picture Sleeves
RCA 3-4 81-86
LPs: 10/12-inch
RCA 5-10 81-86
Also see GALWAY, James, & Sylvia

SYLVIA & MICHAEL JOHNSON C&W '85
Singles: 7-inch
RCA 3-4 86
Also see JOHNSON, Michael
Also see SYLVIA (Sylvia Kirby Allen)

SYLVIA, Carmil
Singles: 7-inch
GEDINSON 4-8 62

SYLVIA, Margo, & Tune Weavers: see TUNE WEAVERS

SYLVIE & HER SILVER DOLLAR BAND C&W '89
Singles: 7-inch
PLAYBACK 3-4 89

SYLVIA & SADDLE-LITES
Singles: 7-inch
CUCA (6554 "Poor Nates Mt. Dew") 8-12 65

SYMBA R&B '80
Singles: 7-inch
VENTURE 3-5 80

SYMBOL 8 R&B '77
Singles: 7-inch
SHOCK 3-5 77-78

SYMBOLIC THREE R&B '85
(Featuring D.J. Dr. Shock)
Singles: 7-inch
REALITY 3-4 85

SYMBOLS
Singles: 7-inch
STANSON (502 "Blue Autumn") 100-150 58

SYMBOLS
Singles: 7-inch
DORE 10-15 63

SYMBOLS
Singles: 7-inch
JCP (1040 "Give Me Time") 10-20 65

SYMBOLS
Singles: 7-inch
MGM 5-10 65-66

SYMBOLS
Singles: 7-inch
LAURIE 5-10 67-68
PRESIDENT 5-10 66

SYMBOLS
Singles: 7-inch
IMPERIAL 4-6 69

SYMBOLS
Singles: 7-inch
JCP (1040 "Give Me Time") 10-20 60s

SYMBOLS
Singles: 7-inch
VINTAGE 3-5 73

SYMON & PI
Singles: 7-inch
CAPITOL 4-8 68

SYMPHONIC SLAM
LPs: 10/12-inch
A&M 5-10 76

SYMPHONICS
Singles: 7-inch
ENRICA (1002 "Come on Honey") .15-25 59
Member: Freddy Scott.
Also see SCOTT, Freddie

SYMPHONICS
Singles: 7-inch
ABC 4-8 68
BRUNSWICK 5-10 66-67
DEE-JON (001 "All Roads Lead to Heartbreak") 15-25 64
TRU-LITE (116 "Our Love Will Grow") 10-20 63

SYMPHONIES
Singles: 7-inch
CARNIVAL 3-6 69

SYMS, Sylvia P&R '56
Singles: 78 rpm
ATLANTIC 3-6 52-53
DECCA 3-6 56-57
Singles: 7-inch
ATLANTIC 5-10 52-53
COLUMBIA 4-8 59-65
DECCA 4-10 56-64
PRESTIGE 4-6 67
RORI 4-6 62
EPs: 7-inch
ATLANTIC 5-15 56
DECCA 5-15 55
LPs: 10/12-inch
A&M 5-10 78

ATLANTIC (137 "Songs By Sylvia Syms") 50-100 53
(10–inch LP.)
ATLANTIC (1243 "Songs By Sylvia Syms") 20-40 56
(Has Atlantic logo at top of label.)
ATLANTIC (1243 "Songs By Sylvia Syms") 15-25 60
(Has Atlantic logo on side of label.)
ATLANTIC (18000 series) 5-10 76
COLUMBIA 20-30 60
DECCA (8188 "Sylvia Sings") 35-45 55
DECCA (8639 "Song of Love") 30-40 58
KAPP 15-25 61
MOVIETONE 10-15 67
PRESTIGE 15-25 65-67
REPRISE 5-10 82
20TH FOX 10-20 64
VERSION (103 "After Dark") 40-50 54
(10–inch LP.)

SYN

Singles: 7–inch
DERAM (7510 "Grounded") 10-15 67

SYNCAPATES

Singles: 7–inch
TIMES SQUARE (7 "Your Tender Lips") 10-20 63
(Colored vinyl.)

SYNCH P&R '86

(Jimmy Hamen & Synch)
Singles: 7–inch
COLUMBIA (05788 "Where Are You Now") 3-4 86
MICKI (001 "Where Are You Now") 10-15
WTG (68625 "Where Are You Now") 3-4 89
Member: Jimmy Hamen.

SYNCOPATERS

Singles: 78 rpm
NATIONAL (9093 "Mule Train") 50-75 49
NATIONAL (9095 "River, Stay Away from My Door") 50-75 49

SYNDA

Singles: 7–inch
PEPPER 4-8 68

SYNDICATE

Singles: 7–inch
EBB TIDE 4-8 62

SYNDICATE

Singles: 7–inch
DORE (743 "My Baby's Barefoot") 20-40 65
DOT (16807 "Egyptian Thing") 20-40 66

SYNDICATE

(Cobblers)
Singles: 7–inch
TEE PEE (45 "Next 21st of May") 10-20 68
Members: Ron Spanbauer; Pat Nugent; Mike Meidl; Bob Weisapple; Bob Misky; Nick Christas.
Also see COBBLERS

SYNDICATE OF SOUND P&R/LP '66

Singles: 7–inch
BELL 4-8 66-67
BUDDAH 3-5 70
CAPITOL 3-6 69
DEL-FI (4304 "Prepare for Love") ..10-20 65
HUSH (228 "Little Girl") 20-30 66
SCARLET (5-3 "Prepare for Love") 15-25 65
LPs: 10/12–inch
BELL (LP-6001 "Little Girl") 25-35 66
(Monaural.)
BELL (SLP-6001 "Little Girl") 30-45 66
(Stereo.)
PERFORMANCE 5-8 88
Members: Jim Sawyers; Bob Gonzalez; John Sharkey; Don Baskin; John Duckworth; Larry Roy; Carl Scott; Barrie Thompson; Dennis Tracy.

SYNERGY LP '75

Singles: 7–inch
PASSPORT 3-5 76
LPs: 10/12–inch
PASSPORT (Black vinyl) 5-10 75-84
PASSPORT (Clear vinyl) 8-12 78

SYREETA LP '72

(Syreeta Wright)
Singles: 7–inch
MOTOWN 3-5 74-80
MOWEST 3-5 72
TAMLA 3-5 80-83
LPs: 10/12–inch
MOTOWN 5-10 74-81
MOWEST 8-12 72
TAMLA 5-10 77-81
Also see JENNIFER / Syretta
Also see PRESTON, Billy, & Syreeta
Also see WRIGHT, Rita

SYSTEM

Singles: 7–inch
VINEYARD (444 "One in a Million") 15-25 60s

SYSTEM P&R/R&B/D&D/LP '83

Singles: 12–inch
MIRAGE 4-6 83-86
Singles: 7–inch
ATCO 3-4 88
ATLANTIC 3-4 87
MIRAGE 3-4 83-86
Picture Sleeves
ATCO 3-4 88
ATLANTIC 3-4 87

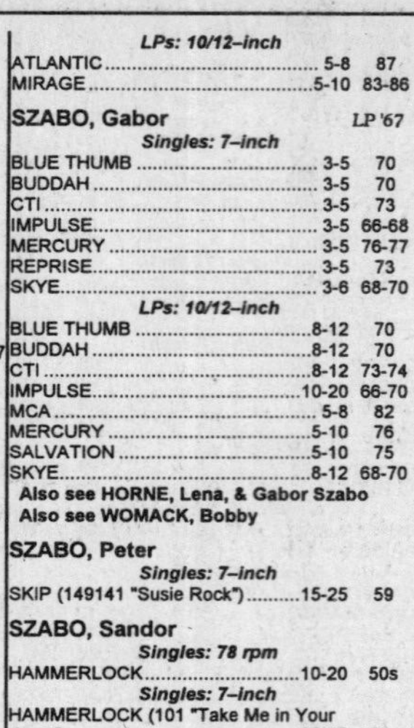
LPs: 10/12–inch
ATLANTIC 5-8 87
MIRAGE 5-10 83-86

SZABO, Gabor LP '67

Singles: 7–inch
BLUE THUMB 3-5 70
BUDDAH 3-5 70
CTI 3-5 73
IMPULSE 3-5 66-68
MERCURY 3-5 76-77
REPRISE 3-5 73
SKYE 3-6 68-70
LPs: 10/12–inch
BLUE THUMB 8-12 70
BUDDAH 8-12 70
CTI 8-12 73-74
IMPULSE 10-20 66-70
MCA 5-8 82
MERCURY 5-10 76
SALVATION 5-10 75
SKYE 8-12 68-70
Also see HORNE, Lena, & Gabor Szabo
Also see WOMACK, Bobby

SZABO, Peter

Singles: 7–inch
SKIP (149141 "Susie Rock") 15-25 59

SZABO, Sandor

Singles: 78 rpm
HAMMERLOCK 10-20 50s
Singles: 7–inch
HAMMERLOCK (101 "Take Me in Your Arms" 25-35 50s

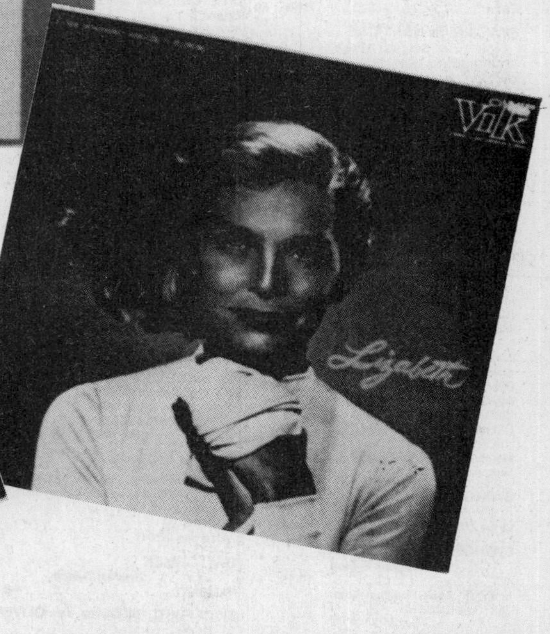

T

T, Dave & Del-Rays: see DAVE T & DEL-RAYS

T BONES P&R '65
(T-Bones)
Singles: 7-inch
LIBERTY ... 5-10 64-66
EPs: 7-inch
LIBERTY ... 8-12 65
(Juke box issues only.)
LPs: 10/12-inch
LIBERTY ... 15-25 64-66
SUNSET ... 10-20 66
Members: Dan Hamilton; Gene Pello; Joe Frank Carollo; Tom Reynolds; Judd Hamilton; Richard Torres; George Dee.
Also see HAMILTON, JOE FRANK & REYNOLDS

T. BOXES
Singles: 7-inch
MERCURY ... 3-5 72

T. LIFE
Singles: 7-inch
ARISTA ... 3-5 81
LPs: 10/12-inch
ARISTA ... 5-10 81

T.P. & INDIANS
Singles: 7-inch
DELLWOOD (3239 "Ally Or Enemy") ... 15-25 67

T. REX P&R/LP '71
(Tyrannosaurus Rex)
Singles: 7-inch
A&M ... 5-10 68
BLUE THUMB ... 4-8 71-72
CASABLANCA ... 3-5 75
REPRISE ... 3-6 71-74
LPs: 10/12-inch
A&M (3000 series) ... 10-15 72
A&M (4000 series) ... 15-20 68
BLUE THUMB (7 "Unicorn") ... 10-20 71
BLUE THUMB (18 "Beard of Stars") ... 10-20 72
(Add $5 to $10 if accompanied by the bonus single *Ride a White Swan*.)
CASABLANCA ... 8-10 74
REPRISE ... 8-12 71-73
Members: Marc Bolan; Steve Peregrine Took; Mickey Finn; Bill Legend; Dino Dines; Steve Currie; Jack Green; Gloria Jones. Session: Howard Kaylan; Marc Volman.
Also see BOLAN, Marc
Also see GREEN, Jack
Also see KAYLAN, Howard, & Marc Volman

T. SWIFT: see SWIFT, Tom

T&T
Singles: 7-inch
W.B. ... 4-8 63

T.C. ATLANTIC
Singles: 7-inch
AESOPS (6044 "Once Upon a Melody") ... 25-35 65
B. SHARP (272 "Mona") ... 40-60 66
CANDY FLOSS (101 "20 Years Ago") ... 30-40 68
PARAMOUNT (0098 "Judgement Train") ... 10-20 71
PARROT (330 "20 Years Ago") ... 20-25 68
PARROT (338 "Faces") ... 20-25 68
TURTLE (1103 "Faces") ... 150-175 66
TURTLE (1105 "Shake") ... 25-35 66
LPs: 10/12-inch
DOVE (4459 "T.C. Atlantic") ... 15-25 67
(Price reduced since recent boot availability.)
Members: Bob Wells; Rod Eaton; Fred Freeman; Joe Kanan.
Also see MARSHALL, Eric, & Chimes

T.C.F. CREW
LPs: 10/12-inch
W.B. ... 8-10 90s

T-CONNECTION P&R/R&B/LP '77
Singles: 12-inch
CAPITOL ... 4-6 81-84
Singles: 7-inch
CAPITOL ... 3-5 81-84
DASH ... 3-5 77-79
LPs: 10/12-inch
CAPITOL ... 5-10 81-84
DASH ... 5-10 77-79
Members: Theophilus T. Coakley; David Mackey; Anthony Flowers; Kirkwood Coakley.

T.D. & CHECKMATES
Singles: 7-inch
PARLIAMENT (9770 "Dark Alley") .. 8-12

TJ'S
Singles: 7-inch
LINDY (740 "Party Party") ... 30-50 57
LINDY (741 "I Got a Baby") ... 50-75 57
LINDY (1124 "Baby Doll") ... 30-50 58
Members: Tom Terry; Jack Roubik; Duane Schroeder; Bill Weigel; Ronnie Hagaland; Guy Buchalou.
Also see CARAVANS

T.F.O. R&B '80
Singles: 7-inch
VENTURE ... 3-5 80-81

THP ORCHESTRA R&B/LP '78
Singles: 7-inch
ATLANTIC ... 3-5 79
BUTTERFLY (Black vinyl) ... 3-4 77-78
BUTTERFLY (Colored vinyl) ... 3-5 77-78
LPs: 10/12-inch
ATLANTIC ... 5-8 79
BUTTERFLY ... 8-10 77

T.I.M. LOVE
Singles: 7-inch
ASCOT ... 4-8 67

T.I.M.E.
(Trust in Men Everywhere)
Singles: 7-inch
LIBERTY ... 5-10 68
Picture Sleeves
LIBERTY ... 10-15 68
LPs: 10/12-inch
LIBERTY ... 12-15 68-69
Also see HARD TIMES
Also see NEW PHOENIX
Also see STEPPENWOLF

T.J. & FORMATIONS
Singles: 7-inch
LIBERTY ... 4-8 67

T.J.K. & P.S. 13 BLUES BAND
Singles: 7-inch
PARKWAY ... 4-8 66

T.J.M.
Singles: 7-inch
CASABLANCA ... 3-5 79
LPs: 10/12-inch
CASABLANCA ... 5-10 79

T-Js
Singles: 7-inch
LINDY ... 8-12 59

TKA P&R/R&B '86
(Total Knowledge in Action)
Singles: 12-inch
TOMMY BOY ... 4-6 86
Singles: 7-inch
TOMMY BOY ... 3-4 86-88
LPs: 10/12-inch
TOMMY BOY ... 5-8 86-88

TKO LP '79
Singles: 7-inch
INFINITY ... 3-5 79
LPs: 10/12-inch
INFINITY ... 5-10 79

T.K.O.'s R&B '66
Singles: 7-inch
TEN STAR ... 4-8 65-67

T.M.G. P&R '79
Singles: 7-inch
ATCO ... 3-5 79
LPs: 10/12-inch
ATCO ... 5-10 79

TMP BAND R&B '86
Singles: 7-inch
CRITIQUE ... 3-4 86

TNJs
Singles: 7-inch
NEWARK ... 4-8 68

TNT LP '87
LPs: 10/12-inch
MERCURY ... 5-8 84-89

TNT BAND R&B '69
Singles: 7-inch
COTIQUE ... 3-5 69

TNT ROCK
Singles: 7-inch
MAUER BROS. ("Shake Baby Shake") ... 4-6 70s
(Selection number not known.)
Picture Sleeves
MAUER BROS. ... 5-10 70s

TNT TRIBBLE: see TRIBBLE, TNT

T.P. & INDIANS
Singles: 7-inch
DELLWOOD (3239 "Goodbye Good Times") ... 15-25 60s

T.R. & YARDSMEN
Singles: 7-inch
HIDEOUT (1105 "I Tried") ... 15-25 65

T-R'S
Singles: 7-inch
WEST-END (001 "The Vam") ... 10-20 66

TR-4
Singles: 7-inch
VELVET TONE ... 4-8 66-68

TR-5
Singles: 7-inch
KAPP ... 4-8 69

T.S.O.L.
LPs: 10/12-inch
FRONTIER ... 5-10 81

TSOL LP '87
(True Sounds of Liberty)
LPs: 10/12-inch
ENIGMA ... 5-8 87

T.S.U. TORONADOS P&R/R&B '69
(Tornados)
Singles: 7-inch
ATLANTIC ... 4-8 68-69
OVIDE (227 "You're Mine") ... 15-25 67
OVIDE (250 "Nothing Can Stop Me") ... 10-20 68
VOLT ... 4-6 69-70
Note: We're told there is a connection between this group and Archie Bell & the Drells.
Also see BELL, Archie

TTF R&B '80
(Today, Tomorrow, Forever)
Singles: 7-inch
CURTOM ... 3-5 80
GOLD COAST ... 3-5 81
RSO ... 3-5 80
LPs: 10/12-inch
GOLD COAST ... 5-10 81

TTT: see TONGUE TWISTIN' TEN

T2
LPs: 10/12-inch
LONDON (583 "It's All Work Out in Boomland") ... 20-30 71

T.U.M.E.
(The Ultimate Musical Experience)
Singles: 7-inch
MGM ... 3-5 75
LPs: 10/12-inch
MGM ... 8-10 75

T.V. & TRIBESMEN
LPs: 10/12-inch
HBR ... 10-20 66

T.V. MAMA JEAN
Singles: 7-inch
KENT ... 3-5 71

T.V. SLIM
(With His Heartbreakers; with His Bluesmen; with His Good Rocking Band; Oscar Wills; Oscar "TV" Wills)
Singles: 78 rpm
CHECKER (870 "Flat Foot Sam") .. 25-50 57
CLIFF (103 "Flat Foot Sam") ... 50-100 57
Singles: 7-inch
CHECKER (870 "Flat Foot Sam") .. 40-60 57
CLIF (103 "Flat Foot Sam") ... 100-200 57
(First issue.)
EXCELL (104 "TV Man") ... 30-40 66
IDEEL (581 "You Won't Treat Me Right") ... 8-12 60s
PZAZZ ... 5-10 69
SPEED (703 "Don't Reach 'Cross My Plate") ... 20-30 59
SPEED (704 "Flat Foot Sam Met Jim Dandy") ... 20-30 59
SPEED (705 "My Ship Is Sinking") .. 10-20 60s
SPEED (706 "My Baby Is Gone") ... 10-20 60s
SPEED (708 "Mean Woman Blues") ... 10-20 60s
SPEED (710 "Dancing Senorita") ... 10-20 60s
SPEED (711 "My Baby Is Gone") ... 10-20 60s
SPEED (714 "Dream Girl") ... 10-20 60s
SPEED (715 "Gravy Around Your Steak") ... 10-20 60s
SPEED (803 "The Big Fight") ... 10-20 60s
SPEED (807 "Boogie Woogie Guitar Twist") ... 10-20 60s
SPEED (808 "Hen Peck Joe") ... 10-20 60s
SPEED (810 "Hold Me Close to Your Heart") ... 10-20 60s
SPEED (6865 "To Prove My Love") ... 40-60 58
TIMBRE (510 "Can't Be Satisfied") .. 8-12 66
U.S.A. (739 "Hold Me Close to Your Heart") ... 8-12
Also see WILLS, Oscar (With Fats Domino's Band) / Paul Gayten

T.Z. D&D '83
Singles: 12-inch
STREET SOUND ... 4-6 83

TA MARA & SEEN P&R/R&B/D&D '85
Singles: 12-inch
A&M ... 4-6 85-86
Singles: 7-inch
A&M (Black vinyl) ... 3-4 85-88
A&M (4402 "Blueberry Gossip") ... 8-12 88
(Lips-shaped picture disc.)
Picture Sleeves
A&M ... 3-4 85
LPs: 10/12-inch
A&M ... 5-8 85

TABB, Jimmy, & Little Boppers
Singles: 7-inch
TIFCO (828 "Pink Scarf") ... 15-25

TABBY & HIS MELLOW, MELLOW MEN
(Tabby Thomas)
Singles: 78 rpm
DELTA (416 "Thinking Blues") ... 25-50 53
Singles: 7-inch
DELTA (416 "Thinking Blues") ... 75-100 53
Also see THOMAS, Tabby

TABBYS
Singles: 7-inch
TIME (1008 "My Darling") ... 25-50 59
(Blue label.)
TIME (1008 "My Darling") ... 20-30 59
(Red label.)

TABBYS
Singles: 7-inch
CLEOPATRA ... 5-10 63
METRO ... 5-10 63

TA'BOO D&D '84
Singles: 12-inch
ACME ... 4-6 84

TABOOS
Singles: 7-inch
LA SALLE (382 "So Sad") ... 15-25

TABOR, Jeff
Singles: 7-inch
DOLTON ... 5-10 60

TABRON
Singles: 7-inch
IN SEASON ... 3-4 83

TABS
Singles: 7-inch
DOT (15887 "First Star") ... 10-20 58
GARDENA (110 "Never Forget") ... 25-50 60
NASCO (6016 "Still Love You Baby") ... 20-30 58
NOBLE (719 "Never Forget") ... 100-200 59
(First pressed crediting the Marquis.)
NOBLE (720 "Oops") ... 1000-2000 59
VEE JAY (418 "Dance Party") ... 8-12 61
VEE JAY (446 "Mash Dem Tatters") ... 8-12 61
WAND (130 "Two Stupid Feet") ... 5-10 63
WAND (139 "I'm with You") ... 5-10 63
Members: Bill Gardner; John Johnson; Jim Tanlin; Herb Northern; Ted Forbes.
Also see MARQUIS

TABULATIONS / Cordells: see CORDELLS / Tabulations

TACKER, Dick
Singles: 7-inch
KINGSTON (1364 "Rock All Night with Me") ... 300-400 59

TACKETT, Marlow C&W '80
Singles: 7-inch
KARI ... 3-5 80
PALACE ... 3-5 80
RCA ... 3-4 82-83

TACO P&R/D&D/LP '83
(Taco Ockerse)
Singles: 12-inch
RCA ... 4-6 83-84
Singles: 7-inch
RCA ... 3-4 83-84
LPs: 10/12-inch
RCA ... 5-8 83-84

TAD & SMALL FRY
Singles: 7-inch
LE CAM ... 15-25 62

TADS
(With the Jimmy Wilcox Band)
Singles: 78 rpm
DOT ... 10-20 56
LIBERTY BELL ... 25-50 56
Singles: 7-inch
DOT (15518 "Your Reason") ... 25-50 56
LIBERTY BELL (9010 "Your Reason") ... 50-100 56
REV (3513 "She Is My Dream") ... 50-75 58

TAFF, Russ
Singles: 7-inch
HORIZON ... 3-4 85-86
LPs: 10/12-inch
MYRRH ... 5-8 80s

TAFFYS
Singles: 7-inch
AMY ... 4-8 65
FAIRMOUNT ... 4-8 63
PAGEANT ... 4-8 63

TAFOYA, Ernest
Singles: 7-inch
BANDBOX ... 4-8 64

TAGES
Singles: 7-inch
VERVE ... 5-10 68
Also see FRAMPTON, Peter

TAGGET
Singles: 7-inch
U.A. ... 3-5 75
LPs: 10/12-inch
U.A. ... 8-10 75

TAIL FEATHERS
Singles: 7-inch
UPTITE ... 15-25 67

TAIL GATORS
LPs: 10/12-inch
RESTLESS ... 5-8 88
WRESTLER ... 5-8 87

TAJ MAHAL LP '69
Singles: 7-inch
COLUMBIA (10000 series) ... 3-5 75
COLUMBIA (44000 series) ... 4-8 67-69
COLUMBIA (45000 series) ... 3-6 69-74
Picture Sleeves
COLUMBIA ... 4-8 67
LPs: 10/12-inch
COLUMBIA ... 6-12 68-81
W.B. ... 5-10 77
Also see RISING SONS
Also see SPRINGSTEEN, Bruce / Albert Hammond / Loudon Wainwright III / Taj Mahal

TAK TIKS
Singles: 7-inch
GUYDEN ... 4-8 67
Also see KIT KATS

TAKA BOOM: see BOOM, Taka

TAKANAKA R&B '86
Singles: 7-inch
AMHERST ... 3-4 86

TAKE FIVE
Singles: 12-inch
DESTINY ... 4-6
Singles: 7-inch
DESTINY ... 3-4
LPs: 10/12-inch
DESTINY ... 5-8

TAKE 6 LP '89
LPs: 10/12-inch
REPRISE ... 5-8 89-90

TAKEOFFS
Singles: 7-inch
FORD ... 5-10 65

TAKERS
Singles: 7-inch
INTERPHON ... 4-8 64

TALBERT, Bubba C&W '83
Singles: 7-inch
RANGER ... 3-4 83

TALBERT, Wayne
LPs: 10/12-inch
PULSAR ... 5-8

TALBOT, John Michael
LPs: 10/12-inch
BIRDWING ... 10-15
SPARROW ... 10-15
Also see TALBOT BROTHERS

TALBOT, Johnny
(With De-Thangs)
Singles: 7-inch
JASMAN (2 "Pickin Cotton") ... 10-15 60s
MODERN (1002 "Never Make Your Baby Cry") ... 5-10 65
RED FIRE (1002 "What You Want to Do") ... 8-12 64

TALBOT, Ross
Singles: 7-inch
BOBBIE ... 4-8 62

TALBOT, Terry
Singles: 7-inch
AUDIO FIDELITY ... 3-4
LPs: 10/12-inch
AUDIO FIDELITY ... 5-10
SPARROW ... 5-8 70s
Also see TALBOT BROTHERS

TALBOT BROTHERS
LPs: 10/12-inch
SPARROW ... 5-8 70s
W.B. ... 5-10 74
Members: Terry Talbot; John Michael Talbot.
Also see MASON PROFFIT
Also see TALBOT, John Michael
Also see TALBOT, Terry

TALBOYS, Lee
Singles: 7-inch
PALLADIUM ... 4-8 61
SPINNING ... 5-10 59

TALBURT, Gus
Singles: 7-inch
PINE (1001 "I'm in Love") ... 75-100

TALENT, Tony
Singles: 7-inch
VANDO ... 4-8 67

TALENTS
Singles: 7-inch
SKYLARK ... 5-10 61
TWINK ... 5-10 60s

TALES OF JONATHAN
Singles: 7-inch
MGM ... 4-8 67

TALFORD, Wanda
Singles: 7-inch
DOME (1242 "Hep to Your Jive") ... 5-10 60s

TALISMAN
Singles: 7-inch
AMERICAN ARTS ... 4-8 65
DOT ... 5-10 60
PRESTIGE ... 4-8 65
LPs: 10/12-inch
BLUE STAR ... 10-20 64
PRESTIGE ... 10-20 65

TALISMEN
Singles: 7-inch
RAMPRO (115 "Glitter & Gold") ... 15-25 66
Members: Paul Beneke; Bill Sherek; John Javorsky; Russ Loniello.
Also see TIKIS

TALISMEN
Singles: 7-inch
HIDEOUT (1226 "Vintage NSU") ... 10-20 67
JULIAN (105 "She Was Good") ... 8-12
RAIO & RAIO (1005 "Good Bye My Love") ... 100-200

TALISMEN
Singles: 7-inch
UA ... 8-12 60s
Also see ROE, Marlys

TALK OF THE TOWN
Singles: 7-inch
T.S.O.P. ... 4-8 74

TALK TALK *P&R/LP '82*
Singles: 12-inch
EMI AMERICA.......... 4-8 82-86
Singles: 7-inch
EMI AMERICA.......... 3-5 82-86
Picture Sleeves
EMI AMERICA.......... 3-5 84-86
LPs: 10/12-inch
EMI AMERICA.......... 5-10 82-86

TALKABOUTS
Singles: 78 rpm
REGENCY (792 "Sweet Lovin' Baby").......... 50-75 59
(Canadian.)
Singles: 7-inch
POPLAR (117 "Sweet Lovin' Baby").......... 20-30 59
REGENCY (792 "Sweet Lovin' Baby").......... 20-30 59
(Canadian.)

TALKING HEADS *LP '77*
Singles: 12-inch
SIRE.......... 4-8 79-86
Singles: 7-inch
SIRE.......... 3-5 77-88
Picture Sleeves
SIRE.......... 3-5 78-86
LPs: 10/12-inch
SIRE (Except 23771).......... 5-10 77-88
SIRE (23771 "Speaking in Tongues").......... 20-30 83
(Promotional issue only.)
W.B. (104 "Live on Tour").......... 25-45 79
(Promotional issue only.)
Members: David Byrne; Jerry Harrison; Tina Weymouth; Brian Eno; Robert Fripp; Chris Frantz.
Also see BYRNE, David
Also see MODERN LOVERS
Also see TOM TOM CLUB

TALKING JUKE BOX
Singles: 7-inch
REPUBLIC (1974 "Talking Juke Box").......... 4-6 74

TALL, Tom *C&W '64*
Singles: 78 rpm
FABOR ("Hot Rod Is Her Name")...30-50 58
Singles: 7-inch
CHART.......... 4-6
CREST (1038 "Stack-a-Records").......... 50-100 58
CREST (1052 "High School Love").......... 15-25 58
FABOR (132 "Hot Rod Is Her Name").......... 30-50 56
PETAL.......... 5-8 63
SAGE (305 "This Island").......... 10-15 59
SUNDOWN (133 "Yukon Trail").......... 5-8 63
Also see WRIGHT, Ginny, & Tom Tall

TALL BOYS
Singles: 7-inch
BRAVE DOG (21065 "Hugs Not Drugs").......... 8-10 88
(Complete press kit, includes color photo-insert, cardboard disc-invitation, R.S.V.P. card and envelope, three page news release, cassette and record of the song.)
BRAVE DOG (21065 "Hugs Not Drugs").......... 3-5 88
(Price for record only.)
Members: Wayne "Tree" Rollins; Jon Koncak; Cliff Levingston; Kevin Willis (all members of the Atlanta Hawks in 1988).

TALL PAUL
Singles: 7-inch
ATOMIC H.......... 15-25

TALL TOPS
EPs: 7-inch
AMAZING.......... 5-8 85

TALLEY, James *C&W '76*
Singles: 7-inch
CAPITOL.......... 3-5 76-77

TALLEY, Johnny T.
Singles: 78 rpm
MERCURY.......... 10-15 56
Singles: 7-inch
MERCURY.......... 20-30 56

TALLEY, Peggy
Singles: 7-inch
MERLENE.......... 4-8 63

TALLWATER, Jimmy
Singles: 7-inch
RAVEN-MAD.......... 3-5

TALLYMEN
Singles: 7-inch
A&M.......... 4-8 63
INFINITY.......... 4-8 62

TALLYSMEN
Singles: 7-inch
TALLY (200,688 "Little By Little")...15-25 65

TALMADGE, Jill
Singles: 7-inch
COLPIX.......... 4-8 61
MAY.......... 4-8 62

TALON BROTHERS
Singles: 7-inch
COLUMBIA.......... 4-8 66

TALTON, Troy
Singles: 7-inch
CREST.......... 4-8 62

TAM, Red, see RED TAM

TAMALPAIS EXCHANGE
Singles: 7-inch
ATLANTIC.......... 3-5 70
LPs: 10/12-inch
ATLANTIC.......... 5-10 70

TAMANEERS
Singles: 7-inch
BRAMLEY (102 "Searching").....200-300 60

TAMANGO, Kim
Singles: 7-inch
FUNTOWN.......... 3-6 69

TAMARA: see TA MARA

TAMBLYN, Larry
(With the Standells)
Singles: 7-inch
FARO (601 "Dearest").......... 20-40 60
FARO (603 "My Bride to Be").....50-100 60
FARO (612 "This Is the Night").....50-100 61
(Purple & silver label.)
FARO (612 "This Is the Night").....30-50 61
(Green label.)
LINDA (112 "Girl in My Heart").......10-20 65
Also see STANDELLS

TAMBLYN, Russ
Singles: 7-inch
BOSCO/MGM (225 "Tom Thumb's Tune").......... 5-10 58
(Promotional issue made for Bosco.)
Picture Sleeves
BOSCO/MGM (225 "Tom Thumb's Tune").......... 10-15 58
(Promotional issue made for Bosco.)

TAMBOURINES
Singles: 7-inch
EPIC.......... 4-8 66

TAME, Johnny
Singles: 7-inch
WORLD PACIFIC.......... 4-8 67

TAMES, Jackie
Singles: 7-inch
FTP.......... 4-8 61

TAMI SHOW *P&R '88*
Singles: 7-inch
CHRYSALIS.......... 3-4 88
Picture Sleeves
CHRYSALIS.......... 3-4 88

TAMIKO
(Tamiko Jones)
Singles: 7-inch
ATCO (6298 "Don't Laugh if I Cry at Your Party").......... 20-30 64
CHECKER (1041 "It's a Sin").......... 10-15 63
Also see JONES, Tamiko

TAMKIN, Robert
Singles: 7-inch
DATE.......... 4-8 68

TAMMI & BACHELORS
Singles: 7-inch
BANGAR (00610 "My Summer Love").......... 15-25

TAMMY JO *C&W '80*
(Tammy Jo Whitehead)
Singles: 7-inch
RIDGETOP.......... 3-5 80

TAMMY & BACHELORS
Singles: 7-inch
BANGAR.......... 10-20 64

TAMMY & CAROLINAS
Singles: 7-inch
LARSON.......... 5-10 61

TAMMYS
Singles: 7-inch
U.A.......... 5-10 63-64
VEEP.......... 5-10 65

TAMPA RED *P&R '36*
(Hudson Whittaker)
Singles: 78 rpm
BLUEBIRD.......... 20-50 44-45
RCA.......... 15-25 45-54
Singles: 7-inch
RCA (47-4000 & 47-5000 series) ...25-45 51-54
RCA (50-0000 series).......... 50-100 49-51
LPs: 10/12-inch
BLUEBIRD.......... 10-15 75
BLUES CLASSICS.......... 5-10
PRESTIGE BLUESVILLE.......... 20-35 61-62
YAZOO.......... 10-15
Also see BIG MACEO
Also see EAGER, Jimmy

TAMRONS
Singles: 7-inch
PYRAMID (7381 "Wild Man").......... 20-30 67

TAMS
Singles: 7-inch
MINK (22 "Memory Lane").......... 30-40 59
(*Memory Lane* was first issued in 1959, showing the group as the Stereos. The same track was reissued in 1963, shown first as by the Tams and then by the Hippies.)
PARKWAY (863 "Memory Lane") ..10-20 63
Also see HIPPIES / Reggie Harrison
Also see STEREOS

TAMS *P&R/R&B '62*
Singles: 7-inch
ABC.......... 3-6 68-73
ABC-PAR.......... 5-10 63-64
APT/ABC.......... 3-5 72
ARLEN (711 "Disillusioned").......... 10-20 62
ARLEN (717 "Deep Inside Me").......... 10-20 62
ARLEN (720 "You'll Never Know") 10-20 62
ARLEN (729 "Find Another Love") 10-20 62
CAPITOL.......... 3-6 71
COLLECTABLES.......... 3-4 80s
COMPLEAT.......... 3-5 83
DAISY.......... 5-10 60s
DUNHILL.......... 3-5 71
GENERAL AMERICAN (714 "Find Another Love").......... 10-15 62
GUSTO.......... 3-5 80
HERITAGE (101 "Vacation Time").......... 150-250 61
1-2-3.......... 3-5 70
KING.......... 5-10 65
MCA.......... 3-4 80s
RIPETE.......... 3-5 82
ROULETTE.......... 3-4 70s
SOUTH.......... 3-5 73
SWAN (4055 "Sorry").......... 30-40 60
WONDER.......... 3-5 82
LPs: 10/12-inch
ABC.......... 10-15 67-69
ABC-PAR.......... 20-30 64
BRYLEN.......... 5-10 84
CAPITOL.......... 5-10 79
COMPLEAT.......... 5-8 83
1-2-3.......... 8-10 70
SOUNDS SOUTH.......... 8-10 77
Members: Joe Pope; Charles Pope; Robert Lee Smith; Horace Key; Floyd Ashton; Albert Cottle.

TAN, Roy: see TANN, Roy

TAN TRUM
LPs: 10/12-inch
OVATION.......... 5-10 78

TANDI & TEAMATES
Singles: 7-inch
EMBER.......... 10-15 60

TANEGA, Norma *P&R '66*
Singles: 7-inch
ABC.......... 3-5 73
ERIC.......... 3-4 70s
NEW VOICE.......... 4-8 66-67
VIRGO.......... 3-4 73
LPs: 10/12-inch
NEW VOICE.......... 15-20 66

TANGEERS
Singles: 7-inch
OKEH (7319 "Let My Heart and Soul Be Free").......... 20-30 69

TANGENTS
(With the Rene Hall Orchestra)
Singles: 7-inch
FRESH (1 "I Can't Live Alone")......25-35 60

TANGENTS
Singles: 7-inch
U.A. (201 "The Wiggle").......... 10-15 60
Also see HALL, Rene

TANGENTS
Singles: 7-inch
MASTERTONE.......... 5-10 64
Members: Sonny Threatt; Murry Judy; Tony Compton; Ross Bolin; Andy McKinney; Land Ligon.
Also see NOMADS
Also see THREATT, Sonny

TANGENTS
Singles: 7-inch
IMPRESSION (111 "Hey Joe")......15-25 66

TANGERINE DREAM *LP '74*
Singles: 7-inch
EMI AMERICA.......... 3-4 84
VIRGIN.......... 3-5 75-77
LPs: 10/12-inch
EMI AMERICA.......... 5-8 84
ELEKTRA.......... 5-10 81
MCA.......... 5-10 77-86
VIRGIN.......... 8-12 74-77
Members: Peter Baumann; Chris Franks; Ed Froese.
Also see BAUMANN, Peter

TANGERINE DREAM / Jon Anderson / Bryan Ferry
LPs: 10/12-inch
MCA (6165 "Legend").......... 8-10 86
(Soundtrack.)
Also see ANDERSON, Jon
Also see FERRY, Bryan
Also see TANGERINE DREAM

TANGERINE ROOF
Singles: 7-inch
ROOF (1 "Back in My Arms").......... 15-25 68

TANGERINE ZOO
Singles: 7-inch
MAINSTREAM (682 "One More Heartache").......... 10-15 68
MAINSTREAM (690 "Like People") 10-15 68
LPs: 10/12-inch
MAINSTREAM (6107 "Tangerine Zoo").......... 25-35 68
MAINSTREAM (6116 "Outisde Looking In").......... 35-55 69
Members: Tony Tavares; Don Smith; Robert Benevides; Ron Medeiros; Wayne Gagnon.
Also see EBB TIDES

TANGERINES
Singles: 7-inch
WILDCAT.......... 10-15 61

TANGIER *P&R/LP '89*
Singles: 7-inch
ATCO.......... 3-4 89-90
Picture Sleeves
ATCO.......... 3-4 89
LPs: 10/12-inch
ATCO.......... 5-8 89-90

TANGIERS
(Hollywood Flames)
Singles: 78 rpm
DECCA.......... 50-100 56
Singles: 7-inch
A-J (905 "The Plea").......... 25-35 62
CLASS (224 "Don't Try").......... 30-40 58
DECCA (29603 "I Won't Be Around").......... 100-150 55
DECCA (29971 "Remember Me").......... 100-150 56
Also see HOLLYWOOD FLAMES

TANGIERS
Singles: 7-inch
STRAND (25039 "Ping Pong").......15-25 61

TANGIERS & JETSON BAND
Singles: 7-inch
DATE.......... 5-10 67
Also see JETSONS & Tangiers

TANGO
Singles: 7-inch
A&M.......... 3-5 74-78
LPs: 10/12-inch
A&M.......... 5-10 78

TANK
Singles: 7-inch
BANG.......... 3-5 73

TANN, Roy
(Roy Tan)
Singles: 78 rpm
DOT.......... 5-10 57
TAN.......... 10-15 57
Singles: 7-inch
DOT (15000 series).......... 5-10 57
DOT (16000 series).......... 4-8 64
TAN.......... 10-15 57

TANNER, Fargo *C&W '75*
Singles: 7-inch
AVCO.......... 3-5 75

TANNER, Gary *P&R '78*
Singles: 7-inch
20TH FOX.......... 3-5 78

TANNER, Joe
Singles: 7-inch
COLONIAL.......... 5-10 61
Also see DEE, Johnny

TANNER, Kid
Singles: 78 rpm
MODERN (889 "Wino").......... 10-20 53
Singles: 7-inch
MODERN (889 "Wino").......... 25-35 53

TANNER, Marc, Band *P&R/LP '79*
Singles: 7-inch
ELEKTRA.......... 3-5 79
PRIVATE I.......... 3-4 80s
LPs: 10/12-inch
ELEKTRA.......... 5-10 78-80
PRIVATE I.......... 5-10 80s

TANNER, R. Wolfe
Singles: 7-inch
LIN.......... 5-10 62

TANNER, Robert
Singles: 7-inch
MEGATONE (111 "Tell Me Your Name").......... 8-12

TANNER, Sammy
Singles: 7-inch
KCM.......... 10-15 59

TANNER, William V.
Singles: 7-inch
LIN.......... 5-10 61

TANNO, Marc
Singles: 7-inch
PRESIDENT.......... 10-15 62
20TH FOX.......... 10-20 60
WHALE (501 "Angel").......... 30-50 61

TANNY, Ric
Singles: 7-inch
TARGET.......... 5-10 60

TANTONES
Singles: 78 rpm
LAMP.......... 40-60 56
Singles: 7-inch
LAMP (2002 "No Matter What") .100-150 56
LAMP (2008 "Tell Me").......... 100-150 56

TANTRUM *LP '80*
Singles: 7-inch
OVATION.......... 3-5 79
LPs: 10/12-inch
OVATION.......... 5-10 79

TANYET
LPs: 10/12-inch
VAULT.......... 10-15 68

TAOS
LPs: 10/12-inch
MERCURY.......... 8-10 70

TAPES
LPs: 10/12-inch
PASSPORT.......... 5-10 80
PVC.......... 5-10 82

TAPESTRY
Singles: 7-inch
CAPITOL.......... 5-10 76
COMPASS.......... 4-8 67-68

TAPESTRY
Singles: 7-inch
AMJO.......... 8-12
PHILLY GROOVE.......... 8-12

TAPIA, Larry
Singles: 7-inch
TALENT.......... 5-10 59

TAPP, Demetriss *C&W '73*
Singles: 7-inch
ABC.......... 3-5 73
BRUNSWICK (55251 "Lipstick Paint a Smile on Me").......... 10-15 63
BRUNSWICK (55257 "Let Go of My Heart").......... 10-20 64
BRUNSWICK (55274 "Ring Dang Doo").......... 10-15 65

TAPP, Dora
Singles: 7-inch
ARROW.......... 3-5

TARANTULA
Singles: 7-inch
A&M.......... 3-6 69
LPs: 10/12-inch
A&M.......... 10-15 69

TARANTULAS
Singles: 7-inch
ATLANTIC (2102 "Tarantula").......... 15-20 61
(Without "fan" logo.)
ATLANTIC (2102 "Tarantula").......... 10-15 61
(With "fan" logo.)
FERNWOOD.......... 5-10 60
SILVER DOLLAR.......... 5-10 61
STOP.......... 4-8 64
Member: Bob Tucker.
Also see TUCKER, Bob

TARBUTTON, Jim
Singles: 7-inch
GEAR (100 "Stinger").......... 10-20 66

TARGET
Singles: 7-inch
A&M.......... 3-5 76-77
LPs: 10/12-inch
A&M.......... 5-10 76-77

TARGETS
Singles: 7-inch
KING (5538 "It Doesn't Matter").....20-30 61

TARHEEL SLIM: see TARHEEL SLIM & LITTLE ANN

TARHEEL SLIM & LITTLE ANN *R&B '59*
(Slim & Ann; Slim & Little Ann; Tarheel Slim & Lil' Annie)
Singles: 78 rpm
FIRE (1000 "Don't Ever Leave Me").......... 50-100 59
Singles: 7-inch
ATCO (6259 "TwoTime Loser").......... 8-12 63
ENJOY (2014 "You Make Me Feel So Good").......... 8-12 65
FIRE (503 "It's a Sin").......... 10-20 61
FIRE (506 "Can't Stay Away from You").......... 10-20 62
FIRE (1000 "Don't Ever Leave Me").......... 15-25 59
FIRE (1009 "Much Too Late").......... 15-25 60
FIRE (1017 "Can't Stay Away").......... 15-25 60
FIRE (1021 "I'll Be Yours").......... 15-25 60
FIRE (1030 "Security").......... 15-25 60
FURY (1068 "I Love You Because").......... 15-25 62
PORT (3001 "Close to You").......... 5-10 65
Also see BUNN, Allen
Also see LITTLE ANN
Also see LOVERS

TARNEY - SPENCER BAND *P&R/LP '78*
Singles: 7-inch
A&M.......... 3-5 78-81
PRIVATE STOCK.......... 3-5 76
LPs: 10/12-inch
A&M.......... 5-10 78-79
Members: Alan Tarney; Trevor Spencer.

TARO, Frankie
Singles: 7-inch
G&G (111 "Suzy Ann").......... 75-100 58

TARRIERS *P&R '56*
Singles: 78 rpm
GLORY.......... 8-12 56
Singles: 7-inch
DECCA.......... 5-10 63-64
GLORY.......... 10-20 56
U.A.......... 8-12 59
LPs: 10/12-inch
ATLANTIC.......... 15-25 60
DECCA.......... 10-20 62-64
GLORY (1200 "The Tarriers").......... 40-60 57
KAPP.......... 10-20 63
U.A.......... 15-25 59
Members: Erik Darling; Alan Arkin; Bob Carey.
Also see MARTIN, Vince
Also see ROOFTOP SINGERS
Also see WEISSBERG, Eric

TARRYTONS
Singles: 7-inch
DOT.......... 5-10 63
EXCLUSIVE.......... 10-15 63

TARTAGLIA
(With the Space Angels)
Singles: 7-inch
CAPITOL....4-6 69
MCA....3-5 78
LPs: 10/12-inch
CAPITOL....10-15 69

TARTANS
(With Kaddo Strings)
Singles: 7-inch
IMPACT (1010 "Nothing But Love")....10-20 66

TARTANS OF LAVENDER LAND
Singles: 7-inch
CAPITOL (2019 "Lovers of the World Unite")....20-25 67

TARVER, Leon
(With the Chordones; Leon D. Tarver)
Singles: 78 rpm
BLUE LAKE....20-30 55
CHECKER....50-75 54
Singles: 7-inch
BLUE LAKE (118 "Somebody Help Me")....50-75 55
CHECKER (791 "I'm a Young Rooster")....150-250 54

TASAVALLAN PRESIDENTI
LPs: 10/12-inch
JANUS....8-10 74

TASHER, Les
Singles: 7-inch
CANADIAN INT'L....5-10 60

TASMANIANS
Singles: 7-inch
CONDA (101 "Baby")....20-30 66
POWER (4933 "I Can't Explain This Feeling")....10-20 67

TASSELLS
Singles: 7-inch
GOLDISC....10-15 63

TASSELS P&R '59
Singles: 7-inch
AMY (946 "To a Soldier Boy")....8-12 66
MADISON (117 "To a Soldier Boy")....15-25 59
MADISON (121 "To a Young Lover")....10-20 59

TASSO, Julian
Singles: 7-inch
KAIN....10-20

TASSO, Vicki
Singles: 7-inch
COLPIX....4-8 62
JEFFREY....10-15 61

TASSO - CAIN & MATADORS
Singles: 7-inch
CAIN (9219 "Castro's Beat")....10-15 59
CY (0001 "Viet Nam Beat")....5-10 66
(Same track as *Castro's Beat*.)

TASSO THE GREAT
Singles: 7-inch
B&F....5-10 60
UNITED....10-15 53

TASTE LP '69
Singles: 7-inch
ATCO....3-5 69-70
LPs: 10/12-inch
ATCO....10-15 69-70
Member: Rory Gallagher.
Also see GALLAGHER, Rory

TASTE OF HONEY P&R/R&B/LP '78
Singles: 12-inch
CAPITOL (Except 9572)....4-8 78-79
CAPITOL (9572 "Sukiyaki")....8-10 80
(Fan shaped disc. Promotional issue only.)
MCA....4-6 84
Singles: 7-inch
CAPITOL....3-5 78-82
MCA....3-4 84
Picture Sleeves
CAPITOL....3-5 78-82
LPs: 10/12-inch
CAPITOL....5-10 78-82
Members: Janice Marie Johnson; Hazel Payne.
Also see FELDER, Wilton
Also see JOHNSON, Janice Marie

TASTY LICKS
LPs: 10/12-inch
ROUNDER....5-10 80

TATE, Billy
Singles: 78 rpm
IMPERIAL....40-60 54
PEACOCK....10-15 56
Singles: 7-inch
IMPERIAL (5337 "Single Life")....100-200 54
(With script style logo.)
PEACOCK (1671 "Don't Call My Name")....15-25 56

TATE, Bobby
Singles: 7-inch
AVA....4-8 63

TATE, Eric Quincy
Singles: 7-inch
CAPRICORN....3-5 70-72
LPs: 10/12-inch
CAPRICORN....8-10 70-72

TATE, Howard P&R/R&B '66
Singles: 7-inch
ATLANTIC....3-6 71-72
EPIC....3-5 74
TURNTABLE....5-10 69-70
UTOPIA (510 "Half a Man")....15-25 66
VERVE....4-8 66-68
LPs: 10/12-inch
ATLANTIC....10-20 71
TURNTABLE....8-10 70
VERVE....10-20 67-68
Also see DOGGETT, Bill
Also see GAINORS

TATE, Joe
Singles: 7-inch
ROULETTE (4059 "Satellite Rock")....15-20 58

TATE, Laurie
(With Joe Morris Blues Cavalcade)
Singles: 78 rpm
ATLANTIC....25-35 52
Singles: 7-inch
ATLANTIC (965 "Rock Me Daddy")....50-75 52
Also see MORRIS, Joe, & His Orchestra

TATE, Michael C&W '81
Singles: 7-inch
OAK....3-5 81

TATE, Paul
Singles: 7-inch
FALCON (1012 "Dance On")....8-12 58

TATE, Tommy R&B '72
Singles: 7-inch
ABC-PAR (10626 "What's the Matter")....15-25 65
JACKSON SOUND....8-10 70
KOKO....3-6 72-76
OKEH....8-12 66

TATER, Kid, & Cheaters
Singles: 7-inch
RIPSAW....3-5 79

TATTLETALES
Singles: 7-inch
W.B....5-10 59

TATTOO
LPs: 10/12-inch
PRODIGAL....8-10 76
Members: Wally Bryson; Jeff Hutton; Dan Klawson; David Allen Thomas; Thom Mooney.
Also see RASPBERRIES

TATUM, Danny
Singles: 7-inch
ROULETTE....4-8 61

TAUPIN, Bernie
LPs: 10/12-inch
ASYLUM....5-10 80
ELEKTRA....8-12 72
RCA....5-10 87

TAURUS
Singles: 7-inch
TOWER....5-10 69
Member: Johnny Cymbal.
Also see CYMBAL, Johnny

TAV FALCO'S PANTHER BURNS
Singles: 7-inch
ROUGH TRADE....4-6
Picture Sleeves
ROUGH TRADE....4-6
LPs: 10/12-inch
ANIMAL....8-10 82
ROUGH....8-10 81

TAVARES P&R/R&B '73
Singles: 12-inch
CAPITOL....4-8 77-79
RCA....4-6 82-84
Singles: 7-inch
CAPITOL....3-5 73-80
RCA....3-4 82-84
LPs: 10/12-inch
CAPITOL....8-10 73-81
RCA....5-10 82-83
Also see CHUBBY & TURNPIKES

TAVARES, Ernie, Trio: see BONAIRS / Ernie Tavares Trio

TAVENER, John
LPs: 10/12-inch
APPLE (3369 "The Whale")....10-15 72

TAWATHA R&B '87
Singles: 7-inch
EPIC....3-4 87

TAWNEY, Jerry
Singles: 7-inch
BELL....4-6 72
LIBERTY....5-8 66
Also see PORTRAITS
Also see YELLOW HAND

TAX FREE
Singles: 7-inch
POLYDOR....3-5 71
LPs: 10/12-inch
POLYDOR....5-10 71

TAXI BOYS
LPs: 10/12-inch
BOMP....5-10 80

TAXXI LP '82
Singles: 7-inch
FANTASY....3-5 82

LPs: 10/12-inch
FANTASY (9617 "States of Emergency")....20-30 82
MCA....10-15 85

TAYLES
Singles: 7-inch
AGE of AQUARIUS (1548 "She Made Me That Way")....10-15 70s
AGE of AQUARIUS (1549 "It's High Time")....10-15 70s
Picture Sleeves
AGE of AQUARIUS....10-20 70s
(1548 and 1549 were both issued in same gatefold picture sleeve.)
LPs: 10/12-inch
CINE VISTA (1001 "Who Are These Guys")....100-150 72
Members: Scott Eakin; Rick Markstrom; Bob Schmitke; Jeremy Wilson.

TAYLOR, Adam
Singles: 7-inch
LEHARVE (1028 "Yvonne")....50-75

TAYLOR, Al, & Poodles
Singles: 7-inch
U.A. (105 "The Ripple")....5-10 58

TAYLOR, Alex LP '71
Singles: 7-inch
BANG....3-5 78-79
CAPRICORN....3-5 71
DUNHILL....3-5 74
LPs: 10/12-inch
CAPRICORN....8-10 71
DUNHILL....8-10 74

TAYLOR, Andrew
Singles: 7-inch
GONE (5109 "That's How I Feel About You")....125-175 61
Also see INDIVIDUALS / Andrew Taylor

TAYLOR, Andy P&R '86
Singles: 12-inch
ATLANTIC....4-6 86
Singles: 7-inch
ATLANTIC....3-4 86
MCA....3-4 86-87
Picture Sleeves
ATLANTIC....3-4 86
MCA....3-4 86
LPs: 10/12-inch
MCA....5-8 87
Also see DURAN DURAN
Also see POWER STATION

TAYLOR, Ann
Singles: 7-inch
WIZARD....4-8 67

TAYLOR, Annabelle
Singles: 7-inch
VILLAGE....4-8 65

TAYLOR, Austin P&R '60
Singles: 7-inch
LAURIE....5-10 60-61
Also see TAYLOR, Ted

TAYLOR, B.E., Group P&R '84
Singles: 12-inch
EPIC....4-6 84
Singles: 7-inch
EPIC....3-4 84-86
MCA....3-5 83-84
Picture Sleeves
EPIC....3-4 86
LPs: 10/12-inch
MCA....5-10 82
Members: B.E. Taylor; Dave Kerr; Rick Withowski; Joe Macre; Joe D'Amico.
Also see CRACK the SKY

TAYLOR, Big John
Singles: 7-inch
RAM (1107 "Money, Money")....15-25 59
Also see JOY, Benny

TAYLOR, Bill
Singles: 7-inch
CITATION (5002 "Income Taxes and You")....10-15 62

TAYLOR, Bill, & Smokey Jo
(With Clyde Leoppard's Snearly Ranch Boys)
Singles: 78 rpm
FLIP (502 "Split Personality")....200-300 55
Singles: 7-inch
FLIP (502 "Split Personality")....500-700 55
Members: Bill Taylor; Smokey Joe Baugh; Clyde Leoppard; Stan Kesler; Buddy Holobaugh.
Also see SMOKEY JOE

TAYLOR, Billy
(With the Teardrops; Billy Taylor Trio; Bill Taylor)
Singles: 78 rpm
ABC-PAR....5-10 55
Singles: 7-inch
ABC-PAR....10-20 55
FELCO....8-12 59
FELSTED....10-15 59
TOWER....4-8 68
TROPHY (500 "Nelda Jane")....20-30 58
LPs: 10/12-inch
ABC-PAR (112 "Evergreens")....30-50 55
BELL....8-12 70
Also see MITCHELL, Willie

TAYLOR, Bobby
(With Charlie & the Jives; Bob Taylor)
Singles: 7-inch
ASTRA (1016 "Seven Steps to an Angel")....8-12 65
CALDWELL (402 "Frankie & Johnny")....15-25 59
CHYTOWN (104 "A Stranger")....8-12
DO-RA-ME (1432 "Samson & Delilah")....10-15 63
GUYDEN (2031 "Night Express")....10-20 60
HOUR (102 "Seven Steps to an Angel")....35-50 62
KAJO (2201 "It's Funny")....50-100 61
STACY (953 "After Hours")....8-12 62
YUCCA (110 "Don't Be Unfair")....75-125 59

TAYLOR, Bobby P&R/R&B '68
(With the Vancouvers)
Singles: 7-inch
BUDDAH....4-6 72
GORDY (Black vinyl, except 7088)....10-20 68-69
GORDY (7088 "Oh I've Been Blessed")....300-400 69
GORDY (Colored vinyl)....10-20 68
(Promotional issue only.)
HOUR....10-15
INTEGRA (103 "This Is My Woman")....50-75 68
MOWEST....4-8 71
PLAYBOY....3-6 75
SUNFLOWER (126 "There Are Roses Somewhere in This World")....15-25 72
TOMMY....3-6 73
V.I.P. (25053 "Blackmail")....10-20 69
(Same track on both sides. Promotional issue only.)
V.I.P. (25053 "Oh I've Been Blessed")....10-20 69
(Black vinyl.)
V.I.P. (25053 "Oh I've Been Blessed")....20-40 69
(Colored vinyl. Promotional issue only.)
LPs: 10/12-inch
GORDY (930 "Bobby Taylor & the Vancouvers")....40-60 68
GORDY (942 "Taylor Made Soul")....40-60 69
Members: Bobby Taylor; Wes Henderson; Eddie Patterson; Robbie King; Ted Lewis; Tommy Chong.
Also see CHEECH & CHONG
Also see COLUMBUS PHARAOHS
Also see FOUR PHARAOHS
Also see HENDERSON, Wes

TAYLOR, Burt
Singles: 7-inch
EAST WEST (118 "Long Lost Love")....10-20 58

TAYLOR, Carmen
(With the Boleros; with Orchestra; "Billboard's 1954 Disc-Jockey Poll Winner")
Singles: 78 rpm
APOLLO (489 "Oh Please")....15-25 56
ATLANTIC (Except 1041)....10-20 53
ATLANTIC (1041 "Freddie")....25-50 54
GUYDEN....10-15 54
TIN PAN ALLEY....10-15 54
Singles: 7-inch
APOLLO (489 "Oh Please")....40-50 56
ATLANTIC (1002 "Lovin' Daddy")....20-40 53
ATLANTIC (1015 "Big Mamou Daddy")....20-40 53
ATLANTIC (1041 "Freddie")....75-100 54
GUYDEN (100 "Let Me Go Lover")....15-25 54
KAMA SUTRA....4-8 65
TIN PAN ALLEY (130 "Love Is Everything")....15-25 54

TAYLOR, Carmol C&W '75
Singles: 7-inch
ELEKTRA....3-5 75-77
SHERBA (1501 "Street of Broken Hearts")....10-15 59
TAGG (504 "Free As a Breeze")....10-15 59

TAYLOR, Carmol, & Stella Parton C&W '77
Singles: 7-inch
ELEKTRA....3-5 76
Also see PARTON, Stella
Also see TAYLOR, Carmol

TAYLOR, Cathie
Singles: 7-inch
CAPITOL (4565 "Bobby Boy")....8-12 61
TOPPA (1006 "Tree Near My House")....10-15 59
Picture Sleeves
CAPITOL (4565 "Bobby Boy")....10-20 61
LPs: 10/12-inch
CAPITOL (1359 "Little Bit of Sweetness")....15-25 60
CAPITOL (1448 "Tree Near My House")....15-25 60

TAYLOR, Chet C&W '79
Singles: 7-inch
VISTA....3-5 79

TAYLOR, Chip C&W '75
(With Ghost Train)
Singles: 7-inch
CAPITOL....3-5 79
COLUMBIA....3-6 69-77
EPIC....4-6 69
MGM....4-8 61
MALA....4-8 64
RAINY DAY....4-8 67
W.B. (5000 series)....4-8 62
W.B. (7700 series)....3-5 73-76
LPs: 10/12-inch
CAPITOL....5-10 79
COLUMBIA....5-10 76
W.B....8-10 73-75
Also see GORGONI, Martin, & Chip Taylor
Also see JUST US

TAYLOR, Chuck
Singles: 7-inch
COLUMBIA....3-5 76
DECCA (31099 "Little Lover")....10-15 60
VEE JAY (388 "Road Runner")....8-12 61

TAYLOR, Danny
Singles: 7-inch
JO-PAR (518 "Things Are Tough")....8-12 60

TAYLOR, Danny "Run Joe"
(With the Louis Payne Orchestra)
Singles: 78 rpm
RCA....10-15 53
SAXONY....10-15 53
Singles: 7-inch
RCA (5558 "You Look Bad")....20-30 53
SAXONY (101 "I Know What I Want")....20-30 55
WHEELER....30-35 50s
Also see PAYNE, Louis, Orchestra

TAYLOR, Dave, & Clique
Singles: 7-inch
ZODIAC....4-6

TAYLOR, Debbie R&B '68
Singles: 7-inch
ARISTA....3-5 75-76
DECCA....4-6 68
GWP....4-6 69
POLYDOR....3-5 74
TODAY....3-5 72
LPs: 10/12-inch
TODAY....6-10 72

TAYLOR, Eddie
Singles: 78 rpm
VEE JAY....20-40 55-56
Singles: 7-inch
VEE JAY (149 "Bad Boy")....50-100 55
VEE JAY (185 "Big Town Playboy")....50-100 55
VEE JAY (206 "You'll Always Have a Home")....40-60 56
VEE JAY (267 "I'm Gonna Love You")....25-35 57
VIVID (104 "I'm Sitting Here")....10-20 64
Session: Jimmy Reed.
Also see PRYOR, Snooky
Also see REED, Jimmy
Also see SUNNYLAND SLIM

TAYLOR, Elaine, & Mastertones
Singles: 7-inch
BAND BOX (233 "Baby, Won't You Please Come Home")....20-25 60
Also see SCOTTY & BOBO with the Mastertones

TAYLOR, Faith, & Sweet Teens
Singles: 7-inch
BEA & BABY (104 "I Need Him to Love Me")....25-50 59
FEDERAL (12334 "Your Candy Kisses")....25-50 58

TAYLOR, Faron
Singles: 7-inch
COLUMBIA....4-6 68

TAYLOR, Felice P&R/R&B '67
Singles: 7-inch
KENT....4-8 68
MUSTANG....5-10 67
Also see SWEETS

TAYLOR, Frank C&W '63
Singles: 7-inch
PARKWAY....4-8 63

TAYLOR, Frank "Czech"
Singles: 7-inch
LOST GOLD (1013 "Let's Play This Tune")....3-4 90
(Gold vinyl.)
Picture Sleeves
LOST GOLD (1013 "Let's Play This Tune")....3-4 90

TAYLOR, Gary R&B '88
Singles: 7-inch
VIRGIN....3-4 88

TAYLOR, Gene
Singles: 7-inch
KENT....5-10 65
MINIT....4-8 69

TAYLOR, Gerri
Singles: 7-inch
CONSTELLATION....10-20 65

TAYLOR, Gloria P&R/R&B '69
(Gloria Ann Taylor)
Singles: 7-inch
COLUMBIA....3-5 74
GLO-WHIZ....4-8 69
KING SOUL (493 "Poor Unfortunate Me")....15-25 68
SELECTOR SOUND (0352 "World That's Not Real")....4-6 70s
SILVER FOX....4-8 69

TAYLOR, Guy, & Phantoms
Singles: 7-inch
LOOP (800 "Lesa")....100-200 58

TAYLOR, Hound Dog
(With the Houserockers)
Singles: 7-inch
BEA & BABY (112 "Take Five")....15-25 60
CJ (626 "Christine")....15-25 62
FIRMA (626 "Christine")....10-20 62
KEY (112 "Take Five")....10-20 62
MARJETTE (1102 "Baby's Coming Home")....20-25

LPs: 10/12-inch
ALLIGATOR (Except 4701)............ 6-12 74-82
ALLIGATOR (4701 "Hound Dog Taylor & the Houserockers")..........10-20 71
(Alligator's first LP release.)
Also see WILLIAMS, Willie

TAYLOR, Hound Dog / Robert Nighthawk / John Littlejohn / Earl Hooker
LPs: 10/12-inch
CHICAGO SLIDE (005 "Slide Guitar Classics")..........................10-15
Also see HOOKER, Earl
Also see NIGHTHAWK, Robert
Also see TAYLOR, Hound Dog

TAYLOR, James *P&R/LP '70*
(With the Original Flying Machine)
Singles: 7-inch
APPLE (1805 "Carolina in My Mind"/"Taking It In")..........................200-300 69
APPLE (1805 "Carolina in My Mind"/"Something's Wrong")................ 5-10 70
(Note different flip side.)
APPLE (PRO-1805 "Carolina on My Mind")...................................25-35 70
(Note title variance. Promotional issue only.)
APPLE (4675 "More Apples, Radio Co-Op Ads")...........................150-200 69
(Single-sided disc. Promotional issue only.)
CAPITOL................................... 3-5 76
COLUMBIA................................. 3-5 77-88
EUPHORIA................................. 3-5 71
W.B. 3-5 70-76
Picture Sleeves
COLUMBIA................................. 3-4 81-88
LPs: 10/12-inch
APPLE.......................................20-30 69-70
COLUMBIA................................. 5-10 77-88
EUPHORIA.................................12-15 71
SPRINGBOARD............................ 5-10 70s
TRIP... 8-10 73
W.B. 8-10 70-77
Also see DOOBIE BROTHERS, James Hall & James Taylor
Also see DOOBIE BROTHERS / Kate Taylor & Simon-Taylor Family
Also see FLYING MACHINE
Also see GARFUNKEL, Art, James Taylor & Paul Simon
Also see KING DREAM CHORUS & HOLIDAY CREW
Also see KORTCHMAR, Danny
Also see SIMON, Carly, & James Taylor

TAYLOR, James, & J.D. Souther *P&R '81*
Singles: 7-inch
COLUMBIA................................. 3-5 81
Also see SOUTHER, J.D.
Also see TAYLOR, James

TAYLOR, Jim *C&W '78*
Singles: 7-inch
CHECKMATE.............................. 3-5 78

TAYLOR, Joanie, & Tabs
Singles: 7-inch
HERALD....................................15-25 61

TAYLOR, Joe, & Dominoes
Singles: 7-inch
HMF (2002 "You Don't Love Me")...50-100 60s

TAYLOR, Joe, & Hitch Hikers
Singles: 7-inch
MARBLE................................... 4-8 67

TAYLOR, John *P&R '86*
(With Jonathan Elias)
Singles: 12-inch
CAPITOL................................... 4-6 86
Singles: 7-inch
CAPITOL................................... 3-4 86
LPs: 10/12-inch
CAPITOL................................... 5-8 86
Also see DURAN DURAN
Also see POWER STATION

TAYLOR, Johnnie *P&R/R&B '63*
(Johnny Taylor; the "Soul Philosopher")
Singles: 7-inch
BEVERLY GLEN.......................... 3-5 82
COLUMBIA................................. 3-5 76-80
DERBY..................................... 4-8 63-64
MALACO................................... 3-4 83-87
RCA... 3-5 77
SAR (Except 131).......................10-15 61-65
SAR (131 "Never Never")............15-25 61
STAX....................................... 3-6 66-77
LPs: 10/12-inch
BEVERLY GLEN.......................... 5-10 82
COLUMBIA................................. 6-10 76-81
MALACO................................... 5-8 83-86
RCA... 8-10 77
STAX....................................... 6-10 67-83
Also see FIVE ECHOES
Also see SOUL STIRRERS

TAYLOR, Johnnie, & Carla Thomas
Singles: 7-inch
STAX....................................... 4-6 69
Also see TAYLOR, Johnnie
Also see THOMAS, Carla

TAYLOR, Josephine
Singles: 7-inch
MAR-V-LUS (6011 "What Is Love")...................................10-20 66
MAR-V-LUS (6013 "What Is Love")...................................10-20 66
MAR-V-LUS (6016 "Ordinary Guy")...................................10-20 66

TWINIGHT..................................5-10 69

TAYLOR, Judy *C&W '82*
Singles: 7-inch
W.B. 3-4 82

TAYLOR, Karen *C&W '82*
(Karen Taylor-Good)
Singles: 7-inch
MESA....................................... 3-4 82-84
LPs: 10/12-inch
MESA.......................................5-10 84

TAYLOR, Kate *LP '71*
Singles: 7-inch
COLUMBIA................................. 3-5 77-79
COTILLION................................ 3-5 71
LPs: 10/12-inch
COLUMBIA.................................5-10 78-79
COTILLION................................5-10 71
Also see DOOBIE BROTHERS / Kate Taylor & Simon-Taylor Family

TAYLOR, King Size, & Dominoes
Singles: 7-inch
MIDNIGHT................................. 5-8 64
LPs: 10/12-inch
MIDNIGHT.................................20-25 65

TAYLOR, Kirk
Singles: 7-inch
BANDERA..................................5-10 60
SALEM...................................... 4-8 65

TAYLOR, Koko *P&R/R&B '66*
(Cocoa Taylor; Ko Ko Taylor)
Singles: 7-inch
CHECKER..................................8-15 66-68
U.S.A. (745 "Like Heaven to Me") .10-20 63
YAMBO.....................................10-15 60s
LPs: 10/12-inch
ALLIGATOR...............................8-15 76-89
CHESS......................................10-15 69-72
Session: Willie Dixon; Walter Horton; Lafayette Leake; Buddy Guy; Robert Nighthawk; Jack Meyers; Clifton James.
Also see DIXON, Willie
Also see GUY, Buddy
Also see HORTON, Big Walter, & His Combo
Also see NIGHTHAWK, Robert

TAYLOR, Leroy
(With the Four Kays)
Singles: 7-inch
BRUNSWICK...............................10-15 67
COLPIX.....................................8-12 64
COLUMBIA.................................8-12 62
SHRINE (101 "Taking My Time")..200-300 65

TAYLOR, Les *C&W '89*
Singles: 7-inch
EPIC.. 3-4 89-91
Also see EXILE
Also see LYNNE, Shelby, & Les Taylor
Also see TOMORROW'S WORLD

TAYLOR, Linwood
Singles: 7-inch
JAMECO................................... 4-8 64

TAYLOR, Little Archie: see BLAZER & LITTLE ARCHIE TAYLOR

TAYLOR, Little Eddie
Singles: 7-inch
PEACOCK (1949 "I Had a Good Life")..50-75 67

TAYLOR, Little Johnny *P&R/R&B/LP '63*
(With Paul Clifton & His Band)
Singles: 7-inch
GALAXY....................................8-15 63-66
RONN....................................... 3-6 71-79
SWINGIN' (624 "Looking at the Future")...............................15-25 60
SWINGIN' (629 "One More Chance").............................15-25 61
LPs: 10/12-inch
BEVERLY GLEN.......................... 5-8 87
ICHIBAN...................................5-10
GALAXY (203 "Little Johnny Taylor")...................................25-45 63
RONN.......................................5-10 72-79
Also see CLIFTON, Paul

TAYLOR, Little Johnny, & Ted Taylor
LPs: 10/12-inch
RONN.......................................5-10 73
Also see TAYLOR, Little Johnny
Also see TAYLOR, Ted

TAYLOR, Livingston *LP '70*
Singles: 7-inch
CAPRICORN.............................. 3-5 70-73
EPIC.. 3-5 78-80
LPs: 10/12-inch
ATCO.......................................8-12 70
CAPRICORN..............................5-10 71-79
EPIC..5-10 78
Also see DOOBIE BROTHERS / Kate Taylor & Simon-Taylor Family

TAYLOR, Livingston, & Leah Kunkel *C&W '88*
Singles: 7-inch
CRITIQUE................................. 3-4 88
Also see KUNKEL, Leah
Also see TAYLOR, Livingston

TAYLOR, Lynn, & Peachettes
Singles: 7-inch
CLOCK......................................8-12 60

TAYLOR, Mad Man
Singles: 7-inch
EAST-WEST (117 "Rumble Tumble")...50-60 58

TAYLOR, Mark
Singles: 7-inch
JUDD..5-10 59

TAYLOR, Mary *C&W '67*
Singles: 7-inch
CAPITOL....................................4-6 66-67
DOT..4-6 68-69
LPs: 10/12-inch
DOT..8-10 67

TAYLOR, Mel
(With the Darts; with Magics)
Singles: 7-inch
RENDEZVOUS.............................5-10 62
TOPPA......................................5-10 62
W.B. 4-8 65-66
LPs: 10/12-inch
W.B. 10-20 66
Also see VENTURES

TAYLOR, Mick *LP '79*
Singles: 7-inch
COLUMBIA.................................3-5 79
LPs: 10/12-inch
COLUMBIA.................................5-10 79
Also see MAYALL, John
Also see ROLLING STONES

TAYLOR, Mike
Singles: 7-inch
DREAM ("He a Lover")...............150-250 62
(No selection number used.)
Also see CAMERONS

TAYLOR, Montana
Singles: 78 rpm
CIRCLE.....................................15-25 46-47

TAYLOR, Montana, & Clarence Lofton
LPs: 10/12-inch
RIVERSIDE................................15-25 61
Also see TAYLOR, Montana

TAYLOR, Morris
Singles: 7-inch
KEY (5718 "Look at What My Baby Done")...50-100 58

TAYLOR, R. Dean *P&R '70*
Singles: 7-inch
AUDIO MASTER (1 "At the High School Dance")...100-150 60
BARRY (3023 "At the High School Dance")..75-125 60
(Canadian.)
FARR..3-5 76
JANE..3-5 77
MALA (444 "I'll Remember")..........25-50 62
MOTOWN...................................3-5
RAGAMUFFIN.............................3-5 79
RARE EARTH (Black vinyl)...........3-5 70-72
RARE EARTH (Colored vinyl)........5-10 70-71
STRUMMER...............................3-4 83
20TH FOX..................................3-5 81
V.I.P. 10-20 65-68
Picture Sleeves
RARE EARTH.............................3-5 71
LPs: 10/12-inch
RARE EARTH.............................10-15 70

TAYLOR, Randy
Singles: 7-inch
UPTOWN...................................4-8 65

TAYLOR, Ray
Singles: 7-inch
CLIX (801 "Clocking My Card")..250-350
CLIX (802 "My Hamtrack Baby")...250-350
CLIX (2207 "Connie Lou").........100-200

TAYLOR, Renee
Singles: 7-inch
FELSTED (8620 "Hello Pigs").........5-10 61

TAYLOR, Robby
Singles: 7-inch
INTEGRA...................................4-8

TAYLOR, Robert
(With the Soul Exciters; with HPJ'S)
Singles: 7-inch
SONIC (33075 "Memories of Yesterday")...................................20-30 60s
(Promotional issue only.)
SONIC (111776 "Somebody Have Mercy")...................................15-25 60s
SONIC (121974 "Let Me Love You")...................................15-25 60s
SONIC (478486 "A Change Gonna Come")...................................15-25 60s

TAYLOR, Rod
LP: 10/12-inch
ASYLUM....................................8-12 73

TAYLOR, Roger *LP '81*
Singles: 7-inch
CAPITOL...................................3-4 84
ELEKTRA...................................3-5 81
LPs: 10/12-inch
CAPITOL...................................5-8 84
ELEKTRA...................................5-10 81
Also see ARCADIA
Also see QUEEN

TAYLOR, Rosemary
Singles: 7-inch
ABC..4-6 68

TAYLOR, Sam Jr.
Singles: 7-inch
GRT (12 "The Stinger")...............4-8 69
Picture Sleeves
GRT (12 "The Stinger")...............4-8 69

TAYLOR, Sam "The Man"
Singles: 78 rpm
ABBEY......................................10-20 49
MGM..10-15 54-56
Singles: 7-inch
MGM..15-25 54-56
EPs: 7-inch
MGM (293 "Music with the Big Beat")..25-50 56
(Two discs. "Produced Under the Supervision of Alan Freed.")
MGM (1181/1182/1183 "Blue Mist")...15-25 55
(Price is for any of three volumes.)
MGM (1272/1273/1274 "Out of This World")...15-25 56
(Price is for any of three volumes.)
MGM (1417/1418/1419 "Music for Melancholy Babies")............................15-25 57
(Price is for any of three volumes.)
MGM (1484/1485/1486 "Rockin' Sax & Rollin' Organ")...............................15-25 57
(Price is for either volume.)
MGM (1515/1516/1517 "Prelude to Blues")...15-25 57
(Price is for any of three volumes.)
LPs: 10/12-inch
MGM (293 "Music with the Big Beat")..50-100 56
(10-inch LP. "Produced Under the Supervision of Alan Freed.")
MGM (3292 "Blue Mist")..............30-60 55
MGM (3380 "Out of This World")...30-60 56
MGM (3473 "Music with the Big Beat")..50-75 56
MGM (3482 "Music for Melancholy Babies")..30-60 57
MGM (3553 "Rockin' Sax & Rollin' Organ")..30-60 57
MGM (3573 "Prelude to Blues").....30-60 57
Also see FREED, Alan
Also see MR. BEAR

TAYLOR, Sam "The Man," & Dick Hyman
Singles: 78 rpm
MGM..5-8 56
Singles: 7-inch
MGM..8-12 56
Also see HYMAN, Dick
Also see TAYLOR, Sam "The Man

TAYLOR, Sammy
(With the Trailers)
Singles: 7-inch
ATLANTIC (2209 "She Rocks My Soul")..8-12 63
ENJOY......................................8-12 62
JALYNNE (109 "Switchin' in the Kitchen")..10-15 61
MAY (123 "Friday the 13th").........10-15 62

TAYLOR, Sandee
Singles: 7-inch
V-TONE (224 "Love Bird")............5-10 61

TAYLOR, Sean
Singles: 7-inch
MAGIC TOUCH...........................8-12 67
Also see ESQUIRES

TAYLOR, Shelly
Singles: 7-inch
SOUND STAGE 7.........................4-8 64

TAYLOR, Sherri
Singles: 7-inch
GLORECO (1002 "I've Got a Crush")..30-50 60s
Also see TAYLOR TONES

TAYLOR, Sherri, & Singin' Sammy Ward
Singles: 7-inch
MOTOWN (1004 "Lover")..............25-35 60
Also see TAYLOR, Sherri
Also see WARD, Singin' Sammy

TAYLOR, Slim
Singles: 7-inch
NU KAT (719 "The Fly").................8-12 60

TAYLOR, Susan
Singles: 7-inch
PRIVATE STOCK.........................3-5 75

TAYLOR, Sydna
Singles: 7-inch
PEPPER.....................................3-5

TAYLOR, Ted *P&R/R&B '65*
(With the Bob Reed Orchestra; Ted Taylor Combo)
Singles: 7-inch
ALARM......................................4-6 76
APT (25063 "Little Things Mean a Lot")..8-12 62
ATCO.......................................5-10 65-66
DADE (5000 "If You Must Leave")...8-12 63
DUKE (304 "Since You're Home") ..10-20 59
DUKE (308 "Count the Stars")........10-20 59
EBB (132 "Keep Walkin' On").........15-25 58
EPIC...4-8 66
GOLD EAGLE (1805 "My Darling") 10-15 61
GOLD EAGLE (1808 "Bandstand Drag")..10-15 61
GOLD EAGLE (1810 "I Don't Care")..10-15 61
GOLD EAGLE (1812 "Never in My Life")..10-15 61
JEWEL.......................................5-10 66-67
LAURIE (3076 "You've Been Crying")..10-20 61
MELATONE (1003 "I'm Leaving You")..8-12 60s
OKEH..6-12 62-65
RONN..4-8 67-72
SONCRAFT (400 "Anytime, Anyplace, Anywhere")..10-20 61
TOP RANK (2011 "I'm Saving My Love")..15-25 59
TOP RANK (2048 "I Need You So")..15-25 60
TOP RANK (2076 "Look Out")........15-25 60
TOP RANK (3001 "Someday").......15-25 61
(First issue.)
U.A. (452 "Pretending Love")..........8-12 62
WARWICK (628 "Someday")...........10-15 61
WATTS CITY (1003 "I'm Leaving You")..4-6 83
LPs: 10/12-inch
OKEH..20-40 63-66
MCA..5-10 78
RONN..8-15 69-72
Also see CADETS
Also see REED, Bob
Also see TAYLOR, Austin
Also see TAYLOR, Little Johnny & Ted Taylor

TAYLOR, Terry
Singles: 7-inch
ACCENT.....................................5-10 60
POINT.......................................5-10

TAYLOR, Tommy, & Five Knights
Singles: 7-inch
MINIT (636 "I Want Somebody")....15-25 61
Also see FIVE KNIGHTS

TAYLOR, True
(Paul Simon)
Singles: 7-inch
BIG (614 "Teenage Fool")............20-40 58
Also see SIMON, Paul

TAYLOR, Vernon
Singles: 78 rpm
DOT (15632 "I've Got the Blues")..50-75 57
Singles: 7-inch
DOT (15632 "I've Got the Blues")..50-75 57
SUN..15-20 59

TAYLOR, Vince
Singles: 7-inch
PALETTE...................................5-10 60-61

TAYLOR, William Tell
Singles: 7-inch
D (1051 "I Like It").....................25-50 59
D (1080 "Uh Huh")......................20-30 59

TAYLOR, Zola
Singles: 78 rpm
RPM (405 "Make Love to Me")..100-200 54
Singles: 7-inch
RPM (405 "Make Love to Me")..150-250 54
Also see GUNTER, Shirley
Also see PLATTERS

TAYLOR BROTHERS
Singles: 7-inch
JOY..4-8 64
UNITED.....................................10-15 60s

TAYLOR TONES
Singles: 7-inch
STARMAKER (1926 "Poor Little Girl")..40-60 61
Member: Sherri Taylor.
Also see TAYLOR, Sherri

TAYLOR-GOOD: Karen: see TAYLOR, Karen

TAYLORTOPS
Singles: 7-inch
ALTON......................................10-15 59

TAZMANIAN DEVILS
Singles: 7-inch
W.B. 3-5 80-81
LPs: 10/12-inch
W.B. 5-10 81

TAZMEN
("Guitar Solo By Joe Rumoro")
Singles: 7-inch
ABC-PAR (9812 "Easy Pickin' ")....10-15 57
TAZ ("Gobo").............................30-40 57
(No selection number used.)
TAZ (1003 "Crackajack")...............15-25 57
TAZ (9015 "Easy Pickin' ")............20-30 58
(Same track as *Gobo*.)
Member: Joe Rumoro.

T-BIRDS
Singles: 7-inch
CASTLE (641 "Thunder Rock")......15-25 59
NEW TALENT (101 "Thunder Rock")..15-25 59
(Canadian.)

T-BIRDS
Singles: 7-inch
CHESS (1778 "Green Stamps")......10-15 61
GONE (5141 "Wild Stomp")............8-12 63
T-BIRD (101 "Green Stamps")........25-50 61
(First issue.)
VEGAS (720 "Nobody But Me").......25-50
Members: Jimmy Norman; Jesse Belvin.
Also see BELVIN, Jesse
Also see NORMAN, Jimmy

T-BONES: see T BONES

TCHAIKOVSKY, Bram P&R/LP '79
Singles: 7-inch
ARISTA ... 3-5 81
POLYDOR ... 3-5 79
LPs: 10/12-inch
ARISTA ... 5-10 81
POLYDOR ... 5-10 79-80
Also see MOTORS

TEA COMPANY
Singles: 7-inch
SMASH (2176 "Come and Have Some Tea with Me") ... 5-10 68
LPs: 10/12-inch
SMASH (67105 "Come and Have Some Tea") ... 15-20 68

TEACHERS
Singles: 7-inch
ABC-PAR ... 4-8 65
PTA ... 5-10 67

TEACHERS EDITION
Singles: 7-inch
HI ... 3-5 72-73

TEACHERS PET
Singles: 7-inch
B-ROD ... 3-5

TEACHO & STUDENTS
Singles: 7-inch
FELSTED (8517 "Rock-et") ... 15-25 58
OKEH (7234 "Chilis & Fever") ... 15-25 65
Member: Teacho Wilshire.
Also see WILTSHIRE, Teacho

TEAGARDEN, Jack
(With the Five Keys)
LPs: 10/12-inch
CAPITOL (820 "Swing Low, Sweet Spiritual") ... 150-250 54
Also see FIVE KEYS

TEAGUE, Susan
Singles: 7-inch
ACCENT ... 4-8 65

TEAM MATES
(Teamates)
Singles: 7-inch
ABC-PAR (10760 "You Must Pay") ... 10-20 66
LE CAM (701 "Sooner Or Later"/"If Only I Had Known") ... 20-30 59
LE CAM (701 "Sooner Or Later"/"I Just Might") ... 15-25 59
LE CAM (706 "You Must Pay") ... 15-25 59
LE CAM (707 "Once There Was a Time"/"Come On Baby") ... 15-25 60
LE CAM (707 "Once There Was a Time"/"Blue Mist") ... 15-25 60
LE CAM (707 "Once There Was a Time"/"Never Believed in Love") ... 15-25 60
LE CAM (709 "Sylvia") ... 20-30 60
PAULA (220 "Most of All") ... 50-75 65
PHILIPS (40029 "Once There Was a Time") ... 10-15 62
SOFT (104 "Most of All") ... 75-125 62
(First issued as by the Danes.)
Also see DANES

TEAR GAS
LPs: 10/12-inch
PARAMOUNT ... 10-15

TEARDROP EXPLODES LP '81
Singles: 7-inch
MERCURY ... 3-5 81-82
LPs: 10/12-inch
MERCURY ... 5-10 81-82
Member: Julian Cope.
Also see COPE, Julian

TEARDROPS
Singles: 78 rpm
SAMPSON ... 50-75 52
Singles: 7-inch
SAMPSON (634 "Come Back to Me") ... 150-250 52

TEARDROPS
Singles: 78 rpm
JOSIE ... 25-75 54
Singles: 7-inch
JOSIE (766 "The Stars Are Out Tonight") ... 100-150 54
JOSIE (771 "My Heart") ... 75-125 54
800 series issues are by a different group and are listed below.

TEARDROPS
Singles: 78 rpm
KING ... 10-20 56-57
Singles: 7-inch
KING (5004 "My Inspiration") ... 15-20 56
KING (5037 "After School") ... 15-20 57

TEARDROPS
Singles: 78 rpm
DOT (15569 "Bridge of Love") ... 10-15 57
Singles: 7-inch
DOT (15569 "Bridge of Love") ... 10-15 57
RENDEZVOUS ... 5-10 58
Members: Tony; Paul.

TEARDROPS
Singles: 7-inch
JOSIE (856 thru 873) ... 10-20 59-60
(700 series issues are by a different group and are listed above.)

TEARDROPS
Singles: 7-inch
DORE (679 "Little Orphan Boy") ... 5-10 63

TEARDROPS
LPs: 10/12-inch
20TH FOX (5011 "At Trinchi's") ... 15-25 63

TEARDROPS
Singles: 7-inch
MUSICOR (1218 "I Will Love You Dear Forever") ... 8-12 93
SAXONY (1007 "That's Why I'll Get By") ... 50-75 64
SAXONY (1008 "I'm Gonna Steal Your Boyfriend") ... 15-25 65
SAXONY (1009 "Tears Come Tumbling") ... 10-15 65
SAXONY (2002 "I Will Love You Dear Forever") ... 4-6 93
Members: Dorothy Dyer; Pat Strunk; Linda Schroeder; Wanda Sheriff

TEARDROPS
Singles: 7-inch
MUSICOR ... 5-10 65

TEARDROPS
Singles: 7-inch
004 (101 "Armfull of Teddy Bear") 10-15 60s
004 (102 "You Go Your Way") ... 10-15 60s
Picture Sleeves
004 (101 "Armfull of Teddy Bear") 15-25 60s
004 (102 "You Go Your Way") ... 15-25 60s

TEARDROPS
Singles: 7-inch
LAURIE ... 4-8 77

TEARDROPS
Singles: 7-inch
COLVIN (777 "I Know") ... 100-200

TEARJERKERS
Singles: 7-inch
SUNDAY ... 3-5 80

TEARS
Singles: 78 rpm
DIG (112 "Nothing But Love") ... 15-25 56
Singles: 7-inch
DIG (112 "Nothing But Love") ... 30-50 56

TEARS
Singles: 7-inch
ASTRONAUT (5001 "Hurt") ... 50-75 61

TEARS
Singles: 7-inch
SMASH (1981 "Good Luck, My Love") ... 15-25 65

TEARS
Singles: 7-inch
SCORPIO ... 5-10 67

TEARS
LPs: 10/12-inch
BACKSTREET ... 5-10 79

TEARS & LAUGHTER
Singles: 7-inch
ALEXIS ... 3-4 85

TEARS for FEARS P&R/LP '83
Singles: 12-inch
MERCURY ... 4-6 83-86
Singles: 7-inch
FONTANA ... 3-4 89
MERCURY ... 3-4 83-86
Picture Sleeves
FONTANA ... 3-4 89
MERCURY ... 3-4 85-86
LPs: 10/12-inch
FONTANA ... 5-8 89
MERCURY ... 5-8 83-86
SELECT ONE ... 12-18

TEARS for FEARS & OLETA ADAMS
Singles: 7-inch
FONTANA ... 3-4 90
Also see ADAMS, Oleta
Also see TEARS for FEARS

TEASE R&B '86
Singles: 12-inch
EPIC ... 4-6 86
RCA ... 4-6 83
Singles: 7-inch
EPIC ... 3-4 86-88
RCA ... 3-4 83
LPs: 10/12-inch
EPIC ... 5-8 86
RCA ... 5-8 83

TEASERS
Singles: 78 rpm
CHECKER ... 100-150 54
Singles: 7-inch
CHECKER (800 "How Could You Hurt Me So") ... 300-500 54
(Black vinyl.)
CHECKER (800 "How Could You Hurt Me So") ... 800-1200 54
(Red vinyl.)
Also see BINKLEY, Jimmy

TEAZE
Singles: 7-inch
CAPITOL ... 3-5 79
LPs: 10/12-inch
CAPITOL ... 5-10 79

TECHNICS
Singles: 7-inch
CHEX (1012 "Cause I Really Love You") ... 10-20 63
CHEX (1013 "Hey Girl Don't Leave Me") ... 20-30 63
Also see TONY & TECHNICS

TECHNIQUE D&D '83
Singles: 12-inch
ARIAL ... 4-6 83

TECHNIQUES P&R '57
Singles: 78 rpm
ROULETTE ... 10-15 57
Singles: 7-inch
ROULETTE ... 10-15 57-58
STARS ... 15-25 57

TECHNIQUES
Singles: 7-inch
VENUS ("Dream Theme") ... 10-15 60s
(No selection number used. Identification number, shown on label, is 8540.)

TECHNIQUES
Singles: 7-inch
LOCKET ... 5-10 61

TECHNOTRONIC P&R/LP '89
(Featuring Felly)
Singles: 7-inch
SBK ... 3-4 89-90
Picture Sleeves
SBK ... 3-4 89
LPs: 10/12-inch
SBK ... 5-8 89-90

TECHNOTRONIC Featuring Ya Kid K / Baltimora
Singles: 7-inch
EMI (17320 "Rockin' over the Beat") .. 4-6 93
(Colored vinyl. "For Jukeboxes Only.")
Also see BALTIMORA
Also see TECHNOTRONIC

TED & JOHNNY
Singles: 7-inch
PEACH ... 5-10 59

TEDDY & CLOCK WATCHERS
Singles: 7-inch
W.B. ... 4-8 65

TEDDY & COLLEEN
Singles: 7-inch
MIRA ... 4-8 66

TEDDY & CONTINENTALS
Singles: 7-inch
RAGO (201 "Tick Tick Tock") ... 15-25 62
RICHIE (445 "Do You") ... 50-75 61
(Label makes no reference to distribution by Roulette.)
RICHIE (445 "Do You") ... 25-40 61
(Label indicates distribution by Roulette.)
RICHIE (453 "Crying Over You") ... 25-50 63
RICHIE (1001 "Tick Tick Tock") ... 40-60 60
Member: Teddy Henry.

TEDDY & DARREL
Singles: 7-inch
MIRA ... 4-8 67
LPs: 10/12-inch
MIRA ... 10-20 66

TEDDY & HIS PATCHES
Singles: 7-inch
CHANCE (101 "Suzy Creemcheese") ... 30-40 67
CHANCE (669 "Haight Ashbury") ... 30-40 67

TEDDY & PANDAS
Singles: 7-inch
CORISTINE ... 8-12 66
MUSICOR ... 8-12 66
TIMBRI ... 8-12 67
TOWER ... 5-10 68
LPs: 10/12-inch
TOWER ... 10-20 68

TEDDY & ROUGH RIDERS
Singles: 7-inch
HURON (22002 "Dream Come True") ... 10-15 61
HURON (22008 "Money & Gold") .. 10-15 61
TILT (778 "Tomahawk") ... 15-25 61

TEDDY & TWILIGHTS P&R '62
Singles: 7-inch
SWAN (4102 "Woman Is a Man's Best Friend") ... 15-20 62
SWAN (4115 "Running Around Town") ... 15-20 62
SWAN (4126 "I'm Just Your Clown") ... 10-20 62
Also see TIFFANYS

TEDDY BEARS P&R/R&B '58
Singles: 78 rpm
DORE (503 "To Know Him Is to Love Him") ... 50-100 58
(Canadian.)
Singles: 7-inch
COLLECTABLES ... 3-4 80s
DORE (503 "To Know Him Is to Love Him") ... 20-25 58
DORE (520 "Wonderful Loveable You") ... 15-25 59
IMPERIAL (5562 "Oh Why") ... 15-20 58
IMPERIAL (5581 "You Said Goodbye") ... 15-20 59
IMPERIAL (5594 "Don't Go Away") ... 15-20 59
LPs: 10/12-inch
IMPERIAL (9067 "The Teddy Bears Sing") ... 200-300 59
(Monaural.)
IMPERIAL (12010 "The Teddy Bears Sing") ... 450-650 59
(Stereo.)
Members: Phil Spector; Annette Kleinbard; Marshall Leib.
Also see CONNORS, Carol
Also see HARVEY, Phil
Also see NELSON, Sandy

TEDDY BOYS
Singles: 7-inch
NORTHLAND (7005 "Jody") ... 25-50 58
Members: Don Uglow; Leo Weidenfeld; Allen Bauman; Glen Zastrow; Ron Bass.

TEDDY BOYS
Singles: 7-inch
(1616 "Don't Mess with Me") ... 20-30 65
(No label name used.)
CAMEO ... 10-15 66-67
MGM (13515 "Jezebel") ... 10-15 66
Also see MORTIMER

TEDDY BOYS
Singles: 7-inch
RICKY DOG ... 10-20 81
LPs: 10/12-inch
RICKY DOG ... 10-15 82

TEDESCO, Tommy
Singles: 7-inch
IMPERIAL ... 4-8 65
LPs: 10/12-inch
DISCOVERY ... 5-10
DOT ... 15-25 62
IMPERIAL ... 10-20 65-66
TREND ... 5-10 79
Also see ANNETTE
Also see AVALANCHES
Also see CATALINAS
Also see FIREBALLS
Also see KNIGHTS
Also see MARKETTS
Also see MONTEZ, Chris
Also see RIP CHORDS

TEE, Willie P&R/R&B '65
(Wilson Turbinton)
Singles: 7-inch
A.F.O. (307 "All for One") ... 15-25 62
ATLANTIC (2273 "Teasin' You") ... 8-10 65
ATLANTIC (2302 "You Better Say Yes") ... 8-10 65
CAPITOL ... 4-8 68-70
CINDERELLA (1202 "Foolish Girl") ... 20-30
GATOR (509 "First Taste of Love") ... 10-20
GATOR (701 "She Really Did Surprise Me") ... 20-30 71
GATOR (8001 "Get Up") ... 10-20
HOT LINE ... 4-8
NOLA (708 "Teasin' You") ... 30-40 64
NOLA (737 "Please Don't Go") .. 100-200 65
U.A. ... 3-5 76
LPs: 10/12-inch
CAPITOL ... 10-15 69
U.A. ... 5-10 76

TEE & CARA
LPs: 10/12-inch
U.A. ... 8-12 69
Members: Tee Sapoff; Cara Beckenstein.

TEE CEES
LPs: 10/12-inch
A.V.I. ... 5-10 78

TEE SET P&R/LP '70
Singles: 7-inch
COLLECTABLES ... 3-4 80s
COLOSSUS ... 3-5 70-71
Picture Sleeves
COLOSSUS ... 3-5 70
LPs: 10/12-inch
COLOSSUS ... 10-15 70

TEEGARDEN & VAN WINKLE P&R '70
Singles: 7-inch
ATCO ... 4-8 68
PLUMM (68102 "God, Love & Rock & Roll") ... 8-12 70
WESTBOUND ... 4-8 69-72
Picture Sleeves
WESTBOUND ... 3-5 70
LPs: 10/12-inch
ATCO ... 10-15 68
WESTBOUND ... 8-12 69-72
Members: David Teegarden; Skip Knape.

TEELEY, Tom
Singles: 7-inch
A&M ... 3-5 83
LPs: 10/12-inch
A&M ... 5-10 83

TEEMATES
Singles: 7-inch
AUDIO FIDELITY (104 "Dream on Little Girl") ... 8-12 64
AUDIO FIDELITY (105 "Night Fall") ... 8-12 64
Picture Sleeves
AUDIO FIDELITY (105 "Night Fall") ... 15-20 64
LPs: 10/12-inch
AUDIO FIDELITY (7042 "Jet Set Dance Discotheque") ... 30-50 64

TEEN, Sandra
Singles: 7-inch
IMPACT ... 5-10 60

TEEN BEATS
LPs: 10/12-inch
LONDON (83 "Guitar Boogie") ... 20-30 61
(Canadian.)

TEEN BEATS
Singles: 7-inch
MYRL ... 5-10 61
ORIGINAL SOUND ... 10-20 60-64

TEEN BEATS
LPs: 10/12-inch
NORTON ... 8-10 90s

TEEN BUGS
Singles: 7-inch
BLUE RIVER ... 10-15 64

TEEN DREAM R&B '87
(With Valentino)
Singles: 7-inch
W.B. ... 3-4 87-88

TEEN DREAMS
(Debbie & Teen Dreams)
Singles: 7-inch
VERNON ("The Time") ... 35-45 62
(No selection number used. Credits the Teen Dreams.)
VERNON (101 "The Time") ... 15-20 62
(Credits Debbie & Teen Dreams.)
Members: Dorothy Yutenkas; Joan Yutenkas; Marie Broncotti.
Also see DEBBIE & DARNELS

TEEN 5: see GENTS / Teen 5

TEEN KINGS
Singles: 78 rpm
JE-WEL (101 "Ooby Dooby") ... 200-300 56
Singles: 7-inch
JE-WEL (101 "Ooby Dooby") ... 500-750 56
(May read "Vocal Roy Oribson," instead of "Orbison," on some labels. Beware since some counterfeits exist that are difficult to identify. Consult an expert if in doubt.)
Members: Roy Orbison; Johnny "Peanuts" Wilson; Billy Par Ellis; James Monroe; Jack Kennelly.
Also see ORBISON, Roy
Also see ROGERS, Weldon

TEEN KINGS
Singles: 7-inch
RAGO ... 15-25 62
WILLETT (118 "My Greatest Wish") ... 150-250 59

TEEN KINGS
Singles: 7-inch
SARA (6342 "It's Too Late") ... 15-25 63
Members: Tom Shills; Richie Ehler; Mike Mellenhoeft; Darrell Mand; Wayne Ehler; Bob Castellan; Tom Kuck.

TEEN KINGS & PRINCE
Singles: 7-inch
5 RECORDS ... 3-5 70s
(S-80 579-3107 "16 Candles") ... 3-5 70s
(No label name used.)
EPs: 7-inch
("Buddy Holly Medley") ... 8-12 70s
(No label name nor selection number used.)
LPs:10/12-inch
TEEN KING ... 8-12 70s

TEEN NOTES
Singles: 7-inch
DEB (121 "Precious Jewel") ... 10-20 60
DEB (127 "Hi-Fi Sweetie") ... 10-20 61

TEEN QUEENS P&R/R&B '56
Singles: 78 rpm
RPM ... 10-25 56-57
Singles: 7-inch
ANTLER (4014 "There's Nothing on My Mind") ... 10-15 60
ANTLER (4015 "I'm a Fool") ... 10-15 60
ANTLER (4016 "Donny") ... 10-15 61
ANTLER (4017 "I Heard Violins") ... 10-15 61
COLLECTABLES ... 3-4 80s
KENT (359 "Eddie My Love") ... 8-12 61
RCA (7206 "Dear Tommy") ... 10-20 58
RCA (7396 "First Crush") ... 10-20 58
RPM (453 "Eddie My Love") ... 20-30 56
RPM (460 "So All Alone") ... 15-25 56
RPM (464 "Billy Boy") ... 15-25 56
RPM (470 "Red Top") ... 15-25 56
RPM (484 "My Heart's Desire") ... 15-25 56
RPM (500 "I Miss You") ... 15-25 57
Picture Sleeves
ANTLER ... 25-35 60
LPs: 10/12-inch
CROWN (5022 "Eddie My Love") ... 50-100 56
CROWN (5373 "Teen Queens") ... 20-30 63
UNITED ... 8-12
Members: Rose Collins; Betty Collins.

TEEN ROCKERS
Singles: 7-inch
COOL (146 "Road Block") ... 10-15 60
DELTONE (5015 "Rinky-Dink Blues") ... 10-15 60
ELDO (116 "Rattlesnake") ... 10-15 61

TEEN STARLETS
Singles: 7-inch
MGM ... 5-10 61
RPC ... 10-15 61

TEEN TONES
("Lead Vocal Gerald Powers")
Singles: 7-inch
NU-CLEAR (2 "Faded Love") ... 50-100 57
WYNNE (107 "Faded Love") ... 25-50 59

TEEN TONES
(Teen-Tones; Teentones)
Singles: 7-inch
CUCA ... 10-15 63
DANDY DAN (2 "Darling I Love You") ... 75-125 63
DEB (132 "Susan Ann") ... 10-15 60
DECCA (30895 "Yes You May") ... 15-25 59
DON & MARIE ... 10-20
GONE (5061 "Rockin' Rumble") ... 15-25 59

NU-CLEAR ("Faded Love")..........75-100
(No selection number used.)
SONIC..................................10-15
SWAN (4040 "My Little Baby").......15-25 59
T&T.....................................5-10 65

TEEN TONES
Singles: 7-inch
TRI DISC (102 "I Feel So Happy") 15-25 61

TEEN TONES
Singles: 7-inch
CUCA...................................10-15 63
SONIC..................................10-15

TEEN TURBANS
Singles: 7-inch
LOMA...................................10-20 66

TEEN'S MEN
Singles: 7-inch
CUCA (1021 "Spin Out")................15-25 61

TEENA MARIE: see MARIE, Teena

TEENAGE MOONLIGHTERS
Singles: 7-inch
MARK (134 "Sorry, Sorry").....1000-2000 59

TEENAGE REBELS
Singles: 7-inch
REELFOOT..............................15-25 60s

TEENAGERS
Singles: 78 rpm
GEE (1046 "Flip-Flop")..................15-25 57
Singles: 7-inch
END (1071 "Crying")......................30-40 60
END (1076 "Can You Tell Me")......20-30 60
GEE (1046 "Flip-Flop")..................15-25 57
ROULETTE (4086 "Broken
Heart")....................................35-50 58
Members: Billy Lobrano; Herman Santiago; Sherman Games; Jim Merchant; Joe Negroni.
Also see JOEY & TEENAGERS
Also see LYMON, Frankie

TEENAGERS
Singles: 7-inch
TAHOE..................................4-8

TEENANGELS
Singles: 7-inch
SUN (388 "Tell Me My Love")........25-35 63
(Promotional issue only.)

TEENBEATS
Singles: 7-inch
TEENBEAT ("Surf Bound")...........25-35 63
(No selection number used. Also issued as *Russian Roulette* by the Nevegans.)
Also see NEVEGANS

TEENERS
Singles: 7-inch
VISCOUNT (532 "Don't Mess
Around")..................................15-25 58

TEENETTES
Singles: 7-inch
BRUNSWICK (55125 "I Want a Boy with a Hi-Fi")......................................10-20 59
GOAL (704 "Story")..................100-200 64
JOSIE (830 "My Lucky Star").........25-50 57
SANDY (250 "Bye Bye Baby").......15-25 63

TEEN-KINGS
Singles: 7-inch
BEE (1115 "Tell Me If You
Know")................................1000-1500 59
(Black vinyl.)
BEE (1115 "Tell Me If You
Know")......................................4-6 96
(Red vinyl.)

TEENMAKERS
Singles: 7-inch
JAMIE.......................................4-6 69

TEENOS
Singles: 7-inch
DUB (2839 "Love Only You").........20-30 58

TEENTONES
("Featuring Arnold Malone with Larry Luple Orchestra)
Singles: 7-inch
KAREN ("Love Is a Vow")...............25-50 59
REGO (1004 "Love Is a Vow")...500-750 58

TEEN-TONES
Singles: 7-inch
DANDY DAN (2 "Darling I Love
You")......................................50-75 58

TEIG, Dave
Singles: 7-inch
SIGNATURE................................5-10 60

TEJUNS
Singles: 7-inch
100-PROOF (144 "Girl")...........500-750

TELEVISION
Singles: 7-inch
ELEKTRA....................................3-5 78
ORK...3-5 75
LPs: 10/12-inch
ELEKTRA..................................5-10 76-78
Member: Tom Verlaine.
Also see VERLAINE, Tom

TELEX
LPs: 10/12-inch
PVC...5-8 82
SIRE..5-10 80

TELLERS
Singles: 7-inch
FIRE (1038 "Tears Fell from My
Eyes")......................................25-35 60

TELL-TALE HEARTS
Singles: 12-inch
VOXX..4-6
LPs: 10/12-inch
VOXX..5-10

TELSTARS
Singles: 7-inch
GLUIDE......................................5-10
IMPERIAL (5905 "Continental
Mash")....................................10-15 62
TEEN (510 "Continental Mash")......15-25 62
TEEN (513 "Pow Wow")...............15-25 63
TEEN (516 "Topless")..................15-25 64
TEEN (51 "Tough George")..........15-25 64

TELSTARS
Singles: 7-inch
COLUMBIA..................................10-15 67

TEMKIN, Gary
Singles: 7-inch
ABC-PAR....................................4-8 61

TEMPER R&B/D&D '84
Singles: 12-inch
MCA..4-6 84
Singles: 7-inch
MCA..3-4 84
Member: Anthony Malloy.
Also see ANTHONY & CAMP

TEMPEST
Singles: 7-inch
W.B. 3-5 73
LPs: 10/12-inch
W.B. 10-12 73

TEMPESTS
Singles: 7-inch
WILLAMETTE (103 "Never Let You
Go")......................................50-100 59

TEMPESTS
Singles: 7-inch
CENTURY.................................10-15 61

TEMPESTS
Singles: 7-inch
FUJIMO (6946 "Look Away").........15-25 63
FUJIMO (7701 "Love I'm In").........15-25 60s
FUJIMO (8126 "Looking Out the
Window")..................................15-25 60s

TEMPESTS
Singles: 7-inch
REFLECTION...............................3-5 77
SARA (6453 "I Wanna Love My Life
Away")....................................10-15 64
SARA (6561 "Hello Amy")...........10-15 65
Members: Dan Fendt; Mike Fendt; Jim Rosenow; Ron Fendt; Danny Kopp.

TEMPESTS
Singles: 7-inch
POLYDOR....................................3-5 71
SMASH.......................................4-8 67
SOUTHERN WING..........................3-5 74
LPs: 10/12-inch
SMASH.....................................15-25 66
Members: Roger Branch; Mike Branch; Mike Williams; Bill Lynch; Ken Baker; Manny Rojas; Rick White; Hazel Martin; Otis Adams.
Also see ARP, James, & Tempest
Also see WILLIAMS, Mike
Also see WARNER, Sonny

TEMPESTS
Singles: 7-inch
PANORAMA (30 "Our Lovin'
Ways")....................................15-25 60s

TEMPESTS
Singles: 7-inch
HALF-LIFE (100 "Rockin'
Rochester")................................4-8

TEMPLE, Bob
Singles: 78 rpm
FRATERNITY...............................8-12 57
KING.......................................10-15 56
Singles: 7-inch
FRATERNITY (762 "Gonna See My
Baby")....................................10-20 57
KING (4958 "Vim Vam Vamoose").20-30 56

TEMPLE, Johnny
Singles: 78 rpm
KING.......................................15-25 46
MIRACLE (156 "Sit Right on
It")..20-30 49

TEMPLE, Little: see LITTLE TEMPLE

TEMPLE, Pick
LPs:10/12-inch
PRESTIGE (13008 "Pick of the
Crop")......................................20-30 60s

TEMPLE, Stevie, Jr.
Singles: 7-inch
DOT..4-8 61

TEMPLES
Singles: 7-inch
DATE (1004 " Whispering
Campaign")..............................50-100 58

TEMPLET, Doyle
Singles: 7-inch
ALART (501 "Waiting All Alone")...15-25

TEMPLETON, Joe
Singles: 7-inch
AMY..4-8 62

TEMPLETON TWINS
(With Teddy Turner's Bunsen Burners)
LPs: 10/12-inch
JAS..5-10 76
VAULT......................................8-12 69

TEMPO, Nick
LPs: 10/12-inch
LIBERTY (3023 "Rock N' Roll Beach
Party")....................................30-40 58

TEMPO, Nino P&R '73
(With 5th Ave. Sax)
Singles: 7-inch
A&M..3-5 73-74
RCA...5-10 59-60
TOWER......................................4-6 67
U.A. 5-10 60
LPs: 10/12-inch
A&M...8-10 74
ATCO......................................10-15 66
Also see ARCHIES
Also see CANO, Eddie, & Nino Tempo
Also see CORCORAN, Noreen
Also see KINGBEES

TEMPO, Nino, & April Stevens P&R '62
Singles: 7-inch
A&M..3-5 72-75
ABC..3-5 73
ATCO..4-8 62-66
BELL...3-6 69
CHELSEA...................................3-5 76
MARINA.....................................3-5 72
WHITE WHALE.............................4-6 66-68
LPs: 10/12-inch
ATCO......................................10-15 63-66
CAMDEN..................................10-15 64
WHITE WHALE...........................10-15 69
Also see PEWTER, Jim
Also see STEVENS, April
Also see TEMPO, Nino

TEMPO TOPPERS
(Featuring Little Richard)
Singles: 78 rpm
PEACOCK.................................20-40 53-54
Singles: 7-inch
PEACOCK (1616 "A Fool at the
Wheel")....................................50-75 53
PEACOCK (1628 "Always")............40-60 54
Members: Richard Penniman; Jimmy Swan; Barry Gilmore; Bill Brooks.
Also see DUCES of RHYTHM & TEMPO TOPPERS
Also see LITTLE RICHARD

TEMPOMEN
Singles: 7-inch
S-K-E (517 "Midnight on Pier 13") .20-30 60s

TEMPO-MENTALS
Singles: 78 rpm
EBB (112 "Dearest")....................30-50 57
Singles: 7-inch
EBB (112 "Dearest")....................30-50 57
Also see PYRAMIDS

TEMPOS
Singles: 7-inch
RHYTHM (121 "Promise
Me")....................................500-1000 58
Members: Marvin Smith; Jewel Jones; James Maddox; Louis Bradley; Dick Nichens.
Also see EL DORADOS
Also see SMITH, Marvin

TEMPOS P&R '59
Singles: 78 rpm
KAPP.......................................10-20 57
Singles: 7-inch
CLIMAX (102 "See You in
September")..............................10-15 59
CLIMAX (105 "Crossroads of
Love")......................................10-15 59
KAPP (178 "Kingdom of Love")......10-20 57
KAPP (199 "Prettiest Girl in
School")...................................10-20 57
KAPP (213 "I Got a Job")..............10-20 58
PARIS (550 "Look Homeward
Angel")...................................10-15 59
ROULETTE..................................3-5 70s

TEMPOS
Singles: 7-inch
HI-Q (100 "It's Tough")..................25-50 59
HI-Q (5005 "I'm Laughing at You") 50-75 59
OASIS (105 "It's Tough")...............25-50 59

TEMPOS
Singles: 7-inch
FREDLO (6202 "Only One")...........15-25 50s

TEMPOS
Singles: 7-inch
FAIRMOUNT..................................4-8 63

TEMPOS
Singles: 7-inch
ASCOT.....................................10-15 65
BOFUZ (1106 "Why Don't You Write
Me")..50-75 63
CANTERBURY..............................5-10 67
MONTEL.....................................5-10 66
RILEY'S (5 "Don't Act That Way") 10-20 66
RILEY'S (8781 "I Need You")........10-20 66
RILEY'S (8782 "Lonely One").........10-20 66
U.S.A. (810 "Why Don't You Write
Me")..20-30 64

TEMPOS
LPs: 10/12-inch
CRYPT (10 "The Tempos")............10-15 87
JUSTICE (104 "Speaking of the
Tempos")...............................450-550 66

TEMPO-TONES
(Featuring Richard Lanham; Tempo Tones; Tempotones)
Singles: 7-inch
ACME (713 "Get Yourself Another
Fool")....................................100-125 57
ACME (715 "In My Dreams")......300-400 57
ACME (718 "Come Into My
Heart")...................................300-400 57
ACME (722 "The Day I Met
You")....................................200-300 57
Also see LANHAM, Richard

TEMPREES P&R '72
Singles: 7-inch
EPIC..3-5 76
STAX..3-4 84
WE PRODUCE..............................3-4 72-74
LPs: 10/12-inch
STAX..5-8 84
WE PRODUCE..............................5-10 72-74
Members: Del Juan Calvin; Jasper Phillips; Harold Scott.

TEMPTASHUNS
Singles: 7-inch
FEDERAL....................................5-10 64

TEMPTATIONS
Singles: 7-inch
KING (5118 "Standing Alone")....150-200 58
Also see VAN DYKES

TEMPTATIONS
Singles: 7-inch
SAVOY (1532 "Mad at Love")........10-20 58
SAVOY (1550 "Don't You Know")..10-20 58

TEMPTATIONS
Singles: 7-inch
PARKWAY (803 "Birds 'N' Bees")...15-25 59

TEMPTATIONS P&R '60
Singles: 7-inch
GOLDISC (3001 "Barbara")...........15-25 60
(Black label.)
GOLDISC (3001 "Barbara")...........10-15 60
(Multi-color label.)
GOLDISC (3007 "Fickle Little
Girl")......................................15-25 60
ROULETTE...................................3-5 71
Also see DREAMERS / Temptations
Also see STEVENS, Neil

TEMPTATIONS R&B '62
Singles: 7-inch
ATLANTIC....................................3-5 77-78
GORDY (1631 thru 1933)................3-4 82-88
GORDY (7001 "Dream Come
True")....................................25-30 62
GORDY (7010 "Paradise")............20-25 62
GORDY (7015 "I Want a Love I Can
See").......................................15-20 63
GORDY (7020 "Farewell My
Love").......................................15-20 63
GORDY (7028 thru 7081)..............8-15 64-68
GORDY (7082 "Rudolph the Red-Nosed
Reindeer")..................................5-10 68
GORDY (7084 thru 7213)...............3-8 69-81
MIRACLE (5 "Oh Mother of
Mine")....................................50-100 61
MIRACLE (12 "Check Yourself")....40-60 62
MOTOWN.....................................3-4 84-87
MOTOWN/TOPPS (4 "My Girl").....50-75 67
MOTOWN/TOPPS (13 "The Way You Do the Things You Do")........................50-75 67
(Topps Chewing Gum promotional item. Single-sided, cardboard flexi, picture disc. Issued with generic paper sleeve.)
Picture Sleeves
GORDY (7038 "My Girl")...............25-50 65
GORDY (7055 "Beauty Is Only Skin
Deep")......................................10-20 66
GORDY (7099 "Ball of Confusion") 10-20 70
EPs: 7-inch
GORDY (60914 "Tempting
Temptations")............................15-25 65
GORDY (60918 "Getting Ready")..15-25 66
GORDY (60919 "Greatest Hits")....15-25 66
MOTOWN (2004 "Temptations")....15-25 60s
MOTOWN (2010 "It's the
Temptations").............................15-25
LPs: 10/12-inch
ATLANTIC...................................5-10 77-78
GORDY (911 "Meet the
Temptations")............................20-30 64
GORDY (S-911 "Meet the
Temptations")............................25-35 64
GORDY (912 "The Temptations Sing
Smokey")..................................15-25 65
GORDY (914 "The Tempting
Temptations")............................15-25 65
GORDY (918 "Gettin' Ready").......15-25 66
GORDY (919 Greatest Hits)..........15-20 66
GORDY (921 "Live")....................15-25 67
GORDY (922 "With a Lot O'
Soul")......................................15-25 67
GORDY (924 "In a Mellow Mood").15-25 67
GORDY (927 "Wish It Would
Rain")......................................15-25 68
GORDY (933 thru 1006)................8-18 69-80
GORDY (6000 series)....................5-8 82-86
KORY..8-10 77
MOTOWN (100 & 200 series).........5-10 81-82
MOTOWN (782 "Anthology").........15-20 73
(Three-disc set. Includes 12-page booklet.)
MOTOWN (998 "Give Love at
Christmas")..............................12-18 80
(Promotional issue only.)
MOTOWN (5389 "25th
Anniversary").............................10-15 86
(Includes eight-page booklet.)
MOTOWN (6246 "Together Again")...5-8 87
NATURAL RESOURCES..................5-10 78
Members: David Ruffin; Eddie Kendricks; Melvin Franklin; Otis Williams; Paul Williams; Damon Harris; Dennis Edwards.
Also see DISTANTS
Also see EDWARDS, Dennis
Also see FOUR TOPS / Temptations
Also see HARRIS, Damon
Also see KENDRICKS, Eddie
Also see LANDS, Liz, & Temptations
Also see PIRATES
Also see ROBINSON, Smokey
Also see ROSS, Diana
Also see RUFFIN, David
Also see STREET, Richard, & Distants
Also see SUPREMES & TEMPTATIONS

TEMPTATIONS & FOUR TOPS
LPs: 10/12-inch
MOTOWN (134 "Battle of the
Champions")..............................10-20
(Promotional issue only.)
SILVER EAGLE (1052 "T N T")......10-15 87
(Three-disc set.)
Also see FOUR TOPS

TEMPTATIONS / Finis Henderson
Singles: 12-inch
MOTOWN (119 "Surface Thrill").......4-8
(Promotional issue only.)
Also see HENDERSON, Finis

TEMPTATIONS & Rick James R&B '82
Singles: 12-inch
GORDY.......................................4-6 82
Singles: 7-inch
GORDY.......................................3-4 82
Also see JAMES, Rick

TEMPTATIONS / Stevie Wonder
LPs: 10/12-inch
GORDY/TAMLA/MOTOWN (100 "The Sky's the Limit")..............................15-25 71
(Promotional issue only.)
Also see TEMPTATIONS
Also see WONDER, Stevie

TEMPTATIONS
Singles: 7-inch
CUCA (1094 "Call of the Wind").....15-25 62
Members: Ricky Lee Smolinski; Roger Loos.

TEMPTATIONS
Singles: 7-inch
P&L (0001 "Blue Surf")................15-25 63

TEMPTATIONS
Singles: 7-inch
MOON (8687 "Hey Bo Diddley")....10-20 60s

TEMPTATIONS
Singles: 7-inch
COTTON (1005 "Peppermint
Cane").......................................5-10

TEMPTERS
Singles: 78 rpm
EMPIRE (105 "I'm Sorry Now")......10-20 56
Singles: 7-inch
EMPIRE (105 "I'm Sorry Now")......25-35 56
Also see YOUNGSTERS

TEMPTERS
Singles: 7-inch
LINK (708 "I Will Go")..................20-30 60s

TEMPTONES
Singles: 7-inch
ARCTIC.....................................10-15 66
Member: Daryl Hall.
Also see HALL, Daryl

TEMPTORS
Singles: 7-inch
HALL of FAME.............................10-20 60s
Member: Terry Klein.
Also see DEE JAY & RUNAWAYS

10CC P&R '73
Singles: 7-inch
MERCURY...................................3-5 75-77
POLYDOR....................................3-5 78
UK...3-5 72-74
Picture Sleeves
MERCURY...................................5-8 75-77
LPs: 10/12-inch
MERCURY.................................10-15 75-77
POLYDOR....................................5-8 78-79
UK...10-15 73-75
W.B. 8-10 80
Members: Kevin Godley; Lol Creme; Graham Gouldman; Eric Stewart; Paul Burgess; Rick Fenn; Tony O'Malley; Stuart Tosh.
Also see GODLEY, Kevin, & Lol Creme
Also see GOULDMAN, Graham
Also see HOTLEGS
Also see KASENETZ-KATZ SINGING ORCHESTRAL CIRCUS
Also see KOKOMO
Also see MOCKINGBIRDS
Also see OHIO EXPRESS
Also see PILOT
Also see SEDAKA, Neil
Also see SILVER FLEET
Also see WAX

10DB
Singles: 7-inch
CRUSH..3-4 88

TEN BROKEN HEARTS
Singles: 7-inch
DIAMOND (123 "Ten Lonely Guys")....25-35 62
Member: Neil Diamond.
Also see DIAMOND, Neil

10 SPEED R&B '84
Singles: 12-inch
QUALITY/RFC....4-6 83
Singles: 7-inch
QUALITY/RFC....3-5 83

10,000 MANIACS LP '87
Singles: 7-inch
ELEKTRA....3-4 87-89
Picture Sleeves
ELEKTRA....3-5 88-89
LPs: 10/12-inch
ELEKTRA....5-10 87-90
MARK (20247 "Human Conflict No. 5")....100-150 82
MARK (20389 "Secrets of the I Ching")....75-100 83
(Includes lyrics/print insert.)
Members: Natalie Merchant; Robert Buck; Dennis Drew; Steven Gustafson; John Lombardo; Robert Wachter; Jerome Augustyniak.

TEN TONS OF LIES
Singles: 7-inch
VOXX....3-4 85

TEN TUFF GUITARS
Singles: 7-inch
COLUMBIA....4-8 65

TEN WHEEL DRIVE P&R/LP '70
(With Genya Ravan)
Singles: 7-inch
CAPITOL....3-5 73
POLYDOR....4-6 69-71
LPs: 10/12-inch
CAPITOL....8-10 73
POLYDOR....10-12 69-71
Member: Genya Ravan.
Also see RAVAN, Genya
Also see ZAGER, Michael, Band

TEN YEARS AFTER LP '68
Singles: 7-inch
COLUMBIA....3-5 71-73
DERAM....4-6 68-70
Picture Sleeves
DERAM....4-6 68
LPs: 10/12-inch
CHRYSALIS....5-10 83-89
COLUMBIA....8-12 71-76
DERAM....8-12 68-75
LONDON....5-10 77
Member: Alvin Lee.
Also see LEE, Alvin

TENANT, Jimmy: see TENNANT, Jimmy

TENDER SLIM P&R '60
Singles: 7-inch
GREY CLIFF....5-10 59
HERALD....4-8 62
Also see GROUND HOG

TENDER TONES
Singles: 7-inch
DUCKY (713 "Just for a Little While")....500-750 59

TENDER TOUCH
Singles: 7-inch
PARAMOUNT (0252 "You Were Never Mine to Begin With")....10-20

TENDERFOOTS
Singles: 78 rpm
FEDERAL....50-100 55
Singles: 7-inch
FEDERAL (12214 "Kissing Bug")....100-150 55
FEDERAL (12219 "My Confession")....100-200 55
FEDERAL (12225 "Those Golden Bells")....100-200 55
FEDERAL (12228 "Sindy")....200-300 55
Members: Carl White; Al Frazier; Sonny Harris; Matt Nelson; Harold Lewis.
Also see LAMPLIGHTERS
Also see RIVINGTONS

TENNANT, Barbara
Singles: 7-inch
KUDO (665 "Rock, Baby, Rock")....25-35 58

TENNANT, Jimmy
(Jimmy Tenant; with Buddy Lucas & Dynatones)
Singles: 7-inch
AMP (790 "Heartbreak Avenue")....10-20 59
THUNDER (1000 "The Witness")....30-50 59
WARWICK (533 "Salute")....10-15 60
Also see GENE & GARE & Velvet Tones
Also see KITT 'N KORY
Also see VELVET, Jimmy

TENNESSEANS C&W '78
Singles: 7-inch
CAPITOL....3-5 78
Members: Willie Wynn; Tony King.
Also see OAK RIDGE BOYS
Also see SWEETWATER

TENNESSEE DRIFTERS
Singles: 78 rpm
DOT....5-10 52-54
Singles: 7-inch
DOT (1098 "Boogie Beat Rag")....15-25 52
DOT (1166 "Boogie Woogie Baby")....15-25 54

TENNESSEE ERNIE: see FORD, "Tennessee" Ernie

TENNESSEE EXPRESS C&W '81
Singles: 7-inch
RCA....3-4 81-83

TENNESSEE GUITARS
Singles: 7-inch
BELL....4-6 67
SSS INT'L....4-6 68
SUN....4-6 69
LP: 10/12-inch
BELL....6-12 67
PLANTATION....6-12 81
SSS INT'L....6-12 68

TENNESSEE JIM
Singles: 7-inch
CHOICE (852 "My Baby, She's Rockin' ")....150-250 57

TENNESSEE PULLYBONE C&W '73
Singles: 7-inch
JMI....3-5 73
Also see BARE, Bobby

TENNESSEE TWO & FRIEND
Singles: 7-inch
COLUMBIA....10-20 60-61
Session: Jerry Lee Lewis.
Also see LEWIS, Jerry Lee

TENNESSEE THREE
Singles: 7-inch
COLUMBIA....8-12 65-67

TENNILLE, Toni LP '84
Singles: 7-inch
MIRAGE....3-5 84
LPs: 10/12-inch
GAIA....5-8 87
MIRAGE....5-8 84
Also see CAPTAIN & TENNILLE

TENSION
Singles: 7-inch
POISON RING....4-8 69-71
Members; Johnny Paris; Paul Miranda; Steve Russo; Dave Marteeny; Bob Costello; John Zeiborn; Vinnie Punzel; Fred Russo; Ralph Onofrio.

10TH ST. STICKBALL TEAM
Singles: 7-inch
DORADO....4-8 69

TEO, Roy
Singles: 7-inch
NASCO....5-10 59

TEOLA
Singles: 7-inch
HALL WAY....4-8 62

TEPPER, Robert P&R/LP '86
Singles: 7-inch
SCOTTI BROTHERS....3-4 85-86
Picture Sleeves
SCOTTI BROTHERS....3-4 86
LPs: 10/12-inch
SCOTTI BROTHERS....5-8 85-86

TERENCE
LPs: 10/12-inch
DECCA....10-15 69

TERESA
LPs: 10/12-inch
DREAM....5-10 80

TERESA, Claire
Singles: 7-inch
CORSAIR....5-10 60

TERMINAL BARBERSHOP
LPs: 10/12-inch
ATCO....10-15 69

TERMINATORS OF ENDEARMENT
Singles: 7-inch
SUBTERRANEAN (64 "Stranger in the Manger")....3-5 88
Picture Sleeves
SUBTERRANEAN (64 "Stranger in the Manger")....3-5 88
EPs: 7-inch
METICULOUS (1 "Let Icons Be Icons")....4-8 80s
(Without cover.)
METICULOUS (1 "Let Icons Be Icons")....8-10 80s
(With wrap-around paper cover.)
Members: Michael Monahan; Steven Strauss.

TERMITES
Singles: 7-inch
BEE (1825 "Give Me Your Heart")....50-100 64

TERRA, Andy
Singles: 7-inch
DAUPHIN....5-10 59

TERRACE, Pete
Singles: 7-inch
A/S....4-6 67
LPs: 10/12-inch
SOMERSET....8-10 68
TICO....8-10

TERRACE, Ray
Singles: 7-inch
JUBILEE (5515 "Ray's Beat")....8-12 65
LPs: 10/12-inch
TOWER....10-20 68

TERRACETONES
Singles: 7-inch
APT (25016 "Words of Wisdon")....50-75 58
Members: Andy Cheatham; Len Walker; Pat Johnson; Ed Johnson; James Ashley; Carl Foushee.

TERRATTACK
LPs: 10/12-inch
IRON WORKS (1008 "Terrattack")....5-10 88
(Picture disc. 500 made.)

TERRELL, Clyde
Singles: 7-inch
EXCELLO....5-10 59

TERRELL, Ernie
Singles: 7-inch
ARGO....5-10 65

TERRELL, Ernie & Jean
Singles: 7-inch
CALLA (132 "Prayer of Love")....5-10 67
Also see TERRELL, Ernie
Also see TERRELL, Jean

TERRELL, Jean R&B '78
Singles: 7-inch
A&M....3-6 78
LPs: 10/12-inch
A&M....8-10 78
Also see SUPREMES
Also see TERRELL, Ernie & Jean

TERRELL, Phil
Singles: 7-inch
CARNIVAL (513 "I'm Just a Boy") 20-30

TERRELL, Tammi P&R/R&B '66
Singles: 7-inch
MOTOWN (1086 thru 1138)....5-10 65-69
LPs: 10/12-inch
MOTOWN (200 series)....5-10 82
MOTOWN (652 "Irresistible")....40-60 66
Also see GAYE, Marvin, & Tammi Terrell
Also see JACKSON, Chuck, & Tammi Terrell
Also see MONTGOMERY, Tammy

TERRELL, Ty
Singles: 7-inch
LUTE....5-10 60

TER-RELLS
Singles: 7-inch
ABC....4-8 67-68

TERRI, Darlene
Singles: 7-inch
COLUMBIA....5-10 64
POCONO....4-8 60s

TERRI & JANE
Singles: 7-inch
FREEDOM....5-10 59

TERRI & KITTENS
Singles: 7-inch
IMPERIAL (5728 "Wedding Bells") 15-20 61

TERRI & TRITONES
Singles: 7-inch
KAY BEE....10-20 60s

TERRI & VELVETEENS
Singles: 7-inch
ARC (6534 "I'm Waiting")....5-10 66
KERWOOD (711 "Bells of Love")....30-50 62

TERRIFIC, Timi, & Redheads
Singles: 7-inch
OCEAN (101 "You Are My Christmas Tree")....8-12 60s

TERRIFIC TABORS
Singles: 7-inch
APPLAUSE....5-10 61

TERRIFICS
Singles: 7-inch
DEMON....10-20 59
VALOR....10-20 58
Member: Ray Stanley.
Also see STANLEY, Ray

TERRIFICS
Singles: 7-inch
FIG (301 "Lover's Plea")....15-25 68

TERRIFS
Singles: 7-inch
DIAMOND JIM....4-8 67

TERRI-TONES
Singles: 7-inch
CORTLAND (105 "Go")....10-20 62

TERRORISTS
Singles: 7-inch
MAX'S (1002 "Riis Park")....4-6 80
Member: John Collins

TERRY
Singles: 7-inch
SEVILLE....4-8 64

TERRY, Al C&W '54
(With the La. Hayriders)
Singles: 78 rpm
ACE....10-15 54
HICKORY....8-10 54-57
Singles: 7-inch
ACE (502 "Shoot Me a Line")....15-25 54
HICKORY....10-20 54-60
LPs: 10/12-inch
INDEX....5-10
LA LOUISIANNE....5-10

TERRY, Dan, Band
Singles: 78 rpm
COLUMBIA....3-5 54
Singles: 7-inch
COLUMBIA....5-10 54
DEVERE (317 "Coca-Cola Rock")....8-15 58
EPs: 7-inch
COLUMBIA....10-15 54
LPs: 10/12-inch
COLUMBIA (6288 "Teen-Age Dance Session")....25-50 54
(10-inch LP.)

TERRY, Dewey
LPs: 10/12-inch
TUMBLEWEED....10-15
Also see DON & DEWEY

TERRY, Don
(With the Strikes; Don Alexander)
Singles: 7-inch
LIN (5018 "Knees Shakin' ")....75-125 59
Also see STRIKES

TERRY, Dossie
(Dossie "Georgia Boy" Terry)
Singles: 78 rpm
CHICAGO....15-25 45
KING (5072 "Thunderbird")....25-35 57
RCA....10-20 51
Singles: 7-inch
AMP 3 (2113 "Skinny Ginny")....20-30 58
BONUS (101 "No Other Love")....20-30 50s
KING (5072 "Thunderbird")....20-40 57
RCA (4474 "Didn't Satisfy You")....20-40 51
RCA (4684 "When I Hit the Number")....20-40 51
RCA (4864 "Lost My Head")....20-40 51
X-TRA (103 "Railroad Section Man")....20-40 57

TERRY, Flash
Singles: 7-inch
KENT (310 "One Thing We Know")....50-75 61
INDIGO....15-25 61
LAVENDER (5 "Cool It")....20-30 61

TERRY, Gene
(With His Down Beats)
Singles: 7-inch
GOLDBAND (1066 "Cindy Lou")....75-100 58
GOLDBAND (1081 "No Mail Today")....20-30 59
GOLDBAND (1088 "Cinderella, Cinderella")....10-20 59
SAVOY....10-15 59

TERRY, George
Singles: 7-inch
SPHERE SOUND (711 "Dreamy Eyes")....10-15 66

TERRY, Gordon C&W '70
(With the Tennessee Guitars; with Tennessee Fiddles)
Singles: 78 rpm
CADENCE....5-10 57-58
COLUMBIA....4-8 55-56
Singles: 7-inch
CADENCE....5-10 57-58
CAPITOL....3-5 70
CHART....4-6 68
COLUMBIA....5-10 55-56
LIBERTY....4-8 62-63
RCA (Except 7632)....10-20 58-62
RCA (7632 "Lotta Lotta Woman")....30-40 59
LPs: 10/12-inch
CHART....10-15 68
LIBERTY....10-20 62
PLANTATION....5-10 77-81
RCA....10-20 62

TERRY, Larry
Singles: 7-inch
TESTA (006 "Hep Cat")....250-350 61

TERRY, Marlene
Singles: 7-inch
MARIA....10-15

TERRY, Mark
Singles: 7-inch
JANARD....4-8 63

TERRY, Maureen
Singles: 7-inch
MARIA....8-12

TERRY, Nat
Singles: 78 rpm
IMPERIAL (5150 "Take It Easy")....50-75 51

TERRY, Ron
Singles: 78 rpm
MERCURY....4-8 56
Singles: 7-inch
MERCURY....5-10 56
LPs: 10/12-inch
WING....10-20 59

TERRY, Sonny
(Sonny "Hootin' " Terry & His Night Owls; with His Buckshot Five)
Singles: 78 rpm
ASCH....15-25 45
CAPITOL....15-40 47-50
GOTHAM....15-25 51
GRAMERCY....15-25 52
GROOVE....15-25 54-55
HARLEM....15-25 52
JACKSON....25-50 52
JOSIE....15-25 56
OLD TOWN....15-25 56
RCA....25-50 53
RED ROBIN....25-50 53
SAVOY....15-25 48
SOLO....15-25 49
Singles: 7-inch
CAPITOL (931 "Telephone Blues")....50-100 50
CHESS (1860 "Dangerous Woman")....10-15 63
CHOICE (15 "Hootin' ")....10-15 61
GOTHAM (517 "Baby, Let's Have Some Fun")....20-30 51
GOTHAM (518 "Harmonica Rumbo")....20-30 51
GRAMERCY (1004 "Hootin' Blues")....25-35 52
(Black vinyl.)
GRAMERCY (1004 "Hootin' Blues")....50-75 52
(Colored vinyl.)
GROOVE (0015 "Lost Jawbone")....25-35 55
GROOVE (0135 "Ride & Roll")....25-35 55
HARLEM (2327 "Dangerous Woman")....40-50 52
JACKSON (2302 "That Woman Is Killing Me")....50-100 52
(Red vinyl.)
JAX (305 "I Don't Worry")....200-300 53
(Red vinyl.)
JOSIE (828 "Fast Freight Blues")....15-25 56
OLD TOWN (1023 "Uncle Bud")....20-30 56
RCA (5492 "Hootin' & Jumpin' ")....50-100 53
RCA (5577 "Sonny Is Drinkin' ")....50-100 53
RED ROBIN (110 "Harmonica Hop")....75-125 53
LPs: 10/12-inch
ARCHIVE of FOLK MUSIC....15-25 65
EVEREST....5-10 70s
FOLKWAYS (35 "Harmonica and Vocal Solos")....50-75 51
(10-inch LP.)
PRESTIGE BLUESVILLE....20-30 61-63
WASHINGTON (702 "Talkin' About the Blues")....25-35 61
Session: Mickey Baker; Brownie McGhee.
Also see BAGBY, Doc
Also see BAKER, Mickey
Also see HOPKINS, Lightnin,' & Sonny Terry
Also see LEADBELLY / Josh White / Sonny Terry
Also see McGHEE, Brownie, & Sonny Terry
Also see SELLERS, Johnny
Also see SONNY & JAYCEE
Also see WALTON, Square

TERRY, Suzanne
Singles: 7-inch
COLUMBIA....3-6 66
Picture Sleeves
COLUMBIA....4-8 66

TERRY, Todd, Project
LPs: 10/12-inch
FRESH....5-8 88

TERRY, Tex
(With the Big Jim DeNoon Band; Ferlin Husky)
Singles: 78 rpm
4 STAR ("Ozark Waltz")....15-25
(Selection number not known.)
Also see HUSKY, Ferlin

TERRY, Tony P&R/R&B '87
Singles: 7-inch
EPIC....3-4 87-90
Picture Sleeves
EPIC....3-4 88
LPs: 10/12-inch
EPIC....5-8 87-91

TERRY, Wiley
Singles: 7-inch
U.S.A.....8-12 65

TERRY & ANNE
Singles: 7-inch
TOWNE HOUSE....4-8 64

TERRY & JERRY
Singles: 7-inch
CLASS....8-10 58

TERRY & BELLES
Singles: 7-inch
DUCKY (711 "I'll Always Be Nearby")....40-60 59

TERRY & CHAIN REACTION
Singles: 7-inch
U.A.....5-10 68

TERRY & FLIPPERS
Singles: 7-inch
RSVP....10-20 64
Also see FABULOUS FLIPPERS

TERRY & MACS
Singles: 78 rpm
ABC-PAR....5-10 56
Singles: 7-inch
ABC-PAR....10-15 56

TERRY & MELLOS
(Terry Corin)
Singles: 7-inch
AMY (812 "Bells of St. Mary's")....15-25 60
RIDER (108 "Why Did You Do It")....15-25 61
Also see CORIN, Terry

TERRY & PEGGY
Singles: 7-inch
YOLO....5-10

TERRY & PIRATES
Singles: 7-inch
CHESS (1696 "Talk About the Girl")....20-30 59

TERRY & TAGS
Singles: 7-inch
SYLVESTER (100 "Rampage")......15-25 62

TERRY & TOMCATS
Singles: 7-inch
TERRY 8-12 59

TERRY & TOPICS
Singles: 7-inch
CORAL..............................15-25 67

TERRY & TUNISIANS
Singles: 7-inch
SEVILLE (131 "The Street")..........20-30 63

TERRY & TYRANTS
Singles: 7-inch
KENT.............................. 5-10 64

TERRY & TOMMY
Singles: 7-inch
A-OK (1030 "I'm No Fool")............15-25 67

TERRY GIRLS
Singles: 7-inch
MALA 8-10 63

TERRY SISTERS
Singles: 7-inch
20TH FOX 5-10 60
UTONA.............................4-8 64

TERRY TWINS
Singles: 7-inch
ATCO 4-8 55
Singles: 7-inch
ATCO 5-10 55

TERRYS
Singles: 7-inch
GOLDWAX.......................... 4-8 67
RIC................................ 4-8 64

TERRYTONES
Singles: 7-inch
WYE................................10-20 61
Members: Claire Charles; Gayle Fortune.
Also see CHARLES, Claire, & the Terrytones
Also see DOWNEY, Morton, Jr.
Also see FORTUNE, Gayle, & Terrytones

TESLA P&R/LP '87
Singles: 7-inch
GEFFEN........................... 3-4 87-90
Picture Sleeves
GEFFEN........................... 3-4 87
LPs: 10/12-inch
GEFFEN........................... 5-8 87-90
Members: Jeff Keith; Brian Wheat; Frank Hannon; Tommy Skeoch; Troy Luccketta.

TESTAMENT LP '88
LPs: 10/12-inch
MEGAFORCE 5-8 88-90

TETES NOIRES
EPs: 7-inch
RAPUNZEL 4-6 85
LPs: 10/12-inch
RAPUNZEL 5-10 85
ROUNDER 5-8 87
Members: Jennifer Holt; Cindy Bartell; Renee Kayon; Camille Gage; Polly Alexander; Angela Frucci.

TEX, Joe P&R '64
(With the Class Mates; with Vibrators)
Singles: 78 rpm
KING 20-50 55-57
Singles: 12-inch
EPIC 4-8 77
Singles: 7-inch
ACE (544 "Cut It Out")..............40-60 58
ACE (549 "Blessed Are These Tears")..............................40-60 58
ACE (550 "Mother's Advice") 50-75 58
ACE (559 "Charlie Brown Got Expelled")...........................20-30 59
ACE (673 "Boys Will Be Boys")......15-25 60
ANNA (1119 "All I Could Do Was Cry")..............................15-25 60
ANNA (1124 "I'll Never Break Your Heart")...........................15-25 60
ANNA (1128 "Ain't I a Mess")........15-25 61
ATLANTIC 3-5 72
CHECKER (1055 "You Keep Her")..10-15 63
CHECKER (1104 "All I Could Do Was Cry")............................. 8-10 65
(Maroon and silver label. "Checker" at left.)
CHECKER (1104 "All I Could Do Was Cry")............................. 5-10 65
(Multi-color label. "Checker" at top.)
DIAL (1000 series) 3-6 71-76
DIAL (2800 series) 3-5 78
DIAL (3000 series) 5-10 61-64
DIAL (4000 series) 4-8 64-69
EPIC 3-5 77-79
HANDSHAKE 3-5 81
JALYNNE 5-10 61
KING (4840 "Come in This House")..........................40-60 55
KING (4884 "My Biggest Mistake")..........................25-50 56
KING (4980 "Pneumonia")............25-50 56
KING (4911 "She's Mine")............25-50 56
KING (5064 "Ain't Nobody's Business")..........................25-50 57
KING (5981 "Come in This House")............................ 5-10 65
EPs: 7-inch
ATLANTIC (8115 "The New Boss") . 8-12 65
(Juke box issue only. Includes title strips.)
LPs: 10/12-inch
ACCORD 5-10 82
ATLANTIC 10-15 65-72
CHECKER 20-30 64
DIAL...............................8-10 72-79
EPIC...............................5-10 77-78
KING..............................15-25 65
LONDON............................5-10 79
PARROT...........................15-25 65
PRIDE..............................8-10 73
Members: Mike Appell; Rod Bristow.
Also see KELLY, Paul
Also see SOUL CLAN

TEX & CHEX
Singles: 7-inch
ATLANTIC (2116 "I Do Love You")...............................30-40 61
NEWTONE..........................10-15 63
20TH FOX 10-20 63
Also see MAGICIANS

TEX & HORSEHEADS
LPs: 10/12-inch
ENIGMA 5-10 84

TEXANS P&R '61
Singles: 7-inch
GOTHIC (001 "Rockin' Johnny Home")............................15-25 61
INFINITY (001 "Green Grass of Texas")............................20-30 61
VEE JAY (658 "Green Grass of Texas")............................8-12 65
Members: Dorsey Burnette; Johnny Burnette.
Also see BURNETTE, Johnny & Dorsey

TEXAS
Singles: 7-inch
JOX...............................10-15 64

TEXAS
Singles: 7-inch
BELL 3-5 73-74
LPs: 10/12-inch
BELL 8-10 73

TEXAS LP '89
Singles: 7-inch
MERCURY 3-4 89
LPs: 10/12-inch
MERCURY 5-8 89
Members: Sharlene Spiteri; Stuart Kerr; John McElhone.
Also see ALTERED IMAGES
Also see HIPSWAY
Also see LOVE & MONEY

TEXANS
Singles: 7-inch
BLUE STAR (1578 "Walk Don't Run")..............................10-20 60s

TEXAS "GUITAR" SLIM
(Johnny Winter)
Singles: 7-inch
JIN (174 "Broke and Lonely")........30-50 62
(This same number was used for *Something's Wrong*, by Rockin' Sidney.)
MOON-LITE 75-100 60
Also see GUITAR SLIM
Also see WINTER, Johnny

TEXAS PLAYBOYS C&W '77
(Original Texas Playboys)
Singles: 7-inch
CAPITOL 3-5 77
LPs: 10/12-inch
CAPITOL...........................5-10 78-79
DELTA.............................6-12 80s
Member: Leon Rausch.
Also see ASLEEP at the WHEEL
Also see RAUSCH, Leon
Also see WILLS, Bob

TEXAS RAY
(Texas-Ray)
Singles: 7-inch
KAYDEE (3001 "Mary Ann") 15-25 60
LAURIE (3072 "Hackensack")........10-15 60
(Previously issued this same year as by "Gene Franklin, Vocal By Texas Ray.")
Also see FRANKLIN, Gene

TEXAS RED
(Texas Red & Jimmy)
Singles: 78 rpm
BULLSEYE..........................10-15 56
CHECKER...........................10-20 57
VICEROY...........................10-20 57
Singles: 7-inch
BULLSEYE..........................10-20 56
CHECKER...........................10-20 57
VICEROY...........................10-20 57

TEXAS SLIM
(John Lee Hooker)
Singles: 78 rpm
KING (4329 "Heart Trouble Blues")..............................50-75 50
KING (4366 "Don't You Remember Me")..............................50-75 50
KING (4377 "Moaning Blues")......75-125 50
Also see HOOKER, John Lee

TEXAS VOCAL COMPANY C&W '83
Singles: 7-inch
RCA.............................. 3-4 83
Members: Sandy Skinner; Dave Roth; Dick Root.
Also see PRIDE, Charley

TEXTONES LP '84
Singles: 7-inch
GOLD MOUNTAIN 3-4 84
I.R.S./FAULTY PRODUCTS 3-5 80
LPs: 10/12-inch
GOLD MOUNTAIN 5-8 84
Members: Carla Olson; Mark Cuff; Kathy Valentine; David Provost; George Callins; Phil Seymour; Tom Morgan; Joe Read.
Also see CLARK, Gene, & Carla Olson
Also see DREAM SYNDICATE
Also see GO-GOs
Also see SEYMOUR, Phil

THACKERAY ROCKE
Singles: 7-inch
CASTALIA (268 "Tobacco Road")..10-20 67
CASTALIA (671 "Bawling")............10-20 67

THANO
Singles: 7-inch
VERVE (10399 "Gimme Something")........................10-20

THARP, Chuck
(With the Fireballs)
Singles: 7-inch
JARO (77029 "Long Long Ponytail")........................75-100 60
KAPP (248 "I Don't Know")........150-200 58
LUCKY (012 "Long Long Ponytail")........................75-100 60

THARPE, Sister Rosetta
Singles: 78 rpm
DECCA.............................5-10 45-56
MERCURY..........................5-10 56
Singles: 7-inch
DECCA.............................8-12 51-56
MERCURY..........................8-12 56
Also see LITTLE RICHARD / Sister Rosetta

THARPE, Sister Rosetta, & Marie Knight
Singles: 78 rpm
DECCA.............................5-10 54
Singles: 7-inch
DECCA.............................8-12 54
Also see KNIGHT, Marie
Also see THARPE, Sister Rosetta

THAT ENGLISH SOUND
LPs: 10/12-inch
MODERN SOUND......................8-10

THAT ROCKIN' BAND
Singles: 7-inch
DIAMOND 4-8 65

THATCHER, Mark
Singles: 7-inch
DIAMOND 4-6 68
U.A................................4-8 64

THAXTER, Jim, & Travelers
Singles: 7-inch
ARIEL (73060 "Sally Jo")..........350-400 60
(500 made.)
Also see TRASHMEN

THAXTON, Lloyd
Singles: 7-inch
CAPITOL............................5-10 63
DECCA..............................4-8 64
LPs: 10/12-inch
DECCA (4594 "Lloyd Thaxton Presents")..........................20-30 64
(Monaural.)
DECCA (7-4594 "Lloyd Thaxton Presents")..........................25-35 64
(Stereo.)
Also see CHALLENGERS
Also see KNICKERBOCKERS

THAYER, Frank
(With the Lyonals)
Singles: 7-inch
OUTLAW (1 "Long Grey Highway")...........................20-30
EPs: 7-inch
OUTLAW.............................5-8 80
LPs: 10/12-inch
OUTLAW.............................8-10 80

THE, The D&D '83
Singles: 12-inch
EPIC...............................4-6 84-89
SIRE...............................4-6 83-84
Singles: 7-inch
EPIC...............................3-4 83-85
LPs: 10/12-inch
EPIC...............................5-8 84-89

THEATRE OF ICE
EPs: 7-inch
ORPHANAGE 5-10

THEE EYES
Singles
AZRA (35 "Running Naked")............8-12 88
(Shaped picture disc. 500 made.)

THEE IMAGE
Singles: 7-inch
MANTICORE..........................3-5 74
LPs: 10/12-inch
MANTICORE..........................8-10 75
Member: Mike Pinera.
Also see CACTUS
Also see PINERA, Mike

THEE MIDNITERS P&R '65
Singles: 7-inch
CHATTAHOOCHEE (666 "Land of 1000 Dances")......................8-12 65
CHATTAHOOCHEE (674 "Sad Girl")...........................8-12 65
CHATTAHOOCHEE (675 "Sad Girl")...........................8-12 65
CHATTAHOOCHEE (684 "Whitter Boulevard")......................8-12 65
CHATTAHOOCHEE (693 "I Need Someone")........................8-12 65
CHATTAHOOCHEE (694 "It's Not Unusual")........................8-12 66
CHATTAHOOCHEE (706 "Are You Angry")..........................8-12 66
UNI................................5-10 69
WHITTIER (200 "Sad Girl")..........15-25 60s
WHITTIER (201 "That's All")..........15-25 60s
WHITTIER (202 "I Need Someone")........................15-25 60s
WHITTIER (500 thru 509)............10-20 66-67
WHITTIER (511 "You're Gonna Make Me Cry")......................100-200 68
WHITTIER (674 "Sad Girl")............5-10 68
LPs: 10/12-inch
CHATTAHOOCHEE (C-1001 "Thee Midniters")......................20-30 65
(Monaural.)
CHATTAHOOCHEE (CS-1001 "Thee Midniters")......................25-45 65
(Stereo.)
RHINO..............................5-8 83
WHITTIER (5000 "Special Delivery").........................15-25 66
WHITTIER (5001 "Unlimited").......15-25 66
WHITTIER (5002 "Giants")...........15-25 67

THEE MUFFINS
LPs: 10/12-inch
("Pop Up") 100-150
(Fan club issue only. No selection number used.)

THEE PROPHETS P&R/LP '69
Singles: 7-inch
KAPP...............................4-8 68-70
TEE PEE............................5-10 67
LPs: 10/12-inch
KAPP..............................15-20 69
Members: Brian Lake; Jim Anderson; Dave Leslie; Chris Michaels; Mark Sandusky; Tony Gazzana; Joe Kopecky; Jerry George; Jose Salazar; Dave Maciolek; Lee Johnson.

THEE SAINTS & PRINCE OF DARKNESS
Singles: 7-inch
CHAMP (2006 "Hey Girl")..............8-12

THEE SIXPENCE: see SIXPENCE

THEE WYLDE MAIN-IACS
Singles: 7-inch
MAIN-IAC (001 "Why Ain't Love Fair")...........................8-12

THEM P&R/LP '65
(Featuring Van Morrison)
Singles: 7-inch
HAPPY TIGER (525 "Lonely Weekends")........................5-10 69
LOMA (2051 "Gloria's Dream")..........5-8 66
LONDON.............................3-4 70s
PARROT (365 "Gloria")................4-8 72
PARROT (3003 "Don't You Know") 10-15 66
PARROT (3006 "Don't Start Crying Now")..........................10-15 66
PARROT (9702 "Don't Start Crying Now")..........................20-30 64
(Polystyrene.)
PARROT (9702 "Don't Start Crying Now")..........................35-50 64
(Vinyl. Promotional issue only.)
PARROT (9727 "Gloria")..............10-15 65
PARROT (9749 "Here Comes the Night")..........................10-15 65
PARROT (9784 "Gonna Dress in Black")..........................10-15 65
PARROT (9796 "Mystic Eyes").......10-15 65
PARROT (9819 "Call My Name")....10-15 66
RUFF (1088 "Walking in the Queen's Garden")........................10-15 67
SULLY (1021 "Dirty Old Man")........15-25 60s
TOWER (384 "Walking in the Queen's Garden")........................5-10 67
TOWER (407 "But It's Alright")........5-10 68
TOWER (461 "We've All Agreed to Help")............................5-10 69
TOWER (493 "Corinna")...............5-10 69
Picture Sleeves
TOWER (384 "Walking in the Queen's Garden")........................15-25 67
LPs: 10/12-inch
HAPPY TIGER (1004 "Them").......20-30 69
HAPPY TIGER (1012 "In Reality").20-30 71
LONDON..............................5-10 77
PARROT (61005 "Them")............50-100 65
(Cover does not highlight *Gloria*.)
(Monaural.)
PARROT (61005 "Them")............30-35 65
(Cover highlights *Gloria*.)
(Monaural.)
PARROT (61008 "Them Again")....25-30 66
(Monaural.)
PARROT (71005 "Them")............50-100 65
(Cover does not highlight *Gloria*.)
(Stereo.)
PARROT (71005 "Them")..............40-50 65
(Cover highlights *Gloria*.)
(Stereo.)
PARROT (71008 "Them Again")....40-50 66
(Stereo.)
PARROT (71053 "Them Featuring Van Morrison")........................10-15 72
TOWER (5104 "Now and Them") ..25-35 68
TOWER (5116 "Time Out")...........25-35 68
Members: Van Morrison; Billy Harrison; Alan Henderson; Peter Bardens; J. McAuley; John Stark.
Also see BARDENS, Peter
Also see BELFAST GYPSIES
Also see MORRISON, Van

THEM / Marvelettes
Singles: 7-inch
A&M (1201 "Baby, Please Don't Go")............................3-4 88
Picture Sleeves
A&M (1201 "Baby, Please Don't Go")............................3-4 88
Also see MARVELETTES
Also see THEM

THEM
Singles: 7-inch
KING................................8-12 65

THEM FEATURING HIM
Singles: 7-inch
HEG (501 "I'm Sorry Now")............25-50

THEM OTHER BROTHERS
Singles: 7-inch
TOLLIE..............................5-10 64

THEMES
Singles: 7-inch
EXCELLO (2152 "The Magic of You")..............................20-30 59
FIDELITY ("Cross My Heart") 10-20 59
(No selection number used.)

THEMES
Singles: 7-inch
MINIT (32009 "Bent Out of Shape")..............................5-10 66
STORK (001 "There's No Moon Tonight")............................25-35 64

THEMES, INC.
Singles: 7-inch
VEE JAY (635 "Paula's Percussion")........................5-10 65
Members: Phil Sloan; Steve Barri.
Also see FANTASTIC BAGGYS

THEO VANESS LP '79
Singles: 7-inch
PRELUDE.............................3-5 79
LPs: 10/12-inch
PRELUDE.............................5-10 79

THEODORE, Donna
Singles: 7-inch
UNI.................................3-5 72

THEODORE, Mike, Orchestra LP '77
Singles: 7-inch
WESTBOUND...........................3-5 77-79
LPs: 10/12-inch
WESTBOUND...........................5-10 77-79

THERESA R&B '87
Singles: 7-inch
RCA.................................3-4 87-88
Members: Theresa King; Victor Porter.

THERRIEN, Joe
(Joe Therrien Jr. & His Rockets, with the Eckos; Joe Therrien Jr. & Sully Trio)
Singles: 78 rpm
BRUNSWICK..........................20-30 57
LIDO...............................75-125 57
Singles: 7-inch
BRUNSWICK (55005 "Hey Babe, Let's Go Downtown")........................20-30 57
BRUNSWICK (55017 "You're Long Gone")............................50-75 57
JAT (101 "I Ain't Gonna Be Around")...........................50-75 59
LIDO (505 "Hey Babe, Let's Go Downtown")........................75-125 57

THESE FEW
Singles: 7-inch
BLACKNIGHT (901 "Dynamite").....15-25 66
Also see SOUTHWEST F.O.B.

THESE PROSPEROUS TIMES
Singles: 7-inch
20TH FOX............................4-8 67

THESE TRAILS
LPs: 10/12-inch
SINERGIA ("These Trails")........100-150 73
(Selection number not known.)

THESE VIZITORS
Singles: 7-inch
CAPITOL (2163 "For Mary's Sake") 8-12 68

THEUS, Fatso, & Flairs: see FATSO & Flairs

THEY MIGHT BE GIANTS LP '88
LPs: 10/12-inch
BAR NONE............................5-8 88
ELEKTRA.............................5-8 90

THIBADEAUX, R.B.
Singles: 78 rpm
PEACOCK............................15-25 49

THIEVES
Singles: 7-inch
BROADWAY (405 "I'm Not the One")............................20-30 65

THIEVES
Singles: 7-inch
ARISTA..............................3-5 79

THIGPEN, Amanda
Singles: 7-inch
DOT.................................5-10 61

THIN LIZZY P&R/LP '76
Singles: 12-inch
W.B.................................4-8 78
(Promotional only.)
Singles: 7-inch
LONDON..............................3-5 73
MERCURY.............................3-5 76-77
VERTIGO.............................3-5 75
W.B.................................3-5 78-79

Picture Sleeves
VERTIGO 3-5 75
LPs: 10/12-inch
LONDON (500 & 600 series) 10-15 71
LONDON (20000 series) 8-12 72
LONDON (50000 series) 5-10 77
MERCURY 8-12 76-77
VERTIGO 10-12 74-75
W.B. 5-10 78-84
Members: Philip Lynott; Gary Moore; Brian Robertson.
Also see LYNOTT, Philip
Also see MOORE, Gary

THINGIES
Singles: 7-inch
CASINO (2305 "It's a Long Way Down") 15-25 66
SONOBEAT (104 "Mass Confusion") 15-25 68

THINGS
Singles: 7-inch
RAYPRO 4-8 67
LPs: 10/12-inch
VOXX 5-10

THINGS to COME
Singles: 7-inch
STARFIRE (103 "Sweet Gina") 20-30 66
W.B. (7164 "Come Alive") 5-10 68
W.B. (7228 "Hello") 5-10 68
Members: Bryan Garofalo; Russ Ward.

THINGS to COME
Singles: 7-inch
DUNWICH (124 "I'm Not Talkin' ") 10-15 66
Members: Ken Ashely; Keith MacKendrick.
Also see CHAMPS
Also see ROXSTERS

THINK
Singles: 7-inch
COLUMBIA 4-8 68-69

THINK P&R '71
Singles: 7-inch
BIG TREE 3-5 74
LAURIE 3-5 71
LPs: 10/12-inch
LAURIE 8-10 72
Member: Lou Stallman.

THIRD AVENUE BLUES BAND
Singles: 7-inch
REVUE 4-8 68-69

THIRD BARDO
Singles: 7-inch
ROULETTE (4742 "My Rainbow Life") 10-20 67
EPs: 7-inch
SUNDAZED (106 "Third Bardo") 5-10 93
(Colored vinyl.)
Members: Jeff Moon; Ricky Goldclang.

THIRD BASS LP '89
LPs: 10/12-inch
DEF JAM 5-8 89-91

THIRD BOOTH
Singles: 7-inch
INDEPENDENCE (86 "I Need Love") 5-10 68
THUNDER ("Sound Inc.") 15-25 68
(Different title, but same song as *I Need Love*, on Independence.)

THIRD DEGREE
Singles: 7-inch
MUSIC FACTORY 4-8 67-68

THIRD EAR BAND
LPs: 10/12-inch
HARVEST 10-15 69

3RD EVOLUTION
Singles: 7-inch
DAWN (306 "Don't Play with Me") 15-25 66
DAWN (312 "Everybody Needs Somebody") 5-10 67

THIRD GUITAR
Singles: 7-inch
ROJAC 4-6 68

THIRD IMAGE
Singles: 7-inch
AVCO 3-5 71

THIRD POWER LP '70
Singles: 7-inch
BARON (626 "Snow") 10-20 68
VANGUARD 4-8 70
LPs: 10/12-inch
VANGUARD (6554 "Believe") 15-20 70
Members: Jim Craig; Drew Abbott.

THIRD RAIL P&R '67
Singles: 7-inch
CAMEO 4-8 66
EPIC 3-6 67-69
LPs: 10/12-inch
EPIC 20-30 67
Member: Joey Levine; Kris Resnik; Art Resnik.
Also see LEVINE, Joey
Also see SALVATION

THIRD SOUL
Singles: 7-inch
CABELL 8-12

THIRD TUESDAY
Singles: 7-inch
TOWER 4-8 68

THIRD WORLD
Singles: 7-inch
RCA 3-5 71
LPs: 10/12-inch
RCA 10-15 71

THIRD WORLD LP '78
Singles: 12-inch
COLUMBIA 4-6 81-85
ISLAND 4-8 78-80
Singles: 7-inch
ABRAXAS 3-5 76
COLUMBIA 3-5 81-85
ISLAND 3-5 79
LPs: 10/12-inch
COLUMBIA 5-8 81-85
ISLAND 5-10 76-80
MERCURY 5-8 89
Member: Stevie Wonder.
Also see WONDER, Stevie

THIRD WORLD CREATIONS
Singles: 7-inch
SOUL-PO-TION 8-12

THIRTEENTH AMENDMENT
Singles: 7-inch
WHIT 10-15

THIRTEENTH COMMITTEE
Singles: 7-inch
MANHATTAN 4-8 67
Session: Davie Allan.
Also see ALLAN, Davie

THIRTEENTH FLOOR ELEVATORS P&R '66
Singles: 7-inch
CONTACT (5269 "You're Gonna Miss Me") 50-75 66
(First issue of *You're Gonna Miss Me.*)
HBR (492 "You're Gonna Miss Me") 50-75 66
(Third issue of *You're Gonna Miss Me.*)
INTERNATIONAL ARTISTS (107 "You're Gonna Miss Me") 10-20 66
(Second issue of *You're Gonna Miss Me.* May be found with: a) two tone light blue label; b) solid dark blue label [which exists with both "IA" and "AI" at top]; c) green and yellow label; d) white label, promotional issue. We have yet to learn of a noteworthy price difference between these.)
INTERNATIONAL ARTISTS (111 through 130) 10-20 66-68
LPs: 10/12-inch
INTERNATIONAL ARTISTS (1 "Psychedelic Sounds") 75-100 67
(Does NOT have "Masterfonics" stamped in the vinyl trail-off.)
INTERNATIONAL ARTISTS (5 "Easter Everywhere") 40-60 67
(Does NOT have "Masterfonics" stamped in the vinyl trail-off.)
INTERNATIONAL ARTISTS (8 "Live") 40-60 68
(Does NOT have "Masterfonics" stamped in the vinyl trail-off.)
INTERNATIONAL ARTISTS (9 "Bull of the Woods") 40-60 68
(Does NOT have "Masterfonics" stamped in the vinyl trail-off.)
INTERNATIONAL ARTISTS 10-20 79
(Reissues. With "Masterfonics" stamped in the vinyl trail-off.)
INTERNATIONAL ARTISTS (White Label) 150-225 67-68
(Promotional issues only.)
TEXAS ARCHIVE 8-10 85
Members: Roky Erickson; Tommy Hall; Stacy Sutherland; John Ike Walton; Benny Thurman.
Also see ERICKSON, Roky
Also see YA HO WA 13
Also see SPADES

13TH HOUR
Singles: 7-inch
TARGET (10/11 "All Right & About Time") 10-20 66
Members: Ricky Lee Smolinski; Bill Vandenburgt; Jimmy Van Hoof.

13TH HOUR GLASS
Singles: 7-inch
FORMAT ("Do I Have to Come Right Out and Say It") 20-30 60s
(Selection number not known.)
FORMAT (5003 "Keep on Running") 20-30 60s
PRESTIGE ("Try") 20-30 60s
(Selection number not known.)

13TH POWER
Singles: 7-inch
SIDEWALK 5-10 67

13TH PRECINCT
Singles: 7-inch
TRX (5005 "You Gotta Be Mine") 15-25 68

THIRTY DAYS OUT
Singles: 7-inch
REPRISE 3-5 72
LPs: 10/12-inch
REPRISE 8-10 72

31ST OF FEBRUARY
(Allman Brothers Band)
Singles: 7-inch
VANGUARD 5-10 68-69
LPs: 10/12-inch
VANGUARD (6503 "31st of February") 20-25 68
Members: Butch Truchs; Scott Boyer; Dave Brown.
Also see ALLMAN BROTHERS BAND
Also see COWBOY
Also see TIFFANY SYSTEM

.38 SPECIAL LP '77
(Thirty Eight Special)
Singles: 12-inch
A&M 4-6 79-84
Singles: 7-inch
A&M 3-5 77-88
CAPITOL 3-5 84
Picture Sleeves
A&M 3-5 80-83
LPs: 10/12-inch
A&M 5-10 77-88
CAPITOL 5-8 84
Members: Donnie Van Zandt; Don Barnes; Jeff Carlis; Steve Brookins; Jack Grodin; Larry Junstrom; Danny Chauncey; Max Carl.

THIS SIDE UP
Singles: 7-inch
CAPITOL 4-8 68

THOM, Peter
Singles: 7-inch
EPIC 4-8 66

THOMAS, Al
Singles: 7-inch
PACEMAKER (235 "Jealously") 10-15 66
(First issue.)
SCEPTER (12155 "Jealously") 4-8 66
VIRTUE 4-6 68

THOMAS, Alan
LPs: 10/12-inch
SIRE 5-10 81

THOMAS, Alexander "Mudcat"
Singles: 7-inch
NRC 10-20 60
LPs: 10/12-inch
SMASH 15-25 64

THOMAS, Andrew
(Andy Thomas)
Singles: 78 rpm
GOLD STAR 25-50 48-49
SWING with the STARS (1039 "I Love My Baby") 50-75 49
Singles: 7-inch
STARWAY 10-20 60-61
Also see HOPKINS, Lightnin'
Also see SMITH, Thunder

THOMAS, Arthur
Singles: 7-inch
CAPA (126 "A Bee Sticks to Honey") 50-75 65

THOMAS, B.J. P&R '66
(With the Triumphs)
Singles: 7-inch
ABC 3-5 75
BRAGG (103 "Billy & Sue") 10-20 66
CLEVELAND INT'L 3-4 83-84
COLLECTABLES 3-4 80s
COLUMBIA 3-4 83-86
HICKORY 6-12 66
JOED (119 "Keep It Up") 10-15 65
LORI (9547 "Hey Judy") 8-10 64
LORI (9561 "For Your Precious Love") 8-10 64
MCA 3-5 77-82
MYRRH 3-4 77-81
PACEMAKER (227 "I'm So Lonesome I Could Cry") 10-15 64
PACEMAKER (231 "M-a-m-a") 10-15 65
PACEMAKER (234 "Bring Back the Time") 10-15 65
PACEMAKER (239 "Tomorrow Never Comes") 10-15 66
PACEMAKER (247 "Plain Jane") 10-15 66
PACEMAKER (253 "Baby Cried") 10-15 66
PACEMAKER (256 "I Can't Help It") 10-15 66
PARAMOUNT 3-5 73-74
SCEPTER (12100 series) 4-8 66-67
SCEPTER (12200 thru 12364) 3-6 68-72
SCEPTER (21000 series) 3-5 73-74
VALERIE 4-8 60s
W.B. (5491 "Billy & Sue") 15-20 64
Picture Sleeves
MCA 3-5 79
LPs: 10/12-inch
ABC 5-10 74-77
ACCORD 5-10 81-82
BUCKBOARD 5-10
CLEVELAND INT'L 5-10 83
COLUMBIA 5-8 86
DORAL 15-25 60s
(Promotional mail-order issue, from Doral cigarettes.)
EXACT 5-10 80
EXCELSIOR 5-10 80
EVEREST 5-10 81
51 WEST 5-10 79
HICKORY (133 "Very Best") 20-30 66
MCA 5-10 77-82
MCA/SONGBIRD 5-10 80
MYRRH 5-10 78-83
PACEMAKER (3001 "B.J. Thomas and the Triumphs") 40-50 66
PARAMOUNT 5-10 73-74
PHOENIX 20 5-10 81
PICKWICK 5-8 78
PRIORITY 5-8 83
SCEPTER (535 thru 561) 10-20 66-67
SCEPTER (586 thru 597) 8-12 70-71
SCEPTER (5101 "Billy Joe Thomas") 8-12 72
SCEPTER (5108 "Country") 8-12 72
SCEPTER (5112 "Greatest All-Time Hits") 10-15 73
SPRINGBOARD 5-10 73-79
STARDAY 5-10 77
TRIP 5-10 76
U.A. 5-10 74
Also see CHARLES, Ray, & B.J. Thomas
Also see EDDY, Duane

THOMAS, B.J. / Smiley Lewis
Singles: 7-inch
OLDIES 45 3-5
Also see LEWIS, Smiley
Also see THOMAS, B.J.

THOMAS, Ba Ba
Singles: 7-inch
KING 4-8 64

THOMAS, Bennie
Singles: 7-inch
RCA 4-8 65
Also see MARCH, Little Peggy, & Bennie Thomas

THOMAS, Bill
(With Carolyn Sherrard)
Singles: 7-inch
CULLMAN 10-15 58-59

THOMAS, Bill, & Fendells
Singles: 7-inch
SAVOY (1628 "Southern Fried Chicken") 4-8 66

THOMAS, Billy
Singles: 7-inch
PLAYBACK 4-8 63

THOMAS, Bob
Singles: 7-inch
ABEL 4-8 60s
KINGSTON 4-8 63

THOMAS, Bob & Bobbie
Singles: 7-inch
BRAVE 4-6 68

THOMAS, Burt, & His Band
Singles: 78 rpm
JADE 15-25 51

THOMAS, Carl
(With the Fitones)
Singles: 7-inch
CUPID 4-6 70
O-GEE (1004 "I Love You Judy") 20-30 59
STROLL (101 "I Love You Judy") 20-30 59

THOMAS, Carla P&R/R&B '61
Singles: 7-inch
ATLANTIC 4-8 60-65
SATELLITE (104 "Gee Whiz, Look at His Eyes") 40-60 60
STAX 3-8 65-72
Picture Sleeves
STAX (188 "Let Me Be Good to You") 5-10 66
EPs: 7-inch
STAX 10-15 66
(Juke box issues only.)
LPs: 10/12-inch
ATLANTIC (8057 "Gee Whiz") 20-30 61
ATLANTIC (8232 "Best of Carla Thomas") 10-15 69
STAX 10-15 66-71
Also see BELL, William, & Carla Thomas
Also see OTIS & CARLA
Also see REDDING, Otis / Carla Thomas / Sam & Dave / Eddie Floyd
Also see RUFUS & CARLA
Also see TAYLOR, Johnnie, & Carla Thomas

THOMAS, Charles
Singles: 7-inch
LOMA (2031 "Lookin' for Love") 10-20 66

THOMAS, Charlie, & Drifters
Singles: 7-inch
MUSICOR 4-8 74
Also see DRIFTERS
Also see THOMAS, Charles

THOMAS, Cheri
Singles: 7-inch
RAYNARD (10069 "Glory Girl") 15-25 66

THOMAS, Cliff
Singles: 7-inch
PHILLIPS INT'L 10-15 59
SUN 3-5 70s
Members: Ed Thomas; Barbara Thomas.

THOMAS, Cliff & Ed
Singles: 7-inch
ACE 5-10 61
Also see THOMAS, Cliff

THOMAS, Dale
Singles: 7-inch
DOT 10-20 62
WAHOO 4-8 68

THOMAS, Dale
Singles: 7-inch
SKY (12837 "Crocodile Hop") 20-30

THOMAS, Danny
Singles: 78 rpm
DECCA 3-5 55-56
RCA 3-5 53-57
Singles: 7-inch
DECCA 5-10 55-56
MYRRH 3-4 73
RCA 4-10 53-67
Picture Sleeves
RCA 4-6 67
LPs: 10/12-inch
COLUMBIA (60818 "An Evening with Danny Thomas") 15-25 50s
(Promotional issue for Post Cereals.)
MGM (200 series) 20-40 53
(10-inch LP.)
MYRRH 5-10 74
Also see DAY, Doris, & Danny Thomas
Also see MARTIN, Dean

THOMAS, Danny Boy
Singles: 7-inch
GROOVY 4-8 66

THOMAS, Darrell C&W '79
Singles: 7-inch
OZARK OPRY 3-5 79

THOMAS, David Clayton LP '69
(With the Shays; with His Quartet; David Clayton-Thomas)
Singles: 7-inch
ATCO (6347 "Hey Hey Hey") 15-25 65
COLUMBIA 3-6 71
DECCA (32556 "Say Boss Man") 5-8 69
EPIC 3-5 83
RED LEAF (65001 "Hey Hey Hey") 100-150 65
ROMAN (1101 "Take Me Back") 75-100 66
(Black label. Canadian.)
ROMAN (1102 "Born with the Blues") 50-100 66
(Black label. Canadian.)
ROMAN (Blue label) 25-75 67
ROULETTE (7048 "No No No") 5-8 69
TOWER (263 "Born with the Blues") 15-25 66
LPs: 10/12-inch
ABC 5-10 78
COLUMBIA 10-15 72
DECCA (75146 "David Clayton-Thomas") 10-20 69
(Remixed rechanneled reissue of the Roman LP.)
RCA 8-12 73-74
ROMAN (101 "David Clayton Thomas & the Shays") 75-125 67
(Canadian.)
Members ("Quartet"/Shays): Fred Keeler; Scott Richards; John Wetherell; Gord Fleming; Ritchie Oates.
Also see BLOOD, SWEAT & TEARS

CLAYTON-THOMAS, David / Linda Ronstadt
LP: 10/12-inch
CAPITOL ("Back on the Streets") 15-25 69
(Selection number not known.)
PICKWICK (3245 "Back on the Streets") 10-15 70
Also see THOMAS, David Clayton
Also see RONSTADT, Linda

THOMAS, Dee, & Versatiles
Singles: 7-inch
COASTER (800 "In the Garden of Love") 25-40 60

THOMAS, Dick C&W '45
(With His Nashville Ramblers)
Singles: 78 rpm
DECCA 5-10 48-49
NATIONAL 5-10 45-46
LPs: 10/12-inch
VIKING 10-15

THOMAS, Dick
Singles: 7-inch
KAREN (1010 "Number One Doll") 10-15 60
Also see TOPPERS

THOMAS, Don
Singles: 7-inch
CORAL (62418 "Hey Little Dancing Girl") 25-35 64
MINUTEMAN 4-8 65

THOMAS, Eddie
Singles: 7-inch
STEPHENY (1837 "Eight Slow Freights") 25-50 59

THOMAS, Ella
Singles: 7-inch
FLAG 8-12 63
TRIAD 8-12 64-65

THOMAS, Ernest
Singles: 7-inch
CRYIN' in the STREETS 3-5 77

THOMAS, Evelyn P&R/R&B/D&D '84
Singles: 12-inch
TSR 4-6 84
Singles: 7-inch
CASABLANCA 3-5 78
TSR 3-5 84
VANGUARD 3-5 85
LPs: 10/12-inch
A.V.I. 5-10 79
CASABLANCA 5-10 78

THOMAS, Gene P&R '61
Singles: 7-inch
HICKORY 3-5 71
TRX 4-8 69
U.A. 6-12 61-65
VENUS (1439 "Sometime") 20-30 61
VENUS (1441 "Lamp of Love") 10-20 62
VENUS (1444 "Down the Road") 50-75 62
Also see GENE & DEBBE

THOMAS, Gerri
Singles: 7-inch
WORLD ARTISTS (1059 "It Could Have Been Me") 10-20 65

THOMAS, Gil
Singles: 7-inch
MASTER 5-10 60

THOMAS, Henry
LPs: 10/12-inch
ORIGIN 8-10

THOMAS, Herschel
Singles: 7-inch
MADISON.. 5-10 59-61
TODD.. 4-8 67

THOMAS, Ian P&R '73
Singles: 7-inch
ATLANTIC.. 3-5 78
CHRYSALIS.. 3-5 75
JANUS.. 3-5 73-74
MERCURY.. 3-4 84
LPs: 10/12-inch
ATLANTIC.. 5-10 78
JANUS.. 8-10 73-74
MERCURY.. 5-8 84

THOMAS, Irma R&B '60
Singles: 78 rpm
RON (328 "Set Me Free") 50-75 59
Singles: 7-inch
BANDY.. 5-8 60s
BUMPA..10-20
CANYON.. 3-5 70
CHECKER.. 5-10
CHESS.. 4-6 68
COTILLION.. 3-5 71-72
FUNGUS.. 3-5 73
IMPERIAL.. 5-10 64-66
MAISON DE SOUL.. 4-6
MINIT.. 8-12 61-63
RCS.. 3-5 79-81
ROKER.. 4-8 71
RON (328 "Set Me Free") 10-20 59
RON (330 "Good Man") 10-20 59
ROUNDER.. 3-4 84
LPs: 10/12-inch
BANDY (70003 "Irma Thomas")..........10-15 70s
FUNGUS.. 8-10 73
IMPERIAL (266 "Wish Someone Would Care")..20-30 64
IMPERIAL (302 "Take a Look")..........15-20 66
RCS.. 5-10 80
Also see BROWN, Maxine / Irma Thomas

THOMAS, Irma / Ernie K-Doe / Showmen / Benny Spellman
LPs: 10/12-inch
MINIT (0004 "New Orleans, Home of the Blues, Vol. 2")..20-30 64
Vol. 1 is found in the Various Artists chapter.
Also see K-DOE, Ernie
Also see SHOWMEN
Also see SPELLMAN, Benny

THOMAS, Jamo, & Party Brothers P&R '66
Singles: 7-inch
CHESS.. 4-8 66
DECCA.. 4-8 68
SOUND STAGE 7.. 4-8 67
THOMAS.. 4-8 66
Picture Sleeves
THOMAS.. 4-8 66

THOMAS, Jeannie
(Jean Thomas)
Singles: 7-inch
CADENCE.. 4-8 63
FELSTED.. 5-10 59-60
GENIE.. 5-10 60
MGM.. 4-8 64
MINUTEMAN.. 4-8 66
SEECO.. 5-10 59
STRAND.. 5-10 61
LPs: 10/12-inch
RELIABLE..15-25 62
STRAND..15-25 61

THOMAS, Jeff
Singles: 7-inch
W.B. 4-8 69

THOMAS, Jeff C&W '87
Singles: 7-inch
REVOLVER.. 3-4 87

THOMAS, Jerry
Singles: 7-inch
ASCOT.. 5-10 66
KHOURY'S (708 "Baby Please")..........25-35 58
ORCHID (274 "Jungle Dan")..........50-75 60
ORCHID (945 "We Won't Be Sorry").. 5-10 60

THOMAS, Jesse
(The Blues Troubador)
Singles: 78 rpm
CLUB ("I Wonder Why")..........75-100 48
(No selection number used.)
CLUB ("You Are My Dreams")..........75-100 48
(No selection number used.)
ELKO (107 "Another Fool Like Me")..75-100 53
FREEDOM (1513 "Guess I'll Walk Alone")..25-50 49
HOLLYWOOD (1072 "Long Time")..200-300 57
MILTONE (232 "Same Old Stuff")..75-100 48
MILTONE (233 "Zepher Blues")....75-100 48
MODERN (710 "Texas Blues")......25-50 49
SPECIALTY (419 "Jack O'Diamonds")..25-50 52
SWING TIME..25-50 51
Singles: 7-inch
HOLLYWOOD (1072 "Long Time")..75-125 57
SPECIALTY (419 "Jack O'Diamonds")..50-100 52

THOMAS, Jimmy
(With the Ike & Tina Revue)
Singles: 7-inch
B&F..10-15 61
MIRWOOD.. 5-10 66
SONJA.. 5-10 60s
SPUTNIK.. 5-10 60s
SUE.. 5-10 63
Also see RENRUT, Icky

THOMAS, Joe R&B '49
(Joe Thomas Orchestra)
Singles: 78 rpm
KING..10-20 49-51
MERCURY..10-20 51
Singles: 7-inch
KING (4299 "Page Boy Shuffle")....15-25 49
KING (4460 "Jumpin' Joe")..........15-25 51
KING (4474 "You're Just My Kind")..15-25 51
MERCURY (8268 "Everybody Loves My Baby")..15-25 51
PLAYBACK ("Page Boy Shuffle") ..15-25
(Selection number not known.)

THOMAS, Joe R&B '76
Singles: 7-inch
GROOVE MERCHANT.. 3-5 76
LRC.. 3-5 77-79
SUE.. 4-8 64
LPs: 10/12-inch
LRC.. 5-10 77-78
TODAY.. 6-12 72

THOMAS, Joe, & Bill Elliott
LPs: 10/12-inch
SUE..15-25 64
Also see THOMAS, Joe

THOMAS, Joel
Singles: 7-inch
FOREMOST.. 4-8 64

THOMAS, Jon P&R/R&B '60
(John Thomas)
Singles: 78 rpm
CHECKER..10-20 55
MERCURY..10-20 57
NOTE..15-25 55
Singles: 7-inch
ABC-PAR.. 8-12 60-61
CHECKER (809 "Rib Tips")..........15-20 55
JUNIOR.. 5-10 64
MERCURY (71078 "Hard Head")....15-25 57
MERCURY (71151 "Fatback")..........15-25 57
NOTE (1001 "Rib Tips")..........30-40 55
(First issue.)
VEEP.. 5-15 67-68
LPs: 10/12-inch
ABC-PAR (351 "Heartbreak")..........20-30 60
(Monaural.)
ABC-PAR (S-351 "Heartbreak")......30-40 60
(Stereo.)
WING..10-20 63

THOMAS, Judy
Singles: 7-inch
1-2-3.. 4-8 69
PHILIPS.. 5-10 62
REPRISE.. 4-8 63
TOLLIE.. 4-8 64
TOWER.. 4-8 65
U.A. 5-10 62

THOMAS, Kid: see KID THOMAS

THOMAS, L.J.
Singles: 78 rpm
CHESS (1493 "Baby, Take a Chance with Me")..50-100 52

THOMAS, Lafayette
Singles: 78 rpm
JUMPING.. 8-12 55
Singles: 7-inch
JUMPING (5000 "Cockroach Run")..15-25 55
SAVOY..10-15 59
Also see JUMPIN' JUDGE & HIS COURT / Lafayette Thomas
Also see ROBINSON, L.C. / Lafayette 'Thing' Thomas / Dave Alexander

THOMAS, Lee
(With the Don Juans)
Singles: 7-inch
JAGUAR (3020 "Baby, Don't You Care")..35-45 57

THOMAS, Leone R&B '76
Singles: 7-inch
DON.. 3-5 76

THOMAS, Lillo R&B '83
Singles: 12-inch
CAPITOL.. 4-6 83-85
Singles: 7-inch
CAPITOL.. 3-4 83-87
LPs: 10/12-inch
CAPITOL.. 5-8 83-85
Also see LAURENCE, Paul

THOMAS, Lillo, & Melba Moore R&B '84
Singles: 7-inch
CAPITOL.. 3-5 84
Also see MOORE, Melba
Also see THOMAS, Lillo

THOMAS, Mamie
Singles: 78 rpm
MGM..10-20 55
Singles: 7-inch
MGM (55009 "Daddy on My Mind")..25-35 55

THOMAS, Marcellus, & His Rhythm Rockets
Singles: 7-inch
AJAX (104 "Breather Blues")..........20-40
Also see MERCY DEE

THOMAS, Maxine
Singles: 7-inch
BO BO.. 4-8 64

THOMAS, Mickey
Singles: 7-inch
MCA.. 3-5 77
RCA.. 3-5 78
LPs: 10/12-inch
MCA.. 8-10 77

THOMAS, Milton, & Escorts
Singles: 7-inch
BI-MI (101 "Angel of My Dreams") 50-75 61

THOMAS, Minnie
Singles: 78 rpm
METEOR..25-50 56
Singles: 7-inch
METEOR (5036 "What Can the Matter Be")..50-75 56

THOMAS, Mona
Singles: 7-inch
USA (776 "There He Goes")..........25-40 64

THOMAS, Mule
Singles: 7-inch
HOLLYWOOD (1091 "Take Some and Leave Some")..75-125 58

THOMAS, Nancy
Singles: 7-inch
CUB.. 4-8 61

THOMAS, Nolan R&B/D&D '84
Singles: 12-inch
EMERGENCY.. 4-6 84-85
Singles: 7-inch
MIRAGE.. 3-5 84-85
Also see MONET & Nolan Thomas

THOMAS, Pat P&R '62
Singles: 7-inch
MGM.. 3-5 62-63
VERVE.. 3-5 62-64
Picture Sleeves
MGM.. 3-6 62
LPs: 10/12-inch
MGM..10-20 62-64
STRAND..10-20 61

THOMAS, Paul
(Paul Gotteshall Jr.)
Singles: 7-inch
GUYDEN.. 5-10 63
Also see ADMIRAL TONES

THOMAS, Philip-Michael R&B '85
Singles: 7-inch
ATLANTIC.. 3-5 85
LPs: 10/12-inch
ATLANTIC (90468 "Living the Book of My Life").. 5-8 85

THOMAS, Playboy
Singles: 78 rpm
PARROT..50-75 53
SWING TIME..50-75 53
Singles: 7-inch
PARROT (785 "Too Much Pride")..75-125 53
(Black vinyl.)
PARROT (785 "Too Much Pride")..200-300 53
(Colored vinyl.)
SWING TIME (340 "Too Much Pride")..75-125 53
SWING TIME (344 "End of the Road")..75-125 53

THOMAS, Prentice
Singles: 7-inch
JIN.. 4-8 68

THOMAS, Ramblin'
LPs: 10/12-inch
BIOGRAPH..10-15 70

THOMAS, Randy
Singles: 7-inch
FARO.. 4-8 66

THOMAS, Ray LP '75
Singles: 7-inch
THRESHOLD.. 3-5 75-76
LPs: 10/12-inch
THRESHOLD (16 "From Mighty Oaks")..10-15 75
(Gatefold cover.)
THRESHOLD (17 "Hopes, Wishes and Dreams")..10-15 76
THRESHOLD (102 "Ray Thomas Discusses *From Mighty Oaks*")..........15-25 75
(Promotional issue only.)
Also see MOODY BLUES

THOMAS, Ricky
Singles: 7-inch
EPIC.. 4-8 61

THOMAS, Rockin' Tabby: see THOMAS, Tabby

THOMAS, Rufus R&B '53
(Rufus "Bearcat" Thomas; Rufus Thomas Jr.)
Singles: 12-inch
A.V.I. 4-8 78
Singles: 78 rpm
CHESS (1466 "Night Walkin' Blues")..15-25 52
CHESS (1492 "No More Doggin' Around")..15-25 52
CHESS (1517 "Juanita")..........15-25 52
STAR TALENT (807 "I'm So Worried")..20-30 50
SUN (181 "Bear Cat [Answer to Hound Dog]")..75-125 53
(With subtitle.)
SUN (181 "Bear Cat")..........50-75 53
(Without subtitle.)
SUN (188 "Tiger Man")..........50-100 53
Singles: 7-inch
A.V.I. 3-5 77-78
ARTISTS of AMERICA.. 3-5 76
HI.. 3-5 78
METEOR (5039 "I'm Steady Holdin' On")..100-150 56
STAX (100 & 200 series)..........4-8 62-68
STAX (0010 thru 0236)..........3-6 68-75
SUN (181 "Bear Cat [Answer to Hound Dog]")..100-200 53
(With subtitle.)
SUN (181 "Bear Cat")..........75-125 53
(Without subtitle.)
SUN (188 "Tiger Man")..........100-150 53
LPs: 10/12-inch
A.V.I. 5-10 77-78
ARTISTS of AMERICA.. 8-10 76
GUSTO.. 5-10 80
STAX (Except 704).. 6-15 70-79
STAX (704 "Walking the Dog")..25-50 63
Also see RUFUS & CARLA

THOMAS, Rusty
Singles: 7-inch
CLUB (265 "Maybellene")..........75-100

THOMAS, Sean
Singles: 7-inch
CAMEO.. 4-8 62

THOMAS, Susan & Richard
Singles: 7-inch
BLUE HOUR.. 3-5 73

THOMAS, Tabby
(Tab Thomas; Rockin' Tabby Thomas)
Singles: 7-inch
EXCELLO.. 4-8 61-65
FEATURE (3007 "Tomorrow")..........25-35 54
GUTTER.. 3-4 85
ROCKO..10-15 61
ZYNN..10-15 61
Also see TABBY & HIS MELLOW, MELLOW MEN

THOMAS, Tasha R&B '78
Singles: 7-inch
ATLANTIC.. 3-5 78-79
ROULETTE.. 4-8 69

THOMAS, Timmy P&R/R&B '72
Singles: 12-inch
GOLD MOUNTAIN.. 4-6 84
SPECTOR.. 4-6 83
Singles: 7-inch
GLADES.. 3-5 72-77
GOLD MOUNTAIN.. 3-4 84-85
GOLDWAX.. 4-8 67
MARLIN.. 3-5 80-81
SPECTOR.. 3-4 83
TM.. 3-5 78
LPs: 10/12-inch
GLADES.. 8-10 72-76
GOLD MOUNTAIN.. 5-8 84

THOMAS, Tommy
Singles: 7-inch
COED.. 4-8 61

THOMAS, Tracy, & Tru-Sonics
Singles: 7-inch
BOLO.. 5-10 62
Also see TRU-SONICS

THOMAS, Truman
Singles: 7-inch
VEEP.. 3-6 68-69
LPs: 10/12-inch
VEEP..10-12 67

THOMAS, Ural
Singles: 7-inch
UNI.. 4-8 67
LPs: 10/12-inch
REVUE..10-12 68

THOMAS, Vaneese R&B '87
Singles: 7-inch
GEFFEN.. 3-4 87
Also see NAJEE

THOMAS, Vic
(With the 4-Evers)
Singles: 7-inch
PHILIPS (40183 "Marianne")..........25-45 64
PHILIPS (40228 "Village of Love").10-20 64

THOMAS & TOMCATS
Singles: 7-inch
NOLTA.. 5-10 61

THOMAS BROTHERS
("Melvin & Elvin")
Singles: 7-inch
MAR-VEL (355 "Way High, Way Low").. 5-10
Members: Melvin Thomas; Elvin Thomas.

THOMAS EDISON ELECTRICAL BAND
Singles: 7-inch
CAMEO.. 4-8 67

THOMAS GROUP
Singles: 7-inch
DUNHILL.. 4-8 66

THOMASON, Jimmy
Singles: 78 rpm
KING.. 5-10 52
VITA.. 5-10 56
Singles: 7-inch
VITA.. 8-12 56

THOME, Henry
Singles: 7-inch
VIV (3 "Scotch & Soda")..........5-8 62
(Era reissue.)
VIV (5 "Brandy")..........4-8 62
VIV (6 "Scarlet")..........4-8 62
VIV (305 "Scotch & Soda")..........8-10 62
(First issue.)

THOMPSON, Al
Singles: 7-inch
DEBONAIRE..15-25

THOMPSON, Billy
Singles: 7-inch
COLUMBUS (1043 "Black-Eyed Girl")..100-150 66
WAND (1108 "Black-Eyed Girl")....50-75 66

THOMPSON, Bob, Orchestra
Singles: 7-inch
RCA.. 4-6 62
LPs: 10/12-inch
RCA..10-20 61
Also see SPOTLIGHTERS

THOMPSON, Buddy
Singles: 78 rpm
ATCO (6095 "This Is the Night")....20-30 57
RCA.. 5-15 55-56
Singles; 7-inch
ATCO (6095 "This Is the Night")....20-30 57
RCA..12-25 55-56

THOMPSON, Cheryle
Singles: 7-inch
DECCA.. 4-8 66-67
VEE JAY.. 4-6 60s

THOMPSON, Chris, & Night P&R '79
Singles: 7-inch
PLANET.. 3-5 79
Also see MANN, Manfred
Also see NIGHT
Also see WARNES, Jennifer, & Chris Thompson

THOMPSON, Chuck
Singles: 7-inch
GRANITE (560 "I'm Tired of Fooling Around")..50-100

THOMPSON, Claudia
(With Barney Kessel)
Singles: 7-inch
EDISON INT'L.. 4-8 59
LPs: 10/12-inch
EDISON INT'L..15-20 60
Also see NELSON, Ricky

THOMPSON, Cotton
Singles: 78 rpm
GOLD STAR..10-20 49
Also see MULLICAN, Moon / Cotton Thompson

THOMPSON, Dickie
Singles: 78 rpm
DECCA..10-15 53
HERALD..10-15 54
Singles: 7-inch
DECCA..15-25 53
HERALD..15-25 54

THOMPSON, Don
LPs: 10/12-inch
SUNDAY.. 8-10

THOMPSON, Don, & Westchester Singers
Singles: 7-inch
COULEE (127 "Try to Remember").. 8-12 68

THOMPSON, Donnie
(Donnie Thompson Combo, Donnie Thompson Quintet)
Singles: 7-inch
DOT (16082 "Cheeze Blintzes")......10-20 60
V-TONE (209 "Chicken Hop")..........10-20 60

THOMPSON, Ernestine
Singles: 7-inch
BLAST.. 5-10 64

THOMPSON, Gene, & Counts
Singles: 7-inch
ACE.. 5-10 63

THOMPSON, Ginger
Singles: 7-inch
1-2-3.. 4-6 68

THOMPSON, Hank C&W '48
(With the Brazos Valley Boys)
Singles: 78 rpm
BLUE BONNET..25-50 47
(Title and selection number not known.)
CAPITOL..10-25 47-57
GLOBE (124 "Whoa Sailor")......100-200 46
Singles: 7-inch
ABC.. 3-5 75-79
ABC/DOT.. 3-5 74-77
CAPITOL (1000 thru 3000 series)....5-15 50-58
CAPITOL (4000 & 5000 series)..........4-8 58-66
CHURCHILL.. 3-4 81-83

DOT ... 3-5 68-74
MCA ... 3-4 79-80
W.B. ... 4-6 66-67

Picture Sleeves

CAPITOL (4649 "Lost John") ... 5-10 61

EPs: 7-inch

CAPITOL ... 10-20 53-59

LPs: 10/12-inch

ABC ... 5-8 78
ABC/DOT ... 5-10 74-77
CAPITOL (H-418 "Songs of the Brazos Valley") ... 60-80 53
(10-inch LP.)
CAPITOL (T-418 "Songs of the Brazos Valley") ... 50-75 55
(Green label.)
CAPITOL (T-618 "North of the Rio Grande") ... 40-60 55
(Green label.)
CAPITOL (T-729 "New Recordings") ... 30-50 55
CAPITOL (T-826 "Hank!") ... 30-40 57
CAPITOL (T-975 "Dance Ranch") ... 30-40 58
CAPITOL (T-1111 thru T-2154) ... 15-25 59-64
(Monaural.)
CAPITOL (ST-1111 through ST-2154) ... 15-30 59-64
(Stereo.)
CAPITOL (SM-2000 series) ... 5-8 75
CAPITOL (T-2274 thru T-2800) ... 10-20 65-67
(Monaural.)
CAPITOL (ST-2274 through ST-2826) ... 10-25 65-67
(Stereo.)
CAPITOL (H-9111 "Favorites") ... 50-100 52
(10-inch LP.)
CAPITOL (11000 series) ... 5-8 79
CHURCHILL ... 5-8 84
DOT ... 5-15 68-74
GUSTO ... 5-8 80
MCA/DOT ... 5-8
PICKWICK/HILLTOP ... 5-15 67-68
PROVINCIA ... 5-8
SEARS (135 "How Many Teardrops Will It Take") ... 10-15 60s
STEP ONE ... 5-8 87
TOWER ... 8-15 68
WACO (101 "Hank Thompson Sings and Plays Bob Wills") ... 30-50
Session: Buddy Cagle.
Also see CAGLE, Buddy
Also see POTTER, Curtis

THOMPSON, Hank, & Merle Travis

(With the Brazos Valley Boys) C&W '55

Singles: 78 rpm

CAPITOL ... 5-10 55

Singles: 7-inch

CAPITOL ... 8-12 55
Also see THOMPSON, Hank
Also see TRAVIS, Merle

THOMPSON, Hayden

(Haydon Thompson)

Singles: 78 rpm

VON ... 50-100 54

Singles: 7-inch

ARLEN (728 "Queen Bee") ... 10-20 63
B.E.A.T. (1011 "Dream Love") ... 15-25 60
BRAVE ... 4-8 67
EXTREMELY BRAVE ... 3-6 73
H.T. ... 3-6 75
KAPP ... 4-8 66
NASHVILLE NORTH ... 3-6 70-73
PHILIPS INT'L (3517 "Love Me Baby") ... 40-60 57
PROFILE (4015 "Whatcha Gonna Do") ... 50-75 61
VON (1001 "Whatcha' Gonna Do") ... 100-150 54

LPs: 10/12-inch

KAPP ... 12-15 66

THOMPSON, Helen

Singles: 7-inch

STATES (126 "All by Myself") ... 25-35 53
(Black vinyl.)
STATES (126 "All by Myself") ... 60-100 53
(Colored vinyl.)
STATES (138 "My Baby's Love") ... 25-35 53
(Black vinyl.)

THOMPSON, Howard, & Upsetters

Singles: 7-inch

MAJOR (1037 "Can't Go on This Way") ... 30-50

THOMPSON, J.W.

C&W '79

Singles: 7-inch

CENTURY 21 ... 3-4 84
NSD ... 3-5 80-81
SOUTHERN STAR ... 3-5 79
USA COUNTRY ... 3-4 83

THOMPSON, Johnny

Singles: 7-inch

GUITARSVILLE ... 4-8 64

THOMPSON, Juanita

Singles: 7-inch

RAMADA ... 4-8 61

THOMPSON, Junior

(With the Meteors)

Singles: 78 rpm

METEOR ... 100-200 56

Singles: 7-inch

ATCO ... 4-8 67
METEOR (5029 "Mama's Little Baby") ... 250-300 56

THOMPSON, Kay

P&R '56

Singles: 78 rpm

CADENCE ... 3-5 56
MGM ... 3-5 54-55

Singles: 7-inch

CADENCE ... 4-8 56
MGM ... 4-8 54-55

Picture Sleeves

CADENCE ... 5-10 56

THOMPSON, Kid Guitar

Singles: 7-inch

DORE ... 4-8 61

THOMPSON, Loretta

Singles: 78 rpm

UNITED ... 25-35 57

Singles: 7-inch

SKOOP (1050 "Square from Nowhere") ... 40-50 59
UNITED (214 "Hi-De-Ho Rock & Roll") ... 25-35 57

THOMPSON, Lucky

Singles: 78 rpm

ABC-PAR ... 35-55 57
SWING BEAT ... 10-15 49

LPs: 10/12-inch

ABC-PAR (171 "Lucky Thompson") ... 35-55 57
DAWN (1113 "Lucky Thompson") ... 25-50 57
URANIA (1206 "Accent on the Tenor") ... 25-50 57

THOMPSON, Marie

Singles: 7-inch

J.C.D. ... 5-10 59

THOMPSON, Mayo

LPs: 10/12-inch

MUSIC LANGUAGE ... 10-15 76
TEXAS REVOLUTION (2270 "Corky's Debt") ... 20-25 69
Also see RED CRAYOLA

THOMPSON, Paul

Singles: 7-inch

VOLT (4042 "Special Kind of Woman") ... 15-25 60s

THOMPSON, Ray

Singles: 7-inch

ON the SQUARE (315 "Little Eva") ... 30-40 59

THOMPSON, Richard

LP '83

Singles: 7-inch

HANNIBAL ... 3-4 83
POLYDOR ... 3-4 85-86
REPRISE ... 3-5 72

LPs: 10/12-inch

CAPITOL ... 5-8 88
HANNIBAL ... 5-8 83
POLYDOR ... 5-8 85-86
REPRISE ... 8-10 72
Also see FAIRPORT CONVENTION

THOMPSON, Richard & Linda

Singles: 7-inch

CHRYSALIS ... 3-5 78
ISLAND ... 3-5 74-75

LPs: 10/12-inch

CHRYSALIS ... 5-10 78
ISLAND ... 5-10 74-75
Also see THOMPSON, Richard

THOMPSON, Richie, & Jesters

Singles: 7-inch

DIAMOND (103 "Too Late to Worry") ... 20-30 61

THOMPSON, Robbin, Band

P&R/LP '80

Singles: 7-inch

COLPAR ... 4-6
NEMPEROR ... 3-5 76-77
OVATION ... 3-5 80
RICHMOND ... 3-5
SHORT PUMP ... 3-4 80s

LPs: 10/12-inch

NEMPEROR ... 5-10 76
OVATION ... 5-10 80
RICHMOND ... 10-15
Also see SPRINGSTEEN, Bruce

THOMPSON, Rocky

(Goree Carter)

Singles: 78 rpm

JADE (207 "My Wish") ... 25-50 51
Also see CARTER, Goree

THOMPSON, Ron

Singles: 7-inch

DREEM ... 5-10
FINGERPOPPIN ... 5-8

THOMPSON, Ron, & Broughams

Singles: 7-inch

SOMA (1108 "Switchblade") ... 100-125 59
Also see ALLISON, Dick, & Broughams

THOMPSON, Ronnie

Singles: 7-inch

GREAT ... 3-6 68
SELECT ... 4-8 63
SOOZEE ... 4-8 62

THOMPSON, Roy

R&B '67

Singles: 7-inch

OKEH ... 4-8 66-67

THOMPSON, Sandra

Singles: 7-inch

OKEH ... 3-5 60

THOMPSON, Shorty

Singles: 78 rpm

MERCURY ... 8-12 48

THOMPSON, Sonny

P&R/R&B '48

Singles: 78 rpm

CHART ... 10-15 56
KING ... 5-15 50-57
MIRACLE ... 10-15 48

Singles: 7-inch

CHART ... 15-25 56
KING (4400 thru 5300 series) ... 5-15 51-60
KNIGHT ... 5-10 61

EPs: 7-inch

KING ... 20-40 52-54

LPs: 10/12-inch

KING (568 "Moody Blues") ... 75-100 58
KING (655 "Mellow Blues") ... 50-75 59
Also see KING, Freddie / Lulu / Sonny Thompson
Also see REED, Lulu

THOMPSON, Sue

P&R '61/C&W '72

Singles: 78 rpm

DECCA ... 5-10 55
MERCURY ... 5-10 51-54

Singles: 7-inch

DECCA ... 10-15 55
GUSTO ... 3-4 80s
HICKORY (Except 1100 & 1200 series) ... 4-8 66-76
HICKORY (1100 & 1200 series) ... 5-10 61-65
MERCURY ... 10-20 51-54

Picture Sleeves

HICKORY ... 5-8 64

LPs: 10/12-inch

HICKORY (Except 104 through 121) ... 8-15 69-74
HICKORY (104 thru 121) ... 15-25 62-65
WING ... 10-15 66
Also see GIBSON, Don, & Sue Thompson
Also see LUMAN, Bob, & Sue Thompson
Also see MARTIN, Dude

THOMPSON, Tommy

Singles: 7-inch

BIRD ... 4-8 62
TOPPA ... 4-8 63

THOMPSON, Virginia

Singles: 78 rpm

LIN ... 5-10 56

Singles: 7-inch

LIN ... 10-15 56

THOMPSON BROTHERS

Singles: 7-inch

DOT (17072 "Walk Away") ... 4-8 68
IVANHOE (5022 "Walk Away") ... 10-20 67

THOMPSON TWINS

R&B/LP '82

Singles: 12-inch

ARISTA ... 4-6 83-86

Singles: 7-inch

ARISTA ... 3-4 82-87
W.B. ... 3-4 89

Picture Sleeves

ARISTA ... 3-5 83-87
W.B. ... 3-4 89

LPs: 10/12-inch

ARISTA ... 5-10 82-87
Members: Tom Bailey; Alannah Currie; Joe Leeway; Chris Bell.
Also see GENE LOVES JEZEBEL

THOMSON, Ali

P&R/LP '80

Singles: 7-inch

A&M ... 3-5 80-81

Picture Sleeves

A&M ... 3-5 80

LPs: 10/12-inch

A&M ... 5-10 80

THOMSON, Jimmy

Singles: 7-inch

KING ... 4-8 63

THOR

LPs: 10/12-inch

MIDSONG ... 8-10 77

THOR'S HAMMER

Singles: 7-inch

COLUMBIA ... 4-8 67

THOR-ABLES

Singles: 7-inch

TITANIC ("Our Love Song") ... 150-250 62
(No selection number used.)
TITANIC (1002 "My Reckless Heart") ... 150-250 62
Members: Lloyd McCraw; Willie Davis.
Also see CADETS

THOR-ABLES / Aaron Collins

Singles: 7-inch

TITANIC (1001 "Our Love Song") ... 75-125 62
Also see COLLINS, Aaron
Also see THOR-ABLES

THORINSHIELD

Singles: 7-inch

PHILIPS ... 4-8 67-68

LPs: 10/12-inch

PHILLIPS ... 10-15 68

THORNDIKE PICKLEDISH

(Thorndike Pickledish Choir; Thorndike Pickledish Pacifist Choir; Bob Smith)

Singles: 7-inch

ABSURD ... 5-10 66
LO-FI ... 5-10 67-68
MTA ... 5-10 67
PICCADILLY ... 5-10 67

EPs: 7-inch

PICCADILLY ... 8-12
Also see DR. ZINGRR
Also see SMITH, Bob

THORNE

Singles: 7-inch

SCENVILLE ... 4-8 68

THORNE, David

P&R '62

(David Throne)

Singles: 7-inch

ADMIRAL ... 4-8 64-65
CHOICE ... 5-10 60
CREST ... 5-10 69
RIVERSIDE ... 4-8 62
SAVOY ... 5-10 59

THORNE, Del

Singles: 78 rpm

EXCELLO ... 20-30 52

Singles: 7-inch

EXCELLO (2006 "I Let Him Move Me") ... 40-60 52
EXCELLO (2017 "Fly Chicken Blues") ... 40-60 52

THORNE, Woody

Singles: 7-inch

GNP ... 10-15 61

THORNTON, Big Mama: see THORNTON, Willie Mae

THORNTON, Fonzi

R&B '83

Singles: 12-inch

RCA ... 4-6 83

Singles: 7-inch

RCA ... 3-4 83

LPs: 10/12-inch

RCA ... 5-8 83

THORNTON, Les

Singles: 7-inch

DU-WELL ... 5-8 60-61

THORNTON, Marsha

C&W '89

Singles: 7-inch

MCA ... 3-4 89-90

THORNTON, Paul

Singles: 7-inch

MUSTANG ... 4-8 65

THORNTON, Teri

Singles: 7-inch

COLUMBIA (43151 "Secret Life") ... 4-8 64

THORNTON, Willie Mae

R&B '53

(Big Mama Thornton)

Singles: 78 rpm

PEACOCK ... 20-40 5

Singles: 7-inch

ABC ... 3-5 73
ARHOOLIE ... 4-6 68
BAY TONE (107 "You Did Me Wrong") ... 10-20 61
CAROLYN ... 4-8 70s
GALAXY (749 "Life Goes On") ... 8-10 66
KENT (424 "Before Day") ... 5-8 65
MERCURY ... 4-6 69
PEACOCK (1567 "Partnership Blues") ... 50-75 51
PEACOCK (1603 "Mischievous Boogie") ... 50-75 52
PEACOCK (1612 "Hound Dog") ... 50-75 53
PEACOCK (1621 "Cotton Picking Blues") ... 40-60 53
PEACOCK (1626 "I Ain't No Fool Either") ... 40-60 53
PEACOCK (1632 "I've Searched the World Over") ... 40-60 54
PEACOCK (1642 "Stop Hoppin' on Me") ... 40-60 54
PEACOCK (1647 "Walking Blues") ... 25-50 55
PEACOCK (1650 "The Fish") ... 25-50 55
PEACOCK (1654 "Tarzan and the Dignified Monkey") ... 25-50 55
(White label issues of this or earlier numbers are reissues, which Peacock continued carrying in their catalog through the '70s.)
PEACOCK (1681 "Just Like a Dog") ... 20-30 57
ST. CAROLYN ... 4-6
SOTOPLAY (0033 "Summertime") ... 8-12 65
SOTOPLAY (0039 "Tomcat") ... 8-12 65

LPs: 10/12-inch

ARHOOLIE ... 10-15 66-67
BACK BEAT ... 20-25 70
MERCURY ... 10-15 69-70
PENTAGRAM ... 12-25 71
ROULETTE ... 10-15 70
VANGUARD ... 8-10 74-75
Session: Don Johnson; Johnny Otis; George Washington; Pete Lewis; Devonia Williams.
Also see HARLEM STARS
Also see OTIS, Johnny

THORNTON, FRADKIN & UNGER

(With Paul McCartney)

Singles: 7-inch

ESP-DISK ... 8-12 71
Also see McCARTNEY, Paul

THORNTON SISTERS

Singles: 7-inch

BOBSAN ... 4-8 64

THOROGOOD, George

(With the Destroyers) LP '78

Singles: 12-inch

EMI (Black vinyl) ... 4-6 83-85
EMI (9293 "Rock & Roll Christmas") ... 5-10 83
(Colored vinyl. Promotional issue only.)

Singles: 7-inch

EMI (Except 17517) ... 3-5 82-94
EMI (17517 "Get a Haircut") ... 5-10 94
(White label, black vinyl. Reads: "For Juke boxes Only!")
EMI (17517 "Get a Haircut") ... 10-15 94
(White label, colored vinyl. Reads: "For Juke boxes Only!")
MCA ... 3-5 79
ROUNDER ... 3-5 78-80

LPs: 10/12-inch

EMI ... 5-8 82-91
MCA ... 5-10 79
ROUNDER ... 6-12 77-80

THORPE, Billy

P&R/LP '79

Singles: 7-inch

CAPRICORN ... 3-5 79
POLYDOR ... 3-5 79
PASHA (Except "Retail Teaser") ... 3-4 85
PASHA ("Retail Teaser") ... 4-8 85
(Selection number not known.)

LPs: 10/12-inch

CAPRICORN ... 15-20 79
ELEKTRA ... 5-8 80
PASHA ... 8-12 82-85
POLYDOR ... 5-8 79

THORPE, Billy, & Aztecs

Singles: 7-inch

GNP ... 5-10 65
Also see AZTECS

THORPE, Lionel

(Carl "Lionel" Thorpe)

Singles: 7-inch

ROULETTE ... 5-10 59-60
Also see CHORDS

THOSE BOYS

Singles: 7-inch

FED (1012 "Never Go Away") ... 20-30 66
FED (1016 "No Good Girl") ... 20-30 66

THOSE FIVE GUYS

Singles: 7-inch

QUILL ... 5-10 60s

THOSE FOUR ELDORADOS

(El Dorados)

Singles: 7-inch

ACADEMY (8138 "A Lonely Boy") ... 250-500 58
Members: Juell Jones; Louis Bradley; Marvin Smith; James Maddox.
Also see EL DORADOS
Also see SMITH, Marvin

THOSE GUYS

Singles: 7-inch

BLACK SHEEP ... 10-20

THOSE OF US

Singles: 7-inch

IGL (124 "Without You") ... 25-35 60s
Also see GREGORY, Dale, & Shouters

THOUGHTS

Singles: 7-inch

PLANET ... 10-20 66

THOUSAND FACES

Singles: 7-inch

ERA ... 4-8 68

THRASHER, Tommy

Singles: 7-inch

TOM TOM (102 "My Baby Knows") ... 50-75 61
TOPPA ... 4-8 63

THRASHER BROTHERS

C&W '81

Singles: 7-inch

MCA ... 3-4 81-83

LPs: 10/12-inch

MCA ... 5-10 82
PRESTIGE ... 6-12
Also see HALLMARK, Roger, & Thrasher Brothers

THRASHERS

(With Joe Ruffin Band)

Singles: 7-inch

CANDLELITE (421 "Jeannie") ... 10-15 63
MASON'S (02 "Jeannie") ... 250-400 57
(Reads: "Mason's Recording Co. 1630 Amsterdam Ave. N.Y.C." Flip is #01.)
MASON'S (02 "Jeannie") ... 100-150 61
(Reads: "Mason's Records 267 Franklin Ave. Brooklyn 5, N.Y." Flip is #01.)

THRASHERS

Singles: 7-inch

CLEARVIEW ... 4-8 65

THREATT, Sonny

Singles: 7-inch

SOFT ... 4-8 68
Also see SONNY & PHYLLIS
Also see TANGENTS

3

LP '88

Singles: 7-inch

GEFFEN ... 3-4 88

LPs: 10/12-inch

GEFFEN ... 5-8 88
Members: Keith Emerson; Carl Palmer.
Also see EMERSON, LAKE & PALMER

31/2

Singles: 7-inch

CAMEO ... 5-10 66-67

THREE ACES & JOKER

Singles: 7-inch

GRC (104 "Booze Party") ... 100-200

THREE BARONS

(Three Riffs)

Singles: 78 rpm

SAVOY ... 15-25 45
Also see THREE RIFFS

THREE BEAUS & A PEEP

Singles: 78 rpm

ALADDIN ... 5-10 57

COLUMBIA....5-10 53
Singles: 7-inch
ALADDIN....8-12 57
COLUMBIA....8-12 53
Also see VALLO, Rick

THREE BELLES
Singles: 78 rpm
JUBILEE....5-10 55
Singles: 7-inch
JUBILEE....10-15 55

THREE BELLS
Singles: 7-inch
LAWN....8-12 65

THREE BITS OF RHYTHM
Singles: 78 rpm
DECCA....15-25 41
MODERN MUSIC....15-25

THREE BLONDE MICE
Singles: 7-inch
ATCO (6324 "Ringo Bells")....10-15 64
ATCO (6353 "What'd I Say")....4-8 65

THREE CHEERS
Singles: 7-inch
GLORY....5-10 59
PHILIPS....4-8 62

THREE CHIMES
(Three Chymes)
Singles: 7-inch
CROSSWAY (444 "Tears and Pain")....50-100 64
Also see CHIMES

THREE CHUCKLES *P&R '54*
(Featuring Teddy Randazzo)
Singles: 78 rpm
BOULEVARD (100 "Runaround")....20-25 53
VIK....5-10 56
"X"....8-12 54-56
Singles: 7-inch
BOULEVARD (100 "Runaround") 50-100 53
CLOUD (507 "Runaround")....5-10 66
VIK (0186 "Anyway")....10-15 56
VIK (0194 "And the Angels Sing")..10-15 56
VIK (0216 "Gypsy in My Soul")....10-15 56
VIK (0232 "Midnight Till Dawn")....10-20 56
VIK (0244 "Won't You Give Me a Chance")....10-20 56
"X" (0066 "Runaround")....15-20 54
"X" (0095 "Foolishly")....15-20 55
"X" (0134 "So Long")....15-20 55
"X" (0150 "Realize")....15-20 55
"X" (0162 "Times Two, I Love You")....15-20 55
"X" (0186 "Anyway")....15-20 55
"X" (0194 "And the Angels Sing")..15-20 56
"X" (0216 "Gypsy in My Soul")....15-20 56
EPs: 7-inch
RCA (192/193/194 "Three Chuckles")....15-25 55
(Price is for any of three volumes.)
VIK (4 "Three Chuckles")....20-40 57
(Promotional issue only. Not issued with cover.)
LPs: 10/12-inch
VIK (1067 "Three Chuckles")....100-150 55
Members: Teddy Randazzo; Phil Benti; Tom Romano; Russ Gilberto.
Also see CHUCKLES
Also see RANDAZZO, Teddy

THREE COQUETTES
Singles: 7-inch
HOPE....10-15 60

3-D
Singles: 7-inch
POLYDOR....3-5 80
LPs: 10/12-inch
POLYDOR....5-10 80

THREE Ds
Singles: 78 rpm
PARIS....8-12 57
PILGRIM....5-10 56
Singles: 7-inch
BRUNSWICK....10-15 59
PARIS....8-12 57-58
PILGRIM....8-12 56
SQUARE (502 "Squeeze")....50-75
SQUARE (503 "High School Love")....50-75
Also see GINSBURG, Arnie
Also see PINARD, Henry, & Three Ds

THREE Ds
Singles: 7-inch
CAPITOL....4-8 64-65
LPs: 10/12-inch
CAPITOL....12-25 64-65

THREE Ds
Singles: 7-inch
PHOENIX....3-5

THREE DEES
Singles: 7-inch
DEAN....10-20

THREE DEGREES *P&R '65*
Singles: 7-inch
ARIOLA AMERICA....3-5 78-80
EPIC....3-5 76
ICHIBAN....3-4 89
METROMEDIA....4-6 69
NEPTUNE....3-5 70
PHILADELPHIA INT'L....3-5 73-76
ROULETTE....3-5 70-73
SWAN....6-12 64-66
W.B.....4-8 68
LPs: 10/12-inch
ARIOLA AMERICA....5-10 78-81
EPIC....8-10 77
PHILADELPHIA INT'L....8-10 74-76
ROULETTE....10-20 70-75
Also see MFSB & Three Degrees

THREE DIMENSIONS
(With the Don Ralke Orchestra)
Singles: 7-inch
CASCADE (5903 "Nightfall")....50-100 59
Also see RALKE, Don

THREE DIMENSIONS
Singles: 7-inch
RCA....5-8 65

THREE DOG NIGHT *P&R/LP '69*
(3 Dog Night)
Singles: 7-inch
ABC....3-5 70-76
DUNHILL (Except 4168)....3-8 69-75
DUNHILL (4168 "Nobody")....5-10 68
PASSPORT....3-5 83
Picture Sleeves
DUNHILL (4168 "Nobody")....20-30 68
(Promotional issue only.)
DUNHILL (4239 "Mama Told Me")....4-6 70
EPs: 7-inch
ABC (40014 "Hard Labor")....10-20 74
(Quadraphonic. Juke box "Special Promotional Record." Includes title strips.)
DUNHILL (PRO-50158 "Cyan")....8-12 73
(Promotional only issue.)
LPs: 10/12-inch
ABC (888 "Coming Down Your Way")....8-12 75
ABC (928 "American Pastime")....8-12 76
ABC/COMMAND (40014 "Hard Labor")....15-25 74
(Quadraphonic.)
ABC/COMMAND (40018 "Dog Style")....15-25 74
(Quadraphonic.)
ABC/COMMAND (40019 "Coming Down Your Way")....15-25 75
(Quadraphonic.)
DUNHILL (50048 thru 50068)....10-15 68-69
DUNHILL (50078 "It Ain't Easy")..50-100 70
(Cover pictures nude people.)
DUNHILL (50078 "It Ain't Easy")....10-12 70
(Cover doesn't show nudes.)
DUNHILL (50088 thru 50158)....10-15 70-73
DUNHILL (50168 "Hard Labor")....15-20 74
(With baby delivery cover.)
DUNHILL (50168 "Hard Labor")....10-12 74
(With Band-Aid cover.)
DUNHILL (50178 "Joy to the World")....8-10 74
K-TEL....5-10
MCA....5-8 82
PASSPORT....5-8 83
PICKWICK....5-8 79
Members: Danny Hutton; Cory Wells; Chuck Negron; Mike Allsup; Jimmy Greenspoon; Joe Schermie; Floyd Sneed.
Also see HUTTON, Danny
Also see WELLS, Cory

THREE DOLLS
Singles: 78 rpm
MGM....5-10 57
Singles: 7-inch
MGM....5-10 57

THREE DONS & GINNY
Singles: 7-inch
BLUE RIVER....4-8 63

THREE DOTS
Singles: 7-inch
BUZZ....10-20 59
RICH....5-10 60

THREE DOTS & DASH
Singles: 78 rpm
IMPERIAL....50-75 51
Singles: 7-inch
IMPERIAL (5164 "I'll Never Love Again")....150-250 51
Member: Jesse Belvin.
Also see BELVIN, Jesse, & Three Dots and a Dash
Also see McNEELY, Big Jay

THREE EMOTIONS
Singles: 7-inch
FURY (1026 "The Night We Met")....25-30 59

THREE FACES WEST
LPs: 10/12-inch
OUTPOST....15-20

THREE FLAMES *P&R/R&B '47*
Singles: 78 rpm
COLUMBIA....15-25 47-51
GOTHAM....15-25 46
HARMONY....10-20 49
MGM....10-20 50
LPs: 10/12-inch
MERCURY (20239 "At the Bon Soir")....25-50 57
Member: Tiger Haynes; Rill Pollard; Roy Testamark.
Also see BARNES, Mae

3 FRIENDS
Singles: 78 rpm
LIDO....15-25 56-57
Singles: 7-inch
BRUNSWICK (55032 "Chinese Tea Room")....15-25 57
LIDO (500 "Blanche")....50-75 56
(Gray label. With straight horizontal lines.)
LIDO (500 "Blanche")....25-50 50s
(Gray label. With wavy horizontal lines.)
LIDO (500 "Blanche")....30-40 57
(Blue label.)
LIDO (502 "I'm Only a Boy")....25-50 57
LIDO (504 "Now That You're Gone")....20-35 57
RELIC....4-8 72
Members: Tony Grochowski; Dom Bartolomeo; Joe Buono; Joey Villa; Frankie Starro. Session: Mickey Baker.
Also see BAKER, Mickey
Also see EMANONS
Also see HEARTBEATS
Also see ILLUSIONS
Also see REARDON, Eddie

3 FRIENDS *P&R '61*
(Three Friends)
Singles: 7-inch
CAL-GOLD (169 "Blue Ribbon Baby")....100-150 61
IMPERIAL (5763 "Dedicated [To the Songs I Love]")....20-30 61
IMPERIAL (5773 "Go on to School")....15-20 61

THREE Gs *P&R '58*
Singles: 7-inch
COLUMBIA....10-15 58
Members: Jerry Glasser; Ted Glasser; Robert Glasser.

3 GIRLS
LPs: 10/12-inch
PHANTOM....8-10 75
Members: Helen Hooke; Anne Bowen; Pam Brandt.
Also see CAVALIERE, Felix

THREE GRACES
Singles: 7-inch
GOLDEN CREST....8-12 59-60

THREE GRACES / Wailers
EPs: 7-inch
GOLDEN CREST (88601/2 "Four Songs on 45 rpm")....75-125 60
(With paper sleeve-mailer. Both sides have label pictures.)
Also see THREE GRACES
Also see WAILERS

THREE HAIRCUTS
Singles: 78 rpm
RCA....4-8 55
Singles: 7-inch
RCA....8-12 55
Members: Sid Caesar; Carl Reiner; Howie Morris.

THREE HEADS
Singles: 7-inch
CHART....4-8 68

THREE HONEYDROPS
Singles: 7-inch
MUSIC CITY....20-30 57

THREE JADES
Singles: 7-inch
MAURICI....8-12

THREE JAYS
Singles: 7-inch
NOVA (120 "Pool Party")....5-8 66

THREE JOKERS
Singles: 7-inch
MERCURY (72345 "He's a Bum") 10-20 60s

THREE Ks
Singles: 7-inch
CAROUSEL....5-10 64
DOT....5-10 61

THREE KARATS
Singles: 7-inch
DELRAY....5-8

THREE KEYS
Singles: 78 rpm
BRUNSWICK....15-25 32-43
COLUMBIA....15-25 32
VOCALION....15-25 33-34

THREE KINGS & QUEEN
LPs: 10/12-inch
SPIVEY....10-20 60s
Members: Lonnie Johnson; Roosevelt Sykes; Big Joe Williams; Victoria Spivey.
Also see DYLAN, Bob
Also see JOHNSON, Lonnie
Also see SPIVEY, Victoria
Also see SYKES, Roosevelt
Also see WILLIAMS, Big Joe

THREE KITTENS
Singles: 78 rpm
BRUNSWICK....5-15 57
CORAL....5-10 55
Singles: 7-inch
BRUNSWICK....8-15 57
CORAL....8-15 55

THREE MAN ARMY
LPs: 10/12-inch
KAMA SUTRA (2044 "Third of a Lifetime")....12-15 71
(Pink label. Gatefold cover.)
KAMA SUTRA (2044 "Third of a Lifetime")....10-12 72
(Blue label. Standard cover.)
REPRISE....10-12 73-74
Members: Ginger Baker; Adrian Gurvitz; Paul Gurvitz.
Also see BAKER - GURVITZ ARMY

THREE MAN ISLAND *P&R '88*
Singles: 7-inch
CHRYSALIS....3-4 88
Picture Sleeves
CHRYSALIS....3-4 88
LPs: 10/12-inch
CHRYSALIS....5-8 88

THREE MEN in BLACK
Singles: 7-inch
TWIN TOWN....8-12 60s

THREE MILLION *R&B/D&D '83*
Singles: 12-inch
COTILLION....4-6 84-84
Singles: 7-inch
COTILLION....3-5 83-84

THREE MARTINIS & OLIVE
LPs: 10/12-inch
MIRA....10-20 67

THREE NOTES
(3 Notes)
Singles: 7-inch
TALLY (116 "I've Been Thinking It Over")....15-25 58
TEE GEE (106 "Bertha, My Girl")....50-100 58

THREE O'CLOCK *LP '85*
Singles: 7-inch
I.R.S.....3-4 85
LPs: 10/12-inch
I.R.S.....5-8 85

THREE OCTAVES
Singles: 7-inch
PLEBE....5-10 60

3 OF a KIND
Singles: 7-inch
SUSSEX....3-5 73
Member: Jeff Perry.
Also see PERRY, Jeff

THREE OF US
Singles: 7-inch
KAPP (756 "One Golden Day")....10-15 66

3 OUNCES OF LOVE *R&B '78*
Singles: 7-inch
MOTOWN....3-5 78
LPs: 10/12-inch
MOTOWN....5-10 78
Members: Elaine Alexander; Ann Alexander; Regina Alexander.

THREE PALS
Singles: 7-inch
SYLESE....4-8 63

THREE PELVES: see STRIKES

3 PENNIES
Singles: 7-inch
B.T. PUPPY....5-10 64
GOLDEN CREST....4-8 60s

THREE PEPPERS
Singles: 78 rpm
DECCA....15-25 39-47
GOTHAM....10-20 49
VARIETY....15-25 37
VOCALION....15-25 37

THREE PLAYMATES *P&R '58*
Singles: 7-inch
SAVOY....8-12 58
Also see PLAYMATES

THREE PROPHETS
Singles: 7-inch
TOGETHER....8-10 71
LPs: 10/12-inch
3-P....8-12 74
Members: Billy Scott; Barbara Scott; Janet Helm; Frankie Haywood.
Also see GEORGIA PROPHETS
Also see PROPHETS

THREE RAYS
Singles: 78 rpm
CORAL (61370 "The Wallflower")..10-15 55
Singles: 7-inch
CORAL (61370 "The Wallflower")..15-25 55

THREE REASONS
(With the Highlanders)
Singles: 7-inch
CARNIVAL....8-12 60s
JRE (224 "No Regrets")....25-50 62

THREE RIFFS
Singles: 78 rpm
APOLLO....15-25 50
ATLANTIC....15-25 48-49
DECCA....20-30 39
Members: Joe Seneca; Eddie Parton.
Also see THREE BARONS

THREE RING CIRCUS
Singles: 7-inch
RCA....4-6 68
Picture Sleeves
RCA....4-8 68
LPs: 10/12-inch
RCA....10-15 68

THREE ROYAL CHECKMATES
Singles: 7-inch
FARO....4-8 67

THREE SHADES OF SOUL
Singles: 7-inch
ENJOY....8-12 60s

THREE SHARPS & FLAT
(Three Sharps & the Flats)
Singles: 78 rpm
DECCA....15-25 39
HAMP-TONE....15-25 39
OKEH....15-25 40-41
TOWER....15-25 47

THREE SOULS
Singles: 7-inch
ARGO (5369 "The Horse")....10-20 60
ARGO (5472 "Hi Heel Sneakers") 10-15 64

THREE SOUNDS
Singles: 7-inch
BLUE NOTE....5-10 58-64
LPs: 10/12-inch
BLUE NOTE....15-25 59-64
LIMELIGHT....10-20 65
Members: Gene Harris; Bill Dowdy; Andrew Simpkins.
Also see HARRIS, Gene

3 SOULS
Singles: 7-inch
ARGO....4-8 64-65
NOTE....5-10 59
LPs: 10/12-inch
ARGO....15-25 64-65
Member: Sonny Cox.

3 SPEED
Singles: 7-inch
MCA....3-5 84

THREE STOOGES
LPs: 10/12-inch
RHINO (808 "Madcap Musical Nonsense")....8-12 82
(Picture disc.)

THREE STRANGERS
Singles: 7-inch
ABC-PAR....4-8 66

THREE SUNS *P&R '44*
(With Larry Green)
Singles: 78 rpm
HIT....3-6 44
MAJESTIC....3-6 46
RCA....3-5 47-57
Singles: 7-inch
RCA....4-8 50-64
EPs: 7-inch
RCA....5-10 50-61
ROYALE....5-10 50s
VARSITY....5-10 52
LPs: 10/12-inch
CAMDEN....5-15 60-64
EVON....10-15 50s
GALAXY....5-10
MUSICOR....5-10 66
RCA....5-20 50-76
RONDO....5-15 59
ROYALE....10-15 50s
VARSITY....10-20 50-52
Members: Al Nevins; Marty Nevins; Art Dunn.

THREE SUNS, Rosalie Allen & Elton Britt *C&W '50*
Singles: 78 rpm
RCA....5-10 50
Also see ALLEN, Rosalie
Also see BRITT, Elton
Also see THREE SUNS

THREE TIMES DOPE *LP '89*
LPs: 10/12-inch
ARISTA....5-8 89

THREE TWINS
Singles: 7-inch
BANANA (512 "All My Dreams")....10-15 58

THREE VALES
Singles: 78 rpm
CINDY (3007 "Blue Lights")....75-100 57
Singles: 7-inch
CINDY (3007 "Blue Lights")....75-100 57

THREE WISHES
Singles: 7-inch
DOLTON....4-8 63

3's a CROWD
Singles: 7-inch
DUNHILL....4-8 67
EPIC....4-8 66-67
LPs: 10/12-inch
DUNHILL (50030 "Christopher's Movie Matinee")....10-15 68
Member: Richard Patterson.

THREETEENS
Singles: 7-inch
REV (3516 "Dear 53310761")....10-20 58
REV (3522 "X + Y = Z")....10-20 59
TODD (1021 "X + Y = Z")....5-10 59

THRESHOLD OF SOUNDS
Singles: 7-inch
NETTIE (101 "She's Mine")....15-25 60s

THRETT, Maggie
Singles: 7-inch
DYNO VOICE....4-8 65

THRILLERS
Singles: 78 rpm
BIG TOWN (109 "The Drunkard")....50-100 53
HERALD (432 "Lizabeth")....50-100 54
THRILLER (3530 "I'm Going to Live My Life Alone")....200-300 53
Singles: 7-inch
BIG TOWN (109 "The Drunkard")....250-500 53

HERALD (432 "Lizabeth") 250-500 54
THRILLER (3530 "I'm Going to Live My Life Alone") 500-1000 53
Members: Bill Davis; Carl Stewart; Joe Murphy; John Dorsey.
Also see FIVE JETS
Also see FIVE STARS
Also see WILSON, Jimmy / Thrillers / Little Caesar

THRILLERS
Singles: 7-inch
UPTOWN 5-8 65

THRILLS (on JAB): see ZIMMERAN, George, & Thrills

THRILLS
Singles: 7-inch
CAPITOL 10-20 66-67

THRILLS LP '81
Singles: 7-inch
G&P 3-5 80-81
LPs: 10/12-inch
G&P 5-10 80-81

THROBBING GRISTLE
LPs: 10/12-inch
FETISH 8-12
ROUGH TRADE 5-10 82

THROBBING MASSES
(Featuring Dave Porter)
Singles: 7-inch
SPLEEN 3-5 81

THROCKMORTON, Sonny C&W '76
Singles: 7-inch
MCA 3-4 81
MERCURY 3-5 78-80
STARCREST 3-5 76

THRONE, David: see THORNE, David

THUDPUCKER, Clarence
Singles: 7-inch
BELL 3-5 72

THUDPUCKER, Jimmy
Singles: 7-inch
W.B. 3-5 77
WINDSONG 3-5 78
LPs: 10/12-inch
WINDSONG (2589 "Greatest Hits") 8-10 77
WINDSONG (2750 "Hollywood Bowl Concert") 10-15 78
(Promotional issue only.)

THUMB, Tom
Singles: 7-inch
DECCA 5-10 59

THUMB, Tom, & Casuals
Singles: 7-inch
BOLO 4-8 65
PANORAMA (21 "I Should Know") 15-25 66
VERVE (10478 "I Should Know") 8-12 67

THUMBS
LPs: 10/12-inch
RAMONA 5-10 80

THUMPER
Singles: 7-inch
A&M 3-6 68-69

THUNDER
Singles: 7-inch
CAPITOL 3-5 74
LPs: 10/12-inch
CAPITOL 8-10 74

THUNDER
LPs: 10/12-inch
ATCO 5-10 80-81

THUNDER, Johnny P&R '62
Singles: 7-inch
ABC 3-5 74
CALLA 4-8 69
DIAMOND 5-15 62-68
EPIC (9329 "Ever You Man") 10-20 59
U.A. 4-6 70
Picture Sleeves
DIAMOND (132 "The Rosy Dance") 10-20 63
LPs: 10/12-inch
DIAMOND (D-5001 "Loop De Loop") 35-50 63
(Monaural.)
DIAMOND (SD-5001 "Loop De Loop") 50-75 63
(Stereo.)
REAL RECORDS 10-15
Also see ARCHIES / Johnny Thunder
Also see HAMILTON, Gil

THUNDER, Johnny, & Ruby Winters P&R/R&B '67
Singles: 7-inch
DIAMOND (218 "Make Love to Me") 5-10 67
DIAMOND (238 "Teach Me Tonight") 5-10 68
Also see THUNDER, Johnny
Also see WINTERS, Ruby

THUNDER, Margo R&B '74
Singles: 7-inch
HAVEN 3-5 74

THUNDER & LIGHTNIN'
Singles: 7-inch
TOMMY 3-5 73

THUNDER & ROSES
Singles: 7-inch
U.A. (50536 "Country Life") 5-10 69
LPs: 10/12-inch
U.A. (6709 "King of the Black Sunrise") 15-25 69
Members: Chris Bond; Tom Schaffer.

THUNDER BOLTS
Singles: 7-inch
RONDACK (7546 "Thunder Head") 15-25 61

THUNDER HEADS
Singles: 7-inch
CARTWHEEL (100 "Thunder Head") 20-25 66

THUNDER MOUNTAIN
LPs: 10/12-inch
THUNDER MOUNTAIN 5-10 80

THUNDER MOUNTAIN BOYS
Singles: 7-inch
CAPEHART (5002 "Olita") 10-15 60

THUNDER ROCKS
Singles: 7-inch
ROSELAWN (501 "What's the Word") 10-15 60s
SABRE (100 "Warpath") 10-15 60

THUNDERBIRD SINGERS
LPs: 10/12-inch
THUNDERBIRD PROD. 10-15

THUNDERBIRDS
(With Art Harris & His Orchestra)
Singles: 78 rpm
DELUXE 30-50 55
G.G. 25-40 55
Singles: 7-inch
DELUXE (6075 "Pledging My Love") 75-125 55
G.G. (518 "Love Is a Problem") ...50-100 55

THUNDERBIRDS
Singles: 78 rpm
ERA 5-10 55
Singles: 7-inch
ERA (1000 "Blueberries") 10-15 55
ERA (1004 "Beguine") 10-15 55

THUNDERBIRDS
Singles: 78 rpm
HOLIDAY 50-100 57
Singles: 7-inch
HOLIDAY (2609 "In My Thunderbird") 100-150 57
(Glossy red label.)
HOLIDAY (2609 "In My Thunderbird") 25-50 50s
(Flat red label.)

THUNDERBIRDS
Singles: 7-inch
BUFFALO ("Flying Saucers") 200-400 59
(No selection number used. Only promo copies made.)

THUNDERBIRDS
Singles: 7-inch
DELTA 5-10 62
MELBOURNE 5-10 63
UNITED SOUTHERN ARTISTS (115 "T-Bird Rock") 10-15 62
LPs: 10/12-inch
RED FEATHER (1 "Meet the Fabulous Thunderbirds") 150-200 64

THUNDERBIRDS
Singles: 7-inch
CORTLAND (51 "Steel") 10-20 64
DELAWARE (1706 "Take a Look at Me") 10-20 66
DELAWARE (1710 "Is It Wrong") ...10-20 66
IVANHOE (50000 "Cindy, Oh Cindy") 10-20
ERMINE (51 "Stalking the Thunderbird") 20-30 63
ERMINE (54 "Simmering") 20-30 63
ERMINE (56 "Crater Soda") 20-30 64

THUNDERBOLTS
Singles: 7-inch
DOT (16496 "Lost Planets") 5-10 63
STAR SATELLITE (1020 "Battle Hymn Twist") 5-10 63

THUNDERCLAP NEWMAN: see NEWMAN, Thunderclap

THUNDERFLASH R&B '83
Singles: 7-inch
JAMPOWER 3-5 83

THUNDERGRIN
Singles: 7-inch
EPIC 4-8 67

THUNDERHEAD
LPs: 10/12-inch
ABC 8-10 75

THUNDERKLOUD, Billy, & Chieftones C&W/P&R '75
Singles: 7-inch
CLAREMONT 5-10
POLYDOR 3-5 76-78
SCEPTER 8-12 68
STABLE 3-5 75
SUPERIOR 3-5 74
20TH FOX 3-5 74-75
YOUNGSTOWN 8-12 68
LPs: 10/12-inch
SUPERIOR 8-12 74
20TH FOX 6-12 74-75
Members: Jack Wolf; Barry Littlestar; Richard Grayowl.
Also see CHIEFTONES

THUNDERMAMA
Singles: 7-inch
MARINA 3-5 72

THUNDERMEN
Singles: 7-inch
(Al & Gerry Jay & Thundermen)
Singles: 7-inch
CUCA (6372 "Night Train") 10-15 63
SOMA (1194 "Flyin' High") 5-10 62
THUNDERMEN 3-5 82-89
LPs:10/12-inch
THUNDERMEN 5-10 82-86
Members: Rick Hoehn; Al Fremstad; Rick Gerry Johnson; Mickey Lynnes; Mike Marx; Chuck Solberg.

THUNDERMEN
Singles: 7-inch
KISKI (2066 "Thunderbeat") 10-15 63

THUNDERMUG
(Thundermugs)
Singles: 7-inch
ALL AMERICAN 4-8 67
AVCO EMBASSY 3-6 71
BIG TREE 3-5 72
EPIC 3-5 73-74
MERCURY 3-5 75
LPs: 10/12-inch
EPIC 10-12 73
MERCURY 8-10 75

THUNDERPUSSY
LPs: 10/12-inch
MRT (31748 "Documents of Captivity") 100-150 73
Members: Steven Jay Morris; Ben Russell; George Tutko.

THUNDERTONES
Singles: 7-inch
DOT (16137 "Jungle Fever") 15-25 60
Member: Lenny Drake.
Also see BROWN, Doug
Also see LENNY & THUNDERTONES

THUNDERTONES
Singles: 7-inch
DONNA (1343 "Thunder Rhythm") 15-25 61

THUNDERTONES
LPs: 10/12-inch
AURORA 10-15

THUNDERTRAIN
LPs: 10/12-inch
JELLY 10-12 77

THUNDERTREE
Singles: 7-inch
ROULETTE 5-10 70
LPs: 10/12-inch
ROULETTE (42038 "Thundertree") 20-30 70
Member: Devin Wallin.

THURMOND, Duff
Singles: 7-inch
NEW VOICE 10-20 66

THURSDAY'S CHILDREN
Singles: 7-inch
INTERNATIONAL ARTISTS (110 "Air Conditioned Man") 40-60 66
INTERNATIONAL ARTISTS (115 "Help, Murder, Police") 40-60 66
KIDD (1334 "You'll Never Be My Girl") 30-50 66
PARADISE (1022 "You'll Never Be My Girl") 20-30 66

THURSDAY'S CHILDREN
Singles: 7-inch
N-JOY 5-10 66

THURSTON, Bobby R&B '80
Singles: 7-inch
PRELUDE 3-5 80

THYME
Singles: 7-inch
A^2 (201 "Somehow") 25-40 60s
A^2 (202 "Time of the Season") 25-40 60s
BANG (546 "Love to Love") 10-20 67

TIA P&R '87
Singles: 7-inch
RCA 3-4 87
Picture Sleeves
RCA 3-4 87

TIARAS
Singles: 7-inch
VALIANT 8-10 63
Member: Don Cole.
Also see COLE, Don

TIARAS
Singles: 7-inch
ALLIANCE (1934 "Mexican Rock") ..5-10 64
Also see DALLAS, Jackie

TIARAS
Singles: 7-inch
DORE (783 "Wild Times") 10-20 67
RUFF (1019 "Southern Love") 10-20 66

TIATT, Lynn, & Comets
Singles: 7-inch
PUSSY CAT (1 "Dad Is Home") 1000-2000

TIBBS, Andrew R&B '49
(With the Dozier Boys)
Singles: 78 rpm
ARISTOCRAT 15-25 47-49
PEACOCK 10-20 52
Singles: 7-inch
M-PAC 4-8 66
PEACOCK (1597 "Mother's Letter") 25-35 52
Also see DOZIER BOYS
Also see TIBBS BROTHERS

TIBBS, Kenneth
(With the Jokers; Kenneth Tibbs)
Singles: 7-inch
FEDERAL (12335 "No More Tears") 40-60 58
Also see TIBBS BROTHERS

TIBBS BROTHERS
Singles: 78 rpm
ATCO (6074 "I'm Going Crazy") 10-20 56
Singles: 7-inch
ATCO (6074 "I'm Going Crazy") 25-50 56
Members: Andrew Tibbs; Kenneth Tibbs.
Also see TIBBS, Andrew
Also see TIBBS, Kenny

TIBOR BROTHERS C&W '76
Singles: 7-inch
ARIOLA AMERICA 3-5 76
JOMAR 3-5 74
LPs: 10/12-inch
JOMAR 5-10 74
Members: Larry Tibor; Kurt Tibor; Harvey Tibor; Francis Tibor; Gerard Tibor.

TIC TOCS
("Featuring Johnny Williams")
Singles: 78 rpm
BACK BEAT 10-20 57
Singles: 7-inch
BACK BEAT (502 "Walking Alone") 15-25 57
RUSH (1042 "True By You") 20-30 62

TICKER TAPES
Singles: 7-inch
GO GO (103 "Her Own Imagination") 10-20 67

TICKLERS
Singles: 7-inch
MUSTANG 5-10 65

TICO & TRIUMPHS P&R '62
(Featuring Paul Simon)
Singles: 7-inch
AMY (835 "Motorcycle") 15-25 62
AMY (845 "Wild Flower") 15-25 62
AMY (860 "Cry Little Boy") 15-25 62
AMY (876 "Cards of Love") 30-40 62
MADISON (169 "Motorcycle") 20-30 61
Also see SIMON, Paul

TICTOC D&D '84
Singles: 12-inch
RCA 4-6 84
Singles: 7-inch
RCA 3-4 84
LPs: 10/12-inch
RCA 5-8 84

TIDAL WAVE
Singles: 7-inch
BUDDAH 4-8 68

TIDAL WAVES
Singles: 7-inch
TIDE (0020 "The Clock") 8-12 61

TIDAL WAVES
Singles: 7-inch
HBR (482 "Farmer John") 8-12 66
HBR (501 "Big Boy Pete") 8-12 66
HBR (515 "Action") 8-12 67
PLYMOUTH (2968 "Little Boy Sad") 15-20 67
RIGHT (6607 "Farmer John") 15-25 66
SVR (1007 "Farmer John") 15-25 66
(We're not sure which of the above two came first, but both probably preceded the HBR.)
STRAFFORD (6503 "You Name It") 15-25 65

TIDBITS
LPs: 10/12-inch
FAMILY PRODUCTIONS 10-12 73

TIDE
Singles: 7-inch
MOUTH (513 "Cowboy Song") 5-10 71
MOUTH (875 "I'm in a Dancing Mood") 5-10 72
LPs: 10/12-inch
MOUTH (7237 "Almost Live") 30-45 71

TIDE, Ripp
Singles: 7-inch
JOSIE 4-8 67

TIDES
(With the Merry Melody Singers; with Jerry Kennedy Orchestra)
Singles: 7-inch
DORE 8-12 59-61
MERCURY 5-10 62
LPs: 10/12-inch
MERCURY 15-20 62-63
WING 15-20 63
Also see KENNEDY, Jerry

TIDES
Singles: 7-inch
WARWICK (653 "Stranger") 10-15 61

TIDES
Singles: 7-inch
620 (1007 "Bring It on Home") 25-35 64
Member: Willie Sullivan.
Also see UNIQUES

TIDE'S IN
Singles: 7-inch
SANFRIS (18 "Trip with Me") 20-30 67

TIDWELL, Billy
Singles: 7-inch
KO CO BO (1009 "Folsom Prison Blues") 25-35

TIDWELL, Bobby
Singles: 7-inch
SKIPPY (108 "Cherokee Stomp") 20-30 59

TIDWELL, Harold
Singles: 7-inch
CJ (605 "Sweet Suzie") 15-25 59

TIEKEN, Freddie, & Rockers
Singles: 7-inch
IT (2302 "Humpty Jump") 10-20 57
LPs: 10/12-inch
IT (2301 "By Popular Demand") 30-50 57
IT (2304 "Live") 30-50 58
Also see GIPSON, Wild Child
Also see GONN
Also see ILMO SMOKEHOUSE

TIENO, Al
Singles: 7-inch
RUST 4-8 61

TIERNY, Patti C&W '73
Singles: 7-inch
MGM 3-5 73

TIERRA P&R/R&B/LP '80
Singles: 7-inch
ASI 3-5 80
BOARDWALK 3-5 80-82
SALSOUL 3-5 81
MCA 3-5 79
TODY 3-5
LPs: 10/12-inch
ASI 5-10 80
BOARDWALK 5-10 80
SALSOUL 5-10 81
Members: Salas Brothers.
Also see EL CHICANO
Also see SALAS BROTHERS

TIFANOS
Singles: 7-inch
TIFCO (822 "It's Raining") 30-50 60
(Label name takes up about half the top portion of the label—between hole and edge of disc.)
TIFCO (822 "It's Raining") 20-40 60
(Label name takes up about 2/3 the top portion of the label—between hole and edge of disc.)

TIFFANIES: see TIFFANYS

TIFFANY P&R/LP '87
(Tiffany Darwisch)
Singles: 7-inch
MCA 3-4 87-89
Picture Sleeves
MCA 3-4 87-89
LPs: 10/12-inch
MCA 5-8 87-88

TIFFANY SHADE
Singles: 7-inch
MAINSTREAM 8-12 68
LPs: 10/12-inch
MAINSTREAM (6105 "The Tiffany Shade") 20-30 68
Members: Michael Barnes; Bob Leonard.

TIFFANY SYSTEM
Singles: 7-inch
MINARET (128 "Let's Get Together") 10-15 60s
Members: Scott Boyer; Dave Brown.
Also see 31ST of FEBRUARY

TIFFANYS
(Tiffany's)
Singles: 7-inch
ROCKIN-ROBIN (1 "I've Got a Girl") 400-600 63

TIFFANYS
Singles: 7-inch
SWAN (4104 "The Peasure of Love") 15-25 62
Also see TEDDY & TWILIGHTS

TIFFANYS
Singles: 7-inch
ATLANTIC (2240 "Please Tell Me") 10-20 64
MRS (777 "Please Tell Me") 50-75 64

TIFFANYS
(Tiffanies)
Singles: 7-inch
ARCTIC 10-20 64
JOSIE 5-10 65-66
KR 10-20 67
RKO 4-8 60s

TIFFIN, Barry
Singles: 7-inch
TIFFIN INT'L 4-8 77

TIG, Jimmy
(With the Rounders; with Louise & Co.)
Singles: 7-inch
BELL 5-10 68
SPAR (779 "Small Town Girl") 100-200

TIGER

LPs: 10/12-inch

EMI....5-10 77
W.B....5-10 76

TIGERMEN

Singles: 7-inch

BUFF (1005 "Close That Door")....15-25 65
BUFF (1006 "Tiger Girl")....15-25 65

TIGERS

Singles: 7-inch

RAYNARD (602 "Flip Side")....10-20 64
(Also issued as by the Apollos.)
Also see APOLLOS

TIGERS

Singles: 7-inch

COLPIX (773 "GeeTO Tiger"/"Big Sounds of the GeeTO Tiger")....20-30 65
COLPIX (773 "GeeTO Tiger"/"The Prowl")....15-25 65
SUMPTHIN' ELSE (3929 "I See the Light")....15-25 65

Picture Sleeves

COLPIX (773 "GeeTO Tiger")....20-30 65
Member: Danny Peil.
Also see PEIL, Danny

TIGERS

Singles: 7-inch

ZIMBY (301 "There She Goes")....8-12 60s

TIGERS

LPs: 10/12-inch

A&M....5-10 80

TIGERS TWO

Singles: 7-inch

VEE JAY....4-8 65

TIGGI CLAY P&R '84

Singles: 7-inch

MOROCCO (1716 "Flashes")....3-5 84
(Black vinyl.)
MOROCCO (1716 "Flashes")....4-6 84
(Colored vinyl. Promotional issue only.)

LPs: 10/12-inch

MOROCCO....5-10 84
Members: Romeo McCall; Fizzy Quick; Billy Peaches.

TIGHT FIT P&R '81

Singles: 12-inch

ARISTA....4-6 81
JIVE....4-6 81

Singles: 7-inch

ARISTA....3-5 81
JIVE....3-5 81

TIGRE, Terry

Singles: 7-inch

GUSTO-STARDAY....4-8 77-78

LPs: 10/12-inch

GUSTO-STARDAY....10-15 77
Session: Scotty Moore; D.J. Fontana; Bob Moore; Jordanaires.
Also see FONTANA, D.J., Band
Also see JORDANAIRES
Also see MOORE, Bob
Also see MOORE, Scotty

TIGRO, Al

Singles: 7-inch

CUPPY (112 "Yvonne")....50-75

TIJUANA BEATLES

LPs: 10/12-inch

ALSHIRE....10-15 69

TIJUANA BRASS: see ALPERT, Herb

TIJUANA BRATS

Singles: 7-inch

RCA....5-10 68

TIKARAM, Tanita LP '89

Singles: 7-inch

REPRISE....3-4 89

Picture Sleeves

REPRISE....3-4 89

TIKIES

Singles: 7-inch

WRIGHT SOUND (0001 "Steam")....40-60 62

TIKIS

Singles: 7-inch

FUJIMO (6139 "Show You Love")....15-25 66

TIKIS

Singles: 7-inch

ASCOT....5-10 65-66
AUTUMN....5-10 65
DIAL....5-10 66
MINARET (115 "One More Chance")....5-8 63
MINARET (116 "Popsicle")....5-8 64
W.B....4-6 66
Also see HARPERS BIZARRE
Also see OTHER TIKIS
Also see WADE, Len

TIKIS

Singles: 7-inch

SARA (6641 "We're on the Move")....15-25 66
Members: Hugh Pearl; Bill Sherek.
Also see TALISMEN

TIKIS

Singles: 7-inch

TRECO....8-12

TIKIS

Singles: 7-inch

THERMIDOR (427 "Surfadelic")....8-12

TIKIS & FABULONS

Singles: 7-inch

PANORAMA (13 "Take a Look")....8-12 65
REX....8-12 60s
TOWER (181 "Take a Look")....5-10 65
Members (Tikis): Dale Colama; Ollie Smith. (Fabulons): Ron Ferrante; Terry McKinley; Mike Roholt; John Chassaign; John Goldman; Dan Shillings; John Duval; Jim Wilson; Gary Welk; Bill Higginbotham.
Also see FABULONS

TIL, Sonny

(With Buddy Lucas Orchestra; with Sid Bass Orchestra; Sonny Till)

Singles: 78 rpm

JUBILEE....50-75 52-53

Singles: 7-inch

CLOWN (3061 "I Gave It All Up")....5-10 60s
JUBILEE (5066 "For All We Know")....150-200 52
(Black vinyl.)
JUBILEE (5066 "For All We Know")....500-650 52
(Red vinyl.)
JUBILEE (5076 "Proud of You")....150-200 52
JUBILEE (5112 "Have You Heard")....150-200 52
(Black vinyl.)
JUBILEE (5112 "Have You Heard")....500-650 52
(Red vinyl.)
JUBILEE (5118 "Congratulations to Someone")....100-200 53
RCA....4-8 69-72
ROULETTE (4079 "Shy")....15-25 58

LPs: 10/12-inch

DOBRE....5-10 78
RCA....10-20 70-71
Also see McGRIFF, Edna, & Sonny Til
Also see ORIOLES

TILL, Sonny / Sonny & Virgil

Singles: 7-inch

DADE (5002 "Someone Up and Told Me")....10-20
Also see TIL, Sonny

'TIL TUESDAY P&R/LP '85

Singles: 7-inch

EPIC....3-4 85-89

Picture Sleeves

EPIC....3-4 89
Members: Aimee Mann; Michael Hausman; Robert Holmes; Joey Pesce.

TILLERY, Linda, & Loading Zone

Singles: 7-inch

RCA....4-8 68
Also see LOADING ZONE

TILLIS, Big Son, & D.C. Bender

Singles: 78 rpm

ELKO....25-50 53

TILLIS, Mel C&W '58

(With the Statesiders; with Sue York)

Singles: 78 rpm

COLUMBIA (40944 "Juke Box Man")....10-20 57
COLUMBIA (41000 series except 41026)....8-12 57
COLUMBIA (41026 "Hearts of Stone")....15-25 57

Singles: 7-inch

COLUMBIA (40944 "Juke Box Man")....10-20 57
COLUMBIA (41000 series except 41026)....8-12 57
COLUMBIA (41026 "Hearts of Stone")....15-25 57
COLUMBIA (41100 series except 41115 & 41986)....5-10 58-61
COLUMBIA (41115 "Teen Age Wedding")....15-25 58
COLUMBIA (3-41986 "Hearts of Stone")....20-30 61
(Compact 33 Single.)
COLUMBIA (4-41986 "Hearts of Stone")....10-15 61
ELEKTRA....3-5 79-82
GUSTO....3-4 80s
KAPP....4-8 65-71
MCA....3-4 73-84
MGM....3-5 70-76
RCA....3-4 85-86
RADIO....3-4 89
RIC....5-10 65

LPs: 10/12-inch

COLUMBIA (1724 "Heart Over Mind")....15-25 62
(Monaural.)
COLUMBIA (1724 "Heart Over Mind")....20-30 62
(Stereo.)
COLUMBIA (30253 "Heart Over Mind")....8-10 70
CORAL....5-10 73
ELEKTRA....5-10 79-83
GUSTO....5-8 80s
HARMONY....10-20 66-72
KAPP....8-15 66-71
MCA....5-12 73-84
MGM....5-12 70-78
PICKWICK....5-10 73
POWER PAK....5-8
STARDAY....8-10 72
TEE VEE....8-10 70s
VOCALION....5-10 70-72
Also see EARWOOD, Mundo
Also see FELTS, Narvel / Red Sovine / Mel Tillis
Also see PIERCE, Webb, & Mel Tillis
Also see WILLS, Bob, & Mel Tillis

TILLIS, Mel, & Sherry Bryce C&W '71

Singles: 7-inch

MGM....3-5 71-75

LPs: 10/12-inch

MGM....6-12 71-74
Also see BRYCE, Sherry

TILLIS, Mel, & Glen Campbell C&W '84

Singles: 7-inch

MCA....3-4 84
Also see CAMPBELL, Glen

TILLIS, Mel, & Bill Phillips C&W '59

Singles: 7-inch

COLUMBIA....5-10 59-60
Also see PHILLIPS, Bill

TILLIS, Mel, & Nancy Sinatra C&W '81

Singles: 7-inch

ELEKTRA....3-5 81

LPs: 10/12-inch

ELEKTRA....5-10 81
Also see SINATRA, Nancy
Also see TILLIS, Mel

TILLIS, Pam C&W '84

Singles: 7-inch

ARISTA....3-4 90-91
W.B....3-4 84-87
Also see TOMORROW'S WORLD

TILLISON, Roger

Singles: 7-inch

WORLD PACIFIC....4-8 66
Also see LEATHERCOATED MINDS

TILLMAN, Bertha P&R '62

Singles: 7-inch

BRENT (7029 "Oh My Angel")....15-20 62
BRENT (7032 "I Wish")....20-30 62
JOCKO (599 "What Am I Trying to Prove")....10-15 60s

TILLMAN, Floyd C&W '44

(With His Favorite Playboys)

Singles: 78 rpm

COLUMBIA....4-8 46-49
DECCA....4-8 44-45

Singles: 7-inch

CIMARRON....4-8 62
COLUMBIA....5-15 51-61
LIBERTY....5-10 60-61
SIMS....4-8 63

LPs: 10/12-inch

BAGATELLE....8-12 71
CIMARRON (2003 "Let's Make Memories")....20-30 62
COLUMBIA....5-10 76
CRAZY CAJUN....5-10 75
51 WEST....5-9 79
GILLEY'S....10-15 81
HARMONY....10-15 69
MUSICOR....10-20 67-68
PICKWICK/HILLTOP....8-10 65
RCA (1686 "Floyd Tillman's Greatest Hits")....30-40 58
STARDAY (310 "Let's Make Memories")....15-20 65

TILLMAN, Lee

Singles: 7-inch

MONTEL....5-10 66
RON (341 "Will Travel")....10-15 61
SONORA (211 "Here I Go Again")....50-100

TILLMAN, Mickey

Singles: 7-inch

VEE JAY....10-15 58

TILLOTSON, Johnny P&R '58

Singles: 7-inch

AMOS....3-5 69-70
BARNABY....3-5 76
BUDDAH....3-5 71-73
CADENCE (1300 series)....5-10 58-61
CADENCE (1400 series)....4-8 61-63
COLUMBIA....3-5 73-75
ERIC....3-4 70s
MGM....4-8 63-68
REWARD....3-4 82-84
U.A....3-5 76-77

Picture Sleeves

CADENCE....10-15 60
MGM....5-8 63-66

EPs: 7-inch

CADENCE (114 "Dreamy Eyes")....25-35 60
CADENCE (33-1 "This Is Johnny Tillotson")....15-25 61
("Cadence Little LP." With cardboard insert in clear cover.)
CADENCE (33-2 "Music by Johnny Tillotson")....15-25 61
("Cadence Little LP." With cardboard insert in clear cover.)

LPs: 10/12-inch

ACCORD....5-10 82
AMOS....10-15 69
BACK-TRAC....5-8 85
BARNABY....8-10 77
BUCKBOARD....5-10 80s
BUDDAH....10-15 72
CADENCE....25-40 61-63
EVEREST....5-8 82
METRO....10-15 66
MGM....12-20 64-71
ROWE/AMI....5-8 66
("Play Me" Sales Stimulator promotional issue.)
U.A....8-10 77
Session: Boots Randolph.
Also see GENEVIEVE
Also see IVAN / Johnny Tillotson
Also see RANDOLPH, Boots

TILLOTSON, Johnny / J.D. Souther

Singles: 7-inch

BUDDAH....3-5 71
Also see SOUTHER, J.D.
Also see TILLOTSON, Johnny

TILT

LPs: 10/12-inch

PARACHUTE....5-8 78

TILTON, Sheila C&W '76

Singles: 7-inch

CON BRIO....3-5 76
Also see TILTON SISTERS

TILTON, Muriel

Singles: 7-inch

BERTRAM INT'L (224 "Bird Dog")....15-20 63
Also see TILTON SISTERS

TILTON SISTERS

Singles: 7-inch

BERTRAM INT'L (214 "Why Won't He Call Me")....15-20 60
BERTRAM INT'L (217 "He Knows")....15-20 61
BERTRAM INT'L (220 "Yellow Bird")....15-20 61
DOT (15939 "Why Why Why")....25-35 59
Members: Sheila Tilton; Gwen Tilton; Muriel Tilton.
Also see TILTON, Sheila
Also see TILTON, Muriel

TIM

(Tim Smith)

Singles: 7-inch

CELTEX (102 "I Need Your Love")....10-20

TIM DAWE

LPs: 10/12-inch

STRAIGHT....10-15 69

TIM TAM & TURN-ONS P&R '66

Singles: 7-inch

PALMER (5002 "Wait a Minute")....8-12 66
PALMER (5003 "Cheryl Ann")....20-30 66
PALMER (5006 "Kimberly")....20-30 66
PALMER (5014 "Don't Say Hi")....5-10 67
Also see DIFFERENT STROKES

TIMBER

LPs: 10/12-inch

ELEKTRA....8-10 71

TIMBERLAND FOUR

Singles: 7-inch

JAMIE (1236 "Hummingbird")....10-15 62
Members: Robert Gunerare; Fred Gunerare; Steve Young; Charles Peterson; Ronald Stoddard.

TIMBERLINE

LPs: 10/12-inch

EPIC (34681 "Timberline")....8-12 77
(Black vinyl.)
EPIC (34681 "Timberline")....15-15 77
(Colored vinyl.)

TIMBUK 3 P&R/LP '86

Singles: 7-inch

I.R.S....3-4 86-88

LPs: 10/12-inch

I.R.S....5-8 86-88

TIME R&B/LP '81

Singles: 12-inch

W.B....4-6 82-84

Singles: 7-inch

W.B....3-5 81-84

LPs: 10/12-inch

PAISLEY PARK....5-8 90
W.B....5-8 81-84
Members: Morris Day; Jesse Johnson; Jimmy Jam; Monte Moir; Jellybean Johnson; Stacy Adams; Terry Lewis; Paul Peterson.
Also see DAY, Morris
Also see JOHNSON, Jesse
Also see ST. PAUL
Also see VANITY 6

TIME BANDITS D&D '85

Singles: 12-inch

COLUMBIA....4-6 85

TIME BOX

Singles: 7-inch

DERAM....3-5 68

LPs: 10/12-inch

PETERS INT'L....8-10 76

TIME OF YOUR LIFE

Singles: 7-inch

IONIC (101 "Ode to a Bad Dream")....20-30 67

TIME PIECE

Singles: 7-inch

GREAT NORTHERN (1001 "Can't Be So Bad")....15-25 60s

TIME ZONE

Singles: 7-inch

WHITE WHALE....4-8 68

TIME ZONE D&D '84

Singles: 12-inch

CELLULOID....4-6 84

TIMEBOX

Singles: 7-inch

DERAM....4-8 68

TIMELORDS P&R '88

Singles: 7-inch

TVT....3-4 88

Singles: 7-inch

TVT....3-4 88

TIMERS

Singles: 7-inch

REPRISE (231 "No Go Showboat")....25-45 63
Members: Gary Usher; Brian Wilson; Chuck Girard.
Also see GIRARD, Chuck
Also see USHER, Gary
Also see WILSON, Brian

TIMES TWO P&R/LP '88

Singles: 7-inch

REPRISE....3-4 88

Picture Sleeves

REPRISE....3-4 88

LPs: 10/12-inch

REPRISE....5-8 88

TIMESTOPPERS

Singles: 7-inch

HBR (516 "I Need Love")....10-20 66

TIMETAKERS

Singles: 7-inch

AUDIO DYNAMICS (190 "At Least I'll Try")....10-20 67

TIMETONES P&R '61

Singles: 7-inch

ATCO (6201 "I've Got a Feeling")....15-25 61
GREENE STONE....4-8
LOST-NITE (406 "I've Got a Feeling")....4-8
RELIC (526 "House Where Lovers Live")....5-10 65
TIMES SQUARE (26 "Sunday Kind of Love")....15-20 64
TIMES SQUARE (34 "House Where Lovers Dream")....30-40 64
TIMES SQUARE (421 "Here in My Heart")....20-30 61
TIMES SQUARE (421 "In My Heart")....10-20 61
(Note shortened title.)
Member: Slim Rose.
Also see SLIM from TIMES

TIMEX SOCIAL CLUB P&R/R&B '86

Singles: 12-inch

DANYA....4-6 86
JAY....4-6 86

Singles: 7-inch

DANYA....3-4 86-87
JAY....3-4 86

TIMKIN, Garry

Singles: 7-inch

ABC-PAR....4-8 61

TIMMY & PERSIANETTES

Singles: 7-inch

OLYMPIA....10-15 63
Member: Timmy Carr.
Also see CARR, Timmy, & Persianettes
Also see PERSIANETTES

TIMMY T. LP '91

LPs: 10/12-inch

QUALITY....5-8 90

TIMMY THE TINY TIGER

Singles: 7-inch

YELLOW DOOR (1002 "Tiger Meat")....3-5 81

Picture Sleeves

YELLOW DOOR (1002 "Tiger Meat")....3-5 81

TIMON

Singles: 7-inch

THRESHOLD....3-5 70

TIMOTHY

Singles: 7-inch

TEE PEE (200 "What Good Will Crying Do Me Now")....10-15 69

TIN HOUSE

Singles: 7-inch

EPIC....3-5 71

LPs: 10/12-inch

EPIC....8-10 71
Also see DERRINGER, Rick

TIN HUEY

Singles: 7-inch

W.B....3-5 79

LPs: 10/12-inch

W.B....5-10 79

TIN MACHINE LP '89

LPs: 10/12-inch

EMI....5-8 89

TIN MEN

Singles: 7-inch

SAXONY (1010 "Rolling Stone")....5-10 65

TIN TIN P&R/LP '71

Singles: 12-inch

SIRE....4-6 81-83

Singles: 7-inch

ATCO....3-5 71

LPs: 10/12-inch

ATCO....10-15 70-71
Members: Steve Kipner; Steve Groves.
Also see KIPNER, Steve

TINA

Singles: 7-inch

HARLAN....4-8 63

TINA & DADDY: see JONES, George

TINA & MUSTANGS

Singles: 7-inch

CAPITOL....4-8 66
Also see MUSTANGS

TINA B. D&D '84
Singles: 12-inch
ATLANTIC....4-6 82-84
ELEKTRA....4-6 83-84
Singles: 7-inch
ATLANTIC....3-4 82
ELEKTRA....3-4 83
LPs: 10/12-inch
ATLANTIC....5-8 82
ELEKTRA....5-8 83

TINA LOUISE
Singles: 7-inch
U.A. (127 "I'll Be Yours")....10-15 58
Also see LIGHT, Enoch, & His Orchestra

TINDLEY, George R&B '69
(With the Modern Red Caps; George Tinley)
Singles: 7-inch
DOO-WOP....4-8
EMBER....10-20 60
HERALD....10-20 61
ROWAX....8-12 63
PARKWAY....5-10 62
SMASH....5-10 62
WAND....4-6 69-70
Also see DREAMS
Also see MODERN RED CAPS

TINGLES
Singles: 7-inch
ERA....5-10 61

TINGLING MOTHERS' CIRCUS
Singles: 7-inch
MUSICOR....8-12 68
ROULETTE (4758 "Face in My Mind")....10-15 67
LPs: 10/12-inch
MUSICOR (3167 "Circus of the Mind")....15-25 68

TINGSTAD, Eric, & Nancy Rumbel
LPs: 10/12-inch
SONA GAIA....5-8 88

TINKER, Bill
LPs: 10/12-inch
TOWER....10-15 69

TINKERBELLS
Singles: 7-inch
HAMILTON (50007 "Hazel Eyes")..10-15 58
HANOVER....5-10 60

TINKERS
Singles: 7-inch
STOP....4-8 65

TINLEY, George: see TINDLEY, George

TINO
(Tino & Revlons)
Singles: 7-inch
DEARBORN (525 "Rave On")....15-25 65
DEARBORN (530 "I'm Coming Home")....15-25 65
DEARBORN (540 "Lotta Lovin' ")...15-25 66
MARK (154 "Story of Our Love")..75-125 60
MAY (103 "Rave On")....50-75 61
PIP (4000 "Wedding Bells Will Ring")....25-50 63
LPs: 10/12-inch
DEARBORN (1004 "By Request at the Sway-Zee")....100-200 66

TINO, Babs
Singles: 7-inch
KAPP....4-8 62

TINO, Freddie, & Twisting Cyclones
Singles: 7-inch
RIC (988 "Shoestring Twist")....10-15 62

TINO, Johnny
Singles: 7-inch
CROSBY (16 "I Want Some Lovin' ")....50-75

TINORY, Rick
Singles: 7-inch
AMY....4-8 62
SEQUEL....5-10 61

TINSON, Paul
Singles: 7-inch
FEDERAL (12418 "Crazy Sadie")..50-75 61

TINT OF DARKNESS
Singles: 7-inch
ROTA....3-5 81
STARFIRE....3-5 79-80
XCLUSIVE....4-8 78
Picture Sleeves
STARFIRE....3-5 79-80
Members: L.C. Coney; Fred Pittman; Ray Morris; Barry Williams; Rick Alexander.

TINTYPES
Singles: 7-inch
CANADIAN AMERICAN....4-8 64

TINY
Singles: 7-inch
KING....4-8 63

TINY ALICE
Singles: 7-inch
KAMA SUTRA....3-5 72
LPs: 10/12-inch
KAMA SUTRA....8-10 72

TINY JOE
Singles: 7-inch
DANBAR....4-8 63

TINY & TIM
Singles: 7-inch
OKEH (7105 "Bo-a-Diddy Do")....10-20 58

TINY TIM
Singles: 7-inch
DELUXE (6184 "Face to Face")....10-20 59
TEEN'S CHOICE (8 "My One Desire")....10-20 60

TINY TIM P&R/LP '68
(Herbert Khaury)
Singles: 7-inch
BLUE CAT (127 "Little Girl")....8-12 65
CLOUDS....3-5 79
NLT....3-4 88
REPRISE....4-8 68-71
SCEPTER....3-6 72
VIC TIM....3-6 71
LPs: 10/12-inch
BOUQUET....10-12
REPRISE....10-20 68

TINY TIM & MISS VICKI
Singles: 7-inch
REPRISE....3-6 71

TINY TIM / Michelle Ramos / Bruce Haack
LPs: 10/12-inch
RA-JO INT'L....5-8 86
Also see TINY TIM

TINY TIM & HITS
Singles: 7-inch
ROULETTE (4123 "Wedding Bells")....35-50 58

TINY TIP & TIP-TOPS
("Tiny Tip [14 yrs. Old]")
Singles: 7-inch
CHESS (1822 "Matrimony")....15-25 62
SCARLET (4129 "I Said a Prayer")....200-300 60

TINY TONY & STATICS
Singles: 7-inch
BOLO (734 "I Wanna Hold Your Hand")....10-20 62
Members: "Tiny" Tony Smith; Merrilee Rush.
Also see GALLAHADS
Also see RUSH, Merrilee
Also see STATICS

TINY TOPSY
Singles: 7-inch
ARGO (5383 "How You Changed")....10-15 61
FEDERAL (12302 "Miss You So")....50-75 57
FEDERAL (12309 "Come On, Come On")....50-75 57
FEDERAL (12357 "Just a Little Bit")....20-30 59
Session: Charms.
Also see CHARMS

TINY TRUST
Singles: 7-inch
ATCO....3-5 70

TIP, Tiny: see TINY TIP

TIP TOES
Singles: 7-inch
KAPP....4-8 65

TIP TOP BAND
Singles: 7-inch
TIP TOP (725 "The Doctor and the Monks")....15-20 59

TIP TOPS
Singles: 7-inch
PARKWAY (868 "He's Braggin' ")....5-8 63
Also see BLACKMAN, Hank / Tip Tops

TIP TOPS
Singles: 7-inch
ROULETTE (4684 "A Little Bit More")....10-15 66

TIPPIE & CLOVERMEN
Singles: 7-inch
STENTON (7001 "Please Mr. Sun")....35-50 62
Member: Roosevelt "Tippie" Hubbard.

TIPPIE & CLOVERS
Singles: 7-inch
TIGER (201 "Bossa Nova Baby")....35-50 62
Member: Roosevelt "Tippie" Hubbard.
Also see TIPPIE & CLOVERMEN

TIPPIN, Aaron C&W '90
Singles: 7-inch
RCA....3-4 90-91

TIPTON, John
Singles: 7-inch
DATE....4-6 69

TIPTOP, Seymour: see MALLARD, Earl, & His Web Feet of Rhythm

TIR NA NOG
Singles: 7-inch
CHRYSALIS....3-5 72-73
LPs: 10/12-inch
CHRYSALIS....10-15 72-73

TIRCUIT, Billy
Singles: 7-inch
BONATEMP....10-20
PONTCHARTRAIN (400 "Face the Facts")....25-50

TIRINO, Tom
Singles: 7-inch
TIRINO....3-5 73

TISDOM, James
Singles: 78 rpm
UNIVERSAL-FOX (100 "Model-T Boogie")....75-125 48
UNIVERSAL-FOX (101 "Throw This Dog a Bone")....75-125 48
UNIVERSAL-FOX (102 "I Feel So Bad")....75-125 48

TITANS
Singles: 78 rpm
SPECIALTY (614 "Sweet Peach") 20-30 57
SPECIALTY (625 "Don't You Just Know It")....25-50 58
SPECIALTY (632 "Arlene")....50-100 58
VITA (158 "Look What You're Doing")....40-60 57
Singles: 7-inch
CLASS (244 "No Time")....30-40 59
FIDELITY (3016 "What Have I Done")....30-50 60
SPECIALTY (614 "Sweet Peach") 25-50 57
SPECIALTY (625 "Don't You Just Know It")....25-50 58
SPECIALTY (632 "Arlene")....25-50 58
VITA (148 "So Hard to Laugh")....75-100 57
VITA (158 "Look What You're Doing")....60-80 57
Also see DON & DEWEY

TITANS
Singles: 7-inch
NOLTA (351 "A-Rab")....10-20 61

TITANS
Singles: 7-inch
MGM....4-8 64
LPs: 10/12-inch
MGM....15-20 61
Also see DAVIS, Danny, & Titans

TITANS
(Titens)
Singles: 7-inch
BANGAR (611 "Motivation")....20-25 64
DUFFS....8-12 67
METROBEAT....15-20 67
SOMA....10-20 63-64
SOUND of MUSIC....8-12 67
STUDIO CITY (1008 "Noplace Special")....15-25 63
Picture Sleeves
SOUND of MUSIC....40-60 67
Member: Rick Colburn.
Also see ALLEN, Dale, & Rebel Rousers

TITENS: see TITANS

TITO & NITO OCTET
Singles: 7-inch
AMBASSADOR....4-8 66

TITO & SILHOUETTES
Singles: 7-inch
RIVAL (03 "Baby Doll")....75-125 50s

TITONES
Singles: 7-inch
SCEPTER (1206 "Symbol of Love")....25-35 59
(White label.)
SCEPTER (1206 "Symbol of Love")....10-20 60
(Red label.)
WAND (105 "Symbol of Love")....8-12 60

TITTLEY, Simon
LPs: 10/12-inch
APEIRON....5-10 93

TITUS, Libby
LPs: 10/12-inch
COLUMBIA....8-10 77
HOT BISQUIT....10-15 68
Also see DR. JOHN & Libby Titus

TITUS GROAN
LPs: 10/12-inch
JANUS....10-12 71

TITUS OATES
LPs: 10/12-inch
LIPS ("Jungle Lady")....100-200 74
Members: Rick Jackson; Lou Tielli; Bill Beaudet; Chris Eigenmann.

TIU, Ginny
Singles: 7-inch
AMARET....5-10

TJADER, Cal LP '63
Singles: 78 rpm
FANTASY....3-5 54-57
SAVOY....3-5 53-54
Singles: 7-inch
FANTASY....3-8 54-71
SAVOY....4-8 53-54
SKYE....3-5 68
VERVE....3-6 61-66
EPs: 7-inch
FANTASY (Black vinyl)....10-25 54-55
FANTASY (Colored vinyl)....20-40 54-55
SAVOY....10-20 54
LPs: 10/12-inch
BUDDAH....8-12 70
CLASSIC JAZZ....5-8 80
CONCORD JAZZ....5-8 80-82
FANTASY (3-9 "Cal Tjader Trio")....75-125 54
(10-inch LP.)
FANTASY (3-17 "Ritmo Caliente")....75-125 54
(10-inch LP.)
FANTASY (3200 series)....25-75 54-60
(Numbers may be shown as 3-200. Double price range for colored vinyl pressings.)
FANTASY (3300 series)....25-35 60-65
FANTASY (8000 & 8100 series, except 8030)....35-45 58-61
FANTASY (8030 "Tjader Goes Latin")....75-125 59
(Colored vinyl.)
FANTASY (8300 series)....20-30 65
FANTASY (8400 series)....8-15 71-72
FANTASY (9000 series)....6-12 72-77
GALAXY....5-10 78-79
METRO....10-15 67
PRESTIGE....5-10 73
SAVOY (9036 "Cal Tjader Quartet")....75-125 54
(10-inch LP.)
SAVOY (12054 "Vib-Rations")....50-100 56
SAVOY (12000 series)....20-40 56
SKYE....8-12 68-69
VERVE....10-30 61-69
(Reads "MGM Records - A Division of Metro-Goldwyn-Mayer, Inc." at bottom of label.)
VERVE....5-12 73-84
(Reads "Manufactured By MGM Record Corp.," or mentions either Polydor or Polygram at bottom of label.)
Also see BRUBECK, Dave, Quartet
Also see O'DAY, Anita, & Cal Tjader

TJADER, Cal, & Stan Getz
LPs: 10/12-inch
FANTASY (3266 "Cal Tjader and Stan Getz")....35-45 58
FANTASY (3300 series)....15-25 65
FANTASY (8005 "Cal Tjader and Stan Getz")....45-55 58
FANTASY (8300 series)....15-25 65
Also see GETZ, Stan
Also see TJADER, Cal

TOAD HALL
LPs: 10/12-inch
LIBERTY....10-15 68

TOADS
Singles: 7-inch
CREW (342 "A Little at a Time")....4-8 70
DECCA (31847 "Leaving It All Behind")....8-12 65
LPs: 10/12-inch
RITE....20-35
WIGGINS (64021 "The Toads")....50-75 65

TOADS / Golden Boys
Singles: 7-inch
BRENT....10-15 65
Also see TOADS

TOALSON SISTERS
Singles: 7-inch
S.I.N.A....5-10 59

TOAST
Singles: 7-inch
JAMIE (1391 "Flowers Never Bend")....4-6 71

TOBER, Ronnie
Singles: 7-inch
GUY....4-8 61

TOBIAS
Singles: 7-inch
MGM....3-5 72
LPs: 10/12-inch
MGM....8-10 72

TOBIN, J.J.
Singles: 7-inch
CLARIDGE....4-8 66

TOBIN, Louise
Singles: 7-inch
AVANTE GARDE (104 "Scatterbrain")....5-10 65

TOBY & RAY WITH THE MARGILATORS
Singles: 7-inch
BLUE MOON (411 "Just Waiting for You")....30-50 59

TOBY BEAU P&R/LP '78
Singles: 7-inch
RCA....3-5 78-80
LPs: 10/12-inch
RCA (Except 2994)....5-10 78-81
RCA (2994 "Three You Missed, One You Didn't")....10-15 78
(Promotional issue only.)

TOBY BEN BLUES BAND
Singles: 7-inch
COLUMBIA....10-15 66

TODAY
Singles: 7-inch
BURDETTE....4-8 69

TODAY LP '89
LPs: 10/12-inch
MOTOWN....5-8 89-90

TODAY & TOMORROW
Singles: 7-inch
NOOSE (812 "Dooley Swings")....20-30 59

TODAY'S CHILDREN
Singles: 7-inch
MINARET (153 "Midnight Strangers")....5-8 69

TODAY'S PEOPLE P&R '73
Singles: 7-inch
20TH FOX....3-5 73

TODAY'S SPECIAL
Singles: 7-inch
DECCA....4-6 68

TODAY'S TOMORROW
Singles: 7-inch
BANG (577 "Witchi Tai To")....8-12 70
TEEN TOWN (118 "You've Gone Away")....10-20 71
TEEN TOWN (125 "Smile Away")..10-20 72
Members: Chuck Holzer; Alex Campbell; Ralph Russell; Eric Melby; Mark Melby; Randy Taylor; Clare Troyanek.
Also see LADDS
Also see SILVER BULLETS

TODD, Art & Dotty P&R/R&B '58
Singles: 78 rpm
DIAMOND....5-10 56
LONDON (17040 "Chanson d'Amour")....15-25 58
(Canadian.)
Singles: 7-inch
CAPITOL....5-10 62
COLLECTABLES....3-4 80s
DAKAR....5-8 63
DART....5-15 59-67
DECCA....5-10 61
DIAMOND (3003 "But Only for Me")....15-25 56
DOT....4-8 66
ERA....10-20 58-59
LONDON (17040 "Chanson d'Amour")....10-20 58
(Canadian.)
M.O.L....4-8 68
SIGNET....5-10 65
LPs: 10/12-inch
BEVERLY HILLS....8-10 73
DART (444 "Black Velvet Eyes")...25-40 60
DOT (3742 "Chanson d'Amour")....20-30 66
REPRISE....10-20 65

TODD, Dick, & Appalachian Wildcats C&W '67
Singles: 7-inch
DECCA....4-6 67

TODD, Don
Singles: 7-inch
DALE....3-5 77

TODD, Dylan
Singles: 78 rpm
RCA....8-15 56
Singles: 7-inch
RCA (6463 "Ballad of James Dean")....10-20 56
Picture Sleeves
RCA (6463 "Ballad of James Dean")....15-20 56

TODD, Fuller
Singles: 78 rpm
KING....10-20 57
Singles: 7-inch
KING....10-20 57-58

TODD, Greg, & Jacks
Singles: 7-inch
HOLIDAY INN....8-12 68

TODD, Johnny
Singles: 78 rpm
MODERN (1003 "Pink Cadillac")...25-50 56
Singles: 7-inch
MODERN (1003 "Pink Cadillac")....50-100 56

TODD, Nick P&R '57
Singles: 78 rpm
DOT....10-20 57
Singles: 7-inch
DOT....10-20 57-60

TODD, Scotty
Singles: 7-inch
PHILIPS....4-8 67

TODD, Shane
Singles: 7-inch
DUTCH (1061 "Today")....15-25 61
Also see CORVETTES & TODDETTES

TODD, Sharkey, & Monsters
Singles: 7-inch
CAPITOL....10-15 59

TODD & DEVIN
Singles: 7-inch
BRAGG (208 "You Make the Decisions")....10-20 60s

TODD BROTHERS
Singles: 7-inch
TREND....8-12

TODDS
Singles: 7-inch
TODD....10-15 61

TODDS
Singles: 7-inch
TODDLIN' TOWN (102 "I Want Her Back")....10-20 67

TODDY, Trudy
Singles: 7-inch
SIGNET (277 "Bandido")....5-10 60

TODES
Singles: 7-inch
EMANON (102 "Good Things")....15-25 66

TOE FAT
Singles: 7-inch
RARE EARTH (Blacy vinyl)....3-5 70-71

RARE EARTH (Colored vinyl)........... 4-8 70
(Promotional issue only.)
LPs: 10/12-inch
RARE EARTH 10-15 70-71
Members: Cliff Bennett; Ken Hensley; Lee Kerslake; Joe Konas.
Also see BENNETT, Cliff, & Rebel Rousers
Also see HENSLEY, Ken

TOGAS
Singles: 7-inch
CHALLENGE 4-8 65
Also see MORGAN, Chris, & Togas

TOGETHER
Singles: 7-inch
AMERICAN WORM........................ 8-10 72

TOGGERTY FIVE
Singles: 7-inch
TOWER..8-12 65

TOHBI, Esther
Singles: 7-inch
HERITAGE 4-6 69

TOKAYS
Singles: 7-inch
BONNIE (102 "Lost and Found")..50-100 62

TOKAYS
Singles: 7-inch
BRUTE (1 "Baby, Baby, Baby")....50-100 67
SCORPIO (403 "Now")...................10-15 65
TO-KAY (273 "Out of Hand") 10-15 60s

TOKENS P&R '61
Singles: 12-inch
DOWNTOWN (103 "The Lion Sleeps Tonight") 8-12 88
(Issued with cover.)
Singles: 78 rpm
MELBA (104 "While I Dream").......30-50 56
Singles: 7-inch
ABC 3-5 73
ATCO (7009 "Penny Whistle Band") . 4-6 74
B.T. PUPPY (500 "A Girl Named Arlene")...10-15 64
B.T. PUPPY (502 "He's in Town") ... 6-12 64
B.T. PUPPY (502 "He's in Town") ... 6-12 64
B.T. PUPPY (505 "Mr. Cupid")........ 6-12 64
B.T. PUPPY (507 "Sylvie Sleepin' ") 6-12 65
B.T. PUPPY (512 "Only My Friend") 6-12 65
B.T. PUPPY (513 "Just One Smile") 6-12 65
B.T. PUPPY (516 "Three Bells") 6-12 65
B.T. PUPPY (518 "I Hear Trumpets Blow").. 5-8 66
B.T. PUPPY (519 "Breezy")............ 6-12 66
B.T. PUPPY (525 "Saloogy")........... 6-12 67
B.T. PUPPY (552 "Get a Job")........ 6-12 69
BELL (190 "You and Me")................. 4-6 72
BUDDAH (151 "She Lets Her Hair Down")... 4-8 69
BUDDAH (159 "Don't Worry Baby") .. 4-8 70
BUDDAH (174 "Both Sides Now")...... 4-8 70
BUDDAH (187 "Listen to the Words") 4-8 70
COLLECTABLES................................. 3-4 84
LAURIE (3180 "Please Write").......10-15 63
MELBA (104 "While I Dream")........30-50 56
RCA (37-7896 "When I Go to Sleep at Night")..25-40 61
(Compact 33 Single.)
RCA (47-7896 "When I Go to Sleep at Night")..10-20 61
RCA (37-7925 "Sincerely")............25-35 61
(Compact 33 Single.)
RCA (47-7925 "Sincerely").............10-20 61
RCA (37-7954 "The Lion Sleeps Tonight")..25-35 61
(Compact 33 Single.)
RCA (47-7954 "The Lion Sleeps Tonight") 8-12 61
RCA (37-7991 "B'Wa Nina")............25-35 62
(Compact 33 Single.)
RCA (47-7991 "B'Wa Nina")............10-15 62
RCA (37-8018 "The Riddle") 20-30 62
(Compact 33 Single.)
RCA (47-8018 "The Riddle")............ 8-12 62
RCA (8052 "La Bomba") 8-12 62
RCA (8089 "I'll Do My Crying Tomorrow").. 8-12 62
RCA (8114 "A Bird Flies Out of Sight").. 8-12 63
RCA (8148 "Tonight I Met an Angel").. 8-12 63
RCA (8210 "Here the Bells") 8-12 63
RCA (8309 "Two Cars") 8-12 64
RCA (8309 "Two Cars") 8-12 64
RCA (8749 "Re-Doo-Wopp")................ 3-5 88
RCA GOLD STANDARD (0702 "The Lion Sleeps Tonight")............................... 4-6 60s
RADIO ACTIVE GOLD 3-4
W.B. 4-8 67-69
WARWICK (615 "Tonight I Fell in Love")..15-20 61
Picture Sleeves
B.T. PUPPY (591 "Greatest Moments in a Girl's Life") 10-15 66
RCA (7896 "When I Go to Sleep at Night")..10-20 61
RCA (7991 "B'Wa Nina")..................10-20 62
(Orange sleeve. No mention of *The Lion Sleeps Tonight* LP.)
RCA (7991 "B'Wa Nina")................... 8-12 62
(Orange and white sleeve. Plugs *The Lion Sleeps Tonight* LP.)
RCA (8018 "The Riddle") 10-20 62
RCA (8052 "La Bomba")...................10-15 62
RCA (8089 "I'll Do My Crying Tomorrow")..10-20 62
RCA (8114 "A Bird Flies Out of Sight") 10-20 63
RCA (8148 "Tonight I Met an Angel") 10-20 63
RCA (8210 "Hear the Bells") 10-15 63
W.B. (5900 "Portrait of My Love")....5-10 67
LPs: 10/12-inch
B.T. PUPPY..15-25 66-78
BUDDAH (5059 "Both Sides Now") 15-20 70
DOWNTOWN...................................... 5-8 88
RCA (LPM-2514 "The Lion Sleeps Tonight") 30-50 61
(Monaural.)
RCA (LSP-2514 "The Lion Sleeps Tonight") 50-75 61
(Stereo.)
RCA (LPM-2631 "We The Tokens Sing Folk")..20-40 62
(Monaural.)
RCA (LSP-2631 "We The Tokens Sing Folk")..25-50 62
(Stereo.)
RCA (LPM-2886 "Wheels")..............20-40 64
(Monaural.)
RCA (LSP-2886 "Wheels")...............25-50 64
(Stereo.)
RCA (LPM-3685 "The Tokens Again") 20-40 66
(Monaural.)
RCA (LSP-3685 "The Tokens Again") 20-40 66
(Stereo.)
RCA (8534 "Re-Doo-Wopp")............ 5-8 88
W.B. (1685 "It's a Happening World")..15-25 67
Members: Jay Siegel; Mitchell Margo; Philip Margo; Henry Medress.
Also see BUDDIES
Also see CHRISTIE, Lou / Len Barry & Dovells / Bobby Rydell / Tokens
Also see COEDS
Also see CROSS COUNTRY
Also see DAMPHIER, Tom
Also see DARRELL & OXFORDS
Also see FOUR WINDS
Also see KEITH
Also see MARGO, MARGO, MEDRESS & SIEGEL
Also see NEW TOKENS
Also see SEDAKA, Neil
Also see SANDS of TIME
Also see U.S. DOUBLE QUARTET

TOKENS / Happenings LP '67
LPs: 10/12-inch
B.T. PUPPY..15-25 67
Also see HAPPENINGS
Also see TOKENS

TOKENS
Singles: 7-inch
DATE (2737 "Oh What a Night")....25-35 61
GARY (1006 "Come Dance with Me")...75-125 61
(Company address is shown as on Broadway.)
Me")...50-100 61
(Company address is shown as on W. 49th St.)

TOLBERT, Israel "Popper Stopper" P&R/R&B '70
Singles: 7-inch
WARREN 3-5 70-71
LPs: 10/12-inch
WARREN 10-15 71

TOLBERT, Johnny
Singles: 7-inch
JASMAN..5-10

TOLBERT, Moss
Singles: 7-inch
VEE JAY 4-8 63

TOLEDO'S BOBBY JACOBS: see JACOBS, Bobby

TOLEDOS
Singles: 7-inch
DOWN (2003 "This Is Our Night") 25-35 61
END (1094 "This Is Our Night")......10-15 61

TOLIVER, Bo, & Timers
Singles: 7-inch
AIRWAY (105 "Beggin' ")..............25-35 58

TOLIVER, Donny, & Renegades
Singles: 7-inch
IMPACT (16 "Little Boy Blue") 15-25 64

TOLIVER, Jimmy
(With His California Blues Men)
Singles: 78 rpm
CHIMES 25-50 50s
Singles: 7-inch
T&T (102 "Breaking Out")...............15-25 63

TOLIVER, Mickey, & Capitols
Singles: 7-inch
CINDY (3002 "Rose-Marie")........100-150 57

TOLLAND, Pat
Singles: 7-inch
KINGSTON.. 4-8 63

TOLLESON, Tommie
Singles: 7-inch
KOOL...10-15 60

TOLLISON, Johnny
Singles: 7-inch
KLUB...5-10 77

TOLLIVER, Danny
Singles: 7-inch
DANNY..5-10 62

TOLLIVER, Kay
Singles: 7-inch
LUCKY ELEVEN.................................. 4-8 66

MUSICOR 3-6 68
NORTH LAKE 4-8 65-66
SURE SHOT 4-6 67
LPs: 10/12-inch
MUSICOR 10-15 68

TOLONEN, Jukka
LPs: 10/12-inch
JANUS 8-10 76

TOLSON, Bill, & Jordanaires
Singles: 7-inch
EASTERN 3-4 78
Also see JORDANAIRES

TOM & CATS
Singles: 7-inch
JEWEL 4-8 65
PAULA 4-8 66

TOM & CLARENCE
Singles: 7-inch
ERA..4-8 67

TOM & DICK
Singles: 7-inch
MERCURY (72573 "Lark Day")........8-10 66
(May have been promotional only.)
Members: Tom Smothers; Dick Smothers.
Also see SMOTHERS BROTHERS

TOM & JERRIO P&R/R&B '65
Singles: 7-inch
ABC-PAR 4-8 65
Members: Eddie Thomas; Jerry Murray.
Also see JERRYO

TOM & JERRY P&R '57
Singles: 78 rpm
BIG (613 "Hey, Schoolgirl")........100-200 57
Singles: 7-inch
ABC-PAR (10363 "Surrender, Please Surrender") 15-25 62
ABC-PAR (10788 "This Is My Story")..10-15 66
BIG (613 "Hey, Schoolgirl")............20-30 57
BIG (616 "Two Teenagers") 20-30 58
BIG (618 "Don't Say Goodbye")......20-30 58
EMBER (1094 "I'm Lonesome").......25-35 59
HUNT (319 "Don't Say Goodbye")..20-25 58
KING (5167 "Hey, Schoolgirl")........35-45 58
Members: Paul Simon; Art Garfunkel.
Also see SIMON & GARFUNKEL

TOM & JERRY / Ronnie Lawrence
Singles: 7-inch
BELL (120 "Baby Talk") 20-30 60
Picture Sleeves
BELL (120 "Baby Talk")...................30-50 60
Also see TOM & JERRY

TOM & JERRY
Singles: 7-inch
MERCURY 4-6 61-63
LPs: 10/12-inch
MERCURY (Except 842)...............15-20 61-62
MERCURY (842 "Surfin' Hootenanny")...................................20-25 63
WING...10-15 67
Members: Charlie Tomlinson; Jerry Kennedy.
Also see KENNEDY, Jerry
Also see TOMLINSON & BAKER

TOM & TEMPESTS
Singles: 7-inch
ALCO (1004 "Play It Cool")............15-25 60s

TOM & WAYNE
Singles: 7-inch
GAMA (707 "I Have Some Love") 10-20

TOM BEE: see BEE, Tom

TOM, PAUL, & JONES
Singles: 7-inch
ADVENTURE (285 "Dance Little Girl")..15-25

TOM TOM CLUB LP '81
Singles: 12-inch
SIRE...4-8 81-83
Singles: 7-inch
SIRE...3-5 81-89
LPs: 10/12-inch
SIRE...5-10 81-89
Members: Chris Frantz; Tina Weymouth.
Also see TALKING HEADS

TOM TOMS
Singles: 7-inch
LAUREL (1011 "Pandemonium") ...15-25 59

TOM TOMS
Singles: 7-inch
SULTAN 10-15 60s

TOM TOMS
Singles: 7-inch
RODEO (247 "Corsicana")...............8-12

TOM TONES
Singles: 7-inch
DEE DEE 15-25 60s

TOMACK, Mike
Singles: 7-inch
BLUE RIVER 4-8 65

TOMANGOES
Singles: 7-inch
WASHPAN (3125 "I Really Love You")...100-200

TOMBOYS
Singles: 7-inch
SWAN 5-8 64

TOMBSTONES
Singles: 7-inch
GRAVE (1001 "I Want You") 10-20 60s

TOMCATS
Singles: 7-inch
TERRY (103 "Saxy Boogie")..........10-20 61
Member: Tommy Wills.
Also see WILLS, Tommy

TOMKOS
(Tomko Trio)
Singles: 7-inch
ARTISTIQUE (607 "Get with It") 6-12 62
ARTISTIQUE (5003 "Spook"/"Spook Pt. 2")...5-10 63
ARTISTIQUE (5003 "Spook"/ "Carol")...5-10 63
(Issued with different flip side.)

TOMKOS
Singles: 7-inch
ARTISTIQUE (5003 "Spook") 5-10 60s

TOMLIN, Lily LP '71
Singles: 7-inch
POLYDOR...3-5 73-75
LPs: 10/12-inch
ARISTA 5-10 77
POLYDOR 5-10 71-75

TOMLIN, Willie
Singles: 7-inch
PEACOCK...4-8 68

TOMLINSON, Malcolm
LPs: 10/12-inch
A&M 5-10 79

TOMLINSON, Michael
Singles: 7-inch
CYPRESS 3-4 88

TOMLINSON & BAKER
LPs: 10/12-inch
SUTTON 10-15
Members: Charlie Tomlinson; Billy Baker.
Also see TOM & JERRY

TOMMY & CHESSMEN
Singles: 7-inch
A-BET 4-8 67

TOMMY & CLEVE
Singles: 7-inch
CHECKER 4-8 66-67

TOMMY & DEL ROYALS
Singles: 7-inch
DESTINY (101 "Trust in Love")..100-200 60

TOMMY & DONNA C&W '88
Singles: 7-inch
OAK 3-4 88

TOMMY & EDDIE
Singles: 7-inch
FINCH 10-15 59

TOMMY & HUSTLERS
Singles: 7-inch
FANTASY 5-10 63

TOMMY & LEON
Singles: 7-inch
DORE...5-10 63

TOMMY & RIVIERAS
Singles: 7-inch
CAMEO (461 "Messing with the Kid")...10-20 67
P'ZAZZ..4-8 66
Members: Tommy Dee; Johnny Ferrari; Dennis Dean; Buddy Tinari; Pete Ream; Ellie DeLieto; Cathy DeSanto; Sue Johnson.

TOMMY & True Blue Facts
Singles: 7-inch
A&M 4-8 68

TOMMY & TWISTERS
Singles: 7-inch
REGENT 4-8 62

TOMMY G.
(With the Charms)
Singles: 7-inch
HOLLYWOOD 4-8 66
RANWOOD 3-6 69

TOMMY GUN & HIT SQUAD
LPs: 10/12-inch
SPIT (1690 "Tommy Gun and the Hit Squad")...8-10 90
(Includews 20" x 25" poster.)
Members: Steve Sukapdjo; Paul Barron; Joey Roberts.

TOMMY T'S FEDERAL RESERVE
Singles: 7-inch
CADET 4-8 67-68

TOMMY TUTONE P&R/LP '80
Singles: 7-inch
COLUMBIA 3-5 80-83
LPs: 10/12-inch
COLUMBIA (Except 1461)...............5-10 80-83
COLUMBIA (1461 "Alive and Almost Dangerous")...................................10-15 82
(Promotional issue only.)

TOMORROW
Singles: 7-inch
NEW VOICE 5-10 67

TOMORROW
LPs: 10/12-inch
SIRE..10-15 68
VISA...8-10

Also see MFSB

TOMORROW'S CHILDREN
Singles: 7-inch
RAYNARD (10065 "In the Midnight Hour")..40-60 65
Also see FARM BAND

TOMORROW'S EDITION R&B '82
Singles: 7-inch
ATLANTIC...3-5 82
GANG 3-5 75

TOMORROW'S PEOPLE
Singles: 7-inch
COLUMBIA 5-10 66

TOMORROW'S PROMISE R&B '73
Singles: 7-inch
CAPITOL..4-8 73-74
MERCURY 3-5 75

TOMORROW'S WORLD
Singles: 7-inch
ERA 4-8 67

TOMORROW'S WORLD C&W '90
Singles: 7-inch
W.B. 3-4 90
Members: Lynn Anderson; Butch Baker; Shane Barmby; Billy Hill; Suzy Bogguss; Kix Brooks; T. Graham Brown; Burch Sisters; Holly Dunn; Foster & Lloyd; Vince Gill; Rusty Golden; William Lee Golden; Highway 101; Shelby Lynne; Johnny Rodriguez; Dan Seals; Les Taylor; Pam Tillis; Kevin Welch; Mac Wiseman.
Also see ANDERSON, Lynn
Also see BAKER, Butch
Also see BARMBY, Shane
Also see BILLY HILL
Also see BOGGUSS, Suzy
Also see BROOKS, Kix
Also see BROWN, T. Graham
Also see BURCH SISTERS
Also see DUNN, Holly
Also see FOSTER & LLOYD
Also see GILL, Vince
Also see GOLDEN, William Lee
Also see GOLDENS
Also see HIGHWAY 101
Also see LYNNE, Shelby
Also see RODRIGUEZ, Johnny
Also see SEALS, Dan
Also see TAYLOR, Les
Also see TILLIS, Pam
Also see WELCH, Kevin
Also see WISEMAN, Mac

TOMPALL & GLASER BROS. P&R '69
(Tompall & Glasers; Tompall Glaser)
Singles: 7-inch
DECCA 5-10 59-65
ELEKTRA...3-5 80-82
MGM 3-8 66-71
RICH (1004 "Yakety-Yak")...............15-25 61
ROBBINS (1006 "I Want You")......50-75 57
LPs: 10/12-inch
DECCA (DL-4041 "This Land")......20-40 60
(Monaural.)
DECCA (DL7-4041 "This Land") 30-50 60
(Stereo.)
ELEKTRA...5-10 81
MGM 10-20 67-75
U.A. (3540 "Ballad of *Namu the Killer Whale* and Others")....................................25-35 66
(Monaural.)
U.A. (6540 "Ballad of *Namu the Killer Whale* and Others")....................................30-40 66
(Stereo.)
VOCALION (3807 "Country Folk")....8-12 67
Members: Tompall Glaser; Jim Glaser; Chuck Glaser.
Also see GLASER, Chuck
Also see GLASER, Jim
Also see GLASER, Tompall

TOMPKINS PARK SINGERS
Singles: 7-inch
RSVP 4-8 66

TOMS
(The Toms)
LPs: 10/12-inch
BLACK SHEEP (10903 "Yawning for Pleasure")...5-10 86
BLACK SHEEP (11177 "The Toms")...20-30 79
Member: Thomas J. Marolda.

TOMS, Gary P&R/R&B/LP '75
(Gary Toms' Empire)
Singles: 12-inch
MCA..4-8 77
Singles: 7-inch
MCA..3-5 77
MERCURY 3-5 78
P.I.P. 3-5 75-76
LPs: 10/12-inch
MCA..5-10 77
MERCURY 5-10 78
P.I.P. 5-10 75

TOMSCO, George, & Dots
Singles: 7-inch
DOT (16691 "Mexican Fun")............5-10 65
Also see FIREBALLS
Also see GEORGE & BABS

TONE LOC P&R '88
Singles: 7-inch
DELICIOUS...3-4 89
Picture Sleeves
DELICIOUS...3-4 89
LPs: 10/12-inch
DELICIOUS...5-8 89

TONEBENDERS
Singles: 12-inch
HEAD FLIES (10003 "Toin Coss")..... 5-8 88
Members: Michael Corcoran; Douglas Davis; Mick Hargrave; Charlie Servello.

TONER, Efrem, Jr.
Singles: 7-inch
GROW 3-6 68

TONES
(With the Al Cailoa Orchestra)
Singles: 7-inch
BATON (265 "We")........................10-20 58
Also see CAIOLA, Al
Also see SANTOS, Larry

TONES R&B '83
Singles: 7-inch
CRIMINAL 3-5 83

TONETTES
(With Sammy Lowe Orchestra)
Singles: 78 rpm
MODERN 10-15 56
Singles: 7-inch
ABC-PAR (9905 "Oh What a Baby") 15-25 58
DOE (101 "Oh What a Baby").........50-75 58
DOE (103 "Uh-Oh")........................35-55 58
DYNAMIC (103 "I Gotta Know").......15-25 59
MODERN (997 "Tonight You Belong to Me") 15-25 56
VOLT (101 "Please Don't Go").......10-20 62
VOLT (104 "Stolen Angel") 10-20 63

TONEY, Oscar, Jr. P&R/R&B/LP '67
Singles: 7-inch
ATCO (6933 "Everything I Own")...10-15 74
BELL 5-10 67-69
CAPRICORN 10-20 71-72
CONTEMPO (7702 "Is It Because I'm Black") 5-10 74
KING (5906 "You Are Going to Need Me") 10-20 64
LPs: 10/12-inch
BELL 10-20 67

TONEY LEE: see LEE, Toney

TONGUE
Singles: 7-inch
HEMISPHERE.................................. 3-5 70
LPs: 10/12-inch
HEMISPHERE................................15-20 70

TONGUE & GROOVE
Singles: 7-inch
FONTANA 4-8 69
LPs: 10/12-inch
FONTANA 15-20 69
Members: Michael Ferguson; Lynne Hughes.
Also see HUGHES, Lynne

TONGUE TWISTIN' TEN
(TTT)
Singles: 12-inch
EARTHTONE 5-8 83

TONGUES OF TRUTH / Grodes
Singles: 7-inch
CURRENT (112 "Let's Talk About Girls") 15-25 66
Also see GRODES

TONI & LYNNE
Singles: 7-inch
BLUE ROCK....................................... 4-6 68

TONI & TERRI
Singles: 7-inch
MERCURY 4-8 65
MONUMENT 4-8 67

TONICS
Singles: 7-inch
FONTANA 3-6 69

TONIGHT SHOW BAND: see SEVERINSEN, Doc

TONIO K
Singles: 7-inch
EPIC... 3-5 79
LPs: 10/12-inch
EPIC.. 5-10 79

TONTO & RENEGADES
(Tonto & Renigades)
Singles: 7-inch
SOUND of the SCEEN (2178 "Easy Way Out") 10-20 67
SOUND of the SCEEN (2212 "Little Boy Blue") 15-25 67

TONTO'S EXPANDING HEAD BAND
LPs: 10/12-inch
EMBRYO......................................10-15

TONY & BANDITS
Singles: 7-inch
CORAL... 4-8 65-66
FLO-ROE 4-8 65

TONY & CAROL R&B '72
Singles: 7-inch
KING 4-6 70
ROULETTE 3-5 72
Members: Tony Issac; Carol McLean.

TONY & CAROLYN
Singles: 7-inch
V.I.P. 8-12 70

TONY & DAYDREAMS
Singles: 7-inch
PLANET (1008 "Why Don't You Be Nice") 60-80 58
PLANET (1054 "Christmas Lullabye") 100-150 61
Member: Tony Carmen.
Also see CARMEN, Tony, & Spitfires

TONY & HOLIDAYS
Singles: 7-inch
ABC-PAR (10295 "Those Goes My Heart Again") 150-200 62
Member: Buddy Sheppard.
Also see SHEPPARD, Buddy, & Holidays

TONY & JEFF
Singles: 7-inch
COOKIN' 4-8 64
DING DONG..................................... 4-8 63

TONY & JOE P&R '58
Singles: 7-inch
DORE.. 4-8 61-62
ERA.. 5-10 58
FLYTE 5-10 59
GARDENA....................................... 5-10 60
Members: Tony Savonne; Joe Saraceno.
Also see BEACH BOYS / Tony & Joe

TONY & JOHNNY
(With the Rextones)
Singles: 7-inch
MILO 8-10 58
Members: Tony Passarella; Johnny Moccia.

TONY & MASQUINS
Singles: 7-inch
RUTHIE (1000 "My Angel Eyes") 75-100 61

TONY & MONSTROSITIES
Singles: 7-inch
CRYPT (107 "Igor's Party") 10-20 60

TONY & NORM
Singles: 7-inch
POPLAR... 4-8 62

TONY & RAINDROPS
Singles: 7-inch
CHESAPEAKE (609 "While Walking") 50-100 62
CROSLEY (340 "My Heart Cried") 500-1000 61

TONY & ROCKIN' ORBITS
Singles: 7-inch
AISLE (001 "Twenty Flight Rock")..... 3-5 92
(Black vinyl. 900 made.)
AISLE (001 "Twenty Flight Rock")....5-10 92
(Gold vinyl. 100 made.)
Picture Sleeves
AISLE (001 "Twenty Flight Rock")..... 3-5 92
Member: Tony Puglisi (a.k.a. Tony Maserati).
Also see KARI, Sax & Rockin' Jukes / Seven Secrets / Tony & Rockin' Orbits

TONY & SIEGRID
Singles: 7-inch
RCA.. 4-8 66-67

TONY & TANDY
Singles: 7-inch
COTILLION 3-4 69

TONY & TECHNICS
Singles: 7-inch
CHEX (1010 "Work Out")..............10-15 63
Also see TECHNICS

TONY & TERRI
(With the Pirates)
Singles: 7-inch
MERCURY (72489 "I Want You") 8-12 65
MONUMENT 4-8 66-68

TONY & TYRONE
Singles: 7-inch
COLUMBIA.. 5-8 65
STON-ROC 12-18
Members: Tony Johnson; Tyrone Pickens.

TONY & TWILIGHTERS
(Anthony & Sophmores)
Singles: 7-inch
COLLECTABLES................................ 3-4 80s
JALYNNE (106 "Be My Girl") 50-75 60
RED TOP (127 "Key to My Heart") 150-175 60
Member: Anthony "Tony" Maresco.
Also see ANTHONY & SOPHOMORES
Also see DYNAMICS, Featuring Tony Maresco

TONY & VELVETS
Singles: 7-inch
ZOOM (9606 "Sunday") 75-125 63

TONY & VIZITORS
Singles: 7-inch
SIDEWALK.....................................10-20 67
Session: Davie Allan.
Also see ALLAN, Davie

TONY & TYRONE
Singles: 7-inch
ATLANTIC (2458 "Please Operator") 15-25 67
COLUMBIA..8-12 65

TONY, BOB & JIMMY
Singles: 7-inch
CAPITOL.. 4-8 62
Members: Tony Butala; Bob Engemann; Jim Pike.
Also see LETTERMEN

TONY! TONI! TONE! P&R/R&B/LP '88
Singles: 7-inch
WING 3-4 88-90
Picture Sleeves
WING 3-4 88

TONY, VIC & MANUEL
Singles: 7-inch
REPRISE 4-8 64
LPs: 10/12-inch
REPRISE 15-20 64

TONY IV
Singles: 7-inch
CO-OP 4-8 68
Members: Tony Pragano; Tony Gargano; Bob DeMartino; George Gould.

TONY'S TYGERS
(Tygers)
Singles: 7-inch
A&M (921 "Little By Little")................4-8 68
JAMIE (1378 "Resurrection") 5-10 69
TEEN TOWN (102 "Little By Little") 8-10 68
TEEN TOWN (105 "I Can't Believe") 8-10 68
TEEN TOWN (107 "Debbie on My Mind") 8-10 68
Members: Tony Dancy; Dave Kuck; Craig Fairchild; Joe Turano; Lanny Hale; Fred Euler; Dennis Duchrow.
Also see PASSION

TONY'S TYGERS / Skunks / Robbs
EPs: 7-inch
WRIT RADIO (1340 "WRIT Sampler") 15-25 68
Also see ROBBS
Also see SKUNKS
Also see TONY'S TYGERS

TOO SHORT LP '89
LPs: 10/12-inch
DANGEROUS 5-8 89
JIVE 5-8 90

TOOK, Ben, & Investas
Singles: 7-inch
DART 5-10 60

TOOMBS, Jackson
Singles: 78 rpm
EXCELLO......................................10-20 56
Singles: 7-inch
EXCELLO (2083 "Kiss-A Me Quick") 35-50 56

TOOMORROW
Singles: 7-inch
KIRSHNER (5005 "Going Back")....15-25 71
Member: Olivia Newton-John.
Also see NEWTON-JOHN, Olivia

TOONE, Gene
Singles: 7-inch
ANNETTE (1001 "You're My Baby") 10-20 64
SIMCO 8-12 60s

TOOTIE & BOUQUETS
Singles: 7-inch
PARKWAY.....................................15-20 63

TOOTS & MAYTALS LP '75
Singles: 12-inch
MANGO...4-6 82
Singles: 7-inch
MANGO...3-5 76-82
LPs: 10/12-inch
ISLAND 5-10 75
MANGO..5-10 76-82
Members: Toots Hibbert; Nathaniel Mathias; Releigh Gordon; Paul Douglas; Jackie Jackson; Winston Wright.
Also see WINWOOD, Steve

TOOTSIE & VERSATILES
Singles: 7-inch
ELMOR (6000 "I've Got a Feeling") 25-50 62

TOP BAND
Singles: 7-inch
TIP TOP 5-10 59

TOP DRAWER
LPs: 10/12-inch
WISHBON (207 "Solid Oak").....300-400 69
Members: Steve Geary; John Baker; Alan Berry; Ray Herr; Ron Linn.

TOP HATS
Singles: 7-inch
CANE 10-20 60s

TOP HATTERS
Singles: 78 rpm
CADENCE...5-10 54
Singles: 7-inch
CADENCE (1243 "Dim, Dim the Lights") 10-15 54

TOP HITS
Singles: 7-inch
NORMAN (504 "Love No One") 150-250 61

TOP NOTCHMEN
Singles: 7-inch
TOP NOTCH 5-10 70s

TOP NOTES
("Derek Ray, Guy Howard & Co."; Topnotes)
Singles: 7-inch
ABC-PAR (10399 "I Love You So Much") 10-15 63
ATLANTIC (2066 "Wonderful Time") 10-20 60
ATLANTIC (2080 "Say Yes") 10-20 60
ATLANTIC (2097 "Hearts of Stone") 10-20 61
ATLANTIC (2115 "Twist & Shout") 10-20 61
FESTIVAL (1021 "Come Back, Cleopatra") 15-25 62
Members: Derek Ray; Guy Howard.

TOP SHELF R&B '70
Singles: 7-inch
LO LO 4-6 69-70
SOUND TOWN 3-5 80

TOP SIX
Singles: 7-inch
P.D.Q. 10-15 60s

TOPAZ
LPs: 10/12-inch
COLUMBIA......................................8-10 77

TOPEL & WARE C&W '87
Singles: 7-inch
RCI 3-4 87
Members: Michael Topel; James Ware.

TOPICS
Singles: 7-inch
CROSS COUNTRY (102 "What Now") 8-12 59

TOPICS
(4 Seasons)
Singles: 7-inch
PERRI (1007 "The Girl in My Dreams") 50-100 61
Also see DIXON, Billy, & Topics
Also see 4 SEASONS

TOPICS
Singles: 7-inch
CARNIVAL 5-10 66
CHADWICK (102 "Hey Girl") 50-75 67
HEAVY DUTY 5-10 60s
TOPIC (100 "The Devil") 10-15 60s
LPs: 10/12-inch
TOPIC ("Living Evidence") 15-25 60s
(Selection number not known.)
VANCO (1002 "Topics for Tonight") 15-25 60s

TOPNOTES: see TOP NOTES

TOPPER, Greg
LPs: 10/12-inch
MAD DOG 8-10

TOPPERS
Singles: 78 rpm
REGENT 10-20 48
SAVOY...10-20 48
Members: Steve Gibson; Dave Patillo; Emmett Matthews; Romaine Brown.
Also see GIBSON, Steve

TOPPERS
Singles: 78 rpm
AVALON (63707 "I Love You") 10-20 54
Singles: 7-inch
AVALON (63707 "I Love You") 20-30 54

TOPPERS
(With Orchestra)
Singles: 78 rpm
JUBILEE..25-50 54
Singles: 7-inch
JUBILEE (5136 "Let Me Bang Your Box") 75-125 54
Members: Sam Fickling; Fred Williams; Vernon Britton; Jerry Half hide; Henry Austin.
Also see HURRICANES

TOPPERS
Singles: 78 rpm
DECCA..5-10 57
Singles: 7-inch
DECCA..5-10 57

TOPPERS
Singles: 7-inch
STACY 8-12 62

TOPPERS
(Dick Thomas & Toppers)
EPs: 7-inch
TOPS (61 "Once Upon a Time")....15-25 61
(Not issued with cover.)
Also see THOMAS, Dick

TOPPS
Singles: 78 rpm
RED ROBIN 50-75 54
Singles: 7-inch
RED ROBIN (126 "What Do You Do") 100-200 54
RED ROBIN (131 "I Got a Feeling") 100-200 54

TOPS
Singles: 78 rpm
SINGULAR...................................50-100 57
Singles: 7-inch
SINGULAR (712 "An Innocent Kiss") 100-200 57

TOPS
Singles: 7-inch
V-TONE (102 "Puppy Love") 100-150 61
(Repressed as by Little Jimmy & Tops.)
Also see LITTLE JIMMY & TOPS

TOPSIDERS
Singles: 7-inch
JOSIE (907 "Heartbreak Hotel")........5-10 63
LPs: 10/12-inch
JOSIE (4000 "Rock Goes Folk") 15-25 63

TOPSIDERS
Singles: 7-inch
ATLANTIC (2115 "Baby Be Mine")....5-10 64

TOPSY, Tiny: see TINY TOPSY

TOPSY TURBYS
Singles: 7-inch
LIBERTY BELL (102 "Hey Tiger")....8-12

TORA TORA LP '89
LPs: 10/12-inch
A&M 5-8 89

TORCH D&D '83
Singles: 12-inch
PACIFIC..4-6 83

TORCH SONG D&D '84
Singles: 12-inch
I.R.S. 4-6 83-84
Singles: 7-inch
I.R.S. 3-4 83-84
LPs: 10/12-inch
I.R.S. 5-8 83

TORCHES
Singles: 7-inch
RING-O 20-25

TOREADORS
Singles: 7-inch
MIDAS (1001 "Do You Remember") 40-50
PAWN (1202 "Ring-a-Leevio")........5-10 63

TOREADORS
Singles: 7-inch
MIDAS (1001 "Do You Remember") 50-100 60s

TORKAYS
Singles: 7-inch
STACY (9960 "Karate") 8-10 63
Members: Keith Murphy.
Also see O'CONNER, Keith

TORKAYS
Singles: 7-inch
COULEE (112 "Linda, I'm Worried So") 8-12 65
Members: Ken Cunningham; Jerry Upson.

TORME, Mel P&R '45
(With the Meltones)
Singles: 78 rpm
BETHLEHEM 4-10 56-57
CAPITOL (1000 & 2000 series) 4-8 50-53
Singles: 7-inch
ATLANTIC...4-6 62-64
BETHLEHEM 5-10 56-58
CAPITOL (1000 & 2000 series) 5-10 50-53
(Purple labels.)
CAPITOL (2000 series) 3-6 69-70
(Orange labels.)
COLUMBIA 3-6 64-67
CORAL..5-10 53-56
LIBERTY 3-6 68
VERVE...4-8 59-61
EPs: 7-inch
CAPITOL...5-15 50
P.R.I. (9 "The Touch of Your Lips")...5-10
LPs: 10/12-inch
ATLANTIC (8000 series)...............12-25 62-64
ATLANTIC (18000 series)...............5-10 75
ATLANTIC (80000 series)................5-8 83
BETHLEHEM (34 "It's a Blue World") 25-50 55
BETHLEHEM (52 "Mel Torme")......25-50 56
BETHLEHEM (4000 series)...........10-20 65
BETHLEHEM (6000 series) 20-40 58-60
(Maroon labels.)
BETHLEHEM (6000 series) 5-10 77-78
(Gray labels.)
CAPITOL (200 "California Suite") 50-100 50
(10-inch LP.)
CAPITOL (300 & 400 series) 8-12 69-70
COLUMBIA (2000 series) 10-20 64-66
(Monaural.)
COLUMBIA (9000 series) 10-20 64-66
(Stereo.)
CONCORD JAZZ 5-8 82
CORAL (57012 "At the Crescendo") 50-100 54
CORAL (57044 "Musical Sounds") 50-100 54
EVEREST 5-10 76
GLENDALE 5-8 78-79
GRYPHON 5-8 79
HALO (50243 "Mel Torme Sings") 25-50 57
LIBERTY 8-15 68
MGM (552 "Songs by Mel Torme") 50-100 52
(10-inch LP.)
MAYFAIR 25-35 58
METRO 10-20 65
MUSICRAFT 5-8 83
STRAND 12-25 60
VERVE 20-35 58-60
(Reads "Verve Records, Inc." at bottom of label.)
VERVE..10-20 61-72
(Reads "MGM Records - A Division of Metro-Goldwyn-Mayer, Inc." at bottom of label.)
VERVE..5-10 73-84
(Reads "Manufactured By MGM Record Corp.," or mentions either Polydor or Polygram at bottom of label.)
VOCALION...5-10 70
Also see CROSBY, Bing, & Mel Torme
Also see LEE, Peggy, & Mel Torme
Also see RICH, Buddy
Also see WHITING, Margaret

TORMENTORS
Singles: 7-inch
KERWOOD (712 "Didn't It Rain") .. 15-25 60s
ROYAL (002 "She's Gone") 10-20 67
ROYAL (003 "Merry-Go-Round") 10-20 67
ROYAL (003-1 "Sounds of Summer") 10-20 67

LPs: 10/12-inch
EVA (12055 "Hanging 'Round") 8-10 88
ROYAL (111 "Hanging 'Round") 100-200 67
Members: Tim Daley; Dan Davis; Mark Davis; Lee Harper.

TORNADER *R&B '77*
Singles: 7-inch
POLYDOR 3-5 77

TORNADOES
Singles: 7-inch
ABC-PAR (10174 "Like a Frog") 8-10 60

TORNADOES
Singles: 7-inch
AERTAUN (100 "Bustin' Surfboards") 10-20 62
AERTAUN (101 "The Gremmie") ... 10-20 62
AERTAUN (102 "Shootin' Beaver"/"Phantom Surfer") 15-25 63
AERTAUN (102 "Lightnin'"/"Phantom Surfer") 10-20 64
(Issued with different flip side.)
LPs: 10/12-inch
JOSIE (4005 "Bustin' Surfboards") 50-100 63
Members: Gerald Sanders; Norman Sanders; Jesse Sanders; George White; Leonard Delany.
Also see HOLLYWOOD TORNADOES

TORNADOES *P&R/R&B '62*
Singles: 7-inch
LONDON 4-8 62-63
TOWER 4-8 65
LPs: 10/12-inch
LONDON 25-35 62-63
Members: Heinz Burt; Alan Caddy; Clem Cattini; George Bellamy.
Also see HEINZ

TORNADOES
Singles: 7-inch
CUCA (1099 "Loneliest Guy in Town") 15-25 62
SOMA (1182 "You're Too Late") 15-25 61
Members: Bill Velline; Richie Wynn; Chet Priewe; Terry Erdman;. Al Johnson; Freddie Swenson; Mark Rowe.
Also see STRANGERS
Also see WYNN, Richie, & Tornadoes

TORNADOS
Singles: 7-inch
BUMBLE BEE (503 "Love in Your Life") 20-25 59

TORNADOS
Singles: 7-inch
CUCA (1092 "Scalping Party") 15-25 62
CUCA (6361 "Last Date") 15-25 63
Members: Gordy Hastreiter; Bob Olson; Teddy Vernick; Denny Hastreiter; Dan Peterson; Dick Saykally; Cookie Bushar.

TORNADOS
Singles: 7-inch
VOX 8-12 60s

TORNADOS
Singles: 7-inch
NEW WORLD (100 "A World That's Free") 10-20 60s

TORNADOS
Singles: 7-inch
PHALANX (1004 "Alone") 50-100 66
PHALANX (1014 "Rainy Day Fairy Tales") 50-100 66

TORNADOS
Singles: 7-inch
HEAD (2001 "The Hawk") 8-12 68
TORNADO (975 "Riot") 8-12

TORONADOES
Singles: 7-inch
VULCO (2 "Ramblin' Man") 10-15 62

TORONADOS
Singles: 7-inch
DATE (1519 "Next Stop, Kansas City") 10-20 66

TORNAY, Sue, & Four Kings
Singles: 7-inch
DORE 5-10 61

TOROK, Mitchell *C&W/P&R '53*
(With the Louisiana Hayride Band; with Matches; with Ramona Redd)
Singles: 78 rpm
ABBOTT 10-20 53-54
DECCA 5-15 57-58
FBC (102 "Nacogdoches County Line") 15-25 48
FBC (115 "Piney Woods Boogie") .. 15-25 49
Singles: 7-inch
ABBOTT 12-25 53-54
CALICO 3-5
CAPITOL 4-8 62-63
DECCA 5-10 57-59
GUYDEN 5-10 59-60
INETTE 4-8 63
MERCURY 4-8 61
RCA 4-8 65
REPRISE 4-6 66-67
Picture Sleeves
GUYDEN 10-20 59-60
LPs: 10/12-inch
CALICO 10-15
GUYDEN (502 "Caribbean") 25-45 60
(Monaural.)
GUYDEN (ST-502 "Caribbean") 50-75 60
(Stereo.)
REPRISE 10-15 66
Also see GREAT PRETENDER & Tennessee Two and a Half
Also see MITCH & GAIL

TORONTO *LP '80*
Singles: 7-inch
NETWORK 3-5 82
SOLID GOLD 3-5
LPs: 10/12-inch
A&M 5-10 80-81
NETWORK 5-10 82
SOLID GOLD 5-10

TORPEDOS
Singles: 7-inch
FOUR WINDS 3-5 80
EPs: 7-inch
FOUR WINDS 5-10 79
Members: Johnny Angelos; Robert Gillespie; Mike Marshall; Tom Curry; Jim Banner; Ralph Serafino.
Also see RED RIDER

TORPEY, Pat
Singles: 7-inch
EPIC 4-8 62-65

TORQUAYS
Singles: 7-inch
WHIRL 8-12 62

TORQUAYS
Singles: 7-inch
GEE GEE CEE (8163 "Escondido") 15-25 63

TORQUAYS
Singles: 7-inch
AERTAUN (103 "Phantom Surfer") 15-25 64

TORQUAYS
Singles: 7-inch
ARA (219 "Find a New Love") 5-10 65

TORQUAYS
Singles: 7-inch
COLPIX (782 "Image of a Girl") 8-12 65

TORQUAYS
Singles: 7-inch
GYPSY (265 "Busting Point") 15-25 67
ORIGINAL SOUND 10-20 67

TORQUAYS
Singles: 7-inch
TEE PEE (43 "I'll Never Forget") 15-25 68
Members: Jim Chase; Paul Smith; Alan Ives; Tom Guenther.

TORQUAYS
Singles: 7-inch
HIDEOUT (1002 "Shake It Tail Feather") 20-30 60s

TORQUAYS
Singles: 7-inch
ROCK-IT 15-20 60s

TORQUAYS
(Torquay's)
Singles: 7-inch
HOLLY (4701 "Pineapple Moon") ... 50-75 60s

TORQUES
Singles: 7-inch
CHESTERFIELD 10-15 63
LEMCO (890 "Bumpin' ") 10-15 65
LPs: 10/12-inch
LEMCO (604 "Live") 50-75 66
WIGGINS (64010 "Zoom") 50-75 67

TORQUETTS
Singles: 7-inch
SANTA CRUZ (002 "Any More") 10-20 65
TORQUETT (005 "Feedback") 15-25 60s
TORQUETT (007 "Side Swiped") 15-25 60s

TORRANCE, George *P&R/R&B '68*
(With the Naturals; with Dippers)
Singles: 7-inch
DUO DISC 4-8 66
EPIC 5-10 61
KING 5-10 60
SHOUT 4-6 68

TORRANCE, Johnny: see TORRENCE, Johnny

TORRANCE, Richard *LP '75*
(With Eureka)
Singles: 7-inch
CAPITOL 3-5 77-79
SHELTER 3-5 75
LPs: 10/12-inch
CAPITOL 5-10 77
SHELTER 5-10 74-75

TORREES
Singles: 7-inch
ICL (114 "Didn't You Know") 25-40 60s

TORRELLS
Singles: 7-inch
SOMA (1186 "Lost Love') 25-35 63

TORRENCE, Johnny
(With the Jewels; Johnny Torrance)
Singles: 78 rpm
IMPERIAL (5230 "Sad Day") 25-50 53
R&B (1306 "Rosalie") 50-100 54
Singles: 7-inch
IMPERIAL (5230 "Sad Day") 100-200 53
IMPERIAL (5897 "Rat Race") 10-20 62
R&B (1306 "Rosalie") 200-300 54
Also see JEWELS

TORRENCE, Lionel
Singles: 7-inch
EXCELLO (2218 "Flim Flam") 8-10 62
ZYNN (1008 "Rockin' Jole Blon") ... 25-45 59
ZYNN (1023 "Rooty Tooty") 15-25 59

TORRES: see TORRIES

TORRENT, Shay
Singles: 7-inch
HEARTBEAT (1 "Rock a-Boogie") 15-25 59

TORRES, Jim, & Sidemen
Singles: 7-inch
ALLIED (6341 "Wheels") 10-20 61
(Canadian.)

TORRES, Liz
Singles: 7-inch
RCA 3-5 75-76

TORRIE, Bill
Singles: 7-inch
ABC-PAR 5-10 61
ALTON 10-20 60

TORRIES
(Torres)
Singles: 7-inch
IGL 10-20 60s
SOMA 10-20 60s

TORROS, El: see EL TORROS

TORTILLA, Pete
Singles: 7-inch
IMPERIAL (5502 "Corrido Rock") ... 15-25 58

TOSH, Peter *LP '76*
Singles: 12-inch
EMI AMERICA 4-6 83
Singles: 7-inch
COLUMBIA 3-5 76-77
EMI AMERICA 3-5 81-84
ROLLING STONES 3-5 78-79
Picture Sleeves
ROLLINS STONES 3-6 78
EPs: 7-inch
COLUMBIA 4-8 76
(Promotional issue only.)
LPs: 10/12-inch
COLUMBIA 5-10 76-77
EMI AMERICA 5-8 81-84
ROLLING STONES 5-10 79

TOSH, Peter, & Mick Jagger
Singles: 7-inch
ROLLING STONES (19308 "Don't Look Back") 4-6 78
(With "Rolling Stones" at top of label.)
ROLLING STONES (19308 "Don't Look Back") 3-5 78
(Without "Rolling Stones" at top of label.)
Promotional Singles
ROLLING STONES (130 "Don't Look Back") 10-20 78
ROLLING STONES (7500 "Don't Look Back") 5-10 78
LPs: 10/12-inch
ROLLING STONES 5-10 78
Also see JAGGER, Mick
Also see MARLEY, Bob, & Wailers

TOTAL COELO *P&R/D&D '83*
Singles: 12-inch
CHRYSALIS 4-6 83
Singles: 7-inch
CHRYSALIS 3-4 83
Picture Sleeves
CHRYSALIS 3-5 83

TOTAL CONTRAST *R&B/D&D '85*
Singles: 12-inch
LONDON 4-6 85-86
Singles: 7-inch
LONDON 3-4 85-88
LPs: 10/12-inch
LONDON 5-8 86

TOTAL ECLIPSE
LPs: 10/12-inch
IMPERIAL 10-15 67

TOTO *P&R/LP '78*
(With the Vienna Symphony Orchestra; with Jean-Michel Byron)
Singles: 12-inch
COLUMBIA 4-8 79-85
Singles: 10-inch
COLUMBIA (168065 "Gift with the Golden Gun"/"Goodbye Elenore") 5-10 81
(Two-discs, songs from *Turn Back*.)
Picture Disc Singles
COLUMBIA (6784 "Hold the Line") 15-25 78
(Picture disc. Has same picture on both sides. Includes card insert autographed by band member.)
COLUMBIA (ZSS-165008 "Hold the Line") 10-15 78
(Licorice Pizza logo picture disc.)
COLUMBIA (ZSS-165008 "Hold the Line") 15-20 78
(KRBE logo picture disc.)
COLUMBIA (ZSS-165009"Hold the Line") 15-20 78
(Roxy Invitation picture disc.)
COLUMBIA (ZSS-165009 "Hold the Line") 15-20 78
(Licorice Pizza or Wherehouse logo picture disc.)
COLUMBIA (165 792 "Georgy Porgy") 25-30 79
(Octagon picture disc. Promotional issue only.)
COLUMBIA (166 516/17 "Hydra") 80-100 79
(Square picture disc. Promotional issue only. 100 made. Includes folder. Some have KORL Channel 65 logo.)
COLUMBIA (166 518/19 "St. George and the Dragon") 80-100 80
(Square picture disc. Promotional issue only.)
COLUMBIA (169-156/109 "Africa"/"We Made It") 15-20 82
(Africa-shaped picture disc. Promotional issue only.)
COLUMBIA (169-156/157 "Africa"/"Good for You") 15-20 82
(Africa-shaped picture disc. Promotional issue only.)
COLUMBIA (8C8-38685 "Africa"/ "Rosanna") 15-20 82
(Africa-shaped picture disc.)
Singles: 7-inch
COLUMBIA 3-5 78-88
Picture Sleeves
COLUMBIA 3-6 82-88
LPs: 10/12-inch
COLUMBIA (30000 series) 5-10 78-86
(Black viny—no picture discs.)
COLUMBIA (9C9-39911 "Isolation") 12-18 84
(Picture disc.)
COLUMBIA (PJC-35317 "Toto") 25-35 79
(Picture disc. Same value for promotional issue. Add $10 if with die-cut cover.)
COLUMBIA (37928 "Toto IV") 20-30 82
(Picture disc. Promotional issue only.)
COLUMBIA (37928 "Toto IV") 25-35 82
(Picture disc. Promotional issue only with *Strawberries*, with WBCN logo.)
COLUMBIA (37928 "Toto IV") 30-40 82
(Picture disc. Promotional issue only, with "Turtles Annual Getaway" logo.)
COLUMBIA (PD-36813 "Turn Back") 35-45 79
(Picture disc. Promotional issue only. Includes calendar insert. 400 made.)
COLUMBIA (47728 "Toto IV") 10-15 83
(Half-speed mastered.)
MFLS (250 "Toto IV") 15-25
POLYDOR 5-8 84
Members: Steve Porcaro; David Paich; Steve Lukather; David Hungate; Jeffrey Porcaro; Bobby Kimball.
Also see FAR CORPORATION
Also see VOICES OF AMERICA / U.S.A. for Africa

TOTTY
LPs: 10/12-inch
OUR FIRST RECORD 5-10 80-81

TOUCH
Singles: 7-inch
MAINLINE ("Light My Fire") 100-200 69
(Selection number not known.)
MAINLINE ("Stormy Monday Blues") 100-200 69
(Selection number not known.)
LPs: 10/12-inch
MAINLINE (2001 "Street Suite") 2000-3000 69
(Reportedly 100 made.)
Members: Ray Stone; Jerry Schulte.

TOUCH *R&B '77*
Singles: 7-inch
ATCO 3-5 80-81
BRUNSWICK 3-5 77
COLISEUM 4-6 69
LECASVER 5-8 69
PUBLIC (103 "No Shame") 5-10 60s
LPs: 10/12-inch
ATCO 5-10 80
COLISEUM (51004 "20/20 Sound") 15-20 68
Members: Don Gallucci; Jeff Hawks; Joe Newman; Bruce Hauser; John Bordonaro.
Also see DON & GOODTIMES

TOUCH *R&B '87*
Singles: 7-inch
SUPERTRONICS 3-4 87
Member: Eric McCaine.
Also see ENTOUCH

TOUCH OF CLASS *R&B '75*
Singles: 12-inch
NEXT PLATINUM 4-6 84
Singles: 7-inch
ATLANTIC 3-5 82
MIDLAND INT'L 3-5 75-77
ROADSHOW 3-5 79-84
LPs: 10/12-inch
MIDLAND INT'L 5-10 76
ROADSHOW 5-10 79

TOUCH OF COUNTRY *C&W '88*
Singles: 7-inch
OL 3-4 88-89

TOUCHABLES
Singles: 7-inch
ROULETTE 5-10 60

TOUCHSTONE
Singles: 7-inch
SOUND MACHINE (10051 "Walk Out in the Rain") 8-12 68

TOUCHSTONE
Singles: 7-inch
COULEE (131 "Sweet 'N Tender") 10-15 69
TRANSACTION (708 "The Show") 10-15 69
Picture Sleeves
COULEE (131 "Sweet 'N Tender") 10-20 69
Members: Janet Evans; Tom Schmidt; Dave Schwandt; Bill Menke; George Swan.

TOUCHSTONE
Singles: 7-inch
U.A. 4-8 72
LPs: 10/12-inch
U.A. (5563 "Tarot") 15-20 72

TOUCHSTONE, Joanne
Singles: 7-inch
SOUND STAGE 7 .... 4-8 64-65

TOUPS, Wayne *LP '89*
(With Zydecajun)
LPs: 10/12-inch
MERCURY 5-8 89

TOURISTS *P&R '80*
Singles: 7-inch
EPIC 3-5 80
LPs: 10/12-inch
EPIC 5-10 81
Members: Annie Lennox; David Stewart; Ed Chin; Pete Coombes; Jim Toomey.
Also see EURYTHMICS

TOUSSAINT, Allen
(Al Tousan)
Singles: 7-inch
ALON (9021 "Go Back Home") 8-12 65
BELL (782 "Tequila") 5-8 68
CAYENNE 5-10
RCA (7192 "Happy Times") 15-25 58
REPRISE (1334 "When the Party's Over") 3-5 75
SCEPTER (12317 "From a Whisper to a Scream") 3-6 71
SEVILLE (103 "Sweetie-Pie") 8-12 60
SEVILLE (110 "Naomi") 8-12 60
SEVILLE (113 "Blue Mood") 8-12 61
SEVILLE (124 "20 Years Later") 8-12 63
TIFFANY (9015 "From a Whisper to a Scream") 5-8 70
LPs: 10/12-inch
ART (26 "Live at La Fin") 15-25 60s
BANDY (70017 "Allen Toussaint Sings with Billy Fayard & the Stokes") 10-15 70s
RCA (1767 "The Wild Sounds of New Orleans") 150-200 58
REPRISE 10-15 72
SCEPTER 10-15 71
W.B. 5-10 78
Also see LENNEAR, Claudia
Also see STOKES
Also see YOUNG ONES

TOW-AWAY ZONE
Singles: 7-inch
EPIC 4-8 68

TOWER, Kenny
Singles: 7-inch
TOWER 4-8 65

TOWER OF POWER *LP '71*
Singles: 7-inch
COLUMBIA 3-5 76-78
SAN FRANCISCO 4-8 64-73
W.B. 4-8 72-75
EPs: 7-inch
SAN FRANCISCO (7-204 "East Bay Grease") 15-25 71
(Promotional issue only.)
LPs: 10/12-inch
COLUMBIA 5-10 76-79
SAN FRANCISCO (204 "East Bay Grease") 10-20 71
W.B. 8-15 72-76
Members: Greg Adams; Mic Gillette; Steve Kupka; Emilio Castillo; Lenny Pickett; Chester Thompson; Francis Prestia; Edward McGhee; Rufus Miller; Lenny Williams.
Also see LITTLE FEAT
Also see WILLIAMS, Lenny

TOWERS
Singles: 7-inch
STUART (427 "Sham-Rock") 15-25 58

TOWERS
Singles: 7-inch
ERA 5-10 63
Also see HUNTERS
Also see SCI-FI's
Also see SOUND OFFS

TOWERS, Bobby
Singles: 7-inch
STYLO (2108 "Gone Gone Dreams") 30-40 60

TOWLES, Fred
Singles: 7-inch
WAY OUT 4-8 68

TOWN, Chris
(With the Townsmen; Chris Town's Unit)
Singles: 7-inch
COTILLION 4-8 68-69
PORT 10-20 67

TOWN CRIERS
Singles: 7-inch
CINEMA (005 "I Think of You and Cry") 5-10
NACIO (100 "My Baby") 5-10 61

TOWN CRIERS
Singles: 7-inch
GET HIP 3-4 89

TOWN THREE
Singles: 7-inch
DE LUXE (6176 "Midnight Blues") 15-25 58
Member: Wes Voight.
Also see VOIGHT, Wes

TOWNES, Carol Lynn *P&R/R&B/D&D '84*
Singles: 12-inch
POLYDOR 4-6 84-85

Singles: 7-inch
POLYDOR ... 3-4 84-85
LPs: 10/12-inch
POLYDOR ... 5-8 84

TOWNES, Jerry
Singles: 7-inch
PENNY ... 8-12

TOWNLEY, John
Singles: 7-inch
CAPITOL ... 3-5 80

TOWNLEY, John, & Apostolic Family
Singles: 7-inch
VANGUARD ... 4-8 69
Also see FAMILY of APOSTOLIC

TOWNS, Chris, & Townsmen
Singles: 7-inch
COTILLION ... 8-15 68-69

TOWNS, Eddie R&B '86
(ET)
Singles: 12-inch
TOTAL EXPERIENCE ... 4-6 86
Singles: 7-inch
TOTAL EXPERIENCE ... 3-4 86
LPs: 10/12-inch
TOTAL EXPERIENCE ... 5-8 86

TOWNS, Ned
Singles: 7-inch
ATLANTIC (2343 "B-I-n-g-o") ... 5-10 66
SKILLET (3609 "I Just Can't Let You Go") ... 10-15 60s

TOWNSEND, Bob
Singles: 7-inch
MINARET (106 "Christmas Message from Space") ... 5-10 62

TOWNSEND, Ed P&R/R&B '58
Singles: 7-inch
ALADDIN (3373 "Love Never Dies") ... 15-25 57
CAPITOL (3926 "For Your Love") ... 10-20 58
CAPITOL (4048 "When I Grow Too Old to Dream") ... 10-20 58
CAPITOL (4104 "Richer Than I") ... 10-15 58
CAPITOL (4171 "Lover Come Back to Me") ... 10-15 59
CAPITOL (4240 "Hold On") ... 10-15 59
CAPITOL (4314 "Be My Love") ... 10-15 59
CAPITOL STARLINE (3926 "For Your Love") ... 4-8 63
CHALLENGE (9118 "Ed Townsend's Boogie Woogie") ... 8-12 61
CHALLENGE (9129 "And Then Came Love") ... 10-15 61
CHALLENGE (9144 "I Love to Hear That Beat") ... 8-12 62
DYNASTY (643 "I Can't Leave You Alone") ... 10-15 60
GLO-TOWN (1008 "Don't Lead Me On") ... 5-8 66
KT (502 "Get Myself Together") ... 5-10 60s
LIBERTY (55516 "Down Home") ... 8-12 62
LIBERTY (55517 "Tell Her") ... 8-12 62
LIBERTY (55542 "There's No End") ... 10-15 63
MGM ... 5-10 67
MAXX (325 "I Love You") ... 10-20 64
POLYDOR ... 4-6 70
W.B. (5174 "I Love Everything About You") ... 10-20 60
W.B. (5200 "Dream World") ... 10-15 61
EPs: 7-inch
CAPITOL (985 "New in Town") ... 20-40 58
(Promotional issue only.)
CAPITOL (1091 "Ed Townsend") ... 20-40 58
LPs: 10/12-inch
CAPITOL (1140 "New in Town") ... 40-60 59
CAPITOL (1214 "Glad to Be Here") ... 40-60 59
CURTOM ... 8-12 76

TOWNSEND, Frank
Singles: 7-inch
SEECO ... 5-10 59

TOWNSEND, Henry
Singles: 78 rpm
COLUMBIA (14491 "Mistreated Blues") ... 100-200 29
LPs: 10/12-inch
PRESTIGE BLUESVILLE ... 25-35 62

TOWNSEND, Henry, & Backwards Sam Firk
LPs: 10/12-inch
ADELPHI ... 8-10 74
Also see FIRK, Backwards Sam

TOWNSEND, Jerry
Singles: 7-inch
MASTER (1012 "Cold Cold Day") ... 15-25

TOWNSEND, Sherrell
Singles: 7-inch
GONE ... 8-12 62
LITTLE STAR ... 20-30 61
LUTE ... 15-25 61

TOWNSEND, Tony
LPs:10/12-inch
ADVENT ... 15-25

TOWNSENDS
Singles: 12-inch
PRIVATE I ... 4-6 84
Singles: 7-inch
MCA ... 3-4 84
PRIVATE I ... 3-4 84

TOWNSHEND, Pete LP '72
Singles: 7-inch
ATCO ... 3-5 80-85
Picture Sleeves
ATCO ... 3-5 85
LPs: 10/12-inch
ATCO ... 5-10 80-87
ATLANTIC ... 5-8 89
DECCA/TRACK ... 10-12 72
Also see ANGIE
Also see WHO

TOWNSHEND, Pete, & Ronnie Lane LP '77
Singles: 7-inch
MCA ... 3-5 77-78
LPs: 10/12-inch
MCA ... 8-10 77
Also see CLAPTON, Eric
Also see ENTWISTLE, John
Also see LANE, Ronnie
Also see TOWNSHEND, Pete
Also see WOOD, Ron, & Ronnie Lane

TOWNSHEND, Simon LP '83
Singles: 12-inch
POLYDOR (357 "Moving Target") ... 5-10 85
(Clear vinyl. Promotional issue only.)
Singles: 7-inch
21 ... 3-4 83
LPs: 10/12-inch
21 ... 5-8 83

TOWNSMEN
Singles: 7-inch
VANITY ... 5-10 60
W.B. ... 4-8 61

TOWNSMEN
Singles: 7-inch
COLUMBIA ... 4-8 65
HERALD ... 10-15 63
JOEY ... 10-20 63

TOWNSMEN / Louie Lymon
Singles: 7-inch
P.J. (1340 "I Can't Go") ... 150-250 63
Also see LYMON, Lewis, & Teenchords
Also see TOWNSMEN

TOWNSMEN
LP: 10/12-inch
COULEE (1009 "I Believe") ... 10-15 70s
Also see JERRY & SILVERTONES

TOY DOLLS P&R '62
Singles: 7-inch
ERA ... 5-10 62

TOY FACTORY
Singles: 7-inch
JUBILEE ... 4-8 69
Member: Eric Olson.
Also see NEXT FIVE

TOY FACTORY
Singles: 7-inch
AVCO EMBASSY ... 4-8 70
LPs: 10/12-inch
AVCO EMBASSY (33013 "Toy Factory") ... 10-15 70

TOY MATINEE LP '91
LPs: 10/12-inch
REPRISE ... 5-8 90

TOYS P&R/R&B '65
Singles: 7-inch
ABC ... 3-5 73
DYNO VOICE ... 4-8 65-66
ERIC ... 3-4 70s
GUSTO ... 3-4 80s
MUSICOR ... 4-8 68
PHILIPS ... 4-8 67
VIRGO ... 3-5 72
LPs: 10/12-inch
DYNO VOICE (9002 "A Lover's Concerto"/"Attack") ... 25-35 66
(Monaural.)
DYNO VOICE (9002-S "A Lover's Concerto"/"Attack") ... 20-30 66
(Stereo.)
SECTET ... 5-10 81
Members: Barbara Harris; June Montiero; Barbara Parritt.

TOYS
Singles: 7-inch
KAY BROTHERS ... 3-6 83
(Promotional issue only.)

T'PAU P&R/LP '87
Singles: 7-inch
VIRGIN ... 3-4 87
Picture Sleeves
VIRGIN ... 3-4 87
LPs: 10/12-inch
VIRGIN ... 5-8 87

TRACE
LPs: 10/12-inch
SIRE ... 8-10 74-75

TRACERS
Singles: 7-inch
SOLLY (928 "She Said Yeah") ... 10-20 66
(Label name misspelled.)
SULLY (928 "She Said Yeah") ... 10-20 66
(Label name correct.)
Also see STONES

TRACES
Singles: 7-inch
LAURIE ... 5-10 69
Member: Sal Corrente.
Also see CORRENTE, Sal

TRACEY, Bill: see TRACY, Bill

TRACEY, Ellen
Singles: 7-inch
HARMON ... 4-8 62

TRACEY, Lee
Singles: 7-inch
MR. MAESTRO ... 4-8 65

TRACEY, Norma
Singles: 7-inch
DAY DELL ... 4-8 64-65

TRACEY, Wreg
Singles: 7-inch
ANNA (1105 "All I Want Is You") ... 15-25 59
ANNA (1126 "Take Me Back") ... 15-25 60

TRACEY TWINS
Singles: 7-inch
EAST WEST (108 "Heartbreak Hill") ... 10-20 58
RESERVE (104 "Every Little Now & Then") ... 10-15
RESERVE (114 "Do You Ever Think of Me") ... 10-15

TRACIE
Singles: 12-inch
A&M ... 4-6 85
Singles: 7-inch
A&M ... 3-4 85
LPs: 10/12-inch
A&M ... 5-8 85

TRACKER
Singles: 7-inch
ELEKTRA ... 3-5 82
LPs: 10/12-inch
ELEKTRA ... 5-10 82

TRACKERS
Singles: 7-inch
LANDA (101 "You Are My World") ... 15-25 66
WHIP ... 10-20 65

TRACKS
Singles: 7-inch
CAPITOL ... 3-5 72
LPs: 10/12-inch
CAPITOL ... 8-10 72

TRACY, Bill
(Billy Tracy; Bill Tracey)
Singles: 78 rpm
RPM (489 "Kiss at Daybreak") ... 20-30 57
Singles: 7-inch
DEL-FI ... 10-15 59
DOT (15797 "One Chance") ... 25-50 58
RPM (489 "Kiss At Daybreak") ... 20-30 57
RADIANT ... 5-10 61
STARFIRE ... 5-10

TRACY, Gloria
Singles: 7-inch
HBR ... 4-8 66
Picture Sleeves
HBR ... 5-10 66

TRACY, Jeanie D&D '84
(Jeanne Tracy)
Singles: 12-inch
MEGATONE ... 4-6 84-85
Singles: 7-inch
FANTASY ... 3-5 83
SMOGSVILLE ... 4-8 67

TRACY, Wendell
Singles: 7-inch
CONCERT-DISC ... 4-6
RESERVE ... 8-12

TRADE WINDS P&R '65
Singles: 7-inch
ERIC ... 3-5 70s
KAMA SUTRA (212 "Mind Excursion") ... 15-20 66
KAMA SUTRA (218 "Catch Me in the Meadow") ... 10-15 66
KAMA SUTRA (234 "Mind Excursion") ... 8-12 67
RED BIRD (020 "New York's a Lonely Town") ... 8-12 65
RED BIRD (028 "The Girl from Greenwich Village") ... 10-20 65
RED BIRD (033 "Summertime Girl") ... 40-60 65
LPs: 10/12-inch
KAMA SUTRA ... 25-35 67
Members: Pete Anders; Vinnie Poncia.
Also see ANDERS & PONCIA

TRADEMARKS
Singles: 7-inch
JUBAL (100 "Baha-Ree-Ba") ... 10-20 63

TRADEMARKS
Singles: 7-inch
MOONGLOW ... 5-10 64

TRADEMARKS
Singles: 7-inch
PALMER (5018 "If I Was Gone") ... 10-20 67

TRADER HORNE
LPs: 10/12-inch
JANUS ... 10-12 70

TRADER - PRICE C&W '89
Singles: 7-inch
UNIVERSAL ... 3-4 89

TRADEWINDS P&R '59
Singles: 7-inch
RCA (7511 "Twins") ... 8-12 59
RCA (7553 "Furry Murray") ... 8-12 59
Members: Ralph Rizzoll; Angel Cifelli; Sal Capriglione; Phil Mehill.

TRADEWINDS
Singles: 7-inch
UNITED SOUTHERN ... 4-8 64

TRADEWINDS
Singles: 7-inch
DAWN CORY (1005 "Gotcha") ... 20-30 64

TRADEWINDS
Singles: 7-inch
BRANDYWINE (1001 "Jump") ... 8-12
BRANDYWINE (1004 "Raw-Hide") ... 8-12
DAN-TONE (1001 "Congo Beat") ... 8-12
TRIUMPH (301 "Strange") ... 8-12

TRADITIONS
Singles: 7-inch
BELL (616 "Forever and Always") ... 8-12 65

TRADITIONS / Ditalians
SAXONY (2004 "Forever and Always"/"I Gotta Go") ... 4-6 96
Also see DITALIANS
Also see TRADITIONS

TRADITIONS
Singles: 7-inch
A-BET ... 3-6 69
BELL ... 4-8 65

TRAFALGAR SQUARE
Singles: 7-inch
USA (890 "Till the End of the Day") ... 15-25 67
Members: Tim Eifler; Steve Grim; John Marselli.

TRAFFIC P&R '67
(Traffic Etc.)
Singles: 7-inch
ASYLUM ... 3-5 74
ISLAND ... 3-5 72-73
U.A. ... 5-10 67-72
Picture Sleeves
U.A. ... 8-10 67
LPs: 10/12-inch
ASYLUM ... 10-15 74
ISLAND (Except 9000 series) ... 5-8 83
ISLAND (9000 series) ... 10-15 71-75
MFSL (209 "The Low Spark of High Heeled Boys") ... 20-30 94
(Half-speed mastered.)
U.A. ... 10-20 68-75
Members: Jim Capaldi; Dave Mason; Steve Winwood; Chris Wood.
Also see CAN
Also see CAPALDI, Jim
Also see MASON, Dave
Also see WINWOOD, Steve

TRAGICALLY HIP LP '90
LPs: 10/12-inch
MCA ... 5-8 90

TRAIL, Buck
Singles: 7-inch
ART (103 "The Knocked Out Joint on Mars") ... 5-10
TRAIL (100 "Honky Tonk on 2nd Street") ... 150-250
TRAIL (103 "Knocked Out Joint on Mars") ... 200-300
TRAIL (105 "Chattanooga Drummer Man") ... 50-100

TRAIL BLAZERS
Singles: 7-inch
ABC-PAR ... 5-10 61

TRAILBLAZERS
Singles: 7-inch
WATSON (500 "Grandpa's Rock") ... 150-200

TRAIL BROTHERS
Singles: 7-inch
LITTLE CROW ... 4-8 60s

TRAIN
Singles: 7-inch
FULLTONE (1002 "I Want Sunshine") ... 60-80 60s

TRAIN
LPs: 10/12-inch
VANGUARD ... 10-15 70

TRAINS
Singles: 7-inch
SWAN ... 4-8 64-65

TRAITS P&R '66
Singles: 7-inch
ASCOT (2108 "Linda Lou") ... 10-20 62
GARRISON (3007 "Too Good to Be True") ... 10-20 60s
PACEMAKER ... 10-15 67
RENNER (221 "Linda Lou") ... 15-25 62
RENNER (229 "Got My Mojo Working") ... 10-20 62
(Black vinyl.)
RENNER (229 "Got My Mojo Working") ... 20-30 62
(Colored vinyl. Promotional issue only.)
SCEPTER (12169 "Harlem Shuffle") ... 5-8 66
TNT (164 "Don't Be Blue") ... 15-25 59
TNT (175 "Live It Up") ... 15-25 59
TNT (177 "My Baby's Fine") ... 15-25 60
UNIVERSAL ... 10-15 66
LPs: 10/12-inch
TNT (101 "Roy Head and the Traits") ... 100-150 65
Member: Roy Head.
Also see HEAD, Roy

TRAITS
Singles: 7-inch
CONTACT (4058 "Some Day, Some Way") ... 25-30
QUEEN'S CITY (101 "Nobody Loves the Hulk") ... 10-20 68

TRAKSTOD
Singles: 7-inch
PHILIPS ... 4-6 70

TRAMA
Singles: 12-inch
SPECTOR ... 4-6
Singles: 7-inch
SPECTOR ... 3-5

TRAMAINE R&B/D&D '85
(Tramaine Hawkins)
Singles: 12-inch
A&M ... 4-6 85-86
Singles: 7-inch
A&M ... 3-4 85-87
LPs: 10/12-inch
A&M ... 5-8 86

TRAMLINE
LPs: 10/12-inch
A&M ... 10-15 69

TRAMMELL, Bobby Lee C&W '72
Singles: 7-inch
ABC-PAR (9890 "Shirley Lee") ... 50-75 58
ALLEY ... 15-25 62-63
ATLANTA ... 15-25 62
ATLANTIC ... 5-10 66
CAPITOL (3718 "Love") ... 4-6 73
CAPITOL (3801 "You Mostest Girl") ... 5-8 73
CONFEDERATE (125 "Shake Me Baby") ... 30-40
COUNTRY ... 4-8 66
FABOR (127 "You Mostest Girl") ... 5-10 64
FABOR (4038 "Shirley Lee") ... 75-125 57
HOT (101 "Shimmy Lou") ... 20-30 59
HOT (102 "Betty Jean") ... 20-30 59
RADIO (102 "You Mostest Girl") ... 30-40 58
RADIO (114 "My Susie Jane") ... 30-40 58
SANTO ... 10-20
SIMS ... 5-10 63-65
SKYLA (1107 "You Mostest Girl") ... 10-20 61
(Also issued as by Bob Lee.)
SOUNCOT ... 3-5 71-72
VADEN (304 "Hi-O Silver") ... 15-25 60
WARRIOR (1554 "Woe Is Me") ... 50-75 59
LPs: 10/12-inch
ATLANTA (1503 "Arkansas Twist") ... 75-100 62
SOUNCOT ... 10-20 71-72
Also see LEE, Bob
Also see ROE, Tommy / Bobby Lee Trammell

TRAMMELL, Bobby Lee, & Jean Steakley
Singles: 7-inch
SOUNCOT ... 3-5 72
Also see TRAMMELL, Bobby Lee

TRAMMPS P&R/R&B '72
(Tramps)
Singles: 7-inch
ATLANTIC ... 3-5 75-80
BUDDAH ... 4-8 72-76
ERIC ... 3-5 78
GOLDEN FLEECE ... 3-6 73-75
Picture Sleeves
ATLANTIC (3389 "Disco Inferno") ... 3-6 77
LPs: 10/12-inch
ATLANTIC ... 5-10 76-80
BUDDAH ... 5-10 75
GOLDEN FLEECE ... 5-10 75
PHILADELPHIA INT'L ... 5-10 77
Also see B-H-Y
Also see EXCEPTIONS
Also see MFSB

TRAMPS
Singles: 7-inch
ARVEE (548 "Ride On") ... 10-15 59
ARVEE (570 "Your Love") ... 20-30 59

TRAMPS
Singles: 7-inch
KING (5572 "Tomahawk") ... 8-10 61

TRAMPS R&B '83
Singles: 7-inch
VENTURE ... 3-5 83

TRANE
Singles: 7-inch
CREATIVE TALENT ... 3-5

TRANELLS
Singles: 7-inch
CHELTEN (090 "Come on and Tell Me") ... 50-75 56

TRANQUILITY
Singles: 7-inch
EPIC ... 3-5 72
LPs: 10/12-inch
EPIC ... 8-10 72

TRANQUILITY BASE
Singles: 7-inch
RCA ... 3-5 70

TRANQUILS
Singles: 7-inch
HAMILTON (50005 "You're Such a Much") ... 15-25 58

TRANSACTIONS
Singles: 7-inch
BRC (3294 "Spooky")..........10-20 67

TRANS-ATLANTIC RAILROAD
Singles: 7-inch
PHOENIX..........4-8 68

TRANSATLANTIC WINKHAM CHICKEN #5
Singles: 7-inch
SILVERADO..........10-15 60s

TRANS-ATLANTIC SUBWAY
Singles: 7-inch
LIGHTFOOT (100,333 "Servent of the People")..........10-20 68

TRANSATLANTICS
Singles: 7-inch
JUBILEE..........4-8 65-66

TRANSFORMER
LPs: 10/12-inch
ELEKTRA..........10-15 68
Members: Joe Livolsi; Mal Mackenzie; John Nicholls; Devi Klate; David Stoughton; Peter Chapman; Steve Tanzer.

TRANSIENTS
LPs: 10/12-inch
HORIZON..........15-25 63
Member: Billy Strange.
Also see STRANGE, Billy

TRAN-SISTERS
Singles: 7-inch
IMPERIAL..........4-8 63
PICKWICK CITY..........5-10 60s

TRANSLATOR
Singles: 12-inch
COLUMBIA..........4-6 82
Singles: 7-inch
COLUMBIA..........3-5 82
LPs: 10/12-inch
COLUMBIA..........5-10 82

TRANSPLANT
Singles: 7-inch
LEJAC..........15-25 60s

TRANSVISION VAMP P&R/LP '88
Singles: 7-inch
UNI..........3-4 88
Picture Sleeves
UNI..........3-4 88
LPs: 10/12-inch
UNI..........5-8 88

TRANS-X P&R '86
Singles: 12-inch
ATCO..........4-6 86
MIRAGE..........4-6 86
Singles: 7-inch
ATCO..........3-4 86

TRANTHAM, Carl
Singles: 7-inch
STARDAY (361 "Deedle Deedle Dum")..........30-50 58

TRAPE, Mary Jo
Singles: 7-inch
SHERRY..........5-10 60

TRAPEZE LP '74
Singles: 7-inch
PAID..........3-5 81
THRESHOLD..........4-8 72
W.B...........3-5 74-75
LPs: 10/12-inch
PAID..........5-10 81
POLYDOR ("Medusa")..........50-100 71
(Selection number not known.)
SHARK..........8-10
THRESHOLD (2 "Trapeze")..........25-50 71
THRESHOLD (4 "Medusa")..........75-100 71
THRESHOLD (8 "You Are the Music, We're Just the Band")..........25-50 72
THRESHOLD (11 "Final Swing")..........25-50 72
W.B...........8-10 74-75
Also see DEEP PURPLE

TRAPP, Sandy
Singles: 7-inch
PARKWAY..........4-8 62

TRAPPER
Singles: 7-inch
BOSSTOWN (1001 "It's All in Your Head")..........4-6 81
Picture Sleeves
BOSSTOWN (1001 "It's All in Your Head")..........4-6 81

TRASH
Singles: 7-inch
APPLE (1804 "Road to Nowhere")..........75-100 69
APPLE (1811 "Golden Slumbers") 15-20 69
APPLE (4671 "Road to Nowhere") 60-80 69
(Promotional issue only.)

TRASH CAN SINATRAS LP '91
LPs: 10/12-inch
LONDON..........5-8 91

TRASH SITE BLUES BAND
Singles: 7-inch
SQUID..........3-4 85

TRASHMEN P&R '63
Singles: 7-inch
APEX (Except 76925)..........15-25 63-65
APEX (76925 "New Generation")..........25-35 64
ARGO (5516 "Bird '65")..........50-75 65
BEAR..........10-20 66
ERA..........3-5 72
ERIC..........3-4 70s
GARRETT..........10-20 63-64
LANA..........3-6 60s
METROBEAT..........12-18 68
SOMA..........4-8
TRIBE (8315 "Same Lines")..........25-35 66
Picture Sleeves
GARRETT (4012 "Whoa Dad")..........60-80 64
GARRETT (4013 "Real Live Doll")..........100-125 64
LPs: 10/12-inch
SOMA/GARRETT (GA-200 "Surfin' Bird")..........50-75 64
(Monaural.)
SOMA/GARRETT (GAS-200 "Surfin' Bird")..........100-150 64
(Stereo.)
SUNDAZED..........5-10 90s
Members: Tony Andreason; Bob Reed; Dal Winslow; Steve Wahrer; Gary Nielsen.
Also see STRING KINGS
Also see THAXTER, Jim, & Travelers

TRASHMEN / Castaways
Singles: 7-inch
SOMA..........4-6 60s
Also see TRASHMEN

TRASK, Diana C&W '68
Singles: 7-inch
ABC/DOT..........3-5 74-75
COLUMBIA..........5-8 61-62
DIAL..........4-8 68
DOT..........3-6 68-75
KARI..........3-4 81
ROULETTE..........10-15 59
LPs: 10/12-inch
ABC..........5-10 76-77
ABC/DOT..........6-12 74-75
COLUMBIA..........15-25 61
DOT..........8-15 69-73

TRASS, Wylie
Singles: 7-inch
ABC..........4-6 69

TRAVEL AGENCY
Singles: 7-inch
HILLPORT (1002 "Until the Day")..........8-12
TANQUERAY (20102 "Time")..........10-20 67
VIVA (637 "What's a Man")..........8-12 69
ZORDAN (107 "Jailbait")..........10-20
LPs: 10/12-inch
VIVA (36017 "Travel Agency")..........15-25 68
Members: Frank Davis.
Also see FEVER TREE

TRAVELAIRES
Singles: 7-inch
ARCADE..........4-6 68

TRAVELERS
Singles: 78 rpm
OKEH..........5-10 53
Singles: 7-inch
OKEH..........10-15 53

TRAVELERS
(Frank Lopez & Travelers)
Singles: 78 rpm
ATLAS (1086 "Betty Jean")..........50-100 57
Singles: 7-inch
ATLAS (1086 "Betty Jean")..........50-100 57
Member: Frank Lopez.

TRAVELERS
Singles: 7-inch
ANDEX (2011 "I'll Be Home for Christmas")..........25-35 57
ANDEX (4006 "Why")..........25-35 58
ANDEX (4012 "He's Got the Whole World in His Hands")..........15-25 58
ANDEX (4033 "I Go for You")..........25-35 58

TRAVELERS
Singles: 7-inch
ABC-PAR..........10-15 60
DECCA..........10-15 61
DON RAY..........8-12 62
GASS (1000 "In the Pines")..........10-20 63
KNIGHT..........5-10 63-64
MG..........10-15 59
MAGIC LAMP..........5-10 64
PRINCESS (52 "Spanish Moon")..........15-25 63
VAULT..........5-10 64
YELLOW SAND..........8-12 63-65
Member: Ron Story.
Also see RIC-A-SHAYS

TRAVELERS
("Vocal By Tom Morgan")
Singles: 7-inch
MIDWEST (4004 "Keep Your Money")..........8-10
Member: Tom Morgan.

TRAVELERS IV
Singles: 7-inch
WORLD-WIDE (8511 "Too Young")..........75-125 62

TRAVELERS IV
Singles: 7-inch
ROX..........5-10 60s

TRAVELERS THREE
(Travelers 3)
Singles: 12-inch
CAPITOL..........3-6 64
LPs: 10/12-inch
CAPITOL..........8-15 65
ELEKTRA..........15-25 62
Members: Dick Shirley; Charlie Oyama; Pete Apo.

TRAVELIN' BAND
Singles: 7-inch
T.B...........5-8
LPs:10/12-inch
LITTLE CROW..........8-12 72

TRAVELING SALESMEN
Singles: 7-inch
RCA..........10-15 67

TRAVELING WILBURYS P&R/LP '88
Singles: 7-inch
WILBURY (27732 "Handle with Care")..........4-8 88
(Commercial issue.)
WILBURY (27732 "Handle with Care")..........10-20 88
(Promotional issue.)
WILBURY (27637 "End of the Line")..........10-15 88
(Commercial issue.)
WILBURY (27637 "End of the Line")..........10-20 88
(Promotional issue.)
Picture Sleeves
WILBURY (27732 "Handle with Care")..........4-8 88
WILBURY (27637 "End of the Line")..........10-20 88
LPs: 10/12-inch
WILBURY..........8-15 88-90
Members: George Harrison; Bob Dylan; Roy Orbison; Tom Petty; Jeff Lynne.
Also see DYLAN, Bob
Also see HARRISON, George
Also see LYNNE, Jeff
Also see ORBISON, Roy
Also see PETTY, Tom, & Heartbreakers

TRAVELLERS
Singles: 7-inch
IMAGE..........4-8 61

TRA-VELLES
Singles: 7-inch
DEBONAIR (101 "Can't Got forThat")..........75-125

TRAVELLING MAGIC
Singles: 7-inch
DOT..........4-6 69

TRAVERS, Jesse
Singles: 7-inch
D'ARCY..........4-8 64

TRAVERS, Mary P&R/LP '71
Singles: 7-inch
CHRYSALIS..........3-5 78-79
W.B...........3-5 71-73
LPs: 10/12-inch
CHRYSALIS..........5-10 78
W.B...........6-12 71-74
Also see DENVER, John
Also see PETER, PAUL & MARY

TRAVERS, Pat LP '77
(Pat Travers Band; Black Pearl)
Singles: 7-inch
POLYDOR..........3-5 77-80
LPs: 10/12-inch
POLYDOR..........5-10 76-84

TRAVIS, Christopher
Singles: 7-inch
RCA..........3-6 69

TRAVIS, Chuck
Singles: 7-inch
ENERGY (105 "Gone Too Soon")..........5-10 75
ROUND UP..........5-10 71-76
Also see WANTED

TRAVIS, Danny
Singles: 7-inch
BENN-X (54 "Ever Since")..........200-250 62

TRAVIS, Dave
Singles: 7-inch
BAGDAD..........4-8 63
U.S.P...........4-8 66

TRAVIS, Diane
Singles: 7-inch
MUSTANG..........5-10 61

TRAVIS, Doug
Singles: 7-inch
NEWHALL..........4-8 67

TRAVIS, McKinley P&R/R&B '70
(With Art Freeman, Bobby Sanders & Bobby Sanders Singers)
Singles: 7-inch
MARINA (602 "Need Your Love")..........4-6 70s
(Remake of Soultown 13: *I Need Your Love.*)
PRIDE (2 "Baby, Is There Something on Your Mind")..........4-6 70
SOULTOWN (11 "Why Do You Have to Go")..........4-6 70s
SOULTOWN (13 "I Need Your Love")..........4-8 70s
Also see FREEMAN, Arthur
Also see SANDERS, Bobby

TRAVIS, Merle C&W/P&R '46
Singles: 78 rpm
CAPITOL..........4-10 46-57
CAPITOL (1100 thru 3100 series)..........5-15 50-55
CAPITOL (5600 series)..........4-6 66
EPs: 7-inch
CAPITOL..........10-20 56-57
LPs: 10/12-inch
CMH..........8-15 79-81
CAPITOL (T-650 "Guitar")..........50-80 56
CAPITOL (SM-650 "Guitar")..........5-10 75
CAPITOL (891 "Back Home")..........50-60 57
CAPITOL (1391 "Walkin' the Strings")..........50-60 60
CAPITOL (1664 "Travis")..........30-40 62
CAPITOL (1956 "Songs of the Coal Mine")..........50-60 57
CAPITOL (T/ST-2662 "Best of Merle Travis")..........15-25 67
CAPITOL (SM-2662 "Best of Merle Travis")..........5-10 75
CAPITOL (2938 "Strictly Guitar")..........20-30 69
PICKWICK/HILLTOP..........10-15 66
PREMIER..........5-8
SHASTA..........10-15
SPIN-O-RAMA..........8-12 60s
Also see RITTER, Tex / Merle Travis
Also see THOMPSON, Hank, & Merle Travis

TRAVIS, Merle, & Johnny Bond
LPs: 10/12-inch
CAPITOL..........10-20 69
Also see BOND, Johnny

TRAVIS, Merle, & Joe Maphis
LPs: 10/12-inch
CMH..........8-12
CAPITOL (T-2102 "Merle Travis & Joe Maphis, Two Great Guitars")..........40-50 64
(Monaural.)
CAPITOL (ST-2102 "Merle Travis & Joe Maphis, Two Great Guitars")..........50-60 64
(Stereo.)
CAPITOL (SM-2102 "Merle Travis & Joe Maphis, Two Great Guitars")..........5-10 78

TRAVIS, Merle, & Mac Wiseman
LPs: 10/12-inch
CMH..........8-12 82
Also see TRAVIS, Merle
Also see WISEMAN, Mac

TRAVIS, Randy C&W '85
(Randy Traywick)
Singles: 7-inch
W.B...........3-4 85-91
LPs: 10/12-inch
W.B...........5-8 85-91
Also see TRAYWICK, Randy
Also see WYNETTE, Tammy, & Randy Travis

TRAVIS, Randy, & George Jones C&W '90
Singles: 7-inch
W.B...........3-4 90

TRAVIS, Tony
Singles: 78 rpm
RCA..........5-10 55
Singles: 7-inch
RCA..........10-15 55
VERVE..........5-10 57

TRAVIS & BOB P&R/R&B '59
Singles: 7-inch
BARREL..........10-15 59
(Canadian.)
BIG TOP..........5-10 60
MERCURY..........5-10 61
SANDY (1017 "Tell Him No")..........10-15 59
(No "Distributed By Dot" on label.)
SANDY (1017 "Tell Him No"..........5-10 59
(Has "Distributed By Dot" on label)
SANDY (1019 thru 1029)..........8-12 59
Members: Travis Pritchett; Bob Weaver.

TRAVIS & PRENTISS
Singles: 7-inch
ARA..........4-6

TRAVOLTA, Joey P&R '78
Singles: 7-inch
CASABLANCA..........3-5 78-79
MILLENIUM..........3-5 78
Picture Sleeves
MILLENNIUM..........3-5 78
LPs: 10/12-inch
CASABLANCA..........5-10 78-79
MILLENNIUM..........5-10 78

TRAVOLTA, John P&R/LP '76
Singles: 7-inch
MIDLAND INT'L..........3-5 76-80
RCA..........3-5 77
RSO..........3-5 78-79
Picture Sleeves
MIDLAND INT'L (Except 10623)..........3-5 76-80
MIDLAND INT'L (10623 "Let Her In")..........4-8 76
RCA..........3-5 77
RSO..........3-5 78-79
LPs: 10/12-inch
MIDLAND INT'L..........5-10 76-77
MIDSONG INT'L..........5-10 78
Also see NEWTON-JOHN, Olivia, & John Travolta

TRAVOLTA, John / Sha Na Na
Singles: 7-inch
RSO..........3-5 78
Also see SHA NA NA
Also see TRAVOLTA, John

TRAX
Singles: 7-inch
POLYDOR..........3-5 77
LPs: 10/12-inch
POLYDOR..........5-10 77

TRAYLOR, Jack, & Steelwind
Singles: 7-inch
GRUNT..........4-8

TRAYLOR, Pearl
(With Chuck Thomas & His All Stars)
Singles: 78 rpm
OKEH (6822 "Come On Daddy")..........10-20 51
Singles: 7-inch
OKEH (6822 "Come On Daddy")..........25-50 51

TRAYNOR, Jay
Singles: 7-inch
ABC-PAR (10845 "Up and Over")..........20-30 66
ROARING (800 "Dusty Said Goodbye")..........10-15 67
Also see JAY
Also see JAY & AMERICANS

TRAYWICK, Randy C&W '79
Singles: 7-inch
PAULA (429 "Dreamin' ")..........8-12 78
PAULA (431 "She's My Woman")..........5-10 78
Also see TRAVIS, Randy

TREACHEROUS THREE
Singles: 12-inch
SUGAR HILL..........4-6 82
Also see KOOL MOE DEE

TREADWAY, Dicky
Singles: 7-inch
T.S.M...........4-8 67

TREADWAY, Dicky, & Mark Scott
Singles: 7-inch
T.S.M...........4-8 68
Also see TREADWAY, Dicky

TREADWELL, Irene
Singles: 78 rpm
JAY-DEE..........5-10 53
Singles: 7-inch
JAY-DEE..........10-15 53

TREADWELL, Margo
Singles: 7-inch
LENOX..........4-8 63

TREASURE
Singles: 7-inch
EPIC..........3-5 78
LPs: 10/12-inch
EPIC..........8-10 77
Member: Felix Cavaliere.
Also see CAVALIERE, Felix

TREASURERS
Singles: 7-inch
CROWN (005 "I Walk with an Angel")..........200-300 61

TREASURES
Singles: 7-inch
VALOR (47900 "Minor Chaos")..........50-75 64
(Black vinyl. 250 made.)
VALOR (47900 "Minor Chaos")..........75-125 64
(Colored vinyl. 250 made.)
Member: Paul M. Hubbard.

TREASURES
Singles: 7-inch
SHIRLEY (500 "Hold Me Tight")..........15-25 64
Members: Pete Anders; Vinnie Poncia.
Also see ANDERS & PONCIA

TREASURES R&B '76
Singles: 7-inch
EPIC..........3-5 77
MERCURY..........3-5 76
LPs: 10/12-inch
EPIC..........5-10 77

TREAT, Londa
Singles: 7-inch
CHAMPION (805 "We Can Make It")..........4-8 60s

TREAT HER RIGHT LP '88
LPs: 10/12-inch
RCA..........5-8 88

TREBLE CHORDS
Singles: 7-inch
DECCA (31015 "Teresa")..........40-60 59

TREBLE TONES
Singles: 7-inch
ATLAS..........5-10 60
SOUVENIR (1010 "Little Laurie")..........10-20 62

TREBLEMAKERS
Singles: 7-inch
SPARTIE (200 "Spartan Stomp")..........8-12

TREBUS, Bob, & Fender Benders
Singles: 7-inch
SOMA..........8-12 60s
Also see FENDERBENDERS

TREE
Singles: 7-inch
BARVIS (7010 "No Good Woman")..........15-25 67
LPs: 10/12-inch
GOAT FARM (580 "Tree")..........40-60 70
Member: Chris Roach.

TREE, Henry: see HENRY TREE

TREE STUMPS
(Tree-Mendous-Stumps)
Singles: 7-inch
RECORD (20013 "Listen to Love")..........15-25 66
Picture Sleeves
RECORD (20013 "Listen to Love")..........15-25 66
Member: Michael Stanley.
Also see SILK
Also see STANLEY, Michael, Band

TREE SWINGERS P&R '60
Singles: 7-inch
BIG TOP (3058 "Only Forever") ... 5-10 60
GUYDEN (2036 "Kookie Little Paradise") ... 8-12 60
Members: Art Polhemus; Terry Byrnes; Kenny Bolognese.
Also see CHANDLER, Kenny

TREE TOPS
(Featuring Jerry Doell)
Singles: 7-inch
ZERO ... 10-15 60

TREES
LPs: 10/12-inch
MCA ... 5-10 82

TREES
Singles: 7-inch
BALI-HI (808 "Your Life") ... 15-25 60s
MUM ... 10-20 60s

TREEZ
Singles: 7-inch
HARLEQUIN (72566 "You Lied to Me Before") ... 15-25 66

TREETOP, Bobby
Singles: 7-inch
TUFF (415 "So Sweet") ... 25-35 65
TUFF (417 "Wait Till I Get to Know Ya") ... 25-35 65

TREETOPS
Singles: 7-inch
TOWER ... 4-8 68

TREFETHEN
LPs: 10/12-inch
PACIFIC ARTS ... 5-10 80
Also see AMBROSIA
Also see PACK, David
Also see PARSONS, Alan, Project

TRE-J'S
Singles: 7-inch
TEE GEE ... 8-12

TRELLS
(With the Soulful Saxons)
Singles: 7-inch
PORT CITY (1112 "Bad Weather") ... 50-75 60s

TREMAINE, Willie
(Willie Tremaine's Thunderbirds)
Singles: 7-inch
CUCA (1001 "Midnight Express") ... 25-50 59
SWASTIKA (1001 "Midnight Express") ... 50-100 59
(First issue.)

TREMAINES
(With "Orchestra")
Singles: 7-inch
CASH (100 "Moon Shining Bright") ... 300-500 58
(First issue.)
KANE (008 "Heavenly") ... 30-50 59
(First issue.)
OLD TOWN (1051 "Jingle Jingle") ... 30-40 58
VAL (100 "Moon Shining Bright") ... 200-300 58
V-TONE (507 "Heavenly") ... 15-25 59

TREMBLERS
LPs: 10/12-inch
JOHNSTON ... 5-10 80

TREMELOES P&R/LP '67
Singles: 7-inch
DJM ... 3-5 74-75
EPIC ... 4-8 66-70
Picture Sleeves
EPIC ... 4-8 67
LPs: 10/12-inch
DJM ... 8-10 74
EPIC ... 15-25 67-68
Also see POOLE, Brian

TREMELOES / Hollies
Singles: 7-inch
EPIC (10184 "Silence is Golden"/"Carrie-Anne") ... 10-20 67
(Colored vinyl. Promotional issue only.)
Also see HOLLIES
Also see TREMELOES

TREMELOES
Singles: 7-inch
ROCKLAND (102 "Jaguar") ... 15-25 60s

TREM-LOS
Singles: 7-inch
NOLTA (350 "Silly Affair") ... 25-35 61
Picture Sleeves
NOLTA (350 "Silly Affair") ... 50-75 61

TREMOLONS
Singles: 7-inch
WILDWOOD ... 10-20 65

TREMONT, Jimmy, & Bronx Dukes
Singles: 7-inch
STREET CORNER ... 3-5 79
Members: Steve Valentino; Ron West; Gary Alfano; Mike Corso; Tommy Lauria; J. Turner; Ron Blair.

TREMONTS
("Featuring Joe Dee"; with Joe Dee & Top Hands)
Singles: 7-inch
BRUNSWICK (55217 "Legend of Love") ... 20-30 61
PAT RICCIO (101 "Legend of Love") ... 50-100 61
Also see CHICAGO, Artie
Also see CURTISS, Jimmy
Also see DEE, Joe, & Top Hands
Also see JOYCE & PRIVATEERS
Also see REGENTS
Also see RIVERS, Johnny / Tremonts / Luke Gordon / Charlie Francis

TREMORS
Singles: 7-inch
LODE (2005 "Yucatan") ... 10-15 58

TREMORS
Singles: 7-inch
CATALINA ... 8-12

TRENCHMEN
Singles: 7-inch
IMPACT SOUND (236678 "Chains on My Heart") ... 25-35 60s

TREND
Singles: 7-inch
FONTANA ... 4-8 67

TREN-DELLS
(Trend-els)
Singles: 7-inch
BOSS (9919 "Love") ... 20-30 65
BOSS (9921 "That's My Desire") ... 20-30 65
CAPITOL (4852 "Night Owl") ... 8-12 62
JAM (100 "Night Owl") ... 15-25 62
JAM (111 "Hey Da-Da-Dow") ... 15-25 62
SOUND 7 STAGE ... 5-10 63
SOUTHTOWN ... 5-10 64
TILT (779 "I'm So Young") ... 20-30 61
TILT (788 "I Miss You So") ... 20-30 62

TRENDS
Singles: 7-inch
ARGO (5341 "I'll Be True") ... 20-30 59
RCA (7733 "The Beard") ... 8-12 60
SCOPE (102 "Once Again") ... 50-100 59

TRENDS
Singles: 7-inch
RECORD CENTER ... 8-12 63

TRENDS
Singles: 7-inch
ABC (10731 "Not too Old to Cry") ... 15-25 65
ABC (10817 "A Night for Love") ... 15-25 66
ABC (10881 "No One There") ... 15-25 66
ABC (10993 "Thanks for a Little Lovin'") ... 10-20 67
ABC (11091 "Soul Clap") ... 10-20 68
ABC (11150 "Not Another Day") ... 20-30 68
ABC-PAR (10731 "Not Too Old to Cry") ... 25-35 65
SMASH (1914 "Dance with Me Baby") ... 10-20 64
SMASH (1933 "Get Something Going") ... 10-20 64

TREND-TONES
Singles: 7-inch
SUPERB (100 "This Is Love") ... 75-125 61
(First issued as by the Paradons.)
Also see PARADONS

TRENIER, Milton
Singles: 78 rpm
GROOVE ... 5-10 54
RCA ... 5-10 53
Singles: 7-inch
DOT (15922 "Gonna Catch Me a Rat") ... 15-25 59
GROOVE ... 10-20 54
RCA ... 10-20 53
Also see TRENIERS

TRENIER, Milton, & Micki Lynn
LPs: 10/12-inch
CADET ... 10-15 67

TRENIER, Skip, & Fabulous Treniers
Singles: 7-inch
RONN ... 3-5 71
Also see FABULOUS TRENIERS

TRENIER TWINS
Singles: 78 rpm
CORAL ... 10-20 49
MERCURY ... 15-25 47-48
Members: Claude Trenier; Cliff Trenier.
Also see TRENIERS

TRENIERS R&B '51
Singles: 78 rpm
BRUNSWICK ... 10-20 57-58
EPIC ... 5-15 54-56
LONDON ... 10-15 50
OKEH ... 10-15 51-55
VIK ... 8-12 56
Singles: 7-inch
BRUNSWICK ... 10-20 57-58
DOM ... 4-8 68
DOT ... 8-12 58-59
EPIC ... 10-20 54-56
OKEH ... 15-30 51-55
VIK ... 10-20 56
EPs: 7-inch
EPIC (7014 "Go Go Go") ... 35-50 56
EPIC (7103 "On TV") ... 35-50 56
EPIC (7014 "Go Go Go") ... 35-50 57
LPs: 10/12-inch
DOT (3257 "Souvenir Album") ... 50-75 60
EPIC (3125 "On TV") ... 100-150 56
Members: Milt Trenier; Cliff Trenier; Claude Trenier.
Also see MAYS, Willie, & Treniers
Also see TRENIER, Milt
Also see TRENIER, Skip, & Fabulous Treniers
Also see TRENIER TWINS

TRENSATIONS
Singles: 7-inch
MINIT ... 4-8 67

TRENT, Barbara
Singles: 7-inch
RED LABEL (38 "One Child") ... 10-15 60s
TERRY (108 "Come On Home") ... 10-15 61

TRENT, Charles
Singles: 7-inch
DEL-FI ... 5-10 60
TENDER ... 8-12 59
TIDE ... 5-10 60

TRENT, Jackie
Singles: 7-inch
A&M ... 4-8 69
KAPP ... 4-8 64
PARKWAY ... 4-8 65
W.B. ... 4-8 65-68

TRENT, Kenneth
Singles: 7-inch
VEEDA (4008 "I Feel About You") ... 20-30 60s

TRENT, Tommy
Singles: 7-inch
ALLSTAR ... 5-10 59-60

TREN-TEENS
Singles: 7-inch
CARNIVAL (501 "My Babys [sic] Gone") ... 50-75 64

TRENTONS
Singles: 7-inch
SHEPHERD (2204 "All Alone") ... 100-200 62
Also see HI-TONES
Also see SHY TONES

TRES FEMMES
Singles: 7-inch
PHIL-L.A. of SOUL ... 3-6 69
20TH FOX ... 4-8 68

TRES HOMBRES
LPs: 10/12-inch
TRIGGER ... 10-15 83

TRESPASSERS
Singles: 7-inch
SILVER SEAL (1020 "Come with Me") ... 15-25 60s

TRETONES
Singles: 7-inch
B-W (604 "Blind Date") ... 10-20 60

TREVOR, Jean
Singles: 7-inch
NORMAN ... 4-8 63

TREVOR, Van C&W '66
(With the Saturday Knights)
Singles: 7-inch
ATLANTIC ... 4-8 63
BAND BOX ... 8-15 66-67
CANADIAN AMERICAN ... 5-10 64
CORSICAN ... 10-15 61
DATE ... 4-8 67-68
VIVID (1004 "C'mon Now Baby") ... 15-20 63
(With the 4 Seasons.)
ROYAL AMERICAN ... 4-6 69-71
LPs: 10/12-inch
BAND BOX ... 10-15 67
DATE ... 10-15 67
ROYAL AMERICAN ... 8-12 70
Also see 4 SEASONS
Also see SATURDAY KNIGHTS

T-REX: see T. REX

TREXLER, Gary
Singles: 78 rpm
REV ... 10-15 57
Singles: 7-inch
REV ... 10-15 57

TREY TONES
Singles: 7-inch
SUNLINER (101 "Nonymous") ... 15-25 64

TREYSZ
Singles: 7-inch
BELLA ... 10-20 60s

TRI FIVE
Singles: 7-inch
DENMARK ... 4-8 63

TRIADS
Singles: 7-inch
RINGO (111 "Bacon Fat") ... 10-20 60

TRIADS
Singles: 7-inch
ENCINO (1002 "One More Kiss") ... 50-60

TRIALS & TRIBULATIONS
LPs: 10/12-inch
VANGUARD ... 8-10 71

TRIANGLE
Singles: 7-inch
FUN ("Why") ... 15-25 67
(No selection number used.)

TRIANGLE
Singles: 7-inch
AMARET ... 8-12 69
LPs: 10/12-inch
AMARET (5001 "How Now Blue Cow") ... 15-25 69
Members: Michael Carelli; Ty Grimes.
Also see CAPTAIN BEEFHEART

TRIANGLE
Singles: 7-inch
PARAMOUNT ... 8-10 72
Member: Vinny Corella.
Also see MADISON STREET
Also see RANDY & RAINBOWS

TRIANGLES
Singles: 7-inch
FARGO ... 4-8 62
FIFO (107 "Really I Do") ... 50-100 64
HERALD (549 "Savin' My Love") ... 15-25 60

TRIBBLE, Mark C&W '89
Singles: 7-inch
PALOMA ... 3-4 89

TRIBBLE, TNT, with Frank Motley & His Crew
Singles: 78 rpm
GOTHAM ... 10-15 53-54
RCA ... 10-20 52
Singles: 7-inch
CHART (638 "T.N.T.") ... 15-25 57
EAST WEST (125 "Madison Beat") ... 15-25 59
GOTHAM (288 "Twin-H Jump") ... 20-30 53
GOTHAM (294 "Hamburger") ... 20-30 54
GOTHAM (300 "Hot Heat!") ... 20-30 54
RCA (4460 "T.V. Boogie Blues") ... 25-50 52
Also see MOTLEY, Frank

TRIBE
Singles: 7-inch
FENTON (2088 "Try Try") ... 20-30 67

TRIBE R&B '73
Singles: 7-inch
ABC ... 3-5 73-74
C & CT ... 3-5 71
LPs: 10/12-inch
ABC ... 5-10 73-74
FARR ... 5-10 77
PICKWICK ... 10-15 75

TRIBE CALLED QUEST LP '90
LPs: 10/12-inch
JIVE ... 5-8 90

TRIBESMEN
Singles: 7-inch
SEMINOLE ... 4-8 69

TRIBU TERRYS
Singles: 7-inch
PRISM (1951 "Leavin' to Stay") ... 15-20 60s

TRIBULATIONS
Singles: 7-inch
IMPERIAL (66416 "Mama's Love") ... 15-25 69

TRIBUNES
Singles: 7-inch
DERRICK (502 "Now That You're Gone") ... 25-35 62
TEEN (1008 "Hearts Are Not Made") ... 30-40

TRIBUTES
Singles: 7-inch
DONNA ... 10-15 64

TRICE, Willie
LPs: 10/12-inch
TRIX ... 10-15

TRICKER, David White
LPs: 10/12-inch
BELL ... 8-10 71

TRICKLES
Singles: 7-inch
GONE (5078 "With Each Step a Tear") ... 100-150 59
POWER (250 "With Each Step a Tear") ... 200-300 58

TRICKS
Singles: 7-inch
DATE ... 4-6 69

TRICKSTER
Singles: 7-inch
JET ... 3-5 78
LPs: 10/12-inch
JET ... 8-10 78-80

TRICYCLE
LPs: 10/12-inch
ABC ... 10-15 69

TRI-DELLS
Singles: 7-inch
ELDO ... 10-15 60

TRIDELS
Singles: 7-inch
SAN-DEE (1009 "Land of Love") ... 50-100 64

TRIDER, Larry
Singles: 7-inch
AMY ... 6-12 68
CORAL (62362 "Note Under My Door") ... 25-35 63
CORAL (62391 "Carbon Copy") ... 50-75 64
DOT (16727 "New Orleans") ... 15-25 65
ROULETTE (4362 "Don't Stop") ... 15-20 61

TRI-FIVE
Singles: 7-inch
DAMARK (2400 "Like Chop") ... 10-20 62

TRIGENTS
Singles: 7-inch
IMPALA ... 4-8 64

TRI-GERIANS
Singles: 7-inch
MARLO (1529 "Kingdom of Love") ... 75-125 63

TRIGGER
Singles: 7-inch
CASABLANCA ... 3-5 78
LPs: 10/12-inch
CASABLANCA ... 5-10 78

TRI-LADS
Singles: 7-inch
BULLSEYE (1003 "Cherry Pie") ... 25-35 59

TRILARK
LPs: 10/12-inch
HANDSHAKE ... 5-10 82

TRI-LITES
Singles: 7-inch
ENITH INT'L (721 "Hot Dog! Here He Comes") ... 10-20 63
Session: Gaynel Hodge.
Also see HODGE, Gaynel

TRILLION
Singles: 7-inch
EPIC ... 3-5 79
LPs: 10/12-inch
EPIC ... 5-10 79-80

TRILLS
LPs: 10/12-inch
G&P ... 5-10 81

TRILOGY
Singles: 7-inch
G.W.P. ... 4-6 60s
MERCURY ... 3-5 70
SUSSEX ... 3-5 71
LPs: 10/12-inch
G.W.P. (2031 "It Starts Again") ... 10-20 60s
MERCURY ... 10-15 70

TRILONS
Singles: 7-inch
TAG ... 10-15 62

TRILYTERS
Singles: 78 rpm
TRILYTE (#100) ... 25-50 56
(Title not known.)

TRINA, Marguerite
Singles: 7-inch
BELLA ... 5-10 59

TRINADADS: see TRINIDADS

TRINERE R&B '85
Singles: 7-inch
JAM PACKED ... 3-4 85-87
LPs: 10/12-inch
JAM PACKED ... 5-8 86

TRINERE / Freestyle / Debbie Deb LP '89
(Trinere & Friends)
LPs: 10/12-inch
PANDISC ... 5-8 89
Also see DEBBIE DEB
Also see FREESTYLE
Also see TRINERE

TRINIDADS
(Trinadads)
Singles: 7-inch
FORMAL (1005 "Don't Say Goodbye") ... 2000-4000 59
FORMAL (1006 "When We're Together") ... 300-400 60

TRINITY, Bobby C&W '77
Singles: 7-inch
GRT ... 3-5 77

TRINITY LANE C&W '88
Singles: 7-inch
CURB ... 3-4 88

TRINITY RIVER BOYS
LPs: 10/12-inch
PROSPECTOR (1 "Trinity River Boys") ... 30-40 64
Also see MURPHEY, Michael
Also see NESMITH, Michael

TRINKETS
Singles: 7-inch
CORTLAND (111 "Nobody But You") ... 10-15 62
IMPERIAL (5497 "Little Boy") ... 15-25 58

TRIO
Singles: 7-inch
MERCURY ... 3-5 80-83
Picture Sleeves
MERCURY ... 3-5 83
LPs: 10/12-inch
MERCURY ... 5-8 82
POLYDOR ... 5-8 85

TRIO+ : see LEWIS, Jerry Lee, Carl Perkins & Charlie Rich

TRIOLO, Frank
Singles: 7-inch
FLAGSHIP (106 "Ice Cream Baby") ... 150-250 58

TRIOTONES
("Vocal Larry Puma with Chuck Ray & His Gang")
Singles: 7-inch
INTRASTATE (43 "Valerie Jo") ... 100-200 58

TRIPJACKS
Singles: 7-inch
SQUIRE 4-8 60s

TRIPLE "S" CONNECTION R&B '80
Singles: 12-inch
20TH FOX 4-6 79-80
Singles: 7-inch
20TH FOX 3-5 79-80
LPs: 10/12-inch
20TH FOX 5-10 79
Also see LIVIN' PROOF
Also see SKOOL BOYZ

TRIPLETS
Singles: 7-inch
BLUE ROCK 4-8 65
DORE 5-10 60
MGM 5-10 59

TRIPP, Allen C&W '82
Singles: 7-inch
NASHVILLE 3-4 82

TRIPPERS
Singles: 7-inch
DOT 5-10 66
GNP 4-8 67
KAY GEE 5-10 65
RUBY-DOO 5-10 67

TRIPPERS
Singles: 7-inch
FULLTONE 20-25 68
MILLTOWN 20-25 69

TRIPPS
Singles: 7-inch
SOUNDSVILLE 8-12
VICTORIA 4-8 67

TRIPPS
Singles: 7-inch
VICTORIA 4-8 67

TRIPSICHORD MUSIC BOX
Singles: 7-inch
SAN FRANCISCO (115 "Times and Season") 8-12 70
LPs: 10/12-inch
JANUS (3016 "San Francisco Sound") 50-100 71

TRIPTIDES
Singles: 7-inch
OFFICIAL (1001 "Lonely Beachcomber") 20-30 60s

TRIS, Berry E.
Singles: 7-inch
WARNOCK (3373 "Rebel") 10-15

TRITONES
Singles: 78 rpm
GRAND (126 "Blues in the Closet") 15-25 54
JAMIE (1035 "Blues in the Closet") 15-25 57
Singles: 7-inch
GRAND (126 "Blues in the Closet") 40-50 54
JAMIE (1035 "Blues in the Closet") 15-25 57

TRI-TONES
Singles: 7-inch
RANGER (9650 "Chicken in the Basket") 100-150 57

TRI-TONES
Singles: 7-inch
RAYCRAFT 10-15 60s
TWILIGHT (406 "Surf-A-Nova") 15-20 63
(First issued on Twilight 405, as by the Parallels.)
Also see PARALLELS

TRI-TONES
Singles: 7-inch
MISS JULIE (6501 "Teardrops") 150-250 64

TRITT, Travis C&W '89
Singles: 7-inch
W.B. 3-4 89-91

TRITT, Travis, & Marty Stuart C&W '91
Singles: 7-inch
W.B. 3-4 91
Also see STUART, Marty
Also see TRITT, Travis

TRIUMPH P&R/LP '79
Singles: 7-inch
MCA (Black vinyl) 3-4 85-86
MCA (Colored vinyl) 3-5 85-86
RCA 3-5 78-84
Picture Sleeves
MCA 3-4 85-86
RCA 3-5 79
LPs: 10/12-inch
MCA 5-8 85-87
RCA 5-10 78-84
Members: Mike Levine; Gil Moore; Rik Emmett.

TRIUMPHS
Singles: 7-inch
DANTE (3002 "The Lazy Man") 10-20 61
DANTE (3011 "You're Mine Tonight") 10-20 62
GENUINE (152 "It's So Easy") 10-20 67
GENUINE (163 "The Walk") 10-20 67
JOED (117 "Garner State Park") 15-25 60s
KAB 5-10 63
OKEH (7272 "Workin' ") 8-12 67
OKEH (7273 "Memories") 8-12 67
OKEH (7291 "I'm Comin' to Your Rescue") 15-25 67
SWAN 5-10 63
TRIUMPH (1001 "Fender Bender") 20-25 61
VERVE 4-8 66
VOLT 8-12 61

TRIUMPHS
Singles: 7-inch
VOLT (100 "Burnt Biscuits") 10-20 62
Member: Booker T.
Also see BOOKER T. & MGs
Also see MAR-KEYS

TRIUMPHS
Singles: 7-inch
IFF (151 "Susie in My History Class") 20-30 63
Members: Jim Peterson; Tom Runte; Jerry George; Mike Prescott; Bob Hahm; Tony Gazzana; Bruce Cole.

TRIUMPHS
Singles: 7-inch
BARCLAY 10-15 64
Member: Pat Farrell.
Also see FARRELL, Pat, & Believers
Also see RAZOR'S EDGE

TRIUMVIRAT LP '74
Singles: 7-inch
CAPITOL 3-5 79
LPs: 10/12-inch
CAPITOL 5-10 74-80
HARVEST 10-12 74

TRIXIES
Singles: 7-inch
TWIN HIT 5-10 64

TRIXONS
Singles: 7-inch
PARAMOUNT 3-6 69

TRIXXX
Singles: 12-inch
COTILLION 4-6 86
Singles: 7-inch
COTILLION 3-4 86

TROCHIANS
Singles: 7-inch
SATIN (4 "Phantom") 8-12

TRODDEN PATH
Singles: 7-inch
NIGHT OWL (6711 "Don't Follow Me") 15-25 67
Members: Tim Urban; Mike Frommer; Steve Turner; Tom Szymarek.

TROGGS P&R/LP '66
Singles: 7-inch
ATCO (6415 "Wild Thing"/"With a Girl Like You") 10-15 66
(Writer credited is "Presley.")
ATCO (6415 "Wild Thing"/"With a Girl Like You") 5-10 66
(Writer credited is "Taylor.")
ATCO (6415 "I Want You") 5-10 66
(Same number used twice.)
ATCO (6444 "I Can't Control Myself") 5-10 66
BELL 3-5 73
FONTANA 4-8 66-69
PAGE ONE 3-6 69-70
PRIVATE STOCK 3-5 77
PYE 3-5 75-76
LPs: 10/12-inch
ATCO (33-193 "Wild Thing") 35-45 66
(Monaural.)
ATCO (SD-33-193 "Wild Thing") 25-35 66
(Stereo.)
FONTANA (27556 "The Troggs") 25-35 66
(Monaural.)
FONTANA (67556 "The Troggs") 20-30 66
(Stereo.)
FONTANA (67576 "Love Is All Around") 20-30 68
LIBERTY (3472 "You're Gonna Hear from Me") 25-35 66
(Monaural.)
LIBERTY (7472 "You're Gonna Hear from Me") 25-35 66
(Stereo.)
MKC 8-10 80
PRIVATE STOCK 10-15 76
PYE 10-15 75
RHINO 5-8 84
SIRE 10-15 76

TROGGS / Brook Benton
Singles: 7-inch
MILLER BEER (621 "Radio Spots") 5-10 60s
Picture Sleeves
MILLER BEER (621 "Radio Spots") 10-15 60s
Also see BENTON, Brook
Also see TROGGS

TROIANO, Domenic
(Domenic Troiano Band)
Singles: 7-inch
CAPITOL 3-5 79
MERCURY 3-5 73
LPs: 10/12-inch
CAPITOL 4-8 78-79
MERCURY 4-8 73
Also see GUESS WHO

TROJANS
Singles: 78 rpm
RPM 40-60 55
Singles: 7-inch
FELSTED (8534 "Make It Up") 15-25 58
RPM (446 "As Long As I Have You") 100-200 55

TROJANS
Singles: 7-inch
TENDER (516 "Don't Ask Me to Be Lonely") 25-50 58
(Previously issued as by the 5 Trojans.)
Also see 5 TROJANS

TROJANS
Singles: 7-inch
TRIANGLE (51317 "All Night Long") 100-150 60

TROJANS
(Mighty Trojans)
Singles: 7-inch
AIR TOWN 5-10 60s
DODGE (804 "Just About Daybreak") 8-12 61
JOED (711 "Just About Daybreak") 5-10 62
TRIANGLE (51317 "All Night Long") 15-25 60

TROJANS OF EVOL
Singles: 7-inch
T.O.E. (125970 "Through the Night") 20-30 67
(Identification number shown since no selection number is used.)

TROLINDER, Delbert
Singles: 7-inch
MIST (1012 "So We Walked") 20-30

TROLL, The
Singles: 7-inch
SMASH 5-10 69
LPs: 10/12-inch
SMASH (67114 "Animated Music") 20-30 69
Members: Richard Gallagher; Richard Clark; Max Jordan; Ken Cortese.
Also see TROLLS

TROLLEY
Singles: 7-inch
PICCADILLY 10-15 68

TROLLEY
Singles: 7-inch
COSMOPOLITAN (1006 "Who's Gonna Sing") 4-8 77
(Includes bonus photo/lyrics insert.)

TROLLS
Singles: 7-inch
PEATLORE (23267 "Walkin' Shoes") 10-20 66

TROLLS
Singles: 7-inch
RUFF (1010 "That's the Way Love Is") 20-30 66
WARRIOR (173 "Stupid Girl") 5-10 67
Picture Sleeves
WARRIOR (173 "Stupid Girl") 10-20 67

TROLLS P&R '66
Singles: 7-inch
ABC 5-10 66-67
U.S.A. 10-20 68
Also see CARNIVAL of SOUND
Also see TROLL

TROMBONES
Singles: 7-inch
CHARTMAKER 3-6 69
LPs: 10/12-inch
CHARTMAKER 8-10 69

TRONICS
Singles: 7-inch
LANDA (676 "Pickin' & Stompin' ") 8-12 61
LANDA (680 "The Big Scroungy") 8-12 62
Members: Baker Knight, Rene Hall.
Also see HALL, Rene
Also see KNIGHT, Baker
Also see PAYMENTS

TROOP R&B/LP '88
Singles: 7-inch
ATLANTIC 3-4 88-90
LPs: 10/12-inch
ATLANTIC 5-8 88-90

TROOPER P&R/LP '78
Singles: 7-inch
LEGEND 3-5 75-77
MCA 3-5 77-78
LPs: 10/12-inch
LEGEND 8-10 75-76
MCA 5-10 78-80
RCA 5-8 82

TROOPERS
Singles: 7-inch
LAMP (2009 "My Resolution") 75-100 57

TROPAY, Mary Jo
Singles: 7-inch
WORLD 4-8 63

TROPEA LP '76
(John Tropea)
Singles: 7-inch
MARLIN 3-5 76-77
LPs: 10/12-inch
MARLIN 8-10 76-77
Also see DEODATO

TROPHIES
Singles: 7-inch
CHALLENGE (9133 "Desire") 35-45 61
CHALLENGE (9149 "Peg o' My Heart") 10-20 62
CHALLENGE (9170 "Felicia") 10-20 62
Members: Dave Burgess; Jimmy Seals; Dash Crofts.
Also see BURGESS
Also see SEALS & CROFTS

TROPHIES
Singles: 7-inch
KAPP 5-10 65-66
NORK (79907 "Walkin' the Dog") 10-15 65
Member: Richard Eriksen.
Also see BUSTERS

TROPICS
Singles: 7-inch
CARNIVAL (She's So Fine") 20-30
(Selection number not known.)
COLUMBIA 4-8 67
FREEPORT 5-10 60s
MALACO 5-10 60s
THAMES 4-8 60s
TOPIC (551 "Happy Hour") 25-35

TROTTER, Don, & Eighth Wonder
Singles: 7-inch
JOSIE 3-5 69

TROTTER, Jimmy
Singles: 7-inch
PEL 5-10 60
SWADE 5-10 59

TROUBADOURS DU ROI BAUDOUIN LP '69
LPs: 10/12-inch
PHILIPS 5-10 63-69

TROUBLE R&B '80
Singles: 7-inch
AL & KIDD 3-5 80
U.A. 3-5 77
LPs: 10/12-inch
U.A. 8-10 77

TROUBLE FUNK R&B/LP '82
Singles: 12-inch
ISLAND 4-6 85-86
SUGAR HILL 4-6 82
Singles: 7-inch
D.E.T.T. 3-4 83
ISLAND 3-4 85-86
TF 3-5 80
LPs: 10/12-inch
ISLAND 5-8 86
SUGAR HILL 5-8 82

TROUP, Bobby
LPs: 10/12-inch
LIBERTY (3078 "Here's to My Lady") 15-25 57

TROUP OF LOVE
Singles: 7-inch
EPOCH (801 "Raining in the North End") 5-10 67

TROUT
Singles: 7-inch
MGM 3-6 69
LPs: 10/12-inch
MGM 10-15 68

TROUTMAN, Tony R&B '75
Singles: 7-inch
GRAM-O-PHONE 3-5 75
T. MAIN 3-4 82-83

TROWER, Robin LP '73
Singles: 12-inch
GNP (2 "No Time") 5-8 87
(Promotional issue only.)
Singles: 7-inch
CHRYSALIS 3-5 72-78
LPs: 10/12-inch
ATLANTIC 5-8 88
CHRYSALIS 5-12 73-82
GNP 5-8 83-87
PASSPORT 5-10 85
Also see PROCOL HARUM

TROXEL, Gary
Singles: 7-inch
DOT 4-8 68
Also see FLEETWOODS

TROY
Singles: 7-inch
ALHAMBRA (001 "Amnesia") 10-20 69

TROY
Singles: 7-inch
COLUMBIA 4-6 72

TROY, Benny R&B '75
(With Maze)
Singles: 7-inch
DE-LITE 3-5 75
20TH FOX 3-5

TROY, Billy
Singles: 7-inch
BARNABY 3-5 71
LPs: 10/12-inch
CMH 5-10 81

TROY, Bo, & His Hot Rods / Dick Dale
LPs: 10/12-inch
DIPLOMAT (2304 "Wild Hot Rod Wails") 10-20 63
(Cover gives Dick Dale top billing, but LP has only two Dale tracks.)
Also see DALE, Dick

TROY, Bobby
Singles: 7-inch
MOHAWK 4-8 63

TROY, Doris P&R/R&B '63
Singles: 7-inch
APPLE 5-10 70
ATLANTIC 5-10 63-65
CALLA (114 "Heartaches") 10-20 66
CAPITOL 5-10 67
MIDLAND INT'L 3-6 76
LPs: 10/12-inch
APPLE (3371 "Doris Troy") 15-20 70
ATLANTIC (8088 "Just One Look") 20-30 64

TROY, J.B.
Singles: 7-inch
MUSICOR (1188 "Ain't It the Truth") 5-10 66
MUSICOR (1210 "Live On") 10-20 66

TROY, Kelly
(With the 3 Jays)
Singles: 7-inch
CORVETTE (100 "Remember When") 10-15 60
TAD (101 "You're Lucky in Love") 100-200 61
TAD (102 "You're Lucky in Love") 100-200 62

TROY, Riki
Singles: 7-inch
CEVETONE 4-8 63

TROY, Roger
Singles: 7-inch
RCA 3-5 76
LPs: 10/12-inch
RCA 8-10 76

TROY & HELEN
Singles: 78 rpm
SIERRA 10-20

TROY & T-BIRDS
Singles: 7-inch
SEVEN ARTS 5-10 61

TROYER, Eric P&R '80
Singles: 7-inch
CHRYSALIS 3-5 80
LPs: 10/12-inch
CHRYSALIS 5-10 80

TROYES
Singles: 7-inch
PHALANX (1008 "Rainbow Chaser") 25-35 66
SPACE (7001 "Rainbow Chaser") 10-20 66
SPACE (7002 "Love Comes, Love Dies") 10-20 67

TROYKA
Singles: 7-inch
COTILLION 3-5 70
LPs: 10/12-inch
COTILLION 8-10 70

TROYS
Singles: 7-inch
HI-HAT (137 "I Was Dreaming") 50-75 50s
OKEH (7120 "Ding-A-Ling-A-Ling") 15-25 59
Also see DELL, Dickey & Bing Bongs

TROYS
Singles: 7-inch
TOWER 5-8 68

TRUANTS
Singles: 7-inch
ROCK-IT (1002 The Truant") 15-25 63
Members: Eddie Rea; Dick Zeiner; Ed Puchalski; Larry Taylor.

TRUBEE, John, & Ugly Janitors of America
LPs: 10/12-inch
ENIGMA 5-8 84

TRUBERT BROTHERS
Singles: 7-inch
SASHAY 5-10 67

TRUC
Singles: 7-inch
U.A. 3-5 73
ZERO 5-8 72
Member: Bob Krause.
Also see WREST

TRUCKAWAY, William
Singles: 7-inch
REPRISE 3-5 72
LPs: 10/12-inch
REPRISE 8-10 71

TRUDY & LOUISE
Singles: 7-inch
FLIP (362 "Teenage Promise") 10-15 63
Members: Trudy Williams; Louise Williams.
Also see SIX TEENS

TRUE, Andrea P&R/R&B/LP '76
(Andrea True Connection)
Singles: 7-inch
BUDDAH 3-5 76-78
ERIC 3-5 78
Picture Sleeves
BUDDAH 4-8 76
LPs: 10/12-inch
BUDDAH 5-10 76-78

TRUE LOVE R&B '87
Singles: 7-inch
CRITIQUE 3-4 87

TRUE LOVES: see TRUELOVES

TRUE REFLECTION
LPs: 10/12-inch
ATCO 8-10 73

TRUE TONES: see TRU-TONES

TRUE WEST
LPs: 10/12-inch
PVC 5-8 84

TRUELEERS
Singles: 7-inch
CHECKER 8-12 62

TRUELOVES
(Lovenotes)
Singles: 7-inch
PREMIUM (611 "A Love Like Yours") 200-300 57
(Previously issued as by the Lovenotes.)
Member: David Haywood.
Also see LOVE NOTES

TRUETONES
(True Tones)
Singles: 7-inch
FELSTED (8625 "Blushing Bride") 75-125 61
JOSIE (950 "That's Love") 10-20 65
JOSIE (1003 "That's Love") 10-15 65
SOULVILLE (2871-53 "That's Love") 50-75 65
(First issue.)

TRUITT, Johnny
(Little Johnny Truitt)
Singles: 7-inch
A-BET 10-15 66-69

TRUJILLO, Orlie
Singles: 7-inch
DEL-FI 10-20 59

TRUK
LPs: 10/12-inch
COLUMBIA 8-10 70

TRUMAININS
Singles: 7-inch
RCA (11117 "Mr. Magic Man") 10-20 77

TRUMPETEERS R&B '48
Singles: 78 rpm
KING 10-15 50
SCORE 10-25 48
LPs: 10/12-inch
GRAND 25-40
SCORE (4021 "Milky White Way") 100-150 56

TRUMPETEERS P&R '59
Singles: 7-inch
SPLASH 8-10 59
Member: Billy Mure.
Also see MURE, Billy

TRUNZO, Phil, & Counts
Singles: 7-inch
EUPHON ("Teardrops in My Heart") 25-35
(No selection number used.)

TRU-SONICS
Singles: 7-inch
BOLO 8-10 61
Also see THOMAS, Tracy, & Tru-Sonics

TRUSSELL R&B '80
Singles: 7-inch
ELEKTRA 3-5 80
LPs: 10/12-inch
ELEKTRA 5-10 80

TRUSTIN' HOWARD
Singles: 7-inch
REPRISE 15-20 62

TRUTH
Singles: 7-inch
ABC-PAR 4-8 66
W.B. 4-8 68

TRUTH
Singles: 7-inch
DERAM (7503 "Hey Gyp") 10-20 67
Also see KENNY & KASUALS

TRUTH
Singles: 7-inch
CADET (5627 "I Can") 8-12 68

TRUTH
Singles: 7-inch
DRIVING WHEEL (7302 "Around and Around") 5-10 73
LPs: 10/12-inch
PEOPLE (5002 "Truth") 20-30 70

TRUTH R&B '74
Singles: 7-inch
ROULETTE 3-5 74-75
SOC 3-5
LPs: 10/12-inch
PARAGON 5-10 78
ROULETTE 5-10 75

TRUTH R&B '80
Singles: 7-inch
DEVAKI 3-5 80-81

TRUTH P&R/LP '87
Singles: 7-inch
I.R.S. 3-4 87
Picture Sleeves
I.R.S. 3-4 87
LPs: 10/12-inch
I.R.S. 5-8 87

TRUTH & JANEY
Singles: 7-inch
SOUND (81472 "Under My Thumb") 8-10 72
LPs: 10/12-inch
MONTROSS (376 "No Rest for the Wicked") 40-60 76
Member: Bill Janey.

TRUTHS
Singles: 7-inch
CIRCLE (953 "Pending") 8-12 65

TRU TONES
Singles: 7-inch
SPOT (1115 "Never Had a Chance") 10-20 64
SPOT (1121 "Little Hit & Run Darling") 15-25 65

TRU-TONES
(True Tones)
Singles: 7-inch
CHART (634 "Tears in My Eyes") 450-650 56
MONUMENT (4501 "Honey Honey") 150-250 58

TRU-TONES
Singles: 7-inch
TRU ("Darling I'm Sorry") 15-25
(Selection number not known.)

TRY CERZ
Singles: 7-inch
JAN-GI (91 "Almost There") 10-20 66

TRYANO, Joyce
Singles: 7-inch
20TH FOX 4-8 64

TRYFLES
LPs: 10/12-inch
MIDNIGHT 5-8

TRYTHALL, Gil LP '70
Singles: 7-inch
ATHENA 3-6 69-70
LPs: 10/12-inch
ATHENA 5-10 69-70
PANDORA 5-8 81

TSCHANN & BURNHAM
Singles: 7-inch
COULEE (139 "Everything I Do") 5-10 60s

TUBB, Ernest P&R '41/C&W '44
(With the Texas Troubadours; with "Friends")
Singles: 78 rpm
BLUEBIRD (6693 "The Passing of Jimmie Rodgers") 200-400 30s
BLUEBIRD (7000 "T.B. Is Whipping Me") 100-200 30s
BLUEBIRD (8899 "Married Man Blues") 100-150 30s
BLUEBIRD (8966 "Right Train to Heaven") 100-150 30s
DECCA 10-20 40-57
Singles: 7-inch
CACHET 3-5 79
DECCA (28067 thru 30872) 5-10 52-59
DECCA (30952 thru 33014) 3-8 59-72
DECCA (46000 series) 5-15 50-52
1ST GENERATION 3-5 77
MCA 3-5 73
RHINO (74415 "Walking the Floor Over You") 3-5 91
(Gold vinyl.)
RHINO (74415 "Walking the Floor Over You") 4-6 91
(Blue vinyl.)
RHINO (74415 "Walking the Floor Over You") 8-12 91
(Black vinyl.)
Picture Sleeves
RHINO (74415 "Walking the Floor Over You") 4-6 91
EPs: 7-inch
DECCA 15-30 51-65
LPs: 10/12-inch
ACM 8-12
CACHET 8-12 79
CASTLE 5-10
CORAL 5-10 73
DECCA (159 "Ernest Tubb Story") 25-45 58
(Monaural. Includes booklet.)
DECCA (7-159 "Ernest Tubb Story") 30-60 58
(Stereo. Includes booklet.)
DECCA (5301 "Ernest Tubb Favorites") 50-75 51
(10-inch LP.)
DECCA (5334 "Old Rugged Cross-Favorite Sacred Songs") 40-60 51
(10-inch LP.)
DECCA (5497 "Sing a Song of Christmas") 40-60 54
(10-inch LP.)
DECCA (8291 "Ernest Tubb Favorites") 40-60 56
DECCA (8553 "Daddy of 'Em All") 35-55 56
DECCA (8834 "The Importance of Being Ernest") 35-55 59
FIRST GENERATION (001 "Living Legend") 8-12 77
FIRST GENERATION (0002 "The Legend and the Legacy") 75-125 79
(Back cover mentions "Ernest Tubb's Record Shop," "Gray Line Tours" and "Grand Ole Opry Tickets.")
FIRST GENERATION (0002 "The Legend and the Legacy") 60-80 79
(No mention on back cover of "Ernest Tubb's Record Shop," "Gray Line Tours" or "Grand Ole Opry Tickets.")
FIRST GENERATION (0002 .... 10-20 79
MCA 5-12 73-84
PICKWICK/HILLTOP 8-12
RADIOLA 5-10 83
RHINO (70902 "Live") 5-10 91
ROUNDER 5-10 82
TV (1033 "The Legend and the Legacy") 40-50 79
(TV mail order offer.)
VOCALION 10-15 66-69
Session: Cal Smith; Jack Greene; Willie Nelson; Merle Haggard; Chet Atkins; Charlie Daniels; Jordanaires; Waylon Jennings; Vern Gosdin; Johnny Paycheck; Loretta Lynn; Marty Robbins; Wilburn Brothers; George Jones; Johnny Cash; Ferlin Husky/Simon Crum; Charlie Rich; Conway Twitty; Justin Tubb; Charlie McCoy; Jerry Kennedy; Grady Martin; Billy Grammer; Billy Byrd; Buddy Emmons; Pete Mitchell; Pete Drake; Kitty Wells; Webb Pierce; Patsy Cline.
Also see ANDREWS SISTERS & Ernest Tubb
Also see ATKINS, Chet
Also see CASH, Johnny
Also see CLINE, Patsy
Also see DANIELS, Charlie
Also see DRAKE, Pete
Also see FOLEY, Red, & Ernest Tubb
Also see GOSDIN, Vern
Also see GRAMMER, Billy
Also see GREENE, Jack
Also see HAGGARD, Merle
Also see HUSKY, Ferlin
Also see JENNINGS, Waylon
Also see JONES, George
Also see JORDANAIRES
Also see MARTIN, Grady, & His Slew Foot Five
Also see McCOY, Charlie
Also see NELSON, Willie
Also see PAYCHECK, Johnny
Also see RICH, Charlie
Also see ROBBINS, Marty
Also see SMITH, Cal
Also see STATLER BROTHERS
Also see TWITTY, Conway
Also see WELLS, Kitty

TUBB, Ernest, & Loretta Lynn C&W '69
Singles: 7-inch
DECCA 4-8 65-69
LPs: 10/12-inch
DECCA 15-25 65-69
MCA 8-12 73
Also see LYNN, Loretta

TUBB, Ernest / Justin Tubb
EPs: 7-inch
DECCA (2422 "Jimmie Rodgers Favorites") 20-30 57
Also see TUBB, Justin

TUBB, Ernest, & Wilburn Brothers C&W '58
Singles: 7-inch
DECCA 5-10 58
EPs: 7-inch
DECCA 10-15 59
Also see TUBB, Ernest
Also see WILBURN BROTHERS

TUBB, Justin C&W '55
(With Norma Gallant)
Singles: 78 rpm
DECCA 5-15 53-57
Singles: 7-inch
CHALLENGE 5-10 60
CUTLASS 3-5 72-73
DECCA 5-15 53-59
DOT 3-6 69
FIRST GENERATION 3-5 78-81
GROOVE 4-8 63-64
HILLTOP 3-5 75
RCA 4-8 65-67
2ND GENERATION 3-5 77
STARDAY 5-10 60-62
EPs: 7-inch
DECCA 10-20 57
LPs: 10/12-inch
CUTLASS (123 "Travelin' Singin' Man") 20-30 72
(Interestingly, reissued circa 1983 on cassette only, which credits Justin but pictures Ernest Tubb.)
DECCA (8644 "Country Boy in Love") 30-50 57
DOT 15-20 69
FIRST GENERATION (01 "Justin Tubb") 8-10 81
HILLTOP (102 "Hilltop Country Presents Justin Tubb") 5-8
(Mail order repackage of Hilltop 209.)
HILLTOP (209 "A New Country Heard From") 8-12 74
PHONORAMA (5565 "What's Wrong with the Way We're Doing It Now") 5-8 83
(Repackage of First Generation 01.)
RCA 15-25 65
STARDAY (160 "Star of the Grand Ole Opry") 20-30 62
STARDAY (198 "Modern Country Music Sound") 20-30 62
STARDAY (334 "Best of Justin Tubb") 20-30 65
VOCALION 10-15 65-67
Also see HILL, Goldie, & Justin Tubb
Also see TUBB, Ernest, & Justin Tubb

TUBB, Justin, & Lorene Mann C&W '65
Singles: 7-inch
RCA 4-6 65-66
LPs: 10/12-inch
RCA (3591 "Together & Alone") 20-30 66
Also see MANN, Lorene

TUBB, Justin / Roger Miller
Singles: 7-inch
DECCA 5-10 58
Also see MILLER, Roger
Also see TUBB, Justin

TUBB, Mack, & Shades
Singles: 7-inch
HUB (1 "You Keep Me Going") 20-30

TUBES LP '75
Singles: 12-inch
CAPITOL 4-6 83
Singles: 7-inch
A&M 3-5 75-79
CAPITOL 3-4 81-85
Picture Sleeves
A&M 4-6 75
CAPITOL 3-5 81-85
LPs: 10/12-inch
A&M 5-10 75-81
CAPITOL 5-8 81-85
Members: Fee Waybill; Roger Steen.
Also see FANN BAND
Also see NEWTON-JOHN, Olivia, & Electric Light Orchestra
Also see WAYBILL, Fee

TUCK, Duncan
Singles: 7-inch
BAND BOX 4-6 67

TUCK & PATTI LP '89
LPs: 10/12-inch
WINDHAM HILL 5-8 88-90

TUCKER, Anita
Singles: 78 rpm
CAPITOL 5-10 55-56
GUYDEN 5-10 55
Singles: 7-inch
CAPITOL (3277 "Let's Make Love") 10-15 55
CAPITOL (3376 "Trying to Get to You") 10-15 56
CAPITOL (3452 "Hop Skip & Jump") 10-15 56
GUYDEN (105 "Ring-Aling-Aling") 10-15 55

TUCKER, Annette
Singles: 7-inch
PIPER 4-8 61

TUCKER, Barney
Singles: 78 rpm
TUCKER 10-20

TUCKER, Billy Joe
Singles: 7-inch
DOT (16240 "Boogie Woogie Bill") 50-75 61
MAHA (103 "Boogie Woogie Bill") 100-200 61
MID WAY (2013 "Tiny Tears") 10-20

TUCKER, Bob
Singles: 7-inch
SILVER-DOLLAR (1002 "Down and Dirty") 10-20 61
Also see TARANTULAS

TUCKER, Bobby
Singles: 7-inch
MALA 8-12

TUCKER, Ernie
(With the Operators; Ernest Tucker)
Singles: 7-inch
EARTH 5-10 60
JUBILEE 5-10 58-59
MUSICOR 5-10 61

TUCKER, George / Coney Island Kids
Singles: 7-inch
JUBILEE (5430 "I Remember Moonlight Beach") 10-15 62
Also see CONEY ISLAND KIDS

TUCKER, Jack
Singles: 78 rpm
DOWNBEAT 5-10 56
Singles: 7-inch
DOWNBEAT 5-10 56

TUCKER, Jack
Singles: 78 rpm
"X" 5-10 54
Singles: 7-inch
BEL-AIRE 5-10
FOUR STAR 5-10
IMPERIAL 10-15 59
OZARK (960 "Honeymoon Trip to Mars") 50-75 58
OZARK (962 "Lonely Man") 25-40 59
TOPPA 4-8 60s
"X" 5-10 54
YOUNG 4-8 60s

TUCKER, Johnny, & Pastels
Singles: 7-inch
SONIC (30864 "Mr. Kennedy") 10-15 64
Picture Sleeves
SONIC (30864 "Mr. Kennedy") 10-15 64

TUCKER, Junior R&B '83
Singles: 7-inch
GEFFEN 3-4 83
LPs: 10/12-inch
GEFFEN 5-8 83

TUCKER, Jerry Lee C&W '88
Singles: 7-inch
OAK 3-4 88-89

TUCKER, Jimmy C&W '79
Singles: 7-inch
GAR-PAX 3-5 79
NSD 3-5 79-80

TUCKER, La Costa: see LA COSTA

TUCKER, Les
Singles: 7-inch
HEP (2144 "Wrong Kinda Lovin' ") 30-50 58

TUCKER, Louise P&R/LP '83
Singles: 7-inch
ARISTA 3-4 83
LPs: 10/12-inch
ARISTA 5-8 83

TUCKER, Mark, & Beach
Singles: 7-inch
TETRAPOD SPOOLS (99752 "Sultry Summer Siren") 4-6 79
(Orange vinyl.)
LPs: 10/12-inch
BALKIN 10-12 72
DOWNEY 10-15 76
(Promotional issues only.)
RPC 12-15 68-71
TETRAPOD 8-10 75-83

TUCKER, Marshall: see MARSHALL TUCKER BAND

TUCKER, Mickey
Singles: 7-inch
ATLANTIC 4-8 64

TUCKER, Monroe
(Monroe Tucker's Orchestra)
Singles: 78 rpm
IMPERIAL (5109 "Kinfolks") 25-50 51
Singles: 7-inch
IMPERIAL (5109 "Kinfolks") 75-100 51

TUCKER, Orrin
Singles: 7-inch
WHITE ROCK (1115 "Been Lookin' for Love") 60-80 58

TUCKER, Rick C&W '89
Singles: 78 rpm
COLUMBIA (41041 "Patty Baby") 50-100 57
Singles: 7-inch
COLUMBIA (41041 "Patty Baby") 50-100 57
HITSVILLE 3-5 76
OAK 3-4 89
VEEDA (4005 "I'll Be There") 30-50 60
LPs: 10/12-inch
HITSVILLE 5-10 76
Session: Rick Tucker; Roy Orbison; Buddy Holly; Don Guess; Bo Clark; Bill Pickering & Picks.
Also see PICKS

TUCKER, Tanya C&W/P&R '72
Singles: 7-inch
ARISTA 3-5 82-84
CAPITOL 3-4 85-88
COLUMBIA 3-5 72-77
MCA 3-5 75-81
Picture Sleeves
COLUMBIA 3-6 72-75
MCA 3-5 75-81
LPs: 10/12-inch
ARISTA 5-8 82-84
CAPITOL 5-8 86
COLUMBIA ("KC" series) 5-10 72-75
COLUMBIA ("PC" series) 5-8 77
MCA 5-10 75-81
Sessions: John Prine; Jimmy Seals; Dash Crofts.
Also see AXTON, Hoyt
Also see CAMPBELL, Glen, & Tanya Tucker
Also see HARRIS, Emmylou
Also see SEALS & CROFTS

TUCKER, Tanya, & T. Graham Brown C&W '90
Singles: 7-inch
CAPITOL 3-4 90
Also see BROWN, T. Graham

TUCKER, Tanya, & Glen Campbell C&W '80
(Glen Campbell & Tanya Tucker)
Singles: 7-inch
CAPITOL 3-4 81
Also see CAMPBELL, Glen

TUCKER, Tanya, Paul Davis & Paul Overstreet C&W '87
Singles: 7-inch
CAPITOL 3-4 87
Also see DAVIS, Paul
Also see OVERSTREET, Paul
Also see TUCKER, Tanya

TUCKER, Tee: see TUCKER, Tommy

TUCKER, Tommy P&R/R&B '64
(Tee Tucker)
Singles: 7-inch
ATCO (6208 "My Girl") 10-20 61
CADET (5584 "Take the Midnight Train") 4-8 67
CADET (5622 "Someday") 4-8 68
CHECKER (1067 "Hi-Heel Sneakers") 5-10 64
CHECKER (1075 "Long Tall Shorty") 5-10 64

CHECKER (1112 "Alimony")........... 5-10 65
CHECKER (1133 "I've Been a Fool") 5-10 66
CHECKER (1178 "I'm Shorty")........ 5-10 67
CHECKER (1186 "A Whole Lot of Fun") 5-10 67
ELBAM (70 "I'll Be Gone") 5-10 66
FESTIVAL (704 "That's Live")........ 5-10 66
HI (2014 "Man in Love")................20-30 59
HI (2020 "Miller's Cave")..............15-25 60
SUNBEAM (128 "Man That Comes Around")..............15-25 59

LPs: 10/12-inch

CHECKER (2990 "Hi-Heel Sneakers")..............40-60 64

Also see DUSTERS

TUCKER, Tommy

Singles: 7-inch

RCA (47-7838 "Return of the Teenage Queen")........... 5-10 61
RCA (37-7838 "Return of the Teenage Queen")..............10-20 61
(Compact 33 Single.)
RCA (68-7838 "Return of the Teenage Queen")..............15-25 61
(Stereo Compact 33 Single.)

TUCKER, Tommy

Singles: 7-inch

XL (355 "Old Devil Memory")........... 5-10 66

TUCKER, Tommy, & Lullabyes

Singles: 7-inch

EMBASSY (204 "You Belong to Me")..............40-60 62

TUCKER, Tommy, & Esquires

Singles: 7-inch

IGL (121 "Don't Tell Me Lies")........15-25 66

TUCKER, Tony

Singles: 7-inch

PAGE (2001 "Jane") 5-10 70s

TUCKY BUZZARD

Singles: 7-inch

PASSPORT........... 3-5 74

LPs: 10/12-inch

CAPITOL..............10-15 71
PASSPORT..............10-15 73-74

TUDOR MINSTRELS

Singles: 7-inch

LONDON (1012 "The Family Way")..............30-40 67
(Promotional issue only.)
Also see McCARTNEY, Paul

TUESDAY CLUB

Singles: 7-inch

PHILIPS........... 5-8 67

TUESDAY'S CHILDREN

Singles: 7-inch

COLUMBIA........... 4-8 66-67

TUFANO & GIAMMARESE *P&R '73*

Singles: 7-inch

ODE 3-5 73-76

LPs: 10/12-inch

EPIC/ODE........... 8-10 76-77
ODE..............10-15 73-74
Members: Dennis Tufano; Carl Giammarese.
Also see BUCKINGHAMS
Also see J.T. CONNECTION

TUFF, Jack

LPs: 10/12-inch

CAPITOL..............10-20 62

TUFF DARTS *LP '78*

Singles: 7-inch

SIRE........... 3-5 78

Picture Sleeves

SIRE........... 3-6 78

LPs: 10/12-inch

SIRE........... 5-10 78

TUFFS

(With Kay Bell)

Singles: 7-inch

DORE (757 "I Only Cry Once a Day Now")..............10-20 66
DOT (16304 "Surfer's Stomp").......10-20 61
Also see BELL, Kay

TUGA

Singles: 12-inch

MCA........... 4-6 84

TUGGLE, Bobby

Singles: 78 rpm

CHECKER........... 5-10 55-56

Singles: 7-inch

CHECKER..............10-20 55-56

TULIPS

Singles: 7-inch

MGM........... 4-8 65

TULL, Jethro: see JETHRO TULL

TULLY, Lee, & Milt Moss

Singles: 78 rpm

FLAIR-X........... 5-10 56

Singles: 7-inch

FLAIR-X..............15-25 56

EPs: 7-inch

JUBILEE (5005 "Comedy") 10-20 54

TULSA, Johnny

Singles: 7-inch

KING..............10-15 61

TULU BABIES

Singles: 7-inch

TEMA (125 "Debbie")..............10-15 65
TEMA (817 "The Hurtin' Kind").......10-15 65
(Copies on Mar—crediting the "Talula Babies"—are bootlegs.)
Also see BASKERVILLE HOUNDS

TUMBLERS

Singles: 7-inch

POCONO..............10-15 65

TUMBLEWEEDS

Singles: 7-inch

TEE PEE (1001 "Truck Driver's Wife")..............10-20 69

TUMBLEWEEDS

LPs: 10/12-inch

BASF........... 8-10

TUNE BLENDERS

Singles: 78 rpm

FEDERAL..............50-75 54

Singles: 7-inch

FEDERAL (12201 "Oh Yes I Know")..............150-250 54

TUNE DROPS: see TUNEDROPS

TUNE ROCKERS *P&R '58*

Singles: 7-inch

PET (804 "No Stoppin' This Boppin' ")..............20-30 58
U.A. (139 "Green Mosquito")..........15-25 58

TUNE SHARKS

Singles: 7-inch

SO-RE-CO (501 "Party Time")......10-20 64

TUNE TAILORS

(With the Pete Pecorara Quintet)

Singles: 7-inch

CENTURY (4158 "Beverly")...........15-25 58

TUNE TIMERS

Singles: 7-inch

COMMAND PERFORMANCE 3-5 79

TUNE TONES

Singles: 7-inch

HERALD (524 "Please Baby, Please")..............20-30 58
HERALD (539 "She's Right with Me")..............15-25 59

TUNE WEAVERS *P&R/R&B '57*

(Margo Sylvia & Tune Weavers; with Paul Gayten Orchestra; Tune Weavers / Paul Gayten & Tone Weavers)

Singles: 78 rpm

CASA GRANDE 20-50 57
CHECKER..............15-25 57

Singles: 7-inch

CASA GRANDE (101 "Little Boy")..............20-25 59
CASA GRANDE (3038 "My Congratulations Baby")..............20-25 60
CASA GRANDE (4037 "Happy, Happy Birthday Baby")..............35-50 57
CASA GRANDE (4038 "I Remember Dear")..............20-25 57
CASA GRANDE (4040 "There Stands My Love")..............20-30 58
CHECKER (872 "Happy, Happy Birthday Baby")..............15-20 57
(Checkerboard top label. Can be found with either of two flips: *Ol Man River* or *Yo Yo Walk*.)
CHECKER (872 "Happy, Happy Birthday Baby")........... 5-8 58
(No Checkerboard at top.)
CHECKER (880 "Ol Man River")....10-15 57
(Flip side credits Paul Gayten & the Tone [sic] Weavers.)
CHECKER (1007 "Congratulations on Your Wedding")..............15-20 62
CHESS........... 3-5 73
CLASSIC ARTISTS (104 "Come Back to Me")........... 4-6 88
CLASSIC ARTISTS (107 "Merry Merry Christmas Baby")........... 4-6 89
COLLECTABLES........... 3-4 80s
ERIC........... 3-5 70s

LPs: 10/12-inch

CASA GRANDE..............10-15 73
Members: Margo Sylvia; Charlotte Davis; Gil Lopez; John Sylvia.
Also see GAYTEN, Paul

TUNEDROPS

(Tune Drops)

Singles: 78 rpm

GONE (5003 "Rosie Lee")..............15-25 57

Singles: 7-inch

GONE (5003 "Rosie Lee") 25-50 57
GONE (5072 "Smoothie")..............15-25 59
METRO (20028 "Smoothie")..........30-40 59
Also see DODDS, Malcolm

TUNEMASTERS

Singles: 78 rpm

MARK..............100-200 57

Singles: 7-inch

ASKEL (2 "Down the Line")..........75-125
MARK (7002 "Sending This Letter")..............300-500 57
Also see WILSON, Willie, & Tunemasters

TUNES

Singles: 7-inch

PEL........... 8-12 59
SWADE (102 "Close the Door") 15-25 59

TUNESMITHS

Singles: 78 rpm

COLUMBIA........... 4-8 56

Singles: 7-inch

COLUMBIA (21485 "Outlaw") 8-12 56

TUNESMITHS with Rosemary Clooney & Don Cherry

EPs: 7-inch

COLUMBIA (8941 "Carl Smith's Tunesmiths")..............10-20 56
Also see CHERRY, Don
Also see CLOONEY, Rosemary
Also see SMITH, Carl
Also see TUNESMITHS

TUNESTERS

Singles: 7-inch

KLUB..............10-15
TIARA..............10-15 59

TUNESTERS

Singles: 7-inch

CORDON 8-12 60s

TUNETOPPERS: see BROWN, Al, & His Tunetoppers

TUNNELL, Jimi *D&D '84*

Singles: 12-inch

MCA........... 4-6 84

Singles: 7-inch

MCA........... 3-4 84

TUNSTALL, Arkey

Singles: 7-inch

BRAND X 3-5 78

TURASSO, Wayne

Singles: 7-inch

PERRY..............20-25 60s
TWAYNE..............20-25 60s

Picture Sleeves

TWAYNE..............25-35 60s

TURBA, Frank

LPs: 10/12-inch

MAINSTREAM/RED LION........... 8-10 74

TURBANS *P&R/R&B '55*

Singles: 78 rpm

HERALD..............20-40 55-57
MONEY..............50-75 55

Singles: 7-inch

ABC........... 3-5 73
COLLECTABLES........... 3-4 80s
FLASHBACK........... 4-8 65
HERALD (458 "When You Dance")..............50-75 55
(Script print/flag logo.)
HERALD (458 "When You Dance")..............15-25 57
(Block print logo.)
HERALD (469 "Sister Sookey")......25-50 55
HERALD (478 "I'm Nobody's") 25-50 56
HERALD (486 "All of My Love")......25-50 56
HERALD (495 "Valley of Love")......25-50 57
HERALD (510 "Congratulations")....25-50 57
(Script print/flag logo.)
HERALD (510 "Congratulations")....15-25 57
(Block print logo.)
HERALD (510 "Congratulations")....25-35 57
(Single sided. Promotional issue only.)
HI-OLDIES........... 3-4 80s
IMPERIAL (5807 "Six Questions")..............25-50 61
IMPERIAL (5828 "This Is My Story")..............15-25 62
IMPERIAL (5847 "I Wonder")..........10-20 62
MONEY (209 "No, No Cherry") .. 100-200 55
PARKWAY (820 "When You Dance")..............15-25 61
RED TOP (115 "I Promise You Love")..............25-50 59
ROULETTE (4281 "Diamonds and Pearls")..............10-20 60
ROULETTE (4326 "I'm Not Your Fool Anymore")..............10-20 61

LPs: 10/12-inch

COLLECTABLES........... 5-8 84
LOST-NITE........... 8-12 81
RELIC..............10-15 70s
Members: Al Banks; Matt Platt; Andrew Jones; Charles Williams.
Also see TURKS / Turbans

TURBO-JETS

Singles: 7-inch

FEDERAL (12349 "Bingo")........... 5-8 59
(Monaural.)
FEDERAL (12349 "Bingo") 10-15 59
(Stereo.)
FEDERAL (12353 "So Sassy")........5-10 59

TURBULATIONS

Singles: 7-inch

GUAVA........... 8-12 69
Also see ESSENCE

TURCO, Ann, & Dream Boys

Singles: 7-inch

MILO (111 "I Don't Know Why")......5-10

TURDZ

Singles

NSFD (8839 "Shithouse Blues")........4-8 88
(Outhouse-shaped picture disc. 500 made.)

TURFITS

Singles: 7-inch

CAPITOL (2018 "If It's Love You Want")..............20-25 67

TURGEN, Hank

Singles: 7-inch

BOSS (101 "I've Got to Hand It to You")..............10-15 61

TURKS

Singles: 78 rpm

BALLY..............10-20 56
CASH..............10-15 56
MONEY..............10-15 56

Singles: 7-inch

BALLY (1017 "This Heart of Mine")..............25-35 56
CASH (1042 "It Can't Be True")......20-30 56
CLASS..............10-15 59
IMPERIAL........... 5-10 61
KEEN..............10-20 58
KNIGHT..............10-20 58
MEMORY PAIN........... 3-5
MONEY (215 "I'm a Fool")..............25-35 56
Member: Gaynel Hodge.
Also see HODGE, Gaynel
Also see HOLLYWOOD FLAMES
Also see TURKS / Seniors

TURKS / Seniors

Singles: 7-inch

BALL (001 "Emily")..............15-20 59

TURKS / Turbans

Singles: 78 rpm

MONEY (211 "Emily")..............10-20 55

Singles: 7-inch

MONEY (211 "Emily")..............30-50 55
(Orange label.)
MONEY (211 "Emily")..............10-20
(Yellow label.)
Also see TURBANS
Also see TURKS

TURKS

Singles: 7-inch

D.J.O. (113 "Let It Flame") 10-20 70
DARAN........... 5-10 69

TURKS

Singles: 7-inch

P.B.D. (112 "Baja")..............15-25 64
P.B.D. (113 "Wipe Out")..............15-25 64

TURLEY, Duane, & Tads

Singles: 7-inch

VIV (103 "Devil's Den")..............10-20 58

TURLEY, Richard

(With the All American Boy's Orchestra)

Singles: 7-inch

DOT (16231 "I Wanna Dance")........25-35 61
FRATERNITY (845 "Makin' Love with My Baby")..............25-35 59
Also see RICHARDS, Turley

TURMAN, Don

(With the Vibra Sonics)

Singles: 7-inch

CANDY (101 "Ram Charger '64")....15-25 64
HART........... 5-10 61

TURN AROUNDS

Singles: 7-inch

ERA (3137 "Ain't Nothin' Shakin' ") 15-25 64

TURNABOUTS

Singles: 7-inch

PRANN (5002 "Cott'n Pick'n' ") 10-15 63
Member: Ike Turner.
Also see TURNER, Ike

TURNAROUNDS

(Turn-A-Rounds)

Singles: 7-inch

MINIT........... 4-8 68
TANGERINE........... 4-6 69

TURNAROUNDS & STINGERS

Singles: 7-inch

DE VILLE (133 "Salt'N'Pepper")......5-10 65

TURNBOW, Jeanne

Singles: 7-inch

BEN-RON........... 5-10 64

TURNER, Baby Face

Singles: 78 rpm

MODERN (882 "Blue Serenade")..............100-150 52

Singles: 7-inch

MODERN (882 "Blue Serenade")..............500-1000 52
Session: Ike Turner.
Also see BLAIR, Sunny
Also see TURNER, Ike

TURNER, Bake

Singles: 7-inch

KAPP........... 3-5 70

Picture Sleeves

KAPP........... 3-5 70

TURNER, Benny

(With the Armourettes; Bernie Turner)

Singles: 7-inch

M-PAC (7215 "Love Me")........... 8-12 64
M-PAC (7219 "Good to Me").......... 8-12 65
ONE-DERFUL (4807 "When I'm Gone")..............10-15 62
SKYMAC (1003 "No More Crying")..............15-25 63
SKYMAC (1005 "I Want to Know")..............30-50 64

TURNER, Betty

(With the Chevelles)

Singles: 7-inch

CRESCENT (631 "Blue Star")..........10-20 63
CRESCENT (637 "The Wind Kept Laughing")..............100-200 63
CRESCENT (6501 "Tell Yourself a Lie")..............10-20 65
INFINITY (008 "I Believe in You")..10-20 61
INFINITY (019 "Stay Away from Jim")..............10-20 61
LIBERTY (55861 "Be Careful Girl")..............20-30 66
Also see CHEVELLES

TURNER, Bill, & Blue Smoke: see BLUE SMOKE

TURNER, Billy

Singles: 7-inch

ROULETTE........... 5-10 63
TACIT........... 5-10 62

TURNER, Bobby

Singles: 7-inch

DECCA........... 5-10 62

TURNER, Bonnie & Ike

Singles: 78 rpm

RPM (362 "Looking for My Baby") 15-25 52

Singles: 7-inch

RPM (362 "Looking for My Baby") 50-75 52

TURNER, Cile

Singles: 7-inch

COLONIAL........... 8-10 59

TURNER, Dale

Singles: 7-inch

COLUMBIA........... 4-8 67

TURNER, Dave

Singles: 78 rpm

DREXEL..............10-15 55

Singles: 7-inch

DREXEL (906 "I'm All Yours, Sugar")..............20-30 55

TURNER, Dennis

Singles: 7-inch

LOUIS..............12-25 61-62

TURNER, Denny

Singles: 7-inch

DIAMOND..............10-20 66

TURNER, Duke

(With the Chi-Towns)

Singles: 7-inch

OMEGA (1101 "Put Soul in Your Dance")..............10-20
OMEGA SOUND (23147 "Put Some Soul In Your Dance")..............10-20
SPINNING TOP (42170 "Let Me Be Your Babysitter")..............20-30

TURNER, Dwight

Singles: 7-inch

CHATOK (1001 "You're Alone").....50-75 60s
Also see TURNER, Spyder

TURNER, Ernest

Singles: 7-inch

HOLLYWOOD........... 4-8 68

TURNER, Grant *C&W '64*

Singles: 7-inch

CHART........... 4-6 64

TURNER, Houston, & Dixielanders

Singles: 7-inch

DO-RA-ME (1416 "Uncle John's Bongos")..............20-30 60

TURNER, Ike

(With the Kings of Rhythm; with His Orchestra; with Dee Dee Johnson)

Singles: 78 rpm

CHESS (1459 "Heartbroken and Worried")..............20-40 51
FEDERAL (12297 "Do You Mean It")..............20-30 57
FEDERAL (12304 "Rock-A-Bucket")..............25-75 57
FLAIR..............20-40 52
RPM (356 "You're Driving Me Insane")..............25-50 52

Singles: 7-inch

ARTISTIC (1504 "Down & Out") 10-20 59
COBRA (5033 "Box Top")..............10-20 59
FEDERAL (12297 "Do You Mean It")..............50-75 57
FEDERAL (12304 "Rock-A-Bucket")..............20-40 57
FLAIR (1040 "Cubano Jump")........40-60 52
FLAIR (1059 "Cuban Getaway") 40-60 52
INNIS (3002 "The Drag")........... 4-6
KING (5553 "Big Question")..........10-15 61
LIBERTY........... 3-5 70
RPM (356 "You're Driving Me Insane")..............50-75 52
SUE (100 series)........... 4-8 66
SUE (722 "My Love")..............10-20 59
U.A........... 3-5 71-74

LPs: 10/12-inch

CROWN (367 "Ike Turner Rocks the Blues")..............50-100 63
POMPEII..............10-15 69
U.A........... 6-12 72-73
Also see BLAND, Bobby, & Ike Turner
Also see BRENSTON, Jackie
Also see EMERSON, Billy 'The Kid'
Also see HOWLIN' WOLF
Also see JOHNSON, Ike & Dee Dee
Also see KING, B.B.
Also see LANE, Willie
Also see RENRUT, Icky
Also see RUSH, Otis
Also see TURNABOUTS
Also see TURNER, Baby Face
Also see TURNER, Bonnie & Ike

TURNER, Ike & Tina *P&R/R&B '60*

(With the Ikettes; with Home Grown Funk; "Featuring Tina")

Singles: 7-inch

A&M (1118 "River Deep, Mountain High")........... 5-10 69

A&M (1170 "A Love Like Yours")....5-10 69
BLUE THUMB....4-6 69-71
CENCO (112 "You Weren't Ready")....5-10 67
COLLECTABLES....3-4 80s
FANTASY....3-5 80
INNIS....4-8 68-71
KENT (402 "My Baby Now")....5-10 64
KENT (409 "Please Please Please")....5-10 64
KENT (418 "Chicken Shack")....5-10 65
KENT (457 "Flee Flu Fla")....5-10 66
KENT (4500 series)....4-6 70
LIBERTY....4-6 70-71
LOMA (2011 "I'm Through with Love")....5-10 65
LOMA (2015 "Just to Be with You") 5-10 65
MINIT....4-8 69-70
MODERN (1007 "Goodbye, So Long")....5-10 65
MODERN (1012 "Gonna Have Fun")....5-10 65
PHILLES (131 "River Deep, Mountain High")....10-15 66
PHILLES (134 "A Man Is a Man Is a Man")....10-20 66
PHILLES (135 "I'll Never Need More Than This")....10-20 66
PHILLES (136 "A Love Like Yours")....10-20 67
POMPEII....4-8 68-70
SONJA (2001 "If I Can't Be First")... 8-10 63
SONJA (2005 "You Can't Miss Nothin' That You Never Had")....8-10 64
SUE (100 series)....5-8 65-66
SUE (730 "Fool in Love")....10-15 60
SUE (734 "Fool Too Long")....10-15 60
SUE (735 "I Idolize You")....10-15 60
SUE (740 "I'm Jealous")....10-15 61
SUE (749 "It's Gonna Work Out Fine")....10-15 61
SUE (753 "Poor Fool")....10-15 61
SUE (757 "Tra La La La")....10-15 62
SUE (760 "It's Gonna Work Out Fine")....8-10 62
SUE (765 "You Should'a Treated Me Right")....8-12 62
SUE (768 "I Idolize You")....8-12 62
SUE (772 "Mind in a Whirl")....8-12 62
SUE (774 "Please Don't Hurt Me") .. 8-12 62
SUE (784 "Don't Play Me Cheap") .. 8-12 63
TRC....3-5 71
TANGERINE (963 "Beauty Is Only Skin Deep")....5-8 66
TANGERINE (967 "Dust My Broom")....5-8 66
U.A.....3-5 71-75
W.B.....5-10 64

Picture Sleeves

MINIT....5-8 69
POMPEII....5-8 69
W.B. (5433 "A Fool for a Fool")....10-20 64

LPs: 10/12-inch

A&M (3179 "River Deep, Mountain High")....8-12 82
A&M (4178 "River Deep, Mountain High")....15-25 69
ABC....8-10 70s
ACCORD....5-10 81
BLUE THUMB....8-12 69-73
CAPITOL (500 series)....5-10 75
(With "SM" prefix.)
CAPITOL (500 series)....10-15 69
(With "ST" prefix.)
CENCO....15-20 60s
COLLECTABLES....5-8 88
FANTASY....5-10 80
HARMONY (11000 series)....10-12 69
HARMONY (30000 series)....8-10 71
KENT (519 "Soul of Ike & Tina")....25-35 61
KENT (538 "Festival of Live Performances")....25-35 62
KENT (550 "Please Please Please")....25-35 62
KENT (5014 "Ike & Tina Revue")....15-25 64
LIBERTY (7000 series)....10-12 70
LIBERTY (51000 series)....5-8 85
LOMA....10-20 66
MINIT....10-15 69
PHILLES (4011 "River Deep, Mountain High")....10000-15000 66
(Covers for a U.S. pressing on Philles are not known to exist. British pressings [London/ Philles SHU-8298] do exist with covers.)
PICKWICK....5-10 70s
POMPEII....10-15 68-69
SUE (2001 "The Sound of Ike & Tina Turner")....200-300 61
SUE (2003 "Dance with Ike & Tina Turner's Kings of Rhythm")....100-200 62
(Instrumentals by Ike & Tina Turner's band.)
SUE (2004 "Dynamite")....250-350 63
SUE (2005 "Don't Play Me Cheap")....100-200 63
SUE (2007 "It's Gonna Work Out Fine")....100-200 63
SUE (1038 "Greatest Hits")....35-45 65
SUNSET....8-12 69-70
UNART....5-10 70s
U.A.....8-12 71-78
UNITED SUPERIOR....8-10
W.B.....10-20 65-69
Session: Vernon Guy; Stacy Johnson.
Also see BLAND, Bobby, & Ike Turner
Also see GUY, Vernon
Also see IKETTES
Also see JOHNSON, Stacy
Also see RAELETTES
Also see SYLVIA
Also see TURNER, Ike
Also see TURNER, Tina

TURNER, Jack
(With His Granger Gang)

Singles: 78 rpm

HICKORY....40-60 56
RCA....10-15 53-55

Singles: 7-inch

HICKORY (1050 "Everybody's Rockin' But Me")....50-100 56
MGM....10-20 58
RCA....15-25 53-55

TURNER, Jesse Lee — *P&R '59*

Singles: 7-inch

CARLTON....10-20 59
FRATERNITY....10-20 59
GNP (184 "All You Gotta Do")....4-8 62
GNP (188 "Shotgun Boogie")....40-60 62
IMPERIAL....8-12 60
SUDDEN....4-6
TOP RANK....8-12 60

Picture Sleeves

CARLTON (509 "Baby Please Don't Tease")....15-25 59
FRATERNITY (855 "Teenage Misery")....35-50 59

TURNER, Joe — *R&B '46*
(With His Blues Kings; with Pete Johnson & His Orchestra; with Van "Piano Man" Walls & His Orchestra; Big Joe Turner)

Singles: 78 rpm

ALADDIN (3013 "Morning Glory")....50-100 49
ALADDIN (3070 "Back Breaking Baby")....50-100 50
ATLANTIC....10-30 51-57
BAYOU....10-20 53
COLONY....10-20 52
CORAL (65000 series)....10-20 48
DECCA....10-20 41-56
DOOTONE (305 "I Love Ya, I Love Ya, I Love Ya")....50-100 51
DOWN BEAT....10-20 48
EXCELSIOR....10-20 49
FIDELITY....10-20 51-52
FREEDOM....10-20 50
IMPERIAL....10-20 50
MGM....10-20 48-50
NATIONAL....10-20 46-51
RPM....25-50 51
SWING BEAT....10-20 49
VOCALION....15-25 39

Singles: 7-inch

ATLANTIC (939 "Chains of Love")....50-100 51
ATLANTIC (949 "Bump Miss Susie")....50-75 51
ATLANTIC (960 "Sweet Sixteen")..50-75 52
ATLANTIC (970 "Don't You Cry")...50-75 52
ATLANTIC (982 "Still in Love")....40-60 52
ATLANTIC (1001 "Honey Hush")...20-30 53
ATLANTIC (1016 "TV Mama")....30-40 53
ATLANTIC (1026 thru 1184)....15-30 54-58
ATLANTIC (2000 series)....8-15 59-60
BAYOU (015 "The Blues Jumped a Rabbit")....100-200 53
BLUESTIME (45001 "Two Loves Have I")....25-50
BLUESWAY....4-8 67
CORAL (62000 series)....5-8 64
DECCA (29000 series)....15-25 55-56
KENT....3-6 69-71
RPM (345 "Ridin' Blues")....100-150 51
RONN....4-6 69

EPs: 7-inch

ATLANTIC (536 "Joe Turner Sings")....50-75 55
ATLANTIC (565 "Joe Turner")....50-75 56
ATLANTIC (586 "Joe Turner")....50-75 56
ATLANTIC (606 "Rock with Joe Turner")....50-75 56
EMARCY (6132 "Joe Turner and Pete Johnson")....50-75 56

LPs: 10/12-inch

ARHOOLIE....15-25 62
ATCO....8-12 71
ATLANTIC (1234 "Boss of the Blues")....100-150 58
ATLANTIC (1332 "Big Joe Rides Again")....50-75 60
ATLANTIC (8005 "Joe Turner")..100-200 57
(Black label.)
ATLANTIC (8005 "Joe Turner")....50-100 59
(Red label.)
ATLANTIC (8023 "Rockin' the Blues")....100-150 58
(Black label.)
ATLANTIC (8023 "Rockin' the Blues")....50-75 59
(Red label.)
ATLANTIC (8033 "Big Joe Is Here")....100-150 59
(Black label.)
ATLANTIC (8033 "Big Joe Is Here")....50-75 59
(Red label.)
ATLANTIC (8081 "Best of Joe Turner")....30-50 63
ATLANTIC (8812 "Boss of the Blues")....5-10 81
BIG TOWN....5-10 78
BLUES SPECTRUM....10-12
BLUESTIME (9002 "The Real Boss of the Blues")....20-30 60s
BLUESWAY....8-12 67-73
CHIARDSCURO....8-10 76
CLASSIC JAZZ....5-10 79
EMARCY (36014 "Joe Turner with Pete Johnson")....100-200 56
INTERMEDIA....5-8 83-84
KENT....8-12 70s
LMI....8-10 74
MCA....5-10 80
PABLO....5-10 76-83
SAVOY (14012 "Blues Can Make You Happy")....100-150 58
SAVOY (14106 "Carless Love")....50-75 64
SAVOY (2223 "Big Joe Is Here")....5-10 77
UNITED....8-10
Session: King Curtis.
Also see BIG VERNON
Also see FLENNOY TRIO & JOE TURNER
Also see JOHNSON, Pete
Also see KING CURTIS
Also see WILLIAMS, Dootsie

TURNER, Joe / Jimmy Nelson

LPs: 10/12-inch

CROWN....15-25 62
Also see NELSON, Jimmy

TURNER, Joe, & Roomful of Blues

LPs: 10/12-inch

MUSE (5293 "Blues Train")....5-10 83
Also see ROOMFUL of BLUES
Also see TURNER, Joe

TURNER, Joe Lynn — *LP '85*

LPs: 10/12-inch

ELEKTRA....5-8 85

TURNER, Johnny

Singles: 7-inch

JAKE LEG....15-20
(Compact 33 single.)

TURNER, Kylo

Singles: 7-inch

SAR....4-8 60

TURNER, Marie

Singles: 7-inch

QUEEN....5-10 61

TURNER, Mary Lou — *C&W '74*

Singles: 7-inch

CHURCHILL....3-4 79-80
MCA....3-5 74-78
Also see ANDERSON, Bill, & Mary Lou Turner

TURNER, Maurice

Singles: 7-inch

STUDIO CITY....8-12 60s
UA....4-8 60s

Picture Sleeves

STUDIO CITY....10-20 60s

TURNER, Mickey

Singles: 7-inch

REVOLVO....5-10 60
VELLEY (1403 "Rock with a Redhead")....50-100 58

TURNER, Nate, & Mirettes
(With Venetta Fields & Mirettes)

Singles: 7-inch

UNI....4-6 69
Also see FIELDS, Venetta

TURNER, Ned

Singles: 7-inch

ARBET (1018 "Didn't I Mean Anything to You")....6-10

TURNER, Odelle

Singles: 78 rpm

ATLANTIC....50-75 52

Singles: 7-inch

ATLANTIC (964 "Alarm Clock Boogie")....100-125 52

TURNER, Pete, & His Blues Band

Singles: 78 rpm

HAVEN....15-25 47

TURNER, Rocky

Singles: 7-inch

PROGRESS (101 "Slow Jerkin' ")..10-15 65
(First issue.)
W.B. (5603 "Slow Jerkin' ")....5-8 65

TURNER, Ruby — *LP '90*
(Featuring Jonathan Butler)

Singles: 7-inch

JIVE....3-4 86-90

LPs: 10/12-inch

JIVE....5-8 86-90
Also see BUTLER, Jonathan

TURNER, Sammy — *P&R/R&B '59*
(With the Twisters)

Singles: 7-inch

BIG TOP (3007 & 3016)....5-10 59
BIG TOP (3029 "Always")....5-10 59
(Monaural.)
BIG TOP (3029 "Always")....15-25 59
(Stereo.)
BIG TOP (3032 thru 3070)....5-10 60-61
BIG TOP (3089 "Falling")....10-15 61
ERIC....3-4 70s
MILLENNIUM....3-4 78
MOTOWN....10-20 64
PACIFIC (3016 "Lavender Blue")...25-35 59
PACIFIC (3029 "Always")....20-30 59
20TH FOX....4-8 65
VERVE (10465 "A Child Is Born")..12-25 66

EPs: 7-inch

BIG TOP (101 "Lavender Blue Moods")....40-60 60
(Not issued with standard cover. Plain paper 45-type sleeve has rubber stamped on both sides: A Special Promotional EP for D.J. use only.")

LPs: 10/12-inch

BIG TOP (1301 "Lavender Blue Moods")....30-50 60
(Monaural.)
BIG TOP (ST-1301 "Lavender Blue Moods")....40-60 60
(Stereo.)
Session: King Curtis.
Also see KING CURTIS

TURNER, Sammy / Ivory Joe Hunter

Singles: 7-inch

GOLD SOUL....3-5
Also see HUNTER, Ivory Joe
Also see TURNER, Sammy

TURNER, Scott
(Scotty Turner)

Singles: 7-inch

ALMO....4-8 64
IMPERIAL....4-6 69

TURNER, Smiley

Singles: 78 rpm

MERCURY....15-25 49

TURNER, Sonny, & Sound Ltd.

LPs: 10/12-inch

SONNY (1000 "Standing Ovation") 10-15 74
Members: Sonny Turner; Leonard Veal; Paul; Jay; Terry; Jeff; Joe.
Also see HESITATIONS
Also see PLATTERS

TURNER, Spyder — *P&R/R&B '66*
(Dwight Turner)

Singles: 7-inch

KWANZA....3-5 73
MGM....5-15 66-71
POLYDOR....3-4 84
WHITFIELD....3-5 78-79

LPs: 10/12-inch

MGM....15-20 67
WHITFIELD....5-10 78-79
Also see BRISTOL, Johnny, & Spyder Turner
Also see TURNER, Dwight

TURNER, Terry

Singles: 7-inch

M.C.M.....4-8 77
S.D.B.....4-8 77

TURNER, Tina — *R&B/LP '75*

Singles: 12-inch

CAPITOL....4-6 84-87

Singles: 7-inch

CAPITOL....3-4 84-89
POMPEII....4-8 68
U.A.....3-5 75-78
WAGNER....3-5 79

Picture Sleeves

CAPITOL....3-5 84-89

LPs: 10/12-inch

AUDIO FIDELITY (100 "Tina Turner")....25-35 84
(Picture disc.)
CAPITOL....5-8 84-89
FANTASY....5-10
SPRINGBOARD....8-10 72
U.A. (Except 200)....8-10 75-78
U.A. (200 "Tina Turner Turns the Country On")....10-15 67
WAGNER....5-8 79
Also see ADAMS, Bryan, & Tina Turner
Also see BASS, Fontella, & Tina Turner
Also see BOWIE, David
Also see CLAPTON, Eric, & Tina Turner
Also see JOHN, Elton / Tina Turner
Also see TURNER, Ike & Tina
Also see U.S.A. for AFRICA

TURNER, Titus — *P&R/R&B '59*

Singles: 78 rpm

ATLANTIC....15-25 57
OKEH....10-20 52-54

Singles: 7-inch

ATCO (6310 "Baby Girl")....5-10 64
ATLANTIC (1127 "A-Knocking at My Baby's Door")....15-25 57
BELL (620 "Sportin' Tom")....4-8 65
COLUMBIA (42873 "Goodbye Rose")....5-10 63
COLUMBIA (42947 "Make Someone Love You")....5-10 64
ENJOY (1005 "My Darkest Hour")...8-12 62
ENJOY (1015 "My Darkest Hour")...5-10 64
ENJOY (2010 "Bow Wow")....5-10 64
GLOVER (200 "Run Home Little Girl")....10-15 59
GLOVER (201 "Taking Care of Business")....10-15 59
GLOVER (202 "When the Sergeant Comes Marching Home")....15-20 60
GLOVER (206 "Cool Down")....10-15 60
JAMIE (1174 "Sound Off")....8-10 60
JAMIE (1184 "Hey Doll Baby")....10-15 61
JAMIE (1189 "Horsin' Around")....8-12 61
JAMIE (1202 "Shake the Hand of a Fool")....8-12 61
JAMIE (1213 "Twistin' Train")....5-10 62
JOSIE....4-8 68-69
KING (Except 5213)....10-25 57-61
KING (5213 "Fall Guy")....10-20 59
(Monaural.)
KING (5213 "Fall Guy")....25-35 59
(Stereo.)
MURBO (1001 "Hoop Hoop Hoop a Hoopa Doo")....4-8 65
OKEH (6844 "The Same Old Feeling")....20-40 52
OKEH (6883 "What'cha Gonna Do")....20-40 52
OKEH (6907 "Jambalaya")....20-40 52
OKEH (6929 "Be Sure You Know") 20-40 52
OKEH (6938 "My Plea")....20-40 53
OKEH (6961 "Big Mary")....20-40 53
OKEH (7027 "Over the Rainbow") 20-40 54
OKEH (7038 "Hello Stranger")....20-40 54
OKEH (7244 "Eye to Eye")....5-8 66
PHILIPS....4-8 67
WING (90006 "Around the World") 15-25 55
WING (90058 "Get on the Right Track, Baby")....15-25 56

LPs: 10/12-inch

JAMIE (3018 "Sound Off")....25-50 61
Session: Mickey Baker.
Also see BAKER, Mickey

TURNER, Tommy

Singles: 7-inch

ELBAM (70 "Lady")....15-25 66

TURNER, Tony

Singles: 7-inch

CUCA (67410 "Carefree")....8-12 67

TURNER, Velvert, Group

LPs: 10/12-inch

FAMILY....10-12 72

TURNER, Zeb — *C&W '49*

Singles: 78 rpm

KING....5-8 49-50

LPs: 10/12-inch

AUDIO LAB (1537 "Country Music in the Zeb Turner Style")....30-40 59

TURNER & KIRWAN

Singles: 7-inch

PETERS INT'L....3-5 77

LPs: 10/12-inch

PETERS INT'L....8-10 77
Members: Pierce Turner; Larry Kirwan.

TURNER BROTHERS

Singles: 7-inch

CARNIVAL....5-10 68
MB (572-19 "Let's Go Fishing")....15-25

TURNERS, Nat
(Nat Turners Rebellion)

Singles: 7-inch

PHILLY GROOVE....3-5 70s

TURNEY, Gene

Singles: 7-inch

ACCENT....4-8 65

TURNPIKES

Singles: 7-inch

CAPITOL....10-20 68

TURNQUIST REMEDY

LPs: 10/12-inch

PENTAGRAM (10004 "Turnquist Remedy")....15-20 70
Members: Scott Harder; John Maggi; Michael Woods.
Also see STRING CHEESE

TURNSTALL, Arkey

Singles: 7-inch

BRAND X (00 "Is the King Dead")....8-12 78

TURRENTINE, Stanley — *LP '67*

Singles: 7-inch

BLUE NOTE....3-8 61-69
CTI....3-5 72
ELEKTRA....3-4 79-81
FANTASY....3-5 74-78
IMPULSE....3-5 67

LPs: 10/12-inch

BAINBRIDGE....5-8 81
BLUE NOTE....25-50 60-61
(Label gives New York street address for Blue Note Records.)
BLUE NOTE....15-30 62-65
(Label reads "Blue Note Records Inc. - New York, U.S.A.")
BLUE NOTE....8-18 65-85
(Label shows Blue Note Records as a division of either Liberty or United Artists.)
CTI....8-12 71-75
ELEKTRA....5-8 79-81
FPM....5-8 75
FANTASY....8-12 74-78
IMPULSE....8-15 67-78
MAINSTREAM....15-25 65
PRESTIGE....6-12 70-71
SUNSET....8-12 69
TIME....25-50 62-63
UPFRONT....6-12 72
Also see BYRD, Donald
Also see FULSON, Lowell
Also see GILBERTO, Astrud, & Stanley Turrentine
Also see HUBBARD, Freddie, & Stanley Turrentine
Also see SILVER, Horace, Quintet, & Stanley Turrentine

TURTLES

Singles: 78 rpm

RCA (6356 "Mystery Train")....5-10 55

Singles: 7-inch

RCA (6356 "Mystery Train")....10-20 55

TURTLES — *P&R/LP '65*

Singles: 7-inch

BUCCANEER (3002 "Happy Together")....5-10
COLLECTABLES....3-4 80s
LOST-NITE....3-5
WHITE WHALE....5-15 65-70

Picture Sleeves

WHITE WHALE....10-15 67-69

EPs: 7-inch

RHINO (RNPD-901 "Turtles 1968")....8-10 83
(Picture disc.)

LPs: 10/12-inch

RHINO....5-8 82-86
SIRE....10-15 74
TRIP....5-10 70s
WHITE WHALE....15-30 65-71
Members: Howard Kaylan; Mark Volman; Chuck Portz; Al Nichol; Don Murray; Jim

Tucker; John Barbata; John Seiter; Jim Pons; Chip Douglas.
Also see CHRISTMAS SPIRIT
Also see CROSSFIRES
Also see FLO & EDDIE
Also see KAYLAN, Howard, & Marc Volman
Also see LEAVES
Also see MODERN FOLK QUARTET

TURZY, Jane
Singles: 78 rpm
DECCA 3-6 51-54
Singles: 7-inch
B&F 10-20 59
CORAL 5-10 58
DECCA 5-10 51-54

TUTONE, Tommy: see TOMMY TUTONE

TU-TONES
Singles: 7-inch
LIN (5021 "Saccharin Sally") 40-50 59

TUTOR, Tim
LPs: 10/12-inch
PLAYBOY 8-10 73

TUTT, Gregory
LPs: 10/12-inch
KENT 8-10 73

TUTTI FRUTTI
Singles: 7-inch
REPRISE 4-8 69

TUTTLE, Wesley, & His Texas Stars *C&W '45*
(With Marilyn Tuttle)
Singles: 78 rpm
CAPITOL 4-8 45-54
Singles: 7-inch
CAPITOL 6-12 52-54
SACRED 10-20

TUXEDO
Singles: 7-inch
HI 3-5 75

TUXEDO JUNCTION *P&R/LP '78*
Singles: 12-inch
BUTTERFLY 4-8 78-80
Singles: 7-inch
BUTTERFLY (Black vinyl) 3-5 78-80
BUTTERFLY (Colored vinyl) 4-6 78
LPs: 10/12-inch
BUTTERFLY (Black vinyl) 5-10 77-79
BUTTERFLY (Colored vinyl) 10-12 77
(Promotional issues only.)

TUXEDOS
Singles: 7-inch
FORTÉ (1414 "Yes It's True") 100-150 60
(Gold label.)
FORTÉ (1414 "Yes It's True") 25-35 60
(Yellow label.)
Also see PORTRAITS

TUXEDOS
Singles: 7-inch
ABC-PAR 4-8 63
SEAGRAVE 4-8

TWANGY REBELS
Singles: 7-inch
GENERAL AMERICAN (719 "Rebel Rouser 65") 5-10 65
Member: Frank Virtuoso.
Also see VIRTUOSO, Frank

TWANS
Singles: 7-inch
DADE (1903 "I Can't See Him Again") 150-250 60s

TWAS BRILLIG
Singles: 7-inch
DATE (1550 "Dirty Old Man") 40-60 67
SCOTTY (6620 "You Love") 60-80 67
Members: Earl Bulinski; Bill Bulinski; Jerry Fink; Gary Omerza; Tim Elving.
Also see ELECTRAS

TWEEDS
Singles: 7-inch
CORAL 4-8 67-68

TWEEDY & TWAYNE
Singles: 7-inch
ARVEE 5-10 60

TWEENS
Singles: 7-inch
DC 4-8 60s

TWEETERS
Singles: 7-inch
DECCA (30725 "Mascara Mama") 15-25 58

12 A.M.
Singles: 7-inch
GROOVY (102 "The Way I Feel") .. 15-25 67

TWENNYNINE *R&B/LP '79*
(Featuring Lenny White)
Singles: 7-inch
ELEKTRA 3-5 79-81
LPs: 10/12-inch
ELEKTRA 5-10 79-81
Also see WHITE, Lenny

TWENTIE GRANS
Singles: 7-inch
COLUMBIA (44239 "Giving Up Your Love") 15-25 67
(Also issued as by the Players.)
Member: Herman Griffin.
Also see GRIFFIN, Herman

Also see PLAYERS

TWENTIETH CENTURY ZOO
Singles: 7-inch
CAZ (103 "You Don't Remember") ... 8-12 67
VAULT 5-10 69
LPs: 10/12-inch
VAULT (122 "Thunder on a Clear Day") 15-25 68

20-20 *LP '79*
Singles: 7-inch
PORTRAIT 3-5 79
EPs: 7-inch
BOMP 5-10
LPs: 10/12-inch
ENIGMA 5-8 83
PORTRAIT 5-10 79-81

21ST CENTURY *P&R/R&B '75*
Singles: 7-inch
RCA 3-5 75
Members: Fred Williams; Tyrone Moores; Alphonso Smith; Piere Johnson; Alonzo Martin.
Also see 21ST CREATION

21ST CREATION
Singles: 7-inch
GORDY 3-5 78
LPs: 10/12-inch
GORDY 5-10 78
Members: Fred Williams; Tyrone Moores; Alphonso Smith; Piere Johnson; Alonzo Martin.
Also see 21ST CENTURY

24 CARAT BLACK
Singles: 7-inch
ENTERPRISE 3-5 73
LPs: 10/12-inch
ENTERPRISE 8-10 73

24 - 7 SPYZ *LP '89*
LPs: 10/12-inch
IN-EFFECT 5-8 89-90

27th SUBMARINE AIRBORNE
Singles: 7-inch
WESTCHESTER 8-12 60s

$27 SNAP-ON FACE
LPs: 10/12-inch
HETRODYNE (001 "Hetrodyne State Hospital") 35-55 77
(Colored vinyl.)

TWICE AS MUCH
Singles: 7-inch
MGM 4-8 66
Picture Sleeves
MGM 8-10 66

TWIGGS
Singles: 7-inch
JERDEN (917 "Flowers & Beads") ... 5-10 66
TRAFF (001 "Letters & Pictures") 5-10 60s

TWIGGY
Singles: 7-inch
BELL 4-8 71
CAPITOL 4-8 67
MERCURY 3-5 76
Picture Sleeves
CAPITOL 5-10 67
LPs: 10/12-inch
MERCURY 8-12 76

TWIGGY & FRIENDS
Singles: 7-inch
BELL (45,115 "Zoo De Zoo Zong") 4-6 71

TWIGS
Singles: 7-inch
DOT 4-8 66

TWILETTES
Singles: 7-inch
DARCEY (5002 "Boss Town Shuffle") 15-25 65

TWILIGHT
Singles: 7-inch
C&J (122652 "What a Surprise") 4-6 82
LPs: 10/12-inch
JADE 5-10 85
Member: Joel Katz.

TWILIGHT STRINGERS
Singles: 7-inch
VALE (1 "Pale Face Twist") 10-15 62
VALE (2 "Cherokee Twist") 10-15 62

TWILIGHT 22 *P&R/R&B/D&D '83*
Singles: 12-inch
VANGUARD 4-6 83-84
Singles: 7-inch
VANGUARD 3-4 83-84
LPs: 10/12-inch
VANGUARD 5-8 84

TWILIGHTERS
(With "Frank Motley [Dual Trumpeter] & His Crew")
Singles: 78 rpm
MARSHALL 50-75 53
Singles: 7-inch
MARSHALL (702 "Please Tell Me You're Mine") 100-200 53
(Black vinyl.)
MARSHALL (702 "Please Tell Me You're Mine") 500-1000 53
(Red vinyl.)
Also see MOTLEY, Frank

TWILIGHTERS
Singles: 78 rpm
SPECIALTY (548 "It's True") 20-30 55
Singles: 7-inch
SPECIALTY (548 "It's True") 40-50 55

Also see ALLEN, Tony

TWILIGHTERS
(Twi-Lighters)
Singles: 78 rpm
DOT (15526 "Eternally") 10-20 56
EBB (117 "Pride and Joy") 20-30 57
MGM (55011 "Little Did I Dream") 40-60 55
MGM (55014 "Lovely Lady") 50-75 55
Singles: 7-inch
BUBBLE (1334 "My Silent Prayer") 25-45 62
CHESS (1803 "She Needs a Guy") 15-25 61
CHOLLY (712 "Let There Be Love") 500-750 58
COLLECTABLES 3-4 80s
DOT (15526 "Eternally") 25-35 56
EBB (117 "Pride and Joy") 20-30 57
ELDO (115 "Do You Believe") 15-25 61
IMPERIAL 5-10 66
J-V-B (83 "How Many Times") . 500-1000 57
MGM (55011 "Little Did I Dream") 100-200 55
MGM (55014 "Lovely Lady") 150-250 55
PICO (2801 "Eternally") 50-75
PLA-BAC (1113 "Eternally") 75-100 57
RED TOP (127 "The Key to My Heart") 150-250 60
RICKI (907 "Help Me") 50-75 61
SUPER (1003 "Please Come Home") 50-100 60

TWILIGHTERS / Little Cholly Wright
Singles: 7-inch
CADDY (103 "Eternally") 150-250 57
Also see TWILIGHTERS
Also see WRIGHT, Little Cholly

TWI-LIGHTERS
Singles: 7-inch
FRATERNITY (889 "Beginning of Love") 15-25 61
SAXONY (2003 "Beginning of Love") 4-8 94

TWILIGHTERS
Singles: 7-inch
BETHLEHEM (3002 "Just Like Before") 15-25 61
BETHLEHEM (3004 "It Hurts Me So") 15-25 62

TWI-LIGHTERS
Singles: 78 rpm
GROOVE 15-25 56
Singles: 7-inch
GROOVE (0154 "Sittin' in a Corner") 35-50 56

TWILIGHTERS
Singles: 7-inch
SARA (1048 "Restless Love") 35-45 61

TWILIGHTERS
Singles: 7-inch
BELL (624 "Be Faithful") 10-15 64
MARK VII 5-10 68

TWILIGHTERS Featuring Donald Richards
Singles: 7-inch
SPIN (1 "Yes You Are") 150-250 60

TWILIGHTS
Singles: 7-inch
FINESSE (1717 "My Heart Belongs to Only You") 30-50 59

TWILIGHTS
Singles: 7-inch
AQUA 5-10 60s
FELICE (713 "Believe It Or Not") ... 30-50 63
(Colored vinyl.)
HARTHON (134 "It's Been So Long") 10-20 64
HARTHON (135 "Shipwreck") 10-20 64
PARKWAY 8-12 67
PARROT 5-10 65
ROULETTE 10-20 64
6 STAR (1001 "Little Richard") 15-25 63
TWILIGHT (1028 "It Could Be True") 15-25 62

TWILIGHTS
Singles: 7-inch
BANGAR 10-20 64
CUCA 10-20 65
Members: Gene Frazier; Dan Dernbach; Bob Grizb; Donnie Winget.

TWILIGHTS
Singles: 7-inch
CAPITOL 5-10 67

TWILIGHTS
Singles: 7-inch
HARTHON (134 "It's Been So Long") 10-20

TWILIGHTS Featuring Tony Richards
(With the Richard Wolfe Orchestra)
Singles: 7-inch
COLPIX (178 "Paper Boy") 75-125 60

TWILITERS
Singles: 7-inch
FLIPPIN' (106 "Infatuation") 10-15 61
NIX (102 "Hey There") 30-50 61
NIX (103 "Back to School") 20-30 61

TWILITERS
Singles: 7-inch
PALOMA (100 "You Better Make It") 25-50 64

TWI-LITES
Singles: 7-inch
KING 8-12 61

TWILLEY, Dwight *P&R '75*
(Dwight Twilley Band)
Singles: 7-inch
ARISTA 3-5 77-79
EMI AMERICA 3-4 82-84
SHELTER 3-5 75-76
Picture Sleeves
EMI AMERICA 3-4 84
SHELTER 3-5 75-76
LPs: 10/12-inch
ARISTA 5-10 77-79
EMI AMERICA 5-8 82-84
SHELTER 5-10 75-76
Also see SEYMOUR, Phil

TWIN CONNEXION
LPs: 10/12-inch
DECCA 15-25 68

TWIN HYPE *LP '89*
LPs: 10/12-inch
PROFILE 5-8 89

TWIN IMAGE *R&B '85*
Singles: 12-inch
CAPITOL 4-6 84-85
Singles: 7-inch
CAPITOL 3-4 84-85
LPs: 10/12-inch
CAPITOL 5-8 84

TWIN TONES: see TWINS

TWIN TUNES QUINTET
Singles: 7-inch
RCA (7091 "Baby Lover") 10-20 60s

TWIN-DELLS
Singles: 7-inch
TWIN DELL (201,022 "Nancy") 15-25 66
Members: Charlie Basile; Paul Basile; Bobby Pano.

TWINK
LPs: 10/12-inch
SIRE 10-15 70

TWINKLE
Singles: 7-inch
AURORA (163 "What Am I Doing Here with You") 5-10 60s
TOLLIE (9040 "Terry") 5-8 64
TOLLIE (9047 "Ain't Nobody Home But Me") 5-8 65
Picture Sleeves
TOLLIE (9040 "Terry") 10-20 64

TWINKLES
(With Al Browne & His Band)
Singles: 7-inch
MUSICOR 5-10 63
PEAK (5001 "Bad Motorcycle") 25-45 58
Also see BROWNE, Al

TWINKLETONES: see HOMBS, Jimmie / Twinkletones

TWINN CONNEXION
LPs: 10/12-inch
DECCA 10-15 68

TWINS
(Twin Tones)
Singles: 7-inch
LANCER 8-12 59
MONTE CARLO 10-15 57
RCA 5-10 58
Picture Sleeves
RCA 10-20 58
EPs: 7-inch
RCA 15-25 57-58
LPs: 10/12-inch
RCA (1708 "Teenagers Love the Twins") 35-45 58
Members: Jim; John.

TWINS *D&D '83*
Singles: 12-inch
QUALITY/RFC 4-6 83

TWINTONES
Singles: 7-inch
BANNER 5-10 60

TWIST, Johnny
Singles: 7-inch
CHECKER 5-8 66

TWIST, Oliver
Singles: 7-inch
EPIC 4-6 69

TWISTED SISTER *LP '83*
Singles: 7-inch
ATLANTIC 3-4 83-87
Picture Sleeves
ATLANTIC 3-4 84-87
LPs: 10/12-inch
ATLANTIC 5-8 83-87
Members: Dee Snider; Jay Jay French; A.J. Pero; Eddie Ojeda; Mark Mendoza.

TWISTER, Big Bill, & His Minters
LPs: 10/12-inch
INT'L AWARD (187 "Do the Twist") 10-15 62

TWISTER, Eddie
Singles: 7-inch
PHILIPS 4-8 62

TWISTERS
Singles: 7-inch
APT 10-15 60
CAMPUS 10-15 61
CAPITOL 10-15 60
FELCO 5-10 59
HULL 5-10 60

TWISTERS
(With the Shades)
Singles: 7-inch
SUN-SET (501 "This Is the End") 300-400 61

TWISTERS
Singles: 7-inch
DUAL 8-10 61
Also see JOEY & TWISTERS

TWISTERS
(Bobby Smith Combo)
Singles: 7-inch
GEMINI (101 "Run Little Sheba") 200-300 62
(Reissued as by the Rebels.)
Also see REBELS
Also see SMITH, Bob

TWISTERS
LPs: 10/12-inch
TREASURE 15-25 62

TWISTERS
LPs: 10/12-inch
GOODS RECORDS 5-10 82
RHINO 5-10 80

TWISTIN' HARVEY
(Harvey Scales)
Singles: 7-inch
CUCA (1132 "The Clock") 5-10 63
Also see SCALES, Harvey

TWISTIN' KINGS
Singles: 7-inch
MOTOWN (1022 "Xmas Twist") 15-25 61
MOTOWN (1023 "Congo") 15-25 62
LPs: 10/12-inch
MOTOWN (601 "Twistin' Around the World") 30-40 61

TWITTY, Conway *P&R '57/C&W '66*
Singles: 78 rpm
MGM (12677 "It's Only Make Believe") 100-150 58
(Canadian.)
MERCURY 25-75 57
Singles: 7-inch
ABC-PAR (10507 "Go on and Cry") 15-25 63
ABC-PAR (10550 "My Baby Left Me") 20-30 64
CONWAY TWITTY FAN CLUB ("It's Only Make Believe") 10-20
(Promotional, fan club issue only.)
DECCA 3-8 65-72
ELEKTRA 3-4 82-83
MCA 3-5 73-90s
MGM (500 series) 3-5 78
MGM (12000 series) 15-25 58-61
MGM (13000 series) 8-12 62
MGM (14000 series) 3-5 71-72
MGM (50000 series) 30-40 58-59
(Stereo.)
MGM GOLDEN CIRCLE 3-5
MERCURY (71086 "I Need Your Lovin'") 30-40 57
MERCURY (71148 "Shake It Up") . 30-40 57
MERCURY (71384 "Why Can't I Get Through to You") 30-40 58
MUSIGRAM 3-6
(Flexi-disc.)
POLYDOR 3-4 80s
W.B. 3-4 83-86
Picture Sleeves
ELEKTRA (47302 "The Clown") 4-6 82
MGM (12886 "What Am I Living For") 20-30 60
MGM (12911 "Is a Blue Bird Blue") 20-30 60
MGM (12969 "C'est Si Bon") 20-30 60
MGM (12998 "The Next Kiss") 20-30 61
MGM (13034 "It's Drivin' Me Wild") 20-30 61
EPs: 7-inch
DECCA (34437 "Look Into My Teardrops") 10-20 66
(Juke box issue only. Includes title strips.)
MGM (1623 "It's Only Make Believe") 30-50 58
MGM (1640/1641/1642 "Conway Twitty Sings") 20-30 59
(Price is for any of three volumes.)
MGM (1678/1679/1680 "Saturday Night with Conway Twitty") 20-30 59
(Price is for any of three volumes.)
MGM (1701 "Lonely Blue Boy") 20-30 60
LPs: 10/12-inch
ACCORD 5-10 82
ALLEGIANCE 5-8 84
CT (1001 "Solid Gold") 8-12
CANDLELITE ("Living Legend") 30-50 70s
(No selection number used.)
CONWAY TWITTY/MCA (1002 "Conway Twitty") 8-10
CORAL 5-8 73
CUTLASS 40-50 72
(Title and selection number not known.)
DECCA 8-18 66-72
DEMAND 8-12 72
ELEKTRA 5-8 82-83
MCA 5-15 73-85
MGM (110 "Conway Twitty") 15-20 70
MGM (3744 "Conway Twitty Sings") 50-100 59
MGM (E-3786 "Saturday Night with Conway Twitty") 50-75 59
(Monaural.)

MGM (SE-3786 "Saturday Night with Conway Twitty")....75-100 59
(Stereo.)
MGM (E-3818 "Lonely Blue Boy")...50-75 60
(Monaural.)
MGM (SE-3818 "Lonely Blue Boy")....75-100 60
(Stereo.)
MGM (E-3849 "Conway Twitty's Greatest Hits")....50-75 60
(Monaural. Black label. With gatefold cover and poster.)
MGM (SE-3849 "Conway Twitty's Greatest Hits")....75-100 60
(Stereo. With gatefold cover and poster.)
MGM (3849 "Conway Twitty's Greatest Hits")....15-20 68
(Blue and yellow label. With standard cover.)
MGM (E-3907 "The Rock and Roll Story")....50-75 61
(Monaural.)
MGM (SE-3907 "The Rock and Roll Story")....75-100 61
(Stereo.)
MGM (E-3943 "The Conway Twitty Touch")....30-40 61
(Monaural.)
MGM (SE-3943 "The Conway Twitty Touch")....35-50 61
(Stereo.)
MGM (E-4019 thru E-4217)....20-40 62-64
(Monaural.)
MGM (SE-4019 thru SE-4217)....25-50 62-64
(Stereo.)
MGM (4650 thru 4884)....10-20 69-73
METRO....15-25 65
OPRYLAND (12636 "Conway Twitty, Then and Now")....75-100
(Six-disc set. Promotional issue only.)
PICKWICK....10-15 72
SUNRISE MEDIA....5-10 81
TEE VEE....5-10 78
TROLLY CAR....5-10
TWITTY BIRD (1001 "Solid Gold")....10-12 82
(Two-discs.)
W.B.....5-10 83-86
Session: Fred Carter Jr.; Anthony Armstrong Jones; Joni Lee.
Also see CARTER, Fred, Jr.
Also see JONES, Anthony Armstrong
Also see LEE, Joni
Also see LYNN, Loretta, & Conway Twitty
Also see MARTIN, Dean
Also see McDOWELL, Ronnie
Also see MILLER, Buddy
Also see TUBB, Ernest

TWITTY, Kathy C&W '85
Singles: 7-inch
PERMIAN....3-4 85
Also see JAMES, Jesseca

TWO BITS
Singles: 7-inch
BIG DEAL....4-8 66

TWO BOBS
Singles: 7-inch
ENVOY....5-10 60

TWO BROTHERS
Singles: 7-inch
IMPERIAL....4-8 61-62

TWO CHAPS
Singles: 7-inch
ATLANTIC (1195 "Forgive Me")....10-20 59
Member: Jay Black.
Also see BLACK, Jay

TWO COOL
Singles: 7-inch
MOONSTAR ("Rock & Roll News")....4-6 84

TWO DOLLAR QUESTION
Singles: 7-inch
INTREPID....4-8 69
Member: Ron Dante.
Also see DANTE, Ron

TWO DONS
Singles: 7-inch
GUYDEN....5-10 60

TWO FACES
Singles: 7-inch
LMI....4-8 65

TWO FRIENDS
Singles: 7-inch
HPC (1001 "Just Too Much to Hope For")....40-60 60
Members: Clyde Wilson (a.k.a. Steve Mancha); Wilbert Jackson.
Also see MANCHA, Steve

TWO GUITARS, PIANO, DRUM & DARRYL
Singles: 7-inch
ATLANTIC....4-8 68

TWO GUNS
Singles: 7-inch
CAPRICORN....3-5 79
LPs: 10/12-inch
CAPRICORN....5-10 79

TWO GUYS
Singles: 7-inch
APT....4-8 65

TWO GUYS from BOSTON
Singles: 7-inch
SCEPTER....4-8 65

TWO HEARTS C&W '85
Singles: 7-inch
MDJ....3-4 85-86
Members: Jama Bowen; Cathy Bowen.

2 LIVE CREW LP '87
(Luke Featuring 2 Live Crew)
Singles: 12-inch
LUKE SKYWALKER....4-8 88-89
Singles: 7-inch
LUKE SKYWALKER....3-4 88-89
LPs: 10/12-inch
LUKE SKYWALKER....5-8 87-90

TWO MAN SOUND
Singles: 12-inch
JDC....4-8

TWO NOTES
Singles: 7-inch
CORAL....5-10 59

2 OF CLUBS P&R '67
Singles: 7-inch
FRATERNITY....5-10 66-67

TWO OF US
Singles: 7-inch
CAMEO....4-8 66

TWO PEOPLE
Singles: 7-inch
A&M....4-8 65
LIBERTY....4-8 65-66
REVUE....4-8 68

TWO PLUS TWO
Singles: 7-inch
DITTO (108 "High Rise")....50-75 68
RCA....15-20

TWO SHAYS
Singles: 7-inch
W.B.....3-5 65

TWO SISTERS D&D '83
Singles: 12-inch
SUGARSCOOP....4-6 83

TWO TONS O' FUN R&B/LP '80
(Two Tons)
Singles: 12-inch
FANTASY....4-6 80
Singles: 7-inch
FANTASY....3-5 80
HONEY....3-5 80-81
LPs: 10/12-inch
FANTASY....5-8 80
HONEY....5-8 80
Members: Martha Wash; Izora Armstead.
Also see WEATHER GIRLS

TWO'S COMPANY
Singles: 7-inch
RCA....3-5 69

TWOVOICE, Johnny
(With the Medallions)
Singles: 78 rpm
DOOTONE....10-20 55
Singles: 7-inch
DOOTONE (373 "My Pretty Baby")....30-50 55
SPECIALTY....5-10 59-60
Also see GREEN, Vernon, & Medallions

TWYLIGHTS
Singles: 7-inch
ROCK'N (102 "Darling Lets [sic] Fall in Love")....50-100 61
Session: Van McCoy
Also see McCOY, Van

TY, Jimmy
Singles: 7-inch
BELLA (607 "Mary Jane")....25-35 62

TY B. & JOHNNY: see B., Ty, & Johnny

TYCE, Napoleon
Singles: 7-inch
NORWOOD (105 "Sitting Here")....150-200 60

TYCOON P&R/LP '79
Singles: 7-inch
ARISTA....3-5 79
LPs: 10/12-inch
ARISTA....5-10 78-81

TYDE, Hy
Singles: 7-inch
GET IT....4-8 66

TYFFANY
Singles: 7-inch
SSS INT'L (Colored vinyl)....5-10 71

TYGERS: see TONY'S TYGERS

TYGERS OF PAN TANG
LPs: 10/12-inch
MCA....5-10 80-82

TYGH & CRITERIONS
Singles: 7-inch
FLITE (101 "To Be Mine")....75-125 63

TYLA GANG
Singles: 7-inch
BESERKLEY....3-4 78
LPs: 10/12-inch
BESERKLEY....5-8 78
Member: Sean Tyla.

TYLE, Teddy
Singles: 7-inch
GOLDEN CREST (500 "Drifting and Dreaming")....10-20 58
GOLDEN CREST (549 "Way Out Upon the Swanee River")....10-20 60

TYLER, Alvin "Red"
(Red Tyler & Gyros)
Singles: 7-inch
ACE....5-10 59
LPs: 10/12-inch
ACE (1006 "Rockin' & Rollin' ")....30-40 60

TYLER, Big T.
Singles: 78 rpm
ALADDIN....25-50 56
Singles: 7-inch
ALADDIN (362 "Looking for a Baby")....50-100 56
ALADDIN (3384 "Sadie Green")....50-100 57

TYLER, Bonnie P&R/C&W/LP '78
Singles: 7-inch
CHRYSALIS....3-5 77
COLUMBIA....3-4 83-86
RCA....3-5 78-79
Picture Sleeves
COLUMBIA....3-4 83-86
RCA....3-5 78
LPs: 10/12-inch
CHRYSALIS....8-12 77
COLUMBIA....5-8 83-86
RCA....5-10 78-81
Also see RUNDGREN, Todd

TYLER, Charles
Singles: 7-inch
LANOR....4-8 63

TYLER, Chip
Singles: 7-inch
CHICORY (401 "I Love You Yvonne")....15-25 66

TYLER, Chuck, & Royal Lancers
Singles: 7-inch
FENWAY (7004 "She's All Mine")..25-35 61
Also see GRECCO, Tony
Also see PREMIERE, Ronnie

TYLER, Frankie
(Frankie Valli)
Singles: 7-inch
OKEH (7103 "I Go Ape")....50-75 58
Promotional Singles
OKEH (7103 "I Go Ape")....40-60 58
Also see VALLI, Frankie

TYLER, Gladys
Singles: 7-inch
ASCOT (2130 "Pack Up")....8-12 63
BROOKS (101 "One Man's Woman")....15-25 64
CORAL (62389 "I'm in the Mood for Love")....10-15 63
DECCA....5-10 66-67

TYLER, Jim
LPs: 10/12-inch
TIME....10-20 62

TYLER, Jimmy
Singles: 78 rpm
FEDERAL (12080 "Take It Away")....20-30 52
FEDERAL (12100 thru 12200 series)....10-25 54-57
Singles: 7-inch
FEDERAL (12080 "Take It Away")....50-75 52
FEDERAL (12100 thru 12200 series)....15-25 54-57
ORIGINAL SOUND....8-10 62

TYLER, Joey
Singles: 7-inch
REPRISE....4-8 64

TYLER, Johnny
Singles: 78 rpm
DECCA....5-10 54
EKKO (1000 "Devil's Hot Rod")....20-40 55
EKKO (1001 "Where You Gonna Hide")....15-25 55
LIBERTY....8-12 55
STARDAY....20-30 56
Singles: 7-inch
DECCA....5-10 54
EKKO (1000 "Devil's Hot Rod")....50-100 55
EKKO (1001 "Where You Gonna Hide")....25-50 55
LIBERTY....10-20 55
RURAL RHYTHM (515 "Lie to Me Baby")....75-125 59
STARDAY (263 "Lie to Me Baby")....50-75 56
(Black vinyl.)
STARDAY (263 "Lie to Me Baby")....100-150 56
(Colored vinyl.)

TYLER, Kip
(With the White Fronts; with Flips)
Singles: 7-inch
CHALLENGE (1014 "She's Got Eyes")....15-25 58
CHALLENGE (59008 "Jungle Hop")....15-25 58
EBB (154 "Rumble Rock")....25-35 58
EBB (156 "Oh Linda")....25-35 59
GYRO DISC....10-15 63
STARLA....10-20 57
Picture Sleeves
GYRO DISC....15-25 63
Members: Kip Tyler; Steve Douglas.
Also see DOUGLAS, Steve
Also see KIPPER & EXCITER
Also see KIPSTERS
Also see TYLER & FLIPS

TYLER, Little Johnny
Singles: 7-inch
ME MEOW....4-8 69

TYLER, Red: see TYLER, Alvin "Red"

TYLER, Ronnie, & Knight Hawks
Singles: 7-inch
AVANT GARDE....5-10 60

TYLER, Ruckus
Singles: 78 rpm
FABOR (135 "Rockin' & Rollin' ")....25-45 56
Singles: 7-inch
FABOR (135 "Rockin' & Rollin' ")....50-75 56

TYLER, T. Texas C&W '46
(With His Oklahoma Melody Boys)
Singles: 78 rpm
DECCA....4-8 53-54
4 STAR....5-10 46-54
Singles: 7-inch
DECCA....5-10 53-54
4 STAR....10-20 53-54
KING....5-10 59-60
RCA....5-10 53-54
LPs: 10/12-inch
CAPITOL....15-25 62-65
DESIGN....10-20 62
INTERNATIONAL AWARD....8-12 60s
KING (664 "T. Texas Tyler")....30-50 59
KING (689 "The Great Texan")....25-40 60
KING (721 "T. Texas Tyler")....15-25 61
KING (734 "Songs Along the Way")....20-30 61
NASHVILLE....5-10 72
PICKWICK/HILLTOP....10-15 67
SOUND (607 "Deck of Cards")....35-55 58
STARDAY (379 "The Man with a Million Friends")....20-30 66
WRANGLER (1002 "T. Texas Tyler")....10-20 62
Also see CLINE, Patsy / T. Texas Tyler / Bill Taylor / Eddie Marvin
Also see PIERCE, Webb / Patsy Cline / T. Texas Tyler

TYLER, Terry
Singles: 7-inch
LANDA....5-10 61
SUNLAND....4-8 62

TYLER, Tod
Singles: 7-inch
DITTO (129 "Inside a Teardrop")...30-60

TYLER & FLIPS
Singles: 7-inch
STARLA (2 "Let's Monkey Around")....10-20
Members: Kip Tyler, Sandy Nelson.
Also see NELSON, Sandy
Also see TYLER, Kip

TYME
Singles: 7-inch
GARLAND....10-15

TYME OF DAY
Singles: 7-inch
MERCURY (72861 "Listen to What Is Never Said")....5-10 68

TYMES P&R/R&B/LP '63
Singles: 7-inch
ABKCO....3-5 74
COLUMBIA....5-10 68-70
MGM (13536 "Pretend")....10-20 66
MGM (13531 "A Touch of Baby")....10-20 66
PARKWAY (871 "So in Love")....10-20 63
PARKWAY (871 "So Much in Love")....5-10 63
PARKWAY (884 "Wonderful, Wonderful")....8-10 63
PARKWAY (891 "Somewhere")....8-10 63
PARKWAY (908 "To Each His Own")....8-10 64
PARKWAY (919 "The Magic of Our Summer Love")....8-10 64
PARKWAY (924 "Here She Comes")....8-10 64
PARKWAY (933 "The Twelfth of Never")....8-10 64
PARKWAY (7039 "Isle of Love")....8-10
RCA....4-8 74-77
WINCHESTER (1002 "These Foolish Things")....8-10 67
Picture Sleeves
PARKWAY....10-20 63-64
LPs: 10/12-inch
ABKCO (4228 "Best of the Tymes")....8-10 74
COLUMBIA (9778 "People")....10-15 69
PARKWAY (7032 "So Much in Love")....40-60 63
(Covers has silhouette drawing of couple walking, with group's picture over the drawing.
PARKWAY (7032 "So Much in Love")....20-40 63
(Cover pictures only the group, checking the "time" on their watches.)
PARKWAY (7038 "Sound of the Wonderful Tymes")....20-40 63
PARKWAY (7039 "Somewhere")....20-40 64
RCA (0727 "Trustmaker")....8-12 74
RCA (1835 "Turning Point")....8-10 77
WYNCOTE....10-20 60s
Members: George Williams Jr; Donald Banks; Al Berry; Norman Burnett; George Hilliard.
Also see MAESTRO, Johnny, & Tymes
Also see WILLIAMS, George, & Tymes

TYNDALL, Lynne C&W '87
Singles: 7-inch
EVERGREEN....3-4 87-89

TYNER, McCoy LP '75
(McCoy Tyner Trio)
Singles: 7-inch
COLUMBIA....3-4 82
IMPULSE....4-8 65
LPs: 10/12-inch
BLUE NOTE....8-15 66-76
COLUMBIA....5-8 82
FPM....5-10 75
IMPULSE....10-30 62-78
MCA....5-10 81
MILESTONE....5-12 72-82
PAUSA....5-8 82

TYNES, Maria
Singles: 7-inch
UPTOWN....10-20 67

TYPHOONS
Singles: 7-inch
CASH....5-10 60

TYPICALLY TROPICAL
Singles: 7-inch
GULL....3-5 75

TYRANNIES
Singles: 7-inch
WATCH (1903 "Little Girl")....15-25 65

TYRANNOSAURUS REX: see T. REX

TYRELL, Danny, & Cleeshays
Singles: 7-inch
EASTMAN (784 "You're Only 17")....25-30 58
Also see KNIGHT, Sonny

TYRELL, Steve
Singles: 7-inch
PHILIPS....4-8 63

TYRODS
Singles: 7-inch
MARK....4-8 67

TYRONE, Janice
Singles: 7-inch
PZAZZ (041 "Meet Me Baby")....10-20

TYRONE (The Wonder Boy)
(Tyrone Davis)
Singles: 7-inch
4 BROTHERS (447 "Try Me")....10-15 65
4 BROTHERS (450 "Good Company")....10-15 66
FOUR BROTHERS (453 "Please Consider Me")....10-15 67
(Note slight change in how label name is shown.)
Also see DAVIS, Tyrone

TYRONE A'SAURUS: see A'SAURUS, Tyrone

TYRONE & NU PORTS
(With the Joseph Ricci Orchestra)
Singles: 7-inch
DARROW (20 "Feel Like a Million")....35-50 60
(First issued as by the Mystery Men.)
DARROW (71 "Look at Her Eyes")....35-50 63
Also see GERRY & GEMS / Tyrone & Nu Ports
Also see MYSTERY MEN

TYRONES
Singles: 78 rpm
MERCURY....10-20 56-57
WING....10-15 56
Singles: 7-inch
DECCA (30559 "Giggles")....15-25 58
DECCA (30643 "Blast Off")....15-25 58
MERCURY (70939 "My Rock & Roll Baby")....15-25 56
MERCURY (71104 "Pink Champagne")....15-25 57
WING (90072 "Campus Rock")....15-25 56

TYROS
Singles: 7-inch
RONDACK (9780 "Torquay")....15-25 63
(Colored vinyl.)

TYSON, Clay
Singles: 7-inch
KING....5-10
WINLEY....5-10 60

TYSON, J.J.
Singles: 7-inch
THUNDERHEAD (7012 "Dirty, Dirty Feeling")....10-15

TYSON, Moses
LPs: 10/12-inch
LIBERTY....5-10 82

TYSON, Roy
Singles: 7-inch
DOUBLE L (723 "Oh What a Night for Love")....50-75 63
DOUBLE L (733 "The Girl I Love")....75-100 63

TYTON
LPs: 10/12-inch
IRON WORKS (17886 "Castle Donnington")....10-15 84
(Picture disc.)

TYZIK R&B/D&D/LP '84
(Jeff Tyzik)
Singles: 12-inch
POLYDOR....4-6 84
Singles: 7-inch
CAPITOL....3-4 82

POLYDOR ... 3-4 84
LPs: 10/12-inch
CAPITOL ... 5-8 82
POLYDOR ... 5-8 84

TZUKE, Judie
Singles: 7-inch
ROCKET ... 3-5 79
LPs: 10/12-inch
ROCKET ... 5-10 80

U

U & I
Singles: 7-inch
BLACK PATCH (1 "Report to the People") ... 4-8 76

UB40 *LP '83*
(With Chrissie Hynde)
Singles: 12-inch
A&M ... 4-6 83-86
Singles: 7-inch
A&M ... 3-4 83-88
Picture Sleeves
A&M ... 3-4 85
LPs: 10/12-inch
A&M ... 5-8 83-88
VIRGIN ... 5-8 89
Also see PRETENDERS

UFO *LP '75*
Singles: 7-inch
CHRYSALIS (Black vinyl) ... 3-5 73-86
CHRYSALIS (2157 "Too Hot to Handle") ... 3-6 77
(Colored vinyl.)
Picture Sleeves
CHRYSALIS (2157 "Too Hot to Handle") ... 3-5 77
LPs: 10/12-inch
CHRYSALIS ... 5-12 74-86
RARE EARTH ... 10-15 71
Also see SCHENKER, Michael, Group

U.K. *LP '78*
Singles: 7-inch
POLYDOR ... 3-5 78-79
LPs: 10/12-inch
POLYDOR ... 5-10 78-79
Members: John Wetton; Eddie Jobson; Terry Bozzio; Bill Bruford; Allan Holdsworth.

U.K. BABY
Singles: 7-inch
IMPERIAL ... 4-8 69

U.K. SQUEEZE: see SQUEEZE

U-KREW *LP '90*
LPs: 10/12-inch
ENIGMA ... 5-8 90

U.K.s
Singles: 7-inch
CAMEO ... 4-8 64

U.S. BEATLEWIGS
Singles: 7-inch
ORBIT ... 8-10 64

U.S. BONDS: see Bonds, Gary U.S.

U.S. DOUBLE QUARTET
(United States Double Quartet)
Singles: 7-inch
B.T. PUPPY ... 4-8 66-67
LPs: 10/12-inch
B.T. PUPPY (1005 "Life Is Groovy") ... 10-15 69
Members: Tokens; Kirby Stone Four.
Also see STONE, Kirby, Four
Also see TOKENS

U.S. GROUP
Singles: 7-inch
UPTOWN ... 10-15 66

U.S. MALES
Singles: 7-inch
BRITANIA ... 5-10 68
MGM ... 5-10 67
SPECIAL DELIVERY (1005 "I Don't Want to Know") ... 15-20 60s

U.S. 1 *P&R '75*
Singles: 7-inch
PRIVATE STOCK ... 3-5 75

U.S. RADIO BAND
Singles: 7-inch
ABC ... 3-5 76

U.S. SIX
Singles: 7-inch
ASCOT ... 4-8 65

U.S.A.- EUROPEAN CONNECTION *LP '78*
Singles: 7-inch
MARLIN ... 3-5 78-79
LPs: 10/12-inch
MARLIN ... 5-10 78-79

USA for AFRICA / Quincy Jones *P&R/R&B/D&D/C&W/LP '85*
(United Support of Artists for Africa)
Singles: 12-inch
COLUMBIA ... 4-6 85
Singles: 7-inch
COLUMBIA ... 3-4 85
Picture Sleeves
COLUMBIA ... 3-4 85
LPs: 10/12-inch
COLUMBIA ... 5-8 85
Members: Dan Aykroyd; Kim Carnes; Ray Charles; Bob Dylan; Daryl Hall; James Ingram; Michael Jackson; Jean-Michael Jarre; Al Jarreau; Waylon Jennings; Billy Joel; Quincy Jones; Cyndi Lauper; Huey Lewis; Kenny Loggins; Bette Midler; Steve Perry; Lionel Richie; Smokey Robinson; Kenny Rogers; Diana Ross; Paul Simon; Bruce Springsteen; Tina Turner; Dionne Warwick; Stevie Wonder.
Also see AYKROYD, Dan, & Pattie Brooks
Also see CARNES, Kim
Also see CHARLES, Ray
Also see DYLAN, Bob
Also see HALL, Daryl
Also see INGRAM, James
Also see JACKSON, Michael
Also see JARRE, Jean-Michael
Also see JARREAU, Al
Also see JENNINGS, Waylon
Also see JOEL, Billy
Also see JONES, Quincy
Also see LAUPER, Cyndi
Also see LEWIS, Huey, & News
Also see LOGGINS, Kenny
Also see MIDLER, Bette
Also see PERRY, Steve
Also see RICHIE, Lionel
Also see ROBINSON, Smokey
Also see ROGERS, Kenny
Also see ROSS, Diana
Also see SIMON, Paul
Also see SPRINGSTEEN, Bruce
Also see TURNER, Tina
Also see VOICES of AMERICA / U.S.A. for AFRICA
Also see WARWICK, Dionne
Also see WONDER, Stevie

U.T.s
Singles: 7-inch
U.A. ... 3-5 74
LPs: 10/12-inch
U.A. ... 8-10 74

UTFO *P&R/R&B/D&D/LP '85*
Singles: 12-inch
SELECT ... 4-6 85-86
Singles: 7-inch
SELECT ... 3-4 85-89
LPs: 10/12-inch
SELECT ... 5-8 85-89
Also see ROXANNE with UTFO

U2 *LP '81*
Singles: 12-inch
ISLAND ... 4-6 83
Singles: 7-inch
ISLAND ... 3-5 81-93
Picture Sleeves
ISLAND ... 3-8 81-93
EPs: 7-inch
ISLAND (99385 "Joshua Tree") ... 5-10 87
LPs: 10/12-inch
ISLAND (Except 314-510347) ... 5-10 81-91
ISLAND (314-510347 "Achtung Baby") ... 15-20 91
(With "naked" cover.)
ISLAND (314-510347 "Achtung Baby") ... 5-10 91
(Without "naked" cover.)
MFSL (207 "The Unforgettable Fire") ... 20-25 94
POLYDOR ... 8-10 90s
Members: Paul "Bono Vox" Hewson; David "The Edge" Evan; Adam Clayton; Larry Mullen.
Also see BAND AID

U2 & B.B. KING *P&R '89*
Singles: 12-inch
ISLAND ... 4-6 89
Singles: 7-inch
ISLAND ... 3-4 89
Picture Sleeves
ISLAND ... 3-4 89
Also see KING, B.B.
Also see U2

U.W. WANKESKA ROCK BAND
Singles: 7-inch
SARA (1543 "Spinning Wheel") ... 4-8 70s

U.X.A.
LPs: 10/12-inch
POSH BOY ... 8-15

UBANS
Singles: 7-inch
RADIANT (102 "Gloria") ... 100-125 64

UBIQUITY *LP '78*
Singles: 7-inch
ELEKTRA ... 3-5 78
LPs: 10/12-inch
ELEKTRA ... 5-10 78
Also see AYERS, Roy

UGGAMS, Leslie *P&R '59*
Singles: 7-inch
ATLANTIC ... 5-15 65-70
COLUMBIA ... 5-10 59-64
GORDY ... 3-5 76
MGM ... 5-15 54-55
SONDAY ... 3-5 71
EPs: 7-inch
MGM ... 5-10 54
LPs: 10/12-inch
ATLANTIC ... 5-15 66-69
COLUMBIA ... 15-30 59-63
MOTOWN ... 5-10 75
SONDAY ... 5-10 72

UGLY DUCKLINGS
Singles: 7-inch
RAZOR (2 "Pain Is Alright") ... 3-4 80
YORKTOWN (45001 "Nothin' ") ... 50-75 66
(Black and silver label. Canadian)
YORKTOWN (45001 "Nothin' ") ... 20-30 66
(Multi-color label. Canadian)
YORKTOWN (45002 "10:30 Train") ... 25-40 66
(Canadian.)
YORKTOWN (45003 "Just in Case You Wonder") ... 25-40 66
(Canadian.)
YORKTOWN (45005 "Postman's Fancy") ... 20-30 67
(Canadian.)
YORKVILLE (45013 "Gaslight") ... 15-25 67
(Canadian.)
YORKVILLE (45017 "I Know What to Say") ... 15-25 67
(Canadian.)
Picture Sleeves
RAZOR (2 "Pain Is Alright") ... 3-5 80
LPs: 10/12-inch
YORKTOWN (50001 "Somewhere Outside") ... 175-225 67
(Canadian.)

UGLYS
(Ugly's)
Singles: 7-inch
ABC-PAR ... 5-10 65-66

UGLIES: see UNBELIEVABLE UGLIES

ULLANDA *R&B '79*
Singles: 7-inch
OCEAN ... 3-5 79

ULLMAN, Tracey *P&R/LP '84*
Singles: 7-inch
MCA ... 3-5 84-85
Picture Sleeves
MCA ... 3-5 84-85
LPs: 10/12-inch
MCA ... 5-10 84

ULTIMATE *P&R/LP '79*
Singles: 7-inch
CASABLANCA ... 3-5 78-80
LPs: 10/12-inch
CASABLANCA ... 5-10 78-80

ULTIMATE TRUTH
Singles: 7-inch
J CITY ... 5-10

ULTIMATE SPINACH *LP '68*
Singles: 7-inch
MGM ... 5-10 68-69
LPs: 10/12-inch
MGM (4518 "Ultimate Spinach") ... 20-30 68
MGM (4570 "Behold & See") ... 20-30 68
MGM (4600 "Ultimate Spinach") ... 15-25 69
Members: Barbara Hudson; Ian Bruce Douglas; Richard Nese; Jeff Baxter; Ted Myers; Tony Scheuren; Mike Levine; Russ Levine.
Also see CHAMAELEON CHURCH
Also see STEELY DAN

ULTIMATES
Singles: 7-inch
ENVOY (2302 "I Can Tell You Love Me Too") ... 15-25 61
Also see EXCELLENTS

ULTIMATES
Singles: 7-inch
ULTIMA (707 "Autumn Wind") ... 10-15 64
Also see MESSINA, Jim

ULTIMATES
Singles: 7-inch
BR. ROMA (101 "Girl I've Been Trying to Tell You") ... 10-15
LAVENDER (2001 "Little Girl") ... 15-25 60s

ULTIMATIONS
Singles: 7-inch
MAR-V-LOUS ... 8-12 67

ULTRA MATES
Singles: 7-inch
CHARTER ... 4-8 63

ULTRAFUNK
Singles: 7-inch
CONHEADO ... 3-5 77

ULTRAMAGNETIC MC'S
LPs: 10/12-inch
NEXT PLATEAU ... 5-8 88

ULTRATONES
(Ultra Tones)
Singles: 7-inch
CARY (2001 "Locomotion") ... 8-12 62
SAN TANA (101 "Chain Reaction") ... 10-20 60

ULTRAVOX *LP '80*
Singles: 12-inch
CHRYSALIS ... 4-6 83
Singles: 7-inch
ANTILLES ... 3-5 78-80
CHRYSALIS ... 3-4 80-84
ISLAND ... 8-10 77
LPs: 10/12-inch
ANTILLES ... 5-10 78-80
CHRYSALIS ... 5-8 80-84
ISLAND ... 8-10 77
Also see BAND AID

ULTTMATTONS
Singles: 7-inch
MAR-V-LUS (6020 "Would I Do It Over") ... 10-20

ULYSSES
LPs: 10/12-inch
20TH FOX (Except 101) ... 10-12 78
20TH FOX (101 "Greek Suite") ... 25-30 79
(Picture disc. Promotional issue only.)

UMEKI, Miyoshi
Singles: 7-inch
MERCURY (71215 "Ooh What Good Company We Could Be") ... 10-15 57
MERCURY (71216 "Sayonara") ... 10-20 57
MERCURY (71243 "Sayonara") ... 10-15 58

UMILANI, Piero *P&R '69*
(Sweden Heaven & Hell Soundtrack)
Singles: 7-inch
ARIEL ... 3-5 69
LPs: 10/12-inch
ARIEL ... 8-12 69

UNBEATABLES
("Gene Cornish & His Orchestra")
Singles: 7-inch
DAWN (552 "I Love Paris") ... 25-50 64
LPs: 10/12-inch
DAWN (5050 "Live at Palisades Park") ... 50-100 64
Member: Gene Cornish.
Also see CORNISH, Gene

UNBELIEVABLE UGLIES
(Uglies)
Singles: 7-inch
CARDINAL (0071 "Off My Hands") ... 20-30 65
INDEPENDENCE (42767 "Spiderman") ... 80-120 67
LIBERTY (55935 "Sorry") ... 10-20 67
MUSIC MASTERS (72164 "Judy Angel") ... 20-30 64
SOMA (1451 "Keep Her Satisfied") ... 10-20 65
SOUND ... 20-25 69-70
UGLIES ... 12-18 78
UA ... 20-25 68-69
Also see FRIENDSHIP
Also see JAY, Robbie
Also see ST. PIERRE, Alan

UNBELIEVABLES
Singles: 7-inch
ERA ... 5-10 65
Also see SKUNKS

UNCALLED FOR
Singles: 7-inch
DOLLIE (509 "Do Like Me") ... 10-20 67
LAURIE (3394 "Do Like Me") ... 8-12 67

UNCHAINED MYNDS
Singles: 7-inch
BUDDAH (111 "We Can't Go on This Way") ... 5-10 69
BUDDAH (119 "Everyday") ... 5-10 70
BUDDAH (140 "Everyday") ... 5-10 70
TEEN TOWN (109 "We Can't Go on This Way") ... 15-25 69
TRANSACTION (705 "We Can't Go on This Way") ... 5-10 69
TRANSACTION (707 "Hole in My Shoe") ... 5-10 69
Picture Sleeves
TRANSACTION (705 "We Can't Go on This Way") ... 50-75 69
Members: Randy Purdy; Wayne Bentzen; Clare Troyanek; Dan Hansen;Doug Krupinski.

UNCLAIMED
Singles: 7-inch
PHILIPS ... 4-8 67

UNCLE & ANTEATERS
Singles: 7-inch
HUNT ... 8-12
NATIONAL ... 8-12

UNCLE DOG *P&R '73*
Singles: 7-inch
MCA ... 3-5 73
LPs: 10/12-inch
MCA ... 5-10 73

UNCLE JIM'S MUSIC
LPs: 10/12-inch
KAPP ... 8-10 71-72

UNCLE LAR' & Li'l Tommy
(Larry Lujack)
LPs: 10/12-inch
WLS (890 "Animal Stories, Vol. II") ... 15-25 82
WLS (847 "Animal Stories, Vol. III") ... 15-25 83
WLS (1001 "Animal Stories") ... 15-25 81
Also see LUJACK, Larry, "Superjock"

UNCLE LOUIE *R&B '79*
Singles: 7-inch
MARLIN ... 3-5 79
LPs: 10/12-inch
MARLIN ... 5-10 78

UNCLE NED
Singles: 7-inch
HOT TODDY (1002 "Two Eggs Over") ... 100-150

UNCLE SAM
Singles: 7-inch
JAMIE (1428 "Bicentennial Ball") ... 4-6 76

UNCLE SAM & WAR MACHINE
Singles: 7-inch
BLUE ONION (103 "Spy Girl") ... 15-25 67

UNCLE SCOTTY & VOCAL CHORDS
Singles: 7-inch
JOKER ... 3-4 85

UNCLE SOUND
Singles: 7-inch
W.B. ... 5-10 68
Member: Jimmy Seals.
Also see SEALS, Jimmy

UNCLE WIGGLY'S HOT SHOES BLUES BAND
Singles: 7-inch
MISTER DELUXE ... 4-8 80-82
Picture Sleeves
MISTER DELUXE ... 4-8 80-82
LP: 10/12-inch
MISTER DELUXE ... 8-12 80
Members: Mark Comerford; Mark Johnson; Norm Piercy; Ike Leonhardt; Dave Rowse; B.J. Hutchinson.

UNDECIDED
Singles: 7-inch
DEARBORN (542 "Make Her Cry") ... 20-30 66

UNDERBEATS
Singles: 7-inch
APEX ... 20-25 64
BANGAR (0632 "Annie Do the Dog") ... 30-60 64
BANGAR (0657 "Little Romance") ... 30-60 64
GARRETT (4004 "Foot Stompin' ") 15-25 64
METROBEAT (4449 "It's Gonna Rain Today") ... 15-25 67
SOMA (1449 "Darling Lorraine") ... 15-25 66
SOMA (1458 "I Can't Stand It") ... 40-60 66
TWIN TOWN (706 "Our Love") ... 20-30 65
Picture Sleeves
SOMA (1449 "Darling Lorraine") ... 25-35 66
Also see GYPSY
Also see SMITH, Jojo

UNDERDOGS
Singles: 7-inch
HIDEOUT (1001 "The Man in the Glass") ... 25-35 65
(First issue.)
HIDEOUT (1004 "Little Girl") ... 25-35 66
(First issue.)
HIDEOUT (1011 "Surprise, Surprise") ... 25-35 66
REPRISE (0422 "The Man in the Glass") ... 10-15 65
REPRISE (0446 "Little Girl") ... 10-15 66
V.I.P. (25040 "Love's Gone Bad") ... 15-25 67
(Black vinyl.)
V.I.P. (25040 "Love's Gone Bad") ... 25-35 67
(Colored vinyl. Promotional issue only.)

UNDERGRADS
Singles: 7-inch
AUDIO SPECTRUM ... 5-8 64

UNDERGROUND
Singles: 7-inch
MAINSTREAM ... 10-15 66
LPs: 10/12-inch
WING (12337 "Psychedelic Visions") ... 15-20 67
(Monaural.)
WING (16337 "Psychedelic Visions") ... 20-25 67
(Stereo.)

UNDERGROUND ALL STARS
LPs: 10/12-inch
DOT ... 10-15 69

UNDERGROUND BALLOON CORPS.
Singles: 7-inch
SCOPE (1/2 "Made of Soul") ... 15-25 60s

UNDERGROUND LITE BULB CO.
Singles: 7-inch
RED LITE (118 "Happy People") ... 10-20 68

UNDERGROUND SUNSHINE *P&R/LP '69*
Singles: 7-inch
EARTH ... 8-12 69
INTREPID ... 5-10 69-70
LPs: 10/12-inch
INTERPID ... 15-25 69
Members: Rex Rhode; Jane Little Whirry; Bert Hohl; Frank Kohl; Chris Connors; Dave Wayne; Mike Hollihan.

UNDERPRIVILEGED
Singles: 7-inch
SMASH (2051 "You Hurt Me") ... 10-20 66

UNDERTAKERS
Singles: 7-inch
PARKWAY ... 8-10 64

UNDERTAKERS
Singles: 7-inch
PINE HILLS (110 "Searching") ... 15-25 67
PINE HILLS (115 "Love So Dear") ... 15-25 67

UNDERTAKERS
Singles: 7-inch
STUDIO 7 (101 "Unchain My Heart") ... 15-25 67

UNDERTAKERS
LPs: 10/12-inch
MIDNIGHT ... 5-8

UNDERTAKERS / Spirits
Singles: 7-inch
SCENE ("Rosalyn")....15-25 66
(No selection number used.)

UNDERTONES LP '80
Singles: 7-inch
CAPITOL.... 3-4 84
HARVEST.... 3-5 81
SIRE.... 3-5 80
LPs: 10/12-inch
CAPITOL.... 5-8 84
HARVEST.... 5-10 81
SIRE.... 5-10 80
Member: Feargal Sharkey.
Also see SHARKEY, Feargal

UNDERWOOD, Carl
(With Zeke Strong Band; with Dealia Copeland)
Singles: 7-inch
CEE JAM (90053 "The Hurt Is On").... 8-12 65
CELESTE (320 "Don't Ever Stop").10-15 64
KUJINGA (101 "Every Woman Has a Right").... 8-12
NORTH AMERICAN (101 "The Hurt Is On")....15-25 65
PROGRESS (320 "Don't Ever Stop")....10-20 63
Also see STRONG, Zeke

UNDERWOOD, Shorty
Singles: 7-inch
TNT.... 8-12 60

UNDERWOOD, Veronica R&B '85
Singles: 7-inch
PHILLY WORLD.... 3-4 85

UNDERWORLD
Singles: 7-inch
REGENCY (979 "Bound")....100-150 68
(Canadian.)

UNDERWORLD P&R/LP '88
Singles: 7-inch
SIRE.... 3-4 88-89
Picture Sleeves
SIRE.... 3-4 88-89
LPs: 10/12-inch
SIRE.... 5-8 88

UNDESYDED
Singles: 7-inch
READING (666 "Freedom of Love") 8-12

UNDISPUTED TRUTH P&R/R&B/LP '71
Singles: 12-inch
WHITFIELD.... 4-8 77-79
Singles: 7-inch
GORDY (Black vinyl).... 3-5 71-75
GORDY (Colored vinyl).... 5-8 71-72
MOTOWN.... 3-4
WHITFIELD.... 3-5 76-79
LPs: 10/12-inch
GORDY....10-20 71-75
WHITFIELD.... 5-10 77-79
Members: Joe Harris; Brenda Evans; Billie Calvin; Carl Smalls; Tyrone Berkley; Tyrone Douglas; Virginia McDonald; Calvin Stevens; Melvin Stuart; Marcy Thomas; Hershel Kennedy; Taka Boom.
Also see BOOM, Taka
Also see DRAMATICS
Also see LITTLE JOE & MORROCOS
Also see MAGIC TONES
Also see OHIO PLAYERS
Also see PEPS

UNEEKS: see UNIQUES

UNFOLDING
LPs: 10/12-inch
AUDIO FIDELITY (6184 "How to Blow Your Mind")....50-75 68
Members: David Dalton; Andrea Ross; Victoria Sackville; Steve Kapovitch.

UNFORGETTABLES
Singles: 7-inch
COLPIX (192 "It Hurts")....20-30 61
PAMELA (204 "Oh, Wishing Well")....150-200 61
(Black vinyl.)
PAMELA (204 "Oh, Wishing Well")....300-400 61
(Colored vinyl.)
TITANIC (5012 "Oh There He Goes")....20-30 63

UNFORGIVEN LP '86
LPs: 10/12-inch
ELEKTRA.... 5-8 86

UNFORSCENE
Singles: 7-inch
MOMENTUM.... 4-8 67
SIDEWALK.... 4-8 67-68

UN-FOUR-GIVEN
Singles: 7-inch
DOT.... 4-8 66

UNICE & EDDIE
Singles: 7-inch
STARFIRE.... 4-8 62

UNICORN LP '74
Singles: 7-inch
CAPITOL.... 3-5 74-77
LPs: 10/12-inch
CAPITOL.... 8-10 74-77

UNIFICS P&R/R&B '68
Singles: 7-inch
FOUNTAIN.... 3-5 71
KAPP.... 4-8 68-69
MCA.... 3-4 73
Picture Sleeves
KAPP.... 4-8 68-69
LPs: 10/12-inch
KAPP....10-15 68
Members: Al Johnson; Michael Ward; Greg Cook; Harold Worthington; Tom Fauntleroy; Marvin Brown.

UNION
Singles: 7-inch
PORTRAIT.... 3-5 81
LPs: 10/12-inch
PORTRAIT....5-10 81

UNION
Singles: 7-inch
RADEL (108 "I Sit and Cry")....10-15

UNION, Johnny, & Pickets
Singles: 7-inch
IMPERIAL.... 4-8 65

UNION GAP: see PUCKET, Gary

UNION JACKS
Singles: 7-inch
RAMPRO (116 "I Gotta Go")....25-35 66

UNION PACIFIC BAND
LPs: 10/12-inch
ECI....5-10 81

UNIPOP P&R '82
Singles: 7-inch
KAT FAMILY.... 3-4 82
LPs: 10/12-inch
KAT FAMILY.... 5-8 82

UNIQUE R&B/D&D '83
Singles: 12-inch
PRELUDE.... 4-6 83
Singles: 7-inch
PRELUDE.... 3-4 83

UNIQUE ECHOES
Singles: 7-inch
SOUTHERN SOUND (108 "Zoom")....25-35 61

UNIQUE TEENS
Singles: 7-inch
DYNAMIC (110 "Run Fast")....50-100 59
HANOVER (4510 "Jeannie")....30-50 58
IVY (112 "Jeannie")....50-75 58

UNIQUES
(With the John W. Pate Orchestra)
Singles: 7-inch
PEACOCK (1677 "Somewhere")....20-30 57
PEACOCK (1695 "Picture of My Baby")....15-25 60
Member: Earl King; Johnny Taylor; Charles Jordan; Leonard Garr; Bob Morland.
Also see KING, Earl
Also see PATE, Johnny

UNIQUES
Singles: 7-inch
WORLD PACIFIC (808 "I Cross My Fingers")....300-500 59

UNIQUES
(With the Outlaws)
Singles: 7-inch
C-WAY (2676-01 "Let Me Weep Let Me Cry")....30-50 59

UNIQUES
Singles: 7-inch
GLORY (289 "The Rocking Toy Soldier")....10-20 59

UNIQUES
("Uneeks Featuring Tiny Valentine")
Singles: 7-inch
BLISS (1004 "I'm So Unhappy") 250-350 60
(First issue.)
END (1012 "Tell the Angels")....100-150 58
GONE (5074 "Sabby")....15-25 59
GONE (5113 "I'm So Unhappy"/"I'm Confessin' ")....150-200 61
(Has playing time on right side.)
GONE (5113 "I'm So Unhappy"/"I'm Confessin' ")....100-150 61
(Has playing time on left side.)
GONE (5113 "I'm So Unhappy"/"It's Got to Come")....50-75 61
(Note different flip.)
FLIPPIN' (202 "Come Marry Me")..25-50 59
MR. CEE (100 "Look at Me")....200-400 60
PRIDE (1018 "I'm So Unhappy")....150-250 60
TEE KAY (112 "A Million Miles Away")....25-50 62
TOLEDO (1501 "Look at Me")....500-750 60
(First issue.)
Also see ADDEO, Nicky

UNIQUES
Singles: 7-inch
AMBER (2004 "Taboo")....15-25 61
UNITED SOUTHERN ARTISTS (104 "Renegade")....15-25 61

UNIQUES
Singles: 7-inch
JASON SCOTT....5-10
LUCKY FOUR (1024 "Silvery Moon")....150-250 62
TEE KAY (112 "A Million Miles Away")....25-50 62
Also see GLIDERS / Uniques

UNIQUES
Singles: 7-inch
620 (1003 "Pretty Baby")....75-125 63
620 (1006 "Cry Cry Cry")....35-50 63
Member: Willie Sullivan.

UNIQUES
("Vocal by Stuffy")
Singles: 7-inch
DEMAND (2936 "Merry Christmas Darling")....50-75 63
(First issue.)
DEMAND (2940 "Times Change") .20-30 64
DEMAND (3950 "Merry Christmas Darling")....40-60 63
DOT (16533 "Merry Christmas Darling")....25-35 63
Member: Stuffy.

UNIQUES
Singles: 7-inch
CAPITOL....5-10 63
ROULETTE....8-12 63

UNIQUES
Singles: 7-inch
ASTRA (1022 "I'm Confessin' ")....5-10 66

UNIQUES
Singles: 7-inch
BANGAR....12-18 67
Also see ARNOLD BROTHERS

UNIQUES P&R '65
Singles: 7-inch
PARAMOUNT....3-5 70-72
PAULA....4-8 65-70
LPs: 10/12-inch
PAULA....12-25 66-70
Members: Joe Stampley; Bobby Stampley; Jim Woodfield; Mike Love; Ray Mills; Bobby Sims; Ronnie Weiss.
Also see MOUSE
Also see RIO GRANDE
Also see STAMPLEY, Joe

UNIQUES
Singles: 7-inch
DAPPER....5-8

UNIQUES Featuring Nickie Addeo: see ADDEO, Nicky

UNIT GLORIA
Singles: 7-inch
ELEKTRA....5-10 69

UNIT 4+2 P&R '65
Singles: 7-inch
LONDON....4-8 65-66
LPs: 10/12-inch
LONDON (427 "Unit 4+2")....25-35 65
(Monaural.)
LONDON (3427 "Unit 4+2")....25-40 65
(Stereo.)
Member: Russ Ballard.
Also see BALLARD, Russ

UNIT PLUS
Singles: 7-inch
VERVE....4-8 69

UNIT 3
Singles: 7-inch
MOONSTONE....8-12

UNITED FOUR
Singles: 7-inch
HARTHON (139 "Go On")....8-12 67
HARTHON (143 "One More Year")..8-12 68

UNITED FRUIT CO.
Singles: 7-inch
LAURIE....4-8 68
YORK....4-8 67

UNITED SONS OF AMERICA
LPs: 10/12-inch
MERCURY....8-12 70

UNITED STATES AIR FORCE BAND LP '63
LPs: 10/12-inch
RCA....5-10 63

UNITED STATES DOUBLE QUARTET: see U.S. DOUBLE QUARTET

UNITED STATES MARINE BAND LP '63
LPs: 10/12-inch
RCA....5-10 63

UNITED STATES NAVY BAND LP '63
LPs: 10/12-inch
RCA....5-10 63

UNITED STATES OF AMERICA LP '68
LPs: 10/12-inch
COLUMBIA (9619 "United States of America")....20-30 68
(With stenciled title brown wrapper.)
COLUMBIA (9619 "United States of America")....10-20 68
(Without wrapper.)
Members: Dorothy Moskowitz; Joseph Byrd; Gordon Marron; Rand Forbes; Craig Woodson.
Also see BYRD, Joe, & Field Hippies

UNITED TRAVEL SERVICE
Singles: 7-inch
RUST....10-20 67

UNITONES
Singles: 7-inch
CANDY....10-15 60

UNITS D&D '83
Singles: 12-inch
EPIC....4-6 83-84
UPROAR....4-6 83
Singles: 7-inch
EPIC....3-4 84
LPs: 10/12-inch
EPIC....5-8 84

UNITY
LPs: 10/12-inch
U.A.....5-10 80

UNIVERSAL LOVE
Singles: 7-inch
GLADES....3-6 77

UNIVERSAL MIND
Singles: 7-inch
RED COACH....3-5 74

UNIVERSAL ROBOT BAND P&R/R&B '77
Singles: 7-inch
RED GREG....3-6 77
LPs: 10/12-inch
RED GREG....5-10 77
Also see KLEEER

UNIVERSALS
("With Rhythm Acc.")
Singles: 7-inch
ASCOT (2124 "Dear Ruth")....30-50 63
CORA-LEE (501 "The Picture")...50-100 58
FESTIVAL (1601 "[I'll Just Have to Go On] Dreaming")....75-125 61
FESTIVAL (25001 "Dreaming")....25-50 61
(Note shorter title and number change.)
MARK-X (7004 "Again")....100-200 57
SHEPHERD (2200 "A Love Only You Can Give")....100-200 62
SOUTHERN (102 "Prayer of Love")....50-75 63
LPs: 10/12-inch
RELIC....8-12 73
Member: Sis Watkins.
Also see WATKINS, Sis

UNIVERSALS
Singles: 7-inch
MODERN (1057 "New Lease on Life")....5-10 68

UNIVERSALS
Singles: 7-inch
COOKING....8-12

UNIVERSE
LPs: 10/12-inch
PBR....8-10 77

UNIVERSE CITY
Singles: 7-inch
MIDLAND INT'L....3-5 76
LPs: 10/12-inch
MIDLAND INT'L....5-10 76

UNIVERSITY FOUR
Singles: 7-inch
CHAIRMAN....4-8 63
LAURIE....4-8 63

UNKNOWN, The
(Jimmy Fields)
Singles: 7-inch
AUTOGRAPH (206 "I Have Returned")....20-30 60
SVR (1008 "Shake a Tail Feather")....20-30

UNKNOWN IV
Singles: 7-inch
JCP (1017 "I Want You to Be Mine")....10-20 64
JCP (1019 "Give Me a Chance")....10-20 64

UNKNOWN KIND
Singles: 7-inch
STAR TREK (3405 "Who Cares")..10-15

UNKNOWN STRANGER
Singles: 12-inch
SALSOUL....4-6 85

UNKNOWNS
Singles: 7-inch
X-TRA (102 "One More Chance")....500-1000 57
SHIELD (7101 "One More Chance")....100-200 62

UNKNOWNS P&R '66
Singles: 7-inch
MARLIN (16008 "Tighter")....10-15 67
PARROT (307 "Melody for an Unknown Girl")....8-12 66
Members: Keith Allison; Mark Lindsay; Steve Alaimo
Also see ALAIMO, Steve.
Also see ALLISON, Keith
Also see LINDSAY, Mark

UNKNOWNS
Singles: 7-inch
LPs: 10/12-inch
SIRE....8-10 81
INVASION....8-10 83

UNKNOWNS
Singles: 7-inch
TRANS WORLD SOUND....8-10 60s

UNLIMITED
Singles: 7-inch
MARINA (504 "Gone Away")....20-30 66
Also see ROYAL FLAIRS

UNLIMITED FOUR
Singles: 7-inch
CHANSON (1178 "Calling")....10-20
CHANSON (1180 "Walk Away Lover")....10-20
CHANSON (1811 "Somebody Help Please")....10-20
Member: Mel Hueston.
Also see HUESTON, Mel

UNLIMITED TOUCH R&B/LP '81
Singles: 12-inch
PRELUDE....4-6 81-84
Singles: 7-inch
PRELUDE....3-5 81-84
LPs: 10/12-inch
PRELUDE....5-10 81-84
Also see LORBER, Jeff

UNLUV'D
Singles: 7-inch
MGM....4-8 68
PARKWAY....4-8 67

UNRELATED SEGMENTS
Singles: 7-inch
HBR (514 "Story of My Life")....10-15 66
LIBERTY (55992 "Where You Gonna Go")....10-15 67
LIBERTY (56062 "Cry Cry Cry")....15-25 68

UNSANE
LPs: 10/12-inch
("Inverted Crosses")....10-15
(Picture disc. No label name or selection number used.)

UNSETTLED SOCIETY
Singles: 7-inch
CHARM....8-12

UNSPOKEN WORD
Singles: 7-inch
U.A.....5-10 66-67
LPs: 10/12-inch
ASCOT....10-15 68
ATCO....8-10 70

UNSUNG HEROS
Singles: 7-inch
20TH FOX....4-8 66

UNTAMED
Singles: 7-inch
PLANET....5-10 66

UNTAMED YOUTH
Singles: 7-inch
NORTON....3-4 89
Picture Sleeves
NORTON....3-4 89
Members: Derek Dickerson; Steve Mace; F. Clarke Marty; Steve Rager.

UNTOUCHABLES
(Chavelles)
Singles: 7-inch
LIBERTY (55335 "You're the Top")....20-30 61
LIBERTY (55432 "Medicine Man")....15-20 62
MADISON (128 "Poor Boy Needs a Preacher")....20-30 59
MADISON (134 "Goodnight Sweetheart")....20-30 60
MADISON (139 "Sixty Minute Man")....20-30 60
MADISON (147 "Raisin' Sugar Cane")....15-25 60
Also see CHAVELLES

UNTOUCHABLES
Singles: 7-inch
RELLO (2 "Benny the Beatnik")....10-20 61
RELLO (5 "Deacon's Walk")....10-20 62

UNTOUCHABLES
Singles: 7-inch
ALAN K (6901 "Funny What a Little Kiss Can Do")....100-200 62
(Reissued as by Little John & Unforgettables.)
Also see LITTLE JOHN & UNFORGETTABLES

UNTOUCHABLES
Singles: 7-inch
DOT....5-10 62
FAAP (26579 "Dragster Boy")....15-25 60s
NAU-VOO....5-10 60

UNTOUCHABLES
Singles: 7-inch
HUNT (450 "Church Key")....10-20 66
Member: Al Huntzinger.
Also see AL'S UNTOUCHABLES

UNTOUCHABLES
Singles: 7-inch
WASP (105 "Don't Go I'm Beggin' ")....15-25 67

UNTOUCHABLES
Singles: 7-inch
MCA....3-4 86
Picture Sleeves
MCA....3-4 86

UNTOUCHABLES LP '89
LPs: 10/12-inch
ENIGMA....5-8
RESTLESS....5-8 89

UNUSUAL ME
LPs: 10/12-inch
PULSAR....10-15 69

UNUSUALS
Singles: 7-inch
MAINSTREAM (653 "Summer Is Over")....12-20 66
PANORAMA (23 "I'm Walkin' Baby")....15-25 65

Members: Pat Jerns; Laurie Vitt; Bill Capp; Vic Bundy; Harvey Redman; Kathi McDonald; Gary Ramsey.
Also see BELLINGHAM ACCENTS
Also see McDONALD, Kathi

UNWANTED CHILDREN
Singles: 7-inch
MURBO (1031 "Without You") 15-25 69

UNYQUE
LPs: 10/12-inch
DJM.. 5-10 80

UP, The
Singles: 7-inch
RAINBOW (22191 "Free John Now") 125-150 71
SUNDANCE (22190 "Just Like an Aborigine")................................50-75 60s
(Colored vinyl.)
Picture Sleeves
SUNDANCE (22190 "Just Like an Aborigine")..............................75-125 60s
LPs: 10/12-inch
ALIVE/TOTAL ENERGY................. 5-10 95
(10-inch LP.)

UP 'N' ADAM
Singles: 7-inch
EARTH 3-6 69

UP with PEOPLE *LP '66*
LPs: 10/12-inch
PACE 5-10 64-70

UPBEATS *P&R '58*
Singles: 7-inch
JOY (223 "Oh What It Seemed to Be")..10-20 58
JOY (227 "You're the One I Care For")..10-20 59
PREP (119 "I Don't Know") 10-20 57
PREP (131 "Will You Be Mine")......10-20 58
SWAN (4010 "My Foolish Heart") ..10-20 58

UPCHURCH, Phil *P&R '61*
(Phil Upchurch Combo)
Singles: 7-inch
BOYD (3398 "You Can't Sit Down") 10-20 61
(No mention of U.A. distribution on label.)
BOYD (3398 "You Can't Sit Down") 8-12 61
(Indicates distribution by United Artists.)
BOYD (1026 "You Can't Sit Down") .. 4-8 66
GOLDEN FLEECE............................ 3-5 74
MARLIN.. 3-4 79
U.A. 5-10 61-62
LPs: 10/12-inch
BLUE THUMB 8-10 73
BOYD (B-398 "You Can't Sit Down") 20-25 61
(Monaural.)
BOYD (BS-398 "You Can't Sit Down") 25-30 61
(Stereo.)
CADET 8-10 69
MILESTONE.. 5-8
U.A. 15-20 61-62
Also see ADAMS, Arthur
Also see CLARK, Dee
Also see REED, Jimmy

UPCHURCH, Phil, & Tennyson Stephens
LPs: 10/12-inch
KUDU.. 8-10 75
Also see STEPHENS, Tennyson
Also see UPCHURCH, Phil

UPFRONT *D&D '83*
Singles: 12-inch
SILVER CLOUD 4-6 83

UPFRONTS
Singles: 7-inch
LUMMTONE (103 "It Took Time")..40-50 60
LUMMTONE (104 "Too Far to Turn Around")....................................25-35 60
LUMMTONE (106 "Little Girl") 35-45 61
LUMMTONE (107 "Send Me Someone to Love")..35-45 61
(White label.)
LUMMTONE (107 "Send Me Someone to Love")..20-25 62
(Black label.)
LUMMTONE (107 "I Stopped the Duke of Earl")..100-150 62
LUMMTONE (108 "It Took Time") 15-20 62
LUMMTONE (114 "Do the Beetle")..40-50 60

UPHORIA
LP: 10/12-inch
RAINBON 10-15 72

UPNILONS: see SMITH, Lester, Jr., & Upnilons

UPP
Singles: 7-inch
EPIC... 3-5 75
LPs: 10/12-inch
EPIC... 8-10 75

UPPER CLASS
Singles: 7-inch
SMASH.. 4-8 67

UPPER DIVISION & TRUE DON BLEU
LPs:10/12-inch
U-D..10-20 70s

UPPER HAND
Singles: 7-inch
EPIC... 4-8 66

UPPERCLASSMEN
Singles: 7-inch
FREEDOM 5-10 59

UPROAR
Singles: 7-inch
EAST COAST..................................5-10

UP-SET
Singles: 7-inch
AMM...5-10

UPSETS
Singles: 7-inch
HARWOOD 8-12

UPSETTERS
(Little Richard's band)
Singles: 7-inch
FALCON...10-15 57
FIRE..10-15 60
GEE 10-15 60
LEE 10-15 60s
PALM 10-15 60
ZANETTE...10-15 60s

UPSETTERS Featuring Little Richard
Singles: 7-inch
LITTLE STAR 10-20 62
Also see LITTLE RICHARD
Also see UPSETTERS

UPSETTERS
Singles: 7-inch
AUTUMN (4 "Draggin the Main")....15-25 64

UPSETTERS
Singles: 7-inch
ABC.. 4-8 68

UPSTAIRS
Singles: 7-inch
CUCA (1309 "Operator Please") 5-10 67
Also see JAGUARS

UPSTARTS
Singles: 7-inch
TOP TEN (7000 "Lovely Dream") ..25-50 60s
Members: Jack Calvert; Jon Battle; Bobby Carrol; Rusty Rutledge.

UPTIGHT SOUND CREATION
Singles: 7-inch
MERCURY 4-8 69

UPTIGHTS
Singles: 7-inch
COLUMBIA (44243 "Shy Guy")......20-30 67
MALA (528 "Academy Awards of Love")..15-20 66

UPTITES
Singles: 7-inch
RA-SEL (2 "Philly Bound") 50-75 60s

UPTIGHTS
Singles: 7-inch
UNI (55233 "Thang")........................5-10 70

UPTON, Pat
Singles: 7-inch
COLUMBIA.. 4-8 71
PLAYBOY (50002 "Higher & Higher")...5-10 72
Also see SPIRAL STARECASE

UPTONES
Singles: 7-inch
COLLECTABLES................................ 3-4 80s
LUTE (6225 "No More") 25-35 62
(Black label.)
LUTE (6225 "No More") 15-25 62
(Multi-color label.)
LUTE (6229 "Be Mine")....................25-35 62
MAGNUM (714 "Wear My Ring")....10-20 63
WATTS (1080 "Wear My Ring")......20-30 63
(First issue.)
Also see DANDEVILLES
Also see GUIDES

UPTOWN *P&R '86*
Singles: 12-inch
SILVER SCREEN 4-6 83
Singles: 7-inch
OAK LAWN 3-4 86

UPTOWN CREW
LPs: 10/12-inch
MCA 5-8 86

UPTOWN EXPRESS
Singles: 12-inch
SUTRA... 4-8
LPs: 10/12-inch
PALO ALTO 5-10

UPTOWN GIRLS
Singles: 7-inch
PICKWICK CITY 5-10 60s

UPTOWN SYNDICATE
Singles: 7-inch
FAT CITY 5-8

UPTOWNS
Singles: 7-inch
LAURIE 8-12 63
SHANGRI-LA.....................................8-12 65

UPTOWNERS
Singles: 7-inch
LE CAM.. 4-8 64
MAJOR.. 4-8 68
RAGE 8-12 59
TIRIS (707 "She's Mine") 15-25 65

UPTOWNERS / Ron-Dels
Singles: 7-inch
CHARAY 58 "She's Mine")................5-10
CHARAY 86 "She's Mine")..................4-8
Also see RON-DELS
Also see UPTOWNERS

UP-TUNES
Singles: 7-inch
GENIE (103 "I Wanna Love Just You")...20-25

URBAN, Al
Singles: 7-inch
FANG (1001 "Lonely Life")..............20-30 59
SARG (148 "Lookin' for Money") 100-150 57
SARG (158 "Won't Tell You Her Name")..100-150 58
SARG (174 "Last Heartache")........20-30 60

URBAN DANCE SQUAD *LP '90*
LPs: 10/12-inch
ARISTA 5-8 90

URBAN HEROES
LPs: 10/12-inch
HANDSHAKE 5-10 80

URBAN RENEWAL
Singles: 7-inch
ST. GEORGE INT'L (202,270 "Love Eyes") 10-20 68

URBAN ROOTS
Singles: 7-inch
RCA 4-8 66

URBAN VERBS
LPs: 10/12-inch
W.B. 5-10 80-81

URCHINS
Singles: 7-inch
MAJESTY...5-10 64

URE, Midge *P&R/LP '89*
Singles: 7-inch
CHRYSALIS...3-4 89
LPs: 10/12-inch
CHRYSALIS...5-8 89

URGENT *P&R '85*
Singles: 7-inch
MANHATTAN 3-4 85
Picture Sleeves
MANHATTAN 3-4 85

URIAH HEEP *LP '70*
Singles: 7-inch
CHRYSALIS...3-5 78
MERCURY 3-5 70-83
W.B. 3-5 73-78
Picture Sleeves
MERCURY 3-5 70-82
EPs: 7-inch
W.B. 8-12 73
(Juke box issue only.)
LPs: 10/12-inch
CHRYSALIS...5-10 78-79
MERCURY 5-10 70-83
W.B. 5-10 73-81
Also see HENSLEY, Ken
Also see ROUGH DIAMOND

URNESS, Harvey
Singles: 7-inch
STUDIO CITY (1018 "Never Been Blue")...25-35 60s

URSA MAJOR
Singles: 7-inch
RCA 3-5 72
LPs: 10/12-inch
RCA 8-10 72
Member: Dick Wagner.
Also see WAGNER, Dick

URUBAMBA
LPs: 10/12-inch
COLUMBIA...8-10 74
Also see SIMON, Paul

US
Singles: 7-inch
ERA 4-8 68
PATTY 10-15 64

US
Singles: 7-inch
FEATURE (102 "Summertime").....15-25 65

US
Singles: 7-inch
HOUR (31137 "You Say")...............15-25 67
Picture Sleeves
HOUR (31137 "You Say")...............25-50 67

US
Singles: 7-inch
SOUTH..3-5 74
SPRING 3-5 74

US FOUR
Singles: 7-inch
RISING SONS (701 "By My Side")..15-25 67

US KIDS
Singles: 7-inch
REX...8-12 67

US '69
LPs: 10/12-inch
BUDDAH 8-12 69

US TOO GROUP
(Us Too)
Singles: 7-inch
HI (2133 "I'll Leave You Crying")......8-12 67
JYNX ("I'll Leave You Crying").......15-25 66
(No selection number used.)

USHER, Gary
(With the Usherettes)
Singles: 7-inch
CAPITOL (5128 "Jody")...................15-25 64
CAPITOL (5193 "Sacramento") 25-30 64
CAPITOL (5403 "Jody")...................15-25 65
DOT (16158 "Three Surfer Boys") 50-75 63
LAN-CET (144 "Tomorrow")............25-50 61
TITAN (1716 "You're the Girl")........50-75 61
(With Ginger Blake.)
Also see DEVONS
Also see FOUR SPEEDS
Also see GINGER
Also see HONDELLS
Also see HONEYS
Also see KICKSTANDS
Also see KNIGHTS
Also see L.A. TEENS
Also see ROAD RUNNERS
Also see SAGITTARIUS
Also see SUNSETS
Also see SUPER STOCKS
Also see SURFARIS
Also see WHEELEMEN

USSERY
Singles: 7-inch
MERCURY 3-5 73
LPs: 10/12-inch
MERCURY 8-10 73

UTMOSTS
Singles: 7-inch
PAN-OR (1123 "I Need You") 75-125 62
Member: Oma Heard.
Also see HEARD, Oma

UTOPIA
LPs: 10/12-inch
KENT (566 "Utopia")........................30-50 73

UTOPIA *LP '77*
Singles: 7-inch
BEARSVILLE 3-5 76-80
NETWORK..3-4 82
PASSPORT..3-4 84-85
LPs: 10/12-inch
BEARSVILLE 5-12 77-82
NETWORK..8-10 82
PASSPORT..5-8 84-85
Members: Todd Rundgren; Willie Wilcox; Roger Powell; Kasim Sulton.
Also see CASSIDY, Shaun, & Todd Rundgren's Utopia
Also see RUNDGREN, Todd

UTOPIANS
Singles: 7-inch
IMPERIAL (5861 "Dutch Treat")......15-25 62
IMPERIAL (5876 "Along My Lonely Way")..200-300 62
IMPERIAL (5891 "Let Love Come Later")..15-25 62

UTOPIAS
Singles: 7-inch
FORTUNE 10-15 65
HI-Q 10-15 60s
LA SALLE (0072 "Girls Are Against Me")..200-300 60s
Picture Sleeves
FORTUNE...10-20 65

V

V & B.B.
Singles: 7-inch
J&S (1623 "They're Just Rocking & Rolling")..20-30 58

V CASHMERES: see FIVE CASHMERES

V CLASSICS: see FIVE CLASSICS

V., Sonny: see SONNY V

V-8's: see V-EIGHTS

V.I.P.s
(V.I.P.'s)
Singles: 7-inch
CARMEL (44 "Fall Guy") 50-100 63

V.I.P.s
Singles: 7-inch
BIG TOP (518 "Flashback")..............5-10 64
BIG TOP (521 "I'm on to You Baby")..5-10 64
CONGRESS (211 "My Girl Cried").10-15 64
DARROW (16013 "Den Yen")..............8-12
GUITARSVILLE (2123 "Don't Turn Around")..8-12

V - NOTES
Singles: 7-inch
VOLK (102 "Get a Baby Like Mine")..50-100 58

V.S.O.P. *LP '77*
(Very Special One-time Performance)
LPs: 10/12-inch
COLUMBIA 5-10 77
Members: Herbie Hancock; Wayne Shorter; Freddie Hubbard; Tony Williams.

VAC, Ricky, & Rock-A-Ways
Singles: 7-inch
HILLTOP (1871 "Colleen")......... 100-200 61

VACANT LOT
Singles: 7-inch
ROULETTE (4740 "I Blew It") 5-10 67
STUDIO 5 ....5-10 70

VACCO, Bobby
Singles: 7-inch
IMPALA...5-10 60

VACELS *P&R '65*
Singles: 7-inch
KAMA SUTRA..4-8 65
Also see RICKY & VACELS

VADEN, Butch
Singles: 7-inch
FORTUNE..5-10 63
Also see NITE SOUNDS

VADEN, Clark, & Crescents
Singles: 7-inch
DOLLY (5578 "You Can Make It if You Try").. 750-1000 61
(Identification number shown since no selection number is used.)

VAGABONDS
Singles: 78 rpm
UNIQUE 5-10 57
Singles: 7-inch
UNIQUE 8-12 57
VIVA...5-10 59
LPs: 10/12-inch
UNIQUE (112 "The Vagabonds")......15-25 57
Members: Attilo Risso; Dom Germano; Al Torriere; Pete Peterson.

VAGABONDS
Singles: 7-inch
ABCO (1001 "Night Drag")..............10-20 64
(Also issued as by the Lincolns.)
Also see LINCOLNS

VAGABONDS (Four Vagabonds): see FOUR VAGABONDS

VAGRANTS
Singles: 7-inch
ATCO 5-10 66-68
SOUTHERN SOUND (204 "Oh, Those Eyes")..15-25 66
VANGUARD (35038 "Young Blues")...10-15 66
VANGUARD (35042 "Final Hour") ..10-20 66
LPs: 10/12-inch
ARISTA (8459 "Great Lost Album")10-20 87

VAILON, Bobby
Singles: 7-inch
CAMELOT (118 "Surfin' Alone") 15-25 60s

VAILS
Singles: 7-inch
BELMONT (4002 "Great Somewhere")......................................40-60 60
BELMONT (4004 "There'll Come a Time")..40-60 60
Also see SCOTT, Sherman, & Vails

VAIN *LP '89*
LPs: 10/12-inch
ISLAND..5-8 89

VAL, Frankie
Singles: 7-inch
FEE (1002 "Mr. Echo") 10-20 62

VAL, Joe
Singles: 7-inch
JOC (100 "Baby of Mine")..............30-40

VAL, Johnny
Singles: 7-inch
SOMA 20-25 60s

VAL, Tommy
Singles: 7-inch
ABS..4-8 67

VALA QUONS
(Valaquons; Vala-Quons)
Singles: 7-inch
LAGUNA (102 "Teardrops")....... 125-150 64
RAYCO (516 "Jolly Green Giant")...20-30 65
TANGERINE (951 "I Want a Woman")...15-25 65

VALADIERS *P&R '61*
Singles: 7-inch
GORDY (7003 "While I'm Away") ..25-50 62
GORDY (7013 "I Found a Girl") 25-50 63
MIRACLE (6 "Greetings") 50-75 61
MIRACLE (6 "Greetings [This Is Uncle Sam]")...25-50 61
(Note longer title.)
Member: Paul Kelly.
Also see KELLY, Paul

VALAIRES
(With Tom Everett & Orchestra; Val-Aires)
Singles: 7-inch
CORAL (62177 "Launie, My Love")..50-100 60
WILLETT (114 "Launie, My Love").. 500-1000 59
Also see VOGUES

VALAQUONS: see VALA QUONS

VALARONS
Singles: 7-inch
ATCO 4-8 66

VAL-CHORDS
("Vocal Tommy Drumgoole")
Singles: 7-inch
GAMETIME (104 "Candy Store Love") 50-75 57
(Horizontal lines on label. No sword pictured.)
GAME TIME (104 "Candy Store Love") 20-40 57
(No lines on label. Sword is pictured.)
Member: Tommy Drumgoole.

VALDEZ, Daniel
LPs: 10/12-inch
A&M 8-10 74

VALDEZ, Sonny / Stream of Consciousness
Singles: 7-inch
CAPITOL 4-8 69

VALDONS
Singles: 7-inch
TWIN CITY MOVEMENT 10-15 60s

VAL DOROS Featuring Charles Pryor
("With Gene Preston & His Band Featuring Erwin Kalcks")
Singles: 78 rpm
SILHOUETTE 20-30 56
Singles: 7-inch
SILHOUETTE (517 "Don't Open the Grave") 50-75 56

VALDY
Singles: 7-inch
A&M 3-5 75-76

VALDEZ, Gloria: see BASCOMB, Paul, & Five Arrows

VALE, Blacky
Singles: 7-inch
HURRICANE (100 "If I Had Me a Woman") 200-300 58

VALE, Bobby
Singles: 7-inch
LAWN 10-20 63

VALE, Dick
Singles: 78 rpm
CORAL 20-40 57
Singles: 7-inch
CORAL (61844 "Rockabilly Blues") 20-40 57

VALE, Jerry P&R '53
Singles: 78 rpm
COLUMBIA 3-5 51-57
Singles: 7-inch
BUDDAH 3-5 78
COLUMBIA 3-10 51-74
Picture Sleeves
COLUMBIA 5-10 64-65
EPs: 7-inch
COLUMBIA 5-15 56-59
LPs: 10/12-inch
COLUMBIA 5-20 58-75
HARMONY 5-10 69-74
Also see CLARK, Dave, Five / New Christy Minstrels / Bobby Vinton / Jerry Vale
Also see MATHIS, Johnny / Tony Bennett / North Carolina Ramblers / Ray Conniff & Jerry Vale with Eugene Ormandy

VALE, Jerry, Peggy King & Felicia Sanders
LPs: 10/12-inch
COLUMBIA 10-20 56
Also see KING, Peggy
Also see SANDERS, Felicia
Also see VALE, Jerry

VALE, Ricky, & His Surfers
LPs: 10/12-inch
STRAND 20-25 63
Members: Ricky Vale; Mark Pastner; Benjie Lipman.

VALE, Sandy
(With the Valiants)
Singles: 7-inch
DECCA 5-10 59
INTERNATIONALE 4-8 63

VALEN, Tex
Singles: 7-inch
COUNSELLOR 4-8 65

VALENS, Ritchie P&R/R&B '58
Singles: 12-inch
DEL-FI (1287 "La Bamba") 15-25 87
Singles: 78 rpm
APEX (76402 "Donna") 100-200 58
(Canadian.)
Singles: 7-inch
ABC 3-5 74
APEX (76402 "Donna") 15-30 58
(Canadian.)
DEL-FI (1287 "La Bamba '87") 3-4 87
DEL-FI (4106 "C'mon Let's Go") 15-25 58
DEL-FI (4110 "Donna") 15-25 58
(Solid green label with black print.)
DEL-FI (4110 "Donna") 10-15 58
(Has rows of circles on label.)
DEL-FI (4110 "Donna") 5-10 61
(Black label with sawtooth circle.)
DEL-FI (4111 "Fast Freight") 10-20 59
(First issued as by Arvee Allens.)
DEL-FI (4114 "That's My Little Suzie") 10-20 59
DEL-FI (4117 "Little Girl") 10-20 59
(Del-Fi "Limited Valens Memorial Series.")
DEL-FI (4128 "Stay Beside Me") 10-20 60
DEL-FI (4133 "Paddiwack") 10-20 60
ERIC 3-5 70s
GOODIES 3-5
KASEY (7040 "Donna") 5-10
LANA 4-6 60s
LOST-NITE 4-8
Picture Sleeves
DEL-FI (4114 "That's My Little Suzie") 25-50 59
DEL-FI (4117 "Little Girl") 20-40 59
(With explanatory "Concerning This Record" insert.)
DEL-FI (4117 "Little Girl") 15-25 59
(Without insert.)
DEL-FI (4128 "Stay Beside Me") 15-25 60
KASEY (7040 "Donna") 5-10
EPs: 7-inch
DEL-FI (1 "Ritchie Valens") 50-75 59
(Promotional issue only.)
DEL-FI (101 "Ritchie Valens") 50-75 59
DEL-FI (111 "Ritchie Valens Sings") 50-75 59
LPs: 10/12-inch
DEL-FI (1201 "Ritchie Valens") .. 150-200 59
(Back cover shows *That's My Little Suzie* as "I Got a Gal Named Sue.")
DEL-FI (1201 "Ritchie Valens") 50-100 59
(Back cover properly shows *That's My Little Suzie.*)
DEL-FI (1206 "Ritchie") 50-100 59
DEL-FI (1214 "Ritchie Valens in Concert") 100-200 61
DEL-FI (1225 "Greatest Hits") 50-100 63
DEL-FI (1247 "Greatest Hits, Vol. 2") 50-100 65
GUEST STAR (1484 "The Original La Bamba") 15-25 64
GUEST STAR (1489 "The Original Ritchie Valens") 15-25 64
MGM (117 "Ritchie Valens") 10-20 70
RHINO (200 "Best of Ritchie Valens") 5-8 81
RHINO (2798 "History of Ritchie Valens") 20-30 81
(Boxed, three-disc set.)
Also see ALLENS, Arvee

VALENS, Ritchie / Jerry Kole
LPs: 10/12-inch
CROWN (5336 "Ritchie Valens & Jerry Kole") 20-30 63
Also see COLE, Jerry

VALENTE, Caterina P&R '55
Singles: 78 rpm
DECCA 3-5 54-57
Singles: 7-inch
DECCA 5-10 54-59
LONDON 3-6 60-68
RCA 4-8 59
TELEFUNKEN 4-8 59
EPs: 7-inch
DECCA 5-10 55
LPs: 10/12-inch
DECCA 5-15 55-64
LONDON 5-15 59-72
RCA 5-15 60-61

VALENTE, Dino
Singles: 7-inch
ELEKTRA 5-8 64
LPs: 10/12-inch
EPIC 15-20 68
Also see QUICKSILVER MESSENGER SERVICE

VALENTI, Bobby
Singles: 7-inch
GORHAM 5-10 60

VALENTI, John P&R/R&B '76
Singles: 7-inch
ARIOLA AMERICA 3-5 76-77

VALENTIN, Dave R&B/LP '80
Singles: 7-inch
GRP 3-5 80-81
LPs: 10/12-inch
GRP 5-10 80-81

VALENTINE
Singles: 7-inch
BIG TOP 5-10 63

VALENTINE
Singles: 7-inch
U.A. 3-5 77

VALENTINE, Alvin
Singles: 7-inch
BRUNSWICK 3-6 69

VALENTINE, Billy
(Billy Valentine Trio)
Singles: 78 rpm
CAPITOL 5-15 55-56
DECCA 5-10 51-52
MERCURY 8-12 49
PRESTIGE 5-10 53
Singles: 7-inch
CAPITOL 15-25 55-56
DECCA 15-25 51-52
FEDERAL 10-15 59
PRESTIGE 15-25 53
Session: Mickey Baker.
Also see BAKER, Mickey
Also see WASHBOARD BILL

VALENTINE, Cal
Singles: 7-inch
LYONS 4-8 62

VALENTINE, Floyd
Singles: 78 rpm
VEE JAY (113 "Off Time") 10-20 54
Singles: 7-inch
VEE JAY (113 "Off Time") 15-25 54
(Black vinyl.)
VEE JAY (113 "Off Time") 30-50 54
(Colored vinyl.)

VALENTINE, Hilton
LPs: 10/12-inch
CAPITOL 10-20 69
Also see ANIMALS

VALENTINE, Ida: see Lyrics

VALENTINE, Jeffrey
Singles: 7-inch
DARAN 4-6

VALENTINE, Jesse
Singles: 7-inch
THUNDERHEAD 5-8

VALENTINE, Jimmy
Singles: 7-inch
CUB (9024 "Rockin' Hula") 10-15 59
LPs: 10/12-inch
JUBILEE 20-30

VALENTINE, Joe
Singles: 7-inch
RONN 4-8 67-69

VALENTINE, Judy
Singles: 7-inch
ABC-PAR 5-10 59

VALENTINE, Kid Thomas: see KID THOMAS

VALENTINE, Leo: see Lyrics

VALENTINE, Lezli R&B '68
Singles: 7-inch
ALL PLATINUM 3-6 68

VALENTINE, Louie
Singles: 7-inch
GREAT 4-8 68

VALENTINE, Marty
Singles: 7-inch
MALA 5-10 60

VALENTINE, Patience
Singles: 7-inch
SAR (111 "In the Dark") 10-20 61
SAR (119 "I Miss You So") 10-20 61
SAR (142 "Ernestine") 10-20 63
Also see FLAIRS

VALENTINE, Penny
Singles: 7-inch
LIBERTY 5-10 65

VALENTINE, Rose
Singles: 7-inch
RCA (9276 "When the Heartaches End") 15-25 67

VALENTINE, Rudy
Singles: 7-inch
REGALIA 4-8 61

VALENTINE, T.D.
Singles: 7-inch
EPIC 3-6 69

VALENTINE, Tony
Singles: 7-inch
GOOD LUCK 4-8 64

VALENTINE BROTHERS R&B '82
Singles: 12-inch
SOURCE 4-6 78
Singles: 7-inch
A&M 3-4 84
BRIDGE 3-4 82
SOURCE 3-5 79
LPs: 10/12-inch
A&M 5-8 84
BRIDGE 5-8 82
SOURCE 5-10 79
Members: John Valentine; Billy Valentine.
Also see YOUNG-HOLT UNLIMITED

VALENTINES
(With Jimmy Wright & His Orchestra)
Singles: 78 rpm
OLD TOWN 150-250 54
RAMA 50-100 55-57
Singles: 7-inch
OLD TOWN (1009 "Tonight Kathleen") 500-750 54
RAMA (171 "Lily Maebelle") 100-200 55
(Blue label.)
RAMA (171 "Lily Maebelle") 25-50 57
(Red label.)
RAMA (181 "Love You, Darling") 100-150 56
RAMA (186 "Christmas Prayer") 300-500 56
(Blue label.)
RAMA (186 "Christmas Prayer") 25-50 57
(Red label.)
RAMA (196 "Woo Woo Train") 50-100 56
(Blue label.)
RAMA (196 "Woo Woo Train") 25-50 57
(Red label.)
RAMA (201 "Twenty Minutes") 50-100 56
RAMA (208 "Nature's Creation") .. 50-100 56
RAMA (228 "Don't Say Goodnight") 100-200 57
ROULETTE 3-5 70s
Members: Richard Barrett; Mickey Francis; Ray Briggs; Ron Bright; Don Raysor; Ed Edgehill; Dave "Baby" Cortez; Carl Hogan.
Also see BARRETT, Richard
Also see CORTEZ, Dave "Baby"
Also see WRIGHT, Jimmy

VALENTINES
Singles: 7-inch
LUDIX (102 "Johnny One Heart") ... 15-25 62

VALENTINES
Singles: 7-inch
BETHLEHEM (3055 "I'll Forget You") 15-25 62
KING (5338 "Please Don't Leave, Please Don't Go") 15-25 60
KING (5433 "Hey Ruby") 15-25 60
KING (5830 "I Have Two Loves") ... 15-25 63
U.A. (764 "Alone in the Night") 10-15 64

VALENTINES
Singles: 7-inch
LEE (5465 "Beautyful [sic]") 20-30 65

VALENTINES
Singles: 7-inch
SOUND STAGE 7 .... 5-15 69-70

VALENTINES
Singles: 7-inch
KING BEE (103 "This Is My Story") 25-35

VALENTINES
Singles: 7-inch
IONA 5-10

VALENTINO
Singles: 7-inch
PINKY 5-10 59

VALENTINO C&W '81
(Valentino Enrique Hernandez)
Singles: 7-inch
GAIEE 3-5 75
RCA 3-4 81

VALENTINO, Bobby
Singles: 7-inch
LITA (1003 "Special Delivery") 5-10 62
Also see RELF, Bobby

VALENTINO, Danny P&R '60
Singles: 7-inch
CONTRAST 5-10 67
MGM 10-20 59-60

VALENTINO, Mark P&R '62
Singles: 7-inch
SWAN 5-10 62-63
(Shown as "Mark Valentinon" on some labels.)
LPs: 10/12-inch
SWAN (508 "Mark Valentino") 30-50 63

VALENTINO, Sal
Singles: 7-inch
FALCO 10-20 62
W.B. 5-10 69-70
Also see BEAU BRUMMELS
Also see ELLIOTT, Ron
Also see NAGLE, Ron
Also see STONEGROUND

VALENTINO, Tony
Singles: 7-inch
SWAN 4-8 62

VALENTINO & LOVERS
Singles: 7-inch
DONNA (1345 "One Teardrop Too Late") 30-40 61

VALENTINOS
Singles: 7-inch
BRUNSWICK (55171 "A Kiss from Your Lips") 10-15 60

VALENTINOS P&R/R&B '62
Singles: 7-inch
ABKCO 3-5 70s
ASTRA (1026 "Looking for a Love") 5-10 66
CHESS 5-10 66
CLEAN 5-10 73
JUBILEE 5-10 68-69
SAR (132 "Looking for a Love") 10-20 62
SAR (137 "Darling Come Back Home") 10-20 62
SAR (144 "She's So Good to Me") 10-20 63
SAR (152 "It's All Over Now") 10-15 64
SAR (155 "Bitter Dreams") 10-15 64
Members: Bobby Womack; Curtis Womack.
Also see WOMACK, Bobby
Also see WOMACK BROTHERS

VALENTINOS
Singles: 7-inch
LINE (114 "Hey Girl") 5-10

VALENTION, Mark: see VALENTINO, Mark

VALERIE & NICK
Singles: 7-inch
GLOVER (3000 "Lonely Town") 10-15 64
Members: Valerie Simpson; Nick Ashford.
Also see ASHFORD & SIMPSON

VALERY, Dana P&R '76
Singles: 7-inch
ABC 5-10 68-69
COLUMBIA (44004 "Having You Around") 15-25 67
LIBERTY 4-6 70
PHANTOM 3-6 75
SCOTTI BROS 3-6 79
Picture Sleeves
PHANTOM 3-5 75
LPs: 10/12-inch
BRUNSWICK 5-10
PHANTOM 5-10 75

Also see SIMON, Paul

VALETS
(With Sammy Lowe Orchestra)
Singles: 7-inch
JON (4025 "I Need Someone") 75-100 58
JON (4219 "Sherry") 25-50 59
VULCAN (135 "Sherry") 150-200 58
Also see LOWE, Sammy, Orchestra

VALHALLA
LPs: 10/12-inch
U.A. 10-15 69

VALIANTS P&R '57
(With the Bumps Blackwell Orchestra; Featuring Billy Storm)
Singles: 78 rpm
KEEN 20-40 57
Singles: 7-inch
ANDEX (4026 "Please Wait My Love") 100-125 58
(First issue.)
KEEN (4008 "Temptation of My Heart") 25-50 58
KEEN (4026 "Please Wait My Love") 40-60 58
KEEN (34004 "This Is the Night") .. 20-40 57
KEEN (34007 "Lover Lover") 20-40 58
KEEN (82120 "This Is the Night") .. 10-20 60
SHAR-DEE (703 "Dear Cindy") 75-125 59
(Reads: "Made in U.S.A." at bottom. No mention of distribution by London.)
SHAR-DEE (703 "Dear Cindy") 25-50 59
(Reads "Distributed by London Records, Inc." at bottom)
Also see CHAVELLES
Also see STORM, Billy

VALIANTS
Singles: 7-inch
SPECK (1001 "Wedding Bells") 2000-3000 59

VALIANTS
Singles: 7-inch
NEW PHOENIX (102 "I Had a Dream") 25-35 60
Members: Paul Stefen; Jim Bing; Tony Kern; Gene Stankowski; Ralph Stevens; Paul Yopps.
Also see STEFAN, Paul

VALIANTS
(Dixieaires)
Singles: 7-inch
JOY (235 "Let Me Go Lover") 10-20 60
Also see BELLS
Also see DIXIEAIRES
Also see VAN LOAN, Joe

VALIANTS
Singles: 7-inch
FAIRLANE 10-15 61
IMPERIAL 10-15 62-63
KC 10-15 62

VALIANTS
Singles: 7-inch
FREDLO (6208 "Twistin' Til the End") 10-20 62

VALIANTS
Singles: 7-inch
ROULETTE 8-12 63

VALIANTS
Singles: 7-inch
SABRE (103 "Wild Party") 10-20 63

VALIANTS
Singles: 7-inch
AMCAN (404 "Moonflight") 10-15 64
AMCAN (404 "Moonflight") 15-25 64
(Single-sided. Promotional issue only.)
DOT 5-8 66
NEW PHOENIX (102 "Mutha") 15-25 66

VALIANTS
Singles: 7-inch
VALOR (101 "The Valiant") 10-15 60s

VALIANTS
Singles: 7-inch
VALOR 5-10 60s

VALIANTS
Singles: 7-inch
EV 8-12
FIDELITY (4057 "Slogian") 8-12
RIDGE (1091 "Jack the Ripper") 8-12
VB (2 "Dawn") 8-12

VALIDS
Singles: 7-inch
AMBER 8-10 65-66
LPs: 10/12-inch
AMBER 15-25 66

VALIENTS
Singles: 7-inch
BANGAR (00601 "Backlash") 10-20 63
GARRETT 10-20 60s

VALINO, Joe P&R '56
Singles: 78 rpm
U.A. 8-12 57
VIK 5-10 56
Singles: 7-inch
BANDBOX 5-10 61
CLEARVIEW 5-10
CROSLEY 5-10 59-60
DEBUT 4-6 67-68
RCA 8-12 59
U.A. 10-15 57-58
VIK 10-20 56
Picture Sleeves
U.A. (101 "Legend of the Lost") 20-30 57

LPs: 10/12-inch
DEBUT 8-12 67

VALJEAN P&R/LP '62
(Valjean Johns)
Singles: 7-inch
CARLTON 4-8 62-63
Picture Sleeves
CARLTON 5-10 62
LPs: 10/12-inch
CARLTON 15-25 62-63

VAL-JEENS
("Vocal Jim Young")
Singles: 7-inch
PEE VEE (141 "Darlene") 100-200 60s

VALKYRIES
Singles: 7-inch
CORI (31003 "Love You Like I Do") 10-20 65

VALLA, Tony
(With the Alamos)
Singles: 7-inch
FORTUNE 10-15 61
HI-Q 8-12 63

VALLET, Gary
Singles: 7-inch
BISON ("Guitar Bass Boogie") 20-25 60
(Selection number not known. Later issued as *The Shock*, by the Quarter Notes.)

VALLEY, Frankie: see VALLI, Frankie

VALLEY, Jim
(Jim "Harpo" Valley; with Don & Goodtimes)
Singles: 7-inch
DUNHILL 5-10 67
JERDEN 5-10 67
Picture Sleeves
DUNHILL 3-6 67
LPs: 10/12-inch
PANORAMA (104 "Harpo") 20-30 68
Also see DON & GOODTIMES
Also see REVERE, Paul, & Raiders
Also see VICEROYS

VALLEY, Jim, & Steve Schurr
LPs: 10/12-inch
LIGHT 10-15
Also see VALLEY, Jim

VALLEY GIRLS
Singles: 12-inch
RHINO 4-6 83

VALLI
(With the Shirelles)
Singles: 7-inch
SCEPTER 10-15 62
Also see SHIRELLES

VALLI, Frankie P&R '66
(With the Travelers; Frankie Valle; Frankie Vally; Frankie Valley; with Romans)
Singles: 10/12-inch
MOTOWN 15-20 73
PRIVATE STOCK 10-15 77
Singles: 78 rpm
MERCURY 50-75 54
Singles: 7-inch
CINDY 75-100 59
COLLECTABLES 3-4 80s
CORONA (1234 "My Mother's Eyes") 300-500 53
DECCA (30994 "Please Take a Chance") 75-100 59
MCA/CURB 3-5 80
MERCURY (70381 "Forgive and Forget") 100-125 54
(Maroon label.)
MERCURY (70381 "Forgive and Forget") 50-75 54
(Black label.)
MOTOWN 8-12 73
MOWEST 5-10 72
PHILIPS (40407 thru 45098, except 40500) 4-8 66-70
PHILIPS (40500 "Donnybrook") 20-40 67
PHILIPS (40661 & 40680) 10-12 69-70
PRIVATE STOCK 3-5 74-78
RSO 3-5 78
SEASONS 3-5
SMASH 5-10 65-66
W.B./CURB 3-5 78-80
Promotional Singles
BOB CREWE PRESENTS (1 "The Girl I'll Never Know") 25-35 69
DECCA (30994 "Please Take a Chance") 50-75 59
MERCURY (70381 "Forgive and Forget") 50-75 54
MOWEST (5025 "The Night") 12-15 71
PHILIPS 8-12 66-70
PRIVATE STOCK 8-10 74-78
SMASH 8-12 65-66
Picture Sleeves
PHILIPS 8-15 66-69
LPs: 10/12-inch
MCA 5-10 79-80
MOTOWN (100 series) 5-8 81
MOTOWN (800 series) 8-12 75
PHILIPS (200247 "Solo") 30-40 67
(Monaural.)
PHILIPS (600000 series) 20-25 67-68
(Stereo.)
PRIVATE STOCK 8-10 75-78
W.B. 8-10 78
Also see BEACH BOYS with Frankie Valli & 4 Seasons
Also see FOUR LOVERS
Also see 4 SEASONS
Also see HARTFORD, Ken
Also see LEE, Larry
Also see NOLAN, Frankie
Also see REID, Matthew
Also see TYLER, Frankie

VALLI, Frankie, & Chris Forde P&R '80
Singles: 7-inch
MCA 3-5 80

VALLI, Frankie, & Cheryl Ladd
Singles: 7-inch
CAPITOL 3-5 82
Also see LADD, Cheryl
Also see VALLI, Frankie

VALLI, June P&R '52
(With Joe Reisman's Orchestra)
Singles: 78 rpm
RCA 3-5 52-56
Singles: 7-inch
ABC-PAR 4-6 63
DCP 4-6 64
MERCURY 4-8 58-61
RCA 5-10 52-56
U.A. 4-6 62
Picture Sleeves
MERCURY 4-8 61
EPs: 7-inch
RCA 5-10 55-56
LPs: 10/12-inch
AUDIO FIDELITY 5-10 69
MERCURY 8-15 60
RCA 12-25 55-56
Also see PIANO RED / June Valli
Also see ZABACH, Florian

VALLIE, Frankie: see VALLI, Frankie

VALLIER, Geneva
Singles: 78 rpm
CASH 15-20 50s

VALLIN, Sylvia
Singles: 7-inch
VALTONE 5-10 63

VALLO, Rick
(With Three Beaus & a Peep; Ricky Vallo)
Singles: 78 rpm
MGM 4-6 53
Singles: 7-inch
MGM 5-10 53
VERVE (10148 "Rockin' River") 10-15 58
VERVE (10149 "Could I Love You More") 10-15 58
Also see THREE BEAUS & A PEEP

VALLONE, Alan
Singles: 7-inch
PHILIPS 4-8 63-64
BVC 5-10 61

VALLY, Frankie: see VALLI, Frankie

VALONS
Singles: 7-inch
MARK III 10-20 60s

VALOR, Tim
Singles: 7-inch
RCA 8-12 62

VALOR, Tony
Singles: 7-inch
MUSICTONE (1119 "Story in My Heart") 50-75 63

VALQUINS
Singles: 7-inch
GAITY (162 "Falling Star") 500-750 59
(Black vinyl.)
GAITY (162 "Falling Star") 1500-2500 59
(Gold vinyl.)

VALRAYS
Singles: 7-inch
PARKWAY (880 "Get a Board") 10-20 63
PARKWAY (904 "Yo Me Pregunto [I Ask Myself]") 10-20 64

VAL-RAYS
Singles: 7-inch
U.A. 4-8 67

VALS
Singles: 7-inch
UNIQUE LABORATORIES/THERON ("The Song of a Lover") 1000-2000 61
(No selection number used.)
Members: Bill Gibson; David Wilkerson Jr.; Ernie Morris; Bill Taylor; Clarence Green.
Also see JOHNSON, Vicki

VALS
Singles: 7-inch
ASCOT 10-20 65

VALTAIRS
Singles: 7-inch
SELSOM (101 "Soul") 8-12 64
SELSOM (106 "Moonlight in Vermont") 10-20 65

VAL-TONES
Singles: 78 rpm
DELUXE 40-60 55
Singles: 7-inch
DELUXE (6084 "Tender Darling") 75-125 55

VALTONE BAND
Singles: 7-inch
BOSS (103 "Norma's Bues") 15-25 63
VALTONE (103 "Norma's Bues") 10-20 65
(Rerecorded version.)
VALTONE (106 "Norma's Bues") 10-20 65
(Reissued with different flip side.)

VALTONES
Singles: 78 rpm
GEE 50-75 56
Singles: 7-inch
GEE (1004 "You Belong to My Heart") 150-200 56

VALUES
Singles: 7-inch
INVICTA (1000 series) 15-20 62
INVICTA (9000 series) 4-8 65

VALUMDEARS
Singles: 7-inch
MART (3517 "King Bee") 15-25 59

VALUMES
(Valume's; Volumes)
Singles: 7-inch
CHEX (1000 "I Love You") 200-300 62
Also see VOLUMES

VAMPIRE STATE BUILDING
Singles: 7-inch
ROULETTE 4-8 69

VAMPIRES
LPs: 10/12-inch
U.A. 20-25 64

VAMPIRES
Singles: 7-inch
CARROLL (104 "Why Didn't I Listen to Mother") 200-300 64
(Reissued as by the Bentleys.)
Also see BENTLEYS

VAN, Billy
(Billy Van Four)
Singles: 7-inch
DRA 4-8 61
LAGREE (705 "I Miss You") 5-10 60

VAN, Gary
Singles: 7-inch
INTRO (9000 "Rockin' Too Much") 50-75 58

VAN, Gloria
Singles: 7-inch
NORMAN 4-8 63

VAN, Ila
(Ila Vann)
Singles: 7-inch
ARNOLD 5-10 63
LIBERTY 5-10 63
ROULETTE 5-15 67-69

VAN, Steve & Bernie
Singles: 7-inch
VAN (107 "Dream Train") 10-15 61

VAN, Trudy, & Realm
Singles: 7-inch
VJV (301 "Surf Is Up") 15-25 60s

VAN & GRACE
Singles: 7-inch
SSS INT'L 3-4

VAN & TITUS R&B '68
Singles: 7-inch
ELF (90016 "Cry Baby Cry") 10-15 68

VAN BEETHOVEN, Camper: see CAMPER VAN BEETHOVEN

VAN BECK, Doug
(Doug Van Beck Trio)
Singles: 7-inch
FARGO (1064 "Surfin' Little Girl") 10-20 63
JUDI (6500 "Sweet Lucy's Kiss") 15-25 64

VAN BERGEYK, Ton
LPs: 10/12-inch
KICKING MULE 5-10
Also see MILLER, Dale / John James / Sam Mitchell / Ton Van Bergeyk

VAN BROTHERS
(Norman Walton & Van Brothers; Arnold & Lee)
Singles: 7-inch
POOR BOY (111 "Servant of Love") 500-750 60
WALTON (2500 "Uncle Jim Riggs Will") 50-75 65
EPs: 7-inch
WALTON (003 "Too Many Women") 300-350 62
(Title shown is the Van Brothers track on side A. Actual EP title is not yet known.)
Members: Arnold Van Winkel; Lee Van Winkle; Norman Walton.
Also see WINKLE, Arnold Van

VANCE, Al
Singles: 7-inch
GOLDWAX (116 "Every Woman I Know") 20-30 65
Also see SCALES, Harvey

VANCE, Billy
Singles: 7-inch
AUGUST 5-10
KAYO (926 "Innocent") 15-25 58
MAP (502 "Drop Me a Line") 8-12

VANCE, Chico
(With the Nocturnals)
Singles: 7-inch
REVIVE 8-12 63
STACY (967 "Why Wait for Winter") 8-12 63
Also see CHEEK-O-VASS
Also see NOCTURNALS

VANCE, Frankie
Singles: 7-inch
REVUE 3-6 69

VANCE, Joel
LPs: 10/12-inch
CADET CONCEPT 8-12 69

VANCE, Kenny
Singles: 7-inch
ATLANTIC 5-10 75
W.B. 5-8 77
LPs: 10/12-inch
ATLANTIC 10-15 75
GOLD CASTLE (171011 "Short Vacation") 5-8 88
ROCK-A-WAY (1457 "Short Vacation") 10-15
Also see HARBOR LIGHTS
Also see JAY & AMERICANS
Also see PLANOTONES with Prof. LaPlano
Also see ROCKAWAYS

VANCE, Larry
(With Delmonacos)
Singles: 7-inch
FOCUS (7137 "Diary of a Broken Heart") 8-12

VANCE, Paul P&R '66
Singles: 7-inch
ROULETTE 4-8 62
SCEPTER 4-8 66
LPs: 10/12-inch
SCEPTER 10-20 66
Also see LEE & PAUL
Also see PAUL'S HIGH SCHOOL BAND

VANCE, Sammy
Singles: 7-inch
EBB 10-20 58

VANCE, Tommy
(With the Checkmates)
Singles: 7-inch
JERDEN 4-8 66
Also see KING GEORGE & CHECKMATES

VANCE, Vince, & Valiants
Singles: 7-inch
PAID (109 "Bomb Iran") 4-6 80
TOWEL (1000 "Bomb Iran") 8-12 80
(Towel is the original issue. Paid track is remixed. No artist credit is shown on the label.)
VALIANT ("All I Want for Christmas Is You") 3-4 89
(Selection number not known.)
Picture Sleeves
VALIANT ("All I Want for Christmas Is You") 3-5 89
Members: Vince Vance; Vickie Valiantette; Troy Powers; Tony King; Katherine Farmer; Darren Pair.

VANCE BROTHERS
Singles: 78 rpm
MACY'S 8-12 50

VANDALL, Glenn
Singles: 7-inch
DIAL 4-8 66

VANDALS
Singles: 7-inch
PAROLE ("Mystery") 20-30 65
(No selection number used.)
TIARA (200 "I Saw Her in a Mustang") 15-25 66
EPs: 7-inch
GOLDEN GATE (0011 "It's Like Now Baby") 30-40 66
(Promotional issue, made for Macy's/Seven-Up.)
Members: George Terry; Johnny Sambataro; Augie Bucci; Richie Kutcher; Bill Cosford; Russ Septilli.

VANDALS
Singles: 7-inch
G.A.R. (105 "You Lied to Me") 200-300 67
Members: Jim Walden; Bob Liles; Craig Strong; Charlie Dionisio.
Also see NORSEMEN

VANDALS
Singles: 7-inch
T-NECK 4-6 70

VAN DELLOS
Singles: 7-inch
CARD (558 "Bring Back") 100-200 61

VAN DELLES
Singles: 7-inch
BOLO (731 "Time After Time") 10-20 62

VANDELLS
Singles: 7-inch
ABC-PAR 5-10 64

VAN-DELLS
(Booker T's MGs)
Singles: 7-inch
STAX (145 "The Honeydripper") 10-15 64
Also see MGs

VANDELLS
Singles: 7-inch
BAY TOWN 10-20
Member: Billy Sherrill.
Also see SHERRILL, Billy

VANDELS
(Vandel's)
Singles: 7-inch
USA (758 "A Small Silver Ring") 75-125 63

VANDELS
Singles: 7-inch
SOULED OUT 5-10 68

VANDENBERG P&R/LP '83
(Adrian Vandenberg)
Singles: 7-inch
ATCO 3-4 83-84
LPs: 10/12-inch
ATCO 5-8 83-84

VAN DER GRAAF GENERATOR
Singles: 7-inch
MERCURY 3-6 69-70
LPs: 10/12-inch
CHARISMA 10-15 71
DUNHILL 10-15 70
MERCURY (1000 series) 8-10 76
MERCURY (61000 series) 15-18 69
PROBE 10-15 70

VANDERBILTS
Singles: 7-inch
CAMEO 4-8 63

VANDERPOOL, Sylvia: see LITTLE SYLVIA

VAN DOREN
Singles: 7-inch
HICKORY 8-12 64

VAN DOREN, Mamie
Singles: 7-inch
DOT 5-10 59
EPs: 7-inch
PREP (1 "Untamed Youth") 50-75 57
LPs: 10/12-inch
CHURCHILL 8-12 85

VAN DOREN, Mamie, & June Wilkinson
Singles: 7-inch
JUBILEE 5-10 64
Also see VAN DOREN, Mamie

VAN DORN SISTERS
Singles: 7-inch
PHILTONE 5-10 62

VANDROSS, Luther R&B '76
Singles: 12-inch
EPIC 4-6 82-85
Singles: 7-inch
COTILLION 3-5 76
EPIC 3-5 81-90
Picture Sleeves
EPIC 3-4 85-87
LPs: 10/12-inch
EPIC 5-10 81-90
Also see BOWIE, David
Also see CHANGE
Also see LUTHER
Also see LYNN, Cheryl, & Luther Vandross
Also see PRESTON, Billy
Also see ROUNDTREE
Also see WARWICK, Dionne, & Luther Vandross

VANDROSS, Luther, & Gregory Hines P&R/R&B '87
Singles: 7-inch
EPIC 3-4 87
Also see HINES, Gregory

VAN DYKE, Bruce C&W '89
Singles: 7-inch
ARIA 3-4 89

VAN DYKE, Connie
(Conny Van Dyke)
Singles: 7-inch
MOTOWN (1041 "Oh Freddy") 25-35 62
WHEELSVILLE (112 "Don't Do Nothing I Wouldn't Do") 75-125 60s

VAN DYKE, Dick
(With the Jack Halloran Singers)
Singles: 7-inch
BUENA VISTA (441 "Chim Chim Cheree") 4-6 65
JAMIE (1256 "Three Wheels on My Wagon") 4-8 61
U.A. (50486 "Hushabye Mountain") 4-8 68
Picture Sleeves
BUENA VISTA (441 "Chim Chim Cheree") 4-8 65
JAMIE (1256 "Three Wheels on My Wagon") 5-10 61
LPs: 10/12-inch
COMMAND 10-20 64

VAN DYKE, Dick, & Julie Andrews
Singles: 7-inch
BUENA VISTA 4-6 65
Picture Sleeves
BUENA VISTA 4-8 65
Also see ANDREWS, Julie
Also see VAN DYKE, Dick

VAN DYKE, Earl
(With the Soul Brothers; with Motown Brass)
Singles: 7-inch
RENAISSANCE (5000 "September Song") 50-75
SOUL (Except 35009) 10-20 64-69
SOUL (35009 "All for You") 100-200 65
LPs: 10/12-inch
MOTOWN (631 "Motown Sound") 20-40 65
SOUL (715 "Earl of Funk") 25-50 69
Also see WALKER, Junior

VAN DYKE, Jerry
Singles: 7-inch
COLUMBIA 4-6 65-66

VAN DYKE, Leroy P&R '56/C&W '57
Singles: 78 rpm
DOT (Except 15561) 10-15 56-57
DOT (15561 "Honky Tonk Song") 20-30 57
Singles: 7-inch
ABC 3-5 74-75
ABC/DOT 3-5 75-77
DECCA 3-5 70-72
DOT (Except 15561 & 15698) 10-20 56-57
DOT (15561 "Honky Tonk Song") 25-35 57
DOT (15698 "Leather Jacket") 50-75 58
KAPP 4-6 68-70
MCA 3-5 73
MERCURY 4-8 61-64
MOUNTAIN DEW 5-10
PLANTATION 3-5 78
SUN 3-5 79
W.B. 4-6 65-67
Picture Sleeves
MERCURY (72232 "Night People") 5-10 64
LPs: 10/12-inch
DECCA 8-10 72
DOT 20-30 60s
HARMONY 8-12 69
KAPP 8-15 68-69
MCA 5-10 73
MERCURY 12-25 62-64
PLANTATION 5-10 77-79
SUN 5-8 74
W.B. 10-15 65-66
WING 8-15 65-66

VAN DYKE FIVE: see VAN DYKES

VAN DYKES
Singles: 7-inch
DECCA (30654 "Run Betty, Run") 25-35 58
DECCA (31036 "Better Come Back to Me") 25-35 59
DECCA (30762 "Come on Baby") 40-60 59

VAN DYKES P&R '61
Singles: 7-inch
DELUXE (6193 "Bells Are Ringing") 10-15 61
DONNA (1333 "Gift of Love") 20-30 60
FELSTED (8565 "Once Upon a Dream") 15-20 59
KING (5158 "Bells Are Ringing") 30-40 58
(Blue label.)
KING (5158 "Bells Are Ringing") 10-15 60s
(Yellow label.)
SPRING (1113 "Gift of Love") 75-125 59
Also see TEMPTATIONS

VAN DYKES
(Calvin & Van Dykes)
Singles: 7-inch
ATLANTIC (2161 "Stupidity") 25-50 62

VAN DYKES
(Van Dyke Five)
Singles: 7-inch
CO-OP 5-10 68
CORNER CLOSET 5-10 67
GREEN SEA 8-12 65-67
Members: Frank Ruggiero; Bob Picagli; Russ Griffith; Tom Juliano; Art DeNicholas.
Also see CATALINAS

VAN DYKES P&R/R&B '66
Singles: 7-inch
HUE (6501 "No Man Is an Island") 15-25 65
MALA (520 "No Man Is an Island") 5-8 65
MALA (530 "What Will I Do") 5-10 66
MALA (539 "Never Let Me Go") 5-10 66
MALA (549 "You're Shakin' Me Up") 5-10 66
MALA (566 "A Sunday Kind of Love") 5-10 66
MALA (584 "Tears of Joy") 20-30 67
LPs: 10/12-inch
BELL (6004 "Tellin' It Like It Is") 15-25 67
Members: Ron Tandy; Wenzon Mosley; Jimmy May.

VAN EATON, Jimmy, & Untouchables
Singles: 7-inch
NITA (1004 "Bo Diddley") 10-20 62
RITA (1004 "Beat-Nik") 10-20 60

VAN EATON, Lon & Derrek
Singles: 7-inch
A&M 3-5 75-77
APPLE (1845 "Sweet Music") 5-10 72
Picture Sleeves
A&M 3-5 76
APPLE (1845 "Sweet Music") 8-12 72
LPs: 10/12-inch
A&M 8-10 75
APPLE (3390 "Brother") 10-15 72
Also see JACOBS CREEK

VANELL, Charles
Singles: 7-inch
ORIOLE (1319 "Knowing the Part") 35-45 59

VANELLI, Johnny
Singles: 7-inch
LITTLE APPLES 5-10 65
NAME 10-15 61

VANESS, Theo
LPs: 10/12-inch
PRELUDE 5-10 79

VANGELIS P&R/LP '81
Singles: 7-inch
POLYDOR 3-4 81
RCA 3-5 78
Picture Sleeves
POLYDOR 3-5 81
LPs: 10/12-inch
POLYDOR 5-10 81-86
RCA 5-10 78-82
Also see APHRODITES CHILD
Also see JON & VANGELIS

VAN GIVENS
Singles: 7-inch
PAULA 4-8 67

VANGUARDS
Singles: 78 rpm
DERBY (854 "So Live") 50-100 54
Singles: 7-inch
DERBY (854 "So Live") 200-250 54
DOT (15791 "Baby Doll") 10-20 58

VANGUARDS
(With B.B. Butler & Orchestra)
Singles: 7-inch
COLLECTABLES 3-4 80s
IVY (103 "Moonlight") 100-150 58
(White label. Promotional issue only.)
IVY (103 "Moonlight") 75-125 58
(Also credits Billy Butler's Orchestra.)
IVY (103 "Moonlight") 25-35 58
(No mention of Butler's Orchestra.)

VANGUARDS
Singles: 7-inch
REGENCY (743 "I Love You Darling") 50-100 50s
(Canadian.)
RUTH (439 "Last Night") 100-200

VANGUARDS
Singles: 7-inch
ENSIGN 5-10 62
W.B. 4-8 66

VANGUARDS R&B '69
Singles: 7-inch
INDIE (91 "Woman Come Home") 6-10
LAMP (81 "Girl Go Away") 6-10 70
LAMP (652 "It's To [sic] Late for Love") 6-10 70
(Shown in some catalogs as Lamp 80. We're not yet aware if copies exist with this number.)
WHIZ (612 "Somebody Please") 8-12 69

VANGUARDS IV
Singles: 7-inch
CHARIOT, INC ("Blue Skies") 5-8 60s
(No selection number used.)

VAN HALEN P&R/LP '78
Singles: 12-inch
W.B. (Commercial issues.) 4-6 83-84
W.B. (Promotionall issues.) 6-12 83-84
Singles: 7-inch
PALM TREE 4-8
W.B. 3-5 78-90
Promotional Singles
W.B. 5-10 78-90
Picture Sleeves
W.B. (Except 8556 & 8823) 3-8 79-88
W.B. (8556 "Running with the Devil") 20-30 78
W.B. (8823 "Dance the Night Away") 8-12 79
LPs: 10/12-inch
W.B. 5-10 78-90
W.B./LOONEY TUNES (705 "Van Halen") 10-20 78
(Colored vinyl. Promotional issue only.)
Members: David Lee Roth; Edward Van Halen; Alex Van Halen; Michael Anthony; Sammy Hagar.
Also see HAGAR, Sammy
Also see MAY, Brian
Also see ROTH, David Lee
Also see VAN HALEN, Edward

VAN HALEN, Edward
LPs: 10/12-inch
MCA 5-8 86
Also see JACKSON, Michael
Also see VAN HALEN

VAN HATTUM, Peter
Singles: 7-inch
PANORAMA 5-10 60

VAN HOLLEBEKE, Jim
(With the Barra-Tone Orchestra)
Singles: 7-inch
CAN-O-VAN 3-5 80

VAN HORN, John
Singles: 7-inch
MERCURY 3-5 72
MOONGLOW 4-8 63
RUMBLE (1958 "Eyes Afire") 3-5 84
LPs: 10/12-inch
MERCURY 8-10 72

VAN HOY, Rafe
LPs: 10/12-inch
MCA 5-10 80

VANILLA FUDGE P&R/LP '67
Singles: 7-inch
ATCO 5-10 67-70
LPs: 10/12-inch
ATCO (224 "Vanilla Fudge") 15-25 68
ATCO (237 "The Beat Goes On") 15-25 68
ATCO (244 "Renaissance") 15-25 68
ATCO (278 "Near the Beginning") 15-25 69
ATCO (303 "Rock 'N' Roll") 15-25 69
ATCO (90006 "Best of Vanilla Fudge") 8-10 82
Members: Mark Stein; Tim Bogert; Vinnie Martell; Carmine Appice.
Also see BECK, BOGERT & APPICE
Also see CREAM / Vanilla Fudge
Also see PIGEONS

VANILLA ICE LP '90
LPs: 10/12-inch
SKB 5-8 90

VANILLA TRAINWRECK
Singles: 7-inch
OTIS (001 "Galvanized") 3-4 90
(White vinyl.)
Picture Sleeves
OTIS (001 "Galvanized") 3-4 90

VANILLI, Milli: see MILLI VANILLI

VANITY P&R/R&B/D&D/LP '84
(Denise Matthews)
Singles: 12-inch
MOTOWN 4-6 84-86
Singles: 7-inch
MOTOWN 3-4 84-86
Picture Sleeves
MOTOWN 3-4 84-86
LPs: 10/12-inch
MOTOWN 5-8 84-86
Members: Denise Matthews; Brenda Bennett; Susan Moonsie.
Also see VANITY 6

VANITY / Smokey Robinson
LPs: 10/12-inch
MOTOWN (179 "Superstar Interviews") 10-15 84
(Promotional issue only.)
Also see ROBINSON, Smokey
Also see VANITY

VANITY FARE P&R '69
Singles: 7-inch
BRENT 4-8 67
DJM 3-5 75
PAGE ONE 3-6 68-70
SOMA 8-12 68
20TH FOX 3-5 73
LPs: 10/12-inch
PAGE ONE 10-15 70

VANITY 6 R&B/LP '82
Singles: 12-inch
W.B. 4-6 82-83
Singles: 7-inch
W.B. 3-4 82-83
LPs: 10/12-inch
W.B. 5-8 82
Member: Denise Matthews.
Also see APOLLONIA 6
Also see TIME
Also see VANITY

VAN LOAN, Jamie
Singles: 7-inch
BLUE BELL 5-10 60

VAN LOAN, Joe
(Joe Van Loan Quartet; Joe VanLoan)
Singles: 78 rpm
CARVER (1402 "Trust in Me") 50-75 54
Singles: 7-inch
CARVER (1402 "Trust in Me") 100-150 54
FORD 10-15 63
PARKWAY 10-15 61
SUDAJA 5-10 60s
V-TONE (200 "Forever") 100-150 59
Also see BACHELORS
Also see BELLS
Also see BROWN, Wini
Also see COBB, Arnett
Also see DIXIEAIRES
Also see DU DROPPERS
Also see INK SPOTS
Also see KINGS
Also see POWELL, Chris, & Five Blue Flames
Also see RAVENS
Also see VALIANTS

VANN, Dickie
Singles: 7-inch
CHEROKEE (501 "The Girl Next Door") 10-20

VANN, Donnie
Singles: 7-inch
GAMBLE 3-5 70

VANN, Ila: see VAN, Ila

VANN, Joey
(Joe Canzano)
Singles: 7-inch
CHUBBY 3-5 82
COED 8-10 65
Also see DUPREES

VANN, Nikki
Singles: 7-inch
FAME (703 "Jade") 10-20 60s

VANN, Paul
Singles: 7-inch
SOUND STAGE 7 3-6 69-70

VANN, Teddy P&R '61
Singles: 7-inch
CAPITOL 3-6 67
COLUMBIA 4-8 61
END 5-10 59
JUBILEE 4-8 62
ROULETTE 4-8 60
TRIPLE-X 5-10 60
Also see WHEELS

VANN, Tommy
(With the Echoes; with Professionals)
Singles: 7-inch
ACADEMY 5-10 66
CAPITOL 4-8 68
HOLLYWOOD (101 "I'm Hopin' You'll Be Mine") 15-25 60s
Members: Tommy Vann; George Dochterman.

VANN WALLS & ROCKETS: see WALLS, Van

VANNELLI, Gino P&R/LP '74
Singles: 12-inch
HME 4-6 85
Singles: 7-inch
A&M 3-5 74-79
ARISTA 3-5 81-82
CBS ASSOCIATES 3-4 85-87
HME 3-4 85
Picture Sleeves
A&M 3-5 76-79
ARISTA 3-5 81-82
CBS ASSOCIATES 3-4 85-87
HME 3-4 85
LPs: 10/12-inch
A&M (3600 series) 5-10 74
A&M (3700 series) 5-8 81
A&M (4000 series) 8-10 74-78
ARISTA 5-10 81-82
CBS ASSOCIATES 5-8 87
HME 5-10 85
MFSL (041 "Powerful People") 25-35 80
NAUTILUS 15-20 81
(Half-speed mastered.)

VAN PEEBLES, Melvin
LPs: 10/12-inch
A&M 10-15 68-71
ATLANTIC 8-10 73
STAX 10-15 71

VAN RONK, Dave
(With the Hudson Dusters)
Singles: 7-inch
VERVE/FORECAST 4-8 67
LPs: 10/12-inch
MERCURY (20908 "Just Dave Van Ronk") 10-20 64
(Monaural.)
MERCURY (60908 "Just Dave Van Ronk") 15-25 64
(Stereo.)
VERVE/FORECAST 10-15 67

VAN SHELTON, Ricky: see SHELTON, Ricky Van

VAN-TELS
Singles: 7-inch
CITE (5009 "Baby, What You Want") 15-25 64
RAYNARD (1085 "Ain't Too Proud to Beg") 10-20 68
Members: Jerry Trado; Joey Piccolo; Gary Jay; Chris King; Skip Kamrath; Bruce Cole; Brad Craig; Steve Fromm; Bob Hershley; Gene Recob; Dennis Pleskechek; Carl Biancuzzo; Dave Zylka.

VAN TIEGHEM, David D&D '84
Singles: 12-inch
W.B. 4-6 84
Singles: 7-inch
W.B. 3-4 84
LPs: 10/12-inch
W.B. 5-8 84

VAN TONGEREN, John, & Jerry Hey
Singles: 12-inch
QWEST 4-6 82

VAN VALKENBURGH, Deborah
Singles: 7-inch
CASABLANCA 3-5 81

VAN VOOREN, Monique
EPs: 7-inch
RCA (1553 "Mink in Hi-Fi") 10-15 57
LPs: 10/12-inch
RCA (1553 "Mink in Hi-Fi") 20-30 57

VAN WALLS: see WALLS, Van

VANWARMER, Randy C&W/P&R/LP '79
Singles: 7-inch
BEARSVILLE 3-5 79
16TH AVE. 3-4 88
LPs: 10/12-inch
BEARSVILLE 5-10 79-83

VAN WINKLE, Arnold
(With Rainbow Rhythmaires)
Singles: 7-inch
RUBY (540 "An Old Rusty Dime") 50-100 57
Also see VAN BROTHERS

VAN ZANT, Johnny, Band LP '80
(Van-Zant)
Singles: 7-inch
POLYDOR 3-5 80-82
LPs: 10/12-inch
ATLANTIC 5-8 90
GEFFEN 5-8 85
POLYDOR 5-10 80-82
Also see LYNYRD SKYNYRD

VAN ZANDT, Townes
Singles: 7-inch
B.T. PUPPY 4-8 68
POPPY 3-6 69-73
TOMATO 3-5 78
LPs: 10/12-inch
POPPY 8-12 69-73
TOMATO 5-10 77-78

VAPORS
Singles: 7-inch
BELL (607 "Jump Out") 10-15 64

VAPORS P&R/LP '80
Singles: 7-inch
LIBERTY 3-5 81
U.A. 3-5 80
LPs: 10/12-inch
LIBERTY 5-10 81
U.A. 5-10 80

VAPOUR TRAILS
LPs: 10/12-inch
W.B. 5-10 79

VAQUEROS
Singles: 7-inch
AUDITION (6102 "Desert Wind") 10-20 64

VAQUEROS
Singles: 7-inch
BANGAR (647 "Birds & Bees") 25-50 64
STUDIO CITY (1049 "Growing Pains") 25-50 66
STUDIO CITY (1059 "Mustang Sally") 75-100 66

VARATONES
Singles: 7-inch
KAY (101 "Repeto") 8-12

VARDAS, Peter
Singles: 7-inch
PHASE 5-10 59

VARE, Ronnie, & Inspirations
(Ronnie Vare & Inspirators with Silver String Trio)
Singles: 7-inch
DELL (5202 "Let's Rock Little Girl") 75-125 59
(Has label's Hartford address under name.)
DELL (5202 "Let's Rock Little Girl") 50-100 59
(No address shown on label.)
GLO (5201 "Let Me Be Your Love") 100-200 60

VAREEATIONS
Singles: 7-inch
DIONN 10-15 68

VARETTA
Singles: 7-inch
BRENT 4-8 63

VARIANT CAUSE
LPs: 10/12-inch
KDT 5-8 87

VARIATIONS
Singles: 7-inch
AMOUR 4-8 70s
BON-JOY 8-12
JUSTICE 50-75 60s
(Selection number not known.)
MTA (121 "Will You Be Mine") 100-200 67
OKEH 5-10 69
POW! 4-8
VEE 4-8
LPs: 10/12-inch
JUSTICE (212 "Dig 'Em Up") 300-400 60s

VARIETEERS
Singles: 78 rpm
HICKORY 50-75 54-55
MGM (10888 "I'll Try to Forget I Loved You") 75-100 51
Singles: 7-inch
HICKORY (1004 "I've Got a Woman's Love") 200-250 54
HICKORY (1014 "I Pay with Every Breath") 200-300 54
HICKORY (1025 "Call My Gal, Miss Jones") 150-200 55
Member: Jimmy Sweeney.
Also see SWEENEY, Jimmy

VARIETY BOYS
Singles: 78 rpm
DECCA 15-25 41

VARIOS
Singles: 7-inch
AMY 4-8 62

VARISCO, Paul, & Milestones
Singles: 7-inch
DATE 3-6 69

VARJU BROTHERS
Singles: 7-inch
MERCURY 4-8 62

VARNELLS
Singles: 7-inch
ARNOLD (1003 "Who Created Love") 25-50 61
ARNOLD (1006 "All Because") 25-50 61
Also see VERNALLS

VARNER, Don
Singles: 7-inch
QUINCY (8002 "Tear-Stained Face") 150-250 69
VEEP (1296 "Tear-Stained Face") 100-200 69

VARSITY MEN
Singles: 7-inch
STAFF (86536 "Please Don't Cry") 100-150 62
(Identification number shown since no selection number is used.)

VARTAN, Sylvie
Singles: 12-inch
RCA (11594 "I Don't Want the Night to End") 10-15 79
Singles: 7-inch
RCA (8520 "I Made My Choice") 8-12 65
RCA (11578 "I Don't Want the Night to End") 3-5 79

LPs: 10/12-inch
RCA (3015 "I Don't Want the Night to End")....10-15 79

VASEL, Marianne, & Erich Storz P&R '58
Singles: 7-inch
MERCURY....4-8 58
LPs: 10/12-inch
DANA....10-20 59

VASHONETTES
Singles: 7-inch
CHECKER (1195 "Love")....10-20 68

VASQUEZ, Ray
Singles: 7-inch
TROPICANA....5-8 61

VASS, Cheek-O: see CHEEK-O-VASS

VASSER, Dave
(With the Muleskinners)
Singles: 7-inch
SARA (63102 "New Orleans")....15-25 63
Also see MULESKINNERS

VASSY, Kin C&W '79
Singles: 7-inch
EPIC....4-8 67
IA....3-5 79-80
LIBERTY....3-4 81-83
UNI....3-6 69
Also see EDDY, Duane
Also see ROGERS, Kenny, & First Edition

VAUGHAN, Frankie P&R '58
Singles: 7-inch
COLUMBIA....4-8 59-60
EPIC....4-8 58
PHILIPS....3-6 62-66
LPs: 10/12-inch
COLUMBIA....10-20 60
PHILIPS....10-15 62

VAUGHAN, Sarah P&R '47
Singles: 78 rpm
COLUMBIA....3-6 49-53
CONTINENTAL....5-10 45
MGM (Except 71)....3-6 50-51
MGM (71 "Sarah Vaughan Sings")....40-60 51
(Boxed, four-disc set.)
MERCURY....3-6 53-57
MUSICRAFT....4-8 47-48
Singles: 7-inch
ATLANTIC....3-5 81
COLUMBIA (38000 & 39000 series)....5-10 51-53
MGM (10000 & 30000 series)....5-10 50-51
MAINSTREAM....3-5 71-74
MERCURY (70000 series)....4-8 53-66
ROULETTE....4-6 60-64
W.B.....3-5 81
Picture Sleeves
MERCURY....4-8 65
EPs: 7-inch
ATLANTIC (527 "Sarah Vaughan Sings")....30-40 55
COLUMBIA....10-20 50-56
EMARCY....10-20 54-56
MGM....10-20 52-55
MERCURY....8-15 53-59
REMINGTON....5-10
ROYALE....5-10 50s
LPs: 10/12-inch
ALLEGRO....5-10
ATLANTIC....5-8 81
COLUMBIA (660 "After Hours")....35-45 55
COLUMBIA (745 "Sarah in Hi-Fi")....35-45 55
COLUMBIA (914 "Linger Awhile")....25-35 57
COLUMBIA (6133 "Sarah Vaughan")....50-100 50
(10-inch LP.)
COLUMBIA (37000 series)....5-8 82
CONCORD....15-25 56
CORONET....8-10 60s
EMARCY (400 series)....8-12 77
EMARCY (1000 series)....5-10 81
EMARCY (26005 "Images")....50-75 54
(10-inch LP.)
EMARCY (36000 series)....30-40 54-57
EVEREST....5-10 70-76
FORUM....8-12
GALAXY....8-12
GUEST STAR....8-12
HARMONY....5-15 59-69
MGM (165 "Tenderly")....50-100 51
(10-inch LPs.)
MGM (544 "Sarah Vaughan Sings")....50-100 54
(10-inch LP.)
MGM (3274 "My Kinda Love")....50-75 55
MAINSTREAM....6-12 71-75
MERCURY (100 "Great Songs")....25-35 57
MERCURY (101 "Gershwin Songs")....25-35 57
MERCURY (1000 series)....5-8 82
MERCURY (20000 series)....15-30 58-64
MERCURY (21000 series)....10-20 65-67
(Monaural.)
MERCURY (25188 "Divine Sarah")....60-80 53
(10-inch LP)
MERCURY (60000 series)....15-25 59-64
MERCURY (61000 series)....10-25 65-67
(Stereo.)
METRO....8-15 65
MUSICRAFT....5-8 83-84
PABLO....5-10 78-82
PALACE....5-10
REMINGTON (1024 "Hot Jazz")....50-100 53
(10-inch LP.)
RIVERSIDE (2511 "Sarah Vaughan Sings")....40-60 55
RONDO....20-40 59
RONDOLETTE....20-40 59
ROULETTE (100 series)....8-15 71
ROULETTE (52000 series, except 52082)....10-25 60-67
(Black vinyl.)
ROULETTE (52082 "You're Mine")....15-25 62
(Black vinyl.)
ROULETTE (52082 "You're Mine")....35-55 62
(Colored vinyl.)
SCEPTER....5-10 74
SPIN-O-RAMA....8-12 60s
SUTTON....5-10 70s
TRIP....5-10 74-76
WING....5-15 63-68
Also see BASIE, Count, & Sarah Vaughan
Also see DIAMONDS / Georgia Gibbs / Sarah Vaughan / Florian Zabach
Also see ECKSTINE, Billy, & Sarah Vaughan
Also see LEGRAND, Michel
Also see WASHINGTON, Dinah, & Sarah Vaughan

VAUGHAN, Sarah, & Quincy Jones
LPs: 10/12-inch
MERCURY....15-25 59
Also see JONES, Quincy
Also see VAUGHAN, Sarah

VAUGHAN, Stevie Ray LP '83
(With Double Trouble)
Singles: 7-inch
COLUMBIA....3-4 87
EPIC....3-4 85
LPs: 10/12-inch
COLUMBIA....5-8 87
EPIC (Except 8E8-39609)....5-10 84-89
EPIC (8E8-39609 "Couldn't Stand the Weather")....70-80 84
(Picture disc.)
Members: Stevie Ray Vaughan; Tommy Shannon; Chris Layton; Reese Wynans.
Also see COBRAS Featuring Stevie Ray Vaughan

VAUGHAN, Stevie Ray, & Dick Dale
Singles: 7-inch
COLUMBIA (07340 "Pipeline")....3-4 87
Picture Sleeves
COLUMBIA (07340 "Pipeline")....3-5 87
Also see DALE, Dick

VAUGHAN BROTHERS P&R/LP '90
Singles: 7-inch
CBS ASSOCIATED....3-4 90
EPIC....3-4 89
LPs: 10/12-inch
EPIC....5-8 89
Members: Stevie Ray Vaughan; Jimmie Vaughan.
Also see FABULOUS THUNDERBIRDS
Also see VAUGHAN, Stevie Ray

VAUGHN, Billy, Orchestra P&R '54
(With the Billy Vaughn Singers)
Singles: 78 rpm
DOT....3-5 54-57
Singles: 7-inch
ABC....3-4 74
DOT....3-8 54-70
PARAMOUNT....3-4 70-72
Picture Sleeves
DOT....3-8 58-67
EPs: 7-inch
DOT....4-8 55-59
LPs: 10/12-inch
ABC....5-8 74
DOT....5-15 55-70
HAMILTON....5-10 65-66
MCA....5-8 83
MISTLETOE....4-8 76
MUSICOR....4-8 77
PARAMOUNT....5-8 70-74
PICKWICK....5-8 68
RANWOOD....4-8 83
Also see BRENNAN, Walter
Also see HILLTOPPERS
Also see NORDINE, Ken
Also see STEVENS, Dodie
Also see STORM, Gale

VAUGHN, Bobby
Singles: 7-inch
WHIZ (503 "Good Good Lovin' ")....25-35 57

VAUGHN, Dale
Singles: 7-inch
VON (480 "High Steppin' ")....150-250

VAUGHN, Dell
Singles: 7-inch
FORTUNE (205 "Rock the Universe")....75-100 60

VAUGHN, Denny P&R '56
Singles: 78 rpm
KAPP....3-6 56
Singles: 7-inch
KAPP....5-10 56

VAUGHN, Jimmy
Singles: 7-inch
CAB....4-8 64

VAUGHN, Morris
Singles: 7-inch
FONTANA....3-6 69

VAUGHN, Sammy C&W '78
Singles: 7-inch
ALPINE....3-5 78
OAK....3-5 79

VAUGHN, Sammy, & Star Marks
Singles: 7-inch
STARDOM (0012 "Always Be Mine")....100-200

VAUGHN, Sharon C&W '74
Singles: 7-inch
ABC/DOT....3-5 75
CINNAMON....3-5 74
Also see FELTS, Narvel, & Sharon Vaughn

VAUGHN, Shirley
Singles: 7-inch
DOUBLE RR....10-15
FAIRMOUNT....8-12

VAUGHN, Walter
Singles: 7-inch
DUCHESS....10-15 60
LIBERTY....5-10 61

VAUGHN, Yvonne
Singles: 7-inch
DOT (16751 "Lonely Little Girl")....100-150 65

VAUGHT, Bob
(With the Renegades; with Renegaids; with Wheels)
Singles: 7-inch
BAMBOO (520 "Church Key Twist")....10-15 62
FELSTED (8682 "Doin' the Surf")....10-20 63
GNP....10-15 63
IMPACT (24 "Church Key Twist")....15-20 63
LPs: 10/12-inch
GNP (GNP-83 "Surf Crazy")....20-25 63
(Monaural.)
GNP (GNPS-83 "Surf Crazy")....25-30 63
(Stereo.)
Members: Bob Vaught; Dave Vaught; Jerry Feliciello; J. Gordon Smith; Neal Nissenson.
Also see RENEGADES

VAUGHT, Freddy
Singles: 7-inch
FRATERNITY....4-8 63

VEACH, Gail C&W '87
Singles: 7-inch
CHOICE....3-4 88
PRAIRIE DUST....3-4 87

VECTORS
Singles: 7-inch
DELIC....5-10

VEE, Bobby P&R '59
(With the Shadows; with Eligibles; with Strangers; with Johnny Mann Singers; Robert Thomas Velline)
Singles: 7-inch
COGNITO....3-5 81
LIBERTY (3331 "How Many Tears")....20-25 61
(Stereo Compact 33 Single.)
LIBERTY (55208 "Suzie Baby")....10-20 59
LIBERTY (55234 thru 55325)....5-8 60-61
LIBERTY (55331 thru 56208)....3-6 61-70
SHADYBROOK....3-5 75-77
SOMA (1110 "Susie Baby")....40-60 59
U.A.....3-5 71-78
Picture Sleeves
LIBERTY....5-10 60-68
EPs: 7-inch
LIBERTY....25-35 60-62
U.A.....10-12 72
LPs: 10/12-inch
LIBERTY (3165 thru 3534)....20-30 60-67
(Monaural.)
LIBERTY (7165 thru 7534)....20-40 60-67
(Stereo.)
LIBERTY (7554 thru 7612)....10-20 68-69
LIBERTY (1000 series)....5-8 80
LIBERTY (10000 series)....5-8 84
SUNSET....10-15 66-67
U.A. (25-G2 "Legendary Masters")....250-350 73
(Includes bound-in booklet. Withdrawn before release, with only two or three copies surviving.)
U.A. (332 "Very Best")....8-10 73
U.A. (1008 "Golden Greats")....5-8 80
Members (Shadows): Bill Velline; Bob Korum; Jim Stillman; Dick Dunkirk; Ken Harvey. Session: Johnny Mann Singers.
Also see ASSOCIATION / Bobby Vee / Mike Love / Mary MacGregor
Also see DE SHANNON, Jackie / Bobby Vee / Eddie Hodges
Also see DUNKIRK, Dick
Also see MANN, Johnny, Singers
Also see STRANGERS
Also see VELINE, Bill, & Shadows

VEE, Bobby / Johnny Burnette / Ventures / Fleetwoods
LPs: 10/12-inch
LIBERTY (5503 "Teensville")....20-30 61
Also see BURNETTE, Johnny
Also see FLEETWOODS

VEE, Bobby, & Crickets LP '62
Singles: 7-inch
LIBERTY....4-8 62
Picture Sleeves
LIBERTY....10-15 60-63
LPs: 10/12-inch
LIBERTY....20-25 62
Also see CRICKETS

VEE, Bobby / Diamonds / Drifters
Singles: 7-inch
MINDSCAPE ("Mindscape and Rock'n'roll Are Here to Stay")....5-10 84
(Soundsheet. Promotional issue only.)
Also see DIAMONDS
Also see DRIFTERS

VEE, Bobby, & Ventures LP '63
LPs: 10/12-inch
LIBERTY....20-25 63
Also see VEE, Bobby
Also see VENTURES

VEE, Cee
Singles: 7-inch
CARROLTON (800 "Lonely Street")....25-35

VEE, Joey, & Raiders
Singles: 7-inch
PROMOTIONAL (102 "Acts of Love")....50-100 62

VEE JAYS
Singles: 7-inch
Richie (456 "Don't Let Me Go")....20-30

VEERS, Russ
Singles: 7-inch
TREND (10 "Warm As Toast")....300-400 58

VEGA, Carol
Singles: 7-inch
CONSTELLATION....5-8 64

VEGA, Suzanne LP '85
Singles: 7-inch
A&M....3-4 85-90
Picture Sleeves
A&M....3-4 87
LPs: 10/12-inch
A&M....5-8 85-90
Also see DNA Featuring Suzanne Vega
Also see GLASS, Philip

VEGA, Tata R&B '76
Singles: 12-inch
TAMLA....4-8 79
Singles: 7-inch
TAMLA....3-5 76-80
LPs: 10/12-inch
TAMLA....5-10 76-80
Also see EARTHQUIRE
Also see RAWLS, Lou

VEGA BROTHERS C&W '86
Singles: 7-inch
MCA....3-4 86
Members: Robert Vega; Ray Vega.

VEGAS
Singles: 7-inch
CLE-AN-THAIR....10-20

VEGAS, Lolly
Singles: 7-inch
AUDIO INTERNATIONAL (202 "It's Love")....25-35 61
Also see VEGAS, Pat & Lolly

VEGAS, Pat
Singles: 7-inch
UNITY....10-20
Also see AVANTIES
Also see PAT & WILDCATS
Also see REDBONE
Also see SHARKS
Also see VEGAS, Pat & Lolly

VEGAS, Pat, & Lolly
Singles: 7-inch
APOGEE....5-10 64
MERCURY....4-8 66
REPRISE....4-8 63
LPs: 10/12-inch
MERCURY....25-35 66
Members: Pat Vasquez; Lolly Vasquez
Also see AVANTIES
Also see INDIVIDUALS
Also see REDBONE
Also see SHARKS
Also see VEGAS, Lolly
Also see VEGAS, Pat

VEHICLE
LPs: 10/12-inch
ROADSHOW....5-10 77

V-EIGHTS
(V-8's)
Singles: 7-inch
ABC-PAR (10201 "My Heart....10-15 61
AURA (101 "Chasin' the Blues")....15-25 50s
MOST (713 "Please Come Back")....100-125 59
VIBRO (4005 "My Heart")....100-200 60
VIBRO (4006 "Guess What")....150-250 61

VEJTABLES P&R '65
Singles: 7-inch
AUTUMN....5-10 65-66
UPTOWN....4-8 67

VEL-AIRES
(Bel-Aires)
Singles: 78 rpm
FLIP....10-15 56
Singles: 7-inch
FLIP (303 "This Paradise")....15-25 56
FLIP (306 "Man from Utopia")....15-25 56
Also see BEL-AIRES

VEL AIRES
Singles: 7-inch
DINO (100 "Forever Always")....200-300 61

VELAIRES P&R '61
Singles: 7-inch
BRENT....5-10 60s
HI-MAR....4-8 65
JAMIE (1198 "Roll Over Beethoven"/"Brazil")....10-20 61
(First issued as by the Flairs.)
JAMIE (1198 "Roll Over Beethoven"/"Frankie & Johnny")....10-20 61
JAMIE (1203 "Dream")....10-15 61
JAMIE (1211 "Ubangi Stomp")....10-15 61
JAMIE (1223 "Memory Tree")....10-15 62
MERCURY....5-10 69
PALMS (730 "Summertime Blues")....30-60 61
RAMCO....5-10 60s
Also see FLAIRS
Also see SCREAMERS
Also see SUNDOWN

VELAIRS
Singles: 7-inch
MGM....8-12 58

VELAR, Dolores
Singles: 7-inch
CORAL....4-8 62

VELASCO, Vi
Singles: 7-inch
MTA....4-6 67
VEE JAY....4-8 65
LPs: 10/12-inch
VEE JAY....10-20 65

VELEBNY, Karel
LPs: 10/12-inch
ESP....10-12

VELEZ, Martha LP '76
Singles: 7-inch
MCA....3-4 80
POLYDOR....3-5 73
SIRE....3-5 69-76
LPs: 10/12-inch
SIRE (6040 "American Heartbeat")....8-10 76
SIRE (7000 series)....8-10 74-76
SIRE (97000 series)....10-12 69

VELL, Gene
Singles: 7-inch
WHIZ....8-12

VELLINE, Bill, & Shadows
Singles: 7-inch
VEE (1001 "Leave Me Alone")....50-75 60
VEE (1110 "Suzie Baby")....80-120 60
Also see VEE, Bobby

VELLINE, Robert Thomas: see VEE, Bobby

VELLO, Lee
Singles: 7-inch
UNIVERSAL ARTISTS....10-15

VELLS
(Vandellas)
Singles: 7-inch
MEL-O-DY (103 "There He Is")....25-50 62
Members: Glorie Williamson; Martha Reeves; Annette Beard; Rosalind Ashford.
Also see DEL-PHIS
Also see MARTHA & VANDELLAS

VEL-MARS
Singles: 7-inch
CONTINENTAL ARTS....4-8 64

VELONS
Singles: 7-inch
BJM....10-15
BLAST (216 "Shelly")....50-100 64
Members: Patsy Bello; Tom Scott; Ray Vitolo; Ron Auriemma; Paul Auriemma.

VELONS
Singles: 7-inch
MAXI (003 "Steamboat")....10-15
MAXI (004 "Hearts Desire")....10-15
STAR FIRE....5-8
LPs: 10/12-inch
MAXI....10-15

VELORE & DOUBLE-O
Singles: 7-inch
VIRGIN....3-4 87
Picture Sleeves
VIRGIN....3-4 87

VELOURS P&R '57
(With Sammy Lowe Orchestra)
Singles: 78 rpm
ONYX....50-100 56-57
Singles: 7-inch
CUB (9001 "Can I Walk You Home")....20-30 58
CUB (9014 "I'll Never Smile Again")....20-30 58
CUB (9029 "Blue Velvet")....15-25 59
END (1090 "Lover Come Back")....15-25 61
GOLDISC (3012 "Sweet Sixteen")....25-35 60
GONE (5092 "Can I Come Over Tonight")....10-15 60
ONYX (501 "My Love Come Back")....100-200 56
ONYX (508 "Romeo")....500-700 57
ONYX (512 "Can I Come Over Tonight")....100-200 57
ONYX (515 "This Could Be the Night")....75-125 57
ONYX (520 "Can I Walk You Home")....75-125 58
(Black and orange label.)
ONYX (520 "Can I Walk You Home")....50-100 58
(Green label.)
ORBIT (9001 "Can I Walk You Home")....50-75 58
(Green label.)

ORBIT (9001 "Can I Walk You Home")....30-50 58
(Red label.)
RELIC (504 "Can I Come Over Tonight")....10-15 64
RELIC (516 "This Cjould Be the Night")....10-15 64
ROULETTE....3-5 70s
STUDIO (9902 "I Promise")....25-50 59
Members: Jerome Ramos; Pete Winston; John Pearson; Don Heywoode; John Cheatdom; Charles Moffett; Keith Williams; Troyce Key.
Also see FANTASTICS
Also see KEY, Troyce
Also see LOWE, Sammy, Orchestra

VELOURS
Singles: 7-inch
MGM (13780 "Don't Pity Me")....15-25 67
RONA (010 "Woman for Me")....10-20 66

VELS
(With the Tim Whitsett Imperials)
Singles: 7-inch
EPs: 7-inch
TREBCO (702 "Please Be Mine")....75-125 61

VELS
Singles: 7-inch
AMY (881 "Do the Walk")....10-15 63

VELS D&D '84
Singles: 12-inch
MERCURY....4-6 84-85
Singles: 7-inch
MERCURY....3-4 84-85
LPs: 10/12-inch
MERCURY....5-8 84

VEL-TONES
Singles: 7-inch
FEE BEE (1 "Broken Heart")....10-20
GOLDWAX....10-15
VEL (9178 "Broken Heart")....1000-2000 58
(Identification number shown since no selection number is used.)

VEL-TONES
(With the Blue Shields)
Singles: 7-inch
COY (101 "Playboy")....200-300 58
KAPP (268 "Playboy")....75-125 59

VELTONES
Singles: 7-inch
MERCURY (71526 "Fool in Love")....25-50 59
SATELLITE (100 "Fool in Love")....150-250 59

VELTONES
(With Al Brown & His Band; Vel-Tones)
Singles: 7-inch
LOST NITE (103 "Now")....75-125 61
(First issue.)
ZARA (901 "Now")....50-75 61
Also see BROWNE, Al

VELTONES
Singles: 7-inch
WEDGE (1013 "I Want to Know")....100-200 64

VELUZAT, Renaud
Singles: 7-inch
DIXIE (880 "Race Track Boogie")...40-60
SUNDOWN (1001 "Surf Zone")....10-20 60s

VELVATONES
Singles: 78 rpm
METEOR....100-200 57
Singles: 7-inch
METEOR (5042 "Real Gone Baby")....100-200 57

VELVATONES
(With Richmond's Lil Walters Band)
Singles: 7-inch
NU KAT (110 "Impossible")....25-35 59

VELVATONES / Continentals
Singles: 7-inch
CANDLELITE (412 "Impossible")....8-12 63
Also see VELVATONES
Also see CONTINENTAL 5

VELVATONES FIVE
Singles: 7-inch
KODIAK (1601 "Freeloader")....10-20 63

VELVEDERES
Singles: 7-inch
COBRA (1601 "Daiquiri")....8-12 63

VELVELETTES P&R/R&B '64
Singles: 7-inch
I.P.G. (1002 "There He Goes")....50-75 63
SOUL (35025 "These Things Will Keep Me Loving You")....10-20 66
V.I.P. (25007 "Needle in a Haystack")....10-25 64
V.I.P. (25013 "He Was Really Saying Something")....10-25 65
V.I.P. (25017 "Lonely Lonely Girl Am I")....10-25 65
V.I.P. (25021 "Bird in the Hand")....300-500 66
V.I.P. (25030 "Bird in the Hand")....15-25 66
V.I.P. (25034 "These Things Will Keep Me Loving You")....15-25 66
Members: Carolyn Gill, Sandra Tilley; Betty Kelly; Bertha McNeal; Mildred Gill; Norma Barbee.
Also see BARBEES
Also see MARTHA & VANDELLAS

VELVET, Chuck
Singles: 7-inch
USA (1224 "Red Lipstick")....8-12 60

VELVET, Jimmy P&R '63
(Jimmy Velvet Five; James Velvet; Jimmy Tennant)
Singles: 7-inch
ABC-PAR....10-20 63-64
BELL....4-8 67
CAMEO (464 "Take Me Tonight")....15-25 67
CORREC-TONE (502 "When I Needed You")....50-100 62
CUB....5-10 61-62
DIVISION....10-20 61
MUSIC CITY....4-6 70
PHILIPS....10-20 65
ROYAL AMERICAN....4-6 68-69
SUNDI....3-6 71
TOLLIE....5-10 64
U.A.....10-20 68
VELVET (201 "You're Mine")....50-75 61
VELVET TONE....10-20 64-68
EPs: 7-inch
VELVET TONE (201 "Golden Hits")....15-25 60s
LPs: 10/12-inch
MUSIC CITY (502 "Jimmy Velvet with Kathy Scott")....10-15 73
U.A. (6653 "A Touch of Velvet")....15-25 68
VELVET TONE (501 "A Touch of Velvet")....20-30 68
WITCH....5-10 62
(Though the artist shown on Bi, Blue, and Teardrop releases is Jimmy Velvet, the singer is actually Jimmy Velvit. Those issues are in his section.)
Also see TENNANT, Jimmy
Also see VELVET VIEW
Also see VELVIT, Jimmy

VELVET ANGELS
Singles: 7-inch
CO-OP....8-10 65
MEDIEVAL....5-8 60s
LPs: 10/12-inch
RELIC....10-15

VELVET CREST
Singles: 7-inch
BOLD (8732 "Na Na Song")....15-20
HARBOUR....5-10 69
LIBERTY....4-8 69

VELVET ELVIS
Singles: 12-inch
ENIGMA....4-8 88
LPs: 10/12-inch
ENIGMA....5-10 88

VELVET HAMMER
Singles: 7-inch
EPIC....3-5 70

VELVET ILLUSIONS
(Georgy & Velvet Illusions)
Singles: 7-inch
METRO MEDIA (307 "Acid Head")....25-30 67
METRO MEDIA (309 "Velvet Illusions")....20-25 67
TELL INT'L (700 "Acid Head")....30-40 67

VELVET KEYS
Singles: 78 rpm
KING (5090 "My Baby's Gone")....25-45 57
Singles: 7-inch
KING (5090 "My Baby's Gone")....25-45 57
KING (5109 "The Truth About Youth")....25-45 58

VELVET NIGHT
Singles: 7-inch
METROMEDIA....4-6 69
LPs: 10/12-inch
METROMEDIA....10-15 70

VELVET SATINS
Singles: 7-inch
GENERAL AMERICAN (006 "Nothing Can Compare to You")....20-30 65
GENERAL AMERICAN (716 Cherry")....20-30 64
GENERAL AMERICAN (720 "Angel Adorable")....25-35 64
Also see CAPRI, Bobby

VELVET SEED
Singles: 7-inch
MAI....4-8

VELVET SOUNDS
(With the Cosmopolites; "Featuring Oliver Johnson & Earl Robbins")
Singles: 78 rpm
COSMOPOLITAN....250-500 53
Singles: 7-inch
COSMOPOLITAN (101 "Silver Star")....1500-2500 53
(Colored vinyl.)
COSMOPOLITAN (105 "Pretty Darling")....1000-2000 53
COSMOPOLITAN (530 "Sing a Song of Christmas Cheer")....1000-2000 53
Members: Oliver Johnson; Earl Robbins.

VELVET UNDERGROUND LP '68
Singles: 12-inch
POLYGRAM....5-10 85
Singles: 7-inch
ASPEN ("Loop")....20-40 66
(Single-sided soundsheet. Promotional issue only.)
COTILLION (44107 "Who Loves the Sun")....20-40 71
INDEX ("Interview")....30-50 67
(Single-sided picture disc soundsheet. Promotional issue only.)
MGM (14057 "What Goes On")....25-50 69
VERVE (10560 "White Light/White Heat")....25-50 68
LPs: 10/12-inch
COTILLION (9034 "Loaded")....15-20 70
COTILLION (9500 "Live")....15-20 70
MGM (131 "Velvet Underground")....8-10 71
MGM (4950 " Archetypes")....10-15 69-74
MERCURY (7504 "Velvet Underground")....12-15 72
PRIDE....10-15 73
VERVE (5046 "White Light/"White Heat")....30-40 67
VERVE (800000 series)....5-10 84-85
Members: Lou Reed; John Cale; Sterling Morrison; Maureen Tucker; Doug Yule.
Also see AMERICAN FLYER
Also see CALE, John
Also see REED, Lou

VELVET UNDERGROUND & NICO LP '67
Singles: 7-inch
VERVE (10427 "All Tomorrow's Parties")....25-50 66
(Blue label.)
VERVE (10427 "All Tomorrow's Parties")....50-75 66
(White label. Promotional issue only.)
VERVE (10466 "Sunday Morning")....25-50 66
Picture Sleeves
VERVE (10427 "All Tomorrow's Parties")....100-150 66
(Promotional issue only.)
LPs: 10/12-inch
VERVE (5008 "Velvet Underground & Nico")....100-200 67
(Monaural. With banana sticker on front cover. Back cover pictures an upside-down torso of a man behind the photo of Andy Warhol. Thus far, all copies meeting this description have been mono.)
VERVE (5008 "Velvet Underground & Nico")....50-75 67
(Stereo. With adhesive banana sticker on front cover. If a stereo copy with the upside-down male torso photo behind Andy Warhol exists, its value would approximately double.)
VERVE (5008 "Velvet Underground & Nico")....50-100 67
(With banana sticker on front cover. Back cover has a sticker above the photo of the group on stage, which reads: "The Velvet Underground & Nico.")
VERVE (5008 "Velvet Underground & Nico")....30-60 60s
(With adhesive banana sticker on front cover. Does not picture the upside-down male torso.)
VERVE (5008 "Velvet Underground & Nico")....25-35 67
(No banana sticker on front cover.)
VERVE (800000 series)....5-10 84
Also see NICO
Also see VELVET UNDERGROUND

VELVET VIEW
Singles: 7-inch
VELVET TONE....4-8 69
Member: Jimmy Velvet.
Also see VELVET, Jimmy

VELVETEEN
Singles: 7-inch
ATLANTIC....3-5 82
LPs: 10/12-inch
ATLANTIC....5-10 82

VELVETEENS
("Ronnie Baker with Monty & the Specialties")
Singles: 7-inch
GOLDEN ARTISTS....5-10 65
LAURIE (3126 "I Thank You")....10-20 62
STARK (102 "Teen Prayer")....20-30 61
(Has only "Stark" at top. *Teen Prayer* is *Please Holy Father* retitled.)
STARK (102 "Teen Prayer")....15-20 61
(Reads: "Stark Records" at top.)
STARK (102 "Teen Prayer")....10-15 61
(Reads: "Stark Distributed By Triway Record Co." at top.)
STARK (12591 "Please Holy Father")....50-100 60
(First issue.)
VELVET (1001 "Please Don't Let Me Go")....10-20 63

VELVETEERS
Singles: 78 rpm
MANOR (1190 "Fine Like Wine")....50-100 49
SPITFIRE (15 "Tell Me You're Mine")....200-400 56
Singles: 7-inch
SPITFIRE (15 "Tell Me You're Mine")....1000-2000 56

VELVETIERS
Singles: 7-inch
RIC (958 "Oh Baby")....150-250 58

VELVETONES
Singles: 78 rpm
COLUMBIA (30206 "How I Miss You")....25-35 50
COLUMBIA (30224 "I'm Disillusioned")....25-35 50
CORONET (1 "One Day")....20-30 46
CORONET (2 "Sweet Lorraine")....20-30 46
CORONET (3 "Swing Out, It Don't Cost Nothing")....20-30 46
CORONET (4 "Don't Say You're Sorry Again")....20-30 46
CORONET (5 "Singing River")....20-30 46
RONDO (1554 "Can You Look Me in the Eyes")....15-25 49
SONORA (2014 "Ask Anyone Who Knows")....20-30 47
SONORA (2015 "Can You Look Me in the Eyes")....20-30 47
SONORA (3010 "It's Written All Over Your Face")....20-30 46
SONORA (3012 "It Just Ain't Right")....20-30 46
SUPER DISC (1055 "Find My Baby Blues")....15-25 48

VELVETONES
(With Tommy Hudson & Savoys)
Singles: 78 rpm
ALADDIN....100-200 57
Singles: 7-inch
ALADDIN (3372 "Glory of Love")....150-200 57
ALADDIN (3391 "I Found My Love")....150-200 57
ALADDIN (3463 "My Every Thought")....200-300 60
(Black label.)
D (1049 "Come Back")....100-150 59
D (1072 "Worried Over You")....50-100 59
DEB (1008 "Who Took My Girl")....100-150 59
IMPERIAL (5878 "Glory of Love") 20-30 62
Member: J.R. Bailey
Also see BAILEY, J.R.

VELVETONES
Singles: 7-inch
ASCOT....8-12 62

VELVETONES
Singles: 7-inch
GLENN (309 "Doheny Run")....15-25 63
VELVET (101 "Doheny Run")....20-30 63

VELVETONES
Singles: 7-inch
G.A.R.P. (102 "Mister X")....15-25 65
(Black vinyl.)
G.A.R.P. (102 "Mister X")....30-50 65
(Colored vinyl.)

VELVETONES
Singles: 7-inch
VERVE....4-8 67

VELVETONES
Singles: 7-inch
JAC-OBE ("Beetle Walk")....10-20 60s

VELVETS
Singles: 78 rpm
FURY....25-50 57
PILGRIM....15-25 56
RED ROBIN....20-50 53
Singles: 7-inch
EVENT....3-5
FURY (1012 "I-I-I")....25-35 57
PILGRIM (706 "I")....20-40 56
PILGRIM (710 "I Cried")....20-40 56
RED ROBIN (120 "They Tried")..100-150 53
RED ROBIN (122 "I")....75-125 53
RED ROBIN (127 "I Cried")....75-125 54
Members: Charles Sampson; Berle Ashton; Don Raysor; Joe Raysor. Session: Ray Stevens; Boots Randolph.

VELVETS P&R '61
("Featuring Virgil Johnson")
Singles: 7-inch
MONUMENT (435 "That Lucky Old Sun")....20-30 61
MONUMENT (441 "Tonight")....20-30 61
MONUMENT (448 "Laugh")....20-30 61
MONUMENT (458 "The Love Express")....15-25 62
MONUMENT (464 "The Lights Go on, the Lights Go Off")....15-25 62
MONUMENT (810 "Crying in the Chapel")....10-20 64
MONUMENT (810 "Crying in the Chapel")....10-20 64
MONUMENT (961 "If")....10-15 66
PLAID (101 "Everybody Knows")...50-75 59
(Features Jerry Sharell.)
20TH FOX (165 "Happy Days Are Here Again")....20-30 59
Members: Virgil Johnson; Will Soloman; Mark Prince; Bob Thursby; Clarence Rigby; Jerry Sharell; Steve Novosel.
Also see SHARELL, Jerry

VEL-VETS
Singles: 7-inch
DORE....8-12 66
20TH FOX (6676 "What Now My Love")....15-25 67

VELVIT, Jimmy
(Jimmy Velvet; James Mullins)
Singles: 7-inch
ALTA....10-15 62
BI....4-8 60s
BLUE....4-8 60s
SHANE....4-8 60s
STARTIME....4-8 60s
TEARDROP....4-8 60s
LPs: 10/12-inch
TEARDROP....10-20 60s
(Though shown as Jimmy Velvet on Bi, Blue, and Teardrop, the singer is James Mullins a.k.a. Jimmy Velvit.)
Also see BELL, James
Also see HENDRICKS, Bobby
Also see CLARK, Bobby
Also see VELVET, Jimmy

VELVITONES
Singles: 7-inch
MILMART (113 "Little Girl I Love You So")....150-250 59

VENDETTA
LPs: 10/12-inch
EPIC....5-10 82

VENDORS
Singles: 7-inch
VICTORIO (128 "Where All Lovers Meet")....450-650 63
(Actually a '62 Invictors' issue [TPE 8221] but with the Victorio/Vendors label on top.)
Also see INVICTORS

VENDORS
Singles: 7-inch
MGM (13133 "Stepping Stones")....5-10 63

VENEERS
Singles: 7-inch
PRINCETON (102 "Believe Me")...25-35 60
TREYCO....10-15 60s
Also see CHANTELS

VENET, Nick
Singles: 7-inch
DECCA....4-8 66
IMPERIAL....10-15 58
EPs: 7-inch
RCA (4100 "Flippin' ")....20-30 57

VENET, Steve
Singles: 7-inch
DORE....5-10 60

VENETIANS P&R '87
Singles: 7-inch
CHRYSALIS....3-4 87

VENICE
(Veniece Stalks)
Singles: 7-inch
HI....5-8 65
Also see STALKS, Veniece

VENNY & MELVIN
Singles: 7-inch
LAURIE....4-8 71
Members: Neil Levenson; Billy Carl.

VENOM
Singles: 7-inch
IOM (1 "Acid Queen")....15-20 83
(Picture disc.)

VENSON, Darlene
Singles: 7-inch
SOMA....8-12 60s

VENT, Joanne
Singles: 7-inch
A&M....3-6 69
LPs: 10/12-inch
A&M....10-15 69

VENTRILLS
Singles: 7-inch
IVANHOE....10-20 67
LITTLE FORT....10-20 65-67
PARKWAY....5-10 67
Members: Frank Vale Ellefson; Jan Hassman; Dave Lexington Hansen; Bob Bellard; Tommy Lee; Donnie Ray Rousch.

VENTURA, Carol
Singles: 7-inch
CAPITOL....4-8 62
PRESTIGE....4-8 66
LPs: 10/12-inch
PRESTIGE....10-15 66

VENTURA, Jesse
Singles: 12-inch
RHINO (6000 "The Body")....5-10 80s
(Picture disc.)
TWIN TONE (8442 "Body Rules")....5-10 84
(Picture disc.)

VENTURAS
Singles: 7-inch
DONNA (1352 "Corrido Twist")....10-20 62
SUGAR (223 "Corrido Twist")....15-25 61

VENTURAS
Singles: 7-inch
DRUM BOY (107 "Apache")....10-20 64
LPs: 10/12-inch
DRUM BOY (DB-1003 "Here They Are")....40-50 64
(Monaural.)
DRUM BOY (DBS-1003 "Here They Are")....50-75 64
(Stereo.)
Members: Ken Ciezek; Jim Radomski; Roman Woprych; Roger Weir.
Also see LI'L WALLY & VENTURAS

VENTURAS
Singles: 7-inch
GREEN LIGHT....8-12

VENTURES P&R/R&B/LP '60
Singles: 12-inch
TRIDEX (1245 "Surfin' & Spyin' ")....5-10 81
(Vocals by Charlotte Caffey and Jane Weidlin.)
Singles: 78 rpm
REO (8497 "Walk – Don't Run")..50-100 60
(Canadian.)
Singles: 7-inch
BLUE HORIZON (100 "Real McCoy")....40-60 59
BLUE HORIZON (101 "Walk Don't Run")....40-60 60
DOLTON (25 "Walk – Don't Run"/"Home")....10-20 60

DOLTON (25-X "Walk – Don't Run"/"The McCoy") ... 8-12 60
DOLTON (28 thru 327) ... 5-15 60-66
LIBERTY ... 4-8 66-70
QUALITY ("Walk – Don't Run") ... 8-12 60s
(Canadian. Reissue of Reo 8497. Selection number not known.)
REO (8497 "Walk – Don't Run") ... 15-25 60
(Canadian.)
TRIDEX ... 3-5 81
U.A. ... 3-6 70-78
Picture Sleeves
DOLTON ... 8-15 60-66
TRIDEX ... 3-5 81
EPs: 7-inch
DOLTON (503 "Walk – Don't Run") ... 20-30 60
LPs: 10/12-inch
AWARD ... 8-12 84
DOLTON (2003 "Walk Don't Run") ... 25-35 60
(Light blue label. Monaural.)
DOLTON (2003 "Walk Don't Run") ... 15-25 61
(Dark blue label. Monaural.)
DOLTON (2004 thru 2050) ... 20-25 61-67
(Monaural.)
DOLTON (8003 "Walk Don't Run") ... 30-40 60
(Light blue label. Stereo.)
DOLTON (8003 "Walk Don't Run") ... 20-30 61
(Dark blue label. Stereo.)
DOLTON (8004 thru 8050) ... 20-30 61-67
(Stereo.)
DOLTON (16500 series) ... 25-35 60s
DOLTON (17000 series) ... 15-20 65-66
LIBERTY (2000 & 8000 series) ... 10-20 67-70
LIBERTY (10000 series) ... 5-10 81-84
LIBERTY (35000 series) ... 10-15 70
SUNSET ... 10-15 66-71
TRIDEX ... 5-10 81-83
U.A. ... 10-15 71-77
Members: Don Wilson; Bob Bogle; Mel Taylor; Nokie Edwards; Jerry McGee; Skip Moore; Howie Johnson; John Durrill.
Also see GO-GOs
Also see LOPEZ, Trini, with the Ventures & Nancy Ames
Also see MARKSMEN
Also see McGEE, Jerry
Also see MOON STONES
Also see TAYLOR, Mel
Also see VEE, Bobby, & Ventures
Also see WILSON, Don

VENTURIE "5"
Singles: 7-inch
VENTURIE (1001 "Good 'N Bad") 10-20 60s

VENUS
Singles: 12-inch
COLUMBIA ... 4-6 83
Singles: 7-inch
COLUMBIA ... 3-4 83

VENUS, Vic *P&R '69*
Singles: 7-inch
BUDDAH (118 "Moonflight") ... 4-8 69
BUDDAH (138 "Moonjack") ... 4-8 69

VENUS & RAZORBLADES
EPs: 7-inch
BOMP ... 8-10 76

VENUS FLYTRAP
Singles: 7-inch
JAGUAR ("103 "Have You Ever") ... 15-20 66
MIJJI ("3005 "Have You Ever") ... 10-20 67

VENUTI, Nick
Singles: 7-inch
IMPALA (5522 "Love in Be-Bop Time") ... 20-30 61

VERA, Billy *P&R '67*
(With the Contrasts; with Beaters; with Blue Eyed Soul)
Singles: 7-inch
ATLANTIC ... 4-6 68-69
FLAVOR ... 10-20 64
MACOLA ... 3-4 87
MIDSONG ... 3-5 75-76
ORANGE ... 4-8 73
RHINO ... 3-4 86-87
RUST (5051 "All My Love") ... 15-25 62
Picture Sleeves
RHINO ... 3-5 86
LPs: 10/12-inch
ATLANTIC ... 10-15 68
CAPITOL ... 5-8 88
MACOLA ... 5-8 87
MIDSONG INT'L ... 8-12 77
RHINO ... 5-8 86
Also see BILLY & BEATERS
Also see BLUE EYED SOUL
Also see KNIGHT RIDERS
Also see RESOLUTIONS

VERA, Billy & Judy Clay *P&R/R&B '67*
Singles: 7-inch
ATLANTIC ... 4-8 67-68
LPs: 10/12-inch
ATLANTIC ... 10-15 68
Also see CLAY, Judy

VERA LYNN: see LYNN, Vera

VERBATIM
Singles: 7-inch
METROMEDIA ... 4-8 69

VERDELL, Jackie
Singles: 7-inch
CORAL ... 3-6 68
DECCA ... 3-6 67

PEACOCK ... 4-8 62-64

VERDI, Joe
Singles: 7-inch
KP (1002 "Arlene") ... 20-40 59

VERDICTS
(With Al Browne's Orchestra)
Singles: 7-inch
EAST COAST (103 "My Life's Desire") ... 150-200 61
O'DELL ... 10-15 60s
RELIC (507 "My Life's Desire") ... 10-15 63
VINTAGE ... 4-6 73
Also see BROWNE, Al

VERITY, John
(John Verity Band)
LPs: 10/12-inch
DUNHILL ... 15-20 74
Also see ARGENT

VERLAINE, Tom *LP '81*
Singles: 7-inch
ELEKTRA ... 3-5 80
W.B. ... 3-5 81-84
LPs: 10/12-inch
ELEKTRA ... 5-10 80
W.B. ... 5-10 81-84
Also see HELL, Richard, & Voidoids
Also see NEON BOYS
Also see TELEVISION

VERNA, Frank
Singles: 78 rpm
DECCA ... 5-8 55
Singles: 7-inch
DECCA ... 8-12 55
JUBILEE ... 4-8 62

VERNALLS
(Varnells)
Singles: 7-inch
RU LU (6753 "Why Can't You Be True") ... 200-300 58
Also see VARNELLS

VERNE, Bobby
Singles: 7-inch
DOC HOLIDAY (101 "Red Hot Car") ... 100-200

VERNE, Larry *P&R/R&B '60*
Singles: 7-inch
COLLECTABLES ... 3-4 80s
ERA ... 5-8 60-64
Picture Sleeves
ERA ... 10-15 60
LPs: 10/12-inch
ERA (104 "Mister Larry Verne") ... 25-35 60

VERNEE, Yvonne
Singles: 7-inch
CORREC-TONE (3178 "Does He Love Me Anymore") ... 20-30 60s
SONBERT (3475 "It's Been a Long Time") ... 25-35 60s
SONBERT (5842 "Just Like You Did Me") ... 500-750 60s

VERNON, Babs
Singles: 7-inch
DOT ... 4-8 64

VERNON, Bobby
Singles: 7-inch
DE VILLE ... 5-10 64

VERNON, Joe
Singles: 7-inch
INTERN ... 4-8 63

VERNON, Kenny *C&W '66*
Singles: 7-inch
CAPITOL ... 3-5 72-74
CARAVAN ... 4-8 66
CHART ... 4-8 68-71
EPIC ... 4-8 66-67
LPs: 10/12-inch
CAPITOL ... 5-10 73
CHART ... 8-12 71
Also see LINDSEY, LaWanda, & Kenny Vernon

VERNON, Lynn
Singles: 7-inch
COVER (5932 "Moon Rocket") ... 15-25 59
Also see B-B / Lyn Vernon

VERNON, Mike
LPs: 10/12-inch
SIRE ... 8-10 74

VERNON, Millie
Singles: 7-inch
ARGO ... 10-15 59
COLPIX ... 5-10 62-63

VERNON, Paul
Singles: 7-inch
LOVE (821 "Keeps My Mind a Wonderin' ") ... 10-20 60s

VERNON, Ray
(With the Raymen; Vernon Wray)
Singles: 7-inch
CAMEO ... 15-25 57-58
LIBERTY ... 10-15 59
MALA ... 8-12 62
MARK ... 10-20 58
RUMBLE ... 10-20 61
SCOTTIE ... 10-20 60
VERNON (100 "Here Was a Man") 15-25 60
Also see WRAY BROTHERS

VERNON & CLIFF
Singles: 7-inch
DOOTO (443 "You Came Along") .20-30 59

Members: Vernon Green; Cliff Chambers.
Also see CHAMBERS, Cliff
Also see GREEN, Vernon, & Medallions

VERNON & JEWELL
(Vernon & the Jewels; Vernon & Jewel)
Singles: 7-inch
KAYO (5104 "The Thought of You"/"Baby, You Got What It Takes") ... 10-15 63
KENT (405 "That's a Rockin' Good Way") ... 10-20 64
PAM MAR (611 "My Every Thought"/"You've Got What It Takes") ... 10-15 60s
(Identical to tracks on Kayo, though titles differ slightly. We don't know yet which disc came first. This one is credited to "Vernon & Jewell," whereas Kayo credits "Vernon & the Jewels.")
Member: Vernon Garrett; Jewell.
Also see GARRETT, Vernon
Also see JACQUET, Russell, Orchestra, & Vernon Garrett

VERNON'S GIRLS
Singles: 7-inch
CHALLENGE (59234 "Stupid Little Girl") ... 15-25 64
Members: Lyn Cornell; Betty Prescott.
Also see BREAKAWAYS
Also see CAREFREES

VERO, Frank
Singles: 7-inch
PIC HIT ... 5-10 61

VERONICA
(Veronica "Ronnie" Spector)
Singles: 7-inch
PHIL SPECTOR (1 "So Young") ... 25-50 64
PHIL SPECTOR (2 "Why Don't They Let Us Fall in Love") ... 40-60 64
Also see NITZSCHE, Jack
Also see SPECTOR, Ronnie

VERROS, Karen
Singles: 7-inch
DOT ... 5-15 65-66

VERSAILLES
Singles: 7-inch
HARLEQUIN ... 8-12 57

VERSAILLES
Singles: 7-inch
OLD TIMER (607 "Lorraine") ... 15-20 65
(Colored vinyl.)
Member: Joey Spano.

VERSALES & TORQUAYS
Singles: 7-inch
MENTOR (4 "Drop Out") ... 10-15 60s

VERSALETTES
Singles: 7-inch
WITCH ... 8-12 63

VERSATILE FOUR
Singles: 7-inch
U.A. ... 4-8 62

VERSATILES
Singles: 7-inch
ATLANTIC (2004 "Passing By") ... 15-25 58
CHECKER (886 "Half Moon") ... 20-40 58
PEACOCK (1910 "White Cliffs of Dover") ... 15-25 62
RO-CAL (1002 "Lundee Dundee") 50-75 60

VERSATILES
Singles: 7-inch
KIN-GAR (104 "Summer Date") ... 10-20 64

VERSATILES
Singles: 7-inch
BRONCO ... 5-10 66
RICH TONE ... 5-10 67
SEA CREST ... 5-10 60s

VERSATILES
Singles: 7-inch
CHEECO (779 "Oh Yeh") ... 25-30 60s

VERSATILES
Singles: 7-inch
RICKARBY (106 "Cyclothymia") ... 8-12

VERSATILES
Singles: 7-inch
STAFF (210 "Cry Like a Baby") ... 25-35

VERSATILES
Singles: 7-inch
COASTER (800 "In the Garden of Love") ... 25-35

VERSATILES & Mike Metko Combo
Singles: 7-inch
RAMCO (3717 "Blue Feeling") ... 75-125 62
Also see VICEROYS

VERSATONES
Singles: 78 rpm
RCA ... 5-10 57
Singles: 7-inch
RCA ... 5-10 57
EPs: 7-inch
RCA ... 15-20 57
LPs: 10/12-inch
RCA (1538 "The Versatones") ... 30-40 57

VERSATONES
Singles: 7-inch
ALL STAR (501 "Tight Skirt and Sweater") ... 20-30 58
ATLANTIC (2211 "Tight Skirt and Sweater") ... 10-15 63
FENWAY (7001 "Tight Skirt and Sweater") ... 15-20 60

MAGIC CITY (4 "Rockin' and Rollin' ") ... 40-60

VERSA-TONES
Singles: 7-inch
KENCO (5015 "Cobra") ... 10-15 61
TIFCO (831 "Heartbeat") ... 10-15 62

VERSATTLES
Singles: 7-inch
CHEECO (780 "Where Did You Go") ... 10-20
STAFF (210 "Cry Like a Baby") ... 10-20

VERSATONES
Singles: 7-inch
RICHIE (4081 "Will She Return") ... 100-150 63

VERSITILES
Singles: 7-inch
AMAKER ... 5-10 62

VERTICAL HOLD
Singles: 7-inch
CRIMINAL ... 3-4 88

VERTUES FOUR
Singles: 7-inch
SEA SEVEN (22 "Angel Baby") ... 20-25 63

VERY STRANGE BREW
LPs: 10/12-inch
ABC ... 10-15 69

VERY-ATIONS
Singles: 7-inch
RINK (542 "I'm So Lonely") ... 10-20 60s

VESPE, Little Joey
Singles: 7-inch
PARKWAY ... 3-5 63

VESPERS
Singles: 7-inch
SWAN (4156 "My Cupid") ... 50-75 63
Also see FOUR EPICS

VESSEL
Singles: 7-inch
VIRTUE (82373 "Purple People Eater Blues") ... 4-8 73

VESTEE, Russ
Singles: 7-inch
AMY (833 "Teardrops") ... 15-25 62
NERO (17000 "Shy Guy") ... 15-25 61

VESTELLES
Singles: 7-inch
DECCA (30733 "Come Home") ... 15-25 58

VESTELLS
Singles: 7-inch
BO JO (1 "Won't You Tell Me") ... 10-20 67

VETS
Singles: 7-inch
SWAMI (551 "Natural Born Lover") ... 15-20 60s

VETTES
Singles: 7-inch
MGM ... 10-20 63
LPs: 10/12-inch
MGM (E-4193 "Rev-Up") ... 30-40 63
(Monaural.)
MGM (SE-4193 "Rev-Up") ... 40-50 63
Members: Bruce Johnston; Steve Douglas.
Also see DOUGLAS, Steve
Also see JOHNSTON, Bruce

VI AUTIO: see AUTIO, Vi

VIA AFRIKA *D&D '84*
Singles: 12-inch
EMI AMERICA ... 4-6 84
Singles: 7-inch
EMI AMERICA ... 3-4 84
LPs: 10/12-inch
EMI AMERICA ... 5-8 84

VIBES
("Formerly the Vibranaires")
Singles: 78 rpm
AFTER HOURS ... 200-300 54
CHARIOT ... 200-300 54
Singles: 7-inch
AFTER HOURS (105 "Stop Torturing Me!") ... 500-1000 54
CHARIOT (105 "Stop Torturing Me!") ... 500-1000 54
Also see VIBRANAIRES

VIBES
Singles: 78 rpm
ABC-PAR (9810 "Darling") ... 25-35 57
Singles: 7-inch
ABC-PAR (9810 "Darling") ... 25-35 57

VIBES
("Vocal By Ronnie Franklin")
Singles: 7-inch
PERSPECTIVE (5858 "Pretty Baby") ... 50-100 58
Member: David Gates as Ronnie Franklin.
Also see GATES, Ronnie

VIBES
Singles: 7-inch
ALLIED (10006 "What's Her Name") ... 35-45 58
ALLIED (10007 "Misunderstood") ... 25-35 59

VIBES
Singles: 7-inch
STARFIRE ... 3-5 79
Picture Sleeves
STARFIRE ... 4-6 79

VIBES
Singles: 7-inch
RAYNA (103 "You Got Me Crying") ... 25-35

VIBRAHARPS
(Vibra-Harps)
Singles: 78 rpm
BEECH (713 "Walk Beside Me") ... 25-50 56
Singles: 7-inch
ATCO (6134 "It Must Be Magic") ... 15-25 59
BEECH (713 "Walk Beside Me") ... 50-100 56
FURY (1022 "The Only Love of Mine") ... 150-200 59
Also see ELBERT, Donnie

VIBRANAIRES
(With Eddie Swanston Quintette; Vibes)
Singles: 78 rpm
AFTER HOURS ... 200-400 54
CHARIOT ... 200-400 54
Singles: 7-inch
AFTER HOURS (103 "Doll Face") ... 1000-1500 54
(Red vinyl.)
CHARIOT (103 "Doll Face") .. 2000-2500 54
LPs: 10/12-inch
LIRRA (500 "Vibranaires Live") ... 20-30 82
(10-inch LP.)
Members: Bobby Thomas; Jimmy Roache; Cleveland Dickerson; Dornell Chavous; Matthew McKnight.
Also see VIBES

VIBRANTS
(Vibrents)
Singles: 7-inch
TRIUMPH (101 "Wildfire") ... 10-20 62
Also see VIBRENTS

VIBRA-SONICS
Singles: 7-inch
IDEAL ("Thunder Storm") ... 15-25 64
(No selection number used.)
Members: George Tweedy; Bob Tweedy; Bill Sabo; Joe Colner; Joey Covington.
Also see FENWAYS
Also see JEFFERSON AIRPLANE
Also see RACKET SQUAD

VIBRASONICS
Singles: 7-inch
MARJON (511 "Don't Go") ... 10-20 66

VIBRATIONS *P&R/R&B '61*
Singles: 7-inch
ABC ... 3-5 74
AMY ... 5-10
ARGO ... 5-10
ATLANTIC (2204 "Between Hello and Goodbye") ... 8-12 63
ATLANTIC (2221 "My Girl Sloopy") ... 10-20 64
BET (0001 "So Blue") ... 75-125 60
CHECKER (954 "So Blue") ... 25-50 60
CHECKER (961 "Feel So Bad") ... 15-25 60
CHECKER (967 "Doing the Slop") 10-20 60
CHECKER (969 "Watusi") ... 10-20 61
CHECKER (974 "Continental") ... 10-20 61
CHECKER (982 "Don't Say Goodbye") ... 10-20 61
CHECKER (987 "All My Love Belongs to You") ... 10-20 61
CHECKER (990 "Let's Pony Again") ... 10-20 61
CHECKER (1002 "Oh Cindy") ... 10-20 61
CHECKER (1011 "New Hully Gully") ... 10-20 62
CHECKER (1022 "Hamburgers on a Bun") ... 10-20 62
CHECKER (1038 "Since I Fell for You") ... 10-20 63
CHECKER (1061 "Dancing Danny") ... 10-20 63
CHESS (2151 "Make It Last") ... 4-6 74
EPIC (10418 "Cause You're Mine") 10-20 68
MANDALA (2511 "Wind Up Toy") ... 4-6 72
NEPTUNE (19 "Expressway to Your Heart") ... 4-8 69
NEPTUNE (21 "Smoke Signals") ... 4-8 70
NEPTUNE (28 "Right On Brother") ... 3-6 70
NORTH BAY (307 "Sneakin' ") ... 5-10
OKEH ... 10-15 64-68
LPs: 10/12-inch
CHECKER (2978 "Watusi") ... 50-75 61
MANDALA (3006 "Taking a New Step") ... 10-15 72
OKEH (14111 "Shout") ... 25-40 65
OKEH (14112 "Misty") ... 25-40 66
OKEH (14129 "Greatest Hits") ... 35-50 69
Also see JAYHAWKS
Also see MARATHONS

VIBRATONES
Singles: 7-inch
MASTERTONE (3075 "Moanin' Bass") ... 50-75 60s

VIBRATONES
Singles: 7-inch
CUCA (1073 "Side-Winder") ... 8-12 62
RAYNARD (10032 "Eventually") ... 8-12 65
RAYNARD (10044 "I Remember Yesterday") ... 8-12 65
Members: Jim Maas; Jerry Schroeder; Roger Bader; Reggie Roznowski; Dickie Leigh; Gary Van Sistine.

VIBRATONES
Singles: 7-inch
STATE ("Half Tuff") ... 8-12
(Selection number not known.)

VIBRATORS
Singles: 7-inch
BROOKE (106 "Way Out") ... 8-12 59

VIBRATORS
Singles: 7-inch
COLUMBIA ... 3-5 77
LPs: 10/12-inch
COLUMBIA ... 5-10 77

VIBRENTS
(Vibrants)
Singles: 7-inch
BAY TOWNE (409 "The Breeze and I") ... 10-15 63
Also see VIBRANTS

VIC & CATALINAS
Singles: 7-inch
BAR CLAY ... 5-10

VIC & GENTS
Singles: 7-inch
DORANA (1170 "Lydia") ... 100-200 62

VIC, BEN & DICK
Singles: 7-inch
ENTERPRISE ... 4-8 67

VICE-ROYS
Singles: 78 rpm
ALADDIN ... 50-100 55
Singles: 7-inch
ALADDIN (3273 "Please Baby, Please") ... 150-250 55

VICEROYS
(With the Mike Metko Combo; Vice-Roys)
Singles: 7-inch
LITTLE STAR (107 "I'm So Sorry") ... 50-75 61
ORIGINAL SOUND (15 Dreamy Eyes") ... 15-25 61
RAMCO (3715 "My Heart") ... 1000-2000 62
SMASH (1716 "I'm So Sorry") ... 15-20 61
Also see VERSATILES
Also see PENGUINS

VICEROYS
Singles: 7-inch
E'DEN (9001 "Don't Let Go") ... 8-10 62

VICEROYS
(Vice-Roys)
Singles: 7-inch
BETHLEHEM ... 8-12 62-65
DVC ... 5-10 60s
U.S.A. (761 "Liverpool") ... 5-10 64
Members: Richard P. Giannini; Larry Holmes; Rick Emerson; Harry Kawolski; Ron Emerson; Jon Ehlers; Frank Giannini; William Morales.
Also see BALLARD, Hank, & Midnighters / Viceroys

VICEROYS
Singles: 7-inch
BOLO ... 6-12 63-65
DOT ... 4-8 63
LPs: 10/12-inch
BOLO (8000 "At Granny's Pad") ... 30-50 63
Member: Jim Valley.
Also see AMERICAN EAGLE
Also see SURPRISE PACKAGE
Also see VALLEY, Jim
Also see WINK & JUDY with the Viceroys Five

VICEROYS
Singles: 7-inch
IMPERIAL (66058 "Earth Angel") ... 5-10 64

VICIOUS BASE Featuring D.J. Magic Mike LP '91
LPs: 10/12-inch
CHEETAH ... 5-8 91
Also see D.J. Magic Mike

VICIOUS PINK
Singles: 12-inch
MANHATTAN ... 4-8

VICK, Jimmy
Singles: 7-inch
CHERRY ... 4-8 63

VICK & JOHN
Singles: 7-inch
ALLERT ... 4-8 65

VICKERS, Charles
Singles: 7-inch
NATIONAL GUILD ... 8-12

VICKERS, Mike
Singles: 7-inch
CAPITOL (5890 "Proper Charles Batman") ... 8-12 67

VICKERS, Vic
(Mac Vickery)
Singles: 7-inch
JAMIE ... 15-25 64
Also see VICKERY, Mack

VICKERY, Mack C&W '77
(Mac Vickery)
Singles: 7-inch
AFCO ... 4-8 66
GONE ... 8-12 59
PLAYBOY ... 3-5 77
PRINCETON (101 "High School Blues") ... 50-100 60
LPs: 10/12-inch
MEGA ... 10-15 70
Also see ATLANTA JAMES
Also see VICKERS, Vic

VICKI
Singles: 7-inch
PARKTOWNE ... 4-8

VICKI DAWN
(Vicki Dawn Sanders)
Singles: 7-inch
BOUNDRY ... 4-6
Also see SANDERS

VICKY
(Vicky Leandros)
Singles: 7-inch
PHILIPS (40546 "Dance with Me Until Tomorrow") ... 10-15 68
VICKY ... 4-8 68
LPs: 10/12-inch
PHILIPS ... 8-12 68
Also see LEANDROS, Vicky

VICKY D R&B '82
Singles: 7-inch
SAM ... 3-4 82

VI-COUNTS
Singles: 7-inch
ACE ... 5-10 60
DONICK ... 5-10 59
VI-COUNTS ... 5-10

VI-COUNTS
Singles: 7-inch
SALESMAKER ... 10-15 65

VICT, Ray
Singles: 7-inch
GOLDBAND (1042 "We're Gonna Bop, Stop, Rock") ... 50-80 57
ZIP (1042 "We're Gonna Bop, Stop, Rock") ... 100-150 57

VICTIMS FAMILY
LPs: 10/12-inch
MORDAM ... 5-8 88

VICTIMS OF CHANCE
LPs: 10/12-inch
CRESTVIEW (3052 "Victims of Chance") ... 35-55 60s

VICTONES
Singles: 7-inch
FRONT PAGE (1001 "My Baby Changes") ... 5-10
FRONT PAGE (2302 "Two Sides to Love") ... 5-10

VICTOR, Johnny
Singles: 7-inch
DOLTON ... 4-8 62

VICTOR, King: see KING VICTOR

VICTOR, Ray
Singles: 7-inch
CORSAIR ... 15-20

VICTOR, Roy
Singles: 7-inch
PHARAOH ... 10-20

VICTOR & SPOILS
Singles: 7-inch
PHILIPS ... 4-8 66

VICTORIA
Singles: 7-inch
SAN FRANCISCO ... 4-6 70
LPs: 10/12-inch
SAN FRANCISCO ... 10-15 70-71

VICTORIA, C.B.
Singles: 7-inch
20TH FOX ... 3-5 75

VICTORIALS
Singles: 78 rpm
IMPERIAL ... 25-40 56
Singles: 7-inch
IMPERIAL (5398 "I Get That Feeling") ... 50-100 56

VICTORIANS
Singles: 78 rpm
SPECIALTY (411 "I Guess You're Satisfied") ... 75-125 50
SPECIALTY (420 "Naturally Too Weak for You") ... 250-500 51
Singles: 7-inch
SPECIALTY (411 "I Guess You're Satisfied") ... 1500-2500 50

VICTORIANS
Singles: 78 rpm
SAXONY (103 "Heartbreaking Moon") ... 100-200 56
Singles: 7-inch
SAXONY (103 "Heartbreaking Moon") ... 300-400 56
SELMA (103 "Wedding Bells") ... 150-250 58
Members: Cas Bridges; Bobby Thompson; Bill Carey; Donny Miles.
Also see CLEFFTONES

VICTORIANS
Singles: 7-inch
HERCULES ... 10-20 60
ROEWANA ... 8-12

VICTORIANS
Singles: 7-inch
END (1033 "Cowbell Rock") ... 10-15 63

VICTORIANS
Singles: 7-inch
LIBERTY (55574 "What Makes Little Girls Cry") ... 15-20 63
LIBERTY (55656 "You're Invited to a Party") ... 10-15 64
LIBERTY (55693 "Happy Birthday Blue") ... 10-15 64
LIBERTY (55728 "If I Loved You") ... 10-15 64

VICTORIANS
Singles: 7-inch
BANG ... 10-15 67
REPRISE ... 10-15 66
Member: Nick Massi.
Also see MASSI, Nick

VICTORIANS
Singles: 7-inch
ARNOLD J. ... 5-10 68

VICTORS
Singles: 7-inch
DOT ... 5-10 63
JACKPOT ... 5-10 59

VICTORS
Singles: 7-inch
ALPHA (603 "We Struck a Match") ... 10-20 66

VICTORS
Singles: 7-inch
PHILIPS (40475 "Hurt") ... 20-30 67

VICTORY LP '89
LPs: 10/12-inch
RHINO ... 5-8 89

VICTORY FIVE
Singles: 7-inch
TERP (101 "I Never Knew") ... 300-400 57
(Colored vinyl.)

VIDAL, Maria P&R/D&D '84
Singles: 12-inch
EMI AMERICA ... 4-6 84
Singles: 7-inch
EMI AMERICA ... 3-4 84
Picture Sleeves
EMI AMERICA ... 3-4 84
Also see CHILD, Desmond, & Rouge

VIDALTONES
Singles: 7-inch
JOSIE (900 "Forever") ... 25-35 62

VIDEEO R&B '82
Singles: 7-inch
H.C.R.C. ... 3-5 82

VIDELS
Singles: 7-inch
DUSTY DISC ("I Wish") ... 5-8
EARLY (702 "I Wish") ... 1000-2000 60

VIDELS P&R '60
(With Joe Sherman & His Orchestra; with Frank Spino & His Orchestra; Vi-Dels; Videls')
Singles: 7-inch
COLLECTABLES ... 3-4 80s
DUSTY DISC ... 5-8
JDS (5004 "Mister Lonely") ... 30-40 60
(Gray label. Reads: "Distributed by United Telefilm Records.")
JDS (5004 "Mister Lonely") ... 15-25 60
(Multi-color label. No mention of distribution by United Telefilm.)
JDS (5005 "She's Not Coming Home") ... 30-40 60
(Gray label. Reads: "Distributed by United Telefilm Records.")
JDS (5005 "She's Not Coming Home") ... 20-30 60
(Yellow label. Reads: "Distributed by United Telefilm Records.")
JDS (5005 "She's Not Coming Home") ... 10-20 60
(Multi-color label. No mention of distribution by United Telefilm.)
KAPP (361 "Streets of Love") ... 15-25 61
KAPP (405 "A Letter from Ann") ... 25-35 61
MEDIEVAL (203 "Be My Girl") ... 15-25 59
MUSICNOTE (117 "We Belong Together") ... 20-30 63
RHODY (2000 "Be My Girl") ... 50-75 59
(First issue.)
TIC-TAC-TOE (5005 "Now That Summer Is Here") ... 75-125 62
LPs: 10/12-inch
MAGIC CARPET (1005 "A Letter from the Videls") ... 8-10
Members: Pete Anders; Vinnie Poncia.
Also see ANDERS & PONCIA
Also see SHERMAN, Joe, & His Orchestra

VIDEOS
Singles: 7-inch
BIM BAM BOOM (101 "Love Or Infatuation") ... 5-10 72
CASINO (102 "Trickle, Trickle") ... 30-50 58
(Label name in shadow print. Does not have six ace playing cards. No mention of distribution by Gone.)
CASINO (102 "Trickle, Trickle") ... 10-15 58
(Has six ace playing cards.)
CASINO (102 "Trickle, Trickle") ... 15-25 61
(Label name in block, shadowless print. Does not have six ace playing cards. Indicates distribution by Gone.)
CASINO (105 "Love Or Infatuation") ... 200-300 59
Members: Ron Woodall; John Jackson; Clarence Bassett; Charles Baskerville; Ron Cuffey.
Also see FIVE SHARPS

VIDLETTES
Singles: 7-inch
HERALD ... 5-10 63

VIDONE, Bob
Singles: 7-inch
FLEETWOOD ... 10-20 58
SENTRY ... 10-20 59

VIEW FROM THE HILL
Singles: 7-inch
CAPITOL ... 3-4 88

VIGILANTES
Singles: 7-inch
CUCA (1042 "Ramblin' On") ... 10-20 61
CUCA (1042 "Travelin' On") ... 10-20 61
(Retitled reissue.)
CUCA (1064 "Highland Fling") ... 20-30 61
HER MI (001 "Warm Wind") ... 10-20 62
Members: James Brogan;Don Hermanson; Greg Coby; Don Kaekala; Jay Mihelich; Lee Sterbenz; John Mitchell; Lloyd Hugo.

VIGILANTES
Singles: 7-inch
JCP (1010 "Notice Me") ... 15-25 67

VIGRASS & OSBORNE P&R '72
Singles: 7-inch
EPIC ... 3-5 74
UNI ... 3-5 72
LPs: 10/12-inch
EPIC ... 8-10 74
UNI ... 8-15 71
Members: Paul Vigrass; Gary Osborne.

VIGUEN
LPs: 10/12-inch
SOUNDEX ... 5-10 79

VI-KINGS
Singles: 7-inch
DEL-MANN (544 "Rock a Little Bit") ... 15-25 60

VIKINGS
Singles: 7-inch
ALTA (105 "Big Squeaky") ... 10-20 62
LIBERTY (55295 "Cliff Dweller") ... 10-20 61
NATIONWIDE (11 "The Viking Twist") ... 10-20 62
MONUMENT (839 "Tradewinds") ... 10-20 64
Members: Leon Halverson; Cliff Hanson; Carl Hintz; Bob Hinze; Tom Stubler.

VIKINGS
Singles: 7-inch
ATHENS (201 "Nicotine") ... 20-30 62

VIKINGS
Singles: 7-inch
SALEM (007 "You Can't Do That") ... 15-25 65

VIKINGS
Singles: 7-inch
CUCA (1096 "Rawhide") ... 10-20 65

VIKINGS
Singles: 7-inch
VALHALLA (661 "Boo-Hoo-Hoo") ... 100-200 66
VIKING (1000 "Come on and Love Me") ... 20-30 66

VILADOS
Singles: 7-inch
STREN (102 "Wild Party") ... 50-75 63

VILLA, Claudio
LPs:10/12-inch
CORAL (57281 "Sings") ... 20-30 58
CORAL (57373 "Romantic Moods Italiano") ... 20-30 58

VILLA, Danny
Singles: 7-inch
DANCO ... 4-8 64-65

VILLA, Joey
(Joe Villa; Joey & the Original 3 Friends)
Singles: 7-inch
CAPITOL (4484 "All American Girl") ... 10-15 60
CHEVRON (500 "Blanche") ... 10-20
DE-LITE ... 8-12
MF (101 "Blanche") ... 25-50
Also see BLUETONES
Also see ROYAL TEENS

VILLA, Pancho
Singles: 7-inch
ARLISS ... 4-8 61
CHANCELLOR ... 5-10 60
MAINLINE ... 10-15 57
PEE VEE ... 4-8 64
SYMBOL ... 4-8 63

VILLAGE CALLERS
Singles: 7-inch
RAMPART ... 4-8 68-69
LPs: 10/12-inch
RAMPART ... 10-15 68

VILLAGE FUGS see FUGS

VILLAGE PEOPLE LP '77
Singles: 12-inch
CASABLANCA ... 4-8 78-79
Singles: 7-inch
CASABLANCA ... 3-5 78-79
RCA ... 3-5 81
Picture Sleeves
CASABLANCA ... 3-5 78-79
RCA ... 3-5 81
LPs: 10/12-inch
CASABLANCA (Except NBPIX series) ... 5-10 77-80
CASABLANCA (NBPIX series) ... 15-25 78
(Picture discs.)
RCA ... 5-10 81
Members: Victor Willis; Alexander Briley; Felipe Rose; Randy Jones; David Hodo; Glenn Hughes.

VILLAGE SOUL CHOIR P&R/R&B '70
Singles: 7-inch
ABBOTT ... 4-6 69-70
SCM (1000 "Talk to Me Sometimes") ... 8-12 60s

VILLAGE SOUND
Singles: 7-inch
HIP ... 5-10 69
ONYX (102 "These Windows") ... 30-40 60s

VILLAGE STOMPERS P&R/R&B/LP '63
Singles: 7-inch
EPIC ... 4-8 63-67
Picture Sleeves
EPIC ... 5-10 63-65
LPs: 10/12-inch
EPIC ... 10-20 63-67
Also see VINTON, Bobby, & Village Stompers

VILLAGE VOICES
Singles: 7-inch
TOPIX (6000 "Red Lips") ... 25-35 61
(Yellow and black label.)
TOPIX (6000 "Red Lips") ... 20-25 61
(Yellow, black and white label.)
Also see 4 SEASONS

VILLAGERS
Singles: 7-inch
ATCO ... 4-8 68
FAME ... 10-20 66
PETAL ... 5-10 63

VILLAGERS
Singles: 7-inch
JCP (1005 "C.C. Rider") ... 10-20 64
JCP (1012 "I Won't Cry") ... 10-20 64

VILLANO, Louie
Singles: 7-inch
AMBER ... 5-10

VILLARI, Guy
Singles: 7-inch
COUSINS (1004 "I'm All Alone") ... 20-30 61
Also see REGENTS

VILLETTE SISTERS
Singles: 7-inch
MGM ... 5-10 60

VILLIANS
Singles: 7-inch
BULLETS ... 4-8 66

VILONS
Singles: 7-inch
ALJON (1259 "Mother Nature") ... 20-30 63
BIM BAM BOOM ... 4-8 72
LAKE ... 10-15 60s
VINTAGE ... 4-8 73
Member: Bob Alveray.

VINA, Joe
Singles: 7-inch
ALLIED (7778 "That's Alright") ... 5-10 59
WEBBER (5001 "Take This Heart") 5-10 60

VINCE & VICTORS
Singles: 7-inch
JERDEN ... 5-10 65
Member: Vince Gerber.
Also see GERBER, Vince

VINCE & WAIKIKI RUMBLERS
Singles: 7-inch
BIG BEN (1003 "Waikiki Rumblers") ... 10-20 65
ZODIAC (1004 "Waikiki Rumblers") ... 15-25 65

VINCENT, Danny
Singles: 7-inch
ROULETTE ... 5-10 61

VINCENT, Darryl
Singles: 7-inch
SANDY (1016 "Mercy Me") ... 35-45 58
SANDY (1020 "Wild Wild Party") ... 45-55 58

VINCENT, Gene P&R/R&B/C&W/LP '56
(With His Blue Caps)
Singles: 78 rpm
CAPITOL ... 50-100 56-57
Promotional Singles: 78 rpm
CAPITOL ... 75-125 56-57
(White or yellow labels.)
Singles: 7-inch
CAPITOL (3450 "Be-Bop-a-Lula") ... 30-40 56
CAPITOL (3530 "Race with the Devil") ... 30-40 56
CAPITOL (3558 "Bluejean Bop") ... 30-40 56
CAPITOL (3617 "Crazy Legs") ... 30-40 57
CAPITOL (3678 "B-I-Bickey-Bi, Bo-Bo-Go") ... 30-40 57
CAPITOL (3763 "Lotta Lovin' ") ... 30-40 57
CAPITOL (3839 "Dance to the Bop") ... 30-40 57
CAPITOL (3874 "Walkin' Home from School") ... 20-30 58
CAPITOL (3959 "Baby Blue") ... 20-30 58
CAPITOL (4010 "Rocky Road Blues") ... 20-30 58
CAPITOL (4051 "Little Lover") ... 20-30 59
CAPITOL (4105 "Say Mama") ... 20-30 59
CAPITOL (4153 "Who's Pushin' Your Swing") ... 20-30 59
CAPITOL (4237 "Right Now") ... 20-30 60
CAPITOL (4313 "Wild Cat") ... 20-30 60
CAPITOL (4442 "Pistol Packin' Mama") ... 15-25 60
CAPITOL (4525 "Mister Lonliness") ... 15-25 61
CAPITOL (4665 "Lucky Star") ... 15-25 61

CAPITOL STAR LINE (6042 "Be-Bop-a-Lula") 4-8 60s
CHALLENGE (59337 "Bird Doggin' ") 15-20 66
CHALLENGE (59347 "Lonely Street") 15-20 66
CHALLENGE (59365 "Born to be a Rolling Stone") 15-20 67
FOREVER (6001 "Story of the Rockers") 10-20 69
KAMA SUTRA (514 "Sunshine") 8-12 70
KAMA SUTRA (518 "High on Life") . 8-12 70
PLAYGROUND (100 "Story of the Rockers") 150-175 68

Promotional Singles: 7-inch

CAPITOL 50-100 56-61
(White or yellow labels.)

Picture Sleeves

CAPITOL (4237 "Right Now") ...800-1000 60

EPs: 7-inch

CAPITOL (438 "Dance to the Bop") 150-200 57
(Promotional issue only. Not issued with cover.)
CAPITOL (764 "Bluejean Bop") 75-125 57
(Price is for any of three volumes.)
CAPITOL (811 "Gene Vincent & His Blue Caps") 75-125 57
(Price is for any of three volumes.)
CAPITOL (970 "Gene Vincent Rocks & Bluecaps Roll") 75-125 58
(Price is for any of three volumes.)
CAPITOL (985 "Hot Rod Gang") 350-400 58
(Green label. Soundtrack.)
CAPITOL (985 "Hot Rod Gang") 400-450 58
(White label. Promotional issue.)
CAPITOL (1059 "Record Date") ...75-125 58
(Price is for any of three volumes.)

LPs: 10/12-inch

CAPITOL (DKAO-380 "Gene Vincent's Greatest") 15-25 69
CAPITOL (SM-380 "Gene Vincent's Greatest") 5-10 78
CAPITOL (764 "Bluejean Bop") 200-300 56
CAPITOL (811 "Gene Vincent & His Blue Caps") 200-300 57
CAPITOL (970 "Gene Vincent Rocks") 200-300 58
CAPITOL (1059 "Gene Vincent Record Date") 200-300 58
CAPITOL (1207 "Sounds Like Gene Vincent") 200-300 59
CAPITOL (T-1342 "Crazy Times") 150-250 60
(Monaural.)
CAPITOL (ST-1342 "Crazy Times") 250-350 60
(Stereo.)
CAPITOL (11000 series) 8-12 74
CAPITOL (16000 series) 5-10 81
COLUMBIA HOUSE (516208 "Gene Vincent's Greatest") 8-12
DANDELION 10-20 70
KAMA SUTRA 10-20 70-71
ROLLIN' ROCK 5-10 80-81
Also see BATTIN, Skip
Also see CHAMPS
Also see FACENDA, Tommy
Also see MERRITT, Jerry
Also see MEYERS, Augie
Also see PRESLEY, Elvis
Also see SUPER-PHONICS / Gene Vincent

VINCENT, Gene / Tommy Sands / Sonny James / Ferlin Husky

LPs: 10/12-inch

CAPITOL (1009 "Teen Age Rock") 50-100 58
Also see HUSKY, Ferlin
Also see SANDS, Tommy

VINCENT, Gene / Frank Sinatra / Sonny James / Ron Goodwin

EPs: 7-inch

CAPITOL (437 "Special Hit Pressing") 75-100 57
(Promotional issue only. Not issued with cover.)
Also see GOODWIN, Ron
Also see JAMES, Sonny
Also see SINATRA, Frank

VINCENT, Gene / Super-Phonics

Singles: 7-inch

MEAN MOUNTAIN (1425 "Interview with Gene Vincent") 5-10
Also see SUPER-PHONICS
Also see VINCENT, Gene

VINCENT, Holly Beth

Singles: 12-inch

EPIC 4-6 82
Also see HOLLY & ITALIANS

VINCENT, James

Singles: 7-inch

BIG TREE 3-6 71

LPs: 10/12-inch

CARIBOU 8-10 74-76

VINCENT, Ronnie

Singles: 7-inch

FM 4-8 64

VINCENT, Rudy, Jr., & His Rockin' Crickets

Singles: 7-inch

END (1042 "Rockin' Crickets") 10-15 59
Also see HOT TODDYS

VINCENT, Stan

(Stanley Vincent)

Singles: 7-inch

BEE 5-10 60s
DWAIN 10-20 60
FELICE 5-10 63
GOLD (101 "Runnin' Scared") 15-25 60
MGM 5-10 64
MARLU (7003 "Little Teardrops") ...50-75 61
Also see PARAMOUNTS

VINCENT, Vinnie, Invasion *LP '86*

Singles: 7-inch

CHRYSALIS 3-4 86-88

Picture Sleeves

CHRYSALIS (43253 "All Systems Go Medley") 3-5 88
(Promotional issue only.)

LPs: 10/12-inch

CHRYSALIS 5-8 86-88
Members: Dana Strum.
Also see KISS
Also see SLAUGHTER

VINE, Joe

Singles: 7-inch

HERCULES 4-8 65

VINE, Marty

Singles: 7-inch

EPIC 5-10 60
MASTERMADE 4-8 61

Picture Sleeves

EPIC 8-12 60

VINE STREET BOYS

Singles: 7-inch

ERA 5-10 63

VINEGAR JOE

LPs: 10/12-inch

ATCO 8-12 73
Members: Robert Palmer; Elkie Brooks; Roger Ball; Dave Brooks; Pete Gage; Steve York; John Woods.

VINES

Singles: 7-inch

CEE=JAY (582 "Love So Sweet")..30-50 61

VINNIE & SUE

Singles: 7-inch

SPRING 20-25

VINNY & NITELITES

(With the Nitelites)

Singles: 7-inch

KC (107 "Poppin' Popcorn") 8-12 62

VINNY & KENNY

Singles: 7-inch

FIRE 10-15 59

VINO, Jack

Singles: 7-inch

BELL 3-5 72

VINSON, Don

Singles: 7-inch

MGM 5-10 58

VINSON, Eddie *R&B '47*

(Eddie "Cleanhead" Vinson)

Singles: 78 rpm

KING 15-25 50-52
MERCURY 10-25 46-55

Singles: 7-inch

BETHLEHEM (11097 "Cherry Red") 8-12 61
BLUESWAY 4-8 67
KING (4563 "Good Bread Alley") ...30-50 52
KING (4582 "Lonesome Train") 30-50 52
MERCURY (70334 "Old Man Boogie") 50-100 54
MERCURY (70525 "Anxious Heart") 50-75 54
MERCURY (70621 "Anxious Heart") 50-75 55
RIVERSIDE 5-10 62

LPs: 10/12-inch

AAMCO (312 "Eddie "Cleanhead" Vinson Sings") 25-35
BETHLEHEM (5005 "Eddie "Cleanhead" Vinson Sings") 50-75 57
BETHLEHEM (6000 series) 5-10 78
BLUES TIME 10-15 69
BLUESWAY (6007 "Cherry Red") ..10-20 67
DELMARK 5-10 80
KING (634 "Eddie Vinson") 40-60 60
KING (1087 "Cherry Red") 10-15 69
MUSE 5-10 78-83
REGGIES 5-10 81
RIVERSIDE (3502 "Backdoor Blues") 30-40 62
Also see BROWN, Roy
Also see HARRIS, Wynonie / Roy Brown / Eddie Vinson
Also see WILLIAMS, Cootie
Also see WITHERSPOON, Jimmy / Eddie Vinson

VINSON, Eddie "Cleanhead," & Roomful of Blues

LPs: 10/12-inch

MUSE 5-10 82
Also see ROOMFUL of BLUES
Also see VINSON, Eddie

VINSON, Smith

Singles: 7-inch

STATUE (20 "The Trials of a Flower Child") 50-75 71

LPs: 10/12-inch

PLAYBOY 15-20 70s

VINTON, Bobby *P&R/R&B/LP '62*

(Bobby Vinton Orchestra)

Singles: 7-inch

ABC 3-5 74-77
ALPINE 10-15 59
AURAVISION (6722 "Rain, Rain Go Away") 8-12 64
(Cardboard flexi-disc, one of six by six different artists. Columbia Record Club "Enrollment Premium." Set came in a special paper sleeve.)
CURB 3-4 88-89
ELEKTRA 3-5 78
EPIC (9000 series) 4-8 60-66
(Black vinyl.)
EPIC (9000 series) 8-10 64
(Colored vinyl.)
EPIC (10000 series) 3-6 66-75
EPIC MEMORY LANE 3-5 87
LARC 3-4 83
MELODY 10-15 59
TAPESTRY 3-5 79-82

Picture Sleeves

EPIC 3-8 62-72
TAPESTRY 3-5 80

EPs: 7-inch

EPIC 6-12 63-65
(Juke box issues.)

LPs: 10/12-inch

ABC 8-10 74-77
CSP 5-10 80s
COLUMBIA 8-10 73
EPIC (500 series) 20-25 60
EPIC (3000 series) 15-20 60
EPIC (20000 series) 8-15 62-70
(Black vinyl.)
EPIC (20468 "Blue on Blue") 20-40 63
(Colored vinyl. Promotional issue only.)
EPIC (30000 series) 5-10 72-79
HARMONY 5-10 70
TAPESTRY 5-10 80
Also see CLARK, Dave, Five / New Christy Minstrels / Bobby Vinton / Jerry Vale
Also see JAN & DEAN / Bobby Vinton / Andy Williams

VINTON, Bobby / Chuck & Johnny

Singles: 7-inch

DIAMOND (121 "I Love You the Way You Are") 5-8 62

VINTON, Bobby, & Village Stompers

LPs: 10/12-inch

EPIC 10-20 66
Also see VILLAGE STOMPERS
Also see VINTON, Bobby

VIN-ZEE *R&B '81*

Singles: 7-inch

EMERGENCY 3-5 81

VIOLA CRAYOLA

LPs: 10/12-inch

FAUTRA 10-12 74
Members: Ron Viola; Anthony Viola.

VIOLATIONS

Singles: 7-inch

DOT 5-10 66

VIOLATORS

Singles: 7-inch

BONZO (7180 "It's a Crime") 6-10

VIO-LENCE *LP '88*

LPs: 10/12-inch

MECHANIC 5-8 88

VIOLENT FEMMES *LP '86*

Singles: 7-inch

SLASH 3-4 83-90

LPs: 10/12-inch

SLASH 5-8 83-91
Members: Gordon Gano; Brian Ritchie; Victor DeLorenzo.

VIOLETS

Singles: 7-inch

HERALD 5-10 64

VIOLETTS

Singles: 7-inch

DIAMOND (343 "I Won't Cry") 10-20 68

VIOLINAIRES

Singles: 78 rpm

DRUMMOND 75-125 54

Singles: 7-inch

CHECKER (5063 "Salt of the Earth") 4-8
DRUMMOND (4000 "Another Soldier Gone") 250-350 54

VIOLINS

(With Al Browne's Orchestra)

Singles: 7-inch

LAKE (713 "What Kind of Fool Am I") 40-60 62
Also see BROWNE, Al

VIOLINSKI

Singles: 7-inch

JET 3-5 79

LPs: 10/12-inch

JET 5-10 79
Member: Mik Kominski.
Also see ELECTRIC LIGHT ORCHESTRA

VIOT, Russ

Singles: 7-inch

NOSE 4-8 67
Session: Davie Allan.
Also see ALLAN, Davie

VIPERS

Singles: 7-inch

DUCHESS (102 "Little Miss Sweetness") 40-60 60s

VIPERS

Singles: 12-inch

MIDNIGHT 4-6 88

Singles: 7-inch

MIDNIGHT 3-4 84-88

LPs: 10/12-inch

MIDNIGHT 5-8 84-88
PVC 5-8 85
SKYCLAD 5-8 89
Members: David Andrew Mann; Graham May; Paul Monroe Martin; Patrick Allen Brown; Jonithan Adam Weiss; John England; Bill McGarvey; Anders Thomsen.
Also see FLESHTONES

VIPPS

Singles: 7-inch

PHILIPS 4-8 66

VIRG, MURF & PROF.

Singles: 7-inch

DECCA (30612 "Way Out") 10-15 58

VIRGIL & 4 CHANELS

Singles: 7-inch

DEB (508 "Waiting") 25-50 59
Also see CHANNELS

VIRGIL BROTHERS

Singles: 7-inch

RARE EARTH 3-6 69

VIRGIN INSANITY

LPs: 10/12-inch

FUNKY (71411 "Illusions of the Maintaince Man") 75-100 60s

VIRGIN SLEEP

Singles: 7-inch

DERAM ("Love") 10-20 67

VIRGINIA

Singles: 7-inch

CRIMSON 4-8

VIRGINIA FOUR

Singles: 78 rpm

DECCA (7662 "Dig My Jelly Roll") 50-75 39
DECCA (7808 "I'd Feel Much Better") 50-75 39
VICTOR (23376 "Don't Leave Me Behind") 50-75 30
VICTOR (38569 "Since I Been Born") 50-75 30

VIRGINIA WOLVES

Singles: 7-inch

ABC 4-8 67
AMY 4-8 66

VIRGINIANS

Singles: 7-inch

DIAMOND (120 "There Goes My Baby") 10-20 62
Member: Bill Ramal.

VIRGINIANS

Singles: 7-inch

COLPIX 4-8 62

VIRGINIANS

Singles: 7-inch

CUCA 8-12 65

VIRGINIANS

Singles: 7-inch

EPIC 4-8 66-67
Member: Bill Swofford.
Also see OLIVER

VIRGOS

Singles: 7-inch

PIONEER 8-12 65

VIRTAMEN, Kalney

Singles: 7-inch

4 CORNERS 4-8 65

VIRTUE, Frank

(Frank Virtue Combo; Frank Virtuoso)

Singles: 78 rpm

ARCADE 5-10 55

Singles: 7-inch

ARCADE 10-15 55
JOY 5-10 63

LPs: 10/12-inch

FAYETTE 25-35 64
Also see VIRTUES
Also see VIRTUOSO, Frank

VIRTUES *P&R/R&B '59*

(With the Virtues; Frank Virtuoso & Virtues; Frank Virtuoso & His Quintet; Fantastic Virtues)

Singles: 7-inch

ABC 3-5 73
ABC-PAR 5-10 59
ARCADE 8-12 50s
B.V.D. 5-10
FAYETTE 4-8 64
HIGHLAND 10-15 60
HUNT (Monaural) 5-10 59
HUNT (Stereo) 15-25 59
RHYTHM 8-12 50s
SURE (500 series) 8-12 59
SURE (1700 series) 4-8 62
VIRNON 5-10 60
VIRTUE 5-10 66-69
WYNNE 5-10 60

LPs: 10/12-inch

STRAND 20-25 60
WYNNE 25-30 60

Also see VIRTUE, Frank

VIRTUOSO, Frank

Singles: 7-inch

LIBERTY (55706 "Move On") 10-20 64
REFRESHMENT (1 "Mountaineer Mashed Potatoes") 25-50 60s
RHYTHM (13 "Rollin' & Rockin' ") ..20-30
TONE-CRAFT (206 "San Antonio Rose") 10-20
TONE-CRAFT (207 "Rollin' and Rockin' ") 50-75
Also see VIRTUE, Frank

VISAGE *LP '81*

Singles: 12-inch

POLYDOR 4-6 80-82

Singles: 7-inch

POLYDOR 3-5 81

LPs: 10/12-inch

POLYDOR 5-10 80-82

VISAS

Singles: 7-inch

TIMELY (904 "Night Train") 10-20 65

VISCAYNES

Singles: 7-inch

TROPO (101 "Stop What You Are Doing") 150-250 61
(Credits "The Viscaynes and the Ramblers.")
TROPO (101 "Stop What You Are Doing") 50-100 61
(Credits only "The Viscaynes.")

VISCAYNES

Singles: 7-inch

VPM (1006 "Hevenly Angel") 15-25 61
VEEP 5-10 65

VISCOS

Singles: 7-inch

JCP (103 "Midnight in Madrid") 8-12 60s

VISCOUNT V

Singles: 7-inch

LAVETTE (5003 "Cherry Red Vette") 10-20 60s
LAVETTE (5010 "She Doesn't Know") 10-20 60s

VISCOUNTS

Singles: 78 rpm

MERCURY (71073 "My Girl") 15-25 57

Singles: 7-inch

MERCURY (71073 "My Girl") 15-25 57
VEGA 10-15 59

VISCOUNTS

Singles: 7-inch

STAR-FAX (1002 "Wandering") 450-650 50s

VISCOUNTS *P&R '59*

(Vicounts)

Singles: 7-inch

AMY 5-10 65-66
CORAL 4-8 66-67
MADISON 10-15 59-61
MR. PEACOCK 8-12 61
MR. PEEKE 5-10 63
REO (8435 "Harlem Nocturne") 10-15 59
(Canadian.)

LPs: 10/12-inch

AMY (8008 "Harlem Nocturne") 20-30 65
MADISON (1001 "Viscounts") 50-100 60
Members: Bobby Spievak; Joe Spievak; Harry Haller; Larry Vecchio; Clark Smith; Mike De Stefano.

VISCOUNTS

Singles: 7-inch

A&R 5-10 64

VISION OF SUNSHINE

LPs: 10/12-inch

AVCO EMBASSY 8-10 70

VISIONS

Singles: 7-inch

WARWICK (108 "Darling Dear") 30-50 59

VISIONS

Singles: 7-inch

R&R (3002 "It's You I Love") 800-1200 60

VISIONS

Singles: 7-inch

BIG TOP (3092 "Tell Me You're Mine") 15-25 61
BIG TOP (3119 "Secret World of Tears") 15-25 62
BRUNSWICK (55206 "There'll Be No Next Time") 15-25 61
COED (598 "Tell Her Now") 10-15 64
CORAL (65575 "Vision of Love") ...10-15 63
ELGEY (1003 "Teenager's Life") 50-75 60
LOST NITE (102 "Teenager's Life") 20-30 61
MERCURY (72188 "Oh Boy What a Girl") 10-15 63
ORIGINAL SOUND (32 "Look at Me Now") 10-15 63

VISIONS

Singles: 7-inch

VIMCO (20 "Take Her") 20-40 65
VIMCO (20 "Route 66") 30-50 65
(Same number used twice.)
VIMCO (21 "Humpty Dumpty") 30-50 66

VISIONS

Singles: 7-inch

UNI 5-10 67
W.B. 5-10 67

VISIONS OF NEW 'OUR

Singles: 7-inch

CAPITOL 5-10 69

VISITORS
Singles: 7-inch
TOWER.......................................8-10 66
Session: Davie Allan.
Also see ALLAN, Davie

VISITORS
Singles: 7-inch
DAKAR.......................................4-8 68
TANGERINE.......................................4-6 69

VISITORS
LPs: 10/12-inch
COBBLESTONE.......................................8-12 72
MONTAGE.......................................5-10 81
MUSE.......................................5-10 76
Members: Earl Grubbs; Carl Grubbs.

VISITORS
Singles: 7-inch
BASHIE.......................................8-12

VISTAS
Singles: 7-inch
REBEL (77755 "Ghost Wave").......15-25 63
VENPRO (1000 "Ghost Wave").....25-35 63
(First issue.)

VISTAS
Singles: 7-inch
TUFF (990 "No Return")..................15-25 64

VISUAL R&B/D&D '83
Singles: 12-inch
PRELUDE.......................................4-6 83-84
Singles: 7-inch
PRELUDE.......................................3-4 83-84

VISUALS
Singles: 7-inch
JASON SCOTT.......................................5-10
POPLAR (115 "Maybe You")..........30-50 62
POPLAR (117 "My Juanita")..........30-50 63
POPLAR (121 "Please Don't Be Mad at Me")..........250-350 63

VITALE, Don
Singles: 7-inch
CONQUEST.......................................4-8 62

VITALE, Jo Jo
Singles: 7-inch
MAY.......................................5-10 62

VITALE, Joe LP '81
Singles: 7-inch
ASYLUM.......................................3-5 81-82
ATLANTIC.......................................3-5 74
LPs: 10/12-inch
ASYLUM.......................................5-10 81
ATLANTIC.......................................5-10 74
Also see EAGLES
Also see WALSH, Joe

VITA-MEN
Singles: 7-inch
CHALLENGE.......................................4-8 66

VITAMIN A
Singles: 12-inch
CHESS.......................................4-8

VITAMIN E R&B '77
Singles: 7-inch
BUDDAH.......................................3-5 77

VITAMIN Z P&R/D&D/LP '85
Singles: 12-inch
GEFFEN.......................................4-6 85
Singles: 7-inch
GEFFEN.......................................3-4 85
Picture Sleeves
GEFFEN.......................................3-4 85
LPs: 10/12-inch
GEFFEN.......................................5-8 85
Member: Geoff Barradale.
Also see PARSONS, Alan, Project

VITAMINS
Singles: 7-inch
CAMERICA.......................................4-6

VITELLS
Singles: 7-inch
DECCA (31362 "Shirley")..............20-30 62

VITO: see PICONE, Vito

VITO, Gene
(With the Playboys)
Singles: 7-inch
BLAST.......................................5-10 64
DECCA.......................................4-6 67

VITO, Sonny
Singles: 7-inch
ABC-PAR.......................................5-10 58
CHANCELLOR.......................................8-12 62
STRAND.......................................5-10 61

VITO & HANDS
Singles: 7-inch
LIVING LEGEND.......................................5-8

VITO & SALUTATIONS P&R '63
Singles: 7-inch
APT (25079 "Walkin' ")..............25-35 65
BOOM (60020 "Bring Back Yesterday")..............15-25 66
CRYSTAL BALL.......................................4-8 78
HERALD (583 "Unchained Melody")..............15-25 63
HERALD (586 "Extraordinary Girl")..............20-30 63
KRAM (1202 "Your Way")............50-100 62
(First issue. Reissue label is "Kran.")
KRAN (125 "Your Way")..............25-30 62
(At least one source shows this number as 5002.)
RAYNA (5009 "Gloria")..............25-40 62
RED BOY (1001 "So Wonderful")..15-25 66
RED BOY (5009 "Gloria")..............15-25 66
REGINA (1320 "Get a Job")..........15-25 64
RUST (5106 "Can I Depend on You")..............15-25 66
SANDBAG (103 "So Wonderful")...10-20 68
STOOP SOUNDS (103 "Be My Girlfriend")..............100-150 96
(Limited edition. Estimates range from less than 10 to a few dozen made.)
WELLS (1008 "Can I Depend on You")..............20-40 64
(Black vinyl.)
WELLS (1008 "Can I Depend on You")..............40-60 64
(Colored vinyl.)
LPs: 10/12-inch
KAPE (1002 "Greatest Hits")..........10-15 73
RED BOY (200/201 "Greatest Hits")..............20-30 81
(Two-disc set, each with a different number.)
ROYAL-T (404 "Unchained Memories")..............10-15 89
Members: Vito Balsamo; Shelly Buchansky; Randy Silverman; Len Citrin; Frank Fox.
Also see KELLOGS
Also see MAGIC TOUCH
Also see POSSESSIONS
Also see SOUL POTION

VITRONES
Singles: 7-inch
AUDITION (6104 "London Fog")....10-20 65

VIVABEAT
Singles: 7-inch
CHARISMA.......................................3-5 80
LPs: 10/12-inch
CHARISMA.......................................5-10 80

VIVIENNE
Singles: 7-inch
VIP (1003 "Light a Candle")..........10-20 60s

VIXEN
LPs: 10/12-inch
AZRA (64 "Made in Hawaii")..........20-25 82
(Picture disc. Issued in boxed set with photo and bio. 150 made.)

VIXEN P&R/LP '88
Singles: 7-inch
EMI.......................................3-4 88-90
Picture Sleeves
EMI.......................................3-4 88-89
LPs: 10/12-inch
EMI.......................................5-8 88-90
Members: Janet Gardner; Share Pedersen; Jan Kuehnemund; Roxy Petrucci.

VOCAL LORDS
Singles: 7-inch
ABLE ("At Seventeen")..............100-150 59
(First issue. No selection number used.)
TAURAS (2968 "At Seventeen")..75-125 59
(Identification number shown since no selection number is used.)

VOCAL TONES
Singles: 7-inch
JUANITA (100 "Walkin' with My Baby")..............50-80 58
Members: Roland Martinez; Bobby Moore; Bobby Robinson; Irving Lee Gail.
Also see PRETENDERS
Also see VOCALTONES

VOCALAIRES
Singles: 7-inch
HERALD (573 "Dance Dance")......20-30 62
Member: Eric Nathanson.
Also see BLUE SONNETTS
Also see REYNOLDS, Ricky

VOCALAIRES / Actuals
Singles: 7-inch
RONNIE.......................................3-5 76
Also see DUBS / Actuals

VOCALEERS R&B '53
("Vocaleers and Joe Duncan"; "with Rhythm Accompaniment")
Singles: 78 rpm
RED ROBIN..............25-75 52
Singles: 7-inch
OLD TOWN (1089 "This Is the Night")..............15-25 60
OLDIES 45.......................................4-6 65
PARADISE (113 "Have You Ever Loved Someone")..............50-75 59
RED ROBIN (113 "Be True").....300-400 52
RED ROBIN (114 "Is It a Dream")..............200-300 52
RED ROBIN (119 "I Walk Alone")..............300-400 53
RED ROBIN (125 "Will You Be True")..............300-400 54
RED ROBIN (132 "Angel Face")..............300-400 54
TWISTIME (11 "A Golden Tear")....15-25 62
VEST (832 "Hear My Plea")......150-225 60
LPs: 10/12-inch
RELIC (5084 "Is It a Dream")..........5-10 92
Members: Joe Duncan; Curtis Dunham; Ted Williams; Mel Walton; Bill Walker; Lamarr Cooper; Joe Powell; Richard Blandon; Leo Fuller; Curtis Blandon; Caesar Williams.
Also see BLENDERS
Also see LITTLE ESTHER & Junior with the Johnny Otis Orchestra / Johnny Otis Orchestra with the Vocaleers

VOCALEERS / Mango Jones
Singles: 7-inch
OLDIES 45.......................................4-6 65
Also see VOCALEERS

VOCALS
Singles: 7-inch
TANGERINE.......................................4-8 64

VOCAL-TEENS
Singles: 7-inch
DOWNSTAIRS.......................................4-8 73

VOCALTONES
APOLLO.......................................20-30 56
Singles: 7-inch
APOLLO (488 "My Girl")..............50-100 56
APOLLO (492 "Darling")..............75-100 56
APOLLO (497 "My Version of Love")..............75-100 56
CINDY (3004 "Walkin' My Baby")..30-40 57
Members: Roland Martinez; Eddie Quintones; Wynn Porter; Tom Grate; Bobby Robinson.
Also see VOCAL TONES
Also see 5 WINGS

VO-DE-O-DOES
Singles: 7-inch
CLASS.......................................4-8 67

VOGGUE
Singles: 12-inch
RED ROCK.......................................4-8 81
Singles: 7-inch
ATLANTIC.......................................3-4 82
LPs: 10/12-inch
ATLANTIC.......................................5-8 82

VOGT, Les
Singles: 7-inch
APT (25042 "Moon Rocketin' ")......15-25 60
IONA (1001 "Moon Rockin' ")......35-50 60

VOGUES
Singles: 7-inch
SURF.......................................10-15 58

VOGUES P&R '65
Singles: 7-inch
ABC.......................................3-5 73
ABC-PAR.......................................4-8 65
ASTRA (1029 "You're the One").........4-6 73
(Black vinyl.)
ASTRA (1029 "You're the One").........5-8 73
(Colored vinyl.)
ASTRA (1030 "Five O'Clock World")..............4-6 73
BELL.......................................4-6 71
BLUE STAR (229 "You're the One")..............15-25 65
CASCADE (5908 "Ev'ry Day, Ev'ry Night")..............15-25 59
CO & CE.......................................5-10 65-67
COLLECTABLES.......................................3-4 80s
DOT (15798 "Love Is a Funny Little Game")..............15-25 58
DOT (15859 "Try Baby Try")..........15-25 58
ERA.......................................3-5 70s
GOLDIES 45.......................................3-5 73
GUSTO.......................................3-4 81
MGM.......................................4-8 67
MAINSTREAM.......................................3-5 72
REPRISE (Except 0663)..............3-6 68-71
REPRISE (0663 "Just What I've Been Looking For")..............5-10 68
REVUE.......................................4-8 68
ROCK'N MANIA.......................................3-4
SSS INT'L.......................................3-4 77
SUN.......................................3-5 77-79
20TH FOX.......................................3-5 73-74
LPs: 10/12-inch
CSP.......................................5-8 82
CO & CE.......................................25-35 65-66
51 WEST.......................................5-10 80s
PICKWICK.......................................8-10 71
PLANTATION (43 "Golden Hits").........5-8 81
REPRISE.......................................10-15 68-70
RHINO.......................................5-8 88
SSS INT'L (34 "Greatest Hits")..........5-10 77
SEARS.......................................15-20 60s
Members: Bob Bush; Bill Burkette; Hugh Geyer; Chuck Blasko; Don Miller. SSS Int'l/Plantation/51 West/CSP line-up: Charly Tichenor; Dick Stevens; Kelly Goad; Bill Packard; Bill Davidson.
Also see ATLANTA
Also see VAL-AIRES

VOGUES
Singles: 7-inch
KEY.......................................4-8

VOICE
LPs: 10/12-inch
MCA.......................................5-10 82

VOICE BOX
Singles: 7-inch
LOMA.......................................4-8 68

VOICE in FASHION
Singles: 7-inch
ATLANTIC.......................................3-4 87

VOICE MASTERS R&B '70
Singles: 7-inch
ANNA (101 "Hope and Pray")......50-100 59
ANNA (102 "Needed")..............50-100 59
BAMBOO.......................................8-15 68-70
FRISCO (15235 "In Love in Vain")..............75-125 60
(Identification number shown since no selection number is used.)
Members: Ty Hunter; C.P. Spencer; Lamont Dozier; David Ruffin; Freddie Gorman.
Also see DOZIER, Lamont
Also see HUNTER, Ty
Also see ORIGINALS
Also see RUFFIN, David

VOICES
Singles: 78 rpm
CASH (1011 "Why")..............15-25 55
Singles: 7-inch
CASH (1011 "Why")..............50-75 55
Members: Earl Nelson; Bobby Byrd; Ernie Freeman.
Also see BYRD, Bobby
Also see FREEMAN, Ernie
Also see NELSON, Earl

VOICES FIVE: see Budd Johnson

VOICES OF AMERICA / U.S.A. for Africa P&R '86
Singles: 7-inch
EMI AMERICA.......................................3-4 86
Picture Sleeves
EMI AMERICA.......................................3-4 86
Also see TOTO
Also see U.S.A. for AFRICA

VOICES OF EAST HARLEM LP '70
Singles: 7-inch
ELEKTRA.......................................3-5 70-72
JUST SUNSHINE.......................................3-5 73-74
LPs: 10/12-inch
ELEKTRA.......................................8-10 70
JUST SUNSHINE.......................................5-10 73-74

VOIDS
Singles: 7-inch
MARLU.......................................4-8 67

VOIGHT, Wes
(Chip Taylor)
Singles: 7-inch
DELUXE (6176 "Midnight Blues")..............50-100 58
DELUXE (6180 "Little Joan").........25-35 58
KING (5211 "I'm Movin' In")..........40-60 59
(Monaural.)
KING (S-5211 "I'm Movin' In") ...100-150 59
(Stereo.)
KING (5231 "I'm Ready to Go Steady")..............25-35 59
(Monaural.)
KING (S-5231 "I'm Ready to Go Steady")..............50-80 59
(Stereo.)
Also see TOWN THREE

VOIT, Johnny
Singles: 7-inch
OXBORO.......................................4-8 60s

VOIVOD LP '89
EPs: 12-inch
COMBAT (8124 "Thrashing Rage")..............15-20
(Picture disc.)
LPs: 10/12-inch
MECHANIC.......................................5-8 89
("Too Scared to Scream")..............15-25 89
(Picture disc. No label name or selection number used.)

VOLCANICS
Singles: 7-inch
PARKWAY.......................................5-10 67

VOLCANOES
Singles: 7-inch
EPIC (9490 "Shotgun")..............10-15 62

VOLCANOS
Singles: 7-inch
TAILSPIN.......................................10-15 60

VOLCANOS R&B '65
Singles: 7-inch
ARCTIC.......................................4-8 65-67
VIRTUE.......................................3-5 70
Member: Gene Faith.
Also see FAITH, Gene
Also see MFSB

VOLCHORDS
Singles: 7-inch
REGATTA.......................................10-15 61

VOLK, Val
Singles: 7-inch
ROCKET (1050 "A Rockin Party Tonight")..............100-200 59
Also see VOLK BROTHERS

VOLK BROTHERS
Singles: 7-inch
CLOVER (1003 "Ducks Flying Backward")..............15-25 60
(No artist credit shown on label.)
Member: Val Volk.
Also see VOLK, Val

VOLKSWAGONS
Singles: 7-inch
DO-RE-MI (201 "The Astronaut")...10-15 60s

VOLLENWEIDER, Andreas LP '84
Singles: 12-inch
CBS/COLUMBIA.......................................4-6 86
Singles: 7-inch
CBS/COLUMBIA.......................................3-4 86
LPs: 10/12-inch
CBS/COLUMBIA.......................................5-8 84-89

VOLPE, Al
Singles: 7-inch
DI VENUS.......................................4-8 66-68
DOMINO.......................................3-6 69

VOLTAGE BROTHERS R&B '86
Singles: 12-inch
MTM.......................................4-6 86
Singles: 7-inch
LIFESONG.......................................3-4 78
MTM.......................................3-4 86
LPs: 10/12-inch
LIFESONG.......................................5-8 78
MTM.......................................5-8 86

VOLTAIRES
Singles: 7-inch
BACONE (9468 "My My Baby").....50-75

VOLUMATIX
LPs: 10/12-inch
REPUBLIC.......................................5-8 83

VOLUMES
Singles: 78 rpm
JAGUAR.......................................50-100 54
Singles: 7-inch
JAGUAR (3004 "I Won't Tell a Soul")..............200-250 54
KAREN.......................................10-20
Also see WATKINS, Lacille, & Volumes

VOLUMES P&R '62
Singles: 7-inch
ABC.......................................3-5 73
AMERICAN ARTS (6 "Gotta Give Her Love")..............20-30 64
AMERICAN ARTS (18 "I Just Can't Help Myself")..............20-30 65
ASTRA (1020 "Gotta Give Her Love")..............8-12 65
CHEX (1002 "I Love You")............25-50 62
(First issued crediting the "Valume's.")
CHEX (1005 "The Bell")..............25-50 62
IMPACT (1017 "That Same Old Feeling")..............25-50 66
INFERNO.......................................10-20 67-68
JUBILEE (5446 "Sandra")..............20-30 63
JUBILEE (5454 "Our Song")..............15-25 63
OLD TOWN (1154 "Why")..............10-20 64
TWIRL (2016 "I Got Love")..............25-50 61
VIRGO.......................................3-5 73
LPs: 10/12-inch
RELIC.......................................5-10 85
Also see NUTMEGS / Volumes
Also see VALUMES

VOLUNTEERS
Singles: 7-inch
ARISTA.......................................3-5 77
LPs: 10/12-inch
ARISTA.......................................5-10 77

VOLZ, Ron, & Rockin' R's
Singles: 7-inch
TEMPUS (1515 "I'm Still in Love with You")..............75-125 59
Also see ROCKIN' R's

VON, Bobby
Singles: 7-inch
GATEWAY.......................................4-8 63

VON, Gary
Singles: 7-inch
DOT.......................................4-8 65
LTD.......................................4-8 66
RE-VON.......................................4-8 64

VON, Tawny
Singles: 7-inch
ENTRE.......................................4-8 66

VON, Vicki Rae C&W '87
Singles: 7-inch
ATLANTIC AMERICA.......................................3-4 87

VON & VOYAGERS
Singles: 7-inch
FLAME (7301 "Shortest Way to Wealth")..............10-20 60s

VONASTICS
Singles: 7-inch
MOON SHOT (6702 "When My Baby Comes Back Home")..............15-20
SATELLITE.......................................5-10
TODDLIN' TOWN.......................................5-10
Members: Bobby Newsome; Jose Holmes; Kenneth Golar; Raymond Penn.

VON CARL, Jimmy
(With the June Voices, Sax Kari & Orchestra)
Singles: 7-inch
FLICK (002 "Lonely Night")............40-60 59
Also see KARI, Sax

VON GAYELS
Singles: 7-inch
DORE (544 "The Twirl")..............15-25 60
U.S.A. (1221 "Loneliness")............35-50 64
Members: Joe Brackenridge; Stacy Steel Jr.; Jimmy Washington; Willie C. Robinson; Charles Johnson.
Also see CASCADES

VON ILG, Gary
Singles: 7-inch
CAPITOL.......................................4-8 59

VONNAIR SISTERS
Singles: 7-inch
BUENA VISTA.......................................4-8 61-63

VONNS
Singles: 7-inch
KING.......................................10-15 63

VON RUDEN
(Rudy Von Ruden)
Singles: 7-inch
IVANHOE (101 "Spider & the Fly") 10-20 70
IVANHOE (503 "Spider & the Fly") 10-20 70
Also see JOHNNY & SHY GUYS

VONDELLS
Singles: 7-inch
AIRTOWN 8-12
MARVELLO (5006 "Leonora") 50-70

VONDORS
Singles: 7-inch
HOLIDAY 8-12

VONN, Gary
Singles: 7-inch
ELF (90029 "Love You Baby") 10-20

VON RYAN'S EXPRESS
LPs: 10/12-inch
MGM 8-10 71

VON SCHMIDT, Eric
Singles: 7-inch
SMASH 4-6 69
LPs: 10/12-inch
PHILO 5-10 78
POPPY 8-12 72
PRESTIGE 10-15 69
SMASH 10-15 69

VONTASTICS P&R/R&B '66
Singles: 7-inch
CHESS 4-8 67
ST. LAWRENCE 4-8 65-66
SATELLITE (2002 "I'll Never Say Goodbye") 25-35 65
Also see FANTASTIC VONTASTICS

VOO DOO MEN
Singles: 7-inch
SOMA (1407 "MoJo Workin") 25-50 60s
Also see BUFORD, Mojo

VOODOO DOLLS / Johnny & Jumper Cables / World of Distortion / Ladds from Bellevue
EPs: 7-inch
DIONYSUS 3-5 91
(With paper sleeve. Colored vinyl.)

VOTE, Vicki
Singles: 7-inch
IMPERIAL 4-8 69

VOUDOURIS, Roger P&R/LP '79
Singles: 7-inch
W.B. 3-5 78-79
LPs: 10/12-inch
W.B. 5-10 78

VOWELS
Singles: 7-inch
LEBAM (156 "It's Alright") 20-30 60s
LEBAM (157 "Your Lovin' Kisses") 15-25 60s
Session: Andy Belvin.
Also see BELVIN, Andy

VOWS
Singles: 7-inch
BIG 3 (400 "When a Boy Loves a Girl") 15-25 60s
MARKAY (103 "I Wanna a Chance") 250-350 62
(Black label.)
MARKAY (103 "I Wanna Chance") 30-50 62
(Orange label. Note slight title change.)
RAN-DEE (112 "Girl in Red") 50-75 60s
STA-SET (402 "When a Boy Loves a Girl") 25-50 64
TAMARA (760 "Dottie") 20-30 64
V.I.P. (25016 "Buttered Popcorn") 15-25 65

VOXMEN
Singles: 7-inch
VM (8438 "Good Things") 50-75 67

VOXPOPPERS P&R/R&B '58
Singles: 7-inch
AMP 3 (1004 "Wishing for Your Love") 30-40 58
MERCURY (71282 "Wishing for Your Love") 10-20 58
MERCURY (71315 "Pony Tail") 10-15 58
POPLAR (107 "Come Back Little Girl") 15-25 58
POPLAR (112 "Come Back Little Girl") 15-25 58
(Each of the Poplar discs has a different flip.)
VERSAILLES (200 "A Blessing After All") 20-40 59
EPs: 7-inch
MERCURY (3391 "Voxpoppers") .75-125 58

VOYAGE R&B/LP '78
Singles: 7-inch
ATLANTIC 3-5 82
MARLIN 3-5 78-79
LPs: 10/12-inch
ATLANTIC 5-8 82
MARLIN 5-10 78

VOYAGER
Singles: 7-inch
ELEKTRA 3-5 79
LPs: 10/12-inch
ELEKTRA 5-10 79
RCA 5-10 80

VOYAGERS
Singles: 7-inch
ENSIGN 5-10 61

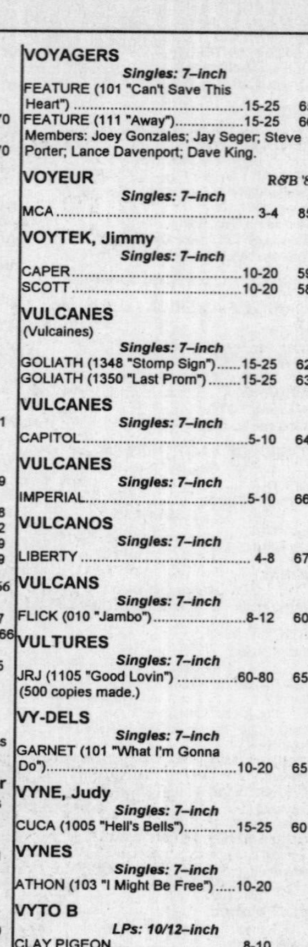

VOYAGERS
Singles: 7-inch
FEATURE (101 "Can't Save This Heart") 15-25 65
FEATURE (111 "Away") 15-25 66
Members: Joey Gonzales; Jay Seger; Steve Porter; Lance Davenport; Dave King.

VOYEUR R&B '85
Singles: 7-inch
MCA 3-4 85

VOYTEK, Jimmy
Singles: 7-inch
CAPER 10-20 59
SCOTT 10-20 58

VULCANES
(Vulcaines)
Singles: 7-inch
GOLIATH (1348 "Stomp Sign") 15-25 62
GOLIATH (1350 "Last Prom") 15-25 63

VULCANES
Singles: 7-inch
CAPITOL 5-10 64

VULCANES
Singles: 7-inch
IMPERIAL 5-10 66

VULCANOS
Singles: 7-inch
LIBERTY 4-8 67

VULCANS
Singles: 7-inch
FLICK (010 "Jambo") 8-12 60

VULTURES
Singles: 7-inch
JRJ (1105 "Good Lovin") 60-80 65
(500 copies made.)

VY-DELS
Singles: 7-inch
GARNET (101 "What I'm Gonna Do") 10-20 65

VYNE, Judy
Singles: 7-inch
CUCA (1005 "Hell's Bells") 15-25 60

VYNES
Singles: 7-inch
ATHON (103 "I Might Be Free") 10-20

VYTO B
LPs: 10/12-inch
CLAY PIGEON 8-10

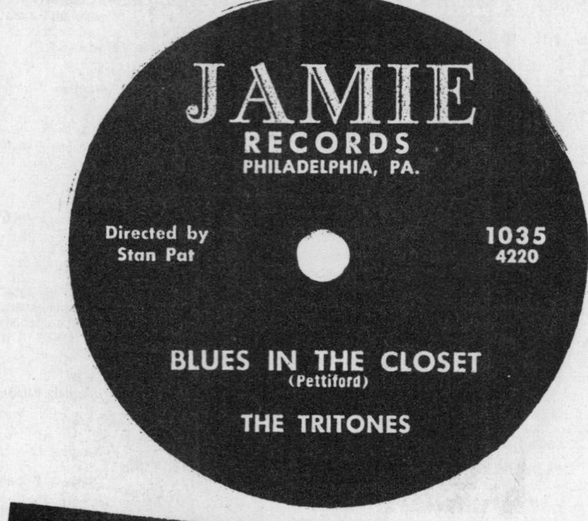

JAMIE
RECORDS
PHILADELPHIA, PA.
Directed by
Stan Pat
1035
4220
BLUES IN THE CLOSET
(Pettiford)
THE TRITONES

jubilee
Record No.
45 - 5136
45 R.P.M.
(45 - JB - 1 - 266)
Vocal
(I Love To Play Your Piano)
LET ME BANG YOUR BOX
(T. McCrae - S. Wyche)
THE TOPPERS
with Orchestra

.38 SPECIAL
WILD-EYED SOUTHERN BOYS
FANTASY GIRL

JESSE LEE TURNER
THAT'S MY GIRL s/w TEENAGE MISERY

TAZ
KEITH MUSIC
ASCAP
TIMING-2:03
GUITAR SOLO
BY
JOE RUMORO
GREEN LIGHT
(Rumoro)
THE TAZMEN
T - 1003 B
ZTSC-9394
TAZ RECORDING CORP. 222 W. NORTH AVE. CHICAGO 10, ILLINOIS

TIN PAN ALLEY
45 RPM
Records
Mfg. By
TIN PAN ALLEY,INC.,
1650 Broadway,N.Y.C.
Trademark Reg.
U.S. Pat. Off.
RECORD NO.
TPA-130
(B M I)
Juke Box Alley
Time: 2:35
LOVE IS EVERYTHING
(Grimm-Covais)
Featuring Billboard's 1954
disc-Jockey poll winner
CARMEN TAYLOR
AND ORCHESTRA

RCA VICTOR
45 RPM
47-4460
(E1VW-4638)
T. V. BOOGIE BLUES
(John Ferrell)
TNT Tribble
with Frank Motley
and his Crew
RCA VICTOR DIVISION, RADIO CORPORATION OF AMERICA, CAMDEN N.J. MADE IN U.S.A.

OKeh
RHYTHM and BLUES
45 RPM
4-6822
COME ON DADDY (Let's Go Play Tonight)
PEARL TRAYLOR

KAYDEE
RECORDS
66 W. 139th St., N.Y.C. - Phone WA 6-4841
Progressive
Music - BMI
Time 2:17
45 R.P.M.
K-3001
"MARY ANN"
(Ray Charles)
TEXAS-RAY

dooto
RECORDS
Ballad
45—443-A
Dootsie Williams,
Inc.
YOU CAME ALONG
(Green & Marshall)
VERNON & CLIFF

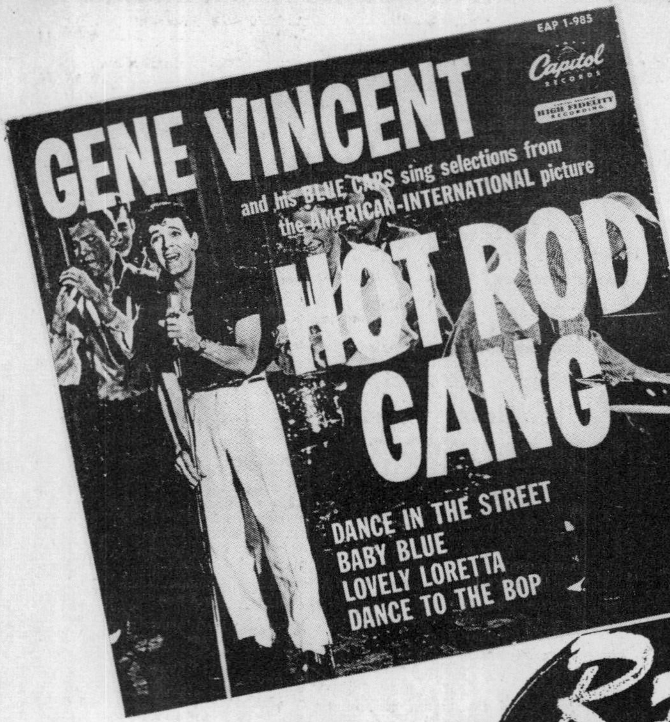

EAP 1-985
Capitol Records
HIGH FIDELITY RECORDING

GENE VINCENT
and his BLUE CAPS sing selections from the AMERICAN-INTERNATIONAL picture
HOT ROD GANG
DANCE IN THE STREET
BABY BLUE
LOVELY LORETTA
DANCE TO THE BOP

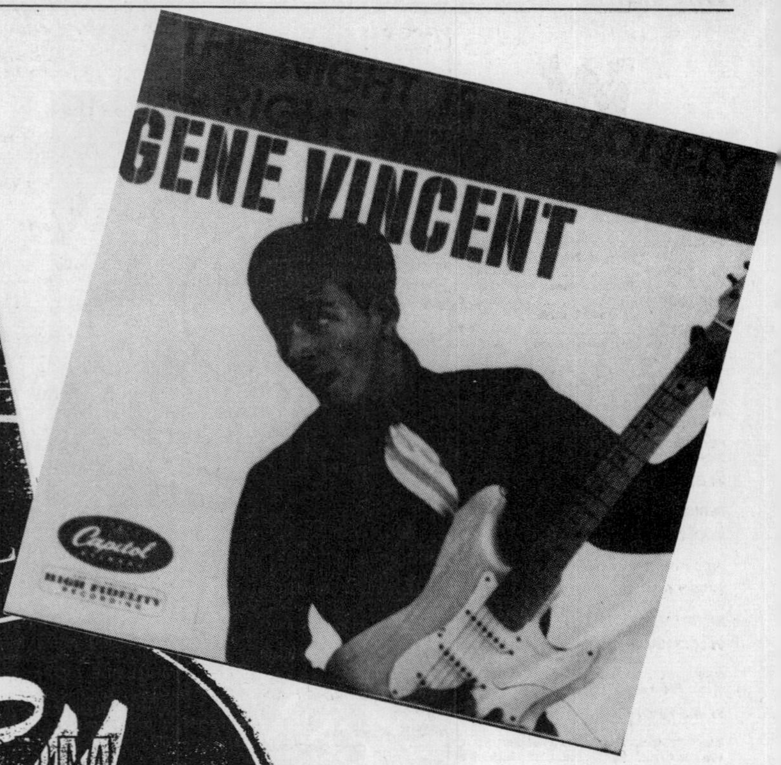

GENE VINCENT
Capitol
HIGH FIDELITY RECORDING

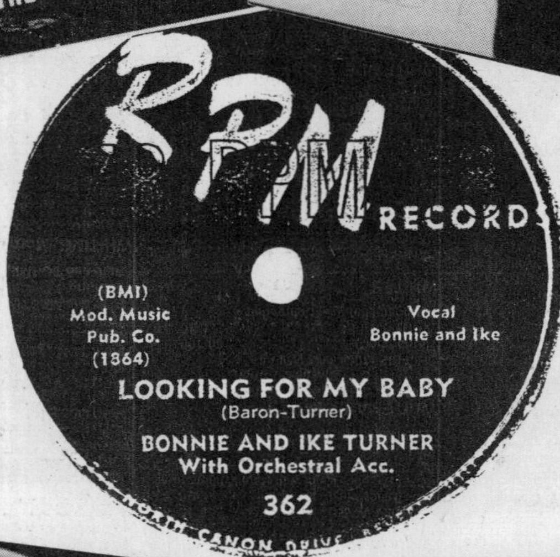

RPM RECORDS
(BMI)
Mod. Music
Pub. Co.
(1864)
Vocal
Bonnie and Ike
LOOKING FOR MY BABY
(Baron-Turner)
BONNIE AND IKE TURNER
With Orchestral Acc.
362

W

W.A.G.B. P&R '82
Singles: 7-inch
STREET SOUNDS 3-4 82

W.A.S.P. LP '84
Singles: 7-inch
CAPITOL 3-4 84-89
Picture Sleeves
CAPITOL 3-4 84-87
LPs: 10/12-inch
CAPITOL 5-8 84-89
Members: Blackie Lawless; Randy Piper; Chris Holmes; Steve Riley.
Also see L.A. GUNS
Also see NEW YORK DOLLS

W.B., Danny
Singles: 7-inch
REPRISE 4-8 66
SMASH 4-8 67

W.B., Eddie
Singles: 7-inch
BERRY 4-8 63

W.C. DORNS
Singles: 7-inch
WCD (1001 "I Need You") 8-12

WDGY RADIO
Singles: 7-inch
WONDERFUL WDGY 5-10 60s

WDSM RADIO
Singles: 7-inch
GRC 5-10 60s
(Promotional only.)

W-RIT RADIO
Singles: 7-inch
WRIT ("Birthday Message to a Harried Housewife") 10-20 60s
(Promotional issue only.)

WA WA NEE P&R/LP '87
Singles: 7-inch
EPIC 3-4 87-88
Singles: 7-inch
EPIC 3-4 87
Picture Sleeves
EPIC 3-4 87
LPs: 10/12-inch
EPIC 5-8 87

WACK CLACKERS
Singles: 7-inch
ENTERPRISE 3-5 71

WACKER, Willy
Singles: 7-inch
FEATHER (6712 "Big Texas Bird") ... 4-6

WACKERS P&R '72
Singles: 7-inch
BOMP 3-5 75
ELEKTRA 3-5 71-73
LPs: 10/12-inch
ELEKTRA 5-10 71-72
Member: Spence Earnshaw.
Also see BIG FOOT

WADDELL, Bob
Singles: 78 rpm
JOY 5-10 57
Singles: 7-inch
DECCA 5-10 58
JOY 5-10 57

WADDELL, Hugh
Singles: 7-inch
LIN 5-10 61

WADDELL, Phil
Singles: 7-inch
LUPINE (122 "Rocket Walk") 15-25 64

WADDLESWORTH
LPs: 10/12-inch
MARTIN 10-15 68

WADDY, Sandy
Singles: 7-inch
S.O.S. 5-10
WAND (1169 "Secret Love") 4-8 68

WADE, Adam P&R '60
(With George Paxton, His Orchestra and the Bel-Aire Singers)
Singles: 7-inch
COED 10-15 59-61
DALYA 4-6 70s
EPIC 5-8 62-66
KIRSHNER 3-5 77
REMEMBER 4-6 69
W.B. 4-8 67-68
Picture Sleeves
COED 10-20 60-61
EPIC 5-10 62-63
EPs: 7-inch
COED (102 "Adam Wade") 10-20 60
(Promotional issue only.)
LPs: 10/12-inch
COED 25-35 60
EPIC 15-20 62
KIRSHNER 5-10 77

WADE, Billy
(With the Third Degrees)
Singles: 7-inch
ABC 4-8 67

WADE, Bobby
Singles: 7-inch
DELUXE 4-6
WAY OUT 10-15

WADE, Don
Singles: 7-inch
SAN (206 "Gone Gone Gone") ... 150-250 58
SAN (207 "Forever Yours") 15-25 59

WADE, Earl
Singles: 7-inch
SEVILLE 5-10 61
SWAN (4008 "I Dig Rock & Roll") .. 20-30 58

WADE, Elvis
Singles: 7-inch
MEMORY (244 "Memories of the King") 4-8 77
SAHARA (301 "Memories of the King") 8-12 77
(First issue.)

WADE, Emmitt
Singles: 7-inch
EMITT WADE 4-6

WADE, J.W. R&B '83
Singles: 7-inch
LARC 3-4 83

WADE, Jake, & Soul Searchers
Singles: 7-inch
MUTT 8-12

WADE, Len
(With the Tikis)
Singles: 7-inch
MINARET (111 "My Bonnie") 5-10 64
U.A. 4-8 65-66
Also see TIKIS

WADE, Lindy
Singles: 7-inch
TENDER 10-20 58

WADE, Norman C&W '79
Singles: 7-inch
ARTIC 4-8
CMI 4-8
NSD 3-5 79
LPs: 10/12-inch
ARTIC 8-10

WADE, Roger
Singles: 7-inch
HARMON (1003 "Little Girl") 50-100 62
THELMA (42282 "Little Girl") 25-50 62

WADE, Ronny
Singles: 78 rpm
KING (5099 "Annie Don't Work") ... 30-40 57
KING (5061 "Gotta Make You Mine") 50-75 57
Singles: 7-inch
KING (5099 "Annie Don't Work") ... 30-40 57
KING (5061 "Gotta Make You Mine") 50-75 57

WADE, Tommy
Singles: 7-inch
THUNDERBOLT 5-10 59

WADE, Wilbert
Singles: 7-inch
LIBERTY 4-8 65

WADE & DICK
(With the College Kids)
Singles: 78 rpm
SUN (269 "Bop Bop Baby") 15-25 57
Singles: 7-inch
SUN (269 "Bop Bop Baby") 20-30 57

WADSWORTH MANSION P&R '70
Singles: 7-inch
SUSSEX 3-5 70
LPs: 10/12-inch
SUSSEX 10-20 71
(Mistakenly shown as "Wadsworth Manison" on some issues.)

WAGES, Ben
Singles: 7-inch
INTERNATIONAL 3-5 78

WAGGONER, Charlie
Singles: 7-inch
LINCO (503 "One Eyed Sam") 50-75 58

WAGGONER, David
LPs:10/12-inch
AMARET 8-12 72
Also see CROW

WAGGONER, Mike, & Bops
Singles: 7-inch
DOVE (1101 "Blue Days Black Nights") 50-75 60s
VEE (7002 "Basher #5") 250-275 59

WAGNER, Cliff
Singles: 7-inch
JEWEL (777 "Exception to the Rule") 10-15 67
JOLUM (105-2509 "When You're Dancin' ") 15-25 64

WAGNER, Danny, & Kindred Soul
Singles: 7-inch
IMPERIAL (66305 "I Lost a True Love") 15-25 68
IMPERIAL (66327 "Harlem Shuffle") 10-15 68
LPs: 10/12-inch
IMPERIAL (12405 "Kindred Soul of Danny Wagner") 20-30 68

WAGNER, Dick
(With the Frost)
Singles: 7-inch
DATE (1577 "Rainy Day") 8-12 68
DATE (1596 "Sunshine") 20-30 68
Picture Sleeves
DATE (1577 "Rainy Day") 10-20 68
Also see FROST
Also see JUST US GIRLS
Also see URSA MAJOR

WAGNER, Jack P&R/LP '84
Singles: 7-inch
QWEST 3-4 84-87
Picture Sleeves
QWEST 3-4 84-87
LPs: 10/12-inch
QWEST 5-8 84-87

WAGNER, John, Foundation
Singles: 7-inch
LOOK 4-6 68-69

WAGNER, Ty, & Scotchmen
Singles: 7-inch
ERA (3168 "Slander") 5-10 66
CHATTAHOOCHEE (699 "I'm a No Count") 5-10 66

WAGONEERS C&W '88
Singles: 7-inch
A&M 3-4 88-89

WAGONER, Porter C&W '54
Singles: 78 rpm
RCA 5-10 53-57
Singles: 7-inch
RCA (0013 thru 1007) 3-6 69-74
RCA (5086 thru 7638) 5-15 53-59
RCA (7708 thru 9979) 3-8 60-71
RCA (10124 thru 11998) 3-5 74-79
W.B. 3-4 82-83
EPs: 7-inch
RCA 8-15 56
LPs: 10/12-inch
ACCORD 5-8 82
CAMDEN 5-15 63-73
COUNTRY FIDELITY 5-8 82
H.S.R.D. (782 "Natural Wonder") ... 15-25 81
MCA/DOT 5-8 86
MUSIC MASTERS 5-10
PICKWICK 5-10 75-77
RCA (Except 1300 through 2900 series) 5-15 66-79
RCA (1358 "A Satisfied Mind") 30-40 56
RCA (LPM-2447 thru LPM-2960) ... 10-20 62-65
(Monaural.)
RCA (LSP-2447 thru LSP-2960) 15-25 62-65
(Stereo.)
TUDOR 5-8 84
W.B. 5-8 83
Also see HUNLEY, Con
Also see NORMA JEAN
Also see SNOW, Hank / Hank Locklin / Porter Wagoner

WAGONER, Porter, & Skeeter Davis
LPs: 10/12-inch
RCA 10-20 62
Also see DAVIS, Skeeter

WAGONER, Porter, & Dolly Parton C&W '67
Singles: 7-inch
RCA 3-6 67-80
LPs: 10/12-inch
RCA (Except 3926 thru 4841) 5-10 74-80
RCA (LPM-3926 "Just Between You and Me") 30-40 68
(Monaural.)
RCA (LSP-3926 thru LSP-4841) ... 10-20 68-73
(Stereo.)
Also see PARTON, Dolly
Also see WAGONER, Porter

WAHLS, Shirley
(With Spouse)
Singles: 7-inch
BLUE ROCK 4-8 68
KING 4-8 67
SMASH 4-6 69

WAIKIKIS P&R '64
Singles: 7-inch
KAPP 3-6 64-68
PALETTE 3-6 62-63
LPs: 10/12-inch
BOOT 5-8 78
KAPP 8-15 64-69
MCA 5-8 80s

WAILERS
Singles: 78 rpm
COLUMBIA (40288 "Hot Love") 25-35 54
PARADISE (102 "Guitar Shuffle") 10-15 55
Singles: 7-inch
COLUMBIA (40288 "Hot Love") ... 75-100 54
PARADISE (102 "Guitar Shuffle") 20-25 55

WAILERS P&R/R&B '59
Singles: 7-inch
BELL 4-8 67
ETIQUETTE 5-15 63-66
GOLDEN CREST 10-20 59
(Label pictures the group.)
GOLDEN CREST 5-10 60-64
(No group picture on label.)
IMPERIAL 5-10 64
U.A. 4-8 67
VIVA 4-6 67
LPs: 10/12-inch
BELL (6016 "Walk Thru the People") 10-15 68
ETIQUETTE (1 "The Fabulous Wailers at the Castle") 75-100 66
ETIQUETTE (022 "The Wailers and Company") 40-60 66
ETIQUETTE (023 "Wailers Wailers Everywhere") 75-100 66
ETIQUETTE (026 "Out of Our Tree") 40-60 60s
(Reissues of Etiquette LPs have a 1980s date on back cover.)
ETIQUETTE (1100 series) 5-8 86
ETIQUETTE (22296/97 "The Wailers and Their Greatest Hits") 10-20 79
(Two discs. Includes a note from Etiquette's
GOLDEN CREST (3075 "The Fabulous Wailers") 100-150 60
(Color cover photo.)
GOLDEN CREST (3075 "The Fabulous Wailers") 40-60 60
(Black and white cover.)
GOLDEN CREST (3075 "The Wailers Wail") 25-35 60s
IMPERIAL 15-20 64
U.A. (3557 "Outburst!") 25-35 67
(Monaural.)
U.A. (6557 "Outburst!") 35-45 67
(Stereo.)
Members: Kent Morrill; Robin Roberts; Gail Harris; Mark Marush; Rich Dangel; John "Buck" Ormsby; Mike Burk; Neil Anderson; Ron Gardner; Dave Roland.
Also see BREAKERS
Also see MORRILL, Kent
Also see SONICS / Wailers
Also see SONICS / Wailers / Galaxies
Also see THREE GRACES / Wailers

WAILING BETHEA & CAP-TANS
Singles: 7-inch
HAWKEYE 4-8 62
Also see BETHEA & CAP-TANS

WAINER, Cherry
Singles: 7-inch
PARIS (533 "Iced Coffee") 15-25 59

WAINWRIGHT, Loudon, III P&R/LP '73
Singles: 7-inch
ARISTA 3-5 76-78
COLUMBIA 3-5 73
LPs: 10/12-inch
ARISTA 5-10 76-78
ATLANTIC 10-15 70-71
COLUMBIA ("KC" series) 10-15 72-73
COLUMBIA ("PC" series) 5-10 75
ROUNDER 5-10 80-83
Also see SPRINGSTEEN, Bruce / Albert Hammond / Loudon Wainwright, III / Taj Mahal

WAITE, John LP '82
Singles: 12-inch
EMI AMERICA 4-6 84
Singles: 7-inch
CHRYSALIS 3-4 82-85
EMI AMERICA 3-4 84-87
Picture Sleeves
CHRYSALIS 3-4 85
EMI AMERICA 3-5 84-87
LPs: 10/12-inch
CHRYSALIS 5-8 82
EMI AMERICA 5-8 84-87
Also see BABYS

WAITRESSES P&R/LP '82
Singles: 7-inch
ANTILLES 3-5 80
POLYDOR 3-4 82
LPs: 10/12-inch
POLYDOR 5-8 82-83

WAITS, Tom LP '75
Singles: 7-inch
ASYLUM 3-5 74
ELEKTRA 3-4 83
ISLAND 3-4 83-88
LPs: 10/12-inch
ASYLUM 5-10 73-80
ELEKTRA 5-8 83
ISLAND 5-8 83-88
Also see GAYLE, Crystal, & Tom Waits

WAKEFIELD SUN
Singles: 7-inch
MGM (14028 "Get Out") 10-15 69
MGM (14072 "Trypt on Love") 15-25 69
LPs: 10/12-inch
MGM (4625 "Wakefield Sun") 20-30 69

WAKELY, Jimmy P&R '43/C&W '44
(With Les Baxter Chorus; with Velma Williams)
Singles: 78 rpm
CAPITOL 3-6 48-52
CORAL 3-6 53-55
DECCA 4-8 43-57
JIMMY WAKELY SOUVENIR 5-10 50s
Singles: 7-inch
ARTCO 3-5 74
CAPITOL (1300 thru 2100 series) ... 5-10 50-52
CORAL 4-8 53-55
DECCA 3-8 55-70
DOT 3-6 66
SHASTA (100 series) 3-6 58-67
SHASTA (200 series) 3-4 71
Picture Sleeves
SHASTA 5-10 58
EPs: 7-inch
CAPITOL 10-20 50-53
CORAL 10-15 54
DECCA 8-12 58
LPs: 10/12-inch
ALBUM GLOBE 5-10 81
CAPITOL (4008 "Songs of the West") 25-50 50
(10-inch LP.)
CAPITOL (9004 "Christmas on the Range") 20-40 53
(10-inch LP.)
CORAL 4-8 73
DANNY 8-10
DECCA (8400 thru 8600 series) 20-35 56-57
DECCA (75000 thru 78000 series) ... 8-18 67-70
DOT 10-15 66
MCA 4-8 80s
MCR 10-15 74
SHASTA 5-15 58-75
TOPS 10-15
VOCALION 5-10 68-70
Also see CHANDLER, Karen, & Jimmy Wakely
Also see WHITING, Margaret, & Jimmy Wakely

WAKELIN, Johnny, & Kinshasa Band P&R '75
Singles: 7-inch
PYE 3-5 75

WAKEMAN, Rick LP '73
(With the London Symphony Orchestra & English Chamber Choir; with English Rock Ensemble)
Singles: 7-inch
A&M 3-5 73
LPs: 10/12-inch
A&M (3000 series) 5-10 74
A&M (4000 series) 5-12 73-77
A&M (QU-5000 series) 10-20 74
(Quadraphonic.)
A&M (6000 series) 10-15 79
MFSL (230 "Journey to the Centre of the Earth") 20-25 94
Also see DALTREY, Roger, & Rick Wakeman
Also see STRAWBS
Also see YES

WALAROO
(Walaroo South)
Singles: 7-inch
SIMPLE SOLUTIONS 3-4 94
Picture Sleeves
SIMPLE SOLUTIONS 3-4 94
Members: Jonathan Drexler; Hans Drexler; Rick Pierce; Wendy Kaiser; Dan Stahl.

WALCOES
Singles: 7-inch
DRUM (011 "Tell Me Why") 200-300 59

WALDEN, Carl, & Humans
Singles: 7-inch
A&M 4-8 65
ALMO 4-8 65

WALDEN, Narada Michael R&B '77
(Narada)
Singles: 12-inch
ATLANTIC 4-6 82-83
NARADA (17254 "Narada Sampler") 5-8 86
(Promotional issue only.)
W.B. 4-6 85
Singles: 7-inch
ATLANTIC 3-5 77-83
REPRISE 3-4 88
W.B. 3-4 85
Picture Sleeves
NARADA (17254 "Narada Sampler") 5-10 86
(Promotional issue only.)
LPs: 10/12-inch
ATLANTIC 5-10 79-83

WALDEN, Narada Michael, & Patti Austin R&B '85
Singles: 7-inch
W.B. 3-4 85
Also see AUSTIN, Patti

WALDER, Charles
Singles: 7-inch
ENSIGN (4030 "Got My Eyes on the World") 50-100 58

WALDMAN, Wendy P&R '78
Singles: 7-inch
EPIC 3-4 82-83
W.B. 3-5 77-78
LPs: 10/12-inch
EPIC 5-8 82-83
W.B. 5-10 78
Also see BRYNDLE

WALDO R&B '82
Singles: 7-inch
COLUMBIA 3-5 82
LPs: 10/12-inch
COLUMBIA 5-10 82

WALDO, Dudley & Dora
Singles: 7-inch
AWFUL 5-10 59

WALDRON, Ron
Singles: 7-inch
VIBRA 5-10 61

WALDROOP, Les
Singles: 7-inch
ME TOO 3-6 72

WALE, Steve
Singles: 7-inch
LUTE 5-10 61

WALEEN, Johnny
(Johnny Wallin)
Singles: 7-inch
COULEE (102 "Mystery Train") ... 25-50 64
SOMA (102 "Road of Heartaches") ... 20-30 59
Picture Sleeves
COULEE (102 "Mystery Train") ... 40-60 64
Also see WALLIN, Johnny

WALES, Howard
LPs: 10/12-inch
COSTAL ... 10-12 76

WALES, Howard & Jerry Garcia
Singles: 7-inch
DOUGLAS ... 10-15 72
LPs: 10/12-inch
DOUGLAS (30859 "Hooteroll") ... 40-60 71
Also see GARCIA, Jerry
Also see WALES, Howard

WALKER, Anna, & Crownettes
Singles: 7-inch
AMY ... 3-6 69

WALKER, April, & Jerry Lakes
LP: 10/12-inch
DBL (3001 "All I Ever Need Is You") ... 10-15 74

WALKER, Big Moose
Singles: 7-inch
C.J. ... 10-20

WALKER, Billy — C&W '54
Singles: 78 rpm
COLUMBIA ... 4-8 54-56
Singles: 7-inch
CAPRICE ... 3-4 79-80
CASINO ... 3-5 77
COLUMBIA (21000 series) ... 6-12 54-56
COLUMBIA (33000 series) ... 4-6 60s
COLUMBIA (40000 series) ... 5-10 56-60
COLUMBIA (42000 & 43000 series) ... 4-8 61-65
DIMENSION ... 3-4 83
MCA ... 3-5 77
MGM ... 3-5 70-74
MRC ... 3-4 77-78
MONUMENT ... 3-6 66-70
PAID ... 3-4 80
RCA ... 3-5 75-76
SCORPION ... 3-4 78
TALL TEXAN ... 3-4 85-88
Picture Sleeves
COLUMBIA ... 4-8 63-67
LPs: 10/12-inch
COLUMBIA ... 10-20 63-69
FIRST GENERATION ... 5-10 81
GUSTO ... 5-8 78
H.S.R.D. ... 5-10 84
HARMONY ... 8-15 64-70
MGM ... 6-12 70-74
MONUMENT ... 8-18 66-72
RCA ... 5-10 75-76

WALKER, Billy, & Barbara Fairchild — C&W '80
Singles: 7-inch
PAID ... 3-5 81
LPs: 10/12-inch
PAID ... 5-10 81
Also see FAIRCHILD, Barbara

WALKER, Billy, & Brenda Kaye Perry — C&W '77
Singles: 7-inch
MRC ... 3-5 77
Also see PERRY, Brenda Kaye
Also see WALKER, Billy

WALKER, Bob, & Friend
Singles: 7-inch
DEE GEE ... 4-8 66
Also see WALLEY, Deborah

WALKER, Bobbi — R&B '80
Singles: 7-inch
CASABLANCA ... 3-5 80

WALKER, Boots — P&R '67
Singles: 7-inch
PROVIDENCE ... 4-6 66
RUST ... 4-8 67-68

WALKER, Bryan
Singles: 7-inch
PIPER PLATTERS ... 10-15 59

WALKER, Buddy
Singles: 7-inch
FLOP ... 5-10 61
SANDY ... 5-10 62

WALKER, Charles, & Band
(With the Daffodils)
Singles: 7-inch
CHAMPION (1014 "Slave to Love") ... 25-50 59
ENSIGN (4030 "I've Got My Eyes on the World") ... 10-20 59
HOLIDAY (2604 "Driving Home") ... 15-25 57
VEST (829 "It Ain't Right") ... 10-20 59
Member: James Spruill
Also see SPRUILL, Jimmy

WALKER, Charlie — C&W '56
Singles: 78 rpm
DECCA ... 4-8 54-56
Singles: 7-inch
CAPITOL ... 3-5 74
COLUMBIA ... 5-10 58-63
DECCA ... 5-15 54-56
EPIC ... 3-8 64-72
RCA ... 3-5 72-73
LPs: 10/12-inch
COLUMBIA ... 15-25 61
EPIC ... 8-15 65-71
HARMONY ... 10-15 67
PLANTATION ... 5-10 78-81
RCA ... 6-12 72-73
VOCALION ... 10-15 67
Also see SOME of CHET'S FRIENDS

WALKER, Cindy — C&W '44
Singles: 78 rpm
DECCA ... 4-8 42-44
COLUMBIA ... 5-10 56
Singles: 7-inch
COLUMBIA ... 8-12 56
LPs: 10/12-inch
MONUMENT ... 10-20 64

WALKER, Darrell, & Buddy Conn, with Santa Clara Valley Boys
Singles: 78 rpm
INTRA STATE ... 15-20 54

WALKER, David T. — R&B '69
Singles: 7-inch
ODE ... 3-5 73-76
REVUE ... 4-6 68-69
ZEA ... 4-6 70
LPs: 10/12-inch
ODE ... 8-10 74-76
REVUE ... 10-15 68-69

WALKER, Eddie
(With the Demons; Edie Walker)
Singles: 7-inch
KEET (1000 "Twistin' Your Life Away") ... 15-25 63
MEW (102 "I Don't Need You Anymore") ... 20-30
MEW (103 "Baby Angel") ... 20-30

WALKER, Gary
Singles: 7-inch
MGM ... 5-10 58

WALKER, Gary
Singles: 7-inch
DATE ... 5-10 66
Also see SURFARIS / Biscaynes
Also see WALKER BROTHERS

WALKER, Gene, & Combo
Singles: 7-inch
AROCK (1002 "Empire City") ... 8-12

WALKER, George, Jr.
Singles: 7-inch
CARLTON ... 4-8 61

WALKER, Gloria — P&R/R&B '68
(With the Chevelles)
Singles: 7-inch
FEDERAL ... 5-10 72
FLAMING ARROW ... 4-8 68-69
PEOPLE ... 3-5

WALKER, Hamilton
Singles: 7-inch
JERDEN ... 4-8 66
UNI ... 4-8 67

WALKER, Jackie
Singles: 78 rpm
IMPERIAL ... 10-15 54-57
Singles: 7-inch
EVEREST ... 5-10 62
IMPERIAL ... 15-25 54-58
TIDAL ... 5-10 61

WALKER, Jay
(With the Pedestrians)
Singles: 7-inch
AMY ... 8-12 62
VEE JAY ... 5-10 61

WALKER, Jeri
Singles: 7-inch
SIMS (218 "Once a Day") ... 4-8 64

WALKER, Jerry
Singles: 7-inch
TEN HIGH ... 8-12

WALKER, Jerry Jeff — P&R '68
Singles: 7-inch
ATCO ... 3-6 68-70
MCA ... 3-5 73-80
SOUTH COAST ... 3-4 81
TRIED & TRUE ... 3-4 89
LPs: 10/12-inch
ATCO (Except 297) ... 15-20 68-70
ATCO (297 "Five Years Gone") ... 30-50 69
DECCA ... 10-12 72
ELEKTRA ... 8-10 70s
MCA ... 5-10 73-80
SOUTH COAST ... 5-10 81
VANGUARD ... 10-12 69

WALKER, Jimmy
Singles: 7-inch
WALKER ... 5-8 65
Also see KNICKERBOCKERS
Also see RIGHTEOUS BROTHERS

WALKER, Jimmy
Singles: 7-inch
COLUMBIA (44742 "Dawn") ... 5-10 69

WALKER, Jimmy — LP '75
Singles: 7-inch
BUDDAH ... 3-5 75
LPs: 10/12-inch
BUDDAH ... 8-10 75

WALKER Jimmy, & Erwin Helfer
LPs: 10/12-inch
FLYING FISH ... 5-8
TESTAMENT ... 10-15

WALKER, John
Singles: 7-inch
GREAT MOUNTAIN ... 3-5 73
SMASH ... 4-8 67-69
Also see WALKER BROTHERS

WALKER, Johnnie
Singles: 7-inch
TOLLIE ... 4-8 64

WALKER, Johnny "Big Moose"
LPs: 10/12-inch
BLUESWAY ... 10-15 70

WALKER, Junior — P&R/R&B/LP '65
(With the All Stars; with All the Stars; Junior Walker All Stars; Jr. Walker)
Singles: 12-inch
WHITFIELD ... 4-8 79
Singles: 7-inch
HARVEY ... 10-20 62-64
MOTOWN ... 3-4 83
SOUL (Except 35003) ... 5-12 65-76
(Black vinyl.)
SOUL (35003 "Monkey Jump") ... 10-15 64
SOUL (Colored vinyl) ... 8-12 70-72
(Promotional issues only.)
WHITFIELD ... 3-5 79
Picture Sleeves
SOUL ... 4-8 65-66
EPs: 7-inch
SOUL (69701 "Shotgun") ... 15-25 66
SOUL (69702 "Soul Sessions") ... 15-25 66
SOUL (69703 "Road Runner") ... 15-25 66
LPs: 10/12-inch
MOTOWN (Except 700 series) ... 5-10 80-83
MOTOWN (700 series) ... 8-12 74
SOUL (701 "Shotgun") ... 20-30 66
SOUL (702 "Soul Sessions") ... 20-30 66
SOUL (703 "Road Runner") ... 20-30 66
SOUL (705 "Live") ... 20-30 66
SOUL (710 "Home Cookin' ") ... 15-20 69
SOUL (718 "Greatest Hits") ... 10-20 69
SOUL (718 "Greatest Hits") ... 10-20 69
SOUL (721 "What Does It Take") ... 10-20 69
SOUL (725 thru 750) ... 5-15 70-78
SOUL (35073 "Jr. Walker") ... 15-25 60s
(Colored vinyl. Promotional issue only.)
WHITFIELD ... 8-10 79
Members: Autry Dewalt II (Jr. Walker); Willie Woods; Vic Thomas; James Graves.
Also see FOREIGNER
Also see VAN DKYE, Earl

WALKER, Junior
Singles: 7-inch
DUKE ... 4-8 66

WALKER, Kenny
Singles: 78 rpm
DELUXE ... 10-20 46

WALKER, L.A.
(Lonnie Walker)
Singles: 7-inch
ORIGINAL SOUND ... 4-8 73
Also see WALKER, Lonnie

WALKER, Lanie, & His Black Mountain Boys
Singles: 78 rpm
BLUE HEN ... 25-50 55-56
Singles: 7-inch
BLUE HEN (123 "Drop In") ... 75-125 59
BLUE HEN (209 "Side Track Daddy") ... 50-100 55
BLUE HEN (219 "Eenie Meenie Miney Mo") ... 50-100 56

WALKER, Lawrence
Singles: 7-inch
LA LOUISIANE ... 10-15

WALKER, Lee
Singles: 7-inch
CLARA (110 "Slippin In") ... 20-30 65

WALKER, Lonnie
Singles: 7-inch
CUCA (1111 "I Slipped, I Stumbled, I Fell") ... 30-40 62
Session: Dave Kennedy & Ambassadors.
Also see KENNEDY, Dave
Also see WALKER, L.A.

WALKER, Lucille
LPs: 10/12-inch
CHECKER (1428 "The Best of Lucille Walker") ... 30-50 57

WALKER, Martin
Singles: 7-inch
ABC-PAR ... 4-8 64
PINKY (301 "Love Is Everything") ... 5-10 60
Picture Sleeves
PINKY (301 "Love Is Everything") ... 10-15 60
LPs: 10/12-inch
ABC-PAR (483 "From Scotland with Love") ... 10-20 64

WALKER, Mel
Singles: 78 rpm
MERCURY ... 10-15 53-54
Singles: 7-inch
MERCURY ... 15-25 53-54
Also see LITTLE ESTHER & MEL WALKER
Also see OTIS, Johnny
Also see ROBINS / Mel Walker & His Bluenotes

WALKER, Nats: see LOVE NOTES / Ronald Gill / Nats Walker Orchestra / Margie Anderson

WALKER, Patty
(Patti Walker)
Singles: 7-inch
EPIC ... 4-8 64
RONN ... 4-8 67

WALKER, Peter
LPs: 10/12-inch
VANGUARD ... 20-25 67

WALKER, Phillip
("And Band")
Singles: 7-inch
ELKO (001 "Louisiana Walk") ... 45-55 58
ELKO (002 "Playing in the Dark") ... 45-55 58
FANTASY ... 5-10
GILKEY (345 "Gorrilla" [sic]) ... 10-20
JOLIET ... 4-8 77
VAULT (959 "The Struggle") ... 5-10 69
LPs: 10/12-inch
ALLIGATOR ... 5-10 80
JOLIET ... 15-25 77
PLAYBOY ... 10-15 73
Also see LONESOME SUNDOWN & PHILIP WALKER
Also see PHIL & BEA BOPP

WALKER, Randolph
Singles: 7-inch
BLACK PRINCE (316 "Shindy [sic] Butterfly") ... 5-10
MALA ... 5-10 67
SHOUT ... 4-8

WALKER, Riley
Singles: 7-inch
ATOMIC (701 "Uranium Miner's Boogie") ... 100-200
(Colored vinyl.)

WALKER, Robert
(With the Night Riders; with Soul Strings)
Singles: 7-inch
DETROIT SOUND (224 "Everything's Alright") ... 50-75 67
GNP (2027 "Excuse Me") ... 20-30 66
RCA (9304 "Stick by Me") ... 10-20 67

WALKER, Ronnie
Singles: 7-inch
ABC ... 5-10 69
BELL ... 5-10
NICO ... 5-10
PHILIPS ... 5-10 67

WALKER, Russ
Singles: 78 rpm
HI FI ... 5-10 57
Singles: 7-inch
HI FI ... 5-10 57
PROTONE ... 5-10 59
Picture Sleeves
HI FI ... 10-20 57

WALKER, Sammy
LPs: 10/12-inch
FOLKWAYS ... 8-10 75
W.B. ... 8-10 76

WALKER, Scott
(Scott Engel)
Singles: 7-inch
PHILIPS ... 3-5 71
SMASH ... 4-8 68-69
LPs: 10/12-inch
SMASH ... 15-20 68-69
Also see ENGEL, Scott
Also see WALKER BROTHERS

WALKER, Steve, & Bold
Singles: 7-inch
DYNOVOICE ("Train Kept A Rollin' ") ... 15-20 67
Also see BOLD

WALKER, T-Bone — P&R '47
(With "His Guitar")
Singles: 78 rpm
ATLANTIC ... 10-20 55
BLACK & WHITE ... 15-25 46-48
COMET ... 15-25 48-49
CAPITOL ... 15-25 45-50
IMPERIAL ... 15-25 50-57
MERCURY ... 15-25 46
POST ... 15-25 55
RHUMBOOGIE ... 15-25 45-46
Singles: 7-inch
ATLANTIC (1065 Papa Ain't Salty") ... 30-50 55
ATLANTIC (1074 "Why Not") ... 30-50 55
BLUESWAY ... 4-8 67
CAPITOL (799 "On Your Way Blues") ... 150-250 49
CAPITOL (944 "Too Much Trouble Blues") ... 100-200 50
IMPERIAL (5171 "Cold Cold Feeling") ... 15-25 61
(First issue on 45 rpm.)
IMPERIAL (5202 "Street Walkin' Woman") ... 75-125 52
IMPERIAL (5216 "Blue Mood") ... 75-125 53
IMPERIAL (5228 "Railroad Station Blues") ... 50-75 53
IMPERIAL (5239 "Party Girl") ... 50-75 53
IMPERIAL (5247 "Everytime") ... 50-75 53
IMPERIAL (5261 "I'm About to Lose My Mind") ... 50-75 53
IMPERIAL (5264 "Pony Tail") ... 50-75 54
IMPERIAL (5274 "Vida Lee") ... 50-75 54
IMPERIAL (5284 "Bye Bye Baby") ... 50-75 54
IMPERIAL (5299 "Teenage Baby") ... 50-75 54
IMPERIAL (5311 "Love Is a Gamble") ... 35-50 55
IMPERIAL (5330 "I'll Understand") ... 35-50 55
IMPERIAL (5384 "Welcome Blues") ... 35-50 56
IMPERIAL (5695 "Travelin' Blues") ... 15-25 60
IMPERIAL (5171 "Cold Cold Feeling") ... 15-25 61
IMPERIAL (5832 "Evil Hearted Woman") ... 15-25 62
IMPERIAL (5962 "Doin' Time") ... 15-25 63
JET STREAM (730 "Reconsider Baby") ... 8-12 66
JET STREAM (738 "She's a Hit") ... 8-12 66
MODERN (1004 "Hey Hey Baby") ... 8-12 65
POST (2002 "I Get So Weary") ... 25-50 55
EPs: 7-inch
CAPITOL (370 "Classics in Jazz") ... 100-150 53
LPs: 10/12-inch
ATLANTIC (8020 "T-Bone Blues") ... 100-200 59
(Black label.)
ATLANTIC (8020 "T-Bone Blues") ... 75-125 60
(Red label.)
ATLANTIC (8256 "T-Bone Blues") ... 10-15 70
BLUE NOTE ... 8-12
BLUESTIME ... 8-12 73
BLUESWAY ... 10-15 67-73
BRUNSWICK ... 10-15 68
CAPITOL (H-370 "Classics in Jazz") ... 250-350 53
(10-inch LP.)
CAPITOL (T-370 "Classics in Jazz") ... 150-250 56
CAPITOL (1958 "Great Blues Vocals and Guitar") ... 40-60 63
DELMARK ... 8-10
FLYING DUTCHMAN/ BLUESTIME ... 10-15 69
HOMECOOKING ... 8-12
IMPERIAL (9098 "T-Bone Walker Sings the Blues") ... 75-150 59
IMPERIAL (9116 "Singing the Blues") ... 50-100 60
IMPERIAL (9146 "I Get So Weary") ... 50-100 61
POLYDOR ... 10-15 70-73
REPRISE ... 10-15 73
WET SOUL ... 10-20 67
Also see GLENN, Lloyd
Also see McCRACKLIN, Jimmy / T-Bone Walker / Charles Brown
Also see WITHERSPOON, Jimmy
Also see X-RAYS

WALKER, T-Bone, Jr.
Singles: 7-inch
DOT (16441 "Empty Feeling") ... 8-12 63
MIDNITE (101 "Empty Feeling") ... 10-20 62

WALKER, Terry
Singles: 7-inch
UNITED (0589 "TCB") ... 4-8

WALKER, Troy
Singles: 7-inch
GNP ... 5-10 62
TRANS WORLD ... 5-10 61
LPs: 10/12-inch
HI FI ... 10-15 64

WALKER, Van
Singles: 7-inch
MERCURY ... 8-10 60

WALKER, Wayne
Singles: 78 rpm
ABC-PAR ... 15-25 56
CHESS ... 10-15 54
COLUMBIA ... 10-20 57
Singles: 7-inch
ABC-PAR (9735 "It's My Way") ... 35-55 56
BRUNSWICK (55133 "You've Got Me") ... 20-30 59
CHESS ... 15-25 54
COLUMBIA ... 10-20 57-58
CORAL ... 5-10 62
EVEREST ... 5-10 60
Also see LEE, Jimmy, & Wayne Walker

WALKER, Wee Willie
Singles: 7-inch
GOLDWAX ... 5-8 65

WALKER, Willie
(With the Alpacas)
Singles: 7-inch
CHECKER ... 5-10 68-69
FREEDOM ... 15-20 59
HI ... 3-5 78
MOTIF ... 10-15 59
PAWN ... 8-12

WALKER, Willie Tee, & Magnificents
Singles: 7-inch
RED COACH ... 8-12

WALKER, Wilmar
Singles: 7-inch
PHILIPS ... 4-8 62

WALKER BROTHERS
Singles: 7-inch
KAY-Y (66785 "Beautiful Brown Eyes") ... 25-50 60

WALKER BROTHERS — P&R '65
Singles: 7-inch
SMASH ... 4-8 64-66
Picture Sleeves
SMASH ... 5-10 65-66
LPs: 10/12-inch
SMASH ... 20-25 66-67
Members: Scott Engel; John Maus; Gary Leeds.

Also see ENGEL, Scott, & John Stewart
Also see WALKER, Gary
Also see WALKER, John
Also see WALKER, Scott

WALKERS
Singles: 7-inch
SOMA (1187 "Time Trap") 10-20 63

WALKERS
Singles: 12-inch
LONDON 4-8

WALKIN' WILLIE
Singles: 7-inch
R.S.V.P. 5-10 61
WEBCOR 8-12

WALKING STICKS
Singles: 7-inch
RAYNARD (10042 "Why") 15-25 65
Members: Bob Barian; Keith Dreher; Kurt Kronhelm; Dick Schurk; Paul Spencer; Gary Josing; Mike Welch; J.D. Harper; Norm Drifka; Denny Schuenemann.
Also see RENEGADES

WALL, Bobby
Singles: 7-inch
ALADDIN 10-20 58

WALL, Shady
Singles: 78 rpm
DECCA (30539 "New Raunchy") 15-25 57
Singles: 7-inch
DECCA (30539 "New Raunchy") 15-25 57

WALL OF SOUND
Singles: 7-inch
BIG BIRD 10-15 67
TOWER 5-10 67

WALL OF VOODOO *LP '81*
Singles: 12-inch
I.R.S. 4-6 83
Singles: 7-inch
I.R.S. 3-5 81-83
Picture Sleeves
I.R.S. 3-5 83
LPs: 10/12-inch
I.R.S. 5-10 81-83
Member: Stan Ridgway.
Also see COPELAND, Stewart, & Stan Ridgway
Also see RIDGWAY, Stan

WALLACE, Billy
Singles: 78 rpm
BLUE HEN 25-50 55
MERCURY 25-50 56
Singles: 7-inch
BLUE HEN 50-75 55
DEB (882 "Wolf Call") 50-75 57
DEB (1003 "Don't Flirt with My Baby") 50-75 59
MERCURY (70876 "Mean Mistreatin' Baby") 50-75 56
MERCURY (70957 "What'll I Do") 50-75 56
PACE ("Gotta Keep Ridin' ") 20-30 59
(Selection number not known.)

WALLACE, Bobby
Singles: 7-inch
OKIE 3-5 78

WALLACE, Esko
Singles: 7-inch
GRAHAM 4-8 63

WALLACE, Eugene
LPs: 10/12-inch
ABC 8-12 74

WALLACE, Fonda
Singles: 7-inch
WINSTON 10-15 57

WALLACE, George, Jr.
Singles: 7-inch
SUNDI 3-5
Picture Sleeves
SUNDI 3-5

WALLACE, Jack
Singles: 7-inch
ZOOM 5-10 59

WALLACE, Jean
Singles: 7-inch
U.A. 4-8 67

WALLACE, Jerry *P&R '54*
(With the Jewels; with Jay Rand Orchestra & Chorus)
Singles: 78 rpm
ALLIED 5-15 51-54
ALPHA 4-8
CHALLENGE 10-20 57
CLASS 5-10 53
MERCURY 5-10 55-56
TOPS 5-10 53
VOGUE 5-10 52
WING 5-10 56
Singles: 7-inch
ALLIED 10-20 54
BMA 3-5 77-78
CHALLENGE (1000 series) 10-15 57
CHALLENGE (9100 series) 5-10 61-63
CHALLENGE (59000 through 59098) 10-20 58-60
CHALLENGE (59223 "Auf Wiedersehn") 5-10 63
CHALLENGE (59246 "In the Misty Moonlight"/"Even the Bad Times Are Good") 5-10 64
(Reissued [Challenge 59249] with a Soul Surfers track on B-side.)
CHALLENGE (59278 "Helpless") 5-10 65
CHALLENGE (59265 "Even the Bad Times Are Good") 5-10 65
CLASS 10-20 53
DECCA 3-5 71-72
DOOR KNOB 3-5 79-80
ERIC 3-4 70s
4-STAR 3-5 78-79
GLENOLDEN 4-6 68
GUSTO 3-4 80s
LIBERTY 4-6 67-70
MCA 3-4 73-74
MGM 3-5 75-76
MERCURY (70000 series) 10-20 55-56
MERCURY (72000 series) 5-8 64-66
SUNSET 5-10
TOPS 10-20 53
U.A. 3-5 72-75
VOGUE 10-20 52
WING 10-15 56
Picture Sleeves
CHALLENGE (59013 thru 59098) 10-20 58-60
CHALLENGE (59200 series) 5-10 63-65
EPs: 7-inch
CHALLENGE 15-25 60
LPs: 10/12-inch
BMA 8-10 77
CHALLENGE (606 "Just Jerry") 30-35 59
CHALLENGE (612 "There She Goes") 20-25 61
CHALLENGE (616 "Shutters and Boards") 15-25 63
CHALLENGE (619 "In the Misty Moonlight") 15-25 64
CHALLENGE (2002 "Greatest Hits") 10-15 69
DECCA 8-12 71-72
4-STAR 5-8 83
LIBERTY 10-12 68
MCA 8-10 73-74
MGM 8-10 75
MERCURY 10-20 66
PICKWICK 5-10 70s
U.A. 8-12 72-75
WING 10-12 68
Also see BARE, Bobby / Donna Fargo / Jerry Wallace

WALLACE, Jerry / Soul Surfers
Singles: 7-inch
CHALLENGE (59249 "In the Misty Moonlight"/"Cannonball") 5-10 64
Also see SOUL SURFERS / Delicates
Also see WALLACE, Jerry

WALLACE, Jimmy
Singles: 7-inch
DON-EL (109 "If I Were Free") 10-20 61

WALLACE, Joe
Singles: 7-inch
MOON (304 "Leopard Man") 25-35 59

WALLACE, John & Bill
Singles: 7-inch
A-B-S (133 "Blinded By Your Love") 5-10 62
Also see WALLACE BROTHERS

WALLACE, Pat
(With the Rock'n Ravens)
Singles: 7-inch
ASTERISK 10-15
BISHOP 4-6 80
ST. CLAIR (007 "Fill the Hole") 15-25

WALLACE, Richard
(Richie Wallace)
Singles: 7-inch
ENSIGN 5-10 61
FEDERAL 5-10 63-64

WALLACE, Sippie
Singles: 78 rpm
MERCURY 10-15 45

WALLACE, Sonny
Singles: 7-inch
YUCCA (127 "Black Cadillac") 50-100 61

WALLACE, Wales
Singles: 7-inch
BASHIE 8-12
BRC 8-12

WALLACE BROTHERS *P&R '64*
Singles: 7-inch
JEWEL 4-8 68-69
SIMS 5-10 63-67
LPs: 10/12-inch
SIMS (128 "Soul, Soul & More Soul") 15-25 65
Members: John Wallace; Ervin Wallace; John Simon.
Also see NATURALS
Also see WALLACE, John & Bill

WALLACE COLLECTION
Singles: 7-inch
CAPITOL 3-6 69
LPs: 10/12-inch
CAPITOL 10-15 69

WALLER, Carole
Singles: 7-inch
U.S.A. (863 "This Love of Mine") 15-25 67

WALLER, Gordon
Singles: 7-inch
BELL 3-6 70
CAPITOL 4-8 67-68
LPs: 10/12-inch
ABC 10-15 72
Also see PETER & GORDON

WALLER, Jim, & Deltas
Singles: 7-inch
ARVEE (5072 "Surfin' Wild") 15-25 64
CAMBRIDGE (124 "Goodnight My Love") 20-30 64
TRAC (502 "I've Been Blue") 30-40 61
LPs: 10/12-inch
ARVEE (A-432 "Surfin' Wild") 25-35 63
(Monaural.)
ARVEE (AS-432 "Surfin' Wild") 35-45 63
(Stereo.)
Members: Jim Waller; Roy Carlson; Ed Atkinson; Jeff Christensen; Terry Christofferson.
Also see JAY & DELTAS
Also see BREAKERS

WALLEY, Deborah
Singles: 7-inch
DEE GEE 5-10 66
Also see WALKER, Bob, & Friend

WALLIN, Johnny
(Johnny Waleen)
Singles: 7-inch
SOMA (1120 "The Road to Heartaches") 8-12 70
Also see WALEEN, Johnny

WALLIS, Ronnie
(With the Rajahs)
Singles: 7-inch
DECCA 4-8 65-67

WALLIS, Ruth *P&R '53*
(With the Deluxe Rhumba Band)
Singles: 78 rpm
DE-LUXE 5-10 47
KING 5-10 52-53
MONARCH 5-10 53-54
WALLIS ORIGINAL 5-10 55-57
Singles: 7-inch
DE-LUXE 15-25 51
KING 10-20 52-53
MONARCH 10-15 53-54
WALLIS ORIGINAL 10-20 55-57
(Some – or all – in this series are red vinyl.)
EPs: 7-inch
KING (215/216/217 "House Party") 15-25 52
(Price is for any of three volumes.)
LPs: 10/12-inch
KING (6 "Rhumba Party") 75-100 52
(10-inch LP.)
KING (9 "House Party") 75-100 52
(10-inch LP.)
KING (507 "House Party") 50-100 56
WALLIS ORIGINAL (2 "Ruth Wallis") 20-30 57

WALLIS, Shani
Singles: 7-inch
LONDON 4-8 63

WALLIS, Suzy
Singles: 7-inch
RCA 5-10 65-66

WALLS, Ann, & Ernie Fields
Singles: 7-inch
RENDEZVOUS 4-8 61
Also see FIELDS, Ernie

WALLS, Bill
Singles: 7-inch
ACCENT 5-10 65

WALLS, Jimmy
Singles: 7-inch
WALTON 4-8 66

WALLS, Van
(Van "Piano Man" Walls & His Orchestra)
Singles: 78 rpm
ATLANTIC (980 "After Midnight") 25-50 52
Singles: 7-inch
ATLANTIC (980 "After Midnight") 60-90 52
Also see BROWN, Clarence "Gatemouth" / Camille Howard / Bill Johnson Quartet / Van "Piano Man" Walls
Also see SPIDER SAM
Also see TURNER, Joe

WALLY
LPs: 10/12-inch
ATLANTIC 8-10 74

WALLY & KNIGHTS
Singles: 7-inch
VEEP 5-10 67

WALLY & RIGHTS
Singles: 7-inch
GM (113 "Hey Now Little Girl") 15-25 66

WALRUS
LPs: 10/12-inch
JANUS 8-12 73

WALSH, Andy
Singles: 78 rpm
SOMA (1013 "Guitar Boogie") 10-20 56
Singles: 7-inch
FM (338 "Guitar Boogie") 40-60 56
(First issue.)
SOMA (1013 "Guitar Boogie") 25-50 56

WALSH, David *C&W '85*
Singles: 7-inch
CHARTA 3-4 85-89

WALSH, James, Gypsy Band
Singles: 7-inch
RCA 3-5 78-79
LPs: 10/12-inch
RCA 5-10 79
Also see GYPSY

WALSH, Joe *LP '72*
Singles: 7-inch
ABC 3-5 75-78
ASYLUM 3-5 78-81
DUNHILL 3-6 73-75
FULL MOON 3-5 80-83
MCA 3-5 79
Picture Sleeves
FULL MOON 3-6 80-83
EPs: 7-inch
ABC/COMMAND (40016 "The Smoker You Drink, the Player You Get") 10-20 74
(Quadraphonic. Juke box "Special Promotional Record." Includes title strips.)
LPs: 10/12-inch
ABC 5-10 76-78
ABC/COMMAND (40016 "The Smoker You Drink, the Player You Get") 15-25 74
(Quadraphonic.)
ABC/COMMAND (40017 "So What") 15-25 75
(Quadraphonic.)
ASYLUM 5-10 78-81
DUNHILL 8-12 72-74
MCA 5-10 79
W.B. 5-8 83-87
Also see BARNSTORM
Also see EAGLES
Also see JAMES GANG
Also see SIMPSONS
Also see VITALE, Joe

WALSH, Johnny
Singles: 7-inch
BUENA VISTA 5-10 59
COLUMBIA 4-8 66
DOT 5-10 60
W.B. 5-10 61-62
EPs: 7-inch
W.B. 10-15 61

WALSH, Steve *LP '80*
Singles: 7-inch
KIRSHNER 3-5 80
LPs: 10/12-inch
KIRSHNER 5-10 80
Also see KANSAS

WALT & SATANS
Singles: 7-inch
EMKAY 4-8 65

WALT, PERCY & TRACERS
Singles: 7-inch
THREE RIVERS ("Wishing") 500-1000
(No selection number used. Reissued as by the Roberson Bro's.)
Also see ROBERSON BRO'S

WALTER & FANCY
Singles: 7-inch
MAGIC LAMP (612 "Campaign Trail") 5-10 64
Members: Walter Crankcase; Fancy Flickerson.

WALTERS, Bucky & Jukes
Singles: 7-inch
NU-PHI ("Crusin' ") 20-30 60s
(Selection number not known.)

WALTERS, Denny
Singles: 7-inch
MASTER (1050 "I Miss You") 10-20

WALTERS, Tommy
Singles: 7-inch
LIMELIGHT (771 "That's Love") 5-10
Picture Sleeves
LIMELIGHT (771 "That's Love") 10-15

WALTERS, Muddy
Singles: 7-inch
FEDERAL 4-8 61

WALTON, J.
(James Walton & His Blues Kings)
Singles: 7-inch
BIG STAR (003 "Tell Me What You Got") 15-25 64
HI-Q 10-15 63

WALTON, Kip
Singles: 7-inch
DECCA (31383 "La Plume De La Ma Tante-Cha Cha") 10-20 62

WALTON, Little Daddy
Singles: 7-inch
BIG HIT 10-20

WALTON, Shirley
Singles: 7-inch
ENTERPRISE 8-12 68

WALTON, Mercy Dee: see MERCY DEE

WALTON, Norman: see VAN BROTHERS

WALTON, Square
(With Sonny Terry)
Singles: 78 rpm
RCA 25-50 54
Singles: 7-inch
RCA (5584 "Bad Hangover") 75-100 54
RCA (5493 "Gimme Your Bank Roll") 75-100 54
Also see TERRY, Sonny

WALTON, Wade
Singles: 7-inch
ARHOOLIE (1005 "Rooster Blues") 10-15 60
LPs: 10/12-inch
PRESTIGE BLUESVILLE (1060 "Shake 'Em on Down") 20-40 62

WALTON, Wilbur, Jr.
(With the James Gang)
Singles: 7-inch
1-2-3 8-15 68-69

WALTON & SILVER LAKE BOYS
Singles: 7-inch
LAEL (1137 "Man, What a Party") 150-200

WALTON BROTHERS
Singles: 7-inch
BIG HIT (300 "Funky Soul") 10-15

WAMMACK, Travis *P&R '64*
Singles: 7-inch
ARA 5-10 64-65
ATLANTIC 4-8 66
CAPRICORN 3-5 75
CONGRESS 4-6
FAME 3-5 72-73
FRATERNITY (103 "Rock & Roll Blues") 50-100 58
LPs: 10/12-inch
CAPRICORN 5-10 75
FAME 8-12 72
PHONORAMA 5-10

WAMPUS CATS
Singles: 7-inch
PSYKOROK (701 "Great Balls of Taxes") 3-5 89
Picture Sleeves
PSYKOROK (701 "Great Balls of Taxes") 3-5 89

WAN, Don
Singles: 7-inch
LAUREL-LI 4-6 59

WANDERER
Singles: 7-inch
STUDIO 5-10 59

WANDERER'S REST
Singles: 7-inch
WRIGHT (6771 "The Boat That I Row") 10-20 67
WRIGHT (6813 "Temptation") 10-20 68
WRIGHT (67101 "You'll Forget") 10-20 67
Members: Richard Podraza; Michael Podraza; Michael Milonszyk; Stanley Starich.

WANDERERS *P&R '61*
(With the Sammy Lowe Orchestra)
Singles: 78 rpm
ONYX (518 "Thinking of You") 30-50 57
SAVOY (1109 "We Could Find Happiness") 50-100 53
Singles: 7-inch
CUB (9003 "Teenage Quarrel") 15-25 58
CUB (9019 "Collecting Hearts") 25-35 58
CUB (9023 "Please") 15-25 58
CUB (9035 "I'm Not Ashamed") 15-25 59
CUB (9054 "I Walked Through a Forest") 15-25 59
CUB (9075 "I Need You More") 15-25 60
CUB (9089 "For Your Love") 15-25 61
CUB (9094 "I'll Never Smile Again") 15-25 61
CUB (9099 "She Wears My Ring") 20-40 61
CUB (9109 "As Time Goes By") 15-25 62
MGM (13082 "As Time Goes By") 10-15 62
ONYX (518 "Thinking of You") 30-50 57
ORBIT (9003 "A Teenage Quarrel") 50-75 58
(Green label.)
ORBIT (9003 "A Teenage Quarrel") 30-50 58
(Red label.)
SAVOY (1109 "We Could Find Happiness") 200-300 53
U.A. (570 "After He Breaks Your Heart") 10-15 62
U.A. (648 "I'll Know") 15-25 62
Members: Ray Pollard; Bob Yarborough; Sheppard Grant; Frank Joyner.
Also see COOPER, Dolly
Also see POLLARD, Ray
Also see SINGING WANDERERS

WANDERERS
Singles: 7-inch
PANAMA 5-10 60

WANDERERS
Singles: 7-inch
BANNER (4601 "Delta Airlines") 10-20 60s

WANDERERS
Singles: 7-inch
TEXAS RECORD CO. (2067 "Higher Education") 15-25 67

WANDERERS
Singles: 7-inch
CAGG ("What's Right") 10-15 67
(No selection number used.)

WANDERERS THREE
Singles: 7-inch
DOLTON 4-8 62-63
MGM 4-8 64
LPs: 10/12-inch
DOLTON 10-20 63

WANDERLEY, Walter *P&R/LP '66*
Singles: 7-inch
A&M 3-5 69
GNP 3-4 81
TOWER 3-6 66-67
VERVE 3-6 66-68
WORLD PACIFIC 3-6 66
LPs: 10/12-inch
A&M 5-10 69

CAPITOL ... 10-15 63
GNP ... 5-8 81
PHILIPS ... 8-12 67
TOWER ... 8-15 66-67
VERVE ... 8-15 66-68
WORLD PACIFIC ... 8-15 66-67
Also see GILBERTO, Astrud

WANG CHUNG *P&R/D&D/LP '84*
(Huang Chung)
Singles: 12-inch
GEFFEN ... 4-6 84
Singles: 7-inch
GEFFEN ... 3-4 84-89
Picture Sleeves
GEFFEN ... 3-4 84-89
LPs: 10/12-inch
ARISTA ... 5-8 83
GEFFEN ... 5-8 84-89

WANKERS
LPs: 10/12-inch
POP (1204 "Breakfast of Champions") ... 8-12 88
(Picture disc.)

WANKTONES
EPs: 7-inch
FOUNTAIN of YOUTH ... 5-8 85
LPs: 10/12-inch
MIDNIGHT ... 8-10 85

WANSEL, Dexter *R&B '76*
Singles: 12-inch
PHILADELPHIA INT'L ... 4-8 79
Singles: 7-inch
PHILADELPHIA INT'L ... 3-5 76-79
LPs: 10/12-inch
PHILADELPHIA INT'L ... 5-10 76-79
Also see MFSB

WANTED
Singles: 7-inch
DEMO (1046 "The Wanted") ... 10-15 66
Members: Chuck Travis; Harry Mccullough; Tony Wells; Paul Leaken; Paul Polizak.
Also see TRAVIS, Chuck

WANTED
Singles: 7-inch
A&M ... 4-8 67
DETROIT SOUND (Except 222) ... 5-10 66-67
DETROIT SOUND (222 "Here to Stay") ... 15-25 66

WAR *P&R '70*
Singles: 12-inch
MCA ... 4-8 78-79
Singles: 7-inch
BLUE NOTE ... 3-5 77
COCO PLUM ... 3-4 85
LAX ... 3-5 81
MCA ... 3-5 77-82
PRIORITY ... 3-4 87
RCA ... 3-5 82-83
U.A. ... 3-6 71-78
WAR ... 3-5 77
Picture Sleeves
MCA ... 3-5 77
U.A. ... 3-5 71-75
EPs: 7-inch
U.A. (92 "The World Is a Ghetto") ... 10-15 72
(Promotional issue only. With paper cover.)
LPs: 10/12-inch
ABC ... 8-10 76
BLUE NOTE ... 8-10 76
MCA ... 8-10 77-82
PRIORITY ... 5-10 87
RCA ... 5-10 82-83
U.A. (Except 103) ... 8-10 71-78
U.A. (103 "Radio Free War") ... 15-20 74
(Colored vinyl. Promotional issue only.)
Members: Howard Scott; Lonnie Jordan; Dee Allen; B.B. Dickerson; Lee Oskar; Charles Miller; Harold Brown.
Also see AALON
Also see BURDON, Eric, & War
Also see JORDAN, Lonnie
Also see OSKAR, Lee

WAR BABIES
Singles: 7-inch
UNI ... 4-6 69

WARD, Anita *P&R/R&B/LP '79*
Singles: 12-inch
T.K. DISCO (124 "Ring My Bell") ... 4-8 79
Singles: 7-inch
JUANA ... 3-5 79
LPs: 10/12-inch
JUANA ... 5-10 79

WARD, Billy, & Dominoes *R&B '51*
Singles: 78 rpm
DECCA ... 15-30 56-57
FEDERAL ... 50-100 52-57
KING (Except 1281) ... 20-30 53-57
KING (1281 "Christmas in Heaven") ... 30-40 53
LIBERTY ... 20-30 57
QUALITY/KING ... 50-100 53
(Canadian.)
Singles: 7-inch
ABC-PAR (10128 "You're Mine") ... 20-30 60
ABC-PAR (10156 "You") ... 20-30 60
DECCA (29933 "St. Theresa of the Roses") ... 25-50 56
DECCA (30043 "Will You Remember") ... 25-50 56
DECCA (30149 "Evermore") ... 25-50 56
DECCA (30199 "Rock, Plymouth Rock") ... 25-50 56
DECCA (30420 "To Each His Own") ... 25-50 57
DECCA (30514 "September Song") ... 25-50 57
FEDERAL (12105 "I'd Be Satisfied") ... 200-300 52
FEDERAL (12106 "Yours Forever") ... 200-300 52
FEDERAL (12114 "Pedal Pushin' Papa") ... 200-300 52
FEDERAL (12129 "These Foolish Things") ... 300-500 53
(Gold top label.)
FEDERAL (12129 "These Foolish Things") ... 100-200 53
(Silver top label.)
FEDERAL (12129 "These Foolish Things") ... 25-50 50s
(Green label.)
FEDERAL (12139 "Where Now, Little Heart") ... 150-250 53
FEDERAL (12162 "My Baby's 3-D") ... 150-250 53
FEDERAL (12178 "Tootsie Roll") ... 150-250 54
FEDERAL (12184 "Handwriting on the Wall") ... 200-300 54
FEDERAL (12193 "Above Jacob's Ladder") ... 75-125 54
FEDERAL (12209 "Can't Do Sixty No More") ... 150-250 55
FEDERAL (12218 "Cave Man") ... 75-125 55
FEDERAL (12263 "Bobby Sox Baby") ... 75-125 57
FEDERAL (12301 "St. Louis Blues") ... 75-125 57
GUSTO ... 3-5 80s
JUBILEE (5163 "Come to Me, Baby") ... 40-60 54
JUBILEE (5213 "Sweethearts on Parade") ... 40-60 55
KING (1280 "Rags to Riches") ... 100-150 53
KING (1281 "Christmas in Heaven") ... 200-300 53
KING (1342 "A Little Lie") ... 100-150 54
KING (1364 "Three Coins in the Fountain") ... 75-125 55
KING (1368 "Little Things Mean a Lot") ... 50-100 55
KING (1492 "Learnin' the Blues") ... 50-100 55
KING (1502 "Over the Rainbow") ... 50-100 55
KING (5322 "Have Mercy Baby") ... 20-30 60
KING (5463 "Lay It on the Line") ... 20-30 61
KING (6002 "This Love of Mine") ... 15-25 65
KING (6016 "Oh Holy Night") ... 15-25 65
LIBERTY (55071 "Stardust") ... 20-30 57
LIBERTY (55099 "Deep Purple") ... 20-30 57
LIBERTY (55111 "My Proudest Possession") ... 15-25 57
LIBERTY (55126 "Solitude") ... 15-25 58
LIBERTY (55136 "Jenny Lee") ... 15-25 58
LIBERTY (55181 "Please Don't Say No") ... 15-25 58
QUALITY/KING (4227 "These Foolish Things") ... 200-300 53
(Canadian.)
QUALITY/KING (4266 "My Baby's 3-D") ... 150-250 53
(Canadian.)
RO-ZAN (10001 "My Fair Weather Friend") ... 25-35 62
UNDERGROUND (6736 "Star Dust") ... 4-6
Picture Sleeves
LIBERTY (55071 "Stardust") ... 50-75 57
EPs: 7-inch
DECCA (2549 "Billy Ward & His Dominoes") ... 100-200 58
FEDERAL (212 "Billy Ward & His Dominoes, Vol. 1") ... 200-300 55
(Silver top label.)
FEDERAL (262 "Billy Ward & His Dominoes, Vol. 2") ... 200-300 55
(Silver top label.)
FEDERAL (269 "Billy Ward & His Dominoes, Vol. 3") ... 200-300 55
(Silver top label.)
FEDERAL (212 "Billy Ward & His Dominoes, Vol. 1") ... 100-150 57
(Green label.)
FEDERAL (262 "Billy Ward & His Dominoes, Vol. 2") ... 100-150 57
(Green label.)
FEDERAL (269 "Billy Ward & His Dominoes, Vol. 3") ... 100-150 57
(Green label.)
LIBERTY (1/2/3-3083 "Yours Forever") ... 50-100 59
(Price is for any of three volumes.)
LPs: 10/12-inch
DECCA (8621 "Billy Ward & His Dominoes") ... 300-500 58
FEDERAL (94 "Billy Ward & His Dominoes") ... 7500-10000 54
(10-inch LP.)
FEDERAL (548 "Billy Ward & His Dominoes") ... 1000-1500 57
FEDERAL (559 "Clyde McPhatter with Billy Ward & His Dominoes") ... 1000-1500 57
KING (548 "Billy Ward & His Dominoes") ... 300-500 58
KING (559 "Clyde McPhatter with Billy Ward & His Dominoes") ... 200-400 61
KING (733 "Billy Ward & His Dominoes Featuring Clyde McPhatter & Jackie Wilson") ... 200-300 61
KING (952 "24 Songs") ... 25-50 66
KING/GUSTO ... 5-10
LIBERTY (3056 "Sea of Glass") ... 100-150 58
LIBERTY (3083 "Yours Forever") ... 100-150 59
LIBERTY (3113 "Pagan Love Song") ... 100-150 59
(Monaural.)
LIBERTY (7113 "Pagan Love Song") ... 200-400 59
(Stereo.)
Members: Clyde McPhatter; Jackie Wilson; Billy Ward; Gene Mumford; Milton Merle; Milton Grayson; William Lamont; Cliff Givens.
Also see DOMINOES
Also see MUMFORD, Gene
Also see WILSON, Jackie

WARD, Burt
Singles: 7-inch
MGM (13632 "Boy Wonder, I Love You") ... 20-30 66

WARD, Clifford T.
LPs: 10/12-inch
FAMOUS CHARISMA ... 8-10 73

WARD, Dale *P&R '63*
(With Robin Ward)
Singles: 7-inch
BIG WAY (001 "River Boat Annie") ... 5-10 60s
BOYD (118 "Big Dale Twist") ... 5-10 62
BOYD (150 "Shake Rattle & Roll") ... 5-10 65
BOYD (152 "I Tried") ... 5-10 65
BOYD (154 "I Didn't Know") ... 5-10 65
DOT (247 "A Letter from Sherry") ... 5-10 65
DOT (16520 "A Letter from Sherry") ... 5-10 64
DOT (16590 "Crying for Laura") ... 5-10 64
DOT (16632 "I'll Never Love Again") ... 5-10 64
DOT (16672 "One Last Kiss Cherie") ... 5-10 64
DOT (16704 "Dirty Old Town") ... 5-10 65
DOT (16759 "Lonely Mary Ann") ... 5-10 65
DOT (17000 series) ... 3-5 71-72
MONUMENT ... 4-8 66-69
PARAMOUNT ... 4-6 69-70
Picture Sleeves
BOYD (118 "Big Dale Twist") ... 10-20 62
Also see WARD, Robin

WARD, Dart, & Cut-Ups
Singles: 7-inch
RIP ... 4-8

WARD, Harold "Thunderhead"
Singles: 7-inch
ALLAN ... 8-12 59

WARD, Herb
Singles: 7-inch
ARGO (5510 "Strange Change") ... 50-75 65
RCA (9688 "Honest to Goodness") ... 40-60 68

WARD, Ivan
(With the Swingsters)
Singles: 7-inch
SAVOY ... 4-8 60-61

WARD, Jacky *C&W '72*
Singles: 7-inch
ASYLUM ... 3-4 82
ELECTRIC ... 3-4 87-88
MEGA ... 3-5 73
MERCURY ... 3-5 75-81
SUNBIRD ... 3-5 80
TARGET (0146 "Big Blue Diamond") ... 5-8 72
W.B. ... 3-4 83
LPs: 10/12-inch
ASYLUM ... 5-10 82
MERCURY ... 6-12 77-80
SUNBIRD ... 5-10 80
TARGET ... 5-10 72

WARD, Jacky, & Reba McEntire *C&W '79*
Singles: 7-inch
MERCURY ... 4-8 79
Also see McENTIRE, Reba
Also see WARD, Jacky

WARD, Janice
Singles: 7-inch
MONUMENT ... 10-20 61

WARD, Joe *P&R '55*
Singles: 78 rpm
KING ... 5-10 55-56
Singles: 7-inch
KING ... 10-20 55-56

WARD, Joey
Singles: 7-inch
COLPIX ... 5-10 60

WARD, Lee
Singles: 7-inch
GAIT (407 "The Defense Rest") ... 50-75 62
(Also issued on the same label, by the Chevrons.)
Also see CHEV-RONS

WARD, Little Sammy
(With Alley Kats & Kitty - Sax Kari Orchestra)
Singles: 7-inch
P-C (103 "Begging for Love") ... 1000-2000
Also see KARI, Sax
Also see WARD, Singin' Sammy

WARD, Pattie
Singles: 7-inch
ROAD ... 4-6 69

WARD, Richard, & Hustlers
Singles: 7-inch
DOWNEY ... 5-10 64

WARD, Robert, & Ohio Untouchables
Singles: 7-inch
THELMA (601 "Your Love Is Real") ... 15-25 64
THELMA (602 "Your Love Is Real") ... 15-25 64
Also see OHIO UNTOUCHABLES

WARD, Robin *P&R/R&B '63*
Singles: 7-inch
DOT ... 4-8 63-64
SONGS UNLIMITED ... 4-8 63
Picture Sleeves
SONGS UNLIMITED ... 5-10 63
LPs: 10/12-inch
DOT (3555 "Wonderful Summer") ... 25-35 63
(Monaural.)
DOT (25555 "Wonderful Summer") ... 35-45 63
(Stereo.)
Also see BOONE, Pat
Also see MARTINDALE, Wink, & Robin Ward
Also see ROBIN
Also see WARD, Dale

WARD, Sam
Singles: 7-inch
GROOVE CITY (205 "Sister Lee") ... 50-100 60s

WARD, Singin' Sammy *R&B '61*
(Sammy Ward)
Singles: 7-inch
SOUL (35004 "You've Got to Change") ... 20-30 64
TAMLA (54030 "What Makes You Love Him") ... 50-100 60
(With horizontal lines. Same number used twice.)
TAMLA (54030 "That Child Is Really Wild") ... 50-100 60
(With horizontal lines.)
TAMLA (54030 "What Makes You Love Him") ... 25-50 61
(With Tamla globe logo.)
TAMLA (54030 "That Child Is Really Wild") ... 25-50 61
(With Tamla globe logo.)
TAMLA (54049 "What Makes You Love Him") ... 20-40 62
TAMLA (54057 "Everybody Knew It") ... 30-40 62
TAMLA (54071 "Part Time Love") ... 25-35 62
Also see TAYLOR, Sherri, & Singin' Sammy Ward
Also see WARD, Little Sammy

WARD, Walter, & Challengers
Singles: 7-inch
MELATONE (1002 "I Can Tell") ... 300-500 58
Also see OLYMPICS

WARD, Willie
(With the Warblers)
Singles: 7-inch
FEE BEE (233 "I'm a Madman") ... 20-30 58
STAR (229 "Iggy Joe") ... 50-100 57

WARDELL & SULTANS
Singles: 7-inch
IMPERIAL ... 10-15 62

WARDEN, J.W., & Jokers
Singles: 7-inch
SIMPSON (11301 "Only a Tear") ... 50-75 59

WARDEN & His Fugitives
Singles: 7-inch
BING (302 "The World Ain't Changed") ... 15-25 65

WARE, Curtis, & Four Do Matics
Singles: 7-inch
KAY BEE (101 "Flame in My Heart") ... 300-400 61

WARE, Delores
Singles: 78 rpm
MERCURY ... 5-10 55
Singles: 7-inch
MERCURY ... 10-15 55
SHARON ... 4-8 62

WARE, Eddie
Singles: 78 rpm
CHESS (1461 "Lima Beans") ... 20-30 51
CHESS (1507 "Jealous Woman") ... 20-30 52
STATES ... 25-35 53
Singles: 7-inch
STATES (130 "That's the Stuff I Like") ... 50-100 53

WARE, Leon *R&B '79*
Singles: 7-inch
ELEKTRA ... 3-5 81
FABULOUS ... 3-5 79
U.A. ... 3-5 72
LPs: 10/12-inch
FABULOUS ... 5-10 79
GORDY ... 5-10 76
U.A. ... 8-12 72
Also see ROMEOS

WARFIELD, Peter
Singles: 78 rpm
MILTONE (5249 "Morning Train Blues") ... 25-50 48

WARINER, Steve *C&W '78*
Singles: 7-inch
ARISTA ... 3-4 91
MCA ... 3-4 84-90
RCA ... 3-5 78-84
LPs: 10/12-inch
MCA ... 5-8 87-90
RCA ... 5-10 81-83
Also see CAMPBELL, Glen, & Steve Wariner
Also see LARSON, Nicolette

WARING, Fred *P&R '23*
(With the Pennsylvanians)
Singles: 78 rpm
CAPITOL ... 3-5 57-58
DECCA ... 3-6 50-57
Singles: 7-inch
CAPITOL ... 3-6 57-59
DECCA ... 3-8 50-68
REPRISE ... 3-6 64
EPs: 7-inch
CAPITOL ... 4-8 57-58
DECCA ... 5-10 50-59
SHAWNEE PRESS ("Excerpts from the Fred Waring Band Book") ... 10-15 50s
(Includes 18-page "Band Book." Promotional issue only.)
LPs: 10/12-inch
CAPITOL ... 5-15 57-69
DECCA ... 5-20 50-68
HARMONY ... 5-10 69
MCA ... 5-8 77
MEGA ... 5-8 71
REPRISE ... 5-15 64-65
RCA ... 5-10 68
Also see SINATRA, Frank, Bing Crosby, & Fred Waring

WARLOCK
Singles: 7-inch
EX-PLO (009 "In a Dream") ... 10-20 69
Members: Henry Rice; Bob Lawler; Frank Pederson; Larry Threadgill.

WARLOCK
Singles: 7-inch
MUSIC MERCHANT ... 3-5 72
LPs: 10/12-inch
MUSIC MERCHANT ... 10-15 72

WARLOCK *LP '87*
LPs: 10/12-inch
MERCURY ... 5-8 87

WARLOCKS
Singles: 7-inch
DECCA (31806 "I'll Go Crazy") ... 8-15 65
WASHINGTON SQUARE ... 10-15 60s

WARLOCKS
Singles: 7-inch
BIG ROCK ... 10-15 60s
PARADISE (1021 "Life's a Misery") ... 10-20 65

WARLOCKS
Singles: 7-inch
ARA (1017 "If You Really Want Me to Stay") ... 100-150 66
Also see AMERICAN BLUES
Also see ZZ TOP

WARLORDS
Singles: 7-inch
AGR (0759 "Real Fine Lady") ... 20-30 66

WARLORDS
Singles: 7-inch
NIGHT OWL (6816 "My Girl") ... 10-15 68
Members: James White; Kurt Kuzalka; Steve Beau; George Barrahas; Randy Lindert; Larry Williams; Bill Shupe.

WARM DUST
LPs: 10/12-inch
UNI ... 10-15 71

WARM SOUNDS
Singles: 7-inch
DERAM ... 4-8 67

WARMER, Faron / Slim Marbles
(Gary Seger)
Singles: 7-inch
JO-REE (501 "Cruisin' Central") ... 20-25 59

WARMEST SPRING
Singles: 7-inch
PARKWAY ... 5-10 66

WARNER, Danny, & Sessions
Singles: 7-inch
CHATTAHOOCHEE (675 "Big Boss Man") ... 10-20 66

WARNER, Merrill
Singles: 7-inch
TRAVEL (505 "Don't Let Me Dream Tonight") ... 75-125

WARNER, Sonny
(Little Sonny Warner)
Singles: 7-inch
CHECKER ... 5-10 66
CONCERTONE ... 5-10 61
FREEDOM ... 10-15 59
Also see McNEELY, Big Jay
Also see TEMPESTS

WARNER, Sonny, & Marie Allen
Singles: 7-inch
BEE BEE ... 5-10 61
Also see ALLEN, Little Marie
Also see WARNER, Sonny

WARNER, Virgil *C&W '67*
Singles: 7-inch
LHI ... 4-6 67-68

WARNER, Virgil, & Suzi Jane Hokum *C&W '67*
Singles: 7-inch
LHI ... 4-6 67-68
Also see HOKUM, Suzi Jane
Also see WARNER, Virgil

WARNER BROTHERS
Singles: 7-inch
BALANCE...10-15 66
DESTINATION...10-20 65-66
DUNWICH...10-15 66
EVEREST...10-15 64-65
KANDY KANE...10-15 67
RAMPAGE (1702 "Beauty & the Beast")...15-25 60s

WARNER MACK: see MACK, Warner

WARNES, Jennifer P&R/C&W/LP '77
(Jennifer Warren)
Singles: 12-inch
20TH FOX ("It Goes Like It Goes")...4-8 79
(Shown as by Jennifer Warnes. No selection number used.)
20TH FOX (379 "It Goes Like It Goes")...8-10 79
(Shown as by Jennifer Warren.)
Singles: 7-inch
ARISTA...3-4 77-82
CYPRESS...3-4 87
PARROT...3-6 68
W.B....3-5 83
LPs: 10/12-inch
ARISTA...5-10 76-82
CYPRESS...5-8 87
REPRISE...5-10 72
Also see COCKER, Joe, & Jennifer Warnes
Also see GILLETTE, Steve, & Jennifer Warnes
Also see JENNIFER
Also see MEDLEY, Bill, & Jennifer Warnes

WARNES, Jennifer, & Chris Thompson P&R '83
Singles: 7-inch
CASABLANCA...3-4 83
Also see THOMPSON, Chris, & Night

WARP 9 R&B '82
Singles: 12-inch
PRISM...4-6 83-84
Singles: 7-inch
PRISM...3-4 82-84

WARRANT P&R/LP '89
Singles: 7-inch
COLUMBIA...3-4 89-90
LPs: 10/12-inch
COLUMBIA...5-8 89-90

WARREN, Annette
Singles: 78 rpm
BLACK & WHITE...10-20 47

WARREN, Baby Boy
(With His Buddy [Charlie Mills]; Robert Warren)
Singles: 78 rpm
BLUE LAKE...50-100 55
DRUMMOND...50-100 54
EXCELLO (2211 "Sanafee")...15-25 53
FEDERAL (12008 "Forgive Me Darling")...50-75 49
GOTHAM (507 "Nervy Woman Blues")...50-75 49
J.V.B. (26 "Sanafee")...50-100 53
SAMPSON (633 "Taxi Driver")...100-200 54
STAFF (707 "Don't Want No Skinny Woman")...100-200 49
STAFF (709 "Forgive Me Darling")...100-200 49
Singles: 7-inch
BLUE LAKE (106 "Mattie Mae")...200-250 55
(Colored vinyl.)
DRUMMOND (3002 "Chicken")...250-350 54
DRUMMOND (3003 "Somebody Put Bad Luck on Me")...250-350 54
EXCELLO (2211 "Sanafee")...50-75 53
Also see WILLIAMS, Johnny

WARREN, Beverly
Singles: 7-inch
B.T. PUPPY...5-10 66-67
RUST...5-10 65
Also see CARROLL, Andrea / Beverly Warren

WARREN, Bobbie
Singles: 7-inch
PAMCO...5-10 60

WARREN, Bobby, Five
Singles: 7-inch
JORDAN (119 "Nite-Beat")...15-25 61

WARREN, Doug
(With the Rays)
Singles: 7-inch
IMAGE...15-25 60
Also see WARREN, Gary

WARREN, Fran
Singles: 78 rpm
MGM...4-8 56
Singles: 7-inch
MGM...5-10 56
EPs: 7-inch
MGM...5-15 56
LPs: 10/12-inch
MGM (3394 "Mood Indigo")...20-30 56
TOPS (1585 "Hey There")...10-20 50s
VENISE (10019 "Fran Warren")...50-75 50s
(Colored vinyl.)
Also see CHRISTY, June / Fran Warren

WARREN, Gary
Singles: 7-inch
IMAGE...5-10 60
NASCO...5-10 58
SOUTHERN SOUND...5-10 62
Also see WARREN, Doug

WARREN, Jennifer: see WARNES, Jennifer

WARREN, Jerry
(With the Pets)
Singles: 7-inch
ARWIN...8-12 59
DORSET...5-10 60
Also see PETS

WARREN, Joel
Singles: 7-inch
KAPP...4-8 62

WARREN, Junior
Singles: 7-inch
SHERBA (1500 "Rock & Roll Fever")...200-300

WARREN, Kelly C&W '79
(Kelli Warren)
Singles: 7-inch
RCA...3-5 78-79
Also see NAYLOR, Jerry, & Kelli Warren

WARREN, Randy
(With the Roland James Orchestra)
Singles: 7-inch
GOOD...10-20
Also see JANES, Roland

WARREN, Rusty LP '60
Singles: 7-inch
JUBILEE...5-10 60
EPs: 7-inch
JUBILEE...10-15 62
LPs: 10/12-inch
GNP...5-12 74-77
JUBILEE...10-20 60-68

WARREN, Shorty & Smokey
Singles: 7-inch
FLAME...5-10 59

WARREN, Shorty / Smokey & Dottie Mae Warren
Singles: 7-inch
YALE...5-10 60

WARREN, Smokey
Singles: 7-inch
FLAMINGO...5-10 63
Also see WARREN, Shorty & Smokey

WARREN, Terry
Singles: 7-inch
RIC TIC (106 "I Don't Know")...20-30 62

WARREN, Travis
Singles: 7-inch
VEE TONE...5-10 60

WARRIOR
LPs: 10/12-inch
MCA...5-8 85

WARRIOR, Jade: see JADE WARRIOR

WARRIORS
Singles: 7-inch
MAYFLOWER...8-12 59
Also see ISLANDERS

WARWICK, Dee Dee P&R/R&B '65
(With the Dixie Flyers)
Singles: 7-inch
ATCO...4-8 70-71
BLUE ROCK (4008 "Happiness")...8-12 65
BLUE ROCK (4027 "I Want to Be with You")...8-12 65
BLUE ROCK (40322 "Baby I'm Yours")...8-12 65
HURT (79 "I")...8-12 66
JUBILEE (5459 "You're No Good")...10-20 63
MERCURY...5-10 66-69
PRIVATE STOCK...3-6 75
SUTRA...3-5
TIGER (103 "I Don't Think My Baby's Coming Back")...10-20 64
LPs: 10/12-inch
ATCO...8-12 70
HERITAGE SOUND...5-8 83
MERCURY...10-20 67-69

WARWICK, Dionne P&R '62
(Dionne Warwicke)
Singles: 12-inch
ARISTA...4-6 84
Singles: 7-inch
ARISTA...3-5 79-90
COLLECTABLES...3-4 80s
ERIC...3-4 70s
FOREVER...3-4 80s
MUSICOR...3-5 77
SCEPTER (1200 series)...5-10 62-65
SCEPTER (12000 series)...4-8 65-71
W.B....3-6 72-78
Picture Sleeves
SCEPTER...5-10 63-71
LPs: 10/12-inch
ARISTA...5-8 79-90
CIRCA...5-8
EVEREST...5-8 81
51 WEST...5-8 80s
MFSL...25-50 82
MUSICOR...5-10 77
PHOENIX...5-8 81
PICKWICK...5-10 70s
RHINO...5-8 80s
SCEPTER (Except 200)...10-25 64-72
SCEPTER (200 "March Is Dionne Warwick Month")...20-30 67
(Promotional issue only.)
SCEPTER/COLUMBIA (5139/40 "Dionne")...15-25 67
(Record club issue.)
U.A....8-10 74
TRIP...8-10 76
W.B....8-10 72-77
Also see BROWN, Nappy
Also see CAMPBELL, Glen / Dionne Warwick / Burt Bacharach
Also see DIONNE & FRIENDS
Also see DIONNE & KASHIF
Also see GIBB, Barry
Also see HAYES, Isaac, & Dionne Warwick
Also see MATHIS, Johnny, & Dionne Warwick
Also see U.S.A. for AFRICA
Also see WONDER, Stevie / Dionne Warwick

WARWICK, Dionne, & Howard Hewett R&B '88
Singles: 7-inch
ARISTA...3-4 88
Also see HEWETT, Howard

WARWICK, Dionne, & Glenn Jones R&B '85
Singles: 7-inch
ARISTA...3-4 85
Also see JONES, Glenn

WARWICK, Dionne, & Jeffrey Osborne P&R/R&B '87
Singles: 7-inch
ARISTA...3-4 87
Picture Sleeves
ARISTA...3-4 87
Also see OSBORNE, Jeffrey

WARWICK, Dionne, & Spinners P&R/R&B '74
Singles: 7-inch
ATLANTIC...3-5 74
Picture Sleeves
ATLANTIC...3-5 74
Also see SPINNERS

WARWICK, Dionne, & Luther Vandross P&R/R&B '83
Singles: 7-inch
ARISTA...3-4 83
Picture Sleeves
ARISTA...3-4 83
Also see VANDROSS, Luther
Also see WARWICK, Dionne

WAS (NOT WAS) R&B '82
Singles: 12-inch
ISLAND...4-6 82
Singles: 7-inch
CHRYSALIS...3-4 88-90
GEFFEN...3-4 83
ISLAND...3-5 81-82
ZE...3-4 82
Picture Sleeves
CHRYSALIS...3-4 88-90
LPs: 10/12-inch
CHRYSALIS...5-8 88-90
GEFFEN...5-8 83
ISLAND...5-8 81
Members: Don Fagenson; David Weiss.

WASDEN, Jaybee
Singles: 7-inch
TREPUR (1011 "Elvis in the Army")...15-25 59

"Wash, Don't Soak": see VOLK BROTHERS

WASHBOARD BILL
(Bill Valentine)
Singles: 78 rpm
KING...8-12 56-57
Singles: 7-inch
KING...10-20 56-57
Session: Mickey Baker; King Curtis.
Also see BAKER, Mickey
Also see KING CURTIS
Also see VALENTINE, Billy

WASHBOARD PETE
(Pete Sanders)
Singles: 78 rpm
SAVOY...25-50 48
Member: Ralph Willis.
Also see WILLIS, Ralph

WASHBOARD SAM
(Robert Brown)
Singles: 78 rpm
BLUEBIRD...15-25 43
CHESS (1545 "Bright Eyes")...25-50 53
RCA...10-15 47-50
Singles: 7-inch
CHESS (1545 "Bright Eyes")...75-125 53
RCA (0023 "I'm Just Tired")...50-100 49
(Colored vinyl.)
RCA (0048 "You Said You Love Me")...50-100 50
(Colored vinyl.)
RCA (0090 "Gamblin Man")...50-100 50
(Colored vinyl.)
LPs: 10/12-inch
BLUES CLASSICS...5-10
RCA...10-15 71
Also see BROONZY, Big Bill, & Washboard Sam
Also see DIXON, Willie
Also see SYKES, Roosevelt

WASHBOARD WILLIE & HIS SUPER SUDS OF RHYTHM
Singles: 78 rpm
J.V.B....25-50 56
Singles: 7-inch
HERCULON...10-15 66
J.V.B. (59 "Cherry Red Blues")...75-125 56
J.V.B. (70 "Washboard Blues")...75-125 56
VON...10-15 64

WASHBURN, Beverly
Singles: 7-inch
SMASH...4-8 63

WASHBURN, Frank, & His Orchestra
LPs: 10/12-inch
PROMENADE (2052 "I'm in the Mood for Love")...25-50 50s
(Cover pictures Jayne Mansfield, although she is not heard on the disc.)
Also see MANSFIELD, Jayne

WASHBURN, Lalomie
Singles: 7-inch
PARACHUTE...3-5 77-78
LPs: 10/12-inch
PARACHUTE...5-10 77

WASHBURN, Perry
Singles: 7-inch
MUSTANG (300 "Pocahontas Baby")...20-30 60s

WASHER WINDSHIELD
Singles: 7-inch
INDIGO ("Kathy Young Finds the Innocents Guilty")...30-50 61
Picture Sleeves
INDIGO ("Kathy Young Finds the Innocents Guilty")...35-60 61
(Promotional issue only.)
Members: Kathy Young; Innocents.
Also see INNOCENTS
Also see YOUNG, Kathy

WASHINGTON, Albert
(With the Kings)
Singles: 7-inch
DELUXE...4-6 71
FINCH (10990 "You Gonna Miss Me")...20-30 65
FRATERNITY...10-20 67-70
JEWEL...4-8 73
L&W...8-12
VLM...10-20 64
WESTWORLD...4-6
LPs: 10/12-inch
EASTBOUND...10-15 74

WASHINGTON, Andy
Singles: 7-inch
CHRISTY...5-10 60

WASHINGTON, Baby R&B '59
(Jeanette "Baby" Washington; Justine Washington)
Singles: 7-inch
ABC-PAR (10223 "My Time to Cry")...15-25 61
ABC-PAR (10245 "There You Go Again")...10-20 61
A.V.I. (253 "I Wanna Dance")...4-6 78
CHECKER (918 "I Hate to See You Go")...15-25 59
CHECKER (1105 "Is It Worth It")...8-12 65
CHESS (2099 "Is It Worth It")...4-8 70
COLLECTABLES...3-4 80s
COTILLION...4-8 69-70
J&S (1001 "It's Been a Long Time")...10-20 63
J&S (1604 "There Must Be a Reason")...40-60 57
J&S (1607 "Ah-Ha")...40-60 58
J&S (1619 "Hard Way to Go")...40-60 58
J&S (1632 "I Hate to See You Go")...20-30 59
J&S (1656 "Every Day")...50-75 57
LAWTON (1600 "Come See About Me")...3-5 81
MASTER FIVE (1001 "Crying in the Midnight Hour")...3-5 88
MASTER FIVE (1800 "Tear After Tear")...3-6 78
MASTER FIVE (3500 "Can't Get Over Losing You")...4-6 74
MASTER FIVE (3502 "Tell Me a Lie")...4-6 75
MASTER FIVE (9104 "Just Can't Get You Out of My Mind")...4-6 73
MASTER FIVE (9107 "I've Got to Break Away")...4-6 73
MASTER FIVE (9110 "Lay a Little Lovin' on Me")...4-6 74
NEPTUNE (101 "The Time")...25-50 58
NEPTUNE (104 "The Bells")...20-25 59
NEPTUNE (116 "Deep Down Love")...15-25 60
NEPTUNE (120 "Medicine Man")...15-25 60
NEPTUNE (121 "Too Late")...15-25 60
NEPTUNE (122 "Nobody Cares")...15-25 61
7L (3000 "Turn Your Boogie Loose")...3-6 79
SIXTH AVENUE (10816 "Either You Love Me Or You Don't")...4-6 76
SUE (4 "I Know")...5-10 69
SUE (104 thru 150)...8-15 64-67
SUE (764 thru 797)...10-20 62-63
VEEP (1274 "White Christmas")...8-12 67
VEEP (1297 "Hold Back the Dawn")...5-10 69
LPs: 10/12-inch
A.V.I....8-12 78
COLLECTABLES...5-8 87-88
SUE...20-40 63-65
TRIP...8-12 71
UNART...10-20 67
VEEP...10-20 68
Also see DEL PRIS
Also see HEARTS

WASHINGTON, Baby, & Don Gardner R&B '73
Singles: 7-inch
MASTER FIVE (9103 "Forever")...4-6 73-74
LPs: 10/12-inch
MASTER FIVE...8-12 74
Also see GARDNER Don
Also see WASHINGTON, Baby

WASHINGTON, Betty Jean
Singles: 78 rpm
PEACOCK...10-20 51

WASHINGTON, Billy
Singles: 7-inch
BETHLEHEM...4-8 62
CIGAR...4-8 63
D'ORO...4-8 64

WASHINGTON, Cecil
Singles: 7-inch
PROPHONICS (2029 "I Don't Like to Lose")...100-200

WASHINGTON, Connie
Singles: 7-inch
CENTRAL...5-10 60

WASHINGTON, D.C.
(D.C. Bendy)
Singles: 78 rpm
GOLD STAR (661 "Rebob Boogie")...25-50 49
Singles: 7-inch
FELSTED...5-10 62
Also see BENDER, D.C.

WASHINGTON, Deborah R&B '78
Singles: 7-inch
ARIOLA...3-5 78
LPs: 10/12-inch
ARIOLA...5-10 78

WASHINGTON, Dinah R&B '48
Singles: 78 rpm
APOLLO...10-25 45-47
KEYNOTE...20-40 44
MERCURY...5-15 46-57
Singles: 7-inch
MERCURY (5000 series)...15-25 50-52
MERCURY (7200 series)...10-15 62
(Compact 33 singles.)
MERCURY (8100 & 8200 series)...15-25 50-52
MERCURY (10008 "What a Difference a Day Makes")...10-20 59
(Stereo.)
MERCURY (70046 thru 70968)...10-20 52-56
MERCURY (71000 & 72000 series)...5-15 57-63
MERCURY CELEBRITY SERIES...4-6 60s
ROULETTE...4-8 62-63
Picture Sleeves
MERCURY...8-12 61-62
EPs: 7-inch
EMARCY...15-25 54-56
MERCURY (3000 thru 3200 series)...15-25 51-57
MERCURY (3300 series)...10-15 60
MERCURY (4000 series)...10-15 61
LPs: 10/12-inch
EMARCY (400 series)...8-12 76
EMARCY (26032 "After Hours")...50-100 54
(10-inch LP.)
EMARCY (36011 "For Those in Love")...50-75 55
EMARCY (36028 "After Hours")...50-75 55
EMARCY (36065 "Dinah")...50-75 56
EMARCY (36073 "In the Land of Hi-Fi")...50-75 56
EMARCY (36119 "Dinah Sings Fats Waller")...50-75 57
EMARCY (36130 "Dinah Sings Bessie Smith")...50-75 58
EVEREST...8-10 75
MERCURY (103 "This Is My Story")...20-30 63
MERCURY (121 "Original Queen of Soul")...12-15 69
MERCURY (603 "This Is My Story")...20-30 63
MERCURY (20100 & 20200 series)...40-60 55-58
MERCURY (20400 thru 20900 series)...20-30 59-63
(Monaural.)
MERCURY (21100 series)...10-20 67
MERCURY (25060 "Dinah Washington")...50-100 50
(10-inch LP.)
MERCURY (25138 "Dynamic Dinah")...50-100 51
(10-inch LP.)
MERCURY (25140 "Blazing Ballads")...50-100 51
(10-inch LP.)
MERCURY (25138 "Dynamic Dinah")...50-100 51
(10-inch LP.)
MERCURY (60100 thru 60900 series)...20-40 59-63
(Stereo.)
MERCURY (61100 series)...10-15 67
PICKWICK...5-10
ROSETTA...5-8 84
ROULETTE (100 series)...10-12 71-72
ROULETTE (25000 series)...15-30 62-65
TRIP...8-10 73-78
WING...15-30 59-64
Also see BENTON, Brook, & Dinah Washington
Also see CHAMBLEE, Eddie
Also see HAMPTON, Lionel & Dinah Washington
Also see JONES, Quincy
Also see RAVENS & Dinah Washington

WASHINGTON, Dinah / Ink Spots
EPs: 7-inch
WALDORF...10-20 55
Also see INK SPOTS

Also see WASHINGTON, Dinah

WASHINGTON, Dinah / Joe Williams / Sarah Vaughan
LPs: 10/12-inch
ROULETTE 15-25 64
Also see VAUGHAN, Sarah
Also see WASHINGTON, Dinah
Also see WILLIAMS, Joe

WASHINGTON, Donna R&B '81
Singles: 7-inch
CAPITOL 3-5 81
LPs: 10/12-inch
CAPITOL 5-10 81

WASHINGTON, Earl
Singles: 7-inch
CHECKER (905 "Miserlou") 8-12 58

WASHINGTON, Ella P&R/R&B '69
Singles: 7-inch
ATLANTIC 4-8 67
SOUND STAGE 4-6 67-69
LPs: 10/12-inch
SOUND STAGE 10-15 69

WASHINGTON, Ernie
Singles: 7-inch
CHATTAHOOCHEE 8-12 60s

WASHINGTON, Freddy, Band
Singles: 7-inch
ATLAS (1026 "8-9-10") 8-12 69

WASHINGTON, Geno
(With the Ramjam Band)
Singles: 7-inch
DJM (1011 "You Lovely Witch") 3-5 76
KAPP (796 "All I Need") 5-10 66
LPs: 10/12-inch
KAPP (1515 "Live") 10-20 67
(Monaural.)
KAPP (3515 "Live") 10-20 67
(Stereo.)

WASHINGTON, George
(With the Cherry Bombs; with Cherry Stompers)
Singles: 78 rpm
ACE 15-25 58
Singles: 7-inch
ACE 15-25 58
MGM 4-8 66
SEAELL (101 "Back Shelf of Your Mind") 15-25 67

WASHINGTON, Gino
Singles: 7-inch
AMON (90580 "Out of This World") 8-12
ATAC (101 "Doin' the Popcorn") 15-25 69
ATAC (102 "I'll Be Around") 25-35 69
ATAC (2743 "It's Winter") 8-12
ATAC (2829 "You Got Me in a Whirlpool") 8-12 75
ATAC (2830 "Rat Race") 10-20
ATAC (7823 "Like My Baby") 25-35
CONGRESS (269 "Understanding") 5-10 66
CONGRESS (273 "Beach Bash") 5-10 66
CORREC-TONE (503 "Gino Is a Coward") 35-45 62
CREED (1051 "Romeo") 10-20 65
DO DE RE (358 "Gino Is a Coward") 10-15 64
MALA (12029 "I'll Be Around") 20-30 68
RIC TIC (100 "Gino Is a Coward") 10-15 64
SIDRA (9005 "Romeo") 10-20
SONBERT (3770 "Gino Is a Coward") 10-20 64
WAND (147 "Out of This World") 10-15 64
WAND (155 "Baby Be Mine") 10-15 64
WASHPAN (32937 "Do the Frog") 8-12
WIG (9005 "Romeo") 10-20
Picture Sleeves
ATAC (2743 "It's Winter") 20-30

WASHINGTON, Grover, Jr. R&B/LP '72
Singles: 7-inch
COLUMBIA 3-4 87
ELEKTRA 3-4 79-84
KUDU 3-5 71-78
MOTOWN 3-4 78-83
Picture Sleeves
ELEKTRA 3-5 80-82
LPs: 10/12-inch
COLUMBIA 5-8 87
ELEKTRA 5-10 79-84
KUDO 8-12 71-77
MOTOWN 5-10 78-83
Also see COSBY, Bill
Also see LABELLE, Patti, & Grover Washington Jr.
Also see MATTHEWS, David
Also see WITHERS, Bill

WASHINGTON, Jeanette: see WASHINGTON, Baby

WASHINGTON, Jerry R&B '73
Singles: 7-inch
EXCELLO 4-8 73-74

WASHINGTON, Jimmy
Singles: 7-inch
BACK BEAT 4-8 65

WASHINGTON, Jon C&W '88
Singles: 7-inch
DOOR KNOB 3-4 88-89

WASHINGTON, Justine: see WASHINGTON, Baby

WASHINGTON, Lee
Singles: 7-inch
FAT FISH (8006 "Little Girl") 20-25

WASHINGTON, Leroy
Singles: 7-inch
EXCELLO 10-20 58-60
REO (8299 "Wild Cherry") 15-25 58
(Canadian.)

WASHINGTON, Little Joe
Singles: 7-inch
FEDERAL 8-12 63-64

WASHINGTON, Lou
(Lou D. Washington & the Professionals)
Singles: 7-inch
STEELTOWN 10-20 69
U.S.A. (831 "Any Old Time") 15-25 66
Also see GAINES, Fats, Band

WASHINGTON, Ray
Singles: 7-inch
VIN 5-10 59

WASHINGTON, Roger
Singles: 7-inch
BURDETTE (1912 "I Won't Never Make You Cry") 10-20 66
JOE DAVIS (7121 "You're Too Much") 15-25 66

WASHINGTON, Sherry, & Chromatics
Singles: 78 rpm
MILLION (2016 "Honey Bug") 15-25 56
Singles: 7-inch
MILLION (2016 "Honey Bug") 25-50 56
Also see CHROMATICS

WASHINGTON, Teddy
Singles: 7-inch
MAXX 4-8 64

WASHINGTON, Toni
Singles: 7-inch
KON-TI (1063 "Dear Diary") 10-20 66
KON-TI (1170 "Satisfaction") 15-25 66

WASHINGTON, Tony
Singles: 7-inch
PEACOCK 4-8 61

WASHINGTON D.C.s
Singles: 7-inch
DATE 5-10 66
FLIP 10-15 64

WASHRAG
Singles: 7-inch
TMI 3-5 72-73
LPs: 10/12-inch
TMI 8-10 73

WASSON, Ben
Singles: 7-inch
NORMAN (519 "It's Springtime Baby") 10-15 62

WASTERS
Singles: 7-inch
UNI 3-6 69

WATANABE, Sadao, & Roberta Flack R&B '84
Singles: 7-inch
ELEKTRA 3-4 84
Also see FLACK, Roberta

WATANABE KAZUMI
LPs: 10/12-inch
GRAMA VISION 5-8 88

WATCHBAND
Singles: 7-inch
STANAL (7137 "No Dice") 50-75 67

WATCHPOCKET
LPs: 10/12-inch
TMI 8-10 72

WATER into WINE BAND
LPs: 10/12-inch
WORD 5-10 70s

WATER WITCH
Singles: 7-inch
MCS 3-5 74
Members: Ralph Sacco; Roger Deleskis; Richard Gribinias; Al Grella; Frank Kosko; Fred Leskowitz; Paul Opoztner.

WATERBOYS LP '88
Singles: 7-inch
ISLAND 3-4 83
LPs: 10/12-inch
CHRYSALIS 5-8 88-90
ISLAND 5-10 83

WATERFORD, Crown Prince
(With His Twistologists; Charles Waterford)
Singles: 78 rpm
ALADDIN 15-25 47
CAPITOL 10-20 48
EXCELLO 10-20 56
HYTONE 15-25 47
KING 10-20 49-50
TORCH 15-25 50
Singles: 7-inch
EXCELLO (2065 "Driftwood Blues") 20-30 56
ORBIT (6943 "I Don't Wanna Get Married") 8-12 62
Also see McSHANN, Jay
Also see MILBURN, Amos / Wynonie Harris / Crown Prince Waterford

WATERFRONT P&R/LP '89
Singles: 7-inch
POLYDOR 3-4 89
Picture Sleeves
POLYDOR 3-4 89
LPs: 10/12-inch
POLYDOR 5-8 89

WATERFRONT HOME D&D '83
Singles: 12-inch
BOBCAT 4-6 83

WATERPROOF CANDLE
Singles: 7-inch
DUNHILL 8-10 68

WATERPROOF TINKERTOY
Singles: 7-inch
CAITLIN 10-20 68
LAURIE 8-12 68

WATERS
Singles: 7-inch
HIP 3-6 69

WATERS
Singles: 7-inch
W.B. 3-5 77
LPs: 10/12-inch
W.B. 5-10 77

WATERS, Chris C&W '80
Singles: 7-inch
RIO 3-4 80-81

WATERS, Clear
Singles: 7-inch
ATOMIC (905 "A-Minor Cha-Cha") 20-30

WATERS, Ethel P&R '21
Singles: 78 rpm
BLACK SWAN 10-20 21-23
BRUNSWICK 10-15 33-34
COLUMBIA 10-15 25-33
CONTINENTAL 4-8 46-47
DECCA 8-12 34-38
EPs: 7-inch
CHANCEL 10-20 50s
MERCURY 15-25 55
LPs: 10/12-inch
BIOGRAPH 8-10 70
COLUMBIA 8-12 68-72
CONTINENTAL 15-25 61
JAY (3010 "Sings Her Best") 20-40 57
MERCURY (20051 "Favorites") 30-50 54
REMINGTON ("Shades of Blue") 50-75 50
(10-inch LP.)
WORD 10-15 62
"X" (1009 "Ethel Waters") 25-50 55

WATERS, Freddie R&B '77
Singles: 7-inch
KARI 3-5 81
OCTOBER 3-5 77

WATERS, Hal
Singles: 7-inch
LIBERTY 3-5 63

WATERS, Joe C&W '81
Singles: 7-inch
NEW COLONY 3-4 81-84

WATERS, Junior
Singles: 7-inch
ABC-PAR 5-10 60
BERNLO 10-15 57
MGM 5-10 61-62

WATERS, Larry
Singles: 78 rpm
DIG (108 "Full Grown Woman") 15-25 56
Singles: 7-inch
DIG (108 "Full Grown Woman") 25-35 56

WATERS, Mira
Singles: 7-inch
GORDY 3-5

WATERS, Muddy R&B '48
Singles: 78 rpm
ARISTOCRAT (406 "Sneakin' and Cryin'") 25-50 50
ARISTOCRAT (412 "Rollin' and Tumblin'") 25-50 50
ARISTOCRAT (1302 "Gypsy Woman") 25-50 48
ARISTOCRAT (1305 "I Can't Be Satisfied") 25-50 48
ARISTOCRAT (1306 "Train Fare Home") 25-50 48
ARISTOCRAT (1307 "You're Gonna Miss Me") 25-50 49
ARISTOCRAT (1310 "Streamline Woman") 25-50 49
ARISTOCRAT (1311 "Little Geneva") 25-50 49
CHESS (1426 "Rollin' Stone") 25-50 50
CHESS (1434 "You're Gonna Need My Help I Said") 25-50 50
CHESS (1441 "Louisiana Blues") 25-50 50
CHESS (1452 "Long Distance Call") 25-50 51
CHESS (1468 "Appealing Blues") 25-50 51
CHESS (1480 "My Fault") 25-50 51
CHESS (1490 "Early Morning Blues") 25-50 51
CHESS (1509 thru 1630) 15-30 52-56
Singles: 7-inch
CHESS (1509 "Country Boy") 50-100 52
CHESS (1514 "Looking for My Baby") 50-100 52
CHESS (1526 "Standing Around Crying") 50-100 52
CHESS (1537 "She's All Right") 50-75 53
CHESS (1542 "Who's Gonna Be Your Sweet Man") 50-75 52
CHESS (1550 "Mad Love") 40-60 53
CHESS (1560 "I'm Your Hootchie Coochie Man") 40-60 53
CHESS (1571 "Just Make Love to Me") 40-60 54
CHESS (1579 "I'm Ready") 40-60 54
CHESS (1585 "I'm a Natural Born Lover") 25-50 54
CHESS (1596 "I Want to Be Loved") 25-50 55
CHESS (1602 "Mannish Boy") 25-50 55
CHESS (1612 "Trouble No More") 25-50 55
CHESS (1620 "Forty Days & Forty Nights") 25-50 56
CHESS (1630 "Don't Go No Farther") 25-50 56
CHESS (1704 "Close to You") 20-30 58
CHESS (1718 "Walkin' Thru the Park") 20-30 59
CHESS (1733 "Take the Bitter with the Sweet") 20-30 59
CHESS (1748 "I Feel So Good") 20-30 60
CHESS (1752 "I'm Your Doctor") 20-30 60
CHESS (1765 "Tiger in Your Tank") 20-30 60
CHESS (1774 "Woman Wanted") 20-30 60
CHESS (1796 "Lonesome Room Blues") 20-30 61
CHESS (1800 & 1900 series) 8-15 62-66
CHESS (2000 series) 4-8 67-73
LPs: 10/12-inch
BLUE SKY (37064 "King Bee") 8-12 81
CADET CONCEPT (314 "Electric Mud") 10-20 68
(Includes eight-page booklet.)
CADET CONCEPT (320 "After the Rain") 10-15 69
CHESS (127 "Fathers and Sons") 15-25 69
CHESS (1427 "The Best of Muddy Waters") 100-200 57
CHESS (1444 "Muddy Waters Sings Big Bill") 50-100 60
CHESS (1449 "Muddy Waters at Newport") 20-30 64
CHESS (1483 "Folk Singer") 15-25 64
CHESS (1500 "Real Folk Blues of Muddy Waters") 15-20 66
CHESS (1507 "Muddy, Brass, and the Blues") 15-20 66
CHESS (1511 "More Real Folk Blues") 15-20 67
CHESS (1539 "Sail On") 15-20 69
CHESS (1553 "They Call Me Muddy Waters") 15-20 69
CHESS (8202 "Rollin' Stone") 5-10 83
CHESS (9000 series) 5-10
CHESS (50023 "Can't Get No Grindin'") 10-12 73
CHESS (50033 "Fathers & Sons") 10-15 75
CHESS (60006 "McKinley Morganfield A.K.A. Muddy Waters") 10-12 71
CHESS (60013 "The London Muddy Waters Sessions") 10-12 72
CHESS (60031 "Unk in Funk") 8-10 74
CHESS (60035 "Muddy Waters at Woodstock") 10-12 75
DOUGLAS 10-15 68
MFSL (201 "Folk Singer") 20-25 94
(Half-speed mastered.)
TESTAMENT (2210 "Down on Stovall's Plantation") 10-15 60s
Session: Little Walter; Otis Spann; Jimmy Rogers; Willie Dixon; Elgin Evans; James Cotton; Earl Hooker; Willie Smith; Pat Hare.
Also see COTTON, James
Also see DIXON, Willie
Also see FOSTER, Leroy, & Muddy Waters
Also see HOOKER, Earl
Also see HORTON, Walter
Also see JONES, Little Johnny
Also see ROGERS, Jimmy
Also see SPANN, Otis
Also see SUNNYLAND SLIM
Also see WELLS, Junior
Also see WILLIAMSON, Sonny Boy
Also see WINTER, Johnny

WATERS, Muddy, & Howlin' Wolf
LPs: 10/12-inch
CHESS 10-15 74
Also see DIDDLEY, Bo, Howlin' Wolf & Muddy Waters
Also see HOWLIN' WOLF
Also see WATERS, Muddy

WATERS, Ozie
Singles: 78 rpm
COAST 10-15 46

WATERS, Patty
LPs: 10/12-inch
ESP 10-15 66

WATERS, Rene
Singles: 7-inch
SOMA (1432 "Zoomerang Jungle Fever") 5-10 65

WATERS, Roger LP '84
(With Madeline Bell, Katie Kissoon, Eric Clapton & Doreen Chanter; with Bleeding Heart Band)
Singles: 12-inch
COLUMBIA 4-6 84
Singles: 7-inch
COLUMBIA 3-4 84
LPs: 10/12-inch
COLUMBIA 5-10 84-87
Also see BELL, Madeline
Also see CLAPTON, Eric
Also see GEESIN & WATERS
Also see KISSOON, Mac & Katie
Also see PINK FLOYD

WATERS, Vic, & Entertainers
Singles: 7-inch
CAPITOL 4-8 69
RCA 4-8 69
Also see IMPACS

WATERSONS
LPs: 10/12-inch
ELEKTRA 10-15 67

WATKINS, Billy
(Bill Watkins)
Singles: 7-inch
CHALLENGE 10-20 59-60
CHART MAKER 8-12 66
CHESS (1810 "Crackin' Up") 15-25 63
ERA (3183 "The Ice-Man") 20-30 67
IMPERIAL 5-10 69
KENT 8-12 64
TIP-TOE (14321 "I Got Troubles") 75-125 64

WATKINS, Katie / Texas Red & Jimmy
Singles: 78 rpm
CHECKER 10-20 57
VICEROY 15-25 57
Singles: 7-inch
CHECKER 10-20 57
VICEROY 15-25 57
Also see KARI, Sax

WATKINS, Lacille, & Volumes
Singles: 78 rpm
JAGUAR 50-100 54
Singles: 7-inch
JAGUAR (3006 "You Left Me Lonely") 150-200 54
Also see VOLUMES

WATKINS, Lovelace
Singles: 7-inch
GROOVE (0016 "Tender Love") 10-15 63
GROOVE (0023 "I Won't Believe It") 15-25 63
MGM 8-12 60
SUE 8-12 64
UNI 5-10 69
LPs: 10/12-inch
MGM (E-3831 "The Voice of Lovelace Watkins") 20-25 60
(Monaural.)
MGM (E-3831 "The Voice of Lovelace Watkins") 25-35 60
(Stereo.)
UNI 10-20 69

WATKINS, Sis
Singles: 7-inch
DIPLOMACY 8-10 62
Also see UNIVERSALS

WATKINS, Tiny
(E. Tiny Watkins)
Singles: 7-inch
EXCELLO 10-15 67-69
RIM (4112 "Can't Take It with You") 8-12
SANDY (1009 "Rocking Satellite") 20-30 58
TEIA 10-15 64

WATKINS, Tip R&B '77
Singles: 7-inch
H&L 3-5 77

WATKINS, Viola
(With the Honey Drips; with Otis Blackwell Quintet)
Singles: 78 rpm
JUBILEE 10-20 49-52
MGM 5-15 48-49
RAMA 10-20 52
SUPER DISC 5-10 47-48
Singles: 7-inch
EBONY 10-20 58
JUBILEE (5095 "Really Real") 25-35 52
RAMA (8 "Real Fine Man") 50-75 52
(Black vinyl.)
RAMA (8 "Real Fine Man") 150-250 52
(Colored vinyl.)
Also see BLACKWELL, Otis
Also see CROWS

WATLEY, Jody P&R/R&B/LP '87
(With Eric B. & Rakim)
Singles: 7-inch
MCA 3-4 87-90
Picture Sleeves
MCA 3-4 87-89
LPs: 10/12-inch
MCA 5-8 87-89
Also see CYMONE, Andre
Also see SHALAMAR

WATSON, Alabama
Singles: 7-inch
BLUESTOWN 10-15 65

WATSON, Anthony R&B '85
Singles: 7-inch
SRO 3-4 85
LPs: 10/12-inch
SRO 5-10 85

WATSON, Big John
Singles: 7-inch
CAPA 4-8 62

WATSON, Bruce
Singles: 7-inch
PIC-A-TUNE 4-8 62

WATSON, Bunny Foote
Singles: 7-inch
BIG HAWK 5-10 66

WATSON, Clayton
Singles: 7-inch
LAVENDER (2454 "Everybody's Boppin' ") ... 250-350
Also see LORD DENT & INVADERS

WATSON, Clyde C&W '77
Singles: 7-inch
GROOVY ... 3-5 77

WATSON, David
Singles: 7-inch
TOWER ... 4-8 66

WATSON: Deek: see BROWN DOTS; FOUR DOTS

WATSON, Dick
Singles: 7-inch
GONE ... 4-8 63

WATSON, Doc C&W '73
(With Merle Watson)
Singles: 7-inch
POPPY ... 3-5 72-74
U.A. ... 3-5 73-79
LPs: 10/12-inch
FLYING FISH ... 5-8 81
FOLKWAYS ... 10-20 63-69
LIBERTY ... 5-8 83
POPPY ... 6-12 72
U.A. ... 8-15 75-76
VANGUARD ... 8-18 64-77
VERVE/FOLKWAYS ... 10-15 66
Also see ATKINS, Chet, & Doc Watson
Also see FLATT, Lester, Earl Scruggs & Doc Watson
Also see STUART, Marty

WATSON, Gene C&W '75
(With the Farewell Party Band)
Singles: 7-inch
CAPITOL ... 3-5 75-80
CURB/MCA ... 3-4 85
DIXIE (2003 "I'll Always Love You") ... 20-30 58
EPIC ... 3-4 85-87
MCA ... 3-4 81-84
RESCO ... 4-6 75
TONKA ... 5-10 65
TRI DEC (8357 "My Rockin' Baby") ... 100-200 58
W.B. ... 3-4 81-89
WIDE WORLD ... 3-5 72
LPs: 10/12-inch
CAPITOL ... 5-12 75-84
MCA ... 5-10 81-84
STONEWAY ... 5-10
Session: Tony Booth.
Also see BOOTH, Tony

WATSON, Jimmy
Singles: 7-inch
BRUNSWICK ... 10-20 58

WATSON, John L., & Hummelfugs
Singles: 7-inch
PARKWAY ... 5-10 65

WATSON, Johnny R&B '55
(Johnny Guitar Watson; Young John Watson; Johnny Watson Trio)
Singles: 78 rpm
FEDERAL ... 40-60 53-54
KEEN ... 20-30 57
RPM ... 25-40 55-56
Singles: 7-inch
ALL STAR (7167 "Darling of My Dreams") ... 25-35 58
ARVEE (5016 "Untouchable") ... 20-30 60
CACTUS (118 "Let's Rock") ... 75-125 59
CLASS (246 "One More Kiss") ... 15-25 59
DJM ... 3-6 77
ESCORT ... 5-10
FANTASY ... 3-6 73-75
FEDERAL (12120 "Highway 60") ... 100-200 53
FEDERAL (12131 "Motor Head Baby") ... 100-200 53
FEDERAL (12143 "I Got Eyes") ... 100-200 53
FEDERAL (12157 "What's Going On") ... 100-200 53
FEDERAL (12175 "Half Pint of Whiskey") ... 100-200 54
FEDERAL (12183 "Gettin' Drunk") ... 100-200 54
GOTH (101 "Falling in Love") ... 75-125 60
HIGHLAND ... 10-20 60s
KEEN (4005 "Gangster of Love") ... 30-50 57
KEEN (4023 "Deana Baby") ... 30-50 57
KENT ... 8-12 60
KING (5536 "Embraceable You") ... 10-20 61
KING (5579 "Broke & Lonely") ... 10-20 61
KING (5607 "Nearness of You") ... 10-20 62
KING (5666 "Sweet Lovin' Mama") ... 10-20 62
KING (5716 "Cold Cold Heart") ... 10-20 62
KING (5774 "Gangster of Love") ... 10-20 63
KING (5833 "I Say I Love You") ... 10-20 64
OKEH ... 5-15 66-67
RPM (423 "Hot Little Mama") ... 50-75 55
RPM (431 "Too Tired") ... 50-75 55
RPM (436 "Those Lonely, Lonely Nights") ... 50-75 55
RPM (447 "Oh, Baby") ... 50-75 55
RPM (455 "Three Hours Past Midnight") ... 50-75 55
RPM (471 "She Moves Me") ... 50-75 55
VALLEY VUE ... 3-4 84
LPs: 10/12-inch
A&M ... 5-10 81
BIG TOWN ... 8-10 77
CADET ... 10-15 67
CHESS (1490 "Blues/Soul") ... 50-100 64
DJM ... 5-10 76-81
FANTASY ... 5-10 73-81
KING (857 "Johnny Guitar Watson") ... 50-100 63
OKEH ... 10-15 67
MCA ... 5-10 81
Also see BLAND, Bobby / Johnny Guitar Watson
Also see LARRY & JOHNNY
Also see OTIS, Johnny
Also see SHIELDS
Also see WATSONIAN INSTITUTE
Also see WILLIAMS, Larry, & Johnny Watson

WATSON, K.C.
(Mojo Watson)
Singles: 7-inch
ATLAS (1080 "All Alone") ... 25-50 57
NANC (003 "Love Bloodhound") ... 20-30 61

WATSON, Les
(With the Panthers.)
Singles: 7-inch
POMPEII ... 8-12 68-69

WATSON, Miles
Singles: 12-inch
PROFILE ... 4-6 83
Singles: 7-inch
PROFILE ... 3-4 83

WATSON, Paula R&B '48
Singles: 78 rpm
MONOGRAM ... 5-10 49
SUPREME ... 5-10 48-49

WATSON, Phil / Ron-Dels
Singles: 7-inch
CHARAY (97 "Jan") ... 4-8
Also see RON-DELS

WATSON, Romance
Singles: 7-inch
CORAL (62133 "Until the Real Thing Comes Along") ... 10-20 59
CORAL (62442 "Where Does That Leave Me") ... 40-60 65

WATSON, Susan
Singles: 7-inch
PALETTE ... 4-8 60

WATSON, Young John: see WATSON, Johnny

WATSONIAN INSTITUTE LP '78
Singles: 7-inch
DJM ... 3-5 78
LPs: 10/12-inch
DJM ... 5-10 78
Also see WATSON, Johnny

WATTA, Maxine
Singles: 7-inch
ROCSCHIRE ... 3-4 81

WATTERSON, Henry, Expressway
Singles: 7-inch
TRX (5020 "Ob-La-Di, Ob-La-Da") ... 4-8 68

WATTRELL, Bobby
Singles: 7-inch
MAGNASOUND ... 3-6

WATTS, Alan
LPs: 10/12-inch
ASCENSION ... 10-20 70
TOGETHER ... 10-20 70

WATTS, Annie
Singles: 7-inch
ELGIN (1030 "Do Me a Favor") ... 25-35

WATTS, Bette
Singles: 7-inch
WAND ... 8-12 60

WATTS, Ernie LP '82
(Ernie Watts Encounter)
Singles: 7-inch
QWEST ... 3-5 82
VAULT (970 "Never Had a Dream Come True") ... 5-10 71
LPs: 10/12-inch
QWEST ... 5-10 82

WATTS, Glenn
Singles: 7-inch
BUNKY ... 8-10

WATTS, Louis
Singles: 7-inch
VAL-UE ... 5-10 60

WATTS, Noble P&R '57
(Noble "Thin Man" Watts & His Rhythm Sparks; Noble Watts Quintet; with Paul "Hucklebuck" Williams)
Singles: 78 rpm
BATON (246 "Easy Going") ... 15-25 57
BATON (249 "The Slop") ... 15-25 57
BATON (249 "Hard Times") ... 10-20 57
(Note title change.)
DELUXE ... 10-15 54
VEE JAY ... 10-15 56
Singles: 7-inch
BATON (246 "Easy Going") ... 15-25 57
BATON (249 "The Slop") ... 15-25 57
BATON (249 "Hard Times") ... 10-20 57
(Note title change.)
BATON (251 thru 266) ... 10-20 57-59
BRUNSWICK ... 4-8 68
CLAMIKE ... 5-10 63-64
CUB (9078 "The Beaver") ... 8-10 60
DELUXE (6066 "Mashing Potatoes") ... 15-25 54
DELUXE ... 8-12 54
ENJOY ... 5-10 63
JELL ("Florida Shake") ... 5-10 62
(No selection number used.)
SIR (273 "Mashed Potatos") ... 8-12 60
VEE JAY (268 "South Shore Drive") ... 10-20 56
Also see WILLIAMS, Paul

WATTS, Noble, & June Bateman
Singles: 7-inch
ENJOY ... 4-8 63
Also see WATTS, Noble

WATTS, Tommy
Singles: 7-inch
CAPITOL (3726 "Grasshopper") ... 15-25 58

WATTS, Wortham
Singles: 7-inch
D (1002 "Cotton Picker") ... 15-25 58
(First issue.)
ORBIT (517 "Cotton Picker") ... 10-20 58

WATTS LINE
Singles: 7-inch
BULLET ... 8-12

WATTS 103rd ST. RHYTHM BAND P&R/R&B '67
(Featuring Charles Wright)
Singles: 7-inch
KEYMEN (108 "Spreadin' Honey") ... 15-20 67
W.B. ... 5-10 68-71
LPs: 10/12-inch
W.B. ... 10-20 68-71
Also see SOUL RUNNERS
Also see WRIGHT, Charles

WATTS PROPHETS
LPs: 10/12-inch
ALA ... 8-12 71

WATUSI WARRIORS
Singles: 7-inch
PRINCE (1206 "Wa-Chi-Bam-Ba") ... 10-15 59

WAUGH, Donny B.
Singles: 7-inch
U.A. ... 10-15 69

WAUGH, Jerry, & Skeptics
Singles: 7-inch
THRUSH (1002 "For My Own") ... 10-15 65
Also see SKEPTICS

WAVE
Singles: 7-inch
BLACK CAT ... 3-4 85

WAVE, Cosmo: see COSMO WAVE

WAVE CRESTS
LPs: 10/12-inch
VIKING (6606 "Surftime USA") ... 25-35 63

WAVERIDERS
Singles: 7-inch
GUYDEN ... 10-20 63
TENER ... 15-25 60s

WAVERLY CONSORT
LPs: 10/12-inch
VANGUARD ... 5-10

WAVES
Singles: 7-inch
POLYDOR ... 3-5 77
LPs: 10/12-inch
POLYDOR ... 5-10 77

WAX R&B '81
Singles: 12-inch
RCA ... 4-6 86
Singles: 7-inch
RCA ... 3-4 81-86
LPs: 10/12-inch
COTILLION ... 5-10 80
RCA ... 5-8 81-86
Members: Graham Gouldman; Andrew Gold.
Also see GOLD, Andrew
Also see 10CC

WAY, Jerry, & Way Outs
Singles: 7-inch
COULEE (101 "Castaway of Love") ... 15-25 63

WAYBILL, Fee LP '84
Singles: 7-inch
CAPITOL ... 3-4 84
LPs: 10/12-inch
CAPITOL ... 5-8 84
Also see MARX, Richard
Also see TUBES

WAYFARERS
Singles: 78 rpm
RCA ... 5-10 56
Singles: 7-inch
LONDON (9510 "Whistle Down Wind") ... 4-8 62
RCA ... 5-10 56-63
Picture Sleeves
LONDON (9510 "Whistle Down Wind") ... 15-25 62
(Sleeve pictures Hayley Mills.)
LPs: 10/12-inch
RCA ... 10-20 63-64
Also see MILLS, Hayley

WAYLON & WILLIE: see JENNINGS, Waylon, & Willie Nelson

WAYNE, Allen
Singles: 7-inch
KAPP ... 4-8 63
TRY ... 4-8 65

WAYNE, Alvis
Singles: 78 rpm
WESTPORT ... 50-100 56-58
Singles: 7-inch
WESTPORT (132 "Swing Bop Boogie") ... 150-200 56
WESTPORT (138 "Don't Mean Maybe Baby") ... 100-150 57
WESTPORT (140 "You Are the One") ... 150-200 58

WAYNE, Artie
(Art Wayne)
Singles: 78 rpm
LIBERTY ... 5-10 56
Singles: 7-inch
LIBERTY (Except 55625) ... 10-15 56-63
LIBERTY (55625 "I Hurt That Girl") ... 15-25 63
SMASH ... 4-8 67

WAYNE, Bernie
Singles: 7-inch
HANOVER ... 10-20 59
IMPERIAL ... 8-12 59
RUST ... 5-10 63
LPs: 10/12-inch
ICE BLUE ... 10-20 63

WAYNE, Billie
Singles: 7-inch
DEE-LARK ... 4-6

WAYNE, Billy
Singles: 7-inch
FEDORA ... 5-10 62
HILLCREST (778 "Walking and Strollin' ") ... 100-150 58

WAYNE, Bobby
Singles: 78 rpm
MERCURY ... 4-8 51-54
Singles: 7-inch
MERCURY ... 5-10 51-54
EPs: 7-inch
MERCURY ... 5-10 53

WAYNE, Bobby
Singles: 7-inch
A&M ... 4-8 63
JERDEN ... 8-12 64
LA VAL ... 5-10
LJV (101 "Sally Ann") ... 25-50 61
W.B. ... 4-8 64
LPs: 10/12-inch
CROWN ... 10-15 60s
JERDEN ... 15-25 64
Members: Bobby Wayne; Dennis Roberts; Vince Gerber.

WAYNE, Bobby C&W '71
Singles: 7-inch
CAPITOL ... 3-5 71
Also see HAGGARD, Merle

WAYNE, Buddy
(With the Vi-Dells; Buddy Wayne Stokes)
Singles: 7-inch
CAPITOL ... 4-8 68-70
GARDENA ... 8-12 64-66
GARPAX (44182 "I'd Fight for My Baby") ... 8-12 62
SATELLITE ... 5-10
LPs: 10/12-inch
CAPITOL ... 8-12 70

WAYNE, Carl, & Vikings
Singles: 7-inch
ABC-PAR ... 5-10 65

WAYNE, Chuck
Singles: 78 rpm
CAVALIER ... 25-50 54
Singles: 7-inch
CAVALIER (836 "Mean Mean Mean") ... 50-100 54

WAYNE, Danny
Singles: 7-inch
CARD (101 "You're Wrong") ... 40-60

WAYNE, Don
Singles: 7-inch
LOOK ... 5-10 59
MERCURY ... 4-8 68
SWAN (4024 "Head Over Heels") ... 50-75 58
U.A. ... 4-8 66

WAYNE, Eddie
LPs: 10/12-inch
CORONET ... 8-12

WAYNE, Francis
LPs: 10/12-inch
ATLANTIC (1263 "Warm Sound") ... 40-50 57
(Black & silver label.)

WAYNE, Gary: see LEAK, Sid / Gary Wayne

WAYNE, Gaylon
Singles: 7-inch
COUNTRY SOUND ... 4-8 70
DELTA ... 4-8 72-73
HARVESTER ... 10-15 68
SENSATION ... 3-5 76-77
UNIVERSAL ARTIST (7172 "I'm Gonna Love the Devil Out of You") ... 10-20 72
UNIVERSAL ARTIST (52071 "High School's on Fire") ... 50-75 71
Also see WILLIAMS, Wayne, & Sure Shots

WAYNE, Hal, & Pee Wee King
Singles: 7-inch
CUCA ... 4-8 67
Also see KING, Pee Wee

WAYNE, James R&B '51
(With the Kidds; James Waynes; Wee Willie Wayne)
Singles: 78 rpm
ALADDIN ... 10-20 54
IMPERIAL ... 15-30 51-57
MILLION ... 15-25 54
PEACOCK ... 15-25 57
SITTIN' IN WITH (573 "Gypsy Blues") ... 20-40 50
SITTIN' IN WITH (588 "Love Me Blues") ... 20-40 51
SITTIN' IN WITH (607 "Junco Partner") ... 20-40 51
SITTIN' IN WITH (622 "Please Baby Please") ... 20-40 52
SITTIN' IN WITH (639 "Money Blues") ... 20-40 52
Singles: 7-inch
ANGELTONE (540 "This Little Letter") ... 10-20 60
ALADDIN (3234 "Cryin' in Vain") ... 40-60 54
IMPERIAL (5258 "I'm in Love with You") ... 40-60 53
IMPERIAL (5355 "Travelin' Mood") ... 40-60 55
IMPERIAL (5368 "Good News") ... 40-60 55
IMPERIAL (5696 "Hard to Handle") ... 20-30 60
IMPERIAL (5725 "Travelin' Mood") ... 15-25 61
IMPERIAL (5737 "Woman") ... 15-25 61
MILLION (2009 "Junco's Return") ... 40-60 54
PEACOCK (1672 "Yes I Do") ... 25-35 57
LPs: 10/12-inch
IMPERIAL (9144 "Travelin' Mood") ... 200-300 61
Also see CHARLES, Ray / Arbee Stidham / Li'l Son Jackson / James Wayne
Also see HOKE, Billy
Also see EVANS, Larry

WAYNE, Jeff
(With Justin Hayward)
Singles: 7-inch
COLUMBIA ... 4-6 78
LPs: 10/12-inch
COLUMBIA ... 20-30 78
Also see HAYWARD, Justin

WAYNE, Jerry
Singles: 7-inch
MGM ... 5-10 58

WAYNE, Jimmy
Singles: 7-inch
CORWIN (6618 "You Shake Me") ... 100-200

WAYNE, John LP '73
(With Hank Levine Orchestra & Chorus)
Singles: 7-inch
CASABLANCA ... 3-4 79
LIBERTY (55399 "I Have Faith") ... 5-10 61
RCA ... 3-5 73
LPs: 10/12-inch
RCA (3000 series) ... 5-10 79-81
RCA (4828 "America") ... 15-25 73
Also see LEVINE, Hank

WAYNE, Kenny
(With the Kamotions)
Singles: 7-inch
AMSTAR ... 3-5 81
CANDY ... 3-4 84
HARE ... 3-5 74
SOUNDWAVES ... 3-4 83
LPs: 10/12-inch
CANDY ... 5-8 84

WAYNE, Larry
Singles: 7-inch
SANTO ... 4-8 62

WAYNE, Lenny, & Hi Tones
Singles: 7-inch
SKY LINE ... 4-8 64

WAYNE, Lorrie
Singles: 7-inch
DALE ... 5-10 60

WAYNE, Luther
Singles: 7-inch
TOPPA ... 5-10 60

WAYNE, Mark
Singles: 7-inch
CT ... 5-10 60
W.B. ... 4-8 62

WAYNE, Nancy C&W '74
Singles: 7-inch
20TH CENTURY ... 3-5 74-75

WAYNE, Pat
Singles: 7-inch
TOWER ... 4-8 65

WAYNE, Paula
Singles: 7-inch
COLUMBIA ... 4-6 66
MONOCLE ... 4-6
Picture Sleeves
COLUMBIA ... 4-8 66

WAYNE, Russ
Singles: 7-inch
SAMTER ... 4-8 63-64

WAYNE, Scotty
(Baldemar Huerta)
Singles: 7-inch
TALENT SCOUT (1008 "Only One") ... 20-30 62
Also see FENDER, Freddy

WAYNE, Susan
Singles: 7–inch
COLUMBIA ... 4-8 64-65

WAYNE, Tammy
Singles: 7–inch
BOOM ... 4-8 66

WAYNE, Terry
Singles: 7–inch
COLUMBIA ... 5-10 59
COTCO ... 5-10 62
TREND ... 10-15

WAYNE, Thomas P&R/R&B '59
(With the DeLons)
Singles: 7–inch
CAPEHART ... 4-8 61
CHALET ... 3-5 69
COLLECTABLES ... 3-4 80s
ERIC ... 3-4 70s
FERNWOOD (Except 106) ... 10-20 59-60
FERNWOOD (106 "You're the One That Done It") ... 50-75 58
MERCURY (71287 "You're the One That Done It") ... 30-50 58
MERCURY (71454 "You're the One That Done It") ... 20-30 59
OLDIES 45 ... 4-6 64
PHILLIPS INT'L ... 5-10 62
RACER ... 4-8 65
SANTO ... 5-10 62

WAYNE, Vince
Singles: 7–inch
BANDSTAND ... 5-10 63
RAVEN ... 8-12 63
STARDUST ... 4-8 65

WAYNE, Wee Willie: see WAYNE, James

WAYNE & DWAIN
Singles: 7–inch
CRUSADER ... 10-20 64

WAYNE & EXCEPTIONS
Singles: 7–inch
LAURIE ... 4-8 67

WAYNE & GARY
Singles: 7–inch
MEDIA ... 4-8 64

WAYNE & MIKE
Singles: 7–inch
ADONIS ... 8-12 60s

WAYNE & RAY
Singles: 7–inch
ADONIS (109 "I've Got Your Love on My Mind") ... 10-15 60
ADONIS (110 "For Your Precious Love") ... 10-15 60
MUTUAL (104 "Be My Honey Bee") ... 10-15 60
TWENTIETH CENTURY (1211 "Sweet Lou") ... 5-10

WAYNES, James: see WAYNE, James

WAYORES
Singles: 7–inch
COLT ... 4-8 67

WAYSTED LP '87
LPs: 10/12–inch
CAPITOL ... 5-8 87

WAYWARD BUS
Singles: 7–inch
RCA ... 4-6 68

WAZOO
Singles: 7–inch
R&R ... 4-6 69
LPs: 10/12–inch
ZIG ZAG ... 10-15

WE BELIEVE
Singles: 7–inch
DUNHILL ... 4-8 68

WE FIVE P&R/LP '65
Singles: 7–inch
A&M ... 4-8 65-69
MGM ... 3-5 73
VAULT ... 4-8 67
VERVE ... 3-5 68-73
LPs: 10/12–inch
A&M ... 15-20 65-69
A.V.I. ... 5-10 77
VAULT ... 10-15 70
Members: Mike Stewart; Pete Fullerton; Beverly Bivens; Bob Jones; Jerry Burgan.

WE in a NUTSHELL
Singles: 7–inch
VILLA (68017 "Never Fade Away") 15-25 68

WE TALKIES
Singles: 7–inch
EPIC ... 4-8 67

WE THE PEOPLE
Singles: 7–inch
CHALLENGE (59333 "Mirror of Your Mind") ... 10-20 66
CHALLENGE (59340 "You Burn Me Up and Down") ... 10-20 66
CHALLENGE (59351 "In the Past") 10-20 67
DJ (251 "Point Panic") ... 20-25 65
HOTLINE (3680 "My Brother the Man") ... 20-30 66
RCA ... 8-12 67-68

WE THE PEOPLE R&B '72
Singles: 7–inch
DAVEL ... 4-8 75
IMPERIAL ... 4-8 69
LION ... 3-6 72-74
MAP CITY ... 4-8 69
REENA ... 4-8 68
VERVE ... 4-6 71
LPs: 10/12–inch
CENTURY ADVENT (5262 "We the People") ... 10-15 73
Members: Terri Gonzalez; Robert Taylor; Shabi Weems; Billy McKeechun.

WE THREE
Singles: 7–inch
COURTNEY ... 4-8 63
DOT ... 4-8 63

WE THREE
Singles: 7–inch
CUCA (6841 "Our Graduation Song") ... 10-15 68

WE THREE TRIO
LPs:10/12–inch
MAINSTREAM ... 15-20

WE TWO
Singles: 7–inch
ABC (10930 "Magic Moments") ... 10-20 67

WE UGLY DOGS
Singles: 7–inch
B.T. PUPPY ... 6-10 68

WE WHO ARE
Singles: 7–inch
LOVE (6739 "Last Trip") ... 150-200 67

WEADS
Singles: 7–inch
DUANE (1042 "Today") ... 10-20 65

WEADS
Singles: 7–inch
TRUMP ... 4-8 60s

WEAPONS OF PEACE R&B '76
Singles: 7–inch
PLAYBOY ... 3-5 76-77
Picture Sleeves
PLAYBOY ... 3-5 76
LPs: 10/12–inch
PLAYBOY ... 5-10 77
Members: Finis Henderson; David Johnson; Lonell Dantzler; Bill Leathers; Randy Hardy.
Also see HENDERSON, Finis

WEASELS
LPs: 10/12–inch
WING ... 20-30 64

WEATHER GIRLS R&B '82
Singles: 12–inch
COLUMBIA ... 4-6 83-85
Singles: 7–inch
COLUMBIA ... 3-4 83-85
LPs: 10/12–inch
COLUMBIA ... 5-10 84
Member: Martha Wash.
Also see BLACK BOX
Also see TWO TONS O' FUN

WEATHER REPORT LP '71
Singles: 7–inch
COLUMBIA ... 3-5 73-84
LPs: 10/12–inch
ARC/COLUMBIA ... 5-10 78-82
COLUMBIA ... 5-10 71-86
Also see PASTORIUS, Jaco
Also see SHORTER, Wayne

WEATHERBEE, Alfy
Singles: 78 rpm
ROULETTE ... 5-10 57
Singles: 7–inch
ROULETTE ... 5-10 57

WEATHERLY, Jim P&R/LP '74
Singles: 7–inch
ABC ... 3-5 76-77
BUDDAH ... 3-5 74-75
ELEKTRA ... 3-5 79-80
ERIC ... 3-5 78
RCA ... 3-5 72-74
20TH FOX ... 4-8 65
Picture Sleeves
BUDDAH ... 3-5 74
LPs: 10/12–inch
ABC ... 5-10 77
BUDDAH ... 5-10 74-75
RCA ... 8-12 72

WEATHERS, Carl R&B '81
Singles: 7–inch
MIRAGE ... 3-5 81

WEATHERS, Oscar R&B '70
Singles: 7–inch
BLUE CANDLE ... 4-6 73
SIRLOIN (009 "When You See What You Want") ... 4-8 75
TOP & BOTTOM ... 5-10 69-72

WEAVER, Curley
Singles: 78 rpm
SITTIN' IN WITH (547 "My Baby's Gone") ... 30-40 50

WEAVER, Darry
Singles: 7–inch
CAPEHART (5001 "Sweet Mary Jo") ... 15-20 60
Also see GAMBLERS

WEAVER, Dennis LP '72
(With the Good Time People)
Singles: 7–inch
CASCADE ... 8-12 59
CENTURY CITY ... 4-6 69
EVA ... 5-10 63
IM'PRESS ... 3-5 72
OVATION ... 3-5 75
W.B. ... 5-10 63
LPs: 10/12–inch
IM'PRESS ... 8-10 72
OVATION ... 5-10 75

WEAVER, Donnie
Singles: 7–inch
14 KARAT ... 8-12

WEAVER, Earl
LPs: 10/12–inch
LIFESONG (8138 "Earl of Baltimore") ... 15-25 82
(Picture disc.)

WEAVER, Gil
Singles: 7–inch
JCP (1056 "Do Like I Do") ... 5-10 60s

WEAVER, Jackie
Singles: 7–inch
CHESS ... 4-8 61

WEAVER, J.C.
TURKEY (712 "Elvis, Coming on Strong") ... 8-12 77

WEAVER, Joe
(With the Blue Notes; with Don Juans)
Singles: 78 rpm
DELUXE ... 20-30 53
FORTUNE ... 15-35 56-57
JAGUAR ... 15-25 55
Singles: 7–inch
DACO (1307 "Farm Boy") ... 20-30 50s
DELUXE (6006 "Soft Pillow") ... 50-75 53
DELUXE (6021 "J.D. Boogie") ... 50-75 53
FORTUNE (820 "Loose Caboose") ... 20-40 55
FORTUNE (825 "Baby, I Love You So") ... 20-40 56
FORTUNE (832 "Looka Here, Pretty Baby") ... 20-40 57
JAGUAR ... 20-40 55
Also see KENT, Al
Also see LAKE, Don, & Don Juans

WEAVER, Patty
Singles: 7–inch
W.B. ... 3-4 82
Picture Sleeves
W.B. ... 3-4 82
LPs: 10/12–inch
W.B. ... 5-10 82

WEAVER, Wee Willie
Singles: 7–inch
TANDY ... 4-8 65

WEAVERS P&R '50
(With Gordon Jenkins' Orchestra)
Singles: 78 rpm
DECCA ... 4-8 50-57
Singles: 7–inch
DECCA (27000 thru 29000 series) 10-20 50-55
DECCA (31000 series) ... 4-8 62
MCA ... 3-5 73
NSD ... 3-5 82
VANGUARD ... 4-8 60-62
EPs: 7–inch
DECCA ... 10-25 51-52
LPs: 10/12–inch
DECCA (173 "Best of the Weavers") ... 10-20 65
(Monaural.)
DECCA (7173 "Best of the Weavers") ... 10-20 65
(Stereo.)
DECCA (5285 "Folk Songs") ... 25-50 51
(10–inch LP.)
DECCA (5373 "Merry Christmas") ... 20-40 52
(10–inch LP.)
DECCA (8893 "Best of the Weavers") ... 15-25 59
DECCA (74277 "Weavers Gold") ... 10-15 70
VANGUARD (15-16 "Greatest Hits") ... 12-18 71
VANGUARD (2000 series) ... 15-25 59-63
VANGUARD (3000 thru 6000 series) ... 8-15 67-70
VANGUARD (9000 series) ... 15-35 56-63
VANGUARD (9100 series) ... 12-25 65
Members: Pete Seeger; Lee Hays; Fred Hellerman; Ronnie Gilbert.
Also see ALMANAC SINGERS
Also see JENKINS, Gordon, & His Orchestra
Also see SEEGER, Pete

WEAVERS & TERRY GILKYSON C&W '51
Singles: 7–inch
DECCA ... 4-8 51
Singles: 7–inch
DECCA ... 8-10 51
Also see GILKYSON, Terry
Also see WEAVERS

WEAVILS
Singles: 7–inch
LORI (9550 "We're the Weavils") ... 20-30 65

WEB
LPs: 10/12–inch
DERAM ... 10-15 68

WEB, Ebony: see EBONEE WEBB

WEBB, Betti
Singles: 7–inch
MGM ... 3-8 70-78

WEBB, Billy
Singles: 7–inch
ADKORP ... 4-6 71

WEBB, Bobby
Singles: 7–inch
ACE (542 "Hear Me") ... 20-30 58

WEBB, Boogie Bill
Singles: 78 rpm
IMPERIAL (5257 "Bad Dog") ... 50-75 53
Singles: 7–inch
IMPERIAL (5257 "Bad Dog") ... 150-200 53

WEBB, Dick
Singles: 7–inch
EPIC ... 8-15 60
MADISON ... 5-10 59
Picture Sleeves
EPIC ... 10-15 60

WEBB, Don
Singles: 7–inch
BRUNSWICK (55158 "Little Bitty Baby") ... 20-30 59

WEBB, Doris
Singles: 7–inch
AVA ... 4-8 63

WEBB, Ebonee: see EBONEE WEBB

WEBB, Gary
(Gary "Spider" Webb)
Singles: 7–inch
BAMBOO ... 4-8 61
DONNA ... 5-10 60
Also see HOLLYWOOD ARGYLES

WEBB, Hoyt
Singles: 7–inch
COTTON CLUB (177 "Baby, Won't You Slow It Down") ... 150-250 57
RUBY (320 "Baby, Won't You Slow It Down") ... 75-125 57

WEBB, Jack LP '55
(With Jazz Combo; with Billy May's Orchestra)
Singles: 7–inch
W.B. (5003 "You'd Never Know the Old Place Now") ... 5-10 58
EPs: 7–inch
RCA (0342/3 "Christmas Story") ... 15-25 50s
RCA (1126 "Pete Kelly's Blues") ... 20-35 55
RCA (3199 "Christmas Story") ... 50-100 53
LPs: 10/12–inch
RCA (1126 "Pete Kelly's Blues") ... 30-50 55
RCA (2053 "Pete Kelly's Blues") ... 20-30 59
RCA (3199 "Christmas Story") ... 75-125 53
(10–inch LP.)
W.B. (B-1207 "You're My Girl") ... 30-50 58
(Monaural.)
W.B. (BS-1207 "You're My Girl") . 50-100 58
(Stereo.)
W.B. (B-1217 "Pete Kelly Lets His Hair Down") ... 30-50 58
(Monaural.)
W.B. (BS-1217 "Pete Kelly Lets His Hair Down") ... 50-100 58
(Stereo.)
Members: Jack Webb; Matty Matlock; Dick Cathcart; Nick Fatool; Elmer "Moe" Schneider; George Van Eps; Ray Sherman; Jud DeNaut.

WEBB, Jay Lee C&W '67
(Jack Webb)
Singles: 7–inch
DECCA ... 3-6 67
LPs: 10/12–inch
DECCA ... 10-15 67-69
Also see LYNN, Loretta

WEBB, Jim
Singles: 7–inch
SUNDANCE ... 5-10 59

WEBB, Jim "Spider"
Singles: 7–inch
SELECT HITS ... 3-4
Picture Sleeves
SELECT HITS ... 3-4

WEBB, Jimmy
(Jim Webb)
Singles: 7–inch
ASYLUM ... 3-5 74
ATLANTIC ... 3-5 77
BELL ... 3-5 70
DUNHILL ... 4-8 68
EPIC ... 5-10 68
REPRISE ... 3-5 70-72
LPs: 10/12–inch
ASYLUM ... 8-10 74
ATLANTIC ... 8-12 77
COLUMBIA ... 5-10 82
EPIC (26401 "Jim Webb Sings Jim Webb") ... 15-20 68
REPRISE ... 5-10 70-72
Also see MIDNIGHT MAIL
Also see STRAWBERRY CHILDREN

WEBB, Johnny
Singles: 7–inch
JIN ... 5-10 59

WEBB, Joyce
Singles: 7–inch
DOMINO (600 "Just Like a Man") ... 30-40 58
GOLDEN WORLD (108 "Laughing to Keep from Crying") ... 10-20 63
LEE RAY (502 "Tears on My Pillow") ... 40-60
PROBE (473 "If I Can't Have You") ... 10-20 60s
RIC TIC (102 "You've Got a Whole Lot of Living to Do") ... 10-20 62

WEBB, June C&W '58
Singles: 7–inch
HICKORY ... 5-10 58

WEBB, Lance R&B '84
Singles: 7–inch
BEANTOWN ... 3-5 84

WEBB, Paula P&R '75
Singles: 7–inch
WESTBOUND ... 3-5 75

WEBB, Spider, & Insects
Singles: 7–inch
LUGAR ... 10-15 63

WEBB, Stanley
Singles: 7–inch
VANDAN ... 4-8 63

WEBB, Walter, & Highlighters
Singles: 7–inch
CHESS (2091 "Your Time Is Gonna Come") ... 15-25 70

WEBBER, Andrew Lloyd LP '91
Singles: 7–inch
MCA ... 3-5 78
LPs: 10/12–inch
MCA ... 5-10 91

WEBBER, Lee
Singles: 7–inch
CHESS ... 4-8 68
EXCELLO (2332 "Seventh Son") ... 5-10 73

WEBBER, Rollie
Singles: 7–inch
COUNTRY ("Tired of Livin' ") ... 25-35
(Selection number not known.)
Members: Rollie Webber; Buck Owens; Don Rich.
Also see OWENS, Buck

WEBER, Joan P&R '54
Singles: 78 rpm
COLUMBIA ... 3-5 54-56
Singles: 7–inch
COLUMBIA ... 5-10 54-56
CROSLEY ... 4-6 63
MAPLE ... 4-6 61
EPs: 7–inch
COLUMBIA ... 5-10 55

WEBER, Lewis
Singles: 7–inch
MAGNUM (82260 "Jean") ... 10-20 60
SCOTTIE (1304 "Judy") ... 150-250 59
TATTOO (7453 "Tell Me Baby") ... 50-75 58
TODD (1061 "Someone") ... 10-20 61

WEBER, Tracy
Singles: 12–inch
QUALITY/RFC ... 4-6 83

WEBS
Singles: 7–inch
SOTOPLAY (006 "Do I Have a Chance") ... 350-500 58
(Reissued on Sotoplay's next number, 007, credited to the Notemakers.)
Also see NOTEMAKERS

WEBS R&B '67
Singles: 7–inch
GUYDEN (2090 "Question") ... 15-25 63
MGM ... 5-10 66
POPSIDE ... 8-15 67-68
VERVE ... 5-10 68

WEBS
Singles: 7–inch
HEART ... 10-20 61-62
LITE ... 10-20 62
Member: Bobby Goldsboro.
Also see GOLDSBORO, Bobby

WEBSPINNERS
Singles: 7–inch
BUDDAH ... 3-5 72
LPs: 10/12–inch
BUDDAH ... 8-12 72
Member: Ron Dante.
Also see DANTE, Ron

WEBSTER, Chase C&W '70
Singles: 7–inch
DOT ... 4-8 61-63
CAMEO ... 4-8 63-64
SOUTHERN SOUND ... 5-10 61
SHOW BIZ ... 3-5 70
SPUR ... 8-10

WEBSTER, John & Anna
Singles: 7–inch
FREEDOM ... 5-10 59

WEBSTER, Katie
Singles: 7–inch
A-BET ... 8-10 67
ACTION (1000 "Close to My Heart") ... 10-20 61
DECCA (30945 "Sea of Love") ... 20-25 59
GOLDBAND (1200 series) ... 6-12 62
QUEEN (24002 "Close to My Heart") ... 10-20 61
ROCKO (503 "Open Arms") ... 15-25 61
ROCKO (513 "Goodbye Baby, I'm Still Leavin' You") ... 10-20 61
SPOT (1000 "Glory of Love") ... 10-20 60s
ZYNN (505 "Sweet Daddy") ... 50-100 58
Also see LAZY LESTER

WEBSTER, Katie, & Ashton Conroy
Singles: 7–inch
KRY (100 "Baby Baby") ... 20-30 58

WEBSTER, Mamie
LPs: 10/12-inch
CUB (8002 "The Blues") ... 100-150 59

WEBSTER, Max: see MAX WEBSTER

WEBSTER'S NEW WORD
Singles: 7-inch
COLUMBIA ... 4-8 66
RCA ... 4-8 67

WEBTONES
Singles: 7-inch
MGM ... 10-20 58
Members: Louis Williams; Terry Wilson; Frank Clemens
Also see DANLEERS

WEDGE
LPs: 10/12-inch
RHINO ... 5-10 80

WEDGES
LPs: 10/12-inch
TIME ... 15-25 63

WEDGWOODS
Singles: 7-inch
LIMELIGHT ... 10-15 60s

WEDLAW, Frankie
Singles: 7-inch
SKYLA ... 10-15 62

WEDNESDAY *P&R '73*
Singles: 7-inch
BUDDAH ... 3-5 75
CELEBRATION ... 3-5 76
SKY ... 3-5 76
SUSSEX ... 3-5 73-74
LPs: 10/12-inch
SUSSEX ... 8-10 74

WEE FOUR
Singles: 7-inch
NU SOUND LTD ... 5-10 66

WEE GEE *R&B '78*
Singles: 7-inch
COTILLION ... 3-5 80
JUNEY ... 3-5 78

WEE WILLIE & MELLODIERS
Singles: 7-inch
WOW (110 "When") ... 500-750

WEED, Gene
Singles: 7-inch
20TH FOX ... 8-12 63
Also see BAGGYS

WEEDS
Singles: 7-inch
N.W.I. (2745 "No Good News") ... 10-15 69
TEENBEAT (1006 "Little Girl") ... 20-30 67
Picture Sleeves
N.W.I. (2745 "No Good News") ... 15-25 69
Members: Ron Buzzel; Bob Atkins; Edward Bowen; Fred Cole; Carl Fortina; Tim Rockson.
Also see LOLLIPOP SHOPPE

WEEJUNS
Singles: 7-inch
JAGUAR ... 5-10 66

WEEKENDS
Singles: 7-inch
COLUMBIA ... 5-10 66
LE-MANS ... 8-12 64

WEEKENDERS
Singles: 7-inch
VOGT ... 10-20

WEEKS & CO. *R&B '81*
Singles: 12-inch
SALSOUL ... 4-6 83
Singles: 7-inch
CHEZ RO ... 3-5 81
SALSOUL ... 3-4 83
LPs: 10/12-inch
SALSOUL ... 5-8 83
Member: Richie Weeks.

WEEMS, Ritchie, & Continental Five
Singles: 7-inch
DUNHILL ... 4-8 65
SPOT ... 5-10 65

WEHBA, Dale
Singles: 7-inch
KINGS X ... 5-10 59

WEIDER, John
LPs: 10/12-inch
ANCHOR ... 8-10 76
GOLD CASTLE ... 5-8 88
Also see ANIMALS
Also see FAMILY

WEIGAND, Jack
Singles: 7-inch
CAMEO ... 5-10 60
LPs: 10/12-inch
WYNCOTE ... 10-15 64

WEIGHT, The
Singles: 7-inch
BERTRAM INT'L (230 "Flip, Flop, and Fly") ... 10-20 64

WEINBERG, Elyse
Singles: 7-inch
TETRAGRAMMATON ... 3-6 69
LPs: 10/12-inch
TETRAGRAMMATON ... 8-10 69

WEINBERG METHOD
LPs: 10/12-inch
ANVIL ... 8-10 70

WEINRIB, Len
Singles: 7-inch
CAPITOL ... 5-10 62

WEINSTEIN & STROLL
Singles: 7-inch
CHIPS ... 3-5 70
LPs: 10/12-inch
CHIPS ... 10-15 70
Members: Bobby Weinstein; Jon Stroll.

WEIR, Bob *LP '72*
Singles: 7-inch
ARISTA (315 "Bombs Away") ... 4-6 77
ARISTA (336 "I'll Be Doggone") ... 10-15 77
(Promotional issue only.)
W.B. ... 8-12 72
LPs: 10/12-inch
ARISTA ... 5-10 78
W.B. (2627 "Ace") ... 25-30 72
Also see BOBBY & MIDNITES
Also see GRATEFUL DEAD
Also see KINGFISH

WEIR, Frank, Orchestra *P&R '54*
Singles: 78 rpm
CAPITOL ... 3-5 56
COLUMBIA ... 3-5 57
LONDON ... 3-5 54-57
Singles: 7-inch
CAPITOL ... 4-8 56
COLUMBIA ... 4-8 57
LONDON ... 4-8 54-63
EPs: 7-inch
LONDON ... 5-10 54-55
LPs: 10/12-inch
COLUMBIA ... 10-20 57
LONDON ... 10-20 54

WEIRD STREET CARNIVAL
Singles: 7-inch
COPRA (2305 "The Subterranean Edible Fungus") ... 20-30 60s

WEIRD-OHS
Singles: 7-inch
MERCURY (72410 "Digger") ... 5-10 65
LPs: 10/12-inch
MERCURY (20976 "New Sounds") ... 30-50 65
(Monaural.)
MERCURY (60976 "New Sounds") ... 20-30 65
(Stereo.)
Also see SILLY SURFERS / Weird-Ohs

WEIRDOS
Singles: 7-inch
LAN-CET ... 5-10 61

WEIRDOS
EPs: 7-inch
BOMP ... 5-10 79
LPs: 10/12-inch
BOMP ... 5-8 80
RHINO ... 5-8 80

WEIRZ
Singles: 12-inch
MCA ... 4-6 83
Singles: 7-inch
MCA ... 3-4 83
LPs: 10/12-inch
BONSALL ... 8-12 75
PRELUDE-WEST ... 5-8 79

WEISBERG, Tim *LP '73*
Singles: 7-inch
A&M ... 3-5 71-79
MCA ... 3-5 79
U.A. ... 3-5 77-80
LPs: 10/12-inch
A&M ... 5-10 73-79
MCA ... 5-10 79-80
NAUTILUS ... 10-15 80
U.A. ... 5-10 77-78
Also see FOGELBERG, Dan, & Tim Weisberg

WEISE, Don
Singles: 7-inch
JERDEN ... 8-12 64

WEISS, Donna
Singles: 7-inch
ATCO ... 3-5 70

WEISS, Doug
Singles: 7-inch
DINAMO (1001 "Do You Love Another") ... 15-25 59
Also see HAHN, Tommy, & Mojo Men

WEISSBERG, Eric, & Marshall Brickman
LPs: 10/12-inch
ELEKTRA (EKL-238 "New Dimensions in Banjo & Bluegrass") ... 15-25 63
(Monaural.)
ELEKTRA (ESK7-238 "New Dimensions in Banjo & Bluegrass") ... 20-30 63
(Stereo.)
Also see TARRIERS

WEISSBERG, Eric, & Deliverance
Singles: 7-inch
EPIC ... 3-5 75
W.B ... 3-5 73
LPs: 10/12-inch
W.B. (2720 "Rural Free Delivery") ... 5-10 73

WEISSBERG, Eric, & Steve Mandell *P&R/C&W/LP '73*
Singles: 7-inch
W.B. (7659 "Dueling Banjos") ... 4-6 72
(Reads: "From the Warner Bros. Film Deliverance." No specific artist credited other than mention of "Arranged by Eric Weissberg.")
W.B. (7659 "Dueling Banjos") ... 3-5 72
(Credit: "Eric Weissberg from the Warner Bros. Film Deliverance.")
LPs: 10/12-inch
W.B. (2683 "Dueling Banjos") ... 5-10 73
Also see WEISSBERG, Eric, & Marshall Brickman

WELCH, Bob *P&R/LP '77*
Singles: 7-inch
CAPITOL ... 3-5 77-81
RCA ... 3-4 81-83
Picture Sleeves
CAPITOL ... 3-5 78-81
LPs: 10/12-inch
CAPITOL (Except 16000 series) ... 8-10 77-80
CAPITOL (16000 series) ... 5-8 80-82
RCA ... 5-10 81-83
Promotional LPs
CAPITOL (11663 "French Kiss") ... 15-25 79
(Picture disc.)
Also see FLEETWOOD MAC
Also see PARIS

WELCH, Bruce
Singles: 7-inch
EMI ... 3-5 74
Also see SHADOWS

WELCH, Ernie *C&W '89*
Singles: 7-inch
DUCK TAPE ... 3-4 89

WELCH, Honey
Singles: 7-inch
CHEVELL ... 4-8 65

WELCH, Kevin *C&W '89*
Singles: 7-inch
REPRISE ... 3-4 90
W.B. ... 3-4 89-90
Also see TOMORROW'S WORLD

WELCH, Lenny *P&R/R&B '60*
(Lenny & the Storks)
Singles: 7-inch
ATCO ... 3-5 72
BARNABY ... 3-5 76
BIG TREE ... 3-5 78-83
CADENCE (Except 1399 & 1422) ... 8-15 59-64
CADENCE (1399 "Boogie Cha Cha") ... 15-25 60
CADENCE (1422 "Congratulations Baby") ... 15-25 62
COLUMBIA ... 4-8 67
COMMONWEALTH UNITED ... 4-6 69
DECCA ... 5-10 59
JASON SCOTT ... 4-8
KAPP ... 5-15 65-67
MAINSTREAM ... 3-5 73-74
MERCURY ... 4-8 68
ROULETTE ... 3-6 71
LPs: 10/12-inch
CADENCE ... 15-25 64
COLUMBIA ... 10-20 65
KAPP ... 10-20 66-67

WELCH, Raquel
Singles: 12-inch
COLUMBIA (07622 "Girl's Back in Town") ... 10-15 87
(Includes cover.)
Singles: 7-inch
COLUMBIA (07622 "Girl's Back in Town") ... 3-5 87
Picture Sleeves
COLUMBIA (07622 "Girl's Back in Town") ... 3-5 87

WELCH, Tim
(Timmy Welch)
Singles: 7-inch
ATTRACK ... 3-5 70s
EDIT ... 5-10 60
REPRISE ... 4-8 62-63

WELD, Tuesday
Singles: 7-inch
PLAZA (508 "Are You the Boy") ... 8-12 62

WELDON, Danny
Singles: 7-inch
ENITH ... 8-10 63

WELDON, Eddie
Singles: 7-inch
MARLY ... 5-10 59

WELK, Lawrence, & His Orchestra *P&R '38*
Singles: 78 rpm
CORAL ... 3-5 50-57
DECCA ... 3-6 42-45
MERCURY ... 3-5 50-55
OKEH ... 3-6 41
VOCALION ... 3-8 38-39
Singles: 7-inch
CORAL ... 3-8 50-66
DOT ... 3-8 59-67
MERCURY ... 3-8 50-55
RANWOOD ... 3-8 68-77
EPs: 7-inch
CORAL ... 4-8 50-58
DOT ... 4-8 59-60
MERCURY ... 4-8 50-55
LPs: 10/12-inch
CORAL ... 5-15 50-65
DECCA ... 5-10 72
DOT ... 5-15 59-67
HAMILTON ... 4-8 64-66
HARMONY ... 4-8 68-70
MCA ... 4-8 74-76
PICKWICK ... 4-8
RANWOOD ... 4-8 68-85
SUNNYVALE ... 4-6 79
TRADITION ... 4-8 75
VOCALION ... 4-8 59-70
WING ... 4-8 60-62
Also see FOLEY, Red
Also see HODGES, Johnny, & Lawrence Welk
Also see HOOPER, Larry
Also see HUDSON, Emperor Bob, & Lawrence Welk
Also see LENNON SISTERS
Also see McGUIRE SISTERS
Also see PRESLEY, Elvis / Lawrence Welk

WELL RED *R&B '87*
Singles: 7-inch
VIRGIN ... 3-4 87

WELLER, Freddy *C&W/LP '69*
Singles: 7-inch
ABC/DOT ... 3-5 75
APT ... 4-8 65
COLUMBIA ... 3-6 69-80
DORE ... 5-10 61
LPs: 10/12-inch
ABC/DOT ... 5-10 75
COLUMBIA ... 5-12 69-80
EPIC ... 8-12 74
51 WEST ... 5-8 80s
Also see REVERE, Paul, & Raiders
Also see SPURZZ

WELLES, Orson *LP '70*
LPs: 10/12-inch
MEDIARTS ... 8-12 70
Also see CROSBY, Bing, and Orson Welles

WELLINGTON, Mary Sue
Singles: 7-inch
TUFF ... 4-8 64

WELLINGTON, Rusty
(With the Travelaires; with Shorty Long's Santa Fe Rangers)
Singles: 78 rpm
ARCADE ... 10-20 53-57
MGM ... 100-200 57
Singles: 7-inch
ARCADE (116 "Doggone It Baby, I'm in Love") ... 15-35 53
ARCADE (124 "I Want a Little Lovin' ") ... 15-35 54
ARCADE (140 "Jump Jump Honey") ... 15-35 56
ARCADE (144 "I Ain't A-Movin' No More") ... 15-35 57
ARCADE (184 "The Allagash") ... 10-20 65
ARCADE (185 "Soft Shoulders") ... 10-20 65
MGM (12581 "Rocking Chair on the Moon") ... 15-25 57
Also see LONG, Shorty

WELLINGTON ARRANGEMENT
Singles: 7-inch
DECCA ... 5-10 71

WELLINGTONS
Singles: 7-inch
ASCOT ... 4-8 66
BUENA VISTA ... 4-8 63

WELLMAN, Tiny *C&W '88*
Singles: 7-inch
LEE ANN ... 3-4 88

WELLS, Ardis
Singles: 7-inch
AZALEA ... 5-10 60
FEDERAL ... 4-8 61

WELLS, Barbara
Singles: 7-inch
CORAL ... 4-8 64

WELLS, Billy, & Crescents
Singles: 78 rpm
RESERVE (105 "Julie") ... 100-200 56
Singles: 7-inch
RESERVE (105 "Julie") ... 300-500 56

WELLS, Bobby
Singles: 7-inch
MERCURY ... 4-8 64

WELLS, Brandi *R&B '81*
Singles: 7-inch
WMOT ... 3-5 81-82
Also see BREEZE
Also see SLICK

WELLS, Cory
(With the Enemys)
Singles: 7-inch
A&M ... 3-5 78
VALIANT ... 8-12 65
LPs: 10/12-inch
A&M ... 5-10 77-79
Also see ENEMYS
Also see THREE DOG NIGHT

WELLS, Dennis
Singles: 7-inch
CREST ... 5-10 60

WELLS, Donnie
Singles: 7-inch
SCEPTER ... 10-20 65

WELLS, Eddie
Singles: 7-inch
CELMAR ... 5-10 60

WELLS, Fargo
Singles: 7-inch
RING-A-DING ... 4-8 63

WELLS, Garry
Singles: 7-inch
ARWIN ... 8-12 58
MGM ... 8-12 59

WELLS, Glenn, & Blends
Singles: 7-inch
JIN (122 "Write Me a Letter") ... 15-25 60
JIN (139 "As My Tears Fall") ... 15-25 61
U.A. (244 "Written in the Stars") ... 10-15 60

WELLS, Jean *R&B '67*
Singles: 7-inch
ABC-PAR (10745 "Don't Come Running to Me") ... 10-20 65
CALLA ... 5-10 67-68
CANYON (39 "Somebody's Been Lovin' You") ... 5-10
QUAKER TOWN ... 4-8
T.E.C. ... 4-6 79
VOLARE ... 5-10 69

WELLS, Johnny
Singles: 7-inch
ASTOR (1001 "Lonely Moon") ... 10-15 59
ASTOR (1002 "For Everyone") ... 10-15 60

WELLS, Junior *R&B '60*
(With His Eagle Rockers; Junior Wells' Chicago Blues Band)
Singles: 78 rpm
STATES ... 25-50 52-53
Singles: 7-inch
ALL POINTS (2000 "Little By Little") ... 10-15 66
BLUE ROCK ... 8-12 68-69
BRIGHT STAR (146 "I'm Losing You") ... 8-12 66
BRIGHT STAR (149 "Up in Heah") ... 8-12 66
BRIGHT STAR (152 "I'm Gonna Cramp Your Style") ... 8-12 67
BRIGHT STAR (504 "I Found Out") ... 8-12 67
CHIEF (7005 "Two-Headed Woman") ... 20-30 57
CHIEF (7021 "Messin' with the Kid") ... 15-25 58
CHIEF (7030 "I'm a Stranger") ... 10-20 61
CHIEF (7034 "You Sure Look Good to Me") ... 10-20 61
CHIEF (7035 "It Hurts Me Too") ... 10-20 61
CHIEF (7037 "So Tired") ... 10-20 61
CHIEF (7038 "I Need Me a Car") ... 10-20 61
HIT SOUND (223 "It's All Soul") ... 5-10 68
KAPP (270 "So Tired") ... 8-12 59
MEL ... 10-15
PROFILE (4005 "I Could Cry") ... 10-20 59
PROFILE (4011 "Come on in This House") ... 10-20 60
PROFILE (4013 "You Don't Care") ... 10-20 60
SHAD (5010 "So Tired") ... 10-20 59
STATES (122 "Cut That Out") ... 100-200 52
(Red vinyl.)
STATES (134 "Hodo Man") ... 100-200 53
(Red vinyl.)
STATES (139 "Lawdy Lawdy") ... 100-200 53
(Red vinyl.)
STATES (143 "So All Alone") ... 150-250 53
(Red vinyl.)
U.S.A. (736 "Every Goodbye Ain't Gone") ... 8-12 63
U.S.A. (742 "She's a Sweet One") ... 8-12 63
U.S.A. (790 "Come on in This House") ... 8-12 64
VANGUARD ... 5-10 67
LPs: 10/12-inch
BLUE ROCK ... 10-20 68
DELMARK ... 10-20 66-69
VANGUARD ... 12-25 66-68
Also see COTTON, James, Carey Bell, Junior Wells & Billy Branch
Also see DIXON, Willie
Also see HOOKER, Earl / Junior Wells
Also see LENOIR, J.B.
Also see SPANN, Otis
Also see WATERS, Muddy

WELLS, Junior, & Buddy Guy
LPs: 10/12-inch
ATCO ... 8-12 72
BLIND PIG ... 5-8 82
INTERMEDIA ... 5-8
Also see GUY, Buddy
Also see WELLS, Junior

WELLS, Karen
Singles: 7-inch
CUCA (1035 "Believe Him") ... 5-10 61

WELLS, Kenny
Singles: 7-inch
NEW VOICE (812 "I Can't Stop") ... 30-50 66

WELLS, Kitty *C&W/P&R '52*
Singles: 78 rpm
DECCA ... 4-10 52-57
RCA ... 6-12 50
Singles: 7-inch
CAPRICORN ... 3-5 74-76
DECCA (28000 & 29000 series) ... 5-15 52-56
DECCA (30000 thru 32000 series) ... 3-10 56-71
MCA ... 3-4 73
RCA (0333 "Make Up Your Mind") ... 15-25 50
(Colored vinyl.)
RUBOCA ... 3-5 79-80
Picture Sleeves
DECCA ... 4-6 69
EPs: 7-inch
DECCA ... 5-15 55-65
LPs: 10/12-inch
BULLDOG ... 5-10
CAPRICORN ... 5-10 74

CORAL/MCA ... 5-8 84

DECCA (174 "Kitty Wells Story") ... 15-25 63

(Monaural. Includes booklet.)

DECCA (7-174 "Kitty Wells Story") ... 20-30 63

(Stereo. Includes booklet.)

DECCA (4075 thru 4929) ... 10-25 61-67

(Monaural.)

DECCA (7-4075 thru 7-4929) ... 15-30 61-67

(Stereo.)

DECCA (7-4961 thru 7-5350) ... 10-15 68-72

(Stereo.)

DECCA (8293 "Country Hit Parade") ... 35-45 56

(Monaural.)

DECCA (7-8293 "Country Hit Parade") ... 15-25 68

(Stereo.)

DECCA (8552 "Winner of Your Heart") ... 35-45 56

DECCA (7-8552 "Winner of Your Heart") ... 10-15 65

DECCA (8732 "Lonely Street") ... 30-40 58

(Monaural.)

DECCA (7-8732 "Lonely Street") ... 10-15 65

(Stereo.)

DECCA (8858 "Dust on the Bible") ... 25-35 59

(Monaural.)

DECCA (7-8858 "Dust on the Bible") ... 10-15 68

(Stereo.)

DECCA (8888 "After Dark") ... 30-40 59

(Monaural.)

DECCA (7-8888 "After Dark") ... 10-15 68

(Stereo.)

DECCA (8979 "Kitty's Choice") ... 25-35 59

(Monaural.)

DECCA (7-8979 "Kitty's Choice") ... 30-40 59

(Stereo.)

EXACT ... 5-10 80

GOLDEN COUNTRY ... 5-10

IMPERIAL HOUSE ... 5-10 80

KOALA ... 5-10 79

MCA ... 4-8 73-83

MISTLETOE ... 5-8 80s

PICKWICK/HILLTOP ... 5-10 70s

ROUNDER ... 5-8 82

RUBOCA ... 8-12 79

SUFFOLK MARKETING ... 5-10 80

VOCALION ... 8-15 66-69

Also see ACUFF, Roy, & Kitty Wells

Also see ANTHONY, Rayburn, & Kitty Wells

Also see JOHNNIE & JACK

Also see PARTON, Dolly / Kitty Wells

Also see PIERCE, Webb, & Kitty Wells

Also see TUBB, Ernest

WELLS, Kitty / Bill Anderson

LPs: 10/12-inch

MCA (734584 "Collector's Album") ... 8-12

Also see ANDERSON, Bill

WELLS, Kitty, & Roy Drusky C&W '60

Singles: 7-inch

DECCA ... 4-8 60

LPs: 10/12-inch

PLAYBACK ... 5-10

Also see DRUSKY, Roy

WELLS, Kitty, & Red Foley C&W '54

Singles: 78 rpm

DECCA ... 4-10 54-56

Singles: 7-inch

DECCA (29000 series) ... 5-15 54-56

DECCA (32000 series) ... 3-6 67-69

EPs: 7-inch

DECCA ... 8-12 59

LPs: 10/12-inch

DECCA ... 12-25 61-67

Also see FOLEY, Red

WELLS, Kitty / Bill Phillips / Bobby Wright / Johnny Wright

LP: 10/12-inch

DECCA (74831 "The Kitty Wells Show") ... 10-20 66

Also see PHILLIPS, Bill

Also see WRIGHT, Bobby

Also see WRIGHT, Johnny

WELLS, Kitty, & Webb Pierce C&W '57

Singles: 78 rpm

DECCA ... 5-10 57

Singles: 7-inch

DECCA ... 5-10 57-64

EPs: 7-inch

DECCA ... 10-15 59

Also see PIERCE, Webb

WELLS, Kitty, & Johnny Wright C&W '68

Singles: 7-inch

DECCA ... 3-6 68-72

LPs: 10/12-inch

DECCA ... 10-20 68-72

Also see WELLS, Kitty

Also see WRIGHT, Johnny

WELLS, Mary R&B '60

Singles: 12-inch

EPIC ... 4-8 82

Singles: 7-inch

ATCO ... 10-20 66-67

EPIC ... 3-4 82

JUBILEE ... 5-15 68-71

MOTOWN (1003 "Bye Bye Baby") ... 15-25 60

(Pink label.)

MOTOWN (1011 "I Don't Want to Take a Chance") ... 10-20 61

(Pink label.)

MOTOWN (1011 "I Don't Want to Take a Chance") ... 8-12 61

(Blue label.)

MOTOWN (1016 thru 1056) ... 10-20 62-64

MOTOWN (1061 "When I'm Gone") ... 100-200 65

MOTOWN (1065 "I'll Be Available") ... 15-25 65

REPRISE ... 5-10 71-74

20TH FOX ... 10-20 64-66

Picture Sleeves

MOTOWN (1003 "Bye Bye Baby") ... 50-75 61

MOTOWN (1011 "I Don't Want to Take a Chance") ... 25-50 61

MOTOWN (1024 "The One Who Really Loves You") ... 20-40 62

MOTOWN (1032 "You Beat Me to the Punch") ... 20-30 62

20TH FOX (590 "He's a Lover") ... 5-10 65

EPs: 7-inch

MOTOWN (60616 "Greatest Hits") ... 25-50 64

LPs: 10/12-inch

ALLEGIANCE ... 5-10 84

ATCO ... 15-20 66

EPIC ... 5-10 81

51 WEST ... 5-8 83

JUBILEE ... 10-20 68

MOTOWN (100 & 200 series) ... 5-10 82

MOTOWN (600 "Mary Wells") ... 200-300 61

(White label with blue print.)

MOTOWN (605 "The One Who Really Loves You") ... 100-200 62

MOTOWN (607 "Two Lovers") ... 75-125 63

MOTOWN (611 "On Stage") ... 40-60 64

MOTOWN (616 "Greatest Hits") ... 25-35 64

MOTOWN (617 "My Guy") ... 40-60 64

MOTOWN (653 "Vintage Stock") ... 40-60 66

MOVIETONE ... 15-20 66

POWER PAK ... 5-8

20TH FOX ... 20-30 65

Also see GAYE, Marvin, & Mary Wells

Also see MARVELETTES / Mary Wells / Miracles / Marvin Gaye

WELLS, Mike C&W '75

Singles: 7-inch

PLAYBOY ... 3-5 75-76

WELLS, Terri R&B/D&D '84

Singles: 12-inch

PHILLY WORLD ... 4-6 84

Singles: 7-inch

PHILLY WORLD ... 3-4 84

Also see MFSB

WELLS, Terry

Singles: 7-inch

RAMCO ... 4-8 62

RAMCO ... 4-8 62

WELTON, Danny

Singles: 7-inch

DOT (15559 "Calypso Melody") ... 15-25 57

ENITH (715 "Surf Dreamin'") ... 10-20 63

Also see NEW MARKETTS

WELLS, Wes, & Steelers

Singles: 7-inch

TORRID ... 8-12

WELZ, Joey

(With the Kidd Brothers; with New Century Singers; with Link Wray)

Singles: 7-inch

AUDIO FIDELITY ... 3-6 69

BAT (1001 "Boppin' the Stroll") ... 15-25 59

BAT (1002 "Mystery of Love") ... 5-10 63

BAT (1003 "Let's Bop and Stroll Again") ... 5-10 64

BAT (1004 "Maybe") ... 4-8 64

(Reissued in 1967 using the same number.)

BAT (4000 series) ... 4-6 67

CANADIAN AMERICAN ... 4-8 64-68

CAPRICE ... 3-4 86-92

GAME TIME ... 4-8 65

LEEDLE ... 5-10

LEFEVRE ... 4-8 66

MONUMENTAL ... 4-8 64

MUSIC CITY ... 4-6 78

PALMER ... 4-8 67-69

SWAN ... 4-8 66

TEARDROP ... 4-8 65-67

Picture Sleeves

CAPRICE ... 3-4 86-92

LPs: 10/12-inch

MUSIC CITY ... 5-10 78

PALMER ... 10-15 70

Also see HALEY, Bill

Also see WRAY, Link

WELZ, Joey, & Dew Watson

Singles: 7-inch

BOLD (888 "Somewhere Elvis Is Smiling") ... 3-4 92

Picture Sleeves

BOLD (888 "Somewhere Elvis Is Smiling") ... 3-4 92

(Wrap-around insert sleeve.)

Also see WELZ, Joey

WENCE, Bill C&W '79

Singles: 7-inch

RUSTIC ... 3-5 79-80

WENCES, Señor

Singles: 7-inch

JOY (228 "Deefeecult for You") ... 5-10 59

Picture Sleeves

JOY (228 "Deefeecult for You") ... 10-20 59

WENDEL, Will, & Aktones

Singles: 7-inch

TRANS AMERICAN (10,000 "Lonely Blue Boy") ... 100-200 62

WENDELL, Glen

Singles: 7-inch

THREE RIVERS (101 "That's It") ... 75-100

WENDELL & DREAMERS

Singles: 7-inch

REON (1305 "That's Love") ... 40-60

WENDI

Singles: 7-inch

CHAMP ... 4-8 67

WENDIGO

Singles: 7-inch

COUSINS ... 10-15 68

SCEPTER ... 5-10 68

WENDLAND, Gerhard

Singles: 7-inch

PHILIPS ... 4-8 62

WENDROFF, Michael

LPs: 10/12-inch

ARIOLA-AMERICA ... 5-10 78

BUDDAH ... 8-10 73-76

Also see SLY BOOTS

WENDRY, Bill, & Boss Tweeds

Singles: 7-inch

COLUMBIA ... 4-6 68-69

WENDY & LISA P&R/LP '87

Singles: 7-inch

COLUMBIA ... 3-4 87-89

Picture Sleeves

COLUMBIA ... 3-4 87

LPs: 10/12-inch

COLUMBIA ... 5-8 87-89

WENDY & ROCKETS

Singles: 7-inch

A&M ... 3-4 84

LPs: 10/12-inch

A&M ... 5-8 84

WENDY & SCHOOLGIRLS

(With Blackie Scheckner & Orchestra)

Singles: 7-inch

GOLDEN CREST (502 "My Guy") ... 100-200 58

WENNER, Mark, & Switchblade

LPs: 10/12-inch

WHITEWALL (001 "Fugitive") ... 10-20 60s

(Limited autographed edition.)

WHITE LINE ... 5-8 86

Also see NIGHTHAWKS

WEREWOLVES

Singles: 7-inch

RCA ... 3-5 78

LPs: 10/12-inch

RCA ... 5-10 78

WERLEY, Coy, & Blackjacks

Singles: 7-inch

SUNDOWN ... 10-20 59

WERNER, David LP '79

Singles: 7-inch

EPIC ... 3-5 79

RCA ... 3-5 74-76

LPs: 10/12-inch

EPIC ... 5-10 79

RCA ... 5-10 75

WERNER, Max P&R '81

Singles: 7-inch

RADIO ... 3-5 81

Also see KAYAK

WERPS

Singles: 7-inch

W.G.W. (Love's a Fire") ... 20-30 67

WERT, Jimmy

Singles: 7-inch

SKYLINE (752 "Bingo Blues") ... 150-250 59

WERTH, Howard, & Moonbeams

Singles: 7-inch

ROCKET ... 3-5 76

Also see AUDIENCE

WES, Johnny

Singles: 7-inch

ROSE (101 "Hully Gully") ... 10-20 62

WESLEY, Fred R&B '73

(With the Horny Horns; with J.B.s)

Singles: 7-inch

ATLANTIC ... 3-5 77

PEOPLE ... 4-6 72-74

RSO ... 3-5 80

LPs: 10/12-inch

ATLANTIC ... 8-10 77

Also see BROWN, James, Band

Also see FRED & NEW J.B.s

Also see J.B.s

Also see PARLIAMENT

WESLEY, Gate

Singles: 7-inch

ATLANTIC ... 4-8 66

WESLEY, Gene

Singles: 7-inch

SESSION ... 5-10 59

WESLEY, John

Singles: 7-inch

MELIC (4170 "You Still Need Me") ... 15-25

MELIC (4195 "Love Is Such a Funny Thing") ... 10-20

VIVID ... 5-10 65

WESS, Jill

Singles: 7-inch

MARLU ... 4-8 61

WESS, Jimmy, & Upsetters

LPs: 10/12-inch

ABC ... 10-15 68

WEST

Singles: 7-inch

EPIC ... 4-8 68

LPs: 10/12-inch

EPIC ... 10-15 68-69

WEST, Adam

Singles: 7-inch

20TH FOX ... 5-10 66

Picture Sleeves

20TH FOX ... 10-20 66

WEST, Alvis

Singles: 7-inch

ROBIN RED (002 "Do You Remember Buddy Holly") ... 5-10 85

WEST, Barbara

Singles: 7-inch

RONN ... 4-8 68

WEST, Belinda R&B '80

Singles: 7-inch

PANORAMA ... 3-5 80

WEST, Clint

Singles: 7-inch

JIN (179 thru 279) ... 5-10 65-69

WEST, Dr: see DR. WEST

WEST, Dottie C&W '63

(With Dale West)

Singles: 7-inch

ATLANTIC ... 4-8 62

LIBERTY ... 3-4 80-83

PERMIAN ... 3-4 84-85

RCA (Except 8000 series) ... 3-6 66-81

RCA (8000 series) ... 4-8 63-66

STARDAY (500 series) ... 4-8 60-61

STARDAY (700 series) ... 3-6 65

U.A. ... 3-4 76-80

Picture Sleeves

LIBERTY ... 3-5 80-81

LPs: 10/12-inch

CAMDEN ... 5-10 71-73

COLUMBIA ... 5-10 80

GUSTO ... 5-8 82

LIBERTY ... 5-8 81-82

NASHVILLE ... 8-12 70s

PERMIAN ... 5-8 85

PICKWICK ... 5-10 75

POWER PAK ... 5-10 70s

RCA ... 8-18 65-75

STARDAY ... 10-20 64-65

U.A. ... 5-10 73-80

Session: Jordanaires.

Also see DEAN, Jimmy, & Dottie West

Also see JORDANAIRES

Also see REEVES, Jim, & Dottie West

Also see ROGERS, Kenny, & Dottie West

WEST, Dottie, & Don Gibson C&W '70

Singles: 7-inch

RCA ... 3-5 69-70

LPs: 10/12-inch

RCA ... 8-12 69

Also see GIBSON, Don

WEST, Dottie / Melba Montgomery

LPs: 10/12-inch

STARDAY ... 10-20 65

Also see MONTGOMERY, Melba

Also see WEST, Dottie

WEST, Gene

Singles: 7-inch

ORIGINAL SOUND ... 3-5

WEST, Guy

Singles: 7-inch

ERA ... 4-8 66

WEST, Jim C&W '79

(With Carol Chase; with Stephanie Winslow)

Singles: 7-inch

MACHO ... 3-5 79-81

LPs: 10/12-inch

HOME COMFORT ... 5-10 77

Also see CHASE, Carol

WEST, Jimmy

Singles: 78 rpm

SANDEE ... 25-50 56

Singles: 7-inch

SANDEE (315 "Bringing Home the Bacon") ... 50-100 56

WEST, Johnny

Singles: 7-inch

SOUL (841 "Tears Baby") ... 15-25 60s

WEST, Keith

Singles: 7-inch

NEW VOICE ... 4-8 67

WEST, Leslie LP '69

(Leslie West Band)

Singles: 7-inch

PHANTOM ... 3-5 75-76

LPs: 10/12-inch

PHANTOM ... 8-10 75-76

WINDFALL ... 10-15 69

Also see JAGGER, Mick

Also see MOUNTAIN

Also see WEST, BRUCE & LAING

WEST, Little Willie

Singles: 7-inch

RUSTONE ... 5-10 60

WEST, Lynette

Singles: 7-inch

JOSIE ... 4-8 63

WEST, Mae P&R '33

(With Somebody's Chyldren)

Singles: 78 rpm

BRUNSWICK ... 10-30 33

Singles: 7-inch

MGM (14491 "Great Balls of Fire") ... 4-8 73

PLAZA ... 5-10 62

TOWER ... 5-10 66

20TH FOX (6718 "Hard to Handle") ... 15-30 70

EPs: 7-inch

DECCA (838 "Fabulous Mae West") ... 50-75 55

(Three-disc set.)

LPs: 10/12-inch

DAGONET ... 10-15 66

DECCA (9016 "Fabulous Mae West") ... 40-60 55

DECCA (79016 "Fabulous Mae West") ... 10-15 70

MGM (4869 "Great Balls of Fire") ... 10-20 72

TOWER ... 15-25 66

Also see FIELDS, W.C.

WEST, Norm

(Norman West)

Singles: 7-inch

HI ... 5-8 64-65

M.O.C. (664 "Baby Please") ... 10-20 67

SMASH ... 10-15 67

WEST, Red

(Red West Combo)

Singles: 7-inch

DOT (16268 "Midnight Ride") ... 10-15 61

JARO (77031 "F.B.I. Story") ... 10-20 60

LOMA ... 5-8 65

SANTO (9006 "My Babe") ... 5-10 63

SONNET (2960 "My Thanks to You") ... 10-20 60

WEST, Rick

(With the Red Hots)

Singles: 7-inch

CENTRAL (314010 "Cop Car") ... 10-20 60s

SOLLY (930 "Crackin' Up") ... 5-10 66

WEST, Rudy

Singles: 7-inch

KING (5276 "Just to Be with You") ... 15-25 59

KING (5305 "The Measure of My Love") ... 15-25 59

Also see FIVE KEYS

WEST, Shelly C&W '83

Singles: 7-inch

VIVA ... 3-4 83-85

W.B. ... 3-4 83-86

LPs: 10/12-inch

VIVA ... 5-10 83

W.B. ... 5-10 83

Also see FRIZZELL, David, & Shelly West

WEST, Sonny

(Sonee West)

Singles: 7-inch

ATLANTIC (1174 "Rave On") ... 25-50 58

NOR-VA-JAK (1956 "Rock-Ola Ruby") ... 300-500 59

WEST, Speedy

(Speedy West & Jimmy Bryant)

LPs: 10/12-inch

CAPITOL (H-520 "2 Guitars") ... 45-55 55

(10-inch LP.)

CAPITOL (T-520 "2 Guitars") ... 30-50 55

CAPITOL (956 thru 1835) ... 15-25 58-62

WEST, Tabby

Singles: 78 rpm

DECCA ... 5-10 55

Singles: 7-inch

DECCA ... 10-15 55

WEST, Tom

Singles: 7-inch

DOT ... 4-6 68

MOMENTUM ... 4-8 66

WEST, Tommy

Singles: 7-inch

LIFESONG ... 3-6 76-77

LPs: 10/12-inch

LIFESONG ... 8-10 76

Also see CASHMAN & WEST

Also see CRITERIONS

Also see SALT WATER TAFFY

WEST, Willie

Singles: 7-inch

CHECKER (964 "Did You Have Fun") ... 20-30 60

DEESU ... 5-10 67

JOSIE (1019 "I Sleep with the Blues") ... 4-8 70

W.B. ... 3-6 75

WEST, BRUCE & LAING LP '72

Singles: 7-inch

COLUMBIA ... 3-5 73

LPs: 10/12-inch

COLUMBIA ... 8-10 74

COLUMBIA/WINDFALL ... 8-12 72-74

Members: Leslie West; Jack Bruce; Corky Laing.

Also see BRUCE, Jack

Also see LAING, Corky

Also see MOUNTAIN

Also see WEST, Leslie

WEST COAST
Singles: 7-inch
DEE JAY ... 3-6 88-89
(Colored vinyl.)
Members: Darrell Smith; Gentry Bradley; Ken Klein.

WEST COAST BRANCH
Singles: 7-inch
A&M ... 4-8 67
VALIANT (753 "Linda's Gone") ... 10-20 66

WEST COAST CREW R&B '86
Singles: 7-inch
KMA ... 3-4 86

WEST COAST 5
Singles: 7-inch
BOOM ... 5-10 60s

WEST COAST POP ART EXPERIMENTAL BAND
Singles: 7-inch
AMOS ... 8-12 69
REPRISE (0552 "1906") ... 15-25 67
REPRISE (0582 "Help I'm a Rock") ... 15-25 67
REPRISE (0776 "Smell of Incense") ... 15-25 68
LPs: 10/12-inch
AMOS (7004 "Where's My Daddy") ... 30-40 68
FIFO (101 "West Coast Pop Art Experimental Band") ... 200-400 66
REPRISE (6247 "West Coast Pop Art Experimental Band Part One") ... 50-100 67
REPRISE (6270 "West Coast Pop Art Experimental Band Volume Two") ... 50-100 67
REPRISE (6298 "A Child's Guide to Good and Evil") ... 50-100 68
Members: Don Harris; Shaun Harris; Bob Markley; Michael Lloyd; Bayard Jones; Jim Wessely.
Also see BYRDS
Also see HARRIS, Shaun
Also see MARKLEY, Bob

WEST COAST RAP ALL STARS LP '90
LPs: 10/12-inch
W.B. ... 5-8 90

WEST COAST WORKSHOP
LPs: 10/12-inch
CAPITOL (T-2776 "Wizard of Oz") ... 15-25 67
(Monaural.)
CAPITOL (ST-2776 "Wizard of Oz") ... 15-25 67
(Stereo.)

WEST MINIST'R
Singles: 7-inch
MAGIC (7432 "My Life") ... 15-25 67
MAGIC (45001 "Sister Jane") ... 15-25 67
RAZZBERRY (2975 "Bright Lights, Windy City") ... 10-20 60s

WEST POINT
Singles: 7-inch
PARROT ... 4-8 70

WEST SIDERS: see WESTSIDERS

WEST STREET MOB P&R/R&B '81
Singles: 12-inch
SUGAR HILL ... 4-6 81-83
Singles: 7-inch
SUGAR HILL ... 3-4 81-83
LPs: 10/12-inch
SUGAR HILL ... 5-10 82
Members: Reggie Griffin.
Also see GRIFFIN, Reggie, & Technofunk

WEST TEXAS SLIM
(Ernest Lewis)
Singles: 78 rpm
FLAME (1007 "Lou Della") ... 50-100 53
Also see LEWIS, Ernest

WEST WINDS
Singles: 7-inch
KAPP ... 4-8 63

WEST WOODS
Singles: 7-inch
A&M ... 15-25 65

WESTBERRY, Kent, & Shaperones
(Kent Westbury)
Singles: 7-inch
ART (172 "My Baby Don't Rock Me Now") ... 100-200 58
ART (174 "Turkish Doghouse Rock") ... 100-200 58

WESTBROOK, Walter J., & His Phantom Five
Singles: 7-inch
BOBBIN ... 10-20 59

WESTBROOKS
Singles: 7-inch
MIRCO (8004 "Travelin' Pain") ... 5-8 66

WESTBURY, Kent: see WESTBERRY, Kent

WESTERMAN, Floyd
Singles: 7-inch
PERCEPTION ... 5-8

WESTERN, Johnny
Singles: 7-inch
COLUMBIA ... 8-12 58
LPs: 10/12-inch
COLUMBIA (1788 "Have Gun, Will Travel") ... 20-25 62
(Monaural.)
COLUMBIA (8588 "Have Gun, Will Travel") ... 30-35 62
(Stereo.)

WESTERN FOUR
Singles: 7-inch
KRAMER (1001 "Mathilda") ... 5-10 60s

WESTERN UNION BAND C&W '88
Singles: 7-inch
SHAWN-DEL ... 3-4 88

WESTFAUSTER
LPs: 10/12-inch
NASCO (9008 "In a King's Dream") ... 50-75 71
Member: C.W. Fauster

WESTLEY, Tarry
(With Yesterday & Today)
Singles: 7-inch
CHAPMAN (1118 "He Lives") ... 3-5 77
(Includes insert photo/sticker.)

WESTMORELAND, Kathy
Singles: 7-inch
AGE of WOMAN (7144 "My Father Watches Over Me") ... 4-8 78
Picture Sleeves
AGE of WOMAN (7144 "My Father Watches Over Me") ... 4-8 78
Also see McDOWELL, Ronnie
Also see PRESLEY, Elvis

WEST-SIDERS
Singles: 7-inch
INFINITY (031 "Candy Yams") ... 10-20 62

WESTON, Billy
Singles: 7-inch
EP-SOM (1002 "I Need You") ... 15-25

WESTON, George
Singles: 7-inch
CHALLENGE ... 15-25 60
GLENN ... 5-10 65
JACKPOT (48013 "Hey Little Car Hop") ... 50-75 58
JACKPOT (48017 "Shelley, Shelley") ... 10-20 59

WESTON, Kim P&R/R&B '63
Singles: 7-inch
BANYAN TREE ... 5-10 69
ENTERPRISE ... 4-6 74
GORDY ... 10-20 65-66
MGM ... 10-20 67-68
MIKIM ... 3-5 71-72
NIGHTMARE ... 3-5 87-88
PEOPLE ... 6-12 69-70
PRIDE ... 4-6 70
RAHKIM ... 4-8 75
TAMLA ... 15-25 63-65
VOLT ... 10-15 71-72
Picture Sleeves
MGM (13720 "I Got What You Need") ... 10-15 67
EPs: 7-inch
MOTOWN (2005 "Kim Weston") ... 15-25
MOTOWN (2015 "Rock Me a Little While") ... 15-25
LPs: 10/12-inch
ENTERPRISE ... 8-12 74
MGM ... 15-25 67-68
VOLT ... 10-15 71
Also see GAYE, Marvin, & Kim Weston
Also see NASH, Johnny, & Kim Weston
Also see WRIGHT SPECIALS

WESTON, Kim / Marvelettes
Singles: 7-inch
TAMLA/MOTOWN (1000 "Do I Like It") ... 3-6 80
Also see MARVELETTES
Also see WESTON, Kim

WESTON, Paul, Orchestra LP '55
Singles: 78 rpm
CAPITOL ... 3-5 45-57
COLUMBIA ... 3-4 50-56
Singles: 7-inch
CAPITOL ... 4-8 57-60
COLUMBIA ... 4-8 50-56
EPs: 7-inch
COLUMBIA ... 5-10 50-56
LPs: 10/12-inch
CAPITOL ... 5-15 57-61
COLUMBIA ... 5-15 50-56
CORINTHIAN ... 4-8 78
HARMONY ... 4-8 72
Also see EDWARDS, Jonathan & Darlene
Also see STAFFORD, Jo

WESTPORT KIDS
Singles: 78 rpm
WESTPORT ... 15-25 56
Singles: 7-inch
WESTPORT (128 "Mama, I Won't Rock It") ... 25-50 55
WESTPORT (130 "You Can't Take It with You") ... 20-35 56

WESTSIDE
Singles: 12-inch
MCA ... 4-6 84

WESTSIDERS
(West Siders)
Singles: 7-inch
LEOPARD (5004 "Don't You Know") ... 15-25 63
U.A. (600"Don't You Know") ... 8-12 63
Members: Edward Alston; Nelson Shields; Joe Sheppard; Ronald Judge; Prince McKnight; Bill Fiason.
Also see LEADERS

WESTWOODS
Singles: 7-inch
A&M ... 4-8 65

WESTWOODS
Singles: 78 rpm
KEM (2763 "Limbo") ... 15-25 55
Singles: 7-inch
KEM (2763 "Limbo") ... 30-60 55

WET, Kevin
LPs: 10/12-inch
VISUAL VINYL (1003 "Wet") ... 20-30 81
(Picture disc. 1000 made.)
VISUAL VINYL (1004 "Hard Attack") ... 20-30 81
(Picture disc. Canadian. 1000 made.)
WET (Except 002) ... 8-10 81
WET (002 "Hard Attack") ... 20-30 81
(Picture disc.)

WET WET WET P&R/LP '88
Singles: 7-inch
UNI ... 3-4 88
Picture Sleeves
UNI ... 3-4 88
LPs: 10/12-inch
UNI ... 5-8 88

WET WILLIE LP '73
Singles: 7-inch
CAPRICORN ... 3-5 74-78
EPIC ... 3-5 77-79
LPs: 10/12-inch
CAPRICORN ... 5-10 71-78
EPIC ... 5-10 78-79
Member: Jimmy Hall; Ricky Hirsch; Jack Hall; John Anthony; Lewis Ross.
Also see HALL, Jimmy

WETBACKS
Singles: 7-inch
WILDCAT ... 5-10 60

WHA-KOO
Singles: 7-inch
EPIC ... 3-5 79
LPs: 10/12-inch
EPIC ... 5-10 79
Also see BIG WHA-KOO

WHALEFEATHERS
Singles: 7-inch
NASCO (026 "It's a Hard Road") ... 8-12 73
LPs: 10/12-inch
NASCO (9003 "Declare") ... 50-100 69
NASCO (9005 "Whalefeathers") ... 50-100 70
Members: Lennie LeBlanc; Stephen Bacon; Michael Jones; M.E. Blackmon; Alex Spence.
Also see LE BLANC, Lenny

WHALEN, Bobby
Singles: 7-inch
KING ... 4-8 61
MUSIC NOTE (123 "Pool of Love") ... 15-25 64

WHALIN, Jimmy
Singles: 7-inch
ROULETTE ... 5-10 59

WHALUM, Kirk LP '88
LPs: 10/12-inch
COLUMBIA ... 5-8 88

WHAM! P&R/D&D/LP '83
(Wham! U.K.; Featuring George Michael)
Singles: 12-inch
COLUMBIA ... 4-6 82-86
Singles: 7-inch
COLUMBIA ... 3-4 83-86
Picture Sleeves
COLUMBIA ... 3-5 82-86
LPs: 10/12-inch
COLUMBIA (Except 40062) ... 5-8 83-86
COLUMBIA (40062 "Make It Big") ... 15-20 84
(Picture disc.)
Members: George Michael; Andrew Ridgely.
Also see MICHAEL, George
Also see PEPSI & SHIRLIE
Also see RIDGELEY, Andrew

WHAMMIES
Singles: 7-inch
BETHLEHEM (3023 "Double Whammy") ... 10-20 61

WHAT FOUR
(What For; Whatt Four)
Singles: 7-inch
CAPITOL ... 5-10 65
COLUMBIA ... 5-10 66
DESTINATION ... 5-10 67
ESP (109 "Our Love Should Last Forever") ... 15-25 66
MERCURY (72716 "Dandelion Wine") ... 10-20 67
REPRISE (0387 "Gemini 4") ... 10-20 65
TOWER ... 5-10 68

WHAT FOURS
Singles: 7-inch
FLEETWOOD (4571 "Basement Walls") ... 15-25 66

WHAT IS THIS P&R/LP '85
Singles: 7-inch
MCA ... 3-4 85
LPs: 10/12-inch
MCA ... 5-8 85

WHAT KNOTS
Singles: 7-inch
DIAL (4067 "I Ain't Dead Yet") ... 10-20 67

WHAT NOTS
Singles: 7-inch
AMBER (101 " Anybody Else") ... 15-25 66
AMBER (102 "Morning") ... 15-25 66

WHAT'S HAPPENING
Singles: 7-inch
CORECO (101 "Baby You're Hurtin' ") ... 20-30 66

WHAT'S IT to YA
LPs: 10/12-inch
HUH ... 8-10 75

WHAT'S LEFT
Singles: 7-inch
CAPRI (520 "Girl Said No") ... 15-25 66

WHAT'S LEFT
Singles: 7-inch
CANDY ... 4-6 73
Member: Scotty Moore.
Also see MOORE, Scotty

WHATNAUTS R&B '70
(With the Whatnaut Band)
Singles: 7-inch
A&I ... 3-5 70
DIAL ... 3-5
GSF ... 3-5 73
HARLEM INT'L ... 3-4 82
STANG ... 3-5 71
LPs: 10/12-inch
STANG ... 10-20 70-71
Members: Billy Herndon; Garrett Jones; Gerald Pinkney.
Also see MOMENTS & WHATNAUTS

WHATSITS
Singles: 7-inch
FINCH ... 15-20 60s

WHATT FOUR: see WHAT FOUR

WHAZOOS
Singles: 7-inch
NATIONAL ... 4-8 68

WHEAT, Elsie
Singles: 7-inch
JAB ... 4-8 61

WHEAT, Peter, & Breadmen
Singles: 7-inch
AMBER ... 5-10 60s

WHEATON, Little David
Singles: 78 rpm
CAPITOL ... 10-20 47-48

WHEATON, Winston
Singles: 7-inch
DONNA ... 5-10 60
Also see KNIGHT, Alan

WHEATSTRAW, Peetie
Singles: 78 rpm
DECCA ... 25-50 34-40
VOCALION ... 40-60 32-44

WHEATSTRAW, Peetie, & Kokomo Arnold
LPs: 10/12-inch
ARHOOLIE ... 10-20 64
BLUES CLASSICS ... 5-10
Also see ARNOLD, Kokomo

WHEATSTRAW, Peetie, & Rudy Ray Moore
LPs: 10/12-inch
KENT ... 8-12 71
Also see MOORE, Rudy Ray
Also see WHEATSTRAW, Peetie

WHEATSTRAW'S BUDDY, Peetie: see PEETIE WHEATSTRAW'S BUDDY

WHEEL
LPs: 10/12-inch
COBURT (1001 "The Wheel") ... 15-25
Member: Bernie Schwartz.
Also see ATELLO, Don

WHEEL MEN
Singles: 7-inch
W.B. (5480 "Hon-Da Beach") ... 10-20 64
Member: Gary Usher.
Also see USHER, Gary

WHEEL OF FORTUNE
Singles: 7-inch
JAMIE ... 4-6 68

WHEEL-A-WAYS
Singles: 7-inch
AURORA ... 4-8 66

WHEELER, Art
Singles: 7-inch
CEE JAM (4 "Walk On") ... 15-25 66
DOT ... 5-10 68
SABRINA (332 "The Plea") ... 15-25 60
SWINGIN' (642 "Jo Jo") ... 10-15 62

WHEELER, Billy Edd C&W '64
(With Rashell Richmond; with Joan Sommer; with Shelly Manne)
Singles: 7-inch
CAPITOL ... 3-5 75-76
KAPP ... 4-8 63-68
NSD ... 3-4 80-81
RCA ... 3-5 70-73
RADIO CINEMA ... 3-5 79
U.A. ... 3-6 69
Picture Sleeves
KAPP ... 4-8 67
LPs: 10/12-inch
AVALANCHE ... 8-10 73
FLYING FISH ... 5-10 79
KAPP ... 10-20 64-68
MONITOR ... 15-25 61-62
RCA ... 8-10 71
U.A. ... 8-15 69
Also see SOME OF CHET'S FRIENDS

WHEELER, Bobby, & His B-Bops
Singles: 7-inch
DIAMOND ... 10-20 61

WHEELER, Caron LP '90
LPs: 10/12-inch
EMI ... 5-8 90
Also see COSTELLO, Elvis

WHEELER, Chuck
Singles: 7-inch
MARLO ... 10-15 60
STEVENS (103 "Cherokee Rock") 15-25 59

WHEELER, Clarence, & Enforcers
LPs: 10/12-inch
ATLANTIC ... 8-10 72-73

WHEELER, Dennis
Singles: 7-inch
KING ... 5-10 64

WHEELER, Karen C&W '72
Singles: 7-inch
CHART ... 3-5 72
RCA ... 3-5 74
Also see HARDEN TRIO

WHEELER, Larry
Singles: 7-inch
GLORY ... 5-10 58

WHEELER, Lin
Singles: 7-inch
ROULETTE ... 10-15 58

WHEELER, Mary, & Knights
Singles: 7-inch
ATOM (701 "A Falling Tear") ... 50-75 60s

WHEELER, Onie C&W '73
Singles: 78 rpm
COLUMBIA ... 10-30 55-57
OKEH ... 5-10 52-54
ORGANA ... 10-15 51
Singles: 7-inch
COLUMBIA ... 15-30 55-57
EPIC ... 4-8 62
OKEH ... 10-20 52-54
OLE WINDMILL ... 3-5 73
ROYAL AMERICAN ... 3-5 73
SUN (315 "Jump Right Out of This Juke Box") ... 15-25 59
Picture Sleeves
EPIC ... 4-8 62
LPs: 10/12-inch
BRYLEN ... 5-10
ONIE ... 8-12 73

WHEELERS
Singles: 7-inch
CENCO (107 "Once I Had a Girl") ... 75-100 50s

WHEELS
Singles: 78 rpm
PREMIUM (405 "My Heart's Desire") ... 15-25 56
PREMIUM (408 "Teasin' Heart") ... 25-50 56
PREMIUM (410 "I Can't Forget") ... 50-75 56
Singles: 7-inch
EARLY BIRD (1006 "Where Were You") ... 4-6 96
(Colored vinyl.)
PREMIUM (405 "My Heart's Desire") ... 25-50 56
PREMIUM (408 "Teasin' Heart") ... 50-75 56
PREMIUM (410 "I Can't Forget") ... 75-125 56
Members: Randy Anderson; Allen Bunn; Jim Pender; Ken Fox; Lorenzo Cook.
Also see BUNN, Allen
Also see FEDERALS
Also see LAKE, Arthur

WHEELS
Singles: 7-inch
TIME (1003 "Where Were You") ... 50-75 58

WHEELS
Singles: 7-inch
FOLLY (800 "Clap Your Hands") ... 8-12 59
Member: Teddy Vann.
Also see VANN, Teddy

WHEELS
Singles: 7-inch
ROULETTE (4271 "No One But You") ... 15-20 60

WHEELS
LPs: 10/12-inch
MONTGOMERY WARD (010 "Sounds of the Hot Rods") ... 15-25 63

WHEELS
Singles: 7-inch
ARA (1913 "Rolls Royce")............... 8-12
AURORA (1258 "Bad Little Woman")......................................10-20 68
IMPACT (1029 "Dancing in the Street")..10-20 67
SIDEWALK..10-15 69

WHEELS
Singles: 7-inch
ATCO (7062 "Skateboard USA")....... 4-6 76

WHEELS, Helen
Singles: 7-inch
FILMORE 3-5 72

WHEELS OF FORTUNE
Singles: 7-inch
RIDON... 8-12

WHELAN, Jim, & Beau Havens
Singles: 7-inch
GAMA.. 5-10

WHEN IN ROME P&R/LP '88
Singles: 7-inch
VIRGIN.. 3-4 88-89
Picture Sleeves
VIRGIN.. 3-4 88-89
LPs: 10/12-inch
VIRGIN.. 5-8 88

WHETHER BUREAU
Singles: 7-inch
LAURIE 10-15 68

WHIFFENPOOFS
Singles: 7-inch
LPs: 10/12-inch
CARILLON (115 "Whiffenpoofs of 1960-'61")..................................10-20 61

WHIGS
Singles: 7-inch
TWO PLUS TWO 4-8 66

WHIPPETS
Singles: 7-inch
JOSIE... 8-10 64

WHIPPLE, Sterling C&W '78
Singles: 7-inch
W.B. 3-5 78-79

WHIPOORWILLS
(With the Joy Vendors)
Singles: 7-inch
DOOTONE (1201 "I Want My Love")..10-20
DOOTONE (1202 "Take Time to Pray")..10-20

WHIPPOORWILLS
Singles: 7-inch
JOSIE (892 "Deep Within' ") 45-55 61

WHIPS
(Flairs)
Singles: 78 rpm
FLAIR (1025 "Pleadin' Heart")....150-250 54
Singles: 7-inch
FLAIR (1025 "Pleadin' Heart")....500-750 54
Also see FLAIRS

WHIPS
Singles: 7-inch
DORE...10-15 58

WHIPS
Singles: 7-inch
MGM 4-8 65

WHIRLERS
Singles: 7-inch
PORT (70025 "Tonight and Forever")..10-15 61
WHIRLIN' DISC (108 "Tonight and Forever")..50-75 57
Members: John Barnes; Les Cooper; Bobby Dunn; Bill Toddman.
Also see COOPER, Les
Also see EMPIRES

WHIRLWIND P&R/R&B '76
Singles: 12-inch
ROULETTE 4-8 77
Singles: 7-inch
ROULETTE 3-5 76

WHIRLWINDS
Singles: 7-inch
GUYDEN (2052 "Angel Love").......20-25 61
PHILIPS (40139 "Heartbeat").......75-125 63

WHIRLWINDS
Singles: 7-inch
AOBA (730 "Darkness on the Delta")... 8-12

WHISK KIDS
Singles: 7-inch
REPRISE... 4-8 65

WHISKEY RIVER
Singles: 7-inch
NORTHLAND 3-5 78

WHISNANT, Ray
Singles: 7-inch
ORBIT 4-8 62

WHISPERING WILL C&W '79
Singles: 7-inch
VISTA... 3-5 79

WHISPERING WINDS
Singles: 7-inch
MGM 4-8 65

WHISPERING SMITH
Singles: 7-inch
EXCELLO (2232 "Hound Dog Twist")...10-15 62
EXCELLO (2237 "Live Jive") 10-15 62

WHISPERS
Singles: 78 rpm
APOLLO (1156 "I've Got No Time")..25-35 50

WHISPERS
Singles: 78 rpm
GOTHAM (309 "Fool Heart")........50-100 53
GOTHAM (312 "Are You Sorry")..100-150 53
Singles: 7-inch
GOTHAM (309 "Fool Heart")......200-300 53
GOTHAM (312 "Are You Sorry")..300-500 53

WHISPERS
Singles: 7-inch
LAURIE (3344 "Here Comes Summer")..10-15 66

WHISPERS R&B '69
Singles: 12-inch
SOLAR 4-6 80-84
Singles: 7-inch
COLLECTABLES.............................. 3-4 80s
DORE..10-20 65-66
FONTANA.......................................10-20 66
JANUS 3-6 70-75
SOLAR 3-5 79-88
SOUL CLOCK 4-8 69-70
SOUL TRAIN 3-6 75-77
LPs: 10/12-inch
ACCORD.. 5-10 81
ALLEGIANCE.................................... 5-8 84
CAPITOL.. 5-8 90
DORE.. 5-10 80
JANUS 8-10 72-75
SOLAR 5-10 78-87
SOUL TRAIN 5-10 76-77
Members: Walter Scott; Wallace Scott; Nicholas Caldwell; Marcus Hudson; Leaveil DeGree.
Also see LUCAS, Carrie, & Whispers

WHISTLE R&B '86
Singles: 12-inch
SELECT 4-6 86
Singles: 7-inch
SELECT 3-4 86-89
LPs: 10/12-inch
SELECT 5-8 86-88

WHISTLE STOP
Singles: 7-inch
SPUNK (2222 "Boogie Music") 5-10 60s

WHISTLER, Chaucer
LPs: 10/12-inch
UNI 8-10 69

WHITAKER, Ruby, & Chestnuts: see CHESTNUTS

WHITAKER, Ruby, & Pyramids
Singles: 7-inch
MARK-X (7007 "I Get the Feeling")..200-300 57
Also see PYRAMIDS

WHITAKER, Sammy, & Tribesmen
Singles: 7-inch
AFFCAN (378 "Hypo") 15-25 57

WHITCOMB, Ian P&R/LP '65
(With Bluesville; with Somebody's Chyldren)
Singles: 7-inch
JERDEN 5-10 64-65
TOWER.. 4-8 65-68
U.A. 3-5 73
Picture Sleeves
TOWER.. 4-8 66
LPs: 10/12-inch
FIRST AMERICAN 5-10 78-82
SIERRA... 5-10 80
TOWER..15-20 65-68
U.A. 8-10 72
Also see SOMEBODY'S CHYLDREN

WHITE, Alan
Singles: 7-inch
ATLANTIC....................................... 3-5 76
LPs: 10/12-inch
ATLANTIC....................................... 8-10 76
Also see YES

WHITE, Artie "Blues Boy" R&B '77
Singles: 7-inch
ALTEE... 3-5 77
RONN.. 3-5 70s
LPs: 10/12-inch
ICHIBAN.. 5-10

WHITE, Barry P&R/R&B/LP '73
(With Love Unlimited & Love Unlimited Orchestra; with Glodean)
Singles: 12-inch
20TH FOX 4-8 73-78
UNLIMITED GOLD 4-6 83
Singles: 7-inch
A&M 3-4 87
BRONCO.. 5-10 67
CASABLANCA 3-5 70s
20TH FOX 3-6 73-78
UNLIMITED GOLD 3-4 79-83
LPs: 10/12-inch
A&M 5-8 87
SUPREMACY...................................10-15 74
20TH FOX (Except 1) 5-10 73-81
20TH FOX (1 "Barry White Radio Special")..10-20 70s
(Promotional issue only.)
UNLIMITED GOLD 5-10 79-82
Also see BOB & EARL
Also see BURNETT, Carl, & Hustlers
Also see JONES, Quincy, James Ingram, Al B. Sure, El DeBarge & Barry White
Also see LEE, BARRY
Also see LOVE UNLIMITED

WHITE, Barry, & Atlantics / Atlantics
Singles: 7-inch
FARO 5-10 63
Also see WHITE, Barry

WHITE, Ben, & Darchaes
Singles: 7-inch
ALJON (1247 "Jocko Sent Me")..200-250 62
Also see ADDEO, Nicky

WHITE, Bergen
Singles: 7-inch
MONUMENT 4-8 67
PRIVATE STOCK.............................. 3-5 75-76
SSS INT'L.. 3-5 70
LPs: 10/12-inch
SSS INT'L.. 5-10 70s
Also see CURRY, Clifford

WHITE, Beverly R&B '43
Singles: 78 rpm
BEACON..10-20 43
DAVIS 10-20 46
Singles: 7-inch
PHILIPS 5-10 62
Also see WHITE, Josh, & Family

WHITE, Bill
Singles: 7-inch
AC'CENT (1058 "Leave My Gal Alone")..15-25 58

WHITE, Bill C&W '78
Singles: 7-inch
PRAIRIE DUST 3-5 78

WHITE, Bob
Singles: 7-inch
CLOWN.. 5-10 60

WHITE, Bob / Jane White
(With the Sunset Playboys)
Singles: 7-inch
EVANA... 5-10
Also see WHITE, Bob

WHITE, Bobby
Singles: 7-inch
END 8-12 61

WHITE, Boyd
Singles: 7-inch
MERCURY 4-8 60

WHITE, Brian C&W '88
Singles: 7-inch
OAK 3-4 88

WHITE, Buddy
(With the Bell Hops)
Singles: 7-inch
MILESTONE (2006 "Betty Jean")....10-15 61
MURCO (1017 "Teenage Ball")......50-75 59
WHEELER DEALERS (501 "For Your Love")..100-200

WHITE, Bukka
(Booker White)
Singles: 7-inch
ARHOOLIE....................................... 4-8 65
TAKOMA 5-10 63
LPs: 10/12-inch
ARHOOLIE.......................................10-20 65
BLUE HORIZON...............................10-15
COLUMBIA.......................................10-15 70
HERWIN 10-15
TAKOMA 10-15

WHITE, Butch
Singles: 7-inch
POP 5-10 59

WHITE, Charley C&W '79
Singles: 7-inch
NSD 3-5 79

WHITE, Danny
Singles: 7-inch
ABC-PAR (10525 "One Little Lie") ...8-12 64
ABC-PAR (10589 "Moonbeam") 8-12 64
ATLAS (1257 "I'm Dedicating My Life")..10-20 66
ATTERU (2001 "I'm Dedicating My Life")..20-30 66
(Much higher quality than Atlas pressing.)
DECCA (32048 "Taking Inventory")..5-10 66
DECCA (32106 "Kiss Tomorrow Goodbye")..5-10 67
DOT (16188 "Give and Take") 15-25 61
FRISCO (104 "Kiss Tomorrow Goodbye")..15-25 63
FRISCO (106 "Make Her Mine") 15-25 63
FRISCO (109 "Twitch")...................15-25 63
FRISCO (110 "Miss Fine, Miss Fine")...15-25 63
FRISCO (114 "My Living Doll").......15-25 63
KASHE (443 "Never Like This")........8-12 65
KING (5122 "That's My Doll")..........25-35 58
SSS INT'L (754 "Natural Soul Brother")... 4-8 69

WHITE, Danny P&R '77
Singles: 7-inch
ROCKY COAST 3-5 77

WHITE, Danny, & Linda Nail C&W '83
Singles: 7-inch
GRAND PRIX 3-4 83
Also see NAIL, Linda

WHITE, Dave
Singles: 7-inch
PINK.. 8-10 60
LPs: 10/12-inch
BELL 10-15
Also see DANNY & JUNIORS

WHITE, Don
Singles: 7-inch
CAROL... 4-6

WHITE, Donnie
Singles: 7-inch
FELSTED... 4-8 61
RIDGEWAY 5-10 59

WHITE, E.T., & His Great Potential Band
Singles: 7-inch
GREAT POTENTIAL (136 "Psycho")..20-30
GREAT POTENTIAL (12962 "Loosen Up")..10-15 68

WHITE, Eddy
Singles: 7-inch
BLUE HORIZON 4-8 66

WHITE, Evelyn
Singles: 7-inch
DESS (7016 "Mind Your Own Business")..40-60

WHITE, Floyd, & Dealers
Singles: 7-inch
CRITERION (1 "Cinderella") 25-50 58

WHITE, Georgia
Singles: 78 rpm
DECCA... 5-15 30s-40s
LPs: 10/12-inch
ROSETTA 5-8 84

WHITE, India
Singles: 7-inch
JUANITA 5-10 59

WHITE, James
(With the Blacks; with Contortions)
LPs: 10/12-inch
PVC... 5-10
ZE 5-10 79

WHITE, Jane
Singles: 7-inch
DAUNTLESS (033 "Alas, No Gas")....5-8 63
Also see WHITE, Bob / Jane White

WHITE, Jim
Singles: 7-inch
GREGG.. 4-8 67

WHITE, Jim
Singles: 7-inch
UBC (1020 "Teenage Doll") 25-35

WHITE, John R&B '87
Singles: 7-inch
GEFFEN 3-4 87

WHITE, Johnny
Singles: 7-inch
BROWNFIELD 4-8 65
DEBONAIR 4-8 66

WHITE, Josh
Singles: 78 rpm
ASCH 10-20 44-45
DECCA...10-20 46-47
LONDON.. 5-15 50-52
MAYOR 10-15 52
V-DISC 10-15 44-45
VOGUE 10-20 50
Singles: 7-inch
DECCA (25000 series) 4-8 64
LONDON..10-20 50-52
MERCURY 4-8 62-63
EPs: 7-inch
DECCA...15-25 50
EMARCY..10-25 55-56
LONDON..10-25 54-55
LPs: 10/12-inch
ABC-PAR (124 "Stories")...............40-50 55
ABC-PAR (166 "Stories, Vol. 2")....20-40 57
ABC-PAR (407 "Josh White Live")..15-25 62
ARCHIVE of FOLK MUSIC...............10-15 67
DECCA (5082 "Ballads & Blues")...50-100 49
(10-inch LP.)
DECCA (5247 "Ballads & Blues, Vol. 2")...50-100 50
(10-inch LP.)
DECCA (8665 "Josh White")..........20-30 58
ELEKTRA (100 series)....................20-30 56-58
ELEKTRA (200 series)....................15-25 62
ELEKTRA (701 "Story of John Henry")..25-35 55
ELEKTRA (75000 series)................10-15 70
EMARCY (26010 "Josh White Sings")...25-35 55
EVEREST 5-8
51 WEST.. 5-8 86
LONDON (341 "A Josh White Program")......................................25-35 54
LONDON (1057 "Josh White Sings, Vol. 2")...25-35 55
MERCURY (20203 "Josh White's Blues")...20-30 57
MERCURY (20821 "Beginning") 12-25 63
(Monaural.)
MERCURY (21022 "I'm on My Own Way")..12-25 63
(Monaural.)
MERCURY (25014 "Josh Sings") 50-100 50
(10-inch LP.)
MERCURY (60821 "Beginning") 12-25 63
(Stereo.)
MERCURY (61022 "I'm on My Own Way")..12-25 63
(Stereo.)
PERIOD (1115 "Josh Comes A-Visiting")......................................30-40 56
STINSON (14 "Josh White Sings the Blues")..35-55 50
(10-inch LP.)
STINSON (15 "Josh White Sings Folk Songs")..35-55 50
(10-inch LP.)
SUPER MAJESTY 8-12
TRADITION..................................... 8-10 70
Also see LEADBELLY / Josh White / Sonny Terry

WHITE, Josh & Big Bill Broonzy
LPs: 10/12-inch
Mercury (36052 "Jazz Great Folk Blues")...25-35
Also see BROONZY, Big Bill

WHITE, Josh / Leadbelly / Bill Broonzy
LP: 10/12-inch
DESIGN (903 "Three of a Kind")....10-20
Also see BROONZY, Big Bill
Also see LEADBELLY

WHITE, Josh, & Family
(Josh White, Sr; Josh White, Jr.; Beverly White)
LPs: 10/12-inch
MERCURY..12-25 62
Also see WHITE, Beverly
Also see WHITE, Josh
Also see WHITE, Josh, Jr.

WHITE, Josh, Jr.
Singles: 7-inch
DECCA 4-8 59
MERCURY 4-8 62-64
U.A. 4-6 68
LPs: 10/12-inch
U.A. 10-15 68-69
Also see WHITE, Josh, & Family

WHITE, Judy
Singles: 7-inch
BUDDAH.. 4-8 68
T-NECK... 4-8 69
Also see ISLEY BROTHERS / Brooklyn Bridge

WHITE, Karyn P&R '86
Singles: 7-inch
W.B. 3-4 86-89
Picture Sleeves
W.B. 3-4 86-89
LPs: 10/12-inch
W.B. 5-8 88
Also see LORBER, Jeff

WHITE, Kitty P&R '55
Singles: 78 rpm
DECCA 3-5 51
MERCURY 3-5 55-56
Singles: 7-inch
CLOVER 3-6 66
DECCA 5-10 51
DOT 4-8 60
GNP 4-8 59
MERCURY 4-8 55-56
EPs: 7-inch
EMARCY.. 5-15 54
PACIFIC JAZZ 8-15 54
LPs: 10/12-inch
EMARCY..30-40 54
CLOVER 6-12 66
MERCURY 20-30 55
PACIFIC JAZZ 30-40 54-55

WHITE, L.E., & Lola Jean Dillon C&W '77
Singles: 7-inch
EPIC 3-5 77

WHITE, Lee
Singles: 7-inch
RIVIERA.. 4-8 66

WHITE, Lenny LP '76
Singles: 7-inch
ELEKTRA... 3-5 78-83
NEMPEROR 3-5 76
LPs: 10/12-inch
ELEKTRA... 5-8 78-83
NEMPEROR 8-10 75-77
Also see RETURN to FOREVER
Also see TWENNYNINE

WHITE, Lucky
Singles: 7-inch
CANYON (18 "Ponderosa Rock")...20-30 62
CONTACT.. 4-6 68

WHITE, Lynn
Singles: 7-inch
ALA-MISS 3-5 81
BUSTOUT.. 5-8
DARBY... 5-8
WAYLO.. 4-6 82

WHITE, Mack C&W '73
Singles: 7-inch
COMMERCIAL.................................. 3-6 73-82
MICHELLE 4-8 64
PLAYBOY 3-5 74

LPs: 10/12-inch
COMMERCIAL 5-10 77-78

WHITE, Margo
Singles: 7-inch
JIN 10-15 60
KHOURY'S 8-12 61

WHITE, Maurice P&R/R&B/D&D/LP '85
Singles: 12-inch
COLUMBIA 4-6 86
Singles: 7-inch
COLUMBIA 3-4 85-86
ELEKTRA 3-5 78
GOLD 8-12 59
PRIDE 10-20 60
Picture Sleeves
COLUMBIA 3-4 85-86
LPs: 10/12-inch
COLUMBIA 5-8 85-86

WHITE, Otis
Singles: 7-inch
GALA 5-10 59

WHITE, Perry
Singles: 7-inch
JET SOUNDS 3-5 77

WHITE, Paul
Singles: 7-inch
COUNTRY JUBILEE 5-10 77

WHITE, Roger C&W '67
Singles: 7-inch
BIG A 3-5 67
BLUE GIANT (001 "Somebody's Stealing My Baby") 40-60

WHITE, Ronnie
Singles: 7-inch
BRENT 4-6 60s

WHITE, Sam
Singles: 7-inch
SHASTA (111 "Rock Baby Rock") 20-30 59
SHASTONE (101 "Rock Baby Rock") 50-75 58

WHITE, Sir, & His Sounds
Singles: 7-inch
REDBUG 10-15 61

WHITE, Snow, & Dwarfs
Singles: 7-inch
ZODIAC 4-6 69

WHITE, Tony Joe P&R/LP '69
(With the Mojos; with Waylon Jennings)
Singles: 7-inch
ARISTA 3-5 79
CASABLANCA 3-5 80
COLUMBIA 3-4 83-85
J-BECK 5-8
MONUMENT 4-8 67-70
20TH FOX 3-5 76
LPs: 10/12-inch
CASABLANCA 5-10 80
COLUMBIA 5-8 83
MONUMENT 8-15 69-70
20TH FOX 5-10 77
W.B. 8-10 71-73
Session: Waylon Jennings.
Also see JENNINGS, Waylon

WHITE, Wilbur "Hi-Fi"
Singles: 7-inch
BANDERA (3301 "Don't Look Now") 20-30
SANDMAN 4-8

WHITE, Willie
Singles: 7-inch
IMPERIAL 4-8 62
SHAW 4-8 65

WHITE, Yolanda
Singles: 7-inch
DECCA 4-8 61

WHITE BUCKS
Singles: 7-inch
DOT 5-10 59

WHITE CANE
LPs: 10/12-inch
LION 8-10 72

WHITE CAPS
Singles: 7-inch
BLUE RIVER (201 "Fender Vendor") 10-20 60s

WHITE CAPS (on Northland): see EDWARDS, Johnny & White Caps

WHITE CHOCOLATE
Singles: 7-inch
RCA 3-5 73
LPs: 10/12-inch
RCA 8-10 73
Member: Charlie Karp.
Also see KARP, Charlie

WHITE CLOUD
Singles: 7-inch
GOOD MEDICINE 3-5 72
TAMMY JO (002 "Paper Caper") 4-6 84
LPs: 10/12-inch
GOOD MEDICINE 10-12 72

WHITE DOOR
Singles: 12-inch
PASSPORT 4-6
LPs: 10/12-inch
PASSPORT 5-8

WHITE DUCK
Singles: 7-inch
UNI 3-5 72
LPs: 10/12-inch
UNI 10-15 71-72
Member: Doug Yankus.
Also see SOUP

WHITE ELEPHANT
LPs: 10/12-inch
JUST SUNSHINE 10-15 73

WHITE FLAG
LPs: 10/12-inch
GASA TANKA 10-15 84

WHITE FLUFF
Singles: 7-inch
EAB (1112 "Vegetable Binge") 15-25 69
Picture Sleeves
EAB (1112 "Vegetable Binge") 25-35 69

WHITE HAVEN PILLOW
Singles: 7-inch
MTA 4-8 68

WHITE HEAT
Singles: 7-inch
RCA 3-5 75
LPs: 10/12-inch
MYRRH 4-8
RCA 8-10 75

WHITE HORSE
Singles: 7-inch
CAPITOL 3-5 77
LPs: 10/12-inch
CAPITOL 8-10 77

WHITE KNIGHTS
Singles: 7-inch
GAIETY (117 "Run Baby Run") 15-25 60s
GAIETY (121 "Promise Her Love") 15-25 60s

WHITE LIE
Singles: 7-inch
WHITE LIE 3-4 79

WHITE LIGHT
LPs: 10/12-inch
CENTURY (39955 "White Light") 200-300 69
(Front cover is identical to *After Sundown*, by the Philosophers.)

WHITE LIGHTING
Singles: 7-inch
HEXAGON (944 "William") 15-25 68
ISLAND 3-5
Member: Tom "Zippy" Caplan.
Also see LIGHTING
Also see LITTER

WHITE LIGHTING
Singles: 7-inch
ATCO (6660 "Of Paupers and Poets") 30-40 69
HEXAGON ("Of Paupers and Poets") 40-60 69
(First issue.)
Member: Zip Kaplan.
Also see LITTER

WHITE LIGHTNIN'
LPs: 10/12-inch
ABC 10-15 69
ISLAND 8-10 75

WHITE LION LP '87
Singles: 7-inch
ATLANTIC 3-4 87-90
Picture Sleeves
ATLANTIC 3-4 87-89
LPs: 10/12-inch
ATLANTIC 5-8 87-90
GRAND SLAM 5-8 88
Members: Mike Tramp; Greg D'Angelo; Jim Lomenzo; Vito Bratta.
Also see ANTHRAX

WHITE NOISE
(David Vorhaus)
LPs: 10/12-inch
ANTILLES 5-10
ISLAND 10-12 71

WHITE PLAINS P&R/LP '70
Singles: 7-inch
DERAM 3-6 70-73
LONDON 3-5 70s
LPs: 10/12-inch
DERAM 10-15 70
Members: Tony Burrows; Ricky Wolff; Roger Greenaway; Robin Box; Robin Shaw; Pete Nelson; Roger Hills.
Also see BURROWS, Tony
Also see FLOWERPOT MEN
Also see PIPKINS

WHITE TIGER
LPs: 10/12-inch
E.M.C. (3653 "Year of the Tiger") .. 15-20 86
Member: Mark St. John.
Also see KISS

WHITE WATER
Singles: 7-inch
RCA 3-5 73
LPs: 10/12-inch
RCA 8-10 73

WHITE WATER JUNCTION C&W '84
Singles: 7-inch
JUNGLE ROGUE 3-4 84

WHITE WITCH
Singles: 7-inch
CAPRICORN 3-6 73-74
LPs: 10/12-inch
CAPRICORN 10-20 73-74

WHITE WOLF LP '85
Singles: 7-inch
RCA 3-4 85-86
LPs: 10/12-inch
RCA 5-8 85-86

WHITE ZOMBIE
LPs: 10/12-inch
MCA (24806 "Astro Creep: 2000") ... 8-10 90s
(Colored vinyl.)

WHITEFACE
Singles: 7-inch
MERCURY 4-6 79
LPs: 10/12-inch
MERCURY (103 "Live at the Agora") 20-25 79

WHITEHEAD, Benny C&W '73
Singles: 7-inch
REPRISE 3-5 73

WHITEHEAD, Charles R&B '75
(With the Swamp Dogg Band)
Singles: 7-inch
ISLAND 3-5 75
LPs: 10/12-inch
FUNGUS 10-15
WIZARD 5-10 78

WHITEHEAD, Col.
Singles: 7-inch
COUNSEL 5-10

WHITEHEAD, John R&B '88
Singles: 7-inch
MERCURY 3-4 88
Also see McFADDEN & WHITEHEAD

WHITEHEAD, Kenny & Johnny R&B '86
Singles: 12-inch
PHILADELPHIA INT'L 4-6 86
Singles: 7-inch
PHILADELPHIA INT'L 3-4 86
LPs: 10/12-inch
PHILADELPHIA INT'L 5-8 86
Also see KENNY & JOHNNY

WHITEHOUSE, Bill
Singles: 7-inch
INDEPENDENT SOUND 3-5 78

WHITEHURST, Floyd
Singles: 7-inch
SANDY (1012 "Brand New Baby") 25-35 58

WHITEMAN, Paul, Orchestra P&R '20
Singles: 78 rpm
CAPITOL 3-5 42-43
COLUMBIA 3-6 28-32
CORAL 3-5 50-56
DECCA 3-5 38-39
VICTOR (Black Plastic) 3-8 20-36
VICTOR (39000 "Night with Paul Whiteman at the Biltmore") 300-400 30s
(Picture disc.)
Singles: 7-inch
CORAL 3-6 50-56
WORLD'S FAIR (82083/84 "Conducts Rhapsody 21") 20-25 62
(Picture disc. Souvenir from Seattle World's Fair.)
EPs: 7-inch
CORAL 4-8 50-56
LPs: 10/12-inch
CAPITOL 5-10 62
CORAL 5-15 50-56
GRAND AWARD 5-15 56-59
RCA (Black vinyl) 4-8 68-69
RCA (67-2000 "Night with Paul Whiteman at the Biltmore") 400-600 30s
(Picture disc.)
WESTMINSTER 4-8 74

WHITEMAN, Stark
(With His Crowns & the Veltones)
Singles: 7-inch
SHO-BIZ (1004 "We Will All Remember") 50-100 59
WHITE CLIFFS 5-10 67
Member: Henry G. Schroeder.

WHITES C&W '81
Singles: 7-inch
CANAAN 3-4 89
CAPITOL 3-5 81
ELEKTRA 3-4 82
MCA/CURB 3-4 84-87
W.B. 3-4 83
LPs: 10/12-inch
MCA 5-10 84
W.B. 5-10 83
Members: Buck White; Patty White; Sharon White; Cheryl White.
Also see HARRIS, Emmylou

WHITESIDE, Bobby
Singles: 7-inch
DESTINATION 5-10 65
PHILIPS 5-10 65
U.S.A. 5-10 64-67
LPs: 10/12-inch
CURTOM 8-12 74
Also see RIVIERAS

WHITESIDEWALLS
(Whitesidewalls Rock'n Roll Review)
Singles: 7-inch
SPIFF-OLA (839 "Clear Lake Medley") 8-12 82
LPs: 10/12-inch
SPIFF-OLA (897 "Whitesidewalls") 15-20 82
SPIFF-OLA (4954 "Whitesidewalls") 15-20 81
(A different collection than on Spiff-Ola 897.)

WHITESNAKE P&R/LP '80
Singles: 12-inch
GEFFEN 4-6 86
Singles: 7-inch
GEFFEN 3-4 82-89
MIRAGE 3-5 80
U.A. 3-5 79
Picture Sleeves
GEFFEN 3-4 87-88
MIRAGE 3-5 80
LPs: 10/12-inch
GEFFEN 5-8 82-89
MIRAGE 5-10 80-81
U.A. 5-10 79
Members: David Coverdale; Jon Lord; Aynsley Dunbar; John Sykes; Neil Murray; Tommy Aldridge; Rudy Sarzo; Vivian Campbell; Adrian Vandenberg; Steve Vai.
Also see COVERDALE, David
Also see DEEP PURPLE
Also see DUNBAR, Aynsley
Also see LORD, Jon

WHITFIELD, Barrence, & Savages
Singles: 7-inch
ROUNDER 5-10 86-87
Members: Barrance Whitfield; Lorne Entress; Bruce Katz; Milton Reder; Richie Robertson; David Sholl.

WHITFIELD, David P&R '54
Singles: 78 rpm
LONDON 3-5 53-57
Singles: 7-inch
LONDON 3-8 53-63
EPs: 7-inch
LONDON 4-8 54
LPs: 10/12-inch
LONDON 5-15 54-66
Also see MANTOVANI

WHITFIELD, Smoki
Singles: 7-inch
CREST (Black vinyl) 8-10 58
CREST (Colored vinyl) 15-20 58

WHITFIELD, Wilbur, & Pleasers
(Little Wilbur & the Pleasers)
Singles: 78 rpm
ALADDIN 25-50 57
Singles: 7-inch
ALADDIN (3381 "The One I Love") 25-50 57
ALADDIN (3396 "I Don't Care") 25-50 57
ALADDIN (3402 "Heart to Heart") .. 25-50

WHITHERSPOONE
Singles: 7-inch
WHITE WHALE 4-8 69

WHITING, Doyle, Band
LPs: 10/12-inch
BLUE WAVE 5-8 86

WHITING, Joe, & Bandit Band
Singles: 7-inch
SCATTER TOONES 3-5 82
Also see PUBLIC EYE

WHITING, Margaret P&R '46
Singles: 78 rpm
CAPITOL 3-8 46-56
DOT 3-8 57
Singles: 7-inch
CAPITOL 5-10 50-56
DOT 5-8 57-59
LONDON 3-6 66-70
VERVE 4-6 60
EPs: 7-inch
CAPITOL 5-10 50-56
LPs: 10/12-inch
CAPITOL 12-25 50-56
DOT 8-18 57-67
HAMILTON 5-15 59-65
LONDON 5-15 67-68
VERVE 10-20 60
Also see MARTIN, Dean, & Margaret Whiting
Also see TORME, Mel

WHITING, Margaret, & Jimmy Wakely C&W '49
Singles: 78 rpm
CAPITOL 3-8 49-51
Singles: 7-inch
CAPITOL 5-10 49-51
EPs: 7-inch
CAPITOL 8-15 53
LPs: 10/12-inch
PICKWICK 8-12 67
Also see WHITING, Margaret
Also see WAKELY, Jimmy

WHITLEY, Jackie
Singles: 7-inch
EDA (1743 "Mean Man Blues") 20-30

WHITLEY, Keith C&W '84
(With Patty Loveless)
Singles: 7-inch
RCA 3-4 84-89
LPs: 10/12-inch
RCA 5-8 84-89
Also see LOVELESS, Patty
Also see McENTIRE, Reba
Also see SKAGGS, Ricky, & Keith Whitley

WHITLEY, Keith, & Lorrie Morgan C&W '90
Singles: 7-inch
RCA 3-4 90
Also see MORGAN, Lorrie
Also see WHITLEY, Keith

WHITLEY, Ray
Singles: 7-inch
APT 4-8 65
ATTARACK 4-8
COLUMBIA 4-8 66-67
1-3-4 .... 4-6 69
TRX 4-8 68
VEE JAY (Except 433) 5-10 62-64
VEE JAY (433 "Yessiree Yessiree") 10-20 62

WHITLOCK, Bobby LP '72
Singles: 7-inch
DUNHILL 3-5 72
LPs: 10/12-inch
CAPRICORN 8-10 76
DUNHILL 10-12 72
Also see BELL, Maggie, & Bobby Whitlock
Also see DELANEY & BONNIE
Also see DEREK & DOMINOES

WHITLOCK, Hunter
Singles: 7-inch
SARDIS (2937 "She Went Away") ... 5-10

WHITMAN, Slim C&W/P&R '52
Singles: 78 rpm
IMPERIAL 5-15 52-57
Singles: 7-inch
CLEVELAND INT'L 3-4 80-82
EPIC 3-4 84
IMPERIAL (5000 series) 5-10 61-63
IMPERIAL (8000 thru 8200 series) 10-25 52-58
IMPERIAL (8300 series) 8-12 59-60
IMPERIAL (50000 series) 3-5 70-71
IMPERIAL (65000 & 66000 series) 3-8 61-69
U.A. 3-8 70-77
EPs: 7-inch
IMPERIAL 30-50 54-65
RCA (3217 "Slim Whitman Sings and Yodels") 100-150 54
LPs: 10/12-inch
CAMDEN 8-12 66
CLEVELAND INT'L (Except AS-99875) 5-10 80-81
CLEVELAND INT'L (AS-99875 "Songs I Love to Sing") 30-35 80
(Picture disc. Promotional issue only. Reportedly 1,600 made.)
EPIC 5-8 84
IMPERIAL (3004 "America's Favorite Folk Artist") 550-650 54
(10-inch LP. Colored vinyl.)
IMPERIAL (9000 series) 35-50 56-60
(Maroon or black label with "Imperial" at top.)
IMPERIAL (9000 series) 8-15 66
(Black label with "Imperial" on left side.)
IMPERIAL (9100 series) 20-40 60-62
(Black label with "Imperial" at top.)
IMPERIAL (9100 series) 8-15 66
(Black label with "Imperial" on left side.)
IMPERIAL (9200 & 9300 series) 15-25 63-67
IMPERIAL (12100 series) 20-30 62
(Black label with "Imperial" at top.)
IMPERIAL (12100 series) 8-15 66
(Black label with "Imperial" on left side.)
IMPERIAL (12200 & 12300 series) 12-25 65-68
IMPERIAL (12400 series) 8-12 68-69
LIBERTY 5-10 80-82
PICKWICK 5-10 70s
RCA (3217 "Slim Whitman Sings and Yodels") 250-350 54
RCA (3700 series) 5-8 80
SUFFOLK MARKETING 8-12 79-82
SUNSET 8-12 66-70
U.A. 6-12 70-80
Also see WILLIAMS, Hank / Slim Whitman

WHITNEY, Eli
EPs: 7-inch
PROMENADE 5-10 59

WHITNEY, Gladys
Singles: 7-inch
SUNDIAL 4-6 88

WHITNEY, Grace Lee
Singles: 7-inch
GLW STAR 4-8 77

WHITNEY, Louise
Singles: 7-inch
WHIZ 4-8 67

WHITNEY, Marva P&R/R&B '69
Singles: 7-inch
EXCELLO (2328 "Don't Let Our Love Fade Away") 5-10 73
FEDERAL 5-10
KING 5-10 67-69
T-NECK 4-6 70
LPs: 10/12-inch
KING 10-15 69
Session: Ellis Taylor.
Also see BROWN, James, & Marva Whitney

WHITNEY, Mary Lee
Singles: 7-inch
LOMA 4-8 66

WHITNEY, Ty
Singles: 7-inch
CARMEL (22 "Big Brown Eyes") 8-12 61

DENNY (4466 "Other Side of Love") 5-10 62
MGM 3-5 72
20TH FOX (447 "Move Over Darling") 5-10 63
20TH FOX (448 "Surfin' Santa Claus") 10-20 63

WHITNEY SUNDAY

LPs: 10/12-inch

DECCA (75239 "Whitney Sunday") 10-15 70

Members: Joe Hinchliffe; Doug Jacobs; Bill White; Larry Scarano; Lester Figarsky; Bill Gallagher.

WHITNEYS

Singles: 7-inch

JOSIE 4-8 65

WHITSETT, Tim, & Imperials

Singles: 7-inch

ACE (665 "Monkey Man") 5-10 63
IMPERIAL (5757 "Jive Harp") 8-12 61
RIM 5-10 63
TREBCO (701 "Jive Harp") 10-20 61
(First issue.)
TREBCO (703 "I Don't Care") 15-25 61

WHITTAKER, Roger P&R/LP '75

Singles: 7-inch

MAIN STREET 3-4 83-84
RCA 3-5 70-86

Picture Sleeves

RCA 3-5 80

LPs: 10/12-inch

MAIN STREET 5-8 84
RCA 5-12 70-86

WHITTINGTON, Dick, & Cats

Singles: 7-inch

ROUND (1003 "Midnight Hour") 10-20 60s

WHITTINGTON, Jim

Singles: 7-inch

LEW BREYER PRODUCTIONS 4-6 77

WHIZ KID R&B '85

Singles: 7-inch

TOMMY BOY 3-4 85

WHIZ KIDS

Singles: 7-inch

DISCREET 5-8 73
MERCURY 4-6 73

LPs: 10/12-inch

KASABA 8-12 74

WHO P&R '65

Singles: 7-inch

ATCO (6409 "Substitute") 20-30 66
ATCO (6509 "Substitute") 10-15 67
DECCA (31725 "I Can't Explain") 15-20 64
DECCA (31801 "Anyway Anyhow Anywhere") 15-25 65
DECCA (31877 "My Generation") 15-25 65
DECCA (31988 "The Kids Are Alright") 15-25 66
DECCA (32058 "I'm a Boy") 15-25 66
DECCA (32114 "Happy Jack") 8-12 67
DECCA (32156 "Pictures of Lily") 8-12 67
DECCA (32206 "I Can See for Miles") 5-10 67
DECCA (32288 "Call Me Lightning") 8-12 68
DECCA (32362 "Magic Bus") 5-10 68
DECCA (32465 "Pinball Wizard") 4-8 69
DECCA (32519 "I'm Free") 4-8 69
DECCA (32670 "The Seeker") 5-10 70
DECCA (32708 "Summertime Blues") 5-10 70
DECCA (32729 "See Me, Feel Me") 5-10 70
DECCA (32737 "Young Man Blues") 50-75 70
DECCA (32846 "Won't Get Fooled Again") 5-10 71
DECCA (32888 "Behind Blue Eyes") 5-10 71
DECCA (32983 "Join Together") 5-10 72
DECCA (33041 "The Relay") 5-10 72
LIFE 20-30
MCA 3-5 74-79
POLYDOR 3-5 75-79
TRACK 4-8 72-74
W.B. 3-5 81-83

Picture Sleeves

DECCA (32114 "Happy Jack") 10-20 67
DECCA (32465 "Pinball Wizard") 8-12 69
DECCA (32729 "See Me, Feel Me") 8-12 70
DECCA (32737 "Young Man Blues") 75-125 70
POLYDOR 4-6 75-79
W.B. 3-5 81-83

Promotional Singles

ATCO (6409 "Substitute") 25-35 66
ATCO (6509 "Substitute") 10-20 67
DECCA (31725 "I Can't Explain") 20-25 64
DECCA (31801 "Anyway Anyhow Anywhere") 20-30 65
DECCA (31877 "My Generation") 20-30 65
DECCA (31988 "The Kids Are Alright") 20-30 66
DECCA (32058 "I'm a Boy") 20-30 66
DECCA (32114 "Happy Jack") 10-20 67
DECCA (32156 "Pictures of Lily") 10-20 67
DECCA (32206 "I Can See for Miles") 10-15 67
DECCA (32288 "Call Me Lightning") 10-15 68
DECCA (32362 "Magic Bus") 8-12 68
DECCA (32465 "Pinball Wizard") 5-10 69
DECCA (32519 "I'm Free") 5-10 69
DECCA (32670 "The Seeker") 10-15 70
DECCA (32708 "Summertime Blues") 10-15 70
DECCA (32729 "See Me, Feel Me") 8-12 70
DECCA (32737 "Young Man Blues") 50-75 70
DECCA (32846 "Won't Get Fooled Again") 8-12 71
DECCA (32888 "Behind Blue Eyes") 8-12 71
DECCA (32983 "Join Together") 8-12 72
DECCA (33041 "The Relay") 8-12 72
DECCA (34444 "Happy Jack") 20-30 67
DECCA ("Excerpts from *Tommy*") 25-35 69
(Boxed set for radio programming. Includes inserts. No number used.)
LIFE 20-30
MCA (Except 8559) 5-10 74-79
MCA (8559 "Long Live Rock") 90-120 79
(Picture disc. Has National Record Mart or NARM logo on back. Promotional issue only.)
MCA (8559 "Long Live Rock") 70-90 79
(Picture disc. With any logo other than NARM's on back.)
POLYDOR 5-10 75-79
TRACK 5-10 72-74
W.B. 4-8 81-83

LPs: 10/12-inch

DDL/MCA (16610 "Who Are You") 40-50 78
(Half-speed mastered.)
DWJ ("Musical Biography") 30-50 78
(Promotional issue only. Not issued with cover.)
DECCA (DL-4664 "My Generation") 50-75 66
(Monaural.)
DECCA (DL-4664 "My Generation") 75-100 66
(White label. Promotional issue only.)
DECCA (DL7-4664 "My Generation") 40-60 66
(Stereo.)
DECCA (DL-4892 "Happy Jack") 50-75 67
(Monaural.)
DECCA (DL-4892 "Happy Jack") 75-100 67
(White label. Promotional issue only.)
DECCA (DL7-4892 "Happy Jack") 40-60 67
(Stereo.)
DECCA (DL-4950 "The Who Sell Out") 30-40 67
(Monaural.)
DECCA (DL-4950 "The Who Sell Out") 50-75 67
(White label. Promotional issue only.)
DECCA (DL7-4950 "The Who Sell Out") 20-30 67
(Stereo.)
DECCA (DL-5064 "Magic Bus") 50-75 68
(Monaural. White label. Promotional issue only.)
DECCA (DL7-5064 "Magic Bus") 25-30 68
DECCA (DXW-7205 "Excerpts from Tommy") 100-150 69
(Monaural. White label. Promotional issue only. Includes 12-page booklet.)
DECCA (DXSW-7205 "Tommy") 25-35 69
(Stereo. Includes 12-page booklet.)
DECCA (79175 "Live at Leeds") 50-75 70
(White label. Promotional issue only.)
DECCA (79175 "Live at Leeds") 20-30 70
(Includes insert pages.)
DECCA (79182 "Who's Next") 15-20 71
DECCA (79184 "Meaty Beaty Big and Bouncy") 15-20 71
MCA (1496 "Who's Greatest Hits") 5-10 83
MCA (1578 "Meaty Beaty Big and Bouncy") 5-10 80
MCA (1987 "Who Are You") 15-25 78
MCA (2000 series) 15-25 74
MCA (2161 "Who by Numbers") 8-10 75
MCA (3050 "Who Are You") 8-10 78
(Black vinyl.)
MCA (3050 "Who Are You") 15-20 78
(Colored vinyl.)
MCA (4067 "Happy Jack"/"The Who Sell Out") 15-25 74
MCA (4068 "My Generation"/"Magic Bus") 15-25 74
MCA (5000 series) 5-8 83-85
MCA (6000 series) 10-12 74
MCA (6895 "Quadrophenia") 8-10 80
(Does not have booklet.)
MCA (8000 series) 10-12 84
MCA (10004 "Quadrophenia") 10-12 81
MCA (10005 "Tommy") 10-12 77
MCA (11005 "The Kids Are Alright") 10-20 79
(Price includes 18-page booklet.)
MCA (12001 "Hooligans") 10-12 81
MCA (14950 "Who Are You") 12-15 79
(Picture disc.)
MCA (19501 "Join Together") 8-12 90
MCA (37000 series) 5-8 79
MFSL (115 "Face Dances") 20-30 84
POLYDOR 5-10
TRACK/MCA (2126 "Odds and Sods") 10-20 74
(Includes insert.)
TRACK/MCA (4000 series) 10-12 74
TRACK/MCA (10004 "Quadrophenia") 15-20 73
(Includes 44-page booklet.)
W.B. 5-10 81-82

Members: Roger Daltrey; Pete Townshend; John Entwistle; Keith Moon; Kenny Jones.

Also see DALTREY, Roger
Also see ENTWISTLE, John
Also see HIGH NUMBERS
Also see McCARTNEY, Paul / Rochestra / Who / Rockpile
Also see MOON, Keith
Also see SMALL FACES
Also see TOWNSHEND, Pete

WHO / Strawberry Alarm Clock

LPs: 10/12-inch

DECCA (734586 "The Who/Strawberry Alarm Clock") 50-75 69
(Philco-Ford Special Products promotional issue.)

Also see STRAWBERRY ALARM CLOCK
Also see WHO

WHODINI R&B '82

Singles: 12-inch

JIVE 4-6 82-86

Singles: 7-inch

JIVE 3-4 82-87

LPs: 10/12-inch

JIVE 5-8 84-87

Members: Jalil Hutchins; John Fletcher; Drew Carter.

Also see JACKSON, Millie
Also see KING DREAM CHORUS & HOLIDAY CREW

WHODINI & MILLIE JACKSON

Singles: 7-inch

JIVE 3-4 87

Also see JACKSON, Millie
Also see WHODINI

WHOLE DARN FAMILY R&B '76

Singles: 7-inch

SOUL INT'L 3-5 76-77

LPs: 10/12-inch

SOUL INT'L 8-10 76

WHOLE GROUP

Singles: 7-inch

S-A 4-6 68

WHOLE OATS

Singles: 7-inch

ATLANTIC 4-8 72

Members: Daryl Hall; John Oates.

Also see HALL, Daryl, & John Oates

WHOLLY GHOST

Singles: 7-inch

CREAM 3-5 71

WHY FOUR

Singles: 7-inch

RAMPRO (118 "Hard Life") 15-25 66

Members: Drew Lund; Gerry Cain; Ken Stoneberner; Terry Lund.

WHYTE BOOTS

Singles: 7-inch

PHILIPS (40422 "Nightmare") 30-50 67

WICHITA LINEMEN C&W '77

(Featuring Greg Stevens)

Singles: 7-inch

LINEMEN 3-5 77-79

WICHITA TRAIN WHISTLE LP '68

Singles: 7-inch

DOT 5-8 68

LPs: 10/12-inch

DOT 15-20 68
PACIFIC ARTS 8-10 78

Member: Michael Nesmith.

Also see NESMITH, Michael

WICK, Craig, & Auto Cords

Singles: 7-inch

COOL (154 "Auto Hop") 20-30 60

WICK, Jimmy

Singles: 7-inch

LENOX 4-8 63

WICK, Johnny, & His Swinging Ozarks

Singles: 78 rpm

UNITED 20-30 52

Singles: 7-inch

UNITED (116 "Jockey Jack Boogie") 35-50 52
UNITED (126 "Glasgow, Kentucky Blues") 35-50 52

WICKED

Singles: 7-inch

ISABELLE 3-5 80

WICKED TRUTH

Singles: 7-inch

TERV (1119 "Take a Chance") 10-15

WICKED WAY

Singles: 7-inch

PIECE (1009 "Complete Control") 15-25 60s

WICKER, Carolyn

Singles: 7-inch

KON-TI (1158 "Prison Blues") 15-25

WICKHAM, Lewie C&W '70

Singles: 7-inch

MCA 3-5 78
STARDAY 3-5 70

WICKLINE C&W '81

(Wickline Band Featuring Scott Gavin)

Singles: 7-inch

CASCADE MOUNTAIN 3-4 81-84

WIDE BOY AWAKE D&D '83

Singles: 12-inch

RCA 4-6 83

Singles: 7-inch

RCA 3-5 83

LPs: 10/12-inch

RCA 5-10 83

WIDESPREAD DEPRESSION

LPs: 10/12-inch

STASH 5-10 79

WIDNER, Jimmie

Singles: 7-inch

IMPERIAL 10-15 53

WIDOWMAKER LP '77

Singles: 7-inch

JET 3-5 76-77

LPs: 10/12-inch

U.A. 8-10 76-77

Members: John Butler; Aerial Bender.

Also see GROSVENOR, Luther
Also see LOVE AFFAIR

WIDSITH

LPs: 10/12-inch

ALTHIA 8-10 73

WIEDLIN, Jane P&R '83

Singles: 7-inch

EMI 3-4 88
I.R.S. 3-4 85

Picture Sleeves

EMI 3-4 88
I.R.S. 3-4 85-88

LPs: 10/12-inch

EMI 5-8 88
I.R.S. 5-8 85

Also see GO-GOs
Also see SPARKS & Jane Wiedlin

WIER, Rusty P&R/LP '75

Singles: 7-inch

ABC 3-5 74
BLACK HAT 3-4 87
COLUMBIA 3-5 76
COMPLEAT 3-4 83-84
LONGHORN 4-8 65
20TH FOX 3-5 75-76

LPs: 10/12-inch

ABC 8-12 74
COLUMBIA 8-10 76
20TH FOX 8-10 75

WIERVILLE, Victor Paul

LPs: 10/12-inch

W.O.W. (117 "Love Letters") 10-20 79
(Picture disc. Promotional issue only.)

WIG

Singles: 7-inch

BLACKKNIGHT (903 "Crackin' Up") 20-30 67
EMPIRE (1 "Crackin' Up") 20-30 67
(Colored vinyl.)
GOYLE (101 "Drive It Home") 20-30 66

WIG & GEORGETOWN MEDICAL BAND

LPs: 10/12-inch

TEXAS ARCHIVE 8-10 85

WIG WAGS

Singles: 7-inch

ERA 5-10 60
SAMA (1002 "I'm on My Way Down the Road") 30-40 60s

WIGFALL, William, & Lyrics

Singles: 7-inch

SKYLIGHT (202 "Got to Get Along") 1000-2000 62

Also see LYRICS

WIGGINS, Ben

Singles: 7-inch

ALMERIA (4004 "It's All Over") 4-8 78

WIGGINS, Gerald

(Jerry Wiggins)

LPs: 10/12-inch

DIG (102 "Wiggin' with Wig") 35-55 56
HI-FI (618 "Wiggin' Out") 25-35 61

WIGGINS, Jay

Singles: 7-inch

AMY (955 "Sad Girl") 5-10 66
ERIC 3-5 70s
I.P.G. (1008 "Sad Girl") 15-25 63
SOLID SOUND (3001 "You're on My Mind") 10-20 60s

WIGGINS, Percy

Singles: 7-inch

A-BET (9434 "Look What I've Done") 15-25 69
ATCO (6479 "Book of Memories") 5-10 67
ATCO (6520 "They Don't Know") 5-10 67
RCA (8915 "Work of a Woman") 15-25 66
RCA (9838 "Singing a Song") 8-12 70

WIGGINS, Ron

Singles: 7-inch

A.P.I. 5-8 65

WIGGINS, Spencer R&B '70

Singles: 7-inch

FAME 4-8 69-70
GOLDWAX 5-10 66-69

WIGGINS, Wally

Singles: 7-inch

MERCURY (Except 71645) 5-15 60-62
MERCURY (71645 "I Need You") 50-75 60

WIGGLES & WAGGLES

Singles: 7-inch

CORAL (61943 "Rock & Roll Session") 15-25 58

WIGGS, Charlie

Singles: 7-inch

D'ARCY 4-8 64
MUSIC TOWN 4-6 69

WIGGS OF 1666

Singles: 7-inch

MERCURY 5-10 66

WIGGY BITS

Singles: 7-inch

POLYDOR 3-5 76

LPs: 10/12-inch

POLYDOR 8-10 76

WIGHTMAN, Steve

Singles: 7-inch

FARR 3-5 76

WIGWAM

Singles: 7-inch

VERVE/FORECAST 3-5 71

LPs: 10/12-inch

VERVE/FORECAST 15-20 71

WILBOURN, Bill, & Kathy Morrison C&W '68

(Bill Wilbourne & Kathy Morrison)

Singles: 7-inch

U.A. 3-6 68-70

LPs: 10/12-inch

U.A. 8-10 69

WILBURN BROTHERS C&W '55

Singles: 78 rpm

DECCA 5-15 54-57

Singles: 7-inch

DECCA (29190 thru 30428) 8-15 54-57
DECCA (30591 "Oo Bop Sha Boom") 15-25 58
DECCA (30686 thru 33027) 3-8 58-72
MCA 3-5 73

EPs: 7-inch

DECCA 5-15 57-62

LPs: 10/12-inch

CORAL 5-8 80s
DECCA (4142 thru 4645) 10-20 61-65
DECCA (4721 "Wilburn Brothers Show") 50-75 66
(With Loretta Lynn, Ernest Tubb & Harold Morrison.)
DECCA (4817 thru 5291) 8-15 67-71
DECCA (8774 "Side By Side") 30-40 58
(Monaural.)
DECCA (78774 "Side By Side") 50-75 58
(Stereo.)
DECCA (8959 "Livin' in God's Country") 20-30 59
(Monaural.)
DECCA (78959 "Livin' in God's Country") 30-40 59
(Stereo.)
DESIGN 8-12 60s
FIRST GENERATION 5-10 81
KING (746 "The Wonderful Wilburn Brothers") 25-35 61
PHONORAMA 5-8 83
STETSON 5-10
VOCALION 5-15 62-70
WORD 5-8

Members: Teddy Wilburn; Doyle Wilburn. Session: Anita Kerr Singers.

Also see KERR, Anita
Also see LYNN, Loretta
Also see PIERCE, Webb, & Wilburn Brothers
Also see TUBB, Ernest, & Wilburn Brothers

WILCOX, Coye

Singles: 7-inch

AZALEA 8-10 60

WILCOX, David

LPs: 10/12-inch

CAPITOL (6513 "Bad Reputation") 20-30 84
(Canadian.)
CAPITOL (45551 "Breakfast at the Circus") 10-20 87
(Canadian.)
FREEDOM (010 "Out of the Woods") 30-40 80
(Canadian.)

WILCOX, Eddie, Orchestra R&B '52

(Featuring Sunny Gale)

Singles: 78 rpm

DERBY 5-10 52

Singles: 7-inch

DERBY 10-20 52
(Colored vinyl.)

Also see GALE, Sunny
Also see SUNSETS

WILCOX, Harlow C&W/P&R '69

(With the Oakies)

Singles: 7-inch

IMPEL (002 "Groovy Grubworm") 15-25 68
PLANTATION 4-8 69-70
SSS INT'L 3-5 70s

Picture Sleeves

PLANTATION 4-6 69

LPs: 10/12-inch

PLANTATION 5-10 70-71

WILCOX, Nancy

Singles: 7-inch

RCA (9233 "Coming On Strong") 10-20 67

WILCOX, Pete: see WILLCOX, Pete

WILCOX THREE

LPs: 10/12-inch

CAMDEN (669 "Greatest Folk Songs Ever Sung") 20-30 61

Member: Chip Douglas.

Also see MODERN FOLK QUARTET

WILD, The

EPs: 12-inch

ERIKA (104 "Get Wild Tonight") 5-10 83
(Picture disc. 500 made.)

WILD, Jack P&R '70
Singles: 7-inch
BUDDAH 3-5 71
CAPITOL 3-5 70
Picture Sleeves
CAPITOL 3-5 70

WILD AFFAIR
Singles: 7-inch
MGM 4-8 66

WILD BEES
Singles: 7-inch
RCA (7275 "Doctor Rock") 15-25 58

WILD BILL & Blue Denims
Singles: 7-inch
GONE 5-10 59

WILD BLUE P&R '86
Singles: 12-inch
CHRYSALIS 4-6 86
Singles: 7-inch
CHRYSALIS 3-4 86
Picture Sleeves
CHRYSALIS 3-4 86
LPs: 10/12-inch
CHRYSALIS 5-8 86

WILD BROTHERS
Singles: 7-inch
CO-RO-SOL ("Kickin' Pebbles on the Beach") 8-10
(No selection number used.)

WILD BUTTER
Singles: 7-inch
U.A. 3-5 70
LPs: 10/12-inch
U.A. 10-15 70

WILD CATS: see WILD-CATS

WILD CHERRIES
Singles: 7-inch
KAPP 8-12 70

WILD CHERRY P&R/R&B/LP '76
Singles: 12-inch
EPIC 4-8 76-79
Singles: 7-inch
A&M 3-5 75
BROWN BAG 3-5 72-73
EPIC/SWEET CITY 3-5 76-79
LPs: 10/12-inch
EPIC/SWEET CITY 5-10 76-79
Members: Robert Parissi; Allen Wentz; Ronald Beitle; Bryan Bassett.

WILD CHILDS
Singles: 7-inch
CASCADE (102 "Rockin' Heart") 25-35 59

WILD CHOIR C&W '86
Singles: 7-inch
RCA 3-4 86
Member: Gail Davies
Also see DAVIES, Gail

WILD COUNTRY
Singles: 7-inch
LSI (75-12-1 "Sweet Country Woman") 25-35 70
LPs: 10/12-inch
LSI (0275 "Wild Country") 500-1000 70
Members: Randy Owen; Jeff Cook; Teddy Gentry; John B. Vartanian.
Also see ALABAMA

WILD COUNTRY
Singles: 7-inch
CENTURY 100 .... 4-8 60s

WILD FLOWERS
Singles: 7-inch
ASTER (01 "On a Day Like Today") 15-25 66
ASTER (02 "More Than Me") 15-25 66

WILD GOOSE
Singles: 7-inch
AGAPE 3-5 72

WILD HONEY SINGERS
LPs: 10/12-inch
KID STUFF 10-15

WILD LIFE
Singles: 7-inch
COLUMBIA 4-8 67

WILD MAGNOLIAS R&B '74
Singles: 7-inch
POLYDOR 3-5 74
LPs: 10/12-inch
POLYDOR 8-10 74

WILD MAN REPORTER RALPH
Singles: 7-inch
SISTER UGLY'S (1 "The Big Race") 4-8 74

WILD MAN STEVE LP '69
(Steve Gallon)
LPs: 10/12-inch
RAW 5-12 69-70

WILD OATS
LPs: 10/12-inch
ALSHIRE 8-10 71

WILD ONES
Singles: 7-inch
S.P.Q.R. (3316 "I've Been Crying") 10-20 64

WILD ONES LP '65
Singles: 7-inch
MAINLINE 4-8 65
MALA 4-8 67
U.A. 4-8 65-66
LPs: 10/12-inch
U.A. 15-20 65
Also see ANTELL, Peter

WILD ONES
Singles: 7-inch
SEARS (2180 "Come on Back") 5-10 66
Picture Sleeves
SEARS (2180 "Come on Back") 10-15 66

WILD ONES
Singles: 7-inch
ORLYN (66791 "Tale of a City") 10-20 66

WILD ONES
LPs: 10/12-inch
POW WOW 5-8 87

WILD ROSE C&W '89
Singles: 7-inch
CAPITOL 3-4 90
UNIVERSAL 3-4 89

WILD SEEDS
LPs: 10/12-inch
JUNGLE 5-8 86

WILD SILK
Singles: 7-inch
KAPP 5-10 69

WILD SOULS
Singles: 7-inch
STRAWBERRY 10-20 60s

WILD TCHOUPITOULAS
Singles: 7-inch
ISLAND 3-5 76
LPs: 10/12-inch
ISLAND 8-10 76
Also see NEVILLE BROTHERS

WILD THING
Singles: 7-inch
ELEKTRA 4-6 70
S.P.Q.R. 4-6
LPs: 10/12-inch
ELEKTRA 10-15 69

WILD THINGS
Singles: 7-inch
BLUE ONION (101 "Summer's Gone") 10-20 67
BLUE ONION (104 "Acid") 10-20 67

WILD THINGS
Singles: 7-inch
DAMON (12680 "Tell Me") 15-25 60s

WILD TONES
Singles: 7-inch
MADISON 15-20 58

WILD TURKEY LP '72
Singles: 7-inch
CHRYSALIS 3-5 72-73
REPRISE 3-5 72
LPs: 10/12-inch
CHRYSALIS 8-10 72-73
REPRISE 8-12 72
Also see JETHRO TULL

WILD UNCERTAINTY
Singles: 7-inch
PLANET 5-10 66-67

WILD WIND
LPs: 10/12-inch
SOUND TRIANGLE 8-10 74

WILDARE EXPRESS
Singles: 7-inch
BRUNSWICK 4-8 67-70
LPs: 10/12-inch
BRUNSWICK 10-15 70

WILDCARD, Johnny
Singles: 7-inch
GULF REEF 10-15

WILD-CATS P&R '59
Singles: 7-inch
U.A. (1154 "Gazachstahagen"/"Billy's Cha Cha") 15-25 58
(Monaural.)
U.A. (1154 "Gazachstahagen"/"?????????????????????????????????????") 20-30 59
(Monaural. Flip side, a novelty, has no credits—only lots of question marks on label.)
U.A. (169 "King Size Guitar") 10-20 59
U.A. (1154 "Gazachstahagen") 20-30 58
(Stereo [reprocessed].)
LPs: 10/12-inch
U.A. (3031 "Bandstand Record Hop") 35-45 59
Also see MURE, Billy

WILDCATS
Singles: 78 rpm
RCA (6386 "Keep Talking") 10-15 56
Singles: 7-inch
RCA (6386 "Keep Talking") 15-25 56

WILDCATS
(Blossoms)
Singles: 7-inch
REPRISE (0253 "3625 Groovy Street") 10-15 64
Also see BLOSSOMS

WILDCATS
Singles: 7-inch
COUNSEL (1301 "The Swim") 10-20 64

WILDE, Bobby
Singles: 7-inch
SOUTHSIDE 4-8 62

WILDE, Danny LP '88
LPs: 10/12-inch
GEFFEN 5-8 88
ISLAND 5-8 86

WILDE, Eugene R&B '84
Singles: 12-inch
PHILLY WORLD 4-6 84-86
Singles: 7-inch
MCA 3-4 86
PHILLY WORLD 3-4 84-86
Picture Sleeves
PHILLY WORLD 3-4 85
LPs: 10/12-inch
PHILLY WORLD 5-8 84-86

WILDE, Jimmy
Singles: 7-inch
CHELSEA 10-15 62

WILDE, Johnny
Singles: 7-inch
CORONET (1302 "Pearl of My Heart") 10-20 59

WILDE, Kim P&R/LP '82
Singles: 12-inch
MCA 4-6 85
Singles: 7-inch
EMI AMERICA 3-5 82
MCA 3-4 85-88
Picture Sleeves
EMI AMERICA 3-5 82
MCA 3-4 85-88
LPs: 10/12-inch
EMI AMERICA 5-10 82
MCA 5-8 85-88

WILDE, Lady
Singles: 7-inch
CHICORY 4-8 66

WILDE, Marty P&R '60
Singles: 7-inch
BELL 3-5 74
EPIC 5-10 58-60
LPs: 10/12-inch
EPIC (575 "Wilde About Marty") 30-40 60
(Stereo.)
EPIC (3686 "Bad Boy") 30-40 60
EPIC (3711 "Wilde About Marty") 25-35 60
(Monaural.)
Also see SHANNON

WILDE, Ricky
Singles: 7-inch
UK 3-5 72-74

WILDE, Tim
Singles: 7-inch
TOWER 4-8 67

WILDE KNIGHTS
Singles: 7-inch
MODERN (1014 "Beaver Patrol") 10-15 65
STAR-BRIGHT (3051 "Beaver Patrol") 25-35 65
LPs: 10/12-inch
VOXX 5-10
Also see AMERICAN CHEESE

WILDER, Matthew P&R/R&B '83
Singles: 12-inch
PRIVATE I 4-6 83-85
Singles: 7-inch
PRIVATE I 3-4 83-85
Picture Sleeves
PRIVATE I 3-4 84
LPs: 10/12-inch
PRIVATE I 5-8 83-85

WILDER, Vic
Singles: 7-inch
DECCA (31001 "My Love For You") 15-20 59
RIC 10-20 59

WILDER, Walt
Singles: 7-inch
HOMA 4-8 73-74
SOUND VALUE 3-5 74

WILDERNESS ROAD
Singles: 7-inch
COLUMBIA (45565 "Bounty Man") 4-6 72
EPs: 7-inch
REPRISE (PRO-556 "Three Genuine Transparent") 25-50 73
(Promotional issue only.)
LPs: 10/12-inch
COLUMBIA (31118 "Wilderness Road") 10-20 72
REPRISE (2125 "Sold for the Prevention of Disease Only") 10-20 73

WILDFIRE P&R '77
Singles: 7-inch
CASABLANCA 3-5 77

WILDFLOWER
Singles: 7-inch
MAINSTREAM 4-8 68
U.A. 4-8 69

WILDFLOWER / Harbinger Complex / Euphoria / Other Side
LPs: 10/12-inch
MAINSTREAM (56100 "With Love: A Pot of Flowers") 25-35 68
(Monaural.)
MAINSTREAM (S-56100 "With Love: A Pot of Flowers") 25-35 68
(Stereo.)
Also see EUPHORIA
Also see HARBINGER COMPLEX
Also see OTHER SIDE

WILDING, Bobby
Singles: 7-inch
ABC-PAR 4-8 61
DCP (Except 1009) 4-8 64
DCP (1009 "I Want to Be a Beatle") 10-20 64
MAY 4-8 62

WILDING BONUS
LPs: 10/12-inch
VISA (7003 "Pleasure Signals") 10-15 78
(Picture disc.)

WILDLIFE
Singles: 7-inch
SWAN SONG 3-5 83
LPs: 10/12-inch
SWAN SONG 5-10 83

WILDROOT, Raven
Singles: 7-inch
JARO 5-10 60

WILDWEEDS P&R '67
Singles: 7-inch
CADET 4-8 67-68
CADET CONCEPT 4-8 68
VANGUARD 3-5 71
LPs: 10/12-inch
VANGUARD 10-15 70
Also see ANDERSON, Al

WILDWOOD
Singles: 7-inch
MAGNUM 8-10 60s

WILDWOODS
Singles: 7-inch
CAPRICE (101 "When the Swallows Come Back to Capistrano") 100-125 59
MAY (106 "Here Comes Big Ed") 10-20 61
Members: Fred Parris; Johnny Seastrand; Johnny Fisko; Jerry Greenberg.
Also see FIVE SATINS
Also see FIVE SATINS / Gerry Granahan & Five Satins

WILEY, Arnold
(Doc Wiley)
Singles: 78 rpm
APOLLO 15-25 47
BULLET 15-25 50
CHICAGO 20-30 45
KING 15-25 48
Singles: 7-inch
ACE (111 "It'll Be a Long Time") 15-25 59

WILEY, Chuck
(Charles Wiley)
Singles: 7-inch
CARIB 5-10 64
JAX (1004 "I Love You So Much") 50-75 59
MUSIC CENTER (3101 "Come Back Baby") 20-30 60
U.A. (113 "Tear It Up") 40-60 58
U.A. (131 "Shake It Up") 30-40 58

WILEY, Doc: see WILEY, Arnold

WILEY, Ed R&B '50
(With His After Hour Rhythm; with Teddy Reynolds & King Tut)
Singles: 78 rpm
ATLANTIC 15-25 51
SITTIN' IN WITH 15-25 50
Singles: 7-inch
ATLANTIC (959 "So Glad I'm Free") 100-150 51
SITTIN' IN WITH (545 "Cry, Cry Baby") 100-200 50
Members: Teddy Reynolds; King Tut.
Also see KING TUT
Also see REYNOLDS, Teddy

WILEY, Irene
Singles: 78 rpm
DIAMOND 10-20 46

WILEY, Major
Singles: 7-inch
VERVE/FORECAST 3-6 69

WILEY, Michelle R&B '77
Singles: 7-inch
20TH FOX 3-5 77

WILEY, Reid
Singles: 7-inch
GUYDEN (2118 "Say Girl") 10-20 64

WILEY, Sheron
Singles: 7-inch
FREE FLIGHT 3-4 79

WILEY, Shirley Jean
Singles: 7-inch
MYRL 10-20

WILEY, Skip
Singles: 7-inch
MOJO (2169 "Fast Livin' ") 25-35
Also see RILEY, Billy Lee

WILEY & GENE C&W '46
Singles: 78 rpm
COLUMBIA 4-8 45-46
Members: Wiley Walker; Gene Sullivan.
Also see SULLIVAN, Gene

WILEY WOLVERINE: see WOLVERINE, Wiley

WILHELM
(Mike Wilhelm)
LPs: 10/12-inch
ZIG ZAG (221 "Wilhelm") 15-25 76
Also see CHARLATANS

WILK, Scott, & Walls
LPs: 10/12-inch
W.B. 5-10 80

WILKE, Corky
Singles: 7-inch
HBR 4-8 65

WILKERSON, Rocky
Singles: 7-inch
GLOVER 5-10 60

WILKERSON, Sheila
Singles: 7-inch
RFT 4-8 68

WILKES, Willie
Singles: 7-inch
EARL'S 8-12 66

WILKERSON, Don
Singles: 7-inch
TOMEL 4-6

WILKERSON, Jimmy
LPs: 10/12-inch
SPAR 8-12

WILKINS, Artie, & Palms
Singles: 78 rpm
STATES 100-200 56
Singles: 7-inch
STATES (157 "Darling Patricia") 400-500 56
Also see PALMS

WILKINS, Buddy
Singles: 7-inch
TRIESS 5-10 60

WILKINS, David
Singles: 7-inch
PHILLIPS INT'L 4-8 62

WILKINS, David C&W '69
(Little David Wilkins)
Singles: 7-inch
EPIC 3-5 78
JERE 3-4 86
MCA 3-5 73-77
PLANTATION 3-6 69
PLAYBOY 3-5 77-78
LPs: 10/12-inch
MCA 6-12 74-76
PLAYBOY 5-10 77
Also see RUSSELL, Johnny, & Little David Wilkins

WILKINS, John Buck
LPs: 10/12-inch
LIBERTY 10-15 70

WILKINSON, John
Singles: 7-inch
RCA 4-6 68-70
Also see PRESLEY, Elvis

WILKINSON TRI-CYCLE
LPs: 10/12-inch
DATE (4016 "Wilkinson Tri-Cycle") 15-20 69

WILKS & WILKERSON
Singles: 7-inch
BAMBOO 4-8 62

WILL & THE KILL LP '88
LPs: 10/12-inch
MCA 5-8 88

WILL OF THE PEOPLE
Singles: 7-inch
FIREBIRD 5-10 70

WILL POWERS D&D '83
Singles: 12-inch
ISLAND 8-10 83

WILL TO POWER P&R/R&B '87
Singles: 7-inch
EPIC 3-4 87-90
LPs: 10/12-inch
EPIC 5-8 87-90

WILLCOX, Pete C&W '82
Singles: 7-inch
M&M (105 "The King") 5-10 82

WILLESDEN–DODGERS D&D '84
Singles: 12-inch
JIVE 4-6 83-84
Singles: 7-inch
JIVE 3-4 83-84

WILLETT, Slim C&W '52
(With the Brush Cutters; Slim Willet; Winston Moore)
Singles: 78 rpm
FOUR STAR 5-10 52-56
SLIM WILLET (133 "Four Hand Blues") 20-40 53
STAR TALENT 10-20 50
Singles: 7-inch
EDMORAL (1010 "I've Been a Wonderin' ") 15-25 50s
FOUR STAR 10-20 52-56
LPs: 10/12-inch
AUDIO LAB (1542 "Slim Willett") 30-40 60
Also see MILS, Telli .W.

WILLETTE, Baby Face
LPs: 10/12-inch
ARGO...15-25 64

WILLETTE, Wally
(With the Telecaster Cats)
Singles: 7-inch
FLAG (118 "Eenie Meenie")...200-300 59
EPs: 7-inch
SMUDGE...5-10 80
LPs: 10/12-inch

WILLIAM & CONQUERORS
Singles: 7-inch
BIG SOUND...20-25 60s

WILLIAM THE WILD ONE
Singles: 7-inch
FESTIVAL...8-12

WILLIAMS, Al
Singles: 7-inch
LABEAT...8-12
PALMER...8-12

WILLIAMS, Alaine
Singles: 7-inch
PARKWAY...4-8 64

WILLIAMS, Alyson
Singles: 7-inch
DEF JAM/COLUMBIA...3-4 89

WILLIAMS, Andre R&B '57
(With the Don Juans; with Five Dollars; with Diablos; with Gino Purifoy; Andre "Bacon Fat" Williams & Inspirations; Andre "Mr. Rhythm" Williams)
Singles: 78 rpm
EPIC...10-20 57
FORTUNE...10-30 55-57
Singles: 7-inch
AVIN (103 "Rib Tips")...5-10 66
AVIN (105 "Hard Hustling")...5-10 66
CHECKER (1205 "Mrs. Mother Usa")...8-12 68
CHECKER (1214 "Do the Popcorn")...5-10 69
CHECKER (1219 "Girdle Up")...5-10 69
EPIC (9196 "Bacon Fat")...20-30 56
(Different take than first issued on Fortune.)
FORTUNE (824 "Pulling Time")...25-50 55
FORTUNE (828 "It's All Over")...25-50 56
FORTUNE (831 "Bacon Fat")...20-40 56
(Blue label.)
FORTUNE (831 "Bacon Fat")...15-25 57
(Orange label.)
FORTUNE (834 "Mean Jean")...20-30 57
FORTUNE (837 "Jail Bait")...20-30 57
FORTUNE (839 "Come On Baby")..15-25 57
FORTUNE (839X "Don't Touch")...20-25 58
FORTUNE (842 "My Last Dance with You")...15-20 58
FORTUNE (842 "My Last Dance with You")...20-40 58
FORTUNE (1986 "Bacon Fat [86]")...4-6 86
(Rerecorded version.)
RIC TIC (124 "You Got It and I Want It")...10-20 67
RONALD (1001 "Please Give Me a Chance")...50-100 50s
MIRACLE (4 "Rosa Lee")...300-500 60
SPORT (105 "Pearl Time")...10-20 67
WINGATE (014 "Loose Juice")...8-12 66
WINGATE (021 "Do It")...8-12 66
LPs: 10/12-inch
FORTUNE...5-10 86
Also see FIVE DOLLARS
Also see KAY, Gary

WILLIAMS, Andre, & Gino Parks
Singles: 7-inch
FORTUNE (839 "Don't Touch")...35-55 57
FORTUNE (851 "Movin' ")...25-50 60
Also see PARKS, Gino
Also see WILLIAMS, Andre

WILLIAMS, Andy P&R '56
Singles: 12-inch
COLUMBIA...4-6 79
Singles: 78 rpm
CADENCE...5-10 56-57
Singles: 7-inch
AURAVISION (6727 "Tammy")...5-10 64
(Cardboard flexi-disc, one of six by six different artists. Columbia Record Club "Enrollment Premium." Set came in a special paper sleeve.)
CADENCE...5-15 56-64
COLUMBIA...3-8 61-79
Picture Sleeves
CADENCE...10-20 59
COLUMBIA...3-5 61-76
EPs: 7-inch
CADENCE...10-15 57-59
COLUMBIA...5-10 62-66
(Juke box issues only.)
COLUMBIA/KFC (679 "Taste of Honey")...5-10 60s
(Promotional issue, made for Kentucky Fried Chicken.)
COLUMBIA SPECIAL PRODUCTS 4-6 60s
LPs: 10/12-inch
CADENCE...20-30 58-62
COLUMBIA...5-15 62-77
COLUMBIA SPECIAL PRODUCTS 5-10
Also see WILLIAMS, Andy & David
Also see JAN & DEAN / Bobby Vinton / Andy Williams

WILLIAMS, Andy, & Cavaliers
Singles: 7-inch
OUR (305 "You Must Be Born Again")...1000-2000 57

WILLIAMS, Andy & David P&R '74
Singles: 7-inch
BARNABY...3-5 74-75
KAPP...3-5 72-73
LPs: 10/12-inch
KAPP...5-10 72
Also see WILLIAMS, Andy

WILLIAMS, Annie
Singles: 7-inch
U.A....5-8 61

WILLIAMS, Anson P&R '77
Singles: 7-inch
CHELSEA...3-5 77
Picture Sleeves
CHELSEA...3-5 77

WILLIAMS, B.
Singles: 78 rpm
TOP TUNES (101 "You're So Near to Me")...50-75 50

WILLIAMS, Beau R&B '84
Singles: 7-inch
CAPITOL...3-4 84-87

WILLIAMS, Becky C&W '88
Singles: 7-inch
COUNTRY PRIDE...3-4 88

WILLIAMS, Ben E.
(With the Steps Four & Del-Reys)
Singles: 7-inch
RIFF (6102 "Nay-Oy-Gwor")...500-750 61

WILLIAMS, Benny
Singles: 7-inch
ROBEN...5-10 63

WILLIAMS, Bernie
Singles: 78 rpm
IMPERIAL...25-50 55
Singles: 7-inch
BELL (768 "Ever Again")...100-200 69
DEL-VAL...10-20
IMPERIAL (5360 "Don't Tease Me")...50-100 55

WILLIAMS, Beth C&W '86
Singles: 7-inch
BGM...3-4 86-87

WILLIAMS, Big Joe
(Joe Lee Williams)
Singles: 78 rpm
TRUMPET...10-20 52
LPs: 10/12-inch
ARCHIVE of FOLK MUSIC...10-15 68
ARHOOLIE...8-12 70
BLUES on BLUE...10-15
BLUESWAY...8-10 75
DELMARK...20-35 60-62
EVEREST...8-10 70s
FOLKWAYS...15-25 62-67
MILESTONE...10-20 66
PRESTIGE...25-40 62
PRESTIGE BLUESVILLE...15-25 63-64
STORYVILLE...5-8 82
TESTAMENT...15-25 64
WORLD PACIFIC...10-15 69
Also see McCOY, Rube
Also see THREE KINGS and a QUEEN
Also see WILLIAMS, Joe (Joe Lee Williams)
Also see WILLIAMSON, Sonny Boy, & Big Joe Williams

WILLIAMS, Big Joe, & J.D. Short
LPs: 10/12-inch
DELMARK...10-20 66

WILLIAMS, Big Joe, & Sonny Boy Williamson
LPs: 10/12-inch
BLUES CLASSICS (21 "Big Joe Williams & Sonny Boy Williamson")...15-25 60s
Also see WILLIAMSON, Sonny Boy

WILLIAMS, Big Joe, & Johnny Young
LPs: 10/12-inch
DELMARK...15-25 62
Also see YOUNG, Johnny

WILLIAMS, Big Joe, & Short Stuff Macon
LPs: 10/12-inch
FOLKWAYS...15-25 62-67
Also see MR. SHORT STUFF
Also see MR. SHORT STUFF & BIG JOE WILLIAMS
Also see WILLIAMS, Big Joe

WILLIAMS, Bill
LPs: 10/12-inch
BLUE GOOSE...10-15

WILLIAMS, Billy P&R '47
(Billy Williams Quartet)
Singles: 78 rpm
CORAL...5-10 54-57
RCA...5-10 47
Singles: 7-inch
CORAL (61212 thru 62069)...20-40 54-59
CORAL (62101 Red Hot Love")...25-50 59
CORAL (62140 thru 65500 series)...10-20 59-64
MCA...3-5 70s
MGM (10000 & 11000 series)...15-25 50-52
MGM (12000 series)...10-15 57
MERCURY...10-20 52-54
EPs: 7-inch
CORAL...15-25 57
MGM...15-25 57
MERCURY...15-25 53-55
LPs: 10/12-inch
CORAL (57184 "Billy Williams")...35-45 57
CORAL (57251 "Half Sweet Half Beat")...30-40 59
CORAL (57343 "The Billy Williams Revue")...30-40 60
MGM (3400 "The Billy Williams Quartet")...35-45 57
MERCURY (20317 "Oh Yeah!")...35-45 58
WING (12131 "Vote for Billy Williams")...30-40 59
Members: Billy Williams; Claude Riddick; John Ball; Eugene Dixon.
Also see CHARIOTEERS

WILLIAMS, Billy Dee
LPs: 10/12-inch
PRESTIGE...20-30 61

WILLIAMS, Blind Boy
(With His Blues Band; Brownie McGhee)
Singles: 78 rpm
SITTIN' IN WITH (538 "Just Drifting")...15-25 48
Also see McGHEE, Brownie

WILLIAMS, Bob
(With the Cyclones)
Singles: 7-inch
DEBONAIR (161 "My Goose Is Cooked")...15-25
LEDO (1680 "My Goose Is Cooked")...25-35 60
SPIN (989 "Hot Rod Race")...15-25 60
TROPHY (503 "You Can't Make Me Cry")...40-60

WILLIAMS, Bobby
(With the Nightliters)
Singles: 7-inch
CORT (1314 "If Dreams Could Come True")...75-100 58
CORT (1315 "Lost My Job")...40-60 59
DECK (142 "Chapel of Love")...75-125 58

WILLIAMS, Bobby R&B '76
(Bobby Williams Group)
Singles: 7-inch
CAPITOL...5-10 68
ROCK 'N' ROLL...3-6 76
SEVEN B (7018 "Boogaloo Mardi Gras")...8-12 60s
SURE SHOT (5003 "Try Love")...10-20 64
SURE SHOT (5005 "Keep on Loving Me")...10-20 65
SURE SHOT (5013 "When You Play")...10-20 65
SURE SHOT (5025 "Try It Again")...10-20 66
SURE SHOT (5031 "I'll Hate Myself Tomorrow")...25-50 67

WILLIAMS, Bobby, & Mystics
Singles: 7-inch
MGM...5-10 67

WILLIAMS, Bobby, & Royal Flairs
Singles: 7-inch
SAM (119 "Let's Go")...20-30 63

WILLIAMS, Bobby Earl R&B '74
Singles: 7-inch
IV CHAINS...3-5 74

WILLIAMS, Calvin
Singles: 7-inch
ATCO...5-10 66

WILLIAMS, Candy
Singles: 7-inch
REQUEST...5-10 62

WILLIAMS, Carol
Singles: 7-inch
RAM (101 "Just for Awhile")...15-25

WILLIAMS, Carol R&B '76
Singles: 12-inch
VANGUARD...4-6 83
Singles: 7-inch
SALSOUL...3-5 76

WILLIAMS, Charles
(With Paul Gayten Orchestra)
Singles: 78 rpm
CHECKER...10-15 57
Singles: 7-inch
CHECKER (831 "So Glad She's Mine")...15-25 56
CHECKER (866 "Darling")...15-25 57
(Checkerboard top label.)
Also see GAYTEN, Paul

WILLIAMS, Charles
LPs: 10/12-inch
MAINSTREAM...8-10 73

WILLIAMS, Cheryl
Singles: 7-inch
MAXX...4-8 64

WILLIAMS, Chickie
Singles: 7-inch
WHEELING (1019 "Storm")...5-8 50s

WILLIAMS, Christopher P&R '89
Singles: 7-inch
GEFFEN...3-4 89
Picture Sleeves
GEFFEN...3-4 89

WILLIAMS, Clarence
Singles: 7-inch
CHANCELLOR...8-12 62
THRONE...5-10 63
LPs: 10/12-inch
ACCENT...8-10 70

WILLIAMS, Colly
Singles: 7-inch
RY-AN (501 "You Know I'll Love You Tomorrow")...5-10 61

WILLIAMS, Cootie R&B/C&W '44
(With Eddie "Cleanhead" Vinson)
Singles: 78 rpm
CAPITOL...10-20 46
DERBY...15-30 51
HIT...15-30 44-45
Singles: 7-inch
DERBY (756 "Shotgun Boogie")..50-100 51
RCA (6899 "Rinky Dink")...15-25 57
LPs: 10/12-inch
MOODSVILLE (27 "Solid Trumpet")...20-30 62
(Monaural.)
MOODSVILLE (27-SD "Solid Trumpet")...25-35 62
(Stereo.)
RCA (1718 "In Hi-Fi")...40-60 58
WARWICK (2027 "Do Nothing Till You Hear from Me")...40-60 59

WILLIAMS, Cootie, & Wini Brown
LPs: 10/12-inch
JARO (5001 "Around Midnight")...40-60 60
Also see BROWN, Wini
Also see VINSON, Eddie

WILLIAMS, Cootie / Jimmy Preston
LP: 10/12-inch
ALLEGRO (4109 "Rock 'N' Roll")...15-25
Also see PRESTON, Jimmy
Also see WILLIAMS, Cootie

WILLIAMS, Cora, & Four Jacks / Shirley Haven & Four Jacks
Singles: 78 rpm
FEDERAL...100-200 52
Singles: 7-inch
FEDERAL (12079 "I Ain't Coming Back Anymore")...300-500 52
Also see FOUR JACKS
Also see HAVEN, Shirley, & Four Jacks

WILLIAMS, Curtis E.
Singles: 7-inch
SKYWAY...8-10 59

WILLIAMS, Cynthia
Singles: 7-inch
ABCO...4-8 65

WILLIAMS, Dan, & Freelancers
Singles: 7-inch
BETH (20 "High School Flame")...50-100
(Also issued as by the Freelancers.)
Also see FREELANCERS

WILLIAMS, Danny P&R/R&B/LP '64
Singles: 7-inch
PILOT...4-8 62
U.A....4-8 61-66
LPs: 10/12-inch
U.A....15-25 63-66

WILLIAMS, Darnell R&B '83
Singles: 7-inch
MY DISC...3-4 83

WILLIAMS, David R&B '84
Singles: 7-inch
OCEAN FRONT...3-5 84

WILLIAMS, Dee, Sextet R&B '49
Singles: 78 rpm
SAVOY...15-25 49

WILLIAMS, Deniece P&R/R&B '76
Singles: 12-inch
COLUMBIA...4-8 77-86
Singles: 7-inch
ARC...3-5 79-82
COLUMBIA...3-5 76-88
TODDLIN' TOWN...4-8 60s
Picture Sleeves
COLUMBIA...3-5 84-88
LPs: 10/12-inch
ARC (Except 1432)...5-10 79-82
ARC (1432 "Niecy")...20-25 82
(Picture disc. Promotional issue only.)
COLUMBIA...5-10 76-88
Also see MATHIS, Johnny, & Deniece Williams
Also see WONDER, Stevie

WILLIAMS, Des, & Red Coats
Singles: 7-inch
KING...5-10 59

WILLIAMS, Diana C&W/P&R '76
Singles: 7-inch
CAPITOL...3-5 76
LITTLE GEM...3-5 77

WILLIAMS, Dickie
(Dick Williams)
Singles: 78 rpm
RCA...5-15 56
Singles: 7-inch
AURORA...5-10 63
PLEDGE...5-10 63
RCA...10-20 56
VIN...10-15 60

WILLIAMS, Dicky
Singles: 7-inch
BAD (1003 "In the Same Motel")...4-8
LPs: 10/12-inch
BAD (30002 "Red Negligee, White Whiskey & Blue Lights")...10-2-

WILLIAMS, Doc
Singles: 78 rpm
WHEELING...15-20 50

WILLIAMS, Don C&W '72
Singles: 7-inch
ABC...3-5 75-78
ABC/DOT...3-5 74-77
CAPITOL...3-4 86
DOT...3-5 74
JMI...3-5 72-74
MCA (Except 1763)...3-4 79-85
MCA (1763 "Special Message from Don Williams for Your Radio Station")...4-8 82
(Promotional issue only.)
LPs: 10/12-inch
ABC (Except 28 & 44)...5-10 77-78
ABC (28 "Don Williams")...10-15 77
(Promotional issue only.)
MCA (44 "Expressions")...15-20 78
(Picture disc. Promotional issue only.)
ABC/DOT...8-10 74-77
CAPITOL...5-8 86
JMI...15-20 73-74
K-TEL...5-8 78
MCA (Except 44)...5-10 75-85
MCA (44 "Expressions")...15-20 78
(Picture disc.)
Also see HARRIS, Emmylou, & Don Williams
Also see POZO SECO SINGERS

WILLIAMS, Donnie
Singles: 7-inch
PURE GOLD...4-8 65

WILLIAMS, Dootsie, & His Orchestra
Singles: 78 rpm
COAST...10-20 48
DOOTONE...10-20 52-54
Also see PENGUINS
Also see TURNER, Joe

WILLIAMS, Dorothy
Singles: 7-inch
GOLDWAX (115 "Country Style")...8-12 65
VOLT (118 "Closer to My Baby")...8-12 64

WILLIAMS, Doug, & Mell-O-Tones
Singles: 7-inch
HY-TONE (103 "Sorrow Valley")...50-75 58
HY-TONE (122 "Sorrow Valley")...30-40 59
HY-TONE (125 "Send Me")...30-50 59

WILLIAMS, Duke & Extremes
LPs: 10/12-inch
CAPRICORN...8-10 73-74

WILLIAMS, Earl
Singles: 7-inch
ABC-PAR...15-20 57
ACE...10-15 59

WILLIAMS, Eddie R&B '49
(With His Brown Buddies)
Singles: 78 rpm
CRYSTAL...10-20 50
DISCOVERY...10-20 50
SELECTIVE...10-20 50
SUPREME...10-20 49
SWING TIME...10-20 49
Also see DIXON, Floyd
Also see MOORE, Johnny

WILLIAMS, Eddie
Singles: 7-inch
BARONET (4 "Just One More")...8-12 62
CORSAIR (402 "Tears Had Fallen")...25-35 64
DOT (16149 "Peace of Mind")...8-12 60
EXCELLO (2158 "You Broke Your Vows")...10-20 59
EXCELLO (2180 "It's Too Late Baby")...10-20 60
ROULETTE (4237 "Sad and Lonely")...10-15 60

WILLIAMS, Eddy
Singles: 7-inch
ALCOR (2013 "Have a Heart")...20-40 63

WILLIAMS, Esther R&B '76
Singles: 7-inch
FRIENDS & CO....3-5 76-78
KENT (438 "This Life of Mine")...5-10 65

WILLIAMS, Floyd (Horsecollar)
Singles: 7-inch
THAT'S IT (226 "Thru-Way")...25-35

WILLIAMS, Frank, & Rocketeers
Singles: 7-inch
PHIL-L.A. of SOUL...4-8 67

WILLIAMS, Freddie
Singles: 7-inch
BARONET (9 "Can't You See")...15-25 62
HOLLYWOOD (1114 "Name in Lights")...10-20 67
HOLLYWOOD (1121 "Heart Can You Hear Me")...25-50 67
HOLLYWOOD (1129 "Sea of Love")...10-20 68

WILLIAMS, Garrett
Singles: 7-inch
AIRWAY (104 "Little Darling")...25-35 58
AIRWAY (106 "Linda")...10-15 58

WILLIAMS, Geoffrey
Singles: 7-inch
ATLANTIC...3-4 88

WILLIAMS, Gary
Singles: 7-inch
CONNIE SUE...4-8 69

WILLIAMS, George, & Tymes
Singles: 7-inch
COLUMBIA 3-6 71
Also see SWEET TYMES
Also see TYMES

WILLIAMS, Hank C&W '47
(With the Drifting Cowboys; Hank Williams as "Luke the Drifter;" with Audrey Williams)
Singles: 78 rpm
MGM 20-30 47-55
STERLING (201 "Calling You") 300-400 47
STERLING (204 "Wealth Won't Save Your Soul") 250-300 47
STERLING (208 "I Don't Care") 200-250 47
STERLING (210 "Honky Tonkin' ") 200-250 47
Singles: 7-inch
MGM (100 series) 5-8 60s
MGM (10000 & 11000 series) 10-20 50-55
MGM (12000 series) 5-15 55-59
MGM (13000 series) 3-6 64-67
EPs: 7-inch
ARHOOLIE 4-6 83
(Not issued with cover.)
MGM (100 & 200 series) 25-50 52-54
MGM (1000 thru 1600 series) 15-30 55-60
LPs: 10/12-inch
ACM 5-10 83
BLAINE HOUSE 15-20 72
BOLL WEEVIL 8-12 76
CMF 5-10
CANDLELITE ("Golden Dream of Hank Williams") 15-20 70s
(Boxed, three-disc set.)
CANDLELITE ("1951-52: Golden Dream of Hank Williams") 8-12 76
COLUMBIA (5616 "Hank Williams Treasury") 35-45 60s
(Boxed, four-disc set. Columbia House Record Club issue.)
GOLDEN COUNTRY 5-8 82
JAMBALAYA 5-10
MGM (2 "36 of Hank Williams' Greatest Hits") 80-100 57
(Three discs.)
MGM (4 "36 More of Hank Williams' Greatest Hits") 80-100 58
(Three discs.)
MGM (107 "Hank Williams Sings") 50-100 51
(10-inch LP.)
MGM (168 "Moanin' the Blues") ... 50-100 52
(10-inch LP.)
MGM (202 "Memorial Album") 50-100 53
(10-inch LP.)
MGM (203 "Hank Williams As Luke the Drifter") 50-100 53
(10-inch LP.)
MGM (240-2 "24 Karat Hits, Hank Williams") 15-20 68
MGM (242 "Honky Tonkin' ") 50-100 54
(10-inch LP.)
MGM (243 "I Saw the Light") 50-100 55
(10-inch LP.)
MGM (291 "Ramblin' Man") 50-100 54
(10-inch LP.)
MGM (912 "Hank Williams . . . Reflections By Those Who Loved Him") 100-200 75
(Boxed, three-disc set. Promotional issue only. Includes guest speakers: Roy Acuff, Little Jimmy Dickens, Lefty Frizzell, Pee Wee King, George Morgan, Bill Monroe, Minnie Pearl, Wesley Rose, Ernest Tubb, Grant Turner, Audrey Williams, Faron Young, and Hank Williams Jr.)
MGM (1000 series) 8-10 76
(Special Products issue.)
MGM (3219 "Ramblin' Man") 50-75 55
(Blue "sketch" cover.)
MGM (3219 "Ramblin' Man") 25-45
(Yellow "suit" cover.)
MGM (3330 "Moanin' the Blues" 100-150 56
(Yellow label.)
MGM (E-3200 thru 3900 series) 25-50 55-61
(Monaural. Through 3733, first issues have a yellow label.)
MGM (SE-3200 thru 3900 series) ... 10-20 63-70
(Reprocessed stereo. Through 3733, first issues have a yellow label.)
MGM (4000 thru 4700 series, except 4267) 10-20 63-71
MGM (4267 "The Hank Williams Story") 50-75 66
(Boxed, four-disc set.)
MGM (4900 thru 5400 series) 5-10 75-77
METRO 10-15 65-67
POLYDOR 5-15 83-84
SUNRISE MEDIA 8-10 81
TIME-LIFE (Except LCW-01) 5-8 81-82
TIME-LIFE (LCW-01 "Hank Williams") 10-15 81
(Boxed, three-disc set.)
Also see DRIFTING COWBOYS
Also see PRESLEY, Elvis / Hank Williams

WILLIAMS, Hank / Roy Acuff
LPs: 10/12-inch
LAMB & LION 8-12
(Three discs. Two by Hank Williams, one by Roy Acuff.)
Also see ACUFF, Roy

WILLIAMS, Hank / Slim Whitman
LPs: 10/12-inch
SUNRISE MEDIA 8-10 81
Also see WHITMAN, Slim

WILLIAMS, Hank, & Hank Williams Jr. LP '65
(Hank Williams / Hank Williams Jr.; Hank Williams Jr. & Hank Williams Sr.)
Singles: 7-inch
W.B. 3-4 89
LPs: 10/12-inch
COLUMBIA HOUSE ("Hank's Place") 5-10 81
(One side by each artist. Bonus LP with boxed set below. Selection number not known.)
COLUMBIA HOUSE "Hank Williams / Hank Williams Jr.) 20-25 81
(Boxed, five-disc record club set. Selection number not known.)
MGM (4200 series) 15-25 65
MGM (4300 thru 4900 series) 10-15 66-74
Also see WILLIAMS, Hank
Also see WILLIAMS, Hank, Jr.

WILLIAMS, Hank, Jr. C&W/P&R '64
(With the Cheatin' Hearts; with Mike Curb Congregation; Luke the Drifter Jr.)
Singles: 7-inch
CONSOL 10-20
(Promotional issue from Consolidation Coal.)
ELEKTRA/CURB 3-4 79-82
MGM (13000 series) 4-8 64-68
MGM (14000 series) 3-5 68-76
MGM GOLDEN CIRCLE 3-5 70s
W.B./CURB (Except 8000 series) 3-4 82-88
W.B./CURB (8000 series) 3-4 77-78
Picture Sleeves
MGM (13000 series) 5-10 64-68
LPs: 10/12-inch
CURB 5-8 83-84
ELEKTRA 5-8 79-83
MGM (Except 5009) 10-20 64-76
MGM (5009 "Hank Williams Jr. and Friends") 25-50 75
POLYDOR 5-8
W.B. (Except 2092) 5-10 77-87
W.B. (2092 "Interview") 8-12 83
(Promotional issue only.)
W.B./CURB 5-8 85-91
Also see BOCEPHUS
Also see CASH, Johnny, & Hank Williams Jr.
Also see CHARLES, Ray, & Hank Williams Jr.
Also see CURB, Mike
Also see FRANCIS, Connie, & Hank Williams Jr.
Also see JENNINGS, Waylon, & Hank Williams Jr.
Also see JONES, George
Also see KERSHAW, Doug, & Hank Williams Jr.
Also see KILGORE, Merle
Also see WILLIAMS, Hank, & Hank Williams Jr.

WILLIAMS, Hank, Jr., & Lois Johnson C&W '72
Singles: 7-inch
MGM 3-5 70-72
LPs: 10/12-inch
MGM 6-12 70-72
Also see JOHNSON, Lois
Also see WILLIAMS, Hank, Jr.

WILLIAMS, Harmonica, & Little Freddie King
LPs: 10/12-inch
AHURA MAZDA 8-10 71

WILLIAMS, James "D-Train" R&B '86
Singles: 12-inch
COLUMBIA 4-6 86
Singles: 7-inch
COLUMBIA 3-4 86-88
LPs: 10/12-inch
COLUMBIA 5-8 86
Also see "D" TRAIN

WILLIAMS, Jason D. C&W '89
Singles: 7-inch
RCA 3-4 89

WILLIAMS, Jeanette R&B '69
Singles: 7-inch
BACK BEAT 10-20 66-69

WILLIAMS, Jerry
(Jerry Williams, Jr.)
Singles: 7-inch
CALLA 10-20 66-67
COTILLION 4-8 69
8730 RECORDS 5-10 67
MUSICOR 5-10 68
V-TONE (501 "You Call it Love") ... 15-25 63
Also see BROOKS & JERRY
Also see LITTLE JERRY
Also see SWAMP DOGG
Also see WILLIAMS, Little Jerry

WILLIAMS, Jerry
Singles: 7-inch
LAURIE 5-10 66
MOONGLOW (1001 "Twistin' Patricia") 5-10 63

WILLIAMS, Jerry, & Rockets
Singles: 7-inch
ROCKET (001 "Blueberry Lane") ... 15-25 62
Members: Jerry Van Dynhoven; Cliff Peranto; Larry Russell; Denny Noie; Bill Pable; Roger Loos; Donnie Van Dynhoven; Carol Van Dynhoven; Denny Hymmerman; Bob Timmers; Jerry Cole.

WILLIAMS, Jerry Lee
Singles: 7-inch
SOLID GOLD (778 "The Go-Tune") 15-20 59

WILLIAMS, Jessie
Singles: 7-inch
CARLTON 5-10 63

WILLIAMS, Jim
Singles: 78 rpm
SUN 10-20 57
Singles: 7-inch
SUN (270 "Please Don't Cry Over Me") 25-40 57

WILLIAMS, Jimmie
Singles: 7-inch
TIDE 4-8 67

WILLIAMS, Jimmy
Singles: 7-inch
ABC 5-10 63
ATLANTIC 5-10 65
CUB 10-20 59
DON-EL 5-10 61
DUB (2842 "You're Always Late") .. 50-75 58
DYNOVOICE 4-8 69
HULL 5-10 64
LIMELIGHT 5-10 64
ORBIT 10-20 58
ROULETTE 10-15 60

WILLIAMS, Jimmy
Singles: 12-inch
SALSOUL 4-6 83

WILLIAMS, Jo Jo
(Joseph Williams)
Singles: 7-inch
ATOMIC ("Rock & Roll Boogie") 30-50 59
(Selection number not known.)
ATOMIC (917 "Afro Shake Dance") 5-10 72

WILLIAMS, Jody
(Joseph Leon Williams)
Singles: 7-inch
ARGO (5274 "You May") 15-25 57
NIKE 10-20 63
SMASH 10-15 63
YULANDO 10-20 62
Also see LITTLE PAPA JOE
Also see WILLIAMS, Sugar Boy

WILLIAMS, Joe
(Joe Lee Williams)
Singles: 78 rpm
BLUEBIRD 15-25 45
BULLET (337 "Jivin' Woman") ... 100-150 50
COLUMBIA 10-20 47-48
Also see WILLIAMS, Big Joe
Also see WILLIAMS, Po' Joe

WILLIAMS, Joe / James McCain
Singles: 78 rpm
CHICAGO (103 "Good Mr. Roosevelt") 50-75 45
Also see WILLIAMS, Joe (Joe Lee Williams)

WILLIAMS, Joe R&B '52
(Joseph Goreed)
Singles: 78 rpm
BLUE LAKE 50-75 54
CHECKER 15-25 52
ROULETTE 5-10 57
SAVOY 10-15 55
TRUMPET 20-30 52
Singles: 7-inch
BLUE LAKE (102 "Tired of Moving") 150-300 54
CHECKER (762 "Every Day I Have the Blues") 25-50 52
RCA 4-8 62-66
ROULETTE 5-10 57-62
SAVOY 10-20 55
SOLID STATE 4-8 66
TEMPONIC 3-6 72
EPs: 7-inch
RCA (2762 "At Newport '63") 8-12 63
LPs: 10/12-inch
RCA 10-15 63-65
REGENT (6002 "Everyday") 35-45 56
ROULETTE 15-30 58-64
SOLID STATE 10-15 66
Also see BASIE, Count
Also see WASHINGTON, Dinah / Joe Williams / Sarah Vaughan

WILLIAMS, Joe, & Rhythmaires
Singles: 78 rpm
NASHBORO 10-20 51

WILLIAMS, Joe, & Three Chocolates
Singles: 78 rpm
CINCINATTI 10-20

WILLIAMS, John, Orchestra P&R '75
Singles: 7-inch
ARISTA 3-4 77-80
COLUMBIA 3-4 83
MCA 3-4 74-76
RCA 3-4 79
20TH FOX 3-4 77-78
W.B. 3-4 79
Picture Sleeves
ARISTA 3-4 77
20TH FOX 3-4 77-78
W.B. 3-4 79
LPs: 10/12-inch
CAPITOL 5-10 71
COLUMBIA (31091 "Changes") 5-10 71
COLUMBIA (37000 series) 5-8 81
DISCOVERY 4-8 84
RCA 5-8 77
For a complete listing of soundtracks by this artist, consult *The Official Price Guide to Movie/TV Soundtracks and Original Cast Albums.*
Also see BOSTON POPS ORCHESTRA

WILLIAMS, Johnny
(John Lee Hooker)
Singles: 78 rpm
GOTHAM (509 "Questionnaire Blues") 15-25 52
GOTHAM (513 "Little Boy Blue") ... 15-25 53
PRIZE (704 "Miss Rosie Mae") 75-125 49
STAFF (710 "Wandering Blues") ... 50-75 50
STAFF (718 "Prison Bound") 50-75 50
SWING TIME 15-25 50
Also see HOOKER, John Lee

WILLIAMS, Johnny
(Robert Warren)
Singles: 78 rpm
STAFF (717 "I Got Lucky") 50-100 50
SWING TIME (225 "I Got Lucky") .. 25-50 50
Also see WARREN, Baby Boy

WILLIAMS, Johnny
LPs: 10/12-inch
CROWN 10-20 60s

WILLIAMS, Johnny R&B/C&W '72
Singles: 7-inch
BASHIE 3-5 70
CUB 4-6 68
EPIC 3-5 72
PHILADELPHIA INT'L 3-5 73

WILLIAMS, Johnny
Singles: 7-inch
CY (001 "Don't Call for Me") 50-100 61
(First issued as by the Implacables.)
Also see IMPLACABLES

WILLIAMS, Johnny
Singles: 7-inch
CINEMA 4-8
TWINIGHT (109 "Maggie") 5-10

WILLIAMS, Johnny, & Jokers
Singles: 7-inch
PIC-1 10-15

WILLIAMS, Johnny Lee
Singles: 7-inch
LOUIS 4-8 62

WILLIAMS, Juan
Singles: 7-inch
BLUE SOUL (101 "My Girl Has Gone") 15-25

WILLIAMS, Juanita
Singles: 7-inch
GOLDEN WORLD (18 "Baby Boy") 10-20 65
WINGATE (008 "Some Things You Never Get Used To") 10-20 65

WILLIAMS, Ken
Singles: 7-inch
OKEH (7303 "Come Back") 20-30 67
SARG (219 "Hey, Leroy") 10-20 65

WILLIAMS, Kenny
Singles: 7-inch
BEN MORE (1001 "Old Fashioned Christmas") 3-5 73
CARLTON (578 "Sugar Lumps") 10-20 62

WILLIAMS, King
Singles: 7-inch
MGM (13259 "Patience Baby") 8-12 64

WILLIAMS, L.C. R&B '49
(With Conney's Combo)
Singles: 78 rpm
BAYOU 10-20 53
FREEDOM 10-20 49-50
GOLD STAR 10-20 48
IMPERIAL 8-15 52
JAX 10-20 52
MERCURY 8-15 52
SITTIN' IN WITH 10-20 52
Singles: 7-inch
BAYOU (008 "My Darkest Hours") 50-100 53
Also see CONNEY'S COMBO
Also see LIGHTNIN' JR.
Also see McBOOKER, Connie
Also see WILLIAMS, Lightnin' Jr.

WILLIAMS, Larry P&R/R&B '57
Singles: 78 rpm
SPECIALTY 15-35 57-58
Singles: 7-inch
CHESS 10-15 59-60
EL BAM (69 "Call On Me") 8-12 65
MERCURY 5-10 63
OKEH 5-10 66-67
SMASH 5-10 66
SPECIALTY (597 thru 658) 20-35 57-59
SPECIALTY (665 thru 682) 15-25 59-60
SPECIALTY (SPBX series) 12-15 85
(Boxed set of six colored vinyl discs.)
VEE JAY 15-25 57
VENTURE 5-8 68
Picture Sleeves
SPECIALTY (626 "Slow Down") 25-50 58
LPs: 10/12-inch
OKEH (12123 "Greatest Hits") 10-15 67
SPECIALTY (2109 "Here's Larry Williams") 50-75 59
SPECIALTY (2109 "Here's Larry Williams") 8-10 86
(Has '80s information and copyright date on back cover.)
SPECIALTY (2158 "Unreleased Larry Williams") 8-10 86
SPECIALTY (2162 "Hocus Pocus") 8-10 86
Session: Art Neville; Rene Hall; Earl Palmer; Plas Johnson; Jewell Grant; Ted Brinson; Alvin Tyler; Roy Montrell.
Also see COOKE, Sam / Lloyd Price / Larry Williams / Little Richard
Also see JOHNSON, Plas
Also see NEVILLE, Art
Also see PALMER, Earl

WILLIAMS, Larry, & Johnny Watson P&R/R&B '67
Singles: 7-inch
BELL (813 "I Could Love You Baby") 5-10 69
OKEH (7274 "A Quitter Never Wins") 10-20 67
OKEH (7281 "Too Late") 10-20 67
OKEH (7300 "Nobody") 15-25 67
(With Kaleidoscope.)
LPs: 10/12-inch
OKEH (14122 "Two for the Price of One") 10-20 67
Also see KALEIDOSCOPE
Also see LARRY & JOHNNY
Also see WATSON, Johnny
Also see WILLIAMS, Larry

WILLIAMS, Lawton C&W '61
(With the Anita Kerr Singers)
Singles: 7-inch
D 5-10 60
LE BILL 5-10
MEGA 3-5 71
MERCURY 4-8 61
RCA (7000 series) 5-10 58
RCA (8000 series) 4-6 64
LPs: 10/12-inch
MEGA 6-10 71
Also see KERR, Anita

WILLIAMS, Lee R&B '67
(With the Moonrays; with Cymbals; Lee "Shot" Williams)
Singles: 7-inch
BLACK CIRCLE 4-8
CARNIVAL 5-10 66-69
FEDERAL 10-15 63-64
GAMMA (101 "Love Now, Pay Later") 25-35
KING (5409 "I'm So in Love") 50-100 60
PM (101 "I Found a Love") 8-12
RAPDA 4-8
SHAMA 5-10 69
TCHULA 4-8
TRUE 10-20
U.A. 4-8

WILLIAMS, Lenny R&B '75
Singles: 12-inch
ABC 4-6 78
ROCSHIRE 4-6 83-84
Singles: 7-inch
ABC 3-5 77-78
ATCO 3-5 72
GALAXY 5-10
KNOBHILL 3-4 86
MCA 3-5 79-81
MOTOWN 3-4 75
ROCSHIRE 3-4 83-84
LPs: 10/12-inch
ABC 8-10 77-78
MCA 5-8 79-81
MOTOWN 8-10 75
ROCSHIRE 5-8 83-84
W.B. 8-12 74
Also see KENNY G. & LENNY WILLIAMS
Also see TOWER of POWER

WILLIAMS, Leon
Singles: 7-inch
JOSIE 5-10 59

WILLIAMS, Leona C&W '69
Singles: 7-inch
ELEKTRA 3-4 81
HICKORY 3-6 69-73
MCA 3-5 78-79
LPs: 10/12-inch
HICKORY 10-20 70-72
MCA 5-10 76
MERCURY 5-10 84
Also see HAGGARD, Merle, & Leona Williams

WILLIAMS, Lester
(With His Band)
Singles: 78 rpm
DUKE 15-20 54
IMPERIAL 15-25 56
MACY'S 10-20 49-50
SPECIALTY 25-50 52-53
Singles: 7-inch
DUKE (123 "Let's Do It") 20-30 54
DUKE (131 "Crazy 'Bout My Baby") 20-30 54
IMPERIAL (5402 "McDonald's Daughter") 25-40 56
SPECIALTY (422 "I Can't Lose with the Stuff I Use") 50-75 52
SPECIALTY (431 "Let Me Tell You a Thing Or Two") 75-100 52
SPECIALTY (437 "Sweet Lovin' Daddy") 75-100 52
SPECIALTY (450 "Brand New Baby") 50-75 53

WILLIAMS, Lew
Singles: 78 rpm
IMPERIAL 50-75 56
Singles: 7-inch
IMPERIAL (5394 "Cat Talk") 75-100 56
IMPERIAL (5411 "Bop Bop Ba Doo Bop") 75-100 56
IMPERIAL (5429 "Centipede") 75-100 57
IMPERIAL (8306 "I'll Play Your Game") 75-100 56

WILLIAMS, Lightnin', Jr.
(L.C. Williams)
Singles: 78 rpm
GOLD STAR....................................20-30 48
Also see WILLIAMS, L.C.

WILLIAMS, Linda R&B '79
Singles: 7-inch
ARISTA... 3-5 79

WILLIAMS, Little Cheryl
Singles: 7-inch
KAPP.. 4-8 62

WILLIAMS, Little Jerry
Singles: 7-inch
ACADEMY.. 8-12 64
CALLA... 8-12 65-66
COTILLION.. 4-8 69
LOMA.. 8-12 64
SOUTHERN SOUND.........................10-20 64-65
Also see WILLIAMS, Jerry

WILLIAMS, Lois C&W '69
Singles: 7-inch
STARDAY... 3-6 69-70
LPs: 10/12-inch
STARDAY... 8-12 70

WILLIAMS, Lonnie
Singles: 78 rpm
SITTIN' IN WITH (567 "Tears in My Heart")....................................15-25 50
SITTIN' IN WITH (593 "Wavin' Sea Blues")..15-25 51

WILLIAMS, Lord, & His Court
Singles: 7-inch
APPLAUSE... 8-12 68

WILLIAMS, Mark, & Kingsmen
Singles: 7-inch
SHELBY (2 "Honey Honey")...........10-20 60s

WILLIAMS, Mary Lou, Trio
Singles: 7-inch
SUE "715 "Chunk A Lunk").............. 8-12 59

WILLIAMS, Mason P&R/LP '68
Singles: 7-inch
W.B. 3-6 68-71
LPs: 10/12-inch
EVEREST... 6-12 69
FLYING FISH..................................... 5-10 78
VEE JAY.. 10-20 64
W.B. 6-12 68-71

WILLIAMS, Mason, & Mannheim Steamroller LP '87
LPs: 10/12-inch
AMERICAN G.................................... 5-8 87

WILLIAMS, Mason / Smothers Brothers
EPs: 7-inch
W.B./7 ARTS (283 "Scope Box") ...20-40 70
(Promotional issue only.)
Also see SMOTHERS BROTHERS
Also see WILLIAMS, Mason

WILLIAMS, Maurice P&R/R&B '60
(With the Zodiacs; with Inspirations)
Singles: 7-inch
ATLANTIC (2741 "Sweetness")........... 4-6 70
CANDI (1031 "Never Leave You Again")..30-40 63
COLLECTABLES................................. 3-4 80s
ERIC.. 3-5 70s
FLASHBACK....................................... 4-8 65
HERALD (552 "Stay")......................15-25 60
HERALD (556 "I Remember")...........15-25 60
HERALD (559 "Come Along")...........15-25 61
HERALD (563 "Someday")...............15-25 61
HERALD (565 "Please")...................15-25 61
OWL.. 3-5 73
SEASIDE (115 "Shaking and Breaking")... 5-10
SELWYN (5121 "College Girl").........25-50 59
SPHERE SOUND (707 "So Fine") .. 8-12 65
LPs: 10/12-inch
COLLECTABLES................................. 6-8 84
HERALD (1014 "Stay") 75-125 61
LOST-NITE.. 5-10 80s
RELIC..10-15
SNYDER...25-30
SPHERE SOUND..............................15-25 66
Also see GLADIOLAS
Also see SWAYZE, Patrick, & Wendy Fraser / Maurice Williams & Zodiacs
Also see ZODIACS

WILLIAMS, Mel
(With the Montclairs)
Singles: 78 rpm
DECCA...15-25 55
DIG..15-25 56-57
FEDERAL..20-40 56
RAGE...50-100 54
Singles: 7-inch
BIT...10-15 64
DECCA (29370 "Lessons in Love")...75-125 55
DECCA (29499 "Eternal Love")....75-125 55
DECCA (29554 "God Gave Me You")...75-125 55
FEDERAL (12236 "Soldier Boy")..100-150 56
DIG (107 "Talk to Me")..................50-100 56
DIG (114 "Here in My Heart").......50-100 56
DIG (123 "My Love")......................50-100 56
DIG (128 "All Through the Night")...50-100 57
DIG (136 "It's You")........................50-100 57
DIG (140 "Stand There, Mountain").......................................50-100 57
MODERN..10-20 66
RAGE (101 "Fools Fall in Love")...300-500 54
(Also issued as by the Capris.)
TASTY HASTY (4 "Fattenin' Frogs")...10-20
LPs: 10/12-inch
DIG (103 "All Through the Night")...100-200 56
Also see BARONS / Mel Williams & Montclairs
Also see OTIS, Johnny

WILLIAMS, Mike P&R/R&B '66
Singles: 7-inch
ATLANTIC... 5-8 65-66
KING... 5-8 66
Also see TEMPESTS

WILLIAMS, Morry, & Kids
Singles: 7-inch
CARLTON (477 "Oh Louise").........30-50 58
LUCK (102 "Time Runs Out") 75-125 59
(Maroon label.)
LUCK (102 "Time Runs Out") 50-75 59
(Yellow label.)
TEE VEE (301 "Oh Louise").......150-200 58

WILLIAMS, Nat, & Mello-Tones
Singles: 7-inch
ARIES (1014 "You Excite Me")......25-35 59

WILLIAMS, Nate
Singles: 7-inch
BACK BEAT....................................... 5-8 62

WILLIAMS, Otis C&W '71
(With the Midnight Cowboys)
Singles: 7-inch
STOP (388 "I Wanna Go Country")... 4-6 71
LPs: 10/12-inch
STOP (1022 "Otis Williams & the Midnight Cowboys")...10-15 71
Note: These are country music releases. Solo R&B Deluxe releases credited either to "Otis Williams," or "Otis Williams & His New Group," are in the "Charms" section.
Also see CHARMS

WILLIAMS, Pat, Band
Singles: 7-inch
VERVE.. 4-6 69
Picture Sleeves
VERVE.. 5-8 69
LPs: 10/12-inch
VERVE..10-15 69

WILLIAMS, Patrick R&B '83
Singles: 7-inch
PCM.. 3-4 83

WILLIAMS, Paul R&B '48
(With His Orchestra)
Singles: 78 rpm
CAPITOL...5-10 55
CLEF...5-10 52
GROOVE...5-10 54
JOSIE...5-10 56
MERCURY...5-10
RAMA..20-30 55
SAVOY..5-10 48-57
Singles: 7-inch
ASCOT (2114 "I Can't Stand It").......8-12 62
CAPITOL (3205 "Rock It Davy Crockett")..10-20 55
CAPITOL (3255 "It's Over")............10-20 55
GROOVE (0014 "Women Are the Root of All Evil")..15-25 54
("Vocal refrain by Jimmy Brown.")
JAX (313 "Thin Man") 50-75 54
(Red vinyl.)
JOSIE (806 "Once Upon a Time")..15-25 56
RAMA (167 "Ring-A-Ling")..............50-75 55
(Vocalist, though not credited, is believed to be Little Willie John.)
SAVOY...10-30 51-59
SEVEN ARTS (713 "Back to Back").5-10 61
VEE JAY (234 "Give It Up")............10-20 57
VEE JAY (268 "South Shore Drive")..10-20 57
Also see DALE, Larry
Also see JOHN, Little Willie
Also see McNEELY, Big Jay / Paul Williams
Also see McPHERSON, Wyatt "Earp," & Paul Williams
Also see MOORE, Bill
Also see WATTS, Noble

WILLIAMS, Paul LP '71
Singles: 7-inch
A&M... 3-4 72-77
PAID.. 3-4 81
PORTRAIT.. 3-4 79
REPRISE.. 3-4 70
LPs: 10/12-inch
A&M...6-10 71-77
PAID.. 5-8 81
PORTRAIT.. 5-8 79
REPRISE..8-12 70
Also see HOLY MACKEREL

WILLIAMS, Po' Joe
(Joe Lee Williams)
Singles: 78 rpm
VEE JAY...15-25 56
Singles: 7-inch
VEE JAY (227 "Going Back Home")...30-50 56
Also see WILLIAMS, Joe (Joe Lee Williams)

WILLIAMS, R.G.
Singles: 78 rpm
77...15-25 51

WILLIAMS, Ray
Singles: 7-inch
ALA (1171 "Tell Me Now") 4-6
LE CAM (717 "I Want to Know") 8-12 61
SPACE (1011 "Hen & Rooster").......5-10 67

WILLIAMS, Richard
(With the Flame Tones)
Singles: 7-inch
BELL...4-6 72
FORWARD...5-8 69
QUAD..4-6 70

WILLIAMS, Robert
Singles: 7-inch
TIP TOP (730 "Loud Mufflers") 10-20 59

WILLIAMS, Robert Pete
LPs: 10/12-inch
AHURA MAZDA 8-10 71
ARHOOLIE...8-10 71
PRESTIGE BLUESVILLE 15-25 61
TAKOMA...10-15 70s

WILLIAMS, Robert Pete, & Snooks Eaglin
LPs: 10/12-inch
FANTASY..8-10
Also see EAGLIN, Snooks
Also see WILLIAMS, Robert Pete

WILLIAMS, Roberta
Singles: 7-inch
UPTOWN...4-8 65

WILLIAMS, Robin LP '79
Singles: 12-inch
CASABLANCA......................................4-8 79
Singles: 7-inch
BOARDWALK.......................................3-5 80
Picture Sleeves
BOARDWALK.......................................3-5 80
LPs: 10/12-inch
CASABLANCA 5-10 79-83

WILLIAMS, Robin & Linda
LPs: 10/12-inch
FLASHLIGHT......................................8-10 75

WILLIAMS, Roger P&R '55
Singles: 78 rpm
KAPP...3-5 55-57
Singles: 7-inch
KAPP...3-8 55-72
MCA..3-4 73-78
W.B...3-4 80
Picture Sleeves
KAPP...5-15 55-66
EPs: 7-inch
KAPP...4-8 55-58
LPs: 10/12-inch
KAPP...5-20 55-72
MCA..4-8 73-83
PICKWICK..4-8
VOCALION..4-8 71

WILLIAMS, Roger, & Jane Morgan
Singles: 78 rpm
KAPP...3-5 56
Singles: 7-inch
KAPP...5-15 56
Also see MORGAN, Jane
Also see WILLIAMS, Roger

WILLIAMS, Ron
Singles: 7-inch
IMPERIAL (5729 "On Top of Old Smokey")...15-25 61
IMPERIAL (5800 "Don't You Tell Me Maybe")..20-30 61
MERCURY..4-8 63
PASTEL...4-8 64
TY-TEX (100 "Sue Sue Baby")...100-150 60
TY-TEX (106 "Wine Wine Wine") ..25-35 61

WILLIAMS, Roxie
Singles: 7-inch
LUCKY ELEVEN (1112 "15 Seconds")..50-75 61

WILLIAMS, Roy
Singles: 7-inch
W.B. COUNTRY SOUND.....................3-5 77

WILLIAMS, Sam
Singles: 7-inch
TOWER (367 "Let's Talk It Over") 40-60 67
UPTOWN (742 "Miracle Worker") 10-20 67

WILLIAMS, Sandy
Singles: 7-inch
FOUR CORNERS 10-20 66
OLIVER...8-12 66

WILLIAMS, Scotty
Singles: 7-inch
JUBILEE...10-20 67
MONA LEE..10-20 60s

WILLIAMS, Sebastian
(With the Soul Men)
Singles: 7-inch
COTILLION...5-10 69
OVIDE (249 "Get Your Point Over")..5-10
SOUND OF SOUL (102 "Too Much")..50-75 65

WILLIAMS, Sherman, Orchestra: see FOUR FLAMES / Sherman Williams Orchestra

WILLIAMS, Shirley
Singles: 7-inch
IMPERIAL 5-10 60

WILLIAMS, Smitty
Singles: 7-inch
MGM 5-10 62

WILLIAMS, Sonny
Singles: 7-inch
COIN..5-10 59

WILLIAMS, Sonny Boy R&B '43
Singles: 78 rpm
DECCA..15-25 43

WILLIAMS, Sugar Boy
(Joseph Leon Williams)
Singles: 7-inch
HERALD..15-25 60
RAINES...10-20 65
Also see WILLIAMS, Jody

WILLIAMS, Sunny, Trio
(Enoch Williams)
Singles: 78 rpm
SUPER DISC 15-25 47-48

WILLIAMS, T.J., & Two Shades of Soul
(Timothy "T.J." Williams & Two Shades of Soul)
Singles: 7-inch
JOSIE (995 "My Life")....................10-20 67
JOSIE (1000 "Baby I Need You")...15-25 68
Member: Timmy Williams.

WILLIAMS, Tawny: see WILLIAMS, Toni

WILLIAMS, Terry
Singles: 7-inch
REPRISE...3-5 70-71
Also see FIRST EDITION

WILLIAMS, Tex C&W '46
(With His Western Caravan; with Spade Cooley; with California Express)
Singles: 78 rpm
CAPITOL...4-8 46-51
COLUMBIA 4-8 46
DECCA...4-8 53-55
Singles: 7-inch
BOONE 4-6 65-68
CAPITOL..5-10 51-60
DECCA...5-10 53-55
DOT 4-6 66
GRANITE 3-5 74
LIBERTY...4-8 63-65
MONUMENT...3-5 70-72
SHASTA..4-8 60-61
EPs: 7-inch
CAMDEN...8-12 58
CAPITOL..10-15 56-57
DECCA...10-15 55
LPs: 10/12-inch
BOONE...10-15 66
CAMDEN (363 "Tex Williams' Best")..20-40 58
CAPITOL (1463 "Smoke! Smoke! Smoke!")..20-40 60
DECCA (4295 "Country Music Time")..15-25 62
DECCA (5565 "Dance-O-Rama")...40-60 55
(10-inch LP.)
GARU...5-10 81
GRANITE 6-12 74
IMPERIAL...10-15 66
LIBERTY...15-25 63
MONUMENT.......................................8-12 71
SHASTA...8-12
SUNSET...10-15 66
Also see COOLEY, Spade, & His Orchestra
Also see STARR, Kay

WILLIAMS, Tim
LPs: 10/12-inch
EPIC..10-15 69

WILLIAMS, Timmy
Singles: 7-inch
MALA (515 "Competition").........150-250 65
Also see WILLIAMS, T.J., & Two Shades of Soul

WILLIAMS, Tom B.
Singles: 7-inch
TOPIX (6009 "Wishing Well").........20-25 62

WILLIAMS, Tommy
(With the Fingerpoppers)
Singles: 7-inch
BACK BEAT (561 "Going Crazy")......5-10 66
FORTE..10-20 60
SUE (747 "I'll Follow You") 10-15 61
ULTRASONIC (111 "Strange Are the Ways of Love")...5-10
VICA (101 "Late, Late Last Night") 15-25 59

WILLIAMS, Toni
(Tawny Williams)
Singles: 7-inch
DELUXE...5-10 69
TUFF (1824 "Oh Baby")..................25-35 62
TUFF (1836 "Pretty Little Words") 25-35 62

WILLIAMS, Tony
Singles: 7-inch
MERCURY...10-20 57-59
PHILIPS...4-8 62-63
REPRISE...5-10 61-62
LPs: 10/12-inch
MERCURY...20-30 59
PHILIPS...15-25 62
REPRISE...20-25 61
Also see PLATTERS

WILLIAMS, Tony LP '79
LPs: 10/12-inch
COLUMBIA 5-10 79

WILLIAMS, Tracey
Singles: 7-inch
DORE...5-10 63

WILLIAMS, Trudy, & Six Teens: see SIX TEENS

WILLIAMS, Tucker C&W '80
Singles: 7-inch
YATAHEY 3-4 80

WILLIAMS, Vanessa P&R/R&B/LP '88
Singles: 7-inch
WING..3-4 88-89
Picture Sleeves
WING..3-4 88-89
LPs: 10/12-inch
WING..5-8 88

WILLIAMS, Verna
Singles: 7-inch
BELINDA...5-8 62

WILLIAMS, Vesta R&B '86
(Vesta)
Singles: 12-inch
A&M..4-6 86
Singles: 7-inch
A&M..3-4 86-89
LPs: 10/12-inch
A&M..5-8 86-89

WILLIAMS, W.W.: see WILLIAMS, Willie

WILLIAMS, Wayne, & Sure Shots
(Gaylon Wayne)
Singles: 7-inch
SURE (1001 "Red Hot Mama").. 150-250 57
Also see WAYNE, Gaylon

WILLIAMS, Wendy O.
LPs: 10/12-inch
PASSPORT...5-10 84
Also see PLASMATICS

WILLIAMS, Willie
(W.W. Williams)
Singles: 7-inch
ABC 6-12 66-67
RCA 5-10 69
SUPREME (777 "38 Woman").........5-10
SUPREME (778 "Black Diamond Rattler")...5-10
SUPREME (1001 "Wine Headed Woman")...5-10 73
LPs: 10/12-inch
SUPREME (1001 "Raw Unpolluted Soul")..10-15 73
Also see TAYLOR, Hound Dog

WILLIAMS, Wilson R&B '78
Singles: 7-inch
ABC 3-5 78

WILLIAMS BROTHERS C&W '63
Singles: 7-inch
DEL-MAR 4-8 63
Members: Jimmy Williams; Bobby Williams.

WILLIAMSON, Chris
Singles: 7-inch
AMPEX 3-5 71
LPs: 10/12-inch
AMPEX 8-10 71

WILLIAMSON, James, & His Trio
Singles: 78 rpm
CHANCE...50-100 52-53
Singles: 7-inch
CHANCE (1131 "Homesick")......150-250 53
Also see HOMESICK JAMES

WILLIAMSON, Joe
Singles: 7-inch
GNP..4-8 64

WILLIAMSON, Sonny Boy R&B '47
(John Lee Williamson)
Singles: 78 rpm
BLUEBIRD (0736 "Miss Stella Brown Blues")..25-50 45
BLUEBIRD (0744 "Elevator Woman")...25-50 46
RCA (0001 "Wonderful Time").........20-40 49
RCA (0021 "Little Girl")..................20-40 49
RCA (0046 "Southern Dream") 20-40 49
RCA (1875 "Early in the Morning")..20-40 46
RCA (2056 "Mean Old Highway") ..20-40 46
RCA (2184 "Hoodoo Hoodoo")........20-40 47
RCA (2521 "Polly Put Your Kettle On")..20-40 47
RCA (2369 "G, M & O Blues") 20-40 47
RCA (2623 "Sugar Gal")................20-40 47
RCA (2796 "I Have Got to Go") 20-40 48
RCA (2893 "Apple Tree Swing") 20-40 48
RCA (3047 "Stop Breaking Down") 20-40 48
RCA (3218 "The Big Boat")............20-40 48
Singles: 7-inch
RCA (0005 "Little Girl")..............100-200 49
RCA (0030 "Southern Dream") .. 100-200 49
LPs: 10/12-inch
BLUES CLASSICS (3 "Blues Classics By Sonny Boy Williamson")...............15-25 60s
BLUES CLASSICS (20 "Blues Classics By Sonny Boy Williamson, Vol. 2")...15-25 60s
Session: Blind John Davis; Big Bill Broonzy; Al Elkins; Charles Sanders; Tampa Red; Judge Riley.
Also see WILLIAMS, Big Joe, & Sonny Boy Williamson

WILLIAMSON, Sonny Boy R&B '55
(Aleck "Rice" Miller; Aleck Ford)
Singles: 78 rpm
ACE 20-40 55
CHECKER..10-25 55-57
RAM...15-20 54
TRUMPET..20-40 51-54
Singles: 7-inch
ACE (511 "Boppin' with Sonny")...50-100 55

CHECKER (824 "Don't Start Me Talkin' ")....25-50 55
CHECKER (834 "Let Me Explain") 25-50 56
CHECKER (847 "Keep It to Yourself")....25-50 56
CHECKER (864 "I Don't Know")....25-50 57
CHECKER (883 "Born Blind")........25-50 57
CHECKER (894 "Born Blind")........25-50 58
CHECKER (910 "Cross My Heart") 10-15 58
CHECKER (927 "Let Your Conscience Be Your Guide")....10-15 59
CHECKER (943 "The Goat")..........10-15 60
CHECKER (956 "Lonesome Cabin")....10-15 60
CHECKER (963 "Trust Me Baby") .10-15 60
CHECKER (975 "Stop Right Now")....10-15 61
CHECKER (1002 thru 1134) 6-12 61-66
RAM (2501 "Mailman Mailman")....25-50 54
TRUMPET (129 "Eyesight to the Blind")....50-100 51
TRUMPET (139 "Do It if You Wanta")....50-100 51
TRUMPET (140 "Stop Crying") 50-100 51
TRUMPET (144 "I Cross My Heart")....50-100 52
TRUMPET (145 "Pontiac Blues") .50-100 52
TRUMPET (166 "Mighty Long Time")....50-100 52
TRUMPET (212 "Too Close Together")....50-75 53
TRUMPET (215 "She Brought Life Back to the Dead")....50-75 54
TRUMPET (216 "Red Hot Kisses").50-75 54
TRUMPET (228 "Empty Bedroom")....50-75 54

EPs: 7-inch

CHESS (1437 "Down and Out Blues")....75-125 60
(Stereo. Juke box issue only. Includes title strips.)

LPs: 10/12-inch

ARHOOLIE.... 8-12
BLUES CLASSICS (9 "The Original Sonny Boy Williamson")....15-25 60s
CHESS (206 "Sonny Boy Williamson")....15-25 76
CHESS (417 "One Way Out")........10-12 74
CHESS (1437 "Down and Out Blues")....50-100 60
CHESS (1503 "Real Folk Blues")...10-20 66
CHESS (1509 "More Real Folk Blues")....10-20 66
CHESS (1536 "Bummer Road")......10-20 69
CHESS (9000 series).................... 5-10
CHESS (50027 "This Is My Story") 15-25 72
STORYVILLE 5-10 80
Session: Muddy Waters; Otis Spann; Jimmy Rogers; Fred Below; Willie Dixon.
Also see DIXON, Willie
Also see MEMPHIS SLIM
Also see PAGE, Jimmy, & Sonny Boy Williamson
Also see ROGERS, Jimmy
Also see SPANN, Otis
Also see WATERS, Muddy
Also see YARDBIRDS

WILLIAMSON, Sonny Boy
Singles: 7-inch
RAM (2501 "Pretty Li'l Thing")........25-35 61

WILLIE, Wet: see WET WILLIE

WILLIE & ALLEN
Singles: 7-inch
SANSU....15-25

WILLIE & ARLENE: see WILSON, Willie, & Tunemasters

WILLIE & HANDJIVES
Singles: 7-inch
VEEP (1227 "Runnin' Girl")..........15-25 66

WILLIE & MIGHTY MAGNIFICENTS
Singles: 7-inch
ALL PLATINUM 4-6 69-72
LPs: 10/12-inch
ALL PLATINUM 8-12 72

WILLIE & POOR BOYS LP '85
Singles: 7-inch
PASSPORT (7928 "Baby Please Don't Go")....3-5 85
PASSPORT (7929 "These Arms of Mine")....3-5 85
Picture Sleeves
PASSPORT (7928 "Baby Please Don't Go")....4-6 85
PASSPORT (7929 "These Arms of Mine")....4-6 85
LPs: 10/12-inch
PASSPORT (6047 "Willie & Poor Boys").... 5-10 85
Members: Andy Fairweather-Low; Mickey Gee; Kenny Jones; Jimmy Page; Chris Rea; Paul Rodgers; Geraint Watkins; Charlie Watts; Bill Wyman.
Also see FAIRWEATHER-LOW, Andy
Also see FREE
Also see PAGE, Jimmy
Also see REA, Chris
Also see ROLLING STONES

WILLIE & RED RUBBER BAND
Singles: 7-inch
RCA.... 4-6 68-69
LPs: 10/12-inch
RCA....10-15 68-69

WILLIE & RUTH
(Willy & Ruth)
Singles: 78 rpm
SPARK....15-35 54
Singles: 7-inch
SPARK (101 "Come a Little Bit Closer")....35-55 54
SPARK (105 "Love Me")....50-75 54
Member: Willie Egans.
Also see EGANS, Willie

WILLIE & TRAVELAIRES
Singles: 7-inch
MILKY WAY (007 "Firey Stomp")....75-100 66

WILLIE & WALKERS
Singles: 7-inch
CAPITOL.... 4-8 66
U.A.... 4-8 68

WILLIE & WEST
LPs: 10/12-inch
STANG....8-10 71

WILLIE & WHEELS
Singles: 7-inch
DUNHILL (4002 "Skateboard Crazy")....10-15 65
Members: Phil Sloan; Steve Barri.
Also see FANTASTIC BAGGYS

WILLIE & ZERKONS
Singles: 7-inch
CUCA (1163 "Out of Here") 10-20 64

WILLIE C.
(Willie Cobbs)
Singles: 7-inch
RULER....8-10 63
Also see COBBS, Willie

WILLIE G.
Singles: 7-inch
RIC TIC (125 "Meet Me Halfway")..10-15 66

WILLIE JOE: see JOE, Willie

WILLIES
Singles: 7-inch
BLUE RIVER.... 4-6 65
CO & CE 3-5 66

WILLING, Foy, & His Riders of the Purple Sage C&W '44
Singles: 78 rpm
CAPITOL.... 4-8 44-49
DECCA.... 4-8 45-46
MAJESTIC.... 4-8 46
LPs: 10/12-inch
ALLEGRO 5-8
BIG BOSS....8-10 77
CROWN....8-10 60s
CUSTOM....8-10 60s
JUBILEE....15-25 62
ROULETTE (25035 "Cowboy") 25-35 58
ROYALE (6032)....15-25
(10-inch LP.)
Session: Red River Dave.

WILLING, Foy, Eddie Dean & His Riders of the Purple Sage
LPs: 10/12-inch
ROYALE (6987 "Foy Willing & Eddie Dean")....25-50
Also see DEAN, Eddie
Also see WILLING, Foy, & His Riders of the Purple Sage

WILLING WIND
Singles: 7-inch
CUCA (6912 "Can I Get to Know You Better")....10-15 69

WILLINGS, Glenn
Singles: 7-inch
COMBO....5-10

WILLIS, Allee
Singles
W.B. (20405 "Big Adventure")......50-100 85
(Pee Wee Herman-shaped picture disc.)

WILLIS, Andra C&W '73
Singles: 7-inch
CAPITOL.... 3-5 73
Also see FORD, Tennessee Ernie, & Andra Willis

WILLIS, Betty
Singles: 7-inch
MOJO....5-10 68
RENDEZVOUS....8-12 62

WILLIS, Bill
Singles: 7-inch
DIXIE (825 "Boogie Woogie All Night")....150-250
DIXIE (845 "Boogie Woogie on a Saturday Night")....50-100

WILLIS, Bruce P&R/R&B/LP '87
Singles: 7-inch
MOTOWN 3-4 87
Picture Sleeves
MOTOWN 3-4 87
LPs: 10/12-inch
MOTOWN 5-8 87

WILLIS, Chick
(Robert Willis)
Singles: 7-inch
ATLAS (2009 "Twistin' in the Hospital")....8-12 62
LA VAL (865 "Things I Used to Do").8-10 64
LA VAL (871 "Stoop Down Baby")..... 4-6 71
LA VAL (874 "Stoop Down Shuffle").... 4-6 74
STOOP DOWN (0011 "I Hear You Knocking")....8-10 60s
STOOP DOWN (0012 "You're Gonna Miss Me")....8-10 60s
LPs: 10/12-inch
LA VAL....15-20
Also see WILLIS, Robert

WILLIS, Chuck R&B '52
(With the Royals; with Sandmen)
Singles: 78 rpm
ATLANTIC....10-30 56-57
COLUMBIA....15-25 51
OKEH....10-25 53-56
Singles: 7-inch
ATLANTIC (1000 & 2000 series)....10-25 56-59
COLUMBIA (30238 "Can't You See")....25-50 51
OKEH (6810 "I Tried") 25-40 51
OKEH (6841 "Let's Jump Tonight")....25-40 51
OKEH (6873 "Loud Mouth Lucy")...25-35 52
OKEH (6905 "My Story")..............25-35 52
OKEH (6930 "Wrong Way to Catch a Fish")....25-35 52
OKEH (6952 "Going to the River") 25-35 53
OKEH (6985 "Don't Deceive Me")..25-35 53
OKEH (7004 "My Baby's Coming Home")....25-35 53
OKEH (7015 "What's Your Name")....25-35 53
OKEH (7029 "I Feel So Bad") 25-40 54
OKEH (7041 "Change My Mind")...25-35 54
OKEH (7048 "Give and Take") 25-35 54
OKEH (7051 "Lawdy Miss Mary")...25-35 55
OKEH (7055 "I Can Tell") 20-30 55
OKEH (7062 "Search My Heart") ...20-30 55
OKEH (7067 "Come on Home").....20-30 56
REGINALD....10-15
EPs: 7-inch
ATLANTIC (591 "Chuck Willis")....50-75 57
ATLANTIC (609 "Rock with Chuck Willis")....50-75 58
ATLANTIC (612 "What Am I Living For")....50-75 58
EPIC (7070 "Sings the Blues")......50-75 56
LPs: 10/12-inch
ATCO....10-12 71
ATLANTIC (8018 "King of the Stroll")....50-100 58
(Black label.)
ATLANTIC (8018 "King of the Stroll")....25-50 59
(Red label.)
ATLANTIC (8079 "I Remember Chuck Willis")....50-100 63
COLUMBIA....5-8 80
EPIC (3425 "Chuck Willis Wails the Blues")....100-200 58
EPIC (3728 "A Tribute to Chuck Willis")....100-200 58
ICHIBAN (1106 "Back to the Blues")....5-10
Also see BARGE, Gene
Also see COOKIES
Also see ROYALS
Also see SANDMEN

WILLIS, Dan: see SPELLING on the STONE

WILLIS, Don
Singles: 7-inch
STYLE (1921 "Mar's Dame")........50-100
SATELLITE (101 "Boppin' High School Baby")....300-400 59

WILLIS, Freddie
Singles: 7-inch
DORE....5-10 60

WILLIS, Gene
(With the Aggregation)
Singles: 7-inch
CORONADO (139 "Shing-a-Ling's the Thing")....5-10
HOLLYWOOD....4-8 68

WILLIS, Hal C&W '64
Singles: 78 rpm
ATLANTIC....150-200 57
Singles: 7-inch
ATHENS (704 "Crazy Little Mama")....75-125 58
ATLANTIC (1114 "Bop-A-Dee Bop-A-Doo")....150-200 57
DECCA....6-12 59
MERCURY....5-10 62
SIMS (Except 288)....4-8 64-66
SIMS (288 "Doggin' in the U.S. Mail")....8-10 66
LPs: 10/12-inch
ARC....10-15
BONANZA....10-15

WILLIS, Herman
Singles: 7-inch
B&C (100 "Forever in Love") 150-250 50s
(Reissued in 1961 as by the Five Blacks.)

WILLIS, Little Son
(Mac Willis)
Singles: 78 rpm
SWING TIME....25-50 52-53
Singles: 7-inch
SWING TIME (304 "Bad Luck and Trouble")....50-100 52
SWING TIME (305 "Harlem Blues")....50-100 52
SWING TIME (306 "Nothing But the Blues")....50-100 52
SWING TIME (341 "Roll Me Over Slow")....50-100 53
Also see WILLIS, Mac

WILLIS, M-D-L-T R&B '74
Singles: 7-inch
IVORY TOWER....3-4 74
Members: Maxine Willis; Diane Willis; Lavern Willis; Tina Willis.
Also see WILLIS SISTERS

WILLIS, Mac
Singles: 78 rpm
ELKO (254 "Pretty Woman") 50-100 50
Also see WILLIS, Little Son

WILLIS, Marlene
Singles: 7-inch
ERA....5-10 60

WILLIS, Milton, Combo
Singles: 78 rpm
LUCKY 7....10-20 49

WILLIS, Pete, & Four Royals
Singles: 7-inch
R.F.H. (001 "What's Your Point of View")....200-300

WILLIS, Ralph
(With His Alabama Trio; Ralph "Bama" Willis; Ralph Willis Country Boys)
Singles: 78 rpm
ABBEY....10-20 49
JUBILEE....10-15 50-52
KING (4611 "Do Right")..............25-50 53
KING (4631 "Gonna Hop on Down the Line")....25-50 53
PAR....15-25 52
PRESTIGE....10-20 51-52
REGIS....15-25 44
SIGNATURE....10-20 47-49
20TH CENTURY....10-20 46
Singles: 7-inch
KING (4611 "Do Right")..............100-150 53
KING (4631 "Gonna Hop on Down the Line")....100-150 53
LPs: 10/12-inch
BLUES CLASSICS....15-25 64
Also see ALABAMA SLIM
Also see McGHEE, Brownie, & Sonny Terry
Also see SLEEPY JOE'S WASHBOARD BAND
Also see WASHBOARD PETE

WILLIS, Ray
Singles: 7-inch
JANE (103 "Patricia Darling") 15-25 58

WILLIS, Robert
(Robert "Chick" Willis)
Singles: 7-inch
BAY-TONE (104 "Pleading")..........30-50 60
Session: Fabulous Flames.
Also see FABULOUS FLAMES
Also see WILLIS, Chick

WILLIS, Rod
Singles: 7-inch
CHIC (1010 "Somebody's Been Rockin' My Baby")....25-50 59
NRC (020 "The Cat")..................100-200 59

WILLIS, Rollie, & Contenders
(With the Matadors)
Singles: 7-inch
SAXONY (1001 "Whenever I Get Lonely")....500-750 62
SAXONY (2001 "Whenever I Get Lonely")....4-6 93
Also see CHARMS
Also see MARTIN, Fred, & Matadors

WILLIS, Ron
Singles: 7-inch
ACE (588 "Someday") 10-20 60

WILLIS, Slim
Singles: 7-inch
C.J....10-15 61-62

WILLIS, Timmy R&B '68
Singles: 7-inch
JUBILEE....5-10 69
SIDRA (9013 "I'm Wondering")........8-12 67
VEEP (1279 "I'm Wondering")..........8-12 67

WILLIS, Vic, Trio
LPs: 10/12-inch
FIRST GENERATION....5-10 81
Also see WILLIS BROTHERS

WILLIS, Willy
Singles: 7-inch
DOT (16018 "Catawampus")..........10-20 59
RITA (1002 "Catawampus")............15-25 59
(First issue.)

WILLIS BROTHERS C&W '64
Singles: 7-inch
STARDAY....4-6 62-70
LPs: 10/12-inch
CORONET (150 "Gunfighter Ballads of the Badmen")....10-20
(The Willis Brothers are not credited on this LP, though they do one side.)
MASTERPIECES....5-10
NASHVILLE....10-15 60s
PICKWICK/HILLTOP....10-15 65
STARDAY (163 "In Action")..........20-30 62
STARDAY (229 "Code of the West")....25-35 63
STARDAY (306 thru 466)..........10-25 65-70
Members: Vic Willis; Guy Willis; Charles Willis.
Also see WILLIS, Vic, Trio

WILLIS "THE GUARD" & VIGORISH
Singles: 7-inch
HANDSHAKE....3-4 80
Members: Jerry Buckner; Gary Garcia.
Also see BUCKNER & GARCIA

WILLIS SISTERS
Singles: 7-inch
ABC-PAR....4-8 63-64
RCA....4-8 62
REJO....4-8 63
REKNOWN....5-10 60
Also see LITTLE CINDY & WILLIS SISTERS
Also see WILLIS, M-D-L-T

WILL-O-BEES P&R '68
Singles: 7-inch
DATE....3-5 67
SGC....3-5 68-69

WILLOUGHBY, Chuck
Singles: 7-inch
REPUBLIC (2029 "Stop the World")....30-40 60

WILLOUGHBY, Larry C&W '83
Singles: 7-inch
ATLANTIC AMERICA....3-4 83-84

WILLOUGHBY - WILSON BAND
Singles: 7-inch
FRONT LINE....3-5 74
EPs: 7-inch
FRONT LINE....5-10 74

WILLOW
LPs: 10/12-inch
20TH FOX....8-12 73-73

WILLOW GREEN
Singles: 7-inch
WHIZ (619 "Fields of Peppermint")....10-20 67

WILLOWBY SINGERS
Singles: 7-inch
EPIC....4-8 64

WILLOWS P&R/R&B '56
Singles: 78 rpm
CLUB (1014 "This Is the End").......15-25 56
MELBA (102 "Church Bells Are Ringing")....50-75 56
MELBA (102 "Church Bells May Ring")....25-35 56
MELBA (106 "Do You Love Me) 15-25 56
MELBA (115 "Little Darlin' ")..........50-75 57
Singles: 7-inch
ABC....3-5 73
CLUB (1014 "This Is the End").....75-100 56
(Orange label.)
CLUB (1014 "This Is the End").......35-45 56
(Blue label.)
COLLECTABLES....3-4
MELBA (102 "Church Bells Are Ringing")....150-250 56
MELBA (102 "Church Bells May Ring")....50-100 56
(Note slight title change.)
MELBA (106 "Do You Love Me) ..50-100 56
(Black label.)
MELBA (106 "Do You Love Me) 25-50 56
(Red label.)
MELBA (115 "Little Darlin' ")........50-100 57
(Red label.)
Members: Tony Middleton; Richard Davis; Ralph Martin; Joe Martin; John Steele; Richard Simon; Dotty Martin.
LPs: 10/12-inch
ELDORADO (1000 "The Willows")...8-12
Also see FIVE WILLOWS
Also see MIDDLETON, Tony
Also see SEDAKA, Neil

WILLOWS
Singles: 7-inch
4 STAR (1753 "Now That I Have You")....100-200 61

WILLOWS
Singles: 7-inch
HEIDI (103 "Tears in Your Eyes")..10-15 64
HEIDI (107 "Such a Night")............10-15 64

WILLOWS
Singles: 7-inch
MGM....5-10 66-67

WILLS, Billy Jack, & His Western Swing Band
Singles: 78 rpm
MGM....15-25 55-56
Singles: 7-inch
MGM (11966 "There's Good Rocking Tonight")....50-75 55
MGM (12034 "Hey Lula")..............50-75 55
MGM (12172 "All She Wants to Do Is Rock")....50-75 56

WILLS, Bob P&R '39/C&W '44
(With His Texas Playboys; with Rusty McDonald; with Tommy Duncan)
Singles: 78 rpm
ANTONES....15-25
CAPITOL....3-5 76
COLUMBIA....5-10 43-48
DECCA....4-8 55-56
MGM....5-10 47-55
OKEH....5-10 40-45
VOCALION....10-20 33-39
Singles: 7-inch
DECCA....5-10 55-56
LIBERTY....4-8 60-64
LONGHORN....4-6 64
MGM....5-15 50-55
EPs: 7-inch
COLUMBIA....10-20 57
DECCA....10-20 55
MGM....10-20 56
RHINO (284 "Greatest Hits of Texas")....15-20 84
(Texas-shaped picture disc.)
LPs: 10/12-inch
ANTONES (6000 "The Texas Playboys")....100-200
(10-inch LP. Fan club issue.)

ANTONES (6010 "The Texas Playboys")....100-200
(10-inch LP. Fan club issue.)
AUDIO/VIDEO....5-8 82
CAPITOL....10-20 76
COLUMBIA (Except 9003)....6-12 73-82
COLUMBIA (9003 "Round-Up")....50-75 50
(10-inch LP.)
CORAL (20109 "Swing Along")....5-10 73
CORONET....8-12 60s
DECCA (5562 "Dance-O-Rama")...50-75 55
(10-inch LP.)
DECCA (DL-8727 "Bob Wills & His Texas Playboys")....35-55 57
(Monaural.)
DECCA (DL7-8727 "Bob Wills & His Texas Playboys")....15-25 66
(Reprocessed stereo.)
DELTA....5-10 81-83
ENCORE....?? 79
HARMONY (Except 7036)....10-20 63-69
HARMONY (7036 "Bob Wills Special")....15-25 57
KAPP....8-12 66-71
KALEIDOSCOPE....5-10 82-83
LARIAT (1 "The Tiffany Transcriptions")....50-75 77
LIBERTY....20-30 60-63
LONGHORN (001 "Bob Wills Keepsake Album, #1")....50-75 65
LONGHORN (007 "Bob Wills Collector's Series")....10-15
LONGHORN (011 "31st St. Blues")....10-15
MCA....6-12 73-80s
MGM (91 "Ranch House Favorites")....75-100 51
(10-inch LP.)
MGM (141 "Tribute to Bob Wills")...8-12 71
MGM (3352 "Ranch House Favorites")....50-75 56
MGM (4866 "History of Bob Wills")....10-15 73
MGM (5303 "24 Great Hits")....8-12 77
METRO....10-15 67
PICKWICK....5-10 70s
RHINO (284 "Greatest Hits of Texas")....8-12 85
(Texas-shaped, picture disc. Promotional issue only.)
STARDAY (375 "San Antonio Rose")....15-25 65
STARDAY (469 "Bob Wills Story")...8-12 70
SUNSET....8-12 66-69
TEXAS ROSE....5-10
TIME-LIFE....5-10 81
TIME-LIFE ("Bob Wills")....10-15 82
(Boxed 3-LP set.)
TISHOMINGO (1 "The Tiffany Transcriptions, 1945-1948")....30-50 78
U.A.....8-15 71-74
VOCALION (3735 "Swing Along")..10-20 65
VOCALION (3922 "San Antonio Rose")....10-20 71
WESTERN HERITAGE....5-10 76
Also see DUNCAN, Tommy
Also see FORT WORTH DOUGHBOYS
Also see McAULIFFE, Leon
Also see TEXAS PLAYBOYS
Also see WILLS, Johnnie Lee, & His Boys

WILLS, Bob, & Mel Tillis
LPs: 10/12-inch
KAPP (3523 "King of Western Swing")....15-25 67
KAPP (3639 "In Person")....15-25 68
Also see TILLIS, Mel
Also see WILLS, Bob

WILLS, David C&W '74
Singles: 7-inch
EPIC....3-5 74-88
RCA....3-4 83-84
U.A.....3-5 77-80
LPs: 10/12-inch
EPIC....5-10 75-88
RCA....5-10 84
Also see RICH, Charlie

WILLS, Johnnie Lee, & His Boys C&W '50
Singles: 78 rpm
BULLET....4-8 49-50
LPs: 10/12-inch
CROWN....10-15 60s
DELTA....5-10 80s
FLYING FISH....5-10 80s
ROUNDER....5-10 80s
SIMS (101 "Where There's a Wills There's a Way")....15-25 62
SIMS (108 "Johnnie Lee Willis at the Tulsa Stampede")....15-25 62
SIMS (129 "Blub Twist")....10-20 62
Also see WILLS, Bob

WILLS, Mary
Singles: 7-inch
CRESTMORE....4-6 60s

WILLS, Maury
Singles: 7-inch
DOT....5-10 63
GLAD HAMP....8-12 62

WILLS, Oscar (With Fats Domino's Band) / Paul Gayten
Singles: 78 rpm
ARGO (5277 "Flat Foot Sam")....10-20 57
Singles: 7-inch
ARGO (5277 "Flat Foot Sam")....15-25 57
Also see DOMINO, Fats
Also see GAYTEN, Paul
Also see T.V. SLIM

WILLS, Tommy C&W '79
(With His Twisting Tomcats; with Marti Maes)
Singles: 7-inch
AIR TOWN....4-8 66
CLUB MIAMI (501 "Let 'Em Roll")....200-250
GOLDEN MOON....3-5 79
GREGORY....5-10 63
NORMAN....5-10 60
TERRY (110 "Aw Shucks")....5-10 62
EPs: 7-inch
TERRY-GREGORY (1000 "Man with a Horn")....8-12 62
(Juke box issue.)
LPs: 10/12-inch
COUNTRY INT'L....5-10 75
GOLDEN MOON....5-10 78
Also see TOMCATS

WILLS, Viola
Singles: 7-inch
BRONCO....5-10 67

WILLSIE, T.R.
LPs: 10/12-inch
LIVERPOOL....10-15 67

WILLY & RUTH: see WILLIE & RUTH

WILMA LEE
(Wilma Lee Cooper)
Singles: 78 rpm
COLUMBIA....5-10 50-53
Singles: 7-inch
COLUMBIA....8-15 50-53
Also see COOPER, Wilma Lee & Stoney

WILMER & THE DUKES P&R '68
Singles: 7-inch
APHRODISIAC....3-6 69
LPs: 10/12-inch
APHRODISIAC....10-15 69
Member: Wilmer Alexander Jr.
Also see ALEXANDER, Wilmer, Jr.

WILMINGTONS
Singles: 7-inch
MGM....4-8 67

WILSON, Adah
Singles: 7-inch
ARRAWAK....4-8 62

WILSON, Al P&R/R&B '68
Singles: 7-inch
BELL....4-6 70
BELL GOLD....3-4 70s
CAROUSEL....3-5 71
PLAYBOY....3-5 76
ROADSHOW....3-4 79
ROCKY ROAD....3-6 72-75
SOUL CITY....4-8 67-69
WAND (1135 "Help Me")....15-25 66
LPs: 10/12-inch
PLAYBOY....8-10 76
ROADSHOW....5-8 79
ROCKY ROAD....8-12 73-74
SOUL CITY....10-15 69
Also see ROLLERS

WILSON, Andy
Singles: 7-inch
ATHENS (700 "Little Mama")....30-40 57
BACK BEAT....4-8 65
BULLSEYE....10-20 58-59
DESTINY....5-10 61

WILSON, Ann P&R '86
(With the Daybreaks)
Singles: 7-inch
CAPITOL....3-4 86
TOPAZ (1311 "Standin' Watchin' You")....50-100 67
(Reportedly 500 made.)
TOPAZ (1312 "Through Eyes and Glass")....50-100 67
(Reportedly 500 made.)
Picture Sleeves
CAPITOL....3-4 86
Also see HEART
Also see RENO, Mike, & Ann Wilson

WILSON, Ann, & Robin Zander P&R '88
Singles: 7-inch
CAPITOL....3-4 88
Also see WILSON, Ann

WILSON, Art R&B '83
Singles: 7-inch
TABU....3-4 83

WILSON, Artie
Singles: 7-inch
KENT....5-10 58
TALENT....5-10

WILSON, Barbara
Singles: 7-inch
AURA....4-8 64

WILSON, Barry, & Camelots
Singles: 7-inch
DOT....5-10 63

WILSON, Benny C&W '85
Singles: 7-inch
COLUMBIA....3-4 85-86
Also see FRICKE, Janie

WILSON, Betty, & Four Bars
Singles: 7-inch
DAYCO (1631 "I'm Yours")....25-50 62
Also see FOUR BARS

WILSON, Beverly Mae
Singles: 7-inch
IMPACT....4-8 61

WILSON, Bill
Singles: 7-inch
BROOKE....5-10 60

WILSON, Bill
LPs: 10/12-inch
BAR B-Q....8-10 76

WILSON, Bob
(With the Easy Dealers)
Singles: 7-inch
DECCA....5-10 61
ERA....5-10 60
SOUND STAGE 7....4-8 66
TREY....5-10 60
Also see WILSON, Easy Deal

WILSON, Bobby
Singles: 7-inch
20TH FOX (108 "Posse")....10-20 59

WILSON, Bobby R&B '73
Singles: 7-inch
BUDDAH....3-5 75
CHAIN....3-5 73
VOLT (144 "Let Me Down Slow")....5-10 66

WILSON, Brian P&R '66
Singles: 7-inch
CAPITOL (5610 "Caroline, No")....15-20 66
SIRE (27694 "Melt Away")....3-5 88
SIRE (27814 "Love and Mercy")....3-5 88
SIRE (28350 "Let's Go to Heaven in My Car")....3-5 87
Promotional Singles
SIRE (27694 "Melt Away")....4-8 88
SIRE (27787 "Night Time")....4-8 88
SIRE (27814 "Love and Mercy")....4-8 88
SIRE (28350 "Let's Go to Heaven in My Car")....5-10 87
Picture Sleeves
SIRE (27787 "Night Time")....8-12 88
SIRE (27814 "Love and Mercy")....4-8 88
SIRE (28350 "Let's Go to Heaven in My Car")....4-8 87
LPs: 10/12-inch
SIRE (3248 "Brian Wilson: Words and Music")....15-20 88
SIRE (225669 "Brian Wilson")....5-10 88
Also see BEACH BOYS
Also see BERRY, Jan
Also see BLOSSOMS
Also see BOB & SHERI
Also see CAMPBELL, Glen
Also see CASTELLS
Also see CURRY, Tim
Also see DeSHANNON, Jackie
Also see HALE & HUSHABYES
Also see HONDELLS
Also see LEGENDARY MASKED SURFERS
Also see LOVE, Mike
Also see RIVERS, Johnny
Also see SAHANAJA, Darian
Also see TIMERS

WILSON, Brian, & Mike Love
Singles: 7-inch
BROTHER (1002 "Gettin' Hungry")....15-25 67
Also see LOVE, Mike
Also see WILSON, Brian

WILSON, Bud
Singles: 7-inch
MOHAWK (1043 "Rattle Snake Daddy")....25-35

WILSON, Carl LP '81
Singles: 7-inch
CARIBOU....3-5 81-83
LPs: 10/12-inch
CARIBOU....5-10 81-82
Also see ANGEL
Also see BEACH BOYS
Also see CASSADY, David
Also see KING HARVEST
Also see NEWTON-JOHN, Olivia

WILSON, Colleen
Singles: 7-inch
JERDEN....4-8 66

WILSON, Coleman C&W '61
Singles: 7-inch
KING....5-8 61

WILSON, Curtis
Singles: 7-inch
CANARY (6417 "Teenage Party Line")....50-75 66
CHERRY (1014 "My Heart Is Made of the Blues")....15-25 60

WILSON, Dallas
(With His Western Troubadours)
Singles: 78 rpm
PEP....15-25 56
Singles: 7-inch
PEP (104 "You'll Never Know")....20-40 56
RODEO (127 "Hi-Steppin' Daddy")....40-60 57

WILSON, Dennis LP '77
Singles: 7-inch
CARIBOU (9023 "You and I")....4-8 77
LPs: 10/12-inch
CARIBOU (34353 "Pacific Ocean Blue")....20-30 77
Also see BEACH BOYS
Also see FOUR SPEEDS

WILSON, Dennis / Ram Jam / Joan Baez
EPs: 7-inch
COLUMBIA (1128 "Music for Every Ear")....15-25 77
(Promotional issue only.)
Also see BAEZ, Joan
Also see CUMMINGS, Burton / Cheap Trick / Crawler
Also see WILSON, Dennis
Also see RAM JAM

WILSON, Dennis William
Singles: 7-inch
ELEKTRA....3-5 79
LPs: 10/12-inch
ELEKTRA....5-10 79

WILSON, Don
Singles: 7-inch
BLUE HORIZON (6054 "Twomp")....8-12 62
Also see VENTURES

WILSON, Don Lee
Singles: 7-inch
IMPERIAL....5-10 64-65
LIBERTY....4-8 66-67

WILSON, Doyle
Singles: 7-inch
LAMP (2015 "Hey Hey")....25-35 58

WILSON, Easy Deal
Singles: 7-inch
PARK AVENUE....5-10 63
SIMS....8-12 60
VIV....5-10 61-62
Also see WILSON, Bob

WILSON, Eddie
Singles: 7-inch
BACK BEAT....5-10 68-69
TOLLIE (9033 "Toast to the Lady")....10-20 64

WILSON, Fats
(Honorable Fats Wilson)
Singles: 7-inch
ROBBEE....5-10 61

WILSON, Faye
(With the Johnny Otis Orchestra)
Singles: 7-inch
HIP (401 "Playing Me for a Fool")....150-250 57
Also see OTIS, Johnny

WILSON, Flip LP '87
Singles: 7-inch
FLIP WILSON (SK-1 "Flip Wilson")..5-10 60s
(Promotional issue only. No title or label shown.)
LITTLE DAVID....3-4 72-75
LPs: 10/12-inch
ATLANTIC....8-15 67-68
IMPERIAL....10-20 61
LITTLE DAVID....5-10 70-72
MINIT....8-15 68
SUNSET....8-10 70

WILSON, Frank
Singles: 7-inch
SOUL (35019 "Do I Love You")....7500-10000 66

WILSON, G., & Genies
Singles: 7-inch
KING....8-10
Also see GENIES

WILSON, Gary
LPs: 10/12-inch
GW....8-10

WILSON, Glorious, & Belles
Singles: 7-inch
FAIRBANKS....5-10 61

WILSON, Hank LP '73
(Leon Russell)
Singles: 7-inch
SHELTER....3-4 73-74
LPs: 10/12-inch
SHELTER....8-10 73
Also see NELSON, Willie, & Hank Wilson
Also see RUSSELL, Leon

WILSON, Henry
(With the Bluenotes)
Singles: 7-inch
COLONIAL (7778 "Are You Ready")....75-125 58
DOT (15692 "Mighty Low")....50-100 58

WILSON, Honorable Fats: see WILSON, Fats

WILSON, Hop, & His Two Buddies
(With the Chickens; Harding Wilson)
Singles: 78 rpm
GOLDBAND....25-35 58
Singles: 7-inch
GOLDBAND (1071 "Chicken Stuff")....15-25 58
GOLDBAND (1078 "Broke and Hungry")....15-25 58
Also see POPPA HOP

WILSON, J. Frank P&R/LP '64
(With the Cavaliers)
Singles: 7-inch
ABC....3-5 73
APRIL (1 "Tell Laura I Love Her")....4-6
CHARAY (13 "Last Kiss '69")....4-6 69
CHARAY (80 "The Clown")....4-6 69
COLLECTABLES....3-4 80s
ERIC....3-4 70s
JOSIE (923 "Last Kiss")....5-10 64
JOSIE (926 "Hey Little One")....5-10 64
JOSIE (929 "Six Boys")....5-10 65
JOSIE (931 "Open Your Eyes")....5-10 65
JOSIE (938 "Forget Me Not")....5-10 65
JUBILEE (923 "Last Kiss")....5-10 64
(Blue label. Canadian – made by Quality.)
JUBILEE (923 "Last Kiss")....4-6 64
(Black label. Canadian – made by Phonodisc.)
LE CAM (500 series)....3-5 81
LE CAM (722 "Last Kiss")....15-25 64
LE CAM (1015 "Kiss and Run")....5-10 65
LE CAM (12000 series)....3-4
QUALITY (049 "Last Kiss")....4-6 67
(Canadian.)
SOLLY (927 "Me & My Teardrops")...5-8 66
TAMARA (761 "Last Kiss")....10-20 64
VIRGO....3-4 72
LPs: 10/12-inch
DILL PICKEL....8-10 71
JOSIE (4006 "Last Kiss")....50-75 64
Also see CAVALIERS

WILSON, Jackie P&R '57
(With Dick Jacobs & His Orchestra)
Singles: 78 rpm
BRUNSWICK....35-65 57-58
Singles: 7-inch
BRUNSWICK (7-38000 series)....40-50 60
(Stereo compact 33 singles. Titles and numbers still needed.)
BRUNSWICK (55024 "Reet Petite")....20-30 57
BRUNSWICK (55052 "To Be Loved")....20-30 58
BRUNSWICK (55070 "I'm Wandering")....30-40 58
BRUNSWICK (55086 "We Have Love")....20-30 58
BRUNSWICK (55105 "Lonely Teardrops")....15-25 58
BRUNSWICK (55121 "That's Why")....15-25 59
BRUNSWICK (55136 "I'll Be Satisfied")....15-25 59
BRUNSWICK (55149 "You Better Know It")....15-25 59
BRUNSWICK (55165 "Talk That Talk")....15-25 59
BRUNSWICK (55166 "Night")....10-20 60
BRUNSWICK (55167 "All My Love")....10-20 60
BRUNSWICK (55170 "Alone At Last")....10-20 60
BRUNSWICK (55201 "My Empty Arms")....10-20 61
BRUNSWICK (55208 "Please Tell Me Why")....10-20 61
BRUNSWICK (55216 "I'm Comin' On Back to You")....10-20 61
BRUNSWICK (55219 "Years from Now")....10-20 61
BRUNSWICK (55220 "The Way I Am")....10-20 61
BRUNSWICK (55221 "The Greatest Hurt")....10-20 62
BRUNSWICK (55225 "Hearts")....10-20 62
BRUNSWICK (55229 "I Just Can't Help It")....10-20 62
BRUNSWICK (55233 "Forever and a Day")....10-20 62
BRUNSWICK (55236 "What Good Am I Without You")....15-25 62
BRUNSWICK (55239 "Baby Workout")....10-15 63
BRUNSWICK (55246 "Shake! Shake! Shake!")....10-15 63
BRUNSWICK (55250 "Baby Get It")....10-15 63
BRUNSWICK (55254 "Silent Night")....15-20 63
BRUNSWICK (55260 "I'm Travelin' On")....15-20 63
BRUNSWICK (55263 "Call Her Up")....15-20 63
BRUNSWICK (55266 "Big Boss Line")....8-12 64
BRUNSWICK (55269 "Squeeze Her, Tease Her")....8-12 64
BRUNSWICK (55273 "She's All Right")....10-15 65
BRUNSWICK (55277 "Danny Boy")....8-12 65
BRUNSWICK (55280 "No Pity")....8-12 65
BRUNSWICK (55283 "I Believe I'll Love On")....8-12 65
BRUNSWICK (55289 "I've Got to Get Back")....8-12 66
BRUNSWICK (55290 "Brand New Things")....8-12 66
BRUNSWICK (55294 "Be My Love")....8-12 66
BRUNSWICK (55300 "Whispers")..5-10 66
BRUNSWICK (55309 "Just Be Sincere")....5-10 67
BRUNSWICK (55321 "I've Lost You")....5-10 67
BRUNSWICK (55336 "Higher and Higher")....5-10 67
BRUNSWICK (55354 "Since You Showed Me How to Be Happy")....5-10 67
BRUNSWICK (55381 "I Get the Sweetest Feeling")....5-10 68
BRUNSWICK (55392 "For Once in My Life")....5-10 68
BRUNSWICK (55402 "I Still Love You")....5-10 69
BRUNSWICK (55418 "Helpless")....5-10 69
BRUNSWICK (55423 "With These Hands")....5-10 70
BRUNSWICK (55435 "Let This Be a Letter")....5-10 70
BRUNSWICK (55443 "This Love Is Real")....5-10 70

BRUNSWICK (55449 "This Guy's in Love with You") 5-10 71
BRUNSWICK (55454 "Say You Will") 5-10 71
BRUNSWICK (55461 "Love Is Funny That Way") 5-10 71
BRUNSWICK (55467 "You Got Me Walking") 5-10 72
BRUNSWICK (55475 "The Girl Turned Me On") 5-10 72
BRUNSWICK (55480 "You Left the Fire Burning") 5-10 72
BRUNSWICK (55490 "Beautiful Day") 5-10 73
BRUNSWICK (55495 "Because of You") 5-10 73
BRUNSWICK (55499 "Sing a Little Song") 5-10 73
BRUNSWICK (55504 "Shake a Leg") 5-10 73
BRUNSWICK (55536 "Nobody But You") 4-8 76
COLUMBIA 3-4 87
ERIC 3-4 83
GUSTO 3-4

Picture Sleeves

BRUNSWICK (55121 "That's Why") 15-25 59
BRUNSWICK (55165 "Talk That Talk") 15-25 59
BRUNSWICK (55166 "Night") 10-20 60
BRUNSWICK (55170 "Alone At Last") 10-20 60
BRUNSWICK (55201 "My Empty Arms") 10-20 61
BRUNSWICK (55220 "The Way I Am") 10-20 61
BRUNSWICK (55221 "The Greatest Hurt") 10-20 62
BRUNSWICK (55236 "What Good Am I Without You") 15-25 62
BRUNSWICK (55435 "Let This Be a Letter") 5-10 70
COLUMBIA 3-5 87

EPs: 7-inch

BRUNSWICK (71040 "Jackie Wilson – To Be Loved") 25-50 60
BRUNSWICK (71042 "Jumpin' Jack") 25-50 60
BRUNSWICK (71045 "That's Why") 25-50 60
BRUNSWICK (71046 "Jackie Wilson – Talk That Talk") 25-50 60
BRUNSWICK (71047 "Mr. Excitement") 25-50 60
BRUNSWICK (71048 "Jackie Wilson – So Much") 25-50 60
BRUNSWICK (71049 "Jackie Wilson -- Night") 25-50 60
BRUNSWICK (71101 "Jackie Wilson – The Greatest Hurt") 20-40 62
BRUNSWICK (71102 "Jackie Wilson – I Just Can't Help It") 20-40 62
BRUNSWICK (71103 "Baby Workout") 20-40 63
BRUNSWICK (771045 "That's Why") 40-60 60
(Stereo.)

LPs: 10/12-inch

BRUNSWICK (111 "Solid Gold") 10-15
(Brunswick Special Products, mail-order offer.)
BRUNSWICK (54045 "Lonely Teardrops") 75-125 59
BRUNSWICK (54042 "He's So Fine") 50-100 59
BRUNSWICK (54050 "So Much") 40-80 60
BRUNSWICK (54055 "Jackie Sings the Blues") 30-50 60
BRUNSWICK (54058 "My Golden Favorites") 30-40 60
BRUNSWICK (54059 "A Woman, a Lover, a Friend") 30-40 60
BRUNSWICK (54100 "You Ain't Heard Nothin' Yet") 25-30 61
BRUNSWICK (54101 "By Request") 25-30 61
BRUNSWICK (54105 "Body and Soul") 25-30 62
BRUNSWICK (54106 "The World's Greatest Melodies") 25-30 62
BRUNSWICK (54108 "At the Copa") 25-30 62
BRUNSWICK (54110 thru 54130, except 54118) 20-25 63-67
BRUNSWICK (54118 "Soul Time") 30-50 66
(Beginning with 54050, Brunswick indicated stereo LPs with a "7" preceeding the selection number. Numbers after 54130 were available as stereo issues only, and are shown here as the 75000 series.)
BRUNSWICK (754138 thru 754167) 15-25 68-71
BRUNSWICK (754185 thru 754212) 10-20 72-77
COLUMBIA 5-8 87
DISCOVERY 8-10 78
EPIC 10-12 83
TELE-HOUSE 10-15

Also see FREED, Alan
Also see WARD, Billy, & Dominoes
Also see WILSON, Sonny

WILSON, Jackie, & Lavern Baker *P&R/R&B '66*

Singles: 7-inch

BRUNSWICK (55287 "Think Twice") 5-10 66
Also see BAKER, Lavern

WILSON, Jackie, & Count Basie *P&R/R&B/LP '68*

Singles: 7-inch

BRUNSWICK (1013 "For Your Precious Love") 3-5
BRUNSWICK (55365 "For Your Precious Love") 5-10 68
BRUNSWICK (55373 "Chain Gang") 5-10 68

LPs: 10/12-inch

BRUNSWICK 15-25 68
Also see BASIE, Count

WILSON, Jackie, & Chi-Lites *R&B '75*

Singles: 7-inch

BRUNSWICK (55522 "Don't Burn No Bridges") 4-6 75
Also see CHI-LITES

WILSON, Jackie, & Linda Hopkins *P&R '62*

Singles: 7-inch

BRUNSWICK (55224 "I Found Love") 8-12 62
BRUNSWICK (55243 "Shake a Hand") 8-12 63
BRUNSWICK (55278 "Yes Indeed") 5-10 65

EPs: 7-inch

BRUNSWICK (71104 "Shake a Hand") 20-30 63

LPs: 10/12-inch

BRUNSWICK 25-35 68
Also see HOPKINS, Linda
Also see WILSON, Jackie

WILSON, Jerry

Singles: 7-inch

PRANN 5-8 63

WILSON, Jim *C&W '55*
(With June Wilson)

Singles: 78 rpm

MERCURY 5-8 56

Singles: 7-inch

MERCURY 6-12 56
REED 5-10 59

WILSON, Jimmy *R&B '53*
(With His All Stars; with Blues Blasters)

Singles: 78 rpm

ALADDIN 25-50 51-54
BIG TOWN 20-40 53-54
CAVATONE 15-25 51
CHART 15-25 56
IRMA 15-25 55
RHYTHM 15-25 50-54
7-11 50-75 53

Singles: 7-inch

ALADDIN (3140 "Mistake in Life") 50-100 51
ALADDIN (3169 "Every Dog Has His Day") 50-100 53
ALADDIN (3241 "It's Time to Change") 50-100 54
BIG TOWN (101 "Tin Pan Alley") 50-75 53
BIG TOWN (103 "Call Me a Hound Dog") 50-75 53
BIG TOWN (107 "Blues at Sundown") 50-75 53
BIG TOWN (113 "Teardrops on My Pillow") 50-75 54
BIG TOWN (115 "Trouble in My House") 50-75 54
BIG TOWN (123 "I've Found Out") 50-75 54
CHART (610 "Louise") 50-75 56
CHART (629 "Send Me the Key") 25-50 56
DUKE (331 "Easy Easy Baby") 10-20 61
DUKE (339 "I Don't Care") 10-20 61
GOLDBAND (1091 "Don't You Know") 15-25 59
IRMA (107 "Blues in the Alley") 25-50 55
7-11 (2104 "Ethel Lee") 100-150 53
7-11 (2105 "Baby Don't Want Nobody But Me") 100-150 53

WILSON, Jimmy / Thrillers / Little Caesar

LPs: 10/12-inch

BIG TOWN (1001 "Big Town Sampler") 150-250 53
(Promotional issue only.)
Also see LITTLE CAESAR
Also see THRILLERS
Also see WILSON, Jimmy

WILSON, Joe
(With Sabers)

Singles: 7-inch

DYNAMO 8-12
WILDCAT (53 "Fast-Slow") 10-20 60

WILSON, Joey

Singles: 7-inch

ATCO 3-4 81

WILSON, Johnny

Singles: 7-inch

ARNOLD 5-10 63
ENJOY 5-10 63

WILSON, Joni
(Joni Wilson's Debonaries)

Singles: 7-inch

FENWAY (1712 "Holly Lynn") 8-12 60s

WILSON, Kathy, & Kwils *D&D '83*

Singles: 12-inch

COLUMBIA 4-6 83

WILSON, L.B.

Singles: 7-inch

VIVID 4-8 63

WILSON, Larry, & Continentals

Singles: 7-inch

SHANE (36 "All of Your Love") 15-25 60

WILSON, Larry Jon *C&W '76*

Singles: 7-inch

MONUMENT 3-5 76

LPs: 10/12-inch

MONUMENT 5-10 76-78
Also see COE, David Allan

WILSON, Lloyd

Singles: 7-inch

ROULETTE 4-8 63

WILSON, Marie

LPs: 10/12-inch

DESIGN (76 "Gentlemen Prefer Marie Wilson") 25-50 57

WILSON, Marty
(With the Lover Boys; with Strat-O-Lites)

Singles: 7-inch

DECCA (30544 "I'm All Woke Up") 15-25 58
DECCA (30644 "Po-Go") 15-25 58
MASTER SOUND (1008 "Carol Ann") 200-300 59
TEL (1008 "Hot Foot") 10-20 59
TROPICAL ISLE (1008 "Carol Ann") 250-350 59
W.B. (5120 "Jungle Fantasy") 10-15 59

LPs: 10/12-inch

20TH FOX (3101 "Young America Dances to Golden Goodies") 15-20 63
(Monaural.)
20TH FOX (4101 "Young America Dances to Golden Goodies") 20-30 63
(Stereo.)

WILSON, Mary *R&B '79*

Singles: 7-inch

MOTOWN 3-4 79

LPs: 10/12-inch

MOTOWN 5-8 79
Also see SUPREMES

WILSON, Meri *P&R/R&B/C&W '77*

Singles: 7-inch

BNA (8248 "Peter, the Meter Reader") 5-10 81
GRT 3-4 77

LPs: 10/12-inch

GRT 5-10 77

WILSON, Murray
(Murry Wilson)

Singles: 7-inch

CAPITOL 5-10 67

LPs: 10/12-inch

CAPITOL 25-50 67

WILSON, Nancy *LP '62*

Singles: 12-inch

CAPITOL 4-6 79

Singles: 7-inch

CAPITOL (Except 4000 & 5000 series) 3-5 68-79
CAPITOL (4000 & 5000 series) 3-6 59-67
(Includes both purple and orange/yellow labels.)

Picture Sleeves

CAPITOL 3-5 65

LPs: 10/12-inch

ASI 5-8 81
CAPITOL (100 thru 800 series) 5-12 69-71
CAPITOL (1300 thru 1700 series) 15-30 59-62
CAPITOL (1800 thru 2900 series) 8-18 63-68
(With "T," "ST" or "SKAO" prefix.)
CAPITOL (1800 thru 2900 series) 5-8 78
(With "SM" prefix.)
CAPITOL (11000 & 12000 series) 5-10 74-80
CAPITOL (16000 series) 5-8 80
COLUMBIA 5-8 84
PICKWICK 5-8
Also see CAPITOL'S MYSTERY ARTIST
Also see LEWIS, Ramsey, & Nancy Wilson

WILSON, Nancy, & Julian "Cannonball" Adderley *R&B/LP '62*

Singles: 7-inch

CAPITOL 3-5 62

LPs: 10/12-inch

CAPITOL (1657 "Nancy Wilson & Cannonball Adderley") 15-25 62
(With "T" or "ST" prefix.)
CAPITOL (1657 "Nancy Wilson & Cannonball Adderley") 5-8 75
(With "SM" prefix.)
CAPITOL (16000 series) 4-8 81
Also see ADDERLEY, Cannonball

WILSON, Nancy, & George Shearing

Singles: 7-inch

CAPITOL 3-5 61

LPs: 10/12-inch

CAPITOL (1524 "Swingin's Mutual") 15-25 61
(With "T" or "ST" prefix.)
CAPITOL (1524 "Swingin's Mutual") 5-8 75
(With "SM" prefix.)
Also see SHEARING, George
Also see WILSON, Nancy

WILSON, Nancy / Red Hot Chili Peppers

Singles: 7-inch

WTG (68678 "All for Love") 5-10 89
(Colored vinyl.)
Also see HEART
Also see KNIGHT, Holly

WILSON, Naomi

Singles: 7-inch

SWAN 4-8 65

WILSON, Norro *C&W '69*
(Norris Wilson)

Singles: 7-inch

CAPITOL 3-5 74
HICKORY 4-8 66
MGM 4-8 65-69
MERCURY 3-5 70
MONUMENT 4-8 62
RCA 3-5 72-73
SMASH 4-6 68-69

LPs: 10/12-inch

SMASH 8-12 69
Also see SMITH, Margo, & Norro Wilson
Also see SOME of CHET'S FRIENDS

WILSON, Obrey

Singles: 7-inch

BELL 8-10
COLUMBIA 8-10 66
EPIC 10-15
LIBERTY 8-10 62
MERCURY 8-10
PHILIPS 8-10

WILSON, Ormond, & Basin Street Boys

Singles: 78 rpm

MERCURY 15-25 48
Also see BASIN STREET BOYS

WILSON, Peanuts
(Johnny Wilson)

Singles: 12-inch

BRUNSWICK (55039 "Cast Iron Arm") 75-125 58
Also see ORBISON, Roy

WILSON, Phill *P&R '61*

Singles: 7-inch

HURON 3-5 61

WILSON, Precious *R&B '86*

Singles: 7-inch

JIVE 3-4 86

LPs: 10/12-inch

JIVE 5-8 86
Also see ERUPTION

WILSON, Ralph
(Ralph Wilson Quintet; Ralph Wilson Orchestra)

Singles: 78 rpm

LUCKY 10-15 48-49

Singles: 7-inch

TIARA (6110 "What's Shakin' ") 10-20 58

WILSON, Robin

Singles: 7-inch

MONUMENT 10-15 60

WILSON, Ron

Singles: 7-inch

COLUMBIA 10-15 68

WILSON, Ronnie

Singles: 7-inch

KARATE 4-8 65
REED 5-10 59

WILSON, Roosevelt

Singles: 7-inch

BULLS EYE 4-8 61

WILSON, Shanice *P&R/R&B/LP '87*

Singles: 7-inch

A&M 3-4 87-88

Picture Sleeves

A&M 3-4 87

LPs: 10/12-inch

A&M 5-8 87
Also see KIARA with Shanice Wilson

WILSON, Smiley

Singles: 7-inch

FREEDOM 5-10 60

WILSON, Smokey

Singles: 7-inch

BIG TOWN 3-5 77-78

LPs: 10/12-inch

BIG TOWN 5-10 77-78

WILSON, Sonny
(Jackie Wilson)

Singles: 78 rpm

DEE GEE (4000 "Rainy Day Blues") 50-75 52
DEE GEE (4001 "Danny Boy") 50-75 52

Singles: 7-inch

DEE GEE (4000 "Rainy Day Blues") 75-125 52
DEE GEE (4001 "Danny Boy") 75-125 52
Also see WILSON, Jackie

WILSON, Sonny

Singles: 7-inch

CANDIX 10-15 61
PLAZA 5-10 61
SUN 5-10 60
VALLEY 3-6 85

WILSON, Stan

LPs:10/12-inch

CAVALIER 20-30
CLEF 20-30
FANTASY 15-25
VERVE 15-25

WILSON, Steve

Singles: 7-inch

PAMELA (205 "Oh-De-Dum") 150-250 61
(Black vinyl.)
PAMELA (205 "Oh-De-Dum") 300-400 61
(Colored vinyl.)

WILSON, Teddy

Singles: 78 rpm

CLEF 5-10 52-54
MERCURY 5-10
MUSICRAFT 5-10 45-47

LPs: 10/12-inch

ALLEGRO (4024 "All Star Sextet") 50-75 54
ALLEGRO (4031 "All Star Sextet") 50-75 54
COLUMBIA (1300 & 1400 series) 20-30 59-60
(Monaural.)
COLUMBIA (8100 & 8200 series) 25-35 59-60
(Stereo.)
COMMODORE (20,029 "Town Hall Concert") 75-125 50
(10-inch LP.)
DIAL (213 "All Stars") 75-125 50
(10-inch LP.)
MGM (129 "Runnin' Wild") 75-125 51
(10-inch LP.)
VERVE (8200 & 8300 series) 20-35 59-60
Also see FITZGERALD, Ella / Teddy Wilson / Lena Horne
Also see HOLIDAY, Billie

WILSON, Timothy *R&B '67*

Singles: 7-inch

BLUE ROCK (6 "Cross My Heart") 10-20 69
BLUE ROCK (4090 "Cross My Heart") 10-20 69
BUDDAH 10-20 67-68
VEEP (1213 "Hey Girl, Do You Love Me") 25-50 65
VEEP (1223 "He Will Break Your Heart") 15-25 65
Also see SERENADERS

WILSON, Tom

Singles: 78 rpm

CREST (1007 "Can You Bop") 15-25 55

Singles: 7-inch

CREST (1007 "Can You Bop") 25-50 55

WILSON, Tommy
(With the Tomcats)

Singles: 7-inch

COOL 10-20 62
NORMAN 5-10 61
TERRY 5-10 61

WILSON, Tony

Singles: 7-inch

BEARSVILLE 3-5 77
Also see HOT CHOCOLATE

WILSON, U.P.

Singles: 7-inch

PEE WEE (10014 "Mean Old World") 3-5
(Disc credits "V.P. Wilson.")

Picture Sleeves

PEE WEE (10016 "Mean Old World") 4-6
(Sleeve, which credits "U.P. Wilson," is numbered differently than disc.)
Session: U.P. Wilson; Matt McCabe; Eddie Stout; Fredde Walden.

WILSON, Wally

Singles: 78 rpm

SABRE 100-200 54

Singles: 7-inch

SABRE (106 "If You Don't Love Me") 400-500 54
Also see SPRIGGS, Wally

WILSON, Wally

Singles: 7-inch

COMPLEAT (154 "How Do You Spell Quadaffi, Khadafy?") 3-6 86

WILSON, Willie, & Tunemasters
(Willie & Arlene with the Tunemasters; with Soul Prospectors)

Singles: 7-inch

DAGGER 10-20
END (1011 "I've Lied") 50-75 58

WILSON BROTHERS *P&R '79*

Singles: 7-inch

ATCO 3-5 79
BIG TREE 3-5 78
RCA 3-5

LPs: 10/12-inch

ATCO 5-10 79
Members: Steve Wilson; Kelly Wilson.

WILSON PHILLIPS *LP '90*

Singles: 7-inch

SBK 3-4 90

Picture Sleeves

SBK 3-4 90

LPs: 10/12-inch

SBK 5-10 90
Members: Wendy Wilson; Carnie Wilson; Chynna Phillips.

WIL-SONES

Singles: 7-inch

HIGHLAND (1020 "Let Me Help You") 100-150 61

WILTON PLACE STREET BAND *P&R/R&B '77*

Singles: 7-inch

ISLAND 3-5 77

WILTSHIRE, Teacho
(With the Clef Clubs; with Tin Pan Alley Trio; with His Piano & Orchestra)

Singles: 78 rpm

TIN PAN ALLEY 10-15 56

Singles: 7-inch

EPIC (9830 "Tell Him") 5-10 65

NOEL (108 "Glamour") 20-30 50s
SAVOY (1551 "It Don't Hurt Anymore") 10-20 58
TIN PAN ALLEY (141 "Love Your Loved One") 20-30 56
TIN PAN ALLEY (143 "Working Overtime") 20-30 56
Also see ADELPHIS
Also see BENNETT, Eddie
Also see COUSINS
Also see FORTUNEERS
Also see LARKTONES
Also see MR. BEAR
Also see PITT, Eugene
Also see SAMMY & DEL LARKS
Also see TEACHO & STUDENTS

WILTSHIRE, Teacho, & Melloharps
Singles: 7-inch
TIN PAN ALLEY (159 "My Bleeding Heart") 350-450 56
Also see MELLOHARPS
Also see WILTSHIRE, Teacho

WIMBERLY, Maggie Sue
Singles: 78 rpm
SUN (229 "How Long") 10-20 55
Singles: 7-inch
SUN (229 "How Long") 25-50 55
Also see RICHARDS, Sue

WINAN, BeBe & CeCe *R&B '87*
Singles: 12-inch
CAPITOL 4-6 87
Singles: 12-inch
CAPITOL 3-4 87
LPs: 10/12-inch
CAPITOL 5-8 87-89

WINANS *R&B '85*
Singles: 12-inch
QWEST 4-6 86
Singles: 7-inch
QWEST 3-4 85-86
LPs: 10/12-inch
LIGHT 4-8 75-85
QWEST 5-8 85-90
Members: Marvin Winan; Carvin Winan; Michael Winan; Ronald Winan.
Also see JACKSON, Michael
Also see McDONALD, Michael
Also see WINAN, BeBe & CeCe

WINANS & ANITA BAKER *R&B '87*
Singles: 7-inch
QWEST 3-4 87
Also see BAKER, Anita

WINBURN, Randy
EPs: 7-inch
BOMP 5-8

WINBUSH, Angela *R&B/LP '87*
Singles: 7-inch
MERCURY 3-4 87-89
LPs: 10/12-inch
MERCURY 5-8 87-89

WINCHELL, Danny
(With Nino & Ebbtides)
Singles: 7-inch
RECORTE (406 "Jeannie") 25-35 58
RECORTE (410 "Don't Say You're Sorry") 25-35 59
RECORTE (415 "Come Back My Baby") 25-35 59
Also see NINO & EBBTIDES

WINCHELL, Paul, & Jerry Mahoney
Singles: 78 rpm
DECCA (308 "Hooray Hooray") 5-10 50s
Singles: 7-inch
DECCA (308 "Hooray Hooray") 5-10 50s
Picture Sleeves
DECCA (308 "Hooray Hooray") 10-15 50s

WINCHESTER, Jesse *LP '72*
Singles: 7-inch
AMPEX 3-4 70
BEARSVILLE 3-4 76-81
LPs: 10/12-inch
BEARSVILLE/AMPEX 15-20 70
BEARSVILLE 6-12 71-81
Promotional LPs
BEARSVILLE (692 "Live at the Bijou") 20-25 75
BEARSVILLE (693 "Live at the Bijou/Live Interview") 30-40 75
Also see HARRIS, Emmylou
Also see LARSON, Nicolette
Also see MURRAY, Anne

WIND
Singles: 7-inch
BLACKNIGHT (900 "Don't Take Your Love Away") 10-20 66

WIND *P&R '69*
Singles: 7-inch
LIFE 4-6 69
LPs: 10/12-inch
LIFE 15-20 69
Member: Tony Orlando.
Also see COOL HEAT
Also see ORLANDO, Tony

WIND
Singles: 7-inch
SOUND HOUSE 8-12 60s
Picture Sleeves
SOUND HOUSE 10-20 60s

WIND
LPs: 10/12-inch
MIDNIGHT 5-10

WIND, Adam
Singles: 7-inch
VALANE 3-5

WIND CHILL FACTOR
LPs: 10/12-inch
REDMARK 5-10 78

WIND HARP
LPs: 10/12-inch
U.A. 10-15 72

WIND IN THE WILLOWS *LP '68*
Singles: 7-inch
CAPITOL (2274 "Uptown Girl") 5-10 68
LPs: 10/12-inch
CAPITOL (2956 "The Wind in the Willows") 40-75 68
Members: Deborah Harry; Paul Klein; Peter Brittain; Anton Carysforth; Steve DePhillips.
Also see HARRY, Debbie

WINDING, Kai, & His Orch. *P&R/LP '63*
(With J.J. Johnson)
Singles: 7-inch
BETHLEHEM 4-8 60
COLUMBIA 5-10 56-59
IMPULSE 3-4 61
MGM 3-5 78
VERVE (Except 10258) 4-6 62-67
VERVE (10258 "Experiment in Terror") 10-15
EPs: 7-inch
COLUMBIA 5-15 58-59
SAVOY 10-20 53
LPs: 10/12-inch
A&M 8-12 68
COLUMBIA (900 thru 1300 series) 15-30 56-59
COLUMBIA (8100 series) 15-25 59
GLENDALE 5-8 76-77
IMPULSE 15-25 61
PICKWICK 5-10 65-70
ROOST (400 series) 60-80 52
(10-inch LPs.)
SAVOY (9000 series) 50-75 53
(10-inch LPs.)
VERVE 10-25 61-67
(Reads "MGM Records - a Division of Metro-Goldwyn-Mayer, Inc." at bottom of label.)
VERVE 5-10 73-84
(Reads "Manufactured By MGM Record Corp.," or mentions either Polydor or Polygram at bottom of label.)
VIK (1040 "Afternoon at Birdland") 40-60 57
(With J.J. Johnson.)
WHO'S WHO in JAZZ 5-8 78
Also see STITT, Sonny, & Kai Winding

WINDJAMMER *R&B '83*
Singles: 7-inch
MCA 3-4 83-85
LPs: 10/12-inch
MCA 5-8 83

WINDJAMMERS
Singles: 7-inch
ARGO 4-8 65
MUSIC FACTORY 4-6 68

WINDMILL
Singles: 7-inch
DECCA 4-6 69

WINDS OF NOTRE DAME
Singles: 7-inch
FANTASY (596 "Radiation Baby") 100-150 65

WINDSOR TUNNEL
LPs: 10/12-inch
AVCO EMBASSY 8-10

WINDSORS
Singles: 7-inch
WIG-WAG (103 "Carol Ann") 100-200 59

WINDSORS
Singles: 7-inch
ABC-PAR 5-10 64

WINDSTORM *R&B '80*
Singles: 7-inch
POLYDOR 3-4 80

WINDY CITY *R&B '80*
Singles: 7-inch
CHI-SOUND 3-4 77
KELLI-ARTS 3-4 80

WINE, April: see APRIL WINE

WINE, Toni
Singles: 7-inch
ATCO (6736 "Take a Little Time Out for Love") 4-8 70
ATCO (6773 "Let's Make Love Tonight") 4-8 70
ATCO (6800 "I Want to See Morning with Him") 4-8 71
COLPIX (715 "My Boyfriend's Coming Home for Christmas") 5-10 63
COLPIX (732 "I Love That Boy") 5-10 64
COLPIX (742 "A Boy Like You") 5-10 64
COLPIX (756 "A Girl Is Not a Girl") 5-10 64
ENTRANCE 3-5 71
SENATE 4-8 67
Picture Sleeves
COLPIX (742 "A Boy Like You") 10-15 64
(Includes promotional insert card.)
Also see ARCHIES

WINE, Toni, & Billy Joe Royal
Singles: 7-inch
KAT FAMILY (2074 "You Really Got a Hold on Me") 5-8 81
KAT FAMILY (2297 "Wasted Time") 5-8 81
Also see ROYAL, Billy Joe
Also see WINE, Toni

WINFIELD, John, Jr.
Singles: 7-inch
DORE 4-8 66

WINFIELD ROAD
Singles: 7-inch
DESMOND 3-5 76

WINFORD, Sue
Singles: 7-inch
JAMIE 4-8 62
20TH FOX 4-8 63

WING & A PRAYER FIFE & DRUM CORPS *P&R/R&B '75*
Singles: 7-inch
WING and a PRAYER 3-4 75-77
LPs: 10/12-inch
WING and a PRAYER 5-8 76-77

WINGATE LOVE-IN STRINGS
Singles: 7-inch
RIC TIC 5-10 60s

WINGED VICTORY CHORUS
Singles: 7-inch
20TH FOX 4-8 60

WINGER *LP '88*
Singles: 7-inch
ATLANTIC 3-4 88-89
Picture Sleeves
ATLANTIC 3-4 89
LPs: 10/12-inch
ATLANTIC 5-8 88-90
Members: Kip Winger; Reb Beach; Rod Morgenstein; Paul Taylor.

WINGERT, Wally, & Caped Club
Singles: 7-inch
BAT NEWS ("Adam West") 5-10

WINGFIELD, Pete *P&R/R&B/LP '75*
Singles: 7-inch
ISLAND 3-4 75-77
LPs: 10/12-inch
ISLAND 5-8 75
Also see OLYMPIC RUNNERS

WINGS
Singles: 7-inch
DUNHILL 3-5 68
LPs: 10/12-inch
DUNHILL 10-12 68

WINGS over JORDAN
Singles: 78 rpm
KING 10-15 47-54
Singles: 7-inch
KING (4677 "I Cried and I Cried") 20-40 53
KING (4694 "Trying to Get Ready") 20-40 54

WINGS with Paul McCartney: see McCARTNEY, Paul

WINK & JUDY WITH THE VICEROYS FIVE
Singles: 7-inch
SEAFAIR 4-8 63
Also see VICEROYS

WINKLE, Danny
Singles: 7-inch
VILLAGE 4-8 63

WINKLE PICKERS
Singles: 7-inch
COLPIX 4-8 66

WINKLER, Judy
Singles: 7-inch
JDS 5-10 59

WINKLY & NUTLEY
Singles: 7-inch
MK (101 "Report to the Nation") 15-25 60
(No mention of distribution by Roulette.)
MK (101 "Report to the Nation") 10-15 60
(Reads: "Dist. by Roulette Records, Inc.")
Members: Jim Stag; Bob Mitchell.

WINLEY, Paul, & Rockers
Singles: 78 rpm
PREMIUM (401 "My Confession") 15-25 55
Singles: 7-inch
PORWIN (1003 "Party with Paul") 10-20 63
PREMIUM (401 "My Confession") 35-50 55

WINNERS
("With Rhythm Accomp.")
Singles: 78 rpm
DERBY 25-50 52
Singles: 7-inch
DERBY (802 "To Think We're Only Friends") 100-200 52

WINNERS
Singles: 78 rpm
RAINBOW 50-100 56
Singles: 7-inch
RAINBOW (331 "Can This Be Love") 200-300 56

WINNERS
Singles: 7-inch
VEE JAY 5-10 63
LPs: 10/12-inch
CROWN 15-25 63

WINNERS *R&B '78*
Singles: 7-inch
ARIOLA-AMERICA 3-4 78
LPs: 10/12-inch
ARIOLA-AMERICA 5-8 78
ROADSHOW 5-10 78

WINSKI, Colin
LPs: 10/12-inch
TAKOMA 8-12 80

WINSLOW, Barry
Singles: 7-inch
BIG TREE 3-6 73
LAURIE 4-8 69
Also see ROYAL GUARDSMEN

WINSLOW, Bobby, & Fabulons
Singles: 7-inch
FABULOUS (1001 "Miss Fabulous") 10-15

WINSLOW, Stephanie *C&W '79*
Singles: 7-inch
CURB/MCA 3-4 83-84
OAK 3-4 83
PRIMERO 3-4 81-82
W.B./CURB 3-5 79-81

WINSTON, George *LP '84*
Singles: 7-inch
WINDHAM HILL 3-4 84
LPs: 10/12-inch
TAKOMA (9016 "Piano Solos") 5-10 73
WINDHAM HILL 5-8 83-88
Also see STREEP, Meryl, & George Winston

WINSTON, Jack, & Hi Jacks
Singles: 7-inch
JAY WING (5806 "It's Rock & Roll") 125-175 58

WINSTON, Roger, & Plaids
Singles: 7-inch
NORTHLAND (7003 "I Want to Be Loved by You") 8-12 58
Also see LEE, Robin

WINSTON, Vic
Singles: 7-inch
BIG TOP 5-10 61

WINSTONS *P&R/R&B/LP '69*
Singles: 7-inch
CURTOM 10-15
METROMEDIA 4-6 69
LPs: 10/12-inch
METROMEDIA 8-12 69
Members: Richard Spencer; Ray Martiano; Phil Tolotta; Quincy Mattison; Sonny Peckrol; G.C. Coleman.
Also see SPENCER, Richard, & Winstons

WINSTONS Featuring Bob Bartel
Singles: 7-inch
CINEMASOUND (92057 "To the Aisle") 200-400 57

WINTER, Cyril
Singles: 7-inch
M&L 8-12 60s
Session: Myron Lee; Caddies.
Also see LEE, Myron

WINTER, Edgar *LP '70*
(Edgar Winter Group; Edgar Winter's White Trash)
Singles: 12-inch
BLUE SKY 4-6 80
BODY ROCK 4-6 83
Singles: 7-inch
BLUE SKY 3-5 75-81
EPIC 4-8 70-75
LPs: 10/12-inch
BACK-TRAC 5-10 85
BLUE SKY (PZ-33483 "Jasmine Nightdreams") 8-10 75
(Stereo.)
BLUE SKY (PZQ-33483 "Jasmine Nightdreams") 15-25 75
(Quadraphonic.)
BLUE SKY (34858 "Re-Cycled") 6-10 77
BLUE SKY (35989 "Edgar Winter Album") 6-10 79
BLUE SKY (36494 "Standing on Rock") 6-10 81
EPIC (26503 "Entrance") 10-20 70
EPIC (30512 "Edgar Winter's White Trash") 10-20 71
EPIC (31249 "Roadwork") 15-20 72
(Two discs.)
EPIC (KE-31584 "They Only Come Out at Night") 10-20 72
(Stereo.)
EPIC (KEQ-31584 "They Only Come Out at Night") 15-25 73
(Quadraphonic.)
EPIC (PE-32461 "Shock Treatment") 10-20 74
(Stereo.)
EPIC (PEQ-32461 "Shock Treatment") 15-25 74
(Quadraphonic.)
EPIC (33770 "Entrance"/"White Trash") 10-20 75
(Two discs.)
Also see HARTMAN, Dan
Also see LA CROIX, Jerry
Also see MONTROSE, Ronnie
Also see SWEATHOG / Free Movement / Bob Dylan / Edgar Winter's White Trash
Also see WINTER, Johnny & Edgar

WINTER, Edgar, & Rick Derringer
LPs: 10/12-inch
BLUE SKY (PZ-33798 "Edgar Winter Group with Rick Derringer") 8-12 75
(Stereo.)
BLUE SKY (PZQ-33798 "Edgar Winter Group with Rick Derringer") 15-25 75
(Quadraphonic.)
Also see DERRINGER, Rick
Also see WINTER, Edgar

WINTER, Jimmy: see WINTER, Johnny

WINTER, Johnny *LP '69*
(With the Crystaliers; Jimmy Winter)
Singles: 7-inch
ATLANTIC (2248 "Gangster of Love") 10-20 64
BLUE SKY (2754 "Raised on Rock") 3-6 75
COLUMBIA 4-8 69-74
FROLIC (503 "Voo Doo Twist") 75-125 62
FROLIC (509 "Gangster of Love") 75-125 62
GRT 4-8 69
IMPERIAL 4-8 69
KRCO (107 "One Night of Love") 50-100 61
MGM (13380 "Gone for Bad") 10-15 65
PACEMAKER (243 "Leavin' Home") 10-15 66
SONOBEAT (107 "Rollin' & Tumblin' ") 10-15 68
TODD (1084 "The Girl You Left Behind") 8-10 63
Picture Sleeves
SONOBEAT (107 "Rollin' & Tumblin' ") 50-75 68
(Some sleeves picture the Vulcan Gas Co., an Austin nightclub, and those are at the high end of the price range given. Sleeves that do not picture the club are priced at the lower end.)
LPs: 10/12-inch
ACCORD (7135 "Ready for Winter") 5-10 81
ALLIGATOR 5-8 84-85
BLUE SKY (PZ-33292 "John Dawson Winter III") 8-12 74
(Stereo.)
BLUE SKY (PZQ-33292 "John Dawson Winter III") 15-25 74
(Quadraphonic.)
BLUE SKY (33944 "Captured Live") 8-12 76
BLUE SKY (34575 "White, Hot & Blue") 8-12 78
BLUE SKY (34813 "Nothin' But the Blues") 8-12 77
BLUE SKY (36343 "Raisin' Cain") 6-10 80
BUDDAH (7513 "First Winter") 15-20 69
CBS ASSOCIATED 5-8
COLUMBIA (9826 "Johnny Winter") 15-20 69
COLUMBIA (9947 "Second Winter") 20-15 69
(Two discs.)
COLUMBIA (30221 "Johnny Winter And") 10-15 70
COLUMBIA (KC-32188 "Still Alive & Well") 10-15 73
(Stereo.)
COLUMBIA (CQ-32715 "Still Alive & Well") 15-25 73
(Quadraphonic.)
COLUMBIA (KC-32715 "Saints & Sinners") 10-15 74
(Stereo.)
COLUMBIA (CQ-32715 "Saints & Sinners") 15-25 74
(Quadraphonic.)
COLUMBIA (30475 "Johnny Winter Live") 10-15 71
COLUMBIA (33651 "Johnny Winter Live"/"Johnny Winter And") 10-20 75
(Two discs.)
CRAZY CAJUN 8-10
GRT (10010 "The Johnny Winter Story") 10-15 69
IMPERIAL (12431 "Progressive Blues Experiment") 15-25 69
JANUS (3008 "About Blues") 15-20 69
JANUS (3023 "Early Times") 15-20 69
JANUS (3056 "Before the Storm") 15-20 70
(Two discs.)
SONOBEAT ("Progressive Blues Experiment") 150-200 68
(Limited edition, autographed issue.)
SONOBEAT ("Progressive Blues Experiment") 75-125 68
(Limited edition, NOT autographed.)
U.A. (139 "Austin, Texas") 8-12 74
Also see COLE, Junior
Also see JOHNNY & JAMMERS
Also see GREAT BELIEVERS
Also see GUITAR SLIM
Also see MIZZELL, Bobby
Also see SPRINGSTEEN, Bruce / Johnny Winter / Hollies
Also see TEXAS "GUITAR" SLIM
Also see WATERS, Muddy

WINTER, Johnny / Argent / Chambers Brothers / John Hammond
EPs: 7-inch
COLUMBIA/PLAYBACK (14 "Good Morning Little Schoolgirl") 15-25 72
Also see ARGENT
Also see CHAMBERS BROTHERS
Also see HAMMOND, John

WINTER, Johnny & Edgar *LP '76*
Singles: 7-inch
BLUE SKY 3-5 76
CASCADE 35-45 64
LPs: 10/12-inch
BLUE SKY (242 "Johnny & Edgar Winter Discuss *Together*") 15-20 76
(Promotional issue only.)
BLUE SKY (34033 "Together") 8-10 76
Also see LA CROIX, Jerry
Also see WINTER, Edgar
Also see WINTER, Johnny

WINTER, Paul *LP '62*
(With Winter Consort; Paul Winter Sextet)
Singles: 7-inch
A&M 3-4 69-77
COLUMBIA 3-5 62
EPIC 3-4 72-73
LPs: 10/12-inch
A&M 8-12 69-78
COLUMBIA 10-20 62-65
EPIC 8-10 72
LIVING MUSIC 5-8 83-86
Also see WINTER CONSORT

WINTER, Ruby: see WINTERS, Ruby

WINTER CONSORT
Singles: 7-inch
A&M 3-5 69
Also see WINTER, Paul

WINTERHALTER, Hugo, & His Orchestra *P&R '49*
Singles: 78 rpm
COLUMBIA 3-5 49-50
RCA 3-5 50-57
Singles: 7-inch
ABC-PAR 3-5 63
COLUMBIA 5-8 50
KAPP 3-5 64-65
MUSICOR 3-5 68-70
RCA 4-10 50-63
EPs: 7-inch
RCA 3-6 50-59
LPs: 10/12-inch
ABC-PAR 5-10 63
CAMDEN 4-8 69-72
KAPP 5-10 65
MUSIC DISC 4-8 69
MUSICOR 5-10 68-71
RCA 5-15 50-77
TRIP 4-8 76
Also see COMO, Perry
Also see DE CASTRO SISTERS / Hugo Winterhalter & His Orchestra
Also see HEYWOOD, Eddie

WINTERMUTE, Joann *C&W '89*
Singles: 7-inch
CANYON CREEK 3-4 89
DOOR KNOB 3-4 89

WINTERS, Chuck
Singles: 7-inch
REGAL (7505 "Buckskin") 15-25 58

WINTERS, David
Singles: 7-inch
ADDISON (15004 "Sunday Kind of Love") 30-50 59
MERCURY 5-10 66
RORI (703 "Bye Bye") 15-25 62

WINTERS, Don *C&W '61*
Singles: 78 rpm
COIN (102 "Be My Baby") 20-30 56
Singles: 7-inch
COIN (102 "Be My Baby") 50-75 56
DECCA 5-10 60-62
HAMILTON 4-8 63
ROBBINS (2005 "You're Right") 10-20

WINTERS, Eddie "Doodie Pickle"
Singles: 78 rpm
GRAND 10-20 53
Singles: 7-inch
GRAND 20-30 53

WINTERS, Jonathan *LP '60*
EPs: 7-inch
VERVE (5077 "Another Day, Another World") 8-10 62
(Promotional issue only.)
LPs: 10/12-inch
COLUMBIA 8-15 68-73
VERVE 15-30 59-60
(Reads "Verve Records, Inc." at bottom of label.)
VERVE 10-20 61-67
(Reads "MGM Records - a Division of Metro-Goldwyn-Mayer, Inc." at bottom of label.)
VERVE 5-10 73-84
(Reads"Manufactured By MGM Record Corp.," or mentions either Poly dor or Polygram at bottom of label.)

WINTERS, Lee
Singles: 78 rpm
CROWN (142 "The Wallflower") 10-15 55
Singles: 7-inch
CROWN (142 "The Wallflower") 20-30 55

WINTERS, Robert, & Fall *R&B '80*
Singles: 7-inch
BUDDAH 3-4 80-81
CASABLANCA 3-4 82-84
LPs: 10/12-inch
BUDDAH 5-8 80-81
CASABLANCA 5-8 82-83

WINTERS, Rog, & Plainsmen
Singles: 7-inch
CUCA 8-12 67
Also see KENNY BEE

WINTERS, Ron
Singles: 7-inch
DIMENSION 10-15 64
SMASH 10-15 65

WINTERS, Ruby *R&B '67*
(Ruby Winter)
Singles: 7-inch
CERTRON (10027 "It's Not Easy Baby") 5-10 71
DIAMOND (207 "In the Middle of a Heartache") 20-30 66
DIAMOND (223 "Try Me") 15-25 67
DIAMOND (230 "I Want Action") 10-20 67
DIAMOND (255 "I Don't Want to Cry") 10-20 69
DIAMOND (258 "Just a Dream") 10-20 69
DIAMOND (265 "Always David") 10-20 69
DIAMOND (269 "Guess Who") 10-20 69
MILLENNIUM (612 "I Will") 4-6 78
(Rerecorded version of Polydor hit.)
PLAYBOY (6048 "Without You") 5-10 75
POLYDOR (14202 "I Will") 5-10 73
POLYDOR (14249 "Love Me Now") 5-10 74
LPs: 10/12-inch
DIAMOND ("Ruby Winters") 100-200 60s
(Exact title and selection number not known. May have been promo only.)
MILLENNIUM 8-10 78
Also see THUNDER, Johnny, & Ruby Winters

WINTERS, Tommy
Singles: 7-inch
DOTTIE 5-10 60

WINTERS, Wyoma
Singles: 7-inch
RCA 4-6 54
Singles: 7-inch
RCA 5-10 54

WINTERS BROTHERS BAND
Singles: 7-inch
ATCO/RABBIT 3-5 77

WINWOOD, Steve *LP '71*
Singles: 7-inch
ISLAND 3-4 77-87
U.A. 4-8 71
VIRGIN 3-4 88-90
Picture Sleeves
ISLAND 3-4 80-88
VIRGIN 3-4 88-89
LPs: 10/12-inch
ISLAND 5-8 77-87
U.A. (5550 "Welcome to the Canteen") 8-12 71
U.A. (9950 "Winwood") 20-30 71
(With liner notes by Bobby Abrahms.)
U.A. (9964 "Winwood") 10-15 71
(Without liner notes.)
VIRGIN 5-8 88-90
Also see BAKER, Ginger
Also see BLIND FAITH
Also see DAVIS, Spencer
Also see McDONALD & GILES
Also see TOOTS & MAYTALS
Also see TRAFFIC
Also see YAMASHTA, Stomu

WIPPO
LPs: 10/12-inch
MANMADE (Black vinyl) 5-10 80
MANMADE (1 "Totally Hip") 10-12 80
(Promotional only picture disc. 1000 made.)

WIRE
LPs: 10/12-inch
HARVEST 5-10 78
W.B. 5-10 79

WIRE *LP '89*
LPs: 10/12-inch
MUTE 5-8 89
Members: Graham Lewis; Colin Newman; Robert Gotobed.

WIRE TRAIN *LP '84*
Singles: 12-inch
COLUMBIA 4-6 84
Singles: 7-inch
COLUMBIA 3-4 84
LPs: 10/12-inch
COLUMBIA 5-8 84-87
MCA 5-8 90
Members: Jeffrey Trott; Brian MacLeod; Anders Rundblad; Kevin Hunter.

WIRELESS
LPs: 10/12-inch
MERCURY 5-10 79

WIRTZ, Mark
Singles: 7-inch
BOMP 3-5 80
CAPITOL 3-5 72-73
LPs: 10/12-inch
CAPITOL 5-10 72-73
MARDI GRAS 10-15

WISDOM
Singles: 7-inch
MALA 4-8 67

WISDOMS
Singles: 7-inch
GAITY (169 "Two Hearts Make One Love") 500-1000 59

WISE, Wild Willie
Singles: 7-inch
BAJA 4-8 68

WISEMAN, Mac *C&W '55*
(With Sonny Osborne; with Tommy Jackson; with Shenandoah Cut-ups; with Johnny Gimble; with Osborne Brothers; with "Friend")
Singles: 78 rpm
DOT 5-10 55-57
Singles: 7-inch
CAPITOL 4-8 62-63
CHURCHILL 3-5 78-79
DOT 5-10 55-59
MGM 4-6 68
RCA 3-6 69-73
EPs: 7-inch
DOT 10-20 55
LPs: 10/12-inch
ABC 10-15 74-77
CMH 5-10 76-82
CAPITOL (1800 "Bluegrass Favorites") 25-40 62
DOT (3084 "Tis Sweet to Be Remembered") 25-50 58
DOT (3135 thru 3697) 15-30 59-66
(Monaural.)
DOT (25135 thru 25896) 15-35 59-68
(Stereo.)
GILLEY'S 10-20
GUSTO 5-10
HAMILTON 10-20 64-66
MCA 5-10
PICKWICK/HILLTOP 10-15 67
RCA 6-12 70-75
RIDGE RUNNER 5-10
RURAL RHYTHM 10-20
VETCO 10-20
Also see HERMAN, Woody
Also see OSBORNE BROTHERS & Mac Wiseman
Also see SOME of CHET'S FRIENDS
Also see TOMORROW'S WORLD

WISH *R&B/D&D '84*
(Featuring Fonda Rae)
Singles: 12-inch
KN 4-6 84
Singles: 7-inch
PERSONAL 3-4 84-85
Also see RAE, Fonda

WISHBONE
Singles: 7-inch
FONTANA 4-8 69
SCEPTER 3-6 71

WISHBONE ASH *LP '71*
Singles: 7-inch
ATLANTIC 3-4 77
DECCA 3-4 71-72
MCA 3-4 73-78
Picture Sleeves
MCA 3-4 78
LPs: 10/12-inch
ATLANTIC 6-10 76
DECCA (Except 1922) 10-15 71-72
DECCA (1922 "Live from Memphis") 15-20 72
(Promotional issue only.)
FANTASY 5-8 82
I.R.S./NO SPEAK 5-8 90s
MCA 5-10 73-82
Members: Steve Upton; Andy Powel; Ted Turner; Martin Turner; Laurie Wisefield.
Also see FOGHAT

WISHFUL THINKING
LPs: 10/12-inch
AMPEX 8-12 71

WISNER, Jimmy
Singles: 7-inch
CAMEO (373 "A Walk in Space") 10-15 65
Also see BIG J.J.
Also see KNIGHTS
Also see KOKOMO
Also see PARISIANS

WISPER
Singles: 7-inch
FRATERNITY 3-5
SCEPTER 3-5 72

WITCH HAZEL & WARLOCKS
Singles: 7-inch
PHANANA 5-10 82
(Picture disc.)

WITCH QUEEN *P&R/LP '79*
Singles: 7-inch
ROADSHOW 3-4 79
LPs: 10/12-inch
ROADSHOW 5-8 79

WITCHER, Norman
Singles: 7-inch
POOR BOY (102 "Somebody's Been Rockin' My Boat") 150-200 58

WITCHES
Singles: 7-inch
BANG (505 "My Little Baby") 20-30 65

WITCHES & WARLOCKS
(Witches and a Warlock)
Singles: 7-inch
CALLA 5-10 65
SEW CITY 4-8 66-68

WITCHKILLER
LPs: 10/12-inch
ENIGMA 5-8

WITHERS, Bill *P&R/R&B/LP '71*
Singles: 12-inch
COLUMBIA 4-6 79
Singles: 7-inch
COLUMBIA 3-4 75-85
SUSSEX 3-4 71-75
Picture Sleeves
SUSSEX 3-4 72
LPs: 10/12-inch
COLUMBIA 5-8 75-85
SUSSEX 8-12 71-75
Also see MacDONALD, Ralph, & Bill Withers
Also see WASHINGTON, Grover, Jr.
Also see WOMACK, Bobby, & Bill Withers

WITHERSPOON, Deacon
Singles: 7-inch
INNER SOUL 3-5 66

WITHERSPOON, Jimmy *R&B '49*
(With Groove Holmes; with Jay McShann & His Band; with Ben Webster; with Panama Francis & Savoy Sultans; with Wilbur de Paris.)
Singles: 78 rpm
CHECKER 20-30 54-55
FEDERAL 20-30 52-53
DOWN BEAT 15-25 48-49
MODERN 15-25 49-53
RCA 15-25 57
SUPREME 25-35 48-49
SWING BEAT 15-25 49
SWING TIME 15-25 51
Singles: 7-inch
ABC 4-6 71
ATCO (6084 "Still in Love") 15-25 57
BLUE NOTE 3-5 75
BLUESWAY 4-6 69
CAPITOL 3-5 74
CHECKER (798 "Big Daddy") 25-50 54
(Black vinyl.)
CHECKER (798 "Big Daddy") 100-200 54
(Colored vinyl.)
CHECKER (810 "Time Brings About a Change") 25-50 55
CHECKER (826 "It Ain't No Secret") 25-50 55
DISCOS RAFF (501 "When My Heart Beats Like a Hammer") 5-10
FEDERAL (12095 "Two Little Girls") 25-50 52
FEDERAL (12099 "Lucille") 25-50 52
FEDERAL (12107 "Corn Whiskey") 25-50 52
FEDERAL (12128 "One Fine Gal") 25-50 53
FEDERAL (12138 "Back Door Blues") 25-50 53
FEDERAL (12155 "Fast Woman, Slow Gin") 25-50 53
FEDERAL (12180 "It") 25-50 54
FEDERAL (12189 "I Done Told You So") 25-50 54
GNP (156 "Ain't Nobody's Business") 10-20 59
HI FI (954 "Every Time I Feel the Spirit") 10-15 60
KENT (20 "She Moves Me") 10-20 60s
(Stereo 33.)
KENT (23 "Boogie Woogie Woman") 10-20 60s
(Stereo 33.)
KENT (4551 "Ain't Nobody's Business") 4-6 71
KING (5997 "Foolish Prayer") 8-10 65
MODERN (877 "Love My Baby") 25-50 52
MODERN (895 "Baby Baby") 25-50 53
MODERN (903 "Each Slip of the Way") 20-40 53
MODERN (909 "I'll Be Right on Down") 25-50 53
PACIFIC JAZZ (327 "Ain't Nobody's Business") 10-15 62
PRESTIGE (266 "Baby Baby Baby") 8-10 63
PRESTIGE (274 "Mean Ole Frisco") 8-10 63
PRESTIGE (341 "You're Next") 8-10 64
PRESTIGE (355 "One Last Chance") 8-10 65
RCA (6977 "Ain't Nobody's Business") 15-25 57
RCA (7075 "All Right, Miss Moore") 15-25 57
RCA (7377 "Ooh Wee, When the Lights Go Out") 15-25 58
REPRISE (275 "Key to the Highway") 10-15 64
REPRISE (20013 "I Don't Know") 10-15 61
REPRISE (20029 "Hey, Mrs. Jones") 10-15 61
RIP (126 "Endless Sleep") 20-30 58
TRIO (711 "You Can Make It if You Try") 5-10
VEE JAY (322 "Everything But You") 10-20 59
VERVE 5-10 66-67
WORLD PACIFIC (327 "Ain't Nobody's Business") 10-15 62
WORLD PACIFIC (807 "When the Lights Go Out") 10-20 59
EPs: 7-inch
ATLANTIC (600 "New Orleans Blues") 50-100 57
LPs: 10/12-inch
ABC 8-12 70
ATLANTIC (1266 "New Orleans Blues") 100-200 57
BLUE NOTE 8-12 75
BLUESWAY 8-15 69-73
CAPITOL 8-10 74
CONSTELLATION 15-25 64
CROWN (215 "Jimmy Witherspoon Sings the Blues") 20-30 61
(Stereo. Black Vinyl.)
CROWN (215 "Jimmy Witherspoon Sings the Blues") 50-100 61
(Stereo. Colored Vinyl.)
CROWN (5156 "Jimmy Witherspoon") 30-40 60
(Monaural selection number not known.)
CROWN (5192 "Jimmy Witherspoon Sings the Blues") 20-30 61
(Monaural.)
FANTASY 10-15 72
HI FI (422 "Feelin' the Spirit") 35-50 59
HI FI JAZZ (426 "At the Renaissance") 75-100 60
INNER CITY 5-10 81
MCA 5-8 83
MUSE 5-8 83
OLYMPIC 8-10 73
PRESTIGE 10-20 64-69
RCA (1048 "Goin' to Kansas City Blues") 8-12 75
RCA (1639 "Goin' to Kansas City Blues") 50-100 58
REPRISE (2008 "Spoon") 25-35 61
REPRISE (6012 "Hey, Mrs. Jones") 25-35 62
REPRISE (6057 "Roots") 25-35 62
SURREY 12-15 65
SUTTON 10-20 60s
UNITED 8-15
VERVE (5000 series) 12-15 66-68
VERVE (8000 series) 8-10 74
VERVE/FOLKWAYS (3011 "Blues Box") 25-30 66
WORLD PACIFIC (1267 "Singin' the Blues") 40-60 59
WORLD PACIFIC (1402 "There's Good Rockin' Tonight") 30-40 61
Also see BURDON, Eric, & Jimmy Witherspoon
Also see CHARLES, Ray, & Jimmy Witherspoon
Also see FREEMAN, Ernie
Also see HASKELL, Jimmy
Also see HOLMES, Richard "Groove"
Also see McSHANN, Jay
Also see WALKER, T-Bone

WITHERSPOON, Jimmy, & Wilbur DeParis
LP: 10/12-inch
ATLANTIC 10-20

WITHERSPOON, Jimmy, & Lamplighters
Singles: 78 rpm
FEDERAL 10-20 52
Singles: 7-inch
FEDERAL (12156 "Sad Life") 25-50 52
FEDERAL (12173 "24 Sad Hours") 25-50 52
Also see LAMPLIGHTERS

WITHERSPOON, Jimmy, & Quintones
Singles: 78 rpm
ATCO (6084 "My Girl Ivy") 25-35 57
Singles: 7-inch
ATCO (6084 "My Girl Ivy") 25-35 57
Also see QUINTONES

WITHERSPOON, Jimmy / Eddie Vinson
LPs: 10/12-inch
KING (634 "Battle of the Blues, Vol. 3") 200-300 59
Also see VINSON, Eddie
Also see WITHERSPOON, Jimmy

WITNESS INC.
Singles: 7-inch
APEX (7706 "Not You Girl") 20-30 68
DECCA 8-12 68
Picture Sleeves
APEX (7706 "Not You Girl") 25-35 68

WITT, Joachim *D&D '83*
Singles: 12-inch
W.E.A. INTERNATIONAL 4-6 83-84

WITTER, Jimmy, & Shadows *P&R '61*
Singles: 7-inch
ELVIS (900 "If You Love My Woman") 200-300 57
NEPTUNE (118 "My Kind of Woman") 50-75 61
U.A. (301 "Pretty Little Girl") 8-12 61
Members: Jimmy Witter; Sidney Smith.

WIZARD
Singles: 7-inch
KAPP 4-6 71
MCA 4-6 70

WIZARD
LPs: 10/12-inch
PEON (1069 "Original Wizard") 150-200 71

WIZARD
Singles: 7-inch
STARDUST 3-5 80s

WIZARDS
Singles: 7-inch
C&J (122651 "Guardian Angel") 3-5 82
GRECO (624 '50s Come Alive") 3-5 81
Picture Sleeves
GRECO (624 '50s Come Alive") 3-5 81
LPs: 10/12-inch
JADE (8002 "50s Come Alive") 5-10 81
Members: Joel Katz; Jeff See.

WIZARDS
Singles: 7-inch
ERA 4-8 66

WIZARDS from KANSAS
LPs: 10/12-inch
MERCURY (61309 "The Wizards from Kansas") 50-100 70
Members: Robert Menadier; John Coffin; Marc Caplan; Robert Crain.

WIZZ
Singles: 7-inch
CAPITOL 3-5 73

WIZZARD
Singles: 7-inch
U.A. 4-8 73

WOBBLERS
Singles: 7-inch
KING 5-10 61

WOFFORD, E.D. C&W '78
Singles: 7-inch
MC....3-5 78

WOLCOTT, Charles, Orchestra P&R '60
Singles: 7-inch
MGM....3-4 60

WOLF
Singles: 7-inch
LONDON....3-5 74
LPs: 10/12-inch
LONDON....8-10 74
Member: Daryl Way.

WOLF P&R/R&B '82
(Bill Wolfer)
Singles: 7-inch
CONSTELLATION....3-4 81-83
Picture Sleeves
CONSTELLATION....3-4 82
LPs: 10/12-inch
CONSTELLATION....5-8 83

WOLF, Dick
Singles: 7-inch
DALE (101 "Spine Tinglin' Love")...15-25 57

WOLF, Gary C&W '82
Singles: 7-inch
COLUMBIA....3-4 82-83
MERCURY....3-4 84-85

WOLF, Howlin: see HOWLIN' WOLF

WOLF, Mike
Singles: 7-inch
(5053 "Like Magic")....10-20 60s
(No label named used. Single-sided. Promotional issue only.)

WOLF, Peter P&R/D&D/LP '84
Singles: 12-inch
EMI AMERICA....4-6 84-85
Singles: 7-inch
EMI AMERICA....3-4 84-87
Picture Sleeves
EMI AMERICA....3-4 84-87
LPs: 10/12-inch
EMI AMERICA....5-8 84-87
MCA....5-8 90
Also see FRANKLIN, Aretha
Also see GEILS, J., Band

WOLF, Peter, & Mick Jagger
Singles: 12-inch
EMI AMERICA....8-10 84
Singles: 7-inch
EMI AMERICA....3-4 84
LPs: 10/12-inch
EMI AMERICA....8-10 84
Also see JAGGER, Mick
Also see WOLF, Peter

WOLF, Philip
Singles: 7-inch
SIMS....4-8 65

WOLF & WOLF
Singles: 7-inch
MOROCCO (1729 "Don't Take the Candy")....3-4 84
(Colored vinyl.)
Picture Sleeves
MOROCCO (1729 "Don't Take the Candy")....3-4 84
LPs: 10/12-inch
MOROCCO (6046 "Wolf & Wolf")...5-10 84
Members: Peter Wolf; Ina Wolf.

WOLF MOON
LPs: 10/12-inch
FUNGUS....8-10 73

WOLF PACK
Singles: 7-inch
INCREDIBLE (101 "Baddest Wolf") 8-12

WOLFE
Singles: 7-inch
HERITAGE....3-5 71
LPs: 10/12-inch
RARE EARTH....8-10 72

WOLFE, Danny
Singles: 78 rpm
DOT....20-60 57
Singles: 7-inch
DOT (15591 "Pretty Blue Jean Baby")....20-40 57
DOT (15667 "Let's Flat Git It")....40-60 57
DOT (15715 "Pucker Paint")....20-40 57

WOLFE, Dick
Singles: 7-inch
ADMIRAL (104 "Sigma 7")....10-15 63

WOLFE, George
Singles: 7-inch
ULTRA....4-8 64

WOLFE, Jim, & T-Towners
Singles: 7-inch
T-TOWN (1001 "Inner Sanctum")...8-12

WOLFE, Richard, Orchestra
Singles: 7-inch
CONTEMPO....5-10 63

WOLFF, Henry, Nancy Hennings & Mickey Hart
LPs: 10/12-inch
PACIFIC ARTS....5-10 83
Also see HART, Mickey

WOLFMAN
Singles: 7-inch
OKEH....10-20 66

WOLFMAN JACK
(Bob Smith)
Singles: 7-inch
AGC....4-8
WOODEN NICKEL....3-4 72-73
LPs: 10/12-inch
COLUMBIA....8-10 75
WOODEN NICKEL....8-10 72-73
Also see FLASH CADILLAC & CONTINENTAL KIDS
Also see GUESS WHO
Also see STAMPEDERS

WOLFMAN JACK & WOLF PACK
Singles: 7-inch
BREAD (71 "Wolfman Boogie")....25-30 65
BREAD (73 "New Orleans")....25-30 65
LPs: 10/12-inch
BREAD (0170 "Wolfman Jack and the Wolf Pack")....150-250 65

WOLFORD, Jimmy
Singles: 7-inch
4 STAR (1714 "My Name Is Jimmy")....75-125 58

WOLFPACK C&W '82
Singles: 7-inch
LOBO....3-5 82
Members: Narvel Felts; Lobo; Kenny Earl.
Also see EARL, Kenny
Also see FELTS, Narvel
Also see LOBO

WOLVERINE, Wiley
Singles: 7-inch
BOX (5005 "The Big Event")....5-10 77

WOMACK, Bobby P&R/R&B/LP '68
(With the Brotherhood; with Peace)
Singles: 12-inch
ELEKTRA/WOMACK....4-6 83
Singles: 7-inch
ARISTA....3-5 79
ATLANTIC....5-8 67
ARISTA....3-5 79
ATLANTIC....4-8 67
BEVERLY GLEN....3-4 81-84
CHECKER....5-10 65
COLUMBIA....3-5 76-78
COLUMBIA/BROTHERHOOD....3-5 76-77
HIM....3-5
ELEKTRA/WOMACK....3-4 83
KEYMEN....3-5
LIBERTY....3-5 70
MCA....3-4 86
MINIT....4-8 67-70
SOUFFLE....3-5
U.A.....3-5 71-76
Picture Sleeves
MCA....3-4 86
EPs: 7-inch
U.A.....10-15 72
(Promotional issue only.)
LPs: 10/12-inch
ARISTA....5-8 79
BEVERLY GLEN....5-8 81-84
COLUMBIA....8-10 75-78
COLUMBIA/BROTHERHOOD....8-10 76
ELEKTRA/WOMACK....5-8 83
LIBERTY (7600 series)....8-10 70
LIBERTY (10000 series)....5-8 80s
MCA....5-8 85
MINIT....10-12 68-70
U.A.....8-10 71-76
Also see BROTHERHOOD
Also see FELDER, Wilton, & Bobby Womack
Also see SUGAR & SPICES
Also see SZABO, Gabor
Also see VALENTINOS
Also see WOMACK BROTHERS

WOMACK, Bobby, & Patti Labelle P&R/R&B '84
Singles: 7-inch
BEVERLY GLEN....3-4 84
Also see LABELLE, Patti
Also see WOMACK, Bobby

WOMACK, Bobby, & Bill Withers R&B '75
Singles: 7-inch
U.A.....3-4 75
Also see WITHERS, Bill

WOMACK, Leon
Singles: 7-inch
EIFFERT....3-5 71

WOMACK & WOMACK R&B/D&D '84
Singles: 7-inch
ELEKTRA....3-4 84-85
LPs: 10/12-inch
ELEKTRA....5-8 84-85
Members: Linda Womack; Cecil Womack.

WOMACK BROTHERS
Singles: 7-inch
SAR (118 "Somebody's Wrong")....5-10 61
Members: Bobby Womack; Cecil Womack; Curtis Womack; Friendly Womack, Jr.; Warris Womack.
Also see VALENTINOS
Also see WOMACK, Bobby

WOMB
Singles: 7-inch
DOT....5-10 69
LPs: 10/12-inch
DOT....10-20 69

WOMBATS
Singles: 7-inch
VOXX....3-4 82
LPs: 10/12-inch
VOXX....5-8 82

WOMBLES P&R '74
Singles: 7-inch
COLUMBIA....3-4 74-75
LPs: 10/12-inch
COLUMBIA....8-10 74
Member: Mike Batt.

WOMENFOLK P&R/LP '64
Singles: 7-inch
RCA....3-4 64-66
LPs: 10/12-inch
RCA....10-15 63-66

WONDER, Dee, & Rhythm Fame
Singles: 7-inch
WARE (6003 "What You've Done")....10-20 65

WONDER, Rufus, & Additions
Singles: 7-inch
LANDO....8-12

WONDER, Stevie P&R/R&B/LP '63
(Little Stevie Wonder)
Singles: 12-inch
MOTOWN....4-8
TAMLA....4-8
Singles: 7-inch
MOTOWN....3-4 84-88
(Black vinyl.)
MOTOWN....4-6 87
(Colored vinyl.)
MOTOWN/TOPPS (8 "Fingertips Part 2")....50-75 67
MOTOWN/TOPPS (10 "Uptight")...50-75 67
(Topps Chewing Gum promotional items. Single-sided, cardboard flexi, picture discs. Issued with generic paper sleeve.)
TAMLA (1600 thru 1800 series)....3-4 82-86
TAMLA (54061 "I Call It Pretty Music")....25-35 62
TAMLA (54074 "Contract on Love")....25-35 63
TAMLA (54080 "Fingertips")....5-10 63
TAMLA (54086 "Workout Stevie, Workout")....5-10 63
TAMLA (54090 "Castles in the Sand")....8-12 64
TAMLA (54096 "Hey Harmonica Man")....8-12 64
TAMLA (54103 "Happy Street")....10-20 64
TAMLA (54119 thru 54139)....5-10 65-66
(Black vinyl.)
TAMLA (54139 "A Place in the Sun")....10-15 66
(Colored vinyl. Promotional issue only.)
TAMLA (54142 "Some Day at Christmas")....8-12 66
TAMLA (54147 thru 54323)....3-6 67-81
(Black vinyl.)
TAMLA (54147 thru 54323)....8-12 69-78
(Colored vinyl. Promotional issues only.)
MOTOWN....3-4 82
Picture Sleeves
MOTOWN....3-4 87
TAMLA (1639 thru 1846)....3-6 82-86
TAMLA (54061 "I Call It Pretty Music")....25-50 62
TAMLA (54080 "Fingertips")....15-25 63
TAMLA (54136 "Blowin' in the Wind")....15-25 66
TAMLA (54139 "A Place in the Sun")....15-25 66
TAMLA (54281 thru 54317)....4-8 77-80
EPs: 7-inch
MOTOWN (2006 "Stevie Wonder")....15-25 60s
MOTOWN (2020 "Songs in the Key of Life")....10-15 76
TAMLA (340 "Something Extra for *Songs in the Key of Life*")....5-8 76
TAMLA (60272 "Stevie Wonder")...15-25 67
LPs: 10/12-inch
MOTOWN (100 & 200 series)....5-8 82
MOTOWN (800 series)....12-15 77
MOTOWN (6000 series)....5-8 84-91
TAMLA (232 "Tribute to Uncle Ray")....50-80 63
TAMLA (233 "The Jazz Soul of Stevie Wonder")....50-80 63
TAMLA (240 "Little Stevie Wonder")....40-50 63
TAMLA (250 "With a Song in My Heart")....35-55 64
TAMLA (255 "At the Beach")....35-55 64
TAMLA (268 thru 279)....15-20 66-67
TAMLA (281 "Someday at Christmas")....30-40 67
TAMLA (282 thru 371)....8-15 68-79
TAMLA (373 "Hotter Than July")....5-8 80
TAMLA (6000 series)....10-12 82-85
Promotional LPs
MOTOWN (PR-77 "Hotter Than July")....10-15 80
TAMLA (PR-61 "Stevie Wonder's Journey Through the Secret Life of Plants")....10-15 79
TAMLA (PR-98/99 "Radio Programmer's Special")....15-20 80s
Also see CHARLENE & Stevie Wonder
Also see DIONNE & FRIENDS
Also see IGLESIAS, Julio, & Stevie Wonder
Also see JACKSONS
Also see JOHN, Elton
Also see KHAN, Chaka
Also see LENNON, Julian, & Stevie Wonder
Also see McCARTNEY, Paul, & Stevie Wonder
Also see REDNOW, Eivets
Also see ROSS, Diana, Stevie Wonder, Marvin Gaye & Smokey Robinson
Also see TEMPTATIONS / Stevie Wonder
Also see THIRD WORLD
Also see U.S.A. for AFRICA
Also see WILLIAMS, Deniece

WONDER, Stevie / John Denver
Singles: 7-inch
WHAT'S IT ALL ABOUT....4-8 80
(Public service, radio station issue.)
Also see DENVER, John

WONDER, Stevie, & Michael Jackson P&R '88
Singles: 7-inch
MOTOWN....3-4 88
Picture Sleeves
MOTOWN....3-4 88
Also see JACKSON, Michael

WONDER, Stevie, & Clarence Paul
(Little Stevie Wonder & Clarence Paul)
Singles: 7-inch
TAMLA (54070 "Little Water Boy")....25-35 62
Also see PAUL, Clarence

WONDER, Stevie / Dionne Warwick LP '84
LPs: 10/12-inch
MOTOWN....5-8 84
Also see WARWICK, Dionne
Also see WONDER, Stevie

WONDER BAND P&R '79
Singles: 7-inch
ATCO....3-4 79
LPs: 10/12-inch
ATCO....5-8 79

WONDER DOGS
Singles: 7-inch
PARIS TOWER (140 "Bo Diddley")....10-20 60s

WONDER LAND, Alice: see ALICE WONDER LAND

WONDER WHO? P&R '67
(4 Seasons)
Singles: 7-inch
COLLECTABLES....3-4 80s
PHILIPS....3-5 65-67
VEE JAY....12-15 64
Picture Sleeves
PHILIPS....15-20 65-67
Also see 4 SEASONS

WONDERETTES
Singles: 7-inch
ENTERPRISE....10-20 64
RUBY (5065 "I Feel Strange")....20-30 65
U.A. (944 "I Feel Strange")....10-20 65
Also see ST. JOHN, Rose, & Wonderettes

WONDERFUL ONES
Singles: 7-inch
LAURIE....4-8 65

WONDERGAP
LPs: 10/12-inch
A&M....5-10 77

WONDERLAND BAND
LPs: 10/12-inch
ROADSHOW....5-10 79

WONDERLAND DISCO BAND
Singles: 7-inch
RS INT'L....3-5 78

WONDERLING, John
Singles: 7-inch
LOMA....4-8 69

WONDERS
Singles: 7-inch
FORWARD (601 "Tell Me")....100-150 58
Also see ALLEN, Tony

WONDERS
Singles: 7-inch
DEOWEE (6132 "Strings-A-Plenty")....10-15 61

WONDERS
Singles: 7-inch
BAMBOO (523 "With These Hands")....100-150 62
CHESAPEAKE (604 "I Wonder")....25-35 62
COLPIX (699 "Say There")....10-20 63
EMBER (1051 "I'll Write a Book")..15-25 59
SIANA....5-10 65

WOO, Gerry R&B '87
Singles: 7-inch
POLYDOR....3-4 87-88

WOOD, Anita
Singles: 7-inch
SANTO....5-10 63-64
SUN....10-15 61

WOOD, Art
Singles: 78 rpm
RCA (6972 "Hey Jibbo")....10-15 57
Singles: 7-inch
RCA (6972 "Hey Jibbo")....10-15 57

WOOD, Austin
Singles: 7-inch
SURE (5015 "Theres' a Big Rock in the Road")....15-25
SURE (5102 "So Let's Rock")....50-100

WOOD, Bill
Singles: 7-inch
AUDAN....5-10 61

WOOD, Billy, & Skylighters
Singles: 7-inch
PEN (110 "Look a Here")....10-20 62
(First issue.)
W.B. (5291 "Look a Here")....8-12 62

WOOD, Bobby P&R '64
(Bobby "Guitar" Wood)
Singles: 7-inch
CHALLENGE....3-5 62
CINNAMON....3-4 74
COLT....3-5
JOY....5-10 63-65
LUCKY ELEVEN....3-4 73
MALA....3-5 66
MGM....3-4 67-69
SUN (369 "Everybody's Searchin'")....50-100 61
LPs: 10/12-inch
JOY (1001 "Bobby Wood")....20-30 64
Also see PRESLEY, Elvis

WOOD, Brenton P&R/R&B/LP '67
Singles: 7-inch
BRENT (7052 "Good Lovin'")....8-12 66
BRENT (7057 "Cross the Bridge") 10-20 66
BRENT (7068 "I Want Love")....8-12 67
CREAM....3-4 76-78
DOUBLE SHOT....4-6 67-71
FIRST PRESIDENT (428 "The Kangaroo")....10-15 60
MR. WOOD....3-5 72-73
PROPHESY....3-4 73
WAND (145 "Mr. Schemer")....25-35 64
W.B.....3-6 75
LPs: 10/12-inch
CREAM....5-8 77
DOUBLE SHOT....10-20 67
Also see LITTLE FREDDY & ROCKETS

WOOD, Chuck
Singles: 7-inch
ERA....4-8 65
MERCURY....4-8 66
ROULETTE....4-8 67
SSS INT'L....4-8 68
W.B.....4-8 61

WOOD, Clara
Singles: 7-inch
IMPERIAL....4-8 65

WOOD, Danny C&W '76
Singles: 7-inch
LONDON....3-5 76-77
RCA....3-4 80-81

WOOD, Del P&R/C&W '51
Singles: 78 rpm
DECCA....3-4 53-54
MERCURY....3-4 62-64
RCA....3-4 55-59
REPUBLIC....3-4 51-54
TENNESSEE....3-6 51
Singles: 7-inch
CHART....3-4 71-72
DECCA....3-5 53-54
MERCURY....3-4 62-64
PICKWICK....5-10 70s
RCA....3-5 55-59
REPUBLIC....3-8 51-54
TENNESSEE....5-10 51
EPs: 7-inch
RCA....5-12 55-60
REPUBLIC....4-10 54-57
LPs: 10/12-inch
AMBASSADOR....5-10
CAMDEN....5-12 62-64
CHART....5-8 71
COLUMBIA....8-12 66
LAMB & LION....5-8
MERCURY....5-12 62-64
PICKWICK....5-8 70s
RCA....5-15 55-60
REPUBLIC....5-15 54-57
VOCALION....5-10 60s

WOOD, Eddie
Singles: 7-inch
EMBER (1064 "Girl of My Best Friend")....10-20 60

WOOD, Glen
Singles: 7-inch
VANDAN....4-8 64

WOOD, Gloria, & Afterbeats
Singles: 7-inch
BUENA VISTA....5-10 60
Also see ANNETTE

WOOD, Jack
Singles: 7-inch
JAB....4-6
LOOK....4-6 69

WOOD, Jimmy, & Changers
Singles: 7-inch
JAMAKA (1010 "That's Why I Love You")....50-75

WOOD, Lauren P&R '79
Singles: 7-inch
W.B.....3-4 79-81
Picture Sleeves
W.B.....3-4 81
LPs: 10/12-inch
W.B.....5-8 81
Also see McDONALD, Michael

WOOD, Lori, & Belmonts
Singles: 7-inch
AMY (842 "But That Was Long Ago")....50-75 62

WOOD, Mickey
Singles: 7-inch
TAMLA (54052 "Please Mr. Kennedy")....40-60 62

WOOD, Nancy C&W '81
Singles: 7-inch
MONTAGE....3-4 81

WOOD, Natalie / Sal Mineo
Singles: 7-inch
RAINBBO ("Natalie Wood & Sal Mineo")....30-40 57
(Cardboard picture disc. No selection number used.)
Also see MINEO, Sal

WOOD, Ron LP '75
(Ronnie Wood)
Singles: 7-inch
COLUMBIA....3-5 79
W.B....3-5 75-76
Promotional Singles
COLUMBIA....4-8 79
W.B....4-8 75-76
LPs: 10/12-inch
COLUMBIA....5-8 79-81
W.B....8-10 74-75
Also see BECK, Jeff
Also see FACES
Also see ROLLING STONES
Also see SEXTON, Charlie, & Ron Wood
Also see STEWART, Rod, & Ronnie Wood

WOOD, Ron, & Ronnie Lane
(With Pete Townshend)
LPs: 10/12-inch
ATCO (126 "Mahoney's Last Stand")....10-15 76
(Soundtrack.)
Also see TOWNSHEND, Pete, & Ronnie Lane
Also see WOOD, Ron

WOOD, Roy LP '73
(Roy Wood's Wizzard; Roy Wood Wizzo Band)
Singles: 7-inch
U.A....3-4 73-76
LPs: 10/12-inch
U.A....8-10 73-74
W.B....5-8 79
Members: Roy Wood; Rick Price; Nick Pentelow; Mike Burney; Keith Smart; Charlie Grima; Bill Hunt; Bob Brady.
Also see ELECTRIC LIGHT ORCHESTRA
Also see MOVE

WOOD, Scott
Singles: 7-inch
BEAT....8-12 59

WOOD, Tommy
Singles: 7-inch
D (1000 "Can't Play Hookey")....50-75 58

WOOD SISTERS
Singles: 7-inch
PHILIPS....4-8 65

WOOD U BELIEVE
Singles: 7-inch
EPIC....4-8 66

WOODALL, Boots, & Radio Wranglers
Singles: 78 rpm
KING (616 "Rattle Snakin' Daddy") 15-25 47

WOODALL, Jimmy, & His Tarpins
Singles: 7-inch
JEM (27396 "Uncle Sam's Call")....50-75 58
(Identification number shown since no selection number is used.)

WOODARD, Jerry
(With the Esquires; with Nuggets)
Singles: 78 rpm
FAD....20-40 50s
Singles: 7-inch
ARGO (5435 "Boat of Love")....8-12 63
CENTURY LIMITED (603 "You Just Wait")....10-20 63
CHANT (518 "Sweet Woman")....15-25
DIAL (3017 "I May Never Get to Heaven")....5-10 63
FAD (301 "Where Is Judy")....25-35
FAD (901 "Six Long Weeks")....100-200 56
FAD (902 "Downbeat")....35-45 57
FAD (903 "Pappy's Club")....10-15 50s
HEART....20-25 60
RCA (7616 "Who's Gonna Rock My Baby")....10-20 59
REED (601 "Who's Gonna Rock My Baby")....100-200 59
(First issue.)
REED (605 "Don't Make Me Lonely")....25-50 59
Also see MIZZELL, Bobby

WOODARD, Mildred
Singles: 7-inch
EXCELLO....4-8 67

WOODARD, Victor
Singles: 7-inch
C-C....3-5 70

WOODBINE
Singles: 7-inch
BLUE HOUR....8-12 70s

WOODBURY, Gene
Singles: 7-inch
DEL-VAL (1005 "Ever Again")....100-125

WOODBURY, Woody LP '60
LPs: 10/12-inch
STEREODDITIES....10-25 59-63

WOODCHUCKS
Singles: 7-inch
PRINCE (6514 "Angry Generation")....10-15 65
Member: Lee Hazlewood.
Also see HAZLEWOOD, Lee

WOODELL, Pat
Singles: 7-inch
COLPIX (772 "What Good Would It Do")....5-10 65
Picture Sleeves
COLPIX (772 "What Good Would It Do")....10-15 65

WOODEN HORSE
Singles: 7-inch
DERAM....4-6 72

WOODEN NICKELS
Singles: 7-inch
OMEN....10-20
PHILIPS....5-10 69
VAULT....8-12 66

WOODENTOPS LP '86
Singles: 7-inch
COLUMBIA....3-4 86
LPs: 10/12-inch
COLUMBIA....5-8 86

WOODFORD, Terry
Singles: 7-inch
FAME....4-8 66

WOODMAN, Brother: see CHANTERS

WOODS
Singles: 7-inch
TRIUMPH....4-8 65

WOODS, Bennie
(With Five Dukes; with Rockin' Townies)
Singles: 78 rpm
ATLAS (1040 "I Cross My Fingers")....200-300 54
(Credits Bennie Woods & Five Dukes.)
ATLAS (1040 "I Cross My Fingers")....100-200 54
(Credits Bennie Woods & Rockin' Townies.)
Singles: 7-inch
ATLAS (1040 "I Cross My Fingers")....500-750 54
(Credits Bennie Woods & Five Dukes.)
ATLAS (1040 "I Cross My Fingers")....450-650 54
(Credits Bennie Woods & Rockin' Townies.)

WOODS, Bill
Singles: 78 rpm
FIRE (100 "Bop")....50-100 56
Singles: 7-inch
BAKERSFIELD (125 "Phone Me Baby")....75-100 57
FIRE (100 "Bop")....150-250 56
GLOBAL (740 "Story of Susie")....10-20 60

WOODS, Billy
Singles: 7-inch
SUSSEX (213 "Let Me Make You Happy")....100-200 71
VERVE....5-10 66-67
Also see McCoy, Van

WOODS, Billy Woods, & Emeralds
Singles: 7-inch
DOT (16053 "Falling Rain")....20-30 60

WOODS, Bobby
Singles: 7-inch
VIN (1009 "Kiss Me Quick")....15-25 59

WOODS, Cora
Singles: 78 rpm
FEDERAL....15-25 55
Singles: 7-inch
FEDERAL (12223 "I Don't Want to Cry")....50-75 55
FEDERAL (12229 "Ooh La La")....50-75 55

WOODS, Danny
Singles: 7-inch
CORREC-TONE (1052 "You Had Me Fooled")....100-125
INVICTUS....5-10 72
SMASH (2106 "90 Days in the County Jail")....15-25 67
SMASH (2140 "To Be Loved")....10-20 67
SMASH (2159 "Come on and Dance")....10-15 68

WOODS, Darlene, & Starlings
Singles: 7-inch
DATE (2736 "All I Want")....10-20 60
WORLD PACIFIC (811 "All I Want")....20-30 59

WOODS, Debby
Singles: 7-inch
EPIC....5-10 62-63

WOODS, Donald
(With the Vel-Aires; with Earl Palmer & Band; with Ray Johnson Combo)
Singles: 78 rpm
FLIP....15-30 55-56
Singles: 7-inch
ALADDIN (3412 "Memories of an Angel")....20-30 58
FLIP (306 "Death of an Angel")....20-30 55
FLIP (309 "Stay with Me Always")....20-30 55
FLIP (312 "Heaven in My Arms")....40-50 56
GOOD OLD GOLD....4-6
Also see BEL-AIRES
Also see PALMER, Earl
Also see SIX TEENS / Donald Woods / Richard Berry
Also see VEL-AIRES

WOODS, Ed
(With the Afro '70)
Singles: 7-inch
YEW....3-5 70

WOODS, Eddie, & Gemtones
Singles: 78 rpm
GEM (204 "Heaven Was Mine")....15-25 53
Singles: 7-inch
GEM (204 "Heaven Was Mine")....20-40 53

WOODS, Gene C&W '60
Singles: 7-inch
HAP....5-10 60

WOODS, Kenni
Singles: 7-inch
PHILIPS....4-8 63

WOODS, Little Eddie
Singles: 7-inch
COMET....8-10 64

WOODS, Lonnie, Trio
Singles: 7-inch
PEACOCK....4-8 66

WOODS, Maceo R&B '69
(With the Christian Tabernacle Choir)
Singles: 78 rpm
VEE JAY (100 series)....5-10 55-56
Singles: 7-inch
ABC....3-4 73
VEE JAY (100 series)....4-8 55-56
VOLT....3-4 69
LPs: 10/12-inch
GOSPEL TRUTH....4-8 72-74
SAVOY....4-8 76-83
STAX....4-8 78
TRIP....4-8 73
VEE JAY....5-15 60-65
VOLT....5-12 69

WOODS, Mickey
Singles: 7-inch
TAMLA (54039 "They Rode Through the Valley")....25-35 61
TAMLA (54052 "Please Mr. Kennedy")....15-25 61

WOODS, Millard
Singles: 7-inch
DEL-FI....5-10 60

WOODS, Mitch
(With the Rocket 88's)
LPs: 10/12-inch
BLIND PIG....8-12

WOODS, Nick
Singles: 7-inch
EPIC....4-8 64
JOEY....4-8 62

WOODS, Orville
Singles: 7-inch
LIBERTY....5-10 64

WOODS, Pearl
Singles: 7-inch
CRACKERJACK....10-15
DAWN....5-10
MALA....4-8 65
WALL (551 "I'll Be a Cry Baby")....10-20 62

WOODS, Ren R&B '79
Singles: 7-inch
ARC....3-4 79
ELEKTRA....3-4 82

WOODS, Sonny
(With the Four Winds; with Twigs)
Singles: 78 rpm
HOLLYWOOD....20-30 54
MIDDLETONE....25-50 56
Singles: 7-inch
HOLLYWOOD (1015 "Chapel of Memories")....100-150 54
HOLLYWOOD (1026 "Wonderful World")....100-150 54
MIDDLETONE (008 "I Promise")....150-200 56
MIDDLETONE (013 "Living in a Dream")....150-200 56
Also see DOWNBEATS
Also see HAYES, Linda
Also see HUGHES, Ben
Also see MOORE, Johnny

WOODS, Stevie P&R/R&B/LP '81
Singles: 7-inch
COTILLION....3-4 81-83
LPs: 10/12-inch
COTILLION....5-8 81-82

WOODS BROTHERS
Singles: 7-inch
AT LAST....4-8 62

WOODS EMPIRE R&B '81
Singles: 12-inch
TABU....4-6 81
Singles: 7-inch
TABU....3-4 81
LPs: 10/12-inch
TABU....5-8 81
Members: Tommy Woods; Linda Woods; Rhonda Woods; Idris Woods; Judy Woods.

WOODSIDE SISTERS
(With "Vocal Quartet" [Harptones] and Instrumental Accompaniment")
Singles: 78 rpm
"X" (0049 "So Soon")....10-15 55
Singles: 7-inch
"X" (0049 "So Soon")....20-40 55
Also see HARPTONES

WOODSON, Cash T.
Singles: 7-inch
HARVEY....10-15

WOODSON, Johnny, & Crescendos
(Johnny Woodson & His Orchestra)
Singles: 7-inch
SPRY (108 "Dreamer from My Heart")....800-1200 57
SPRY (1008 "Don't Say Goodbye")....300-400 60

WOODWARD, Mick
Singles: 78 rpm
SHERATON....5-10 55
Singles: 7-inch
SHERATON....10-15 55
Also see WOODWARD BROTHERS

WOODWARD BROTHERS
Singles: 78 rpm
SHERATON....5-10 55
Singles: 7-inch
SHERATON....10-15 55
Member: Mick Woodward.
Also see WOODWARD, Mick

WOODY, Bill C&W '79
Singles: 7-inch
MCA....3-5 79

WOODY, Don
Singles: 78 rpm
DECCA....50-100 57
Singles: 7-inch
ARCO (4623 "Not I")....20-40 58
DECCA (30277 "You're Barking Up the Wrong Tree")....100-150 57
(Black label.)
DECCA (30277 "You're Barking Up the Wrong Tree")....50-100 57
(Pink label. Promotional issue only.)

WOODY WAGGERS
Singles: 7-inch
DAYTONE (6407 "Sahara Hop")....15-25 64

WOODY'S TRUCK STOP
Singles: 7-inch
SMASH....4-6 68-69
LPs: 10/12-inch
SMASH....10-15 69

WOODYS
(Ozarks)
Singles: 7-inch
CALIFORNIA (304 "The Saints Go Surfin' In")....10-15 63
Previously issued as *The Saints* and shown as by the Ozarks.)

WOOFERS
LPs: 10/12-inch
WYNCOTE....15-20 64

WOOFING COOKIES
Singles: 7-inch
MIDNIGHT....3-5
LPs: 10/12-inch
MIDNIGHT....5-10

WOOL
Singles: 7-inch
ABC....4-8 68-69
COLUMBIA....3-5 70-72
LPs: 10/12-inch
ABC....10-15 69

WOOL, Ed, & Nomads
Singles: 7-inch
RCA....5-10 66
Also see WOOL

WOOLERY, Chuck C&W '77
Singles: 7-inch
EPIC....3-4 80
RCA....4-6 72
W.B....3-5 77

WOOLEY, Amy C&W '82
Singles: 7-inch
MCA....3-4 81-82
LPs: 10/12-inch
MCA....5-10 81

WOOLEY, Sheb P&R '55/C&W '62
Singles: 78 rpm
BLUEBONNET....20-30 54
BULLET (603 "I Can't Live Without You")....25-50 45
MGM....5-15 48-57
Singles: 7-inch
BLUEBONNET (125 "Peepin' Thru the Keyhole")....30-60 54
BLUEBONNET (130 "Too Long with the Wrong Woman")....30-50 54
MGM (11000 series)....10-20 52-55
MGM (12000 series)....5-15 55-61
MGM (13000 series)....4-8 61-68
MGM (14000 series)....3-6 68-75
POLYDOR....3-4
Picture Sleeves
MGM....4-8 59-62
EPs: 7-inch
MGM....10-20 56-58
LPs: 10/12-inch
LAKESHORE (621-2-3 "Ben Colder and Sheb Wooley")....10-20 70s
MGM (3299 "Blue Guitar")....30-50 56
MGM (3904 "Days of Rawhide")....20-25 56
MGM (4136 thru 4026)....15-20 61-62
MGM (4275 thru 4615)....8-15 65-69
Also see COLDER, Ben

WOOLIES P&R '67
Singles: 7-inch
DUNHILL....4-8 66-67
SPIRIT....10-15 65-66
TTP (156 "Black Crow Blues")....15-20 65
LPs: 10/12-inch
SPIRIT (2001 "Basic Rock")....20-30 71
SPIRIT (2005 "Live at Lizard's")....20-30 73
Members: Stormy Rice; Ron English; Jeff Baldori; Bob Baldori.
Also see RICE, Stormy

WOOLLEY, Bruce, & Camera Club LP '80
Singles: 7-inch
COLUMBIA....3-4 80
Picture Sleeves
COLUMBIA....3-4 80
EPs: 7-inch
COLUMBIA (11264 "Bruce Woolley and the Camera Club")....4-8 80
(Issued with paper sleeve. Promotional issue only.)
LPs: 10/12-inch
COLUMBIA (36301 "Bruce Woolley and the Camera Club")....5-8 80

WOOTEN, Willis
Singles: 7-inch
VIRTUE....4-8 68

WOPAT, Tom C&W '86
Singles: 7-inch
CAPITOL....3-4 88
EMI AMERICA....3-4 86-87
EMI MANHATTAN....3-4 87-88

WORD
Singles: 7-inch
BRENT....4-8 65

WORD
Singles: 12-inch
SUGAR HILL....4-6

WORD OF MOUTH R&B/D&D '85
(Featuring D.J. Cheese)
Singles: 12-inch
BEAUTY & BEAST....4-6 85
PROFILE....4-6 86

WORDD
Singles: 7-inch
CAPRICE....10-15 66

WORDS OF LUV
Singles: 7-inch
HICKORY....10-15 67

WORK, Jimmy C&W '55
Singles: 78 rpm
DOT....4-8 55
Singles: 7-inch
ALL....4-8 61
DOT....5-10 55

WORKDOGS
Singles: 7-inch
OKRA ("Roberta")....4-8 89
(Selection number not known.)
Picture Sleeves
OKRA ("Roberta")....4-8 89

WORKMAN, Nanette
Singles: 7-inch
ATCO....3-5 75
BIG TREE....3-5 76
LPs: 10/12-inch
BIG TREE....5-8 76

WORKMAN BROTHERS
Singles: 7-inch
POPPY....4-8 59

WORKS
Singles: 7-inch
PRIORITY....3-5 80

WORKSHOP
Singles: 7-inch
ERA....4-8 67

WORLD
Singles: 7-inch
COBBLESTONE....4-6 69

WORLD D&D '84
Singles: 12-inch
ELEKTRA....4-6 83

WORLD CLASS
Singles: 7-inch
EPIC....3-4 86

WORLD CLASS WRECKIN CRU P&R/R&B '88
Singles: 7-inch
KRU'CUT....3-4 88

WORLD COLUMN
Singles: 7-inch
ATCO (6604 "Midnite Thoughts")....10-15 68
TOWER (510 "It's Not Right")....8-12 69

WORLD of DISTORTION: see VOODOO DOLLS / Johnny & Jumper Cables / World of Distortion / Ladds from Bellevue

WORLD of MILAN: see MILAN

WORLD OF OZ
Singles: 7-inch
DERAM ... 4-8 68-69
LPs: 10/12-inch
DERAM ... 10-15 69

WORLD OF TEARS
Singles: 7-inch
BELLA ... 4-8

WORLD PARTY LP '86
Singles: 7-inch
CHRYSALIS ... 3-4 86-87
Picture Sleeves
CHRYSALIS ... 3-4 87
LPs: 10/12-inch
CHRYSALIS ... 5-8 86
ENSIGN ... 5-8 90

WORLD PREMIER R&B/D&D '84
Singles: 12-inch
CAPITOL ... 4-6 84
Singles: 7-inch
CAPITOL ... 3-4 84

WORLD PREMIERE
Singles: 7-inch
EAST STREET ... 3-4 84

WORLD'S FAMOUS SUPREME TEAM R&B/D&D '84
Singles: 12-inch
ISLAND ... 4-6 84
Singles: 7-inch
ISLAND ... 3-4 84
Also see McLAREN, Malcom

WORLD'S FARE
Singles: 7-inch
AMARET ... 3-5 70

WORLEY, Wayne
Singles: 7-inch
BRENT (7024 "Red Headed Woman") ... 35-45 61
ELBRIDGE (11016 "Red Headed Woman") ... 75-125 61

WORRELL, Bernie R&B '79
Singles: 7-inch
ARISTA ... 3-4 79
LPs: 10/12-inch
ARISTA ... 5-8 79
Also see McLAREN, Malcom
Also see PARLIAMENT

WORRYIN' KIND
Singles: 7-inch
TRIM (350 "Wild About You") ... 15-25 66

WORTH
Singles: 7-inch
EPIC ... 4-6 72

WORTH, Debby
Singles: 7-inch
TITANIC ... 5-10 63

WORTH, Howard, & Moonbeams
Singles: 7-inch
MCA ... 3-5 76
LPs: 10/12-inch
MCA ... 5-10 76

WORTH, Marion C&W '59
Singles: 7-inch
CHEROKEE ... 5-10 59
COLUMBIA ... 4-8 60-67
DECCA ... 3-6 67-70
GUYDEN ... 5-10 59-60
Picture Sleeves
COLUMBIA ... 3-5 61-62
LPs: 10/12-inch
COLUMBIA ... 10-20 63-64
DECCA ... 8-12 67
Also see MORGAN, George, & Marion Worth

WORTH, Ronnie
Singles: 78 rpm
UNIVERSAL (1010 "Office Girl") ... 10-15 56
Singles: 7-inch
UNIVERSAL (1010 "Office Girl") ... 10-20 56

WORTH, Stan
Singles: 7-inch
ENITH ... 4-8 63
L.A. ... 4-8 67-68
RCA ... 4-8 64
LPs: 10/12-inch
L.A. ... 10-15 67
RCA ... 10-15 64-65

WORTHAN, Johnny
(Johnny Wortham)
Singles: 7-inch
PEACH (567 "Dream Boy Dream") ... 20-25 59
PEACH (711 "Too Too Many") ... 25-50 59
PEACH (722 "The Cats Were Jumpin' ") ... 150-200 59
PEACH (732 "Strange Woman's Love") ... 50-75 60
PEACH (2617 "Strange Woman's Love") ... 40-60 60

WORTHINGTON, Oliver
Singles: 7-inch
COMPASS ... 4-8 67

WOTNOT, Ollie
Singles: 7-inch
CINEMA ... 4-8

WOULD
LPs: 10/12-inch
PERCEPTION ... 8-10 72

WOW WOWS
Singles: 7-inch
CHALLENGE (59046 "Count Down") ... 5-10 59
Member: Ronnie Isle.
Also see ISLE, Ronnie

WOWERS
Singles: 7-inch
CONDOR ... 5-10 61

WOWO HOOSIER HOP GANG
Singles: 78 rpm
VOGUE (V-105 "Rural Rhythms") ... 400-500 47
(Two discs [R736 by Downhomers; R744 by Nancy Lee & Hilltoppers] in boxed set with sleeves.)
Also see DOWNHOMERS

WRABIT LP '82
Singles: 7-inch
MCA ... 3-4 82
LPs: 10/12-inch
MCA ... 5-8 82

WRANGLERS
Singles: 7-inch
CUCA (1049 "A Lonely Game") ... 15-20 61
Also see MILLER, Dick

WRATH, Jasper: see JASPER WRATH

WRATHCHILD AMERICA LP '89
LPs: 10/12-inch
ATLANTIC ... 5-8 89

WRAY, Bill P&R '79
Singles: 7-inch
ABC ... 3-5 79

WRAY, Doug
Singles: 7-inch
EPIC ... 5-10 59
Also see WRAY BROTHERS

WRAY, Link P&R/R&B '58
(With His Ray Men; with His Wray Men; Link Ray)
Singles: 78 rpm
CADENCE ... 20-40 58
Singles: 7-inch
ATLAS ... 4-6 62
BARNABY ... 3-4 76
CADENCE ... 10-15 58
EPIC ... 5-8 59-61
HEAVY ... 3-5 68
KAY (3690 "I Sez Baby") ... 50-100 58
MR. G ... 3-5 69
NORTON ... 3-4 89
OKEH ... 3-5 67
POLYDOR ... 3-4 70-74
RUMBLE (1000 "Jack the Ripper") ... 15-25 61
SWAN (4137 "Jack the Ripper") ... 10-15 63
SWAN (4154 "Week End") ... 6-12 63
SWAN (4163 thru 4187) ... 5-10 63-64
SWAN (4201 "Good Rockin' Tonight") ... 10-15 65
SWAN (4211 thru 4232) ... 4-8 65
SWAN (4239 "Ace of Spades") ... 10-12 65
SWAN (4244 "Batman Theme") ... 5-8 66
SWAN (4261 "Ace of Spades") ... 8-10 66
SWAN (4273 thru 4282) ... 4-6 66-67
TRANS ATLAS (687 "Big City Stomp") ... 10-15 62
Picture Sleeves
EPIC ... 20-35 59
LPs: 10/12-inch
EPIC (3661 "Link Wray and the Wraymen") ... 40-50 60
NORTON ... 5-10 90s
POLYDOR ... 8-10 71-74
RECORD FACTORY ... 20-25 74
SWAN ... 50-60 63
VERMILLION ... 20-25 75
VISA ... 5-8 79-80
Also see BERT & RAY
Also see DUDLEY, Dave / Link Wray
Also see GORDON, Robert
Also see GRAMMER, Billy / Judy Lynn / Link Wray
Also see MOON MEN
Also see PACK
Also see RAYMEN
Also see SPIDERS
Also see WELZ, Joey
Also see WRAY, Lucky
Also see WRAY, Vernon
Also see WRAY BROTHERS

WRAY, Link / Red Saunders
Singles: 7-inch
OKEH (7100 series) ... 4-6 63
OKEH (7200 series) ... 3-5 67

WRAY, Lucky
(Link Wray)
Singles: 78 rpm
STARDAY (500 series) ... 10-20 56
STARDAY (608 "Teenage Cutie") ... 150-200 57
Singles: 7-inch
STARDAY (500 series) ... 20-30 56
STARDAY (608 "Teenage Cutie") ... 150-200 57
(These 500 and 600 series numbers should not be confused with a similar series from the '60s.)

WRAY, Vernon
(With Link Wray)
LPs: 10/12-inch
VERMILLION ... 20-25
Also see WRAY BROTHERS

WRAY BROTHERS
(Wray Family)
Singles: 7-inch
INFINITY ... 6-10 62
LAWN ... 6-10 63
Members: Link Wray; Doug Wray; Vernon Wray.
Also see VERNON, Ray
Also see WRAY, Doug
Also see WRAY, Link

WRAYS, The C&W '83
(Wray Brothers Band)
Singles: 7-inch
CIS ... 3-4 83
MERCURY ... 3-4 86-87
SASPARILLA ... 3-4 85
Also see RAYE, Collin

WRECK-A-MENDED
Singles: 7-inch
BELL ... 10-20 68
U.A. ... 15-25 67

WRECKING CREW
Singles: 7-inch
O'DELL (107 "Demolition") ... 10-20 62
TRUTH (3214 "Bump & Boogie") ... 8-12

WRECKING CREW R&B '83
Singles: 12-inch
ERECT ... 4-6 83
Singles: 7-inch
ERECT ... 3-4 83
SOUND of FLORIDA ... 3-4 83

WRECKING CRU
Singles: 7-inch
EPIC ... 3-4 86

WRECKLESS ERIC
Singles: 7-inch
STIFF/EPIC ... 3-5 80
LPs: 10/12-inch
STIFF/EPIC ... 5-10 80
Members: Wreckless Eric; Martin Ace; Steve Currie; John Brown; Steve Goulding; John Earle; Nick Lowe; Dave Payne; David Witton.
Also see LOWE, Nick

WRECKX-N-EFFECT LP '90
(Wrecks-N-Effect)
LPs: 10/12-inch
MOTOWN ... 5-8 89

WREN, Larry C&W '77
Singles: 7-inch
50 STATES ... 3-5 77

WRENCH
Singles: 7-inch
DORE ... 4-6 69

WRENS
("Featuring Bobby Mansfield")
Singles: 78 rpm
RAMA (Except 65) ... 50-100 55
RAMA (65 "Come Back My Love"/"Eleven Roses") ... 50-100 55
RAMA (65 "Come Back My Love"/"Beggin' for Love") ... 25-50 55
Singles: 7-inch
RAMA (53 "Love's Something That's Made for Two") ... 1000-2000 54
RAMA (65 "Come Back My Love"/"Eleven Roses") ... 300-500 55
RAMA (65 "Come Back My Love"/"Beggin' for Love") ... 75-125 55
(Blue label.)
RAMA (65 "Come Back My Love"/"Beggin' for Love") ... 35-45 55
(Red label.)
RAMA (65 "Will You Come Back My Love"/"Beggin' for Love") ... 50-70 55
(Blue label. Note slight title variation.)
RAMA (110 "Eleven Roses") ... 200-300 55
RAMA (174 "Hey Girl") ... 200-300 55
RAMA (184 "I Won't Come to Your Wedding") ... 800-1200 55
(Rama 194 is in the following section for WRENS / Jimmy Wright.)
ROULETTE ... 3-5 72
Members: Bobby Mansfield; Frenchie Concepcion; George Magnezid; Rocky.

WRENS / Jimmy Wright
Singles: 78 rpm
RAMA (194 "C'est La Vie") ... 50-100 56
Singles: 7-inch
RAMA (194 "C'est La Vie") ... 300-500 56
Also see WRENS
Also see WRIGHT, Jimmy

WREST
Singles: 7-inch
TARGET ... 5-10 69-70
TOWER ... 4-6 69
Members: Bob Krause; Tom Witter; Bob Sowinski; Carl Mussman; Ed Wegner; Randy Fare.
Also see TRUC

WRIGHT, Arthur
Singles: 78 rpm
SPITFIRE ... 5-10 55
Singles: 7-inch
HANGAR (100 "Monkey Hips & Rice") ... 8-12
SPITFIRE ... 10-15 55

WRIGHT, B.J. C&W '78
Singles: 7-inch
SOUNDWAVES ... 3-5 78-80

WRIGHT, Bernard R&B/LP '81
Singles: 12-inch
ARISTA ... 4-6 83
MANHATTAN ... 4-6 85
Singles: 7-inch
ARISTA ... 3-4 83-84
GRP ... 3-4 81-82
MANHATTAN ... 3-4 86
LPs: 10/12-inch
ARISTA ... 5-8 83
GRP ... 5-8 81
MANHATTAN ... 5-8 86

WRIGHT, Betty P&R/R&B '68
Singles: 12-inch
EPIC ... 4-6 81
JAMAICA ... 4-6 84-85
Singles: 7-inch
ALSTON ... 3-8 68-79
ATCO ... 3-4 83
DEEP CITY ... 10-20 66
EPIC ... 3-4 81-83
FANTASY ... 3-5 82
FIRST STRING ... 3-4 86
JAMAICA ... 3-4 84-85
MS. B. ... 3-4 88
TK ... 3-4
LPs: 10/12-inch
ALSTON ... 6-10 72-79
ATCO ... 10-15 68
COLLECTABLES ... 5-8 88
EPIC ... 5-8 81-83
MS. B. ... 5-8 88
Also see ALAIMO, Steve, & Betty Wright
Also see BROWN, Peter, & Betty Wright
Also see HENRY, Freddy, & Betty Wright
Also see HUGH, Grayson, & Betty Wright
Also see KC & SUNSHINE BAND
Also see LITTLE BEAVER

WRIGHT, Beverly
Singles: 7-inch
TIME ... 8-12 60

WRIGHT, Billy R&B '49
Singles: 78 rpm
REGENT ... 10-20 51
SAVOY ... 10-20 49-52
Singles: 7-inch
CARROLLTON (801 "Have Mercy Baby") ... 10-20 59
CHRIS (102 "If I Didn't Love You") ... 10-20
SAVOY (776 "Mean Old Wine") ... 40-60 51
SAVOY (827 "Drinkin' and Thinkin' ") ... 40-60 52

WRIGHT, Bobby C&W '67
Singles: 7-inch
ABC ... 3-5 73-75
DECCA ... 3-6 67-73
U.A. ... 3-5 77-79
LPs: 10/12-inch
ABC ... 5-10 74
DECCA ... 8-12 71
Also see WELLS, Kitty / Bill Phillips / Bobby Wright / Johnny Wright

WRIGHT, Buddy
Singles: 7-inch
UPTOWN ... 4-8 66

WRIGHT, Charles
Singles: 7-inch
PHILIPS ... 4-8 66

WRIGHT, Charles, & Malibus
Singles: 7-inch
TITANIC (5003 "Latinia") ... 15-25 60s

WRIGHT, Charles, & Watts 103rd Street Rhythm Band R&B/LP '69
Singles: 7-inch
ABC ... 3-4 75
DUNHILL ... 3-5 73-74
W.B. ... 4-6 70-71
LPs: 10/12-inch
ABC ... 6-10 75
DUNHILL ... 6-10 73-74
W.B. ... 8-12 70-72
Also see SHIELDS
Also see SOUL RUNNERS
Also see WATTS 103RD STREET RHYTHM BAND

WRIGHT, Chuck
Singles: 7-inch
EMBER ... 10-20 62-64

WRIGHT, Curtis C&W '89
Singles: 7-inch
AIRBORNE ... 3-4 89
Also see GOSDIN, Vern
Also see SUPER GRIT COWBOY BAND

WRIGHT, Dale P&R '58
(With the Rock-Its; with Wright Guys & the Dons)
Singles: 7-inch
ALCAR (1503 "My Heart") ... 10-15 60
FRATERNITY (792 "She's Neat") ... 10-20 58
FRATERNITY (818 "Please Don't Do It") ... 15-25 59
QUEEN-B ... 8-12
STARBURST (1 "Egg Beater") ... 50-75 50s
Also see ROCK-ITS

WRIGHT, Don, & Housebreakers
Singles: 7-inch
BOLO (100 "Corn Bread") ... 8-12 60s

WRIGHT, Duke
Singles: 7-inch
MOOLA ... 4-6 60

WRIGHT, Earl
Singles: 7-inch
CAPITOL (5516 "Thumb a Ride") ... 10-20 65

WRIGHT, Florence
Singles: 78 rpm
SAVOY ... 5-10 52
Singles: 7-inch
SAVOY ... 10-15 52

WRIGHT, Gary LP '75
(With Spooky Tooth)
Singles: 7-inch
A&M ... 3-4 70-72
W.B. ... 3-4 75-81
LPs: 10/12-inch
A&M ... 8-12 70-76
W.B. ... 5-8 75-81
Also see SPOOKY TOOTH
Also see WRIGHT'S WONDERWHEEL

WRIGHT, George
Singles: 7-inch
ORBIT (712 "Aunt Blanche's Boogie") ... 8-12

WRIGHT, Ginny C&W '54
(With Jim Reeves)
Singles: 78 rpm
FABOR (101 "I Love You") ... 10-15 53
FABOR (130 "Please Leave My Darlin' Alone") ... 8-12 55
Singles: 7-inch
FABOR (101 "I Love You") ... 15-20 53
FABOR (130 "Please Leave My Darlin' Alone") ... 10-15 55
Also see REEVES, Jim

WRIGHT, Ginny, & Tom Tall C&W '55
Singles: 78 rpm
FABOR (117 "Are You Mine") ... 5-8 54
FABOR (127 "Come with Me") ... 8-12 55
Singles: 7-inch
FABOR (117 "Are You Mine") ... 10-15 54
FABOR (127 "Come with Me") ... 10-15 55
ZERO (106 "Are You Mine") ... 5-10 60
Also see TALL, Tom
Also see WRIGHT, Ginny

WRIGHT, Hank
Singles: 7-inch
MOON ... 5-10 59

WRIGHT, Janet D&D '84
Singles: 12-inch
COTILLION ... 4-6 84

WRIGHT, Jerry
(With the Damans Vocal Group & Phil Meeks Combo)
Singles: 7-inch
LANJO (2394 "Do You Remember") ... 30-40 60

WRIGHT, Jimmy
(Jimmy Wright Orchestra; with Merry Dee)
Singles: 78 rpm
ALADDIN ... 10-15 57
CASH ... 10-15 54
METEOR ... 15-25 53
RAMA ... 10-20 56
Singles: 7-inch
ALADDIN ... 10-15 57
CASH (1001 "Jimmy's Boogie") ... 15-25 54
LUCKY (007 "Blow Jimmy Blow") ... 8-12 60
METEOR (5007 "Porky Pine") ... 25-50 53
METEOR (5011 "Slow Down Daddy") ... 25-50 53
RAMA (205 "Move Over") ... 15-25 56
Also see ANGELS
Also see FIVE CROWNS
Also see LYMON, Frankie
Also see VALENTINES
Also see WRENS / Jimmy Wright

WRIGHT, Johnny
Singles: 78 rpm
DELUXE (6029 "I Stayed Down") ... 10-15 54
RPM (443 "Suffocate") ... 10-20 55
Singles: 7-inch
DELUXE (6029 "I Stayed Down") ... 25-35 54
RPM (443 "Suffocate") ... 30-40 55

WRIGHT, Johnny
(With Cora Bennette)
Singles: 7-inch
MAGNIFICENT (109 "Who Was") ... 20-30 50s
STEVENS (1001 "Look at That Chick") ... 15-25 59

WRIGHT, Johnny C&W '64
Singles: 7-inch
DECCA ... 4-6 64-68
LPs: 10/12-inch
DECCA ... 10-20 65-68
RUBOCA ... 5-8
Also see JOHNNY & JACK
Also see WELLS, Kitty / Bill Phillips / Bobby Wright / Johnny Wright
Also see WELLS, Kitty, & Johnny Wright

WRIGHT, Justin C&W '89
Singles: 7-inch
BEAR ... 3-4 89

WRIGHT, Lee C&W '78
Singles: 7-inch
POMPEII ... 4-8 68
PRAIRIE DUST ... 3-5 78-85

WRIGHT, Leo
(With the El-Jays)
Singles: 7-inch
ATLANTIC ... 5-10 63
CB (5008 "I Wonder") ... 100-150 62
PERICO ... 5-10 65
LPs: 10/12-inch
ATLANTIC ... 15-25 61-62
VORTEX ... 10-15 70

WRIGHT, Little Cholly
Singles: 7-inch
CHOLLY (7093 "Eternally")........300-400 56
Also see TWILIGHTERS / Little Cholly Wright

WRIGHT, Lonnie
Singles: 7-inch
FREE FORM (502 "Hot Rod")........15-20

WRIGHT, Lorna
Singles: 7-inch
ROCKET.............................. 3-5 77-78
LPs: 10/12-inch
ROCKET.............................. 5-10 78

WRIGHT, Marvin "Lefty"
Singles: 7-inch
BLUE STAR (1000 "Run Run Run").. 4-8 64
EPs: 7-inch
X (54/55 "Boogie Woogie Piano") ..10-20 54
LPs: 10/12-inch
X (3028 "Boogie Woogie Piano") ...25-50 54
(10-inch LP.)

WRIGHT, Mary
(With Budd Johnson Orchestra)
Singles: 7-inch
KIM (101 "One Guy")....................25-20 60

WRIGHT, Michelle C&W '90
Singles: 7-inch
ARISTA.............................. 3-4 90

WRIGHT, Milton, & Terra Shirma Strings
Singles: 7-inch
CARLA (1902 "The Gallop")..........15-25 60s

WRIGHT, O.V. P&R/R&B '65
Singles: 7-inch
ABC.............................. 3-4 75-76
BACK BEAT.............................. 3-8 65-74
GOLDWAX.............................. 5-10 64
HI.............................. 3-6 76-79
LPs: 10/12-inch
BACK BEAT..............................10-20 65-72
HI.............................. 5-10 78-79

WRIGHT, Priscilla P&R '55
Singles: 78 rpm
UNIQUE.............................. 4-8 55
Singles: 7-inch
20TH FOX.............................. 5-10 59
UNIQUE.............................. 5-10 55

WRIGHT, Randy C&W '83
Singles: 7-inch
MCA.............................. 3-4 83-84
SKIDMORE (1001 "Fifty-Fifty")......15-25
Also see MANDRELL, Barbara
Also see NIXON, Nick

WRIGHT, Rebel
Singles: 7-inch
LINDA (002 "Long Gone Daddy")...50-75

WRIGHT, Rena
Singles: 7-inch
TIDE (1000 series).......................... 5-10 61
TIDE (2000 series).......................... 4-8 68

WRIGHT,Reuben: see WRIGHT, Ruben

WRIGHT, Richard
(With the Star-Vells)
Singles: 7-inch
ME-O (1001 "Give Your Love to Me").............................15-25 65

WRIGHT, Richard
LPs: 10/12-inch
COLUMBIA (35559 "Wet Dream") 10-15 78
Also see PINK FLOYD

WRIGHT, Rita
(Syreeta Wright)
Singles: 7-inch
GORDY.............................. 4-8 68
Also see SYREETA

WRIGHT, Roy: see ROBBINS, James / Roy Wright

WRIGHT, Ruben R&B '66
(Reuben Wright)
Singles: 7-inch
CAPITOL.............................. 3-5 64-67
WYNNE.............................. 3-5 60

WRIGHT, Ruby P&R '57
(With the Bello Larks; with Dick Pike; with Ruth Lyons)
Singles: 78 rpm
FRATERNITY.............................. 5-10 57
Singles: 7-inch
CANDEE (501 "Poor Butterfly")....... 8-12 59
CANDEE (502 "This Is Christmas")..............................10-20 59
COLUMBIA.............................. 4-8 60
FRATERNITY.............................. 5-10 57
KING (5192 "Three Stars")..........10-15 59
KING (5208 "Goodbye, Jimmy, Goodbye").............................. 5-10 59
(Monaural.)
KING (5208 "Goodbye, Jimmy, Goodbye")..............................15-20 59
(Stereo.)
KING (5225 "Don't Take Me for Granted").............................. 5-10 59
(Monaural.)
KING (5225 "Don't Take Me for Granted")..............................15-20 59
(Stereo.)
KING (5261 "Sweet Night of Love").............................. 5-10 59
KING (5297 "When You're Away") .. 5-10 60

WRIGHT, Ruby C&W '64
Singles: 7-inch
EPIC.............................. 4-6 66-67
KAPP.............................. 4-6 66
RIC.............................. 4-8 64
LPs: 10/12-inch
KAPP..............................10-15 66

WRIGHT, Sam, Group
Singles: 7-inch
BIG (17 "Telstar")..............................5-10 62
PEAK (7 "Green Onions")..............................5-10 62

WRIGHT, Sonny C&W '77
Singles: 7-inch
ATLANTIC..............................5-10 60
DOOR KNOB.............................. 3-5 77-80
KAPP.............................. 3-6 69
LPs: 10/12-inch
KAPP..............................10-15 69
Also see PEGGY SUE & Sonny Wright

WRIGHT, Steve
(With the Lin-Airs)
Singles: 7-inch
CUSTOM.............................. 4-8 64
DOT..............................5-10 62
LIN (5022 "Wild Wild Woman")..100-200 59
LIN (5024 "Silver Bells")..........15-25 60
LIN (5025 "Far and Distant Lands")..............................25-50 60
THUNDERBALL.............................. 4-8 67
Session: Mike Danbom.

WRIGHT, Steven LP '85
LPs: 10/12-inch
W.B.............................. 5-8 85

WRIGHT, Stevie
LPs: 10/12-inch
ATCO.............................. 3-5 75

WRIGHT, Tommy
Singles: 7-inch
SOUNDTRACK (1012 "We've Lost It")..............................10-15 66

WRIGHT, Willie
(With the Sparklers)
Singles: 7-inch
FEDERAL (12372 "Your Letter")....25-50 60
FEDERAL (12382 "What Will I Say")..............................25-50 60
FEDERAL (12406 "I'm Gonna Leave You")..............................25-50 61
HOTEL (539 "Right On for the Darkness")..............................8-12 60s
LPs: 10/12-inch
ARGO (4024 "I'm on My Way")......15-25 63
CONCERT DISC (45 "I Sing Folk Songs")..............................30-40 60
(Stereo.)
CONCERT DISC (1045 "I Sing Folk Songs")..............................20-30 60
(Monaural.)

WRIGHT BROTHERS C&W '81
Singles: 7-inch
AIRBORNE.............................. 3-4 88
MERCURY.............................. 3-4 84-85
W.B.............................. 3-4 81-83

WRIGHT SISTERS
Singles: 7-inch
CADENCE.............................. 5-8 61

WRIGHT SOUNDS
Singles: 7-inch
KEE VEE (101 "For Sale").........100-200 64
(Reissued as by the Electrons.)
Also see ELECTRONS

WRIGHT SPECIALS
Singles: 7-inch
DIVINITY..............................8-12 60s
Also see WESTON, Kim

WRIGHT TONE
Singles: 7-inch
RENDEZVOUS.............................. 5-8 62

WRIGHT'S WONDERWHEEL
Singles: 7-inch
A&M.............................. 3-5 72
Member: Gary Wright.
Also see WRIGHT, Gary

WRITERS R&B '79
Singles: 12-inch
COLUMBIA.............................. 4-6 79
Singles: 7-inch
COLUMBIA.............................. 3-4 78-79
LPs: 10/12-inch
COLUMBIA.............................. 5-8 79

WRITUS, Arthur, & Nagging Pains
Singles: 7-inch
REPRISE.............................. 4-6 67

WRONG BLACK BAG
Singles: 7-inch
MAINSTREAM..............................5-10 67
Members: Christine Bernardoni; Tom Meccariello; Ellsworth Apgar; Victor Bernardoni; Al Ranaudo.

WRONG NUMBERS
Singles: 7-inch
HITT CART ("I Wonder Why") 25-35 65
(No selection number used.)
PARIS TOWER (111 "I'm Your Puppet")..............................15-25 67

WU, Larry
Singles: 12-inch
ATLANTIC.............................. 4-6 81

WUF TICKET R&B '82
Singles: 12-inch
PRELUDE..............................4-6 81
Singles: 7-inch
PRELUDE..............................3-4 81

WURZELS
Singles: 7-inch
ABC/DOT..............................3-5 76

WYATT, Don
Singles: 7-inch
COLPIX..............................8-12 60
ERA..............................10-20 58
GARPAX..............................5-10 63
ROSCO..............................8-12 59
RUBY (270 "You Broke a Date")....15-25 57

WYATT, Gene C&W '68
Singles: 7-inch
EBB (123 "Love Fever")..............50-75 57
LUCKY SEVEN (101 "Prettiest Girl at the Dance")..............................40-60 59
MERCURY..............................4-8 67-68
PAULA..............................4-6 68

WYATT, J.D. & Thunderbolts
Singles: 7-inch
G.A.R. (106 "How Do You Lose a Girl")..............................10-20 67
Also see SWINGSTERS

WYATT, Johnny
(With the Hightones)
Singles: 7-inch
BIG TIME (1927 "We Met at a Dance")..............................50-75 59
BRONCO..............................10-15 66
CHALLENGE (9172 "I'll Stand by You")..............................15-25 62
CHALLENGE (9207 "I Wouldn't Change a Thing About You")..............................25-35 63
CHALLENGE (59242 "Hang Up the Phone")..............................15-25 64
MAGNUM..............................10-15 66
SWINGIN' (643 "Goodnight")........15-25 62
Also see ROCHELL & CANDLES

WYATT, Nina C&W '88
Singles: 7-inch
CHARTA..............................3-4 88

WYATT, Robert
Singles: 7-inch
VIRGIN..............................3-5 74
LPs: 10/12-inch
VIRGIN..............................8-10 74
Also see SOFT MACHINE

WYATT BROTHERS C&W '86
Singles: 7-inch
WYATT..............................3-4 86

WYCOFF, Michael R&B '80
Singles: 12-inch
RCA..............................4-6 83
Singles: 7-inch
RCA..............................3-4 80-84
LPs: 10/12-inch
RCA..............................5-8 83
Also see CLAYTON, Merry

WYDELL, George
Singles: 7-inch
TANGERINE..............................10-20 65

WYLD
Singles: 7-inch
CHARAY ("Know a Lot About Love")..............................15-25 66
(Selection number not known.)
CHARAY (28 "Lost One")..............15-25 66
Also see ROOTS

WYLD, Bob
Singles: 7-inch
ACADEMY (107 "Roses Are Blooming")..............................10-15
FORD..............................4-8 63

WYLDE HEARD
Singles: 7-inch
PHILIPS (40454 "Stop It Girl")........5-10 67
Picture Sleeves
PHILIPS (40454 "Stop It Girl").......10-15 67
Also see HEARD

WYLDE MAIN-IACS, Thee: see THEE WYLDE MAIN-IACS

WYLES, Gene
Singles: 7-inch
COLUMBIA..............................4-8 66

WYLIE, Richard R&B '71
(Richard "Popcorn" Wylie; Popcorn Wylie & the Mohawks)
Singles: 7-inch
ABC..............................3-4 75
EPIC (9543 "Come to Me")...........15-25 62
EPIC (9575 "Brand New Man").......15-25 63
EPIC (9611 "Head Over Heels in Love")..............................15-25 63
KAREN (1542 "Rosemary, What Happened")..............................15-25 68
MOTOWN (1009 "Money") 30-40 61
NORTHERN (3732 "Pretty Girl")....15-25 60s
SOUL..............................3-5 71
Picture Sleeves
EPIC..............................4-8 62
LPs: 10/12-inch
ABC..............................8-10 74
Also see AMES, Stewart
Also see POPCORN & MOHAWKS

WYMAN, Bill P&R '67
Singles: 12-inch
A&M (12041 "Je Suis Un Rock Star")..............................6-10 81
Singles: 7-inch
A&M (2367 "Je Suis Un Rock Star") ..3-4 81
ROLLING STONES..............................4-6 74-75
Promotional Singles
A&M (2367 "Je Suis Un Rock Star") ..4-6 81
A&M (12041 "Je Suis Un Rock Star")..............................15-20 81
(12-inch single.)
Picture Sleeves
A&M (2367 "Je Suis Un Rock Star") ..3-5 81
LPs: 10/12-inch
ROLLING STONES..............................8-10 74-76
(Stereo.)
ROLLING STONES (QD 79100 "Monkey Grip")..............................15-20 74
(Quadraphonic.)
Also see HAMMOND, John

WYMAN, Bill / Rolling Stones
Singles: 7-inch
LONDON (907 "In Another Land") 4-6 67
Promotional Singles
LONDON (907 "In Another Land") ...8-10 67
Picture Sleeves
LONDON (907 "In Another Land")..............................10-15 67
Also see ROLLING STONES
Also see WYMAN, Bill

WYMORE, Buddy, & Knaves
Singles: 7-inch
MITCHELL..............................8-12

WYND CHYMES R&B '83
Singles: 7-inch
RCA..............................3-4 82-83
LPs: 10/12-inch
RCA..............................5-8 82

WYNDER K. FROG: see FROG, Wynder K.

WYNETTE, Tammy C&W '66
(With Ricky Skaggs; with Emmylou Harris)
Singles: 7-inch
EPIC (Except 1)..............................3-8 66-86
EPIC (1 "Wonders You Perform")....5-10 70
(Colored vinyl. Promotional issue only.)
Picture Sleeves
EPIC..............................3-4 69-76
LPs: 10/12-inch
COLUMBIA (Except "EQ" series).....5-10 72-73
COLUMBIA (EQ-30658 "We Sure Can Love Each Other")..............................10-15 71
(Quadraphonic.)
COLUMBIA HOUSE (5856 "Tammy Wynette")..............................25-35 73
(Boxed, six-disc set.)
COLUMBIA SPECIAL PRODUCTS 5-8 77-82
EPIC..............................5-15 68-86
HARMONY..............................5-10 70-71
TIME-LIFE..............................5-8 81
Session: Sue Richards.
Also see CASH, Johnny / Tammy Wynette
Also see GRAY, Mark, & Tammy Wynette
Also see HOUSTON, David, & Tammy Wynette
Also see JONES, George, & Tammy Wynette
Also see LYNN, Loretta / Tammy Wynette
Also see NEWTON, Wayne, & Tammy Wynette
Also see RICHARDS, Sue

WYNETTE, Tammy, & Randy Travis C&W '91
Singles: 7-inch
EPIC..............................3-4 91
Also see TRAVIS, Randy
Also see WYNETTE, Tammy

WYNN, Jim
Singles: 78 rpm
MODERN MUSIC..............................10-20

WYNN, Lee, & Chromatics
Singles: 78 rpm
MILLION..............................25-50 56
Singles: 7-inch
MILLION (2013 "I Couldn't Take It")..............................50-100 56
Also see CHROMATICS

WYNN, Mel
Singles: 7-inch
ROULETTE..............................4-8 66

WYNN, Michael, Band
LPs: 10/12-inch
ARIOLA AMERICA..............................5-10 78

WYNN, Nan
Singles: 78 rpm
RCA..............................3-5 56
Singles: 7-inch
RCA..............................5-10 56

WYNN, Richie, & Tornadoes
Singles: 7-inch
SOMA (1182 "Spookin") 20-25 62
Also see TORNADOES

WYNN, Paul: see BELL, Benny

WYNN, Ricky
Singles: 7-inch
CAMPBELL..............................10-20

WYNNE, Philippe R&B '77
Singles: 12-inch
FANTASY..............................4-6 83
Singles: 7-inch
COTILLION..............................3-4 77
FANTASY..............................3-4 83
SUGAR HILL..............................3-4 83
UNCLE JAM..............................3-4 80
LPs: 10/12-inch
COTILLION..............................5-8 77
Also see DUNLAP, Gene
Also see SPINNERS

WYNNE, Roberta
Singles: 7-inch
JUBILEE..............................4-8 61

WYNNEWOODS
Singles: 7-inch
WYNNE (108 "Is That Wrong")......15-25 59

WYNNS, Sandy
(Edna Wright)
Singles: 7-inch
CHAMPION (14001 "A Lover's Quarrel")..............................10-20 64
CHAMPION (14002 "Yes I Really Love You")..............................10-20 65
DOC (103 "A Lover's Quarrel")......20-30 64
(First issue.)
Also see HONEY CONE

WYNTER, Mark
Singles: 7-inch
GUYDEN..............................5-8 64
SCEPTER..............................5-8 65

WYNTER, Pat
Singles: 7-inch
TAKE FIVE..............................8-12 64

WYNTERS, Gail
Singles: 7-inch
HICKORY..............................3-5 68
LPs: 10/12-inch
RCA..............................5-10 77

WYNTERS, Stormy
Singles: 7-inch
MERCURY (72505 "Life Saver")....10-20 65

WYRICK, Jim, & Union Gold C&W '83
Singles: 7-inch
NSD..............................3-4 83

WYTE, Marty
Singles: 7-inch
BRUSH (7000 "Queen of the Mardi-Gras")..............................15-25 50s
SHAMMY (501 "Queen of the Mardi-Gras")..............................15-25 50s

X

X LP '81
Singles: 7-inch
ELEKTRA..............................3-4 82-83
MERCURY (Black vinyl)..............................3-4 93
MERCURY (1036 "Country at War")..3-4 93
(Colored vinyl. Promotional issue only.)
Picture Sleeves
ELEKTRA..............................3-4 83
MERCURY (1036 "Country at War")..3-4 93
LPs: 10/12-inch
ELEKTRA..............................5-8 82-88
ROCSHIRE..............................5-8 83
SLASH (104 "Los Angeles")..........10-20 80
SLASH (107 "Wild Gift")..............10-20 81
Members: Dave Alvin; Exene Cervenka; John Doe; D.J. Bonebrake; Tony Gilkyson.
Also see ALVIN, Dave
Also see BLASTERS
Also see CERVENKA, Exene, & Wanda Coleman
Also see DOE, John
Also see LONE JUSTICE

X, Malcolm: see MALCOLM X

X LINCOLN
Singles: 7-inch
DOT..............................4-8 68

XIT
Singles: 7-inch
CANYON..............................4-8 75
MOTOWN..............................3-6 74
RARE EARTH..............................5-10 72-73
LPs: 10/12-inch
CANYON (7114 "Entrance")..........25-45 74
CANYON (7121 "Relocation")........25-35 77
RARE EARTH (536 "Plight of the Red Man")..............................15-25 72
RARE EARTH (545 "Silent Warrior")..............................15-25 73
Members: Michael Martin; Lee Herrere; Mac Sauzo; R.C. Garliss, Jr.
Also see BEE, Tom
Also see LINCOLN STREET EXIT

XLs
Singles: 7-inch
CBC..............................8-12
MMC..............................8-12 68
STRACK..............................8-12

XL-5
Singles: 7-inch
FOUR (004 "Miserlou")..............................5-10
LPs:10/12-inch
XL..............................5-10 69

XL-5 MINUS 1
Singles: 7-inch
COVE ... 4-8 67

XS BAGGAGE
Singles: 7-inch
MGM ... 3-5 70

XTC LP '80
Singles: 7-inch
EPIC ... 3-4 82
GEFFEN (Except "PRO" series) ... 3-4 83-89
GEFFEN ("PRO" series) ... 3-5 83-84
(Promotional issues only.)
RSO ... 3-4 81
VIRGIN ... 3-4 79-81
Picture Sleeves
GEFFEN ... 3-4 89
VIRGIN ... 3-4 79
LPs: 10/12-inch
EPIC ... 5-10 82
GEFFEN ... 5-8 84-89
RSO ... 5-10 81
VIRGIN ... 5-10 78-82
Members: Andy Partridge; Barry Andrews; Colin Moulding;
Terry Chambers; Dave Gregory.
Also see DUKES of STRATOSPHERE
Also see SHRIEKBACK

XYZ LP '89
Singles: 7-inch
GRASS ROOTS ... 3-6 72
LPs: 10/12-inch
ENIGMA ... 5-8 89
Members: Anka Wolbert; Ronny Moorings; Pieter Nooten.

XAVIER R&B/LP '82
(Xavier Smith)
Singles: 12-inch
LIBERTY ... 4-6 82
Singles: 7-inch
LIBERTY ... 3-4 82
LPs: 10/12-inch
LIBERTY ... 5-8 82

XAVION R&B '85
Singles: 7-inch
ASYLUM ... 3-4 84-85
LPs: 10/12-inch
ASYLUM ... 5-8 84

X-CELLENTS
(E-Cellents)
Singles: 7-inch
SMASH (1966 "Hey Little Willie") ... 10-15 65
SURE PLAY (0002 "And I'm Cryin' ") ... 15-25 66
(Mistakenly credits group as "E-Cellents.")
SURE PLAY (0003 "Hang It Up") ... 15-25 66
LP: 10/12-inch
PRISM ... 10-20

X-CEPTIONS
Singles: 7-inch
DECEMBER ... 4-8 67

X-CESSORS
Singles: 7-inch
LU TALL ... 3-5 74

XCITERS
Singles: 7-inch
JAGUAR (200 "Upsetter") ... 15-25 65

X-CITERS
Singles: 7-inch
SOUND of BIRMINGHAM ... 3-5 82

X-CITERS UNLIMITED
Singles: 7-inch
ABC ... 4-8 68

X-CITERS VOCAL GROUP
Singles: 7-inch
CARTER (2764 "As We Dance") ... 250-500 50s

X-CLAN LP '90
LPs: 10/12-inch
4TH & BROADWAY ... 5-8 90

XCURSION
LPs: 10/12-inch
RAMPAGE ... 5-10

XENA D&D '83
Singles: 12-inch
EMERGENCY ... 4-6 83

XENOS, Dax
Singles: 7-inch
MR. G ... 3-5 72

X-RAYS R&B '49
Singles: 7-inch
SAVOY ... 10-15 48-49
Also see JACQUET, Illinois
Also see WALKER, T-Bone

XTREEMS
Singles: 7-inch
STAR TREK (1221 "Substitute") ... 15-25 60s

X-25 BAND R&B '82
Singles: 7-inch
H.C.R.C. ... 3-4 82

XYMOX LP '89
Singles: 12-inch
4AD ... 4-8 85-88
WING/POLYGRAM ... 5-8 89
LPs: 10/12-inch
4AD ... 5-10 85-87
WING/MERCURY ... 5-8 91
WING/POLYGRAM ... 5-8 89

Y

Y & T LP '83
(Yesterday & Today)
Singles: 7-inch
A&M ... 3-4 81-85
LPs: 10/12-inch
A&M ... 5-8 81-85
GEFFEN ... 5-8 87-89
LONDON ... 8-10 78

YBS
LPs: 10/12-inch
ARIOLA AMERICA ... 5-10 79
GEFFEN ... 5-8 89

YA HO WA 13
(Father Yod & Spirit of '76; Yod Aquarian)
LPs: 10/12-inch
HIGHER KEY ("Principles of the Children") ... 600-800 78
(Selection number not known.)
HIGHER KEY ("Contraction") ... 400-500 76
HIGHER KEY ("Expansion") ... 400-500 76
HIGHER KEY (3301 "Kohoutek") ... 300-400 73
HIGHER KEY (3304 "All Or Nothing at All") ... 300-400 74
HIGHER KEY (3306 "The Savage Sons of Ya Ho Wa") ... 300-400 74
HIGHER KEY (3307 "Penetration") ... 300-400 74
HIGHER KEY (3309 "I'm Gonna Take You Home") ... 500-750 75
Also see THIRTEENTH FLOOR ELEVATORS

YA HO WA 13 & Sky Saxon
LPs: 10/12-inch
PSYCHO (2 "Golden Sunrise") ... 15-25 82
(Colored vinyl. Reportedly 300 made.)
Also see SAXON, Sky
Also see YA HO WA 13

YA YA
Singles: 7-inch
ROCK 'N' ROLL ... 3-5 84
LPs: 10/12-inch
ROCK 'N' ROLL ... 5-10 84

YACHTS LP '79
Singles: 7-inch
POLYDOR ... 3-4 79
LPs: 10/12-inch
POLYDOR ... 5-8 79-80
RADAR ... 6-10

YACHTSMEN
Singles: 7-inch
DESTINY (402 "It's So Hard to Be Young") ... 50-75 59
HAR-GLO (420 "Our Future") ... 100-150 58
(Shows company address and phone.)
HAR-GLO (420 "Our Future") ... 75-125 61
(No address and phone shown.)
Also see LONDON, Lloyd, & Yachtsmen

YACHTSMEN
LPs: 10/12-inch
BUENA VISTA ... 10-20 62

YAEGER, Atlee
LPs: 10/12-inch
CHELSEA ... 8-10 73

YAGAMI, Junko
Singles: 12-inch
VANGUARD ... 4-6
Singles: 7-inch
VANGUARD ... 3-4

YAGER, Laura
LPs: 10/12-inch
OVATION ... 8-10 72

Y'ALLS
Singles: 7-inch
RUFF (1016 "Run for Your Life") ... 15-25 66
Also see KITCHEN CINQ

YAMA & Karma Dusters
LPs: 10/12-inch
MANHOLE ("Up from the Sewers") ... 100-200 70
(No selection number used.)

YAMASHTA, Stomu LP '76
(With Steve Winwood & Michael Shrieve)
LPs: 10/12-inch
ARISTA ... 5-8 77
ISLAND ... 5-8 76-78
VANGUARD ... 8-10 71-74
Also see WINWOOD, Steve

YAMBU R&B '75
Singles: 7-inch
MONTUNO GRINGO ... 3-4 75

YANCEY, Jimmy
(With Mama Yancy)
Singles: 78 rpm
COLUMBIA ... 5-10 47
Singles: 7-inch
BLACK GOLD (600 "Lion's Den") ... 8-12
EPs: 7-inch
ATLANTIC (525 "At the Piano") ... 15-25 51
LPs: 10/12-inch
ATLANTIC (130 "Yancy Special") ... 50-100 51
(10-inch LP.)
ATLANTIC (134 "Piano Solos") ... 50-100 51
(10-inch LP.)
ATLANTIC (1283 "Pure Blues") ... 50-75 58
ATLANTIC (7229 "Blues Originals") ... 10-15 72
PARAMOUNT (101 "Yancy Special") ... 50-100 51
(10-inch LP.)
PAX (6007 "Jimmy & Mama Yancy") ... 50-75 53
(10-inch LP.)
PAX (6011 "Yancy's Mixture") ... 40-60 57
PAX (6012 "Evening with the Yancys") ... 40-60 57
RCA (3000 "Blues & Boogies") ... 75-100 51
(10-inch LP.)
RIVERSIDE (123 "Yancey's Greeting") ... 25-35 58
RIVERSIDE (124 "Yancey's Getaway") ... 25-35 58
RIVERSIDE (1028 "Last Recording Date") ... 50-75 54
(10-inch LP.)
RIVERSIDE (1061 "Yancey's Getaway") ... 50-75 55
(10-inch LP.)

YANCEY, Jimmy / Cripple Clarence Lofton
LP: 10/12-inch
JAZZTONE (224 "Pioneers of Boogie Woogie") ... 15-25 56
Also see LOFTON, Cripple Clarence

YANCEY, Mama, & Art Hodes
LPs: 10/12-inch
VERVE/FOLKWAYS ... 12-15 65
Also see MONTGOMERY, Little Brother, & Mama Yancey
Also see YANCEY, Jimmy

YANCEY, Vernon, Combo
Singles: 7-inch
CUCA (1146 "Crazy Rock") ... 10-20 63

YANCY DERRINGER
LPs: 10/12-inch
HEMISPHERE ... 10-15 75

YANKEE DOLLAR
Singles: 7-inch
DOT ... 4-8 68-69
LPs: 10/12-inch
DOT ... 15-25 69

YANKEES
LPs: 10/12-inch
BIG SOUND ... 8-10

YANKOVIC, "Weird Al" P&R/LP '83
Singles: 12-inch
ROCK 'N' ROLL ... 4-6 84
Singles: 7-inch
CAPITOL ... 3-4 79
ROCK 'N' ROLL ... 3-4 83-89
SCOTTI BROS./CBS (2105 "Like a Surgeon") ... 30-40 85
(Picture disc. Promotional issue only.)
TK ... 3-4 81
Picture Sleeves
ROCK 'N' ROLL ... 3-4 83-89
LPs: 10/12-inch
ROCK 'N' ROLL ... 5-8 83-89

YANNI LP '90
LPs: 10/12-inch
PRIVATE ... 5-8 90
Also see CHAMELEON

YANOVSKY, Zalman
Singles: 7-inch
BUDDAH ... 4-8 67
LPs: 10/12-inch
BUDDAH ... 10-15 68
KAMA SUTRA ... 8-10 71
Also see LOVIN' SPOONFUL
Also see MUGWUMPS

YARBROUGH, Bob C&W '71
(Bob Yarborough)
Singles: 7-inch
MUSIC MILL ... 3-5 76
SUGAR HILL ... 3-5 71

YARBROUGH, Glenn LP '64
Singles: 7-inch
PRIDE ... 3-4 72
RCA ... 3-4 64-68
STAX ... 3-4 73-74
W.B. ... 3-4 68-71
Picture Sleeves
RCA ... 3-6 65
LPs: 10/12-inch
ELEKTRA (135 "Here We Go, Baby") ... 20-30 57
FIRST AMERICAN ... 8-12 81
IMPRESS ... 8-10 71
RCA ... 12-25 64-69
STACK-O-HITS ... 10-20
STAX ... 8-10 74
TRADITION ... 8-15 67-70
W.B. ... 8-12 68-71
Also see LIMELITERS

YARBROUGH, Lafayette
Singles: 7-inch
BART (7625 "Cool Cool Baby") ... 100-200 57

YARBROUGH & PEOPLES R&B/LP '80
Singles: 12-inch
TOTAL EXPERIENCE ... 4-6 82-86
Singles: 7-inch
MERCURY ... 3-4 80-81
TOTAL EXPERIENCE ... 3-4 82-86
LPs: 10/12-inch
MERCURY ... 5-8 80
TOTAL EXPERIENCE ... 5-8 82-86
Members: Calvin Yarbrough; Alisa Peoples.

YARDBIRDS P&R/LP '65
Singles: 7-inch
CAPITOL (72274 "Heart Full of Soul") ... 20-40 65
(Canadian.)
EPIC (9709 "I Wish You Could") ... 15-20 64
EPIC (9790 thru 10204) ... 5-8 65-67
EPIC (10248 "Ten Little Indians") ... 10-15 67
EPIC (10303 "Goodnight Sweet Josephine") ... 15-20 68
Picture Sleeves
EPIC (Except 9709) ... 10-15 65-66
EPIC (9709 "I Wish You Could") ... 75-125 64
(Promotional issue only.)
LPs: 10/12-inch
ACCORD ... 5-8 81-83
COLUMBIA (11311 "Live Yardbirds") ... 25-35 72
(Columbia Special Products issue.)
COMPLEAT ... 8-12 86
EPIC (24167 "For Your Love") ... 50-100 65
(Monaural.)
EPIC (24177 "Having a Rave Up") ... 40-60 65
(Monaural.)
EPIC (24210 "Over Under Sideways Down") ... 40-60 66
(Monaural.)
EPIC (24246 "Greatest Hits") ... 30-40 66
(Monaural.)
EPIC (24313 "Little Games") ... 40-60 67
(Monaural.)
EPIC (26167 "For Your Love") ... 30-40 65
(Stereo.)
EPIC (26177 "Having a Rave Up") ... 30-40 65
(Stereo.)
EPIC (26210 "Over Under Sideways Down") ... 30-45 66
(Stereo.)
EPIC (26246 "Greatest Hits") ... 30-40 66
(Stereo.)
EPIC (26313 "Little Games") ... 35-50 67
(Stereo.)
EPIC (30135 "The Yardbirds Featuring Performances by Jeff Beck, Eric Clapton, Jimmy Page") ... 75-100 70
EPIC (30615 "Live Yardbirds") ... 50-75 71
EPIC (34490 "Yardbirds Favorites") ... 8-12 77
(Orange label.)
EPIC (34490 "Yardbirds Favorites") ... 5-8
(Black label.)
EPIC (34491 "Great Hits") ... 8-10 77
EPIC (38455 "The Yardbirds") ... 5-8 83
EPIC (48455 "The Yardbirds") ... 12-15 83
(Half-speed mastered.)
MERCURY (21271 "Eric Clapton & Yardbirds Live with Sonny Boy Williamson") 20-30 66
(Monaural.)
MERCURY (61271 "Eric Clapton & Yardbirds Live with Sonny Boy Williamson") 30-40 66
(Stereo. Red label.)
MERCURY (61271 "Eric Clapton & Yardbirds Live with Sonny Boy Williamson") ... 5-8
(Black label.)
RHINO (Black vinyl) ... 6-10 82-86
RHINO (253 "Afternoon Tea") ... 10-15 82
(Picture disc.)
SPRINGBOARD ... 8-10 72
Members: Eric Clapton; Jeff Beck; Keith Relf; Jimmy Page; Jim McCarty; Chris Dreja.
Also see ARMAGEDDON
Also see BECK, Jeff
Also see BOX of FROGS
Also see CLAPTON, Eric
Also see CLARK, Dave, Five / Simon & Garfunkel / Yardbirds / New Christy Minstrels
Also see PAGE, Jimmy
Also see RELF, Keith
Also see RENAISSANCE
Also see WILLIAMSON, Sonny Boy

YARROW, Peter P&R/LP '72
Singles: 7-inch
W.B. ... 3-4 68-75
LPs: 10/12-inch
W.B. ... 8-10 72-75
Also see PETER, PAUL & MARY

YATES, Bill
Singles: 7-inch
SUN ... 10-15 64-66
EMERY ... 3-5 78

YATES, Billy
Singles: 7-inch
BETHLEHEM ... 4-8 62
1ST ... 4-8 61

YATES, Count
Singles: 7-inch
NEW BAG ... 5-10 67
REGIS (1 "Golden Key") ... 10-15

YATES, Duane, & Capris
Singles: 7-inch
N-JOY ... 5-10 65

YATES, Jenny C&W '87
Singles: 7-inch
MERCURY ... 3-4 87

YATES, Little Sammy
Singles: 7-inch
GENIE ... 5-10 59

YATES, Lori C&W '88
Singles: 7-inch
COLUMBIA ... 3-4 88-89

YATES, Ruby, & Swinging Rocks
Singles: 7-inch
HIT PRODUCTIONS (3588 "It's Been a Long Time") ... 40-60

YATES, Tommy
Singles: 7-inch
VERVE (10556 "Darling, Something's Gotta Give") ... 10-20 67

YAZ P&R/R&B/LP '82
(Yazoo)
Singles: 12-inch
SIRE ... 4-6 82-84
Singles: 7-inch
SIRE (Except 29953) ... 3-4 82-84
SIRE (29953 "Situation") ... 4-6 82
(Credited to Yazoo.)
SIRE (29953 "Situation") ... 3-4 82
(Credited to Yaz.)
Picture Sleeves
SIRE ... 3-4 82
LPs: 10/12-inch
SIRE ... 5-8 82-83
Members: Alison Moyet; Vince Clarke.
Also see ERASURE
Also see MOYET, Alison

YAZZ & PLASTIC POPULATION P&R '88
Singles: 7-inch
ELEKTRA ... 3-4 88
Picture Sleeves
ELEKTRA ... 3-4 88

YEAR 2000
Singles: 7-inch
AMY ... 4-8 68
RAMA RAMA ... 4-6 69

YEAR ZERO
Singles: 7-inch
CHRYSALIS ... 3-4 87
Picture Sleeves
CHRYSALIS ... 3-4 87

YELLEN, Peter, & Breakers
Singles: 7-inch
OK PROD. ... 3-4
Picture Sleeves
OK PROD. ... 3-4 84

YELLO D&D/LP '83
Singles: 12-inch
ELEKTRA ... 4-6 83-85
RALPH ... 5-8 81
STIFF ... 4-8
Singles: 7-inch
ELEKTRA ... 3-4 83-85
MERCURY ... 3-4 87-89
RALPH ... 3-4 81
STIFF (Picture discs) ... 4-8
Picture Sleeves
MERCURY ... 3-4 87
LPs: 10/12-inch
ELEKTRA ... 5-8 83-85
MERCURY ... 5-8 87-89
RALPH ... 8-10 81

YELLOW BALLOON P&R '67
Singles: 7-inch
CANTERBURY ... 4-8 67-68
LPs: 10/12-inch
CANTERBURY ... 15-20 67
Members: Alex Valdez; Don Grady; Don Braucht; Forrest Green; Paul Cannella; Darryl Dragon.
Also see CAPTAIN & TENNILLE
Also see GRADY, Don
Also see SPIRIT

YELLOW BRICK ROAD
Singles: 7-inch
LAURIE ... 4-6 69

YELLOW HAIR
Singles: 7-inch
BELL ... 4-8 69
PACIFIC AVENUE ... 5-10 60s
Member: Scott McCarl.
Also see RASPBERRIES

YELLOW HAND
Singles: 7-inch
CAPITOL ... 3-5 70
LPs: 10/12-inch
CAPITOL ... 10-15 70
Members: Jerry Tawney; Pat Flynn; Mickey Armstrong; Kenny Trujillo; Oscar Vildasolo.
Also see TAWNEY, Jerry

YELLOW JACKETS
Singles: 7-inch
SMASH ... 3-5 68

YELLOW MAGIC ORCHESTRA P&R/R&B/LP '80
Singles: 12-inch
A&M ... 4-6 80
Singles: 7-inch
A&M ... 3-4 80
HORIZON ... 3-4 80
Picture Sleeves
HORIZON ... 3-4 80
LPs: 10/12-inch
A&M ... 5-8 80-81
HORIZON ... 5-8 80

YELLOW PAYGES
Singles: 7-inch
SHOWPLACE (216 "Sleeping Minds")....................15-25 67
SHOWPLACE (217 "Love in the Making")....................10-15 67
UNI....................10-15 67-70
LPs: 10/12-inch
UNI (73045 "The Yellow Payges, Volume 1"....................20-30 69
Also see NOMADS

YELLOW POWER
Singles: 12-inch
ROCSHIRE....................4-6
Singles: 7-inch
ROCSHIRE....................3-4

YELLOW SUNSHINE
Singles: 7-inch
TSOP....................3-5 73
LPs: 10/12-inch
GAMBLE....................8-10 73

YELLOWJACKETS LP '83
Singles: 7-inch
MCA....................3-4 86
W.B. 3-4 81-85
LPs: 10/12-inch
MCA....................5-8 86
W.B. 5-8 81-85

YELLOWMAN D&D '84
Singles: 12-inch
COLUMBIA....................4-6 84
Singles: 7-inch
COLUMBIA....................3-4 84
LPs: 10/12-inch
COLUMBIA....................5-8 84
SUNSPLASH....................5-8

YELLOWSTONE & VOICE
Singles: 7-inch
RED BUS....................3-5 73

YELVINGTON, Malcolm
(With the Star Rhythm Boys)
Singles: 78 rpm
SUN....................25-50 56
Singles: 7-inch
SUN (211 "Drinkin' Wine Spo-Dee-O-Dee")....................75-125 54
(Counterfeits exist of this release.)
SUN (246 "Rockin' with My Baby")....................50-75 56
Also see BURLISON, Paul

YEOMAN
Singles: 7-inch
MAINSTREAM....................3-5 69

YEOMANS
Singles: 7-inch
HEIDI....................10-15 60s

YEOMEN
LPs: 10/12-inch
HI-TOP (6201 "Session One")........25-50 62
Members: Bob Finkenaur; Jack Otterness; Keith Critchlow; Don Bennett.

YES P&R/LP '71
Singles: 12-inch
ATCO....................4-6 83-86
Singles: 7-inch
ATCO....................3-4 83-87
ATLANTIC (Black vinyl)....................3-6 70-78
ATLANTIC (Colored vinyl)....................4-8 70-78
Picture Sleeves
ATCO....................3-4 83-87
LPs: 10/12-inch
ARISTA....................5-8 91
ATCO....................5-8 83-87
ATLANTIC (100 series)....................10-15 73
ATLANTIC (500 series)....................6-12 80
ATLANTIC (900 series)....................10-15 74
ATLANTIC (7000 series)....................8-12 71-72
ATLANTIC (8000 series)....................10-15 69-71
ATLANTIC (16000 thru 19000 series)....................5-10 74-82
MFSL (077 "Close to the Edge")....35-50 82
Promotional LPs
ATLANTIC ("Solos")....................30-40 76
Members: Jon Anderson; Rick Wakeman; Steve Howe; Chris Squire; Tony Kaye; Alan White; Bill Bruford; Patrick Moraz; Geoff Downes; Trevor Horn.
Also see ANDERSON, Jon
Also see ANDERSON, BRUFORD, WAKEMAN, HOWE
Also see BANKS, Peter
Also see BRUFORD, Bill
Also see BUGGLES
Also see HOWE, Steve, Band
Also see KING CRIMSON
Also see MORAZ, Patrick
Also see PAVLOV'S DOG
Also see SIMON, Paul
Also see SQUIRE, Chris
Also see WAKEMAN, Rick
Also see WHITE, Alan

YES IT IS
Singles: 7-inch
STUDIO CITY (1046"Walking the Dog")....................20-30 66
STUDIO CITY (1052 "That Summer")....................10-15 66

YESTER, Jerry
Singles: 7-inch
DUNHILL....................4-8 66-67
Also see HENSKE, Judy, & Jerry Yester
Also see LOVIN' SPOONFUL

YESTERDAY & TODAY
LPs: 10/12-inch
LONDON....................5-8 76

YESTERDAY'S CHILDREN
Singles: 7-inch
PARROT (314 "To Be Or Not to Be")....................10-15 66

YESTERDAY'S CHILDREN
Singles: 7-inch
SHOWCASE (9812 "Wanna Be with You")....................15-25 67

YESTERDAY'S CHILDREN
LPs: 10/12-inch
MAP....................8-10 70s

YESTERDAY'S FOLK
LPs: 10/12-inch
BUDDAH....................10-15 69

YESTERDAY'S NEWS
LPs: 10/12-inch
ANGELA (100 "Good Old Acapella")....................5-10 80s
(Colored vinyl.)
Members: Tony Delvecchio; Vic Spina; Vinnie Gallo; Charlie Rocco; Dennis Elber.

YESTERDAY'S NEWS / Poppit Brothers
Singles: 7-inch
CRYSTAL BALL (148 "Countdown to Love")....................3-5 85
Picture Sleeves
CRYSTAL BALL (148 "Countdown to Love")....................3-5 85
Also see YESTERDAY'S NEWS

YESTERDAY'S OBSESSION
Singles: 7-inch
PACEMAKER (262 "Complicated Music")....................15-25 66

YESTERDAY'S RHYTHM
LPs: 10/12-inch
YESTERDAY'S RHYTHM....................5-8 80s
Members: Joe Grzybowski; Bob Friedman; Mike Whitmore; Lester Williams; George Carl.

YETTI-MEN / Uppa-Trio
LPs: 10/12-inch
LAK (4348 "The Yetti-men")......500-650 64
(Each group has one side of the LP.)

YIPES!! LP '79
Singles: 7-inch
MILLENNIUM....................3-4 79-80
LPs: 10/12-inch
MILLENNIUM....................5-8 79-80

YO YOs
(Yo-Yos)
Singles: 7-inch
CORAL....................15-25 66
GOLDWAX....................10-20 66
PINCUS (100 "The Nightmare") 100-200 60s

YOAKAM, Dwight C&W/LP '86
Singles: 7-inch
OAK....................15-25 86
REPRISE....................3-4 86-90
LPs: 10/12-inch
OAK (2356 "Guitars, Cadillacs, Etc.")....................500-750 84
REPRISE....................5-8 86-90

YOAKAM, Dwight, & Buck Owens C&W '88
Singles: 7-inch
REPRISE....................3-4 88
Also see OWENS, Buck
Also see YOAKAM, Dwight

YOCHANAN, Muck Muck
Singles: 7-inch
SATURN (4237 "Hot Skillet Momma")....................25-35

YODER, Gary Lee
Singles: 7-inch
EPIC....................3-4 70
Also see OXFORD CIRCLE

YOHO THE PHAROAH
Singles: 7-inch
COLLECTOR (11 "Part One")........30-40 80
(Picture disc. Includes picture sleeve. Promotional issue only.)

YOKOHAMA KNIGHTS
LPs: 10/12-inch
GRT....................8-10 69

YOKOHAMA RAMBLERS
Singles: 7-inch
TOWER....................4-8 66

YOLANDA
(With the Naturals; with Charmanes; with Castanets)
Singles: 7-inch
KIMLEY (923 "My Memories of You")....................50-100 62
SMASH (1777 "Hootchy Cootchy Girl")....................10-20 62
TANDEM (7002 "Meet Me After School")....................20-30 61

YONAH
Singles: 7-inch
FREE FLIGHT....................3-5 70

YONKER, David
Singles: 7-inch
AUDIO UNLIMITED (6359 "A Song")....................15-25 67

YORE, Joseph
Singles: 7-inch
SILVERTIP....................4-8 62

YOREY, Bobby
Singles: 7-inch
SOOZEE....................4-8 62

YORGESSON, Yogi P&R '49
(With the Johnny Duffy Trio; Harry Stewart)
Singles: 78 rpm
CAPITOL....................4-8 49-55
S&H (3009 "My Clam Digger Sweetheart")....................10-20
Singles: 7-inch
CAPITOL (700 thru 3000 series)......5-10 49-55
EPs: 7-inch
CAPITOL....................10-15 52-53
LPs: 10/12-inch
CAPITOL (336 "Family Album").....30-50 53
(10-inch LP.)
Also see KARI, Harry, & His Six Saki Sippers

YORK, Dave, & Beachcombers P&R '62
Singles: 7-inch
LANCELOT (6 "Beach Party")........15-25 62
P-K-M. (6700 "Beach Party")..........8-12 62
Session: Glen Campbell; Gary Paxon; Steve Douglas; Jerry Reaple; Ray Polman.
Also see CAMPBELL, Glen
Also see DOUGLAS, Steve
Also see PAXTON, Gary

YORK, Fred: see JALOPY FIVE

YORK, Johnny
Singles: 7-inch
BEV MAR (605 "True Lovers").......25-35 60s

YORK, Laura Sue
Singles: 7-inch
PHILIPS....................3-5 64-65

YORK, Rusty P&R '59
(With J.D. Jarvis)
Singles: 7-inch
CAPITOL....................3-5 61
CHESS....................5-8 59
GAYLORD....................3-5 63
KING (5100 series)....................5-8 58
KING (5500 series)....................4-6 61-62
MERCURY....................15-25 58
NOTE....................20-30 59
P.J.....................10-15 59
SAGE....................10-15 60
EPs: 7-inch
BLUE GRASS....................10-15 61
JEWEL....................8-12 61
LPs: 10/12-inch
QUEEN CITY....................10-15
RURAL RHYTHM....................8-12
Also see CAJUNS
Also see MACK, Lonnie, & Rusty York

YORK BROTHERS
Singles: 78 rpm
DECCA....................20-30 57
KING....................5-10 52
Singles: 7-inch
DECCA (30473 "Everybody's Tryin' to Be My Baby")....................20-30 57
KING....................10-15 52
EPs: 7-inch
KING....................10-15 57
LPs: 10/12-inch
KING....................20-40 58-63
Member: Leslie York.

YORKSHIRE PUDDING
Singles: 7-inch
DELLWOOD (1 "Black Jacket Woman")....................10-20 67
DELLWOOD (3932 "Good Night Day")....................10-20 67

YORKSHIRES
Singles: 7-inch
WESTCHESTER (1000 "Tossed Aside")....................10-20 60s

YORKVILLE EVOLUTION
LPs: 10/12-inch
YORKVILLE....................5-8

YOST, Dennis
Singles: 7-inch
MGM....................3-4 75
ROBOX....................3-4 81
LPs: 10/12-inch
ACCORD....................5-8 81
PHONORAMA....................10-15 82
ROBOX....................10-15 81
Also see CLASSICS IV

YOU & ME
Singles: 7-inch
CHARTMAKER (409 "I Got That Feeling")....................10-20

YOU KNOW WHO GROUP P&R '64
Singles: 7-inch
CASUAL....................4-6 65
4 CORNERS....................4-6 64
INT'L ALLIED....................5-10 65
Picture Sleeves
INT'L ALLIED (823 "This Day Love")....................10-15 65
LPs: 10/12-inch
INT'L ALLIED....................15-20 65

YOULDEN, Chris
LPs: 10/12-inch
LONDON....................8-10 73-74
Also see SAVOY BROWN

YOUNG, April
Singles: 7-inch
COLUMBIA....................4-8 64-65

YOUNG, Barry P&R '65
Singles: 7-inch
COLUMBIA (43584 "A Heart Without a Home")....................4-8 66
DOT....................5-10 65-66
EVA (102 "Come on Pretty Baby")...8-12 63
HOOKS BROTHERS....................4-6 66
Picture Sleeves
COLUMBIA....................4-8 66
LPs: 10/12-inch
DOT....................15-25 65

YOUNG, Beamon
Singles: 7-inch
ARVEE....................5-10 59

YOUNG, Betty
Singles: 7-inch
RISING SONS....................4-8 67

YOUNG, Billy
Singles: 7-inch
CHESS (1961 "You Left the Water Running")....................8-12 66
JOTIS (429 "Sloopy")....................8-12 65
MERCURY (72693 "Nothing's Too Much")....................10-15 67
MERCURY (72769 "Let Them Talk")....................8-12 68
ORIGINAL SOUND (29 "Are You for Me")....................8-12 63
SHOUT (236 "I'm Available")..........8-12 68

YOUNG, Billy Joe
Singles: 7-inch
JEWEL....................4-8 66
PAULA....................4-8 66

YOUNG, Bob
Singles: 7-inch
PACIFIC CHALLENGER....................4-8 67

YOUNG, Bobby
Singles: 7-inch
FOXIE....................4-8 62

YOUNG, Bobby
(With Rick & the Masters)
Singles: 7-inch
GUYDEN (2087 "To Each His Own")....................150-200 63
Also see RICK & MASTERS

YOUNG, Cathy
Singles: 7-inch
MAINSTREAM....................3-6 69
LPs: 10/12-inch
MAINSTREAM....................8-10

YOUNG, Cecil
(Cecil Young Quartet)
Singles: 78 rpm
KING....................10-15 52-54
Singles: 7-inch
KING (4604 "That Old Black Magic")....................20-40 53
KING (4638 "Fish Net")....................20-40 53
KING (4692 "Ooh Diga-Gow")........20-40 54
KING (4749 "Who Parked the Car")....................20-40 54
KING (15165 "Tea for Two")..........20-40 52
KING (15174 "Night & Day")..........20-40 52
KING (15175 "Rushin' on Home")..20-40 52
KING (15192 "South of the Border")....................20-40 52
EPs: 7-inch
KING (247 "Cecil Young Quartet")....................30-40 53
KING (277 "Cecil Young Quartet, Vol. 2")....................30-40 53
KING (374 "Modern Sounds")........20-30 56
LPs: 10/12-inch
AUDIO LAB (1516 "Jazz on the Rock")....................30-40 59
KING (1 "Cecil Young Quartet")....50-100 52
(10-inch LP.)
KING (505 "Concert of Cool Jazz")....................40-60 56
Also see STARGLOWS / Rock-A-Bouts / Cecil Young Quartet

YOUNG, Chip
Singles: 7-inch
ESCO....................15-25 60

YOUNG, Cole C&W '83
Singles: 7-inch
EVERGREEN....................3-4 83

YOUNG, Colin
Singles: 7-inch
UNI....................3-6 72
Also see FOUNDATIONS

YOUNG, Cortez
Singles: 7-inch
GOLD (101 "Everybody's Going")..50-75

YOUNG, De De
(Dee Dee Young)
Singles: 7-inch
ASCOT....................4-8 62
CHALLENGE....................4-8 64

YOUNG, Debbie
Singles: 7-inch
SOUL TIME....................4-8 60s

YOUNG, Don
Singles: 7-inch
BANG....................4-6 69

YOUNG, Don, & Memory Machine
LPs: 10/12-inch
PROJECT THREE....................8-10 77

YOUNG, Donna Jean
Singles: 7-inch
LAD....................5-10 59

YOUNG, Donny
Singles: 7-inch
DECCA (Except 31077)....................10-15 61
DECCA (31077 "Shakin' the Blues")....................20-25 60
MERCURY....................5-10 61-62
TODD....................4-8 64
Also see PAYCHECK, Johnny

YOUNG, Donny, & Roger Miller
Singles: 7-inch
DECCA (30763 "On This Mountain Top")....................15-25 58
Also see MILLER, Roger
Also see YOUNG, Donny

YOUNG, Eve P&R '48
(Karen Chandler)
Singles: 78 rpm
RCA....................4-8 48-49
Also see CHANDLER, Karen

YOUNG, Faron C&W '53
(With Margie Singleton; with Anita Kerr Singers; with Jordanaires)
Singles: 78 rpm
CAPITOL....................5-10 53-57
Singles: 7-inch
CAPITOL (2200 thru 3900 series)...5-10 53-58
CAPITOL (4000 thru 4800 series).....4-8 58-62
MCA....................3-5 79-80
MERCURY....................3-6 63-78
Picture Sleeves
CAPITOL....................5-10 61
MERCURY....................4-8 62-68
EPs: 7-inch
CAPITOL....................8-15 54-61
REPERTORY (1 "And Now")..........10-15
LPs: 10/12-inch
ALBUM GLOBE....................5-8 81
ALLEGIANCE....................5-8 84
BULLDOG....................5-10
CBS....................5-8 83
CAPITOL (778 "Sweethearts Or Strangers")....................30-50 57
CAPITOL (1004 "Object of My Affection")....................30-50 58
CAPITOL (1096 "This Is Faron Young")....................30-50 58
CAPITOL (1185 "My Garden of Prayer")....................30-50 59
CAPITOL (1245 "Talk About Hits") 30-40 59
CAPITOL (1450 thru 2536)..........12-25 60-66
(With "T," "DT" or "ST" prefix.)
CAPITOL (1500 series)....................5-8 75
(With "SM" prefix.)
CASTLE....................5-8
EXACT....................5-8 80
FARON YOUNG (001 "20 Great Hits")....................10-20
FARON YOUNG (003 "Family Favorites")....................10-15
FARON YOUNG (004 "Faron Young Presents the Country Deputies")....................10-15
FARON YOUNG (4-22-82 "Fortunes in Music")....................8-15 82
IMPACT....................5-10
K-TEL....................5-10 77
MCA....................4-8 79-83
MARY CARTER PAINTS (1000 "Faron Young Sings on Stage")....................20-30
(Promotional issue only.)
MERCURY....................5-15 63-77
MOUNTAIN DEW....................5-10
PHONORAMA....................5-8 82
PICADILLY....................5-10 80
PICKWICK/HILLTOP....................8-12 66-68
REALM....................5-8 81
SEARS....................8-12
TOWER....................12-15 66-68
WING....................8-12 68
Session: Don Adams; Jordanaires.
Also see ADAMS, Don
Also see ATKINS, Chet, Faron Young, & Anita Kerr Singers
Also see CLEMENTS, Vassar
Also see FRANKS, Tillman
Also see JORDANAIRES
Also see KERR, Anita
Also see MORRIS, Lamar
Also see NELSON, Willie / Faron Young
Also see OWENS, Buck / Faron Young / Ferlin Husky

YOUNG, Faron / Carl Perkins / Claude King
LPs: 10/12-inch
PICKWICK/HILLTOP....................8-15 65
Also see KING, Claude
Also see PERKINS, Carl

YOUNG, Faron / Jean Shepard
EPs: 7-inch
CAPITOL CUSTOM (118-30 "Recorded Especially for Ballard Flour")....................10-20
(Promotional issue, made for Ballard Flour.)
Also see SHEPARD, Jean
Also see YOUNG, Faron

YOUNG, Faron, & Margie Singleton C&W '64
Singles: 7-inch
MERCURY....................4-6 64

Also see SINGLETON, Margie
Also see YOUNG, Faron

YOUNG, Freddy
Singles: 7-inch
FRIENDLY FIVE ... 10-15 63

YOUNG, George, & Sidemen
Singles: 7-inch
KAPP ... 3-5 65

YOUNG, Georgie P&R '58
(With the Rockin' Bocs; George Young)
Singles: 7-inch
CAMEO ... 4-6 58-59
CHANCELLOR ... 3-5 61
COLUMBIA (42773 "Supercar") ... 10-20 63
FORTUNE ... 5-8 57
MERCURY (71259 "Can't Stop Me") ... 30-40 58
PACE SETTER ... 5-8
PARKWAY (809 "Gold Rush") ... 10-15 60
SWAN ... 4-6 60

YOUNG, Gordon
Singles: 7-inch
FELSTED ... 5-10 59

YOUNG, Greg
Singles: 7-inch
KENT ... 5-10 60

YOUNG, James "Big Sambo"
Singles: 7-inch
JET STREAM ... 4-8

YOUNG, Jerry
Singles: 7-inch
CALLENDER ... 5-8 61

YOUNG, Jesse Colin LP '72
(With the Youngbloods)
Singles: 7-inch
ELEKTRA ... 3-4 78
REPRISE ... 3-4 73
W.B. ... 3-4 70-77
LPs: 10/12-inch
CAPITOL (2000 series) ... 20-25 64
CAPITOL (11000 series) ... 8-10 74
CAPITOL (16000 series) ... 5-8 80
ELEKTRA ... 5-8 78
MERCURY (61005 "Young Blood") ... 20-25 65
MERCURY (61273 "Two Trips") ... 10-15 70
W.B. ... 8-10 72-77
Also see YOUNGBLOODS

YOUNG, Jimmy
Singles: 78 rpm
EMBER (1003 "Need Your Love") ... 8-12 56
Singles: 7-inch
EMBER (1003 "Need Your Love") ... 20-25 56

YOUNG, John Paul P&R '75
Singles: 7-inch
ARIOLA AMERICA ... 3-4 75-76
SCOTTI BROTHERS ... 3-4 78
LPs: 10/12-inch
SCOTTI BROTHERS ... 5-8 78

YOUNG, Johnny
(Man Young)
Singles: 78 rpm
OLD SWINGMASTER (19 "My Baby Walked Out on Me") ... 50-100 48
ORA NELLE (712 "Worried Man Blues") ... 50-100 47
PLANET (103 "My Baby Walked Out on Me") ... 100-150 48
LPs: 10/12-inch
ARHOOLIE ... 10-15
BLUE HORIZON ... 10-20
BLUESWAY ... 8-12 73
Also see PRYOR, Snooky
Also see WILLIAMS, Big Joe, & Johnny Young
Also see YOUNG, Man

YOUNG, Johnny, & Big Walter
LPs: 10/12-inch
ARHOOLIE ... 10-15
Also see BIG WALTER
Also see YOUNG, Johnny

YOUNG, Jonathan
Singles: 7-inch
ARVEE ... 4-8 61

YOUNG, Karen P&R/R&B '78
Singles: 7-inch
WEST END ... 3-4 78

YOUNG, Kathy P&R '60
(With the Innocents)
Singles: 7-inch
COLLECTABLES ... 3-4 80s
ERA ... 3-4 72
ERIC ... 3-4 70s
INDIGO ... 10-15 60-62
MONOGRAM ... 8-10 62
STARFIRE ... 3-6 79
VIRGO ... 3-4 72
Picture Sleeves
INDIGO ... 6-12 60-61
EPs: 7-inch
INDIGO (1001 ""Kathy Young") ... 50-75 61
LPs: 10/12-inch
INDIGO (504 "The Sound of Kathy Young") ... 50-100 61
STARFIRE (1000 "Our Best to You") ... 12-18 81
(Picture disc on one side, black vinyl on flip.)
Also see CHRIS & KATHY
Also see INNOCENTS
Also see WASHER WINDSHIELD

YOUNG, Kathy / Innocents
Singles: 7-inch
TRIP ... 3-5 70s
Also see INNOCENTS
Also see YOUNG, Kathy

YOUNG, Kenneth, & English Muffins
Singles: 7-inch
DIAMOND ... 5-8 65

YOUNG, Kenny
Singles: 7-inch
ATCO ... 5-10 64
MGM ... 4-8 63
SHARE ... 4-6 69
U.A. ... 4-8 66
W.B. ... 3-5 72
LPs: 10/12-inch
W.B. ... 8-12 72

YOUNG, Leon
Singles: 7-inch
ATCO (6301 "John, Paul, George & Ringo") ... 5-10 64
LPs: 10/12-inch
ATCO (163 "Liverpool Sound") ... 15-25 64

YOUNG, Lester R&B '44
(With His Kansas City Five; Lester Young Quartet)
Singles: 78 rpm
ALADDIN ... 5-10 46-47
KEYNOTE ... 5-10 44
MERCURY ... 5-10 44
SAVOY ... 4-8 45-46
Singles: 7-inch
ALADDIN ... 20-30 53-54
EPs: 7-inch
ALADDIN ... 35-55 53
CLEF ... 25-50 51-53
EMARCY ... 25-50 54
MERCURY ... 35-55 50
NORGRAN ... 35-55 52-54
SAVOY ... 20-40 51
LPs: 10/12-inch
ALADDIN (706 "Lester Young and His Tenor Sax") ... 150-250 53
(10-inch LP.)
ALADDIN (801 "Lester Young and His Tenor Sax, Vol. 1") ... 75-125 56
ALADDIN (802 "Lester Young and His Tenor Sax, Vol. 2") ... 75-125 56
AMERICAN RECORDING SOCIETY (8205 "Pres & Teddy") ... 35-50 57
CHARLIE PARKER (402 "Pres") ... 30-50 62
CHARLIE PARKER (405 "Pres Is Blue") ... 30-50 62
CLEF (104 "Lester Young Trio") ... 100-200 51
(10-inch LP.)
CLEF (10 "Lester Young Collates") ... 100-200 52
(10-inch LP.)
CLEF (10 "Lester Young Collates No. 2") ... 100-200 53
(10-inch LP.)
CLEF (135 "Lester Young Trio, No. 2") ... 100-200 53
(10-inch LP.)
COMMODORE (20021 "Kansas City Style") ... 100-200 50
(10-inch LP.)
COMMODORE (30014 "Kansas City Style") ... 50-75 59
EMARCY (26021 "Pres Meets Vice-Pres") ... 100-200 54
(10-inch LP.)
EPIC (3107 "Lester Leaps In") ... 50-100 56
EPIC (3168 "Let's Go to Prez") ... 50-100 56
EPIC (3576 "Memorial Album, Vol 1") ... 40-60 59
EPIC (3576 "Memorial Album, Vol 2") ... 40-60 59
EPIC (6031 "Memorial Album") ... 50-100 59
(Two discs.)
INTRO (602 "Swinging") ... 50-100 57
INTRO (603 "The Greatest") ... 50-100 57
JAZZTONE (1218 "Prez & Chu") ... 50-75
MAINSTREAM (6012 "Prez") ... 25-35 65
(Stereo.)
MAINSTREAM (56012 "Prez") ... 25-35 65
(Monaural.)
MERCURY (25015 "Lester Young Quartet") ... 150-250 50
(10-inch LP.)
NORGRAN (1005 "The President") ... 50-100 54
NORGRAN (1022 "Lester Young") ... 50-100 54
NORGRAN (1043 "Pres & Sweets") ... 50-100 55
NORGRAN (1071 "Lester' Here") ... 50-75 55
NORGRAN (1072 "Pres") ... 50-75 55
NORGRAN (1074 "Lester Young & the Buddy Rich Trio") ... 50-75 55
NORGRAN (1093 "Lester Swings Again") ... 40-60 56
SAVOY (9002 "All Star Be-Bop") ... 150-250 51
SAVOY (12068 "Blue Lester") ... 40-60 56
SAVOY (12071 "Master's Touch") ... 40-60 56
SAVOY (12155 "Immortal") ... 30-50 59
SAVOY (1109 "Lester Young") ... 10-15 77
SCORE (4028 "Swinging") ... 40-60 58
SCORE (4029 "The Greatest") ... 40-60 58
VSP (27 "Pres & His Cabinet") ... 20-30 66
VERVE (2516 "Lester Swings") ... 10-20 77
(Two discs.)
VERVE (2518 "Bird & Pres") ... 10-20 77
(Two discs.)
VERVE (6054 "Laughin' to Keep from Crying") ... 50-70 59
(Stereo.)
VERVE (8161 "Lester' Here") ... 40-60 57
VERVE (8162 "Pres") ... 40-60 57
VERVE (8164 "Lester Young & the Buddy Rich Trio") ... 40-60 57
VERVE (8181 "Lester Swings Again") ... 40-60 57
VERVE (8187 "It Don't Mean a Thing") ... 40-60 57
VERVE (8205 "Pres & Teddy") ... 40-60 57
VERVE (8298 "Going for Myself") ... 40-60 59
VERVE (8303 "The Lester Young Story") ... 40-60 59
VERVE (8316 "Laughin' to Keep from Crying") ... 40-60 59
(Monaural.)
VERVE (8378 "In Paris") ... 40-60 59
VERVE (8398 "The Essential Lester Young") ... 30-50 61
Session: Red Callender; Howard McGhee; Paul Quinchette; Buddy Rich; Ray Brown; John Lewis; Connie Kay; Harry Edison; Chu Berry; Kenny Clarke; Roy Eldridge; Teddy Wilson; Count Basie; Coleman Hawkins.
Also see BASIE, Count
Also see CALLENDER, Red
Also see JACQUET, Illinois / Lester Young

YOUNG, Lester, & Nat "King" Cole
Singles: 78 rpm
PHILCO ... 5-10 42
EPs: 7-inch
ALADDIN ... 20-40 53
LPs: 10/12-inch
ALADDIN (705 "Lester Young Trio with Nat 'King' Cole") ... 100-200 53
(10-inch LP.)
SCORE (4019 "Lester Young Trio with Nat 'King' Cole") ... 50-75 58
Also see COLE, Nat "King"
Also see PETERSON, Oscar

YOUNG, Lester, Nat "King" Cole & Buddy Rich
LPs: 10/12-inch
VSP (30 "Giants 3") ... 20-30 66
Also see RICH, Buddy
Also see YOUNG, Lester, & Nat "King" Cole

YOUNG, Lester, & Oscar Peterson
EPs: 7-inch
NORGRAN ... 20-40 52
LPs: 10/12-inch
NORGRAN (5 "Lester Young with Oscar Peterson") ... 100-150 52
(10-inch LP.)
NORGRAN (6 "Lester Young with Oscar Peterson, No. 2") ... 100-150 52
(10-inch LP.)
NORGRAN (1054 "The President Plays with the Oscar Peterson Trio") ... 50-100 55
VERVE (8144 "The President Plays with the Oscar Peterson Trio") ... 50-75 57
Also see PETERSON, Oscar
Also see YOUNG, Lester

YOUNG, Lester
(With the California Playboys)
Singles: 7-inch
ANGLE TONE ... 5-10 60s
BARRY (1009 "Stop") ... 10-15 66
CHASE (1200 "Wobble Time") ... 5-10 63
OLD TOWN (1186 "I Got the Right") ... 5-10 65
UNITY ... 4-8 68

YOUNG, Mae
Singles: 7-inch
KARATE ... 10-20 66

YOUNG, Man: see YOUNG, Johnny

YOUNG, Mighty Joe
Singles: 78 rpm
JIFFY ... 10-20 56
Singles: 7-inch
JIFFY ("Broke, Downhearted and Disgusted") ... 20-40 56
(Selection number not known.)
USA ... 5-10 60s
WEBCOR (102 "Hey Baby") ... 8-12 65
WET SOUL (3 "The Rains Came") ... 4-8
LPs: 10/12-inch
DELMARK ... 8-12 71
OVATION ... 5-10 74

YOUNG, Monalisa
Singles: 7-inch
MOTOWN ... 3-4 83
LPs: 10/12-inch
MOTOWN ... 5-8 83

YOUNG, Neil LP '69
(With Crazy Horse; with Shocking Pinks; with Bluenotes)
Singles: 12-inch
GEFFEN ... 4-6 86
Singles: 7-inch
GEFFEN ... 3-4 83-86
REPRISE (0785 thru 0898) ... 3-5 68-70
REPRISE (0911 thru 1396) ... 3-5 70-79
(Black vinyl.)
REPRISE (1395 "Comes a Time") ... 250-300 78
(Picture disc. 200 numbered copies made. Promotional issue only.)
REPRISE (49000 series, except 49895) ... 3-5 79-81
REPRISE (49895 "Southern Pacific") ... 250-350 81
(Triangular picture disc. Promotional issue only. Green vinyl. 25 made.)
REPRISE (49895 "Southern Pacific") ... 250-350 81
(Auto- or train-shaped picture disc. Promotional issue only. 10 made of each shape.)
REPRISE (49895 "Southern Pacific") ... 15-25 81
(Triangular picture disc. Promotional issue only. With either red or black vinyl.)
Picture Sleeves
GEFFEN ... 3-4 83
REPRISE ... 3-4 78-81
EPs: 7-inch
REPRISE ... 10-15 72
(Juke box issue only.)
LPs: 10/12-inch
GEFFEN ... 5-8 83-87
MFSL (252 "Old Ways") ... 15-25 95
REPRISE (2000 series, except 2257 & 2296) ... 5-8 72-90
REPRISE (2257 "Decade") ... 12-15 77
REPRISE (2296 "Live Rust") ... 10-12 79
REPRISE (6317 "Neil Young") ... 50-100 68
(Front cover does NOT have Neil Young's name.)
REPRISE (6317 "Neil Young") ... 8-12 68
(Front cover shows Neil Young's name.)
REPRISE (6349 "Everybody Knows This Is Nowhere") ... 10-12 69
REPRISE (6383 "After the Gold Rush") ... 10-12 70
REPRISE (6480 "Journey Through the Past") ... 12-15 72
REPRISE (25000 thru 46000 series) ... 5-12 88-96
W.B. ... 6-15 72-79
Session: Waylon Jennings.
Also see BUFFALO SPRINGFIELD
Also see CASCADES
Also see CRAZY HORSE
Also see CROSBY, STILLS, NASH & YOUNG
Also see DANNY & MEMORIES
Also see HARRIS, Emmylou
Also see JENNINGS, Waylon
Also see LARSON, Nicolette
Also see SQUIRES
Also see STILLS - YOUNG BAND

YOUNG, Neil, & Jim Messina
Singles: 7-inch
REPRISE ... 3-5 70
Also see MESSINA, Jim

YOUNG, Neil, & Graham Nash P&R '72
Singles: 7-inch
REPRISE ... 3-4 72
Also see NASH, Graham
Also see YOUNG, Neil

YOUNG, Nelson
(With the Sandy Valley Boys)
Singles: 7-inch
LUCKY (0002 "Rock Old Sputnik") ... 150-200 59
MADISON (3003 "Charlie Brown's Mule") ... 50-100 59
RUBY (310 "Hillybilly Rock & Roll") ... 50-100 57
VETCO (526 "Big Pipeline") ... 25-50

YOUNG, Patti
Singles: 7-inch
ERNSTRAT (495 "Head and Shoulders") ... 100-150

YOUNG, Paul P&R '83
Singles: 12-inch
COLUMBIA ... 4-6 83-86
Singles: 7-inch
COLUMBIA ... 3-4 83-86
EPIC (Except 11116) ... 3-4 86
EPIC (11116 "Every Fool Has His Reasons") ... 4-6 74
Picture Sleeves
COLUMBIA ... 3-4 83-86
LPs: 10/12-inch
COLUMBIA ... 5-8 84-90
Also see BAND AID
Also see MIKE + THE MECHANICS
Also see SAD CAFE

YOUNG, Paul, & Versatones
Singles: 7-inch
BECK ... 8-10 63

YOUNG, Reggie
Singles: 7-inch
SCEPTER ... 4-6 71

YOUNG, Retta R&B '75
Singles: 7-inch
ALL PLATINUM ... 3-4 75

YOUNG, Roger C&W '79
Singles: 7-inch
DESSA ... 3-5 79

YOUNG, Roy
Singles: 7-inch
20TH FOX ... 4-8 61
LPs: 10/12-inch
KAPP ... 8-10 72

YOUNG, Sonny
Singles: 7-inch
S.P.Q.R. ... 4-8 64

YOUNG, Steve C&W '77
Singles: 7-inch
RCA ... 3-5 76-78
LPs: 10/12-inch
A&M ... 10-15 69
RCA ... 10-15 68

YOUNG, Tami
Singles: 7-inch
MODERN ... 4-8 68

YOUNG, Tommie R&B '73
Singles: 7-inch
MCA ... 3-5 78
SOUL POWER ... 3-5 73-75
LPs: 10/12-inch
MCA ... 5-10 78

YOUNG, Tony
Singles: 7-inch
CAMEO ... 4-8 62

YOUNG, Val R&B/D&D '85
Singles: 12-inch
GORDY ... 4-6 85-86
Singles: 7-inch
AMHERST ... 3-4 87
GORDY ... 3-4 85-86
LPs: 10/12-inch
GORDY ... 5-8 85-86
Also see BRIDES OF FUNKENSTEIN
Also see GAP BAND

YOUNG, Vern
(With the Ambassadors)
Singles: 7-inch
CHORDS (101 "Cindy Lou") ... 5-10 60

YOUNG, Vicki
Singles: 78 rpm
BRUNSWICK ... 5-10 57
CAPITOL ... 5-10 54-56
Singles: 7-inch
BRUNSWICK ... 5-10 57
CAPITOL ... 8-15 54-56
EPs: 7-inch
CAPITOL (593 "Riot in Cell Block #9") ... 20-40 54

YOUNG, Vicki, & Joe Carr
(With the Joy Riders)
Singles: 78 rpm
CAPITOL ... 5-8 56
Singles: 7-inch
CAPITOL ... 8-12 56
Also see CARR, Joe "Fingers"
Also see YOUNG, Vicki

YOUNG, Victor P&R '31
Singles: 78 rpm
BRUNSWICK ... 3-5 31-34
DECCA ... 3-4 34-57
Singles: 7-inch
DECCA ... 3-4 50-57
EPs: 7-inch
DECCA ... 3-6 50-57
LPs: 10/12-inch
DECCA ... 5-15 50-59
Also see CROSBY, Bing
Also see GARLAND, Judy

YOUNG, William, & Jamaicans
Singles: 7-inch
DIMENSION ... 5-10 63

YOUNG ALLEY CATS
Singles: 7-inch
ROBIN (100 "Since You Been Gone") ... 10-15 66

YOUNG AMERICANS LP '69
LPs: 10/12-inch
ABC ... 5-10 69

YOUNG & COMPANY
Singles: 7-inch
ATLANTIC ... 3-4 86
BRUNSWICK ... 3-5 81
RCA ... 4-6 69
LPs: 10/12-inch
BRUNSWICK ... 5-8 81

YOUNG & RESTLESS LP '90
LPs: 10/12-inch
PANDISC ... 5-8 90

YOUNG ARISTOCRACY
Singles: 7-inch
ACROPOLIS (6721 "Don't Lie") ... 10-20 67

YOUNG AT HEART
Singles: 7-inch
FOUR WAYS ... 4-8 67

YOUNG BROTHERS
Singles: 7-inch
SOUL POWER ("What's Your Game") ... 350-400
(Selection number not known.)

YOUNG CALIFORNIANS
Singles: 7-inch
FLICK CITY ... 4-8 69

YOUNG CANADIANS
Singles: 7-inch
FILMWAYS (109 "Making My Mind Up") ... 15-25 60s

YOUNG CHICAGOANS
Singles: 7-inch
DESTINATION (636 "Summertime Blues") ... 10-15 67

YOUNG ENTERPRISE
Singles: 7-inch
FONTANA ... 4-8 69
RUST (5111 "Think I'm Gonna Make It") ... 5-10 65

YOUNG EXECUTIVES
Singles: 7-inch
MERCURY ... 5-10 66

YOUNG FOLKS
Singles: 7-inch
MAR-V-LUS (6017 "Lonely Girl") ... 8-15 67

YOUNG FRESH FELLOWS
Singles: 7-inch
POPLLAMA ... 3-4 85-86
EPs: 7-inch
POPLLAMA ... 3-5 87
LPs: 10/12-inch
POPLLAMA ... 5-8 84-86

POPLLAMA/FRONTIER ... 5-8 87
Members: Scott McCaughey; Tad Hutchison; Jim Sangster; Chuck Carroll.

YOUNG GENERATION
Singles: 7-inch
CAPTAIN ... 8-12
RED BIRD ... 8-12 66
Member: Janis Siegel.
Also see MANHATTAN TRANSFER

YOUNG GENTS
Singles: 7-inch
BUDDAH ... 4-8 69

YOUNG HEARTS P&R/R&B '68
(Younghearts)
Singles: 7-inch
AVCO EMBASSY (4554 "Change of Mind") ... 5-10 70
MINIT (32039 "Oh, I'll Never Be the Same") ... 5-10 68
MINIT (32049 "I've Got Love for My Baby") ... 20-30 69
SOULTOWN (3000 "I've Got Dancing Fever") ... 10-20
20TH FOX (2080 "Me & You") ... 4-6 74
20TH FOX (2130 "Wake Up and Start Sanding") ... 4-6 75
LPs: 10/12-inch
MINIT ... 15-25 69
Members: Ronald Preyer; Earl Carter; James Moore; Charles Ingersoll; Bob Solomon.
Also see NEW YOUNG HEARTS

YOUNG - HOLT UNLIMITED
(Young-Holt Trio) P&R/R&B '66
Singles: 7-inch
BRUNSWICK ... 4-6 66-69
COTILLION ... 3-5 70-71
ERIC ... 3-4 83
PAULA ... 3-5 73
LPs: 10/12-inch
ATLANTIC ... 8-10 73
BRUNSWICK ... 10-20 67-69
COTILLION ... 8-12 70-71
PAULA ... 5-10 73
Members: Eldee Young; Isaac Holt; Floyd Morris.
Also see LEWIS, Ramsey
Also see VALENTINE BROTHERS

YOUNG IDEA
Singles: 7-inch
CAPITOL ... 4-8 67-68

YOUNG IDEAS
Singles: 7-inch
SWAN ... 5-10 59

YOUNG IDEAS
Singles: 7-inch
ABC ... 4-6 68
DATE ... 4-6 68

YOUNG IMAGINATION
Singles: 7-inch
(S-80 142 "Your Friend") ... 4-8 60s
(No label name used.)

YOUNG JESSIE
(Obediah Jessie)
MODERN ... 8-12 54-56
Singles: 7-inch
ATLANTIC ... 15-25 58
CAPITOL ... 10-15 59
DCP ... 5-10 65
MERCURY ... 5-10 61-63
MODERN (921 "I Smell a Rat") ... 30-50 54
MODERN (961 "Mary Lou") ... 30-50 55
MODERN (973 "Nothing Seems Right") ... 30-50 55
MODERN (1002 "Hit, Git & Split") ... 30-50 56
MODERN (1010 "Oochie Coochie") ... 30-50 57
VANESSA (101 "Brown Eyes") ... 15-20
Also see FLAIRS
Also see JACKS
Also see JACKSON, Chuck / Young Jessie

YOUNG LADS
Singles: 78 rpm
NEIL (100 "Moonlight") ... 25-50 56
Singles: 7-inch
NEIL (100 "Moonlight") ... 50-100 56

YOUNG LADS
Singles: 7-inch
FELICE (712 "Graduation Kiss") ... 50-100 63

YOUNG LIONS
Singles: 7-inch
DOT (16172 "Little Girl") ... 30-40 60

YOUNG LIONS
Singles: 7-inch
LOMA ... 4-8 65

YOUNG MC P&R/LP '89
Singles: 7-inch
DELICIOUS ... 3-4 89-90
Picture Sleeves
DELICIOUS ... 3-4 89-90
LPs: 10/12-inch
DELICIOUS ... 5-8 89-90

YOUNG MEN
Singles: 7-inch
BOLO ... 8-15 63-64
CAMELOT ... 5-10
Members: Ron Wilderman; Rainier Rey; Larry Wilber; Tom Severns.

YOUNG MEN
Singles: 7-inch
VIVA ... 5-10 68

YOUNG MEN
Singles: 7-inch
MALTESE (105 "A Young Man's Problem") ... 15-25 60s
MALTESE (108 "Go Away Girl") ... 50-75 60s

YOUNG MEN FOUR: see FOUR YOUNG MEN

YOUNG MONKEY MEN
Singles: 7-inch
JADE (101 "Bald Headed Woman") ... 15-25 66
P&M (3648 "I'm Waitin' for the Letter") ... 15-25 67

YOUNG ONES
(Stokes)
Singles: 7-inch
ALON (9025 "Sawdust Floor") ... 8-12 65
Members: Allen Toussaint; Billy Fayard; Al Fayard.
Also see STOKES

YOUNG ONES
(Youngones)
Singles: 7-inch
YUSSELS (7701 "Marie") ... 30-50 62
YUSSELS (7703 "I'm in the Mood for Love") ... 25-40 62
YUSSELS (7704 "Diamonds and Pearls") ... 25-40 62

YOUNG ONES / El Sierros
Singles: 7-inch
RELIC (516 "Sweeter Than"/"Picture of Love") ... 15-25 65
TIMES SQUARE (28 "Gloria") ... 15-25 64
Also see EL SIERROS
Also see YOUNG ONES

YOUNG ONES
Singles: 7-inch
COLUMBIA (43788 "Sour Grapes") ... 8-12 66
Picture Sleeves
COLUMBIA (43788 "Sour Grapes") ... 10-15 66

YOUNG ONES
Singles: 7-inch
SUPER-COOL (7337 "Too Much Lovin' ") ... 30-40 67
Also see CYKLE

YOUNG RASCALS: see RASCALS

YOUNG ROX
Singles: 7-inch
ROX (2014 "Penetration") ... 10-20 60s

YOUNG SAVAGES
Singles: 7-inch
DYNAMIC SOUND (2006 "The Invaders Are Coming") ... 15-25 67
DYNAMIC SOUND (2007 "I Love You Oh So Much") ... 15-25 67
Member: Doc Couty.
Also see COUTY, Doc

YOUNG SAVAGES
Singles: 7-inch
ROULETTE ... 10-15 67-68

YOUNG SISTERS
Singles: 7-inch
MALA ... 4-8 63
PHILIPS ... 3-5 75
TWIRL ... 10-15 60-61

YOUNG TURKS
Singles: 7-inch
ODYSSEY ... 4-8 69

YOUNG TYRANTS
Singles: 7-inch
IN (67101 "She Don't Got the Right") ... 10-20 67
TRY (101 "I Try") ... 15-25 67

YOUNG VANDALS R&B '70
Singles: 7-inch
T-NECK ... 3-5 70

YOUNG VOYAGERS
Singles: 7-inch
RUST ... 4-8 64

YOUNG WILLIAM & JAMAICANS
Singles: 7-inch
DIMENSION (1005 "Limbo Drum") ... 10-20 63

YOUNG WOLF
(Gus Jenkins)
Singles: 78 rpm
COMBO ... 15-25 55
Singles: 7-inch
COMBO (88 "Worries and Troubles") ... 30-50 55
Also see JENKINS, Gus

YOUNG WORLD SINGERS
Singles: 7-inch
DECCA (31660 "Ringo for President") ... 8-12 64

YOUNGBLOOD
Singles: 7-inch
TANGERINE (96 "I Had a Dream") ... 5-10 66

YOUNGBLOOD, Edison
Singles: 7-inch
COMET (101 "Big Bad Betty") ... 25-35 60
HANOVER ... 5-10 59
HERALD ... 5-10 59

YOUNGBLOOD, Freddy
Singles: 7-inch
SOUL SOUND ... 8-10 66

YOUNGBLOOD, Lonnie R&B '72
(Lonnie Youngblood's Combo)
Singles: 7-inch
CAMEO ... 5-10 65
EARTH ... 4-8 60s
LOMA ... 5-10 67-68
RADIO ... 3-5 81
SHAKAT ... 3-5 74
SILVER-TONE ... 4-6
TURBO ... 3-5 71-73
VIBRATION ... 3-5 76
LPs: 10/12-inch
RADIO ... 5-8 81
TURBO ... 8-10 71
Also see HENDRIX, Jimi, & Lonnie Youngblood

YOUNGBLOOD, Oscar
Singles: 7-inch
TOWER ... 4-6 69

YOUNGBLOOD, Sydney P&R/LP '90
Singles: 7-inch
ARISTA ... 3-4 90
LPs: 10/12-inch
ARISTA ... 5-8 90

YOUNGBLOOD, Tommy
Singles: 7-inch
CHATTAHOOCHEE (654 "Hello Darling") ... 10-20 64
CHATTAHOOCHEE (679 "Lonesome for You") ... 10-15 65
CHATTAHOOCHEE (699 "Lonesome for You") ... 5-10 66
J-R-M (004 "Caress Me My Love") ... 5-10 67
KENT ... 3-5 70
NEWPORT (100 "I'm a Man") ... 10-20 62
RAYCO (518 "Now That You're on Your Own") ... 10-15 64
LPs: 10/12-inch
UNITED SUPERIOR ... 8-10

YOUNGBLOODS P&R '66
(Featuring Jesse Colin Young)
Singles: 7-inch
MERCURY ... 5-8 66-69
RCA ... 4-6 66-71
W.B./RACCOON ... 3-4 70-72
Picture Sleeves
RCA ... 4-6 66
LPs: 10/12-inch
RCA (3000 series) ... 5-8 80
(With "ALY1" prefix.)
RCA (3000 series) ... 12-15 67
(With "LPM" or "LSP" prefix.)
RCA (4000 series) ... 10-15 69-71
(With "LPM" or "LSP" prefix.)
RCA (6000 series) ... 12-15 72
W.B./RACOON ... 10-12 70-72
Members: Jesse Colin Young; Jerry Corbit; Joe Bauer; Lowell "Banana" Levinger.
Also see BANANA & BUNCH
Also see BOWIE, David / Joe Cocker / Youngbloods
Also see YOUNG, Jesse Colin

YOUNGER, Cole
LPs: 10/12-inch
ANCHOR ... 8-10 75

YOUNGER, James & Michael: see YOUNGER BROTHERS

YOUNGER, Johnny
Singles: 7-inch
LAURIE ... 5-10 60

YOUNGER, Louis
Singles: 7-inch
FESTIVAL ... 4-8 67

YOUNGER, Scotty, & Outlaws
Singles: 7-inch
DOBROY ... 5-10 61

YOUNGER BROTHERS
Singles: 7-inch
ROULETTE ... 4-8 68
SCEPTER ... 4-8 65
W.B. ... 4-8 63-64
WENDY ... 4-8 67
Also see ORANGE COLORED SKY

YOUNGER BROTHERS C&W '82
(James & Michael Younger)
Singles: 7-inch
AIR ... 3-4 86
MCA ... 3-4 82-83
PERMIAN ... 3-4 85
Members: James Younger; Michael Younger.

YOUNGER BROTHERS BAND C&W '84
Singles: 7-inch
ERP ... 3-4 86
Member: Terry Gehman.

YOUNGER GENERATION
Singles: 7-inch
EPIC ... 4-6 69

YOUNGER SOCIETY
Singles: 7-inch
SMASH ... 4-8 69

YOUNGFOLK
(Young Folk)
Singles: 7-inch
DOUBLE SHOT ... 4-8 67
MERCURY ... 4-8 67

YOUNGHEARTS
Singles: 7-inch
INFINITY (006 "Do Not Forsake Me") ... 150-200 61

YOUNGHEARTS
Singles: 7-inch
ABC ... 3-5 77
CANTERBURY ... 4-6 67
20TH FOX ... 3-5 73-76
LPs: 10/12-inch
ABC ... 5-8 77
20TH FOX ... 8-10 73-74

YOUNGHEARTS (on Minit): see YOUNG HEARTS

YOUNGONES: see YOUNG ONES

YOUNGSTERS
Singles: 78 rpm
EMPIRE ... 25-50 56
Singles: 7-inch
EMPIRE (104 "Shattered Dreams") ... 50-100 56
EMPIRE (107 "You're an Angel") ... 50-100 56
EMPIRE (109 "Dreamy Eyes"/"Dreamy Eyes") ... 150-250 56
EMPIRE (109 "Dreamy Eyes"/"I'm Sorry Now") ... 50-100 56
EMPIRE (109 "Dreamy Eyes"/"Christmas in Jail") ... 40-60 56
Members: Charles Everidge; Harold Murray; James Warren; Homer Green.
Also see FIVE SATINS / Youngtones / Youngsters / Shells
Also see TEMPTERS

YOUNGSTERS
Singles: 7-inch
APT (25021 "Sweet Talk") ... 20-30 58
CHECKER (917 "Lucky Sixteen") ... 15-20 59

YOUNGSTERS
Singles: 7-inch
CANDELITE (428 "You Told Another Lie") ... 8-12 63
Also see LITTLE PETE & YOUNGSTERS

YOUNGSTERS
Singles: 7-inch
BLUE BERRY SUNSHINE ... 8-12 69
JUBILEE ... 8-12 69
YOUNSTERS (8478 "Telling Lies") ... 40-60 67

YOUNGSTERS
Singles: 7-inch
MELIC (4115 "Organ Grinder") ... 10-15 61

YOUNGSTERS / Danny Zella
Singles: 7-inch
SHOW-BIZ (555 "Zebra") ... 8-12 60s
Also see ZELLA, Danny

YOUNGTONES
Singles: 7-inch
BRUNSWICK (55089 "Come On Baby") ... 50-75 58

YOUNGTONES
Singles: 7-inch
CANDLELITE (417 "You I Adore") ... 10-15 63
TIMES SQUARE (13 "Patricia") ... 10-12 63
(Black vinyl.)
TIMES SQUARE (13 "Patricia") ... 12-18 63
(Colored vinyl.)
TIMES SQUARE (28 "Gloria") ... 10-12 64
X-TRA (104 "You I Adore") ... 100-150 57
(Titles and artists in 1/8-inch letters. Label also has double horizontal lines.)
X-TRA (110 "Patricia") ... 50-75 58
(Titles and artists in 1/8-inch letters. Label also has double horizontal lines.)
X-TRA (120 "Can I Come Over") ... 150-200 59
(Titles and artists in 1/8-inch letters. Label also has double horizontal lines.)
X-TRA (120 "Can I Come Over") ... 30-40 59
(Titles and artists in 1/4-inch letters.)
Member: Ron Jackson.
Also see FIVE SATINS / Youngtones / Youngsters / Shells

YOUNGTONES / Blasters
Singles: 7-inch
TIMES SQUARE (31 "I Do") ... 10-12 64
Also see YOUNGTONES

YOUNG'UN
Singles: 7-inch
MERCURY ... 3-5 75

YOUNG-UNS
EPs: 7-inch
FENTON ... 25-35 66

YOUR FRIENDS
Singles: 7-inch
SOLA (14 "Sun Burned Idol") ... 10-15 67

YOUR GANG
LPs: 10/12-inch
MERCURY ... 10-20 66

YO-YOZ
Singles: 7-inch
IKON ... 4-8

YUKON
Singles: 7-inch
SUSSEX ... 3-5 71

YUKON, Johnny
Singles: 7-inch
VERSATILE ... 5-10 59-60

YUM YUM KIDS
LPs: 10/12-inch
MGM ... 10-15 66

YUM YUMS
Singles: 7-inch
ABC-PAR (10697 "Looky Looky") ... 10-20 65

YUMMIES
Singles: 7-inch
SUNFLOWER (103 "Hippie Lady") ... 15-25 60s

YUNIS, George
Singles: 7-inch
TOWER TOWNE ... 3-4 80
Picture Sleeves
TOWER TOWNE ... 3-5 80

YURO, Timi P&R/R&B/LP '61
Singles: 7-inch
FREQUENCY (101 "Nothing Takes the Place of You") ... 5-10 60s
LIBERTY (55000 series) ... 10-20 61-64
LIBERTY (56000 series) ... 4-8 68
MERCURY ... 5-10 64-67
PLAYBOY ... 4-6 75
EPs: 7-inch
LIBERTY ... 10-20 61
(Juke box issues only.)
LPs: 10/12-inch
COLGEMS ... 8-10 68
LIBERTY (Except 7500 series) ... 20-30 61-63
LIBERTY (7500 series) ... 8-10 68
MERCURY ... 10-20 65
SUNSET ... 8-12 66-70
U.A. ... 5-8 75-76
WING ... 8-10 68
Session: Willie Mitchell.
Also see MITCHELL, Willie
Also see RAY, Johnnie, & Timi Yuro

YUTAKA P&R/R&B/LP '81
(Yukata Yokokura)
Singles: 7-inch
ALFA ... 3-4 81
Picture Sleeves
ALFA ... 3-4 81
LPs: 10/12-inch
ALFA ... 5-8 81
Also see AUSTIN, Patti

YVETTE & LORDS
Singles: 7-inch
YVETTE ... 4-8 66

YVONNE & VIOLETS
Singles: 7-inch
BARRY ... 8-12

Z

Z., Johnny: see JOHNNY Z.

Z DEBS
Singles: 7-inch
ROULETTE ... 5-10 64

Z ROCKS
LPs: 10/12-inch
Z ... 5-8 83

Z III
Singles: 12-inch
W.B. ... 4-6 82
Singles: 7-inch
W.B. ... 3-5 82

ZZ TOP P&R/LP '72
Singles: 12-inch
W.B. ... 4-6 84-86
Singles: 7-inch
LONDON ... 3-8 70-77
SCAT (500 "Salt Lick") ... 100-200
W.B. ... 3-4 80-90
Picture Sleeves
LONDON ... 3-4 75-76
W.B. ... 3-4 83-90
LPs: 10/12-inch
LONDON (Except 1001) ... 8-12 71-77
LONDON (1001 "World Wide Texas Tour") ... 10-20 76
(Promotional issue only.)
W.B. ... 5-15 79-90
Members: Bill Gibbons; Frank Beard; Dusty Hill.
Also see AMERICAN BLUES
Also see MOVING SIDEWALKS
Also see WARLOCKS

ZABACH, Florian P&R '51
Singles: 78 rpm
DECCA ... 3-5 51-54
MERCURY ... 3-5 56-57
Singles: 7-inch
CADENCE ... 4-8 61
DECCA ... 5-10 51-54
MERCURY ... 5-10 56-58
EPs: 7-inch
DECCA ... 5-10 51-54
MERCURY ... 5-10 56-58
LPs: 10/12-inch
DECCA ... 5-15 51-65
MERCURY ... 5-15 56-60
VOCALION ... 4-8 63-66
WING ... 4-8 63
Also see DIAMONDS / Georgia Gibbs / Sarah Vaughan / Florian Zabach

Also see VALLI, June

ZABE, Dick

Singles: 7-inch

PIO........4-8 61

ZACA CREEK C&W '89

Singles: 7-inch

COLUMBIA........3-4 89-90

ZACHARIAH

Singles: 7-inch

BLACK MARKET........5-10 73
JEANNIE HITMAKER........3-5 80

ZACHARIAS, Helmut P&R '56

(Helmut Zacharias' Magic Violins)

Singles: 78 rpm

DECCA........3-4 56-57

Singles: 7-inch

CAPITOL........3-4 69
DECCA........3-4 56-64

EPs: 7-inch

DECCA........3-6 56-58

LPs: 10/12-inch

CAPITOL........4-8 69
DECCA........5-15 56-61
PHILIPS........4-8 62
RCA........4-8 66

ZACHERIAS & TREE PEOPLE

Singles: 7-inch

VIKING........10-20 69

ZACHERLE, John P&R/R&B '58

(Zacherle; Zacherley; John Zacherlie "Cool Ghoul")

Singles: 78 rpm

CAMEO........25-50 58

Singles: 7-inch

ABKCO........3-4 80s
CAMEO........10-15 58
COLPIX........4-6 64
ELEKTRA........4-6 60
PARKWAY........3-5 62

LPs: 10/12-inch

CRESTVIEW........25-35 63
ELEKTRA........25-35 60
PARKWAY........25-35 62-63

ZACK, Eddie, & Cousin Richie

Singles: 78 rpm

COLUMBIA........30-60 55

Singles: 7-inch

COLUMBIA (21387 "Rocky Road Blues")........100-150 55
COLUMBIA (21441 "I'm Gonna Rock & Roll")........100-150 55
Members: Eddie Zack; Dick Richards.
Also see RICHARDS, Dick

ZACKERY, Jan

Singles: 7-inch

TOGA........4-8 61

ZADORA, Pia C&W '79

(With the London Symphony Orchestra)

Singles: 12-inch

MCA........4-6 83

Singles: 7-inch

CURB........3-4 83
ELEKTRA........3-4 82-83
MCA........3-4 83-84
W.B./CURB........3-4 78-80

LPs: 10/12-inch

CBS ASSOCIATED........5-8 86
ELEKTRA........5-8 82
Also see JACKSON, Jermaine, & Pia Zadora
Also see LITTLE PIA

ZADORA, Pia, & Lou Christie

Singles: 7-inch

MIDSONG (72013 "Don't Knock My Love")........15-20 80
Also see CHRISTIE, Lou
Also see ZADORA, Pia

ZAGER, Michael, Band P&R/R&B/LP '78

Singles: 12-inch

CBS ASSOCIATED........4-6 84
COLUMBIA........4-6 79-80

Singles: 7-inch

BANG........3-4 78
CBS ASSOCIATED........3-4 84
PRIVATE STOCK........3-4 78

LPs: 10/12-inch

COLUMBIA........5-8 79
PRIVATE STOCK........5-8 78
Also see TEN WHEEL DRIVE

ZAGER, Michael, Moon Band, & Peabo Bryson P&R/R&B '76

Singles: 7-inch

BANG........3-4 76
Also see BRYSON, Peabo
Also see ZAGER, Michael, Band

ZAGER & EVANS P&R/LP '69

Singles: 7-inch

RCA........3-5 69-70
TRUTH........8-12 69
VANGUARD........3-4 71

Picture Sleeves

VANGUARD........4-8 71

LPs: 10/12-inch

RCA (1000 series)........8-10 75
RCA (4000 series)........12-15 69-70
VANGUARD........10-12 71
WHITE WHALE........12-15 69
Members: Denny Zager; Rick Evans.

ZAHND, Ricky, & Blue Jeaners P&R '55

Singles: 78 rpm

COLUMBIA........4-6 55-56

Singles: 7-inch

COLUMBIA........5-10 55-56

Picture Sleeves

COLUMBIA........8-12 55-56

ZAHARA

LPs: 10/12-inch

ANTILLES........5-10 83

ZAKARY THAKS

Singles: 7-inch

CEE BEE (1005 "Everybody Wants to Be Somebody")........10-20 69
J-BECK (1006 "I Need You")........20-30 66
J-BECK (1009 "Face to Face")........20-30 67
J-BECK (1101 "Won't Come Back")........20-30 67
J-BECK (1103 "Mirror of Yesterday")........20-30 67
MERCURY (72633 "I Need You")........10-15 66
THAK (1001 "My Door")........15-25 68

ZAKATEK, Lenny

Singles: 7-inch

A&M........4-6 79
LONDON........3-5 82

LPs: 10/12-inch

A&M........5-10 79
Also see PARSONS, Alan, Project

ZAKONS

Singles: 7-inch

CUCA (1033 "Trackin' ")........25-35 61
Members: Larry Krecowski; Bill Joswick; Tom Kropp; Ronnie Pagel; Billy Lee King; Bill Anderson; Bob Bierd.

ZAMBON, Francis, & Naturals

Singles: 7-inch

VAMALCO........15-20 59

ZAMOT, Johnny

Singles: 7-inch

DECCA........4-8 67
GEMA........3-5 70
GRANDE........4-8 68

LPs: 10/12-inch

DECCA........10-15 67

ZANE, Herb

Singles: 78 rpm

DELUXE........5-10 57

Singles: 7-inch

ARROW (718 "Love Love, Crazy Love")........10-20 57
DELUXE........10-15 57
20TH FOX........5-10 62

ZANG, Tommy

Singles: 7-inch

CANADIAN AMERICAN........5-10 59
HICKORY........4-8 64

ZANGO, Willie

Singles: 7-inch

GIZMO (66435 "Nancy Jane")........25-50 60
(Identification number shown since no selection number is used.)

ZANICCHI, Iva

LPs: 10/12-inch

U.A. (15502 "Cara Mio")........30-40

ZANIES

Singles: 7-inch

DORE (509 "Do You Dig Me Mister Pigmy")........10-20 58
DORE (515 "Mad Scientist")........10-20 59
DORE (597 "It's Love")........10-15 61
DORE (632 "Frustration")........8-12 62
DORE (638 "London Rock")........8-12 62
DORE (647 "Sleepwalker")........8-12 62
DORE (655 "Hello Jackie")........8-12 62
DORE (658 "Russian Roulette")........8-12 63
DORE (683 "Chicken Surfer")........10-20 63
DORE (693 "Get Your Good Good Lovin' from Me")........8-12 64
DORE (734 "Last Dance at the Prom")........5-10 65
DORE (853 "Will the Real Frankenstein Please Stand Up")........10-15 71
DORE (875 "Mr. President to Be")........4-8 72
DORE (889 "Let Out a Scream")........4-8 73
DORE (900 "Let Out a Scream")........4-8 74
DORE (979 "It's a Million Miles to Paradise")........3-5 83
ERA (1080 "The Blob")........10-20 58

LPs: 10/12-inch

DORE (321 "The Zanies")........10-20 69
DORE (337 "The Zanies")........5-10 79
Session: Davie Allan.
Also see ALLAN, Davie
Also see JIGGLES & ZANIES
Also see LUBY DUBY DOO & ZANIES

ZANTEES

Singles: 12-inch

MIDNIGHT........4-8

Singles: 7-inch

LITTLE RICKY........3-6

LPs: 10/12-inch

BOMP........5-10 82
MIDNIGHT........5-10
Also see DONNER, Ral / Zantees

ZAP

Singles: 7-inch

POLYDOR........3-5 77

ZAP POW

Singles: 7-inch

MANGO........3-5 73

LPs: 10/12-inch

MANGO........5-10 79
RHINO........5-10 80

ZAPATA

Singles: 7-inch

ATCO........4-6 69
ORIGINAL SOUND........4-6 60s

ZAPP P&R/R&B/LP '80

Singles: 12-inch

REPRISE (40982 "Zapp & Roger")........4-8 93

Singles: 7-inch

W.B.........3-4 80-89

LPs: 10/12-inch

W.B.........5-8 80-89
Members: Roger Troutman; Shirley Murdock; Lester Troutman; Larry Troutman; Tony Troutman.
Also see BOOTSY'S RUBBER BAND
Also see MURDOCK, Shirley
Also see ROGER

ZAPPA, Dweezil & Moon

(Dweezil)

Singles: 7-inch

BARKING PUMPKIN (03366 "My Mother Is a Space Cadet")........3-5 83

Picture Sleeves

BARKING PUMPKIN (03366 "My Mother Is a Space Cadet")........3-5 83
Also see ZAPPA, Frank & Moon

ZAPPA, Frank LP '70

(With the Mothers; Francis Vincent Zappa)

Singles: 12-inch

BARKING PUMPKIN (1114 "Goblin Girl")........20-30 79
(Picture disc. Promotional issue only.)
BARKING PUMPKIN (1115 "Baby Snakes")........40-50 82
(Picture disc.)
RHINO/DEL-FI (604 "Rare Meat")........10-20 83
(Cover has portrait of Zappa.)
RHINO/DEL-FI (604 "Rare Meat")........5-10 83
(Plain cover, no portrait of Zappa.)
ZAPPA (1001 "I Don't Want to Get Drafted")........8-10 80

Singles: 7-inch

BARKING PUMPKIN........3-4 82
BIZARRE/REPRISE (0800 series)........10-15 69-70
BIZARRE/REPRISE (0900 series)........6-10 70
DISCREET........3-5 73-74
ROTATE........3-5
U.A.........5-8 71
VERVE........8-12 66-68
W.B.........4-6 76-77
ZAPPA........3-5 79-80

Promotional Singles

DISCREET (586 "Cosmik Debris")........10-12 74

EPs: 7-inch

REPRISE (336 "Hot Rats")........35-40 72
(Promotional issue only.)
U.A. ("200 Motels")........35-40 71
(Promotional issue only.)

Picture Sleeves

ZAPPA........3-5 80

LPs: 10/12-inch

BARKING PUMPKIN (37000 series)........10-15 81
BARKING PUMPKIN (38000 series)........5-10 82-83
BARKING PUMPKIN (74000 series)........5-10 84-88
BIZARRE (2030 "Chunga's Revenge")........15-25 70
(Blue label.)
BIZARRE (2030 "Chunga's Revenge")........5-10 70s
(Brown label.)
BIZARRE (2094 "Waka Jawaka")........15-25 70
(Blue label.)
BIZARRE (2094 "Waka Jawaka")........5-10 70s
(Brown label.)
BIZARRE (6356 "Hot Rats")........15-25 69
(Blue label.)
BIZARRE (6356 "Hot Rats")........5-10 70s
(Brown label.)
DEL-FI (604 "Rare Meat")........35-45 83
DISCREET (DS-2175 "Apostrophe")........15-25 74
DISCREET (DS4-2175 "Apostrophe")........30-40 74
(Quardophonic.)
DISCREET (DSK-2175 "Apostrophe")........8-10 79
DISCREET (2202 "Roxy and Elsewhere")........20-30 74
DISCREET (2216 "One Size Fits All")........15-25 75
DISCREET (2234 "Bongo Fury")........15-25 75
DISCREET (2290 "Zappa in New York")........300-400 78
(Has *Punky's Whips* and a full-length *Titties and Beer*. May have been on test pressings only.)
DISCREET (2290 "Zappa in New York")........100-200 78
(Cover indicates *Punky's Whips* and a full-length *Titties and Beer*, though discs have neither.)
DISCREET (2290 "Zappa in New York")........20-30 78
(Omits *Punky's Whips* and has an edited *Titties and Beer*.)
DISCREET (2291 "Studio Tan")........10-15 78
DISCREET (2294 "Orchestral Favorites")........10-15 79
EMI/ANGEL (38170 "Boulez Conducts Zappa")........10-15 84
REPRISE........8-12 72
RHINO (70907 "Beat the Boots")........100-175 91
(Boxed, eight-disc set. Includes button and T-shirt.)
VERVE (8741 "Lumpy Gravy")........25-30 68
U.A.........20-30 71
ZAPPA (1501 "Sheik Yerbouti")........10-20 79
ZAPPA (1502 "Joe's Garage, Acts I & III")........10-20 79
ZAPPA (1603 "Joe's Garage, Act I")........10-15 79
W.B.........5-10 76

Promotional LPs

BARKING PUMPKIN (1111 "Shut Up 'N' Play Yer Guitar")........15-20 81
(Mail-order LP offer.)
BARKING PUMPKIN (1112 "Shut Up 'N' Play Yer Guitar Some More")........15-20 81
(Mail-order LP offer.)
BARKING PUMPKIN (1113 "Return of Shut Up 'N' Play Yer Guitar")........15-20 81
(Mail-order LP offer.)
BIZARRE (368 "Zapped")........30-40 69
(Photo collage cover with title in red. Also has tracks by Alice Cooper; Captain Beefheart & His Magic Band; Judy Henske & Jerry Yester; Tim Buckley; Wild Man Fischer; Tim Dawe; Lord Buckley; Jeff Simmons; & GTO's.
BIZARRE (368 "Zapped")........20-30 69
(Cover pictures only Frank Zappa. Title in black.)
BIZARRE (2030 "Chunga's Revenge")........30-40 70
ZAPPA (78 "Sheik Yerbouti, Clean Cuts")........20-30 79
ZAPPA (129 "Joe's Garage, Acts I, II & III")........30-40 79
Session: Howard Kaylan; Marc Volman.
Also see BABY RAY & FERNS
Also see FANKHAUSER, Merrell
Also see G.T.O.
Also see GROUP 87
Also see GUY, Bob
Also see HOGS
Also see HEARTBREAKERS
Also see HOLLYWOOD PERSUADERS
Also see KAYLAN, Howard, & Marc Volman
Also see LORD, Brian, & Midnighters
Also see MINTZ, Junior
Also see MR. CLEAN
Also see MOTHERS of INVENTION
Also see NED & NELDA
Also see ROMAN, Don

ZAPPA, Frank & Moon

Singles: 12-inch

BARKING PUMPKIN (03069 "Valley Girl")........5-8 82

Singles: 7-inch

BARKING PUMPKIN (02972 "Valley Girl")........3-4 82

Picture Sleeves

BARKING PUMPKIN (02972 "Valley Girl")........3-4 82

Promotional Singles

BARKING PUMPKIN (1490 "Valley Girl")........4-6 82
Also see ZAPPA, Dweezil & Moon
Also see ZAPPA, Frank

ZAPPACOSTA

Singles: 7-inch

CAPITOL........3-4 84

LPs: 10/12-inch

CAPITOL........5-8 84

ZARA, Michael, & Compliments

(With Bill Ramal & Orchestra)

Singles: 7-inch

SHELL (313 "Angels of Mercy")........20-30 63

ZARIO, Tex

Singles: 78 rpm

ARCADE........8-15 54-57

Singles: 7-inch

ARCADE........10-20 54-60
SKYROCKET (Except 1001)........10-20 59-60
SKYROCKET (1001 "Go Man")........50-75 58

ZAVAL, Dave

Singles: 7-inch

SQUARE........5-10 60

ZAVARONI, Lena P&R '74

Singles: 7-inch

STAX........3-5 74

LP: 10/12-inch

STAX........5-10 74

ZAZU

LPs: 10/12-inch

WOODEN NICKEL........8-10 75

ZE MAJESTICS

(Ze-Majestics)

Singles: 7-inch

ABC-PAR (10318 "Sapphire")........10-20 62
FOX (5014 "Bobbi Ann")........50-100

ZEAMER, Will, & Northerly Winds

Singles: 7-inch

TARGET........5-10 72

ZEBRA

Singles: 7-inch

BLUE THUMB........4-6 69
PHILIPS........4-8 68
VORTEX........4-8 68
WHITE WHALE........4-8 69

ZEBRA

Singles: 7-inch

PRO-GRESS........5-10 72

ZEBRA P&R/LP '83

Singles: 7-inch

ATLANTIC........3-4 83-84

LPs: 10/12-inch

ATLANTIC........5-8 83-84

ZEBULONS

Singles: 7-inch

CUB (9069 "Falling Water")........40-50 60

ZED

Singles: 7-inch

ATLANTIC........3-5 81

LPs: 10/12-inch

ATLANTIC........5-10 81

ZEE, Ginny

Singles: 7-inch

ATCO........10-15 62

ZEE, Kathy

Singles: 7-inch

LAURIE (3020 "Buzzin' ")........10-20 58

ZEE, Tommy

Singles: 7-inch

AMY (815 "Rebecca Remember") 25-35 61
(At least one source says this artist is Johnny Zee. We don't know yet who's right.)

ZEE, Vin

Singles: 7-inch

EMERGENCY........3-5 81

ZEE-BRASS

Singles: 12-inch

ATLANTIC........4-6 83

Singles: 7-inch

ATLANTIC........3-4 83

ZEET BAND

Singles: 7-inch

CHESS........8-10 67

ZEILER, Gayle C&W '82

Singles: 7-inch

EQUA........3-5 80-81
Also see ETHEL & SHAMELESS HUSSIES

ZEINER, Ray

Singles: 7-inch

POISON RING........8-12

ZEITGEIST

Singles: 7-inch

RCA........3-6 70

ZEKE & GENEVA

(With the Zeke Strong Band)

Singles: 7-inch

SWINGIN'........5-10 61
Member: Zeke Strong.

ZEKES

Singles: 7-inch

BEVERLY HILLS (9353 "Leaving You")........15-25 60s

ZELLA, Danny P&R '59

(With the Larados & His Zell Rocks)

Singles: 7-inch

DIAL (100 "Sapphire")........100-150 59
FOX ("Black Sax")........30-50 58
(No selection number used. First issue.)
FOX (10057 "Wicked Ruby")........20-30 59
RED ROCKET (475 "Black Sax")........15-25 58
Also see DANNY & ZELTONES
Also see LARADOS
Also see YOUNGSTERS / Danny Zella

ZE-MAJECTICS: see ZE MAJESTICS

ZEN

Singles: 7-inch

PHILIPS........4-6 69
PIP........3-5 70

ZEN IDOLS

Singles

ERIKA (18411 "Rub the Buddha")........10-15 84
(Buddha-shaped picture disc.)

ZENDIK

Singles: 7-inch

PSLHRTZ........15-25

ZENITH

Singles: 7-inch

LYNX........3-5 81

LPs: 10/12-inch

LYNX........5-10 81

ZENO LP '86

LPs: 10/12-inch

MANHATTAN........5-8 86
Member: Zeno Roth; Michael Flexig.

ZENTNER, Si, & His Orchestra P&R/LP '61

(With the Johnny Mann Singers)

Singles: 7-inch

BEL CANTO........5-10 59
LIBERTY........5-10 59-67
RCA........4-6 64-66

Picture Sleeves

LIBERTY........5-10 62

EPs: 7-inch

LIBERTY........5-10 59-67

LPs: 10/12-inch

BEL CANTO........10-20 59
LIBERTY........10-20 59-67
RCA........5-10 65-66
SUNSET........5-10 66
Also see CARPENTER, Ike
Also see DENNY, Martin
Also see MANN, Johnny, Singers
Also see MARTIN, Dean / Patti Page
Also see SINATRA, Frank

ZEP, Jo Jo, & Falcons

LPs: 10/12-inch

COLUMBIA........3-5 80-81

ZEPHYR LP '69
Singles: 7-inch
PROBE....5-8 70
W.B. 3-4 70
Promotional Singles
PROBE....10-12 70
LPs: 10/12-inch
PROBE (4510 "Zephyr") 30-40 69
RED SNEAKERS....5-10 82
W.B. 25-30 71-72
Members: Candy Givens; Tommy Bolin.
Also see BOLIN, Tommy

ZEPHYRS
Singles: 7-inch
AMBER....8-15 64-66
ROTATE....5-10 65
Picture Sleeves
AMBER (214 "She's Mine")....10-15 65

ZEPPA, Ben
(With the 4 Jacks; with Zephers; Ben Joe Zeppa; with Pharaohs)
Singles: 78 rpm
SPECIALTY....10-20 56
Singles: 7-inch
AWARD (124 "Shame on You Miss Lindy")....25-35 59
ERA (1042 "Topsy Turvy")....25-35 57
GILMAR (278 "No Not Much")....100-150 57
HUSH (1000 "Young Heartaches")..10-20 58
METRO (9001 "Shame on You Miss Lindy")....50-75 58
SPECIALTY (577 "Foolish Fool")...40-50 56
TOPS....15-25 56
EPs: 7-inch
TOPS (278 "Why Do Fools Fall in Love")....30-50 56

ZEPPELIN, Led: see LED ZEPPELIN

ZEPPERS
Singles: 7-inch
LONGFIBER (202 "Let's Forget the Past")....75-125 66

ZERFAS
LPs: 10/12-inch
700 WEST (730710 "Zerfas")....350-450 73
Members: Herman Zerfas; David Zerfas; Bill Rice; Steve Newbold; Mark Tribby.

006
Singles: 7-inch
HARLEQUINN (606415 "Like What, Me Worry")....20-30 66
RED BIRD (066 "Like What, Me Worry")....10-20 66

ZERO HOUR
Singles: 12-inch
VANGUARD....4-6 83
LPs: 10/12-inch
VANGUARD....3-4 83

ZEROES
Singles: 7-inch
TY-TEX (105 "Flossie Mae")....100-200 62

ZEROS
Singles: 7-inch
KAM....5-10 69
EPs: 7-inch
BOMP....8-10

ZEV
Singles: 7-inch
FETISH (13 "Wipe Out")....10-20 60s

ZEVON, Warren LP '76
(Zevon)
Singles: 7-inch
ASYLUM....3-4 76-80
CHRYSALIS....3-4 87
Picture Sleeves
CHRYSALIS....3-4 87
LPs: 10/12-inch
ASYLUM....5-8 76-82
ELEKTRA (11386 "Werewolves of London")....70-90 78
(Picture disc. Promotional issue only.)
IMPERIAL....10-12 70
VIRGIN....5-8 87
Members: Richard Hayward; Kenny Gradney; Greg Beck; Karen Childs.
Also see HINDU LOVE GODS
Also see LITTLE FEAT
Also see LYME & CYBELLE

ZIG ZAG PEOPLE
Singles: 7-inch
BELL....4-8 68
DECCA....4-6 69-70
LPs: 10/12-inch
DECCA....10-15 69

ZIG-ZAGS
Singles: 7-inch
TANGENT (104 "Why Oh Why")....4-8 60s

ZIGGURAT
Singles: 7-inch
ROBOX....3-5 79-81
LPs: 10/12-inch
ROBOX....5-10 79-82

ZIGGY & ZEU
(With Ena Anka)
Singles: 7-inch
ZEU (5011 "Da-Doo-Ron-Ron")....20-30 70s
ZEU (5011 "Little Star")....20-30 70s
(Same selection number used twice.)

ZILL, Pat P&R '61
Singles: 7-inch
BIG C....3-5 62
ERA....3-5 63
INDIGO....3-5 61
SAND....5-8 61

ZIMMERAN, George, & Thrills
(With Bubby Cypers Band)
Singles: 78 rpm
JAB....100-200 56
Singles: 7-inch
JAB (103 "Whose Baby Are You")....500-750 56
Session: Bubby Cypers; L.D. Williams; Herb Adams; Guy Richard Jones; Vonnie Holte; Jimmy Nolan.

ZINC
LPs: 10/12-inch
JIVE....5-8

ZINE, Ben
Singles: 7-inch
PARKWAY (996 "Village of Tears")....40-60 66

ZINGA
Singles: 7-inch
MY DISC....3-4 82
LPs: 10/12-inch
MY DISC....5-8 82

ZINGARA R&B '80
Singles: 7-inch
WHEEL....3-4 80-81
LPs: 10/12-inch
WHEEL....5-8 81

ZINO D&D '84
Singles: 12-inch
PACIFIC 6....4-6 84

ZION BAPTIST CHURCH CHOIR
Singles: 7-inch
MYRRH....5-8 73

ZION TRAVELERS
Singles: 78 rpm
DOOTONE....10-15 56
Singles: 7-inch
DOOTO (400 series)....5-10 59-63
DOOTONE (389 "Two Little Fishes")....15-25 56
DOOTONE (399 "Soldier of the Cross")....15-25 56

ZIP, Danny
Singles: 7-inch
MGM....5-10 64

ZIP & ZIPPERS
Singles: 7-inch
PAGEANT (607 "Where You Goin' Little Boy")....10-20 63
Members: Shirley Brickley; Rosetta Hightower; Steve Caldwell; Marlena Davis.
Also see ORLONS

ZIP CODES
Singles: 7-inch
BETTER....8-12 60s
LIBERTY (55703 "Run Little Mustang")....10-15 64
LPs: 10/12-inch
LIBERTY (3367 "Mustang")....40-50 64
(Monaural.)
LIBERTY (7367 "Mustang")....50-60 64
(Stereo.)

ZIPPERMAN, Stan
LPs: 10/12-inch
STANZA....8-10

ZIPPERS
Singles: 7-inch
HICKORY....4-8 64

ZIPPERS
Singles: 12-inch
RHINO (601 "Six Song Mini Album")....20-30 81

ZIRCONS
Singles: 7-inch
DE VILLE (120 "Frog in the Fog")..10-20
DOT (15724 "Only One Love")....25-35 58
FEDERAL (12452 "No Twistin' on Sunday")....20-30 62
FEDERAL (12478 "Mr. Jones")....20-30 62
WINSTON (1020 "Only One Love")....75-100 57
WINSTON (1022 "Crazy Crazy")..75-125 58
Picture Sleeves
DE VILLE (120 "Frog in the Fog")..20-40

ZIRCONS
Singles: 7-inch
BAGDAD (1007 "Surfing in the Sunset")....15-25 60s

ZIRCONS
Singles: 7-inch
AMBER (851 "One Summer Night")....10-15 66
COOL SOUND (1030 "Silver Bells")....20-30 64
MELLOMOOD (1000 "Lonely Way")....15-25 63
OLD TIMER (602 "Silver Bells")....10-15 64
OLD TIMER (603 "Sincerely")....10-15 64
OLD TIMER (606 "Remember Then")....20-30 64
(Colored vinyl.)
SIAMESE (403 "Sincerely")....10-15 65
LPs: 10/12-inch
SNOWFLAKE (1003 "The Crown Kings of Acappella")....45-65

ZIRCONS / Destinaires
Singles: 7-inch
OLD TIMER (602 "Silver Bells")....10-15 64
Also see DESTINAIRES
Also see ZIRCONS

ZIRCONS
Singles: 7-inch
CAPITOL (2667 "Finders Keepers")....20-30 69
HEIGH-HO (607 "Where There's a Will")....20-30 67
HEIGH-HO (608 "I Couldn't Stop Crying")....20-30 67
HEIGH-HO (646 "Go On and Cry")....20-30 67

ZISKA, Stosh
Singles: 7-inch
AVCO....4-6 70
Also see DEL SATINS

ZITTS
Singles: 7-inch
O&W (76 "Surfin' & Sleepin' ")....10-20 60s

Z'LOOKE
Singles: 7-inch
ORPHEOUS....3-4 88

ZNOWHITE
LPs: 10/12-inch
ENIGMA....5-8

ZODIAC
Singles: 7-inch
UNI....4-8 69

ZODIAC MINDWARP & LOVE REACTION LP '88
LPs: 10/12-inch
VERTIGO....5-8 86

ZODIACS
Singles: 7-inch
ATLANTIC (2199 "Lonliness")....10-20 63
COLE (100 "Golly Gee")....50-75 59
COLE (101 "She's Mine")....50-75 59
DEE-SU (304 "May I")....10-20 67
DEE-SU (309 "Surely")....10-20 67
DEE-SU (311 "How to Pick a Winner")....10-20 68
DEE-SU (318 "Stay")....8-12 68
PLUS (4401 "Try")....8-10
SCEPTER (12113 "Lonliness")....8-10 65
SEA HORN (503 "Return")....8-10 64
Also see WILLIAMS, Maurice

ZODIACS
Singles: 7-inch
VEE JAY (678 "May I")....8-10 64
VEEP (1294 "The Four Corners")....5-10 68

ZODIACS
Singles: 7-inch
SOMA (1410 "Lita")....40-60 64
SOMA (1418 "Anything")....60-80 64

ZOE
Singles: 12-inch
POSSE....4-6 83

ZOGHBY, Emil Dean
Singles: 7-inch
COTILLION....3-4 71

ZOLTON, Frank
Singles: 7-inch
DIXIE (1056 "Cat Eyes")....50-75

ZOMBIES P&R '64
Singles: 7-inch
DATE....4-8 68-69
EPIC....3-5 74
ERIC....3-4 83
LONDON....3-5
PARROT....5-10 64-66
(U.S. issues.)
PARROT (9695 "She's Not There")....15-25 64
(Blue label. Canadian.)
PARROT (9695 "She's Not There") 5-10 60s
(Black label. Canadian.)
Picture Sleeves
PARROT....10-20 65
LPs: 10/12-inch
BACK-TRAC....5-8 85
DATE (4013 "Odessey & Oracle")....20-25 68
(No promotional mention of *Time of the Season* on front cover.)
DATE (4013 "Odessey & Oracle")..15-20 68
(With promo for *Time of the Season* on front cover.)
EPIC....10-15 74
LONDON....10-15 69
PARROT....30-35 65
RHINO....5-8
Members: Colin Blunstone; Rod Argent.
Also see ARGENT
Also see BLUNSTONE, Colin

ZON
Singles: 7-inch
EPIC....3-5 79
LPs: 10/12-inch
EPIC....5-10 79

ZONE 26
Singles: 7-inch
WORLD PACIFIC....3-6 68

ZONE V
Singles: 7-inch
CARAVAN (21449 "Black Jacket Woman")....15-25

ZONK
Singles: 7-inch
U.A. 3-5 71

ZOO
Singles: 7-inch
PARKWAY (147 "She Said-Good Day Sunshine")....8-10 67
SEASCAPE (502 "Feeling")....8-12
SUNBURST....5-10 68-69
LPs: 10/12-inch
MERCURY....10-15 70
SUNBURST (7500 "Chocolate Moose")....15-25 68
Also see BEAU DENTURIES

ZOO
Singles: 7-inch
PKC (1013 "Gonna Miss Me")....10-20 68

ZOO
Singles: 7-inch
RCA....3-4 83
Picture Sleeves
RCA....3-4 83
Member: Mick Fleetwood.
Also see FLEETWOOD, Mick

ZOOFS
Singles: 7-inch
DEESU (310 "Not So Near")....10-15 67

ZOOGZ RIFT
LPs: 10/12-inch
NSFD (8401 "Ipecac")....5-10 84
(Picture disc.)

ZOOKIE & POTENTATES
Singles: 7-inch
COCONUT GROOVE (2017 "Banana Man")....15-25 60s
NU-SOUND (711 "Telephony")....8-12 60s
Member: Gary "Zookie" Story.
Also see PLAIN BROWN WRAPPER

ZOOM R&B '81
Singles: 7-inch
MCA....3-4 83
POLYDOR....3-4 81-82
LPs: 10/12-inch
A&M....8-10 74
MCA....5-8 83
POLYDOR....5-8 81

ZORO & ZIPS
Singles: 7-inch
SPOT (1002 "Frankie & Johnny")..10-15 60s
Member: Bobby McBride.

ZORRO
Singles: 7-inch
MASKE (702 "Somebody Cares")..30-40 61

ZORRO, Johnny
Singles: 7-inch
AVA....5-10 63
BRAVO ("Road Hog"/"Coesville")..15-25 59
(No selection number used.)
BRAVO (123 "Road Hog"/"Camel Train")....10-20 59
(Note different flip.)
INFINITY....5-10 61
JOCKO....5-10 64
W.B. 5-10 59-60

ZORROS, Keith, & Energy
Singles: 7-inch
RCA....3-5 80
LPs: 10/12-inch
RCA....5-10 81

ZORY, Cathy
Singles: 12-inch
BUDDAH....4-8 79
Singles: 7-inch
BUDDAH....3-5 79

ZOSER
Singles: 7-inch
HEXAGON....10-15 70

ZOT
LPs: 10/12-inch
ELEKTRA....5-8

ZOTS
Singles: 7-inch
O.E.K. 5-10 61

ZU ZU BAND
Singles: 7-inch
A&M....4-8 66

ZUCKERMAN'S DREAM
Singles: 7-inch
COLUMBIA....4-6 69

ZUIDER ZEE
LPs: 10/12-inch
COLUMBIA....8-10 75

ZULEMA R&B '73
(Zulema Cusseaux)
Singles: 7-inch
LE JOINT....3-4 78-79
RCA....3-4 74-76
SUSSEX....3-4 72-73
LPs: 10/12-inch
LE JOINT....5-8 78
RCA....5-8 75-76
SUSSEX....8-10 72-74
Also see FAITH, HOPE & CHARITY

ZUMMOS
LPs: 10/12-inch
A&M....5-8 85
Members: Vinnie Zummo; Janice Zummo.

ZWERLING, Andy
LPs: 10/12-inch
KAMA SUTRA....8-10 71

ZWOL P&R '78
(Walter Zwol)
Singles: 7-inch
EMI AMERICA (Except 8905)....3-4 78-79
EMI AMERICA (8905 "New York City")....4-8 78
(Alternate version on white vinyl. Promotional issue only.)
LPs: 10/12-inch
EMI AMERICA....5-8 78-79

ZYDECO, Buckwheat: see BUCKWHEAT ZYDECO

ZYDIAK, Marc
LPs: 10/12-inch
NIRVANA....5-10 77

ZZEBRA
LPs: 10/12-inch
POLYDOR....5-10 75

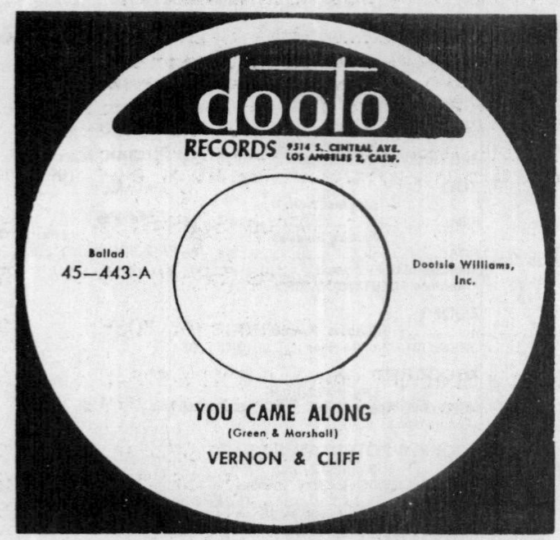
dooto
RECORDS 9514 S. CENTRAL AVE. LOS ANGELES 2, CALIF.
Ballad
45—443-A
Dootsie Williams, Inc.
YOU CAME ALONG
(Green & Marshall)
VERNON & CLIFF

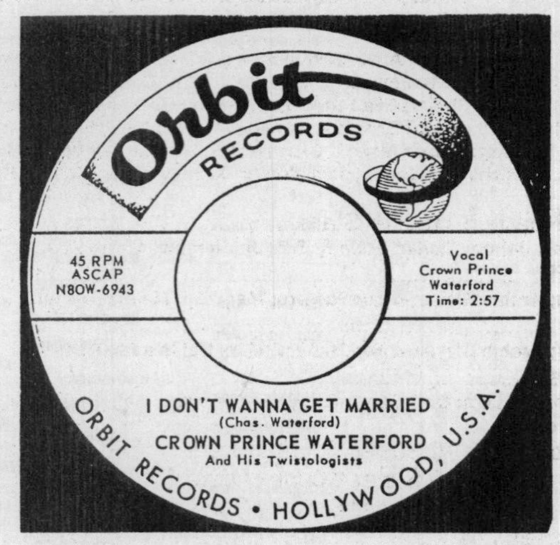
Orbit
RECORDS
45 RPM
ASCAP
N8OW-6943
Vocal
Crown Prince
Waterford
Time: 2:57
I DON'T WANNA GET MARRIED
(Chas. Waterford)
CROWN PRINCE WATERFORD
And His Twistologists
ORBIT RECORDS • HOLLYWOOD, U.S.A.

TREBCO
T-801
Angle-
Anderson
Pub.,-BMI
45-701
Time: 2:15
JIVE HARP
(Whitsett)
TIM WHITSETT
and
The Imperials
TREBCO RECORDS INC. · 117 W. CAPITOL ST. · JACKSON, MISSISSIPPI

ember
RECORDS
Manufactured by Herald Records
45 RPM
45 RPM
(E-1222)
Angel Music (BMI)
Vocal
Time: 2:27
DISC
JOCKEY
COPY
NEED YOUR LOVE
(W. Spriggs)
JIMMY YOUNG
E-1003

LEOPARD
RECORDS
RECORDS
(JR-1660)
Leopard Music, Inc.
(BMI) 2:29
Vocal Group
with Orch.
Prod. & A r. by
Joe Rene
DON'T YOU KNOW
(Nelson Shields)
WEST SIDERS
45-5004
DIVISION OF LEOPARD MUSIC INC., NEW YORK, N.Y.

The Who
You Better
You Bet

Various Artists Compilations

5 Golden Records (5 LP) … RCA (S) DKS-002 20-25 70s

(Boxed set.) Frank Sinatra; Ames Brothers; Ed Ames; Eddy Arnold; Harry Belafonte; Boston Pops; Fanny Brice; Eddie Cantor; Carol Channing; Rosemary Clooney; Russ Columbo; Perry Como; Don Cornell; Bing Crosby; Vernon Dalhart; Tommy Dorsey; Ronald Dyson; Nelson Eddy; Eddie Fisher; Ella Fitzgerald; George Gershwin; Benny Goodman; Cole Porter; Perez Prado; David Rose; Artie Shaw; Dinah Shore; Sinfonia of London; Ernest Gold; Rudy Vallee; Paul Whiteman; Hugo Winterhalter; Henry Mancini; Freddy Martin; Mary Martin; Billy May; Ethel Merman; Robert Merrill; Glenn Miller; Vaughn Monroe; Helen Morgan; Peter Nero; Helen O'Connell; Guess Who; Florence Henderson; Al Hirt; Allan Jones; Jack Jones; Sammy Kaye; Richard Kiley; Mario Lanza; Norman Luboff; Jeanette MacDonald. (Made for Avon.)

6 Days on the Road - 6 Trucker Stars … Hilltop (S) JS-6134 5-10 70s

Dave Dudley; Johnny Dollar; Johnny Exit; Jim Nesbitt; Charlie Wiggs; Jimmy Gately.

8 Top Hits (2 EP) … Cadence (EP) 4058/9 15-25 55

Chordettes; Archie Bleyer; 4 Top Hatters; Mary Del; Maddy Russell.

8 Top Hits … Cadence (M) 3055 20-30 60

Chordettes; Archie Bleyer; 4 Top Hatters; Mary Del; Maddy Russell.

10 Favorite Hits … Columbia Special Products (M) XTV-67845 5-10

Paul Weston; Hi-Lo's; Dino Martinelli; Earl Wrightson; Lois Hunt; Liberace; Percy Faith; Norman Luboff Choir; Michel Legrand; Andre Kostelanetz.

10 Giant Country Hits - 10 Super Country Stars, Vol. 2 … MGM (S) SE-4921 5-10 72

10 Giant Country Hits - 10 Super Country Stars, Vol. 3 … MGM (S) SE-4922 5-10 72

10 Giant Country Hits - 10 Super Country Stars, Vol. 4 … MGM (S) SE-4923 5-10 72

10 Golden Encores … Longines/Decca (S) SYS-5134 10-15

Eddie Cantor; Andrews Sisters; Sophie Tucker; Larry Alder; Ted Lewis; Jimmy Durante; Pearl Bailey; George Jessel; Ames Brothers; Ben Bernie.

10 Golden Years (36 Great Motion Picture Themes) (2 LP) … United Artists (S) UXS 68 10-20 60s

George Martin; Al Caiola; John Addison; Ferrante & Teicher; Joohn Barry; Ennio Morricone; Manos Hadjidakis; Ernest Gold; Jerome Moross; Ken Lauber; Leroy Holmes; Duke Ellington; Count Basie; Riz Ortolani; Henry Jerome; Johnny Williams; Andre Previn; Neil Hefti; Elmer Bernstein; Zero Mostel & Co.; Monty Norman; Francis Lai; Mikis Theodorakis; Johnny Mandel; Hollywood Studio Orchestra; West One Orchestra; Buddy Morrow.

10 Great Bands … RCA (M) LPM-6702 15-25 57

Glenn Miller; Benny Goodman; Tommy Dorsey; Lionel Hampton; Artie Shaw; Duke Ellington; Louie Armstrong; Count Basie; Larry Clinton; Hal Kemp.

10 Great Country Hits, 10 Super Country Stars Vol. 1, … MGM (M) SE-4920 5-10 72

Hank Williams Jr.; Tompall & Glaser Brothers; Billy Walker; Jeannie C. Riley; Mel Tillis; Sherry Bryce; Mel Tillis & Statesiders; Pat Boone & First Nashville Jesus Band; Conway Twitty; Don Gibson; Sheb Wooley.

10 Great Rock and Roll Hits … Columbia House (M) D-1027 10-20 70s

(Columbia Record Club issue.) Jimmie Rodgers; Carl Mann; Carl McVoy; Johnny Preston; Jerry Lee Lewis; Roy Orbison; Carl Perkins; Wilbert Harrison.

10 More Monster Hits … Columbia House (S) DS 1001 5-10 72

(Mail order offer.) Mark Lindsay; Johnnie Taylor; Ronnie Dyson; Addrisi Brothers; Spiral Staircase; Sly & Family Stone; Cliff Noble; Gary Puckett & Union Gap; Buckinghams; Booker T. & MGs; Tymes.

10 More Monster Hits … Columbia House (S) XSM 156776 5-10 72

10 Runaway Hits … United Artists/Columbia House (S) P 16014 5-10

Fats Domino; Little Anthony & Imperials; Nancy Ames; Bobby Goldsboro; Highwaymen; Jay & Americans; Patience & Prudence; Mel Carter; Vic Dana.

10 Song Hits That Sold One Million Records … Guest Star (M) GS-1474 10-20 60s

10 Song Hits That Sold One Million Records … Guest Star (S) GS-1474 10-20 60s

Ritchie Valens; Penguins; Platters; Faye Adams; Hollywood Argyles; Roy Milton; Crescendos; Monarchs; Bill Haley & His Comets; Shirley & Lee.

10 Top Chart Hits of Today Vol. 1 … Alshire (S) ???? 6-12 70

10 Top Chart Hits of Today Vol. 2 … Alshire (S) 5186 6-12 70

10 Top Hits of 1974 (American Music Awards Presents) … Columbia Special Products (S) P-12664 8-12 74

Charlie Rich; Mac Davis; Roy Clark; Four Tops; Ray Stevens; Curtis Mayfield; David Essex; Hollies; Clint Holmes; Johnny Nash.

12 Big Hits … Columbia (M) CL-1617 15-25 61

12 Big Hits … Columbia (S) CS-8417 20-30 61

Marty Robbins; Johnny Horton; Mitch Miller; Buzz Clifford; Jerry Murad's Harmonicats; Norman Luboff Choir; Stonewall Jackson; Mandrake; Aretha Franklin; Johnny Williams; Valiants.

12 Big Ones … RCA (M) LPM-2232 20-25 60

12 Big Ones … RCA (S) LSP-2232 25-30 60

Sam Cooke; Jim Reeves; Don Gibson; Chet Atkins; Henry Mancini; Eddy Arnold; Floyd Cramer; Jim Ed Brown; Marty Gold; Neil Sedaka; Della Reese.

12 By Six … Decca (S) DL-75186 8-12 70

Pearl Bailey; Ella Fitzgerald; Peggy Lee; Sammy Davis Jr.; Al Hibbler; Mel Torme.

12 Collector's Goodies … Camay (M) CA-3012 10-20

12 Collector's Goodies … Camay (S) CA-3012-S 10-20

Five Discs; Donnie & Dreamers; Excellents; Magnificent 4; Ronnie & Hi-Lites; Court Jesters; Emblems; Performers; Roaches.

12 Flip Hits: see SIX TEENS / Donald Woods / Richard Berry

12 Great Country Hits 12 Great Country Artists … Showcase (S) CPR-9007 8-12

Webb Pierce; Ferlin Husky; Patsy Cline; George Jones; Cowboy Copas; Carl Belew; Hank Locklin; Jimmy Dean; Justin Tubb; T. Texas Tyler; Red Sovine; Slim Willet.

12 Great Country Hits 12 Great Country Artists … Hilltop (S) JS-6000 8-12 60s

Patsy Cline; Carl Belew; Hank Locklin; Ferlin Husky; Justin Tubb; Webb Pierce; Slim Willet; George Jones; T. Texas Tyler; Cowboy Copas; Red Sovine; Jimmy Dean.

12 Great Guys .... RCA (M) PRM-161 10-15 64
Ed Ames; Eddy Arnold; Chet Atkins; Brook Benton; Eddie Fisher; Sergio Franchi; John Gary; Al Hirt; Mario Lanza; Tony Martin; Peter Nero; Andy Williams.

12 Great Rock & Roll Love Songs .... Era (S) BU 5250 5-10 83
Everly Brothers; Teddy Bears; Pat Boone; Patti Page; Marcels; Shirelles; Frankie Avalon; Phil Phillips; Fleetwoods; Drifters; Dale & Grace; Nino Tempo & April Stevens.

12 Greatest Golden Oldies in the Whole World Ever .... Parkway (M) P-7031 75-125 63
Superiors; Fabulaires; Nightcaps; Bluenotes; Desires; Metallics; Universals; Frankie Lymon; Bostones; Jimmy Rivers; Carnations.

12 Hits of Christmas .... United Artists (S) UA-LA-669 5-10 76
Nat King Cole; Bing Crosby; Gene Autry; Bobby Helms; David Seville & Chipmunks; Harry Simeone Chorale; Jimmy Boyd; Brenda Lee; Eartha Kitt; LeRoy Anderson; Spike Jones & His City Slickers.

12 Million Record Sellers .... Camay (SE) CA 3010 8-12 60s
Shep & Limelites; Bobby Hendricks; Slades; Three Friends; Desires; Spaniels; Dells; Little Anthony & Imperials; Harptones; Videos; Ike & Tina Turner.

12 Million Sellers .... Forum (M) F 9057 25-35 62
12 Million Sellers .... Forum (SE) SF 9057 20-30 62
Joey Dee & Starliters; Playmates; Frankie Lymon; Ronnie Hawkins; Eddie Cooley; Regents; Jimmie Rodgers; Cathy Carr; Buddy Knox; Cleftones; Heartbeats; Rock-A-Teens.

12 Million Sellers, Vol. 2 .... Forum (M) F 9103 25-35 60s
12 Million Sellers, Vol. 2 .... Forum (SE) SF 9103 20-30 60s
Joey Dee & Starliters; Bill Haley & His Comets; Count Basie; Joann Campbell; Chantels; Playmates; Regents; Isley Brothers; Little Anthony & Imperials; Jimmie Rodgers; Imperials; Flamingos.

12 Original Artist Hits, Vol. 1 .... Custom (M) CM 2041 10-20 60s
12 Original Artist Hits, Vol. 1 .... United (S) US-7704 10-20 60s
Teen Queens; B.B. King; young Jessie; Cadets; Joe Houston; Roscoe Gordon; Marvin & Johnny; Jesse Belvin; Jacks; Etta James; Queens; Jimmy Beasley.

12 Original Artist Hits, Vol. 2 .... United (S) US-7706 10-20 60s
B.B. King; Jesse Belvin; Richard Berry; Marvin & Johnny; Saunders King; Jacks; Etta James; Joe Turner; Teen Queens; Jimmy Witherspoon; Cadets; Jimmy Nelson.

12 Original Artist Hits, Vol. 2 .... Souffle (S) SO 2018 10-15 69
B.B. King; Jesse Belvin; Richard Berry; Marvin & Johnny; Saunders King; Jacks; Etta James; Joe Turner; Teen Queens; Jimmy Witherspoon; Cadets; Jimmy Nelson.

12 + 3 = 15 Hits .... End (M) 310 30-50 60
Little Anthony & Imperials; Jo Ann Campbell; Chantels; Dubs; Channels; Flamingos; Dubs; Temptations; Shirelles; Bobbettes.

12 Smokin' Joints (Disco Party Freaks) .... Paul Winley (S) 125 5-10 75
Ohio Players; Isley Brothers; George McCrae; B.B. King; Ben E. King; Carol Douglas; Barry White; B.T. Express; Mighty Tom Cats; Rufus Thomas; Bill Withers; Staple Singers.

12 String Story .... Horizon (M) WP-1626 10-20 63
12 String Story .... Horizon (S) ST-1626 15-25 63
Glen Campbell; Joe Maphis; Bob Gibson; others.

12 String Story, Vol. 2 .... Horizon (M) WP-1635 15-25 63
12 String Story, Vol. 2 .... Horizon (S) ST-1635 25-35 63
James McGuinn; Glenn Campbell; Billy Strange; Frank Hamilton; Dick Rosmini; Tommy Tedesco; Joe Maphis; Mason Williams; Jim Helms; Howard Roberts; Fred Gerlack.

12 Top Hits .... Modern Sound (SE) MS 1049 10-15
Chords; Bobby Sims; Fantastics; Kathy Shannon; Chellows; Flowers; Jalopy Five; Sherrie York.

12 Top Hits .... Tops (M) L-1510 8-12
Ted Weaver; Dick Heller; Mike Page; Jerry Case; Antonio Paladino; Sandy Beaumont; Streamers Trio; Jimmy Morris; Dominic Gianelli; Walter Kent; Toppers; Jerry Evans.

12 Top Teen Dances, 1961-1962 .... Cameo (M) C-1016 15-25 62
12 Top Teen Dances, 1961-1962 .... Cameo (S) CS-1016 15-25 62
Dovells; Chubby Checker; Dreamlovers; Lavenders; Apple Jacks.

13 Hits, Vol. 1 .... Grant (M) GLP-3001 10-15
Fiestas; Arthur Alexander Ivory Joe Hunter; Del-Vikings; Shields; Jimmie Dee; Tab Hunter; Sanford Clark; Gladiolas; Fontaine Sisters; Nervous Norvis.

14 By Request .... Tilt (M) TLP-1201 50-75 59?
Tren-Dells; Sultans; Carnations; Cosmo; Paul Penny; others.

14 Chart Toppers .... United Artists (M) UAL-3440 15-25 65
14 Chart Toppers .... United Artists (S) UAS-6440 20-30 65
Johnny Rivers; Frankie Avalon; Jay & Americans; Bobby Goldsboro; Manfred Mann; Danny Williams; Garnet Mimms & Enchanters.

14 Golden Recordings (From the Historic Vaults of Duke/Peacock) .... ABC (S) ABCX-784 10-20 73
Bobby Bland; Casuals; Johnny Ace; O.V. Wright; Rob Roys; Willie Mae Thornton; Junior Parker; El Toros; Clarence Gatemouth Brown; Roy Head; Roy Hinton.

14 Golden Recordings (From the Historic Vaults of Duke/Peacock) Vol. 2 .... ABC (S) ABCX-789 10-20 73
Bobby Bland; Johnny Ace; Roy Head; O.V. Wright; Ernie K-Doe; Junior Parker; John Roberts; Lamp Sisters; Paulette Parker; Clarence & Calvin; Jeanne Williams; Insights.

14 Golden Recordings (From the Historical Vaults of Vee Jay) .... ABC (S) ABCX-785 10-20 73
Dells; Gene Chandler; Betty Everett; Jerry Butler; Gladys Knight & Pips; Dee Clark; Jimmy Reed; John Lee Hooker; Eddie Harris.

14 Hit Flashbacks from the Golden Group Era .... King (M) 893 30-40 64
14 Hit Flashbacks from the Golden Group Era .... King (SE) KS-893 30-40 64
Chanters; Royals; Strangers; Checkers; Strangers; Swallows; Van Dykes; Platters; Hurricanes; Mascots.

14 More Newies But Goodies .... Mercury (M) MG-20581 20-30 60
Patti Page; Platters; Dinah Wahington; Johnny Preston; Brook Benton; Sarah Vaughan; Jivin' Gene & Jokers; Rusty Draper; Sil Austin; Ernestine Anderson; Johnny Yuma; George Jones; Elton Anderson.

14 More Newies But Goodies .... Mercury (S) SR-60241 25-35 60
(Has nine tracks in true stereo, and one in mono. Same LP as MG-20581 above.)

14 Newies But Goodies .... Mercury (M) MG-20493 25-35 60
Brook Benton; Boyd Bennett; Platters; Dinah Washington; Sarah Vaughan; Phil Phillips; Diamonds; Rod Bernard; Jivin' Gene & Jokers; Sil Austin; Ralph Marterie; Jimmy McCracklin; David Carroll.

14 No. 1 Country Hits .... RCA (S) AHL1-7004 5-10 85
Dolly Parton; Sylvia; Earl Thomas Conley; Alabama; Waylon Jennings; Steve Wariner; Ronnie Milsap; Razzy Bailey; Jerry Reed; Eddy Raven; Charley Pride.

15 Country Greats .... Columbia Musical Treasury (S) DS 556 5-10 60s
Marty Robbins; Jimmy Dean; Tammy Wynette; Bob Luman; Van Trevor; Johnny Cash; Judy Lynn; George Morgan; David Houston; Terry White; Melba Montgomery; Hank Locklin; George Jones; Johnny Horton; Stonewall Jackson.

15 Country Hits - 15 Country Stars .... Hilltop (SE) JS-6064 5-10 60s
Glen Campbell; Hank Locklin; Patsy Cline; Ferlin Husky; Wynn Stewart; Johnny Horton; Dave Dudley; Jerry Smith; Jimmy Dean; Charlie Ryan; Stuart Hamblen; Hal Willis; Stewart Family; Webb Pierce; Floyd Cramer.

15 Golden Hits .... United Artists (M) UAL-3192 20-25 62

15 Golden Hits .... United Artists (S) UAS-6192 30-35 62
Gene Pitney; Highwaymen; Ferrante & Teicher; Steve Lawrence; Don Costa; Al Caiola; Clovers; Marv Johnson; Phil Upchurch.

15 Great Country Artists, 15 Great Country Hits .... Pickwick Special Products (M) RMP 0101 10-20 68
T. Texas Tyler; Stuart Hamblen; Patsy Cline; Floyd Tillman; Charli Ryan; Carl Belew; Hank Locklin; Slim Willet; Jimmy Dean; Johnny Cash; Sonny James; Ferlin Husky; Floyd Cramer; Dave Dudley; Maddox Bros. & Rose.

15 Greatest Songs of the Beatles .... Vee Jay (M) VJLP 1101 75-100 64

15 Greatest Songs of the Beatles .... Vee Jay (S) VJLPS 1101 150-200 64

15 Hits: see Original Hits, Vol. 5

15 Number 1 Hits: see Original Hits, Vol. 10

15 Original Big Hits: see Stax 15 Original Big Hits

15 Original Rock and Roll Biggies, Vol. 2 .... American Variety Int'l (S) AVSM-9002 8-12
Platters; Little Anthony & Imperials; Gloria Jones; Standells; Chocolate Watchband; Tradewinds; Shangri-Las; Dixie Cups; E-Types; El Coco; Day By Day Original Cast; Brenton Wood; Forum; Bobby Fuller Four.

15th Anniversary Country Music Awards .... Ronco (S) 3220 5-10 80
Mickey Gilley; Statler Brothers; Tanya Tucker; Cal Smith; Freddy Weller; Barbara Mandrell; Roger Miller; John Conlee; Charlie Rich; Linda Ronstadt; Ray Price; Donna Fargo; Freddy Fender; Tammy Wynette; Merle Haggard.

15th Annual Academy of Country Music Awards .... Columbia (S) P-15419 5-10 80
(Special products release for Ronco.) Mickey Gilley; Statler Brothers; Tanya Tucker; Cal Smith; Freddy Weller; Barbara Mandrell; Roger Miller; John Conlee; Charlie Rich; Linda Ronstadt; Johnny Paycheck; Ray Price; Donna Fargo; Freddy Fender; Tammy Wynette; Merle Haggard.

16 Big Hits: see 16 Original Big Hits [Motown series.]

16 Boss Oldies (Jack Diamond Remembers) .... Eric (S) 1600 5-10
Bobby Fuller Four; Santo & Johnny; Duprees; Terry Stafford; Shelley Fabares; Little Eva; Ronnie & Hi Lites; Dubs; Jay Wiggins; Marcels; Tymes; Paris Sisters; J. Frank Wilson; Gene Chandler; Freddy Scott; Angels.

16 Collectors Goodies: see Blasts from the Past

16 Country Gospel Hits .... Everest (SE) CML 5 8-12 80
Roy Acuff; T. Texas Tyler; Patsy Cline; Miller Family; Carl Story; Texas Jim Robertson; Maddox Brothers & Rose; Texas Jim Robertson.

16 Fiddler's Greatest Hits .... Gusto (S) SD-3014 5-10 77
Scotty Stoneman; Howdy Forrester; Chubby Wise; Buck Ryan; Buddy Spicher; Shorty Lavender; Ken Clark; Harry Choates; Mac Magaha; Benny Martin; Fiddlin' Arthur Smith; Curly Fox; Jerry Rivers; Fiddlin' Red Herron; Joe "Red" Hayes; Tommy Jackson.

16 Golden Grooves for Collectors Only (Charlie Apple Presents) .... Pantomime (M) 999 8-12
Flourescents; Continental Five; Lovelarks; Infascinations; Kacties; Screaming Jay Hawkins; Chevrons; Capris; Orbits; Five Roses; Five Sounds; Vitones; Zircons; Velvetones; Roxie & Daychords.

16 Golden Oldies, Vol. 1 .... Trip (S) TLP-8001 8-12 72
Turtles; Beach Boys; Chad & Jeremy; Cascades; Terry Stafford; John Fred; Soul Survivors; Aaron Neville; Brenton Woods; Count Five; Dells; Shangri-Las.

16 Golden Oldies, Vol. 2 .... Trip (S) TLP 8002 8-12 72

16 Golden Oldies, Vol. 3 .... Trip (S) 8003 8-12 72

16 Golden Oldies, Vol. 4 .... Trip (S) TLP-8004 8-12 72
Embers; Johnny & Joe; Wilbert Harrison; Gladys Knight & Pips; Charts; Starlights; Lloyd Price; Patti LaBelle & Blue Belles; Five Satins; Jive Five; Lee Andrews & Hearts; Fireflies; Bobby Day; Maxine Brown.

16 Golden Oldies, Vol. 5 .... Trip (S) TLP-8005 8-12 72
Dale & Grace; Jackie Lee; Leaves; Forum; Ad Libs; Shangri-Las; Inez Foxx; Dixie Cups; Seeds; Boby Fuller Four; Dobie Gray; Patti LaBelle & Blue Belles; Barbara Lynn; Lloyd Price; Betty Everett.

16 Golden Oldies, Vol. 6 .... Trip (S) TLP-8006 8-12 72
Elmore James; Buster Brown; Tousaint McCall; Bobby Powell; Don Gardner & Dee Dee Ford; Lee Dorsey; Wilson Pickett; Ike & Tina Turner; Barbara George; Jimmy Hughes; Lloyd Price; Maxine Brown.

16 Golden Oldies, Vol. 7 .... Trip (S) 8022 8-12 72
Skyliners; Jesters; Cadillacs; Dubs; Channels; Classics; Paragons; Spaniels; Teen Queens; El Dorados; Kodaks; Moonglows; Roomates; Volumes.

16 Golden Oldies, Vol. 8 .... Trip (S) 80?? 8-12 72

16 Golden Oldies, Vol. 9 .... Trip (S) 80?? 8-12 72

16 Golden Oldies, Vol. 10 .... Trip (S) 8031 8-12 72
Chiffons; Dion & Belmonts; Dee Clark; Gerry & Pacemakers; Dixie Cups; Jack Scott; Dave "Baby" Cortez; Raindrops; Jerry Butler & Betty Everett; Happenings; Turtles; Jimmy Charles; Duals; Bobby Freeman.

16 Golden Oldies, Vol. 11 .... Trip (S) 8032 8-12 72
Mystics; Happenings; Olympics; Beach Boys; Angels; Chiffons; Les Cooper; Jerry Butler; Angels; Dion; Gerry & Pacemakers; Anita Bryant; Paul Evans; Little Richard; Chris Kenner; Lloyd Price; Johnny & Hurricanes.

16 Greatest Country Hits .... Trip (S) TOP-16-26 5-10 76
Sammi Smith; Ronnie Milsap; Buck Owens; Patsy Cline; George Jones; Orville Couch; Dave Dudley; Henson Cargill; Roger Miller; B.J. Thomas; Rex Allen; Melba Montgomery; Roy Drusky; Harold Dorman; Tex Ritter.

16 Greatest Truck Driver Hits .... Gusto (S) SD-3024 5-10 78
Claude Gray; Willis Brothers; Red Sovine; Pete Drake; Jimmy Martin; Stanley Brothers; Charlie Moore; Hylo Brown; Del Reeves; Reno & Smiley; Slim Jacobs; Bobby Sykes; Moore & Napier; Coleman Wilson; Benny Martin; Tommy Hill Music Festival.

16 #1 Hits of the Early Sixties........Motown (S) 5248ML 5-10 82
Smokey Robinson & Miracles; Marvelettes; Contours; Stevie Wonder; Martha & Vandellas; Mary Wells; Diana Ross & Supremes; Temptations; Jr. Walker & All Stars; Four Tops.

16 #1 Hits of the Late Sixties........Motown (S) 5249ML 5-10 82
Diana Ross & Supremes; Isley Brothers; Elgins; Jimmy Ruffin; Stevie Wonder; Monitors; Jr. Walker & All Stars; Temptations; Jackson Five.

16 Original Big Hits, Vol. 1........Tamla (M) TM-??? 10-20 64
(Has yellow label with globe logo.)

16 Original Big Hits, Vol. 1........Motown (M) MT-614 10-20 64

16 Original Big Hits, Vol. 1........Motown (S) MS-614 10-20 64
Miracles; Marvelettes; Barrett Strong; Marvin Gaye; Martha & Vandellas; Eddie Holland; Supremes; Mary Wells; Kim Weston; Contours; Little Stevie Wonder.

16 Original Big Hits, Vol. 2........Tamla (M) TM-256 10-20 64
Martha & Vandellas; Mary Wells; Supremes; Marvin Gaye; Contours; Stevie Wonder; Miracles; Eddie Holland; Temptations; Mrvelettes; Marvin Gaye; Kim Weston; Valadiers. (Has yellow label with globe logo.)

16 Original Big Hits, Vol. 3........Motown (M) MT-624 10-20 65

16 Original Big Hits, Vol. 3........Motown (S) MS-624 10-20 65
Miracles; Brenda Holloway; Temptations; Marvelettes; Martha & Vandellas; Stevie Wonder; Contours; Supremes; Spinners; Mary Wells; Marvin Gaye.

16 Original Big Hits, Vol. 4........Motown (M) M-633 10-20 65

16 Original Big Hits, Vol. 4........Motown (S) MS-633 10-20 65
Four Tops; Supremes; Mary Wells; Temptations; Martha & Vandellas; Jr. Walker & All Stars; Marvin Gaye & Mary Wells; Marvelettes; Miracles; Shorty Long; Contours.

16 Original Big Hits, Vol. 5........Motown (M) M-651 10-20 66

16 Original Big Hits, Vol. 5........Motown (S) MS-651 10-20 66
Jr. Walker & All Stars; Marvin Gaye; Temptations; Four Tops; Supremes; Martha & Vandellas; Miracles; Kim Weston; Brenda Holloway; Stevie Wonder; Marvelettes; Contours.

16 Original Big Hits, Vol. 6........Motown (M) M-655 10-20 67

16 Original Big Hits, Vol. 6........Motown (S) MS-655 10-20 67
Supremes; Miracles; Marvin Gaye; Jr. Walker & All Stars; Martha & Vandellas; Marvelettes; Jimmy Ruffin; Tammi Terrell; Isley Brothers; Kim Weston; Temptations; Stevie Wonder; Contours; Spinners; Velvelettes.

16 Original Big Hits, Vol. 7........Motown (M) M-661 10-20 67

16 Original Big Hits, Vol. 7........Motown (S) MS-661 10-20 67
Supremes; Stevie Wonder; Jr. Walker & All Stars; Elgins; Temptations; Marvelettes; Shorty Long; Tammi Terrell; Martha & Vandellas; Jimmy Ruffin; Smokey Robinson & Miracles; Marvin Gaye; Kim Weston; Four Tops.

16 Original Big Hits, Vol. 8........Motown (M) M-666 10-20 67

16 Original Big Hits, Vol. 8........Motown (S) MS-666 10-20 67
Stevie Wonder; Martha & Vandellas; Marvin Gaye; Diana Ross & Supremes; Temptations; Four Tops; Jimmy Ruffin; Jr. Walker & All Stars; Monitors; Gladys Knight & Pips; Isley Brothers; Elgins; Smokey Robinson & Miracles.

16 Original Big Hits, Vol. 9........Motown (M) M-668 10-20 68

16 Original Big Hits, Vol. 9........Motown (S) MS-668 10-20 68
Temptations; Diana Ross & Supremes; Impressions; Marvin Gaye & Tammi Terrell; Four Tops; Miracles; Stevie Wonder; Martha Reeves & Vandellas; Jr. Walker; Marvelettes; Gladys Knight & Pips; Smokey Robinson & Miracles; Jimmy Ruffin.

16 Original Big Hits, Vol. 10........Motown (M) M-684 10-20 69

16 Original Big Hits, Vol. 10........Motown (S) MS-684 10-20 69
Diana Ross & Supremes; Gladys Knight & Pips; Temptations; Martha & Vandellas; Four Tops; Stevie Wonder; Marvin Gaye; Brenda Holloway; Marvin Gaye & Tammi Terrell; Isley Brothers; Spinners; Edwin Starr; Barbara Randolf.

16 Original Big Hits, Vol. 11........Motown (M) M-693 10-20 69

16 Original Big Hits, Vol. 11........Motown (S) MS-693 10-20 69
Stevie Wonder; Marvin Gaye & Tammi Terrell; Supremes; Tamptations; Miracles; Bobby Taylor & Vancouvers; Four Tops; Marvelettes; Isley Brothers.

16 Original Golden Oldies, Vol. 1........Jocko (S) LPS-965-1 8-12
Charts; Channels; Five Satins; Capris; Little Caesar & Romans; Johnny & Joe; Danleers; Ad Libs; Paradons; Wilbert Harrison; Dave "Baby" Cortez; Patty LaBelle & Blue Belles; Del Shannon; Dubs; Roomates.

16 Original Golden Oldies, Vol. 2........Jocko (S) LPS-965-2 8-12
Penguins; Lee Andrews & Hearts; Ritchie Valens; Jive Five; Mello Kings; Tommy Edwards; Jimmy Charles; Dee Clark; Chantels; Jaguars; Dion; Teen Queens; Jerry Butler; Carla Thomas; Dixie Cups; Bobby Day.

16 Rock Guitar Greats........Trip (S) TOP-16-27 5-10 76
Jeff Beck; Jimi Hendrix; Yardbirds; Spencer Davis Group; Elmore James; Rory Gallagher; Canned Heat; others.

16 Rock Vocal Greats........Trip (S) TOP-16-30 5-10 76
Rod Stewart; John Baldry; Brian Auger; Jimi Hendrix; Eric Clapton; Rory Gallagher; Animals; others.

16 Successful Sounds: see Godfrey Presents 16 Successful Sounds

18 Country Legends........DMG (S) 4133 8-12 81
Johnny Cash; Dave Dudley; Slim Whitman; Jeannie C. Riley; Roger Miller; Flatt & Scruggs; Wynn Stewart; Johnny Paycheck; Carlisles; Jimmy Dean; Carl Belew; Patsy Cline; Floyd Tillman; Charlie Ryan; Moon Mullican; Hank Locklin; Carl Perkins; Red Simpson.

18 Great Hits of the '30s & '40s........Homestead/Pickwick (SE) HOM-18 5-10 70s
Pied Pipers; Artie Shaw; Connie Boswell; Three Suns; Ray Eberle; Kate Smith; Tony Pastor; Maxine Sullivan; Woody Herman; Ink Spots; Charlie Barnet; Ginny Sims; Clyde McCoy; Frankie Laine; Dorsey Brothers; Kay Starr; Duke Ellington; Raymond Scott.

18 King-Size Country Hits........Columbia (M) CL-2668 10-20 67

18 King-Size Country Hits........Columbia (S) CS-9468 10-20 67
Cowboy Copas; Grandpa Jones; Stanley Brothers; others.

18 King-Size Rhythm and Blues Hits........Columbia (M) CL-2667 20-30 67

18 King-Size Rhythm and Blues Hits........Columbia (S) CS-9467 20-30 67
Platters; Earl Bostic; Otis Williams; Hank Ballard & Midnighters; Little Willie John; James Brown & Famous Flames; Freddy King; Joe Tex; Bill Doggett; Wynonie Harris; Sonny Thompson; Ivory Joe Hunter; Bullmoose Jackson; Five Royales; Billy Ward & Dominoes; Lonnie Johnson; Otis Williams & Charms; Otis Redding.

18 Original Rock and Roll Biggies (2 LP)........American Variety Int'l (S) BAVL-1038 8-12 75
Ad Libs; Standells; Hannibal; Shangri-Las; Joshua; Jelly Beans; Tune Weavers; Gloria Jones; Harptones; Forum; Sopwith Camel; E Types; Sir Douglas Quintet; Robert Parker; Aaron Neville; Dixie Cups; Standells; Joshua.

19 Hot Country Requests .... Epic (M) FE-39597 5-10 84
Merle Haggard; Mickey Gilley; Willie Nelson; Ricky Skaggs; George Jones; B.J. Thomas; David Allan Coe; Merle Haggard; Willie Nelson; George Jones; Janie Fricke; Ronnie McDowell; B.J. Thomas; Mickey Gilley; Charly McClain; Larry Gatlin & Gatlin Brothers.

19 Hot Country Requests, Vol. 2 .... Epic (M) FE-40175 5-10 85
Ricky Skaggs; Merle Haggard; Exile; George Jones; Willie Nelson; B.J. Thomas; Ronnie McDowell; Charly McClain; Crystal Gayle; Lacy J. Dalton; David Allan Coe; Johnny Rodriguez; Janie Fricke; Mickey Gilley; Roasanne Cash.

20/20: Twenty No. 1 Hits from Twenty Years at Motown (2 LP) .... Motown (S) MS-937 8-12 80
Jackson 5; Smokey Robinson & Miracles; Michael Jackson; Eddie Kendricks; Diana Ross; Miracles; Stevie Wonder; Diana Ross & Supremes; Temptations; Marvin Gaye; Commodores.

20 All Star Country Hits (2 LP) .... RCA (S) R 214225 8-12 77
Ronnie Milsap; Dottsy; Floyd Cramer; Dickey Lee; Chet Atkins; Eddy Arnold; Bobby Bare; Dave & Sugar; Vernon Oxford; Willie Nelson; Jim Reeves; Billy Walker; Jim Ed Brown; Helen Cornelius; Gary Stewart; Danny Davis; Charley Pride; Hank Snow; Jerry Reed; Dottie West; Charlie Rich.

20 All Time Greats of the '50s .... K-Tel NU-413 5-10 71
Mitch Miller; Johnnie Ray; Johnny Mathis; Marty Robbins; Johnny Cash; Four Lads; Louis Armstrong; Vic Damone; Guy Mitchell; Frankie Laine; Stonewall Jackson; Tony Bennett; Doris Day; Les Paul & Mary Ford; Patti Page.

20 All Time No. 1 Hits .... Roulette (M) R-25290 20-25 65
20 All Time No. 1 Hits .... Roulette (SE) SR-25290 20-25 65
Buddy Knox; Joey Dee; Essex; Jimmie Rodgers; Frankie Lymon; Chantels; Crows; Little Anthony & Imperials; Playmates; Lee Dorsey; Joe Jones; Buster Brown; Heartbeats.

20 "Big Boss" Favorites (10 Great Hits of 1964 - 10 Great Oldies Hits) .... Roulette (M) R-25304 15-20 65
20 "Big Boss" Favorites (10 Great Hits of 1964 - 10 Great Oldies Hits) .... Roulette (S) SR-25304 15-20 65
Chubby Checker; Patti LaBelle & Blue Belles; J. Frank Wilson; Bobby Rydell; Little Anthony & Imperials; Beau Brummels; Harptones; Lou Christie; Ray Barretto; Channels; Bobby Lewis; Dale & Grace; Chartbusters; Joey Dee & Starliters; Eddie Cooley; Hullaballoos; Jimmy Bowen; Cadillacs; Classics.

20 Big Country Artists - 27 Hits (2 LP) .... GRT (SE) 2103-704 8-12 74
Johnny Cash; Charlie Rich; Jeannie C. Riley; Bill Justis; Carl Perkins; Roy Orbison; Jerry Lee Lewis; Donna Fargo; Johnny Tillotson; Mel Street; Ferlin Husky; Roy Clark; Jan Howard; Hagers; Lefty Frizzell; Bobby G. Rice; Johnny Carver; Stonewall Jackson; Ray Stevens; Billy Crash Craddock.

20 Collector's Records of the '50s & '60s, Vol. 2 .... Laurie (S) R 170231 5-10 89
Music Explosion; Petula Clark; Coasters; Drifters; Dion & Belmonts; Mystics; Tokens; Passions; Dean & Jean; Chiffons; Four Epics; Reparata & Delrons; Ray-Vons; Ernie Maresca; Demilles; Harps.

20 Chartstoppers, Vol. 1 .... Salem-Select (S) SA-1001 8-12 74
Lobo; B.J. Thomas; Dave & Ansil Collins; Stylistics; James Brown; Joe Jeffrey Group; Glass Bottle; Bells; Jim Stover; Bullet; Manfred Mann; Neighborhood; Mel & Tim; Morning Mist; Magic Lanterns.

20 Country Artists Singing Their Original Hits .... Artistic (S) LP-711 8-12 69
Patsy Cline; Jimmy Dean; Wynn Stewart; Hank Locklin; Cowboy Copas; Johnny Bond; George Jones; Arthur "Guitar" Smith; Eddie Dean; Webb Pierce; Jerry Wallace; Hylo Brown; Red Sovine; Jan Howard; Sunshine Boys; Moon Mullican; String Bean; Carl Story; Willis Brothers; Justin Tubb; Archie Campbell

20 Dynamic Hits: see Top Star Festival 20 Dynamic Hits

20 Electrifying Hits (2 LP) .... Commonwealth (S) MO 333 8-12 72
Ray Stevens; Tokens; Raiders; Turtles; Dixie Cups; Joe Jones; others.

20 Explosive Hits .... Crystal (S) 1500 8-12 71
Mungo Jerry; Edison Lighthouse; Stairsteps; Box Tops; Classics IV; Who; Alive 'N Kicking; Jaggerz; Tee Set; Bob Lind; Shocking Blue; Hugh Masekela; Cufflinks; Tommy James & Shondells; Canned Heat; Bee Gees; Intruders; Bill Deal.

20 Explosive Original Hits .... K-Tel (S) TU-220 8-12 71
Mungo Jerry; Edison Lighthouse; Stairsteps; Box Tops; Classics IV; Who; Alive 'N Kicking; Jaggerz; Tee Set; Bob Lind; Shocking Blue; Hugh Masekela; Cufflinks; Tommy James & Shondells; Canned Heat; Three Degrees; Intruders; Bill Deal.

20 Famous Country Hits .... Crystal (S) CR 1400 5-10
Johnny Cash; George Jones; Henson Cargill; Patsy Cline; Conway Twitty; Ray Charles; Loretta Lynn; Bill Anderson; Lefty Frizzell; Hank Williams; Red Foley; Jack Greene; Kitty Wells; Jimmy Rodgers; Buck Owens; Ernest Tubb; Johnny Bond.

20 Famous Country Hits, Vol. 4 .... K-Tel (S) WV 320 5-10
Johnny Cash; George Jones; Henson Cargill; Patsy Cline; Conway Twitty; Ray Charles; Loretta Lynn; Bill Anderson; Lefty Frizzell; Hank Williams; Red Foley; Johnny Bond; Jack Greene; Kitty Wells; Jimmy Rodgers; Buck Owens; Ernest Tubb.

20 Golden Nuggets (Jimmy Bishop Presents) .... Antique (S) 1000 10-15 68
Aretha Franklin; Lee Dorsey; Impressions; Poets; Gene Chandler; Olympics; Five Stairsteps; Barbara Mason; Aaron Neville; Volcanos; Otis Redding; Sam & Dave; Capitols; Intruders; Bar-Kays; Mad Lads; Gladys Night & Pips; Esquires; Freddie Scott.

20 Golden Souvenirs Of Music City U.S.A., Vol. 2 .... Plantation (S) PLP-533 5-10 78
(Green vinyl.) Johnny Cash; Jerry Lee Lewis, Rita Remington; Jeannie C. Riley; Leroy VanDyke; Charlie Rich; Jimmy C. Newman; Hank Locklin; Charlie Walker; John Wesley Ryles; Willie Nelson; Dave Dudley; David Allan Coe; Jeannie C. Riley; James O'Gwynn; Murry Kellum; Gordon Terry; Paul Martin; Rufus Thibodeaux; Rex Allen Jr.; Jimmy Davis.

20 Great Hits, 20 Great Artists .... Plantation (S) PLP-521 5-10 77
Jimmy C. Newman; David Allan Coe; Rex Allen Jr. Maxine Brown; James O'Gwynn; John Wesley Ryles; Linda Martel; Tennessee Guitars; Robbie Harden; Eddie Burns; Ruby Wright; Sleepy LaBeef; Ray Pillow; Debbie Lori Kaye; Harlow Wilcox; Little David Wilkins; George Kent; Tokyo Matsu.

20 Great Hits - Country Sounds, Vol. 1 .... Ronco/Columbia Special Products (S) CS1-1001 5-10 72
Sammi Smith; Tommy Overstreet; George Jones; Tammy Wynette; Henson Cargill; Lynn Anderson; Faron Young; Roy Drusky; Marty Robbins; Dave Dudley; David Houston; Johnny Cash; Roger Miller; Tom T. Hall; Statler Brothers; Jeannie Seely; Ray Price; Hank Thompson; Roy Clark.

20 Great Memories .... Fat John (S) 2003 5-10
Crystals; Gene Chandler; Angels; Echoes; Fireflies; Dixie Cups; Gladys Knight; Otis Redding; Johnny Thunder; Blue Bells; Little Caesar & Romans; Charts; Richard Fields; Jerry Butler; Maxine Brown; Channels; Yvonne Carroll; Danleers; Classics; Shep & Limelites.

20 Great Stars Perform 20 Great Hits of the '60s .... Columbia (S) GP-25 10-15 70
Andy Williams; Robert Goulet; Tony Bennet; Jim Nabors; Aretha Franklin; Barbara Streisand; O.C. Smith; Johnny Cash; Percy Faith; Jerry Vale; Johnny Mathis; Charlie Byrd; Eydie Gorme; Steve Lawrence; Ray Conniff; Andre Kostelanetz; Aretha Franklin; John Davidson..

20 Greatest Blues Hits .... United (S) US-7748 10-15 70s
20 Greatest Blues Hits By the Original Artists .... Kent (M) 527/5027 8-12 60s
20 Greatest Blues Hits By the Original Artists .... Custom (M) RB-1 10-15 60s
B.B. King; Jimmy Witherspoon; Elmore James; Roosevelt Sykes; Jimmy McCracklin; Pee Wee Crayton; Howlin' Wolf; Saunders King; Smokey Hogg; Lowell Fulson; John Lee Hooker; Lightnin' Hopkins; Jimmy Nelson; Roscoe Gordon; Jimmy Beasley.

20 Heavy Hits .... Crystal (S) S-600 8-12
(Mail order offer. Same as below, Adam VIII (S) 600.)

20 Heavy Hits .... Adam VIII (S) 600 5-10
Janis Joplin; Impressions; Tommy James & Shondells; Strawberry Alarm Clock; Len Barry; Delfonics; Intruders; Ohio Express; Who; Richardo Ray; 1910 Fruitgum Company; Turtles; Amboy Dukes; Happenings; Lemon Pipers; Sonny & Cher.

20 Knocked Out Nifties of the Past (Joe Niagara Presents) .... Lost-Nite (M) LP-106 8-12
Dovells; Lee Andrews & Hearts; Bobby Lewis; Duprees; Gary "U.S." Bonds; Capris; Collegians; Ritchie Valens; Cobras; Little Anthony & Imperials; Isley Brothers; Jive Five; Boss Tones; Little Caesar & Romans; Orlons; Crests; Coasters; Drifters; Shirelles.

20 Monster Hits (2 LP) .... Columbia Musical Treasury (S) DS 951-2 10-15 72

20 Monster Hits (2 LP) .... Columbia House (S) P2S-5760 10-15 72
(Mail order offer.) Donovan; Paul Revere & Raiders; Dr. Hook; Laura Nyro; Big Brother & Holding Company; Stephen Stills/Al Kooper; Lookig Glass; Red Bone; Blood, Sweat & Tears; Argent; Hollies; Pacific Gas & Electric; Santana; Ten Years After; Zombies; Byrds; Sweathog; Chase; Poco; Buckinghams.

20 of the Greatest Dance Records of All Times .... Scepter (SE) SPS-5106 8-12 72
Major Lance; Hank Ballard & Midnighters; Olympics; Robert Parker; Bob & Earl; Jackie Lee; Du-Tones; Joey Dee & Starliters; Little Richard; Mel & Tim; Little Eva; Lee Dorsey; Lloyd Price; Larks; Ray Barretta; Bobby Freeman.

20 Oldies But Goodies, Vol. 1 .... Rare Bird (S) 8003 8-12
Five Delights; Willows; Don Julian & Meadowlarks; Genies; Crests; Jesters; Paragons; Scarlets; Shirley & Lee; Hearts; Untouchables; Bluenotes; Valiants; Quintones; Penguins; Moonglows; Spinners; Maurice Williams & Zodiacs.

20 Original Country Classics .... Mercury (S) MERC 301 5-10 73
Tom T. Hall; Faron Young; Jerry Lee Lewis; Dave Dudley; Roger Miller; Roy Druskey; Statler Brothers.

20 Original Golden Oldies, Vol. 1 .... Mr. Maestro (M) LP-1001 15-25 63
El Dorados; Cashmeres; others.

20 Original Golden Oldies, Vol. 2 .... Mr. Maestro (M) LP-1010 15-25 63
Royal Teens; Dave "Baby" Cortez; Angels; Bobby Lewis; Jimmy Charles; Echoes; Ivy Three; Dee Clark; Cadillacs; Magnificents; Bobby Freeman; Channels; Cashmeres; Jerry Butler & Impressions; Al Brown's Tune Toppers; Fireflies; Ike & Tina Turner; El Dorados; Fidelitys; Patty Labelle & Blue Belles.

20 Original Golden Oldies, Vol. 3 .... Mr. Maestro (M) LP-1111 15-25 63
Gene Chandler; Crests; Orioles; Three Friends; Willows; Lee Andrews & Hearts; Harptones; Bobby Lewis; Excellents; King Curtis; Johnnie & Joe; Contours; Shirelles; Jerry Butler; Billie & Lillie; Janie Grant; Cadillacs; Marvelettes; Angels; Claudine Clark.

20 Original Golden Oldies, Vol. 4 .... Mr. Maestro (M) LP-1112 15-25 63
Lee Dorsey; Percells; Johnny Thunder; Rosie & Originals; Wilbert Harrison; Gladys Knight & Pips; Les Cooper; Crests; Gary "U.S." Bonds; Dee Clark; Dells; Don Gardner & Dee Ford; Danleers; Charts; Champs; Cupids; Deltairs; Bobby Marchan; Shep & Limelites.

20 Original Golden Oldies, Vol. 5 .... Mr. Maestro (M) LP-1113 15-25 63
Mongo Santamaria; Crescendos; Larry Hall; Troy Shondell; Jack Scott; Jimmy Reed; Jerry Butler; Anita Bryant; Eddie Harris; Hollywood Argyles; Pastel Six; Jerry Wallace; Paul Evans; Rocketones; Dee Clark; Spaniels; Patsy Cline; Gene Chandler; Cannonball Adderley; Gladys Knight & Pips.

20 Original Hits .... Mark-Fi (M) LP-999 15-25 63
Penguins; Innocents; Jerry Butler; Little Anthony; Ray Sharpe; Dubs; Dee Clark; Harptones; Paris Sisters; Kathy Young & Innocents; Jesse Belvin; Youngsters; Rosie & Originals; Crystals; Flamingos; Bobby Day; Eugene Church; Crystals; Jimmy Norman; Marvin & Johnny.

20 Original Hits of the '70s .... TVP (S) TVP-1024 5-10 77
(Mail order offer.) Melanie; Three Dog Night; Hamilton, Joe Frank & Reynolds; Love Unlimited featuring Barry White; Billy Paul; Billy Paul; Hot Butter; Dobie Gray; Stories; Vicki Lawrence; Gladys Knight & Pips; O'Jays; Sylvia; MFSB; Linda Ronstadt; Three Degrees; Rufus (featuring Chaka Khan); Van McCoy; Rhythm Heritage; Walter Murphy; Stylistics.

20 Original Hits from the Soundtrack of Hometown U.S.A.: see Hometown U.S.A.

20 Original Oldies .... Almor (M) A-100 10-20 64

20 Original Oldies .... Almor (S) AS-100 10-20 64
Faye Adams; Three Friends; Willows; Shepherd Sisters; Tokens; Quintones; Eternals; Fireflies; Dubs; Jesters; Del-Vikings; Neil Sedaka & Tokens; Harptones; Monarchs; Videls; Medallions; Halos; Cufflinks; Fireballs; Angels.

20 Original Winners, Vol. 1 .... Roulette (M) R-25249 15-20 64
Wilbert Harrison; Bobby Lewis; Joe Jones; Joey Dee; Chantels; Little Joey & Flips; Eddie Cooley; Chubby Checker; Cleftones; Crows; Penguins; Billy Bland; Lee Dorsey; Moonglows; Little Eva; Dovells; Cadillacs; Drifters; Lou Christie.

20 Original Winners, Vol. 2 .... Roulette (M) R-25251 15-20 64
Frankie Lymon; Channels; Maxine Brown; Spaniels; Maurice Williams; Little Anthony; Five Satins; Lee Allen; Regents; Coasters; Ben E. King; Jerry Butler; Flamingos; Joe Henderson; Fiestas; Moonglows; Turbans; Cadillacs; Monotones.

20 Original Winners, Vol. 3 .... Roulette (M) R-25263 15-20 64
Etta James; Coasters; Ruth Brown; Lou Christie; Harptones; Robert & Johnny; Chuck Berry; Little Richard; Edsels; Ral Donner; Shirley & Lee; Eternals; Chuck Willis; Devotions; Heartbeats; Dion & Belmonts; Jesse Belvin; Buster Brown; Faye Adams; Joey Dee & Starliters.

20 Original Winners, Vol. 4 .... Roulette (M) R-25264 15-20 64
Carla Thomas; Joey Dee; Crystals; Sonny Til & Orioles; Little Anthony & Imperials; Lee Dorsey; Tune Weavers; Cleftones; Lee Andrews & Hearts; Bobbettes; Johnny & Hurricanes; Jack Scott; Crests; Neil Sedaka & Tokens; Ruth McFadden; Bo Diddley; Cadets; Moonglows; Paul Evans; String-A-Longs.

20 Original Winners of 1964 .... Roulette (M) R-25293 10-15 65

20 Original Winners of 1964 .... Roulette (S) SR-25293 10-15 65
Drifters; Marvin Gaye; Millie Small; Martha & Vandellas; Patty & Emblems; Jerry Butler; Barbara Lewis; Reflections; Mary Wells; Rivieras; Betty Everett; Gene Chandler; Detergents; Exciters; Bobby Freeman; Honeycombs; Jimmy Hughes; Raindrops; Miracles.

20 Power Hits, Vol. 1 .... K-Tel (S) ???? 5-10
Sly & Family Stone; Gary Puckett & Union Gap; Santana; Janis Joplin; Mark Lindsay; Spirit; Pacific Gas & Electric; Byrds; Blood, Sweat & Tears; Hollies; Spiral Staircase; Poco; Billy Joe Royal; It's a Beautiful Day; Chambers Brothers; Big Brother & Holding Company.

20 Power Hits, Vol. 2 .... K-Tel (S) TU-222 5-10 71
Tommy James; Dawn; Partridge Family; Wadsworth Family Mansion; Delfonics; Isley Brothers; Dells; Melanie; Ocean; Bells; Sugarloaf; Guess Who; Fuzz; Brian Hyland; Ray Charles; Curtis Mayfield; Edwin Hawkins Singers; Joe Simon; Dawn.

20 Rock Revival Greats .... K-Tel (S) NI-4750 5-10 70s
Platters; Lloyd Price; Silhouettes; Timi Yuro; Chad Allen; Guess Who; Coasters; Freddy Cannon; Jimmy Gilmer; Ray Peterson; Jimmy Clanton; Buddy Knox; Troy Shondell; Mel & Tim; Dee Clark.

20 Rockin' Originals (2 LP) .... Pickwick (S) PTP-2060 8-12
Chuck Berry, Jerry Lee Lewis; Fats Domino; Platters; Bill Haley & His Comets; Big Bopper; 5 Satins; Wilbert Harrison; Tommy Roe; Bobby Day; Diamonds; Jimmy Clanton; Charlie Ryan; Paragons; Crew-Cuts; Champs; Dusty Springfield; Ray Stevens; Frankie Ford.

20 Rockin' Originals (2 LP)....Pickwick (S) PTP-2082 8-12
Hondells; Left Banke; Poni-Tails; Paul & Paula; Penguins; Royal Teens; Angels; Diamonds; Elegents; Lloyd Price; Sparkletones; Danny & Juniors; George Hamilton IV; Muvva "Guitar" Hubbard; Tommy Roe; Del-Vikings; Steve Gibson & Redcaps; Blues Magoos; Spanky & Our Gang.

20 Solid Gold Hits....Crystal (S) S-1200 10-15 60s
Tommy James & Shondells; Vanilla Fudge; Animals; Brooklyn Bridge; Bee Gees; Cowsills; Derek; Lovin' Spoonful; Turtles; Righteous Brothers; Dionne Warwick; J.J. Jackson; Miracles; Joe Tex; Ben E. King; Janis Joplin; Young Rascals; Johnny Nash. (Songs are reportedly edited versions, not full length.)

20 Solid Gold Hits....Adam VIII (S) A-8016 5-10 74
(Mail order offer.) Love Unlimited Orchestra; Carl Douglas; Bachman-Turner Overdirve; Stylistics; Gladys Knight & Pips; Spinners; George McCrae; Jim Weatherly; Fancy; Truth; others.

20 Soulful Oldies, Vol. 1....Vee Jay Vintage/Oldies (SE) 1001 10-15 72
Olympics; Capris; Little Richard; Dee Clark; Quintones; Spaniels; Maurice Williams; Joe Simon; Richard Berry; Impressions; Gladys Knight & Pips; Jimmy Charles; Scarlets; Marvin & Johnny; Harptones; Joe Jones; Flamingos; Dubs; Angels; Mark II.

20 Soulful Oldies, Vol. 2....Vee Jay Vintage/Oldies (SE) 1002 10-15 72
Little Richard; Olympics; Lee Dorsey; Dee Clark; Gene Chandler; Dells; Willows; Bob & Earl; Flamingos; Buster Brown; Gene Chandler; Betty Everett & Jerry Butler; John Lee Hooker; Gladys Knight & Pips; Skyliners; Eldorados; Harptones; Jackie Lee.

20 Soulful Oldies, Vol. 3....Vee Jay Vintage/Oldies (SE) 1003 10-15 72
John Lee Hooker; Jimmy Reed; Jimmy Hughes; Billy Preston; Dells; Betty Everett & Jerry Butler; Betty Everett; Jerry Butler; Wilbert Harrison; Chris Kenner; Bobby Lewis; Jennell Hawkins; Jessie Belvin; Etta James; Faye Adams; Buster Brown; Roscoe Gordon; Bob & Earl; Wade Flemmons.

20 Soulful Oldies, Vol. 4....Vee Jay Vintage/Oldies (SE) 1004 10-15 72
Jennell Hawkins; Olympics; Jerry Butler; others.

20 Soulful Oldies, Vol. 5....Vee Jay Vintage/Oldies (SE) 1005 10-15 72
Ritchie Valens; Dee Clark; others.

20 Soulful Oldies, Vol. 6....Vee Jay Vintage/Oldies (SE) 1006 10-15 72
Jimmy Reed; Maxine Brown; Bob & Earl; others.

20 Spotlight Hits....Columbia (S) DS-78 10-20 68
Bob Dylan; Dave Clark Five; Major Lance; Rip Chords; Dion; New Christy Minstrels; Aretha Franklin; Bobby Vinton; Village Stompers; Chuck Bene & Mice; Paul Revere & Raiders; Byrds. (Columbia Record Club issue.)

20 Super Rhythm and Blues Hits, Vol. 2....United (S) US-7751 10-20 70s

20 Unforgetable Oldies, Vol. 1....UFO (M) 1001 10-15 73
(Mail order offer.) Little Richard; Olympics; Capris; Dee Clark; Quintones; Spaniels; Maurice Williams; Joe Simon; Richard Berry; Impressions; Gladys Knight & Pips; Jimmy Charles; Scarletts; Marvin & Johnny; Harptones; Joe Jones; Flamingos; Dubs; Angels; Mark II.

20 Unforgetable Oldies, Vol. 2....UFO (M) 1002 10-15 73
(Mail order offer.) Little Richard; Olympics; Lee Dorsey; Dee Clark; Dells; Willows; Betty Everett; Jerry Butler; Bob & Earl; Flamingos; Buster Brown; Gene Chandler; Betty Everett & Jerry Butler; John Lee Hooker; Gladys Knight & Pips; Skyliners; El Dorados; Harptones; Jackie Lee.

20 Unforgetable Oldies, Vol. 3....UFO (M) 1002 10-15 73
(Mail order offer.) John Lee Hooker; Jimmy Reed; Jimmy Hughes; Billy Preston; Jimy Reed; Dells; Betty Everett & Jerry Butler; Betty Everett; Jerry Butler; Wilbert Harrison; Chris Kenner; Bobby Lewis; Jennell Hawkins; Etta James; Faye Adams; Buster Brown; Roscoe Gordon; Bob & Earl; Wade Flemmons.

20 Unforgetable Oldies, Vol. 5....???? 10-15
Eddie Holman;Festivals; Barbara Mason; Ballads; Cruisers; Scott English; Little Anthony; Billy Abbott; Dells; Donnie Elbert;Jewels; Billy Stewart; Intruders;Bobby Marchan;Barbara Lynn; Masqueraders; Metallics; Sa-Shays; Blendells; Brenton Wood.

20 Unforgetable Oldies, Vol. 6....???? 10-15
Eddie Holman; Aaron Neville; James & Bobby Purify; Delfonics; Jerry Butler; Barbara Lewis; Marvelos; Don & Juan; Intruders; Bobby Taylor; Moonglows; Robert & Johnny; Lee Andrews & Hearts; Shells; Baby Washington; Velvetones; Donnie Elbert; Sharps; Perez Brothers; Jesse Belvin.

20 Unforgetable Oldies, Vol. 7....???? 10-15
Dreamlovers; Van McCoy; Barbara Lewis; Students; Moonglows; Johnny & Joe; Chantels; Shirelles; Jivin' Gene & Jokers; Julie Stevens; Delicates; Monitors; Paragons; Shirley & Lee; Tiny Time & Hits; Sam & Bill; Lenny Welch; Santo & Johnny; Elgins.

20 Years of Hits....Acuff-Rose (M) 102 20-25 68
(Promotional issue only.) Jim Reeves; Carl Smith; Eddy Arnold; Pee Wee King; Don Gibson; Ernest Ashworth; Rusty & Doug; George Morgan; Marvin Rainwater; Marty Robbins.

20 Years of No. 1 Hits....Columbia (S) KG-32007 10-15 73
Marty Robbins; Johnnie Ray; Simon & Garfunkel; Percy Faith; Janis Joplin; Mac Davis; others.

20 Years of Rock and Roll (Dick Clark's) (2 LP)....Buddah (S) BDS-5133 15-20 73
(Gatefold cover. Without 24-page booklet and bonus record *Inside Stories*.) Orioles; Crew-Cuts; Carl Perkins; Fats Domino; Brenda Lee; Dion; Joey Dee; Lovin' Spoonfull; Rascals; Al Green; Melanie; Gallery; Bill Haley & His Comets; Johnny Cash; Duane Eddy; Everly Brothers; Paul Anka; Frankie Avalon; Shirelles; Kingsmen; Shangri-Las; Sam the Sham & Pharaohs; Righteous Brothers; McCoys; Van Morrison; Otis Redding; Tommy James & Shondells; Edwin Hawkins Singers; Curtis Mayfield; Jerry Lee Lewis.

20 Years of Rock and Roll (Dick Clark's) (2 LP)....Buddah (S) 5133 15-20 73
(Standard cover.) Orioles; Crew-Cuts; Carl Perkins; Fats Domino; Brenda Lee; Dion; Joey Dee; Lovin' Spoonfull; Rascals; Al Green; Melanie; Gallery; Bill Haley & His Comets; Johnny Cash; Duane Eddy; Everly Brothers; Paul Anka; Frankie Avalon; Shirelles; Kingsmen; Shangri-Las; Sam the Sham & Pharaohs; Righteous Brothers; McCoys; Van Morrison; Otis Redding; Tommy James & Shondells; Edwin Hawkins Singers; Curtis Mayfield; Jerry Lee Lewis.

21 All Time Golden Oldies....Take 6 (S) 2025 10-15 67

21 All Time Hits: see KDWB 21 All Time Hits

21 Gold Rocks - Original Oldies....Tunedex (S) TD-1000 5-10
Del-Vikings; Fats Domino; Coasters; Platters; Jackie Wilson; Johnnie & Joe; Drifters; Chantels; Dells; Little Anthony & Imperials; Chuck Berry; Tune Weavers; Moonglows; Robert & Johnny; Timi Yuro; Shells; Dubs; Clovers; Gene Chandler; Rosie & Originals.

21 Golden Rocks: see KFRC (The Big 610) 21 Golden Rocks

21 Golden Gate Greats: see KYA's 21 Golden Gate Greats

21 Great Stars Sing the All Time Gospel Hits....RCA Special Products (S) DVL-1-0421 5-10 79
Dolly Parton; Jim Reeves; Webb Pierce; Tammy Wynette; Red Foley; Jimmy Davis; Charley Pride; Ray Price; Ernie Ford; Eddy Arnold; Carl Smith; Hank Snow; Connie Smith; Ernest Tubb; Kitty Wells; Porter Wagoner; George Jones; David Houston; Hank Williams; Johnny Cash.

21 Gun Salute to '61....MGM (M) 9/10 15-25 61
(Promotional issue only.) Conway Twitty; Connie Francis; Tommy Edwards; others.

21 Ice Breaker Hits (Vol. 2 from WCFL)....Take 6 (S) 2012-CHI 8-12 67
John Fred; Van Morrison; Neil Diamond; Bobby Fuller Four; Sopwith Camel; Knickerbockers; Flock; Jon & Robin; Jay & Americans; American Breed; Bob Lind; Esquires; Brenton Wood; Lee Dorsey; McCoys; Otis Redding; Ray Charles; James & Bobby Purify; Casinos; Michael & Messengers; Viscounts.

21 Jump Street....I.R.S. (S) IRS-6270 10-15 89
(TV Soundtrack.) Alarm; Reckless Sleepers; One Nation; Holly Robinson; Peter Bernstein; Hunters & Collectors; dBs; Ranking Rogers; Timbuk 3.

21 of the Greatest Popular Songs of all Time .... Pickwick/Motorola (SE) BL-21 8-12
Tony Pastor; Connie Boswell; Charlie Spivak; Mel Torme; Marty Paich; Gordon Jenkins; Raymond Scott; Dennis Day; Dean Franconi; Sarah Vaughan; George Auld; Louis Prima; Larry Clinton; Kay Starr; Eddie Condon; Al Donahue; Gloria Lynne; Artie Shaw; Russ Morgan; Duke Ellington; Gene Autry.

21 Sounds for the Sunset (As advertised on WCFL) ....Take 6 (S) 2006 8-12 67
Lovin' Spoonful; Standells; Royal Guardsmen; B.J. Thomas; Shangri-Las; Slim Harpo; Premiers; Tommy James & Shondells; Music Machine; Count Five; Association; Yellow Balloon; Sunrays; Davie Allan; Ian Whitcomb; Cannibal & Headhunters; Chiffons; Brenton Wood; Seeds; Five Americans.

21 Very Important Platters: see KGFJ

22 Explosive Hits, Vol. 2.... K-Tel (S) TU-224 5-10 72
Sammy Davis Jr.; Gallery; Lobo; Olivia Newton-John; Osmonds; Fortunes; Pop Tops; Hamilton, Joe Frank & Reynolds; Daddy Dewdrops; April Wine; Hot Butter; Derek & Dominos; Flash; Giorgio; Danyel Gerard; Sugar Bears; James Last; Detroit Emeralds; Chi-Lites; Millie Jackson; James Brown; Joe Simon.

22 Fantastic Hits....K-Tel (S) TU-233 5-10 73
Dawn; Elton John; Focus; Sweet; Bill Withers; Raspberries; Albert Hammond; Foster Sylvers; Jerry Jeff Walker; New York City; Barry White; Maureen McGovern; Rod Stewart; Vicki Lawrence; Donny Osmond; First Choice; Lobo; Blue Mink; Gunhill Road; Gary Glitte; Cliff Richard.

22 Golden Oldies: see WPRO Radio 630

22 Good Guy Goodies, Vol. 1 (Gary Stevens Presents) .... Lost-Nite (M) LP-114 8-12 70s
Curtis Lee; Shangri-Las; Don & Juan; Chiffons; Ronny & Daytonas; Shirelles; Tymes; Dixie Cups; Jackie Lee; Fontella Bass; Velvets; Dovells; Dion; Billy Stewart; Del Shannon; Gene Chandler; Isley Brothers; Reflections; Little Caesar; Orlons; Ad Libs; J. Frank Wilson.

22 Greatest Hit Folk Songs .... Vanguard SPV-8/Columbia Musical Treasury (S) 1P 6015 8-12 73
Weavers; Joan Baez; Rooftop Singers; Buffy Sainte-Marie; Phil Ochs; Mimi & Richard Farina; Ian & Slvia; Country Gentlemen; Leon Bibb; Pete Seeger; Johnny Cash; Brothers Four; Burl Ives; Leonard Cohen; Byrds; Mahalia Jackson; Carter Family; Flatt & Scruggs; New Christy Minstrels.

22 High Ballin Hits .... GRT (S) 2103-709 5-10 76
Red Sovine; Webb Pierce; Connie Eaton; Dave Peel; Johnny Dollar; Jim Gately; Roger Miller; Dave Dudley; Conway Twitty; Roy Drusky; Bob Wills; Jimmy Dean; Jack Reno; Michael Parks; Ray Pillow; Henson Cargill; Kitty Wells; Jim Nesbit; Hank Williams; Johnny Exit; Tom T. Hall; Bobby Edwards; Clay Hart.

22 Hits by the Original Artists (Frank X. Feller. Made in Philadelphia).... Post (M) 674 5-10
Billy Harner; Orlons; Dreamlovers; Patty & Emblems; Majors; Candy & Kisses; Videos; Blue-belles; Contenders; Saphires; Dovells; Keith; Hippies (listed as the Tams); Del-fonics; Diane Renay; Tymes; Three Degrees; Billy Abbott; Dawn; Intruders; Maureen Gray; Lee Andrews & Hearts.

22 Hot Heavy Weights, Vol. 2 ....No Label (M) 22-1810 8-12
Monotones; Crows; Ritchie Valens; Peppermint Harris; Del-Vikings; Tony Allen; Shirley & Lee; Gene Chandler; Jive Bombers; Faye Adams; Robert & Johnny; Jaguars; Carla Thomas; Heartbeats; Shep & Limelites; Little Anthony; Rays; Paradons; Flamingos; Dubs; Dells; Sixteens.

22 More Good Guy Goodies, Vol. 2 (Gary Stevens Presents) .... Lost-Nite (M) LP-123 8-12 70s
Marcels; Bobby Lewis; Duprees; Chiffons; Trashmen; Slim Harpo; Syndicate Of Sound; B.J. Thomas; Joe Cuba; Cascades; McCoys; Larks; Jive Five; Shirelles; Jaynetts; Castaways; Freddie Scott; Del Shannon; Happenings; Shangri-Las; Knickerbockers.

22 Original Winners, (Good Guy - Jack Spector Presents).... Roulette (M) R 25254 10-15 65
Dovells; Vibrations; Little Eva; Joey Dee; Rays; Tempos; Crystals; Wilbert Harrison; Lee Dorsey; Shirley & Lee; Penguins; Chubby Checker; Coasters; Little Richard; Bobby Lewis; Joe Jones; Regents; Bo Diddley; Essex; Drifters; Robert & Johnny; Chuck Berry.

24 Country & Western Greats, Vol. 6 ....K-Tel (S) WU 321 5-10 72
Anne Murray; Glen Campbell; Sonny James; Ferlin Husky; Faron Young; Hank Thompson; Roy Clark; Burl Ives; Loretta Lynn; Jeannie C. Riley; Hank Williams Jr.; Patsy Cline; Wanda Jackson; Kitty Wells; Bill Anderson; Bobby Helms; Red Foley; Mel Tillis; Johnny Cash; Webb Pierce.

24 Golden Greats, WMEE 1380 (2 LP) ....Custom Fidelity (S) 2315-2 8-12 71
Shocking Blue; Classics IV; Billy Stewart; Clique; James & Bobby Purify; Barry McGuire; Mungo Jerry; Music Explosion; Lee Dorsey; Turtles; Intruders; Bob Lind; Jay & Americans; Bobby Goldsboro; Sunshine Company; Mel Carter; T-Bones; Gary Lewis; Canned Heat; Bobby Vee; Nitty Gritty Dirt Band; Gene McDaniels; Little Anthony & Imperials; Jackie DeShannon.

24 Great Heartbreakers and Tear Jerkers (2 LP)....Excelsior (S) 2XMP-4405 8-12 80

24 Great Tear Jerkers ....K-Tel (S) NC-9130 5-10 76
(Canada issue.)

24 Great Tear Jerkers ....K-Tel (S) NU-9130 5-10 76
Dion; Ray Peterson; Paul Anka; Everly Brothers; Lou Christie; Timi Yuro; Teddy Bears; Donnie Brooks; Pat Boone; Bobby Edwards; Dee Clark; Mark Dinning; Ritchie Valens; Little Anthony & Imperials; Dicky Lee; Orioles; Shangri-Las; Jackie Wilson; Ronnie Dove; Troy Shondell; Leslie Gore; Shirelles; Tony Williams; Paul Robi.

24 Great Truck Drivin' Songs .... K-Tel (S) 3320 5-10 76
C.W. McCall; Dave Dudley; Hank Snow; Johnny Dollar; Willis Brothers; Bill Carlisle; Connie Eaton & Dave Peel; Roy Drusky; Johnny Paycheck; Roger Miller; Porter Wagoner; Johnny Horton; Carl Smith; Jim Nesbitt; Lavon Lyle; Jim & Jesse; Stoney Cooper & Wilma Lee; Red Sovine.

24 Greatest Dumb Ditties ....K-Tel (M/SE) NU 9330 8-12 77
Chuck Berry; Bobby "Boris" Pickett; David Seville & Chipmunks; Tom Glazer; Serendipity Singers; Leroy Pullins; Jimmy James; Tom Katz; Lucy Diner; Gingerbread; Paul Evans; Kingsmen; Jimmy Soul; Barry Mann; Dodie Stevens; Johnny Cymbal; Ray Stevens; Frank Gallop; Galaxies; Bobby Biggs; Billy Pressman; Bermudas; Leapy Lee.

24 Groovy Greats .... Crystal LP 714 10-15 60s

24 Groovy Greats (2 LP) ....Telerad/Columbia (M) HLP-714 10-15 60s
(Mail order offer.) Little Eva; Ronnie Dove; Tommy James & Shondells; Little Anthony & Imperials; James Brown; Toys; Drifters; Dixie Cups; Coasters; Ramsey Lewis; Lee Dorsey; Dave Clark 5; Ray Barretto; Wilbert Harrison; Ike & Tina Turner; 4 Seasons; Percy Sledge; Fontella Bass; Toys; Vogues. (Columbia Special Products. Made for Telerad Inc., Hollywood Album Center.)

24 Happening Hits (2 LP) ....Crystal (S) GT-9000 15-20 66
(Mail order offer.) Tommy James & Shondells; Buckinghams; Neil Diamond; Cyrkle; Mitch Ryder & Detroit Wheels; Love; Sam the Sham & Pharaohs; J.J. Jackson; Syndicate of Sound; Tempos; Shep & Limelites; Frankie Lymon; Five Americans; Bobby Hebb; Lovin' Spoonful; Young Rascals; Sonny & Cher; Seeds; Wilson Pickett; Critters; Terry Knight & Pack; 4 Seasons; Crows; Chantels.

24 Happening Hits (2 LP) .... Columbia (S) GT-9000 15-20 66
(Mail order offer.) Tommy James & Shondells; Buckinghams; Neil Diamond; Cyrkle; Mitch Ryder & Detroit Wheels; Love; Sam the Sham & Pharaohs; J.J. Jackson; Syndicate of Sound; Tempos; Shep & Limelites; Frankie Lymon; Five Americans; Bobby Hebb; Lovin' Spoonful; Young Rascals; Sonny & Cher; Seeds; Wilson Pickett; Critters; Terry Knight & Pack; 4 Seasons; Crows; Chantels.

24 Heavy Hits .... Crystal (S) S-600 8-12 70s
(Mail order offer.) Janis Joplin; Impressions; Ohio Express; Len Barry; Delfonics; Tommy James & Shondells; Strawberry Alarm Clock; Who; Intruders; Ricardo Ray; Turtles; Amboy Dukes; Lemon Pipers; Happenings; Sonny & Cher; 1910 Fruitgum Company.

24 Karat Gold from the Country (2 LP) .... MGM (S) SE-241-2 8-12 70s
Hank Williams; Arthur Smith; Conway Twitty; Johnny Tillotson; Marvin Rainwater; Roy Acuff; Ben Colder; Jimmy Newman; Merle Kilgore; Osborne Brothers; Carson Robinson; Tompall & Glaser Brothers; Sheb Wooley.

24 More Great Heartbreakers and Tear Jerkers (2 LP) .... Excelsior (S) 2XMP-4406 8-10 80
(Rerecorded versions of hits by the original artists.)

24 Original Happening Hits (2 LP) .... Columbia Special Products (S) GT-9000 8-12 66
(Mail order offer.) Tommy James & Shondells; Buckinghams; Neil Diamond; Cyrkle; Love; Sam the Sham; J.J. Jackson; Syndicate of sound; Tempos; Frankie Lymon & Teenagers; Shep & Limelites; others. (Special products. Made for Telerad Inc., Hollywood Album Center.)

24 Solid Hits .... Crystal (S) LP 500 8-12 70s
Barbara Mason; Peaches & Herb; Happenings; Sam & Dave; Little Anthony & Imperials; Loved Ones; Young Rascals; Lovin' Spoonful; Neil Diamond; Spanky & Our Gang; Esquires; Byrds; Mitch Ryder & Detroit Wheels; Jay & Americans; Tommy James & Shondells; Brenton Wood; Bobby Goldsboro; Cowsills; John Fred; Box Tops; Buckinghams; Soul Survivors.

25 Artists and Tunes Shindig .... Guest Star (M) G-1488 10-20 60s
Meadowlarks; Lloyd Price; Platters; Chuck Jackson; 4 Seasons; Julie London; Tokens; Steve Lawrence; Penguins; Monarchs; Bill Haley & His Comets; Arthur Prysock; Shirley & Lee; Neil Sedaka; Al Martino; Mel Torme; Billy Eckstine; Bobbettes; Johnny Rivers; Maxine Brown; Little Esther; Cuff Links; Willows; Ray Charles; Fireflies.

25 Big Hits .... Jafco (M) 101 10-15 60s
Bobby Freeman; Eugene Church; Dorsey Burnette; Donnie Brooks; Frankie Avalon; Gene Chandler; Dee Clark; Marketts; Routers; Dion & Belmonts; B.B. King; Marvin & Johnny; Etta James; Della Reese; Ernie Fields; John Lee Hooker; Chuck Jackson; Shirelles; Bobby Day; Jerry Wallace; Champs; Hollywood Argyles; Fendermen.

25 Country Music Greats .... Starday (M) CMG-1 10-20 70s
Johnny Cash; Buck Owens; Cowboy Copas; George Jones; Moon Mullican; Hank Locklin; Floyd Tillman; Dottie West; Patsy Cline; Webb Pierce; Tommy Hill; Blue Sky Boys; Justin Tubb; Rex Allen; Jimmy Dean; Pee Wee King; Roger Miller; Willis Brothers; Smiley Burnette; Joe Maphis; Johnny Bond; Roy Drusky; Pete Drake; Blue Boys; Lonzo & Oscar.

25 Country Music Greats, 2rd Anniversary Album .... Homestead (S) AC 1-2 8-12
Johnny Cash; Buck Owens; Cowboy Copas; George Jones; Moon Mullican; Hank Locklin; Floyd Tillman; Dottie West; Patsy Cline; Webb Pierce; Tommy Hill; Blue Sky Boys; Justin Tubb; Rex Allen; Jimmy Dean; Pee Wee King; Roger Miller; Willis Brothers; Smiley Burnette; Joe Maphis; Johnny Bond; Roy Drusky; Pete Drake; Blue Boys; Lonzo & Oscar.

25 Country Music Greats, 3rd Anniversary Album .... Homestead (S) AC 1-2 8-12
Archie Campbell; Moon Mullican; Cowboy Copas; Roger Miller; Justin Tubb; Guy Mitchell; Patsy Cline; Charley Walker; Webb Pierce; Pee Wee King; Jimmy Dean; Buck Owens; George Morgan; Willis Brothers; Johnny Bond; Minnie Pearl; Carl Story; George Jones; Sonny James; Dave Dudley; Stoneman Family; Stanley Brothers; Dottie West; Leon McAuliffe; Red Sovine.

25 Golden Years - 25 Golden Hits (2 LP) .... Lowery Group (S) No Number Used 25-35 71
(Promotional issue only.) Beatles; Lynn Anderson; Friend & Lover; Billy Joe Royal; Deep Purple; Dennis Yost & Classics IV; others.

25 Golden Years in Lowrey Country (2 LP) .... Lowery Group (S) LG-1 50-60 80
(Promotional issue only.) Elvis Presley; Sonny James; Hank Snow; Gene Vincent; Red Foley; Kitty Wells; Wilburn Brothers; Jimmy Dean; Bill Lowery & Smith Brothers; Leroy Van Dyke; Ray Stevens; Brenda Lee; Johnny Cash; Porter Wagoner; Joe South; Freddy Weller; Billy Joe Royal; Lynn Anderson; Sandy Posey; Roy Drusky; Dickey Lee.

25 Great Country Artists .... Artistic (M) 711 8-12
Patsy Cline; Jimmy Dean; Wynn Stewart; Hank Locklin; Cowboy Copas; Johnny Bond; Moon Mullican; George Jones; Arthur "Guitar" Smith; Eddie Dean; Webb Pierce; Jerry Wallace; Archie Campbell; Hylo Brown; Red Sovine; Jan Howard; Sunshine Boys; Stringbean; Carl Story; Willis Brothers; Justin Tubb; Lonesome Pine Fiddlers; Tommy Hill; Leon Payne; Bobby Austin.

25 Great Country Artists .... Country Music Association (S) CMA 712 8-12 77
Roy Acuff; Bill Anderson; Eddy Arnold; Bobby Bare; Johnny Bond; Johnny Cash; Patsy Cline; Dave Dudley; Red Foley; Lefty Frizzell; Don Gibson; Pee Wee King; Roger Miller; George Morgan; Buck Owens; Ray Price; Jim Reeves; Tex Ritter; Marty Robbins; Hank Snow; Hank Thompson; Merle Travis; Ernest Tubb; Kitty Wells; Hank Williams.

25 Great Country Stars and Hits .... Pickwick (S) PTP-2085 8-12
George Jones; Patsy Cline; Johnny Cash; Carl Belew; Dave Dudley; Merle Kilgore; Jimmy Dean; Roy Drusky; Del Wood; Bobby Bare; Anita Carter; T. Texas Tyler; Sue Thompson; Maddox Brothers & Rose; Roger Miller; Rusty Draper; Faron Young; Leroy Van Dyke; Conway Twitty; Webb Pierce; Charlie Rich; Ferlin Husky; Hank Locklin; Rex Allen; Jan Howard.

25 Great Hits of the '30s & '40s .... Pickwick (SE) LCA-0003 5-10 70s
Three Dog Night; Russ Morgan; Fran Warren; Louis Prima; Dick Stabile; Eddie Condon; Merry Macs; Jimmie Lunceford; Charlie Ventura; Beatrice Kay; Harry Horlick; Lani McIntire; Teddy Powell; Lena Horne; Jerry Gray; Charlie Spivak; Ray Charles; Earl Fatha Hines; Boyd Raeburn; Judy Canova; Ink Spots; Will Osborne; Morton Downey; Russ Case.

25 Great Hits of the '30s & '40s, Vol. 2 .... Pickwick (SE) LCA-0004 5-10 70s
Claude Thornhill; Kay Starr; Red Norvo; Phil Brito; Ted Straeter; Teddy Wilson; Nat Brandywynne; Al Hibbler; Les Elgart; Dizzie Gillespie; Matty Matlock; Johnny Desmond; Gisele MacKenzie; Jan Garber; Art Mooney; Dorothy Lamour; Buddy Cole; Red Nichols; D'Artega; Ray Heatherton; Billie Holiday; Fletcher Henderson; Pee Wee King; Roberta Sherwood; Percy Faith.

25 Great Country Music Artists .... Country Hall of Fame (S) CMA 712 8-12
Roy Acuff; Bill Anderson; Eddy Arnold; Bobby Bare; Johnny Bond; Johnny Cash; Patsy Cline; Dave Dudley; Red Foley; Lefty Frizzell; Don Gibson; Pee Wee King; Roger Miller; George Morgan; Buck Owens; Ray Price; Jim Reeves; Tex Ritter; Marty Robbins; Hank Snow; Hank Thompson; Merle Travis; Ernest Tubb; Kitty Wells; Hank Williams.

25 Hit Tunes .... ???? (S) HT-25 8-12
Nancy Martin; Poodles; Vines; Christopher; Carlocks; L.H. & Memphis Sounds; Dion & Belmonts; Bobby Goldsboro; Bill Doggett; Jan & Dean; Robin & Hoods; Paul Revere & Raiders; Baby Dolls; Tommy Roe; Orioles; Shangri-Las; Simon & Garfunkel; Lou Rawls; Slim Harpo; Bobby Freeman; J. Frank Wilson; Trini Lopez; Champs; Spads.

25 No. 1 Hits from 25 Years (2 LP) .... Motown (S) 5308 8-12 83
Stevie Wonder; Diana Ross & Supremes; Temptations; Marvin Gaye; Jackson Five; Eddie Kendricks; Smokey Robinson & Miracles; Marvelettes; Four Tops; Thelma Houston; Commodores; Rick James.; others

25 Original Big Hits .... Homestead (S) H-1001 10-15
Steppenwolf; Grass Roots; Mama Cass; Impressions; Tams; O'Kaysions; B.B. King; Animals; Hombres; Friend & Lover; Everly Brothers; Association; Sonny & Cher; Deep Purple; Andy Kim; Bob Lind; Peggy Scott & Jo Jo Benson; Lovin' Sponful; Sir Douglas Quintet; Professor Morrison's Lollipops; Mickey Murray; James & Bobby Purify.

25 Polka Waltz Greats, Vol. 2 .... K-Tel (S) ???? 5-10 71
Frankie Yankovic; Polka Padre; Myron Floren; Six Fat Dutchmen; Deutchmeisters; Bernie Roberts; Stan Freeze; Lawrence Welk.

25 Rock Revival Greats (2 LP) .... K-Tel (S) S 10966/RR-2 8-12 72
Bill Haley & His Comets; Chuck Berry; Everly Brothers; Lloyd Price; Monotones; Crew-Cuts; Sparkletones; Little Richard; Fats Domino; Poni-Tails; Bo Diddley; Big Bopper; Bobby Day; Beach Boys; Safaris; Jimmy Gilmer; Jerry Lee Lewis; Lloyd Price; Clovers; Jewel Akens; Tommy Roe; Dave Clark Five; Donnie Brooks; Shirelles; Roy Orbison.

25 Years of Country and Western Sacred Songs .... King (M) 807 20-30 63

25 Years of Country and Western Sacred Songs .... King (S) 807 20-30 63
Reno & Smiley; Cowboy Copas; T. Texas Tyler; Parker Family; others.

25 Years of Grammy Greats .... Motown (S) 5309 8-12 83

25 Years of Recorded Comedy (3 LP) .... Warner Bros. (M) 3BX-3131 10-20 77
Lenny Bruce; Shelley Berman; Richard Pryor; Lily Tomlin; Carl Reiner; Mel Brooks; Gabriel Kaplan; Stan Freberg; Cheech & Chong; National Lampoon; Alan Sherman; Monty Python; Firesign Theater; Marty Allen & Steve Rossi; Eddie Lawrence; David Frye.

25 Years of Rhythm and Blues .... King (M) 725 25-35 61
LaVern Baker; Earl Bostic; Roy Brown; Champion Jack Dupree; others.

25 Years of Rhythm and Blues, Vol. 2 .... King (M) 749 25-35 61
Earl Bostic; Bobby Lewis; Chanters; Tiny Bradshaw; Billy Ward & Dominoes; Ivory Joe Hunter; Hank Ballard & Midnighters; Platters; Bill Doggett; Little Willie John; James Brown & Famous Flames; Otis Williams & His Charms; Bullmoose Jackson; Henry Booth & Midnighters; Roy Brown.

26 Nonstop Sing Along Honky Tonk .... K-Tel NU-423 5-10 71
(Mail order offer. Includes two-page songbook.) Jo Ann Castle; Del Wood; Joe "Fingers" Carr; Charlie Young; Johnny Maddox.

26 Top Hits .... Hit (M) 446 10-15 68

30 Golden Country Hits (2 LP) .... RCA Special Products (S) DVL2-0447 8-12 80
(Mail order offer.) Hank Locklin; Connie Smith; George Jones; Hank Thompson; Jimmie Rodgers; Dave Dudley; Bobby Bare; Hank Williams; Bobby Helms; Jim Reeves; Kitty Wells; Porter Wagoner; Stuart Hamblen; Carl Butler; Don Gibson; Hank Snow; Webb Pierce; Ernest Ashworth; Skeeter Davis; Johnny Cash; Faron Young; Bill Anderson; Roger Miller; George Hamilton IV; Ray Price; Wanda Jackson; Pee Wee King; Carl Smith; Browns.

30 Grand Ole Country & Western Favorites .... Syndicate (S) SCW-30 10-20 64
Patsy Cline; Wilburn Brothers; Faron Young; Hank Locklin; George Jones; Floyd Tillman; Jan Howard; Ferlin Husky; Charlie Ryan; Stuart Hamblen; Sonny James; Maddox Brothers & Rose; Dave Dudley; Wally Fowler; Floyd Cramer; Johnny Horton; Webb Pierce; Rex Allen; Carl Belew; Billy Grammer; Bobby Austin; Wynn Stewart; Del Reeves; Johnny Sea; Champ Butler; David Houston; Claude King; Johnny Cash; Melba Montgomery; T. Texas Tyler.

30 Great Hits by 30 Great Country Artists: 30 X 30 .... Columbia Musical Treasury (S) DS 342 10-15 68
David Houston; Statler Brothers; Jimmy Dean; Claude King; Stonewall Jackson; Carl Smith; Mel Tillis; Don Gibson; Marty Robbins; Little Jimmy Dickens; Carl & Pearl Butler;. Tammy Wynette; Billy Walker; Johny Bond; George Morgan; Jordanaires; Johnny Cash; Ray Price; Carter Family; Harden Trio; Johnny Horton; Lefty Frizzell; Norma Jean; Flatt & Scruggs; Marion Worth; Bobby Lord; Carl Perkins; Skeets McDonald; Roy Drusky; Hawkshaw Hawkins.

30 Great Hits by 30 Great Country Artists, 30 X 30, Vol. 2 .... Columbia Musical Treasury (S) DS 365 10-15 68
David Houston; Marty Robbins; Van Trevor; Ray Price; Patsy Cline; Johnny Cash; June Carter; George Morgan; Johnny Dollar; Johnny Horton; Faron Young; Stonewall Jackson; George Jones; Sonny James; T. Texas Tyler; Gene Autry; Tammy Wynette; Carl Smith; Claude King; Charlie Walker; Ferlin Husky; Statler Brothers; Jimmy Dean; Floyd Tillman; Carter Family; Melba Montgomery; Merle Kilgore; Hank Locklin; Wynn Stewart; Webb Pierce; Lucille Starr.

30 Great Hits by 30 Great Country Artists (2 LP) .... Columbia (S) P2S 5218 10-20 68
(Columbia Record Club issue.) David Houston; Statler Brothers; Jimmy Dean; Claude King; Stonewall Jackson; Carl Smith; Mel Tillis; Don Gibson; Marty Robbins; Little Jimmy Dickens; Carl & Pearl Butler; Tammy Wynette; Billy Walker; Johny Bond; George Morgan; Jordanaires; Johnny Cash; Ray Price; Carter Family; Harden Trio; Johnny Horton; Lefty Frizzell; Norma Jean; Flatt & Scruggs; Marion Worth; Bobby Lord; Carl Perkins; Skeets McDonald; Roy Drusky; Hawkshaw Hawkins.

30 Great Hits by 30 Great Country Artists, Vol. 2 (2 LP) .... Columbia Musical Treasury (S) P2S 5220 8-12 68
(Columbia Record Club issue.) David Houston; Marty Robbins; Van Trevor; Ray Price; Patsy Cline; Johnny Cash; June Carter; George Morgan; Johnny Dollar; Johnny Horton; Faron Young; Stonewall Jackson; George Jones; Sonny James; T. Texas Tyler; Gene Autry; Tammy Wynette; Carl Smith; Claude King; Charlie Walker; Ferlin Husky; Statler Brothers; Jimmy Dean; Floyd Tillman; Carter Family; Melba Montgomery; Merle Kilgore; Hank Locklin; Wynn Stewart; Webb Pierce; Lucille Starr.

30 Great Hits by 30 Great Country Artists, Vol. 3 (2 LP) .... Columbia Musical Treasuries (M) D 408 8-12 68
Marty Robbins; Jimmy Dean; Tammy Wynette; Bob Luman; Van Trevor; Flatt & Scruggs; Patsy Cline; Johnny Cash; Charlie Walker; George Jones; Stonewall Jackson; Judy Lynn; George Morgan; Johnny Horton; Charlie Rich; David Houston; Terry White; Mel Tillis; Wynn Stewart; Carl Smith; Jan Howard; Ray Price; Hank Locklin; Melba Montgomery; Chuck Wagon Gang; T. Texas Tyler; Faron Young; Lew DeWitt; Ferlin Husky; Webb Pierce.

30 Great Love Songs of the '60s, '70s, & '80s (3 LP) .... CBS Special Products (S) P3 18655 10-20 85
Bobby Vinton; Gary Puckett & Union Gap; Turtles; Dionne Warwick; Blood, Sweat & Tears; Steve Lawrence; Classics IV; Jackie DeShannon; Association; Gene Pitney; Charlie Rich; Morris Albert; Jennifer Warnes; Hollies; Meatloaf; Crystal Gayle; Mac Davis; Emotions; Hamilton, Joe Frank & Reynolds; Lou Rawls; Willie Nelson; Bertie Higgins; Paul Carrack; Peter Allen; Air Supply; Engelbert Humperdinck; Teddy Pendergrass; Champaign; Dr. Hook; Toto.

30 Now Goldens (68/WRKO) (2 LP) .... Post (SE) 68 10-15 68
Association; Tommy James & Shondells; Bob Lind; Sam & Dave; Cascades; Ad-Libs; Keith; Standells; Bobby Hebb; Beau Brummels; Count Five; Dixie Cups; Bobby Fuller Four; Del Shannon; Lovin' Spoonful; Ritchie Valens; Tradewinds; Shirley Ellis; Critters; Shangri-Las; B.J. Thomas; Neil Diamond; Happenings; Vogues; Barbara Mason; Knickerbockers; Ketty Lester; Wildweeds; McCoys.

30 Now Goldens (68/WRKO), Vol. 2 (2 LP) .... Post (SE) 747 10-15 70
Animals; Turtles; O'Kaysions; Chuck Berry; 1910 Fruitgum Co.; B.J. Thomas; Strawberry Alarm Clock; ? & Mysterians; Deep Purple; Paris Sisters; Tommy Roe; Bo Diddley; Hugh Masekela; Skyliners; Delfonics; Mamas & Papas; James & Bobby Purify; Van Morrison; Buckinghams; Robert Parker; Shirelles; Johnny Nash; Lemon Pipers; Tommy James & Shondells; Lovin' Spoonful; James Brown; Terry Stafford; Crests; Soul Survivors; Righteous Brothers.

30 Years of Bluegrass (2 LP) .... Gusto/Lake Shore (M) GT-101 10-15 77
Stanley Brothers; Flatt & Scruggs; Reno & Smiley; Country Gentlemen; Hylo Brown; Tommy Jackson; Jim & Jesse; Bill Clifton; Mac Wiseman; Bill Emerson; Allen Shelton; Red Allen; New Grass; Revival; Kentucky Travelers; Grandpa Jones; Bill Harell; Jim Eanes; Stringbean; Stoneman Family; Charles Moore; Moore & Napier; Buzz Busby; Carl Story.

30 Years of No. 1 Country Hits (7 LP) .... Reader's Digest (S) RBA-215-A 40-50 86
(Boxed set. Mail order offer.) Elvis Presley; George Hamilton IV; Jack Greene; B.J. Thomas; John Conlee; Everly Brothers; Eddy Arnold; Red Foley; Merle Haggard; Loretta Lynn; Roy Clark; Faron Young; Roger Miller; Jean Shepard; Ferlin Husky; Statler Brothers; Crystal Gayle; Hank Williams Jr.; Bill Anderson; Jan Howard; Donna Fargo; Glen Campbell; Red Sovine; Del Reeves; Waylon Jennings; Willie Nelson; Jerry Lee Lewis; Johnny Cash; Kendalls; Jim Reeves; Conway Twitty; Sammi Smith; Dolly Parton; Bobby Goldsboro; Hank Snow; Patsy Cline; Don Williams; Kitty Wells; Hank Williams Sr.; Charley Pride; Hawkshaw Hawkins; Ronnie Milsap; Don Gibson; Tom T. Hall; Connie Smith; Hank Locklin; Tennessee Ernie Ford; George Jones; Pee Wee King; Bill Anderson; Sonny James; Browns; Leroy Van Dyke; Linda Ronstadt; Jerry Reed; Webb Pierce; Hank Thompson.

32 Original Hits (2 LP) .... Sessions (S) ARI 1020 8-12 80
Bobby Day; Dion & Belmonts; Everly Brothers; Chordettes; Donnie Brooks; Jackie Wilson; Connie Francis; Crescendos; Mark Dinning; Phil Phillips; Danleers; Chuck Berry; Bobby Freeman; Dodie Stevens; Buddy Knox; Jimmie Rodgers; Buddy Holly; McGuire Sisters; Del-Vikings; Elegants; Pat Boone; Poni-Tails; Kalin Twins; Ritchie Valens; Lloyd Price; Robin Luke; Randy & Rainbows; Jarmels; Kathy Young; Patti Page; Bobby Rydell; Fats Domino.

33 Golden Hits (3 LP) .... Warner Special Products/Sessions (S) ARI-1012 10-15 70s
Byrds; Buckinghams; Billy Paul; Minnie Riperton; Aretha Franklin; Jeannie C. Riley; Vikki Lawrence; Shirelles; Melanie; Lulu; Blood, Sweat & Tears; Gary Puckett & Union Gap; O.C. Smith; Lesley Gore; Michael Murphey; Marcie Blane; Dusty Springfield; Dave Loggins; Barbara Mason; Hollies; Merrilee Rush; Judy Collins; Barbara Lynn; Julie Rogers; Dionne Warwick; Sandy Posey; Janis Ian; Charlie Rich; Chi Coltrane; Springfields; Delaney & Bonnie; Joan Baez.

34 Original Hits (3 LP) .... Sessions/Warner Special Products (S) OP-3508 10-15 82
Beach Boys; Tommy Boyce & Bobby Hart; Chris Kenner; Isley Brothers; Sonny & Cher; John Fred; Bobby Lewis; Del Shannon; Robin Luke; Bobby Rydell; Chiffons; Vogues; Harpers Bizarre; Association; Rascals; New Seekers; Temptations; Kenny Rogers & First Edition; Drifters; R.B. Greaves; Peaches & Herb; Neon Philharmonic; Barbara Lewis; Cascades; Everly Brothers; Robert John; Sweet Inspirations; Tymes; Turtles; Chris Montez; Fantastic Johnny C.; Doris Troy; Joanie Sommers; Wilson Pickett.

35 Golden Hits (2 LP) .... K-Tel (S) ???? 15-25

36 Great Motion Picture Themes: see 10 Golden Years

36 Rockin' Oldies (3 LP) .... Readers Digest (S) SH-3306 10-20 70s
(Mail order offer.) Bill Haley & His Comets; Platters; Wilbert Harrison; Fats Domino; Tommy Roe; Jerry Butler; Ray Stevens; Jerry Lee Lewis; Champs; Fendermen; Dusty Springfield; Maurice Williams; Maxine Brown; Lee Dorsey; Lou Rawls; Johnny Rivers; Chuck Jackson; Vogues; Neil Sedaka; Bobby Rydell; Lloyd Price; Trashmen; Garnet Mimms; Silhouettes; Gaylords; Jan & Dean; Clyde McPhatter; Lee Allen; Little Richard; Diamonds; Baby Cortez; Gene Pitney; Clovers; Isley Brothers.

36 Super Gold Hits (2 LP) .... K-Tel (S) TU-2470 15-25 76

40 Country Hits of the '40s (3 LP) .... Gusto (S) GTV-108 10-15 78
Cowboy Copas; Wayne Raney; Delmore Brothers; Little Jimmie Dickens; Patsy Montana; Tex Ritter; Jimmie Davis; Roy Acuff; Jimmy Osborne; Pop Eckler; Gene Autry; Rose Maddox; Pee Wee King; Redd Stewart; Moon Mullican; George Morgan; Bob Wills; Tommy Duncan; Hank Penny; Grampa Jones; York Brothers; Kenny Roberts; Arthur Smith; T. Texas Tyler; Leon Payne; Floyd Tillman; Rock Bill Ford; Farley Holden; Homer & Jethro; Lulu Belle & Scotty; Clyde Moody; Hawkshaw Hawkins; Carlisle Brothers.

40 Funky Hits (3 LP) .... Longines Symphonette (S) SQ-95837 10-20 74
(Mail order offer.) Little Anthony & Imperials; Olympics; Little Richard; Little Jimmy Dickens; Royal Guardsmen; Gene Chandler; Hollywood Argyles; Dyke & Blazers; Ed Byrnes; Joe Jones; Joe South; Lee Dorsey; Bill Haley & His Comets; Cannibal & Headhunters; Standells; Fendermen; Trashmen; Ray Stevens; Playmates; Jewel Akens; Pastel Six; Castaways; Premiers; Little Caesar & Romans; Billy Joe & Checkmates; Paul Evans & Curls; Turbans; Little Richard; Dave Dudley; Jayhawks; B. Bumble & Stingers; Dave "Baby" Cortez; Jarmels; Ritchie Valens; Lloyd Price.

40 Great Folk Songs (4 LP) .... Vanguard/Radio Shack (S) RS 50-2031 15-25 74
Weavers; Flatt & Scruggs with the Foggy Mountain Boys; Odetta; Ian & Sylvia; John Hammond; Joan Baez; Jack Elliott; Ed McCurdy; Jose Feleciano; Patrick Sky; Cisco Houston; Jim Kweskin; Leon Bibb; Bob Gibson; Mike Seeger; Greenbriar Boys; Paul Robeson; Doc Watson; Arbors; Mississippi John Hurt; Sonny Terry; Brownie McGhee; Clara Ward; Ronnie Gilbert; Pete Seeger; Rooftop Singers; Reverend Gary Davis; John Lee Hooker; Staple Singers; Hedy West; Buffy Sainte-Marie; Babysitters.

40 Hits (2 LP) .... K-Tel (S) ???? 10-15

40 No. 1 Original Country Goldies (3 LP) .... Adam VIII Ltd. (S) 8001 10-20
(Mail order offer.) Jeannie C. Riley; Carl Smith; Johnny Cash; Moon Mullican; Marty Robbins; George Jones; Leroy Van Dyke; Everly Brothers; Henson Cargill; Jerry Lee Lewis; Red Foley; Red Sovine; Webb Pierce; Lefty Frizzell; Roy Drusky & Priscilla Mitchell; Ray Price; Del Reeves; Ernest Tubb; Cowboy Copas; Bobby Helms; Roger Miller; Jim Reeves; Johnny Horton; Jimmie Rodgers; Stonewall Jackson; Kitty Wells; Hawkshaw Hawkins; Tom T. Hall.

40 Original Hits (3 LP) .... Sessions/RCA (S) DPL3-0171 15-20 76
Chuck Berry; Dion; Linda Scott; Bobby Rydell; Blues Magoos; Donnie Brooks; Thomas Wayne; Dovells; Don & Juan; Del-Vikings; Shirelles; Bill Justis; Shangri-Las; Jim Reeves; Lloyd Price; Robin Luke; Dixie Cups; ? & Mysterians; Little Willie John; Sam Cooke; Jewel Akens; Tony Bellus; Permiers; Cannibal & Headhunters; Dee Dee Dharp; Jimmy Clanton; Platters; Bobby Day; Mystics; Rosie & Originals; Neil Sedaka; Ray Peterson; Jody Reynolds; Del Shannon; Della Reese; Cascades; Maurice William & Zodiacs; Guess Who; Ray Smith; Harold Dorman. (Mail order offer. Special products. Made for Sessions.)

40 Shades of Green .... London (S) SW-99531 8-12 71

44 Happy Hits of the Fun '40s (4 LP) .... Good Music/BMG/MCA (M) GMR 80041 10-20 89
(Mail order offer.) Merry Macs; Danny Kaye; Andrews Sisters; Mills Brothers; Mel Blanc & Sportsmen; Dinah Shore; Guy Lombardo; Peggy Lee; Alvino Rey; Red Foley; Ames Brothers; Jo Stafford; Hoagy Carmichael; Frankie Laine; Pee Wee Hunt; Johnny Mercer; Russ Morgan; Art Mooney; Carlton Carpenter; Debbie Reynolds; Arthur Godfrey & Two Rat Trio; Red Ingle; Jerry Colonna; Eileen Barton; Bing Crosby; Evelyn Knight; Betty Hutton; Dinah Shore; Kenny Roberts; Two-Ton Baker & His Music Makers; Dorothy Shay; Kay Kyser; Sammy Kaye; Phil Harris; Count Basie; Perry Como with the Fontane Sisters; Glahe Musette Orchestra; Spike Jone & His City Slickers; Alvino Rey; Merv Griffin; Freddy Martin; Tex Beneke & Glenn Miller; Vaughn Monroe.

45 of the Best 45's (3 LP) .... Fairway (S) ???? 10-20 79
(Mail order offer.) Little Richard; Olympics; Dee Clark; Gene Chandler; Dells; Leaves; Spaniels; Chimes; Crests; Isley Brothers; Richie Valens; Duprees; Shirelles; Jesse Belvin; Jerry Butler & Impressions; Casinos; Cannibal & Headhunters; Rocky Fellers; Turtles; Dobie Gray; Shepard Sisters; Teen Queens; Bob & Earl; Jimmy Dorsey; Fred Hughes; Gladys Knight & Pips; Lee Dorsey; Marvin & Johnny; Maxine Brown; Skyliners; Jimmy Clanton; Terry Stafforrd; Huey "Piano" Smith: Jody Reynolds; Tee Set; Maurice Williams; Bobby Lewis; Betty Everett; Harptones; Willows.

45 of the Greatest Rock & Roll 45s (3 LP) .... Vee Jay (S) VJSP-711 20-25
(Mail order offer.) Little Richard; Olympics; Lee Dorsey; Dee Clark; Gene Chandler; Dells; Willows; Betty Everett; Jimmy Charles; Marvin & Johnny; Harptones; Joe Jones; Flamingos; Dubs; Leaves; Orioles; Teen Queens; Mello Kings; Nutmegs; Crests; Cadillacs; Heartbeats; Regents; Cleftones; Bobby Lewis; Skyliners; Wilbert Harrison; Maurice Williams; Spaniels; Isley Brothers; Ritchie Valens; Duprees; Shirelles; Jesse Belvin; Jerry Butler; Paul Evans; Casinos; Cannibal & Headhunters; Turtles; Dobie Gray; Shephard Sisters; Rocky Fellers.

50th Anniversary Show .... RCA (M) LOC-1037 20-30 58
(TV Soundtrack.) Pat Boone; Carol Burnett; Dan Daily; Dinah Shore; Doretta Morrow; Steve Lawrence; Howard Keel; Cyril Ritchard; Claudia Crawford; Hugo Winterhalter.

50 Beloved Songs of Faith (Album No. 1) .... Reader's Digest (S) BMR3-100 5-8 89
Elvis Presley; Loretta Lynn; Porter Wagoner; Scott Singers; Guy & Ralna; Red Foley; Kate Smith; Pat Boone; Jim Reeves; Statler Brothers; Cristy Lane; Jack Halloran Male Chorus; Charley Pride; Norma Zimmer; Jim Roberts; Perry Como.

50 Beloved Songs of Faith (Album No. 2) .... Reader's Digest (S) BMR3-100 5-8 89
Dolly Parton; Jimmy Dean; Doris Ackers; Hank Williams Jr.; Browns; Jimmy Davis; Johnson Family; George Beverly Shea; Eddy Arnold; Three Suns; Floyd Cramer; Don Hustad Chorale; Bill Gaither Trio; Oak Ridge Boys; Tennessee Ernie Ford.

50 Beloved Songs of Faith (Album No. 3) .... Reader's Digest (S) BMR3-100 5-8 89
(Mail order offer.) Johnny Cash; Tammy Wynette; George Jones; Willie Nelson; Roy Rogers; Dale Evans; Carter Family; Roy Acuff; Marty Robbins; Jim Roberts; Burl Ives; Mike Curb Congregation; David Houston; Anita Kerr; Ray Price; Larry Gatlin; Wayne Newton; B.J. Thomas; George Jones; Anita Bryant; Jim Nabors; Mormon Tabernacle Choir. (Three individual LPs but sold as a set. We value the set at $15 to $25.)

50 Country Greats (3 LP) .... Starday (S) P3S-5292 10-20
(Box set.) Glen Campbell; George Jones; Dolly Parton; Guy Mitchell; Webb Pierce; June Stearns; Gene Martin; Clyde Moody; Lonzo & Oscar; Red Sovine; Bobby Sykes; Melba Montgomery; Dave Dudley; Pee Wee King; Red Stewart; Patsy Cline; Jimmie Skinner; Minnie Pearl; Willis Brothers; Justin Tubb; T. Texas Tyler; Johnny Horton; Lulu Belle & Scotty; Grandpa Jones; Roy Wiggins; George Morgan; Flatt & Scruggs; Archie Campbell; Boots Randolph; Jimmy Richardson; Wilf Carter; Stonemans; Hawkshaw Hawkins; Arthur "Guitar" Smith; Stanley Brothers; Leon McAuliffe; Johnny Bond; Dottie West; Wynn Stewart; Sonny James; Roger Miller; Jimmy Dean; Carl Story; Johnny Cash; Snooky Lanson; Charlie Walker; Buck Owens; Pete Drake; Pop Stoneman; Kenny Roberts; Cowboy Copas.

50 Golden Years .... Columbia Special Products (S) P-12840 5-10 75
King Family; Anita Bryant; Burl Ives; Jim Nabors; Philadelphia Orchestra; Mahalia Jackson; Johnny Cash; Rosemary Clooney; Robert Goulet; Ray Conniff. (Made for Baptist Book Stores.)

50 of the Greatest Rock and Roll Groups (2 LP) .... Realm (S) 2V-8005 10-20
Flamingos; Diamonds; Chordettes; Orlons; Shirelles; Monotones; Impressions; Hollywood Argyles; Crystals; Cadillacs; Crests; Kingsmen; Fifth Estate; Regents; Angels; Tommy James & Shondells; Tymes; Dixie Cups; Chantels; McCoys; Capris; Maurice Williams & Zodiacs; Dubs; Dion & Belmonts; Shep & Limelites; Silhouettes.

50 of the Most Famous Records Ever Made, Album #1 .... Suffolk (M) SMI-1-86 5-10 85
Jo Stafford; Ink Spots; Gordon Jenkins; Stan Kenton; Glen Gray; Margaret Whiting; Art Mooney; Nat King Cole; Kitty Kallen; Dick Haymes; Count Basie; Art Lund; Judy Garland; Johnny Mercer.

50 of the Most Loved Records of Your Life, Vol. 1 .... SMI/CBS P 17691 5-10 84
(Mail order offer.) Englebert Humperdinck; Patti Page; Platters; Harmonicats; Ink Spots; Bing Crosby; Kitty Kallen; Four Aces featuring Al Alberts; Tom Jones; Vera Lynn; Nat King Cole; Frank Ifield; Al Martino; Margaret Whiting; Edith Piaf; Billy Vaughn.

50 of the Most Loved Records of Your Life, Vol. 2 .... SMI/CBS P 17692 5-10 84
(Mail order offer.) Eddy Arnold; Ray Price; Jim Reeves; Four Lads; Browns; Johnnie Ray; Rosemary Clooney; Eddie Fisher; Guy Mitchell; Ray Conniff; Frankie Laine; Bobby Darin; Doris Day; Ames Brothers; Johnny Mathis; Bobby Vinton; Jane Morgan; Tony Bennett; Three Suns.

50 of the Most Loved Records of Your Life, Vol. 3 .... SMI P 17692 5-10 84
(Mail order offer.) Jo Stafford; Brook Benton; Vic Damone; Billy Eckstine; Roger Williams; Mills Brothers; Gordon Jenkins; Les Paul & Mary Ford; Dean Martin; Fats Domino; Art Mooney; Georgia Gibbs; Al Hibbler; Teresa Brewer; Bobby Helms.

50 Oldies A Go-Go (5 LP) .... Somerset (S) SF-109 25-35 60s
Otis Redding; Hollywood Argyles; Tony Butala; Danny the Dreamer; Monorails; Ty Tyrell; Uptones; Nairobi River Boys; Sparkletts; Billy & Kids; Emily Parker; Innocents; Ribbons; Bobby Lile; Breakers; Cyd & Sheri; Sherrell Townsend; Downbeats; Gil Shelton; Rockin' Sidney; Starr Sisters.

50 Romantic Records, #1 .... CBS Special Products/Suffolk (S) P 20344 5-10 88
(Mail order offer.) Neil Sedaka; Bobby Helms; Shirelles; Del-Vikings; Percy Faith; Moonglows; Johnny Mathis; Four Lads; Lettermen; Bobby Vinton; Gene Pitney; Tune Weavers; Buddy Holly & Crickets; Everly Brothers; Four Aces; Harold Melvin & Blue Notes; Jackie Wilson; others.

50 Romantic Records, #2 .... Warner Special Products/Suffolk (S) OP-1563 5-10 88
(Mail order offer.) Association; Brook Benton; Marvin Gaye & Tammi Terrell; Temptations; Lenny Welch; Bobby Darin; Gladys Knight & Pips; Drifters; Frankie Valli & 4 Seasons; Jerry Butler & Betty Everett; Jim Croce; Four Tops; Fifth Dimension; Righteous Brothers; Supremes; Percy Sledge.

50 Romantic Records, #3 .... Suffolk/SMI (S) 1-135 5-10 88
(Mail order offer.) Capris; Ritchie Valens; Skyliners; Classics; Chiffons; Fats Domino; Marcels; Frankie Lymon & Teenagers; Dion & Belmonts; Penguins; Tommy Edwards; Mel Carter; Platters; Crests; Little Anthony & Imperials; Frankie Avalon; Johnny Tillotson.

50 Song Favorites (2 LP) .... RCA Camden (S) ADL2-0180 8-12 73
Charlie Barnet; Lena Horne; Lana Cantrell; Eddie Fisher; John Gary; Living Strings; Living Voices; Ethel Ennis.

50 Stars! 50 Hits (2 LP) .... Homestead (SE) 0008 8-12
Glen Campbell; Dolly Parton; Guy Mitchell; Wynn Stewart; Snooky Lanson;Melba ontgomery; Moon Mullican; Homesteaders; Grandpa Jones; Stonemans; Ray King; Kenny Roberts; Red Sovine; Pee Wee King; Justin Tubb; Clyde Moody; George Riddle; Texas Ruby; Pop Stoneman; Jim & Jesse; Dottie West; Webb Pierce; Dave Dudley; Johnny Cash; Bobby Sykes; Carl Story; Jim Glaser; Hylo Brown; Warren Robb; Patsy Cline; Stanley Brothers; Merle Kilgore; Minnie Pearl; Buck Owens; George Jones; Willis Brothers; Arthur Smith; Tommy Hill; Flatt & Scruggs; Jimmie Skinner; Cowboy Copas; Jan Howard; T. Texas Tyler; Boots Randolph; Jimmy Richardson; Lulu Belle & Scotty; Archie Campbell; Jackie Phelps; Roger Miller; Johnny Bond; George Morgan.

50 Stars! 50 Hits of Country Music (2 LP) .... Starday (M) CMS-1/4 10-15 60s
Justin Tubb; Benny Martin; George Riddle; Pete Drake; Red Hayes; Stanley Brothers; Carl Story; Texas Ruby; Tommy Hill; Sunshine Boys; Frankie Miller; Sonny James; T. Texas Tyler; Red Sovine; Cowboy Copas; David Houston; Johnny Horton; Minnie Pearl; Pee Wee King; Redd Stewart; Betty Amos; Archie Campbell; Melba Montgomery; Del Reeves; Denny Roberts; Moon Mullican; Arthur (Guitar Boogie) Smith; Homesteaders; Buddy Starcher; Willis Brothers; Jimmy Dean; Roger Miller; Dottie West; Johnny Bond; Hylo Brown; Rose Lee Maphis; Howard Vokes; Clyde Moody; Jim & Jesse; Lulu Belle & Scotty; Duke of Paducah; Jackie Phelps.

50 Years of Country Music (2 LP) .... Camden (S) ADL2-0782 8-12 74
Chet Atkins; Carter Family; Waylon Jennings; Skeeter Davis; Porter Wagoner; Don Gibson; Dottie West; Sons of the Pioneers; others.

50 Years of Film Music (3 LP) .... Warner Bros. (S) 3XX 2736 10-20

50 Years of Hit Songs (2 LP) .... Camden (S) ADL2-0779 8-12 74
Ames Brothers; Paul Anka; Allan Jones; Helen Morgan; Kay Starr; others.

50 Years of Jazz Guitar (2 LP) .... Columbia (S) CG-33566 10-20 76
Sam Moore; Lonnie Johnson; Eddie Land; Benny "King" Nawahi; Bobby Leecan; Teddy Bunn; Otto "Coco" Heimal; Dick McDonough; Carl Kress; Leon McAuliffe; Oscar "Buddy" Woods; Joe Sodja; Charlie Christian; Slim Gaillard; Memphis Minnie; Django Reinhardt; George Van Eps; Hark Garland; Kenny Burrell; Eddie Durham; Herb Ellis; George Benson; Charlie Byrd; John McLaughlin.

50 Years of Million Sellers (2 LP) .... Camden (S) CCL2-0620 6-12 74
Gene Austin; Elton Britt; Ames Brothers; Eddie Fisher; Vaughn Monroe; Perez Prado; Jerry Reed; Harry Belafonte; Vernon Dalhart; Friends of Distinction; Glahe Musette Orchestra; Spike Jones & His City Slickers; Pee Wee King; Freddy Martin; Jim Reeves; Ssgt. Barry Sadler; Kay Starr; Tokens; Paul Whiteman.

50 Years of Movie Music (2 LP) .... Camden (S) ADL2-0756 6-12 74
Ames Brothers; Living Strings; Norman Luboff Choir; Living Voices; Tony Martin; Melachrino Strings; Peter Nero; Ragtimers; Kate Smith; others.

'50s Explosion! Original Artists .... Exact (S) EX 245 5-10 81
Jimmy Clanton; Clovers; Drifters; Frankie Ford; Johnny Otis; Lloyd Price; Ritchie Valens; Shirelles.

'50s Greatest Love Songs; Greatest Hits to Remember Them By .... Columbia House (S) DS 718/724 5-10 70s
(Record club issue.) Tony Bennett; Joan Weber; Edith Piaf; Sammy Kaye; Guy Mitchell; Percy Faith; Johnny Mathis; Rosemary Clooney; Jerry Vale; Les Paul & Mary Ford; Mitch Miller; Doris Day; Marty Robbins; Four Lads; Frankie Laine; Johnny Horton. (Also packaged as two single LPs; *The Fifties: Golden Hits to Remember Them By* & *Fifties: Greatest Love Songs*.)

55 Original Country Classics (4 LP) .... RCA/Sessions (S) ???? 10-20
(Mail order offer.) Don Gibson; Johnny Cash; Jim Reeves; Eddy Arnold; Kitty Wells; Rex Allen; George Jones; Patsy Cline; Roy Clark; Red Foley; Ernest Ashworth; Ray Price; Sonny James; Jimmie Rodgers; Carl Perkins; Hank Williams; Loretta Lynn; Red Sovine; Webb Pierce; others. (Special products. Made for Sessions.)

55 Original Hits (3 LP) .... Columbia Special Products/Sessions (S) P3 12660 10-15 75
Frankie Lymon & Teenagers; Fireflies; Angels; Joey Dee & Starliters; Paul & Paula; Mitch Ryder & Detroit Wheels; Teen Queens; J.J. Jackson; Blood, Sweat & Tears; Byrds; Lou Christie; Tune Weavers; Tommy James & Shondells; Essex; Cleftones; Paul Revere & Raiders; Toys; Elegants; Lee Dorsey; Classics; Roy Hamilton; Keith; Little Anthony & Imperials; Swingin' Medallions; Alive 'N Kicking; Sandy Nelson; Walker Brothers; J. Frank Wilson; Billy Joe Royal; Gary Puckett & Union Gap; Buckinghams; Joe Jones; Shep & Limelights; Buster Brown; Happenings; Hollywood Argyles; Buddy Knox; Jimmie Rodgers; Willows; Playmates; Cathy Jean & Roomates; Huey Smith & Clowns; Olympics; Preston Epps; Frankie Ford; Dion; Left Banke; Skyliners.

55 Years of Great Hits .... Mark 56 (S) 523 5-10
Kirby Stone Four; Bonnie Baker; Dick Cathcart & New Dixieland Band; Dorothy Provine; Cindyapple Singers; Tex Beneke & Modernaires; Pinky Tomlin; Pete Kelly's Big Seven; Edgar "Stardust" Hayes.

59/WOW Presents Solid Gold (2 LP) .... Custom Fidelity (S) S3309 10-20 70s
Donny Osmond; Five Man Electrical Band; Daddy Dewdrop; Lighthouse; Grass Roots; Bobby Bloom; Smith; Osmonds; Ides of March; Stepenwolf; Mamas & Papas; Flying Machine; Cufflinks; Mouth & McNeal; Tee Set; Rod Stewart; Brian Hyland; O'Kaysions; Sammy Davis Jr.; Cowsills; B.B. King; Tommy Roe; Eddie Holman; Hamilton, Joe Frank & Reynolds.

60 Flashback Greats of the '60s (5 LP) .... K-Tel (S) ???? 30-40 73
(Boxed set.) Beatles with Tony Sheridan; Buddy Holly; Dion; Terry Stafford; Chad & Jeremy; Left Banke; Ray Charles; Joe South; others.

60 Monster Hits (6 LP) .... Columbia House (S) P6S-5908 35-45 72
(Boxed set. Mail order offer.) Santana; Byrds; Buckinghams; Dr. Hook & Medicine Show; Argent; Chase; Ten Years After; Hollies; Donovan; Redbone; Tymes; Looking Glass; Blood, Sweat & Tears; Pacific Gas & Electric; Byrds; Zombies; Paul Revere & Raiders; Laura Nyro; Big Brother & Holding Company; Sweathog; Poco; Stephen Stills/Al Kooper; Johnny Nash; Loggins & Messina; Delaney & Bonnie; Chi Coltrane; Mac Davis; Carlos Santana; Buddy Miles; Sly & Family Stone; Mark Lindsay; Addrisi Brothers; Mott the Hoople; Janis Joplin; Yardbirds; Scott McKenzie; David Bromberg; Johnnie Taylor; Ronnie Dyson; Spiral Staircase; Cliff Nobles; Gary Puckett & Union Gap; Johnny Cash; Mongo Santamaria..

60 Rock & Roll Smash Hits (Series A) (5 LP) .... Roulette (M) 665-A 100-150 66
(Boxed set. Reissue of the *Golden Goodies* series.)

60 Rock & Roll Smash Hits (Series B) (5 LP) .... Roulette (M) 665-B 100-150 66
(Boxed set. Reissue of the *Golden Goodies* series.)

60 Rock & Roll Smash Hits (Series C) (5 LP) .... Roulette (M) 665-C 100-150 66
(Boxed set. Reissue of the *Golden Goodies* series.)

60 Rock & Roll Smash Hits (Series D) (5 LP) .... Roulette (M) 665-D 100-150 66
(Boxed set. Reissue of the *Golden Goodies* series.)

60 Second Airplay Special .... Mercury (EP) DJ-115 10-15 69
(7 inch promotional issue only.Issued with paper sleeve.) New Colony Six; Aquarian Age; Manfred Mann; Jerry Butler; Mother Earth; Buddy Miles.

60 Top of the Chart Hits, #1 Country (6 LP) .... Columbia (S) P 6682 20-30 77
(Mail order offer.) Al Dexter; George Morgan; Hank Williams; Margaret Whiting; Jimmy Wakely; Lefty Frizzell; Ray Price; Everly Brothers; Sonny James; Carl Smith; Marty Robbins; Johnny Horton; Faron Young; Stonewall Jackson; Leroy Van Dyke; Billy Walker; Carl & Pearl Butler; Claude King; Johnny Cash; Flatt & Scruggs; Jimmy Dean; David Houston; Little Jimmy Dickens; Glen Campbell; Lynn Anderson; Hank Williams Jr.; Donna Fargo; Barbara Fairchild; Mel Tillis; Tom T. Hall; George Jones; Tammy Wynette; Charlie Rich; Tanya Tucker; Willie Nelson; Johnny Rodriguez; Freddy Fender; Johnny Duncan; B.J. Thomas.

60 Years of Country Music (2 LP) .... RCA (S) CPL2-4351 10-20 82
Elvis Presley; Henry C. Gilliland & A.C. (Eck) Robertson; Vernon Dalhart; Jimmie Rodgers; Carter Family; Wilf Carter; Milton Brown & His Musical Brownies; Bill Boyd & His Cowboy Ramblers; Blue Sky Boys; Hackberry Ramblers; Bill Monroe & His Bluegrass Boys; Elton Britt; Sons of the Pioneers; Hank Snow; Don Gibson; Jim Reeves; Chet Atkins; Eddy Arnold; Jerry Reed; Charley Pride; Waylon Jennings; Dolly Parton; Ronnie Milsap; Alabama.

60 Years of Grand Ole Opry (2 LP) .... RCA (S) CPL2-9507 10-20 86
Uncle Dave Macon; Crook Brothers; DeFord Bailey; Paul Warmack & Gully Jumpers; Theron Hale & Daughters; Vagabonds; Asher Sizemore & Little Jimmie; Bradley Kincaid; Delmore Brothers with Fiddlin' Arthur Smith; Bill Monroe; Ernest Tubb; Eddy Arnold; Pee Wee King; Willis Brothers; Johnnie & Jack with Kitty Wells; Del Wood; Minnie Pearl; Grandpa Jones; Chet Atkins; Hank Snow; Jordanaires; Don Gibson; Hank Locklin; Jim Reeves; Dottie West; Porter Wagoner; Browns; Billy Walker; Connie Smith; Justin Tubb; George Hamilton IV; Bobby Bare; Skeeter Davis; Archie Campbell; Lester Flatt; Willie Nelson; Dolly Parton; Ronnie Milsap; Osborne Brothers.

60 Years of Music America Loves Best, Golden Performances That Will Live Forever .... (2 LP) RCA (S) SM-0700 15-25
Enrico Caruso; Paul Whiteman; Wanda Landowska; Gene Austin; Sergei Rachmaninoff; Marian Anderson; Ignace Paderewski; Hoagy Carmichael; Artie Shaw; Arthur Fiedler; Fritz Kreisler; Glenn Miller; Leopold Stokowski & Philadelphia Orchestra; Leontyne Price; Benny Goodman; Duke Ellington; Freddy Martin; Tommy Dorsey; Frank Sinatra; Perry Como; Jan Peerce; John McCormack; Pablo Casals; Eddy Arnold; Mario Lanza; Arturo Toscanini & NBC Symphony Orchestra; Perez Prado; Risë Stevens; Hugo Winterhalter; Sons of the Pioneers; Harry Belafonte.

60 Years of Music America Loves Best, Vol. 1 (2 LP) .... RCA (M) LM-6074 15-25 59
Enrico Caruso; Harry Belafonte; Paul Whiteman; Gene Austin; Artie Shaw; Benny Goodman; Duke Ellington; Tommy Dorsey; Frank Sinatra; Vladimir Horowitz; Sergei Rachmaninoff; Jeanette MacDonald; Nelson Eddy; Marian Anderson; Ignace Paderewski; Jascha Heifetz; Arthur Fiedler; Glenn Miller; Freddy Martin; Perry Como; Jan Peerce; Three Suns; Arthur Rubenstein; Eddy Arnold; Mario Lanza; Arturo Toscanini & NBC Symphony Orchestra; Perez Prado; Ames Brothers; Hugo Winterhalter; Jose Iturbi; Leopold Stokowski; Fritz Kreisler; Boston Pops.

60 Years of Music America Loves Best, Vol. 2 (2 LP) .... RCA (M) LM-6088 15-25 60
Eddie Fisher; John Phillip Sousa; Perry Como; Guy Lombardo; Vaughn Monroe; Spike Jones; Robert Merrill; Mario Lanza; Enrico Caruso; Maurice Chevalier; Allan Jones; Leonard Warren; Mischa Elman; Artie Shaw; Wayne King; Larry Clinton; Grace Moore; Glenn Miller; Tommy Dorsey; David Rose; Sergei Rachmaninoff; Lucretia Bori; L. Stokowski; Pablo Casals; Harry Belafonte; Arthur Fiedler; Fritz Kreisler; Will Glahe; Risě Stevens; Toscannini.

60 Years of Music America Loves Best, Vol. 3 (Popular)..RCA (M) LOP-1509 15-25 61
Frank Sinatra; Harry Belafonte; Benny Goodman; Glenn Miller; Artie Shaw; Tommy Dorsey; Bunny Berigan; Ted Weems; Hal Kemp; Bing Crosby; Harry Lauder; Vernon Dalhart; Ella Fitzgerald; Marian Anderson; John Barrymore; Jusci Bjoerling; E. Caruso; Arthur Fiedler; Kirsten Flagstad; Horowitz; Serge Koussevitzky; Fritz Kreisler; Ezio Pinza; Lily Pons; Tonscannini.

60 Years of Music America Loves Best (Classical)...RCA (M) LM-2574 10-20 59

61 More Hits...Screen Gems/Columbia (M) 1002 20-30

62 Golden Greats (4 LP)...Sessions/RCA (S) SRL-4-0266 20-30 77
(Gatefold cover. Mail order offer.) Frankie Avalon; Freddy Cannon; Charlie Rich; Dave "Baby" Cortez; Spanky & Our Gang; Brooklyn Bridge; Happy Day; Vogues; Sam Cooke; Shirelles; Cowsills; Neil Sedaka; Lemon Pipers; Skeeter Davis; Casinos; Hues Corp.

62 Golden Greats..K-Tel (S) ???? 20-25

64 of the Greatest Motown Original Hits (4 LP)..Motown (S) No Number Used 20-30 72
(Mail order offer from Cimco.) Diana Ross; Jackson 5; Michael Jackson; Supremes; Marvin Gaye; Temptations; Smokey Robinson & Miracles; Stevie Wonder; Four Tops; Gladys Knight & Pips; Rare Earth; Marvelettes; Undisputed Truth; Martha & Vandellas; Jr. Walker & All-Stars; Tammi Terrell; Jimmy Ruffin; Edwin Starr; David Ruffin; Mary Wells.

'70s Gold (2 LP)..Warner Special Products/Sessions (S) OP 2523 8-12 80
Abba; Dire Straits; Harry Chapin; Seals & Crofts; Spinners; Orleans; Sister Sledge; Nicollette Larson; Fire Fall; Night; Robert John; Stylistics; Leo Sayer; Ian Matthews; Exile; England Dan & John Ford Coley; Blondie; Gary Wright; Dr. Hook; Andrew Gold; Stephen Bishop; Yvonne Elliman; John Stewart; Charlie Dore; Alice Cooper; Nick Gilder; Shaun Cassidy; KC & Sunshine Band.

72 Top Original Hits by the Original Artists (4 LP)..............................Columbia Special Products (S) C-10568/71 15-25 70s
(Box set.) Ad Libs; Ray Barretto; Fontella Bass; Box Tops; James Brown; Buckinghams; Byrds; Chantels; Lou Christie; Dave Clark Five; Coasters; Cowsills; Critters; Crows; Cyrkle; Neil Diamond; Dixie Cups; Lee Dorsey; Ronnie Dove; Drifters; Esquires; Five Americans; 4 Seasons; Inez Foxx; John Fred; Bobby Goldsboro; Happenings; Wilbert Harrison; Bobby Hebb; J.J. Jackson; Tommy James; Jay & Americans; Jay & Techniques; Terry Knight & Pack; Ramsey Lewis Trio; Little Anthony; Little Eva; Love; Loved Ones; Lovin' Spoonful; Frankie Lymon; Barbara Mason; Peaches & Herb; Wilson Pickett; Rascals; Mitch Ryder & Detroit Wheels; Sam & Dave; Sam the Sham; Seeds; Shep & Limelites; Percy Sledge; Sonny & Cher; Soul Survivors; Spanky & Our Gang; Syndicate Of Sound; Tempos; Toys; Ike & Tina Turner; Vogues; Brenton Wood.

80 Biggest Hits by the Stars that Made Them Famous (4 LP)...Columbia (S) ???? 15-20
Ray Barretto; Beau Brummels; Chuck Bene & Mice; Jimmy Bowen; Buster Brown; Jerry Butler; Byrds; Cadillacs; Gene Chandler; Channels; Chantels; Chartbusters; Chubby Checker; Lou Christie; Dave Clark Five; Classics; Eddie Cooley; Crows; Dale & Grace; Joey Dee & Starliters; Detergents; Dion; Lee Dorsey; Drifters; Bob Dylan; Essex; Betty Everett; Exciters; Aretha Franklin; Bobby Freeman; Marvin Gaye; Harptones; Heartbeats; Honeycombs; Jimmy Hughes; Hullaballoos; Joe Jones; Buddy Knox; Patti LaBelle & Blue Belles; Major Lance; Barbara Lewis; Bobby Lewis; Little Anthony & Imperials; Frankie Lymon; Martha & Vandellas; Miracles; New Christy Minstrels; Patty & Emblems; Playmates; Raindrops; Reflections; Paul Revere & Raiders; Rip Chords; Rivieras; Jimmie Rodgers; Bobby Rydell; Millie Small; Village Stompers; Bobby Vinton; Mary Wells; J. Frank Wilson. (Reissue of *20 Spotlight Hits* [Col. 78], *20 Original Winners of 1964* [Rou. 25293], *20 All Time No. 1 Hits* [Rou. 25290]; and *20 "Big Boss" Favorites* [Rou. 25304].)

80 Minutes in Lovers Lane (2 LP)..Columbia (M) XTV 28701/4 10-15 50s
Rhonda Flemming; Doris Day; Harry James; Don Cherry; Jerri Adams; Xavier Cugat with Abbe Lane; Rosemary Clooney & Percy Faith; Benny Goodman; Norman Luboff; Les Elgart; Erroll Garner; Otto Cesana; Mitch Miller; Hi-Lo's; Sammy Kaye; Michel Legrand; Claude Thornhill; Art VanDamme Quintet. (Made for Lane Company, Makers of Sweetheart Chests.)

93/KHJ Sound of the Sixties: see KHJ

93Q Morning Zoo (KKBQ Houston), Greatest Hits, Vol. 1...Arista (S) ALB-8414 5-10 84
John Lander; John Rio; Dr. Dave Kolin; Mr. Leonard; Cleat; Pumpster; Jackie Robbins; Archer Dusablon.

96X Home Grown..Phoenix (S) 76 5-10
Blues Image; others.

96X Stereo FM..Columbia/RKO (S) No Number Used 20-25 78
(Picture disc. Promotional issue only.) Boston; Ringo Starr; others.

97 (KSSR) Rocks - Houston Home Cooking Album...Columbia/ABS (S) KSSR-001 15-20 82
(Picture disc. Promotional issue only.)

99X Rocking the Apple...Columbia (S) No Number Used 5-10 78

100 All Time Country Hall of Fame Hits, Vol. 1 (2 LP)..TVP (S) TVP-1017 10-15 77
Patsy Cline; Bobby Helms; Jan Howard; Jack Greene; Burl Ives; Conway Twitty; Johnny Wright; Bill Anderson; Kitty Wells; Red Sovine; Henson Cargill; B.J. Thomas; Sammi Smith; Ronnie Milsap; Orville Couch; Dave Dudley; Roger Miller; George Jones; Rex Allen; Melba Montgomery; Roy Drusky; Tex Ritter; Frankie Laine; Tex Williams; Jeanne Pruitt; Wilma Burgess; Bill Monroe; Ernest Tubb; Red Foley; Webb Pierce; Sons of the Pioneers; Brenda Lee; Billy Grammer; Hoosier Hot Shots; Buck Owens; Mac Davis.

100 All Time Country Hall of Fame Hits, Vol. 2 (2 LP)..TVP (S) TVP-1017 10-15 77
Carl Belew; Sammi Smith; George Jones; Ronnie Milsap; B.J. Thomas; Henson Cargill; Jimmy Dean; Anitha Bryant; Don Gibson; Tommy Cash; Tex Ritter; Mac Davis; Patsy Cline; Dave Dudley; Buck Owens; Nashville Singers; Roy Drusky; Jerry Wallace; Johnny Bond; Dorsey Burnette; Lonnie Mack; George Jones; Gene Pitney.

100 Hall of Fame Oldies (5 LP)...Vee Jay (M) HHF 6833-6837 35-45 70s
Marvin & Johnny; Flamingos; Mark II; Capris; Spaniels; Richard Berry; Jimmy Charles; Dubs; Little Richard; Dee Clark; Maurice Williams; Impressions; Scarlets; Joe Jones; Angels; Olympics; Quin-Tones; Joe Simon; Buster Brown; Gene Chandler; Betty Everett; Jerry Butler; John Lee Hooker; Gladys Knight & Pips; Skyliners; El Dorados; Harptones; Jackie Lee; Lee Dorsey; Dells; Willows; Bob & Earl; Betty Everett & Jerry Butler; Chris Kenner; Billy Preston; Jimmy Hughes; Wilbert Harrison; Bobby Lewis; Jennell Hawkins; Jesse Belvin; Etta James; Faye Adams; Roscoe Gordon; Wade Flemons; Jimmy Reed; Gary LeMel; Jimmy Conwell; Performers; Earl Crosby; Bobby Garrett; Mirettes; Five Echos; Orchids; Delegates; Bobby Jamison.

100 Proof Country..Hilltop (S) JS-6176 8-12 60s
George Jones; Statler Brothers; Tom T. Hall; Roger Miller; Flatt & Scruggs; Leroy Van Dyke; Roy Drusky.

100 Songs...Columbia Special Products (S) CSS-1492 10-15 70
Lulu; Aretha Franklin; Jimmy Dean; Patti Page; Gary Puckett & Union Gap; New Christy Minstrels; Steve Lawrence; others. (Made for Benson & Hedges.)

101 FM K-EARTH: see KRTH

101 FM WCBS History of Rock: see WCBS

102.3 WBAB: see WBAB

200 Years of American Heritage in Music..CMH (S) 1776 8-12 76
Don Ange; Benny Martin; Arthur Smith; Maggie Griffin; others.

200 Years of Gospel Music, Vol. 2...Gospel Time (S) GT-5032 8-12 76
Jerry Goff & Singing Goffs; Oak Ridge Quartet; Georgians; Pine Ridge Boys; Carl Story & Mountaineers; Jake Hess & Jordanaires; Dixie Echoes & Hal Kennedy; J.T. Adams & Men of Texas; Sunshine Girls; Sego Brothers & Naomi.

212 Hits..Screen Gems/Colgems (S) 212 20-30 84
(Promotional issue only.) Beatles; others.

610 KFRC: see KFRC
610 WRKO: see WRKO
1133 (Opening of the Inmont Building in NY, NY) .... RCA Special Products (S) PRS 281 5-10 68
Duke Ellington; Peter Nero; Eddie Heywood; Earl Hines & His Boys; Skitch Henderson; Claus Ogerman; Paul Desmond; Anita Kerr Singers.
1220 - WGAR Means Music (2 LP) .... Lost Nite (S) 5053 10-15
Bill Haley & His Comets; Paris Sisters; Wilbert Harrison; Little Caesar & Romans; Jimmy Jones; Bobby Helms; Buddy Holly; Tommy Edwards; Jerry Butler; Capris; Lou Christie; Everly Brothers; Bobby Lewis; Gene Chandler; Marcels; Ritchie Valens; Dee Clark; Righteous Brothers; Silhouettes; Don & Juan; Bobby Fuller Four; Crests; Del Shannon; Ruby & Romantics.
1927 .... RCA (M) LPV-545 10-15 67
George Olsen; Gertrude Lawrence; Paul Whiteman; others.
1928 .... RCA (M) LPV-523 10-15 66
Helen Kane; George Olsen; Jesse Crawford; Gene Austin; Irving Aaronson; Relelers; Leo Reisman; Johnny Hamp's Kentucky Serenaders; Duke Ellington; Helen Morgan; Roger Wolfe Kahn; Vaughn Dedeath; Paul Whiteman; Fred Waring; Jack Smith; Irene Bordoni.
1930's Big Bands .... Columbia (M) CJ 40651 8-12
1930's Small Combos .... Columbia (M) CJ 40833 8-12
1940's the Small Groups: New Directions .... Columbia (M) CJ 44222 8-12
Woody Herman; Gene Krupa; Harry James; others.
1945-1946 New Year's Radio Dancing Party #31 .... Radiola (M) MR 1031 5-10 74
Guy Lombardo; Harry James; Count Basie; Freddy Martin; Woody Herman; Gene Krupa; Henry King; Louis Armstrong; Jimmy Dorsey; Les Brown; Artie Shaw; Stan Kenton; Tommy Dorsey; Carmen Cavallero; Louis Prima; Benny Goodman; Duke Ellington.
1950's Rock and Roll Revival .... Kama Sutra (S) KSBS-2015 20-25 70
(With program booklet.)
1950's Rock and Roll Revival .... Kama Sutra (S) KSBS-2015 15-20 70
(Without program booklet.) Bill Haley & His Comets; Five Satins; Mello Kings; Shep & Limelites; Penguins; Capris; Spaniels; Gary "U.S." Bonds.
1950's Rock 'N' Roll (Cruisin' Lovers Lane) (3 LP) .... Candlelite (S) 719 10-15 83
(Boxed set with 12-page booklet.) Jerry Butler; Chordettes; Everly Brothers; El Dorados; Blue Jays; Dells; Dee Clark; Gary "U.S." Bonds; Spaniels; Gene Chandler; Flamingos; Johnny Tillotson;; Paris Sisters; Lenny Welch; Link Wray; Little Richard; Betty Everett.
1950's Rock 'N' Roll (Jukebox Saturday Night) (3 LP) .... Candlelite (S) 718 10-15 83
(Boxed set with 12-page booklet.) Paradons; Barbara George; Lenny Welch; Billie & Lillie; Dion & Belmonts; Cathy Jean & Roomates; Little Richard; Casinos; Johnny Preston; Phil Phillips; Huey Smith & Clowns; Little Caesar & Romans; Chubby Checker; Barbara Lewis; Johnny "Piano" Wilson; Dee Clark; Penguins; Ron Holden; Troy Shondell; Harold Dorman; Mystics; Fire Flies; Bobby Vee; Brook Benton; Jarmels; Ritchie Valens; Kathy Young & Innocents.
1950's Rock 'N' Roll (Rock 'N' Roll Kingdom) (3 LP) .... Candlelite (S) 717 10-15 83
(Boxed set with 12-page booklet.) Platters; Impalas; Tommy Edwards; Jimmy Jones; Danleers; Gino & Gina; Conway Twitty; Sarah Vaughan; Clyde McPhatter; Diamonds; Stereos; Crew-Cuts; Red Prysock; Dinah Washington; Fats Domino; Vox-Poppers; Big Bopper.
1950's Treasure of Love (2 LP) .... RCA Special Products (S) SVL2-0574 10-15 82
(Mail order offer.) Clyde McPhatter; Platters; Five Satins; Teddy Bears; Penguins; Phil Phillips; Ritchie Valens; Floyd Cramer; Jack Scott; Pony-Tails; Dion & Belmonts; Flamingos; Heartbeats; Dubs; Connie Stevens; Crests; Sam Cooke; Mello Kings; Everly Brothers; Ivory Joe Hunter; Chantels; Bobby Helms; Tommy Edwards; Danleers; Kathy Young & Innocents; Paul Anka; Jean Weber; ; Jimmy Rodgers; Sonny James; Kitty Kallen; Little Anthony & Imperials; Robert & Johnny; Harptones; Johnny Ace; Fleetwoods.
1961 Original Artists Super Hits .... Gusto (S) GT-009 5-10 79
Coasters; Dick & Deedee; Curtis Lee; Bobby Edwards; Angels; Dovells; Bobby Lewis; Sandy Nelson; Clarence "Frogman" Henry; Hank Ballard & Midnighters; Bill Doggett.
1964 - Year in Review .... Gateway (M) LP-9004 35-55 65
Paul McCartney; John Lennon; Ringo Starr; Cassius Clay; others.
1966 Grammy Award Winners .... NARAS (S) XTV-123942 40-60 67
(Promotional issue only.) Beatles; Louis Armstrong; Ella Fitzgerald; Ray Charles; Wes Montgomery; New Vaudeville Band; John Gary; Eydie Gorme; Anita Kerr Singers; David Houston.
1967 Grammy Award Winners .... Grammy (S) 2236/2237 40-60 68
1968 Grammy Awards Show .... NARAS (S) 144949/50 40-60 69
Beatles; others.
1969 .... Polydor (S) 837362-1 8-10 88
(Soundtrack.) Jimi Hendrix; Cream; Animals; Creedence Clearwater Revival; Canned Heat; Zombies; Jesse Colin Young; Blind Faith; Moody Blues; Crosby, Nash & Young; Pretenders.
$64,000 Jazz .... Columbia (M) CL-777 40-60 55
Benny Goodman; Louis Armstrong; Eddie Condon; Harry James; Buck Clayton; Duke Ellington; Dave Brubeck; Pete Rugolo; Sarah Vaughan; J.J. Johnson; Kai Winding; Erroll Garner; Woody Herman. (Tie-in with *$64,000 Question* TV program.)
A&M Bootleg Album .... A&M (S) SP-8022 15-20 73
(Promotional issue only.) Joe Cocker; Leon Russell; Captain Beefheart & His Magic Band; Dillard & Clark; Flying Burrito Brothers; Move; Larry Marks; Lee Michaels; Procol Harum; Tyrannosaurus Rex.
A&M Foreplay: see Foreplay
A&M Million Dollar Sound Sampler .... A&M (S) 19001 8-12 60s
Herb Alpert & Tijuana Brass; Chris Montez; Sandpipers; Sergio Mendes; Baja Marimba Band; We Five; Claudine Longet; Canadian Sweet Hearts.
A&M Pre Release Sampler (April 1980): see Foreplay, Vol. 31
A&M Propaganda .... A&M (S) SP-4786 5-10 79
(Standard LP.) Granati Brothers; Joe Jackson; Police; Reds; Bobby Henry; Squeeze; David Kubinek; Shrink.
A&M Propaganda .... A&M (S) SP-4786 40-50 80
(Picture disc. Has same picture on both sides.) Granati Brothers; Joe Jackson; Police; Reds; Bobby Henry; Squeeze; David Kubinek; Shrink.
A&M Propaganda .... A&M (S) SP-4786 20-30 80
(Picture disc. Has a different picture on each sides.) Granati Brothers; Joe Jackson; Police; Reds; Bobby Henry; Squeeze; David Kubinek; Shrink.
A&M Summer Spectacular .... A&M (S) SP 8653 8-12 75
Joan Baez; Cat Stevens; Carpenters; Billy Preston; Captain & Tennille; Gino Vannelli; Tubes; Hummingbird; Pablo Cruise; Head East; Hudson-Ford.
A&M - the Album .... A&M (S) SP 8096 8-12
(Made to promote voter registration.)

ABC Album Release Sampler, July 1976 .... ABC (S) SPABC-776 8-10 76
John Mayall; Delbert McClinton; Flamin' Groovies; Christine McVie; Larry Hosford; Randy Cornor; Buck Trent.
ABC Album Release Sampler, August 1976 .... ABC (S) 876 8-10 76
(Promotional issue only.) J.J. Cale; Hank Thompson; Tommy Overstreet; Wade Marcus; Dalton & Dubarri; Nektar; Fireballet; Kraan; Johnny Carver; John Klemmer; Marilyn McCoo & Billy Davis Jr.; Crown of Glory; Biblical Gospel Singers.
ABC Album Sampler, January 1977 (2 LP) .... ABC (S) SP ABC 177 8-12 77
Rufus; Ace; Tompall Glaser; Rhythm Heritage; Shotgun; Jim Weatherly; Keith Jarrett; Big Wha-Koo; Tommy Overstreet; Tessie Hall; Dirk Hamilton; Tom Sullivan; Street Corner Symphony; Cado Belle; Harold Melvin & Blue Notes; Avalanche; Isaac Hayes; Dionne Warwick; Martin Mull; Don Everly; Mighty Clouds of Joy; Anthony Phillips; B.B. King; Mildred Clark; Lakeside; Booty People.
ABC Presents 14 Golden Recordings: see 14 Golden Recordings
ABC Spring of '73 Sampler .... ABC RPRO 102 5-10 73
Steely Dan; Diamond Head; John Kurtz; William St. James; Genya Ravan; Jim Croce; Rufus; Tim Moore; Dusty Springfield; Thomas Jefferson Kaye.
Aberbach Presents All Time Greats, Vol 1 .... ATG (S) VOL-1 10-15
Aberbach Presents All Time Greats, Vol 2 .... ATG (S) VOL-2 10-15
Aberbach Presents All Time Greats, Vol 3 .... ATG (S) VOL-3 10-20
Elvis Presley; others.
About Last Night .... EMI America (S) SV-17210 8-10 86
(Soundtrack.) Sheena Easton; John Oates; Jermaine Jackson; J.D. Souther; Bob Seger; Nancy Shanks; Michael Henderson; Paul Davis; Del Lords; John Waite.
Absolute Beginners .... EMI America (S) SV-17182 8-10 86
(Soundtrack.) David Bowie; Sade; Style Council; Ray Davies; Gil Evans; Eighth Wonder; Working Week; Slim Gaillard; Jerry Dammers.
Academy Awards Presentation .... Columbia (S) LSS-1006/7 10-20
(Soundtrack.) Anita Bryant; Jerry Vale; John Davidson; Eydie Gorme; Doris Day; Julie Andrews; others. (Made for General Electric.)
Acid Visions (Best of Texas Punk & Psychedelic) .... Voxx (SP) VHM 2000,008 8-12 83
Great Believers; Scotty McKay Quintet; A-440; Things; Stoics; Satori; Neal Ford & Ramadas; Roy Head; Johnny Winter; Pandas; Bad Roads; Amos Boynton & ABCs.
Action Jackson .... Lorimar (S) 7 90886-1 8-12 88
(Soundtrack.) Pointer Sisters; Madame X; Levert; Vanity; Sister Sledge; David Koz; Skyy; M.C. Jam & Pee Wee Jam.
Admiral Million Dollar Look in Color TV .... Columbia Special Products (S) CSS-465 5-10 60s
Barbra Streisand; Percy Faith; Doris Day; Robert Goulet; Eydie Gorme; Steve Lawrence; New Christy Minstrels; Tony Bennett; Andre Kostelanetz; Jerry Vale; Leslie Uggams;
Admiral Quality Solid-State Stereophonic High Fidelity .... Admiral/RCA (S) PRS-218 10-15 66
Leo Addeo; Arthur Fiedler & Boston Pops; Three Suns; John Gary; Arthur Murray; Chet Atkins; Carol Channing; Claus Ogerman; Sid Ramin; Frankie Carle; Bill Gale. (Special products. Made for Admiral.)
Admiral Stereo Demonstration Record Featuring Amazing Phantom 3rd Channel .... Decca (S) 738241 10-20 60s
Bill Haley & His Comets; Henry Jerome; Rosemary Clooney; Warren Covington & Tommy Dorsey Orchestra; Lenny Dee; Mishel Piastro; Carol Burnette; Irving Fields Trio; Wayne King; Jan Garber; Stratford Strings; Lionel Newman; 20th Century-Fox Orchestra.
Adventures in Paradise, Vol. 3 .... ABC-Paramount (M) ABC-414 8-12 60s
Islanders; Roy Smeck; Alfred Apaka; Terorotua & His Tahitians.
Adventures in Sound .... Manhattan (M) 548 8-12 50s
Dick Haymes; Carmen McCrae; Pupi Campo; Bill Briscoe; Max Matthews; others.
Adventures of Ford Fairlane .... Elektra (S) 60952-1 8-10 90
(Soundtrack.) Yello; Billy Idol; Motley Crue; Ton Loc; Andrew Dice Clay; Sheila E.; Queensryche; Richie Samboro; Teddy Pendergrass; Lisa Fisher; Dion.
After Hours - the Chart Soaring Hits of Today .... K-Tel (S) PTU 2920 5-10 82
Rick Springfield; Journey; Little River Band; Abba; Barry Manilow; Donnie Iris; LeRoux; George Benson; Charlene; Air Supply; Quincy Jones with James Ingram; Greg Guidry; Eddie Rabbitt; Lindsay Buckingham; Paul Davis.
After Hours .... King (M) 395-528 100-150 57
After Hours .... King (SE) 528 20-30 61
Sonny Thompson; Ace Harris; Earl Bostic; Bill Jennings; Pete "Guitar" Lewis; Jimmy Nolen; Bill Doggett; Todd Rhodes; Washboard Bill.
After the Riot at Newport: see NASHVILLE ALL-STARS
After You've Gone .... Concord (S) CJ-6 10-15
Against All Odds .... Atlantic (S) 80152-1-E 8-10 84
Against All Odds .... Atlantic (S) A1 80152 5-8 84
(Soundtrack.) Phil Collins; Stevie Nicks; Jimmy Iovine; Peter Gabriel; Big Country; Mike Rutherford; Kid Creole & Coconuts; Larry Carlton; Michel Columbier.
Age of Rock .... EMR Enterprises (M) RH-8 100-125 69
(Promotional issue only) Elvis Presley; others. (Made for Random House and Vintage Books.)
Age of Television – a Chronicle of the First 25 Years. .... RCA (S) LL-8 10-20 72
(Soundtrack.) (Selections are excerpts. Includes booklet.) Milton Berle; Hugh Downs; Howdy Doody Time; Harry S Truman; First Moon Walk; Greal Gildersleeve; Your Hit Parade; Giants vs. Dodgers; Kukla, Fran & Ollie; Arlene Francis; Strike It Rich; People Are Funny; Fred Allen; Pat Weaver; Roy Rogers; Gene Autry; All Star Review; Dwight D. Eisenhower; Texaco Star Theatre; John F. Kennedy; Today; Captain Kangaroo; Assassination of Lee Harvey Oswald; My Little Margie; Life of Riley; Dick Van Dyke Show; Lyndon B. Johnson; Beverly Hillbillies; Secret Storm; Guiding Light; Doctors; Let's Make a Deal; Hubert H. Humphrey; What's My Line; Sesame Street; Moon Trek; Superman; Spiro T. Agnew; Ding Dong School; Ben Casey; Peter Pan; Ed Sullivan; Tonight Show with Jack Paar; Tonight Show with Johnny Carson; Apollo 15.
Air America .... MCA (S) 6467 8-10 90
(Soundtrack.) Aerosmith; B.B. King; Bonnie Raitt; Charles Sexton; Steely Dan; Edgar Winter; Rick Derringer; Mamas & Papas; Four Tops; Temptations; Fontella Bass; Seeds.
Air Force Sound Flights into Jazz, Vol. 3 .... ???? 15-25 59
Chubby Jackson; Hank D'Amico; Jimmy Nottingham; Art Farmer; George Auld; Elliott Lawrence.
Akron Compilation .... Stiff (S) GET 3 8-12
A La Carte: see Warner Bros. Promotional Releases/Samplers
Al Brown's New York Sound, Volume 1 .... Crystal Ball (S) 116 8-12 84
Eddie & Starlights; Lunar & Planets; Mellow Tones; Jell Tones; Crescents; Passions; Donnie & Chappells; Gaytunes; Charlets; Vilons.
Alabama State Troupers .... Elektra (S) 75022 8-12 72
Alabama State Troupers; Don Nix; Jeanie Greene; Furry Lewis; others.

Alan Freed's Golden Pics .... End (M) 313 45-55 62
Cadets; Turbans; Flamingos; Little Richard; Nutmegs; Magnificants; Gloria Mann; El Dorados; Hearts; Rivileers; Chuck Berry; Jimmy McCracklin; Little Walter; Willows; Chantels.

Alan Freed Rock'n Roll Show: see FREED, Alan

Alan Freed's Memory Lane .... End (M) LP-314 50-75 62
Alan Freed; Sonny Til & Orioles; Rays; Jerry Butler; Crests; Moonglows; Dells; Flamingos; Jacks; Five Satins; Teen Queens; Robert & Johnny; Little Anthony & Imperials; Jesse Belvin; Mello Kings.

Alan Freed's Memory Lane .... Roulette (SE) R-42041 10-15 70s
(Reissue.) Alan Freed; Sonny Til & Orioles; Rays; Jerry Butler; Crests; Moonglows; Dells; Flamingos; Jacks; Five Satins; Teen Queens; Robert & Johnny; Little Anthony & Imperials; Jesse Belvin; Mello Kings.

Alan Freed's Rock 'N' Roll Dance Party, Vol. 2 .... WINS (M) 1011 15-25
Alan Freed Band; Flamingos; Flairs; Big Maybelle; Clyde McPhatter; Valentines; Gene Vincent & Blue Caps; Bonnie Sisters.

Alan Freed's Rock 'N' Roll Dance Party, Vol. 3 .... WINS (M) 1012 15-25
Alan Freed Band; Bill Haley & His Comets; Cleftones; Four Fellows; Etta James; Jacks; Platters; Gloria Mann.

Alan Freed's Rock 'N' Roll Dance Party, Vol. 4 (Recorded Live on Stage) .... WINS (M) 1013 15-25
Frankie Lymon & Teenagers; LaVern Baker; Little Richard; Clovers; Otis Williams & Charms; Three Chuckles; Chuck Willis; Five Keys with Alan Freed Orchestra.

Alan Freed's Top 15 .... End (M) LP-315 30-40 62
Lloyd Price; Dee Clark; Etta James; Santo & Johnny; Nutmegs; Silhouettes; Charlie & Ray; Cadillacs; Shirelles; Guitar Slim; Spaniels; Rivileers; Edna McGriff; Faye Adams; Larry Williams.

Alan Freed's Top 15 .... Roulette (M) 42042 10-15
(Reissue.) Wilbert Harrison; Dee Clark; Etta James; Santo & Johnny; Nutmegs; Silhouettes; Charlie & Ray; Cadillacs; Shirelles; Buster Brown; Spaniels; Lee Dorsey; Rivileers; Edna McGriff; Faye Adams.

Album .... A&M (S) 10-15 72
(Mail order LP promoting voter registration.)

Album, The .... Columbia Special Products (S) CSS-1217 8-12
Paul Revere & Raiders; Flock; Byrds; Gary Puckett & Union Gap; Chicago; Chambers Brothers; Sly & Family Stone; Pacific Gas & Electric; Spirit; Illinois Speed Express.

Alivemutherforya .... Columbia (S) 35349 5-10 78
Billy Cobham; Steve Khan; Alphonso Johnson; Tom Scott. (Live recordings.)

All Aboard .... Starday (M) S-170 15-25 62
Moon Mullican; Jim Glaser; Stanley Brothers; Wayne Raney; others.

All About Rain .... Capitol (S) STB 138/8 8-12
Four Freshmen; Keely Smith; Nancy Wilson; Ray Anthony; Jo Stafford; Stan Kenton; Kay Starr; Jackie Gleason; George Shearing; Jonah Jones. (Made for U.S. Royal/Uniroyal Tires.)

All American Country (5 LP) .... Sessions (S) OP 5506 20-25 84
(Mail order offer. Box set.) Charly McClain; Willie Nelson; Merle Haggard; Janie Fricke; George Jones; Lacy J. Dalton; Gatlin Brothers; David Allen Coe; B.J. Thomas; Roseanne Cash; Waylon Jennings; Deborah Allen; Eieran Kane; Rex Allen Jr.; Margo Smith; Earl Thomas Conley; Judds; Razzy Bailey; Debby Boone; Jerry Lee Lewis; Johnny Lee; Whites; Vern Gosdin; Con Hunley; Bobby Goldsboro; Gail Davies; Conway Twitty; Eddie Rabbitt; Tompall & Glaser Bros.; Mel Tillis; Sylvia; John Anderson; Ronnie Milsap; Donna Fargo; T.G. Sheppard; Emmylou Harris; Wright Brothers; Diana; Hank Williams Jr.; Crystal Gayle; Gary Morris; Eddy Raven; Statler Brothers; Reba McEntire; Bellamy Brothers; Karen Brooks; Susie Allanson; Steve Wariner.

All American Hits .... Parrot (M) PA-61023 15-25 64
All American Hits .... Parrot (SE) PAS-71023 10-15
Marcie Blane; Bobby "Boris" Pickett; Sir Douglas Quintet; Kathy Linden; Willie Mitchell; Flares; Jimmy Soul; G-Clefs; Murry Kellum; Bill Black Combo; Ernie Maresca.

All American Pop Collection, Vol. 1 .... Impact (S) BC 285 5-10 80
Crystals; Jimmy Gilmer; Duane Eddy; Bobby Vee; Chubby Checker; Marcels; Exciters; Gary "U.S." Bonds; Angels; Danny & Juniors.

All American Pop Collection, Vol. 2 .... Impact (S) BC 286 5-10 80
Kingsmen; Bobby Lewis; Jan & Dean; Del Shannon; Chiffons; Chris Montez; Bobby Fuller Four; Cascades; Ritchie Valens; Bobby Day.

All American Pop Collection, Vol. 3 .... Impact (S) BC 287 5-10 80
Box Tops; Bobby Vee; B.J. Thomas; Oliver; Original Cast; Brooklyn Bridge; Casinos; Gary Lewis & Playboys; Del Shannon; Little Anthony & Imperials.

All American Pop Collection, Vol. 4 .... Impact (S) BC 288 5-10 80
Joey Dee & Starliters; Lou Christie; Drifters; Frankie Ford; Chubby Checker; Dee Clark; Chantays; Ray Peterson; Jaynetts.

All American Pop Collection, Vol. 5 .... Impact (S) BC 289 5-10 80
Leslie Gore; J. Frank Wilson; Shirelles; Duane Eddy; Coasters; others.

All Day Thumb Sucker .... Blue Thumb (S) BTS-2000 10-15 71
Southwind; Sammy Lay; Fred McDowell; Robbie Basha; T Rex; Ike & Tina Turner; Love; Nathan Beauregard; Aynsley Dunbar; Albert Collins; Earl Hooker; Chicago Bluestars; Bossa Rio.

All Ears .... Realistic (S) 50-6002 5-10 70s
Shirley & Squirrely; Randy Goodrum; Bob Gelotte; Ed Bernet; Johnny Hemphill; Mac Wiseman; Curtis Young; Oscar Ray. (Special products release.)

All Girl Million Sellers .... Ascot (M) M-13007 25-35 63
All Girl Million Sellers .... Ascot (S) S-16007 25-35 63
Linda Scott; Angels; Janie Grant; Shepherd Sisters; Chiffons; Chantels; Carousels; Storey Sisters; Anita Bryant; Faye Adams.

All Gold .... Sunset (S) SL-4023 10-15 60s
Little Anthony & Imperials; Timi Yuro; Clovers; Del Shannon; Fleetwoods; Jay & Americans; Sandy Nelson; Fats Domino; Dick & Deedee.

All God's Children Got Rhythm .... Prestige (M) PR-7248 15-20 63
All God's Children Got Rhythm .... Prestige (S) PRS-7248 20-25 63
Sonny Stitt; Bud Powell; J.J. Johnson; others.

All Meat: see Warner Bros. Promotional Releases/Samplers

All Music 93 KHJ: see KHJ

All Night Sing .... Camden (M) CAL-767 5-10
Blackwood Brothers; Speer Family; Original Carter Family; Statesmen Quartet; Porter Wagoner; Stuart Hamblen.

All Night Sing, Vol. 2 .... Camden (M) CAL-832 5-10 64
Harmoneers; Weatherford Quartet; Blackwood Brothers; Stamps-Baxter Quartet; Statesmen.

All Platinum Gold....All Platinum (S) 3016 5-10 76
Donnie Elbert; Rhetta Young; Hank Ballard & Midnighters; Chuck Jackson; Linda Jones; Derek Martin; Rimshots; Sylvia; George Kerr; Moments; Seldon Powell; Brother to Brother; Whatnauts.
All Singing, All Talking, All Rocking: see Warner Bros. Promotional Releases
All Star All Time Folk Festival....Camden (M) CAL-817 10-20 64
All Star All Time Folk Festival....Camden (S) CAS-817 10-20 64
Browns; Elton Britt; Limeliters; Browns; Buchanan Brothers; Jimmie Driftwood; Walter Forbes; Homer & Jethro; Raftsmen; Wayfarers; Windjammers.
All Star Cast....ABC-Paramount (M) ABC-423 15-25 62
All Star Cast....ABC-Paramount (S) ABCS-423 20-30 62
Ray Charles; Lloyd Price; Eddie Fisher; Paul Anka; Johnny Nash; Four Aces; Steve Lawrence; Don Costa; Teddy Randazzo; Ferrante & Teicher; Brian Hyland; Eydie Gorme.
All Star Children's Album, Vol. 1....Harmony (M) 9552 10-20 50s
Doris Day; Gene Kelly; Rosemary Clooney; Red Buttons; Arthur Godfrey; Julie Andrews; Art Carney; Gene Autry; Polly Bergen; Burl Ives.
All Star Christmas Columbia....Columbia (M) CL 1699 8-12 61
All Star Christmas Columbia....Columbia (S) CS 1699 8-12 61
Doris Day; Harmonicats; Aretha Franklin; Bobby Hackett; Johnny Cash; Jesus & Mary Choral Group; Ray Conniff; Frankie Laine; Brothers Four; Andre Previn; Les Paul & Mary Ford; Les Brown.
All-Star Color TV Review, Vol. 1....Hollywood (M) LPH 110 10-15
(TV Soundtrack.) Vic Damone; Charles Magnante; Mullen Sisters; Lanny Ross; Peggy Mann; Camarata Orchestra.
All-Star Color TV Review, Vol. 2....Hollywood (M) LPH 126 10-15
(TV Soundtrack.) Vic Damone; Lawrence Brooks; Allen Roth; Glenn Osser; others.
All Star Country....MGM (S) SE-4690 8-12 70
Hank Williams; Hank Williams Jr.; Mel Tillis; Billy Walker; Sheb Wooley; Luke the Drifter; Luke the Drifter Jr.; Ben Colder; Tompall & Glaser Brothers.
All Star Country....Harmony (S) 11296 6-12 69
Roy Acuff; Norma Jean; Johnny Cash; Marty Robbins; Carl & Pearl Butler; Lefty Frizzell; Stonewall Jackson; Ray Price.
All Star Country Christmas....Capitol (S) STBB-348 6-12 69
Buck Owens; Glen Campbell; Tennessee Ernie Ford; Faron Young; Ferlin Husky; Sonny James; Tex Ritter; Roy Rogers & Dale Evans; Louvin Brothers.
All Star Country Hits....MGM (S) SE-4787 6-12 71
Conway Twitty; Billy Walker; Hank Williams; others.
All Star Festival....United Nations (M) UN-1 10-20 63
All Star Festival....United Nations (S) UNS-1 10-20 63
Doris Day; Patti Page; Maurice Chevalier; Ella Fitzgerald; Louis Armstrong; Nat King Cole; Nana Mouskouri; Mahalia Jackson; Bing Crosby; Edith Piaf; Katherine Valente; Anne Shelton; Luis Alberto Del Parana. (Made to aide the World's Refugees.)
All Star Four: see CHRISTIE, Lou / Len Barry & Dovells / Bobby Rydell / Tokens
All Star Golden Oldies....Spin-O-Rama (M) M-142 10-15 60s
All Star Golden Oldies....Spin-O-Rama (S) S-142 10-15 60s
Nutmegs; Bobbettes; Faye Adams; Isley Brothers; Chiffons; Chuck Jackson; Dave "Baby" Cortez; Brook Benton; Jo Ann Campbell; Del-Vikings.
All Star Golden Oldies....Coronet (SE) CXS-217 15-25 60s
Del-Vikings; Bobbettes; Five Satins; Little Richard; Lee Allen; Isley Brothers; Belmonts; Turbans.
All Star Gospel Favorites, Vol. 1....QCA (S) LP-305 5-10
Blackwood Brothers; Blue Ridge Quartet; Dixie Echoes; Jerry & Singing Goffs; Kingsmen; Winston Miller & Singing Millers; London Parris & Apostles; Prophets Quartet; Statesmen Quartet; Thrasher Brothers; Weatherford Quartet; Butch Williams Singers.
All Star Hootenanny....Riverside (M) RM-7539 10-20 63
All Star Hootenanny....Riverside (S) RS9-7539 10-20 63
Odetta; Bob Gibson; Sonny Terry; Homesteaders; Oscar Brand; Cynthia Gooding; Staple Singers; Billy Faier; Lonesome River Boys; Memphis Slim; Eric Weisberg & Dick Rosmini; John Lee Hooker.
All Star Hootenanny, Vol. 2....Riverside (M) RM-7543 10-20 64
All Star Hootenanny, Vol. 2....Riverside (S) RS9-7543 10-20 64
Oscar Brand; Odetta; Bob Gibson; Ed McCurdy; Billy Faler; Staple Singers; Memphis Slim; John Lee Hooker; Home Steaders; Lonsome River Boys; Millburnaires; Carolina Freedom Fighters.
All Star Hootenanny....Columbia (S) CS-149 15-20 60s
Bob Dylan; Pete Seeger; Orriel Smith; Clancy Brothers & Tom Makem; others.
All Star Hootenanny....Columbia (M) CL-2122 25-35 63
All Star Hootenanny....Columbia (S) CS-8922 30-40 63
Bob Dylan; Johnny Cash; New Christy Minstrels; Pete Seeger; Carolyn Hester; Flatt & Scruggs with Mother Maybelle Carter; Clancy Brothers & Tommy Makem; Leon Bibb; Orriel Smith; Brothers Four.
All Star Parade....Columbia (S) CS 8218 10-20 60
Tony Bennett; Bing Crosby; Vic Damone; Doris Day; Duke Ellington; Percy Faith; Four Lads; Norman Luboff Choir; Richard Maltby; Johnny Mathis; Mitch Miller.
All Star Parade, Hits from the Movies....Columbia (M) CL-1421 10-15
(Soundtrack.) Johnny Mathis; Doris Day; Percy Faith; Norman Luboff Choir; Bing Crosby; Frank DeVol; Duke Ellington; Four Lads; Tony Bennett; Vic Damone; Mitch Miller; Richard Maltby.
All Star Piano (6 LP)....Columbia (S) 6P 6624 25-30
(Boxed set.)
All Star Rock, Vol. 1....Original Sound Recordings (S) OSR-1 8-12 72
All Star Rock, Vol. 2....Original Sound Recordings (S) OSR-2 8-12 72
All Star Rock, Vol. 3....Original Sound Recordings (S) OSR-3 8-12 72
All Star Rock, Vol. 4....Original Sound Recordings (S) OSR-4 8-12 72
All Star Rock, Vol. 5....Original Sound Recordings (S) OSR-5 8-12 72
All Star Rock, Vol. 6....Original Sound Recordings (S) OSR-6 8-12 72
All Star Rock, Vol. 7....Original Sound Recordings (S) OSR-7 8-12 72
All Star Rock, Vol. 8....Original Sound Recordings (S) OSR-8 8-12 72
All Star Rock, Vol. 9....Original Sound Recordings (S) OSR-9 8-12 72

All Star Rock, Vol. 10 .... Original Sound Recordings (S) OSR-10 8-12 72
All Star Rock, Vol. 11 .... Original Sound Recordings (S) OSR-11 20-25 72
(Mail order offer.) Elvis Presley; Don McLean; Melanie; Al Green; Badfinger; Three Dog Night; Raiders; Cher; Carpenters; Apollo 100; Bee Gees; Bread; Joe Cocker; Osmonds.
All Star Rock and Roll .... Atlantic (EP) EP-575 35-50 56
LaVern Baker; Ivory Joe Hunter; Clyde McPhatter; Ruth Brown.
All Star Rock and Roll Revue .... King (M) KLP-513 10-20 87
All Star Rock and Roll Revue .... King (M) 395-638 50-75 59
Platters; Otis Williams & Charms; Lucky Millinder; Earl Bostic; Tiny Bradshaw; Little Willie John; Midnighters; Billy Ward & Dominoes; Cathy Ryan; Bill Doggett; Swallows; Earl King.
All Star Rock and Roll Revue, Vol. 2 .... King (M) 654 40-60 60
Otis Williams & Charms; Billy Ward & Dominoes; Hank Ballard & Midnighters; Annie Laurie; others.
All Star Salute, the Very Best of Cole Porter .... MGM (M) E 4244 10-20 64
All Star Salute, the Very Best of Cole Porter .... MGM (S) SE 4244 10-20 64
Kathryn Grayson & Howard Keel; Artie Shaw; Louis Armstrong; David Rose; Margaret Whiting; Lisa Kirk; Eartha Kitt; Cyril Ornadel.
All Star Salute, the Very Best of George Gershwin .... MGM (M) E 4242 10-20 64
All Star Salute, the Very Best of George Gershwin .... MGM (S) SE 4242 10-20 64
David Rose; Judy Garland; Oscar Peterson; Bing Crosby; Jaye P. Morgan; Maurice Chevalier; Ray Charles Singers; Larry Elgart; Georges Guetary; Art Tatum; Anna Maria Alberghetti.
All Star Salute, the Very Best of Irving Berlin .... MGM (M) E 4240 10-20 64
All Star Salute, the Very Best of Irving Berlin .... MGM (S) SE 4240 10-20 64
Judy Garland; Bing Crosby; Howard Keel; Fred Astaire; Kate Smith; Louis Armstrong; Irene Reid; Artie Shaw; Dancing Voices; Jaye P. Morgan; Louis Calhern; Keenan Wynn & Betty Hutton.
All Star Salute, the Very Best of Jerome Kern .... MGM (M) E 4241 10-20 64
All Star Salute, the Very Best of Jerome Kern .... MGM (S) SE 4241 10-20 64
Cyril Ornadel; Judy Garland; Oscar Peterson; Lena Horne; David Rose; Kathryn Grayson & Howard Keel; Ava Gardner; Art Tatum; Margaret Whiting.
All Star Salute, the Very Best of Lerner & Loewe .... MGM (M) E 4243 10-20 64
All Star Salute, the Very Best of Lerner & Loewe .... MGM (S) SE 4243 10-20 64
David Rose; Maurice Chevalier; Mel Torme; Gene Kelly; Leslie Caron; Robert Farnon; J. Gustafson; Margaret Whiting; Cyril Ornadel.
All Star Salute, the Very Best of Rodgers & Hart .... MGM (M) E 4238 10-20 64
All Star Salute, the Very Best of Rodgers & Hart .... MGM (S) SE 4238 10-20 64
Judy Garland; Bing Crosby; Lena Horne; Maurice Chevalier; David Rose; Mel Torme; Louis Armstrong; Larry Elgart; Bess Myerson; Margaret Whiting; Anna Maria Alberghetti; Cyril Ornadel.
All Star Salute, the Very Best of Sigmund Romberg .... MGM (M) E 4239 10-20 64
All Star Salute, the Very Best of Sigmund Romberg .... MGM (S) SE 4239 10-20 64
Helen Traubel; Tony Martin; Howard Keel; Vic Damone; Rosemary Clooney; Gene Kelly; Ann Miller; Jose Ferrer; William Olvis; Adolph Deutsch.
All Star Shindig .... Spin-O-Rama (M) M-154 10-15 60s
All Star Shindig .... Spin-O-Rama (S) S-154 10-15 60s
4 Seasons; Bobby Rydell; Jo Ann Campbell; John Gary; Johnny Rivers.
All Star Show .... Royale (M) 1808 10-20 54
(10–inch LP.) Jane Froman; Lanny Ross; Thelma Carpenter & Ames Brother; Ella Logan; others.
All Star Showcase .... Atlantic (M) AT-1 20-30 65
All Star Showcase .... Atlantic (S) ATSD-1 25-35 65
(Promotional issue only.) Mr. Acker Bilk; Ray Charles; Bobby Darin; Wilbur de Paris; Drifters; Bent Fabric; Barbara Lewis; Herbie Mann; Modern Jazz Quartet; Otis Redding; Sonny & Cher; Joe Tex.
All Star Soul .... Harmony (S) 11400 8-12 70
Peaches & Herb; Ike & Tina Turner; Aretha Franklin; Little Richard; Major Lance; Shirley Ellis; Four Tops; Walter Jackson; Vibrations.
All Star Spectacular .... RCA Camden (M) SP-33-18 10-15 59
(Promotional issue only. Sampler.) Tony Martin; Guy Lombardo; Eddie Fisher; Count Basie; Artie Shaw; Perez Prado; Three Suns; Arturo Toscannini; Arthur Fiedler; Mario Lanza; Jeanette McDonald; Ezio Pinza.
All Star Spectacular .... Reprise (M) R-6028 20-25 62
All Star Spectacular .... Reprise (S) R9-6028 25-30 62
Frank Sinatra; Dean Martin; Sammy Davis Jr.; Al Hibbler; Billy May; Mort Sahl; Neal Hefti; Lou Monte; Soupy Sales; Mavis Rivers; Calvin Jackson; Barney Kessel; Leo Diamond.
All Star Surprise Party .... Kapp (M) KL-1282 8-12 60s
All Star Surprise Party .... Kapp (S) KS-1282 8-12 60s
Chad Mitchell Trio; Roger Williams; Pete King; Gordon Jenkins; Freddy Martin; Julius LaRosa; Jane Morgan; Vardi; Jack Jones; Fortune Tellers; Andrew Sisters; Four Lads.
All the Comedy Hits .... Capitol (S) DT 1854 8-12
All the Hits By All the Stars, Vol. 1 .... Parkway (M) 7013 20-30 61
Chubby Checker; Bobby Rydell; Dovells; Orlons; Dee Dee Sharp.
All the Hits By All the Stars, Vol. 2 .... Parkway (M) 7016 20-30 62
Chubby Checker; Bobby Rydell; Dovells; Orlons; Dee Dee Sharp; Jo Ann Campbell (shown as Judy Campbell).
All the Hits with All the Stars, Vol. 1 .... Wyncote (M) W-9029 10-15 63
All the Hits with All the Stars, Vol. 1 .... Wyncote (S) W-9029 10-15 63
Chubby Checker; Bobby Rydell; Dee Dee Sharp; Dovells; Orlons; Tymes; Rocky Fellers; Lee Andrews; Dovells.
All the Hits with All the Stars, Vol. 2 .... Wyncote (M) W-9054 10-15 63
All the Hits with All the Stars, Vol. 2 .... Wyncote (S) SW-9054 10-15 63
Bobby Freeman; Tokens; Johnny Cymbal; Chimes; Don Covay; Frankie Lymon; Mystics; Billy Abbott & Jewels; Charlie Gracie
All the Hits with All the Stars, Vol. 2 .... Wyncote (M) W-1029 10-15 63
Tymes; Bobby Rydell; Chubby Checker; Rocky Fellers; Dee Dee Sharp; Orlons; Dovells; Lee Andrews.
All the Hits with All the Stars, Vol. 3 .... Wyncote (M) W 90?? 10-15 63
All the Hits with All the Stars, Vol. 4 .... Wyncote (M) W-9082 10-15 63
Jimmy Dean; Denise Darcel; Billy Scott; Merv Griffin; Charlie Gracie; Clint Eastwood; Peggy King; Skyliners.
All the Hits with All the Stars, Vol. 5 .... Wyncote (M) W-9095 10-15 63

Brook Benton; Lloyd Price; Chuck Jackson; Betty Everett.

All the Hits with All the Stars, Vol. 6 .... Wyncote (M) W-9113 10-15 64

John Gary; Jimmy Dean; Teddy Wilson; Merv Griffin; Ray Charles; Maynard Ferguson; Frankie Laine; Brook Benton.

All the Stars Biggest Hits .... Parkway (M) 7033 15-25 63

Chubby Checker; Bobby Rydell; Dee Dee Sharp; Dovells; Tymes; Orlons.

All the Stars Biggest Hits, Vol. 2 .... Parkway (M) 7034 15-25 63

Chubby Checker; Bobby Rydell; Dee Dee Sharp; Dovells; Orlons; Hippies. (Includes peel-off pictures.)

All These Things .... Bandy S) 7007 5-10 80s

Art Neville; Lee Dorsey; Chris Kenner; Roger & Gypsies; Pitter Pats; Aaron Neville; Stokes; Willie Harper; Raymond Lewis; Ernie K-Doe.

All These Things .... Instant (M) LP-71000 25-35 60s

Lee Dorsey; Aaron Neville; Chris Kenner; Stokes; Art Neville; Pitter Pats; Rogers & Gypsies.

All This and World War II (2 LP) .... 20th Fox (S) 2T-522 10-12 76

(Soundtrack. Boxed set with booklet, a T-shirt ad flyer.) Ambrosia; Elton John; Bee Gees; David Essex; Frankie Laine; 4 Seasons; Henry Gross; Tina Turner; Leo Sayer; Rod Stewart; Keith Moon; Helen Reddy; Status Quo; Frankie Valli; Bryan Ferry; Jeff Lynne; Roy Wood; Brothers Johnson; Richard Cocciante; London Symphony Orchestra.

All Time Christmas Favorites (5 LP) .... Collector's Edition (S) CE-505 200-300 78

(Boxed set.) Elvis Presley; Frank Sinatra; Dean Martin; Glen Campbell; Tammy Wynette; Charley Pride; Johnny Mathis; Andy Williams; Barbra Striesand; Lynn Anderson.

All Time Country and Western .... Decca (M) DL-4010 20-30 60
All Time Country and Western .... Decca (SE) DL7-4010 20-30 60

Jimmie Davis; Ernest Tubb; Sons of the Pioneers; Red Foley; Bill Monroe; Webb Pierce; Kitty Wells; Goldie Hill; Justin Tubb; Bobby Helms; Patsy Cline.

All Time Country and Western, Vol. 2 .... Decca (M) DL-4090 20-25 61
All Time Country and Western, Vol. 2 .... Decca (SE) DL7-4090 20-25 61

Jimmie Davis; Ernest Tubb; Kitty Wells; Webb Pierce; Red Foley; Bill Monroe; Warner Mack; Goldie Hill & Justin Tubb; Carl Belew; Tex Williams; Wilburn Brothers.

All Time Country and Western, Vol. 3 .... Decca (M) DL-4134 20-25 62
All Time Country and Western, Vol. 3 .... Decca (SE) DL7-4134 20-25 62

Ernest Tubb; Kitty Wells; Webb Pierce; Red & Betty Foley; Bill Monroe; Bob Wills; T. Texas Tyler; Roy Acuff & Kitty Wells; Jimmie Davis; Jenny Lou Carson; Wilburn Brothers.

All Time Country and Western, Vol. 4 .... Decca (M) DL-4359 15-25 63
All Time Country and Western, Vol. 4 .... Decca (SE) DL7-4359 15-25 63

Red Foley; Ernest Tubb; Kitty Wells; Webb Pierce; Loretta Lynn; Bill Monroe; Jimmy Martin; Patsy Cline; Jimmie Davis; Bill Anderson; Roy Drusky; Wilburn Brothers; Sons of the Pioneers.

All Time Country and Western, Vol. 5 .... Decca (M) DL-4549 15-25 64
All Time Country and Western, Vol. 5 .... Decca (SE) DL7-4549 15-25 64

Rex Allen; Johnnie & Jack; Red Foley; Patsy Cline; Webb Pierce; Bobby Helms; Ernest Tubb; Bill Anderson; Jimmie Davis; Bill Monroe; Roy Drusky; Kitty Wells.

All Time Country and Western, Vol. 6 .... Decca (M) DL-4657 15-20 65
All Time Country and Western, Vol. 6 .... Decca (SE) DL7-4657 15-20 65

Webb Pierce; Kitty Wells; Red Sovine; Goldie Hill; Loretta Lynn; Bill Anderson; Jimmie Davis; Patsy Cline; Kitty Wells & Red Foley; Bill Monroe; Wilburn Brothers; Red Foley; Ernest Tubb.

All Time Country and Western, Vol. 7 .... Decca (M) DL-4775 10-20 66
All Time Country and Western, Vol. 7 .... Decca (SE) DL7-4775 10-20 66

Ernest Tubb; Kitty Wells; Webb Pierce; Roy Drusky; Loretta Lynn; Red & Betty Foley; Bill Monroe; Bob Wills; Patsy Cline; Jimmy Martin; Billy Grammer; Red Foley.

All Time Country and Western, Vol. 8 .... Decca (M) DL-???? 10-20 67
All Time Country and Western, Vol. 8 .... Decca (S) DL-7???? 10-20 67
All Time Country and Western, Vol. 9 .... Decca (S) DL-75025 10-20 68

Loretta Lynn; Webb Pierce; Patsy Cline; Red Foley; Wilburn Brothers; Bill Monroe; Kitty Wells; Johnny Wright; Bill Anderson; Jimmy Martin; Jimmy Newman.

All Time Country and Western Hits .... King (M) 395-537 50-75 57
All Time Country and Western Hits .... King (M) 710 30-40 60

Stanley Brothers; Webb Pierce; Hawkshaw Hawkins; others.

All Time Country Hit Review .... K-Tel (S) BU 4560 5-10 77

Ferlin Husky; Bobby Helms; Del Wood; Jimmy C. Newman; Tommy Collins; Skeeter Davis; Carl Belew; Mitchell Torok; Charlie Walker; Warner Mack; Bill Carlisle; Roy Drusky; Marvin Rainwater; Stoney Cooper & Wilma Lee; Pee Wee King; Claude Gray.

All Time Great Country and Western Songs .... Guest Star (M) G 1415 8-12

Benny Martin; George Jones; Benny Barnes; Leon Payne; Red Sovine; Willis Brothers; Jim Glaser; Cowboy Copas; Moon Mullican; Frankie Miller; Benny Martin.

All Time Greatest Hits of Country Music (3 LP) .... RCA Special Products (S) DVL4-0629 15-20 83

Johnny Cash; Sons of the Pioneers; Elton Britt; Roy Acuff; Hank Williams; Eddy Arnold; Jimmy Rodgers; Davis Sisters; Tex Ritter; Vaughn Monroe & Quartet; Stuart Hamblen; Homer & Jethro; Chet Atkins; Pee Wee King & His Band featuring Redd Stewart; Porter Wagoner; Hank Snow; Don Gibson; Jim Reeves; Slim Whitman; Connie Smoth; Ernest Ashworth; Hank Locklin; Ferlin Husky; Red Sovine; Tennessee Ernie Ford; Jerry Reed; Hankshaw Hawkins; Bobby Bare; Sheb Wooley; Carlisles; Skeeter Davis; Browns; George Hamilton IV; Dottie West & Jordanaires; Hank Thompson; George Jones; Barry Sadler; Sonny James; Moon Mullican.

All Time Greats, Vol. 1 .... Promo (S) ???? 30-50

Elvis Presley; others.

All Time Greats, Vol. 3 .... Promo (S) ???? 30-50

Elvis Presley; others.

All Time Hits .... Artistic (S) 500 10-20
All Time Hits .... Click (EP) 101 15-25

Danny & Juniors; Johnny & Joe; Chuck Willis; Chuck Berry; Billie & Lillie; Coasters.

All Time Hits, Vol. 2 .... No Label Name (EP) SL-102 15-25

Silhouettes; Diamonds; Jimmy Clanton; Huey "Piano" Smith & Clowns; Rays; Timmie Rogers.

All Time Hits, Vol. 3 .... No Label Name (EP) SL-103 15-25 60s

Duane Eddy; Crests; Frankie Avalon; others.

All Time Hits, Vol. 4 .... No Label Name (EP) SL-104 15-25 60s

Paradons; Dovells; Conway Twitty; others.

All Time Hits on the "In" Side .... Decca (M) DL-34469 10-20
Pete Fountain; Debbie Reynolds; Four Aces; Les Brown; Judy Garland; Peggy Lee; Mills Brothers; Brenda Lee; Ted Weems; Louis Armstrong.

All Time Hootenanny .... Decca (M) DL-4469 10-20 63
All Time Hootenanny .... Decca (S) DL-74469 15-25 63
Weavers; Josh White; Bob Gibson; Tarriers; Oscar Brand; Bill Monroe; Tompall & Glaser Brothers; Gateway Singers; Wilburn Brothers; Ivy League Trio; Sam Hinton; Richard Dyer-Bennett.

All Time Hootenanny Folk Favorites, Vol. 2 .... Decca (M) DL-4485 10-20 64
All Time Hootenanny Folk Favorites, Vol. 2 .... Decca (S) DL-74485 15-25 64
Weavers; Josh White with Sonny Terry & Brownie McGhee; Bob Gibson; Oscar Brand; Gateway Singers; Bob Gibson; Tompall & Glaser Brothers; Sam Hinton; Ivy League Trio; Bill Monroe & His Blue Grass Boys; Osborne Brothers; Tarriers; Wilburn Brothers.

All Time Original Hits .... Dot (S) DLP 25818 10-15
Eddie Fisher; Tony Martin; Jimmy Dorsey; Don Cornell; Francis Craig; Art & Dotty Todd; Vaughn Monroe; Debbie Reynolds; Gene Austin; Andrews Sisters; Mills Brothers; Johnny Maddox.

All Time Smash Hits .... Smash (M) MGS-27052 20-30 64
All Time Smash Hits .... Smash (S) SRS-67052 20-30 64
Angels; Bruce Channel; Caravelles; Dickie Lee; Matt Lucas; Joe Dowell; Rick & Keens; Jerry Kennedy; Joe Barry; Jerry Lee Lewis; Bill Justis.

All Time Standards .... Columbia (S) P 14922 5-10 79
Andre Kostelanetz; Tony Bennett; Mel Torme; Percy Faith; Jerry Vale; Leslie Uggams; Ray Conniff; Bobby Vinton.

All Year Party, Vol. 1 (Rodney Bingenheimer Presents) .... Martian (S) LP 1714 5-10 84
Rodney & Brunettes; Ventures; Cheri Gage; Blake Xolton; Dave Raeder; Screamin' Sirens; Martians; Unit Three with Venus; Nikki & Corvettes; Phast Phreddie & Thee Precisions; Marsupials; Annette Funacello & Frankie Avalon with the Ventures.

Allegro Jazz Sampler .... Allegro (M) 1910 15-25 56
Jack Teagarden; Pee Wee Hunt; Coleman Hawkins; Duke Ellington; Georgie Auld; Dizzy Gillespie; Sarah Vaughan; Boogie Beat; Teddy Wilson; Joe Bushkin; Sidney Bechet; All Stars.

Almost Persuaded .... Nashville (SE) NLP-2099 5-10 71
Rose Maddox; Lois Williams; Dolly Parton; others.

Almost Summer .... MCA (S) MCA-3037 10-20 78
(Soundtrack.) Mike Love; Celebration; High Inergy; Fresh.

Alphabet Rock (2 LP) .... Tee Vee/Warner Special Products (S) OP 2517 8-12 80
Barry Mann; Brenda Lee; Little Anthony & Imperials; Bobby Rydell; Manfred Mann; Daddy Dewdrop; Brian Hyland; Brenton Wood; Lee Dorsey; Otis Redding; Dixie Cups; Coasters; LaVern Baker; Major Lance; Cadillacs; Rock-A-Teens; Chords; Edsels; Billy & Lillie; Blendells; Playmates; Bobby Darin; Rivingtons; Dicky Doo & Don'ts; Sam the Sham & Pharaohs; Freddie Cannon; Roy Orbison; Gene Vincent; Larry Williams; Little Richard.

Alternatives .... Warner Bros. (S) WS-1873 20-25 70
Neil Young & Crazy Horse; Jimi Jendrix Experience; James Taylor; John Sebastian; Van Morrison; Small Faces; Grateful Dead; Arlo Guthrie; Tim Buckley; Joni Mitchell; Graham Bond; Mothers; Gordon Lightfoot; Jethro Tull.

Always .... MCA (S) 8036 8-10 90
(Soundtrack.) J.D. Souther; Jimmy Buffett; Lyle Lovett; Denette Hoover; Michael Smotherman; Platters; John Williams.

America I Hear You Singing .... Reprise (S) FS 2020 5-10
America Jazz Men in Europe .... Vantage (S) LP 512 8-12
America Salutes the Beatles .... Capitol 31712 8-10 90s
America Sings .... Columbia Special Products (S) P-12706 5-10 75
Anita Bryant; Mormon Tabernacle Choir; Kate Smith; Andre Kostelanetz; Mahalia Jackson; New Christy Minstrels; Mitch Miller; Robert Goulet.

America the Beautiful .... World Communications (S) UN-542 WCL 5-10 85
Kingston Trio, others.

America the Beautiful .... Harmony (S) H-30278 5-10 70
Anita Bryant; Burl Ives; Jerry Vale; others.

America the Beautiful (Let's Keep It That Way) (2 LP) .... RCA (S) PRS 330-2 8-12
Robert Shaw Chorale; Richard Kiley; Chet Atkins; Norman Luboff Choir; Eddy Arnold; Peter Nero; Perry Como; Al Hirt; Ann Margret; Ed Ames; Arthur Fiedler with Boston Pops; Della Reese; Morton Gould; John Gary; Floyd Cramer; Jimmy McPartland; Jack Jones; Kate Smith.

America's Favorite Country and Western Stars .... Design (M) DLP-635 10-15 60s
America's Favorite Country and Western Stars .... Design (S) DLP-635 10-15 60s
Johnny Horton; Frankie Miller; Jimmy Dean; Webb Pierce; Wilburn Brothers.

America's Favorites .... RCA (M) LM-2991 10-15 68
America's Favorites .... RCA (S) LSC-2991 10-15 68
Kate Smith; Arthur Fiedler & Boston Pops; others.

America's Folk Heritage .... Everest (S) 3301 8-10 70
Pete Seeger; Leadbelly; Josh White; Lightnin' Hopkins; Odetta; others.

America's Greatest Country Stars Live and in Person .... Harmony (M) 7414 8-15 67
America's Greatest Country Stars Live and in Person .... Harmony (S) 11214 8-15 67
Stonewall Jackson; Carl Smith; Johnny Cash; Billy Walker; Lefty Frizzell; Harold Bradley; Carl & Pearl Butler; Statler Brothers; June Carter.

America's Greatest Gospel Favorites .... Canaan (S) CTV-904 5-10
Happy Goodman Family; Blue Ridge Quartet; Florida Boys; Joel & LaBreeska; Dixie Echoes; Rebels Quartet; Coy Cook; Steve Sanders; Couriers; Jack Holcomb; Harvesters Quartet.

America's Greatest Music Makers .... Decca (S) DL-74126 8-12
Guy Lombardo; Brazen Brass & Henry Jerome; Ralph Flanagan; Wayne King; Pete Fountain; Irving Fields Trio; Carmen Cavallaro with Jack Pleis Orchestra; Sammy Kaye; Big Tiny Little; Jan Garber; Warren Covington; Liberace.

America's Musical Roots - the Blues .... Festival (M) FR-1008 8-12 76
Little Walter; Howlin' Wolf; Muddy Waters; Sonny Boy Williamson; Lowell Fulson; John Lee Hooker; Bo Diddley; Chuck Berry; Elmore James; Memphis Slim.

American Anthem .... Atlantic (S) 7 81661-1-E 8-12 86
(Soundtrack.) Stevie Nicks; Graham Nash; John Parr; Mr. Mister; Andy Taylor; Chris Thompson; Alan Silvestri; INXS.

American Bandstand Favorites (Brought to You By Cheerios) .... Cherrios (EP) CH-1001 15-25 58
(Mail-order offer.) McGuire Sisters; Bill Haley & His Comets; Bill Doggett; Jim Lowe; Charlie Gracie; Pat Boone; Timmie Rodgers; Ames Brothers. (Special products. Made for Cheerios.)

American Banjo - Scruggs Style............Folkways (M) FA 2314 10-20 60s
Junie Scruggs; Joe Stewart; Snuffy Jenkins; Oren Jenkins; Eugene Cox; Veronica Cox; J.C. Sutphin; Larry Richardson; Don Bryant; Smiley Hobbs; Tom Morgan; Pete Roberts; Bob Baker & Pike County Ramblers; Kenny Miller; Mike Seeger; Eric Weissberg; Ralph Rinzler.

American Christmas (From the Archives of Saturday Evening Post) (12 LP)...........Otis Conner Prod. (SP) 1A-12B 125-200 84
(Boxed set. Includes programming inserts. Promotional issue only.) Elvis Presley; others.

American Country............Capitol Creative Products (SP) SE-6900 8-12
Tex Ritter; Sonny James; Glen Campbell; Anne Murray; Roy Rogers; Bobbie Gentry; Roy Acuff; Roy Clark; Ferlin Husky. (Made for American Motors Dealers.)

American Country Gold: see Country Music Cavalcade, American Country Gold

American Dream, Great Folk Songs & Ballads............Imperial House (S) NU 9790 8-12 81
Brothers Four; Byrds; Donovan; Mama Cass Elliot; Highwaymen; Kingston Trio; Bob Lind; Lovin' Spoonful; New Christy Minstrels; Nitty Gritty Dirt Band; Pozo-Seco Singers; Merrilee Rush; Sandpipers; Spanky & Our Gang; We Five; Glenn Yarbrough.

American Dream - the '60s............Excelsior (S) XMP-6017 5-10 80
Crystals; Leslie Gore; Freddie Gore; Freddie Cannon; Angels; Chiffons; Dixie Cups; Jan & Dean; Martha Reeves; Drifters; Jimmy Gilmer; Coasters; Marcels.

American Dreamer............Mediarts (S) 41-12 10-15 71
(Soundtrack.) Gene Clark; Hello People; John Manning; John Buck Wilkins; Abbey Road Singers.

American Flyers............GRP (S) AP-2001 8-10 85
(Soundtrack.) Lee Ritenour; Greg Mathieson; Creedence Clearwater Revival; Glenn Shorrock; Danny Hutton; Chris Isaak.

American Folk Blues Festival............Exodus (S) EXS 302 15-25
Memphis Slim; Willie Dixon; Big Joe Williams; Bill Stepney; Lonnie Johnson; Muddy Waters; Victoria Spivey; Matt Murphy; Sonny Boy Williamson.

American Folk Blues Festival............Excello (M) 8029 10-15 72

American Folk Blues Festival............Decca (M) DL-4392 15-25 63

American Folk Blues Festival............Decca (S) DL-74392 20-30 63
Memphis Slim; Sonny Terry & Brownie McGhee; T-Bone Walker; Joh Lee Hooker; Shaky Jake; Jump Jackson; Willie Dixon.

American Folk Music (The Life Treasury of)............Life Treasury (M) L 1001 20-30 61
Leadbelly; Woody Guthrie; Cisco Houston; Hermes Nye; Gene Bluestein; Alan Mills; Kid Clayton; Logan English; Pete Seeger; Mickey Miller; Fort Wingate Indian Children.

American Folk Singers and Balladeers (4 LP)............Vanguard (SP) RL-5644 20-30 64
(Boxed set. Mail order offer.) Joan Baez; Maybelle Carter; Flatt & Scruggs; Jack Elliott; Doc Watson; Sonny Terry & Brownie McGhee; others.

American Folk Theater Hootenanny............Alzazar (S) ALC-102 5-10 87
Theodore Bikel; Gene & Francesca; Joyce James; Brownie MacIntosh; Eric Weissberg.

American - French Music of the Bayous of Louisiana............Goldband (M) GR-7738 15-25 63
Le Roy Broussard; Iry Le June; Linus Touchet; others.

American Gigolo............Polydor (S) PD 1-6259 8-10 80

American Gigolo............Polydor (S) 2391 447 5-8 Re
(Soundtrack.) Giorgio Moroder; Blondie; Cheryl Barnes; Harold Faltermeyer.

American Graffiti (2 LP)............MCA (S) 2-8001 10-12 73
(Gatefold cover.)

American Graffiti (2 LP)............MCA (S) 2-8001 6-10 73
(Standard cover.) (Soundtrack.) Bill Haley & His Comets; Buddy Holly; Crests; Beach Boys; Fats Domino; Buster Brown; Chuck Berry; Platters; Flamingos; Silhouettes; Five Satins; Bobby Freeman; Buddy Knox; Del-Vikings; Johnny Burnette; Lee Dorsey; Mark Dinning; Flash Cadillac & Continental Kids; Monotones; Big Bopper; Sonny Til & Orioles; Spaniels; Booker T. & MGs; Fleetwoods; Diamonds; Clovers; Joey Dee & Starliters; Tempos; Heartbeats; Frankie Lymon & Teenagers; Regents; Skyliners; Del Shannon; Wolfman Jack.

American Graffiti, Vol 2: see More American Graffiti

American Graffiti, Vol. 3 (2 LP)............MCA (S) 2-8008 10-12 76
Dorsey Burnette; Hollywood Argyles; El Dorados; Jimmy Reed; Ritchie Valens; Toni Fisher; Jewel Akens; Jody Reynolds; Jerry Butler; Jimmie Rodgers; Wilbert Harrison; Chris Montez; Little Richard; Bobby Helms; Johnny Tillotson; Beach Boys; Teddy Bears; Everly Brothers; Olympics; Joe Jones; Ronnie Hawkins; Kathy Young; Ritchie Valens; Lenny Welch; Little Anthony; Fendermen; Buddy Holly.

American Hot Wax (2 LP)............A&M (SP) SP-6500 15-20 78
(Soundtrack. Stereo disc has 'live' tracks. Mono disc has original versions.) Chuck Berry; Buddy Holly; Jerry Lee Lewis; Bobby Darin; Little Richard; Jackie Wilson; Delights; Chesterfields; Professor LaPlanto & Planatones; Clark Otis; Tammy & Tulips; Screamin' Jay Hawkins; Spaniels; Moonglows; Drifters; Mystics; Maurice Williams & Zodiacs; Elegents; Turbans; Frankie Ford; Spaniels; Big Beat Band; Delights.

American Hot Wax, Vol. 2............A&M (S) SP-???? 15-25 78
Chuck Berry; Buddy Holly; Bobby Darin; Little Richard; Jackie Wilson; Moonglows; Drifters; Mystics; Maurice Williams & Zodiacs; Cadillacs; Turbans; Frankie Ford; Spaniels.

American Music Awards Present: see 10 Top Hits of 1974

American Music: the 1950's (Collectors History of) (5 LP)............Columbia (SE) P5 15547 20-25 81
(Boxed set.) Rosemary Clooney; Four Lads; Tony Bennett; Joan Weber; Johnny Mathis; Patti Page; Mitch Miller; Roy Hamilton; Mindy Carson; Johnnie Ray; Vic Damone; Four Coins; Champ Butler; Guy Mitchell; Frankie Laine; Toni Arden; Johnny Horton; Percy Faith; Les Paul & Mary Ford; Fess Parker; Sammy Kaye; Jerry Murad's Harmonicats; Rosemary Clooney & Guy Mitchell. (Made for Publishers Central Bureau.)

American Pop............MCA (S) 5201 20-25 81
(Soundtrack.) Pat Benatar; Big Brother & Holding Company; Mamas & Papas; Peter, Paul & Mary; Marcy Levy; Jimi Hendrix Experience; Dave Brubeck Quartet; Sam Cooke; Fabian; Doors.

American Pop Classics (2 LP)............I & M (S) I-016 10-15 79
(Mail order offer.) Ben E. King; Bobby Darin; Drifters; Shirelles; Everly Brothers; Platters; Paul Anka; Sam Cooke; Five Satins; Brian Hyland; Capris; Tymes; Gene McDaniels; Jay & Americans; Fleetwoods; Little Anthony & Imperials; Duprees; Dionne Warwick; Jimmy Rodgers; Jimmy Charles; Freddie Scott; Flamingos.

American Rock Anthology............MGM (S) SE 4687 10-15 70
Ritchie Valens; Lou Christie; Gentrys; Friend & Lover; Every Mother's Son; Royalettes; Sam the Sham & Pharaohs; Hombres; Bobby Fuller Four; Johnny Crawford.

American Rock 'N' Roll Classics, Vol.1............ABZ/Roulette SR 59054 5-10 80s
Bobby Darin; Fontella Bass; Thurston Harris; Jimmy Bowen; Rock-A-Teens; Petula Clark; Bo Diddley; Clovers; Smith; Drifters.

American Rock 'N' Roll Classics, Vol. 2............ABZ/Roulette SR 59055 5-10 80s
Shangri-Las; Freddie Scott; Drifters; Ray Barretto; Association; Jerry Lee Lewis; Bill Haley & His Comets; Del-Vikings; Cher; Ike & Tina Turner.

American Rock 'N' Roll Classics, Vol. 3 .... ABZ/Roulette SR 59056 5-10 80s
Carl Perkins; Sonny & Cher; Tommy James & Shondells; Bill Justis; Jay & Americans; Archie Bell & Drells; Happenings; Ohio Express; Fleetwoods; Brooklyn Bridge.

American Rock 'N' Roll Classics, Vol. 4 .... ABZ/Roulette SR 59057 5-10 80s
Lovin' Spoonful; Ad Libs; Bobbettes; Shangri-Las; Jerry Butler & Betty Everett; Playmates; Lemon Pipers; Jay & Americans; Jerry Lee Lewis; Bobby Darin.

American Rock 'N' Roll Classics, Vol. 5 .... ABZ/Roulette SR 59058 5-10 80s
Isley Brothers; Dixie Cups; Fats Domino; Mamas & Papas; Ned Miller; Fontane Sisters; Jelly Beans; Dells; Gladys Knight & Pips; Fifth Estate.

American Rock 'N' Roll Classics, Vol. 6 .... ABZ/Roulette SR 59059 5-10 80s
Spencer Davis Group; LaVern Baker; Jan Bradley; Clyde McPhatter; Bobby Vee; Ronnie Hawkins; Bobby Scott; Edwin Hawkins Singers; Jerry Butler; Lovin' Spoonful.

American Rock 'N' Roll Classics, Vol. 7 .... ABZ/Roulette SR 59060 5-10 80s
Bill Haley & His Comets; El Dorados; Five Keys; Betty Everett; Ray Peterson; Dave "Baby" Cortez; Jimmy McCracklin; Jimmy Rodgers; Bobby Freeman; Fats Domino.

American Rock 'N' Roll Classics, Vol. 8 .... ABZ/Roulette SR 59061 5-10 80s
Shirley & Lee; Penguins; Five Keys; Gene Chandler; Bobby Vee; Little Peggy March; Dee Clark; James Darren; Paul Peterson; Spaniels.

American Rock 'N' Roll Classics, Vol. 9 .... Roulette SR 59062 5-10 80s
Johnny Otis Show; Ray Charles; Jerry Butler; Frankie Lymon & Teenagers; Bobby Helms; Gene Vincent; Cheers; Mickey & Sylvia; 1910 Fruitgum Company; Chips.

American Song Festival .... ASF (S) 101 5-10

American Song Festival: Winners! .... Buddah (S) BDS 5624 5-10 74
Judy Kaye; Molly Bee; Rev. James Cleveland; Stephan Geyer; Stampeders; Etta James; Al Wilson; Hagers; Oak Ridge Boys; Glenn Yarbrough & Limeliters; Sanford & Townshend; Lettermen.

American Tail .... MCA (S) 39096 8-10 86
(Soundtrack.) Linda Ronstadt; James Ingram; Dom Deluise; Philip Glasser; Nehemiah Persoff; John Guarnieri; Warren Hays; Christopher Plummer; Betsy Cathcart.

American Top 40 (2 LP) .... Custom Fidelity (S) CFS 2315-2 8-12 71
Shocking Blue; Classics IV; Billy Stewart; Clique; James & Bobby Purify; Barry McGuire; Mungo Jerry; Music Explosion; Lee Dorsey; Turtles; Intruders; Bob Lind; Jay & Americans; Bobby Goldsboro; Sunshine Company; Mel Carter; T-Bones; Gary Lewis; Canned Heat; Bobby Vee; Nitty Gritty Dirt Band; Gene McDaniels; Little Anthony & Imperials; Jackie DeShannon. (Also issued as *24 Golden Greats, WMEE 1380.*)

Americana (2 LP) .... Columbia Special Products (S) XTV 82068 8-12 60s
Mitch Miller; Anita Bryant; Andre Kostelanetz; New Christy Minstrels; Mormon Tabernacle Choir; Jerry Vale; Brothers Four; Percy Faith; Norman Luboff Choir; Johnny Cash; Robert Goulet; Billy Butterfield; John Davidson; Gordon Jenkins; Mahalia Jackson; Louis Armstrong; Doris Day.

Americathon .... Lorimar (S) JS-36174 10-12 79
(Soundtrack.) Beach Boys; Elvis Costello; Nick Lowe; Eddie Money; Tom Scott; Harvey Korman; Zane Buzby.

An Album of WMEX Solid Gold: see WMEX Solid Gold

An All Star Parade, Hits from the Movies: see All Star Parade

& Winner Is: see Winner Is

Anatomy of Dancing, Vol. 3, the Twistin' & Swingin' Mood .... MGM (M) E 4038 10-15 61
Leroy Holmes; Morty Craft; Danny Davis; Ray Ellis; Skip Martin; Al Hirt; Pete Fountain.

Angel Heart .... Antilles New Directions (S) 91035 8-10 87
(Soundtrack.) Bessie Smith; Brownie McGhee; Courtney Pine; LaVern Baker; Lilian Boutte; Glen Gray.

Angels Die Hard .... UNI (S) 73091 20-25 70
(Soundtrack.) Fever Tree; Sylvanus; Dewey Martin & Medicine Ball; East-West Pipline; Mark Eric; Rabbit MacKay.

Angels from Hell .... Tower (S) ST-5128 35-50 68
(Soundtrack.) Stu Phillips; Peanut Butter Conspiracy; Lollipop Shoppe; Ted Marckland.

Animal House: see National Lampoon's Animal House

Annual Report for Fiscal Year Ended Jan. 31, 1962 .... Liberty (M) LAR-3/4 15-25 62
(10-inch LP.) Felix Slatkin; Thomas Garrett; Johnny Mann; Si Zentner; Martin Denny; Bobby Vee; Timi Yuro; Gene McDaniels.

Another Collection of Golden Hits .... Mercury (M) MG-20541 20-30 60

Another Collection of Golden Hits .... Mercury (S) SR-60256 25-35 60

Another Day in the Big World .... Columbia (S) AS 1949 5-10 84
Wham; Eurogliders; Romeo Void; Red Rockers; Dave Edmunds; Bangles; Iam Siam.

Anthology - Duane Allman, Vol. 2 (2 LP) .... Capricorn (S) 2CP-0139 10-15 74
Duane Allman; Aretha Franklin; Otis Rush; Lulu; Hourglass; Herbie Mann; others.

Anthology of Folk Music (5 LP) .... Sine Qua Non (S) SQN-102 25-35
(Boxed set) Glen Campbell; Woody Guthrie; Rooftop Singers; Leadbelly; Sonny Terry & Brownie McGhee; Odetta; Rod McKuen; others.

Anthology of British Blues, Vol. 1 (2 LP) .... Immediate (S) Z12-52006 10-15 68

Anthology of British Blues, Vol. 2 (2 LP) .... Immediate (S) Z12-52014 10-15 69

Anthology of British Rock - the Pye Years (2 LP) .... Compleat (S) 672011-1 10-20 85
David Bowie; Donovan; Mungo Jerry; Status Quo; Sandie Shaw; Kinks; Searchers; Foundations; Honeycombs; others.

Anthology of Rhythm & Blues, Vol. 1 .... Columbia (S) CS-9802 10-15 69
James Brown & Famous Flames; Hank Ballard & Midnighters; Bill Doggett; LaVern Baker; Tiny Bradshaw; Five Royales; Bullmoose Jackson; Little Willie John; Champion Jack Dupree; Billy Ward & Dominoes; Charles Brown; Annie Laurie; Otis Williams & Charms; Wynonie Harris; Donnie Elbert; Freddy King.

Anthology of the 12 String Guitar .... Tradition/Everest (S) TR-2071 10-15 60s
James McGuinn; Glen Campbell; Mason Williams; Bob Gibson; Howard Roberts; Joe Maphis; Billy Strange.

Any Which Way You Can .... Warner Bros. (S) HS-3499 8-10 80
(Soundtrack.) Ray Charles; Clint Eastwood; Glen Campbell; David Frizell; Shelly West; Fats Domino; Sondra Locke; Jim Stafford; Johnny Duncan; Gene Watson; Cliff Crofford; John Durrill; Texas Opera Company.

Apocalypse Now .... Elektra (S) DP-90001 20-25 79
(Soundtrack.) Doors; Vienna Philharmonic Orchestra; Flash Cadillac; others.

Apollo Acapella Audition Album .... Relic (M) 5075 8-10 88
Avalons; Casanovas; Mirian Grate & Dovers; Gentlemen; Keynotes.

Apollo Saturday Night .... Atco (M) 159 20-30 64

Apollo Saturday Night .... Atco (S) SD-159 20-30 64
Ben E. King; Coasters; Falcons; Doris Troy; Rufus Thomas; Otis Redding.

Apollo Yesterdays ....Harlem Hitparade (SE) HHP-5008 10-20 72
Wilbert Harrison; Clovers; Platters; Moonglows; Lloyd Price; Huey "Piano" Smith; Jesters; Harptones; Paragons; Don Covay.

Approved By 10,000,000 ....Teem (M) LP-5004 15-25

April Fools ....Columbia (S) OS-3340 10-15 69
(Cover without clipped corners.)

April Fools ....Columbia (S) OS-3340 5-10 69
(Soundtrack. Cover with clipped corners.) Chambers Brothers; Mongo Santamaria; Taj Mahal; Robert John; Percy Faith; others.

April Samplers (RCA): see RCA April Samplers

Arista Winter Sampler 1976-'77 ....Arista (S) ALS-03 8-12 77
(Promotional issue only.)

Arista's Greatest Hits: Portrait of a Decade 1975 - 1985 (3 LP) ....Arista (S) SE-10383 20-25 85
Aretha Franklin; Dionne Warwick; Barry Manilow; Outlaws; Kinks; Melissa Manchester; Jennifer Warnes; Air Supply; Grateful Dead; Lou Reed; Angela Bofill; Alan Parsons Project; Flock of Seagulls; Thompson Twins; Al Stewart; Ray Parker Jr. & Raydio; G.Q.; Haircut 100; Krokus; Kenny G.; Kashif; Billy Ocean; Dregs; Paul Davis; Gino Vannelli; Eric Carmen; Patti Smith Group; Graham Parker; Tom Browne; Gil Scott-Heron; Jermaine Jackson.

Arista Holiday Sampler ....Arista (S) ADP 9552 10-15 86
(Promotional issue only.) Monkees; Jermaine Stewart; Aretha Franklin; Billy Ocean; Whitney Houston; George Michael; Kenny G.; Whodini; Jermaine Jackson; KBC Band; GTR.

Arista Power/R&B Sampler ....Arista (S) SP-50 8-12 79
(Promotional issue only.) Raydio; Breakwater; Harvey Mason; Bobby Womack; Angela Bofill; Fiesta; Ohio Players; Bernie Worrell; Mandrill; Phyliss Hyman; GQ; Galaxy. (Cover reads *The Arista Power Sampler* but label says *R&B Sampler*.)

Armed and Dangerous ....Manhattan (S) SJ-53041 8-10 86
(Soundtrack.) Atlantic Starr; Escapades; Maurice White; Cheryl Lynn; Tito Puente & His Latin Ensemble; Glenn Burtrick; Eve; Sigue Sigue Sputnik; Michael Henderson; Bill Meyers.

Army of Stars - Christmas Greetings from Salvation Army ....RCA (M) LPM-2723 10-15 60s

Army of Stars - Christmas Greetings from Salvation Army ....RCA (S) LSP-2723 10-15 60s
Maralin Niska; Azusa Pacific College Choir; Jeanette Scovotti; Stuart Burrows; Raymond Burr.

Army ROTC Presents "Country Line" ....No Label/Number Used 15-30 78
Vernon Presley; Col. Tom Parker; Drifting Cowboys; Olivia Newton-John; Asleep at the Wheel; Bill Anderson; Jim Glaser; Merle Haggard; Johnny Paycheck; Ray Price Alumni; Vern Gosdin.

Arrival ....Nu (S) 5650 5-10 82
Amy Grant; B.J. Thomas; Silverwind; Imperials; Sweet Comfort Band; David Meece; Phil Keagy; Keith Green; 2nd Chapter; john Michael & Terry Talbot; Dallas Holm & Praise; Evie & Don Francisco.

Around the Christmas Tree ....Decca (M) DL 38170 5-10 63
Four Aces; Own Bradley Quintet; Dick Haymes; Columbus Boys Choir; Axel Stordahl; Vincent Lopez; Shulmerich Carillon Bells.

Art of the Ballad 2 ....VSP (M) 38 10-15 67

Art of the Ballad 2 ....VSP (S) 38 10-15 67
Charlie Parker; Stan Getz; Sonny Stitt; others.

Art Laboe's Memories of El Monte: see Memories of El Monte

Arthur Godfrey and His Friends ....Columbia (M) CL 6113 15-25
(TV Soundtrack.) (Possibly different from LP below.)

Arthur Godfrey and His Friends ....Columbia (M) CL 2514 20-30 56
(TV Soundtrack.) Arthur Godfrey; Janette Davis; Mariners; Marion Marlowe & Frank Parker; Lu Ann Simms; Haleloke Kahauolopua.

Arthur Godfrey's TV Calendar Show ....Columbia (M) CL-521 25-35 53
(TV Soundtrack.) Arthur Godfrey; Julius LaRosa; Lu Ann Simms; Marion Marlowe; Frank Parker; Jeanette Davis; Mariners; Haleloke Kahauolopua; Chordettes.

Arthur Murray Presents Discotheque Dance Party ....RCA (M) LPM-2998 25-30 64

Arthur Murray Presents Discotheque Dance Party ....RCA (S) LSP-2998 30-35 64
Hip City Five; others.

Artistry in Music ....Capitol (S) PRO 1386-87 8-12

Assault of the Killer Bimbos ....Rhino (S) R1-70311 8-10 88
(Soundtrack.) Knight & Day; Fierce; Linda Strick; Attila the Hun; Billion Dollar Babies; Lois Blaisch; Andy Landis & Rockslide; Third Language; Mavis Vegas Davis; Idolls.

Assorted Flavors of Pacific Jazz (a Hi-Fi Sampler) ....Pacific Jazz (M) HFS-1 25-35 56
Cy Touff Octet; Gerry Mulligan; Bud Shank & Shorty Rogers Quintet; Chet Baker; Ensemble Sextet; Laurindo Almeida; Richard Twardzik Trio; Bill Perkins Quintet; Chico Hamilton Quintet; Frank Evans (narrator; KHJ).

At the Hootenanny ....Kapp (M) KL-1330 10-20 63

At the Hootenanny ....Kapp (S) KS-3330 15-25 63
Chad Mitchell Trio; Jo March; Marais & Miranda; Betty & Duke; Jo Mapes; David Hill; Samplers; Terry Gilkyson.

At the Hootenanny, Vol. 2 ....Kapp (M) KL-1343 10-20 63

At the Hootenanny, Vol. 2 ....Kapp (S) KS-3343 15-25 63
Chad Mitchell Trio; Alan Lomax; Jo Mapes; Betty & Duke; Marais & Miranda; Samplers; Alan Lomax; Lincolns; Hillel; Terry Gilkyson; David Hill; Travellers.

At the Hootenanny, Vol. 3 ....Kapp (M) KL-1344 10-20 64

At the Hootenanny, Vol. 3 ....Kapp (S) KS-3344 15-25 64
Chad Mitchell Trio; Travellers; Tom Glazer & Samplers; Betty & Duke; Joe Mapes; Lincolns; Peggy Seeger; David Hill; Alan Lomax; Greg Winkfield.

At the Hop ....Coronet (M) CX-244 10-15 64

At the Hop ....Coronet (S) CXS-244 10-15 64
4 Seasons; Charles Francis; Buggs; Barbara Brown.

At the Hop ....Forum Circle (S) FCS-9102 ?? 65
Chantels; Flamingos; Imperials; others.

At the Hop (Collection of Classic Oldies) (2 LP) ....ABC (S) AA-1111/2 10-15 78
Danny & Juniors; Jimmie Rodgers; Elegants; Pat Boone; Fontaine Sisters; Sony James; Gale Storm; Del-Vikings; Lloyd Price; Poni-Tails; George Hamilton IV; Barry Mann; Shields; Royal Teens; Del Shannon; Tommy Roe; Chantays; Surfaris; Barry McGuire; Tams; Impressions; Mamas & Papas; Grass Roots; Steppenwolf; O'Kaysions; Eddie Holman; Richard Harris; Three Dog Night.

At the Hop (3 LP) ....Brookville (S) BR 4600 15-20 75

At the Hop (3 LP)..MCA/Brookville (S) DXS-528 15-20 75
(Mail order offer.) Beach Boys; Buddy Holly & Crickets; Cozy Cole; Coasters; Surfaris; Teddy Bears; Kathy Young & Innocents; Tommy Roe; Jody Reynolds; Drifters; Jerry Keller; Danny & Juniors; Lesley Gore; Angels; Monotones; Chiffons; Wilbert Harrison; Jewel Akens; Silhouettes; Hollywood Argyles; Sandy Nelson; Music Machine; Bobby Lewis; Chris Montez, Preston Epps, Cascades; Rays; Dion; Clovers; Maurice Williams & Zodiacs; Tokens; Brian Hyland; Fendermen; Olympics. (Special products. Made for Brookville.)

At the Hop (5 LP).. CBS/Columbia Special Products (SE) P5-14747 30-40 78
(Boxed set. Mail order offer.) Danny & Juniors; Chantels; Jimmy Clanton; Bobby Day; Diamonds; Mark Dinning; Fleetwoods; Sandy Nelson; Duane Eddy; Four Aces; Frankie Ford; Huey "Piano" Smith; Coasters; Bobby Freeman; Robin Luke; Little Richard; Bobby Helms; Paul Evans; Four Preps; Jimmie Rodgers; Sammy Turner; Jerry Wallace; Gaylords; Jack Scott; Kingston Trio; Lloyd Price; Crests; Hilltoppers; Dave "Baby" Cortez; Gene & Eunice; Johnny & Hurricanes; Buddy Knox; Bill Doggett; Skyliners; Mystics; Penguins; Olympics; Bill Justis; Johnny Otis; Sonny Til & Orioles; Carl Dobkins Jr.; Dee Clark; Fiestas.

Atco Sales Meeting, Summer 1969 (2 LP)..Atco (S) ? 10-20 69
(Promotional issue only.) Aretha Franklin; Archie Bell & Drells; Jimmy Ellis; Ars Nova; Arif Marden; Rascals; Sweet Inspirations; Marion Wilkins; Roberta Flack; Joe Tex; David Newman; Carla Thomas; Don Covay; Clarence Carter; Phil Moore Jr.; Herbie Mann.

Atco Sales Meeting, Winter 1970..Atco (S) 2 10-12 70
(Promotional issue only.) Blues Image; others.

Athens, Ga. – Inside/Out..I.R.S. (S) RS-6185 8-10 87
(Soundtrack.) Squalls; Flat Duo Jets; R.E.M.; Love Tractor; Kilkenny Cats; Time Toy; Pylon; Bar-B-Q Killers; Dreams So Real.

Atlanta Blues.. RBF (M) RF-15 10-20 66
Charlie Lincoln; Peg Leg Howell; Alec Johnson; Buddy Moss; Barbecue Bob; Lonnie Coleman; Tampa Red; Blind Willie McTell.

Atlanta Blues 1933..JEMF (M) JEMF-106 10-20 79
Georgia Browns; Blind Willie McTell; Curley Weaver; Buddy Moss.

Atlantic/Atco - All Star Showcase: see All Star Showcase

Atlantic Blues: Guitar (2 LP)..Atlantic (S) 81695 10-15 86
John Lee Hooker; Blind Willie McTell; Mississippi Fred McDowell; Stick McGhee; T-Bone Walker; Texan John Brown; T-Bone Walker; Chuck Norris; Guitar Slim; Cornell Dupree; Big Joe Turner; Al King; Mickey Baker; Ike & Tina Turner; B.B. King; Albert King; John Hammond Jr.; Stevie Ray Vaughn.

Atlantic Blues: Piano (2 LP).. Atlantic (S) 81694 10-15 86

Atlantic Family Live at Montreaux..Atlantic (S) SD2-3000 8-12 77
Average White Band; Klaus Doldinger; Don Ellis; Sonny Fortune; Ben E. King; Herbie Mann; Luther Vandross; others.

Atlantic Heavies for February '73..Atlantic (S) PR-181 15-20 73
(Promotional issue only.) Dr. John; Duke Ellington; Allman Brothers; Black Oak Arkansas; Modern Jazz Quartet.

Atlantic Heavies for January..Atlantic (S) PR-180 15-20 74
(Promotional issue only.) Bee Gees; others.

Atlantic Heavies for June '73..Atlantic (S) PR-187 15-20 73
(Promotional issue only.) Badger; Bee Gees; Blue; Aaaaretha Franklin; Wayne Davis; Willie Nelson; Nikki Giovanni; Donny Hathaway; Ray Charles; others.

Atlantic Heavies for September from Atlantic, Atco, Rolling Stones, Little David, Virgin, Clean, Manticore (2 LP)..Atlantic Promotional (S) PR-194 10-20 73
Rolling Stones; Bette Midler; Crosby, Stills, Nash & Young; John Prine; Black Oak Arkansas; Delbert & Glen; George Carlin; Burns & Schreiber; Committee; Mike Oldfield; Barnaby Bye; Billy Cobham; True Reflection; Hanson; Hall & Oates; Gil Evans; Robin Renyatta; Jelly Roll Morton; Eddie Condon & Bud Freeman; Don Byas Slam Stewart Duo; Gary Farr; Buffalo Springfield.

Atlantic Honkers, a Rhythm & Blues Saxophone Anthology (2 LP)..Atlantic (M) 81666-1 8-12 86
Arnett Cobb; Frank Culley; King Curtis; Tiny Grimes; Willis Jackson; Joe Morris; Jesse Stone; others.

Atlantic Jazz Anthology Sampler..Atlantic (S) PR-2006 10-15

Atlantic Jazz Singers (2 LP)..Atlantic (S) 81706-1 10-15

Atlantic Records History of Rhythm & Blues Vocal Groups..Atlantic (M) 90132 8-10 83
(Promotional issue only.) Chords; Cardinals; Clovers; Royal Jokers; Drifters; Robins; Sensations Featuring Yvonne Mills; Bobbettes; Coasters.

Atlantic Rhythm & Blues, 1947-1952, Vol. 1, (2 LP).. Atlantic (SP) 781293-1 8-12 85
Joe Morris; Tiny Ggrimes; Frank Culley; Stick McGhee; Ruth Brown; Professor Longhair; Harry Van Walls; Clovers; Cardinals; Joe Turner; Willis Jackson; Ray Charles.

Atlantic Rhythm & Blues 1952-1955, Vol. 2, (2 LP).. Atlantic (SP) 781294-1 8-12 85
Diamonds; Ruth Brown; Clovers; Ray Charles; LaVern Baker; Clyde McPhatter & Drifters; Professor Longhair; Joe Turner; Chords; Tommy Ridgley; Cardinals; Drifters; Robins.

Atlantic Rhythm & Blues 1955-1958, Vol. 3, (2 LP).. Atlantic (SP) 781295-1 8-12 85
Drifters; Cookies; Joe Turner; Clovers; Ray Charles; LaVern Baker; Coasters; Clyde McPhatter; Chuck Willis; Ivory Joe Hunter; Ruth Brown; Bobbettes.

Atlantic Rhythm & Blues 1958-1962, Vol. 4, (2 LP).. Atlantic (SP) 781296-1 8-12 85
LaVern Baker; Ray Charles; Coasters; Drifters; Ben E. King; Carla Thomas; Solomon Burke; Mar-Keys; Ikettes; William Bell; Falcons; Booker T. & MGs.

Atlantic Rhythm & Blues, 1962-1966 Vol. 5, (2 LP).. Atlantic (SP) 781297-1 8-12 85
LaVern Baker; Drifters; Ben E. King; Solomon Burke; Otis Redding; Barbara Lewis; Doris Troy; Nat Kendricks & Swans; Chris Kenner; Rufus Thomas; Esther Phillips; Don Covay; Drifters; Joe Tex; Wilson Pickett; Don Covay; Sam & Dave; Percy Sledge; Capitols; Jimmy Hughes.

Atlantic Rhythm & Blues, 1966-1969, Vol. 6, (2 LP).. Atlantic (SP) 781298-1 8-12 85
Wilson Pickett; Eddie Floyd; Otis Redding; Sam & Dave; Arthur Conley; Aretha Franklin; Joe Tex; Carla Thomas; Booker T. & MGs; Bar-Kays; King Curtis; Archie Bell & Drells; Clarence Carter; Roberta Flack; R.B. Greaves; Brook Benton.

Atlantic Rhythm & Blues, 1969-1974, Vol. 7, (2 LP)..Atlantic (S) 781299-1 8-12 85
Donny Hathaway; Tyrone Davis; Les McCann & Eddie Harris; Aretha Franklin; Clarence Carter; Beginning of the End; Persuaders; Roberta Flack; Betty Wright; Spinners; Major Harris.

Atlantic Sales Meeting - Winter 1970..Atlantic (S) SD-JSM-1 10-15
(Promotional issue only.)

Attack of the Killer B's.. Warner Bros. (S) 23837-1 5-10 83
Ramones; Marshall Crenshaw; Pretenders; Blasters; John Hiatt; Roxy Music; Peter Gabriel; Time; Talking Heads; Gang of Four; T-Bone Burnett; Laurie Anderson.

Audio Fidelity Stereodisc..Audio Fidelity (S) AFSD 5890 8-12
(Sound effects. No music.)

August Sampler (RCA): see RCA August Sampler

Austin Rhythm & Blues Christmas .... Epic (S) E-40576 5-10 86
Angela Strehli; Fabulous Thunderbirds; Lou Ann Barton; Sarah Brown; Paul Ray; Kaz Jazz Quartet; Charles Sexton.

Autumn Leaves (3 LP) .... MCA Special Markets/Brookville (S) 34902 5-10 73
(Mail order offer.) Bobby Helms; Carl Dobkins Jr.; Peggy Lee; Teresa Brewer; Don Cornell; McGuire Sisters; Four Aces; Lennon Sisters; Earl Grant; Al Hibbler; Owen Bradley; Tommy Dorsey Orchestra with Warren Covington; Bobby Helms; Richard Chamberlain; Florian Zabach; Jerry Lewis; Weavers; San Fernando Brass; Freddy Martin; Roger Williams; Jack Jones; Dimitri Tiomkin; Ruby & the Romantics; Brenda Lee; Kalin Twins; Jane Morgan; Chad & Jeremy; Vic Damone; Gogi Grant; Eddie Fisher; Jerry Wallace; Champs; Patti Page; Rusty Draper; Tommy Edwards; Kitty Kallen; Four Lads..

Autumn Leaves (3 LP) .... MCA Special Markets/Brookville (S) DXS 7-526/13173 10-15 70s
Jack Jones; Dimitri Tiomkin; Ruby & Romantics; Brenda Lee; Kalin Twins; Jane Morgan & Troubadors; Jerry Lewis; Florian Zabach; Weavers & Terry Gilkyson; San Fernando Brass; Freddy Martin; Roger Williams; Peggy Lee; Four Aces; Teresa Brewer; Don Cornell; McGuire Sisters; Carl Dobkins Jr.; Lennon Sisters; Earl Grant; Al Hibbler; Bobby Helms; Owen Bradley Quintet; Tommy Dorsey Orchestra with Warren Covington; Vic Damone; Chad & Jeremy; Gogi Grant; Eddie Fisher; Jerry Wallace; Champs; Patti Page; Rusty Draper; Tommy Edwards; Kitty Kallen; Richard Chamberlain; Four Lads.

Avon Valentine Favorites .... RCA (S) DPL1-0751 10-15 86
Elvis Presley; Kenny Rogers; Perry Como; Tony Bennett; Henry Mancini; Peabo Bryson & Roberta Flack; Jose Feliciano; Johnny Mathis; Alabama. (Special products. Made for Avon.)

Award Winners .... Columbia Special Products (M) C 10391 8-12 60s
Andre Kostelanetz; Jerry Vale; Les & Larry Elgart; Modernaires & Paula Kelly; Bobby Hackett; New Christy Minstrels; Jane Morgan; Ray Conniff; Anita Bryant; Joe Harnell.

Award Winners .... RCA (S) APL1-2262 5-10 77
Charley Pride; Chet Atkins; Dolly Parton; Dickey Lee; others.

Award Winners of the Country Music Association 1968-1977 .... RCA (S) DPL 0305 5-10 78
Glen Campbell; Johnny Cash; Merle Haggard; Sammi Smith; Charley Pride; Danny Davis; Ronnie Milsap; Freddy Fender; Dolly Parton; Crystal Gayle.

B.F. Goodrich - Something Festive .... A&M (S) SP-19003 8-12
Herb Alpert & Tijuana Brass; Julius Wechter & Baja Marimba Band; Sergio Mendes; Burt Bacharach; Liza Minnelli; Pete Jolly; Claudine Longet; We Five. (Special products. Made for B.F. Goodrich.)

Baby Don't Go .... Reprise (S) R 6177 10-20 60s
Sonny & Cher; Caesar & Cleo; Bill Medley; Lettermen; Blendells.

Bacharach Songbook .... Columbia (S) C 10262 5-10

Bachelor Party .... I.R.S. (S) 70047 8-10 84
(Soundtrack.) Fleshtones; Oingo Boingo; R.E.M.; Jools Holland; Alarm.

Back to Cool .... Capitol Creative Products (S) SL-6535 10-15 68
Peter & Gordon; Lettermen; Lou Rawls; Chad & Jeremy; Outsiders. (Special products. Made for Sears and for Florsheim stores.)

Back to School .... MCA (S) 6175 8-10 86
(Soundtrack.) Jude Cole; Bobby Caldwell; Tyson & Schwartz; Michael Bolton; Philip Ingram; Rodney Dangerfield; Aretha Franklin.

Back to the Beach .... Columbia (S) JS-40892 10-12 87
(Soundtrack.) Annette Funicello; Frankie Avalon; Eddie Money; Stevie Ray Vaughan; Dick Dale; Aimee Mann; Private Domain; Pee-Wee Herman; Marti Jones; Fishbone; Herbie Hancock; Dweezil Zappa; Terry Bozzio; Dave Edmunds.

Back to the Fabulous Fifties .... Panaural (M) PA 3-81 ?? 60s
Jolly Jax; Demons; Isley Brothers; Dolls; Johnny Honeycut; R Kai Ray.

Back to the Future .... MCA (S) 6144 8-10 85
(Soundtrack.) Huey Lewis & News; Outatime Orchestra; Eric Clapton; Lindsay Buckingham; Etta James; Marty McFly (Michael J. Fox) & Starlighters.

Backstage at the Grand Old Opry .... RCA (S) AHL1-4350 5-10 83
Po' Folks; Roy Acuff; John Conlee; Dottie West; Osborne Brothers; Jimmy C. Newman; Connie Smith; Hank Snow; Boxcar Willie; B.J. Thomas; Bill Anderson. (From Nashville Network TV.)

Bad Boys .... Capitol (S) ST-12272 8-10 83
(Soundtrack.) Ebonee Webb; Melba Moore; T-Connection; others.

Bad Guys .... Casablanca (S) 826610-1 8-10 86
(Soundtrack.) Spyder Turner; Precious Metal; Kane Gang; Paul Chiten; Redskins; Hand Tools; William Goldstein; Robert John; Stars on 45; Jeff Tyzik.

Bad Influence .... Mango (S) MLPS-9860 5-10 90
(Soundtrack.) Toots; Nana Vasconcelos & Bushdancers; Lloyd Cole; Etta James; Chaba Fadela; Thomas Mapfump; Skinny Puppy; Les Negresses Vertes; Gavin Friday & Man; Trevor Jones.

Bad Luck and Trouble .... Arhoolie F-1018 10-20 65
Lightnin' Hopkins; Clifton Chenier; others.

Badger A-Go-Go .... Cuca/Night Owl (M) KTV-3 25-45
Betty Moore with the Esquires; Seven Sounds; Dave Kennedy & Ambassadors; Centurys; Chieftones; Grapes of Wrath; Mule Skinners; Rod Means; War Lords; Jerry & Continentals; Del Rays; Robin Lee & Lavenders; Kiriae Crucible; Voodoos. (Cover shows Cuca but label reads Night Owl.)

Badmen (2 LP) .... Columbia (M) L2L-1011 15-20 63

Badmen (2 LP) .... Columbia (S) L2S-1012 15-25 63
Pete Seeger; Ed McCurdy; Harry Jackson; Jack Elliott; others.

Balanced for Broadcast: see Capitol Promotional Releases/Samplers

Ballads and Breakdowns of the Golden Era .... Columbia (S) CS-9660 10-15 68
Charlie Poole; Dock Walsh; Gid Tanner; others.

Ballads and Songs .... Old Timey (M) LP-102 5-10

Band of the Hand .... MCA (S) 6165 8-21 86
(Soundtrack.) Bob Dylan with the Heartbreakers; Shriekback; Reds; Andy Summers; Tiger Tiger; Michael Rubini.

Banded Together .... Epic (S) JE 36177 5-10
Johnny Cash; Willie Nelson; David Allan Coe; Johnny Paycheck; Charlie Daniels Band; Bobby Bare; George Jones.

Banded Together .... Columbia (S) ???? 5-10
Johnny Cash & Waylon Jennings; Willie Nelson; David Allan Coe; Johnny Paycheck; Charlie Daniels Band; Bobby Bare; George Jones & James Taylor.

Bang and Shout Super Hits .... Bang (S) LPS-220 10-20 58

Banjo (3 LP) ....Murray Hill (S) S-5395 X/3 12-20
(Box set.) Jim McGuinn; Flatts & Scruggs; Eric Weissberg & Marshall Brickman; Dick Rossini; Mike Seeger; Pete Seeger; Joe Maphis; David Lindley; Erik Darling; Billy Cheatwood.
Banjo Bonanza (2 LP) .... Columbia Special Products (S) P-11890 8-12 74
Banjoman .... Sire (S) SA-7527 12-18 77
(Soundtrack.) Bob Dylan; Jimmy Driftwood; Byrds; Joan Baez; Nitty Gritty Dirt Band; Earl Scruggs Revue; Doc & Merle Watson; Jack Elliot.
Banjo Story..Horizon (M) WP-1623 10-20 64
Banjo Story..Horizon (S) ST-1623 10-20 64
Mason Williams; Joe Maphis; Mike Seeger; others.
BankAmericard Music Box .... A&M (S) SP-19006 10-15 69
Herb Alpert & Tijuana Brass; Sergio Mendes; Wes Montgomery; Sandpipers; Julius Wechter & Baja Marimba Band; Claudine Longet. (Special products. Made for BankAmericard.)
Barefoot Rock and You Got Me.. Duke (M) LP-72 40-50 58
Bargain Day!.. EmArcy (M) MG 36087 10-15
Barrel of Oldies.. Del-Fi (M) DFLP-1219 40-50 61
Ritchie Valens; Ron Holden; Bo Diddley; Lee Andrews & Hearts; Gallahads; Pentagons; Carlos Brothers; Twiliters; Rosie & Ron; Johnny Flamingo.
Baseball Tips from the Stars ....Mars 1-3 25-50
(Three-disc promotional set.) Includes tips from Lou Boudreau and other players as well as space for their autographs. (If set includes authentic autographs, price would increase significantly. Made for Mars Candy.)
Basic Black - 25 Hits (2 LP)... GRT (S) 2103-705 10-15 75
Fontella Bass; Bobby Moore; Ramsey Lewis; Sensations; Etta James; Billy Stewart; Clarence Henry; Pigmeat Markham; Dells; Laura Lee; Bobby Bland; Tony Clark; Jackie Ross; Vibrations; Impressions; Bo Diddley; B.B. King; Lloyd Price; Dave "Baby" Cortez; Gene Chandler; Eddie Holman.
Bass, The (3 LP) ....ABC Impulse (S) ASY 9284-3 10-20
(Boxed set.)
Battle of the Bands ....Star (M) 101 50-100 64
Lepricons; Escorts; Arcades; Frolic Five; Rivals; Duples; Thunderbird; Kona Casuals; Statics; Renegades; Raiders; Dimensions; Impacts; Majestics; Star Lighters; Adventurers; Checkmates; Sensations; Royal Malads; Infasions.
Battle of the Bands ....SRM 101 5-10 90s
Battle of the Bands 1966 (Recorded Almost Live) .... Onyx (M) ES-80689 30-40 66
Poets of Merit; Fugitives, Inc.; Apaches; Vibrants; Satisfactions; Hearts of Darkness; Here They Are; Mods; Stolen Minutes.
Battle of the Bands ....Ren Vell (M) LP-317 10-20
Battle of the Bands, Vol. 1..Panorama (M) 103 20-25 66
Don & Goodtimes; Sonics; Live Five; Bandits; Dynamics.
Battle of the Bands, Vol. 2..Panorama (M) 108 20-25 67
Battle of the Beat...California Recording Service (M) 101 75-125 64
Blazers; Exiles; Torques; Del Pierce & Knockouts; Showmen; Continentals; Viscounts; Bonnevilles; Apollos; Aquanauts; Debonairs; Lad Teens; Vestells.
Battle of the Blues, Vol. 1 ....King (M) 395-607 100-200 58
Battle of the Blues, Vol. 2 ....King (M) 395-627 100-200 59
Battle of the Blues, Vol. 3 ....King (M) 395-634 100-200 59
Battle of the Blues, Vol. 4 ....King (M) 395-668 300-400 59
Battle of the Groups (Round 1) .... End (EP) R-1 10-20 59
(Issued with paper sleeve.) Dubs; Flamingos; Chantels; Rockin' Ronald.
Battle of the Groups (Round 2) .... End (EP) R-2 10-20 59
(Issued with paper sleeve.) Little Anthony & Imperials; Dubs; Richard Barrett; Flamingos.
Battle of the Groups (Round 3) .... End (EP) R-3 10-20 59
(Issued with paper sleeve.) Little Anthony & Imperials; Flamingos; Velours; Channels.
Battle of the Groups (Round 4) .... End (EP) R-4 10-20 59
(Issued with paper sleeve.) Little Anthony & Imperials; Sam Hawkins; Dubs; Jo Ann Campbell.
Battle of the Groups (Round 5) .... End (EP) R-5 10-20 59
(Issued with paper sleeve.) Little Anthony & Imperials; Richard Barrett; Chantels; Flamingos.
Battle of the Groups (Round 6) .... End (EP) R-6 10-20 59
(Issued with paper sleeve.) Little Anthony & Imperials; Flamingos; Chantels; Jo Ann Campbell.
Battle of the Groups (Round 7) .... End (EP) R-7 10-20 59
(Issued with paper sleeve.)
Battle of the Groups (Round 8) .... End (EP) R-8 10-20 59
(Issued with paper sleeve.) Little Anthony & Imperials; Flamingos; Neons; Chantels.
Battle of the Groups (Round 9) .... End (EP) R-9 10-20 59
(Issued with paper sleeve.)
Battle of the Groups (Round 10) .... End (EP) R-10 10-20 59
(Issued with paper sleeve.) Flamingos; Jo Ann Campbell; Dubs; Little Anthony & Imperials.
Battle of the Groups .... End (M) LP-305 40-50 59
Isley Brothers; Dubs; Flamingos; Little Anthony & Imperials.
Battle of the Groups, Vol. 2 .... End (M) LP-309 40-50 60
Dubs; Flamingos; Little Anthony & Imperials; Chantels.
Battle of the Surfing Bands.. Del-Fi (M) DFLP-1235 35-45 63
Battle of the Surfing Bands.. Del-Fi (S) DFST-1235 45-55 63
Bruce Johnston; Lively Ones; Challengers; Jim Waller & Deltas; Sentinels; Kings; Impacts; Biscaynes; Charades.
Bawdy Blues.. Prestige Bluesville (M) BV-1055 15-25 63
Lonnie Johnson; Memphis Slim; Memphis Willie B.; Blind Willie McTell; Tampa Red; Victoria Spivey; Pink Anderson.
Be a Hit at School (From Your Remington Portable Typewriter Dealer) ....RCA (EP) SP-45-93 25-35 60
(Has paper cover. Promotional issue only.) Neil Sedaka; Henry Mancini; Sam Cooke; Della Reese; Browns; Jeannie Johnson; Neal Hefti.
Be Our Guest (Sampler)...Gene Norman Presents (M) GNP-20 20-30 50s
Charlie Ventura; Buddy DeFranko; Gerry Mulligan; Dizzy Gillespie; Lyle Murphy; Max Roach & Clifford Brown; Lionel Hampton; Rene Touzet; Corky Hale; Marty Paich; Billy Daniels; Frank Morgan.

Beach Beat .... Atlantic (M) 8140 20-30 67
Clovers; Coasters; Barbara Lewis; Chuck Willis; Clyde McPhatter; Drifters; Willie Tee; Doris Troy; Stick McGhee.

Beach Beat, Vol. 2 .... Atlantic (S) SD-8191 15-25 68
Clovers; Coasters; Barbara Lewis; Clyde McPhatter; Willie Tee; Bobby Moore & Rhythm Aces; Billy Stewart; King Curtis & Kingpins; Maurice Williams & Zodiacs; Lenny O'Henry; Tony Clarke; Ben E. King.

Beach Beat Classics .... Ripete (S) 392146 8-12 80
Catalinas; Tymes; Fantastic Shakers; Band of Oz; Bob Collins & Fabulous Five; Cannonball; Tempests; Swinging Medallions; Showmen; Willie Tee; Billy Stewart; Garnett Mimms & Enchanters; Lenny O'Henry; Prophets; Ernie K-Doe; Chairmen of the Board.

Beach Blow-Out .... PRI/Capitol (S) SL 9304 5-10 85
David Lee Roth; Jan & Dean; Trashmen; Ventures; Beach Boys; Sandals; Surfaris; Chantays; Chris Montez.

Beach Classics .... Surfside (S) SR 1002 5-10 82
Carolina Beach Music; Gen. Johnson & Chairmen; Band of Oz; Showmen; Tempest.

Beach Party .... G.S.P. (M) 6901 75-100 63
Surf Bunnies; Charades; Gary Paxton; Surfaris; Dave Kinzie; Revels; Kenny & Sultans; Judy Russell; Sandford & Sandles.

Beat, The .... K-Tel (S) TU-5040 5-10 82
Go Go's; Bow Wow Wow; Duran Duran; Billy Idol; Thompson Twins; Depeche Mode; Orchestral Manoeuvers in the Dark; Flock of Seagulls; Kim Wilde; Haircut One Hundred; Sparks; Split Enz; Graham Parker; Waitress& His Orchestra.

Beat Battle of the World .... Groovemaster (M) GR-140 20-30 64

Beat Battle of the World .... Groovemaster (SE) GR-140 20-30 64
Dave Clark Five; Tottenhamers; Chuck Jackson; Miller Sisters; Dick Dale; Jades; Angels; Neil Sedaka with the Tokens.

Beat of the Beach (2 LP) .... Arista (S) A2L-8503 10-15 82
Lee Dorsey; Showmen; Clifford Curry; Aaron Neville; Garnet Mimms; Box Tops; Don Gardner & Dee Dee Ford; Wilbert Harrison; General Johnson; James & Bobby Purify; Drifters; Patty & Emblems; Shirley & Shirelles; Nino Tempo & April Stevens; O'Jays; Trammps; Van Dykes; Gladys Knight & Pips.

Beat of the Bahamas .... Bahamas (M) No Number Used 5-10

Beat of the Traps, MSR Madness, Vol. 1 (Tom Ardolino Presents) .... Carnage Press (M) CP-714 8-10 92
Gary Roberts & Satellites; Rod Rogers & Swinging Strings; Rodd Keith; Rodd, Terri, & M.S.R. Singers; Rod Rogers, Teri Summers & Librettos; Bob Lloyd; Gene Marshall; Norm Burns & Five Stars; Music Magicians.

Beat Street .... Atlantic (S) 80154-1 8-10 84
(Soundtrack.) Grandmaster Melle Mel & Furious Five; System; Jenny Burton & Patrick Jude; Juicy; Sharon Green; Lisa Counts & Debbie D; Cindy Mizelle; Arthur Baker; Ruben Blades; Afrika Bambastaa & Soul Sonic Force + Shango.

Beat Street, Vol. 2 .... Atlantic (S) 80158-1 8-10 84
(Soundtrack.) Jazzy Jay; Juicy; Tina B.; Jenny Burton; others.

Beatle Originals .... Rhino (S) RNLP-70071 8-12 86
Larry Williams; Carl Perkins; Donays; Shirelles; Dr. Feelgood & Interns; Arthur Alexander; Little Richard; Buddy Holly & Crickets; Buck Owens.

Beatlesongs .... Rhino (S) RNLP-803 15-20
(Cover pictures Mark Chapman.)

Beatlesongs .... Rhino (S) RNLP-803 5-10
(Mark Chapman not pictured.)

Beautiful Hair Breck Presents a Hootenanny .... Audio Premium/Decca (M) MG 79571-2 10-20 63
Rooftop Singers; Weavers; Ian & Sylvia; Dillards; Theodore Bikel. (Special products. Made for Breck.)

Beautiful People .... Harmony (S) HS-11383 8-10 70
John Kay; Ravi Shankar; Byrds; Electric Flag; Grace Slick & Great Society; Rising Sons; United States of America; Tim Rose; Don Ellis..

Be-Bop Era .... RCA (M) LPV-519 10-20 65
Charlie Ventura; Illinois Jacquet; Count Basie; others.

Bechet of New Orleans .... RCA (M) LPV-510 10-20 65
Sidney Bechet; Jelly Roll Morton; others.

Beginning British Blues (2 LP) .... Immediate (S) Z12-52018 10-15 69
Santa Barbera; Machine Head; Jeff Beck; Cyril Davies; All Stars; Stuff Smith; Eric Clapton & Jimmy Page.

Believe in Music .... K-Tel (S) TU-227 5-10 73
Looking Glass; Daniel Boone; Lighthouse; Mouth & MacNeil; Hollies; Donny Osmond; O'Jays; Raspberries; Andy & David Williams; Rod Stewart; Bobby Vinton; Cher; Dr. Hook & Medicine Show; Argent; Eric Clapton; Slade; Bulldog; Five Man Electrical Band; Rick Springfield; Albert Hammond; Gallery.

Benjamin's After Dark Live (2 LP) .... Thunderstruck (S) BADO 101 8-12 81
Andrea Re & Clouds; Searsmost St. Band; Randy Hawks; Quetones; Blues Over Easy.

Bent, Batty and 'Bnoxious .... Torture (M) TORT-000-NO 8-10
Baby Huey & Baby Sitters; Sal Masi's Untouchables; Johnny & Baa-Baas; Kwentin Qwisp; Alfred A. Alfa; Lalo Guerrero; Charlie & Chan; Rumblers; Phil Campos; Bob Ridgley; Don Miller; Sticks Evans; Gunga Din; Marty Neon; Big Daddy; Little Sisters; Singing Dogs; Stu Mitchell; Johnny Buckett.

Berkeley Blues Festival .... Arhoolie (M) 1030 10-15 67
Mance Lipscomb; Clifton Chenier; others.

Berkeley Farms .... Folkways (M) FA 2436 10-15 72
Larry Hanks; Holly Tanner; Bayou Croakers; New Tranquility String Band; Phil Marsh; Hank Bradley; Jody Stecher.

Beserkley Chartbusters - Home of the Hits, Vol. 1: see KIHN, Greg, Band / Earthquake / Rubinoos / Jonathan Richman

Best Disco in Town (2 LP) .... Adam VIII (S) 8033 8-12
Dr. Buzzard's Original Savannah Band; Jakki; Lou Courtney; Bay City Rollers; Double Exposure; Salsoul Orchestra; Whirlwind; Carol Douglas; Marilyn Chambers; Gary Glitter; D.C. Larue; Faith, Hope & Charity; Donna Summer; Stravarious; Camoflage; Ritchie Family; Crown Heights Affair; Walter Murphy & Big Apple Band; Rim Shots; Kool & Gang; Candi Staton; Spinners; Norman Connors.

Best from Buddah .... Buddah (S) BDS-5000 10-15 69
Ohio Express; 1910 Fruitgum Co.; Lemon Pipers; Shadows of Knight; Melanie; Barry Goldberg Band; Kasenetz-Katz Super Circus.

Best of '57, (Red Seal Preview Album) .... RCA (M) SRL-12-49 10-15 57
Charles Munch & Boston Symphone Orchestra; Robert Russell Bennett & RCA Victor Symphony; Symphony of the Air with Arthur Rubinstein & Josef Krips; Fritz Reiner & Chicago Symphony Orchestra; Pierre Monteux & Paris Conservatoire Orchestra; Arthur Fiedler & Boston Pops; Rome Opera House with Janel Perlea & Robert Merrill; Morton Gould. (Made for Heinz 57.)

Best of '66, Vol. 1 .... Columbia (M) TB-1 10-15 66

Best of '66, Vol. 1 .... Columbia (S) TBS-1 10-15 66
Brothers Four; Byrds; Chad & Jeremy; Crykle; John Davidson; Bob Dylan; New Christy Minstrels; Pozo Seco Singers; Paul Revere & Raiders; Billy Joe Royal; Simon & Garfunkel.

Best of '66, Vol. 2 .... Columbia (M) AB-1 10-15 66
Best of '66, Vol. 2 .... Columbia (S) ABS-1 10-15 66
Tony Bennett; Ray Conniff; Percy Faith; Eydie Gorme; Robert Goulet; Andre Kostelanetz; Steve Lawrence; Barbra Streisand; Jerry Vale; Andy Williams.
Best of 1967 .... ARP (S) LP-101 10-15 60s
Beatles; Monkees; Doors; Jefferson Airplane; Janis Ian; Procol Harum; Aretha Franklin; Rascals; Supremes; Happenings; Marvin Gaye; Association. (A question about the legitimacy of this LP has been raised. We're not yet sure.)
Best of a Great Year, Vol. 1 .... RCA (M) LM 6074 5-10 72
Jerry Reed; Eddy Arnold; Charley Pride; Porter Wagoner; others.
Best of a Great Year, Vol. 2 (2 LP) .... RCA (S) LSP-6088 8-12 72
Charley Pride; Jim Ed Brown; Pat Daisy; Eddy Arnold; Hank Snow; Dolly Parton; Porter Wagoner; Chet Atkins; Dickey Lee; Skeeter Davis; Jerry Reed; Lester Flatt & Mac Wiseman; Dallas Frazier; Waylon Jennings; Nat Stuckey; Floyd Cramer; Dottie West; Kenny Price; Jim Reeves; Danny Davis & Nashville Brass; George Hamilton IV; Connie Smith; George Jones.
Best of a Great Year, Vol. 3 (2 LP) .... RCA (S) CPL-2-0449 8-12 74
Eddy Arnold; Chet Atkins; Dolly Parton; Connie Smith; Dottie West; Hank Snow; Charlie Rich; others.
Best of Acapella, Vol. 1 .... Relic (M) 101 10-15 65
Zircons; Nutmegs; Kooltones; Velvet Angels; Excellons; Pretenders; Young Ones; Barons; Delstars; Chessmen; Savoy 5; Camelots.
Best of Acapella, Vol. 2 .... Relic (M) 102 10-15 65
Chessmen; Citadels; Delstars; Holidays; Shadows; Youngones; Velvet Angels.
Best of Acapella, Vol. 3 .... Relic (M) 103 10-15 65
Quotations; Nicky & Naks; Count 5; Islanders; Citadels; Durhams; Enchantments; Horizons; Apparitions.
Best of Acapella, Vol. 4 .... Relic (M) 104 10-15 65
Ginger & Adorables; Durhams; Islanders; Little Joe & Majestics; Nicky & Nacks; Notations; Quotations; Rondells; Semesters; Tremonts.
Best of Acapella, Vol. 5 .... Relic (M) 105 10-15 65
Apparitions; Chessmen; Count Five; Islanders; Citadels; Majestics; Nicky & Nacks; Quotations; Sintells; Uniques.
Best of Acapella, Vol. 6 .... Relic (M) 108 10-15 67
Apparitions; Five Jades; Islanders; Kac-Ties; Knick-Knacks; Quotations; Spirals; Uniques; Velvet Angels; Vibraharps.
Best of Acapella, Vol. 7 .... Relic (M) 109 10-15 67
Apparitions; Five Jades; Quotations; Velvet Angels; Vibraharps; Chevieres; Creations; Del-Vikings; Reminiscents.
Best of Alan Freed Oldies .... United International (S) 101 10-15
Marcels; Bobby Lewis; Olympics; Pagents; Flares; Ad Libs; Gary "U.S." Bonds; Curtis Lee; Fiestas; Angels; Jerry Butler; Maxine Brown; Jive Five; Jesse Belvin; Dells; Robert & Johnny; Jody Reynolds; Visions; Tony Dale.
Best of Argo .... Argo (S) ALPS-1 10-15
Ahmad Jamal; Jazztet; Lorez Alexandria; Al Grey; Milt Buckner; Buddy Rich; Benny Golson; Ramsey Lewis Trio; James Moody; Art Farmer; Roland Kirk.
Best of Atlanta, Vol.1 .... Mine (S) 1108 8-10 70s
Joe South; freddie Weller; Ray Whitley; Mac Davis.
Best of Atlanta, Vol.2 .... Mine (S) 1109 8-10 70s
Best of Atlanta, Vol.3 .... Mine (S) 1110 8-10 70s
Best of Atlanta, Vol.4 .... Mine (S) 1111 8-10 70s
Best of Bakersfield .... Capitol (S) ST-1111 5-10 72
Buck Owens; Susan Raye; Freddie Hart; others.
Best of Blue Note (2 LP) .... Blue Note (M) BST2-84429 10-15 84
Bud Powell; James Moody; Thelonious Monk; Milt Jackson; Clifford Brown; Miles Davis; John Coltrane; Herbie Hancock; Donald Byrd; Art Blakey & Jazz Messengers; Lou Donaldson; Horace Silver; Jimmy Smith; Kenny Burrell; Lee Morgan.
Best of Bluegrass .... Wing (M) MGM-12267 10-15 60s
Best of Bluegrass .... Wing (S) SRW-16267 10-15 60s
Jeffery Null & Denver Duke; Lew Childre; Benny Martin; Stanley Brothers; Carl Story & Rambling Mountaineers; Flatt & Scruggs; Jimmie Skinner.
Best of Bomp .... Bomp (S) LP-4002 10-15 78
(White vinyl.) Iggy & Stooges; Weirdos; Venus & Razor Blades; Flamin' Groovies; DMZ; Zeros; 20/20; Willie Alexander & Boom Boom Band; Snatch; Wackers; Poppees; Shoes.
Best of Britain .... K-Tel (S) TU-2380 5-10 70s
Searchers; Wayne Fontana & Mindbenders; Billy J. Kramer & Dakotas; New Vaudeville Band; Crazy World of Arthur Brown; Cilla Black; Sandie Shaw; Kinks; Gerry & Pacemakers; Zombies; Honeycombs; Dave Clark Five; Swinging Blue Jeans; Freddie & Dreamers; Georgie Fame; Donovan; Foundations; Mungo Jerry; Adam Faith; Vanity Fare.
Best of Broadway .... Disneyland (M) DQ-1267 10-20 65
Annette; Darlene Gillespie; others.
Best of Buddah (2 LP) .... Buddah/Pear (S) PDL-2-1202 8-12 88
(Same tracks as Buddah 2103-713. See below.)
Best of Buddah (2 LP) .... Buddah (S) 2103-713 10-15 76
Isley Brothers; Gladys Knight & Pips; Lovin' Spoonful; Curtis Mayfield; New Birth; Jim Weatherly; Melanie; Five Stairsteps; Honey Cone; Flaming Ember; Lemon Pipers; Ohio Express; 100 Proof Aged in Soul; Ocean; Jaggerz; Brewer & Shipley; Brooklyn Bridge; Motherlode; Sopwith Camel; Stories; Edwin Hawkins Singers; Lou Christie.
Best of Buddah - Tailored Music (2 LP) .... GRT (S) 2103-713 10-15 76
Isley Brothers; Gladys Knight & Pips; Lovin' Spoonful; Curtis Mayfield; New Birth; Jim Weatherly; Melanie; Five Stairsteps; Honey Cone; Flaming Ember; Lemon Pipers; Ohio Express; 100 Proof Aged in Soul; Ocean; Jaggerz; Brewer & Shipley; Brooklyn Bridge; Motherlode; Sopwith Camel; Stories; Edwin Hawkins Singers; Lou Christie.
Best of Burt Bacharach .... Scepter Citation CTN 18012 8-12 72
Dionne Warwick; B.J. Thomas; Tommy Hunt; Shirelles; Chuck Jackson; Buddy Greco.
Best of Burt Bacharach .... Trip (S) X-3503 5-10 75
Dionne Warwick; Jackie DeShannon; Chuck Jackson; Timi Yuro; Tommy Hunt; Gene Pitney; Shirelles; others.
Best of Chess Blues (2 LP) .... Chess/MCA (S) CH2-6023 10-15 87
Muddy Waters; Robert Nighthawk; Eddie Boyd & His Chessmen; Willie Mabon; Lowell Fulson; Howlin' Wolf; Little Walter & His Night Cats; J.B. Lenoir; Jimmy Rogers; Elmore James; Sonny James; Little Milton; Koko Taylor.
Best of Chess/Checker/Cadet Doo Wop .... Chess (M) CH-9120 8-12 84
Sensations; Marathons; Ideals; Moonglows; Dream Kings; Students; Lee Andrews & Hearts; Revels; Flamingos; Johnnie & Joe; Tune Weavers; Pastels; Rays; Blue Jays.
Best of Chess/Checker/Cadet Rhythm & Rock .... Chess/PRT (M)CXMP 2002 8-12 81

Little Tommy Tucker; Clarence Henry; Dale Hawkins; Bo Diddley; Jackie Brenston; Koko Taylor; Dave Baby Cortez; Chuck Berry; Jimmy McCracklin; Eddie Fontaine; Rusty York; Little Walter.

Best of Chess Jazz (2 LP) .... Chess (S) CH2-6025 10-15 80s

Best of Chess Rhythm & Blues (2 LP) .... Chess (S) CH2-6022 10-15 87

Moonglows; Miracles; Jimmy McCracklin; Corsairs; Vibrations; Clarence "Frogman" Henry; Bobby Moore & Rhythm Aces; Jan Bradley; Billy Stewart; Little Milton; Tony Clarke; Mitty Collier; Radiants; Dells; Fontella Bass; Ramsey Lewis Trio; Sugar Pie DeSanto; Jackie Ross; Etta James.

Best of Chess Rock and Roll (2 LP) .... Chess/MCA (S) CH2 6024 10-15 87

Chuck Berry; Bo Diddley; Dale Hawkins; Bobby Charles; Jackie Brenston & His Delta Kings; Moonglows; Flamingos; Clarence "Frogman" Henry; Tune Weavers; Students; Monotones; Lee Andrews & Hearts; Sensations; Johnnie & Joe; Tommy Tucker; Dave "Baby" Cortez; Jaynetts.

Best of Chess Vocal Groups (2 LP) .... Chess/MCA (S) CH2 6029 10-15 88

Moonglows; Dozier Boys; Four Tops; Flamingos; Ravens; Monotones; Lee Andrews & Hearts; Gems; Students; Marathons; Pastels; Knight Brothers; Sensations; Miracles; Dells; Radiants; O'Jays.

Best of Chicago Blues (2 LP) .... Vanguard (S) VSD-1/2 15-20

Jimmy Cotton; Junior Wells; Otis Spann; Buddy Guy; J.B. Hutto; Big Walter Horton; Homesick James; Johnny Young.

Best of Christmas .... Capitol (S) STBB-2979 5-10 68

Bing Crosby; Jackie Gleason; Peggy Lee; Al Martino; David Rose; Nat King Cole; Nancy Wilson; Dean Martin.

Best of Christmas (2 LP) .... Capitol (S) STBB-502979 8-12 68

Bing Crosby; Jackie Gleason; Peggy Lee; Al Martino; David Rose; Nat King Cole; Nancy Wilson; Dean Martin; Hollyridge Strings; Wayne Newton; Lou Rawls; Tennessee Ernie Ford; Sandler & Young; Ella Fitzgerald; Guy Lombardo; Lettermen; Fred Waring; Marlene Dietrich; Glen Campbell; Hollywood Bowl Symphony Orchestra.

Best of Christmas .... RCA (S) CPL1-7013 5-10 85

Elvis Presley; Dolly Parton; Willie Nelson; Alabama; Earl Thomas Conley; Waylon Jennings; Ronnie Milsap; Judds.

Best of Christmas, Vol. 1 .... Capitol (S) SM-11833 5-10 78

Nat King Cole; Peggy Lee; Jackie Gleason; Sandler & Young; Glen Campbell; Al Martino; Jo Stafford; Bing Crosby; Dean Martin; Wayne Newton.

Best of Christmas, Vol. 2 .... Capitol (S) SM-11839 5-10 78

Dean Martin; others.

Best of Christmas .... Mistletoe (S) 1209 5-8 70s

Gene Autry; Harry Simeone Chorale; Liberace; Brook Benton; Bobby Helms.

Best of Christmas, Vol. 2 .... Mistletoe (S) 1221 5-8 75

Chipmunks; Robert Rheims; Ferrante & Teicher; Liberace; Lawrence Welk.

Best of Country .... MCP (S) 8009 5-10

Sonny James; Roy Acuff; Jimmy Newman; Hawshaw Hawkins; Cowboy Copas; Don Gibson; Jimmy Dean.

Best of Country (4 LP) .... Columbia (M) P4M-5061 15-20

Best of Country (4 LP) .... Columbia (S) P4S-5062 15-20

(Box set.) Marty Robbins; Carl Smith; Ray Price; Johnny Bond; Al Dexter; Johnny Cash; George Morgan; Claude King; Carl Perkins; Charlie Walker; Molly O'Day; David Houston; Marion Worth; Floyd Tillman; Stonewall Jackson; Carl & Pearl Butler; Don Gibson; Statler Brothers; Bob Atcher; Norma Jean; Carter Family; Billy Walker; Bob Wills; Bill Monroe; Gene Autry; Bob Lord; Rose Maddox, Jimmy Dean; Little Jimmy Dickens; Flatt & Scruggs; Johnny Norton; Hawkshaw Hawkins; Skeets McDonald; Chuck Wagon Gang.

Best of Country Comedy .... RCA (S) LSP-4126 10-20 68

Archie Campbell; Bob Corley; Don Bowman; Junior Samples; Dave Gardner; Homer & Jethro; Fannie Flagg; Junior Samples & Archie Campbell.

Best of Country Crossovers, Vol. 1 .... Excelsior (S) XLP-88000 5-10 79

Kenny Rogers; Anne Murray; Bobby Goldsboro; Billie Jo Spears; Glen Campbell; Jessi Colter; Crystal Gayle;; Willie Nelson; Bobbie Gentry; Joe South; Linda Ronstadt; Asleep at the Wheel.

Best of Country Music (2 LP) .... Capitol (S) SQB-91184 8-12

Buck Owens; Sonny James; Roy Clark; Jean Shepard; Hank Thompson; Ferlin Husky; Tex Ritter; Wynn Stewart; Wanda Jackson; Charlie Louvin; Rose Maddox; Tommy Collins; Leon McAuliffe; Glen Campbell; Faron Young; Bobby Durham; Mary Taylor; Ira Louvin; Merle Travis; Neal Merritt; Ray Pillow; Mac Wiseman; Walter Hensley.

Best of Country Music .... Columbia Special Products (M) CL-243 8-12 66

Best of Country Music .... Columbia Special Products (S) CSP-243 10-15 66

Jimmy Dean; Ray Price; Collins Kids; Marion Worth; Stonewall Jackson; Carl Smith; Marty Robbins; Johnny Cash; Lefty Frizzell; Bob Atcher; Little Jimmy Dickens; Carl Butler. (Made for Shurfine Quality Foods.)

Best of Country Music, Vol. 7 .... K-Tel (S) WU 325 8-12 73

Susan Raye; Roy Clark; Leroy Van Dyke; Sonny James; Ned Miller; Patsy Cline; Kitty Wells; Donna Fargo; Commander Cody; George Jones; Marvin Rainwater; Buck Owens; Hank Williams; Webb Pierce; Johnny Paycheck; Wanda Jackson; Wynn Stewart; Johnny Cash; Freddie Hart; Hank Thompson; LaWanda Lindsey.

Best of Cousins Records .... Crystal Ball (S) 121 8-12 80s

Original Camerons; Regents; Camerons; Consorts; Guy Vilari; Dreamers.

Best of Dixieland .... RCA (S) LSP-2982 5-10

Louis Armstrong; Turk Murphy; Muggsy Spanier; Bourbon Street All Star Dixielanders; Henry "Red" Allen; Bunk Johnson; Dukes of Dixieland; Bob Scobey; Pete Kelly & His Big Seven; Jimmy McPartland; Tony Almerico; Original Dixieland Jazz Band.

Best of Grand Ole Opry .... Columbia Special Products (M) CSM 1047 8-12 60s

Marty Robbins; George Morgan; Flatt & Scruggs; Marion Worth; Jimmy Dean. (Made for Shurfine Foods. Advertised in *Life* magazine.)

Best of Heart and Soul .... Musico (S) MDS-1019 10-15 70s

Jerry Butler; Platters; Inez & Charlie Foxx; Sam Cooke; Tommy Hunt.

Best of Holiday Records .... Holiday (M) H-1000 8-12 70s

Bop-Chords; Thunderbirds; Harmonaires; Love Notes; Pretenders; Ladders.

Best of Holiday Records: see Golden Groups (Best of Holiday Records)

Best of Jocko's .... Memory Disc (M) 696 10-20 60s

Shirelles; Johnny & Joe; Dubs; Smokey & Miracles; Rochell & Candles; School Boys; Harptones; Blue Jays; Carousels; Channels; Crests; Jackie & Starlites; Patti LaBelle & Blue Belles; Deltairs; Fire Flies; Dion & Belmonts; Embers; Lee Andrews & Hearts; Cupids; Chantels; Kathy Jean & Roomates; Montclairs.

Best of Joyce (Al Brown Presents) .... Crystal Ball (S) 117 8-10 84

Gaytunes; Crescents; Crests; Love Notes; Starlites; others.

Best of La Bamba .... Rhino (S) R1-70617 5-10
Ritchie Valens; Crickets; Mariachi Vargas; Big Daddy; Conjunto Medellin De Lino Chavez; Tonio K.; Rice University Marching Owl Band; Draive; Mormon Tabernacle Choir.

Best of Laurie, Vol. 1 .... Laurie (S) LES-4003 15-20 70s
Chiffons; Mystics; Dion; Royal Guardsmen; Dean & Jean; Bernadette Carroll; Music Explosion; Dion & Belmonts; Randy & Rainbows; Jarmels; Passions.

Best of Laurie, Vol. 2 .... Laurie (S) LES-???? 10-15 70s

Best of Laurie, Vol. 3 .... Laurie (S) LES-4026 10-15 79
Dion; Chiffons; Skyliners; Passions; Mystics; Five Discs; Ernie Maresca; Carlo; Belmonts; Curtis Lee.

Best of Louie Louie .... Rhino (S) RNEP-605 5-10 80s
Kingsmen; Rice University Marching Owl Band; Richard Berry; Rockin' Robin Roberts; Sonics; Sandpipers; Last; Black Flag; Les Danz; Impossibles.

Best of Mohawk .... Crystal Ball (S) 110 8-10 83
Radiants; Ricky Reynolds; Intruders; Lonnie of the Carrolons; Joey & Ovations; Del-Terriers; Belmonts; Dion & Belmonts; Marco; Companions; MelloKings; Demensions.

Best of Music & Rhythm .... PVC (S) 6902 5-10 82
Peter Gabriel; XTC; Ekome; Mighty Sparrow; Prince; Nico; Mbarga & Rocafil Jazz; David Byrne; Pete Townshend; English; Rico; Shankar & Bill Lovelady.

Best of Old Time Radio .... Columbia Musical Treasuries (M) 558 8-12
Will Rogers; Bing Crosby; Eddie Cantor; Jimmy Durante; Clayton, Jackson & Durante; Harry Hershfield; Kate Smith; W.C. Fields; Al Jolson; Burns & Allen.

Best of Original Records .... Original (M) OR-1000 10-15 81
Don Julian & Meadowlarks; Penguins; Originals; Jaguars; Sonny Knight; Viceroys; Charades; Hitmakers.

Best of Party Rock .... Columbia Special Products (S) P 17210 5-10 83
Dion; Chiffons; Maurice Williams & Zodiacs; Little Eva; Fats Domino; Gary Lewis & Playboys; Box Tops; Diana Ross & Supremes; Four Tops; Marvelettes; Lovin' Spoonful; Young Rascals; Monkees; Archies; Turtles; Everly Brothers; Shelly Fabres; Shirelles; Drifters.

Best of Quartets All Night Sing, Vol. 2 .... RCA Camden (M) CAL-832 8-12 64
Harmoneers Quartet; Weatherford Quartet; Blackwood Brothers; Stamps-Baxter Quartet; Statesmen Quartet.

Best of Ralph (2 LP) .... Ralph (S) Rockin' Records 8251 15-20 82
Residents; Fred Frith; Tuxedo Moon; Yello; Art Bears; Renaldo & Loaf; others.

Best of Rhythm and Blues .... Jubilee (M) 1014 100-200 55
(Black vinyl.) Four Tunes; Orioles; Ravens; Dominoes.

Best of Rhythm and Blues .... Jubilee (M) 1014 300-400 55
(Red vinyl.) Four Tunes; Orioles; Ravens; Dominoes.

Best of Rhythm and Blues .... Warwick (M) W-2026 30-50 60

Best of Rhythm and Blues .... Warwick (S) W-2026ST 50-75 60
Shirley & Lee; Roy Milton; Faye Adams; Bullmoose Jackson; Little Esther; Ann Cole.

Best of RSO .... RSO (S) RPRO 1006 8-12 78
Eric Clapton; Bee Gees; Frankie Valli; Andy Gibb; Yvonne Elliman; John Travolta & Olivia Newton-John; Robin Gibb; Player.

Best of the 1950s Rock & Roll Revival (3 LP) .... Candelite (M) 8818-8820 10-20
Belmonts; Jerry Lee Lewis; Rocky Barra & Barratones; Bruce Channell; Quin-Tones; Del-Vikings; Shells; Four Coins; Jimmy Clanton; Platters; Jerry Lee Lewis; Twilights; Paul & Paula; Possessions; Dickey Lee; Guitar Champs; Superiors; Diamonds; Johnny Preston; Fabulous Cruisers; Starglows; Passions; Clyde McPhatter; Little Richard; Blenders; Gino & Gina; Dinah Washington; Barratones with Rocky Barra;Crew-Cuts; Schoolboys; Chiffons; Frankie Valley & Travelers; Joe Dowell; Sarah Vaughan; Diamonds; Kitty White; Twilights; Jerry Butler; Red Prysock; Crimson Townes; Rebels; Dion & Belmonts; Clyde McPhatter; Gadabouts; Carollons; Conway Twitty; Fats Domino; Shells; Voxpoppers; A Street Choir.

Best of the '50s .... RCA (M) LPM-3934 10-15 68

Best of the '50s .... RCA (SE) LSP-3934 10-15 68
Ames Brothers; Perez Prado; Eartha Kitt; Kay Starr; Mario Lanza; Jaye P. Morgan; Sammy Kaye; Hugo Winterhalter; Tony Martin; Jine Valli; Vaughn Monroe.

Best of the '50s .... RCA (SE) AEL1-5800 8-12 86
Elvis Presley; Jim Reeves; Eddy Arnold; Hank Snow; Don Gibson; Porter Wagoner; Browns; Pee Wee King; Hank Locklin.

Best of the '60s .... RCA (S) AEL1-5802 8-12 86
Elvis Presley; Jim Reeves; Eddy Arnold; Hank Snow; Jim Ed Brown; Hank Locklin; Charley Pride; Skeeter Davis; Barry Sadler; George Hamilton IV.

Best of the '70s .... RCA (S) AEL1-5837 8-12 86
Elvis Presley; John Denver; Dolly Parton; Ronnie Milsap; Waylon & Willie; Jerry Reed; Waylon Jennings; Charley Pride; Gary Stewart; Dave & Sugar.

Best of the '50s, '60s and '70s .... RCA (S) AEL1-5838 8-12 86
Elvis Presley; Eddy Arnold; Hank Snow; Don Gibson; Dolly Parton; Ronnie Milsap; Charley Pride; Jerry Reed; Skeeter Davis.

Best of the All Time Heavyweight Tournament (2 LP) .... ???? (M) ???? 20-30 66
John L; Jack Dempsey; Cassius Clay; Rocky Marciano; others.

Best of the Best .... Capitol (M) T-1654 15-25 62

Best of the Best .... Capitol (S) ST-1654 20-30 62
Wanda Jackson; Hank Thompson; Faron Young; others.

Best of the Best .... Relativity (S) 88561-1034-1 10-20 89
(Soundtrack.) Paul Gilman; Jim Capaldi; Charlie Major; Stubblefield & Hall; Kirsten Nash; Golden Earring.

Best of the Best of . . . . RCA (M) LPM-3632 15-20 66

Best of the Best of . . . . RCA (S) LSP-3632 15-25 66
Al Hirt; Eddy Arnold; Sam Cooke; Neil Sedaka; Paul Anka; Henry Mancini; Jim Reeves; Lorne Greene; Floyd Cramer; Chet Atkins; Harry Belafonte; Perry Como.

Best of the Big Band Singers .... Columbia Musical Treasuries (M) D 295 10-15 68
Harry James; Helen Forrest; Dick Haymes; Frank Sinatra; Les Brown; Doris Day; Claude Thornhill; Fran Warren; Tony Pastor; Orrin Tucker; Wee Bonnie Baker; Benny Goodman; Peggy Lee; Kay Kyser; Harry Babbitt; Gloria Wood; Joe Bushkin; Bobby Hackett; Lee Willey; Skinnay Ennis; Hal Kemp; Glen Gray; Kenneth Sargent; Guy Lombardo; Bing Crosby.

Best of the Big Band Singers .... Columbia Musical Treasuries (M) D 405 10-15 68
Dick Haymes; Harry James; Doris Day; Les Brown; Frank Sinatra; Kitty Kallen; Fran Warren; Claude Thornhill; Saxie Dowell; Hal Kemp; Wee Bonnie Baker; Orrin Tucker; Peggy Lee; Benny Goodman; Sully Mason; Playmates; Kay Kyser; Lee Wiley & Bobby Hackett; Joe Bushkin & Swinging Strings; Skinnay Ennis; Hal Kemp; Ginny, Harry, Jack & Max; Kenny Sargent; Glen Gray; Roy Eldridge & Anita O'Day; Gene Krupa.

Best of the Big Band Singers, Vol. 1 .... Tulip (M) TLP 106 5-10
Connie Haines & Tommy Dorsey; Kathleen Lane & Bunny Berigan; Helen Forrest & Artie Shaw; Ivie Anderson & Duke Ellington; Peggy Lee & Benny Goodman; Helen Hand & Teddy Wilson; June Hutton & Artie Shaw Grammercy Five; Kitty Kallen & Harry; Kay Starr & Charlie Barnet.
Best of the Big Band Vocalists, Vol. 1 .... Columbia (S) P 16780 8-12
Best of the Big Band Vocalists, Vol. 2 .... Columbia (S) P 16781 8-12
Best of the Big Band Vocalists, Vol. 3 .... Columbia (S) P 16782 8-12
Best of the Big Bands (2 LP) .... Columbia Musical Treasuries (M) P2M 5193 10-15 70s
Best of the Big Bands (2 LP) .... Columbia Musical Treasuries (M) D403/D404 10-15 68
Benny Goodman; Harry James; Les Brown; Gene Krupa; Anita O'Day; Tommy Dorsey; Jimmy Dorsey; Woody Herman; Duke Ellington; Sammy Kaye; Modernaires; Charlie Spivak; Will Bradley with Ray McKinley; Artie Shaw; Raymond Scott; Eddie Duckin; Henry Busse; Lionel Hampton; Charlie Barnet; Tony Pastor; Orrin Tucker & Wee Bonnie Baker; Count Basie; Frankie Carle; Glenn Miller; Claude Thornhill; Clyde McCoy; Russ Morgan & Mullin Sisters.
Best of the Big Bands from the Vaults of Decca Records .... MCA (M) 27094 5-10 80
Charlie Barnet; Count Basie; Woody Herman; Lionel Hampton; Glen Gray; Les Brown with Joann Greer; Jimmy Dorsey with Bob Eberle & Helen O'Connell; Artie Shaw; Chick Webb with Ella Fitzgerald; Glenn Miller; Tommy Dorsey.
Best of the Big Name Bands .... RCA Camden (M) CAL 368 8-12
Best of the Biggest .... Custom (M) CM 2056 10-20
Ray Charles; B.B. King; John Lee Hooker; Bobby Bland; Elmore James; Howling Wolf.
Best of the Biggest .... United (S) US-7718 10-20 70s
Best of the Blues .... Day Dream (S) 1012 8-12
B.B. King; Bobby Bland; Joe Hinton; Junior Parker; O.V. Wright; Jimmy McCracklin; Otis Rush; Johnny Ace; Big Walter.
Best of the Blues, Vol. 1: see McCRACKLIN, Jimmy / T-Bone Walker / Charles Brown
Best of the Blues, Vol. 2 .... Imperial (M) LP-9259 20-30 64
Lightnin' Hopkins; Amos Milburn; Katie May; Floyd Dixon; Peppermint Harris; Fats Domino.
Best of the British Invasion .... Pye (S) 506 5-10 75
Lonnie Donegan; Searchers; Honeycombs; Rockin' Berries; Sandie Shaw; Kinks; Ivy League; Foundations; Long John Baldry; Status Quo.
Best of the Bunch - WGRD FM, Grand Rapids .... Phoenix (S) P-791 5-10 79
KC & Sunshine Band; Van McCoy; Walter Murphy; Grank Funk; Creedence Clearwater Revival; Three Dog Night; Samantha Sang; Dorothy Moore; Austin Roberts; Bread; Climax; Rod Stewart.
Best of the California Central Coast .... Ocean (S) 8703 8-10 90
Merrell Fankhauser; John Bankston; Living Water; Allen Freeman; Michelle Marie; Tim Fankhauser; Shock Value; Gordon Scott; Chris Leitz; T.W. Rush; Impacts.
Best of the Chicago Blues (2 LP) .... Vanguard (S) VSD 1-2 10-20 70
Jimmy Cotton; Junior Wells; Otis Spann; Buddy Guy; J.B. Hutto; Big Walter Horton; Homesick James; Johnny Young.
Best of the Easy Sounds - in a Mellow Mood .... Capitol (S) 6602 5-10
Best of the Girl Groups .... Pricewise (M) 4004 15-25
Shangri-Las; Shirelles; Orlons; Angels; Blue Belles; Goldie & Gingerbreads.
Best of the Gold '50s, Vol. 1 .... Columbia (S) C-32389 5-10 73
Rosemary Clooney; Johnnie Ray; Frankie Laine; Four Lads; others.
Best of the Gold '50s, Vol. 2 .... Columbia (S) C-32390 5-10 73
Rosemary Clooney; Johnnie Ray; Frankie Laine; Four Lads; Marty Robbins; Guy Mitchell; Tony Bennett; Terry Gilkyson & Easy Riders; Don Cherry.
Best of the Gold '50s, Vol. 3 .... Columbia (S) C-32391 5-10 73
Best of the Gold '50s, Vol. 4 .... Columbia (S) C-32392 5-10 73
Best of the Gold '50s, Vol. 5 .... Columbia (SE) P 13800 5-10 73
Rosemary Clooney; Frankie Laine & Jimmy Boyd; Guy Mitchell; Tony Bennett; Johnnie Ray; Kirby Stone Four; Jimmy Carroll; Four Lads; Johnny Cash; Les Compagons de la Chanson; Louis Armstrong.
Best of the Gold '50s, Vol. 5 .... Columbia (S) C-32393 5-10 73
Best of the Gold '60s, Vol. 6 .... Columbia (S) C-32394 5-10 73
Paul Revere & Raiders; Dion; Gary Puckett & Union Gap; Percy Faith; Claude King; Marty Robbins; Jimmy Dean; Bill Pursell; Patti Page; Johnny Horton.
Best of the Gold '60s, Vol. 7 .... Columbia (S) C-32395 5-10 73
Best of the Gold '60s, Vol. 8 .... Columbia (S) C-32396 5-10 73
Blood, Sweat & Tears; Buckinghams; Jimmy Dean; Paul Revere & Raiders; Buzz Clifford; Gary Puckett & Union Gap; Billy Joe Royal; O.C. Smith; Cyrkle; Statler Brothers.
Best of the Gold '60s, Vol. 9 .... Columbia (S) C-32397 5-10 73
Byrds; Buckinghams; Gary Puckett & Union Gap; Paul Revere & Raiders; Brothers Four; Dion DiMucci; Cyrkle; Patti Page; Billy Joe Royal; Sprial Staircase.
Best of the Gold '60s, Vol. 10 .... Columbia (S) C-32398 5-10 73
New Christy Minstrels; Gary Puckett; Robert Goulet; Brothers Four; O.C. Smith.
Best of the Goodies (Bobby Vann) .... Vann (S) LP 101 15-25 60's
Johnny Adams; Teen Queens; Jerry McClain; Robert & Johnny; Earl Connelly King; Little Walter; Big Walter; James "Sugarboy" Crawford; Ernie K-Doe; Students; Clarence "Frogman" Henry.
Best of the Great Continental Favorites .... Capitol (S) SL 6740 8-12
Best of the Great Song Stylists .... Capitol (S) SL 6603 8-12
Dean Martin; others.
Best of the Great Songs with a Folk Accent: see Zenith Presents the Best of the Great Songs with a Folk Accent
Best of the Great Songs with a Folk-Country Accent, Vol. 3 .... Capitol Creative Prod. (S) SL 6599 8-12
Glen Campbell; Ella Fitzgerald; Kingston Trio; Peggy Lee; Al Martino; Rod McKuen; Andy Russell; Seekers; Jo Stafford; Kay Starr.
Best of the Greatest Songs of Christmas .... Columbia (S) CSS 1478 5-10
Petula Clark; Tony Bennett; Percy Faith; Andy Williams; Doris Day; Steve Lawrence; Ray Conniff; John Davidson; New York Philharmonic; Anna Moffo; Richard Tucker; Mahalia Jackson; Isaac Stern; Barbra Streisand. (Made for Goodyear.)
Best of the Groups .... Scepter/Citation (S) CTN-18007 8-12 72
Best of the Hideouts .... Hideout (M) HLP-1002 150-250 66
Underdogs; Four of Us; Pleasure Seekers; Yorkshires; Henchmen; Doug Brown.

Best of the Hit Parade (2 LP) .... Columbia House (SE) P2S 5652 8-12 73
Patti Page; Dinah Shore; Kate Smith; Frankie Laine; Kay Kyser; Les Brown; Sammy Kaye; Ken Griffin; Harry James; Buddy Clark; Xavier Cugat; Tony Bennett; Burl Ives; Duke Ellington; Horace Heidt; Frankie Carle; Arthur Godfrey; Anton Karas. (Record club issue.)

Best of the Hit Parade, the Early Years (2 LP) .... Columbia House (SE) P2S 5654 8-12 73
Fred Astaire with Johnny Green; Benny Goodman (vocal by Peggy Lee); Buddy Clark; Dorothy Shay; Les Brown (vocal by Doris Day); Kay Kyser; Dinah Shore; Kate Smith; Harry James (vocal by Helen Forrest); Gracie Fields; Gene Autry; Dick Powell; Frankie Carle; Gene Krupa; Billie Holiday; Dorothy Lamour with Cy Feller; Orrin Tucker; Marilyn Raye with David Rose Orchestra; Mildred Bailey; Hal Kemp. (Record club issue.)

Best of the Lot .... Circlon (SE) 40003 8-10
Gladys Knight & Pips; Intruders; Bill Deal; Brooklyn Bridge; Casinos; Delfonics; Brenda & Tabulations; Unifics; Moments; Foundations; Temptations; Madaline Bell; Jerry Butler; Joe Simon; Impressions; Dells.

Best of the Movie Greats .... Metro (S) MS-600 10-15
John Barry; Metropolitan Pops Orchestra; Alfred Newman & MGM Studio Orchestra; Ornadel & Starlight Symphony; Symphony of Rome; David Rose; Joe Cain; Lennie Hayton & MGM Studio Orchestra.

Best of the Oldies But Goodies .... Crown (M) CLP-5144 10-20 60s
Cadets; Teen Queens; Marvin & Johnny; Etta James; B.B. King; Joe Houston; Jesse Belvin; Queens; Young Jessie; Roscoe Gordon.

Best of the R&B Groups .... Warwick (M) W-2025 35-55 60
Harptones; Genies; Willows; Nutmegs; Fidelitys; Eternals.

Best of the UGHA Groups .... Crystal Ball (S) 113 8-10 83
Computones; Valentinos; Yesterday's News; Patty & Street-Tones; Reality; Endings; Emerys; Uniques; Street Corner Memories.

Best of Today .... Columbia (S) CSS 1342 10-20 68
Blood, Sweat & Tears; Sly & Family Stone; Chicago; Chambers Brothers; Spiral Staircase; Aretha Franklin; Hollies; Union Gap; Moby Grape; Donovan. (Special product for Magnavox.)

Best of Today's Country Hits (2 LP) .... RCA (S) UPS-6017 8-12
Jim Reeves; Porter Wagoner; Dolly Parton; Don Gibson; Lynn Anderson; John Hartford; Chet Atkins; Skeeter Davis; Hank Snow; Jim Ed Brown; George Hamilton IV; Jerry Reed; Charley Pride; Connie Smith; Bobby Bare; Norma Jean; Jimmy Dean; Floyd Cramer; Dottie West; Waylon Jennings; Hank Locklin; Liz Anderson; Leon Ashley.

Best of Twist-A-Rama, U.S.A. .... Tar (M) 1000 10-15

Best of Vee Jay Jazz .... Vee Jay (S) ???? 8-10 74
(Promotional issue for 1974 National Record Convention.)

Best Plucking in Town: see KESSEL, Barney / Grant Green / Oscar Moore / Mundell Lowe

Best Twenty Original Oldies .... Almor (M) A-101 15-25 64

Best Twenty Original Oldies .... Almor (S) AS-101 15-25 64
Hollywood Argyles; Angels; Harptones; Dave "Baby" Cortez; Collegians; String-Alongs; Penguins; Dubs; Buchanan & Goodman; Janie Grant; Matt Monro; Bob Crewe; Eternals; Meadowlarks; Rocketones; Spaniels; Gene & Eunice; Videls; Shirley & Lee.

Best Vocal Groups - Rhythm and Blues: see PENGUINS / Meadowlarks / Medallions / Dootones

Best Vocal Groups in Rock 'N' Roll .... Dooto (M) DL-224 50-100 57
(Yellow label.) Meadowlarks; Romancers; Penguins; Medallions; Calvanes; Cuff Links; Souvenirs; Birds; Pipes.

Best Vocal Groups in Rock 'N' Roll .... Dooto (M) DL-224 25-50
(Maroon label.) Meadowlarks; Romancers; Penguins; Medallions; Calvanes; Cuff Links; Souvenirs; Birds; Pipes.

Best Vocal Groups in Rock 'N' Roll .... Dooto (M) DL-224 20-30
(Multi-color label.) Meadowlarks; Romancers; Penguins; Medallions; Calvanes; Cuff Links; Souvenirs; Birds; Pipes.

Best Vocal Groups in Rock and Roll .... Authentic (M) AUL-224 10-15
Meadow Larks; Pipes; Romancers; Penguins; Medallions; Calvanes; Cuff Links; Souvenirs; Birds.

Best of Whirlin' Disc Records: see Golden Groups (Best of Whirlin' Disc Records)

Bethlehem's Best (3 LP) .... Bethlehem (M) EXLP 6 30-50 56
Chris Connor; Sy Oliver; Conte Candoli; Joe Derise; Charlie Mariano; Frances Jaye; Chico Hamilton; Mel Torme; Kai Winding & J.J. Johnson; Russ Garcia; Bobby Scott; Australian Jazz Quartet; Julie London; Charlie Shavers; Herbie Mann; Stu Williamson; Red Mitchell; Johnny Hartman; Frances Faye; Oscar Pettiford; Howard McGhee; Milt Hinton; Hal McKusick; Max Bennett; Ruby Braff; Bobby Troup; Herbie Harbor; others. (Also issued as EXLP 3.)

Bethlehem's Grab Bag .... Bethlehem (M) EXLP 2 20-30
Mel Torme & Frances Faye; Carmen McRae; Australian Jazz Quintet; Pat Moran Quartet; Betty Roche; Sam Most's Quartet; Duke Ellington's Quartet; Betty Roche; Sam Most's Quartet; Duke Ellington; Claude Williamson's Trio; San Salvador's Quartet; Herbie Mann's Quartet; Frank Rosolino's Quartet.

Beverly Hills Cop .... MCA (S) MCS-5547 8-10 84

Contains *BHC (I Can't Stop)* by Rick James.Beverly Hills Cop .... MCA (S) MCS-5553 8-10 84
(Soundtrack. *Emergency* by Rockie Robbins replaces the Rick James track.) Patti LaBelle; Shalamar; Junior; Rick James; Pointer Sisters; Glenn Frey; Danny Elfman; System; Harold Faltermeyer.

Beverly Hills Cop II .... MCA (S) MCS-6207 8-10 87
(Soundtrack.) Bob Seger; Charlie Sexton; Corey Hart; Jets; Pointer Sisters; Sue Ann; Jermaine Jackson; James Ingram; George Michael; Pebbles; Ready for the World.

Beyond the Calico Wall .... Voxx (SP) VXS 200,051 5-10 90
Park Avenue Playground; Hoooterville Trolley; Afterglow; Flower Power; Pulse; Alvasnelling; Rasputin & Mad Monks; Spontanneous Generation; Cosmic Rockshow; Greek Fountains; Duffy; Pebble Episode; Bohemian Vendetta; Demons of Negativity.

Beyond the Valley of the Dolls .... 20th Century-Fox (S) TFS-4211 100-150 70
(Soundtrack.) Sandpipers; Strawberry Alarm Clock; Carrie Nations; others.

Beyond the Wildwood (Tribute to Syd Barrett) .... Communion COMM-14 5-10 87
Mock Turtles; Plasticland; SS-20; Paul Roland; Fit & Limo; Shamen; Opal; Ashes in the Morning; Lobster Quadrile; Paint Set; Tropicana Fishtank; TV Personalities; Soup Dragons; Green Telescope;

Big Bad Boss Beat .... Original Sound (M) LPM-5008 15-25 64

Big Bad Boss Beat .... Original Sound (SE) LPS-8871 15-25 64
Champs; Dee Dee Sharp; B. Bumble & Stingers; Sandy Nelson; Gary "U.S." Bonds; Preston Epps; Bill Doggett; Ernie Fields; Revels.

Big Band Christmas .... Columbia (S) PC 40948 5-10 88
Les Brown with Doris Day; Russ Morgan; Red Norvo with Mildred Bailey; Artie Shaw with Peg La Centra; Harry James with Marion Morgan; Benny Goodman with Peggy Lee & Art Lund; Frankie Carle with Marjorie Hughes; Lester Lanin; Sammy Kaye & Kaydettes; Tex Beneke; Ray Noble with Cathy & Elliot Lewis.

Big Band Christmas (2 LP) .... Bigbandarch (S) LP 2203 8-12

Big Band Era - Vol. 2 .... Mac (S) LSP-4602 5-10 78
(Rerecordings.) Louis Armstrong; Tommy Dorsey; Johnny Desmond; Glenn Miller; Harry James; Benny Goodman; Ink Spots; Les Brown; Mel Torme; Norman Brooks; Judy Garland; New Orleans Jazz Band; Artie Shaw.

Big Band Scene (2 LP) .... Bigbandarch (S) LP 2204 8-12

Big Band Sound (2 LP) .... Pickwick (SE) DL2-0619 8-12 74
Artie Shaw; Duke Ellington; Bunny Berigan; Count Basie with Jimmy Rushing; Charlie Barnet; Guy Lombardo; Sammy Kaye with Tony Alamo; Wayne King; Les Brown with Miriam Shaw; Hal Kemp with Bob Allen; Blue Barron Orchestra with Charles Fisher; Hal Kemp with Skinny Ennis; Frank MacCormack.

Big Bands (3 LP) .... Mac Millan Co. (M) 48987 10-20 70s
(Boxed set. Sold with book, *The Big Bands* by George T. Simon. Includes albums; Columbia CSM 661; RCA PRM 261; Decca DL 34503.) Al Hibbler; Harry James with Helen Forrest; Duke Ellington with Al Hibbler; Les Brown with Doris Day; Will Bradley with Ray McKinley; Kay Kyser with Harry Babbitt & Trudy Erwin; Woody Herman; Hal Kemp with Skinnay Ennis; Red Norvo with Mildred Bailey; Claude Thornhill; Jack Teagarden; Horace Heidt with Donna & Her Don Juans; Gene Krupa with Roy Eldridge & Anita O'Day; Bob Crosby; Chick Webb with Ella Fitzgerald; Glen Gray with Kenny Sargent; Jan Savitt with Bon Bon; Guy Lombardo; Carmen Lombardo; Count Basie; Jimmy Dorsey with Bob Eberle & Helen O'Connell; Ted Weems; Jimmy Lunceford Trio; Johnny Long with the Glee Club; Stan Kenton; Lionel Hampton; Artie Shaw; Tommy Dorsey with Frank Sinatra & Pied Pipers; Freddy Martin; Larry Clinton with Bea Wain; Vaughn Monroe; Benny Goodman; Martha Tilton; Bunny Berigan; Glenn Miller with Tex Beneke; Ray Noble with Al Bowly; Shep Fields; Sammy Kaye with Don Cornell; Charlie Barnet.

Big Bands .... Columbia (M) CSM-661 5-10 70s
(One of three albums issued in *Big Bands* 3 LP and book set.) Al Hibbler; Harry James with Helen Forrest; Duke Ellington with Al Hibbler; Les Brown with Doris Day; Will Bradley with Ray McKinley; Kay Kyser with Harry Babbitt & Trudy Erwin; Woody Herman; Hal Kemp with Skinnay Ennis; Red Norvo with Mildred Bailey; Claude Thornhill; Jack Teagarden; Horace Heidt with Donna & Her Don Juans; Gene Krupa with Roy Eldridge & Anita O'Day.

Big Bands .... Decca (M) DL 34503 5-10 70s
(One of three albums issued in *Big Bands* 3 LP and book set.) Bob Crosby; Chick Webb with Ella Fitzgerald; Glen Gray with Kenny Sargent; Jan Savitt with Bon Bon; Guy Lombardo; Carmen Lombardo; Count Basie; Jimmy Dorsey with Bob Eberle & Helen O'Connell; Ted Weems; Jimmy Lunceford Trio; Johnny Long with the Glee Club; Stan Kenton; Lionel Hampton.

Big Bands .... RCA (M) PRM 261 5-10 70s
(One of three albums issued in *Big Bands* 3 LP and book set.) Artie Shaw; Tommy Dorsey with Frank Sinatra & Pied Pipers; Freddy Martin; Larry Clinton with Bea Wain; Vaughn Monroe; Benny Goodman; Martha Tilton; Bunny Berigan; Glenn Miller with Tex Beneke; Ray Noble with Al Bowly; Shep Fields; Sammy Kaye with Don Cornell; Charlie Barnet.

Big Bands Greatest Hits (2 LP) .... Columbia (SE) CG 30009 8-12 72
Glenn Miller; Frankie Carle; Clyde McCoy; Modernaires; Les Brown; Claude Thornhill; Harry James; Russ Morgan; Count Basie; Lawrence Welk; Ray Noble; Woody Herman; Benny Goodman; Orrin Tucker; Bunny Berigan; Duke Ellington; Eddie Duchin.

Big Bands Greatest Hits, Vol. 2 (2 LP) .... Columbia (S) G 31213 8-12 72
Lionel Hampton; Charlie Spivak; Les Brown; Duke Ellington; Claude Thornhill; Freddy Martin; Ray Noble; Kay Kyser; Harry James; Sammy Kaye; Glen Gray; Woody Herman; Guy Lombardo; Tony Pastor; Will Bradley; Henry Busse; Fran Warren; Elmer Feldkamp; Snooky Lanson; Harry Babbit & Gloria Wood; Harry James; Helen Forrest; Tony Russo; Kenneth Sargent; Bing Crosby; Ray McKinley; Freddie Slack.

Big Band Sound .... Columbia Special Products (S) CSP 296 8-12

Big Band Sound (2 LP) .... RCA/Camden (SE) CCL 2-0619 8-12 74
Artie Shaw; Bunny Berigan; Charlie Barnet; Guy Lombardo; Sammy Kaye; Hal Kemp; Wayne King; Larry Clinton; Count Basie; Les Brown; Blue Barron; Duke Ellington.

Big Band Stereo .... Capitol (S) SW 1055 8-12

Big Bands Greatest Vocalists .... Joyce (M) 6047 8-12

Big Bands Greatest Hits, Vol. 2 (2 LP) .... Columbia (SE) G 31213 8-12 72
Harry James; Woody Herman; Glen Gray; Henry Busse; Freddy Martin; Ray Noble; Guy Lombardo; Sammy Kaye; Claude Thornhill; Duke Ellington; Kay Kyser; Lionel Hampton; Les Brown; Charlie Spivak; Tony Pastor; Will Bradley.

Big Bands Revisited (7 LP) .... Columbia Musical Treasury (S) P7S 5122 20-30
Kay Kyser; Sammy Kaye; Freddy Martin; Eddy Howard; Frankie Masters; GlenGray; Lionel Hamilton; Ray Noble; Tommy Tucker; Abe Lyman; Henry Busse; Count Basie; Gene Krupa; Charlie Barnet; Duke Ellington; Glenn Miller; Benny Goodman; Harry James; Woody Herman; Artie Shaw; Charlie Spivak; Hal McIntyre; Les Brown; others.

Big Bands Theme Songs .... Pickwick (M) SPC 3235 5-10
Benny Goodman; Ray Anthony; Guy Lombardo; Les Brown; Glen Gray; Clyde McCoy; Harry James; Freddy Martin; Duke Ellington; Kay Kyser.

Big Chill .... Motown (S) 6062 8-10 83
(Soundtrack.) Marvin Gaye; Three Dog Night; Rascals; Smokey Robinson & Miracles; Procol Harum; Exciters; Aretha Franklin; Temptations.

Big Chill (More Songs from the Original Soundtrack) .... Motown (S) 6094ML 8-10 84
(Soundtrack.) Creedence Clearwater Revival; Beach Boys; Four Tops; Percy Sledge; Martha Reeves & Vandellas; Marvin Gaye; Rascals; Steve Miller; Spencer Davis Group; Marvelettes; Band.

Big Country (13 LP) .... No Label Used (S) SH-3307 40-60
(Box set.) Glen Campbell; Bobbie Gentry; Sonny James; Merle Haggard & Bonnie Owens; Jean Shepard; Tennessee Ernie Ford; Buck Owens; Wanda Jackson; Hank Thompson; Tex Ritter; Roger Miller; Carlisles; George Jones; Johnny Horton; Benny Barnes; Rusty Draper; Roy Drusky; Leroy Van Dyke; Jimmie Skinner; Faron Young Merle Kilgore; Flatt & Scruggs; Country Road; Patsy Cline; Ferlin Husky; Dave Dudley; Stuart Hamblen; T. Texas Tyler; Slim Willet; Jimmy Dean; Carl Belew; Texas Jim Robertson; Floyd Tillman; Jan Howard; Hank Locklin.

Big Country (2 LP) .... Mercury (S) SRP-2-605 10-20 60s
Roger Miller; Roy Drusky; Pete Drake; Anita Carter; Faron Young; Rex Allen; Dave Dudley; Margie Singleton; George Jones; Mother Maybelle Carter; James O'Gwynn; Claude Gray; Pricella Mitchell; Leroy Van Dyke; Johnny Sea; Flatt & Scruggs; Jimmie Skinner; Tom T. Hall.

Big Country Hits, Vol. 1 .... RCA (M) LPM-3603 10-15 66

Big Country Hits, Vol. 1 .... RCA (S) LSP-3603 15-20 66
Jim Reeves; Don Gibson; Norma Jean; Connie Smith; Bobby Bare; Hank Snow; Chet Atkins; Dottie West; Waylon Jennings; Bobby Bare & Skeeter Davis; Porter Wagoner; Bobbi Staff.

Big Country Hits .... Pickwick (S) JS-6166 10-20 75
Elvis Presley; others.

Big Easy .... Antilles (S) AN-7087 8-12 87
(Soundtrack.) Dixie Cups; Professor Longhair; Buckwheat Zydeco; Zachary Richard; Aaron Neville & Neville Brothers; Beausoleil; Terrance Simien & Mallet Playboys; Wild Tchoupitoulas; Dennis Quaid; Swan Silvertones.

Big Hit Country Songs .... Alshire (S) 5169 5-10 70

Big Hits .... Columbia (EP) B-13152 10-15 59

Big Hits .... Columbia (EP) B-13531 10-15 59
Johnny Horton; Lefty Frizzell; Carl Perkins; Johnny Cash.

Big Hits .... Columbia (M) CL-1353 20-30 59

Big Hits .... Columbia (S) CS-8161 30-40 59

Johnny Horton; Lefty Frizzell; Carl Perkins; Johnny Cash; Ray Price; Charlie Walker; Stonewall Jackson; George Morgan; Carl Smith; Freddie Hart.

Big Hits .... Columbia (EP) B-2108 10-15 56
Big Hits .... Columbia (M) CL-2574 25-35 56
Big Hits from England and U.S.A. .... Capitol (M) T-2125 30-45 64
Big Hits from England and U.S.A. .... Captiol (SE) DT-2125 25-35 64
Beatles; Beach Boys; Nat King Cole; Al Martino; Peter & Gordon; Cilla Black.
Big Hits of 1959 .... London (M) LL-3200 20-25 61
Tommy Steele; Vera Lynn; Barry Sisters; others.
Big Hits of 1960 .... London (M) LL-3201 20-25 61
Anthony Newley; Ted Heath; Bob Cort; Wee Willie Harris; Alex Murray; Lyn Cornell; Rhet Stoller; Mark Wynter; Lindys; Sally Kelly; Jess Conrad.
Big Hits of Mid-America, Vol. 3 (2 LP) .... Twin-Tone (S) TTR-7907/7908 15-25
Pistons; Swingers; Commandos; Buzz Barker & Atomic Bums; Hypstrz; Jets; Suburds; NNB; Fingerprints; Curtis & Originals; Yipes; Robert Ivers & Ice Stars; Wad; Swan Lake 6; Suburbs; NNB; Pistons; Robert Ivers & Ice Stars; Jets; Finger Prints; Curtis A & Originals; Yipes.
Big Hits of Mid-America, Vol. 1 .... Soma (M) MG-1245 50-75 65
Underbeats; Accents; Gregory Dee & Avanties; others.
Big Hits of Mid-America, Vol. 2 .... Soma (M) MG-1246 50-75 65
Castaways; Chancellors; Gestures; High Spirits; others.
Big Hits of Mid-America, Vol. 1 .... Garrett 201 15-25 64
Big Hits of the '70s .... Project 3 (S) PRO-6027/6028 SD 5-10 77
(Promotional issue only.) Enoch Light; others.
Big Hits Now .... Dunhill (S) DS-50085 15-20 70
Three Dog Night; Eddie Holman; Grass Roots; B.B. King; Mama Cass; Tommy Roe; Steppenwolf; Smith; Tyrone Davis.
Big Hootenanny .... In (M) 1001 10-20 64
Shenandoah Trio; Rod McKuen; Barbara Dane; others.
Big Hot Rod Hits .... Capitol (M) T-2024 25-30 63
Big Hot Rod Hits .... Capitol (S) ST-2024 25-35 63
Dick Dale; Beach Boys; Super Stocks; Cheers; Jimmy Dolan; Hot Rod Rog.
Big Itch .... Mr. Manicotti (SP) MM 328 5-10 80s
Bobby Lee Trammell; Trashmen; Chord-R-Notes; Lindy Blaskey & Lavells; Dinks; Elite; Del Tinos; Gregory Dee & Avanties; Torques; Freddie & Ravens; Deacons; Arch Hall Jr.; Four Dimensions; Society; Larry & Loafers; Glenn Mooney & Ferraris; Andy & Classics; Trez Trezo; King Usniewicz & Uszniewictones.
Big Itch, Vol. 2 .... Mr. Manicotti (SP) MMLP 340 5-10 90s
Joe E. Ross; Rock-Fellers; Bob Lee; Johnny Litrell; Jimmy Knight; Vladimir & Grave Diggers; Mike Fern; Metropolitans; Tommy Hancocck; Tremolons; Brotther Zee & Red Tos; Slough Boys; Tony & Runaways; Bill Jamaes & Hex-o-tones; Archie Pier & Rhyhm Aires; Ron Robbins.
Big Itch, Vol. 3 .... Mr. Manicotti (SP) MM 341 5-10 90s
Rock Roll; Glenn & Christy; Gary Shelton; Warlocks; Tommy Bee & Juarez Tones; Three D's; Joe & Furies; Wayne Sherwood; Tirads; Jerry Coulston; McHale's Navy Cast; Rex Johnson; Billy & Mickey; Mad Mike & Maniacs; Fantstic Emanons; Dinks; Terry Teene; Vancie Flowers; Crew; T. Valentine..
Big John .... RCA Special Products (S) DPL1-0089 5-10 74
Eddie Bruce; Danny Davis; Eddy Arnold; Marilyn Maye; Kenny Price; Ragtimers; Don Gibson; Dottie West; Floyd Cramer; Dickey Lee. (Made for John Deere Snowmobile.)
Big Red Music .... Columbia (S) AS-536 10-15 78
(Colored vinyl. Promotional issue only.) Dane Donohue; Eddie Money; Jules & Polar Bears; Phoebe Snow; Flint; Boomtown Rats; Jan Punk Band; Valerie Carter; David Holster; Bliss Band.
Big Seven Stars Songs .... Bert Tanzer Productions (M) 1013 8-12
Mel Torme; Lena Horne; Gordon MacRae; Sarah Vaughan; Frankie Laine; Georgia Gibbs; Andre Previn; Bert Tenzer (narrator).
Big Sixteen Country and Western Favorites .... Musicor (M) MM-2076 10-20 66
Big Sixteen Country and Western Favorites .... Musicor (S) MS-3076 15-20 66
George Jones; Roger Miller; Melba Montgomery; Gene Pitney; others.
Big Sixteen Golden Oldies .... Scepter (M) 519 20-30 63
Shirelles; Eternals; Maxine Brown; Willows; Harptones; Del-Vikings; Three Friends; James McArthur; Shirley & Lee; Hearts; Angels; Monarchs; Faye Adams.
Big Sound Stars Intl. Inc. Presents Radio Temperature (Readings 100-109) .... Big Sound (M) BS 17 8-12
Dean Martin; others.
Big Sounds of the Drags .... Capitol (M) T-2001 10-20 63
Big Sounds of the Drags .... Capitol (S) ST-2001 15-25 63
(Sound effects album—no music.)
Big Sounds of the Sports Cars .... Capitol (M) T-2004 10-20 63
Big Sounds of the Sports Cars .... Capitol (S) ST-2004 15-25 63
(Sound effects album—no music.)
Big Stars & Big Hits of Country Music .... Starday (M) 407 10-15 67
Big Stars & Big Hits of Country Music .... Starday (S) 407 10-15 67
Buck Owens; Dottie West; Dave Dudley; others.
Big Sur Festival (Celebration) .... Ode '70 (S) SPX-77008 15-25 70
Joan Baez; Kris Kristofferson; Mickey Newbury; Taj Mahal; Blood, Sweat & Tears; Beach Boys; Merry Clayton.
Big Sur Festival .... Columbia (S) KC-31138 10-20 72
Joan Baez; Kris Kristofferson; Mickey Newbury; Taj Mahal; Blood, Sweat & Tears.
Big Surf Hits .... Del-Fi (M) DFLP-1235 35-45 63
Big Surf Hits .... Del-Fi (S) DFST-1235 45-55 63
Lively Ones; Sentinels; Surf Stompers; Dave Myers & Surftones; Impacts; Centurions; Surf Mariachis..
Big Town .... Atlantic (S) 81769-1 8-10 87
(Soundtrack.) Little Willie John; Drifters; Ray Charles; Bobby Darin; Johnny Cash; Ivory Joe Hunter; Big Joe Turner; Jesse Belvin; LaVern Baker; Ronnie Self.

Big Train Express Railroad Songs - Country Style .... Nashville (M) NLP 2019 10-15
Jim Glaser; Curly Fox; Rainbow Ranch Boys; Jimmy Williams; Red Ellis; Benny Martin; Phipps Family; Stanley Brothers; Clinch Mountain Boys; Bill Clifton & Dixie Mountain Boys; Country Gentlemen; Lew Childre; Howard Yokes; Moon Mullican; Lonesome Pine Fiddlers.
Big Van Sounds .... Mark 56 (M) 527 10-20 60s
Tex Beneke & Modernaires; Larry Clinton; Woody Herman; Jerry Grey & Pied Pipers; Russ Morgan; Charlie Barnet; Bonnie Baker; Glenn Miller; Bob Eberly & Helen O'Connell; Gus Bivona. (Made for Allied Van Lines.)
Biggest Hits of '55 .... RCA Camden (M) CAL-294 10-15 56
Gisele MacKenzie; Snooky Lanson; Jose Melis; Bob Carroll; Johnny Guarnieri; Jack Haskell; Charlie Spivak; Honey Dreamers.
Biggest Hits of '56, Vol. 1 .... RCA Camden (M) CAL-318 10-15 57
Tex Beneke; Honey Dreamers; Earl Sheldon; Guy Lupar; Bob Carroll; Domenico Savino.
Biggest Hits of '56, Vol. 2 .... RCA Camden (M) CAL-331 10-15 57
Polly Bergen; Kyle Kimbro; Jack Say; Johnny Guarnieri; Townsmen; Connie Haines; Earl Grant; Van Alexander.
Biggest Hits of '57, Vol. 1 .... RCA Camden (M) CAL-362 10-15 58
Robert Alda; Tex Beneke; Stuart Foster; Peter Ricardo; Johnny Guarnieri; Townsmen; Earl Sheldon.
Biggest Hits of '57, Vol. 2 .... RCA Camden (M) CAL-400 10-15 58
Earl Sheldon; George DeWitt; Tex Beneke; Peter Ricardo; Jim Storer; Robert Alda; Stuart Foster.
Biggest Hits of '58, Vol. 1 .... RCA Camden (M) CAL-431 10-15 59
Hill Bowen; Stuart Foster; Earl Sheldon; Dave Martin; Strollers.
Biggest Hits of '58, Vol. 2 .... RCA Camden (M) CAL-435 10-15 59
RCA Camden Rockers; Larry Green; others.
Big Three: see BIG THREE (in "B" section)
Bill & Ted's Excellent Adventure .... A&M (S) SP-3915 8-10 89
(Soundtrack.) Extreme; Vital Signs; Glen Burtnick; Tora Tora; Shark Island; Big Pig; Bricklin; Robbie Robb; Power Tool.
Bill Graham Presents: see Fillmore - the Last Days
Bill Wright Presents a Gold Mine of All Time Hits: see Gold Mine of All Time Hits
Billboard Great Christmas Hits (1935-1954) .... Rhino (S) DLP1-0884 5-10 89
Bing Crosby; Vaughn Monroe; Gene Autry; Nat King Cole; Spike Jones & His City Slickers; Jimmy Boyd; Andrews Sisters & Guy Lombardo; Eartha Kitt.
Billboard Great Christmas Hits (1955-Present) .... Rhino (S) DLP1-0885 5-10 89
Elvis Presley; Bobby Helms; Brenda Lee; Chipmunks with David Seville; Harry Simeone Chorale; Harry Belafonte; Barry Gordon; Charles Brown; Drifters; Elmo 'N Patsy.
Billboard Top R&B Hits - 1955 .... Rhino (S) R1-70641 5-10 89
Johnny Ace; Little Walter & His Jukes; Etta James & Peaches; Fats Domino; Bo Diddley; Shirley & Lee; Smiley Lewis; Joe Turner; Nutmegs; Turbans.
Billboard Top R&B Hits - 1956 .... Rhino (S) R1-70642 5-10 89
Fats Domino; Platters; Teenagers featuring Frankie Lymon; Shirley & Lee; Clyde McPhatter; Little Richard; Teen Queens; Cadillacs; Five Satins.
Billboard Top R&B Hits - 1957 .... Rhino (S) R1-70643 5-10 89
Fats Domino; Bobbettes; Micky & Sylvia; Bobby Blue Bland; Little Richard; Del-Vikings; Thurston Harris; Johnnie & Joe.
Billboard Top R&B Hits - 1958 .... Rhino (S) R1-70644 5-10 89
Jackie Wilson; Cozy Cole; Bobby Day; Ernie Freeman; Bobby Freeman; Fats Domino; Chantels; Little Anthony & Imperials; Johnny Otis Show; Monotones.
Billboard Top R&B Hits - 1959 .... Rhino (S) R1-70645 5-10 89
Brook Benton; Coasters; Lloyd Price; James Brown & Famous Flames; Fats Domino; Phil Phillips with the Twilights; LaVern Baker; Jackie Wilson; Falcons; Dee Clark.
Billboard Top R&B Hits - 1960 .... Rhino (S) R1-70646 5-10 89
Dinah Washington & Brook Benton; Brook Benton; Jerry Butler; Jackie Wilson; Buster Brown; Bobby Marchan; Barrett Strong; Marv Johnson; Fats Domino.
Billboard Top R&B Hits - 1961 .... Rhino (S) R1-70647 5-10 89
Miracles; Ben E. King; Jive Five; Lee Dorsey; Gladys Knight & Pips; Chris Kenner; Bobby Blue Bland; Fats Domino; Impressions; Dee Clark.
Billboard Top Rock and Roll Hits - 1955 .... Rhino (S) R1-70598 5-10 88
Bill Haley & His Comets; Fontane Sisters; Platters; Chuck Berry; Cheers; Penguins; Fats Domino; LaVern Baker; El Dorados; Moonglows.
Billboard Top Rock and Roll Hits - 1956 .... Rhino (S) R1-70599 5-10 88
Elvis Presley; Jim Lowe; Carl Perkins; Fats Domino; Buchanan & Goodman; Bill Haley & His Comets; Frankie Lymon & Teenagers; Gene Vincent & His Blue Caps; Sanford Clark.
Billboard Top Rock and Roll Hits - 1957 .... Rhino (S) R1-70618 5-10 88
Elvis Presley; Everly Brothers; Paul Anka; Buddy Knox; Crickets; Diamonds; Buddy Holly; Chuck Berry; Jerry Lee Lewis.
Billboard Top Rock and Roll Hits - 1958 .... Rhino (S) R1-70619 5-10 88
Danny & Juniors; Champs; Teddy Bears; Conway Twitty; Silhouettes; Elegants; Everly Brothers; Coasters; Jerry Lee Lewis.
Billboard Top Rock and Roll Hits - 1959 .... Rhino (S) R1-70620 5-10 88
Elvis Presley; Bobby Darin; Frankie Avalon; Lloyd Price; Paul Anka; Santo & Johnny; Wilbert Harrison; Dave "Baby" Cortez; Coasters; Crests.
Billboard Top Rock and Roll Hits - 1960 .... Rhino (S) R1-70621 5-10 88
Elvis Presley; Everly Brothers; Johnny Preston; Drifters; Chubby Checker; Hollywood Argyles; Maurice Williams & Zodiacs; Jimmy Jones; Ventures.
Billboard Top Rock and Roll Hits - 1961 .... Rhino (S) R1-70622 5-10 88
Bobby Lewis; Del Shannon; Tokens; Marcels; Bobby Vee; Dion; Gary "U.S." Bonds; Shirelles; Ernie K-Doe; Marvelettes.
Billboard Top Rock and Roll Hits - 1962 .... Rhino (S) R1-70623 5-10 88
Neil Sedaka; 4 Seasons; Joey Dee & Starliters; Shirelles; Gene Chandler; Shelley Fabares; Tommy Roe; Little Eva; Dion; Freddy Cannon.
Billboard Top Rock and Roll Hits - 1963 .... Rhino (S) R1-70624 5-10 88
Jimmy Gilmer; Chiffons; Angels; Little Stevie Wonder; 4 Seasons; Jan & Dean; Lesley Gore; Essex; Kingsmen; Beach Boys.
Billboard Top Rock and Roll Hits - 1964 .... Rhino (S) R1-70625 5-10 89
Beach Boys; Manfred Mann; 4 Seasons; Shangri-Las; Newbeats; J. Frank Wilson & Cavaliers; Zombies; Terry Stafford; Marketts; Jan & Dean.
Billboard Top Rock and Roll Hits - 1965 .... Rhino (S) R1-70626 5-10 88
Byrds; Righteous Brothers; Gary Lewis & Playboys; Beach Boys; McCoys; Barry McGuire; Sam the Sham & Pharaohs; Roy Head; Len Barry.
Billboard Top Rock and Roll Hits - 1966 .... Rhino (S) R1-70627 5-10 88
Monkees; Righteous Brothers; Mamas & Papas; Lovin' Spoonful; Supremes; Troggs; Four Tops; Tommy James & Shondells; Nancy Sinatra; Beach Boys.

Billboard Top Rock and Roll Hits - 1967 ....Rhino (S) R1-70628 5-10 88
Monkees; Association; Box Tops; Turtles; Buckinghams; Strawberry Alarm Clock; Music Explosion; Paul Revere & Raiders; Tommy James & Shondells; Spencer Davis Group.

Billboard Top Rock and Roll Hits - 1968 ....Rhino (S) R1-70629 5-10 88
Marvin Gaye; Diana Ross & Supremes; John Fred; Hugh Masekela; Lemon Pipers; Cliff Nobles & Co.; Steppenwolf; Box tops; Tommy James & Shondells; Ohio Express.

Billboard Top Rock and Roll Hits - 1969 ....Rhino (S) R1-70630 5-10 88
5th Dimension; Archies; Tommy Roe; Temptations; Tommy James & Shondells; Steam; Cowsills; Foundations; Zombies; Youngbloods.

Billboard Top Rock and Roll Hits - the Early Years (3 LP) ....Rhino (S) RNTV-76600 10-20 88
Bill Haley & His Comets; Platters; Gene Vincent & His Blue Caps; Fats Domino; Buddy Knox; Diamonds; Jerry Lee Lewis; Crickets; Buddy Holly; Danny & Juniors; Silhouettes; Chuck Berry; Little Richard; Ricky Nelson; Everly Brothers; Conway Twitty; Eddie Cochran; Ritchie Valens; Frankie Avalon; Coasters; Wilbert Harrison; Drifters; Gary "U.S." Bonds; Dion; Chiffons; Kingsmen.

Billie Holiday Revisited ....Mainstream (S) 409 5-10 74
Sarah Vaughn; Carmen McRae; Dinah Washington; Morgana King.

Billy Jack ....Warner Bros. (S) BJS-1001 15-20 73
(Soundtrack.) Coven; Teresa Kelly; Lynn Baker; Gwen Smith; Katy Moffatt.

Billy Williams Revue ....Coral (M) CRL-57343 10-15 60

Billy Williams Revue ....Coral (S) CRL7-57343 ?? 60
Billy Williams; Fats Hudson; Clora Bryant; Four Dukes; Tommy Butler with Don Nero; Bob Bryant; Skip Cunningham.

Bionic Gold ....Big Sound (S) BSLP-001 5-10 78
Robert Orsi; Scratch Band; Mick Farren; Vince Whirlwind; Philip Rambow; Nelson Adelard Band; Hilly Michaels; Fran Koualski; Roger C. Reale.

Bird Lives! (Music of Charlie Parker) ....Milestone (S) M-9166 8-12
Art Pepper; others.

Birdland Stars on Tour, Vol. 2 ....RCA (M) LPM-1328 20-40 56
Al Cohn; Conte Condoli; Phil Woods; Kenny Durham; John Simmons; Kenny Clarke; Hank Jones.

Birdland Story (2 LP) ....Roulette (M) RB-2 10-20
(Box set.) Harry Belafonte; John Coltrane; Miles Davis; Stan Getz; Dizzie Gillespie; Charlie Parker; Machito; Johnny Smith; Lee Morgan; Max Roach; Don Lamond; Bud Powell; F. Wess; H. Jones; T. Jones; Eddie Safranski; Richard Davis; Al Grey; Osie Johnson; Billy Mitchell; Brew Moore; Art Taylor; Bobby Timmons; Curly Russell; Al Haig; Tommy Potter; Duke Jordon; Sanford Gold.

Birdlanders ....Everest (S) 275 5-10 73
J.J. Johnson; Milt Jackson; Kai Winding; Max Roach; Oscar Pettiford.

Birth of a Label Introducing Judson Records ....Judson (M) J-1 15-25 50s
Vienna State Opera Orchestra; Chauncey Gray; Francoise Prevost; Will Rogers Jr. & Tom Scott; Kenny Drew; Herb Straus; Dylan Todd; Lenny Herman; Henry Morgan; Steel Drum Trio; Emil Cole Choir.

Birth of Bop....Savoy (M) MG 9022 150-250 50s
(10-inch LP.) Charlie Parker; Dexter Gordon; J.J. Johnson; Milt Jackson; Leo Parker; Stan Getz.

Birth of Rock....Scepter (S) SPS-5103 10-15 72
Dionne Warwick; Lloyd Price; Shirelles; Chuck Jackson; Bobby Lewis; King Curtis; Shirelles; Timmy Shaw; Chuck Jackson; Maxine Brown; Esquires; Gene Chandler; Theola Kilgore; Kingsmen; Mel & Tim.

Birth of Soul....Decca (S) DL-79245 8-12 69
Louis Armstrong; Ella Fitzgerald; Billie Holiday; others.

Bitter End Years ....Roxbury (S) RLX-101 5-10 75
Carly Simon; Arlo Guthrie; Jerry Jeff Walker; John Prine; Van Morrison; Curtis Mayfield; Melanie; Bette Midler; James Taylor; John Sebastian; Isley Brothers; John Denver.

Bitter End Years (3 LP)....Roxbury (S) RLX-300 15-20 74
Judy Collins; Everly Brothers; Limeliters; Phil Ochs; Tom Paxton; Woody Allen; George Carlin; David Frye; Robert Klein; John Denver; Dion; Arlo Guthrie; Isley Brothers; Curtis Mayfield; Melanie; Bette Midler; Van Morrison; John Prine; John Sebastain; James Taylor; Jerry Jeff Walker; Theodore Bikel; Peter, Paul & Mary; Tom Rush; Pete Seeger; Simon Sisters; Josh White; David Steinberg; Lily Tomlin; Joan Rivers.

Black California ....Savoy (S) SJL-2215 10-15 76
Slim Gaillard; Helen Humes; Sonny Criss; Roy Porter Big Band; Eric Dolphy; Harold Land; Hampton Hawes; Art Pepper.

Black California, Vol. 2 - Anthology....Savoy (S) SJL-2242 10-15 80
Kenny Clarke All-Stars; Helen Humes; Slim Gaillard; Wardell Gray; Russell Jacquet; Wild Bill Moore.

Black Caucus Concert....Chess (S) CH-60037 5-10 75
Gladys Knight & Pips; Curtis Mayfield; Kool & Gang; Jimmy Witherspoon; War.

Black Giants ....Columbia (S) PG-33402 212 5-10 75
Miles Davis; Ramsey Lewis; Duke Ellington; Erroll Garner; Quincy Jones; Charles Mingus.

Black Gold 24 Carats (2 LP)....Warrner Special Products (SP) SP 2000-3 10-15 73
Aretha Franklin; Percy Sledge; Roberta Flack & Donny Hathaway; Otis Redding; Jackie Moore; Booker T. & MGs, R.B. Greaves; Drifters; Sam & Dave; Persuaders; Clarence Carter; Manu Dibango; Donny Hathaway; Betty Wright; Ben E. King; Joe Tex; Carla Thomas; Brook Benton; King Curtis; Roberta Flack; King Floyd; Spinners; Beginning of the End; Wilson Pickett.

Black Is Beautiful....Musico (S) MDS-1046 10-15 70s
Pearl Bailey; Inez Foxx; Melba Moore; Marie Knight; Eartha Kitt, Maxine Brown; Sarah Vaughn.

Black Music Month Sampler ....Arista (S) 9503 5-10 86
Aretha Franklin; J. Stewart; Billy Ocean; J. Jackson; P. Wilson; Whitney Houston; Whodini.

Black Rain ....Virgin (S) 91292-1 8-10 89
(Soundtrack.) Gregg Allman; UB40; Iggy Pop; Soul II; Soul with Caron Wheeler; Les Rita Mitsouko & Sparks; Ryuichi Sakamoto.

Blame It on the Blues ....Collectables (S) COL-5050 5-10 80s
Willie Headen; Roy Milton; Chuck Higgins; Filmore Slim.

Blast Off....K-Tel (S) TU 2960 5-10 82
Melissa Manchester; Ray Parker Jr.; Billy Idol; Genesis; Van Halen; A Flock of Seagulls; Steel Breeze; .38 Special; Kansas; Tane Cain; Haircut One Hundred; Joan Jet & Blackhearts; John Cougar.

Blasts from the Past ....Blast (M) BLP-6803 25-45 63
(Red and white cover with text only.) Shep & Limelites; Bobby Hendricks; Slades; Three Friends; Desires; Spaniels; Dells; Little Anthony & Imperials; Videos; Ike & Tina Turner; Harptones. (May have either a red and white label or a black and white one.)

Blasts from the Past (Clay Cole Presents) ....Blast (M) BLP-6803 40-50 63
(Cover pictures deejay Clay Cole.) Shep & Limelites; Bobby Hendricks; Slades; Three Friends; Desires; Spaniels; Dells; Little Anthony & Imperials; Videos; Ike & Tina Turner; Harptones.

Blasts from the Past (Jim Lounsbury Presents) ... Blast (M) BLP-6803 40-50 63
(Cover pictures deejay Jim Lounsbury.) Shep & Limelites; Bobby Hendricks; Slades; Three Friends; Desires; Spaniels; Dells; Little Anthony & Imperials; Videos; Ike & Tina Turner; Harptones.

Blasts from the Past ... Blast (M) BLP-6805 40-50 60s
Excellents; Donnie & Dreamers; Magnificent Four; Ronnie & Hi-lites; Court Jesters; Emblems; Performers; Harptones.

Blaze ... A&M (S) SP-3932 8-10 89
(Soundtrack.) Bennie Wallace; Fats Domino; Hank Williams, Sr.; Bonnie Sheridan; Randy Newman.

Bless This House ... Capitol Creative Products (S) SL-6748 5-10
Capitol Symphony Orchestra; Fred Waring; Roger Wagner Chorale; Tennessee Ernie ford; Hollywood Bowl Symphony Orchestra; Ralph Carmichael.

Blind Date ... Rhino (S) RNIN-70705 8-10 87
(Soundtrack.) Jennifer Warnes; Billy Vera & Beaters; Keith L'Neire; Hubert Tubbs; Henry Mancini; Stanley Jordan.

Blind Gary Davis and Others ... Continental (M) 15
Blind Gary Davis; others

Blitz ... RCA (S) DJL1-4182 5-10
Bow Wow Wow; Polyrock; Landscape; Robert Ellis Orrall; Slow Children; Sparks; Shock.

Block Buster ... K-Tel (S) TU 2430 5-10 76
War; Average White Band; Gladys Knight & Pips; Alice Cooper; Hollies; Edgar Winter Group; Leon Haywood; Sammy Johns; David Geddes; Frankie Valli; Carol Douglas; Johnny Rivers; Kool & Gang; B.T. Express; 5000 Volts; Silver Convention; Jigsaw; David Loggins; KC & Sunshine Band.

Blow-Up ... MGM (M) E-4447 25-30 67
Blow-Up ... MGM (S) SE-4447 30-35 67
(Soundtrack.) Herbie Hancock; Yardbirds; others

Blowin' in the Wind (5 LP) ... Reader's Digest (S) RBA-183 25-35 88
(Boxed set. Mail order offer.) Kingston Trio; others. (Includes booklet.)

Blue Christmas ... Welk Music Group (S) WM-3002 60-80 84
(Promotional issue only.) Elvis Presley; Living Voices; Chet Atkins; Willie Nelson; Mickey Gilley; Lawrence Welk; Jim Reeves; Ernest Tubb; Tammy Wynette; Jackie Gleason; Glen Campbell; Beach Boys; Danny Davis & Nashville Brass; Johnny Mathis; Merle Haggard; Percy Faith; Bing Crosby; Lynn Anderson.

Blue Iguana ... Polydor (S) 835592-1 8-10 88
(Soundtrack.) Kurtis Blow; Zodiac Mindwarp & Love Reaction; Fat Boys; Del-Vikings; Chuck Brown & Soul Searchers; James Brown; L.A. Guns; White Boys; Fela Anikulapo Kuti; Platters; Ethan James; Dirge.

Blue Monday ... Stax (S) MPS 8528 5-10 84
Albert King; Freddie Robinson; Little Sonny; Little Milton; others.

Blue Montreaux 2 ... Arista (S) AB 4245 8-12
Blue Note Gems of Jazz ... Blue Note (M) BLP 2001 10-15
Blue Note Live at the Roxy (2 LP) ... Blue Note (S) BN-LA-663-J2 8-12 76
Alphonse Mouzon; Carmen McRae; Blue Note All Stars; Donald Byrd; Ronnie Laws; Earl Klugh.

Blue Note's Three Decades of Jazz (2 LP) ... Blue Note (S) BST (M) 89903 10-15
Blue Ribbon Country (2 LP) ... Capitol (S) STBB-2969 10-15 69
Buck Owens; Sonny James; Bobbie Gentry; Johnny & Jonie Mosby; Wynn Stewart; Merle Haggard; Glen Campbell; Jean Shepard; Dick Miles; Ferlin Husky; Tex Ritter; Bonnie Owens; Wanda Jackson; Charlie Louvin; Chaparral Brothers.

Blue Ribbon Country, Vol. 2 (2 LP) ... Capitol (S) STBB-217 10-15 69
Glen Campbell; Merle Haggard; Wanda Jackson; others.

Blue Ribbon Country, Vol. 3 ... Capitol (S) SJA 7912 5-10 82
Jimmy C. Newman; Bobby Helms; Roy Drusky; Price Mitchell; Pee Wee King; Claude Grey; Johnny Dollar; Kirk Hansard.

Blue Ridge Mountain Music ... Atlantic (M) 1347 25-35 60
Blue Ridge Mountain Music ... Atlantic (S) SD-1347 30-40 60
Bluebird Blues ... RCA (M) LPV-518 15-20 65
Joe Williams; Tampa Red; Lonnie Johnson; Blind Willie McTell & Kate McTell; Poor Joe Williams; Sonny Boy Williamson; Tommy McClennan; Sleepy John Estes & Son Bond; Arthur Crudup.

Bluegrass! ... Hilltop (S) PTP 2069-2 8-12
Flatt & Scruggs; Denver Duke; Jeffery Null; John Duffy & Country Gentlemen; Jimmie Skinner; Lew Childre; Benny Martin.

Bluegrass and Country By These Famous Artists ... Rural Rhythm (M) RR 155 8-12 60s
Wear Family; Ray Godfrey; Ernie Cook; Boys from Shioio; Autry Inman; Billy Carter; Johnny Tyler.

Bluegrass for Collectors ... RCA (M) APM1-0568 8-12 74
J.E. Mainer & His Mountaineers; Bill Monroe's Bluegrass Boys; Charlie Monroe & Kentucky Pardners; Riley Puckett; Gid Tanner & His Skillet Lickers.

Bluegrass Hall of Fame ... Starday (M) S-181 15-25 62
Bluegrass Hall of Fame ... Starday (M) S-296 10-20 64
Flatt & Scruggs; Hylo Brown; Stanley Brothers; others.

Bluegrass Oldies But Goodies ... Smash (M) MGS-27028 10-20 63
Bluegrass Oldies But Goodies ... Smash (S) SRS-67028 10-20 63
Stanley Brothers; Carl Story; Hylo Brown; Red Allen; Stringbean; others.

Bluegrass Oldies But Goodies ... Cumberland (M) 29520 10-15 65
Bluegrass Oldies But Goodies ... Cumberland (S) 69520 10-15 65
Stanley Brothers; Carl Story; Hylo Brown; Red Allen; Stringbean; others.

Bluegrass Special ... Starday (M) S-115 15-25 60
Bluegrass Special ... Starday (S) SLP-115 15-25 60
Bluegrass Special ... World Pacific (S) 21898 8-12 69
Folkswingers; Kentucky Colonels; Tut Taylor; others.

Bluegrass Spectacular ... Starday (M) S-232 15-20 63
Bluegrass Spectacular ... Starday (S) SLP-232 15-20 63
Flatt & Scruggs; Carl Story; Stanley Brothers; others.

Blues ... Asch (M) 101 8-10
(Soundtrack.) J.D. Short; Pink Anderson; Furry Lewis; Baby Tate; Memphis Willie B.; Gus Cannon; Sleepy John Estes.

Blues .... Folkways (M) FS-3817 15-25 59
Sonny Terry & Brownie McGhee; Big Bill Broonzy.
Blues .... World Pacific (S) WST-1021 15-25 59
Gerry Mulligan; Chico Hamilton; others.
Blues .... Vee Jay (M) VJLP-1020 25-35 60
Priscilla Bowman; Jimmy Reed; Roscoe Gordon; John Lee Hooker; Gene Allison; Billy Boy; Memphis Slim; J.B. Lenore; Harold Burrage; Elmore James; Jimmy Witherspoon.
Blues .... Pacific Jazz (M) JWC 502 10-20
(Issued in plain cover.)
Blues (Vol. 1) .... Argo (M) LP-4026 20-25 63
Sonny Boy Williamson; Buddy Guy; Chuck Berry; Little Walter; John Lee Hooker; Lowell Fulson; Howlin' Wolf; Jimmy Witherspoon; Muddy Waters.
Blues (Vol. 1) .... Cadet (M) LP-4026 10-15 67
Sonny Boy Williamson; Buddy Guy; Chuck Berry; Little Walter; John Lee Hooker; Lowell Fulson; Howlin' Wolf; Jimmy Witherspoon; Muddy Waters.
Blues (Vol. 1) .... Trip (M) X-7503 5-10 75
B.B. King; Buster Brown; Memphis Slim; Elmore James; Jimmy Reed; Arthur Crudup; Slim Harpo; others.
Blues (Vol. 2) .... Argo (M) LP-4027 20-25 63
Sonny Boy Williamson; Buddy Guy; Chuck Berry; Little Walter; John Lee Hooker; Lowell Fulson; Howlin' Wolf; Jimmy Witherspoon; Muddy Waters; Otis Rush.
Blues (Vol. 2) .... Cadet (M) LP-4027 10-15 67
Sonny Boy Williamson; Buddy Guy; Chuck Berry; Little Walter; John Lee Hooker; Lowell Fulson; Howlin' Wolf; Jimmy Witherspoon.
Blues (Vol. 2) .... Trip (M) X-7504 5-10 76
Lightnin' Hopkins; Elmore James; Arthur Crudup; Jimmy Reed; John Lee Hooker; Memphis Slim; others.
Blues (Vol. 3) .... MCA/Chess (S) CH 9276 5-10 80s
Washboard Sam; Willie Dixon; Little Milton; Howlin' Wolf; Elmore James; etc.
Blues (Vol. 3) .... Argo (M) LP-4034 20-25 64
Blues (Vol. 3) .... Cadet (M) LP-4034 10-15 67
Blues (Vol. 4) .... Argo (M) LP-4042 20-25 65
Billy Stewart; Little Walter; Lowell Fulson; Larry Williams; Eddie Boyd; Willie Mabon; Betty James; Muddy Waters; TV Slim; Memphis Slim; John Lee Hooker.
Blues (Vol. 4) .... Cadet (M) LP-4042 10-15 67
Billy Stewart; Little Walter; Lowell Fulson; Larry Williams; Eddie Boyd; Willie Mabon; Betty James; Muddy Waters; TV Slim; Memphis Slim; John Lee Hooker.
Blues (Vol. 5) .... Cadet (M) LP-4051 10-15 67
Little Walter; John Lee Hooker; Lowell Fulson; Howlin' Wolf; Muddy Waters; Jimmy Rogers; Jimmy Nelson; Percy Mayfield; Willie Mabon; Memphis Minnie; Eddie Boyd.
Blues - a Real Summit Meeting (2 LP) .... Buddah (S) BDS 5144-2 10-15 73
Muddy Waters; B.B. King; Big Mama Thornton; Lloyd Glenn; Eddie "Cleanhead" Vinson; Jay McShann; Clarence "Gatemouth" Brown; Arthur "Big Boy" Crudup.
Blues and Folk .... Bethlehem (M) BCP-6071 20-30 63
Memphis Slim; Lonnie Johnson; Texas Slim; others.
Blues Are Back .... Columbia Special Products (SP) P 13211 5-10 76
Mississippi John Hurt; Blind Lemon Jefferson; Leadbelly; Bessie Smith; Robert Johnson; Billie Holiday; Elmore James; Mose Allison; Taj Mahal; Blood, Sweat & Tears. (Made for Sedgefield Jeans.)
Blues at Midnight .... International Award (S) AK-243 10-15
Ray Charles; Jimmy Rushins; Ivory Joe Hunter; others.
Blues at Newport, 1964, Part 1 .... Vanguard (M) VRS-9180 10-20 65
Blues at Newport, 1964, Part 1 .... Vanguard (S) VSD-79180 10-20 65
Sleepy John Estes; Fred McDowell; Hammy Nixon; Yank Rachel; Doc Reese; Robert Pete Williams.
Blues at Newport, 1964, Part 2 .... Vanguard (M) VRS-9181 10-20 65
Blues at Newport, 1964, Part 2 .... Vanguard (S) VSD-79181 10-20 65
Elizabeth Cotton; Willy Doss; Mississippi John Hurt; Skip James; Rev. Robert Wilkins.
Blues Avalanche (2 LP) .... Chess (S) 2CH-60015 15-20 72
Bo Diddley; Muddy Waters; Koko Taylor; T-Bone Walker; Willie Dixon; Lafayette Leake; Aces.
Blues Bash .... Olympic (S) 7115 5-10 73
Big Joe Williams; Lightnin' Hopkins; Brownie McGhee & Sonny Terry; others.
Blues Book .... Prestige (M) PR-7340 15-20 65
Blues Book .... Prestige (S) PRS-7340 20-25 65
Booker Ervin; Richard Davis; others.
Blues Box .... Verve/Folkways (M) FV-3011 10-20 66
Blues Box .... Verve/Folkways (S) FVS-3011 10-20 66
Lightnin' Hopkins; Sonny Terry; Jimmy Witherspoon; others.
Blues Brothers .... Atlantic (S) SD-16017 8-10 80
(Soundtrack.) James Brown; Cab Calloway; Ray Charles; Aretha Franklin; Dan Aykroyd; John Belushi.
Blues Classics, Vol. 1 .... Bluesway (S) 6061 8-12 73
Ray Charles; John Lee Hooker; T-Bone Walker; Archie Shepp; others.
Blues Classics, Vol. 2 .... Bluesway (S) 6062 8-12 73
Jimmy Reed; Charles Brown; B.B. King; Jimmy Rushing; others.
Blues Deluxe .... XRT Records 9301 10-15 80
Lonnie Brooks Blues Band; Son Seals Blues Band; Mighty Joe Young; Muddy Waters; Koko Taylor & Her Blues Machine; Willie Dixon & Chicago Allstars.
Blues Festival (Second Annual) .... Arhoolie (S) F-1030 8-12
Mance Lipscomb; Clifton Chenier; Lightnin' Hopkins; others.
Blues Folk Series, Vol. 4 (Ray Charles) .... Time (M) N9OP-1386 10-20
Ray Charles; Peppermint Harris; James Wayne; Brownie McGhee & Sonny Terry; Arbee Stidham; Lil Son Jackson.
Blues for Collectors: see British Archives
Blues for Tomorrow .... Riverside (M) RLP 12-243 10-20

East Coast All Stars; Sonny Rollins Quartet; Bobby Jaspar Quartet; Herbie Mann's Californians; Mundell Lowe Quartet.

Blues from Big Bill's Copacabana .... Chess (S) 1533 10-15 69
Muddy Waters; Buddy Guy; Howlin Wolf; Sonny Boy Williams; Willie Dixon.

Blues from Chicago .... Cherry Red (S) CR-5104 8-12
Barry Goldberg; Harvey Mandell; Charlie Musselwhite; Neil Merryweather.

Blues Guitar Killers .... Barrelhouse (M) BH-012 5-10 77
L.C. Green & Sam Kelly; Johnny Howard; Rocky Fuller; Henry Smith; Eddie Burns.

Blues Hoot: see HOPKINS, Lightnin; / Brownie McGhee & Sonny Terry

Blues in Baton Rouge .... Excello (S) 8021 8-12 72

Blues in Modern Jazz .... Atlantic (M) 1337 30-40 60

Blues in the Mississippi Night .... United Artists (M) UAL 4027 10-20

Blues Jam in Chicago, Vol. 1 .... Blue Horizon (S) 4803 10-15 70
Fleetwood Mac; Otis Spann; Willie Dixon; others.

Blues Jam in Chicago, Vol. 2 .... Blue Horizon (S) 4805 10-15 70
Fleetwood Mac; Otis Spann; Willie Dixon; others.

Blues Never Die .... Prestige (M) PR-7391 15-20 65

Blues Never Die .... Prestige (S) PRS-7391 20-25 65
Otis Spann; James Cotton; others.

Blues Oldies and Goodies .... Crown (M) 5238 30-40 60s

Blues Oldies and Goodies .... Crown (M) CLP-5405 15-25 60s

Blues Oldies and Goodies .... Crown (S) CST-405 15-25 60s
B.B. King; Etta James; John Lee Hooker; Bobby Blue Bland; Jimmy Witherspoon.

Blues Originals, Vol. 3: Texas Guitar from Dallas to L.A. .... Atlantic (S) SD-7226 10-15 72
T-Bone Walker; Guitar Slim; Lawyer Houston; Al King; Ray Agee; R.S. Rankin.

Blues Originals, Vol. 4: Blues Piano - Chicago Plus .... Atlantic (S) SD-7227 10-15 72
Little Johnny Jones; Floyd Dixon; Little Brother Montgomery; Frank "Sweet" Williams; Meade Lux Lewis. (Four of the six volumes in this series are by solo artists.)

Blues Project .... Elektra (M) EKL-264 15-20 64

Blues Project .... Elektra (S) EKS7-264 15-25 64
Dave Van Ronk; Danny Kalb; Dave Ray; others.

Blues Rocks .... Bluestime (S) 29010 8-12 73
Otis Spann; Joe Turner; Eddie Vinson; T-Bone Walker.

Blues Roll On .... Atlantic (M) 1352 30-40 61

Blues Roll On .... Atlantic (S) SD-1352 35-45 61
Boy Blue; Willie Jones; Forest City Joe; Sonny Boy Rogers; Fred McDowell; Lonnie Young; John Dudley; Joe Lee; Rosalie Hill.

Blues Roots .... Poppy (S) 60003 10-15 69
Joe Williams; Lightnin' Hopkins; Lowell & Martin Fulson; others.

Blues Sampler Series .... Fantasy (S) 4 10-15
(Promotional issue only.) Jimmy Witherspoon; Lightnin' Hopkins; John Lee Hooker; Sonny Terry & Brownie McGhee; Memphis Slim; others.

Blues Singers .... Halo (M) 50280 10-20 57
Bob Mitchell; Big Sheba & Freddie Mitchell Orchestra; Valaida Snow & Jim Mundy's Orchestra.

Blues That Gave America Soul .... Duke (M) DLP-82 10-20 66
Bobby Bland; Johnny Ace; Junior Parker; Roscoe Gordon; Larry Davis; Jackie Verell; Little Frankie Lee; Arthur Prysock; Marie Adams; Sonny Parker; Memphis Slim; Jimmy McCracklin.

Blues-A-Rama, Vol. 2 .... Blacktop (S) 1045 5-10 80s

Bob Livorio, Vol. 2 .... WKPA (M) No Number Used 15-20
Metallics; Pyramids; Surfaris; Harlequins; Anthony & Sophomores; Malcolm Dodd; Initials; Flamingos; Billy Vera & Contrasts; Bill & Doree Post; Rosie & Originals.

Body by Jake ('Don't Quit') .... MCA (S) 5505 5-10 84
Bobby Caldwell; Maxayne Lewis; Michael Sembello; Joseph Williams; Leslie Smith; Kamau Peterson.

Body Rock .... EMI America (S) SO-17140 8-10 84
(Soundtrack.) Maria Vidal; David Lasley; Laura Branigan; others.

Body Slam .... MCA (S) 6197 8-10 87
(Soundtrack.) Bachman-Turner Overdrive; Kick; Frankie Valli & 4 Seasons; Jimmy Scarlet & Dimensions; others.

Bolo Bash .... Bolo (M) BLP-8002 20-25 64
Viceroys; Tiny Tony & Statics; Exotics; Billy Saint; Dynamics; Jimmy Hanna; Dave Lewis; Chanteurs.

Bonanza of Country .... Hilltop (S) JS-6107 5-10
George Jones; Leroy Van Dyke; Carlisles; Faron Young; Johnny Horton; Benny Barnes; Merle Kilgore; Rusty Draper; Jimmie Skinner.

Boogie Nights .... Ronco (S) 2240 5-10 78
Heatwave; Eruption; Tavares; Commodores; Atlanta Rhythm Section; Stargard; Emotions; Hot; Chic; Trammps; Ram Jam; Donna Summer; Belle Epoch; Mandrill; Rick James; Len Boone; Odyssey; Gene Page.

Boogie Nights .... Ronco (S) RTL 2027 5-10 78
Abba; Boz Scaggs; Noosha Fox; David Essex; Tina Charles; Ram Jam; Bruce Johnston; Dead End Kids; Dooleys; Sutherland Brothers & Quiver; Heat Wave; Billy Ocean; Deneice Williams; Joe Tex; Lou Rawls; Biddu Orchestra; Manhattans; Billy Paul; Philadelphia All Stars; Wild Cherry.

Boogie Woogie Greatest Hits .... BW (M) 1000 5-10
Pinetop Smith; Cripple Clarenc Lofton; Joe Sullivan; Meade Lux Lewis; Art Hodes; Louis Jordan; Red Nelson; Honey Hill; Pete Johnson; Albert Ammons; Bob Zurke; Freddie Slack.

Boogie Woogie Rarities, 1927-1932 .... Milestone (M) MLP-2009 8-10 72

Boogie Woogie Revisited .... RCA (M) LPM-2321 15-25 60

Boomtown Party 1959 .... Share (M) No Number Used 10-15

Bop (4 LP) ....Sessions/Warner Special Products OP-4518 10-20 89
(Mail order offer.) Jerry Lee Lewis; Little Richard; Danny & Juniors; Monotones; Bobby Day; Shirelles; Bill Haley & His Comets; Chuck Berry; Diamonds; Neil Sedaka; Billy Bland; Buddy Holly; Jackie Wilson; Mickey & Sylvia; Isley Brothers; Buddy Knox; Bobby Darin; Earls; Dion; Coasters; Connie Francis; Lloyd Price; Johnny Otis Show; Kalin Twins; Jimmy Jones; Barry Mann; Bobby Lewis; Silhouettes; Eddie Cochran; Robin Luke; Dodie Stevens; Bobby Day; Freddy Cannon; Everly Brothers; Curtis Lee; Johnny Tillotson; Fats Domino; Bobby Freeman; Annette; Paul Anka; Clovers; Dion; Linda Scott; Del-Vikings; Big Bopper.

Bop Lives....................Harlem Hitparade (SE) HHP-5011 8-12
Dizzy Gillespie; Charlie Parker; Erroll Garner; Coleman Hawkins; Cannonball Adderley; Barney Bigard Sextette; Art Tatum; Sonny Rollins; Eric Dolphy; Teddy Wilson; Ben Webster.

Boppin'....................Jubilee (M) JGM-1118 50-75 60
Orioles; Toppers; Emanons; Coney Island Kids; Marylanders; Deke Watson & Brown Dots.

Border....................Backstreet (S) BSR-6105 8-10 82
(Soundtrack.) Ry Cooder; John Hiatt; Jim Dickinson; Sam "Sam the Sham" Samudio; Dan Penn; Brenda Patterson; Bobby King; Willie Greene Jr.

Border Radio ....Enigma (S) SJ-73221 8-10 87
(Soundtrack.) Divine Horsemen; Green on Red; Dave Alvin; John Doe; Chris D.; Tonys.

Born Losers....................Tower (M) T-5082 15-20 67

Born Losers....................Tower (S) DT-5082 20-25 67
(Soundtrack.) Mike Curb; Terry Stafford; Sidewalk Sounds; Summer Saxophones; others.

Born on the Fourth of July ....MCA (S) 6340 8-10 90
(Soundtrack.) Edie Brickell & New Bohemians; Broken Homes; Van Morrison; Don McLean; Temptations; Shirelles; Frankie Avalon; Henry Mancini.

Born to Be Country Boys....................Share (S) JS-6104 5-10

Boss Goldies (Sounds from the Grooveyard)....................Columbia (M) CL-2559 10-20 66

Boss Goldies (Sounds from the Grooveyard)....................Columbia (S) CS-9359 10-20 66
Dion; Johnny Tollotson; Anita Bryant; Rip Chords; Four Tops; Everly Brothers; Aretha Franklin; Rene & Rene; Chordettes; Townsmen; Buzz Clifford.

Boss Groups (3 LP)....................Mad Bag (SE) MB-278/279/280 15-25 70
Shirley & Lee; Del-Vikings; Monarchs; Cadets; Angels; Tommy Edwards; Moonglows; Johnny & Hurricanes; Cufflinks; Five Satins; Eternals; Genies; Tokens; Harptones; Neil Sedaka & Tokens; Silhouettes; Paragons; Flamingos; Fireflies; Tune Weavers; Faye Adams; Gladys Knight & Pips; Bobby Day; Three Friends; Maxine Brown; Buchanan & Goodman; Nutmegs; Quintones; Collegians.

Bossa Nova ....Grand Prix (M) K-400 8-12
Osie Johnson; Ted Sommer; Bill Lavorgna; Sam Most; Mat Mathews; Hank Jones; Jimmy Jones; Louis Metcalf; Buster Harding; Al Hall.

Boston Does the Beatles (2 LP) ....Fast Track (S) FT-100 10-15 88
Lenny Gardino; Beat Surrender; Further Adventures of Ken Scales; I-Tones; Mata Hari; Jeanne French & Hot Wire; Didi Stewart; Powerglide; Barry Cowsill; One Four Five; Blaros; Bishop Desmond & Tutus; Bentmen; Capitol Gain; A.K.A.; Mr. Curt's Camaraderie; Big Woods; Funky Young Monks; Tax Collectors; Memphis Rockabilly; Rugbeaters; Chris Martin Mainfesto; Apples; Trap the Clown; Joanne Victoria; Me & Boys; KGB; Bim Skala Bim; Bruce Marshall & Clue; Berlin Airlift; Triage.

Boston Incest Album ....Sounds Interesting SILP 005 8-12
Marshalls; Willie Alexander; Peytons; Sidewinders with the Paley Brothers; Fugitives; Professor Anonymous; Reflectors; Eric Ross; Lynch & Mob.

Bottleneck Blues (Guitar Classics 1926-1937)....................Yazoo (M) L-1026 8-10
King Solomon Hill; Barbecue Bob; Shreveport Home Wreckers; Robert Johnson; Black Ace; Ruth Willis; Jim & Bob; Bo Weavil Jackson; Weaver & Beasley; Ramblin' Thomas; Kansas Joe & Memphis Minnie; Oscar Woods; Bukka White; Irene Scruggs.

Bottleneck Guitar: see ARNOLD, Kokomo / Casey Bill Weldon

Bourbon Street ....Louisiana Tourist Development Commission (S) No Number Used 10-15 70
(Promotional issue only.) Pete Fountain; Thomas Jefferson; Danny Barker; Al Hirt; Murphy Campo; Dukes of Dixieland; Your Father's Mustache Orchestra; Arm& Hug; Louis Cottrell Jr.; Ronnie Cole; Leon Kelner & Blue Room Orchestra.

Bowling Balls from Hell, Vol. 1 ....Clone (S) CLO-11 5-10
Waitresses; Denis DeFrange; Ralph Carney; Ralph Carney & David Thomas; Denis DeFrange & Mark Frazier; Haff Notz; Hurricane Bob.

Bowling Balls from Hell, Vol. 2 ....Clone (S) CL-013 5-10
Susan Schmidt & Debbie Smith; Unit 5; Bizarros; Hammer Damage; Tim Huey; Totsuzen Danball; Waitresses.

Boy Friends ....Harmony (M) HL 7147 10-15 50s
Bing Crosby; Snookie Lanson; Jack Paar; Tony Martin; Frank Parker.

Boy - Girl - Boy: see KING, Freddie / Lulu Reed / Sonny Thompson

Boy Meets Girl....................Stax (S) STS 2-2024 10-20 60s
William Bell; Eddie Floyd; Cleotha Staples; Mavis Staples; Rervis Staples; Johnnie Taylor; Carla Thomas.

Boy Named Sue (And Other Country Hits)....................Somerset (S) 34500 5-10 70

Boys and Girls Together....................Columbia (M) CL 2530 15-20
(10–inch LP.)

Braintree Battle of the Bands ....Normandy (S) No Number Used 20-30
Immortals; others.

Brazil Classics 2 - O Samba....................Luka Bop/Warner (S) 26019 5-10 89
Clara Nunes; Zeca Pagodinho; Alcione; Ciro Monteiro; Beth Carvalho; Neguinho Da Beija Flor; Almir Guineto; Agapé; Martinho Da Vila; Paulinho Da Viola.

Brazil's Super Hits ....Atlantic (S) SD 8167 8-12

Bread and Roses Festival of Music (2 LP) ....Fantasy (S) 7011 10-15 80
Joan Baez; Hoyt Axton; Joel Bernstein; Bread & Roses Dixielland Band; Norton Buffalo; Chambers Brothers; Chick Corea; David Crosby; Mimi Farina; Freebo; John Hammond; Kris Kristofferson; Leah Kunkel; Maria Muldaur; Graham Nash; Roches; Pete Seeger; Paul Siebel.

Breakfast Club....................A&M (S) SP-3294 5-8

Breakfast Club....................A&M (S) SP-5045 8-10 85
(Soundtrack.) Simple Minds; Elizabeth Daily; Wang Chung; Jesse Johnson; Stephanie Spruill; Karla DeVito; Joyce Kennedy.

Breakin'....................Polydor (S) 821919-1 8-10 84
(Soundtrack.) Bar-Kays; Carol Lynn James; Rufus; Chaka Khan; Chris Taylor & David Storrs; Ollie & Jerry; Hotstreak; 3V; Fire Fox; Re-Flex.

Breakin' 2 - Electric Boogaloo ....Polydor (S) 823696-1 8-12 84
(Soundtrack.) Ollie & Jerry; Fire Fox; George Krantz; Steve Donn; Carol Lynn Townes; Mark Scott; Rags & Riches.

Breakout: Top 40 Hits of Today..........Columbia (S) KC-32519 8-12 73
Mott the Hoople; Ten Years After; Andy Pratt; Looking Glass; Edgar Winter Group; Hollies; Argent; Dr. Hook & Medicine Show; Chi Coltrane; Loggins & Messina; Loudon Wainwright III.

Breast of Soul..........Pompeii (S) 6005 8-12
Ike & Tina Turner; Les Watson; Fontella Bass; Leroy Horne; Roger Collins; others.

Breck Presents a Hootenanny: see Beautiful Hair Breck Presents a Hootenanny

Bright Lights & Country Music, Nashville Sound, Vol. 7..........Columbia Musical Treasury (SE) 1P 6086 5-10 74
Ray Price; Barbara Mandrell; Charlie Rich; Tanya Tucker; Freddy Weller; George Jones; Tammy Wynette; Mac Davis; Lynn Anderson; Johnny Cash. (Columbia House Record Club issue.)

Bright Lights and Honky Tonks..........Starday (M) S-239 15-20 63

Bright Lights and Honky Tonks..........Starday (S) SLP-239 15-20 63

Bright Lights, Big City..........Warner Bros. (S) 1-25688 8-10 86
(Soundtrack.) Prince; New Order; Narada; Bryan Ferry; Depeche Mode; Donald Fagen; Noise Club; Konk; Jennifer Hall; M/A/R/R/S.

Bright Side of Music..........K-Tel (S) TU-230 5-10 73
Hurricane Smith; Raspberries; Gallery; Sailcat; Sam Neely; Timmy Thomas; Eric Clapton; Lobo; Skylark; Donny Osmond; New Seekers; Osmonds; Jud Strunk; Brighter Side of Darkness; Joe Simon; Wayne Newton; James Brown.

Brighten the Corner Where You Are..........New World (S) 224 5-10

Brightest Stars of Christmas..........RCA (S) DPL1-0086 5-10 74
Elvis Presley; Eugene Ormandy & Philadelphia Orchestra; Danny Davis & Nashville Brass; Perry Como; Henry Mancini; Julie Andrews; Ed Ames; Arthur Fiedler & Boston Pops; Charley Pride; Robert Shaw; Sergio Franchi. (Special products. Made for J.C. Penney stores.)

Brimstone & Treacle..........A&M (S) SP-3945 8-12 82
(Soundtrack.) Sting; Police; Go-Go's; Squeeze; Brimstone Chorale; Finchley Children's Music Group.

Brite-Stars Pick Hits of the Greats..........Brite Star (S) 2628 8-12 70

British Archives Vol. 1..........RCA (SE) LSP-4409 15-20 70
John Mayall & Bluesbreakers; Eric Clapton; Savoy Brown Blues Band; others.

British Archives Vol. 2..........RCA (SE) LSP-4455 15-20 71
T.S. McPhee; Eric Clapton; Dharma Blues Band; Jeremy Spencer; others.

British Archives Vol. 3..........RCA (SE) LSP-4488 15-20 71
Jeff Beck; Jimmy Page; Stuff Smith; Cyril Davies & All Stars; Santa Barbera Machine Head; Eric Clapton; Nicky Hopkins.

British Archives Vol. 4..........RCA (SE) LSP-4549 15-20 71
Albert Lee; Dave Kelly; Rod Stewart; Eric Clapton; others.

British Beat A-Go-Go..........Majorette (M) M-305A 10-20 65
All Instrumentals. No artists credited.

British Go-Go (Mickie Most Presents)..........MGM (M) E-4306 15-25 65

British Go-Go (Mickie Most Presents)..........MGM (S) SE-4306 20-30 65
Herman's Hermits; Animals; Symbols; Cherokees; Moqettes.

British Gold..........Sire (S) R-224095 10-20 78
(RCA Record Club issue.) Beatles; Derek & Dominos; Peter & Gordon; Freddie & Dreamers; Elton John; Rod Stewart; Chad & Jeremy; Mindbenders; Van Morrison; Kinks; Hollies; Wayne Fontana & Mindbenders; Troggs; Olivia Newton-John; Fleetwood Mac; Manfred Mann; Deep Purple; Searchers; Cream.

British Rock Classics (2 LP)..........Sire (S) R-234021 10-15 78
(RCA Record Club issue.) Beatles with Tony Sheridan; Kinks; Peter & Gordon; Honeycombs; Gerry & Pacemakers; Bee Gees; Rod Stewart; Uriah Heep; Cream; Troggs; Elton John; Zombies; Eric Burdon & Animals; Billy J. Kramer & Dakatos; Crazy World of Arthur Brown; Fleetwood Mac; Caravelles; Searchers; Deep Purple; Tornadoes.

British Sixties..........Warner/JCI (S) 3107 8-12 85
Donovan; Peter & Gordon; Fortunes; Marianne Faithful; Manfred Mann; Kinks; Hollies; Gerry & Pacemakers; Small Faces; Billy J. Kramer & Dakotas; Them.

British Sterling..........Lakeshore (S) LSM-811 15-25 81
Beatles; Mindbenders; Billy J. Kramer & Dakotas; Fortunes; Chad & Jeremy; Sandie Shaw; Spencer Davis Group; others.

Broadside Ballads..........Broadside (M) BR-301 25-35 63
Blind Boy Grunt (Bob Dylan);New World Singers; Pete Seeger; Peter LaFarge; Phil Ochs; Gil Tanner; Happy Traum; Matt McGinn; Mark Spoelstra.

Broadside Ballads, Vol. 1..........Folkways (M) FH 5301 25-35 64
Blind Boy Grunt (Bob Dylan);New World Singers; Pete Seeger; Peter LaFarge; Phil Ochs; Gil Tanner; Happy Traum; Matt McGinn; Mark Spoelstra.

Broadside Reunion..........Folkways (M) FR 5315 15-25 72
Blind Boy Grunt (Bob Dylan); Phil Ochs; Tom Paxton; Mike Millins; Eric Anderson; Peter LaFarge; Len Chandler; Sis Cunningham; others.

Broadway & Hollywood Now!..........Columbia (S) CSS 755 8-12

Broadway & Hollywood Show Stoppers..........Capitol (S) SL 6645 8-12
Jackie Gleason; Gordon MacRae; Al DeLory; Sandler & Young; David Rose; Nancy Wilson; Matt Monro; Alfred Newman.

Broadway Magic..........Columbia (S) JS-36282 8-10 79
(Soundtrack.) Joel Grey; Priscilla Lopez; Angela Lansbury; Elaine Stritch; Ethel Merman; Gwen Verdon; Larry Kert; Julie Andrews; Carol Lawrence; Betty Wolfe; others.

Broadway Magic, Vol. 2 (The Great Performers)..........Columbia (S) JS-36409 8-10 80
(Soundtrack.) Debbie Reynolds; Danny Kaye; John Travolta; Barbra Streisand; Ruby Keeler; Angela Lansbury; Ethel Merman; Beatrice Arthur; Julie Andrews; Rex Harrison.

Broadway Magic, Vol. 5 (The Great Performances)..........Columbia (S) JS-36859 8-10 81
(Soundtrack.) Ethel Merman; Jack Klugman; Sandra Church; Gwen Verdon; Richard Burton; Pat Suzuki; Larry Blyden; Donna McKechnie; Leslie Uggams; Patricia Neway; Judy Holliday; Dorothy Loudon; Rex Harrison.

Broadway Magic Collection, Vols. 1-6..........Columbia (S) C6X-37642 ?? 81
(Soundtrack.) Joel Grey; Priscilla Lopez; Angela Lansbury; Elaine Stritch; Ethel Merman; Gwen Verdon; Larry Kert; Julie Andrews; Carol Lawrence; Betty Wolfe; Debbie Reynolds; Danny Kaye; John Travolta; Barbra Streisand; Ruby Keeler; Rex Harrison; Beatrice Arthur; Chita Rivera; Stanley Holloway; Helen Gallagher; Stubby Kaye; Mary Martin; Adolph Green; Jill Haworth; Sandra Church; Larry Blyden; Pat Suzuki; Leslie Uggams; Donna McKechnie; Dorothy Loudon; Judy Holliday; Richard Burton; Patricia Neway.

Broadway Opening Night, Vol. 1, the '60s..........RCA (S) ARL1-4049 8-10 81
(Soundtrack.) Zero Mostel; Lucille Ball & Paula Stuart; John Cullum; Liza Minelli; Jeannie Carson; John Raitt & Eileen Christy; Lee Venora; Richard Banke; Ethel Merman; Ronn Carrol & Children.

Broadway Opening Night, Vol. 2, the '70s..........RCA (S) ARL1-4050 8-10 81

Broadway Show Stoppers .... Columbia Special Products (S) CSP-168 5-10
Tony Bennett; Ray Conniff; Rosemary Clooney; Vic Damone; Andre Previn; Jerry Vale; Andre Kostelanetz; Anita Bryant; Lester Lanin; Buddy Greco; Aretha Franklin; Merrill Staton Choir. (Special products release for Sandy's.)

Broken Heart for Every Guitar in Nashville .... ???? 5-10
Willie Nelson; Freddy Fender; Wilma Burgess; Jack Scott; B.J. Thomas; George Jones; Barbara Mandrell; Johnny "Piano" Wilson; Statler Brothers; Jack Greene.

Bronco Billy .... Elektra (S) 5E-512 8-10 80
(Soundtrack.) Ronnie Milsap; Penny DeHaven; Merle Haggard; Clint Eastwood; Reinsmen.

Brothers in Song (16 Original Hits) .... Trolley Car (M) TC-5004 10-15
Isley Brothers; Chuck Berry; Lloyd Price; Jimi Hendrix; Jerry Butler; Ray Charles; Brook Benton; Chuck Jackson.

Brothers, Sisters, Aces and Spots .... Decca (S) DL-75187 8-12 70
Mills Brothers; Ames Brothers; McGuire Sisters; Andrew Sisters; Four Aces; Ink Spots.

Brunswick's Greatest Hits .... Brunswick (S) BL-754186 8-12 70s

Bubble Gum Greatest Hits, Vol. 1 .... Accord (S) SN-7136 ?? 81
Ohio Express; Lemon Pipers; 1910 Fruitgum Co.; others.

Bubble Gum Greatest Hits, Vol. 2 .... Accord (S) SN-7137 ?? 81
Ohio Express; Lemon Pipers; 1910 Fruitgum Co.; others.

Bubble Gum Music Is—the Naked Truth, Vol. 1 .... Buddah (S) BDS-5032 20-25 69
Ohio Express; Lemon Pipers; 1910 Fruitgum Company; Shadows of Knight; Kastenetz Katz Super Cirkus.

Buddah's 360° Dial-A-Hit .... Buddah (S) BDS-5039 20-25 70
1910 Fruit Gum Company; Brooklyn Bridge; Ohio Express; Five Stairsteps; Smoke Ring; Elephants Memory; Impressions; Lovin' Spoonful; Melanie; Barry Goldberg; U.S. '69; Road.

Buddah 1970 (2 LP) .... Buddah (S) NEC 1970 20-25 70

Bull Durham .... Capitol (S) C1-90586 8-10 88
(Soundtrack.) George Thorogood & Destroyers; Fabulous Thunderbirds; House of Schock; Los Lobos; John Fogerty; Pat Laughlin; Dr. Bennie Wallace; Blasters.

Bumpers (2 LP) .... Island (S) IDP-1 10-20 70s
Traffic; Bronco; Spooky Tooth; Quintessence; Mott the Hoople; Jethro Tull; Jimmy Cliff; Bloodwyn Pig; Dave Mason; John & Beverly Martin; King Crimson; If; Free; Nick Drake; Fairport Convention; Cat Stevens; Renaissance; Fotheringay; Clouds.

Bunch of Goodies .... Chess (M) LP-1441 50-75 59
(Black vinyl.)

Bunch of Goodies .... Chess (M) LP-1441 500-750 59
(Multi-color vinyl. Promotional issue only.) Harvey & Moonglows; Lee Andrews & Hearts; Miracles; Orchids; Coronets; Moonglows.

Burghers, Vol. 1 .... No Label/No Number Used (S) 8-12 80s
Swamp Rats; Peters Pipers; Arondies; Fenways; Grains of Sand; Marshmellow Steamshovel; Fantastic Dee Jays; Napoleonic Wars.

Burglar .... MCA (S) MCA-6201 8-10 87
(Soundtrack.) Sly Stone; Belinda Carlisle; Jets; Smithereens; Wax; Jacksons; Distance; Belle Stars; Bobcat Goldthwait.

Burt Bacharach & Friends .... A&M (S) 19007 5-10

Burton Lane in Hollywood (2 LP) .... JJA (S) JJA 19824 10-15

Bushel of Five String Banjos .... Pickwick (M) 6111 8-12
Flatt & Scruggs; Stanley Brothers; Carl Story; Denver Duke; Jeffery Null.

Bushel of Top Country Hits! .... Design (M) DLP 642 10-15 60s

Bushel of Top Country Hits! .... Design (SE) SDLP 642 10-15 60s
Ferlin Husky; Hank Locklin; Jan Howard; Del Reeves; Stewart Family; Larry Steele; Floyd Tillman; T. Texas Tyler; Hal Willis; Wilburn Brothers.

Buster .... Atlantic (S) 81905-1 8-10 88
(Soundtrack.) Phil Collins; Hollies; Anne Dudley; Sonny & Cher; Spencer Davis Group; Four Tops; Gerry & Pacemakers; Dusty Sprngfield; London Film Orchestra; Searchers.

Bustin' Loose .... MCA (S) 5141 8-10 81
(Soundtrack.) Roberta Flack; Peabo Bryson; Eric Mercury; Luther Vandross; others.

Bustin' Surfboards .... GNP/Crescendo (S) GNPS-2152 5-10 82
Beach Boys; Marketts; Ritchie Valens; Challengers; Surf Raiders; Bobby Fuller; Neil Norman; Rockin' Rebels; Dick Dale & His Deltones; Tornadoes; Gamblers; Jim Messina & Jesters; Lively Ones; Jack Nitzsche.

By Invitation Only (2 LP) .... Atlantic (SP) K 60112 15-25 74
Led Zeppelin; Rolling Stones; Stephen Stills; Average White Band; Buffalo Springfield; Fornerra; Marconi; Heavy Metal Kids; Yes; Roberta Flack; Emerson, Lake & Palmer; Pretty Things; Delaney & Bonnie; Aretha Franklin; others.

Bye Bye Birdie .... Colpix (M) CP-454 25-30 64

Bye Bye Birdie .... Colpix (S) SCP-454 30-40 64
(Soundtrack.) James Darren; Paul Petersen; Shelley Fabares; Marcels; Stu Phillips.

CKLW Solid Gold (2 LP) .... Post (SP) 8 10-20 60s
(Mail order offer.) Association; Tommy James & Shondells; Flying Machine; Brooklyn Bridge; Animals; Shelly Fabares; J. Frank Wilson; Bob Seger; Robert Knight; James Brown; Johnny Nash; Foundations; Shangri-Las; Winstons; Funkadelic; Rightwous Brothers; Intruders; Dells; Shirelles; Aaron Neville; Crests; Delfonics; Tommy Roe; 1910 Fruitgum Company; Turtles; Cowsills; Surfaris; Neil Diamond; Shocking Blue; Cowsills.

CKLW Solid Gold, Vol. 2 (2 LP) .... Post (SP) 7108 10-20 70s
(Mail order offer.) Osmond Brothers; Bells; Chi-Lites; Brian Hyland; Edison Lighthouse; Buoys; Guess Who; Five Stairsteps; Tee Garden & Van Winkle; Oliver; George Baker; Daddy Dewdrop; Ocean; Gordon Lightfoot; Chairmen of the Board; Vanity Fare; Dells; Steam; Poppy Family; Tommy James & Shondells; James Brown; Andy Kim; Moments; Alice Cooper.

CTI Summer Jazz at the Hollywood Bowl .... CTI (S) 7076 8-12 77
Hubert Laws; Grover Washington Jr.; Stanley Turrentine; Deodato; Milt Jackson; Johnny Hammond; Joe Farrell; George Benson; Hank Crawford; Freddie Hubbard; Airto; Esther Phillips; Ron Carter; Jack DeJohnette; Bob James.

CTI Summer Jazz at the Hollywood Bowl (Live Three) .... CTI (S) 7078 8-12 77
CTI All Stars; Hubert Laws; Grover Washington Jr.; Stanley Turrentine; Deodato; Milt Jackson; Johnny Hammond; Joe Ferrell; George Benson; Hank Crawford; Freddie Hubbard; Airto; Esther Phillips; Ron Carter; Jack DeJohnette; Bob James.

Caddyshack 2 .... Columbia (S) SC-44317 5-8 88
(Soundtrack.) Tamara Champlin; Cheap Trick; Earth, Wind & Fire; Lisa Lisa; Cult Jam; Full Force; Kenny Loggins; Michael Dilbeck; Andy Johns; Ira Newborn; Pointer Sisters; Patty Smyth; Eric Martin.

Cadence Classics Series, Vol. 1 .... Barnaby (S) BR-4000 8-12 75
Everly Brothers; Johnny Tillotson; Chordettes; Eddie Hodges; Link Wray.

Cadence Classics Series, Vol. 2 .... Barnaby (S) BR-4001 8-12 75
Everly Brothers; Johnny Tillotson; Chordettes; Eddie Hodges; Link Wray; Charlie McCoy.

Cadence Classics Series, Vol. 3 .... Barnaby (S) BR-4002 8-12 76
Everly Brothers; Johnny Tillotson; Chordettes; Lenny Welch; Marion Marlowe; Lulius La Rosa; Bill Hayes; Don Shirley Trio; Archie Bleyer.

Cajun Music - the Early '50s .... Arhoolie (M) 5008 8-12 69
Shuk Richard & His Louisiana Aces; Texas Melody Boys; Floyd LeBlanc & His French Fiddle; Nathan Abshire; Lawrence Walker & His Wandering Aces; Elsie Deshotel & His Louisiana Rhythmaires; Amar DeVillier & His Louisiana Jambaleers; Wallace LaFleur; Sandy Austin; Harry Choates.

Cajun Swamp Pop Super Hits .... Jin (S) 9028 5-10 80s

California Christmas .... Capitol (S) ST-11226 5-10 73
Buck Owens; Lawanda Lindsey; Buddy Alan; Susan Raye; Freddie Hart; others.

California Dreaming .... Casablanca/American International (S) AILP 3001 8-12 79
(Soundtrack.) America; Henry Small; Burton Cummings; Flo & Eddie; FDR; Michelle Phillips; Pat Upton.

California Jam 2 .... Columbia (S) PC2-35389 15-20 78
Aerosmith; Heart; Santana; Ted Nugent; Dave Mason; Frank Marino & Mahogany Rush; Jean Michel Jarre; Heart; Rubicon. (Live concert.)

California, U.S.A. (2 LP) .... Columbia (S) C2-37412 8-12 83
Bruce & Terry; Rick Henn; Sparks; Euclid Beach Band; Northern Light; Inconceivables; Lou Christie; Roger McGuinn; Rip Chords; Surfer Girls; Walter Egan; Ricci Martin; Jan & Dean; Fresh; Hondells; Flo & Eddie; American Spring; Jackie De Shannon; Keller & Webb; Blue Rose; Minnesota.

Calypso Carnival (2 EP) .... Decca (EP) ED 624 10-20

Camp .... Capitol (M) 2472 8-12
Dean Martin; others.

Campus Beat .... MCA Special Products (S) DL-734634 8-12

Campus Hootenanny .... RCA (M) LPM-2829 15-20 64

Campus Hootenanny .... RCA (S) LSP-2829 15-25 64
Jabberwocks; Krokodiloes; Cayuga's Waiters; others.

Campus Jazz Festival, Viceroy Cigarettes .... RCA Custom (M) 1543 20-30 59
Red Norvo; Bob Scobey; Erroll Garner; Dukes of Dixieland; Duke Ellington; Jonah Jones; Big 18; Shorty Rogers; Louis Armstrong; Benny Goodman.

Candlelight and Wine Album .... ???? (S) ???? 5-10
Lou Rawls; Ray Conniff; Roger Whittaker; Gladys Knight & Pips; Arpin; B.J. Thomas; Vikki Carr; Charlie Rich; Hagood Hardy; Three Degrees; Ray Price; Manny Kellem; Gilbert Becaud; Minnie Riperton; Andy Williams; Johnny Mathis; Samatha Sang.

Candy .... ABC (S) ABCS-OC-9 12-18 68
(Soundtrack.) Dave Grusin; Steppenwolf; Byrds; others.

Cannes Jazz Festival .... RCA Custom (M) ???? 15-20 59
Benny Goodman; Louis Armstrong; Shorty Rogers; Red Norvo; Jonah Jones; Duke Ellington; Dukes of Dixieland; Bob Scobey; Big 18; Erroll Garner. (Made for Viceroy Cigarettes.)

Cannonball Run .... Warner Bros. (S) HS-3580 10-15 81

Cannonball Run .... RCA (S) VIP-28036 8-10 81
(Soundtrack.) Ray Stevens; Lou Rawls; Chuck Mangione; Al Capps; California Childrens Chorus.

Can't Stop the Music .... Casablanca (S) NBLP-7220 8-10 80
(Soundtrack.) David London; Ritchie Family; Village People; others.

Cape Breton Jamboree .... Celtic (M) CX-1 5-10

Capitol Classics 1942-1950 .... Capitol (SP) MFP 5610 5-10 84
Lou Busch; Jane Froman; Judy Garland; Dick Haymes; Pee Wee Hunt; Kingston Trio; Nellie Lutcher & Her Rhythm; Dean Martin; Al Martino; Johnny Mercer & Pied Pipers; Ella Mae Morse; Tex Ritter; Freddie Slack; Jo Stafford.

Capitol Hi-Fi Demonstration Record .... Capitol (M) PRO 138 15-25 50s
(10–inch LP.) French National Symphony Orchestra; Hollywood String Quartet; Leonard Pennario; Los Angeles Orchestra; Ballet Theatre Orchestra; Pittsburgh Symphony Orchestra; Stan Kenton; Les Paul; Nat King Cole; Joe "Fingers" Carr; Alex Stordahl; Ray Anthony; Gordon MacRae.

Capitol Promotional Releases/Samplers (Listed by catalog number. All are promo only.)

Capitol Son of Singles Sampler 8-10 74

Capitol 6 New Spirit of Capitol 10-15
Steve Miller; Hedge & Donna; Joe South; Linda Ronstadt; John Stewart; David Axelrod; Edgar Brighton Band; Grand Funk; Sons; Pink Floyd; Guitar Jr.; Bob Seger System; Mississippi Fred McDowell.

Capitol 103 (b/w 104) Capitol Cavalcade (Capitol's 10th Anniversary, 1942-1952) (10 inch LP) 50-75 52
Dave Barbour; Les Baxter; Mel Blanc; Billy Butterfield; Nat King Cole; Frank DeVol; Tennessee Ernie; Mary Ford; Pee Wee Hunt; Betty Hutton; Red Ingle; Stan Kenton; Peggy Lee; Nellie Lutcher; Billy May; Johnny Mercer; Ella Mae Morse; Les Paul; Pied Pipers; Bobby Sherwood; Freddie Slack; Kay Starr; Jimmy Wakely; Paul Weston; Margaret Whiting; Tex Williams; Yogi Yorgesson. (Narrated by Dave Dexter Jr.)

Capitol 138 (b/w 139) Excerpts from Popular Music 50-75 53
Stan Kenton; Les Paul; Nat King Cole; Joe "Fingers" Carr; Strings of Stordahl; Ray Anthony; Gordon MacRae; George Fenneman. Side 1 has "Capitol Classics."

Capitol 197 (b/w 198) The Capitol Story (EP) 500-750 54
Frank Sinatra; Dean Martin; Nat King Cole; Peggy Lee; Stan Kenton; Yma Sumac; Jerry Lewis; Johnny Mercer; Jackie Gleason; Billy May; Kay Starr; George Fenneman. (Sleeve says "The Capitol Story," but disc reads "The Capitol Record." 100 copies made.)

Capitol 201 (b/w 202) Christmas LP for Deejays 30-50
Frank Sinatra; Nat King Cole; Billy May; Les Paul; others.

Capitol 215 (216/217/218) Recorded Highlights of Glenn Wallichs Day, September 27, 1954 (2 LP) 300-500 54
(10–inch LPs.) Frank Sinatra; Dean Martin; Peggy Lee; Nat King Cole; Johnny Mercer; Ella Mae Morse; Tex Williams; Glen Wallichs; others.

Capitol 246 (b/w 247) Selections from New Capitol Albums, March 1956 .... 25-50 56
Frank Sinatra; Tennessee Ernie Ford; Franck Pourcel; Joe Bushkin; Harry James; others.

Capitol 254 (b/w 255) The Capitol Record - A Souvenir of the Capitol Tower (EP) 250-500 56
Frank Sinatra; Dean Martin; Nat King Cole; Peggy Lee; Stan Kenton; Johnny Mercer; Jackie Gleason; Gordon MacRae; Les Brown; George Fenneman.

Capitol 268 (269/270/271) Salesmen's Demonstration Records, August 1956 (2 LP) 40-60 56
Frank Sinatra; Franck Pourcel; June Christy; John Raitt; Stan Kenton; Guy Lombardo; Four Freshmen; George Shearing; others.

Capitol 271 (272/273/274) Salesmen's Demonstration Record - New Album Releases, August-September 1956 (2 LP) 40-60 56
Frank Sinatra; Ray Anthony; Woody Herman; Billy May; Jane Froman; Franck Pourcel; June Christy; John Raitt; Stan Kenton; Guy Lombardo; Four Freshmen; George Shearing; Lucho Gatica; Ruby Murray; Ray Martin; others.

Capitol 280/281: see SINATRA, Frank
Capitol 299 (b/w 300) Salesmen's Demonstration Record, November 1956 .... 30-50 56
Frank Sinatra; Les Brown; Nelson Riddle; Jackie Gleason; Guy Lombardo; Paul Smith; Roger Wagner Chorale; others.
Capitol 301 (302) New Album Preview 25-50 56
Frank Sinatra; Les Brown; Nelson Riddle; Jackie Gleason; Guy Lombardo; Paul Smith; Roger Wagner Chorale; others.
Capitol 304 (b/w 305) Triple Hit Preview for Billboard Readers (EP) 50-100 56
Frank Sinatra; Dean Martin; Nat King Cole; Peggy Lee; Stan Kenton; Johnny Mercer; Jackie Gleason; Gordon MacRae; Les Brown; George Fenneman. (Available only through Billboard magazine.)
Capitol 311 (312/313/314) New Album Preview - Capitol's February Releases, February 1957 (2 LP) 50-100 57
Frank Sinatra; Andrews Sisters; Billy May; Les Baxter; George Shearing; All Stars; Les Baxter; Berkes Bela Orchestra; Big Ben Banjo Band; Serge Chaloff; Miles Davis; Woody Herman; Hollywood Bowl Symphony Orchestra; Gordon Jenkins with Ralph Brewster Singers; Guy Lombardo; Kenny Gardner; Marimba Chiapas; Ray Martin; Billy May; Red Nichols; Dino Oliver; Line Renaud.
Capitol 324, January 1957 Capitol Salesman Demo Record 20-30 57
Dean Martin; others.
Capitol 325 (326/327/328) New Album Preview, March 1957 (2 LP) 50-100 57
Gene Vincent; Five Keys; Don Baker; Frank Barber; Les Baxter; Nat King Cole; Det Er Det Samme Hvor Jeg Drar; Raphael Farina; Glasgow Police Pipe Band; Philip Green; King Sisters; Lord Beginner; Harry Owens; Billy May; Marian McPartland; Lizzie Miles; Les Paul & Mary Ford; Sharkey; Torpedo; Rolf Van Der Linden.
Capitol 329 (330/331/332) New Album Preview (2 LP) 50-100 57
Capitol 333 (b/w 334) New Album Preview, April 1957 .... 10-20 57
Les Brown; Eve Boswell; Jackie Davis; Ken Errair; Tennessee Ernie Ford; Jackie Gleason; Lord Flea; Ray Martin; Mariachi Mexico; Orkiestra Sekcji Polskiej Radia Francuskiego; Nino Posadas; Nelson Riddle; Voices of the Atolls with Zizou Bar Trio.
Capitol 339 (340/341/342) Maytime in Music Time on Capitol - New Album Preview, May 1957 (2 LP) 25-50 57
Frank Sinatra; Judy Garland; June Christy; Gordon MacRae; Kate Smith; Norrie Paramor; Louis Prima; Lucho Gatica; Li Li Hua & Tung Pei Pei; Mexican National Symphony; others.
Capitol 347 (348/349/350) Salesmen's Demonstration Records, May 1957 (2 LP) 25-50 57
Frank Sinatra; Jonah Jones; Joe Bushkin; Jack Teagarden; Ray Anthony; Paul Smith; Coleman Hawkins; Judy Garland; June Christy; Gordon MacRae; Kate Smith; Louis Prima; others.
Capitol 363 (b/w 364) Spectacular! New Album Preview, August 1957 (2 LP) 20-30 57
Nat King Cole; James Dean Story; Fred Waring; Peggy Lee; Jackie Gleason; Joe "Fingers" Carr; Glen Gray; Bobby Hackett; Vincente Bianchi & Los Jaranistas; Los Centauros with Dora Maria; Ron Goodwin; Sonny James; Merry Macs; Jula de Palma & Enzo Amadori; Norrie Paramor; Trudy Richards; George Shearing; Leith Stevens.
Capitol 373 (b/w 374) Popular Classics Album Spectacular, September 1958 (2 LP) 15-30 57
Laurindo Almeida; Rudolf Firkusny; Sascha Gorodnitzki; Hollywood Bowl Symphony Orchestra; Leonard Pennario; Roger Wagner Chorale.
Capitol 391 (392/393/394) There's Magic in Music on Capitol - New Album Preview, September 1957 (2 LP) 25-50 57
Frank Sinatra; Ray Anthony; Gordon MacRae; Ferlin Husky; Gordon Jenkins; Andrews Sisters; Harry James; Four Freshmen & Pete Rugolo; Dakota Staton; Franck Pourcel; Johnny Pecon; others.
Capitol 398 (399/400/401) Capitol's All-Star Line-Up, October 1957 (2 LP) 25-50 57
Frank Sinatra; Tennessee Ernie Ford; Nelson Riddle; Les Baxter; Guy Lombardo; others.
Capitol 424 (b/w 425) Christmas Around the World - 13 Christmas Albums, December 1957 .... 25-50 57
Frank Sinatra; Fred Waring; Jackie Gleason; Roger Wagner Chorale; Carmen Dragon; Hollywood Bowl Symphony Orchestra; others.
Capitol 426/427: see SINATRA, Frank / Roger Wagner Chorale / Hollywood Bowl Symphony Orchestra
Frank Sinatra; Roger Wagner Chorale; Hollywood Bowl Symphony Orchestra.
Capitol 434/435: see SINATRA, Frank
Capitol 437/438: see VINCENT, Gene / Frank Sinatra / Sonny James / Ron Goodwin
Capitol 439 (440/441/442) Salesmen's Demonstration Records, January 1958 (2 LP) 25-50 58
Frank Sinatra; Ray Anthony; Tommy Sands; Guy Lombardo; Louvin Brothers; others.
Capitol 443 (444/445/446) I Love Music - Preview of January Albums from Capitol (2 LP) 25-50 58
Frank Sinatra; Ray Anthony; Tommy Sands; Guy Lombardo; Louvin Brothers; Billy May; Freddy Martin; Dave Pell; King Sisters; Hans Conreid; Pee Wee Hunt; Keely Smith; others.
Capitol 500: see SINATRA, Frank / Nat King Cole
Capitol 502: see FIVE KEYS / Ferlin Husky
Capitol 511 (EP) 10-15
Johnny Otis Show; Four Preps; Faron Young; Carlson's Raiders.
Capitol 564 (565/566/567) Salesmen's Demonstration Records, April 1958 (2 LP) 25-50 58
Frank Sinatra; Sonny James; Jackie Davis; Webley Edwards; Pee Wee Hunt; Joe Bushkin; Ferlin Husky; Gordon MacRae; Les Baxter; Peggy Lee; Andrews Sisters; others.
Capitol 568 (b/w 569) Hi-Fi Esta - Capitol New Album Preview, April 1958 .... 25-50 58
Frank Sinatra; Sonny James; Jackie Davis; Webley Edwards; Pee Wee Hunt; Joe Bushkin; Ferlin Husky; Gordon MacRae; Les Baxter; Peggy Lee; Andrews Sisters; others.
Capitol 617 (b/w 618) Salesmen Demonstration Record, June 1958 .... 25-50 58
Kingston Trio; Don Baker; Woody Herman; Les Paul & Mary Ford; Nat Cole; Jordanaires; Paul Smith; Guy Lombardo; Glen Gray; Gordon Jenkins; Jackie Gleason; 6 International Artists; Joe "Fingers" Carr; Bobby Hackett; Page Cavanaugh; Mickey Katz.
Capitol 642 (643/644/645) New Worlds of Music from the Capitol Tower, August 1958 (2 LP) 25-50 58
Frank Sinatra; others.
Capitol 696 (b/w 697) New Album Preview for September 1958 .... 25-50 58
Frank Sinatra; others.
Capitol 727 (728/729/730) Christmas Around the World, December 1958 (2 LP) 25-50 58
Frank Sinatra; Dean Martin; Nat King Cole; Jackie Gleason; Johnny Mercer; Tennessee Ernie Ford; Fred Waring; others.
Capitol 736 (737/738/739) International Festival of Music, September 1958 (2 LP) 25-50 58
June Christy; Lou Busch; Sam Butera; Del Courtney; Ethel Ennis; Four Freshmen; Jackie Gleason; Bobby Hackett; Pee Wee Hunt; Stan Kenton; Maderas De Mi Tierra Orchestra; Freddy Martin; Billy May; Miguel de Molina; Red Nichols & Five Pennies; Norrie Paramour; Tommy Sands; Keely Smith; Cliffie Stone; Fred Waring.
*Capitol 758 (b/w 759) Salesman's Stereo Demonstration Record, New Albums for Nov. 1958 - International Festival of Music*25-50 58
Frank Sinatra; Billy May; Stan Kenton; Fred Waring; Ray Anthony; others.
Capitol 766 (767/768/769) International Festival of Music, November 1958 (2 LP) 25-50 58
Ray Anthony; Don Baker Trio; Les Baxter; Molly Bee; Joe Bushkin; William Clauson; Nat King Cole; Webley Edwards; Fairuz; Four Preps; Judy Garland; Harry James; Jonah Jones; Peggy Lee; Los Macarenos; Mariano Mores; Ray Martin; Louis Prima with Sam Butera & Witnesses; Alvino Rey; Ann Richards; Johnny Richards; Tex Ritter; George Shearing Quintet; Jack Teagarden; Faron Young.
Capitol 801 (b/w 802) Merry Christmas from [Capitol Artists] (EP) 15-25 58
Frank Sinatra; Fred Waring; Tennessee Ernie Ford; Jackie Gleason.

Capitol 846 (b/w 847) Untitled 25-50 58
Frank Sinatra; others.
Capitol 896 (b/w 899) Sounds Unlimited '59 (2 LP) 20-30 59
Nat King Cole; Jonah Jones; Les Baxter; Peggy Lee; George Shearing; Judy Garland; others.
Capitol 967 (968/969/970) Sounds Unlimited - New Album Preview for March 1959 (2 LP) 25-50 59
Frank Sinatra; Dean Martin; others.
Capitol 987: see MARTIN, Dean
Capitol 1033 (b/w 1034) Sounds Unlimited April 1959 .... 20-30 59
Dakota Staton; Red Nichols; Stan Kenton; Yma Sumac; Hank Jones; others.
Capitol 1116 (b/w 1117) From Capitol, June 1959 .... 20-30 59
Kingston Trio; others.
Capitol 1166 (1167/1168/1169) Kaleidoscope, August 1959 (2 LP) 25-50 59
Frank Sinatra; Larry Hovis; Jack Marshall; Jack Fascinato; Ed Townsend; Peggy Lee; George Shearing; Four Preps; Dorothy Donegan; Joe "Fingers" Carr; Tennessee Ernie Ford; Paul Weston; Andy Griffith; Webley Edwards; Cliffie Stone; Renato Carosone; Adi Cakobau Girls School Choir.
Capitol 1223 (1224/1225/1226) Capitol Kaleidoscope, September 1959 (2 LP) 20-40 59
Van Alexander; Les Baxter; Nat King Cole; Stan Freberg; Jackie Gleason; Glen Gray; Bobby Hackett; Kenyon Hopkins; John LaSalle Quintet; Guy Lombardo; Katyna Ranieri & Riz Ortolani; Tommy Sands; Felix Slotkin; Dakota Staton; Gigi Stok; Hank Thompson; Faron Young.
Capitol 1253 (b/w 1254) Merry Christmas from Capitol 25-50 59
Frank Sinatra; others.
Capitol 1263 (b/w 1264) the Gift of Music: Excerpts from New Albums, October 1959 .... 15-25 59
Ray Anthony; Susan Barrett; Elmer Bernstein; Alfred Drake & Patricia Morrison; Four Freshmen; Pee Wee Hunt; Jonah Jones; Mickey Kartz; Gordon MacRae; Alvino Rey; Semprini; Dinah Shore.
Capitol 1298 (b/w 1299) New Preview Albums: the Gift of Music November 1959 .... 20-30 59
Kay Starr; Nat King Cole; Dean Martin; George Shearing; Tennessee Ernie Ford & Jordanaires; Stan Kenton; Jeri Southers; Paul Weston; Freddy Martin; Donna Hightower; Laurindo Almeida; Ruth Welcome; Muzzy Marcellino; Jack Jones; Plas Johnson; Max Jaffa.
Capitol 1390 (b/w 1391) I Feel a Song Comin' On - Capitol Records Tribute to Jimmy McHugh 25-50 59
Frank Sinatra; Dean Martin; Judy Garland; Keely Smith; Peggy Lee; June Christy; Ann Richards; Gordon MacRae; Nat King Cole; Ray Anthony; Tommy Sands; Nelson Riddle.
Capitol 1444 (b/w 1445) Artistry in Music, February 1960 .... 15-25 60
Ray Anthony; Les Baxter; June Christy; Les Compagnos De La Chanson; Four Freshmen; Jordanaires; Stan Kenton; Guy Lombardo; Enric Madriguera & Chuy Reyes; Billy May; Curt Massey; Dave Pell; Kay Starr; Ruth Welcome.
Capitol 1539 (b/w 1540) Reach for a Star on Capitol - New Album Preview, May 1960 .... 25-50 60
Frank Sinatra; others.
Capitol 1549/1550: see SINATRA, Frank
Capitol 1585 (b/w 1666) Reach For a Star! July 1960 .... 15-25 60
Dean Martin; others.
Capitol 1665 (b/w 1666) Reach For a Star! October 1960 .... 15-25 60
Dean Martin; Van Alexander; Rene Bloch; Nat King Cole; Ron Goodwin; Stan Kenton; Alfred Newman & Ken Darby; Fred Waring; Nancy Wilson.
Capitol 1685 (b/w 1686) Reach For a Star! 15-25 60
Dean Martin; others.
Capitol 1725 (b/w 1726) New from the Sound Capitol of the World, January 1961 .... 25-50 61
Frank Sinatra; Nat King Cole; Les Baxter; Four Freshmen; Jonah Jones; Gordon MacRae; Dakota Staton; Freddy Martin; Martha Carson; Los Churum Beles; Maurice Evans; Tammy Grimes; Phil Napoleon; Pastors; Ann Richards & Stan Kenton; Dick Sinclair.
Capitol 1759 (b/w 1760) Great New Releases from the Sound Capitol of the World, February 1961 .... 15-25 61
Ray Anthony & Anita Ray; Bob Bain; June Christy; Benny Goodman; Glen Gray; Ferlin Husky; Wanda Jackson; Harry James; Plas Johnson; Kingston Trio; Buck Owens; Louis Prima & Keely Smith; Kay Starr; Fred Waring.
Capitol 1775 (b/w 1776) Capitol's Winners in the Billboard 13th Annual Disc Jockey Poll 25-50 61
Frank Sinatra; Nat King Cole; Four Freshmen; Jonah Jones; Dinah Shore; Stan Kenton; Nancy Wilson; Peggy Lee; Kingston Trio; June Christy; Ray Anthony; others.
Capitol 1797 (b/w 1798) New Releases from the Sound Capitol of the World, March 1961 .... 15-20 61
Ray Anthony; Les Baxter; Sam Butera; Nat King Cole; Jackie Davis; Webley Edwards; Jackie Gleason; Pee Wee Hunt; Bob Melvin; Dave Pell Octet; George Shearing & Nancy Wilson; Jean Shepard; Voices of Hope; Ruth Welcome; Stanley Wilson; Faron Young.
Capitol 1834 (b/w 1835) Goin' Places with Capitol: Minute Masters 15-20 61
Kingston Trio; others.
Capitol 1864: see SINATRA, Frank
Frank Sinatra; Out Islanders; others.
Capitol 1898 (b/w 1899) Do Not Open Before Christmas 25-50 61
Frank Sinatra; June Christy; Stan Kenton; Peggy Lee; Dinah Shore; Louvin Brothers; Kingston Trio; Nat King Cole; Jackie Gleason; Fred Waring; Guy Lombardo; others.
Capitol 1958 (b/w 1959) Great New Releases from the Sound Capitol of the World, February 1962 .... 15-25 62
Kingston Trio; Dean Martin; others.
Capitol 1970 (b/w 1971) Instant Instrumentals - Minute Masters 15-25 62
Ray Anthony; Jackie Davis; Benny Goodman; Glen Gray; Woody Herman; Harry James; Jonah Jones; Stan Kenton; Billy May; Red Nichols; Nelson Riddle; Shorty Rodgers; George Shearing & Nancy Wilson; George Shearing.
Capitol 1974 (b/w 1975) Great New Releases from the Sound Capitol of the World, April 1962 .... 20-30 62
Frank Sinatra; Kay Starr; Peggy Lee; Nat King Cole; Woody Herman; Guy Lombardo; Stan Kenton; others.
Capitol 2036 (b/w 2037) Silver Platter Service 15-25 62
Vic Damone; Tennessee Ernie Ford; Four Freshmen; Pee Wee Hunt; Dave Pell; George Shearing; Ginny Simms & Harry Babbitt; Roger Wagner Chorale; Nancy Wilson & Cannonball Adderley.
Capitol 2068 (b/w 2069) Great New Releases from the Sound Capitol of the World, July 1962 .... 20-30 62
Frank Sinatra; Peggy Lee; Nat King Cole; Cy Coleman; Glen Gray; Jordanaires; Van Alexander; Norrie Paramor; Guy Lombardo; Jordanaires; Ralph Carmichael.
Capitol 2081 (b/w 2082) Full Dimensional Sound 20-40 62
Kingston Trio; others.
Capitol 2085 (b/w 2086) Silver Platter Service, Sides 9 & 10, July 1962 .... 20-40 62
Frank Sinatra; others.
Capitol 2097 (b/w 2098) Silver Platter Service, Sides 11 & 12, July 1962 .... 20-40 62
Frank Sinatra; others.

Capitol 2123 (b/w 2124 Silver Platter Service, August 1962 .... *20-30* *62*
Les Baxter; George Chakiris; Nat King Cole; Vic Damone; Kingston Trio; Peggy Lee; Roger Wagner; Nancy Wilson.
Capitol 2125 (b/w 2126) Great New Releases from the Sound Capitol of the World, August 1962 .... *15-25* *62*
George Chakiris; Nat King Cole; Vic Damone; Judy Garland; Kingston Trio; Nancy Wilson.
Capitol 2143 (b/w 2144) Campus Crowd Pleasers, September 1962 .... *20-40* *62*
Lettermen; Barbara Dane; Four Freshmen; Fantastic Five Keys; Tex Ritter with Stan Kenton; June Christy; George Shearing; Journeymen; Pilgrim Travelers featuring Lou Rawls.
Capitol 2155 (b/w 2156) Silver Platter Service, September 1962 .... *15-25* *62*
Les Baxter; George Chakiris; June Christy; Vic Damone; Four Freshmen; Arch Oboler; Nelson Riddle; Nancy Wilson.
Capitol 2159 (b/w 2160) Silver Platter Service, Sides 19 & 20, September-October 1962 .... *20-30* *62*
Frank Sinatra; Steve Allen; Jackie Gleason; June Christy; Peggy Lee; Jack Marshall; others.
Capitol 2163 (2164/2165/2166) Selections from Sinatra: the Great Years *and* Rodgers and Hammerstein Deluxe Set *(2 LP)25-45* *62*
Frank Sinatra; others.
Capitol 2181 (b/w 2182) Sales Meeting Demonstration Record for October 1962 .... *20-30* *62*
Frank Sinatra; Roy Clark; Wanda Jackson; Buck Owens; Peggy Lee; Bobby Darin; Jonah Jones; Jackie Gleason; Al Martino; others.
Capitol 2195 .... *20-30* *62*
Dean Martin; others.
Capitol 2209 (b/w 2210) A Merry Christmas from Capitol *20-30* *62*
Frank Sinatra; others.
Capitol 2229: see KINGSTON TRIO / Frank Sinatra
Capitol 2233 (b/w 2234) Excerpts from Popular Albums from December 1962 (EP) *20-30* *62*
Frank Sinatra; others.
Capitol 2237 (b/w 2238) Ten Winners from Capitol's Deck of Cards for '63, January 1963 .... *15-25* *63*
Glen Gray; Vic Damone; Ralph Carmichael; Dean Elliott; George Chakiris; Nelson Riddle; Lou Rawls; Jimmy Pruett; Lionel Long with the Noel Gilmour Sextet & Dell Tones.
Capitol 2280 (b/w 2281) Great New Releases from the Sound Capitol of the World, February 1963 .... *15-25* *63*
Joe Bucci; Peggy Lee; Van Alexander; Jimmie Rowles; George Shearing Trio; Bobby Darin; Jonah Jones; Semprini; Al White; Lettermen.
Capitol 2292 (b/w 2293) Silver Platter Service Instant Music, March/April 1963 .... *15-25* *63*
June Christy; Jackie Gleason; John Gray; Kingston Trio; Franck Pourcel; Jack Sheldon; Nancy Wilson; Lettermen; Bobby Darin; Peggy Lee; Vic Damone; Frank Sinatra; Journeymen; Cy Coleman; Laurindo Almeida; George Shearing; Stan Kenton; Billy May; Charlie Shavers; Jonah Jones.
Capitol 2304 (b/w 2305) Great New Releases from the Sound Capitol of the World, March 1963 .... *15-25* *63*
June Christy; Lee Evans; Four Preps; Jackie Gleason; John Gray; Kingston Trio; Franck Pourcel; Jack Sheldon; Nancy Wilson; Walter Wanderly.
Capitol 2308 (b/w 2309) Instant Music, April 1963 .... *10-20* *63*
Laurindo Almeida; Lee Evans Trio; Howard Roberts; Nelson Riddle; Walter Wanderly; Pee Wee Hunt.
Capitol 2328 (b/w 2329) Great New Releases from the Sound Capitol of the World, April 1963 .... *15-25* *63*
Laurindo Almeida; Judy Garland; Howard Roberts; Nat King Cole; Nelson Riddle; Frank Fontaine; Johnny Mercer; Four Freshmen; Ruth Welcome; Francis Langford; Gateway Trio.
Capitol 2375 (b/w 2376) Balanced for Broadcast, June 1963 .... *15-25* *63*
Legends; others.
Capitol 2377 (b/w 2378) Demonstration Disc *15-25* *63*
Capitol 2414 (b/w 2415) Great New Releases from the Sound Capitol of the World, August 1963 .... *15-25* *63*
Frank Sinatra; Bobby Darin; Kingston Trio; Nancy Wilson; Lettermen; Vic Damone; Glen Gray; Tennessee Ernie Ford.
Capitol 2424 (b/w 2425) Great New Releases from the Sound Capitol of the World, 1962 .... *15-25* *63*
Kingston Trio; others.
Capitol 2416 (b/w 2417) Excerpts from Popular Albums for August 1963 .... *15-25* *63*
Frank Sinatra; Bobby Darin; Kingston Trio; Nancy Wilson; Lettermen; Tennessee Ernie Ford; Glen Gray; others.
Capitol 2430 (b/w 2431) Instant Music - Minute Masters - September 1963 .... *15-25* *63*
Frank Sinatra; Bobby Darin; Kingston Trio; Nancy Wilson; Lettermen; Vic Damone; others.
Capitol 2436 (b/w 2437) Excerpts from Great New Releases from the Sound Capitol of the World, September 1963 .... *15-25* *63*
Laurindo Almeida; June Christy; Roy Clark; Cy Coleman; Four Freshmen; Judy Garland; Jonah Jones; Journeymen; Guy Lombardo; Wayne Newton; Howard Roberts; Merle Travis; T-Bone Walker; Fred Waring.
Capitol 2463 (b/w 2464) Demonstration Disc *15-25* *63*
Capitol 2474 (b/w 2475) Sounds of the Holiday Season from the Sound Capitol of the World *15-25* *63*
Frank Sinatra; Nat King Cole; Tennessee Ernie Ford; Peggy Lee; Guy Lombardo; Roger Wagner Chorale; Fred Waring; others.
Capitol 2476 Great New Releases from the Sound Capitol of the World, November 1963 .... *15-25* *63*
Earl "Fatha" Hines; Marion Montgomery; George Shearing; Stan Kenton; Four Preps; Joe Graves; Les Baxter; Dean Elliott; Tex Ritter; Ruth Welcome; Martial Solal; Gordon MacRae & Dorothy Kirsten; Webley Edwards; Ferlin Husky; Danny Long Trio.
Capitol 2479 (b/w 2480) Demonstration Disc *15-25* *63*
Capitol 2493 (b/w 2494) Demonstration Disc *15-25* *63*
Capitol 2505 (2506/2507/2508) Instant Hits from Capitol's Star Line Series, January 1964 (2 LP) *25-35* *63*
Frank Sinatra; Dean Martin; Nat King Cole; Four Freshmen; Dinah Shore; Peggy Lee; Judy Garland; Les Baxter; June Christy; Billy May; Kingston Trio; Kay Starr; Jonah Jones; Andy Griffith; Guy Lombardo.
Capitol 2510: see Star Lines (Artist Introductions to) Instant Hits
Capitol 2519 (b/w 2520) Great New Releases from the Sound Capitol of the World, January 1964 .... *15-25* *64*
Kingston Trio; Big Ben Banjo Band; Good Time Singers; Jeannie Hoffman; Lettermen; Billy Liebert; Nils Lindberg; Freddy Martin; Al Martino; Leon McAuliffe; Jo Stafford; Nancy Wilson.
Capitol 2537 (b/w 2538) Great New Releases from the Sound Capitol of the World, February 1964 .... *75-100* *64*
Beatles; Frank Sinatra; Wayne Newton; Freddy Martin; Wanda Jackson; Len Weinrab & Joyce; Dick Weissman; Nat King Cole; Peggy Lee; others.
Capitol 2556 (b/w 2557) Great New Releases from the Sound Capitol of the World, March 1964 .... *15-25* *64*
Glen Gray; Stan Kenton & Jean Turner; Ray Anthony; Al Martino; Fred Waring; Guy Lombardo; Richard & Jim; Mr. Gasser & Weirdos; Beach Boys; Super Stocks; Dick Dale & Del-Tones; Jerry Cole & Spacemen.
Capitol 2578 (b/w 2579) Great New Releases from the Sound Capitol of the World, April 1964 .... *15-25* *64*
Judy Garland; George Shearing; Jackie Gleason; Bob Flanigan & John Gray; Four Freshmen; Laurindo Almeida; Norrie Paramor; Jimmie Haskell; Rod McKuen; Glen Campbell; Ketty Lester; Red Nichols & Five Pennies; Jesse Colin Young; Andy Griffith.
Capitol 2614 (b/w 2615) Great New Releases from the Sound Capitol of the World, May 1964 .... *15-25* *64*
Tex Beneke & Modernaires; Nancy Wilson; Junior Mance; Jonah Jones; Blossom Dearie; Lettermen; Alfred Apaka; Kingston Trio; Nat King Cole; King Curtis; Earl Taylor; Hank Thompson.
Capitol 2634 (b/w 2635) Great New Releases from the Sound Capitol of the World, June 1964 .... *15-25* *64*

Jack Jones; George Shearing; Kay Starr; Hollyridge Stings; Al Martino; Freddy Martin; Tennessee Ernie Ford; Onzy Matthews; Donna Lynn.

Capitol 2658 (b/w 2659) Great Surfin' Hits - July 1964 .... 40-50 64
Beach Boys; Dick Dale; others.

Capitol 2685 (b/w 2686) Great New Releases from the Sound Capitol of the World, August 1964 .... 20-30 64
Beach Boys; Nancy Wilson; Nat King Cole; Peggy Lee; Gilberto & Jobim; Jimmie Haskell; Peter & Gordon; Regents; Johnny Rivers.

Capitol 2698 (b/w 2699) Balanced for Broadcast, September 1964 .... 15-25 64
Roy Clark; Vic Damone; Benny Goodman; Glen Gray; Walter Hensley; Hollyridge Strings; Stan Kenton; Russ Morgan; Wayne Newton; Clliffie Stone Singers.

Capitol 2722 (b/w 2723) Great New Releases from the Sound Capitol of the World, October 1964 .... 15-25 64
Goodtime Singers; George Shearing; Four Freshmen; Liza Minnelli; Lettermen; Shelly Manne; Three D's; Gallants; Four Preps; Pete Seeger.

Capitol 2744 (b/w 2745) Programming Aids from Capitol 15-25 64

Capitol 2732 (b/w 2733) Merry Christmas from Capitol 15-25 64
Frank Sinatra; Fred Waring; Tennessee Ernie Ford; Jackie Gleason.

Capitol 2784 (b/w 2785) Great New Releases from the Sound Capitol of the World, January/February 1965 .... 15-25 64
H.B. Barnum; Roger Bourdin; Nat King Cole; Fred E. Finn; Hollyridge Strings; Lettermen; Junior Mance; Al Martino; Lou Rawls; Don Scarletta Trio; George Shearing; Travelers Three; Nancy Wilson.

Capitol 2808 (b/w 2809) Great New Releases from the Sound Capitol of the World, March 1965 .... 15-25 65
Bobby Rydell; Cannonball Adderley & Ernie Andrews; H.B. Barnum; Peter Brandy; Wanda de Sah; Benny Goodman Quartet; Kingston Trio; Frankie Laine; Buck Owens; Howard Roberts.

Capitol 2821 (b/w 2822) Great New Releases from the Sound Capitol of the World, April 1965 .... 15-25 65
Dean Martin; Peggy Lee; Guy Lombardo; Jackie Gleason; Bing Crosby; Rosemary Clooney; others.

Capitol 2879 (b/w 2880) Great New Releases from the Sound Capitol of the World, June 1965 .... 15-25 65
Dean Martin; others.

Capitol 2905: see Capitol Souvenir Record

Capitol 2966 Excerpts from Great New Releases form the Sound Capitol of the World, Nov. 1965 .... 10-20 65
Lettermen; Laurindo Almeida; Jody Miller; Howard Roberts; Jackie Gleason; N. Fontaine & Ensemble; Jackie Gleason; Peggy Lee; Lou Rawls; King Sisters; Howard Roberts; June Christy.

Capitol 3021 (b/w 3022) Silver Platter Service, Sides 21 & 22, October 1962 .... 20-30 62
Frank Sinatra; Peggy Lee; Andy Griffith; Jonah Jones; Fred Waring; Jackie Gleason; others.

Capitol 3023 (b/w 3024) Silver Platter Service, Sides 23 & 24, October 1962 .... 20-30 62
Frank Sinatra; others.

Capitol 3025 (b/w 3026) Silver Platter Service, Sides 25 & 26, November 1962 .... 20-30 62
Frank Sinatra; others.

Capitol 3027 (b/w 3028) Silver Platter Service, Sides 27 & 28, November 1962 .... 20-30 62
Frank Sinatra; Stan Kenton; Carmen Dragon; Laurindo Almeida; Les Baxter; Tony Renis; George Shearing.

Capitol 3029 (b/w 3030) Silver Platter Service, Sides 29 & 30, December 1962 .... 20-30 62
Frank Sinatra; Dean Martin; Stan Kenton; Roger Wagner; June Christy; Peggy Lee; Nat King Cole; Jackie Gleason; others.

Capitol 3031 (b/w 3032) Silver Platter Service, Sides 31 & 32, December 1962 .... 15-25 62

Capitol 3033 (b/w 3034) Silver Platter Service, Sides 33 & 34, January 1963 .... 15-25 63

Capitol 3035 (b/w 3036) Silver Platter Service, Sides 35 & 36, January 1963 .... 15-25 63

Capitol 3037 (b/w 3038) Silver Platter Service, Sides 37 & 38, February 1963 .... 15-25 63
Van Alexander; Les Baxter; Joe Bucci Duo; Peggy Lee; Jimmie Rowles; Semprini; George Shearing.

Capitol 3039 (b/w 3040) Silver Platter Service, Sides 39 & 40, February 1963 .... 15-25 63

Capitol 3041 (b/w 3042) Silver Platter Service, Sides 41 & 42, March 1963 .... 15-25 63
Les Baxter; June Christy; Four Preps; Jackie Gleason; John Gray; Granck Pourcel; Nelson Riddle; Nancy Wilson.

Capitol 3043 (b/w 3044) Silver Platter Service, Sides 43 & 44, March 1963 .... 15-25 63
June Christy; Lee Evans Trio; Jackie Gleason; John Gray; Franck Pourcel; Nancy Wilson.

Capitol 3045 (b/w 3046) Silver Platter Service, Sides 45 & 46, April 1963 .... 15-25 63
Les Baxter; Frank Fontaine; Four Freshmen; Pee Wee Hunt; Frances Langford; Johnny Mercer; Robert Morse & Charles Reilly; Howard Roberts; George Shearing.

Capitol 3047 (b/w 3048) Silver Platter Service, Sides 47 & 48, April 1963 .... 15-25 63
Laurindo Almeida; Les Baxter; Nat King Cole; Four Freshmen; Johnny Mercer; Nelson Riddle; Howard Roberts; George Shearing.

Capitol 3049 (b/w 3050) Silver Platter Service, Sides 49 & 50, May 1963 .... 15-25 63
Laurindo Almeida; Alfred Apaka; Les Baxter; Webley Edwards; Frances Langford; Charlie Shavers; George Shearing.

Capitol 3051 (b/w 3052) Silver Platter Service, Sides 51 & 52, May 1963 .... 15-25 63
Laurindo Almeida; Gateway Trio; Jackie Gleason; Marian Montgomery; Charlie Shavers; George Shearing; Jack Sheldon.

Capitol 3053 (b/w 3054) Silver Platter Service, Sides 53 & 54, June 1963 .... 15-25 63
Alfred Apaka & Weblet Edwards; Jackie Gleason; Stan Kenton; Peggy Lee; Marian Montgomery; Charlie Shavers; George Shearing; Paul Weston.

Capitol 3055 (b/w 3056) Silver Platter Service, Sides 55 & 56, June 1963 .... 15-25 63
Frank Sinatra; Billy May; Stan Kenton; Peggy Lee; others.

Capitol 3057 (b/w 3058) Silver Platter Service, Sides 57 & 58, June-July 1963 .... 15-25 63
Frank Sinatra; Al Martino; others.

Capitol 3059 (b/w 3060) Silver Platter Service, Sides 59 & 60, July 1963 .... 15-25 63
Frank Sinatra; Nat King Cole; Les Brown; Freddy Martin; others.

Capitol 3061 (b/w 3062) Silver Platter Service, Sides 61 & 62, July 1963 .... 15-25 63
Frank Sinatra; Bobby Darin; others.

Capitol 3063 (b/w 3064) Silver Platter Service, Sides 63 & 64, August 1963 .... 15-25 63
Frank Sinatra; Kingston Trio; Nancy Wilson; others.

Capitol 3065 (b/w 3066) Silver Platter Service, Sides 65 & 66, August 1963 .... 15-25 63
Frank Sinatra; Shorty Rogers; Jack Lemmon; Lucho Gatica; others.

Capitol 3067 (b/w 3068) Silver Platter Service, Sides 67 & 68, September 1963 .... 15-25 63
Laurindo Almeida; June Christy; Cy Coleman; Vic Damone; George Eiferman; Four Freshmen; Jonah Jones; Journeymen; Howard Roberts.

Capitol 3067 (b/w 3068) Silver Platter Service, Sides 67 & 68, September 1963 .... 15-25 63
Laurindo Almeida; Cy Coleman; Jack Lemmon; Kay Starr; Inca Taqui; Howard Roberts; June Christy. (Note two different line-ups of artists were issued for same month.)

Capitol 3069 (b/w 3070) Silver Platter Service, Sides 69 & 70, September 1963 .... 15-25 63

Capitol 3071 (b/w 3072) Silver Platter Service, Sides 71 & 72, October 1963 .... 15-25 63

Capitol 3073 (b/w 3074) Silver Platter Service, Sides 73 & 74, October 1963 .... 15-25 63

Capitol 3075 (b/w 3076) Silver Platter Service, Sides 75 & 76, November 1963 .... *15-25* *63*
Frank Sinatra; Les Baxter; Nat King Cole; Cindy Malone; George Shearing; Nelson Riddle; Jackie Gleason; Cy Coleman; others.
Capitol 3077 (b/w 3078) Silver Platter Service, Sides 77 & 78, November 1963 .... *15-25* *63*
Frank Sinatra; Les Baxter; Benny Goodman; Four Preps; Glen Gray; others.
Capitol 3079 (b/w 3080) Silver Platter Service, Sides 79 & 80, November 1963 .... *15-25* *63*
Frank Sinatra; Wayne Newton; Lettermen; Four Freshmen; George Chakiris; Howard Roberts; Jackie Gleason; Peggy Lee; Bobby Darin; Judy Garland; Stan Kenton; others.
Capitol 3081 (b/w 3082) Silver Platter Service, Sides 81 & 82, December 1963 .... *15-25* *63*
Frank Sinatra; Bobby Darin; Kingston Trio; Nelson Riddle; Benny Goodman; Les Baxter; George Chakiris; Frank Cordell; Dean Elliott; Johnny Mercer; Nancy Wilson.
Capitol 3083 (b/w 3084) Silver Platter Service, Sides 83 & 84, December 1962 .... *15-25* *62*
Capitol 3085 (b/w 3086) Silver Platter Service, Sides 85 & 86, January 1964 .... *15-25* *64*
Stan Freberg; Andy Griffith; Jeannie Hoffman; Kingston Trio; Billy Liebert; Lou Rawls; Jo Stafford; Nancy Wilson.
Capitol 3087 (b/w 3088) Silver Platter Service, Sides 87 & 88, January 1964 .... *15-25* *64*
Capitol 3089 (b/w 3090) Silver Platter Service, Sides 89 & 90, February 1964 .... *15-25* *64*
Frank Sinatra; Peggy Lee; Nat King Cole; others.
Capitol 3091 (b/w 3092) Silver Platter Service, Sides 91 & 92, February 1964 .... *15-25* *64*
Frank Sinatra; Freddy Martin; Nat King Cole; Jo Stafford; Luis Arcaraz; others.
Capitol 3093 (b/w 3094) Silver Platter Service, Sides 93 & 94, March 1964 .... *10-20* *64*
Capitol 3095 (b/w 3096) Silver Platter Service, Sides 95 & 96, March 1964 .... *10-20* *64*
Capitol 3097 (b/w 3098) Silver Platter Service, Sides 97 & 98, April 1964 .... *10-20* *64*
Capitol 3099 (b/w 3100) Silver Platter Service, Sides 99 & 100, April 1964 .... *10-20* *64*
Capitol 3101 (b/w 3102) Silver Platter Service, Sides 101 & 102, May 1964 .... *10-20* *64*
Capitol 3103 (b/w 3104) Silver Platter Service, Sides 103 & 104, May 1964 .... *10-20* *64*
Capitol 3105 (b/w 3106) Silver Platter Service, Sides 105 & 106, June 1964 .... *10-20* *64*
Capitol 3107 (b/w 3108) Silver Platter Service, Sides 107 & 108, June 1964 .... *10-20* *64*
Capitol 3109 (b/w 3110) Silver Platter Service, Sides 109 & 110, July 1964 .... *10-20* *64*
Four Freshmen; Hollyridge Strings; Kingston Trio; Junior Mance; Freddy Martin; Ozny Matthews; George Shearing; Nancy Wilson.
Capitol 3111 (b/w 3112) Silver Platter Service, Sides 111 & 112, July 1964 .... *10-20* *64*
Jimmie Haskell; Hollyridge Strings; Kingston Trio; George Shearing; Barbra Streisand; Len Weinrib & Joyce Jameson; Nancy Wilson.
Capitol 3113 (b/w 3114) Silver Platter Service, Sides 113 & 114, August 1964 .... *10-20* *64*
Capitol 3115 (b/w 3116) Silver Platter Service, Sides 115 & 116, August 1964 .... *10-20* *64*
Capitol 3117 (b/w 3118) Silver Platter Service, Sides 117 & 118, September 1964 .... *10-20* *64*
Capitol 3119 (b/w 3120) Silver Platter Service, Sides 119 & 120, September 1964 .... *10-20* *64*
Vic Damone; Glen Gray; Hollyridge Strings; Stan Kenton; Peggy Lee; Russ Morgan; Nancy Wilson.
Capitol 3121 (b/w 3122) Silver Platter Service, Sides 121 & 122, October 1964 .... *10-20* *64*
Capitol 3123 (b/w 3124) Silver Platter Service, Sides 123 & 124, October 1964 .... *10-20* *64*
Capitol 3125 (b/w 3126) Silver Platter Service, Sides 125 & 126, November 1964 .... *10-20* *64*
Capitol 3127 (b/w 3128) Silver Platter Service, Sides 127 & 128, November 1964 .... *10-20* *64*
Four Freshmen; Four Preps; Goodtime Singers; Shelly Manne; Freddy Martin; Marian Montgomery; Wayne Newton; Franck Pourcel; George Shearing.
Capitol 3129 (b/w 3130) Silver Platter Service, Sides 129 & 130, December 1964 .... *10-20* *64*
Capitol 3131 (b/w 3132) Silver Platter Service, Sides 131 & 132, December 1964 .... *10-20* *64*
Hollyridge Strings; Bobby Darin; Laurindo Almeida.
Capitol 3133 (b/w 3134) Silver Platter Service, Sides 133 & 134, December 1964 .... *10-20* *64*
Capitol 3135 (b/w 3136) Silver Platter Service, Sides 135 & 136, January 1965 .... *10-20* *65*
Capitol 3137 (b/w 3138) Silver Platter Service, Sides 137 & 138, January 1965 .... *10-20* *65*
Capitol 3139 (b/w 3140) Silver Platter Service, Sides 139 & 140, February 1965 .... *10-20* *65*
Capitol 3141 (b/w 3142) Silver Platter Service, Sides 141 & 142, February 1965 .... *10-20* *65*
Capitol 3143 (b/w 3144) Silver Platter Service, Sides 143 & 145, March 1965 .... *10-20* *65*
Capitol 3145 (b/w 3146) Silver Platter Service, Sides 145 & 146, March 1965 .... *10-20* *65*
Capitol 3147 (b/w 3148) Silver Platter Service, Sides 147 & 148, April 1965 .... *10-20* *65*
Frank Sinatra; Dean Martin; Stan Kenton; Bing Crosby; Jackie Gleason; Benny Goodman; Bill Taylor.
Capitol 3149 (b/w 3150) Silver Platter Service, Sides 149 & 150, April 1965 .... *10-20* *65*
Frank Sinatra; Billy Taylor; Dean Martin; others.
Capitol 3151 (b/w 3152) Silver Platter Service, Sides 151 & 152, May 1965 .... *10-20* *65*
Capitol 3153 (b/w 3154) Silver Platter Service, Sides 153 & 154, May 1965 .... *10-20* *65*
Capitol 3155 (b/w 3156) Silver Platter Service, Sides 155 & 156, June 1965 .... *10-20* *65*
Capitol 3157 (b/w 3158) Silver Platter Service, Sides 157 & 158, June 1965 .... *10-20* *65*
Capitol 3159 (b/w 3160) Silver Platter Service, Sides 159 & 160, July 1965 .... *10-20* *65*
Capitol 3161 (b/w 3162) Silver Platter Service, Sides 161 & 162, July 1965 .... *10-20* *65*
Capitol 3163 (b/w 3164) Silver Platter Service, Sides 163 & 164, August 1965 .... *10-20* *65*
Capitol 3165 (b/w 3166) Silver Platter Service, Sides 165 & 166, September 1965 .... *10-20* *65*
Capitol 3167 (b/w 3168) Silver Platter Service, Sides 167 & 168, September 1965 .... *10-20* *65*
Capitol 3169 (b/w 3170) Silver Platter Service, Sides 169 & 170, October 1965 .... *10-20* *65*
Capitol 3171 (b/w 3172) Silver Platter Service, Sides 171 & 172, October 1965 .... *10-20* *65*
Capitol 3173 (b/w 3174) Silver Platter Service, Sides 173 & 174, November 1965 .... *10-20* *65*
Capitol 3175 (b/w 3176) Silver Platter Service, Sides 175 & 176, November 1965 .... *10-20* *65*
Capitol 3177 (b/w 3178) Silver Platter Service, Sides 177 & 178, December 1965 .... *10-20* *65*
Capitol 3179 (b/w 3180) Silver Platter Service, Sides 179 & 180, December 1965 .... *10-20* *65*
Dean Martin; others.
Capitol 3181 (b/w 3182) Silver Platter Service, Sides 181 & 182, January 1966 .... *10-20* *66*
Frank Sinatra; Nancy Wilson; Lettermen; Peggy Lee; others.
Capitol 3183 (b/w 3184) Silver Platter Service, Sides 183 & 184, January 1966 .... *10-20* *66*
Frank Sinatra; David McCallum; Maria Cole; Nat King Cole; Nancy Wilson.
Capitol 3185 (b/w 3186) Silver Platter Service, Sides 185 & 186, January 1966 .... *10-20* *66*
Frank Sinatra; Nancy Wilson; Lettermen; Peggy Lee; others.

Capitol 3187 (b/w 3188) Silver Platter Service, Sides 187 & 188, February 1966 .... 10-20 66
Frank Sinatra; Lettermen; Nancy Wilson; Peggy Lee; Elliot Fisher; Al Martino; Tennessee Ernie Ford; Beach Boys; Jackie Gleason; Wayne Newton; George Shearing; Ray Anthony; Lou Rawls; others.

Capitol 3189 (b/w 3190) Silver Platter Service, Sides 189 & 190, February 1966 .... 10-20 66
Frank Sinatra; Al Martino; Nancy Wilson; David McCallum; Jack Marshall; others.

Capitol 3191 (b/w 3192) Silver Platter Service, Sides 191 & 192, March 1966 .... 10-20 66

Capitol 3193 (b/w 3194) Silver Platter Service, Sides 193 & 194, March 1966 .... 10-20 66

Capitol 3195 (b/w 3196) Silver Platter Service, Sides 195 & 196, April 1966 .... 10-20 66

Capitol 3197 (b/w 3198) Silver Platter Service, Sides 197 & 198, April 1966 .... 10-20 66

Capitol 3199 (b/w 3200) Silver Platter Service, Sides 199 & 200, May 1966 .... 10-20 66

Capitol 3201 (b/w 3202) Silver Platter Service, Sides 201 & 202, May 1966 .... 10-20 66

Capitol 3203 (b/w 3204) Silver Platter Service, Sides 203 & 204, June 1966 .... 10-20 66

Capitol 3205 (b/w 3206) Silver Platter Service, Sides 205 & 206, July 1966 .... 10-20 66
Frank Sinatra; Lettermen; Ray Anthony; George Van Eps; others.

Capitol 3207 (b/w 3208) Silver Platter Service, Sides 207 & 208, July 1966 .... 10-20 66

Capitol 3209 (b/w 3210) Silver Platter Service, Sides 209 & 210, August 1966 .... 10-20 66
Frank Sinatra; Billy May; Nancy Wilson; Ray Anthony; Nat King Cole; Matt Monro; Lettermen; others.

Capitol 3211 (b/w 3212) Silver Platter Service, Sides 211 & 212, June 1966 .... 10-20 66

Capitol 3213 (b/w 3214) Silver Platter Service, Sides 213 & 214, June 1966 .... 10-20 66

Capitol 3215 (b/w 3216) Silver Platter Service, Sides 215 & 216, June 1966 .... 10-20 66

Capitol 3217 (b/w 3218) Silver Platter Service, Sides 217 & 218, June 1966 .... 10-20 66

Capitol 3219 (b/w 3220) Silver Platter Service, Sides 219 & 220, October 1966 .... 10-20 66
Frank Sinatra; Webley Edwards; Stan Kenton; Jackie Gleason; Gordon MacRae; Jonah Jones; others.

Capitol 3221 (b/w 3222) Silver Platter Service, Sides 221 & 222, November 1966 .... 10-20 66
Frank Sinatra; Hank Levine; George Shearing; Peggy Lee; Jackie Gleason; others.

Capitol 3223 (b/w 3224) Silver Platter Service, Sides 223 & 224, November 1966 .... 10-20 66

Capitol 3225 (b/w 3226) Silver Platter Service, Sides 225 & 226, November 1966 .... 10-20 66

Capitol 3227 (b/w 3228) Silver Platter Service, Sides 227 & 228, December 1966 .... 10-20 66

Capitol 3229 (b/w 3230) Silver Platter Service, Sides 229 & 230, December 1966 .... 10-20 66

Capitol 3231 (b/w 3232) Silver Platter Service, Sides 231 & 232, January 1967 .... 10-20 67

Capitol 3233 (b/w 3234) Silver Platter Service, Sides 233 & 234, January 1967 .... 10-20 67

Capitol 3235 (b/w 3236) Silver Platter Service, Sides 235 & 236, February 1967 .... 10-20 67

Capitol 3237 (b/w 3238) Silver Platter Service, Sides 237 & 238, February 1967 .... 10-20 67

Capitol 3239 (b/w 3240) Silver Platter Service, Sides 239 & 240, March 1967 .... 10-20 67

Capitol 3241 (b/w 3242) Silver Platter Service, Sides 241 & 242, March 1967 .... 10-20 67

Capitol 3243 (b/w 3244) Silver Platter Service, Sides 243 & 244, April 1967 .... 10-20 67

Capitol 3245 (b/w 3246) Silver Platter Service, Sides 245 & 246, April 1967 .... 10-20 67

Capitol 3247 (b/w 3248) Silver Platter Service, Sides 247 & 248, May 1967 .... 10-20 67

Capitol 3249 (b/w 3250) Silver Platter Service, Sides 249 & 250, May 1967 .... 10-20 67

Capitol 3251 (b/w 3252) Silver Platter Service, Sides 251 & 252, June 1967 .... 10-20 67
Frank Sinatra; Webley Edwards; Nancy Wilson; Matt Monro; Peggy Lee; Ray Anthony; Howard Roberts; others.

Capitol 3253 (b/w 3254) Silver Platter Service, Sides 253 & 254, June-July 1967 .... 10-20 67

Capitol 3255 (b/w 3256) Silver Platter Service, Sides 255 & 256, July 1967 .... 10-20 67

Capitol 3257 (b/w 3258) Silver Platter Service, Sides 257 & 258, July-August 1967 .... 10-20 67
Frank Sinatra; David Rose; David McCallum; Wayne Newton; Jackie Gleason; Ray Anthony; Fred Waring; others.

Capitol 4030 (b/w 4031) Capitol Pops for March '66 .... 10-20 66
Tennessee Ernie Ford; Guitars Unlimited; Peggy Lee; Ray Anthony; Al Martino; George Shearing; Hollyridge Strings; Jackie Gleason; Webley Edwards.

Capitol 4075 (b/w 4076) Capitol Pops for May 1966 .... 10-20 66
David McCallum; Lettermen; Howard Roberts; Wayne Newton; Nancy Wilson; New Classic Singers; Ruth Welcome.

Capitol 4095 Capitol Pops for June '66 .... 10-15 66
Ray Anthony; Lettermen; George VanEps; Nat King Cole Trio; Cannonball Adderley; Roy Clark; Al Martino.

Capitol 4111 (4112/4113/4114) FM Stereo Silver Platter Service (2 LP) 10-20 67
Frank Sinatra; Nat King Cole; Nancy Wilson; Peggy Lee; Jackie Gleason; Laurindo Almeida; others.

Capitol 4123 (b/w 4124) Balanced for Broadcast, September 1966 .... 10-20 66
Bobby Darin; Webley Edwards; Lettermen; Gordon MacRae; Wayne Newton; Norrie Paramor; George Shearing.

Capitol 4155 (b/w 4156) Capitol Pops for October 1966 .... 10-20 66
Frank Sinatra; Dean Martin; Hollyridge Strings; Jonah Jones; Jackie Gleason; others.

Capitol 4174 (4175/4176/4177) Remember How Great (2 LP) 15-25 66
Frank Sinatra; Dean Martin; Judy Garland; Nelson Riddle; Jo Stafford; Four Freshmen; Kingston Trio; Lettermen; Dinah Shore; Nat King Cole; Nancy Wilson; Peggy Lee; Wayne Newton; others.

Capitol 4196 (b/w 4197) Balanced for Broadcast, November 1966 .... 10-20 66
Howard Roberts; Peggy Lee; Matt Monro; Four Amigos; Mexican Golden Violins; Mrs. Miller; David Rose; Peggy Lee; Liza Minelli; Manne/Marshall.

Capitol 4210 (b/w 4211) Music for Christmas Shoppers Only 10-20 66
Frank Sinatra; Buck Owens; Dean Martin; Peggy Lee; Nat King Cole; Jackie Gleason; Lettermen; Tennessee Ernie Ford; Wayne Newton; others.

Capitol 4237 (b/w 4238) Capitol Disc Jockey Album, January 1967 .... 15-25 67
George Shearing; Lou Rawls; Nancy Wilson; Lettermen; David McCallum; Wayne Newton.

Capitol 4370 (b/w 4371) Capitol Disc Jockey Album - Balanced for Broadcast, August 1967 .... 15-25 67
Sandler & Young; Nancy Wilson; Nat King Cole; Lou Rawls; Jackie Gleason; Matt Monro; Milt Buckner.

Capitol 4404 (b/w 4405) Capitol Disc Jockey Album, October 1967 .... 15-25 67
Murry Wilson; Eddie Heywood; Ann Dee, Al Martino; Dave Cavanaugh; Bobbie Gentry.

Capitol 4411 (b/w 4412) Capitol's 25th Anniversary Celebration 25-35 67
Beatles; Frank Sinatra; others.

Capitol 4470 (b/w 4471) The Compleat Little Drummer Boy 250-300 67
Frank Sinatra; Peggy Lee; Tennessee Ernie Ford; Lou Rawls; Sonny James; Lettermen; Al Martino; Marlene Dietrich; Nat King Cole; Ella Fitzgerald. (Seven-inch single. Includes picture sleeve.)

Capitol 4472 (b/w 4473) Short Playing Christmas Favorites (EP) 15-25 67
Frank Sinatra; Ella Fitzgerlad; Nat King Cole; others

Capitol 4566 (b/w 4567) Capitol Disk Jockey Album, June 1968 .... **10-20** **68**

Capitol 4582 (b/w 4583) Capitol Dee Jay Album - Balanced for Broadcast, July 1968 .... **20-30** **68**
Frank Sinatra; Wind in the Willows; Tony Bruno; Nancy Wilson; Nat King Cole; Al Mar; Lou Rawls; Marion Love.

Capitol 4607 (b/w 4608) Capitol Disk Jockey Album, August 1968 .... **10-20** **68**

Capitol 4633 (b/w 4634) Capitol Dee Jay Album - Balanced for Broadcast, October 1969 .... **10-20** **69**
Glen Campbell; Bettye Swann; James Taylor; Mary Hopkin; Hollyridge Strings; Letta; Roy Meriwether Trio; Four King Cousins; Line Renaud; Cannonball Adderley.

Capitol 4650 (b/w 4651) Capitol Disk Jockey Album, November 1968 .... **10-20** **68**

Capitol SPRO-4673 Capitol Disc Jockey Album 2/69 .... **10-20** **69**
Beach Boys; Eddie Heywood; Sandler & Young; Guitars Unlimited; Clara Ward; Tennessee Ernie Ford; Patti Drew; Cannonball Adderley.

Capitol SPRO-4684 (b/w 4685) Capitol Disc Jockey Album, March 1969 .... **10-20** **69**
Mary Hopkin; Bettye Swann; Lettermen; Anthony Quinn; James Taylor.

Capitol SPRO-4698 Capitol Disc Jockey Album **10-20**
Glenn Campbell; Brian Auger & Trinity; Ray Brown; Sounds of Our Times; Cashman, Pistilli & West; John Andrew Tartaglia; Nat King Cole; Os Tres Brazileirds.

Capitol SPRO 4710 (b/w 4711) Capitol Disc Jockey Album - May 1969 .... **5-10** **69**
John Stewart; Peggy Lee; Garaldo Vespar; Bobby Engmann; Tom Vaughn.

Capitol 4724 (b/w 4725) Capitol Hits Through the Years **40-50** **69**
Beatles; Frank Sinatra; Gene Vincent; Nat King Cole; Dean Martin; Beach Boys; Jeanne Black; Mel Blanc; Stan Freberg; Wanda Jackson; Ferlin Husky; Mary Hopkin; Nancy Wilson; Al Martino; Bob Seger; Joe South; Kay Starr; Ray Anthony; Les Baxter; Glen Campbell; Senator Everett M. Dirkson; Four Preps; Tennessee Ernie Ford; Jane Froman; Bobbie Gentry; Pee Wee Hunt; Red Ingle; Betty Hutton; Sonny James; Grace Kelly & Bing Crosby; Stan Kenton; Peggy Lee; Lettermen; Laurie London; Nellie Lutcher; Gordon MacRae; Johnny Mercer; Jody Miller; Ella Mae Morse; Wayne Newton; Outsiders; Buck Owens; Les Paul; Les Paul & Mary Ford; Peter & Gordon; Pied Pipers; Frank Purcell; Lou Rawls; Nelson Riddle; Tex Ritter; Andy Russell; Kyu Sakamoto; Seekers; Bobby Sherwood; Fred Slack; Jo Stafford; Johnny Standley; Jimmy Wakely; Paul Whiteman; Margaret Whiting; Tex Williams; Yogi Yorgesson; Faron Young. (Samples 133 Capitol releases, 1942 to 1969.)

Capitol SPRO 4774 Silver Platter Service, July 1969 .... **5-10** **69**
Al Martino; George Van Eps; Bobbie Gentry; Joe South; Comon People; Betsy Chapman.

Capitol 4934 (b/w 4935) Capitol Disk Jockey Album, February 1970 .... **10-20** **70**

Capitol 5003 (b/w 5004) Listen in Good Health **20-30** **70**
Beatles; David Axelrod; Sons; Quicksilver Messenger Service; Fred Neil; Roy Harper; Steve Miller; John Stewart; the Band; Buddy Miles; Pink Floyd.

Capitol 6743 Singles Only Sampler **10-15** **73**
Pink Floyd; 10 Wheel Drive; Tavares; Anne Murray; Sutherland Brothers & Quiver; Helen Reddy; Grand Funk Railoroad; Skylark; Alex Harvey; Edward Bear; Flying Circus; Lori Lieberman; Raspberries; Renaissance.

Capitol 6471 (b/w 6472) Tower Gives Good Records **10-15** **73**
(Special products. Made for Tower Records stores.)

Capitol 6630 (b/w 6631) Son of Singles Only Sampler **10-20** **73**
Helen Reddy; Raspberries; Sam Neely; Hamlet; Fortunes; Barclay James Harvest; Skylark; Hurricane Smith; Lattermen; Times; Johnny Farnham; Flying Circus; Marcus Hook Roll Band; Edward Bear.

Capitol 6743 (b/w 6744) Singles Only Sampler **10-20** **73**
Pink Floyd; Tavares; Anne Murray; Edward Bear; Helen Reddy; Grand Funk Railroad; Skylark; Alex Harvey; Flying Circus; Lori Lieberman; Raspberries; Renaissance; Sutherland Brothers & Quiver; 10 Wheel Drive.

Capitol 8168 (b/w 8169) Summer Trip **10-15** **76**
Bob Seger; Sweet; Brewer & Shipley; Status Quo; Dr. Hook; Triumvirat. (May have local radio station tie-in on cover.)

Capitol 8511 (b/w 8512) Greatest Music Ever Sold **20-30** **76**
Beatles; John Lennon; Ringo Starr; Glen Campbell; Beach Boys; Helen Reddy; Leo Kottke; Bob Seger; Steve Miller.

Capitol 8552 (b/w 8553) What's in Store for You, Vol. 2 .... **10-15** **76**
Steve Miller; Steve Harley & Cockney Rebel; Bob Seger; Sammy Hagar; Gentle Giant; Little River Band; Maze.

Capitol 8708 (b/w 8709) CAP-FM/What's in Store for You #3 .... **10-15** **77**
Bob Welch; Little River Band; Rhead Brothers; Klaatu; Gentle Giant; Mink Deville; Dr. Hook; Bebop Deluxe. (Simulated radio show, with announcer.)

Capitol 8802 (b/w 8803 CAP-FM/What's in Store for You #4 .... **10-15** **78**
Sweet; Status Quo; Starz; Bebop Deluxe; Tom Robinson Band; No Dice; Crane; Maze. (Simulated radio show, with announcer.)

Capitol 9303 (9304/9305/9306) A Rocking Christmas Stocking - in Store Sampler (2 LP) **10-20** **84**
Frank Sinatra; Nat King Cole; Bing Crosby; Joe Cocker; Peter Wolf; Anne Murray; Duran Duran; Eramus Hall; Bob Seger; J. Geils Band; Ashford & Simpson; Lillo Thomas; Tina Turner; Sheena Easton; David Bowie; Corey Hart; Kenny Rogers; .38 Special.

Capitol SPRO 9039A (9039B, 9040A/9040B) Fresh Air (2 LP) **10-20** **80s**
Bob Seger; Anne Murray; Kim Carnes; Little River Band; McGuinn, Clark & Hillman; Marshall Hain; Bob Welch; Tavares; Chip Taylor; Peabo Bryson; Alley & Soul Sneekers; Desmond Child & Rogue; Gonzales; Moon Martin; J. Geils Band; Barooga Bandit; April Wine.

Capitol TW 9122 Today's Top Hits, Vol. 12 (M) **10-20**

Capitol SPRO 9481 .... **10-15** **85**
Power Station; Freddie Jackson; ; Heart; Tina Turner; Helix; others.

Capitol 9864 Hits on Board **10-15** **82**
Beatles; others.

Capitol 9867 Capitol In-Store Sampler **10-15** **82**
Beatles; America; Juice Newton; Billy Squire; Steve Miller; Missing Persons; Motels; Little River Band; Duran Duran; Plasmatics.

Capitol SPRO-9937, Plenty Good Music from Capitol **10-15** **80s**
Bob Seger; Duran Duran; Tubes; Sheriff; Little River Band; Maze; Strange Advance; Marillion; Burning Sensations; George Clinton.

Capitol ????, Balanced for Broadcast, Songs of Celebration, April 1970 .... **20-30** **70**
Beatles; David Axelford; Sons; Quicksilver; Fred Neil; Roy Harper; Steve Miller; John Stewart; Band; Buddy Miles, others.

Capitol Souvenir Record .... Capitol (EP) SPRO-2905 50-100 65
Beatles; Frank Sinatra; Nat King Cole; George Shearing Quintet; Lettermen; Robert Preston; Buck Owens; Judy Garland. Compact 33. Promotional issue only.)

Capitol's Country Faith .... Capitol (S) SQ-91655 10-15 69
Buck Owens; Sonny James; Ferlin Husky; Houie Lister & Statemen Quartet; T. Texas Tyler; Louvin Brothers; Roy Acuff; Dale Evans; Jordanaires; Rose Maddox; Tennessee Ernie Ford. (Capitol Record Club issue.)

Capitol's Country Jamboree .... Capitol (S) SQ-91654 10-15 69
Sonny James; Glen Campbell; Wanda Jackson; Buck Owens; Merle Haggard; Charlie Louvin; Wynn Stewart; Ned Miller; Jody Miller; Ray Pillow; Bobby Austin; Jean Shepard; Ferlin Husky; Tex Ritter. (Capitol Record Club issue.)

Car Wash (2 LP) .... MCA (S) 2-6000 12-15 76
(Soundtrack.) Rose Royce; Pointer Sisters; Spinners; Hot Chocolate; Jane Rose; others.

Car Wash (Mini-Wash) .... MCA (EP) 1947 10-15 76
(Soundtrack. Promotional issue only.) Rose Royce; Pointer Sisters; others.

Caribou Sampler Fall Release .... Caribou (S) CABPU 40-60 77
(Promotional only picture disc.) L.A. Express; O.C. Smith; others.

Carlito's Way .... Epic (S) E-57620 ?? 93
(Soundtrack.) Patti LaBelle; Carlos Santana; KC & Sunshine Band; Ray Barretto.

Carload O' Hits .... Muse (EP) MEP-250 40-60 60
Silhouettes; Five Satins; Turbans; Charlie & Ray; Nutmegs; Faye Adams.

Carload O' Hits .... Muse (M) 500 50-100 60
Silhouettes; Nutmegs; Charlie & Ray; Five Satins; Mello-Kings; Lee Allen; Turbans; Billy Myles; Faye Adams.

Carnival Copacabana De 1955 .... SOM (M) CLP 2004 10-20 55
(10–inch LP.)

Carnival of Songs .... King (M) 819 40-55 63
James Brown; Platters; Nina Simone; Sonny Thompson; Hank Ballard & Midnighters; Bill Doggett; Five Royales; Earl Bostic; Little Willie John; Billy Eckstine; Dominoes; Freddy King.

Carnival Rock .... ???? (M) ???? 800-1000 57
(Soundtrack. Promotional issue only. Colored vinyl.) Platters; David Houston; Bob Luman; others. (Label name and number, if any, are not yet known.)

Carols & Candlelight .... Columbia (S) P1 2525 5-10 74
Andre Kostelanetz; Kate Smith; John Davidson; Julie Andrews; Mahalia Jackson; Harry Belafonte; Leonard Bernstein; Doris Day; Stan Getz; Percy Faith; Yank Lawson & Bob Haggart; Tony Bennett; Enoch Light; Andy Williams.

Carols of Christmas .... Hallmark 629XPRO 9732 5-10 89
Mormon Tabernacle Choir; Sarah Vaughan; Samuel Ramey; others.

Cashbox, Jan. 1981 .... Han-O-Disc (S) No Number Used 20-30 81
(Picture disc. Promotional issue only.)

Cat Meets Chick: see RUSHING, Jimmy, Ada Moore and Buck Clayton

Catch My Soul .... Metromedia (S) BML 1-0176 8-12 73
(Soundtrack.) Ritchie Havens; Tony Joe White; Lance LeGault; Delaney Bramlett; Bonnie Bramlett; Susan Tyrell.

Cavalcade of Stars .... Mohawk (S) MH-T1-1/2/3 10-15
Steve Lawrence; John Gary; Jimmy Smith; Count Basie; Lena Hrone; Al martino; Nina Simone; Cam Cooke; Lou Rawls; Duke Ellington; Eddie Fisher; Harry Belafonte; Lawrence Welk; Frankie Valli; Ray Charles.

Cavalcade of Stars .... RCA Camden (S) CAS 781 5-10 60s
Limeliters; Peter Nero; Al Hirt; Della Reese; Eddie Fisher; Chet Atkins; Dinah Shore; Floyd Cramer; Ann Margret; Lou Monte; Hugo Winterhalter.

CBS Salutes Country Music Month .... Columbia (S) AS 2535 5-10 86
(Promotional issue only. Issued without cover.) George Jones; Ricky Skaggs; Exile; Charly McClain; Willie Nelson; John Conlee; Rosanne Cash; Willie Nelson & Johnny Cash & Waylon Jennings & Kris Kristofferson; Sweethearts of the Rodeo; Marty Stuart.

Celebrate the Season with Tupperware .... RCA (S) DPL1-0803 20-40 87
Elvis Presley; Arthur Fiedler & Boston Pops; Dolly Parton; Perry Como; Johnny Mathis; Alabama; Nat King Cole; Anne Murray; Jose Feliciano; Henry Mancini.

Celebration: see Big Sur Festival (Celebration)

Certified Gold (2 LP) .... K-Tel (S) TU 2930 8-12 81
Kenny Loggins; Gino Vannelli; Aretha Franklin; Phil Seymour; John Cougar; Police; Blondie; Pure Prairie League; Poco; Ambrosia; Devo; Joe Dolce; Air Supplly; Tierra; Ray Parker Jr. & Raydio; Stephanie Mills; 38 Special; Pat Benatar; Pretenders; Prince; Benny Mardones; Robby Dupree; Alan Parsons Project; Kiss.

Cha-Cha Jubilee .... Jubilee (M) 1097 10-15

Changing Face of Harlem .... Savoy (M) SJL-2208 10-15 77
Buck Ram All-Stars; Earl Bostic; Don Byas; Red Norvo; Cozy Cole; Hot Lips Page; Jesse Brown; Ben Webster; Slam Stewart; Charlie Parker; Miss Rhapsody; Herbie Fields; Budd Johnson; Lionel Hampton; Floyd "Horsecollar" Williams; Foots; Thomas; Chuck Wayne; Teddy Wilson; Pete Brown; Frankie Newton; Remo Palmieri; others.

Changing Face of Harlem, Vol. 2 .... Savoy (M) SJL-2224 10-15 77
Nat King Cole; Oscar Moore; Johnny Miller; Frankie Newton; Don Byas; Hank D'Amico; Dave Rivera; Cozy Cole; Dave Page; Herbie Fields; Lionel Hampton; George Jones; Stuff Smith; Jimmy Jones; Emmett Berry; Illionis Jacquet; Bill Doggett; Pete Brown; Leonard Hawkins; Courtney Williams; Lem Davis; others.

Charlie Apple Presents: see 16 Golden Grooves for Collectors Only

Chart Busters .... Columbia (S) ???? 8-12 60s
Earl Scruggs; Vikki Carr; Village Stompers; Tammy Wynette & George Jones; Jim Nabors; Andre Kostelanetz; Joe Harnell; Percy Faith; Jerry Vale.

Chart Winners .... Mercury (M) MG-20651 20-30 61

Chart Winners .... Mercury (S) SR-60651 25-35 61
Brook Benton; Platters; Damita Jo; Clebanoff Strings; Abbe Lane; Diomonds; George Jones; Dinah Washington; Jose Melis; LeRoy Van Dyke; Clyde McPhatter; Claude Gray.

Chartbusters .... Harmony (S) H-30023 20-30 66
Joe South & Believers; Neil Diamond; Lulu; Hollies; Dion; Sonny & Cher; Everly Brothers.

Chartbusters .... Vernon (S) 521 25-40 62
Tony Orlando; Bobbettes; Birdwatchers; Nomads; Mylos.

Chartbusters '62 .... Capitol (M) T-1837 25-35 63

Chartbusters '62 .... Capitol (S) ST-1837 30-40 63
Beach Boys; Bobby Darin; Lettermen; Kingston Trio; Nat King Cole; Faron Young; Nelson Riddle; Ray Anthony; Four Preps; Ferlin Husky; Tex Ritter. (Title actually shown as *Chart Busters '62*.)

Chartbusters, Vol. 2 .... Capitol (M) T-1945 25-35 63

Chartbusters, Vol. 2 .... Capitol (S) ST-1945 30-40 63
Beach Boys; Nat King Cole; Kingston Trio; Kyu Sakamoto; Bobby Darin; Al Martino; Roy Clark.

Chartbusters, Vol. 2 .... Motown (S) MS-715 8-12
Four Tops; Temptations; Diana Ross & Supremes; Jackson Five; Martha Reeves & Vandellas; Marvelettes; Smokey Robinson & Miracles; Gladys Knight & Pips; Jr. Walker & All Stars; Temptations; Marvin Gaye; Isley Brothers.

Chartbusters, Vol. 3 ... Capitol (M) T-2006 25-35 63

Chartbusters, Vol. 3 ... Capitol (S) ST-2006 30-40 63

Beach Boys; Wayne Newton; Nat King Cole; Bobby Darin; Sonny James; Kingston Trio; Al Martino; Nancy Wilson; Frank Ifield.

Chartbusters, Vol. 3 ... Motown (S) MS-732 8-12 71

Supremes; Four Tops; Jackson 5; Temptations; Spinners; Originals; Edwin Starr; Stevie Wonder; Diana Ross & Supremes; Gladys Knight & Pips; Martha Reeves & Vandellas; Jr. Walker & All Stars.

Chartbusters, Vol. 4 ... Capitol (M) T-2094 30-40 64

Chartbusters, Vol. 4 ... Capitol (S) ST-2094 50-60 64

Beatles; Beach Boys; Drew-Vels; Al Martino; Nat King Cole; Kingston Trio; Donna Lynn; Jody Miller.

Chartbusters, Vol. 4 ... Motown (S) 734 8-12 71

Edwin Starr; Originals; Marvin Gaye; others.

Chess Rockabillies, Vol. 1 ... Chess/MCA (M) CH 9173 8-10 84

Chess Rockabillies, Vol. 1 ... Chess (M) CH 92000 8-10 84

Bobby Sisco; Dale Hawkins; Billy Barrix; Larry Diamond; Rusty York; Mel Robbins; Lou Josie; Bobby Dean; Silvatones; Rod Bernard; Jet Tones; Del Saint & Devils; Johnny Fuller; Eddie Fontaine; Jimmy Lee & Wayne Walker; G.L. Crockett.

Chess Sisters of Soul, Vol. 1 ... Chess (S) CH 9140 8-12 84

Koko Taylor; Jackie Ross; Jan Bradley; Etta James; Fontella Bass; Jaynetts; Mitty Collier; Aretha Franklin.

Chicago Ain't Nothin' But a Blues Band ... Delmark (S) 624 10-15 72

Sunny & Slim; J.T. Brown; Eddie Clearwater; Jo Jo Williams; Morris Pejoe; Marmonica George.

Chicago Blues Anthology (2 LP) ... Chess (2 LP) (S) 2CH-60012 10-15

Elmore James; Eddie Boyd; Robert Nighthawk; Washboard Sam; Johnny Saines; J.B. Lenoir; Jimmy Rogers; Memphis Slim; Otis Rush; Floyd James; John Brim; Big Boy Spires; Big Bill Broonzy.

Chicago Blues at Home ... Advent (S) 2806 5-10 77

Louis Myers; Eddie Taylor; others.

Chicago Blues Today, Vol. 1 ... Vanguard (S) VSP 79216 10-20 66

Junior Wells Chicago Blues Band; J.B. Hutto & His Hawks; Otis Spann's South Side Piano.

Chicago Blues Today, Vol. 2 ... Vanguard (S) VSP 79217 10-20 66

Otis Rush Blues Band; Jimmy Cotton Blues Quartet; Homesick James & His Dusters.

Chicago Blues Today, Vol. 3 ... Vanguard (S) VSP 79218 10-20 66

Johnny Young's South Side Blues Band; Big Walter Horton's Blues Harp Band with Memphis Charlie.

Chicago Garage Band Greats - Best of Rembrandt Records 1966-1968 ... Cicadelic (S) CICLP 983 8-12 80s

Lemon Drops; Nuchez; Nite Owls; Mind Distortions; Nickel Bag; Watermelon; Inifinite Pyramid; Circus.

Chicago Guitar Killers ... Blue Night (S) BN-073-1669 10-20 79

Otis Rush; Robert Nighthawk; Albert King; B.B. King; Earl Hooker; Buddy Guy.

Chicago Jazz Album ... Decca (M) DL 8029 25-40 51

Eddie Condon & His Chicagoans; Jimmy McPartland; George Nettling's Chicago Rhythm Kings; others.

Chicago Plus ... Atlantic (S) 7227 8-12 70s

Chicago Soul: Legendary Brunswick/Dakar Hits (2 LP) ... Epic (S) PE2-39895 10-15 85

Barbara Acklin; Artistics; Young-Holt Unlimited; Young-Holt Trio; Willie Henderson; Lost Generation; Tyrone Davis; Chi-Lites; Gene Chandler.

Chicagoans (1928-1930) ... Decca (M) DL-9231 10-20 67

Chicagoans (1928-1930) ... Decca (S) DL-79231 10-20 67

Frank Teschemacher; Joe Mannone; others.

Chicken Chronicles ... United Artists (S) UA-LA830-H 8-10 77

(Soundtrack.) Classics IV; Nitty Gritty Dirt Band; Canned Heat; Jackie De Shannon; Boffalongo; Kutee.

Child's Christmas ... Harmony (S) HS-14563 5-10 68

Gene Autry; Art Carney; Burl Ives; others.

Child's Introduction to Jazz ... Wonderland (S) RLP 1435 8-12

Cannonball Adderley; others.

China Beach - Music and Memories ... SBK (S) K1-93744 10-15 90

(TV Soundtrack.) John Lennon; others.

Christine ... Motown (S) M-6086 8-10 83

(Soundtrack.) George Thorogood & Destroyers; Buddy Holly & Crickets; Johnny Ace; Robert & Johnny; Little Richard; Dion & Belmonts; Viscounts; Thurston Harris; Danny & Juniors; Larry Williams.

Christmas, Vol. 2 ... Capitol (S) SM-11834 5-10 78

Bing Crosby; Nancy Wilson; Tennessee Ernie Ford; David Rose; Lettermen; Dean Martin; Margaret Whiting; Jimmy Wakely; Jackie Gleason; Nat King Cole; Ella Fitzgerald.

Christmas - A Gift of Music ... Capitol (S) SL-6687 5-10

Glen Campbell; Nat King Cole; Ella Fitzgerald; Hollywood Bowl Symphony Orchestra; Peggy Lee; Al Martino; David Rose's; Sandler & Young; Voices of Christmas.

Christmas - A Gift of Music ... Zenith/Capitol (S) SL-6544 5-10

Roger Wagner Chorale; Hollywood Bowl Symphony Orchestra & Carmen Dragon; Peggy Lee; Jackie Gleason; Bing Crosby; Fred Waring; Korean Orphan Choir; Franco Corelli.

Christmas Album ... Columbia (SE) PC 39466 5-10 84

Frank Sinatra; Andy Williams; Johnny Mathis with Percy Faith; Mitch Miller; Tony Bennett; Barbra Streisand; Jim Nabors; Mormon Tabernacle Choir; Robert Goulet; Andre Kostelanetz.

Christmas Album (2 LP) ... Columbia (S) CG-30763 10-15 60s

Frank Sinatra; Andy Williams; Mitch Miller; Doris Day; Ray Conniff; Tony Bennett; Johnny Cash; Jerry Vale; Anita Bryant; Andre Kostelanetz; Jim Nabors; Barbra Streisand; Burl Ives; Robert Goulet; Marty Robbins; Mormon Tabernacle Choir; Johnny Mathis; Patti Page; Percy Faith; Mahalia Jackson.

Christmas America ... Columbia (S) SL-6884 8-12 73

Bing Crosby; Glen Campbell; Peggy Lee; Nat King Cole; Dinah Shore; Dean Martin; Tennessee Ernie Ford; Ella Fitzgerald; Fred Waring; Hollywood Pops Orchestra. (Special Products release.)

Christmas America ... Capitol Special Market (S) SL 6950 5-10 74

Bing Crosby; Anne Murray; Roy Clark; Merle Haggard; Lettermen; Glen Campbell; Donna Fargo; Nat King Cole; Wayne Newton; Fred Waring. (Made for Firestone.)

Christmas Carousel (2 LP) ... Capitol (S) SQBE-94406 8-12 72

Christmas Country Style ... Capitol Creative Products (S) SL 6581 5-10

Roy Rogers & Dale Evans; Ferlin Husky; Glen Campbell; Sonny James; Buck Owens; Louvin Brothers.

Christmas Day .... Pickwick (S) SPC 1010 10-15
Beach Boys; Tennessee Ernie Ford; Sandler & Young; Al Martino; Guy Lombardo; Nat King Cole; Peggy Lee; Roger Wagner Chorale; Ella Fitzgerald.
Christmas Favorites .... Columbia (S) A 21273 5-10
Christmas Festival of Songs & Carols .... RCA (S) PRM 170 8-12
Marian Anderson; Arthur Fiedler & Boston Pops; Eddie Fisher; Hugo & Luigi Children's Chorus; Ralph Hunter Choir; Mario Lanza; Jim Reeves; Robert Shaw Chorale.
Christmas Festival of Stars! .... Columbia (M) CL 1394 8-12
Mitch Miller; Johnny Mathis; Bing Crosby & Frank DeVol; Norman Luboff Choir; Percy Faith; Hi-Lo's & Frank DeVol; Ed Kenny & Luther Henderson.
Christmas Gift for You: see RONETTES / Crystals / Darlene Love / Bob B. Soxx & Blue Jeans
Christmas Gift of Music, Vol.3 .... Capitol (S) SL 6659 8-12
Dean Martin; others.
Christmas Gift 'Rap .... Motown (S) 725 30-50 71
Diana Ross & Supremes; Four Tops; Temptations; Smokey Robinson & Miracles; Stevie Wonder.
Christmas Greetings .... Columbia Special Products (S) CSS-1499 5-10
Ray Conniff; Andre Kostelanetz; Barbra Streisand; Johnny Mathis; Steve Lawrence; Eydie Gorme; Mitch Miller; New York Philharmonic with Leonard Bernstein; Mormon Tabernacle Choir with Richard P. Condie; Tammy Wynette; Percy Faith; Robert Goulet; Mahalia Jackson.
Christmas Greetings, Vol. 2 .... Columbia Special Products (SP) P-10398 5-10 70s
Johnny Cash; Lynn Anderson; Bobby Vinton; Johnny Mathis; Andre Kostelanetz; Ray Conniff; Barbra Streisand; Mitch Miller; Jim Nabors; Leonard Bernstein; Percy Faith; Robert Goulet; Mahalia Jackson; Steve Lawrence & Eydie Gorme. (Made for A&P.)
Christmas Greetings, Vol. 3 .... Columbia Special Products (SP) P-11383 5-10 72
Anna Moffo; Johnny Mathis; Carol Burnett; Johnny Cash; Vikki Carr; Tony Bennett; Andre Kostelanetz; Barbra Streisand; Eugene Ormandy & Philadelphia Orchestra; Lynn Anderson; Mark Lindsay; Doris Day; Cary Grant.
Christmas Greetings, Vol. 4 .... Columbia Special Products (SP) P-11987 5-10 73
Debbie Reynolds; Julie Andrews; Johnny Mann Singers; Andy Williams; Barbra Streisand; New York Philharmonic with Leonard Bernstein; Mormon Tabernacle Choir with Richard P. Condie; Vikki Carr; Tonny Bennett; Percy Faith; Robert Merrill; Ray Price; Guy Lombardo. (Made for A&P.)
Christmas Greetings from Nashville .... Camden (S) ACL1-0256 5-10 73
Eddy Arnold; Floyd Cramer; Porter Wagoner; others.
Christmas Greetings from Nashville .... RCA (S) ANL1-1953 5-10 76
Eddy Arnold; Chet Atkins; Dottie West; Floyd Cramer; Jim Reeves; Skeeter Davis; Hank Snow; others.
Christmas Holiday Favorites .... National Guard (S) XPD-1212 10-20 63
(Promotional issue only.) Kingston Trio; others.
Christmas in California .... RCA (S) PRS-276 5-10
Christmas in New York .... RCA (S) PRS-257 5-10
Kate Smith; Henry Mancini; Morton Gould; Arthur Fiedler & Boston Pops; Norman Luboff Choir; Vic Damone; Ed Ames; Robert Shaw chorale; Marian Anderson; Mario Lanza; Sir Thomas Beecham & Royal Philharmonic Orchestra & Chorus; Jan Peerce & Columbus Boy Choir.
Christmas in New York, Vol. 2 .... RCA (S) PRS-270 5-10
Christmas in the Country .... Camden (S) ACL1-0256 5-10 73
Blackwood Brothers Quartet; Anita Kerr Singers; Jim Reeves; others.
Christmas Is .... Columbia Special Products (SE) P-11417 5-10 72
Barbra Streisand; Jo Stafford; Frank Sinatra; Tony Bennett; Carpenters; Julie Andrews; Andy Williams; Hillside Singers; Doris Day; Bing Crosby; Patti Page; Vikki Carr; Judy Garland; Mills Brothers.
Christmas Music Festival .... Capitol (S) SL 6688 8-12
Dean Martin; others.
Christmas Programming from RCA Victor .... RCA (M) SP-33-66 1000-1200 59
(Includes paper sleeve. Promotional issue only.) Elvis Presley; Perry Como; J. Klein; Boston Pops; Arthur Fiedler; R. Elias & G. Tozzi; Esquivel; Ralph Hunter; Three Suns; Mario Lanza; Royal Philharmonic Orchestra; George Melachrino; Beorge Beverly Shea.
Christmas Programming Special: see MCA Promotional Releases/Samplers
Christmas Remembrance .... Columbia (S) C-10442 5-10
Robert Goulet; Andre Kostelanetz; Doris Day; Jerry Vale; Mormon Tabernacle Choir; Leonard Bernstein; Jim Nabors; Rita Ford Music Boxes; Mahalia Jackson; Mike Douglas; Eugene Ormandy & Philadelphia Orchestra. (Special Products release.)
Christmas Seal Campaign .... Decca (M) M6-79606 10-15 63
Kingston Trio; others.
Christmas Sing with Bing (Around the World) .... Decca (M) DL-8419 10-20 56
Christmas Sing with Bing (Around the World) .... MCA (S) 15018 5-10 77
(Radio soundtrack. From International broadcast of *CBS Radio's 1955 Christmas Show*.) Bing Crosby; Paul Weston; Norman Luboff Choir; St. Louis Carol Association; Little Singers of Granby, Quebec; Salt Lake City Tabernacle Choir; Voices of Christmas (Hollywood); Delores Short; Village of Neuilly Children's Choir (France); Reed Warbler's Choir (Holland); Vatican Choir; Dedham Choral Society (England).
Christmas Song and Other Favorites .... Columbia Special Products (S) P-12446 5-10 74
Christmas Songs by These Famous Country Artists .... King (S) 811 50-75 63
Cowboy Copas; Reno & Smiley; others.
Christmas Soul Special .... QAG (S) 1600 5-10 82
Wilson Pickett; Mary Wells; Ben E. King; Martha Reeves; Shirley; Sam Moore.
Christmas Sound of Music .... Capitol (S) SL 6996 5-10
Christmas Sound of Music .... Capitol Creative Products (S) SL 6643 5-10 60s
Glen Campbell; Ella Fitzgerald; Bobbie Gentry; Lettermen; Sadler & Young.
Christmas Star Time .... CBS (SP) P-15756 5-10 81
Robert Goulet; Jerry Vale; Woody Herman; Ray Price; Barbra Streisand; Julie Andrews; Doris Day; Anita Bryant; Ray Conniff; Lynn Anderson; Bing Crosby; Mitch Miller; Bobby Vinton; Charlie Byrd.
Christmas Stocking .... Capitol (S) SNP-90494 10-15
Kingston Trio; others.
Christmas Through the Years .... MCA (SP) DL 734596 5-10 70s
Lawrence Welk; Bing Crosby; Roger Williams; Trapp Family Singers; Texas Boys Choir; Four Aces; Ethel Smith; Columbus Boychoir; Jack Jones; Jo Stafford; Ames Brothers; Fred Waring; McGuire Sisters. (Produced for First Financial Marketing Group.)

Christmas Through the Years (5 LP) .... Readers Digest (S) RDA-143 15-25 84
Arthur Fiedler; Perry Como; Harry Simeone Chorale; Kate Smith; Bing Crosby; Freddy Martin; Vaughn Monroe; Ames Brothers; Harry Belafonte; Lawrence Welk; Dennis Day; Gary, Lindsay, Dennis, & Bing Crosby; Guy Lombardo; Eddie Fisher; Fontane Sisters; Spike Jones; Bobby Helms; Stan Freberg; Lettermen; Ed Ames; Jim Reeves; Fireside Singers; Roy Orbison; Singing Dogs; Brenda Lee; Jose Feliciano; Dick Haymes & Song Spinners; Russ Morgan; Fred Waring; Glenn Miller; Yogi Yorgesson; John McCarthy Chorale; Royal Philharmonic.

Christmas Time .... Decca (M) CL 34037 10-15

Christmas Time .... Vocalion (M) VL-3812 8-10 67

Christmas Time .... Vocalion (S) VL7-3812 8-10 67
Loretta Lynn; Webb Pierce; Red Foley; Jimmie Davis; Kitty Wells; Ernest Tubb; Bobby Helms; Elton Britt; Maddox Brothers & Rose; Lonzo & Oscar.

Christmas to Remember .... Capitol (S) SL 6573 5-10
Al Martino; Peggy Lee; Nat King Cole; Tennessee Ernie Ford; Lettermen; Fred Waring; Guy Lombardo; Roger Wagner Chorale; Hollywood Bowl Symphony Orchestra. (Made for Montgomery Ward.)

Christmas Treasury of Classics from Avon .... RCA (S) DPL1-0716 8-12 85
Elvis Presley; Dolly Parton; Bing Crosby; Nat King Cole; Julie Andrews; Kenny Rogers; Jose Feliciano; John Denver & Muppets; Anne Murray; Perry Como.

Christmas Wishes .... Columbia Special Products (S) 13844 5-10 77
Mormon Tabernacle Choir; Tony Bennett; Robert Goulet; Johnny Mathis; Bobby Vinton; Percy Faith; Andre Kostelanetz; Jim Nabors; Steve Lawrence & Eydie Gorme; Ray Conniff.

Christmas with Arthur Godfrey .... Columbia (M) CL-540 20-30 54
(TV Soundtrack.) Arthur Godfrey; Jeanette Davis; Mariners; Julius LaRosa; McGuire Sisters; Frank Parker; Marion Marlowe; Haleloke Kahauolopua; Lu Ann Simms.

Christmas with the Johnny Cash Family .... Columbia (S) KC 31754 8-12 72
Johnny Cash; June Carter; Statler Brothers; Carter Family; Tommy Cash; Carl Perkins; Tennessee Three; Larry Butler.

Christmas with the Stars .... Capitol Special Markets (S) SL 6931 5-10 77
Nelson Riddle; Peggy Lee; Bing Crosby; Glen Campbell; Fred Waring; David Rose; Ella Fitzgerald; Tennessee Ernie Ford; Nat King Cole.

Christmas Wonderland .... RCA Special Products (SP) DPL 1-0717 5-10
John Gary; Lang Cantrell; Norman Luboff Choir; Freddy Martin; Merv Griffin & Martin Men; Kate Smith; Yuletide Choristers; Vic Damone; Peggy Lee; Ed Ames; Perry Como with the Ray Charles Singers.

Christmastime in Carol and Song .... RCA (S) PRS 289 5-10

Chuck and His Friends .... Brookville/Aristocrat (S) 1274/BR-100 10-20 74
(Mail order offer.) Chuck Berry; Little Richard; Billy Stewart; Teen Queens; Platters; Dale Hawkins; Chiffons; Moonglows; Kingsmen; Penguins; Johnny Ace; Champs; Fontella Bass; Hank Ballard & Midnighters; Little Willie John; Ramsey Lewis; Shangri-Las; Shirelles; Bo Diddley. (Special products. Made for Brookville. Cover shows Brookville but label is Aristocrat.)

Church in the Wildwood, Vol. 1 .... Capitol (EP) EPA-1-1113 5-10 59

Church in the Wildwood, Vol. 2 .... Capitol (EP) EPA-2-1113 5-10 59

Church in the Wildwood, Vol. 3 .... Capitol (EP) EPA-3-1113 5-10 59

Church in the Wildwood .... Capitol (M) T-1113 20-25 59
Sonny James; Jordanaires; Tex Ritter; Tommy Collins; Statesmen; others.

Cicadelic '60s — Don't Put Me On .... Cicadelic (S) CICLP-998 15-25 84
Pagens; Kings Court; Innsmen; Hearsemen; House of Commons; Lykes of Us; Solitary Confinement.

Cincinnati Rock and Roll, 1950s .... Lee (M) JRC 869 10-15
Bill Watkins; Dillard Anderson; Johnny Northside; Ray Pennington; Orangie Ray Hubbard; Pete Nantz; Ray Moore; Nelson Young.

Circuit Breaker .... K-Tel (S) TU-2760 5-10 79
Leif Garrett; Ian Matthews; Bobby Caldwell; Anne Murray; Patti Smith Group; Gerry Rafferty; Foreigner; Nigel Olson; Babys; Firefall; Rick James; Chanson; Raes; Sylvester.

Circus Royale .... Rhino (S) RNLP 007 5-10

Citizens on Patrol – Police Academy 4: see Police Academy IV – Citizens on Patrol

Class of '62 (5 LP) .... RCA (S) DML5-0540 ?? 84
(Contains 75 hits from 1958-1962 by original artists.)

Class of '74 .... K-Tel (S) TU-2346 5-10 74

Classic Blues, Vol. 1 .... Bluesway (S) BLS-6061 8-12 73
Ray Charles; John Lee Hooker; Johnny Walker; T-Bone Walker; Mel Brown; Roy Brown; George Smith; Jimmy Witherspoon; Andrew Odom; Archie Shepp.

Classic Blues, Vol. 2 .... Bluesway (S) BLS-6062 8-12 73

Classic Country .... 4 Star (S) 4S-SP-105 5-10 77
Jan Howard; Wynn Stewart; Johnny & Jonie; Carl Belew; George Morgan; Jimmy Elledge; Mary Ford; Billy Don Burns; Jeannie Seely; Betty Jean Robinson.

Classic Country Duets .... MCA (S) 5599 5-10 85
Don Williams & Emmylou Harris; Barbara Mandrell & Steve Wariner; Bill Anderson & Jan Howard; Jack Greene & Jeannie Seely; Loretta Lynn & Ernest Tubb; Barbara Mandrell & Lee Greenwood; Loretta Lynn & Conway Twitty; Kitty Wells & Roy Acuff; Kendalls; Merle Haggard & Leona Williams.

Classic Country Music (8 LP) .... Smithsonian Institute (S) PB 15640 35-50 81
(Box set. Includes 56-page booklet.) Eck Robertson; Fiddlin John Carson; Grayson & Whitter; Uncle Dave Macon; Vernon Dalhart; Charlie Poole; Gid Tanner & His Skillet Lickers; Smith's Sacred Singers; East Texas Serenaders; Darby & Tarlton; Buell Kazee; Bradley Kincaid; Carl Sprague; Ernest V. Stoneman; Carter Family Jimmy Rodgers; Arthur Smith; Riley Puckett; Cliff Carlisle; Coon Creek Girls; Mac & Bob; Callahan Brothers; Blue Sky Boys; Delmore Bros.; Monroe Bros.; Rouse Bros.; Red Foley; Karl & Harty; Lulu Belle & Scotty; J.E. Mainer's Mountaineers; Rex Griffin; Roy Acuff; Carter Family; Gene Autry & Jimmy Longs; Sons of Pioneers; Patsy Montana; Montana Slim; Stuart Hamblen; Light Crust Doughboys & Leon Huff; Shelton Bros.; Jimmie Davis; Bill Boyd; Milton Brown & His Brownies; Bob Wills & His Texas Playboys; Leo Soileau; Woody Guthrie; Chuck Wagon Gang; Cliff Bruner's Texas Wanderers; Bob Wills & Texas Playboys; Gene Autry; Ernest Tubb; Wiley Walker & Gene Sullivan; Ted Daffan's Texans; Elton Britt; Al Dexter; Tex Ritter; Molly O'Day; Jack Guthrie; Bailes Brothers; Roy Acuff; Merle Travis; Tex Ritter; Eddy Arnold; Tex Williams; Johnny & Jack; Jimmy Dickens; Maddox Brothers & Rose; Red Foley; Grandpa Jones; Cowboy Copas; Blue Sky Boys; Moon Mullican; Slim Whitman; Hank Snow; Leon Payne; Pee Wee King; Martha Carson; Floyd Tillman; Lefty Frizzell; Carl Smith; Hank Thompson; Kitty Wells; Wilma Lee & Stoney Cooper; Hank Williams; Webb Pierce; Johnny Cash; Tennessee Ernie Ford; Everly Bros.; Chet Atkins; Jim Reeves; Ray Price; Bobby Helms; Louvin Bros.; Johnny Horton; Marty Robbins; Rusty & Doug; Patsy Cline; Buck Owens; George Jones & Melba Montgomery; Bill Monroe & His Blue Grass Boys; Flatt & Scruggs; Stanley Bros.; Mac Wiseman; Jim & Jesse & Virginia Boys; Osborne Brothers; Bill Clifton; Reno & Smiley; Lilly Brothers; Hylo Brown; Jimmy Martin; Kenny Baker; Doc Watson; Charlie Moore; Cliff Waldron & New Shades of Grass; Country Gentlemen; Seldom Scene; Dave Dudley; Bobby Bare; Porter Wagoner; Roger Miller; Charley Pride; Tom T. Hall; Dolly Parton; Merle Haggard; Loretta Lynn; Tammy Wynette; Moe Bandy; Flying Burrito Bros.; Willie Nelson.

Classic Pianos....................Doctor Jazz (M) EW 38851 8-12 70s
James P. Johnson; Art Hodes Trio; Earl Hines Trio; Erroll Garner; others.
Classic Rock, Vol. 1....................MCA (S) MCA-25185 5-10 88
Joe Walsh; Steely Dan; Dobie Gray; Dave Mason; Lynyrd Skynyrd; Steppenwolf; Elton John; Rossington Collins Band; Bo Diddley; Golden Earring.
Classic Rock – 1964 (2 LP)....................Time-Life/Warner (S) SCLR-03 ?? 84
Classic Rock – 1965 (2 LP)....................Time-Life/Warner (S) SCLR-01 ?? 84
Classic Rock – 1966 (2 LP)....................Time-Life/Warner (S) SCLR-02 ?? 84
Classmates....................Buddah (S) BDS-5017 10-15
Five Stairsteps; Judy White; Timothy Wilson; Henry Lumpkin; Tony Lamarr; Mama & Papa Stairstep.
Clay Cole Presents Blasts from the Past: see Blasts from the Past
Cleveland Metal....................Clubside (S) 0001 5-10 83
Black Death; Sacred Few; Cerberus; Jagged Edge; Mistreater; Breaker; Shok Paris; Sorcerer.
Club 15....................Decca (M) DL-5155 40-45 49
(Soundtrack. 10-inch LP.) Jerry Gray; Dick Haymes; Andrews Sisters; Evelyn Knight; Modernaires.
C'mon Let's Live a Little: see DE SHANNON, Jackie / Bobby Vee / Eddie Hodges
CM Collection: see Curtis Mathis Collection
Coal Miner's Daughter....................MCA (S) 5107 8-10 80
Coal Miner's Daughter....................MCA (S) 1699 5-8 Re
(Soundtrack.) Sissy Spacek; Levon Helm; Beverly D'Angelo; Jordanaires.
Coast to Coast....................Full Moon (S) FM-3490 8-10 80
(Soundtrack.) Rita Coolidge; Johnny Lee; Ambrosia.
Cobra....................Scotti Bros. (S) SZ 40325 8-10 86
(Soundtrack.) John Cafferty & Beaver Brown Band; Jean Beauvoir; Gladys Knight; Bill Medley; Sylvester Levay; Gary Wright; Miami Sound Machine; Robert Tepper; Carmen Twillie; Little Richard; Beach Boys.
Cocktail....................Elektra (S) 60806-1 8-10 88
(Soundtrack.) Starship; Robbie Nevil; Fabulous Thunderbirds; Beach Boys; Ry Cooder; Little Richard; Bobby McFerrin; Georgia Satellites; Preston Smith; John Cougar Mellencamp.
Coffee Break with a Latin Beat....................Columbia (M) XTV-82075 5-10
Ray Conniff; Michel Legrand; Norman Luboff; Percy Faith; Tommy Dorsey; Andre Kostelanetz; Xavier Cugat; Les Elgart; Les Brown; Art Van Damme; Sammy Kaye.
Coffee House Blues....................Vee Jay (M) VJLP-1138 10-20 65
Coffee House Blues....................Vee Jay (S) VJSR-1138 15-25 65
Lightnin' Hopkins; Brownie McGhee & Sonny Terry; others.
Cole Porter's *Out of This World* (7 EP)....................Columbia (EP) A-980 15-25 50
Cole Porter's *Out of This World*....................Columbia (M) ML-54390 20-25 50
(Disc label reads "ML-4390.")
Cole Porter's *Out of This World*....................Columbia (M) OL-4390 15-18 Re
Cole Porter's *Out of This World*....................Columbia Special Products (M) COL-4390 8-10 Re
(Original Broadway Cast.) Charlotte Greenwood; William Eythe; Priscilla Gillette; William Redfield; Barbara Ashley; George Jongeyans; David Burns.
Colgate Presents: see Geat Sounds and New Sounds from Columbia
Collectables Presents Great Groups of the Fifties, Vol. 1....................Collectables (M) COL 5037 5-10 88
Five Satins; Roulettes; Scarlets; Spaniels; Starlarks; Vocaleers; Veltones; Lewis Lymon & Teenchords; Kings; Kodaks; Castells; Channels; Whispers; Avalons.
Collectables Presents Great Groups of the Fifties, Vol. 2....................Collectables (M) COL 5038 5-10 88
Five Satins; Kodaks; Baltineers; Continentals; Videos; Cherokees; Cherokees; Capris; Charts; El Dorados; Angels; Silhouettes; Spaniels; Scarlets; Skylarks.
Collectables Presents Great Groups of the Fifties, Vol. 3....................Collectables (M) COL 5039 5-10 88
Channels; Flamingos; Hide-A-Ways; Five Satins; El Dorados; Gazelles; Skyhawks; Mello Moods; Jackie & Starlites; Spaniels; Charts; Castelles; Hemlocks; Idols.
Collection of Classic Oldies: see At the Hop (a Collection of Classic Oldies)
Collection of Golden Hits....................Mercury (M) MG-20213 30-40 60
Platters; Gaylords; Crew-Cuts; Diamonds.
Collection of Golden Hits....................Mercury (S) SR-60234 15-25 61
Platters; Diamonds; Crew-Cuts; Gaylords; others.
Collection of Los Angeles Bands, Vol. 2....................Rhino (S) RNLP 009 8-12
Kats; Oingo Biongo; Charm School; Rubber City Rebels; Low Numbers; Denny Ward; Weasels; Twisters; Surf Punks; Ravers; Droogs; Spock; Furys.
Collection of Million Sellers for the Entire Family (2 LP)....................MGM (M) 2E-7 25-40 60
Conway Twitty; Hank Williams; Sheb Wooley; Billy Eckstine; Tommy Edwards; Arthur "Guitar Boogie" Smith; David Rose; Carlton Carpenter; Debbie Reynolds; Blue Barron; Leslie Caron; Mark Dinning; Lenny Hayton; Leroy Holmes; Dick Hyman; Jimmy Jones; Art Lund; Silvana Mangano; Art Mooney; Jaye P. Morgan; George Shearing.
Collection of New Folk Music - Legacy....................Windham Hill (S) WH6-1086 5-10 89
Pierce Pettis; Cliff Eberhardt; Rebecca Jenkins; David Massengill; Blue Rubies; Bill Morrissey; Lillie Palmer; John Gorka; Uncle Bonsai; Steven Roback; Anne Bourne; Kirk Kelly; Ian Matthews; Sara Hickman; Milo Bender.
Collection of Popular Recordings, Vol. 1....................Modern (M) MOD-2001 35-55 51
(10–inch LP.)
Collection of Popular Recordings, Vol. 2....................Modern (M) MOD-2002 35-55 51
(10–inch LP.)
Collection of Popular Recordings, Vol. 3....................Modern (M) MOD-2003 35-55 51
(10–inch LP.)
Collection of Popular Recordings, Vol. 4....................Modern (M) MOD-2004 35-55 51
(10–inch LP.)
Collection of Popular Recordings, Vol. 5....................Modern (M) MOD-2005 35-55 51
(10–inch LP.) Pee Wee Crayton; Hadda Brooks; Jimmy Witherspoon; Little Willie Littlefield; Little Esther; Gene Phillips; Jimmy Girssom.

Collection of Popular Recordings, Vol. 6 .... Modern (M) MOD-2006 35-55 51
(10-inch LP.)
Collection of Popular Recordings, Vol. 7 .... Modern (M) MOD-2007 35-55 51
(10-inch LP.)
Collection of Popular Recordings, Vol. 8 .... Modern (M) MOD-2008 35-55 51
(10-inch LP.)
Collection of Popular Recordings, Vol. 9 .... Modern (M) MOD-2009 35-55 51
(10-inch LP.)
Collection of Popular Recordings, Vol. 10 .... Modern (M) MOD-2010 35-55 51
(10-inch LP.)
Collection of Popular Recordings, Vol. 11 .... Modern (M) MOD-2011 35-55 51
(10-inch LP.)
Collection of Popular Recordings, Vol. 12 .... Modern (M) MOD-2012 35-55 51
(10-inch LP.)
Collection of Popular Recordings, Vol. 13 .... Modern (M) MOD-2013 35-55 51
(10-inch LP.)
Collection of 16 Original Big Hits: see 16 Original Big Hits
Collectors Album of All Time Hits Sweet & Cool .... Columbia Special Products (M) XTV 86071 8-12
Kirby Stone Four; Tony Bennett; Polly Bergen; Les Elgart; Luther Henderson; Jo Stafford; Lester Lanin; Andre Previn; Ray Conniff; Dukes of Dixieland.
Collectors Delight .... Dore (S) LP 401 5-10 81
Collectors History of Classic Jazz (5 LP) .... Murray Hill (SE) 927942 25-35
(Boxed set.) Blind Lemon; Harlem Christian; Fred Van Epps; New Orleans Military Band; Kerry Mills; Scott Joplin; James Scott; Jelly Roll Morton; Mead Lux Lewis; Lucky Roberts; Original Dixieland Band; King Oliver's Creole Jazz Band; Louis Armstrong & His Hot Seven; Blunk Johnson; Kid Ory; Jimmy Noone; Sidney Bechet; George Lewis; Pee Wee Russell; Eddie Condon; Jess Stacy; Billy Butterfield; Bobby Haggart; Geoorge Wettling; Max Kaminsky; Jo Jones; Pete Fountain; Jack Teagarden; Lawson-Haggart Sextet; Bessie Smith; Leadbelly; Brownie & Sonny; Muggsy Spanier; Lightnin' Hopkins; Big Joe Williams; Josh White; Big Bill Broonzy; John Lee Hooker; Ray Charles; Billie Holiday; Memphis Slim; Jimmy Reed; Fletcher Henderson; Duke Ellington; James P. Johnson; Charlie Christian; Charlie Parker; Fats Waller; Dizzie Gillespie; Ella Fitzgerald; Charlie Mingus; Eric Dolphy; Sonny Rollins; Cannonball Adderley; Miles Davis; Benny Goodman; Woody Herman; Charlie Barnet; Artie Shaw; Tommy Dorsey; Duke Ellington; Jimmy Dorsey; Roy Eldridge, Flip Phillips; Clyde McCoy; Teddy Wilson; Sarah Vaughan; Count Basie..
Collectors Records of the '50s and '60s .... Laurie (S) SLP-2051 10-15 77
Five Discs; Passions; Chiffons; Randy & Rainbows; Mystics; Dimensions; Dion; Carlo; Del-Satins; Jarmels; Dino & Diplomats; Dion & Belmonts; Bobby Goldsboro; Skyliners; Tokens.
Collectors Records of the '50s and '60s, Vol. 2 .... Laurie (S) LES-4009 10-15 78
Five Discs; Passions; Chiffons; Mystics; Carlo; Del-Satins; Skyliners; Demilles; Vito & Salutations; Enchords; Elegants; Bon Aires; Four Graduates; Harps.
Collectors Records of the '50s and '60s, Vol. 3 .... Laurie (S) LES-4011 10-15 78
Five Discs; Chiffons; Mystics; Four Graduates; Billy Vera & Contrasts; Dion & Belmonts; Emotions; Larry & Standards; Four Epics; Carlo; Ray Vons; Four Pennies; Randy & Rainbows; Jarmels.
Collectors Records of the '50s and '60s, Vol. 4 .... Laurie (S) LES-4018 10-15 79
Chiffons; Mystics; Dion; Four Pennies; Dion & Belmonts; Skyliners; Carlo; Del Satins; Jimmy Clanton; Bernadette Carroll; Curtis Lee; Delrons; Ernie Maresca; Demilles.
Collectors Records of the '50s and '60s, Vol. 5 .... Laurie (S) LES-4021 10-15 79
Platters; Chiffons; Dion & Belmonts; Four Pennies; Isley Brothers; Dionne Warwick; Ernie Maresca; Bill Haley & His Comets; Dean & Jean; B.J. Thomas; Shirelles; Del Satins; Dino & Diplomats; Dion & Del Satins.
Collectors Records of the '50s and '60s, Vol. 6 .... Laurie (S) LES-4022 10-15 79
Chiffons; Mystics; Dion & Belmonts; Ernie Maresca; B.J. Thomas; Beach Boys; Platters; Gene Pitney; Carlo; Barbarians; Bobby Goldsboro; Bobby Hebb; Boots Walker; Dion.
Collectors Records of the '50s and '60s, Vol. 7 .... Laurie (S) LES-4023 10-15 79
Chiffons; Mystics; Dion; Ernie Maresca; Gene Pitney; Carlo; Bobby Goldsboro; Boots Walker; Shirelles; Brook Benton; Passions; Bill Haley & His Comets; Dionne Warwick; Dean & Jean.
Collectors Records of the '50s and '60s, Vol. 8 .... Laurie (S) LES-4024 10-15 79
Chiffons; Dion; Dino & Diplomats; Ernie Maresca; Carlo; Shirelles; Dionne Warwick; Tune Weavers; Platters; Chuck Jackson; 1929 Depression; Skyliners; Barbarians; Four Coins; Rivingtons.
Collectors Records of the '50s and '60s, Vol. 9 .... Laurie (S) LES-4025 10-15 79
Mystics; Maxine Brown; Cardboard Zeppelin; Bernadette Carroll; Shirelles; Del Shannon; Carlo; Dion; Belmonts; Don & Juan; Jim Campbell; Ernie Maresca; Sundae.
Collectors Records of the '50s and '60s, Vol. 10 .... Laurie (S) LES-4026 10-15 79
Criterions; Ersel Hickey; Four Coins; Teardrops; Dion; Skyliners; Demotrons; Casualeers; Dionne Warwick; Emotions; Del Shannon; Chiffons; Brook Benton; Mystics; Sundae.
Collectors Records of the '50s and '60s, Vol. 11 .... Laurie (S) LES-40?? 10-15 79
Collectors Records of the '50s and '60s, Vol. 12 .... Laurie (S) LES-40?? 10-15 79
Collectors Records of the '50s and '60s, Vol. 13 .... Laurie (S) LES-4046 10-15 82
Everly Brothers; Don & Juan; Johnny Tillotson; Marcie Blaine; Dion; Del Shannon; Carlo; ernie Maresca; Regents; Foreign Intrigue; Dean & Jean; Chiffons; Spiedels; Belmonts.
Collectors Records of the '50s and '60s, Vol. 14 .... Laurie (S) LES-4047 10-15 82
Everly Brothers; Gene Chandler; Richie Valens; Bobby Hebb; Del Shannon; Jeans; California; Dion; Traces; Ernie Maresca; Dean & Jean; Four Coins.
Collectors Records of the '50s and '60s, Vol. 15 .... Laurie (S) LES-4048 10-15 83
Everly Brothers; Bobby Fuller; Olympics; Johnny Tillotson; Dion & Belmonts; Russ Damon; Yellow Brick Road; Bernadette Carroll; Traces; Frank Lyndon.
Collectors Records of the '50s and '60s, Vol. 16 .... Laurie (S) LES-4051 10-15 83
Everly Brothers; Lenny Welch; Dee Clark; Jerry Butler; Reparata; Ray Stevens; Dion; Terra & Cook; Karl Hammel Jr.; Casualeers; Hubcaps; Traces.
Collectors Records of the '50s and '60s, Vol. 17 .... Laurie (S) LES-4052 10-15 83
Everly Brothers; Dee Clark; Betty Everett & Jerry Butler; Dion; Five Discs; Bernadette Carroll & Ernie Maresca; Magic; Carlo; Terra & Cook; Chiffons; Andrew; Ernie Maresca & Del Satins; Freddy; Belmonts.

Collectors Records of the '50s and '60s, Vol. 18 .... Laurie (S) LES-4053 10-15 83
Jerry Butler; Lenny Welch; Chordettes; Jarmels; Carlo; Del Shannon; Five Discs; Kenny Chandler; Cardboard Zeppelin; Belmonts; Ernie Maresca & Del Satins; Bernadette Carroll; Boots Walker.

Collectors Records of the '50s and '60s, Vol. 19 .... Laurie (S) LES-4054 10-15 83
Everly Brothers; Five Discs; Royal Guardsmen; Bobby Shafto; Del Shannon; Frank Lydon of the Belmonts; Slim Jim; Dean & Jean; Music Explosion; Cardboard Zeppelin; Foreign Intrigue; Dion; Ernie Maresca & Belmonts.

Collectors Records of the '50s and '60s, Vol. 20 .... Laurie (S) LES-4055 10-15 83
Everly Brothers; Ernie Maresca; Barbarians; Brooklyn Boys; Dion; Belmonts; Boots Walker; Traces; Del Shannon; Chimes; Warren Gardus of the Belmonts; After Hours; Terry & Cooke.

Collectors Roots - Chicago Blues .... Blue Flame (M) 10 5-10
Hound Dog Taylor; Little Mack; Betty Everett; others.

Collectors Set, Vol. 1 .... Capitol (S) SL 6552 5-10 60s
Nat King Cole; George Shearing; Nancy Wilson; Hollyridge Strings; Matt Monro; Lettermen; Stan Kenton.

Collectors Showcase - Aces Three .... Constellation (M) CS-7 15-20 64
Jimmy Clanton; Frankie Ford; Huey "Piano" Smith; others.

Collectors Showcase - Bucket of Blues .... Constellation (M) CS-6 15-20 64
John Lee Hooker; T-Bone Walker; others.

Collectors Showcase - Groups Three, Vol. 5: see BLUENOTES / Five Echoes / Five Chances

Collectors Showcase - Ya Ya .... Constellation (M) CS-1 15-20 64
Lee Dorsey; Don Gardner & Dee Dee Ford; King Curtis; others.

Colliers Encyclopedia 1965 Edition - the Year in Sound .... Radio Press Int'l (M) No Number Used 15-20 65
(Promotional issue only.) Interviews with John Lennon, Paul McCartney and others.

Color Me OBG (Radio Station WDRC) .... Roulette (M) R-25347 10-15 67
Little Eva; Five Satins; Crystals; Les Cooper; Reflections; Patty & Emblems; Raindrops; Honeycombs; Lou Christie; Joey Dee & Starliters; Tommy James & Shondells; Bobby Lewis; Barbara Lewis; Essex; Edsels; Bobby Freeman; Billy Bland; Rivieras; Betty Everett; Dovells.

Color My Soul .... Sunset (S) SVS 5314 8-10 71
Fats Domino; O'Jays; Isley Bros; Ike & Tina Turner; Jimmy McCracklin.

Color of Money .... MCA (S) 6189 8-10 86
(Soundtrack.) Don Henley; Warren Zevon; Robert Palmer; Eric Clapton; Mark Knopfler; Willie Dixon; B.B. King; Robbie Robertson.

Colors .... Warner Bros. (S) 1-25713 8-10 88
(Soundtrack.) 44 Mag Mix; Decadent Dub Team; Salt-N-Pepa; Big Daddy Kane; Eric B.; Kool G.; 7A3; Roxanne Shante; M.C.; Rick James.

Colossus Gold .... Colossus (S) 5001 8-12 70
Shocking Blue; Tee Set; Bill Deal; Shannon; Cherry People; George Baker Selection; Show Stoppers; Duprees; Jerry Ross Symposium; Festival.

Columbia Basic Library of Great Jazz .... Columbia (M) K3L-236 10-15
Mahalia Jackson; Buck Clayton & His All Stars; Sarah Vaughan; Bessie Smith; Billie Holiday; Pete Rugolo; Wally Rose; Count Basie; Chet Baker; Turk Murphy & His Jazz Band; Jimmie Lunceford; Calvin Jackson Quartet; Kid Ory's Creole Jazz Band; Harry James; Lenny Hambro Quintet; Pete Johnson; Benny Goodman Sextet; Johnny Eaton Quartet; Louis Armstrong & His Hot Five; Villegas; McKenzie & Condon's Californians; Erroll Garner; Ted Macero; Frankie Trumbauer; Gene Krupa; Bob Prince; Duke Ellington; Woody Herman; Rampart Street Paraders; Dave Brubeck Quartet.

Columbia Dateline August .... Columbia (EP) ZEP 36309 10-15 50s
Michel Legrand; Peggy King; Jerry Vale; Percy Faith; Les Elgart; Eugene Ormandy & Philadelphia Orchestra; Art Linkletter; Louis Armstrong & His All Stars; others.

Columbia Hall of Fame, Vol. 1 (1951) .... Columbia (S) AE2-1012 10-20 60s
Columbia Hall of Fame, Vol. 2 (1952) .... Columbia (S) AE2-1013 10-20 60s
Columbia Hall of Fame, Vol. 3 (1953 - 1954) .... Columbia (S) AE2-1014 10-20 60s
Columbia Hall of Fame, Vol. 4 (1955 - 1956) .... Columbia (S) AE2-1015 10-20 60s
Columbia Hall of Fame, Vol. 5 (1957 - 1959) .... Columbia (S) AE2-1016 10-20 60s
Columbia Hall of Fame, Vol. 6 (1960 - 1963) .... Columbia (S) AE2-1017 10-20 60s
Buzz Clifford; Brothers Four; Johnny Horton; Percy Faith; Jimmy Dean; Marty Robbins; Steve Lawrence; Claude King; Andy Williams; Dion DiMucci; Johnny Mathis; Bill Pursell.

Columbia House Party .... Columbia (S) XLP 36209/36210 10-15 60s
Jo Stafford; Paul Weston; Frankie Laine; Liberace; Norman Luboff Choir; Dave Brubeck Quartet; Mitch Miller; Guy Mitchell; Four Lads; Rosemary Clooney. Tony Bennett; Louis Armstrong.

Columbia Jazz Festival .... Columbia (M) J-1 15-25 60
Columbia Jazz Festival .... Columbia (S) JS-1 15-25 60
Duke Ellington; Gerry Mulligan Quartet; Lionel Hampton; Teddy Wilson & His Trio; Joe Wilder Quartet; Benny Goodman; Miles Davis; Dave Brubeck Quartet; Buck Clayton & All Stars; J.J. Johnson.

Columbia Record Club Bonus Record .... Columbia (S) CB-12 8-12
Columbia Record Club Demonstration Record .... Columbia (S) D-7 8-12
Columbia Records Fall 1975: the Heavy Weights (2 LP) .... Columbia (S) S2S 174 15-30 75
(Promotional only issue.) Pink Floyd; Bruce Springsteen; Janis Ian; New Riders of the Purple Sage; Paul Simon; Dave Mason; Herbie Hancock; Mott; Art Garfunkel; Ramsey Lewis; Chicago; Taj Mahal; Loggins & Messina; Tony Williams; Barbra Streisand; Bill Withers; Flying Burrito Band.

Columbia Rock .... Columbia Special Products (S) P 16399 5-10
Molly Hatchett; Eddie Money; Journey; Southside Johnny & Ashbury Jukes; Santana; Nick Lowe; REO Speedwagon; Ian Gomm; Steve Forbert.

Columbia Sound (A Collection of 16 Original Big Hits) .... Columbia Special Products (S) DS-486 10-15 68
(Mail order offer.) Peaches & Herb; Aretha Franklin; United States of America; Chambers Brothers; Grace Slick & Great Society; Union Gap; Cryan' Shames; Electric Flag; Ravi Shankar; Peanut Butter Conspiracy; Buckinghams; Leonard Cohen; Moby Grape; Paul Revere & Raiders; Byrds; Tremeloes.

Columbia Star Time, Vol. 1 & 2 (2 LP) .... Columbia (M) ST-1 15-20
Les Elgart; Frankie Laine; Les Brown; Percy Faith; Art Van Damme Quintet; Norman Paris Trio; Chet Baker; Norman Luboff Choir; Benny Goodman; Morton Gould; Dan Terry; Marek Weber; Harry James; Liberace; Sammy Kaye; Andre Kostelanetz; Jo Stafford; Eugene Ormandy & Philadelphia Orchestra; Tony Bennett; Isaac Stern; Guy Mitchell; Bruno Walter & Philharmonic Symphony of New York; Mitch Miller; Paul Weston; Doris Day.

Columbia Stereophonic Phonograph Demonstration Record ....Columbia (S) CPSP-1 15-20 50s
Kirby Stone Four; Frank DeVol; Ray Conniff; Percy Faith; Frank Comstock; New York Phiharmonic; Andre Kostelanetz; Leonard Bernstein; Eugene Ormandy & Philadelphia Orchestra; Les & Larry Elgart; Red Allen & All Stars; Original Broadway Cast of *West Side Story*; Art Hannes (narrator.)

Columbia's All New Time - Release Capsule, Vol. 3 ....Columbia (S) AS 271 8-12 76
Sutherland Brothers & Quiver; Dave Mason; Sparks; Rex; Phoebe Snow; Hubert Laws; Ned Doheny; Bobby Scott.

Columbia's 21 Top 20 (2 LP) ....Columbia (S) A2S-700 15-25 79
(Promotional only issue.) Paul McCartney; others.

Columbia's 24 Top Hits in the Top 20 for 1982 (2 LP) ....Columbia (S) A2S-1558 15-25 82
Promotional only issue.) Paul McCartney; others

Come Dance at My Party ....Epic (M) LN-3712 20-30 60

Come Dance at My Party ....Epic (S) BN-576 20-30 60
Lester Lanin; Chuck Sagle; Francis Bay; Link Wray; others.

Come Dance with Me (Rama/Gee Archives) ....Murray Hill (M) 001101 5-10 88
Vocaltones; Heartbeats; Rainbows; Crows; Little Butchie Saunders; Jets; Rosebuds; Debonaires; Limelighters; Valtones; Mellow Keys; Joytones.

Come Dance with Me ....Columbia (M) PC 36743 5-10 80
Benny Goodman; Harry James; Les Brown; Charlie Barnet; Gene Krupa.

Come, Josephine, in My Flying Maching ....New World (S) 233 5-10 77
Eddie Morton; Elida Morris; Sam Ash; Harry Ash; American Quartet; Will Haley; others.

Come One, Come All, Hoot ....Warner Bros. (M) W-1512 10-20 63

Come One, Come All, Hoot ....Warner Bros. (S) WS-1512 15-20 63

Come to a Shindig Dance Party ....Custom (M) CS1038 10-20 60s
Steve Alaimo; Trini Lopez; Johnny Rivers; Ray Charles; Brook Benton; Jerry Cole; Neil Sedaka; Dave Clark Five; Little Richard; Ritchie Valens.

Comedy Caravan ....Capitol (M) T-732 50-75 56
Stan Freberg; Andy Griffith; Johnny Standley; Hari Kari; Yogi Yorgesson.

Comedy Hits ....Capitol (M) T-1854 15-20 63

Comedy Hits ....Capitol (S) ST-1854 20-25 63
Stan Freberg; Frank Fontaine; Andy Griffith; Carl Reiner & Mel Brooks; Johnny Standley; Yogi Yorgesson.

Coming Home (2 LP) ....RCA (S) DVL2-0869 10-20 88
(Mail order offer.) Elvis Presley; Dolly Parton; Hank Williams; Charley Pride; Wink Martindale; Jim Reeves; Johnny Cash; Kris Kristofferson; Original Carter Family; Porter Wagoner; Tom T. Hall; Cristy Lane; Red Foley; Willie Nelson; Walter Brennan; Ferlin Husky; Kitty Wells & Carol Sue; Roy Acuff; Marty Robbins; Molly O'Day; Merle Haggard; George Jones; Melba Montgomery; Tennessee Ernie Ford. (LPs packaged individually but sold as a set.)

Coming to America ....Atco (S) 0-90958/DMD 1189 10-15 88
(Promotional issue only.)

Coming to America ....Atco (S) 90958-1 8-10 88
(Soundtrack.) System; Cover Girls; Chico DeBarge; Michael Rodgers; Laura Branigan; Joe Esposito; JJ Fad; Mell & Kim; Levert; Sister Sledge; Nona Hendrix.

Command Performance ....Pickwick (S) SHM 912 5-10
Tony Bennett; Johnny Cash; June Carter; Vikki Carr; Mario Lanza; Frankie Vaughn; Des O'Connor; Jim Reeves; Dionne Warwick.

Command Performance ....Ronco (SE) MSD 2005 (TV) 10-20 73
(Live recordings from Ed Sullivan Show.) Barbra Streisand; Tony Bennett; Nancy Wilson; Johnny Mathis; Sammy Davis Jr.; Connie Francis; Harry Belafonte; Peggy Lee; Robert Goulet; Judy Garland; Louis Armstrong; Eartha Kitt; Nat King Cole; Patti Page; Maurice Chevalier; Trini Lopez; Tony Martin; Frankie Laine; Gordon MacRae; Lena Horne.

Command Sampler, Vol. 6 ....Command (S) COM-6 8-12 60s

Command Sampler, Vol. 11 ....Command (S) COM-11SD 8-12 60s
Enoch Light; Alfred Drake & Roberta Peters; Ray Charles Singers; Tony Mottola; Robert de Cormier Folk Singers; Lew Davies; Dick Hyman; Charles Magnante.

Command Sampler, Vol. 12 ....Command (S) COM-1250 8-12 60s
Enoch Light; Ray Charles Singers; Tony Mottola; Dick Hyman; Doc Severinsen; Lew Davies; Robert de Cormier Folk Singers; Dick Van Dyke; Lee Evans.

Command Sampler, Vol. 16 ....Command (S) COM-1650 8-12 60s
Mitchell Ayres; Ray Charles Singers; Dick Hyman; Tony Mottola; Robert de Cormier Singers; Doc Severinsen & His Sextet; Bobby Byrne; Count Basie; Toots Thielemans; Donald O'Connor; Phyllis Newman; Larry Blyden; Eddie Foy Jr.

Comparative Blue ....Jazztone (M) Jazztone J 1258 15-25 57
Buck Clayton; Sidney Bechet; Jimmy Yancey; Maxie Kaminsky; Jack Teagarden; Joe Newman & Count's Men; Dizzy Gillespie; Charlie Parker; Eddie Bert.

Compatible Stereo/Quadraphonic Sound ....Ovation (Q) OD/1 10-15

Compositions of Dizzy Gillespie ....Riverside (M) RLP 93508 10-20

Concert for Bangla Desh: see HARRISON, George

Concerts for the People of Kampuchea (2 LP) ....Atlantic (S) SD-2-7005 10-15 81
Paul McCartney & Wings; Who; Pretenders; Elvis Costello & Attractions; Rockpile; Robert Plant; Queen; Clash; Ian Dury & Blockheads; Specials; Rockestra.

Concord Sound, Vol. 1 ....Concord (S) CJ-278 5-10

Concussion! ....Mr. Manicotti (M) MM-342 5-10 80s
Holidays; Ree-Gents; Downbeats; Nautiloids; Jeujene & Jaybops; Glenrays; Ben Leonard & Furies; Jerry & Casuals; Zakons; Jack & Rippers; Four Unknowns; Punk Carson & Chucklers; Bop-Kats; Emanons; Rockin' Rebels; Teen Rockers; Aldon & E.C.'s.

Connecticut's Greatest Hits ....Co-Op/Phase One (S) CP-101 10-20
Van Dykes; Chosen Few; Majenics; Pearlean Gray & Passengers; Fred Parris & Restless Hearts; Leo & Duets; Tony IV Featuring Tony Pagano.

Contact Sounds of Mod ....Columbia Special Products (S) CSP-314 10-15 60s
Bob Dylan; Bobby Vinton; Chad & Jeremy; Yardbirds; Dave Clark Five.

Contemporary Guitar ....Takoma (M) C-1006 10-15 67
Robbie Basho; John Fahey; Max Ochs; Harry Taussig; Bukka White.

Cookie ....UNI (S) 600 8-10
(Soundtrack.) Holly Johnson; Transvision Vamp; Bobby Helms; Nanci Griffith; Thomas Newman.

Cookin' with Country .... Hilltop (S) PTP 2074 8-12
Glen Campbell; Bobbie Gentry; Sonny James; Tennessee Ernie Ford; Jean Shepard; Buck Owens; Roy Clark; Wanda Jackson; Hank Thompson; Tex Ritter; Patsy Cline; Hank Locklin; Wynn Stewart; Ferlin Husky; Johnny Horton; Dave Dudley; Jerry Smith; Jimmy Dean; Charlie Ryan; Stuart Hamblen; Hal Willis; Stewart Family; Webb Pierce; Floyd Cramer.

Cool and Carefree .... Columbia Special Products (S) CSP-119 8-12 60s
Dorsey Brothers; Frankie Carle; Jo Stafford; Louis Armstrong; Sarah Vaughan; Dukes of Dixieland; Rosemary Clooney; Duke Ellington; Eddie Duchin; Walter Huston. (Made for Carrier Air Conditioning Company.)

Cool and Clear .... Columbia Special Products (S) CSP-197 10-20 66
Bruce & Terry; Rip Chords; Bobby Vinton; Major Lance; Johnny Mathis; New Christy Minstrels; Damita Jo; Jerry Vale; Aretha Franklin; Village Stompers.

Cool Box Lunch .... TY-CA (S) 1001 5-10 77
Al Mehaffey; Joe Hudson; Jan Deneau; Paul Kreibich; others.

Cool Playing Blues .... Relic (M) 8025 5-10 89
Jojo Adams; Curtis Jones; Little Papa Joe; L.C. McKinley; Nature Boy Brown; Jody Williams; Curtis Jones; St. Louis Jimmy.

Cool Runnings .... Chaos (S) 57553 ?? 93
(Soundtrack.) Jimmy Cliff; Diana King; Tony Rebel; Super Cat; Tiger; Wailing Souls; Worl-A-Girl; Hans Zimmer.

Cool Scene .... Warner Bros. (M) W-1328 15-25 59
Cool Scene .... Warner Bros. (S) WS-1328 20-30 59
Trombones; Marty Paich; Frank Comstock; Don Ralke; Signatures; Smart Set; Robert Price; Marty Wilson; Guitars, Inc.; Warren Barker; Chico Hamilton Quintet.

Cool Yule .... Rhino (S) RNLP-70073 5-10 86
Chuck Berry; Drifters; Ike & Tina Turner; James Brown; Surfaris; Booker T. & MGs; Marquees; Solomon Burke; Jack Scott; Bud Logan; Clarence Carter; Paul & Paula; Edd "Kookie" Byrnes.

Cool Yule, Vol. 2 .... Rhino (S) RNLP-70193 5-10 88
Johnny Preston; Brenda Lee; Uniques; Harmony Gritts; Jack Scott; Martels; Chuck Berry; Marcels; Gary Walker; Huey "Piano" Smith & Clowns; Honey & Bees; Gary "U.S." Bonds; Sonics; Davy Jones, Mickey Dolenz & Peter Tork.

Cooley High .... Motown (S) M7-840R2 15-20 75
(Soundtrack.) Diana Ross & Supremes; Stevie Wonder; Four Tops; Luther Allison; Martha Reeves & Vandellas; Marvelettes; Smokey Robinson & Miracles; Jr. Walker & All-Stars; Barrett Strong; Mary Wells; Freddie Perren.

Co-op Hootenanny .... Century Custom (M) 22912 10-15 65
(Live at Berkeley Community Theater, Oct. 9, 1965.) Village Five &n Some; Corly Collier; Jim Stein; Nikki Vilas; Vangie Elkins; Bandells; Betty Reid; Stanley Franks; Crabgrassers; Hebrew Boys; Glenn Myles; Carol Pierson; Leroy Taylor; Dev Singh; Kelly Girls.

Copulatin' Blues .... Stash (M) ST-101 10-15 76
Lil Johnson; Sidney Bechet & His New Orleans Feetwarmers; Bessie Smith; Oscar's Chicago Swingers; Johnny Temple & Harlem Hamfats; Merline Johnson (The Yas Yas Girl); Coot Grant & Kid Wesley Wilson; Tampa Red's Hokum Jug Band; Jelly Roll Morton; Lucille Bogan; Bessie Jackson; Georgia White.

Copulatin' Blues, Vol. 2 .... Stash (S) ST-122 8-10 76
Eddie Johnson & His Crackerjacks; Unknown Cowboy; Lucille Bogan & Walter Roland; Cliff "Ukulele Ike" Edwards; Light Crust Doughboys; Art McKay; Clovers; Claude Hopkins & His Band; Hokum Boys; Harry Roy & His Bat Club Boys; Butterbeans & Susie; Clara Smith; Bessie Jackson.

Core of Jazz (Bottled by MGM) .... MGM (S) SE-47 8-12
Core of Rock .... MGM (S) SE-4669 10-15 70
Richie Havens; Tim Hardin; Janis Ian; Enemies; Blues Project; Van Dyke Parks.

Core of Rock, Vol. 2 .... MGM (S) SE-4718 10-15 70
Richie Havens; Eric Burdon & Animals; Freda Payne; Michael Parks; Enemies; Blues Project; A.B. Skhy; Tommy Edwards; Simon Stokes & Nighthawks.

Core of Rock, Vol. 3 .... MGM (S) SE-4779 10-15 71
Richie Havens; Eric Burdon & Animals; Orpheus; others.

Counter Revolutions in Rock .... Mercury (S) 118 10-20 79
(Promotional issue only. Plays from inside to outside.) Carolyne Mas; Larry Raspberry; Scorpions; John Cougar; Southside Johnny & Asbury Jukes.

Country All Star Festival (3 LP) .... Plaza House (S) ???? 10-15
Buck Owens; Tennessee Ernie Ford; Merle Haggard; Sonny James; others.

Country All Star Festival .... Capitol Creative Products (S) SLB-6721 8-12
Roy Rogers; Susan Raye; Ferlin Husky; Buddy Alan; Jean Shepard; Dick Curless; Tex Ritter; Rose Maddox; Buck Owen's Buckaroos; Anne Murray; Wynn Stewart; Wanda Jackson; Hagers; Charlie Louvin; Melba Montgomery; Roy Clark; Billie Jo Spears; Johnny & Jonie Mosby; Merle Haggard's Strangers; Linda Ronstadt.

Country and Hillbilly .... Capitol (M) 9107 30-40 56
Hank Thompson; Tennessee Ernie Ford; Jimmy Wakely; Tex Ritter; Merle Travis; others.

Country and Western .... Wrangler (M) 1001 10-20 62
Country and Western .... Wrangler (S) 1001 10-20 62
Patsy Cline; Hank Locklin; others.

Country and Western All Star Instrumentals .... Guest Star (S) GS-1497 10-20 60s
Moon Mullican; Arthur Smith; Roy Wiggins; Jackie Phelps; Tommy Hill; Benny Martin; Crook Brothers; Dean Manuel; Ken Clark.

Country and Western All Stars .... Modern Sound (SE) MS-579 5-10
Moon Mullican; Carl Story; Jack Rogers; Kathy Taylor; Chase Webster; Bill Pursell; Jimmy Wilkerson; Tommy Downs; Jack Bond; Katy Richards.

Country and Western Award Winners .... Decca (M) DL-4837 10-20 67
Country and Western Award Winners .... Decca (S) DL-74837 10-20 67
Loretta Lynn; Jimmy C. Newman; Kitty Wells; others.

Country and Western Award Winners '64 .... Decca (M) DL-4622 10-20 65
Country and Western Award Winners '64 .... Decca (S) DL-74622 10-20 65
Loretta Lynn; Kitty Wells; Webb Pierce; Wilburn Brothers; Bill Anderson; Ernest Tubb; Patsy Cline; Jimmy Martin; Jimmy C. Newman; Ernest Tubb; Loretta Lynn.

Country and Western Bonanza .... Camay (M) CA-3001 8-12
Don Gibson; Roy Acuff; Jimmy Newman; Bob Luman; Bill Haley & His Comets; Billy Byrd; Tennessee Ernie Ford; Bob Wills; Wesley Tuttle; Merle Travis; Tex Williams; Weavers; Brad Randy; Cass County Boys.

Country and Western Bonanza .... Design (S) SDLP-638 8-12 60s

Country and Western Bonanza .... Nouveau (SE) SDLP-638 8-12
Faron Young; Wilburn Brothers; Bobby Austin; Hank Locklin; Del Reeves; Bobby Bare.
Country & Western Cavalcade .... Gladwynne (M) 2006 50-100
Hawkshaw Hawkins; others.
Country and Western Caravan .... RCA (EP) EPB-3220 15-25 54
Country and Western Caravan .... RCA (M) LPM-3220 35-50 54
(10–inch LP.)
Country and Western Classics (1955) .... Economic Consultants (M) 1955 20-40 73
(Mail order offer.) Elvis Presley; others.
Country and Western Classics (1956) .... Economic Consultants (M) 1956 20-40 73
(Mail order offer.) Elvis Presley; others.
Country and Western Classics (1957) .... Economic Consultants (M) 1957 20-40 73
(Mail order offer.) Elvis Presley; others.
Country and Western Classics (1958) .... Economic Consultants (M) 1958 20-40 73
(Mail order offer.) Elvis Presley; others.
Country and Western Favorites .... Capitol Creative Products (S) SL 6555 8-12
Buck Owens; Sonny James; Glen Campbell; Tex Ritter.
Country and Western Favorites .... Metro (M) M-530 10-20 65
Country and Western Favorites .... Metro (S) MS-530 10-20 65
Hank Williams; Marvin Rainwater; others.
Country and Western Favorites, Vol. 2 .... Metro (M) M-572 10-20 66
Country and Western Favorites, Vol. 2 .... Metro (S) MS-572 10-20 66
Hank Williams; Floyd Cramer; Jimmy Newman; others.
Country and Western Golden Goodies .... Custom (S) CS 1095 8-12
Bud Titus; Goldie Fields; Doye O'Dell; Lonnie Barron; Tom T. Hall; Ray Lunsford; Kelleys; Larry Thornton; Rovers; Casey Clark; Evelyn Harlene; Whitey Knight.
Country and Western Golden Hit Parade .... Starday (S) SLP 245 10-20 60s
Cowboy Copas; Red Sovine; Texas Ruby; Archie Campbell; Curly Fox; Justin Tubb; Johnny Bond; Benny Martin; Willis Brothers; Dottie West; Dean Manuel; Buck Owens; Bobby Sykes; Arthur Smith; Hylo Brown; Leon Payne; George Jones; Jimmie Skinner; Cathy Copas; Glenda Raye; Tom O'Neal; others.
Country and Western Golden Hits .... Mercury (M) MG-21034 15-20 65
Country and Western Golden Hits .... Mercury (S) SR-61034 15-25 65
Claude Gray; Patti Page; George Jones; others.
Country and Western Golden Hits .... Wing (S) 16368 8-12 68
George Jones; Claude Gray; Rex Allen; others.
Country and Western Greats .... Rondo (M) R-2024 10-15 50s
Country and Western Greats .... Rondo (S) RS-2024 10-15 50s
Patsy Cline; Webb Pierce; Eddie Dean; others.
Country and Western Guitars, Vol. 1 .... Time (S) S-303 5-10
Country and Western Guitars, Vol. 2 .... Time (S) S-303 5-10
Kelso Herston & His Guitar Kings; Bobby Bond; Rick Hardin; Lloyd Green; Hargus Robbins; Hugo Montenegro; Billy Hutch & His Harmonica & Band; Faye Tucker. (Vol. 2 has same record number as Vol. 1.)
Country and Western Hall of Fame .... Design (S) SDLP-605 10-15 60s
Patsy Cline; Jimmy Dean; Ferlin Husky; Johnny & Jonie Mosby; Maddox Brothers & Rose; Marvin Rainwater; Bobby Austin.
Country and Western Hits, Vol. 1 .... Bud-Jet (S) 301 8-12 65
Country and Western Hits, Vol. 2 .... Bud-Jet (S) 302 8-12 65
Country and Western Hits, Vol. 3 .... Bud-Jet (S) 303 8-12 65
Country and Western Hits, Vol. 14 .... Mountain Dew (S) S7060 10-15 72
Elvis Presley; Donna Fargo; Tom T. Hall; Billy "Crash" Craddock; Freddie Hart; Sonny James; Faron Young; Charley Pride; Sonny James; Johnny Cash.
Country and Western Hits Made Famous by America's Greatest Singers.... Somerset/Stereo Fidelity (S) SE-18400 10-20
Jerry Shook; Red Sovine; others.
Country and Western Jamboree: see DEAN, Jimmy / Marvin Rainwater / Rusty Evans
Country and Western Jamboree .... Design (M) DLP-619 10-15 60s
Country and Western Jamboree .... Design (S) SDLP-619 10-15 60s
Floyd Cramer; Carl Belew; Stewart Family; Wynn Stewart; Jan Howard; T. Texas Tyler; Johnny Sea; David Houston; Ferlin Husky; Johnny Horton.
Country and Western Jamboree .... Palace (M) M-718 8-12 60s
Lonzo & Oscar; Red Sovine; Gene Pierce; Woody & Sam Jones; Jack Todd & Hometowners; Red Henderson; Leon Jackson; Stanley Alpine; Morgan Woodward; Ned Miles; Hank Payne.
Country and Western Jamboree .... King (M) 697 40-50 60
Hank Locklin; T. Texas Tyler; others.
Country and Western Jamboree (2 LP) .... Camden (S) ADL2-0579 8-12 74
Rosalie Allen; Gene Autry; Bill Boyd; Dale Evans; Roy Rogers; Sons of the Pioneers; Three Suns; others
Country and Western Jamboree .... Custom Records (S) CS-1092 5-10 72
Country and Western Jubilee .... Guest Star (SE) GS 1478 10-15 60s
Willie Nelson; David Houston; Jim Reeves; Ginny Wright; Warner Mack; Zeke Clements.
Country and Western Kings .... Pentagon (M) A-114 5-10
Country and Western Kings .... Pentagon (S) AS-114 5-10
Sonny James; Roy Acuff; Jimmy Newman; others.
Country and Western Music, Vol. 5 .... Design (M) DLP-609 10-20 60s
Charlie Ryan; Frankie Miller; T. Texas Tyler; Maddox Brothers & Rose; Stuart Hamblen; Slim Willet; Ferlin Husky; Carl Belew.
Country & Western Original Recordings .... Camay (M) CA-3001 15-25
Country & Western Original Recordings .... Camay (S) CA-3001-S 15-25
Don Gibson; Roy Acuff; Bob Luman; Bill Haley; Billy Bryd; Jimmy Newman.
Country and Western Sacred Song Greats .... Rondo (M) R-2025 10-15 50s

Country and Western Sacred Song Greats......Rondo (S) RS-2025 10-15 50s
T. Texas Tyler; Stewart Family; others.
Country and Western Star Jamboree, Vol. 2......Hurrah (M) H-1040
Country and Western Star Jamboree, Vol. 2......Hurrah (S) HS-1040
Patsy Cline; Ferlin Husky; Wynn Stewart; Jimmy Dean; Marvin Rainwater; Webb Pierce; Carl Belew; Hank Locklin; T. Texas Tyler; Bobby Austin.
Country and Western Stars......Design (M) DLP-601 10-20 62
Country and Western Stars......Design (S) SDLP-601 10-20 62
Patsy Cline; Jimmy Dean; Carl Belew; Ferlin Husky; Maddox Brothers & Rose.
Country and Western Stars......Pickwick (S) SDLP-601 5-10 75
Ferlin Husky; Patsy Cline; Bobby Austin; Johnny & Jonie; Jimmy Dean; Maddox Brothers & Rose; Marvin Rainwater.
Country and Western Stars......Design (M) DLP-605 10-20 62
Country and Western Stars......Design (S) SDLP-605 10-20 62
Jimmy Dean; Maddox Brothers & Rose; Bobby Austin; Patsy Cline; Ferliln Husky; Johnny & Jonie; Marvin Rainwater.
Country and Western Stars......Pickwick (S) SDLP-605 5-10 75
Ferlin Husky; Patsy Cline; Bobby Austin; Johnny & Jonie; Jimmy Dean; Maddox Brothers & Rose; Marvin Rainwater.
Country and Western Stars......Design (M) DLP-606 10-20 64
Country and Western Stars......Design (S) SDLP-606 10-20 64
Wynn Stewart; Billy Brown; Johnny & Jonie; Jan Howard; Marvin Rainwater; Ferlin Husky; Jimmy Dean; Patsy Cline.
Country and Western Stars......Pickwick (M) SDLP-606 5-10 75
Wynn Stewart; Billy Brown; Johnny & Jonie; Jan Howard; Marvin Rainwater; Ferlin Husky; Jimmy Dean; Patsy Cline.
Country and Western Stars......Design (M) DLP-608 10-20 62
Country and Western Stars......Design (S) SDLP-608 10-20 62
Slim Willet; Rocky Bill Ford; Charlie Ryan; T. Texas Tyler; Maddox Brothers & Rose; Ferlin Husky; Frankie Miller; Carl Belew; Stuart Hamblen.
Country Artists Int'l Presents......Country Artists (S) 1003 5-10 71
Jim Foster; Lorita Barlow; Bill Floyd; others.
Country Blues Classics......RBF (S) 1 15-20 59
Blind Lemon Jefferson; Lonnie Johnsonn; Cannon's Jug Stompers; Peg Leg Howell; Willie McTell; Willie Johnson; Leroy Carr; Sleepy John Estes; Big Bill; Bukka White; Robert Johnson; Tommy McClennan; Washboard Sam.
Country Blues Classics......Blues Classics (M) BC-5 10-20 65
Willie Baker; Elmore James; others.
Country Bound......Columbia Special Products (M) WU 3580 5-10 81
Don Williams; Willie Nelson; Lacy J. Dalton; Statler Brothers; Tanya Tucker; Tammy Wynette; George Jones; Kendalls; Barbara Mandrell; Merle Haggard; Johnny Duncan; Crystal Gayle; John Conlee; Jennifer Warnes; Moe Bandy & Joe Stampley; Conway Twitty.
Country Boy - Country Girl......Decca (M) DL-4201 15-25 62
Country Boy - Country Girl......Decca (S) DL-74201 20-30 62
Kitty Wells; Webb Pierce; Goldie Hill; Red Sovine; Red Foley; Betty Foley; Billy Gray; Mimi Roman; Justin Tubb; others.
Country Boy - Country Girl......RCA (S) APL1-1244 5-10 76
Jim Reeves & Dottie West; Bobby Bare & Skeeter Davis; Waylon Jennings & Anita Carter; other duets.
Country Boys - Country Girls......Wing (M) MGW-12275 10-20 64
Country Boys - Country Girls......Wing (S) SRW-16275 10-20 64
George Jones; James O'Gwynn; Connie Hall; Jeanette Hicks; Virginia Spurlock; Margie Bowes; Betty Amos; Jimmy Skinner.
Country Cavalcade, Vol .1......Longines Symphonette (M) SQ-93087 5-10 60s
Buck Owens; Bonnie Owens; Merle Haggard; Buddy Alan; Jody Miller; Wynn Stewart; Bobbie Gentry; Jean Shepard; Ferlin Husky; Linda Ronstadt; Sonny James; Jody Miller; Wanda Jackson.
Country Cavalcade, Vol .2......Longines Symphonette (M) SQ-93088 5-10 60s
Tennessee Ernie Ford; Dale Evans; T. Texas Tyler; Dick Curless; Buck Owens; Rose Maddox; Ferlin Husky; Louvin Brothers; Jordanaires; Houie Lister.
Country Chart Busters......Columbia (S) 1P 6683 5-10 77
(Columbia Record Club issue.) Marty Robbins; Tammy Wynette; Carl Smith; Tanya Tucker; Ray Price; Lynn Anderson; Stonewall Jackson; Johnny Cash.
Country Chart Busters Vol. 1......Columbia (S) KC-32720 5-10 73
Freddy Weller; Lynn Anderson; Bob Luman; Sonny James; others.
Country Chart Busters Vol. 2......Columbia (S) KC-32718 5-10 73
Marty Robbins; Tammy Wynette; Carl Smith; Tanya Tucker; Ray Price; Lynn Anderson; Stonewall Jackson; Johnny Cash; Jody Miller; Earl Scruggs.
Country Chart Busters Vol. 3......Columbia (S) KC-32721 5-10 73
Lynn Anderson; Sonny James; Ray Price; Tammy Wynette; others.
Country Chart Busters Vol. 4......Columbia (S) KC-32723 5-10 73
Charlie McCoy; George Jones; Jody Miller; Tommy Cash; others.
Country Chart Busters Vol. 5......Columbia (S) KC-32724 5-10 73
Freddy Weller; Johnny Cash; Lynn Anderson; Connie Smith; others.
Country Christmas......Decca (S) DL-74343 10-20 60s
Jimmie Davis; Roy Drusky; Red Foley; Bobby Helms; Jimmy Martin; Bill Monroe; Jimmy Newman; Webb Pierce; Ernest Tubb; Kitty Wells; Wilburn Brothers.
Country Christmas......Epic (S) PE-36823 5-10 80
Charlie Rich; Johnny Cash & Tommy Cash; Tanya Tucker; Ray Price; Bobby Vinton; Tammy Wynette; Connie Smith; George Jones; Marty Robbins; George Jones & Tammy Wynette.
Country Christmas......King (M) 811 20-25 62
Country Christmas......Monument (S) 18125 5-10 69
Billy Walker; Linda Webb; Harold Bradley; Leamon Sisters; Ray Penninton; Grandpa Jones; others.
Country Christmas......Columbia (S) CS-9888 5-10 69
Johnny Cash; Tammy Wynette; Marty Robbins; Carl Smith; Gene Autry; others.
Country Christmas (3 LP)......Time-Life (S) STL-109 15-20 88
(Boxed set. Mail order offer.) Elvis Presley; Loretta Lynn; George Strait; Gene Autry; Willie Nelson; Buck Owens; Merle Haggard; Roy Orbison; Marty Robbins; George Jones & Tammy Wynette; Bill Monroe; Statler Brothers; Reba McEntire; Alabama; Roger Miller; Jerry Lee Lewis; Jim Reeves; Davis Sisters; Chet Atkins; Charley Pride; Tammy Wynette; Ernest Tubb; Freddy Fender; Louvin Brothers; Dwight Yoakam; Red Simpson; Homer & Jethro; Hank Snow; Ronnnie Milsap; George Jones; Johnny Cash; Eddy Arnold; Mickey Gilley; Dolly Parton.

Country Christmas, Vol. 2 .... RCA (S) AYL1-4809 8-10 83
Elvis Presley; Earl Thomas Conley; Dolly Parton; Jerry Reed; Eddy Arnold; Sylvia; Louise Mandrell; Alabama.

Country Christmas with Loretta Lynn and Friends .... MCA Special Products (S) 34979 8-12 70s
Loretta Lynn; Burl Ives; Brenda Lee; Ernest Tubb; Bill Anderson; Voices of Christmas.

Country Classics, 40 Original Hits by Original Artists (3 LP) .... Adam VIII Ltd A-8024 10-20 76
Jeannie C. Riley; Eddy Arnold; Johnny Cash; Moon Mullican; Hank Snow; George Jones; Leroy Van Dyke; Everly Brothers; Hank Locklin; Jerry Lee Lewis; Red Foley; Red Sovine & Webb Pierce; Don Gibson; Roy Drusky & Priscilla Mitchell; Pee See King; Del Reeves; Cowboy Copas; Bobby Helms; Roger Miller; Jim Reeves; Davis Sisters; Connie Smith; Jimmie Rodgers; Porter Wagoner; Jerry Reed; George Hamilton IV; Kitty Wells; Hawkshaw Hawkins; George Jones; Red Foley; Tom T. Hall.

Country Classics .... Columbia Special Products (S) P 13612 5-10 76
Johnny Cash; Bill Anderson; Tammy Wynette; Red Foley; Lynn Anderson; George Jones; Jeannie C. Riley; Jack Greene; Kitty Wells; David Houston; Tanya Tucker; Conway Twitty; Loretta Lynn; Charlie Rich; Patsy Cline; Ray Price; Barbara Mandrell; Johnny Paycheck.

Country Classics .... Longines Symphonette (S) SYS-5445 5-10 76
(Mail order offer.) Tex Williams; T. Texas Tyler; Al Dexter; Harlan Howard; Tex Ritter; Wanda Jackson; Geezinslaw Brothers; Jean Shepard; Ferlin Husky; Ned Miller.

Country Classics .... RCA (M) LPM-2313 15-25 61

Country Classics .... RCA (S) LSP-2313 20-30 61
Eddy Arnold; Jim Reeves; Hank Snow; Porter Wagoner; Elton Britt; Skeeter Davis; Don Gibson; Three Suns; Johnnie & Jack; Browns; Hank Locklin; Sons of the Pioneers; Rosalie Allen & Elton Britt.

Country Classics (4 LPs) .... RCA (S) DPL4-0081 15-20 73
Don Gibson;.Norma Jean; Browns; Johnny Cash; Skeeter Davis; Sonny James; Connie Smith; Roger Miller; Boots Randolph; Lorne Greene; Jimmy Dean; Dottie West; Duane Eddy; George Hamilton IV; Dolly Parton; Bobby Bare; Nashville String Band; Kenny Price; Liz Anderson; Floyd Cramer; Jerry Reed; Jeannie C. Riley; Connie Smith; David Houston; Danny Davis; Dottie West; Roger Miller; Bonnie Guitar; John Hartford; Dickey Lee; Blue Boys; Waylon Jennings & Jessi Colter; Willie Nelson.

Country Classics (90 Minutes of) (2 LP) .... Fleetwood (S) FMS 1022 10-15
Skeeter Davis; Jeannie C. Riley; Willis Brothers; Kendalls; Henson Cargill; Johnny Paycheck; Sammi Smith; Jerry Lee Lewis; Bob Luman; Jack & Misty; Red Sovine; Don Gibson; Tommy Cash; Justin Tubb; Little Jimmy Dickens; Kenny Price; Claude King; Charlie Walker; Dave Dudley; Stoney Cooper & Wilma Lee; Roy Orbison; Ferlin Husky; Marvin Rainwater; Johnny Cash; Ned Miller; Ernie Ashworth; Carl Perkins; Roy Drusky; Bob Gallon; Claude Gray; Jan Howard; Bobby Helms.

Country Comes to Carnegie Hall .... ABC/Dot (S) 20879 8-10 77
Hank Thompson; Freddy Fender; Roy Clark; Don Williams; others.

Country Cousins .... Musicor (S) MS-3053 10-20 65
George Jones; Gene Piney; Connie Hall; others

Country Cream, 18 Country Hits, Famous Country Artists .... Columbia (S) C-10422 5-10
Lynn Anderson; Jerry Lee Lewis; Hank Thompson; Roger Miller; Faron Young; Leroy Van Dyke; Anita Kerr Sisters; Dave Dudley; Ray Price; Tammy Wynette; Tommy Overstreet; Roy Drusky; Roy Clark; Marty Robbins.

Country Cream .... Ford (M) 723 5-10 74
Dolly Long; Shorty Long; Dickson Hall; Lila Lou; Paul Tannen; others.

Country Delight .... Epic (S) KE-33165 5-10 74
Charlie McCoy; Kris Kristofferson; George Jones; Tammy Wynette; David Houston & Barbara Mandrell; Tina & Mommy; Jody Miller & Johnny Paycheck; Charlie Rich; Bob Luman; Tina & Daddy.

Country Duets .... RCA (S) LSP-4082 10-15 68
Jim Reeves & Dottie West; Hank Snow & Anita Carter; Hank Snow & Chet Atkins; Porter Wagoner & Dolly Parton; others

Country Duos .... K-TEL (S) WU-3540 5-10 81
Willie Nelson & Leon Russell; Johnny Duncan & Janie Fricke; Jim Ed Brown & Helen Cornelius; Bellamy Brothers; Rita Coolidge & Glen Campbell; Moe Bandy & Joe Stampley; George Jones & Johnny Paycheck; Moe Bandy & Tammy Wynette; Dave & Sugar; Johnny Rodriguez & Charly McClain; Louise Mandrell & R.C. Bannon; Johnny Cash & George Jones; Loretta Lynn & Conway Twitty; Porter Wagoner & Dolly Parton.

Country Dynamite .... Columbia (EP) AS-5 5-15
Freddy Weller; Tommy Cash; David Rogers; Bob Luman; Claude King; Arlene Hardin; Charlie Rich.

Country Dynamite from Nashville .... Nashville (SE) NLP-2101 5-10 71
Dottie West; Rose Maddox; Red Sovine; others.

Country Express .... Commonwealth (S) WU-3380 5-10 77
Sammi Smith; Kenny Price; Claude Gray; Roy Drusky; Jan Howard; Bob Gillion; Jimmy C Newman; Merle Kilgore; Claude King; Warner Mack; Ferlin Husky; Marvin Rainwater; Bobby Helms; Skeeter Davis; Ned Miller; Henson Cargill; Tommy Collins; Margie Bowes; Mitchell Torok; Pee Wee King.

Country Express .... Nashville (M) NLP-2006 10-15 64

Country Express .... Starday (M) SLP-109 20-30 59
Wayne Raney; Stanley Brothers; Bill Wimberly; Bill Clifton; Jim & Jesse; Tommy Jackson; Country Gentlemen; Herbie Remington; Wally Traugutt; Buzz Busby; Ken Clark.

Country Fair .... Capitol (S) SWBB-562 8-10 70
Glen Campbell; Joe South; Jean Shepard; Sonny James; Ferlin Husky; Buck Owens.

Country Favorites .... Somerset (S) 34300 5-10 70

Country Favorites .... Buckboard (S) 1038 5-10 76
George Jones; Roger Miller; Rex Allen; Don Gibson; Wanda Jackson; Merle Haggard; Bobbie Gentry; Johnny & Jonie Mosby; Charlie Louvin.

Country Favorites .... Musico (S) MDS-1017 10-15 70s
George Jones; Roger Miller; Gene Pitney; Melba Montgomery; Rex Allen; Don Gibson.

Country Favorites .... Wyncote (M) W-9016 10-20 64

Country Favorites .... Wyncote (S) SW-9016 10-20 64
George Jones; Bill Mack; Claude Gray; others.

Country Gals - Country Hits (2 LP) .... Camden (S) ALD2-0177 8-12 73
Liz Anderson; Martha Carson; Davis Sisters; Skeeter Davis; Norma Jean; Dolly Parton; Dottie West; others.

Country Get-Together .... Sunset (S) 5283 5-10 70

Country Giants (2 LP) .... Mercury (S) SRM-2-606 10-15 70
Jerry Lee Lewis; Faron Young; Roger Miller; others.

Country Girl Hall of Fame .... Starday (M) SLP 313 10-20 60s
Dottie West; Texas Ruby; Jonie Mosby; Sue Thompson; Margie Singleton; Rose Maddox; June Stearns with Pete Drake's Talking Steel Guitar; Rose Lee Maphis; Helen Carter with Bobby Sykes; Patsy Cline; Cathy Copas; Lulu Belle Wiseman; Betty Amos; Connie Hall.

Country Girl Sing Me A Song .... Nashville (M) NLP-2029 5-10 70s

Country Girl Sing Me A Song .... Nashville (S) NLP-2029 5-10 70s
Lulu Belle Wiseman; Betty Amos; Patsy Cline; Molly O'Day; Glenda Raye; Jeanette Hicks; Dottie West; Rose Lee Maphis; June Stearns; Margie Singleton; Texas Ruby; Minnie Pearl.

Country Girls .... Camden (S) CAS-2403 5-10 70
Dottie West; Connie Smith; Norma Jean; Dolly Parton; Bonnie Guitar; Martha Carson; Lorene Mann; Skeeter Davis; Wendy Dawn.

Country Girls .... Commonwealth (S) BU-4800 5-10 78
Faron Young; David Houston; Tommy Overstreet; Billy "Crash" Craddock; Bobby Helms; Bob Luman; Bobby Lewis; Del Reeves; Johnny Darrell; Joe Stampley; Compton Brothers; Justin Tubb; Charlie Walker; Jimy Skinner.

Country Girls Sing Country Songs .... Camden (M) CAL-959 10-15 66

Country Girls Sing Country Songs .... Camden (S) CAS-959 10-15 66
Kitty Wells; Dottie West; Connie Smith; Norma Jean; Skeeter Davis; Liz Anderson.

Country Gold (2 LP) .... Columbia (S) DS 491 10-15 69
Tammy Wynette; David Houston; Johnny Cash; Leon Ashley; Glen Campbell; Charlie Walker; Margie Singleton; Marty Robbins; Boots Randolph & Jimmy Richardson; Claude King; George Jones; Jimmy Dean; Cowboy Copas; David Rogers; Johnny Horton; Leon Ashley; Jeannie C. Riley; Carl Smith; Autry Inman; Billy Walker; Flatt & Scruggs & Foggy Mountain Boys; Bobby Barnett; Lucille Star; Johnny Seay; Johnny Duncan; Red Sovine; Lefty Frizzell; Ray Price; Stonewall Jackson; Bob Wills.

Country Gold (2 LP) .... Columbia (M) P2M-5176 10-15 67

Country Gold (2 LP) .... Columbia (S) P2S-5176 10-15 67
(Columbia Record Club issue.) David Houston; Tammy Wynette; Jimmy Dean; Claude King; Johnny Horton; George Morgan; Roy Drusky; Jim & Jesse; Little Jimmy Dickens; Ray Price; Norma Jean; Statler Brothers; Bobby Lord; Freddie Hart; Marty Robbins; Carl Smith; Johnny Cash; Flatt & Scruggs; Harden Trio; Johnny Bond; Lefty Frizzell; Charlie Walker; Stonewall Jackson; Jordanaires; Carl Perkins; Hawkshaw Hawkins; Billy Walker.

Country Gold .... Sunset (S) 5259 5-10 69
Buddy Cagle; Johnny Carver; Slim Whitman; Larry Butler; others.

Country Gold (2 LP) .... RCA (S) R 233899 (e) 8-12 77
Hank Snow; Uncle Dave Macon; Jimmie Rodgers; Minnie Pearl; Pee Wee King; Jim Reeves; Carter Family; Eddy Arnold; Grampa Jones; Bobby Bare; Don Gibson; Browns; Bill Monroe; Porter Wagoner; Chet Atkins; Charley Pride; Willie Nelson; Charlie Rich; Gary Stewart; Dottie West. (RCA Record Club issue. Mail order.)

Country Gold .... RCA (S) DPL1-0561 20-25 82
Elvis Presley; Dolly Parton; Razzy Bailey; Earl Thomas Conley; Waylon Jennings; Ronnie Milsap; Alabama; Juice Newton & Silver Spur; Charley Pride & Cherry Singers; Sylvia.

Country Gold .... Harmony (SE) HS-11378 5-10 70
Carl Smith; Johnny Cash; Johnny Horton; Tammy Wynette; Lynn Anderson; Jimmy Dean; Claude King; Leroy Van Dyke; David Houston.

Country Gold, Vol. 1 .... Plantation (S) 5 8-10 69
Jeannie C. Riley; Becki Bluefield; David Wilkins; Teresa Brewer; Marcie Dickerson; George Kent; others.

Country Gold, Vol. 1 .... United Artists (S) UA-LA412-E 5-10 75
Johnny Cash; Cowboy Copas; Hank Cochran; Jan Howard; Dave Dudley; others.

Country Gold, Vol. 2 .... Harmony (S) H-30018 5-10 70
Johnny Cash & Carter Family; Marty Robbins; others.

Country Gold, Vol. 1 .... Buckboard (SE) BBS 1005 5-10 70s
Patsy Cline; Dave Dudley; Johnny Tillotson; Jerry Wallace; Orville Couch; Jack Scott; Anita Bryant.

Country Gold, Vol. 2 .... Buckboard (SE) BBS 1006 5-10 70s
Patsy Cline; Jack Scott; Anita Bryant; Orville Couch; Johnny Tillotson; Jerry Wallace; Johnny Bond.

Country Gold, Vol. 5 .... Buckboard (SE) BBS 1018 5-10 70s
Johnny Cash; Charlie Rich; Sammi Smith; Jeannie C. Riley; Jerry Lee Lewis; Carl Belew; Bill Black's Combo.

Country Gospel .... Gusto (S) GT-0069 5-10 70s
Wanda Jackson; Claude Gray; Mac Wiseman; George Jones; Carl Smith; Tex Ritter; T. Texas Tyler; Ferlin Husky; Little Jimmy Dickens.

Country Gospel Favorites .... Rural Rhythm (M) RR 149 8-12 60s
G.M. Farley; Gospeletts; Martin; Bill Carter & Cooper Brothers; Billy & Gordon Hemrick; Owen & Mack; Charlie & Lee Cline; Happy Four; Masters Quartet.

Country Gospel Greats .... Rural Rhythm (M) RR 138 8-12 60s
Onie Wheeler; Ray Baker; Jackie & Arlin Vaden; others.

Country Gospel Meeting .... Somerset (S) 34100 5-10 69

Country Gospel Songs .... Folkways (M) RBF-19 5-10 71

Country Greats .... Rural Rhythm (M) RR 155 8-12 60s
Hall Wallis; Vandergrift Brothers; Salty Dog; Tony Douglas; Swaney Caldwell; Boys from Shilo; De Wayne Wear; James Worley; Doug La Vall; Dub Dickerson; others.

Country Greats .... Harmony (S) KH-30346 5-10 70
Johnny Cash; Tammy Wynette; Marty Robbins; others.

Country Guitar .... Nashville (M) NLP-2021 10-15 66
Billy Byrd & Jimmy Capps; Hardrock Gunter; Eddie Eddings; Thumbs Carlisle; Arthur "Guitar Boogie" Smith.

Country Guys & Gals .... Hilltop/Pickwick (SE) JS-6096 8-12 60s
Buck Owens; Glen Clampbell; Roy Clark; Bobbie Gentry; Tex Ritter; Hank Thompson; Sonny James; Tennessee Ernie Ford; Wanda Jackson; Jean Shepard.

Country Hall of Fame .... Musico (S) MDS-1027 10-15 70s
George Jones; Tommy Cash; Don Gibson; Marvin Rainwater, Jimmy Dean.

Country Hall of Fame, Vol. 1 .... Country Music Association (S) CMA 712 5-10 60s
Roy Acuff; Bill Anderson; Eddy Arnold; Bobby Bare; Johnny Bond; Johnny Cash; Patsy Cline; Dave Dudley; Red Foley; Lefty Frizzell; Don Gibson; Pee Wee King; Roger Miller; George Morgan; Buck Owens; Ray Price; Jim Reeves; Tex Ritter; Marty Robbins; Hank Snow; Hank Thompson; Merle Travis; Ernest Tubb; Kitty Wells; Hank Williams.

Country Hall of Fame, Vol. 2 .... Country Music Association (S) CMA-800 5-10 60s
Roger Miller; Patsy Cline; Leroy Van Dyke; Johnny Horton; Ferlin Husky; Sonny James; Floyd Cramer; Johnny Cash; Tex Williams; Del Wood; Jimmy Wakely; Chet Atkins; Faron Young; Buck Owens; Hank Williams; Webb Pierce; Loretta Lynn; Lefty Frizzell; Ray Price; George Jones; Rex Allen; Jimmie Rodgers; Flatt & Scruggs; Grandpa Jones; Kitty Wells.

Country Hall of Fame, Vol. 2 .... Telerad (S) CMA-800 5-10 60s
(Mail order offer.) Roger Miller; Patsy Cline; Leroy Van Dyke; Johnny Horton; Ferlin Husky; Sonny James; Floyd Cramer; Johnny Cash; Tex Williams; Del Wood; Jimmy Wakely; Chet Atkins; Faron Young; Buck Owens; Hank Williams; Webb Pierce; Loretta Lynn; Lefty Frizzell; Ray Price; George Jones; Rex Allen; Jimmie Rodgers; Flatt & Scruggs; Grandpa Jones; Kitty Wells. (Special products. Made for Telerad Inc., Hollywood Album Center.)

Country Harvest........ K-Tel (S) BU 4160 5-10 81
Billy Crash Craddock; Crystal Gayle; Willie Nelson; Jessi Colter; Melba Montgomery; Gene Watson; Mel Tillis; Barbara Mandrell; Ray Price; Ed Bruce; David Houston; Loretta Lynn; John Conlee.

Country Heaven (3 LP)........ RCA Special Products/Teledisc (M) TD19/DVL3-0888 10-20 89
Ernest Tubb; Hank Williams; Patsy Cline; Leon Payne; Lefty Frizzell; Bob Wills; George Morgan; Johnny Bond; Stuart Hamblen; Bob Luman; Jack Guthrie; Kenny Price; Skeets McDonald; Merle Travis; Vernon Hal Hart; Jimmy Wakely; T. Texas Tyler; Red Foley; Jimmie Rodgers; Red Sovine; Texas Jim Robertson; Johnny Horton; Wynn Stewart; Tex Williams; Al Dexter; Homer & Jethro; Lester Flatt; Nat Stuckey; Hawkshaw Hawkins; Delmore Brothers; Sons of the Pioneers; Carter Family; Elton Britt; Marty Robbins; Tex Ritter.

Country Hit Parade........ Chart (S) 3000 5-10 69
Lynn Anderson; Kenny Vernon; Johnny Dollar; Gene Hood; Vince Bulla; Joe Gibson.

Country Hit Parade........ Starday (S) SLP-110 20-30 59
Lois Williams; Willis Brothers; Red Sovine; others.

Country Hit Parade........ Nashville (SE) NLP-2089 5-10 70
Lois Williams; Willis Brothers; Red Sovine; others.

Country Hits........ Columbia Special Products (S) CSS 1519 5-10
Marty Robbins; Ray Price; David Houston; Carter Family; Flatt & Scruggs; Johnny Cash; Tammy Wynette.

Country Hits........ Petal (M) 2000 5-10

Country Hits, Vol. 2........ United Artists (M) UAL-3185 15-20 62

Country Hits, Vol. 2........ United Artists (S) UAS-6185 20-25 62
George Jones; Claude Gray; Jape Richardson; Bill Mack; Carl Sauceman; Leon Payne; Johnny Mathis; Herby Remington; Benny Barnes; James O'Gwynn; Jimmy Blakely; Tony Douglas.

Country Hits By Country Stars........ Capitol (M) T-1912 15-20 63

Country Hits By Country Stars........ Capitol (S) ST-1912 15-25 63
Ferlin Husky; Faron Young; Rose Maddox; Sonny James; others.

Country Hits for Highway and Home........ Mega (S) 1022 5-10 73
Jack Reno; Alice Creech; Jackie Ward; Linda Gayle; Shoji Tabuchi.

Country Hits of the '40s........ Capitol (S) ST-884 5-10 72
Tennessee Ernie Ford; Tex Ritter; Jimmy Wakely; Jimmie Davis; Tex Williams; Margaret Whiting & Jimmy Wakely; Merle Travis; Al Dexter; Leon Payne; Jack Guthrie.

Country Hits of the '50s........ Capitol (M) SM-885 8-12 72

Country Hits of the '50s........ Capitol (S) ST-885 5-10 72
Tennessee Ernie Ford; Ferlin Husky; Sonny James; Jean Shepard; Hank Thompson; Freddie Hart; Faron Young; Tommy Collins; Skeets McDonald.

Country Hits of the '60s........ Capitol (S) ST-886 8-10 72
Glen Campbell; Wanda Jackson; Buck Owens; Merle Haggard; Wynn Stewart; Faron Young; Tex Ritter; Roy Clark; Sonny James; Ferlin Husky.

Country Hits Parade........ RCA (M) LPM-3452 10-20 66

Country Hits Parade........ RCA (S) LSP-3452 15-20 66
Hank Snow; Eddy Arnold; Connie Smith; Roger Miller; Norma Jean; Hank Locklin; George Hamilton IV; Bobby Bare; Jim Reeves; Skeeter Davis; Porter Wagoner; Dottie West.

Country Hits Parade........ RCA (S) VLP-3452 5-10 66
(Juke box issue; includes title strips.) Jim Reeves; Eddy Arnold; Connie Smith; Bobby Bare; Dottie West; Porter Wagoner.

Country Hits with Vocals........ Alshire (S) 2-119 5-10

Country Holiday........ Columbia Musical Treasuries (SE) DS-467 5-10 68
Jimmy Dean; Johnny Cash; Marty Robbins; Gene Autry; Chuck Wagon Gang; Anita Bryant; Stuart Hamblen; David Houston; Little Jimmy Dickens; Patti Page.

Country Humble Pie........ Koala (S) AW 14110 8-10 79
Jerry Lee Lewis; Platters; Carl Perkins; Etta James; Merrill E. Moore; Roy Orbison; Jordanaires; Richard Berry & Pharaohs; Bill Haley & His Comets.

Country Hymns........ Columbia (S) C 30324 8-12
Johnny Cash; Marty Robbins; Ray Price; Chuck Wagon Gang; Carl Smith; Jimmy Dean; Anita Bryant; Flatt & Scruggs; Statler Brothers; Carl & Pearl Butler; Stonewall Jackson.

Country Inspirations........ Lotus (M) BU-1983 5-10 83
Tom T. Hall; Stuart Hamblen; Hank Williams; Danny Davis & Nashville Brass; Statler Brothers; Cristy Lane; Larry Gatlin; Anne Murray; B.J. Thomas; Mahalia Jackson; Tennessee Ernie Ford; Don Gibson; Kris Kristofferson; Johnny Cash; Roy Acuff; Oak Ridge Boys.

Country Inspirations........ Lotus (M) BU-5780 5-10 83
Tom T. Hall; Stuart Hamblen; Hank Williams; Danny Davis & Nashville Brass; Statler Brothers; Cristy Lane; Larry Gatlin; Anne Muray; B.J. Thomas; Mahalia Jackson; Tennessee Ernie Ford; Don Gibson; Kris Kristofferson; Johnny Cash; Roy Acuff; Oak Ridge Boys.

Country Instrumentals........ Starday (EP) S-45-440 5-10 59
Stanley Brothers; Wayne Raney; others.

Country Instrumentals, Vol. 1........ RCA (S) LSP-4380 8-10 70
Boots Randolph; Chet Atkins; Floyd Cramer; others.

Country Instrumentals, Vol. 2........ RCA (S) LSP-4494 8-10 71
Jerry Reed; Lester Flatt; Chet Atkins; others

Country Instrumentals, Vol. 3........ RCA (S) LSP-4728 8-10 72
Chet Atkins; Floyd Cramer; Boots Randolph; Jerry Reed; others.

Country Jamboree........ Capitol (S) 91654 8-10
(Capitol Record Club issue.) Merle Haggard; Buck Owens; Sonny James; Glen Campbell; Wanda Jackson; Charlie Louvin; Wynn Stewart; Ned Miller; Jody Miller; Ray Pillow; Bobby Austin; Jean Shepard; Ferlin Husky; Tex Ritter.

Country Jubilee........ Decca (M) DL-4172 20-30 61

Country Jubilee........ Decca (M) 38237 20-30 61
Red Foley; Bill Monroe; Grady Martin; Mervin Shiner & Jordanaires; Milton Brown & Brownies; Jimmy Wakely; Red Sovine & Gadabouts; Jimmy Wakely; Clayton McMichen's Georgia Wildcats; Webb Pierce; Shelton Brothers; Tompall & Glaser Brothers; Rex Allen.

Country Jubilee of Stars........ Guest Stars (M) G-1444 10-20 63

Country Jubilee of Stars........ Guest Stars (S) GS-1444 10-20 63
Link Wray; others.

Country Jukebox........ Pickwick (S) JS-6183 5-10 70s
Roger Miller; Tom T. Hall; Roy Drusky; George Kent; Norro Wilson.

Country Kings .... Hass (S) 14074 5-10 78
Joe South; Buddy Mize; others.

Country Line .... K-Tel (S) WU 3450 5-10 79
Don Williams; Mel Tillis; Conway Twitty; Jim Ed Brown; Helen Cornelius; John Conlee; Larry Gatlin; Tany Tucker; Kendalls; Oak Ridge Boys; Crystal Gayle; Kenny Rogers; Barbara Mandrell; Anne Murray; Statler Brothers; Eddie Rabbitt.

Country Love .... Harmony (S) KH-30608 5-10 71
Tammy Wynette; Johnny Cash; Marty Robbins; others.

Country Love, Vol. 1 & 2 (2 LP) .... RCA (SE) PRS-392 8-12 72
(Mail order offer.) Don Gibson; Norma Jean; Jim Ed Brown; Floyd Cramer; Dickey Lee; Dottie West; Connie Smith; Danny Davis; Hank Snow; Skeeter Davis; John Hartford; Roger Miller; Browns; George Hamilton IV; Liz Anderson; Waylon Jennings; Porter Wagoner; Dolly Parton; Hank Locklin; Jim Reeves; Bobby Bare; Sonny James; Chet Atkins; Jerry Reed; Charley Pride.

Country Love, Vol. 1 .... Columbia (S) KG-30326 5-10 70
Charlie Rich; Johnny Cash; Lynn Anderson; Johnny Horton; others.

Country Love, Vol. 2 .... Columbia (S) KG-32010 5-10 73
Ray Price; Patti Page; Tommy Cash; Tammy Wynette; others.

Country Love, Vol. 3 .... Columbia (S) KG-32725 5-10 73
Arlene Harden; Lynn Anderson; Marty Robbins; George Jones; Charlie Rich; Ray Price; Freddy Weller; others.

Country Magic (3 LP) .... Telehouse (S) CD 2005 10-15 73
Lynn Anderson; Jerry Lee Lewis; Roger Miller; Leroy Van Dyke; Dave Dudley; Ray Price; Tammy Wynette; Tommy Overstreet; Faron Young; Roy Drusky; Marty Robbins; Johnny Cash; Arthur Smith; George Morgan; Hank Thompson; David Houston & Tammy Wynette; Lynn Anderson; June Carter; Jim Nabors; Cowboy Copas; George Morgan; Buck Owens; Johnny Bond.

Country Memories .... ???? 5-10
Louvin Brothers; Tex Ritter; Jean Shepard & Ferlin Husky; Skeeter Davis; Pee Wee King; Wayne Raney; Moon Mullican; Red Sovine; Hawkshaw Hawkins; Cowboy Copas.

Country Memories (7 LP) .... Reader's Digest/BMG (S) RBA-037 40-55 89
(Boxed set. Mail order offer. Includes booklet.) Elvis Presley; others.

Country Memories (7 LP) .... Reader's Digest/BMG (S) RBA-066 40-55 89
(Boxed set. Mail order offer. Includes six songs by Elvis, and 11 'live' tracks by Hank Williams.) Elvis Presley; Carl Perkins; Gene Vincent; Vaughn Monroe; Hank Williams; Eddy Arnold; Bing Crosby; Andrew Sisters; Frankie Laine; Cowboy Copas; Moon Mullican; Ella Mae Morse; Red Ingle & Natural Seven; Webb Pierce; Slim Whitman; Rusty Draper; Red Foley; Murv Shiner; Conway Twitty; Sonny James; Jimmie Rodgers; Bill Justis; Everly Brothers; Billy Grammer; Marvin Rainwater; Wink Martindale; Bobby Bare; Lorne Greene; Jim Reeves; Floyd Cramer; Roger Miller; Ned Miller; Charlie Rich; Joe Barry; Gale Barnett; Kenny Rogers & First Edition; Bobbie Gentry; Hugo Montenegro; Sandy Posey; Bobby Goldsboro; Jewel Akens; Pete Drake; Donna Fargo; Jerry Reed; Freddy Fender; Charlie Pride; Waylon Jennings; Sylvia; C.W. McCall; Oak Ridge Boys; Ronnie McDowell; Bob Wills; Kitty Wells; Tennessee Ernie Ford; Jim Reeves; Everly Brothers; Leroy Van Dyke; Glen Campbell; Dave Dudley; Jimmy Dean; B.J. Thomas.

Country Music All Time Favorites .... RCA (S) ???? 5-10
Charley Pride; Ronnie Milsap; Dave & Sugar; Willie Nelson; Jim Ed Brown & Helen Cornelius; Razzy Bailey; Zella Lehr; Jerry Reed; Dickey Lee; Bobby Bare.

Country Music by the Wayside .... Wayside (M) 1013 5-10 68

Country Music Cannonball .... Starday (M) S-276 10-20 64

Country Music Cavalcade - American Country Gold (3 LP) .... Candlelite (S) CU-161 10-20 80
(Box set.) Buddy Holly & Crickets; Don Williams; Jimmie Rodgers; Red Foley & Betty Foley; Brenda Lee; Freddy Fender; Wilma Burgess; Narvel Felts; Jack Greene; Webb Pierce; Carl Dobkins Jr.; Patsy Cline; Billy "Crash" Craddock; Ernest Tubb & Texas Troubadors; Barbara Mandrell; Tanya Tucker; Conway Twitty; Kitty Wells; B.J. Thomas; Bill Anderson & Jan Howard.

Country Music Cavalcade - Midnight in Memphis (3 LP) .... Candlelite (S) 1/2/3 10-20 75
(Mail order offer.) Conway Twitty; Jimmy Clanton; Patti Page; Rusty Draper; Tommy Edwards; Ray Peterson; Nightriders; Marvin Rainwater; Champs; Hank Williams; Jerry Lee Lewis; Mark Dinning; Pete Drake; Leroy Van Dyke; Joey Heatherton; Statler Brothers; Frank Slades & Cahpparell; Dicky Lee; Roger Miller.

Country Music Cavalcade - Nashville Graffiti, Vol. 1 (3 LP) .... Candlelite (S) P3 13235 10-20 76
Johnny Cash; Bobby Helms; Link Wray; Frank Slader & Chaperal; Statler Brothers; Marty Robbins; Buzz Clifford; Billy Grammer; Patti Page; Bobby Vinton; Johnnie Ray; Ersel Hickey; Stonewall Jackson; Claude Kings; Guy Mitchell; Mindy Carson; Johnny Carson; Ray Price; Tennessee Saxes Plus Two; Carl Perkins; Jimmy Dean.

Country Music Cavalcade - Nashville Graffiti (3 LP) .... Candlelite (S) CU-750 10-20 85
Johnny Cash; Timi Yuro; Duane Eddy; Wink Martindale; Guy Mitchell; Jerry Lee Lewis; Patti Page; Carl McCoy; Sandy Posey; Johnnie Ray; Margo Smith; Jimmy Dean; Bobby Helms; Roy Orbison; Frankie Laine; Dickey Lee; Claude King; Stonewall Jackson; Pat Boone; Jivin' Gene & Jokers; Carl Mann; Jim Ed Brown; Carl Perkins; Jody Miller; Del Reeves.

Country Music Express .... Unart (S) S 21016 8-12 60s
George Jones; Melba Montgomery; Judy Lynn; Al Caiola; Leroy Holmes; Bill Harell.

Country Music Festival .... Starday (M) S-274 10-20 64

Country Music Festival, Vol. 2 .... Starday (M) S-362 10-20 66
Willis Brothers; Joe & Rose Maphis; Johnny Bond; others.

Country Music Goes to War .... Starday (M) S-374 10-20 66
Willis Brothers; Jimmy Blakely; Dottie West; others.

Country Music Hall of Fame .... Design (S) SDLP-620 10-15 60s
Roger Miller; Johnny Cash; Webb Pierce; Carl Belew; Jimmy Dean; Dave Dudley; Buck Owens; Del Reeves; George Jones; Sonny James.

Country Music Hall of Fame .... Starday (S) 9-468 10-20 70
Buck Owens; Dolly Parton; George Jones; others.

Country Music Hall of Fame, Vol. 1 (2 LP) .... Starday (M) S-164 20-30 62

Country Music Hall of Fame, Vol. 1 (2 LP) .... Starday (S) SLP-164 20-30 62
Cowboy Copas; George Jones; Hank Locklin; others.

Country Music Hall of Fame, Vol. 2 .... Starday (M) S-190 15-25 62

Country Music Hall of Fame, Vol. 2 .... Starday (S) SLP-190 15-25 62
Johnny Cash; Jimmy Dean; Red Sovine; George Jones Johnny Horton; Sue Thompson; Cowboy Copas; Rod Brasfield; Flatt & Scruggs; Buck Owens; A.P. Carter & Carter Family; Jimmie Skinner; Roy Drusky; Roger Miller; Leon McAuliffe; Lulu Belle & Scotty; Blue Sky Boys; Arthur "Guitar Boogie" Smith; Johnny Bond; Moon Mullican; Smiley Burnette; Lew Childre; others.

Country Music Hall of Fame, Vol. 3 (2 LP) .... Starday (M) S-256 15-25 63

Country Music Hall of Fame, Vol. 3 (2 LP) .... Starday (S) SLP-256 15-25 63
Buck Owens; Jimmy Dean; Rex Allen; Minnie Pearl; Roger Miller; Jimmie Skinner; Red Sovine; Blue Sky Boys; Arthur "Guitar Boogie" Smith; T. Texas Tyler; Maddox Brothers & Rose; Johnny Horton; Hank Locklin; Flatt & Scruggs; Cowboy Copas; Patsy Cline; Hawshaw Hawkins; George Jones; Webb Pierce; Patsy Cline; others.
Country Music Hall of Fame, Vol. 4 (2 LP) .... Starday (M) S-295 15-25 64
Patsy Cline; Flatt & Scruggs; Bob Wills; others.
Country Music Hall of Fame, Vol. 5 .... Starday (M) 360 10-20 66
Floyd Tillman; Dottie West; Charlie Walker; others.
Country Music Hall of Fame, Vol. 6 .... Starday (M) 390 10-15 67
Country Music Hall of Fame, Vol. 6 .... Starday (S) 390 10-15 67
George Morgan; Roger Miller; Melba Montgomery; others.
Country Music Hall of Fame, Vol. 7 .... Starday (S) 409 10-15 69
Country Music Hall of Fame, Vol. 8 .... Starday (S) 430 10-15 69
Glen Campbell; Wynn Stewart; Jan Howard; others.
Country Music Hall of Fame, Vol. 9 .... Starday (S) 9-449 10-15 70
Buck Owens; Minnie Pearl; Jimmy Dean; Red Sovine; Dolly Parton; others.
Country Music Hits .... Camden (M) CAL-686 10-20 62
Country Music Hits .... Camden (S) CAS-686 10-20 62
Eddy Arnold; Jim Reeves; Don Gibson; Hank Snow; others.
Country Music Hits By Country Music Stars, Vol. 2, ... Camden (M) CAL-689 10-20 63
Country Music Hits By Country Music Stars, Vol. 2 .... Camden (SE) CAS-689 10-20 63
Jim Reeves; Eddy Arnold; Davis Sisters; Hank Locklin; Don Gibson; Pee Wee King; Slim Whitman; Hal "Lone" Pine; Grandpa Jones; Elton Britt; Hank Snow; Gid Tanner.
Country Music Hootnenanny .... Capitol (M) T-2009 20-25 63
Country Music Hootnenanny .... Capitol (S) ST-2009 25-30 63
Buck Owens; Merle Travis; Rose Maddox; others.
Country Music in the Modern Era (1940s - 1970s) .... New World (S) NW-207 50-70 76
(Indended for library use only.) Elvis Presley; Eddy Arnold; Jim Reeves; Lefty Frizzell; Ray Price; Patsy Cline; Hank Snow; Kitty Wells; Ernest Tubb; Marty Robbins; Loretta Lynn; Johnny Cash; Buck Owens; Roger Miller; Merle Haggard; Dolly Parton; Kris Kristofferson.
Country Music Jamboree .... Mercury (M) MG-20350 30-40 58
Country Music Just for You .... Capitol ???? 10-15
Faron Young; Ferlin Husky; others. (Made for Coca-Cola.)
Country Music Laugh-Out .... Starday (S) 452 5-10 70
Buck Owens; Junior Samples; Grandpa Jones; Archie Campbell; others.
Country Music Like You Want to Hear it .... Somerset (S) 34700 5-10 70
Country Music Memorial (2 LP) .... Starday (S) 9-451 8-12 70
Cowboy Copas; Stanly Bros.; Johnny Horton; Patsy Cline; Jimmy Osborne; Delmore Brothers; Phil Sullivan; Texas Ruby; Lonzo & Oscar; Moon Mullican; Dean Manuel & Blue Boys; Smiley Burnette; Pop Stoneman; Tommy Duncan with Bob Wills; Eddie McDuff; A.L. Phipps Family; Robert Lunn; Rod Brasfield; Lonnie Irving; Adrian Roland; Hawkshaw Hawkins; Jimmy Osborne; Lew Childre; Leon Payne.
Country Music Memorial Album .... Starday (M) SLP 291 15-20 64
Cowboy Copas; Patsy Cline; Demore Brothers; Johnny Horton; Lew Childre; Texas Ruby; Lonnie Irving; Phil Sullivan; Phipps Family; Hawshaw Hawkins; Rod Brasfield.
Country Music on the Go, Vol. 1 .... Sage & Sand (M) C-18 10-20 61
Eddie Dean; Charlie Williams; Les York; others.
Country Music on the Go, Vol. 2 .... Sage & Sand (M) C-20 10-20 61
Goldie Fields; Bud Titus; Casey Clark; others.
Country Music on the Go, Vol. 3 .... Sage & Sand (M) C-22 10-20 61
Tex Carman; Jimmy Patton; Wayne West; others.
Country Music on the Go, Vol. 4 .... Sage & Sand (M) C-24 10-20 61
Bud Titus; Goldie Fields; Rovers; Casey Clark; others.
Country Music Spectacular .... Starday (M) S-117 25-35 61
George Jones; Cowboy Copas; James O'Gwynn; Frankie Miller; others.
Country Music Spectacular (4 LP) .... Starday (M) SYM-6401 15-25 67
Country Music Spectacular (4 LP) .... Starday (S) SYS-6401 15-25 67
Cowboy Copas; George Jones; Dave Dudley; Maddox Brothers & Rose; Jimmie Skinner; Red Sovine; Johnny Bond; Roger Miller; Merle Kilgore; Flatt & Scruggs; Boots Randolph; Jimmy Richardson; Minnie Pearl; Willis Brothers; Webb Pierce; Sonny James; Roy Drusky; Hawkshaw Hawkins; Patsy Cline; George Morgan; Buck Owens; Johnny Horton; Ferlin Husky; Stoneman Family; Faron Young; Texas Ruby; Moon Mullican; Stringbean; Wayne Raney; Frankie Miller; Margie Singleton; Joe & Rose Lee Maphis; Mac Wiseman; Stanley Brothers; Carl Story; Grandpa Jones; Melba Montgomery; Carter Family; Leon Payne; Bill Carlisle; Wilf Carter; Lonzo & Oscar.
Country Music Star Spectacular .... Hickory (M) 116 10-20 64
Country Music Story [Narrated] By Minnie Pearl .... Starday (M) SLP-397 10-15 60s
Minnie Pearl; Carter Family; George Jones; Leon McAuliffe; Dottie West; Flatt & Scruggs; Cowboy Copas; Willis Brothers; Johnny Cash; Buck Owens; others.
Country Music Time .... Decca (M) DL 34057 10-20 60s
Jimmie Davis; Bill Monroe; Webb Pierce; Tommy Jackson; Montana Slim; Rex Allen; Red Foley; Red Sovine; Billy Grammer; Roy Drusky; Bill Anderson; Ernest Tubb.
Country Music USA .... Candelite (S) CM 1/3 10-20 80
(Box set.) Troy Shondell; Jack Scott; Donnie Brooks; Sanford Clark; Buddy Knox; Duane Eddy; Robin Luke; Ray Smith; J. Frank Wilson; Wanda Jackson; Kenny Price; Jimmy Clanton; Patti Page; Henson Cargill; Jeannie Seely; Lonnie Mack; Kingston Trio; Memphis Blue; Ned Miller; Johnny & Hurricanes; Wynn Stewart; Jan Howard; Jimmy Gilmer; Dorsey Burnette; Sue Thompson; Gene Simmons; Faron Young; Harden Trio.
Country Music USA .... Readers Digest/RCA (S) RD4-193 10-20 77
(Boxed set.) Glen Campbell; Bobbie Gentry; Buck Owens; Anne Murray; Freddie Hart; Tennessee Ernie Ford; Roy Clark; Jody Miller; Sonny James; Jimmy Wakely & Margaret Whiting; Hank Thompson; Tex Ritter; Roy Acuff; Jean Shepard; Faron Young; Louvin Brothers; Ferlin Husky; Merle Travis; Hank Thompson; Tex Williams; Charlie Louvin & Melba Montgomery; Wanda Jackson; Billie Jo Spears; Johnny & Jonie Mosby; Ned Miller; Susan Raye; Buddy Alan; Merle Haggard; Roy Clark; Harlan Howard; Dick Curless; Red Simpson; Roy Drusky; Buck Owens & Susan Raye; Jan Howard; Linda Ronstadt; Tony Booth; LaWanda Lindsey; Melba Montgomery; Roy Rogers & Dale Evans; Jordanaires.
Country Music Who's Who .... Starday (M) SLP-304 15-20 64

Willis Brothers; Jimmy Dean; Joe Maphis; Johnny Cash; Roger Miller; Cowboy Copas; George Jones; Dottie West; Jimmie Skinner; Dean Manuel; Duke of Paducah; Buck Owens; Pee Wee King; Pete Drake.

Country Music Who's Who .... Starday (M) SLP-304 20-25 64

(Issued with 52-page booklet, also "premium certificate" coupon.) Willis Brothers; Jimmy Dean; Joe Maphis; Johnny Cash; Roger Miller; Cowboy Copas; George Jones; Dottie West; Jimmie Skinner; Dean Manuel; Duke of Paducah; Buck Owens; Pee Wee King; Pete Drake.

Country Music's Greatest Stars .... Nashville (M) NLP 2028 5-10

George Jones; Dottie West; Dave Dudley; Johnny Bond; Roy Drusky; Pete Drake & Talking Steel Guitar; Willis Brothers; Buck Owens; Charlie Walker; Roger Miller; Archie Campbell; Jimmy Dean.

Country Music's Top 14 .... CBS (S) P 15829 5-10

Charlie Rich; Ray Price; Willie Nelson; Tammy Wynette; etc.

Country My Way (4 LP) .... Columbia Musical Treasury (SE) 4P 6212 15-20 75

(Boxed set. Record club issue.) Charlie Rich; David Houston; Lynn Anderson; Johnny Cash; Tanya Tucker; Tammy Wynette; Roy Clark.

Country Negro Jam Session .... Arhoolie (M) 2018 10-15

Butch Cage; Robert Pete Williams; Clarence Edwards; Ben Douglas; Sally Dotson; Willie B. Thomas; Rebecca Smith; Smoky Babee; Leon Strickland.

Country Oldies But Goodies .... Smash (M) MGS-27016 10-20 62

Country Oldies But Goodies .... Smash (S) SRS-67016 10-20 62

Cowboy Copas; Justin Tubb; Stanley Brothers; others.

Country Oldies You Know and Love .... Somerset (S) 33700 5-10 69

Country-Politan Hits .... Crystal (S) LP-1100 5-10

(Mail order offer.) Johnny Darrell; Jeannie C. Riley; Jack Greene; George Jones; Kitty Wells; Bobby Lewis; Red Foley; Linda Manning; Bobby Helms; Jimmie Rodgers; Glen Campbell; Henson Cargill; Jeannie Seely; Red Sovine; Burl Ives; Patsy Cline; Robert Mitchum; Buck Owens; Webb Pierce; Del Reeves; Loretta Lynn.

Country Pop, Vol. 1 & 2 (2 LP) .... Capitol/Telehouse (S) SLB-6872 8-12 73

(Mail order offer.) Glen Campbell; Johnny Cash; Sonny James; Jeannie C. Riley; Roy Clark; Anne Murray; Ferlin Husky; Wanda Jackson; Faron Young; Tex Ritter; Bobbie Gentry; Wynn Stewart; Freddie Hart; Susan Raye; Tennessee Ernie Ford; Dick Curless; Dorsey Burnett; Anne Murray; Charlie Louvin & Melba Montgomery; Billie Jo Spears; Joe South; Linda Ronstadt.

Country Proud .... K-Tel WU 3670 5-10 84

Gary Morris; Crystal Gayle; John Conlee; Earl Thomas Conley; Deborah Allen; Janie Fricke; Willie Nelson; Lee Greenwood; Sylvia; Ronnie Milsap; Alabama; George Strait; Lynn Anderson; Jim Glaser; Ricky Scaggs; Don Williams.

Country Road .... K-Tel WU 3270 5-10 75

Charlie Rich; Mel Tillis; George Jones; Tammy Wynette; Sonny James; Barbara Mandrell; Ray Price; Lynn Anderson; David Houston; Billy Walker; Sheb Wooley; Carl Smith; Jody Miller; Stonewall Jackson; Johnny Horton; Carl Butler; Jud Strunk.

Country Roundup .... Epic (S) EGP-504 5-10 70

Tammy Wynette; Bob Luman; David Houston; Goldie Hill; Autry Inman; Jim & Jesse & Virginia Boys; others.

Country Salute to Hank Williams .... Harmony (M) HL-7265 15-20 60

Carl Perkins; Roy Acuff; Rose Maddox; others.

Country Side of Christmas .... Capitol Creative Products (S) SL 6586 5-10

Sonny James; Glen Campbell; Roy Rogers; Buck Owens; Hollywood Pops Orchestra; Al Martino; Roger Wagner Chorale; Korean Orphan Choir.

Country Sides (2 LP) .... MCA (S) 1929 8-12 70s

Osborne Brothers; Tennessee Hound Dog; others.

Country Soft and Mellow (7 LP) .... Reader's Digest/BMG (SP) RB4-200 40-55 89

(Boxed set. Mail order offer. Includes booklet.) Elvis Presley; others.

Country Songs .... Camden (S) CAS-2333 8-10 69

Eddy Arnold; Bobby Bare; Don Gibson; Hank Snow; Porter Wagoner.

Country Sounds, Vol. 1 .... Ronco/Columbia Special Products (S) CS 10847 5-10 72

Sammi Smith; Tommy Overstreet; George Jones & Tammy Wynette; Henson Cargill; Lynn Anderson; Faron Young; Roy Drusky; Marty Robbins; Dave Dudley; David Houston; Johnny Cash; Roger Miller; Tammy Wynette; Tom T. Hall; George Jones; Statler Brothers; Jeannie Seely; Ray Price; Hank Thompson; Roy Clark.

Country Special .... Capitol (S) STBB-402 8-12 69

Glen Campbell; Ferlin Husky; Faron Young; Johnny & Jonie Mosby; Charlie Louvin; Buck Owens; Jody Miller; Sonny James; Wynn Stewart; Wanda Jackson; Louvin Brothers; Roy Acuff; Merle Haggard; Jean Shepard; Tennessee Ernie Ford; Jeannie Black; Hank Thompson.

Country Special .... Columbia House (SP) DS-994 5-10 72

(TV offer.) Sammi Smith; Dave Dudley; George Jones; Jerry Lee Lewis; Tammy Wynette; Johnny Paycheck; Lynn Anderson; Mel Tillis & Sherry Bryce; Freddy Weller; Hank Williams Jr.

Country Spectacular .... Columbia (M) CL-894 30-50 56

Rosemary Clooney; Gene Autry; Carl Smith; Don Cherry; Tunesmiths; Collins Kids.

Country Star Parade, Vol. 1 .... Vocalion (M) VL-3768 10-15 66

Country Star Parade, Vol. 1 .... Vocalion (S) VL 73768 10-15 66

Roger Miller; Roy Acuff; Wanda Jackson; Red Sovine; Louvin Brothers.

Country Star Parade, Vol. 2 .... Vocalion (M) VL-3804 10-15 67

Country Star Parade, Vol. 2 .... Vocalion (S) VL73804 10-15 67

Roger Miller; Ernest Ashworth; Jenny Lou Carson; Justin Tubb; Mitchell Torok; Jason Fleming; Roger Miller.

Country Star Parade, Vol. 3 .... Vocalion (S) VL 73836 10-15 69

Country Stars, Country Hits .... Camden (M) CAL-793 10-20 64

Country Stars, Country Hits .... Camden (S) CAS-793 10-20 65

Eddy Arnold; Hank Snow; Don Gibson; Chet Atkins; Homer & Jethro; Elton Britt; Jim Reeves; Pee Wee King; Red Stewart; Gid Tanner; Porter Wagoner; Montana Slim; Bill Boyd.

Country Stars of Today .... Power Pak (S) PO-287 5-10 75

Freddy Fender; Jean Shepard; Johnny Paycheck; Mike Lunsford; Barbara Fairchild; Billy "Crash" Craddock; Narvel Felts; Buck Owens; Pozo Seco Singers; Stella Parton.

Country Stars Sing Sacred Songs .... Camden (M) CAL-2136 10-15 67

Country Stars Sing Sacred Songs .... Camden (S) CAS-2136 10-15 67

Bobby Bare; Connie Smith; Hank Snow; Martha Carson; Browns; Kitty Wells; George Hamilton IV; Don Gibson; Sons of the Pioneers; Porter Wagoner.

Country Standards from House of Bryant, Vol. 1 .... HB (S) 1001 10-15
(Promotional issue only.) Glen Campbell & Bobbie Gentry; Bob Moore; Jim Reeves; Everly Brothers; Osborne Brothers; Eddy Arnold; Lynn Anderson; Chet Atkins; Ray Price.

Country Style .... Design (SE) SDLP-641 10-15
Patsy Cline; Maddox Brothers & Rose; Jimmy Dean; Ferlin Husky; Melba Montgomery; Lonzo & Oscar.

Country Style (2 LP) .... RCA/Telehouse (S) PRS-439 8-12 73
(Mail order offer.) Jim Reeves; Chet Atkins; Hank Locklin; Don Gibson; Skeeter Davis; Porter Wagoner; Norma Jean; Floyd Cramer; Bobby Bare; Liz Anderson; Jim Ed Brown; Danny Davis & Nashville Brass; Hank Snow; Dickie Lee; Connie Smith; Bobby Bare; Skeeter Davis; Waylon Jennings; Leon Ashley; Dolly Parton; Jerry Reed; Dottie West; Jimmy Dean; Browns.

Country Sunshine (2 LP) .... Adam VIII Ltd. (S) A8R-8011 8-10 74
(Mail order offer.) Dottie West; Bobby Bare; Donna Fargo; Tommy Overstreet; Brenda Lee; Johnny Rodriguez; Tom T. Hall; Marty Robbins; Kenny Price; Porter Wagoner; Charlie Rich; Olivia Newton-John; Eddy Arnold; Dolly Parton; Jerry Reed; Faron Young; Roy Clark; Waylon Jennings; Johnny Bush; Jim Ed Brown.

Country Super Sounds (1956) .... Omega Sales (M) O-6-1956 20-40 73
(Mail order offer.) Elvis Presley; others.

Country Super Sounds (1957) .... Omega Sales (M) O-6-1957 20-40 73
(Mail order offer.) Elvis Presley; others.

Country Super Sounds (1958) .... Omega Sales (M) O-6-1958 20-40 73
(Mail order offer.) Elvis Presley; others.

Country Teardrops .... K-Tel (S) BU 4760 5-10 78
Ferliln Husky; Webb Pierce; Warner Mack; Merle Kilgore; Claude King; Bobby Edwards; Bill Phillips; Bobby Helms; Marvin Rainwater; Skeeter Davis; Sammi Smith; Ned Miller; Charlie Louvin; Carl Belew; Webb Pierce; Margie Bowes; Warner Mack; Ernest Ashworth; Roy Drusky.

Country Time .... ???? 5-10
Jody Miller; Willie Nelson; George Jones; Boots Randolph; David Wills; Mac Davis; Moe Bandy; Charlie McCoy; Tammy Wynette; Charlie Rich.

Country Time .... Columbia (S) ???? 5-10 73
(TV offer.) Ray Price; Faron Young; Jim Rodgers; Hank Thompson; Jimmy Wakely; Stonewall Jackson; Roger Miller; Johnny Cash; Arthur Smith; George Morgan; David Houston & Tammy Wynette; Lynn Anderson.

Country Times (2 LP) .... Columbia/Dynamic House (S) P-11797-A 8-12 73
(Mail order offer.) Ray Price; Faron Young; Jimmie Rodgers; Hank Thompson; Jimmy Wakely; Stonewall Jackson; Roger Miller; Johnny Cash; Arthur Smith; George Morgan; David Houston & Tammy Wynette; Lynn Anderson.

Country Time Music .... Maverick (S) 1002 10-20
Danny Darren; Skip & Gail; Billy B. & Impressions; Kenny Christensen.

Country USA 1968 (2 LP) .... Time-Life (S) STL-11/CTR-06 8-12 89
Waylon Jennings; Jerry Lee Lewis; Conway Twitty; George Jones; Osborne Brothers; Tammy Wynette; Merle Haggard; Buck Owens & His Buckaroos; Porter Wagoner & Dolly Parton; Charley Pride; Jeannie C. Riley; Glen Campbell; Johnny Cash; Loretta Lynn; Porter Wagoner; Flatt & Scruggs; Del Reeves; Henson Cargill.

Country Wine, 100 Proof Country Hard Drinkin' Hits (2 LP) .... Polystar (S) ?? 8-12
Mel Tillis; Hank Williams Jr.; Ben Colder; C.W. McCall; Billy Walker; Del Reeves; Doc & Merle Watson; Wanda Jackson; Freddy Weller; David Wills; Johnny Cash; George Jones; Roger Miller; Tom T. Hall; Roy Drusky; Faron Young; Johnny Rodriguez; Patti Page; Cledus Maggard & Citizens Band.

Country Winners '73 .... Columbia (S) 1P-6067 5-10 73
Tanya Tucker; David Houston; Mac Davis; Tammy Wynette; Freddy Weller; Charlie Rich; Lynn Anderson; Johnny Cash; Barbara Mandrell; Johnny Duncan.

Country's Best, Vol. 1 .... Capitol (EP) EAP 1-1179 5-10 59
Skeets McDonald; Jean Shepard; Tommy Collins; Hank Thompson.

Country's Best, Vol. 2 .... Capitol (EP) EAP 2-1179 5-10 59

Country's Best, Vol. 3 .... Capitol (EP) EAP 3-1179 5-10 59

Country's Best .... Capitol (M) T-1179 20-30 59
Faron Young; Skeets McDonald; Louvin Brothers; Jean Shepard & Ferlin Husky; Tex Ritter; Tommy Collins; Freddie Hart; Hank Thompson; Wynn Stewart.

Country's Gospel (2 LP) .... Word/Capitol (S) SL 6894/5 10-15 70s
Johnny Cash; Loretta Lynn; Jimmie Davis; Inspirations; Redd Harper; Marty Robbins; Cliff Barrows; Ray Price; Pat Boone; Patsy Cline; Ernest Tubb; Joe Maphis; Bob Daniels; Wilburn Brothers; Anita Bryant; Red Foley; Glen Campbell; Norma Zimmer; Jim Roberts; Alan McGill; Happy Goodman Family; Roy Acuff; Burl Ives; Mary Jayne; Wayne Newton; J.T. Adams; Wanda Jackson; Sonny James; Blue Ridge Quartet; Ferlin Husky; Roy Rogers; Dale Evans & Tennessee Ernie Ford.

Country's Greatest Hits .... Columbia (S) 465 5-10 69
(Columbia Record Club issue.) Johnny Cash; Johnny Horton; others.

Country's Greatest Hits, Vol. 1 .... Columbia (S) GP-9 5-10 69
Johnny Cash; George Morgan; Johnny Horton; Little Jimmy Dickens; Lonzo & Oscar; Roy Acuff; Billy Walker; Jimmy Dean; Carl Smith; Flatt & Scruggs; Charlie Walker; Tommy Collins; Statler Brothers; Marty Robbins; Ray Price..

Country's Greatest Hits, Vol. 2 (2 LP) .... Columbia (S) GP-19/CS 9930 8-12 69
Johnny Cash; Marty Robbins; Ray Price; Carl Smith; Stonewall Jackson; Carl Butler; Flatt & Scruggs; Johnny Horton; Freddie Weller; Carl Perkins; Lefty Frizzell; Jimmy Dean; Little Jimmy Dickens; Johnny Bond; Harden Trio; Claude King; Gene Autry; George Morgan; Floyd Tillman; Bob Wills.

Country's Greatest Love Songs, 10 Years of Country Gold (2 LP) .... Columbia (SE) P2S 5644 8-12 70s
(Mail order. Columbia House Record Club issue.) Ray Price; Johnny Cash; June Carter; David Houston & Tammy Wynette; Dave Dudley; Leon Ashley; Marty Robbins; Charlie Rich; George Morgan; Roy Drusky; Jimmy Dean; Carl Smith; Johnny Cash; Lynn Anderson; Claude King; Johnny Horton; Leroy Van Dyke; Tammy Wynette.

County Bound .... Columbia/Imperial House WU 3580 5-10 81
(Mail order offer.) Don Williams; Wille Nelson; Lacy J. Dalton; Statler Brothers; Tanya Tucker; Tammy Wynette & George Jones; Moe Bandy & Joe Stampley; Kendalls; Barbara Mandrell; Merle Haggard; Johnny Duncan; Crystal Gayle; John Conlee; Jennifer Warnes; Conway Twitty.

Coupe de Ville .... Cypress (S) 71334 8-10 90
(Soundtrack.) Kingsmen; Dion; Flamingos; Temptations; Cadillacs; Joey Dee & Starliters; Chips; Everly Brothers; Nervous Norvous; Young MC.

Courier .... Virgin Movie Music (S) 90954-1 8-10
(Soundtrack.) Dangerous Games; Cry Before Dawn; Declan MacManus; Something Happens; Hothouse Flowers; Lord John White; U2.

Cousin Brucie's Rock 'N Roll Dedications .... Hall of Music (S) HL 007 5-10 81
Jimmy Charles; Adam Wade; Mel Carter; Casinos; Little Caesar & Romans; Dee Clark; Safaris; Gladys Knight & Pips; Sammy Turner; Lenny Welch; Classics; Paradons; Shells.

Cowboy! .... Design (M) DLP-189 10-15

Gene Autry; Smiley Burnette; Eddie Dean; Foy Willing; Bradley Kincaid.

Cowboy Songs for Children .... Harmony (M) HL-9512 10-20 60
Fess Parker; Jerry Blaine; others.

Cowpoke .... Camay (S) CA 3040 5-10 60s
Tex Ritter; Tennessee Ernie Ford; Merle Travis; Wesley Tuttle; Tex Williams; Wlton Britt; Hank Fort; others.

Crash Tops, Vol. III .... Crash (S) 1003 5-10 70s
Beatles; Tony Joe White; Jaggerz; Zager & Evans; Joe Jeffrey Group; 5 Stairsteps; Gene Chandler; Jimmy Ruffin; Classics IV; Zombies; Syndicate of Sound; Crosby, Stills, Nash & Young.

Cream of the Country Crop .... Starday (M) S-394 10-15 67
Buck Owens; Johnny Cash; Sonny James; Dottie West; others.

Cream of the Crop .... Epic (M) LN-3701 25-35 60
Johnnie Ray & Four Lads; De John Sisters; Ahmad Jamal Trio; Brook Benton; Roy Hamilton; Chuck Willis; Four Coins; Link Wray; Sal Mineo; Somethin' Smith & Redheads.

Creepers .... Enigma (S) SJ-73205 8-10 86
(Soundtrack.) Claudio Simonetti; Ron Maiden; Goblin; Sex Gang Andi; Bill Wyman; Terry Taylor; Simon Boswell; Motorhead.

Critic's Choice .... Takoma (S) 1062 5-10 78
Mike Auldridge; Rose Maddox; Tut Taylor; Lawrence Hammond; others.

Cross Section .... MCA (S) L33 1819 5-10

Crossroads .... Warner Bros. (S) OP 2515 8-12
Spencer Davis Group; Alive 'N Kicking; Box Tops; American Breed; Steam; Zombies; Eric Burdon & Animals; Santana; Grass Roots; Rascals; Left Banke; Kinks; Outsiders; Steppenwolf; Mitch Ryder & Detroit Wheels; Electric Prunes; Vanilla Fudge; Blues Magoos; Strawberry Alarm Clock; Iron Butterfly.

Crowd Pleasers .... Columbia Special Products (SE) CSS 670 5-10 60s
Robert Goulet; Jerry Vale; Diahann Carroll; Steve Lawrence; Ray Conniff; Andre Kostelanetz; Mel Torme; Eydie Grome; Doris Day; New Christy Minstrels.

Cruisin' (5 LP) .... Warner Special Products/Sessions OP 5055 20-30 84
Beach Boys; Orleans; Doobie Brothers; Eddie Cochran; Allman Brothers; Jan & Dean; Bobby Fuller Four; Sam & Dave; Tommy James & Shondells; Mason Williams; Bay City Rollers; Steppenwolf; Dion; Supremes; America; Monkees; Box Tops; Syndicate of Sound; Aretha Franklin; Ronny & Daytonas; Dwight Twilley Band; Gete Pitney; Contours; Wilson Pickett; American Breed; Guess Who; Fleetwood Mac; Ventures; Leslie Gore; Paul Revere & Raiders; Connie Francis; Creedence Clearwater Revival; Chuck Berry; Soul Survivors; Booker T. & MGs; Edwin Starr; Everly Brothers; Golden Earring; Rivieras; Zager & Evans; Little Eva; J.J. Jackson; Freddy Cannon; Buddy Holly; Grass Roots.

Cruisin' 1955 ("Jumpin" George Oxford, KSAN-FM San Francisco) .... Increase (M) IN-2000 10-15 72
Ray Charles; Hank Ballard & Midnighters; Moonglows; Charms; Little Walter; Penguins; Chuck Berry; Platters; Fats Domino; Nutmegs; Bo Diddley; Johnny Ace.

Cruisin' 1956 (Robin Seymour, WKMH Detroit) .... Increase (M) IN-2001 10-15 70
Chuck Berry; Teen Queens; Frankie Lymon & Teenagers; Mello-Kings; Little Willie John; Platters; Little Richard; Cadets; Cadillacs; Crowns; Five Satins; Bill Doggett.

Cruisin' 1957 (Joe Niagra, WIBG Philadelphia) .... Increase (M) IN-2002 10-15 70
Dale Hawkins; Tune Weavers; Chuck Berry; Heartbeats; Spaniels; Buddy Knox; Diamonds; Johnnie & Joe; Larry Williams; Five Satins; Jimmie Rodgers; Lee Andrews & Hearts.

Cruisin' 1958 (Jack Carney, WIL St. Louis) .... Increase (M) IN-2003 10-15 70
Danny & Juniors; Monotones; Chuck Berry; Jimmie Rodgers; Royalteens; Big Bopper; Bobby Freeman; Bobby Day; Silhouettes; Harvey & Moonglows; Duane Eddy.

Cruisin' 1959 (Hunter Hancock, KGFJ Los Angeles) .... Increase (M) IN-2004 10-15 70
Olympics; Big Jay McNeeley; Skyliners; Chuck Berry; Dinah Washington; Bo Diddley; Crests; Lloyd Price; Brook Benton; Phil Phillips; Flamingos; Wilbert Harrison.

Cruisin' 1960 (Dick Biondi, WKBW Buffalo) .... Increase (M) IN-2005 10-15 70
Joe Jones; Little Anthony & Imperials; Brook Benton & Dinah Washington; Jack Scott; Hank Ballard & Midnighters; Tempos; Hollywood Argyles; Maurice Williams; Johnny Preston; Miss Toni Fisher; Duane Eddy; Buster Brown.

Cruisin' 1960 .... Ruby (M) RR 3-4083 5-10 81
Wilbert Harrison; Jack Scott; Dorsey Burnette; Impalas; Frankie Avalon; Maurice Williams; Thomas Wayne; Jerry Wallace; Fabian; Donnie Brooks.

Cruisin' 1961 (Arnie "Woo Woo" Ginsburg, WMEX Boston) .... Increase (M) IN-2006 10-15 70
Marcels; Jive Five; Chuck Berry; Shep & Limelites; Joe Dowell; Del Shannon; Clarence Frogman Henry; Playmates; Bobby Lewis; Freddy Cannon; Regents; Lee Dorsey; Freddie King.

Cruisin' 1962 (Russ "Weird Beard" Knight, KLIF Dallas) .... Increase (M) IN-2007 10-15 70
Joey Dee & Starliters; Shirelles; Don Gardner & Dee Dee Ford; Bruce Channel; Sensations; Shelley Fabares; Gene Chandler; Barbara Lynn; Dion; James Darren Brian Hyland; Little Eva.

Cruisin' 1963 (B. Mitchell Reed, WMCA New York) .... Increase (M) IN-2008 10-15 72
Red Prysock; Essex; Jaynetts; Chiffons; Isley Brothers; Shirelles; Lesley Gore; Rooftop Singers; Freddie Scott; Randy & Rainbows; Jan Bradley; Paul & Paula; Kingsmen.

Cruisin' 1964 (Johnny Holliday, WHK Cleveland) .... Increase (M) IN-2009 10-15 73
Bob & Earl; Shirley Ellis; Roger Miller; Shangri-Las; others.

Cruisin' 1965 (Robert W. Morgan, KHJ Los Angeles) .... Increase (M) IN-2010 10-15 73
McCoys; Sam the Sham & Pharaohs; Petula Clark; Righteous Brothers; others.

Cruisin' 1966 (Pat O'Day, KJR Seattle) .... Increase (M) IN-2011 10-15 73
Mitch Ryder & Detroit Wheels; Sufaris; Tommy James & Shondells; Tommy Roe; others.

Cruisin' 1967 (Dr. Don Rose, WQXI Atlanta) .... Increase (M) IN-2012 10-15 73
John Fred; Jay & Techniques; Blues Magoos; Brenton Wood; Royal Guardsmen; Strawberry Alarm Clock; Cowsills; Music Explosion; Keith; Tommy James; Turtles; Janis Ian.

Cruisin' 1968 (Johnny Dark) .... Increase (M) ???? 5-10 88
Steppenwolf; Temptations; Classic IV; Box Tops; Bobby Goldsboro; Merrilee Rush; O'Kaysions; Grass Roots; Supremes; Marvin Gaye.

Cruisin' 1969 (Harv Moore) .... Increase (M) ???? 5-10 88
Groovers; Champs; Clyde McPhatter; Fifth Dimension; Sunny & Sunglows; Smokey Robinson & Miracles; Angels; Desmond Dekker; Seeds; Stevie Wonder.

Cruisin' Ann Arbor ....Ann Arbor Music Project (S) AAMP-982 15-20 82
George Bedard & Bonnevilles; Blue Front Persuaders; Urbations; Ranger Kvaran; Steve Newhouse Band; Peter "Madcat" Ruth; Non-Fiction; VVT; Cult Heroes; It Play; SKL; Mike Gould & Gene Pool Band.

Cruisin' Lovers Lane (3 LP) ....Candlelite (S) CU 719 10-15 83
(Boxed set.) Jerry Butler & Impressions; Chordettes; Everly Brothers; El Dorados; Blue Jays; Dells; Dee Clark; Gary "U.S." Bonds; Spaniels; Gene Chandler; Flamingos; Johnny Tillotson; Paris Sisters; Lenny Welch; Link Wray; Jimmy Dorsey; Little Richard; Betty Everett.

Cruisin' Series ....Increase (S) CSTM 4452 15-20
(Promotional issue only.)

Cruisin' the Drag: see SONICS / Flash Terry / Crowns / Vibes

Cruisin' with the Cadillacs 'N Cats Like That ....Harlem Hit Parade (SE) HH-5009 10-20 72
Cadillacs; Desires; Charades; Del-Vikings; Ivory Joe Hunter.

Cruisin' Years ....Increase (S) INC 1000 5-10 85
(One song from each of the Cruisin' series LPs from 1955-1963.

Cruising ....Columbia (S) JC-36410 30-35 80
(Soundtrack.) Willy DeVille; Cripples; John Hiatt; Madelynn Von Ritz; Mutiny; Rough Trade; Germs.

Cub Koda Crazy Show ....Ace (M) CH 108 8-12 84
Frankie Ford; Pat Cupp; Dee & Patty; Little Junior Parker; Etta James; Richard Berry; Howlin' Wolf; Punk Carson; Everly Brothers; Link Wray; Diz & Doormon Poorboys; Chan Romero; Arthur Alexander; Young Jessie; Elmore James; King Hszniewicz.

Current Audio Magazine (August-September 1972) ....Current Audio Magazine (M) 1 45-55 72
Elvis Presley; Mick Jagger; Angela Davis; Ted Kennedy; others.

Current Country Hits ....Harmony (EP) 16 10-20 56
Current Country Hits ....Harmony (M) HL-9008 30-50 56
Current Country Hits, Vol. 1 ....Harmony (M) HL-9011 30-50 56
Current Country Hits, Vol. 2 ....Harmony (M) HL-9016 30-50 56
Current Country Hits, Vol. 3 ....Harmony (M) HL-9020 30-50 56
Current Country Hits, Vol. 4 ....Sutton (M) SU-323 15-25 66
Current Craze ....Sutton (S) SSU-323 15-25 66
Current Craze ....Arista (S) SP-150 ?? 83
Current Events (Arista's Guide to New Rock) ....
(Promotional issue.)

Current Events (Arista's Guide to New Rock) ....Arista (S) SP-150 5-10 83
Thompson Twins; Heaven 17; Pete Shelley; Alex Call; Krokus; Flock of Seagulls; Ministry; Q-Feel.

Current Hits ....CTI (S) CTS-1 5-10

Curtis in Chicago ....Curtom (S) 8018 5-10 73
Curtis Mayfield; Jerry Butler; others.

Curtis Mathis Collection of Stereo Music, Album 6 ....Columbia (S) XSV 86078 8-12 60s
Les Brown; Polly Bergen; Lionel Hampton; Four Lads; Banjo Barons; Frankie Laine; Percy Faith; Si Rady Voices; Duke Ellington; Romanoff Singers. (Made for Curtis Mathis Manufacturing Co.)

Curtis Mathis Collection of Stereo Music, Album 10 ....Columbia (S) XSV 86086 8-12 60s
Merrill Staton Choir; Brothers Four; Norman Luboff Choir; Dukes of Dixieland; Dave Brubeck & Carmen McRae; Richard Maltby; Four Lads; Lester Lanin; Ray Conniff. (Made for Curtis Mathis Manufacturing Co.)

Custom Fidelity Promotions ....Custom Fidelity (S) CFS-3281 15-25 70s
Beatles; others.

D.C. Cab ....MCA (S) MCA-5469 8-10 84
(Promotional issue only.)

D.C. Cab ....MCA (S) 6128 8-10 84
(Soundtrack.) Irene Cara; Peabo Bryson; Shalamar; others.

DMM - Direct Metal Mastering - Demo LP ....DMM (S) 66-22981 10-15

Daddy-O Presents Two Dozen Oldies ....Hammer (M) 5007 10-15
Danleers; Dubs; Dells; Harptones; Channels; Cufflinks; Del-Vikings; Kodoks; Quin-Tones; Meadowlarks; Corvells; Spaniels; Jimmy Charles & Reveletts; Medallions; ; Bel-Larks; Pyramids; Excellents.

Dance A-Go-Go with All the Stars, Vol. 1 ....Wyncote (M) W-9111 10-20 64
Chubby Checker; Dovells; Orlons; Dee Dee Sharp; Tymes; Bobby Rydell; Don Covay.

Dance A-Go-Go with All the Stars, Vol. 2 ....Wyncote (M) W-9121 10-20 64
Chubby Checker; Dee Dee Sharp; Don Covay; Dovells; Orlons; Tymes.

Dance, Be Happy! ....Columbia (M) CL 967 5-10 57
Percy Faith; Boyd Raeburn; Xavier Cugat; Les Elgart; Sammy Kaye; Claude Thornhill; Benny Goodman; Paul Weston; Art Van Damme; Duke Ellington; Belmonti; Les Brown.

Dance Craze ....Capitol (EP) EPA-1-927 5-10 58
Dance Craze ....Capitol (EP) EPA-2-927 5-10 58
Dance Craze ....Capitol (EP) EPA-3-927 5-10 58
Dance Craze ....Capitol (M) T-927 20-30 58
Dance Craze ....Capitol (SE) DT-927 5-10 69
Ray Anthony; Pee Wee Hunt; Stan Kenton; Plas Johnson; Nelson Riddle; Les Brown; Dave Cavanaugh; Lord Flea; Billy May; Guy Lombardo.

Dance Craze ....Chrysalis (S) PV 41299 8-10 81
(Soundtrack.) Specials; English Beat; Bad Manners; Madness; Selector; Bodysnatchers.

Dance Dance Dance (4 LP) ....Telehouse (S) CD-2023 20-25 71
Wilson Pickett; Fantastic Johnny C.; Dee Dee Sharp; Rivingtons; Cliff Nobles & Co.; Little Eva; Diamonds; Jackie Lee; Rufus Thomas; Dovells; Shirley Ellis; Chubby Checker; Ray Baretto; Joey Dee & Starliters; Rufus Thomas; Hank Ballard & Midnighters; Wilson Pickett; Dovells; Little Joey & Flips; Champs; Larks; Isley Brothers; Vibrations; Tommy James & Shondells; Jimmy cCracklin; Olympics; Rufus Thomas; Huey Smith & Clowns. (LPs packaged individually, not as a boxed set.)

Dance Discotheque ....Decca (M) DL-4556 10-20 64
Dance Discotheque ....Decca (S) DL-74556 10-20 64
Peter Duchin; Tommy Dorsey; Discotheque Orchestra; Emilio Reyes; others.

Dance Hall Reggae ....Cosmic Force (S) 8002 5-10
Sanchez; Robert Lee; Dickie Rankin; Frankie Paul; Linval Thompson; Shabba Ranks; Chaka Demus; Good Times; Little Harry; Cornel Campbell.

Dance Machine .... K-Tel (S) NU 9090 5-10 76
KC & Sunshine Band; B.T. Express; Van McCoy; Soul City Symphony; Jim Gilstrap Johnny Bristol; Little Beaver; Gwen McCrae; Trammps; Black Byrds; Silver Convention; LaBelle; Ritchie Family; Kool & Gang; James Brown; Hamilton Bohannon; George McCrae; Betty Wright; Miami; Jimmie Bo Home.

Dance Party.. Dance Party (M) DL 34033 10-15

Dance Party.. Libra (M) 6001 5-10

Dance Sampler for College Radio.. Columbia (S) AS 1766 5-10 83
Philip Bailey; Herbie Hancock; Ellison Chase; Carol McQuade; Jimmy the Hoover; Third World; Jimmy Cliff; Weather Girls; Andre Cymone/

Dance Sixties .... Warner Special Products (S) OP 1543 5-10 85
Ike & Tina Tuner; Mitch Ryder & Detroit Wheels; Eddie Floyd; Fontella Bass; Jackie Wilson; Spencer Davis Group; Knickerbockers; Aretha Franklin; Otis Redding; Pacific Gas & Electric; Cannibal & Headhunters.

Dance the Fox Trot.. Columbia (M) CL-533 10-15 50s
Dick Jurgens; Harry James; Tony Pastor; Les Brown; George Siravo; Hal McIntyre; Woody Herman; Ray Noble; Kitty Kallen; Buddy James; Sammy Kaye.

Dance the Night Away.. Columbia (M) PC 36742 5-10 80
Charlie Barnet; Les Brown; Benny Goodman; Gene Krupa; Harry James.

Dance the Rock and Roll.. Atlantic (M) 8013 50-100 57
Willis Jackson; Chuck Calhoun; Tommy Ridgley; Arnett Cobb; Joe Morris; Johnny Griffin; Frank Culley; Van "Piano Man" Walls; Tiny Grimes Quintet.

Dance to the Themes of the Greatest Bands .... Columbia Special Products (S) XTV 68511 8-12
Duke Ellington; Frankie Carle; Eddy Duchin; Woody Herman; Claude Thornhill; Kay Kyser; Harry James; Les Brown; Glen Gray; Gene Krupa; Count Basie; Charlie Spivak.

Dance Tunes from the Vault.. Chess (M) LP-1476 20-30 63
Al Brown's Tunetoppers Featuring Cookie Brown; Vibrations; Steve Alaimo; Dells; Gene & Wendell; Nat Kendricks & Swans; Jimmy McCracklin; Lamont Anthony. (Volume one is titled *Treasure Tunes from the Vault*.)

Dancer.. K-Tel (S) TU-2790 5-10 81
Kool & Gang; Whispers; Sister Sledge; Gap Band; Con Funk Shun; Brothers Johnson; Diana Ross; Lipps Inc.; Yarbrough & Peoples; Quincy Jones; Frankie Smith; Lakeside; SOS Band; Pointer Sisters.

Dancin' Hits .... Wyncote (M) W-9027 10-20 64

Dancin' Hits .... Wyncote (S) SW-9027 10-20 64
Chubby Checker; Bobby Rydell; Dovells; Dee Dee Sharp; Orlons.

Dancing After Dark .... Columbia (M) CB-18 10-20 50s
Les Brown; Paul Weston & His Music from Hollywood; Felicia Sanders; Woody Herman; Pete Rugolo; Les Elgart; Jerry Vale & Peggy King; Percy Faith; Erroll Garner; Peter Barclay; Dick Jurgens at the Aragon Ballroom; Claude Thornhill.

Dancing Cheek to Cheek .... RCA Special Products (M) BU 5800 5-10 83
Eddy Duchin with Lew Sherwood; Glenn Miller with Ray Eberle & Modernaires; Gene Krupa; Guy Lombardo; Carmen Lombardo; Benny Goodman Quartet; Hal McIntyre; Hal Kemp with Skinnay Ennis; Tommy Dorsey.

Dancing Discotheque .... Mercury (M) MG 20964 10-15 65

Dancing Discotheque .... Mercury (S) SR 60964 10-15 65
Quincy Jones; Tornadoes; David Carrol; Jeff Bowen; others.

Dangerously Close .... Enigma (S) SJ-73204 8-10 86
(Soundtrack.) Smithereens; Black Uhuru; Green on Red; T.S.O.L.; Lords of the New Church; Lost Pilots; Michael McCarty.

Dark Muddy Bottom Blues.. Specialty (M) SPS-2149 5-10 72
John Lee Hooker; Pinebluff Pete; Big Joe Williams; Lightnin' Hopkins; Clarence London; Country Jim; Mercy Dee.

Date with Riverside.. Riverside (S) S-4 15-25
Coleman Hawkins; Chauncey Gray; Bob Gibson; Clark Terry; Mundell Lowe; Geoffrey Holder; Gin Bottle Seven; Kenny Drew; Jean Ritchie & Oscar Brand; George Lewis; Lenny Herman; Ed McCurdy.

Day in the Country.. Audio Lab (M) 1519 25-35 59
Bob Newman; Clyde Moody; Jack Cardwell; Harvie June; others.

Day the Music Died .... Silhouette (S) SM-10003 8-10
Familee; Rubettes; Tommy Dee; Ray Campi; Kittens; Loretta Thompson; Beat Buddies; Pilot; Donna Dameron; Lee Davis; Ruby Wright.

Days Of Thunder.. David Geffen Co. (S) DGC 24294-D1 10-15 90
(Soundtrack.) Cher; Chicago; David Coverdale; Guns N' Roses; Joan Jett & Blackhearts; Elton John; Maria McKee; Terry Reid; Apollo Smile; Tina Turner; John Waite.

Dealer's Prevue (SDS-7-2): see PRESLEY, Elvis / Martha Carson / Lou Monte; / Herb Jeffries

Dealer's Prevue.. RCA (EP) SDS-57-39 900-1200 57
(Includes envelope/sleeve. Promotional issue only.) Elvis Presley; Stuart Hamblen; Statesmen Quartet; Kathy Barr; Perry Como; Eddie Fisher.

Death, Glory & Retribution.. EMI America (S) SQ-17187 5-10 85
Jody Reynolds; Jan & Dean; Bloodrock; Bob Gibson; Glen Campbell; Jody Miller; Johnny Burnette; Beach Boys; Jeanne Black; Weird Al Yankovic; Sammi Lynn; Wendy Hill; Geraldine Stevens; Isley Brothers.

Debut Records Autobiography in Jazz .... Debut (M) DEBN 198 10-20 50s
Max Roach Septet; Jackie Paris with Charlie Mingus; Lee Konitz with Charlie Mingus; Janet Thurlow; Paul Bley Trio; Gordons; Jazz Workshop; Thad Jones; Honey Gordon; Sam Most Quartet; Don Senay; Hank Jones; Bud Powell;

Decade of Broadway and Cinema.. Decca (S) DL-734094 15-20 61
(Soundtrack.) Lawrence Welk; Wayne King; Four Aces; Peter Duchin; Carol Burnett; Liberace; Teresa Brewer.

Decade of Gold .... Columbia Special Products (S) P 14228 5-10 77
Hollies; Looking Glass; O'Jays; Santana; Spiral Staircase; Buckinghams; Three Degrees; Gary Puckett & Union Gap; Blood, Sweat & Tears; Mark Lindsay; Peter Nero; Dave Loggins.

Decade of Gold (1955 - 1965).. Era (S) E-602 10-15 72
Gogi Grant; Teddy Bears; Donnie Brooks; Jewel Akens; Chris Montez; Castells; Castaways; Dorsey Burnette; Art & Dottie Todd; Castaways; Hollywood Argyles; Pastel Six; Dave Dudley; Fendermen; Larry Verne..

Decade of Golden Groups (2 LP).. Mercury (S) SRM-2-602 10-20 69
Platters; Diamonds; Cardigans; Angels; Paul & Paula; Spanky & Our Gang; Gaylords; Del-Vikings; Penguins; Crew-Cuts; Rick & Keens; Hondells; Wayne Fontana & Mindbenders; Left Banke; Manfred Mann; Troggs; Blues Magoos.

Decade of the '30s (2LP).. RCA (M) VPM 6058 10-15 72
Tony Martin; Melachrino Strings; Ames Brothers; Tommy Dorsey; Phil Harris; Lena Horne; Hugo Montenegro; Glahe Musette Orchestra; Allan Jones; Jeanette McDonald & Nelson Eddy; Art Mooney; Eddie Fisher; Vaughn Monroe; Perez Prado; Sons of the Pioneers; Glenn Miller.

Decade of the '40s (2 LP) ... RCA (M) VPM 6059 10-15 72
Perry Como; Sons of the Pioneers; Vaughn Monroe; Art Mooney; Glenn Miller; Ames Brothers; Duane Eddy; Tommy Dorsey; Dinah Shore; Spike Jones; Crew-Cuts; Pat Suzuki.

Decade of the '50s (2 LP) ... RCA (M) VPM 6060 10-15 72
Phil Harris; Eddy Arnold; Hugo Winterhalter; Catrina Valente & Werner Muller; Domenico Modugno; Harry Belafonte; Browns; Perez Prado; Ames Brothers; Eddie Fisher; Melachrino Strings; Perry Como; Kay Starr; Tommy Leonetti; Sam Cooke.

Decade of the '60s (2 LP) ... RCA (M) VPM 6061 10-15 72
Carol Channing & Company; Zager & Evans; Living Pianos; Tokens; Barry Sadler; Jimmy Dean; Guess Who; Floyd Cramer; Connie Smith; Youngbloods; Eddy Arnold; Friends of Distinction; Dolly Parton; Living Voices; Carol Burnett.

Decca Cavalcade of Stars ... Decca (M) DL-34289 10-15 66
Decca Cavalcade of Stars ... Decca (S) DL-734289 10-15 66
Brenda Lee; Loretta Lynn; Pete Fountain; Bing Crosby; Guy Lombardo; Red Foley; Ethel Smith; Leroy Anderson; Al Jolson; Carmen Cavallaro; Weavers; Bert Kaempfert.

Decline of Western Civilization ... Slash (S) 1-23934 8-10 81
(Soundtrack.) Black Flag; X; Circle Jerks; Fear; Catholic Discipline.

Dedicated Jazz ... Jazztone (M) J 1250 20-30 56
Rex Stewart with Lawrence Brown; Hilton Jefferson; Danny Bank; Hank Jones; Milt Hinton; Osie Johnson; Peanuts Hueko with Billie Butterfield; Boomie Richmond; Hank Jones; Mundell Lowe; Jack Lesberg; Morey Feld.

Dedication, Vol. 1 ... Silhouette (S) SM 1006 5-10 82
Alan Freed's Moondog House Radio Show; Sam "The Man" Taylor; Bill Haley & His Comets; Gloria Mann; Jimmy Cavello & House Rockers; Moonglows; Big Maybelle.

Dedication, Vol. 2 ... Silhouette (S) SM 1007 5-10 82
Alan Freed; Sam "The Man" Taylor; Clyde McPhatter & Drifters; Bonnie Sister; Johnny Burnette; Four Fellows; Faye Adams.

Dedication, Vol. 3 ... Silhouette (S) SM 1008 5-10 82
Alan Freed; Penguins; Robins; Gene Vincent & Blue Caps; Flairs; Valentines.

Dee Jay Sampler ... A&M (S) SP-19004 8-12
Dee Jay's Choice (2 LP) ... Dot (M) DPR-1A 10-20 60s
(Promotional issue only.) Billy Vaughn; Pat Boone; Helen Traubel; Johnny Maddox; Fontane Sisters; Gale Storm; Paul Horn; Ken Nordine; Don Bagley; Pete & Conte Condoli; Hilltoppers; Frank Fields; Bonnie Guitar; Babe Russin; Margaret Whiting; Eddie Peabody.

Definitive Jazz Scene, Vol. 1 ... Impulse (S) AS-99 10-15
Duke Ellington; Eddie Delange; Irving Mills; Thad Jones; Terry Gibbs; Shirley Scott; John Coltrane; Desylva; A. Jolson; Vincent Rose; Charlie Mingus; Bob Hammer; McCoy Tyner.

Definitive Jazz Scene, Vol. 2 ... Impulse (S) A-100 10-15
Definitive Jazz Scene, Vol. 3 ... Impulse (S) A-9101 10-15
John Coltrane; Chico Hamilton; Elvin Jones; Oliver Nelson; Russian Jazz Quartet; Shirley Scott; Archie Shepp; McCoy Tyner.

Del-Fi Album Sampler ... Del-Fi (M) 00 250-350 59
(Green vinyl. Paper sleeve/cover.) Ritchie Valens; Balladeers; Bob Keene Quintet; Tony "Pepino" Martinez.

Del-Fi Record Hop ... Del-Fi (M) DFLP-1210 75-100 59
Chan Romero; Ritchie Valens; Bill Tracy; Buddy Landon; Balladeers; Rookies; Prentice Moreland; Addrisi Brothers; Nitehawks.

Delightfully Light ... Jazztone (M) J 1277 15-25 57
Red Norvo Trio with Tal Farlow; Cal Tjader Quartet; Gerry Wiggins; Gene Wright; Bill Douglass.

Demand Performances ... Monument (M) MLP-8010 15-25 64
Demand Performances ... Monument (S) SLP-8010 15-25 64
Billy Grammer; Jerry Byrd; Velvets; Bob Moore; Roy Orbison; Jack Eubanks.

Demonstration of 33mm Magnetic Film ... Mercury (M) MGD 15 10-15
Demonstration of 33mm Magnetic Film ... Mercury (S) SRD 15 10-15
Descargas at the Village Gate - Live, Vol. 1 ... Tico (S) SLP 1135 8-12
Destination Victoria Station ... Columbia (S) VS 150 8-12
Johnny Cash; others.

Detroit Defaces the '80s ... Tremor (S) TRLP-101 8-10 80
Cinecyde; Cubes; Ivories; Twenty-Seven; Rushlow-King Combo; Mark J. Norton; Service.

Detroit Girl Groups ... Relic (M) 8004 5-10 85
Clevers; Clara Hardy; Kittens; La Dolls; Primettes; Satin Angels; Ruby & Her Swinging Rocks; Taylor Tones; Conquerors; Corvells.

Detroit on a Platter ... Automotive (S) Auto LP-1000 10-15 81
Mutants; Zooks; Reruns; Ivories; Destroy All Monsters; Torpedos; Cinecyde; Master Cylinder; Coldcock; Sillies; Stirling Silver.

Detroit Sound ... Wyncote (M) W-9208 10-20 64
Dial-A-Hit ... Bell (S) 6030 15-20 69
Box Tops; Bobby Russell; James & Bobby Purify; O'Jays; Masqueraders; Delfonics; Merrilee Rush; Al Greene.

Dial-A-Hit: see Buddah's 360° Dial-A-Hit

Diamond Jubilee Showcase (For Rexall 60th Birthday) (2 LP) ... Columbia (S) XTV-86088-86091 15-20
Bix Beiderbecke; Dukes of Dixieland; Louis Armstrong; Duke Ellington; Gerry Mulligan; Dave Brubeck; Tommy & Jimmy Dorsey; Frankie Carle; Woody Herman; Harry James; Les Brown; Les Elgart; Ezio Pinza; Jo Stafford; Andy Williams; Rosemary Clooney; Sarah Vaughan; Tony Bennett; Andre Kostelanetz; Jerry Murad's Harmonicats; Ray Conniff; Percy Faith; Andre Previn; Norman Luboff.

Diamonds By the Dozen ... RCA (M) LPM-2632 10-15 63
Diamonds By the Dozen ... RCA (S) LSP-2632 10-20 63
Chet Atkins; Ames Brothers; Peter Nero; Frankie Carle; Sid Ramin; Morton Gould; Hugo Winterhalter; Robert Merrill; Floyd Cramer; Armando Trovajoli; Rosemary Clooney; Melachrino Strings.

Diamonds By the Dozen - Country Style ... RCA (M) LPM-2668 15-20 63
Diamonds By the Dozen - Country Style ... RCA (S) LSP-2668 20-25 63
Don Gibson; Eddy Arnold; Chet Atkins; Browns; Gene Autry; Jim Reeves; Skeeter Davis; Sons of the Pioneers; Hank Locklin; Hank Snow; Del Wood; Porter Wagoner; Gene Autry.

Dick Clark New 20 Years of Rock N' Roll, Volume 3 ... Columbia Special Products (S) P 13045 8-12 70s
Johnny Rivers; Major Lance; Platters; Byrds; Fats Domino; Champs; Everly Brothers; Jamie; Dion; Shirelles; Neil Sedaka; Bobby Day; Lloyd Price; Bobby Hebb.

Dick Clark Presents All Time Hits: see All Time Hits

Dick Clark Presents American Bandstand Favorites: see American Bandstand Favorites

Dick Clark's 25th Anniversary Collection (5 LP) ....Imperial House (S) NU 9420 20-30 78
(Boxed set with booklet.)

Dick Clark's Rock and Roll (1955 - 1975) .... Columbia (S) P213044 8-12 76
(Mail order offer.)

Dick Clark's Rock, Roll and Remember, Vol. 2 ....Columbia (S) 17212 8-12 83
(Mail order offer. Soundtrack.) Tony Orlando & Dawn; Supremes; Jackson Five; Blood, Sweat & Tears; Hollies; Chuck Berry; Jackie Wilson; Temptations; Barry Manilow; Santana.

Dick Clark's Rock, Roll and Remember ....Columbia (S) 17213 8-12 83
(Mail order offer.) Jackie Wilson; Temptations; Barry Manilow; Byrds; Santana; Martha & Vandellas; Everly Brothers; Del Shannon; Dawn; Five Satins; Box Tops; Jackson 5; Blood, Sweat & Tears; Dion; Hollies; Dawn; B.J. Thomas.

Dick Clark's Rock, Roll and Remember (3 LP).................... Heartland Music/Columbia (SP) 17213 10-20 83
Turtles; Mamas & Papas; Everly Brothers; Association; Hollies; Lovin' Spoonful; Byrds; Zombies; Buckinghams; Sonny & Cher; Beach Boys; Box Tops; B.J. Thomas; Del Shannon; Dion; Bobby Hebb; Gary Puckett; Dionne Warwick; Dawn; Barry Manilow; Fifth Dimension; Otis Redding; Percy Sledge; Supremes; Blood, Sweat & Tears; Temptations; Jackson Five; Smokey Robinson & Miracles; Four Tops; Jackie Wilson.

Diesel Smoke, Dangerous Curves (And Other Truck Driver Favorites) .... Starday (M) S-250 15-20 60s

Diesel Smoke, Dangerous Curves (And Other Truck Driver Favorites) ....Starday (S) SLP-250 15-20 60s

Different Strokes....................Columbia (S) AS-12 8-12 71
Johnny Winter And; Tom Rush; Poco; Dreams; Big Brother & Holding Co.; Miles Davis; Spirit; It's a Beautiful Day; Chambers Brothers; Laura Nyro; Ballin' Jack; N.Y. Rock & Roll Ensemble; Hollies; Redbone; Elvin Bishop; Fraser & DeBolt; Bill Puka; Soft Machine; Flock.

Different Strokes....................Columbia (S) XSM-153777 8-12
Johnny Winter Band; Tom Rush; Poco; Dreams; Big Brother & Holding Co.; Miles Davis; Spirit; It's a Beautiful Day; Chambers Brothers; Laura Nyro; Ballinjack; N.Y. Rock & Roll Ensemble; Hollies; Redbone; Elvin Bishop; Fraser & DeBolt; Bill Puka; Soft Machine; Flock.

Dig This .... Columbia (EP) AS-1 5-10 70
(Promotional issue only; 7 inch, 33 rpm.) Pacific Gas & Electric; Moondog; Nick Gravenites; Pete Seeger; Santana; New Don Ellis Band; Raven; Firesign Theatre; Tony Kosi.

Dig This .... Columbia (EP) AS-3 5-10 70
(Promotional issue only; 7 inch, 33 rpm.) Carl Perkins & NRBQ; Electric Lucifer; Good News; Tom Rush; Illinois Speed Press; Bobby Lester.

Diggin' Out....................Mr. Manicotti (M) MM-329 5-10 80s
Illusions; Vistas; Avengers; Dave & Customs; Nation Rockin'; Shadows; Newport Nomads; Goldtones; Chevells; Progressives; Gestics; Phantoms; Irridescents; New Dimensions; Tommy & Hustlers; Lonely Ones.

Dimension Dolls: see COOKIES / Little Eva / Carole King

Dimensions....................K-Tel (S) TU 2900 5-10 81
Juice Newton; Rick Springfield; Billy Squier; Pat Benatar; Climax Blues Band; Gary Wright; Manhattan Transfer; Hall & Oates; Greg Kihn Band; Pablo Cruise; Air Supply; Alan Parsons Project; Stars on 45; Oak Ridge Boys.

Dimensions in Dynagroove ....RCA (S) PRS 180 5-10 65
Sid Ramin; Melachrino Strings; Si Zentner; Marty Gold; Frankie Carle; Hugo Montenegro; Norman Luboff Choir; Morton Gould; Robert Brereton; Arthur Fiedler & Boston Pops; Boston Symphony. (Made for RCA's Solid State Stereo.)

Diner....................Elektra (S) E1-60107E (2 LP) 10-15 82
(Soundtrack.) Elvis Presley; Jerry Lee Lewis; Dion & Belmonts; Heartbeats; Eddie Cochran; Carl Perkins; Fleetwoods; Lowell Fulson; Clarence Henry; Del-Vikings; Bobby Darin; Jane Morgan; Dick Haymes; Tommy Edwards; Fats Domino; Jimmy Reed; Jack Scott.

Direct Hits....................Columbia (S) C-30603 5-10 71
Mashmakhan; Mark Lindsay; Ronnie Dyson; Chambers Brothers; Hollies; Pacific Gas & Electric; Byrds; Santana; Christie; Blood, Sweat & Tears.

Dirty Dancing....................RCA Victor (S) 6408-1 8-10 87

Dirty Dancing.................... RCA Victor (S) R-8209 5-8 Re

Dirty Dancing, Vol. 2 (More Dirty Dancing)....................RCA Victor (S) 695-1 8-10 88

Dirty Dancing, Vol. 2 (More Dirty Dancing).................... RCA Victor (S) ST-46 8-10 Re
(Soundtrack.) Ronettes; Patrick Swayze; Maurice Williams & Zodiacs; Merry Clayton; Blow Monkeys; Bruce Channel; Mickey & Sylvia; Zappacosta; Tom Johnson; Five Satins; Bill Medley; Jennifer Warnes.

Disco Boogie, Vol. 1 ....Salsoul (S) 0101 5-10 78

Disco Boogie, Vol. 2....................Salsoul (S) 0102 5-10 78
Double Exposure; Claudia Barry; Salsoul Orch.; Silvetti; others.

Disco Express, Vol. 1 .... RCA (S) APL1-1401 5-10 76
Blood Hollins; Jean Lang; Main Ingredient; Labelle; Sunny Gale; others.

Disco Fever .... Ronco (M) R-2180 5-10 78
(Mail order offer.) Donna Summer; Johnny Taylor; Thelma Houston; Walter Murphy; Gloria Gaynor; Andrea True Connection; Maxine Nightingale; Labelle; Silver Convention; Ritchie Family; George McCrae; Hues Corporation; Vicki Sue Robinson; Gladys Knight & Pips; Wild Cherry; Van McCoy; Salsoul Orchestra; Shirley & Co.

Disco Fire (2 LP) ....K-Tel (S) TU-2590 8-12 78
Chic; Meco; Barry White; Stargard; C.J. & Co.; T.H.P. Orchestra; Donna Summer; Parliament; KC & Sunshine Band; Rhythm Heritage; Samantha Sang; Eruption; Trammps; Brick; Bionic Boogie; Jimmie "Bo" Horne; Santa Esmeralda; Emotions; Roy Ayers; Boney M; Tuxedo Junction; Michael Zager Band; Peter Brown.

Disco Funk .... RCA (S) ANL1-1118 5-10 75
Brother Soul; Lillian Hale; T.C.B.; Madeira; People; others.

Disco Gold.................... Scepter (S) 5120 5-10 75

Disco Hustle (2 LP) ....Adam VIII (S) A 8029 8-12 76
Donna Summer; Andrea True Connection; Silver Convention; Gary Toms Empire; Ecstacy, Passion & Pain; D.C. Larue; Melba Moore; Crown Heights Affair; Brothers; Yambu; Moments of Truth; Salsoul Orchestra; Softones; Carol Williams; Louis Ramirez; Ritchie Family; Frankie Avalon; Gloria Gaynor; Vicki Sue Robinson; Richael Zager's Moon Band; Pat Lundy.

Disco Mania....................K-Tel (S) TU 2410 5-10 75
Van McCoy & Soul City Symphony; Blackbyrds; Gwen McCrae; Sugarloaf; Disco Tex & Sex-O-Lettes; Stylistics; Hot Chocolate; Bachman-Turner Overdrive; Gloria Gaynor; Carol Douglas; Shirley & Company; Carl Douglas; Kool & Gang; Billy Preston; George McCrae; Jim Gilstrap; Hues Corporation; Kiss; B.T. Express.

Disco Motion.................... Commonwealth (S) TU 2540 5-10 77
(Mail order offer.) Andrea True Connection; Salsoul Orchestra; Ritchie Family; Gwen McCrae; Kool & Gang; Walter Murphy Band; KC & Sunshine Band; George McCrae; Crown Heights Affair; Flash Cadillac & Continental Kids; Ecstacy, Passion & Pain.

Disco Nights ......K-Tel (S) TU 2610 5-10 79
Chanson; Evelyn "Champagne" King; Peter Brown; Foxy; Len Boone; Cissy Houston; Village People; Rick James; KC & Sunshine Band; Lenny Williams; Andy Gibb; Sylvester.
Disco Party ......Marlin (S) 2207/2208 5-10 78
T-Connection; Ritchie Family; Foxy; George McCrae; Peter Brown; Eli's Second Coming; KC & Sunshine Band; Ralph McDonald; Celi Bee; Jimmy Bo Horne; Betty Wright.
Disco Party ......Adam VIII (S) A-8021 5-10 75
(Mail order offer.) Van McCoy & Soul City Symphony; Stylistics; Gloria Gaynor; Hues Corporation; Shirley & Company; Barry White; Carol Douglas; George McCrae; Bachman-Turner Overdrive; Paper Lace; Rufus; Main Ingredient; Carl Carlton; Moment of Turth; Ecstasy, Passion & Pain; Love Child's Afro Cuban Blues Band; Three Degrees; Styx; Chi-lites; Gladys Knight & Pips.
Disco Party ......Profile (S) PRO-12001 5-10 83
Class Action; Sharon Redd; Sinnamon; Man Parrish; Margie Joseph; Rockers Revenge; Donnie Calvin; Sharon Brown; Toney Lee; Forrest; Menage.
Disco Par-r-r-ty ......Spring (S) SPR 6705 5-10 75
Lyn Collins; Millie Jackson; Fred Wesley & JB's; Main Streeters; Maceo & Macks; Joe Simon; Act I; Chakachas; Mandrill; Peppers; James Brown; Hank Ballard & Midnighters; Timmy Thomas; Barry White.
Disco Rocket (2 LP) ......K-Tel (S) TU 2570 5-10 78
Wild Cherry; Andrea True Connection; Tavares; Eddie Kendricks; Normon Conners; Addrisi Brothers; Rose Royce; Melba Moore; Supremes; Timmy Thomas; Salsoul Orchestra; KC & Sunshine Band; Wilton Place Street Band; T-Connection; Miracles; Celi Bee & Buzzy Bunch; Sylvers; George McCree; Bebu Silvetti; Diana Ross; Kebekelektric; Originals.
Disco Rocket, Vol. 2 (2 LP) ......K-Tel (S) TU 2572 5-10 78
Disco Spectacular (Inspired By the Film *Hair*) ......RCA (S) 3356 5-10 79
Evelyn King; Vicki Sue Robinson; others.
Disco Teen '66......Columbia (M) D-155 10-20 66
Disco Teen '66......Columbia (S) DS-155 10-20 66
(Columbia Record Club issue.) Paul Revere & Raiders; Simon & Garfunkel; Bob Dylan; Dave Clark Five; Bobby Vinton; Ventures; Cyrkle; Billy Joe Royal; Major Lance; Chad & Jeremy; Byrds; Yardbirds.
Disco Tex & Sex-O-Lettes Review ......Chelsea (S) 505 10-15 75
Disco Tex & Sex-O-Lettes; Chocolate Kisses; Lu Ann Simms; Freddie Cannon; Jam Band; others.
Disco Trek ......Atlantic (S) SD 18158 8-12 76
Blue Magic; Sister Sledge; Jackie Moore; Valentinos; Sons of Robin Stone; Clyde Brown; Sweet Inspirations; United Eight.
Discomania 2......Juke Box Int'l (S) TVLP-177601 5-10 76
(Mail order offer.) Donna Summer; Ohio Players; Esther Phillips; Johnny Bristol; Hot Cocholate; Labelle; Ralph Carter; Carl Carlton; Silver Convention; Crown Heights Affair; Moment of Truth; South Shore Commission; Gloria Gaynor; Al Downing; Stylistics; B.T. Express; Bimbo Jet; Pete Wingfield.
Disco-Ring, Vol. 1 ......Virgin (S) VD1 101 8-12 80s
Culture Club; Heaven 17; I Level; Simple Minds; Human League; Toto Coelo; Devo; Orchestral Manoeuvers in the Dark; Toni Basil.
Discotech Vol. 1 ......Motown (S) M6-824 8-12 75
Stevie Wonder; Martha & Vandellas; Jr. Walker & All Stars; Gladys Knight & Pips; Spinners; Temptations; Jackson Five; Marvin Gaye; Eddie Kendricks; Supremes; Shorty Long; Miracles.
Discotech Vol. 2 ......Motown (S) M6-831 8-12 75
Commodores; Temptations; Eddie Kendricks; Supremes; Jackson Five; Undisputed Truth; Rare Earth; Gladys Knight; Willie Hutch; G.C. Cameron; Miracles.
Discotheque Au Go Go ......Design (M) DLP-194 10-20 64
Johnny Rivers; Betty Everett; Roy Orbison; Johnny Cymbal; Don Covay; Irma Thomas; Clovers; Paragons; Tommy Roe; Gene Pitney.
Discotheque Dance Album......Command (M) R-892 5-10 66
Discotheque Dance Album......Command (S) RS-892 5-10 66
Tony Mottola; Dick Hyman; Doc Severinsom; Bob Haggard; others.
Discotheque Dance Music......Columbia Special Products (EP) 10-20 60s
(7-inch 33 RPM EP.) Dutones; Ernie Heckscher; Dreamlovers; Aretha Franklin; Ray Conniff; Lester Lanin. (Made for Wurlitzer.)
Discotheque in Astrosound ......Clarion (M) 509 30-40 66
Discotheque in Astrosound ......Clarion (S) 509 50-60 66
Beatles with Tony Sheridan; Ray Charles; Swallows; LaVern Baker; Bobby Darin; Carl Holmes & Commanders; Chris Kenner; Ben E. King; Drifters; Rene Bloch.
Discotheque Jet Set, Vol. 2 ......Audio Fidelity (S) DFS-7040 15-25
Jim Messina & Jesters; others.
Discotheque with the Stars......Wyncote (M) W-9125 10-15 64
Discotheque with the Stars......Wyncote (S) SW-9125 10-15 64
Chubby Checker; Bobby Rydell; Dee Dee Sharp; Orlons; Dovells; Tymes.
Disorderlies ......Tin Pan Apple (S) 833274-1 8-10 87
(Soundtrack.) Fat Boys; Bananarama; Latin Rascals; Cashflow; Anita; Bon Jovi; Art of Noise; Tom Kimmel; Gwen Guthrie; Laura Hunter.
Dixieland......Goltentone (M) C 4021 8-12
Matty Matlock & His Dixie-Men; Morty Corb & His Dixie All Stars; Pee Wee Hunt.
Dixieland All Stars ......Audio Lab (M) AL 1509 10-20
Billy Butterfield; others.
Dixieland Classics ......Jazztone (M) J-1216 20-25 50s
Eddie Condon; Jam Session with Bobby Hackett; George Brunies; Pee Wee Russell; Bud Freeman; Jess Stacy; Artie Shapiro; George Wettling.
Dixieland Now &n ......Jazztone (M) J1241 20-35 56
Jimmy McPartland's Chicago Rompers; Paul Barbarin's New Orleans Stompers; others.
Dixieland Sampler ......Riverside (M) S-1 10-20
(Promotional issue only. Possibly issued without custom cover.) Tony Parenti; Wild Bill Davison; Red Onion Jazz Band; Bob Helm; Ralph Sutton; Lu Watters; Sidney Bechet; Joe Sullivan; George Lewis; Dixieland Rhythm Kings; Dick Wellstood; Yank Lawson.
Dixieland Swing & All That Jazz ......RCA (M) PRM 178 10-20 65
Louis Armstrong; Mildred Bailey; Count Basie; Sidney Bechet; Tex Beneke; Bunny Berigan; Nat Cole; Tommy Dorsey; Duke Ellington; Ziggy Elman; Benny Goodman; Lionel Hampton; Coleman Hawkins; Al Hibbler; Billie Holiday; Jimmy McPartland; Glenn Miller; King Oliver; Tony Pastor; Ben Pollack; Buddy Rich; Artie Shaw; Art Tatum; Fats Waller; Metronome All Stars.
(Produced for Barrett Division of Allied Chemical.)

Do It Now - 20 Giant Hits .... Ronco LP-1001 10-20 70
(Yellow label.) Beatles; Neil Diamond; Janis Joplin; Jimi Hendrix; Melanie; Richie Havens; Donovan; Jefferson Airplane; Eric Burdon; Association; Ides of March; B.J. Thomas; Teagarden & Van Winkle; Byrds; Crazy Elephant; Five Stairsteps; Mel & Tim; Buffalo Springfield; Turtles; Steam.

Do It Now - 20 Giant Hits .... Ronco LP-1001 10-15 70
(Green label.) Beatles; Neil Diamond; Janis Joplin; Jimi Hendrix; Melanie; Richie Havens; Donovan; Jefferson Airplane; Eric Burdon; Association; Ides of March; B.J. Thomas; Teagarden & Van Winkle; Byrds; Crazy Elephant; Five Stairsteps; Mel & Tim; Buffalo Springfield; Turtles; Steam.

Do It With Music .... Decca (M) DL 34106 10-15
Peggy Lee; Steve Lawrence; Eydie Gorme; Ames Brothers; Theresa Brewer; McGuire Sisters; Lawrence Welk; Tommy Dorsey Orchestra with Warren Covington; Liberace; Carmen Cavallaro; Les Brown; Henry Jerome.

Do the Right Thing .... Motown (S) MOT-6272 10-15 89
(Soundtrack.) Public Enemy; Teddy Riley; EU; Steel Pulse; Perri; Take 6; Keith John; Al Jarreau; Ruben Blades.

Dr. Demento's Delights .... Warner Bros. (S) BS-2855 8-12 75
Allan Sherman; Possum; Spike Jones; Jim Kweskin Jug Band; Napoleon XIV; Holy Modal Rounders; Ben Gay & Silly Savages; Harry Gibson; Jef Jaison; Doodles Weaver; Robert Crumb.

Dr. Demento's Dementia Royale .... Rhino (S) RNLP-010 5-10 80
Toons; Barnes & Barnes; Yiddish People; "Weird Al" Yankovic; Damaskas; Scott Beach; Fred Blassie; Ruth Wallis; Red Bovine; Mark Zydiak; Wild Man Fisher; Bobby Pickett; Peter Ferrara; Dr. Demento.

Dr. Demento's Mementos .... Eccentric (M) PVC-8912 8-12 82
(Standard LP.) Dr. Demento; Barnes & Barnes; John W. Christensen; Tim Cavanagh; Carlos Borzenie, Sr.; Other Half; Uncle Vic; Showdown; Purvis; Pickett & Punk-a-billies; Three Stooges; Steve Lisenby; Dickie Goodman; Gary Muller; Doug Robinson; Tom Fenton & Ice-Nine; Travesty Ltd.; Jason & Strap-Tones.

Dr. Demento's Mementos .... Eccentric (M) PVC-8912 12-18 82
(Picture disc.)

Dr. Demento's Mementos .... Eccentric (M) PVC-8912 20-25 82
(Promotional picture disc, with KMET logo on back.)

Doctor Detroit .... Backstreet (S) 6120 8-10 83
(Soundtrack.) Dan Aykroyd; Devo; T. Carter; James Brown; Pattie Brooks; others.

Doctor Goldfoot & Girl Bombs .... Tower (M) T-5053 12-15 66

Doctor Goldfoot & Girl Bombs .... Tower (SE) DT-5053 15-25 66
(Soundtrack.) Sloopys; Mad Doctors; Terry Stafford; Bobby Lile; Paul & Pack; Candles.

$ (Dollars) .... Reprise (S) MS-2051 8-12 71
(Soundtrack.) Quincy Jones; Little Richard; Doug Kershaw; Roberta Flack; Don Elliott Voices.

Don Bombard Presents: see Pittsburgh's Hall of Fame

Don't Knock the Twist .... Parkway (M) P-7011 20-40 62
(Soundtrack.) Chubby Checker; Dovells; Carroll Brothers; Dee Dee Sharp.

Doo Wop .... Specialty (S) SPS-2114 15-25 68
(Gatefold cover.) Chimes; Monitors; Larry Williams; Vernon Green & Phantoms; Jesse & Marvin; Marvin & Johnny; Four Flames; Roddy Jackson; Bob "Froggy" Landers & Willie Joe; Roy Montrell; Jimmy Liggins & His 3-D Music; King Perry & His Pied Pipers; Rene Hall; Joe Lutcher.

Doo Wop, Vol. I .... Classic Artists (S) 3055 8-10
Earl Lewis & Channels; Herb Cox & Cleftones; Arthur Lee Maye; Vocaleers; Johnny Staton & Feathers; Richard Blandon & Dubs; Leon Peels & Bluejays; Jaguars & Charles Middleton; Calvanes; Wrens & Bobby Mansfield; Vernon Green & Medallions; Storytellers.

Doo Wop Ballads .... Rhino (M) RNLP-70181 5-10 87
Five Satins; Dells; Crests; Jive Five; Passions; Dion & Belmonts; Moonglows; Jerry Butler & Impressions; Penguins; Blue Jays; Rosie & Originals; Tune Weavers; Mello-Kings; Spaniels.

Doo Wop Ballads, Vol. 2 .... Rhino (M) R1-70904 5-10 89
Flamingos; Cadillacs; Clovers; Dion & Belmonts; Velvetones; Heartbeats; Shep & Limelites; Lee Andrews & Hearts; Pastels; Jive Five; Safaris; Skyliners; Danleers; Harvey & Moonglows.

Doo-Wop Christmas Album (and a Happy New Year!) .... Promotional (M) PRX-100 10-20 80s
(Limited numbered edition, 500 made. "Promotional" is the label name.) Uniques; Four Pennies; Falcons; Penguins; Melodeers; Shantons; Dynamics; Lonnie & Crisis; Martels.

Doo Wop Delights .... Savoy Jazz (M) SJL-1185 8-12
Falcons; Gaylords; Wanderers; Dreams; Roamers; Debutantes; Playmates; Cubs; Billy Nelson & Five Wings; Temptations.

Doo Wop Diner, Vol. II .... Classic Artists (S) 3056 8-10
Wrens & Bobby Mansfield; Earl Lewis & Channels; George Grant & Castelles; Storytellers; Arhur Lee Maye; Margo Sylvia & Tuneweavers; Leon Peel & Bluejays; Richard Blandon & Dubs; Herb Cox & Cleftones; Jaguars & Val Poliuto; Rudy West & Five Keys; Don Julian & Meadowlarks; Johnny Staton & Feathers; Vernon Green & Medallions.

Doo Wop Gold, Vol. 1 (2 LP) .... Rare Bird (S) ???? 8-12

Doo Wop Honor Roll of Girl Names .... Adam & Eve (S) 502 8-10 80s
Sunsets; Fabulous Four; Impalas; Treble-chords; Mon-vales; Vibraharps; Little Julian Herrera & Tigers; Trade & Tantones; Vitells; Tim Tam & Turn-ons; Fiestas; Frank Lopez & Travelers; Chancers; Saucers.

Doo Wop Rock (3 LP) .... WCI (S) UR-520 10-15 86
Moonglows; Don & Juan; Diamonds; Crew-Cuts; Monotones; Regents; Platters; Skyliners; Marcels; Dion; Cleftones; Penguins; Crystals; Drifters; Dovells; Chantels; Bobbettes; Fiestas; Ad Libs; Del-Vikinggs; Olympics; Elegants; Danny & Juniors; Little Caesar & Romans; Capris; Crests; Duprees; Belmonts; Jarmels; Jive Five; Clovers; Innocents; Jay Black; Fleetwoods.

Doo Wop Uptempo .... Rhino (M) RNLP-70182 5-10 87
Del-Vikings; Edsels; El Dorados; Willows; Hollywood Flames; Dion & Belmonts; Vito & Salutations; Monotones; Silhouettes; Turbans; Elegants; Crests; Tokens.

Doo Woppin' the Blues .... Rarin' (M) 777 8-12
Dozier Boys; Larks; Clouds; Moonlights; Arbee Stidham & Group; Leon Tarver & Cordones.

Doo Wops Greatest Hits (Vee Jay Presents) .... Vee Jay (S) VJLP 1144 5-10 86
Jerry Butler & Impressions; El Dorados; Dells; Spaniels; Magnificents; Flamingos; Moonglows; Gladys Knight & Pips; Gene Chandler.

Double Golden (OR-FM) .... Post (S) 987 10-15 68
Association; Five Satins; Sam & Dave; Bob Lind; Angels; Crests; Keith; Mello Kings; Lovin' Spoonful; Ritchie Valens; Eddie Floyd; Shirelles; Del Shannon; Gene Chandler; Tommy Edwards; McCoys; Rays; Cascades; Dixie Cups; Critters; Dubs; Dion & Belmonts; Freddy Scott; Penguins; Happenings; Jimmy Charles; Ad Libs; Little Caesar & Romans; Duprees; Bobby Hebb.

Down a Country Road ....Columbia Musical Treasury (SE) 1P 6112 5-10 75
(Columbia House Record Club issue.) Tanya Tucker; Mac Davis; Tammy Wynette; Jody Miller; Charlie Rich; Roger Miller; Lynn Anderson; Ray Price; Flatt & Scruggs; Freddy Weller.
Down and Out in Beverly Hills ....MCA (S) MCA-6160 8-10 87
(Soundtrack.) Little Richard; David Lee Roth; Mariachi Vargas de Tecalitian; Randy Newman.
Down Home Gospel (2 LP) .... Fairway (S) ???? 5-10 77
(Mail order offer.) Marty Robbins; Tammy Wynette; Bill Monroe & Bluegrass Boys; Statler Brothers; Anita Bryant; Ray Price; Burl Ives; Johnny Cash; Andy Griffith; Flatt & Scruggs; Roy Acuff; Little Jimmy Dickens; Andy Griffith; Jim Nabors; David Houston; Carter Family; Stonewall Jackson; Sonny James.
Down Home Stomp: see Rural Blues, Vol. 3
Down South Summit Meeting ....World Pacific (M) WP-1296 15-20 60
Down South Summit Meeting ....World Pacific (S) ST-1296 20-25 60
Sonny Terry; Brownie McGhee; Lightnin' Hopkins; Joe Williams.
Do-Wop Gold, Vol. 1 ....Laurie (S) LES-4014 8-10 79
Vito & Salutations; Carlo; Mystics; Passions; Del Satins; DeMilles; Del Rons; Dion & Belmonts; Music Explosion; Five Discs; Dino & Diplomats; Barbarians.
Do-Wop Gold, Vol. 2 ....Laurie (S) LES-4017 8-10 79
Curtis Lee; Chiffons; Dion; Del Satins; Mystics; Dean & Jean; Ernie Maresca; Passions; Randy & Rainbows; Belmonts; Dion & Belmonts; Jarmels; Four Pennies; Ray Vons; Four Epics; Skyliners.
Do-Wop Gold, Vol. 3 ....Laurie (S) LES-4025 8-10 79
Chiffons; Carlo; Jimmy Clanton; Dino & Diplomats; 1929 Depression; Ernie Maresca; Dion & Belmonts; Mystics; Dean & Jean; Five Discs.
D'oze Crazy Oldies .... Oldies 33 (M) OL-8007 15-20 64
Ray Stevens; Little Anthony & Imperials; Hollywood Argyles; Playmates; Turbans; Cadets; John Zacherle; Bop- Chords; Cadillacs; John Lee Hooker; Collegians.
Dragnet (1987) ....MCA (S) MCA-6210 10-15 87
(Soundtrack.) Patti LaBelle; Dan Aykroyd; Tom Hanks; Art of Noise; New Edition; Peter Aykroyd; Pat Thrall; Ira Newborn.
Dream a Little Dream ....Cypress (S) YL9-0125 8-10 89
(Soundtrack.) Mike Reno; R.E.M.; Michael Damian; Fee Waybill; Chris Thompson; Otis Redding.
Dreamin' .... I&M (S) 1-012 5-10 79
Samatha Sang; Dan Hill; Gladys Knight & Pips; David Soul; Paul Anka; Kenny Nolan; Atlanta Rhythm Section; Mary MacGregor; Jessi Colter; Roberta Flack; Dorothy Moore; Spinners; Peter McCann; Eric Carmen; Jennifer Warnes; LeBlanc & Carr; England Dan & John Ford Coley; Hall & Oates.
Dreams (60 Songs of Love) (6 LP) ....Columbia (S) 6P 7033 20-30
(Boxed set.)
Drugstore Cowboy ....Novus (S) 3077-1-N9 8-10
(Soundtrack.) Bobby Goldsboro; Abbey Lincoln; Jackie De Shannon; John Fred; Desmond Dekker & Aces; others.
Drummin' the Blues .... Liberty (M) RLP-3064 30-50 57
Drumology ....RCA (EP) EPAT 437 10-15
Drums, the (3 LP) .... ABC Impulse (S) ASH 9272-3 10-20
(Boxed set.)
Dueling Banjos ....Pickwick (S) SPC 3340 8-12 73
Bob & Sam Springer; Flatt & Scruggs; Stanley Brothers; John Duffy & Country Gentlemen; Bill Emerson & His Country Banjo.
Duet Country .... Chart (S) 1014 5-10 69
Lynn Anderson & Jerry Lane; Gordon Terry & Maxine Brown; Kenny Vernon & Lawanda Lindsey; others.
Duke Ellington & Others ....Guest Star (M) 1427 10-15
Duke Ellington; Lionel Hampton; Art Mooney; Ray Bloch; Johnny Long.
Duke's Hand .... Epic (EP) EG 7104 10-15
Dukes of Hazzard ....Scotti Bros. (S) FZ-37712 15-25 82
(Soundtrack.) Catherine Bach; James Best; Johnny Cash; Sorrell Booke; Doug Kershaw; John Schneider; Tom Wopat; Hazzard County Boys.
Dunwich Story ....Voxx 200063 5-10 90s
Duophonic Story ....Capitol (S) PRO 1836 10-15
Dusty and Sweets McGee .... Warner Bros. (S) WS-1936 15-20 71
(Soundtrack.) Van Morrison; Monotones; Marcels; Gene Chandler; Del Shannon; Little Eva; Blues Image; Bruce Channel; Jimmy Forest; Harry Nilsson; Jake Holmes.
Dutch Explosion ....White Whale (S) WW-7130 15-25 70
Dynamic Sound .... K-Tel (S) TU-235 5-10 74
Bachman-Turner Overdrive; Gladys Knight & Pips; DeFranco Family; Ronny Dyson; Moments; Mocedades; Stylistics; First Choice; Incredible Bongo Band; Chi-Lites; Wednesday; Love Unlimited; Donny Osmond; Tom T. Hall; Five Man Electrical Band; James Brown; Dobie Gray; Marie Osmond; Bill Amesbury; Looking Glass; Helen Reddy; Dawn with Tony Orlando.
Dynamite: see 20 Original Hits, 20 Original Stars
Dynamite ....K-Tel (S) TU 236 5-10 74
Paper Lace; Bachman-Turner Overdrive; Nazareth; William DeVaughn; Eric Clapton; Kool & Gang; Stealers Wheel; Albert Hammond; George McCrae; Elton John; Terry Jacks; Rick Derringer; Peter Noone; DeFranco Family; Lobo; Sister Janet Mead; Love Unlimited Orchestra; Al Wilson; Gladys Knight & Pips; Stylistics.
Dynamite Country Duets (Nashville's Best Songs/Performances) ....Harmony (SP) KH-32479 5-10 73
Johnny Cash & June Carter; Tammy Wynette & George Jones; Carl & Pearl Butler; Agnes & Orville; Lynn Anderson & Glenn Sutton; Johnny Duncan & June Stearns; Arlene Harden & Frank Jones; George Morgan & Marion Worth; Jody Miller & Johnny Paycheck; David Houston & Barbara Mandrell.
Dynamite Instrumentals .... Exact (S) EX-210 5-10 80
B. Bumble & Stingers; Chantays; Duane Eddy; Preston Epps; Surfaris; Bill Black's Combo; Bill Justis; Bill Pursell.
Dynamite Doo-Wops, Vol. 1 .... No Label Name (S) D-1101 8-12 70s
Capitols; Logics; Pretenders; Dino Matthews; Extremes; Freddy Schaefer; Tony Lamar; Joey & Teenagers; Blue Lights; Roulettes; Cordials; Rick & Masters; Nick & Nacks; Del-Aires; Videls; Tri-Tones; Tex & Chex; Spirals.
Dynamite Doo Wops, Vol. 2 .... No Label Name (S) D-1002 8-12 70s
Three Friends; Raindrops; Jimmy Jones & Jones Boys; Calendars; Hi Tensions; Upfronts; Caleb & Playboys; Temptations; Five Chestnuts; Memories; Gabriel & Angels; Bel-Larks; Catalinas; Squires; Joey Dee & Starliters; Montereys; Profiles; Five Trojans.

Dynamite Doo-Wops, Vol. 3 .... No Label Name (S) D-1103 8-12 70s
Farris Hill & Madison Brothers; Johnny Darling & Hurricanes; Little Clydie & Teens; Universals; Carter Rays; Georgia Harris & Hy-Tones; Masters; Yachtsmen; Velons; Billy the Kid; Supremes; Larry Lee & Four Bel-Aires; Gothics; Velvet Keys; Four Cheers; Danny Winchel & Ebb Tides; Gallahads; Enchantments.

Dynamite Doo-Wops, Vol. 4 .... No Label Name (S) D-1104 8-12 79
Viscayayanes; Corvells; Wheels; Belvederes; Elroy & Excitements; Infatuators; Vampires; Note-Torials; Parktowns; Holidays; Classic IV; Gothics; Del Shays; Uniques; Magnets; Markels.

Dynamite Doo-Wops, Vol. 5 .... No Label Name (S) D-1105 8-12 80s
Creations; Uniques; Gales; Swinging Hearts; Convincers; Stringbeans; Four Horsemen; Wanderers; Elements; Accents; Dicky Doyle & Casualaires; Chateaus; Whalers; Lovers.

Dynamite Doo-Wops, Vol. 6 .... No Label Name (S) D-1106 8-12 86
Sedates; Tabs; Bill Baker; Esquires; Castaleers; Individuals; Starlighters; Chimes; Elgins; Fairlanes; Dovers; Holidays; Danny Zip & Zippers; Extremes; David Winters; Disires; Raindrops; Fabulous Four.

Dynamite Doo-Wops, Vol. 7 .... No Label Name (S) D-1107 8-12 92
Norvells; Initials; Classicals; Fabulous Valients; Lucien Farrar & Lifesavers; Eddie Williams & Group; Tytones; Montereys; Hi-Tones; Sunny & Horizons; Re-Vels; Bobby Starr & Group; Darts; Chanticleers; Star Steppers; Leroy Parker & Group; Magics.

EMI America — Various Artists .... EMI America (S) SPRO 9078 5-10
(Promotional issue only.) Kate Bush; Dwight Twilley; Elbow Bones & Racketeers; Via Afrika; Jon St. James; Great White; Jason & Scorchers; Kim Carnes; Jules Shear; Talk Talk.

ESP Sampler ESP-1051 8-10

E-Z Country Programming, No. 2 .... RCA (M) No. 2 250-300 55
(10–inch LP. Promotional issue only. Not issued with special cover.) Elvis Presley; Eddy Arnold; Nita, Rita & Ruby; Chet Atkins; Hank Snow; Sons of the Pioneers; Anita Carter; Skeeter Brown; Homer & Jethro; Hank Locklin; Stuart Hamblen.

E-Z Country Programming, No. 3 .... RCA (M) No. 3 250-300 55
(10–inch LP. Promotional issue only. Not issued with special cover.) Elvis Presley; Eddy Arnold; Chet Atkins; Hank Snow; Hawkshaw Hawkins; Johnnie, & Jack & Ruby Wells; Jim Reeves; Dorothy Olsen; Porter Wagoner.

E-Z Pop Programming - You Can't Have Too Many Hits! .... RCA (M) No Number Used 15-25 55
(Promotional issue only. Not issued with special cover.) Eddie Fisher; Perry Como; Jaye P. Morgan; Henri Rene; Ertha Kitt; Kay Starr; Vaughn Monroe; Lou Monte; LaFalce Brothers.

E-Z Pop Programming, No. 5 .... RCA (M) No. 5 250-300 55
(Promotional issue only. Not issued with special cover.) Elvis Presley; Eddie Fisher; Dinah Shore; Rhythmettes; Jaye P. Morgan; Vaughn Monroe; Kay Starr; Henri Rene; Mike Pedicin; Perry Como; Eddy Arnold; Chet Atkins.

E-Z Pop Programming, No. 6 .... RCA (M) No. 6 250-300 55
(10–inch LP. Promotional issue only. Not issued with special cover.) Elvis Presley; Julius La Rosa; Teddi King; Billy Eckstine; Ames Brothers; Jaye P. Morgan; Eddy Arnold; Perry Como; Dorothy Olsen; Singing Dogs.

Eagle .... Condor (S) 100A 5-10
Lou Christie; Leslie Gore; Thee Midnighters; Lovin' Spoonful; Shirelles; Essex; Shelly Fabares; Left Banke; Gary Lewis; Cookies; Peggy March; Chiffons; Cyrkle; Johnny Rivers; Little Eva; Jeannie C. Riley; Cascades; Vibrations.

Early and Rare .... Riverside (M) 134 20-25 60
Jelly Roll Morton; Ma Rainer; Fats Waller; others.

Early Bones (2 LP) .... Prestige (S) P 24067 10-20

Early Chicago, Vol. 1 .... Happy Tiger (S) 1017 10-15 71
Mauds; American Breed; De-Vetts; Shadows of Knight; George Edwards & Friends; Cryan' Shames; Flock; Saturday's Children; Trolls; H.P. Lovecraft; Little Boy Blues. Rovin' Kind.

Early Country Music .... Historical (S) 2 8-10 67
Joe Evans; John Dilleshaw; Hap Hayes; others.

Early Jazz Greats .... Jazztone (M) J 1249 15-25 56
Sidney Bechet; Original Dixieland Jazz Band; Jelly Roll Morton; Johnny Dodds; King Oliver; Jean Goldkette with Bix Beiderbecke; Mound City Blue Blowers; Earl Hines; Mezz Mezzrow; Jimmy Yancy; Joe Venute & Eddie Lang; Napolean's Emperors.

Early L.A. (Archive Series, Vol. 4) .... Together (S) ST-T-1014 10-15
Leadbelly; Dino Valente; Hoyt Axton; Ray Charles; Jim McGuinn & Gene Clark; Ruth Talley; Gene Clark; Dillard & Martin; Canned Heat.

Early Rural String Bands .... Victor (M) LPV-552 8-10 68

Early '60s: see These Were Our Songs

Earth Angel .... Guest Star (M) G 1432 10-20 60s

Earth Angel .... Guest Star (SE) GS 1432 10-20 60s
Penguins; Dave "Baby" Cortez; Monarchs; Medallions; Paragons; Inspirations; Willows; Bob Crewe; Eternals; Meadowlarks.

Earth Girls Are Easy .... Sire/Reprise (S) 25835 8-10 89
(Soundtrack.) Darryl Hall; John Oates; Royalty; Information Society; Jill Jones; "N"; B-52s; Depeche Mode; Jesus & Mary Chain; Stewart Copeland; Julie Brown.

East and West of Jazz .... MGM/Charlie Parker (S) PLP-805 15-20 62
Sadim Hakim; Duke Jordan; others.

East Memphis Music - Hits from the Stax Era .... Irving (S) EM-50009 15-25 84
(Promotional issue only. Irving Music Publishing sampler.) Otis Redding; Al Green; Luther Ingram; Carla Thomas; Sam & Dave; Shirley Brown; Ann Peebles; Eddie Floyd; Aretha Franklin; Staple Singers; Wilson Pickett; Booker T. & MGs; Isaac Hayes; Johnny Taylor.

East Side Revue (1963-1965) .... Rampart (S) 3303 20-30 66
Cannibal & Headhunters; Premiers; Blendells; Jaguars; others.

East Side Revue (1965-1968) .... Rampart (S) ???? 20-30 69
(Multi-colored vinyl.)

East Side Revue (1965-1968) .... Rampart (S) 3305 15-25 69
(Includes 24" x 30" color poster. Multi-color vinyl.) Village Callers; Thee Royal Checkmates; Aldermen; Premiers; Thee Epics; Back Seat; Sammy Lee & Summits; Thee Flurtations; Sunday Funnies; Romancers; Little Ray; David & Ruben; Thee Runabouts; Thee Impalas; Pagents; Salas Brothers with the Jaguars; Thee Ambertones; East Side Kids; Thee Midniters.

East Side Story, Vol. 1 .... East Side (S) LP 2001 8-12 70s
Tony Allen; Thee Midniters; Johnny & Express; Sunny & Sunliners; Intruders; Shirley & Lee; Larks; Chantels; Van McCoy; Persuaders; Players.

East Side Story, Vol. 2 .... East Side (S) LP 2002 8-12 70s
Sunny; Little Royal; Lloyd Price; Don & Juan; Chantels; Notations; Thee Midniters; Shirelles; Brenda & Tabulations; Orlons; Donnie Elbert; Shells.

East Side Story, Vol. 3 .... East Side (S) LP 2003 8-12 70s
Frankie Karl; Thee Midniters; Crests; Sunglows; Shirelles; Billy Stewart; Shields; Etta James; Brenda & Tabulations; Delfonics; Robert & Johnny; Lovelites.

East Side Story, Vol. 4 .... East Side (S) LP 2004 8-12 70s
Vanguards; Jewels; Bertha Tillman; Barbara Mason; Radiants; Miracles; Intruders; Percy Sledge; Flamingos; Cruisers.

East Side Story, Vol. 5 .... East Side (S) LP 2005 8-12 70s
Elgins; Heartbeats; Brenda & Tabulations; Masqueraders; Nutmegs; Dubs; Impressions; Aaron Neville; Sapphires; Jackie Ross; Clovers; Jimmy Clanton.

East Side Story, Vol. 6 .... East Side (S) LP 2006 8-12 70s
Ralphi Pagan; Whispers; Danleers; Billy Stewart; Johnny Flamingo; Donnie Elbert; Uptones; Johnny Ace; Moments; Dubs; Delicates; Little Anthony.

East Side Story, Vol. 7 .... East Side (S) LP 2007 8-12 70s
Gene Chandler; Billy Stewart; Students; Incredibles; Linda Jones; Carla Thomas; Rosie & Ron; Five Satins; Superbs; Chris & Kathy; Ritchie Valens; Originals.

Eastman Kodak Album (Academy Award Winning Songs) .... Columbia Special Products (S) CSM 467 10-15 60s
Patti Page; Ray Conniff; New Christy Minstrels; Andre Kostelanetz; Eydie Gorme; Percy Faith; Doris Day; Robert Goulet; Steve Lawrence.

Easy Does It .... Columbia Special Products (S) CSS 873 5-10 60s
Ray Conniff; Johnny Mathis; Eydie Gorme; Andy Williams; Barbra Streisand; Robert Goulet; John Davidson; Brothers Four; Gary Puckett & Union Gap; New Christy Minstrels. (Made for Sherwin-Williams.)

Easy Does It, 2nd Great Edition .... Columbia Special Products (S) CSS 1111 5-10
Patti Page; Percy Faith; Robert Goulet; Johnny Mathis; Jim Nabors; Peter Nero; Jerry Vale; Aretha Franklin; Bobby Martin; Blood, Sweat & Tears. (Made for Sherwin-Williams.)

Easy Jazz .... Capitol Creative Products (S) SL-6652 10-15
Cannonball Adderley; Sergio Mendes; Shelly Manne; Jack Marshall; Howard Roberts; Eddie Heywood.

Easy Listening .... Decca (S) DL-75045 8-12

Easy Listening (2 LP) .... Tele House (S) CD 2019 10-15
Trini Lopez; Carole King; Grass Roots; Joe Simon; Vogues; Classics IV; Mac Davis; Mark Lindsay; Merrilee Rush; Norman Greenbaum; Hamilton, Joe Frank & Reynolds; Mama Cass; Love Unlimited; Paul Mauriet; Dionne Warwick; Ferrante & Teicher; Billy Paul; Lulu; Ray Charles Singers; Van Morrison; Mamas & Papas; Dawn; R.B. Greaves; Bob Lind; Melanie; Oliver; Highwaymen; Vikki Carr; Spiral Staircase; Kenny Rogers & First Edition; Jackie DeShannon; Bobby Vinton; B.J. Thomas; Sylvia; Ocean; O.C. Smith; Association; Happenings; B.B. King; T-Bones.

Easy Listening Hits of the '60s and '70s (7 LP) .... Reader's Digest (S) RBA-040-A 40-55 89
(Boxed set. Mail order offer. Includes booklet.) Elvis Presley; Debby Boone; Eric Carmen; Diana Ross; Leo Sayer; Helen Reddy; Anne Murray; Randy Van Warmer; Natalie Cole; Sonny & Cher; Dionne Warwick; Mama Cass; Cher; Tom Jones; Glen Campbell & Anne Murray; 5th Dimension; Beach Boys; Harry Nilsson; Petula Clark; Oliver; Everly Brothers; Engelbert Humperdinck; Lionel Richie & Commodores; Rita Coolidge; Joe Cocker; Bobby Goldsboro; Starland Vocal Band; Ronnie Milsap; Keith Carradine; Dolly Parton; Commodres; Captain & Tennille; Neil Sedaka; Cindi Grecco; Rupert Holmes; Tony Orlando & Dawn; Sergio Mendes; Vikki Carr; Kingston Trio; Chad & Jeremy; Kenny Rogers & First Edition; Glen Campbell & Bobbie Gentry; Roger Whittaker; Henry Mancini; Chuck Mangione; Michel Legrand; Frank Mills; Al De Lory; Diana Ross & Supremes; Al Wilson; Gladys Knight & Pips; Supremes & Temptations; Marvin Gaye; Louis Armstrong; Bobby Darin; Jim Croce; Paul Anka; Richard Chamberlain.

Easy Money .... Columbia (S) JS-38968 8-10 83
(Soundtrack.) Billy Joel; Scandal; Heaven; Nick Lowe; Weather Girls.

Easy Rider .... Dunhill (S) DSX 50063 15-20 69
(Soundtrack.) Steppenwolf; Smith; Byrds; Holy Modal Rounders; Fraternity of Man; Jimi Hendrix Experience; Kyrie Eleison; Electric Prunes; Roger McGuinn.

Easy Sounds - in a Mellow Mood, Vol. 9 .... Capitol (S) 4XL-6619 5-10

Easy to Love .... ???? 5-10
Bobby Vinton; Vikki Carr; Peter Nero; Johnny Mathis; Andre Kostelanetz; Terry Baxter; Tony Bennett; Ronnie Aldrich; Jerry Vale; Percy Faith.

Echoes of a Rock Era - Birdland All Stars Live at Carnegie Hall .... Roulette (SE) RE-127 8-12 75
Count Basie; Charlie Parker; Dan Terry; Billie Holiday; Lester Young & Count Basie; Sarah Vaughan.

Echoes of a Rock Era - Early Years (2 LP) .... Roulette (SE) RE-111 10-15 71
Faye Adams; Bo Diddley; Chuck Berry; Sonny Till & Orioles; Penguins; Moonglows; Nutmegs; Jesse Belvin; Cadillacs; Heartbeats; Frankie Lymon; Crows; Chuck Willis; Tune Weavers; Jimmie Rodgers; Rays; Buddy Knox.

Echoes of a Rock Era - Later Years (2 LP) .... Roulette (SE) RE-113 10-15 71
Maxine Brown; Shirelles; Chubby Checker; Carla Thomas; Cleftones; Chantels; Dreamlovers; Lee Dorsey; Joey Dee & Starliters; Joe Henderson; Lou Christie; Essex; Mary Wells; Stringalongs; Bobby Lewis; King Curtis; Spaniels; Little Eva; Ben E. King; Dave "Baby" Cortez.

Echoes of a Rock Era - Middle Years (2 LP) .... Roulette (SE) RE-112 10-15 71
Monotones; Silhouettes; Chantels; Jimmy Rodgers; Little Anthoney & Imperials; Moonglows; Dee Clark; Flamingos; Wilbert Harrison; Johnny & Hurricanes; Crests; Fiestas; Billy Bland; Maurice Williams & Zodiacs; Joe Jones; Maxine Brown; Dovells; Joey Dee & Starliters.

Echoes of a Rock Era - the Groups (2 LP) .... Roulette (SE) RE-114 10-15 72
Crows; Harptones; others.

Echoes of a Rock Era - the Groups (2 LP) .... Roulette (SE) RE-115 10-15 72
Shep & Limelites; Heartbeats; others.

Echoes of an Era .... Elektra (S) 60021 5-10 82
Chaka Khan; Freddie Hubbard; Chick Corea; others.

Echoes of an Era - Count Basie, Vocal Years .... Roulette (S) RE-110 8-12 71
Art Tatum; Erroll Garner; Bud Powell; Billy Taylor.

Echoes of an Era - Count Basie, Vocal Years .... Roulette (S) RE-107 8-12 71
Count Basie; Tony Bennett; Sarah Vaughn; Joe Williams; Billy Eckstine.

Echoes of the '20s & '30s (2 LP) .... Columbia Special Products (M) 10-15 73
Billie Holiday; Russ Columbo; Connie Boswell; Fred Astaire; Ethel Merman; Alice Faye; Gene Austin; Duke Ellington; Bing Crosby; Boswell Sisters; Mary Martin; Frances Langford; Eddie Cantor; Ruth Etting; Louis Armstrong; Bix Beiderbecke; Lee Morse; Buck & Bubbles; Bessie Smith; George Gershwin; Isham Jones; Blossom Seeley; Helen Morgan; Miff Mole; Tess Gardella; Rudy Vallee; Ethel Waters.

Echoes of the Ozarks, Vol. 1 .... County (M) 518 8-12 70s
Pope's Arkansas Mountaineers; Morrison Twin Brothers String Band; Ashley's Melody Men; Carter Brothers & Son; Arkansas Barefoot Boys; Dutch Coleman & Red Whitehead.

Echoes of the Ozarks, Vol. 2 .... County (M) 519 8-12 70s

Echoes of the Ozarks, Vol. 3 .... County (M) 520 8-12 70s

Edison Originals (1878-1956, 78th Anniversary)........ Edison (M) 30-50 56
Carmen Melis; Marie Rappold; Lucett Korsoff; Celestina Boninsegna; Emmy Destinn & Dinh Gilly; Maria Galvany.

Elected Performers of the Country Music Hall of Fame (2 LP)........ Columbia Special Products (S) P 12824 10-15 75
Jimmie Rodgers; Eddy Arnold; Jim Reeves; Original Carter Family; Chet Atkins; Pee Wee King; Hank Williams; Fred Rose; Roy Acuff; Tex Ritter; Ernest Tubb; Uncle Dave Macon; Red Foley; Bob Wills; Gene Autry; Bill Monroe; Jimmie Davis; Patsy Cline; Owen Bradley.

Electric Breakdance .... Dominion (S) 2320 5-10 84

Electric Dreams .... Virgin (S) SE-39600 8-10 84
(Soundtrack.) Giorgio Moroder; Philip Oakey; Jeff Lynne; Culture Club; Helen Terry; Heaven 17; P.P. Arnold.

Electric Seventies........ Warner/JCI (S) 3302 8-12 86
Grand Funk; Manfred Mann; Black Sabbath; Allman Brothers Band; Edgar Winter Group; Mountain; Santana; Uriah Heep; Mott the Hoople; Brownsville Station; Alice Cooper; Focus.

Electric Sixties .... Warner/JCI (SP) 3103 8-12 85
Steppenwolf; Santana; Blind Faith; Humble Pie; Traffic; Chambers Brothers; Cream; Velvet Underground; Byrds; Quicksilver; Spirit; Big Brother.

Elektra/Asylum Fall 1973 Releases........ Elektra (S) EK-Promo 22 8-12 73
Atomic Rooster; Jo Jo Gunne; Harry Chapin; Casey Relly; Jobraith; Skymonters with Hamid; Hamilton Camp; Mickey Newberry; Painter; Joni Mitchell.

Elektra Promotional Releases/Samplers (Listed by catalog number. All are promo only.)

Elektra EK-6 - 8-71 (September Releases) *8-12* *71*
Wackers; Jeannie Greene; Lindisfarne; Lonnie Mack.

Elektra EK-Promo-8, January Releases (2 LP)........ *20-35* *72*
(Includes extended version of *Taxi* by Harry Chapin.) Doors; Harry Chapin; Bernie Taupin; John Kongos; Incredible String Band; Atomic Rooster; Lindisfarne; Carol Hall; Alabama State Troopers; New Seekers; J.F. Murphy & Salt; Timber; Bread.

Elektra EK-11 - March 1972 Sampler........ *8-12* *72*
Audience; J.F. Murphy & Salt; Carol Hall; Wackers; Butterfield Blues Band.

Elektra EK-15 - August 1972 Sampler........ *8-12* *72*
Ship; Casey Kelley; Atomic Rooster.

Elektra EK-16 - September 1972 Sampler........ *8-12* *72*
Harry Chapin; Lindisfarne; Good Thunder; Electric Prunes: Seeds; Ship. (From *Nuggets - Original Artyfacts from the First Psychedelic Era 1965-1968*.)

Elektra EK-23 - Summer 1973 Sampler........ *8-12* *73*
Bob Dylan & Band; Queen; Souther-Hillman-Furray Band; Harry Chapin; Eagles; Cris Jagger; Jobraith; Rod Taylor; Dick Feller; Melba Montgomery; Mickey Newbury; Eddie Rabbitt.

Elektra EK-19 - July Releases, 1973........ *8-12* *73*
Courtland Pickett; Capital City Rockets; Linda Hargrove; Ian Matthews.

Elektra EK-24 - Fall 1974 Sampler........ *8-12* *74*
Joni Mitchell; Tim Moore; Hagers; Larry Ballard; Jackson Browne; Tom Waits; David Gates; Gene Clark; Traffic; Jo Jo Gunn; Lindisfarne; Jack the Lad; Bob Neuwirth; Dennis Linde; A Foot in Coldwater; Essra Mohawk; Linda Hargrove.

Elektra EX-13 - May Releases........ *8-12*
Judy Collins; Audience; Sailcat; John Kongos.

Elektra EX-17 - October Releases........ *8-12*
Bread; Sweet Salvation; Plainsong; Wackers.

Elektrock: the Sixties (4 LP) .... Elektra (S) 9 60403-1-V 15-25 85
Holy Modal Rounders; Beefeaters; Luke & Apostles; Ars Nova; Clear Light; Earth Opera; Eclection; David Peel & Lower East Side; Wild Thing; Roxy; Crabby Appleton; Rhinoceros; Gulliver; Voices of East Harlem; Delany & Bonnie; Stalk-Forrest Group; Nico; Butterfield Blues Band; Incredible String Band; Love; Tim Buckley; MC5; Stooges

Elite, The .... K-Tel (S) TU 3000 5-10 81
Bee Gees; Diana Ross; Michael Jackson; James Taylor; Kenny Rogers; Supertramp; Neil Diamond; Barbra Streisand; Billy Joel; Earth, Wind & Fire; Boz Scaggs; Dr. Hook; Cliff Richard; Anne Murray; Abba.

Elvira Presents Haunted Hits (2 LP)........ Rhino (M) R1-71492 10-15
Bobby "Boris" Pickett; Jumpin' Gene Simmons; Ray Parker Jr.; Marketts; Five Blobs; Dave Edmunds; Sheb Wooley; Vic Mizzy; Lewis Lee; Alice Cooper; Oingo Boingo; Neil Norman & Cosmic Orchestra; Screamin' Jay Hawkins; Tubes; Big "T" Taylor; Jayhawks; Lambert, Hendricks & Ross; Skyhooks; Cramps; LaVern Baker; Ran-Dells; Elvira.

Elvis Presley Years (7 LP)........ Reader's Digest/BMG (S) RBA-236 40-60 91
(Boxed set. Mail order offer. Includes booklet.) Elvis Presley; Buddy Holly; Chuck Berry; Beach Boys; Linda Ronstadt; Donna Summer; Supremes; others.

Elvis Will Live On! .... Royal Master (S) No Number Used 5-8 70s
Jim Ward; Matt Vincent; Gina Val; Jay Pauley.

Emotions .... K-Tel (S) NU 9390 5-10 78
Dan Hill; Paul Davis; LeBlanc & Carr; Barry Manilow; Player; Paul Anka; Crystal Gayle; Mary MacGregor; David Soul; Commodores; Kenny Nolan; JenniferWarnes; Seals & Crofts; England Dan & John Ford Coley; Yvonne Elliman; Samantha Sang.

Empire Jazz........ RSO (S) 3085 5-10 80

Enchantment of Christmas........ MCA (S) 734662 5-10

Enchanted Evenings with Rogers & Hamerstein (2 LP) .... RCA/Columbia (S) ???? 8-12 85
Ezio Pinza; Eileen Christy; John Raitt; Julie Andrews & Jon Cypher; Yul Brynner; James Melton; Florence Henderson; Ed Ames; Dinah Shore; Bill Lee; Mary Martin; Patricia Northul; Juanita Hall; Constance Towers; Mens Chorus. (Made for Sea Lion Films, Inc.)

Encores from the '30s (1930-1935), Vol. 1 (2 LP)........ Epic (S) L2N-6072 10-20 69
Ethel Waters; Paul Whiteman; Frankie Trumbauer; Isham Jones; Ruth Etting; Louis Armstrong & Cotton Club Orchestra; Dorsey Brothers; Ted Lewis; Bing Crosby; Kate Smith; Harry Richman; Al Jolson; Eddie Duchin; Lee Sims; Gene Austin; Frances Williams; Lee Wiley; Boswell Sisters; Joe Sullivan; Mildred Bailey; Karl Kress & Dick McDonough; Fred Astaire; Guy Lombardo; Dick Powell; Hal Kemp; Lanny Ross; Leo Reisman; Connie Boswell; Mills Brothers; Carl Brisson; Ozzie Nelson; Helen Morgan.

Encyclopedia of 100 Rock & Roll Super Hits (5 LP)........ TVP TVP-1009 20-30
Dixie Cups; Beach Boys; Shirelles; Gladys Knight; Gene Pitney; Turtles; Patti LaBelle; B.J. Thomas; Dells; Mitch Ryder; Chiffons; Manhattans; Lonnie Mack; Kingsmen; Tommy James; Coasters; Sam Cooke; Dion; Little Ceasar; Bill Haley & His Comets; Jelly Beans; Happenings; Dixie Cups; Hot Butter; Brook Benton; Angels; King Curtis; Lloyd Price; Shirelles; Chuck Jackson; Wilson Pickett; Platters; Staple Singers; Coasters; Ike & Tina Turner; Billy Preston; Jesse Belvin; Isley Brothers; Kathy & Roomates; Turtles; Crests; Brook Benton; Mac Davis; Bill Parsons; Drifters; Platters; Manhattans; Ike & Tina Turner; Shangri-Las; Cascades; Mongo Santamaria; Jimi Hendrix; Ronnie Milsap; King Curtis; Toys; O'Jays; Kingsmen; Inez & Charlie Foxx; Jerry Butler; Dion & Belmonts; Guess Who; Joe Jeffrey; Ohio Players; Brenton Wood; Curtis Mayfield; Sly Stone; Count Five; Animals.

Endless Beach (2 LP)........Epic (SP) EG-37915 8-12 82
Robert John; Spellbinders; Major Lance; Tymes; Tower of Power; Otis Leavill; Ron Moody & Centaurs; Billy Butler & Enchanters; Spiral Starecase; Essence; Wild Cherry; Tyrone Davis; Tina Charles; Jimmy Hall.

Endless Love........Mercury (S) SRM-2001 8-10 81
(Soundtrack.) Diana Ross; Lionel Richie; Kiss; Cliff Richard.

England Rocks........Epic (S) PE 37332 5-10 80s
Zombies; Cafe Jacques; Crawler; Colin Blunstone; Russ Ballard; Tourists; Fabulous Poodles; Sailor; After the Fire; Argent.

England's Greatest Hitmakers........London (M) LL-3430 15-20 65

England's Greatest Hitmakers........London (S) PS-430 15-20 65
Rolling Stones; Tom Jones; Zombies; Lulu & Lovers; Applejacks; Bachelors; Dave Berry; Bern Elliott; Billy Fury; Johnny Howard Band; Tom Jones; Kathy Kirby; Mike Leander; Them; Unit Four Plus Two.

England's Greatest Hits........Fontana (M) MGF-27570 15-25 67

England's Greatest Hits........Fontana (S) SRF-67570 10-20 67
(Includes Union Jack insert.) Troggs; Manfred Mann; Dave Dee, Dozy, Beaky, Mick & Tich; Millie Small; Springfields; Wayne Fontana & Mindbenders; New Vaudeville Band; Walker Brothers; Dusty Springfield; Silkie.

English Cats and Others (2 LP)........Brookville (S) BR-3400 10-15 74
(Mail order offer.) Zombies; Los Bravos; Them; Poppy Family; Marmalade; Cat Stevens; Whistling Jack Smith; White Plains; Nashville Teens; Unit 4 + 2; Brotherhood of Man; Dave Edmunds; Jonathan King; Frijid Pink; Fortunes; Lulu.

English Freak Beat, Vol. 1........Archive International (S) AIP 10039 5-10 80s
Gound Hogs; Johnny Neal & Starliners; In-betweens; Betterdays; Rebounds; Primitives; Beat Merchants; Steve Davis; Loot; Miki Dallon; Chasers; Sheffields; Couriers; Rats; Wild Ones.

English In-Groups (Mickie Most Presents)........Metro (M)M-577 10-20 66

English In-Groups (Mickie Most Presents)........Metro (SE) MS-577 10-20 66
Symbols; Animals; Herman's Hermits; Moquettes; Cherokees.

English Music Hall........Capitol (M) T-10273 10-15

English Music Hall........Capitol (S) ST-10273 10-20

Enigma Variations (2 LP)........Enigma (S) 72001-1 10-15 85
Screamin' Sirens; Jet Black Berries; Naked Prey; Tex & Horseheads; Greg Sage; Chris D., Divine Horseman; John Trubee; Rain Parade; Plasticland; Pandoras; Get Smart; Leaving Trains; Green on Red; Game Theory; 45 Grave; Effigies; Kraut; Redd Kross; TSOL; Channel 3; Cathdral of Tears; Passionnel; Untouchables; Pool; SSQ; Scott Goddard.

Epic Memory Lane Series........Epic (M) No Number Used 15-25 64
(Promotional issue only.) Tony Orlando; Roy Hamilton; Link Wray; Schoolboys; Jamies; Lillian Briggs; Screamin' Jay Hawkins; Four Coins; Adam Wade; Bobby Vinton; Buddy Greco; Dave Clark Five; Rolf Harris; Jane Morgan; Major Lance; Yardbirds; Litle Joe & Thrillers; Ersel Hickey. (Both LPs are in individual, soft cardboard sleeves. Price is for either LP. Disc identification numbers are 77715 and 77716.)

Epic Records Sampler........Epic (S) AS 537 20-30 78
(Promotional only picture disc. 1500 made.) Tonio K; Brownsville Station; Trillion; Fabulous Poodles.

Epic Rockbusters........Epic (SP) XSB 139674 10-20
Terry Reid; Kak; Gentle Soul; Chicken Shack; Sly & Family Stone; Kaleidoscope; Dino Valente; Jeff Beck; Anna Black; Screamin' Jay Hawkins; Fleetwood Mac; others.

Epitaph for a Legend (6 LP)........International Artists (S) 13 25-40 79
(Boxed set. Includes booklet.) Chaynes; Patterns; Chapparrals; Thursday's Children; Electric Rubayyat; Sonny Hall; Inner Scene; Red Crayola; Emperors; Lost & Found; Big Walter; Dave Allen; Lightnin' Hopkins; Roky Erickson; Spades; Roky Erickson & Clementine Hall; 13th Floor Elevators.

Ertegun's New York - New York Cabaret Music........Atlantic (S) 81817-1 30-40 87
Mae Barnes; Joe Bushkin; Barbara Carroll; Eddie Condon; Chris Connor; Jimmy Daniels; Goldie Hawkins; Greta Keller; Jimmy Lyon; Carmen McRae; Mabel Mercer; Joe Mooney; Hugh Shannon; Bobby Short; Ted Straeter; Sylvia Syms; Billy Taylor; Mel Torme; Cy Walter; Joe Bushkin.

Escalator over the Hill........JCOA (S) EOTH 15-25 72
Don Cherry; Linda Rondstadt; Carla Bley.

Escapade Reviews the Jazz Scene........Liberty (S) SL-9005 20-30

Essential Jazz Vocals........Verve (M) V-8505 10-20 63

Essential Jazz Vocals........Verve (S) V6-8505 15-25 63

Everlasting Love........???? 5-10
Benny Goodman; Mantovani; Patti Page; Jan August; Tony Bennett; Tony Mottola; Lawrence Welk; Percy Faith; Jo Stafford; Harry James.

Everlasting Love........Sessions (S) AR1-1019 5-10 80
(Mail order offer.) Johnny Tillotson; Gale Garnett; Lemon Pipers; Dee Clark; Chad & Jeremy; Mamas & Papas; Brian Hyland; Ruby & Romantics; Al Martino; Glen Campbell; Bob Lind; Ray Charles Singers; Spanky & Our Gang; Seekers; Keith; Gerry & Pacemakers; Toys; Murmaids; Casinos.

Everlasting Sacred Songs by Country Stars........Camden (M) CAL-880 10-20 65

Everlasting Sacred Songs by Country Stars........Camden (S) CAS-880 10-20 65
Eddy Arnold; Hank Snow; Stuart Hamblen; others.

Every Man Has a Woman........Polydor (S) 823490 1-Y-1 8-12 84
John Lennon; Sean Ono Lennon; Harry Nilsson; Elvis Costello; Eddie Money; Rosanne Cash; Roberta Flack; Trio; Spirit Choir; Alternating Boxes.

Every Great Motown Songs (the First 25 Years, Vol. 1)........Motown (S) 5343ML 5-10 84
Diana Ross & Supremes; Smokey Robinson & Miracles; Martha Reeves & Vandellas; Four Tops; Kim Weston; Gladys Knight & Pips; Marvin Gaye; Temptations; Marvelettes.

Every Which Way But Loose........Elektra (S) SE-503 8-10 79
(Soundtrack.) Eddie Rabbitt; Mel Tillis; Cliff Crofford; Charlie Rich; Larry Collins; Carol Chase; Sondra Locke; Phil Everly; Hank Thompson.

Everybody Digs........Winley (M) 6001 35-55
Paragons; Jesters; Quinns; others.

Everybody Rocks........Capitol (M) T-1025 35-55 58
Five Keys; Nat King Cole; Beavers; Big Dave; Tommy Sands; Gene Vincent; Johnny Otis; Sonny James; Nick Greene; Bob Bain; Ray Stevens; Four Preps.

Everybody's All-American........Capitol (S) C1-91184 8-10 88
(Soundtrack.) Nat King Cole; Shirley & Lee; Lloyd Price; Jesse Hill; Hank Ballard & Midnighters; Jaguars; Barbara Lynn; Smiley Lewis; Dietra Hicks & Evan Rogers; Don Gardner & Dee Dee Ford.

Everybody's Favorite Blues........King (M) 875 20-30 63

Everybody's Favorite Blues .... King (S) KS-875 20-30 63
Ivory Joe Hunter; John Lee Hooker; others.
Everybody's Goin' Surfin' .... Parkway (M) 7035 20-40 63
Chubby Checker; Bobby Rydell; Dee Dee Sharp; Orlons; Dovells; Tymes.
Everybody's Surfin' .... Parkway (M) 7036 20-40 63
Chubby Checker; Bobby Rydell; Dee Dee Sharp; Orlons; Dovells; Tymes.
Everyday Is A Holly Day .... Eergo (S) EM 9465 5-10 89
Imitation Life; Shoes; Red River; LMNOP; Classic Ruins; Ted & Talltops; Willie Alexander; Paul Roland; Country Rockers; Lolitas; Elliot Murphy; Tav Falco's Panther Burns; Speedy Sparks; Slickee Boys; Chris Speeding; OFB; Chris Bailey.
Everything's Beautiful (Columbia Musical Treasury) .... Columbia House (S) IP-6581 5-10
Lynn Anderson; Marty Robbins; Johnny Cash; June Carter Cash; Mac Davis; Jim Nabors; Patti Page; Statler Brothers; Tammy Wynette; Flatt & Scruggs; Ray Price.
Everything New Is Old...Everything Old Is New .... Ambient Sound (S) BL-37911 5-10 82
(Rerecordings.) Jive Five; Mystics; Randy & Rainbows; Harptones.
Evolution of the Blues Song .... Columbia (M) CL-1583 20-30 60
Evolution of the Blues Song .... Columbia (S) CS-8383 25-35 60
Excello Story .... Excello (S) 8023 8-12 72
Excerpts from *Tommy* .... Pickwick (S) SPC-3339 5-10
Exciting New Liverpool Sound (Authentic Mersey Best) .... Columbia (M) CL-2172 20-30 64
Sonny Webb & Cascades; Ian & Zodiacs; Del Renas; others.
Exposed (A Cheap Peek at Today's Provocative New Rock) (2 LP) .... CBS (S) X2-37124 8-12 81
Ian Gomm; Rosanne Cash; Steve Forbert; Ellen Foley; Romantics; Judas Priest; Adam & Ants; Loverboy; Sorrows; Boomtown Rats; Garland Jeffreys.
Exposed II .... CBS (S) X2-37601 5-10 81
Billy Thorpe; Gary Myrick & Figures; Harlequin; Hitmen; Holly & Italians; Jo Jo Zep & Falcons; Karla DeVito; Orchestral Manoeuvres in the Dark; Psychedelic Furs; Tommy Tutone; Whitford-St. Holmes Band.
FM (2 LP) .... MCA (S) MCA2-12000 10-12 78
FM (2 LP) .... MCA (S) 2-6900 5-10 78
(Soundtrack.) Boston; Jimmy Buffett; Doobie Brothers; Eagles; Dan Fogelberg; Foreigner; Billy Joel; Randy Meisner; Steve Miller; Tom Petty & Heartbreakers; Queen; Boz Scaggs; Bob Seger & Silver Bullet Band; Steely Dan; James Taylor; Joe Walsh; Linda Ronstadt.
Fabulous '50s (2 LP) .... Columbia Musical Treasuries (SE) P2S 5510 10-15 71
Fess Parker; Dinah Shore; Vic Damone; Arthur Godfrey; Marlene Dietrich; Rosemary Clooney; Stonewall Jackson; Sammy Kaye; Louis Armstrong; Patti Page; Red Buttons; Terry Gilkyson & Easy Riders; Frankie Laine; Four Lads; Johnnie Ray; Mitch Miller; Doris Day; Jimmy Dorsey; Johnny Mathis; Paul Weston; Tony Bennett; Les Compagnons de la Chanson. (Columbia House Record Club issue.)
Fabulous '50s: see Fifties Greatest Love Songs
Fabulous Baker Boys .... GRP (S) GR-2002 8-10
(Soundtrack.) Dave Grusin; Michelle Pfeiffer; Duke Ellington; Benny Goodman; Earl Palmer Trio.
Fabulous Bubble Gum Years .... Kory (S) KK-3001 5-10 76
Lemon Pipers; 1910 Fruitgum Co.; Ohio Express; Music Explosion; Kasenetz-Katz Singing Orchestral Circus; Crazy Elephant; Jaggerz.
Fabulous Favorites of Our Time .... Liberty (M) LRP-3223 15-25 62
Fabulous Favorites of Our Time .... Liberty (S) LST-3223 20-30 62
Felix Slatkin; Si Zentner; Julie London; Martin Denny; Jimmy Dorsey; Cy Coleman Trio; Gene McDaniels. (Also has soundtrack music from *Gigi, One-Eyed Jacks, The Alamo, El Cid* and *Bonanza*.)
Fabulous Fifties (2 LP) .... Columbia (S) DS716/DS717 8-12
(Columbia Record Club issue.) Johnny Mathis; Paul Weston; Tony Bennett; Patti Page; Rosemary Clooney; Les Compagnons De La Chanson; Four Lads; Dinah Shore; Johnnie Ray; Mitch Miller; Doris Day; Jimmy Dorsey; Red Buttons; Fess Parker; Easy Riders; Frankie Laine; Vic Damone; Arthur Godfrey; Marlene Dietrich & Rosemary Clooney; Stonewall Jackson; Sammy Kaye; Louis Armstrong.
Fabulous Oldies in Stereo, Vol. 1 .... Fabulous Sound (SE) FS-1001 8-10
Jimy Reed; Vibrations; Cannibal & Headhunters; Shep & Limelites; Mello-Kings; Johnnie & Joe; Carlos Brothers; Metallics; Blendells; Castaleers.
Fabulous Oldies in Stereo, Vol. 2 .... Fabulous Sound (SE) FS-1002 8-10
Ronnie & Hi-Lites; Rivieras; Jimmy Norman; Rosei & Ron; Joe Houston; Diplomats; Little Julian Herrea; Rainbow; Jimmy Hughes; Sapphires.
Fabulous Oldies in Stereo, Vol. 3 .... Fabulous Sound (SE) FS-1003 8-10
Premiers; Huey "Piano" Smith & Clowns; Cathy Jean & Roomates; Turks; Hollywood Saxons; Perez Brothers; Resonics; Hey Girl; Count Five; Crests.
Fabulous Oldies in Stereo, Vol. 4 .... Fabulous Sound (SE) FS-1004 8-10
Fireflies; Wilson Pickett & Falcons; Scott English; Marcels; Five Satins; Jesse Belvin & Cliques; Sa-Shays; Rosie & Ron; Richard "Dimples" Fields; Arthur Lee Maye & Crowns.
Fabulous Oldies in Stereo, Vol. 5 .... Fabulous Sound (SE) FS-1005 8-10
Jimmy Charles; Angels; Paris Sisters; Yvonne Carroll; Cadillacs; Uptones; Midniters; Z.Z. Hill; Martinels; Alfred & Joe.
Fabulous Oldies in Stereo, Vol. 6 .... Fabulous Sound (SE) FS-1006 8-10
Duprees; McKinley Mitchell; Lee Andrews & Hearts; Jesse Belvin & Gassers; Chris Montez; Oscar McLollie; Blendtones; Carol Hughes; Thee Midniters.
Fabulous Oldies in Stereo, Vol. 7 .... Fabulous Sound (SE) FS-1007 8-10
Packers; Sammy Turner; Wallace Brothers; Baby Washington; Beau Brummels; El Dorados; Nutmegs; Johnny Ace; Tears; Ambertones.
Face to Face .... Decca (M) DXD-166 20-30 61
Perry Como; Bing Crosby; Bob Hope; Sammy Davis Jr; Danny Kaye; Ethel Merman; Mary Martin; others.
Fair Sex-Tette .... Everest (M) 1202 10-20 63
Fair Sex-Tette .... Everest (S) 1202 10-20 63
Patsy Cline; Gloria Lynne; Ketty Lester; Gisele MacKenzie; Della Reese; Joya Sherrill.
Fairy Tales, Nursery Rhymes & Doo Wops .... Wizard (S) 5002 8-10
Admirations; Spaniels; Corvairs; Ideals; Troupers; Billy & Essentials; Fraternity Men; Valaquans; Chargers; Marty & Symbols; Roulettes; Colonials; Emblems; Devotions.
Falcon .... Condor (S) 100 5-10
Orlons; Billy Stewart; Medallions; Dale & Grace; Jimmy Clanton; Frankie Carle; Esquires; Len Barry; Gallahads; Jerry Butler; Patti Drew; Diamonds; J.J. Jackson; Lee Andrews & Hearts; Ruby & Romantics; Falcons; Newbeats; Johnnie & Joe; Ike & Tina Turner; Marvelettes.
Family Christmas Collection (3 LP) .... Time-Life (S) STL-131 25-35 90
(Boxed set. Mail order offer.) Elvis Presley; others.

Family Christmas Package.. Mercury (S) PKW-110 10-15 68
Family Portrait... A&M (S) SP-19002 10-20 67
Herb Alpert & Tijuana Bass; Wes Montgomery; Chris Montez; Sandpipers; Burt Bacharach; Sergio Mendes; Tommy Boyce & Bobby Hart; Herbie Mann; Liza Minnelli; Tamba 4; Merry-Go-Round; Phil Ochs; Claudine Longet; Antonio Carlos Jobim; Jimmie Rodgers; Julius Wechter.
Famous Original Hits by 25 Great Country Music Artists ....Country Music Assoc. CMA (M) 712 8-12 65
Roy Acuff; Bill Anderson; Eddy Arnold; Bobby Bare; Johnny Bond; Johnny Cash; Patsy Cline; Dave Dudley; Red Roley; Lefty Frizzell; Don Gibson; Pee Wee King; Roger Miller; George Morgan; Buck Owens; Ray Price; Jim Reeves; Tex Ritter; Marty Robbins; Hank Snow; Kitty Wells; Hank Williams.
Famous Torch Songs of the '20s.. Columbia Special Products (M) XTV 82077/8 8-12
Polly Bergen; Frankie Laine; Helen Morgan; Sarah Vaughan; Harry James with Helen Forrest; Maysa; Peggy Lee with Benny Goodman; Lena Horne.
Fanfare of Hits...Argo (M) 656 15-25 63
Fantastic...K-Tel (S) TU 233 5-10 73
Dawn; Elton John; Focus; Sweet; Lobo; Bill Withers; Raspberries; Albert Hammond; Sylvers; Blue Mink; Jerry Jeff Walker; New York City; Cliff Richard; Maureen McGovern; Gunhill Road; Barry White; Rod Stewart; Vicki Lawrence; Donny Osmond; First Choice; Gary Glitter.
Fantastic Country, Vol. 1 ....RCA Special Products (S) PRS-387 8-12 72
Michael Nesmith; Duane Eddy; Liz Anderson; Chet Atkins; Bobby Bare; Skeeter Davis; Jimmy Dean; Norman Luboff; Lorne Greene; George Hamilton IV; John Hartford; Pat McKinney; Roger Miller; Jerry Reed; Connie Smith; Sammi Smith; Hank Snow; Porter Wagoner. (Made for Salem-Select Distribution.)
Fantastic Fifties, Vol. 1 (2 LP) ....Columbia Special Products (SE) C2-10236 10-15
Rosemary Clooney; Guy Mitchell; Dinah Shore; Four Lads; Bobby Hackett; Jerry Vale; Frankie Laine; Ray Conniff; Doris Day; Vic Damone; Johnny Mathis; Patti Page; Bobby Vinton; Sammy Kaye; Eddie Layton; Joan Weber; Mitch Miller; Judy Garland; Roy Hamilton; Johnnie Ray; Les & Larry Elgart; Four Lads; Louis Armstrong; Doris Day. (Also issued as *Great Hits of the Fantastic Fifties*.)
Fantasy Blues Twofer Giants ....Fantasy (M) FP-4 10-15 73
Jimmy Witherspoon; Jesse Fuller; Memphis Slim; Dave Van Ronk; others.
Far Out ....Ronco (S) R-1975-915 5-10 75
(Mail order offer.) Hot Chocolate; Styx; Tony Orlando & Dawn; Barry Manilow; Sweet Sensations; Joe Simon; Frankie Valli; Shirley & Co.; Isaac Hayes; Neil Sedaka; Ray Stevens; Disco Tex & Sex-O-Lettes; B.T. Express; Dave Loggins; Gloria Gaynor; Moments; Lobo; Johnny Taylor; Jim Stafford; Ace.
Far Out Man ....Chameleon (S) D1-74829 10-15 90
(Soundtrack.) DV8; Kool Moe Dee; Bobby Dee; Bobby Taylor & Carolyn Majors; Bonedaddys; Samantha Fox; Tommy Chong; Don Dokken.
Fast Times at Ridgemont High ....Full Moon/Island (S) 982 15-25 82
(Six-track picture disc sampler. Promotional issue only.)
Fast Times at Ridgemont High ....Full Moon/Island (S) 99246 5-10 82
(Single disc.)
Fast Times at Ridgemont High (2 LP) .... Full Moon/Asylum (S) 4-60158 10-15 82
(Soundtrack.) Jackson Browne; Jimmy Buffett; Don Felder; Go-Go's; Louise Goffin; Sammy Hagar; Don Henley; Gerard McMahon; Graham Nash; Oingo Boingo; Palmer-Jost; Poco; Quarterflash; Ravyns; Timothy B. Schmit; Stevie Nicks; Billy Squier; Donna Summer; Joe Walsh.
Fatal Beauty ....Atlantic (S) 81809-1 8-10 87
(Soundtrack.) Donna Allen; Le Vert; Madam X; Miki Howard; Shannon; Debbie Gibson; War; System.
Favorite Gospel Quartets .... Modern Sound (S) MS 800 5-10
Speer Family; others.
Favorite Songs of Christmas ....Capitol (M) T-2176 8-12 65
Favorite Songs of Christmas ....Capitol (S) ST-2176 8-12 65
Nat King Cole; Bing Crosby; Carmen Dragon; Eddie Dunstedter; Tennessee Ernie Ford; Virgil Fox; Kingston Trio; Peggy Lee; Guy Lombardo; Roger Wagner Chorale; Nancy Wilson.
Favorite Western Songs...Rural Rhythm (M) FW 2114 8-12 60s
Patsy Montana; De Wayne Wear; Roy Scott; Kenny Roberts; Jimmy Payton; Hall Wallis.
Favorites from Broadway & Hollywood.. Capitol (S) SL-6513 5-10 65
Nat King Cole; Lettermen; Nancy Wilson; Matt Monro; George Shearing; Les Baxter.
Favorites from Nashville...Camden (S) X-9019 5-10 72
Eddy Arnold; Sonny James; Norma Jean; Dottie West; Chet Atkins; Floyd Cramer; Jim Ed Brown; Skeeter Davis; Waylon Jennings; Roger Miller; Dolly Parton; Boots Randolph; Charlie Rich; Connie Smith; Hank Snow; Porter Wagoner.
Favorites Performed By 20 Great Artists... Columbia (S) KG-30763 8-12 71
Andy Williams; Barbra Streisand; Johnny Cash; Anita Bryant; Robert Goulet; Marty Robbins; others.
Favorites with a Foreign Accent .... Capitol (S) SL 6649 8-12 60s
Sounds of Our Times; New Classic Singers; Howard Roberts; Jackie Gleason; Lettermen; Eddie Heywood; Al Martino; Laurindo Almeida; Ray Anthony.
Features from Mercury's LP Albums ....Mercury (EP) MEP 74 10-15
February Sampler (RCA): see RCA February Sampler
'Feds .... GNP/Crescendo (S) GNPS-8014 8-10 88
(Soundtrack.) Albert Collins; Roy Gaines; Barry Goldberg; Electric Boys; Joe Louis Walker.
Feelings...Adam VIII (S) A 8035 5-10 77
Eddie Holman; Morris Lambert; Stairsteps; Hamilton, Joe Frank & Reynolds; Four Tops; Bloodstone; B.J. Thomas; Johnny Nash; Chilites; Sammy Davis Jr.; Bobby Bloom; Freddy Fender; Hurricane Smith; Andy Kim; Hollies; Main Ingredient; Lou Rawls; Hues Corporation; Gladys Knight & Pips; Lettermen; Looking Glass; Daddy Dewdrop; Minnie Riperton; Bells.
Feelings... K-Tel (S) ???? 5-10 70s
Feminine Touch (2 EP) .... Decca (EP) ED-537 10-15
Festival of RCA Victor Artists Gospel Sing... RCA (M) LPM-2330 15-20 61
Festival of RCA Victor Artists Gospel Sing... RCA (S) LSP-2330 15-25 61
Jim Reeves; Blackwood Brothers; Statesmen; Don Gibson; others.
Festival of RCA Victor Artists Religious Concert..................................... RCA (M) LPM-2329 15-20 61
Festival of RCA Victor Artists Religious Concert..................................... RCA (S) LSP-2329 15-25 61
Harry Belafonte; George Beverly Shea; Jerome Hines; others.
Festival Tapes .... Flying Fish (S) 068 5-10 78
Byron Berline; Sundance; Bryan Bowers; John Hartford; New Grass Revival; others.
Feudin' Banjos..Olympic (S) OL-7105 5-10 73
Eric Weissberg; Mason Williams; Mike Seeger; Joe Maphis; Eric Darling; Jim Helms; Jim McGuinn; Dick Rosmin.

Fiddler's Hall of Fame........ Starday (M) S-209 15-20 63
Fiddler's Hall of Fame........ Starday (S) SLP-209 15-20 63
Fiddlin' Country Style........ Wyncote (S) SW-9077 8-12 64
Stanley Brothers; Tommy Hill; Lonesome Pine Fiddlers; Ken Clark; Benny Martin; Chubby Wise; Herbie Remington; Wayne Raney; Eddie Eddings; Tommy Hill.
Fiddlin' Country Style........ Starday (M) S-114 15-25 60
Fiddlin' Country Style........ Starday (S) SLP-114 15-25 60
Fiddlin' Country Style........ Nashville (M) NLP-2015 10-15 65
Fifties........ Decca (M) DL 4009 15-20
Carl Dobkins Jr.; Jerry Lewis; Four Aces; Toni Arden; Louis Armstrong; Bill Kenny & Song Spinners; Florian Zabach; Tommy Dorsey; Victor Young & His Swinging Strings; Dream Weavers; Sylvia Syms; Carmen Cavallaro.
Fifties........ RCA (M) VPM-6060 8-12 72
Eddy Arnold; Harry Belafonte; Sam Cooke; Kay Starr; Domenico Dodugno; Caterina Valente; others.
Fifties: Golden Hits to Remember Them By........ Columbia Musical Treasury (S) DS 724 5-10
(Columbia House Record Club issue.) Frankie Laine; Percy Faith; Johnny Horton; Mitch Miller; Doris Day; Marty Robbins; Four Lads.
Fifties Greatest Hits (2 LP)........ Columbia (M) G-30592 8-10 70
Fifties Greatest Hits (2 LP)........ Columbia (S) G-30592 8-10 72
Four Lads; Les Paul & Mary Ford; Guy Mitchell; Patti Page; Rosemary Clooney; Joan Weber; Kirby Stone Four; Louis Armstrong; Marty Robbins; Johnny Mathis; Mitch Miller; Johnny Horton; Doris Day; Vic Damone; Johnnie Ray; Les Compagnons de la Chanson; Frankie Laine.
Fifties Greatest Love Songs (2 LP)........ Columbia Musical Treasury (S) P2S-5514 8-12 71
Percy Faith; Johnny Mathis; Rosemary Clooney; Jerry Vale; Les Paul & Mary Ford; Tony Bennett; Joan Weber; Edith Piaf; Sammy Kaye; Guy Mitchell; Mitch Miller; Doris Day; Marty Robbins; Four Lads; Frankie Laine; Johnny Horton; Dinah Shore; Johnnie Ray; Jimmy Dorsey; Patti Page; Les Compagnons de la Chanson.
Fifties Greatest Love Songs........ Columbia Musical Treasury (S) DS 718 5-10
Percy Faith; Johnny Mathis; Rosemary Clooney; Jerry Vale; Les Paul & Mary Ford; Tony Bennett; Joan Weber; Edith Piaf; Sammy Kaye; Guy Mitchell. (Columbia House Record Club issue.)
Fillet of Soul........ Stax (S) STS 3021 10-15 73
Issac Hayes; Staple Singers; Rufus Thomas; Little Milton; Johnnie Taylor; Mavis Staples; Dramatics; Mel & Tim; Frederick Knight; Bar-Kays.
Fillmore - the Last Days (Bill Graham Presents in San Francisco) (3 LP)........ CBS/Fillmore (S) Z3X-31390 40-50 72
(Boxed set. Includes bonus interview 45, poster and souvenir ticket.) Lamb; Elvin Bishop Group; Malo; Taj Mahal; Boz Scaggs; Sons of Champlin; It's a Beautiful Day; Quicksilver Messenger Service; Tower of Power; Cold Blood; Stoneground; New Riders of the Purple Sage; Grateful Dead; Hot Tuna; Santana.
Fillmore - the Last Days (3 LP)........ Warner Bros. (S) 3XS-2637 30-40 72
(Reissue.) Lamb; Elvin Bishop Group; Malo; Taj Mahal; Boz Scaggs; Sons of Champlin; It's a Beautiful Day; Quicksilver Messenger Service; Tower of Power; Cold Blood; Stoneground; New Riders of the Purple Sage; Grateful Dead; Hot Tuna; Santana.
Fine Mess........ Motown (S) 6180 8-10 86
(Soundtrack.) Temptations; Mary Jane Girls; Chico De Barge; Henry Mancini; Smokey Robinson; Nick Jameson; Keith & Darryl; Los Lobos; Christine McVie.
Finest of Folk Bluesmen........ Bethlehem (S) 6017 5-10 76
Lonnie Johnson; John Lee Hooker; Piney Brown; Texas Slim; others.
Fink Along with Mad........ Big Top (M) 1306 30-50 63
Dellwoods; Mike Russo; Jeannie Hayes.
Fire & Ice........ Warner/Realistic (S) OP 1525 5-10 82
Diana Ross; Donna Summer; Rickie Lee Jones; Manhattan Transfer; Kim Carnes; Pat Benatar; Heart; Blondie; Carly Simon; Irene Cara; Pretenders; Bonnie Raitt; Abba; Pointer Sisters.
Fire into Music........ CTI/Salvation/Kudu (S) CTS-2 8-12 76
Grover Washington Jr.; Freddie Hubbard; stanley Turrentine; Bob James; Hubert Laws; Deodato; Hubert Laws; Deodato; Esther Phillips; George Benson; Hank Crawford.
Fire on the Strings........ Starday (M) M-221 10-20 67
Fire on the Strings........ Starday (M) S-221 10-20 67
Bob Wills; Boots Randolph with Jimmy Richardson; Flatt & Scruggs; Leon McAuliffe & His Cimarron Boys; Arthur Smith; Tommy Hill; Reno & Smiley; Tommy Jackson; Pete Drake.
Fire on the Strings........ Starday (M) SYM-0127 10-20 67
Fire on the Strings........ Starday (S) SYS-0127 10-20 67
(RCA Record Club issue.) Bob Wills; Boots Randolph with Jimmy Richardson; Flatt & Scruggs; Leon McAuliffe & His Cimarron Boys; Arthur Smith; Tommy Hill; Reno & Smiley; Tommy Jackson; Pete Drake.
Firestone 5 Star Fiesta........ Capitol Custom (M) CSD-1001 15-20 62
Dean Martin; Jackie Gleason; Nat King Cole; Kay Starr; Guy Lombardo.
First Annual Rock 'N' Roll Convention Show........ Post (SE) P-1950 8-12
Duprees; Olympics; Rivieras; Shangri-Las; Lee Andrews & Hearts; Crests; Del Shannon; Jerry Butler; Jimmy Charles; Dells.
First Authentic 1950's Rock & Roll Collection (4 LP)........ JBR (M) SQ 95717 20-30 70s
(Mail order.) Pentagons; Carolonns; Clyde McPhatter; Shells; Dion & Belmonts; Parktownes; Meadowlartks; Lonnie & Carolonns; Capris; Diamonds; Dubs; Ivy-Tones; Crew-Cuts; Four Counts; Edsels; Platters; Wheels; Quin-Tones; Chifons; Penguins; Edsels; Platters; Wheels; Quin-Tones; Chiffons; Penguins; Half-Notes; Passions; Cuff-Links; Students; Moonglows; Dion; Heartbeats; Angels; Mellowkings; Zirkons; Youngsters; Danleers; Crests; Majestics; Delacardos; Quotations; Five Satins; Tokens; Shields; Guitar Kings; Hearts; Virtues; Five Discs; King Curtis; Tony Orlando; Wailers; Graduates; Mystics; Jerry Lee Lewis; Formations; Phil Phillips & Twilights; Fascinations; Harptones.
First Authentic 1950's Rock & Roll Collection (4 LP)........ Jukebox (M) SQ 95717 20-30
First Authentic 1950's Rock & Roll Collection (4 LP)........ Jukebox (M) SQ 94986/94989 20-40 60s
(Mail order.) Danleers; Graduates; Tony Orlando: Passions; Penguins; Capris; Clyde McPhatter; Velvetones; Tokens; Platters; Jarmels; Five Satins; Diamonds; Wheels; Chiffons; Cuff Links; Admirations; Dion; Dion & Belmonts; Harptones; Shells; Belmonts; Crew-Cuts; Fascinations; Meadow Larks; Wailers; Youngsters; Lee Andrews & Hearts; Studets; Shields; Arrogants; Quin-Tones; Five Discs; Crests; Dubs; Bluenotes; Jerry Lee Lewis; Jordan & Fascinations; Mystics; Phil Phillips; King Curtiss; Delacardos; Heartbeats; Moonglows; Quotations; Shantones; Zircons; Formations; Vibraniques; Doe-vells; Counts.
First Christmas Record for Children........ Harmony (S) 14554 5-10 68
Doris Day; Jimmy Boyd; Red Skelton; others.
First Edition Golden 20 Awards........ Gilmor (S) GT-900 5-10
First Generation - Soul........ Buddah (S) BDS-7504 8-12 69
Jerry Butler; Betty Everett; Jesse Belvin; Gladys Knight & Pips; Jimmy Hughes; Gene Chandler; Jimmy Charles; Dee Clark; Maxine Brown; Chris Kenner; Lee Dorsey; Bobby Lewis; Gene Allison.

First Great Rock Festivals of the '70s - Isle of Wright Atlantic Pop Festival (3 LP)............ Columbia (S) G3X-30805 15-25 71
Jimi Hendrix; Allman Brothers; Johnny Winter And; Kris Kristofferson; Miles Davis; Ten Years After; Sly & Family Stone; Mountain; Poco; Procol Harum; Chambers Brothers; Cactus; Leonard Cohen; David Bromberg.

First Meetin' .... World Pacific (M) WP-1817 10-20 64
First Meetin' .... World Pacific (S) ST-1817 10-20 64
Lightnin' Hopkins; Brownie McGhee & Sonny Terry; Joe Williams; others.

First of the Famous .... Capitol (M) T-2275 15-25 65
Hank Thompson; Sonny James; Tex Ritter; Faron Young; Wanda Jackson; Ferlin Husky; Buck Owens; Jean Shepard; Tennessee Ernie Ford; Jimmy Wakely; Tex Williams; Merle Travis.

First Vibration .... Do It Now (S) LP-5000 10-20 69
Beatles; Animals; Hoyt Axton; Buffalo Springfield; Byrds; Canned Heat; Chad & Jeremy; Donovan; Genesis; Jefferson Airplane; Jimi Hendrix; Peanut Butter Conspiracy; Ravi Shankar; Things to Come.

Five Kings of the Country World .... Harmony (S) KH-31561 6-12 72
Johnny Cash; Ray Price; Marty Robbins; Jerry Reed; David Houston.

Five Queens of Country Music .... Nashville (S) NLP 2057 8-12
Patsy Cline; Dottie West; Jan Howard; Melba Montgomery; Margie Singleton.

Five Queens of the Country World .... Harmony (S) KH-31535 6-12 72
Lynn Anderson; Tammy Wynette; Arlene Harden; Barbara Mandrell; Sammi Smith.

Five Star Fiesta: see Firestone 5 Star Fiesta

Five String Banjo Jamboree .... Mercury (M) MGW-12299 10-20 65
Five String Banjo Jamboree .... Mercury (S) SRW-16299 15-20 65
Flatt & Scruggs; Stanley Brothers; Carl Story; others.

Flamingo Kid .... Varèse Sarabande (S) STV-81232 25-30 84
Flamingo Kid .... Motown (S) 6131ML 10-15 84
(Soundtrack.) Jesse Frederick; Martha Reeves & Vandellas; Chiffons; Acker Bilk; Dion; Little Richard; Barrett Strong; Impressions; Hank Ballard & Midnighters; Silhouettes; Maureen Steele; Crystals.

Flappers, Speakeasies & Bathtub Gin .... Warner Bros. M/S 1425 10-20 61
Ira Ironstrings; Matty Matlock & Paducah Patrol; Dorothy Provine; Eddie Condon & Chicagoans; Joe Fingers Carr; Gus Farney.

Flash Fearless vs. the Zorg Women, Parts 5 & 6 .... Chrysalis (S) CHR-1072 8-12 75
(Soundtrack.) Elkie Brooks; Alice Cooper; James Dewar; Jim Dandy; John Entwistle; Eddie Jobson; Frankie Miller; Carmen Appice; Bill Bruford; Justin Hayward; Nicky Hopkins; Keith Moon; John Weider; James Dewar.

Flashback '50s .... K-Tel/Era (S) BU 4520 5-10 77
Jim Lowe; Little Richard; Coasters; Jack Scott; Duane Eddy; Diamonds; Sammy Turner; Frankie Ford; Buddy Knox; Carl Dobkins Jr.; Jimmie Rodgers; Platters; Johnny & Hurricanes; Fiestas; Jimmy Clanton; Lloyd Price.

Flash-Back Greats of the '60s .... K-Tel (S) TU-229 8-12 72
Joanie Somers; Dion; Gene Pitney; Ron Holden; Chris Montez; Sam the Sham & Pharaohs; Jay & Techniques; Chiffons; Ruby & Romantics; Bobby Hebb; Dobie Gray; New Vaudeville Band; Jewel Akens; Donnie Brooks; Teddy Bears. (Apparently there are three different LPs with the number 229.)

Flash-Back Greats of the '60s .... K-Tel (S) TU-229 8-12 73
Beatles with Tony Sheridan; Buddy Holly; Dion; Terry Stafford; Chad & Jeremy; Left Banke; Ray Charles; Joe South. (Apparently there are three different LPs with the number 229.)

Flash-Back Greats of the '60s .... K-Tel (S) TU-229 8-12 73
Len Barry; Strawberry Alarm Clock; Cuff Links; Peggy March; Cowsills; Fontella Bass; Ramsey Lewis Trio; Stone Poneys; Neil Sedaka; Peter & Gordon; Leslie Gore; Shangri-Las; Beach Boys; O'Kaysions. (Apparently there are three different LPs with the number 229.)

Flash-Back Greats of the '60s (2 LP) .... K-Tel (S) TU-228 10-15 73
Steam; Lobo; Ides of March; Bullit; Joe Simon; Bells; Teegarden & Van Winkle; Wadsworth Mansion; Brian Hyland; Dennis Coffee; Olivia Newton-John; Hot Butter; Sly & Family Stone; Honeycone; Georgio; Five Man Electrical Band; Who; Flash; Raiders; Hamilton, Joe Frank & Reynolds; Fortunes; Osmonds; Lighthouse; Daddy Dewdrops.

Flashbacks from the Golden Group Era: see 14 Flashbacks from the Golden Group Era

Flashdance .... Casablanca (S) NBLP-7278 8-10 83
Flashdance .... Casablanca (S) 422-811-492-1 8-10 83
(Soundtrack.) Irene Cara; Shandi; Helen St. John; Karen Kamon; Joe Esposito; Laura Branigan; Donna Summer; Cycle V; Kim Carnes; Michael Sembello.

Fletch .... MCA (S) 6142 8-10 85
(Soundtrack.) Stephanie Mills; Dan Hartman; John Farnum; Fixx; Kim Wilde; Harold Faltermeyer.

Folk '66 .... Design (M) DLP-207 8-12 66
Folk '66 .... Design (S) SDLP-207 8-12 66
Hoyt Axton; Judy Henshe; Limeliters; Barry McGuire; New Christy Minstrels.

Folk A-Go-Go .... Verve/Folkways (M) FV-9011 10-20 65
Folk A-Go-Go .... Verve/Folkways (S) FVS-9011 10-20 65
Woody Guthrie; Pete Seeger; Jean Ritchie; others.

Folk and Popular Blues Styles .... New World (S) 290

Folk Blues .... Continental (M) C-16003 15-25 62
Big Boy Ellis; Sonny Boy & Sam; others.

Folk Blues Song Fest .... Aravel (M) AB-1004 10-20 64
Leadbelly; Big Bill Broonzy; Memphis Slim; Brownie McGhee; Sonny Terry; Lightnin' Hopkins; Arbee Stidham; Cisco Houston; Woody Guthrie; Memphis Slim; Jack Dupree.

Folk Concert .... Onacrest (S) ONA-5004 10-20

Folk Favorites .... Wyncote (M) W-9010 10-20 63
Folk Favorites .... Wyncote (S) SW-9010 10-20 63
Villagers; Raun MacKinnon; Three Young Men from Montana.

Folk Festival .... MCA (S) 9113 5-10 80s
Folk Festival .... ABC-Paramount (M) ABC-408 15-20 62
Folk Festival .... ABC-Paramount (S) ABCS-408 15-25 62
Oscar Brand; Jean Ritchie; others.

Folk Festival .... Legacy (S) LEG-110 8-10 70
Judy Collins; Glen Campbell; Theodore Bikel; Rod McKuen; Oscar Brand; Dillards; Will Holt; Lightnin' Hopkins; Ed McCurdy; Odetta; Pete Seeger; Sonny Terry & Brownie McGee; Mason Williams; Glenn Yarbrough.

Folk Festival at Newport, Vol. 1 .... Vanguard (S) VRS-9062 20-30 60

Folk Festival at Newport, Vol. 2 .... Vanguard (S) VRS-9063 20-30 60
Odetta; Joan Baez; Bob Gibson; New Lost City Ramblers; Barbara Dane; Sonny Terry & Brownie McGhee.

Folk Festival of the Blues .... Argo (M) LP-4031 30-50 64
Muddy Waters; Buddy Guy; Howlin' Wolf; Sonny Boy Williamson; Willie Dixon.

Folk Heroes .... Disneyland (M) 3921 10-20 64

Folk Heroes .... Disneyland (S) ST-3921 10-20 64
Fess Parker; Wellingtons; Rex Allen; others.

Folk Jamboree .... Columbia Special Products (S) CSP-205 10-20 60s
Bob Dylan; Village Stompers; Johnny Cash; New Christy Minstrels; Les & Larry Elgart; Flatt & Scruggs; Clancy Brother; Tommy Makem; Pete Seeger; Brothers Four; Banjo Barons. (Made for Philco.)

Folk Music of Newport Folk Festival, 1959-1960, Vol. 1 .... Folkways (M) FA-2431 20-25 61
Pat Clancy; Pete Seeger; Frank Hamilton; others.

Folk Music of Newport Folk Festival, 1959-1960, Vol. 2 .... Folkways (M) FA-2432 20-25 61
Sonny Terry; Brownie McGhee; Guy Carawan; others.

Folk, Pop 'N' Jazz Sampler .... Elektra (M) SMP-3 15-20 57
Jazz Messengers; Norene Tate; Teddy Charles; Josh White; Cynthia Gooding; Clarence Cooper; Ed McCurdy; Sabicas; Susan Reed; Glenn Yarbrough; New York Jazz Quartet.

Folk Scene .... Elektra (M) MP-6 15-20 62

Folk Scene .... Elektra (S) SMP-6 20-25 62
Limeliters; Josh White; Theodore Bikel; others.

Folk Singers of Washington Square .... Continental (M) C-2010 10-20 62

Folk Singers of Washington Square .... Continental (S) CS-2010 10-20 62
Anne Bird; Martin Lorin; Molly Scott; others.

Folk Sixties Baby Boomer Classics .... JCI (S) 3109 5-10 85
Joan Baez; Brothers Four; Highwaymen; Kingston Trio; New Christy Minstrels; Rooftop Singers; Sandpipers; Pete Seeger; Seekers; Serendipity Singers; Weavers; We Five.

Folk Song and Minstrelsy (4 LP) .... Vanguard (S) SRL-7624 ?? 62
(Boxed set includes 26-page booklet.) Joan Baez; Leon Bibb; Deller Consort; Jimmy Driftwood; Bob Gibson; Ronnie Gilbert; Cisco Houston; Ewan MacColl; Ed McCurdy; Tommy Makem; Alan Mills; John Jacob Niles; Odetta; Pete Seeger; Weavers.

Folk Sound .... Columbia Special Products (S) CSP-299 10-15 67
New Christy Minstrels; Johnny Cash; Brothers Four; Statler Brothers; Simon & Garfunkel; Flatt & Scruggs; Marty Robbins; Bob Dylan; Jimmy Dean; Banjo Barons.

Folked Again - Best of Mountain Railroad, Vol. 1 .... Mountain Railroad (S) MR 52671 8-12 87
Tom Paxton; Bob Gibson; Josh White Jr.; Gamble Rogers; Rod MacDonald; Free Hot Lunch; Dick Pinney; Steve Young; Betsy Kaske; Jim Post; Gibson & Camp; Dave Snaker Ray.

Folksingers 'Round Harvard Square: see BAEZ, Joan, Bill Wood and Ted Alevizos

Folksong '65 .... Elektra (M) S-8 10-20 65
Tom Rush; Judy Collins; Koerner; Ray & Glover; Hamilton Camp; Dick Rosmini; Tom Paxton; Paul Butterfield Blue Band; Kathy & Carol; Mark Spoelstra; Fred Neil; Bruce Murdock; Phil Ochs.

Folkways: a Vision Shared, a Tribute to Woody Guthrie & Leadbelly .... Columbia (S) OC 44034 5-10 88
Bob Dylan; Sweet Honey in the Rock; John Mellencamp; Bruce Springsteen; U2; Little Richard; Fishbone; Arlo Guthrie; Willie Nelson; Emmylou Harris; Taj Mahal; Brian Wilson; Pete Seeger; Doc Watson; Little Red Schoolhouse Chorus.

Follow that Bird .... RCA Victor (S) CBL1-5475 8-10 85
(Soundtrack.) Van Dyke Parks; Waylon Jennings; Alabama; Ronnie Milsap; Sesame Street Cast; Frank Oz; Muppets.

Folsom Prison Blues .... Nashville (SE) NLP-2059 5-10 68
Johnny Cash; Flatt & Scruggs; Joe Maphis; Billie Morgan; Carl Story; Bill Dudley; Hylo Brown; Pee Wee King.

Folsom Prison Blues and Other Country Hits .... Modern Sound (S) MS-599 5-10 69

Fonzie Favorites .... Ahed (S) TVLP-177602R 8-10 76
(Mail order offer.) Pratt & Mclain; Coasters; Bobby Darin; Everly Brothers; Joe Jones; Genents; Jerry Lee Lewis; Bill Haley & His Comets; Frankie Lymon; Heyettes; Dubs; Flamingos; Little Anthony & Imperials; Chantels; Jimmy Charles; Rays; Five Satins; Cleftones; Lee Dorsey.

Fonzie Favorites .... Juke Box International (S) TVLP-177602 RJ 8-12 76
(Mail order offer.) Pratt & Mclain; Coasters; Bobby Darin; Everly Brothers; Joe Jones; Genents; Jerry Lee Lewis; Bill Haley & His Comets; Frankie Lymon; Heyettes; Dubs; Flamingos; Little Anthony & Imperials; Chantels; Jimmy Charles; Rays; Five Satins; Cleftones; Lee Dorsey.

Fool Britannia .... Acapella (M) 1 5-10

Fools .... Reprise (S) RS-6429 12-15 71
(Soundtrack.) Kenny Rogers & First Edition; Mimi Farina; Shorty Rogers; Katherine Ross.

Footloose .... Columbia (S) JS-39242 8-10 84

Footloose (Picture disc) .... Columbia (S) 9C9-39404 10-15 84
(Soundtrack.) Kenny Loggins; Shalamar; Deniece Williams; Mike Reno & Ann Wilson; Bonnie Tyler; Sammy Hagar; Karla Bonoff; Moving Pictures.

Footprints in Time .... White Whale (S) W-7125 15-25 70
Packers; Ad Libs; Shangri-Las; Sir Douglas Quintet; Wailers; Barbara Lynn; Romeos; Dixie Cups; Trade Winds; Cascades.

For a Musical Merry Christmas .... RCA (M) PRM 163 5-10 64

For a Musical Merry Christmas .... RCA (SE) PRS 163 5-10 64
Hugo Winterhalter; Tony Martin; Three Suns; Ames Brothers; Rosalind Elias; Giorgio Tozzi; Eddie Fisher; Hugo & Luigi with Their Children's Chorus; Dick Leibert; Gisele MacKenzie; Augustana Choir; Melachrino Strings; Jan Peerce & Columbus Boys Choir. (Made for B.F. Goodrich.)

For a Musical Merry Christmas .... RCA (S) PRS 253 5-10 67
Vic Damone; Melachrino Strings; Anita Kerr Singers; Floyd Cramer; Hugo Winterhalter; John Gary; Dick Leibert; Living Strings; Jim Reeves; Hugo & Luigi Children's Chorus; Arthur Fiedler & Boston Pops; Norman Luboff Choir; Three Suns.

For Free Form Radio Stations .... Motown (S) 101 8-12
(Promotional issue only.) Stevie Wonder; others.

For Jazz Lovers .... EmArcy (M) M 36086 20-30 50s
Cannonball Adderley; Sarah Vaughn; Terry Gibbs; Dinah Washington; Clifford Brown; Eddie Heywood; Helen Merrill; Erroll Garner.

For Ladies Only .... Columbia Special Products (S) CSP 12943 10-15
Aretha Franklin; Leslie Gore; Jeannie C. Riley; Dionne Warwick; Vikki Lawrence; Dusty Springfield; Barbara Lynn; Shirelles; Marcie Blane; Julie Rogers; Barbara Mason; Delaney & Bonnie; Sandy Posey; Chi Coltrane; Joan Baez; Lynn Anderson; Melanie; Lulu; Springfields; Janis Ian; Judy Collins; Merrilee Rush.

For Segregationists Only .... Rebel (S) 1000 20-30 67
Johnny Rebel; others.

For the Collector (4 LP) .... Laurie (SP) SLP 7000 15-20 81
(Boxed set.) Del Satins; Dino & Diplomats; Mystics; Skyliners; Four Epics; Billy Vera & Contrasts; Carlo; Criterions; Four Pennies; Five Discs; Harps; DeMilles; Reparata & Del Rons; Bernadette Carroll; Four Graduates; Ernie Maresca; Jimmy Curtiss; Slim Jim; Capris; Dream Weavers; Chimes; Ersel Hickey; Music Explosion; Scott Garrett; Jarmels; Curtis Lee; Dean & Jean; Randy & Rainbows; Traces; Boots Walker; Barbarians; Jimmy Clanton; Rayons.

For the Good Times .... ???? 5-10
(Label name missing, but likely Columbia or Epic.) David Houston; Lynn Anderson; Larry Gatlin; Connie Smith; Joe Stampley; Sonny James; Johnny Cash; Charlie Rich; David Allen Coe; Tammy Wynette.

For the in Crowd .... Capitol (S) SL 6537 10-15 66
Peter & Gordon; Lettermen; New Classic Singers; Nancy Wilson; Lou Rawls; Hollyridge Strings.

For the Love of Elvis (Elvis Novelties) .... Superstar (S) SS-110 10-15
Bill Parsons; Jim Ford; Stan Freeburg; Holly Twins; Carl Perkins; Sonny Cole; Sophisticates; Bobby Bare; Genee Harris; Jerry Reed; Thirteens; Greats; the Unknown.

For the Young at Heart: see ROE, Tommy / Bobby Rydell / Gene Pitney

For the Young at Heart .... Columbia Special Products (S) CSPS 388 8-12 70s
Brothers Four; Gary Puckett & Union Gap; Diahann Carroll; Ray Conniff Singers; Aretha Franklin; Percy Faith; O.C. Smith; Anita Bryant; Steve Lawrence & Eydie Gorme.

For Twisters Only .... Ace (M) LP-1021 20-30 62

For You Alone .... Columbia Limited Edition (M) GB-2 8-12 50s

For You Alone .... Columbia Limited Edition (S) GB-2 8-12 50s
Frank DeVol; Percy Faith; Otto Cesana; Mitch Miller; Sammy Kaye; Richard Maltby; Norman Luboff Choir; Paul Weston; Andre Kostelanetz; Ray Conniff.

For Young Lovers Only: see Jerry Blavat Presents for Young Lovers Only

For Young Teenagers Only: see Jerry Blavat Presents for Yon Teenagers Only

For Your Precious Love 1950's (2 LP) .... RCA (S) SUL2-0691 8-12 84
Paul Anka; Dion & Belmonts; Patience & Prudence; Fleetwoods; Mystics; Three Chuckles; Moonglows; Cadillacs; Tempos; Frankie Avalon; Neil Sedaka; Skyliners; Ferlin Husky; Ruth McFadden; Four Freshmen; Solitaires; Spaniels; Jerry Butler & Impressions; Mickey & Sylvia; Channels; Platters; Fats Domino; Della Reese; Crows; Tune Weavers; Thomas Wayne; Drifters; Johnnie & Joe; Sixteens; Jimmy Rodgers; Crew-Cuts; Teen Queens; Jesse Belvin; Everly Brothers; Five Satins.

Foreplay, Vol. 1 .... A&M (S) SP-17015 5-10 78
(Promotional issue only.) Airwaves; Billy Swan; Wondergap; Bryan Haworth; Craig Nuttycombe; .38 Special; Letta Mbulu; Garland Jeffreys; Chuck Berry; Chesterfields; Delights; Jerry Lee Lewis; Timmy & Tulips; Big Beat Band.

Foreplay, Vol. 1 (Horizon Music Records & Tapes, Sampler 1) .... A&M (S) SP-17038 5-10 78
(Promotional issue only.) Dr. John; Neil Larsen; Mark Almond Band.

Foreplay, Vol. 4 .... A&M (S) SP-17092 5-10 79
(Promotional issue only.) Neil Larsen; Brenda Russell.

Foreplay, March 1978, FPS #6 .... A&M (S) SP-4684 5-10 78
Airwaves; Billy Swan; Wondergap; Bryn Haworth; Craig Nuttycombe; 38 Special; Letta Mbulu; Garland Jeffreys; American Hot Wax.

Foreplay, Vol. 7 .... A&M (S) SP-17018 5-10 78
(Promotional issue only.) Pablo Cruise; Quincy Jones; Stranglers; Tarney Spencer Band; Gap Mangione; Sylvia Sims; LTD; Rita Coolidge; Paul Winter; Vic Squires; William B. Smith.

Foreplay, Vol. 9 .... A&M (S) SP-17032 5-10 78
(Promotional issue only. Single-sided disc.) Ozark Mountain Daredevils; Chuck Mangione; Alessi; Tim Cutty; Dirty Angels.

Foreplay, Vol. 10 .... A&M (S) SP-17036 5-10 78
(Promotional issue only. Single-sided disc.) Booker T. Jones; Richard Kee; Peter C. Johnson; Les McCann; Randall Chowning Band.

Foreplay, Vol. 17 .... A&M (S) SP 17074 5-10 79
Tarney/Spencer Band; Chris DeBurgh; U.K. Squeeze; Tim Weisburg.

Foreplay, Vol. 20 .... A&M (S) SP-17088 5-10 79
(Promotional issue only.) Nils Lofgren; Lazy Racer; David Kubinec; Airwaves; LTD; Tim Curry; Marc Benno; Rick Wakeman.

Foreplay, Vol. 24 .... A&M (S) SP 17096 5-10 79
Ben Sidran; Bell & James; Rita Coolidge; Sad Cafe; Les McCann; 1994; Dr. John; Halloween Horrors.

Foreplay, Vol. 29 .... A&M (S) SP 17110 5-10 79
Brothers Johnson; Private Lighting; Matthew Fisher; Booker T. Jones; Bryan Adams.

Foreplay, Vol. 31 (A&M Pre Release Sampler April 1980) .... A&M (S) SP-17113 5-10 80
Rockie Robbins; Sterling; Collins & Collins; Lazy River; Humans.

Foreplay, Vol. 32 .... A&M (S) SP-17116 5-10 80
(Promotional issue only. Single-sided disc.) Joan Armatrading; Rockie Robbins; Mark Andrews; Gents.

Foreplay, Vol. 36 .... A&M (S) SP 17124 5-10 80
Head East; Seawind; Stranglers; Chelsea; Oingo Boingo.

Foreplay, Vol. 37 .... A&M (S) SP-17128 5-10 80
(Promotional issue only. Single-sided disc.) Peter Allen; Athetico; Spizz; Fist.

Foreplay, Vol. 38 .... A&M (S) SP-17132 5-10 80
(Promotional issue only.) Albert Lee; Emmylou Harris; Johnny Cash; Charlie Daniels; Levon Helm; Tommy Dee; Darlene Love; Dean Conn; Wall of Voodoo.

Foreplay, Vol. 40 .... A&M (S) SP-17144 5-10 81
(Promotional issue only.) Rita Coolidge; Doc Holliday; Ali Thomson; Dennis Brown; Jerry Knight; Atlantic Starr; Passage; John Cale; Patrick Martin.

Foreplay, Vol. 43 .... A&M (S) SP-17134 5-10 81
(Promotional issue only.) Peter Frampton; Chas Jankel; Oingo Boingo; Robert Williams; Zeyder Zar; Payolas.

Foreplay, Vol. 45 .... A&M (S) SP-17162 5-10 81
(Promotional issue only.) Herb Alpert; Joe Jackson's Jumpin' Five; Tim Curry; Bryan Adams; Tubes; Go-Go's; others.

Forever Blues Original Hits, Vol. I .... Forever (SE) FR-104 8-10 70
John Lee Hooker; Jimmy McCracklin; Junior Parker; Howlin' Wolf; Lightning Hopkins; Sonny Boy Williamson; Bobby Marchan; Lowell Fulson; Little Walter; Muddy Waters; Gene Allison; Bobby Bland.

Forever Country .... Columbia Special Products (S) 13613 5-10 76
Lynn Anderson; Ray Price; Loretta Lynn; David Houston; Johnny Cash; June Carter; Barbara Mandrell; Webb Pierce; Barbara Fairchild; George Jones; Tanya Tucker; Sonny James; Tammy Wynette; Henson Cargill; Jody Miller; Kitty Wells; Bill Anderson; George Morgan; Patsy Cline.

Forever Country Original Hits, Vol. I .... Forever (SE) 105 8-10 70
Rex Allen; Rusty Draper; George Jones; Johnny Preston; Ned Miller; Jerry Wallace; Leroy Van Dyke; Claude Gray; Faron Young; Patsy Cline; others.

Forever Gold Groups Original Hits, Vol. I .... Forever (SE) FR-102 8-10 70
Mello-Kings; Platters; Cuff Links; Silhouettes; Five Satins; Pastels; Turbans; Magnificants; Fireflies; Del-Vikings; El Dorados; Nutmegs; Monotones; Contours; Spaniels; Diamonds.

Forever Gold Groups Original Hits, Vol. II .... Forever (SE) FR-103 8-10 70
Capris; Danleers; Channels; Crew-Cuts; Pastels; Three Friends; Baysiders; Penguins; Platters; Orioles; Gadabouts; Zodiacs Featuring Maurice Williams; Five Satins; Echoes.

Forgotten Hits: Unforgettables .... Forget-Me-Not (M) LPF-101 15-25 60

Forgotten Million Sellers .... King (M) 792 20-30 62
Hank Ballard & Midnighters; James Brown; Billy Ward & Dominoes; Wynonie Harris; Ivory Joe Hunter; Lonnie Johnson; Earl King; Otis Williams; Freddie King; Little Willie John; Five Royales; Bill Doggett; Bull Moose Jackson; Lulu Reed.

Foster Brooks' Roasts .... Roast (S) RR-1002 10-15 76
Dean Martin; Foster Brooks; Hubert Humphrey; Joe Namath; Carroll O'Connor; Johnny Carson; Ralph Nader; Don Rickles; others.

Foundations of Modern Jazz .... Everest (S) FS 229 10-15
Charlie Mingus; others.

Four Big Hits: see PRICE, Ray / Johnny Horton / Carl Smith / George Morgan

Four Decades of Jazz (2 LP) .... Xanadu (S) 5001 10-15

Four Kings of Country Music: JONES, George / Buck Owens / David Houston / Tommy Hill.

Four Trombones .... Fantasy (S) 86005 25-40 62
(Blue vinyl.) J.J. Johnson; Kai Winding; Bennie Green; Willie Dennis; Charlie Mingus; Art Taylor; John Lewis.

Four Trombones, Vol. 2 .... Fantasy (M) 6008 15-20 60s
Cannonball Adderley; Clifford Brown; Sarah Vaughan; Eddie Haywood; Terry Gibbs; Helen Merrill; Dinah Washington; Erroll Garner.

Fourth of July – a Rockin' Celebration of America .... Love Foundation (S) No Number Used 10-15 86
Ringo Starr & Beach Boys; Mike Love; Oak Ridge Boys; Beach Boys & Oak Ridge Boys; Joe Ely; Four Tops; Three Dog Night; America; Bellamy Brothers; Beach Boys with Julio Iglesias; Beach Boys & Jimmy Page & Friends.

Frank Guida Presents Greatest Hits .... Legrand (M) LFG-1000 10-15 79
Gary "U.S." Bonds; Frank Guida & Swedish All Star Orchestra; Jimmy Soul; Gregory Cafone; Church Street 5; Tommy Facenda; Lenis Guess. (Also issued as *Rock's World Revolution - the Roots*.)

Frank Sinatra & His Friends Want You to Have Yourself a Merry Little Christmas .... Reprise (S) R9-50,0001 25-30 61
Dean Martin; Frank Sinatra; Jo Stafford; Billy May; McGuire Sisters; Keely Smith; Hi-Lo's; Sammy Davis Jr.; Les Baxter's Balladeers; Mavis Rivers; Lou Monte; Nelson Riddle; Rosemary Clooney.

Frank X. Feller Strikes Back .... Post (S) 671 8-12 60s
Dixie Cups; Gary "U.S." Bonds; Shangri-Las; Cascades; Inez Foxx; Ivy Tones; Claudine Clark; Ad Libs; Tina Brett; Exceptions; Anthony & Sophomores; Barbara George; Duprees; Sheppards; Quintones; Moonglows; Dreamlovers; Sapphires; Baby Washington; Blue Notes; Crests.

Frank X. Feller Made in Philadelphia: see 22 Hits by the Original Artists

Frankie Laine & His Guests .... Wyncote W-9161 10-15
Frankie Laine; John Gary; Merv Griffin; Teddy Wilson; Maynard Ferguson.

Frantic Fifties as Broadcast in "The World Today" .... Mutual Broadcasting System (M) RW-4082 200-300 59
(Promotional issue only.) Elvis Presley; others. (News highlights LP.)

Frat Rock .... Rhino (S) RNLP-70136 5-10 87
Kingsmen; Sam the Sham & Pharaohs; Swingin' Medallions; Human Beinz; Isley Brothers; McCoys; Troggs; Strangeloves; Righteous Brothers; Gentrys; Surfaris; Dynatones.

Freakout U.S.A. .... Sidewalk (M) T-5901 15-20 67

Freakout U.S.A. .... Sidewalk (SE) DT-5901 15-20 67
Aftermath; Mugwumps; Mom's Boys; Glass Family; Jesters; International Theatre Foundation; Everybodys Children; Hands of Time.

Free to Be...You and Me .... Arista (S) AL 8-8044 8-12
New Seekers; Mel Brooks; Marlo Thomas; Diana Ross; Billy DeWolfe; Harry Belafonte; Carol Channing; Tom Smothers;Rosey Grier; Dick Cavett; Alan Alda; Diana Sands; Jack Cassidy; Shirley Jones; Bobby Morse. (One source shows this number as 4003. We're not sure which is correct.)

Freedom (2 LP) .... Sessions/RCA (S) DPL2-0110 10-15 75
Who; Jefferson Airplane; Barry McGuire; Ocean; Country Joe & Fish; Norman Greenbaum; Doors; Otis Redding; Linda Ronstadt; Friend & Lover; Animals; Joan Baez; Nilsson; BTO; Coven; Cowsills; Cream; Jimi Hendrix; Brotherhood of Man; Guess Who; Steppenwolf; Merrilee Rush; Dion; Uriah Heep. (Mail order offer. Special products. Made for Sessions.)

Freedom Rock (4 LP) .... Sessions/Warner Bros. (SP) OP 4510 15-20 87
Byrds; Ten Years After; Jethro Tull; Joan Baez; Edwin Starr; Santana; Harry Nilsson; Deep Purple; Otis Redding; Brotherhood of Man; Jefferson Airplane; Canned Heat; Friend & Lover; America; Lynyrd Skynyrd; Allman Brothers; Guess Who; Elton John; Ocean; Three Dog Night; Derek & Dominos; Moody Blues; Five Man Electrical Band; Jonathan Edwards; O'Jays; Cream; Judy Collins; Seals & Crofts; Zager & Evans; Alice Cooper; Youngbloods; Sonny & Cher; Dion; Melanie; Spirit; James Taylor; Lobo; Coven.

Freedomland, U.S.A. .... Columbia (M) CL-1484 20-25 60

Freedomland, U.S.A. .... Columbia (S) CS-8275 20-30 60
Johnny Horton; Jill Corey; others.

Friday at the Cage A-Go-Go: see FUGITIVES/ Oxford Five / Lourds / Individuals

Friday Night Forever .... Candelite (M) CU-154 5-10 82
Four Tops; Marvelettes; Miracles featuring Smokey Robinson; Mary Wells; Jimmy Ruffin; Supremes featuring Diana Ross; Martha & Vandellas; Contours; Temptations.

Friends .... A&M (S) SP-8021 10-15 71
(Promotional sampler.) Cat Stevens; Humble Pie; Blodwyn Pig; Free; Spooky Tooth; Lee Michaels; Move; Fairport Convention; Ron Davies; Lambert & Nuttycombe; Quincy Jones; Fotheringay.

Fright Night........Private I (S) SZ 40087 8-10 85
(Soundtrack.) J. Geils Band; Autograph; Ian Hunter; April Wine; Devo; Sparks; Evelyn "Champagne" King; White Sister; Fabulous Fontaines; Brad Fiedel.
Fritz the Cat........Fantasy (M) F-9405 20-25 72
Fritz the Cat........Fantasy (M) MPF-4532 10-12 Re
(Soundtrack.) Bo Diddley; Alice Stuart; Innocent; Bystanders; Cal Tjader; Watson Sisters; others.
From Broadway to Hollywood........Columbia Special Products (M) CSP-213 15-20 60s
From Fortune's Treasure Chest of Musty Dusties: see Treasure Chest of Musty Dusties
From Hot to Cold........RCA (EP) SPA 73 10-15
From Nashville with Love (3 LP)........RCA (S) R 213764-1-2-3 10-20 72
(RCA Record Club issue.) Jim Reeves; Dottie West; George Hamilton IV; Archie Campbell & Lorene Mann; Jimmy Dean; Floyd Cramer; Porter Wagoner & Skeeter Davis; Browns; Sonny James; Homer & Jethro; Willie Nelson; Anita Kerr Singers; Eddy Arnold; Liz Anderson; Nat Stuckey; Wendy Dawn; Justin Tubb; Roger Miller; John D. Loudermilk; Norma Jean; Jim Ed Brown; Chet Atkins; Connie Smith; Hank Snow; Don Bowman; Stuf Phillips; Don Gibson; Waylon Jennings; Hank Locklin; Bobby Bare.
From New Orleans to Chicago........London (S) 553 8-10 70
Champion Jack Dupree; John Mayall; Eric Clapton; Keef Hartley; others.
From the Historic Vaults of Duke/Peacock, Vol. 1........ABC (M) ABCX-784 8-12
From the Vaults........Natural Resources (S) NR 4014 5-10 79
Monitors; Marvin Gaye; Marvellettes; Diana Ross & Supremes; Mary Wells; Temptations; Gladys Knight & Pips; Martha Reeves & Vandellas; Smokey Robinson & Miracles; Spinners; Marvelettes; Spinners.
From the Vaults of Duke/Peacock, Vol. 2........ABC (M) ABCX-789 8-12
Fujitsu - Concord Jazz Festival, Vol. 3........Concord (S) CJ 347 8-12
Full House........Crystal Ball (S) 106 8-12 80s
Motions; Jimmy Curtiss & Regents; Del-Rios; Joe & Continentals; Paramounts; Scott Garrett & Mystics; Holidays; Al Tenio & Teenagers; Ovations; Premiers; Rusty Lane & Mystics; Monograms; Ronnie Baker & Deltones; Montclairs.
Full Metal Jacket........Warner Bros. (S) 9-25613-1 10-15 87
(Soundtrack.) Abigail Mead; Nigel Goulding; Johnny Wright; Dixie Cups; Sam the Sham & Pharaohs; Chris Kenner; Nancy Sinatra; Trashmen; Goldman Band.
Full Tilt........K-Tel (S) TU-2770 5-10 81
Blondie; Pete Townsend; Devo; Robbie Dupree; SOS Band; Jimmy Hall;Larsen-Feiten Band; Pointer Sisters; Ambrosia; Manhattans; Al Stewart; Genesis; Cheap Trick; Pat Benatar.
Fun House........Harmony/Columbia (M) HL-7224 10-15
Red Buttons; Art Carney; Robert Q. Lewis; Molly Goldberg; Abe Burrows.
Fun Rock (4 LP)........Warner Special Products/Heartland (S) HL-1042-4 15-20 86
(Mail order offer.) Jan & Dean; Royal Teens; Mitch Ryder & Detroit Wheels; Lou Christie; McCoys; Sam the Sham & Pharaohs; Marcels; Ronny & Daytonas; Jimmy Jones; John Fred; Millie Small; Archies; Newbeats; Bobby Darin; Steam; Del Shannon; Shirelles; Gene Chandler; Joe Jones; Coasters; Freddy Cannon; Champs; Coasters; Ernie K-Doe; Jimmy Soul; Hollywood Argyles; Bobby "Boris" Pickett; Sheb Wooley; Trashmen; Brian Hyland; Troggs; Wilson Pickett; Kingsmen; Contours; Gary "U.S." Bonds; Allan Sherman; Johnny Cash; Shirley Ellis; Lonnie Donegan; Napolean XIV.
Fun Rock........Ronco (S) P 12629 5-10 75
(Mail order offer.) Sammy Davis Jr.; 1910 Fruitgum Co.; Brian Hyland; Sheb Wooley; Ray Stevens; New Vaudeville Band; Sam the Sham & Pharaohs; Little Eva; Archies; Ohio Express; Barry Mann; Tokens; Johnny Preston; Lemon Pipers; Shirley Ellis; Tommy Roe; Monkees.
Fun Songs........Alshire (S) 2-122 5-10 75
Fun Time........Coral (M) CRL-57072 10-20 56
(Comedy.) Buddy Hackett; Steve Allen; Myron Cohen; Henny Youngman; Bob & Ray; Hermion Gingold; Billy DeWolfe; Phil Foster; Harvey Stone; Hal March; Tom D'Andrea.
Funk/Fusion........Elektra/Asylum (S) E/A Promo 10-78 5-10 78
(Promotional issue only.) Lenny White; Aquarian Dream; Patrice Rushen; Donald Byrd; Lee Oskar; Joe Cocker.
Funky Blues........Verve (M) V-8486 15-25 62
Oscar Peterson; Charlie Parker; Benny Carter; Johnny Hodges; Ben Webster.
Funky Christmas........Cotillion (S) 9911 8-10 76
Lou Donaldson; John Edwards; Willis Jackson; Impressions; Margie Joseph; others.
Funky Favorites........Ronco (S) R-2150 5-10 78
(Mail order offer.) Bobby "Boris" Pickett; Playmates; Lee Dorsey; Royal Guardsmen; 1910 Fruitgum Co.; Detergents; Brian Hyland; Coasters; Chuck Berry; Alan Sherman; Larry Groce; Sam the Sham & Pharaohs; Sheb Wooley; Little Anthony & Imperials; Ohio Express; Tom Glazer & Children's Chorus; Cadillacs; Jim Stafford.
Funky '50s........Harlem Hit Parade (SE) HHP-5001 10-15 72
Platters; Bobby Day; Jesters; Harptones; Turbans; Clovers; Bobby Freeman; Paragons; Five Satins.
Funky '69........Toddlin' Town (S) TTS 3001 10-15 70
Bull & Matadors; Otis Clay; Alvin Cash; Five DuTones; others.
Funny Bone Favorites........Ronco (S) R-2210 10-15 78
Debbie Reynolds; Carleton Carpenter; Hollywood Argyles; Coasters; Cadets; Phil Harris; Reunion; Ray Stevens; Larry Verne; Rick Dees & His Cast of Idiots; John Zacherle; Shirley Ellis; Buzz Clifford; Clovers; Olympics; Little Jimmy Dickens; David Seville & Chipmunks.
Gabe's Dirty Blues........King/Gusto (M) GTS-110 10-15 78
Little Willie John; Champion Jack Dupree; Lulu Reed; Roy Brown; Midnighters; Little Esther Phillips; Billy Ward & Dominoes; Lamplighters; Wynonie Harris; Todd Rhodes & Connie Allen; Bull Moose Jackson; Five Royales; Tiny Bradshaw; Freddy King.
Galaxy of Country & Western Golden Hits........Mercury (S) SRD-12 15-25 60s
George Jones; Claude Gray; Leroy Van Dyke; James O'Gwynn; Jimmy Skinner; Margie Bowes; George Jones & Margie Singleton; Margie Singleton; Benny Barnes; Merle Kilgore; Lawton Williams; Rex Allen.
Galaxy of Golden Hits........Mercury (M) MGD-9 20-25 64
Galaxy of Golden Hits........Mercury (S) SRD-9 25-30 64
Brook Benton; Xavier Cugat; Platters; David Carroll; Damita Jo; Clebanoff Strings; Dinah Washington; Quincy Jones; Billy Eckstine; Jose Melis; Eddy Howard; Jan August; George Jones; Griff Williams; Eddie Heywood; Dick Contino.
Galaxy of Golden Hits........Mercury (M) MGD-11 20-25 65
Galaxy of Golden Hits........Mercury (S) SRD-11 25-30 65
Patti Page; Brook Benton; Platters; Dinah Washington; Eddy Howard; Richard Hayman; Frankie Laine; Sarah Vaughan; Tony Martin; Diamonds; Tiny Hill; George Jones.
Galaxy of Golden Hits........Mercury (M) PPMD 3-12 10-15 60s

Galaxy of Golden Hits.......... Mercury (S) SD 3-12 10-15 60s
Xavier Cugat; Pete Rugolo; David Carroll; George Barnes; Mike Simpson; Quincy Jones; Clebanoff Strings; Hal Mooney; Richard Hayman; Fredrick Fennell.
Galaxy 30 (2 LP).......... Mercury (M) MGD 2-13 15-25 60s
Galaxy 30 (2 LP).......... Mercury (S) SRD 2-13 15-25 60s
Xavier Cugat; Brook Benton; David Carroll; Patti Page; Jan August; Dinah Washington; Richard Hayman; Clebanoff Strings; Sarah Vaughan; Jose Melis; Billy Eckstine; Dick Contino; Quincy Jones; Platters; Eddie Layton; George Jones; others.
Gamble Record All-Stars.......... Gamble (S) LP-SG-5007 8-12 70
Intruders; Frank Beverly & Butlers; Baby Dolls; Brothers of Hope; Gail Anderson; Jaggerz; Cruisers; Dee Dee Sharp; Billy Paul; Panic Buttons; Bobby Marchan.
Gang at Bang: see Golden Hits from the Gang at Bang
Neil Diamond; McCoys; others.
Garbage Pail Kids .... MCA (S) 6221 8-10 87
(Soundtrack.) David Lawrence; Beat Farmers; Ed Keupper; Hakim & Lady Dianna; Jimmy Scarlett & Dimensions; Debbie Lytton; Garbage Pail Kids.
Garden of Delights (2 LP).......... Elektra (S) ESP-9001 10-15
Love; Bamboo; Koerner-Murphy; Zodiac; Tim Buckley; Earth Opera; Incredible String Band; Delaney & Bonnie; Tom Paxton; Roxy; Lonnie Mack; Paul Siebel; Farquahr; Eric Clapton; Stooges; Butterfield Blues Band; Tom Rush; Bread; Rhinoceros; David Ackles; Crabby Appleton; Voices of East Harlem; Judy Collins.
Garden of Delights (3 LP).......... Elektra (S) S3-10 10-20 71
Butterfield Blues Band; Spider John Koerner & Willie Murphy; Paul Seibel; Don Nix; Carol Hall; Tim Buckley; Bread; Beefeaters; Love; Clear Light; Crabby Appleton; Show of Hands; Stooges; Voices of East Harlem; Joshua Rifkin; Even Dozen Jug Band; Josh White; Roxy; Lonnie Mack; Lord Buckley; New Seekers; Farquahr; Rhinoceros; Swamp Dogg; Wackers; Diane Hildebrand; Rainbow Band; Siren; Incredible String Band; Lindisfarne; Audience; Atomic Rooster; Renaissance; Timber; Tom Paxton; Quinaimes Band; Judy Collins; David Ackles; Jeannie Greene; Earth Opera.
Gary Stevens in London.......... Lost-Nite (M) LP-129 8-12 70s
Gary Stevens' 22 Good Guy Goldies: see 22 Good Guy Goodies
Gathering.......... Coliseum (S) 711 20-30 71
Danny & Aces; Parabolic Rush; Wizzard; I.D.E.C.; Myrckwode.
Gathering at the Depot.......... Beta (S) 1414 25-35 70
Deadeye; Crockett; System; Thunderstorm; Danny's Reasons; Litter; Grizzly; Free & Easy; Kiwani; Pepper Fog; Chesterfield Gathering.
Gems.......... Gems One 5-10
Pussycats; Honey Bees; Fortune Cookies; Rev-Lons; Angels; Alice Wonderland; Diane Renay; Christine Quaite; Little Eva; Halos; Noreen Corcoran; Good Girls; Pin-Ups; Hedy Sontag; Three Bells; Short Cuts; Cinders; Candies; Love Exchange; Butterflys.
Gems of Jazz, Vol. 1 .... Decca (M) DL 5133 20-30 49
(10-inch LP.) Mildred Bailey; Jess Stacy; Gene Krupa; Israel Crosby; Meade "Lux" Lewis; Joe Marsala; Bud Freeman; "All Star Personel.")
Gems of Jazz, Vol. 2 .... Decca (M) DL 5134 20-30 49
(10-inch LP.) Gene Krupa; Ray Baudac; Bunny Berigan; Dick Clark; Israel Crosby; Benny Goodman; Joe Harris; Cliff Jackson; Nate Kazebier; Eddie Miller; Allan Reuss; Edgar Sampson; Jess Stacy.
General Electric Presents a Stereo Parade of Stars.......... Columbia Special Products (S) XSV 86013 8-12
Frankie Laine; Percy Faith; Jimmy Dean; Harmonicats; Diana Trask; Brothers Four; Ray Conniff; Robert Goulet; Polly Bergen; Andy Williams; Buddy Greco; Frank DeVol's Rainbow Strings & Golden Voices.
General Electric Presents a Stereo Show Case of Stars .... Columbia (SE) 82009/10 8-12
Eugene Ormandy & Philadelphia Orchestra; Diana Trask; Count Basie; Duke Ellington; Frankie Laine; Brothers Four; Lionel Hampton; Guy Mitchell; Miles Davis; Norman Luboff Choir; Hi-Lo's; Les Brown; Four Lads.
General Electric Presents "All Together Now".......... Capitol Custom (EP) 15-25 60s
(7-inch Compact Double 33.) Kingston Trio; Stan Kenton; Gordon MacRae; June Christy; Jonah Jones; George Shearing.
Gentlemen's Choice (Country Hits By Nashville's Top Male Vocalists).......... Harmony (S) KH-32480 5-10 73
Ray Price; Marty Robbins; Claude King; Sonny James; others.
Genuine House Rockin' Music, Vol. 1 .... Alligator (S) AL-101 5-10 87
Johnny Winter; Koko Taylor; Lonnie Mack; Collins Cray Copeland; Son Seals; Lonnie Brooks; Roy Buchanan; Fenton Robinson; Jimmy Johnson; James Cotton; Hound Dog Taylor.
Genuine House Rockin' Music, Vol. 2 .... Alligator (S) AL-102 5-10 87
Albert Collins; Big Twist & Mellow Fellows; Koko Taylor; Lil' Ed & Blues Imperials; Little Charlie & Nightcaps; Donald Kinsey; Johnny Winter; Lonnie Brooks; Lonnie Mack; James Cotton; Roy Buchanan with Delbert McClinton; Clarence "Gatemouth" Brown.
Genuine House Rockin' Music, Vol. 3 .... Alligator (S) AL-103 5-10 87
George Jones & His Country Cousins - Salute to the Grand Ole Opry.......... United Artists (M) UAL-3309 15-20 63
George Jones & His Country Cousins - Salute to the Grand Ole Opry.......... United Artists (S) UAS-6309 20-25 63
George Jones; Sonny Burns; Kathy Dee; others.
Gerry Goffin and Carole King: Solid Gold.......... Screen Gems/Columbia (S) CLP-713 20-30 70
(Promotional issue only).Beatles; Cookies; Tony Orlando; James Darren; Freddie Scott; Blood, Sweat & Tears; Hermans' Hermits; Little Eva; Maxine Brown; Chiffons; Monkees; Bobby Vee; Drifters; Shirelles.
Get a Board.......... Satan 1007 5-10 90s
Get Crazy.......... Morocco (S) 6065CL 8-10 83
(Soundtrack.) Sparks; Lori Eastside & Nada; Ramones; Marshall Crenshaw; Lou Reed; Malcolm McDowell; Bill Henderson; Fear with Lee Ving; Michael Boddicker; Howard Kaylan & Cast.
Get Dancin' — Hot Hits to Get You Movin' .... K-Tel (S) TU-3110 5-10 '83
Kool & Gang; Jermaine Jackson; Patrice Rushen; Luther Vandross; Aretha Franklin; Laura Branigan; Toni Basil; Pointer Sisters; Q Feel; Grandmaster Flash; Jeffrey Osborne; Evelyn King.
Get It On.......... Ronco/Columbia (S) P-12101 5-10 74
(Mail order offer.) Brownsville Station; Ohio Players; Jim Stafford; Johnny Nash; Barry White; Jerry Lee Lewis; B.B. King; Clint Holmes; Dr. Hook & Medicine Show; Stylistics; Lobo; Four Tops; Deodato; Dobie Gray; Pointer Sisters; Maureen McGovern; O'Jays; Donna Fargo; Billy Paul; Ian Thomas.
Get It Together .... Mainstream (S) 350 5-10 72
Charles McPherson; Dave Hubbard; Johnny Coles; Charles Kynard; others.
Get It Together (2 LP).......... Sessions/RCA (S) DPL2-0045 10-15 73
(Mail order offer.) Youngbloods; Buddy Miles; Steppenwolf; Jefferson Airplane; Iron Butterfly; Guess Who; Original Broadway Cast of *Hair*; John Fred; Zager & Evans; Music Explosion; Four Jacks & a Jill; Vanilla Fudge; Grass Roots; Shocking Blue; Cream; Who; Kinks; Monkees; Los Bravos; Gene Pitney; Rascals. (Special products. Made for Sessions.)

Get Off..........NAPRA, Inc. (M) No Number Used 10-20 73
(Promotional, anti-drug message issue.) Harry Chapin; Doobie Brothers; B.B. King; Ringo Starr; Judy Collins; Eagles; Al Kooper; Ravi Shanker; Alice Cooper; Bob Weir; Spence Dryden; Frank Zappa; William Shatner; Leonard Nimoy; Nichelle Nichols.

Get Together..........Verve/Folkways (M) FV-9010 10-20 65
Get Together..........Verve/Folkways (S) FVS-9010 10-20 65
Sonny Terry; Pete Seeger; Woody Guthrie; others.

Get Yourself a College Girl..........MGM (M) E-4273 12-18 65
Get Yourself a College Girl..........MGM (S) SE-4273 20-30 65
(Soundtrack.) Dave Clark Five; Animals; Stan Getz; Astrud Gilberto; Jimmy Smith Trio; Mary Ann Mobley; Standells; Freddie Bell & Bell Boys; Roberta Linn.

Getting Together with the Jackson 5..........Music Records (S) MDS-1047 50-100 67
Jackson 5; Platters; Brook Benton; Inez & Charlie Foxx; Jerry Butler; Frankie Lymon & Teenagers; Tommy Hunt.

Ghostbusters..........Arista (S) AL8-8246 8-10 84
(Soundtrack.) Ray Parker Jr.; Busboys; Alessi; Thompson Twins; Air Supply; Laura Branigan; Mick Smiley.

Ghostbusters 2..........MCA (S) MCA-6306 8-10 89
(Soundtrack.) Bobby Brown; New Edition; James Taylor; Doug E. Fresh & Get Fresh Crew; Run DMC; Oingo Boingo; Elton John; Glenn Frey; Howard Huntsberry.

Giant Box (2 LP)..........CTI (S) X-6031 8-12 73
Don Sebesky; Molt Jackson; Paul Desmond; Freddie Hubbard; others.

Giant Country..........United Artists (S) UAS-6745 5-10 70
Del Reeves; George Jones; Johnny Darrell; Bobby Lewis.

Giant Instrumental Rhythm & Blues Hits..........Imperial (M) LP 9271 15-20
Ernie Freeman; Lloyd Glenn; Illinois Jacquet; Erskine Hawkins; Lynn Hope; Bo Rhambo.

Giants of Country Music..........Design (S) SDLP-643 8-12 60s
Carl Belew; Patsy Cline; Ferlin Husky; Hank Locklin; Webb Pierce; Rocky Bill Ford; Claude King; T. Texas Tyler; Slim Willet; Hal Willis.

Giants of Jazz..........American Recording Society (M) 401 15-25 50s
Gene Krupa; Oscar Peterson Quartet; Billie Holiday; Buddy DeFranco Quartet; Count Basie; Dizzy Gillespie; Stan Getz; Johnny Hodges.

Giants of Jazz (2 LP)..........Atlantic (S) SD-2-905 8-12
Thelonius Monk; Dizzy Gillespie; Sonny Stitt; others.

Giants of Jazz..........Columbia (M) CL 1970 10-20 63
Giants of Jazz..........Columbia (S) CS 8770 10-20 63
Dave Brubeck; Chico Hamilton; Carmen McRae; Miles Davis; Lionel Hampton; Quincy Jones; Jimmy Guiffre; Duke Ellington; Thelonius Monk; Bill Doggett; J.J. Johnson; Bud Powell; others.

Giants of Jazz & Blues in Concert..........Masters (S) MA 281285 8-12
Dave Brubeck; B.B. King; others.

Giants of Jazz - the Guitarists (3 LP)..........Time-Life (S) STL J12 10-20
(Boxed set.)

Giants of Rock..........Scepter (S) SPS-5107 8-12 72
Tommy James & Shondells; Dionne Warwick; Del-Vikings; Chiffons; Barbara Lynn; Angels; Eternals; Dixie Cups; B.J. Thomas; Duprees; Aaron Neville; Shirelles; Bobby Freeman; Shangri-Las; Betty Everett; Dubs; Ad Libs; Don & Juan; Buoys; Shep & Limelights.

Gibson Gold (2 LP)..........RCA Special Products (S) DPL 20778 30-40 87
Elvis Presley; others.

Gift of Christmas, Vol. 1..........Columbia (S) CSS 706 5-10 70s
Ray Conniff; Steve Lawrence; Philadelphia Brass Ensemble; Anita Bryant; Jimmy Dean; Doris Day; Glad Singers; Patti Page; Mitch Miller; Bobby Vinton; Norman Luboff; Eugene Ormandy & Philadelphia Orchestra.
f

Gift of Music (QSP Presents)..........RCA (S) QSP1-0034 40-60 84
(Mail order offer.) Kenny Rogers & Dolly Parton; Eurythmics; Perry Como; James Galway & Sylvia; Hall & Oates; Charles Gerhardt & National Philharmonic; Alabama; Larry Elgart & His Manhattan Swing Orchestra; Charley Pride; Joe Reisman; Leontyne Price. (Special products. Made for QSP/Reader's Digest.)

Gift of Music (QSP Presents)..........RCA (S) QSP1-0037 40-60 84
Elvis Presley; others.

Gigantic Stars of Rock and Roll..........Crown (M) CLP-5013 50-75 56
Gilbey's Gin, Gilbey's Vodka Rock Opera Mix..........RCA Special Products (S) PRS-403 8-10 72
(Special products. Made for Gilbey's.)

Girl Groups: *the* Story of a Sound..........Motown (S) 5322ML 8-12 83
(Soundtrack.) Shangri-Las; Supremes; Mary Wells; Dixie Cups; Shirelles; Marvelettes; Angels; Martha & Vandellas; Velvelettes.

Girls...and More Girls..........Lion (M) L-70018 20-30
(Soundtrack.) Jane Powell; Debbie Reynolds; Judy Garland; Ann Blyth; June Allyson; Lena Horne; Esther Williams; Ava Gardner; Susan Hayward; Betty Hutton; Jane Russell; Kathryn Grayson; Johnny; David Rose; MGM Studio Orchestra.

Girls Girls Girls..........K-Tel (S) ???? 8-12 76
(Mail order offer.) Regents; Neil Sedaka; Randy & Rainbows; Paul & Paula; Robin Luke; Dion; Little Richard; Ronnie Hawkins; Ray Peterson; Wilson Pickett; Tommy Roe; Paul Anka; Everly Brothers; Jimmy Clanton; Fats Domino; Bobby Darin; Swinging Blue Jeans.

Girls Girls Girls..........Plantation (S) 519 5-10 77
Carol Channing; Betty Lavette; Gloria Taylor; Rita Remington; others.

Girls Girls Girls Around the World..........Adam & Eve (S) 504 8-12 90
Crystalairs; Vic Fontaine & Futures; Four Dates; Four Imperials; Hi-Fives; Celtics; Enchanters; Matthew Reid & Seasons; Four Cents; Four Gents; Billy Barnette & Group; Little Freddie & Gents; Enchantments; Steve Colt & Blue Knights; Statlers.

Girls Girls Girls & More Girls..........Adam & Eve (S) 501 8-12 80s
Elgins; Val-Airs; Gleems; Dynamics; Four Temptations; Little Sammy Rossi & Guys; Corvells; Mike & Utopians; Litterbugs; Squires; Valets; Valiants; Precisions; Velons.

Girls in the Garage, Vol. 3..........Roulan (S) UFOX04 5-10 80s
Laurie; Luv'd Ones; Heartbeats; Patti's Groove; Liverbirds; Plommons; Mandy & Girl Friends; Jean & State Siders; Tone Benders; Las Dilly Sisters; Ace of Cups; Jacqueliine Taieb.

Girls Just Want to Have Fun..........Mercury (S) 422-824 10-12 85
Girls Just Want to Have Fun..........Mercury (S) 824510-1 8-10 Re
(Soundtrack.) Alex Brown; Chris Farren; Rainey; Q-Feel; Deborah Galli; Tami Holbrook; Meredith Marshall; Animotion; Amy Hart; Holland.

Give a Little Love (Boy Scouts of America)........ Comin (S) 1187-002 10-15 87
George Harrison; Ringo Starr; others.

Give Joy to the World with Music (2 LP)........ WEA (S) SMP-4 10-15 77
Alan O'Day; Rod Stewart; Queen; C.J. & Co.; Chris Hillman; Ramones; Cate Brothers; Fleetwood Mac; Firefall; Steve Goodman; Debby Boone; Foreigner; Jay Ferguson; Leo Sayer; Johnny Rivers; Terence Boylan; Rolling Stones; Doobie Brothers; Harry Chapin; Rowans; Randy Newman; Crosby, Stills & Nash; Tom Waits; Spinners; Shaun Cassidy; Abba.

Give Love for Christmas........ Holland Sound (S) 1 15-25 86
Synch; Dakota; TNT; John Nasser & Don't Walk Band; Asylum Blue; Mark Wanko; Rudi & Living Dolls; Bobby Ross.

Glasnost........ MCA (S) 6358 5-10 88
Cruise; Alla Pugachova; Time Machine; Bravo; Forum; Sofia Rotaru; Creators; EVM; Autograph.

Go for the Geffen Gold........ Geffen (S) PRO-A 2670 8-12 87
Wang Chung; Ric Ocasek; Lone Justice; Berlin; Levi Stubbs; Tesla; Steve Martin; Debbie Harry.

Go, Johnny, Go!........ No Label Name Used (EP) No Number Used 200-300 60
(Soundtrack. Promotional issue only.) Jimmy Clanton.

Go, Johnny, Go!........ No Label Name Used (M) No Number Used 500-750 60
(Soundtrack. Promotional issue only.) Jimmy Clanton; Sandy Stewart; Jackie Wilson; Chuck Berry; Cadillacs; Flamingos; Eddie Cochran; Ritchie Valens; Harvey Fuqua; Jo Ann Campbell.

Go, Johnny, Go!........ Reel 'N' Rock (M) JN 5705 10-20 80s
(Soundtrack. Reissue.) Jimmy Clanton; Sandy Stewart; Jackie Wilson; Chuck Berry; Cadillacs; Flamingos; Eddie Cochran; Ritchie Valens; Harvey Fuqua; Jo Ann Campbell.

Go West Man!........ Jasmine (S) JASM 1048 8-12

Go with the Greats........ Naras (M) XTV 86076 10-15 62
Benny Goodman; Ella Fitzgerald; Paul Weston; Nat King Cole; Jo Stafford; Count Basie; Peggy Lee; Perry Como; Judy Garland; Roger Williams; Johnny Mercer; Woody Herman. (Made for Chevrolet.)

Go with the Greats........ Naras (M) XTV 86077 10-15 62
Benny Goodman; Ella Fitzgerald; Paul Weston; Nat King Cole; Jo Staffford; Count Basie; Peggy Lee; Perry Como; Judy Garland; Roger Williams; Johnny Mercer; Woody Herman. (Made for Chevrolet.)

Godfrey Presents 16 Successful Sounds (Vol. 1)........ Flashback (M) FBL-603 10-20
Cannibal & Headhunters; Thee Midniters; Z.Z. Hill; Count Five; Carol Hughes; Scott English; Beau Brummels; Chris Teller; McKinley Mitchell; Blendells; Diplomats; Casinos; Premiers; Richard "Dimples" Fields; Ambertones; Godfrey.

Godfrey Presents 18 R&B Flashbacks (Vol. 2)........ Flashback (M) FBL-602 10-20
Vibrations; Castaleers; Hollywood Saxons; Sa-Shays; Jimmy Hughes; Jesse Belvin; Resonics; Thee Midniters; Arthur Lee Maye & Crowns; Falcons Featuring Wilson Pickett; Blendtones; El Dorados; Perez Brothers; Rosie & Ron; Metallics; Alfred & Joe; Godfrey; Joe Houston. (Selection number is correct, Vol. 2 is one number lower than Vol. 1.)

Goin' to Chicago........ Testament (M) T-2218 8-10

Going Down the Valley........ New World (S) 236 5-10 77
Shortbuckle Roark & Family; Shelor Family; Pope's Arkansas Mountaineers; Allen Bros.; others.

Gold and Platinum........ Realm/Columbia (S) 1P 7679 5-10 84

Gold and Platinum........ Realm (S) R-172499/LP-7679 5-10 84
Paul McCartney & Michael Jackson; Dan Fogelberg; Toto; Journey; Cyndi Lauper; Hall & Oates; Asia; Pat Benatar; Quiet Riot; Police; Men at Work; Billy Joel; Cars; Nena; Olivia Newton-John. (RCA Record Club issue.)

Gold and Platinum........ Realm (S) LP-7679 5-10 84
Paul McCartney; Cyndi Lauper; Pat Benatar; Men at Work; Hall & Oates; Journey; Michael Jackson; Billy Joel; Police. (Columbia House Record Club issue.)

Gold and Platinum........ Columbia (S) 1P 7726 5-10 86
Pointer Sisters; Huey Lewis & News; Cyndi Lauper; Bruce Springsteen; Lionel Richie; Tears for Fears; Bryan Adams; Wham!; Paul Young; John Waite; Sade; Til Tuesday; Hall & Oates; REO Speedwagon. (Made for T.J. Martell Foundation for Leukemia & Cancer.)

Gold Guitar Awards 1957-1963........ Columbia (M) D2J-1 15-30 63
(Promotional issue only. Special commemorative album, WSM Grand Ole Opry's 38th Birthday Celebration.) Ray Price; Marty Robbins; Johnny Cash; Johnny Horton; Stonewall Jackson; Jimmy Dean; Claude King; Bill Pursell.

Gold Hits........ Warwick (M) W-2008 50-75 59
Moonglows; Willows; Flamingos; Harptones; Hearts; Shepherd Sisters; Rod Bernard; Rivileers. (Reissued as *Goodies But Oldies, Vol. 2*.)

Gold Hits, Vol. 2........ RCA (M) LPM-2775 10-20 63

Gold Hits, Vol. 2........ RCA (S) LSP-2775 15-25 63
Perry Como; Tommy Dorsey; Eddie Fisher; Artie Shaw; Browns; Vaughn Monroe; Glenn Miller; Mario Lanza; Ames Brothers; Pee Wee King; Spike Jones. (See *Golden Hits, Vol. 1* for first volume in this series.)

Gold Mine of All Time Hits (Bill Wright Presents)........ Lost-Nite (M) LP-111 8- 12 70s

Gold Mine of All Time Hits (Bill Wright Presents)........ Lost-Nite (SE) LP-111 8- 12 70s
Ritchie Valens; Jimmy Rodgers; J. Frank Wilson; Gene Vincent; Mark Dinning; Del Shannon; Everly Brothers; Thomas Wayne; Buddy Knox; Bill Wright, Sr.; Conway Twitty; Shelly Fabares; Charlie Gracie.

Gold Record........ Capitol (M) T-830 35-45 57

Gold Record........ Capitol Starline (M) T-830 25-30 61

Gold Record........ Capitol (SE) DT-830 10-20 63
Nat King Cole; Peggy Lee; Les Paul & Mary Ford; Les Baxter; Dean Martin; Kay Starr; Sonny James; Nelson Riddle; Tennessee Ernie Ford; Pee Wee Hunt.

Gold Record Hits........ Columbia Special Products (S) CSP-XTV-82067 8-12 60s
Les Brown; Frankie Carle; Woody Herman; Eddy Duchin; Harry James; Louis Armstrong; Jo Stafford; Tony Bennett; Frankie Laine; Percy Faith.

Gold Rocks: see 21 Gold Rocks

Gold Rush 79 (2 LP)........ K-Tel (S) TU 2660 8-12 79
Blondie; Ian Matthews; Gerry Rafferty; Babys; Orleans; John Paul Young; Al Stewart; Little River Band; Dr. Hook; Raydio; Nick Gilder; Amii Stewart; Peaches & Herb; Rick James; Foxy; Andy Gibb; G.Q.; Melissa Manchester; Natalie Cole; Bob Welch; Player; Firefall; Hot Chocolate.

Gold Soul........ Stax (S) STS-2031 8-12 70s
Johnnie Taylor; Mavis Staples; Isaac Hayes; Booker T. & MGs; Albert King; Judy Clay & William Bell; Rufus Thomas; William Bell; Eddie Floyd; Carla Thomas; David Porter; Soul Children.

Golden Age Christmas........ Victrola (M) 1682 5-10 72
Enrico Caruso; Richard Crooks; John McCormack; Rosa Ponselle; Ernestine Schumann-Heink; others.

Golden Age of Comedy (5 LP) ....Longines Symphonette (S) SYS-5277 20-30

Eddie Cantor & Bert Gordon; Ed Gardner; W.C. Fields; Edgar Bergen; Charlie McCarthy; Tallulah Bank Head; Fred Allen; Ed Wynn; George Burns; Gracie Allen; Carl Reiner; Mel Brooks; Fanny Brice; Hanley Stafford; Red Skelton; Allan Sherman; Mike Nichols; Elaine May; George Burns; Milton Berle; Dick Gregory; Oscar Levant; Betty Walker; Buddy Hackett; Don Ameche; Frances Langford; Sid Caesar; Omigene Coca; Stiller & Meara; Ernie Kovaks; Andy Griffith; Jonathan Winters; Leonard Barr; Norm Crosby; Woody Woodbury; Frank Gallop; Lou Jacobi; George Gobel; Morey Amsterdam; David Frye; Pat Paulsen; Bob & Ray; Milt Kamen; Hal Holbrook; Bob Hope; David Steinberg; Smothers Brothers; Jack Gilford; David Frost; Orson Bean; George Kirby; Herschel Bernardi; Uanand Schenck; Moms Mabley; Jimmy Joyce; Myron Cohen; Godfrey Cambridge; Joan Rivers; Pat McCormick; Shelly Berman; Pete Barbutti; Jack Benny; Kenny Delmar; Jack Pearl; Victor Borge; Fibber McGee & Molly; Bob "Bazooka" Burns.

Golden Age of Country Music (6 LP)....................Columbia Musical Treasury (S) P6S 5614 15-25 70s

Johnny Cash; David Houston & Barbara Mandrell; Charlie Rich; Lynne Anderson; Bob Luman; Ray Price; Stonewall Jackson; Roy Clark; Johnny Horton; Jeannie C. Riley; John Wesley Ryles; Tammy Wynette; Johnny Cash; David Houston; Lefty Frizzell; Sandy Posey; George Jones; Statler Brothers; Conway Twitty; Tom T. Hall; Harden Trio; Claude King; Billy Walker; Dave Dudley; Hank Williams, Sr.; Bonnie Guitar; Roger Miller; Marty Robbins; George Morgan; Johnny Cash; June Carter; Jim Nabors; Leroy Van Dyke; Roy Acuff; Jerry Lee Lewis; Flatt & Scruggs; Arlene Harden; Roy Drusky; Jimmy Dickens; George Jones; Lynn Anderson; Carl Butler; Patti Page; Merle Kilgore.

Golden Age of Country Music, 1940-1970 (7 LP)....................Readers Digest (S) RB4-005 20-30 87

Jimmie Davis; Bob Wills & His Texas Playboys; Roy Acuff & His Smoky Mountain Boys; Elton Britt; Arthur Guitar Boogie Smith; Ernest Tubb; Merle Travis; Eddy Arnold; Zeke Manners & His Band; Red Foley; Hank Thompson; Hank Williams; Jimmy Wakely & Margaret Whiting; Wayne Raney; Patti Page; Hank Snow; Moon Mullican; Tennessee Ernie Ford; Webb Pierce; Slim Whitman; Red Foley; Davis Sisters; Kitty Wells; Johnny Cash; Faron Young; Everly Brothers; Ferlin Husky; Patsy Cline; Jim Reeves; Don Gobson; Bobby Helms; Hank Locklin; Tex Ritter; George Jones; Roy Drusky; Sheb Wooley; Roy Clark; Porter Wagoner; George Jones & Melba Montgomery; Roger Miller; Del Reeves; Charley Pride; Glen Campbell; Eddy Arnold; Bill Andrews with the Po' Boys; Hank Williams, Sr.; Sonny James.

Golden Age of Dance Bands....................Somerset (M) P-9500 10-15 60s

Golden Age of Dance Bands....................Somerset/Stereo Fidelity (S) SF-9500 10-15 60s

Golden Age of Movie Musicals (2 LP)....................MGM (S) SQBO 93890 10-20 60s

(Soundtrack.) Judy Garland; Vic Damone; Ann Blyth; Fred Astaire; Leslie Caron; Mel Ferrer; Bert Lahr; Kathryn Grayson; Betty Hutton; Howard Keel; Keenan Wynn; Louis Calhern; Jane Powell; Ava Gardner; Gene Kelly; Georges Guetary; June Allyson; Peter Lawford; Debbie Reynolds; Carleton Carpenter; Red Skelton; Anita Ellis; Mickey Rooney; Ann Miller; Jane Russell; Esther Williams; Ricardo Montalban.

Golden Age of Rhythm & Blues (2 LP)....................Chess (S) 2CH-50030 30-50 72

Bluejays; Coronets; El-Rays; Moonglows; Moonlighters; Orchids; Flamingos; Five Notes; Ravens; Quintones; Tornadoes; Sentimentals; Lee Andrews & Hearts; Monotones; Students; Pastels; Re-Vels; Sonics; Miracles.

Golden Age of Rock 'N' Roll (6 LP)....................Columbia Special Products (SE) 6P-7035 20-30 80

(Boxed set.) Kingston Trio; Little Richard; Crew-Cuts; Ron Holden; Carl Dobkins Jr.; Larry Williams; Johnny Otis; Exciters; Johnnie Ray; Fleetwoods; Bill Black Combo; Mark Dinning; Gaylords; Bobby Vee; Drifters; Shirelles; Jack Scott; Del Shannon; Frankie Ford; Skyliners; Chubby Checker; Hank Ballard & Midnighters; Rivingtons; Crests; B. Bumble & Stingers; Duane Eddy; Bobby Freeman; Chimes; Dovells; Sonny Til & Orioles; Angels; Buddy Knox; Dick & DeeDee; Gaylords; Curtis Lee; Robin Luke; Coasters; Dee Clark; Clarence "Frogman" Henry; Chantels; Lloyd Price; Sammy Turner; Chiffons; Diamonds; Gary "U.S." Bonds; Jimmy Clanton; Crystals; Jimmy Charles; Bobby Lewis; King Curtis; Four Lads; Kingston Trio; Four Preps; Four Aces.

Golden Anniversary Album....................RCA (S) PR-111 15-20 61

Tommy Dorsey; Rosemary Clooney & Perez Prado; Artie Shaw & His Gramercy Five; Larry Clinton; Louis Armstrong; Charlie Barnet; Helen O'Connell; Bunny Berigan; Duke Ellington; Benny Goodman; Guy Lombard; Glenn Miller. (Made for Chevrolet.)

Golden Child....................Capitol (S) SJ-12544 8-10 87

(Soundtrack.) Ann Wilson; Melissa Morgan; Ashford & Simpson; Martha Davis; Ratt; Marlon Jackson; Robbie Buchanan; Michel Colombier; John Barry.

Golden Circle....................Columbia Special Products (S) CSP 287 8-12 60s

Simon & Garfunkel; Steve Lawrence; Robert Goulet; Barbra Streisand; Eydie Gorme; Johnny Mathis; Jane Morgan; New Christy Minstrels; Theodore Bikel; Jimmy Dean; Ramsey Lewis Trio; Mike Douglas.

Golden Classics 42 (3 LP)....................Warner Special Products/Sessions ???? 10-15 70s

Angels; Belmonts; Billy Bland; Bobby Bland; Pat Boone; Eric Burdon & Animals; Capris; Casinos; Claudine Clark; Danny & Juniors; Carl Dobkins Jr.; Earls; Elegants; Everly Brothers; Larry Finnegan; Richard Harris; Connie Francis; Brian Hyland; Andy Kim; Lonnie Mack; Tommy James & Shondells; Mamas & Papas; Robin McNamara; Wilson Pickett; Mindbenders; Rod Stewart; Strawberry Alarm Clock; Brenton Wood; others.

Golden Classics, Vol. 1....................Golden Classics (S) 103 5-10 70

Golden Classics, Vol. 2....................Golden Classics (S) 104 5-10 70

Golden Classics, Vol. 3....................Golden Classics (S) 105 5-10 70

Golden Classics, Vol. 4....................Golden Classics (S) 106 5-10 70

Golden Classics, Vol. 5....................Golden Classics (S) 107 5-10 70

Golden Classics, Vol. 6....................Golden Classics (S) 108 5-10 70

Golden Classics, Vol. 7....................Golden Classics (S) 109 5-10 70

Golden Classics, Vol. 8....................Golden Classics (S) 110 5-10 70

Golden Classics, Vol. 9....................Golden Classics (S) 111 5-10 70

Golden Classics, Vol. 10....................Golden Classics (S) 112 5-10 70

George Morgan; Dottie West; Buck Owens; Flatt & Scruggs; George Jones; others.

Golden Country....................Wyncote (M) W-9159 8-12 60s

Golden Country....................Wyncote (S) SW-9159 8-12 60s

Jimmy Dean; George Jones; Country Johnny Mathis; Stoneman Family; Deputies.

Golden Country and Western Hits....................RCA (M) CPM-500 10-15 65

Golden Country and Western Hits....................RCA (S) CSP-500 10-15 65

Hank Snow; Jim Reeves; Don Gibson; Floyd Cramer; Porter Wagoner; Eddy Arnold; Gene Autry; Skeeter Davis; Hank Locklin; Chet Atkins; George Hamilton IV; Bobby Bare.

Golden Country Hits, Vol. 2....................Artistic (EP) 224 15-25 65

(7 inch, 33 rpm. Also issued as *Western, Vol. 2*, and also as *Original Country Hits*.) Maddox Brothers & Rose; Pete Pike; Ferlin Husky; T. Texas Tyler; Jimmy Dean; Webb Pierce; Hank Locklin; Slim Willet.

Golden Country Hits....................United Artists (M) UAL-3327 10-15 64

Golden Country Hits....................United Artists (S) UAS-6327 15-20 64

George Jones; Burl Ives; Judy Lynn; others.

Golden Country Hits....................Harmony (M) HL-7362 10-15 66

Golden Country Hits .... Harmony (S) HS-11162 10-15 66
Ray Price; Flatt & Scruggs; Stonewall Jackson; Billy Walker; Bobby Helms; Freddie Hart; Little Jimmy Dickens; Mel Tillis; Carl Butler; Lefty Frizzell.

Golden Country Hits, Vol. 2 .... Harmony (M) HL-7391 10-15 66
Golden Country Hits, Vol. 2 .... Harmony (S) HS-11191 10-15 66
Johnny Horton; Jimmy Dean; Marion Worth.

Golden Days of British Rock (4 LP) .... Sire (S) V-8046 25-35 76
(Boxed set.) Beatles; Swinging Blue Jeans; Springfields; Pretty Things; Derek & Dominos; Billy J. Kramer; Status Quo; Cream; Troggs; David & Jonathan; Foundations; Donovan; Python Lee Jackson; Dusty Springfield; Eric Burdon & Animals; Manfred Mann; Kinks; Mongo Jerry; Merseys; Fleetwood Mac; Gerry & Pacemakers; Freddie & Dreamers; Cilla Black; Bee Gees; Searchers; Vanity Fare; Chad & Jeremy; Peter & Gordon; Honeycombs; Sandie Shaw.

Golden Dozen .... Columbia (M) CL-1462 15-20 60
Johnny Mathis; Doris Day; Four Lads; others.

Golden Dozen .... Columbia Special Products (M) CSP-167 10-15 60s
Vic Damone; Patti Page; Bobby Hackett; Eydie Gorme; Percy Faith; Robert Goulet; Bobby Vinton; Barbra Streisand; Tonny Bennett; Gordon Jenkins; Steve Lawrence; Louis Armstrong. (Made for National Tea Company.)

Golden Dozen .... Columbia Special Products (M) CSP-181 10-15 60s
Vic Damone; Patti Page; Bobby Hackett; Eydie Gorme; Percy Faith; Robert Goulet; Bobby Vinton; Barbra Streisand; Tonny Bennett; Gordon Jenkins; Steve Lawrence; Louis Armstrong.

Golden Dozen, Volume 2 .... Jin (S) LP9004 5-10
Uniques; Shelton Dunaway; Boogie Kings; Charles Mann; John Fred; Bobby Charles; Johnnie Allan; Clint West; Tousaint McCall.

Golden Echoes .... Arvee (M) A 433 25-35 62
Bel-Airs; Olympics; Marathons; Dudley; Fugitives.

Golden Encore .... Columbia Special Products (S) CSP-248 10-20 65
Steve Lawrence; Eydie Gorme; Johnny Mathis; Doris Day; Barbra Streisand; Tony Bennett; Robert Goulet; Julie Andrews; Chad & Jeremy; Andre Kostelanetz; Patti Page; Dave Clark Five. (Made for Stop & Shop.)

Golden Encores .... Cadence (M) CLP-3043 30-50 60
Chordettes; Archie Bleyer; Alfred Drake; Andy Williams; Julius LaRosa; Marion Marlowe; Genevieve; Stephen Douglas.

Golden Era of Dance and Songs (2 LP) .... Mercury (S) SRM-2-601 10-20 69
Patti Page; Lesley Gore; Bobby Hebb; Brook Benton; Dinah Washington; Richard Hayman; Dusty Springfield; Teresa Brewer; Sarah Vaughan; Vic Damone; Harmonicats; Frankie Laine; Eddy Howard; David Carroll; Dick Contino; Robert Maxwell; Georgia Gibbs; Billy Eckstine.

Golden Era of Hits (2 LP) .... London (S) LS-3128/1-2 10-15
Champs; Velvets; Duane Eddy; Chris Kenner; Kalin Twins; Sir Douglas Quintet; Roy Orbison; Dennis Turner; Isley Brothers; Ned Miller; Buddy Holly; Sanford Clark; Billy Bland; Shirelles; Jerry Keller; Len Barry; Brian Hyland; Terry Stafford; Johnny Cymbal; Bill Haley & His Comets; Chris Montez.

Golden Era (3 LP) .... ERA (S) 123 35-45 69
Kathy Young; Chris Montez; Richard Berry; Gogi Grant; Donnie Brooks; Dorsey Burnette; Innocents; Castells; Larry Verne; Russell Arms; Ketty Lester; Jewel Akens; Donald Woods; Six Teens; Leon Peels; Dave Dudley; Paragons; Castaways; Incredibles; Uptones. (The LPs in this set were also issued separately and are listed below.)

Golden Era, Vol. 1 .... ERA (SP) VOL-1 10-15 69
Gogi Grant; Dorsey Burntt; Castells; Donnie Brooks Larry Verne; Jewel Akens; Teddy Bears; Russell Arms.

Golden Era, Vol. 2 .... ERA (S) VOL-2 10-15 69
Golden Era, Vol. 3 .... ERA (S) ESVOL-3 10-15 69
Richard Berry; Donald Woods; Chris Montez; Sixteens; Jewel Aikens; Leon Peels; Dave Dudley; Paragons; Castaways; Kathy Young; Incredibles; Uptones.

Golden Galaxie of Rhythm & Blues Hits .... Hollywood (M) HLP 503 25-35 60s
Red Callender; Linda Hayes; Jimmy McCracklin; Jacks; Pee Wee Crayton; Jessie Belvin; Ray Charles; Feathers; Lloyd Glenn; Lowell Fulsom; King Perry; Johnny Fuller; Jessie Thomas; Tal Miller; Johnny Moore & Blazers.

Golden Gassers .... Capitol (M) T-1561 20-30 61
Sam Cooke; Ferlin Husky; Four Preps; Ed Townsend; Thomas Wayne; Bill Parsons; Sonny James; Valiants (with Billy Storm); Harold Dorman; Cathy Carr; Johnny Morsette.

Golden Gassers .... Chess (M) LP-1458 30-40 61
Robert & Johnny; Moonglows; Students; Flamingos; Monotones; Tune Weavers; Billy Bland; Johnnie & Joe; Lee Andrews & Hearts. (Also issued as *Murray the K's Golden Gassers* as *KYA Golden Gate Greats* and as *WAMO's Golden Gassers*. There are probably other editions of this same LP with radio station/dee jay tie-ins.)

Golden Gassers for a Dance Party: see Murray the K's Golden Gassers for a Dance Party

Golden Gassers for Hand Holders .... Roulette (M) R-25191 20-30 62
Dion & Belmonts; Chantels; Capris; Flamingos; Harptones; Three Friends; Darrell & Oxfords; Drifters; Ruth McFadden.

Golden Girls Sing the Golden Hits of the '50s & '60s .... Laurie (S) LES 4019 8-12 79
Maxine Brown; Chiffons; Petula Clark; Reperata & Delrons; Brenda Lee Jones; Bernadette Carroll; Dionne Warwick.

Golden Girls Sing the Golden Hits of the '50s & '60s, Vol. 2 .... Laurie (S) LES 4031 8-12 81
Dionne Warwick; Shirelles; Petula Clark; Chiffons; Four Pennies; Brenda Lee Jones; Linda Laurie; Cathy Carr.

Golden Glow of Christmas .... Columbia (SP) C-10925 5-10 72
Leonard Bernstein; Johnny Mathis; Doris Day; Percy Faith; Julie Andrews; Jerry Vale; Ray Conniff; Arthur Fiedler Tony Bennett; Andre Kostelanetz; Robert Goulet & Carol Lawrenc; Barba Streisand. (Made for J.C. Penney.)

Golden Goodies .... Mercury (M) MG-20511 25-35 60
Golden Goodies .... Mercury (S) SR-60217 30-40 60
Brook Benton; Dinah Washington; Sarah Vaughn; Patti Page; Sil Austin; Phil Phillips; Platters; Diamonds; June Valli.

Golden Goodies .... Time (M) T-52082 25-35 63
Golden Goodies .... Time (SE) ST-2082 25-35 63
Golden Goodies, Vol. 1 .... Roulette (M) R-25207 15-25 63
Heartbeats; Angels; Harptones; Echoes; Frankie Lymon; Devotions; Tiny Tim & Hits; Valentines.

Golden Goodies, Vol. 2 .... Roulette (M) R-25210 15-25 63
Frankie Lymon; Chantels; Coasters; Sonny Til & Orioles; Eddie Cooley; Little Anthony & Imperials; Flamingos; Cleftones; Heartbeats; Dubs; Crows.

Golden Goodies, Vol. 3 .... Roulette (M) R-25218 15-25 63
Drifters; Moonglows; Flamingos; El Dorados; Chantels; Lee Andrews & Hearts; Temptations; Bobbettes; Crests; Cadillacs.

Golden Goodies, Vol. 4 .... Roulette (M) R-25209 15-25 63
Joey Dee & Starliters; Little Joey & Flips; Dovells; Chubby Checker; Vibrations; Little Eva; Jive Five; Bobby Freeman; Etta James.

Golden Goodies, Vol. 5 .... Roulette (M) R-25215 15-25 63
Monotones; Nutmegs; Dells; Spaniels; Dion & Belmonts; Pastels; Cadillacs; Fiestas; Heartbeats; Moonglows; Channels.

Golden Goodies, Vol. 6 .... Roulette (M) R-25216 15-25 63
Spaniels; Dells; Turbans; Five Satins; Magnificents; Robert & Johnny; Chantels; Flamingos; Nutmegs; Moonglows.

Golden Goodies, Vol. 7 .... Roulette (M) R-25212 15-25 63
Dion & Belmonts; Moonglows; Mello Kings; Silhouettes; Four Tunes; Playmates; Regents; Rock-A-Teens; Cleftones; Little Anthony & Imperials; 4 Seasons; Harptones.

Golden Goodies, Vol. 8 .... Roulette (M) R-25214 15-25 63
Maxine Brown; Faye Adams; Jimmie Rodgers; Chuck Berry; Bo Diddley; Ronnie Hawkins; Jesse Belvin; Ral Donner; Dee Clark.

Golden Goodies, Vol. 9 .... Roulette (M) R-25213 15-25 63
Joey Dee & Starliters; Maxine Brown; Lee Allen; Buddy Knox; Chuck Berry; Lou Christie; Frankie Lymon; Jimmie Rodgers; Jimmy Bowen; Ral Donner; Dee Clark.

Golden Goodies, Vol. 10 .... Roulette (M) R-25217 15-25 63
Moonglows; Spaniels; Edsels; Chantels; Little Anthony & Imperials; Tune Weavers; Jacks; Dubs.

Golden Goodies, Vol. 11 .... Roulette (M) R-25219 15-25 63
Dreamlovers; Valentines; Five Satins; El Dorados; Moonglows; Pastels; Chantels; 4 Seasons; Willows; Spaniels; Channels.

Golden Goodies, Vol. 12 .... Roulette (M) R-25211 15-25 63
Bobby Lewis; Maurice Williams; Ruth McFadden; Faye Adams; Billy Myles; Ben E. King; Jerry Butler; Edna McGriff; Billy Bland; Joe Jones; Sam Hawkins; Joe Henderson.

Golden Goodies, Vol. 13 (Instrumental Golden Goodies) .... Roulette (M) R-25238 15-25 64
Johnny & Hurricanes; King Curtis; Stringalongs; Dave "Baby" Cortez; Joey Dee; Spacemen; Les Cooper Ray Barretto.

Golden Goodies, Vol. 14 .... Roulette (M) R-25239 15-25 64
Penguins; Four Esquires; Beverly Anne Gibson; Larry Williams; Lloyd Price; Paragons; G-Clefs; Monarchs; Meadowlarks; Little Richard; Five Channels; Sheps (Shepherd Sisters).

Golden Goodies, Vol. 15 .... Roulette (M) R-25240 15-25 64
Eternals; Collegians; Penguins; Medallions; Beverly Anne Gibson; G-Clefs; Cuff Links; Four Esquires; Guitar Slim; Paragons.

Golden Goodies, Vol. 16 .... Roulette (M) R-25241 15-25 64
Paul Evans; Rays; Echoes; Jack Scott & Chantones; Rosemary June; Sparkeltones; Crystals; Gloria Mann; Neil Sedaka & Tokens; Tempos.

Golden Goodies, Vol. 17 .... Roulette (M) R-25242 15-25 64
Wilbert Harrison; Tom & Jerry; Buster Brown; Jesters; Don Gardner & Dee Dee Ford; Lee Dorsey; Harptones; Cadets; Crests; Shirley & Lee; Neil Sedaka.

Golden Goodies, Vol. 18 .... Roulette (M) R-25247 15-25 64
Essex; Lou Christie; Joey Dee & Starliters; Gene Chandler; Debbie Dovale; Ben E. King; Ray Barretto; Jerry Butler.

Golden Goodies, Vol. 19 .... Roulette (M) R-25248 15-25 64
Frankie Lymon; Flamingos; Regents; Crests; Crows; Fiestas; Penguins; Monotones; Drifters; Moonglows; Tune Weavers; Cleftones.

Golden Gospel Jubilee (2 LP) .... Savoy (S) 7022 8-12 76
James Cleveland; Rosie Wallace; Shirley Caesar; S.W. Michigan Choir; Angelic Choir; Oneal Twins; Clara Ward; Harrison Johnson; Sara Jordan Powell; Roberta Martin; Esther Rolle; Blind Boy of Alabama; Inez Andrews; Davis Sisters; Rosetta Tharpe; Staple Singers.

Golden Gospel Jubilee (2 LP) .... Nashco (S) 5140 8-12 80s
Swanee Quintet; James Cleveland; Consolers; Brooklyn All Stars; Rev. Milton Brunson; Gospel Keynotes; Rev. Isaac Douglas; Mahalia Jackson; Supreme Angels; others.

Golden Graffitti Greats .... Music Productions Corp. (S) 5000 8-12
Chuck Berry; Association; Joanie Sommers; Jody Reynolds; Cascades; Gene Chandler; Little Richard; Dee Clark; Duprees; Ides of March; Terry Stafford; Vogues; Olympics; Bob & Earl; Bo Diddley; Jerry Butler; Crests.

Golden Greats .... Columbia Special Products (S) CSP-291 10-15 67
Barbra Streisand; Louis Armstrong; Robert Goulet; Leonard Bernstein; Doris Day; Dave Brubeck; Andy Williams; Mormon Tabernacle Choir; Mahalia Jackson; Tony Bennett; Percy Faith; Richard Tucker. (Special products. Made for the American Freedom from Hunger Foundation.)

Golden Groups .... Specialty (M) SP 2155 8-12 85
Chimes; Dukes; Arthur Lee Maye & Crowns; Tony Allen & Champs; Crystals; Ben Zeppa & Zephers; Crowns; Metronomes; Tropicals; Pharaohs; Twilighters; Byron Slick Gipson & Sliders.

Golden Groups (Best of Holiday Records) .... Relic (M) 5090 8-10 90

Golden Groups (Best of Whirlin' Disc Records) .... Relic (M) 5089 8-10 90

Golden Groups, Vol. 1 (Best of Onyx Records) .... Relic (M) 5005 8-10 72
Velours; Pearls; Marquis; Montereys; Impressors; Joyettes; Chordells.

Golden Groups, Vol. 2 (Best of Vita Records) .... Relic (M) 5007 8-10 73
Chevelles; Aquires; Colts; Vitamins (Titans).

Golden Groups, Vol. 3 (Best of Angeltone/Atlas Records) .... Relic (M) 5012 8-10 73
Revels; Chandeliers; Parakeets; Travelers; Four Haven Knights; Little Butchie & Vells; Vic Donna & Parakeets.

Golden Groups, Vol. 4 (Best of Celeste Records) .... Relic (M) 5014 8-10 74
Mellows; Four Sounds; Minors; Mellows with Lillian Leach.

Golden Groups, Vol. 5 (Best of Herald Records) .... Relic (M) 5015 8-10 74
Mello-Kings; Debonairs; Mint Juleps; Little Butchie Saunders & His Buddies; Five Willows; Loungers; Sunbeams; Royal Holidays; Cashmeres; Nutmegs; Premiers; Smart Tones; Heralds; Concords; Thrillers.

Golden Groups, Vol. 6 (Best of Ember Records) .... Relic (M) 5016 8-10 74
Lee Allen; Starlarks; Silhouettes; Marktones; Camelots; Illusions; Smoothtones; Edsels Fabulons; Embers; Barries.

Golden Groups, Vol. 7 (Best of Winley Records) .... Relic (M) 5019 8-10 74
Duponts; Paragons; Jesters; Collegians; Quinns; Calanders; Persuaders.

Golden Groups, Vol. 8 (Best of Red Top Records) .... Relic (M) 5021 8-10 74
Quintones; Tony & Twilighters; Students; Blue Notes; Ivytones.

Golden Groups, Vol. 9 (Best of Club Records) .... Relic (M) 5022 8-10
Willows; Jay Saunders; Crescents; Duvals; Pageants; Relations; Cherlos; Little Freddy & Gents.

Golden Groups, Vol. 10 (Best of Tip Top Records) .... Relic (M) 5026 8-10
Performers; Three Friends; Jumping Jacks; Emblems; Mastertones; Eddie Robbins; Versatones; Creations; Mistakes; Five Vets.

Golden Groups, Vol. 11 (Best of Relic Records) .... Relic (M) 5027 8-10
Four Most; Teenos; Verdicts; Starlarks; Academics; Darvels; Illusions; Unique Teens; Melloharps; Martels.

Golden Groups, Vol. 12 (Best of Beltone Records) .... Relic (M) 5028 8-10
Carnations; Corvairs; Jive Five; Leopards; Mello-Kings; Dean Barlow; George Jackson & Unisons; Headliners; Johnny & Jokers; Cameos; Meteors; Dontells.

Golden Groups, Vol. 13 (Best of X-Tra Records) .... Relic (M) 5029 8-10
Collegians; Youngtones; Unknowns; Belairs; Heartspinners; Admirations; Sonics.

Golden Groups, Vol. 14 (Best of Johnson Records) .... Relic (M) 5031 8-10
Cordovans; Dubs; Shells; Carribians; Cleo & Crystaliers; Arcades; Nate & Chryslers; Cameos; Bobby Capri & Velvet Angels; King Curtis.

Golden Groups, Vol. 15 (Best of Times Square Records) .... Relic (M) 5032 8-10
Five Sharks; Decoys; Timetones; Summits; Jaytones; Pharotones.

Golden Groups, Vol. 16 (Best of Rainbow Records) .... Relic (M) 5034 8-10
Clovers; Lovenotes; Hearts; Swans; Dappers; Marquis; Winners; Jets; Startones.

Golden Groups, Vol. 17 (Best of Relic Records, Vol. 2) .... Relic (M) 5036 8-10
Five Crystals; Dee Vines; Vilons; Excels; Starlites; Newtones; Nutones; Quinns; Kents (Criterions); Continentals.

Golden Groups, Vol. 18 (Best of Premium Records) .... Relic (M) 5037 8-10
Wheels; True Loves; Montclairs; Escorts; Paul Winley & Rockets; Copesetics.

Golden Groups, Vol. 19 (Best of Jay-Dee Records) .... Relic (M) 5038 8-10
Chestnuts; Scaletones; Sparrows; Pyramids; Dovers; Goldentones; Romancers; Continentals; Blenders.

Golden Groups, Vol. 20 (Best of Valmor Records) .... Relic (M) 5042 8-10
Roomates; Embers; Cathy Jean & Roomates; Twilights; Paramounts & Eddie Saxon.

Golden Groups, Vol. 21 (Best of LuPine Records) .... Relic (M) 5043 8-10
Marv Johnson; Conquerors; Bumble Bees; Falcons; Tornados; Rivals; Little Joe & Morrocos; Sonny Woods Group; Bob Hamilton's Group; Five Masters; Professor Hamilton & tyhe Schoolboys; Minor Chords; Brian Holland.

Golden Groups, Vol. 22 (Best of Klik Records) .... Relic (M) 5044 8-10
Nobles; Centuries; Shades; Revlons; Anglones; Memories.

Golden Groups, Vol. 23 (Best of Showtime Records) .... Relic (M) 5045 8-10
Feathers; June Moy & Feathers; Five Stars; Individuals; John & Louis Staton.

Golden Groups, Vol. 24 (Best of Bruce Records) .... Relic (M) 5046 8-10
Laurels; Corvells; Johnny Angel; Premiers; Eddie Robbins; Four of Us; Shy-Tones; Versatones; Van Dykes; Five Vets; Herb Lance; Jumping Jacks; Kingsmen; Creations.

Golden Groups, Vol. 25 (Best of Herald Records, Vol. 2) .... Relic (M) 5047 8-10
Debonaires; Five Willows; Thrillers; Rocketeers; Heralds; Loungers; Cashmeres; Mint Juleps; Little Butchie Saunders & Buddies; Sonnets; Desires; Smart Tones; Dale & Del-Hearts; Dynamics; Vocalaires.

Golden Groups, Vol. 26 (Best of Ember Records, Vol. 2) .... Relic (M) 5048 8-10
Skarlettones; Boptones; Starlites; Wonders; Fashions; Paramounts; Barries; Silhouettes; David Clowney; Concords; Colonairs; Roger & Travelers.

Golden Groups, Vol. 27 (Best of Flash Records) .... Relic (M) 5049 8-10 85
Jayhawks; Hornets; Emanon Four; Arrows; Poets; Cubans.

Golden Groups, Vol. 28 (Best of Onyx Records) .... Relic (M) 5050 8-10 85
Velours; Pearls; Impressors; Montereys; Wanderers; Carvels; Marquis.

Golden Groups, Vol. 29 (Best of Atlas/Angeltone Records, Vol. 2) .... Relic (M) 5051 8-10 85
Little Butchie & Vells; Lincolns; Five Dukes; Chandeliers; Charmers; Angle-tones; Travelers; Parakeets; Fabulous Fabuliers; Gypsies; Haven Knights.

Golden Groups, Vol. 30 (Best of Dig Records) .... Relic (M) 5052 8-10 85
Arthur Lee Maye & Crowns; Premiers; Mel Williams & Jayos; Julian Herrera & Tigers; Tears; Cell Foster & Audios; Tony Allen & Night Owls; Gladiators.

Golden Groups, Vol. 31 (Best of Specialty Records) .... Relic (M) 5054 8-10 85
Chimes; Dukes; Arthur Lee Maye & Crowns; Tony Allen & Champs; Crystals; Ben Zeppa & Zephyrs; Metronomes; Tropicals; Pharaohs; Twilighters; Byron Slick & Sliders.

Golden Groups, Vol. 32 (Best of Class Records, Vol. 1) .... Relic (M) 5055 8-10 85
Richard Berry & Pharaohs; Sputniks; Intervals; Earl Nelson & Pelicans; Classics; Bobby Day & Satellites; Blenders; Oscar McLollie; Paul Clifton.

Golden Groups, Vol. 33 (Best of the Los Angeles Groups) .... Relic (M) 5056 8-10 85
Rocketeers; Strands; Ebbtides; Cadets; Peacocks; Jayhawks; Castle-tones; Thrills; Marvells; Gassers.

Golden Groups, Vol. 34 (Best of Class Records, Vol. 2) .... Relic (M) 5057 8-10 85
Searchers; Titans; Richard Berry & Pharaohs; Blenders; Bobby Day & Satellites; Paul Clifton; Sputniks; Steve Kass & Lovelarks; Eugene Church & Fellows; Earl Nelson & Pelicans; Intervals; Classics; Rollettes; Tangiers.

Golden Groups, Vol. 35 (Best of Club 51 Records) .... Relic (M) 5059 8-10 85
Four Buddies; Kingsmen; Rudy Greene; Bobby James; others.

Golden Groups, Vol. 36 (Best of Swingin' Records) .... Relic (M) 5060 8-10 85
Rochelle & Candles; Hollywood Saxons; Paradons; Hollywood Saxons.

Golden Groups, Vol. 37 (Best of Milestone Records) .... Relic (SP) 5061 8-10 86
Paradons; HI Tensions; Metronomes; Angels; Wil-sons.

Golden Groups, Vol. 38 (Best of Chex Records) .... Relic (M) 5063 8-10 86
Majestics; Othea George; Donald Richards & Volumes; Bohemians; Tony & Technics.

Golden Groups, Vol. 39 (Best of Nu-Kat Records) .... Relic (SP) 5065 8-10 87
Continental Five; Orbits; Velvatones; Five Roses.

Golden Groups, Vol. 40 (Best of Len Records) .... Relic (M) 5066 8-10 87
Herb Johnson & Premiers; Dreamlovers; Four Bars; Marquees; Herb Johnson & Cruisers; Masters; Little Jimmy Rivers & Tops; Parliaments.

Golden Groups, Vol. 41 (Best of V-Tone Records) .... Relic (M) 5067 8-10 87
Fashions; Clefts; Farris Hill & Madisons; Dreamlovers; Joe Van Loan; Boss-Tones; Cruisers; Tremains.

Golden Groups, Vol. 42 (Best of Lummtone Records) .... Relic (M) 5068 8-10 87
Upfronts; Elgins; Five Ramblers; Colognes; Troopers.

Golden Groups, Vol. 43 (Best of Combo Records) .... Relic (M) 5069 8-10 87
Sharps; Savoys; Native Boys; Kokos; Nutones; Blenders; Chanters & Gene Ford; Buddies & Carl Ell; Echoes; Debonaires; Blenders & Ray Frazier; Paramounts; Laurels; Chimes & Gene Moore.

Golden Groups, Vol. 44 (Best of Combo Records, Vol. 2) .... Relic (M) 5070 8-10 87
Sharps; Debonaires; Bative Boys; Starliters; Savoys; Buddies & Carl Ell; Chanters & Gene Moore; Squires; Nutones; Echoes; Paramounts.

Golden Groups, Vol. 45 (Best of Timely/Luna Records) .... Relic (M) 5071 8-10 87
Ambassadors; Charmers; Crystals; Gaytunes.

Golden Groups, Vol. 46 (Best of Combo Records, Vol. 3) .... Relic (M) 5076 8-10 87
Chanters; Ebonaires; Native Boys; Chimes & Gene Moore; Squires; Echoes; T.L. Clemons & Sir Nites; Combonettes.

Golden Groups, Vol. 47 (Best of Apollo Records) ... Relic (M) 5077 8-10 89
Mel-O-Dots; Hearts; Opals; Jumping Jacks; Lydia Larson & River Rovers; Larks.
Golden Groups, Vol. 48 (Best of Apollo Records, Vol. 2) ... Relic (M) 5078 8-10 89
Gentlemen; Larks; Dovers; Nite Riders; Romeos.
Golden Groups, Vol. 49 (Best of the Times Square, Vol. 2) ... Relic (M) 5079 8-10 89
Vitones; El Sierros; Crests; Camelots; Timetones; Flamingos; Lytations; Youngones; Teen Five; Gents; Fairlanes.
Golden Groups, Vol. 50 (Best of Apollo Records, Vol. 3) ... Relic (M) 5080 8-10 89
Sparks of Rhythm; Inspirations; Lillian Leach; Mellows; Keynotes.
Golden Groups, Vol. 51 (Best of Apollo Records, Vol. 4) ... Relic (M) 5081 8-10 89
Delroys; Tonettes; Brochures; Casanovas; La Fits & Kitty; Chesters; Claremonts; Ann Ford.
Golden Groups, Vol. 52 (Best of Parrot/Blue Lake Records, Vol. 1) ... Relic (M) 5086 8-10 90
Orchids; Flamingos; Five Thrills; Rockettes; Earls.
Golden Groups, Vol. 53 (Best of Parrot/Blue Lake Records, Vol. 2) ... Relic (M) 5088 8-10 90
Flamingos; Fascinators; Swans; Five Chances; Clouds; Pelicans; Fortunes; Parrots.
More volumes now exist in the *Golden Groups* series from Relic, although the specifics were unavailable at press time. We are lacking the years of release for Volumes 9 through 27, although they did come out between 1974 and 1985.
Golden Groups, Golden Memories (8 LP) ... Reader's Digest (S) RD-0581 25-35 80
(Boxed set. Mail order.) Kingston Trio; Modernaires; Mills Brothers; Andrew Sisters; Merry Macs; Ink Spots; Song Spinners; Pied Pipers; King Sisters; Sportsmen; Ames Brothers; Jubilaires; Weavers & Gordon Jenkins; Four Aces; Pine Toppers; Gaylords; Sonny Till & Orioles; Four Knights; Four Tunes; Hilltoppers; Chordettes; Crew-Cuts; De Castro Sisters; Fontane Sisters; Drifters; Platters; Four Freshmen; Everly Brothers; Crickets; Fleetwoods; Flamingos; Four Preps.
Golden Hit Parade ... Pickwick/Camden (M) ACL 7030 5-10 76
Ames Brothers; Kay Starr; Jaye P. Morgan; Sammy Kaye with Don Cornell; Hugo Winterhalter; Perez Prado; Tony Martin; June Valli; Vaughn Monroe; Eartha Kitt.
Golden Hits ... Decca (M) DL 34399 10-15
Brenda Lee; Les Brown & Ames Brothers; Debbie Reynolds; Tommy Dorsey; Ted Weems; Peggy Lee; Gordon Jenkins; Mills Brothers; Claude Thornhill; Dick Haymes; Louis Armstrong & All Stars.
Golden Hits ... Cameo (M) 1063 15-25 63
Chubby Checker; Bobby Rydell; others.
Golden Hits - the Golden Instrumentals: see Golden Instrumentals - the Golden Hits
Golden Hits ... Wyncote (M) W-9012 10-20 63
Golden Hits ... Wyncote (S) SW-9012 10-20 63
Chubby Checker; Bobby Rydell; Orlons; Dovells; Dee Dee Sharp; Jo Ann Campbell.
Golden Hits, Vol. 1 ... RCA (M) LPM-2774 10-20 63
Golden Hits, Vol. 1 ... RCA (S) LSP-2774 15-25 63
Perry Como; Eddie Fisher; Artie Shaw; Freddy Martin; Perez Prado; Tommy Dorsey; Vaughn Monroe; Harry Belafonte; Ames Brothers. (See *Gold Hits, Vol. 2* for second volume in this series.)
Golden Hits, Vol. 2: see Gold Hits, Vol. 2
Golden Hits, Vol. 2 ... Cameo (M) 1067 15-25 63
Dovells; Orlons; others.
Golden Hits - All Time Original Hits ... Dot (M) DLP-3818 10-20 67
Golden Hits - All Time Original Hits ... Dot (S) DLP-25818 10-20 67
Eddie Fisher; Debbie Reynolds; Mills Brothers; .
Golden Hits from the Gang at Bang ... Bang (M) 215 10-20 67
Golden Hits from the Gang at Bang ... Bang (S) 215 10-20 67
Golden Hits of the 40's ... Harmony (M) HL-7373 10-15 66
Buddy Clark; Harry James; Dinah Shore; Les Brown; Kitty Kallen; Three Flames; others.
Golden Hits of the Golden Groups, Vol. 1 ... SSS Int'l (S) 32 8-10 76
Ad Libs; Jelly Beans; Butterflys; Shangri-Las; Tradewinds.
Golden Hollywood Themes ... Decca (M) DL-4362 10-15 63
Golden Hollywood Themes ... Decca (S) DL-74362 15-20 63
(Soundtrack songs from 12 1950's movies.) Victor Young; Morris Stoloff; Alex North; Alfred Newman; Joseph Gershenson; Elmer Bernstein.
Golden Instrumental Hits ... Warner Bros. (M) W-1725 10-20 67
Golden Instrumental Hits ... Warner Bros. (S) WS-1725 10-20 67
Marketts; Fireballs; Champs; others.
Golden Instrumentals Country Style ... Wing (M) MGW-12261 10-20 64
Golden Instrumentals Country Style ... Wing (S) SRW-16261 10-20 64
Golden Instrumentals - *the* Golden Hits ... Dot (M) DLP-3820 15-20 67
Golden Instrumentals - *the* Golden Hits ... Dot (S) DLP-25820 15-20 67
Santo & Johnny; Surfaris; Sandy Nelson; Chantays; Dave "Baby" Cortez; Champs; Lonnie Mack; Cozy Cole; Dartells; Preston Epps; Fireballs; Johnny & Hurricanes.
Golden Memories of the Past, Vol. 1 ... Musictone (M) 7000 20-30 64
Quin-Tones; Eternals; Paragons; Tokens; Chimes; Classics; Crests (shown as "The Crest"); Harptones; Elchords; Jimmy Charles; Rocketones; Videls.
Golden Memories of the Past, Vol. 2 ... Musictone (M) 7001 15-25 64
Beverly Ann Gibson; Faye Adamss; Little Esther; Ann Cole; Maxine Brown.
Golden Moments of Country and Western Music (2 LP) ... Capitol (S) SQBO-90985 8-12 67?
Hank Thompson; Jean Shepard; Sonny James; Merle Haggard; Red Simpson; Buck Owens; Wanda Jackson; Ned Miller; Tex Ritter; Ferlin Husky; Tennessee Ernie Ford.
Golden Motion Picture Themes and Original Soundtracks ... United Artists (M) UAL-3376 8-10 64
Golden Motion Picture Themes and Original Soundtracks ... United Artists (S) UAS-6376 8-10 64
(Soundtrack.) Ferrante & Teicher; Riz Ortolani; Hollywood Studio Orchestra; Al Caiola; Leroy Holmes; Ken Lauber; Billy May; John Barry; John Addison; Frank DeVol; Ernest Gold.
Golden Movie Greats ... Liberty (M) LRP-3306 10-20 63
Golden Movie Greats ... Liberty (S) LST-7306 15-25 63
Felix Slatkin; Martin Denny Eddie Heywood; others.

Golden Oldies....Decca (M) DL-4036 40-60 60
Bobby Darin; Flamingos; Crickets (with Buddy Holly); Kalin Twins; Paul Evans; Bill Haley & His Comets; Shirelles; Carl Dobkins Jr.; Dreamweavers; Bobby Helms.
Golden Oldies, All Star....Coronet (SE) CXS-217 20-30
Golden Oldies, Vol. 1....International Award Series (S) AKS-221 5-10 63
Bobby Day; Googie Rene; Billy Myles; Wilbert Harrison; Turbans; Ann Cole; Cap-Tans.
Golden Oldies, Vol. 2....International Award Series (S) AKS-222 5-10 63
Stingers; Googie Rene; Ernie Fields; Glenn Miller; Vikki Carr; Petula Clark; Johnny Rivers; Fifth Dimension; Glen Campbell; Longines Symphonette.
Golden Oldies, Vol. 1....Strand (M) SL-1129 20-30 60s
Golden Oldies, Vol. 1....Strand (S) SLS-1129 20-30 60s
Angels; Brook Benton; Cashmeres; Chris Columbo; Dave "Baby" Cortez; Gary Criss; Fiestas; Fireflies; Larry Hall; Harptones.
Golden Oldies, Vol. 3....International Award Series (M) AK-229 5-10
Silhouettes; Fidelities; Lee Dorsey; Angel Face; Ernie Fields; Maurice Williams; Fabulous Cyclones; Noble Watts; Jackie McLean; Dynasaurs.
Golden Oldies - Original Hits, Vol. 1....Design (M) DLP-701 15-20 63
Golden Oldies - Original Hits, Vol. 1....Design (S) DLP-701 15-20 63
Wilbert Harrison; Five Satins; Fidelities; Nobel Watts; Turbans; Jackie McLean; Fabulous Cyclones; Teacho Wiltshire.
Golden Oldies - Original Hits, Vol. 1....Pickwick (M) SDLP-701 5-10 75
Wilbert Harrison; Five Satins; Fidelities; Nobel Watts; Turbans; Jackie McLean; Fabulous Cyclones; Teacho Wiltshire.
Golden Oldies - Original Hits, Vol. 2....Design (M) DLP-702 15-20 63
Silhouettes; Lee Allen; Lee Dorsey; Hearts; Fabulous Cyclones; Ray Charles; Jackie McLean; Rivileers.
Golden Oldies - Original Hits, Vol. 2....Pickwick (M) SDLP-702 5-10 75
Silhouettes; Lee Allen; Lee Dorsey; Hearts; Fabulous Cyclones; Ray Charles; Jackie McLean; Rivileers.
Golden Oldies - Original Hits, Vol. 3....Design (M) DLP-703 15-20 63
Maurice Williams; Billy Myles; Five Satins; Lee Dorsey; Ann Cole; Margie Anderson; Ink Spots; Fabulous Cyclones; Jackie McLean.
Golden Oldies - Original Hits, Vol. 3....Pickwick (M) SDLP-703 5-10 75
Maurice Williams; Billy Myles; Five Satins; Lee Dorsey; Ann Cole; Margie Anderson; Ink Spots; Fabulous Cyclones; Jackie McLean.
Golden Oldies - Original Hits, Vol. 4....Design (M) DLP-704 15-20 63
B. Bumble & Stingers; Googie Rene; Ernie Fields; Eugene Church; Jesse Belvin; Angel Face; Henry Curtis; Cap-Tans; Veronnee; Clyde Crawford.
Golden Oldies - Original Hits, Vol. 4....Pickwick (M) SDLP-704 5-10 75
B. Bumble & Stingers; Googie Rene; Ernie Fields; Eugene Church; Jesse Belvin; Angel Face; Henry Curtis; Cap-Tans; Veronnee; Clyde Crawford.
Golden Oldies - Original Hits, Vol. 5....Design (M) DLP-705 15-20 63
Ernie Fields; Dynasaurs; Jesse Belvin; Bobby Day; Mello-Kings; Angel Face; Henry Curtis; Cap-Tans; Frank Motley; T.N.T. Tribble.
Golden Oldies - Original Hits, Vol. 5....Pickwick (M) SDLP-705 5-10 75
Golden Oldies - Original Hits, Vol. 6....Design (M) DLP-706 15-20 63
Golden Oldies - Original Hits, Vol. 6....Design (S) SDLP-706 15-20 63
Sunny Gale; Frankie Laine; Eugene Church; Wilbert Harrison; Starlites; Lee Allen; Jackie Fontaine; Marilyn Maxwell; Lloyd Schaffer; Frank Motley.
Golden Oldies - Original Hits, Vol. 6....Pickwick (M) SDLP-706 5-10 75
Sunny Gale; Frankie Laine; Eugene Church; Wilbert Harrison; Starlites; Lee Allen; Jackie Fontaine; Marilyn Maxwell; Lloyd Schaffer; Frank Motley.
Golden Ones....Columbia Special Products (M) CSP-121 5-10
Ray Conniff; Tony Bennett; Kirby Stone Four; Percy Faith; Les Paul & Mary Ford; Guy Mitchell; Four Lads; Vic Damone; Andre Kostelanetz; Jo Stafford; Harry James; Don Costa.
Golden Ones (NARAS Presents) '59 Edition, Vol. 1....Naras (M) 1000 10-20 59
Chordettes; Nat King Cole; Perry Como; Doris Day; Fats Domino; Ella Fitzgerald; Edward "Kookie" Byrnes; Julie London; Patti Page; Debbie Reynolds; Carlton Carpenter; Billy Vaughn; Roger Williams. (Made for Watchmakers of Switzerland.)
Golden Performances That Will Live Forever: see 60 Years of Music America Loves Best
Golden Rock 'N' Rollers....Pickwick (S) ACL-7032 5-10 76
(Reissue of *Old 'N' Golden Goodies, Vol. 2*, RCA 3641.) Duane Eddy; Paul Anka; Peggy March; Isley Brothers; Tokens; Dave "Baby" Cortez; Jesse Belvin; Neil Sedaka; Skeeter Davis; Boots Randolph.
Golden Soul....Kapp (S) 3643 8-12 71
Chicano; Unifics; Hesitations; others.
Golden Soul (In Aid of the World's Refugees)....Atlantic (S) 18198 8-10 76
Otis Redding; Ray Charles; Roberta Flack; Drifters; Aretha Franklin; Spinners; King Curtis; Wilson Pickett; Ben E. King; Sam & Dave; Percy Sledge; Joe Tex.
Golden Sounds of Country Music....Harmony (M) HL-7449 8-10 68
Golden Sounds of Country Music....Harmony (S) HS-11249 8-10 68
Ray Price; Johnny Cash; Carl Smith; Johnny Horton; George Morgan; others.
Golden Souvenirs: see ADAMS, Faye / Little Esther / Shirley and Lee
Golden Souvenirs....United Artists (M) UAL-3317 15-25 63
Golden Souvenirs....United Artists (S) UAS-6317 20-30 63
Golden Summer (2 LP)....United Artists (SE) UA-LA627-H2 15-25 76
Beach Boys; Ventures; Surfaris; Jan & Dean; Frankie Avalon; Jack Nitzsche; Annette Funicello; Marketts; Fantastic Baggys; Frogmen; Dick Dale & His Del-Tones; Trashmen; Tradewinds; Routers.
Golden Teen Hits....Liberty (M) L-5505 20-30 62
Golden Throats - the Great Celebrity Sing Off....Rhino (S) R1 70187 5-10
Leonard Nimoy; Sebastian Cabot; Eddie Albert; William Shatner; Noel Harrison; Frankie Randall; Jack Webb; Mae West; Andy Griffith; Jim Nabors; Joel Gray.
Golden Treasure Chest....United Artists (M) UAL-3314 15-25 63
Golden Treasure Chest....United Artists (S) UAS-6314 20-30 63
Penguins; Medallions; Dave Baby Cortez; Chuck Jackson; Brook Benton; Del-Vikings; Meadowlarks; Neil Sedaka; Joe Houston; Jimmy Soul; Tokens; Hollywood Argyles.

Golden Treasures (3 LP) .... Ruby (S) PC3-0002 10-15 81
Little Caesar & Romans; Angels; Jimmy Clanton; Gary "U.S." Bonds; Dee Clark; Coasters; Johnny Maestro; Freddie Cannon; Mark Dinning; Chubby Checker; Crystals; Drifters; Clovers; Jimmy Gilmer; Jan & Dean; Bobby Day; Kingston Trio; Jim Lowe; Bobby Lewis; Happenings; Rosemary Clooney; Johnnie Ray; Marcels; Lloyd Price; Crew-Cuts; Gary Lewis & Playboys; Joey Dee & Starliters; Mary Wells; DelShannon; Leslie Gore; Hondells; Dovells; Billy Joe Royal; Association; Fontella Bass; Classics IV; Ad Libs; Cowsills; Archie Bell & Drells; Gerry & Pacemakers; John Fred; Vogues; Gary Puckett & Union Gap; Oliver; Martha Reeves; Jeannie C. Riley; Bobby Vee; B.J. Thomas; Percy Sledge.

Golden Treasury of Christmas Music (2 LP) .... Columbia Musical Treasury (SE) P2S 5270 10-15 60s

Golden Treasury of Greatest Hits .... Columbia (M) C2X-3 15-25 61
Johnny Mathis; Johnny Horton; Marty Robbins; Doris Day; Tony Bennett; Mitch Miller; Frankie Laine; Les Brown; Rosemary Clooney; Percy Faith; Four Lads; Benny Goodman; Harry James; Johnnie Ray; Dinah Shore; Jo Stafford; Arthur Godfrey.

Golden Treasury of Hymns .... Word (S) SPL-110 5-10
(Mail order offer.) Eddy Arnold; Dave Boyer; Pat Boone; Anita Bryant; Ralph Carmichael; Evie; Guy & Ralna; Burl Ives; Wanda Jackson; Kurt Kaiser; Anita Kerr Singers; Norman Luboff Choir; Jim Nabors; Wayne Newton; Patti Page; Bill Pearce; Ray Price; Roy Rogers & Dale Evan; George Beverly Shea; Norma Zimmer.

Golden Turkey Album, Best Songs from the World's Worst Movies .... Rhino (SP) RNSP 307 10-12 85
(Soundtrack.) Gordon Zahler; Five Blobs; Arch Hall Jr.; Carol Kay & Stone Tones; Bobby & Benny Belew; Pleasant Valley Boys; Don Snyder; "Peewee" Flynn; Linda & Tickles Steckler; Milton Delugg; Little Eskimos; Johnnie Fern; Dr. Frederick Kopp; Harold "Duke" Lloyd Jr.; Page Cavanaugh & His Trio; Ron Haydock & Boppers.

Golden 20 Oldies .... Lost Night (M) 109 5-10
Rivieras; Versatones; Chantels; Skip & Flip; Dion; Dreamlovers; Mellokings; Ron Holden; Don & Juan; Regents; Frankie Lymon; 5 Satins; Pentagons; Jive Five; Crystsals; Bellnotes; Heartbeats; Charts; Velvets.

Golden Winners .... Capitol (M) T-1892 15-20 63

Golden Years of Gospel Greats .... Modern Sound (S) MS-815 5-10
J.T. Adams; Wally Fowler; John Daniels Quartet; Speer Family; Florida Boys; Sons of Song; Sego Brothers & Naomi; Wendy Bagwell; Jake Hess; Oak Ridge Quartet.

Gone But Not Forgotten .... Class (M) CL-5004 45-55 60
Bobby Day; Oscar McLollie; Jeanette Baker; Bob & Earl; Eugene Church; Googie Rene.

Gone But Not Forgotten .... Starday (M) SLP-346 10-20 65
Cowboy Copas; Patsy Cline; Hawkshaw Hawkins; others.

Good Friends Are Made for Keeps .... United Artists (S) No Number Used 8-12 76
Max Morath; Dinah Shore; Glenn Miller; Vicki Carr; Petula Clark; Johnny Rivers; Fifth Dimension; Glen Campbell; Longines Symphonette. (Made for Bell System's 100th Anniversary.)

Good Guy Jack Spector Presents 22 Original Winners .... Roulette (M) R-25254 8-12
Dovells; Vibrations; Little Eva; Joey Dee; Rays; Tempos; Crystals; Wilbert Harrison; Lee Dorsey; Shirley & Lee; Penguins; Chubby Checker; Coasters; Little Richard; Bobby Lewis; Joe Jones; Regents; Bo Diddley; Essex; Drifters; Robert & Johnny; Chuck Berry.

Good Morning, Vietnam .... A&M (S) SP-3913 8-10 87
(Soundtrack.) Martha Reeves & Vandellas; Beach Boys; Wayne Fontana & Mindbenders; Searchers; Castaways; James Brown; Them; Marvelettes; Vogues; Rivieras; Louis Armstrong.

Good Old Boys .... Columbia (S) P 14583 8-12 78
(Country Music Magazine.) David Wills; Freddy Fender; Johnny Paycheck; Freddy Weller; David Allen Coe; Tommy Cash; Sonny James; Joe Stampley; Ray Price; Bob Luman; Moe Bandy; B.J. Thomas; Marty Robbins; David Houston; Billy "Crash" Craddock; George Jones; Narvel Felts; Johnny Cash; Charlie Rich; Billy Swan.

Good Old Country Boys (5 LP) .... Mercury/Columbia House (S) 5P 6000 20-30 73
(Boxed set. Record club issue.) Faron Young; Tom T. Hall; Roger Miller; Jerry Lee Lewis; others.

Good Old Country Gospel .... Country Music (S) CM-1036 5-10 75
Loretta Lynn; Jimmie Davis; Red Foley; Bill Monroe; Ernest Tubb; Bill Anderson; Webb Pierce; Kitty Wells; Wilburn Brothers; Jimmy Martin.

Good Old Country Gospel .... Green Valley (S) MSM-35008 8-12
Bill Anderson; Jimmie Davis; Red Foley; Bill Monroe; Loretta Lynn; Ernest Tubb; Kitty Wells; Webb Pierce; Wilburn Brothers; Jimmy Martin.

Good Old Country Gospel .... RCA (S) LSP-4778 5-10 72
Chet Atkins; Floyd Cramer; Dolly Parton; Dottie West; Charley Pride; Porter Wagoner; Connie Smith; Hank Snow; Skeeter Davis; Jim Reeves.

Good Old Fifties .... Atco (M) 33-118 30-40 60
Bobby Darin; Coasters; Paul Evans; King Curtis; Sandy Stewart; Hollywood Flames; Hutch David; Chordcats; Jackson Brothers.

Good Old Oldies (By Rhythm and Blues Groups) .... Davis (M) LP-206 10-15 74
Millionaires; Sparrows; Crickets; Chestnuts; Deep River Boys; Mellows; Scaletones; Pyramids; Goldentones.

Good Old Rock & Roll (2 LP) .... Lakeshore/Gusto (S) Gt-105 10-15 78
Thurston Harris; Ray Peterson; Jimmy Gilmer; Sam the Sham; Carl Dobkins Jr.; Barbara Mason; Gary Lewis; Billy Joe Royal; Crests; Gene Simmons; Jack Scott; Sandy Nelson; Bobby Day; Impalas; Olympics; Jewel Akens.

Good Time Music .... K-Tel 9268 10-15 78
Harry Belafonte; Brothers Four; Gale Garnett; Highwaymen; Kingston Trio; Trini Lopez; New Christy Minstrels; New Seekers; Pozo Seco Singers; Sandpipers; Seekers; Tokens; We Five; Glenn Yarbrough.

Good Time Music .... Imperial House (S) 466 10-15
Paper Lace; Rubettes; Rod Stewart; Jud Strunk; Ray Stevens; Freddy Fender; Johnny Rivers; Johnny Nash; Lynn Anderson; Gallery; Hollies; Ray Price; Oliver; American Breed; Mr. K; Mel & Tim; Tremeloes; Austin Roberts; B.J. Thomas; Clint Holmes; Ad Libs; Brewer & Shipley; First Class; Jigsaw.

Good Times in Country Music (2 LP) .... Columbia/Tampa (SE) C2-10419 8-12 70s
Ray Price; Faron Young; Jim Rodgers; Hank Thompson; Jimmy Wakely; Stonewall Jackson; Arthur Smith; Roger Miller; Lynn Anderson; Johnny Cash; Cowboy Copas; George Morgan; Kenny Roberts; Andy Wilson; David Houston & Tammy Wynette; Johnny Cash; June Carter; Grandpa Jones; Bill Clifton; Jim Nabors; Carl Story; Carl Smith; Roy Clark; Buck Owens; Johnny Bond; Dottie West; Jimmy Dean.

Good to Go .... Island (S) 90509-1 8-10 86
(Soundtrack.) Trouble Funk; Hot Cold Sweat; Sly Dunbar & Robbie Shakespeare; E.U.; Wally Baradou; Chuck Brown & Soul Searchers; Donald Banks; Ini Kamoze; Redds & Boys.

Good Vibrations .... Centron (S) PSLP-002 8-10
Joe Simon; Mandrill; Eric Clapton; Roy Buchanan; Millie Jackson; John Mayall; James Brown; Slade; Manfred Mann; Rory Gallagher; Lyn Collins; Cat Mother & All Night Newsboys.

Good Vibrations .... Ronco/Columbia Special Products (S) P 11773 5-10 73
(Mail order offer.) Johnny Nash; Chi Coltrane; Harold Melvin & Blue Notes; Blood, Sweat & Tears; Poco; Hollies; Rod Stewart; Sly & Family Stone; Association; Ramsey Lewis; Raiders; Albert Hammond; Mac Davis; King Harvest; Red Bone; O'Jays; James Brown; Loudon Wainwright III; Melanie; Johnny Williams; Mott the Hoople; Looking Glass.

Good Vibrations (Rock of Ages): see Rock of Ages–Sounds of Top 40 Radio: 1964-1967 (Good Vibrations)

Goodbye to the '40s, Hello to the '50s .... Relic (M) 8018 5-10 89

Striders; Larks; Melody Masters; Four Blues; Rivals; Rhythm Kings.

Goodbye to the '40s, Hello to the '50s, Vol. 2 .... Relic (M) 8019 5-10 89

Striders; Melody Masters; Rhythm Kings; Three Riffs; Four Blues.

Goodies, Vol. 1 .... Warner Bros. (S) BS-2575 8-10 72

Van Morrison; Dion; Faces; Gordon Lightfoot; Jesse Colin Young; Jimi Hendrix Experience; Tony Joe White; Jethro Tull; Fleetwood Mac; Grateful Dead; T Rex.

Goodies But Oldies, Vol. 2 .... Warwick (M) W-2008 35-55 60

Moonglows; Willows; Flamingos; Harptones; Hearts; Tune Weavers; Shepherd Singers; Rod Bernard; Rivileers. (First issued as *Gold Hits.*)

Goodies for LP Fans .... RCA (M) LPM-2210 20-30 60

Neil Sedaka; Browns; Rod Lauren; Ray Peterson; Jim Reeves; Della Reese.

Goodies Old and New .... Time (M) 10000 30-40 59

Skip & Flip; Chevrons; Knockouts; Bell Notes; Rusty Isabel; Genies; Garry Lee; Lee Greenlee.

Goodtime Music .... K-Tel (S) NU-9260 5-10 77

Kingston Trio; New Christy Minstrels; We Five; Brothers Four; Harry Belafonte; Trini Lopez; Tokens; Highwaymen; Seekers; Gale Garnett; New Seekers; Pozo-Seco Singers; Glenn Yarbrough; Sandpipers.

Goofy Gold .... Exact (S) EX-204 5-10 80

Sue Thompson; Coasters; Sheb Wooley; Lonnie Donegan; Sam the Sham & Pharaohs; Johnny Cymal; Rufus Thomas; Paul Evans.

Goofy Gold .... HRB (S) 5000 5-10 78

Bobby Pickett; Sheb Wooley; Sam the Sham & Pharaohs; Johnny Preston; Playmates; Johnny Horton; Coasters; Lou Monte; Jimmy Dean.

Goofy Greats .... K-Tel (S) NU 9030 8-12 75

(Mail order offer.) Royal Guardsmen; Brian Hyland; Newbeats; Fendermen; Bobby Day; Hollywood Argyles; Johnny Thunder; Ohio Express; George Baker Selection; Tokens; Trashmen; Ray Stevens; Shirley Ellis; Lemon Pipers; 1910 Fruitgum Company; Piero Umiliani; Bill Haley & His Comets; Playmates; Jewel Akens; Lovin' Spoonful; Larry Verne; Larry Williams.

Goonies .... Epic (S) SE-40067 8-10 85

(Soundtrack.) Cyndi Lauper; REO Speedwagon; Luther Vandross; Joseph Williams; 14K; Philip Bailey; Bangles; Dave Grusin.

Gospel .... Diplomat (M) 2602 5-10

Sunshine Boys; Wally Fowler; Kirby Buchanan; Old Hickory; Oak Ridge Quartet.

Gospel According to Music .... Canaan (S) CAS-9787 5-10 76

Happy Goodmans; Inspirations; Florida Boys; Kingsmen; Wendy Bagwell & Sunliters; Jimmie Davis; Cathedral Quartet; LeFevres; Thrasher Brothers; Reverend Cleavant Derricks & Family; Lewis Family; Singing Christians; Windy Johnson & Messengers.

Gospel Favorites .... Wyncote (M) W 9067 10-15 64

Carl Storey; Wally Fowler; Stanley Brothers; Sunshine Boys; Oak Ridge Quartet; Kirby Buchanan; Old Hickory Singers.

Gospel Gathering .... Harmony (S) KH-32082 5-10 73

Patti Page; Chuck Wagon Gang; Mormon Tabernacle Choir; Ray Price; others.

Gospel Hootenanny .... Imperial (M) 9240 10-15 63

Gospel Hootenanny .... Imperial (S) 12240 10-15 63

Soul Stirrers; Traveling Four; others.

Gospel Music, Vol. 1 .... Imperial (M) LP-94007 10-15

Gospel Music Association's Top Ten Songs for 1976 .... Canaan (S) CAS-9802 5-10 77

Florida Boys; Kingsmen; Inspirations; Blackwood Brothers; Imperials; Sego Brothers & Naomi; Jerry & Goffs; Marijohn Wilkin; Cathedrals; Rambos.

Gospel Music's Top Ten for 1970 .... Heartwarming (S) 3103 5-10 71

Singing Rambos; Imperials; Oak Ridge Boys; others.

Gospel Music's Top Ten for 1971 .... Heartwarming (S) 3169 5-10 72

Florida Boys; Speer Family; Stamps Quartet; Oak Ridge Boys; Statesmen Quartet; LeFevres; Blackwood Brothers; Gaither Trio; Singing Rambos; Blue Ridge Quartet.

Gospel Music's Top Ten for 1971 .... Canaan (S) CAS-9710 5-10

Florida Boys; Speer Family; Stamps Quartet; Oak Ridge Boys; Statesmen Quartet; LeFevres; Blackwood Brothers; Gaither Trio; Singing Rambos; Blue Ridge Quartet.

Gospel Music's Top Ten for 1976 .... Canaan (S) 9802 5-10 77

Florida Boys; Kingsmen; Singing Rambos; Marijohn; others.

Gospel Singing Caravan .... Sing (M) MFLP 557 5-10

LeFevres; Blueridge Quartet; Johnson Sisters; Prophets; others.

Gospel Singing Caravan .... Sing (M) MFLP 558 5-10

LeFevres; Blueridge Quartet; Johnson Sisters; Prophets; others.

Gospel Singing Jubilee .... Canaan (M) CA-4602 5-10

Happy Goodman Family; Florida Boys; Couriers; Hal Kennedy; Dixie Echoes; Dale Shelnut; Duane Nicholson; Coy Cook; Rusty Goodman.

Gospel Singing Jubilee .... Canaan (M) CA-4618 5-10

Happy Goodmans; Dixie Echoes; Florida Boys; Hal Kennedy; Glen Allred.

Gospel Singing from the Heart .... Modern Sound (S) MS-809 8-12

Florida Boys; Dixie Echoes; Clyde Beavers; Travelers Quartet; Sons of Song; Sego Brothers & Naomi; McCormick Gospel Singers; Sunshine Girls; Wally Fowler; Georgians.

Gospel Sound, Vol. 1 .... Columbia (S) KG-31086 5-10 72

Mahalia Jackson; Staple Singers; Dorothy L. Coates; others.

Gospel Sound, Vol. 2 (2 LP) .... Columbia (S) KG-31595 8-12 72

Mahalia Jackson; Marion Williams; Blind Willie Johnson; Pilgrim Travelers; Eddie Head & Fammily; Golden Gate Jubilee Quartet; Arizona Dranes; Mitchell's Christian Singers; Rev. J.M. Gates; Staple Singers; Bessie Griffin; R.H. Harris & Christ Land Singers; Dorothy Love Coates & Original Gospel Harmonettes.

Gospel Special 20 Great Songs by 20 Great Artists .... Power Pak (S) PO-292 5-10 76

Wilma Lee & Stoney Cooper; Archie Campbell; Masters Family; Oak Ridge Quartet; Carl Story; Sunshine Boys; Stamps Quartet; Red Sovine; Reno & Smiley; Sego Brothers & Naomi; George Jones; Statesmen Quartet; Blue Ridge Quartet; T. Texas Tyler; Blackwood Singers; Speer Family; Prophets Quartet.

Gospel's Top 20 All Time Favorites .... Columbia Special Products (S) P 13429 5-10 76

(Mail order.) Charlie Rich; Johnny Cash; Tammy Wynette; Statler Brothers; Kitty Wells; Jim Reeves; David Houston; Loretta Lynn; Roy Rogers; Chuck Wagon Gang; Marilyn Sellars; Roy Acuff; Hank Williams; Billy Walker; Carter Family.

Got a Feeling (2 LP) .... Warner Bros./Tee Vee (S) TV-1043 8-12 79

(Mail order offer.)

Gotcha .... MCA (S) 5596 8-10 85

(Soundtrack.) Thereza Bazar; Giuffria; Camelflage; Hubert Kah; Joan Jett & Black Hearts; Bill Conti; Bronski Beat; Nik Kershaw.

Graffiti Bridge (2 LP)....Paisley Park (S) 1-27493 8-12 90
(Soundtrack.) Prince, Tevin Campbell, Morris Day, Jerome Benton & Time, Jill Jones, Mavis Staples, George Clinton, Ingrid Chavez, Robin Power, T.C. Ellis.

Graffiti Gold (2 LP) ....Vee Jay (M) VJ-2-9000 15-20 73
Spaniels; Crests; Buster Brown; Olympics; Regents; Lee Dorsey; Buddy Knox; Joey Dee & Starliters; Frankie Lymon; Little Anthony & Imperials; Heartbeats; Flamingos; Bobby Freeman; Tempos; Sonny Til & Orioles; Johnny Bond; Joe Jones; Dubs; Big Wheelie & Hubcaps; Playmates; Wilbert Harrison; J. Frank Wilson & Cavaliers; Doug Clark & Hot Nuts; Jimmy Clanton; Frankie Ford; Jimmy Charles; Little Richard; Jerry Butler; Dee Clark; Gene Chandler; El Dorados; Kathy Young & Innocents; Teen Queens; Betty Everett..

Graffiti Gold (3 LP) ....Brookville (S) T-1008 10-15 70s
(Mail order offer.) Crests; Buster Brown; Cleftones; Regents; Lee Dorsey; Buddy Knox; Joey Dee & State Siders; Frankie Lymon; Little Anthony & Imperials; Heartbeats; Flamingos; Tempos; Bobby Freeman; Johnny Bond; Joe Jones; Sonny Til & Orioles; Dubs; Big Wheelie & Hubcaps; Joey Dee & Starliters; Playmates; Wilbert Harrison; J. Frank Wilson & Cavaliers; Jimmy Clanton; Betty Everett; Gene Chandler; Jimmy Charles; Jerry Butler; Dee Clar; El Dorados; Little Richard; Kathy Young & Innocents; Frankie Ford; Teen Queens; Olympics; Spaniels.

Graffiti Scrapbook (3 LP)....Fairway (S) TC 1000 10-15 79
(Mail order offer.) Chubby Checker; Tymes; Dee Dee Sharp; Thomas Wayne; Bobby Rydell; Spaniels; Nutmegs; Silhouettes; Five Satins; Turbans; Mello Kings; Dale & Grace; Tommy Edwards; Mark Dinning; Conway Twitty; Cadillacs; Danleers; Shirelles; Fats Domino; Chuck Berry; Shells; Fireflies; Shangri-Las; Dixie Cups; Fiestas; Billy Bland; Capris; Penguines; Jimmy Clanton; Little Richard; Moonglows; Monotones; Johnny Ace; Classics; Chimes; Thurston Harris.

Graffiti Scrapbook, Vol. 1 ....Fairway (S) GFS 1001 5-10 80
(Mail order offer.) Chubby Checker; Tymes; Dee Dee Sharp; Tommy Wayne; Bobby Rydell; Spaniels; Nutmegs; Silhouettes; Five Satins; Turbans; Mello Kings; Dale & Grace.

Graffiti Scrapbook, Vol. 2 ....Fairway (S) GFS 1002 5-10 80
(Mail order offer.) Tommy Edwards; Mark Dinning; Conway Twitty; Cadillacs; Danleers; Shirelles; Fats Domino; Chuck Berry; Shells; Fireflies; Shangri-Las; Dixie Cups.

Graffiti Scrapbook, Vol. 3 ....Fairway (S) GFS 1003 5-10 80
(Mail order offer.) Fiestas; Billy Bland; Capris; Penguins; Jimmy Clanton; Little Richard; Moonglows; Monotones; Johnny Ace; Classics; Chimes; Thurston Harris.

Grand Ole Country (8 LP)....Columbia Special Products/Readers Digest RDA-122 25-40 74
Lynn Anderson; Johnny Cash; Tammy Wynette; David Houston; Marty Robbins; Johnny Horton; Charlie Rich; Tanya Tucker; Ray Price; Statler Brothers; Mac Davis; Flatt & Scruggs; June Carter; Mother Maybelle Carter; Tommy Cash; Carter Family; George Jones; Roger Miller; Jim & Jesse; George Hamilton IV; Stonewall Jackson; Statler Brothers; Terri Lane; Charlie Walker; Carl & Pearl Butler; Lefty Frizzell; Barbara Mandrell; Charlie McCoy; Charlie Rich; Jeannie Seely; Bob Luman; Carl Smith; Billy Walker; Boots Randolph; Bonnie Lou; Mel Tillis; Flatt & Scruggs; Arthur Smith; Lloyd Green; Jimmy Dean; Jack Cardwell; Claude King; Barbara Fairchild; Sonny James; Jody Miller; Johnny Paycheck; Connie Smith; Carl Perkins; Patti Page; Freddy Weller; Little Jimmy Dickens; Jody Miller; Anita Bryant; Faron Young; Johnny Bond; Dolly Parton; George Morgan; Floyd Tillman; Roy Acuff; Gene Autry; Moon Mullican.

Grand Ole Country ....Hilltop (S) JS-6157 5-10
Charlie Rich; Johnny Cash; T. Texas Tyler; Roy Orbison; Jerry Lee Lewis; Carl Belew; Conway Twitty; Patsy Cline; Webb Pierce; Jan Howard; Carl Perkins; Ferlin Husky; Jimmy Dean; Hank Locklin; Maddox Brothers & Rose.

Grand Ole Country Hits ....Camden (M) CAL-737 10-20 63

Grand Ole Country Hits ....Camden (SE) CAS-737 10-15 66
Hank Snow; Chet Atkins; Eddy Arnold; Pee Wee King; Lone Pine; Jimmie Rodgers; Don Gibson; Hank Locklin; Homer & Jethro; Jim Reeves; Gid Turner & Skillets; Roy Rogers & Sons of the Pioneers.

Grand Ole Country Hits ....Pickwick/Spectrum (S) ACL-7054 5-10 63
Hank Snow; Chet Atkins; Eddy Arnold; Pee Wee King; Redd Stewart; Jimmie Rodgers; Rainbow Ranch Boys; Don Gibson; Hank Locklin; Homer & Jethro; Jim Reeves; Roy Rogers; Sons of the Pioneers.

Grand Ole Opry Past and Present....Hilltop (S) JS-6022 8-12 60s
Uncle Jimmy Thompson & Eva Thompson Jones; Webb Pierce; Faron Young; Carl Belew; Wilburn Brothers; Billy Grammer; Lonzo & Oscar.

Grand Ole Opry Spectacular (2 LP) ....Starday (M) S-242 15-20 63

Grand Ole Opry Spectacular (2 LP) ....Starday (S) SLP-242 15-20 63
George Jones; Grandpa Jones; Red Sovine; Margie Singleton; Jimmy Skinner; Dottie West; Leon Payne; Tommy Jackson; Archie Campbell; Hawshaw Hawkins; Texas Ruby; Jim & Jesse.

Grease (2 LP)....RSO (S) RS 2-4002 10-12 78
(Soundtrack.) Frankie Valli; John Travolta; Olivia Newton-John; Frankie Avalon; Stockard Channing; Jeff Conaway; Cindy Bullens; Sha-Na-Na; Louis St. Louis.

Grease 2....RSO (S) RS 1-3803 8-10 82
Four Tops; others.

Greasy Kid Stuff ....United Artists (S) UXS-90 8-10 72
Dick & Deedee; Exciters; Falcons; Sandy Nelson; others.

Great All Time Country Hits, Vol. 1....Harmony (M) HL-7292 15-20 61
Bob Wills; Floyd Tillman; Louise Massey; others.

Great American Rock 'N' Roll Revival (2 LP) ....Laurie (S) LES 4029 8-12 80
Del Shannon; B.J. Thomas; Dion; Shirelles; Dionne Warwick; Billy Haley & His Comets; Skyliners; Curtis Lee; Gene Pitney; Dion & Belmonts; Beach Boys; Chiffons; Five Discs; Ernie Maresca; Ernie Maresca & Belmonts.

Great American Rock 'N' Roll Revival, Vol. 3 (2 LP) ....Laurie (S) LES 4032 8-12 81
Shirelles; Skyliners; Dion & Belmonts; Maxine Brown; Platters; Petula Clark; Brook Benton; Del Shannon; Chiffons; Royal Guardsmen; Mystics; Belmonts; Carlo; Cardboard Zeppelin; Jarmels; Four Pennies; Rany & Rainbows; Dean & Jean; Boots Walker; Ernie Maresca; Sundae.

Great Artists at Their Best....RCA Camden (S) SLC 12-8 8-12
Festival Concert Orchestra; On the Town Orchestra; Leonard Bernstein; Richard Crooks; Luboshutz & Nemenoff; John Charles Thomas; Cromwell Symphony Orchestra; Gisele MacKenzie; Johnny Desmond & Page Cavanaugh Trio; Guy Lombardo; Marjorie Lawrence; Erica Morini; Artur Balsam; Star Symphone Orchestra; Goldman Band & Edwin Franko Goldman.

Great Artists at Their Best, Vol. 2, Pop Singers ....RCA Camden (M) CAL-342 10-15 56
Polly Bergen; Bob Carroll; Mindy Carson; Don Cornell; Johnny Desmond; Connie Haines; Jack Haskell; Lena Horne; Snooky Lanson; Gisele MacKenzie; Dinah Shore; Fred Warren.

Great Artists of the 20th Century - the Great Rock Stars ....Columbia (S) CSS-1504 8-12 60s
Hollies; Chicago; Santana; Laura Nyro; Big Brother & Holding Company; Chambers Brothers; Pacific Gas & Electric; Blood, Sweat & Tears; Lulu; Mark Lindsay.

Great Balls of Fire .... Polydor (S) 839516-1 ?? 89
(Soundtrack.) Jerry Lee Lewis; Jackie Brenston & Delta Cats; Booker T. Laury; Valerie Wellington.
Great Band Era (10 LP) .... Readers Digest/RCA Custom (M) RD-25-K 30-40 65
(Boxed set.) Ozzie Nelson & Harriet Hilliard; Duke Ellington; Tony Pastor; Charlie Spivak; Alvino Rey & Yvonne King; Charlie Barnet & Barnet Modernaires; Lionel Hampton; Claude Thornhill; Guy Lombardo; Fats Waller; Eddy Duchin & Lew Sherwood; Tommy Dorsey & Sentimentalists; Artie Shaw & Imogene Lynn; Freddy Martin & Clyde Rogers; Charlie Spivak & Irene Rogers; Hal McIntire; Benny Goodman & Martha Tilton; Shep Fields; Glenn Miller & Ray Eberle; Earl Hines & Madeline Green & Three Varieties; Hal McIntyre & Ruth Gaylor; Four King Sisters & Male Chorus; Sammy Kaye & Billy Williams; David Rose; Hal Kemp & Bob Allen; Benny Goodman & Betty Van; Rudy Vallee & His Connecticut Yankees; Tommy Dorsey & Frank Sinatra; Sammy Kaye & Freddie Stewart; Vaughn Monroe & Norton Sisters & Rosemary Calvin; Artie Shaw & Helen Forrest; Larry Clinton & Bea Wain; Hal Kemp & Judy Starr; Abe Lyman & Bill Sherman; Tommy Dorsey & Jo Stafford; Glenn Miller & Skip Nelson; Ernie Madriguera; Jan Savitt & His Top Hatters & Carlotta Dale; Sammy Kaye & Three Kadets; Teddy Powell & Peggy Mann; Freddy Martin & Jack Leonard; Les Brown & Miriam Shaw; Freddy Martin & Glen Hughes; Skinnay Ennis; Ziggy Elman; Bunny Berigan & Kathleen Lane; Sammy Kaye & Three Barons; Artie Shaw & Paula Kelly; Alvino Rey & Skeets Hertfurt & Bill Schallen; Earl Hines & Billy Eckstine; Freddy Martin & Eddie Stone; Charlie Barnet & Larry Taylor; Bob Chester & Dolores O'Neill; Gray Gordon & His Tic-Toc Rhythm & Meredith Blake; Charlie Barnet & Bob Carroll; Larry Clinton & Helen Southern; Glenn Miller & Marion Hutton; Glenn Miller & Dorothy Claire & Modernaires; Artie Shaw & Bonnie Lake; Jan Savitt & His Top Hatters & Allen Dewitt; Xavier Cugat & Dinah Shore.
Great Bands .... Harmony (M) HL-7238 10-20 60
Harry James; Jimmy Dorsey; Les Brown; Woody Herman; Gene Krupa.
Great Bands and Jazz (2 LP) .... Columbia Special Products (M) XSV 86476-83 10-20
Louis Armstrong & Carmen McRae; Chico Hamilton Quintet; Xavier Cugat; Duke Ellington; Gerry Mulligan; Lester Lanin; Dukes of Dixieland; Hi-Lo's; Billy Butterfield; Count Basie & Tony Bennett; Carmen McRae; Lee Castle & Dorsey Orchestra; Bill Doggett; Dave Brubeck & Jimmie Rushing; Johnny Williams; Miles Davis; Lambert, Hendricks & Ross; Stereo Brass Choir; Andre Previn; Art Van Damme; Eddie Condon; J.J. Johnson; Charlie Mingus; Luther Henderson; Dave Brubeck; Hank Garland; Ray Bryant; Les Elgart. (Made for General Electric.)
Great Bands of Our Times .... RCA Camden (SE) CAS 811 8-12 64
Artie Shaw; Charlie Barnet; Ray Noble; Lonel Hampton; Glen Gray; Hal Kemp; Shep Fields; Gene Krupa.
Great Big Band Vocalists .... Columbia Special Products (S) CSS 1507 8-12
Les Brown & Doris Day; Guy Lommbardo & Bing Crosby; Harry James & Helen Forrest; Kay Kyser & Harry Babbit & Gloria Wood; Gene Krupa & Roy Eldridge & Anita O'Day; Harry James & Dick Haymes; Jo Bushkin & Bobby Hackett & Lee Wiley; Kay Kyser & Trudy & Harry; Orrin Tucker & Wee Bonnie Baker; Claude Thornhill & Fran Warren.
Great Big Bands .... Columbia Special Products (S) CSS 1506 8-12
Harry James; Clyde McCoy; Jimmy Lunceford; Gene Krupa & Charlie Ventura; Tommy Dorsey; Bunny Berigan; Benny Goodman; Tommy & Jimmy Dorsey; Duke Ellington; Woody Herman.
Great Blues Men .... Vanguard (S) VSM 73104 8-12 84
Homesick James; Mississippi John Hurt; John Lee Hooker; Junior Wells; Sleepy John Estes; Johnny Shines; Muddy Waters; Son House; Jessie Fuller; Sonny Terry; Mance Lipscomb; Joe Turner & Pete Johnson; Rev. Gary Davis.
Great Blues Men .... Vanguard (S) VSD-25/26 8-10 72
Homesick James; Muddy Waters; Johnny Shives; Johnny Young; others.
Great Bluesmen at Newport .... Vanguard (S) VSD-77/78 5-10 76
John Lee Hooker; Rev. Gary Davis; Lightnin' Hopkins; Brownie McGhee; Sonny Terry; Skip James; others.
Great Boy Oldies: see We Like Boys
Great British Reggae .... I.R.S. (S) 82029 5-10 90
Pato Banton; Tippa Irie; Papa Levi; Nerious Joseph; Major Popular; Peter Spence; Phillip Leo; C.J. Lewis; Winsome; Charisma; Lytie; Dee Sharpe.
Great Country and Western Hits .... Hilltop/Pickwick (S) JS-6088 8-12 60s
Johnny Horton; Sue Thompson; Faron Young; Flatt & Scruggs; Jimmy Dean; Anita Carter; Leroy Van Dyke; Carlisles; Rex Allen; Del Wood; Margie Bowes.
Great Country and Western Hits (10 EP) .... RCA (EP) SPD-26 800-1000 56
(Boxed set. Includes insert/separator sheets.) Elvis Presley; Eddy Arnold; Chet Atkins; Johnnie & Jack; Homer & Jethro; Jim, Edward & Maxine Brown; Jim Reeves; Hank Snow; Sons of the Pioneers; Porter Wagoner; Del Wood.
Great Country and Western Stars .... MGM (M) 2E-12 15-25 64
Great Country and Western Stars .... MGM (S) S2E-12 20-30 64
Hank Williams; Sheb Wooley; Roy Acuff; others.
Great Country and Western Stars .... Wing (M) MGW-12268 10-20 64
Great Country and Western Stars .... Wing (S) SRW-16268 10-20 64
Johnny Horton; Jimmy Dean; Sue Thompson; Rex Allen; Carlisles.
Great Country Duets .... Columbia (S) C-30896 5-10 71
Johnny Cash; June Carter; Carl & Pearl Butler; others.
Great Country Favorites .... MGM (M) E-4211 10-20 64
Great Country Favorites .... MGM (S) SE-4211 15-20 64
Sheb Wooley; Hank Williams; Ben Colder; others.
Great Country Folk .... Harmony (S) KH-31109 5-10 72
Sammi Smith; Tommy Cash; Johnny Cash; others.
Great Country Folk, Vol. 2 .... Harmony (S) KH-31389 5-10 72
Carl Smith; Carl Butler; Johnny Cash; Lynn Anderson; others.
Great Country Gospel Groups .... Wing (M) MGW-12262 8-12 64
Great Country Gospel Groups .... Wing (S) SRW-16262 8-12 64
Flatt & Scruggs; Stanley Brothers; Masters Family; Carl Story & Rambling Mountaineers; Tammy & Jim Wilson with the Chanters; Stamps Quartet.
Great Country Hits .... United Artists (M) UAL-3159 15-25 61
Bill Mack; Jim Blakley; others.
Great Country Hits .... Epic (S) BN 26550 5-10 70
Tammy Wynette; David Houston; Jim & Jesse & Virginia Boys; Charlie Walker; Stan Hitchcock; Tommy Cash; Mac Curtis; David Houston & Tammy Wynette; Bob Luman; Charlie Rich; Autry Inman.
Great Country Hits of the Year (3 LP) .... RCA Victor (S) CPL3-0697 10-20 74
Eddy Arnold; Chet Atkins; George Jones; Dottie West; Karen Wheeler; Skeeter Davis; Floyd Cramer; Dolly Parton; Charlie Rich; Bobby Bare; Jim Ed Brown; Josie Brown; Johnny Bush; Danny Davis; Willie Nelson; George Hamilton IV; Waylon Jennings; George Jones; Dickey Lee; Ronnie Milsap; Kenny Price; Jerry Reed; Jim Reeves; Johnny Russell; Brian Shaw; Connie Smith; Hank Snow; Nat Stuckey; Porter Wagoner; Charlie Walker.

Great Country Love Songs (4 LP) .... Columbia Musical Treasury (SE) P4S 5400 15-20
(Boxed set. Record club issue.) Roger Miller; Ray Conniff; Tammy Wynette;Marty Robbins; Johnny Cash; Dave Dudley; David Houston; Freddie Weller; Patti Page; Ray Price; Leon Ashley; Bobby Vinton; John Wesley Ryles; Jerry Lee Lewis; Jimmy Dean; O.C. Smith; Roy Drusky; Frankie Laine; Bonnie Guitar; Jim Nabors; Stonewall Jackson; Roy Clark; Johnny Horton; Johnny Cash; June Carter; Carl Smith; Jerry Vale; Lefty Frizzell; Flatt & Scruggs.

Great Country Music.. Dot (M) DLP-3732 10-20 66
Great Country Music.. Dot (S) DLP-25732 10-20 66
Cowboy Copas; Hank Garland; others.

Great Country Singers.. Columbia Special Products (S) CSS 1503 5-10
Johnny Cash; Tammy Wynette; Anita Bryant; Marty Robbins; Chuck Wagon Gang; David Houston; Carl Smith; Roy Acuff; Ray Price; Stonewall Jackson.

Great Country Stars Singing Their Biggest Hits (4 LP) .... Capitol/Tampa (S) SLD-6870 20-25
(Mail order offer.) Buck Owens; Wanda Jackson; Hobby Helms; Sonny James; Patsy Cline; Tex Ritter; Red Foley; Wayne Rancy; Moon Mulligan; Merle Travis; Jimmy Wakely; T. Texas Tyler; Pete Seeger; Tennessee Ernie Ford; Hank Thompson; Ferflin Husky; Faron Young; Sonny James; Bill Anderson; Ernest Ashworth; Wynn Stewart; Conway Twitty; Jody Miller; Roy Clark; Leroy Van Dyke; Jeannie C. Riley; Billie Jo Spears; Glen Campbell; Bobbie Gentry; Susan Raye; Freddie Hart; Buddy Alan; Anne Murray; Joe South.

Great Country Stars Sing Their Great Country Hits.. Capitol (M) T-2739 10-20 67
Great Country Stars Sing Their Great Country Hits.. Capitol (S) ST-2739 10-20 67
Buck Owens; Jean Shepard; Wanda Jackson; others.

Great Folk Country Hits.. Capitol Creative Products (S) SL 6647 8-12 60s
Lettermen; Hedge & Donna; Al De Lory; Nancy Wilson; Glen Campbell; Ella Fitzgerald; Tennessee Ernie Ford; Kingston Trio.

Great Girl Singers (2 LP)... Capitol (S) SLB 6952 5-10 74
Margaret Whiting; Jo Stafford; Helen O'Connell; Helen Forrest; Jane Froman; Billie Holiday; Frances Langford; June Hutton; Kay Starr; Peggy Lee; Edith Piaf; Betty Hutton; June Christy; King Sisters; Dinah Shore; Martha Tilton; Andrews Sisters; Ella Mae Morse; Anita O'Day; Ella Fitzgerald; Judy Garland.

Great Golden Grooves .... Epic (M) LN-24040 20-30 63
Tony Orlando; Roy Hamilton; Link Wray; Schoolboys; Lillian Briggs; Screamin' Jay Hawkins; Hearts; DeJohn Sisters; Little Joe & Thrillers; Rivileers; Ersel Hickey.

Great Gospel Quartets .... Columbia Special Products (S) P-13967 5-10 77
(Produced by Country Music Magazine.) Imperials; Sego Brothers & Naomi; Floriday Boys; LeFevres; Stamps; Foggy River Boys; Blackwood Brothers; Oak Ridge; Wendy Bagwell & Sunliters; Statesmen; Sons of Song; Jordanaires; Pine Ridge Boys; Trav'lers; Plainsmen; Rebels; Blue Ridge; Swanee River Boys; Gospel Singing Caravan; J.T. Adams & Men of Texas; Speer Family; Dee White Chorale; Jerry & Singing Goffs.

Great Gospel Songs.. Word (S) 8698 5-10 76
Anita Kerr; Walt Mills; Norma Zimmer; Ray Price; Roy Clark; Carol Lawrence; Mary Jayne; Dale Evans; others.

Great Gospel Songs Encore! (2 LP).. Word (S) WST-8645 8-12 76
Danny Thomas; Wanda Jackson; Anita Bryant; Roy Rogers & Dale Evans; Dino; Happy Goodman Family; Kurt Kaiser; Gene Gaither & Mary Jane; Thrasher Brothers; Cliff Barrows; Love Song; Norma Zimmer; Evie; Ray Price; Ken Medema; Marijohn; Andrae Crouch; Pat Boone Family; 2nd Chapter of Acts; Dave Boyer; Ralph Carmichael; Inspirations; Barry McGuire; Jimmie Davis.

Great Group Goodies .... Atco (M) 33-143 30-40 62
Ikettes; Hollywood Flames; Robins; Harptones; Coasters; Superiors; Royal Jokers; Solitaires; Sensations; Prophets.

Great Group Oldies, Vol. 1 .... Oldies 33 (M) OL-8003 10-20 60s
Great Group Oldies, Vol. 1 .... Vee Jay (M) VJLP-8003 15-20 64
Dells; El Dorados; Capris; Magnificents; Flamingos; Channels (actually Mary Wells); Quintones; El Dorados; Moonglows; Dubbs (sic, actually Channels); Spaniels.

Great Group Oldies, Vol. 2 .... Oldies 33 (M) OL-8006 10-20 60s
Great Group Oldies, Vol. 2 .... Vee Jay (M) VJLP-8006 15-20 64
Mellow Kings; Pentagons; Willows; Impressions; Robert & Johnny; Spaniels; Nutmegs; Dukays; Marvin & Johnny;Genies; Gladys Knight & Pips; Skyliners.

Great Groups.. Buddah (S) BDS-7509 8-12 69
Dells; Skyliners; Nutmegs; Spaniels; Rosie & Originals; Flamingos; Quintones; Moonglows; Magnificents; El Dorados; Dubs; Jive Five.

Great Groups (2 LP)... RCA/Brookville (SE) DLP 2-0068 10-15 74
(Mail order offer.) King Sisters with the Rhythm Reys; Ames Brothers with Hugo Winterhalter; Tommy Dorsey & Pied Pipers; Andrews Sisters; Mills Brothers; Mello-Larks; Three Suns; Harmonicats; Limeliters; King Sisters with Buddy Cole; Ames Brothers. (Special products. Made for Brookville.)

Great Groups (3 LP)... Adam VIII (S) 8032 10-15 76
Shirelles; Shep & Limelites; Frankie Lymon & Teenagers; Chantels; Flamingos; Little Anthony & Imperials; Everly Brothers; Platters; Earls; Fiestas; Robert & Johnny; Harptones; Capris.

Great Groups Are Back (2 LP).. Brookville/RCA (S) 8-12 75
Ames Brothers; Platters; Ink Spots; Crew-Cuts; Three Suns; Andrews Sisters; Tommy Dorsey with Frank Sinatra & Pied Pipers; Chordettes; Mello Larks; Mills Brothers; King Sisters; Nat King Cole Trio.

Great Groups, Great Records .... Laurie (M) LLP-2010 20-30 62
Dion & Belmonts; Skyliners; Five Satins; Mystics; Passions; Turbans; Dimensions; Five Discs; Belmonts.

Great Groups, Vol. 2 .... Laurie (M) LES 4015 8-12 79
Skyliners; Passions; Dion & Belmonts; Mystics; Tokens; Randy & Rainbows; Jarmels; Four Coins; Harps.

Great Guitars of Jazz... MCM (S) SE-4691 8-12
Kenny Burrell; Herb Ellis; Barney Kessel; Howard Roberts; Wes Montgomery; Tal Farlow; Oscar Moore.

Great Hits of 1964 and Other Great Goodies.. Vee Jay (M) VJLP-1136 20-30 64
Great Hits of 1964 and Other Great Goodies.. Vee Jay (S) VJSR-1136 25-35 64
4 Seasons; Jerry Butler; Betty Everett; Jimmy Hughes; Terry Stafford; Terry Black; Joe Simon; Honeycombs; Flamingoes; Little Richard; Gene Chandler; Skyliners; Bobby Day; Don Gardner & Dee Dee Ford; Joe Jones.

Great Hits of R&B (2 LP) .... Columbia/Brookville (S) G-30503 30-50 71
James Brown; Bill Doggett; Platters; Earl Bostic; Otis Williams; Hank Ballard & Midnighters; Little Willie John; James Brown & Famous Flames; Freddy King; Joe Tex; Bill Doggett; Wynonie Harris; Sonny Thompson; Ivory Joe Hunter; Bullmoose Jackson; Five Royales; Billy Ward & Dominoes; Lonnie Johnson; Otis Williams & Charms; Donnie Elbert; LaVern Baker; Champion Jack Dupree.

Great Hits of the Big Bands... RCA/Readers Digest(S) RDA-44D1/2 8-12
Glenn Miller; Artie Shaw; Tommy Shaw; Guy Lombardo; Sammy Kaye; Charlie Barnet; Bunny Berigan; Hal Kemp; Wayne King; Benny Goodman; Duke Ellington; Vaughn Monroe.

Great Hits of the Fantastic '50s (2 LP) ....Brookville/Columbia Special Products (SE) C2-10236 10-15
Rosemary Clooney; Guy Mitchell; Dinah Shore; Four Lads; Bobby Hackett; Jerry Vale; Frankie Laine; Ray Conniff; Doris Day; Vic Damone; Johnny Mathis; Patti Page; Bobby Vinton; Sammy Kaye; Eddie Layton; Joan Weber; Mitch Miller; Judy Garland; Roy Hamilton; Johnnie Ray; Les & Larry Elgart; Four Lads; Louis Armstrong; Doris Day. (Also issued as *Fantastic Fifties*.)

Great Hits of the Great Bands ....RCA (S) RD4-44-2 8-12 69
(RCA Custom for Reader's Digest.) Artie Shaw; Glenn Miller; Hal Kemp; Tommy Dorsey; Duke Ellington; Charlie Barnet; Bunny Berigan; Freddy Martin; Guy Lombardo; Sammy Kaye; Vaughn Monroe.

Great Hits of the Great Bands, 12 All Time Favorites ....RCA (S) RD4-44-1 8-12 69
Glenn Miller; Artie Shaw; Tommy Dorsey; Guy Lombardo; Sammy Kaye & Billy Williams Choir; Charlie Barnet; Bunny Berigan; Hal Kem p & Skinny Ennis; Wayne King; Benny Goodman & Martha Tilton; Duke Ellington; Vaughn Monroe.

Great Hits of the '60s.......... Era (S) BU-4530 8-12 77
Box Tops; Gary "U.S." Bonds; Casinos; Five Americans; Lou Christie; Ray Peterson; Sandy Posey; John Fred; Chubby Checker; American Breed; Tremeloes; Sam & Dave; Gary Lewis & Playboys; Oliver; Brooklyn Bridge; Del Shannon.

Great Hits of the '60s..........RCA Custom (S) XRIS 9709 5-10 70
Johnny Gibbs; Jo Stafford & Pied Pipers; Vic Damone; Joe Reisman; Chet Atkins; Les Brown; Les Reed; Ray Eberle & Modernaires; Vaughn Monroe; Bob Crosby.

Great Hits on Dot.......... Dot/Seeco (M) DLP-3049 25-40 57
Jim Lowe; Rusty Bryant; Francis Craig; Billy Vaughn with Ken Nordine; Elmo Tanner; Joe Liggins; Naomi Ford; Jimmy "Nervous Norvus" Drake; Sanford Clark; Dan Belloc.

Great Hits on Dot..........Dot (M) DLP-3677 10-20 66
Great Hits on Dot.......... Dot (S) DLP-25677 10-20 66
Jim Lowe; Rusty Bryant; Francis Craig; Billy Vaughn with Ken Nordine; Elmo Tanner; Joe Liggins; Naomi Ford; Jimmy "Nervous Norvus" Drake; Sanford Clark; Dan Belloc.

Great Ideas: see KIHN, Greg, Band / Earthquake / Modern Lovers / Rubinoos

Great Instrumental Hits (3 LP)..........RCA (SP) DVL3-0173 10-15 76
(Mail order offer.) Henry Mancini; Bert Kaempfert; Arthur Lyman; Roger Williams; Apollo 100; Floyd Cramer; Kai Winding; Vincent Bell; Mantovani; Kenny Bell; Hugo Winterhalter; Los Indios Tabajaras; Ferrante & Teicher; Bill Black's Combo; Hot Butter; Ramsey Lewis; Santo & Johnny; Mason Williams; David Rose; Joe Harnell; Perez Prado; Bent Fabric; Hugh Masekela; Vince Guaraldi Trio; Martin Denny; Chris Barber's Jazz Band; Arthur Lyman; Tornadoes; Elmer Bernstein; Billy Vaughn; Eric Weissberg; Royal Scots Dragoon Guards. (Special products. Made for Sessions.)

Great Instrumental Oldies ....Vee Jay (M) VJLP-8005 15-25 64
Great Jazz Artists Play Compositions of Cole Porter ....Riverside (M) RM 3515 15-20 60s
Great Jazz Artists Play Compositions of Cole Porter ....Riverside (S) RS 3515 15-20 60s
George Shearing & Wes Montgomery; Cannonball Adderley; Sonny Rollins; Johnny Griffin; Herbie Mann; Milt Jackson; Bill Evans; Clark Terry; Eddie "Lockjaw" Davis & Johnny Griffin.

Great Jazz Artists Play Compositions of George Gershwin ....Riverside (M) RM 3517 15-20 60s
Great Jazz Artists Play Compositions of George Gershwin ....Riverside (S) RS 3517 15-20 60s
Cannonball Adderley; Thelonious Monk; George Shearing & Wes Montgomery; Bill Evans; Charlie Byrd; Junior Mance; Harry Edison & Eddie Davis; Billy Taylor; John Lytle.

Great Jazz Artists Play Compositions of Harold Arlen ....Riverside (M) RM 3518 15-20 60s
Great Jazz Artists Play Compositions of Harold Arlen ....Riverside (S) RS 3518 15-20 60s
Great Jazz Artists Play Compositions of Jerome Kern..........Riverside (M) RM 3516 15-20 60s
Great Jazz Artists Play Compositions of Jerome Kern..........Riverside (S) RS 3516 15-20 60s
Sonny Rollins; Wes Montgomery; Blue Mitchell; Red Garland; Chet Baker; Cannonball Adderley; Bill Evans; Bobby Timmons; Nat Adderley.

Great Jazz Artists Play Compositions of Richard Rodgers ....Riverside (M) RM 3514 15-20 60s
Great Jazz Artists Play Compositions of Richard Rodgers ....Riverside (S) RS 3514 15-20 60s
Great Jazz Brass..........RCA (M) CAL-383 8-12
Louis Armstrong & His All Stars; Bix Beiderbecke; Buck Clayton; Lee Collins; Ziggy Elman; Harry James; J.J. Johnson & Kai Winding; Tommy Ladrier; Wingy Manone; King Oliver; Muggsy Spanier; Jack Teagarden.

Great Jazz of All Time (10 LP) ....Pickwick (S) SSH-102 30-50 62
(Boxed set.) Ray Charles; Jimmy & Marian McPartland; Dizzy Gillespie; Andre Previn; Lionel Hampton; Si Zentner; Charlie Shavers; Stan Getz; Lucky Thompson;Charlie Mingus; Al Hibbler; Tyree Glenn; Tommy & Jimmy Dorsey; Ben Webster; Della Reese; Earl Fatha Hines; Maxine Sullivan; Kai Winding; J.J. Johnson; Billy Taylor; Don Elliott; Django Reinhardt; Ralph Burns; Jack Teagarden; others.

Great Jazz Brass..........RCA Camden (M) CAL-383 10-15 59
J.J. Johnson & Kai Winding; Tommy Ladnier; Wingy Manone; King Oliver; Muggsy Spanier; Jack Teagarden; Louis Armstrong; Bix Biederbecke; Buck Clayton; Lee Collins; Ziggy Elman; /Harry James.

Great Jazz Pianists ....RCA Camden (M) CAL-328 10-15 58
Oscar Peterson; Earl Hines; Meade Lux Lewis; Jelly Roll Morton; Albert Ammons & Pete Johnson; Fats Waller; Art Tatum; Jess Stacy; Errol Gardner; Duke Ellington; James P. Johnson; Mary Lou Williams.

Great Jazz Reeds..........RCA Camden (M) CAL-339 10-15 58
Sidney Bechet; Chu Berry; Barney Bigard; Johnny Dodds; Irving Fazola; Bud Freeman; Coleman Hawkins; Mezz Mezzrow; Jimmy Noone; Charlie Parker; Pee Wee Russell; Ben Webster.

Great Love Songs of the Fabulous '40s ....Columbia (SE) 1P 6265 5-10 74
Kitty Kallen; Harry James; Buddy Clark & Ray Noble; Art Mooney; Doris Day; Perry Como; Marjorie Hughes & Frankie Carle; Andrews Sisters; Blue Barron; Art Lund; Dick Haymes; Helen Forrest.

Great Love Songs of the Fabulous '40s, Long Ago & Far Away (2 LP)..........Columbia (SE) 2P 6264 8-12 74
Hoagy Carmichael; Sammy Kaye; Dinah Shore; Jimmy Dorsey; Judy Garland & Gene Kelly; Xavier Cugat; Ink Spots; Charlie Spivak; Evelyn Knight; Bing Crosby; Les Brown with Doris Day; Ella Fitzgerald; Glen Gray; Ken Griffin; Dick Haymes; Frankie Laine; Doris Day & Buddy Clark; Benny Goodman; Russ Morgan; Kay Kyser. (Record club issue.)

Great Love Songs of the Fabulous '50s ....Columbia House (S) D5 830 5-10
Percy Faith; Roy Hamilton; Rosemary Clooney; Johnny Mathis; Georgia Gibbs; Platters; Tommy Edwards; Doris Day; Jan August. (Record club offer.)

Great Love Songs of the '50s & '60s ....Laurie (S) LES 4020 5-10 79
Platters; Gene Pitney; Dion & Belmonts; Passions; Brook Benton; Dionne Warwick.

Great Love Songs of the '50s & '60s, Vol. 3 ....Laurie (S) LES 4072 5-10 80s
Skyliners; Jerry Butler; Everly Brothers; Cathy Carr; etc.

Great Memories from Old Time Radio..........Columbia (S) DS-515 5-10
(Mail order offer.)

Great Men of Music (4 LP) .... Time Life (S) STL 541 10-20 74
(Boxed set with 24-page booklet.) Van Cliburn; Kiril Kondrashin; Leontyne Price; Jascha Heifetz; Chicago Symphony Orchestra; Eugene Ormandy & Philadelphia Orchestra; Boston Symphony Orchestra; others.

Great Million Sellers .... Strand (M) SL-1043 25-35 60s
Ted Weems; Larry Hall; Don Cherry; Candido; Billy Mure; Jack Haskell; Los Espanoles; Ken Karen; Karen Chandler; Joe Zawinul.

Great Millions .... Dot (M) DLP-3181 20-30 59
Pat Boone; Gale Storm; Billy Vaughan; Jim Lowe; Francis Craig; Mills Brothers; Hilltoppers; Fontane Sisters; Mr. Ford & Mr. Goon Bones.

Great Millions .... Dot (SE) DLP-25181 10-15 66
Pat Boone; Gale Storm; Billy Vaughn; Jim Lowe; Francis Carig; Mills Brothers; Hilltoppers; Fontane Sisters; Mr. Ford & Mr. Goon Bones.

Great Moments at the Grand Ole Opry (2 LP) .... RCA (S) CPL2-1904 8-12 77
Minnie Pearl; Connie Smith; Sonny James; Chet Atkins; Don Gibson; Dottie West; Ronnie Milsap; Billy Walker; Jim Ed Brown; Bobby Bare; Hank Snow; Dolly Parton; Porter Wagoner; Jim Reeves; Archie Campbell.

Great Motion Picture Themes .... United Artists (M) UAL-3122 10-15 61
Great Motion Picture Themes .... United Artists (S) UAS-6122 10-20 61
(Soundtrack.) Ferrante & Teicher; Don Costa; Al Caiola; Nick Perito; Gerry Mulligan; Shelly Manne; Jerome Moross; Mario Nascimbene; Ernest Gold; Adolph Deutsch; David Buttolph; Alex North.

Great Motion Picture Themes, Vol. 2 .... United Artists (M) UAM-3625 10-15 67
Great Motion Picture Themes, Vol. 2 .... United Artists (S) UAS-6625 10-20 67
(Soundtrack.) Francis Lai; Leroy Holmes; Georges Garvarentz; Pier Luigi Urbini; Ferrante & Teicher; John Addison; Quincy Jones; John Barry; Dave Grusin; Serendipity Singers.

Great New Stars of Country Music .... Guest Star (M) G-1494 10-15 64
Great New Stars of Country Music .... Guest Star (S) GS-1494 10-15 64
Roger Miller; Clyde Beavers; Dave Dudley; Tibby Edwards; Merle Kilgore; George Jones; Benny Barnes; James O'Gwynn; Dottie West; Frankie Miller.

Great New York Groups, Vol. 1 .... Laurie (S) LES-4012 8-12
Randy & Rainbows; Belmonts; Vito & Salutations; Mystics; Passions; Five Discs; Del Satins; Dion & Belmonts; Tokens; Elegants; Orients; Four Epics; Dino & Diplomats; Four Graduates.

Great Ones .... Capitol (M) T-1718 20-25 62
Great Ones .... Capitol (S) ST-1718 25-30 62
Buck Owens; Faron Young; Jeanne Black; Louvin Brothers; Tennessee Ernie Ford; Rose Maddox; Ferlin Husky; Tex Ritter; Wanda Jackson; Hank Thompson.

Great Ones (2 LP) .... Columbia Special Products/Brookville (S) C2-11003 8-12 72
(Mail order offer.) Tony Martin; Eddie Fisher; Vaughn Monroe; Vic Damone; Frankie Laine; Harry James; Johnny Mathis; Eddy Howard; Tony Bennett; Bing Crosby; Johnnie Ray; Don Cornell; Dinah Washington; Doris Day; Judy Garland; Eileen Barton; Patti Page; Peggy Lee; Jane Morgan; Teresa Brewer; Sarah Vaughan; Dinah Shore; Rosemary Clooney; Georgia Gibbs; Frank Sinatra; Kitty Kallen; Dick Haymes.

Great Original Hits of the '50s and '60s (9 LP) .... Readers Digest (S) RD4-182 30-50 74
(Mail order offer. Boxed set.) Teresa Brewer; Andrews Sisters; Frankie Laine; Weavers; Ames Brothers; Eddie Fisher; Oliver; Diana Ross & Supremes; Youngbloods; Manfred Mann; Henry Mancini; Stevie Wonder; Four Aces; Georgia Gibbs; Don Cornell; Vera Lynn; Eddy Howard; Paul Mauriat; Bobby Goldsboro; Jeannie C. Riley; Otis Redding; Irish Rovers; Hugo Montenegro; Frank Weir; Jim Reeves; Vikki Carr; Association; Bobby Hebb; Dusty Springfield; Aretha Franklin; Bill Haley & His Comets; Patti Page; Perry Como; Gaylords; Horst Jankowski; Supremes; Bert Kaempfert; Searchers; Sonny & Cher; Ramsey Lewis; Roger Williams; Al Hibbler; McGuire; Sisters; Billy Vaughn; Platters; Louis Armstrong; Singin Nun; Al Hirt; Serendipity Singers; Nino Tempo & April Stevens; Carl Perkins; Gogi Grant; Fats Domino; Pat Boone; Rooftop Singers; Brenda Lee; Little Peggy March; Drifters; Paul & Paula; Leslie Gore; Jane Morgan; Bobby Helms; Debbie Reynolds; Paul Anka; Joe Harnell; Kenny Ball; Tokens; Bent Fabric; Ketty Lester; Coasters; Chuck Berry; Diamonds; Sam Cooke; Floyd Cramer; Dinah Washington; Bobby Darin; Sarah Vaughan; Dave "Baby" Cortez; Della Reese; Ferrante & Teicher; Larry Verne; Brian Hyland; Johnny Preston

Great Personalities of Broadway .... Camden (M) CAL-745 10-15 63
Great Personalities of Broadway .... Camden (S) CAS-745 15-20 63
(Soundtrack.) Al Jolson; George M. Cohan; Fanny Brice; Helen Morgan; Rudy Vallee; Harry Lauder; Ethel Merman; Ezio Pinza; Beatrice Lillie.

Great Popular Favorites .... Capitol (S) SL-6644 8-12
Tom Vaughn; Lettermen; Glen Campbell; Romanoff; Mel Torme; Laurindo Almeida; Peggy Lee; Nat King Cole; David Rose

Great Popular Vocalists .... Capitol (S) SL-6648 8-12
Dean Martin; Nat King Cole; Judy Garland; Nancy Wilson; Glen Campbell; Peggy Lee; Sandler & Young; Lou Rawls; Al Martino; Mel Torme.

Great Popular Oldies Volume 2 .... Sutton (M) SU-325 15-25 67
Great Popular Oldies Volume 2 .... Sutton (S) SSU-325 15-25 67
Hollywood Argyles; Starr Sisters; Mairobi River Boys; Bobby Lile; Robbie & Downbeats.

Great Popular Oldies Volume 3 .... Sutton (M) SU-326 15-25 67
Great Popular Oldies Volume 3 .... Sutton (S) SSU-326 15-25 67
Hollywood Argyles; Ty Tyrell; Rockin' Sidney; Cyd & Cherri; Breakers; Mono Rails.

Great Popular Oldies Volume 4 .... Sutton (M) SU-327 15-25 67
Great Popular Oldies Volume 4 .... Sutton (S) SSU-327 15-25 67
Innocents; Billy & Kids; Sherrel Townsend; Uptones; Danny & Dreamers; Sparklets.

Great Popular Oldies Volume 5 .... Sutton (M) SU-328 15-25 67
Great Popular Oldies Volume 5 .... Sutton (S) SSU-328 15-25 67
Hollywood Argyles; Ribbons; Bobby Lile; Shooters; Gil Shelton.

Great Rock Revival .... Columbia Special Products (S) C-10859 5-10 72
Lloyd Price; Everly Brothers; Dodie Stevens; Bo Diddley; Little Richard; Crew-Cuts; Del Shannon; Diamonds; Fats Domino; Big Bopper; Chuck Berry; Jimmy Rodgers; Bobby Day.

Great Rock Revival .... Columbia Special Products (S) C-10850 5-10 72
Diamonds; Jack Scott; Chuck Berry; Jimmy Clanton; Dinah Washington; Del-Vikings; Debbie Reynolds; Art & DottieTodd; Thomas Wayne; Pat Boone; Sarah Vaughn; Chordettes; Platters; Phil Phillips.

Great Rock Revival (2 LP) .... Tampa/Columbia Special Products (SP) C-2 10848 8-12 72
Pat Boone; Platters; Jack Scott; Phil Phillips; Chuck Berry; Jimmy Clanton; Dinah Washington; Del-Vikings; Debbie Reynolds; Diamonds; Art & Dottie Todd; Thomas Wayne; Chordettes; Sarah Vaughan; Lloyd Price; Everly Brothers; Dodie Stevens; Bo Diddley; Little Richard; Crew-Cuts; Del Shannon; Fats Domino; Big Bopper; Jimmy Rodgers; Bobby Day.

Great Singing Groups: see HARPTONES / Paragons / Jesters / Clovers

Great Smash Hits .... Capitol (M) T-1488 20-30 61

Great Smash Hits .... Capitol (S) ST-1488 25-35 61
Frank Sinatra; Tommy Sands; Kingston Trio; Dean Martin; Pee Wee Hunt; Jo Stafford & Red Ingle; Margaret Whiting & Jimmy Wakely; Nat King Cole; Les Paul & Mary Ford; Tex Williams.

Great Songs of America .... Columbia Special Products /Goodyear (M) CSP-133 10-15 60s
Mary Martin; Mitch Miller; Andre Kostelanetz; Mahalia Jackson;Robert Goulet; Theodore Bikel; Brothers Four; New Christy Minstrels; Norman Luboff Choir; Percy Faith. (Special products. Made for Goodyear.)

Great Songs of Christmas .... Columbia/Goodyear (S) XTV 69406 8-12
Mormon Tabernacle Choir; Eileen Farrell & Luther Henderson; Percy Faith; Mitch Miller; Andre Kostelanetz; Leonard Bernstein & New York Philharmonic; Frank DeVol & Rainbow Strings; Burl Ives; Norman Luboff Choir. (Special products. Made for Goodyear.)

Great Songs of Christmas .... Columbia Special Products /Goodyear (S) CSP-2385 8-12 66
Andy Williams; Steve Lawrence & Eydie Gorme; Dinah Shore; Andre Kostelanetz; Anna Maria Alberghetti; Danny Kaye; Richard Tucker; Doris Day; Sammy Davis Jr.; Maurice Chevalier. (Special products made for Goodyear.)

Great Songs of Christmas, Vol. 1 .... Columbia/Goodyear (M) XTV 86100/1 10-15 59
Great Songs of Christmas, Vol. 1 .... Columbia/Goodyear (SE) XTV 86100/1 10-15 59
Leonard Bernstein; Andre Previn; Percy Faith; Eileen Farrell; Mormon Tabernacle Choir; Earl Wrightson; Norman Luboff; Nelson Eddy; Eugene Ormandy & Philadelphia Orchestra; Andre Kostelanetz. (Special products. Made for Goodyear.)

Great Songs of Christmas, Vol. 2 .... Columbia/Goodyear (M) XTV 86100 10-15 60
Great Songs of Christmas, Vol. 2 .... Columbia/Goodyear (SE) XTV 86100 10-15 60
Percy Faith; Mormon Tabernacle Choir; Eileen Farrell; Nelson Eddy; Earl Wrightson; Andre Previn; Leonard Bernstein & New York Philharmonic; Norman Luboff Choir; Eugene Ormandy & Philadelphia Orchestra; Nelson Eddy; Andre Kostelanetz. (Special products. Made for Goodyear.)

Great Songs of Christmas, Vol. 3 .... Columbia Special Products /Goodyear (M) CSP-117-M 10-15 61
Great Songs of Christmas, Vol. 3 .... Columbia Special Products /Goodyear (SE) CSP-117-S 10-15 61
Eugene Ormandy & Philadelphia Orchestra; Julie Andrews; Percy Faith; Mormon Tabernacle Choir; Mitch Miller; Isaac Stern; Robert Goulet; New Christy Minstrels; Leonard Bernstein; Norman Luboff; Andre Previn. (Special products. Made for Goodyear.)

Great Songs of Christmas, Vol. 4 .... Columbia Special Products /Goodyear (M) CSP-155-M 10-15 63
Great Songs of Christmas, Vol. 4 .... Columbia Special Products /Goodyear (SE) CSP-155-S 10-15 63
Mary Martin; New Christy Minstrels; Brothers Four; Percy Faith; Leonard Bernstein & Mormon Tabernacle Choir; Doris Day; New Christy Minstrels; Mitch Miller; Andre Previn; Robert Goulet; Eugene Ormandy & Philadelphia Orchestra; Isaac Stern. (Special products. Made for Goodyear.)

Great Songs of Christmas, Vol. 5 .... Columbia Special Products /Goodyear (M) CSP-238-M 10-15 65
Great Songs of Christmas, Vol. 5 .... Columbia Special Products /Goodyear (SE) CSP-238-S 10-15 65
Andy Williams; Andre Kostelanetz; Anna Maria Alberghetti; Maurice Chevalier; Eugene Ormandy & Philadelphia Orchestra; Richard Tucker; Steve Lawrence & Eydie Gorme; Dinah Shore; Diahann Carroll; Danny Kaye; Doris Day; Sammy Davis Jr. (Special products. Made for Goodyear.)

Great Songs of Christmas, Vol. 6 .... Columbia/Goodyear (M) CSM-388 10-15 66
Great Songs of Christmas, Vol. 6 .... Columbia/Goodyear (SE) CSS-388 10-15 66
Barbra Streisand; Johnny Mathis; Bing Crosby; New Christy Minstrels; Percy Faith; Mormon Tabernacle Choir; Steve Lawrence & Eydie Gorme; Andy Williams; King Family; Pablo Casals; Jan Peerce; Ray Conniff; Mahalia Jackson. (Special products. Made for Goodyear.)

Great Songs of Christmas, Vol. 7 .... Columbia/Goodyear (SE) CSS-547 8-12 66
Tony Bennett; Robert Goulet; New Christy Minstrels; Steve Lawrence; John Davidson; Brothers Four; Barbra Streisand; Harry Simeone Chorale; Jerry Vale; Sally Ann Howes; George Szell; Diahann Carroll. (Special products. Made for Goodyear.)

Great Songs of Christmas, Vol. 8 .... Columbia/Goodyear (SE) CSS-888 8-12 66
Andy Williams; Robert Goulet & Carol Lawrence; Ray Conniff; Tony Bennett; Percy Faith; Johnny Mathis; New Christy Minstrels; Barbra Streisand; Anthony Newley; Sally Ann Howes; Robert Merrill; Anna Moffo; Brothers Four. (Special products. Made for Goodyear.)

Great Songs of Christmas, Vol. 9 .... Columbia/Goodyear (S) CSS-1033 8-12 67
Petula Clark; Bing Crosby; Joan Sutherland; Connie Francis; Richard Kiley; Lawrence Welk; Erich Leinsdorf & London Symphony Orchestra & Roger Wagner Chorale; Mantovani; Lena Horne; Vladimer Horowitz. (Special products. Made for Goodyear.)

Great Songs of Faith and Inspiration (4 LP) .... RCA (S) R 213812 15-20 72
(Boxed set.) Charley Pride; Blackwood Brothers Quartet featuring J.D. Sumner; Jimmy Dean with the Imperials Quartet & Jordanaires; Floyd Cramer; Dolly Parton; Porter Wagoner; Billy Graham Crusade Choir; George Beverly Shea; Chet Atkins; Pat Boone; Jim Reeves; Tony Fontaine; Rex Hubbard Singers; Bobby Bare; Nat Stuckey & Connie Smith; Hank Snow; Statesmen Quartet; Don Gibson; Dottie West; Eddy Arnold; Sons of the Pioneers; Skeeter Davis; Hank Locklin; Danny Davis & Nashville Brass; Doris Akers; Jack Holcomb; Speer Family; Wendy Bagwell & Sunliters; Jerome Hines; Anita Kerr Quartet; Cliff Barrows; Roy Rogers & Dale Evans; Archie Campbell; Norma Jean; Browns; Jake Hess.

Great Songs of the '60s .... Columbia Special Products/Safeway (S) CSP-129 8-12 62
Tony Bennett; Percy Faith; Barbra Streisand; Lester Lanin; Jerry Vale; Andre Kostelanetz; Ernie Heckscher; Anita Bryant; Les & Larry Elgart; Patti Page; Buddy Greco; Skitch Henderson. (Special products. Made for Safeway.)

Great Songs of the '60s .... Columbia Special Products /Kroger (S) CSP-157 8-12 62
Tony Bennett; Percy Faith; Barbra Streisand; Lester Lanin; Jerry Vale; Andre Kostelanetz; Ernie Heckscher; Anita Bryant; Les & Larry Elgart; Patti Page; Buddy Greco; Skitch Henderson. (Special products. Made for Kroger.)

Great Songs of the '60s, Vol. 2 .... Columbia Special Products /Safeway (S) CSP-138 8-12
Barbra Streisand; Jerry Vale; Tony Bennett; Patti Page; Buddy Greco; others. (Special products. Made for Safeway.)

Great Songs of the '60s, Vol. 2 .... Columbia Special Products /Kroger (S) CSP-180 8-12 62
Jerry Vale; Ray Conniff; Eydie Gorme; Vic Damone; Andre Kostelanetz; Lester Lanin; New Christy Minstrels; Patti Page; Steve Lawrence; Buddy Greco; Tony Bennett; Ernie Hecksher. (Special products. Made for Kroger.)

Great Songs of the '60s .... Columbia Special Products /Food Fair (S) CSP-292 8-12 63
Tony Bennett; Percy Faith; Barbra Streisand; Lester Lanin; Jerry Vale; Andre Kostelanetz; Ernie Heckscher; Anita Bryant; Les & Larry Elgart; Patti Page; Buddy Greco; Skitch Henderson. (Special products. Made for Food Fair.)

Great Songs of the '60s (3 LP) .... New York Times (S) MOS-2A/2F 20-25
(Boxed set.) Joan Baez; Byrds; Glen Campbell; Judy Collins; Jackie De Shannon; Kingston Trio; Al Cooper & Mike Bloomfield; Peggy Lee; Lovin' Spoonful; Linda Ronstadt; Bobby Vinton; Tammy Wynette; others.

Great Songs of the Beatles .... Capitol (Q) QL-6735 10-15 72
Peggy Lee; Lettermen; Hollyridge Strings; Tennessee Ernie Ford; Bobbie Gentry; Laurindo Almeida; Tom Vaughn; Sounds of Our Times.

Great Soul Hits .... Brunswick (S) BL-754129 10-15 69
Jackie Wilson; Gene Chandler; Big Maybelle; others.

Great Soul Hits, Vol. 1 .... Soul Parade (SE) HHP-5012 8-12
Little Joe & Thrillers; Titus Turner; Buster Brown; Wilbert Harrison; Lee Dorsey; Bobby Marchan; Don Gardner & Dee Dee Ford; Gladys Knight & Pips; Willie Hightower.

Great Soul Hits of: .... Brunswick (S) BL 754129 15-25

Jackie Wilson; Barbara Acklin; Big Maybelle; Gene Chandler; Artistics; Young-Holt Unlimited.

Great Sounds and New Sounds from Columbia (Colgate Presents)............................Columbia (S) XTV 62320/21 10-20 60s
Les Elgart; Tony Bennett; Andre Kostelanetz; Jo Stafford; Ray Conniff; Mitch Miller; Luther Henderson; Jerry Vale; Norman Luboff; Johnny Cash; Leslie Uggams; Mormon Tabernacle Choir.

Great Stars - Great Songs............................Columbia (M) C10256 5-10
Caravelli & His Magnificant Strings; Ray Conniff; Percy Faith; Jerry Vale; Jane Morgan; Brothers Four.

Great Stars of Christmas............................RCA (S) DLP-0132 5-10 75
Arthur Fiedler; Ed Ames; Ralph Hunter Choir; Florence Henderson; Harry Belafonte; Melachrino Strings; Lorne Greene; Robert Shaw Chorale; Eddy Arnold; Julie Andrews; Eddie Fisher. (Special products release.)

Great Stars of Country & Western, Vol. 2............................Diplomat (S) DS 2408 8-12 60s
Dave Dudley; David Houston; Johnny Sea; Sonny James; Warner Mack; Willie Nelson; Cowboy Copas.

Great Stars of Country & Western, Vol. 3............................Diplomat (M) D 2416 8-12 60s
Cowboy Copas; Johnny Sea; Dave Dudley; Sonny James; Bill Carlisle.

Great Stars of Song............................Musico (S) MDS-1026 10-15 70s
Jerry Butler; Brook Benton; Gene Pitney; Lou Rawls; Al Martino.

Great Stars of Vaudeville............................Columbia Special Products (S) CSS 1509 10-20 60s
Rudy Vallee; Eddie Cantor; Clayton, Jackson & Durante; Burns & Allen; W.C. Fields; Al Jolson; Morton Downey; Baby Rose; Marie; Arthur Tracy; Victor Borge.

Great Stars, Their Greatest Hits: see Great Ones

Great Swing Bands............................Jazztone (M) J 1245 10-20 56
Benny Goodman; Glen Gray; Tommy Dorsey; Artie Shaw; Bunny Berigan; Earl Hines; Count Basie; Jimmie Lunceford.

Great Vocalists of the Big Band Era............................Longines/Decca/MCA Special Products (SE) DL-734655 5-10 70s
Judy Garland; Nat King Cole; Ella Fitzgerald; Bing Crosby; Mary Martin; Jimmy Dorsey; Peggy Lee & Gordon Jenkins; Rudy Vallee; Ethel Merman; Ted Weems; Pearl Bailey; Ink Spots; Andrews Sisters; Weavers & Terry Gilkyson.

Great Vocalists of the Big Band Era............................Longines Symphonette (SE) SY-5207 5-10 70s
Judy Garland; Nat King Cole; Ella Fitzgerald; Bing Crosby; Mary Martin; Jimmy Dorsey; Peggy Lee & Gordon Jenkins; Rudy Vallee; Ethel Merman; Ted Weems; Pearl Bailey; Ink Spots; Andrews Sisters; Weavers & Terry Gilkyson. (Special products release from MCA/Decca.)

Greater Antilles Sampler (2 LP)............................Antilles (S) AX-7000 10-15 76
Quiet Sun; Fripp & Eno; Tim Haselin; Allen Fontenot & Country Cajuns; Martin Carthy; Dave Swarbrick; Gary Shearston; Osamu Kitajima; Tom Newman; White Noise: Don Cherry Trio; Steve Winwood; Remi Kabaka; Abdul Lasisi Amao; Morning Glory; John Cage; Tibetan Bells; Portsmouth Sinfonia & Choir.

Greatest 15 Hits on Ace Records............................Ace (M) LP-1012 30-40 61
Jimmy Clanton; Frankie Ford; Scotty McKay; Jo & Ann; Huey "Piano" Smith; Clowns; Big Boy Myles; Earl King; Bobby Marchan; Ted Tyler; Little "Gonzo" Booker; Eddie Bo; Lloyd Price; Huey & Jerry.

Greatest Bands in All the Land (First Show)............................Bygone (S) BB/SWNG 1501 8-12

Greatest Bands in All the Land (Second Show)............................Bygone (S) BB/SWNG 1502 8-12

Greatest Comedy Stars of the Grand Old Opry............................Guest Star (S) GS-1475 10-20
Homer & Jethro; Cousin Jody; Lonzo & Oscar; Brother Oswald; Unkle Willie Potts.

Greatest Country and Western Hits, No. 3............................Columbia Limited Edition (S) LE 10035 5-10
Ray Price; Billy Walker; George Morgan; Mel Tillis; Carl Butler; Stonewall Jackson.

Greatest Country and Western Hits, No. 3............................Columbia (M) CL-1816 15-25 62

Greatest Country and Western Hits, No. 3............................Columbia (S) CS-8616 15-25 62
Ray Price; Mel Tillis; Carl Butler; Billy Walker; George Morgan; Stonewall Jackson.

Greatest Country and Western Hits, Vol. 4............................Columbia (M) CL-2081 15-25 63

Greatest Country and Western Hits, Vol. 4............................Columbia (S) CS-8881 15-25 63
Jimmy Dean; Marion Worth; Marty Robbins; Ray Price; Carl Smith; Flatt & Scruggs; Johnny Cash; Claude King; Lefty Frizzell; Stonewall Jackson; Little Jimmy Dickens; Carl Butler.

Greatest Country and Western Hits of the '70s............................Columbia (S) JC-36549 5-10 80
Larry Gatlin; Willie Nelson; Johnny Cash; David Allen Coe; Moe Bandy; Johnny Paycheck; Charlie Rich; Joe Stampley; Marty Robbins; Mickey Gilley.

Greatest Country and Western Instrumentals............................Diplomat (S) DS-2600 10-15 60s
Chubby Wise; Eddie Eddings; Herbie Remington; Ken Clark; Lonnie Glosson; Moon Mullican; Bill Boyd; Hardrock Gunter; Lonesome Pine; Riddlers; Cowboy Copas.

Greatest Country and Western Stars (5 LP)............................Showcase (S) SH-1503 15-25
(Boxed set.) Patsy Cline; Ferlin Husky; Carl Belew; T. Texas Tyler; Stuart Hamblen; Charlie Ryan; David Houston; Johnny Horton; others.

Greatest Country and Western Stars & Hits (5 LP)............................Showcase (S) SH-1503 15-25
Patsy Cline; Ferlin Husky; Carl Belew; T. Texas Tyler; Stuart Hamblen; Slim Willet; Charlie Ryan; Frankie Miller; Johnny Sea; David Houston; Johnny Horton; Jan Howard; Rose Maddox; Wynn Stewart; Jimmy Dean; Maddox Brothers & Rose; Hank Locklin; Webb Pierce; Rex Allen, others.

Greatest Country Fiddlers of Our Time............................Starday (S) SLP 294 10-15 60s
Benny Martin; Tommy Hill; Curly Fox; Lonesome Pine Fiddlers; Scotty Stoneman; Jerry Rivers; Howdy Forrester; Chubby Wise; Tommy Jackson; others.

Greatest Country Hits of the '70s............................Columbia (S) JC 36549 5-10 80
Larry Gatlin & Gatlin Brothers; Willie Nelson; Johnny Cash; David Allen Coe; Moe Bandy; Johnny Paycheck; Charlie Rich; Joe Stampley; Marty Robbins; Mickey Gilley.

Greatest Dance Hits Slauson Style (Lloyd Thaxton Presents)............................Domain (M) 101 20-30 63

Greatest Folk Singers of the '60s (2 LP)............................Vanguard (S) VSD-17/18 10-20 72
Bob Dylan; Country Joe & Fish; Ian & Sylvia; Joan Baez; Odetta; Pete Seeger; Doc Watson; Eric Anderson; Joan Baez & Bob Gibson; Theodore Bikel; Oscar Brand & Jean Ritchie; Paul Butterfield Blues Band; Chambers Brothers; Judy Collins; Richard & Mimi Farina; Flatt & Scruggs; Jack Elliott; Jose Feliciano; Bob Gibson; & Hamilton Camp; John Hammond; Cisco Houston; Mississippi John Hurt; Jim Kweskin & Jug Band; Tommy Makem; New Lost City Ramblers; Phil Ochs; Tom Paxton; Rooftop Singers; Buffy Saint-Marie; Peggy Seeger & Ewan MacColl; Staple Singers; Doc Watson; Weavers.

Greatest Golden Goodies............................Laurie (M) 2014 20-25 62
Dion & Belmonts; Five Satins; Jarmels; Mystics; Passions; Skyliners; Turbans; Demensions; Five Discs; Diamonds.

Greatest Golden Oldies in the Whole World Ever!............................Parkway (M) P-7031 10-20

Greatest Gospel Gems, Vol. 1............................Specialty (S) 2144 5-10 71
Sam Cooke & Soul Stirrers; Alex Bradford; others.

Greatest Gospel Gems, Vol. 2............................Specialty (S) ???? 5-10 71
Alex Bradford; Pilgrim Gravelers; James Cleveland; others.

Greatest Gospel Hits, Vol. 1 .... Paula (S) LP-801 5-10 90
Greatest Groups of Rock 'N' Roll (2 LP) .... Fairway (S) TC 1000 8-10 77
(Mail order offer.) Coasters; Shirelles; Drifters; Platters; Beach Boys; Del-Vikings; Five Satins; Dion & Belmonts; Bill Haley & His Comets; Crests; Duprees.
Greatest Hits .... Warner Bros(S) BS-2558 8-12 70
Association; Petula Clark; Trini Lopez; Vogues; Charles Wright; Harpers Bizarre; Norman Greenbaum; Mercy; Miriam Makeba; Kenny Roger & First Edition; Ides of March; Mason Williams.
Greatest Hits - An All Star Parade .... Harmony (M) HL-7255 15-20 60
Count Basie; Les Brown; Buddy Clark; Rosemary Clooney; Xavier Cugat; Benny Goodman; Benny Goodman with Peggy Lee; Woody Herman; Harry James & Frank Sinatra; Sarah Vaughan.
Greatest Hits from England .... Parrot (M) PA-61010 15-25 67
Greatest Hits from England .... Parrot (S) PAS-71010 10-20 67
Them; Zombies; Kathy Kirby; Fortunes; Los Bravos; Nashville Teens; Hedgehoppers Anonymous; Tom Jones; Moody Blues; Unit 4 + 2; Noel Harrison.
Greatest Hits from England, Vol. 2 .... Parrot (M) PA-61017 15-25 68
Greatest Hits from England, Vol. 2 .... Parrot (S) PAS-71017 10-20 68
Procol Harum; Zombies; Tornadoes; Lulu; Englebert Humperdinck; Bachelors; Cat Stevens; Them; Whistling Jack Smith; Marianne Faithfull; Fortunes.
Greatest Hits from Memphis .... Hi (S) SHL-32049 10-15 70
Bill Black Combo; Ace Cannon; Jerry Jaye; Gene Simmons; Murry Kellum; Willie Mitchell.
Greatest Hit from the Fifties to the Sixties .... Musico (S) MDS-1030 10-15 70s
Frankie Lymon; Little Anthony; Revilers; Buddy Knox; Tommy Edwards; Cleftones; Moonglows; Platters; Weavers..
Greatest Hits from the Movies (4 LP) .... Columbia House (S) P4S-5920 15-25 73
(Boxed set. Columbia Record Club issue.) Mantovani; Louis Jordan; Roger Williams; Steve Lawrence; Percy Faith; Joel Gray; Frankie Laine; Andre Kostelanetz; Tony Bennett; Ray Conniff; Peter Nero; John Barry; Miklos Rozsa; Johnny Mathis; Francis Lai; Robert Goulet; Patti Page; Jack Jones; New Christy Minstrels; Sand Pipers; Judy Garland; O.C. Smith; Aretha Franklin; John Davidson; Anita Bryant; Terry Baxter; Andre Previn.
Greatest Hits from the Soul of Texas .... Wand (M) WDM-677 15-20 66
Greatest Hits from the Soul of Texas .... Wand (S) WDS-677 20-25 66
J. Frank Wilson; B.J. Thomas; Roy Head; Sunny & Sunliners; Traits.
Greatest Hits of 1971 .... United Artists (S) UAS-6817 8-10 71
Ike & Tina Turner; Bobby Goldsboro; Canned Heat; others.
Greatest Hits of Rock & Roll. Collectors Edition 8 .... Impact (S) BC-309 5-10
Crystals; Chantays; Leslie Gore; Kingsmen; Surfaris; Chiffons; Dovells; Jaynetts; Barbara Lewis.
Greatest Hits of Rock & Roll: see 20 Oldies But Goodies, Vol. 1
Greatest Hits of the '30s .... Capitol/Plaza House (SE) SL-6716 8-12 70s
Artie Shaw; Andrews Sisters; Benny Goodman; Fred Waring; Nat King Cole; Clyde McCoy; Guy Lombardo; Freddy Martin; Rudy Vallee; Glen Gray; Judy Garland.
Greatest Hits of the '40s .... Capitol/Plaza House (SE) SL-6717 8-12 70s
Freddy Martin; Dinah Shore; Pee Wee Hunt; Harry James; Nat King Cole; Les Brown; Woody Herman; Margaret Whiting; Guy Lombardo; Peggy Lee.
Greatest Hits of the '40s .... Columbia (SE) KG-31216 8-12 72
Kay Kyser; Horace Heidt; Harry James; Doris Day; Kate Smith; others.
Greatest Hits of the '50s and '60s (2 LP) .... Plaza House/Capitol (SE) SL-6718 8-12 70s
Greatest Hits of the '50s and '60s (2 LP) .... Plaza House/Capitol (SE) SLB-6718 8-12 70s
Nelson Riddle; Nat King Cole; Peggy Lee; Duke Ellington; Jackie Gleason; Tennessee Ernie Ford; Kay Starr; Les Paul & Mary Ford; Les Baxter; Kingston Trio; Louis Prima & Keely Smith; Ray Anthony; Ella Mae Morse; Frankie Laine; Glen Campbell; Bobby Gentry; Lettermen; Nancy Wilson; Wayne Newton; Al Martino; Jack Jones.
Greatest Hits of the '60s (3 LP) .... Columbia (S) G3P-23 10-15 70
Andy Williams; Aretha Franklin; Tony Bennett; Marty Robbins; Barbra Streisand; Jerry Vale; Johnny Cash; New Christy Minstrels; Johnny Mathis; Mel Torme; Patti Page; Michele Lee; Jim Nabors; Percy Faith; Eydie Gorme; Robert Goulet; Ray Conniff; Doris Day; Charlie Byrd; Steve Lawrence; Les & Larry Elgar; Skitch Henderson; Andre Previn; John Barry; Andre Kostelanetz; Joe Harnell; Pete Seeger; Burl Ives; Brothers Four; Ed Sullivan Singers; Jerry Murad's Harmonicats; O.C. Smith; Caravelli & His Magnificent Strings; Modernaires; Steve & Eydie; John Davidson; Bobby Hackett; Peter Nero; Anita Bryant; Leslie Uggams.
Greatest Hits of the Big Bands .... Columbia (SE) P-13513 5-10 76
Benny Goodman; Modernaires; Glenn Miller; Woody Herman; Will Bradley; Tommy Dorsey; Les Brown; Count Basie. (Special Products release for Ford.)
Greatest Hits of the Big Band Era (2 LP) .... RCA Special Products (S) DPM2-0813 8-12 88
(Mail order offer. BMG Direct Marketing.) Glenn Miller; Andews Sisters; Dick Haymes; Duke Ellington; Artie Shaw; Tommy Dorsey; Vaughn Monroe; Mills Brothers; Benny Goodman; Martha Tilton; Sammy Kaye; Billy Williams; Dinah Shore; Charlie Barnet; Frank Sinatra & Pied Pipers; Spike Jones & His City Slickers with Carl Grayson; Ink Spots; Perry Como; Tex Beneke & Modernaires.
Greatest Hits of the Century '30s, Vol. 1 .... MCA Special Markets (SE) DL 734892 5-10 70s
Andrews Sisters; Eddie Cantor; Judy Garland; Woody Herman; Artie Shaw; Louis Armstrong; Tommy Dorsey; Tony Martin; Bing Crosby; King Cole Trio; Guy Lombardo; Ella Fitzgerald.
Greatest Hits of the Century '40s, Vol. 2 .... MCA Special Markets (SE) DL 734893 5-10 70s
Jimmy Dorsey; Bob Eberle; Helen O'Connell; Bing Crosby; Ink Spots; Eydie Gorme; Dick Haymes; Freddy Martin; Louis Armstrong; Sammy Kaye; Mills Brothers; Andrews Sisters; Judy Garland; Gene Kelly.
Greatest Hits of the Century '50s - '60s, Vol. 3 & 4 (2 LP) .... MCA (SE) 34894/5 8-12 70s
Teresa Brewer; Peggy Lee; Brenda Lee; Earl Grant; Al Hibbler; Four Aces; Sammy Davis Jr.; Guy Lombardo; Al Hibbler; Kitty Kalen; Don Cornell; Ames Brothers; Lawrence Welk & Lennon Sisters; Leroy Anderson; Billy Williams; Four Aces; Al Hibbler; Debbie Reynolds; Roger Williams; Len Barry; Burl Ives; Irish Rovers; Roger Williams; Bert Kaempfert; Bobby Helms; Bert Kaempfert; Jack Jones; Burt Bacharach; Louis Armstrong.
Greatest Hits of the Era, Part 1 .... Solid Smoke (S) SS-8031 5-10 84
Dion & Belmonts; Five Satins; Del-Vikings; Harptones; Dells; Nutmegs; Hollywood Flames; Danleers; Silhouettes; Mello-Kings; Capris; Edsels; Paradons; Fiestas.
Greatest Hits of the Golden Groups .... Columbia Musical Treasury (M) D-956 8-12 72
Chantels; Rays; Crests; Mello Kings; Little Anthony & Imperials; Champs; Cadillacs; Santo & Johnny; Five Satins; Dion & Belmonts.
Greatest Hits of the War Years (2 LP) .... Tele House Inc. (SE) CD 2035 10-15 74
Ralph Hunter Choir; Harry James; Spike Jones & His City Slickers; Vaughn Monroe; Marlene Dietrich; Kay Kyser; Harry James; Sammy Kaye; Tony Pastor; Tommy Dorsey; Gracie Fields; Kate Smith; Mello-Larks; Barry Wood; King Sisters; Vera Lynn.

Greatest in Person .... Grand Prix (M) K-403 10-15 60s
Ray Charles; Gloria Lynne; Ketty Lester; Lionel Hampton; Sammy Davis Jr.; Ink Spots; Joya Sherrill; Earl "Fatha" Hines.
Greatest Jazz Concert in the World (4 LP) .... Pablo (S) 2625-704 15-25
(Boxed set.)
Greatest Love Songs .... Columbia (S) DS-790 5-10
Gene Pitney; Bobby Vinton; Steve Lawrence; David Houston; Connie Francis; Robert Goulet; Tony Bennett; Jim Nabors; Statler Brothers; Marty Robbins.
Greatest Love Songs of the Century, Vol. 1 .... RCA Special Products (S) PRS-382 5-10 71
Percy Faith; Louis Armstrong; Tommy Dorsey; Frank Sinatra; Bunny Berigan; Jeanette MacDonald & Nelson Eddy; Glenn Miller; Les Brown; Helen O'Connell; Bing Crosby & Rosemary; Xavier Cugat.
Greatest Love Songs of the Century, Vol. 2 .... RCA Special Products (S) PRS-383 5-10 71
Ames Brothers; Artie Shaw; Tommy Dorsey; Frank Sinatra; Dinah Shore; Perry Como; Benny Goodman; Vaughn Monroe; Mario Lanza; Lena Horne; Don Cornell; Tony Martin.
Greatest Love Songs of the Century, Vol. 3 & 4, (2 LP) .... RCA Special Products (S) PRS-384 8-12 71
Eddie Fisher; Kay Starr; Andy Williams; Three Suns; Brook Benton; Gisele MacKenzie; Paul Anka; Melachrino Strings; Sam Cooke; Jaye P. Morgan; Al Hirt; Anthony Newley; John Gary; Henry Mancini; Norman Luboff Choir; Della Reese; Ed Ames; Peter Nero; Jack Jones; Harry Belafonte; Andre Previn; Jose Feliciano.
Greatest Love Songs of the Sensational '60s (2 LP) .... Columbia (S) P2S-5592 10-15
(Columbia Record Club offer.) Bobby Vinton; Steve Lawrence; David Houston; Connie Francis; Robert Goulet; Gene Pitney; Paul Mauriat; Ray Conniff; Tony Bennett; Jim Nabors; Statler Brothers; Marty Robbins; O.C. Smith; Horst Jankowski; Eydie Gorme; Village Stompers; Dusty Springfield; Jimmy Dean; Stan Getz & Astrud Gilberto; Bobby Hebb; Byrds; New Vaudeville Band; Jeannie C. Riley; Charlie Byrd & Stan Getz; Brothers Four; Mike Douglas; Johnny Mathis; New Christy Minstrels; Lulu; John Barry; Percy Faith; John Davidson; Patti Page; Terry Baxter; Maurice Jarre.
Greatest Moments in Sports .... Columbia (EP) AX-5000 15-25
Greatest Moments in Sports (Excerpts) .... Columbia (M) ???? 25-35
(Sampler from Gillette Safety Razor Co.)
Greatest Moments in Sports .... Columbia (M) ML-5000 50-75
Mel Allen; Jack Dempsey; Joe Humphries; Gene Tunney; Jim Corbett; Tommy Farr; Clem McCarthy; Tony Galento; Joe Louis; Grantland Rice; Knute Rockne; Jesse Owens; Roger Bannister; Fred Capossela; Babe Ruth; Johnny Vander Meer; Lou Gehrig; Red Barber.
Greatest Music Available Today .... Time (M) TMD-4 10-15
(Promotional issue only.) Jerry Fielding; Gordon Jenkins; Richard Hayman; Hugo Montenegro; Maury Laws; Manhattan Pops Orchestra; Kermit Leslie; Dominic Cortese; Al Caila; Stanley Wilson.
Greatest Music Ever Sold: see Capitol Promotional Releases/Samplers
Greatest Names in Jazz .... Verve (S) PR-2-3 10-15
Greatest on Stage .... Wand (M) 661 15-20 65
Greatest on Stage .... Wand (S) 661 20-25 65
Kingsmen; Chuck Jackson; Shirelles; Dionne Warwick; Maxine Brown; Tommy Hunt.
Greatest R&B Stars .... Guest Star (M) GS-1906 10-20 60s
Greatest R&B Stars .... Guest Star (S) GS-1906 10-20 60s
Roy Milton; Arthur Alexander; Chuck Jackson; Big Caesar.
Greatest Rhythm and Blues Hits, Vol. 1 .... Amazon (M) AM-1007 25-35 62
Jimmy Norman; Jennell Hawkins; Penguins; Etta James; Gene & Eunice; Jacks; Cadets; Jesse Belvin; others.
Greatest Rhythm and Blues Hits, Vol. 2 .... Amazon (M) AM-1008 20-30 64
Ron Holden; Bobby Blue Bland; Etta James; Joe Houston; Roscoe Gordon; Jesse Belvin; Joe Turner; Jimmy Norman; Ray & Bob; Jennell Hawkins; Turks; Vernon Green & Medallions; Cufflinks; Gus Jenkins; Don Julian & Meadowlarks; Blue Jays; Rochell & Candles; Paradons; Big Jay McNeeley & Little Sonny.
Greatest Rock and Roll .... Atlantic (M) 8001 100-150 56
Ray Charles; LaVern Bkaer; Clovers; Clyde McPhatter; Ruth Brown; Chuck Willis; Joe Turner; Drifters; Ivory Joe Hunter.
Greatest Rock and Roll Hits .... Adam VIII/Roulette (S) ???? 10-20
Isley Brothers; Bill Haley & His Comets; Penguins; Chantels; Wilbert Harrison; Kingsmen; Five Satins; Jimmy Charles; Heartbeats; Crests; Spaniels; Shep & Limelites; Gene Chandler; Frankie Lymon & Teenagers; Silhouettes; Joe Jones; Mello-Kings; Crows; Buddy Knox; Tune Weavers; Jerry Lee Lewis; Chuck Berry; Bobby Lewis; Dubs; Richie Valens; Sonny Til & Orioles; Shirelles; Playmates; Fats Domino; Joey Dee & Starliters; Skyliners; Crew-Cuts; Tempos; Nutmegs; Harold Dorman; Maurice Williams; Platters; Little Anthony & Imperials; Cleftones; Bobby Freeman; Bo Diddley; Fleetwoods; Cadillacs; Bobby Day; Diamonds; Shirley & Lee; Flamingos; Monotones;Capris; Moonglows; Lee Dorsey; Big Bopper.
Greatest Rock and Roll Hits, Original Hits by Original Stars (4 LP) .... Adam VIII (SE) A8R 9001 20-30 70s
Greatest Rock and Roll Hits (4 LP) .... Dynamic House/Roulette (SE) CR-1005/1008 20-30 70s
(Boxed set. Mail order offer.) Frankie Lymon & Teenagers; Heartbeats; Silhouettes; Ritchie Valens; Skyliners; Harold Dorman; Bo Diddley; Maurice Williams; Lee Dorsey; Big Bopper; Isley Brothers; Kingsmen; Spaniels; Joe Jones; Bill Haley & His Comets; Five Satins; Shep & Limelites; Mello-Kings; Penguins; Jimmy Charles; Gene Chandler; Crows; Chantels; Buddy Knox; Wilbert Harrison; Crests; Tune Weavers; Jerry Lee Lewis; Fats Domino; Platters; Diamonds; Chuck Berry; Joey Dee & Starliters; Little Anthony & Imperials; Shirley & Lee; Bobby Lewis; Skyliners; Cleftones; Flamingos; Dubs; Crew-Cuts; Bobby Freeman; Monotones; Tempos; Capris; Sonny Til & Orioles; Nutmegs; Fleetwoods; Moonglows; Shirelles; Cadillacs; Bobby Day; Playmates.
Greatest [Girls] Sing Their Soul Favorites .... Wand (M) LP-660 15-25 65
Theola Kilgore; Dione Warwick; Little Esther Phillips; Big Maybelle; Maxine Brown; Barbara Lynn.
Greatest 64 Motown Original Hits: see 64 of the Greatest Motown Original Hits
Greatest Song Hits of Woody Guthrie (2 LP) .... Vanguard VSD-35/36 10-20
Woody Guthrie; Joan Baez; Babysitters; Country Joe McDonald; Jack Elliott; Cisco Houston; Odetta; Weavers.
Greatest Spiritual Singers .... Apollo (M) LP-489 15-20 60
Mahalia Jackson; others.
Greatest Stars and Songs .... RCA Camden (M) CAL-781 10-15 64
Greatest Stars and Songs .... RCA Camden (S) CAS-781 10-15 64
Peter Nero; Della Reese; Al Hirt; Limeliters; Eddie Fisher; Chet Atkins; Dinah Shore; Floyd Cramer; Ann Margaret; Lou Monte.
Greatest Stars - Wipe Out .... K-Tel/Era (S) BU 4600 5-10 77
(Mail order offer.) Duane Eddy; Surfaris; Virtues; Lonnie Mack; Dave Baby Cortez; Champs; Rockin' Rebels; Chantays; Sputniks; B. Bumble & Stingers; Mongo Santamaria; Santo & Johnny; Johnny & Hurricanes; Ernie Fields; Bill Justis. (Some tracks are rerecordings.)
Greatest Summer of Your Life (WFIL-56): see WFIL-56 Summer Love
Greatest Teenage Hits of All Time .... Teem (M) LP-5003 15-25

Jimmy Clanton; Huey "Piano" Smith; Joe & Ann; Silhouettes; Big Boy Myles; Narvel Felts; Scotty McKinley; Frankie Ford; Johnny Fairchild; Joe Turner.

Greatest Twist Hits .... Atlantic (M) 8058 25-35 62

Clovers; Tommy Ridgely; Tee Tucker; Ray Charles; Bobbettes; Joe Turner; Lloyd Sims; Top Notes; Solomon Burke; Mar-Keys; Clyde McPhatter; LaVern Baker; King Coleman; King Curtis.

Greatest Western Hits: see PRICE, Ray / Lefty Frizzell / Carl Smith

Greatest Western Hits .... Columbia (M) CL-1976 20-30 59

Greatest Western Hits .... Columbia (SE) CS-8776 10-20 63

Ray Price Carl Smith; Lefty Frizzell; Marty Robbins; others.

Greatest Western Hits, Vol. 2 .... Columbia (M) CL-1408 20-30 60

Greatest Western Hits, Vol. 2 .... Columbia (SE) CS-8777 10-20 63

Ray Price; Carl Smith; George Morgan; Little Jimmy Dickens; Marty Robbins; Lefty Frizzell.

Greatest Western Hits, Vol. 3 .... Columbia (M) CL-???? 15-25 63

Greatest Western Hits, Vol. 3 .... Columbia (S) CS-???? 15-25 63

Greatest Western Hits, Vol. 4 .... Columbia (M) CL-2081 15-25 64

Greatest Western Hits, Vol. 4 .... Columbia (S) CS-8881 15-25 64

Greatest Years of Country Music: see History of Country Music, Vol. 5

Greats, the .... United (S) US-7803 8-12

Green Peace .... A&M (S) SP-5091 5-10 85

George Harrison; others.

Griffith Park Collection .... Elektra (S) E1-60025 5-10 82

Stanley Clark; Chick Corea; Joe Henderson; Freddie Hubbard; Lenny White.

Gremlins .... Geffen (S) GHSP-24044 8-10 84

(Soundtrack.) Michael Sembello; Quarter Flash; Peter Gabriel; others.

Grooves, Vol. 1 .... Warner Bros (S) 1933 8-12 71

Gordon Lightfoot; Van Morrison; Dion; others.

Groovin' High with Great Sax Stars .... Coronet (S) CXS 196 8-12

Groovy Greats (2 LP) .... Galaxy (S) SDLP-217 10-15 70

Wilbert Harrison; Maurice Williams; Maxine Brown; Clovers; Silhouettes; Don Covay; Five Satins; Lee Allen; Buddy Miles; Lee Dorsey; Vic Dana; Dave "Baby" Cortez; Dynasaurs; Bobby Day; Jan & Dean; Solomon Burke; Champs; Lou Christie.

Groovy Greats .... Design (S) SDLP-272 8-12 68

Johnny Rivers; Ray Charles; Lou Christie; Bobby Goldsboro; Ronnie Dove; Joe Tex; Chuck Jackson; Bobby Freeman.

Groovy Goodies .... Prestige (M) PR-7313 15-20 64

Groovy Goodies .... Prestige (S) PRS-7313 20-25 64

Etta Jones; Jack McDuff; John Coltrane; others.

Groovy Goodies .... Colpix (M) CP-466 25-35 64

Groovy Goodies .... Colpix (S) SCP-466 35-45 64

Paul Petersen; James Darren; Girlfriends; Marcels; Shelly Fabares; Teddy Randazzo; Sandy Stewart; Freddie Scott; Matadors; Ronettes.

Groovy Sounds .... Columbia (S) CSS-731 10-20 68

Byrds; David Houston; Buckinghams; John Davidson; Arbors; Aretha Franklin; Bobby Vinton; Dave Clark Five; Pozo-Seco Singers; Paul Revere & Raiders. (Special products. Made for Zale's Jewelers.)

Group of Goldies .... Group (M) W-33001 20-30 63

Marcie Blane; Flares; Jimmy Soul; Ernie Maresca; Bobby (Boris) Pickett; G-Clefs; Kokomo; Ace Cannon; Bill Black's Combo; Rays; Kathy Linden; Trumpeterrs.

Group of Goodies .... Chess (M) LP-1478 20-30 63

Moonglows; Sensations; Lee Andrews & Hearts; Pastels; Flamingos; Johnny & Joe; Students.

Group of Goodies, Vol. 2 .... Chess (M) LP-1491 20-30 65

Tune Weavers; Jaynetts; Dave "Baby" Cortez; Corsairs; Jan Bradley; Etta James; Moonglows; Radiants; Sonics; Billy Stewart; Tommy Tucker; Vibrations.

Group Oldies But Goodies .... Smash (M) MGS-27038 20-25 63

Group Oldies But Goodies .... Smash (S) SRS-67038 20-25 63

Shells; Fireflies; Echoes; Tempos; Fascinations; Quintones; Harptones; Angels; Three Friends; Turbans; Embers; Roommates.

Groupquake .... RCA (S) SPS-33-525 10-20 68

(Promotional issue only.) Youngbloods; Status Cymbal; Autosalvage; Sonte Country; Joyfull Noise; Loading Zone; Group Therapy; Family Tree.

Groups Are the Greatest .... Scepter (S) 518 20-25 63

Shirelles; Isley Brothers; Angels; Rocky Fellers; Kingsmen; Blue Belles.

Growing Pains .... Reprise (S) 1-25735 8-12 88

(TV Soundtrack.) B.J. Thomas; Dusty Springfield; Jill Colucci; Take 6; Bill Medley; Eddie Rabbitt; Anne Murray; Kenny Rogers.

Guaranteed to Please Featuring 10 Big Stars .... Teem (M) LP-5002 15-25

Jimmy Clanton; Frankie Ford; Bill Robbin; Lee Dorsey; Scotty McKay; Huey "Piano" Smith; Supremes; Silhouettes; Roland Stone; Alvin "Red" Tyler.

Guest Stars of the Hee Haw Show .... Pickwick (SE) SS 6083 8-12

Sonny James; Ferlin Husky; Faron Young; Buck Owens; Wynn Stewart; George Jones.

Guide to Jazz .... RCA (M) LPM 1393 20-30 56

Louis Armstrong; Count Basie; Sidney Bechet; Johnny Dodds; Johnny Dodds; "Sleepy" John Estes; Duke Ellington; Lionel Hampton; Coleman Hawkins; Fletcher Henderson; Earl Hines; Ladnier-Mezzrow All Stars; Jimmy Lunceford; Jelly Roll Morton; King Oliver; Fats Waller; Jimmy Lunceford.

Guitar Album (2 LP) .... Polydor (S) 2-3008 10-15 74

Eric Clapton; Roy Buchanan; John Mclaughlin; Rory Gallagher; Ellen McIlwaine; Area Code 615; T-Bone Walker; Link Wray; Stone the Crows.

Guitar Album (2 LP) .... Columbia (S) KG-31045 10-15 72

Charlie Byrd; Chuck Wayne; Bucky Pizzarelli; George Barnes; Tiny Grimes; Eve & John McLaughlin.

Guitar Boogie: see CLAPTON, Eric, Jeff Beck and Jimmy Page

Guitar Greats .... Everest (S) FS-243 8-12

Glen Campbell; Mason Williams; Joe Maphis; James McGuinn; Billy Strange.

Guitar Heroes .... Epic (S) JE-36864 5-10 70s

Boston; REO Speedwagon; Molly Hatchet; Johnny Winter; Rick Derringer; Cheap Trick; Russ Ballard; Charlie Daniels Band.

Guitar Player (2 LP) .... MCA (S) MCA2-8012 10-20 77
Guitar Player (2 LP) .... MCA (S) MCA2-6002 10-20 77
B.B. King; Laurindo; Almeida; Irving Ashby; John Collins; Larry Coryell; Herb Ellis; Barney Kessel; Joe Pass; Lee Ritenour.
Guitar Players .... Mainstream (S) 410 8-10 74
Amboy Dukes; Brownie McGhee; Jim Raney; David Spinoza; Jack Wilkins; others.
Guitar Soul .... Status (S) 8318 10-15 65
Kenny Burrell; Bill Jennings; Tiny Grimes; others.
Guitar Tapestry (2 LP) .... Project 3 (S) PR2-6019/20 10-15 76
Chet Atkins; Wes Montgomery; Joe Pass; Charlie Christian; Les Paul; Johnny Smith; Bucky Pizzarelli; Joseph Iadone; Don Arnone; Tony Mottola; Al Caiola; Eric Weissberg; Vinnie Bell; Jay Berliner; Don Young; Al Casamenti.
Guitar Wizards (1926-1935) .... Yazoo (M) L-1016 8-10
Carl Martin; Billy Bird; Blind Blake; Tampa Red; Sam Butler; William Moore.
Guitars That Destroyed the World .... Columbia (S) C-31998 8-12 73
Carlos Santana; Buddy Miles; John McLaughlin; Mountain; Spirit; Johnny Winters; West, Bruce & Lang; Edgar Winter; Blue Oyster Cult.
Gus Gossert Collectors Album, First Edition .... No Label (M) No Number Used 15-25 71
(10–inch LP.) Avalons; Nobles with Nicky; Shells with Nate; Larks; Vernalls; Sonics; Dootones; Capris; Youngtones; Four Pals; Symbals with Lee Ward; Cuff-links.
Gus Gossert Presents the Original New York Doo-Wopp Album, Vol. 1 .... Juke Box (M) 5000 10-15 68
(Colored vinyl.) Anthony & Sophomores; Students; Five Satins; Dubs; Harptones; Nutmegs; Three Friends; Shells; Cordovans; Master-Tones; Dubs; Frankie Lymon & Teenagers; Ocapello's; Airedales; Delacardos; Arrogants; Velours; Quotations.
Gus Gossert Presents the Original New York Doo-Wopp Album, Vol. 2 .... Juke Box (M) 5001 10-15 69
(Colored vinyl.) Tony Williams & Platters; Bagdads; Students; Admirations; Five Discs; Continentals; Arcades; Shells; Youngtones; Jessie Belvin &The Feathers: Smoky Robinson & Miracles: Etta & Harvey; Numegs featuring the late Leroy Griffin; Monotones; Graduates; Flourescents; Dubs; Penguins.
Gus Gossert Presents the Original New York Doo-Wopp Album, Vol. 3 .... Juke Box (M) 5002 10-15 69
(Colored vinyl.) Five Keys; Nobles; Fascinators; Videos; Shells; Youngtones; Nutmegs; Penguins; Cuff Links; Superiors; Videos; Five Satins; Rob Roys; Penguins; Bluenotes; Majestics; Joylarks; Wheels; Hide-A-Ways; Syl Johnson.
Gus Gossert Presents the Original New York Doo-Wopp Album, Vol. 4 .... Juke Box (M) 5003 10-15 70
(Colored vinyl.) Collegians; Quin-Tones; Shells; Youngsters; Medallions; Emblems; Capris; Nutmegs; Lee Andrews & Hearts; Arrogants; Lonnie & Carrolons; Zirkons; Nutmegs; Shells; Jukebox Combo; Five Satins; Penguins; Velvetones; Harptones.
Gus Gossert Presents the Original New York Doo-Wopp Album, Vol. 5 .... Juke Box (M) 5004 10-15 70s
(Colored vinyl.) Vito & Salutations; Belmonts; Shells; Turbans; Lonnie & Carollons; Possessions; Capris; Five Satins; Jordan & Fascinators; Cineramas; Nutmegs; Meadowlarks; Vernalls; King Curtis; Tokens; Quin-Tones; Valchords; Velvet Satins; Shields; Slades.
Gus Gossert Presents the Original New York Doo-Wopp Album, Vol. 6 .... Juke Box (M) 5005 10-15 70s
(Colored vinyl.) Chimes; Jordan & Fascinators; Medallions; Five Satins; Decoys; Dubs; Camelots; Quin-tones; Chuck-A-Luks; Crests; Vita 7 the Elegants; Fascinations; Tony Orlando; Heartbeats.
Gutsy Guitars of… .... Sears (S) SPS 478 8-12
Mason Williams; Glen Campbell; Billy Strange; Howard Roberts; 12 String Guitar Band.
Guys and Dolls .... Harmony (M) CL-2567 20-30 50s
(10-inch LP.) Frankie Laine; Rosemary Clooney; Jo Stafford; Jerry Vale; Harry James.
Guys and Dolls .... Harmony (S) HS-11374 10-20 69
(Soundtrack.) Frank Sinatra; Dean Martin; Sammy Davis Jr.; Bing Crosby; Dinah Shore; Allan Sherman; Debbie Reynolds; McGuire Sisters.
Guys with Soul Are the Greatest .... Wand (M) WDM-666 15-20 65
Chuck Jackson; Solomon Burke; Otis Redding; Tommy Hunt; Timmy Shaw.
Hail! Hail! Rock N' Roll .... MCA (SP) 6217 8-10 87
(Soundtrack.) Keith Richards; Chuck Berry; Eric Clapton; Robert Cray; Etta James; Julian Lennon; Linda Ronstadt.
Hairspray .... MCA (S) 6228 8-10 88
(Soundtrack.) Rachel Sweet; Ray Bryant Combo; Jan Bradley; Gene & Wendell; Flares; Jerry Dallman & Knightcaps; Little Peggy March; Barbara Lynn; Gene Pitney; Ikettes; Toussaint McCall; Five Du-Tones.
Hal Jackson from Palisades Park Presents Golden Oldie Greats .... Rare Bird (S) 8025 10-15
Crests; Dixie Cups; Classics; Bobby Lewis; Angels; Maxine Brown; Betty Everett; Harptones; Mellokings; Cascades; Ike & Tina Turner; Five Satins; Gladys Knight & Pips; Channels; Dobie Gray; Jerry Butler; Dee Clark; Belmonts; Terry Stafford; Capris.
Hall of Fame .... Columbia (M) CL-2600 10-15 66
Hall of Fame Hits .... Columbia (M) CL-1308 20-25 59
Hall of Fame Hits .... Columbia (SE) CS-8640 15-25 62
Four Lads; Doris Day; Vic Damone; Percy Faith; Jo Stafford; Johnnie Ray; Tony Bennett; Johnny Mathis; Guy Mitchell; Rosemary Clooney; Mitch Miller; Frankie Laine. (Reissue of CL-1308.)
Hall of Fame Series .... Columbia (M) CL-613 10-15 50s
Liberace; Tony Bennett; Percy Faith; Rosemary Clooney; Frankie Laine; Buddy Clark & Ray Noble; Doris Day; Guy Mitchell.
Halloween 2 .... Varese Sarabande (S) STV-81152 12-15 81
(Soundtrack.) John Carpenter; Alan Howarth; Chordettes; others.
Hand Me Down Blues .... Relic (M) 8024 5-10 89
John Brim; Dusty Brown; Henry Gray; Albert King; Snooky Pryor; Slim Sunnyland; Little Willie Foster.
Happening, A .... Design (M) DLP-263 10-15 60s
Happening, A .... Design (SE) SDLP-263 8-12 60s
Chuck Jackson; Royo Orbison; April Stevens & Nino Tempo; Johnny Rivers; Lee Dorsey; Simon & Garfunkel; Critters; Vic Dana; Surfaris; Joe Tex.
Happy Birthday U.S.A. (2 LP) .... 20th Fox (S) T2-506 10-15 76
Pat Boone; Donnie Brooks; Randy Nicklaus; Sammy Davis Jr.; Jerry Naylor; Dee Dee Henrichs; Lloyd Schoonmaker; Rick Tucker; Paul Revere & Raiders; Mike Curb Congregation; Dorsey Burnette; Billy Joe Royal; Charles Wright & Watts 103rd St. Rhythm Band; Lyle Countryman; Susie Allanson; Sean Morton Downey Jr.; Tom Sullivan & Up the People; Jerry Cole & Paula Ruffin.
Happy Blend of Stars & Songs .... RCA (M) PRM-171 5-10 65
Pete King Chorale; John Gary; Ann-Margret; Peter Nero; Jonah Jones; Hugo Winterhalter; Bing Crosby & Rosemary Clooney; Dukes of Dixieland; Helen O'Connell; Ed Ames; Melachrino Strings; Carol Channing.

Happy Days - Fonzie Favorites .... Jukebox Int'l TVLP 177602R 5-10 76
(TV mail order offer.) Coasters; Bobby Darin; Everly Brothers; Joe Jones; Regents; Jerry Lee Lewis; Bill Haley & His Comets; Frankie Lyndon; Heyetts; Rays; Dubs; Flamingos; Little Anthony & Imperials; Chantels; Elegants; Jimmy Charles; Five Satins; Skyliners; Cleftones; Lee Dorsey.

Happy Days of Rock 'N' Roll .... Pickwick (S) SPC-3517 5-10
Bobby Day; Platters; Vogues; Chuck Berry; Trashmen; Wilbert Harrison; Tommy Roe; Five Satins; Diamonds; Frankie Ford; Bill Haley & His Comets.

Happy Gospel Songs .... Rural Rhythm (M) RR 141 8-12 60s
Jerry & Sandy Bernard; G.M. Farley; Foggy River Boys; Pilgrim Heirs Quartet; Bill Carter; Jackie & Arlin Vaden.

Happy Holiday .... Columbia Special Products (S) P-12438 5-10 74
Debbie Reynolds; Patti Page; Doris Day; Anita Bryant; Mahalia Jackson.

Happy Holiday .... Mistletoe (S) MLP-1243 5-10 78
Rosemary Clooney; Bing Crosby; Enzo Stuarti; Lou Monte; Frank Sinatra.

Happy Holidays .... Capitol (S) SL-6730 5-10
Tennessee Ernie Ford; William Loose & Hollywood Pops Orchestra; Sandler & Young; New Sounds of Christmas; Peggy Lee; Al Martino; Nat King Cole; Lettermen; Ella Fitzgerald.

Happy Holidays .... Columbia Special Products (M) CSP 242 10-15 66
Les Brown; Billy Butterfield; Ray Conniff; Skitch Henderson; Andre Kostelanetz; Lester Lanin; Norman Luboff; Patti Page; Jo Stafford; Jerry Vale; Bobby Vinton. (Sold only at True Value Hardware Stores.)

Happy Holidays, Vol. 1 .... RCA (S) DPL1-0411 5-10 79
(Sold at V & S Variety Stores.) Perry Como; Arthur Fiedler; Norman Luboff; John Gary; Lana Cantrell; Eugene Ormandy & Philadelphia Orchestra; Bing Crosby; Kate Smith; Robert Shaw Chorale; Jan Peerce; Columbus Boys Choir.

Happy Holidays, Vol. 2 .... Columbia Special Products CSP (M) 348 5-10 67
(Sold only at True Value Hardware Stores.) Andre Kostelanetz; Doris Day; Tony Bennett; Percy Faith; New Christy Minstrels; Frank DeVol; Merrill Staton Choir; Patti Page; Norman Luboff; Tex Beneke; Anita Bryant; Ray Conniff.

Happy Holidays, Vol. 3 .... RCA (S) PRS 255 5-10 67

Happy Holidays, Vol. 4 .... ???? 5-10 69
(Sold only at True Value Hardware Stores.)

Happy Holidays, Vol. 5 .... ???? 5-10 70
(Sold only at True Value Hardware Stores.)

Happy Holidays, Vol. 6 .... ???? 5-10 71
(Sold only at True Value Hardware Stores.)

Happy Holidays, Vol. 7 .... ???? 5-10 72
(Sold only at True Value Hardware Stores.)

Happy Holidays, Vol. 8 .... ???? 5-10 73
(Sold only at True Value Hardware Stores.)

Happy Holidays, Vol. 9 .... ???? 5-10 74
(Sold only at True Value Hardware Stores.)

Happy Holidays, Vol. 10 .... ???? 5-10 75
(Sold only at True Value Hardware Stores.)

Happy Holidays, Vol. 11 .... ???? 5-10 76
(Sold only at True Value Hardware Stores.)

Happy Holidays, Vol. 12 .... ???? 5-10 77
(Sold only at True Value Hardware Stores.)

Happy Holidays, Vol. 13 .... ???? 5-10 78
(Sold only at True Value Hardware Stores.)

Happy Holidays, Vol. 14 .... ???? 5-10 79
(Sold only at True Value Hardware Stores.)

Happy Holidays, Vol. 15 .... ???? 5-10 80
(Sold only at True Value Hardware Stores.)

Happy Holidays, Vol. 16 .... ???? 5-10 81
(Sold only at True Value Hardware Stores.)

Happy Holidays, Vol. 17 .... ???? 5-10 82
(Sold only at True Value Hardware Stores.)

Happy Holidays, Vol. 18 .... RCA (S) DPL1-0608 8-12 83
Elvis Presley; Ed Ames; Harry Belafonte; Nat King Cole; Perry Como; Arthur Fiedler; Harry Simeone Chorale; Jack Jones; Anne Murray; Roger Whittaker. (Sold only at True Value Hardware Stores.)

Happy Holidays, Vol. 19 .... RCA (S) DPL1-0689 5-10 84
(Sold only at True Value Hardware Stores.) Jim Reeves; Willie Nelson; Roger Whittaker; Robert Shaw Chorale; Carpenters; Bing Crosby; Arthur Fiedler; Julie Andrews; Andre Previn; Norman Luboff Choir; Peggy Lee.

Happy Holidays, Vol. 20 .... RCA (S) DPL1-0713 8-12 85
Elvis Presley; Carpenters; Perry Como & Ray Charles Singers; Bing Crosby; Sergio Franchi; Mario Lanza; Mantovani; Ronnie Milsap; Leontyne Price; Robert Shaw Chorale; George Beverly Shea; Kate Smith; Mel Torme; Roger Whittaker. (Sold only at True Value Hardware Stores.)

Happy Holidays, Vol. 21 .... RCA (S) DPL1-0739 8-12 86
Elvis Presley; Alabama; Ames Brothers; Julie Andrews; Canadian Brass; Nat King Cole; Bing Crosby; Tommy Dorsey; James Galway & Royal Philharmonic; Steve Lawrence & Eydie Gorme; Arthur Fiedler; Glenn Miller; Bobby Vinton. (Sold only at True Value Hardware Stores.)

Happy Holidays, Vol. 22 .... RCA (S) DPL1-0777 5-10 87
(Sold only at True Value Hardware Stores.) Perry Como; Alabama; Julie Andrews; Carpenters; Jose Feliciano; Ella Fitzgerald; Crystal Gayle; Lettermen; Ronnie Milsap.

Happy Holidays, Vol. 23 .... MCA Special Products (S) 15042 5-10 88
Andrews Sisters; Chuck Berry; Bing Crosby; Jets; Brenda Lee; Loretta Lynn; Oak Ridge Boys; Harry Simeone; Ray Stevens; George Strait; Trap Family Singers; Roger Williams. (Sold at True Value stores.)

Happy Sing-A-Long .... Crown (S) CST-245 5-10
Sportsmen; Kirby Stone Four; others.

Happy Times .... Commonwealth (S) NU-9200 5-8 76
(Without poster of Fonzie.)

Happy Times ....Commonwealth (S) NU-9200 8-10 76
(Includes poster of Fonzie.) Dovells; Angels; Chubby Checker; Dee Clark; Frankie Ford; Lloyd Price; Fiestas; Carl Dobkins Jr.; Mark Dinning; Jimmy Rodgers; Billy Bland; Jimmy Gilmer; Bobby Vee; Chiffons; Capris; Jim Lowe; Jimmy Clanton; Buddy Knox; Gary "U.S." Bonds; Jack Scott; Bobby Freeman; Johnny & Hurricanes.

Happy Together Tour 1985 ....K-Tel (S) BU 9240 8-12 85
Turtles; Grass Roots; Gary Lewis & Playboys; Buckinghams.

Happy Trails ....United Artists (S) UA-LA766-G2 5-10 77
Slim Whitman; Roy Rogers; Dave Dudley; Bob Wills; Jean Shepard; Bobby Goldsboro; George Jones; Patsy Cline; Del Reeves; others.

Hard Ride ....Paramount (S) PAS-6005 20-25 71
(Soundtrack.) Bill Medley; Thelma Comacho; Junction; Bluewater; Bob Moline; Sounds of Harley.

Hard to Hold ....RCA Victor (S) ABL1-4935 8-10 84
(Soundtrack.) Rick Springfield; Randy Crawford; Graham Parker; Nona Hendryx; Peter Gabriel.

Harder They Come ....Mango/Capitol (S) SMAS 7400 10-12 73

Harder They Come ....Mango/Capitol (S) SMAS 9202 8-12 Re
(Soundtrack.) Jimmy Cliff; Scotty; Melodions; Maytals; Slickers; Desmond Dekker.

Hark the Stars of Hollywood Sing ....Coral (M) CRL-57307 10-15 59

Hark the Stars of Hollywood Sing ....Coral (S) CRL7-57307 10-15 59
Dolores & Bob Hope; Claire & Les Brown; June Hutton; Axel Stordahl; Reginald Owen; Margaret & Barbara Whiting; Ken Lane; Dottie & Sonny Burke; Katie Nero; JoAnn Greer; Ed Platt; Dick Noel; Charles Budant; Lucy Ann Polk; Jack Shabazian; others.

Harlem Holiday, Vol. 4 ....Collectables (M) Col-5054 5-10 90s
Collegians; Jesters; Calendars; Paragons; Quinns; Jesters; Duponts; Quinns.

Harlem Holiday, Vol. 6 ....Collectables (M) Col-5056 5-10 90s
Maurice Williams & Zodiacs; Nutmegs; Five Willows; Five Satins; Sonnets; Turbans; Smart Tones; Five Satins; Starlarks; Desires; Loungers; Five DeBonaires; Vocalaires; Rodger & Travelers.

Harlem Holiday, New York Rhythm & Blue, Vol. 7 ....Collectables (M) Col-5057 5-10 90s
Mello Kings; Mint Juleps; Starlites; Marktones; Desires; Smart Tones; Five Satins; Silhouettes; Nutmegs; Boptones; Starlettones; Fabulons; Turbans.

Harlem N. Y., the Doo-Wop Era (2 LP) ....Collectables (M) Col-7001 8-12 80s
Magnificents; Student;s Rainbows; Collegians; Charts; Love Notes; Kodaks; Lewis Lymon & Teenchords; Fabulaires; Five Discs; Silhouettes; Videos; Collegians; Perfections; Continentals; Ladders; Debonaires; Magnificent Four; Monarchs; Bop Chords; Ivy-Tones; Edsels; El Dorados; Paragons; Charts; Carnations; Revalons; Dells; Eternals; Revels; Quinns; Pyramids; Veltones; Little Bobby Rivera & Hemlocks; Chalets.

Harmony (2 LP) ....Sessions/RCA (S) DPL2-0159 8-15 76
(Mail order offer.) Turtles; B.J. Thomas; Carol Douglas; Guess Who; Kinks; Lobo; Dawn; Bo Donaldson & Heywoods; Crabby Appleton; April Wine; Status Quo; Fifth Dimension; Lovin' Spoonful; Every Mother's Son; Buoys; Silver Convention; Bullet; Chad & Jeremy; Hues Corporation; Foundation; Styx; Gary Glitter; Godspell. (Special products. Made for Sessions.)

Harper Valley P.T.A. ....Nashville (SE) NLP-2109 5-10 73
Jeanne C. Riley; Dottie West; Rose Maddox; Sue Thompson; others.

Harper Valley P.T.A. ....Plantation (S) PLP-700 8-10 78
(Soundtrack. Green vinyl.) Jeannie C. Riley; Nelson Riddle; Jerry Lee Lewis; Johnny Cash; Carol Channing, Rita Remington.

Hats Off to Country ....Columbia Special Products (S) P 15639 5-10 81
(Promotional issue only.) Byrds; Willie Nelson; Johnny Cash; Johnny Paycheck; Charlie Rich; Tammy Wynette; New Riders of the Purple Sage; Earl Scruggs Revue; Lynn Anderson; Tanya Tucker. (Made for Stetson Hat Company.)

Haul Off and Love Me ....Nashville (SE) NLP-2084 5-10 70
Johnny Bond; Frankie Miller; Hank Penny; Willis Brothers; Wayne Raney; George Jones; others.

Have a Merry Chess Christmas ....Chess/MCA (S) CH-25210 5-10 80
Chuck Berry; Gems; Meditation Singers; Moonglows; Ramsey Lewis Trio; Rotary Connection with Minnie Riperton; O'Jays; Salem Travelers; Soul Stirrers.

Have Yourself a Merry Little Christmas ....Columbia (S) CR-21529 5-10 70
Ray Conniff; Gene Autry; Burl Ives; others.

Having Wonderful Time! Wish You Would Hear ....Columbia (M) CZ-1 10-15 50s
(Promotional issue only. Includes 10-page booklet/catalog.) Frank Sinatra; Michel Legrand; Art Van Damme Quintet; Norman Luboff Choir; Les Elgart; Frankie Laine & Buck Clayton; Andre Kostelanetz; Percy Faith; Paul Weston; Sammy Kaye; Erroll Garner; Louis Armstrong & His All Stars.

Hawaiian Guitar Hot Shots ....Yazoo (M) L-1055 5-10
King Benny Nawahi; Sol Hoopii; Kane's Hawaiians; Jim & Bob; Hauulea Entertainers; Pale K. Lua; Roy Smeck; King, Queen & Jack; Hanapi Trio; Franchini & Dettborn; Master's Hawaiians.

Hawaiian Steel Guitar - 1920s to 1950s ....Folklyric (M) 9009 5-10 76
Kalama's Quartete; Sam Ku West; Honolulu Players; Sol Hoopii; Masters's Hawaiians; Tubize Royal Hawaiian Orchestra; Roy Smeck; M.K. Moke; Hoot Gibson; Hawaiian Songbirds; Sol K. Bright; George Keoko Davis; Jenks "Tex" Carman; Jerry Byrd.

Hawk ....Condor (M) 100 10-15 70s
(Mail order offer. Issued without outer cover.) Sam the Sham; Little Anthony; Chris Montez; Dion; Don & Juan; Shades of Blue; Toys; Richard Berry; Safaris; Chuck Berry; Fats Domino; Shirelles; Skyliners; Don & Dewey; ? & Mysterians; Chantels; Betty Everett; Jay & Techniques; Shields.

Hayride Medley ....Osborne Enterprises Ltd. (EP) OE-819 5-10 84
(Promotional issue only. Issued with Jerry Osborne's *Country Music* price guide.) Johnny Horton; George Jones; Loretta Lynn; Ray Price; Marty Robbins; Jim Reeves; Hank Snow; Bob Luman; Ferlin Husky.

He's My Girl ....Scotti Bros. (S) SZ-40906 8-10 87
(Soundtrack.) David Hallyday; Sylvie Vartan; Paul Revere & Raiders; Mountain; Chambers Brothers; Mickey Barrera; Kim Bullard.

Headliners ....Sunset (SE) SUS-5270 10-15
O.C. Smith; Jerry Butler; Fats Domino; Gloria Lynne; O'Jays.

Headliners ....Columbia (M) GB-7 15-20 60

Headliners ....Columbia (S) GS-7 15-20 60
(Columbia Record Club issue.) Tony Bennett; Brothers Four; Dave Brubeck; Ray Conniff; Percy Faith; Four Lads; Lionel Hampton; Andre Kostelanetz; Norman Luboff Choir; Johnny Mathis; Mitch Miller; Marty Robbins.

Headliners, Vol. 2 ....Columbia (M) GB-9 15-20 61

Headliners, Vol. 2 ....Columbia (S) GS-9 15-20 61
(Columbia Record Club issue.) Johnny Cash; Percy Faith; Roger Williams; Mitch Miller; Patti Page; Miles Davis; Quintet Lester Lanin; Brook Benton; Harmonicats; Brothers Four; Dinah Washington; Dave Brubeck.

Headliners, Vol. 3 .... Columbia (M) GB-11 15-20 62
Headliners, Vol. 3 .... Columbia (S) GS-11 15-20 62
(Columbia Record Club issue.) Steve Lawrence; Marty Robbins; Jerry Murad's Harmonicats; Bobby Vee; Andre Previn Trio; Banjo Barons; Ray Conniff; Andy Williams; Ferrente & Teicher; Les Paul & Mary Ford; Roger Williams; Brook Benton; Andre Kostelanetz.
Headliners '63.......... Columbia (M) GB-13 15-20 63
Headliners '63.......... Columbia (S) GS-13 15-20 63
(Columbia Record Club issue.) Tony Bennett; Percy Faith; Bobby Vee; New Christy Minstrels; Dave Brubeck; Ferrante & Teicher; Robert Goulet; Roger Williams; Ventures; Ray Conniff; Marty Robbins; Julie London; Quincy Jones.
Headliners '64.......... Columbia (M) GB-15 15-20 64
Headliners '64.......... Columbia (S) GS-15 15-20 64
(Columbia Record Club issue.) Andy Williams; Ray Conniff; Smothers Brothers; Barbra Striesand; New Christy Minstrels; Johnny Cash; Ventures; Fats Domino; Andre Kostelanetz; Jerry Vale; Bobby Vinton; Thelonious Monk.
Headliners '65.......... Columbia (M) D-80 15-20 65
Headliners '65.......... Columbia (S) DS-80 15-20 65
(Columbia Record Club issue.) Andy Williams; Barbara Streisand; Jerry Vale; Patti Page; Jimmy Dean; Johnny Cash; New Christy Minstrels; Percy Faith; Doris Day; Tony Bennett; Robert Goulet; Andre Previn; Ray Conniff; Andre Kostelanetz.
Headliners '66.......... Columbia (M) D-154 15-20 66
Headliners '66.......... Columbia (S) DS-154 15-20 66
Barbra Streisand; Tony Bennett; Ray Conniff; Andre Kostelanetz; Johnny Mathis; Steve Lawrence; Joe Harnell; Andy Williams; Robert Goulet; Eydie Gorme; Percy Faith; Jerry Vale; Patti Page; Skitch Henderson.
Heads Up .... Columbia (EP) AS-4 5-10 70s
(Promotional issue only.) Argent; Catfish; Shuggie Otis; Jam Factory; Susan Carter; Redbone.
Hear Them Again (10 LP).......... Readers Digest (S) RDA-49A 30-45
(Boxed set.) Andy Williams; Dinah Shore; Bing Crosby; others.
Heart and Soul Fifties.......... Warner/JCI (SE) 3204 5-10 85
Wilbert Harrison; Ivory Joe Hunter; Thurston Harris; Bobby Bland; LaVern Baker; Little Richard; Silhouettes; Clyde McPhatter; Fats Domino; Smiley Lewis; Marv Johnson; Lloyd Price.
Heart Full of Memories .... Pick-A-Hit (S) P 1000 8-12 70
Young Hearts; Boby Sanders; Little Helen; McKinley Travis; Delicates.
Heart of Dixie.......... A&M (S) SP-3930 10-15 89
(Soundtrack.) Elvis Presley; Kenny Vance; Delbert McClinton; Charlie Jacobs; Rebecca Russell; Ivory Joe Hunter; Snakes.
Heart to Heart.......... Columbia (S) 1P-6325 5-10 75
Terry Baxter; Charlie Rich; Dave Loggins; Jerry Vale; Percy Faith; Tony Bennett; Ray Conniff; Vikki Carr; Andre Kostelanetz; Bobby Vinton. (Columbia House Record Club issue.)
Heartbeat.......... I&M (S) I-020 5-10 80
Robert John; Air Supply; KC & Sunshine Band; Dr. Hook; Dionne Warwick; Rupert Holmes; Abba; Suzie Quatro & Chris Norman; Roberta Flack & Donny Hathaway; Al Stewart; Ray, Goodman & Brown; Jennifer Warnes; Gino Vannelli; Kenny Rogers & First Edition; Gloria Gaynor; Bob Welch.
Heartbeat of the '70s .... K-Tel (S) TV-3100 5-10 83
America; Rita Coolidge; Hall & Oates; Carly Simon; Melissa Manchester; Diana Ross; Joe Cocker; Jim Croce; Anne Murray; Leo Sayer; Debby Boone; Peaches & Herb.
Heartbreak Hotel .... RCA (S) 8533-1-R 5-8 88
(Soundtrack.) Elvis Presley; David Keith & T. Graham Brown Band; Dobie Gray; Alice Cooper; Charlie Schlatter & Zulu Time Band.
Hearts of Fire.......... Columbia (S) SC-40870 8-12 87
(Soundtrack.) Bob Dylan; Fiona; Rupert Everett, others.

Heavies: see Atlantic Heavies
Heavenly Bodies .... Private Bodies (S) SZ-39930 8-12 85
(Soundtrack.) Bonnie Pointer; Tubes; Cheryl Lynn; others.
Heavenly Stars (Gospel Series) .... Cotillion (S) SD 052 10-20 71
Wilson Pickett; Solomon Burke; Aretha Franklin; Roberta Flack; Sweet Inspirations; Brook Benton; Myrna Summers & Interdenominational Singers; Marion Williams.
Heavy Guitars.......... Pickwick (S) SPC 3203 8-12
Glen Campbell; Mason Williams; Joe Maphis; Jim McGuinn; Tommy Tedesco.
Heavy Hands .... Columbia (S) CS-1048 8-12 70
Yardbirds & Jeff Beck; Pacific Gas & Electric; Spirit; Santana; Taj Mahal; Freddy King; Nick Gravenites & Mike Bloomfield; Fleetwood Mac; Loose Pages.
Heavy Haulers .... Power Pak (M) PO-290 5-10 75
Red Sovine; Tommy Downs; Bobby Sykes; Frankie Miller; Slim Jacobs; Johnny Bond; Willis Brothers; Betty Amos; Reno & Smiley.
Heavy Heads .... Chess (S) LPS-1522 10-15 69
Howlin' Wolf; John Lee Hooker; Muddy Waters; Little Walter; Sonny Boy Williamson; Bo Diddley; Little Milton; Washboard Sam.
Heavy Heads, Voyage 2.......... Chess (S) LPS-1528 10-15 69
Howlin' Wolf; John Lee Hooker; Willie Mabon; Muddy Waters; Chuck Berry; Little Walter; Lowell Fulson; Sonny Boy Williamson.
Heavy Hits .... Adam VIII (S) A8R-8010 5-10 74
(Mail order offer.) Gladys Knight & Pips; Moments; Kool & Gang; Mocedades; Who; Stories; Impressions; Staple Singers; Olivia Newton-John; Natural Four; El Chicano; Barry White; Johnny Taylor; James Brown; Think; Ecstasy, Passion & Pain; Bill Amesbury; Five Man Electrical Band; Brenda Lee; Marty Robbins.
Heavy Hits .... Columbia (S) CS-9840 10-15 69
Leonard Cohen; Moby Grape; Electric Flag; Taj Mahal; Laura Nyro; Great Society with Grace Slick; Byrds; Mike Bloomfoeld & Al Kooper; Blood, Sweat & Tears; Chambers Brothers; Big Brother & Holding Company.
Heavy Hitters (Radio Sampler).......... Arista (S) SP-73 5-10 79
(Issued in plain white cover with title/time sticker.) Michael Gregory Jackson; David Sancious; John Scofield; Larry Coryell; Air; Baird Hersey.Promotional issue only.
Heavy Metal: see Superstars of the '70s, Vol. 2, Heavy Metal
Heavy Metal – the Score (2 LP) .... Asylum (S) DP-9004 12-15 81
Heavy Metal.......... Asylum (S) 5E-547 35-40 81
(Soundtrack.) Black Sabbath; Blue Oyster Cult; Cheap Trick; Devo; Donald Fagen; Don Felder; Grand Funk Railroad; Sammy Hagar; Journey; Nazareth; Stevie Nicks; Riggs; Trust.

Heavy Metal (Loss Leader): see Warner Bros. Promotional Releases/Samplers
Heavy Mix....Pickwick (S) SPC-3324 5-10 71
Motherlode; Elephant's Memory; Lou Christie; Captain Beefheart; Sopwith Camel.
Heavy Soul....Atlantic (S) 2-500 8-12 72
King Floyd; Tyrone Davis; Persuaders; King Curtis; others.
Heavy Sounds....Columbia (S) CS-9952 10-15 70
(Red "360 Sound" label.) Big Brother & Holding Co.; Blood, Sweat & Tears; Laura Nyro; Electric Flag; It's a Beautiful Day; Taj Mahal; Johnny Winter; Mike Bloomfield & Al Kooper; Byrds; Chicago; Mongo Santamaria.
Heavy Sounds....Columbia (S) CS-9952 8-12 70
(Red and yellow label.) Big Brother & Holding Co.; Blood, Sweat & Tears; Laura Nyro; Electric Flag; It's a Beautiful Day; Taj Mahal; Johnny Winter; Mike Bloomfield & Al Kooper; Byrds; Chicago; Mongo Santamaria.
Heavy Traffic....Fantasy (S) 9436 10-25 73
(Soundtrack.) Sergio Mendes; Chuck Berry; Isley Brothers; Dave Brubeck Quartet; Merl Saunders; Ed Bogas; Ray Shanklin.
Heavyweights (2 LP)....Columbia (S) A2S-174 40-60 75
Bruce Springsteen; others.
Hee Haw: see Stars of Hee-Haw
Hell Broke Loose in Georgia: North Georgia Fiddle Bands....County (M) 514 8-12 70s
Hello Hawaii....Decca (M) DL-8906 20-25 59
Bing Crosby; Andrews Sisters; Ames Brothers; others.
Henry Mancini Selects Great Songs of Christmas by Great Artists....RCA/Goodyear (S) DPL1-0148 5-10 75
Carpenters; Henry Mancini; Robert Shaw Chorale; Julie Andrews; Andre Previn; Perry Como; Mantovani; Leontyne Price; Danny Davis & Nashville Brass; Ed Ames; Ella Fitzgerald; John Gary; Kate Smith; Bing Crosby.
Herald the Beat....Herald (M) HLP-0110 150-175 57
Turbans; Faye Adams; Al Savage; Charlie & Ray; Tommy Ridgley; Nutmegs; Mello Kings.
Here Ain't the Sonics....Popllama/Estrus (S) PL-ES-0024 8-10 89
(Colored vinyl.) Nomads; Girl Trouble; Mono Men; Original Sins; Screaming Trees; Game for Vultures; Surf Trio; Thee Headcoats; Cynics; Young Fresh Fellows; Pippi Eats Cherries; Fallouts; Marshmallow Overcoat; Kings of Rock; Mojo Nixon & Skid Roper.
Here Are the Hits....Fire (M) FLP-100 100-150 59
Scarlets; Velvets; Rainbows; Charts; Channels; Teen Chords; Kodaks.
Here Comes Santa Claus....Harmony (M) HL 7137 5-10
Singing Princess; Tony Mottola; Bob Hannon; Arthur Malvin; Ray Heatherton.
Here Comes Summer....K-Tel (S) NC-471 5-10 77
Mungo Jerry; Billy Stewart; Eddie Cochran; Chad & Jeremy; Jamies; Chilliwack; Shangri-Las; Craig Ruhnke; War; Robin Ward; Lovin' Spoonful; Jan & Dean; First Class; O'Kaysions; Surfers; Johnny Rivers; Sly & Family Stone.
Here Comes the Bride....Design (S) DLP-618 8-12 62
Bobby Austin; Charlie Ryan; Stuart Hamblen; Pete Pike; T. Texas Tyler; Stewart Family; Carl Belew.
Here We Go 'Round the Mulberry Bush....United Artists (M) UAL-5175 10-12 68
Here We Go 'Round the Mulberry Bush....United Artists (S) UAS-5175 10-15 68
(Soundtrack.) Traffic; Spencer Davis Group; Steve Winwood.
Heroes and Cowards....Stiff (S) SEWL-1000 8-10
Elvis Costello; Nick Lowe; Ian Dury; Wreckless Eric; Motorhead; Damned; Adverts; Mick Farren & Deviants; Alberto y Los Trios Paranoias.
Hey, Let's Twist....Roulette (M) R-25168 20-25 62
Hey, Let's Twist....Roulette (S) SR-25168 25-30 62
(Soundtrack.) Joey Dee & Starliters; Jo Ann Campbell; Teddy Randazzo
Hi-Fi All Stars....Halo (M) 50271 10-20 57
Kay Starr; Gordon MacRae; Rose Murphy; Frankie; Deek Watson & Brown Spots; Jaye P. Morgan; Hilltoppers; Fran Allison; Butch Stone; Ames Brothers; Lanny Ross.
Hi-Fi Around the World....Voice of America (M) GB 4052-3 8-12 50s
Harry Sukman; Webley Edwards; Les Baxter; John Raitt; Bobby Hackett; Roger Wagner Chorale; Nelson Riddle; George Shearing; Ray Anthony; Royal Polynesians.
Hi Fi in an Oriental Garden....ABC-Paramount (M) ABC-224 20-30 57
Hi Fi in an Oriental Garden....ABC-Paramount (S) ABCS-224 40-50 57
Hi-Fi Jazz Sampler....Masterseal (M) MS 1001 10-20
Hollywood Transcription Orchestra; David Rose; Sarah Vaughan; Dizzy Gillespie; Dennis Day; Frank DeVol; Fontanna; Eddie "Piano" Miller; Rias Symphony Orchestra; Viennese Symphonic Orchestra; Austrian Symphony Orchestra.
Hi-Fi Jazz Session....Altone (S) AST-230 10-15
Sarah Vaughan; Red Norvo; Rubber Legs Williams; Coleman Hawkins; Hen Gates Combo; Dorothy; Sabby Lewis Band; Eddie South.
Hi-Fi Jazz Session....Masterseal (M) MSLP 5013 15-25 57
Sarah Vaughan; Charlie Ventura; Red Norvo; Don Byas; Dizzy Gillespie; H. Carels; Cozy Cole; Hen Gates; Dorothy Donegan; Sabby Lewis; Eddie South.
Hi-Fi Plus Demonstration Record....Columbia (EP) HF 5-10
(Issued in picture sleeve.) Andre Kostelanetz; Duke Ellington; New York Philharmonic; Eugene Ormandy & Philadelphia Orchestra; Cleveland Orchestra.
Hi-Fi Tribute to Peter De Rose....Everest (S) LPBR-5035 8-12
Tutti Camarata; others.
Hiding Out....Virgin (S) 90661-1 8-10 87
(Soundtrack.) Boy George; Lolita Pop; Pretty Poison; Scarlett & Black; Felix Cavaliere; All That Jazz; Hue & Cry; Roy Orbison; K.D. Lang; Lee Anthony Brisdon; David L. Brisdon; Black Britain; Public Image Limited.
High Energy....K-Tel (S) TU 2620 5-10 79
Blondie; Amii Stewart; Gloria Gaynor; Peaches & Herb; Instant Funk; Chic; Foxy; G.Q.; Ponter Sisters; Foreigner; Orleans; Pablo Cruise; Farragher Brothers; Captain & Tennille; Gino Vannelli; Styx.
High Steppin' Country....Columbia Special Products (S) P-12979 5-10 75
Charlie Rich; Tammy Wynette; Johnny Cash; Barbara Mandrell; Marty Robbins; Statler Brothers; Ray Price; Tanya Tucker; Johnny Horton; Flatt & Scruggs; Jimmy Dean. (Made for Jarman Shoes for Men.)
High Voltage....K-Tel (S) TU 2740 5-10 81
Gino Vannelli; Frankie & Knockouts; Styx; Police; Phil Seymour; Alan Parsons Project; Hall & Oates; Kool & Gang; Heart; Delbert McClinton; Pat Benatar; Lover Boy; Cliff Richard; Eddie Rabbitt.

Highs in the Mid-Sixties, Vol. 1 (LA 65, Teenage Rebellion) .... Archive Int'l (S) AIP 10003 8-12 80s
Avengers; Colony; Sean & Brandy Wines; Epics; Limey & th Yanks; Standells; Spats; Grains of Sand; Gypsy Trips; Rumors; Warden & His Fugitives; Rod Runners; 4 Making Do; Answer; Star Fires; Lyrics.

Highs in the Mid-Sixties, Vol. 6 (Michigan Part 2) .... Archive Int'l (S) AIP-10011 8-12 84
Yorkshires; Underdogs; Jimmy Gilbert; 4 of Us; Masters of Stonehouse; Blues Co.; Blokes; Chosen Few; Bed of Roses; Choclate Pickles; Pleasure Seekers.

Highs in the Mid-Sixties, Vol. 7 (Northwest) .... Archive Int'l (S) AIP-10012 8-12 84
Jack Bedient & Chessmen; Jolly Green Giants; H.B. & Checkmates; Wilde Knights; Chambermen; Jack Eely & Courtmen; Squires; Sires; Lincolns; Express; Pastels; Nightwalkers; Mr. Lucky & Gamblers; Bootmen; Rock-N-Souls.

Highs in the Mid-Sixties, Vol. 10 (Wisconsin, Part 1) .... Archive Int'l (S) AIP-10017 8-12 86
Shag; Wanderer's Rest; Young Savages; Faro's; Lord Bev. Moss & Mossmen; Noblemen; Hinge; Jack & Beanstalks; Joey Gee & Come Ons; Trodden Path; Devrons; Love Society.

Highs in the Mid-Sixties, Vol. 14 (Northwest, Part 2) .... Archive Int'l (S) AIP-10020 8-12 86
Lord Dent & His Invaders; Night People; Volk Brothers; Paymarks; J. Michael & Bushmen; Statics; Talismen; Sir Raleigh & Cupons; Jack Bedient & Chessmen; Tom Thumb & Casuals; Scotsmen; Rooks.

Highs in the Mid-Sixties, Vol. 15 (Wisconsin, Part 2) .... Archive Int'l (S) AIP-10025 8-12 86
Gord's Horde; Baroques; Shaprels; Cannons; Family; Wanderer's Rest; Challengers; Medallions; Fugatives; Joey Gee & Come Ons; Mid-Nighters; Impalas; Spacemen; Mustard Men.

Highs in the Mid-Sixties, Vol. 16 (Northwest, Part 3) .... Archive Int'l (S) AIP-10024 8-12 87
Raymarks; Unusuals; Rocky & His Friends; Dominions; Bumps; Live Five; Express; Navarros; Gentleman Wild; Wheel of Fortune; Prembrook LTD.; City Zu; United Travel Service; International Brick.

Highs in the Mid-Sixties, Vol. 19 (Michigan Part 3) .... Archive Int'l (S) AIP-10028 8-12 87
Yorkshires; Underdogs; Jimmy Gilbert; 4 of Us; Masters of Stonehouse; Blues Co.; Blokes; Chosen Few; Bed of Roses; Chocolate Pickles; Pleasure Seekers.

Highlights Staged for Stereo .... Capitol (S) STAC-1638 10-20 62

Highway of Blues: see McGHEE, Stick / John Lee Hooker

Hillbilly Heaven .... Capitol Special Market (S) SL-8118 8-12 79
Tex Ritter; Johnny Horton; Hank Williams; Red Foley; Patsy Cline; Cowboy Copas; George Morgan; Bob Wills & Tommy Duncan; Johnny Bond; Elton Britt; Jim Reeves; Lefty Frizzell; Moon Mullican; Ira Louvin with the Louvin Brothers; Carter Family; T. Texas Tyler; Skeets McDonald; Leon Payne; Jack Guthrie; Hawkshaw Hawkins.

Hillbilly Hit Parade .... Mercury (M) MG-20282 25-40 57

Hillbilly Hit Parade .... Starday (M) S-102 50-75 56

Hillbilly Hit Parade .... Starday (S) SLP-102 15-25 62
George Jones; Leon Payne; Jeanette Hicks; George Jones & Jeanette Hicks; Benny Barnes; Eddie Blank; Red Hayes; Thumper Jones.

Hillbilly House Party .... Imperial (M) 9124 15-20 63
Charlie Walker; Billy Briggs; others.

Hills and Home (30 Years of Bluegrass) .... New World (S) 225 5-10 77
Bill Monroe's Bluegrass Boys; Osborne Brothers; Country Gentlemen; others.

Hires Presents RCA Victor's Sound Spectaculars for '59 .... RCA (M) SP 33-15 10-15 59
Ames Brothers; Dinah Shore; Harry Belafonte; Skitch Henderson; Big Band of Shorty Rogers; Melachrino Orchestra; Luis Arcaraz; Abbe Lane; Chip Fisher; Bob Scobey's Frisco Jazz Band; Clancy Hayes; Gisele MacKenzie; Band of the Coldstream Guards.

His Sound is Right for Her .... Columbia (S) CSS 893 8-12 60s
Byrds; Cryan Shames; Paul Revere & Raiders; O.C. Smith; Peter Nero; Percy Faith; Diahann Carroll; Bobby Vinton; Chambers Brothers; Mongo Santamaria.

Historic Jazz Concert at Music Inn .... Atlantic (M) 1298 10-20
Jimmy Guiffre; Pee Wee Russell; Rex Stewart; Herbie Mann; Teddy Charles; Dick Katz; George Wein; Percy Heath; Oscar Peterson; Ray Brown; Connie Kay.)

History of Bell U.K. 1970-1975 .... Arista (S) AL-4112 8-10 77
Hello; Glitter Band; Gary Glitter; Showaddywaddy; Slik; Bay City Rollers; Linda Lewis; Pearls; Drifters; Barry Blue.

History of British Blues, Vol. 1 (2 LP) .... Sire (S) SASH-3701 10-15 73
Cyril Davis Rhythm & Blues All-Stars; Yardbirds; Fleetwood Mac; Savoy Brown; Jo Ann Kelly; Key Largo; Climax Blues Band; Alexis Korner Blues Inc.; Spencer Davis R&B Quartet; Graham Bond Organization; Downliners Sect; John Mayall's Bluesbreakers; Aynsley Dunbar; Duster Bennett; Chicken Shack; Christine Perfect; Gordon Smith; Jellybread; Mike Vernon.

History of British Rock, Vol 1 .... Creative Sounds (S) CS-001 8-12 70s
Eric Clapton; Jimmy Page; Rod Stewart; John Mayall; Small Faces; Fleetwood Mac; Savoy Brown; Nice; Crispian St. Peters.

History of British Rock (2 LP) .... Sire (S) SAS-3702 10-15 74
Manfred Mann; Honeycombs; Gerry & Pacemakers; Peter & Golden; Freddie & Dreamers; Searchers; Swingin' Blue Jeans; Walker Brothers; Cliff Richard; Uriah Heep; Rod Stewart; Silkie; Dusty Springfield; Troggs; Kinks; Dave Clark Five; Vanity Fare; Merseys; Bee Gees; Mindbenders; Small Faces; Status Quo; Billy J. Kramer & Dakotas; Hollies; Pretty Things; Wayne Fontana & Mindbenders.

History of British Rock (2 LP) .... Sire (S) 2P-6547 10-20 76
(Columbia Record Club edition.) Beatles; Fleetwood Mac; Mungo Jerry; Donovan; Python Lee Jackson; Chad & Jeremy; Eric Burdon & Animals; Dusty Springfield; Cream; Bee Gees; Manfred Mann; Freddie & Dreamers; ; Searchers; Swingin' Blue Jeans; Walker Brothers; Cliff Richard; Uriah Heep; Rod Stewart; Silkie; Dusty Springfield; Troggs; Kinks; Dave Clark Five; Vanity Fare; Merseys; Bee Gees; Mindbenders; Small Faces; Status Quo; Billy J. Kramer & Dakotas; Hollies; Pretty Things; Wayne Fontana & Mindbenders.

History of British Rock, Vol. 2 (2 LP) .... Sire (S) SASH-3705 10-15 74
Beatles with Tony Sheridan; Billy J. Kramer & Dakotas; Peter & Gordon; Cilla Black; Dave Clark Five; Searchers; Gerry & Pacemakers; Kinks; Donovan; Rod Stewart; Sandy Shaw; Hollies; Chad & Jeremy; Manfred Mann; Tremelos; Troggs; Dusty Springfield; Van Morrison; Cream; Small Faces; Badfinger; Bee Gees; Elton John; Deep Purple; Julie Driscoll with Brian Auger & Trinity; Thunderclap Newman; Crazy World of Arthur Brown; Who.

History of British Rock, Vol. 3 .... Sire (S) SASH-3712 10-15 74
Beatles with Tony Sheridan; David Bowie & Lower Third; Derek & Dominos; Cream; Deep Purple; Bee Gees; Eric Burdon & Animals; Billy J. Kramer; Gerry & Pacemakers; Unit Four + 2; Kinks; Troggs; Donovan; Them; Dusty Springfield; Manfred Mann; Zombies; Peter & Gordon; Dave Clark Five; Badfinger; Matthews Southern Comfort; Olivia Newton-John; Elton John; Python Lee Jackson; Chris Farlowe; Mary Hopkin.

History of Classic Jazz (5 LP)........Riverside (M) SDP-11 40-60
(Boxed set. Includes book.) Blind Lemon Jefferson; Rev. J. M. Gates & Congregation; Sodero's Military Band; Fred Van Eps; Scott Joplin; James Scott; Joseph Lamb; Cow Cow Davenport; Ma Rainey; Bessie Smith; Ida Cox; Chippie Hill; Big Bill Broonzy; King Oliver's Creole Jazz Band; Jelly Roll Morton's Stomp Kings; New Orleans Rhythm Kings; Original Memphis Melody Boys; Red Onion Jazz Babies; Wesley Wallace; Jimmy Yancy; Cripple Clarence Lofton; Meade Lux Lewis; Art Hodes; Pete Johnson; Johnny Dodds; Tiny Parham; Freddie Keppard's Jazz Cardinals; Barrelhouse Five; State Street Ramblers; Lovie Austin's Blues Serenaders; Doc Cook's Dreamland Orchestra; Mugsy Spanier's Stomp Six; Bix Beiderbecke & Wolverines; Original Wolverins; Charles Pierce; Jungle Kings; Wingy Manone; Jame P. Johnson; Fats Waller; Cliff Jackson; Clarence Williams; Euke Ellington's Washingtonians; Fletcher Henderson; Original Memphis Five; California Ramblers; Red & Miff's Stompers; Wild Bill Davison; Yank Lawson; Mugsy Spanier; Kid Ory; Bunk Johnson; George Lewis; Lu Watter's Yerba Buena Jazz Band; Bob Helm's Riverside Roustabouts; Dixieland Rhythm Kings.

History of Country Music, Vol. 1........Radiant (S) RRC 1011 8-12 73
Jimmie Rodgers; Ernest Tubb; Gene Autry; Carter Family; Pee Wee King; Sons of the Pioneers; Homer & Jethro; Elton Britt; Vaughn Monroe; Hank Snow; Chet Atkins; Del Wood; Slim Whitman; Davis Sisters; Stuart Hamblen.

History of Country Music (2 LP)........UMI (S) 1600/1601 10-15 73
Jimmie Rodgers; Ernest Tubb; Gene Autry; Carter Family; Pee Wee King; Sons of the Pioneers; Homer & Jethro; Elton Britt; Vaughn Monroe; Hank Snow; Chet Atkins; Del Wood; Slim Whitman; Davis Sisters; Stuart Hamblen; Roy Acuff; Cowboy Copas; Moon Mullican; Hank Williams; Tennessee Ernie Ford; Patti Page; Carlisles; Hank Thompson; Tex Ritter; Johnny Cash; George Jones.

History of Country Music, Vol. 2........Radiant (S) RRC 1012 8-12 73
Roy Acuff; Cowboy Copas; Moon Mullican; Hank Williams; Tennessee Ernie Ford; Patti Page; Carlisles; Hank Thompson; Tex Ritter; Johnny Cash; George Jones.

History of Country Music, Vol. 2 (2 LP)........UMI (S) 1650 10-15 73
Porter Wagoner; Don Gibson; Browns; Jim Reeves; Jimmy Dean; Bobby Bare; Skeeter Davis; Norma Jean; Connie Smith; Roger Miller; Dottie West; Dolly Parton; Dickie Lee; Jerry Reed; Faron Young; Leroy Van Dyke; Ferlin Husky; Sonny James; Everly Brothers; George Jones; E. Ashworth; Red Sovine; Tom T. Hall; Jerry Lee Lewis; Johnny Cash.

History of Country Music, Vol. 3 (2 LP)........Radiant (S) RRC 1013 10-15 73
Eddie Arnold; Hank Snow; Porter Wagoner; Jim Reeves; Hank Locklin; Bobby Bare; Waylon Jennings; Nat Stuckey; George Morgan; Dorsey Burnett; Gogi Grant; Patsy Cline; Marvin Rainwater; Jerry Wallace; Sheb Wooley; Hankshaw Hawkins; Roy Clark; Sammi Smith; Jacky Ward; Donna Fargo; Hank Thompson.

History of Country Music, Vol. 4........Radiant (S) RRC 1014 8-12 73
Faron Young; Leroy Van Dyke; Ferlin Husky; Sonny James; Everly Brothers; George Jones; E. Ashworth; Roger Miller; Red Sovine; Tom T. Hall; Jerry Lee Lewis; Johnny Cash.

History of Country Music, Vol. 5, Lee Cash Presents........Radiant (S) RRC 1015 8-12 73
(Single LP; same as disc #1 of Vol. 3.; also has same cover.) Eddy Arnold; Hank Snow; Porter Wagoner; Jim Reeves; Hank Locklin; Bobby Bare; Waylon Jennings; Nat Stuckey.

History of Country Music, Vol. 6........Radiant (S) RRC 1016 8-12 73
George Morgan; Dorsey Burnett; Gogi Grant; Patsy Cline; Marvin Rainwater; Jerry Wallace; Sheb Wooley; Hawkshaw Hawkins; Bonny Guitar; Roy Clark; Sammi Smith; Jacky Ward; Hank Thompson; Donna Fargo.

History of Country Music, Vol. 7........Radiant (S) RRC 1019 8-12 81
Johnny Cash; Everly Brothers; Jimmie Rodgers; Ernest Tubb; Ray Price; George Jones; Ferlin Husky; Johnny Horton; Patsy Cline; Bill Anderson.

History of Country Music, Vol. 8........Radiant (S) RRC 1020 8-12 81
Burl Ives; Marty Robbins; Jim Reeves; Roger Miller; Webb Pierce; Slim Whitman; Kitty Wells; Faron Young.

History of Country Music, Vol. 9........Radiant (S) RRC 1021 8-12 81
Buck Owens; Eddy Arnold; Dave Dudley; Sonny James; Merle Haggard; Tammy Wynette; George Jones; Bill Anderson.

History of Country Music, Vol. 10........Radiant (S) RRC 1022 8-12 81
Billie Jo Spears; Charley Pride; Tompall & Glaser Brothers; Bob Wills; Eddy Arnold; Jim Reeves; Browns; Sons of the Pioneers; George Hamilton IV.

History of Country Music, Vol. 11........Radiant (S) RRC 1023 8-12 81
Lonzo & Oscar; Justin Tubb; Jim Reeves; Porter Wagoner; Skeeter Davis; Jim Ed Brown; Maxine Brown; Eddy Arnold; Hank Snow; Johnny & Jack.

History of Country Music, Vol. 12........Radiant (S) RRC 1024 8-12 81
Eddy Arnold; Jim Reeves; Johnny & Jack; Hank Locklin; Faron Young; Tex Williams; Homer & Jethro; Porter Wagoner; George Hamilton IV..

History of Drag Racing........Capitol (M) TAO-2145 10-20 64

History of Drag Racing........Capitol (S) STAO-2145 15-25 64
(Sound effects - no music.)

History of Hi Records Rhythm & Blues, Vol. 1: the Beginnings........MCA (S) 25226 5-10 88
Bill Black Combo; Ace Cannon; Willie Mitchell; Don Bryant; Ann Peebles; Al Green; George Jackson; Otis Clay.

History of Hi Records Rhythm & Blues, Vol. 2: the Glory Years........MCA (S) 25227 5-10 88
Al Green; Otis Clay; Ann Peebles; Syl Johnson; Erma Coffee; Hi Rhythm; O.V. Wright.

History of Jazz, Vol. 1........Capitol (M) T 793 10-20 50s

History of Jazz, Vol. 2........Capitol (M) T 794 10-20 50s

History of Jazz, Vol. 3........Capitol (M) T 795 20-30 57
Glen Gray; Red Norvo's Nine; Benny Goodman Band; Bob Crosby's Dixieland Band; Duke Ellington; Jess Stacy; Art Tatum; Tommy Douglas; International Jazzmen; Rex Stewart's Big Eight; Bobby Hackett.

History of Jazz, Vol. 4........Capitol (M) T 796 20-30 50s

History of Jazz, Vol. 2, the Golden Era........Capitol (M) H 246 20-30 50s
(10–inch LP.) Paul Whiteman; Sonny Greer; Red Nichols; Julie Lee; Jay McShann.

History of Latino Rock—Eastside Sound, Vol. 1 - 1956-1965........Zyanya/Rhino (S) 061 5-10 83
Ritchie Valens; Chan Romero; L'il Juan Herrera; Blendells; Midnighters; Rene & Ray; Ronnie & Pomona Casuals; Salas Brothers; Little Ray; Premiers; Romanciers; Carlo Brothers; Velveteens; Cannibal & Headhunters.

History of New Orleans Rock & Roll, Vol. 1........Ace (M) 7184 8-10 84
Huey "Piano" Smith; Dr. John; Frankie Ford; Scotty McKay; Jimmy Clanton; Joe & Ann; Big Boy Myles; Lee Allen; Earl King; Alvin "Red" Tyler; Bobby Marchan; Professor Longhari; Billy Bland. (Made in conjunction with the 1984 World's Fair in New Orleans.)

History of New Orleans Rock & Roll, Vol. 2........Ace (M) 7284 8-10 84
(Made in conjunction with the 1984 World's Fair in New Orleans.) Clowns; Bobby Marchan; Lee Dorsey; others.

History of New Orleans Rock & Roll, Vol. 3........Ace (M) 7384 8-10 84
(Made in conjunction with the 1984 World's Fair in New Orleans.) Supremes; Frankie Ford; Lloyd Price; Emeralds; etc.

History of New Orleans Rock & Roll, Vol. 4 .... Ace (M) 7484 8-10 84
Huey "Piano" Smith; Little Booker; Dr. John; Frankie Ford; Jimmy Clanton; Joe Tex; Earl King; Clowns; Thomas Brothers; Piano Red; Chuck Carbo; Jerry Byrnes. (Made in conjunction with the 1984 World's Fair in New Orleans.)

History of Northwest Rock, Vol. 1 .... Great Northwest Music Company (S) GNW-4003 15-25 76
Frantics; Dave Lewis; Sonics; Kingsmen; Don & Goodtimes; Sir Raleigh & Coupons; Ian Whitcomb; Bards; Springfield Rifle.

History of Northwest Rock, Vol. 2 .... Great Northwest Music Company (S) GNW-4008 10-20 78
Paul Revere & Raiders; Don & Goodtimes; Sonics; Springfield Rifle; Bards; Kingsmen; Dave Lewis; Dimensions; New Yorkers; Ian Whitcomb.

History of Northwest Rock, Vol. 3 .... Great Northwest Music Company (M) GNW-4009 10-20 80
Springfield Rifle; London Taxi; Bumps; Breakers (Wailers); Jack Horner & Plums; Sonics; Bards; Live Five; Magic Fern; P.H. Phactor; Kingsmen; Brave New World.

History of Northwest Rock, Vol. 4 .... Great Northwest Music Company (S) GNW-4010 10-20 80
Sonics; Bandits; City Limits; Mr. Lucky & Gamblers; Bards; Don & Goodtimes; Dynamics; Liberty Party; Counts; Live Five; Mercy Boys; George Washington & Cherry Bombs.

History of Rhythm & Blues, Vol. 1 - the Roots (1947-52) .... Atlantic (M) 8161 10-20 68
History of Rhythm & Blues, Vol. 1 - the Roots (1947-52) .... Atlantic (SE) SD-8161 10-20 68
Ravens; Orioles; Stick McGhee & His Buddies; Frank Cully; Delta Rhythm Boys; Laurie Tate; Joe Morris; Leadbelly; Clovers; Cardinals; Joe Turner; Edna McGriff; Ruth Brown.

History of Rhythm & Blues, Vol. 2 - the Golden Years (1953-55) .... Atlantic (M) 8162 10-20 68
History of Rhythm & Blues, Vol. 2 - the Golden Years (1953-55) .... Atlantic (SE) SD-8162 10-20 68
Diamonds; Ruth Brown; Clovers; Drifters with Clyde McPhatter; Chords; Joe Turner; Tommy Ridgley; LaVern Baker; Ray Charles; Five Keys.

History of Rhythm & Blues, Vol. 3 - Rock and Roll (1956-57) .... Atlantic (M) 8163 10-20 68
History of Rhythm & Blues, Vol. 3 - Rock and Roll (1956-57) .... Atlantic (SE) SD-8163 10-20 68
Robins; Clovers; Joe Turner; Drifters; Clyde McPhatter; Ivory Joe Hunter; LaVern Baker; Coasters; Chuck Willis.

History of Rhythm & Blues, Vol. 4 - the Big Beat (1958-60) .... Atlantic (M) 8164 10-20 68
History of Rhythm & Blues, Vol. 4 - the Big Beat (1958-60) .... Atlantic (SE) SD-8164 10-20 68
Coasters; Bobby Darin; Clyde McPhatter; LaVern Baker; Drifters; Ray Charles; Ben E. King; Carla Thomas.

History of Rhythm & Blues, Vol. 5 - the Beat Goes On (1961-62) .... Atlantic (SE) SD-8193 10-20 68
Ray Charles; Coasters; Ben E. King; Mar-Keys; Solomon Burke; Ikettes; William Bell; Falcons; Booker T. & MGs; LaVern Baker; Otis Redding; Rufus Thomas; Drifters.

History of Rhythm & Blues, Vol. 6 - On Broadway (1963-64) .... Atlantic (SE) SD-8194 10-20 69
Drifters; Barbara Lewis; Solomon Burke; Doris Troy; Chris Kenner; Nat Kendricks & Swans; Ben E. King; Rufus Thomas; Coasters; Wilson Pickett; Carla Thomas; Don Covay; Joe Tex; Otis Redding.

History of Rhythm & Blues, Vol. 7 - the Sound of Soul (1965-66) .... Atlantic (SE) SD-8208 10-20 69
Willie Tee; Solomon Burke; Barabar Lewis; Otis Redding; Wilson Pickett; Don Covay & Goodtimers; Sam & Dave; Capitols; Percy Sledge; Eddie Floyd.

History of Rhythm & Blues, Vol. 8 - the Memphis Sound (1967) .... Atlantic (S) SD-8209 10-20 69
Sam & Dave; Arthur Conley; Aretha Franklin; Booker T. & MGs; Otis Redding; Carla Thomas; Bar-Kays; Wilson Pickett; King Curtis; Percy Sledge; Joe Tex.

History of Rock .... Collectables (S) COL 5061 5-10 88
Bobby Day; Chuck Berry; Screamin' Jay Hawkins; Frankie Avalon; Music Explosions; Trashmen; Vanity Fare; Chiffons; Moonglows; Dells; Etta James; Jerry Butler & Betty Everett; Casinos; Maurice Williams & Zodiacs.

History of Rock, Vol. 2 .... Collectables (S) COL 5062 5-10 88
Dion; Pastels; Ritchie Valens; Cadets; J. Frank Wilson; Gladys Knight & Pips; Gene Chandler; Thurston Harris; Vogues; Chad & Jeremy; Del-Vikings; Turtles; Little Caesar & Romans; Silhouettes.

History of Rock, Vol. 3 .... Collectables (S) COL 5063 5-10 88
Chiffons; Moonglows; Betty Everett; Teen Queens; Frankie Avalon; Sue Thompson; Dale & Grace; Toni Fisher; Turbans; Dale Hawkins; Capris; Jerry Butler; Chuck Berry; Dion.

History of Rock, Vol. 4 .... Collectables (S) COL 5064 5-10 88
Shirley & Lee; Fendermen; Etta James; Passions; Bruce Channel; Mel & Tim; Marvin & Johnny; Jewel Akens; Dion; Billy Stewart; Sue Thompson; Claudine Clark; Five Satins; Gene & Debbie.

History of Rock, Vol. 5 .... Collectables (S) COL 5065 5-10 88
Del-Vikings; Turtles; Lloyd Price; Chuck Berry; Capitols; Barbara Lynn; Marcie Blaine; Hollywood Argyles; Bo Diddley; Dorsey Burnette; Nutmegs; Corsairs; Royal Guardsmen; Barbara Lewis.

History of Rock, Vol. 6 .... Collectables (S) COL 5066 5-10 88
Dion & Belmonts; Bobby Lewis; Harptones; Fabian; Vanity Fare; Chantels; Edison Lighthouse; Barbara Lewis; Count Five; Mystics; Billy Stewart; Jacks; Vogues; Teddy Bears.

History of Rock, Vol. 7 .... Collectables (S) COL 5067 5-10 88
Cascades; Ernie K-Doe; Brenton Wood; Miracles; O'Kaysions; Dee Clark; Mungo Jerry; Jarmels; Gogi Grant; Lloyd Price; Students; Five Satins; Chuck Berry; Turtles.

History of Rock, Vol. 8 .... Collectables (S) COL 5068 5-10 88
Randy & Rainbows; Fontella Bass; Troy Shondell; Turtles; Swingin' Medallions; Lee Andrews & Hearts; Deon Jackson; Dion & Belmonts; Donnie Brooks; Frank Ifield; Tune Weavers; Paradons; Castaways; Mr. Aker Bilk.

History of Rock, Vol. 9 .... Collectables (S) COL 5069 5-10 88
Newbeats; Jackie Ross; Dells; Royal Guardsmen; Climax; Jan & Dean; Brenton Wood; Chiffons; Esquires; Jan Bradley; Tony Bellus; Blue Jays; Cannibal & Headhunters; Jesse Belvin.

History of Rock, Vol. 10 .... Collectables (S) COL 5070 5-10 88
Soul Survivors; Chuck Berry; Moonglows; Newbeats; Phil Phillips; Ernie Maresca; Turtles; Larry Verne; Sue Thompson; Bill Parsons; Al Wilson; Kathy Young & Innocents; Harold Dorman; Dion & Belmonts.

History of Rock & Roll (2 LP) .... Collectables (S) PDR 1-2500 35-40 82
(Promotional only picture discs.) Chiffons; Dion; others.

History of Rock & Roll, Vol. 1 .... Pickwick (S) SPC 3666 5-10 79
Joe Bennett & Sparkletones; Danny & Juniors; Del-Vikings; Steve Gibson & Redcaps; George Hamilton IV; Sonny James; Jim Lowe; Poni-Tails; Lloyd Price.

History of Rock & Roll, Vol. 2 .... Pickwick (S) SPC 3667 5-10 79
Pat Boone; Grass Roots; Brian Hyland; Mamas & Papas; Barry McGuire; Tommy Roe; Robin Ward; Richard Harris.

History of Rock & Roll, Vol. 3 .... Pickwick (S) SPC 3677 5-10 79
Ventures; Fleetwoods; Bobby Vee; Timi Yuro; Gary Lewis; Jan & Dean; Canned Heat; Classics IV; Cher.

History of Rock & Roll, Vol. 4 .... Pickwick (S) SPC 3678 5-10 79
Ernie K-Doe; O'Jays; Sandy Nelson; Sugarloaf; Bobby Goldsboro; Gary Lewis; Eddie Cochran; Jay & Americans; Bobby Vee.

History of Rock Instrumentals, Vol. 1 .... Rhino (S) RNLP 70137 5-10 87
Surfaris; Sandy Nelson; Routers; Marketts; Ventures; Jack Nitzsche; Santo & Johnny; Preston Epps; Dartells; Dave "Baby" Cortez; B. Bumble & Stingers; Johnny & Hurricanes.

History of Rock Instrumentals, Vol. 2 .... Rhino (S) RNLP 70138 5-10 87
Champs; Duane Eddy; Bill Justis; Lonnie Mack; Link Wray & His Ray Men; Wailers; Alvin Cash & Crawlers; Ramrods; Johnny & Hurricanes; Cozy Cole; Viscounts.

History of Soul .... Pride (S) 0021 5-10 73
Isaac Hayes; Sylvers; Joe Tex; Freda Payne; Solomon Burke; Ollie Nightingale.

History of Surf Music, the Instrumentals, Vol. 1 .... Rhino (S) RNLP 051 8-12 82
Dick Dale; Chantays; Belairs; Blazers; Pyramids; Lively Ones; Original Surfaris; Crossfires; Eddie & Showmen; Sentinals; Tom Starr & Galaxies; Challengers; Surfaris.

History of Surf Music, the Instrumentals, Vol. 2 .... Rhino (S) RNLP 052 8-12 82

History of Syracuse Music, Vol. 1 .... ECEIP (M) PSLP-1000 10-15

History of Syracuse Music, Vol. 2 .... ECEIP (M) PSLP-1003 10-15

History of Syracuse Music, Vols. 3 & 4 .... ECEIP (M) PSLP-1007 10-15

History of Syracuse Music, Vol. 5 .... ECEIP (M) PSLP-1011 10-15

History of Syracuse Music, Vol. 6 .... ECEIP (M) PSLP-1001 10-15

History of Syracuse Music, Vol. 8 & 9 .... ECEIP (M) PSLP-1015/18 15-25 76
John & Yoko (interview); Joe English; others.

History of Syracuse Music, Vol. 10 & 11 (2 LP) .... ECEIP (M) PSLP-1019/22 15-25 80
John & Yoko (interview); others.

History of Vancouver Rock and Roll, Vol. 1, ... VCRA (S) 003 5-10 87
(Canada issue. Has booklet.) Jim Morrison; Les Vogt; Prowlers; Canadian V.I.P.'s; Stripes; Stan Cayer; Gerry Fiander; Classics; Chessmen; Hi-Fives; Valentines; Patty Surbey; Jimmy Morrison & Stripes.

History of Vancouver Rock and Roll, Vol. 2, ... VCRA (S) 002 5-10 85
(Canada issue. Has booklet.) Shockers; Chessmen; Terry Jacks; Pacers; Shadracks; Fred Latremouille; Patty Surby; Canadian V.I.P.'s; Nocturnals; Trials of Jayson Hoover; Night Train Revue; Little Daddy & Bachelors.

History of Vancouver Rock and Roll, Vol. 3, ... VCRA (S) 001 5-10 83
(Canada issue. Has booklet.) Seeds of Time; Spring; Tom Northcott Trio; Painted Ship; Self Portrait; United Empire Loyalists; Winter's Green; Collectors; Northwest Company; Orville Dorp.

History of Vancouver Rock and Roll, Vol. 4, ... VCRA (S) 004 5-10 91
(Canada issue. Has booklet.) Northwest Company; William Tell & Marksmen; Shockers; Eternal Triangle; Long Time Comin'; One Way Street; Mock Duck; Lock; Collectors; Silver Chalice Revue.

Hit A Day in August .... Columbia (EP) ZEP 36309/10 8-12

Hit After Hit .... Ronco (S) R-2080 5-10 76
Johnny Taylor; Andrea True Connection; Vicki Sue Robinson; Hall & Oates; Melissa Manchester; Billy Joel; Smokey Robinson; Salsoul Orchestra; Morris Albert; Silver Convention; Bay City Rollers; Diana Ross; Elvin Bishop; David Ruffin; Commodores; Leo Sayer; Wet Willie; Willie Hutch; Eric Carmen; Brotherhood of Man.

Hit Explosion .... Ronco (S) R-2130 5-10 77
Wild Cherry; Firefall; England Dan & John Ford Coley; Brick; Diana Ross; Parker McGee; Barkays; David Dundas; Barry Manilow; Bay City Rollers; Spinners; William Bell; Diamond REO; Ohio Players; Barry Mann; John Sebastian; Charlie Daniels Band; Orleans.

Hit 45s of the '70s, Vol. 1 .... Epic (S) PE 37329 5-10 81
Hollies; Dave Loggins; Michael Murphey; Charlie Rich; Looking Glass; Johnny Nash; Albert Hammond; Burton Cummings; Englebert Humperdinck.

Hit 45s of the '70s, Vol. 2 .... Epic (S) PE 37330 5-10 81
Wild Cherry; Labelle; Redbone; Johnny Nash; Joe Tex; Johnny Rivers; Hollies; Ram Jam; Argent; Edgar Winter Group.

Hit Kickers Series, Vol. 2 (3 LP) .... FR 1015/1016/1017 10-20 76
Johnny Winter; Boogie Kings; Doug Sahm; Freddy Fender; Moe Bandy; Gaylan Ladd; Buddy Collard; Mickey Gilley; B.J. Thomas; Dale McBride; Ray Rushay; Ronnie Milsap; Floyd Tillman; Doug Kershaw.

Hit Kickers Series, Vol. 8 (3 LP) .... FR 1033/1034/1035 10-20 76
T-Bone Walker; Lee Maye; Johnny Clyde Copeland; Jackie Payne; Ivory Joe Hunter; Jean Knight; Barbara Lynn; Oscar Perry; Sonny Raye & Fancy; Freddy Fender; Johnny Winter; Ron Bernard; Southern Comfort; Clarence Frogman Henry; Johnny Williams; Doug Sahm; Doug Kershaw; Joe Barry; Warren Storm; Jimmy Donley; Ken Lindsey.

Hit Kickers Series, Vol. 9 (3 LP) .... FR 1036/1037/1038 10-20 76
Joe Barry; Clarence Frogman Henry; Floyd Tillman; Johnny Winter; Jean Knight; Oscar Perry; Sonny Raye & Fancy; Warren Storm; T.K. Hulin; Barbara Lynn; Ken Lindsey; Jimmy Dooley; T-Bone Walker; Jimmy Heap; Henry Moore; Johnny Williams; Joe Pips; Lowell Fulson; Doug Sahm; Allison & So. Funk Blues.

Hit Machine .... K-Tel (S) TU 2480 5-10 76
(Mail order offer.) KC & Sunshine Band; Maxine Nightingale; Starbuck; War; Linda Ronstadt; Pratt & McClain; Frankie Valli; Paul Anka; Billy Ocean; Rick Dees & His Cast of Idiots; Elton John; Walter Murphy & Big Apple Band; Bellamy Brothers; John Sebastian; Electric Light Orchestra; Rick Springfield; Kiss; Jessi Colter; 4 Seasons; Johnnie Taylor.

Hit Makers .... Jerden (S) 7005 20-30 60s
Kingsmen; Ian Whitcomb; Paul Revere & Raiders; Don & Goodtimes; Sir Walter Raleigh.

Hit Makers .... Columbia (M) CL-1485 10-15 60

Hit Makers .... Columbia (S) CS-8276 10-15 60
Johnny Mathis; Brothers Four; Percy Faith; Doris Day; Jerry Vale; Mitch Miller; Tony Bennett; Kitty Kallen; Johnny Horton; Frank DeVol; Marty Robins; Ray Bryant.

Hit Makers (Chancellor): see FABIAN / Frankie Avalon

Hit Makers &ir Record Breakers .... King (M) 737 20-30 61
Hank Ballard & Midnighters; James Brown; Bill Doggett; Little Willie John.

Hit Motion Picture Themes .... Mercury (M) MG-20810 12-15 63

Hit Motion Picture Themes .... Mercury (S) SR-60810 12-20 63
(Soundtrack.) Brook Benton; Xavier Cugat; Billy Eckstine; Dick Contino; Shirley Horn; Clebanoff Strings;Caesar Giovannini; Carl Stevens; others.

Hit Parade, Vol. 1 .... Mercury (M) MG-25164 35-50 52
(10-inch LP.)

Hit Parade, Vol. 1 .... Mercury (M) MG-25205 25-50 55
(10-inch LP.)

Hit Parade, Vol. 2 ....Mercury (M) MG-25166 35-50 52
(10–inch LP.)
Hit Parade of American Country Music (2 LP)....Starday (M) S-184 15-25 62
Hit Parade of American Country Music (2 LP)....Starday (S) SLP-184 15-25 62
Buck Owens; George Jones; Cowboy Copas; Moon Mullican; Red Sovine; Frankie Miller; Justin Tubb; Archie Campbell; others.
Hit Parade of Bluegrass Stars ....Starday (M) S-343 15-20 65
Hit Parade of Bluegrass Stars ....Starday (S) SLP-343 15-20 65
Reno & Smiley; Hylo Brown; Flatt & Scruggs; others.
Hit Parade of Country Music....Starday (M) S-184 15-25 62
Hit Parade of Country Music....Starday (S) SLP-184 15-25 62
Hit Power....Columbia House (S) 7290 8-10 81
Ronny & Daytonas; Joey Dee & Starliters; Brooklyn Bridge; Box Tops; Sopwith Camel; Ohio Express; Syndicate of Sound; 1910 Fruitgum Co.; Lemon Pipers; Loggins & Messina.
Hit Singles 1958-1977....Atlantic (S) 81909 5-10 88
Bobby Darin; Nino Tempo & April Stevens; Rascals; Sonny & Cher; Buffalo Springfield; Dusty Springfield; Blues Image; Stephen Stills; Robert John; Brownsville Station; Average White Band; England Dan & John Ford Coley; Hot.
Hit Singles 1980-1988....Atlantic (S) 81910 5-10 88
Bette Midler; Foreigner; Phil Collins; Laura Branigan; John Parr; Genesis; Nu Shooz; INXS; Debbie Gibson.
Hit Sounds of Music City-West....Tower (M) T-5070 10-15 67
Hit Sounds of Music City-West....Tower (SE) DT-5070 10-15 67
Dick Curless; Jan Howard; others.
Hit Sounds of the Young Generation....Capitol (S) SL 6646 8-12 60s
Bobbie Gentry; Hollyridge Strings; Peggy Lee; Sounds of Our Times; Glen Campbell; Lettermen; Tartaglia.
Hitline (2 LP)....K-Tel (S) TU 2800 8-12 80
Michael Jackson; Sister Sledge; Raydio; Carrie Lucas; Jimmy Ruffin; Spinners; Rupert Holmes; Teri De Sario; KC & Sunshine Band; Nigel Olsson; Lobo; Randy Vanwarmer; Brothers; Johnson; Kool & Gang; Isaac Hayes; David Naughton; Bonnie Pointer; Steve Forbert; Suzi Quatro; John Stewart; Little River Band; Babys; Robert Palmer.
Hitline 80 (2 LP)....Columbia A2S-890 15-25 80
(Promotional only issue.) Paul McCartney; others.
Hitmakers ....Jerden (M) JRL-7005 25-35 66
Hitmakers ....Jerden (S) JRLS-7005 35-45 66
Kingsmen; Ian Whitcomb; Paul Revere & Raiders; Don & Goodtimes; Sir Walter Raleigh.
Hitmakers ....Columbia (M) CL 1485 8-12 60
Johnny Mathis; Brothers Four; Percy Faith; Doris Day; Jerry Vale; Mitch Miller; Tony Bennett; Kitty Kallen; Johnny Horton; Frank DeVol; Marty Robbins; Ray Bryant.
Hitmakers, Vol. 11 ....Columbia Special Products (S) CSP-320 5-10 60s
Robert Goulet; Barbra Streisand; Andy Williams; Doris Day; Johnny Mathis.
Hitmakers by Zenith: see Zenith Presents the Hitmakers
Hits A Go-Go with the Stars ....Wyncote (M) W 9143 10-15 60s
Hits A Go-Go with the Stars ....Wyncote (S) SW 9143 10-15 60s
Dee Dee Sharp; Chubby Checker; Don Covay; Orlons; Tymes.
Hits Are on Verve ....Verve (M) VS-201 10-15
Hits Are on Verve ....Verve (S) V6S-201 10-15
Kai Winding; Jimmy Smith; Stan Getz; Bill Evans; Wynton Kelly; Antonio Carlos Jobin; Pat Thomas.
Hits from *Finian's Rainbow*....Harmony (S) HS 11286 10-20
Dean Martin with the Hi-Lo's; others.
Hits from Hollywood Movies ....RCA Special Products (S) PRS 389 8-12 72
Arthur Fiedler & Boston Pops; Ed Ames; Al Hirt; Harry Belafonte; Henry Mancini; Morton Gould; Norman Luboff Choir; Vic Damone; Hugo Montenegro.
Hits from *My Fair Lady* ....Columbia House Party Series (M) CL 2597 10-20 56
Jo Stafford; Percy Faith; Rosemary Clooney; Sammy Kaye; Vic Damone; Paul Weston.
Hits from the Movies....Columbia (M) 8218 15-25 59
Hits from the Movies....Columbia (S) CS-8218 15-25 59
Johnny Mathis; Doris Day; Percy Faith; Tony Bennett; Four Lads; Mitch Miller; Richard Maltby; Bing Crosby; Vic Damone; Duke Ellington; Norman Luboff.
Hits I Forgot to Buy....Swan (M) LP-512 25-35 64
Freddie Cannon; Danny & Juniors; Dickie Doo & Don'ts; Teddy & Twilights; Billie & Lillie; Link Wray; Rockin' Rebels; Bobby Comstock; Gabriel & Angels.
Hits of '64 - '65....Columbia (S) D-65 10-20 65
Hits of the Hops....Warner Bros. (M) W-1448 15-25 62
Hits of the Hops....Warner Bros. (S) WS-1448 20-30 62
Everly Brothers; Jerry Fuller; Jerry Wallace; Champs; Connie Stevens; Bob Luman; Jan & Dean; Joanie Sommers; Don Ralke.
Hits of the Mersey Era....EMI/Capitol (S) M-16077 8-10 77
(Reissue.)
Hits of the Mersey Era....EMI/Capitol (S) M-11690 8-12 77
Gerry & Pacemakers; Billy J. Kramer; Swingin' Blue Jeans; Cilla Black; Freddie & Dreamers; Hollies.
Hits of the '20s, '30s, '40s, '50s, '60s....Columbia (S) CSP 317 8-12 66
("Stone Container Corporation presents 40 years of progress.") Dinah Shore; Jo Stafford; Ray Conniff; Andre Kostelanetz; Michel Legrand; Johnny Mathis; Les & Larry Elgart; Eddy Davis.
Hits of the '20s....RCA Camden (M) CAL-361 10-15 57
Larry Greene; Gene Krupa; Buddy Morrow; Tommy Mercer; Mindy Carson; Jeanette MacDonald; Vaughn Monroe; NBC Chamber Music Society of Lower Basin Street; Dinah Shore; Deep River Boys; Jerry Jerome; Sammy Kaye; Tony Alama; D'Artega Orchestra.
Hits of the '30s....RCA Camden (M) CAL-370 8-12
Claude Thornhill; Jerry Jerome; Fran Warren; Ralph Flanagan; NBC Chamber Music Society Orchestra; Jesse Crawford; David Whitehall; Xavier Cugat; Guy Lombardo; Allen Jones; Vaughn Monroe.
Hits of the '40s....Realistic/Capitol Special Markets (M) SL 6980 5-10 75
Harry James; Johnny Mercer; Pied Piper; Freddy Martin; Andrews Sisters; Helen Forrest; Pee Wee Hunt; Margaret Whiting; Nat King Cole.

Hits of the '40s, Vol. 2 .... Capitol Special Markets (M) SL 8018 5-10 76
Stan Kenton; Nat King Cole; Peggy Lee; Dick Haymes; Ella Mae Morse; Andy Russell; Betty Hutton; Margaret Whiting; Mel Torme; Judy Garland. (Made for Radio Shack.)

Hits of the '50s .... RCA Camden (M) CAL-444 10-20
Dean Martin & His Group with the Strollers; Honey Dreamers; Domenico Savino; Connie Haines with the All Star Band; Bob Carroll; Tony Martin; Earl Sheldon Singers; Gisele MacKenzie; Perter Ricardo & His Calypso; Stuart Foster; Jack Haskell

Hits of the '50s .... Era/K-Tel (S) BU 4510 5-10 77
Bobby Day; Diamonds; Bobby Freeman;Duane Eddy; Freddy Cannon; Bobby Helms; Buddy Knox; Coasters; Robin Luke; Little Richard; Mark Dinning; Jimmie Rodgers; Jimmy Clanton; Johnny & Hurricanes; Dee Clark.

Hits of the '60s .... ???? 8-12
Box Tops; Gary "U.S." Bonds; Casinos; Five Amercians; Lou Christie; Ray Peterson; Sandy Posey; John Fred; Chubby Checker; American Breed; Tremeloes; Sam & Dave; Gary Lewis & Playboys; Oliver; Brooklyn Bridge; Del Shannon.

Hits of the '70s .... ???? 8-12
Hollies; Dave Loggins; Michael Murphey; Charlie Rich; Looking Glass; Johnny Nash; Albert Hammond; Burton Cummings; Charlie Rich; Englebert Humperdinck.

Hits on Board: see Capitol Promotional Releases/Samplers

Hits on Verve .... Verve (M) V6-201 10-20 67
Hits on Verve .... Verve (S) VS-201 10-20 67
Kai Winding; Jimmy Smith; Stan Getz; Bill Evans; Wynton Kelly; Antonio Carlos Jobim; Pat Thomas.

Hits That Jumped .... Checker (M) LP-2975 40-50 60
Tune Weavers; Bobby Lester & Moonlighters; Lewis Sisters; Johnny Fuller; Danny Overbea; Harvey; Jimmy McCraklin; Students; Earl Washington.

Hitsville .... Coral (M) CRL-57269 40-60 59
Hitsville .... Coral (S) CRL7-57269 50-75 59
Buddy Holly; McGuire Sisters; Teresa Brewer; Art Lund; Billy Williams; Jackie Wilson; Al Alberts; Betty Madigan; Rosemary Clooney; Lennon Sisters; Steve Lawrence; Four Knights.

Hitsville .... Mount Vernon Music (M) MVM-109 20-30
Five Satins; Faye Adams; King Curtis; Johnny Hartman; Turbans; Billy Miles; Charlie & Ray.

Hitsville .... Imperial (M) 9084 35-45 59
Wee Willie Wayne; Jewels; Smiley Lewis; Spiders; Bees; Bobby Mitchell & Toppers.

Hitsville, Vol. II .... Imperial (M) 9099 30-45 60
Pee Wee Crayton; Johnny Fuller; Archibald; Lil Son Jackson; Ken Copeland; Ernie Freeman.

Hittin' the Road .... Decca (M) DL-4681 10-20 65
Hittin' the Road .... Decca (S) DL-74681 10-20 65
Ernest Tubb; Carl Smith; others.

Hoagy Carmichael from "Star Dust" to "Ole Buttermilk Sky" (3 LP) .... Book of the Month (M) P3-15343 15-25 80
(Boxed set with libretto. All original versions of his compositions; 36 songs from 1924 to 1951.)

Holiday on Sunday .... Love (S) 1001 10-15
Magnificent Men; Shirelles; Donnie Elbert; Baby Washington; Pentagons; Barbara Lewis; James Brown; Volcanos; Impressions; Drifters; Chantels; Mad Lads; Ketty Lester; Jerry Butler; Delfonics; Frankie Lymon.

Hollywood Hootenanny .... Horizon (M) WP-1631 10-20 63
Hollywood Hootenanny .... Horizon (S) ST-1631 10-20 63
Hoyt Axton; Barbara Dane; Sherwood Singers; others.

Hollywood Knights .... Casablanca (S) 7218 8-10 80
(Soundtrack.) Frankie Valli & 4 Seasons; Martha Reeves & Vandellas; Brooklyn Dreams.

Hollywood Palace .... Zodiak (S) PHS 1 10-20 67
(Cover states "For presentation on ABC-TV".) Bing Crosby; Bing Crosby, Phil Harris & Alice Faye; Ella Fitzgerald; Bing & Ella; Butch Stone; Martha Raye; Helen O'Connell; Alice Faye; Phil Harris.

Hollywood Rock and Roll Record Hop .... Modern (M) LMP-1211 100-125 56
Etta James; Marvin & Johnny; Cadets; Joe Turner; Joe Houston; Jacks; Shirley Gunter; Dolly Cooper; Young Jessie; Cliques.

Hollywood Rock 'N Roll Record Hop .... Crown (M) CLP-5011 75-100 56
Etta James; Marvin & Johnny; Cadets; Joe Turner; Joe Houston; Jacks; Shirley Gunter; Dolly Cooper; Young Jessie; Cliques.

Hollywood Sign (Azra Sampler) .... Azra (S) 004 20-25 80
(Promotional only picture disc.) Centaurus; others.

Home For Christmas (3 LP) .... Columbia Musical Treasury (SE) P3S 5608 10-15 70s
(Boxed set.) Gene Autry; Tony Bennett; Leonard Bernstein & New York Philharmonic; E. Power Biggs; Brothers Four; Anita Bryant; Charlie Byrd; Johnny Cash; Richard P. Condie & Philadelphia Orchestra; Ray Conniff; John Davidson; Doris Day; Percy Faith; Eileen Farrell; Rita Ford's Music Boxes; Robert Goulet; Burl Ives; Mahalia Jackson; Andre Kostelanetz; Peter La Manna; London Pops Orchestra; Johnny Mathis; Mormon Tabernacle Choir; Jim Nabors; Eugene Ormandy & Temple University Choir; Patti Page; Robert Page; Philadelphia Brass Ensemble; Marty Robbins; St. Francis de Sales Boys Choir; Jerry Vale; Earl Wrightson; Tammy Wynette.

Home For Christmas .... Columbia Musical Treasury (S) DS 802 5-10
Doris Day; London Pops Orchestra & Chorus; Eugene Ormandy & Philadelphia Orchestra; John Davidson; Andre Kostelanetz; Leonard Bernstein & New York Philharmonic; Jim Nabors; Rita Ford's Music Boxes; Robert Goulet; Percy Faith.

Home For Christmas (2 LP) .... Realm (S) 2V 8101 8-12 77
(Mail order offer.) Tony Bennett; Jerry Vale; Ray Conniff; Tammy Wynette; Johnny Mathis; Gene Autry; Patti Page; Doris Day; John Davidson; Jim Nabors; Robert Goulet; Johnny Cash; Brothers Four; Percy Faith; Marty Robbins; Rita Ford's Music Boxes; Anita Bryant; Charlie Byrd; Andre Kostelanetz; Burl Ives; Mahalia Jackson.

Home for the Holidays .... MCA (S) MSM 35007 5-10 78
Pat Boone & Family; Bing Crosby; Loretta Lynn; Liberace; Jack Jones; Brady Bunch; Burl Ives; Lawrence Welk; Roger Williams; Pete Fountain; Robert Shaw & Atlanta Symphony Orchestra & Chorus.

Home of Grand Records, Vol. 1 .... Collectables (M) CLP-6004 5-10
Castelles; Belltones; Angels; Cherokees; George Grant; Marquis; Carter-Rays; Castroes.

Home of the Blues: see New Orleans, Home of the Blues

Home Movie Sound Effects .... Audio Fidelity (S) DFS 7018 5-10 63
(42 various sound effects.)

Homecoming 1945 (4 LP) .... Good Music (M) GMR 80037 10-20 88
Russ Morgan; Harry James with Helen Forrest; Dick Haymes & Helen Forrest; Bing Crosby with Carmen Cavallaro; Frankie Carle with Marjorie Hughes; Kay Kyser with Trudy & Harry Babbitt; Nat King Cole; Andrews Sisters; Tommy Dorsey & Sentimentalists; Glen Gray; Artie Shaw; Ink Spots; Woody Herman; Jimmy Dorsey with Bob Eberle & Helen O'Connell; Charlie Barnet with Bob Carroll; Glenn Miller with Marion Hutton & Modernaires; Johnny Mercer; Tommy Dorsey with Frank Sinatra; Benny Goodman; Andy Russell; Dick Jurgens with Buddy Moreno; Tommy Dorsey with Freddie Stewart; Spike Jones & His City Slickers; Freddy Martin with Clyde Rogers; Dinah Shore; Glenn Miller with Ray Eberle & Modernaires; Three Suns; Vaughn Monroe; Mills Brothers; Pied Pipers; Bing Crosby & Andrews Sisters; Tony Pastor with Ruth McCullough; Frank Sinatra with Harry James; Kate Smith; Perry Como with Russ Case.

Homer .... Cotillion (S) SD 9037 10-12 70
(Soundtrack.) Led Zeppelin; Buffalo Springfield; Byrds; Cream; Hearts & Flowers; Lovin' Spoonful; Steve Miller; Don Scardino.

Homespun Humor .... King (M) 726 20-30 60
Grandpa Jones; Charlie Ryan; Stanley Brothers; others.

Hometown U.S.A. .... K-Tel (S) NU-9460 8-10 79
(Soundtrack.) Betty Everett; Ritchie Valens; Little Richard; Five Satins; Chiffons; Skyliners; Del-Vikings; Teen Queens; Dion & Belmonts; Penguins; Jerry Lee Lewis; Rosie & Originals; Paris Sisters; Dion; Willows; Marvin & Johnny.

Honest to Goodness Country Music Hits .... RCA (M) LPM-2564 15-20 62
Honest to Goodness Country Music Hits .... RCA (S) LSP-2564 20-25 62
Hank Snow; Jim Reeves; Eddy Arnold; Porter Wagoner; Skeeter Davis; Jimmie Rodgers; Don Gibson; Browns; Hank Locklin; Pee Wee King; Elton Britt; Homer & Jethro.

Honest to Goodness Country Music Hits, Vol. 2 .... RCA (M) LPM-2633 15-20 63
Honest to Goodness Country Music Hits, Vol. 2 .... RCA (S) LSP-2633 20-25 63
Jim Reeves; Hank Snow; Don Gibson; Pee Wee King; Browns; Porter Wagoner; Chet Atkins; Hank Locklin; Wade Ray; Eddy Arnold; Johnnie & Jack.

Honeysuckle Rose (2 LP) .... Columbia (S) S2-36752 8-10 80
(Soundtrack.) Willie Nelson; Dyan Cannon; Amy Irving; Johnny Gimble; Jody Payne; Hank Cochran; Emmylou Harris; Jeannie Seely; Kenneth Threadgill.

Honkers and Bar Walkers, Vol. 1 .... Delmark (S) DL-438 5-10 88
Jimmy Forrest; Teddy Brannon; Cozy Eggleston; Jimmy Coe; Doc Sausage; Fred Jackson; Fats Noel; Paul Bascomb.

Honkers and Screamers: see Roots of Rock 'N' Roll, Vol. 6

Honky Tonk Angels .... Nashville (SE) NLP-2081 5-10 70
Dolly Parton; June Stearns; Dottie West; Melba Montgomery; Patsy Cline; Jan Howard; others.

Honky Tonk Favorites .... Mercury (M) MGW-12297 10-20 65
Honky Tonk Favorites .... Mercury (S) SRW-16297 15-20 65
Johnny Horton; George Jones; Rex Allen; Betty Amos James O'Gwynn; Sue Thompson; Jimmie Skinner; Claude Gray; Benny Barnes; Jennie Lou Carson.

Honky Tonk Saturday Night .... Warner Special Products (S) OP 1511 5-10 81
Emmylou Harris; Willy Nelson; Conway Twitty; Hank Williams; Gail Davis; Mickey Gilley; Tanya Tucker; Jerry Lee Lewis; John Conlee; Commander C & His Orchestra:

Honkytonk Man .... Warner Bros. (S) 1-23739 8-10 82
(Soundtrack.) Clint Eastwood; Porter Wagoner; Ray Price; Marty Robbins; John Anderson; Linda Hopkins; Johnny Gimble & Texas Swing Band; David Frizzell & Dottie West.

Honor Roll of Hits - 1926 .... RCA (EP) EPA-514 5-10 54
Honor Roll of Hits - 1927 .... RCA (EP) EPA-515 5-10 54
(10–inch LP.) Perry Como; Freddy Martin; Eddie Fisher; Benny Goodman.

Honor Roll of Hits - 1926-1927 .... RCA (M) LPM-3175 25-40 54
(10–inch LP.) Eddie Fisher; Perry Como; Ralph Flanagan; Dinah Shore; Freddy Martin; Benny Goodman; others.

Honor Roll of Hits - 1928 .... RCA (EP) EPA-516 5-10 54
(10–inch LP.) Buddy Morrow; Tony Martin; Larry Green.

Honor Roll of Hits - 1929 .... RCA (EP) EPA-517 5-10 54
Honor Roll of Hits - 1928-1929 .... RCA (M) LPM-3176 25-40 54
(10–inch LP.) Buddy Morrow; Larry Green; Melachrino Strings; James Melton; Tony Martin; Ralph Flanagan.

Honor Roll of Hits - 1930 .... RCA (EP) EPA-518 5-10 54
(10–inch LP.) Perry Como; Vaughn Monroe; Ralph Flanagan; Tommy Dorsey.

Honor Roll of Hits - 1931 .... RCA (EP) EPA-519 5-10 54
Honor Roll of Hits - 1930-1931 .... RCA (M) LPM-3177 25-40 54
(10–inch LP.) Perry Como; Vaughn Monroe; Ralph Flanagan; Tommy Dorsey; Melachrino Strings; Freddy Martin; others.

Honor Roll of Hits - 1932 .... RCA (EP) EPA-520 5-10 54
Honor Roll of Hits - 1933 .... RCA (EP) EPA-521 5-10 54
(10–inch LP.) Tony Martin; Dinah Shore; Ray Noble; Lisa Kirk.

Honor Roll of Hits - 1932-1933 .... RCA (M) LPM-3178 25-40 54
(10–inch LP.) Tony Martin; Eddie Fisher; Sammy Kaye; Dinah Shore; Ray Noble; others.

Honor Roll of Hits - 1934 .... RCA (EP) EPA-522 5-10 54
Honor Roll of Hits - 1935 .... RCA (EP) EPA-523 5-10 54
Honor Roll of Hits - 1934-1935 .... RCA (M) LPM-3179 25-40 54
(10–inch LP.) Henri Rene; Duke Ellington; National Farm & Home Hour Quintet; Ray Noble; Dennis Day; Four King Sisters; Vaughn Monroe; others.

Honor Roll of Hits - 1936 .... RCA (EP) EPA-524 5-10 54
(10–inch LP.) Fats Waller; Ezio Pinza; Phil Harris; Guy Lombardo.

Honor Roll of Hits - 1937 .... RCA (EP) EPA-525 5-10 54
Honor Roll of Hits - 1936-1937 .... RCA (M) LPM-3180 25-40 54
(10–inch LP.) Fats Waller; Guy Lombardo; Phil Harris; Sammy Kaye; Tommy Dorsey; Ralph Flanagan; others.

Honor Roll of Hits - 1938 .... RCA (EP) EPA-526 5-10 54
(10–inch LP.) Hal Kemp; Tony Martin; Larry Clinton; Guy Lombardo.

Honor Roll of Hits - 1939 .... RCA (EP) EPA-527 5-10 54
Honor Roll of Hits - 1938-1939 .... RCA (M) LPM-3181 25-40 54
(10–inch LP.) Hal Kemp; Tony Martin; Guy Lombardo; Larry Clinton; Glahe Musette; Glenn Miller; Hugo Winterhalter.

Honor Roll of Hits - 1940 ... RCA (EP) EPA-528 5-10 54
(10-inch LP.) Glenn Miller; Tommy Dorsey.
Honor Roll of Hits - 1941 ... RCA (EP) EPA-529 5-10 54
Honor Roll of Hits - 1940-1941 ... RCA (M) LPM-3182 25-40 54
(10-inch LP.) Glenn Miller; Tommy Dorsey; Sammy Kaye; Freddy Martin; Artie Shaw.
Honor Roll of Hits - 1942 ... RCA (EP) EPA-530 5-10 54
(10-inch LP.) Glenn Miller; Tommy Dorsey; Freddy Martin.
Honor Roll of Hits - 1943 ... RCA (EP) EPA-531 5-10 54
Honor Roll of Hits - 1942-1943 ... RCA (M) LPM-3183 25-40 54
(10-inch LP.) Glenn Miller; Freddy Martin; Tommy Dorsey; Henri Rene; Hugo Winterhalter.
Honor Roll of Hits - 1944 ... RCA (EP) EPA-532 5-10 54
Honor Roll of Hits - 1945 ... RCA (EP) EPA-533 5-10 54
Honor Roll of Hits - 1944-1945 ... RCA (M) LPM-3184 25-40 54
(10-inch LP.) Hugo Winterhalter; Eddy Arnold; Dinah Shore; Tommy Dorsey; Perry Como; Hal McIntyre; Vaughn Monroe.
Hoot Tonight ... Warner Bros. (M) W-1512 10-20 63
Hoot Tonight ... Warner Bros. (S) WS-1512 15-20 63
Gateway Singers; Lynn Gold; Phoenix Singers; others.
Hootenanny ... Diplomat (S) DS-2299 8-12 60s
Bob Riley Group; Song Spinners; Tex Johnson & His Six Shooters; Sing Alongers; Glitters; Sam Wright Group; Jack Arthur; Billy King & Jacks; Ginny Starr.
Hootenanny ... World Pacific (M) WP-1813 10-20 63
Hootenanny ... World Pacific (S) WP-1813 10-20 63
Bud & Travis; Lightnin' Hopkins; Lynn Gold; Goldcoast Singers; Brownie & Sonny; Folkswingers; Barbara Dand; Bumble Bee Slim.
Hootenanny ... King (M) 862 15-25 63
Hootenanny ... MGM (M) E-4154 15-20 63
Hootenanny ... MGM (S) SE-4154 15-25 63
Mark Dinning; Randy Sparks; Gateway Singers; Addiss & Crofut - the Little Sisters; Stan Wilson; Pickard Family; Ramblers Three.
Hootenanny ... RCA (M) PRM-152 10-20 64
Hootenanny ... Riverside (M) RM-7539 10-20 63
Hootenanny ... Riverside (S) RS9-7539 10-20 63
Hootenanny '64: see Zenith Hootenanny Special
Hootenanny (Kapp): see At the Hootenanny
Hootenanny at Carnegie Hall ... Folkways (M) FN-2512 20-30 60
Rev. Gary Davis; Hally Wood; Pete Seeger; Tony Kraber; Jerry Silverman; Will Geer; Mike Seeger.
Hootenanny at the Limelight (5 LP) ... Somerset (M) SF-108 15-25 63
(Boxed set.) Homer & Barnstormers; Rusty Adams; Appalachians; Don Bailey; Happy Goseplaires; Jerry Shook; Wanderin' Five; Buzz Wilson; Mariachis del Mexico.
Hootenanny at the Troubadour ... Horizon (M) WP-1616 10-20 63
Hootenanny at the Troubadour ... Horizon (S) SWP-1616 10-20 63
Hoyt Axton; Travis Edmonson; Sherwood Singers; Travis; Barry & Barry; Judy Henske; Paul Sykes; Judy Mayhan; Other Singers; Phil Campos.
Hootenanny Bluegrass Style ... Mercury (M) MG-20857 10-20 63
Hootenanny Bluegrass Style ... Mercury (S) SR-60857 10-20 63
Flatt & Scruggs; Stanley Brothers; Anita Carter; others.
Hootenanny Country Style ... Spin-O-Rama (M) M-126 8-12 60s
Wetherly Brothers; Bayou Boys; Sons of the Soil; Virginia Mountaineers.
Hootenanny Hoe Down ... Camay (SE) CA 3036 8-12 60s
Burl Ives; Connie Haines; Weavers; Mitchell Choirboys; Dinning Sisters; Florian Zabach; Robin Roberts; Jordanaires; Mary Mayo.
Hootenanny Hoot ... MGM (M) E-4172 8-15 63
Hootenanny Hoot ... MGM (S) SE-4172 10-25 63
(Soundtrack.) Sheb Wooley; Mark Dinning; Gateway Trio; Chris Crosby; Cathie Taylor; Joe & Eddie.
Hootenanny Jubilee ... Camay (SE) CA 3028 8-12 60s
Burl Ives; Weavers; Hank Fort; Rowena; Robin Roberts.
Hootenanny Live at the Bitter End ... FM (M) FM-309 10-20 63
Hootenanny Live at the Bitter End ... FM (S) FS-309 10-20 63
Jo Mapes; Bob Carey; Fred Neil; Len Chandler; others.
Hootenanny Parade ... Camay (SE) CA 3022 8-12 60s
Weavers; Connie Haines; Mitchell Choirboys; Rowena; others.
Hootenanny Party Pak ... Time (M) T-52091 10-20 63
Hootenanny Party Pak ... Time (S) ST-2091 10-20 63
Sonny Lester; others.
Hootenanny Tonight ... Folkways (M) FN-2511 20-25 59
Pete Seeger; Les Pine; Jean Hart; Al Moss; Laura Duncan; Earl Robinson; Sonny Terry; Betty Sanders; Jackie Berman; Jerry Silverman; Leon Bibb; Elizabeth Knight; Jewish Young Folksingers; Bob & Louise DeCormier; Sylvia Kahn.
Horizons ... K-Tel NU 9530 8-12 81
Stephanie Mills; Hall & Oates; Natalie Cole; Larry Graham; Commodores; Melissa Manchester; Dionne Warwick; Don Williams; Korgis; Stacy Lattisaw; Fred Knoblock; Air Supply; Robbie Dupree; Dirt Band.
Hot Boppin' Girls ... Supersonic Sound (S) FV-1169 10-15 84
Barbara Pitman; Jackie Johnson; Laura Lee Perkins; Georgia Gibbs; Bonnie Guitar; Debbie Stevens; Bunny Paul; Patsy Cline; Katie Webster; Penny Candy; Dorothy Collins; Jamie Horton; Jean Chapel; Dolly Cooper.
Hot Canaries ... Columbia (M) CL-2534 20-30 56
(10-inch LP.)
Hot Chicken ... Jay Jay (M) 5069 8-12 64
Hot Chicken ... Jay Jay (S) 5069 8-12 64
Lil' Wally; Andy Doll; Eddie Blatnick; others.
Hot Dogs Old Gold ... Atlantic (M) 8068 10-20 62

Hot Hits .... Juke Box Int'l (S) TV-DISC-74001 5-10 74
(Mail order offer.)

Hot Hits to Warm Your Winter .... Polygram (S) SA-054 8-12 85
(Promotional issue only. In-store sampler.) Deep Purple; Big Country; Kiss; Martin Briley; Kool & Gang; Carol Lynn Townes; Kurtis Blow; Stephanie Mills; Shakatak; Cosmetic.

Hot Nights & City Lights .... K-Tel (S) TU-2710 5-10 79
Sister Sledge; Anita Ward; Village People; Bionic Boogie; Gonzalles; Amii Stewart; Claudia Barry; Gloria Gaynor; Blondie; Arpeggio; T-Connection; Instant Funk; Evelyn "Champagne" King; Jacksons.

Hot Ones .... EMI (S) SPRO 9865/9866 8-12 82
(Promotional only in-store sampler.) J. Geils Band; Stray Cats; Little Steven & Disciples of Soul; Talk Talk; Michael Stanley Band; George Thorogood; Australian Crawl; Kim Carnes; Kenny Rogers; Sheena Easton; David Lasley; Michael Murphey; Cliff Richard; Gery Rafferty.

Hot Ones (2 LP) .... K-Tel (S) 2750 8-12 78
Abba; Yvonne Elliman; Atlanta Rhythm Section; Andrew Gold; Dave Mason; Dan Hill; England Dan & John Ford Coley; Gene Cotton; Smokie; Jay Ferguson; KC & Sunshine Band; Parliament; Trammps; Player; Emotions; Barry White; B.J. Thomas.

Hot Parts .... Kama Sutra (S) KSBS 2054 12-15 72
(Soundtrack.) Steve Martin; Bert Sommer; Montage; Allan Nicholls; Michael Brown.

Hot Rocks .... Pickwick (S) SPC-3775 5-10 80
Classics IV; Drifters; Bobby Day; ; Sam & Dave; Percy Sledge; Kingston Trio; Shirelles; Little Anthony & Imperials.

Hot Rocks, Epic Sampler .... Epic (S) AS-409 5-10 70s
(Promotional issue only.) Meat Loaf; Wet Willie; Crack the Sky; Network; Edgar Winter; Kansas; Crawler; Charlie Daniels Band; Starcastle; Cheap Trick.

Hot Rod City: see QUADS / Grand Prix / Customs

Hot Rod Drag Races: see DALE, Dick / Surfaris / Fireballs

Hot Rod Magazine Rally: see SUPER STOCKS / Hot Rod Rog / Shutdown Douglas

Hot Rod Rally: see SUPER STOCKS / Hot Rod Rog / Shutdown Douglas

Hot Soul Summer .... Polydor (S) SA 016 8-12 76
Roy Ayers; Joe Simon; Fatback Band; Creative Source; Millie Jackson.

Hot Tracks .... K-Tel (S) TU-2990 5-10 80s
Michael Sembello; Eurythmics; Rick Springfield; Styx; Billy Idol; Chris DeBurgh; Animals; Police; Bryan Adams; Def Leppard; Wall of Voodoo; Naked Eyes; Patrick Simmons; Shalamar.

Hot Tracks .... Hot Tracks (S) SA-3-8 100-150 84
(12-inch EP with remixed versions. Promotional issue only.) Paul McCartney; others.

Hot Wax Greatest Hits .... Hot Wax (S) HA-710 10-15 72
Honey Cone; 100 Proof (Aged in Soul); Flaming Ember; Laura Lee; Silent Majority.

Hotels, Motels and Road Shows (2 LP) .... Capricorn (S) CPN-2-0208 10-20 78
Stillwater; Sea Level; Dixie Dregs; Marshall Tucker Band; Bonnie Bramlet; Grinderswitch; Elvin Bishop; Wet Willie; Richard Betts; Greg Allman; Allman Brothers Band.

Hot'lanta Home Cookin' .... CBS (S) PD9162 20-25 81
(Promotional only picture disc made for WKLS radio. 800 made.)

Hot'lanta Home Cookin' .... CBS (S) PD9162 35-45 81
(Promotional only picture disc made for Turtles Records' Hilton Getaway. 200 made.)

Hound Dog's Old Gold .... Atlantic (M) 8068 30-40 62
Willie Mae Thornton; Mello-Kings; Coasters; Jack Scott; Chuck Willis; Wilbert Harrison; Shirelles; Spaniels; Chuck Berry; Fiestas; Al Brown & Toppers; Clyde McPhatter.

Hour with Irving Berlin .... Royale (M) 1343 8-12
Morton Downey; Jack Smith; Georgia Gibbs; Thelma Carpenter; Danny O'Neil.

House Of Flowers .... Columbia (M) ML-4969 8-12 54
(Soundtrack. Columbia Record Club issue.) Pearl Bailey; Diahann Carroll; Juanita Hall; Rawn Spearman; Ada Moore; Miriam Burton; Dolores Harper; Enid Mosier.

House Party .... Motown (S) MOT-6296 8-10 90
(Soundtrack.) Arts & Crafts; Today; Force MDs; Full Force Family; Flavor Flav; Kid 'N' Play; Kenny Vaughan & Art of Love.

House Party .... Decca (M) DL-38242 15-25 63

House Party .... Decca (M) DL-4206 15-25 60s
Teresa Brewer; Mills Brothers; Russ Morgan; Jimmy Durante; Lawrence Welk; Roberta Sherwood; Four Aces; Percy Faith; Pearl Bailey; Judy Garland; Frankie Carle; Tommy Dorsey.

Houston Home Cookin' .... Columbia/ABS (S) 001 20-25 82
(Promotional only picture made for "Sprite Concert Series.")

How I Got to Be a Mouseketeer .... Disneyland (M) 3916 15-25 62

How I Got to Be a Mouseketeer .... Disneyland (S) ST-3916 20-30 62
Various Mousekeeters speaking.

How the West Was Won .... RCA Victor (M) LOP-6070 25-35 60

How the West Was Won .... RCA Victor (S) LSO-6070 45-55 60
(Soundtrack. Gatefold covers and booklets. Based on a Life Magazine series that inspired the film.) Bing Crosby; Rosemary Clooney; Sam Hinton; Jack Halloran Singers; Jimmie Driftwood; Tarry Town Trio; Mormon Tabernacle Choir.

How to Blow Your Mind and Have a Freak Out Party .... Audio Fidelity (S) AFSD-6184 25-35

How to Get the Most Out of Your Stereo .... Warner Bros. (S) XS-1400 100-125 60
(Soundtrack. Gold vinyl, audiophile issue.) George Greeley; John Scott Trotter; Frank Comstock; Buddy Cole; Ira Ironstrings; Gus Farney; Warner Bros. Military Band; Don Ralke; Matty Matlock & Paducah Patrol; Spike Jones; Warren Barker.

How to Stuff a Wild Bikini .... Wand (M) 671 20-25 65

How to Stuff a Wild Bikini .... Wand (S) S-671 30-40 65
(Soundtrack.) Annette Funicello; Kingsmen; Mickey Rooney; Lu Ann Simms; Brian Donlevy; Harvey Lembeck.

Huggie Boy's Rare R&B Oldies .... Dub Tone (M) LP-1245 20-30 63
Colts; Squires; Phil & Harv; Twilighters; Richard Berry; Cufflinks; Johnnie & Joe; Robert & Johnny; Johnny Flamingo; Pips; Little Julian Herrera; Clovers; Spaniels; Gene & Eunice; Youngsters; Johnny "Guitar" Watson; Medallions; Channels.

Huggie Boy's Rare R-B Oldies, Vol. II .... Original Oldies (M) LP-1247 15-25 63
Buster Brown; Orlons; Rene & Ray; Safaris; Yvonne Carroll; Paradons; Bob & Earl; Capris; Oscar McLollie & Jeanette Baker; Joe & Ann; Passions; Johnny Ace; Quintones; Frankie & Johnny Dubs; Johnny Flamingo; Rosie & Originals; Little Caesar & Romans.

Huggie Boy's Rare R&B Oldies, Vol. III .... Original Oldies (M) LP-1249 15-25 64
Johnnie & Joe; Vito & Salutations; Jerry Glenn; Premiers; Scarlets; Charles McCullough; Perez Brothers; Blendtones; Bob & Earl; Robins; Pentagons; Bo Diddley; Blue Jays; Johnny Flamingo; Baby Washington; Dots.

Huggy (sic) Boy Presents 20 Big Oldies, Vol. 1 .... Hollywood Knickerbocker (M) 1002 10-20 60s
Bobby Day; Jerry Butler; Eugene Church; Rosie & Originals; Johnny "Guitar" Watson; Marvin & Johnny; Jimmy Norman; Gene Allison; Theola Kilgore; Jesse Belvin; El Dorados; Jimmy Reed; Maxine Brown; Innocents; Flamingos; Kathy Young; Dells; Dubs; Phil & Harv; Pentagons.

Huggy (sic) Boy Presents 20 Big Oldies, Vol. 2 .... Hollywood Knickerbocker (M) 1003 10-20 60s
Crystals; Gene Chandler; Angels; Echoes; Fireflies; Dixie Cups; Gladys Knight & Pips; Otis Redding; Johnny Thunder; Charts; Jerry Butler; Blue-Bells; Little Caesar & Romans; Richard "Dimples" Fields; Jerry Butler; Maxine Brown; Channels; Yvonne Carroll; Danleers; Classics; Shep & Limelites. Hollywood Flames; Daylighters.

Hullabaloo .... Design (M) DLP-191 10-20 65
Hullabaloo .... Design (S) SDLP-191 10-20 65
Roy Orbison; Roger Miller; Bobby Freeman; Betty Everett; Gene Pitney; Maxine Brown; Lloyd Price; Garnet Mimms; Brook Benton; Clovers.

Hullabaloo .... Pickwick (S) SDLP-191 5-10 75
Roy Orbison; Roger Miller; Bobby Freeman; Betty Everett; Gene

Hullabaloo Au-Go-Go .... Design (M) DLP-211 10-20 65
Hullabaloo Au-Go-Go .... Design (S) SDLP-211 10-20 65
Barry McGuire; Roy Orbison; 4 Seasons; Gene Pitney; Bobby Rydell; Tommy Roe; Jimmy Smith; Glen Campbell; Ronnie Dove; Freddie Scott; Roger Miller; Bobby Freeman; Brook Benton.

Hullabaloo with the Stars .... Wyncote (M) W-9080 15-20 64
Hullabaloo with the Stars .... Wyncote (S) SW-9080 15-20 64
Chubby Checker; Dovells; Orlons; Dee Dee Sharp; Bobby Rydell; Tymes.

Hullabaloo with the Stars, Vol. 2 .... Wyncote (M) W-9100 15-20 64
Hullabaloo with the Stars, Vol. 2 .... Wyncote (S) SW-9100 15-20 64
Impressions with Jerry Butler; Chubby Checker; Bobby Rydell; Dee Dee Sharp; Tymes; Orlons; Dovells; Jo Ann Campbell; Don Covay.

Human Orchestra Rhythm Quartets in the '30s .... Clanka Lanka (M) CL-144,003 5-10 85
Five Jones Boys; Golden Gate Quartet; Lewis Bronzeville Five; Four Blackbirds; Norfolk Jazz Quartet; Three Peppers; Five Breezes; Rollin Smith's Rascals; Mills Brothers; Three Keys; Ink Spots; Mississippi Mud Mashers; Four Southern Singers; Five Jinks; Jones Boys Sing Band; Cabineers.

Hurt So Bad: see Rock of Ages – Early Sixties Soul: 1960-1975 (Hurt So Bad)

Hungry for Hits (2 LP) .... K-Tel (S) ???? 8-12 84

Hustle Hits .... Delite (S) DEP-2019 5-10 75
Gary Toms' Empire; Crown Heights Affair; Kool & Gang; others.

Hy Lit Presents Collectors Gold .... Collectables (S) 7000 8-12
(Colored vinyl.) Globetrotters; Fidelitys; Corvairs; Lydells; Ivy-Tones; Pentagons; Four J's; Mohawks; Earls; Superiors; Videos; Anthony & Sophomores; Dreamlovers; Dell Vikings; Classics; Blue Notes; Eternals; Lee Andrews & Hearts; Candy & Kisses; Shades of Blue; Danleers.

Hy Lit Show Album .... Post (S) 675 8-12
Bobby Hebb; Association; J.J. Jackson; Beau Brummels; Dobie Gray; Cascades; Bobby Fuller Four; Gene Chandler; Terry Stafford; Neil Diamond; Lovin' Spoonful; Shirelles; B.J. Thomas; Shirley Ellis; Duprees; Shelly Fabres; Billy Stewart; Cathy Jean & Roomates; Ronnie & Hi-Lites; Felice Taylor; Jerry Butler.

Hymns, America's 28 Favorite Hymns (2 LP) .... Word (S) WST 8117/2 8-12 60s
(Includes 12-page booklet.) Claude Rhea & Dick Anthony Choristers; Bill Mann & Earl Backus; Frank Boggs; Ralph Carmichael; Serenaders Quartet; Bill Pearce & Dick Anthony; Lew Charles & Charles & Magnuson; Bill McVey; Flo Price; Haven of Rest Quartet; Billy Graham Crusade a Cappella Choir; Paul Mickelson; Moody Bible Institute Musical Groups; Abilene Christian College a Cappella Choir; Jerry Barnes; Kurt Kaiser Singers.

Hymns of Gold .... Columbia Special Products (S) CSP 10779 5-10 72
(TV offer only.) Jerry Lee Lewis; Johnny Cash; Anita Kerr Singers; Roy Clark; Lynn Anderson; Jimmie Rodgers; David Houston; Jim Nabors; Marty Robbins; Pat Boone; Bob Daniels; Ray Price; George Morgan; Jimmy Dean; Patsy Cline; Patti Page; Charlie Walker; Tammy Wynette; Statler Brothers;

Hymns of Gold, Vol. 2 .... Columbia Special Products (S) CSP 12620 5-10 74
(TV offer only.) Lynn Anderson; Anita Bryant; Wayne Newton; Pat Boone; Johnny Cash; Jordanaires; Jimmy Dean; Jim Nabors; Jo Stafford; Stuart Hamblen; George Jones; Bob Daniels; Roy Clark; Suzy Hamblen; Rosemary Clooney; Wanda Jackson; Tammy Wynette; Statler Bros.; Carter Family.

I.R.S. Greatest Hits, Vol. 2 and 3 (2 LP) .... I.R.S. (S) SP 70800 15-25 81
Police; Cramps; Fleshtones; Brian James; Henry Badowski; Alternative TV; Squeeze; Skarsh; Damned; Klark Kent; Stranglers; Chelsea; Humans; Sector 27; John Cale; Jools Holland; Payolas; Fall; Fashion; Patrick D. Martin; Oingo Boingo; Buzz Cocks; Wazmo Nariz.

I Asked for Water, She Gave Me Gasoline .... Imperial (S) LP-12455 10-15 70
Jim Pitts; Jim & Raphael; Andy Fernbach Connexion; Tony McPhee; Jo-Ann Kelly & Groundhogs; Brett Marvin & Thunderbolts; John Lewis; Graham Hines.

I Believe .... Harmony (S) KH-30480 5-10 71
Frankie Laine; Anita Bryant; Johnny Cash; Jim Nabors; others.

I Believe in Music (6 LP) .... Columbia Musical Treasury (S) 6P 6115 15-25 74
Janis Joplin; Hollies; Ray Conniff; Freddy Weller; Barbara Fairchild; Bobby Vinton; Mac Davis; Charlie Rich; Johnny Mathis; Peter Nero; Vikki Carr; Roy Clark; Lynn Anderson; Sonny James; Tanya Tucker; Earl Scruggs; Jerry Vale; Andre Kostelanetz; Ray Price; Tony Bennett; Percy Faith; Donna Fargo; Johnny Paycheck; Boots Randolph; Ray Stevens; Marty Robbins; Blood, Sweat & Tears; Steve Lawrence & Eydie Gorme; Sammy Davis Jr.; Clint Holmes; Jody Miller; Johnny Cash; June Carter; Jerry Lee Lewis; Staple Singers; Jerry Reed; Tom T. Hall; Tammy Wynette; Jim Nabors.

I Couldn't Believe My Eyes .... Bluesway (S) BLS-6059
I Dig Acapella .... Cat Time (M) 201 8-12
I Dig Acapella .... Cat Time (M) 202 8-12
I Dig Acapella, Vol. 2 .... Score (M) LP-4002 100-150 57
I Dig Rock and Roll
Shirley & Lee; Amos Milburn; Lloyd Glenn; Charles Brown; Lynn Hope; Gene & Eunice; Peppermint Harris; Five Keys; Helen Humes; Richard Lewis.

I Got Rhythm: see MILLER, Dale / John James / Sam Mitchell / Ton Van Bergeyk

I Have to Paint My Face .... Arhoolie (S) F 1005 10-15
Sam Chaman; K.C. Douglas; Sam Chatman; Big Joe Williams; Bukka White; Wade Walton; R.C. Smith; Butch Cage.

I Hear Music .... Sacred (M) LP-7-3021 5-10
Ralph Carmichael; Bob Daniels; Sunday Sing Trio; Lorin Whitney; Norman Nelson; Wesley & Marilyn Tuttle & Charles Magnuson; Patti Stiles; Robert Bowman & Les Barnett; Alan McGill; Bud Tutmarc; Beth Farman; Bob McGrath; Mark Davidson.

I Like Jazz .... Columbia (M) JZ 1 20-30 55
Wally Rose; Bessie Smith; Louis Armstrong; Eddie Condon; Bix Beidrbecke; Phil Napoleon; Duke Ellington; Teddy Wilson & Billie Holiday; Original Benny Goodman Orchestra; Pete Rugolo; Turk Murphy; Dave Brubeck.

I Live for the Sun .... EMI America Treasury (S) ST 17221 8-12 86
Fantastic Baggys; Fender IV; Sunrays; Richie Allen & Pacific Surfers; Superstocks; Frank N. Stein & Dropouts; Wailers; Davie Allan; Jan & Dean; Beach Boys; Ventures; Sandals.

I Love Music .... Ronco (S) R 2120 5-10 76
Diana Ross; England Dan & John Ford Coley; Hall & Oates; Walter Murphy & Big Apple Band; Miracles; Melissa Manchester; Eric Carmen; Ronnie Dyson; Barry Manilow; Spinners; Silver; Aretha Franklin; Bay City Rollers; Starbuck; Outlaws; Lenny LeBlanc; Jackson Five; Manhattans.

I Remember Bebop (2 LP) .... Columbia (S) C2-35381 10-15

I Want to Take You Higher: see Rock of Ages – American Soul: 1961: 1972 (I Want to Take You Higher)

I Was a Teenage Zombie .... Enigma (S) SJ-73296 8-10 87
(Soundtrack.) Smithereens; Los Lobos; Alex Chilton; Ben Vaughn Group; Bob Pfeifer; Fleshtones; Del Fuegos; DB's; Dream Syndicate; Violent Femmes; Waitresses.

I Will Sing .... Columbia Musical Treasury (SE) 1P 6213 5-10 76
Lynn Anderson; George Jones; Barbara Mandrell; Johnny Cash; Rosey Nix; Charlie Rich; Ray Price; Tammy Wynette; David Houston; Tanya Tucker; Roy Clark. (Columbia House Record Club issue.)

I'll Be Home For Christmas .... Pickwick (S) SPC 1009 5-10
Dean Martin; others.

I'll Still Write Your Name in the Sand .... Nashville (SE) NLP-2067 5-10 69
Mac Wiseman; Jim & Jesse; Stanley Brothers; Flatt & Scruggs.

I'm Gonna Git You Sucka .... Arista (S) AL8-8574 8-10 88
(Soundtrack.) Gap Band; Jennifer Holliday; Jermaine Jackson; Curtis Mayfield; Friends of Distinction; Boogie Down Productions; Four Tops; Aretha Franklin; K-9 Posse; Fishbone; Too Nice.

I'm in the Mood for Mod .... Columbia Special Products (S) CSP 343 8-12 60s
Fiesta Brass; Barbra Streisand; Ray Conniff; Andre Kostelanetz; Village Stompers; Ernie Heckscher; Charlie Byrd; Les & Larry Elgart; Brothers Four; Percy Faith.

I'm Telling You Now .... Tower (M) T-5003 15-25 65
I'm Telling You Now .... Tower (SE) DT-5003 15-25 65
Freddie & Dreamers; Linda Laine & Sinners; Four Just Men; Mike Rabin & Demons; Toggerty Five; Heinz.

Ice Cream and Suckers .... Mercury (S) 61213 10-15 69

Idolmaker .... A&M (S) 4840 8-10 80
(Soundtrack.) Darlene Love; Jesse Frederick; Nino Tempo; Colleen Fitzpatrick; Peter Gallagher; Sweet Inspirations & London Fog; Ray Sharkey.

Idols .... Era (S) BU 4140 5-10 81
Frankie Avalon; Bobby Vee; Fabian; Bobby Rydell; Everly Brothers; Mark Dinning; Johnny Tillotson; Tab Hunter; Jimmy Clanton; Ritchie Valens.

Idols of Rock & Roll (3 LP) .... RCA Special Products (S) DVL3-0271 10-15 77
Dion; Neil Sedaka; Tommy James & Shondells; Bobby Vinton; Sam Cooke; Jimmy Rodgers; Fabian; Del Shannon; Paul Anka; Jimmy Clanton; Buddy Knox; Conway Twitty.

If the Shoe Fits .... Warner Bros. (S) PRO-A-2093 5-10 83
Echo & Bunnymen; Laurie Anderson; T-Bone Burnettt; Tim Scott; Gang of Four; Aztec Camera; Juluka.

Images .... K-Tel (S) 9620 5-10 76
Neil & Dara Sedaka; Manhattans; Felix Cavaliere; Andy Gibb; Rita Coolidge; Bernadette Peters; Captain & Tennille; Ali Thomson; Pure Prairie League; Tommy James; Eddie Rabbitt; Kool & Gang; Photo Glo; Lauren Wood.

Images in Dynagroove .... RCA (S) PRS-160 8-12 64
Sid Ramin; Frankie Carle; Dick Schory; Melachrino Strings; Marty Gold; Ann-Margret; Arthur Fiedler; Leonard Pennario; Leontyne Price; Fritz Reiner; Erick Friedman; Erich Leinsdorf. (Special products for New Vista Solid State.)

Immediate A's & B's: the Singles Collection (2 LP) .... Compleat (S) 672010-1 10-20 85
All Stars featuring Jimmy Page; Arnold; Mockingbirds; Duncan Browne; Marquis of Kensington; Billy Nichols; Fifth Avenue; Le Fleurs De Lus; Jimmy Tarbuck; John Mayall & Bluesbreakers; Savoy Brown; Albert Lee.

Imperial Musicians 1951-1962, Rhythm in Rhythm & Blues .... EMI America (S) SQ 17265 8-12 87
Fats Domino; Dave Batholomew; Smiley Lewis; Smilin' Joe; Archibald; Earl King; Huey Smith & Clowns; Ford Eaglin; Joe Houston; Big Jay McNeely.

Imperials Records 1949-1957 .... EMI America (S) ST 17200 8-12 86
Roy Brown; Fats Domino; Joe Turner; Jewel King; Spiders; Smiley Lewis; Bobby Marchan; Tommy Ridgley; Billy Tate.

Improved—Ultra Dance .... RCA (S) AFL-1-5322 5-10 70s
Hues Corporation; Odyssey; Vicki Sue Robinson; Brainstorm; Charme; Keni Burke; Grey & Hanks.

In a Mellow Mood (5 LP) .... MCA Special Products (S) DNX 510 15-25 70s
Pete Fountain; Midas Touch; Bert Kaempfert; Brenda Lee; Burt Bacharach; Pete Fountain; John & Anne Ryder; Peter Duchin; Roger Williams & Salvation Navy Band; Leroy Anderson; Kitty Kallen; Four Aces; Teresa Brewer; Billy Williams; Tommy Dorsey; Peggy Lee & Gordon Jenkins; Mills Brothers; McGuire Sisters; Gordon Jenkins & Weavers; Florence Henderson; Lenny Dee; Roger Williams; Vincent Bell; Jack Jones; Rafael Mendez; Woody Herman; Stan Kenton; Count Basie; Artie Shaw; Bob Crosby; Jimmy Lunceford; Glenn Miller; Les Brown; Tommy James & Shondells; Ed Evanko; Cuff Links; Karen Wyman; Carmen Cavallaro; John Rowles; Lenny Dee.

In a Sentimental Mood .... RCA Special Products (S) PRS 419 5-10 72
Al Hirt; Arthur Fiedler & Boston Pops; Hill Bowen; Norman Luboff Choir; Percy Faith; Skitch Henderson; Melanchrino Strings; Cascading Voices of Hugo & Luigi Chorus; Paul Horn Quintet; Morton Gould.

In Concert .... Ronco (S) R-1975 5-10 74
Hues Corporation; Donny & Marie; O'Jays; Bachman-Turner Overdrive; Jim Weatherly; Red Bone; O.C. Smith; Eric Burdon & Jimmy Witherspoon; Ray Stevens; Lynyrd Skynyrd; Tymes; Johnny Bristol; Jim Stafford; Golden Earring; Brownsville Station; Jimmy Witherspoon; Staple Singers; Mac Davis; Paper Lace; Reunion.

In Concert (2 LP) .... RCA (S) CPL2-1014 5-10 75
Charley Pride; Dolly Parton; Gary Stewart; Ronnie Milsap; Jerry Reed; Chet Atkins.

In Crowd .... Design (M) DLP-252 10-20 65

In Crowd .... Design (S) SDLP-252 10-20 65
Bobby Goldsboro; Jan & Dean; Ronnie Dove; Johnny Rivers; Isley Brothers; Ray Charles; Lou Christie; Paul Revere & Raiders; Chuck Jackson; Joe Tex.

In Crowd .... International Award (S) AKS-296 10-20 65
Bobby Goldsboro; Petula Clark; Ronnie Dove; Johnny Rivers; Isley Brothers; Ray Charles; Lou Christie; Paul Revere & Raiders; Chuck Jackson; Joe Tex.

In Harmony .... Warner/Sesame Street (S) BSK-3481 5-10 80
Doobie Brothers; James Taylor; Carly Simon; Bette Midler; Ernie & Cookie Monster; Al Jarreau; Linda Rondstadt & Wendy Waldman; Libby Titus & Dr. John; George Benson & Pauline Wilson; Lucy Simon; Kate Taylor & Simon-Taylor Family; Livingston Taylor.

In Harmony, Vol. 2 .... Columbia (S) BFC 37641 10-15 81
Billy Joel; James Taylor; Lou Rawls & Deniece Williams; Janis Ian; Crystal Gayle; Dr. John; Kenny Loggins; Carly & Lucy Simon; Bruce Springsteen; Teddy Pendergrass.

In Hollywood .... Columbia Special Products (S) CSS 1340 5-10 60s
Robert Goulet; Andre Kostelanetz; Ray Conniff; Barbra Streisand; Percy Faith.

In Loving Memory, Vol. 1 .... Motown (S) M5-207V1 5-10

In Memory .... King (M) 835 15-25 63

In Memory .... King (S) 835 15-25 63
Hawkshaw Hawkins; Cowboy Copas; others.

In Memory of these Great Artists .... King (M) 887 15-25 64

In Memory of these Great Artists .... King (S) KS-835 15-25 64
Hawkshaw Hawkins; Cowboy Copas; others.

In the Beginning .... Checker (S) 3014 10-20
Harold Smith Majestic Singers; Little Milton; Aretha Franklin; Earnest Franklin; Dorothy Best; Martha Bass; Sammy Lewis.

In the Beginning .... ATV (S) ATV-VM1 25-25 80
(Promotional issue only.) Elvis Presley; Beatles; Rolling Stones; Sam Cooke; Little Richard; Bill Haley & His Comets; Larry Williams; Donny & Marie Osmond; Rascals; Mitch Ryder; Linda Hopkins; Gene Simmons; Everly Brothers; Kingsmen; Buddy Holly.

In the Dancing Mood .... Columbia (M) CB-14 10-20 56
(Record Club issue.) Benny Goodman; Les Brown; Erroll Garner; Les Elgart; Harry James; Art Van Damme; Woody Herman; Claude Thornhill; Jimmie Lunceford; Paul Weston; Percy Faith; Sammy Kaye.

In the Still of the Night: see Rock of Ages – Doo Wop Groups: 1951-1962 (In the Still of the Night)

Inauguration Album (2 LP) .... Columbia (S) JC-1/S 34706 10-20 77
Linda Ronstadt; Paul Simon; Loretta Lynn; Aretha Franklin; Beverly Sills; Shirley MacLaine; others. (ISpecial issue for Jimmy Carter's inauguration.)

Incense and Oldies .... Buddah (SE) BDS-5014 10-15 68
Dixie Cups; Tommy James & Shondells; Tradewinds; Shangri-Las; Sopwith Camel; Jelly Beans; Ad Libs.

Incredible Collection: Dr. Knew's Music .... RCA (S) DJL1-4860 8-10 84
(Promotional issue only.) JoBoxers; Parachute Club; Bongos; Eurythmics; Blue Zoo; Hayse Fantayzee; Wide Boy Awake; Nona Hendryx.

Innerspace .... Geffen (S) GHS-24161 8-10 87
(Soundtrack.) Rod Stewart; Wang Chung; Narada Michael Walden; Berlin; Sam Cooke; Jerry Goldsmith.

Inside Moves .... Full Moon (S) FMH-3506 8-10 80
(Soundtrack.) Spinners; Boz Scaggs; Ambrosia; Lady Sylvia; Leo Sayers; Eagles; Pablo Cruise.

Instant Hits: see Star Lines (Artist Introductions to) Instant Hits

Instant Replay, Vol. 2: see Jerry Steven's Instant Replay, Vol. 2

Instant Replay .... Tower (SE) ST-5157 15-25 69
Arrows; Ian Whitcomb; Sunrays; Standells; Freddie & Dreamers; Eternity's Children.

Instant Replays .... Dimension (S) 16103 5-10
Carol Channing; Peter Duchin; Pete Fountain; Bert Kaempfert; Frankie Laine; Bobby Byrne.

Instant Replays .... Evolution (S) 16103 5-10
Carol Channing; Peter Duchin; Pete Fountain; Bert Kaempfert; Frankie Laine; Bobby Byrne. (Special products release for Voice of Music.)

Instrumental Christmas Favorites .... Capitol (S) STBB-349 8-12 69
David Rose; Guy Lombardo; Jackie Gleason; George Shearing; others.

Instrumental Golden Goodies: see Golden Goodies, Vol. 13

Instrumental Madness .... Ostrich (S) OR-002 8-10 81
Lenny & Thundertones; X-Terminators; Wailers; Shades; Conny & Bell Hops; Eddie Smith & Hornets; Triumphs; Noblemen; Strangers; Velvetones; Thunder Rocks; Jades; Royaltones; Genteels; Tony March & Rockets.

Instrumental Music of Southern Appalachians .... Tradition (M) 1007 25-35 50s
Hobart Smith; Etta Baker; Boone Reid; Edd Presnell; Richard Chase; Lacey Phillips.

Instrumentals: see History of Surf Music (the Instrumentals)

Intensified! Original Ska 1962-66 .... Mango (S) MLPS 9524 8-12 79
Roland Alphonso; Eric Morris; Baba Brooks; Charms; Shenley Duffus; Don Drummond & Drumbago; Skatalites; Maytals; Tommy McCook; Stranger Cole; Derrick & Patsy; Don Drummond; Justin Hines.

International Affair .... RCA Special Products (S) PRS 420 5-10 72
Arthur Fiedler & Boston Pops; Melachrino Strings; Norman Luboff Choir; Al Hirt; Morton Gould; Peter Nero; Living Strings; Robert Shaw Chorale; Sergio Franchi.

Into the Night .... MCA (S) 5561 8-10 85
(Soundtrack.) B.B. King; Patti LaBelle; Thelma Houston; Marvin Gaye; Four Tops.

Introducing . . .. Decca (M) DL-4091 20-25 61

Introducing . . .. Decca (S) DL-74091 25-30 61
Bill Anderson; Roy Drusky; Connie Hall; Ernest Ashworth; Lewis Pruitt; Elmer Snodgrass.

Introducing Command Records .... Command (S) 2 S.D. 8-12
Dixie Rebels; Tony Mottola. (Plus selections from four other Command LP's, whose artists are not named. Stereo demonstration record.)

Introspection: Neglected Jazz Figures of the '50s & Early '60s .... New World (M) NW 275 8-12 77
Herbie Nichols Quartet; Curtis Lance Quintet; Jaki Byard; Serge Chaloff Sextet; Steve Lucy Quartet; Booker Little Sextet.

Invictus' Greatest Hits .... Invictus (S) ST-9807 8-12 72
Freda Payne; 8th Day; Chairmen of the Board; Ruth Copeland; Glass House; Barrino Brothers.

Invisible Moods (2 LP) .... RCA (S) DPL2-0109 10-15 70s
Nilsson; Gale Garnett; Tokens; John Gary; Royal Scots Dragoon Guards; Glenn Yarbrough; B.W. Stevenson; Browns; Hugo Montenegro; Paul Anka; Peggy March; Friends of Distinction; Skeeter Davis; Main Ingredient; Dottie West; Ed Ames; Al Hirt; Guess Who; Bobby Bare; Floyd Cramer; Original Cast of "Hair"; Kitty Kallen.

Iron Eagle .... Capitol (S) SV-12499 8-10 86
(Soundtrack.) George Clinton; Queen; Katrina & Waves; Dio; Helix; King Kobra; Eric Martin; Adrenalin; Urgent; Jon Butcher Axis.

Iron Eagle 2 .... Epic (S) SE-45006 8-10 88
(Soundtrack.) Insiders; Alice Cooper; Mike Reno; Sweet Obsession; Doug & Slugs; Britny Fox; FM/UK; Henry Lee Summer; Ruth Pointer; Billy Vera; Rick Springfield.

Iron Tyrants I .... World Metal (S) WMR 001 10-15 84
(Picture disc. 500 made.)

Iron Tyrants III .... World Metal (S) WMR 003 10-15 89
(Picture disc. 500 made.)

Irrepressible Impulses .... Impulse (S) 1972 5-10 72
John Coltrane; Ahmad Jamal; Chico Hamilton; others.

Irving Berlin: 100th Anniversary Collection .... MCA (S) 39324 10-15 88
(Soundtrack.) Bing Crosby; Al Jolson; Linda Ronstadt; Nelson Riddle; Fred Astaire; Tommy Dorsey; Mills Brothers; Teresa Brewer; Ethel Merman; Andrews Sisters; Dick Haymes; Duke Ellington; Irving Mills; Kate Smith.

Irving Berlin Songs .... Mercury (M) MG-20813 10-20 64

Irving Berlin Songs .... Mercury (S) SR-60813 15-20 64
Clebanoff Strings; Brook Benton; David Carroll; others.

Is It True What They Say About Dixie .... 20th Fox (M) TF-3027 15-25 59

Island People .... Island (S) SPRO-6757 10-15 73
Wailers; Amazing Blondel; Spooky Tooth; John Martyn; Sutherland Brothers & Quiver; Traffic.

It Came from Hollywood .... Capitol (S) SPRO-79199 8-12 87
(Promotional issue only. Capitol Alternative Sampler.) Grapes of Wrath; Fetchin Bones; Kane Gang; Flesh for Lulu; Reivers; New Model Army; Duane Eddy; Belouis Same; Skinny Puppy; Martha Davis; Sounds of Soweto.

It Came from the Garage II .... Wanghead (S) WH-005 10-15 87
Gories; Artphag; Zombie Surfers; Termites of 1939; 3-D Invisibles; Snake Out; Nine Pound Hammer; Elvis Hitler; 52 Dead Babies; Born with Tails; Jerry Vile; Vegas Raz Experience; Lost Patrol; Fishcats; Treblemakers; Natives from Earth.

It Had to Be You .... New World (M) NW 298 8-12 77
Lee Sims; Ohman & Arden; Zez Confrey; Walter Gross; Eddy Duchin; Carmen Cavallaro; Nat Brandywynne; Frankie Carle; Cy Walter; Eddie Heywood Jr.; Liberace; Buddy Weed; George Feyer; Fairchild & Carroll; Roger Williams.

It Takes Two .... Natural Resources (S) NR-4012T1 5-10 79
Marvin Gaye & Tammi Terrell; Thelma Houston & Jerry Butler; Syreeta & G.C. Cameron; Diana Ross; Supremes & Four Tops; Art & Honey; Blinky & Edwin Star; Temptations; Kim Weston.

It Will Stand: Minit Records, 1960-1963 .... EMI America/Minit (S) ST-17202 8-12 86
Ernie K-Doe; Showmen; Aaron Neville; Irma Thomas; Del Royals; Allen & Allen; Benny Spellman; Jessie Hill; Eskew Reeder; Allen Orange; Irma Thomas.

Itcy Twitchy Feelings: Sue Records, 1958-1966 .... EMI America (S) ST-17203 8-12 86
Bobby Hendricks; Poets; Prince La La; Johnny Darrow; Derek Martin; Don Covay; Bobby Lee; Inez Foxx; Baby Washington; Ike & Tina Turner; Tina Britt; Soul Sisters.

It's a Knockout .... Epic/Columbia (S) AS-235 10-15 76
(Includes a black and white, 8" x 10" photo of each artist. Promotional issue only.) Mother's Finest; Gasolin; Herb Pedersen; Boston; Supercharge; Jim Peterik.

It's Christmas .... Columbia Special Products (SE) C-10040 5-10 70s
Eddie Fisher; Jack Halloran Singers; Bonnie Guitar; Billy Vaughn; Anita Kerr Singers; Mills Brothers; George Wright; Pat Boone; Liberace.

It's Christmas Time Again .... Stax (S) MPS 8519 5-10 82
Little Johnny Taylor; Rance Allen Group; Mack Rice; Rufus Thomas; Albert King; Staple Singers; Isaac Hayes; Temprees; Emotions.

It's Dance Time (With All the Stars) .... Cameo (M) 1068 20-30 64
Orlons; Bobby Rydell; Chubby Checker; Tymes; Dovells; Dee Dee Sharp; Don Covay; Dardenelles.

It's For Everybody .... Columbia Special Products (S) C 10007 5-10 70s
(Promotional issue only for Gold Pin Fun Centers.) Johnny Cash; June Carter; Mark Lindsay; Pacific Gas & Electric; Tammy Wynette; Johnny Mathis; Robert Goulet; Ray Conniff; Ronnie Dyson; Jim Nabors; Blood, Sweat & Tears.

It's Happening .... MCA (S) DL-734727 8-10

It's in the Stars .... RCA (S) SP-33-562 15-25
(Promotional issue only.)

It's Love! It's Love! .... Columbia Special Products (M) CSP 127 5-10 60s
Kirby Stone Four; George Maharis; Les Elgart; Vic Damone; Skitch Henderson; Buddy Greco; Hi-Lo's; Adam Wade; Bill Purcell; Tony Orlando.

It's Raining .... Bandy (S) 7700012 5-10 80s
James River; Art Neville; Crescents; Aaron Neville; Barbara George; Lee Diamond; Boogie Kings; Huey Smith & Clowns; Issac Gordon; Irma Thomas.

Jack Diamond Remembers 16 Boss Oldies: see 16 Boss Oldies (Jack Diamond Remembers)

Jack Linkletter Presents a Folk Festival Recorded Live .... Link/GNP Crescendo (S) GNP-95 5-10 60s
Yachtsmen; Jim & Jean; Chloe Marsh; Les Baxter's Balladeers; Jack Linkletter.

Jackpot of Hits, Vol. 1 .... Apollo (M) LP-490 50-100 60
Little Anthony & Chesters; Solomon Burke; Eddie Bo; "Handyman" Jimmy Jones; Keynotes; King Curtis; Delroys; Chuck Edwards; Cellos.

Jam Session, Vol. 1 .... Verve (S) V-8049 35-45 57
Oscar Peterson; Ray Brown; Barney Kessel; J.C. Heard.

Jam Session, Vol. 2 .... Verve (S) V-???? 30-40
Oscar Peterson; Ray Brown; Barney Kessel; J.C. Heard.

Jam Session .... Verve (S) VE-2508 8-10 76
Oscar Peterson; Charlie Parker; Johnny Hodges; Benny Carter; others.

Jamaica Ska .... Atlantic (M) 8098 15-25 64

Jamboree .... Warner Bros. (M) No Number Used 2000-3000 57
(Soundtrack. Promotional issue only.) Fats Domino; Buddy Knox; Jimmy Bowen; Charlie Gracie; Slim Whitman; Jerry Lee Lewis; Connie Francis; Four Coins; Carl Perkins; Frankie Avalon; Jodie Sands; Count Basie; Joe Williams; Andy Martin; Martha Lou Harp; Paul Carr; Lewis Lymon & Teenchords; Ron Coby.

Jamboree .... Warner Bros. (M) No Number Used 10-20 80s
(Soundtrack. Reissue. We are not yet aware of how to distinguish this from an original.)
James Bond – 13 Original Themes .... Liberty (S) LO-51138 10-15 83
James Bond – 13 Original Themes .... Liberty (S) LJ-51138 15-20 80s
James Bond – 13 Original Themes .... Liberty/Columbia House (S) LO-51138 10-15 80s
James Bond – 13 Original Themes .... Liberty/RCA Victor (S) R-151594 10-15 80s
(Soundtrack.) (Above two are record club issues.) Paul McCartney; Sheena Easton; Carly Simon; Lulu; Shirley Bassey; Nancy Sinatra; Louis Armstrong; Tom Jones; Rita Coolidge; Matt Monro.
James Bond – 10th Anniversary .... United Artists (S) UXS-91 20-25 72
(Soundtrack.) John Barry; Matt Monro; Shirley Bassey; Louis Armstrong.
Jane Fonda's Workout Record (2 LP) .... Columbia (S) CX2 38054 5-10 82
Jacksons; REO Speedwagon; Brothers Johnson; Linda Clifford; Billy Ocean; Jimmy Buffett; Boz Scaggs.
January Sampler (RCA): see RCA January Sampler
Jazz a La Midnight .... Hall of Fame (S) JG 608 8-12
Jazz a La Mode .... Jazztone (M) J1254 20-40 52
Coleman Hawkins Quintet; Willie "the Lion" Smith; Jack Teagarden Big Eight; Ernie Royal Sextet; Lucky Thompson Quintet.
Jazz Abstractions .... Atlantic (M) 1365 25-35 61
Jazz at Columbia — Collector's Items .... Columbia (M) CB-16 10-20 50s
(Not for sale. Free to Columbia Record Club members.) Bix Beiderbecke; Louis Armstrong & His Savoy Ballroom Five; Bessie Smith; McKenzie & Condon's Chicagoans; Wally Rose; Bunk Johnson; Harry James; Pete Johnson; Duke Ellington; Louis Armstrong & His Hot Five; Billie Holiday; Jimmie Lunceford.
Jazz at Columbia — Dixieland .... Columbia (M) CB-8 10-20 50s
Louis Armstrong & His All Stars; Eddie Condon & His All Stars; Rampart Street Paraders; Jimmy Dorsey & His Original Dorseyland Jazz Band; Turk Murphy's Jazz Band; Eli's Chosen Six; Phil Napoleon & His Memphis Five; Matty Matlock & His Jazz Band.
Jazz at Columbia — Swing .... Columbia (M) CB-4 10-20 50s
(Not for sale. Free to Columbia Record Club members.) Benny Goodman; Harry James; Gene Krupa Jazz Trio; Duke Ellington; Charlie Barnet; Buck Clayton Jam Session & Woody Herman; New Benny Goodman Sextet; Count Basie; Lionel Hampton.
Jazz at Hollywood Bowl .... Verve (S) MGV 8231-2 10-15
Jazz at the Metropole Cafe, Vol. 1 .... Bethlehem (M) BCP-21 15-20
Red Allen; Charlie Shavers; others.
Jazz at the Philharmonic .... American Recording Society (M) 417 15-25 50s
Oscar Peterson Trio; Gene Krupa Quartet; JATP All Stars.
Jazz Beaucoup .... Columbia (S) AS 1367 5-10 82
Weather Report; Ramsey Lewis; Wynton Marsalis; N.Y. Montreaux Connection; Charles Earland; Marcio Montarroyos; Miles Davis.
Jazz Composers Workshop, Vol. 1 .... Savoy (M) MG-12045 50-75 56
Jazz Composers Workshop, Vol. 2 .... Savoy (M) MG-12059 50-75 56
Jazz Confidential .... Crown (M) 5056 15-25
Dave Brubeck; Cal Tjader; Jim Guiffre; Stan Getz; Shelly Manne; Shorty Rogers; Erroll Garner; Paul Desmond; Sonny Criss; Wardell Gray; Red Norvo; Charlie Shavers; Louis Bellson; Ben Webster; Irving Ashby; Red Callender; Sabu Martinez; Jackie Mills; Willie Smith; Oscar Moore.
Jazz Erotica .... Hi Fi (M) R-604 10-20
Richie Kamuca; Conte Candoli; Frank Rosolini; Ed Leddy; Bill Holman; Vince Guaraldi; Monte Budwig; Stan Levy.
Jazz Festival .... Almor (M) S-110 10-20 64
Jazz Festival .... Almor (S) AS-110 10-20 64
Jimmy Smith; Philly Joe Jones; Donald Byrd; Kai Winding; Paul Chambers; Pepper Adams; Curtis Fuller.
Jazz Festival .... Kapp (M) KS-1 15-25 56
Dave Pell Octet with Ray Sims; Don Fugerquist; Ronny Lang; Hi-Lo's; Don Lodice; Jerry Fielding; Morey Feld Band & Don Elliott; Peanuts Hucko; Art Harris Trio & Clyde Lombardi; Jim Chapin; Johnny Holiday & Dick Nash; Russ Garcia; Harris/Leigh Baroque Band & Sunny Russo; Doc Goldberg; Art Harris; Joe Howard; Buddy Collette; Matt Dennis; George Siraro Band & Billy Butterfield; Bernie Kaufman; Ruth Price & Lou Stein; Milt Hinton; George Wettling Jazz Trio & Pee Wee Russell; Gene Schroeder; Benny Payne & Joe Wilder; Mundell Lowe.
Jazz Festival .... Wyncote (M) W-9031 10-15
Jazz Festival .... Wyncote (S) SW-9031 10-15
Maynard Ferguson; Clark Terry; Rufus Jones; Teddy Wilson.
Jazz Festival in Hi-Fi .... Warner (M) W-1281 15-20
Jazz Festival in Stereo .... Warner (S) WS-1281 15-25
Chico Hamilton Quintet; Trombones Inc.; Ruby Braff; First Jazz Piano Quartet; Dick Cathcart; Bob Prince Tentette; Fred Katz; Jim Timmens & His Jazz All Stars; Morris Nanton Trio; Matty Matlock & Paducah Patrol.
Jazz for Hi-Fi Lovers .... Dawn (M) DLP 1125 10-15 50s
Paul Quinchette; Dick Garcia-Gene Quill; Randy Weston; Mat Mathews; Les Modes; Alex Smith; Zoot Sims; Gene Roland Octet.
Jazz for People Who Hate Jazz .... RCA (M) LJM 1008 15-25 54
Benny Goodman; Duke Ellington; Bunny Berigan; Charlie Barnet; Count Basie; Lionel Hampton; Artie Shaw; John Kirby; Tommy Dorsey; Wingy Manone; Sauter-Finegan; Fats Waller.
Jazz for Playboys .... Savoy (M) MG-12095 40-60 57
Jazz Giants '58 .... Verve (M) MGV-8248 30-40 58
Jazz Greats .... Rondo R (M) 2018 10-15 50s
Woody Herman; Jack Teagarden; Ralph Burns; others.
Jazz Greats, Vol. 1 .... Realistic (S) 50-6010 5-10 70s
Bobby Hackett; Ruby Braff; Earl Hines; Teddy Wilson; Jonah Jones; Buddy Tate; Eddie Condon; Don Ewell.
Jazz Guitar Album .... Verve (S) 2367-196 10-15
Howard Roberts; Kenny Burrell; Billy Bauer; Les Spann; Charlie Christian; Barney Kessel; Herb Ellis; Jim Hall; Bola Sete; Grant Green; Tal Farlow; Laurindo Almeida; Django Reinhardt; George Benson; Wes Montgomery; Johnny Smith; Oscar Moore; Jimmy Raney; Charlie Byrd; John McLaughlin.
Jazz Hall of Fame, Vol. II .... Design (M) DLP-113 10-15
Maxine Sullivan with Charlie Shavers; Django Reinhardt & Quintette of the Hot Club of France; Jac Teagarden; Charles White; Charlie Shavers & Original John Kirby Orchestra; Ralph Burns Quartet; Big Bill Broonzy.
Jazz Jam Session/Rock 'n' Roll Festival .... Paris (M) 3 20-30 56
Sarah Vaughan; Hen Gates & His House Rockers; Dizzy Gillespie; Dono Byas; Red Norvo.

Jazz Makers .... Columbia (M) CL 1036 10-20
Louis Armstrong; Duke Ellington; Billie Holiday; Count Basie; Bessie Smith; Teddy Wilson with Roy Eldridge; Fletcher Henderson; Jones-Smith, Inc.; Louis Prima with Pee Wee Russell; Benny Goodman with Charlie Christian; Earl Hines; Dizzy Gillespie.

Jazz Men .... Savoy (M) MG-12083 40-60 57

Jazz Montage .... Liberty (M) LRP-3292 15-25 63

Jazz Monteray (2 LP) .... PAJ (S) PA-8080-2 10-15

Jazz Music for People Who Don't Care About Money .... Bethlehem (M) BCP-88 15-20

Jazz of Two Decades .... Emarcy (M) DEM-2 25-50 56
Clliford Brown; Max Roach; Sarah Vaughan; Erroll Garner; Clark Terry; Dinah Washington; Julian Adderely; Irving Fazola's Dixielanders; Bud Freeman's All Stars; Joe Turner & Pete Johnson; Billy Taylor with Johnny Hodges; Coleman Hawkins; Charlie Ventura with Kai Winding; Lenny Tristano Trio.

Jazz Omnibus .... Columbia (M) CL-1020 40-50 57
Eddie Condon; Louis Armstrong; Turk Murphy; Erroll Garner; Duke Ellington; Dave Brubeck; J.J. Johnson; Jazz Messengers; Smoke Signal; Miles Davis; Gigi Gryce & Don Byrd.

Jazz Poll Winners .... Columbia (M) CL-1610 20-30 60

Jazz Poll Winners .... Columbia (S) CS-8410 25-35 60
(Package includes portfolio.) Les Brown; Dave Brubeck; Kenny Burrell; Miles Davis; Duke Ellington; Don Elliott; Lionel Hampton; Charlie Mingus; J.J. Johnson; Hi-Los; Lambert, Hendricks & Ross; Gerry Mulligan; Art Van Damme; Paul Desmond.

Jazz: Red Hot & Cool: see Zenith Presents Jazz: Red Hot & Cool

Jazz Salute to Freedom (2 LP) .... Core (S) 100 15-20 60s
Cannonball Adderley; Nat Adderley; Steve Allen; Louis Armstrong; Count Basie; Harry Belafonte; Tony Bennett; Chris Connor; Miles Davis; Billy Eckstine; Duke Ellington; Maynard Ferguson; Erroll Garner; Stan Getz; Dizzy Gillespie; Woody Herman; J.J. Johnson; Lambert, Hendricks, & Ross; Machito; Herbie Mann; Joe Newman; Charlie Parker; Bud Powell; Max Roach; Horace Silver; Zoot Sims; Art Tatum; Sarah Vaughan; Dinah Washington; Joe Williams; Kai Winding.

Jazz Sampler .... Jazztone (M) J-SPECS-100 20-40 55
(10-inch LP.) Sidney Bechet & His New Orleans Feetwarmers; Red Norvo All Stars; Charlie Parker All Stars; Art Tatum; Buck Clayton Quintet; Coleman Hawkin Quartet; Coleman Hawkins Quartet; Jack Teagarden; Erroll Garner; Woody Herman Woodchoppers; Rex Stewart & His Dixieland Jazz Band.

Jazz Scene .... Verve (M) MGV-8060 30-40 57

Jazz Scene .... American Recording Society (M) 419 15-25 50s
George Handy; Bud Powell; Charlie Parker; Neal Hefti; Coleman Hawkins; Lester Young; Machito & Flip Phillips; Ralph Burns; Willie Smith; Duke Ellington.

Jazz Scene at ABC Paramount .... ABC (M) S-1 15-25
Candido; West Coast All Stars & Quincy Jones; Oscar Pettiford; Art Farmer; Urbie Green; Jimmy Raney; Zoot Sims; Jackie & Roy; Billy Taylor Trio; Vinnie Burke; Don Elliott; Quincy Jones with Art Farmer, Phil Woods, & Hank Jones.

Jazz Studio One .... Decca (EP) ED-634 15-20 54

Jazz Studio One .... Decca (EP) ED-2130 15-20 54

Jazz Studio One .... Decca (M) DL-8058 30-50 54

Jazz Studio Two .... Decca (M) DL-8079 30-50 54
Herb Geller; Milt Bernhart; John Grass; Don Faberquist; Marty Paich; Howard Roberts; Curtis Counce; Larry Bunker.

Jazz Swing Session (Montreaux Jazz Festival) .... Blue Jay (S) BJ-8814 8-12

Jazz Tone Society .... Jazz Tone (M) J-Spec 100 25-40 55
Sidney Bechet; Red Norvo; Charlie Parker; Art Tatum; Buck Clayton Quintet; Coleman Hawkins Quartet; Jack Teagarden.

Jazz Wave Ltd. on Tour .... Blue Note (S) BST-89905 10-15

Jerry Blavat for Collectors Only .... Lost-Nite (M) LP-103 10-15

Jerry Blavat for Lovers Only, Vol. 2 .... Lost-Nite (M) LP-107 10-15
Rivieras; Avalons; Moonglows; Dion & Belmonts; Vidaltones; Clovers; Schoolboys; Fidelities; Velours; Bertha Tillman; Companions; Embers; Theola Kilgore; Keytones.

Jerry Blavat "Guess What?" .... Crimson (M) LP-501 20-30 66

Jerry Blavat "Guess What?" .... Crimson (SE) LP-501 15-25 66
Ducanes; Jordan & Fascinations; Five Discs; Five Satins; Crests; Magnificant Four; Louis Lymon the the Teenchords; Cadillacs; Johnny Greco; Roger & Travelers; Pooky Hudson; Duprees; Jackie & Starlites; Charades; Cleftones.

Jerry Blavat Presents for Yon Teenagers Only .... Lost-Nite (M) LP-105 10-15
Desires; Camelots; Superiors; Chanters; Rainbows; Salutations; Tams (Hippies); Paragons; Metallics; Little Anthony & Imperials; Bluenotes; Carnations; Moonglows; Lee Andrews & Hearts; Universals; Fabulaires; Frankie Lymon; Harptones.

Jerry Blavat Presents for Young Lovers Only .... Lost-Nite (M) LP-102 10-15

Jerry Blavat Presents for Young Lovers Only .... Lost-Nite (SE) LP-102 10-15
Lenny Welch; Jesters; Arthur Lee Maye & Crowns; Click-ettes; Capris; Wheels; Lee Andrews; Emotions; Ly-Dells; Quinns; Carousels; Sheppards.

Jerry Blavat Presents the Untouchables .... Old Gold (S) LP-105 5-10 80s
Johnny Greco; Roy Tyson; Coasters; Larry Dale; Oscar Wills; Imaginations; Rob Roys; Elegents; Richie Allen & Ebonistics; 4 Seasons; Metallics; Destinations; Eddie & Starlites; Chesters; Emotions.

Jerry Blavat T.V. Songs Storybook .... Lost-Nite LPC-101 10-15
Candy & Kisses; Astors; Fontella Bass; C.O.D.'s; Toys; Jackie Lee; Capitols; Orlons; Four Shells; Jerry Blavat & Yon Teenagers; Bobby Comstock; Marvelows; Otis Redding; Frankie & Classicals; Bob Brady & Concords; Tymes; Sir Mack Rice; Olympics.

Jerry Osborne's Rockin' Records: see Rockin' Records

Jerry Steven's Instant Replay, Vol. 2 .... Lost Nite (M) LN-119 5-10
Tymes; Patti LaBelle & Blue Belles; Shells; Videos; Turbans; Lee Andrews; Charts; Channels; Velours; Jesse Belvin; Chiffons; Nutmegs; Paragons; Jimmy Rivers; Starlites; Three Friends; Bopchords; Five Satins; Harptones; Crests.
Jetsons: the Movie .... MCA (S) MCA-6431 12-1590(Soundtrack.)

Jewel of the Nile .... Jive/Arista (S) JL9-8406 8-12 85
(Soundtrack.) Billy Ocean; Ruby Turner; Hugh Masekela & Jonathan Butler; Willesden Dodgers; Whodini; Precious Wilson; Mark Shrieve; Nubians; Jack Nitzsche.

Jewels, Vol. 1 .... SSS Int'l (S) 24 5-10 76
Tommy James & Shondells; Peggy Scott & Jo Jo Benson; Jerry Lee Lewis; Rugbys; Ad Libs; Shangri-Las; Alive 'N Kicking; Dixie Cups; Jelly Beans; Three Degrees; Carl Perkins; Bill Justis.

Jewels, Vol. 2 .... SSS Int'l (S) 25 5-10 76
Johnny Adams; Peggy Scott & Jo Jo Benson; George Perkins; Wilbert Harrison; Betty La Vette; Gloria Taylor; Big John Hamilton; Calvin Leavy; Hank Ballard & Midnighters; Mickey Murray; Bill Hemmans;

Jim Lounsbury Presents Blasts from the Past: see Blasts from the Past

Jim Reeves and Some Friends .... RCA (S) LSP-4112 5-10 69
Jim Reeves; Dottie West; Leo Jackson; others.

Jingle Bell Jazz.......... Columbia (S) PC 36803 5-10 80
Duke Ellington; Lionel Hampton; Chico Hamilton; Carmen McRae; Pony Poindexter; Paul Horn; Dave Brubeck Quartet; Lambert, Hendricks & Ross; Herbie Hancock; Manhattan Jazzs All Stars; Marlowe Morris; Miles Davis.

Jingle Bell Rock (The Rock 'N' Roll Era) (2 LP).......... Time Life (S) SRNR XM 10-20 87
(Boxed set. Mail order only. Digital remaster.) Bobby Helms; Chuck Berry; Smokey Robinson & Miracles; Supremes; Drifters; Beach Boys; Booker T. & MGs; Temptations; Carla Thomas; Jackson Five; Jan & Dean; King Curtis; Brenda Lee; Marvin & Johnny; Ventures; O'Jays; Jack Scott; Dodie Stevens; Aretha Franklin; Donny Hathaway; Elton John.

Jo Jo Dancer, Your Life is Calling .... Warner Bros. (SP) 1 25444 8-10 86
(Soundtrack.) Muddy Waters; Chaka Khan; O'Jays; Gladys Knight & Pips; Marvin Gaye; Spinners; Mahalia Jackson; Jr. Walker & All Stars; Herbie Hancock.

Jocko Presents Two Dozen Oldies.......... Hammer (M) 5007 10-15
Danleers; Dubs; Excellents; Harptones; Channels; Cufflinks; Del-Vikings; Kokaks; Quin-Tones; Meadowlarks; Corvells; Spaniels; Jimmy Charles; Dells; Corvells; Medallions; Bell Larks; Pyramids.

Jocko's Choice R&B Oldies.......... Bonded (M) B-777 10-15
Wilbert Harrison; Teen Chords; Dubs; Dee Clark; Harptones; Cathy Jean & Roomates; Tune Weavers; Videos; Lee Andrews; Shells; Passions; Paragons; Silhouettes Velours; Kodaks; Nutmegs; Willows; Collegians; Wheels; Monarchs.

Jocko's New Album Two Dozen Oldies, Vol. 2.......... Hammer (M) LP-5008 10-15
Skyliners; Dream Lovers; Ritchie Valens; Little Caesar & Romans; School Boys; Paradons; Crests; Starlights; Fascinations; Capris; Genies; Channels; Rochelle & Candles; Danleers; Chimes; Dubs; Dells; Quintones; Magnifient 4; Pips; Spaniels.

Joe Niagara Presents 20 Knocked Out Nifties of the Past: see 20 Knocked Out Nifties of the Past

Joe Niagara, 10th Anniversary Album.......... Lost Nite (M) LP-116 8-12
Curtis Lee; Mystics; Rays; Danny & Juniors; Camelots; Del-Vikings; Lee Andrews & Hearts; Wilbert Harrison; Silhouettes; Dixie Cups; Duettes; Cleftones; Dovells; Anthony & Sophomores; Maurice Williams & Zodiacs; Hippies; Bobby Day; Clickettes; Sensations.

Joe Niagara, the Rockin' Bird — More 10th Anniversary .... Lost Nite (M) LP-121 8-12
Randy & Rainbows; Rosie & Originals; Lee Dorsey; Jesters; Teenchords; Ebonaires; Ronny & Daytonas; Shirelles; Teen Queens; Tymes; Charts; Nobles; Lee Allen; Larks; Cadets; Kodacs; Lee Andrews; Billy Myles; Patti Labelle & Blue Belles; Garnet Mimms; Orlons; Classics.

Joel Ray Sprowl's Lincoln Jamboree: see Lincoln Jamboree

Johnny Be Good.......... Atlantic (S) 81837-1 8-10 88
(Soundtrack.) Frozen Ghost & Friends; Bernie Shanahan; Dirty Looks; Judas Priest; Myles Goodwyn; Kix; Fiona; Rick Astley; Saga; Ted Nugent.

Johnny Otis Show Live (2 LP) .... Epic (S) 30473 8-12 71
(Includes poster.) Johnny Otis; Little Esther; Joe Turner; Ivory Joe Hunter; Roy Brown; Pee Wee Crayton; Roy Milton; Eddie Cleanhead Vinson; Margie Evans; Mighty Flea; Mighty Mouth Evans.

Journey into Yesterday (1956) .... Economic Consultants Inc. (M) 1956 20-40 73
(Mail order offer.) Elvis Presley; others.

Journey into Yesterday (1957) .... Economic Consultants Inc. (M) 1957 10-15 73
(Mail order offer.)

Journey into Yesterday (1958) .... Economic Consultants Inc. (M) 1958 10-15 73
(Mail order offer.)

Journey into Yesterday (1959) .... Economic Consultants Inc. (M) 1959 10-15 73
(Mail order offer.)

Journey into Yesterday (1960) .... Economic Consultants Inc. (M) 1960 10-15 73
(Mail order offer.)

Journey into Yesterday (1961) .... Economic Consultants Inc. (M) 1961 10-15 73
(Mail order offer.)

Journey into Yesterday (1962) .... Economic Consultants Inc. (M) 1962 10-15 73
(Mail order offer.)

Journey into Yesterday (1963) .... Economic Consultants Inc. (M) 1963 10-15 73
(Mail order offer.)

Journey into Yesterday (1964) .... Economic Consultants Inc. (M) 1964 10-15 73
(Mail order offer.)

Journey into Yesterday (1965) .... Economic Consultants Inc. (M) 1965 10-15 73
(Mail order offer.)

Journey into Yesterday (1966) .... Economic Consultants Inc. (M) 1966 10-15 73
(Mail order offer.)

Journey into Yesterday (1967) .... Economic Consultants Inc. (M) 1967 10-15 73
(Mail order offer.)

Journey into Yesterday (1968) .... Economic Consultants Inc. (M) 1968 10-15 73
(Mail order offer.)

Journey into Yesterday (1969) .... Economic Consultants Inc. (M) 1969 20-40 73
(Mail order offer.) Elvis Presley; others.

Journey into Yesterday (1971) .... Economic Consultants Inc. (M) 1969 10-15 73
(Mail order offer.) Don McLean; Carpenters; Three Dog Night; Chicago; Joan Baez; Neil Diamond; Tom Jones; Janis Joplin; Lobo; Melanie; Nilsson; Partridge Family; Cat Stevens; Cher; Yvonne Elliman; Murray Head.

Journey to the Center of the Earth .... A&M (S) SP-3621 10-15 74
(Soundtrack. Includes poster.)

Journey to the Center of the Earth .... A&M (Q) QU-53621 20-25 74
(Soundtrack. Includes booklet.) David Hemmings (narration); Rick Wakeman; Garry Pickford-Hopkins; Ashley Holt; Mike Egan; Roger Newell; Barney James; John Cleary; English Chamber Choir; others.

Joy of Christmas.......... Columbia Special Products (S) C-11087 5-10 70s
Marty Robbins; Lynn Anderson; Ray Price; Tammy Wynette; Chuck Wagon Gang; Johnny Cash.

Joyful Moments .... Word (S) WST-8720 5-8 76

Joyous Christmas.......... Columbia Special Products (S) C 10396 5-10 60s
Bing Crosby; Senior Concert Orchestra; Diahann Caroll; Anna Moffo; Tony Bennett; Robert Goulet; Carol Lawrence; Richard Tucker; Beneficial Singers.

Joyous Songs of Christmas.......... Columbia/Goodyear (S) AS-10400

Jubilation.......... Myrrh (S) A-6555 5-10 75
Barry McGuire; Lamb; Sonlight Orchchestra; Ray Hildebrand; Love Song; Walt Mills; Parchment; Larry Norman; others.

Jubilee Monophonic Instrumental & Vocal Sampler.......... Jubilee (M) MSJLP-803 20-30 57
(Promotional issue only.) Cadillacs; Cy Coleman; Lois Kahn; Carl Ravazza; Don Rondo; Moe Koffman; Mark Monte & His Continentals; Ray Martin; Shep Fields; Gray Rains; Mary Ann McCall; Frank Hunter.

Jubilee Surprise Party.......... Jubilee (M) J-1107 20-30 59

Jubilee Surprise Party.......... Jubilee (S) SDJ-1107 30-40 59
Della Reese; Don Rondo; Moe Koffman; Sy Oliver; Marty Holmes; Leroy Lewis; others.

Jud.......... Ampex (S) A-50101 15-20 71
(Soundtrack.) John Hartford; Crow; Mason Proffit; American Breed; Barbara Robison.

Juggernauts of the Early '70s.......... Dunhill (S) DSX-50146 8-12 73
Jim Croce; Three Dog Night; Grass Roots; James Gang; Hamilton, Joe Frank & Reynolds; Steppenwolf; Smith; Eddie Holman; Mama Cass Elliot; Gayle McCormick; Tommy Roe; John Kay.

Jugs, Washboards and Kazoos.......... Victor (M) LPV-540 8-10 67
Dixieland Jug Blowers; Memphis Jug Band; others.

Juke Box Classics.......... Excelsior (S) XMP 6013 5-10 80
Marcels; Kingsmen; Little Anthony & Imperials; Jimmy Gilmer; Platters; Little Richard; Crystals; Lou Christie; Martha & Vandellas; Billy Bland; Archie Bell & Drells; Billy Joe Royal.

Juke Box Jive.......... K-Tel (S) NU-9020 8-10 75
Beau-Marks; Clyde McPhatter; Ronnie Hawkins; Frankie Avalon; Paul Anka; Del Shannon; Mitch Ryder & Detroit Wheels; Tokens; Wilbert Harrison; Joey Dee & Starliters; Lou Christie; Buddy Knox; Chris Montez; Castaways; Clovers; Johnny Thunder; Sue Thompson; Newbeats; Curtis Lee; Bill Haley & His Comets.

Juke Box Saturday Night (3 LP).......... Candlelite (S) CU 718 10-15 83
(Boxed set.) Paradons; Barbara George; Lenny Welch; Billie & Lillie with Billie Ford's Thunderbirds; Dion & Belmonts; Kathy Jean & Roomates; Little Richard; Casinos; Johnny Preston; Phil Phillips & Twilights; Johnny Wilson; Dee Clark; Penguins; Ron Holden & Thunderbirds; Huey Smith & Clowns; Little Caesar & Romans; Chubby Checker; Barbara Lewis; Troy Shondell; Harold Dorman; Mystics; Fireflies; Bobby Vee; Brook Benton; Jarmels; Ritchie Valens; Kathy Young & Innocents.

Juke Box Saturday Night (4 LP).......... Juke Box (S) JBD-95141 15-20
(Boxed set.) Olympics; Time Tones; Decoys; Shells; House Rockers; Tony Orlando; Chimes; Thomas Wayne; Visions; Youngsters; Waiters; Harptones; Collegians; Bellnotes; Marathons; Bill Justis; Dubs; Camelots; Sintells; Rebels; Fascinations; Paradons; Cannibal & Headhunters; Youngtones; Vic Donna; Satins; Royals; Summits; Jimmy Clanton; Bluejays; Elegants; Martian Mad Caps; Sinceres; Classics; Huey Smith & Clowns; Counts; Darvels; Veltones; Admirations; Perfections; Capris; Roy Orbison; Zirkons; Chessmen.

Jukebox Saturday Night.......... RCA (M) LPT-1016 20-35 54
Glenn Millers; Tex Beneke; Dorothy Claire; Ray Eberle; Marion Hutton; Skip Nelson & Modernaires.

Jukebox Saturday Night, 96 Great Jukebox Hits (8 LP).......... RCA/Readers Digest (S) RD4-139 25-40 75
(Boxed set.) Glenn Miller & Marion Hutton; Clyde McCoy; Mills Brothers; Orrin Tucker; Les Paul & Mary Ford; Vic Damone; Margaret Whiting & Jimmy Wakely; Nat King Cole; Kay Starr; Frankie Laine; Benny Moten; Bunny Berigan; Andrews Sister; Shep Fields; Fats Waller; Glen Gray & Kenny Sargent; Peggy Lee; Pee Wee Hunt; Dick Grove & Margaret Whiting; Frankie Laine; Vera Lynn; Guy Lombardo; Eddy Duchin & Patricia Norman; Larry Clinton & Bea Wain; Rudy Vallee; Judy Garland; Peggy Lee; Perry Como; Alvino Rey; Arthur Godfrey; Edith Piaf; Red Ingle; Kay Kyser & Ginny Sims; Eddy Howard; Cab Calloway; Art Mooney; Francis Craig; Nellie Lutcher; Tex Williams; Kate Smith; Harry James & Helen Forrest; Nat Cole Trio; Gracie Fields; Sammy Kaye & Don Cornell; Freddie Slack & Ella Mae Morse; Spike Jones; Paul Weston & Pied Pipers; Peggy Lee; Stan Kenton & June Christy; Andy Russell; Paul Whiteman & Lady Day (Billie Holiday); Perry Como; Louis Prima; Billy Butterfield & Margaret Whiting; Three Suns; Stan Kenton & Anita O'Day; Jo Stafford & Johnny Mercer & Pied Pipers.

Jump 'N Shout New Orleans Rhythm & Blues.......... Pearl (M) PL-15 8-12
Dave Bartholomew; Erline Harris; Johnson Brothers; Combo; Joseph "Googie Eyes" August; Chubby "Hip Shakin'" Newsome; James "Blazer Boy" Locks.

Jumpin'! With Pop Hits of Tomorrow.......... Sutton (M) SU-321 15-25 66

Jumpin'! With Pop Hits of Tomorrow.......... Sutton (S) SSU-321 15-25 66
Diane Coley; Viscaines; Sims Sisters; Sparkplugs; Dal Cory.

Jumpin' Jack Flash.......... Mercury (S) 830545-1 8-10 86
(Soundtrack.) Rene & Angela; Bananarama; Kool & Gang; Gwen Guthrie; Billy Branigan; Rolling Stones; Face to Face; Supremes; Thomas Newman.

Jumpin' Keyboard.......... Guest Star (S) GS-1423 8-12
Eddie Heywood; Earl Hines; Matt Dennis; Mike DiNapoli; Hazel Scott; Barclay Allen.

Jumping '50s (5 LP).......... Columbia Special Products (S) C5 10919 20-30 72
Crew-Cuts; Fats Domino; Pat Boone; Hilltoppers; Tune Weavers; Little Richard; Jim Lowe; Wilbert Harrison; Chordettes; Lloyd Price; Chuck Berry; Del-Vikings; Everly Brothers; Platters; Clyde McPhatter; Jimmy Clanton; Diamonds; Chuck Berry; Dodie Stevens; Jimmy Rodgers; Phil Phillips; Sarah Vaughan; Chordettes; Buddy Knox; Moonglows; Monotones; Paul Evans; Bobby Day; Art & Dottie Todd; Dinah Washington; Lee Andrews & Hearts; Teen Queens; Big Bopper. (Reader's Digest mail order offer.)

June 1, 1974.......... Island (S) 9291 8-10 74
Kevin Ayers; John Cale; Eno; Nico.

Jungle Exotica.......... Strip (S) 005 5-10 90s
Jan Davis; Cherokees; Kookie Joe; Nocabouts; Gaylads; Medallions; Hully Gully Boys; Del Saints; Emanons; Ganim's Asia Minors; Continental Cousins; J.C. Davis; Revels; Diablito; Baby Sticks & Kingtones; Peeple; Enchanters; Majestics; Guitar Gable.

Just Another Pop Album.......... Titan (S) 8001 10-15
Gary Charlson; Boys; J.P. McClain & Intruders; Arlis.

Just for Variety, Vol. 2.......... Capitol (M) ???? 8-12 50s
Dean Martin; others.

Just for Variety, Vol. 3.......... Capitol (M) 946 8-12 50s
Dean Martin; others.

Just for Variety, Vol. 6.......... Capitol (M) 949 8-12 50s
Dean Martin; others.

Just for Variety, Vol. 8.......... Capitol (M) 951 8-12 50s
Dean Martin; others.

Just for Variety, Vol. 10 .... Capitol (M) 953 8-12 50s
Dean Martin; others.

Just for Variety, Vol. 12 .... Capitol (M) 955 8-12 59
Les Baxter; Les Paul; June Christy; Jackie Gleason; Gordon MacRae; Harry James; Billy May; Tennessee Ernie ford; Joe "Fingers" Carr; Nelson Riddle; Margaret Whiting; Lou Busch.

Just for Variety, Vol. 13 .... Capitol (M) 967 8-12
Dean Martin; others.

Just for Variety, Vol. 15 .... Capitol (M) 1007 8-12
Dean Martin; others.

Just for You .... Columbia (S) XTV-86334/5 8-12

Just Let Me Hear Some of That Rock and Roll Music (2 LP) .... Goodman Group (S) GG PRO-1 30-60 79
(Promotional issue only.) Excerpts of 100 songs by : Elvis Presley; Beatles; Dion; Clarence "Frogman" Henry; Chuck Berry; Jackie Wilson; Jorgen Ingmann; El Dorados; Pat Boone; Jimmy Reed; Linda Ronstadt; Bo Diddley; Monotones; John Lee Hooker; Animals; Gene Chandler; Jerry Butler; Spaniels; McGuire Sisters; Tune Weavers; Tony Orlando & Dawn; Charms; Fontane Sisters; Jerry Keller; Rod Stewart; Flamingos; Yardbirds; Rita Coolidge; Little Walter; Gentrys; Peter & Gordon; Sensations; Lee Andrews & Hearts; Johnny Rivers; Lonnie Mack; Mike Douglas; Johnny Cymbal; Spiral Starecase; Moonglows; Dee Clark; Dells; Clovers; Ray Charles; Johnnie & Joe; Otis Redding; Chantays; Bobby Vinton; Fleetwoods; Bill Haley & His Comets; Faye Adams; Rays; Beach Boys; Dale Hawkins; Creedence Clearwater Revival; Pearl Bailey; Aaron Neville; Harvey & Moonglows; Capris; Pozo Seco Singers; Ronnie Hawkins; Jimmy McCracklin; Vibrations; Julie Rodgers; Gene Allison; Dovells.

Just One of the Guys .... Elektra (S) 60426-1 8-10 85
(Soundtrack.) Shalamar; Ronnie Spector; Berlin; others.

KAKC Solid Gold (2 LP) .... Post (S) 97 10-20
Tommy James & Shondells; Frankie Avalon; Barbara Mason; Van Morrison; Esquires; John Fred; Brenton Wood; Knickerbockers; Cannibal & Headhunters; Rivieras; Gene Chandler; Terry Stafford; Dobie Gray; Strawberry Alarm Clock; Count Five; Billy Stewart; Bobby Fuller Four; Chuck Berry; Lemon Pipers; Buckinghams; Syndicate of Sound; Robert Parker; Neil Diamond; Dells; 1910 Fruitgum Co.; James Brown; McCoys; Association.

KATZ Presents Donny Brooks - 8th Wonder of the World .... Lost Nite (S) LN-126 5-10
Jive Five; Soul Survivors; Barbara Greene; Billy Stewart; Starlites; Lee Andrews; James & Bobby Purify; Little Ceasar; Bobby Lewis; Deon Jackson; Patty Labelle; Jay Wiggins; Dreamlovers; Charts; Knight Brothers; Jackie Lee; Olympics

KATZ Soul 16 (22 Soul Survenirs) .... Post (S) 16 10-15
Winstons; James Brown; Tony Joe White; Robert Parker; O'Kaysions; Dobie Gray; Brenton Wood; Esquires; Billy Stewart; Johnny Nash; Hugh Masekela; Delfonics; Dells; Intruders; Joe Simon; Bettye Swann; Aaron Neville; Toussant McCall; Barbara Mason; Tommy Edwards; James & Bobby Purify; Righteous Brothers.

KBOX .... Roulette (M) R-25338 10-20 67

KCBQ Radio 1170 .... Columbia (S) No Number Used 20-25 78
(Picture disc. Promotional issue only.) Boston; Ringo Starr; others.

KDAY Oldies But Goodies, Vol. 9 .... Original Sound (S) 8859 15-25 60s
(Promotional issue only.) Timi Yuro; Casinos; Esther Phillips; Don & Juan; Cathy Jean & Roommates; J. Frank Wilson; Del Shannon; Bobby Fuller Four; Castaways; Jewel Aiken; Bobby Day; Bobby Bland.

KDKB Arizona Sounds .... KDKB (S) 31577 5-10

KDKB Arizona Sounds, Vol. 3 .... KDKB (S) 36674 5-10 79
Loosely Tight; Atrox; Jim Moorhaus; the Now; Whitenoise; Billy Clone & Same; Booth-Davis & Lowe; Llory McDonald; Justin Tyme; Fast Eddie; Stephan Shawn; Nurl Fartley & Original Fartones.

KDWB 21 All Time Hits, Vol. 1 .... Take 6 (S) 2033 15-25 67
Del Counts; Stillroven; T.C. Atlantic.

KDWB Disc/Coveries .... KDWB (M) 63-1 30-40 63
Billy Bland; April Stevens; Viscounts; Johnny Bond; Ernie Fields; Jorgan Ingman; Joanie Sommers; Bobby Vee; Ben E. King; Johnny Burnette; Paris Sisters; Ventures.

KEWB Disc/Coveries .... Liberty KEWB (M) 91 35-45 60
Everly Brothers; Jerry Wallace; Bobby Vee; Santo & Johnny; Ben E. King; Martin Denny; Johnny Burnette; Ventures; Johnny Preston; Paris Sisters; Viscounts; Hollywood Argyles.

KFJZ — Golden Oldies, Vol. 2 .... Karat (S) 71 5-10
Kenny Rogers & First Edition; Eddie Floyd; Uniques; Cornelius Brothers & Sister Rose; Brian Hyland; Van Morrison; Honey Cone; Steam; Ides of March; Lobo; Redeye; Bells; Five Man Electrical Man; 8th Day; Spanky & Our Gang; Gordon Lightfoot.

KFRC 610 .... Columbia (S) No Number Used 20-25 78
(Picture disc. Promotional issue only.) Boston; Ringo Starr; others.

KFRC (The Big 610) 21 Golden Rocks .... Take 6 (S) 2004 10-15 67
Sopwith Camel; Count Five; Jackie Lee; Syndicate of Sound; Standells; Righteous Brothers; Beau Brummels; Leaves; Slim Harpo; Seeds; Young Rascals; Ian Whitcomb; Chiffons; Association; Olympics; McCoys; Barbara Lewis; Love; Neil Diamond; Vogues; Them.

KFWB Disc/Coveries .... KFWB (M) 98 35-45 60
Connie Francis; Pat Boone; Kuff Links; Ernie Fields; Four Preps; Edd Byrnes; Andy Williams; Roy Hamilton; James Darren; Art & Dotty Todd; Coasters; Martin Denny.

KGB 21 Boss Goldens, Vol. 2 .... Take 6 (S) T-6 S 2020 8-12
Bobby Fuller Four; Esquires; Brenton Wood; Jerry Butler; Shangri-Las; Beach Boys; Lee Dorsey; Chiffons; Cannibal & Headhunters; Knickerbockers; Lyrics; Casinos; Sir Douglas Quintet; Neil Diamond; Lovin' Spoonful; Jackie Lee; Tradewinds; Alvin Cash & Crawlers; Innocence.

KGFJ - 20 Super Hits .... Century (S) 43133 5-10 75

KGFJ - 21 Very Important Platters .... KGFJ (S) 1230 10-20 68
(Yellow vinyl.) Barbara Mason; Billy Stewart; Ikettes; O.V. Wright; Gene Chandler; Fantastic Four; Aaron Neville; Fred Hughes; James Brown & Famous Flames; Edwin Starr; Packers; Incredibles; Toussaint McCall; Derek Martin; Bobby Bland; Bobby Moore & Rhythm Aces; Olympics; Freddie Scott; Mike & Censations; Invincibles.

KGFJ Sounds of Success .... Roulette (M) R-25347 15-25 67

KHJ 93 All Music 93 .... Columbia (S) No Number Used 20-25 78
(Promotional picture disc.)

KHJ 30 Boss Goldens (2 LP) .... Pacer (M) 93 10-20 68
Association; James Brown; Bobby Fuller Four; Keith; Tommy James & Shondells; Love; Five Americans; Bobby Hebb; Sam & Dave; Leaves; Danny Hutton; James & Bobby Purify; Mojo Men; Routers; ? & Mysterians; Standells; Bob Lind; Brenton Wood; Beau Brummels; Tommy Roe; Marcia Strassman; Sir Douglas Quintet; Royal Guardsmen; Neil Diamond; Bobby Moore; Happenings; Impressions; Seeds; Freddie Scott; Lovin' Spoonful.

KHJ Boss Goldens, Vol. 1 .... KHJ (M) 9365 10-20 65

KHJ Boss Goldens, Vol. 1 .... KHJ (S) 9365 10-20 65
Them; Knickerbockers; Kingsmen; Wilson Pickett; Zombies; Guess Who; Sonny & Cher; Castaways; Barbara Lewis; Sir Douglas Quintet; Jewel Akens; Barry McGuire.

KHJ Presents 30 Boss Goldens .... Pacer (S) 93 10-20 67
Association; James Brown; Bobby Fuller Four; Keith; Tommy James & Shondells; Love; Five Americans; Bobby Hebb; Sam & Dave; Leaves; Danny Hutton; James & Bobby Purify; Mojo Men; Routers; ? & Mysterians; Standells; Bob Lind; Brenton Wood; Beau Brummels; Tommy Roe; Marcia Strassman; Sir Douglas Quintet; Royal Guardsmen; Lovin' Spoonful; Freddy Scott; Seeds; Impressions; Happenings; Bobby Moore; Neil Diamond.

KHJ Sound of the Sixties (2 LP) .... Pacer (S) 1970 10-20 70
Tommy Roe; Cowsills; Delfonics; Canned Heat; O'Kaysions; Tony Joe White; Tommy James & Shondells; Animals; Classics IV; Joe Simon; Shelley Fabares; Buckinghams; Winstons; Noblemen; Hugh Masekela; Oliver; Turtles; Merrilee Rush; Lovin' Spoonful; Dells; Van Morrison; Strawberry Alarm Clock; Association; Mamas & Papas; Jeannie C. Riley; Shocking Blue; Aaron Neville; Neil Diamond; Barbara Mason; Harpers Bazaar; Righteous Brothers. (Mail order and in-store sales.)

KILT Double Gold (2 LP) .... Post (S) 610 10-20
Association; Animals; Ohio Express; James Brown; Tommy Roe; Johnny Nash; Lemon Pipers; B.J. Thomas; Derek; Foundations; Terry Stafford; Soul Survivors; Chuck Berry; Surfaris; Buckinghams; Tommy James & Shondells; Turtles; Bubble Puppy; Dobie Gray; Fun & Games; Shelly Fabares; Hugh Masekela; Merrilee Rush; Deep Purple; Tommy Edwards; Standells; Arrows; Aaron Neville; Strawberry Alarm Clock; Righteous Brothers.

KILT Double Gold, Vol. 2 (2 LP) .... Phoenix (S) 101 10-20
Tommy Roe; Winstons; Shocking Blue; Canned Heat; Box Tops; Andy Kim; Jeannie C. Riley; 1910 Fruitgum Co.; Joe Simon; Sam the Sham & Pharaohs; Cowsills; Tony Joe White; Alive 'N Kicking; Neil Diamond; Steam; Flying Machine; Moments; Classics IV; Tee Set; Oliver; J. Frank Wilson; Peppermint Rainbow; Wilbert Harrison; Tommy James & Shondells; Delfonics; Turtles; George Baker; Freda Payne; Harpers Bizarre; Righteous Brothers.

K/MEN Rebounds .... K/Men (S) 129 10-20 64
Dee Dee Sharp; B. Bumble & Stingers; Dee Clark; Jerry Butler; Shields; Paris Sisters; Routers; Bobby Rydell; Sandy Nelson; Dobie Gray; Hollywood Persuaders; Connie Stevens. (Also has radio jingles.)

KIMN Gold Mine .... Phoenix (S) 108 10-15 70s
Freda Payne; Mountain; Melanie; Mungo Jerry; Dave & Ansil Collins; Five Man Electrical Band; Osmond Brothers; Lobo; Crow; Mercy; Isley Brothers; Brian Hyland; Andy Kim; Cowsills; Bells; Honey Cone; Tony Joe White; Sugarloaf; Tommy James & Shondells; Ocean; Shocking Blue; Tommy Roe; Turtles; Five Stairsteps.

KING Radio/1090 .... Sound of Seattle (S) ST-1-403 20-25
(Picture disc.)

KISS-FM 98.7 Presents Shep Pettibone's Mastermixes (2 LP) .... Prelude (S) PRL-19100 8-10 82
D-Train; Strikers; France Joli; Gayle Adams; Sharon Redd; Jeanette "Lady" Day; Secret Weapon; Nick Straker Band; Unlimited Touch; Empress; Conquest.

KJR Solid Gold .... KJR (S) No Number Used 10-15 69
Merrilee Rush; Dionne Warwick; Andy Williams; Steppenwolf; Ohio Express; Impressions; Tomy Roe; Neil Diamond; Canned Heat; Lemon Pipers; McCoys; Bobby Goldsboro; Animals; Strawberry Alarm Clock; Zager & Evans; James Brown; J. Frank Wilson; Box Tops; Jose Feliciano; Kingsmen; Three Dog Night; B.J. Thomas; Classics IV: Irish Rovers; Ventures; Glen Campbell.

KLIF Presents 21 KLIF Klassics, Vol. 1 .... Take 6 (S) 2011 8-12
Association; Five Americans; Royal Guardsmen; B.J. Thomas; Syndicate of Sound; Lovin' Spoonful; Dixie Cups; Neil Diamond; Them; Slim Harpo; Happenings; Yellow Balloon; Cannibal & Headhunters; Bobby Fuller Four; Seeds; Music Machine; Premiers; Ad Libs; Chiffons; Beach Boys; McCoys.

KLIF 21 KLIF Klassics, Vol. 2 .... Take 6 (S) T-6-2028 8-12
John Fred; Strawberry Alarm Clock; Sam & Dave; Kenny O'Dell; Tommy James & Shondells; Otis Redding; Bob Lind; Jon & Robin; Bob Kuban; Uniques; American Breed; Lovin' Spoonful; Mojo Men; Eddie Floyd; New Beats; Casinos; Knickerbockers; Shangri-Las; Castaways; Ritchie Valens; Viscounts.

KLIF Klassics, Vol. 5 .... Karat (S) 71-1 8-12 71
Eddie Floyd; Kenny Rogers; Brian Hyland; Van Morrison; Cornelius Brothers; Honey Cone; Steam; Ides of March; Lobo; Redeye; Five Man Electrical Band; Bells; 8th Day; Spanky & Our Gang; Gordon Lightfoot; Uniques.

KRLA, 21 Solid Rocks, Vol. 1 .... Take 6 (M) 2003-LA 8-12 67
Standells; Count Five; Shangri-Las; Rascals; Happenings; Righteous Brothers; Neil Diamond; Premiers; McCoys; Cannibal & Headhunters; Lovin' Spoonful; Tommy James & Shondells; Syndicate of Sound; Ian Whitcomb; Ad Libs; Vogues; Chiffons; Dixie Cups; Slilm Harpo; Jackie Lee; Spencer Davis Group. (Vol. 2 is titled *Son of KRLA Solid Rocks.*)

KRLA 42 Solid Rocks (2 LP) .... Take 6 (S) T6S 2018 10-20 68
Standells; McCoys; Count Five; Cannibal & Headhunters; Shangri-Las; Lovin' Spoonful; Neil Diamond; Rascals; Syndicate of Sound; Premiers; Tommy James; Ian Whitcomb; Happenings; Righteous Brothers; Ad Libs; Vogues; Chiffons; Dixie Cups; Slim Harpo; Jackie Lee; Spencer Davis Group; Sopwith Camel; B.J. Thomas; Leaves; Royal Guradsmen; Yellow Balloon; Trade Winds; Them; Association; Sunrays; Music Machine; Davie Allan; Love; Rainy Daze; Olympics; Seeds; Five Americans. (Reissue of *KRLA 21 Solid Rocks*, and *Son of KRLA 21 Solid Rocks.*)

KRLA Solid Rocks Strikes Again, Vol. 3 .... Take 6 (S) 2009-LA 8-12 68
Van Morrison; Sly & Family Stone; John Fred; Brenton Wood; Otis Redding; Happenings; Hombres; Casinos; Hombres; Eddie Floyd; Billy Stewart; American Breed; Kenny O'Dell; Esquires; Lovin' Spoonful; Sam & Dave; Sir Douglas Quintet; Soul Survivors; Lee Dorsey; Electric Prunes; Innocence; Tokens.

KRLA's Million Dollar Sound .... KRLA (S) 1110 25-35 63
Connie Stevens; Paradons; Paris Sisters; Donnie Brooks; Blue Jays; Skyliners; Routers; Sandy Nelson; Bobby Rydell; Pastel Six; Preston Epps; Hollywood Argyles.

KRTH (K-EARTH) 101 FM .... Columbia (S) No Number Used 20-25 78
(Picture disc. Promotional issue only.) Boston; Ringo Starr; Electric Light Orchestra; others.

KRUX (Radio Phoenix - 1360) .... Flashback (M) K-1360 25-35 62
Dodie Stevens; Rays; Fleetwoods; Hollywood Argyles; Eddie Cochran; Toni Fisher; Cookie & Cupcakes; Crests; Jimmy Charles; Jerry Keller; Big Bopper; Sammy Turner; Buzz Clifford.

KSLQ .... Columbia (S) No Number Used 20-25 78
(Picture disc. Promotional issue only.)

KSOL Radio 1450, Soul Over the City .... KSOL (S) 1450 10-20
(black vinyl.) James Brown; Billy Stewart; Linda Jones; Esther Phillips; Ikettes; Lou Courtney; Manhattans; others.

KSOL Super Soul Souvenirs .... KSOL (S) 1450 15-20
(Colored vinyl.) James Brown; Billy Stewart; Linda Jones; Esther Phillps; Ikettes; Lou Courtney; Manhattans; Little Anthony & Imperials; Freddie Scott; Fontella Bass; Jackie Lee; Joe Tex; Invincibles; Magicians; Alvin Cash & Crawlers; Chuck Jackson & Maxine Brown; Whispers; Barbara Mason; Entertainers IV; Shirley Ellis; Esquires.

KYA Golden Gate Greats .... Chess (M) LP-1458 30-40 61

Robert & Johnny; Moonglows; Students; Flamingos; Monotones; Tune Weavers; Billy Bland; Johnnie & Joe; Lee Andrews & Hearts. (Also issued as *Golden Gassers*.)

KYA 1260 Great Rip Off Album .... Warner/Reprise (S) PRO 509 10-15 71
Beach Boys; Grateful Dead; John Stewart; Youngbloods; Seals & Crofts; John Hartford; Van Morrison; Paul Parrish; Fleetwood Mac; Mothers of Invention.

KYA's 21 Golden Gate Greats, Volume 1 .... Take 6 (S) T6-2019 8-12 67
Association; Five Americans; B.J. Thomas; Lovin' Spoonful; Neil Diamond; Bobby Fuller Four; Esquires; Ad Libs; Lee Dorsey; Richie Valens; Alvin Cash & Crawlers; McCoys; Davie Allan; Yellow Balloon; Brenton Wood; Tommy James & Shondells; Count Five; Cannibal & Headhunters; Music Machine; Knickerbockers; Dixie Cups.

KYA's 21 Golden Gate Greats .... Take 6 (S) T6-2032 8-12 67
Fever Tree; Johnny Nash; Derek; Turtles; John Fred; Sam & Dave; Grass Roots; Van Morrison; Eddie Floyd; Seeds; Bubble Puppy; American Breed; Booker T. & MGs; Soul Survivors; Peggy Scott & Jo Jo Benson; Mojo Men; Bob Lind; Lovin' Spoonful; Deon Jackson; Chad & Jeremy; Electric Prunes.

KYA's Battle of the Surfing Bands .... Del-Fi (M) DFLP-1235 35-45 63
(Also issued as *Battle of the Surfing Bands*.)

KYA's Memories of the Cow Palace .... Autumn (M) 101 25-30 63
Ronettes; Dee Dee Sharp; Righteous Brothers; Freddy Cannon; Bobby Freeman; George & Teddy; Dionne Warwick; Betty Harris.

KYNO-Rock 96 FM, Valley Grown .... KYNO (S) LPs-1978 8-12 78
Avenue; T. Sherman Lewis; Providence; Born Again; Gene Short; TNT; Helena Rocha; Dawn Mallory; Mike Harris; Mush.

KYYX FM — Seattle Grown .... O'Day Broadcasting (S) Promo 1 PREW 10-15 78
Rail & Company; Greg Boehme; Breeze; Ozone Street Band; Pilot; Blueseye; Lana James Band; Clear Logic; Feelings; Epicentre; Nancy & Juvey; Shyanne.

KZEW 98 FM, Zooberry Jam .... KZEW (S) ???? 5-10
Liberation; Hummin' Bird; Karen Bella; Uncle Rainbow; Synthesis; Bee Knees; Pyramid.

Kansas City Jazz .... Decca (M) DL-8044 30-50 53

Kapp Records Presents a Demonstration in Stereophonic Total Sound .... Kapp (S) KST-1 10-15
Vic Shoen; Jane Morgan; Roger Williams; Frank Hunter; Kate Smith; Marty Gold; David Rose; John Garth; New Bijou Orchestra.

Karate Kid .... Casablanca (S) NBLP-7282 8-10 84

Karate Kid .... Casablanca (S) 822213-1 8-10 80s
(Soundtrack.) Jan & Dean; Survivor; Flirts; Broken Edge; Commuter; Paul Davis; Shandi; St. Regis; Baxter Robinson; Gang of Four; Joe "Bean" Esposito.

Karate Kid 2 .... United Artists/Urania (S) SW 40414 8-10 86
(Soundtrack.) Peter Cetera; Moody Blues; Mancrab; Paul Rodgers; Southside Johnny; Dennis DeYoung; New Edition; Carly Simon; Bill Conti.

Karate Kid 3 .... MCA (S) 6308 8-10 89
(Soundtrack.) Little River Band; Glenn Medeiros; Boys Club; Jude Cole; Pointer Sisters; Winger; PBF; Money Talks.

Keep the Dream Alive .... RCA (S) VPSX-6093 8-12 73
Jimmy Castor Bunch; Jose Feliciano; Main Ingredient; Wilson Pickett; Flip Wilson; Linda Hopkins; others.

Kellogg's Presents...Big Band Classics .... RCA Special Products (M) DPL1-0438 8-12 80
Benny Goodman & Ella Fitzgerald; Count Basie & Jimmy Rushing; Glenn Miller; Duke Ellington & Joya Sherrill; Louis Armstrong; Earl Hines & Billy Eckstine; Tommy Dorsey; Artie Shaw.

Kentucky Derby Day: Phillip Morris Derby Festival Show .... Columbia (S) CS 9031 15-25
(Live material.) Johnny Cash; Stonewall Jackson; Billy Walker; Lefty Frizzell; Carl Smith; Carl & Pearl Butler; June Carter; Statler Brothers; Harold Bradley.

Keyboard Kings of Jazz .... RCA (M) LPT-4 15-25 50s
Count Basie; Earl Hines; Pete Johnson & Albert Ammons; Meade "Lux" Lewis; Duke Ellington; Fats Waller.

Kickin' Country .... K-Tel (S) WU 3600 5-10
Willie Nelson; Johnny Paycheck; Bobby Bare; Mickey Gilley; Jerry Reed; Rovers; Moe Bandy & Joe Stampley; Jerry Jeff Walker; New Riders of the Purple Sage; David Alan Coe; Johnny Russell; Ed Bruce; Gary Stewart & Merle Haggard.

Kicks & Chicks, Vol. 1, (Original 1960's Acid Punk) .... Eleventh Hour (SP) ???? 8-12 90
Jikis; Bubble Puppy; Marble Phrogg; Stone Harbour; Rising Four; Rainy Daze; White Light; Scott Beford Four; Bo Allen; Sin-Say-Shuns; Steam Fellow String Balloon.

King Curtis and Others .... Crown (M) CLP-294 10-20

King Curtis and Others .... Crown (S) CST-294 10-20
King Curtis; Etta James; Young Jessie; Shirley Gunter; Teen Queens; Jesse Belvin; Roscoe Gordon.

King - Federal Rockabillys .... King (S) 5016X 20-30 78
Mac Curtis; Charlie Feathers; Joe Penny; Ronnie Molleen; Bob & Lucille; Hank Mizell; Bill Beach.

"King" Kong Compilation .... Mango (M) MLPS-9632 5-10 81
Desmond Dekker & Aces; Maytals; Melodians; Ken Boothe; Tyrone Evans; Pioneers; Delroy Wilson; Burce Ruffin; Ansell Collins.

King of Comedy .... Warner Bros. (S) 9 23765-1 8-10 83
(Soundtrack.) Pretenders; Van Morrison; B.B. King; Talking Heads; Bob James; Rickie Lee Jones; Robbie Robertson; Ric Ocasek; Ray Charles; David Sanborn.

King of Rock and Roll .... Alshire (S) 5202 5-10 70
Bill Haley & His Comets; others.

King of Swing .... Pickwick (S) SPC 2181 10-15
Harry James; Bob Crosby; Billy May; Woody Herman; Artie Shaw; Les Brown; Benny Carter; Benny Goodman; Duke Ellington.

Kings and Queens .... Coronet (M) CX-260 15-20 62

Kings and Queens .... Coronet (S) CXS-260 15-20 62
Ray Charles; Maxine Brown; Jimmy Soul & Belmonts; Lena Horne; Little Richard; Chuck Jackson; Brook Benton.

Kings & Queens of Soul .... Columbia (S) DS 567 5-10 70
Maxine Brown; O.C. Smith; Aretha Franklin; Tymes; Major Lance; Peaches & Herb; Mongo Santamaria; Taj Mahal; Staple Singers; Walter Jackson.

Kings of Comedy .... Longines Symphonette (S) SYS-52882 10-15
George Burns; Abbott & Costello; Will Rogers; Jackie Gleason; Jack Benny; Smith & Dale; Al Jolson; Groucho Marx.

Kings of New Orleans .... Design (M) DLP-213 10-15 60s

Kings of New Orleans .... Design (S) SDLP-213 10-15 60s
Jack Teagarden; Eddie Condon; Earl Bostic; Pee Wee Hunt; Pete Fountain.

Kings of the Keyboard .... American Recording Society (M) 406 15-25 50s
Teddy Wilson; Bud Powell; Meade Lux Lewis; Art Tatum; Oscar Peterson.

Kings of the Rocking Fifties .... Clarion (S) 604 10-15 67
Ray Charles; Clyde McPhatter; Joe Turner; Chuck Willis; Ivory Joe Hunter.

Kings Sing the Blues .... Teem (M) LP-5005 15-25

Kooky Country .... Era (S) PBU 4190 8-12 82
Claude King; Johnny Preston; Jack & Misty; Dick Feller; Guy Drake; Little Jimmy Dickens; Ray Stevens; Hank Thompson; Charlie Walker; Tommy Collins; Billy Edd Wheeler; Larry Verne.

Kooky Tunes .... K-Tel (S) WU 3300 10-15 76
(Mail order offer.) Little Jimmy Dickens; Johnny Bond; Roger Miller; Jack Blanchard & Misty Morgan; Homer & Jethro; Fendermen; Charlie Walker; Murry Kellum; Bill Carlisle; Jr. Samples; Leapy Lee; Lonnie Donegan; Johnny Preston; Tom T. Hall; Olympics; Mel Tillis & Webb Pierce; Larry Verne.

Known Faces - New Faces (2 LP) .... Columbia (M) 42371 50-75 57
(Promotional issue only.) Ronnie Self; Tony Bennett; Mindy Carson; Jill Corey; Johnnie Ray; Marty Robbins; Eilene Rodgers; Jerry Vale; Billy Walker; George Morgan; Jimmy Dean; Billy Brown; Ken Bowers; Paul Hampton; Wayne Walker; Southerners.

Krush Groove .... Warner Bros. (S) 1-25295 8-10 85
(Soundtrack.) Chaka Khan; Beastie Boys; Kurtis Blow; Sheila E.; Fat Boys; Force M.D.'s; Gap Band; Debbie Harry; LL Cool J: Run D.M.C.

K-Tel Presents Country Superstars .... K-Tel (S) WU 3390 5-10 76
Glen Campbell; Freddy Fender; Johnny Rodriguez; George Jones; others.

L.A. Soundtrack '76 .... K-West (S) 43446 5-10 76

La Bamba .... Slash (S) 1-25605 8-15 87

La Bamba .... Slash (S) R-120062 8-10Re(Soundtrack.)

Ladies' Choice (Country Hits of Nashville's Top Female Vocalists) .... Harmony (S) KH-32487 5-10 73
Lynn Anderson; Jody Miller; Tammy Wynette; Tanya Tucker; others.

Lady Rock .... ???? (S) BU 4890 5-10 78
Crystals; Chiffons; Angels; Mary Wells; Sandy Posey; Skeeter Davis; Ketty Lester; Timi Yuro; Exciters; Chantels; Teddy Bears.

Lady Sunbeam Serenade .... Columbia Special Products (S) XTV 86058 8-12 60s
Andy Williams; Andre Previn; Tony Bennett; Four Lads; Ray Conniff; Robert Goulet; Percy Faith; Bobby Hackett; Sammy Kaye; Jerry Vale. (Made for Sunbeam Corporation.)

Larry Aiken's Gold Dust .... KQV (M) Radio Number One 20-30 60s
Gene & Eunice; Tokens; Moonglows; Willows; Flamingos; Hearts; Tune Weavers; Shepperd Sisters; Harptones; Ron Bernard; Rivileers.

Las Vegas Grind! .... Strip (M) 001 8-12
James Holloway; Jesters; Bob Taylor; Phantom; Ken Williams; Buddy Miller; Bob Calloway; Valiants; Crescendos; Wildtones; Zircons; Youngsters; Tic & Toc; Groovers; Tarantula Ghoul; Singing Dogs; Dyna-Sores; Casual-Aires; John & Jackie; Genteels.

Las Vegas Winners .... Spin-O-Rama (M) M-165 10-15 60s

Las Vegas Winners .... Spin-O-Rama (S) S-165 10-15 60s
John Gary; Keely Smith; Ray Charles; Johnny Rivers; 4 Seasons.

Last American Virgin .... Columbia (S) JS-38279 8-10 82
(Soundtrack.) Oingo Boingo; Phil Seymour; Tommy Tutone; others.

Last Dragon .... Motown (S) 6128ML 8-10 85
(Soundtrack.) Dwight David; Vanity; Alfie; Charlene; Willie Hutch; DeBarge; Stevie Wonder; Smokey Robinson & Syretta; Rockwell; Temptations.

Last Picture Show .... Columbia (S) S-31143 10-15 72
(Soundtrack.) Tony Bennett; Eddie Fisher; Pee Wee King; Hank Snow; Frankie Laine; Lefty Frizzell; Johnnie Ray; Jo Stafford.

Last Waltz: see BAND

Laugh of the Party .... Coral (M) CRL-57017 10-20 55
(Comedy.) Steve Allen; Buddy Hackett; Phil Foster; Harvey Stone; Tom D'Andrea & Hal March; Bob & Ray; Jackie Miles; Henny Youngman; Jimmy Komack; Hermione Gingold & Billy DeWolfe; Eddie Lawrence.

Laurie Golden Goodies .... Laurie (S) SLLP 2041 8-12 70s
Music Explosion; Chiffons; Royal Guardsmen; Gary "U.S." Bonds; Dion; Mystics; Dion & Belmonts; Jarmels; Gerry & Pacemakers.

Lawrence Welk Television Show: 10th Anniversary .... Dot (M) DLP-3591 8-12 64

Lawrence Welk Television Show: 10th Anniversary .... Dot (S) DLP-25591 10-15 64
Lawrence Welk; Myron Floren; Lennon Sisters; others.

Lawrence Welk Showcase .... Coral (M) CRL-57383 5-10 61

Lawrence Welk Showcase .... Coral (S) CRL7-57383 ?? 61
Lawrence Welk; Pete Fountain; Dick Kesner; "Big" Tiny Little; Myron Floren; Lennon Sisters; Alice Lon; Jerry Burke.

Lay That New Orleans Rock 'N' Roll Down .... Specialty (M) SP-2167 5-10 88
Ernie K-Doe; Larry Williams; Bobby Marchan; Lloyd Price; Roy Montrell; Li'l Millet; Art Neville; Edgar Blanchard.

Le Menu .... Azra (S) No Number Used 10-15 88
(Menu shaped picture disc. 100 made.)

Leadbelly Sings and Plays .... Stinson (S) 91 8-10 70
Leadbelly; Wood Guthrie; Josh White; Cisco Houston; Sonny Terry.

Leaders of the Pack (3 LP) .... Brookville/Laurie (SE) 8001/2/3 15-25 75
(Mail order offer.) Dion & Belmonts; Jarmels; Frankie Ford; Del Shannon; Dee Clark; Curtis Lee; Johnny & Hurricanes; Gene Chandler; Beach Boys; Duprees; Shangri-Las; Five Satins; Jimmy Clanton; Gary "U.S." Bonds; Lloyd Price; Lee Andrews; Linda Scott; Mystics; Bobby Goldsboro; Don & Juan; Lee Dorsey; Cathy Carr; Little Richard; Skyliners; Chiffons; Royal Guardsmen; Crests; Dean & Jean; Bernadette Carroll; Randy & Rainbows; Music Explosion; Capris; Passions.

Leaders of the Pack, Vol. 1 .... Laurie (S) LES-4049 5-10 83
(RCA Record Club issue.) Shangri-Las; Ritchie Valens; Bobby Fuller; Lenny Welch; Ernie Maresca; Everly Brothers; Dion; Marcie Blane; Chiffons; Del Shannon; Five Discs; Carlo.

Leaders of the Pack, Vol. 3 .... Laurie (S) LES-4063 5-10
Everly Brothers; Shangri-Las; Inez Foxx; Dee Clark; Del Shannon; Chiffons; Olympics; Dion; Jerry Butler; Ernie Maresca; Dion & Belmonts; Brooklyn Boys; Jimmy Curtiss; Frank Lyndon & Belmonts.

Lean on Me .... Warner Bros. (S) 1-25843-1 10-15 89
(Soundtrack.) Thelma Houston; Winans; Guns N' Roses; Stetsasonic; Roxanne Shante; TKA; Siedah Garrett; Force M.D.'s; Riff; Teen Dream; Taja Sevelle; Big Daddy Kane; Sandra Reaves-Phillips.

Leaning on the Lamp Post .... Modern Sound (SE) MS 1031 8-12
Chords; Betty Richards; Fred York; Houstons; Tony Christopher; Leroy Jones; Bobby Brooks; Music City Five Plus Ten; Richie Brown.

Lee Presents the Best of Live from the Lone Star........................ Columbia Special Products (S) P 15946 8-12 81
(Promotional issue only for Lee Jeans.) Moe Bandy & Joe Stampley; Johnny Winter; Asleep at the Wheel; Kinky Friedman; Billy Swan; Charly McClain; Johnny Rodriguez; New Riders of the Purple Sage; Muddy Waters.

Legal Eagles.. MCA (S) MCA-6172 8-10 86
(Soundtrack.) Rascals; Daryl Hannah; Steppenwolf; Elmer Bernstein; United Kingdom Symphony.

Legend of Jesse James .... A&M (S) SP-3718 10-15 80
(Soundtrack.) Levon Helm; Johnny Cash; Emmylou Harris; Charlie Daniels; Albert Lee.

Legendary Masters Series - Rural Blues, Vol. 1: Going Up the Country........................ Imperial (M) LM-94000 30-50 68
Nathaniel Terry; Manny Nichols; Country Jim; Lil Son Jackson; Thunder 'N' Lightnin'; Lightnin' Hopkins; Snooks Eaglin.

Legendary Masters Series - Rural Blues, Vol. 2: Saturday Night Function .... Imperial (M) LM-94001 30-50 68

Legendary Masters Series - Rural Blues, Vol. 3: Down Home Stomp.................................. Imperial (M) LM-94006 30-50 68
Papa Lightfoot; Boogie Bill Webb; J.D. Edwards; Lowell Fulson; Roosevelt Sykes; Manny Nichols; Country Jim; Little Son Jackson.

Legendary Masters Series - Rhythm 'N' Blues, Vol. 1: the End of an Era .... Imperial (M) LM-94003 30-50 68
Shaw-wez; Five Keys; Dukes; Sharp-Tones; Mellow Drops; Kidds (Pelicans) Spiders; Barons; Hawks; Jewels; Bees; Jivers (Centars).

Legendary Masters Series - Rhythm 'N' Blues, Vol. 2: Sweet N' Greasy .... Imperial (M) LM-94005 30-50 68
Shades; Pelicans (Kidds); Sha-Weeze; Savoys; Jewels; Fidelitones; Crystals; Robins; Avalons.

Legendary Masters Series - Urban Blues, Vol. 1: Blues Uptown .... Imperial (M) LM-94002 30-50 68
Fats Domino; Dirty Red; T-Bone Walker; Smiley Lewis; Roosevelt Sykes; Joe Turner; Mercy Dee; Joe Turner & Wynonie Harris.

Legendary Masters Series - Urban Blues, Vol. 2: New Orleans Bounce.............................. Imperial (M) LM-94004 30-50 68
Fats Domino; Smiley Lewis; Archibald; Little Sonny; Fats Matthews; Joe Turner; Wee Willie Wayne; Amos Milburn.

Legendary Song Stylists.. Capitol (S) SL 6706 8-12
Dean Martin; others.

Leonard Feathers Encyclopedia of Jazz of the '60s.. Exodus (S) EXS 6033 15-25 60s
Lightnin' Hopkins; Brownie McGhee; Jimmy Witherspoon; Juanita Hall; Joe Williams; Dinah Washington; Lambert, Hendricks & Ross; Mavis Rivers; Sarah Vaughan; Bill Henderson; Ann Richards.

Less Than Zero .... Def Jam/Columbia (S) SC-44042 5-8 87
(Soundtrack.) Aerosmith; Roy Orbison; Poison; L.; Glen Danzig & Power & Fury Orchestra; Slayer; Public Enemy; Black Flames; Joan Jett & Blackhearts; Oran "Juice" Jones; Alyson Williams; Bangles.

Let the Good Times Roll: see Rock of Ages – Early Rock Classics: 1952-1958 (Let the Good Times Roll)

Let the Good Times Roll.. Arista (S) ABM 2004 5-10 82
Bill Haley & His Comets; Little Richard; Bo Diddley; Danny & Juniors; Fats Domino; Shirelles; Coasters; Chubby Checker; Five Satins.

Let the Good Times Roll.. Guest Star (M) G 1905 10-20 60s

Let the Good Times Roll... Guest Star (S) GS 1905 10-20 60s
Shirley & Lee; Little Esther; Bull Moose Jackson; Dee Dee Evans; Big Caesar.

Let the Good Times Roll (2 LP) .... Bell (S) 9002 20-25 73
(Soundtrack.) Chuck Berry; Chubby Checker; Shirelles; Little Richard; Bo Diddley; Coasters; Five Satins; Fats Domino; Danny & Juniors; Bill Haley & His Comets.

Let Us Entertain You .... RCA (S) PRS-278 5-10 68
Arthur Fiedler & Boston Pops; Marty Gold; Ed Ames; Living Voices; Peter Nero; Henry Mancini; Morton Gould; Si Zentner; Marilyn Maye; Floyd Cramer; Sid Ramin. (Made for Magnavox.)

Let Yourself Go! .... Columbia Special Products (M) CSM-477 5-10
Tony Bennett; Steve Lawrence; Jerry Vale; Bobby Hackett; Julie Andrews; Barbra Streisand; Robert Goulet; Julie Andrews; Ray Conniff; Eydie Gorme; Johnny Mathis; Brothers Four. (Made for American Express.)

Let's Beat It... K-Tel (S) TV-2200 8-10 84
Paul McCartney & Michael Jackson; others.

Let's Celebrate Christmas .... Capitol (S) SL 6923 8-12 70s
Dean Martin; others.

Let's Clean Up the Ghetto .... Philadelphia Int'l (S) JZ-34659 5-10 77
Lou Rawls; Dee Dee Sharp; Teddy Pendergrass; Three Degrees; O'Jays; Billy Paul; Archie Bell & Drells; Intruders; Harold Melvin & Blue Notes.

Let's Dance (2 LP).. Columbia (M) C2 40517 8-12 87
Eddy Grant; Jackie Moore; Deniece Williams; Marlena Shaw; Patrick Hernandez; Sharon Ridley; Chicago; Dan Hartman & Leoleata Holloway; Buddy Miles; Cheryl Lynn; Sarah Dash; Gary' Gang.

Let's Dance.. Columbia (M) JC 36580 5-10 80
Benny Goodman; Les Brown; Harry James; Charlie Barnett; Count Basie; Gene Krupa.

Let's Dance.. K-Tel/Era (S) BU 4580 5-10 77
Chris Montez; Chubby Checker; Billy Bland; Diamonds; Bobby Freeman; Gary "U.S." Bonds; Dovells; Swinging Blue Jeans; Johnny & Hurricanes; Bugs Bower. (Some tracks are rerecordings.)

Let's Go to Church, Vol. 1 .... Capitol (EP) EPA-1-1042 5-8 59

Let's Go to Church, Vol. 2 .... Capitol (EP) EPA-2-1042 5-8 59

Let's Go to Church, Vol. 3 .... Capitol (EP) EPA-3-1042 5-8 59

Let's Go to Church.. Capitol (M) T-1042 15-25 59
Faron Young; Tennessee Ernie Ford; Margaret Whiting; Jane Froman; Gordon MacRae; Jimmy Wakely.

Let's Have a Dance Party .... Ace (M) LP-1019 30-40 61
Huey Smith & Clowns; Clowns; Marvels; Cliff Thomas; Jimmy Clanton.

Let's Have a Party .... Decca (M) DL-8655 30-50 58

Let's Have a Party .... MCA (S) DL-734615 5-10
Bill Haley & His Comets; Roger Williams; Sammy Davis Jr.; Liberace; Pete Fountain; Jack Jones; Ames Brothers; Lawrence Welk & His Champagne Music; Johnny Long; Guy Lombardo.

Let's Have a Party: see Rock of Ages – Rockabilly Influence: 1950-1960 (Let's Have a Party)

Let's Hit the Road .... Starday (M) S-306 10-20 65
Willis Brothers; Jimmy Dean; Joe Maphis.

Let's Live .... Columbia Special Products (M) CSP 106 10-15
Ella Fitzgerald; Dave Brubeck; Buddy Greco; Andre Previn; George Maharis; Judy Garland; Percy Faith; Jerry Vale; Hi-Lo's; Les Elgart.

Let's Party Bacardi .... Capitol Custom (M) CA-1M 10-15 60s

Let's Party Bacardi .... Capitol Custom (S) CA-1S 10-15 60s
Keely Smith; Jack Jones; Four Freshmen; Ray Anthony; Harry James; Jonah Jones; Woody Herman; George Shearing; Laurindo Almeida; Al Martino; Stan Kenton.

Lethal Weapon .... Warner Bros. (S) 1-25561 8-10 87
(Soundtrack.) Eric Clapton; David Sanborn; Michael Kamen; Honeymoon Suite.

Lethal Weapon 2 .... Warner Bros. (S) 1-25985 8-10 89
(Soundtrack.) George Harrison; Eric Clapton; Beach Boys; David Sanborn; Randy Crawford; Michael Kamen.

Letter to Breszhnev .... MCA (S) 6162 8-10 85
(Soundtrack.) Redskins; Fine Young Cannibals; Carmel; Sandie Shaw; Alan Gill; Bronski Beat; Flesh; Certain Ratio; Paul Quinn; Margi Clarke.

Liberty DJ Sampler, January 1963 .... Liberty (M) MM-417 15-20 62
(Promotional issue only.) Ace Cannon; Cozy Cole; Gene McDaniels; Nancy Ames; Martin Denny; Rivingtons; Ernie Freeman; Fleetwoods; Wanderers Three.

Liberty Hootenanny .... Liberty (M) L-5506 15-20 63
Liberty Hootenanny .... Liberty (S) S-6606 15-25 63
Nancy Ames; Bud & Travis; Johnny Mann Singers; Bob Harter; Wanderers Three; Leon Bibb; Walter Raim; Jackie De Shannon; George Mitchell Choir.

Liberty Proudly Presents Stereo - the Visual Sound .... Liberty (S) LST-100 15-25 59?
Billy Ward; Julie London; David Seville & Chipmunks; Sound effects; University Brass Band; Russ Garcia; Invitations; Stanley Johnson; Spencer Hagen Orchestra; Jad Paul's Banjo Magic; Martin Denny; Don Swan; John Buzon Trio; Chick Floyd; Jack Costanzo.

Liberty Records 1958-1964 (More Hits More Often) .... EMI America (S) ST 17204 8-12 86
Eddie Cochran; Johnny Burnette; Ventures; Gene McDaniels; Jackie De Shannon; Jan & Dean; Bobby Vee; Arbogast & Ross; David Seville; Rivingtons; Fleetwoods; Dick & DeeDee; Timi Yuro.

Liberty/United Artists: Teen Rock 1956-1966 .... EMI America (S) SQ 17263 8-12 87
Jay & Americans; Bertell Dache; Johnny Maestro; Belmonts; Patty Duke; Mike Clifford; Gary Lewis & Playboys; Bobby Vee; Fleetwoods; Patience & Prudence; Johnny Burnette; Jan & Dean.

License to Drive .... MCA (S) 6241 8-10 88
(Soundtrack.) Breakfast Club; Belinda Carlisle; Boys Club; Billy Ocean; New Edition; D.J.; Jonathan Butler; Femme Fatale; Slave Raider; Brenda K. Starr.

Life of the Party .... RCA (S) PR S-414 5-10 72
Larry Elgart; Al Hirt; Ralph Finagan; Perez Prado; King Curtis Combo; Jean Goldkitte; Richard Maltby; Bob Scobey; Tito Puente; Aaron Bell Trio.

Light of Day .... CBS/Blackheart (S) ZK-40654 8-10 87
(Soundtrack.) Barbusters; Fabulous Thunderbirds; Ian Hunter; Dave Edmunds; Bon Jovi; Joan Jett & Blackhearts; Michael J. Fox; Rick Cox; Chas Smith; Jon C.

Lightning Strikes .... Columbia Special Products (S) P-12072 8-12 73
Ten Years After; Mott the Hoople; Sly & Family Stone; Byrds; Clint Holmes; Argent; Ronny Dyson; Tommy James; Freda Payne; Edgar Winter; Earth, Wind & Fire; Blood, Sweat & Tears; O'Jays; Redbone; Billy Paul; Looking Glass; Blue Grass Country Boys (shown on cover as C.S. & Co.); Poco; Honeycone; Chairman of the Board.

Lights Out: San Francisco .... Blue Thumb (S) BTS-6004 8-12 72
Dan Hicks & His Hot Licks; Cliff Coulter; John Lee Hooker; Lydia Pense & Cold Blood; Loading Zone; Tower of Power; Pointer Sisters; Sylvester & His Hot Band.

Like 'Er Red Hot .... Duke (M) DLP-73 30-40 60
Bobby Bland; Johnny Ace; Casuals; Rob Roys; El Torros; Little Junior Parker; Paul Perryman; Clarence "Gatemouth" Brown; Ernie Harris; Willie Mae Thornton.

Lincoln Jamboree (Joel Ray Sprowl's) .... Queen City (M) 80415 10-15 68
Glenn & Joyce Phillips; "Boogie" Sherrard; Jack "Cornsilk" Lewis; Bob Jones; Lou Bingham; Becky Sue; Dell Shirley; Jim Curry; Charlie Durham; Ronnie Benningfield.

Listen in Good Health: see Capitol Promotional Releases/Samplers

Listen to Our Story (Panorama of American Balladry) .... Brunswick (M) BL-59001 75-125 50
(10–inch LP.) Buel Kazee; Bascom Lunsford; Frank Boggs; Reinhart; others.

Listen to the Blues .... Vanguard (M) 3007 10-15 67
Listen to the Blues .... Vanguard (S) V7-3007 15-20 67
Jimmy Rushing; Buddy Tate; Jo Jones; others.

Lisztomania .... A&M (S) SP-4546 10-12 75
(Soundtrack.) Roger Daltry; English Rock Ensemble; John Forsythe; Linda Lewis; George Michie; National Philharmonic Orchestra; Paul Nicholas; Rick Wakeman; David Wilde.

Little Bit of Groovy .... Capitol Creative Products (S) SL-6638 8-12 70
Joe South; Bobbie Gentry; Lord Sitar; Lou Rawls; Linda Ronstadt; Glen Campbell; Lettermen; Sounds of Our Times; Nancy Wilson; Linda Ronstadt & Stone Poneys.

Little Bits of Jazz .... Columbia (M) DJ-11 15-25
(Promotional issue only.) Thelonious Monk; Bud Powell; Miles Davis; Dave Brubeck Quartet; Stan Getz & Herbie Hancock; Joe Mooney; Carmen McRae & Dave Brubeck; Charles Lloyd.

Little Club Jazz (Small Groups in the '30s) .... New World (M) NW 250 10-15 76
Joe Venuti's Blue Four; Harlem Footwarmers; Eddie South & His International Orchestra; Henry Allen & Coleman Hawkins; Candy & Coco; Gene Gifford; Red Norvo & His Swing Sextet; Putney Dandridge; Stuff Smith & His Onyx Club Orchestra; Louis Prima & His New Orleans Gang; Roly's Tap Room Gang; Teddy Wilson; Emilio Caceres Trio; Joe Marsala's Chicagoans.

Little Drummer Boy .... Pickwick (S) SPC 3462 5-10
Dean Martin; others.

Little Green Apples .... Sterling (M) 4003 8-12 60s
Little Shot of Rhythm & Blues .... Surrey (S) SS-1042 8-12
Olympics; Earl Crosby; Mirettes; Bob & Earl; Jackie Lee; Belles; Bobby Garrett.

Live and Let Die: see McCARTNEY, Paul

Live at Bill Graham's Fillmore West .... Columbia (S) CS-9893 10-15 69
Mike Bloomfield; Taj Mahal; Nick Gravenites; others.

Live at CBGB's .... CBGB (S) CBGB-315 15-20 76
Tuff Darts with Robert Gordon; Shirts; Laughing Dogs; Manster Sun; Miamis; Mink De Ville; Stuart's Hammer.

Live at CBGB's (2 LP) .... Atlantic (S) 2-508 10-15 76
Tuff Darts with Robert Gordon; Shirts; Laughing Dogs; Manster Sun; Miamis; Mink De Ville; Stuart's Hammer.

Live at Rick's Cafe Americain .... Flying Fish (M) 079 8-12 79
Red Norvo; Urbie Green; Dave McKenna; Buddy Tate; Steve La Spina; Barrett Deems.
Live at the Rat, Vol. 1 .... Rat (S) 528 8-10
Willie Alexander's Boom Boom Band; Susan; Third Rail; DMZ; Real Kids; Thundertrain; Sass; Marc Thor; Boize; Infliktors.
Live at the Roadhouse .... Criminal (S) 33-02 8-12 80s
In Your Face Band; Curtis Salagado; Paul Delay; Tom McFarland; Isaac Scott.
Live at the Whiskey A-Go-Go: see Recorded Entertainment Live at the Whiskey A-Go-Go
Live at Yankee Stadium: see ISLEY BROTHERS
Live! For Life .... I.R.S. (S) 5731 5-10 86
Stewart Copeland & Derek Holt; Bob Marley & Wailers; R.E.M.; Alarm; General Public; Sting; Bangles; Oingo Boingo; Go-Go's; Squeeze. (AMC Cancer Research Center benefit.)
Live from the Silver Slipper .... ABC/Dot (S) DOSD-2038 5-10 75
Tommy Overstreet; Three of a Kind; Linda Hart; Skip Devol.
Live It Up and Laugh It Up .... Starday (M) S-187 15-20 62
Johnny Bond; Cowboy Copas; Justin Tubb; others.
Live Stiffs .... Stiff (S) STF-0001 5-10 70s
Nick Lowe's Last Chicken in the Shop; Wreckess Eric & New Rockets; Larry Wallis' Psychedelic Rowdies; Elvis Costello & Attractions; Ian Dury & Block Heads.
Live - the Best of the Rock 'N' Roll Revival .... De Ja Vu (S) 100 8-12
Harptones; Charts; Channels; Earls; Nutmegs; Shangri-Las; Turbans; Shirley & Lee; Five Keys.
Liverpool Today .... Capitol (M) T-2544 15-20 66
Liverpool Today .... Capitol (S) ST-2544 15-25 66
Living World of SQ Quadraphonic Sound .... Columbia Special Products (Q) PQ 11796 10-20 70s
Blood, Sweat & Tears; Columbia Brass Ensemble; Peter Nero; Johnny Mathis; Percy Faith; Anthony Newman & Friends; Isaac Stern & Columbia Symphony Orchestra; New York Philharmonic; Mormon Tabernacle Choir.
Lloyd Thaxton Presents: see Greatest Dance Hits Slauson Style
London a Go Go, Vol. 1 .... Carnaby (M) CR-VOL I 10-15 66
Artists not identified on disc or cover.
London a Go Go, Vol. 2 .... Carnaby (M) CR-VOL II 10-15 66
Artists not identified on disc or cover.
London Hit Parade .... London (M) LL-1613 35-45 50s
Vera Lynn with Roland Shaw; Frank Chacksfield; Lonnie Donnegan; Mantovani; Gracie Fields; Anton Karas; Stanley Black; David Whitfield; Edmundo Ros; Primo Scala; Frank Weir; Bulawayo Band.
London Hit Parade .... London (SE) PS-525 10-15 68
Vera Lynn with Roland Shaw; Frank Chacksfield; Lonnie Donnegan; Mantovani; Gracie Fields; Anton Karas; Stanley Black; David Whitfield; Edmundo Ros; Primo Scala; Frank Weir; Bulawayo Band.
London Really Swings .... Columbia (M) 0301 10-15
Lonesome Valley .... Guest Star (M) G 1490 8-12
Lonesome Valley .... Guest Star (S) GS 1490 8-12
Carl Story; Lonzo & Oscar; Frankie Miller; Stanley Brothers; Cowboy Copas; Jimmie Williams & Red Ellis; Phipps Family; Lewis Family; Sam & Kirk McGee.
Long Ago and Far Away: see Great Love Songs of the '40s
Long Hit Summer on Epic, Portrait & CBS Associated Labels .... Epic (S) EAS 2118 10-15 85
Beach Boys; Jeff Beck & Rod Stewart; John Cafferty & Beaver Brown Band; REO Speedwagon; Dead or Alive; Luther Vandross; Carly Simon; 'til Tuesday; Sade; Dan Fogelberg.
Look of Love .... Crane/Norris (S) CN 101 8-12 77
David Soul; B.J. Thomas; Barry DeVorzon; Keith Carradine; Michel Legrand; George Benson; Richard Harris; Astrud Gilberto; Claudine Longet; Gladys Knight & Pips; Dorothy Moore; Roberta Flack; Sergio Mendes; Sylvia; Lou Rawls; Maureen McGovern; Rhythm Heritage; Dionne Warwick; Johnny Bristol; Major Harris.
Look Who's Surfin' Now .... King (M) 882 25-35 63
Look Who's Surfin' Now .... King (S) KS-882 25-35 63
James Brown; Little Willie John; Freddy King; Albert King; Hank Moore; King Curtis; Surf Jumpers; King Surfers; Tonni Kalash; Gene Redd; Johnny Otis; Wild Kats.
Lookin' Back .... Columbia (S) 1P 6975 8-12
Little Anthony & Imperials; Kingston Trio; Clarence Carter; American Breed; Bobby Vee; Eddie Floyd; Classics IV: Johnny Cymbol; Lou Christie; Surfaris. (Columbia House Record Club issue.)
Looking Back – The Jumping 50s (5 LP) .... CBS (S) C5-10919 ?? 72
Looking for Mr. Goodbar .... Columbia (S) JS-35029 8-10 77
(Soundtrack.) Donna Summer; Commodores; Thelma Houston; Diana Ross; O'Jays; Bill Withers; Boz Scaggs; Marlena Shaw.
Looney Tunes .... K-Tel (S) NU-9140 5-10 78
Napoleon XIV; Coasters; Allan Sherman; Rivingtons; Edd Byrnes; David Seville & Chipmunks; Buzz Clifford; Nervous Norvus; Joe Perkins; Jumpin' Gene Simmons; Charlie Drake; Ray Stevens; Tiny Tim; Lonnie Donegan; Sam the Sham & Pharaohs; John Zacherle; Susan Christie; Ernie K-Doe.
LOOP-FM 98 (Chicago) .... Loop-FM (S) 20-30 78
(Picture disc.)
Loose Ends .... Union Pacific (S) UP 005 10-15 72
Young John Watson; Scotty Moore Trio; B.B. Cunningham Jr.; Eddie Skelton; Virtues; Vigilantes; Hawk (Jerry Lee Lewis); Viscounts; Duane Eddy; Ronnie & Rainbows; Fendermen; Fireballs.
Lost Angels .... A&M (S) SP-3926 8-10 89
(Soundtrack.) Apollo Smile; Happy Mondays; Cure; Soundgarden; Poghes; Toni Childs; Soul Asylum; Raheem; Royal Court of China; John Williams; Wayne Shorter.
Lost Boys .... Atlantic (S) 7 81767-1 8-10 87
(Soundtrack.) INXS; Jimmy Barnes; Lou Graham; Roger Daltry; Echo & Bunnymen; Gerard McMann; Eddie & Tide; Tim Cappello; Thomas Newman; Mummy Calls.

Lost in Love (4 LP) ....Starland/Warner Special Products (S) 4548 15-20 94
Cars; Eric Carmen; Sheriff; Johnny Hates Jazz; Meat Loaf; Foreigner; Kansas; Atlantic Starr; Alan Parsons Project; Moody Blues; Linda Ronstadt & Aaron Neville; Doobie Brothers; Spandau Ballet; REO Speedwagon; Christopher Cross; Nicolette Larson; Dan Hill; Robbie Dupree; Dan Hartman; Elton John; Lou Gramm; Bangles; Glenn Frey; Donny Osmond; Boy Meets Girl; Air Supply; Expose; Billy Very & Beaters; ELO; Jets; Champaign; Richard Marx; Starship; Kinks; Debbie Gibson; Restless Heart.

Lost in the Stars: the Music of Kurt Weill ....A&M (S) 9-5104 8-12 85
Sting; Steve Weisberg; Fowler Brothers with Stan Bidgway; Marianne Faithfull; Chris Spedding; Van Dyke Parks; Ralph Shucket with Richard Butler; Armadillo String Quartet; John Zorn; Lou Reed; Carla Bley & Phil Woods; Tom Waits; Dagmar Krause; Todd Rundgren; others.

Lost Soul, Vol 1 ....Epic (SP) PE 37730 5-10 82
Brenda & Tabulations; Bill Covay; Gwen McCrae; Jackie Moore; Essence; Soul Children; Z.Z. Hill; Betty LaVette; Mavis Staples & Staple Singers; Vibrations.

Lost Soul, Vol 2 ....Epic (SP) PE 37731 5-10 82
Chairman of the Board; Brenda & Tabulations; Philly Devotions; Joe Tex; Roger Hatcher; Bobby Womack & Brotherhood; Howard Tate; Essence; Gwen McCrae; Don Covay & Goodtimers.

Lost Soul, Vol 3 ....Epic (SP) PE 37732 5-10 82
Tyrone Davis; Bobby Womack; Thelma Jones; Gwen McCrae; Z.Z. Hill; Lou Courtney; Fontella Bass; Obrey Wilson; Laura Lee; Mattie Moultrie.

Lou Chicchetti's Bronx Classics ....Crystal Ball (S) 122 8-12 80s
Cousins; Chuckles; Dials; Chuck Harper; Lee Mareno & Runarounds; Sonny Dee; Al Reno; Darrell & Dreams.

Louisiana Blues ....Arhoolie (S) 1054 10-15 70
Henry Gray; Silas Hogan; Whispering Smith; Guitar Kelley; Clarence Edwards.

Louisiana Cajun Music, Vol. 1 .... Old Timey (M) LP-108 5-10

Louisiana Cajun Music, Vol. 2 .... Old Timey (M) LP-109 5-10

Louisiana Cajun Music, Vol. 3 .... Old Timey (M) LP-110 5-10

Louisiana Cajun Music, Vol. 4 .... Old Timey (M) LP-111 5-10

Louisiana Cajun Music, Vol. 5 .... Old Timey (M) LP-114 5-10

Love in the Afternoon (Soap Opera Stars Singing) ....MCA (S) 5392 8-12 83
Mary Gordon Murray; Stuart Damon; Loanne Bishop; Joel Crothers; Helen Gallagher; Sharon Gabet; Michael Storm; Susan Lucci; John Gabriel; James Mitchell.

Love Italian Style (2 LP ....RCA (S) PRS-438 15-25
Sophia Loren; Frank Sinatra; Louis Prima; Dick Contino; Hugo Winterhalter; Eddie Fisher; Enrico Caruso; Tony Martin with the Interludes; Hugo Montenegro; Lou Monte; Living Strings; Sergio Franchi; Three Suns; Domenico Modugno; Peter Nero; Al Hirt; Vic Damone; Julius LaRosa; Ray Ellis; Frankie Fanelli; Gino Del Vescaro & His Mandolins.

Love Me Tender (2 LP) ....Time-Life (S) STL-133 15-25 91
(Mail order offer.) Elvis Presley; Tommy Edwards; Crests; Platters; Johnny Mathis; Sonny James; Jim Reeves; Tune Weavers; Jerry Butler & Impressions; Five Satins; Capris; Chantels; Penguins; Danleers; Dion & Belmonts; Pat Booner; Shep & Limelites; Flamingos; Jesse Belvin; Santo & Johnny; Brenda Lee; Everly Brothers; Lenny Welch; Little Anthony & Imperials; Johnnie & Joe; Phil Phillips; Sammy Turner; Duprees; Connie Francis; Nino Tempo & April Stevens; Conway Twitty; Bobby Vinton; Jack Scott; Skyliners; Gene Pitney; Skeeter Davis; Floyd Cramer.

Love Rock ....Ronco/Columbia Special Products (S) P 14235 5-10 77
Lou Rawls; Minnie Riperton; Barry White; Hollies; Aretha Franklin; Seals & Crofts; Sylvia; Marvin Gaye; Diana Ross; Love Unlimited; England Dan & John Ford Coley; Melissa Manchester; Starbuck; Bill Withers; Millie Jackson; Hamilton, Joe Frank & Reynolds; Billy Paul; Gladys Knight & Pips.

Love Seventies ....Warner/JCI (S) 3303 8-12 86
Andy Kim; Gladys Knight & Pips; Jim Croce; Lou Rawls; Randy Van Warmer; Brook Benton; Elton John; Al Green; Maria Muldaur; America; Dorothy Moore; Souther, Hillman, Furay Band.

Love Sixties ....Warner/JCI (S) 3102 8-12 85
Gene Pitney; Jerry Butler & Betty Everett; Everly Brothers; James & Bobby Purify; Delfonics; Toys; Walker Brothers; Oscar Tony Jr.; Mel Carter; Dionne Warwick; Shirelles; Gladys Knight & Pips.

Love Songs of the Rock & Roll Era .... Era (S) BU 5260 5-10 82
Frankie Avalon; Jay Black; Ben E. King; Timi Yuro; Johnny Maestro; Gerry & Pacemakers; Roger Williams; Chad & Jeremy; Crystals; Gogi Grant; Shirelles; Barbara Lewis.

Love That Music! ....A&M (S) LTM-1 5-10
Herb Alpert; Carpenters; Nazareth; Joe Cocker; Captain & Tennille; Peter Frampton; LTD; Paul Williams; Peter Allen; Joan Armatrading; Brothers Johnson; Perry Botkin Jr.; Rita Coolidge; Gino Vannelli; Chuck Mangione.

Love Those Goodies .... Checker (M) LP-2973 50-75 59
(Black vinyl.)

Love Those Goodies .... Checker (M) LP-2973 500-750 59
(Multi-color vinyl. Promotional issue only.) Bo Diddley; Sugar Boy; Gene Barge; Jimmy Witherspoon; Little Walter; Eddie Chamblee; Lowell Fulson; Little Walter; Al Kent; Willie Dixon.

Love You New Orleans ....Bandy (S) 70008 5-10 80s
Hueys; Allen Toussaint; Lee Bates; David Batiste & Gladiators; Skip Easterling; Ernie K-Doe; Clint West & Boogie Kings; Eskew Reeder; Chuck Carbo; Kathy Savoy; Little Buck.

Lovedolls Superstar ....SST (S) 062 8-10
(Soundtrack.) Lovedolls; Redo Kross; Black Flag; Sonic Youth; Painted Willie; Lawndale; Gone; Anarchy 6; Meat Puppets; Dead Kennedys.

Loveless ....Roadshow (S) RS-102 8-12 83
(Soundtrack.) Bill Justis; Sandy Nelson; Diamonds; Little Richard; Robert Gordon; Eddy Dixon.

Lovers Concerto ....RCA Special Products (S) PS 418 5-10 72
Peter Nero; Duke Ellington; Ray Hartley; Eddie Heywood; Frankie Carle; Floyd Cramer; Cy Walter; Derek & Ray; Earl Hines; Skitch Henderson.

Lovin' Fifties .... Warner/JCI (SE) 3203 5-10 85
Platters; Tommy Edwards; Fleetwoods; Elegants; Sonny James; Conway Twitty; Buddy Holly; Everly Brothers; Crests; Mark Dinning; Frankie Avalon; Connie Francis.

Loving Couples .... Motown (S) M8-949 8-10 80
(Soundtrack.) Fred Karlin; Greg Wright; Temptations; Billy Preston; Jermaine Jackson; Syreeta.

Loving Memory .... Motown (S) 642 10-15 68
Gladys Knight & Pips; Marvin Gaye; Diana Ross & Supremes; Martha & Vandellas; Four Tops; others.

Low Down Blues .... Continental (M) C-16002 15-20 62
Champion Jack Dupree; Brownie McGhee; Sonny Boy & Lonnie; others.

Low Down Memphis Barrelhouse Blues .... Mamlish (S) 3803 8-10 72
Hattie Hart; John Estes; Memphis Minnie; others.
Low Down Memphis Harmonica .... Nighthawk (S) 103 10-15
Hot Shot Love; Joe Hill Louis; J.D. Horton; Willie Nix; Woodrow Adams; W. Horton.
Lowery Group 25 Golden Years (2 LP) .... JL (S) No Number 20-30
(Promotional only issue.) Sonny James; Ray Stevens; Brenda Lee; Gene Vincent; Tommy Roe; Billy Joe Royal; Joe South; Dizzy; Paul Revere & Raiders; Dennis Yost & Classics IV; Tams; Beatles; Friend & Lover; Deep Purple; Osmonds; Starbuck.
Lullabies of Birdland .... Forum (S) SFC-9056 15-25 60s
Count Basie; Joe Williams; Woody Herman; Sarah Vaughan; Johnny Smith; Charlie Parker; Maynard Ferguson; Lambert, Hendricks & Ross; Billy Exkstine; Dizzy Gillespie; Charlie Parker; Art Tatum; Miles Davis & J.J. Johnson.
M'm! M'm! Good! .... Columbia (S) CSS-918 8-10 69
New Christy Minstrels; Robert Goulet; Steve Lawrence; Eydie Gorme; Charlie Byrd; Jerry Vale; Johnny Mathis; John Davidson; Diahann Carroll; Jim Nabors; Ray Conniff; Lester Lanin. (Special products. Made for Campbell's Soup.)
MCA Christmas Programming Special .... MCA (SP) 1910 8-12 70s
(Promotional issue only.) Bing Crosby; Brenda Lee; Harry Simeone Choral; Bobby Helms; Guy Lombardo; others.
MCA Music (4 LP) .... MCA (S) ???? 25-30
(Promotional issue only.) Beatles; others.
MCA Sound Conspiracy .... MCA/Decca (S) 734837 8-12 71
(Promotional issue only.) Wishbone Ash; Help; Matthews Southern Comfort; Melissa; American Eagle; Fanny Adams; Virgil Fox; Chelsea; Glass Harp; Jeremiah; Raw.
MCA Spring Sampler (2 LP) .... MCA (S) L33-2-1177 5-10
(Promotional issue only.) Joe Ely; Van Stephenson; Tracy Ullman; Ravens; Tony Carey; Chameleons U.K.; Frankie & Knockouts; Rod Falconer; Real Life; Nick Kershaw; End Games.
MCA Vintage Series .... MCA (S) 25121 5-10
Big Danny Oliver; George Hamilton IV: Shields; Carl Dobkins Jr.; Buddy Holly; Woolies; Chuck Berry; Mitty Collier; Three Dog Night.
MCA Vintage Series, Vol. 7 .... MCA (S) 25025 5-10 86
American Breed; Len Barry; Chantays; Bobby Moore & Rhythm Aces; Shirley Ellis; Buddy Holly; Chuck Berry; Tommy Tucker; Roy Head & Traits; Impressions.
MGM DJ Sampler, August 1962 .... MGM (M) E DJ 4 15-20 62
Eileen Farrell; Eartha Kitt; Cyril Ornadel; Sam the Man Taylor; Ramblers Three; David Rose; George Shearing; Connie Francis; Bill Ramal; Jonah Jones; Paul LaValle.
MGM Hits with a Beat, Vol. 1 .... MGM (M) E-3826 20-30 60
Conway Twitty; Impalas; Rocky Hart; Sam the Man Taylor; Clyde McPhatter; Danny Valentino; Sheb Wooley.
MGM Million Sellers, Country and Western Hits Vol. 1 .... MGM (M) E-3825 20-25 60
Hank Williams; others.
MGM Million Sellers, Pop Hits Vol. 1 .... MGM (M) E-3824 15-25 60
Art Lund; Art Mooney; Billy Eckstine; Dick Hyman; David Rose; Blue Barron; Silvana Mangano; Leroy Holmes; Eileen Barton; Lenny Hayton; Ziggy Ellman.
MGM Parade of Stars: see Parade of Stars
MGM Special Disc Jockey Sampler for August & September .... MGM (M) MG DJ2 10-20 58
(Promotional issue only.) Joni James; Hank Williams; Leroy Holmes; Robert Maxwell; Kaye Ballard; Maurice Chevalier; Sheila Gayle; Jimmy Lanin; others.
MGM Star Power Release 1960 (2 LP) .... MGM (M) MGDJ8 20-40 60
(Promotional issue only.) Connie Francis; Conway Twitty; Tommy Edwards; U.S. Coast Guard Academy Singers; Dana de la Plaza de Toros; Sabicas; Robert Stolz; Obadia Sugar Middle East Ensemble; Ornadel; Jaye P. Morgan; Harry James; Rosemary Clooney; Maurice Chevalier; Hank Williams; Clyde McPhatter; Robert Maxwell; Roger King Morgan; Charles Camiller; Joni James; David Rose; Mark Dinning; Ray Ellis.
MGM Star Spectacular, Vol. 1 .... MGM (M) PM-10 8-12 60s
Stan Getz; Judy Garland; Gene Krupa; Debbie Reynolds; Ray Ellis; Count Basie; Ramblers Three; Al Hirt; Anita O'Day; Andre Previn; Mel Torme; David Rose; Bill Walker.
MGM Top Hits, Vol. 1 .... MGM (M) E-3814 20-30 60
Conway Twitty; Jimmy Jones; Jaye P. Morgan; Clyde McPhatter; Tommy Edwards; Mark Dinning.
MGM Years .... MGM (S) PG-5878 18-20
(Soundtrack. Boxed set.) Judy Garland; Betty Hutton; Howard Keel; Fred Astaire; Gene Kelly; Esther Williams; Ricardo Montalban; William Warfield; Leslie Caron; others.
MTV's Rock and Roll to Go .... Elektra (S) 60399 5-10 85
Cars; Cyndi Lauper; Madonna; Police; Thompson Twins; others.
Mad Mike Moldies, Vol. 1 .... N.R.M. (M) 1590 20-40 68
Dyke & Californians; Vito & Salutations; Jimmie Heap; Emcees; Kai Ray; Instrumentals; Aquanites; Harvey; Arabians; Leo Wright & El Jays; Fabulaires; Empires; Swinging Hearts; Hollywood Saxons; Del Cords; Chevrons.
Mad Mike Moldies, Vol. 2 .... N.R.M. (M) 1591 20-40 68
Savoys; Bobby Lee Trammell; Tommy James & Shondells; Big Syl Barnes; Castaways; Blendtones; Andy Charles; Rusty Isabel; Franke Olvera; Rome & Paris; Gay Knights; DeVaurs.
Mad Mike Moldies, Vol. 4 .... N.R.M. (M) 1592 20-40 68
(Black vinyl. There is no Vol. 3 in this series.)
Mad Mike Moldies, Vol. 4 .... N.R.M. (M) 1592 30-50 68
(Colored vinyl.) Sonics; Saxons; J.J. Jackson; Bobby Summers; Saucers; Vic Dana; Fascinators; Contrasts; Del-nites; Five Satins.
Mad Mike Moldies, Vol. 5 .... N.R.M. (M) 1593 20-40 68
Tasso the Great Kain; Ronnie Cook; Corvettes; Jimmie Kelly; Count Ferrell; Baskerville Hounds; Anthony & Sophomores; Monorays; Bobby Taylor; Nino & Ebb Tides; Grand Prees.
Mad Twists Rock and Roll: see DELLWOODS / Mike Russo / Jeanne Hayes
Made in Heaven .... Elektra (S) 60729-1 8-10 87
(Soundtrack.) Martha Davis; R.E.M.; Ric Ocasek; Luther Vandross; Nylons; Buffalo Springfield; Mark Isham.
Made in Philadelphia: see 22 Hits By the Original Artists, Frank Feller
Made in Pittsburgh, Vol. 1 .... Bogus (S) LP-225801 10-15
Eddie & Otters; Empire; Little Ramus; Walk & Roll Brothers; Flashcats; Leslie Smith; Fragile; Rock'n Ravens; Hank Bank; Gravel/Hanner-Corbin Band.
Made in Pittsburgh, Vol. 2 .... Bogus (S) LP-1111801 10-15
Bill Loeffler; Flashcats; Ratriderz; Walk & Roll Brothers; Justin Kase; Lovesick; Empire; Eddie & Otters.

Made in Pittsburgh, Vol. 3 .... Bogus (S) LP-1112801 10-15
Swarm; Hipsters; Whereabouts; Rum Hounds; Dialtones; Down-Town-ers; Modern Anxiety; Sputniks.

Magic Christian.......... Commonwealth United (S) CU-6604 15-20 70
(Soundtrack.) Badfinger; Thunderclap Newman; Ringo Starr; Peter Sellers; Ken Thorne. (With dialogue. Known to have at least three sleeve and label variations.)

Magic Garden of Stanley Sweetheart.......... MGM (S) 1SE-20 10-15 70
(Soundtrack.) Bill Medley; Eric Burdon & War; Mike Curb Congregation; Crow; David Lucas; Wheel; Angeline Butler; Stilroc; Michael Greer; Angeline Butler.

Magic Memories, Vol. 1 .... J&L (S) 1215 5-10 86
Judy Thomas; Van McCoy; Top Hits; Love Notes; Five Superiors; Squires; Dranell & Dreams; Contesters; Resonics; Dimensions; Davi; Nancy Thomas.

Magic Moment (Candlelite Music Proudly Presents) (2 LP) .... RCA Special Products (S) DLP2-0157 10-20 75
(Mail order offer.) Neil Sedaka; Legends Orchestra; Everly Brothers; Kay Starr; Sparkles; Jimmy Elledge; Ray Peterson; Four Lovers; Dubs; Howdy Doody & Buffalo Bob; Sonny Til & Orioles; Wailers; Sam Cooke; Don Gibson; Street Corner Choir; Statler Brothers; Ames Brothers; George Hamilton IV: Perez Prado; Three Chuckles; Rebells; Fess Parker; Twin-Tones (Jim & John).

Magic Moments from the Tonight Show (2 LP) .... Casablanca (S) SPNB-1296 20-40 76
(TV Soundtrack. Includes poster.) Johnny Carson; Ed McMahon; Doc Severinsen; Jay Silverheels; Bette Midler; Groucho Marx; George Carlin; Dean Martin; Pearl Bailey; Lenny Bruce; Billie Holiday; Judy Garland; Aretha Franklin; Smothers Brothers; Richard M. Nixon; Peter Falk; Ike & Tina Turner; Lucille Ball; Desi Arnaz Jr.; Buddy Hackett; Jack Benny; Glen Campbell; Don Rickles Sammy Davis Jr.; George Burns; Joey Bishop; Jerry Lewis; others.

Magic of Christmas (2 LP) .... Capitol (S) SWBB 93810 8-12
Robert Wagner Chorale; Peggy Lee; Nat King Cole; Glen Campbell; Lettermen; Tennessee Ernie Ford; Ella Fitzgerald; Wayne Newton; Al Martino; Bobbie Gentry; Dean Martin; Fred Waring; Nancy Wilson; Bing Crosby; Beach Boys; Sandler & Young; Dinah Shore; Lou Rawls; Voices of Christmas; Jo Stafford.

Magic of Christmas (3 LP) .... Columbia House (SE) P3S 5806 10-15 72
(Boxed set. Record Club issue.) Ronnie Aldrich; Johnny Mathis; Tammy Wynette; E. Power Biggs; Bert Kaempfert; Burl Ives; Mantovani; Philadelphia Orchestra; Eugene Ormandy & Temple University Choir; Robert Page; James Last; Alfred Burt Carols; Bing Crosby; Lennon Sisters; Ray Conniff; Charles Smart & James Blades; Herb Alpert & Tijuana Brass; Lawrence Welk; John Davidson; Mahalia Jackson; Guy Lombardo; Robert Goulet; Terry Baxter; Roger Williams; Gunter Kallmann; Jim Nabors; Fred Waring; Patti Page; Percy Faith; Arthur Fiedler & Boston Pops; Mormon Tabernacle Choir; Richard P. Condie; Alexander Schreiner; Frank Asper; St. Thomas Choir; Tony Bennett; Charlie Byrd; Julius Wechter; Baja Marimba Band; Andre Kostelanetz; Phyllis Curtin with Kilian Boys Choir; Joan Sutherland; Doris Day; New York Philharmonic; Leonard Bernstein.

Magical Memories (2 LP .... Mercury (S) R 214447 8-12 76
Teresa Brewer; Ralph Marterie; New Vaudeville Band; Buddy Morrow; Frankie Laine; Roger Miller; Rusty Draper; Louis Armstrong; Bill Justis; Patti Page; Ted Weems; Soeur Sourire (Singing Nun); Lawrence Welk; Sarah Vaughan; Jan August; Dinah Washington; Horst Jankowski; Eddy Howard; Harmonicats.

Magnavox Award Winners (60th Anniversary) .... Columbia Special Products (S) C 10391 5-10 70s
Charlie Byrd; Percy Faith; Tony Bennett; Lynn Anderson; Bobby Vinton; Ray Conniff; Johnny Mathis; Peter Nero; Jerry Vale; Andre Kostelanetz.

Magnavox Presents A Reprise of Great Hits.......... Reprise (S) PRO-578 10-20 73
(Soundtrack. Promotional issue only.) Frank Sinatra; Association; Count Basie; Harpers Bizarre; Don Ho; Barbara McNair; Nelson Riddle.

Magnificent Moments from MGM Movies .... MGM (M) E-4017 20-25 62
(Soundtrack.) Judy Garland; Gene Kelly; Vic Damone; Louis Jourdan; Howard Keel; Georges Guetary; Adolph Deutsch; Leslie Caron; Mel Ferrer; Kathryn Grayson; Ann Blyth; William Warfield; Lennie Hayton.

Magnificent Movie Music .... United Artists (M) UAL-3476 8-12 66
Magnificent Movie Music .... United Artists (S) UAS-6476 ?? 66
(Soundtrack.) Ferrante & Teicher; Leroy Holmes; John Barry; Elmer Bernstein; Neal Hefti; George Martin; Burt Bacharach; Riz Ortolani; Arnold Goland.

Mahoney's Last Stand .... Atlantic (S) SD-36-126 8-12 76
(Soundtrack.) Ron Wood; Ronnie Lane; Ian McLagan; Bruce Rowlands; Rick Grech; Ian Stewart; Kenney Jones; Pete Townshend; Bubby Keys; Jim Price; Benny Gallagher; Glynis Johns; Billy Nicholls.

Main Event.......... Columbia (S) JS-36115 8-10 79
(Soundtrack.) Barbra Streisand; Frankie Valli & 4 Seasons; Loggins & Messina.

Male Singing Greats .... Rondo R (M) 2017 10-15 50s
Male Singing Greats .... Rondo RS (S) 2017 10-15 50s
Ray Charles; Nat King Cole; Johnny Desmond; Mel Torme; Frankie Laine; Billy Daniels.

Man Behind the Wheel.......... Starday (M) 404 10-15 67
Man Behind the Wheel.......... Starday (S) 404 10-15 67
Dave Dudley; George Morgan; Red Sovine; others.

Man with a Horn .... Decca (M) DL 8250 20-30 50s
Randy Brooks; Jimmy McPartland; Bobby Hackett; Louis Armstrong; Ralph Mendes; Roy Eldridge; Billy Butterfield; Sonny Dunham; Muggsy Spanier; Bunny Berigan; Yank Lawson; Howard McGhee.

Manhunter .... MCA (S) 6182 8-10 86
(Soundtrack.) Iron Butterfly; Prime Movers; Reds; Red 7; Michael Rubini; Shriekback.

Many Moods of Christmas.......... Columbia/Goodyear (S) P-12013 5-10 73
Frank Sinatra; Ella Fitagerald; Barbra Streisand; Pat Boone; Sammy Davis Jr.; Jo Stafford; Doris Day; Tex Beneke; Pete Fountain; Bing Crosby; Julie Andrews; Andy Williams; Tony Bennett. (Special products. Made for Goodyear.)

Many Moods of Music.......... Columbia Special Products (S) CSS 864 5-10
Ray Conniff; Andre Kostelanetz; Percy Faith; Louis Armstrong; Andre Previn Trio; Cleveland Orchestra; New York Philharmonic; Philadelphia Orchestra.

Maple on the Hill.......... Camden (M) CAL-898 10-15 65
Maple on the Hill.......... Camden (S) CAS-898 10-15 65
Delmore Brothers; Uncle Dave Macon; Mainers Mountaineers; Bradley Kincaid; Carlisle Brothers; Riley Puckett.

Mar Y Sol.......... Atco (S) SD 2-705 8-12 72
Dr. John; Osibisa; Cactus; Allman Brothers Band; Herbie Mann; J. Geils Band; Mahavishnu Orchestra; B.B. King; Emerson, Lake & Palmer; Nitzinger; Jonathan Edwards; John Baldry. (Live at Mar Y Sol Festival.)

Mardi Gras in New Orleans .... Mardi Gras (M) MG-1001 5-10 76
Professor Long Hair; Wild Magnolias; Al Johnson; Earl King; Stop Inc.; Hawketts.

Married to the Mob .... Reprise (S) 1-25763 8-10 88
(Soundtrack.) Ziggy Marley & Melody Makers; New Order; Chris Isaak; Debbie Harry; Q. Lazzarus; Voodooist Corporation; Brian Eno; Feelies; Sinead O'Connor; Tom Tom Club.

Marty Thau Presents 2 x 5 .... Red Star (S) RED-100 5-10 80

Mar-Vel Masters .... Cowboy Carl (S) CCLP-100 8-12
Chuck Dallis; Ray Lynn; Billy Hall; Herbie Duncan; Bob Burton; Troy Robinson; Jack Bradshaw; Billy Wax; Bobby Sisco; Harry Carter; Mel Kimbrough; Chuck Dallis.

Maryland Vietnam Veteran Memorial Concert 1986 .... ???? (S) ???? 5-10 86
Paper Cup; Pedestrians; Heat & Cold Sweat Horns; others.

Mastermixes: see KISS-FM 98.7 Presents Shep Pettibone's Mastermixes

Mask .... MCA (S) 6140 8-10 85
(Soundtrack.) Steppenwolf; Gary "U.S." Bonds; Steely Dan; Little Richard; Lynyrd Skynyrd; Grateful Dead.

Master's Collection (Christian Music) .... Myrrh (S) MSB-6724 5-10 82
Amy Grant; Imperials; Steve Camp; Leon Patillo; Benny Hester; B.J. Thomas; Evie; Honey Tree; David Meece; Dion.

Max's Kansas City, 1976 .... Ram (S) ???? 10-15 76
Wayne County; Fast; Harry Toledo; Pere Ubu; Cherry Vanilla; John Collins Band; Suicide.

Max's Kansas City, Vol. 2 - 1977 .... Ram (S) 2213 10-15 77
Philip Rambow; Lance; Andrew Pearson; Just Water; Brats; Grand Slam.

Maxell Jazz Sampler, Vol. 2 .... RCA (S) DPL1-0465 5-10 80
Buddy Rich; Slam Stewart; Bucky Pizzarelli; Ella Fitzgerald; Count Basie; Thad Jones; Mel Lewis; Umo; Jeff Lorber Fusion; Oscar Peterson; Benny Carter; Tom Browne; Spyro Gyra. (Special products. Made for Maxell.)

Maxell Rock Sampler .... RCA (S) DPL1-0400 5-10 79
Triumph; Starbuck; Strawbs; Rufus & Chaka Khan; Odyssey; Omaha Sheriff; Hall & Oates; Harvey Mason; Alan Parsons Project. (Special products. Made for Maxell.)

Maxell Rock Sampler, Vol. 2 .... RCA (S) DPL1-0466 5-10 80
Triumph; Poco; Robert Gordon; Outlaws; Hall & Oates; Airplay; Styx; Michael Stanley Band. (Special products. Made for Maxell.)

Medicine Ball Caravan .... Warner Bros. (S) BS-2565 10-12 71
(Soundtrack.) Youngbloods; B.B. King; Delaney & Bonnie; Alice Cooper; Sal Valentino & Stoneground; Doug Kershaw.

Meditation .... Mainstream (M) 56037 10-20 65

Meditation .... Mainstream (S) 6037 15-20 65
Coleman Hawkins; Art Tatum; Benny Carter; others.

Meet the Artist .... RCA (M) SP-33-21 10-20 59
Juilliard String Quartet; Joseph Eger; Rosalind Elias; Maureen Forrester; Garry Graffman; Antonio Janigro; Byron Janis; Leontyne Price; Henryk Szeryng; Cesare Vallenti.

Meet the Girls .... Aamco (M) ALP 308 10-15
Julie London; Sallie Blair; Carmen McCrae; Maxine Sullivan; Frances Faye.

Meet the Girls .... Halo (M) 50254 15-20 57
Fontaine Sisters; Sunny Gale; Mindy Carson; Jane Froman; Toni Arden; Kitty Kallen.

Meet the Girls (An RCA Victor Showcase) .... RCA Victor (EP) SPA-7-21 20-30 56
(Promotional issue only.With paper sleeve.) Lena Horne; Dinah Shore; Barbara Carroll; Kay Starr; Jaye P. Morgan; Martha Carson; Lurlean Hunter; Teddi King; Gwen Verdon.

Mega Hits 1986 .... MCA (S) 5985 5-10 87
Aretha Franklin; Belinda Carlisle; Mr. Mister; Moody Blues; Patti LaBelle & Michael McDonald; Stevie Wonder; Outfield; Fabulous Thunderbirds; Miami Sound Machine; Don Johnson. (Benefit for T.J. Martell Foundation for Leukemia and Cancer Research.)

Mellow 20 Great Songs, 20 Original Stars .... K-Tel (S) NU 9250 5-10
(Mail order offer.) Morris Albert; Association; B.J. Thomas; Percy Sledge; Paul Anka; Three Dog Night; Vogues; Dorothy Moore; Spinners; Love Unlimited Orchestra; Jackie DeShannon; Aretha Franklin; Kenny Rogers & First Edition; Gladys Knight & Pips; Four Tops; Major Harris; Little Anthony & Imperials; Brooklyn Bridge; Casinos; Dennis Yost & Classics IV.

Mellow Gold (3 LP) .... Sessions/Warner Special Products (M) OP 3503 10-20 76
(Mail order offer.)

Mellow Gold (3 LP) .... Warner Special Products (M) OP 3506 10-20 76
Gordon Lightfoot; Maria Muldaur; Aretha Franklin; Casinos; Doobie Brothers; We Five; Jonathan Edwards; Association; Wilson Pickett; Tee Set; Carly Simon; Abba; Rascals; Spanky & Our Gang; Harry Nilsson; Vogues; Stephen Stills; Otis Redding; Jackson Browne; Roberta Flack; Spinners; Seals & Crofts; Barbara Lewis; Todd Runtgren; Judy Collins; Hall & Oates; Souther, Hillman, Furay Band; Danny O'Keefe; Sonny & Cher; Kenny Rogers & First Edition; Association.

Melody .... Atco (S) SD-33-363 10-12 71
(Soundtrack.) Bee Gees; Crosby, Stills, Nash & Young; Richard Hewson.

Memorable Moments in Musical Comedy .... Decca (M) DL-6019 30-45 51
(Soundtrack. 10–inch LP.) Walter Huston; Julia Sanderson; Mary Martin; Millie Weitz; Ethel Merman; Joan Carroll; Gertrude Niesen; Foursome.

Memories (2 LP) .... Columbia (SP) P2-13239 10-15 76
Tommy Edwards; Johnny Mathis; B.J. Thomas; Billy Paul; Tony Bennett; Bobby Vinton; Tammy Wynette; Clint Holmes; Viki Lawrence; Hollies: Cowsills: Mac Davis; Bill Withers; Dionne Warwick; Ray Price; Spanky & Our Gang; Melanie; Blood, Sweat & Tears; Ray Conniff; Buckinghams; Gary Puckett; Dave Loggins; Charlie Rich.

Memories Are Made of Hits: see Original Hits, Vol. 4

Memories Are Made of These .... Capitol (S) 6520 5-10 60s
Jack Jones; Kay Starr; George Chakiris; Keely Smith; Vic Damone; June Christy.

Memories of El Monte .... Starla (M) LPM-1960 20-30 60
Al Laboe; Paragons; Marvin & Johnny; Chuck Higgins; Don & Dewey; Ron Holden; Jim Balcom; Shields; Gene & Eunice; Sonny Knight; Julie Stevens; Jacks; Little Julian Herrera.

Memories of the Past, Vol. 1 .... Musicraft (M) MLP 600 10-15 61
Eternals; Rocketones; Elchords; Crests; Chimes; Chalets; Classics; Tokens; Paragons; Jimmy Charles; Videls; Harptones.

Memories of the Past, Vol. 2 .... Rare Bird (M) RB 8005 8-12
Maxine Brown; Untouchables; Silhouettes; Chimes; Paragons; Monarchs; Tokens; Fidelities; Genies; Velours; Crests; Five Discs; Three Friends; Belmonts; Wheels.Memory Lane: see Alan Freed's Memory Lane

Memory Lane (Epic): see Epic Memory Lane Series

Memory Lane .... Fire (M) FLP-100 100-200 60
Charts; Rainbows; Scarlets; Velvets; Channels; Kodaks; Teen Chords.

Memory Lane Hits .... Fire (M) FLP-101 100-150 60

Memphis Country ....Sun/SSS Int'l (S) 120 8-10 70
Jerry Lee Lewis; Johnny Cash; Conway Twitty; Charlie Rich; Carl Perkins; Warren Smith; Roy Orbison; Onie Wheeler; Jack Clement; David Houston; Barbara Pittman; Bill Strength.
Memphis Gold, Vol. 1 ....Stax (M) 710 10-20 66
Memphis Gold, Vol. 1 ....Stax (S) S-710 15-25 66
Carla Thomas; Mad Lads; Sam & Dave; Otis Redding; Mar-Keys; Rufus Thomas.
Memphis Gold, Vol. 2 ....Stax (M) 726 10-20 67
Memphis Gold, Vol. 2 ....Stax (S) S-726 15-25 67
Eddie Floyd; Otis Redding; Carla Thomas; Bar-Kays; Albert King; Sam & Dave; Johnnie Taylor; William Bell; Mable John.
Memphis Millions ....Stax (S) STS-3023 8-12 73
Isaac Hayes; Staple Singers; Eddie Floyd; Dramatics; Emotions; Booker T. & MGs; Johnnie Taylor; Soul Children; Carla Thomas; Jean Knight.
Memphis Swamp Jam ....Blue Thumb (S) BTS-8706 8-12
Men in a Country Girls' Heart ....Camden (M) CAL-984 10-15 66
Men in a Country Girls' Heart ....Camden (S) CAS-984 10-15 66
Roger Miller; Hank Snow; Don Gibson; Floyd Cramer; Johnnie & Jack; Hank Locklin; Homer & Jethro.
Mercury Country Sampler ....Mercury (S) 50 5-10 76
(Promotional issue only.) Johnny Rodriquez; Statler Bros; Tom T. Hall; Jerry Lee Lewis; others.
Mercury DJ Special ....Mercury (EP) 36 20-30 57
(Promotional issue only.) Ivories; Johnny Jay; Nick Noble; Sarah Vaughan.
Mercury In-Store Play Special ....Mercury (S) MK-8 10-15 73
(Promotional issue only.) Thin Lizzy; Ray Manzarek; Kraftwerk; Rush; Vassar Clements; Neil Merryweather.
Mercury In-Store Play Special ....Mercury (S) SAMP-6751 10-15 70s
(Promotional issue only.) Spirit; Flock; Grenslde; Nicky Hopkins; Love Craft; Sensational Alex Harvey Band.
Mercury Nashville Package of Country Hits ....Mercury (S) 6499 317 8-10 72
(Promotional issue only.) Jerry Lee Lewis; Faron Young; Roger Miller; Dave Dudley; Roy Drusky; Linda Gail Lewis; Statler Brothers; Tom T. Hall; Johnny Rodriguez; Flatt & Scruggs.
Mercury's Galaxy of Golden Hits: see Galaxy of Golden Hits
Merry Christmas - Sonics / Wailers / Galaxies: see SONICS / Wailers / Galaxies
Merry Christmas ....Columbia Special Products (S) P 15758 5-10 81
Robert Goulet; Anita Bryant; Burl Ives; Barbra Streisand; Mitch Miller; John Davidson; Ray Conniff; Doris Day; Chuck Wagon Gang; Lynn Anderson; Liberace; Patti Page; Johnny Cash; Kate Smith.
Merry Christmas (2 LP) ....Columbia Musical Treasury (S) 2P 7285 8-12
Dean Martin; others.
Merry Christmas ....King (M) 680 40-60 59
Merry Christmas Baby ....Hollywood (EP) EP-501 25-50 56
Merry Christmas Baby ....Hollywood (M) LP-501 100-125 56
Lowell Fulson; Lloyd Glenn; Charles Brown; Mabel Scott; Johnny Moore's Blazers; Jimmy Witherspoon.
Merry Christmas Baby ....Gusto/King (M) K-5018 10-15 78
Lowell Fulson; Bull Moose Jackson; Freddy King; Jackson Trio; Billy Ward & Dominoes; Lloyd Glenn; Charles Brown; Mabel Scott; Johnny Moore's Blazers; Jimmy Witherspoon.
Merry Christmas Baby ....Jewel (S) LPS-5014 5-10 85
Charles Brown; Ronnie Kole Trio; Violinaires; Bobby Powell; Lowell Fulsom; Uniques.
Merry Christmas from [Coral Artists]. ....Coral (M) CRL-57355 15-25 60
McGuire Sisters; Teresa Brewer; Ames Borthers; Lennon Sisters; Mel Torme; Lawrence Welk; Johnny Desmond; Dorothy Collins.
Merry Christmas from... (4 LP) ....Columbia Special Products/Readers Digest (S) ???? 10-20 69
Mormon Tabernacle Choir; Eileen Farrell; Philadelphia Orchestra & Temple University Choir; Richard Tucker; Nelson Eddy; Norman Luboff Choir; Johnny Mathis; E. Power Biggs; Jerry Vale; Andre Kostelanetz; Mitch Miller; Doris Day; New Christy Minstrels; Charlie Byrd; Mahalia Jackson; Burl Ives; Robert Goulet; Doris Day; Frankie Laine; Alexander Schreiner; Ray Conniff; Anita Bryant; Percy Faith; Eydie Gorme & Trio Los Panchos; Steve Lawrence; Gene Autry; Marty Robbins; Jimmy Boyd; Mel Torme; Jerry Murad's Harmonicats; Brothers Four.
Merry Christmas from Motown ....Motown (S) 681 15-25 68
Merry Christmas Music ....Capitol (S) SL 6881 8-12
Dean Martin; others.
Merry Christmas to You ....Capitol (S) W 9028 8-12
Dean Martin; others. (Has 16 tracks.)
Merry Christmas to You ....Capitol (S) W 9028 8-12
Dean Martin; others. (Has 12 tracks.)
Metal Massacre (5 LP) ....Metal Blade (S) MBB 1 60-80 84
(Picture disc set.)
Metal That Matters ....Iron Works (S) 1016 10-15 88
(Promotional only picture disc. 250 made.)
Metalgon: Axemaster ....Azra/Condor Classix (S) No Number Used 8-12 87
(Hexagon shaped picture disc. 500 made.) Mars; Axemasters; Triad; Legend; Coda.
Metropolis ....Columbia (S) JS-39526 8-12 84
Metropolis ....Columbia (S) CK-39526 5-10 Re
(Soundtrack.) Freddie Mercury; Pat Benatar; Jon Anderson; Cycle V; Giorgio Moroder; Bonnie Tyler; Loverboy; Billy Squier; Adam Ant.
Miami Vice ....MCA (S) 6150 8-10 85
(TV Soundtrack.) Jan Hammer; Glenn Frey; Chaka Khan; Phil Collins; Grandmaster Flash; Melle Mel; Tina Turner.
Miami Vice 2 ....MCA (S) 6192 8-10 86
(TV Soundtrack.) Jan Hammer; Phil Collins; Roxy Music; Jackson Browne; Damned; Patti LaBelle; Bill Champlin; Steve Jones; Andy Taylor.
Michigan Mixture, Vol 1 ....Clinging Hysteria (S) CHR-1 10-15 89
Up; Sweet Cherry; Pitche Blende; Glass Sun Dick Rabbit; Popcorn Blizzard; She Devils; Renaissance Fair; Orange Wedge.
Michigan Mixture, Vol 2 ....Clinging Hysteria (S) CHR-2 10-15 89
Clinging Hysteria; Dick Rabbit; 9th Street Market; Ruby; Cambridge; B.C. & Cavemen; Chevrons; Herd; Soulbenders; Bottle Company; Rainy Daze; Geyda.
Michigan Rocks ....Seeds & Stems (S) 77001 20-25 77
MC-5; Stooges; Bob Seger System; Detroit with Mitch Ryder; Frost; Ted Nugent & Amboy Dukes; Third Power; SRC; Rationals.
Michigan Rocks II ....Plastic (S) PR-8203 15-20 82

Grand Funk; Brownsville Station; Rare Earth; Stix & Stones; Teegarden & Van Winkle; Frijid Pink; Woolies; Sunday Funnies; Catfish Hodge.

Mickey Mantle—My Favorite Hits: see My Favorite Hits

Mickey Most Presents English In-Groups: see English In-Groups

Midnight at Eddie Condon's .... Trip (S) 5529 5-10 74
Eddie Condon; Bud Freeman; others.

Midnight Fire (2 LP) .... Tee Vee/Warner Special Products (S) OP 2513 8-12 79
Lou Rawls; Brook Benton; Spinners; Roberta Flack; Drifters; Otis Redding; Aretha Franklin; Clyde McPhatter; Platters; Percy Sledge; Laverne Baker; Drifters; R.B. Greaves; Barbara Lewis; Ben E. King; Blue Magic; Watts 103rd St. Rhythm Band.

Midnight Hoot .... Kapp (M) KL-1357 10-20 64
Midnight Hoot .... Kapp (S) KS-3357 10-20 64
Tarriers; Miriam Makeba; Alan Lomax; others.

Midnight Jamboree .... Decca (M) DL-4045 15-20 62
Midnight Jamboree .... Decca (S) DL-74045 20-25 62
Patsy Cline; Ernest Tubb; Webb Pierce; Kitty Wells; Wilburn Brothers; Jerry Hanlon; Buddy Emmons; Linda Flanagan.

Mighty Quinn .... A&M (S) SP-3924 8-10 89
(Soundtrack.) UB40; Arrow; Michael Rose; Sheryl Lee Ralph; Cedella Marley; Sharon Marley Pendergast; Half Pint; Yello; Neville Brothers; Little Twitch; Seventeen Plus.

Mike & Dean Rock 'N' Roll Show .... Hitbound/Premore (M) PL-983 10-20 83
Mike Love; Dean Torrence; Association; Rip Chords; Paul Revere & Raiders.

Milestone Jazz Stars in Concert .... Milestone (S) 55006 5-10 79
McCoy Tyner; Ron Carter; Sonny Rollins; Al Foster; others.

Milestone Twofer Giants Vol. 1 .... Milestone (M) MSP-1 5-10 73
Wes Montgomer; Bill Evans; Yusef Lateef; Charlie Byrd; Art Blakey; others.

Miller Music .... RCA (S) DPL1-0726 5-10 84
Sugar Creek; Caruso; Steve Smith & Naked; A-Train; Entertainers; DeLuxury; DC Star; Producers; Fayrewether; Del Fuegos; Telluride; King Joe Carrasco; Son Seals; Paris One; James Harmond Band; Magnum.

Million Dollar Hits of the '50s and '60s (6 LP) .... Longines Symphonette (S) LS-223 25-35 72
(Boxed set. Mail order offer.) Ames Brothers; Andrews Sisters; Louis Armstrong; Crickets; Crew-Cuts; Four Aces; Dean Martin; Frankie Laine; Patti Page; Kingston Trio; Platters; Nelson Riddle; Kay Starr; Weavers; Debbie Reynolds; Tommy Dorsey; McGuire Sisters; Billy Williams; Buddy Holly; Teresa Brewer; Leroy Anderson; Sammy Kaye; Dimitri Tiomkin; Bill Haley & His Comets; Eileen Barton; Karen Chandler; Don Cornell; Pearl Bailey; Kitty Kallen; Roger Williams; Joe Harnell; Weavers; Jane Morgan; Ralph Marterie; Pat Boone; Dinah Washington; Diamonds; Sarah Vaughan; Billy Vaughn; Nat King Cole; Al Martino; Bobbie Gentry; Les Paul & Mary Ford; Lawrence Welk; Longines Symphony Orchestra.

Million Dollar Memories .... Laurie (S) LES 4071 5-10 85
Gene Chandler; Dion; Ritchie Valens; Del Shannon; Harps; etc.

Million Dollar Memories (9 LP) .... Columbia Special Products/Readers Digest (S) ? 30-40 72
Johnny Horton; Ray Price; Marty Robbins; Benny Goodman; Peggy Lee; Kay Kyser; Harry James; Frank Sinatra; Al Dexter & His Troopers; Andy Williams; Percy Faith; Johnny Cash; Johnny Mathis; Ray Conniff; Kitty Kallen; Les Brown; Georgia Carroll; Woody Herman; Xavier Cugat; Doris Day; Jim Nabors; Barbra Streisand; O.C. Smith; Frankie Laine; Dinah Shore; Village Stompers; Robert Goulet; Tony Bennett; New Christy Minstrels; Buddy Clark; Ray Noble; Jerry Murad's Harmonicats; Frankie Carle; Marjorie Hughes; Gloria Wood; Brothers Four; Guy Mitchell; Ralph Burns; Jon & Sandra Steele; Harry Babbitt; Patti Page; Vic Damone; Ray Bryant Trio; Frank DeVol; Ezio Pinza; Sammy Kaye; Tony Alamo & Kaydets; Louis Armstrong; Rosemary Clooney; Mitch Miller; Johnnie Ray; Andre Previn Quartet; Four Lads; Erroll Garner; Easy Riders; Felicia Sanders; Les Elgart; Judy Garland; Roy Hamilton.

Million Dollar Vaudeville Show (Lion Records Presents) .... Lion (M) L 70089 15-25 50s
Danny Thomas; Jimmy Durante; Art Mooney; Debbie Reynolds; Carleton Carpenter; Carson Robison; Gene Kelly; Betty Garrett; David Rose; Macklin Marrow; Lionel Barrymore; Leslie Caron; Mel Ferrer; Lionel Hampton.

Million $ Music .... Dot (M) DLP-3425 20-25 62
Del-Vikings; Travis & Bob; Tab Hunter; Jimmy Dee; Jan & Arnie; Sanford Clark; Ronnie Love; Robin Luke; Arthur Alexander; Lonnie Donegan; Carol Jarvis.

Million Dollar Sellers, Vol. 1 .... Longines Symphonette (M) SQ-93925 5-10
Million Dollar Sellers, Vol. 1 .... Longines Symphonette (S) SQ-93925 5-10
(Mail order offer.) Bert Kaempfert; Teresa Brewer; Warren Covington; Four Aces; Leroy Anderson; Ames Brothers; McGuire Sisters; Al Hibbler; Russ Morgan; Alan Dale.

Million Dollar Sellers, Vol. 2 .... Longines Symphonette (M) SQ-93926 5-10
Million Dollar Sellers, Vol. 2 .... Longines Symphonette (S) SQ-93926 5-10
(Mail order offer.) Les Baxter; Nat King Cole; Tennessee Ernie Ford; Kingston Trio; Peggy Lee; Dean Martin; Les Paul & Mary Ford; Nelson Riddle; Jo Stafford; Kay Starr.

Million Dollar Sellers, Vol. 3 .... Longines Symphonette (S) SYS-5390 5-10
Million Dollar Sellers, Vol. 3 .... Longines Symphonette (M) SQ-93927 5-10
Million Dollar Sellers, Vol. 3 .... Longines Symphonette (S) SQ-93927 5-10
(The above three LPs were individually packaged but sold as a set. Mail order offer.) Crew-Cuts; Georgia Gibbs; Ralph Marterie; Frankie Laine; Diamonds; Patti Page; Rusty Draper; Sarah Vaughan; Eddie Heywood; Dinah Washington.

Million Dollar Sound Sampler .... A&M (S) 9001 15-25 66
Chris Montez; Herb Alpert; Sandpipers; Lucille Starr; Sergio Mendes; Baja Marimba Band; Canadian Sweethearts; Claudine Longet; We Five.

Million Dollar Stereo .... MGM (S) SE-3823 20-25 60

Million or More Best Sellers, A .... ABC-Paramount (M) ABC-216 50-75 59
Tommy Roe; Lloyd Price; George Hamilton IV; Danny & Juniors; Elegants; Poni-Tails; Steve Gibson & Red Caps; Eddie Platt; Royal Teens; Sparkletones; Muvva "Guitar" Hubbard; Paul Anka.

Million Performance Songs .... EMI (S) ???? 8-12
(Promotional issue only.) B.J. Thomas; Mac Davis; Donny Osmond; Todd Rundgren; Blue Swede; Gallery; Barry Manilow; Kyu Sakamoto; Drifters; Ocean; Association; Frank Sinatra; Glen Campbell; Jim Reeves; Waylon Jennings; Jessi Colter; Billy "Crash" Craddock; Anne Murray; Roger Williams; Wayne Newton; Bobby Vinton; Al Martino; Dave Mason; James Taylor; Righteous Brothers; Lulu; Andy Williams; Neil Sedaka; Dolly Parton; Bert Kaempfert.

Million Seller, Vol. 11 .... Alshire (S) 5257 5-10 72
Million Seller, Vol. 12 .... Alshire (S) 5259 5-10 72
Million Seller Soul Hits .... Alshire (S) 5221 5-10 71

Million Sellers .... Tops (M) L1647 8-12
Lew Raymond & Hollywood Studio Orchestra; Laine Sisters; Lola Gray; Bill Carlson; Cliff Rogers; Toppers; Norma Zimmer; Ronnie Deauville; Mimi Martel.

Million Sellers Dance Hits .... Parkway (M) P-7028 15-25 63
Chubby Checker; Bobby Rydell; Dovells; Dee Dee Sharp; Orlons.

Million-Airs .... Coral (M) CRL-57310 50-75 60
(Maroon label.) Ames Brothers; Buddy Holly; McGuire Sisters; Jackie Wilson; Teresa Brewer; Billy Williams; Pearl Bailey; Debbie Reynolds; Johnny Desmond, Alan Dale; Don Cornell.

Milwaukee Sentinel Battle of the Bands .... Century (S) 3313 40-60 66
Yorks; 7 Wonders; Coachmen; Shags; Destinations; Overtures; Rogues; Fastbacks; Woodsmen; Ethics; Patriots; Radicals.

Mindbender .... K-Tel TU-2440 5-10 76
Neil Sedaka; Hot Chocolate; Kiss; Labelle; Spinners; Salsoul Orchestra; Jigsaw; War; 10cc; Ozark Mountain Daredevils; George Baker Selection; Ohio Players; Rhythm Heritage; Elton John; Stampeders; KC & Sunshine Band; Blue Magic; Abba; Ace; Amazing Rhythm Aces; C.W. McCall.

Minstrel Men .... Colpix (M) CP-434 15-20 62
Minstrel Men .... Colpix (S) SCP-434 20-25 62
George Burns; Jack Benny; Milton Berle; Phil Silvers; Benny Fields.

Minute Man for Harried Disc Jockeys .... RCA (EP) SP-45-30 20-30 58
(Sampler of tracks from new RCA albums. Has paper cover.)

Mirage! Avant Garde & Third Stream Jazz .... New World (M) NW 216 8-12
Woody Herman; Duke Ellington; Lennie Tristano Quartet; Stan Kenton; Charles Mingus Octet; Jannet Thurlow; George Russell & His Smalltet; Brandeis Jazz Festival Ensemble; John Lewis; Ran Blake; Jeanne Lee.

Mississippi Bottom Blues .... Mamlish (S) 3802 5-10 72
Freddie Spruell; Otto Virgial; others.

Mistletoe and Memories .... RCA (S) 8372-1-R 10-20 88
Elvis Presley; Judds; Alabama; K.T. Oslin; Ronnie Milsap; Michael Johnson; Kenny Rogers; Baillie & Boys; Dolly Parton.

Modern Country Hits of Today .... Starday (M) 9-418 10-15 68
Modern Country Hits of Today .... Starday (S) 9-418 10-15 68
Red Sovine; Guy Mitchell; others.

Modern Moods .... Prestige/Moodsville (M) Vol. 2 15-20
Miles Davis Quintet with Red Garland; Sonny Rollins with Ray Bryant; John Coltrane; Donald Byrd; Modern Jazz Quartet with Milt Jackson & John Lewis; Sonny Stitt; Art Farmer.

Modern Girls .... Warner Bros. (S) 1-25526 8-10 86
(Soundtrack.) Depeche Mode; Anthony & Camp; Fly Joy; Toni Basil; Female Body Inspectors; George Black; Club Nouveau; Ice House; TKA; Jesus & Mary Chain.

Modern Jazz Hall of Fame .... Design (M) DLP-29 20-25 57
Dizzy Gillespie Quintet; Max Roach Septet; Charles Mingus Quintet; Sam Most Quintet; Jazz Workshop; Kai Winding; Bud Powell Trio; Thad Jones.

Modern Jazz Spectacular .... Jazztone (M) J-1231 30-60 56
Kai Winding; Gerry Mulligan; Sonny Stitt; Brew Moore; George Wallington; Curley Russell; Max Roach; Lou Stein; Jack Lesberg; Dom Lamond; George Berg; Sid Cooper; Don Elliott; Horace Silver.

Mom and Dad Songs .... Starday (M) S-329 10-20 65
Moment By Moment .... RSO (S) RS-1-3040 8-12 78
(White label. Promotional issue only.)

Moment By Moment .... RSO (S) RS-1-3040 8-10 78
(Soundtrack.) Yvonne Elliman; Michael Franks; Stephen Bishop; Charles Lloyd; Dan Hill; 10CC.

Moments to Remember .... Candlelite (M) BMLLP-6 8-12 82
Skyliners; Paradons; Dion & Belmonts; Capris; Fireflies; Little Caesar & Romans; Kathy Young & Innocents; Penguins; Phil Philips & Twilights.

Moments to Remember (3 LP) .... Candlelite (SP) CU-725-LP 10-20 83
Dion & Passions; Chiffons; Belmonts; Randy & Rainbows; Ernie Maresca; Enchords; Five Discs; Jarmels; Bon-Aires; Marcia Blaine; Jan & Dean; Mystics; Del Stains.

Moments to Remember .... Era (S) BU-4430 5-10
Four Lads; Patti Page; Brook Benton; Gaylords; Four Aces; Johnnie Ray; Frankie Laine; Rosemary Clooney; Sammy Turner; Four Preps.

Monday Monday .... Modern Sound (S) MS-1030 5-10 66
Jalopy Five; Chellows; Leroy Jones; Ed Hardin; Fred York; Jack White; Farley Wayne; Robby Brooks. (*Monday Monday* is the top song title shown on the front cover, but is not the official LP title. Actually, there doesn't seem to be a title.)

Monday Night at Birdland .... Roulette (M) R-52015 20-40 58
Hank Mobley; Billy Root; Curtis Fuller; Lee Morgan; "Specs" Wright; Ray Bryant; Tommy Bryant.

Money Music .... August (S) 100 200-250 67
Underbeats; Stillroven; H.T. Three; Seraphic Street Sound; T.C. Atlantic; Calico Wall; Castaways; C.A. Quintet; Electras; Bedlam Rock; Hot Half Dozen.

Money For Art's Sake - an Esoteric Collection .... Esoteric (S) EST-004 5-10 87
Martha & Regime; Friction; E-Z Access; Golfers; Worker Burn-out; Blamed; Jemima; Too Normal; Briggs Beall; Das Ubermensch; Thunder Rose; Shout.

Monophonic Instrumental & Vocal Sampler .... Jubilee (M) MSJLP 803 15-20 59
Cadillacs; Cy Coleman; Lois Kahn; Carl Ravazza; Don Rondo; Moe Koffman.

Monster Album .... DCP (M) 6805 10-15
Montana Gold .... Rod (S) KM 5782 8-12
Patriot; Rush Hour; Time; Sonics; Phil & Blanks; Lost Highway; Mission Mountain Wood Band; High Country; Rollers; Dog Water; Home Grown; Bop & Dips; others.

Monterey International Pop Festival .... Dunhill (S) DSX-50100 8-10 71
Montgomery Ward Artist Series (Top 9) .... Montgomery Ward (S) MWS 90 15-20
(Red vinyl.) Andre Previn; Lawrence Welk; Ink Spots; Jaye P. Morgan; Artie Shaw; Lena Horne; Three Suns; Johnny Desmond; David Rose.

Montreux Blues Festival .... Excello (S) 8026 8-10 72
Montreux Jazz Festival .... Warner Bros. (S) 23718 5-10 82

Montreux Summit, Vol. 1 (2 LP) .... Columbia (S) JG 35005 8-12 77
Bob James; George Duke; Billy Cobham; Ralph MacDonald; Steve Khan; Janne Schaffer; Eric Gale; Stan Getz; Woody Shaw; Alphonso Johnson; Dexter Gordon; Benny Golson; Hubert Laws; Bobbi Humphrey; Thijs Van Leer; Maynard Ferguson.

Montreux Summit, Vol. 2 .... Columbia (S) JG-35090 5-10 78

Monumental Country Hits .... Monument (S) SLP-18095 10-20 68
Dolly Parton; Jeannie Seely; Billy Walker; others.

Monumental Pop Hits .... Monument (S) SLP-18096 10-20 68
Roy Orbison; Bob Moore; Don Cherry; Joe Simon; Billy Grammer; Dixie Bells; Rusty Draper.

Mood Music for Dining (10 LP) .... RCA/Readers Digest (S) RDA 47-A 25-35 67
(Boxed set.) Romantic Strings; Norman Percival; Ray Davis; Douglas Gamley; Bob Docker; Robert Mandrell; Douglas Gamley; Ron Playdell; Ken Thorne; Gary Hughes; London Pops; Dick Mahl; others.

Mood Music for Listening and Relaxation (11 LP) .... RCA/Readers Digest (S) RD-43-A 25-35
Daniel Michael; John Norman; Royal Philharmonic Orchestra; Sir Malcolm Sargent; Earl Wild; Al Caiola; Henri Rene; Josef Leo Gruber; others

Mood Music Sampler .... Somerset (M) P-100 10-20 58
Monte Kelly; Ray Charles Chorus; Jay White; Billy Butterfield; Mulcays; Don Costa; Kingsway Strings.

Mood Music Sampler .... Trans-World (M) TWLP-100 5-10 60s
Ray Charles Chorus; Jay White; Billy Butterfield; Mulcays; Don Costa; Kingsway Strings.

More '50s (2 LP) .... Columbia (S) P2S 5606 8-12 72
(Mail order offer.) Johnny Mathis; Arthur Godfrey; Rosemary Clooney; Somethin' Smith & Redheads; Roy Hamilton; Doris Day; Frankie Laine; Tony Martin; Carl Smith; Richard Hayman; Georgia Gibbs; Rusty Draper; Mariners; Tommy Edwards; Jerry Vale; Guy Mitchell; Buddy Clark; Eddy Howard; George Shearing.

More American Graffiti (2 LP) .... MCA (S) 2-8007 15-20 75
Bill Haley & His Comets; Chantels; Little Richard; Little Eva; Carl Dobkins Jr.; Crickets; Danleers; Buddy Holly & Crickets; Cadillacs; Dion & Belmonts; Betty Everett; Brenda Lee; Gene Chandler; Lloyd Price; Carole King; Shirelles; Dubs; Tune Weavers; Larry Williams; Crows; Kingsmen; Jerry Butler; Platters; Coasters; Gene Chandler.

More American Graffiti (2 LP) .... MCA (S) 2-11006 15-20 79
(Soundtrack.) Martha & Vandellas; Andy Williams; Byrds; Angels; Simon & Garfunkel; Donovan; Supremes; Cream; Bob Dylan; Aretha Franklin; Zombies; ? & Mysterians; Chantays; Lenny Welch; Marvelettes; Bobby Vinton; Capitols; S/Sgt. Barry Sadler; Mary Wells; McCoys; Percy Sledge.

More American Graffiti .... MCA (S) No Number Used 25-35 79
(Soundtrack picture disc.)

More Bluegrass .... Starday (S) SLP 296 10-20 60s
Jim & Jesse; Bill Clifton; Bluegrass Champs; Hylo Brown; New River Boys; Carl Story; Red Allen; Stanley Brothers; Country Gentlemen; Benny Martin; Lonesome Pine Fiddlers; Jim Eanes; Jimmie Skinner; Jimmy Martin; Bob Osborne.

More Blues & Abstract Truth .... Impulse (M) A-75 10-20 65

More Blues & Abstract Truth .... Impulse (S) AS-75 10-20 65
Oliver Nelson; Thad Jones; Phil Woods; others.

More Country & Western Favorites! .... Design (M) DLP-637 8-12 60s

More Country & Western Favorites! .... Design (SE) SDLP-637 8-12 60s
Ferlin Husky; Carl Belew; Patsy Cline; Hank Locklin; Rocky Bill Ford.

More Country Classics .... RCA (M) LPM-2467 15-20 61
Hank Snow; Eddy Arnold; Browns; Jim Reeves; Hank Locklin; Skeeter Davis; Del Wood; Don Gibson; Homer & Jethro; Porter Wagoner; Jimmie Driftwood; Johnnie & Jack.

More Country Gold .... Sunset (S) 5290 5-10 70
Bobby Goldsboro; Jerry Wallace; Del Reeves; Johnny Darrell; Willie Nelson.

More Country Music Festival .... Starday (M) S-327 10-20 65

More Country Music Samplers .... Starday (M) SLP-178 10-20
Justin Tubb; Archie Campbell; Willis Brothers; Pete Drake; "Little" Roy Wiggins; Cowboy Copas; Lew Childre; Sunshine Boys; Cathy Copas; Arthur "Guitar Boogie" Smith; Bill Clifton & His Dixie Mountain Boys; George Jones; Chubby Wise; Jim Glaser.

More Country Music Spectacular .... Starday (M) S-140 15-25 61

More For Your Money .... Bell (S) 6009 8-12
Lee Dorsey; Van Dykes; Gladys Knight & Pips; James Carr; James & Bobby Purify; Emperors; Viscounts.

More Gold Hits, Vol.2 .... Warwick (M) W-2044 35-55 61
Melloharps; Monarchs; Willows; Eternals; Neil Sedaka & Tokens; Harptones; Legends; Tokens; Inspirators; Four of a Kind.

More Golden Goodies .... Mercury (M) MG-20583 25-35 60

More Golden Goodies .... Mercury (S) SR-60243 25-35 60
Richard Hayman; David Carroll; Jan August; Dick Contino; Harmonicats; Xavier Cugat; Erroll Garner; Sil Austin; Clyde McCoy; Buddy Morrow; Jack Fina; Eddie Heywood; Jerry Byrd; Ralph Marterie.

More Great Hits of 1964 and Other Golden Goodies .... Vee Jay (M) VJLP-1136 15-20 65

More Great Hits of 1964 and Other Golden Goodies .... Vee Jay (S) VJSR-1136 20-25 65
Jerry Butler; Betty Everett; Flamingos; Terry Black; Joe Simon; Honeycombs; 4 Seasons; Little Richard; Gene Chandler; Skyliners; Bobby Day; Dee Dee Ford; Joe Jones.

More Great Motion Picture Themes .... United Artists (M) UAL-3158 8-10 61

More Great Motion Picture Themes .... United Artists (S) UAS-6158 8-12 61
(Soundtrack.) Marilyn Monroe; Bill Potts; Ferrante & Teicher; Don Costa; Al Caiola; Andre Previn; Louis Armstrong; Melina Mercouri; Modern Jazz Quartet; Elmer Bernstein; Mitchell Powell; Leroy Holmes; Henry Jerome.

More Greatest Hits .... Harmony (M) HL-7277 15-20 60
Dinah Shore; Harry James; Gene Krupa; Frankie Carle; others.

More Heavy Sounds .... Columbia (S) CS-1016 8-12 70
Laura Nyro; Janis Joplin; Chicago; Johnny Winter; Santana; Taj Mahal; NRBQ; Byrds; Pacific Gas & Electric; Al Kooper.

More Hootenanny .... Diplomat (M) DS 2301 5-10 60s
Song Spinners; Bob Riley Group; Bill Baron; Sam Wright; Tex Johnson & His Six Shooters; Sing Alongers; Glitters; Billy King & Jacks.

More Mad Mike Moldies: see Mad Mike Moldies

More Oldies and Goodies .... Crown (M) CLP-5202 15-20 60s
Etta James; Marvin & Johnny; Jimmy Beasley; Joe Turner; Jacks; B.B. King; Jesse Belvin.

More Original Soundtracks & Hit Music from Great Motion Picture Themes .... UA (M) UAL 6158 15-25 61

More Original Soundtracks & Hit Music from Great Motion Picture Themes .... UA (S) UAS 6158 15-25 61
Marilyn Monroe; Ferrante & Teicher; Melina Mercouri; Al Caiola; Louis Armstrong; Andre Previn; Don Costa; Bill Potts; Mitchell Powell; Elmer Bernstein; Modern Jazz Quartet.

More Rockin' Sixties .... Warner/JCI (S) 3111 8-12 85
Music Machine; Spencer Davis Group; Box Tops; Standells; Crow; Sly & Family Stone; Human Beinz; Outsiders; Strangeloves; Syndicate of Sound; Monkees; Lovin' Spoonful.

More Slipping Around Songs .... Starday (M) S-338 10-20 65
Roy Drusky; Patsy Cline; Cowboy Copas; others.

More Solid Gold Programming .... Screen Gems/Colgems (S) EMI-717 20-30
(Promotional only issue.) Beatles; Linda Ronstadt & Stone Poneys; Aretha Franklin; Carole King; Diana Ross; Helen Reddy; Kyu Sakamoto; Outsiders; Grand Funk Railroad; Drifters; Ocean; Association.

More Soul Sauce .... Somerset (S) 74800 5-10 70

More Teenage Triangle: see DARREN, James / Shelley Fabares / Paul Petersen

More! Wonderful World of Country Music, Vol. 2 .... Starday (M) SLP-320 8-12
Joe & Rose Lee Maphis; Wayne Raney; Benny Martin; Jackie Phelps; Dick Flood; Jimmie Skinner; Clyde Moody; Dean Manuel; Cowboy Copas; Pee Wee King; Redd Stewart; June Stearns; Gene Martin; George Jones; Gene Martin; Arthur "Guitar Boogie" Smith.

Most, Vol. 1 .... Forum (S) SF-9064 8-12 60s
Count Basie; Sarah Vaughan; Johnny Smith; Joe Newman; Billy Eckstine; Phineas Newborn; Lambert, Hendricks & Ross; Joe Williams; Maynard Ferguson.

Most, Vol. 1 .... Roulette (M) R-52050 20-25 60
Most, Vol. 1 .... Roulette (S) SR-52050 25-30 60
Sarah Vaughn; Count Basie; Billy Eckstine; Johnny Smith; Lambert, Hendricks, Ross & Williams; Joe Newman; Maynard Ferguson; Joe Williams; Phineas Newhorn.

Most, Vol. 2 .... Roulette (M) R-52053 20-25 60
Most, Vol. 2 .... Roulette (S) SR-52053 25-30 60
Count Basie; Billy Eckstine; Maynard Ferguson; Bill Russo; Sarah Vaughan; Joe Williams; Harry "Sweets" Edison; Cora Lee Day.

Most, Vol. 3 .... Roulette (M) R-52057 20-25 61
Most, Vol. 3 .... Roulette (S) SR-52057 25-30 61
Sarah Vaughan; Billy Eckstine; Joe Williams; Count Basie; Herbie Mann; Johnny Smith; Machito; Sonny Stitt; Maynard Ferguson; Harry "Sweets" Edison.

Most, Vol. 4 .... Roulette (M) R-52062 20-25 61
Most, Vol. 4 .... Roulette (S) SR-52062 25-30 61
Count Basie; Joe Williams; Machito; Billy Eckstine; Maynard Ferguson; Sarah Vaughan; Johnny Smith; John Handy; Lambert, Hendricks & Ross.

Most of the Twist .... Roulette (M) R-25176 15-25 62
Count Basie; Sarah Vaughan; Joey Dee & Starliters; Pearl Bailey; 7 Blends; Maynard Ferguson; Dale Hawkins & His Escapades; Orchids; Machito.

Most Spectacular Latin Dance Rhythms .... Seeco (M) SS-4 10-15 50s
La Plata Sextette; Damiron & Chapuseaux; Cuban All Stars; Jose Valdes; Alberto Beltran; Roberto Faz; Primo Corchia.

Mother, Jugs & Speed .... A&M (S) SP-4590 8-12 76
(Soundtrack.) Steve Marriott; Peter Frampton; Billy Preston; Brothers Johnson; Crusaders; Paul Jabara; Michelle Phillips; Pete Jolly.

Motortown Review, Vol. 1 .... Motown (M) MT-609 15-20 63
Mary Wells; Marvin Gaye; Marvelettes; Stevie Wonder; Miracles; Contours; Supremes.

Motortown Review, Vol. 2 .... Motown (M) MT-615 15-20 64
Mary Wells; Marvin Gaye; Marvelettes; Stevie Wonder; Miracles; Kim Weston; Martha & Vandellas; Temptations.

Motortown Review in Paris .... Tamla (M) 264 15-20 65
Motortown Review in Paris .... Tamla (S) S-264 20-25 65
Supremes; Miracles; Martha & Vandellas; Stevie Wonder; Earl Van Dyke & Soul Brothers.

Motortown Review Live .... Motown (S) MS-688 8-15 69

Motown at the Hollywood Palace .... Motown (S) MS-703 8-12 70
Diana Ross & Supremes; Jackson 5; Stevie Wonder; others.

Motown Chartbusters, Vol. 1 .... Motown (S) MS 707 5-10 70
Temptations; Jr. Walker & All Stars; Marvin Gaye & Tammi Terrell; Smokey Robinson & Miracles; Diana Ross & Supremes; Stevie Wonder; Brenda Holloway; Martha Reeves & Vandellas; Marvelettes.

Motown Chartbusters, Vol. 2 .... Motown (S) MS ???? 5-10 71
Motown Chartbusters, Vol. 3 .... Motown (S) MS 732 5-10 71
Supremes; Jr. Walker & All Stars; Four Tops; Stevie Wonder; Originals; Spinners; Diana Ross & Supremes; Jackson Five; Temptations; Gladys Knight & Pips; Martha & Vandellas; Edwin Starr.

Motown Chartbusters, Vol. 4 .... Motown (S) MS 734 5-10 71
Jackson 5; Gladys Knight & Pips; Jr. Walker; Temptations; Marvin Gaye; Edwin Starr; Diana Ross & Supremes; Smokey Robinson & Miracles; David Ruffin; Stevie Wonder; Four Tops; Originals.

Motown Christmas (2 LP) .... Motown (S) M-795V2 15-25 73
Jackson 5; Stevie Wonder; Temptations; Diana Ross & Supremes; Smokey Robinson & Miracles; Michael Jackson.

Motown Disco, Vol. 3 .... Motown (S) M6-863 5-10 76
Commodores; Miracles; Jackson 5; Eddie Kendricks; Temptations; Diana Ross & Supremes; Marvin Gaye; Smokey Robinson; Willie Hutch.

Motown Disco, Vol. 4 .... Motown (S) No Number Used 5-10 77

Motown Instrumentals .... Natural Resources (S) 4002 5-10 77
San Remo Golden Strings; Jr. Walker; Crusaders; Commodores; Temptations; Jermaine Jackson; Rare Earth.

Motown Legends - Love Songs .... Motown (S) 5367 5-10 85
Diana Ross & Supremes; Temptations; Jackson Five; Smokey Robinson & Miracles; Mary Wells; Syreeta; Jimmy Ruffin; Brenda Holloway; Martha & Vandellas; Gladys Knight & Pips.

Motown's Love Songs, Vol. 2 (Broken Hearts) .... Natural Resources (S) NR 4019T1 5-10
Marvelettes; Smokey Robinson & Miracles; Syreeta; Brenda Holloway; Jimmy Ruffin; Temptations; Marvin Gaye; Eddie Kendricks; Diana Ross; Gladys Knight & Pips.

Motown Mania .... Motown (S) ???? 5-10
Barrett Strong; Contours; Spinners; Marvin Gaye & Tammi Terrell; Edwin Starr; David Buffin; Michael Jackson; Undisputed Truth; Supremes & Temptations.

Motown Monster Hits, Vol. 1....Pickwick (S) SPC-3543 5-10 76
Marvin Gaye; Smokey Robinson & Miracles; Jackson 5; Temptations; Martha Reeves & Vandellas; Gladys Knight & Pips; Four Tops; Junior Walker & All Stars; Diana Ross & Supremes.

Motown Monster Hits, Vol. 2....Pickwick (S) SPC-3546 5-10 76
Jimmy Ruffin; Jackson 5; Temptations; Stevie Wonder; Junior Walker & All Stars; Diana Ross & Supremes; Monitors; Elgins.

Motown Original Versions....Motown (S) M860V1 5-10 76
Martha Reeves & Vandellas; Gladys Knight & Pips; Four Tops; Supremes; Jackson Five; Marvin Gaye & Tammi Terrell; Isley Brothers; Brenda Holloway; Miracles; Marvelettes; Temptations.

Motown Review....Motown (S) PR-43 8-12 78
(Promotional issue only.) Bonnie Pointer; Switch; Rare Earth; Thelma Houston; Smokey Robinson; Grover Washington Jr.

Motown Show Tunes....Natural Recources (S) 4003 5-10 78
Diana Ross; G.C. Cameron; Marvin Gaye; Willie Hutch; others.

Motown Story (3 LP)....Motown (S) 5-726 20-30 71
Marvin Gaye; Martha & Vandellas; Diana Ross & Supremes; Four Tops; Jackson 5; Jr. Walker; Temptations; others.

Motown Story, Vol. 1....Motown (S) MS-727 8-12 71
Berry Gordy Jr.; Barrett Strong; Smokey Robinson & Miracles; Marvelettes; Marvin Gaye; Stevie Wonder; Martha Reeves & Vandellas.

Motown Story, Vol. 2....Motown (S) MS-728 8-12 71
Smokey Robinson & Miracles; Marvin Gaye; Diana Ross & Supremes; Martha Reeves & Vandellas; Four Tops; Temptations; Jr. Walker & All Stars.

Motown Story, Vol. 3....Motown (S) MS-729 8-12 71
Marvin Gaye; Four Tops; Diana Ross & Supremes; Smokey Robinson & Miracles; Stevie Wonder; Martha Reeves & Vandellas; Temptations; Jimmy Ruffin.

Motown Story, Vol. 4....Motown (S) MS-730 8-12 71
Four Tops; Diana Ross & Supremes; Martha Reeves & Vandellas; Marvin Gaye & Tammi Terrell; Gladys Knight & Pips; Smokey Robinson & Miracles; Temptations; Stevie Wonder.

Motown Story, Vol. 5....Motown (S) MS-731 8-12 71
Diana Ross & Supremes; Temptations; Marvin Gaye; Jr. Walker & All Stars; Originals; Jackson Five.

Motown Story: the First 25 Years (5 LP)....Motown (S) 6048 25-35 83
Marvin Gaye; Martha & Vandellas; Diana Ross & Supremes; Four Tops; Jackson 5; Jr. Walker & All Stars; Temptations; Stevie Wonder; Gladys Knight & Pips; Lionel Richie & Commodores; Smokey Robinson & Miracles; Rick James; Dazz Band; Originals; Jimmy Ruffin; Eddie Kendricks. (Includes dialogue segments.)

Motown Superstars....Ronco (S) 2110 5-10

Motown Winners Circle, Vol. 1....Gordy (S) GS-935 10-15 69
Marvelettes; Stevie Wonder; Diana Ross & Supremes; Marvin Gaye; Temptations; Mary Wells; Smokey Robinson & Miracles; Brenda Holloway; Contours; Martha Reeves & Vandellas; Jr. Walker & All Stars; Four Tops; Barrett Strong.

Motown Winners Circle, Vol. 2....Gordy (S) GS-936 10-15 69
Four Tops; Supremes; Mary Wells; Temptations; Contours; others.

Motown Winners Circle, Vol. 3....Gordy (S) GS-943 10-15 69
Mary Wells; Diana Ross & Supremes; Stevie Wonder; Marvin Gaye; Temptations; Smokey Robinson & Miracles; Four Tops; Marvelettes.

Motown Winners Circle, Vol. 4....Gordy (S) 946 10-15 69
Stevie Wonder; Four Tops; Diana Ross & Supremes; Marvin Gaye & Tammi Terrell; Jr. Walker & All Stars; others.

Motown Winners Circle, Vol. 5....Gordy (S) 950 10-15 70
Mary Wells; Smokey Robinson & Miracles; Temptations; Diana Ross & Supremes; Four Tops; Marvin Gaye & Tammi Terrell; Marvelettes; Martha & Vandellas.

Motown's Preferred Stock....Motown (S) M6-881 5-10 77
Gladys Knight & Pips; Spinners; Marvin Gaye & Tammi Terrell; Marvelettes.

Mountain Frolic....Brunswick (M) BL-59000 75-125 50
(10–inch LP.) Bradley Kincaid; Dad Crockett; others.

Move....Status (S) 8307 10-20 65
Hampton Hawes; Freddie Redd; others.

Movie Pop Parade....MGM (EP) X-323 10-15 55

Movie Pop Parade....MGM (EP) X-1157 10-15 55

Movie Pop Parade....MGM (M) E-3220 25-35 55

Movie Pop Parade....MGM (M) E-3294 20-35 56

Movie Pop Parade, Vol. 2....Pickwick (S) CL-001 30-40

Moving Ahead with Music....
Elvis Presley; others.

Mr. Santa Boogie....Savoy Jazz (S) SJL-1157 5-10 85
Ravens; Little Esther Phillips with Johnny Otis; Felix Gross; Jimmy Butler; Dan Grissom; A.B. Green; Big Maybelle; Charlie Parker; Marshall Brothers; Gatemouth Moore; Washboard Pete; Debbie Dabney; Johnny Guarnieri with Slam Stewart.

Mrs. Faruki's Suzuki....Mark 56 (S) 5378 10-20 60s
Olympics; Avengers VI; Marathon; Suzuki Swingers; Chuck Rio & Champs; Barry McGuire; Elmer Bernstein; Marathon.

Murray & Jackie the K's Golden Gassers for a Dance Party....Roulette (M) R-25192 10-20 66
Joey Dee & Starliters; Vibrations; Coasters; Spartans; Jive Five; Little Eva; Chubby Checker; Dovells; Steve Alaimo; Little Joey & Flips.

Murray & Jackie the K's Golden Gassers for Hand Holders....Roulette (M) R-25191 10-20 66
Dion & Belmonts; Chantels; Harptones; Three Friends; Darrell & Oxfords; Capris; Drifters; Flamingos; Ruth McFadden; Valentines.

Murray the K (Live from the Brooklyn Fox in His Record Breaking Show)....KFM (M) 1001 30-40 63
Ronettes; Jan & Dean; Angels; Gene Pitney; Miracles; Shirelles; Chiffons; Dovells; Drifters; Ben E. King; Tymes; Randy & Rainbows; Jay & Americans.

Murray the K Live As It Happened....IBC Distributing (M) MTK-0001-2 15-20 76
Vibrations; Doors; Ronnettes; Dionne Warwick; Patti LaBelle & Blue Belles; Deon Jackson; Shangri-Las; Shirelles; Ben E. King; Drifters; Joe Tex; Chuck Jackson; Jan & Dean; Tymes; Jay & Americans; Gene Pitney; Smokey Robinson & Miracles; Dovells.

Murray the K Presents....Brook-Lyn (M) 302 10-15 68

Murray the K Presents....Brook-Lyn (S) SD-302 10-15 68
Rascals; Joe Tex, Bee Gees; Vanilla Fudge; Royalettes; Janis Ian; Blues Project; Shangri-Las; Deon Jackson. (Side two is live.)

Murray the K, the Fifth Beatle, Gives You Their Favorite Golden Gassers....Scepter (M) 524 15-25 64

Murray the K, the Fifth Beatle, Gives You Their Favorite Golden Gassers....Scepter (S) S-524 15-25 64
Dionne Warwick; Drifters; Chuck Jackson; Jan Bradley; Dale & Grace; Kingsmen; Ben E. King; Little Anthony & Imperials; Chiffons.

Murray the K's 1962 Boss Golden Gassers........ Scepter (M) S-510 15-25 63
Murray the K's 1962 Boss Golden Gassers........ Scepter (S) SPS-510 15-25 63
Shirelles; Johnny Tillotson; Ben E. King; Chuck Jackson; Edsels; Don & Juan; Isley Brothers; Gene Chandler; Etta James; Duprees; Sensations.

Murray the K's Blasts from the Past........ Chess (M) LP-1461 25-35 61
Chantels; Chuck Berry; Bobby Lester & Moonglows; Bo Diddley; Flamingos; Nat Kendrick & Swans; Fiestas; Orchids; Ritchie Valens; Moonglows; Moonlighters; Pastels.

Murray the K's Gassers for Submarine Race Watchers........ Chess (M) CH 9172 8-12 84
Murray the K's Gassers for Submarine Race Watchers........ Chess (M) LP-1470 25-35 62
Shirelles; Chantels; Pastels; Tokens; Harptones; Moonglows; Students; Little Anthony & Imperials.

Murray the K's Golden Gassers........ Chess (M) LP-1458 30-40 61
Robert & Johnny; Moonglows; Students; Flamingos; Monotones; Tune Weavers; Billy Bland; Johnnie & Joe; Lee Andrews & Hearts. (Also issued as *Golden Gassers*.)

Murray the K's Golden Gassers for a Dance Party........ Roulette (M) R-25192 20-25 62
Joey Dee & Starliters; Vibrations; Coasters; Spartans; Jive Five; Little Eva; Chubby Checker; Steve Alaimo; Little Joey & Flips.

Murray the K's Greatest Holiday Show, Live from the Brooklyn Fox........ Brook-Lyn (M) 301 15-25 65
Dionne Warwick; Vibrations; Patti LaBelle & Blue Belles; Dick & Deedee; Shangri-Las; Shirelles; Ben E. King; Drifters; Chuck Jackson.

Murray the K's Sing Along with the Original Golden Gassers........ Roulette (M) R-25159 20-25 61
Murray the K's Sing Along with the Original Golden Gassers........ Roulette (S) SR-25159 20-25 61
Buddy Knox; Jimmie Rodgers; Joe Jones; Continentals; Cleftones; Heartbeats; Frankie Lymon; Playmates; Channels; Sonny Til & Orioles; Crows. (Also issued as *Sing Along with the Original Golden Gassers*.)

Music Avon Grew Up With (5 LP)........ RCA (S) DRS-002 15-30
Frank Sinatra; Ames Brothers; Ed Ames; Eddy Arnold; Harry Belafonte; Boston Pops; Fanny Brice; Eddy Cantor; Carol Channing; Rosemary Clooney; Russ Colombo; Perry Como; Don Cornell; Bing Crosby; Vernon Dalhart; Tommy Dorsey; Ronald Dyson; Nelson Eddy; Eddie Fisher; Ella Fitzgerald; George Gershwin; Benny Goodman; Guess Who; Florence Henderson; Al Hirt; Allan Jones;Jack Jones; Sammy Kaye; Richard Kiley; Mario Lanza; Norman Luboff Choir; Jeanette McDonald; Henry Mancini; Freddy Martin; Mary Martin; Billy May; Ethel Merman; Robert Merrill; Glenn Miller; Vaughn Monroe; Helen Morgan; Peter Nero; Helen O'Connell; Cole Porter; Perez Prado; David Rose; Artie Shaw; Dinah Shore; Sinfonia of London Orchestra; Rudy Vallee; Paul Whiteman; Hugo Winterhalter.

Music Box: see Bankamericard Music Box

Music City USA (6 LP)........ Columbia House (S) 6P 6626 10-20 78
C.W. McCall; Tammy Wynette; George Jones; Freddy Fender; Lynn Anderson; Mickey Gilley; Linda Ronstadt; Sonny James; Ray Price; Donna Fargo; Faron Young; Lynn Anderson & Glenn Sutton; David Houston; Johnny Cash; June Carter; David Houston; Barbara Mandrell; Roy Rogers & Dale Evans; Michael Murphey; Charlie Daniels Band; David Allan Coe; Marshall Chapman; Moe Bandy; Glen Campbell; Bobby Gentry; Lynn Anderson; Marty Robbins; Tex Ritter; Billie Jo Speers; Red Simpson; Dick Curless; Charlie Rich; Jody Miller; Roy Drusky; Jean Shepard; Mac Davis; Tanya Tucker; Statler Brothers; Roy Clark; Charlie McCoy; Wanda Jackson; Melba Montgomery; Wanda Jackson; Ferlin Husky; Roy Acuff; David Houston; Hank Thompson; Ned Miller; Johnny Horton; Bob Wills; Stonewall Jackson.

Music Express........ K-Tel (S) TU-2420 5-10 75
(Mail order offer.) Captain & Tennille; Frankie Valli; KC & Sunshine Band; Elton John Band; Harry Chapin; Barry Manilow; 10cc; Phoebe Snow; Sammy Johns; David Geddes; Austin Roberts; Ozark Mountain Daredevils; Mike Post; Jigsaw; Ritchie Family; Disco Tex & Sex-O-Lettes; Doobie Brothers; Tony Camillo's Bazuka; Johnny Wakelin & Kinshasa Band.

Music Explosion........ Commonwealth Music (S) TU-2520 5-10 77
Music Fit for a King........ Columbia Special Products (S) CSP 260 5-10 60s
Hi-Lo's; Tony Bennett; Four Lads; Frank DeVol; Rosemary Clooney; Jerry Vale; Art VanDamme Quintet; Les Brown.

Music for a Hot Body, Vol. 3........ TSR (S) TLP 1225 5-10 87
Double Take; Lime; Fun Fun; Magazine; Vivien Vee; Lisa Smith; Lana Pellay.

Music for a Mad Ball........ Tops (M) L-1610 35-45 58
Dave Burgess; Scatman Crothers; Neil Hunt; others.

Music for AM, Route 66........ American Motors (S) GPJ 4732 8-12 66
(Automotive Announcement Show.) Sally Ackerman; John C. Becher; Lynne Boyle; Marilyn Cooper; Norma Donaldson; Mary Ehara; Chuck Green; Tommy Karaty; Gloria Lambert; Linda Loftus; Michael Mann; Gary Oakes; Bruce Peyton; Connie Taylor; George Tipton; Carole Woodruff.

Music for Brass........ Columbia (M) CL941 10-20 58
Brass Ensemble of the Jazz & Classical Music Society; J.J. Johnson; John Lewis; Jimmy Guiffre; Miles Davis; Joe Wilder.

Music for Candlelight & Wine........ Capitol (M) PM-21 8-12
Oscar Peterson; Andre Previn; Johnny Hodges; Leroy Holmes; Eddie Heywood; Ray Ellis; Benny Carter; David Rose; George Shearing; Ray Charles Singers.

Music for Everyone........ Columbia (M) XTV 67856 8-12 61
Lee Castle & Jimmy Dorsey; Cleveland Pops; Les Brown; Les Elgart; Buddy Greco; Roy Hamilton; Neal Hefti; Lester Lanin; Somethin' Smith. (Made for Sealy Mattress Co.)

Music for Hand-Jiving........ London (M) LL-3034 30-50 58
Four Jacks; Blue Jeans; Worried Men; Bob Cort Skiffle; Baron; Tommy Steele; Graham Stewart Seven; Terry Dene.

Music for Longhairs........ Design (M) DLP-256 10-20 60s
Music for Longhairs........ Design (S) DLP-256 10-20 60s
Lou Rawls; Young Rascals; Johnny Sea; Chiffons; Robert Parker; Dave "Baby" Cortez; Tommy Roe; Barry McGuire; Impressions with Jerry Butler; Bobby Freeman & Romances.

Music for Lovers Only (Terry Lee Presents)........ Astra (M) ALP 1001 10-20
Avons; Beachcombers; Brightones; Uniques; Ronny & Daytonas; Falcons; Jimmy Dockett; Chants; Revlons; Dee Ervin; Monorays; Starlettes; Four Buddies; O'Capellos; Lou Johnson.

Music for Lovers Only (Terry Lee Presents)........ Airship (M) CS-82742-37 5-10 77
Avons; Beachcombers; Brightones; Uniques; Ronny & Daytonas; Falcons; Jimmy Dockett; Chants; Revlons; Dee Ervin; Monorays; Starlettes; Four Buddies; O'Capellos; Lou Johnson. (Reissue of Astra 1001.)

Music for Lovers Only (Terry Lee Presents)........ Airship (S) CS-82742-34 5-10 77
Skyliners; Johnny Barfield; Ron Holden; Fenways; Tery Klein; Avalons; Starglows; Wheels; Terry Lee with Santo & Johnny; Orchids; Gary Glenn.

Music for Lovers Only (Terry Lee Presents) Vol. 3........ Airship (S) CS-82742-36 5-10 77
Sharades; Scott English; Johnny Barfield; Demons; Brothers of Soul; Barbara Mason; Chuck Corby; Fascinators; Bob Knight Four; Ordells; Empires; Gary Glenn. (reissue of Stone 4001.)

Music for Lovers, (Terry Lee Presents) Vol. 3........ Stone (S) SLP-4001 15-20 60s

Sharades; Scott English; Johnny Barfield; Demons; Brothers of Soul; Barbara Mason; Chuck Corby; Fascinators; Bob Knight Four; Ordells; Empires; Gary Glenn.

Music for Lovers, (Terry Lee Presents) Vol. 4 .... Stone (S) SLP-4002 15-20 60s
Del-Chords; Nino & Ebb Tides; Initials; Avalons; Starglows; Johnny Beecher; Skyliners; True Tones; Matadors; Terry Klein; Anthony & Sophomores.

Music for Lovers, (Terry Lee Presents) Vol. 4 .... Airship (S) CS-82742-35 5-10 77
Del-Chords; Nino & Ebb Tides; Initials; Avalons; Starglows; Johnny Beecher; Skyliners; True Tones; Matadors; Terry Klein; Anthony & Sophomores.

Music for the Boyfriend (He Likes to Go Dancing) .... Decca (M) DL-8313 ?? 56
(Cover features "Petty Girl" pin-up art as featured in *Esquire.*)

Music for the Boyfriend (He Really Digs Jazz) .... Decca (M) DL-8314 20-30 56
(Cover features "Petty Girl" pin-up art as featured in *Esquire.*) Tommy Dorsey's Clambake Seven; John Graas Ensemble; Woody Herman.

Music for the Boyfriend (He Digs Rock and Roll) .... Decca (M) DL-8315 50-100 56
(Cover features "Petty Girl" pin-up art as featured in *Esquire.*) Billy Haley & His Comets; Gloria Mann; Mellotones; Mel Williams; Barons; Sam Taylor.

Music for the Boyfriend (The Feminine Touch) .... Decca (M) DL-8316 ?? 56
(Cover features "Petty Girl" pin-up art as featured in *Esquire.*)

Music for the Easy Hours .... Capital Creative Products (S) SL 6651 5-10 60s
Laurindo Almeida; Jackie Gleason; Hollyridge Strings; Al DeLory; Guitars Unlimited; Ray Anthony.

Music for the Girlfriend (Did Someone Say a Party?) .... Decca (M) DL-8309 ?? 56
(Cover features "Petty Girl" pin-up art as featured in *Esquire.*)

Music for the Girlfriend (She Dotes on Dreamy Music) .... Decca (M) DL-8310 ?? 56
(Cover features "Petty Girl" pin-up art as featured in *Esquire.*)

Music for the Girlfriend (She Adores the Latin Type) .... Decca (M) DL-8311 ?? 56
(Cover features "Petty Girl" pin-up art as featured in *Esquire.*)

Music for the Girlfriend (She Loves the Movies) .... Decca (M) DL-8312 ?? 56
(Cover features "Petty Girl" pin-up art as featured in *Esquire.*)

Music for the Jet Set .... Capitol (M) CA1/CA2 10-15
Four Freshmen; Laurindo Almeida; Benny Goodman; Ray Anthony; Stan Kenton; Al Martino; Jack Jones; Harry James; Keely Smith; Vic Damone. (Made for Northeast Airlines.)

Music for the Twelve Days of Christmas .... RCA (SE) PRS-188 10-20 65
Bonanza TV cast (Lorne Greene; Michael Landon; Dan Blocker); Ralph Hunter Choir; Mario Lanza; Robert Shaw Chorale; RCA Victor Symphony Orchestra; Arthur Fiedler & Boston Pops; John Gary; Melachrino Strings; Norman Luboff Choir; Eddy Arnold; Ames Brothers.

Music for UNICEF Concert .... Polydor (S) PD-1-6214 10-15 79
Earth, Wind & Fire; Andy Gibb; Donna Summer; Olivia Newton-John; Abba; Rod Stewart; John Denver; Rita Coolidge; Kris Kristofferson; Bee Gees.

Music For Your Pleasure (Buick Presents) .... RCA (S) PC8S-518 8-12

Music from Shubert Alley .... Sinclair (?) OSS-2250 10-20
(Soundtrack from 1959 TV special.) Andy Williams; Alfred Drake; Lisa Kirk; Ray Walston; Doretta Morrow; Betty Comden; Adolph Green.

Music from the Dancing Years .... RCA (M) PR-112 10-20 61
Frank Sinatra; Glenn Miller; Gus Arnheim; Duke Ellington; Artie Shaw; Xavier Cugat; Tommy Dorsey; Helen O'Connell; Vaughn Monroe. (Made for Dole Pineapple.)

Music Hall (Country Gold Award Album) (3 LP) .... Plaza House (S) 6719/20/21 10-15 70s
Merle Haggard; Sonny James; Buck Owens; Tennessee Ernie Ford; others.

Music in Depth - F:35d - Perfect Presence Sound Monaural .... Mercury (M) PPMD-4-12 10-15 61
Hal Mooney; Mike Simpson; Quincy Jones; Richard Hayman; Clebanoff Orchestra; Johnny Best; Dick Cathcart All Stars.

Music Lover's Album (3 LP) .... Columbia (S) 3P 6299 10-15
(Boxed set.) Mac Davis; Ray Price; Jerry Vale; Johnny Mathis; Anita Bryant; Ray Conniff; John Davidson; Andre Kostelanetz; Ronnie Dyson; Vikki Carr; Bobby Vinton; Tammy Wynette; Jim Nabors; Tony Bennett; Percy Faith; Charlie; Charlie McCoy; Lynn Anderson; Johnny Cash; Sonny James; Tanya Tucker; Robert Goulet; Steve Lawrence;

Music Machine .... K-Tel (S) TU 2560 5-10 77
Andy Gibb; KC & Sunshine Band; David Soul; Peter McCann; Sylvers; Marvin Gaye; Marilyn McCoo & Billy Davis Jr.; Wild Cherry; Abba; Kiss; Manfred Mann; Rose Royce; Kenny Rogers; Kenny Nolan; Elton John; Alice Cooper; Foreigner.

Music Magic, Hit Sounds of Today .... K-Tel (S) TU-2600 5-10 78
Andy Gibb; Player; Crystal Gayle; High Inergy; Odyssey; Con Funk Shun; Commodores; Santa Esmeralda; Chic; Samantha Sang; Donna Summer; Diana Ross; Eric Carmen; Foreigner; El Coco; Meco; Bay City Rollers; Steely Dan.

Music of Christmas .... Columbia Special Products (M) SP 122 5-10
Norman Luboff; Percy Faith; Jesus & Mary Choral Group; Buddy Cole; Andre Kostelanetz; Ray Conniff; Frank DeVol; Rosemary Clooney; Jimmy Boyd; Harmony Choristers. (Made for Walgreens.)

Music of Cole Porter Played by America's Greatest Jazzmen .... Moodsville (M) MVLP-34 15-25 63
Modern Jazz Quartet; Stan Getz; Gene Ammons; Frank Wess; Coleman Hawkins; Shirley Scott; Billy Taylor; Gil Evans; Red Garland.

Music of George Gershwin Played by America's Greatest Jazzmen .... Moodsville (M) MVLP-33 15-25 63
Gene Ammons; Sonny Rollins; J.J. Johnson; Eddie "Lockjaw" Davis; Red Garland; Billy Taylor; Jaki Byard; Modern Jazz Quartet; Milt Jackson; John Lewis.

Music of Spring .... Columbia Special Products (S) CSP 170 5-10
New Christy Minstrels; Tony Bennett; Rosemary Clooney; Ray Conniff; Leslie Uggams; Skitch Henderson; Jerry Vale; Patti Page; Vic Damone; Andre Kostelanetz; Anita Bryant; Percy Faith. (Made for Scotts.)

Music of Spring .... Columbia Special Products (S) CSP 263 5-10
Barbra Streisand; Johnny Mathis; Percy Faith; Les Elgart; Andre Kostelanetz; Jerry Vale; Tony Bennett; New Christy Minstrels; Andre Previn; Jane Morgan; Ray Conniff; Bobby Hackett. (Made for Scotts.)

Music of Spring, Vol. 3 .... Columbia Special Products (M) CSM 420 5-10
Skitch Henderson & Tonight Show Orchestra; Barbra Streisand; Tony Bennett; Modernaires with Paula Kelly; Brothers Four; Bobby Hackett; Robert Goulet; Julie Andrews; Eydie Gorme; Fiesta Brass; Steve Lawrence; Andre Previn. (Made for Scotts Lawn Care.)

Music of the Yank Years .... RCA Special Products (M) DMM 1-0698 5-10 84
Benny Goodman; Tommy Dorsey with Frank Sinatra & Pied Pipers; Glenn Miller; Duke Ellington; Tommy Dorsey with Jack Leonard & Male Chorus; Artie Shaw; Larry Clinton; Bunny Berigan; Charlie Barnet; Vaughn Monroe with the Norton Sisters; Freddy Martin with Clyde Rogers; Spike Jones & His City Slickers.

Music of Your Life .... CBS Special Products (SE) PM 16905 5-10 83

Jimmy Dorsey with Helen O'Connell & Bob Eberle; Benny Goodman; Mills Brothers; Buddy Clark; Doris Day; Harry James; Dick Haymes; Pied Piper; Dinah Shore; Frankie Laine.

Music of Your Life....CBS Special Products (SE) PM 16906 5-10 83
Dick Haymes; Weavers with Gordon Jenkins; Jo Stafford; Frankie Laine; Four Lads; Guy Lombardo; Tony Bennett; Rosemary Clooney; Guy Mitchell; Kay Starr.

Music of Your Life....CBS Special Products (SE) PM 16907 5-10 83
Peggy Lee; Kay Kyser; Buddy Clark; Doris Day; Dinah Shore; Ames Brothers with Les Brown; Sammy Kaye; Jo Stafford; Bing & Gary Crosby; Les Paul & Mary Ford; Percy Faith.

Music of Your Life....CBS Special Products (SE) PM 16908 5-10 83
Harry James with Dick Haymes; Les Brown with Doris Day; Nat King Cole; Dinah Shore; Buddy Clark; Cab Calloway; Kay Kyser; Woody Herman; George Shearing Quintet; Mitch Miller.

Music of Your Life....CBS Special Products (SE) PM 16909 5-10 83
Billie Holiday; Claude Thornhill with Fran Warren; Vic Damone; Platters; Percy Faith; Art Mooney; Frankie Laine; Patti Page; Harry James; Brothers Four.

Music of Your Life....CBS Special Products (SE) PM 169010 5-10 83
Carmen Cavallaro; Dinah Washington; Lawrence Welk; Patti Page; Tony Bennett; Nat King Cole; Peggy Lee; Andy Williams; Brenda Lee; Charlie Rich.

Music People (3 LP)....Columbia (S) C3X-31280 15-25 72
Wayne Cochran; It's a Beautiful Day; Bob Dylan; Boz Scaggs; Chase; Ten Years After; Santana; Poco; Taj Mahal; Sweathog; Santana; New Riders of the Purple Sage; Genya Raven; Chambers Brothers; REO Speedwagon; Barry Mann; Compost; Johnny Winter; Jeff Beck Group; Byrds; Dreams; Mahavishnu Orchestra; Blue Oyster Cult; Mylon; Colin Blunstone; Bell & Arc; Blood, Sweat & Tears; David Clayton Thomas; Redbone; Spirit; Jake Holmes; Jimmie Spheeris; Dr. Hook & Medicine Show; Blue Rose; Kris Kristofferson; Edgar Winter's White Trash; Kenny Loggins with Jim Messina; Grin; Pamela Pollard; Grootna; Fields.

Music Power....K-Tel (S) TU 234 5-10 74
(Mail order offer.) Brownsville Station; Jim Stafford; Stylistics; Ian Thomas; Sylvia; Millie Jackson; Stories; Lighthouse; Gladys Knight & Pips; Sonny & Cher; Gordon Sinclair; Dawn; Four Tops; Grass Roots; Blue Mink; Chi-Lites; Natural Four; Raspberries; Sweet; Joe Simon; Dobie Gray; Barry White.

Music Row Greats....4 Star (S) 4S-SP-111 5-10 77
George Morgan; Carl Belew; Wynn Stewart; Jerry Fuller; Jan Howard; Mary Ford; Jimmy Elledge; Travis Brothers; Johnny & Jonie; Betty Jean Robinson.

Music 'Til Dawn....Columbia Special Products (M) CSM 386 5-10
Music 'Til Dawn....Columbia Special Products (SE) CSS 386 5-10
Sy Mann; Percy Faith; Andre Kostelanetz; Bobby Hackett with Glenn Miller; Andre Previn; George Szell with Cleveland Orchestra; Leonard Bernstein & New York Philharmonic; Eileen Farrell with Columbia Symphony Orchestra; Max Rudolf; Eugene Ormandy & Philadelphia Orchestra.

Music to Have Fun By....RCA (M) LM-2813 8-12
Music to Have Fun By....RCA (S) LSC-2813 8-12
Boston Pops; Boston Symphony Orchestra; Chicago Symphony Orchestra; RCA Victor Symphony Orchestra; Morton Gould; National Symphony Orchestra.

Music to Live By....Mercury (M) PJC-1 8-12
Ralph Marterie; Dick Contino; David Carroll; Dinah Washington; Jimmy Cleveland; Terry Gibbs. (Side two has various classical selections.)

Music to Paint By....RCA (M) PRM-208 5-10 68
Music to Paint By....RCA (S) PRS-208 5-10 68
Jim Reeves; John Gary; Della Reese; Norman Luboff Choir; Peter Nero; Tony Martin; Lena Horne; Sergio Franchi; Skitch Henderson; Ed Ames.

Music to Party By....RCA (S) PRS-224 10-20 60s
Limeliters; Roger Miller; Carol Channing; Vic Damone; Della Reese; Living Brass; Sid Ramin; Pete Fountain; Dukes of Dixieland. (Special products. Made for George Dickel & Co.)

Music to Read James Bond By....United Artists (M) UAL-3415 15-20 65
Music to Read James Bond By....United Artists (S) UAL-6415 15-25 65
Music to Read James Bond By, Vol. 2....United Artists (M) UAL-3541 15-20 66
Music to Read James Bond By, Vol. 2....United Artists (S) UAS-6541 20-25 66
Music to Relax With....Columbia Special Products (S) CSP 303 5-10 60s
Percy Faith; Tony Bennett; Ray Conniff; Jane Morgan; Marty Robbins; Banjo Barons; Andre Kostelanetz; Vic Damone; Brothers Four; Jerry Vale; Patti Page; Skitch Henderson.

Music to Remember....RCA (SE) PRS-400 5-10 72
Bing Crosby; Kate Smith; Maurice Chevalier; Guy Lombardo; Frank Sinatra; Helen O'Connell; Vaughn Monroe; Tommy Dorsey; Billy Eckstine; Lee Wiley; Tony Martin; Percy Faith. (Made for General Foods.)

Music to Remember from "Lawrence of Arabia" and Other Hits....United Artists (M) UAL-3278 ?? 63
Music to Remember from "Lawrence of Arabia" and Other Hits....United Artists (S) UAS-6278 ?? 63
(Soundtrack.) Marilyn Monroe; Shirley Bassey; Don Costa; Nick Perito; Al Caiola; Leroy Holmes.

Music to Remember from Motion Pictures....United Artists (M) UAL-3249 8-10 63
Music to Remember from Motion Pictures....United Artists (S) UAS-6249 10-12 63
(Soundtrack.) Ferrante & Teicher; Al Caiola; Don Costa; Andre Previn; others.

Music to Shave By....Columbia/Auravision (EP) No Number Used 10-15
(Square cardboard picture disc.) Bing Crosby; Louis Armstrong; Rosemary Clooney; Hi-Los.

Music...the Language of Love (8 LP)....Columbia Special Products (S) P8 14096 30-45 77
(Boxed set.) Nelson Riddle; Ray Eberle & Modernaires with Tex Beneke; Jo Stafford with Paul Weston; Laurindo Almeida; Vic Damone with Nelson Riddle; Pete King; Helen Forrest with Harry James; Charlie Barnet; Bob Crosby with the Bobcats; Frankie Carle; Vaughn Monroe; Hugo Montenegro; Ed Ames with Ken Thorne; Helen O'Connell with Joe Reisman; Jerry Whitman & Tomorrows with Perry Botkin; Marilyn King with Dick Grove; Freddy Martin; King Sisters with Frank DeVol; Billy May; Helen Forrest with Wally Stott; Gene Merlino with Harry James; Helen Forrest with Artie Shaw; Shelby Flint with Perry Botkin Jr.; Jo Stafford & Pied Pipers with Paul Weston.

Music with 58 Musicians: see Warner Bros. Promotional Releases/Samplers

Musical Annual (4 LP) ....Columbia Special Products (S) 10160/10161/600S/S-1200 20-30 72

(Boxed set.) Peaches & Herb; Byrds; Paul Revere & Raiders; Buckinghams; Lulu; Yardbirds; Donovan; Bobby Vinton; Johnny Cash; Gary Puckett & Union Gap; Hollies; Dave Clark Five; Scott McKenzie; Arbors; Al Kooper; Janis Joplin; Santana; Hollies; Sly & Family Stone; Billy Joe Royal; Mark Lindsay; Pacific Gas & Electric; Taj Mahal; Blood, Sweat & Tears; Johnny Winter; Poco; Chambers Brothers; Mongo Santamaria; Tom Rush; Impressions; Tommy James & Shondells; Strawberry Alarm Clock; Len Barry; Delfonics; Intruders; Ohio Express; Who; Ricardo Ray; 1910 Frutigum Co.; Turtles; Amboy Dukes; Happenings; Lemon Pipers; Sonny & Cher. (Repackage that includes *Super Hits* [Col. 10160], *More Super Hits* [Col. 10161], *20 Heavy Hits* [Adam 600S], and *20 Solid Gold Hits* (Crystal 1200].) (Made for Brennan Industries.)

Musical Memories for the Class of '62 (4 LP) ....Columbia Special Products (S) C4 10939 10-20 72

(Boxed set.) Chordettes; Chuck Berry; Paul Anka; Johnny Tillotson; Sam Cooke; Connie Stevens; Bobby Freeman; Frankie Avalon; Curtis Lee; Ritchie Valens; Poni-Tails; Neil Sedaka; Jimmy Charles; Fats Domino; Dovells; Diamonds; Ventures; Dee Dee Sharp; Joey Dee & Starliters; Orlons; Perez Prado; Little Eva; Bent Fabric; Chubby Checker; Dave "Baby" Cortez; Duane Eddy; Isley Brothers; Monotones; Dion; Marvelettes; Floyd Cramer; Fleetwoods; Maurice Williams & Zodiacs; Claudine Clark; Frankie Avalon; Jimmy Clanton; Shirelles; Bobby Vee; Coasters; Tokens; Bobby Darin; Little Richard; Freddy Cannon; Floyd Cramer; Neil Sedaka; Hollywood Argyles; Beach Boys; Silhouettes; Joe Jones; Freddy Cannon; Everly Brothers; Paul Anka; Miracles; Fabian; Della Reese; Donnie Brooks; Jim Reeves; Contours; Don Gibson; Kitty Kallen; Ray Peterson.

Musical Memories for the Class of '72 (4 LP) ....Columbia Special Products (S) C4 10628 10-20 72

(Boxed set.) Gary Puckett & Union Gap; Paul Revere & Raiders; Michele Lee; Big Brother & Holding Co.; Aretha Franklin; O.C. Smith; Donovan; Georgie Fame; Buckinghams; Blood, Sweat & Tears; Johnny Cash; Chambers Brothers; Sly & Family Stone; Mark Lindsay; Spiral Staircase; Christie; Al Kooper; Janis Joplin; Santana; Hollies; Billy Joe Royal; Pacific Gas & Electric; Ray Stevens; Tommy James; Fuzz; Ten Years After; Tina Turner & Ikettes.

Musical Milestones ....Plantation House/Capitol (S) SL-6808 8-12 72

(Mail order offer.) Ella Mae Morse; Johnny Mercer; Margaret Whiting; Nat King Cole; Les Paul & Mary Ford; Jo Stafford; Ray Anthony; Kay Starr; Les Baxter; Dean Martin; Gogi Grant; Tommy Edwards; David Rose; Glen Campbell; Peggy Lee; Al Martino.

Musical Spectrum ....RCA DJL1-5361 5-10 85

(Promotional issue only.) Glenn Jones; Evelyn "Champagne" King; Charme; Skyy; Pointer Sisters; Band of Gold; Richard "Dimples" Fields; Fonzi Thornton.

Musicor Musicale ....Musicor (S) SP-1 10-15 60s

(Promotional issue only.) Gene Pitney; George Jones; Les Barnett; Ralph Marterie; Los Hispanos Quartet; Vinnie Bell; Tito Rodriguez; Al Soyka; Gus Vali.

Musique Boutique ....Capitol Creative Products (S) SL 6536 8-12

Laurindo Almeida; Glen Campbell; Lettermen; Nancy Wilson; Gordon MacRae; Matt Monro; Sounds of Our Times.

My Favorite Hits — Mickey Mantle ....RCA (M) LPM-1704 30-40 58

Artie Shaw; Vaughan Monroe; Eddy Arnold; Glenn Miller; Hal Kemp; Tommy Dorsey; Tony Martin; Hugo Winterhalter; Duke Ellington; Billy Butterfield; Sons of the Pioneers; Ralph Flanagan.

My Favorite Story ....20th Fox (M) TFM-3106 10-20 63

Bob Hope; Bing Crosby; Jack Benny; others.

My Funny Valentine ....MCA Special Markets (S) 7-34690 5-10 70s

Sammy Davis Jr.; Bert Kaempfert; Brenda Lee; Peter Duchin; Percy Faith; Liberace; Louis Armstrong; Midas Touch; Peggy Lee; Pete Fountain.

My Stepmother Is an Alien ....Polydor (S) 837798-1 8-10 88

(Soundtrack.) Animotion; M/A/R/R/S; Ivan Neville; Kim Basinger; Dan Aykroyd; Cameo; Jackie Jackson; Siren.

My Son the Surf-Nut ....Capitol (M) T-1939 20-30 63

My Son the Surf-Nut ....Capitol (S) ST-1939 30-40 63

Frank N. Stein & Abominable Surf Men; Knotknees McGurdy & Drop Outs; Daddie Ho & Hodaddies; Hangten Horwitz; Dingston Trio; Sudsy Shots & Pier-Shooters.

NARAS Presents the Golden Ones, 1959 Edition, Vol. 1 ....No Label Used (M) 1000 BTY 10-20 59

(Promotional issue only.) Chordettes; Nat "King" Cole; Perry Como; Doris Day; Fats Domino; Ella Fitzgerald; Ed "Kookie" Byrnes; Julie London; Patti Page; Debbie Reynolds; Carleton Carpenter; Billy Vaughn; Roger Williams. (Presented by the Watchmakers of Switzerland.)

N.A.R.M.'s Golden Decade ....RCA (S) PRS-264 20-40 69

(Soundtrack. Promotional issue only.) Limeliters; Ann-Margret; Al Hirt; Paul Anka; Homer & Jethro; Peter Nero; Eddy Arnold; John Gary; Chet Atkins; Floyd Cramer; Anita Kerr Singers; Boots Randolph; Myron Cohen; SSGT. Barry Sadler; Henry Mancini; Jack Jones; Harry Belafonte.

NBC's Chamber Music Society of Lower Basin Street ....RCA Camden (M) CAL 321 10-15 56

Dinah Shore; Lena Horne; Henry Levine & His Barefoot Dixieland Philharmonic; Paul Laval & His Woodwindy Ten; NBC Chamber Music Society of Lower Basin Street.

N.E.C. Convention ....Buddah (S) NEC-1970 10-15 70

(Promotional issue only.)

Nashville ....Columbia/Magnavox (S) CSS-1341 8-15 60s

Johnny Cash; June Carter; Flatt & Scruggs; Tammy Wynette; Marty Robbins; Ray Price. (Special products. Made for Magnavox.)

Nashville Bandstand ....King (M) 813 15-25 63

Nashville Bandstand ....King (S) S-813 15-25 63

Hank Locklin; Cowboy Copas; Reno & Smiley; others.

Nashville Bandstand, Vol. 2 ....King (M) 847 15-25 63

Nashville Christmas Party ....RCA (M) LPM-2579 10-15 62

Nashville Christmas Party ....RCA (S) LSP-2579 10-15 62

Skeeter Davis; Eddy Arnold; Porter Wagoner; John D. Loudermilk; Hank Snow; Anita Kerr Singers; Hank Locklin; Floyd Cramer; Jimy Elledge; Jim Edward Brown; Chet Atkins.

Nashville City Limits ....Columbia Musical Treasury (S) 1P-6627 5-10 74

(Columbia Record Club issue.) Bobbie Gentry; Charlie Rich; Jody Miller; Sonny James; Ned Miller; Joe Stampley; Billie Jo Spears; Roy Clark; Melba Montgomery; Faron Young.

Nashville Gold (2 LP) ....RCA R 213295-1-2 8-12 70s

Dolly Parton; Bobby Bare; Chet Atkins; Waylon Jennings; Connie Smith; Nat Stuckey; Jerry Reed; Willie Nelson; Nashville String Band; Jim Reeves; Norma Jean; John Denver; Dottie West; Kenny Price; Danny Davis; George Hamilton IV; Dallas Frazier; Eddy Arnold; Skeeter Davis; Floyd Cramer; Red Lane; Johnny Russell; Porter Wagoner.

Nashville Graffiti (2 LP) ....Candelite/Columbia Special Products (S) P2-12702 10-20 75

Link Wray; Johnny Horton; Bobby Vinton; Ray Price; Buzz Clifford; Johnny Cash; Marty Robbins; Guy Mitchell; Patti Page; Ersel Hickey; Statler Brothers; Carl Perkins; Bobby Helms; Jimmy Dean; Mindy Carson; Claude King; Stonewall Jackson; Johnnie Ray; Billy Grammer.

Nashville Music City USA ....Deltron (S) Q-7701 40-60 76

(Promotional only picture disc.) George Jones; Mel Tillis; Dottie West; others.

Nashville on My Mind ....???? 5-10
Lynn Anderson; Mel Tillis; Jerry Wallace; Jody Miller; Johnny Paycheck; Mac Davis; Barbara Fairchild; David Allen Coe; Roger Miller; George Jones.

Nashville Package of Original Country Hits .... Mercury (S) SR-61375 5-10 72
Jerry Lee Lewis; Roger Miller; George Jones; Statler Brothers; Leroy Van Dyke; Flatt & Scruggs; Faron Young; Roger Miller; Dave Dudley; Tom T. Hall; Bobby Bare; Roy Drusky; Priscilla Mitchell.

Nashville Saturday Night .... Columbia House (SE) 1P 6215 5-10 75
(Record club issue.) Sonny James; Johnny Cash; Marion Worth; Ferlin Husky; Charlie Walker; Judy Lynn; Floyd Tillman; Marty Robbins; Patsy Cline; Johnny Bond.

Nashville Saturday Night .... Starday (M) S-128 20-30 61
Cowboy Copas; George Jones; String Bean; Frankie Miller; Carl Story; Merle Kilgore; Benny Martin; Jim Eanes; Red Sovine; Cousin Jody; Margie Singleton; Lonzo & Oscar; Wally Fowler & Oak Ridge Quartet; Wayne Raney.

Nashville Saturday Night .... Nashville (M) NLP-2009 10-15 64

Nashville Sound: Bright Lights & Country Music (6 LP) .... Columbia Musical Treasury (SE) 6P 6054 20-30 74
(Boxed set. Columbia House Record Club issue.) John Wesley Ryles; Kitty Wells; David Houston; Barbara Fairchild; Johnny Paycheck; Bill Anderson; Freddy Weller; Mac Davis; Bonnie Guitar; Bob Luman; Tanya Tucker; Roger Miller; Donna Fargo; Hank Thompson; Lynn Anderson; Stonewall Jackson; Jerry Lee Lewis; Charlie Rich; Tammy Wynette; Jimmy Dean; Statler Brothers; Johnny Cash; June Carter; Jack Greene; Dave Dudley; Conway Twitty; Lefty Frizzell; Webb Pierce; Sonny James; Marty Robbins; Carl Smith; Mel Tillis; Jerry Wallace; Kris Kristofferson; Pat Boone; Roy Clark; Johnny Horton; Flatt & Scruggs; Jody Miller; Johnny Duncan; George Jones; Judy Lynn; Tom T. Hall; Barbara Mandrell; O.C. Smith; Ray Price; Joan Weber; Pete Drake; Jeannie C. Riley; Carter Family; Earl Scruggs.

Nashville Sound .... Design (S) DLP-634 8-12 66
Patsy Cline; Carl Belew; Rocky Bill Ford; Hank Locklin; Ferlin Husky.

Nashville Sound, Vol. 7: see Bright Lights & Country Music Vol. 7

Nashville Sounds of Country Music .... Rural Rhythm (M) RR 150 8-12 60s
Bob Jennings; Autry Inman; Swanny Caldwell; Kenny Smith; Johnny Tyler; Johnny Skilles; Jo Casey; Skiles-Akins-Cipoll; Bill Carter; Jerrie Walker; Hal Willis; Bobby Barnett;

Nashville Stars .... Crane/Norris (S) CN-100 5-10 70s
(Mail order offer.) Johnny Rodriguez; Billy Crash Craddock; Donna Fargo; Gene Watson; Eddie Rabbitt; Don Williams; Conway Twitty; Barbara Mandrell; Willie Nelson; Joe Stampley; Linda Ronstadt; Waylon Jennings; Freddy Fender; Emmylou Harris; Ronnie Milsap; Glen Campbell; Tom T. Hall; Statler Brothers; Bill Anderson.

Nashville Steel Guitar .... Starday (M) SLP-138 15-20 61
Pete Drake; Little Roy Wiggins; Don Helms; Jimmy Day; Herbie Remington; Dick Stubbs; Al Petty.

Nashville Steel Guitar .... Nashville (M) NLP-2017 10-15 65
Pete Drake; Little Roy Wiggins; Don Helms; Jimmy Day; Herbie Remington; Dick Stubbs; Al Petty.

Nashville Wives .... Nashville (S) NLP-2104 8-12
Judy West; Dolly Parton; Jan Howard; Melba Montgomery; Dottie West; Rose Maddox.

Nashville's Greatest Instrumentalists .... RCA (S) APL1-0167 5-10 73
Chet Atkins; Floyd Cramer; Lester Flatt; Homer & Jethro; others.

Nashville's Greatest Instrumentalists, Vol. 2 .... RCA (S) APL1-0536 5-10 74
Chet Atkins; Floyd Cramer; Jerry Reed; Kossi Gardner; others.

Nashville's Greatest Instrumentalists (With Their Great Hits) .... RCA (S) ANL1-2181 5-10 77
Floyd Cramer; Roddy Bristol; Buck Trent; Jerry Reed; Chet Atkins; others.

Nasty Blues .... Ichiban (S) ICH-1048 5-10 89
Clarence Carter; Trudy Lynn; Chick Willis; Artie White; Gary B.B. Coleman; Little Johnny Taylor; Travis Haddix.

National Gospel Quartet Convention .... RCA (M) LPM-2728 10-20 63

National Gospel Quartet Convention .... RCA (S) LSP-2728 10-20 63
Stamps; Blackwood Brothers; Oak Ridge Quartet; Statesmen; Speer Family; Kingsmen.

National Lampoon Album of the Month .... National Lampoon (S) Jan-76 A/B 20-25 76
John Lennon; others.

National Lampoon In-Store Airplay LP of the Month .... National Lampoon (S) No Number 15-25 79
Promotional only issue.) Paul McCartney; others.

National Lampoon In-Store Promo LP for March 1974 .... National Lampoon (S) No Number 10-15 74
Joni Mitchell; Commander Cody; Donovan; Puzzle; Leo Sayer; Stealers Wheel; Leo Kotke; Carly Simon; Todd Rundgren; Nazareth; Rick Nelson; Dave Mason.

National Lampoon In-Store Promo LP for May 1974 .... National Lampoon (S) No Number 10-15 74
War; Eddie Hendricks; Pointer Sisters; Bachman-Turner Overdrive; Peter Frampton; Alan Price; Paul Simon; Cat Stevens; Grand Funk; Lou Reed; Chicago; Firesign Theatre.

National Lampoon In-Store Promo LP for June 1974 .... National Lampoon (S) No Number 10-15 74
Harry Nilsson; Jefferson Airplane; Rita Coolidge; Frank Zappa; Smokey Robinson; Ozark Mountain Daredevils; Wet Willie; Buzzy Linhart; Boz Scaggs; Rick Derringer; Mott the Hoople; Michael Murphey.

National Lampoon In-Store Promo LP for July 1974 .... National Lampoon (S) No Number 10-15 74
Rick Wakeman; Hollies; Kris Kristofferson; Jesse Colin Young; Kinks; Leon Russell; Golden Earring; Argent; Mary Travers; Kathi McDonald; Guess Who; Save the Children; New Riders of the Purple Sage; Kansas; Loggins & Messina.

National Lampoon In-Store Promo LP for August 1974 .... National Lampoon (S) No Number 10-15 74
Rick Wakeman; Elvis Bishop; Blue Oyster Cult; Kathi McDonald; Sutherland Brothers; Bob Wills; Mary Travers; Save the Children; Bob Dylan; Nitty Gritty Dirt Band; Marvin Gaye; Elton John.

National Lampoon In-Store Promo LP for September 1974 .... National Lampoon (S) No Number 10-15 74

National Lampoon In-Store Promo LP for October 1974 .... National Lampoon (S) OCT-74 10-15 74
(Promotional issue only.) Joe Cocker; Red, White & Bluegrass; Harry Chapin; Little Feat; Jim Capaldi; Mary Travers; Stevie Wonder; Sly & Family Stone; Harry Nilsson; Neil Young; John Stewart. (Labels and back cover are blank.)

National Lampoon's Animal House .... MCA (S) 3046 8-10 78

National Lampoon's Animal House .... MCA (S) 1692 8-10 78
(Soundtrack.) Sam Cooke; Bobby Lewis; Paul & Paula; Chris Montez; Lloyd Williams; Stephen Bishop; John Belushi; Richard Berry; Elmer Bernstein; National Lampoon. (With dialogue.)

National Lampoon's Vacation .... Warner Bros (S) 1-23909 8-10 83
(Soundtrack.) Ramones; Lindsey Buckingham; Fleetwoods; Ralph Burns; Nicolette Larson; June Pointer; Vanity 6.

Native American Ballads .... RCA (M) LPV-548 10-15 67
Hall Brothers; Delmore Brothers; Jimmy Davis; others.

Navy Seals .... Atlantic (S) 82125-1 8-10 90
(Soundtrack.) Mr. Big; Bon Jovi; Richie Havens; Planet 3; Gowan; Vicki Thomas; Lisa Hartman; Blue Rodeo.

Ned Kelly .... United Artists (S) UAS-5213 15-20 70

Ned Kelly .... United Artists (S) UA-LA300-G 10-12 74
(Soundtrack.) Waylon Jennings; Mick Jagger; Kris Kristofferson; Tom Ghent.

Negro Church Music........ Atlantic (M) 1351 20-30 60

Negro Church Music........ Atlantic (S) SD-1351 25-35 60

Nemperor Line........ Nemperor (S) PR 248 5-10 75
Tommy Bolin; Stanley Clarke; Lenny White; Jan Hammer; Jerry Goodman; Raices.

New and Old Sounds........ United Artists (S) UA-LA808-R 5-10 77
Bob Marley; Meditaitions; Dillinger; Elroy Wilson; Ken Boothe; others.

New and Old Time Country & Folk Songs .... Rural Rhythm (M) RR 153 8-12 60s
Ernie Cook; Boys from Shiola; Swanny Caldwell; Bill Carter; Johnny Skiles & Bob Hill; Bob Jennings; Autry Inman; Bobby Barnet; Kentucky Boys; Dewayne Wear; Johnny Tyler.

New August '60 Albums .... Warner Bros. (M) PRO 115 10-20 60
Bill Haley & His Comets; George Greeley; Swe-danes; Raoul Meynard; John Scott Trotter; Joe "Fingers" Carr; Ira Ironstrings; Buddy Cole; Outriggers; John Raitt; Otto Cesana.

New Breed........ RCA (S) CPL1-5491 5-10 85
Juice Newton; Earl Thomas Conley; Gus Hardin; Vince Gill; Restless Heart; Eddy Raven; Judds.

New Country & Western Round-Up (5 LP)........ Capitol (S) SLER 6582 20-30
(Boxed set.) Buck Owens; Merle Haggard; Glen Campbell; Sonny James; Wynn Stewart; Tex Ritter; Geezinslaw Brothers; Buckaroos; Jean Shepard; Wanda Jackson; others.

New Dimensions .... Musak (S) H-1-35 5-10 68
(Promotional issue only.) Phil Bodner; Elliot Lawrence; George Siravo; Charles Grean; Ted Heath; Sid Bass; Earl Sheldon; Dave Terry; Al Caiola; Frank Hunter; Richard Haymen.

New Folks........ Vanguard (S) VSD7-9140 10-20 60s
Eric Anderson; Phil Ochs; Bob Jones; Lisa Kindred.

New Golden Age of Sound Albums .... RCA (S) SPS-33-50 10-15 50s
Melanchrino Strings; Perez Prado; Harry Belafonte; Pat Suzuki; Buddy Morrow; Xavier Cugat; Fritz Reiner; Arthur Fiedler; Mario Lanza; Morton Gould; Kiril Kondrashin. (Made for Breck.)

New Hi .... Tempo (M) 2 150-250 71
Stevie Ray Vaughan; Stone Sypher; Image; Mint; Blue Persuasion.

New Orleans Home of the Blues .... Bandy (S) 700066 5-10 80s

New Orleans, Home of the Blues, Vol. 1 .... Minit (M) 0001 20-30 62
Jessie Hill; Aaron Neville; Ernie K-Doe; Lee Diamond. (For Vol. 2, see THOMAS, Irma / Ernie K-Doe / Showmen / Benny Spellman.)

New Orleans, Home of the Blues, Vol. 2 .... Minit (M) 0004 20-30
Irma Thomas; Benny Spellman; Ernie K-Doe; Showmen.

New Orleans, Our Home Town........ Imperial (M) LP-9260 20-30 64
Fats Domino; Irma Thomas; Spiders; Ernie K-Doe; Jessie Hill; Shirley & Lee.

New Orleans Rhythm & Blues .... Chess (M) CH-9174 8-12 84
Myles & Dupont; Charles Williams; Sugarboy Crawford; Hawkettes; Clarence Henry; T.V. Slim; Allen Brooks; Edgar Blanchard; Reggie Hall; Eddie Bo; Rod Bernard; Bobby Blanquet; Clifton Chenier.

New Orleans Rhythm 'n Blues........ Krazy Kat (M) 7403 5-10
Lloyd Price; Benny Spellman; Jivin' Gene; Dave Bartholomew; Allen Toussaint; Chris Kenner; Professor Longhair; Roy Brown; Joe Barry; Eddie Bo; Huey Smith.

New Orleans Rhythm & Blues Anniversary Album: see Official New Orleans Rhythm & Blues Anniversary Album

New Releases from Atlantic Country........ Atlantic (S) PR 193 10-15 73
(Promotional issue only.) David Rogers; Henson Cargill; Marti Brown; Troy Seals; Terry Stafford; Don Adams.

New Scene .... Capitol (S) SL-6771 5-10 70s
Quicksilver Messenger Service; Joy of Cooking; Glen Campbell; Joe South; Anne Murray; If; Helen Reddy.

New Sensations in Jazz from RCA........ RCA (M) SPL-12-41 15-25
Larry Clinton; George Russell's Smalltet; Red Norvo Quintet; Peanuts Hucko; Bob Scobey's Frisco Jazz Band; Bud Powell Trio; Tito Puente; Tony Scott Quartet; Lou McGarity; Andy Kirk & His Clouds of Joy; Pete Kelly's Big Seven; Hal McKusick; Shorty Rogers & His Giants; Eddie Cano Sextet; Tony Scott; Sauter-Finegan Orchestra; Barbara Carroll Trio; Tommy Dorsey; George Williams; Johnny Hamlin Quintet; Duke Ellington; Cleman Hawkins with Billy Byers; Pete Jolly Trio; Muggsy Spanier's Ragtime Band; Hal McKusiek Ninetet; Lou Levy Quartet; Fletcher Henderson; Dave Pell Octet; Phineas Newborn Jr. Quartet; RCA Victor All Stars./

New Sound America Loves Best .... RCA SP-33-91 8-12 60s
Rosemary Clooney; Henry Mancini; Ralph Hunter Choirs & Sid Ramin; Chet Atkins; Ames Brothers; Perez Prado; Sam Cooke; John Klein; Morton Gould; Robert Shaw Male Chorus; Leontyne Price; Chicago Symphony Orchestra & F. Reiner; Boston Pops with Arthur Fiedler; Mario Lanza; RCA Victor Symphony Orchestra & Band with R.R. Bennett. (Made for Breck.)

New Sound of the Stars Dynagroove .... RCA Red Seal (M) PS 33-223 10-15 63

New Sound of the Stars Dynagroove .... RCA Red Seal (S) SPS 33-223 10-15 63
Sid Ramin; Perry Como; Chet Atkins; Hugo & Luigi Chorus; Eddy Arnold; Floyd Cramer; Marty Gold; Jim Reeves; Peter Nero; Limeliters; Sam Cooke; Al Hirt.

New Sound of the Stars........ RCA Red Seal (M) SP 33-224 5-10 63
Robert Shaw Choral; Chicago Symphony; Boston Symphony; Boston Pops; Leontyne Price; Erick Freidman; Sergio Franchi.

New Sounds America Loves Best .... RCA (S) SPS 33-91 10-15 60s
Sam Cooke; Chet Atkins; Rosemary Clooney; Henry Mancini; Two Ralph Hunter Choirs; Ames Brothers; Perez Prado; John Klein; Morton Gould; Robert Shaw Male Chorus; Leontyne Price; Chicago Symphony Orchestra; Boston Pops; Mario Lanza.

New Spirit of Capitol........ Capitol (S) SNP-6 8-12 70
Steve Miller; Hedge & Donna; Joe South; Linda Ronstadt; John Stewart; David Axelrod; Edgar Broughton Band; Sons; Pink Floyd; Guitar Jr.; Bob Seger System; Mississippi Fred McDowell; Grand Funk Railroad.

New Stars in Action: see Oldsmobile Spotlights the New Stars in Action

New Themes from Motion Pictures .... Time (M) 52065 5-10 60s

New Themes from Motion Pictures .... Time (S) S-2065 10-20 60s
(Soundtrack.) Gordon Jenkins; Billy May; Hugo Montenegro; Maury Laws; Jerry Fielding; Kermit Leslie; Domenic Cortese.

New Tradition Is the Winning Tradition .... W.B./Reprise/Curb (S) PRO A-2744 8-12 87
Michael Martin Murphy; Nitty Gritty Dirt Band; Randy Travis; Dolly Parton; Linda Ronstadt; Emmylou Harris; Hank Williams Jr.; Dwight Yoakum.

New Wave Surf Party .... Ostrich (S) OR-001 8-10
Revels; Surf-Teens; Reveliers; Fender IV; Breakers; Truants; Pyramids; Vistas; Vy-Dels; Creations; Velvetones; Temptations; Tornados; Gamblers.

New York City's Greatest Oldies, Vol. 1 .... Paul Winley (M) LP-1001 50-75 60s
(Album cover says LP-100.) Les Cooper; Maurice Williams & Zodiacs; James Brown; Six-Teens; Jesters; Dave "Baby" Cortez; Channels; Skyliners; Sam Cooke; Little Anthony & Imperials; Students; Jackie & Starlites; Paragons; Velours; Collegians.

New York Stories .... Elektra (S) 60857-1 10-15 89
(Soundtrack.) Kid Creole & Coconuts; Pianosaurus; Frankie Carle; Wilbur De Paris; Bernie Leighton; Procol Harum; Transvision Vamp; Hot Club of France; Bob Dylan; Band.

Newport Folk Festival .... Elektra (M) EKL-189 15-25 60
Newport Folk Festival .... Elektra (S) EKS-7189 20-30 60
Oscar Brand; Geula Gill; Will Holt; Theodore Bikel; others.

Newport Folk Festival, 1960 .... Vanguard (M) VRS-9083 15-20 63
Newport Folk Festival, 1960 .... Vanguard (S) VSD-2087 15-25 63
Newport Folk Festival, 1963 .... Vanguard (M) VRS-9148 10-20 64
Newport Folk Festival, 1963 .... Vanguard (S) VSD-79148 10-20 64
Newport Folk Festival, 1963, Vol. 2 .... Vanguard (M) VRS-9149 10-20 64
Newport Folk Festival, 1963, Vol. 2 .... Vanguard (S) VSD-79149 10-20 64
Newport Folk Festival, 1963 Broadside .... Vanguard (S) VRS-9144 20-30 64
Newport Folk Festival, 1963 Broadside .... Vanguard (S) VSD-79144 20-30 64
Bob Dylan; Pete Seeger; Joan Baez; Tom Paxton; Sam Hinton; Bob Davenport; Freedom Singers; Jim Garland; Ed McCurdy; Phil Ochs; Peter LaFarge.

Newport Folk Festival, 1963 Country Music and Bluegrass .... Vanguard (S) VRS-9146 10-20 64
Newport Folk Festival, 1963 Country Music and Bluegrass .... Vanguard (S) VSD-79146 10-20 64
Newport Folk Festival, 1963 Old Time Music .... Vanguard (S) VRS-9147 10-20 64
Newport Folk Festival, 1963 Old Time Music .... Vanguard (S) VSD-79147 10-20 64
Newport Folk Festival, 1964, Vol. 1 .... Vanguard (M) VRS-9184 10-20 65
Newport Folk Festival, 1964, Vol. 1 .... Vanguard (S) VSD-79184 10-20 65
Sleepy John Estes; Jose Feliciano; Jim Kweskin Jug Band; Hammy Nixon; Phil Ochs; Frank Proffitt; Yank Rachel; Rodriguez Brothers; Buffy Sainte-Marie; Pete Seeger.

Newport Folk Festival, 1964, Vol. 2 .... Vanguard (M) VRS-9185 10-20 65
Newport Folk Festival, 1964, Vol. 2 .... Vanguard (S) VSD-79185 10-20 65
Joan Baez; Theodore Bikel; Jesse Fuller; Greenbriar Boys; Hamza El Din; Phipps Family; Staple Singers.

Newport Folk Festival, 1964, Evening Concerts, Vol. 3 .... Vanguard (M) VRS-9186 10-20 65
Newport Folk Festival, 1964, Evening Concerts, Vol. 3 .... Vanguard (S) VSD-79186 10-20 65
Cajun Band; Gaither Carlton; Koerner, Ray & Glover; Fred McDowell; Tom Paxton; Judy Roderick; Swan Silvertones; Arnold Watson; Doc Watson; Merle Watson; Hedy West.

Newport Folk Festival, 1965 .... Vanguard (M) 9225 10-15 67
Newport Folk Festival, 1965 .... Vanguard (S) 7-9225 10-15 67
Son House; Chambers Brothers; others.

Newport Folk Festival, Vol. 2 .... Vanguard (M) VRS-9063 10-15 60s
Newport Folk Festival, Vol. 2 .... Vanguard (S) VSD-2054 10-15 60s
Newport in New York '72 .... Cobblestone (S) 9028 10-15 72
Newport in New York '72 .... Atlantic (S) 40 439 10-15 72
Roberta Flack; B.B. King; Curtis Mayfield; Herbie Mann; Les McCann; Billy Exkstine.

Nice and Easy .... Columbia House (S) 1P-6565 8-10 70s
(Columbia Record Club issue.) Johnny Mathis; Lynn Anderson; Charlie Rich; Aretha Franklin; Marty Robbins; George Jones; Tammy Wynette; Vikki Carr; Johnny Cash; Ray Conniff; Tanya Tucker.

Nice Price Various Artists .... CBS (S) AS-2131 10-15 85
(Promotional only issue.) Paul McCartney; others.

Night at Studio 54 (2 LP) .... Casablanca (S) NBLP-2-7161 8-12 79
Chic; Michael Zager Band; Village People; G.Q.; Cher; Alicia Birdges; Love & Kisses; Donna Summer; Cheryl Lynn; Instant Funk; Karen Young; Patrick Juvet; Voyage; D.C. Larue; Musique; Dan Hartman; Peaches & Herb.

Night at the Boulevard .... Felsted (M) 7503 30-40 59
Night at the Grand Old Opry, Vol. 1 .... Harmony (S) HS-11169 5-10
Flatt & Scruggs; Carter Family; George Morgan; Marion Worth; Billy Walker.

Night at the Louisiana Hayride .... Wing (M) MGW-12200 20-25 60
Johnny Horton; George Jones; Benny Barnes; Margie Singleton; Gray Bryant, Johnny Mathis; James O'Gwynn; Tibby Edwards; Jeanette Hicks; Eddie Bond.

Night in a Brewery .... Capitol (M) T-1820 15-20 63
Night in a Brewery .... Capitol (S) ST-1820 15-25 63
Night in Heaven .... A&M (S) SP-4966 8-10 83
(Soundtrack.) Mike Des Barres; Holly Knight; Europeans; English Beat; Tom Teeley; Kiddo; Bryan Adams; Jan Hammer & Next; Rita Coolidge; Gary "U.S." Bonds.

Night of the Comet .... Macola (S) MRCO 900 10-15 84
(Soundtrack.) Revolver; Diana DeWitt; Thom Pace; Skip Adams; Chris Farren; John Townsend; Stallion; Amy Holland.

Night Shift .... Warner Bros. (S) 1-23702 8-10 82
Night Shift .... Warner Bros. (S) 92-37021 8-12 82
(Soundtrack.) Quarterflash; Burt Bacharach; Al Jarreau; Pointer Sisters; Rod Stewart; Marshall Crenshaw; Heaven 17; Talk Talk; Rufus with Chaka Khan.

Night the Lights Went Out in Georgia .... Mirage (S) XWTG-16051 10-15 81
(Soundtrack.) Tanya Tucker; Glen Campbell; George Jones; Tammy Wynette; Dennis Quaid; Kristy McNichol; Billy Preston; Syreeta.

Night Train .... King (M) 771 20-30 62
James Brown; Henry Moore; others.
Night Train of Oldies .... Arrawak (M) 100 20-30 60s
Elchords; Shells; Cameos; Arcades; Bonnevilles; Adelphis; Starlights; Chantels; Cordovans.
Nightmare on Elm Street 4: the Dream Master .... Chrysalis (S) OV-41673 8-10 88
(Soundtrack.) Sea Hags; Angels from Angel City; Go West; Divinyls; Jimmy Davis & Junction; Vinnie Vincent Invasion; Vigil; Blondie; Love/Hate; Craig Safan.
Nightmare on Elm Street 5: the Dream Child .... Jive (S) 1258-1-J 8-10 89
(Soundtrack.) Bruce Dickinson; Romeo's Daughter; WASP; Mammoth; Slave Raider; Whodini; Samantha Fox; Kool Moe Dee; Doctor Ice; Schooly D; Jay Ferguson.
Nine ½ Weeks .... Capitol (S) SV-12470 8-10 86
(Soundtrack.) Corey Hart; John Taylor; Eurythmics; Joe Cocker; Luba; Bryan Ferry; Dalbello; Devo; Stewart Copeland.
Nitty Gritty .... Vee Jay (M) VJLP-1084 20-30 63
Nitty Gritty .... Vee Jay (S) VJSR-1084 25-35 63
Jerry Butler; Dee Clark; Roscoe Gordon; Pee Wee Crayton; Billy Emerson; Earl Phillips; Pricilla & Spaniels; Eddie Taylor; Lee Diamond; Crume Brothers; Harold Burrage; Joe Buckner.
Nitty Gritty Guitar of .... Pickwick (SE) SPC-3148 10-15
Glen Campbell; Howard Roberts; Mason Williams; Billy Strange; 12 String Guitar Band.
No New York: see CONTORTIONS / Teenage Jesus & Jerks / Mars / D.N.A.
No Nukes - the MUSE concerts for a Non-Nuclear Future (3 LP) .... Asylum (S) ML-801 15-25 79
Jackson Browne; Bruce Springsteen & E Street Band; Tom Petty & Heartbreakers; Doobie Brothers; Bonnie Raitt; John Hall; James Taylor; Carly Simon; Graham Nash; Nicolette Larson; Ry Cooder; Sweet Honey in the Rock; Gil Scott-Heron; Jesse Colin Young; Raydio; Chaka Khan; Poco; Crosby, Stills & Nash.
No. 1 Country - 60 Top of the Chart Hits: see 60 Top of the Chart Hits, #1 Country
No Small Affair .... Atlantic (S) 78-01891 8-10 84
(Soundtrack.) Fiona; Chrissy Faith; Rupert Holmes; Twisted Sister; Zebra; Paul Delph; Malcolm McLaren & McLarenettes.
No Wave .... A&M (S) SP-4738 15-20 78
(Picture disc. Promotional issue only.) U.K. Squeeze; Police; Joe Jackson; Klark Kent; Secret; Stranglers; Dickies.
No Wave .... A&M (S) SP-4738 15-20 78
(Colored vinyl. Promotional issue only.) U.K. Squeeze; Police; Joe Jackson; Klark Kent; Secret; Stranglers; Dickies. (Has a clear plastic cover.)
Nobody's Perfect .... Sisapa (S) 75782-1 8-10 89
(Soundtrack.) KC & Sunshine Band; Terry Wood; Fee Waybill; Neurotica; Michael Logan; D.B Night; Lorraine Devon; Crybabys; Robert Randeles.
Nocturna (2 LP) .... MCA (S) 2-4121 10-15 79
(Soundtrack.) Gloria Gaynor; Vicki Sue Robinson; Jay Siegel; Heaven & Hell Orchestra & Chorus; Moment of Truth.
Norfolk to Liverpool/Liverpool to New York .... Legrand (S) ???? 8-10 79
Gary "U.S." Bonds; Jimmy Soul; Church Street Five; Twisting Matilda; Tommy Facenda; Lenis Guess.
Norman Granz' Jam Session: see Jam Session
Norman Granz' Jazz at the Philharmonic, Vol. 8 .... Clef (M) MG-Vol.8 50-100 49
Illinois Jacquet; Flip Phillips; Bill Harris; Howard McGhee; Jo Jones; Ray Brown; Hank Jones.
Northwest Collection: see SONICS / Wailers / Galaxies
Nostalgia, Vol. 1 .... Big Tree (S) 2011 8-10 72
Mystics; Dion; Chiffons; Gary "U.S." Bonds; Jarmels; Royal Guardsmen; Music Explosion; Jarmels; Gerry & Pacemakers.
Nothing but a Man .... Motown (M) MT-630 12-15 65
Nothing but a Man .... Motown (S) S-630 15-20 65
(Soundtrack.) Smokey Robinson & Miracles; Little Stevie Wonder; Mary Wells; Martha Reeves & Vandellas.
Nothing in Common .... Arista (S) AL9-8438 8-10 86
(Soundtrack.) Thompson Twins; Kinks; Richard Marx; Carly Simon; Nick Heywood; Christopher Cross; Aretha Franklin; Real to Reel; Cruzados; Pat Leonard.
Now Explosion .... Adam VIII (S) 8008 5-10 74
(Mail order offer.) Four Tops; Ian Thomas; Mandrill; Albert Hammond; Gladys Knight & Pips; Maureen McGovern; Bill Withers; War; Sylvia; Stories; Barry White; Jim Croce; Lighthouse; Steely Dan; Stylistics; Godspell; Charlie Daniels; Billy Paul; Gary Glitter.
Now Hear .... Prestige (M) PR-7346 15-20 65
Andy & Bey Sisters; others.
Now Playing .... Ava (M) A-23 10-20 63
Now Playing .... Ava (S) AS-23 15-25 63
Carol Lawrence; Victor Feldman Trio; Harry Betts; Elmer Bernstein; Pete Jolly Trio; Dick Hazard; B. Brown Singers.
Now Sound! .... Columbia Special Products (S) CSS-672 10-20 60s
Byrds; Paul Revere & Raiders; Cyrkle; Arbors; Buckinghams; Steve Lawrence; Eydie Gorme; Ray Conniff; Percy Faith; New Christy Minstrels; Simon & Garfunkel. (Made for Der Wienerschnitzel Hot Dogs.)
Now Sounds of the New Generation .... Capitol (S) S66600 8-12
Hollyridge Strings; Lettermen; Bobbie Gentry; Glen Campbell; others.
Now That's What I Call Music #2 (2 LP) .... Now (S) 2 10-20 85
Queen; Paul McCartney; Nik Kershaw; Thompson; Matt Bianco; Carmel; Madness; Flying Pickets; Nena; Cyndi Lauper; Tracey Ullman; Matthew Wilder; Julia & Company; Joe Fagin; Hot Chocolate; Snowy White; Frankie Goes to Hollywood; Eurythmics; Howard Jones; Smiths; Fiction Factory; Re-Flex; Thomas Dolby; China Crisis; David Bowie; Culture Club; Big Country; Slade; Duran Duran.
Number One Hits of the '60s (4 LP) .... Tele House (S) 1013/1014/1015/1016 15-20 73
(Boxed set. Mail order offer.) Dave Clark Five; Sly & Family Stone; ? & Mysterians; Percy Sledge; Archie Bell & Drells; Lovin' Spoonful; Dawn; Righteous Brothers; Rascals; McCoys; Box Tops; Monkees; Tommy James; Gary Lewis & Playboys; Turtles; Lemon Pipers; Paul Revere & Raiders; Guess Who; Byrds; Buckinghams; Sonny & Cher; Gene Chandler; Shirelles; Ruby & Romantics; Ray Stevens; Shangri-Las; Lulu; Percy Faith; Dion; Otis Redding; Animals; Tymes; Archies; Brenda Lee; Rascals; Chiffons; Paul & Paula; Tommy James; Little Eva; Shocking Blue; Tokens; Bobby Vinton; Shelly Fabares; Dixie Cups; Essex; Chubby Checker; Steam; Santo & Johnny; Jan & Dean.
Nuggets (Original Artifacts from the First Psychedelic Era) (2 LP) .... Sire (S) SASH 3716-2 10-15 76
(Re-issue of Elektra 7E-2006.)

Nuggets (Original Artifacts from the First Psychedelic Era) (2 LP)... Elektra (S) 7E-2006 20-25 72
Electric Prunes; Standells; Strangeloves; Knickerbockers; Vagrants; Mouse; Blues Project; Shadows of Knight; Seeds; Barbarians; Remains; Magicians; Castaways; Thirteenth Floor Elevators; Count Five; Leaves; Michael & Messengers; Cryan Shames; Amboy Dukes; Blues Magoos; Chocolate Watch Band; Mojo Men; Third Rail; Sagittarius; Nazz; Premiers; Magic Mushrooms.

Nuggets, Vol. 1, the Hits..Rhino (SP) RNLP 025 5-10 84
Leaves; Electric Prunes; Five Americans; Standells; Human Beinz; Blues Magoos; Barbarians; Seeds; Music Machine; Count Five; Balloon Farm; Nazz; Amboy Dukes; Blue Cheer.

Nuggets, Vol. 2, Punk...Rhino (SP) RNLP 026 5-10 84
Love; Shadows of Knight; Seeds; Music Machine; Chocolate Watch Band; Del-Vetts; Vagrants; Standells; Leaves; Sonics; Elastik Band.

Nuggets, Vol. 3, Pop ....Rhino (SP) RNLP 027 5-10 84
Parade; Boyce & Hart; Merry-Go-Round; Cyrcle; Lewis & Clark Expedition; Bobby Fuller Four; Turtles; Spiral Staircase; Outsiders; People; October Country; Knickerbockers; Cryan Shames.

Nuggets, Vol. 4, Pop Part Two ....Rhino (SP) RNLP 028 5-10 84
Merry-Go-Round; Outsiders; Royal Guardsmen; Teddy & Pandas; Parade; E-Types; Rumor; Palace Guard; Yellow Balloon; Knickerbockers; Chartbusters; Long Island Sound; Lyme & Cybelle.

Nuggets, Vol. 5, Pop Part Three..Rhino (SP) RNLP 029 5-10 84
Knickerbockers; Vacels; Vogues; Hackamore Brick; Lovin' Spoonful; Association; Mojo Men; American Breed; Cherokee; Grass Roots; Electric Prunes; Tradewinds; Strawberry Alarm Clock; Primrose Circus.

Nuggets, Vol. 6, Punk, Part Two ....Rhino (SP) RNLP 030 5-10 85
Mouse & Traps; Captain Beefheart; Nightcrawlers; Brogues; Unrelated Segments; Black Pearl; We the People; Shadows of Knight; Steppenwolf; Chocolate Watch Band; Grass Roots; Seeds; Underdogs; Electric Prunes.

Nuggets, Vol. 7, Early San Francisco...Rhino (SP) RNLP 031 5-10 85
Beau Brummels; Mojo Men; Vejtables; Jan Ashton; We Five; Charlatans; Great Society; Country Joe & Fish; Tikis.

Nuggets, Vol. 8, the Northwest..Rhino (SP) RNLP 70032 5-10 80s
Kingsmen; Sonics; Paul Revere & Raiders; Wailers; Initial Shock; Daily Flash; Weeds; Floating Bridge; Surprise Package.

Nuggets, Vol. 10, Folk Rock..Rhino (SP) RNLP 70034 5-10 80s
Byrds; Turtles; Grass Roots; Deep Six; Jake Holmes; Sunshine Company; Scott McKenzie; Barry McGuire; Nitty Gritty Dirt Band; M.F.Q.; Peanut Butter Conspiracy; Love Exchange; P.F. Sloan; Hearts & Flowers.

Nuggets, Vol. 11, Pop Part Four ....Rhino (SP) RNLP 70035 5-10 80s
Grass Roots; Left Banke; Montage; Gene Clark; Sunshine Company; Magicans; Fever Tree; Lee Michaels; Third Rail; Critters; Blues Magoos; Blues Project; American Breed; Keith.

Nuggets, Vol. 12, Punk Part Three...Rhino (SP) RNLP 70036 5-10 80s
Syndicate of Sound; Paul Revere & Raiders; Kenny & Kasuals; Other Half; Spats; Remains; Max Frost & Troopers; Hombres; Woolies; Mouse & Traps; Harbinger Complex; Lollipop Shoppe; Uniques; Unrelated Seqments.

No. 1 Hits!: see Original Hits, Vol. 11

No. 1 Country 60 Top of the Chart Hits (6 LP) .... Columbia (S) 6P 6682 20-30 77
(Columbia Record Club issue.) Al Dexter; George Morgan; Hank Williams, Sr.; Margaret Whiting; Jimmy Wakely; Lefty Frizzell; Ray Price; Everly Brothers; Sonny James; Carl Smith; Marty Robbins; George Jones; Johnny Horton; Faron Young; Stonewall Jackson; Leroy Van Dyke; Billy Walker; Carl & Pearl Butler; Claude King; Johnny Cash; Flatt & Scruggs; Jimmy Dean; David Houston; Tammy Wynette; Little Jimmy Dickens; Glen Campbell; Lynn Anderson; Hank Williams Jr.; Donna Fargo; Barbara Fairchild; Mel Tillis; Tom T. Hall; Charlie Rich; Tanya Tucker; Willie Nelson; Johnny Rodriguez; Freddy Fender; Johnny Duncan; B.J. Thomas.

No. 1 Hits of the '60s (52 Hits By Original Stars) (4 LP) .... Tele House (S) CR1013/1016 20-30 73
(Mail order offer. Boxed set.) Righteous Brothers; Dave Clark Five; Box Tops; ? & Mysterians; Monkees; Guess Who; Otis Redding; McCoys; Shocking Blue; Percy Sledge; Sonny & Cher; Little Eva; Rascals; Angels; Steam; Lovin' Spoonful; Turtles; Sly & Family Stone; Archie Bell & Drells; Dawn; Monkees; Tommy James & Shondells; Gary Lewis & Playboys; Lemon Pipers; Paul Revere & Raiders; Byrds; Shirelles; Gene Chandler; Ruby & Romantics; Ray Stevens; Shangri-Las; Lulu; Percy Faith; Dion; Animals; Tymes; Archies; Brenda Lee; Chiffons; Paul & Paula; Tokens; Bobby Vinton; Shelley Fabares; Dixie Cups; Essex; Chubby Checker; Jan & Dean; Santo & Johnny; John Fred.

No. 1 Hits of the '60s (40 Original Hits By the Original Artists) (3 LP) ....Adam VII Ltd. (S) A-8022 15-20 75
(Mail order offer.) Monkees; Guess Who; Otis Redding; McCoys; Shocking Blue; Percy Sledge; Sonny & Cher; Little Eva; Rascals; Angels; Steam; Lovin' Spoonful; Turtles; others. (Excerpted from the 4 LP set above.)

Nutty Numbers ....K-Tel (S) NC-492 5-10 78

O Holy Night .... Columbia Special Products (S) P 11682 5-10 73
Robert Goulet; Mahalia Jackson; Ray Conniff; John Davidson; Mormon Tabernacle Choir; Jim Nabors; Anita Bryant; Johnny Mathis; Doris Day; Philadelphia Brass Ensemble. (Made for Baptist Book Stores.)

Oakland Blues .... Arhoolie (M) 2008 8-10 71
K.C. Douglas; Jimmy McCracklin; Jimmy Wilson; others.

Ocean Beach Drive, Vol. 3 (2 LP) .... Warner Special Products (S) OP 2526 10-15 81
Tams; Joe Turner; Temptations; Drifters; Bill Deal; Jackie Wilson; Chairmen of hte Board; Robert John; Mary Wells; William Bell; Judy Clay; Dionne Warwick; Patty & Emblems; Intrigues; Elgins; Maurice Williams & Zodiacs; Impressions; Marvin Gaye; Artistics; Coasters; Edwin Starr; James & Bobby Purify; Archie Bell & Drells.

Ocean Drive (3 LP)...???? 10-15
O'Kaysions; Maurice Williams & Zodiacs; Junior Walker & All Stars; Trammps; Impressions; Coasters; Garnett Mimms; Bill Deal; Archie Bell & Drells; Brenton Wood; Drifters; Deon Jackson; Dominoes; Barbara Lewis; Marvin Gaye; Chairman of the Board; Tams; Tymes; Mary Wells; Major Lance; Willie Lee; Four Tops; Platters; Temptations; Bruce Channel; Isley Brothers; Doris Troy; Showmen; Patty & Emblems; Jackie Wilson.

October Samplers (RCA): see RCA October Samplers

Odyssey - Experience Altec .... Altec/A&M (S) SP-19009 10-15 73
(Promotional issue only.) Joan Armatrading; Cheryl Dilcher; Lani Hall; Paul Williams; Quincy Jones; Rick Wakeman; Rita Coolidge; Strawbs; Sonny & Brownie; Sandy Denny; Randy Newman.

Officer and a Gentleman ....Island (S) 90017-1 8-10 82
(Soundtrack.) Joe Cocker; Jennifer Warnes; Van Morrison; ZZ Top; Pat Benatar; Sir Douglas Quintet; Dire Straits.

Official Grammy Awards Archive Collection (Record of the Year)...................................Franklin Mint (S) GRAM-1 50-100 85
(Boxed set. Includes booklet. Colored vinyl.) Beatles; Bobby Darin; Ray Stevens; Toto; Willie Nelson; Perry Como; others.

Official Grammy Awards Archive Collection (All-Time Winners) ....Franklin Mint (S) GRAM-2 50-100 85
(Boxed set. Includes booklet. Colored vinyl.) Johnny Cash; Roger Miller; Paul Simon; Stevie Wonder; Aretha Franklin; others.

Official Grammy Awards Archive Collection (Great Performances of the Rock Era, Vol. 1)...Franklin Mint (S) GRAM-3 50-100 85
(Boxed set. Includes booklet. Colored vinyl.) Beach Boys; Fleetwood Mac; Byrds; Rolling Stones; Jefferson Airplane; others.

Official Grammy Awards Archive Collection (The Great Singers) ....Franklin Mint (S) GRAM-4 100-150 85
(Boxed set. Includes booklet. Colored vinyl.) Elvis Presley; Frank Sinatra; Judy Garland; Billie Holiday; Tony Bennett; Lena Horne; Nat King Cole; Peggy Lee.
Official Grammy Awards Archive Collection (Pop Performances, Vol. 1)..........................Franklin Mint (S) GRAM-5 50-100 85
(Boxed set. Includes booklet. Colored vinyl.) Janis Joplin; Brook Benton; Linda Ronstadt; Carole King; Carpenters; Bread; America; others.
Official Grammy Awards Archive Collection (Best New Artists) ....Franklin Mint (S) GRAM-6 50-100 85
(Boxed set. Includes booklet. Colored vinyl.) Cher; Bobby Darin; Eric Clapton; Cream; Sonny & Cher; others.
Official Grammy Awards Archive Collection (The Big Band Sound)..Franklin Mint (S) GRAM-7 50-100 85
(Boxed set. Includes booklet. Colored vinyl.) Ray Anthony; Count Basie; Les Brown; Quincy Jones; Stan Kenton; Neal Hefti; others.
Official Grammy Awards Archive Collection (Rhythm & Blues, Vol. 1)...................................Franklin Mint (S) GRAM-8 50-100 85
(Boxed set. Includes booklet. Colored vinyl.) Jackie Wilson; Jesse Belvin; Coasters; Temptations; B.B. King; Ike & Tina Turner; Etta James; others.
Official Grammy Awards Archive Collection (Song of the Year)...Franklin Mint (S) GRAM-9 50-100 85
(Boxed set. Includes booklet. Colored vinyl.) Neil Sedaka; Paul Williams; Delfonics; Joe South; Dottie West; Otis Redding; Charlie Rich; Dolly Parton; others.
Official Grammy Awards Archive Collection (Folk Music Classics) ....Franklin Mint (S) GRAM-10 50-100 85
(Boxed set. Includes booklet. Colored vinyl.) Leadbelly; Woody Guthrie; Bob Dylan; Pete Seeger; Joan Baez; Arlo Guthrie; others.
Official Grammy Awards Archive Collection (Stage and Original Cast Recordings) ....Franklin Mint (S) GRAM-11 75-100 85
(Soundtrack.) (Boxed set. Includes booklet. Colored vinyl.) Ethel Merman; Robert Goulet; Pat Suzuki; Mary Martin; Dick Van Dyke; Steve Lawrence; Tommy Steele; Angela Lansbury; Joel Grey; Jack Gilford; Lotte Lenya; Leslie Uggams; Dean Jones; Hal Linden; Theodore Bikel; Sally Ann Howes; Paul Lynde; Zero Mostel; Ronnie Dyson; Andrea McArdle; Glynis Johns; Ken Page; Nell Carter; Robin Lamont; Clifton Davis; Lynn Kellogg; Irving Jacobson; Barbara Harris; Gwen Verdon; Elizabeth Allen; Allen Case; Robert Hooks; Charles Braswell; John Miller; others.
Official Grammy Awards Archive Collection (The Producers Choice) ....Franklin Mint (S) GRAM-12 50-100 85
(Boxed set. Includes booklet. Colored vinyl.) Quincy Jones; Bee Gees; Pointer Sisters; O'Jays; George Jones; Charlie Rich; Johnny Mathis; others.
Official Grammy Awards Archive Collection (Great Jazz Vocalists).................................Franklin Mint (S) GRAM-13 50-100 85
(Boxed set. Includes booklet. Colored vinyl.) Billie Holiday; Sarah Vaughan; Peggy Lee; Jimmy Rushing; Etta Jones; Mel Torme; others.
Official Grammy Awards Archive Collection (Album of the Year)......................................Franklin Mint (S) GRAM-14 50-100 85
(Boxed set. Includes booklet. Colored vinyl.) Andy Williams; Tony Bennett; Peter Frampton; Fifth Dimension; Supertramp; Glen Campbell; others.
Official Music of the XXIIIrd Olympiad, Los Angeles 1984 ....Columbia (S) AS-99 1871 12-15 84
(Soundtrack. Promotional only picture disc.)
Official Music of the XXIIIrd Olympiad, Los Angeles 1984 .... Columbia (S) BJS 39322 8-12 84
(Soundtrack.) Loverboy; Giorgio Moroder; John Williams; Quincy Jones; Bill Conti; Foreigner; Herbie Hancock; Philip Glass.
Official New Orleans Rhythm & Blues Anniversary Album, Vol. 1...Dese Days (M) 101 8-12 84
Johnny Adams; Dixie Cups; Lee Dorsey; King Floyd; Ernie K-Doe; Earl King; Jean Wright; Bobby Marchan; Bobby Mitchell; Robert Parker; Van & Grace. (Rerecorded versions of their hits.)
Oh to Hear Them Again...Columbia Special Products (SP) P-14842 5-10 78
Roy Acuff; Gene Autry; Johnny Cash; Ray Price; Marty Robbins; Lefty Frizzell; Sons of the Pioneers; Patsy Cline; Kitty Wells; Ernet Tubb; Ferlin Husky; Hank Williams; Webb Pierce; Davis Sisters; Jimmy Wakely; Carl Smith; Moon Mullican; Red Foley; Bob Wills; Carter Family.
Okeh Chicago Blues (2 LP)...Epic (S) 37318 10-15 82
Big Boy Edwards; Victoria Spivey & Her Chicago Four; Curtis Jones; Roosevelt Scott; Peter Chatman & His Washboard Band; Brownie McGhee; Champion Jack Dupree; Roosevelt Sykes; Tony Hollins; Peter Cleighton; Memphis Minnie; Little Son Joe; Big Bill & His Rhythm Band; Yas Yas Girls; Johnny Shines; Muddy Waters; Big Joe Williams.
Okeh Rhythm & Blues (2 LP) ....Epic (S) EG 37649 10-15 82
Smiley Lewis; Chuck Willis; Big Maybelle; Screamin' Jay Hawkins; Titus Turner; Larry Darnell; Ravens; Johnnie Ray; Sandmen; Marquees; Billy Stewart; Schoolboys; Sheppards; Treniers; Paul Gayten; Little Joe & Thrillers; Doc Bagby; Red Saunders; Little Richard.
Okeh Soul (2 LP)..Epic (S) EG 37321 10-15 82
Major Lance; Billy Butler & Enchanters; Walter Jackson; Opals; Artistics; Vibrations.
Oklahoma All Night Singing...OK (S) LPS-7160 8-12
Sharver Family; Darby Singers; Bud Chambers; Glaze Family; Siloam Samaritans; Trent Family; Wills Family; Cooley Brothers; Conn Family; Bob Allen Trio; Christians Consolidated; Gospel Light Singers.
Oklahoma Country ....ARI (S) 1025 8-12 82
Sammi Smith; Bob Wills; Jody Miller; Sons of the Pioneers; Wanda Jackson; Kay Starr; Hoyt Axton; Conway Twitty; Carl Belew; Tommy Collins; Merle Travis; Jack Guthrie; Hank Thompson; Cal Smith.
Old and Golden ....Jamie (S) SLP-3031 15-20 68
Fantastic Johnny C; Cliff Nobles & Co.; Crispian St. Peters; Brenda & Tabulations; Tommy McLain; Barbara Mason; Dale & Grace; Sunny & Sunglows; Show Stoppers; James Boys; Volcanoes; Della Humphrey; Helene Smith; Duane Eddy; Kit Kats; Barbara Lynn.
Old and Good Country Hits ....Cumberland (M) 29521 10-15 65
Old and Good Country Hits .... Cumberland (S) 69521 10-15 65
Leon Payne; Leon McAuliffe; Red Sovine; others.
Old and Heavy Gold (1956)...Economic Consultants (M) 1956 20-40 73
Old and Heavy Gold (1957)...Economic Consultants (M) 1957 20-40 73
Old and Heavy Gold (1958)...Economic Consultants (M) 1958 20-40 73
Old and Heavy Gold (1959)...Economic Consultants (M) 1959 10-15 73
Old and Heavy Gold (1960)...Economic Consultants (M) 1960 20-40 73
Old and Heavy Gold (1961)...Economic Consultants (M) 1961 20-40 73
Old and Heavy Gold (1962)...Economic Consultants (M) 1962 20-40 73
Old Country Church.. Rural Rhythm (M) RR 148 8-12 60s
Jackie & Arlin Vaden; Bill Carter; Cooper Crothers; Owen & Mack; George Frace; Johnny Tyler; James Baum.
Old Curiosity Shop ....RCA (M) LCT-1112 30-50 53
Helen Morgan; Helen Kane; Will Rogers; Sophie Tucker; Gloria Swanson; De Wolf Hopper; Marlene Dietrich; Maurice Chevalier; John Barrymore; Fanny Brice; Nora Bayes; Jack Noworth; Enrico Caruso.
Old Favorites By Jim Lowe.. Kats Karavan (M) LP-100 50-75 58
Rusty Bryant & Carolyn Club Band; Spaniels; Clovers; Jimmy Reed; Johnnie & Joe; El Dorados; Drifters; Moonglows; Clyde McPhatter & Drifters; Gene Allison.
Old Favorites By Rock and Roll Stars .... Vee Jay (M) 100 25-35 60

Old Gold .... Sunset (S) SUS-5266 10-15 69
Little Anthony & Imperials; Garnet Mimms; Inez & Charlie Foxx; Barbara George; Bobby Hendricks; Bobby Goldsboro; Jive Five; Johnny Rivers.

Old King Gold, Vol. 1 .... King/Gusto (M) KS-16001 8-12 75
Platters; Hank Ballard & Midnighters; Flamingos; Otis Williams & Charms; Bonnie Lou; Earl Bostic; Bobby Lewis; Wayne Cochrane; Boyd Bennett; Billy Ward & Dominoes; Little Willie John; Sil Austin.

Old King Gold, Vol. 2 .... King/Gusto (M) KS-16002 8-12 75
Bill Doggett; Little Willie John; Dominoes; Patti LaBelle & Blue Belles; Checkers; Earl Bostic; Swallows; Hank Ballard & Midnighters; 5 Royales; Tiny Bradshaw; Annie Laurie.

Old King Gold, Vol. 3 .... King/Gusto (M) KS-16003 8-12 75
Billy Ward & Dominoes; Hurricanes; Hank Ballard & Midnighters; Otis Williams & Charms; Little Willie John; Ivory Joe Hunter; Tiny Bradshaw; Bull Moose Jackson; Five Royales; Lonnie Johnson; Checkers; Charms.

Old King Gold, Vol. 4 .... King/Gusto (M) KS-16004 8-12 75
Billy Ward & Dominoes; Wynonie Harris; Freddy King; Joe Tex; Hank Ballard & Midnighters; Otis Redding; Little Willie John; Todd Rhodes; LaVern Baker; Earl Bostic; Lloyd Glenn; Bull Moose Jackson; Lynn Hope.

Old King Gold, Vol. 5 .... King/Gusto (M) KS-16005 8-12 75
Donnie Elbert; Hurricanes; Hank Ballard & Midnighters; Otis Williams & Charms; Little Willie John; Bill Doggett; Chanters; Sonny Thompson; Charles Brown; Bobby Freeman; Johnny Pate..

Old King Gold, Vol. 6 .... King/Gusto (M) KS-16006 8-12 75
Big Jay McNeely; Wynonie Harris; Billy Ward & Dominoes; Bubber Johnson; Hank Ballard & Midnighters; Sonny Thompson; Johnny Pate; Bill Doggett; Otis Williams & Charms; Eddie "Cleanhead" Vinson; Bill Jennings; Strangers.

Old King Gold, Vol. 7 .... King/Gusto (M) KS-16007 8-12 75
Bull Moose Jackson; Billy Ward & Dominoes; King Pins; Hank Ballard & Midnighters; Otis Williams & Charms; Earl King; Hank Marr; Albert King; Swallows; Sonny Thompson; Billy Gayles; Escos.

Old King Gold, Vol. 8 .... King/Gusto (M) KS-16008 8-12 75
Lulu Reed; Billy Ward & Dominoes; Roy Brown; Little Esther Phillips; Hank Ballard & Midnighters; Otis Williams & Charms; Johnny "Guitar" Watson; Bill Doggett; Gene & Ruth; Sonny Thompson; Tiny Bradshaw; Lucky Millinder; Freddy King.

Old King Gold, Vol. 9 .... King/Gusto (M) KS-16009 8-12 75
Tiny Bradshaw; Bonnie Lou; Hank Ballard & Midnighters; Wynonie Harris; Roy Brown; James Duncan; Little Willie John; Earl Bostic; Earl King; Lulu Reed; Sonny Thompson; Freddie King; Five Royales.

Old King Gold, Vol. 10 .... King/Gusto (M) KS-16010 8-12 75
Donnie Elbert; Hank Ballard & Midnighters; Lloyd Glenn; Earl Bostic; Otis Williams & Charms; Bill Doggett; Roy Brown; Little Esther Phillips; Freddy King; Kenny Martin; Five Royales; Johnny Long.

Old 'N' Golden Goodies, Vol. 1 .... RCA (M) LPM-2740 25-35 63

Old 'N' Golden Goodies, Vol. 1 .... RCA (SP) LSP-2740 35-45 63
Neil Sedaka; Della Reese; Floyd Cramer; Don Gibson; Dave "Baby" Cortez; Ray Peterson; Isley Brothers; Mickey & Sylvia; Brook Benton; Joe Valino; Floyd Robinson; Kay Starr; Boots Brown.

Old 'N' Golden Goodies, Vol. 2 .... RCA (M) LPM-3641 20-30 66

Old 'N' Golden Goodies, Vol. 2 .... RCA (SP) LSP-3641 25-35 66
Duane Eddy; Paul Anka; Peggy March; Isley Brothers; Tokens; Dave "Baby" Cortez; Jesse Belvin; Neil Sedaka; Skeeter Davis; Boots Randolph.

Old Time Classics: Collection of Mountain Banjo Songs and Tunes .... County (M) 515 8-12 75
Uncle Dave Macon; Lano Norris; Marion Underwood; Riley Puckett; R.B. Smith; S.J. Allgood; Red Headed Fiddlers; Bascom Lamar Lunsford; Frank Jenkins; Buell Kazee; Fisher Hendley; J. Small.

Old Time Classics: Collection of Mountain Blues .... County (M) 511 8-12 75
Sam McGee; Lowe Stokes & His North Georgians; Jimmie Tarlton; Leake County Revelers; Carolina Tar Heels; Dock Boggs; Frank Hutchison; Narmour & Smith; Dick Justice; Burnett & Rutherford; Doc Roberts; Clarence Green.

Old Time Music at Clarence Ashley's, Vol. 2 .... Folkways (M) FA 2359 8-12 63
Tom Ashley; Doc Watson; Clint Howard; Fred Price; Gaither Carlton; Arnold Watson; Original Carolina Tar Heels; others.

Old Time Radio (2 LP) .... CBS Direct Marketing Services (M) P2M 5287 10-20 68
Rudy Vallee; Will Rogers; Bing Crosby; Eddie Cantor; Jimmy Durante; Clayton Jackson; Harry Hershfield; Kay Kyser; Kate Smith; W.C. Fields; Al Jolson; Burns & Allen; Authur Tracy; FBI in Peace & War; Mr. Keen, Tracer of Lost Persons; Yours Truly, Johnny Dollar; Whistler; Baby Rose Marie; Uncle Don; Arthur Godfrey; Cliff Edwards; Morton Downey; Our Miss Brooks; Young Widder Brown; Franklin D. Roosevelt (speech excerpt); Eileen Randell; Victor Borge; Wee Bonnie Baker with Orrin Tucker; Ray Noble.

Old Time Religion .... Power Pak (M) PO-254 5-10 75
Charlie Rich; Johnny Cash; Jerry Lee Lewis; Sleepy LeBeef; Dave Rich; Jeannie C. Riley; Eddie Bond; Dee Mullins.

Old Time String Band Classics: Recorded 1927-1933 .... County (M) 531 8-12 75
Luke Highnight & His Ozark Strutters; Alex Hood & His Railroad Boys; Dr. Humphrey Bate & His Possum Hunters; Roanoke Jug Band; Earl Johnson & His Clodhoppers; Fox Chasers; Sharp, Hinman & Sharp; Caplinger's Cumberland Mountain Entertainers' Allen County String Band; Ted Gossett's Band; Booker Orchestra; Floyd County Ramblers.

Old Town Doo Wop (3 LP) .... Murray Hill (M) 000083 10-20 85
(Boxed set.) Harptones; Valentines; Five Crowns; Clefftones; Eugene Mumford & Serenaders; Coeds; Packards; Royaltones; Fi-Tones; Supremes; Universals; Keytones; Bonnevilles; Inspirations; Crowns.

Oldies! Great Vocal Groups .... Dooto (M) DTL 855 10-15 72
Penguins; Souvenirs; Pearls; Calvanes; Romancers; Silks; Medallions; Meadowlarks; Crescendos.

Oldies: see Top Ten Hits By Original Artists

Oldies .... Wyncote (M) W-9008 10-20 64

Oldies .... Wyncote (S) SW-9008 10-20 64
Charlie Greene; Billy Scott; John Zacherle; Applejacks; Georgie Young; Timmie Rodgers.

Oldies A-Go-Go, Vol. 1 .... Somerset (M) P-23900 10-15 60s

Oldies A-Go-Go, Vol. 1 .... Somerset/Stereo-Fidelity (S) SF-23900 10-15 60s
Otis Redding; Hollywood Argyles; Tony Butula; Monorails; Emily Parker.

Oldies A-Go-Go, Vol. 2 .... Somerset (M) P-24000 10-15 60s

Oldies A-Go-Go, Vol. 2 .... Somerset/Stereo-Fidelity (S) SF-24000 10-15 60s
Hollywood Argyles; Bobby Lile; Starr Sisters; Downbeats; Nairobi River Boys.

Oldies A-Go-Go, Vol. 3 .... Somerset (M) P-24100 10-15 60s

Oldies A-Go-Go, Vol. 3 .... Somerset/Stereo-Fidelity (S) SF-24100 10-15 60s
Cyd & Cheri; Monorails; Rockin' Sidney; Breakers; Ty Tyrell.

Oldies A-Go-Go, Vol. 4 .... Somerset (M) P-24200 10-15 60s

Oldies A-Go-Go, Vol. 4 .... Somerset/Stereo-Fidelity (S) SF-24200 10-15 60s
Sherrell Townsend; Innocents; Uptowns; Danny the Dreamer; Sparkletts; Billy & Kids.
Oldies A-Go-Go, Vol. 5 .... Somerset (M) P-24300 10-15 60s
Oldies A-Go-Go, Vol. 5 .... Somerset/Stereo-Fidelity (S) SF-24300 10-15 60s
Otis Redding; Hollywood Argyles; Bobby Lile; Gil Shelton; Ribbons.
Oldies and Goodies (Best of the) .... Crown (M) CLP-5144-2 10-20 60s
Cadets; Teen Queens; Marvin & Johnny; Etta James; B.B. King; Joe Houston; Jesse Belvin; Queens; Young Jessie; Roscoe Gordon.
Oldies and Goodies (Rock 'N' Roll Party) .... Crown (M) CLP-5227 20-25 60s
Teen Queens; Etta James; Jimmy Beasley; Vido Musso; Marvin & Johnny; Johnny Allen; B.B. King; Joe Turner; Joe Houston; Jesse Belvin; Robbie Robinson.
Oldies and Goodies (Country & Western #3) .... Crown (M) CLP-5241 20-25 60s
Gabbard & Holt; Jimmy Patten; Whitey Pullen; Wally & Don; others.
Oldies But Biggies .... Camden (S) CAS-2561 5-10 72
Eddie Fisher; Al Hirt; Julius La Rosa; Vaughn Monroe; Helen O'Connell; Hugo Winterhalter; Browns; Perez Prado.
Oldies But Goodies, Vol. 1 .... Original Sound (M) LPM-5001 25-35 59
Five Satins; Penguins; Teen Queens; Mello Kings; Don Julian; Medallions; Shirley & Lee; Sonny Knight; Cadets; Jaguars; Etta James; Oscar McLollie. (Back cover must picture no other volumes in the series. Reissues in the '70s and later may have completely different tracks than shown in this edition.)
Oldies But Goodies, Vol. 1 .... Original Sound (M) LP-8850 5-10 71
Oldies But Goodies, Vol. 1 .... Original Sound (S) 8850 5-10 66
Five Satins; Penguins; Teen Queens; Mello Kings; Don Julian; Medallions; Shirley & Lee; Sonny Knight; Cadets; Jaguars; Etta James; Oscar McLollie.
Oldies But Goodies, Vol. 1 .... Original Sound (M) 5001 5-10
Five Satins; Penguins; Teen Queens; Mello Kings; Don Julian; Medallions; Shirley & Lee; Sonny Knight; Cadets; Jaguars; Etta James; Oscar McLollie. (Back cover pictures later volumes in the series.)
Oldies But Goodies, Vol. 2 .... Original Sound (M) 5003 15-25 60
Clovers; Heartbeats; Jesse Belvin; Velvetones; Nutmegs; Charts; Joe Turner; Crows; Tony Allen; Turbans; Peppermint Harris; Faye Adams. (Back cover must picture no higher volumes in the series than Vol. 2.)
Oldies But Goodies, Vol. 2 .... Original Sound (M) LP-8852 5-10 66
Oldies But Goodies, Vol. 2 .... Original Sound (S) LPS-8852 5-10 66
Clovers; Heartbeats; Jesse Belvin; Velvetones; Nutmegs; Charts; Joe Turner; Crows; Tony Allen; Turbans; Peppermint Harris; Faye Adams.
Oldies But Goodies, Vol. 2 .... Original Sound (M) 5003 5-10
Clovers; Heartbeats; Jesse Belvin; Velvetones; Nutmegs; Charts; Joe Turner; Crows; Tony Allen; Turbans; Peppermint Harris; Faye Adams. (Back cover pictures later volumes in the series.)
Oldies But Goodies, Vol. 3 .... Original Sound (M) 5004 15-20 61
Flamingos; Shields; Dells; Jerry Butler & Impressions; Little Anthony & Imperials; Gene & Eunice; Del-Vikings; Huey "Piano" Smith; El Dorados; Frankie Ford; Preston Epps; Little Richard. (Back cover must picture no higher volumes in the series than Vol. 3.)
Oldies But Goodies, Vol. 3 .... Original Sound (M) LP-8853 5-10 70
Oldies But Goodies, Vol. 3 .... Original Sound (S) 8853 5-10 66
Flamingos; Shields; Dells; Jerry Butler & Impressions; Little Anthony & Imperials; Gene & Eunice; Del-Vikings; Huey "Piano" Smith; El Dorados; Frankie Ford; Preston Epps; Little Richard.
Oldies But Goodies, Vol. 3 .... Original Sound (M) 5004 5-10
Flamingos; Shields; Dells; Jerry Butler & Impressions; Little Anthony & Imperials; Gene & Eunice; Del-Vikings; Huey "Piano" Smith; El Dorados; Frankie Ford; Preston Epps; Little Richard. (Back cover pictures later volumes in the series.)
Oldies But Goodies, Vol. 4 .... Original Sound (M) 5005 15-20 62
Rays; Six Teens; Dubs; Gloria Mann; Five Satins; Chantels; Mickey & Sylvia; Jerry Lee Lewis; Sandy Nelson; Norman Fox & Rob-Roys; Barrett Strong; Carl Perkins. (Back cover must picture no higher volumes in the series than Vol. 4.)
Oldies But Goodies, Vol. 4 .... Original Sound (S) 8854 5-10 62
Rays; Six Teens; Dubs; Gloria Mann; Five Satins; Chantels; Mickey & Sylvia; Jerry Lee Lewis; Sandy Nelson; Norman Fox & Rob-Roys; Barrett Strong; Carl Perkins.
Oldies But Goodies, Vol. 4 .... Original Sound (M) 5005 5-10
Rays; Six Teens; Dubs; Gloria Mann; Five Satins; Chantels; Mickey & Sylvia; Jerry Lee Lewis; Sandy Nelson; Norman Fox & Rob-Roys; Barrett Strong; Carl Perkins. (Back cover pictures later volumes in the series.)
Oldies But Goodies, Vol. 5 .... Original Sound (M) 5007 10-20 63
Elegants; Rosie & Originals; Skyliners; Paradons; Shep & Limelites; Channels; Hollywood Argyles; Maurice Williams; Dominoes; Bobby Day; Preston Epps; Jewels. (Back cover must picture no higher volumes in the series than Vol. 5.)
Oldies But Goodies, Vol. 5 .... Original Sound (S) 8855 5-10 66
Elegants; Rosie & Originals; Skyliners; Paradons; Shep & Limelites; Channels; Hollywood Argyles; Maurice Williams; Dominoes; Bobby Day; Preston Epps; Jewels.
Oldies But Goodies, Vol. 5 .... Original Sound (M) 5007 5-10
Elegants; Rosie & Originals; Skyliners; Paradons; Shep & Limelites; Channels; Hollywood Argyles; Maurice Williams; Dominoes; Bobby Day; Preston Epps; Jewels. (Back cover pictures later volumes in the series.)
Oldies But Goodies, Vol. 6 .... Original Sound (M) 5011 10-20 63
Little Caesar & Romans; Dion & Belmonts; Gladys Knight & Pips; Safaris; Fireflies; Skyliners; Gary "U.S." Bonds; Bill Doggett; Gene Chandler; Dee Dee Sharp; Dee Clark. (Back cover must picture no higher volumes in the series than Vol. 6.)
Oldies But Goodies, Vol. 6 .... Original Sound (M) LP-8856 5-10 82
Oldies But Goodies, Vol. 6 .... Original Sound (S) 8856 5-10 66
Little Caesar & Romans; Dion & Belmonts; Pips; Safaris; Fireflies; Skyliners; Gary "U.S." Bonds; Bill Doggett; Gene Chandler; Dee Dee Sharp; Dee Clark.
Oldies But Goodies, Vol. 6 .... Original Sound (M) 5011 5-10
Little Caesar & Romans; Dion & Belmonts; Pips; Safaris; Fireflies; Skyliners; Gary "U.S." Bonds; Bill Doggett; Gene Chandler; Dee Dee Sharp; Dee Clark. (Back cover pictures later volumes in the series.)
Oldies But Goodies, Vol. 7 .... Original Sound (M) 5012 10-15 64
Tommy Edwards; Paris Sisters; Ritchie Valens; Mark Dinning; Chimes; Jerry Butler; Jimmy Jones; Gary "U.S." Bonds; Champs; Dion; Barbara George; B. Bumble & Stingers; Gladys Knight & Pips. (Back cover must picture no higher volumes in the series than Vol. 7.)
Oldies But Goodies, Vol. 7 .... Original Sound (M) LP-8857 5-10 82
Oldies But Goodies, Vol. 7 .... Original Sound (S) 8857 5-10 66
Tommy Edwards; Paris Sisters; Ritchie Valens; Mark Dinning; Chimes; Jerry Butler; Jimmy Jones; Gary "U.S." Bonds; Champs; Dion; Barbara George; B. Bumble & Stingers.

Oldies But Goodies, Vol. 7 .... Original Sound (M) 5012 5-10
Tommy Edwards; Paris Sisters; Ritchie Valens; Mark Dinning; Chimes; Jerry Butler; Jimmy Jones; Gary "U.S." Bonds; Champs; Dion; Barbara George; B. Bumble & Stingers. (Back cover pictures later volumes in the series.)
Oldies But Goodies, Vol. 8 .... Original Sound (M) 5014 10-15 66
Oldies But Goodies, Vol. 8 .... Original Sound (M) LP-8858 10-15
Oldies But Goodies, Vol. 8 .... Original Sound (S) 8858 10-15 66
Dixie Cups; Troy Shondell; Dale & Grace; Terry Stafford; Carla Thomas; Blue Jays; Bobby Darin; Coasters; Inez Foxx; Ernie Fields; Ritchie Valens; Ernie Freeman. (Back cover must picture no higher volumes in the series than Vol. 8.)
Oldies But Goodies, Vol. 8 .... Original Sound (M) 5014 5-10
Oldies But Goodies, Vol. 8 .... Original Sound (S) 8858 5-10
Dixie Cups; Troy Shondell; Dale & Grace; Terry Stafford; Carla Thomas; Blue Jays; Bobby Darin; Coasters; Inez Foxx; Ernie Fields; Ritchie Valens; Ernie Freeman. (Back cover pictures later volumes in the series.)
Oldies But Goodies, Vol. 9 .... Original Sound (M) LP-8859 10-15 60s
Oldies But Goodies, Vol. 9 .... Original Sound (S) 8859 10-15 60s
Timi Yuro; Casinos; Esther Phillips; Don & Juan; Cathy Jean & Roommates; J. Frank Wilson; Del Shannon; Bobby Fuller Four; Castaways; Jewel Aiken; Bobby Day; Bobby Bland. (Back cover must picture no higher volumes in the series than Vol. 9.)
Oldies But Goodies, Vol. 9 .... Original Sound (S) 8859 5-10
Timi Yuro; Casinos; Esther Phillips; Don & Juan; Cathy Jean & Roommates; J. Frank Wilson; Del Shannon; Bobby Fuller Four; Castaways; Jewel Akens; Bobby Day; Bobby Bland. (Back cover pictures later volumes in the series.)
Oldies But Goodies, Vol. 10 .... Original Sound (S) 8860 8-12 60s
Righteous Brothers; Shirelles; Frankie Avalon; Tune Weavers; Duprees; Johnny Ace; Chuck Berry; Isley Brothers; Fats Domino; Bo Diddley; Sam the Sham & Pharaohs; Olympics. (Back cover must picture no higher volumes in the series than Vol. 10.)
Oldies But Goodies, Vol. 10 .... Original Sound (M) LP-8860 5-10 71
Oldies But Goodies, Vol. 10 .... Original Sound (S) 8860 5-10
Righteous Brothers; Shirelles; Frankie Avalon; Tune Weavers; Duprees; Johnny Ace; Chuck Berry; Isley Brothers; Fats Domino; Bo Diddley; Sam the Sham & Pharaohs; Olympics. (Back cover pictures later volumes in the series.)
Oldies But Goodies, Vol. 11 .... Original Sound (S) 8861 8-12 60s
Righteous Brothers; Little Anthony & Imperials; Bobby Hebb; Mary Wells; Classics IV; Harvey & Moonglows; Little Richard; Kingsmen; Chuck Berry; Angels; Diamonds; Soul Survivors. (Back cover must picture no higher volumes in the series than Vol. 11.)
Oldies But Goodies, Vol. 11 .... Original Sound (S) 8861 5-10
Righteous Brothers; Little Anthony & Imperials; Bobby Hebb; Mary Wells; Classics IV; Harvey & Moonglows; Little Richard; Kingsmen; Chuck Berry; Angels; Diamonds; Soul Survivors. (Back cover pictures later volumes in the series.)
Oldies But Goodies, Vol. 12 .... Original Sound (M) LP-8862 5-10 70s
Oldies But Goodies, Vol. 12 .... Original Sound (S) 8862 5-10 70s
Everly Brothers; Delfonics; James & Bobby Purify; Lenny Welch; Ruby & Romantics; Impressions; Box Tops; Contours; Chuck Berry; Jerry Lee Lewis; Little Richard; Fontella Bass. (Allowing for those with triskaidekaphobia, Original Sound decided to skip Vol. 13 in this series. Really!)
Oldies But Goodies, Vol. 14 .... Original Sound (S) 8864 5-10 70s
Platters; Dionne Warwick; Crests; Brenda Lee; Lloyd Price; Dinah Washington; Bill Haley & His Comets; Martha & Vandellas; Wilson Pickett; Chiffons; McCoys; Shirelles.
Oldies But Goodies Christmas Album, Vol. 1 .... Lunar #2 (S) 2001 5-10 80s
Oldies But Goodies from the Radio Stations, Vol. 1 (2 LP) .... Laurie (S) LES 4035 8-12 81
Shirelles; Capris; Del Shannon; Dionne Warwick; B.J. Thomas; Isley Brothers; Bill Haley & His Comets; Chuck Jackson; Ernie Maresca; Gene Pitney; Skyliners; Belmonts; Chiffons; Dean & Jean; Brook Benton; Dion & Belmonts; Five Discs; Jimmy Curtiss; Dion; Bernadette Carroll.
Oldies By the Dozen .... Parkway (M) P-7037 20-25 63
Crows; Shirelles; Orlons; Dee Dee Sharp; Chubby Checker; John Zacherle; Rays; Dickie Doo & Don'ts; Timmie Rodgers; Little Anthony & Imperials; Charlie Gracie.
Oldies By the Dozen, Vol. 2 .... Parkway (M) P-7041 20-25 64
Frankie Lymon; Billy & Lillie; Freddy Cannon; Dovells; Bobby Lewis; Chubby Checker; Bobby Rydell; Jive Five; Preston Epps.
Oldies By the Dozen, Vol. 2 .... Parkway (M) P-7041 25-35 64
Frankie Lymon; Billy & Lillie; Freddy Cannon; Dovells; Bobby Lewis; Chubby Checker; Bobby Rydell; Jive Five; Preston Epps. (Package includes a bonus 45 rpm, Parkway 7041, *The Twist* [Chubby Checker]/*Mashed Potato Time* [Dee Dee Sharp].)
Oldies by Various Artists: see Oldies (Wyncote)
Oldies Dance Party, Vol. 1 .... Vee Jay (M) VJLP-8001 15-25 63
Oldies Dance Party, Vol. 1 .... Oldies 33 (M) OL-8001 15-20 64
4 Seasons; Maxine Brown; Dee Clark; Wilbert Harrison; Jimmy Charles; Don Gardner & Dee Dee Ford; Joey Dee; Gladys Knight & Pips; Jimmy Rodgers.
Oldies Dance Party, Vol. 2 .... Vee Jay (M) VJLP-8002 15-25 63
Oldies Dance Party, Vol. 2 .... Oldies 33 (M) OL-8002 15-20 64
Joey Dee; Tony Bellus; 4 Seasons; Jerry Butler; Maxine Brown; Frank Ifield; Lee Dorsey; Jimmy Clanton; Bobby Day; Joe & Ann; Jerry Butler & Impressions; Spaniels.
Oldies Dance Party, Vol. 3 .... Oldies 33 (M) OL-8006 15-20 64
Skyliners; Pentagons; Dukays; Spaniels; Gladys Knight & Pips; Impressions; Genies; Mello Kings; Willows; Marvin & Johnny; Robert & Johnny; Nutmegs.
Oldies, Goodies and Woodies .... Vault (M) LP-103 20-30 65
Oldies, Goodies and Woodies .... Vault (S) VS-103 25-35 65
Challengers; Beach Girls; Vibrents; Gladiators; Busy Bodies; Tom Starr & Galaxies.
Oldies in Hi Fi .... Chess (M) LP-1439 50-75 59
(Black vinyl.)
Oldies in Hi Fi .... Chess (M) LP-1439 500-750 59
(Multi-color vinyl. Promotional issue only.) Buddy & Claudia; Willie Mabon; Dale Hawkins; Jackie Brenston; John Godfrey Trio; Rusty York; Bobby Charles; Johnnie & Joe; Calvin Bostic.
Oldsmobile Spotlights the New Stars in Action .... RCA (M) PRM 167 10-15 64
Oldsmobile Spotlights the New Stars in Action .... RCA (S) PRS 167 10-15 64
Ann-Margret; Sergio Franchi; Peter Nero; Anthony Newley; Ethel Ennis; Dick Schory; Womenfolk; John Gary; Gale Garnett; Ed Ames; Ketty Lester; Glenn Yarbrough.

Oliver & Company .... Disneyland (S) 64101 20-25 88
(Soundtrack.) Huey Lewis; Billy Joel; Ruth Pointer; Bette Midler; Myhann Tran; Ruben Blades.
Olympus 7-0000 .... Command (M) CS-33-07 8-12 66
Olympus 7-0000 .... Command (S) CS-07-SD 10-12 66
(Soundtrack from 1966 TV presentation.) Donald O'Connor; Phyllis Newman; Larry Blyden; Eddie Foy Jr.
On Stage at the Grand Ole Opry .... Decca (M) DL-4393 20-25 64
On Stage at the Grand Ole Opry .... Decca (S) DL-74393 25-30 64
Patsy Cline; Wilburn Brothers; Roy Drusky; others.
On the Move: see BACHARACH, Burt / Glen Campbell / Dionne Warwick
On the Record .... Caedmon (M) TC-1572 60-80 77
(News highlights for radio use.) Elvis Presley; Bing Crosby; Guy Lombardo; Anita Bryant; others.
On the Road .... RCA (M) LPM-3509 10-20 66
On the Road .... RCA (S) LSP-3509 15-20 66
Porter Wagoner; Norma Jean; Speck Rhodes; others.
On the Road Again .... Adelphi (S) 1007 5-10 70
Furry Lewis; Bukka White; Gus Cannon.
On the Road Again, Anthology of Chicago Blues .... Muskadine (M) 100 15-25 71
Floyd Jones; Snooky & Moody; Delta Joe; Liltle Walter Trio; Little Walter; Baby Face Leroy Trio; Othum Brown; Johnny Shines; John Brim Trio; J.B. & His Hawks.
On the Road Again: see Rock of Ages, Rocks New Frontiers: 1966-1970 (On the Road Again)
On the Seventh Day .... Mercury (S) 61248 8-10 70
On the Trail .... Riverside (M) 486 10-15 66
On the Trail .... Riverside (S) 9-486 10-15 66
Jimmy Heath Quintet; Kenny Burrell; Wynton Kelly; others.
Once Bitten .... MCA/Curb (S) MCA-6154 8-10 85
(Soundtrack.) 3 Speed; Hubert Kah; Real Life; Private Domain; Two of Us; Gifthorse; Maria Vidal; Kevin McKnelly; Moses Tyson Jr.; John Du Prez.
Once Upon a Tour .... Cozy (S) TV-2000 12-18 68
Once Upon a Tour .... Premore (S) PL-2000 8-12 Re
(TV Soundtrack.) Dora Hall; Rich Little; Frank Sinatra Jr.; Phil Harris; Oliver; Ben Blue; Rosey Grier; Jack Elliott; Electric Prunes.
One Big Family .... Compleat (45) 679001-7 5-10 85
(With picture sleeve.) Roy Acuff; Rex Allen Jr.; Lynn Anderson; Eddy Arnold; Chet Atkins; Bobby Bare; Lane Brody; T. Graham Brown; Little Jimmy Dickens; Karen Taylor-Good; Dobie Gray; Sonny James; George Jones; Kendalls; Dave Kirby; Neal Matthews; Kathy Mattea; O.B. McClinton; Ronnie McDowell; Colleen Peterson; Boots Randolph; Jerry Reed; Jeannie C. Riley; Ronny Robbins; Ray Sawyer; Troy Seals; Jeannie Seely; Rick Schulman; Gordon Stoker; Tanya Tucker; Mack Vickery; Porter Wagoner; Duane West; Leona Williams; Bergen White; Faron Young.
One Dozen Goldies .... Carlton (M) 12/121 35-45 60
Jack Scott; Nu Tornados; Jesse Lee Turner; Gary Stites; Anita Bryant; Kenny Rogers.
One Funky Album: see Goofy Greats
Only for Teenagers and Real Swinging Adults .... Success-Premier (M) S-LP-1011MX 20-30 60s
Blendtones; Jimmy McHugh; Oscar Boyd; Cicero Blake; Extensions; Martinels.
Only in America: see Rock of Ages – East Coast Rock: 1969-1968 (Only in America)
Only You, the Originals .... Pickwick (SE) SPC 3512 5-10
Platters; Chuck Berry; Jerry Lee Lewis; Fats Domino; Bill Haley & His Comets.
Ooh Child .... Pickwick (S) SPC-3325 5-10
Stairsteps; Isley Brothers; Jimi Hendrix; Baby Huey; Wilbert Harrison; Dorothy Morrison; Impressions; Chee Chee & Peppy.
Open House .... Decca (M) DL 38234 20-30 63
Open House .... Decca (M) DL-4205 20-30 63
Judy Garland; Jimmy Durante; Ames Brothers; Eddie Heywood; McGuire Sisters; Billy Williams; Russ Morgan; Teresa Brewer; Ray Charles Singers; Billy Ward; Roberta Sherwood; Les Brown.
Open House .... Riverside (M) 482 10-15 66
Open House .... Riverside (S) 9-482 10-15 66
Johnny "Hammond" Smith; Thad Jones; Ray Barretto; others.
Open Up Yer Door .... Frog Death (S) 101 15-25
Clefs of Lavender Hill; others.
Opry Album .... Columbia Special Products (M) XTV 86113 10-20 50s
Flatts & Scruggs; Marty Robbins; Stonewall Jackson; Bobby Lord; Billy Walker; Ray Price; George Morgan; Hawshaw Hawkins; Carl Butler; Bill Carlisle.
Opry Old Timers .... Starday (S) SLP-182 15-25 62
Opry Time in Tennessee .... Starday (M) S-177 15-25 62
Opry Time in Tennessee .... Starday (S) SLP-177 15-25 62
George Jones; Flatt & Scruggs; Cowboy Copas; others.
Original, The .... Pickwick (S) SPC-3311 5-10 72
Big Bopper; Diamonds; Bobby Day; Charlie Ryan; Paragons; Crew-Cuts; Five Satins; Frankie Ford; Jimmy Clanton.
Original '50s .... Pickwick (S) SPC-3520 5-10 70s
Royal Teens; Poni-Tails; George Hamilton IV; Tommy Roe; Elegants; Danny & Juniors; Muvva "Guitar" Hubbard; Steve Gibson & Red Caps; Lloyd Price; Sparkletones.
Original '50s and '60s .... Pickwick (S) SPC-3535 5-10 70s
Angels; Penguins; Paul & Paula; Spanky & Our Gang; Cardigans; Diamonds; Del-Vikings; Hondells; Left Banke; Blues Magoos.
Original Amateur Hour 25th Anniversary Album (2 LP) .... United Artists (M) UXL-2 30-40 60
(TV Soundtrack.) Pat Boone; Teresa Brewer; Jerry Vale; others.
Original Beatles Medley: see Beatles
Original Boogie Woogie Piano Giants .... Columbia (M) KC-32708 5-10 74
Meade Lux Lewis; Pete Johnson; Joe Turner; Albert Ammons; Champion Jack Dupree; Jimmy Yancy.
Original Country Hits .... Artistic (EP) 223 15-25 65
(7 inch, 33 rpm. Also issued as Western, Vol. 1.) Eddie Dean; Chuck Hawkins; Rex Trailer; Johnny Williams; Foy Willing & Riders of the Purple Sage; Don Hughes; Sterling Blythe; Doye O'Dell.

Original Country Hits .... Artistic (EP) 224 15-25 65
(7 inch, 33 rpm. Also issued as Western, Vol. 2 and also as Golden Country Hits.) Webb Pierce; Slim Willet; Ferlin Husky; T. Texas Tyler; Jimmy Dean; Rose Maddox; Hank Locklin; Pete Pike.

Original Country Hits, Vol. 1 .... Liberty (M) LRP-3305 15-20 63
Johnny Cash; Joe Carson; Cowboy Copas; George Jones; Bobby Edwards; Walter Brennan; Wynn Stewart; Warren Smith; Jan Howard; Bob Wills; Johnny & Jonie Mosby; others.

Original Country Hits, Vol. 2 .... Liberty (M) LRP-3345 15-20 64

Original Country Hits, No. 3 .... Liberty (M) LRP-3382 15-20 64
George Jones; Patsy Cline; Johnny Cash; Dave Dudley; Slim Whitman; Cowboy Copas; Johnny & Jonie Mosby; Wynn Stewart; Bob Wills & Tommy Duncan; Joe Carson; Pete Drake; Jan Howard.

Original Country Hits of the '50s (8 LP) .... Reader's Digest (M) 446-RM-26040 25-40 78
(Boxed set.) Don Gibson; Red Foley; Hank Williams, Sr.; Kitty Wells; Eddy Arnold; Pee Wee King; Webb Pierce; Everly Brothers; Hank Snow; Jerry Lee Lewis; Elton Britt & Rosalie Allen; Ernest Tubb; Patti Page; Pine Toppers; Carlisles; Davis Sisters; Jim Reeves; Justin Tubb & Goldie Hill; Johnnie & Jack; Stuart Hamblen; Johnny Cash; Jimmie Rodgers; George Jones; Porter Wagoner; Browns; Carl Perkins; Hank Locklin; Bobby Helms; Patsy Cline; Don Gibson; Wilma Lee & Stoney Cooper; Skeeter Davis; Wilburn Brothers.

Original Early Top 40 Hits (2 LP) .... Paramount (S) PAS 1013 8-12 74
Hilltoppers; Billy Vaughn; Pat Boone; Gale Storm; Sanford Clark; Nervous Norvous; Jim Lowe; Chantays; Robin Luke; Shields; Wink Martindale; Del-Vikings; Tab Hunter; Surfaris; Lonnie Donegan; Dodie Stevens; Dartells; Jimmy Gilmer.

Original Folk Blues - Arkansas Blues .... United (S) US-7784 10-20 70s
Robert Dudlow Taylor; James "Peck" Curtis; Sunny Blair; Baby Face Turner; Drifting Slim.

Original Folk Blues - Blues from the Deep South .... United (S) US-7780 10-20 70s
Pinetop Slim; Dixie Blues Boys; Leroy Simpson; Big Bill Dotson; Arkansas Johnny Todd.

Original Folk Blues - California Blues .... United (S) US-7780 10-20 70s
Johnny "Guitar" Watson; George Smith; James Reed; Walter Robinson; Johnny Fuller.

Original Folk Blues - Detroit Blues: see HOOKER, John Lee / Eddie Kirkland / Eddie Burns / Sylvester Cotton

Original Folk Blues - Memphis Blues .... United (S) US-7779 10-20 70s
Howlin' Wolf; Joe Hill Louis; Walter Horton; Bobby Bland; Junior Parker; Willie Nix.

Original Folk Blues - Mississippi Blues: see GILMORE, Boyd / Houston Boines / Charlie Booker

Original Folk Blues - Texas Blues .... United (S) US-7782 10-20 70s
Little Son Jackson; Smokey Hogg; Jesse Thomas; Alexander Moore; Lowell Fulson; Charlie Bradix.

Original Folk Blues - West Coast Blues .... United (S) US-7789 10-20 70s
Mercy Dee; Jimmy Nelson; Pee Wee Crayton; Saunders King; J.W. Walker; James Reed; Roy Hawkins.

Original Gold (3 LP) .... Warner Special Products/Sessions (S) OP 3505 10-15 79
Carly Simon; Righteous Brothers; Arlo Guthrie; Prelude; Joan Baez; Seals & Crofts; Alice Cooper; Orleans; Flying Machine; Gary Wright; Linda Ronstadt; Abba; Association; Candi Staton; Spinners; New York City; Aretha Franklin; Hot; Staple Singers; Dionne Warwick; Spinners; Samantha Sang; Diana Ross; Tim Moore; David Soul; Manfred Mann; England Dan & John Ford Coley; John Sebastian; Todd Rundgren; Lobo; Albert Hammond.

Original Gold – 44 (3 LP) .... Sessions/RCA Special Products (S) 0142 10-15 75
(Mail order offer.) Dale & Grace; Shirelles; Bobby Lewis; Tommy Roe; Chiffons; Everly Brothers; Lloyd Price; Jimmie Rodgers; Paul Anka; Impalas; Cliff Nobles & Co.; Sam Cooke; Everly Brothers; Eddie Holman; Chuck Berry; Phil Phillips; Bobby Rydell; Chairman of the Board; Brian Hyland; Kathy Young & Innocents; Toni Fisher; Happenings; Chris Montez; Ohio Express; Ral Donner; Chiffons; Jimmy Charles; Hondells; Dorsey Burnette; Fifth Estate; Duane Eddy; Jarmels; Poni-Tails; 1910 Fruitgum Co.; Randy & Rainbows; Ritchie Valens; Johnny Cash; Fantastic Johnny C.; Steve Lawrence; Mamas & Papas; Impressions; Jackie Wilson.

Original Gold Soul (2 LP) .... Mercury (S) SRM-2-600 20-25 69
(Red label.) Louis Jordan; Sil Austin; Red Prysock; Buddy Johnson; Dinah Washington; Joe Medlin; Clyde McPhatter; Jimmy McCracklin; Arthur Prysock; Josh White Sr.; Eddie Chamblee; Ruth Brown; Billy Eckstine; Joe Liggins; Eddie Vinson; Penguins; Ivory Joe Hunter; Cannonball Adderley; Bill Samuels; Jay McShann; Big Bill Broonzy.

Original Golden Blues Greats, Vol. 1 .... Liberty (S) LST-7572 10-15 68
Trashmen; Majors; Lloyd Price; Don & Juan; Bobby Day; Lonnie Mack; Billy Ward & Dominoes; Jessie Hill; Fats Domino; Wilson Pickett; Rivingtons; Larry Williams.

Original Golden Country Greats, Vol. 1 .... Liberty (S) LST-7569 10-15 68
Johnny Cash; Bobby Edwards; Walter Brennan; Cowboy Copas; Wynn Stewart; Jan Howard; George Jones; Warren Smith; Bob Wills & Tommy Duncan; Frankie Miller; Johnny & Jonie Mosby.

Original Golden Country Greats, Vol. 2 .... Liberty (S) LST-7570 10-15 68
Dave Dudley; Johnny Cash; Slim Whitman; Cowboy Copas; Hank Cochran; Joe Carson; Walter Brennan; Moon Mullican; Fendermen; Warren Smith; Willie Nelson; Bob Wills & Tommy Duncan.

Original Golden Country Greats, Vol. 3 .... Liberty (S) LST-7571 10-15 68
Dave Dudley; Patsy Cline; George Jones; Slim Whitman; Cowboy Copas; Jerry Wallace; Bob Wills & Tommy Duncan; Pete Drake; Jan Howard; Wynn Stewart; Joe Carson; Johnny & Jonie Mosby.

Original Golden Greats, Vol. 1 .... Liberty (M) LRP-3500 10-15 67

Original Golden Greats, Vol. 1 .... Liberty (S) LST-7500 10-15 67
Gary Lewis & Playboys; Cher; Ventures; Jackie De Shannon; T-Bones; Mel Carter; Hollies; Vic Dana; Bob Lind; Bud Shank; Billy J. Kramer; Johnny Rivers.

Original Golden Greats, Vol. 2 .... Liberty (M) LRP-3543 10-15 67

Original Golden Greats, Vol. 2 .... Liberty (S) LST-7543 10-15 67
Johnny Rivers; Vikki Carr; Sunshine Company; Vic Dana; Jackie De Shannon; 5th Dimension; Cher; Bobby Vee & Strangers; Nitty Gritty Dirt Band; Mel Carter; Del Shannon; Gary Lewis & Playboys.

Original Golden Greats, Vol. 3 .... Liberty (S) LST-7573 10-15 68
Ventures; Ace Cannon; Cozy Cole; Bill Black Combo; Jimmy Dorsey; Johnny & Hurricanes; Preston Epps; Santo & Johnny; Champs; Lee Allen; Sandy Nelson.

Original Golden Greats, Vol. 4 .... Liberty (S) LST-7574 10-15 68
Jan & Dean; Bobby Day; Fleetwoods; Jessie Hill; David Seville; Fats Domino; Bobby Vee; Buddy Knox; Hollywood Argyles; Fendermen; Maurice Williams; Bobby Freeman.

Original Golden Greats, Vol. 5 .... Liberty (S) LST-7575 10-15 68
Ernie K-Doe; Fleetwoods; Ray Peterson; Five Satins; Buchanan & Goodman; Timi Yuro; Dick & Deedee; Troy Shondell; Gene McDaniels; Faye Adams; Bobby Vee; Anita Bryant.

Original Golden Greats, Vol. 6 .... Liberty (S) LST-7576 10-15 68
Bobby Vee; Gene McDaniels; Anita Bryant; Paul Evans; Chantels; Johnny Burnette; Bobby Edwards; Paris Sisters; Billy Bland; Jack Scott; Toni Fisher; Timi Yuro.

Original Golden Greats, Vol. 7 .... Liberty (S) LST-7577 10-15 68

Bobby Lewis; Jody Reynolds; Harold Dorman; Crescendos; Patience & Prudence; Bobby Vee; Silhouettes; Billy Ward & Dominoes; Johnny Burnette; Martin Denny; Eddie Cochran; Ray Sharpe.

Original Golden Greats, Vol. 8 .... Liberty (S) LST-7578 10-15 68
Jerry Lee Lewis; Fats Domino; Little Esther; Olympics; Irma Thomas; Larry Williams; Sammy Turner; Bill Justis; Marvin & Johnny; Little Anthony & Imperials; Five Keys; Thurston Harris.

Original Golden Greats, Vol. 9 .... Liberty (S) LST-7579 10-15 68
Eddie Cochran; Jackie De Shannon; Gene McDaniels; Patience & Prudence; Cadets; Jan & Dean; Johnny Rivers; Curtis Lee; Georgie Fame; Julie London; Turbans; Bobby Vee.

Original Golden Greats, Vol. 10 .... Liberty (S) LST-7619 10-15 69
Bobby Vee; Hollies; Fifth Dimension; Bobby Goldsboro; Canned Heat; Count Five; Classics IV; Brenton Wood; Johnny Rivers; Jackie De Shannon; Cher; Gary Lewis & Playboys.

Original Golden Hits .... Artistic (M) 227 50-100 65
(Mail order offer.) Jan & Dean; Jerry Wallace; Champs; Ray Sharpe; Fireflies; Rosie & Originals; Gene & Eunice.

Original Golden Hits, Vol. 1 .... Artistic (EP) 227 40-50 65
(7 inch, 33 rpm.) Jerry Wallace; Champs; Jan & Dean; Ray Sharpe; Fireflies; Rosie & Originals; Gene & Eunice.

Original Golden Hits, Vol. 2 .... Artistic (EP) 228 40-50 65
(7 inch, 33 rpm.) Hollywood Argyles; Don Julian; Meadowlarks; Jessie Belvin; Penguins; Etta James; Teen Queens; Marvin & Johnny; Chuck Higgins.

Original Golden Hits of the Great Blues Singers .... Mercury (M) MG-20826 15-25 63
Original Golden Hits of the Great Blues Singers .... Mercury (S) SR-60826 20-30 63
Ray Charles; Frankie Lymon; Brook Benton; Clyde McPhatter; Lee Dorsey; Chuck Jackson; Ray Charles; Chuck Willis; Lightning Hopkins; Ivory Joe Hunter; Billy Bland; Elmore James.

Original Golden Hits of the Great Blues Singers, Vol. 2 .... Mercury (M) MGH-25002 15-25 64
Lightnin' Hopkins; Little Junior Parker; Lowell Fulson; Howlin' Wolf; Brook Benton; Gene Allison; Roscoe Gordon; Clyde McPhatter; Muddy Waters; Johnny Adams; Chuck Jackson; Bobby Bland.

Original Golden Hits of the Great Blues Singers, Vol. 3 .... Mercury (M) MGH-25003 15-25 64
John Lee Hooker; Chuck Jackson; Lightnin' Hopkins; Raymond Lewis; Chris Kenner; Bobby Bland; Muddy Waters; Bunker Hill; Ted Taylor; James Booker; Bo Diddley; Bobby Charles.

Original Golden Hits of the Great Blues Singers, Vol. 4 .... Mercury (M) MGH-25011 15-25 64
Phil Phillips; Wilbert Harrison; Faye Adams; Willie Harper; Maxine Brown; Joe Henderson; Jesse Belvin; Della Reese; Lightnin' Hopkins; Lucky Millender; Willie Mabon; Johnny Long.

Original Golden Hits of the Great C&W Stars .... Mercury (M) MG-20825 15-20 63
Original Golden Hits of the Great C&W Stars .... Mercury (S) SR-60825 20-25 63
Faron Young; Rex Allen; Claude Gray; George Jones; Leroy Van Dyke; others.

Original Golden Hits of the Great Groups, Vol. 1 .... SSS Int'l (S) 32 8-10 76
Ad Libs; Jelly Beans; Butterflys; Dixie Cups; Shangri-Las; Tradewinds.

Original Golden Hits of the Great Groups.......... Mercury (M) MG-20809 20-30 63
Original Golden Hits of the Great Groups.......... Mercury (S) SR-60809 25-35 63
Platters; Drifters; Cleftones; Diamonds; Crests; Flamingos; Valentines; Shirelles; Del-Vikings; Clovers; Fiestas; Chantells.

Original Golden Hits of the Great Groups, Vol. 2 .... Mercury (M) MGH-25000 20-30 63
Platters; Mickey & Sylvia; Monotones; Capris; Pastels; Mello-Kings; Cadillacs; Sensations; Turbans; Nutmegs; Five Satins; Fireflies.

Original Golden Hits of the Great Groups, Vol. 3 .... Mercury (M) MGH-25007 20-25 64
Platters; Silhouettes; Moonglows; Contours; Pastels; Spaniels; El Dorados; Danleers; Kuf-Linx; Orioles; Marveletts; Channels.

Original Golden Hits of the Great Groups, Vol. 4 .... Mercury (M) MGH-25010 20-25 64
Crew-Cuts; Platters; Champs; Mark IV; Galens; Diamonds; Magnificents; Moonglows; Gaylords; Fiestas; Baysiders; Cadets.

Original Golden Instrumental Hits, Vol. 1 .... Mercury (M) MGH-25001 15-25 63
Cannonball Adderly; Mongo Santamaria; Lee Allen; Phil Upchurch; Mar-Keys; Ace Cannon; David Carroll; Booker T. & MGs; Les Cooper; Ernie Fields; Ramrods; Champs

Original Golden Instrumental Hits .... Warner Bros. (M) W-1725 10-15 68
Original Golden Instrumental Hits .... Warner Bros. (S) WS-1725 10-15 68
String-A-Longs; Marketts; Ernie Fields; Fireballs; B. Bumble & Stingers; Champs; Routers; Preston Epps; Sandy Nelson; Hollywood Persuaders.

Original Golden Oldies (Clay Cole) .... Jubilee (S) JGM 5026 15-20 63
Dion & Timberlanes; Innocents; Drifters; Bobby Darin; Flamingos; etc.

Original Golden Oldies .... Group (M) W-33002 20-25 63
Frankie Lymon & Teenagers; Moonglows; Little Anthony & Imperials; Collegiates (sic, actually Collegians); Hearts; Willows; Buddy Knox; Moonglows; Shepherd Sisters; others.

Original Golden Oldies, Vol. 1 .... Gozo International Ltd. (S) 797 10-15 64
Angels; Jimmy Soul; Willows; Nutmegs; Teddy Van; Del-Vikings; Bobbettes; Eternals; Penguins; Paragons.

Original Golden Rhythm and Blues Hits, Vol. 1 .... Mercury (M) MGH-25006 20-25 64
(Red label.) Faye Adams; Otis Redding; Clarence Henry; Don Gardner & Dee Dee Ford; Jimmy Holiday; Billy Stewart; Bobby Marchan; Sonny Boy Williamson; Little Walter; Maxine Brown; William Bell; Jimmy McCracklin.

Original Golden Teen Hits, Vol. 1 .... Mercury (M) MGH-25004 20-25 64
Gary "U.S." Bonds; Thomas Wayne; Shirelles; Rosie & Originals; Hollywood Argyles; Sammy Turner; Carla Thomas; Sensations; Maurice & Charms; Johnnie & Joe; Paul Peek; Dickie Doo & Don'ts.

Original Golden Teen Hits, Vol. 2 .... Mercury (M) MGH-25005 20-25 64
Buddy Knox; Al Brown; Ray-O-Vacs; Cleveland Crochet; Bobby Freeman; Gary "U.S." Bonds; Lesley Gore; Johnny Thunder; Johnnie & Joe; Robert & Johnny; Rufus Thomas; Ray Stevens.

Original Golden Teen Hits, Vol. 3 .... Mercury (M) MGH-25009 20-25 64
Gary "U.S." Bonds; Shirelles; Champs; Dicky Doo & Don'ts; Jerry Wallace; Janie Grant; Jan Bradley; Sammy Turner; Jerry Fuller; Troy Shondell; Angels; Johnny Preston.

Original Golden Town and Country Hits, Vol. 1 .... Mercury (M) MGH-25008 15-25 64
Brook Benton; Faron Young; Jerry Wallace; Patti Page; Claude Gray; Jerry Fuller; Rex Allen; Tom & Jerry; Patsy Cline; Rusty Draper; Ned Miller; Leroy Van Dyke.

Original Goldies from the Fabulous Fifties .... Josie (M) 4002 30-40 63
Sonny Til & Orioles; Cookies; Chaperons; Four Tunes; Jimmy Ricks & Ravens; Continentals; Bobby Freeman; Cadillacs; Kathy Young; Bobby Constock.

Original Goldies from the Fabulous Fifties, Vol. 2 .... Josie (M) 4003 30-40 63
Volumes; Bobby Freeman; Channels; Edna McGriff; Cadillacs; Collegians; Chips; Jesters; Joe Henderson; Paragons; Couplings; Night Caps.
Original Goldies from the Fabulous Fifties, Vol. 3 .... Josie (M) 4004 30-40 63
Caddilacs; Chandellors; Channels; Collegians; Impressions; Orioles; Ravens.
Original Goodies .... Time (M) 52082 20-30 63
Skip & Flip; Bell Notes; Hugo Montenegro; Knockouts; Bertha Tillman; Beau Marks; Genies; Chariots; Chevrons.
Original Great Northwest Hits, Vol. 1 .... Jerden (M) JRL-7001 25-35 65
Dave Lewis; Frantics; Adventurers; Exotics; Kingsmen; Little Bill & Bluenotes; Gary Hodge; Bonnie Guitar; Darwin & Cupids.
Original Great Northwest Hits, Vol. 2 .... Jerden (M) JRL-7002 25-35 65
Dave Lewis; Kingsmen; Gentleman Jim & Horsemen; Ron Peterson & Accents; Paul Revere & Raiders; Doug Robertson & Good Guys; Darwin & Cupids; Jack Bedient; Keith Colley; DeVilles; Bobby Wayne.
Original Greatest Hits of the Great .... Mercury (M) W-12325 10-20 66
Original Greatest Hits of the Great .... Mercury (S) 16325 10-20 66
Leroy Van Dyke; George Jones; Faron Young; others.
Original Hit Performances – All Time Country and Western: see All Time Country and Western
Original Hit Performances of the Thirties, Forties & Fifties (3 LP) .... Decca/MCA (M) R-204600 10-20 70s
Clyde McCoy; Riley Farley & His Onyx Club Boys; Andy Kirk & His Twelve Clouds of Joy; Jimmie Lunceford; Judy Garland; Count Basie; Andrews Sisters; Ella Fitzgerald; Ink Spots; Glen Gray; Dick Haymes; Alfred Drake; Guy Lombardo; Ethel Smith; Carmen Cavallaro; Gordon Jenkins; Louis Jordan & His Tympani Five; Hoagy Carmichael; Al Jolson; Bing Crosby; Gary Crosby; Weavers; Leroy Anderson; Louis Armstrong; Four Aces; Peggy Lee; Mills Brothers; Kitty Allen; Bill Haley & His Comets; Sammy Davis Jr.
Original Hit Performances: Rhythm, Blues and Boogie Woogie .... Decca (M) DL-4011 25-50 59
Count Basie; Andy Kirk; Nat King Cole Trio; Buddy Johnson; Jay McShann; Pete Johnson; Lionel Hampton; Ella Fitzgerald; Lucky Millinder; Sister Rosetta Tharpe; Louis Jordan & His Tympany Five; Billie Holiday.
Original Hit Performances: the Late Thirties .... Decca (M) DL-4000 25-50 59
(Black and silver label.)
Original Hit Performances: the Late Thirties .... Decca (M) DL-4000 15-20 65
(Multi-color label.) Clyde McCoy; Riley Farley; Andy Kirk; Jimmie Lunceford; Bing Crosby; Count Basie; Judy Garland; Andrews Sisters; Ella Fitzgerald; Chick Webb; Ink Spots; Glen Gray.
Original Hit Performances: Into the Forties .... Decca (M) DL-4001 25-50 59
(Black and silver label.)
Original Hit Performances: Into the Forties .... Decca (M) DL-4001 15-20 65
(Multi-color label.) Bing Crosby; Judy Garland; Gene Kelly; Andrews Sisters; Mills Brothers; Lionel Hampton; Woody Herman; Johnny Long; Jimmy Dorsey; Bob Crosby.
Original Hit Performances: the Middle Forties .... Decca (M) DL-4002 25-50 59
(Black and silver label.)
Original Hit Performances: the Middle Forties .... Decca (M) DL-4002 15-20 65
(Multi-color label.) Dick Haymes; Alfred Drake & Oklahoma Chorus; Guy Lombardo; Ethel Smith; Ink Spots & Ella Fitzgerald; Andrews Sisters; Carmen Cavallero; Bing Crosby; Gordon Jenkins; Louis Jordan & His Tympany Five; Hoagy Carmichael; Al Jolson.
Original Hit Performances: into the Fifties .... Decca (M) DL-4003 25-50 59
(Black and silver label.)
Original Hit Performances: into the Fifties .... Decca (M) DL-4003 15-20 65
(Multi-color label.) Ted Weems; Bing Crosby; Fred Waring; Dick Haymes; Evelyn Knight; Russ Morgan; Ray Bolger; Andrews Sisters; Louis Armstrong; Guy Lombardo; Ethel Merman; Gordon Jenkins & Weavers.
Original Hit Performances: the Early Fifties .... Decca (M) DL-4004 25-50 59
(Black and silver label.)
Original Hit Performances: the Early Fifties .... Decca (M) DL-4004 15-20 65
(Multi-color label.) Bing Crosby; Gary Crosby; Weavers; Leroy Anderson; Louis Armstrong; Peggy Lee; Mills Brothers; Four Aces; Kitty Kallen; Bill Haley & His Comets; Sammy Davis Jr.
Original Hit Performances: the Late Fifties .... Decca (M) DL-4005 25-50 59
(Black and silver label.)
Original Hit Performances: the Late Fifties .... Decca (M) DL-4005 15-20 65
(Multi-color label.) Bill Haley & His Comets; Al Hibbler; Morris Stoloff; Bobby Helms; Kalin Twins; Warren Covington & Tommy Dorsey Orchestra; Roberta Sherwood; Domenico Modugno; Earl Grant; Victor Young.
Original Hit Performances: the Thirties .... Decca (M) DL-4006 25-50 59
(Black and silver label.)
Original Hit Performances: the Thirties .... Decca (M) DL-4006 15-20 65
(Multi-color label.) Horace Heidt; Bing Crosby; Jimmy Dorsey; Jimmie Lunceford; Johnny Mercer; Mills Brothers; others.
Original Hit Performances: the Forties .... Decca (M) DL-4007 25-50 59
(Black and silver label.)
Original Hit Performances: the Forties .... Decca (M) DL-4007 15-20 65
(Multi-color label.) Woody Herman; Jimmy Dorsey; Merry Macs; Judy Garland; Mills Brothers; Bing Crosby; Eddie Heywood; Ink Spots; Hoagy Carmichael; Andrews Sisters; others.
Original Hit Performances: the Late Forties .... Decca (M) DL-4008 25-50 59
(Black and silver label.)
Original Hit Performances: the Late Forties .... Decca (M) DL-4008 15-20 65
(Multi-color label.) Bing Crosby; Ella Fitzgerald; Russ Morgan; Louis Jordan & His Tympany Five; Evelyn Knight; Guy Lombardo; Gordon Jenkins; Anton Karas; Randy Brooks; Danny Kaye.
Original Hit Performances: the Fifties .... Decca (M) DL-4009 25-50 59
(Black and silver label.)
Original Hit Performances: the Fifties .... Decca (M) DL-4009 15-20 65
(Multi-color label.) Bing Crosby; Bill Kenny & Ink Spots; Florian Zabach; Tommy Dorsey; Dream Weavers; Sylvia Syms; Four Aces; Jerry Lewis; Carl Dobkins Jr.; Louis Armstrong; Victor Young; Carmen Cavallero; Toni Arden.
Original Hit Records .... Roulette (M) R-25106 20-30 60
Original Hit Records .... Roulette (S) SR-25106 25-35 60
Frankie Lymon; Rock-A-Teens; Trade Martin; Jimmie Rodgers; Four Preps; Cathy Carr; others.
Original Hits by Original Artists, Vol. 1 .... Guest Star (M) G 1430 10-20 60s
Harptones; Chants; Frank Gari; Bobbettes; Fireflies; Angels; Janie Grant; Collegians; Neil Sedaka; Dave "Baby" Cortez.

Original Hits, Vol. 1 .... Circa (S) COH-1 15-25 62
Bobby Edwards; Toni Fisher; Metallics; Big Jay McNeeley; Innocents; Jennell Hawkins; Defiants; Kathy Young; Glen Campbell; Blue Jays; Rochelle & Candles; Paradon.
Original Hits, Vol. 1 .... Rondo (M) R-2013 5-10
Original Hits, Vol. 1 .... Rondo (S) RS-2013 5-10
Bobby Day; Googie Rene; Silhouettes; Maurice Williams; Wilbert Harrison; Jackie McLean; Ray Charles; Fabulous Cyclones.
Original Hits, Vol. 2 .... Rondo (M) R-2014 5-10
Original Hits, Vol. 2 .... Rondo (S) RS-2014 5-10
Bobby Day, Teacho Wiltshire; Fabulous Cyclones, Jackie McLean; Turbans; Mello Kings; Fay Adams; Maurice Williams.
Original Hits, Vol. 1 (Past & Present) .... Liberty (M) LRP-3178 20-30 60
Bobby Freeman; Fleetwoods; Larry Williams; Jody Reynolds; Olympics; Crescendos; Champs; Ventures; Garry Miles; Johnny Burnette; Joiner, Arkansas Jr. H.S. Band; Harold Dorman.
Original Hits, Vol. 2 (Past & Present) .... Liberty (M) LRP-3180 15-25 61
Cadets; Fleetwoods; Larry Williams; Highlights; Margie Rayburn; Marvin & Johnny; Eddie Cochran; Johnny Burnette; Ventures; Buddy Knox; Little Dippers; Bill Black Combo; Bobby Vee.
Original Hits, Vol. 3 (Past & Present) .... Liberty (M) LRP-3187 15-25 61
Sammy Turner; Martin Denny; Bobby Vee; Patience & Prudence; Billy Ward & Dominoes; Ray Sharpe; Bill Black Combo; Johnny Burnette; Kathy Young; Gene McDaniels; Rollers.
Original Hits, Vol. 4 (Memories Are Made of Hits) .... Liberty (M) LRP-3200 15-25 61
Bobby Vee; Preston Epps; Patience & Prudence; Ray Smith; Billy Ward & Dominoes; Sammy Turner; Johnny Burnette; Fendermen; Eddie Cochran; Johnny & Hurricanes; Ray Peterson; Fleetwoods.
Original Hits, Vol. 5 (15 Hits) .... Liberty (M) LRP-3235 15-25 62
Bobby Vee; Fleetwoods; Toni Fisher; Bobby Freeman; Ray Peterson; Dick & DeeDee; Ventures; Gene McDaniels; Fendermen; Timi Yuro; Flamingos; Sammy Turner; Johnny Burnette; Troy Shondell; Little Anthony & Imperials.
Original Hits, Vol. 6 .... Liberty (M) LRP-3260 15-25 62
Maurice Williams; Jack Scott; Chantels; Walter Brennan; Timi Yuro; Five Satins; Fleetwoods; Paul Evans; Anita Bryant; Silhouettes; Bobby Vee; Jimmy Dorsey.
Original Hits, Vol. 7 (All-Time Hit Instrumentals) .... Liberty (M) LRP-3274 15-25 63
Cozy Cole; Ace Cannon; Ventures; Johnny & Hurricanes; Sandy Nelson; Bill Black Combo; Preston Epps; Lee Allen; Joiner, Arkansas Jr. High School Band.
Original Hits, Vol. 8 .... Liberty (M) LRP-3288 15-25 63
Hollywood Argyles; Bobby Edwards; Anita Bryant; Billy Bland; Paris Sisters; Bobby Vee; Paul Evans; Shelby Flint; Gene McDaniels; Fireflies; Don & Juan; Faye Adams.
Original Hits, Vol. 9 .... Liberty (M) LRP-3325 15-25 63
Original Hits, Vol. 9 .... Liberty (S) LST-3325 15-25 63
Jan & Dean; Jerry Lee Lewis; B. Bumble & Stingers; Curtis Lee; Johnny Cash; Bobby Day; Ernie Fields; Toni Fisher; Bobby Vee; Mello-Kings; Bill Justis; Turbans; Little Esther.
Original Hits, Vol. 10 (15 Number 1 Hits) .... Liberty (M) LRP-3344 15-25 64
Original Hits, Vol. 10 (15 Number 1 Hits) .... Liberty (S) LST-7344 15-25 64
Jan & Dean; Champs; Bobby Vee; Ventures; Fats Domino; Fleetwoods; Ernie K-Doe; Buchanan & Goodman; Ernie Freeman; Bobby Lewis; David Seville; Hollywood Argyles; Ventures; Bobby Freeman; Fendermen.
Original Hits, Vol. 11 (No. 1 Hits!) .... Liberty (M) LRP-3418 15-25 64
Original Hits, Vol. 11 (No. 1 Hits!) .... Liberty (S) LST-7418 15-25 64
Del Shannon; Gary Lewis & Playboys; Ricky Nelson; Cascades; Kathy Young; Jerry Lee Lewis; Jack Scott; Fats Domino; Ernie Freeman; Maurice Willisms; Cozy Cole.
Original Hits 20 Original Stars, Dynamite .... K-Tel (S) TU 236 5-10 74
Paper Lace; Bachman-Turner Overdrive; Nazareth; William De Vaughn; Eric Clapton; Kool & Gang; Stealers Wheel; Albert Hammond; George McCrae; Elton John; Terry Jacks; Rick Derringer; Peter Noon; DeFranco Family; Lobo; Sister Janet Mead; Love Unlimited Orchestra; Al Wilson; Gladys Knight & Pips; Stylistics.
Original Hits by Original Artists, Vol. 1 .... Guest Star (M) G-1430 10-20 60s
Original Hits by Original Artists, Vol. 1 .... Guest Star (S) GS-1430 10-20 60s
Dave "Baby" Cortez; Neil Sedaka; Collegians; Janie Grant; Angels; Fireflies; Bobbettes; Frank Gari; Chants; Harptones.
Original Hits by Original Artists .... Guest Star (M) G-1432 10-20 60s
Original Hits by Original Artists .... Guest Star (S) GS-1432 10-20 60s
Penguins; Dave "Baby" Cortez; Monarchs; Medallions; Paragons; Inspirations; Willows; Bob Crewe; Eternals; Meadowlarks.
Original Hits of Right Now .... ABC/Dunhill (S) DS-50070 10-12 69
Grass Roots; Three Dog Night; Mama Cass; Robbs; Steppenwolf; Smith; Odetta.
Original Hits Golden Oldies: see Golden Oldies - Original Hits
Original Hootenanny .... Crestview (M) CRV-806 10-20 63
Original Hootenanny .... Crestview (S) CRS-7806 10-20 63
Limeliters; Travelers 3; Theodore Bikel; Ed McCurdy; Will Holt; Judy Collins; Josh White; Bob Gibson; Dillards; Bud & Travis; Judy Henske; Oscar Brand.
Original Hootenanny, Vol. 2 .... Crestview (M) CRV-807 10-20 63
Original Hootenanny, Vol. 2 .... Crestview (S) CRS-7807 10-20 63
(Boxed set.) Bob Gibson; Bob Camp; Josh White; Dian & Greenbriar Boys; Clara Ward Singers; Hoyt Axton; Judy Henske; Theodore Bikel; Limeliters; Glenn Yarbrough; Marilyn Child; Juan Serrano; Erik Darling; Travelers Three.
Original Liverpoole Beat .... 20th Fox (M) TFM-3144 15-25 64
Original Liverpoole Beat .... 20th Fox (S) TFS-4144 20-30 64
Typhoons; Mike Redway; Bobby Stevens; others.
Original Memphis Rock and Roll, Vol. 1 .... Sun/SSS (SE) 116 10-15 70
Carl Perkins; Jerry Lee Lewis; Charlie Rich; Carl McVoy; Warren Smith; Carl Mann; Bill Justis; Roy Orbison; Billy Lee Riley.
Original Million Sellers .... RCA (EP) EPA-5132 5-10 60
Original Million Sellers .... United Artists (M) UAL-3260 15-25 63
Original Million Sellers .... United Artists (S) UAS-6260 25-30 63
Gene Pitney; Exciters; Mike Clifford; Highwaymen; Al Caiola; Ferrante & Teicher; Steve Lawrence; Jimmy Forest; Nathaniel Mayer; Falcons; Clovers. (The Tune Rockers are listed on the front cover, but are not mentioned on the back cover nor are they on the disc.)
Original Motion Picture Themes .... United Artists (M) UAL-3197 10-15 62
Original Motion Picture Themes .... United Artists (S) UAS-6197 15-20 62

(Soundtrack.) Ferrante & Teicher; Al Caiola; Nick Perito; Gene Pitney; Louis Armstrong; Roger Wayne; Ralph Marterie.

Original New York Rock and Roll, Vol. 1 .... SSS Int'l (S) 6 8-12 70

Tradewinds; Ad Libs; Evie Sands; Jelly Beans; Shangri-Las; Alvin Robinson.

Original Nitty Gritty: see Nitty Gritty

Original Old Gold .... Sunset (S) SUS-5274 10-15 60s

Timi Yuro; Exciters; Del Shannon; Little Anthony & Imperials; Clovers; Fleetwoods; Jay & Americans; Sandy Nelson; Dick & Deedee; Fats Domino.

Original Old Gold, Vol. 6 .... ???? 8-12

Percy Sledge; Maurice Williams; Sunny & Sunliners; Joe Barry; Otis Redding; Brenda & Tabulations; Rene & Rene; Peaches & Herb; Mitty Collier; Jimmy Clanton; Wilson Pickett; Dion & Belmonts; Los Bravos; Showmen; Del Shannon; Dovells; Buster Brown; Jay & Techniques; Huey "Piano" Smith.

Original Oldies, Vol 1 .... Springboard (S) SP-2001 10-15 70

Count Five; Cathy Jean; Roommates; Soul Survivors; Johnnie & Joe; Jimmy Charles; Classics; Capris; Music Machine; Chimes.

Original Oldies, Vol 2 .... Springboard (S) SP-2002 10-15 70

Faye Adams; Embers; Harptones; Jesters; Maxine Brown; Brenton Wood; Wilbert Harrison; Gladys Knight & Pips; Collegians.

Original Oldies, Vol 3 .... Springboard (S) SP-2003 10-15 70

Charts; Dave "Baby" Cortez; King Curtis; Gladys Knight & Pips; Paragons; Les Cooper; Baby Washington; Starlights; Brenton Wood.

Original Oldies, Vol 4 .... Springboard (S) SP-2004 10-15 70

Lee Dorsey; Don Gardener & Dee Dee Ford; Bobby Powell; Robert Parker; Elmore James; Buster Brown; Aaron Neville; Tousant McCall.

Original Oldies, Vol 5 .... Springboard (S) SP-2005 10-15 70

Olympics; Bob & Earl; Jackie Lee; Leaves; Forum; Mirettes.

Original Oldies, Vol 6 .... Springboard (S) SP-2006 10-15 70

Don & Juan; Dave "Baby" Cortez; Danleers; Johnny & Hurricanes; Shells; Del Shannon; Rosie & Originals; Classics; Danleers; Patti LaBelle & Blue Belles.

Original Oldies, Vol 7 .... Springboard (S) SP-2007 10-15 70

Ad Libs; Dubs; Ike & Tina Turner; Shangri-Las; Baby Washington; Crests; Jelly Beans; Angels; Five Satins.

Original Oldies, Vol 8 .... Springboard (S) SP-2008 10-15 70

Bobby Lewis; Jack Scott; Lee Andrews & Hearts; Chantels; Embers; Shells; Gladys Knight & Pips; others.

Original Oldies, Vol 9 .... Springboard (S) SP-2009 10-15 70

Crests; Dubs; Duals; Dixie Cups; Janie Grant; Five Satins; Barbara George; Angels; Fireflies; Shangri-Las.

Original Oldies, Vol 10 .... Springboard (S) SP-2010 10-15 70

Gladys Knight & Pips; Buddy Knox; Ike & Tina Turner; others.

Original Oldies, Vol 11 .... Springboard (S) SP-2011 10-15 70

Terry Stafford; Ritchie Valens; Bobby Fuller Four; Dobie Gray; Cascades; John Fred; Beach Boys.

Original Oldies, Vol 12 .... Springboard (S) SP-2012 10-15 70

Spaniels; Dukays; El Dorados; Gene Chandler; Dells; Bobby Day; Gladys Knight & Pips.

Original Oldies, Vol 13 .... Springboard (S) SP-2013 10-15 70

Barbara Lynn; Dells; Patti LaBelle & Blue Belles; Romeros; Paragons; Paradons; Chimes; Ron Holden; Little Caesar & Romans.

Original Oldies, Vol 14 .... Springboard (S) SP-2014 10-15 70

Harptones; Tradewinds; Dixie Cups; Blue Jays; Baby Washington; Wailers; Maxine Brown; Sir Douglas Quintet; Beach Boys.

Original Oldies, Vol 15 .... Springboard (S) SP-2015 10-15 70

Jimmy Reed; Jerry Butler; Dee Clark; Joe Simon; Gene Chandler; Chris Kenner; Jimmy Hughes; Fred Hughes.

Original Oldies, Vol 16 .... Springboard (S) SP-2016 10-15 70

Lloyd Price; Wilson Pickett; Little Richard; Jerry Butler; Gene Allison; Gladys Knight & Pips; Olympics; Baby Washington; Bob & Earl.

Original Oldies, Vol 17 .... Springboard (S) SP-2017 10-15 70

Joe Simon; Gene Chandler; Wade Flemmons; Roscoe Gordon; Betty Everett; Impressions; Dee Clark; Little Richard; Wilson Pickett.

Original Oldies, Vol 18 .... Springboard (S) SPB-2018 10-15 70

Betty Everett; Spaniels; Dee Clark; Harptones; Jerry Butler; Little Richard; Sonny Knight; Flamingos.

Original Oldies, Vol 18 .... Springboard (S) SP-2018 10-15 70

Charts; Rainbows; Velvets; Scarlets; Channels; Kodaks; Teen Chords.

Original Oldies, Vol 19 .... Springboard (S) SP-2019 10-15 70

Trashmen; Shangri-Las; Fendermen; Leaves; Thomas Wayne; Jack Scott; Forum; Jackie Lee.

Original Oldies, Vol 20 .... Springboard (S) SP-2020 10-15 70

Charts; Rainbows; Velvets; Scarlets; Channels; Kodaks; Teen Chords.

Original Oldies, Vol 21 .... Springboard (S) SP-2021 10-15 70

Shangri-Las; Dale & Grace; Brenton Wood; Aaron Neville; Beach Boys; Dells.

Original Oldies, Vol 22 .... Springboard (S) SP-2022 10-15 70

Beach Boys; Turtles; Chad & Jeremy; Del Shannon; Lloyd Price; Jimmy Clanton; Tradewinds.

Original Oldies, Vol 23 .... Springboard (S) SP-2023 10-15 70

Turtles; Lloyd Price Chad & Jeremy; Dixie Cups; Jimmy Clanton; Kathy Young.

Original Oldies, Vol 24 .... Springboard (S) SP-2024 10-15 70

Dion & Belmonts; Mystics; Chiffons; Happenings; Volumes; Randy & Rainbows; Dovells; Gerry & Pacemakers.

Original Oldies, Vol 25 .... Springboard (S) SP-2025 10-15 70

Sam Cooke; Percy Sledge; Gerry & Pacemakers; J. Frank Wilson; Chiffons; Capitols; Dion.

Original Recordings (By the Artists Who Made Them Hits) .... Flip (M) 1002 30-50 62

Richard Berry; Jennell Hawkins; Elgins; Donald Woods; Six Teens; Lena Calhoun.

Original Rhythm & Blues Hits, Vol. 1 .... Liberty (M) LRP-3381 20-25 64

Majors; Fats Domino; Lloyd Price; Rivingtons; Don & Juan; Trashmen; Bobby Day; Lonnie Mack; Larry Williams; Billy Ward & Dominoes; Jessie Hill; Wilson Pickett.

Original Rhythm & Blues Hits by Rhythm & Blues Stars .... RCA Camden (M) CAL-740 15-25 63

Arthur "Big Boy" Crudup; Four Clefs; Big Maceo; Jazz Gillum; Arbee Stidham; Sonny Boy Williamson; Mickey & Sylvia; Lil Green; Tampa Red; Washboard Sam.

Original Rock and Roll .... Power Pak (S) PO-251 5-10 70s

Carl Perkins; Thomas Wayne; Jimmy Clanton; Charlie Rich; Roy Orbison; Dixie Cups; Shangri-Las; Ad Libs; Frankie Ford.

Original Rock and Roll, Vol. 2 .... Power Pak/Gusto (S) PO-294 5-10 76

Bill Doggett; Hank Ballard & Midnighters; Boyd Bennett; Otis Williams; Bobby Lewis; Little Willie John; Platters; Five Royales; Coasters.

Original Rock and Roll Show - Live Recording at the Academy of Music Theatre .... Goldisc (S) GS2-5001 10-15 70

Alan Freed; Danny & Juniors; Harptones; Don & Juan; Del-Vikings; Monotones; Bobbettes; Mystics; Cadillacs; Passions; Dubs; Cleftones; Sonny Til & Orioles; Skyliners.

Original Rock Oldies, Vol. 1 .... Specialty (S) SPS-2129 10-15 70

Little Richard; Larry Williams; Lloyd Price; Monotones; Sam Cooke; Johnnie & Joe; Arthur Lee Maye & Crowns; Tony Allen & Champs; Don & Dewey; Chimes.

Original Rock Oldies, Vol. 2 .... Specialty (S) SPS-2130 10-15 70

Little Richard; Larry Williams; Lloyd Price; Sam Cooke; Tony Allen & Champs; Don & Dewey; Tommy Tucker; Clifton Chenier; Johnny Fuller; Chimes.

Original Rock 'N' Roll Hits of the '50s, Vol. 1 .... Roulette (S) SR 59001 5-10 82

Danny & Juniors; Flamingos; Chuck Berry; Tune Weavers; Maurice Williams; Cleftones; Frankie Lymon & Teenagers; Crows; Elegants; Little Anthony & Imperials; Chantels.

Original Rock 'N' Roll Hits of the '50s, Vol. 2 .... Roulette (S) SR 59002 5-10 82

Jimmie Rodgers; Jimmy Bowen; Chuck Berry; Royal Teens; Flamingos; Brian Hyland; Buddy Knox; Barry Mann; Joe Bennett; Lee Allen; Della Reese.

Original Rock 'N' Roll Hits of the '50s, Vol. 3 .... Roulette (S) SR 59003 5-10 82

Chuck Berry; Frankie Lymon; Moonglows; Bobby Freeman; Pastels; Etta James; Bo Diddley; Lloyd Price; Monotones; Cadets; Jesse Belvin.

Original Rock 'N' Roll Hits of the '50s, Vol. 4 .... Roulette (S) SR 59004 5-10 82

Sonny Til & Orioles; Cadillacs; Silhouettes; Cleftones; Fiestas; Royal Tones; Danny & Juniors; Chuck Berry; Harptones; Jacks; Heartbeats.

Original Rock 'N' Roll Hits of the '50s, Vol. 5 .... Roulette (S) SR 59005 5-10 82

Jimmie Rodgers; Ronnie Hawkins; Frankie Lymon; Wilbert Harrison; Moonglows; George Hamilton IV: Lloyd Price; Chuck Berry; Harptones; Moe Koffman Septette; Paragons.

Original Rock 'N' Roll Hits of the '50s, Vol. 6 .... Roulette (S) SR 59006 5-10 82

Chuck Berry; Five Satins; Dubs; Shep & Limelites; Frankie Lymon & Teenagers; Harptones; Flamingos; Moonglows; Ruth McFadden; Heartbeats; Chantels.

Original Rock 'N' Roll Hits of the '50s, Vol. 7 .... Roulette (S) SR 59007 5-10 82

Moonglows; Ronnie Hawkins; Orioles; Chantels; Valentines; Chuck Berry; Jimmie Rodgers; Playmates; Nutmegs; Channels; Lloyd Price.

Original Rock 'N' Roll Hits of the '50s, Vol. 8 .... Roulette (S) SR 59008 5-10 82

Jimmie Rodgers; Five Satins; Vibrations; Eddie Cooley; Dubs; Lloyd Price; Moonglows; Edsels; Nutmegs; Pastels; Chantels.

Original Rock 'N' Roll Hits of the '50s, Vol. 9 .... Roulette (S) SR 59009 5-10 82

Little Anthony & Imperials; Turbans; Heartbeats; Devotions; Valentines; Tiny Tim & Hits; Lee Andrews & Hearts; Frankie Lymon; Harptones; Cadillacs; Chantels.

Original Rock 'N' Roll Hits of the '50s, Vol. 10 .... Roulette (S) SR 59010 5-10 82

Jimmie Rodgers; Flamingos; Cadillacs; Little Anthony & Imperials; Channels; Heartbeats; Joey Dee & Starliters; Moonglows; Harptones; Chantels; Dubs.

Original Rock 'N' Roll Hits of the '60s, Vol. 11 .... Roulette (S) SR 59011 5-10 82

Shirelles; Chuck Jackson; Chuck Berry; B.J. Thomas; Impressions; Capris; Dionne Warwick; Lloyd Price; Tommy James & Shondells; Little Milton; Tommy Roe.

Original Rock 'N' Roll Hits of the '60s, Vol. 12 .... Roulette (S) SR 59012 5-10 82

Shirelles; Dionne Warwick; Billy Bland; Cleftones; Tommy James & Shondells; Tommy Roe; B.J. Thomas; Kingsmen; Regents; Mamas & Papas; Impressions.

Original Rock 'N' Roll Hits of the '60s, Vol. 13 .... Roulette (S) SR 59013 5-10 82

Kingsmen; Shirelles; Chuck Berry; Dionne Warwick; Impressions; Earls; Tommy Roe; Tommy James & Shondells; Joey Dee & Starliters; Essex; Lou Chrisite.

Original Rock 'N' Roll Hits of the '60s, Vol. 14 .... Roulette (S) SR 59014 5-10 82

Shirelles; Marcels; Dionne Warwick; Tommy Roe; Impressions; Ral Donner; Tommy James & Shondells; Cookies; B.J. Thomas; Joey Dee & Starliters.

Original Rock 'N' Roll Hits of the '60s, Vol. 15 .... Roulette (S) SR 59015 5-10 82

Tommy James & Shondells; Lou Christie; Little Eva; Ral Donner; Tommy Roe; Tams; Shirelles; Mitch Ryder & Detroit Wheels; Mamas & Papas; Impressions; Joe Jones.

Original Rock 'N' Roll Hits of the '60s, Vol. 16 .... Roulette (S) SR 59016 5-10 82

Mamas & Papas; Dionne Warwick; Tommy James & Shondells; Steppenwolf; Grass Roots; Shirelles; Mitch Ryder; Tommy Roe; Okaysions; Impressions; Cookies.

Original Skeets McDonald's *Tattooed Lady* Plus 11 Other Sizzlers .... Fortune (M) 3001 10-20 61

Skeets McDonald; York Brothers; Roy Hall; Rufus Shoffner; Boots Gilbert; Johnny Bucket; Tommy Odim.

Original Solid Gold Hits, Vol. 2 .... MCP (S) MCP 8001 8-12

Harptones; Willows; Tokens; Rocketones; Spaniels; Frankie Lymon & Teenagers; Angels; Buddy Knox; Three Friends; Fireflies.

Original Soundtracks and Music from the Great Motion Pictures .... United Artists (M) UAL-3303 15-20 63

Original Soundtracks and Music from the Great Motion Pictures .... United Artists (S) UAS-6303 15-20 63

(Soundtrack.) Leroy Holmes; Riz Ortolani; Ferrante & Teicher; Hollywood Sound Stage Orchestra; Manos Hadjidakis; Franz Waxman; Andre Previn; Mikis Theodorakis; Elmer Bernstein; Carlo Rustichelli.

Original Soundtracks and Other Music from Great Movies (2 LP) .... MGM (S) 2E-10 20-25 64

Original Soundtracks and Other Music from Great Movies (2 LP) .... MGM (S) 2SE-10 35-40 64

(Soundtrack.) Alfred Newman; David Rose; Robert Armbruster; Carlo Savina; Miklos Rozsa; Cyril Ornadel; Hans Sommer.

Original Stars - Original Hits .... K-Tel (S) TU 2530 5-10 77

10cc; Hall & Oates; Al Stewart; Mary MacGregor; Dr. Hook; Yvonne Elliman; Atlanta Rhythm Section; Cliff Richard; Addrisi Brothers; KC & Sunshine Band; Tavares; Thelma Houston; Stanky Brown Group; War; Quincy Jones; Kiss; William Bell; Climax Blues Band.

Original Stars Sing the Greatest Oldie Hits .... Diplomat (M) D-2312 8-12 60s

Original Stars Sing the Greatest Oldie Hits .... Diplomat (S) DS-2312 8-12 60s

Sheppard Sisters; Tokens; Eternals; Paragons; Jesters; Harptones; Monarchs; Inspirations; Hollywood Argyles; Angels.

Original Supercharged Rock & Roll Hits .... Pickwick (S) SPC-3316 5-10 71

Dixie Cups; Jelly Beans; Carl Perkins; Shangri-Las; Jerry Lee Lewis; Bill Justis; Ad Libs.

Original Surfin' Hits .... GNP/Crescendo (M) GNP-84 20-25 63

Original Surfin' Hits .... GNP/Crescendo (S) GNPS-84 25-35 63

(Includes bonus surfing photos.) Sentinals; Rhythm Kings; Soul Kings; Jim Waller & Deltas; Bob Vaught & Renegaids; Breakers; Dave Myers & Surftones.

Original *Theme from A Summer Place* and Other Great Hits from the Movies: see Hits from the Movies

Original Toga Party (2 LP)....Adam VIII (S) A-8053 8-12 79
Isley Brothers; Sam Cooke; Billy Bland; Dovells; Paul & Paula; Barrett Strong; Regents; Little Eva; Orlons; Jimmy Jones; Chris Montez; Kingsmen; Bobby Lewis; Joey Dee & Starliters; Bobby Freeman; Lee Dorsey; Jimmy Charles; Chips; Tommy James & Shondells; Little Anthony & Imperials; Essex; Flamingos; Royal Teens.

Original Top Hits by the Hit Makers....Columbia (M) CL-1485 15-25 60
Original Top Hits by the Hit Makers....Columbia (S) CS-8276 20-30 60
Tony Bennett; Marty Robbins; Johnny Mathis; Kitty Kallen; Percy Faith; Doris Day; Johnny Horton; Brothers Four; Mitch Miller; Jerry Vale; Frank Ve Vol; Ray Bryant.

Original Torch Singers....Take Two TT 207 5-10 80
Fanny Brice; Libby Holman; Ruth Etting; Helen Morgan.

Our Best to You....Capitol (M) T-1801 15-25 62
Our Best to You....Capitol (S) ST-1801 20-25 62
Kay Starr; Tex Williams; Tex Ritter; others.

Our Best to You....Columbia (S) ABS-2 5-10 67
Tony Bennett; Ray Conniff; John Davidson; Percy Faith; Robert Goulet; Andre Kostelanetz; Jim Nabors; Barbra Streisand; Jerry Vale; Andy Williams.

Our Best to You....Columbia (S) TBS-2 10-20 67
Buckinghams; Byrds; Cryan' Shames; Aretha Franklin; Moby Grape; Paul Revere & Raiders; Peaches & Herb; Simon & Garfunkel; Tremeloes; Yardbirds.

Our Significant Hits: see COOKE, Sam / Lloyd Price / Larry Williams / Little Richard

Out Came the Blues....Decca (M) DL-4434 15-25 63
Lightnin' Hopkins; Big Joe Turner; Trixie Smith; Sleepy John Estes; Cousin Joe; Kokomo Arnold; Gerogia White; Peetie Wheatstraw; Scrapper Blackwell; Rosetta Crawford; Johnnie Temple; Memphis Minnie; Red Nelson; Oscar Woods.

Out of Bounds....I.R.S. (S) 6180 8-10 86
(Soundtrack.) Stewart Copeland; Adam Ant; Cult; Siouxsie & Banshees; Intimate Strangers; Belinda Carlisle; Night Ranger; Tommy Keene; American Girls; Lords of the New Church.

Out of Sight....K-Tel (S) TU-2390 5-10 75
Elton John; Kiki Dee; Reunion; First Class; Paper Lace; Fancy; Kool & Gang; Tymes; Gladys Knight & Pips; Carl Douglas; Bachman-Turner Overdrive; Stealers Wheel; Prelude; Hudson Brothers; Stylistics; Jim Weatherly; DeFranco Family; Brownsville Station; Hues Corporation; Disco Tex & Sex-O-Lettes.

Out of Sight....Design (M) DLP-269 10-20 67
Paul Revere & Raiders; Joe Tex; Vic Dana; J. Brothers; Lou Rawls; Hi-Lifes; Lou Christie; Liberty Men; Tommy Roe; Beachnuts (features Lou Reed).

Out of Sight....Decca (M) DL-4751 12-18 66
Out of Sight....Decca (SE) DL-74751 15-20 66
(Soundtrack.) Gary Lewis & Playboys; Astronauts; Turtles; Freddie & Dreamers; Dobie Gray; Knickerbockers; J. Brothers; Liberty Men; Joe Tex; Lou Christie; Lou Rawls; Vic Dana; Tommy Roe; Hi-Lifes; Beachnuts.

Out of the Storm....Verve (M) 8663 10-15 66
Out of the Storm....Verve (S) 8663 10-15 66
Ed Thigpen; Kenny Burrell; Clark Terry; others.

Outta' Sight!....Capitol/Creative Products (S) SL-6554 8-12 67
Stone Poneys; Standells; Human Beinz; Davie Allan; Peter & Gordon; Glen Campbell; Sounds of Our Times.

Over the Edge....Warner Bros. (S) BSK-3335 8-10 79
(Soundtrack.) Cheap Trick; Cars; Van Halen; Jimi Hendrix; Ramones; Little Feat; Valerie Carter.

Over the Top....Columbia (S) SC-40655 8-10 87
(Soundtrack.) Sammy Hagar; Robin Zander; Larry Greene; Big Trouble; Frank Stallone; Kenny Loggins; Asia; Giorgio Moroder; Eddie Money.

Package of 16 Big Hits: see 16 Original Big Hits

Packed in Surf....Columbia (S) P-16140 10-15 81
(Boomer World Team Surfing Promo.) Beach Boys; Surfaris; Chantays; Jan & Dean; Trashmen; Rivieras; Paul Gilman Band.

Pajama Party....Roulette (M) R-25021 50-75 58
Valentines; Cleftones; Heartbeats; Frankie Lymon & Teenagers; Jimmy Wright.

Pajama Party....Forum (M) 9006 25-35
Pajama Party....Forum (S) SF 9006 25-35
Valentines; Cleftones; Heartbeats; Frankie Lymon & Teenagers; Jimmy Wright.

Panassie Sessions....RCA (M) LPV-542 10-15 67
Tommy Ladnier; Milton Mezzrow; others.

Papa Was a Preacher....Word (S) 7-01-900210-2 8-10 84
(Soundtrack.) Mac Frampton; Sandi Patti; Porter Kids; Robert Pine with Brandon Sokolosky & Choir.

Paper Moon....Paramount (S) PAS-1012 8-10 73
(Soundtrack.) Paul Whiteman; Ozzie Nelson; Leo Reisman; Dick Powell; Bing Crosby; Jimmy Grier; Victor Young; Boswell Sisters; Hoagy Carmichael; Blue Sky Boys; Jimmie Davis; Tommy Dorsey; Enric Madriguera's Hotel Biltmore Orchestra; Johnny Hamp's Kentucky Serenaiders.

Paper Roses....Camden (S) ACLI-0533 5-10 74
Bobby Bare; Al Caiola; Connie Smith; Dottie West; others.

Parade of Hits....MGM (M) E-4078 15-20 62
Parade of Hits....MGM (S) SE-4078 20-25 62
(Soundtrack.) Richard Chamberlain; David Rose; Leroy Holmes; Starlight Symphony; Benton Ames; Andre Previn; Conway Twitty; Wanderers; Elmer Bernstein; Sheb Wooley; Jaye P. Morgan; Sue Lyon.

Parade of Show Stoppers....Columbia Special Products (S) CSP-237 10-15 60s
(Soundtrack.) Barbra Streisand; Ray Conniff; Robert Goulet; Eydie Gorme; Julie Andrews; Vic Damone; Kirby Stone Four; Tony Bennett; Jerry Vale; Percy Faith; Johnny Mathis; Andre Kostelanetz.

Parade of Stars....MGM (M) NP-90569 10-15 65
Parade of Stars....MGM (S) SNP-90569 10-20 65
(Capitol Record Club issue.) Connie Francis; Herman's Hermits; Roy Orbison; Sam the Sham & Pharaohs; Richard Chamberlain; Hank Williams; Johnny Tillotson; Animals; Katyna Raniera; David Rose; Osmond Brothers; Maurice Chevalier.

Parade of Stars....Columbia Special Products (EP) CSP-223 ?? 60s
(Promotional EP w/cardboard picture sleeve for 5th Avenue candy bar.) Dave Clark Five; Bobby Vinton; New Christy Minstrels; Jerry Vale.

Parrot Doowop....Parrot (M) 2120 10-15
Pelicans; Five Arrows; Swans; Fortunes; Clouds; Earls; Rocketts.

Party After Hours: see MILBURN, Amos / Wynonie Harris / Velma Nelson / Crown Prince Waterford

Party Favorites .... Tops (M) L1526 10-15 50s
Buzz Adlam; Henry King; Bob Hayward & Mellotones; Ella Logan; Jeannie McKeon; Jan Garber; Wilbert Baranco; Jack McVea; Gerald Wilson; Sammy Franklin & Atomics.

Party Party....A&M (S) SP-3212 8-12 82
(Soundtrack.) Elvis Costello & Attractions; Dave Edmunds; Altered Images; Bad Manners; Sting; Bananarama; Madness; Modern Romance; Pauline Black; Midge Ure; Chas & Dave.

Party Rock....Lotus (S) BU 5770 5-10
Bobby Freeman; Angels; Little Richard; Sam the Sham & Pharaohs; Bobby Rydell; Sandy Nelson; Freddie Cannon; Lloyd Price; Leslie Gore; Danny & Juniors; Crystals; Guess Who; Johnny & Hurricanes; Dovells; Diamonds; Chiffons.

Party Time Fifties....Warner/JCI (S) 3201 5-10 85
Wanda Jackson; Crickets; Everly Brothers; Dion & Belmonts; Bobby Darin; Little Richard; Bill Haley & His Comets; Freddy Cannon; Fiestas; Chuck Berry; Diamonds; Danny & Juniors.

Patty .... Stang (S) 1027 15-20 76
(Soundtrack.) Moments; Rimshots; Retta Young; Chuck Jackson.

Paul Simon Plus....MCP (S) 8027 15-25
Jerry Landis (Paul Simon); Tony Orlando; Neil Sedaka; Johnny Rivers; 4 Seasons.

Pause That Refreshes....RCA (EP) CEP 6144 8-12
Eddie Fisher; others.

Peace on Earth (2 LP).... Capitol (S) STBB-585 8-12 70
Frank Sinatra; Nat King Cole; Ella Fitzgerald; Lettermen; Glen Campbell; others.

Peaches Pick of the Crop (2 LP) ....Capricorn (S) PRO 588 10-15 74
Richard Betts; Wet Willie; Elvin Bishop; Johnny Darrell; Percy Sledge; Maxayn; Marshall Tucker Band; Cowboy with Boyer & Talton; Johnny Jenkins; Allman Brothers Band; Bobby Thompson; Captain Beyond; Gregg Allman; Larry Henley; Grinder Switch; James Montgomery Band; Arthur Conley; White Witch; Hydra; Duke Williams & Extremes; Kenny O'dell; Kitty Wells; Chris Christian; Duane Allman.

Pebbles .... BFD (M) 5016 8-12 79
Litter; Preachers; Floyd Dakil Combo; Outcasts; Squires; Grains of Sand; Ju Ju's; Haunted; Soupgreens; Wig; Positively 13 O'Clock; Kim Fowley; Elastik Band; Split Ends; Shadows of Knight; Wild Knights.

Pebbles, Vol. 2 .... BFD (M) 5019 8-12 79
Satans; Moving Sidewalks; Sons of Adam; Road; Lyrics; Buddahs; Zackary Thaks; Randy Alvey & Green Fuz; Squires; Little Boy Blues; Dovers; Phil & Frantics; Choir; Bobby Fuller Four; Litter.

Peggy Sue Got Married....Varese Sarabande (S) STV 81295 10-15 86

Peggy Sue Got Married ....That's Entertainment(S) TER-1126 8-10 80s
(Soundtrack.) John Barry; Buddy Holly; Dion & Belmonts; Marshall Crenshaw Band; Nicholas Cage with Pride & Joy.

Penitentiary 3 .... RCA (S) 6663-1 8-10 87
(Soundtrack.) Freda Payne; Lenny Williams; Yarbrough & Peoples; La Rue; Rodney Franklin; Midnight Star; Gap Band; New Choice; Shawnie G.; Lotti Dotti; James Reese; Diabolical.

Pennies from Heaven (2 LP) ....Warner Bros. (S) 2-HW-3639 8-12 81
(Soundtrack.) Elsie Carlisle; Sam Browne; Connie Boswell; Fred Latham; Bing Crosby; Arthur Tracy; Boswell Sisters; Ida Sue McCune; Rudy Vallee; Dolly Dawn; George Hall; Helen Kane; Walt Harrah; Gene Merlino; Vern Rowe; Robert Tebow; Irving Aaronson; Ronnie Hill.

People Got to Be Free....Four Most (S) FM 7230 CS 10-15 72
Steve & Maria; Random Sample; Soul Concern; Under New Management; Master Switch; Young & Free; Finis Fator; New World; Trust Company.

People's Choice of the Greatest Talent....Camden (M) CAL-946 5-10 66

People's Choice of the Greatest Talent....Camden (S) CAS-946 5-10 66
John Gary; Peter Nero; Kitty Kallen; Chet Atkins; Lorne Greene; Eddy Arnold; Charlie Rich; Sammy Kaye; Don Cornell; Della Reese.

Peppermint Twist - the Twisters ....Crown (S) 5249 10-20 60s
Twisters; B.B. King; Marvin & Johnny; Young Jessie; Roscoe Gordon; Shirley Gunter; Flairs; Dreamers; Joe Houston; Jimmy Witherspoon.

Percussion and Brass ....Grand Award (S) GA 255 10-15 60
Grand Award All Stars; Doc Severinson; Mel Davis; Bernie Glow; Bobby Bryne; Nick Hixon; Ezell Watson; Stanley Webb; Bob Haggart; Artie Narotti; Willie Rodriguez; Cliff Leeman; Don Lamond; Phil Bodner; Al Cassamenti; Sol Gubin; Dominic Cortesi.

Percussion on Parade....United Artists (S) WWS-8515 8-12
Ferrante & Teicher; Terry Snyder; Eydie Gorme; Steve Lawrence; Don Costa; Sauter & Finegan; Ralph Marterie; Al Caiola; Nick Perito; Tito Rodriguez.

Perfect....Arista (S) AL6-8278 8-10 85
(Soundtrack.) Jermaine Jackson; Pointer Sisters; Thompson Twins; Wham; Berlin; Jermaine Stewart; Dan Hartman; Nona Hendrix; Lou Reed; Whitney Houston.

Perfect for Dancing – Sambas (2 EP) ....RCA (EP) EPB-1073 10-20 56
Fafa Lemos; Patricia Teixeira; Jose Curbelo; Zaccarias; Noro Morales.

Perfect for Dancing Jitterbug or Lindy....RCA (M) LPM 1071 10-15
Erskine Hawkins; Glenn Miller; Artie Shaw; Boots Brown & His Blockbusters; Ralph Flanagan; Ray McKinley; Tommy Dorsey.

Perfect for Dancing Sampler .... RCA (EP) SPA-7-12 8-12 55
Tito Rodriguez; Henri Rene; Ralph Flanagan; Three Suns; Gene Krupa; others.

Perfect for Parties Highlight Album .... RCA (EP) SPA-7-37 80-120 56
(Promotional, mail order offer. Includes paper cover.) Elvis Presley; Tony Cabot; Tito Puente; Tony Scott; Three Suns; Dave Pell.

Performance....Warner Bros. (S) BS-1846 25-30 70

Performance....Warner Bros. (S) BS-2554 12-18 70
(Soundtrack.) Randy Newman; Mick Jagger; Buffy Sainte-Marie; Merry Clayton; Merry Clayton Singers; Last Poets.

Permanent Record .... Epic (S) SE 40879 8-10 88
(Soundtrack.) Lou Reed; Joe Strummer & Latino Rockabilly War; Godfathers; Bodeans; J.D. Souther; Stranglers.

Permanent Wave .... Epic (S) JE-36136 5-10 79
(Promotional issue only.) Vibrators; Only Ones; Masterswitch; Spikes; After the Fire; Kurssaal Flyers; New Hearts; Diodes.

Personalities....Hamilton (M) 140 15-25 65

Personalities....Hamilton (S) 12140 15-25 65
Debbie Reynolds; Louis Prima; Gene Austin; Eddie Albert; Walter Brennan; Marlene Dietrich; Tab Hunter; Tony Martin; Sophia Loren; Mills Brothers; Vaughn Monroe; Margaret Whiting.
Petal Pushers....Chess (M) LP-1520 15-20 68
Petal Pushers....Chess (S) LPS-1520 15-20 68
Bystanders; Sounds Around; Pennsylvania Sixpence; Ali Ben Dhown; Pinkerton;s Colours; Traffic Jam; Tony Crane.
Peter Drake Show.... Stop (S) 10011 8-10 69
Phil Marks Originals: see Roots, the Rock and Roll Sound of Louisiana and Mississippi
Phil Spector - the Early Productions 1958-1961....Rhino (M) RNDF 203 8-12 83
Teddy Bears; Curtis Lee; Ducanes; Kell Osborne; Spectors Three; Gene Pitney; Paris Sisters.
Phil Spector Spectacular....Philles (M) 100 5000-7500 60s
(Promotional issue only.) With letter signed by Phil Spector.
Phil Spector Spectacular....Philles (M) 100 4000-6000 60s
(Promotional issue only.) Without letter from Phil Spector.
Phil Spector's Christmas Album: see RONETTES / Crystals / Darlene Love / Bob B. Soxx & Blue Jeans
Phil Spector's Greatest Hits (2 LP)....Warner/Spector (S) 2SP-9104 25-35 77
Ronettes; Crystals; Righteous Brothers; Bob B. Soxx & Blue Jeans; Darlene Love; Teddy Bears; Curtis Lee; Paris Sisters; Gene Pitney; Ben E. King; Ike & Tina Turner; Sonny Charles & Checkmates Ltd.
Phil Spector's Top Twenty, Echoes of the '60s....Spector (S) SPS 2307-013 10-15
Philadelphia Classics (2 LPs)....International P2G (S) 34940/42 8-12 77
MFSB; TSOP; Three Degrees; O'Jays; Harold Melvin & Blue Notes; Intruders.
Philadelphia Int'l All-Stars....Philadelphia Int'l (S) JZ-24659 5-10 77
Lou Rawls; Billy Paul; Archie Bell; Teddy Pendergrass; O'Jays; Dee Dee Sharp Gamble; Three Degrees; Intruders; Harold Melvin & Blue Notes.
Philco Invites You to a Stereo Party....Columbia Custom (S) No Number Used 10-15
Percy Faith; Michel Legrand; Jerry Vale; Four Lads; Percussion Goes Dixieland; Andre Previn; Xavier Cugat; Mahalia Jackson; Ray Conniff; Buddy Greco; Diana Trask; Miles Davis.
Philips Dealer Demonstration Disc.... Philips (S) 5 10-20 '60s
(Promotional issue only.) H.P. Lovecraft; Hello People; Blue Cheer; others.
Philip Morris Country Music Show....Columbia (M) CL 1048 8-12
Biff Collie; Carl Smith; Ronnie Self; Shirley Caddell; George Morgan; Goldie Hill; Little Jimmy Dickens; Red Sovine; Mimi Roman; Tunesmiths.
Philip Morris Derby Festival Show: see Kentucky Derby Day
Photoplay Picks the Great Love Themes from Hollywood....Warner Bros. (S) WS 1368 15-25 60
Muir Mathieson; George Greeley; John Scott Trotter; Outriggers; Warren Barker; Buddy Cole; Raoul Maynard; Ray Heindorf.
Piano Greats.... Rondo R (M) 2017 10-15 50s
Piano Greats.... Rondo RS (S) 2017 10-15 50s
Buddy Cole; Teddy Wilson; Joe Bushkin; Mary Lou Williams; Hank Jones; Earl "Fatha" Hines.
Piano Variations....King (M) 395-540 50-75 57
Erroll Garner; Jimmy McPartland; Mary Lou Williams.
Pick Hits of the Radio Good Guys, Vol. 1....Laurie (M) LP-2021 15-20 63
Pick Hits of the Radio Good Guys, Vol. 1....Laurie (S) SLP-2021 15-20 63
Chiffons; Dion; Tokens; Gary "U.S." Bonds; Randy & Rainbows; Mystics; Passions; Demensions; Jarmels.
Pick Hits of the Radio Good Guys, Vol. 2....Laurie (S) SLP-2026 15-20 64
Chiffons; Bernadette Carroll; Dean & Jean; Dion & Belmonts; Bobby Goldsboro; Gary "U.S." Bonds; Cathy Carr; Mustangs; Kenny Chandler.
Pick of the Country....RCA (EP) EPA-5155 5-10 60
Browns; Don Gibson; Porter Wagoner; Davis Sisters.
Pick of the Country.... RCA (M) LPM-2094 15-25 60
Pick of the Country.... RCA (S) LSP-2094 20-30 60
Jim Reeves; Stuart Hamblen; Maxine & Bonnie Brown; Don Gibson; Porter Wagoner; Davis Sisters; Hank Snow; Browns; Eddy Arnold; Hank Locklin; Pee Wee King; Johnnie & Jack; Jimmie Rodgers.
Pick of the Country, Vol. 2.... RCA (M) LPM-2956 10-20 65
Pick of the Country, Vol. 2.... RCA (S) LSP-2956 15-20 65
Eddy Arnold; Jim Reeves; George Hamilton IV; Porter Wagoner; Darrell Glenn; Johnnie & Jack; Skeeter Davis; Hank Snow; Homer & Jethro; Don Gibson; Hank Locklin; Kitty Wells.
Pick of the Crop - Peaches, Vol. 2 (2 LP)....Capricorn (S) PRO 605 10-15 75
Pink Cadillac.... Warner Bros. (S) 1-25922 8-10 89
(Soundtrack.) Michael Martin Murphey; Hank Williams Jr.; Hank Williams Sr.; Jill Hollier; Randy Travis; Southern Pacific; J.C. Crowley; Billy Hill; Dion; Robben Ford.
Pioneers of the Jazz Guitar....Yazoo (M) L-1057 8-10
Lonnie Johnson; Eddie Lang; Dick McDonough; Carl Kress; Nick Lucas; John Cali; Tony Guttuso.
Pirate Movie (2 LP).... Polydor (S) PD-2-9503 8-10 82
(Soundtrack.) Christopher Atkins; Brain Robertson; Pirates & Mike Brady; Kristy McNichol; Ian Mason; Kool & Gang; Peter Cupples Band; Peter Sullivan; Ted Hamilton; Bill Kerr; Gary McDonald & Policemen; The Sisters.
Pitchin' Boogie....Milestone (M) 2018 8-10 72
Meade Lux Lewis; Roosevelt Sykes; Jimmy Blythe; Will Ezell; others.
Pittman Family of Music / Our First 20 Years....CBS (S) AS-15663 15-25 80
(Promotional only issue.) Paul McCartney; others.
Pittsburgh Rocks: see WDVE Pittsburgh Rocks
Pittsburgh's Golden Oldies, Vol. 1....Astra (S) ASLP-1002 15-20
(Colored vinyl.) Wardell & Sultans; Blossoms; Lee Maye; Sparkletones; Fire Balls; Innocents; Marshall & Chi-Lites; Ray Allen & Upbeats; Ray Ethier; Dramatics; Challengers; Jimmy Hanna; Four Dots.
Pittsburgh's Greatest Hits (2 LP)....Itzy (M) ITZY-101 40-60 66
(Gatefold cover.)

Pittsburgh's Greatest Hits (2 LP) .... Itzy (M) ITZ-497/498 10-15 86
(Standard cover.) Romancers; Del Rios; Vows; Donald Jenkins; Blue Sonnets; Starglows; Empires; Burce Clark & Q's; Egyptian Kings; Jimmy & Wayne; Sheppards; Jewels; Charades; Four Evers; Splendors; Royal Jesters; Baby Huey; Premiers; Belltones; Tom & Jerrio; Executioners; Little Ike; King Rock; Lord Rockingham's XI; Mickey Lee Lane; Arondies; Bobby Comstock; Big Bo; Chuck Edwards; John Hammond; Silvertones; Triumphs. (Labeled a "20th Anniversary issue.")

Pittsburgh's Hall of Fame (Don Bombard Presents) .... Sunday Night (S) 100 10-15
Billy Guy; Stereos; Delcos; Teddy & Continentals; Roy Byrd & Blues Jumpers; Thunderbirds; Josh White Jr.; Bruce Clark & Q's; Henrietta; Untouchables; Sultans; Contrails; Luvs.

Planes, Trains and Automobiles .... Hughes/MCA (S) MCA-6223 8-10 88
(Soundtrack.) Dream Academy; Steve Earle & Dukes; Dave Edmunds; Emmylou Harris; Silicon Teens; Stars of Heaven; E.T.A. (Steve Martin & John Candy); Westworld; Balaam & Angel.

Platoon (And Songs from the Era) .... Atlantic (S) 81742-1 8-10 87
(Soundtrack.) Georges Delerue; Vancouver Symphony Orchestra; Smokey Robinson; Merle Haggard; Doors; Jefferson Airplane; Aretha Franklin; Otis Redding; Percy Sledge; Rascals.

Play It Again .... Commonwealth/K-Tel (S) NU 9290 5-10 77
Gary Lewis & Playboys; Rosie & Originals; Box Tops; Larry Finnegan; Exciters; Dovells; Capris; Eddie Hodges; Marcels; Chiffons; Jack Scott; Crystals; Little Anthony & Imperials; Bobby Lewis; Jimmy Clanton; Billy Bland; Crystals; Chubby Checker; Fiestas; Lou Christie; Dorsey Burnette; Bobby Vee; Buddy Knox; Jimmie Rodgers; Sandy Posey.

Play It Loud .... Arista (S) ABM-2002 5-10 82
Lovin' Spoonful; Syndicate of Sound; Jaggerz; Sweet; Monkees; Box Tops; Stories; Dwight Twilley Band; Bay City Rollers; Ramrods.

Play Musical Christmas Gifts .... Epic (M) 2SB 116472 90-100
(33 1/3 single. Promotional only. About 40 seconds per song.) Dave Clark Five; Yardbirds; Nancy Ames; Buddy Hackett; Jane Morgan; Eddie Layton; Bobby Vinton; Enzo Stuarti; David Houston; Luis Bonfa; Walter Jackson; Mike Douglas; Doodletown Pipers; Buddy Greco; Glenn Miller; Lester Lanin.

Play the Blues .... Atco (S) 33-3-64 8-12
Eric Clapton; others.

Playboy Country .... Playboy (S) PB 129 8-12
Mickey Gilley; Barbi Benton; Mike Wells; Wynn Stewart; Brenda Pepper; Boby Borchers; Chuck Price.

Playboy Jazz Allstars .... PB (M) 1957 20-35 58
(Winners of 1957 Playboy Jazz Poll.) J.J. Johnson; Ella Fitzgerald; Dizzy Gillespie; Bud Shank; Barney Kessell; Stan Kenton; Shorty Rogers; Stan Getz; Kai Winding, others.

Playboy Jazz Festival (2 LP) .... Elektra/Musician (S) E1-60298 8-12 84
Pieces of a Dream; Grover Washington Jr.; Dexter Gordon Group; Weather Report; Manhattan Transfer; Art Farmer, Bennie Golson; Nancy Wilson Trio; Great Quartet.

Playboy Music Hall of Fame Winners (3 LP) .... Playboy (S) PB-7473 100-200 78
(Mail order offer.) Elvis Presley; Beatles; Frank Sinatra; Count Basie; Ray Charles; Shelly Manne; Louis Armstrong; Dave Brubeck; Duke Ellington; Ella Fitzgerald; John Coltrane; Wes Montgomery; Duane Allman; Cy Coleman; Paul Desmond; Dizzy Gillespie; Lionel Hampton; Stan Kenton; Herb Alpert.

Playing for Keeps .... Atlantic (S) 81678-1 8-10 86
(Soundtrack.) Peter Frampton; Sister Sledge; Eugene Wilde; Chris Thompson; Pete Townshend; Joe Cruz; Arcadia; Julian Lennon; Phil Collins.

Plaza House Presents Country All-Star Festival (2 LP) .... Capitol Creative Products (SP) SLB 6721 10-15
Roy Rogers; Susan Raye; Ferlin Husky; Buddy Allan; Jean Shepard; Dick Curless; Tex Ritter; Rose Maddox; Buck Owens & His Buckaroos; Anne Murray; Wynn Stewart; Wanda Jackson; Hagers; Charlie Louvin; Melba Montgomery; Roy Clark; Billie Jo Spears; Johnny & Jonie Mosby; Merle Haggard's Strangers; Linda Ronstadt.

Please Say You Want Me .... Epic (M) LN-3702 25-40 60
Schoolboys; Jamies; Sal Mineo; Link Wray & Wraymen; Screamin' Jay Hawkins; Little Joe & Thrillers; Ersel Hickey; Lillian Briggs; Big Maybelle; Chuck Willis.

Plenty More, Keep Score .... Bandy (M) 70011 5-10 80s
Huey Smith & Clowns; Irma Thomas; Allen Toussaint; Chris Kenner; Ernie K-Doe; Showmen; Eddie Bo; Benny Spellman.

Police Academy IV - Citizens on Patrol .... Motown (S) 6235ML 8-10 87
(Soundtrack.) Darryl Duncan; S.O.S. Band; Stacy Lattisaw; Brian Wilson; Michael Winslow & L.A. Dream Team; Family Dream; Chico De Barge; Garry Glenn; Southern Pacific.

Polygram Radio & Store Sampler .... Polygram (S) SA 051 5-10 83
(Promotional issue only.) Trio; Peter Godwin; Comateens; Suburbs; Style Council; Big Country; others.

Pop and Rock Classics, 60 Great Hits (6 LP) .... Columbia House (S) 6P 6974 20-30 73
(Some tracks are rerecordings.) Santana; Dixie Cups; Dale & Grace; Rivingtons; Electric Flag; Mott the Hoople; Dobie Gray; Mary Hopkin; Barry Sadler; Paul Revere & Raiders; Dr. Hook & Medicine Show; Mary Wells; Timi Yuro; Box Tops; Laura Nyro; Poco; John Fred; Tremeloes; Gary Lewis & Playboys; Johnny Nash; Blood, Sweat & Tears; Chiffons; Dennis Yost & Classics IV; Leonard Cohen; Charlie Daniels Band; Nashville Teens; Glenn Yarbrough; Del Shannon; Minnie Riperton; Gary Puckett & Union Gap; Freddie & Dreamers; Brooklyn Bridge; Vogues; Sly & Family Stone; Byrds; Sam the Sham & Pharaohs; Troggs; Gerry & Pacemakers; Hollies; Janis Joplin; Clarence Carter; Drifters; Grass Roots; New York Rock Ensemble; Bobby Vinton; Penguins; Lesley Gore; Sam & Dave; New Riders of the Purple Sage; Tim Hardin; Nino Tempo & April Stevens; J. Frank Wilson; Flying Machine; David Bromberg; Aretha Franklin; Jay & Techniques; Larks; Barbara Lynn; Argent.

Pop and Rock Collection, Vol. 1 .... Gateway (S) GSLP-10101 8-12
Chubby Checker; Red Prysock; Harold Betters; Donnie Elbert; Prez Prado; Human Bienz & Mammals; Marcels; Del-Vikings.

Pop and Rock Collection, Vol. 2 .... Gateway (S) GSLP-10102 8-12
Chubby Checker; Red Prysock; Harold Betters; Donnie Elbert; Prez Prado; Human Bienz & Mammals; Marcels; Del-Vikings.

Pop Country Hits .... RCA (M) LPM-2949 10-20 64

Pop Country Hits .... RCA (S) LSP-2949 15-20 64
Jim Reeves; Hank Locklin; Hank Snow; Don Gibson; George Hamilton IV; John D. Loudermilk; Bobby Bare; Skeeter Davis; Dottie West; Floyd Cramer; Porter Wagoner; Eddy Arnold.

Pop Hits Country Flavored .... RCA (S) PRS-417 5-10 72
Danny Davis; Skeeter Davis; Willie Nelson; Chet Atkins; Dottie West; John Hartford; Nashville String Band; Liz Anderson; Waylon Jennings; Jessi Colter; Floyd Cramer.

Pop Hit Party, Vol. 1 .... Columbia (M) CL-1237 8-12 58
Doris Day; Vic Damone; Johnny Mathis; Four Lads; Sophia Loren; Frankie Laine; Kirby Stone Four; Jill Corey; Jimmy Dean; Tony Bennett; Jeannie Smith; Mary Mayo.

Pop Hit Party, Vol. 2 .... Columbia (M) CL-1269 8-12 58

Pop Hit Party, Vol. 3 .... Columbia (M) CL-1306 8-12 58
Tony Bennett; Polly Bergen; Johnny Cash; Vic Damone; Four Lads; Doris Day; Frankie Laine; Norman Luboff; Johnny Mathis; Mitch Miller.

Pop Hit Party .... Columbia (M) CL-1239 20-30 58
(Boxed set.) Four Lads; Kirby Stone Four; Johnny Mathis; Frankie Laine; Mary Mayo; Jimmy Dean; Doris Day; Vic Damone; Tony Bennett; Sophia Loren; Jill Corey; Jennie Smith.

Pop Instrumentals .... Columbia (M) CL 593 15-25 52
Paul Weston; Wally Stoff; Percy Faith; Morton Gould; Ken Griffin.

Pop Jazz (5 LP) .... World's Greatest Music (SP) WGM 2A 25-35 62
(Boxed set.) Sarah Vaughan; Count Basie; Maynard Ferguson; Erroll Garner; Harry Belafonte; Charlie Parker; Art Tatum; Dizzy Gillespie; Joe Williams; Miles Davis; Randy Weston; Sonny Stitt; Herbie Mann; Bud Powell; Machito; Johnny Smith; Stan Getz; Joe Newman; Eddie Davis; Johnny Griffin; Horace Silver; Lambert, Hendricks & Ross.

Pop Jazz (5 LP) .... World's Greatest Music (SP) WGM 2B 25-35 62
(Boxed set.) Sarah Vaughan; Count Basie; Maynard Ferguson; Dinah Washington; Billy Eckstine; Louis Armstrong; Duke Ellington; Chris Connor; Joe Williams; Candido; Woody Herman; Nat Adderley; Machito; John Coltrane; Illinois Jacquet; Phineas Newborn; Lambert, Hendricks & Ross.

Pop Jazz (10 LP) .... World's Greatest Music (SP) WGM 2AB 60-80 62
(Boxed set includes contents from both of above 5 LP sets, WGM 2A and WGM 2B.)

Pop, Jazz & Classical Selections Demonstrating Mercury Stereo .... Mercury (S) SRD 3 10-20 60
David Carroll; Brook Benton; Griff Williams; Clebanoff Strings; Pete Rugolo; Patti Page; Dick Contino; Lou Stein; Sarah Vaughan; Ramsey Lewis; Buddy Morrow; Pierre Challet; Sister Rosetta Tharpe; Eddie Layton; Clyde Otis; Jerry Murad's Harmonicats; Julian Adderley; Ernestine Anderson; Jan August; Max Roach; Jon Hall; Platters; others.

Pop Origin .... Chess (S) LP-1544 10-20 70
Chuck Berry; Bo Diddley; Lowell Fulsom; Howlin' Wolf; Dale Hawkins; Little Milton.

Pop Parade .... Mercury (M) E211 20-40
(10–inch LP.) Silvana Mangano; Buddy DeFranco; Joni James; Billy Eckstine; Blue Barron; Hank Williams; Lew Douglas; Art Mooney.

Pop Parade .... Mercury (M) MGD-25217 20-40 56
(10–inch LP.)

Pop Parade .... Mercury (M) MGD-25219 20-40 56
(10–inch LP.)

Pop Parade .... Trumpet (M) LP-2007 8-10

Pop Parade .... MGM (M) E-211 30-40 53

Pop Parade .... MGM (EP) X-299 10-15 55

Pop Parade .... MGM (M) E-299 20-35 55
(10–inch LP.)

Pop Parade .... MGM (EP) X-313 10-15 55

Pop Parade, Vol. 9 .... MGM (M) MGD 9 15-25 50s
Gaylords; Richard Haymen; Nick Noble; Georgia Gibbs; Rusty Draper; Diamonds; Chuck Miller; Patti Page; David Carroll; Sarah Vaughan; Crew-Cuts; Platters. (Issued in paper cover.)

Pop Shopper .... RCA (M) SPL 12-13 20-30 55
(Boxed set.) Perry Como; Harry Geller; Jaye P. Morgan; Chet Atkins; Al Cohn; George Melachrino; Eartha Kitt; Perez Prado; Hank Snow; Sauter-Finegan; Eddy Arnold; Milton Hinton.

Pop Singers on the Air .... Radiola (M) MR-1149 5-10 84
(Has four complete broadcasts, 1943-1958.) Perry Como; Vic Damone; Sylan Lavine; Eddie Fisher; Ayel Stordahl; Dick Haymes; Jerry Gray; Andrews Sisters; Evelny Knight & Modernaires.

Pop Sixties .... Warner/JCI (S) 3112 8-12 85
Lou Christie; Bruce Channel; Shirelles; Gene Chandler; Music Explosion; Tornadoes; Everly Brothers; McCoys; Jive Five; Bobby Vee; Seekers; Dion.

Pop Special (Command Records Sampler) .... Command (S) CPS 150 10-20 63
Enoch Light; Tony Mottola; Don Lamond; Ray Charles Singers; Doc Severinsen; Urbie Green.

Pops Concert of American Bon Bons .... Somerset (M) P-3900 5-10
Paris Theatre Orchestra; Hamburg Philharmonic Orchestra; Kingsway Strings; Stockholm Strings.

Pops We Love You.......... Motown (S) M7-921 5-10 79
Diana Ross; Marvin Gaye; Stevie Wonder; Commodores; Smokey Robinson; Jermaine Jackson; Tata Vega.

Popular Christmas Classics .... Capitol Special Markets (M) SL-8100 5-10 77
Gene Autry; Nat King Cole; Leroy Anderson; Harry Simeone Chorale; Bing Crosby; Tennessee Ernie Ford; Burl Ives; Margaret Whiting; Jimmy Wakely; Glen Campbell; Dean Martin.

Popular Favorites, Vol. 2 .... Columbia (M) CL 6119 25-75 50
(10-inch LP.) Frank Sinatra; Xavier Cugat; Dinah Shore; Harry James; Doris Day; Herb Jeffries; Arthur Godfrey; Les Brown.

Popular Favorites, Vol. 3 .... Columbia (M) CL 6150 25-75 50s
(10-inch LP.) Frank Sinatra; Mitch Miller; Percy Faith; Harry James; Sammy Kaye; Mariners; Dinah Shore; Doris Day.

Popular Favorites, Vol. 7 .... Columbia (M) CL 6256 20-30 50s
(10-inch LP.) Percy Faith; Felicia Sanders; Frankie Laine; Paul Weston; Ken Griffin; Jimmy Boyd; Harry James.

Popular Favorites, Vol. 8 .... Columbia (M) CL 6284 20-30 50s
(10-inch LP.) Tony Bennett; Frankie Laine; Les Elgart; Secret Love; Rosemary Clooney; Jose Ferrer; Harry James; Paul Weston.

Popular Gold Album .... Capitol (M) T-972 20-30 58
George Shearing; Tennessee Ernie Ford; Jackie Gleason; Judy Garland; Les Baxter; Nat King Cole; Joe Bushkin; June Christy; Harry James; Tommy Sands; Ray Anthony; Four Freshmen.

Popular Jazz Gold Album .... Capitol (M) T 1034 10-20
Jonah Jones; Jess Stacy; Paul Smith; Nat King Cole; Jack Teagarden; Dakota Staton; Bobby Hackett; George Shearing; Marian McPartland; June Christy; Four Freshmen; Louis Prima; Keely Smith.

Popular Music Hit Parade (9 LP) .... Readers Digest (S) RDA-63 25-35 68
(Boxed set.) Bob Crosby & Bobcats; Vic Damone; Nelson Riddle; Marty Paich; Jo Stafford; Paul Weston; Hank Levine; Bill Lee; Johnny Gibbs; Ray Davis; Marni Nixon; Pete King; Les Brown; Bll & Diana Lee; Frank DeVol; Joy Martell; Robert Mandell; Caballeros; Wayne & Geraldi; Warren Barker; Jerry Reed; Weldon Myrick; Hurshel Wiginton Singers; Joe Babcock; Nashville Sounds & Strings; others.

Popular Pairs in Music.......... RCA (S) CR 156 10-15 60s
Paul Whiteman & Bing Crosby; Glenn Miller & Ray Eberle; Tommy Dorsey & Jo Stafford; Louis Prima & Keely Smith; Xavier Cugat & Abbe Lane; Ted Weems & Elmo Tanner; J.P. Morgan & Hugo Winterhalter; Earl Hines & Billy Eckstine; Larry Clinton & Bea Wain; Lena Horne & Lennie Hayton; Eartha Kitt & Shorty Rogers; Rosemary Clooney & Perez Prado.

Porky Chedwick's Golden Goodies, Vol. 1 .... No Label Used (S) GG-101 10-20 70s
Four Pearls; Precisions; Symphonics; Tojo; Utopians; Hal Davis; Funky Sisters; Poets; El Capris; Ronnie Haig; Four Steps of Rhythm.

Porky Chedwick's Orginals, Vol. 1.......... PCLP (S) 1 20-30 70s

Porky Chedwick's Orginals Collection, Vol. 1 .... No Label Used (S) WL-507 10-20 70s
Five Dollars; Anthony & Sophomores; Dominoes; others.
Porky's Golden Dusties .... Atlantic (M) 8100 20-40 64
Caps; Tony March; Royaltones; Nite Caps; Swingin' Hearts; Dubs; Aladdins; Avalons; Blonde Bomber; Ronnie Jones & Classmates; Jimmy McHugh; Falcons; Clyde McPhatter; Penguins; Clovers; Robbins; Larry Dale; Versatones; Coasters; Superiors.
Porky's Revenge .... Columbia (S) JS-39983 10-15 85
(Soundtrack.) Dave Edmunds; Jeff Beck; Fabulous Thunderbirds; George Harrison; Willie Nelson; Carl Perkins; Clarence Clemons; Crawling King Snakes.
Portraits — Album of Today's Softer Sounds .... Arista (ST 5820 5-10 83
Jennifer Warnes; Eric Carmen; Gino Vannelli; Aretha Franklin; David Gates; Mary MacGregor; Al Stewart; Merrilee Rush; Melissa Manchester; Dionne Warwick; Paul Davis.
Portraits in Jazz .... Reprise R/RS 6084 10-15 60s
Duke Ellington; Mavis Rivers; Shorty Rogers; Sidney Bechet; Django Reinhardt; Dizzy Gillespie; Count Basie; Barney Kessel; Marv Jenkins; Chico Hamilton.
Pot of Golden Goodies, Vol. 1 .... Herald (M) LP-1015 40-50 62
Five Satins; Silhouettes; Nutmegs; Dion & Belmonts; Dubs; Flamingos; Paragons; Cadillacs; Bobby Freeman; Jesters; Chantels; Bobby Hendricks; Mello-Kings; Turbans.
Power Blues .... London (S) PS-579 8-12 70
Keef Hartley Band; Otis Span; Savoy Brown; John Mayall; others.
Power House .... K-Tel (S) TU 2460 5-10 76
Silver Convention; Keith Carradine; Tavares; Hall & Oates; Larry Groce; Morris Albert; Linda Ronstadt; Seals & Crofts; Leon Haywood; Henry Gross; Glen Campbell; Andrea True Connection; Roxy Music; Dorothy Moore; Brotherhood of Man; Styx; Rufus featuring Chaka Khan; Heart; Wing & a Prayer Fife & Drum Band; Hot Chocolate.
Power Play .... K-Tel (S) TU-2630 5-10 80
Power Train '66 .... Columbia Special Products (S) CSP-251 10-15 66
Power Train '66 (John Deere Is Going Places) .... Columbia Special Products (S) XTV 105381 10-15 66
Bob Dylan; Skifflers; New Christy Minstrels; Johnny Horton; Percy Faith; Pete Seeger; Carter Family; Little Jimmy Dickens; Flatt & Scruggs; Johnny Cash.
Praise the Lord .... Design (S) SDLP-615 5-10
Maddox Brothers & Rose; T. Texas Tyler; Wally Fowler; Eddie Dean; Texas Jim Robertson.
Precious Memories .... Camden (S) CXS-9020 5-10 72
Blackwood Brothers; Skeeter Davis; George Beverly Shea; Porter Wagoner; others.
Precious Memories of Sacred Hymns .... Modern Sound (S) MS-802 5-10
Sons of Song; J.T. Adams; Dixie Echoes; Wendy Bagwell & Sunlighters; Wally Fowler & Oak Ridge Quartet; Jake Hess & Jordanaires; Georgians; Plainsmen; Florida Boys; Sego Brothers & Naomi.
Precious Songs of Thomas Dorsey .... Columbia (S) KG 32151 10-15
Premier Spectacular .... Liberty (S) S 6604 8-12
Felix Slatkin; Si Zentner; Johnny Mann Singers; Richard Marino; 50 Guitars of Tommy Garrett; Bessie Griffin & Gospel Pearls.
Premiere 12 Performances .... Philips (S) PHM-PHS-1 8-12 60s
Michel Legrand; Woody Herman; Sviatoslaw Richter; Francis Bay; Vienna Concert Orchestra; Franz Jackson; Skinnay Ennis; Frankie Vaughan; Barrier Brothers; Malando; Julius Watkins; Rawicz & Landaver.
Presenting Jocko's Two Dozen Oldies: see Jocko's New Album
Presenting the Stars of Acapella, Vol. 1 .... Amber (M) LP-801 10-15 60s
Autumns; Valids; Del-Capris; Five Sharks; Zircons.
Pretty in Pink .... A&M (S) SP 3293 8-12 86
Pretty in Pink .... A&M (S) SP 5113 8-10 86
(Soundtrack.) Orchestral Manoeuvers in the Dark; Suzanne Vega; Joe Jackson; INXS; Psychedelic Furs; New Order; Belouis Some; Danny Hutton; Hitters; Echo & Bunnymen; Smiths.
Pretty Woman .... EMI (S) E1-93492 8-10 90
(Soundtrack.) Roy Orbison; Natalie Cole; David Bowie; Go West; Jane Wiedlin; Roxette; Robert Palmer; Peter Cetera; Lauren Wood; Red Hot Chili Peppers; Christopher Ocasek.
Pride of Cleveland Past .... WTLF-FM/WJKW/Scene (S) ???? 8-12 84
Outsiders; Choir; Twilighters; Joey & Continentals; Secrets; Tommy Facenda; Tom King & Starfires; Circus; Raspberries; Tulu Babies; Bocky & Visions; Tree Stumps; Baskerville Hounds; Grasshoppers.
Prime Time Radio Smash Flashbacks .... Laurie (M) LLP-2028 15-20 64
Mystics; Five Discs; Passions; Skyliners; Turbans; Five Satins; Dimensions.
Prime Time Radio Smash Flashbacks .... Laurie (M) LLP-2029 15-20 60s
Dion; Turbans; Five Satins; Mystics; Passions; Dimensions; Five Discs; Skyliners.
Prince's Trust 10th Anniversary Birthday Party .... A&M (S) SP 3906 5-10 87
Paul McCartney; Dire Straits; Midge Ure; Suzanne Vega; Phil Collins; Big Country; Howard Jones; Level 42; Elton John; Joan Armatrading; Tina Turner; Rod Stewart. (Benefit concert.)
Prisoners Songs .... Starday (M) S-207 15-20 63
Johnny Cash; James O'Gwynn; Hylo Brown; others.
Private School .... MCA (S) 36005 8-10 83
(Soundtrack.) Phoebe Cates; Men's Room; Bill Wray; Rick Springfield.
Production, Vol. 3 .... Columbia Special Products (S) CSS 689 5-10 68
Theodore Bikel; Barbara Cook; Jane Morgan; Andre Kostelanetz; Eydie Gorme; Herschel Bernardi; Ezio Pinza; Robert Goulet; John Raitt; Rosemary Clooney.
Program of All Time Favorites (4 EP) .... RCA (EP) 1438 10-15
(Boxed set.) Marian Anderson; Boston Pops; Enrico Caruso; First Piano Quartet; Allan Jones; Jeanette MacDonald; Jan Peerce; Leopold Stokowski.
Progressive Heavies .... United Artists (SP) UAS-5503 8-12 70
Traffic; Bee Gees; Johnny Winter; Canned Heat; Spencer Davis; Cream; Bonzo Dog Band.
Progressives .... Columbia (S) KG-31574 10-20 73
Mahavishnu Orchestra; Weather Report; Matching Mole; Walter Carlos; Ornette Coleman; Soft Machine; Don Ellis; Keith Jarrett; Charles Mingus; Gentle Giant; Compost; Paul Winter & Winter Consort; Paul Horn; Bill Evans.
Propaganda: see A&M Promotional Releases/Samplers

Proudly They Came (2 LP) .... Landmark (S) PR-LP-101 15-20 70
(Soundtrack.) Kate Smith; Bob Hope; Teresa Graves; Young Americans; Jack Benny; Centurymen; Dinah Shore; Glen Campbell; Dorothy Lamour; Red Skelton; Jeannie C. Riley; New Christy Minstrels; Pat Boone; Esther Phillips; Fred Waring; Les Brown; James Stewart; Dr. Billy Graham; Vince Lombardi.

Psychedelic Dreams .... Columbia (S) ???? 8-10 85

Psychedelic Moods .... Cicadelic (M) 976 5-10 87
Hydro; Pyro; Fallen Angels; Electric Prism; Rear Exit; Los Chijuas.

Psychedelic Unknowns, Vol. 3 .... Syn-Sity (M) SS 1 8-12 80s
Loved Ones; Grammy Fones; Luv Bandits; Starfires; Trolls; Touch; Crome Surcus; Pat Farrel & Believers; Wreck-A-Mended; 4 of Us; Bush; Tracers; Dagenites; Flares; Xtreems; Henry the IX; State of Mind; Ognir & Night People.

Psych-Out .... Sidewalk (S) ST-5913 12-15 68
(Soundtrack.) Strawberry Alarm Clock; Seeds; Storybook; Boenzee Cryque.

Pump Up the Volume .... MCA (S) 8039 8-10 90
(Soundtrack.) Concrete Blonde; Ivan Neville; Liquid Jesus; Pixies; Peter Murphy; Bad Brains with Henry Rollins; Above the Law; Soundgarden; Sonic Youth; Cowboy Junkies.

Pumping Iron 2 - the Women .... Island (S) 90273 8-10 85
(Soundtrack.) Art of Noise; Skipworth & Turner; Grace Jones; Will Powers; New York City Peech Boys; Black Uhuru; Roach; Fast Forward.

Punk and Disorderly .... Posh Boy (S) PBS-131 8-10 81
Dead Kennedys; Vice Squad; Addicts; U.K. Decay; Disorder; Peter & Test Tube Babies; Disrupters; Red Alert; Blitz; Partisans; Demob; Insane; Abrasive Wheels; Chaos; U.K. Outcasts; G.B.I.

Pure Disco .... Ronco (S) 2250

Pure Gold, Vol. 1 .... K-Tel (S) TU 2550-1 5-10 77
Maxine Nightingale; Cliff Richard; Mary MacGregor; Al Stewart; Bellamy Brothers; Paul Anka with Odia Coates; Diana Ross; England Dan & John Ford Coley; Addrisi Brothers; 10cc; David Soul; Hall & Oates; Atlanta Rhythm Section; Billy Ocean; Henry Gross; Walter Murphy & Big Apple Band; Abba; Linda Ronstadt.

Pure Power .... K-Tel (S) TU-2510 5-10 77
Kiss; Eylvers; England Dan & John Ford Coley; Gary Wright; Alice Cooper; Heart; Walter Murphy Band; KC & Sunshine Band; Diana Ross; Brass Construction; ELP; Doobie Brothers; Hall & Oates; David Dundas; Dr. Buzzard's Original Savannah Band; Elvin Bishop; Wet Willie; War; Gladys Knight & Pips; Paul Anka; Odia Coates.

Pure Soul .... United (S) US-7738 10-20 70s
B.B. King; Lowell Fulsom; Elmore James; Z.Z. hill; Little Richard; Vernon & Jewell.

Purple People Eater .... AJK (S) A227-1 10-15 88
(Soundtrack.) Little Richard; Jan & Dean; D.K.; Chubby Checker; Sha Na Na; Bobby Day; Mike Harris; Penny & Sondra; Longfellow; Happenings; Bob Summers.

Pursuit of D.B. Cooper .... Polydor (S) PD1-6344 10-15 81
(Soundtrack.) Waylon Jennings; Rita Coolidge; Jessi Colter; Marshall Tucker Band.

Put on Your Dancing Shoes .... Capitol/EMI (S) EG 2605721 5-10 85
Bobby Freeman; Clovers; Fats Domino; Rivingtons; Johnny Darrow; Everglades; Robert Parker; Human Beinz; Beach Boys; Silhouettes; Five Keys; Rollers; Senors; Johnny Otis; Larks; Bobby Fuller Four.

Put the Hammer Down .... Realistic/Capitol Special Markets (S) SL 8017 5-10 70s
Merle Haggard; C.W. McCall; Cledus Maggard & Citizens Band; Dick Curless; Glen Campbell; Red Sovine; Red Simpson.

Q-FM-96 Hometown Album Project #1 .... QFM96 (S) No Number Used 20-25 70s
Frank Pierce Groupe; Gary Whitman; McGuffey Lane; Geoff Tyus; Buttons; Spittin' Image; Champ; Reflection; Muffs; Pagen Brothers Band; Roughrider.

QSP Presents a Gift of Music: see Gift of Music

Quadraphonic (Spectacular Sound of Four Channel Stereo): see SQ Quadraphonic

Quadradisc by Sylvania .... RCA Special Products (?) DPD 1-0084 8-12 70s
Dr. Teleny's Incredible Plugged-In Orchestra; Jerry Reed; Arthur Fiedler & Boston Pops; Friends of Distinction; B.W. Stevenson; Danny Davis & Nashville Brass; Hugo Montenegro; Nilsson; Eugene Ormandy & Philharmonic Orchestra.

Quadrophenia (2 LP) .... Polydor (S) PD-2-6235 10-15 80
(Soundtrack.) Who; High Numbers; Cross Section; James Brown; Kingsmen; Booker T. & MGs; Cascades; Chiffons; Ronettes; Crystals.

Quicksilver .... Atlantic (S) 81631 8-10 86
(Soundtrack.) Roger Daltrey; Fiona; Peter Frampton; Ray Parker Jr.; Helen Terry; Larry John McNally; Thomas Newman; Tony Banks; Fish; John Parr; Marilyn Martin.

Quiet Days in Clichy .... Vanguard (S) VSD-79303 10-12 70
(Soundtrack.) Country Joe McDonald; Ben Webster; Andy Sundstrom; Young Flowers; Papa Blue's Viking Jazz Band.

R&B Hitmakers .... Harlem Hitparade (SE) HHP-5002 5-10 72
Jerry Butler & Impressions; Turbans; Jesters; Paragons; Silhouettes; Harptones; Lee Dorsey; Huey "Piano" Smith; Maurice Williams; Clovers.

R&B Hits .... Hollywood (M) H-503 50-100 58

R&B Super Stars .... Harlem Hitparade (SE) HHP-5003 5-10 72
Rivileers; Five Satins; Fidelities; Hearts; Starlights; Jesters; Platters; Joe Tex.

RCA Untitled, Promotional Releases/Samplers (Listed by catalog number. All are promo only.)

RCA 4 Untitled 1000-1500 56
(Not issued with special cover.) Elvis Presley; Gypsy Sandor; Andy Russell; Bob Scobey; Herb Jeffries; Skitch Henderson; Luis Arcaraz; Beny Moré; Tito Puente; Billo; M. López; Jerome; Hank Snow; La Playa; Tommy Dorsey; Lou Monte; Grant-Martin; Glenn Miller; Fritz Reiner; Heifetz-Primrose; G. Tozzi; W. Landowska; Richard Shaw.

RCA 10 Untitled 900-1200 58
(Not issued with special cover.) Elvis Presley; Dissell & O'Reilly; Clegg; George Feyer; Perez Prado; J. Lewis; Los Indios Tabajaras; Lena Horne; Tony Martin; M. Davis; Xavier Cugat; Johnny Conquet; Dave Peil; Tony Perkins.

RCA 15 Title Unknown (10 EP) (EP) 800-1000 55
(Black label. Box or cover not yet verified.) Elvis Presley; others.

RCA 15 Title Unknown (10 EP) (EP) 800-1000 55
(Gray label. Intended for jukebox use. Box or cover not yet verified.) Elvis Presley; others.

RCA 61 Untitled (EP) 1000-1500 57
(Not issued with special cover.) Elvis Presley; Billy Mure; Sabres; Gogi Grant; Nick Venet; Lane Brothers; Versatones Jeannie Smith; Paul Lavalle; Robert Merrill.

RCA 93 Untitled (EP) 15-25 59
(Not issued with special cover.) Neil Sedaka; Henry Mancini; Jeanie Johnson; others.

RCA 3736: see PRESLEY, Elvis / Vaughn Monroe / Gogi Grant / Robert Shaw Chorale

RCA April '64 Pop Sampler .... RCA (S) SPS-33-272 500-750 64
(Promotional issue only. Not issued with special cover.) Elvis Presley; Henry Mancini; Gale Garnett; Solomon King; Blackwood Brothers; George Beverly Shea; Frankie Fanelli; Miriam Makeba; Carlos Montoya; Ames Brothers; Don Gibson; Joe Williams; Frankie Carle; Chet Atkins; Los Indios Tabajaras.

RCA April '65 Pop Sampler .... RCA (S) SPS-33-331 500-750 65
(Promotional issue only. Not issued with special cover.) Elvis Presley; Juan Serrano; Mariachi Los Camperos of Nati Cano; Connie Smith; Joe Williams; Don Bowman; Don Robertson; John Goldsmith; Ethel Ennis; Frankie Carle; Peter Nero; Paul Desmond; Jim Hall; Miriam Makeba; Melachrino Strings.

RCA April '66 Pop Sampler .... RCA (S) SPS-33-403 500-750 66
(Promotional issue only. Not issued with special cover.) Elvis Presley; Ray Kinney & His Aloha Serenaders; Rod McKuen; Brook Benton; Frankie Carle; George Wilkins; Willie Nelson; Blue Boys with Bud Logan; Charlie Rich; Tommy Leonetti; Marilyn Maye; Hugo Montenegro; Provocative Strings of Zacharias.

RCA August 1959 Sampler .... RCA (SP) SP-33-27 750-1000 59
(Promotional issue only. Not issued with special cover.) Elvis Presley; Jim Reeves; Buddy Morrow; Perez Prado; Pat Suzuki; Harry Belafonte; Hugo Winterhalter; Melachrino Strings; Howard Keel; Anne Jeffreys; Xavier Cugat; Esquivel; Shorty Rogers.

RCA August '65 Pop Sampler .... RCA (S) SPS-33-347 500-750 65
(Promotional issue only. Not issued with special cover.) Elvis Presley; Tahitian Native Group; Carl Belew; Marilyn Maye; Justin Tubb; Paul Lavalle & Band of America; Floyd Cramer; Peggy March; Bennie Thomas; Lorne Greene; Los Indios Tabajaras; Jim Reeves; Duane Eddy.

RCA December '62 Pop Sampler .... RCA (S) SPS-33-191 500-750 62
(Promotional issue only. Not issued with special cover.) Elvis Presley; Gaylord Carter; Hank Jones & Dean Kay; Jimmie Haskell Orchestra & Chorus; Sir Julian; Sacha Distel; Ray Ellis Orchestra; Neil Sedaka; Tokens; Marty Gold Orchestra; Zaccarias.

RCA December '63 Pop Sampler .... RCA (S) SPS-33-247 500-750 63
(Promotional issue only. Not issued with special cover.) Elvis Presley; Jerome Moss; Hank Locklin; Neil Sedaka; Henry Mancini; Joe Daley Trio; Eddie Fisher; Womenfolk; Villagers.

RCA Family Record Center .... RCA (EP) PR-121 1500-2000 62
(Promotional issue only. Not issued with special cover.) Elvis Presley; Peter Nero; Paul Anka; Living Strings; Sam Cooke; Al Hirt; Perry Como; Henry Mancini.

RCA February Sampler 59-7 .... RCA (M) SP-33-59-7 600-800 59
(Promotional issue only. Not issued with special cover.) Elvis Presley; Ray Hartley; Don Walker; Blackwood Brothers; Buddy Morrow; others. (Has RCA Victor black label on one side and RCA Camden label on side 2, thus sampling tunes from LPs on both labels.)

RCA February 1978 Album Sampler .... RCA (M) DJL1-2722 10-15 78
Charley Pride; Perry Como; Helen Schneider; Roger Whittaker; Danny Davis & Nashville Brass; Beaverteeth; Vangelis; First lire.

RCA Introduces a Sherlyn Sampler .... RCA (S) DJL1-1468 8-10
KC & Sunshine Band; Wilson Pickett; Fire; Latimore; Hokis Pokis; Gwen McCrae; George McCrae; Jackie Moore; Betty Wright; Jimmy "Bo" Horne; Milton Wright; Seven Seas; Clarence Reid; Sunshine Band; SOS; Tropea; Alley; Funky Party Band.

RCA January 1978 Sampler .... RCA (S) DJL1-2685 10-20 78
(Promotional issue only.) Scorpions; Vicki Sue Robinson; Dr. Buzzard's Original Savannah Band; Vangelis; Valentine; Waylon & Willie; Aztec Two-Step; Tom T. Hall; Tomita; Steve Young; Floyd Cramer.

RCA March '62 Pop Sampler .... RCA (S) SPS-33-159 20-30 62
(Promotional issue only. Not issued with special cover.) Jimmy Driftwood; Ann-Margret; Sons of the Pioneers; Joe Morello; Floyd Cramer; Jonathan Edwards; Rudy Vallee; Perez Prado; Turk Murphy.

RCA March 1978 Sampler .... RCA (M) DJL1-2723 10-15 78
(Promotional issue only.) Hot Tuna; Jimmy Beaumont & Skyliners; Helen Schneider; Jerry Reed; Jim Reeves; Flame; Renee Armand; Jim Ed Brown & Helen Cornelius.

RCA November/December Sampler 59-44 thru 59-47 .... RCA (S) SPS-33-57 600-750 59
(Promotional issue only. Not issued with special cover.) Elvis Presley; Jerry Byrd; Lena Horne; New Glenn Miller Orchestra; Frankie Carle; Ames Brothers; Kay Starr, Marty Gold's Orchestra; Dave Gardner; Del Wood; Dukes Of Dixieland; Chet Atkins; Tito Puente; Ray Martin Orchestra.

RCA October 1960 Popular Stereo Sampler .... RCA (S) SPS-33-96 500-750 60
(Promotional issue only. Not issued with special cover.) Elvis Presley; Shorty Rogers; Skeeter Davis; Jimmy Driftwood; Frankie Carle; Hugo & Luigi; Miriam Makeba; Ames Brothers; Dick Schory; George Beverly Shea; Blackwood Brothers; Lyman; Laymen Singers; Nashville All-Stars.

RCA October '61 Pop Sampler .... RCA (S) SPS-33-141 500-750 61
(Promotional issue only. Not issued with special cover.) Elvis Presley; Henri Rene; Ray Martin; Jim Reeves; Sam Cooke; Chet Atkins; New Glenn Miller Orchestra with Ray McKinley; Floyd Cramer; Don McNeill; George Beverly Shea; Blackwood Brothers.

RCA October '67 Camden Sampler .... RCA Camden (S) UCRS-6540/SPS-33-489 8-12 67
(Promotional issue only.) Living Voices; Soul Founders; Montana Slim; Wilf Carter; Bobby Dukoff with Ray Charles Chorus; George Beverly Shea with Billy Graham; New York Crusade Chorus.

RCA October '67 Pop Sampler .... RCA (S) SPS-33-487 15-25 67
(One-sided disc.) Peter Nero; Skeeter Davis; Homer & Jethro; Carol Burnett; Chet Atkins; Joe Feeney; Blackwood Brothers Quartet.

RCA October '67 Pop Sampler .... RCA (S) SPS-33-486/JNRS-7909 15-20 67
Bill Dixon; Father Tom Vaughn; Il Groupo; Connie Smith; Spike Jones & His City Slickers; Liz Anderson; Jim Ed Brown; Willie Nelson; Milton DeLugg; Lana Cantrell; Rod McKuen; Youngbloods; Rouvan.

RCA October Christmas Sampler 59-40-41 .... RCA (SP) SPS-33-54 600-750 59
(Promotional issue only. Not issued with special cover.) Elvis Presley; Gisele MacKenzie; J. Klein; Esquival; George Melachrino; Three Suns; Ralph Hunter; George Beverly Shea; Perry Como; Johnson Family; Boston Pops; Mario Lanza; R. Elias; G. Tozzi.

RCA Sampler, Selections from "Best of" Series .... RCA (S) SP 393 10-15
Duane Eddy; Three Suns; Hank Snow; Frankie Carle; Homer & Jethro; Sons of the Pioneers; Bobby Bare; Jim Reeves; Esquivel.

RCA September Album Sampler .... RCA (S) DJL-1-2571 10-15 70s
Bill Quateman; Fandango; Rosie; Redbone; Chocolate Milk; Silverado; Darcus; Rocky & Chy Ann; Michael Smotherman.

RCA September '63 Pop Sampler .... RCA (S) SPS-33-219 500-750 63
(Promotional issue only. Not issued with special cover.) Elvis Presley; Odetta; Limeliters; Duane Eddy; Floyd Cramer; Don Gibson; Hank Snow; Sam Cooke; Three Suns; Sid Ramin; Hugo & Luigi Chorus; Frankie Carle; Peter Nero; Ann-Margret; Kitty Kallen; Della Reese.

RCA Victor Encyclopedia of Recorded Jazz in 12 Great Albums .... RCA (M) G7 OL 4206 20-30 50s
Red Allen; Albert Ammons; Louis Armstrong; Buster Bailey; Mildred Bailey; Count Basie; Sidney Bechet.

RCA Victor Encyclopedia of Recorded Jazz, Album 1 .... RCA (M) LEJ-1 25-45 50s
(10–inch LP.) Red Allen; Albert Ammons; Louis Armstrong; Buster Bailey; Mildred Bailey; Charlie Barnet; Count Basie; Sidney Bechet.

RCA Victor Encyclopedia of Recorded Jazz, Album 2 .... RCA (M) LEJ-2 25-45 50s
(10–inch LP.) Bix Beiderbeck; Bunny Berigan; Chu Berry; Barney Digard; George Brunis; Cab Calloway; Hoagy Carmichael; Barbara Carroll; Benny Carter; Buck Clayton.

RCA Victor Encyclopedia of Recorded Jazz, Album 3 .... RCA (M) LEJ-3 25-45 50s
(10–inch LP.) Larry Clinton; Al Cohn; Lee Collins; Eddie Condon; Wild Bill Davison; Johnny Dodds; Tommy Dorsey.

RCA Victor Encyclopedia of Recorded Jazz, Album 4 .... RCA (M) LEJ-4 25-45 50s
(10–inch LP.) Billy Eckstine; Roy Eldridge; Duke Ellington; Ziggy Elman; Irving Fazola; Bud Freeman; Erroll Garner.

RCA Victor Encyclopedia of Recorded Jazz, Album 5 .... RCA (M) LEJ-5 25-45 50s
(10–inch LP.) Dizzy Gillespie; Benny Goodman; Glen Gray; Lionel Hampton; Coleman Hawkins; Fletcher Henderson; J.C. Higgin Botham.

RCA Victor Encyclopedia of Recorded Jazz, Album 6 .... RCA (M) LEJ-6 25-45 50s
(10–inch LP.) Earl Hines; Johnny Hodges; Billie Holiday; Lena Horne; Harry James; Bunk Johnson; Johnson & Winding.

RCA Victor Encyclopedia of Recorded Jazz, Album 7 .... RCA (M) LEJ-7 25-45 50s
(10–inch LP.) P. Johnson; Max Kaminsky; John Kirby; Gene Krupa; Tommy Ladnier; Eddie Long; Leadbelly; George Lewis.

RCA Victor Encyclopedia of Recorded Jazz, Album 8 .... RCA (M) LEJ-8 25-45 50s
(10–inch LP.)

RCA Victor Encyclopedia of Recorded Jazz, Album 9 .... RCA (M) LEJ-9 25-45 50s
(10–inch LP.)

RCA Victor Encyclopedia of Recorded Jazz, Album 10 .... RCA (M) LEJ-10 25-45 50s
(10–inch LP.)

RCA Victor Encyclopedia of Recorded Jazz, Album 11 .... RCA (M) LEJ-11 25-45 50s
(10–inch LP.)

RCA Victor Encyclopedia of Recorded Jazz, Album 12 .... RCA (M) LEJ-12 25-45 50s
(10–inch LP.)

RCA Victor Pop Shopper (3 EP).......... RCA (EP) SPC-7-13 15-20

RCA Victor Stereo Spectacular .... RCA (S) PRS 249 8-12 67
Ray Martin; Norman Luboff Choir; Living Strings; Derek & Ray; Chet Atkins; Bernie Green; Henry Mancini; Al Hirt; Ragtimers; Morton Gould; Claus Ogerman; Arthur Fiedler & Boston Pops.

RCA's Hottest Tracks (2 LP) .... RCA (S) DJL2-4648 10-20 82
(Promotional issue only.) Pointer Sisters; Steel Breeze; Tane Cain; Rick Springfield; Sylvia; Hall & Oates; Jefferson Starship; Diana Ross; Chilliwack; Tavares; Alabama; Le Roux; Frankie & Knockouts; Ronnie Milsap.

RCA's Sound Spectaculars for '59 (Kellogg's Presents) .... RCA (M) SP-33-16 8-12 59
Dovrak; Puccini; Boston Pops; Morton Gould; Arthur Rubinstein; others.

RSO Chartbusters .... RSO (S) RS-1-3066 5-10 79
Andy Gibb; Frankie Valli; Suzi Quatro; Chris Norman; John Stewart; Yvonne Elliman; Player; David Naughton; Paul Nicholas; Linda Clifford.

Rad .... MCA (S) 6166 8-10 86
(Soundtrack.) John Farnham; Beat Farmers; 3-Speed; Hubert Kah; Real Life; Sparks; Jimmy Haddox.

Radar Blues .... King (S) KLP 1050 8-12 70s
Coleman Wilson; Moore & Napier; Reno & Smiley; Stanley Brothers; Grandpa Jones; Hylo Brown; Willis Brothers; Red Sovine; Johnny Bond; Cowboy Copas; Hawkshaw Hawkins.

Radio Active .... K-Tel TU 2940 5-10 82
(Mail order offer.) Police; Moody Blues; REO Speedwagon; Pat Benatar; Who; Rick Springfield; Hall & Oates; Commodores; Carl Carlton; Rick James; Genesis; Devo; Go-Go's; Blondie.

Radio Active Summer LP .... Epic (S) AS 77 8-12 74
(Promotional issue only.) Badger; Hollies; Edgar Winter Group; Kansas; Argent; Rupert Holmes; Murray McLaughlin; Kris Kristofferson; Chase; Redbone; Michael Murphey; Flash Cadillac; Minnie Riperton; Flash Cadillac; King Biscuit Boy; Poco.

Radio Band Remotes .... Radiola (M) 1314 5-10 70
Russ Morgan; Glen Gray; Jimmy Grier; Jan Garber; Shep Fields; Blue Baron; Del Courtney; Phil Harris; Guy Lombardo; Lionel Hampton; Freddy Martin; Ted Fio Rito; Henry Busse; George Olson.

Radio Classics of the '50s .... Columbia (SE) FC-45017 5-10 89
Johnny Horton; Marty Robbins; Tony Bennett; Rosemary Clooney; Johnny Mathis; Doris Day; Johnnie Ray; Guy Mitchell; Louis Armstrong & His All Stars; Joan Weber; Frankie Laine; Terry Gilkyson & Easy Riders; Brothers Four; Four Lads.

Radio Days (Selections from the Soundtrack) .... Novus/RCA (S) 3917-1-N9 8-10 87
(Soundtrack.) Tommy Dorsey; Sammy Kaye; Guy Lombardo; Glenn Miller; Benny Goodman; Duke Ellington; Xavier Cugat.

Radio Smash Flashbacks Drive Time .... Laurie (S) LLP-2028 8-12
Billy Bland; Dean & Jean; Carla Thomas; Fiestas; Flamingos; Chiffons; Monotones; Clyde McPhatter; Moonglows; Drifters; Jarmels; Tommy Hunt.

Radio Smash Flashbacks Prime Time .... Laurie (S) LLP-2029 8-12
Dion & Belmonts; Five Satins; Mystics; Passions; Turbans; Skyliners; Five Discs; Demensions.

Radio Tokyo Tapes .... Ear Movie (S) EM 0027 8-12 83
The Last; Jane Bond & Undercover Men; Long Ryders; Bangles (Bangs); Choir Invisible; Three O'clock; Rain Parade; Spoiler Project; Minutemen; Savage Republic; Alisha & Nomads; Michael James; Wednesday Week; 100 Flowers; Worm; Action; Now; Harvey Kubernik's Attention Getting Device.

Radio Tokyo Tapes, Vol. 3 .... PVC (S) PVC 8931 8-12 85
Knitters; Balancing Act; Kerry McBride; Revolver; Cindy Lee Berryhill; Chris D. & Divine Horsemen; Alisa; Pop Art; Sandy Bull; Henry Rollins; Beep Sisters; Carmaig de Forest; Linda Albertano; Minutemen; Phranc; Drew Steele.

Radio's Million Performance Songs .... CBS (S) SNGS-101 25-50 84
(Promotional issue only.) Elvis Presley; Beatles; Fats Domino; Jimmy Jones; Fleetwoods; Gale Storm; Inez & Charlie Foxx; Bob Lind; Jim Reeves; Jackie De Shannon; Barry Manilow; Carly Simon; Freddie Fender; Bobby Goldsboro.

Ragtime Piano Originals .... Folkways (M) RF 23 8-12 74
Mike Bernard; Harry Thomas; Malvin M. Franklin; Joseph Batten; others.

Railroad in Folksong .... RCA (M) LPV-532 10-15 66
Carter Family; Jimmie Davis; Monroe Brothers; others.

Railroad Songs .... King (M) 869 20-30 63

Railroad Songs .... King (S) KS-869 20-30 63
Grandpa Jones; Reno & Smiley; Stanley Brothers; others.

Railroad Sounds, Sounds of a Vanishing Era! .... Audio Fidelity (M) AFLP 1843 8-12

Railroad Sounds, Sounds of a Vanishing Era! .... Audio Fidelity (S) AFSD 5843 8-12
(Sound effects. No music.)

Rain Man .... Capitol (S) C1-91866 8-10 89
(Soundtrack.) Delta Rhythm Boys; Etta James; Johnny Clegg & Savuka; Ian Gillan; Roger Glover; Bananarama; Hans Zimmer; Lou Christie; Belle Stars; Rob Wasserman; Aaron Neville.

Raisinets Movie Greats .... Ward-Johnson (S) BU-5400 5-10 82
(Soundtrack.) Maureen McGovern; Rose Royce; Isaac Hayes; Nilsson; Onyx; Opus I; Michel Legrand; Henry Mancini; Oliver; Al Martino; B.J. Thomas.

Ralph Cooper in Person Presents, Vol. 1 .... Jubilee (S) JGM 5012 15-25 63
Cadillacs; Four Tunes; Orioles; Della Reese; Ravens; Channels; others.

Rappin' .... Atlantic (S) 81252-1 8-10 85
(Soundtrack.) Mario Van Peebles; Kadeem Hardison; Eriq La Salle; Tuff Inc.; Warren Mills.

Rap's Greatest Hits .... Priority (S) SL-9466 5-10
Timex Social Club; Run-D.M.C.; Boogie Boys; Real Roxanne with Howie Tee; Fat Boys; Doug E. Fresh & Get Fresh Crew; Joeski Love; Whodini; WTFO; Rockmaster Scott & Dynamic Three.

Rare Dowops .... Wizard (S) 5003 8-10
Billy Dodds & Primes; Lee Adrian & Collegians; Four Epics; Jimmy & Towers; Jimmy Mana & Four Gents; Jimmy Inman & Impalas; Rhythm Stars; Dick Caruso & Clefs; Hy-Tones; Billy Lynn & Lines; Billy Storm & Group; Montgomerys; Fortunes; Rendezvous; Pery Mates; Constellations.

Rare Los Angeles Tracks .... Charade (M) 8301 10-15 83
Ray Agee; Charades; Agnes Duke; Jesse Belvin; Capris; Unknown; Charles Andrea & Hi-Tones; Marc Anthony Band; Chavez & Chaney; Charles Wright; Emmet Lord; Donnie Toliver.

Rare Meat - A Six Song Mini-Album .... Del-Fi/Rhino (M) RNEP-604 5-10 83
Baby Ray & Ferns; Heartbreakers; Boby Guy; others.

Rare Rockabilly, Vol. 3 .... MCA (M) MCL-1757 8-12
Buddy Covelle; Roy Hall; Autrey Inman; Moon Mullican; Billy Harlan; Rockin' Saints; Rex Allen; Jerry Eagle; Red Sovine; Chester Smith; Jerry Kennedy; Chuck & Bill; Roy Hall; Red Foley; Joe Therrian & His Rockets; Vernon Claud; Arthur Osborne; Billy Harlan.

Rare Trax—Timeless Hits Rediscovered .... Era (S) BU-9970 8-12
Strawberry Alarm Clock; John Fred; O'Kaysions; R. Dean Taylor; Brewer & Shipley; Brooklyn Bridge; American Breed; Five Americans; Soul Survivors; Ron Banks.

Rarest of the Rare, Vol. 1 .... Crystal Ball (S) 129 8-10 90
Mustangs; Twisters; DeCoys; Eric & Plazas; Dutch London; John Hurley; Bryan Brent & Cut Outs; Carvettes; Crystalights; Classics; Caprees; Cardinals; Downbeats; Dawns.

Rattles Highway Revisited, Tribute to the Rutles .... Shimmy-Disc (S) 041 5-10 90s
Bongwater; Dog Bowl; Pale Face; Shonen Knife; King Missle; Galaxie 500; Tinklers; Daniel John Ston; Das Damen; Tuli Kupferberg; Unrest; Joey Arias; Lida Husik; Jelly Fish Kiss; Pussywillows; Bongos; Bass & Bob; Uncle Wiggly; Syd Straw; Marc Ribot; Peter Stampfel & Bottle Caps; When People Were Shorter and Lived Near the Water.

Reach Out and Touch (7 LP) .... Reader's Digest/BMG (S) 037 40-55 91
(Boxed set. Mail order offer.) Elvis Presley; others.

Real Ambassadors .... Columbia (M) OL-5850 15-20 63

Real Ambassadors .... Columbia (S) OS-2250 20-25 63
Louis Armstrong; Dave Brubeck; Dave Lambert; Jon Hendricks; Annie Ross; Carmen McRae.

Real Blues .... Excello (S) 8011 10-20
Roscoe Shelton; Blue Charlie; Baby Boy Warren; Earl Gaines; Whispering Smith; Silas Hogan; Jimmy Anderson; Lightnin' Slim; Lazy Lester; Slim Harpo.

Real Summit Meeting Live at Newport: the Blues (2 LP) .... MFSL (S) 2-518 30-40 80s

Realistic Drug Education Album .... Do It Now Foundation (S) DIN-302 8-12 72
Byrds; Alliota Haynes; Hoyt Axton; Canned Heat; Fugs; Genesis; others.

Realistic Jazz Greats, Vol. 2 .... Columbia Special Products (S) P 13230 8-12 76
Louis Armstrong; Dave Brubeck Quartet; Pete Fountain; Erroll Garner; Ella Fitzgerald; Count Basic; Al Hirt; Benny Goodman; Duke Ellington. (Made for Radio Shack.)

Rebel Rouser .... K-Tel (S) NC-451 5-10 70s
Duane Eddy; Surfaris; Champs; Lonnie Mack; Dave "Baby" Cortez; Johnny & Hurricanes; Bill Justis; Santo & Johnny; Mongo Santamaria; Sputnicks; Chantays; Ventures; Rockin' Rebels; Incredible Bongo Band; String-a-Longs; B. Bumble & Stingers; Virtues; Ernie Fields.

Rebirth of Beale St. .... Beale St. (S) No Number Used 200-225 83
(Promotional issue only.) Elvis Presley; Lou Rawls; Handy's Orchestra; Charlie Williamson's Beale St. Frolic; Furry Lewis; Illionis Central Glee Club; Memphis Jug Band; B.B. King; Sunset Travelers; Little Junior's Blue Flames; Rufus Thomas. (Limited edition, 1000 numbered copies.)

Record Hop: see Del-Fi Record Hop

Record of Quality, Vol. 2 .... Columbia Special Products (M) CSP 116 5-10 60s
Andre Kostelanetz; Merrill Staton; George Maharis; Rosemary Clooney; Andre Previn; Tony Bennett; Frank DeVol; Vic Damone; Percy Faith; Four Lads; Jerry Vale. (Made for Sanitone Dry Cleaner.)

Recorded Entertainment Live at the Whiskey A-Go-Go! .... Vee Jay (M) VJLP-1100 20-25 64
Jerry Butler; Betty Everett; Jimmy Reed; Wilbert Harrison; Gladys Knight & Pips; Maxine Brown; Joe & Ann; Eugene Church; John Lee Hooker; Marvin & Johnny. (Studio recordings with audience overdub.)

Recorded Highlights of Glenn Wallichs Day: see Capitol Promotional Releases/Samplers

Recorded Live at Newport in New York .... Buddah (S) 5616 8-10 74
Stevie Wonder; Aretha Franklin; Ray Charles; Donny Hathaway; Staple Singers.

Recorded Live at the Apollo in New York .... Motown (M) 609 15-20 63
Mary Wells; Stevie Wonder; Miracles; Supremes; Marvin Gaye; Marvelettes; Contours.

Records Galore .... A-Bet (M) LP-401 10-15
Radiants; Dave "Baby" Cortez; Guitar Gable; Kelly Brothers; Tony Clark; Wallace Brothers; Carter Brothers; Knight Borthers; Lowell Fulson; B.B. King; Bobby Powell; Teen Queens; Slim Harpo; Bo Diddley; Gladiolas.

Reefer Songs .... Stash (S) ST-100 8-10 80s

Red Bird Goldies .... Red Bird (M) RB 20-102 20-30 65
Dixie Cups; Shangri-Las; Trade Winds; Jelly Beans; Butterflys; Alvin Robinson; Ad Libs.

Red Foley Story .... Decca (M) DL-4341 25-35 63

Red Foley Story .... Decca (S) DL-74341 30-40 63
Red Foley; Patsy Cline; Kitty Wells; Ernest Tubb; Wilburn Brothers; others.

Redneck Mothers .... RCA (S) APL1-2438 5-10 77
Johnny Russell; Gary Stewart; Willie Nelson; Bobby Bare; others.

Redneck Mothers .... RCA (S) AYL1-3674 5-8 80s
Steve Young; Jerry Reed; Tennessee Pulleybone; Vernon Oxford; others.

Reflections....................Columbia (S) 1P 6466 5-10 76
Dinah Shore; Les Brown; Pearl Bailey; Eddy Duchin; Harry James; Jose Powell; Frankie Carle; Peggy Lee; Benny Goodman; Orrin Tucker; Duke Ellington. (Columbia Record Club issue.)

Reflections (2 LP)....................Columbia Special Products/Sessions (S) ???? 8-12 70s
Johnny Mathis; Ray Conniff; Andre Kostelanetz; Vikki Carr; Tony Bennett; Robert Goulet; Brooklyn Bridge; Peter Nero; Mamas & Papas; Lulu; Scott McKenzie; Mama Cass; Jim Nabors.

Reflections....................K-Tel (S) NU 9450 5-10 74
Anne Murray; Roberta Flack; Donny Hathaway; Michael Johnson; Morris Albert; Barry Manilow; Eric Carmen; Crystal Gayle; Harry Nilsson; Natalie Cole; Gene Cotton; Chris Rea; Stephen Bishop; Seals & Crofts; Paul Davis; Toby Beau.

Reggae Spectacular....................A&M (S) 3529 76
Jimmy Cliff; Blue Haze; Glen & Dave; Greyhound; Harry J. & Stars; Bob & Marcia.

Release Me....................Nashville (SE) NLP-2068 5-10 69
Dolly Parton; Dottie West; Jan Howard; June Stearns.

Release Me....................Power Pak (SE) PO 299 5-10
Dolly Parton; Dottie West; Jan Howard; June Stearns.

Remember Christmas....................Columbia (S) CCS 1077 5-10 70s
Eugene Ormandy & Philadelphia Orchestra; Burl Ives; Anita Bryant; Ray Conniff; Jim Nabors; New Christy Minstrels; Robert Goulet; Percy Faith; Steve Lawrence; Eydie Gorme; Skitch Henderson.

Remember How Great, Vol. 1....................Roulette (S) 42027 10-15 69
Heartbeats; Frankie Lymon; Chantels; Chuck Berry; Little Anthony & Imperials; others.

Remember How Great, Vol. 1....................Columbia (M) XTV-66639/66640 10-20
Louis Armstrong; Count Basie; Les Brown; Doris Day; Cab Calloway; Xavier Cugat; Tommy Dorsey; Eddy Duchin; Duke Ellington; Harry James; Andre Kostelanetz; Mary Martin; Dinah Shore. (Special products. Made for Lucky Strike.)

Remember How Great, Vol. 2....................Columbia (M) XTV-69408/69409 10-20
Jo Stafford; Percy Faith; Chordetts; Andy Williams; Gogi Grant; Frankie Laine; Guy Mitchell; Rosemary Clooney; Tony Bennett; Champs; Patti Page; Cab Calloway.

Remember the Night, the Girl & Song....................Warner Bros. (M) W-1426 10-20 61

Remember the Night, the Girl & Song....................Warner Bros. (S) WS-1426 15-25 61
Art Lund; Helen O'Connell; Martha Tilton; Bob Eberly; Ronnie Kemper; Yvonne King; Joe "Fingers" Carr; Jack Leonard; Martha Tilton; Skinnay Ennis; Hoagy Carmichael; Tex Beneke.

Remember the Oldies....................Argo (M) LP-649 100-200 63
(Colored vinyl.)

Remember the Oldies....................Argo (M) LP-649 40-60 63
(Black vinyl.) Clifton Chenier; Jody Williams; Three Souls; Paul Gayten; Eddie McDuff; Kendall Sisters; Clarence Henry; Silla-Tones; Rod Bernard; Monotones.

Remember the '60s, Vol. 1 (2 LP)....................???? 8-12
Dave Berry; Turtles; Overlanders; David Garrick; Flowerpot Man; Byrds; Gerry & Pacemakers; Chrispian St. Peters; Searchers; Jonathan King; Sandy Shaw; Troggs; Fleetwood Mac; Kinks; Love Affair; Tremeloes; Donovan; Desmond Dekker & Aces; Mermaids; Gary Puckett & Union Gap; Clinton Ford; Georgie Fame; Equals; Zombies; Tommy James & Shondells; Dave Berry; Status Quo; Lovin' Spoonful.

Remember the '60s, Vol. 2 (2 LP)....................???? 8-12
Small Faces; Amen Corner; Fleetwood Mac; Barry McGuire; Vincent Edwards; Twice As Much; Billy Joe Royal; Monkees; Zager & Evans; Paul Revere & Raiders; Archies; Gun; Chris Farlowe; Humble Pie; Scorpions; Tommy Roe; Equals; American Breed; Grapefruit; Marmalaide; Tremeloes; Andy Kim; Shocking Blue; Nice; McCoys; Blood, Sweat & Tears; Chicken Shack; Cupid's Inspiration; Mamas & Papas; Small Faces; Donovan.

Remember the '60s, Vol. 3 (2 LP)....................???? 8-12
Rolling Stones; Jimi Hendrix; Them; Marbles; Fortunes; Marmalade; Julie Driscoll; Crazy World of Arthur Brown;. Beatles; Cat Stevens; Honeybus; Bee Gees; Aphrodite's Child; Fat Mattress; Cream; Small Faces; Golden Earring; Dave Dee, Dozy, Beaky, Mick & Tich; Unit 4 + 2; Grignard; New Vaudeville Band; Lulu; Walker Brothers; Pretty Things; Robin Gibb; Herd; Thunderclap Newman; Marianne Faithfull; Mersey Beats; David Bowie; Blue Cheer.

Remember the '60s, Vol. 4 (2 LP)....................???? 8-12
Procol Harum; Mamas & Papas; Dave Dee, Dozy, Beeky, Mick & Tich; Mindbenders; Dave Berry; Whistling Jack Smith; 1910 Gruitgum Co.; Casuals; Scott McKenzie; Dusty Springfield; Lemon Pipers; Herd; Fortunes; Small Faces; Spencer David Group Traffic; Cream; Joe Cocker; Troggs; Dawn Marbles; Blood, Sweat & Tears; Spooky Tooth; Jimi Hendrix; Fleetwood Mac; Free; George Cash; Martha Reeves; Neil Diamond; Royal Guardsmen; Pretty Things.

Remember the '60s, Vol. 5 (2 LP)....................???? 8-12
Monkees; Flowerpot Men; Otis Redding; Moody Blues; Walker Brothers; Wayne Fontana & Mindbenders; Turtles; Oliver; Joe Cocker; Blind Faith; Traffic; Tremeloes; Billie Joe Royal; Mariane Faithfull; Donovan; Bob & Earl; Family Dogg; Kenny Rogers & First Edition; Byrds; Sam & Dave; Sonny & Cher; Ike & Tina Turner; Fortunes; Cat Stevens; Them; Merseys; Freddie & Dreamers; Ohio Express; Dave Dee, Dozy Beeky, Mick & Tich; Procol Harum.

Remember the '60s, Vol. 6 (2 LP)....................???? 8-12
Animals; Donovan; Searchers; Manfred Mann; Honeycombs; Freddie & Dreamers; Sandie Shaw; Beach Boys; Canned Heat; Don Partridge; Peter & Gordon; Jay & Americans; Foundations; Chris Andrews; Ivy League; Dave Davies; Herman's Hermits; Keith; Bonzo Dog Band; Cilla Black; Gerry & Pacemakers; David Gerrick; Scaffold.

Remember the '60s, Vol. 7 (2 LP)....................???? 8-12
Q65; Focus; Bintangs; Cuby & Blizzards; Armand; Buffoons; Motions; Golden Earrings; Sandy Coast; Peter Tetteroo; Shocking Blue; Outsiders; Les Baroques; Groep 1950; Roek's Family; Zen; Cats; Brainbox; Ekseption; Wally Tax; Het; Rodys; Shoes; Earth & Fire; Dizzy Man Band; Swinging Soul Machine; Rudy Bennett; Free; George Baker Selection; Bob Hoeke Rhythm & Blues Group; Boudewijn de Groot.

Remember These (3 LP)....................UMI (S) no number 15-20 70s
Teddy Bears; Chad & Jeremy; June Valli; Perez Prado; Harry Belafonte; Della Reese; Castells; Donnie Brooks; Gogi Grant; Art & Dottie Todd; Russell Arms; Vogues; Jerry Wallace; Jimmie Rodgers; Tommy Edwards; Chordettes; Statler Brothers; Pat Boone; Crew-Cuts; Gaylords; Frankie Laine; David Carroll; Dells; Rusty Draper; San Fernando Voices; Patti Page; Platters; Jim Lowe; Billy Vaughn; Sarah Vaughan; Paris Sisters; Kitty Lester; Hugo Winterhalter.

Remembering Christmas with the Big Bands....................RCA (M) DPM1-0506 5-10 81
Glenn Miller; Sammy Kaye; Fontane Sisters; Larry Clinton; Fats Waller; Ralph Flanagan; Claude Thornhill; Freddy Martin; Henry Mancini.

Remembering the '40s (8 LP) .... Reader's Digest (SE) RDA-053 30-45 77

(Boxed set.) Glenn Miller; Ray Eberle; Tex Beneke; Marion Hutton; Modernaires; Jimmy Dorsey; Tommy Dorsey; Frank Sinatra; Pied Pipers; Bob Eberly; Helen O'Connell; Dinah Shore; Bob Chester; Al Stuart; Judy Garland; Andrews Sisters; Bing Crosby; Ella Fitzgerald; Ink Spots; Wayne King; Buddy Clark; Guy Lombardo; Carmen Miranda; Harry James & Helen Forrest; Eddy Howard; Merry Macs; Billie Holiday; Vaughn Monroe; Norton Sisters; Jimmie Lunceford; Dooley Wilson; Dick Haymes; Song Spinners; Glen Gray; Eugenie Baird; Duke Ellington; Alfred Drake; Joan Roberts; Marlene Dietrich; Russ Morgan; Louis Jordan; Patti Dugan; Carmen Cavallaro; Perry Como; Sammy Kaye; Don Cornell; Billy Williams Choir; Louis Prima; Art Lund; Hoagy Carmichael; Art Mooney; Freddy Martin; Merv Griffin; Clyde Rogers; Glen Hughes & Martian Men; Blue Barron; Carson Robison & Pleasant Valley Boys; Francis Craig; Gordon Jenkins; Charles LeVere; Evelyn Knight & Starlighters; Henri Rene; Tony Martin; Fran Warren.

Remembering the '50s & '60s (3 LP) .... Reader's Digest (S) RDA-030 15-25 79

(Boxed set. Includes booklet. Mail order offer.) Ed Ames; Ames Brothers; Association; Les Baxter; Harry Belafonte; Pat Boone; Teresa Brewer; Browns; Glen Campbell; Cascades; Perry Como; Sam Cooke; Floyd Cramer; Crew-Cuts; Diamonds; Drifters; Everly Brothers; Fifth Dimension; Eddie Fisher; Tennessee Ernie Ford; Four Aces; Gale Garnett; Bobbie Gentry; Harpers Bizarre; Kingston Trio; Peggy Lee; Lettermen; Trini Lopez; Los Indios Tabajaras; Jim Lowe; Mamas & Papas; Henry Mancini; Dean Martin; Tony Martin; Al Martino; Mickey & Sylvia; Mills Brothers; Domenico Modugno; Harry Nilsson; Patti Page; Les Paul & Mary Ford; Emilio Pericoli; Peter & Gordon; Platters; Perez Prado; Jim Reeves; Nelson Riddle; Ruby & Romantics; Kyu Sakamoto; Neil Sedaka; Seekers; Jo Stafford; Kay Starr; Morris Stoloff; Vogues; Weavers; Mason Williams; Roger Williams; Glenn Yarbrough.

Repo Man .... San Andreas/MCA (S) 39019 8-10 84

(Soundtrack.) Iggy Pop; Black Flag; Suicidal Tendencies; Plugz; Juicy Bananas; Circle Jerks; Burning Sensations; Fear.

Reprise All Star Spectacular: see All Star Spectacular

Reprise Record Distributor .... Reprise RD-2 75-125 61

Frank Sinatra; others.

Reprise Record Distributor .... Reprise RD-3 75-125 61

Frank Sinatra; others.

Reprise Record Distributor .... Reprise RD-4 75-125 62

Frank Sinatra; others.

Reprise Record Distributor .... Reprise RD-5 75-125 62

Frank Sinatra; others.

Reprise Record Distributor .... Reprise RD-6 75-125 62

Frank Sinatra; Dean Martin; others. (One-sided record.)

Reprise Record Distributor: 74,000,000 Talent Bonanza, July 1962 .... Reprise RD-7 75-125 63

Frank Sinatra; others.

Reprise Record Distributor .... Reprise RD-8 75-125 63

Frank Sinatra; others.

Reprise Record Distributor: Look Who's Coming to Your House, Jan. 1963 .... Reprise RD-9 20-40 63

Dean Martin; others.

Requested by You, the Billboard .... Columbia (M) CL 607 50-100 53

Frank Sinatra; Paul Weston; Rosemary; Harry James; Xavier Cugat; Woody Herman; Doris Day; Morton Gould; Frank Parker; Benny Goodman; Andre Kostelanetz. (12-inch LP.)

Requested by You, the Billboard .... Columbia (M) CL 6254 50-100 54

(10–inch LP.) Frank Sinatra; Paul Weston; Rosemary Clooney; Harry James; Xavier Cugat; Woody Herman; Doris Day.

Residue .... Ralph (S) RZ-8302 8-10 83

Residents; others.

Return of the Living Dead .... Enigma (S) 72004-1 8-1085(Soundtrack.) C

Return of the Living Dead .... Enigma (S) 72085-1 15-20 85

(Picture disc.)

Return of the Living Dead, Part 2 .... Island (S) 90854-1 8-10 88

Return of the Living Dead, Part 2 .... Island (S) ISTA-17 8-10 88

(Soundtrack.) Julian Cope; Anthrax; Mantronic; Leatherwolf; Lamont; Big O; J. Peter Robinson; Zodiac Mindward & Love Reaction.

Return to Casablanca .... Casablanca (S) NBD-20135 8-12 78

(Promotional issue only.) Sylvers; Stonebolt; Randy Brown; Shel Silverstein; Lori Lieberman.

Return to Casablanca (2 LP) .... Casablanca (S) NBD-2014-2 10-15 78

(Promotional issue only.) Donna Summer; Sheila B. Devotion; Roberta Kelly; Cameo; Parlet; Morris Jefferson; Alec R. Costandinos; Sphinx; Sumeria; Love & Kisses; Parliament; Village People; Santa Esmeralda featuring Jimmy Goings; Meco; Kiss; Angel; Trigger; Stallion; Godz.

Return to Macon County .... United Artists (S) UA-LA-491 8-10 75

(Soundtrack.) Fats Domino; Sandy Nelson; Eddie Cochran; Fleetwoods; Rick Nelson; Freddy Cannon; Ventures; Jimmy Dorsey; Gary Miles.

Reunion 74/1 .... Columbia (S) 2P-6144 12-15

(Two LPs.)

Reunion 74/2 .... Columbia (S) 1P-6144 8-12

(One LP. These two LPs were reissued as _World's Greatest Rock Festival_.)

Reunion Blues .... MPS (S) 20908 8-12 73

Oscar Peterson; Ray Brown; Milt Jackson; Louis Hayes.

Revenge of the Nerds .... Scotti Bros. (S) AL-39599 10-12 84

(Promotional issue only.)

Revenge of the Nerds .... Scotti Bros. (S) BFZ-39599 8-10 84

(Soundtrack.) Andrea & Hot Mink; Ya Ya; Rubinoos; others.

Revenge of the Killer B's .... Warner Bros. (S) 25068-1 5-10 84

Fleetwood Mac; Marshall Crenshaw; Depeche Mode; Rank & File; B 52's; Pretenders; Talking Heads; Madonna; Tom Verlaine; Aztec Camera; Echo & Bunnymen; Kid Creole & Coconuts.

Revolution .... United Artists (S) UAS-5185 20-25 68

Revolution .... United Artists (S) UA-LA296-G 12-15 74

(Soundtrack.) Quicksilver Messenger Service; Steve Miller; Mother Earth; others.

Rhapsody in Hues .... Mark 56 (M) 526 10-15 65

Raoul Ploiakin; Keith Textor Singers; Billy Daniels; Arthur Lyman; George Greely & Warner Brothers Orchestra; Hi-Lo's; Larry Clinton; Bob Prince; Matty Matlock & Paducah Patrol.

Rhino Royale .... Rhino (S) RNLP 002 8-12 78

(Colored vinyl.) Ruben Guevara; Gefilte Joe & Fish; Rockin' Richie Ray; Fred Blassie; Richie Balance; Temple City Kazoo Orchestra; Wild Man Fischer; Little Stevie Weingold; Credibility Gap; Wino.

Rhythm and Blues .... Guest Star (M) G-1900 10-20 60s

Rhythm and Blues ....Guest Star (S GS-1900 10-20 60s
Penguins; Medallions; Platters; Cufflinks; Romancers; Gold Chords; Meadowlarks.

Rhythm and Blues, Vol. 1 - the End of an Era: see Legendary Masters Series

Rhythm and Blues, Vol. 1 ....Savoy (EP) XP-8049 50-100 51

Rhythm and Blues, Vol. 1 ....Savoy (M) MG-15008 150-250 51
(10–inch LP.)

Rhythm and Blues, Vol. 2 ....Savoy (EP) XP-8050 50-100 51

Rhythm and Blues, Vol. 2 - Sweet N' Greasy: see Legendary Masters Series

Rhythm and Blues and Greens: see McPHATTER, Clyde / Little Richard / Jerry Butler

Rhythm and Blues Christmas ....United Artists (S) UA-LA-654-R 8-12 76
(Boxed set.) Charles Brown; Five Keys; Chuck Berry; B.B. King; Lowell Fulson; Amos Milburn; Orioles; Clyde McPhatter & Drifters; Baby Washington; Marvin & Johnny.

Rhythm and Blues Classics ....Rhythm/Starfire (M) RSF-1000 15-25 81
(Picture disc.)

Rhythm and Blues Classics ....Rhythm/Starfire (M) RSF-1000 8-12 81
(Blue vinyl.) Lyrics; Spinners; Alice Jean & Mondellos; Little Willie Littlefield; Tempos; Bob Jeffries & Marcels; Ollie Clay.

Rhythm and Blues Greatest Hits ....Pickwick (S) SPC-3663 5-10 79
Eddie Holman; Lloyd Price; O'Kaysions; Impressions; Carl Carlton; Joe Hinton; Bobby "Blue" Bland; Del-Vikings; Roy Head.

Rhythm and Blues Vocal Groups ....Authentic (M) AULP-501 10-15
Medallions; Penguins; Cufflinx; Romancers; Willie Headen & Birds.

Rhythm and Blues in the Night ....Hollywood (M) 30 20-30
Connie Bennet; Bill Smyth & Harlem-Aires; others.

Rhythm & Booze, Vol. 1 ....Lunar 2 (S) L2M- 2002 8-12 80s
Floyd Dixon; Bel-Aires; Stick McGhee; Lucky Millinger; Robins; Wynonie Harris; Nightcaps; Five Keys; Amos Milburn; Jimmy Liggens; Hot Lips Paige.

Rhythm & Booze, Vol. 2 ....Lunar 2 (S) L2M-2004 8-12 80s
Roscoe Gordon; Hollywood Four Flames; Champion Jack Dupree; Five Owls; Kidds; Thrillers; Screamin' Jay Hawkins; Floyd Dixon; Question Marks; Crickets; Joe Dyson; Echos.

Ride the Wild Surf ....Liberty (M) LPR-3368 20-25 64

Ride the Wild Surf ....Liberty (S) LST-7368 25-30 64
(Soundtrack.) Jan & Dean; Fantastic Baggys; others.

Right Now ....Columbia (S) C 10170 8-12 70
Raiders; Poco; Ray Stevens; Ronnie Dyson; Blood, Sweat & Tears; Al Kooper; Tom Rush; Aretha Franklin; Santana; Barbra Streisand.

Right On ....K-Tel (S) TU 2500 5-10 76
Thin Lizzy; Heart; Firefall; ELO; Barry DeVorzon; Perry Botkin Jr.; Manhattans; Bay City Rollers; Miracles; Diana Ross; Lou Rawls; Elton John; Commodores; Paul Anka; Odia Coates; Abba; Norman Connors; War; Eric Carmen; Pilot; Flash Cadillac & Continental Kids; Brick.

Riot in Blues ....Time (M) T-70006 20-30 60
Ray Charles; Lightnin' Hopkins; Sonny Terry; others.

Riot on Sunset Strip ....Tower (M) T-5065 15-20 67

Riot on Sunset Strip ....Tower (S) ST-5065 20-25 67
(Soundtrack.) Standells; Mugwumps; Chocolate Watch Band; Sidewalk Sounds; Debra Travis; Mom's Boys; Drew.

Rip Roarin' Country ....K-Tel (S) WU 3760 5-10 83
Alabama; Willie Nelson; Hank Williams Jr.; Conway Twitty; Eddie Rabbitt; Moe Bandy; Bellamy Brothers; Mel Tillis; Waylon Jennings; George Jones; George Strait; Mel McDaniel; Johnny Cash; T.G. Sheppard; Delbert McClinton; Bobby Bare.

Ripe Beats ....Columbia (S) AS-548 5-10 79
(Promotional issue only.) Gary's Gang; Cheryl Lynn; John Davis & Monster Orchestra; Keith Barrow; Jackie Moore. (Labeled "Special Limited Edition for Disco D.J.s only.")

Rising Stars of San Francisco ....War Bride (S) WB-9005 10-15
Eye Protection; Fun Addicts; New Romans; Holly Sstanton; Kingsnakes; Barry Bonn; Roy Loney; Imposters; Readymades; Timmy Spence; Pushups.

Risky Blues ....King (M) KS-1133 15-20 71

Risky Blues ....King (SE) KS-1133 15-20 71

Risky Blues ....Gusto (S) KS-1133 8-10 76
(Reissue of King LP.) Midnighters; Dominoes; Wynonie Harris; Bull Moose Jackson; Swallows; Checkers; Lucky Millinder; Robert Henry; Jesse Powell; Fluffy Hunter; Todd Rhodes; Eddie "Lockjaw" Davis.

Risky Business ....Virgin (S) V-2302 10-12 84
(Soundtrack.) Bob Seger; Jeff Beck; Muddy Waters; Tangerine Dream; Prince; Journey; Phil Collins.

River Rat ....RCA (S) CBL1-5310 8-10 84
(Soundtrack.) Alabama; Earl Thomas Conley; Deborah Allen; Bill Medley; Autograph; Joey Scarbury.

River's Edge ....Enigma (S) SJ-73242 8-10 87
(Soundtrack.) Slayer; Agent Orange; Wipers; Burning Spear; Hallows Eve; Fates Warning.

Riverside Folk Song Sampler ....Riverside (M) RLP S-2 10-15
Bob Gibson; Paul Clayton; Margaret Barry; Ewan MacColl; John Greenway; Patrick Galvin; Ed McCurdy; A.L. Lloyd; Obray Ramsey; Milt Okun; Oscar Brand; Erik Darling; Jean Ritchie; Artus Moser; Merrick Jarrett; Rev. Gary Davis.

Road House ....Arista (S) AL9-8576 8-10 89
(Soundtrack.) Jeff Healey Band; Bob Seger; Otis Redding; Little Feat; Patrick Swayze; Kris McKay.

Road Music ....Gusto (S) GTV-107 5-10
Red Sovine; Dave Dudley; Del Reeves; Coleman Wilson; T.H. Music Festival; Willis Brothers; Minnie Pearl; Moore & Napier; Tiny Harris; Rod Hart; Jimmy Martin; Jimmy Griggs; Lonnie Irving; Claude Gray.

Roadie (2 LP) ....Warner Bros. (S) 2HS-3441 10-12 80
(Soundtrack.) Cheap Trick; Pat Benatar; Teddy Pendergrass; Jay Ferguson; Blondie; Styx; Joe Ely Band; Alice Cooper; Eddie Rabbitt; Stephen Bishop; Yvonne Elliman; Sue Sadd & Next; Asleep at the Wheel; Jerry Lee Lewis; Roy Orbison; Emmy Lou Harris; Hank Williams Jr.

Roadie ....Warner Bros. (S) PRO-A-861 15-20 80
(Soundtrack. Promotional issue only.) Alice Cooper; Pat Benatar; Blondie; Stephen Bishop; Yvonne Elliman; Jay Ferguson; Styx; Sue Sadd & Next; Double Yellow Line; Teddy Pendergrass; Roy Orbison; Emmylou Harris; Cheap Trick.

Roadie ....Warner Bros. (S) PRO-A-885 15-20 80
(Soundtrack. Promotional issue only.) Jerry Lee Lewis; Hank Williams Jr.; Blondie; Roy Orbison, Emy Lou Harris; Eddie Rabbitt; Asleep at the Wheel.

Robert W. Sarnoff—25 Years of RCA Leadership .... RCA (SP) RWS-0001 1000-2000 73
(In-house promotional issue honoring Sarnoff's career at RCA.) Elvis Presley; Perry Como; Spike Jones; Mario Lanza; Phil Harris; Eddie Fisher; Vaughn Monroe; Perez Prado; Jascha Heifetz; Artur Rubinstein; Leontyne Price; Vladmir Horwitz; Artur Toscanini; Harry Belafonte; Van Cliburn; John F. Kennedy; Henry Mancini; Little Peggy March; Al Hirt; SSGT. Barry Sadler; Eddy Arnold; Browns; Charley Pride; Jim Reeves; Chet Atkins & Boston Pops; Monkees; Guess Who; José Feliciano; Jefferson Airplane; Neil Armstrong; Friends of Distinction; John Denver; Main Ingredient; Jimmy Castor Bunch; David Bowie; Harry Nilsson; Linda Hopkins; others. (Approximately 50 made.)

Robin & Seven Hoods .... Reprise (M) R-2021 25-35 64

Robin & Seven Hoods .... Reprise (S) FS-2021 40-45 64
(Soundtrack.) Dean Martin with Frank Sinatra & Bing Crosby; Sammy Davis Jr.; Peter Falk; others.

Rock .... Columbia Special Products (S) C 10247 8-12 70s
Blood, Sweat & Tears; Spiral Staircase; Fleetwood Mac; Mark Lindsay; Santana; Gary Puckett & Union Gap; Hollies; Mike Bloomfield & Al Kooper; Raiders; Big Brother & Holding Company.

Rock '80 .... K-Tel (S) TU-2780 5-10 80
Gary Numan; Pretenders; Sniff 'N' the Tears; Nick Lowe; Joe Jackson; Pat Benatar; Blondie; Ramones; Knack; Cheap Trick; Ian Gomm; M.

Rock Album .... K-Tel (S) TU 2680 5-10 80
ELO; Foreigner; Eddie Money; Robin Trower; Blue Oyster Cult; Cheap Trick; Robert Palmer; Styx; Boston; Jethro Tull; Journey; Babys; Kansas; Toto.

Rock All Stars (5 LP) .... Columbia 5P 7289 20-25
(Mail order offer.) Mitch Ryder & Detroit Wheels; Three Dog Night; Creedence Clearwater Revival; Tommy James & Shondells; 5th Dimension; Paul Revere & Raiders; Lovin' Spoonful; Byrds; Monkees; Gary Puckett & Union Gap. (Each album side has tracks by one artist.)

Rock All Night .... Mercury (M) MG-20293 70-80 57
(Soundtrack.) Platters; Blockbusters; Eddie Beal Combo; Nora Hayes.

Rock and Raunchy .... Audio Encores (S) AE1-1007 5-10 80
(Direct-to-disc rerecordings.) Duane Eddy; Bill Justis; Chantays; Johnny & Hurricanes; Bill Doggett; Surfaris.

Rock and Roll .... Grand Award (M) 33-343 10-15

Rock and Roll .... Waldorf Music Hall (S) MHK-33-1210 10-15
Jerry Duane & Light Brigade; Artie Malvin & Rhythm Rockets; Ink Spots; Loren Becker; Rhythm Rockets; Vincent Lopez; Artie Malvin; Enoch Light.

Rock and Roll .... Regent (M) MG-6015 30-60 56
Chuz Alfred Combo; Hal Singer Band; Bobby Banks; Rockin' Brothers Orchestra; Bob Oakes; T.J. Fowler; Paul Williams.

Rock and Roll 2 .... Regent (M) MG-6042 30-60 56

Rock and Roll Bandstand .... Roulette (M) R-25093 30-40 59
Buddy Knox; Jimmy Bowen; Playmates; Ronnie Hawkins; Cathy Carr; Valerie Carr.

Rock and Roll Dance Party .... Modern (M) LMP-1210 75-100 56

Rock and Roll Dance Party .... RPM (M) LRP-3001 150-250 56

Rock and Roll Dance Party .... Crown (M) CLP-5001 50-75 56
Etta James; Marvin & Johnny; Cadets; Teen Queens; Jimmy Beasley; Joe Turner; Joe Houston; Little Clydie; Jacks.

Rock and Roll Dance Party .... King (M) 395-536 100-150 57

Rock and Roll Dance Party .... Somerset (M) P-1300 200-400 58
Bill Haley & His Comets; Dinning Sisters; Bunny Paul; Swingers; Ken Carson; Escorts; Aristocrats; House Rockers.

Rock and Roll: Evolution or Revolution? .... Laurie (M) LLP 2044 10-15 70

Rock and Roll: Evolution or Revolution? .... Laurie (S) SLP 2044 10-15 70
(Narration by Norm N. Nite. Excerpts of 41 songs.) Turbans; Five Satins; Mellow Kings; Maurice Williams & Zodiacs; Robins; Coasters; Drifters; Jive Five; Bill Haley & His Comets; Ron Holden; Little Caesar & Romans; Penguins; Dell-Vikings; Cadillacs; Bobby Freeman; Silhouettes; Hank Ballard & Midnighters; Dion & Belmonts; Mystics; Gary "U.S." Bonds; Chiffons; Music Explosion; Diamonds; Danleers; Etta James; Teen Queens; Smokey Robinson & Miracles; Skyliners; Preston Epps; Crows; Frankie Lymon & Teenagers; Heartbeats; Cleftones; Little Anthony & Imperials; Joe Jones; Little Richard; Isley Brothers.

Rock and Roll Era .... Audio Encores (S) AE1-1006 5-10 80
(Rerecordings by original artists.) Dee Clark; Marcels; Frankie Ford; Bobby Freeman; Diamonds; Randy & Rainbows; Dovells; Bobby Lewis; Jumpin' Gene; Kingsmen.

Rock and Roll Festival, Vol. 1 .... United (S) US-7761 10-20 70s

Rock and Roll Forever (2 LP) .... Forever (S) FR-101 8-12 70
Les Cooper; Bo Diddley; Shirelles; Robert & Johnny; Dan Leers; Gary "U.S." Bonds; Contours; James Booker; Diamonds; Chris Kenner; Howlin' Wolf; Mello-Kings; Bobby Freeman; Sensations; Jan Bradley; Otis Redding; Booker T. & MGs; Johnny Thunder; Clarence Henry; Quin-Tones; Jesse Belvin.

Rock and Roll Forever .... Atlantic (M) 1239 100-150 56

Rock and Roll Forever .... Atlantic (M) 8010 75-125 57
LaVern Baker; Ruth Brown; Ray Charles; Clovers; Clyde McPhatter & Drifters; Joe Turner; T-Bone Walker.

Rock and Roll Forever, Vol. 2 .... Atlantic (M) 8021 50-75 59
LaVern Baker; Ruth Brown; Ray Charles; Clovers; Clyde McPhatter; Drifters; Joe Turner; Ivory Joe Hunter; Jaye Sisters; Chuck Willis.

Rock and Roll Is Here to Stay .... United Artists (S) UAS 29336 10-20
Eddie Cochran; Clovers; Fats Domino; Ventures; Jerry Lee Lewis; Smiley Lewis; Lonnie Mack; Thurston; Hollywood Argyles; Larry Williams.

Rock and Roll Jamboree .... End (M) LP-302 100-150 58
Little Anthony & Imperials; Dubs; Gone Allstars Featuring Buddy Lucas; Ronnie Baxter; Chantels; Jo-Ann Campbell; Eddie Platt.

Rock and Roll Juke Box .... ERA (S) 806 8-12 70
Sandy Nelson; Innocents; Ketty Lester; others.

Rock and Roll New Orleans Blues .... Waldorf (M) MH-33-136 40-60 56
(10–inch LP.) Dave Barton & Royal Playboys; Clarence Samuels; Edgar Blanchard & Gondoliers; Meyer Kennedy; Royal Playboys; Shrewsbury Kid; Helen Marino.

Rock and Roll of the '50s and '60s, Vol. 1 .... MZ (S) 101 8-12
Crystal Tones; Down Beats; Spydels; Larry Lee & Four Bel-Aires; LaSalles; Satellites; Billy James & Crystal Tones.

Rock and Roll Party .... Coral (M) LPCM-97006 15-25
Steve Lawrence; Alan Freed; Lawrence Welk; Don Cornell; George Cates; Georgie Auld; Lancers; McGuire Sisters; Johnny Burnette; Goofers; Freddie Mitchell; George Williams; Sarah McLawler.

Rock and Roll Party .... Guest Star (M) G-1406 10-20 60s

Rock and Roll Party .... Guest Star (S) GS-1406 10-20 60s
Frankie Lymon; Cleftones; Heartbeats; Billy King; Jimmy Vogel; Sammy Greene.

Rock and Roll Party....Regent (M) MG-6042 100-150 56
Nappy Brown; Big Jay McNeeley; T.J. Fowler; Little Esther; Hot Shots; Paul Williams; Hal Singer; Heywood Henry.
Rock and Roll Radio Starring Alan Freed ....Radiola (M) MR-1087 20-30 78
(Radio soundtrack.) Cadillacs; Chordettes; Ivory Joe Hunter; Gene Vincent; LaVern Baker; Etta James; Platters; Chuck Berry; Clyde McPhatter; Penguins; Bill Haley & His Comets; Frankie Lymon & Teenagers; Drifters; Otis Williams & Charms.
Rock and Roll Record Hop....Roulette (M) R-25059 30-40 59
Frankie Lymon & Teenagers; Valentines; Heartbeats; Crows; Playmates; others.
Rock and Roll Revival (3 LP)....Pickwick (S) SH 3306 10-15
(Boxed set.) Bill Haley & His Comets; Platters; Wilbert Harrison; Fats Domino; Tommy Roe; Ray Stevens; Jerry Lee Lewis; Champs; Dusty Springfield; Maurice Williams; Maxine Brown; Lee Dorsey; Lou Rawls; Johnny Rivers; Chuck Jackson; Vogues; Neil Sedaka; Bobby Rydell; Lloyd Price; Trashmen; Garnet Mimms; Silhouettes; Gaylords; Jan & Dean; Clyde McPhatter; Lee Allen; Little Richard; Diamonds; Dave Baby Cortez; Ray Charles; Gene Pitney; Clovers; Isley Brothers.
Rock and Roll Revival ....Pickwick (S) SPC-3280 5-10 70s
Bill Haley & His Comets; Platters; Wilbert Harrison; Fats Domino; Tommy Roe; Ray Stevens; Jerry Lee Lewis; Champs; Dusty Springfield.
Rock and Roll Revue....King (M) 395-513 100-200 56
Rock and Roll Show ....Gusto (SE) GT-0002 5-10 78
Chuck Berry; Jerry Lee Lewis; Coasters; Dominoes; Moonglows; Sammy Turner; Screamin' Jay Hawkins; Bill Dogett; Frankie Ford. (Some tracks are rerecordings.)
Rock and Roll Show (5 LP) ....Gusto (S) GT-0139/0143 15-25 84
(TV mail order offer.) Coasters; Jack Scott; Jay & Techniques; Bill Haley & His Comets; Bull Moose Jackson; Jimmy Clanton; Shirelles; Dee Clark; Jerry Lee Lewis; Van Dykes; Crests; Dorsey Burnette; Cascades; Beach Boys; Midnighters; Dominoes; Charlie Feathers; Sue Thompson; Clarence Carter; American Breed; Sandy Posey; Thomas Wayne; Duane Eddy; Narvel Felts; Ray Peterson; Frankie Ford; Frankie Avalon; Bobby Freeman; Rufus Thomas; Olympics; Ernie K-Doe; Carl Perkins; Swallows; Isley Brothers; Mac Curtis; Climax; Dobie Gray; Hank Ballard & Midnighters; Sam Turner; Freddie King; Little Willie John; Sam & Dave; Del Shannon; Terry Cobb; Lovin' Spoonful; Lee Dorsey; Bobby Day; Bonnie Lou; Gene Pitney; Dixie Cups; Phil Phillips; Joey Dee; Ace Cannon; Boyd Bennett; Wynonie Harris.
Rock and Roll Sock Hop ....Score (M) LP-4018 100-150 58
Rock and Roll Spectacular....Dawn (M) 119 50-75 50s
Sophomores; Royal Jokers; Treniers; others.
Rock and Roll Stars....Buddah (S) BDS-7503 8-12 69
Richie Valens; Bobby Day; Terry Stafford; Jimmy Clanton; Little Richard; Harold Dorman; Maurice Williams; Joe Jones; Frankie Ford; Ron Holden.
Rock and Roll Survival ....Decca (S) DL-75181 10-15 69
Bill Haley & His Comets; Buddy Holly; Kalin Twins; Flamingos; Len Barry; Shirelles.
Rock and Roll - the Early Days....RCA (M) AFM1-5463 8-12 85
Elvis Presley; Chords; Wynonie Harris; Willie Mae Thornton; Muddy Waters; Joe Turner; Bill Haley & His Comets; Carl Perkins; Chuck Berry; Bo Diddley; Little Richard; Jerry Lee Lewis.
Rock and Roll - the Way We Were (2 LP) ....Candlelite/Columbia Special Products (S) P2 13072 15-20 76
Dion; Muhammed Ali; Johnny Mathis; Roy Hamilton; Lenny Welch; Four Lads; Tony Orlando; Percy Faith; Jack Scott; Terry Gilkyson; Billy Joe Royal; Del Shannon; Little Joe & Thrillers; Marty Robbins; Casinos.
Rock and Roll vs. Rhythm and Blues ....Dooto (M) LP-233 50-100 57
Rock and Roll with Buddah (2 LP) ....Buddah (M) 1970 25-35 70
(Promotional issue only.) Bill Haley & His Comets; Brewer & Shipley; Brooklyn Bridge; 1910 Fruitgum Company; Edwin Hawkins Singers; First Generation; Flaming Ember; Impressions; Bengali Bauls; Isley Brothers; Jaggerz; Johnny Winter; Lou Christie; Lovin' Spoonful; Melanie & Hawkins Singers; Motherlode; Myddle Class; Road; Sha Na Na; Silver Metre; Tokens; 1910 Fruitgum Company. (Made for distribution as a souvenir at the N.E.C. convention, February 15-18, 1970 in Memphis.)
Rock and Roll with Rhythm and Blues ....Aladdin (M) LP-710 150-250 56
Rock Around the Clock (3 LP) ....Adam VIII (S) A-8025 10-15 76
Billy Haley & His Comets; Little Anthony & Imperials; Frankie Lymon & Teenagers; Buster Brown; Ronnie Hawkins; Isley Brothers; Kathy Young & Innocents; Shep & Limelites; Dells; Jimmie Rodgers; Buddy Holly & Crickets; Capris; Toys; Jackie Wilson; Lloyd Price; Royal Teens; Poni-Tails; Barry Mann; Elegants; Joe Bennett & Sparkletones.
Rock Baby, Rock It....Rhino (M) RNSP-309 8-10
(Soundtrack.) Johnny Carroll & Hot Rocks; Cell Block Seven; Don Coats & Bon-Aires; Five Stars; Preacher Smith & Deacons; Roscoe Gordon & Red Tops; Belew Twins.
Rock Begins, Vol. 1 ....Atco (SP) SD-33-314 10-15 70
Joe Turner; Ray Charles; Bobby Darin; Chords; LaVern Baker; Coasters; Drifters; Clovers; Clyde McPhatter; Ruth Brown.
Rock Begins, Vol. 2 ....Atco (SP) SD-33-315 10-15 70
Clyde McPhatter & Drifters; Clovers; Ray Charles; Coasters; LaVern Baker; Chuck Willis; Robins; Sensations.
Rock Classics....Columbia (S) P-13867 8-10 70s
Chambers Brothers; Blood, Sweat & Tears; Edgar Winters; Byrds; Buddy Miles; Carlos Santana; Mott the Hoople; Mountain; Electric Flag; Poco; Argent; David Essex; Spirit.
Rock Classics....Warner/Reprise (S) BS 2590 5-10 72
Association; Olympics; Vogues; Harpers Bizarre; Mercy; Everly Brothers; Marketts; Sonny & Cher; Fats Domino; Tokens; Little Richard; Noel Harrison; Dino, Desi & Billy; Watts 103rd St. Band.
Rock Collection ....Columbia Special Products (SP) P-11979 5-10 73
Johnny Winter; Association; Raiders; Byrds; Redbone; Argent; Hollies; Poco; Chase; Mike Bloomfield, Al Kooper; Stephen Stills.
Rock Fantasy ....Columbia Musical Treasury (S) 1P 7230 5-10 81
Spencer Davis Group; Lonnie Mack; Cher; Paul Revere & Raiders; Lovin' Spoonful; Impressions; Castaways; Chris Kenner; Mitch Ryder & Detroit Wheels; ? & Mysterians.
Rock Festival, Elektra-Asylum....Elektra/Asylum/Planet Promo (S) 10-2-79 5-10 79
Gamma; Shoes; Pointer Sisters; Richard Lloyd; Simms Brothers Band; Ritchie Furay; Boulder; Louise Goffin; John Prine.
Rock Festival....MCA Special Products (S) 734748 8-10
Who; Tommy James & Shondells; Strawberry Alarm Clock; David Clayton Thomas; McKendree Spring.
Rock for Amnesty ....Mercury (S) 830 617 5-10 86
Paul McCartney; others.
Rock for Amnesty ....Mercury (S) 830 617 10-15 86
(Promotional only issue.) Paul McCartney; others.
Rock from the Mid-West, the Cuca Story, Volume I....Cuca/White Label (S) 8847 8-12
Jimmy Sun & Radiants; Dick Hiorns; Willie Tremain's Thunderbirds; Don & Dominos; Night Tranes; Montereys; Rock-A-Fellers; Larry Phillipson.

Rock from the Mid-West, the Cuca Story, Volume II........ Cuca/White Label (S) 8848 8-12
Teens Men; Orbits; Jimmy Sun; Zakons; Night Hawks; Steve Sperry; Phaetoms; Furys; Corals; Larry Phillipson.

Rock from the Mid-West, the Cuca Story, Volume III........ Cuca/White Label (S) 8849 8-12
Marv Blihovde; Badgers; Royal Lancers; Teentones; Teen Kings; Night Beats; Bobby Hodge; Vibratones; Mule Skinners; Catalinas.

Rock Gospel (The Keys of the Kingdom)........ Motown (S) M 743L 20-40 71
Supremes; Marvin Gaye; Stony & Meatloaf; Jackson Five; Bobby Taylor; Valerie Simpson; Blinky; Impact of Brass; Ken Christy & Sunday People; Gladys Knight & Pips.

Rock Guitar Greats........ Springboard (S) SPB-4042 8-10 76
Jimi Hendrix; Eric Clapton; Jeff Beck; Jimmy Page; Sonny Boy Williamson.

Rock Guitar Greats Vol. 2........ Springboard (S) 4061 8-10 76
Jeff Beck; Rory Gallagher; Stevie Winwood; Jimi Hendrix; others.

Rock Invasion (1956-1969)........ London (S) LC-60012 5-10 78
Rod Stewart; Lonnie Donegan; Small Faces; Fortunes; Nashville Teens; Joe Cocker; Los Bravos; Marmalade; Graham Bond Organization; Unit Four + Two; Andrew Loog Oldham; Zombies.

Rock Is Here to Stay (3 LP)........ Adam VIII/Roulette SE) A8R-8020 20-25 75
(Same contents as below item, A-8020.)

Rock Is Here to Stay (3 LP)........ Tele House/Dynamic House (SE) A-8020 20-25 75
(TV mail order offer. Boxed set.) Lee Andrews & Hearts; Angels; Paul Anka; Frankie Avalon; Chuck Berry; Billy Bland; Bobbettes; Jerry Butler; Channels; Ray Charles; Chubby Checker; Coasters; Eddie Cochran; Sam Cooke; Bobby Darin; Fats Domino; Dovells; Drifters; El Dorados; Fabian; Five Satins; Flamingos; Harptones; Johnny & Joe; Bill Justis; Gladys Knight & Pips; Jerry Lee Lewis; Little Anthony & Inperials; Frankie Lymon & Teenagers; Magnificents; Marcels; Gene McDaniels; Orlons; Carl Perkins; Platters; Quintones; Rays; Regents; Bobby Rydell; Mitch Ryder & Detroit Wheels; Neil Sedaka; Sensations; Shangri-Las; Dee Dee Sharp; Shirelles; Sonny & Cher; Teen Queens; Turbans; Bobby Vee; Willows; J. Frank Wilson & Cavaliers.

Rock Lives........ Sunset (S) 5281 8-10 70
Fleetwoods; Johnny Burnette; Fats Domino; Buddy Knox; Troy Shondell; Showmen; Billy Ward & Dominoes; Eddie Cochran; Shirley & Lee.

Rock Lives On, Vol. 1........ Sunnyvale (S) SVL-1020 8-10 78
Valentines; Keystones; Larry Finnegan; Capris; Harptones; Earls; Robert & Johnny; Solitaires.

Rock Lives On, Vol. 2........ Sunnyvale (S) SVL-1021 8-10 78
Royaltones; Fiestas; Billly Bland; Mello Kings; Silhouettes; Nutmegs; Turbans; Charlie & Ray; Fay Adams.

Rock Lives On, Vol. 3........ Sunnyvale (S) SVL-1022 8-10 78
Maurice Williams & Zodiacs; Fay Adams; Turbans; Lee Allen; Five Satins; Billy Myles; Bill Baker & Five Satins.

Rock Me All Night Long 1945-1958........ Aladdin (M) ST-17201 5-10 80s
Helen Humes; Peppermint Harris; Louis Jordon; Amos Milburn; Five Keys; Big "T" Tyler; Thurston Harris; Gene & Eunice; Shirley & Lee; Marvin & Johnny.

Rock Menu — Hot Platters of Chrysalis Hits........ Columbia House Rock (S) 1P 7736 5-10
Jethro Tull; Blondie; Huey Lewis & News; Pat Benatar; John Waite; Go West; Ultravox; Billy Idol; Babys; Nick Gilder; Leo Sayer; Toni Basil.

Rock 'N' Country........ Columbia Special Products (S) P 15578 5-10 81
Jody Reynolds; Johnny Burnette; Bill Doggett; Fendermen; Ray Smith; Harold Dorman; Phil Phillips; Claude King.

Rock 'N' Forever........ Excelsior (S) XMP-6011 5-10 80
Box Tops; Bobby Lewis; Little Richard; Kingsmen; Angels; Reflections; Bobby Day; Chiffons; Crystals; Fontella Bass; Martha Reeves; Jaggerz.

Rock 'N' Roll Era 1954-1955........ Time-Life/Warner Special Products (M) OP-2535 8-12 86
(Mail order offer.) Billy Haley & His Comets; Clyde McPhatter & Drifters; Moonglows; Cadillacs; Bo Diddley; Spaniels; Joe Turner; Platters; Smiley Lewis; Thee Midnighters; Penguins; Chuck Berry; Little Richard; LaVern Baker; Fats Domino; Charms; Johnny Ace; Chords; Ray Charles; Ruth Brown; Etta James; Crows.

Rock 'N' Roll Fever, Vol. 1........ K-Tel (S) NU-2890-1 5-10 82
Chris Montez; Chubby Checker; Danny & Juniors; Marcels; Teddy Bears; Cascades; Freddy Cannon; Gary Lewis & Playboys; Angels; Sandy Nelson; Shangri-Las; Little Richard; Diamonds; Bobby Lewis; Wilbert Harrison; Tommy Roe; Jay & Americans; Robin Luke; Leslie Gore; Dovells. (Some tracks are rerecordings.)

Rock 'N' Roll Fever, Vol. 2........ K-Tel (S) NU-2890-2 5-10 82
Trashmen; Chantays; Drifters; Jan & Dean; Frankie Ford; Fendermen; Wanda Jackson; Bobby Rydell; Surfaris; Crystals; O'Kaysions; Billy Joe Royal; Paul Evans; J. Frank Wilson; Bobby Vee; Chiffons; Turtles; Jay & Americans. (Some tracks are rerecordings.)

Rock 'N' Roll Gold (2 LP)........ Mercury (S) R 214379 8-12 76
Crew-Cuts; Paul & Paula; Jay & Techniques; Left Banke; Clyde McPhatter; Johnny Preston; Angels; Phil Phillips; Steam; Platters; Big Bopper; Mouth & McNeil; Joe Dowell; Gene Chandler; Wayne Fontana & Mindbenders; Diamonds; Bruce Channel; Jerry Butler; Caravelles; Ray Stevens.

Rock 'N' Roll High School........ Sire (S) SRK-6070 8-10 79
(Soundtrack.) Ramones; Chuck Berry; Alice Cooper; Todd Rundgren; Paley Brothers; Nick Lowe; Eddie & Hot Rods; Brownsville Station; Devo; R.J. Soles; Brian Eno.

Rock 'N' Roll Idols Sing Their Hits of the '50s and '60s........ Laurie (S) LES 4027 5-10 80
Del Shannon; Bill Haley & His Comets; B.J. Thomas; Gene Pitney; Skyliners; Dion; Ernie Maresca; Dion & Belmonts; Curtis Lee; Music Explosion; Brook Benton; Five Discs.

Rock 'N' Roll Idols Sing Their Hits of the '50s and '60s, Vol. 2........ Laurie (S) LES 4028 5-10 80
Bill Haley & His Comets; Del Shannon; Dionne Warwick; Shirelles; Beach Boys; Chiffons; Five Discs; Platters; Gene Pitney; Randy & Rainbows; Dion & Belmonts; Skyliners.

Rock 'N' Roll Kingdom (3 LP)........ Candlelite (S) CU 717 10-20 83
(Boxed set.) Platters; Impalas; Tommy Edwards; Jimmy Jones; Danleers; Gino & Gina; Conway Twitty; Sarah Vaughn; Clyde McPhatter; Diamonds; Stereos; Crew-Cuts; Red Prysock; Dinah Washington; Fats Domino; Vox-Poppers; Big Bopper.

Rock 'N' Roll Party........ Relic (M) 8008 5-10 86
Jimmy Von Carl; Little Sonny & Corvettes; Herman Griffin; Brian Lolland; Minor Chords; Al Garner & Primettes; Upsetters; Vulcans; Five Masters; Herman Griffin & L.A. Dolls; Majestics; Bob Hamilton & Schoolboys; Sonny Woods.

Rock 'N' Soul (1953-1954-1955)........ ABC (S) ABCX-1955 10-15 73
Turbans; Johnny Ace; Orioles; Cadillacs; Faye Adams; Ravens; Jimmy Reed; Willie Mae Thornton; Four Tunes.

Rock 'N' Soul (1956)........ ABC (S) ABCX-1956 10-15 73
Frankie Lymon & Teenagers; Dells; Shirley & Lee; Little Richard; Eddie Cooley; Five Satins; Sonny Knight; Willows; Channels.

Rock 'N' Soul (1957)........ ABC (S) ABCX-1957 10-15 73
Dubs; Johnny Nash; Lloyd Price; Bobby Bland; Gene Allison; Paragons; Della Reese; Huey "Piano" Smith; Danny & Juniors; Junior Parker; Charts.

Rock 'N' Soul (1958)....ABC (S) ABCX-1958 10-15 73
Elegants; Jimmy Clanton; Olympics; Lloyd Price; Chantels; Billie & Lillie; Silhouettes; Bobby Freeman; Quintones; Jerry Butler; Huey "Piano" Smith.

Rock 'N' Soul (1959)....ABC (S) ABCX-1959 10-15 73
Crests; Dee Clark; Frankie Ford; Lloyd Price; Wilbert Harrison; Jivin' Gene; Flamingos.

Rock 'N' Soul (1960)....ABC (S) ABCX-1960 10-15 73
Olympics; Rosie & Originals; Gary "U.S." Bonds; Ron Holden; Jimmy Charles; Jimmy Reed; Joe Jones; Crests; Buster Brown; Jerry Butler; Bobby Marchan.

Rock 'N' Soul (1961)....ABC (S) ABCX-1961 10-15 73
Jimmy Reed; Impressions; Regents; Dee Clark; Bobby Bland; Cleftones; Gary "U.S." Bonds; Little Caesar & Romans; Shep & Limelites; Gladys Knight & Pips; Lee Dorsey; Slim Harpo.

Rock 'N' Soul (1962)....ABC (S) ABCX-1962 10-15 73
Gene Chandler; John Lee Hooker; Junior Parker; Joe Henderson; Joey Dee & Starliters; Bobby Bland; Gary "U.S." Bonds; Don Gardner & Dee Dee Ford; Les Cooper & Soul Rockers; Jerry Butler.

Rock 'N' Soul (1963)....ABC (S) ABCX-1963 10-15 73
Bob & Earl; Tams; Lonnie Mack; Gene Chandler; Olympics; Bobby Bland; Impressions; Raindrops; Lou Christie; Betty Everett.

Rock Now....Original Sound Recordings (S) ROCK 401 10-15
John Lennon; others.

Rock of Ages – American Soul: 1961: 1972 (I Want to Take You Higher)....Capitol (M) SQ ???? 5-10 85
Sly & Family Stone; others.

Rock of Ages – California Surf Music: 1962-1974 (Summer Means Fun)....Capitol (M) SQ 12456 5-10 85
Beach Boys; Fantastic Baggys; Legendary Masked Surfers; Jan & Dean; Honeys; Survivors.

Rock of Ages – Doo Wop Groups: 1951-1962 (In the Still of the Night)....Capitol (M) SQ ???? 5-10 85

Rock of Ages – Early Rock Classics: 1952-1958 (Let the Good Times Roll)....Capitol (M) SQ 12451 5-10 85
Shirley & Lee; Fats Domino; Jerry Lee Lewis; Merrill Moore; Smiley Lewis; Esquerita; Johnny Otis Show; Larry Williams; Thurston Harris & Sharps.

Rock of Ages – Early Sixties Soul: 1960-1975 (Hurt So Bad)....Capitol (M) SQ ???? 5-10 85
Little Anthony & Imperials; others.

Rock of Ages – East Coast Rock: 1969-1968 (Only in America)....Capitol (M) SQ 12457 5-10 85
Jay & Americans; Royal Teens; Elegants; Clovers; Marv Johnson; Bobbie Smith & Dream Girls; Isley Brothers; Garnet Mimms & Enchanters.

Rock of Ages –Sounds of Top 40 Radio: 1964-1967 (Good Vibrations)....Capitol SQ (S) 12461 10-15
Beach Boys; Johnny Rivers; Jackie DeShannon; Bob Lind; Glen Campbell; P.J. Proby; Cher; Jay & Americans; Classics IV; Bobby Vee & Strangers.

Rock of Ages – Instrumental Rock: 1957-1965 (Teen Beat)....Capitol (M) SQ 12463 5-10 85
Ventures; Lonnie Mack; Piltdown Men; Duals; Bill Justis; Phil Upchurch Combo; Sandy Nelson; Davie Allan; B. Bumble & Stingers; Tune Rockers; Jimmy McGriff.

Rock of Ages – Rocks New Frontiers 1966-1970 (On the Road Again)....Capitol (S) SQ-12460 5-10 85
Standells; Outsiders; Count Five; Canned Heat; Steve Miller; Sugarloaf; the Band; Stone Poneys; Nitty Gritty Dirt Band; Joy of Cooking; Hour Glass; Joe South.

Rock of Ages – Rockabilly Influence: 1950-1960 (Let's Have a Party)....Capitol (M) SQ 12455 5-10 85
Wanda Jackson; Gene Vincent; Dorsey Burnette; Billy Briggs; Jimmy Head & Melody Masters; Eddie Cochran; Johnny Burnette; Bob Luman.

Rock of Ages – West Coast Rock: 1958-1964 (Till My Dreamin' Comes True)....Capitol (M) SQ 12453 5-10 85
Bobby Vee; Dick & DeeDee; Four Preps; Paris Sisters; Gary Lewis & Playboys; Lettermen; Hollywood Argyles; Gene McDaniels; Cascades; Kathy Young & Innocents; Johnny Burnette; Fleetwoods.

Rock On! Golden Rock Greats (3 LP)....Columbia (S) 3P-6222 15-25

Rock On: the Musical Encyclopedia of Rock 'N' Roll (2 LP)....Columbia (S) KG-33390 20-30 75
(Promotional issue only.) Marty Robbins; Stonewall Jackson; Four Lads; Guy Mitchell; Terry Gilkyson & Easy Riders; Don Cherry with Ray Conniff & Columbians; Frankie Laine; Johnny Horton; Percy Faith; Dion; Jimmy Dean; Rip Chords; Tony Orlando; Johnny Mathis; Roy Hamilton; James; Major Lance; Little Joe & Thrillers; Brothers Four; Bobby Vinton.

Rock Power (Don Kirshner Presents)....Ronco (S) P-12417 5-10 74
(Mail order offer.) Barry White; Aretha Frankliln; Stylistics; Grass Roots; Alice Cooper; David Essex; Love Unlimited; Seals & Crofts; Dr. John; Five Man Electrical Band; Al Green; Spinners; First Choice; Gladys; Knight & Pips; Procol Harum; Bachman-Turner Overdrive; Black Sabbath; Faces; Steppenwolf; Doobie Brothers.

Rock Power Music....RCA (S) DPL1-0581 5-10 83
Hall & Oates; Dillman Band; Evelyn King; Alabama; Louis Clark; Franke & Knockouts; Tane Cain; Chilliwack; Toby Beau; Triumph. (Special products. Made for RPM Jeans.)

Rock Pretty Baby (Vol. 1)....Decca (EP) ED 2480 50-75 56

Rock Pretty Baby (Vol. 2)....Decca (EP) ED 2481 50-75 56

Rock Pretty Baby (Vol. 3)....Decca (EP) ED 2482 50-75 56

Rock Pretty Baby....Decca (M) DL-8429 50-100 56
(Black label or pink label promo.)

Rock Pretty Baby....Decca (M) DL-8429 30-35 60s
(Soundtrack.) Jimmy Daley & Ding-A-Lings; Rod McKuen; Alan Copeland; Hal Dickinson; Henry Mancini. Rainbow (or multi-color) label.

Rock, Rhythm & Blues....Warner Bros. (S) 25817 5-10 89
Elton John; Rick James; Michael McDonald; Chaka Khan; Howard Hewett; Manhattan Transfer; Randy Travis; Pointer Sisters; Christine McVie & Friends; El DeBarge.

Rock, Rock, Rock....Chess (M) LP-1425 75-125 58

Rock, Rock, Rock....Roost (M) No Number Used 500-750 58
(Soundtrack. Promotional issue only.) LaVern Baker; Bowties; Jimmy Cavallo; Moonglows; Alan Freed; 3 Chuckles; Frankie Lymon & Teenagers; Johnny Burnette; Connie Francis; Chuck Berry; Flamingos.

Rock, Rock, Rock....Chess/MCA (M) CH-9254 8-12 86
(Soundtrack. Reissue.)

Rock, Rock, Rock (All Star Rock-Vol. 11)....Original Sound Recordings (SP) OSR- 11 40-50 72
Elvis Presley; Don McLean; Melanie; Al Green; Badfinger; Three Dog Night; Raiders; Cher; Carpenters; Apollo 100; Bee Gees; Bread; Joe Cocker; Osmonds. (Also issued as the *All Star Rock* series.)

Rock Rolls On....Pair (S) ARPDL2-1087 8-12 84
Maurice Williams & Zodiacs; Turbans; Nutmegs; Channels; Mello Kings; Silhouettes; Lee Allen; Five Satins; Bill Haley & His Comets; Little Richard; Bo Diddley; Danny & Juniors; Fats Domino; Coasters.

Rock Southern Style........K-Tel (S) NU 5480 5-10 84
Lynyrd Skynyrd; Marshall Tucker Band; Allman Brothers Band; Ozark Mountain Dare Devils; Elvin Bishop; Rossington Collins Band; Charlie Daniels Band; Grateful Dead; Wet Willie; Atlanta Rhythm Section; Outlaws; Molly Hatchett.

Rock! The Stars Do Their Big Ones........RCA (S) PRS-411 8-12 72
Guess Who; Julie Budd; Jerry Reed; Friends of Distinction; Original Cast of *Hair*; Jefferson Airplane; Nilsson; Generation Gap Orchestra; Main Ingredient; Zager & Evans.

Rock! The Stars Do Their Big Ones (5 LP)........RCA Special Products (SP) PRS-411-5 20-30
(Boxed set.) Jefferson Airplane; Guess Who; Living Voices; Hugo Montenegro; Living Voices; Michael Nesmith; Nite Liters; Floyd Cramer; Julie Budd; Jerry Reed; Friends of Distinction; Original Cast - Hair; Nilsson; Generation Gap Orchestra; Main Ingredient; Zager & Evans.

Rock Then & Now........Columbia (SP) P-116777 5-10 73
Blood, Sweat & Tears; Dave Clark Five; Paul Revere & Raiders; Sly & Family Stone; Byrds; Hollies; Looking Glass; Mac Davis; Argent; Albert Hammond.

Rock Vocal Greats........Springboard (S) SPB-4062 8-10 76
Jimi Hendrix; Jeff Beck; Yardbirds; Stevie Winwood; Rod Stewart; Eric Burdon & Animals; Jack Bruce; Ginger Baker; Dick Heckstal Smith; Greg Allman; Duane Allman; Spencer Davis Group; Rory Gallagher.

Rock's Greatest Hits........Columbia (S) DS 1099 8-12 73
Argent; Donovan; Addrisi Brothers; Mott the Hoople; Santana; Janis Joplin; Yardbirds; Laura Nyro; Scott McKenzie; David Bromberg.

Rock's Greatest Hits (2 LP)........Columbia (S) GP-11 10-15 69
Chambers Brothers; Mongo Santamaria; Dion; Byrds; Robert John; Arbors; Gary Puckett & Union Gap; Moby Grape; Cryan' Shames; Crykle; Aretha Franklin; Chad & Jeremy; Peaches & Herb; Paul Revere & Raiders; Rip Chords; Billy Joe Royal; Tymes; Leonard Cohen.

Rock's Greatest Hits (4 LP)........Columbia (S) P4S-5918 20-25 74
(Boxed set. Mail order offer.) Johnny Nash; Hollies; Loggins & Messina; Santana; Blood, Sweat & Tears; Janis Joplin; Dr. Hook & Medicine Show; Laura Nyro; Scott McKenzie; David Bromberg; Looking Glass; Redbone; Argent; Chi Coltrane; Mac Davis; Yardbirds; Carlos Santana; Buddy Miles; Sly & Family Stone; Mark Lindsay; Zombies; Addrisi Brothers; Mott the Hoople; Delaney & Bonnie; Pacific Gas & Electric; Donovan; Bryds; Paul Revere & Raiders; Stephen Stills; Al Kooper; Ten Years After; Sweathog; Chase; Poco.

Rock's Greatest Hits (3 LP)........Columbia (S) 3P-6526 15-20 76
Johnny Nash; Hollies; Loggins & Messina; Santana; Blood, Sweat & Tears; Janis Joplin; Dr. Hook & Medicine Show; Laura Nyro; Scott McKenzie; David Bromberg; Looking Glass; Redbone; Argent; Chi Coltrane; Mac Davis; Yardbirds; Carlos Santana; Buddy Miles; Sly & Family Stone; Mark Lindsay; Zombies; Addrisi Brothers; Mott the Hoople; Delaney & Bonnie; Pacific Gas & Electric; Donovan; Bryds; Paul Revere & Raiders.

Rock's World Revolution - the Roots........Legrand (M) LG-1000 10-15 79
Gary "U.S." Bonds; Frank Guida & Swedish All Star Orchestra; Jimmy Soul; Gregory Cafone; Church Street 5; Tommy Facenda; Lenis Guess. (Also issued as *Frank Guida Presents Greatest Hits*.)

Rock-A-Ballads........Cadence (M) CLP-3041 30-50 60
Everly Brothers; Andy Williams; Chordettes; Johnny Tillotson.

Rock-A-Hits........Cadence (M) CLP-3042 30-50 60
Everly Brothers; Andy Williams; Chordettes; Ernie England; Johnny Tillotson; Link Wray & His Ray Men.

Rockabilly Bash........Bopalacious (M) 100 10-20
Jeff Daniels; Art Adams; Norman Witcher; Tony & Jackie Lane; Jim McDonald; Kingbeats; Cliff Davis; Tommy "Jim" Beam; Al Casey; Tom Dinkins; Eddie & Chuck.

Rockabilly Classics, Vol. 1........MCA (M) MCA-25088 5-10 87
Dale Hawkins; Rickin' Saints; Jo Ann Campbell; Billy the Kid; Robin Luke; Clint Miller; John Ashley; Sanford Clark; Billy Adams; Buddy Holly.

Rockabilly Classics, Vol. 2........MCA (M) MCA-25089 5-10 87
Roy Hall; Bobby Helms; Johnny Carroll & His Hot Rocks; Brenda Lee; Webb Pierce; Johnny Burnette & His Rock & Roll Trio; Justin Tubb; Moon Mullican; Billy Lee Riley & Spooks; Ronnie Self.

Rockabilly Hot........Columbia (S) FC-40904 5-10 87
Rick Nelson; Billy Swan; Marty Stuart; Carl Perkins; Johnny Cash; Steve Earle; Jerry Lee Lewis; Charlie Rich; Marty Robbins; Mickey Gilley.

Rockabilly Stars, Vol. 1 (2 LP)........Epic (S) EG 37618 10-15 81
Carl Smith; Scotty Moore; Bob Luman; Mac Curtis; Carl Perkins; Johnny Cash; Allan Rich; Mickey Gilley; Charlie Rich; Town Hall Party; Everly Brothers; Little Jimmy Dickens; Marty Robbins; Johnny Horton; Collins Kids.

Rockabilly Stars, Vol. 2 (2 LP)........Epic (S) EG 37621 10-15 81
Collins Kids; Everly Brothers; Sid King & Five Strings; Little Jimmy Dickens; Jive After Five; Lorrie Collins; Ronnie Self; Link Wray; Sleepy LaBeef; Carl Perkins; Rick Nelson; Billy Lee Riley; Mickey Gilley; Johnny Cash.

Rockabilly Stars, Vol. 3 (2 LP)........Epic (S) EG 37984 10-15 82
Little Jimmy Dickens; Everly Brothers; Collins Kids; Joe Maphis; Larry Collins; Ronnie Self; John D. Loudermilk; Johnny Cash; Jimmy Murphy; Cliff Johnson; Onie Wheeler; Johnny Horton; Rose Maddox; Jaycee Hill: Carl Perkins; Werly Fairburn; Sid King & Five Strings; Bobby Lord; Lorrie Collins" Leon Smith.

Rockabilly, the Roots of Rock and Roll........Imperial House (S) WU 3590 5-10 82
Carl Perkins; Gene Vincent; Buddy Holly & Crickets; George Jones; Jerry Lee Lewis; Roy Orbison; Conway Twitty; Charlie Rick; Johnny Burnette; Big Bipper; Johnny Cash & Tennessee Two; Chuck Miller; Billy Lee Riley; Guy Mitchell; Ray Campi & His Rockabilly Rebels.

Rockarama, Vol. 1 (2 LP)........Abkco (S) AB 4222 10-15 72
Chubby Checker; Terry Knight; Orlons; Tymes; Dee Dee Sharp; ? & Mysterians; Bobby Rydell; Dovells; Charlie Gracie; Rays.

Rockarama, Vol. 2 (2 LP)........Abkco (S) AB 4223 10-15 72
Orlons; Bobby Rydell; Dee Dee Sharp; John Zacherlie; Chubby Checker; ? & Mysterians; Jo Ann Campbell; Tymes; Don Covay; Dovells; Candy & Kisses; Charlie Gracie.

Rockers........Mango (S) 9587 8-10 80
(Soundtrack.) Inner Circle; Maytones; Junior Murvin; Heptones; Peter Tosh; Jacob Miller; Junior Byles; Bunny Wailer; Gregory Isaacs; Rockers All-Stars; Kiddus I; Burning Spear; Third World; Justin Hines & Dominoes.

Rocket to the Stars........Wand (M) LP-651 20-30 62
Jocko Henderson; Shirelles; Maxine Brown; Shep & Limelites; Wilbert Harrison; Lee Andrews & Hearts; Little Anthony & Imperials.

Rockin' and Rollin' '50s and '60s (2 LP)........MGM/Romar (S) 2RMS-2003 10-15 73
Frankie Avalon; Fabian; Jodie Sands; Lou Christie; Ritchie Valens; Sandy Nelson; Frankie Lymon & Teenagers; Lee Andrews & Hearts; Tommy Edwards; Claudine Clark; Capris; Buddy Knox; Mark Dinning.

Rockin' at Midnight at the Parrot Club........Relic (M) 8020 5-10 89
Five Thrills; Choclateers; Marvin Philips; Maples; Briley Guy; Walter Spriggs & Five Echoes; Lowell Fulsom; Lou Mac; Five Arrows; Mable Scott; Rockettes.

Rockin' at the Drive-In........Combo (M) 400 8-10

Rockin' Blues Featuring Willie Egan........Relic (M) 8002 5-10 84

Rockin' Christmas.......... Columbia Special Products (S) P-12445 10-15 74
Gary Puckett; Bobby Vinton; Everly Brothers; Paul Revere & Raiders; Mark Lindsay.

Rockin' Christmas the Sixties.......... Rhino (S) RNLP 067 5-10 84
Christmas Spirit; Santo & Johnny; Nathaniel Mayer; Turtles; Poets; Barry Richards; Sonics; Trashmen; Paul Revere & Raiders; Aretha Franklin; Bobby Boris Pickett & Crypt Kickers; Wailers; James Brown.

Rockin' Date with the South Louisiana Stars.......... Jin (M) LP-4002 20-30

Rockin' Down the Block (4 LP).......... Silver Eagle/Capitol Special Markets (S) SLD 9724 15-20 87
Aretha Franklin; Swingin' Medallions; Gentrys; Sam the Sham & Pharaohs; Rivingtons; Beach Boys; Vogues; Chris Kenner; Sly & Family Stone; Rascals; Del Shannon; Sir Douglas Quintet; Stevie Wonder; Ernie K-Doe; T-Bones; Kingsmen; Chuck Berry; Spencer Davis Group; Johnny Otis Show; Tommy Tucker; Contours; Bachman-Turner Overdrive; Tommy James & Shondells; Mitch Ryder & Detroit Wheels; James Brown; Ray Charles; Bobby Fuller Four; Three Dog Night; Isley Brothers; Wilson Pickett; Booker T. & MGs; Sam & Dave; Ike & Tina Turner; Clovers; Surfaris; Trashmen; LaBelle; Ventures; Paul Revere & Raiders; Ritchie Valens; Blue Cheer.

Rockin' Down the House (5 LP).......... Silver Eagle (S) OP 5504 20-25 84
Bill Haley & His Comets; Chuck Berry; Sensations; Fleetwoods; Fontella Bass; Fats Domino; Monotones; Drifters; Ernie Maresca; Coaster; Bobby Darin; Impalas; Rays; Bobby Rydell; Kinks; Herman's Hermits; Orlons; Animals; Johnny & Hurricanes; Buddy Holly; Jerry Lee Lewis; Champs; Chubby Checker; Johnny Burnette; Jimmy Jones; Little Anthony & Imperials; Toys; Buddy Knox; Dion; Ritchie Valens; Clyde McPhatter; Billy Bland; Dovells; Diamonds; Roy Head; Lloyd Price; Tymes; Marketts; Gary "U.S." Bond; Dodie Stevens; Larry Finnegan; Joe Turner.

Rockin' Down the Line (5 LP).......... Silver Eagle/Warner (S) OP 5504 15-25 84
(Mail order offer.) Bill Haley & His Comets; Chuck Berry; Sensations; Fleetwoods; Fontella Bass; Fats domino; Johnny Burnette; Jimmy Jones; Little Anthony & Imperials; Toys; Monotones; Drifters; Ernie Maresca; Buddy Knox; Dion; Ritchie Valens; Clyde McPhatter; Billy Bland; Coasters; Bobby Darin; Impalas; Ray; Bobby Rydell; Dovells; Orlons; Diamonds; Chubby Checker; Kinks; Herman Hermits; Animals; Johnny & Hurricanes; Roy Head; Lloyd Price; Tymes; Buddy Holly; Jerry Lee Lewis; Champs; Marketts; Gary "U.S." Bonds; Dodie Stevens; Larry Finnegan; Joe Turner.

Rockin' Easy: see Superstars of the '70s, Vol. 3, Rockin' Easy

Rockin' Fifties.......... Warner/JCI (SE) 3202 5-10 85
Eddie Cochran; Carl Perkins; Big Bopper; Gene Vincent; Frankie Ford; Buddy Holly; Jerry Lee Lewis; Little Richard; Fats Domino; Larry Williams; Johnny Otis Show; Chuck Berry.

Rockin' Little Christmas.......... MCA (M) 25084 5-10 86
Chuck Berry; Moonglows; Bobby Helms; Lord Douglas Byron; Gems; Enchanters; Surfaris; Brenda Lee; Dodie Stevens.

Rockin' On.......... Columbia Musical Treasury (S) IP 7036 5-10 79
Jaynetts; Freddie Cannon; Jim Lowe; Capris; Little Caesar & Romans; Joey Dee & Starliters; Marcels; Little Richard; Cleftones; Johnny & Hurricanes.

Rockin' Originals!.......... Pickwick/Share (S) SPC-3316 5-10 71
Dixie Cups; Jelly Beans; Carl Perkins; Shangri-Las; Jerry Lee Lewis; Bill Justis; Ad Libs. (Reissue of *Orginal Supercharged Rock N' Roll Hits*, Share.)

Rockin' Records, Vol. 1.......... Sun (M) 1032 20-30 86
Dusty Brooks & His Tones; Hardrock Gunter; Billy "The Kid" Emerson; Jones Brothers; Carl Perkins; Sammy Lewis & Willie Johnson Combo; Five Tinos; Miller Sisters; Roy Orbison; Jean Chapel; Rudi Richardson; Dick Penner; Dickey Lee; Ray Smith; Ken Cook; Ernie Barton. (Promotional bonus, offered to *Rockin' Records* book buyers. 600 made.)

Rockin' Records, Vol. 2.......... Sun (M) 1033 10-15 88
Johnny London; Dusty Brooks & His Tones; Hardrock Gunter; Bill Taylor & Smokey Joe; Guitar Red; Red Williams; Sonny Burgess; Tommy Blake & His Rhythm Rebels; Jerry Lee Lewis; Four Dukes; Gene Simmons; Ernie Barton; Brother James Anderson; Load of Mischief. (Promotional bonus, offered to *Rockin' Records* book buyers. 1000 made.)

Rockin' Records, Vol. 3.......... Sun (M) 1034 10-15 88
Prisonaires; Five Tinos; Vel-Tones; Four Dukes; Roscoe Gordon; Bill Pinkney & Turks; Ed Kirby; Hunki Dori. (Promotional bonus, offered to *Rockin' Records* book buyers. 1000 made.)

Rockin' Records, Vol. 4.......... Sun (M) 1035 10-15 89
Walter Horton; Howlin' Wolf; Joe Hill Louis; Willie Nix; B.B. King; Bobby "Blue" Bland; Roscoe Gordon; Rufus Thomas; Tiny Kennedy; Billy Love; Ike Turner; Jackie Brenston. (Promotional bonus, offered to *Picture the Blues* book buyers. 1000 made.)

Rockin' Records, Vol. 5.......... Sun (M) RR-05 10-15 93
Macy "Skip" Skipper; Carl McVoy; Andy Anderson & Rolling Stones; Luke McDaniel; Warren Smith; Jerry Lee Lewis; Sonny Burgess; Roy Orbison; Harold Jenkins (Conway Twitty); Billy Lee Riley; Carl Perkins; Hayden Thompson; Barbara Pittman. (Promotional bonus, offered to *Rockin' Records* book buyers. 1000 made.)

Rockin' Seventies.......... JCI/Warner (S) 3301 5-10 86
Raspberries; Argent; Golden Earring; J. Geils Band; Loggins & Messina; Hollies; Elton John; Eric Clapton; Foghat; Blues Image; Bachman-Turner Overdrive; David Essex.

Rockin' Sixties.......... JCI/Warner (S) 3101 8-12 85
Three Dog Night; Hollies; Rascals; Blue Cheer; Smith; Blood, Sweat & Tears; Spencer Davis Group; Mitch Ryder & Detroit Wheels; Canned Heat; Shocking Blue; Ides of March; Joe Cocker.

Rockin' Slumber Party.......... Famous (M) F-501 10-15 69
Sam Cooke; Herbie Alpert; Lani Kai; Billy Storm; Real Tones; Matt Barris; Bumps Blackwell; Turks; Echoes.

Rockin' Sounds of R & B.......... Columbia Special Products (S) P 14643 5-10 79
Johnnie Taylor; John Handy; Wild Cherry; O'Jays; Rufus; Harold Melvin & Blue Notes; MFSB; Carl Carlton.

Rockin' Together.......... Atco (M) 33-103 40-60 58
Bobby Darin; Coasters; King Curtis; Hutch Davie; Chordcats; Guitar Slim; Jesse Stone; Sensations; Gerry Granahan.

Rocking '50s.......... Atlantic (M) 8037 40-60 60
LaVern Baker; Bobbettes; Ruth Brown; Ray Charles; Clovers; Drifters; Ivory Joe Hunter; Clyde McPhatter; Chuck Willis.

Rocky IV.......... Scotti Bros. (S) SZ-40203 10-15 85
(Soundtrack.) Survivor; John Cafferty; Kenny Loggins; Gladys Knight; James Brown; Robert Tepper; Go West; Touch.

Rods and Drags Forever.......... Battle (M) BM-6134 15-20 64

Rods and Drags Forever.......... Battle (S) BS9-6134 15-25 64

Roller Boogie (2 LP).......... Casablanca (S) NBLP-2-7194 10-12 80
(Soundtrack.) Cher; Johnnie Coolrock; Mavis Vegas Davis; Earth, Wind & Fire with the Emotions; Ron Green; Cheeks; Bob Esty & Cheeks; Michele Allen.

Rollin' the Rock, Vol. 1.......... Rollin' Rock (S) LP-009 10-15 74
Martin "Johnny Legend" Marguiles; Billy Zoom; Ray Campi; Johnny Carroll; Alvis Wayne; Chuck Weiss; Sid King; Colin Winski.

Rollin' the Rock, Vol. 2.......... Rollin' Rock (S) LP-012 10-15 74
Jack "Waukeen" Cochran; Cort Murray; Jerry Sikorski; Colin Winski; Ray Campi; Johnny Legend; Don Sawyer; Kevin Olson; Chuck Weiss; Mac Curtis; John Blair.

Rollin' the Rock, Vol. 3 .... Rollin' Rock (S) LP-015 10-15 74
Mac Curtis; Ray Campi; Sarah Harrie; Cort Murray; Jimmie Lee Maslon; Tony Conn; Johnny Carroll.

Romantic Classics (3 LP) .... World Communications (SE) VE-530 10-20 86
Eddie Fisher; Rosemary Clooney; Liberace; Steve Lawrence; Eydie Gorme; Tony Bennett; Four Lads; Jerry Vale; Andy Williams; Johnny Mathis; Perry Como; Roy Hamilton; Vic Damone; Percy Faith; Robert Goulet; Don Ho; Jim Nabors; Nat King Cole; Judy Garland; Guy Lombardo; Dean Martin; Vaughn Monroe; Mills Brothers; Four Aces; Roger Williams; Pat Boone; Lena Horne; Ames Brothers; Pied Pipers; Tony Martin; Jack Jones; Matt Monro; Al Martino; Modernaires; Bing Crosby; Dick Haymes; Hoagy Carmichael; McGuire Sisters; Tommy Dorsey; Letterman; Al Jolson.

Roof Garden 2nd Annual Jamboree .... IGL (M) LP-103 100-200 67
Trashmen; Senn Men; Yetti Blues Band; Tommy Tucker; Terry Klein; Those of Us; Steve Ellis & Starfires; Marauders; South 40; Chateaux; Madhatters; Activators; Gas Company; Canoise.

Rootin' Tootin' Hootenanny .... FM (M) FM-310 10-20 63

Rootin' Tootin' Hootenanny .... FM (S) FMS-310 10-20 63
Ward Singers; Allen & Grier; others.

Roots .... Fontana (S) 67606 8-12 69
Memphis Slim; Big Joe Williams; Willie Dixon; others.

Roots: the Rock and Roll Sound of Louisiana and Mississippi .... Folkways (M) FJ-2865 15-25 65
Jerry Butler; M. Thomas; Earl Stanley & Stereos; Billy Stewart; Al White & Hi-Liters; Doug & Dave; N. Stewart; L. Bruce; Cookie Gabriel; Perails.

Roots of American Music (2 LP) .... Arhoolie (S) 2001/2002 10-20 68
Fred McDowell; Mance Lipscomb; Black Ace; Alex Moore; Big Joe Williams; Lil Son Jackson; John Jackson; Guitar Slim & Jelly Belly; Lowell Fulsom; Mercy Dee; Juke Boy Bonner; Lightnin' Hopkins; Big Mama Thornton; Clifton Chenier; Larry Williams; Johnny Young; Bukka White; Jesse Fuller; Rev. Overstreet; Robert Shaw; Kid Thomas; Joe Turner; Luna; J.E. Mainer's Mountaineers; Del McCoury; Hodges Brothers; Luderin Darbone; Nathan Abshire; Alice Stuart; Crabgrass; James Campbell.

Roots of British Rock .... Sire (S) SASH-3711 5-10 75
Tommy Steele; Lonnie Donegan; Frank Ifield; Mr. Acker Bilk; Petula Clark; Shadows; Mike Berry; Shane Fenton & Fentones; Tornadoes; Emile Ford & Checkmates; Chas McDevitt Group with Nancy Whiskey; Russ Hamilton; Laurie London; Gary Mills; Kenny Ball; Karl Denver Trio; Helen Shapiro; Adam Faith; Chris Barber; Cliff Richard & Shadows; Drifters; Ricky Valance; Billy Fury; Eden Kane; Jet Harris; Tony Meehan; Craig Douglas; Johnny Kidd & Pirates; Joe Brown; Marty Wilde; Springfields; Caravelles.

Roots of Rhythm and Blues .... RBF (M) RBF-20 20-25 66
Al White & His Hi-Liters; Naomi Bradly; Queenettes; Dominoes; Barons; Louis Armstrong & His Rainbow of Rhythm; Dave Bonds; Phillip & Originals; Johnny Larand & Internes.

Roots of Rhythm and Blues .... Folkways (M) RBF-20 15-20 66
Al White & His Hi-Liters; Naomi Bradly; Queenettes; Dominoes; Barons; Louis Armstrong & His Rainbow of Rhythm; Dave Bonds; Phillip & Originals; Johnny Larand & Internes.

Roots of Rock .... Yazoo (M) 1063 8-10
Kansas Joe; Memphis Minnie; Charley Patton; Bukka White; Skip James; Bo Carter; Blind Blake; Blind Willie McTell; Henry Thomas; Tommy Johnson; Hambone Willie Newbern; Blind Joe Reynolds; Robert Wilkins; Cannon's Jug Stompers.

Roots of Rock & Roll (2 LP) .... Fairway/Temco Ltd. (S) RR 4200 8-12 79
(Mail order offer.) Chuck Berry; Ruth Brown; Ivory Joe Hunter; Fats Domino; Shirley & Lee; Five Keys; Jesse Belvin; B.B. King; Johnny Ace; Mellows; El Dorados; John Lee Hooker; Little Walter; Little Richard; Big Mama Thornton; Faye Adams; Little Willie John; Chords; Lloyd Price; Dells; Charms; Moonglows; Flamingos; Bo Diddley.

Roots of Rock and Roll (2 LP) .... Savoy (M) SJL-2221 20-25 77
Wild Bill Moore; Paul Williams; Big Jay McNeeley; Hal Singer; Sam Price; Johnny Otis; Mel Walker; Nappy Brown; Huey "Piano" Smith; Little Esther; Varetta Dillard; Big Maybelle; Ravens; Robbins; Luther Bond & His Emeralds; Clarence Palmer & Jive Bombers.

Roots of Rock and Roll, Honkers & Screamers, Vol. 6, (2 LP) .... Savoy (M) SJL-2234 10-15 79
Big Jay McNeely; Paul Willaims; Hal Singer; Lee Allen; Sam "The Man" Taylor.

Roots of Rock and Roll, Vocal Group Album, Vol. 8, ... Savoy (M) SJL-2241 10-15 77
Three Barons; Toppers; Syncopaters; Four Buddies; Marshall Brothers; Carols; Dreams; Little David & Harps; Jimmy Jones & Savoys.

Roots of Rock and Roll and Rockabilly .... Imperial House (M) 3590 15-20 82
Carl Perkins; Gene Vincent; Buddy Holly & Crickets; George Jones; Charlie Rich; Johnny Cash; Johnny Burnette; Big Bopper; Ray Campi; Guy Mitchell; Billy Lee Riley; Chuck Miller; Jerry Lee Lewis; Roy Orbison; Conway Twitty.

Roots of Soul (3 LP) .... Imperial House (S) NU 9300 10-15 77
(Mail order offer.) Ray Charles; Fats Domino; B.B. King; Ben E. King; Sam Cooke; Jackie Wilson; Chiffons; Marcels; Crystals; Drifters; Dells; James Brwon; Ike & Tina Turner; Wilson Pickett; Aretha Franklin; Rufus Thomas; Booker T. & MGs; Otis Redding; Arthur Conley; Sam & Dave; Barrett Strong; Diana Ross & Supremes; Temptations; Mary Wells; Smokey Robinson & Miracles; Impressions; O'Jays; Billy Paul; Intruders; Harold Melvin & Blue Notes; KC & Sunshine Band; George McCrae; Gwen McCrae; Timmy Thomas; Quincy Jones.

Roots of the Blues .... Atlantic (M) 1348 40-50 60

Roots of the Blues .... Atlantic (S) SD-1348 45-55 60

Roots of the Blues .... Newworld (SP) NW 252 8-12 77
Henry Ratcliff; Bakari-Bodji; John Dudley; Tangle Eye; Leroy Miller; Fred McDowell; Miles Pratcher; Ed Young; Lonnie Young; Alec Askew; Bob Pratcher; Leroy Gary; Rev. Crenshaw; Forrest City Joe; Fannie Davis; Bessie Jones.

Rosebud .... Reprise (S) RS-6426 8-12 70
Judy Henske; others.

Rosko's Evergreens .... Warner Bros. (M) W-1551 25-30 64
Jimmy Reed; Drifters; Dee Clark; Jerry Butler; Gene Chandler; Shirelles; Ben E. King; Chuck Jackson; Freddie Scott; Yvonne Carroll; Jessie Hill.

Rosko's Evergreens Back on the Scene .... Domain (M) LP-102 25-35 64
Drifters; Shirelles; Jerry Butler; Yvonne Caroll; Dee Clark; Chuck Jackson; Jimmy Reed; Freddie Scott; Ben E. King; Jessie Hill; Gene Chandler; plus *Rosko's Theme*.

Roulette Presents a Demonstration of the New Dimensional Sound of Dynamic Stereo .... Forum (S) SF9001 20-30
Count Basie; Pearl Bailey; Jimmie Rodgers; Machito; Tito Rodriguez; Tyree Glenn; Joe Newman; Joe Williams; Johnny Richards; Maynard Ferguson.

Round-Up .... Capitol (S) SL-6641 8-10
Glen Campbell; Bobbie Gentry; Al Martino; Lettermen; Tennessee Ernie Ford; Glen Campbell; Bobbie Gentry.

Roxy London W.C. 2 .... Harvest (S) SHSP-406 5-10 77
(Live at Roxy Club in 1977.) Slaughter & Dogs; Wire; Unwanted; Adverts; Johnny Moped; Eaters; X-Ray Specs; Buzzcocks.

Rude Awakening .... Elektra (S) 60873-1 8-10
(Soundtrack.) Mike + Mechanics; Sigue Sigue Sputnik; Bill Medley; Frankie & Knockouts; Kim Carnes; Georgia Satellites; Miami Sound Machine; Jefferson Airplane; Grateful Dean; Phoebe Snow; Bob Dylan.

Rudy Harvey Presents: see Greatest Rhythm and Blues Hits

Rumble .... Jubilee (M) JGM-1114 50-100 59
Bop-Chords; Channels; Continentals; Love-Notes.

Rumble .... Josie (M) 4009 30-40 66
Bop-Chords; Channels; Continentals; Love-Notes.

Running Scared .... MCA (S) 6169 10-12 86

Running Scared .... MCA (S) 39321 8-10 86
(Soundtrack.) Michael McDonald; Fee Waybill; Rod Temperton & Beat Wagon; Larry Williams; Ready for the World; Klymaxx; New Edition; Patti LaBelle; Kim Wilde.

Rural Blues, Vol. 2 — Down Home Stomp .... Imperial (M) LM-94006 10-15

Rustler's Rhapsody .... Warner Bros. (S) 1-25284 8-10 85
(Soundtrack.) Gary Morris; Nitty Gritty Dirt Band; John Anderson; Pinkard & Bowden; Charlie McCoy; Pam Tillis; Randy Travis; Karen Brooks; Rex Allen Jr.; Rex Allen Sr.; Roy Rogers.

Ruthless People .... Epic (S) SE-40398 8-10 86
(Soundtrack.) Mick Jagger; Billy Joel; Machinations; Luther Vandross; Dan Hartman; Kool & Gang; Michel Colombier; Bruce Springsteen; Nicole; Paul Young.

SVR Hits of the Sixties, Vol. 1 .... SVR (S) 42441 10-15 85
Unrelated Segments; Tidal Waves; Quintette Plus; Gruve; Four Gents; Boys; Unknowns.

Sacred Concert .... Singspiration (M) LP 137 5-10
George Beverly Shay; Herman Voss; Helen McAlerney Barth; Csehy Musical Messengers; Adora Norlander; George Edstrom.

Sacred Songs .... Diplomat (M) 2603 8-12
Carl Story; Lonzo & Oscar; Stanley Brothers; Cowboy Copas; Frankie Miller; Phipps Family; Lewis Family; Jimmie William & Red Ellis; Sam & Kirk McGee.

Sacred Songs .... Guest Star (S) GS-1498 8-12
Carl Story; Stanley Brothers; Phipps Family; String Bean; Sam & Kirk McGee; Lonesome Pine Fiddlers; Stoneman Family; Hylo Brown; Frankie Miller.

Sacred Songs .... King (M) 395-556 20-30 57

Saint Elmo's Fire .... Atlantic (S) 81261-1 8-10 85
(Soundtrack.) John Parr; Billy Squier; Elefante; Jon Anderson; Fee Waybill; David Foster; Vikki Moss; Airplay; Donny Gerrard; Amy Holland.

Salesmen's Demonstration Record, January 1962 .... Liberty (M) MM-412 10-20 62
Si Zentner; Gene McDaniels; Johnny Mann Singers; Johnny Burnette; Jimmy Dorsey; Blue Grass Gentlemen; Eddie Heywood; Timi Yuro; Bud & Travis; Johnnie Ray; Eddie Cochran.

Salsa .... MCA (S) 6232 8-10 88
(Soundtrack.) Bobby Caldwell; Ben E. King; Marisela with the Edwin Hawkins Singers; Tito Puente; Robby Rosa; Wilkins; Mavis Vegas Davis; Grupo Niche; Laura Branagan; Kenny Ortega.

Salt and Tabasco .... Mango (S) MLPS-9852 5-10 90
Arrow; Los Van Van; LBW; Jorge Ben; Kid Creole; Gibson Brothers; Bandara; Yomo Toro; Third World; Nana Vasconcelos.

Salute to Rock and Roll .... Festival (S) FR-1006 A 10-15 76
Chuck Berry; Sensations; Dale Hawkins; Clyde McPhatter; Mickey & Sylvia; Four Lovers; Angels; Big Bopper; Del-Vikings; Sir Douglas Quintet; Bobby Moore; Clarence Henry; Diamonds; Lee Andrews & Hearts; Monotones; Bobby Hebb; Students; Johnnie & Joe; Jan Bradley.

Sammy Davis Show .... Reprise (S) RS 6188 10-20
Sammy Davis Jr.; Dean Martin; others.

Sample the Magic of Motown .... Motown (S) 35 5-10 78
(Promotional issue only.)

San Antonio Rose Steel Guitar Rag .... Starday (M) 375 10-15 66

San Antonio Rose Steel Guitar Rag .... Starday (S) 375 10-15 66
Leon McAuliffe; Bob Wills with Tommy Duncan; others.

San Francisco .... San Francisco (S) SD-158 10-20

San Francisco Roots .... Vault (S) LP-119 20-30 68
Grace Slick & Great Society; Beau Brummels; Mojo Men; Tikis; Knight Riders; Vejtables.

San Francisco Roots .... JAS (S) JAS-5001 15-25 76
Grace Slick & Great Society; Beau Brummels; Mojo Men; Tikis; Knight Riders; Bobby Freeman.

San Francisco Records Sampler .... San Francisco (S) SD-158 5-10 70
Cold Blood; Hammer; Victoria; Tower of Power; David Lannan. (Sampler made for retail sales.)

San Francisco Sound, Vol. 1 .... Fifth Pipe Dream (S) 11680 50-75 69
It's a Beautiful Day; Indian Puddin' & Pipe; Tripsichord; Music Box; Black Swan.

Santa Claus Blues .... Jass (S) 8 5-10 86
Louis Prima & His New Orleans Gang; Clarence Williams Trio with Louis Armstrong; Johnny Otis with Lem Tally; Dick Robertson; Victoria Spivey; Bob Crosby; Babs Gonzalez; Louis Armstrong; Dick Robertson with Bobby Hackett; Count Basie with Jimmy Rushing; Al Bowlly; Woody Herman; Benny Carter & His Swing Quintet; Lionel Hampton with Sonny Parker; Jack Teagarden.

Saturday Night at the Old Barn Dance .... Kapp (M) KL-1442 8-12 60s
Bob Atcher; Arkie "The Arkansas Woodchopper"; Johnson Sisters, Ruth & Edith; Bob & Bobbie Thomas; Mary Jane Johnson; Red Blanchard; Sage Riders; Dolph Hewitt.

Saturday Night at the Uptown .... Atlantic (M) 8101 20-25 64

Saturday Night at the Uptown .... Atlantic (S) SD-8101 20-25 64
Drifters; Patti LaBelle & Blue Belles; Barbara Lynn; Vibrations; Patty & Emblems; Carltons; Wilson Pickett.

Saturday Night Downtown .... Warner Bros. (S) OP 2509 8-12 72
(Promotional issue only. Special products.) Arthur Conley; Otis Redding; Wilson Pickett; Sam & Dave; Eddie Floyd; Percy Sledge; Sam Cooke; Clarence Carter; Archie Bell & Drells; Marvin Gaye; Joe Tex; Chilites; Jackie Wilson; Miracles.

Saturday Night Fever (2 LP) .... RSO (S) RS-2-4001 10-12 77

Saturday Night Fever (2 LP) .... RSO (S) 825389-1 8-10 Re
(Soundtrack.) Bee Gees; Yvonne Elliman; Walter Murphy; Tavares; Kool & Gang; KC & Sunshine Band; Trammps; MFSB; David Shire; Ralph McDonald.

Saturday Night Grand Ole Opry .... Decca (M) DL-4303 15-25 62

Saturday Night Grand Ole Opry .... Decca (S) DL-74303 20-30 62
Kitty Wells; Roy Drusky; Tommy Jackson; Bill Anderson; Tompall & Glaser Brothers; Jimmy Newman; Ernest Tubb; Patsy Cline; Bill Monroe; Johnny & Jack; Billy Grammer; Wilburn Brothers; Roy Acuff & Smoky Mountain Boys..

Saturday Night Grand Ole Opry (Vol. 2) .... Decca (M) DL-4539 10-20 64
Saturday Night Grand Ole Opry (Vol. 2) .... Decca (S) DL-74539 15-25 64
Bill Anderson; Loretta Lynn; Bill Monroe; Tommy Jackson; Billy Grammer; Johnny Wright; Margie Bowes; Jimmy "C" Newman; Kitty Wells; Ernest Tubb; Tompall & Glaser Brothers; Bill Phillips; Wilburn Brothers.

Saturday Night Jamboree .... Longines Symphonette (S) SYS-5182 8-12
Glen Campbell; Roy Clark; Buckaroos; James Burton; Ralph Mooney; Les Paul; Merle Travis; Buck Owens; Strangers; Walter Hensley; Hank Thompson.

Saturday Night Mood .... Columbia (M) CL 599 8-12 50s
Jimmy Dorsey; Les Elgart; Percy Faith; Paul Weston; Harry James; Les Brown; Benny Goodman; Frankie Carle; Dan Terry; Dick Jurgens; Sammy Kaye; Tony Pastor.

Saturday Night Shindig .... Mercury (M) MG-21036 10-20 65
Saturday Night Shindig .... Mercury (S) SR-61036 10-20 65
Roy Drusky; Margie Singleton; Faron Young; others.

Saturday Pogo .... Rhino (S) RNLP-003 5-10
Winos; Berlin Brats; Droogs; Needles & Pins; Motels; Vom; Low Numbers; Dils; Daddy Mayfield; Young Republicans; Backstage Pass; Dogs; Chainsaw; Hebe Gee Bees.

Savage Seven .... Atco (M) 33-245 20-25 68
Savage Seven .... Atco (SP) SD-33-245 20-30 68
(Soundtrack.) Cream; Barbara Kelly & Morning Good; Iron Butterfly.

Save on Records (Bulletin for June) .... RCA (EP) SPA-7-27 250-300 56
(Mail order offer.) Elvis Presley; Frankie Carle; Al Nevins; Sauter-Finnegan Orchestra; Harry Belafonte; Rubinstein; Risě Stevens; Arturo Toscanini; Arthur Fiedler & Boston Pops; Boston Symphony.

Save the Children (Songs from the Hearts of Women) .... Women Strike For Peace (M) W-001 15-25 67
Joan Baez; Judy Collins; Barbara Dane; Mimi Farina; Janis Ian; Viveca Lindfors; Odetta; Pennywhistlers; Malvina Reynolds; Buffy Sainte-Marie.

Save the Children (2 LP) .... Motown (S) M-800-R2 8-12 73
(Soundtrack. Includes poster.) Matt Robinson; Jackson 5; Nancy Wilson; Roberta Flack; Brenda Lee Eager; James Cleveland; Marvin Gaye; Sammy Davis Jr.; Temptations; Bill Withers; O'Jays; Gladys Knight & Pips; Main Ingredient; Curtis Mayfield; Jerry Butler; Ramsey Lewis Trio; Quincy Jones; Jesse Jackson; Zulema; Cannonball Adderley.

Sax Greats .... Everest (S) 331 5-10 77
Stan Getz; Coleman Hawkins; Don Dyas; Ben Webster; Charlie Ventura; Ted Nash; others.

Saxomaniac .... Apollo (M) LP-477 30-50
Coleman Hawkins; Illinois Jacquet; George Auld; others.

Scarface .... MCA (S) 6126 15-20 83
(Soundtrack.) Paul Engemann; Deborah Harry; Amy Holland; Maria Conchita; Giorgio Moroder; Elizabeth Daily; Beth Anderson.

Schlitz Country .... RCA/Schlitz (S) DPL1-0472 8-10 80
Willie Nelson; Charley Pride; Dottie West; Bobby Bare; Dave & Sugar; Gary Stewart; Dean Dillon; Ronnie Milsap; Tom T. Hall; Sylvia; Razzy Bailey; Jim Ed Brown; Helen Cornelius. (Made for Schlitz Beer.)

Schoner Gigolo – Armer Gigolo (Just a Gigolo) .... Ariola (S) 200 462 320 25-30 79
(Soundtrack.): Marlene Dietrich; Manhattan Transfer; Ragtimers; Pasadena Roof Orchestra; Gunther Fischer; Sydne Rome; Rebels; Barnabas Orchestra; Village People.

School Daze .... EMI (S) E1-48680 8-10 88
(Soundtrack.) E.; Tech & Effx; Rays; Jigaboo & Wannabee Ensemble; Kenny Barron; Terence Blanchard; Morehouse College Glee Club; Keith John; Phyllis Hyman; Pieces of a Dream; Portia Griffin.

Scooby Doo .... Zephyr (M) ZP-12202G 5-10
Scrapbook of Golden Hits .... Wing (S) SRW-16371 10-15 68
Gaylords; Platters; Diamonds; Crew-Cuts; others.

Scrooge's Rock N' Roll Christmas .... Hitbound (SP) HB-1003 10-15
Mike Love; Dean Torrance; Three Dog Night; Merrilee Rush; Paul Revere & Raiders; Mary McGregor; Association; Bobby Goldsboro.

Scrooged .... A&M (S) SP 3921 8-10 89
(Soundtrack.) Annie Lennox; Al Green; Mark Lennon; New Voices of Freedom; Dan Hartman; Denise Lopez; Kool Moe Dee; Miles Davis; Larry Carlton; Paul Shaffer; Robbie Robertson; Buster Poindexter.

Season's Best .... Columbia (S) C-30124 5-10 70
Barbara Streisand; Johnny Cash; Jim Nabors; Andy Williams; others.

Season's Best from Warner/Elektra/Atlantic (2 LP) .... Warner (S) WEA-SMP-2-10-76 15-20 76
(Promotional issue only.) Ringo Starr; Alice Cooper; Orleans; Rod Stewart; Linda Ronstadt; Hall & Oates; Spinners; Elvin Bishop; Average White Band; Fleetwood Mac; Harry Chapin; Cate Brothers; Stills-Young Band; Foghat; Firefall; James Taylor; George Benson; Abba; Gordon Lightfoot; Judy Collins; England Dan & John Ford Coley; Gary Wright; Beach Boys; Jackson Browne; Doobie Brothers; Stanley Clarke; Tom Waits; Jimmy Castor; Johnny Bristol. (Made for In-Store-Airplay.)

Season's Greetings .... Capitol (M) T 1662 8-12
Dean Martin; others.

Season's Greetings .... Columbia (M) CL-1394 15-20 59
Season's Greetings .... Columbia (S) CS-8189 15-20 59
Johnny Mathis; Mitch Miller; Norman Luboff Choir; Percy Faith; Hi-Los; Bing Crosby; Ed Kenney with Luther Henderson.

Season's Greetings from Motown Records .... Motown (S) PR-2-1 ?? 73
(45 rpm. Promotional issue only.) Walter Gaines; Smokey Robinson; Mike Campbell; Eddie Kendricks; Thelma Houston; Gwendolyn Berry; Karin Patterson; Willie Hutch; Michael Jackson; Jermaine Jackson; Tito Jackson; Jackie Jackson; Edwin Starr; Stevie Wonder.

Secret Admirer .... MCA (S) 5611 8-10 85
(Soundtrack.) Van Stephenson; Tony Carey; Kim Wilde; Don Felder; Klymaxx; Nik Kershaw; Rosemary Butler; Arnold McCuller; Timothy B. Schmit; Jan Hammer.

Secret Love (4 LP) .... Warner/Sessions (S) OP-4505 15-25 87
(Mail order offer.) Whitney Houston; Foreigner; Air Supply; Robert John; 5th Dimension; Quincy Jones; James Ingram; Joe Cocker; Jennifer Warnes; James Taylor; England Dan & John Ford Coley; Rita Coolidge; Bee Gees; Moody Blues; Phil Collins; Dionne Warwick; Peaches & Herb; Carly Simon; Eddie Rabbitt; Crystal Gayle; Jack Wagoner; Patti Austin; Commodores; Lobo; Harry Nilsson; Anne Murray; Gary Wright; Klymaxx; Casinos; Brian Hyland; Linda Ronstadt; Leo Sayer; Peabo Bryson; Roberta Flack; Kool & Gang; Joe Cocker; Larry Graham; America; Firefall; Righteous Brothers; Ray Parker & Raydio; Seals & Crofts; Bread; Three Dog Night; Billy Ocean; Ambrosia; Captain & Tennille; Sergio Mendes. (Special products. Made for Sessions.)

Secret of My Success .... MCA (S) 6205 8-10 87
(Soundtrack.) Night Ranger; Pat Benatar; Danny Peck; Nancy Shanks; Bananarama; David Foster; Roger Daltrey; Restless Heart; Taxxi.

Secret Policeman's Ball - the Music .... Island (S) 9630 5-10 81
Pete Townshend; Tom Robinson; Neil Innes; John Williams; others.

Secret Policeman's Other Ball - the Music .... Island (S) 9698 8-12 82
Jeff Beck; Eric Clapton; Phil Collins; Donovan; Sting; Bob Geldof; Johnny Fingers; Secret Police.

Secret Policeman's Third Ball - the Music .... Virgin (S) 7 90643-1 8-12 87
Kate Bush; Duran Duran; Lou Reed; Bob Geldof; Jackson Browne; Erasure; Nik Kershaw; Joan Armatrading; Mark Knopfler; Chet Atkins; Peter Gabriel.

Selections from Hollywood Knights .... Excelsior (S) XMP-6009 5-10 80
Martha Reeves; Capitols; Marcels; Chiffons; Platters; Surfaris; Chiffons; Mark Dinning; Chantays; Curtis Lee; Crystals.

Senior Prom (4 LP) .... Warner Bros./Sessions (S) OP-4508 20-25 87
(Mail order offer.) Ben E. King; Everly Brothers; Poni-Tails; Bobby Vee; Brian Hyland; Pat Boone; Bobby Vinton; Sam Cooke; Platters; Lenny Welch; Shelley Fabares; Righteous Brothers; Four Freshmen; Ritchie Valens; Shirelles; Mark Dinning; Paul & Paula; Paris Sisters; others. (Special products. Made for Sessions.)

Sensational '60s (2 LP) .... Columbia Musical Treasuries (S) P2S 5590/DS 788-9 10-20 71

Sensational '60s (2 LP) .... Columbia Musical Treasury (S) P2S 5590 10-20 71
O.C. Smith; Horst Jankowski; Eydie Gorme; Village Stompers; Tony Bennett; Dusty Springfield; Jimmy Dean; Getz & Gilberto; Cyrkle; Bobby Helms; Byrds; New Vaudville Band; Jeannie C. Riley; Stan Getz & Charlie Byrd; Brothers Four; Gene Pitney; Bobby Vinton; Mike Douglas; Bill Justis; Marty Robbins; New Christy Minstrels; Sandpipers; Pete Seeger; Johnny Horton; David Rose; Dave Clark Five; Johnny Cash; Singing Nun; Gary Puckett & Union Gap; Tammy Wynette; Scott McKenzie; Claude King; Lesley Gore; Roger Williams. (Columbia House Record Club issue.)

September '63 Pop Sampler: see RCA September '63 Pop Sampler

Serenade of Soul: see LYNNE, Gloria / Nina Simone / Billie Holiday

Sessions: JBL Test Record for Demonstration .... ???? (S) ???? 5-10 73
(Promotional issue only.) Hoyt Axton; Alex Harvey; Alex Richman; Dick Rosmini; Rick Ruskin.

Sgt. Pepper's Lonely Hearts Club Band (2 LP) .... RSO (S) R5-24100 10-12 78
(Soundtrack.) Bee Gees; Peter Frampton; Billy Preston; Steve Martin; Earth, Wind & Fire; Paul Nicholas; George Burns; Aerosmith; Alice Cooper; Sandy Farina; Frankie Howard; Dianne Steinberg.

Shades of the Blues .... Relic (M) 8003 5-10 84
Eddie Kirkland with the Falcons; Eddie Kirkland; Mr. Bo; Ohio Untouchables; Robert Ward & Ohio Untouchables.

Shag .... Sire (S) 1-25800 8-10 89
(Soundtrack.) LaVern Baker; K.D. Lang & Reclines; Randy Newman; Ben E. King; Louise Goffin; Charmettes; Hank Ballard & Midnighters; Chris Isaak; Tommy Page; Take 6.

Shake a Hand .... Guest Star (M) G-1904 10-20 60s

Shake a Hand .... Guest Star (S) GS-1904 10-20 60s
Chuck Jackson; Faye Adams; Jesse Belvin; Ann Cole; Tommy Middleton; Tokens; Bobby Troy.

Shake It and Break It .... Capitol (M) TBO-1572 15-20 61
Andrews Sisters; Joe "Fingers" Carr; Pee Wee Hunt; Red Nichols; Pete Dailey; others.

Shake, Shout and Soul .... Impact (M) 2 40-50 60s
Dave Myers & Surftones; Surfaris; New Dimensions; others.

Sharky's Machine .... Warner Bros. (S) BSK-3653 10-15 81
(Soundtrack.) Randy Crawford; Flora Purim; Buddy De Franco; Manhattan Transfer; Chet Baker; Doc Severinsen; Sarah Vaughan; Joe Williams; Julie London; Peggy Lee; Eddie Harris.

Sharp Cuts .... Planet (S) P-6 5-10
Single Bullet Theory; Billy Thermal; Bates Motel; Peter Dayton; Alley Cats; Know; Willys; Fast; DB's; Suburgan Lawns.

Sharp/Optonica .... Direct Disc (S) 09-003 15-20 82
(Picture disc.)

She-Devil .... Polydor (S) 841-583-1 25-35 89
(Soundtrack.) Safire; Carmel; D-Mob; Chubby Checker; Tom Kimmel; Elvis Presley; Jermaine Stewart; Kate Ceberano; Yello; Fatboys.

She's Having a Baby .... I.R.S. (S) 6211 8-10 88
(Soundtrack.) Everything But the Girl; Bryan Ferry; Gene Loves Jezebel; Dr.; XTC; Love & Rockets; Carmel; Dave Wakeling; Kate Bush; Kirsty MacColl.

She's Out of Control .... MCA (S) 6281 8-10 89
(Soundtrack.) Troy Hinton; Brenda K. Starr; Phil Thornalley; Boys Club; Harold Faltermeyer; Jim Ladd; Oingo Boingo; Brian Wilson; Frankie Avalon; Kinks; Jetboy.

Shindig .... Guest Star (M) G-1488 10-20 60s

Shindig .... Guest Star (S) GS-1488 10-20 60s
Platters; Chuck Jackson; 4 Seasons; Julie London; Tokens; Steve Lawrence; Penguins; Monarchs; Bill Haley & His Comets; Arthur Prysock; Shirley & Lee; Neil Sedaka; Al Martino; Mel Torme; Billy Eckstine; Johnny Rivers; Maxine Brown; Little Esther; Cufflinks; Willows; Ray Charles; Fireflies; Meadowlarks; Lloyd Price; Bobbettes.

Shindig .... Spectrum (M) DLP-190 10-20 65

Shindig .... Spectrum (S) DLP-190 10-20 65
Jerry Lee Lewis; Irma Thomas; Chuck Jackson; Solomon Burke; Jimmy Clanton; 4 Seasons; Floyd Cramer; Jan & Dean; Ronnie Dove; Don Covay.

Shindig .... Design (M) DLP-190 10-20 60s
Jerry Lee Lewis; Irma Thomas; Chuck Jackson; Solomon Burke; Jimmy Clanton; 4 Seasons; Floyd Cramer; Jan & Dean; Ronnie Dove; Don Covay.

Shindig .... Kapp (M) KL-1431 15-20 65

Shindig .... Kapp (S) KS-3431 15-25 65
Searchers; Shirley Ellis; Ruby & Romantics; Waikikis; Boss Guitars; Linda Scott; Johnny Cymbal; You Know Who Group.

Shindig (Based on the ABC-TV Shindig) .... ABC-PAR (M) ABC-504 20-25 65

Shindig (Based on the ABC-TV Shindig)..ABC-PAR (S) ABCS-504 25-30 65
Tommy Roe; Impressions; Fats Domino; Tams; Spats; Steve Alaimo; Gauchos; Sapphires; Shin-Diggers.
Shindig Hullabaloo Spectacular: see RIVERS, Johnny / 4 Seasons / Jerry Butler / Jimmy Soul
Shindig with the Stars, Vol. 1 ....Wyncote (M) W-9053 10-20 64
Shindig with the Stars, Vol. 1 ....Wyncote (SE) SW-9053 10-20 64
Chubby Checker; Bobby Rydell; Dee Dee Sharp; Jo Ann Campbell; Orlons; Dovells; Tymes.
Shindig with the Stars, Vol. 2 ....Wyncote (M) W-9070 10-20 65
Shindig with the Stars, Vol. 2 ....Wyncote (SE) SW-9070 10-20 65
Johnny Rivers; Maxine Brown; Neil Sedaka; 4 Seasons; Paragons; Classics.
Shindig with the Stars, Vol. 3 ....Wyncote (M) W-9125 10-20 65
Shindig with the Stars, Vol. 3 ....Wyncote (SE) SW-9125 10-20 65
Shirley Alston with . . .: see ALSTON, Shirley
Shirley Scott & Soul Saxes..Atlantic (S) 1532 10-15 69
Shirley Scott & Soul Saxes; King Curtis; Hank Crawford; David Newman.Christmas Around the World: see Capitol Promotional Releases/Samplers
Shocker..SBK (S) K1-93233 5-10 89
Shocker ....Varèse Sarabande (S) VS-5247 10-1589(Soundtrack.)
Short Cuts, Vol. 1 (2 LP) ....World Pacific Jazz (S) ST-22200 10-15
Buddy Rich Big Band; Richard "Groove" Holmes; Bobby Bryant; Jean-Luc Ponty; Bud Shank; Gerald Wilson; Jazz Crusaders; Ernie Watts Quartet; Wilbert Longmire; Freddy Robinson; Wilton Felder.
Short Playing Christmas Favorites: see Capitol Promotional Releases/Samplers
Shoutin' Swingin' and Makin' Love ....Chess (S) CHV-412 8-12 71
Show Biz from Vaude to Video..RCA (M) LOC 1011 15-25 50s
Gene Austin; Ben Bernie; Fanny Brice; Eddie Cantor; Maurice Chevalier; George M. Cohan; Bing Crosby; Tommy Dorsey; Morton Downey; Jimmy Durante; Eddie Fisher; George Gershwin; Benny Goodman; Hildegarde; Helen Kane; Danny Kaye; Harry Lauder; Beatrice Lillie; Glenn Miller; Helen Morgan; Will Rogers; Kate Smith; Sophie Tucker; Rudy Vallee; Paul Whiteman; George Jessel; others.
Show Stoppers ....Wand (M) 652 20-25 62
Joey Dee; Bobby Lewis; Isley Brothers; others.
Showcase of Country Stars ....Guest Star (S) GS-1426 5-10 60s
Sunshine Boys; Curly Gribbs; Moon Mullican; Red Sovine; Willis Brothers; Brother Oswald; George Jones; Dean Manuel; Sam & Kirk McGee; Cowboy Copas.
Showcase of Stars ....Guest Star (M) G-1424 5-10 60s
Showcase of Stars ....Guest Star (S) GS-1424 5-10 60s
Eddie Heywood; Steve Lawrence; Anita O'Day; Platters; Enzo Stuarti; Joey Dee; Jack Teagarden; Enoch Light; Homer & Jethro; Julie London.
Showcase of Stars, Vol. 2 ....Guest Star (S) GS-1425 10-15 60s
Ferrante & Teicher; Duke Ellington; Mel Torme; Borrah Minevitch; Coleman Hawkins; Alan Dale; Ray Eberle; Cozy Cole; Johnny Long; Betty Clooney.
Showdown: see COLLINS, Albert, Robert Cray and Johnny Copeland
Shower of Stars..Capitol (M) T-90088 15-20 65
Beach Boys; Buck Owens; Nat King Cole; Nancy Wilson; Al Martino; Jackie Gleason; George Shearing; Stan Kenton; Sonny James; Jean Shepherd; Louvin Brothers; Lettermen; Hollyridge Strings. (Capitol Record Club issue.)
Showtime, Best of Broadway..Harmony (SE) KH 30132 10-15 70
(Soundtrack.) Angela Lansbury; Mary Martin; Joel Grey; Barbra Streisand; Ethel Merman; Julie Andrews; Carol Lawrence; Carol Channing; Larry Kert; Judy Holliday; Dick Van Dyke.
Shut Down..Capitol (M) T-1918 35-45 63
Shut Down..Capitol (S) ST-1918 45-55 63
Beach Boys; Super Stocks; Robert Mitchum; Cheers; Piltdown Men; Jimmy Dolan; Eligibles.
Shut Downs and Hill Climbs ....Liberty (M) LRP-3366 15-25 64
Shut Downs and Hill Climbs ....Liberty (S) LST-7366 15-25 64
Jan & Dean; Ventures; T-Bones; Dave Dudley; Strangers; Johnny Bond; Earl Palmer; Paul Evans; Paul Hampton; Danny & Gwen.
Seize the Beat (Dance Ze Dance)..Ze/Island (S) IL 9667 5-10 81
Silent Partner..Pablo Today (S) 2312-103 8-10 78
(Soundtrack.) Oscar Peterson; Benny Carter; Clark Terry; Zoot Sims; Milt Jackson; John Heard; Grady Tate.
Silver Bullets: see Superstars of the '70s, Vol. 4, Silver Bullets
Silver Platter Service: see Capitol Promotional Releases/Samplers
Silver Seal Sampler..Sears Roebuck/Silver Seal (M) UT 59 5-10
Harry Belafonte; Dina Robbins; Kay Starr; London Pops Orchestra; New World Strings; Kings of Polkaland.
Silver Sounds of the Surf..Cloister (M) CLP-6301 20-30 63
Dick Dale; Stompers; others.
Silver Years ....Capitol (S) SNP-91017 10-15 67
Nat King Cole; Peggy Lee; Stan Kenton; Kay Starr; Tennessee Ernie Ford; Dean Martin; Nancy Wilson; Al Martino; Wayne Newton; Lou Rawls; Matt Monro; Sandler & Young. (Capitol Record Club issue.)
Sin Alley (18 Action Packed Rockers 1955-'61) ....Leisure Book (M) ???? 10-15
Dave Travis; Danny Dell; Gradie O'Neal; Frantics 4; Rhythm Rockers; Mel McGonnigle; Myron Lee; Pico Pete; Tony Casanova.
Sincerely (2 LP)..Lake Shore/MCA LSM-106/MSM-35000 8-12 77
Andrews Sisters; Hoagy Carmichael; Ella Fitzgerald; Ink Spots; Four Aces; Kitty Kallen; Judy Garland; Dick Haymes; Helen Forrest; Mills Brothers; Russ Morgan; Jimmy Dorsey; Glen Gray; Ted Weems; Gordon Jenkins & Weavers; Jimmy Lunceford; McGuire Sisters; Merry Macs.
Sing ....Columbia (S) SC-45086 8-10 89
(Soundtrack.) Mickey Thomas; Art Garfunkel; Patti LaBelle; Laurnea Wilkerson; Joe Williams; Bill Champlin; Paul Carrack; Terri Nunn; Michael Bolton; Cast of "Sarafina"; Nia Peeples; Johnny Kemp.
Sing A Song For Heaven's Sake (2 LP) ....Tame (S) LP-1001 8-12 78
Chuck Wagon Gang; Oak Ridge Boys; J.D. Sumner & Stamps; Imperials; Klaudt Indian Family; Sewanee River Boys; Blackwood Brothers; Hovie Lister & Statesmen; Billy Grammer; Rangers; Blue Ridge Quartet; Red Foley.
Sing a Song of Soul..Checker (M) LP 2998 15-25 68
Sing a Song of Soul..Checker (S) LPS 2998 15-25 68
Little Milton; Fontella Bass; Maurice & Radiants; Jackie Ross; Johnny Nash; Bobby Moore; Ko Ko Taylor; Mitty Collier; Knight Brothers; James Phelps; Etta James; Billy Stewart.

Sing All Night........Sims (M) LP-125 10-15
Frost Brothers; Smith Brothers; Happy Goodman Family; Luttrells; Plainsmen.

Sing Along with........Decca (M) DL 38243 15-25 62

Sing Along with........Decca (M) DL-4209 10-20 62
Four Aces; Mills Brothers; Ames Brothers; Ray Charles Singers; Buffalo Bills; Red Foley.

Sing Along with the Oldies........Warner Bros. (M) W-1516 10-20 63

Sing Along with the Oldies........Warner Bros. (S) WS-1516 15-20 63

Sing Along with the Original Golden Gassers: see Murray the K's Sing Along with the Golden Gassers.

Sing Me A Country Song (6 LP)........Columbia Musical Treasury (SE) 6P 6111 20-30 74
(Boxed set. Columbia Record Club issue. Mail order.) Tom T. Hall; Jody Miller; Johnny Duncan; Tammy Wynette; George Jones; Barbara Fairchild; Johnny Paycheck; Connie Smith; Bob Luman; Freddy Weller; Tanya Tucker; Mac Davis; Carl Smith; Marty Robbins; Roy Clark; Ray Price; Johnny Cash; June Carter; Mel Tillis; Charlie Rich; Tommy Cash; Lynn Anderson; Jud Strunk; Donna Fargo; Dave Dudley; David Houston; Jerry Reed; Jerry Lee Lewis; Barbara Mandrell; Ray Stevens; Flatt & Scruggs; Lefty Frizzell; Sonny James; Roy Drusky; Priscilla Mitchell; Jimmy Dean; Charlie McCoy; Johnny Rodriguez; Boots Randolph; Roger Miller.

Sing Out!........Sing Out (EP) (M) SO-1 15-30 61
(Packaged in 10th Anniversary issue of *Sing Out* magazine.) Pete Seeger; Woody Guthrie; Frank Hamilton; Ewan McColl; Peggy Seeger; Ethel Raim; Jerry Silverman; Mickey Miller; Bess Hawes; Big Bill Broonzy; Montgomery Alabama Gospel Choir; Vladimir Troshin.

Sing Out America! (8 LP)........RCA Custom/Readers Digest (S) RDA-037 35-45 80
(Boxed set. Has 16-page booket.) Dottie West; Asleep at the Wheel; Red Foley; Glen Campbell; Kate Smith; Ambrosian Singers; Fireside Singers; Robert Shaw Chorale; Arthur Fiedler & Boston Pops; Tennessee Ernie Ford; Fred Waring; Roland Shaw & Spirit of Freedom Singers; Patti Page; Les Brown; Guy Lombardo; Buddy Bregman; Perry Como; Margaret Whiting; Johnny Gibbs; Andrews Sisters; John Gary; Louis Armstrong; Voices of Robert MacDonald; Pete Fountain; Jimmy Brown; Alan Braden; Wally Scott; Johnny Lawrence; Lamplighters; Johnny Arthey; Bing Crosby & Jesters with Bob Haggart; Frankie Carle; Eddy Arnold; Rosemary Squires; Judy Garland with Georgie Stoll; Vic Flick; Bobby Bare; Robert Q. Lewis; Betty Clooney; Circle Five Orchestra; Alfred Drake; Joan Roberts; Cattlemen; Woody Herman; Mills Brothers; Al Capps; Country Folk; Johnny Mercer; Dukes of Dixieland; Eddy Jones; Louis Nunley; Golden Saxophone & Romantic Strings; Pete King Chorale; Mike Sammes Singers; Nick Ingman; Alvino Rey; Yvonne King; Al Caiola; Buddy Cole Trio; John McCarthy Male Chorus; Burl Ives; Hill Bowen & Royal Philharmonic Orchestra; Merrymacs; Danny Davis & Nashville Brass; Weavers; University of Michigan Band.

Sing Popular Country Songs: see Country Songs

Singer (Stereo Demo Record)........Singer (S) S-301SD 10-15 68
Enoch Light Singers; Tony Mottolo; Guitar Underground; Bobby Hackett; Urbie Green; Free Design; Enoch Light & Light Brigade.

Singer Presents........Columbia (S) CSS-552 10-15 66
Tony Bennett; Count Basie; Percy Faith; Jerry Vale; Doris Day; Ray Conniff; Bobby Hackett; Johnny Mathis; Andre Kostelanetz; Leslie Uggams.

Singer-Songwriter Project........Elektra (M) EKL-299 15-20 65

Singer-Songwriter Project........Elektra (S) EKS7-299 20-25 65
Richard Farina; Patrick Sky; others.

Singin' and Swingin'........Wing (M) MGW 12211 15-25
Platters; Diamonds; Sil Austin; Conway Twitty; Narvel Felts; Big Bopper.

Singin' the Blues (2 LP)........MCA (S) 2-4064 8-12 74
Jimmy Rushing; Ella Fitzgerald; Kay Starr; Lil Armstrong; Wynonie Harris; Dinah Washington; Helen Humes; Billie Holiday; Cousin Joe; Ella Johnson; Louis Jordan; Walter Brown.

Singing the Blues........Aladdin (M) LP-813 100-200 57

Singing the Gospel........Modern Sound (S) MS 509 5-10
Sons of Song; Florida Boys; Wendy Bagwell & Sunliters; Sego Brothers & Naomi; Dixie Echoes; Wally Fowler & Oak Ridge Quartet; Jake Hess; Plainsmen.

Singing the Gospel........Modern Sound (S) MS 805 5-10
Sego Brothers & Naomi; McCormick Singers; Sunshine Girls; Georgians; Wally Fowler & Oak Ridge Quartet; Sons of Song; Florida Boys; Dixie Echoes; Foggy River Boys.

Singing the Gospel........Modern Sound (S) MS 819 5-10
Crusaders; Sego Brothers & Naomi; Clyde Beavers; Travelers Quartet; Sons of Song; McCormick Gospel Singers; Sunshine Girls; Foggy River Boys; Melodymen Quartet; Dixie Echoes.

Sisters in Song (16 Original Hits)........Trolley Car (M) TC-5005 10-15
Gladys Knight; Tina Turner; Sarah Vaughan; Dinah Washington; Betty Everett; Little Esther; Dionne Warwick; Irma Thomas.

Sisters of Soul........Musico (S) MDS-1025 10-15 70s
Dinah Washington; Inez Foxx; Maxine Brown; Irma Thomas; Toys.

Six Pak, Vol. 1........Lone Star (S) L-4600 8-10 78
Willie Nelson; Cooder Browne; Ray Wylie Hubbard; Don Bowman; Steve Fromholz; Geezinslaw Brothers.

Sixteen Candles........MCA (S) 36012 8-10 84
(Soundtrack.) Stray Cats; Annie Golden; Ira Newborn & Geeks; Patti Smith; Thompson Twins.

Sixties........RCA (S) VPS-6061 8-12 72
Guess Who; Carol Burnette; Carol Channing; Floyd Cramer; Dolly Parton; Youngbloods; others.

Skateboard........RCA (S) ABL1-2769 8-10 77
(Soundtrack.) Dr. John; Jefferson Starship; Mickey Thomas; Taro Meyer; Mona Lisa; Terry Young; Roger Jaep.

Skatetown U.S.A.........Columbia (S) JC-36292 8-10 80
(Soundtrack.) Dave Mason; Earth, Wind & Fire; Emotions; Marilyn McCoo & Billy Davis Jr.; Jacksons; Hounds; John Sebastian; Heatwave; Patrick Hernandez.

Slam Dance........Island (S) 90662-1. 8-10 87
(Soundtrack.) Stan Ridgway; Mitchell Froom; Tim Scott; Eddy Howard.

Slaves to Rock........Iron Works (S) 1016B 10-15 88
(Promotional only picture disc. 500 made.)

Sleep Baby Sleep........Columbia Special Products (S) CSP 177 10-20 60s
Doris Day; Anna Maria Alberghetti; Norman Luboff Choir; Andre Kostelanetz; Bing Crosby; Diahann Carroll; Rosemary Clooney; Mitch Miller; Sandpipers; Anne Lloyd; Mary Martin. (Made for Pet Milk Co.)

Slice of Lemon........Columbia Special Products (M) CSM-389 15-25 65

Slice of Lemon........Columbia Special Products (S) CSP-389 15-25 65
(Promotional issue only.) Dick Clark; Dave Clark Five; Brothers Four; Percy Faith; New Christy Minstrels; Tony Bennett; Dave Brubeck; Andre Previn; Doris Day; Bob Dylan; Simon & Garfunkel.

Slide Guitar Classics: see TAYLOR, Hound Dog / Robert Nighthawk / John Littlejohn / Earl Hooker

Slumber Party '57........Mercury (S) SRM-1-1097 8-12 76

(Soundtrack.) Jerry Lee Lewis; Crew-Cuts; Johnny Preston; Paul & Paula; Platters; Angels; Bruce Channel; Danleers; Big Bopper; Phil Phillips; Jivin' Gene & Jokers; David Carroll.

Smash Hits............Smash (M) MGS-27018 20-25 62
Smash Hits............Smash (S) SRS-67018 20-25 62
Billy Myles; Maurice Williams & Zodiacs; Silhouettes; Nutmegs; others.

Smash Sounds............Atco (M) 850 10-20 67
Smash Sounds............Atco (S) SD-850 15-25 67
Ben E. King; Otis Redding; King Curtis; Capitols; Sonny & Cher; Arthur Conley; Shadows of Knight; Buffalo Springfield; Coasters; Deon Jackson; Percy Wiggins; Jimmy Hughes.

Smile and Be Happy............Columbia Special Products (M) C-10698 5-10
Ray Conniff; Bobby Vinton; Lynn Anderson; Percy Faith; Robert Goulet; Johnny Cash; Tammy Wynette; Johnny Mathis; Andre Kostelanetz; Marty Robbins.

Smithsonian Collection of Classic Jazz (6 LP)............Columbia Special Products P-6-118891 30-50 73
(Boxed set with 46-page booklet.) Scott Joplin; Robert Johnson; Bessie Smith; King Oliver's Creole Jazz Band; Jellyroll Morton's Red Hot Peppers; Red Onion Jazz Babies; Sidney Bechet & His Blue Note Jazzmen; James P. Johnson; Louis Armstrong & His Hot Seven; Earl Hines; Frankie Trumbauer; Fletcher Henderson; Benny Motens Kansas City Orchestra; Fats Waller; Meade Lux Lewis; Benny Goodman Trio; Coleman Hawkin Quartet; Billie Holiday; Eddie Heywood; Ella Fitzgerald; Art Tatum; Jimmie Lunceford; Gene Krupa; Roy Eldgridge; Benny Carter; Lionel Hampton; Count Basie's Kansas City Seven; Benny Goodman Sextet & Charlie Christian; Duke Ellington; Don Byas; Dizzy Gillespie Sextet / All Star Quintet; Charlie Parker's Re-Boppers / Quintet / Sextet / All Stars; Erroll Garner; Bud Powell Trio; Sarah Vaughan; Lennie Tristano; Miles Davis Sextet; Tadd Dameron's Sextet; Dexter Gordon Quartet; Thelonius Monk Quartet; Miles Davis & Gil Evans; Sonny Rollins Quartet; Modern Jazz Quartet; Charles Mingus; Sonny Rollins Plus Four; Cecil Taylor; Ornette Coleman; John Coltrane.

Smokey & Bandit 2............MCA (S) 6101 8-10 80
(Soundtrack.) Jerry Reed; Statler Brothers; Don Williams; Roy Rogers & Sons of the Pioneers; Bandit Band; Tanya Tucker; Mel Tillis; Brenda Lee; others (With dialogue.)

Smokey & Bandit 3............MCA (S) 36006 8-10 83
(Soundtrack.) John Stewart; Lee Greenwood; Ed Bruce; others.

Smokey Mountain Ballads............Camden/Pickwick (M) ACL-7022 5-10 76
Uncle Dave Macon; Wade Mainer, Zeke Morris; Steve Ledford; Dixon Brothers; Arthur Smith Trio; Monroe Brothers; Carter Family; J.E. Mainer's Mountaineers; Gid Tanner & His Skillet Lickers.

Smooth & Swinging Jazz............Verve (M) PM-12 15-25 60s
Count Basie; Joe Williams; Gerry Mulligan; Dizzy Gillespie; Roy Eldridge; Bobby Brookmeyer; Johnny Hodge; Billy Strayhorn; Terry Gibbs; Anita O'Day; Ray Brown. (Made for Blended Scotch Whiskey.)

Smooth Country Greats............RCA Special Products (S) DPL1 0092 5-10 74
Jeannie C. Riley; Charlie Rich; Johnny Cash; Dottie West; Don Gibson; Eddy Arnold; Skeeter Davis; Jerry Reed; Porter Wagoner; Hank Snow. (Made for Kessler Whiskey.)

Snowfall............CBS (S) P-18879 5-10 86
Willie Nelson; Johnny Mathis; Mitch Miller; Doris Day; Gene Autry; Andy Williams; Lynn Anderson; Tony Bennett; Percy Faith; Robert Goulet.

Sock Hoppin' Sixties............Warner/JCI (S) 3110 8-12 85
Dion; Shirelles; Shangri-Las; Freddy Cannon; Bobby Lewis; Joey Dee & Starliters; Del Shannon; Angels; Claudine Clark; Chiffons; Sensations; Ernie Maresca.

Soft Pedal............Columbia House Party Series (M) CL 2511 15-25 56
(10-inch LP.) Erroll Garner; Teddy Wilson; Stan Freeman; Eddie Heywood; Joe Bushkin; Joe Reichman.

Solid Gold............MGM (M) E-4352 15-20 65
Solid Gold............MGM (S) SE-4352 15-25 65
Lovin' Spoonful; Royalettes; Cal Tjader; Johnny Tillotson; Gentrys; Sam the Sham & Pharaohs.

Solid Gold (3 LP)............RCA Special Products/Sessions (S) DVL-3 0294 10-15 77
Orlons; Rays; Fontella Bass; Platters; Spanky & Our Gang; Dinah Washington; Turtles; Grass Roots; Every Mother's Son; Gentrys; Lou Christie; Marcie Blane; Beach Boys; Outsiders; Bobby Pickett; G-Clefs; Bobby Bare; Bachelors; Poppy Family; Jerry Lee Lewis; Perez Prado; Tokens; Neil Sedaka; Barry Mann; Tommy Roe; Jimmy Gilmer; Ruby & Romantics; Cuff Links; Brenda Lee; Bobby Freeman; Dion; Ernie Maresca; Don Gibson; Isley Brothers; Mickey & Sylvia; Tommy Edwards; Cowsills.

Solid Gold............SSS Int'l (S) 3 8-12
Johnny Adams; Mickey Murray; Peggy Scott & Jo Jo Benson; Big John Hamilton; Laura Greene; Johnny McKinnie; Sil Austin; Johnny Soul; Betty Harris.

Solid Gold............Warner Lambert (S) BU-5290 5-10 84
Percy Sledge; 5th Dimension; Mel Carter; Shirley & Co.; Shalamar; Taste of Honey; Brook Benton; Delfonics; Gladys Knight & Pips; Four Tops; Cornelius Brothers; Tavares. (Rerecordings. Made for Listerine.)

Solid Gold (2 LP)............Columbia House (S) P2M-5843 10-15 '72
(Columbia Record Club issue.) Everly Brothers; Jimmy Clanton; Cadillacs; Crew-Cuts; Bill Justis; Silhouettes; Lee Dorsey; Diamonds; Sonny Til & Orioles; Santo & Johnny; Eddie Rambeau; Dion & Belmonts; Frankie Lymon & Teenagers; Big Bopper; Mello Kings; J. Frank Wilson; Bill Doggett; Huey "Piano" Smith; Buster Brown; Platters; Joey Dee & Starliters; James Brown & Famous Flames; Mitch Ryder; Five Satins; Little Anthony & Imperials; Shep & Limelites; Crows; Hank Ballard & Midnighters; Channels; Frankie Ford.

Solid Gold 30 Original Rock and Roll Hits (2 LP)............Columbia (S) D1025/1026 10-15 72
Diamonds; Orioles; Eddy Rambeau; Dion & Belmonts; Santo & Johnny; Frankie Lymon; Big Bopper; Mello Kings; Everly Brothers; Jimmy Clanton; Cadillacs; Crew-Cuts; Bill Justis; Silhouettes; Lee Dorsey; Mitch Ryder; Five Satins; Little Anthony & Imperials; Shep & Limelites; Crows; Frankie Ford; Hank Ballard & Midnighters; Channels; J. Frank Wilson; Bill Doggett; Huey Smith; Buster Brown; Platters; Joey Dee; James Brown.

Solid Gold – An Album of "Wife" (2 LP)............Variety Club (S) No Number Used 8-12 70s
Merrilee Rush; Andy Williams; Dionne Warwick; Steppenwolf; Ohio Express; Impressions; Tommy Roe; Neil Diamond; Canned Heat; Lemon Pipers; McCoys; Bobby Goldsboro; Animals; Strawberry Alarm Clock; Zager & Evans; James Brown; J. Frank Wilson; Box Tops; Jose Feliciano; Kingsmen; Three Dog Night; B.J. Thomas; Classics IV; Irish Rovers; Ventures; Glen Campbell. (A promotional, "International Charity Album.")

Solid Gold Country............RCA (S) CPL1-4841 5-10 83
Waylon Jennings; Jerry Reed; Gus Hardin; Earl Thomas Conlin; Troy Seals; Ronnie Milsap; Louise Mandrell; Sylvia; Charley Pride.

Solid Gold Groups............Atlantic (M) 8065 30-40 62
Diamonds; Clovers; Chordcats; Clyde McPhatter & Drifters; Cardinals; Ben E. King & Drifters; Cookies; Penguins.

Solid Gold Hits............Imperial (M) 9230 20-30 63
Fats Domino; April Stevens; others.

Solid Gold Hits, Vol. 1 ....ABC (S) 2271 10-15 69
Elegants; Tommy Roe; Lloyd Price; Frankie Laine; others.
Solid Gold Hits, Vol. 2 ....ABC (S) 2272 10-15 69
Tommy Roe; Impressions; Tams; Brian Hyland; others.
Solid Gold Hits, Vol. 3 ....ABC (S) 2273 10-15 69
Lloyd Price; Royal Teens; Frankie Laine; Gabor Szabo; others.
Solid Gold Old Town, Vol. 1 ....Cotillion (SE) SD-9032 10-15 70
Fiestas; Solitaires; Keystones; Robert & Johnny; Royal Tones; Billy Bland; Ruth McFadden; Valentines; Harptones; Keytones.
Solid Gold Party (5 LP).... Silver Eagle/Warner Bros. (S) OP 5501 20-25 82
(Mail order offer.) Dion; Chiffons; Bobby Darin; Maurice Williams & Zodiacs; Little Eva; Shangri-Las; Fats Domino; Peggy March; Neil Sedaka; Dixie Cups; Bobby Vee; Wilbert Harrison; Chubby Checker; Silhouettes; Dee Dee Sharp; Essex; Gary Lewis & Playboys; Jan & Dean; Association; Box Tops; Diana Ross & Supremes; Archie Bell & Drells; Percy Sledge; Mary Wells; Aretha Franklin; Four Tops; Marvelettes; Martha Reeves & Vandellas; Jackson Five; Temptations; Lovin' Spoonful; Young Rascals; ? & Mysterians; Tommy Roe; Beach Boys; Monkees; Dawn; Tommy James & Shondells; Archies; 5th Dimension; Peter & Gordon; Turtles; Ides of March; Everly Borthers; Shelley Fabares; Shirelles; Ruby & Romantics; Brenda Lee; Connie Francis; Drifters.
Solid Gold Programming ....Screen Gems/Columbia (S) 711 10-20 60s
(Promotional only issue.) Roger Williams; Wayne Newton; Bobby Sherman; Bobby Vinton; Sergio Mendes; Al Martino; Frank Sinatra; Monkees; Mindbenders; Carole King; Aretha Franklin; Drifters; Stone Poneys; Righteous Brothers. Also see *More Solid Gold Programming.*
Solid Gold Rock and Roll, Vol. 1 ....Mercury (S) SR-61371 8-12 72
Crew-Cuts; Big Bopper; Johnny Preston; Del-Vikings; Danleers; Angels; Caravelles; Dickey Lee; Wayne Fontana & Mindbenders; Left Banke; Sir Douglas Quintet; Steam; Diamonds.
Solid Gold Rock and Roll, Vol. 2 ....Mercury (S) SR-61372 8-12 72
Diamonds; Jay & Techniques; Paul & Paula; Jerry Lee Lewis; Phil Phillips; Joe Dowell; Mindbenders; Platters; Del-Vikings; Bruce Channel; Dickey Lee; Lesley Gore; Ray Stevens; Crew-Cuts.
Solid Gold Soul.... Guest Star (M) GS 1503 15-20 60s
Arthur Prysock; Ray Charles; Garnet Mimms; Lloyd Price; Chuck Jackson; Jesse Belvin.
Solid Gold Soul....Stax (S) 2031 8-12 71
Solid Gold Soul....Atlantic (M) 8116 10-20 66
Solid Gold Soul.... Atlantic (S) 8116 10-20 66
Solomon Burke; Wilson Pickett; Joe Tex; Don Covay; Ben E. King; Otis Redding.
Solid Gold Soul, Vol. 2 ....Atlantic (M) 8137 10-20 66
Solid Gold Soul, Vol. 2 .... Atlantic (S) 8137 10-20 66
Solomon Burke; Wilson Pickett; Joe Tex; Ray Charles; Chris Kenner; Percy Sledge; others.
Solitary Dreams (2 LP) ....Sessions/Capitol Special Markets (S) SLB-6991 10-15 75
(Mail order offer.) People; Peter & Gordon; Beach Boys; Paul Mauriet; 5th Dimension; Maureen McGovern; Seekers; Linda Ronstadt; Dionne Warwick; Glen Campbell; Sounds of the '70s Orchestra; Terry Jacks; Tony Orlando & Dawn; Kingston Trio; Lettermen; Nat King Cole; Al Martino; B.J. Thomas; Laurie London. (Special products. Made for Sessions.)
Some Kind of Wonderful .... MCA (S) 6200 8-10 87
(Soundtrack.) Furniture; Lick the Tins; Blue Room; Pete Shelley; Jesus & Mary Chain; Flesh for Lulu; March Violets; Stephen Duffy; Apartments.
Some Like It Cool....United Artists (M) MX-21 10-15 59
Some Like It Cool....United Artists (S) SX-71 15-20 59
Johnny Mandel; Art Farmer Quintet; Diahann Carol; Andre Previn Trio; Herb Pomeroy; Irene Kral; Jazz Combo from *I Want to Live*; Randy Weston Sextet; Big Miller; Bob Brookmeyer's K.C. Seven; Hal Schaefer; Morgana King; Benny Carter; Cecil Taylor Quintet.
Some of the Best of Vocal Group Harmony .... No Label Used (S) No Number Used 8-12 80s
Keynotes; Deltas; Whirlwinds; Rambles; Personalities; Mighty Jupiters; Incredible Upsetters; Swinging Hearts; 5 Playboys; Frankie Greer Quartet; Miriam Grate & Dovers; Metronomes; Ballads; Vala Quons; Sonnets.
Some People Who Play Guitar Like a Lot of Others Who Don't ....Kicking Mule (S) KM-104 5-10 74
Stephan Grossman; Woody Mann; Roy Bookbinder; Larry Sandberg; Rev. Gary Davis.
Someday at Christmas ....Tamla (S) 281 15-25 67
Somethin' Else Again (26 Heavy Sounds) (2 LP)....Columbia Musical Treasury (S) P2S 5386 10-20 70s
Somethin' Else Again (26 Heavy Sounds) (2 LP).... Columbia Musical Treasury (S) DS 569 10-20 70s
(Mail order offer.) Santana; Big Brother & Holding Company; Laura Nyro; Chicago; Spiral Staircase; Pacific Gas & Electric; Sly & Family Stone; Al Kooper; Mike Bloomfield; NRBQ; Aretha Franklin; Gary Puckett & Union Gap; Arbors; Paul Revere & Raiders; Byrds; Taj Mahal; Tim Rose; Chambers Brothers; Linda Divine; Electric; Flag; Jeff Beck; Blood, Sweat & Tears; Kaleidoscope; Johnny Winters; Zombies; Raven; Moby Grape.
Something Festive: see B.F. Goodrich - Something Festive
Something Sentimental: see FISHER, Eddie / Vic Damone / Dick Haymes
Something Special ....Capitol Creative Products (S) SL 6655 5-10 60s
Bobbie Gentry; Lettermen; Nancy Wilson; Al Martino; Al DeLory. (Made for Shurfine.)
Something to Sing About.... Milton Okun (M) MOS-1 8-12
Something Wild .... MCA (S) 6194 8-10 86
(Soundtrack.) Oingo Boingo; UB40; Fine Young Cannibals; Sonny Okkossun; Celia Cruz; Jerry Harrison; New Order; Sister Carol; Steve Jones; Jimmy Cliff.
Son of KRLA, 21 Solid Rocks, Vol. 2 .... Take 6 (S) 2005-LA 8-12 67
Sopwith Camel; Neil Diamond; B.J. Thomas; Leaves; Lovin' Spoonful; Sunrays; Music Machine; Olympics; Royal Guardsmen; Yellow Balloon; Tradewinds; Them; Ian Whitcomb; Association; Tommy James & Shondells; Sunray; Shangri-Las; Music Machine; Davie Allan; Love; Rainy Daze; Olympics; Seeds; Five Americans. (Vol. 1 is titled *KRLA Solid Rocks.*)
Songbird ....K-Tel (S) NU-9730 5-10 81
(Mail order offer.) Air Supply; Champaign; Poco; Phoebe Snow; Tierra; Ambrosia; Don McLean; Leo Sayer; Johnny Lee; Abba; Jim Photoglo; Susan Anton; Fred Knoblock; James Taylor; J.D. Souther; Terri Gibbs.
Songs by Stephen Foster....Nonesuch (S) 71268 5-10 72
Songs for a Summer Night (2 LP) ....Columbia (M) PM-2 10-20 63
Songs for a Summer Night (2 LP) ....Columbia (S) PMS-2 15-20 63
Marty Robbins; Julie Andrews; Doris Day; Robert Goulet; New Christy Minstrels; Clancy Brothers & Tommy Makem; Eydie Gorme; Patti Page; Oscar Brown Jr.; Mahalia Jackson; Barbra Streisand; Leslie Uggams; Jerry Vale; Andy Williams; Earl Wrightson; Mitch Miller; Steve Lawrence; Frankie Laine; Aretha Franklin; Anita Bryant; Brothers Four; Dion; Jimmy Dean.

Songs for Christmas Time .... Golden Tone (M) C 4047 5-10
Martha Tilton; Norma Zimmer; Bill Reeve; Pied Pipers; Marni Nixon; Thurl Ravenscroft; John Gabriel.
Songs for the Christmas Season .... Capitol (S) SL-6541 5-10
Nat King Cole; Fred Waring; Al Martino; Guy Lombardo; Tennessee Ernie Ford; Nancy Wilson; Lettermen; Roger Wagner Chorale.
Songs for the Seventies (2 LP) .... SSS (S) 1 300-400 69
(Promotional issue only.) Elvis Presley; Eddy Arnold; Connie Francis; Johnny Adams; Michael Henry Martin; LaVern Baker; Margaret Whiting; Cookie & Cupcakes; Al Martino; Ella Washington; David Clayton Thomas; Brook Benton; Peggy Scott & Jo Jo Benson; Sylvie Vartan; O.C. Smith; B.J. Thomas; Jesse Pearson; Johnny Mathis; Duane Dee; Stu Phillips; Roy Drusky; Lucille Starr; Ray Pillow; Ben Peters; Jeannie C. Riley; Dave Dudley; George Morgan; Lynn Anderson; Bobby Lewis; Mike Douglas; Connie Smith; Red Sovine; Waylon Jennings; Dee Mullins.
Songs from the Smokey Valley .... Living Room (S) LRR 373 5-10 87
Ramblers; New Villagers; Maria & Delreys; Taco Pronto; Noisy Neighbors; Trade Brothers; Rock & Roll Suicide Band.
Songs of Christmas .... Zip (S) 998 5-10 77
(Special products. Made for Singcord.)
Songs of Faith .... Audio Lab (M) AL-1504 20-30 58
Blue Valley Boys; others.
Songs of Faith, Vol. 2 .... Audio Lab (M) AL-1523 15-25 59
Songs of Faith and Inspiration (3 LP) .... Time-Life (S) STL-127 20-25 89
(Boxed set. Mail order offer.) Elvis Presley; Buck Owens; Don Gibson; George Jones; Johnny Cash; Bill Monroe; Red Foley; Jim Reeves; Webb Pierce; Rex Allen; Ferlin Husky; Hank Williams; Patsy Cline; Roy Acuff; Kitty Wells; Eddy Arnold; Grandpa Jones; Merle Haggard; Porter Wagoner; Tammy Wynette; Stanley Brothers; Dolly Parton; Ray Price; Ricky Skaggs; Tony Rice; Louvin Brothers; Oak Ridge Boys; Loretta Lynn; Wilburn Brothers; Claude Gray; Ernest Tubb; Nitty Gritty Dirt Band.
Songs of Family Faith, Vol. 2 .... Word/Tee Vee WTV-506 5-10 78
Carol Lawrence; Roy Clark; Wanda Jackson; George Beverly Shea; Anita Bryant; Ray Price; Anita Kerr Singers; Danny Thomas; B.J. Thomas; Roy Rogers & Dale Evans.
Songs of Love .... Capitol (S) SL 6941 8-12
Dean Martin; others.
Song of New England .... Columbia (M) XTV 86361/86362 8-12
Hi-Lo's; Norman Petty Trio; Les Elgart; Norman Luboff Choir; Buffalo Bills; Modernaires; Jerri Adams; Percy Faith; Tony Bennett; Kirby Stone Four.
Songs of North America .... RCA (M) PRM 259 8-12 67
Arthur Fiedler & Boston Pops; Robert Shaw Chorale; Al Jolson; Enrico Caruso; Paul Whiteman; George Gershwin; Lena Horne; Tommy Dorsey; Frank Sinatra; Marty Gold.
Songs of Paul Simon – Collection of Hits .... DMG (S) 1 15-20 75
(Promotional issue only.) Paul Simon; Simon & Garfunkel; Aretha Franklin; Yes; Crykle; Booker T. & MGs.
Songs of Paul Simon – Easy Listening Collection .... DMG (S) 2 10-15 75
(Promotional issue only.)
Songs of Randy Newman .... Interworld Music Group (S) IMG-1000 15-20
(Promotional only issue.) Ringo Starr; others.
Songs of the Civil War (3 LP) .... Folkways (M) FH 5717 20-30 60
Pete Seeger; E. Knight; E. Rain; J. Gluck; Jerry Silverman; Hermes Nye; New Lost City Ramblers; Ellen Stekert; Sandy Ives; Cisco Houston; others.
Songs of the Cowboy .... Design/Pickwick (SE) SDLP 189 8-12 62
Gene Autry; Foy Willing; Smiley Burnette; Eddie Dean; Bradley Kincaid.
Songs of the Fabulous Century (Kapp Sampler) .... Kapp (M) KDJS-1 10-20 50s
Roger Williams; Jane Morgan; Troubadors; Vic Shoen; David Rose; Marty Gold; Frank Hunter.
Songs of the Golden West .... Grand Award (M) GA-33-330 10-20
Songs of the Hills .... Audio Lab (M) AL 1515 10-20
Jimmie Osborne; Shorty Long; Clyde Moody; Jack Cardwell; Redd Stewart; Luke McDaniel; Charlie Gore; Ann Jones; Jimmy Martin; Bob Osborne; Pop Eckler; Red Perkins; Harvie June Van.
Songs of the Great Hank Williams .... Alshire (S) 5136 8-10 69
Songs of the Rivers (The Oceans & Seas) .... King (M) 871 15-25 63
Moon Mullican; Cowboy Copas; Delmore Brothers; others.
Songs of the Season, Summertime .... Columbia Special Products (M) XTV 82031 8-12 60s
Songs of the Season, Summertime .... Columbia Special Products (S) XTV 82031 8-12 60s
Polly Bergen; Andy Williams; Percy Faith; Ray Conniff; Dinah Shore; Kirby Stone Four; Dimitri Tiomkin Chorus; Tony Bennett; Banjo Barons; Merrill Staton Choir.
Songs of the Singing Cowboys .... Bruno-Dean Ent. (S) RBS-119 5-10 80
(Mail order offer. Some songs are rerecordings by original artists.) Gene Autry; Foy Willing; Ray Whitley; Bill Boyd's Cowboy Ramblers; Sons of the Pioneers; Walter Brennan; Tex Ritter; Eddie Dean; Roy Rogers & Dale Evans; Jimmy Wakely; Margaret Whiting; Rex Allen; Tex Williams; Johnny Bond.
Sonic Bullets .... Columbia Special Prodcuts (S) P-15850 5-10 81
Santana; Pat Benatar; Journey; Earth, Wind & Fire; Boston; Elvin Bishop; Toto; Cheap Trick; Eddie Money; Dave Mason. (Half-speed mastered sampler made for Radio Shack stores.)
Sonics Boom: see SONICS / Wailers / Galaxies
Sonny and Cher and Friends: see SONNY and CHER / Righteous Brothers / Lettermen
Soul Blues: see CHARLES, Ray / Little Richard / Sam Cooke
Soul .... Original Sound (S) OSR 201 5-10
Marvin Gaye; New Birth; Donnie Elbert; Aretha Franklin; Bill Withers; Frederick; Freda Payne; Jean Knight; Chee-Chee & Peppy; Tyrone Davis; B.B. King; Martha Reeves & Vandellas; Intruders; Delfonics.
Soul Christmas .... Atco (S) SD-33-269 15-25 68
Clarence Carter; King Curtis; Otis Redding; Joe Tex; Booker T. & MGs; Carla Thomas; Solomon Burke; William Bell; King Curtis. Soul Christmas (Promotional, in-store sampler): see Booker T. & MGs.
Soul Clan .... Atco (S) SD-33-281 15-20 69
Joe Tex; Arthur Conley; Solomon Burke; Ben E. King; others.
Soul Explosion .... Musico (S) MDS-1039 10-15 70s
Little Anthony & Imperials; Sam Cooke; Inez Foxx; Joee Tex; Ray Charles; Lou Rawls; Brook Benton; Toys; Jerry Butler; Dinah Washington; Frankie Lymon; Jimmy Soul; Maxine Brown; Tommy Edwards.

Soul Explosion....Stax (S) 2-2007 10-15 69
Johnnie Taylor; Booker T. & MG's; Eddie Floyd; Jimmy Hughes; Carla Thomas; Southwest F.O.B.; Mad Lads; William Bell; Judy Clay; Staple Singers; Ollie & Nightingales; Albert King.

Soul Feelin'....Capitol Special Markets (S) SL 6940 5-10 75
Lloyd Price; Isley Brothers; Cannonball Adderley; Jerry Butler; Shirelles; Lou Rawls; Nancy Wilson; King Curtis; Wilson Pickett; Little Richard.

Soul Gold, Vol. 1 .... SSS Int'l (S) 3 8-12 69
Johnny Adams; Mickey Murray; Peggy Scott & Jo Jo Benson; others.

Soul Groove ....Capitol Special Markets (S) SL-6678 8-12 60s
Nancy Wilson; Cannonball Adderley; Lou Rawls; King Curtis; Bettye Swan.

Soul Man .... A&M (S) SP-3903 8-10 86
(Soundtrack.) Sam Moore; Lou Reed; Models; Nu Shooz; Martha Davis; Sly Stone; Ricky; Brenda Russell; Vesta Williams; Rae Dawn Chong; Tom Scott.

Soul Meeting Saturday Night (Hootenanny Style) ....Vee Jay (M) VJLP-1074 10-20 63
Soul Meeting Saturday Night (Hootenanny Style) ....Vee Jay (S) SR-1074 10-20 63
Soul Meeting Saturday Night (Hootenanny Style) .... Vee Jay (S) VJS-1074 8-12 80s
Jimmy Reed; John Lee Hooker; Bird Legs & Pauline; Roscoe Gordon; Priscilla Bowman; Gene Allison; Memphis Slim.

Soul Monster - Original Rhythm and Blues Hits, Vol. 1 .... Original Oldies (M) LP-007 15-20
Sunny & Sunglows; Barbara Lynn; Bobby Hebb; Chantels; Leon Peels; M&M & Peanuts; Sonny Knight; Incredibles; Billy Abbott; Joe Hinton; Five Du-tones; Thee Midniters; Lonnie Russ; Vibrations; Betty Everett; Wilson Pickett; Fiestas; McKinley Mitchell; Fats Domino.

Soul of Detroit.... Relic (M) 8009 5-10 87
Charles Amos; Conquerors; Eddie Floyd; Betty Lavette; Benny McCain; Don Revel; Gene Martin; Primettes; Mack Rice; Joe Stubbs; Al Garner; Majestics; Minor Chords; Rivals.

Soul of Jazz....World Wide (M) MG-20002 10-20
Soul of Jazz - Riverside.... Riverside (S) S-5 15-25 61
Thelonius Monk; Wes Montgomery; Johnny Griffin; Nat Adderley; Bobby Timmons; Cannonball Adderley Quintet; Bill Evans; Blue Mitchell; Jimmy Heath; Jazz Brother (Mangione Brothers.)

Soul of Minit Records '66-69, Struttin' and Flirtin'....EMI (S) 17262 8-12 80s
Soul Oldies, Vol. 1.... Unart (M) M-20022 10-15 67
Soul Oldies, Vol. 1....Unart (S) S-21022 10-15 67
Marv Johnson; Lee Andrews; Tune Rockers; Garnett Mimms; Ray Baretto; Anthony & Imperials; Exciters; Busters.

Soul Oldies, Vol. 2.... Unart (M) M-20023 10-15 68
Soul Oldies, Vol. 2....Unart (S) S-21023 10-15 68
Clovers; Jimmy Forrest; King Pleasure; Jive Five; Garnett Mimms; Phil Upchurch; Georgie Auld; Little Anthony & Imperials.

Soul Sessions, Vol. 6 ....Cobblestone (S) 9028 8-12 72
Roberta Flack; B.B. King; Curtis Mayfield; Billy Eckstine; others.

Soul Sixties....Warner/JCI (S) 3105 5-10 85
Sam & Dave; J.J. Jackson; Otis Redding; Brenton Wood; James & Bobby Purify; Carla Thomas; Aretha Franklin; Wilson Pickett; Doris Troy; Watts 103rd Street Rhythm Band; Johnnie Taylor; Bar-Kays.

Soul Supreme, Vol. 1 .... Longines/Motown (S) SQ-93752 5-10
Martha & Vandellas; David Ruffin; Temptations; Diana Ross & Supremes;Edwin Starr; Gladys Knight & Pips; Jimmy Ruffin; Shorty Long; Billy Eckstine.

Soul Supreme, Vol. 1 ....Longines Symphonette (S) SYS-5269 5-10
Diana Ross & Supremes; Stevie Wonder; Brenda Holloway; Marvin Gaye & Tammi Terrell; Smokey Robinson & Miracles; Mary Wells; Four Tops; Marvelettes; Contours; Barbara McNair.

Soul Supreme, Vol. 2 .... Longines/Motown (S) SQ-93752 5-10
Soul Supreme, Vol. 2 ....Longines Symphonette (S) SYS-5270 5-10
Martha & Vandellas; David Ruffin; Temptations; Diana Ross & Supremes; Edwin Starr; Gladys Knight & Pips; Junior Walker & All Stars; Jimmy Ruffin; Shorty Long; Billy Eckstine.

Soul to Soul....Atlantic (S) 7207 10-12 71
Soul to Soul.... Atlantic (S) 81674-1 10-12 Re
(Soundtrack.) Wilson Pickett; Ike & Tina Turner; Staple Singers; Eddie Harris; Les McCann; Amoa; Roberta Flack; Voices of East Harlem.

Soul Train.... Avco Embassy (S) 11007 8-12 72
Stylistics; Donnie Elbert; Three Degrees; Continental Four; others.

Soul Train, Hall of Fame....Adam VIII Ltd. (S) AVIII 8004 8-12 73
Mickey & Sylvia; Moments; Frieda Payne; Chairmen of the Board; Honey Cone; Ike & Tina Turner; Isley Brothers; 5 Stairsteps; Betty Wright; Otis Redding; Sam & Dave; Archie Bell & Drells; Shep & Limelites; Frankie Lymon & Teenagers; Edwin Hawkins Singers; Sly & Family Stone; Barbara Lewis; James Brown; Joe Simon; Delphonics; Gladys Knight & Pips; Clarence Carter.

Soul Train Hits That Made It Happen ....Adam VIII Ltd. (S) AVIII 8005 8-12 73
Cornelius Brothers & Sister Rose; Curtis Mayfield; Barbara Mason; Al Green; Timmy Thomas; Cymande; Joe Simon; James Brown; Joe Tex; Independents; Archie Bell & Drells; Four Tops; Candi Staton; Dennis Coffey; Brighter Side of Darkness; Dells; O'Jays; Billy Paul; Main Ingredient.

Soul Train Super Tracks....Adam VII (S) A8R-8012 5-10 74
(Mail order offer.) George McCrae; Four Tops; Isaac Hayes; Curtis Mayfield; Dells; Spinners; B.B. King; Staple Singers; Soul Children; Ecstacy, Passion & Pain; Kool & Gang; Gladys Knight & Pips; Moments; Impressions; Whispers; Natural Four; Bobby Blue Bland; Johnnie Taylor; Sylvia; Honeycone.

Soul Years 1948-1973 (2 LP) ....Atlantic (S) SD2-504 25-35 73
LaVern Baker; Bobbettes; Brook Benton; Booker T. & MGs; Ruth Brown; Ray Charles; Solomon Burke; Clarence Carter; Chords; Clovers; Coasters; Drifters; King Floyd; Arethaa Franklin; Ivory Joe Hunter; Stick McGhee & His Buddies; Wilson Pickett; Otis Redding; Sam & Dave; Percy Sledge; Spinners; Joe Tex; Joe Turner; Chuck Willis; Betty Wright.

Soul's Greatest Hits, Kings & Queens of Soul (2 LP) ....Columbia (S) P2S 5378 10-20
Johnnie Taylor; Booker T. & MGs; Shirley Ellis; Bill Doggett; Albert King; Peggy Scott & Jo Jo Benson; Otis Redding; Fantastic Johnny C.; Sly & Family Stone; Screamin' Jay Hawkins; James Brown; Chamber Brothers; Judy Clay & William Bell; Cliff Nobles; Eddie Floyd; Platters; Maxine Brown; O.C. Smith; Tymes; Major Lance; Peaches & Herb; Mongo Santamaria; Taj Mahal; Staple Singers; Walter Jackson.

Souled Out .... Chess (M) 1546 10-15 69
Tony Clarke; Jackie Ross; Knight Brothers; Mitty Collier; Little Miss Cornshucks; Little Milton; Radiants; Moonglows; Tommy Tucker; Students; Bobby Moore; Ty Hunter; Jan Bradley; Vontastics.

Souled Out Country....Triune (S) 0001 5-10 73
Linda K. Lance; Nashville Brass; Jordanaires; others.

Souled Out Country .... Triune (S) 0004 5-10 74
Lynda K. Lance; Dee Mullins; Bob Langston; Jimmy Dallas; others.
Soulful Christmas .... Mistletoe (M) 1213 8-10 74
Jerry Butler; Brook Benton; Sonny Til & Orioles; Patti LaBelle; Charles Brown.
Soulful Oldies .... Oldies 33 (M) 8005 15-20 64
Jerry Butler; Dee Clark; Dee Clark; Jimmy Reed; Birdlegs & Pauline; Roscoe Gordon; Memphis Slim; Gene Allison; John Lee Hooker.
Sound Effects, Vol. 1 .... Audio Fidelity (M) DFM 3006 8-12
Sound Effects, Vol. 1 .... Audio Fidelity (S) DFS 7006 8-12
(Sound effects. No Music.)
Sound Effects, Vol. 2 .... Audio Fidelity (M) DFM 3010 8-12
Sound Effects, Vol. 2 .... Audio Fidelity (S) DFS 7010 8-12
(Sound effects. No Music.)
Sound Effects, Vol. 3 .... Audio Fidelity (M) DFM 3011 8-12
Sound Effects, Vol. 3 .... Audio Fidelity (S) DFS 7011 8-12
(Sound effects. No Music.)
Sound Effects, Vol. 4 .... Audio Fidelity (M) DFM 3015 8-12
Sound Effects, Vol. 4 .... Audio Fidelity (S) DFS 7015 8-12
(Sound effects. No Music.)
Sound Effects Nuclear Powered Aircraft Carrier .... Audio Fidelity (M) DFM 3014 8-12
Sound Effects Nuclear Powered Aircraft Carrier .... Audio Fidelity (S) DFS 7014 8-12
(Sound effects. No Music.)
Sound Effects U.S. Air Force Firepower .... Audio Fidelity (M) DFM 3012 8-12
Sound Effects U.S. Air Force Firepower .... Audio Fidelity (S) DFS 7012 8-12
(Sound effects. No Music.)
Sound Experience .... Magnavox (S) QL-6953 5-10
Raspberries; Pat Williams; Southland Stingers; Anne Murray; Glen Campbell; Fox Capitol Theater Wurlitzer Pipe Organ; Peggy Lee; John Morell Band; Lettermen; Sounds of the Seventies Orchestra.
Sound Explosion .... Ronco (S) R-1976 5-10 76
Silver Convention; Hot Chocolate; Abba; Michael Murphey; Faith, Hope & Charity; David Geddes; Outlaws; Austin Roberts; Frankie Valli; Melissa Manchester; Barry Manilow; Jig Saw; KC & Sunshine Band; Qwen McCrae; Katfish; Ambrosia; Ray Berruto; Phoebe Snow; Pure Prairie League; Neil Sedaka.
Sound Express .... Ronco (S) P 15447 5-10 80
Rupert Holmes; Toto; Cliff Richard; Chris Thompson; Tom Johnson; Gene Chandler; Robert Palmer; Hall & Oates; Dionne Warwick; Steve Forbert; Cheap Trick; Alan Parsons Project; Santana; Eric Carmen; Kinks; Kool & Gang; Eddie Rabbitt; Nicolette Larson.
Sound Ideas (6 LP) .... Welk Music (S) 5007 50-75 86
(Promotional issue only. All songs are edited versions.) Elvis Presley; Mario Lanza Paul Robeson; Helen Morgan; Frank Parker; Billie Holiday; Fred Astaire; Glenn Miller; Frank Sinatra; Perry Como; T. Texas Tyler; Patti Page; Diamonds; Platters; Brook Benton; Bobby Rydell; Linda Scott; Bobby Vinton; Ventures; Nancy Wilson; Jimmie Rodgers; R.B. Greaves; Johnny Mathis; Gladys Knight & Pips; Waylon Jennings & Willie Nelson; Kenny Rogers; Eric Clapton; Carpenters; Air Supply; Rick Springfield; Diana Ross; Animotion; others.
Sound of Bluegrass .... Camden/Pickwick (S) ACLI-0535 5-10 74
Wade Ray; Bluegrass Banjo Pickers; Country Fiddlers; Living Guitars; Country Pardners & Bill Price; Morris Brothers; Monroe Brothers; Blue Sky Boys; Lonesome Pine Fiddlers; Charlie Monroe.
Sound of Broadway .... RCA (M) PRM-162 15-20 64
(Soundtrack.) Ann-Margret; Pete King Chorale; John Gary; Ed Ames; Alfred Drake; Jane Pickens; Richard Kiley; Florence Henderson; Sergio Franchi; Dick Schory; Cascading Voices of the Hugo & Luigi Chorus.
Sound of Christmas .... Capitol Custom (S) CSD-1001 8-12
Bing Crosby; Carmen Dragon; Hollyridge Strings; Kingston Trio; Al Martino; Alfred Newman; Voices of Walter Schumann; Roger Wagner Chorale; Fred Waring; Nancy Wilson; Hollywood Pops Orchestra.
Sound of Christmas .... Capitol Creative Products (S) SL-6515 5-10
Nat King Cole; Korean Orphan Choir; Tennessee Ernie Ford; Fred Waring; Al Martino; Hollywood Bowl Symphony Orchestra; Dinah Shore; Hollyridge Strings; Bing Crosby; Jo Stafford; Al Newman; Carmen Dragon.
Sound of Deep Ellum .... Island (S) 7-90637-1 8-12
Three on a Hill; Decadent Dub Team; Buck Pets; Shallow Reign; Reverend Horton Heat; New Bohemians; Trees; End Over End; Daylights; Legendary Revelations.
Sound of Folk Music .... Vanguard (M) SRV-125 15-20 61
Joan Baez; Odetta; Weavers; Leon Bibb; Erik Darling; Martha Schlamme; Erich Kunz; Paul Robeson; Nethania Davrath; Shoshana Damari; Ronnie Gilbert; Karmon Israeli Dancers & Singers; Cisco Houston; Germaine Montero; Babysitters; Alfred Deller.
Sound of Jazz .... Columbia (M) CL-1098 25-30 58
Henry "Red" Allen All-Stars; Billie Holiday; Mal Waldron; Count Basie All-Stars; Jimmy Giuffre Trio; Jimmy Rushing.
Sound of Jazz .... Columbia (S) CS-8040 25-35 58
Henry "Red" Allen All Stars; Billie Holiday; Mal Waldron; Count Basie All Stars; Jimmy Giuffre Trio; Jimmy Rushing.
Sound of Leadership (Souvenir of the Miami Meeting, June 1956) (8 EP) .... RCA (EP) 1800-2200 56
(Boxed set. Includes insert/separator sheets. Promotional issue only.) Elvis Presley; Enrico Caruso; Tommy Dorsey; Boston Pops; Glenn Miller; Artie Shaw; Freddy Martin; Perry Como; Vaughn Monroe; Mario Lanza; Eddie Fisher; Ames Brothers; Kay Starr; Gene Austin; Will Glahe; Leopold Stokowski; Robert Merrill; Eddy Arnold; Pee Wee King; Perez Prado.
Sound of Philadelphia (2 LP) .... Columbia/Brookville (S) P2-13924 8-12 77
(Mail order offer.) O'Jays; Harold Melvin & Blue Notes; Lou Rawls; Intruders; MFSB; People's Choice; Johnny Williams; Billy Paul; Three Degrees.
Sound of Philadelphia '73 .... Philadelphia Int'l (S) Z-32713 8-12 73
O'Jays; Ebonys; Johnny Williams; Billy Paul; Bunny Sigler; others.
Sound of Reprise/Sound of Atlantic .... Atlantic/Reprise (45) ???? 10-20
(7-inch promotional only flexi-disc.) Dean Martin; others.
Sound of Richard Rodgers' Music .... RCA (M) PRM 201 5-10 66
Sound of Richard Rodgers' Music .... RCA (S) PRS 201 8-12 66
(Soundtrack.) Richard Kiley; Florence Henderson; John Raitt; Peter Nero; Mary Martin; Norman Luboff Choir; Andre Previn; Sergio Franchi; Lena Horne; Alfred Drake; Arthur Fiedler & Boston Pops; John Gary. (Made for B.F. Goodrich.)
Sound of Tomorrow .... RCA (M) SP 33-204 5-10 70s

Sound of Tomorrow .... RCA (S) SPS 33-204 5-10 70s
Peter Nero; Marty Gold; Hugo & Luigi; Dick Schory; Sid Ramin; Erich Leinsdorf & Boston Symphony Orchestra; Arthur Fiedler & Boston Pops; Robert Shaw Chorale with RCA Victor Symphony Orchestra; Charles Munich with Boston Symphony Orchestra; Leontyne Price. (Made for Buick.)

Sound Off...Softly .... Columbia Special Products (M) CSP 244 8-12
(Promotional issue only.) Saul Goodman; Les & Larry Elgart; Count Basie; Duke Ellington; Les Brown; Percy Faith; Andre Kostelanetz; Tony Bennett; Gordon Jenkins; Ray Conniff; Bobby Hackett; Patti Page. (Made for Gold Bond Ceiling Tile.)

Sound That Takes You There .... Columbia (S) ST-163 10-15 60s
Paul Weston; Vic Damone; Andre Kostelanetz; Norman Luboff Choir; Polly Bergen; Sammy Kaye. (Special products. Made for Columbia Phonographs.)

Sound Waves .... K-Tel (S) TU 2690 5-10 80
Diana Ross; Lipps, Inc.; Spinners; Jermaine Jackson; Prince; Meco; Kiss; Pat Benatar; Robbie Dupree; Rocky Burnette; Pure Prairie League; Captain & Tennille; Air Supply; Ali Thompson; Benny Mardones.

Sounds Fantastic! .... RCA (S) PRS-210 5-10 66
Sid Ramin; Si Zentner; Marty Gold; Claus Ogerman; Chet Atkins; Dick Shory & His Percussion Pops Orchestra; Living Strings; Al Hirt; Frankie Randall; Living Guitars; Three Suns; Esquivel. (Made for RCA Portable Swinging Line Stereo.)

Sounds from True Stories .... Sire (S) 1-25515 8-10 86
(Soundtrack.) David Byrne; Carl Finch; Panhandle Mystery Band; Kronos Quartet; Banda Eclipse; Steve Jordan.

Sounds in Space (Stereophonic Sound Demonstration Record) .... RCA (S) SP-33-13 15-20 58
Ken Nordine (narrator); Pierre Monteaux & Paris Conservatoire Orchestra; Skitch Henderson; Fritz Henderson; Fritz Reiner & Chicago Symphony Orchestra; Ralph Flanagan; Melachrino Orchestra; Lena Horne & Nat Brandwynne's; New Glenn Miller Orchestra; Julie Andrews; Jerome Hines; Paul Mickelson Concert Orchestra; Band of the Coldstream Guards; Charles Munch & Boston Symphony Orchestra; Arthur Fiedler & Boston Pops.

Sounds of 1959 .... MGM (M) 5 25-35 59
(Promotional issue only.)

Sounds of '73 .... Unicom (S) UEC-1000 8-12 73
Pointer Sisters; Stories; Deodato; Dr. John; Sylvia; Aretha Franklin; Spinners; Donna Fargo; Maureen McGovern; Eric Weisberg; Steve Mandell. (Special products. Made for Dr. Pepper.)

Sounds of Asbury Park .... Visa (S) 7014 10-15 80
Lord Gunner Group; Sonny Kenn & Friends; Ken Viola & Friends; Paul Whistler; Kog Nito & Geeks; Lisa Lowell.

Sounds of Christmas (2 LP) .... Capitol STBB (S) 93245 8-12
Bing Crosby; Peggy Lee; Sandler & Young; Jackie Gleason; Lou Rawls; Hollyridge Strings; Nat King Cole; Wayne Newton; Lettermen; Jo Stafford; Nancy Wilson; Dean Martin; Hollywood Pops Orchestra; Al Martino; Ella Fitzgerald; David Rose; Tennessee Ernie Ford; Fred Waring; Eddie Dunstedter; Glen Campbell.

Sounds of Christmas .... MCA Special Markets (S) DL 734735 5-10 70s
(Mail order offer.) Pete Fountain; Mel Torme; Ames Brothers; Kitty Wells; Louis Armstrong; Jack Jones; Columbus Boys Choir; Lawrence Welk; Salt Lake City Tabernacle Choir; Brenda Lee; Weavers; Roger Williams; Bing Crosby; Guy Lombardo.

Sound of Genius, Vol. 2 .... Columbia (M) GB-8 8-12
New York Philharmonic; Alexander Brailowsky; Ivan Davis London Symphony Orchestra; Philippe Entremont; Philadelphia Orchestra; Sviatoslav Richter; Eastman Wind Ensemble.

Sounds of Love .... Columbia Special Products (S) CSS-1511 5-10 70s
John Davidson; Robert Goulet; Aretha Franklin; Peter Nero; Charlie Byrds; Percy Faith; Ray Conniff; Andre Kostelanetz; Caravelli & His Magnificent Strings; Frank DeVol. (Made for 1847 Rogers Brothers Silverware.)

Sounds of San Francisco .... KGO Radio 81 (S) No Number Used 10-20 60s
(Promotional only issue, not banded.) Percy Faith; Johnny Mathis; Ferrante & Teicher; Rosemary Clooney; Les Baxter; Tony Bennett; Don Costa; Vic Damone; Mitch Miller; Doris Day; Al Caiola; Nat King Cole.

Sounds of Success .... Jamie (M) JLP 70-3017 30-45 61
Duane Eddy; Savannah Churchill; Donnie Owens; Jacky Noguez; Inspirations; Geoff Gilmore & Sheiks; Blackwells; Heartbeats; Jordan Brothers; Sharps; Neil Sedaka; Mitchell Torok; Jesse Belvin; Ray Sharpe.

Sound of the City, Acappella .... Times Square (M) 201 10-15
Vitones; Tommy & Tears; Tear Stains; Knick Knoks; Revlons; Memories; El Sierros; Monteys; Nutmegs.

Sounds of the Big Bands .... Columbia Special Products (SE) CSS 322 5-10 60s
Woody Herman; Glenn Miller; Les & Larry Elgart; Les Brown; Ernie Heckscher.

Sounds of the Hit Groups .... United Artists (M) UAL-3322 15-20 64
Sounds of the Hit Groups .... United Artists (S) UAS-6322 20-25 64
Exciters; Isley Brothers; Angels; Highwaymen; Jay & Americans; Garnett Mimms & Enchanters; others.

Sounds of the Now Generation .... Word (S) 8413 5-10 68
Sounds of the Sixties .... United Artists (M) MX-60 15-20 60
Sounds of the Sixties .... United Artists (S) SX-60 20-25 60
Clovers; Marv Johnson; Burl Ives; DeJohnson Sisters; Alexander & Margie King; Ruth Clay; Don Costa; Manny Albam; Diahann Carroll; Andre Previn; Dave Lambert; Stan Rubin; Axidental Angelo; Barbara Russell.

Sounds of the South .... Atlantic (M) 1346 20-25 61
Sounds of the South .... Atlantic (SE) SD-1346 20-25 61
Neil Morris; Lonnie Young; Estil C. Ball; Vera Hall; Mountain Ramblers; Bob Carpenter; Rev. W.A. Donaldson; Viola James & Congregation; Alabama Sacred Harp Singers; Fred McDowell; Sid Hemphill; John Davis; Ed Lewis.

Sounds Spectacular .... K-Tel (S) TU 2400 5-10 75
Gloria Gaynor; Edgar Winter Group; Ohio Players; BTO; Golden Earring; Redbone; Polly Brown; Fanny Rubettes; B.T. Express; Frankie Valli; Shirley & Co.; Disco Tex; Billy Preston; Atlanta Rhythm Section; Charlie Daniels; New Birth; William DeVaughn; Main Ingredient; B.W. Stevenson.

Sounds Terrific .... RCA (S) PRS 268 10-15 68
Al Hirt; Peter Nero; Ray Ellis; Chet Atkins; Frankie Carle; Neal Hefti; Claus Ogerman; Marty Gold; Lana Cantrell; Duke Ellington.

Sounds That Swing .... Columbia Special Products (S) CSP-206 10-20 60s
J.J. Johnson; Andre Kostelanetz; Village Stompers; Glenn Miller; Bobby Hackett; Andre Previn; Percy Faith; Dave Brubeck; Art Van Damme; Neil Wolfe; Duke Ellington. (Made for Philco.)

Soundsville .... Design (M) DLP-187 20-30 60s
Soundsville .... Design (S) SDLP-187 20-30 60s
Beachnuts; Hi-Lifes; Liberty Men; J. Brothers; Roughnecks; Jeannie Larimore; Hollywoods; Connie Carson.

Soup for One .... Atlantic/Mirage (S) WTG 19353 8-12 82
(Soundtrack.) Chic; Carly Simon; Teddy Pendergrass; Fonzi Thornton; Sister Sledge; Deborah Harry.

South Sea Island Magic (4 LP)....RCA Custom/Readers Digest (SE) RDA 67-A 15-20 68
(Boxed set.) Kalua Beach Boys; Douglas Gamley; Johnny Gibb; Islanders; Louis Nunley & Islanders; Robert Mandell; Rosemary Squires; Marie Tarangi Trio; Jack de Mello.

South's Greatest Hits....Capricorn (S) 0187 8-10 76
Elvin Bishop; Outlaws; Dr. John; Gregg Allman; Lynyrd Skynyrd; Charlie Daniels; Marshall Tucker; Amazing Rhythm Aces; Wet Willie; Atlanta Rhythm Section; Allman Brothers.

South's Greatest Hits, Vol. 2....Capricorn (S) CP-0209 8-10
Marshall Tucker Band; Atlanta Rhythm Section; Charlie Daniels; Outlaws; Allman Brothers Band; Elvin Bishop; Sea Level; Stillwater; Wet Willie.

Southbound....Vanguard (M) 9213 8-15 66

Southbound....Vanguard (S) 7-9213 8-15 66
Doc Watson; Merle Watson; others.

Southern Priso Blues....Tradition (M) 2066 10-20

Souvenir of Arizona....LJR-114 75-100 63
Waylon Jennings; Donnie Owens; others.

Souvenirs of Music City U.S.A....Plantation (S) PLP-506 5-10 78
Jeannie C. Riley; Charlie Rich; Jimmy C. Newman; George Jones; Hank Locklin; Leroy Van Dyke; Gordon Terry; James O'Gwynn; Rita Remmington; Roy Orbison; David Allan Coe; Willie Nelson; Carl Perkins; Johnny Cash; Ray Pillow; Rex Allen Jr.; Sleepy LaBeef; David Wilkins; Carl Belew; David Houston.

Souvenirs of Music City U.S.A., Vol. 2....Plantation (S) PLP-533 5-10 78
Johnny Cash; Jerry Lee Lewis; Charlie Rich; LeRoy Van Dyke; Jimmy C. Newman; Hank Locklin; Charlie Walker; John Wesley Ryles; Willie Nelson; Dave Dudley; Jeannie C. Riley; James O'Gwynn; Murray Kellum; Gordon Terry; Paul Martin; Rex Allen Jr.; Rufus Thibodeaux; Jimmie Davis; Rita Remington.

Spaceballs....Atlantic (S) 81770-1 10-15 87
(Soundtrack.) Van Halen; Pointer Sisters; Spinners; Ladyfire; Berlin; Kim Charles; Jeffrey Osborne.

Speaker Death! Heavy Metal Head-Bangers....CBS (S) AS 993 10-15 81
Judas Priest; Frank Marino; Blue Oyster Cult; Joe Perry Project; Ted Nugent; Journey; Ozzy Osborne; Brad Whtford; Derek St. Holmes; Loverboy.

Special Delivery: see ORBISON, Roy / Bobby Bare / Joey Powers

Spectacular....Starday (M) S-345 10-20 65

Spectacular....Starday (S) SLP-140 10-20 65

Spectacular Sampler....Coral (M) 98012 15-25
(Promotional issue only.) Steve Allen; Don Cornell; Edgar Sampson; Ray Bloch; Lynn Taylor; Alan Freed; Lawrence Welk; Johnny Desmond; Dick Jacobs; Larry Sonn; Steve Lawrence; Geroge Cates.

Speed Zone....Grudge (S) 4506-1-F9 8-10 89
(Soundtrack.) Stevie Wonder; Richie Havens; Billy Burnette; David Wheatley; Splash; Ross Vanelli; Felix Cavaliere; Charlie Karp; Omar & Howlers; Will to Power.

Spin Girl for January '58....Mercury (M) LPC-1 15-20 58
(Promotional issue only.) Richard Hayman; Elie Taube; Jan August; Pearl Bailey; David Carroll; Freddie Bell & Bell Boys; Dick Contino; Jon Thomas; Gus Bivona; Florian Zabach; Jerry Murad's Harmonicats; Sil Austin; Marion Evans; Manny Albam; Sarah Vaughan; George Siravo; Blue Stars; Billy Eckstine; Patti Page; Rolf Ericson; Julian Cannonball Adderely; Pete Rugolo; Jack & Jill.

Spirit of America....RCA (S) ANL1-1128 5-10 75
Lorne Green; Limelighters; Kate Smith; Jim Aylward; Robert Shaw Chorale; Paul Lavalle; Living Voices; Living Strings .

Spirit of Charlie Parker....World Wide (M) MG-20003 10-20

Spirit of Christmas....Capitol Creative Products (S) SL 6516 5-10
Lettermen; Hollyridge Strings; Vienna Boys Choir; Al Martino; Peggy Lee; Bing Crosby; Roger Wagner Chorale.

Spirit of Christmas....Columbia (S) C 10389 5-10
New York Philharmonic Orchestra; Mormon Tabernacle Choir; Tony Bennett; Ray Conniff; Patti Page; Johnny Mathis; Percy Faith; Robert Goulet; Mitch Miller; John Davidson; Andre Kostelanetz; Jim Nabors.

Spirit of Christmas, Vol. 2....Columbia (S) CSS-???? 5-10

Spirit of Christmas, Vol. 3....Columbia (SE) CSS-1463 5-10
Johnny Mathis; Anita Bryant; Andre Kostelanetz with Earl Wrightson; Mahalia Jackson; Percy Faith; Johnny Cash; Burl Ives; Ray Conniff; Robert Goulet; Leonard Bernstein & New York Philharmonic; Mormon Tabernacle Choir. (Made for TG & Y.)

Spirituals to Swing (John Hammond's) (2 LP)....Columbia(S) G 30776 10-20 72
Goddard Lierberson; George Benson Quartet; Marion Williams; Cafe Society Band; Joe Turner; Pete Johnson; John Handy Ensemble; Big Mama Thornton; Count Basie; Richard Boone.

Spitballs....Beserkley (S) JBZ-0058 5-10 78

Splendor of the Brass (2 LP)....Camden (S) CSX-9033 8-12 72
Al Hirt; Danny Davis & Nashville Brass; Bunny Berigan; Mel Davis; Charlie Spivak; Living Brass.

Sports Cars in Stereo (Sebring, Florida - 1958)....Riverside (S) 1101 20-30 58

Spotlight....K-Tel (S) TU 2700 5-10 79
Andy Gibb; A Taste of Honey; John Paul Young; Crystal Gayle; Player; Stephen Bishop; Hall & Oates; Alicia Bridges; Commodores; Little River Band; Bob Welch; Paul Davis; Nick Gilder; Kenny Rogers; Chris Rea; Gerry Rafferty.

Spring Band Project....Elektra (M) EKL 292 10-15

Spring Band Project....Elektra (S) EKS 7292 10-15
Uncle Willie's Brandy Sniffers; Stu Jamieson's Boys; Phil Boroff; Dry City Scatt Band; John Cohen; Penny Cohen; Bob Mamis; Mother Bay State Entertainers; Spontaneous String Band; Siegal-Grisman-Rose-Lowinger.

Spring Break....Warner Bros. (S) 1-23826 8-10 83
(Soundtrack.) Cheap Trick; Gerald McMahon; Jack Mack & Heart Attack; Dreamers; Hot Date; NRBQ; Big Spender.

Spring Is Here....Mercury (M) MG-20795 15-25 63
David Carroll; Billy Eckstine; Sarah Vaughan; Platters; Clebanoff Strings; Richard Hayman; Helen Merrill; Buddy Morrow; Eddie Heywood; Xavier Cugat; Hal Mooney; Frank D'Rone; Jan Marek & Vienna Light Orchestra.

SQ Quadraphonic: Spectacular Sound of Four Channel Stereo....Columbia CSQ 10559 10-15 70s
Santana; Barbra Streisand; Johnny Mathis; Percy Faith; Ray Conniff; Ruby Keeler; Lynn Anderson; Andy Williams; Janis Joplin; Ray Price; Dean Jones & Original Cast.

Square Dance Music....King (M) 395-562 20-30 57
Red Herron; Curly Fox; others.

Stage Door Canteen (4 LP)....Heartland Music (S) HL 1051-4 15-20 87
Frank Sinatra; Harry James; Dick Haymes; Bing Crosby; Andrew Sisters; Song Spinners; Ink Spots; Kay Kyser; Jimmy Dorsey; Julie Conway; Bob Eberle; Helen O'Connell; Horace Heidt; Larry Cotton; Donna Wood; Helen Forrest; Kitty Kallen; Russ Morgan; Frankie Carle; Marjorie Hughes; Les Brown; Doris Day; Merry Macs; Al Dexter & His Troopers; Benny Goodman; Peggy Lee; Mills Brothers; Glenn Miller; Marion Hutton; Tex Beneke & Modernaires; Sammy Kaye; Vaughn Monroe; Freddy Martin; Tommy Dorsey; Frank Sinatra; Dinah Shore; Spike Jones; Rudy Vallee; Perry Como.

Stand By Me....Atlantic (S) 81677-1 8-10 86
(Soundtrack.) Ben E. King; Buddy Holly; Shirley & Lee; Del-Vikings; Silhouettes; Chordettes; Coasters; Jerry Lee Lewis; Bobbettes.

Stand Up and Sing....United Artists (M) UAL-3331 10-20 63

Stand Up and Sing....United Artists (S) UAS-6331 15-20 63

Star Fire....Ronco (S) R-3200 5-10 80
(Mail order offer.) Michael Jackson; France Joli; Michael Johnson; Robert John; Lobo; Journey; Melissa Manchester; Robert John; Night; Isaac Hayes; Rupert Holmes; Little River Band; Nick Lowe; Crusaders; Jennifer Warnes; Alton McClain & Destiny; Peaches & Herb; Jacksons; Raydio.

Star Folk....Onacrest (S) ONA-5006 10-20 60s
Hoyt Axton; Barry McGuire; Barbara Dane; Travis Edmonson; Josh White; Travelers Three; Shenandoah Trio; Rod McKuen.

Star Lines (Artist Introductions to) Instant Hits....Capitol (EP) PRO-2510 15-25 63
(Promotional issue only.) Four Freshmen; Stan Freberg; Ray Anthony; Kay Starr; Freddy Martin; others.

Star Power....K-Tel (S) TU-2580 5-10 78
(Mail order offer.) Meco; Foreigner; Firefall; Paul Nicholas; England Dan & John Ford Coley; Bay City Rollers; Stephen Bishop; Paul Davis; Babys; Little River Band; Kiss; David Soul; Hot; Brick; Peter Brown; Sylvers; Floaters; Alan O'Day.

Star Spectacular, Vol. 1....MGM (M) PM-10 10-15 60s
Billy Walker; David Rose; Mel Torme; Andre Previn; Anita O'Day; Al Hirt; Ramblers Three; Count Basie; Ray Ellis; Debbie Reynolds; Gene Krupa; Judy Garland; Stan Getz.

Star Struck....A&M (S) SP-4938 8-10 83
(Soundtrack.) Jo Kennedy; Turnaround; Swinger; Ross O'Donovan; John O'May; Mental As Regular.

Starburst (2 LP)....Columbia Musical Treasury (SP) P2S-5414 5-10
Tony Bennett; Tammy Wynette; Blood, Sweat & Tears; Patti Page; Johnny Cash; Freddie Weller; Jim Nabors; Johnny Mathis; Marty Robbins; Aretha Franklin; Bobby Vinton; Terry Baxter; Robert Goulet; Andre Kostelanetz; Ray Price; Gary Puckett & Union Gap; Michele Lee; Peter Nero; Jerry Vale.

Starburst....K-Tel (S) TU-2650 5-10 78
Andy Gibb; Nick Gilder; Evelyn "Champagne" King; Heatwave; Robert Palmer; Bonnie Tyler; James Taylor; Samanta Sang; Sanford Townsend Band; Meat Loaf; Toby Beau; Johnny Mathis; Deniece Williams; Atlanta Rhythm Section; Peter Brown; Rick James; Stone City Band; Foxy; Eruption; Eddie Money.

Starday - Dixie Rockabillys, Vol. 1....Starday/Gusto (M) GD 5017 8-12 79
Link Davis; "Groovey" Joe Poovey; Rudy "Tutti" Grayzell; Sonny Fisher; Bill Mack; Fred Crawford; Cliff Blakely; Benny Joy.

Starday - Dixie Rockabillys, Vol. 2....Starday/Gusto (M) GD 5031 8-12 79
Link Davis; Bill Mack; Sonny Fisher; Bob Doss; "Groovy" Joe Poovey; Thumper Jones; Rudy "Tutt" Grayzell; Cliff Blakely; Benny Joy.

Stardust (2 LP)....Arista (S) AL-5000 10-12 75
(Soundtrack.) Neil Sedaka; Maxine Brown; Bobby Vee; Zombies; Bobby Darin; Billy J. Kramer & Dakotas; Crystals; Beach Boys; Drifters; Chiffons; Little Eva; Fortunes; Carole King; Gerry & Pacemakers; Jan & Dean; Cat Stevens; Barbara Lewis; Shirelles; Box Tops; Mamas & Papas; Lovin' Spoonful; Monkees; Animals; Hollies; Bee Gees; Righteous Brothers; Barry McGuire; Jefferson Airplane; Aretha Franklin.

Stardust Memories....RCA/Readers Digest (S) BIRS-9621 5-10 72
Hill Bowen; Jim Tyler; Jorge Morel & Bill Walker; Melachrino Strings; Frankie Carle; Los Indios Tabajaras; London Pops Orchestra & Robert Mandell; Harry James; Eddie Heywood Trio; Robert Bentley.

Stardust Memories (8 LP)....Readers Digest (S) RD4-108 25-35 73
Hill Bowen; Jim Tyller; Jorge Morel; Bill Walker; Melachrino Singers; Frankie Carle; Johnny Pearson; Henry Mancini; Floyd Cramer; Johnny Gibbs; Malcolm Lockyer; Les Brown; Diego Lopez-Diaz; Harry Hames; Robert Farnon; Alberto Mendez; Wally Stott; Ronnie Aldrich; Richard Alden; Three Suns; Ken Thorne; Ronnie Ogden; Trio Musette de Paris; Laurindo Almeida; Chet Atkins; Bob Benson; Robert Farnon; Golden Saxophones & Romantic Strings; Johnny Douglas; Billy May; Richard Wayne; Gregg Gallbraith; Royal Philharmonic Orchestra; Earl Wild; Ken Thorne; Billy Nalle; John Gardner; Kalua Beach Boys; Los Indios; London Pops Orchestra; Eddie Heywood Trio; Robert Bentley; Gary Hughes; Hugo Winterhalter; Robert Mondell with the Satin Saxophones; Morton Gould; Marie Goosens; David Snell.

Starfire Best of....Starfire (S) 1003 20-25 82
(Picture disc on one side, black vinyl on otherside.) Ral Donner; Robin Luke; others.

Starflight....K-Tel (S) TU 2920 5-10 79
Robert John; Maxine Nightingale; Elton John; Abba; Foreigner; Cheap Trick; Peter Frampton; M; David Naughton; Peaches & Herb; Atlanta Rhythm Section; Earth, Wind & Fire; McFadden & Whitehead.

Starfolk, Vol. 4....Surrey (S) SS-1023 8-12 60s
Barry McGuire; Josh White; Hoyt Axton; Travis Edmonson; Travelers Three; Shenandoah Trio; Barbara Dane; Rod McKuen.

Stargazing: see BENTON, Brook / Chuck Jackson / Jimmy Soul

Starlight Express....MCA (S) 5972 10-15 87
(Soundtrack.) Josie Aiello; Peter Hewlett; Earl Jordan; Richie Havens; Marc Cohn; Harold Faltermeyer; El Debarge.

Starring Lou Christie & Classics: see CHRISTIE, Lou, & Classics / Isley Brothers / Chiffons

Starring the Young Rascals: see (YOUNG) RASCALS / Buggs / 4 Seasons / Johnny Rivers

Stars....Sun (S) SUN-148 5-10 82
Alabama; Jerry Lee Lewis; Orion; Johnny Cash; Carl Perkins.

Stars and Guests of the Louisiana Hayride....Guest Star (M) G 1492 8-12
Margie Singleton; Country Johnny Mathis; Red Sovine; Sleepy LaBeef; Benny Barnes; Sonny Burns; Tibby Edwards; Hoot & Curly; Merle Kilgore; Eddie Bond.

Stars and Hits of Country Music....Nashville (M) NLP-2012 10-15 64
George Jones; Cowboy Copas; Merle Kilgore; others.

Stars for a Summer Night (2 LP)....Columbia (M) PM-1 10-20 61

Stars for a Summer Night (2 LP)....Columbia (S) PMS-1 15-20 61
Ray Conniff; Dave Brubeck; Frank DeVol; Les Elgart; Percy Faith; Andre Previn; Andre Kostelanetz; Bobby Hackett; Art Van Damme; Les Brown; Billy Butterfield; Andre Previn; Harmonicats; Thomas Schippers New York Philharmonic Orchestra; Eugene Ormandy & Philadelphia Orchestra; Alexander Brailowsky; Eileen Farrell; Philipe Entremont; Mormon Tabernacle Choir; Ivan Davis; Richard Tucker.

Stars in Stereo....Capitol (S) SW 1062 10-15
Frank Sinatra; Harry James; Les Baxter; Nat King Cole; Jackie Gleason; Les Brown; Fred Waring; Nelson Riddle; Gordon Jenkins; Stan Kenton

Stars in Stereo - K 57 (5 LP)....No Label/Number Used (S) 20-30
Ray Charles; Frank Sinatra; Harry Belafonte; Louis Prima; Keely Smith; Pearl Bailey; Tommy Dorsey; others.

Stars in the Night....Columbia Special Products (S) CSP 252 8-12 60s
Tony Bennett; Andre Kostelanetz; Bobby Hackett; Johnny Mathis; Les Elgart; Percy Faith; New Christy Minstrels; Paul Weston; Andre Previn; Ray Conniff; Jerry Vale; Les Brown.

Stars of Christmas....RCA (S) DPL1-0842 15-25 88
Elvis Presley; Johnny Mathis; Pointer Sisters; Roger Whittaker; Jose Feliciano; James Galway; Judy Collins; Andy Williams; Kenny Rogers; Carpenters; Bing Crosby; Forester Sisters. (Includes 20-page booklet. Made for Avon.)

Stars of Hee-Haw, Vol. 1....Capitol (S) ST-437 8-12 70
Stars of Hee-Haw, Vol. 2....Capitol (S) ST-670 8-12 71
Buck Owens; Buddy Alan; Don Rich; Roy Clark; Hagers; Susan Raye.

Stars of Hitsville....Wyncote (M) W-9187 10-20 64
Stars of Hitsville....Wyncote (S) SW-9187 10-20 64
Stars of the Apollo....Columbia (M) KG-30788 8-12 72
Bessie Smith; Cab Calloway; Pearl Bailey; Sarah Vaughan; Ruby Smith; Ella Fitzgerald; Billie Holiday; Count Basie; Mills Brothers; Buck & Bubbles; Mamie Smith; Butterbeans & Susie; Claude Hopkins; Earl Hines; Ida Cox; Duke Ellington; Aretha Franklin; others.

Stars of the Grand Ole Opry (2 LP)....RCA (M) LPM-6015 10-20 67
Stars of the Grand Ole Opry (2 LP)....RCA (S) LSP-6015 10-20 67
(Boxed set with booklet.) Hank Snow; Dottie West; Skeeter Davis; Kitty Wells; Porter Wagoner; Chet Atkins; Bobby Bare; Don Bowman; Browns; Archie Campbell; Martha Carson; Carter Family; Delmore Brothers; Jimmie Driftwood; Don Gibson; George Hamilton IV; Sonny James; Johnnie & Jack; Grandpa Jones; Bradley Kincaid; Pee Wee King; Hank Locklin; Lonzo & Oscar; John D. Loudermilk; Uncle Dave Macon; Roger Miller; Willie Nelson; Norma Jean; Leon Payne; Minnie Pearl; Boots Randolph; Wade Ray; Jim Reeves; Connie Smith; Ernest Stoneman; Justin Tubb; Slim Whitman; Willis Brothers; Del Wood.

Stars of the Grand Ole Opry 1926-1974 (2 LP)....RCA (S) CPL 2-0466 10-15 74
Grandpa Jones; Eddy Arnold; Jim Ed Brown; Chet Atkins; Don Gibson; Kitty Wells; Dotty Parton; Dottie West; Sonny James; Porter Wagoner; Uncle Dave Macon; Pee Wee King; Bill Monroe; Minnie Pearl; Lester Flatt; Lonzo & Oscar; Hank Snow; Carter Family; Del Wood; Martha Carson; Johnnie & Jack; Kitty Wells; Jim Reeves; Archie Campbell; George Hamilton IV; Hank Locklin; Browns; Bobby Bare; Connie Smith; Jeanne Pruett.

Stars of the Silver Screen, 1929-1930....RCA (M) LPV-538 10-15 67
(Soundtrack.) John Boles; Fanny Brice; Maurice Chevalier; Bebe Daniels; Dolores Del Rio; Duncan Sisters; George Jessel; Helen Kane; Charles King; Dennis King; Jeanette MacDonald; Everett Marshall; Helen Morgan; Gloria Swanson; Sophie Tucker; Lupe Velez.

Stars of the Steel Guitar....Starday (M) S-350 10-20 65
Pete Drake; Walter Haynes; Leon McAuliffe; others.

Stars Salute Dr. Martin Luther King....Warner Bros. (M) W-1591 10-15 65
Stars Salute Dr. Martin Luther King....Warner Bros. (S) WS-1591 10-15 65
Louis Armstrong; Count Basie; Harry Belafonte; others.

Starshine....Pickwick (S) SPC 3253 5-10
Nat King Cole; Dean Martin; Glen Campbell; Jackie Gleason; Sergio Mendes; Al Martino; Sandler & Young; Judy Garland; Tennessee Ernie Ford.

Starship, the De-Lite Superstars....De-Lite (S) DE-4004 5-10 70s
Kool & Gang; Frankie Avalon; Crown Heights Affair; Kay-Gees; Benny Troy; Rhythm Makers; Genya Raven; Shelly Black; Street People.

Startracking '76 (2 LP)....Ronco (S) R-1976-2 5-10 76
(Mail order offer.) Jackson 5; Hot Chocoloate; Rhythm Heritage; Blue Magic; Greg Allman; Temptations; Barry Manilow; Abba; Hot Chocolate; Wet Willie; Mellisa Manchester; Salsoul Orchestra; Allman Brothers; Eddie Kendricks; Marshall Tucker; Outlaws; Average White Band; Charlie Ross; Abba; Who; Major Harris; Travis Wammack.

Stash Christmas Album....Stash (S) ST-125 5-10 85
Lightnin' Hopkins; Clarence Williams' Blue Five; Ozie Ware with Duke Ellington's Hot Five; Putney Dandridge & His Swing Band; Harry Reser; Paul Whiteman; Ted Weems; Benny Goodman; Fats Waller; Lionel Hampton; Ella Fitzgerald; Louis Armstrong & Commanders; Benny Carter.

State Fair....Dot (M) DLP-9011 12-15 62
State Fair....Dot (S) DLP-29011 15-18 62
(Soundtrack.) Bobby Darin; Ann-Margret; Pat Boone; Tom Ewell; Anita Gordon; Alice Faye; Bob Smart; David Street.

Stations of the Stars WARM Land....Take (S) 2051 10-15
Shangri-Las; Tommy James & Shondells; John Fred; Esquires; Chiffons; Association; Lovin' Spoonful; McCoys; Five Americans; Happenings; Sir Douglas Quintet; Yellow Balloon; Van Morrison; Casinos; Newbeats; Jon & Robin; Five Dutones; Neil Diamond; Aaron Neville; Dixie Cups; Jerry Butler.

Stax 15 Original Big Hits....Stax (S) MPS-8535 5-10 87
Dramatics; Isaac Hayes; Albert King; Johnnie Taylor; Mad Lads; Booker T. & MGs; Mavis Staples; Rufus Thomas; Soul Children; Emotions; Eddie Floyd; Rance Allen; David Porter; Staple Singers; Margie Joseph.

Stax 15 Original Big Hits, Vol. 2....Stax (S) MPS-8502 5-10 81
Booker T. & MGs; Emotions; Albert King; Carla Thomas; Johnnie Taylor; Judy Clay & William Bell; Temprees; Isaac Hayes; Bar-Kays; Staples; Dramatics; Rufus Thomas; Rance Allen; Shack; Newcomers.

Stax 15 Original Big Hits, Vol. 3....Stax (S) MPS-8516 5-10 82
Johnnie Taylor; Staple Singers; William Bells; Soul Children; Dramatics; Rance Allen; Isaac Hayes; Eddie Floyd; Emotions; Albert Kings; Rufus Thomas; Jimmy Hughes; Hot Sauce; Mavis Staples; Booker T. & MGs.

Stax/Volt Revue, Vol. 1 Live in London....Stax (M) 721 10-20 67
Stax/Volt Revue, Vol. 1 Live in London....Stax (S) 721 15-25 67
Otis Redding; Carla Thomas; Sam & Dave; Eddie Floyd; Mar-Keys; Booker T. & MGs.

Stax/Volt Revue, Vol. 2: see REDDING, Otis / Carla Thomas / Sam & Dave / Eddie Floyd

Stay Awake....A&M (S) SP-3918 8-12 88
Betty Carter; Garth Hudson; Aaron Neville; NRBQ; Harry Nilsson; Sinéad O'Connor; Bonnie Raitt; Ringo Starr; Yma Sumac; Ken Nordine; Tom Waits; Susan Vega; Buster Poindexter; Replacements; James Taylor; Los Lobos; others.

Stay in School - Don't Be a Drop Out....Stax (M) A-11 50-100 67
(Promotional issue only.) Otis Redding; Carla Thomas; Eddie Floyd; William Bell; Sam & Dave; Booker T. & MGs; Mar-keys.

Stay Awake: Various Interpretations of Music From....................A&M (S) SP-3918 8-12 88
Ringo Starr; Ken Nordine; Bill Frisell; Wayne Horvitz; Natalie Merchant; Michael Stipe; Mark Bingham; Roches; Los Lobos; Bonnie Raitt; Was (Not Was); Tom Waits; Suzanne Vega; Syd Straw; Buster Poindexter & Banshees of Blue; Yma Sumac; Aaron Neville; Garth Hudson; NRBQ; Betty Carter; Replacements; Sinead O'Connor; Sun Ra & His Arkestra; Harry Nilsson; James Taylor.

Staying Alive....................RSO (S) 422-813-269-1 8-10 83
(Soundtrack.) Bee Gees; Tommy Faragher; Cynthia Rhodes; Frank Stallone; others.

Stealing Home....................Atlantic (S) 81885-1 8-10 88
(Soundtrack.) Jerry Lee Lewis; Bo Diddley; Everly Brothers; David Foster; Shirelles; Nylons; Marilyn Martin; 4 Seasons.

Steel Guitar and Dobro Spectacular!....................Starday (S) SLP 293 10-15 60s
Buddy Emmons; Jerry Byrd; Cecil Campbell; Leon McAuliffe; others.

Steel Guitar Classics....................Old Timey (M) LP-113 5-10 73
Jimmy Tarlton; Sol Hoopii's Trio; Lemuel Turner; Kanui & Lula; Jenks "Tex" Carman; Cliff Carlisle; Jimmie Davis; Roy Acuff.

Steel Guitar Hall of Fame....................Starday (S) SLP 233 8-12
Jerry Byrd; Leon McAullife; Little Roy Wiggins; Shot Jackson; Buddy Emmons; Don Helms; Jimmy Day; Herbie Remington; Speedy Western; others.

Steel Guitar Hall of Fame....................Nashville (S) NLP-2055 5-10
Pete Drake; Leon McAuliffe; Herbie Remington; Jimmy Day; Shot Jackson; "Little" Roy Wiggins; Buddy Emmons; Jerry Byrd; Don Helms; Bashful Brother Oswald.

Steppin' Out (Disco's Greatest Hits) (2 LP)....................Polydor (S) 2-9007 8-12 78
Charachas; Isaac Hayes; Bionic Boogie; Gloria Gaynor; others.

Steppin' Out....................Midsong Int'l (S) BKL1-2423 5-10 77
Silver Convention; Carol Douglas; Liquid Pleasure; Touch of Class; Andrea True Connection.

Steppin' Out with Girls, Girls, Girls, Vol. #3....................Adam & Eve (S) 503 8-10
Al Tigro & Tigers; Crystal Tones; Adelphies; Chessmen; Shy Tones; Jades; Ricky Vac & Rock-A-Ways; Ralph DeMarco & GP; Little Romeo & Casanovas; Bobby & Consoles; Encores; Endells; Preludes; Jive Tones.

Steppin' to Our Disco....................Polydor (S) PRO-60 5-10 70s
(Promotional issue only.) Gloria Gaynor; Gregg Diamond's Bionic Boogie; Alicia Bridges; Miguel Brown; Arpeggio; Joe Simon; Don Ray; Isaac Hayes; Kikrokos; Peaches & Herb.

Stereo Demonstration Record....................Bel Canto (S) SR 2000 10-20 59
Jack Wagner (narrator); Jack Smith; Orrin Tucker; Larry Fotine; Evelyn Freeman; Si Zentner; others.

Stereo Festival: see ASTRONAUTS / Liverpool Five

Stereo for Swing Season (3 LP)....................RCA (S) PRS-238-1-2-3 10-15 67
(Boxed set.) Roger Miller; Ray Martin; Living Brass; Living Guitars; Living Voices; Si Zentner; Claus Ogerman; Norman Luboff Choir.

Stereo Party (Philco Presents) (5 LP)....................Columbia Record Productions XSV 68712/21 20-30 50s
(Boxed set.) Tony Bennett; Jerry Vale; Jo Stafford; Polly Bergen; Andre Kostelanetz; Norman Luboff Choir; Leonard Bernstein & New York Philharmonic; Eugene Ormandy & Philadelphia Orchestra; George Szell; Hi-Lo's; Les & Larry Elgart; Ray Conniff; Les Brown; Andre Previn; Luther Henderson; Lee Castle; Jimmy Dorsey.

Stereo Sampler, Vol. 1....................Mercury (S) SRD-1 10-20
Richard Hayman; David Carroll; Dick Contino; Griff Williams; Patti Page; Eugene List; Pete Rugolo; Terry Gibbs; Sarah Vaughan; Clebanoff; Rochester Orchestra; London Orchestra.

Stereo Showcase....................Capitol (S) SKAO-1268 15-25 59

Stereo Spectacular....................Audio Fidelity (S) DFS-7777 15-25 63
Jim Messina & Jesters; others.

Stereo Spectacular Demonstration & Sound Effects....................Audio Fidelity (S) DFS-7013 10-20 62

Stereo Test Record, 1st Component Series....................Audio Fidelity (S) FCS 50000 10-15
(Various frequencies, test tones, pitches, and channel tests.)

Stereosonic Jubilee Sampler, Vol. 1....................Jubilee (S) SSJLP-801 15-25 59
(Promotional issue only.) Walter Scharf; Frank Ortega; Heart Strings; Lou Levy; others.

Stereosonic Jubilee Sampler, Vol. 2....................Jubilee (S) SSJLP-802 15-25 59
(Promotional issue only.) Bobby Freeman; Don Rondo; Della Reese; Lu Ann Simms; Gretchen Wyler; Accents.

Sterling Album (Souvenir Album)....................Motown (S) 1047 25-50 71
Diana Ross; Stevie Wonder; Smokey Robinson & Miracles; Marvin Gaye; Joe Hinton; Earl Van Dyke.

Stiffs Live....................Stiff (S) STF-0001 5-10 78
Elvis Costello & Attractions; Ian Dury & Blockheads; Nick Lowe's Last Chicken in the Shop; Wreckless Eric & New Rockets; Larry Wallis' Psychedelic Rowdies.

Still More Gold Hits, Vol. 3....................Warwick (M) W-2048 35-55 61
Johnny & Hurricanes; Collegians; Gene & Eunice; Jesters; Paragons; Bob Crewe; Harptones; Tokens; Three Friends.

Stingiest Man in Town....................Columbia (M) CL-950 15-25 56
Stingiest Man in Town....................Columbia (M) P-12637 5-10Re(Soundtrack fr

Stormy Monday....................Virgin (S) 90962-1 8-10 88
(Soundtrack.) B.B. King; Mike Figgis; Krakow Jazz Ensemble; Linda Taylor; Stephanie De Sykes; Linda Allen.

Story of the Blues (2 LP)....................Columbia (M) G-30008 10-20 70
Leadbelly; Brownie McGhee; Otis Spann; Fra-Fra Tribesmen; Missippi John Hurt; Blind Willie McTell; Charley Patton; Blind Lemon Jefferson; Texas Alexander; Peg Leg Howell; Barbecue Bob/Laughing Charley; Henry Williams/Eddie Anthony; Mississippi Jook Band; Memphis Jug Band; Bessie Smith; Lillian Glinn; Bertha "Chippie" Hill; Butterbeans & Susie; Leroy Carr/Scrapper Blackwell; Faber Smith/Jimmy Yancey; Peetie Wheatstraw; Casey Bill/Black Bob; Bo Carter; Robert Johnson; Bukka White; Memphis Minnie; Blind Boy Fuller/Sonny Terry; Joe Williams/Sonny Boy Williamson; Big Bill Broonzy; Joe Turner/Pete Johnson; Otis Spann; Elmore James; Johnny Shines.

Storytellers....................Warner Special Products (S) OP-2512 5-10 79
Gordon Lightfoot; Clarence Carter; Winstons; Bobby Goldsboro; Bobbie Gentry; Rod Stewart; Nitty Gritty Dirt Band; Judy Collins; Arlo Guthrie; Harry Chapin; Kenny Rogers & First Edition; Vicki Lawrence; Tony Orlando & Dawn; Gladys Knight & Pips; Janis Ian; Drifters; Roberta Flack; Coven.

Straight from the Heart Songs....................Precisions (S) TV-LP-76022 5-10 76
(Mail order offer.)

Straight to Hell....................Enigma (S) SJE-73308 8-10 87
(Soundtrack.) Joe Strummer; Cait O'Riordan; Pogues; Pray for Rain; Zander Schloss.

Straighten Up and Fly Right....................New World (M) 261 5-10 77
Lionel Hampton; Nat King Cole; Louis Jordan; Muddy Waters; others.

Strawberry Statement....MGM (S) 2 SE-14 12-15 70
(Soundtrack.) Buffy Sainte-Marie; Crosby, Stills, Nash & Young; Neil Young; Thunderclap Newman; Red Mountain Jug Band; Berlin Philharmonic Orchestra; MGM Studio Orchestra.
Streak....Power Pak (S) SA-243 5-10
Street Beat (4 LP)....Sugar Hill (S) SH-2-9228 12-15 84
Grandmaster & Melle Mel; Treacherous Three; West Street Mob; Jocko; Sugar Hill Gang; Fine Quality & Cuz; Crash Crew; Farrari; Kevie Kev; Grandmaster Flash & Furious Five; Melle Mel & Duke Bootee.
Street Mix....Dominion (S) 2480 5-10
Streetcorner Heartbreak....Arista Flashback (S) ABM 2003 5-10 82
Maurice Williams & Zodiacs; Turbans; Nutmegs; Channels; Mello Kings; Silhouettes; Starlites; Kodaks; Clarence Palmer & Jive Bombers; Five Satins.
Streets of Fire....MCA (S) 5492 8-10 84
(Soundtrack.) Fire Inc.; Fix; Blasters; Marilyn Martin; Greg Phillingames; Maria McKee; Dan Hartman; Ry Cooder.
Streetwalking Blues.... Stash (M) ST-117 8-12 79
Memphis Minnie; Maggie Jones; Virginia Liston; Lil Johnson; Sam Theard; Billie Pierce; C. Williams; Lonnie Johnson; Georgia White; Ma Rainey; Clara Smith; Irene Scruggs; Bertha "Chippie" Hill; Lucille Bogan.
String Band Project....Electra (M) EKL-292 10-15 65
String Band Project....Electra (S) EKS7-292 10-15 65
Uncle Willie's Brandy Sniffers; Stu Jamieson's Boys; others.
String Bands, Vol. 1....Old Timey (M) LP-100 5-10
String Bands, Vol. 2....Old Timey (M) LP-101 5-10
Stuff This in Your Stocking....Skyclad (S) VEEBL-68 5-10 90
Hello Disaster; French Lemon Santas; Electric Shoes; Leonards; Dirty Dogs; Pink Slip Daddy; Russ Tolman & North Pole Men; Emma Vine & Emotionals; Human Drama; Sterilles; Sky Saxon; Jigsaw Seen; L-Status; Characters.
Styled Just for You....Capitol Custom (M) NLB-2267/8 10-15 50s
Nelson Riddle; Ray Anthony; Les Baxter; Billy May; Alfred Newman.
Sue Story, Chapter 1 (Old Goodies).... Sue (M) LP-1021 25-35 64
Inez Foxx; Jimmy McGriff; Barbara George; Ike & Tina Turner; Bobby Hendricks; Duals; Baby Washington; Soul Sisters; Prince La La; Johnny Darrow; Matadors.
Sugar Mama Blues....Biograph (M) 12009 8-10 69
David Wylie; Frank Edwards; Pee Wee Hughs; Curley Wealer; Dennis McMillian.
Suite Steel (Pedal Steel Guitar)....Electra (S) 74072 8-12 70
Buddy Emmons; Sneaky Pete; Rusty Young; J.D. Maness; Red Rhodes.
Summer Lovers.... Warner Bros. (S) 1-23695 5-8 82
(Soundtrack.) Chicago; Michael Sembello; Depeche Mode; Stephen Bishop; Tina Turner; Nona Hendryx; Heaven 17; Elton John.
Summer Means Fun: see Rock of Ages – California Surf Music: 1962-1974 (Summer Means Fun)
Summer Means Fun (2 LP)....Columbia (S) C2-30869 8-12 82
Rip Chords; Bruce Johnston; Jan & Dean; Johnny Rivers; Hot Doggers; Bruce & Terry; Flash Cadillac & Continental Kids; Islands.
Summer of Love (2 LP).... Rhino (S) 71106 8-12 87
Donovan; Scott McKenzie; Friend & Lover; Youngbloods; Marcia Strassman; Troggs; Young Rascals; Cowsills; 5th Dimension; Spanky & Our Gang; Turtles; Harpers Bizarre; Sunshine Company; Electric Prunes; Strawberry Alarm Clock; Canned Heat; Byrds; Monkees; Sonny & Cher; Hombres; Mamas & Papas; Petula Clark; Grass Roots.
Summer School....Chrysalis (S) OV-41607 8-10 87
(Soundtrack.) Tami Show; Paul Engemann; Billy Burnette; Danny Elfman; Elisa Fiorillo; E.G. Daily; Fabulous Thunderbirds; Tone Norum; Tonio K.
Summer Souvenirs....Bell (S) 6035 8-12 69
Clifford Curry; Five Satins; Lee Dorsey; Syndicate of Sound; James & Bobby Purify; Silhouettes; Maurice Williams & Zodiacs; Don Gardner & Dee Dee Ford; Ronny & Daytonas; Bob Kuban; Buster Brown.
Summer Trip: see Capitol Promotional Releases/Samplers
Summertime on the Pier (Ed Hurst Presents).... Mer-Bri (M) MLP-100 20-30
Frankie Lymon & Teenagers; Little Anthony & Imperials; Cleftones; Moonglows; Flamingos; Hearts; Tune Weavers; Revileers; Buddy Knox; Day Brothers; Rod Bernard; Johnny & Hurricanes; Maxine Brown; Dave (Baby) Cortez; Penguins; Dubs; Shirley & Lee; Willows; Tokens; Del-Vikings; Fireflies.
Summit Meeting....Vee Jay (M) VJLP-3026 15-20
Summit Meeting....Vee Jay (S) VJSR-3026 15-25
Sun Rockabilly....Rounder (M) SS-37 8-12
Billy Lee Riley & Little Green Men; Edwin Bruce; Gene Simmons; Tracy Pendarvis & Swampers; Ernie Barton; Tommy Blake & Rhythm Rebels; Warren Smith; Jack Earls & Jimbos; Hayden Thompson; Ray Harris; Conway Twitty (Harold Jenkins); Slim Rhodes; Sandy Brooks.
Sun Rockabillies, Vol. 1....Sun (M) 1010 8-12 79
(Yellow vinyl.) Junior Thompson; Rhythm Rockers; Sonny Burgers; Smokey Joe Baugh; Vernon Taylor; Hayden Thompson; Ray Smith; E. Bruce; Jimmy Wages; Dick Ponner; Danny Stewart; Don Hosea.
Sun Story (2 LP)....Rhino (M) RNDA-71103 10-15 86
Elvis Presley; Jackie Brenston; Carl Perkins; Junior Parker; Johnny Cash; Five Tinos; Roy Orbison; Jerry Lee Lewis; Charlie Rich; Carl Mann; Sonny Burgess; Billy Riley; Prisionaires; Warren Smith; Rufus Thomas Jr.; Bill Justis.
Sun's Gold Hits.... Sun (M) 1250 50-75 60
Jerry Lee Lewis; Johnny Cash; Carl Perkins; Carl Mann; Charlie Rich; Bill Justis.
Sun's Greatest Hits.... Rhino (S) 256 10-15 86
(Picture disc.) Johnny Cash; Jerry Lee Lewis; Carl Perkins; Roy Orbison; others.
Sunburn.... Arrival (S) NU-9540 20-25 77
(Soundtrack.) Graham Gouldman; 10CC; Heatwave; Kandidate; John Ferrara.
Sunday After Church.... Hilltop (S) JS-6102 8-12
Johnny Cash; Jeannie C. Riley; Jerry Lee Lewis.
Sunday Morning....Trip (S) 7016 5-10 73
Harmonizing Four; Swan Silvertones; Staple Singers; Maceo Woods; Kathy Young & Innocents; others.
Sunday Morning at Our House.... Design (S) SDLP-644 8-12
Patsy Cline; Hank Locklin; Stewart Family; Maddox Brothers & Rose; Wally Fowler.

Sundown .... K-Tel (S) WU 3530 5-10 80
Willie Nelson; Eddie Rabbitt; Moe Bandy; Joe Stampley; Barbara Mandrell; Don Williams; John Conlee; Gene Watson; Charlie Daniels Band; Larry Gatlin; Crystal Gayle; Jennifer Warnes; Conway Twitty; Jim Ed Brown & Helen Cornelius; Dave & Sugar; Kendalls; Statler Brothers.

Sunset Strip .... AL-FI (M) C4079 8-12 60s
Norma Zimmer; Doris Drew; June Hutton; Martha Tilton; Curt Massey; Clark Dennis; Robert Alda; Johnny Desmond.

Sunset Surf .... Capitol (M) T-1915 20-25 63

Sunset Surf .... Capitol (S) ST-1915 25-30 63
John Severson; others.

Super Bad .... K-Tel (S) NU-427 5-10 73
Issac Hayes; Staple Singers; Millie Jackson; Fredrick Knight; Detroit Emeralds; Love Unlimited; Sylvers; Main Ingredient; Jerry Butler; Joe Tex; James Brown; Barbara Mason; Joe Simon; Timmy Thomas; Chi-Lites; Freda Payne; Chairman of the Board; Honey Cone; Presidents; Free Movement.

Super Bad Is Back .... K-Tel (S) NU-430 5-10 73
Joe Simon; Annette Snell; Manhattans; First Choice; Tyrone Davis; Kool & Gang; Barry White; Fred Wesley & JBs;Chakachas; Millie Jackson; Chi-Lites; Curtis Mayfield; Don Covay; Bill Withers; New York City; Mandrill; Lyn Collins; Earth, Wind & Fire; James Brown; O'Jays.

Super Bubble (3 LPs) .... Lakeshore (S) OP 3504 10-20 77
Archies; Tommy Roe; Ohio Express; Bobby Sherman; Vanity Fare; Cuff Links; Monkees; Box Tops; 1910 Fruitgum Company; Dawn; Association; Looking Glass; Lobo; Turtles; Foundations; Flying Machine; Gary Lewis & Playboys; Crazy Elephant; Tommy James & Shondells; Lemon Pipers; Sweet; Daniel Boone; White Plains; Lou Christie.

Super Country '83 .... K-Tel (S) WU 3720 5-10 83
John Anderson; Bellamy Brothers; Earl Thomas Conley; Statler Brothers; Hank Williams Jr.; Mel McDaniel; Jerry Reed; T.G. Sheppard & Karen Brooks; Michael Murphey; Dolly Parton; Conway Twitty; David Frizzell; Ricky Skaggs; Reba McEntire.

Super Girls (3 LP) .... Lakeshore Music/Warner Special Products (S) OP 3507 20-30 79
(Mail order offer.) Shangri-Las; Martha & Vandellas; Joanie Sommers; Cookies; Mary Wells; Essex; Raindrops; Marcie Blaine; Murmaids; Earl Jean; Chordettes; Orlons; Doris Troy; Diane Renay; Skeeter Davis; Supremes; Marvelettes; Shirley Ellis; Dixie Cups; Barbara Lewis; Shelly Fabares; Chiffons; Peggy March; Jelly Beans; Betty Everett; Little Eva; Dee Dee Sharp; Claudine Clark; Brenda Lee; Robin Ward.

Super Golden Hits, Vol. 1 .... Jubilee (S) JGS-8019 10-15 69
Raindrops; Cadillacs; Betty Harris; Johnny & Expressions; Kathy Young & Innocents; Bobby Freeman; J. Frank Wilson; Fifth Estate; Della Reese; Joe Henderson; Blades of Grass; Volumes.

Super Golden Hits, Vol. 2 .... Jubilee (S) JGS-8023 10-15 69
Joey Dee; Little Anthony & Imperials; Volumes; Kathy Young; Ray Barretto; Cleftones; Frankie Lymon & Teenagers; Flamingos; Bobby Darin; Drifters; Innocents; Dion & Timberlanes.

Super Group .... Warner (S) PRO 630 10-15 76
Jorge Calderon; Bootsy's Rubber Band; Leon & Mary Russell; William D. Smith; Miroslay Vitous; Pat Martino; Jesse Colin Young; Todd Rundgren; Roger Cook; 4 Seasons; Doobie Borthers; Phil Cody; Elvin Bishop; Michael Franks; Rahsaan Roland Kirk; Bellamy Brothers; Seals & Crofts; Emmylou Harris; George Benson; Maria Muldaur; Slade; First Choice; John Sebastian.

Super Groups .... Atco (S) SD-33-279 10-20 69
Bee Gees; Rascals; Buffalo Springfield; Cream; Iron Butterfly; Vanilla Fudge.

Super Groups .... Peacock (S) 166 5-10 73
Mighty Clouds of Joy; Dixie Hummingbirds; Highway QCs; others.

Super Groups of the '50s .... Pickwick (S) SPC-3271 5-10 71
Diamonds; Platters; Gaylords; Crew-Cuts.

Super Groups from Holland .... White Whale (S) WW-7129 15-25 70

Super Hits .... Original Sound Recording (S) OSR 301 15-20 70
Paul & Linda McCartney; Bee Gees; Osmonds; Sonny & Cher; Bread; Bobby Sherman; Joan Baez; Les Crane; Carpenters; James Taylor; Five Man Electrical Band; Grass Roots.

Super Hits .... Pickwick (S) SPC-3620 5-10 78
Quicksilver Messenger Service; Linda Ronstadt; Raspberries; Edward Bear; Glen Campbell; Andy Kim; Skylark.

Super Hits 1959 .... Gusto (S) PO 308 5-10 77
(Rerecordings by original artists.) Coasters; Frankie Ford; Carl Dobkins Jr.; Johnny & Hurricanes; Jimmy Clanton; Jack Scott; Thomas Wayne; Sandy Nelson.

Super Hits 1962 .... Gusto (S) PO 308 5-10 77
Jimmy Clanton; Mary Wells; Joey Dee; Del Shannon; Duane Eddy; Clarence "Frogman" Henry; Dee Dee Sharp; Skeeter Davis; Mike Clifford; Crystals.

Super Hits, Vol. 1 .... Atlantic (M) 501 10-20 67

Super Hits, Vol. 1 .... Atlantic (S) SD-501 10-20 67
Aretha Franklin; Wilson Pickett; Sam & Dave; Rascals; Percy Sledge; Booker T. & MGs; Eddie Floyd; Barbara Lewis; Carla Thomas; Mar-Keys; Joe Tex.

Super Hits, Vol. 2 .... Atlantic (S) SD-8188 10-20 68
Wilson Pickett; Aretha Franklin; Rascals; Sam & Dave; Bar-Kays; Joe Tex; Otis Redding; Sonny & Cher; Bee Gees; Buffalo Springfield; Jimmy Gilmer.

Super Hits, Vol. 3 .... Gusto (S) GT-0088 5-10 82
Gary Puckett; Barry Sadler; George Jones; Kingsmen; Sue Thompson; Edwin Hawkins; Jewel Akens; Billy Joe Royal; Ferlin Husky; Bill Blacks Combo.

Super Hits, Vol. 3 .... Atlantic (S) SD-8203 10-20 68
Aretha Franklin; Wilson Pickett; Archie Bell & Drells; Sam & Dave; Cream; Arthur Conley; Rascals; Sweet Inspirations; Percy Sledge; Booker T. & MGs; Vanilla Fudge.

Super Hits, Vol. 4 .... Atlantic (S) SD-8224 10-20 69
Aretha Franklin; Rascals; Clarence Carter; Cream; Bee Gees; Archie Bell & Drells; Tyrone Davis; Arthur Brown; Dusty Springfield; Wilson Pickett.

Super Hits, Vol. 5 .... Atlantic (S) SD-8274 15-20 70
Aretha Franklin; Wilson Pickett; Crosby, Stills, Nash & Young; Blues Image; R.B. Greaves; Tyrone Davis; Lulu; Brook Benton; Led Zeppelin; Thunderclap Newman; Rascals; Nazz.

Super Hits of 1973 .... Power Pak (S) 238 5-10 74

Super Hits of the '50s .... Gusto (S) PO-316 5-10 78
Thurston Harris; Jimmy Clanton; Coasters; Crests; Jack Scott; Bobby Day; Bill Doggett; Sanford Clark; Impalas; Olympics.

Super Hits of the '60s .... Gusto (S) PO-309 5-10 79
Jimmy Clanton; B.J. Thomas; Jimmy Gilmer; Sgt. Barry Sadler; Casinos; Derek; Sam the Sham & Pharaohs; Billy Joe Royal; Hondells; Jumpin' Gene Simmons.

Super Hits of the Superstars (2 LP) ....K-Tel (S) TU 2450 8-12 75
Barry Manilow; Phoebe Snow; Sugarloaf with Jerry Corbetta; Sweet Sensation; Gladys Knight & Pips; Hot Chocolate; Blackbyrds; Gwen McCrae; Ohio Players; Golden Earring; Brother To Brother; Hues Corporation; Disco Tex & Sex-O-Lettes; Van McCoy & Soul City Symphony; Bachman-Turner Overdrive; Kool & Gang; Lighthouse; Stealers Wheel; Reunion; Paper Lace; Elton John; Lobo; Tymes; Billy Preston.

Super Oldies....Piccadilly (S) PIC-3468 5-10 80
Everly Brothers; Charlie McCoy; Eddie Hodges; Chordettes; Link Wray; Johnny Tillotson. (Also issued as Cadence Classics, Vol. 2, Barnaby.)

Super Oldies, Vol. 1 ....Capitol (M) T-2562 10-20 66
Super Oldies, Vol. 1 ....Capitol (S) ST-2562 10-20 66
Dobie Gray; Jody Miller; Chuck Berry; others.

Super Oldies, Vol. 2 ....Capitol (M) T-2565 10-20 66
Super Oldies, Vol. 2 ....Capitol (S) T-2565 10-20 66
Outsiders; Lettermen; Jody Miller; Kyu Sakamoto; others.

Super Oldies, Vol. 3 (2 LP)....Capitol (SP) STBB-2910 10-20 68
Human Beinz; Bobbie Gentry; Joe South; Lou Rawls; Lettermen; Cannonball Adderley; Stone Poneys; Glen Campbell; People; Dallas Frazier; Chad & Jeremy; David & Jonathan; Curtis Knight; Jimi Hendrix; Peter & Gordon

Super Oldies, Vol. 4 (2 LP)....Capitol (SP) STBB-149 10-20 69
Glen Campbell; Steve Miller; Bob Seger; Chad & Jeremy; Bobbie Gentry; Curtis Knight (with Jimi Hendrix); Cannonball Adderley; Joe South; Peter & Gordon; Linda Ronstadt & Stone Poneys; Patti Drew; Swingin' Medallions; John W. Anderson.

Super Oldies, Vol. 5 (2 LP)....Capitol (SP) STBB-216 10-20 69
Glen Campbell; Lettermen; Seekers; Bettye Swann; Jody Miller; Nat King Cole; Joe South; David & Giants; Kingston Trio; Chad & Jeremy; Kyu Sakamoto; Freddie & Dreamers; Vic Waters & Entertainers; Crystal Mansion; Peter & Gordon; Bobbie Gentry.

Super Oldies, Vol. 6 (2 LP)....Capitol (SP) STBB-401 15-25 69
Sam Cooke; Chuck Berry; Beach Boys; Gene Vincent; Bobby Freeman; Jack Scott; Terry Stafford; Peggy Lee; Nelson Riddle; Cilla Black; Sonny James; Peter & Gordon; Ed Townsend; Johnny Otis; Gene Chandler; Beau Brummels; Ferlin Husky; Thomas Wayne; Billy Bland; Bill Parsons.

Super Oldies of the '50s, Vol. 1 (2 LP) ....Trip (M) TOP-50-1 5-12 75
Super Oldies of the '50s, Vol. 1 (2 LP) ....Trip (SE) TOX-50-1 5-12 75
(May have been issued as single LP [TOP prefix] and also sold as a 2 LP sets [TOX prefix]). Penguins; Sonny Til & Orioles; Little Anthony & Imperials; Crows; Five Satins; Chantels; Dubs; Cadillacs; Lloyd Price; Mystics; Richie Valens; Harptones; Danleers; El Doradoes; Little Richard; Lee Andrews & Hearts; Jesters; Jimmy Clanton; Bobby Freeman; Johnny & Joe.

Super Oldies of the '50s, Vol. 2 (2 LP) ....Trip (M) TOP-50-2 5-12 75
Super Oldies of the '50s, Vol. 2 (2 LP) ....Trip (SE) TOP-50-2 5-12 75
(May have been issued as single LP [TOP prefix] and also sold as a 2 LP sets [TOX prefix]). Flamingos; Frankie Lymon & Teenagers; Teen Queens; Heartbeats; Monotones; Wilbert Harrison; Shirelles; Lloyd Price; Charts; Olympics; Dion & Belmonts; Little Richard; Dave "Baby" Cortez; Bobby Day; Sam Cooke; Spaniels; Richie Valens; Dee Clark; Frankie Ford; Dubs.

Super Oldies of the '50s, Vol. 3 (2 LP) ....Trip (M) TOP-50-3 5-12 75
Super Oldies of the '50s, Vol. 3 ....Trip (SE) TOP-50-3 5-12 75
Super Oldies of the '50s, Vol. 3 (2 LP) ....Trip (SE) TOX-50-3 5-12 75
(May have been issued as single LP [TOP prefix] and also sold as a 2 LP sets [TOX prefix]). Platters; Diamonds; Crests; Little Richard; Harptones; Jerry Lee Lewis; Five Satins; Scarlets; Channels; Willows; Little Richard; Bobby Day; Crew-Cuts; Spacemen; Crests; Lloyd Price; Eugene Church; Lee Andrews & Hearts; Continentals; Little Richard.

Super Oldies of the '50s, Vol. 4 (2 LP) ....Trip (M) TOP-50-4 5-12 75
Super Oldies of the '50s, Vol. 4 ....Trip (SE) TOP-50-4 5-12 75
Super Oldies of the '50s, Vol. 4 (2 LP) ....Trip (SE) TOX-50-4 5-12 75
(May have been issued as single LP [TOP prefix] and also sold as a 2 LP sets [TOX prefix]). Moonglows; Tune Weavers; Platters; Crests; Jerry Lee Lewis; Little Richard; Kodaks; El Dorados; Spaniels; Paragons; Harptones; Jacks; Wailers; Channels; Eternals; Platters; Velvets; Marvin & Johnny; Donnie Owens; Skip & Flip.

Super Oldies of the '50s, Vol. 5 (2 LP) ....Trip (M) TOP-50-5 5-12 75
Super Oldies of the '50s, Vol. 5 (2 LP) ....Trip (SE) TOX-50-5 5-12 75
(May have been issued as single LP [TOP prefix] and also sold as a 2 LP sets [TOX prefix]). Platters; Tommy Edwards; Shirley & Lee; Diamonds; Channels; Jack Scott; Anita Bryant; Cadillacs; Fire Flies; Shepherd Sisters; Champs; Phil Phillips; Jerry Wallace; Johnny Preston; Thomas Wayne; Johnny & Hurricanes; Paul Evans; Tony Bellus; Jerry Butler; Della Reese.

Super Oldies of the '50s, Vol. 6 (2 LP) ....Trip (M) TOP-50-6 5-12 75
Super Oldies of the '50s, Vol. 6 (2 LP) ....Trip (SE) TOX-50-6 5-12 75
(May have been issued as single LP [TOP prefix] and also sold as a 2 LP sets [TOX prefix]). Crests; Platters; Three Friends; Moonglows; Little Richard; Del-Vikings; Spaniels; Teen Chords; Faye Adams; Starlights; Jerry Lee Lewis; Little Richard; Cadillacs; Continentals; Crests; Lloyd Price; Sam Cooke; Jimmy Reed; Little Richard; Huey "Piano" Smith.

Super Oldies of the '50s, Vol. 7 (2 LP) ....Trip (M) TOP-50-7 5-12 75
Super Oldies of the '50s, Vol. 7 (2 LP) ....Trip (SE) TOP-50-7 5-12 75
Super Oldies of the '50s, Vol. 7 (2 LP) ....Trip (SE) TOX-50-7 5-12 75
(May have been issued as single LP [TOP prefix] and also sold as a 2 LP sets [TOX prefix]). Big Bopper; Channels; Cadets; Crests; Platters; Diamonds; Jack Scott; Collegians; Little Richard; Paragons; Cadillacs; Moonglows; Jesters; Magnificants; Jessie Belvin; Dells; Etta James; Lloyd Price; Flamingos.

Super Oldies of the '50s, Vol. 8 (2 LP) ....Trip (M) TOP-50-8 5-12 75
Super Oldies of the '50s, Vol. 8 (2 LP) ....Trip (SE) TOP-50-8 5-12 75
(May have been issued as single LP [TOP prefix] and also sold as a 2 LP sets [TOX prefix]). Fats Domino; Eddie Cochran; Santo & Johnny; Fleetwoods; Clovers; Marv Johnson; Bill Haley & His Comets; Frankie Avalon; Penguins; Teen Queens; Bill Doggett; Falcons; Fabian; 5 Satins; Jimmy Clanton; Dubs; Mickey & Sylvia.

Super Oldies of the '60s, Vol. 1 (2 LP) ....Trip (SE) TOP-60-1 5-12 75
(May have been issued as single LP [TOP prefix] and also sold as a 2 LP sets [TOX prefix]). Shirelles; Kingsmen; Jive Five; Dion; Chantels; Kathy Young & Innocents; Dion & Belmonts; Shells; Cascades; Gene Chandler; Dave "Baby" Cortez; Del Shannon; Ron Holden; Troy Shondell; Rosie & Originals; Jimmy Clanton (incorrectly listed as Frankie Avalon); Angels; Les Cooper; Little Caesar & Romans.

Super Oldies of the '60s, Vol. 2 (2 LP) ....Trip (SE) TOX-60-2 5-12 75
(May have been issued as single LP [TOP prefix] and also sold as a 2 LP sets [TOX prefix]). Shep & Limelites; Dale & Grace; Capris; Chiffons; Dee Clark; Lee Dorsey; Blue Jays; Dionne Warwick; Harold Dorman; Paul Evans; Joe Jones; Anita Bryant; Paul Peterson; Shirelles; James Darren; Chimes (incorrectly listed as the Capris); Fendermen; Sam Cooke; Freddie Scott; Dovells.

Super Oldies of the '60s, Vol. 3 (2 LP) ....Trip (SE) TOX-60-3 5-12 75

Super Oldies of the '60s, Vol. 3 (2 LP) .... Trip (SE) TOP-60-3 5-12 75

(May have been issued as single LP [TOP prefix] and also sold as a 2 LP sets [TOX prefix]). Chuck Jackson; Barbara Lynn; Jerry Butler; Ike & Tina Turner; Shirelles; Wilson Pickett; Jimmy Hughes; Maxine Brown; Joe Henderson; Gladys Knight & Pips; Patti LaBelle & Blue Belles; King Curtis; Maxine Brown; Jerry Butler; Betty Harris.

Super Oldies of the '60s, Vol. 4 (2 LP) .... Trip (SE) TOX-60-4 5-12 75

Super Oldies of the '60s, Vol. 4 (2 LP) .... Trip (SE) TOP-60-4 5-12 75

(May have been issued as single LP [TOP prefix] and also sold as a 2 LP sets [TOX prefix]). Bobby Lewis; Dion; Randy & Rainbows; Terry Stafford; Jimmy Charles; Don & Juan; Del Shannon; Trashmen; Barbara George; Volumes; Shirelles; Paradons; Beach Boys; Cathy Jean & Roomates; Dixie Cups; Duals; Don Gardner & Dee Dee Ford; Inez Foxx; Angels; Chris Kenner.

Super Oldies of the '60s, Vol. 5 (2 LP) .... Trip (SE) TOX-60-5 5-12 75

(May have been issued as single LP [TOP prefix] and also sold as a 2 LP sets [TOX prefix]). Toys; Little Eva; B.J. Thomas; Happenings; Beach Boys; Turtles; Robert Parker; Chad & Jeremy; Shelley Fabares; Dionne Warwick; Mitch Ryder & Detroit Wheels; Gerry & Pacemakers; Betty Everett; Raindrops; Cookies; Classics; Shirelles; Shangri-Las; Dobie Gray.

Super Oldies of the '60s, Vol. 6 (2 LP) .... Trip (M) TOP-60-6 5-12 75

Super Oldies of the '60s, Vol. 6 (2 LP) .... Trip (SE) TOX-60-6 5-12 75

(May have been issued as single LP [TOP prefix] and also sold as a 2 LP sets [TOX prefix]). Percy Sledge; Sam & Dave; Don Covay; Bobby Freeman; Otis Redding; Capitols; Dionne Warwicke; Brenton Wood; Slim Harpo; Joe Jeffrey Group; James Brown; Jerry Butler & Betty Everett; Esquires; B.B. King; Alvin Cash; Packers; Tommy Tucker; Fred Hughes; Meters; Maxine Brown.

Super Oldies of the '60s, Vol. 7 (2 LP) .... Trip (SE) TOX-60-7 5-12 75

(May have been issued as single LP [TOP prefix] and also sold as a 2 LP sets [TOX prefix]). J. Frank Wilson; Soul Survivors; Shangri-Las; Gerry & Pacemakers; Chad & Jeremy; Dionne Warwick; Happenings; Dixie Cups; B.J. Thomas; Turtles; Royal Guardsmen; Jackie Lee; Beach Boys; Ad-Libs; Jelly Beans.

Super Oldies of the '60s, Vol. 8 (2 LP) .... Trip (SE) TOP-60-8 5-12 75

Super Oldies of the '60s, Vol. 8 (2 LP) .... Trip (SE) TOX-60-8 5-12 75

(May have been issued as single LP [TOP prefix] and also sold as a 2 LP sets [TOX prefix]). Turtles; B.J. Thomas; Tommy James & Shondells; Dionne Warwicke; Brenton Wood; Deon Jackson; John Fred; Mitch Ryder & Detroit Wheels; Toussaint McCall; Happenings; Chiffons; Aaron Neville; Forum; Leaves; Seeds; Count Five; Bobby Fuller Four.

Super Oldies of the '60s, Vol. 9 (2 LP) .... Trip (M) TOP-60-9 5-12 75

Super Oldies of the '60s, Vol. 9 (2 LP) .... Trip (S) TOP-60-9 5-12 75

(Also issued as single LP [TOP prefix] and sold as 2 LP sets [TOX prefix]). Duprees; Crests; Roomates; Beach Boys; Janie Grant; Chimes; Embers; Premiers; Jan & Dean; Champs; Tradewinds; B.J. Thomas; Johnny Crawford; Raindrops; Evie Sands; Jerry Wallace; Chad & Jeremy; Jack Scott; Dionne Warwick.

Super Oldies of the '60s, Vol. 10 (2 LP) .... Trip (M) TOP-60-10 5-12 75

Super Oldies of the '60s, Vol. 10 (2 LP) .... Trip (SE) TOP-60-10 5-12 75

Super Oldies of the '60s, Vol. 10 (2 LP) .... Trip (SE) TOX-60-10 5-12 75

(May have been issued as single LP [TOP prefix] and also sold as a 2 LP sets [TOX prefix]). Leslie Gore; Dickey Lee; Duprees; Leroy Van Dyke; Vogues; Cowsills; Flares; B.J. Thomas; Cannibal & Headhunters; Jay & Techniques; Every Mothers Son; Roger Miller; Sam the Sham & Pharaohs; Gentrys; Shangri-Las.

Super Oldies of the '60s, Vol. 11 (2 LP) .... Trip (M) TOP-60-11 5-12 75

Super Oldies of the '60s, Vol. 11 (2 LP) .... Trip (SE) TOP-60-11 5-12 75

Super Oldies of the '60s, Vol. 11 (2 LP) .... Trip (SE) TOX-60-11 5-12 75

(May have been issued as single LP [TOP prefix] and also sold as a 2 LP sets [TOX prefix]). Nat Kendircks & Swans; Billy Preston; Patti LaBelle & Blue Belles; John Lee Hooker; Manhattans; Baby Washington; Gene Chandler; Lloyd Price Jimmy Reed; Wilson Pickett; Ike & Tina Turner; Jennell Hawkins; Joe Simon; Gladys Knight & Pips; Jimi Hendrix; Chantels; Manhattans; Baby Washington; Jimmy Reed.

Super Oldies of the '60s, Vol. 12 (2 LP) .... Trip (M) TOP-60-12 5-12 75

Super Oldies of the '60s, Vol. 12 (2 LP) .... Trip (SE) TOP-60-12 5-12 75

(May have been issued as single LP [TOP prefix] and also sold as a 2 LP sets [TOX prefix]). Angels; Platters; Bobby Hebb; Lesley Gore; Standells; Mark Dinning; Left Banke; Knickerbockers; Cowsills; Stan Getz & Astrud Gilberto; Duprees; Crests; B.J. Thomas; Johnny Crawford; David Rose; Friend & Lover; Dionne Warwick; Jerry Butler; Rochelle & Candles.

Super Oldies of the '60s, Vol. 13 (2 LP) .... Trip (M) TOP-60-13 5-12 75

Super Oldies of the '60s, Vol. 13 (2 LP) .... Trip (SE) TOP-60-13 5-12 75

(May have been issued as single LP [TOP prefix] and also sold as a 2 LP sets [TOX prefix]). Bobby Goldsboro; Johnny Burnette; Cher; Dick & Deedee; Turtles; Jay & Americans; Ventures; Exciters; Dennis Yost & Classics IV; Bob Lind; Eric Burdon & Animals; Jackie DeShannon; Little Anthony & Imperials; Buddy Knox; Rivingtons; Buckinghams; Bobby Vee; Capris.

Super Oldies of the '60s, Vol. 14 (2 LP) .... Trip (M) TOP-50-14 5-12 75

Super Oldies of the '60s, Vol. 14 (2 LP) .... Trip (SE) TOP-50-14 5-12 75

(May have been issued as single LP [TOP prefix] and also sold as a 2 LP sets [TOX prefix]). Little Anthony & Imperials; Gene McDaniels; Jay & Americans; Johnny Burnette; Bobby Goldsboro; Jackie DeShannon; Rivieras; Timi Yuro; Cher; C.O.D.'s; Dennis Yost & Classics IV; Bobby Vee; Sugarloaf; Animals; Rivingtons; Fabian; Frankie Avalon; Ernie K-Doe.

Super Pop Rock & Soul (5 LP) .... Columbia (S) P5S 5836 20-30 73

Super Pop Rock & Soul (5 LP) .... Columbia (S) 5P 6042 20-30 73

Chase; Looking Glass; Freddy Weller; Leonard Cohen; Chambers Brothers; Edgar Winter's White Trash; Taj Mahal; Laura; Nyro; Grace Slick; Pacific Gas & Electric; O.C. Smith; Cyrkle; Byrds; Dickie Lee; Caravelles; Tim Hardin; Janis Joplin; Sly & Family Stone; Christie; Buddy Miles & Carlos Santana; Buckinghams; Donovan; Cliff Nobles; Paul & Paula; Leslie Gore; Spiral Staircase; It's a Beautiful Day; Mac Davis; Mongo Santamaria; Kooper, Bloomfield & Stills; Fantastic Johnny C; Barbara Mason; Gene Pitney; James Brown; Free Movement; Bobby Hebb; Angels; Peaches & Herb; Diamonds; Tymes; Big Bopper; Gary Puckett & Union Gap; Addrisi Brothers; Screamin' Jay Hawkins; Paul Revere & Raiders; Zombies; Don Ellis; Aretha Franklin; Santana; Johnny Winter; Fleetwood Mac; Chad & Jeremy; Electric Flag; NRBQ; Johnny Cash; Chi Coltrane; Loggins & Messina; Mott the Hoople. (Columbia Record Club issue.)

Super Rock (2 LP) .... Columbia (S) G-30121 8-12 70

Miles Davis; Santana; Al Kooper; Its A Beautiful Day; Chicago; Laura Nyro; Hollies; Jeff Beck; Johnny Winter; Janis Joplin; Byrds; Poco; NRBQ; Tom Rush; Pacific Gas & Electric; Blood, Sweat & Tears; Flock; Sly & Family Stone; Taj Mahal; Chambers Brothers.

Super Sonic .... Ronco (S) R 3010 5-10 79

(Mail order offer.) Earth, Wind & Fire; Joe Jackson; Blondie; Ambrosia; Jay Ferguson; Toto; Dionne Warwick; Dr. Hook; Charlie Daniels; Robert John; Amii Stewart; Babys; Tycoon; Al Stewart; Cars; Exile.

Super Soul .... Wand (M) 685 10-15 67

Super Soul .... Wand (S) 685 10-20 67

Super Soul-Dees .... Capitol (M) T-2798 10-20 67

Super Soul-Dees .... Capitol (S) ST-2798 10-20 67
Lou Rawls; Nat King Cole; Dobie Gray; Fascinators; Drew-Vels; Milt Buckner; Verdelle Smith; Sam Cooke; Cannonball Adderley; King Curtis; Ed Townsend.

Super Soul-Dees, Vol. 2 (2 LP) .... Capitol (S) STBB-2911 10-20 68
Lou Rawls; Patti Drew; Checkmates; Johnny Otis Show; Willie Hightower; Cannonball Adderley; Curtis Knight; Verdelle Smith; Dobie Gray; Milt Buckner; Sam Cooke; Nancy Wilson; Magnificent Men; Ed Townsend; King Curtis; Billy Preston; Tender Joe Richardson; Art Reynolds Singers.

Super Soul-Dees, Vol. 3 (2 LP) .... Capitol (S) STBB-178 10-20 69
Lou Rawls; Nancy Wilson; Patti Drew; Larks; Bettye Swann; Billy Preston; Clara Ward; Dobie Gray; Willie Hightower; King Curtis; Ohio Players; Cannonball Adderley; Chuck Berry; Salty Peppers; Gene Chandler; KaSandra.

Super Soul Sounds of Today .... Original Sound Recording (S) OSR-31 8-12 70s
Delia Gartrell; Donnie Elbert; Joe Tex; Aretha Franklin; 5th Dimension; Wilson Pickett; Denise LaSalle; Martha Reeves & Vandellas; Chaka Khan; Roberta Flack; Rufus Thomas; Detroit Emeralds; Jackson Five; J.B.'s.

Super Sounds from the Wide World of Music on ABC Records .... ABC/TRG (S) NM 1000 5-10 76
Ace; Pointer Sisters; B.J. Thomas; Cold Blood; Dramatics; Three Dog Night; Duke & Drivers; Isaac Hayes. (Made for Gillette.)

Super Stars (3 LP) .... Sessions (S) ARI 1002 10-15 76
Frankie Avalon; Freddie Cannon; Brenda Lee; Tommy Roe; Fabian; others.

Super Stars in Country Music .... K-TEL (M) WU-3430 5-10 78
Kendalls; Johnny Duncan; Crystal Gayle; Larry Gatlin; Marty Robbins; Joe Stampley; George Jones; Tammy Wynette; Mel Tillis; Oak Ridge Boys; Loretta Lynn; Charlie Rich; Eddie Rabbitt; Roy Clark; Gene Watson; Don Williams; Freddy Fender; Dave & Sugar; Linda Ronstadt.

Super Stars, Super Hits (2 LP) .... Columbia (M) D-348 10-20 68
Super Stars, Super Hits (2 LP) .... Columbia (S) DS-348 10-20 68
(Columbia Record Club issue.) Buckinghams; Count Five; Critters; Joe Cuba; Neil Diamond; Doors; 4 Seasons; Aretha Franklin; Happenings; Bobby Hebb; Chuck Jackson; Maxine Brown; Tommy James & Shondells; Keith; Left Banke; Peaches & Herb; ? & Mysterians; Paul Revere & Raiders; Ronny & Daytonas; Mitch Ryder & Detroit Wheels; Sam & Dave; Sam the Sham & Pharaohs; Simon & Garfunkel; Sonny & Cher; Young Rascals.

Super Stars, Super Hits, Vol. 2 (2 LP) .... Columbia (M) D-400 10-20 68
Super Stars, Super Hits, Vol. 2 (2 LP) .... Columbia (S) DS-400 10-20 68
(Columbia Record Club issue.) 1910 Fruitgum Co.; Sonny & Cher; Brenton Wood; Box Tops; Aretha Franklin; Lovin' Spoonful; Lemon Pipers; Jay & Americans; Tommy James & Shondells; Buckinghams; Spanky & Our Gang; Sandpebbles; Mitch Ryder & Detroit Wheels; Union Gap; Jay & Techniques; Young Rascals; Peaches & Herb; Van Morrison; Sam & Dave; Cowsills; Bobby Goldsboro; James & Bobby Purify; Happenings; Neil Diamond.

Super Super Blues Band: see DIDDLEY, Bo, Howlin' Wolf and Muddy Waters

Superblues - All-Time Classic Blues Hits, Vol. 1 .... Stax (S) MPS-8851 5-10 90
B.B. King; Z.Z. Hill; Ike & Tina Turner; Albert King; Howlin' Wolf; Jimmy Reed; Koko Taylor; Little Johnny Taylor; Bobby "Blue" Bland; Little Milton; Lightnin' Hopkins.

Superstar Collection (2 LP) .... K-Tel (S) TU-2810 10-15 78
Atlantic Rhythm Section; Andy Gibb; Dave Mason; Smokie; Baby; Kiss; Andrew Gold; Bay City Rollers; Starbuck; England Dan & John Ford Coley; Kenny Nolan; Alice Cooper; KC & Sunshine Band; Meco; Sanford-Townsend Band; Hall & Oates; Peter McCann; Michael Zager Band; Paul Nicholas; Peter Brown; Yvonne Elliman; High Inergy; Manfred Mann; Abba; Hot; Marilyn McCoo & Billy Davis Jr.; Player; Johnny Rivers; Anita O'Day; Samantha Sang; Bill Conti; Rubicon; Floaters; Steely Dan.

Superstars .... Ronco (S) R-2170 5-10 78
(Green label.)

Superstars .... Ronco (S) R-2170 5-10 78
(Yellow label.) Donna Summer; Alan O'Day; Eric Carmen; Sylvers; Brick; LeBlanc & Carr; KC & Sunshine Band; Barry Manilow; Kiss; Bay City Rollers; Little River Band; England Dan & John Ford Coley; Alan Parsons Project; Jennifer Warnes; Randy Edelman; Stephen Bishop; Abba.

Superstars Greatest Hits (2 LP) .... K-Tel (S) TU 237 8-12 74
(Mail order offer.) Hollies; Dr. Hook; Gladys Knight & Pips; Chi Coltrane; O'Jays; Brownsville Station; Albert Hammond; Elton John; Tommy James & Shondells; Maureen McGovern; Godspell; Five Man Electrical Band; Vicki Lawrence; Stories; Chi-Lites; DeFranco Family; Lighthouse; Timmy Thomas; Clint Holmes; New York City; Johnny Nash; Apollo 100; Tony Orlando & Dawn; Charlie Daniels; Bill Amesbury; Kool & Gang; Honey Cone; Billy Paul; Bill Withers.

Superstars Greatest Hits, Vol. 2 (2 LP) .... K-Tel (S) TU 237-2 8-12 74
(Mail order offer.) DeFranco Family; Lighthouse; Timmy Thomas; Tommy James & Shondells; Clint Holmes; New York City; Johnny Nash; Apollo 100; Dawn; Charlie Daniels; Bill Amesbury; Kool & Gang; Honeycone; Billy Paul; Bill Withers.

Superstars of the '70s, Vol. 1 .... Warner Special Products (S) SP-2000 10-15 74
(Mail order offer.)

Superstars of the '70s, Vol. 2 (Heavy Metal) (2 LP) .... Warner Special Products (S) SP-2001 10-15 74
(Mail order offer.) Blues Image; MC5; Black Sabbath; Alice Cooper; Jimi Hendrix; James Gang; Deep Purple; T Rex; J. Geils Band; Dr. John; Led Zeppelin; Buffalo Springfield; Faces; Doors; Allman Brothers Band; Delaney & Bonnie; Van Morrison; Eagles; Yes; Golden Earring; Grateful Dead; Foghat; Uriah Heep; War.

Superstars of the '70s, Vol. 3 (Rockin' Easy) (2 LP) .... Warner Special Products (S) SP-2002 10-15 75
(Mail order offer.) Jackson Browne; Stephen Stills; Hall & Oates; Carly Simon; Todd Rundgren; Gordon Lightfoot; Nilsson; Bonnie Raitt; James Taylor; Seals & Crofts; America; Jesse Colin Young; Doobie Brothers; Maria Muldaur; Randy Newman; Eagles; Dionne Warwick; Marshall Tucker Band; Bee Gees; Aretha Franklin; Tim Moore; Blue Magic; Fleetwood Mac; Malo.

Superstars of the '70s, Vol. 4 (Silver Bullets) (2 LP) .... Warner Special Products (S) SP-2003 10-15 75
(Mail order offer.) Abba; Average White Band; Chi-Lites; Deep Purple; Doobie Brothers; Foghat; Aretha Franklin; Friends of Distinction; J. Geils Band; Grateful Dead; Isaac Hayes; Dr. John; Main Ingredient; Harold Melvin & Blue Notes; Van Morrison; Ohio Players; O'Jays; Persuaders; Todd Rundgren; Spinners; Staple Singers; B.W. Stephenson; Stephen Stills; Tower of Power.

Superstars of the '70s (4 LP) .... Warner Special Products (S) SP-4000 30-40 73
(Boxed set, combining 2000, 2001, 2002 and 2003. Mail order only.) Allman Brothers; America; Beach Boys; Bee Gees; Black Sabbath; Jackson Browne; Byrds; Judy Collins; Alice Cooper; Crosby, Stills & Nash; Deep Purple; Doobie Bothers; Doords; Eagles; Emerson, Lake & Palmer; Faces; Roberta Flack; Donny Hathaway; Aretha Franklin; Grateful Dead; Guess Who; Jo Jo Gunne; Arlo Guthrie; Jimi Hendrix; Jefferson Airplane; Kinks; Led Zeppelin; Gordon Lightfoot; Joni Mitchell; Van Morrison; Randy Newman; Wilson Pickett; Otis Redding; Rolling Stones; Todd Rundgren; Seals & Crofts; Carly Simon; Stephen Stills; James Taylor; Yes.

Surf & Drag .... Columbia Special Products (S) P 14439 8-12 78
Beach Boys; Jan & Dean; Surfaris; Kingsmen; Lonnie Mack; Hondells; Rip Chords; Ventures; Chantays; Trashmen; Marketts; Ronny & Daytonas. (Made for KBO Publishers, Inc.)

Surf Battle .... GNP/Crescendo (M) GNP-85 15-25 63
Surf Battle .... GNP/Crescendo (S) GNPS-85 20-30 63
Dave Myers & Surftones; Rhythm Kings; others.

Surf City....................Impact (S) BC 261 5-10 79
Surf Family....................Dub-Tone (M) LP-1246 20-25
Dick Dale; Hollywood Surfers; others.
Surf Kings....................Guest Star (M) G-1433 15-25 63
Surf Kings....................Guest Star (S) GS-1433 15-25 63
Dick Dale; Surfaris; Beach Boys. (Beach Boys credited on LP.)
Surf Kings....................Guest Star (M) G-1433 10-20 63
Surf Kings....................Guest Star (S) GS-1433 10-20 63
Dick Dale; Surfaris; Surf Boys. (No mention of Beach Boys.)
Surf Party....................Ava (M) A-28 15-20 63
Surf Party....................Ava (S) AS-28 20-25 63
Surfaris; Surf Teens; Jesters; others.
Surf Party....................20th Fox (M) TFM-3131 15-20 64
Surf Party....................20th Fox (S) TFS-4131 25-30 64
(Soundtrack.) Jackie De Shannon; Astronauts; Routers; Kenny Miller; Patricia Morrow; Lory Patrick.
Surf War: Battle of the Surf Groups....................Shepherd (M) 1300 25-35 63
Dave Myers & Surftones; Centurions; Bob Vaught & Renegades; Impacts; Jim Waller & Deltas.
Surf's Up at Banzai Pipeline....................Northridge (M) 101 30-40 63
Soul Kings; Dave Myers & Surftones; Doug Hume; Biscaynes; Jim Waller & Deltas; Surfaris; Neal Nissenson; Bob Vaught & Renegades; Bob Hafner.
Surf's Up at Banzai Pipeline....................Reprise (M) R-6094 25-30 63
Surf's Up at Banzai Pipeline....................Reprise (S) RS-6094 30-40 63
Soul Kings; Dave Myers & Surftones; Doug Hume; Biscaynes; Jim Waller & Deltas; Surfaris; Neal Nissenson; Bob Vaught & Renegades; Bob Hafner.
Surfin' Hits....................Rhino (S) R 170089 5-10 89
Surfin' in the Midwest....................Unlimited Productions (M) UNLP-0003 8-10 85
Royal Flairs; Treasures; Emotionals; Shattoes; Little John & Sherwood Men; Rich Clayton & Rumblers; Viscounts; Readymen; Bleach Boys; Citations; Vaqueros; Twilights; Tradewinds; Rockin' Continentals; Titans; Slough Boys.
Surfin' on Wave Nine....................King (M) 855 20-30 63
Vice-Roys; Nutrons; Micker Baker; Tramps; Wobblers.
Surfin' Roots....................Festival (SP) FR-1010 10-15 77
Beach Boys (Original Candix versions); Pyramids; Dick Dale & His Del-Tones; Frogmen; Marketts; Dave Myer & Surftones; Rumblers; Annette & Beach Boys; Chantays; Sentinals; Kenny & Cadets (members of Beach Boys); Surfaris; Denel & Rendezvous. (Dick Dale tracks are rerecordings.)
Surfin' Sixties....................Baby Boomer (S) JCI 3106 5-10 85
Jan & Dean; Sunrays; Marketts; Rivieras; Sandals; Surfaris; Ronny & Daytonas; Chantays; Jack Nitsche.
Surfin' U.S.A.....................Era (S) PBU-4710 8-10 82
Jan & Dean; Beach Boys; Regents; Bobby Freeman; Surfaris; Chantays; Crystals; Trashmen; Hondells.
Surfing with....................Gateway (S) GSLP 10104 8-12 79
Beach Boys; Marketts; Frogmen, others.
Surfing's Greatest Hits....................Capitol (M) T-1995 15-25 63
Surfing's Greatest Hits....................Capitol (S) ST-1995 20-30 63
Beach Boys; Dick Dale & His Del-Tones; Frank N. Stein & Drop-Outs; Jack Marshall.
Swamp Blues....................Excello (S) 8015 10-15 70
Whispering Smith; Silas Hogan; Henry Gray; others.
Swampland Soul from the Bayous of Louisiana....................Goldband (M) LP-7754 8-12
Sweet Chariot....................Columbia (M) CL 2061 15-20 60s
Sweet Lies....................Island (S) 90855-1 8-10 88
(Soundtrack.) Compagnie Creole; Robert Palmer; Trevor Jones; Paul McGovern; Gold; Salif Keita; George Decimus.
Sweet Summer Love....................Columbia Musical Treasury (S) 1P-6583 5-10 70s
Percy Faith; Doodletown Pipers; Johnny Mathis; Vikki Carr; Ray Conniff; Marty Robbins; Doris Day; Bobby Vinton.
Sweetheart Soap Presents Great Songs of Romance....................RCA (M) SP-33-162 10-20 60s
Sweetheart Soap Presents Great Songs of Romance....................RCA (S) SPS-33-162 10-20 60s
Boston Pops; Melachrino Strings; Norman Luboff; Three Suns; Lena Horne; Morton Gould; Henry Mancini; Ann Margret; Al Hirt; Della Reese; Peter Nero; Chet Atkins.
Sweethearts in Heaven....................Starday (S) 446 10-15 69
Buck Owens; Cowboy Copas; Dottie West; others.
Swing Again....................Captiol (M) T-1386 20-25 60
Les Brown; Benny Goodman; Stan Kenton; Harry James; Woody Herman; Glen Gray.
Swing: Best of the Big Bands....................MCA (M) 25196 5-10 88
Tommy Dorsey Orchestra & Warren Covington; Billie Holiday; Count Basie; Ink Spots; Woody Herman & Band that Plays the Blues; Tex Beneke; Charlie Barnet; Mills Brothers; Stan Kenton.
Swing Billies....................Audio Lab (M) LP-1546 20-30 60
Swing Billies, Vol. 2....................Audio Lab (M) LP-1566 20-30 60
Swing Street....................Epic (M) N-4042 15-20 62
Swing Street....................Epic (S) SN-6042 20-25 62
Louis Prima; Fats Waller; Billie Holiday; Woody Herman; Art Tatum; Ella Logan; John Kirby; others.
Swing With, Vol. 1, Vintage Series 1936-'46....................RCA (M) LPV 578 10-15 71
Jam Session at Victor 1937; Gene Krupa's Swing Band; Una Mae Carlisle; Lester Young Orchestra; Chubby Jackson & His Jacksonville Seven; Esquire All Americans 1946; Frankie Newton.
Swingin' and Singin': see Singin' and Swingin'
Swingin' Country, the Big Instrumental Hits from Nashville....................Nashville (S) NLP-2051 8-12
Phil Baugh; Tommy Hill; Leon McAuliffe; Shot Jackson; Thumbs Carlisle; Joe Maphis; Pete Drake; Red Hayes; Jackie Phelps; Little Roy Wiggins.
Swingin' Easy Big Bands and Jazz (2 LP)....................Columbia Special Products (M) CSP 210 8-12
Andre Previn; Paul Winter; Art Van Damme; Terry Snyder; Neil Wolfe; Les Elgart; Bobby Hackett with Glenn Miller Orchestra; Ernie Heckscher; Dukes of Dixieland; Percussion Goes Dixieland; Joe Quijano; Dave Brubeck; Percy Faith; Duke Ellington; Xavier Cugat.

Swingin' Friends .... Brunswick (M) BL-54114 15-25 63
Gene Roland; Al Cohn; Zoot Sims; Clark Terry; others.
Swingin' Shindig .... Coronet (SE) CXS-246 10-20 65
Johnny Rivers; Tremonts; Luke Gordon; Charlie Fransic.
Swingin' Shindig .... Premier (SE) PS-9037 10-20 65
Johnny Rivers; Tremonts; Luke Gordon; Charlie Fransic.
Swingin' Sound .... Columbia Special Products (M) XTV 82029 10-15 60s
Dave Brubeck; Hi-Lo's; Duke Ellington; Gerry Mulligan Quartet; Buddy Greco; Ray Conniff; Brothers Four; Carmen McRae; Roy Hamilton; Andre Previn; Lambert, Hendricks & Ross; Miles Davis. (Made for W.A. Sheafer Pen Co.)
Swingin' Sounds for Secret Agents .... Columbia Special Products (M) CSM 444 5-10 60s
Bobby Vinton; Mel Torme; Percy Faith; Village Stompers; John Barry; David Lloyd; Ray Conniff; Orchestra U.S.A.
Swingin' Stereo .... Capitol (S) SW-1161 20-25 59
Ray Anthony; Billy May; Glen Gray; others.
Swingin' Summer .... HBR (M) H-9500 15-25 65
Swingin' Summer .... HBR (S) HST-9500 20-30 65
(Soundtrack.) Donnie Brooks; Righteous Brothers; Rip Chords; Raquel Welch; Carol Conners; Swingers.
Swinging for the King .... Mercury (M) 20133 10-20 50s
Ralph Marterie; Terry Gibbs; Dinah Washington; Erroll Garner; Lionel Hampton; Sarah Vaughan; Teddy Wilson; Red Norvo.
Switched on Blues .... Motown (S) SS 720 8-12 70
Amos Milburn; Sammy Ward; Gino Parks; Stevie Wonder; Mable John; others.
Swinging Sisters on the Air (3 LP) .... Radiola 3MR-1 10-15
Boswell Sisters; McGuire Sisters; others.
Sylvester .... MCA/Curb (S) MCA-39026 8-10 85
(Soundtrack.) Cruzados; Los Lobos; Textones; Gail Davies; Rank & File.
Symposium in Blues .... RCA (M) PRM 235 10-20 66
(Promotional. A presentation album from Merck, Sharp and Dohme.) Leroy Carr; Duke Ellington; Louis Armstrong; Washboard Sam; Lonnie Johnson; Walter Davis; Leadbelly; Wingy Manone; Mildred Bailey; Artie Shaw; "Hot Lips" Page; Ethel Waters; Joe Williams.
TV Country Jamboree .... Camden (M) CAL-925 10-15 65
TV Country Jamboree .... Camden (S) CAS-925 10-15 65
Eddy Arnold; Connie Smith; Hank Snow; others.
TV Record Hop (Milt Grant, WTTG-TV, Washinton, D.C.) .... RCA (M) LPM-1802 50-75 58
The Twins (Jim & John), Billy Mure's Rocking Guitars; Ellie Gaye; Equadors; Leroy Kirkland's Hi Flyers; Ronnie & Rockin' Kings.
TV Record Hop (RCA Salutes Ron Drake of WHP-TV in Harrisburg, Penn.) .... RCA (M) LPM-1809 50-75 58
The Twins (Jim & John); Equadores; Ronnie & Rockin' Kings; Billy Mure's Rocking Guitars; Ellie Gaye; Leroy Kirkland's Hi-Flyers. personality tie-ins.)
TV Record Hop (RCA Salutes Jim Dunbar of WDSU-TV in New Orleans) .... RCA (M) LPM-1815 50-75 58
The Twins (Jim & John); Equadores; Ronnie & Rockin' Kings; Billy Mure's Rocking Guitars; Ellie Gaye; Leroy Kirkland's Hi-Flyers. (Probably issued with other TV personality tie-ins.)
Take Me Home Country Roads (8 LP) .... Readers Digest (S) RD4-142 25-40 73
(Box set. Mail order offer.) Rex Allen; Lynn & Liz Anderson; Eddy Arnold; Chet Atkins; Bobby Bare; Owen Bradley; Elton Britt; Browns; Wilma Burgess; Johnny Cash; Patsy Cline; Danny Davis & Nashville Brass; Skeeter Davis; Jimmy Dean; Dave Dudley; Duane Eddy; Lester Flatt; Red Foley; Don Gibson; Billy Gray; Jack Greene; Tom T. Hall; George Hamilton IV; Bobby Helms; Homer & Jethro; Wanda Jackson; Sonny James; Waylon Jennings; Johnnie & Jack; George Jones; Anita Kerr Singers; Pee Wee King; Brenda Lee; Jerry Lee Lewis; Loretta Lynn; Warner Mack; Roger Miller; Minnie Pearl; Bill Monroe; Willie Nelson; Norma Jean; Roy Orbison; Osborne Brothers; Dolly Parton; Webb Pierce; Charley Pride; Boots Randolph; Jerry Reed; Jim Reeves; Marty Robbins; Roy Rogers; Connie Smith; Sammi Smith; Hank Snow; Red Sovine; Statler Brothers; Mel Tillis; Ernest Tubb; Conway Twitty; Porter Wagoner; Kitty Wells; Dottie West; Bob Wills; Mac Wiseman; Del Wood; Faron Young.
Taken from the Top .... RCA (M) PR-128 10-15 62
Ann Margret; Limeliters; Al Hirt; Lena Horne; Frankie Carle; Tony Martin; Della Reese; Jan Peerce; Jonah Jones; Louis Prima & Keely Smith; Louis Armstrong.
Taking It Easy .... ???? 5-10
Terry Baxter; Bobby Vinton; Vikki Carr; Percy Faith; Ray Conniff; Jerry Vale; Lester Lanin; Mac Davis; Andre Kostelanetz; Charlie Rich.
Taking Off .... Decca (S) DL-79181 10-12 71
(Soundtrack.) Nina Hart; Susan Chafitz; 48 Girls; Carly Simon; Mary Mitchell; Ike & Tina Turner; Susan Cohen; Incredible String Band; Buck Henry.
Tall Twelve .... Starday (M) S-337 10-20 65
George Jones; Sonny James; Johnny Bond; Jim Reeves Blue Boys; Roger Miller; Willis Brothers; Johnny Cash; Faron Young; Buck Owens; Bobby Bare; Floyd Cramer; Jimmy Dean.
Tapeheads .... Island (S) 91030-1 8-10 88
(Soundtrack.): Swanky Modes; Devo; Bo Diddley; King Cotton; Fishbone.
Tamla/Motown Special 1 .... Tamla (M) TM-224 50-75 62
Miracles; Mary Wells; Barrett Strong; others.
Taste of Bluesway .... Bluesway (S) 1973 8-12 73
Ray Charles; Charles Brown; Jimmy Reed; Jimmy Witherspoon; B.B. King; John Lee Hooker; T-Bone Walker; Earl Hooker; Brownie McGhee & Sonny Terry; Jimmy Rushing.
Taste of MCA .... MCA (S) L33-1803 8-10 79
(Promotional issue only.) Dyan Diamond; Blend; Lane Cauldell; Joe Ely; B.J. Thomas; Chuck Brown & Soul Searchers; Valentine Brothers.
Taste of Strings .... Time (S) S-2111 5-10
Hugo Montenegro; Billy May; Gordon Jenkins; Kermit Leslie; Richard Hayman; Stanley Wilson; Hal Mooney.
Tea Pad Songs, Vol. 2 .... Stash (M) ST 104 8-12
Teachers .... Capitol (S) SV-1-12371 8-10 84
(Soundtrack.) ZZ Top; :38 Special; Roman Holliday; Joe Cocker; Night Ranger; Freddie Mercury; Bob Seger & Silver Bullet Band; Eric Martin & Friends; Motels; Ian Hunter.
Teachin' the Blues .... Guest Star (M) G-1902 10-20 60s
Teen Age Goodies .... Coral (M) CRL-57431 20-30 63
Teen Age Goodies .... Coral (SE) CRL7-57431 20-30 63
(Maroon label.) Fireflies; Harptones; Pyramids; Storey Sisters; Carousels; Chandeliers; Embers; Elchords; 3 Friends; Lonnie & Carralons.

Teen Age Riot .... Atomic Passion (S) AP 1957 5-10 80s
Phil Johns & Lonely Ones; Chuck Harrod & Anteaters; Portuguese Joe; Gene Maltais; Chuck Daniels & Classics; Robert Williams & Groovers; Reggie Perkins; Savoys; Ronnie Allen; Betty Dickson; Barry Weaver; Billy Ledbetter; Steve Carl & Jags; Rip Tyler & Flips; T.V. Slim; Little Johnny & Rumblers.

Teen Age Rock: see VINCENT, Gene / Tommy Sands / Sonny James / Ferlin Husky

Teen Delights .... Vee Jay (M) VJLP-1021 30-45 60
Flamingos; Wade Flemmons; Moonglows; Jerry Butler; Dee Clark; El Dorados; Magnificents; Spaniels; Dells; Orioles; Jimmy Reed.

Teen Delights, Vol. 2 .... Vee Jay (M) VJLP-1036 30-45 61
Jerry Butler; Jimmy Reed; Dee Clark; Rockin R's; Roscoe Gordon; Preston Epps; Sandy Nelson; Pips; Rosie & Originals; Eddie Harris; Lee Diamond.

Teen Bandstand: see SEDAKA, Neil, & Tokens / Angels / Jimmy Gilmer & Fireballs

Teen Beat - Instrumental Rock 1957-1965: see Rock of Ages – Instrumental Rock: 1957-1965 (Teen Beat)

Teen Beat .... Diplomat (SE) 2414 10-15 60s
4 Seasons; Johnny Rivers; Trini Lopez; Ray Charles; Garnett Mimms; Lloyd Price.

Teen Idols (2 LP) .... Warner Special Products (S) OP 2552 10-15 80
Conway Twitty; Fabian; Everly Brothers; Bobby Vee; Brian Hyland; Ritchie Valens; Dion; Neil Sedaka; Johnny Tillotson; Tab Hunter; James Darren; Frankie Avalon; Bobby Darin; Del Shannon; Mark Dinning; Pat Boone; Bobby Rydell; Tommy Sands; Jimmy Clanton; Paul Peterson; Johnny Crawford; Ed Byrnes.

Teen Idols (3 LP) .... Teledisc USA (S) TD-0007 10-20 87
(Boxed set with five tracks by each artist.) Dion; Fabion; Frankie Avalon; Johnny Tillotson; Bobby Vee; Neil Sedaka.

Teen King: Porky Chedwick (2 LP) .... Green Dolphin 1011 40-50
Larry Allan; Jerry Butler; Spaniels; Flamingos; Schoolboys; Keynotes; Bertha Tillna; Charters; Mar-keys; Donald Woods & Vel-Aires; Hank Blackman & Killers; Mattie Jackson & Blue Nighthawks; Novas; Turbans; Lee Diamond; Ralph Naturale.

Teen Scene .... Columbia Special Products (S) CSP-293 10-15 67
Dave Clark Five; Paul Revere & Raiders; Bob Dylan; Bobby Vinton; Brothers Four; Byrds; New Christy Minstrels; Vibrations; Chad & Jeremy; Village Stompers; Byrds.

Teen Sound .... Columbia (S) CSS 523 20-30 60s
Dave Clark Five; Bob Dylan; Byrds; Donovan; Paul Revere & Raiders; Cyrkle; Chad & Jeremy; New Happiness; Bobby Vinton.

Teen Street .... Buena Vista (M) BV-3313 20-30 63
Annette; Billy Storm; Hayley Mills; Style Sisters; others.

Teen Time .... Verve (M) 2083 150-200 57
Ricky Nelson; Randy Sparks; Gary Williams; Jeff Allen; Rock Murphy; Barney Kessel.

Teen Time .... MGM (M) E-4256 15-25 65
Ricky Nelson; Randy Sparks; Gary Williams; Jeff Allen; Rock Murphy; Barney Kessel; Johnny Rivers.

Teen Time Million Seller Hits .... Design/Pickwick Int'l (M) DLP 217 8-12 60s
Wilbert Harrison; Maurice Williams; Maxine Brown; Clovers; Silhouettes; Don Covay; Five Satins; Lee Allen; Billy Miles; Lee Dorsey.

Teen Wolf Too .... Curb (S) CRB-10400 8-10 87
(Soundtrack.) Oingo Boingo; Ragtime; B.G. Vox; Ed Keupper; Mark Goldenberg; Real Life; Beat Farmers; Desert Rose Band.

Teen-Age Cruisers .... Rhino (S) 016 10-12 80
(Soundtrack.) Johnny Legend; Billy Zoom; Blasters; Ray Campi; "Wildman" Tony Conn; Jerry Sikorski; Alvis Wayne; Jackie Lee "Waukeen" Chochran; Charlie Feathers.

Teenage Mutant Ninja Turtles .... SBK (S) K1-91066 8-10 90
(Soundtrack.) Hi Tek 3; Partners in Kryme; M.C.; Riff; Spunkadelic; Johnny Kemp; Investiture & Crime Wave; John Du Prez; Turtles Mutate; Orchestra on the Half Shell.

Teenage Party .... Gee (M) 702 50-75 58
(Red label.) Valentines; Cleftones; Crows; Wrens; Harptones.

Teenage Party .... Gee (M) 702 30-40 61
(Gray label.) Valentines; Cleftones; Crows; Wrens; Harptones.

Teenage Party .... Gee (SE) GLPS-702 10-15
(Silver or white label.) Valentines; Cleftones; Crows; Wrens; Harptones.

Teenage Tragedies .... Rhino (SP) RNEP 611 5-10 84
Jody Reynolds; Mark Dinning; Ray Peterson; Shangri-Las; Dickie Lee; J. Frank Wilson; Jan & Dean; Jimmy Cross; Julie Brown. (Some tracks are rerecordings. Includes tissue paper insert.)

Teenage Triangle: see DARREN, James / Shelley Fabares / Paul Petersen

Teenagers Dance .... RCA (M) LPM-1540 25-35 57

Teensville .... Liberty (M) L5503 20-30 60s
Bobby Vee; Fleetwoods; Ventures; Conway Twitty; Johnny Burnette.

Television's Greatest Hits .... TeeVee Toons (S) TVT 1100 8-12

Ten: see 10

Tell It Like It Is .... Modern Sound (SE) MS 1037 10-15
Jalopy Five; Bobby Sims; Buchanans; Chords; Chellows; Ed Hardin & Cadets; Leroy Jones; Carol Janis; John Pamplin.

Ten for Cocktails .... Columbia Special Products (M) CSM 517 5-10
Skitch Henderson; Andre Kostelanetz; Glenn Miller; Lester Lanin; Andre Previn; Percy Faith; Les Elgart; Art Van Damme; Michel Legrand; Bobby Hackett. (Made for Mr. Boston Distiller.)

Ten from Texas, (Herd it Through the Grapevine) .... Elektra (S) 9 60373-1 5-10 84
Commandos; Random Culture; David Bean; Tribe; Optimystics; Dan Del Santo; Secret Six; Refugee; Vital Signs; Johnny Reno & Sax Maniacs.

Ten Years of #1 Hits .... Philadelphia International (S) PZ 39307 5-10 84
McFadden & Whitehead; MFSB; O'Jays; Teddy Pendergrass; Billy Paul; Lou Rawls; Archie Bell & Drells.

Tender Lovin' Country .... Warner Special Products (M) OP-1540 5-10 84
Bellamy Brothers; Gail Davies; Johnny Lee; Don Williams; T.G. Sheppard with Karen Brooks; Con Hunley; Cary Morris; Emmylou Harris; Conway Twitty; John Anderson; John Conlee; Mel Tillis; Barbara Mandrell.

Tender Moments Original Artists .... Pickwick (S) 3776 5-10 80
Classic IV; Gerry & Pacemakers; Happenings; Bobby Vee; Association; Little Anthony & Imperials; Chad & Jeremy; Keith; Climax.

Tender Moods of Love .... Columbia Special Products (S) CSS 757 5-10 60s
Robert Goulet; Patti Page; Skitch Henderson; Jerry Vale; Tony Bennett; Steve Lawrence; Eydie Gorme; Percy Faith; Ray Conniff; Mike Douglas.

Tenderly ....???? 5-10
Rosemary Clooney; Buddy Clark; Vikki Carr; Peter Nero; Aretha Franklin; Johnny Cash; Eydie Gorme; Tony Bennett; Diahann Carroll; Percy Faith; Ray Conniff; Robert Goulet.
Tennessee Christmas .... MCA (EP) S45-17046 5-8 85
(Colored vinyl. Paper sleeve.) Steve Wariner; Jimmy Buffett; Nicolette Larson; John Schneider.
Tennessee C & W Series .... Design (S) SDLP-611 8-12 60s
Carl Perkins; Hevelyn Duvall; Frank Simon; Carl Belew.
Tennessee Jamboree .... RCA (EP) EPB-3192 15-25 54
Tennessee Jamboree .... RCA (EP) EPB-3192 35-50 54
(10–inch LP.)
Tenor Sax Album .... Savoy (M) 2220 5-10 77
Ben Webster; Ike Quebec; John Hardee; Illinois Jacquet; Coleman Hawkins.
Tequila Sunrise .... Capitol (S) C1-91185 8-10 88
Tequila Sunrise .... Capitol (S) CERS-0106 8-10 88
(Soundtrack.) Ann Wilson; Robin Zander; Crowded House; Everly Brothers; Beach Boys; Andy Taylor; Church; Bobby Darin; Dave Grusin; Lee Ritenour; David Sanborn; Duran Duran; Ziggy Marley & Melody Makers.
Terry Lee Presents: see Music for Lovers Only
Terry Lee Presents the Best of the T.L. Sound .... Astra (S) ALP 1000 10-20
(Black vinyl.)
Terry Lee Presents the Best of the T.L. Sound .... Astra (S) ALP 1000 15-25
(Colored vinyl.) Initials; Flamingos; Del Vetts; Tony & Raindrops; Pookie Hudson; Fortunes; Kingsmen; Avantis; Billy Guy; Hank Blackman; Jimmy Beck; Chip Nelson; Dynamics.
Tex-Arkana-Louisiana Country: 1927-1932 .... Yazoo (M) ???? 8-10
Buddy Boy Hawkins; Henry Thomas; Blind Lemon Jefferson; Little Hat James; Six Cylinder Smith; Sammy Hill; King Solomon Hill; Willie Reed; Texas Alexander.
Texas Chainsaw Massacre, Part 2 .... I.R.S. (S) IRS-6184 8-10 86
(Soundtrack.) Torch Song; Lords of the New Church; Timbuk 3; Cramps; Concrete Blonde; Oingo Boingo; Stewart Copeland.
Texas Farewell - Texas Fiddlers 1922-30 .... County (M) 517 8-12 70s
Texas Flashbacks, Vol 1. - Dallas .... Texas Archive (S) TAR-5 5-10 86
Changing Times; Menerals; Living End; Mankind.
Texas Guitar from Dallas to L.A. .... Atlantic (S) SD-7226 8-12 72
Texas Proud 1836-1986 .... Erika (S) 514745 15-20 86
(Texas-shaped picture disc.) Ernest Tubb; Willie Nelson; Tanya Tucker; Bob Wills; Johnny Bush; Billy Walker; Curtis Potter; Pride of Texas.
Texas Sand .... Rambler (M) 101 10-15
Tune Wranglers; Roy Newman & His Boys; Milton Brown & His Brownies; Cliff Bruner; Prairie Ramblers; Jimmie Revard & His Oklahoma Playboys; Johnny Tyler & His Riders of the Rio Grande; Curley Williams & His Georgia Peach Pickers; Sunshine Boys; Jesse Ashlock; T. Texas Tyler & His Oklahoma Melody Boys.
Thank God It's Friday (3 LP) .... Casablanca (S) NBLP-7099-3 15-20 78
(Soundtrack. Includes 2 LPs and a bonus 12–inch single.) Donna Summer; Commodores; Diana Ross; Thelma Houston; Santa Esmeralda; Pattie Brooks; Paul Jabara; Wright Brothers' Flying Machine; D.C. LaRue; Cameo; Sunshine Natural Juices; Love & Kisses; Marathon.
Thanks for the Memory, Vol. 2 .... Longines Symphonette (S) SYS-5294 8-12
Dick Powell; Harry Richman; Ethel Waters; Fred Astaire; Ruth Etting; Jimmy Dorsey; Frances Langford; Boswell Sisters; Jane Froman; Mills Brothers.
That Christmas Feeling .... Columbia Special Products (S) P-11853 5-10 73
Percy Faith; Leonard Bernstein; Andy Williams; Johnny Mathis; New Christy Minstrels; Ray Conniff; Barbra Streisand; Norman Luboff Choir; Robert Goulet; Eugene Ormandy & Philadelphia Orchestra; Sammy Davis Jr. (Made for J.C. Penney.)
That Dobro Sound's Goin' 'Round .... Starday/Gusto (M) SLP-340 8-10 76
Uncle Josh; Hoss Linneman; Bashful Brother Oswald; Shot Jackson; Deacon Brumfield.
That's Dancing! .... EMI America (S) SJ-17149 8-10 85
(Soundtrack.) Kim Carnes; Ruby Keeler; Wini Shaw; Dick Powell; Fred Astaire; Ginger Rogers; Ray Bolger; Judy Garland; Gene Kelly; Donald O'Connor; Ann Miller; Bobby Van; Tommy Rall; Bob Fosse; Bee Gees; Irene Cara.
That's the Way I Feel Now, Tribute to Thelonious Monk (2 LP) .... A & M (S) SP-6600 10-15 84
NRBQ; Bruce Fowler; Steve Khan; Donald Fagen; Carla Bley Band; Dr. John; Johnny Griffin; Todd Rundgren; Randy Weston; Steve Lacy; Elvin Jones; John Zorn; Arto Lindsay; Wayne Horvitz; M.E. Miller; Terry Adams; Shockabilly; Barry Harriss; Was (Not Was); Charlie Rouse; Mark Bingham; Steve Swallow; Joey Barron; John Scofield; Brenden Harkein; Joe Jackson; Chris Spedding; Peter Frampton; Gil Evans; Bobby McFerrin.
That's Truck Drivin' .... Starday (S) 357 10-20 65
Red Sovine; Johnny Bond; Willis Brothers; others.
That's What I Call Music .... Capitol (M) T-1719 10-20 62
That's What I Call Music .... Capitol (S) ST-1719 10-20 62
Les Paul; Joe "Fingers" Carr; Pee Wee Hunt; Clyde McCoy; others.
Thee Unheard of .... Paradise Lost (M) PLR-001 20-25 89
Underdogs; Aces; Fentons; Cherry Slush; Bells of Rhymney; Headhunters; Shieks; Saharas; Zookie & Potentates.
Them Old Country Songs (2 LP) .... Tampa (S) PRS-404-2 8-12 72
Jim Ed Brown; Davis Sisters; Jim Reeves; Del Wood; Stuart Hamblen; Porter Wagoner; Dolly Parton; Hank Snow; Skeeter Davis; Chet Atkins; Hank Locklin; Jimmy Dean; Homer & Jethro; Connie Smith; Bobby Bare; Waylon Jennings; Hank Snow; Dottie West; Roger Miller; Leon Ashely; Nat Stuckey; Jerry Reed.
Theme Songs .... Columbia (M) CL-6016 15-30 50s
(10–inch LP.) Frankie Carle; Claude Thornhill; Xavier Cugat; Elliot Lawrence; Gene Krupa; Les Brown; Dick Jurgens; Ray Noble.
Theme Songs .... RCA (M) LPM 3007 15-30 50s
(10–inch LP.) Tex Beneke; Tommy Dorsey; Larry Green; Sammy Kaye; Wayne King; Freddy Martin; Vaughn Monroe; Three Suns.
Theme Songs of the Big Bands .... Bright Orange (M) X-BO-725
Theme Songs of the Great Bands .... Harmony (M) HL-7336 8-12 65
Benny Goodman; Count Basie; Artie Shaw; others.
Theme Songs of the Great Name Bands .... Harmony (M) HL-7153 8-12 60s
Frankie Carle; Les Brown; Woody Herman; Gene Krupa;Claude Thornhill; Tommy Tucker; Elliot Lawrence; Kay Kyser; Harry James; Charlie Spivak.

Themes from Great Films............Time (M) 52078 5-10
Themes from Great Films............Time (S) S-2078 5-10
(Soundtrack.) Hugo Montenegro; Don Sebesky; Richard Hayman; Hal Mooney; George Siravo; Dominic Cortese; Maury Laws; Jerry Fielding.
Themes of TV's Greatest Westerns............RCA (M) LBY-1027 35-45 59
(Soundtrack.) Prairie Chiefs; Sons of the Pioneers; Hollywood Sound Stage Orchestra & Chorus; Ernie Felice; Jack Halloran Singers; Johnny O'Neill; Lee Adrian.
There's No Place Like Rome: Best of Rome Records............Crystal Ball (S) 112 8-12 83
Earls; Johnny & Jokers; Del-Escorts; Pretenders; Prince-Tones; Glens.
These Are the Sounds of the Bob Livorio Show............WKPA (S) 1150 5-10
Arondies; Castaways; Saxons; Blue Jays; Scott English; Bertha Tillman; Pat & Californians; Jimmy McHugh; Paragons; Clovers; Rochelle & Candles; Cathy Jean & Roomates.
These Dues............Tru Sound (M) T-15005 10-20 62
These Dues............Tru Sound (S) TS-15005 10-20 62
Clark Terry; Oliver Nelson; Clea Bradford; others.
These Were Our Songs - the Early '60s (7 LP)............Reader's Digest (S) RCA-100-A 40-50 90
(Boxed set. Mail order offer.) Paul Anka; Beach Boys; Brook Benton; Chuck Berry; Marcie Blane; Gary "U.S." Bonds; Johnny Burnette; Jerry Butler; Freddy Cannon; Contours; Cookies; Johnny Cymbal; Skeeter Davis; Joey Dee & Starliters; Dion; Fats Domino; Duprees; Duane Eddy; Betty Everett; Everly Brothers; Shelley Fabares; Four Preps; Connie Francis; Marvin Gaye; Barbara George; Lesley Gore; Clarence "Frogman" Henry; Hondells; Isley Brothers; Jan & Dean; Jarmels; Jimmy Jones; Ernie K-Doe; Kingsmen; Brenda Lee; Curtis Lee; Barbara Lewis; Little Anthony & Imperials; Little Eva; Barry Mann; Marcels; Gene McDaniels; Chris Montez; Ray Peterson; Elvis Presley; Randy & Rainbows; Martha Reeves & Vandellas; Rivieras; Smokey Robinson & Miracles; Tommy Roe; Diana Ross & Supremes; Neil Sedaka; Del Shannon; Shirelles; Terry Stafford; Ray Stevens; Barrett Strong; Surfaris; Temptations; Trashmen; Bobby Vee; Ventures; Dionne Warwick; Dinah Washington; Mary Wells; Jackie Wilson.
They Call It an Accident............Island (S) WB-1457 10-12
They Call It an Accident............Island (S) XILP-9757 8-10 82
They Call It an Accident............Island (S) ILPS-9757 8-10 82
(Soundtrack.) Steve Winwood; U2; Marianne Faithfull; Jess Roden; Peter Wood; Compass Point All Stars; Wallyu Badarou.
They Sang in Brooklyn............Crystal Ball (S) 128 8-10 88
Mystics; Bay Bops; Quotations; Vocal-Airs; Bob Knight 4; Fascinators; Accents; Passions; Zarzana Brothers; Ultimates.
They Sang in Pittsburg, Vol. 1............Crystal Ball (S) 130 8-10 90
Marcels; Laurels; Altairs; Jets; Lou & Sensations; Dynamics; Walt Maddox; Skyliners; Del-Vikings; Chi-Tones; Chapelairs; Embers; Twilighters; Fred & Embers; Fabulous Uptowners.
They Sang in Pittsburg, Vol. 2............Crystal Ball (S) 131 8-10 90
Dynamics; Laurels; Capitols; Jets; Lou & Sensations; Robertson Bro's; Cameos; Skyliners; Jerry Hilton & Diadems; Embers; Enchantments; Four Dots; Ronald Mark & Group; Little Maxine Simmons & Group.
They Sang the Blues............Historical (S) 22 8-12 68
Robert Wilkins; Furry Lewis; others.
They're the Top............RCA (M) PRM 165 10-15 64
Cole Porter; Ethel Merman; Maurice Chevalier; Helen Morgan; Alfred Drake; Fred Astaire; Gertrude Lawrence; George Gershwin; Paul Weston. (Made for Barrett-Allied Chemical.)
Thing with Two Heads............Pride (S) PRD-0005 15-25 72
Thing with Two Heads............Pride (S) LST-7353 15-20 73
(Soundtrack.) Jerry Butler; Billy Butler & Infinity; Sammy Davis Jr.; Ollie Nightingale; others.
Thing-Fish (3 LP)............EMI (S) 24-0294-3 35-40 84
(Soundtrack. Boxed set. With libretto.) Frank Zappa; Ike Willis; Terry Bozzio; Dale Bozzio; Napoleon Murphy Brock; Bob Harris; Johnny "Guitar" Watson; Ray White.
This Country's Gospel (2 LP)............Word (S) SL 6894/5 8-12
Johnny Cash; Loretta Lynn; Jimmie Davis; Inspirations; Redd Harper; Marty Robbins; Cliff Barrows; Ray Price; Pat Boone; Patsy Cline; Ernest Tubb; Joe Maphis; Bob Daniels; Wilburn Brothers; Anita Bryant; Red Foley; Glen Campbell; Norma Zimmer; Jim Roberts; Alan McGill; Happy Goodman Family; Roy Acuff; Burl Ives; Mary Jayne; Wayne Newton; J.T. Adams; Wanda Jackson; Sonny James; Blue Ridge Quartet; Ferlin Husky; Roy Rogers; Dale Evans; Tennessee Ernie Ford.
This is Broadway (2 LP)............RCA (S) VPS-6034 8-12 71
Peter Nero; Ed Ames; Al Hirt; Anthony Newley; Marty Gold; Henry Mancini; Kate Smith; Rouvann; Della Reese; Ray Ellis; Marilyn Maye; Chet Atkins; Florence Henderson; Norman Luboff Choir; Anita Kerr Singers; Floyd Cramer.
This is Broadway's Best (2 LP)............Columbia Masterworks (M) B2W-1 12-15 60s
This is Broadway's Best (2 LP)............Columbia Masterworks (S) B2WS-1 15-20 60s
(Soundtrack.) Jan Clayton & Charles Fredericks; Ella Logan; Anna Belle Hill; Ezio Pinza; Carol Channing; Harold Lang & Beverly Fite; Carol Haney; Alfred Drake; Doretta Morrow; Richard Kiley; Henry Calvin; Enid Mosier & Ada Moore; Shorty Long; John Henson; Alan Gilbert; Roy Lazarus; Irra Petina; George Blackwell; Thomas Pyle; Barbara Cook; Judy Holliday; Carol Lawrence & Larry Kert; Pat Suzuki; Rex Harrison; Julie Andrews; Robert Coote; Ethel Merman; Mary Martin; Paul Lynde & Mari Jane Maricle; Clive Revill & Elizabeth Seal; Adolph Green; John Reardon; Cris Alexander.
This Is Christmas............RCA (S) VPS-6046 5-10 71
Perry Como; Ed Ames; Mario Lanza; Marian Anderson; others.
This Is Country (6 LP)............Columbia House (S) 6P 6515 20-30 76
(Boxed set.) Rusty Draper; Tammy Wynette; George Jones; Charlie Rich; Jody Miller; David Allan Coe; Roy Orbison; Sonny James; Lefty Frizzell; Charlie McCoy; Lynn Anderson; Johnny Cash; June Carter; David Houston; Boots Randolph; Freddy Weller; Johnny Paycheck; George Ray Price; Tom T. Hall; Dolly Parton; Connie Smith; John Wesley Ryles; Dan Fogelberg; Mac Davis; Lynn Anderson; Earl Scruggs Revuew; Barbara Mandrell; Sonny James; Charlie McCoy; Mel Tillis; Statler Brothers; Faron Young; Freddy Weller; Larry Gatlin; Moe Bandy; Jerry Lee Lewis.
This is Dynagroove............RCA (S) PRS-140 8-12 63
Sid Ramon; Marty Gold; Dick Schory; Hugo & Luigi; Peter Nero; Arthur Fiedler & Boston Pops; Boston Symphony; Leontyne Price; Morton Gould.
This Is Epic Stereorama............Epic (S) BN-1 10-15 60s
Lester Lanin; Merrill Stanton Choir; Joe Harnell; Ralph & Buddy Bonds; Jimmy Mundy; Malando & Tango Orchestra; Somethin' Smith & Red Heads; Polka Kings; Dave McKenna; Marine Band of the Royal Netherlands Navy; Joe Glover & His Collegians.
This Is How It All Began, Vol. 1............Specialty (SE) SPS-2117 15-25 69
(Multi-color cover.) Chosen Gospel Singers; Soul Stirrers; Alex Bradford; Swan Silverstones; John Lee Hooker; Frankie Lee Sims; Mercy Dee; Roy Milton; Joe Liggins; Percy Mayfield; Four Flames; Camille Howard; Jimmy Liggins.

This Is How It All Began, Vol. 1 ....Specialty (SE) SPS-2117 10-15 82
(Brown cover.) Chosen Gospel Singers; Soul Stirrers; Alex Bradford; Swan Silverstones; John Lee Hooker; Frankie Lee Sims; Mercy Dee; Roy Milton; Joe Liggins; Percy Mayfield; Four Flames; Camille Howard; Jimmy Liggins.

This Is How It All Began, Vol. 2 ....Specialty (SE) SPS-2118 15-25 69
(Black cover.)

This Is How It All Began, Vol. 2 ....Specialty (SE) SPS-2118 10-15 82
(Brown cover.) Lloyd Price; Guitar Slim; Jesse Belvin & Marvin Phillips; Tony Allen & Champs; Little Richard; Larry Williams; Sam Cooke; Art Neville; Don & Dewey; Jerry Byrne.

This Is Music Country ....Columbia Special Products (S) CSPS-401 8-12
Johnny Cash; Flatt & Scruggs; June Stearns; Ray Price; Marion Worth; Jordanaires; Jimmy Dean; Carl Smith; Johnny Horton; Marty Robbins.

This Is Music from Nashville..Columbia Special Products (S) C-10265 5-10

This Is Rock 'N' Roll (Alan Freed)..Silhouette (S) SM 10016 8-12 85
Buddy Holly interview; Alan Freed's Moondog House Radio Show; Alan Freed; Steve Allen; Al "Jazzbo" Collins; Modernaires; George Cates; Alan Freed's Rock 'N' Roll Dance Party TV Show; Jerry Lee Lewis.

This is Soul..Atlantic (M) 8170 10-20 68

This Is Soul..Atlantic (S) SD-8170 10-20 68
Aretha Franklin; Wilson Pickett; Ray Charles; Joe Tex; Percy Sledge; Solomon Burke; Drifters; Ben E. King; Arthur Conley; Capitols; Esther Phillips; Don Covay.

This Is Stereo ....RCA Camden (S) SP-33-22 8-12 59
John McCromack; Gruner-Hegge Orchestra; Hill Bowen; Oivin Fjelstad & Oslo Philharmonic Orchestra; Lorin Hollander; Fred Astaire Dance Studio Orchestra; Mundell Lowe & His All Stars; Ralph Camargo.

This Is Stereo - Sound of the Sixties .... Liberty (S) LST-101 20-30 62
(Promotional issue only. Blue vinyl.) Narratied by Spike Jones; David Seville & Chipmunks; Si Zentner; Gene McDaniels; Felix Slatkin; Martin Denny; Bud & Travis; Julie London.

This is the Big Band Era (2 LP) .... RCA (M) VPM 6043 8-12 71
Benny Mofens Kansas City Orchestra; Tommy Dorsey; Benny Goodman; Bunny Berigan; Artie Shaw; Ziggy Elman; Lionel Hampton; Charlie Barnet; Glen Miller; Earl "Fatha" Hines; Erksine Hawkins; Duke Ellington; Count Basie; Larry Clinton.

This Is the Blues..Pacific Jazz (M) PJ-30 15-20 61

This Is the Blues.. Pacific Jazz (S) PJS-30 20-25 61
Richard Holmes; Curtis Amy; Les McCann; others.

This Is the Blues.. World Pacific (M) 150 15-25
Sonny Terry & Brownie McGhee; others.

This is the Era of Memorable Song Hits - Decade of the '50s (2 LP) ....RCA (M) 6060 8-12
Phil Harris; Eddy Arnold; Hugo Winterhalter; Catrina Valente; Domenico Modugno; Kay Starr; Perry Como; Perez Prado; Tommy Leonetti; Sam Cooke; Harry Belafonte; Browns; Ames Brothers; Eddie Fisher; Melachrino Strings.

This is the Nashville Sound (2 LP) ....RCA (S) VPS-6037 8-12 71
Charley Pride; Chet Atkins; Waylon Jennings; Connie Smith; Nat Stuckey; Dottie West; Kenny Price; Danny Davis & Nashville Brass; George Hamilton IV; Porter Wagoner; Dolly Parton; Dallas Frazier; Eddy Arnold; Skeeter Davis; Floyd Cramer; Hank Snow; Hank Locklin; Jimmy Dean; Jerry Reed; Willie Nelson; Nashville String Band; Jim Reeves; Norma Jean; Jim Ed Brown.

This is 21 Channel Sound .... MGM (M) E 4094 5-10
David Rose; Kurt Edelhagen; Kurt Wege; Larry Elgart; Manuel & His Strings; Paul Lavalle & Band of America; Monte Carlo Light Symphony.

This Land Is Your Land (4 LP)..Columbia Musical Treasury (S) P4M-5061 15-20
Johnny Horton; Jimmy Dean; Ray Price; Roy Acuff; Marty Robbins; Jordanaires; Johnny Cash; "Little" Jimmy Dickens; Norma Jean; Lefty Frizzell; Carl Smith.

Those Fabulous '50s (3 LP) ....Sessions/RCA (S) DVL2-0887 20-25 89
(Mail order offer.) Elvis Presley; Fats Domino; Four Preps; Patti Page; Sonny James; Patience & Prudence; Jimmie Rodgers; Jo Stafford; Everly Brothers; Gogi Grant; Ferlin Husky; Playmates; Harry Belafonte; Fleetwoods; Sarah Vaughan; Diamonds; Peggy Lee; Domenico Modugno; Crests; Platters; Johnny Preston; Ames Brothers; Connie Francis; Mario Lanza; Bill Haley & His Comets; Pat Boone; Fontane Sisters; Debbie Reynolds; Jim Lowe; Teresa Brewer; Billy Williams; McGuire Sisters; Four Aces; Perry Como; Gale Storm; Bobby Day; Kitty Kallen. (Special products. Made for Sessions.)

Those Faraway Places.. Columbia Special Products (S) CSP 221 8-12 60s
Skitch Henderson; Michel Legrand; Tony Bennett; Norman Luboff Choir; Ernie Heckscher; Anita Bryant.

Those Good Old Memories ....Capitol (M) T-1414 25-35 60
Gene Vincent; Nat King Cole; Four Preps; Royal Teens; Ed Townsend; Sonny James; Five Keys; Cheers; Johnny Otis Show; Tommy Sands.

Those Legendary Leading Ladies of Stage, Screen & Radio..Harmony (M) KH 32422 10-15 73
Mae West; Ruth Etting; Boswell Sisters; Jane Froman; Helen Morgan; Ethel Waters; Lee Wiley; Kate Smith; Marlene Dietrich; Grace Moore.

Those Legendary Leading Ladies of Stage, Screen & Radio, Vol 2 ....Harmony (M) KH 32423 10-15 73
Ethel Merman; Fraces Langford; Irene Dunne; Kay Thmpson; Gertrude Niessen; Dorothy Lamour; Alice Faye; Martha Raye; Ella Logan; Mary Martin.

Those Legendary Leading Men of Stage, Screen & Radio ....Harmony (M) 32424 10-15 73
Louis Armstrong; Harry Richman; Cab Calloway; Eddie Cantor; Rudy Vallee; Bing Crosby; Russ Columbo; Al Jolson; Ben Berne; Gene Austin.

Those Legendary Leading Men of Stage, Screen & Radio, Vol. 2 ....Harmony (M) 32425 10-15 73

Those Memory Years, Vol. 1 ....Longines/Decca (SE) DL-734663 5-10 60s

Those Memory Years, Vol. 1 ....Longines (SE) SY-5205 5-10 60s
Les Brown; Ames Brothers; Ben Bernie; Judy Garland; Gene Kelly; Hoagy Carmichael; Ethel Smith; Artie Shaw; Fred Waring; Woody Herman; Louis Armstrong; Ted Weems; Walter Huston; Clyde McCoy; Glenn Miller.

Those Memory Years, Vol. 2 ....Longines/Decca (SE) DL-734664 5-10 60s

Those Memory Years, Vol. 2 ....Longines Symphonette (SE) SY-5206 5-10 60s
Jimmy Durante; Pearl Bailey; Eddie Cantor; Nat King Cole; Mills Brothers; Modernaires; Carmen Cavallaro; Sammy Kaye; Liberace; Ray Eberle; Count Basie; Four Aces; Wayne King; Ink Spots.

Those Swingin' Days of the Big Bands (3 LP) .... Showcase (S) SH-3301 10-15
(Boxed set.) Benny Goodman; Duke Ellington; Les Brown; Ray Anthony; Bob Crosby; Kay Kyser; Harry James; Fredy Martin; Clyde McCoy; Glen Gray; Stan Kenton; Guy Lombardo; Pied Pipers; Woody Herman; Russ Morgan; Ray Eberle; Abel Lyman; Orrin Tucker; Charlie Barnet; Claude Thornhill; Louis Prima; Charlie Spivak; Lawrence Welk; Artie Shaw; Raymond Scott; Jack Teagarden; Tommy Dorsey; Shep Fields; Joe Reichman; Jimmie Lunceford; David Rose; Jerry Gray; Dick Stabile; Bunny Berigan; Will Osborne; Jan Garber.

Those Were the Days..Columbia Special Products (S) P 15577 5-10 81
Diamonds; Fleetwoods; Leslie Gore; Mary Hopkin; Del Shannon; Drifters; Sam the Sham & Pharaohs; Larks; Little Richard; Huey Piano Smith & Clowns.

Those Were the Days........ Era (S) BU 4920 8-12 78
Mary Hopkin; Vogues; Lou Christie; J. Frank Wilson; Dovells; Crystals; Casinos; Dobie Gray; Drifters; Exciters; Chiffons; John Fred; Five Americans; Lesley Gore; Jimmy Gilmer; Jay & Techniques; Gary Lewis & Playboys; Little Anthony & Imperials.

Those Wonderful Fifties (5 LP) .... Columbia 14663 15-20

Those Wonderful Girls (2 LP)........ Epic (M) N 6059 10-20 67

Those Wonderful Girls (2 LP)........ Epic (S) SN 159 10-20 67
Mary Martin; Mae West; Helen Morgan; Jane Froman; Martha Raye; Kate Smith; Irene Dunne; Ethel Merman; Frances Langford; Ethel Waters; Dorothy Lamour; Kay Thompson; Lee Wiley; Ella Logan; Alice Raye; Marlene Dietrich; Boswell Sisters; Ruth Etting; Grace Moore; Gertrude Niessen.

Those Wonderful Guys (2 LP)........ Epic (M) L2N-6064 10-20 67

Those Wonderful Guys (2 LP)........ Epic (S) B2N-164 10-20 67
Louis Armstrong; Rudy Vallee; Bing Crosby; others.

Those Wonderful Stars of Yesterday (6 LP)........ Columbia (M) P6S-5334 35-45
(Boxed set.)

Those Wonderful Thirties (Stars of Broadway/Clubs/Vaudeville) (2 LP) .... Decca (SE) DEA-7-2 10-15 60s
Joe Lewis; Walter Huston; Mary Martin; Sophie Tucker; George Jessel; Harry Richman; Cab Calloway; Bill "Bojangles" Robinson; Ted Lewis; Ethel Merman; Jane Froman; Ethel Waters; Borrah Minevitch & His Harmonica Rascals; Benny Fields; Frances Raye; Hildegarde; Libby Holman; Foursome; Gene Austin; Clayton Jackson; Jimmy Durante.

Those Wonderful Thirties (Stars of Hollywood's Golden Era) (2 LP) .... Decca (SE) DEA-7-1 10-15 60s
Nick Lucas; Al Jolson; Marlene Dietrich; Mae West; Jimmy Durante with Six Hits & a Miss; James Melton; Louis Armstrong; Kenny Baker; Bob Hope & Shirley Ross; Judy Garland; Wini Shaw; Pinky Tomlin; Grace Moore; Tony Martin; Frances Langford; Bobby Breen; Bing Crosby; Dorothy Lamour; Dick Powell; Deanna Durbin.

Those Wonderful Thirties (Radio Stars/Great Bands/Great Vocalists) (2 LP)........ Decca (SE) DEA-7-3 10-15 60s
Al Jolson; Boswell Sisters; Arthur Tracy; Eddie Cantor; Arthur Godfrey; Henry Busse; Clyde McCoy; Guy Lombardo; Mal Hallett; Ted Weems; Bing Crosby; Mills Brothers; Kate Smith; Rudy Vallee; Andrews Sisters; Wayne King; Ben Bernie; Isham Jones; Glen Gray; Fred Waring.

Those Wonderful Years (4 LP)........ Heartland (S) HL 1082/4 10-20 90
Dean Martin; Percy Faith; Patti Page; Jimmie Rodgers; Jane Morgan & Troubadors; Platters; Terry Gilkyson & Easy Riders; Della Reese; Tony Bennett; Les Baxter; Eddie Fisher; Doris Day; Al Hibbler; Fats Domino; Four Lads; Rosemary Clooney; Johnnie Ray; Georgia Gibbs; Pat Boone; Joan Weber; Don Cherry; Guy Mitchell; Crew-Cuts; Frankie Laine; Teresa Brewer; Nat King Cole; Four Aces; Jo Stafford; Jerry Vale; Guy Lombardo; Eddy Howard; Kay Starr; Les Paul & Mary Ford; Johnny Mathis; Pearl Bailey; Perry Como; Marty Robbins; Sammy Kaye; Four Lads; Andy Williams; McGuire Sisters.

Threads of Glory - 200 Years of America in Words and Music .... London Phase 4 (S) 14000 5-8 75
Ronald Reagan; Henry Fonda; Burt Lancaster; Walter Pedgeon; others.

Three at the Top: see JONES, Tom / Freddie & Dreamers / Johnny Rivers

Three Billion Millionaires .... United Artists (M) UXL-4 15-25 63

Three Billion Millionaires .... United Artists (S) UXS-4 20-30 63
Bing Crosby; Carol Burnett; Jack Benny; George Maharis; Judy Garland; Sammy Davis Jr.; Wally Cox; Danny Kaye; Terry Thomas.

Three Country Gentlemen: see SNOW, Hank / Hank Locklin / Porter Wagoner

Three Great Bands: see HIRT, Al / Henry Mancini / Perez Prado

Three Great Girls: see ANN-MARGRET / Kitty Kallen / Della Reese

Three Great Guys: see ANKA, Paul / Sam Cooke / Neil Sedaka

Three Great Pianos: see CRAMER, Floyd / Peter Nero / Frankie Carle

Three of a Kind: see CHARLES, Ray / Ivory Joe Hunter / Jimmy Rushing

Three Shades of Blue........ Flying Dutchman (S) 120 8-12 70
Johnny Hodges; Leon Thomas; Oliver Nelson; others.

Ticket to Rock........ CBS (S) AS-1525 ?? 82
(White promotional issue.) Saga; Buck Dharma; REO Speedwagon; Clocks; Randy Meisner; Shooting Star; Paul Carrack; Garland Jeffreys; Aldo Nova; Fortnox; Ozzy Osbourne.

Till My Dreamin' Comes True: see Rock of Ages – West Coast Rock 1958-1964 (Till My Dreamin' Comes True)

Till the End of Time, Vol. 2 .... Realm (S) 1V 8031 5-10 76
Jimmy Dorsey; Frankie Laine; Judy Garland; Ink Spots; Bing Crosby; Gordon Jenkins; Evelyn Knight; Guy Lombardo; Mills Brothers; Margaret Whiting.

Time is Running Out, Vol. 5 .... Broadside (S) 312 8-12 71

Time Life Treasury of Christmas .... Time-Life (3 LP) (S) STL-107 15-20 86
(Boxed set. Mail order offer.) Elvis Presley; Bing Crosby; Dolly Parton; Harry Simeon Choral; Andre Previn; Roger Whittaker; Nat King Cole; Perry Como; Carpenters; Robert Shaw Choral; Fred Waring; Beach Boys; Charley Pride; Ed Ames; Jim Reeves; Gene Autry; Jose Feliciano; Morton Gould; Bobby Helms; Arthur Fiedler & Boston Pops; Leontyne Price; Brenda Lee; Luciano Pavarotti; Julie Andrews; Alabama; Glen Campbell; Philadelphia Orchestra Chorus; Judy Garland; Harry Belafonte; Lena Horne; Sergio Franchi; Kate Smith; Burl Ives; Fontane Sisters.

Time Life Treasury of Christmas, Vol. 2 (3 LP) .... Time-Life (S) STL-108 10-15 87
(Boxed set. Mail order offer.) Elvis Presley; Nat King Cole; Bing Crosby & Andrews Sisters; Roger Whittaker; Arthur Fiedler & Boston Pops; Harry Belafonte; Eddy Arnold; Julie Andrews; Chet Atkins; Perry Como; Canadian Brass; Glen Campbell; Red Foley; Jim Reeves; Vienna Choir Boys; Ed Ames; Sergio Franchi; Beach Boys; Alabama; Morton Gould; Choir of Kings College; Luciano Pavarotti; Andrews Sisters; Bing Crosby; Robert Shaw Choral; Al Hirt; Ames Brothers; Supremes; Gladys Knight & Pips; Willie Nelson; Roger Miller; Virgil Fox; Renata Tebaldi.

Time Machine........ Recall (M) OL57 10-15 74
Inspirations; Pentagons; Larks; Heartbeats; Cruisers; Butlers; Tony Allen; 4 Jays; Chords; Billy & Essentials; No Names.

Time Passages (2 LP)........ Sessions (S) ???? 8-12 80
Glen Campbell; Donna Fargo; Tom T. Hall; Gino Vannelli; B.J. Thomas; Sammi Smith; Al Wilson; Paul Anka; Fortunes; Morris Albert; Toby Beau; Main Ingredient; Youngbloods; Genn Yarbrough; Mac Davis; Dolly Parton; Three Degrees; England Dan & John Ford Coley; Jennifer Warnes; Eric Carmen; Bay City Rollers; Maxine Nightingale.

Time Release Capsules, Vol. 1 .... Columbia (S) AS-247 8-10 76
(Promotional issue only.) Herbie Hancock; Tony Williams; Fania All Stars; Deneice Williams; John Reid; Jane Olivor; Freddie Hubbard; Earth, Wind & Fire; Flo & Eddie; Artful Dodger.

Time Release Capsules, Vol. 2 .... Columbia (S) AS-2?? 8-10 76
(Promotional issue only.)

Time Release Capsules, Vol. 3 .... Columbia (S) AS-271 8-10 76
(Promotional issue only.) Sutherland Brothers & Quiver; Dave Mason; Sparks; Rex; Phoebe Snow; Hubert Laws; Ned Doheny; Bobby Scott.

Time to Get It Together .... Capitol (S) SL 6696 8-12

Lothar & Hand People; Quicksilver Messenger Service; Linda Ronstadt; the Sons; Joe South.
Times Square (2 LP) .... RSO (S) RPD-1026 8-10 80
(Promotional issue only.)
Times Square (2 LP) .... RSO (S) RS-2-4203 8-12 80
(Soundtrack.) Suzi Quatro; Pretenders; Roxy Music; Gary Numan; Marcy Levy; Robin Gibb; Robin Johnson; Trini Alvarado; Ruts; Lou Reed; D.L. Byron; Desmond Child; Rouge; Talking Heads; Joe Jackson; XTC; Ramones; Cure; Garland; Feffreys; Patti Smith Group; David Johansen.
Tipalet Experience: see FRANKLIN, Aretha / Union Gap / Blood, Sweat & Tears / Moby Grape
T.L. Sound For Young Lovers, The .... Lost Nite (M) LN-112 10-20 60s
Wheels; Clickettes; Seniors; Orchids; Jive Five; Hideaways; Scarlets; Capris; Five Thrills; Ebonaires; Lydells; Jesters; Baltaneers; Swans.
To Elvis: Love Still Burning .... Fotoplay (S) FSP-1001 20-30 78
(Picture disc. White cover with black print.) Danny Mirror; Bobby Fisher; Leon Everette; Johnny Tollison; Barry Tiffin; Jim Whittington; Ral Donner; Frankie Allen; George Pickard; Michael Morgan; Tony Copeland.
To Elvis: Love Still Burning .... Fotoplay (S) FSP-1001 10-15 78
(Picture disc. Black cover with white print.) Danny Mirror; Bobby Fisher; Leon Everette; Johnny Tollison; Barry Tiffin; Jim Whittington; Ral Donner; Frankie Allen; George Pickard; Michael Morgan; Tony Copeland.
To Mother .... Specialty (S) 2152 5-10 73
Pilgrim Travelers; Alex Bradford; Bessie Griffin; Soul Stirrers; others.
To Mother with Love .... Del-Fi (M) 1207 30-40 59
To My Love .... Columbia (S) P-14328 5-10 78
To the Good Life .... Columbia Special Products (S) P-11744 5-10 70s
Mark Lindsay; Rolf Harris; Tony Bennett; Ray Conniff; Patti Page; Dave Brubeck; Favio; Percy Faith; Julie Andrews; Carol Burnett; Original Cast of *New York, New York*.
Today .... Columbia (S) 1P-6681 5-10 77
(Columbia House Record Club.) Ray Conniff; Bobby Vinton; John Gregory; Johnny Mathis; Andre Kostelanetz; Anita Bryant; Terry Baxter; Ettore Stratta; Columbia Pops Orchestra.
Today's Country (5 LP) .... RCA (S) DML5-0486 20-25 82
(Mail order. Special products. Boxed set.) Willie Nelson; Helen Cornelius; Razzy Bailey; Zella Lehr; Billy Walker; Porter Wagoner; Dottsy; Jim Ed Brown; Dickey Lee; Charley Pride; Dave & Sugar; Dottie West; Don Gibson; Connie Smith; Nat Stuckey; Jimmy Dean; Skeeter Davis; George Hamilton IV; Jim Reeves; Hank Snow; Tom T. Hall; Johnny Russell; Charlie Rich; Chet Atkins; Ray Stevens; Jerry Reed; Danny Davis & Nashville Brass; Johnny Bush; Gary Stewart; Bobby Bare.
Today's Gold .... Columbia (S) P 11525 5-10 72
Carole King; Blood, Sweat & Tears; Sly & Family Stone; Who, Mac Davis; Mama Cass; Chi Coltrane; Looking Glass; Association; Argent; Rascals; Chambers Brothers; Addrisi Brothers; Pacific Gas & Electric; Donnie Brooks; Christie; Hollies; Tommy Roe; Hamilton, Joe Frank & Reynolds; Giorgio.
Today's Hits .... Philles (M) PH-4004 50-100 63
Ronettes; Crystals; Alley Cats; Darlene Love; Bob B. Soxx & Blue Jeans.
Today's Scene .... Pickwick Int'l (M) RMP-0102 8-12 70s
Clovers; Jimmy Clanton; Roy Orbison; Isley Brothers; Bobby Goldsboro; Paul Revere & Raiders; Gene Pitney; Wilbert Harrison; Maurice Williams & Zodiacs; Lou Rawls; Jan & Dean; Dave "Baby" Cortez; Don Covay; Young Rascals; Simon & Garfunkel. (Special products. Made for General Electric.)
Today's Super Greats, Vol. 1 .... K-Tel (S) TU-231-1 5-10 74
Daniel Boone; Lighthouse; Mouth & McNeal; Donny Osmond; Raspberries; Brain Hyland; Cher; Sammy Davis Jr.; Stampeders; Dawn; Olivia Newton-John; Hamilton, Joe Frank & Reynolds; Derek & Dominos.
Today's Super Greats, Vol. 2 .... K-Tel (S) TU-231-2 5-10 74
Hurricane Smith; Tee Set; Shocking Blue; Dawn; Freda Payne; Dennis Coffey; Bells; Gallery; Rod Stewart; Chairman of the Board; Joe Simon; Skylark; Austin Roberts; James Brown.
Today's Super Greats, Vol. 3 .... K-Tel (S) TU-231-3 5-10 74
Jud Strunk; Rick Springfield; Lobo; Edison Lighthouse; Box Tops; New Seekers; Osmonds; Fortunes; Eric Clapton; Wayne Newton; Teegarden & Van Winkle; Steam.
Today's Top Hits by Today's Top Artists, Vol. 1 .... Capitol (M) H 9101 20-30 50s
(10-inch LP.) Les Baxter; Nat King Cole; Peggy Lee; Stan Kenton; Les Paul & Mary Ford; Kay Starr; Bob Crosby.
Today's Top Hits by Today's Top Artists, Vol. 2 .... Capitol (M) H 9102 20-30 50s
(10-inch LP.) Les Paul & Mary Ford; Four Knights; Nat King Cole; Ray Anthony; Bob Sands; Margaret Whiting; Mary Mayo; Helen O'Connell; Tennessee Ernie Fields.
Today's Top Hits by Today's Top Artists, Vol. 3 .... Capitol (M) H 9103 20-30 50s
(10-inch LP.) Billy May; Helen O'Connell; Dick Beavers with Les Baxter; Lou Dinning; Nat King Cole; Four Knights; Clark Dennis.
Today's Top Hits by Today's Top Artists, Vol. 5 .... Capitol (M) H 9106 20-30 50s
(10-inch LP.) Jane Froman; Ray Anthony; Les Baxter; Dick Beavers; Les Paul; Kay Starr; Helen O'Connell; Stan Kenton.
Today's Top Hits by Today's Top Artists, Vol. 6 .... Capitol (M) H 9108 20-30 50s
(10-inch LP.) Al Martino; Kay Starr; Nat King Cole; Les Paul & Mary Ford; Les Baxter; Jane Froman; Dinning Sisters.
Today's Top Hits by Today's Top Artists .... Capitol (M) H 9112 20-30 50s
(10-inch LP.)
Today's Top Hits by Today's Top Artists .... Capitol (M) H 9115 20-30 50s
(10-inch LP.) Frank Sinatra; Les Paul & Mary Ford; Pee Wee Hunt; Kay Starr; Helen O'Connell; Nat King Cole.
Today's Top Hits, Vol. 9 .... Capitol (M) T 911? 20-30 50s
(10-inch LP.) Nat King Cole; Margaret Whiting; Jimmy Wakely; Bob Manning; Jan Garber; Les Paul; Ella Morse; June Hutton; Alex Strodahl; Harry Kari
Today's Top Hits, Vol. 11 .... Capitol (M) T 9116 20-30 50s
(10-inch LP.) Dean Martin; Joe "Fingers" Carr; Gordon MacRae; Vicki Young; Kay Starr; Axel Stordahl; Ray Anthony; Jerry Shard.
Today's Top Hits, Vol. 13 .... Capitol (M) T 9127 15-25 50s
Frank Sinatra; Les Paul & Mary Ford; Les Baxter; Nat King Cole; Ella Mae Morse; Four Freshmen; Cliffie Stone.
Today's Top Hits, Vol. 14 .... Capitol (M) T 9130 15-25 50s
Frank Sinatra; Dean Martin; Nat King Cole; Ray Anthony; Les Paul & Mary Ford; Tennessee Ernie Ford; Nelson Riddle; Kit Carson; Four Freshmen.

Together (2 LP) .... Imperial House (S) NU 9830 8-12 82
Air Supply; Quincy Jones; Dan Hill; Michael Johnson; Don McLean; Rita Coolidge; J.D. Souther; Randy VanWarmer; Crystal Gayle; Burton Cummings; Dave Loggins; Robert John; Al Stewart; Stephen Bishop; Billy Preston; Syreeta; Dionne Warwick; Manhattans; Aretha Franklin; Taste of Honey; Melissa Manchester.

Together .... RCA (S) ABL1-3541 5-10 80
(Soundtrack.) Jackie De Shannon; Burt Bacharach; Paul Anka; Libby Titus; Michael McDonald.

Together Sound of Reading, Pennsylvania .... Airport (S) ???? 50-100 70

Tokyo Pop .... Ric (S) RCR-850 8-10 88
(Soundtrack.) Carrie Hamilton; Red Warriors; Michael Cerveris; Yutaka Todokkor; Papaya Paranoia.

Tommy .... Ode '70 (S) SP-99001 20-25 72
(Soundtrack.) Steve Winwood; Richie Havens; Rod Stewart; Ringo Starr; Richard Harris; Pete Townshend; Roger Daltry; Sandy Denny; Merry Clayton; Graham Bell; Maggie Bell; London Symphony Orchestra.

Tommy Boy's Greatest Beats (2 LP) .... Tommy Boy (S) TBLP-1005 10-15 85
Afrika Bambaataa; Soulsonic Force; Planet Patrol; Jonzun Crew; Pressure Drop; Special Request; Globe & Whiz Kid; Malcolm X & Keith LeBlanc; Force MD's; Beatmaster.

Tomorrow's Golden Oldies .... 20th Fox (M) FXG-5018 15-25 63

Tomorrow's Golden Oldies .... 20th Fox (S) SXG-5018 20-30 63

Tomorrow's Hits .... Vee Jay (M) VJLP-1042 20-30 62
The Duke of Earl (Gene Chandler); Dukays; Sheppards; Rod Bernard; Ray Whitley; Bill Allen & Trio; Jerry Butler; Dee Clark; Wade Flemons; Grover Mitchell; Norman Charles.

Tonight in Person the Gene Pitney Show .... Musicor (M) MM 2101 20-30 60s

Tonight in Person the Gene Pitney Show .... Musicor (S) MS 2101 25-35 60s
Gene Pitney; Platters; Marie Knight; Steve Rossi; Teddy & Pandas; Critters; Bitter End Singers; Danny & Diego.

Tonight's the Night (4 LP) .... Time-Life/Warner Special Products (S) OP 4517 15-20 89
(Mail order offer. Digitally remastered.) Shirelles; Bobby Vinton; Barbara Lewis; Mel Carter; Capris; Jerry Butler; Barbara Lynn; Miracles; Nino Tempo & April Stevens; Jose Feliciano; Ben E. King; Ruby & Romantics; Classics IV; Marvin Gaye & Tammi Terrell; Temptations; Peaches & Herb; Duprees; Deon Jackson; Rascals; Ketty Lester; Dionne Warwick; Righteous Brothers; Barbara Mason; Percy Sledge; Lenny Welch; Delfonics; Jerry Butler & Betty Everett; Dells; Jimmy Charles; Eddie Holman; Aaron Neville; Drifters; Mary Wells; Three Dog Night.

Top 10 Hits By Original Artists .... Wyncote (M) W-9007 10-20 63

Top 10 Hits By Original Artists .... Wyncote (S) SW-9007 10-20 63
Bobby Rydell; Chubby Checker; Dovells; Dee Dee Sharp; Orlons.

Top 10 Songs of the Year .... Heartwarming (S) 3055 5-8 70
Imperials; Speer Family; Bill Gaither Trio; others.

Top 10 with a Bullet! Motown Solo Stars .... Motown (S) 5323ML 5-10 84
Marvin Gaye; Jimmy Ruffin; Jermaine Jackson; Michael Jackson; Stevie Wonder; Smokey Robinson; Edwin Starr.

Top 10 with a Bullet! Motown Love Songs .... Motown (S) 5324ML 5-10 84
Stevie Wonder; Diana Ross; Lionel Richie; Jackson 5; Smokey Robinson; Commodores; Marvin Gaye; Tammi Terrell.

Top 10 with a Bullet! Motown Dance/Love Songs (2 LP) .... Motown (S) 213535 8-12 84
Miracles; Commodores; Dazz Band; Bonnie Pointer; Jackson Five; Diana Ross; Thelma Houston; Martha & Vandellas; Stevie Wonder; Lionel Richie; Smokey Robinson.

Top 12, Vol. 1 .... Columbia (M) CL-937 20-30 57
Doris Day; Vic Damone; Percy Faith; Four Lads; Mitch Miller; Tony Bennett; Rosemary Clooney; De Los Rios; Jerry Vale; Don Cherry.

Top 12, Vol. 2 .... Columbia (M) CL-944 20-30 57
Guy Mitchell; Mindy Carson; Percy Faith; Jo Stafford; Four Lads; Frankie Laine; Tony Bennett; Johnnie Ray; De Los Rios; Frankie Vaughn; David Hughes.

Top 12, Vol. 3 .... Columbia (M) CL-1017 20-30 57
Doris Day; Vic Damone; Four Lads; Frankie Laine; Johnny Mathis; Guy Mitchell; Marty Robbins; Bill McGuffie; Calypso Carnival featuring King Flash.

Top 12, Vol. 4 .... Columbia (M) CL-1057 20-30 57
Johnny Mathis; Ray Ellis; Norman Petty; Vic Damone; Jimmy Dean; Tony Bennett; Marty Robbins; Don Cherry.

Top 18 Hits .... Waldorf (M) 33-TH-11 10-15
Loren Becker; Enoch Light; Joe Pryor; Zig Zags; Jimmy Blaine; Ink Spots; Lois Winter; Artie Malvin; Bob Eberly; Dottie Evans.

Top 18 Hits .... Waldorf (M) 33-TH-09 10-15
Van Alexander ; Loren Becker; Enoch Light; Tommy Turner; Jerry Duane & Zig Zags; Artie Malvin; Lois Winters; Sylvia Textor; Keith Textor; Anita Gordon; Mike Stewart.

Top 18 Hits .... Waldorf (M) 33-TH-157 10-15
Jerry Duane & Zig Zags; Loren Becker; Bob Eberly with Paul Whiteman; Artie Malvin; Monarchs; Enoch Light; Rhythm Rockets; Jerry Duane Brigadiers Quartet; Lois Winters.

Top 20 .... Top 20 (M) 12973 10-15 60s
Danny & Juniors; Clarence Henry; Dion & Belmonts; Paul & Paula; Marcels; Crests; Frankie Avalon; Five Satins; Dubs; Frankie Valli; Paragons; Mello Kings; Bo Diddley; Sonny Knight; Chantels; Royal Jesters; Little Richard; Blue Jays; Ritchie Valens.

Top 40 Gold (2 LP) .... ???? 8-12
Little Anthony & Imperials; Johnny Burnette; Eddie Cochran; Bobby Vee; Crickets; Laurie London; Gene McDaniels; Essex; Gary "U.S." Bonds; Chubby Checker; Exciters; Frankie Ford; Murmaids; Danny Williams; Jan & Dean; Toys; Chad & Jeremy; Jay & Americans; Belmonts; Hollies; Keith; Outsiders; Spanky & Our Gang; American Breed; Eddie Floyd; Seekers; Sam & Dave; Sopwith Camel; Human Beinz; Brian Hyland.

Top 100 Rock N Roll Hits of All Time (5 LP) .... Candlelite (S) DML5-0436 20-30 81
(Mail order offer. Boxed set.) Johnny Ace; Angels; Paul Anka; Frankie Avalon; Chuck Berry; Big Bopper; Browns; Jerry Butler & Impressions; Freddy Cannon; Champs; Gene Chandler; Chantels; Ray Charles; Chubby Checker; Jimmy Clanton; Coasters; Sam Cooke; Crests; Crew-Cuts; Danleers; Danny & Juniors; Bobby Darin; Bobby Day; Dells; Del-Vikings; Diamonds; Mark Dinning; Dion & Belmonts; Fats Domino; Drifters; Duane Eddy; Tommy Edwards; Elegants; Everly Brothers; Flamingos; Fleetwoods; Frankie Ford; Bobby Freeman; Bill Haley & His Comets; Bobby Helms; Buddy Holly & Crickets; Sonny James; Jimmy Jones; Buddy Knox; Brenda Lee; Jerry Lee Lewis; Little Anthony & Imperials; Little Caesar & Romans; Little Richard; Frankie Lymon & Teenagers; Marcels; Clyde McPhatter; Mickey & Sylvia; Penguins; Phil Phillips; Platters; Lloyd Price; Rays; Jim Reeves; Bob Riley; Jimmie Rodgers; Royal Teens; Bobby Rydell; Jack Scott; Neil Sedaka; Shep & Limelites; Shields; Shirelles; Shirley & Lee; Teddy Bears; Tokens; Conway Twitty; Ritchie Valens; Bobby Vee; Sheb Wooley.

Top Chart Hits of Today, Vol. 1 .... Alshire (S) ???? 5-10 71

Top Chart Hits of Today, Vol. 2 .... Alshire (S) ???? 5-10 71

Top Chart Hits of Today, Vol. 3 .... Alshire (S) ???? 5-10 71

Top Chart Hits of Today, Vol. 4 .... Alshire (S) ???? 5-10 71

Top Chart Hits of Today, Vol. 5 .... Alshire (S) ???? 5-10 71
Top Chart Hits of Today, Vol. 6 .... Alshire (S) ???? 5-10 71
Top Chart Hits of Today, Vol. 7 .... Alshire (S) 5217 5-10 71
Top Chart Hits of Today, Vol. 8 .... Alshire (S) 5222 5-10 71
Top Chart Hits of Today, Vol. 9 .... Alshire (S) 5236 5-10 71
Top Country (2 LP) .... Pickwick (M)PTP-2023 ?? ??
Glen Campbell; Ferlin Husky; Webb Pierce; Patsy Cline; Hank Locklin; Stewart Family; Johnny Horton; Floyd Cramer; Wynn Stewart; Jerry Smith; Dave Dudley; Jimmy Dean; Stewart Hamblen; George Jones; Cowboy Copas; Carl Belew; Justin Tubb; T. Texas Tyler; Red Sovine; Slim Willet; Charlie Ryan; Hal Willis.
Top Country (3 LP) .... Showcase (S) SH-3302 10-20
(Boxed set.) Jerry Lee Lewis; Glen Campbell; Roy Clark; Buck Owens; Roy Acuff; Tennesssee Ernie Ford; Dave Dudley; Rusty Draper; Del Wood; Roy Drusky; Roger Miller; Flatt & Scruggs; Patsy Cline; Jimmy Dean; Bobby Bare; Stuart Hamblen; Tex Ritter; Hank Locklin; T. Texas Tyler; Texas Jim Robertson; Floyd Cramer; Cowboy Copas; Slim Willet; Justin Tubb; Jerry Smith; Ferlin Husky; Wanda Jackson; Sonny James; Johnny Horton; Rex Allen; Jean Shepard; Hank Thompson; George Jones; Patti Page; Sue Thompson; Charlie Louvin.
Top Gun .... Columbia (S) SC 40323 8-10 86
(Soundtrack.) Berlin; Kenny Loggins; Loverboy; Cheap Trick; Harold Faltermeyer; Steve Stevens; Miami Sound Machine; Teena Marie; Marietta; Larry Greene.
Top Hits of '54 .... Capitol (EP) EPA-1-9117 10-15 54
Top Hits of '54 .... Capitol (EP) EPA-2-9117 10-15 54
Top Hits of '54 .... Capitol (M) H-9117 25-35 54
(10-inch LP.)
Top Hits of '54, Vol. 2 .... Capitol (EP) EPA-1-9119 10-15 54
Top Hits of '54, Vol. 2 .... Capitol (EP) EPA-2-9119 10-15 54
Top Hits of '54, Vol. 2 .... Capitol (M) H-9119 25-35 54
(10–inch LP.)
Top Hits of the '50s .... Columbia/Realistic (SE) P 12869 5-10 75
Penguins; Monotones; Johnnie Ray; Jamies; Four Lads; Johnny Horton; Everly Brothers; Marty Robbins; Carol Haney & Ensemble; Ray Conniff.
Top Hits of the '60s, Vol. 2 .... Columbia/Realistic (S) P-12872 5-10 75
New Vaudeville Band; Byrds; Bobby Vinton; Turtles; Gary Puckett & Union Gap; Lulu; Jimmy Dean; Paul Mauriat; Johnny Cash; Blood, Sweat & Tears.
Top Hits of the '60s, Vol. 3 .... Capitol/Realistic (S) SL-8020 5-10 76
David Rose; Kyu Sakamoto; Peter & Gordon; Beach Boys; Johnny Preston; Bobbie Gentry; Glen Campbell; Joey Dee & Starliters; Shirelles; Seekers.
Top Hits of the '70s .... Columbia/Realistic (S) P-12873 5-10 75
Santana; Clint Holmes; Argent; Daniel Boone; David Essex; Looking Glass; Dr. Hook & Medicine Show; Mac Davis; Redbone; Billy Joel.
Top of the Pops, Vol. 2 .... Super Beeb (S) BELP 003 5-10 75
Rubettes; Gloria Gaynor; Jim Gilstrap; Glitter Band; Showaddy Waddy; KC & Sunshine Band; Wigan's Chosen Few; Bay City Rollers; Mac & Katie Kissoon; George McCrae; Sweet Sensation; Trammps; Love Unlimited; Slade.
Top of the Rock (2 LP) .... Columbia Musical Treasuries (S) P2S 5428 15-20 71
Janis Joplin; Tim Rose; Spiral Staircase; Johnny Winter; Santana; Laura Nyro; Paul Revere & Raiders; It's a Beautiful Day; NRBQ; Mongo Santamaria; Linda Divine; Moby Grape; Gary Puckett & Union Gap; Nick Gravenites; Al Kooper; Taj Mahal; Byrds; Keith; Barbour; Chambers Brothers; Sly & Family Stone; Mike Bloomfield; Chicago; Jeff Beck; Blood, Sweat & Tears; Tymes; Lulu; Pacific Gas & Electric; Flock; Arbors; Yardbirds.
Top Pop Song Hits, Vol. 2 .... Columbia S) DS 127 10-15 66
Corsairs; Anne Kettle; Murray Head; Russ Loader; Dana Valery; Mark Richardson; Soho Singers; Bill Lesage Quartet. (Columbia Record Club issue.)
Top Pops .... Columbia (M) LP-35228/35229 20-30 50s
(Promotional issue only. Not issued with special cover.) Four Lads; Peggy King; Percy Faith; Frankie Laine; Mindy Carson; Metrotones; Joan Weber; Tony Bennett; Johnnie Ray; Lu Ann Simms; Don Cherry; Tattle Tales.
Top Pops .... RCA (EP) EPB-3282 5-10 54
Top Pops .... RCA (M) LPM-3137 25-40 50s
(10-inch LP.) Ames Brothers; Perry Como; Eddie Fisher; Homer & Jethro; Eartha Kitt; Dinah Shore; Three Suns; June Valli.
Top Pops .... RCA (M) LPM-3282 25-40 54
(10–inch LP.) Homer & Jethro; Ames Brothers; Perry Como; Eddie Fisher; Dinah Shore; Three Suns; June Valli.
Top Pops .... Decca (M) DL-8860 20-30 59
Top Pops in Stereo .... Decca (S) DL-78860 25-40 59
Four Aces; Sonny Burke; Earl Grant; Kalin Twins; Tommy Dorsey; Jack Pleis; Carmen Cavallaro; Malcolm Dodds; Red Foley.
Top Ryhthm and Blues Artists (Do the Greatest Country Songs) .... King (M) 884 20-25 64
Otis Williams & Charms; James Brown & Famous Flames; Earl Bostic; Hank Ballard & Midnighters; Little Willie John; Charles Brown; Freddie King; Eugene Church.
Top Rock Hits, Vol. 1 .... Solo (S) SM 1010 10-15 73
Paul & Linda McCartney; Moody Blues; Elton John; Isaac Hayes; Cat Stevens; Bread; Nilsson; Neil Diamond; Paul Simon; Badfinger.
Top Scoring Hits .... Columbia Special Products (S) P 13823 5-10 70s
Labelle; Manhattans; MFSB; Johnny Mathis; Harold Melvin & Bluenotes; Dave Mason; Lou Rawls; Biddu Orchestra; Blood, Sweat & Tears; Byrds; Santana; Minnie Ripperton; Mott the Hoople; Michael Murphey; New Riders of the Purple Sage; Edgar Winter. (Made for J.G. Companies.)
Top Star Festival 20 Dynamic Hits, Vol. 2 .... K-Tel (S) TU-223 8-12 72
(Mail order offer.) Hillside Singers; Bee Gees; Osmonds; James Taylor; Joan Baez; Bread; Elton John; Donovan; Neil Diamond; Guess Who; Raiders; Delaney & Bonnie; Stampeders; Rod Stewart; Doors; Melanie; Gary Puckett; Aretha Franklin; It's A Beautiful Day; Three Dog Night.
Top Teen Bands, Vol. 1 .... Bud-Jet (S) 311 30-50 65
Rave-Ons; Muleskinners; Kan Dells; Aaron Brothers; Deacons; Corvets; Accents; Underbeats; Avanties; Only Ones.
Top Teen Bands, Vol. 2 .... Bud-Jet (S) 312 30-50 66
Rave-Ons; Deacons; Corvets; Can; Lady Bugs; Novas; Accents; Satisfactions; Underbeats; Avanties; Deacons; Mojo Buford.
Top Teen Bands, Vol. 3 .... Bud-Jet (S) 313 30-50 67
Rave-Ons; Deacons; Accents; Underbeats; Avanties; Only Ones; Can; Lady Bugs; Novas; Bandits.
Top Teen Dances .... Cameo (M) C-1016 15-25 60

Top Teen Dances..Cameo (S) SC-1016 15-25 60
Dovells; Chubby Checker; Dreamlovers; Lavenders; Apple Jacks.

Top Teen Hits: see LEE, Brenda / Bill Haley & His Comets / Kalin Twins / Four Aces

Top Ten Winners '71 Barbershop Quartets..USR (S) 5-10 71
Gentlemen's Agreement; Sundown's Golden Staters; Pacificaires; Far Westerner's; Grandma's Boys' Fanfares; Roaring '20s; Avant Garde; Easternaires.

Tops in Pop Artists..Evon (M) 319 5-10
Pee Wee Hunt; Fred Burton; Ted Nash; Louis Prima; Ivoro Morales; Three Suns; Sarah Vaughn; Larry Ross; Martyn Green; Frank Conners; Lani McIntire.

Tops in Pops: see DIAMONDS / Georgia Gibbs / Sarah Vaughan / Florian Zabach

Topanga's Woody Guthrie Folk Festival One..Sky (S) 5006 5-10 76
Tommy Taylor; Gary White; others.

Torrid Tunes...Audio Lab (M) AL 1534 10-20
April Stevens; Marge Phelan; others.

Touch of Country Love..K-Tel (S) WU 3490 5-10 80
Eddie Rabbitt; Moe Bandy; Crystal Gayle; Lynn Anderson; Don Williams; Charlie Rich; Mickey Gilley; Willie Nelson; Barbara Mandrell; Tammy Wynette; Johnny Duncan; Tom Jones; Gene Watson; Conway Twitty; Billyl "Crash" Craddock; John Conlee.

Tower Gives Good Records: see Capitol Promotional Releases/Samplers
(Promotional issue only.)

Town Hall Party..Columbia (M) CL-1072 30-45 57
Collins Kids; Joe Maphis; Freddie Hart; Dortha Wright; Rose Lee; Tex Ritter; Johnny Bond; Tex Carmen; Les "Carrot-Top" Anderson; Bobby Charles; Town Hall Band.

Toyota Jazz Parade (Rock/Dixie)..RCA (S) DPL1-0008 8-12 73
Al Hirt; Dukes of Dixieland; Louis Armstrong; King Oliver; Jose Feliciano; Jerry Reed; Generation Gap; Guess Who; Jefferson Airplane. (Special products. Made for Toyota.)

Trade Secrets, Vol. 1..Smash (S) 422 830 408-1 5-10
Steve Alaimo; others.

Traditional Country Classics 1927-1929..Historical (S) 8003 10-15 68

Traditional Fiddle Music of Mississippi, Vol. 1...County (M) 528 8-12 70s

Traditional Fiddle Music of Mississippi, Vol. 2...County (M) 529 8-12 70s

Traditional Music at Newport, 1964, Part 1..Vanguard (M) VRS-9182 10-20 65

Traditional Music at Newport, 1964, Part 1..Vanguard (S) VSD-79182 10-20 65
Fred McDowell; Doc Watson; Bill Thatcher; Chet Parker & Elgia Hickok; Sacred Harp Singers; Joe Patterson; Ken & Neriah Benfield; Willy Doss: Cajun Band; Sarah Gunning; Moving Star Hall Singers; Hobart Smith.

Traditional Music at Newport, 1964, Part 2..Vanguard (M) VRS-9183 10-20 65

Traditional Music at Newport, 1964, Part 2..Vanguard (S) VSD-79183 10-20 65
Seamus Ennis; Georgia Sea Island Singers; Hindman School Dancers; Mississippi John Hurt; Clayton McMichen; Glenn Ohrlin, Phoeba & Roscoe Parsons; Phipps Family; Frank Proffitt; Almeda Riddle; Edna Ritchie; Jean Ritchie; Rev. Robert Wilkins; Robert Pete Williams.

Tragic Songs of Death and Sorrow..Starday (S) SLP-168 15-25 62

Transformers..Scotti Bros. (S) SZ-40430 8-10 86
(Soundtrack.) Stan Bush; Vince Di Cola; Spectre General; Weird Al Yankovic; Lion.

Treasure Album..Hickory (S) LPs 154 10-20 69
Sue Thompson; B.J. Thomas; Newbeats; Kris Jensen; Gene & Debbe.

Treasure Chest of Golden Hits...Columbia Special Products (S) CSP 246 8-12 65
New Christy Minstrels; Vic Damone; Glenn Miller; Bobby Hackett; Anita Bryant; Andre Previn; Percy Faith; Ray Conniff; Jerry Vale; Patti Page; Village Stompers; Andre Kostelanetz; Art Van Damme.

Treasure Chest of Goldies...Stax (M) 703 15-25 64
Jerry Lee Lewis; Mar-Keys; William Bell; Carla Thomas; Nick Charles; Charlie Rich; Bill Justis; Thomas Wayne; Carl Mann; Booker T. & MGs.

Treasure Chest of Hits...Swan (M) LP-501 50-75 59
Rays; Billy & Lillie; Applejacks; Dicky Doo & Don'ts; Gloria Mann; Freddy Cannon; Charlie Gracie; Timmie Rogers; Billy Scott; Quaker City Boys.

Treasure Chest of Musty Dusties (From Fortune's)..Fortune (M) 8011 35-45 61

Treasure Chest of Musty Dusties, Vol. 2 (From Fortune's)...Fortune (M) 8017 25-35 64
Delteens; Five Dollars; Monteclairs; Earthquakes; Creators; Nathaniel Mayer & Fabulous Twilights; Royal Jokers; Swans; Four Kings; Centurys; Andre Williams; Gino Parks; Floyd Smith; Del Rios; Constellations; Destinations; Five Jets; Hi Fidelities; Short & Short Stops; Combinations; Fabulous Four; Joe Weaver.

Treasure Chest of Song Hits...Columbia (EP) B-1963 10-15 55

Treasure Chest of Song Hits...Columbia (EP) B-1964 10-15 55

Treasure Chest of Song Hits...Columbia (EP) B-1965 10-15 55

Treasure Chest of Song Hits...Columbia (M) CL-613 25-35 55
Frankie Laine; Tony Bennett; Rosemary Clooney; Doris Day; Liberace; Percy Faith; Guy Mitchell; Buddy Clark.

Treasure Tunes from the Vault (As Advertised on WLS)..Chess (M) LP-1474 20-30 62
Kathy Young; Ritchie Valens; Clarence Henry; Fiestas; Maurice Williams & Zodiacs; Chuck Berry; Tokens; Sammy Turner; Barrett Strong; Crescendos; Monotones; Lee Andrews & Hearts. (Volume two is titled *Dance Tunes from the Vault.*)

Treasured Hits from the South Presented By Nick Adams..Stax (M) 702 10-20 66

Treasures of Love...Hall of Fame/Daydream (S) DD 1017 5-10 80
Clyde McPhatter; Gene Chandler; Maxine Brown; Chuck Jackson; Jimmy Jones.

Treasury of Great Original Hits...ABC/Dunhill (S) DS-50057 8-12 72
Mamas & Papas; Steppenwolf; Grass Roots; Three Dog Night; Barry McGuire; Richard Harris; Mama Cass. (May also be shown as *Treasury of Great Contemporary Hits*. Can be found with either of two covers, each with slight differences.)

Treasury of Great Contemporary Hits...Dunhill (S) DS-50057 10-15 69
Steppenwolf; Mamas & Papas; Grass Roots; Three Dog Night; Barry McGuire; Richard Harris; Mama Cass.

Treasury of Immortal Performances "Theme Songs"...RCA (M) LPT-1 20-30 50s
(10–inch LP.) Charlie Barnet; Lionel Hampton; Louis Armstrong; Duke Ellington; Benny Goodman; Artie Shaw.

Tribute to Billy Joel: see JOEL, Billy

Tribute to Burt Bacharach .... Scepter (S) SPS-5100 10-15 72
Jerry Butler; Bobby Vinton; Jackie DeShannon; Chuck Jackson; Shirelles; Dionne Warwicke; Gene Pitney; Dusty Springfield; B.J. Thomas; Timi Yuro.

Tribute to Woody Guthrie, Part 1 .... Columbia (S) KC-31171 10-15 72
Arlo Guthrie; Odetta; Pete Seeger; Bob Dylan; others.

Tribute to Woody Guthrie, Part 2 (2 LP) .... Columbia (S) B2 586 10-15 72
Judy Collins; Odetta; Jack Elliot; others.

Tribute to Woody Guthrie, Parts 1 & 2 (2 LP) .... Warner Bros. (S) 2W-3007 8-12 77
Arlo Guthrie; Will Geer; Odetta; Bob Dylan; Pete Seeger; Tom Paxton; Joan Baez; Jack Elliott; others.

Triple Hit Preview for Billboard Readers: see Capitol Promotional Releases/Samplers

Truck and Country .... Nashville (SE) NLP-2066 5-10 69
Ray King; Red Sovine; Merle Kilgore; others.

Truck Driver Songs .... King (M) 866 20-25 63

Truck Driver Songs .... King (S) KS-866 20-25 63
Tommy Downs; Bob Newman; Swanee Caldwell; Coleman Wilson; Cowboy Jack Derrick; Charlie Moore; Bill Napier; Jimmy Logsdon.

Truck Driver's Queen .... Nashville (SE) NLP-2075 5-10 70
Moore & Napier; Jimmy Logsdon; Reno & Smiley.

Truck Drivin' Man .... Nashville (M) NLP 2034 5-10
Hylo Brown; Joe & Rose Lee Maphis; Willis Brothers; Tommy Hill's String Band; Johnny Bond; Red Sovine; Betty Amos; Benny Martin; Frankie Miller.

Truck Drivin' Son of a Gun .... Nashville (SE) NLP-2082 5-10 70
Red Sovine; Willis Bros.; George Morgan; others.

Truck Driving Hits .... Exact (S) EX211 5-10 80
Dave Dudley; Kenny Price; Del Reeves; Red Simpson; Willis Brothers.

Truck Stop .... Nashville (SE) NLP-2052 8-12
Tom O'Neal; Frankie Miller; Joe Maphis; Benny Martin; Lonnie Irving; Willis Brothers; Red Sovine; Johnny Bond; George Morgan.

Truck Stop Favorites .... Starday/Power Pak (S) PO 298 5-10 77
Dave Dudley; Johnny Bond; Dollly Parton; Cowboy Copas; Slim Jacobs; Willis Brothers; Red Sovine; Dottie West; Johnny Paycheck; George Morgan.

Truck Stop Favorites .... Nashville (SE) NLP-2096 8-12 71
Dave Dudley; Johnny Bond; Cowboy Copas; others.

Truckin' On, Speed Limit 55 (2 LP) .... Capitol (S) SLB-8016 5-10 76
Merle Haggard; Dick Curless; Dave Dudley; Red Simpson; Glen Campbell; C.W. McCall; Kenny Price; Roy Drusky; George Hamilton IV; Red Sovine; Freddie Hart; Willis Brothers; Cledus Maggard & Citizens Band.

Truth of Truths - A Contemporary Rock Opera .... Oak (S) 1001 8-12 71
Jim Backus; Donnie Brooks; others.

Tuff Turf .... Rhino (S) RNSP-308 8-10 85
(Soundtrack.) Southside Johnny; Jim Carroll Band; Jack Mack & Heart Attack; Lene Lovich; Marianne Faithfull; Dale Gnyea with J.R. & 2-Men.

Tulsa Sampler (2 LP) .... Pilgrim (S) No Number Used 10-20 77
Tulsa; Harry Tucker; Sonny Landreth; Jim Byfield; El Roacho; Guava & Witt Richmond; Jim Sweeney; others.

Tumbleweed Records Sampler .... Tumbleweed (S) ???? 8-12 72

Tunes for Teens .... Decca (M) DL-34441 20-30 65
(Promotional issue only.) Brenda Lee; Bobbie Martin; Spokesmen; Len Barry; Surfaris.

Tunes to Be Remembered .... Excello (M) 8001 30-40 61
Crescendos; Gladiolas; Arthur Gunter; Warren Storm; Skippy Brooks Combo; Ray Norman; Kid King's Combo; Marigolds; Guitar Gable; Slim Harpo; Jimmy Beck.

Tupperware Home Parties .... Tupperware (EP) THP-11973 50-75 73
Elvis Presley; Johnnie Ray; Bobby Darin; Chordettes; Georgia Gibbs; Ernest Tubb. (Special products. Made for Tupperware.)

Turn Back the Clock .... King (M) 859 20-30 64

Turn Back the Clock .... King (SE) KS-859 20-30 64
Memphis Slim; Lonnie Johnson; Pete Lewis; others.

Turn Back the Hands of Time (2 LP) .... RCA/Brookville (SP) PRS-395 8-12 72
(Mail order offer.) Eddie Fisher; Ray Peterson; Ames Brothers; Browns; Hugo Winterhalter; Eddy Arnold; Kay Starr; Neil Sedaka; Eddie Heywood; Joe Valino; June Valli; Mickey & Sylvia; Paul Anka; Jaye P. Morgan; Sam Cooke; Perez Prado; Della Reese; Ernest Gold. (Special products. Made for Brookville.)

Twins .... WTG (S) SP-45036 8-10 88
(Soundtrack.) Bobby McFerrin; Herbie Hancock; 2 Live Crew; Nicolette Larson; Jeff Beck; Terry Bozzio; Tony Hymas; Philip Bailey; Little Richard; Nayobe; Henry Lee Summer; Marilyn Scott; Spinners; Andrew Roachford; Peter Richardson.

Twist Around .... King (M) 771 20-25 62
James Brown; Henry Moore; others. (Repackage of *Night Train*.)

Twist to Radio KRLA: see KEENE, Bob

Twist with the Stars .... Mercury (M) MG-20687 15-25 62

Twist with the Stars .... Mercury (S) SR-60687 20-30 62
Platters; Patti Page; Brook Benton; Quincy Jones; Dinah Washington; Johnny Preston; David Carroll; Billy Eckstine; Richard Hayman; Clyde McPhatter; Tom & Jerry; Damita Jo.

Twistin' All Night Long .... Swan (M) 506 25-35 62
Danny & Juniors; Freddy Cannon; Dicky Doo & Don'ts; Unique Echoes; Frank Slay.

Twistin' Time .... Era (S) PBU 5050 5-10 82
Chubby Checker; Joey Dee & Starliters; Hank Ballard & Midnighters; Dee Dee Sharp; Dovells; Bobby Freeman.

Two Dozen Oldies: see Jocko Presents Two Dozen Oldies

Two in Blues: see BLAND, Bobby / Johnny Guitar Watson

Two of a Kind .... MCA (S) 6127 8-10 83
(Soundtrack.) Olivia Newton-John; John Travolta; Chicago; David Foster; Magness-Ballard; Steve Kipner; Boz Scaggs; Journey.

Two Rooms: Celebrating the Songs of Elton John & Bernie Taupin (2 LP) .... Polydor (S) P1-45750 8-10 91
Eric Clapton; Kate Bush; Sting; Who; Beach Boys; Wilson-Phillips; Joe Cocker; Jon Bon Jovi; Tina Turner; Hall & Oates; Rod Stewart; Oleta Adams; Bruce Hornsby; Sinead O'Connor; Phil Collins & Serious Band; George Michael.

Two Trips .... Mercury (S) SR-61273 10-15 71

Ultimate Party Album (3 LP) .... Warner Special Products (S) 4541 10-15 92
Chic; Blondie; Gap Band; Laura Branigan; Peaches & Herb; Rick James; Pointer Sisters; Trammps; Evelyn Champaign King; Frankie Valli; Bonnie Pointer; Andy Gibb; Yvonne Elliman; Donna Summer.

Ultimate Radio Bootleg - Southeast Edition .... Mercury (S)MK-106 15-25 79
Q Brothers; Southside Johnny; Carolyne Mas; Bob Sherwood; Jim Jeffries; John Long; Rusty Black.

Ultimate Radio Bootleg, Vol. 1 .... Mercury (S) ???? 15-25 79

Ultimate Radio Bootleg, Vol. 2 .... Mercury (S) ???? 15-25 79

Ultimate Radio Bootleg, Vol. 3 .... Mercury (S) MK2-121 20-30 79
Beatles (interview); others

Unavailable 16 Hits of Yesteryear .... Vee Jay (M) VJLP-1051 20-30 62
Moonglows; 5 Echos; Tony Bellus; Impressions; Orchids; Delegates; Quintones; Harold Dorman; Ray Smith; Dells; Rosie & Originals; Magnificents; Flamingos; El Dorados.

Under Cover .... Enigma (S) SJ-73276 10-15 87
(Soundtrack.) Wednesday Week; T.S.O.L.; Todd Rundgren; Agent Orange; Passionnel.

Under Current .... Epic (S) E-30236 8-12 70
Donovan; Sly & Family Stone; Poco; Hollies; Spirit; Catfish; Argent; Shuggie Otis; Edgar Winter; Jeff Beck; Redbone.

Under the Boardwalk .... Enigma (S) D1-73234 8-10 88
(Soundtrack.) Untouchables; Surf Punks; Surf MC's; Del-Lords; Ike Willis; Smithereens; Broadcasters; Wednesday Week; Drifters.

Underground .... Tower (S) ST-5168 10-15 70
Pink Floyd; Chocolate Watchband; Jake Holmes; Them; Kim Fowley.

Underground Blues .... Kent (M) 535 10-20
Jimmy Reed; B.B. King; John Lee Hooker; Lightnin' Hopkins; Howlin' Wolf; Elmore James.

Underground Blues .... United (S) US-7754 10-20 70s
Jimmy Reed; B.B. King; John Lee Hooker; Lightnin' Hopkins; Howlin' Wolf; Elmore James.

Underground Gold .... Liberty (S) LST-7625 5-10 70s
Canned Heat; Traffic; Albert Collins; Spencer Davis Group; Jo-Anne Kelly; Johnny Winter.

Unforgettable (2 LP) .... Capitol (S) SLB-8024 8-12 60s
Acker Bilk; James Last; Stan Getz; Roger Williams; Platters; Sarah Vaughn; Jackie Gleason; Frank Chacsfield; Nat King Cole; Kai Winding; George Shearing; Dinah Washington; Mantovani; Lenny Welch; Bert Kaempfert; Al Hibbler; Matt Monro; Ketty Lester; Stan Getz & Astrud Gilberto; Ed Townsend.

Unforgettable Country Instrumentals .... Starday (M) S-277 15-20 64
Flatt & Scruggs; Curly Fox; Roy Wiggins; Shot Jackson; Thumbs Carlisle; Arthur "Guitar Boogie" Smith; Tommy Hill; Leon McAuliffe; Jackie Phelps; Buddy Emmons; Jerry Rivers.

Unforgettable Fifties, the .... Columbia Special Products (SE) P 14920 5-10 79
Four Lads; Guy Mitchell; Don Cherry; Terry Gilkyson & Easy Riders; Vic Damone; Johnnie Ray; Percy Faith; Mitch Miller; Patti Page.

Unforgettable Fifties (4 LP) .... Heartland (S) HL-1072/1073/1074 15-25 88
(Mail order offer.) Elvis Presley; Crew-Cuts; Perry Como; Eddie Fisher; Doris Day; Don Gibson; Ames Brothers; Nat King Cole; Jo Stafford; Perez Prado; Jim Reeves; Patti Page; Gogi Grant; Tennessee Ernie Ford; Johnny Mathis; Browns; Tony Bennett; Four Aces Featuring Al Alberts; Teresa Brewer; Roger Williams; Pat Boone; Debbie Reynolds; Red Foley; McGuire Sisters; Domenico Modugno; Rosemary Clooney; Pee Wee King; Mario Lanza; Dean Martin; Platters; Kay Starr; Eddy Arnold; Bobby Darin; Chordettes; Guy Mitchell; Sheb Wooley; Morris Stoloff; Leroy Anderson; Fontane Sisters; Kitty Kallen; Gordon Jenkins & Weavers.

Unforgettable Hits of the '40s and '50s (2 LP) .... Decca (S) R 214291 10-20
Woody Herman; Andrews Sisters; Judy Garland; Johnny Long; Bob Crosby; Jimmy Dorsey; Bing Crosby; Mills Brothers; Lionel Hampton; Judy Garland; Gene Kelly; Ted Weems; Gordon Jenkins; Dick Haymes; Russ Morgan; Evelyn Knight; Ray Bolger; Ethel Merman; Louis Armstrong; Guy Lombardo; Weavers.

Unforgettable Oldies .... Unart (M) 20014 10-15 68

Unforgettable Oldies .... Unart (S) 21014 10-15 68
Del Shannon; Volumes; Johnny & Hurricanes; Royaltones; Dream Girls; Johnny Gibson.

Unforgettable Oldies, Vol. 2 .... Unart (M) 20027 10-15 68

Unforgettable Oldies, Vol. 2 .... Unart (S) 21027 10-15 68
Spencer Davis Group; Jay & Americans; Bobby Goldsboro; Frankie Avalon; Mike Clifford; Easybeats.

United Artists Black Singles: 1959-1967 Motor City to Central Park .... EMI America (S) SQ-17266 8-12 87
Exciters; Garnet Mimms & Enchanters; Marv Johnson; Marcels; Isley Brothers; Falcons; Eddie Holland; Clovers; Bill Pinkney & Originals; Five Satins; Little Anthony & Imperials. (Treasury Series.)

United Artists Jazz Sampler .... United Artists (M) UA-91 20-30 62
Herbie Mann; Oliver Nelson; Jerome Richardson; Doug Small; Billie Holiday; Lloyd Mayers; Bill Evans & Jim Hall; Art Blakey & His Jazz Messengers.

United Artists Strings Attached .... United Artists ???? 15-25
Shirley Bassey; Robert Thomas; Velline; Bobby Goldsboro; James Bond; Tommy Garrett; Corvells; Meadowlarks; Medallions; Bel-Larks; Cufflinks; Pyramids; Excellents; Del-Vikings.

United States Air Force Presents Country Music Time (7 LP) .... Series (S) 37 25-35 76
(Boxed set.) Johnny Russell; Leona Williams; Mac Wiseman; Jean Shepard; Charlie McCoy; Ed Bruce; Ronnie Prophet; Rusty Adams; Charlie McCoy; Carl Perkins; Mel Street; Ruby Falls; Sue Richards; Leroy Van Dyke; Wilburn Brothers; Mickey Gilley; Karen Wheeler; Nat Stuckey, others.

Unreleased Gems of the '50s (The Hartford Groups) .... Relic (M) 5085 5-10 90
Henry Hall & Five Bell Aires; Gene Pitney & Embers; Larry Lee & Embers; Larry Lee & Sereneders; John Hall & Five Bell Aires.

Unreleased Vaults of Lou Chicchetti & Cousin Records .... Crystal Ball (S) 124 8-10 87
Darnell & Dreams; Regents; Runarounds; Dials; Ruteens; Bi Tones; Orientals; Excellents; Teardrops.

Unsigned, Vol. 2 .... Epic (S) BFE-40842 5-10 87
Green; New Salem Witch Hunters; Worms; Three Hits; Slab Fashion; Velez Manifesto; Paul Chastain; Big Noise; Basics.

Unstoppables! .... Verve (M) PM-18 15-25
Charlie Parker; Gerry Mulligan; Sam Taylor; Count Basie; George Shearing; Dizzy Gillespie; Harry James; Oscar Peterson; Al Hirt; Pete Fountain; Cal Tjader; Woody Herman.

Unto the Lord .... Modern Sound (S) MS-804 8-12
Sego Brothers & Naomi; McCormick Singers; Sunshine Girls; Wally Fowler & Oak Ridge Quartet; Georgians; Florida Boys; Dixie Echoes; Foggy River Boys; Sons of Song.

Up the Academy .... Capitol (S) SOO-12091 10-15 80
(Soundtrack.) Blondie; Ian Hunter; Babys; Blow-Up; Jonathan Richman & Modern Lovers; Cheeks; Pat Benatar; Sammy Hagar.

Uptight on Fifth Ave. .... Columbia Special Products (S) CSS-789 10-15

Cyrkle; Paul Revere & Raiders Featuring Mark Lindsay; Aretha Franklin; Gary Puckett & Union Gap; Buckinghams; Wilson Pickett; Archie Bell & Drells; Ramsey Lewis; Percy Sledge; Tommy James & Shondells. (Special products. Made for 5th Avenue Candy.)

Urban Cowboy (2 LP) .... Asylum (S) DP-90002 8-15 80

(Soundtrack. Includes poster.) Jimmy Buffett; Joe Walsh; Dan Fogelberg; Bob Seger & Silver Bullet Band; Mickey Gilley; Johnny Lee; Anne Murray; Eagles; Bonnie Raitt; Charlie Daniels Band; Gilley's Urban Cowboy Band; Kenny Rogers; Boz Scaggs; Linda Ronstadt; John David Souther.

Urban Cowboy 2 .... Full Moon/Epic (S) SE-36921 8-10 80

(Soundtrack.) Bayou City Beats; Charlie Daniels Band; Mickey Gilley; Johnny Lee; J.D. Souther.

Urgh! A Music War (2 LP) .... A&M (S) SP-6019 10-15 81

(Soundtrack.) Police; Go-Go's; Devo; Joan Jett & Blackhearts; Alley Cats; Klaus Nomi; Members; XTC; Pere Ubu; Gang of Four; Steel Pulse; Jools Holland; X; 999; Magazine; Skafish; John Otway; Cramps; Athletico Spizz 80; Toyah Wilcox; Wall of Voodoo; Fleshtones; Au Pairs; Echo & Bunnymen; Orchestral Manoeuvres in the Dark; Oingo Boingo; Members; Gary Numan.

Valley Girl .... Epic (M) FE 38623 50-75 83

(Soundtrack. Five tracks from the film. Promotional issue only.)

Valley Girl .... Roadshow (S) RS-101 50-150 83

(Soundtrack.) Bonnie Hayes with the Wild Combo; Sparks; Josie Cotton; Plimsouls. (Six track mini-album. Recalled shortly after production.)

Valley Rock, Z-95 WZZO .... TDK (S) RTR-8257 8-12

Crisis; Daddy Licks; Kings & Queens; Tentatine Relationship; Dee Hart; G Rox Band; Serpent Bullet; Limits; Home Brew Band.

Vanishing Point .... Amos (S) AAS-8002 15-20 71

(Soundtrack.) Jerry Reed; Mountain; Delaney & Bonnie & Friends; J.B. Pickers; Jimmy Walker; Bobby Doyle; Big Mama Thornton; Doug Dillard Expedition; Segarini & Bishop; Eve, Kim & Dave; Jimmy Bowen.

Variety of Country Sacred Songs .... Audio Lab (M) 1557 15-25 60

Brother Claude Ely; Trace Family Trio; others.

Various Country Artists, Vol. 1 .... Dot (S) 3700 10-15 66

Johnny Bond; Cowboy Copas; Hank Garland; others.

Various Country Artists, Vol. 2 .... Dot (M) 3701 10-15 66

Lonzo & Oscar; Bob Lamm; Big Jeff; others.

Various Country Artists, Vol. 3 .... Dot (M) 3702 10-15 66

Mac Wiseman; Tommy Jackson; Roy Wiggins; others.

Various Country Artists, Vol. 4 .... Dot (M) 3703 10-15 66

Joe Allison; Tennessee Drifters; Joe Claire; others.

Velvet Soul .... Prestige (M) PR-7320 15-20 65

Velvet Soul .... Prestige (S) PRS-7320 20-25 65

Gene Ammons; Frank Wess; others.

Verve Disc Jockey Copy (Vol. 1) .... Verve (M) DJ V-1 20-30 57

Verve Disc Jockey Copy (Vol. 2) .... Verve (M) DJ V-2 20-30 57

Verve Disc Jockey Copy (Vol. 3) .... Verve (M) DJ V-3 20-30 57

Ella Fitzgerald; Rudi Vannelli; Jane Powell Charlie Barnet; Benny Carter; Blossom Dearie; Peter Lawford; Joan Holloway; Buster Davis Choir; Anita O'Day; Art Tatum; Benny Carter; Louis Bellson; Dizzy Gillespie; Django Reinhardt; Tal Farlow; Lionel Hampton; Stan Getz; Harry Edison.

Verve Disc Jockey Copy (Vol. 4) .... Verve (M) DJ V-4 20-30 57

Tal Farlow; Bud Powell; Howard Roberts; Count Basie; Art Tatum Trio; Stan Getz; Johnny hodges; Stuff Smith; Woody Herman; Freddy Morgan; Polka Dots Starring Ole Svenson; Josephine Premice; Spike Jones; Bill Thompson Singers; Conrad Salinger; Rose Murphy.

Very Best of Country (2 LP) .... Columbia House (S) DS 907-6 8-12 72

(Same contents as item below, P2S 5706.)

Very Best of Country (2 LP) .... Columbia House (S) P2S 5706 8-12 72

(Columbia House Record Club issue.) Roger Miller; Lynn Anderson; Freddy Weller; Stonewall Jackson; David Houston; Ray Price; Jeannie C. Riley; Barbara Mandrell; Statler Brothers; Billy Walker; Claude King; Johnny Horton; Lefty Frizzell; Tom T. Hall; Johnny Cash; Marty Robbins; George Jones; Tammy Wynette.

Very Best of Country (2 LP) .... Columbia House (S) P2S 5643 8-12 72

(Columbia House Record Club issue.) Roger Miller; Lynn Anderson; Dave Dudley; Freddy Weller; Stonewall Jackson; David Houston; Jimmy Dean; Ray Price; Jeannie C. Riley; David Houston; Barbara Mandrell; Statler Brothers; Flatt & Scruggs; Ian & Sylvia; Billy Walker; Harden Trio; George Jones; Tammy Wynette; Claude King; Johnny Horton; Lefty Frizzell; Tom T. Hall; Johnny Cash; Marty Robbins; Carl Butler; Shel Silverstein.

Very Best of Country Banjo .... United Artists LA 411 10-15 75

Jim McGuinn; Cheatwood; Mike Seeger; Dick Rosmini; Billy Faier; Joe Maphis; Dick Weisman; David Lindley; Mason Williams.

Very Best of Country Gold .... United Artists (S) UA-LA413-E 5-10 75

Willie Nelson; Johnny Cash; Jerry Wallace; Slim Whitman; others.

Very Best of the Big Bands .... MGM (M) E-4219 10-15 64

Very Best of the Big Bands .... MGM (S) SE-4219 10-20 64

Very Best of the Oldies .... Del-Fi (M) DF-1227 30-40 63

Ritchie Valens; Jesse Belvin; Rochell & Candles; Etta James; Ron Holden; Marvin & Johnny; Big Jay McNeely; Pentagons; Cadets; B.B. King; Little Caesar & Romans; Teen Queens; Jacks.

Very Best of the Oldies, Vol. 1 .... United Artists (M) UA-LA256-G 5-10 75

Shirley & Lee; Bobby Hendricks; Marv Johnson; Jesse Hill; Thurston Harris; Falcons; Clovers; Ernie K-Doe; Inez & Charlie Foxx; Phil Upchurch; Barbara George; Garnet Mimms & Enchanters.

Very Best of the Oldies, Vol. 2 .... United Artists (M) UA-LA335-E 5-10 75

Showmen; Benny Spellman; Marv Johnson; Majors; Rivingtons; Shirley & Lee; Dick & DeeDee; Exciters; Gene & Eunice; Ike & Tina Turner.

Very Best of the Oldies, Vol. 3 .... United Artists (M) UA-LA384-E 5-10 74

Very Best of the Oldies, Vol. 3 .... United Artists (S) UA-LA517-E 5-10 75

Shirley & Lee; Falcons; Clovers; Jesse Hill; Ernie K-Doe; Silhouettes; Turbans; Five Satins; Lee Andrews & Hearts; Fireflies; Jerry Lee Lewis; Larry Williams; Claudine Clark; Thurston Harris.

Very Best of the Oldies, Vol. 4 (The Instrumentals) .... United Artists (M) UA-LA518-E 5-10 75

Lonnie Mack; Johnny & Hurricanes; Bill Justis; Cozy Cole; Duals; Ventures; Sandy Nelson; Busters; Lee Allen.

Very Merry Christmas .... Columbia Special Products (SE) CSS-563 10-15 60s

Ray Conniff; Jimmy Dean; Patti Page; Simon & Garfunkel; Johnny Mathis; Jimmy Rodgers; Theodore Bikel; Andre Kostelanetz; Pennywhistlers; Mike Douglas; E. Power Biggs; Burl Ives; Percy Faith; Andre Previn; Bobby Vinton; Mormon Tabernacle Choir; Eugene Ormandy & Philadelphia Orchestra. (Special products for Grants.)

Very Merry Christmas, Vol. 2 .... Columbia Special Products (SE) CSS-788 10-15

Mitch Miller; Robert Goulet; Anita Bryant; Andre Kostelanetz; Steve Lawrence; Mahalia Jackson; New Christy Minstrels; Jim Nabors; Doris Day; Johnny Mathis; Skitch Henderson; Johnny Cash; Eydie Gorme; Bing Crosby; Mormon Tabernacle Choir with Richard Condie; Leonard Bernstein & New York Philharmonic. (Special products for Grants.)

Very Merry Christmas, Vol. 3 .... Columbia Special Products (SE) CSS-997 10-15

Robert Goulet; Leslie Uggams; Percy Faith; Johnny Mathis; Ray Conniff; Jim Nabors; Andre Kostelanetz; Cary Grant; Eugene Ormandy & Philadelphia Orchestra; Burl Ives; Mahalia Jackson; Ed Sullivan; Diahann Carroll; Mitch Miller; Bobby Vinton. (Made for Grants.)

Very Merry Christmas, Vol. 4 .... Columbia Special Products (SE) CSS-1464 10-15

Steve Lawrence; Eydie Gorme; Gary Puckett; Arthur Fiedler & Boston Pops; Mark Lindsay; Mel Torme; Barbra Streisand; Johnny Cash; Tony Bennett; Aretha Franklin; Bing Crosby; Julie Andrews; Peter Nero. (Special products for Grants.)

Very Special Christmas, A .... A&M (S) SP-3911 8-12 87

U2; Bruce Springsteen; Madonna; Bob Seger; Pointer Sisters; Whitney Houston; Pretenders; John Cougar Mellancamp; Sting; Bryan Adams; Bon Jovi; Alison Moyet; Stevie Nicks.

Very Special Love Songs (3 LP) .... ???? 10-15

Charlie Rich; Jody Miller; Jud Strunk; Tom T. Hall; Donna Fargo; Sonny James; Johnny Cash; June Carter; Jerry Reed; Jerry Lee Lewis; Barbara Fairchild; David Houston; Lynn Anderson; Roy Clark; Mac Davis; Earl Scruggs; Marty Robbins; Jim Nabors; Tammy Wynette; George Jones; Johnny Paycheck; Tanya Tucker; Jimmy Dean; Roger Miller; Anita Bryant.

Viceroy Cigarettes "Campus Jazz Festival": see Campus Jazz Festival.

Victory in Review .... London (M) SP-44024 5-10

Vintage Music - Collectors Series, Vol. 4 .... MCA (S) 1432 5-10 87

Chuck Berry; Poni-Tails; Students; Sparkletones; Royal Teens; Buddy Holly & Crickets; Bo Diddley; Fontane Sisters; Lloyd Price; Pastels.

Vintage Music - Collectors Series, Vol. 11 .... MCA (S) 25120 5-10 87

Bill Haley & His Comets; Dells; Chuck Berry; Dartells; Robin Ward; Grass Roots; Impressions; Rumblers; Brenda Lee; Four Knights.

Vintage Music - Collectors Series, Vol. 14 .... MCA (S) 25123 5-10 87

Pat Boone; Demensions; Al Hibbler; Big Mama Thornton; Shirelles; Billy Vaughn; Jerry Keller; Dells; Elegants; Little Richard.

Vintage Music - Collectors Series, Vol. 17 .... MCA (S) 25126 5-10 87

Tyrones; Bill Haley & His Comets; Pat Boone; Danny & Juniors; Critters; Patsy Cline; Sanford Clark; Impressions; Brenda Lee; Bo Diddley.

Vintage Rock (6 LP) .... Columbia (S) 6P 7229 20-30 81

(Boxed set. Columbia Record Club issue.) Jewel Akens; Len Barry; Pat Boone; Brothers Four; Buckinghams; Jerry Butler; Byrds; Capitols; Cascades; Gene Chandler; Ray Charles Singers; Chubby Checker; Chiffons; Classics IV; Claudine Clark; Dee Clark; Jimmy Dean; Dick & DeeDee; Dion; Dovells; Essex; Betty Everett; Bobby Fuller Four; Eddie Hodges; Hollies; Hollywood Argyles; Eddie Holman; Tommy James & Shondells; Major Lance; Ketty Lester; Lovin' Spoonful; Mamas & Papas; Chris Montez; Newbeats; O'Kaysions; Orlons; Outsiders; Peaches & Herb; Gary Puckett & Union Gap; Tommy Roe; Billy Joe Royal; Royal Guardsmen; Ruby & Romantics; Dee Dee Sharp; Sly & Family Stone; Smith; Statler Brothers; Steppenwolf; Strawberry Alarm Clock; Sue Thompson; Three Dog Night; Johnny Tillotson; Tymes; Bobby Vee; Larry Verne; Bobby Vinton; Vogues; Lenny Welch; Timi Yuro.

Vision Quest .... Geffen (S) GHS-24063 8-10 85

(Soundtrack.) Journey; Style Council; Madonna; Don Henley; Dio; John Waite; Red Rider; Sammy Hagar; Foreigner.

Viva! .... Capitol Creative Products (S) SL-6650 8-12 60s

Billy May; Ray Anthony; Sounds of Our Times; Joe Leahy; Guy Lombardo; Sergio Mendes.

Vocal Group Album (2 LP) .... Savoy (M) SJL-2241 8-12 79

Three Barons; Toppers; Syncopators; Four Buddies; Marshall Brothers; Carols; Dreams; Little David & Harps; Jimmy Jones & Savoys; Tiny Grimes; Steve Gibson; Dolly Cooper; Sam Taylor; Mickey Baker.

Vocal Groups 1940s and 1950s .... Yorkshire (M) 782 8-12

Striders; Larks; Billy Bunn & Buddies; Clan-Tones; Virginia Four; Four Vagabonds; Blendres; Four Knights; Savannah Churchill & Striders.

Vocally Speaking .... Columbia Special Products (S) CSS 1338 5-10 70s

Johnny Mathis; Andy Williams; Ray Conniff; John Davidson; New Christy Minstrels.

Voice of the Blues - Bottle Guitar Masterpieces .... Yazoo (M) L-1046 8-10

Barbecue Bob; Georgia Browns; Rambling Thomas; Tampa Kid; Hokum Boys; Too Bad Boys; Sister O.M Terrell; Sam Butler; Oscar "Buddy" Woods; Roy Smeck; Irene Scruggs; Jimmie Davis; Blind Willie Davis; Georgia Cotton Pickers.

Voices of the Civil Rights Movement (1960-1966) (3 LP) .... Smithsonian Collection R 023 10-15 80

(Boxed set with 24-page booklet.) SNCC Freedom Singers; Betty Mae Fikes; Willie Peacock; Hollis Watkins; Amanda Bowens Perdew & Virginia Davis; Fannie Lou Hamer; Integration Grooves; CORE Freedom Singers; Alabama Christian Movement Choir; Jimmy Collier & Movement Singers; Cleo Kennedy; Sam Block; Mabel Hillary; Matthew Jones; Cordell Reagon; Rev. Lawrence Campbell; Bertha Gober; Carlton Reese; Bernice Johnson.

Volunteer Jam .... Capricorn (S) CP-0172 5-10 76

Charlie Daniels Band; Marshall Tucker Band; Dicky Betts; Jimmy Hall; Chuck Leavell.

Volunteer Jam 6 .... Epic (S) 36438 5-10 80

Ted Nugent; Wet Willie; Crystal Gayle; others.

Volunteer Jam 7 .... Epic (S) 37178 5-10 81

WAMO's Golden Gassers (Porky Chedwick) .... Chess (M) LP-1458 30-40 61

Robert & Johnny; Moonglows; Students; Flamingos; Monotones; Tune Weavers; Billy Bland; Johnnie & Joe; Lee Andrews & Hearts. (Also issued as *Golden Gassers*.)

W.A.R.M. Land .... Eric (S) SLP 590 8-12 71

Leer Brothers Band; Underground Sunshine; Shocking Blue; Tommy James & Shondells; Association; Terry Stafford; Freddie Scott; Paris Sisters; Dixie Cups; Dee Clark; Betty Everett & Jerry Butler; Wilbert Harrison; Ritchie Valens; Crests; Claudine Clark.

WBAB 102.3 .... PRI (S) 785 20-25

(Promotional picture disc.)

WBLI Gold Rush (2 LP) .... Custom Fidelity (S) CFS 3268/3269 8-12

Cadets; Dells; Dubs; Little Caesar & Romans; Gene Chandler; Dee Clark; Ritchie Valens; Jerry Butler; Chris Kenner; Fendermen; Cleftones; Chantels; Little Richard; Jack Scott; Ron Holden & Thunderbirds; Lee Dorsey; Wilbert Harrison; Betty Everett; Jimmy Charles; Bobby Freeman; Jive Five; Bobby Lewis; Joe Jones; Olympics; Capris; Playmates; Joey Dee & Starliters; Paul Evans & Curls; Don Gardner & Dee Dee Ford.

WCAU-FM Presents Old Gold from the Fabulous '50s .... WCAU (S) OLD-1001 10-15 70s

Frankie Lymon & Teenagers; Platters; Shields; Johnnie & Joe; Chantels; Olympics; Diamonds; Tommy Edwards; Dion & Belmonts; Chuck Berry; Five Satins; Skyliners; Little Richard; Robert & Johnny; Drifters.

WCBS 101 FM History of Rock - the Doo Wop Ear (2 LP) .... Collectables (S) COL-2507 5-10 82

Capris; Paragons; Lewis Lymon & Teenchords; Passions; Collegians; Kodaks; Dion & Belmonts; Mello Kings; Rainbows; Students; Little Bobby Rivera & Hemlocks; Channels; Five Discs; Shells; Eternals; Chimes; Videos; Excellents; Edsels; Bop Chords; Mystics; Charts; Pyramids; Classics.

WCBS 101 FM History of Rock .... Collectables (S) PDR2-2500 5-10 82

(Promotional, double picture disc set.)

WCBS 101 FM History of Rock - the '60s, Part 2 (2 LP) .... Collectables (S) Col 2501 10-15 80s
Brooklyn Bridge; Music Explosion; Casinos; Ad Libs; Little Anthony & Imperials; Soul Survivors; Jay & Americans; Lovin' Spoonful; Turtles; Mercy; Shocking Blue; Archies; Chiffons; Beau Brummels; Shangri-Las; Outsiders; Dennis Yost & Classics IV; Dion; Five Americans; Aaron Neville; Swingin' Medallions; Tradewinds.

WCBS 101 FM History of Rock - the '60s, Part 4 (2 LP) .... Collectables (S) Col 2504 10-15 80s
Surfaris; Mamas & Papas; Dion; Angels; Tommy Roe; Troy Shondell; John Fred; Barry Mann; Vogues; Jewel Akens; Box Tops; American Breed; Marvelows; Passions; Jerry Butler; Len Barry; Chiffons; Brenton Wood; Jesters; Edsels; Dee Clark; Safaris.

WCBS 101 FM History of Rock - the '50s, Vol. 1 .... Lost-Nite (S) LNLP-5052 8-12
Dion & Belmonts; Elegants; Huey "Piano" Smith; Wilbert Harrison; Crests; Bill Haley & His Comets; Penguins; Harptones; Diamonds; Platters; Del-Vikings; Five Satins; Larry Williams; Dells; Buddy Holly; Mello-Kings; Big Bopper; Paragons; Danny & Juniors; Silhouettes; Tommy Edwards.

WCFL Double Gold (2 LP) .... Post (S) 10 10-20

WCFL Winter Gold: see Winter Gold

WDAS Charities Presents Soul Sounds .... Post (S) 661 8-12
Jackie Wilson; Ben E. King; Betty Everett; Alvin Cash; Billy Bland; Astors; Inez & Charlie Foxx; Shirelles; Falcons; Etta James; Five DuTones; Tom & Jerrio; Chuck Jackson; Rufus Thomas; Booker T. & MGs; Gladys Knight; Ikettes; Barbara Mason; Fiestas; Tommy Hunt; Jerry Butler; Vibrations.

WDGY Radio .... Del-Fi 1222 8-12 63/

WDRQ 93 FM .... Columbia (S) No Number Used 20-25 78
(Picture disc. Promotional issue only.) Boston; Ringo Starr; others.

WDRQ Detroit Graffiti .... Post (S) 7308 8-12
Rod Stewart; Curtis Mayfield; Climax; Sylvia; Focus; Surfaris; Coven; Elton John; Bobby Hebb; others.

WDVE Pittsburgh Rocks .... Nova (S) BMC-80102 10-15
Teaser; Good Neighbors Band; Wizard; Garden; Madhouse; Adam Michaels Band; Sugarcane; Arty Tedesco; Penn Central; Robbers Roost.

WEA Presents CD-4 Channel Discrete Demonstration Quadradisc .... WEA (Q) PR-186 8-12 73
(Promotional issue only.) Aretha Franklin; Bread; Doobie Brothers; Stardrive; Carly Simon; Seals & Crofts; Arlo Guthrie; Bette Midler; Spinners.

WEBN Album Project 2 .... WEBN (S) BFC-1002 10-20 77
Wheels; Meg Davis; Mad Anthony; Tom Martin; Paul Karoly; Nigel & Just Another Band; Essence; Coyote; Paul Patterson; Barb Kushner & Carefree Day; Marty McMullen.

WEBN Album Project 3 - Brute Force Cybernetics .... WEBN (S) 1003 10-20 78
Wheels; Venus; Fast Anny; Deno Koumoutros; Raisins; Danny Morgan; Meg Davis; Coyote; Early Music Consort; George Uetz; Barb Kushner; Michael C. Megler.

WEBN Album Project 9 - Made in the U.S.A. .... WEBN (S) No Number Used 8-12 86
Dave & One Ways; Modulators; Meg Davis; Rubber Soul; Allies; Voyage; Painter; Carp Brothers; Stevie G. & Westside Stompers; Hoodwink; Bill Gwynne; Fried Chicken Brothers.

WFIL-56 Summer Love .... Lost-Nite (S) LN-148 8-12
Shirley Ellis; Lenny Welch; Delphonics; Lettermen; Presidents; Magnificent Men; Billy Stewart; Ruby & Romantics; Osmonds; Bobbi Martin; Dawn; Five Man Electrical Band; Mitch Ryder; Melanie; Lobo; Bobby Bloom. (Also issued as *Greatest Summer of Your Life*.)

WFIL Famous 56 Music Power .... Lost-Nite (S) LP-133 8-12
Tommy James & Shondells; Robert Knight; Paris Sisters; Bill Deal; Johnny Nash; Bobby Comstock; Turtles; Jay & Techniques; Derek; Mel Carter; Gene & Debbie; Bob Kuban & In Men; Showstoppers; Ronnie & Hi Lites; Lemon Pipers; Tommy Roe; Capitols; Hugh Masekela.

WFIL 50th Anniversary — Golden Greats .... Lost-Nite (S) LN-146 8-12
Ides of March; Freda Payne; Peter, Paul & Mary; Edison Lighthouse; Classics IV; Jerry Butler; Van Morrison; Judy Collins; Doors; Robin Ward; Bread; Norman Greenbaum; Five Stairsteps; Daddy Dewdrop; Animals; Bells.

WFIL Getting It Together .... Lost-Nite (S) LP-140 8-12
Box Tops; Oliver; Vogues; Joe Jeffrey; Nazz; Cowsills; New Colony Six; Turtles; Shocking Blue; Brooklyn Bridge; Tommy James & Shondells; Andy Kim; Righteous Brothers; Classics IV; Surfaris; Little Anthony & Imperials.

WFIL History of Rock, the Fifties, Vol. 1 .... Lost-Nite (S) LP 5054 8-12 70s
Frankie Lymon & Teenagers; Five Satins; Del-Vikings; Diamonds; Jerry Lee Lewis; Jimmie Rodgers; Lloyd Price; Conway Twitty; Tommy Edwards; Ritchie Valens; Skyliners; Flamingos; Thurston Harris; Dubs; Lee Andrews & Hearts; Chantels; Tune Weavers; Chuck Berry; Silhouettes; Jerry Butler; Danleers; Crests; Little Anthony & Imperials; Monotones.

WFIL History of Rock, the Fifties, Vol. 2 (2 LP) .... Lost-Nite (S) LP 5055 8-12 70s
Bill Haley & His Comets; Platters; Frankie Ford; Fats Domino; Bobby Day; Jesse Belvin; Buddy Holly; Penguins; Carl Perkins; Jackie Wilson; Shields; Bill Doggett; Big Bopper; Teen Queens; Huey "Piano" Smith; Shirley & Lee; Fleetwoods; Wilbert Harrison; Dion & Belmonts; Del-Vikings; Bobby Helms; Jerry Lee Lewis; Impalas; Everly Brothers.

WFIL History of Rock, the Fifties, Vol. 3 (2 LP) .... Lost-Nite (S) LP 5056 8-12 70s
Johnny Ace; El Dorados; Nutmegs; Willows; Platters; Spaniels; Sonny James; Dells; George Hamilton IV; Tommy Sands; Ferlin Husky; Charts; Paul Anka; Lee Andrews & Hearts; Mello-Kings; Danny & Juniors; Five Satins; Ritchie Valens; Elegants; Videos; Phil Phillips; Lloyd Price; Capris; Sarah Vaughan.

WFIL Non Stop Music .... Lost-Nite (S) LP-142 8-12
Steam; Jaggerz; Association; Tommy James & Shondells; Gerry & Pacemakers; Vanity Fair; Neil Diamond; Tommy Roe; Foundations; Intruders; Flaming Embers; Royalettes; John Fred; Toys; Box Tops; Delfonics.

WFIL Pop Oldies Explosion, Vol. 1 .... Lost-Nite (S) LP-120 8-12 60s
Curtis Lee; Shangri-Las; Don & Juan; Chiffons; Ronny & Daytonas; Shirelles; Tymes; Dixie Cups; Jackie Lee; Fontella Bass; Velvets; Dovells; Dion; Billy Stewart; Del Shannon; Gene Chandler; Isley Brothers; Reflections; Little Caesar & Romans; Orlons; Ad Libs; J. Frank Wilson.

WFIL Pop Oldies Explosion, Vol. 2 .... Lost-Nite (S) LP-127 8-12 60s
McCoys; Shangri-Las; Cascades; Jaynetts; Rockin' Rebels; Shondells; Chiffons; Happenings; Sir Douglas Quintet; ? & Mysterians; Slim Harpo; Marcels; B.J. Thomas; Larks; Strangeloves; Del Shannon; Barry McGuire; Freddie Scott; Syndicate Iof Sound; Trashmen; Shades of Blue; Castaways.

WFIL Pop Oldies Explosion, Vol. 3 .... Lost-Nite (S) LP-131 8-12 60s
Association; Soul Survivors; Casinos; Eddie Floyd; Deon Jackson; Otis Redding; Jimmy Jones; Count Five; Newbeats; Sam & Dave; Billy Stewart; Bob Lind; Everly Brothers; Jellybeans; Lovin' Spoonful; Five Americans; Bobby Fuller Four.

WFIL Rockin' in the Cradle of Liberty .... WFIL (S) WC-56 10-15 73
(Promotional issue only.) George McCrae; First Class; Major Harris; Love Unlimited Orchestra; Terry Jacks; Jim Stafford; Helenn Reddy; Bobby Womack; Tony Orlando & Dawn; Maria Muldaur; Bo Donaldson & Heywoods; Gladys Knight & Pips; Steve Miller; Al Green; Spinners.

WFUN Son of 21 Golden Rocks .... Take 6 (S) 2013 8-12 67
Birdwatchers; Clefs of Lavender Hill; others.

WFYR, Another Time, Another Place .... Vee Jay Special Products (S) CFS-3355 8-12 73

Big Bopper; Freddy Cannon; Angels; Bobby Lewis; Jerry Lee Lewis; Wilbert Harrison; Joey Dee & Starliters; Fats Domino; Platters; Flamingos; Jimmy Charles; Capris; Dickey Lee; Rosie & Originals.

WGH Authenic Virginia Gold 1310 .... (S) No Number Used 8-12
Cannibal & Headhunters; Bill Deal; Five Americans; Aaron Neville; Beau Brummels; Brenton Wood; B.J. Thomas; Jeannie C. Riley; Strawberry Alarm Clock; Soul Survivors; Bobby Moore & Rhythm Aces; ? & Mysterians; Jackie Lee; Shadows of Knight; James Brown; Robert Parker; Freddie Scott; Happenings; Association; Count Five; Bob Marshall & Crystals.

WHBQ .... Columbia (S) No Number Used 20-25 78
(Picture disc. Promotional issue only.) Boston; Ringo Starr; others.

WIBG 22 Big Hits .... Post (S) 22 8-12 70s
O'Kaysions; Bill Deal; 1910 Fruit Gum Company; Johnny Nash; Jamo Thomas; Bubble Puppy; James Brown; Bobby Fuller Four; Jay & Techniques; Brenton Wood; Harpers Bizarre; Tommy James & Shondells; Ronnie & Hi-Lites; Duprees; Dells; Jimmy Charles; Tymes; Lemon Pipers; Freddie Scott; Shelley Fabares; Jerry Butler; Roger Williams.

WILD's Choice R&B Oldies .... Bonded (S) B 777 8-12
Wilbert Harrison; Teen Chords; Dubs; Dee Clark; Shells; etc.

WIXY 1260, Super Oldies .... Post (S) No Number Used 10-15 70s
Association; Tommy Roe; Tony Joe White; O'Kaysions; Bubble Puppy; Peppermint Rainbow; Winstons; Shockng Blue; Cowsills; Turtles; Delfonics; Animals; Hugh Masekela; Alive 'N Kicking; Oliver; Joe Jeffries; Classics IV; Tommy James & Shondells; Deep Purple; Bill Deal; Merrilee Rush; Flying Machine; Canned Heat; Righteous Brothers; Box Tops; Brooklyn Bridge; Mamas & Papas; Strawberry Alarm Clock; Lemon Pipers; Freda Payne.

WIXY 21 Super Oldies, Vol. 2 .... Take 6 (S) S-2014 5-10
Association; Five Americans; Sir Douglas Quintet; McCoys, Cannibal & Headhunters; Esquires, Royal Guardsmen; Lee Dorsey, Alvin Cash & Crawlers; Forum; Ritchie Valens; Van Morrison; Brenton Wood; Lovin' Spoonful; Neil Diamond; Bob Lind; Casinos; Beach Boys; New Beats; Strangeloves; Tokens.

WIXY Super Oldie Hits of the Past, Vol. 1 .... Lost Nite (S) LPS-130 5-10
Dovells; Fontella Bass; Tommy James & Shondells; Dixie Cups; Bobby Fuller Four; Cascades; Ronny & Daytonas; Dion; Shangri-Las; Happenings; Syndicate of Sound; Shirelles; Trashmen; ? & Mysterians; Del Shannon; Castaways; Terry Knight; Ad Libs; J. Frank Wilson; Jaynetts.

WIXY 30 Super Oldies (2 LP) .... Post (S) 1260 10-15
Bill Deal; Merrilee Rush; Flying Machine; Canned Heat; Righteous Brothers; Brooklyn Bridge; Mamas & Papas; Box Tops; Peppermint Rainbow; Winstons; Shocking Blue; Cowsills; Turtles; Delfonics; Animals; Hugh Masekela; Alive 'N Kicking; Tommy James & Shondells; Classics IV; Deep Purple.

WIXY's Top Bananas .... Post (S) 7305 5-10 73
(For Muscular Dystrphy Association.) Stories; Climax; Focus; Sylvia; Gallery; Isley Brothers; Mountain; Curtis Mayfield; Osmond Brothers; War; Melanie; Gary Glitter; Godspell; Charlie Daniels.

WKBW Klassics, Vol. 1 (2 LP) .... Post (S) No Number Used 10-20 70s

WKBW Klassics, Vol. 2 (2 LP) .... Post (S) No Number Used 10-20 70s
Neil Diamond; Alice Cooper; Bread; Buoys; Ides of March; Lobo; Isley Brothers; Sugarloaf; Canned Heat; Freda Payne; Shocking Blue; Amboy Dukes; Mountain; Gordon Lightfoot; Oliver; Soul Survivors; Brian Hyland; Tommy James & Shondells; Bells; Ocean; Judy Collins; Box Tops; Tony Joe White; Crow.

WKEE, 24 of the Greatest: see Flash-Back Greats of the '60s (2 LP)

WKLS 96 Rock .... CBS (S) PD-9162 20-30 81
(Promotional picture disc.)

WKLS 96 Rock .... CBS (S) PO-9162 35-45 81
(Promotional picture disc. Note different prefix.)

WKNR Keener 13 Oldies But Goodies .... WKNR (S) A&B 10-15 60s
Sandy Nelson; Gene Chandler; Dee Dee Sharp; Bobby Rydell; Bobby Day; Hollywood Argyles; Skyliners; Jerry Butler; Paris Sisters; Rosie & Originals; Dee Clark; Ritchie Valens; WKNR Jingle.

WKNR Keener Gold, Vol. 4 .... WKNR (S) Vol. IV 10-15 60s
Association; Fontella Bass; Don & Juan; Bob Lind; Newbeats; Casinos; Jaynetts; Curtiss Lee; Five Amercians; Syndicate of Sound; Lovin' Spoonful; Count Five; James & Bobby Purify; Bobby Lewis; Bobby Fuller Four; B.J. Thomas; Billy Stewart; ? & Mysterians; Del Shannon; Isley Brothers.

WLAV-FM 97, Music to Watch Cartoons .... Phoenix (S) 8406 8-12 84
(Red vinyl.) Human Beinz; Soul Survivors; Kingsmen; J.J. Jackson; Syndicate of Sound; Sam the Sham & Pharaohs; Bobby Fuller Four; Strange Loves; ? & Mysterians; Standells.

WLYV, '71 Solid Gold .... Solid Gold (S) SG 1001 20-30 71
Rolling Stones; George Harrison; Who; Bee Gees; Isaac Hayes; Donny Osmond; Dramatics; Carole King; Three Dog Night; Rod Stewart; Dawn; Aretha Franklin; Murray Head; Sly & Family Stone.

WMEE 1380: see 24 Golden Greats, WMEE 1380

WMEX Solid Gold, (And Album of), (2 LP) .... ???? 10-15
(A Variety Club's International Charity Album.) Merrilee Rush; Dionne Warwicke; Andy Williams; Steppenwolf; Ohio Express; Impressons; Tommy Roe; Neil Diamond; Canned Heat; Lemon Pipers; McCoys; Bobby Goldsboro; Animals; Strawberry Alarm Clock; Zager & Evans; James Brown; J. Frank Wilson; Box Tops; Jose Feliciano; Kingsmen; Three Dog Night; B.J. Thomas; Classics IV; Irish Rovers; Ventures; Glen Campbell.

WMID - the Jersey Giant, Vol. 1 .... Post (S) 7201 10-15 71

WMID - the Jersey Giant, Vol. 2 .... Post (S) 7202 10-15 71
Chuck Berry; Johnnie & Joe; Lee Andrews & Hearts; Santo & Johnny; Shepards; Heartbeats; Five Satins; Quin-Tones; Steam; Intrigues; Tony Joe White; Winstons; Cowsils; Fuzz; Neil Diamond; Runt.

WMYQ Hits .... Post (S) 7109 10-15
Tommy Roe; Bells; Alive 'N Kicking; Cowsills; Tommy James & Shondells; Strawberry Alarm Clock; Steam; Merrilee Rush Rush; Soul Survivors; Shocking Blue; Deep Purple; Oliver; Tony Joe White; Association; Freda Payne; Canned Heat; Flying Machine; Box Tops; Dion; Mungo Jerry.

WNBC 66 - Hometown Album .... WNBC (S) 1000 10-15 80s
Ikabar Krane; U.S. 1; Joe Saint; Jim Bashian; Stephanie Davy; Chailo; Eric Matthew; Ron Rinaldi; Mike Cotter; Aberdeen Street Band.

WNHC (Boss Radio) Presents a Million Dollar Weekend .... Lost Nite (S) LPS-134 10-15 70s
Soul Survivors; Nutmegs; Lee Andrews; Dixie Cups; Jive Five; Mello-Kings; Curtis Lee Happenings; Ritchie Valens; Don & Juan; Silhouettes; Shangri-Las; Little Caesar; J. Frank Wilson; Capris; Five Satins; Crests; Duprees; Ronnie & Hi-Lites; Angels.

WNOX Tennessee Barn Dance .... Golden Crest (M) 3084 10-15

WOKY, 22 Heavy Hits .... Post (S) 92 10-15

Turtles; Tommy Roe; O'Kaysions; Strawberry Alarm Clock; McCoys; Unchained Mynds; Brenton Wood; Shangri-Las; Ohio Express; John Fred; Terry Stafford; 1910 Fruitgum Company; Van Morrison; Robert Knight; Buckinghams; Prophets; Syndicate of Sound; Paris Sisters; Mojo Men; Robert Parker; Frankie Avalon; Tommy James & Shondells.

WOL (Soul Brothers - First Anniversary) .... Roulette (M) R-25337 10-20 67

WOR-FM 98.7 - Solid Gold (2 LP) .... Post (S) No Number Used 10-20 70s

Animals; Delfonics; Little Anthony & Imperials; Flying Machine; James Brown; Merrilee Rush; B.J. Thomas; Turtles; Dells; Shirelles; Orpheus; Hugh Masekela; Brooklyn Bridge; Chuck Berry; Mamas & Papas; Tommy James & Shondells; Skyliners; Ramsey Lewis; Foundations; Duprees; We Five; Casinos; Deep Purple; Flamingos; Vogues; Crests; Shangri-Las; Association; Righteous Brothers.

WOR-FM 98.7 (2 LP) .... Post (S) 7001 10-20 70s

Animals; Delfonics; Little Anthony & Imperials; Flying Machine; James Brown; Merrilee Rush; B.J. Thomas; Turtles; Dells; Shirelles; Orpheus; Hugh Masekela; Brooklyn Bridge; Chuck Berry; Mamas & Papas; Tommy James & Shondells; Skyliners; Ramsey Lewis; Foundations; Duprees; We Five; Casinos; Deep Purple; Flamingos; Vogues; Crests; Shangri-Las; Association; Righteous Brothers.

WONE - the Dayton Scene .... Prism (M) 1966 10-20 66

WOW: see 59/WOW

WPGC Together Gold, Vol. 1 (2 LP) .... Darby (S) 801/802 8-12 60s

Classics IV; Cadets; Brenton Wood; Winstons; Bob Lind; others.

WPGC Cousin Duffy Presents 22 Smash Tracks .... Post (S) 671 8-12 60s

Lovin' Spoonful; Cascades; Dobie Gray; Duprees; Don & Juan.

WPOP - 1410 from Then to Now .... WPOP (S) No Number Used 15-20 68

(Colored vinyl.) Cannibal & Headhunters; Gene Pitney; B.J. Thomas; Jon & Robin; Association; J. Frank Wilson; Five Satins; Music Machine; Wildweeds; Ritchie Valens; Ronnie Dove; James Brown; Count Five; Beau Brummels; Barry McGuire; Shadows of Knight; Five Americans; Brenton Wood; Ronny & Daytonas; ? & Mysterians; Strawberry Alarm Clock.

WPOP, Vol. 2 "Hear Here" .... WPOP (S) 1410 15-20 69

(Multi-color vinyl.) John Fred; Betty Everett & Jerry Butler; Surfaris; Turtles; Bob Kuban & In-Men; Toys; Aaron Neville; Soul Survivors; Deep Purple; Jeannie C. Riley; Small Faces; James Brown; Tommy Roe; Beach Boys; Lemon Pipers; Premiers.

WPRO Radio 630 / 22 Golden Oldies .... Post (S) 63 10-15

Surfaris; B.J. Thomas; James Brown; Buckinghams; Strawberry Alarm Clock; Billy Stewart; Ohio Express; McCoys; Robert Parker; Lemon Pipers; John Fred; Happenings; Tommy James & Shondells; Del Shannon; Robert Knight; Shirelles; Neil Diamond; Shelley Fabares; Bill Deal; Aaron Neville; Bobby Fuller Four; Casinos.

WQAM 560, the Roaring 30 (2 LP) .... Post (S) 560 15-25

Birdwatchers; Wayne Cochran; Association; 1910 Fruitgum Co.; Robert Parker; Wayne Cochran; Love; Aaron Neville; Bird Watchers; Standells; John Fred; Neil Diamond; Barbara Mason; Van Morrison; Brenton Wood; Keith; Tommy James & Shondells; Strawberry Alarm Clock; Bettye Swann; Syndicate of Sound; Dobie Gray; Count Five; Knickerbockers; Esquires; McCoys; Lemon Pipers; Freddie Scott; Fontella Bass; Cannibal & Headhunters; Mojo Men; American Breed; Bobby Hebb.

WRCA Plays the Hits for Your Customers .... RCA (S) DJL1-1785 300-350 76

(Promotional issue only.) Elvis Presley; Hall & Oates; Rosie; Silver Convention; Vicki Sue Robinson; Brothers; Waylon Jennings; Pure Prairie League; D.J. Rogers; Tymes; Choice Four; Scorpions; Vangelis; Henry Mancini; Chet Atkins; Les Paul; Roger Whittaker.

WRKO 610 .... WRKO (S) No Number Used 20-25 78

(Picture disc. Promotional issue only.) Boston; Ringo Starr; others.

WRKO Hall of Fame (2 LP) .... Post (S) 7101 10-15 71

Bill Haley & His Comets; Gogi Grant; Sam Cooke; Rays; Tommy Edwards; Teddy Bears; Frankie Avalon; Wilbert Harrison; Everly Brothers; Bobby Lewis; Del Shannon; Gene Chandler; Little Eva; Paul & Paula; Chiffons; Kingsmen; Sam the Sham & Pharaohs; McCoys; Association; Righteous Brothers; Boxt Tops; Turtles; Jeannie C. Riley; Dion; Flying Machine; Oliver; Tommy Roe; Tommy James & Shondells; Shocking Blue; Moments.

WSAI Command Performance (2 LP) .... Post (S) 1360 10-20 71

Association; Cowsills; O'Kaysions; Turtles; Tony Joe White; Jeannie C. Riley; Classics IV; Tommy Roe; Moments; Canned Heat; Foundations; Shocking Blue; Winstons; 1910 Fruitgum Co.; Righteous Brothers; Tommy James & Shondells; Neil Diamond; Delfonics; Cuff Links; Box Tops; Flying Machine; Animals; Kenny Rogers & First Edition; Freda Payne; Johnny Nash; Merrilee Rush; Hugh Masekela; Strawberry Alarm Clock; Alive 'N Kicking; Oliver.

WVIC, '71 Solid Gold .... Solid Gold (S) SG 1001 20-30 71

Rolling Stones; George Harrison; Who; Bee Gees; Isaac Hayes; Donny Osmond; Dramatics; Carole King; Three Dog Night; Rod Stewart; Dawn; Aretha Franklin; Murray Head; Sly & Family Stone.

WVON Good Guys Holiday Package .... WVON (S) 16382 10-15 60s

Aretha Franklin; Toussaint McCall; Mickey Murray; Jean Wells; Syl Johnson; Bar-Kays; Oscar Toney Jr.; Dyke & Blazers; Peaches & Herb; Darrell Banks; Ruby Andrews; Sand Pebbles; Dells; Esquires; Don Cornelius. (Includes audio history of WVON with short bios of disc jockeys.)

WWIN .... Roulette (M) R-25333 10-20 67

WZZO: see Valley Rock

Wacky Westerns .... K-Tel (S) WU 3280 8-12 75

Little Jimmy Dickens; Johnny Bond; Roger Miller; Jack Blanchard; Misty Morgan; Homer & Jethro; Fendermen; Murry Kellum; Ray Stevens; Junior Samples; Leapy Lee; Lonnie Donegan; Johnny Preston; Tom T. Hall; Olympics; Mel Tillis; Webb Pierce; Larry Verne.

Wagon Train Nuggets .... Camay (S) CA 3023 8-12 60s

Tex Ritter; Tennessee Ernie Ford; Sumpin' Smith & Redhead; Tex Williams; others.

Waikiki Surf Battle, Vol. 1 .... Sounds of Hawaii (M) SH-5014 50-100 63

Delrays; Majestics; Escents; Statics; Stardels; Angie & Originals; Vogues; Shandels; Road Runners; Judy & Belmonts; Spiedels.

Waikiki Surf Battle, Vol. 2 .... Sounds of Hawaii (M) 5014 50-100 63

Bel-Airs; Royal Victors; Regents; Denny & Dukes; Harmonics; Strollers; Vacqueros; Strollers. (Both volumes are separate albums that have the same catalog number.)

Wail on the Beach .... Satan 1004 5-10 90s

Walkin' By Myself .... Chess (M) LP-1446 20-30 60

Eddie Boyd; Washboard Sam; Memphis Slim; Jimmy Rogers; Floyd Jones; Roscoe Gordon; Lulu Reed.

Wally Fowler's All Night Sing, 15th Anniversary .... Modern (S) MS-814 8-12 63

Wally Fowler & Oak Ridge Quartet; Sego Brothers & Naomi; Plainsmen Quartet; Jake Hess & Jordanaires; Florida Boys; Sons of Song; Wendy Bagwell & Sunlighters.

Walt Disney's Merriest Songs .... Disneyland (M) DL-3510 10-20 68

Dick Van Dyke; Julie Andrews; Mary Martin; Mouse Chorus; Burl Ives; Louis Armstrong; Jiminy Cricket; Ed Wynn; Louis Prima; Phil Harris; Sebastian Cabot.

Walt Disney's Wonderful World of Color .... Disneyland (M) DQ-1245 30-35 64

(Soundtrack.) Annette; Hayley Mills; Fess Parker; others.

Wanderers .... Warner Bros. (S) BSK-3359 25-30 79

(Soundtrack.) 4 Seasons; Lee Dorsey; Angels; Shirelles; Ben E. King; Contours; Isley Brothers; Dion.

Wanted! the Outlaws: see JENNINGS, Waylon, Willie Nelson, Jessi Colter, and Tompall Glaser

War (The Jesters vs. the Paragons): see JESTERS / ParagonsIt's a Knockout: see Columbia Promotional Releases/Samplers

War of the Worlds Special Radio Edition .... Columbia (S) AS 454 10-20 78

(Promotional issue only.) Justin Hayward; Richard Burton; Chris Thompson; Phil Lynott; Julie Covington; David Essex.

War of the Worlds (2 LP) .... Columbia (S) PC2-35290 15-20 78

(Soundtrack. Includes booklet. Musical production.) Richard Burton; Justin Hayward; David Essex; Julie Covington; Philip Lynott; Jo Partridge; Chris Thompson; Jeff Wayne.

Warner Bros. Promotional Releases and Lost Leader Samplers (Listed by catalog number. All are promo only.)

Warner Bros. 290 1968 Some of Our Best Friends Are *15-25* *69*

Jimi Hendrix; Kensington Market; Joni Mitchell; Eric Andersen; David Blue; Grateful Dead; Arlo Guthrie; Randy Newman; Fugs; Electric Prunes; Tom Northcut; Van Dyke Parks.

Warner Bros. 331 1969 Warner/Reprise Songbook (2 LP) *25-35* *69*

Electric Prunes; Sal Valentino; Tom Northcott; Van Dyke Parks; Everly Brothers; Wild Man Fischer; Jethro Tull; Pentangle; Van Morrison; Family; Neil Young; Beau Brummels; Randy Newman; Tiny Tim; Mothers of Invention; Fugs; Arlo Guthrie; Sweetwater; Joni Mitchell; Eric Anderson; Kinks; Jimi Hendrix; Miriam Makeba.

Warner Bros. 336 1969 Warner/Reprise Record Show (2 LP) *15-25* *69*

Everly Brothers; Van Dyke Parks; Grateful Dead; Geoff & Maria Muldaur; David Blue; Hamilton Camp; Neil Young; Doug Kershaw; Arlo Guthrie; Blue Velvet Band; Theo Bikel; Joni Mitchell; John Redbourn; Bert Jansch; Pentangle; Peter, Paul & Mary; Sweetwater; Louie Shelton; Lorraine Ellison; Randy Newman; Pearls Before Swine; Ella Fitzgerald; Fugs; Mothers of Invention; Jethro Tull; Mephistopheles; Jimi Hendrix.

Warner Bros. 351 October 10, 1969 .... *10-20* *69*

Frank Zappa; Kinks; Norman Greenbaum; Levitt & McClure; Denny Brooks; Ruthann Friedman; Fleetwood Mac; Eric Anderson; Fifth Avenue Band; Mike Post Coalition.

Warner Bros. 358 The Big Ball (2 LP) *15-25* *70*

Everly Brothers; Fleetwood Mac; Kinks; Fifth Avenue Band; John Sebastain; Beach Boys; Geoff & Maria Muldaur; Arlo Guthrie; Eric Andersen; Norman Greenbaum; Savage Grace; Van Morrison; Pentangle; Jethro Tull; Small Faces; Family; Tim Buckley; Joni Mitchell; Neil Young; Gordon Lightfoot; Randy Newman; James Taylor; Dion; Ed Sanders; GTO's; Captain Beefheart; Mothers of Invention; Wild Man Fischer; Pearls Before Swine; Grateful Dead.

Warner Bros. 359 Schlagers (2 LP) *20-30* *70*

Frank Sinatra; Trini Lopez; Petula Clark; Watts 103rd St. Rhythm Band; Peter, Paul & Mary; Ella Fitzgerald; Glenn Yarbrough; Vogues; Theo Bikel; Joni Mitchell; Gordon Lightfoot; Dion; Everly Brothers; Arlo Guthrie; Harpers Bizarre; San Sebastian Strings; Herbie Hancock; Association; Vince Guaraldi; Neon Philharmonic; Fifth Avenue Band; Mason Williams; Mike Post Coalition; Randy Newman; Doug Kershaw; Kenny Rogers & First Edition.

Warner Bros. 368 Zapped: see ZAPPA, Frank

Warner Bros. 423 Looney Tunes - Merrie Melodies (3 LP) *50-100* *70*

(Boxed set. Includes booklet.) Faces; Small Faces; Black Sabbath; Little Feat; Hard Meat; Fleetwood Mac; Jimi Hendrix; John Simon; Ry Cooder; Randy Newman; Gordon Lightfoot; Jimmy L. Webb; *Performance* (Soundtrack); Little Richard; Grateful Dead; Van Morrison; Kinks; Arlo Guthrie; Youngbloods; Jeffrey Cain; Lovecraft; Sweetwater; Captain Beefheart; Mothers of Invention; Frank Zappa; Beaver & Krause; Pearls Before Swine; James Taylor; Harpers Bizarre; Van Dyke Parks; Persuasions; Turley Richards.

Warner Bros. 443 Non-Dairy Creamer *15-25* *71*

Little Feat; Rosebud; Peter Green; Curved Air; Tony Joe White; John & Beverly Martyn; Ohio Knox; Jeffrey Cain; Zephyr; Ron Nagle; Brownsville Station.

Warner Bros. 463 Warner/Reprise Radio Show *10-20* *71*

Pearls Before Swine; T Rex; Mother Earth; Doobie Brothers; Faces; Crazy Horse; Youngbloods; Ron Nagle; Ohio Knox.

Warner Bros. 474 Menu-Hot Platters (2 LP) *15-25* *71*

Kinks; Ry Cooder; T Rex; Deep Purple; John Baldry; Labelle; Redeye; Randy Newman; Jackie Lomax; Paul Stookey; Norman Greenbaum; Ron Nagle; Gordon Lightfoot; Beach Boys; Fanny; Stovall Sisters; Rosebud; Big Mama Thornton; John D. Loudermilk; Beaver & Krause; Ronnie Milsap; Mother Earth.

Warner Bros. PRO-486 Together *10-20* *71*

Doobie Brothers; Faces; Stoneground; Jackie Lomax; Mother Earth; Earth, Wind & Fire; John Baldry; Crazy Horse; Alice Cooper; T Rex; Mary Travers.

Warner Bros. PRO-496 Super Record-Contemporary (JBL Loudspeakers) *10-15* *70s*

Lovecraft; James Taylor; Mason Williams; Van Dyke Parks; Pentangle; Joni Mitchell; Gordon Lightfoot.

Warner Bros. 508 the Warner/Reprise Display Case, Vol. 2 (2 LP) *10-20* *70s*

Van Morrison; T. Rex; John Stewart; Laurie Styvers; Bert Jansch; Red Wilder Blue; Fleetwood Mac; Dion; Youngbloods; Kindred; Lazarus; William Truckaway; Alice Cooper; Sweetwater; John Hartford; Bonnie Raitt; Little Richard; Jesse Frederick; Curved Air; Seals & Crofts; Daddy Cool; Pentagle; Ronnie Milsap; Colosseum; High Country.

Warner Bros. 512 The Whole Burbank Catalog (2 LP) *10-20* *72*

Jethro Tull; Halfnelson; Themes Like Old Times; Jerry Garcia; Arthur Alexander; Allan Toussaint; Jackie Lomax; Daddy Cool; Faces; Malo; Fleetwood Mac; Bonnie Raitt; William Truckaway; Ramblin' Jack Elliott; Kenny Young; Arlo Guthrie; Alice Cooper; T Rex; Captain Beefheart; Seals & Crofts; Todd Rundgren; America; Walter Carlos; Sesame Street II; Ry Cooder.

Warner Bros. 525 Middle of the Road (2 LP) *20-30* *72*

Frank Sinatra; Fleetwood Mac; John Sebastian; Jennifer; Dion DiMucci; Rod McKuen; Jesse Colin Young; Gordon Lightfoot; James Taylor; Randy Newman; John Stewart; Kenny Rogers & First Edition; Seals & Crofts; Todd Rundgren; Beach Boys; America; Mary Travers; T Rex; Alex Taylor; Pentangle; Peter Yarrow; Tony Joe White; Dionne Warwick; Paul Stookey.

Warner Bros. 529 Burbank (2 LP) *15-25* *72*

Deep Purple; Arlo Guthrie; Jimi Hendrix; Tower of Power; Curved Air; Alice Cooper; Van Dyke Parks; John Cale; Labelle; Fanny; T Rex; Maxayn; Foghat; Meters; Flo & Eddie; Beaver & Krause; Captain Beyond; Bob Weir; John Fahey; Zephyr; Long John Baldry; Martin Mull; John Renbourne; Matthew Ellis; Geoff & Maria Muldaur.

Warner Bros. 530 Display Case #7 (2 LP) *15-25* *72*

Bob Weir; Howard Kaylan; Mark Volman; Tom Paxton; Steve Young; Matthew Ellis; Allen Toussaint; Labelle; Alice Cooper; Van Dyke Parks; Banana & Bunch; Captain Beyond; John Cale; Seanor & Koss; Doobie Brothers; Seals & Crofts; Beaver & Krause; Sparks; Geoff & Maria Muldaur; White Witch; Curved Air; John Renbourn; T Rex; Charles Wright; Thirty Days Out; Martin Mull.

Warner Bros. 532 Display Case #8 (2 LP) *20-30* *72*

T Rex; Tim Buckley; Thirty Days Out; John Fahey; Michael Hurley; Quiver; Martin Mull; Nazareth; Beaver & Krause; Jack Nitzsche; Rod McKuen.

Warner Bros. 538 Display Case #9 (2 LP) *20-30* *72*

Bobby Charles; Memphis Slim; Bonnie Raitt; Dion; Bob Seger; Mickey Hart; Pentangle; Ed Sanders & Hemptones; Miss Abrahams.

Warner Bros. 540 Days of Wine and Vinyl (2 LP)........ 20-30 73
David Bowie; Arlo Guthrie; Harpers Bizarre; Arthur Conley; Tir Na Nog; Tim Buckley; Jesse Winchester; Captain Beefheart & Magic Band; Section; James Taylor; America; Mickey Hart; Dion; Incredible String Band; Bonnie Raitt; Alexis Karner & Snape; Steeleye Span; Jethro Tull; Dick Heckstall-Smith; Sparks; Youngbloods; Bobby Charles; Memphis Slim; Roxy Music; Norman Greenbaum; John Hartford.

Warner Bros. 542 Display Case #10 (3 LP)........ 25-35 73
(Boxed set.) Little Richard; Deep Purple; Gravenites & Bloomfield; Captain Beefheart; Jesse Winchester; Incredible String Band; Black Sabbath; Malo; Christoper Milk; Section; Stoneground; Dick Heckstall-Smith; Memphis Slim; Wet Willie; Gordon Lightfoot; Doug Kershaw; Norman Greenbaum; Mason Profitt; Marjoe; Mystic Moods Orchestra; Electric Co.; San Sebastain Strings; Ry Cooder; John Simon; Dion; John Hartford.

Warner Bros. 548 Burbank's Greatest Hits........ 10-20 73
Alice Cooper; America; T Rex; James Taylor; Jethro Tull; Allman Brothers; Malo; Seals & Crofts; Doobie Brothers; Tower of Power; Todd Rundgren; Arlo Guthrie.

Warner Bros. 550 Hit Sounds of Merrie Melodies (2 LP)........ 20-25 73
Frankie & Johnny; Claudia Lennear; Deep Purple; Linda Lewis; Richard Thompson; Dionne Warwick; Beach Boys; Ralph McTell; Alexis Korner & Snape; Gram Parsons; Wilderness Road; Barbara Keith; Paul Stookey. (Not available by mail like the other Loss Leader LPs. Distributed at in-store promotions.)

Warner Bros. 569 Appetizers (2 LP)........ 15-25 73
Beach Boys; Deep Purple; Linda Lewis; Lorraine Ellison; William Truckaway; Little Feat; Arlo Guthrie; Bert Jansch; Paul Butterfield; Seals & Crofts; Van Morrison; Faces; Todd Rundgren; Fanny; Alice Cooper; John Cole; Procol Harum; Incredible String Band; Steeleye Span; Doobie Brothers; Wet Willie; T Rex; Martin Mull; Flo & Eddie; Seatrain; Foghat.

Warner Bros. 573 All Singing, All Talking, All Rocking (2 LP)........ 15-25 73
Martin Mull; Richard Burton; Elizabeth Taylor; Jimmy Cliff; Maria Muldaur; Strider; Bonnie Raitt; Humphrey Bogart; Alfonzo Bedayo; Allman Brothers Band; JSD Band; Three Man Army; Jethro Tull; James Dean; Back Door; Mothers; Section; Robin Trower; Marshall Tucker Band; Sopwith Camel; Kathy Dalton; Bugs Bunny; Barbra Striesand; Uriah Heep; America; James Cagney; Labat; Gene Parsons; Doobie Brothers; Bedlam; Wendy Waldman; Jesse Colin Young; Tim Buckley; Ingrid Bergman; Peter Yarrow.

Warner Bros. 583 Hard Goods (2 LP)........ 15-25 74
Neil Young; Graham Nash; Denver, Boise & Johnson; Graham Central Station; Montrose; Doobie Brothers; Ted Nugent & Amboy Dukes; Talbot Brothers; Foghat; Van Morrison; Chunky, Navi & Ernie; Deep Purple; Frank Zappa; Todd Rundgren; Bog Seger; KISS; Steeleye Span; Marshall Tucker Band; Gregg Allman; Alan Price; Seals & Crofts; Terry Melcher; Leo Sayer; Beach Boys; Robin Trower; Dooley Wilson.

Warner Bros. 588 Peaches - "Pick of the Crop" (2 LP)........ 15-25 74
Chris Christman; others.

Warner Bros. 591 Deep Ear (2 LP)........ 15-30 74
Van Dyke Parks; Good Rats; James Taylor; Jimmy Cliff; Richard Betts; Jesse Winchester; Elvin Bishop; Doug Sahm Tex Mex Trip; Little Feat; Maria Muldaur; Adam Faith; Ry Cooder; Lorraine Ellison; Wendy Waldman; Frankie Miller; America; Arlo Guthrie; Randy Newman; Jesse Colin Young; Browing Bryant; Ashton & Lord; Bonnie Raitt; Peter Ivers Band; John Hartford; Meters; Wet Willie.

Warner Bros. 596 The Force (2 LP)........ 20-25 74
(Gatefold cover.) Leo Sayer; Jethro Tull; Kenny Rankin; Fleetwood Mac; Percy Sledge; Graham Central Station; Trapeze; Foghat; Montrose; Todd Rundgren's Utopia; Bachman-Turner Overdrive; Deep Purple; Marshall Tucker Band; John Sebastian; Maria Muldaur; Mike McGear; Doobie Brothers; Ron Wood; Tower of Power; Gregg Allman; Van Morrison.

Warner Bros. 596 The Force (2 LP)........ 15-20 74
(Standard, separate covers.) Jan & Dean; Debbie Dawn; others.

Warner Bros. 604 All Meat (2 LP)........ 15-20 75
Faces; Rod Stewart; Doobie Brothers; James Taylor; Wendy Waldman; Cher; Harry Nilsson; Curtis Mayfield; Elvin Bishop; John Hammond; Emmylou Harris; Grinderswitch; Wet Willie; Commander Cody & His Lost Planet Airmen; Allen Toussaint; Gary Wright; Beau Brummels; Peter Yarrow; Geoff Muldaur; John Renton; Martin Mull; Jesse Colin Young; Hirth Mastinez; Todd Rundgren; Earth, Wind & Fire; Labelle; Jimi Hendrix.

Warner Bros. 605 Peaches, Vol. 2 (2 LP)........ 15-20 75
Travis Wammack; Razzy Bailey; Kitty Wells; others.

Warner Bros. 608 I Didn't Know They Still Made Records Like This (2 LP)........ 15-20 75
Seals & Crofts; Bonnie Raitt; Leo Sayer; Dionne Warwick; Van Morrison; Fleetwood Mac; James Taylor; Marcia Waldorf; Arlo Guthrie; Chris Ducey; Joni Mitchell; Randy Newman; John Sebastian; Maria Muldaur; Kenny Rankin; Waldo De Los Rios; San Sebastian Strings; Gordon Lightfoot; Gregg Allman; Rex Allen Jr.; Wendy Waldman; Jesse Colin Young; Rod McKuen.

Warner Bros. 610 The Works (2 LP)........ 15-25 75
Beach Boys; Rod Stewart; Foghat; Jimmy Cliff; Montrose; Tower of Power; Van Dyke Parks; Fleetwood Mac; Al Jarreau; Bonnie Raitt; Roy Wylie Hubbard & Cowboy Twinkies; David Sanborn; Graham Central Station; Meters; Leo Sayer; Little Feat; Commander Cody & His Lost Planet Airmen; Richard Pryor; Frank Zappa; Captain Beefheart; Ronee Blakely; Leon Redbone; Chris Ducy; Black Sabbath; Todd Rundgren's Utopia.

Warner Bros. 611 The Force........ 10-20 75
Leo Sayer; Jethro Tull; Kenny Rankin; Fleetwood Mac; Percy Sledge; Graham Central Station; Trapeze; Foghat; Todd Rundgren's Utopia; Bachman-Turner-Bachman; Deep Purple; Montrose.

Warner Bros. 630 Supergroup (2 LP)........ 15-20 76
George Colderon; William D. Smith; Jesse Colin Young; 4 Seasons; Elvin Bishop; Bellamy Brothers; George Benson; First Choice; Bootsy's Rubber Band; Miroslov Vitous; Todd Rundgren; Doobie Brothers; Michael Franks; Seals & Crofts; Maria Muldaur; John Sebastian; Leon & Mary Russell; Pat Mortino; Roger Cook; Phil Cody; Rahsoon Ruldan Kirk; Slade; Emmylou Harris.

Warner Bros. 645 The People's Record (2 LP)........ 15-20 76
Little Feat; James Taylor; Gordon Lightfoot; Dion; Beach Boys; Arlo Guthrie; Mike Finnigan; Fleetwood Mac; Peter Ivers; Tiger; Alice Cooper; Graham Central Station; Philip Catherine; Nazareth; Lamont Dozier; George Benson; Al Jarreau; Rod Stewart; Billy Joe Shaver; Leon Redbone; Michael Franks; Rex Allen Jr.; Bonnie Bramlet; Ray Stevens; Ron Ranier.

Warner Bros. 660 Cook Book (2 LP)........ 15-20 77
Charles Wright & 103rd St. Rhythm Band; Meters; Graham Central Station; Dionne Warwick; Candi Staton; Staples; Curtis Mayfield; Funkadelic; Ashford & Simpson; Roy Redmond; New Birth; Undisputed Truth; Jimmy Cliff; George Benson; Doobie Brothers; Bootsy's Rubber Band; Banks & Hampton; Crackin; Randy Crawford; Paul Kelly; Tony Wilson; Al Jarreau; Lomont Dozier; Mystique.

Warner Bros. 691 Limo (2 LP)........ 10-20 77
Henhouse Five Plus Too; Ry Cooder; Sanford-Townsend Band; Johathan Cain Band; Bonnie Raitt; Little Feat; Van Morrison; Leo Sayer; Al Jarreau; Kate & Anna McGarrigle; Danny O'Keefe; Eddie Hazel; Fleetwood Mac; Mylon LeFevre; Chunky, Navi & Ernie; Jesse Winchester; Wendy Waldman; Jesse Colin Young; Deaf School; Galby Pahinui Hawaiian Band; Hirth Martinez; Emmylou Harris; Gary Wright; Attitudes; Ted Nugent & Amboy Dukes; Doobie Brothers; Rod Stewart.

Warner Bros. 726 Collectus Interruptus (2 LP)........ 10-20 78
Allen Tousaint; John Handy; Ashford & Simpson; Prince; Etta James; Seals & Crofts; David Sanborn; Dan Hicks; George Benson; Renaissance; Ronnie Montrose; Gary Wright; Deodato; Ambrosia; Van Halen; Sex Pistols; Bootsy's Rubber Band; Manfred Mann; Leo Sayer; Shawn Cassidy; Ramones; Wendy Waldman; Gordon Lightfoot; Randy Newman; Band; Emmylou Harris; Ry Cooder.

Warner Bros. 773 Pumping Vinyl (2 LP)........ 10-20 79
Nicolette Larsen; Rodney Crowell; Michael Franks; Rose Royce; Staples; Thin Lizzy; Larry Graham & Graham Central Station; Larry Carlton; Third World; Fortiene; Van Morrison; Lonete McKee; Donna Fargo; Flora Purim; Carlene Carter; Willie Hutch; Todd Rundgren; Devo; Pirates; Jimmy Cliff; Leon Russell; Captain Beefheart & Magic Band; Bruce Cockburn; Arlo Guthrie.

Warner Bros./Reprise 775 The Warner Bros. Records 20th Anniversary Album in Sound & Picture........ 300-600 78
(Six LPs in slipcase. 3,000 made. Frank Sinatra; others.

Warner Bros. 794 A La Carte (2 LP)........ 10-20 78
St. Paradise; Jr. Walker; Con Hunley; Candi Staton; Adam Mitchell; Robert Palmer; Bellamy Brothers; Danny O'Keefe; Gibson Brothers; Sanford-Townsend Band; Climax Blues Band; Duncan Browne; Madleen Kane; Runner; Roger Vaudauris; Nytro; B-52s; Mavis Staples; Emmylou Harris; Manfred Mann; Maria Muldaur; Bootsy's Rubber Band.

Warner Bros. 796 Monsters (2 LP)........ 15-25 79
Ricki Lee Jones; Doobie Brothers; Asiris; Ashford & Simpson; George Benson; Lowell George; Randy Crawford; George Harrison; Bob Marley & Wailers; Gary Wright; Kate & Anna McGarrigle; Van Halen; Mary Russell; Inner Circle; Chaka Khan; Gino Soccia; American Standard Band; Wornell Jones; Tin Huey; Alice Cooper; Michael Franks; Roches.

Warner Bros. 828 Eclipse (2 LP)........ 10-20 80
Leo Sayer; Tom Johnston; Lauren Wood; Vapour Trails; Danny Daulma; Van Morrison; Roy Wood; Korgis; Ramones; Alda Reserve; Talking Heads; Monty Python; Randy Newman; Nicolette Larson; Ry Cooder; Beau Brummels; Carlene Carter; Bonnie Raitt; Sly & Family Stone; Funkadelic; Little Feat; Dukes; Bob Marley & Wailers.

Warner Bros. 841 Gold Medal Sampler (2 LP)........ 10-20 80
Pearl Harbor & Explosions; Undertones; Dukes; Christopher Cross; Roger Voudouris; Jess Rogen; Pretenders; Utopia.

Warner Bros. 850 Music with 58 Musicians, Vol. 1........ 10-20 80

Warner Bros. 857 Troublemakers........ 15-20 80
Sex Pistols; John Cale; Modern Lovers; Public Image Ltd.; Brian Briggs; Pearl Harbor & Explosions; Urban Verbs; Robin Lane & Chartbusters; Wire; Gang of Four; Devo; Buggles; Nico; Marianne Faithful.

Warner Bros. 981 Vocal Tracks/U.S. Marine Corps/Toys for Tots........ 100-200
(Seven-inch single.) Frank Sinatra; George Harrison; Buck Owens; Glen Campbell; Cathy Lee Crosby; others.

Warner Bros. ??? Record Show........ 10-20
Neil Young; Grateful Dead; Geoff & Maria Muldaur; Everly Brothers; Dough Kershaw; David Blue; Arlo Guthrie; Blue Velvet Band; Theodore Bikel; Joni Mitchell; John Redbourn; Bert Jansch; Pentangle; Peter, Paul & Mary; Sweetwater; Louie Shelton; Lorraine Ellison; Vany Dyke Parsons; Randy Newman; Pearls Before Swine; Hamilton Camp; Ella Fitzgerald; Fugs; Mothers of Invention; Jethro Tull; Mephistopheles; Jimi Hendrix Experience.

Warriors........ A&M (S) SP-4761 12-15 79

Warriors........ A&M (S) SP-3151 8-10 Re
(Soundtrack.) Barry DeVorzon; Kenny Vance; Joe Walsh; Eric Mercury; Desmond Child.

Warriors........ Azra (S) 9342 10-20 82
(Picture disc.)

Washington Committee........ Double L (M) DL-2302 25-35 63
Baby Washington; Lloyd Price; Wilson Pickett; Billy Guy; Pookie Hudson; Wilbert Harrison.

Wattstax (The Living Word) (2 LP)........ Stax (S) STS-2-3010 15-20 73
(Soundtrack.) Isaac Hayes; Staple Singers; Rufus & Carla; Eddie Floyd; Bar-Kays; Albert King; Soul Children.

Wattstax 2 (The Living Word)........ Stax (S) STS-2-3018 15-20 73
(Soundtrack.) Isaac Hayes; Staple Singers; Luther Ingram; Richard Pryor; Rev. Jesse Jackson; Rufus Thomas; Carla Thomas; Bar-Kays; Johnnie Taylor; Emotions; Kim Weston; Eddie Floyd; Albert King; Soul Children.

Way It Was - the Sixties (3 LP)........ CBS (M) F3M-38858 10-15 70
Hosted by Walter Cronkite; interviews and news highlights. Includes: Beatles; Tony Bennett; Bob Dylan; others. (Reissue of *I Can Hear It Now - the Sixties*.)

We Are the World........ Columbia (S) USA 40043 5-10 85
USA For Africa; Bruce Springsteen & E Street Band; Steve Perry; Pointer Sisters; Northern Lights; Prince & Revolution; Chicago; Tina Turner; Huey Lewis & News.

We Cut This Album for Bread........ Bethlehem (M) BCP-86 15-20

We Funk the Best........ Salsoul (S) SA 8527 5-10 79

We Got 'Em Pretty Songs/Rhythm Songs........ Columbia (M) XLP 36099/36100 10-15 50s
(Promotional issue only. Identification number used since no selection number is shown. Issued in plain unmarked cover.) Tony Bennett; Jo Stafford; Jerry Vale; Rosemary Clooney; Percy Faith; Mitch Miller; Doris Day; Les Elgart; Jill Corey; Four Lads; Frankie Laine.

We Like Boys - Great Boy Oldies........ Oldies 33 (M) OL-8004 15-20 64
Wilbert Harrison; Jack Scott; Eugene Church; Jesse Belvin; Jerry Butler; Jimmy Charles; Wade Flemmons; Gene Chandler; Dee Clark; Maurice Williams; Ron Holden; Thomas Wayne.

We Like Boys - Oldies........ Vee Jay (M) VJLP-8004 15-25 64
Wilbert Harrison; Jack Scott; Eugene Church; Jesse Belvin; Jerry Butler; Jimmy charles; Wade Flemmons; Gene Chandler; Dee Clark; Maurice Williams; Ron Holden; Thomas Wayne.

We Shall Overcome........ UCR (M) 1 10-20 63
Joan Baez; Peter, Paul & Mary; others.

We Sing the Blues........ Bandy (S) 70010 5-10 80s
Chris Kenner; Aaron Neville; Showmen; Irma Thomas; Ernie K-Doe; Eskew Reeder; Willie Harper; Benny Spellman; Jessie Hill.

We Sing the Blues........ Bandy (S) 70012 5-10 80s

We Sing the Blues........ Minit (M) LP-0003 20-30 63
Ernie K-Doe; Jessie Hill; Chris Kenner; Irma Thomas; Willie Harper; Aaron Neville; Benny Spellman; Eskew Reeder.

We Three: see WASHINGTON, Dinah / Joe Williams / Sarah Vaughan

We Wish You a Merry Christmas........ Pickwick/Dot (S) SPCX 1004 5-10
Bonnie Guitar; Billy Vaughn; Liberace; Pat Boone; Hollaran Singers; Lawrence Welk; Lennon Sisters; Eddie Fisher; George Wright; Dr. Kendall.

We Wish You a Merry Christmas........ Vocalion (M) VL-3813 8-10 67

We Wish You a Merry Christmas........ Vocalion (S) VL-73813 8-10 67
Brenda Lee; Fred Waring; Earl Grant; Sammy Kaye; Voices of Christmas; Lawrence Welk; Lenny Dee; Pete Fountain; Wayne King; Earl Grant; Columbus Boys Choir .

We Wish You a Merry Christmas........ Natural Resources (S) NR-4011 5-10 78

We Wish You a Merry Christmas........ Harmony (S) KH-31536 5-10 72
Johnny Mathis; Marty Robbins; Jim Nabors; Andre Kostelanetz; others.

We Wish You the Merriest .... Harmony (S) HS-11351 5-10 69
Doris Day; Aretha Franklin; Johnny Cash; Frankie Laine; others.
We Won't Move .... Folkways (M) FS 5287 10-15 83
P. Constantini; Rob Rosenthal; Holy Tannen; M. Rawson; Sunny Bea; others.
We Wrote 'Em and We Sing 'Em .... MGM (M) E-3912 20-30 61
We Wrote 'Em and We Sing 'Em .... MGM (S) SE-3912 25-40 61
Eddie Cooley; Winfield Scott; Lincoln Chase; Otis Blackwell; Billy Dawn Smith; Ollie Jones.
Weird Science .... MCA (S) 6146 8-10 85
Weird Science .... MCA (S) 6152 8-10 85
(Soundtrack.) Oingo Boingo; Max Carl; Taxxi; Cheyne; Kim Wilde; Wall of Voodoo; Broken Homes; Wild Men of Wonga; Lords of the New Church; Killing Joke.
We'll Remember Always .... ???? 5-10
Four Lads; Danny & Juniors; Chris Montez; Chubby Checker; Santo & Johnny; Bobby Darin; Drifters; Lettermen; Jamies; Percy Faith; Brothers Four; Shirelles; Dreamlovers; Tempos; Four Freshmen.
We'll Take Romance .... Stack-O-Hits (S) AG-9010 5-10 81
Louis Armstrong; Charlie Barnet; June Christy; Vic Damone; Sam Fletcher; Robert Goulet; Lena Horne; Kingston Trio; Santo & Johnny; Sarah Vaughan.
We'll Take Romance .... Intermedia (S) QS-5051 5-10 83
Louis Armstrong; Charlie Barnet; June Christy; Vic Damone; Sam Fletcher; Robert Goulet; Lena Horne; Kingston Trio; Santo & Johnny; Sarah Vaughan.
Welcome to Columbia Country .... Columbia (S) CWS-2 10-15 60s
Johnny Cash; Arlene Harden; Stonewall Jackson; Statler Brothers; Carl Smith; Johnny Duncan; Judy Lynn; Marty Robbins; Harden Trio; Tommy Hunter; Ray Price; June Stearns; Flatt & Scruggs; Claude King; Billy Mize; Tommy Collins; Johnny Seay; Carl & Pearl Butler; Sammi Smith; Lefty Frizzell.
Welcome to Music City U.S.A. .... Columbia (M) CL-2590 10-15 66
Welcome to Music City U.S.A. .... Columbia (S) CS-9390 10-15 66
Carl Smith; Little Jimmy Dickens; Billy Mize; Flatt & Scruggs; Del Wood; George Morgan; Marion Worth; Marty Robbins; Stonewall Jackson; Harden Trio; Claude King; Tommy Collins; Carl & Pearl Butler; Carter Family; Johnny Cash; Ray Price.
Welcome to the Wondrous World of Admiral Stereo .... Decca (S) DL 734212 10-15
Brenda Lee; Warren Covington; Bob Rosengarden; Phil Krause; Mishel Piastro; Boss Combo; Teresa Brewer; Jan Garber; Lenny Dee; Bob Gibson; Bert Kaempfert; Carmen Cavallaro; Symphony of the Air with Leopold Stokowski; Pete Fountain & His Mardi Gras Strutters.
Welcome to Tyrol .... Epic (M) LF-18013 10-20
Welcome to Tyrol .... Epic (S) BF-19013 10-20
We're Playing Your Song .... Pickwick (S) RPS-1 20-40 80
Elvis Presley; others.
West Coast Doo Wop! .... Kent (S) KLP 2029 5-10 87
Young Jessie; Marvin & Johnny; Cadets; Jacks; Teen Queens.
West Coast Jazz .... Verve (M) MGV-8028 30-40 57
West Coast Jazz Anthology .... Jazztone (M) J 1243 15-25 56
Bud Shank; Chet Baker; Chico Hamilton; Bill Perkins; Gerry Mulligan; Hampton Hawes; Russ Freeman; Jack Sheldon; Cy Touff.
West Coast Love-In: see PEANUT BUTTER CONSPIRACY / Ashes / Chambers Brothers
Westbound Disco Sizzlers .... Westbound (S) 6107 5-10 78
Fantastic Four; Dennis Coffey; C.J. & Co.; Detroit Emeralds; Mike Theodore.
Western Gentlemen Brand, the Golden Country Hits .... Columbia (S) RS 1 8-12 60s
Flatt & Scruggs; Marty Robbins; Lefty Frizzell; Carl & Pearl Butler; Carm Smith; Marion Worth; Billy Walker; Ray Price; Claude King; Little Jimmy Dickens; George Morgan; Stonewall Jackson; Bob Atcher.
Western Hits .... Sutton (S) SSU 300 8-12
Martha Tilton; Ann Suthern; Dave Denny; Riley Shepard; Santa Fe Rangers.
Westminster Pop Sampler .... Westminster (M) WPS-1 8-12 56
Billy Butterfield; Dick Leibert; Ferrante & Teicher; Edric Connor; Deutschmeister Band; Organ & Carillon; Clara Petraglia; Antal Kocze; Herbert Seiter; Eric Robinson.
Western, Vol. 1 .... Artistic (EP) 223 15-25 65
(7 inch, 33 rpm. Also issued as *Original Country Hits*.) Eddie Dean; Chuck Hawkins; Rex Trailer; Johnny Williams; Foy Willing & Riders of the Purple Sage; Don Hughes; Sterling Blythe; Doye O'Dell.
Western, Vol. 2 .... Artistic (EP) 224 15-25 65
(7 inch, 33 rpm. Also issued as *Golden Country Hits, Vol. 2*, and also as *Original Country Hits*.) Maddox Brothers & Rose; Pete Pike; Ferlin Husky; T. Texas Tyler; Jimmy Dean; Webb Pierce; Hank Locklin; Slim Willet.
Western Hits .... Sutton (SE) SSU 300 5-10
Martha Tilton; Ann Southern; Dave Denny; Riley Shepard; Santa Fe Rangers.
Western Star Parade .... Vocalion (M) VL-3805 8-10 67
Western Star Parade .... Vocalion (S) VL7-3805 8-10 67
Sons of the Pioneers; Bob Wills; others.
Western Swing .... King (M) 876 20-30 64
Al Dexter; Spade Cooley; Red Stewart; Paul Howard; Leon Rusk; Curt Barret; Charlie Linville; Carolina Cotton; Luke Wills; Tex Atchison; Jimmy Widener; Jimmy Thompson.
Western Swing .... Old Timey (M) LP-105 5-10
Western Swing in Hi-Fi .... Decca (M) DL-8730 25-35 58
Westinghouse "All Around" Stereo Sound .... Columbia Special Products (S) CSP-150 10-20 60s
(Special products. Made for Westinghouse.)
Westward Ho .... Camay (M) CA-3029 10-20
Westward Ho .... Camay (S) CA-3029-S 10-20
Tex Ritter; Bob Wills; Tex Williams; Wesley Tuttle; Hank Fort; Cass County Boys; Elton Britt; Katie Lee & Barbara Allen. (Cocredits Tennessee Ernie Ford and Merle Travis instead of Wesley Tuttle and Katie Lee & Barbara Allen.)
What Stuff .... Iloki (S) 1011 5-10 90
Germs; Dils; Eyes; Skulls; Controllers; Kaos; Pandoras; Untold Fables.
What's in Store for You: see Capitol Promotional Releases/Samplers
What's New? Vol. 1 .... Capitol (S) SN-1 15-20 59

What's New? Vol. 4 .... Capitol (S) SN-4 15-20 59
Nat King Cole; Glen Gary; Les Baxter; Van Alexander; John LaSalle Quartet; Tommy Sands; Dakota Staton; Jackie Gleason; Kenyon Hopkins; Bobby Hackett; Guy Lombardo; Hank Thompson.
What's Shakin' .... Elektra (M) EKL-4002 15-20 66
What's Shakin' .... Elektra (S) EKL7-4002 15-25 66
Lovin' Spoonful; Paul Butterfield; others.
Wheelin' and Dealin' .... Prestige (M) 7131 25-35 58
When the Boys Meet the Girls .... MGM (M) E-4334 12-15 65
When the Boys Meet the Girls .... MGM (S) SE-4334 25-30 65
When the Boys Meet the Girls .... MCA (S) 25013 5-10 86
(Soundtrack.) Connie Francis; Harve Presnell; Liberace; Louis Armstrong; Sam the Sham & Pharaohs; Herman's Hermits.
When the Stars Go Marching In .... Camden (S) X-9018 5-10 72
Pete Fountain; Al Hirt; George Girard; Tony Almerico; others.
When the Wind Blows .... Virgin (S) 790599 8-10 87
(Soundtrack.) Roger Waters & Bleeding Hearts; David Bowie; Hugh Cornwell; Genesis; Squeeze; Paul Hardcastle.
When They Brought Down *the* House .... Columbia (M) XTV 69449 10-20 50s
Benny Goodman; Rosemary Clooney; Ezio Pinza; Jo Stafford; Frankie Laine; Mahalia Jackson; Duke Ellington; Charlie Barnett; Xavier Cugat; Maurice Chevalier; Jimmy Durante; Lionel Hampton; Marlene Dietrich. (Made for Dutch Boy Paints.)
When We Were Young (2 LP) .... Columbia Special Products (S) CSS 937 8-12
Doris Day; Mitch Miller; Mahalia Jackson; Gordon Jenkins; Robert Goulet; others.
When We're Together...with the Folk Sound .... Columbia Special Products (S) CSP-280 10-20 60s
Bob Dylan; Johnny Cash; New Christy Minstrels; Brothers Four; Norman Luboff; Village Stompers; Back Porch Majority; Banjo Barons; Pete Seeger.
When We're Together with the Swinging Sounds .... Columbia Special Products (S) CSP-276 10-15 60s
Andre Kostelanetz; Les & Larry Elgart; Bobby Hackett; Dave Brubeck; Jerry Murad's Harmicats; Duke Ellington; Count Basie; Village Stompers; Charlie Byrd; Art Van Damme; Percy Faith.
Where It All Began: see RICHMOND GROUP / Earl Preston's Realms / Michael Allen Group
Where It's At - Live at the Cheetah: see ESQUIRES / Mike St. Shaw & Prophets / Thunder Frog Ensemble
Where It's At, 32 New Affirmations of the Action (2 LP) .... Mills Music (S) 1000 15-20 60s
(Promotional issue only.) Yardbirds; Society's Children; Carmen McRae; Los Pekenikes; Fortunes; David & Jonathan; Earl Wilson Jr.; James Royal; Petula Clark; Gibsons; Life 'N' Soul; Mary Langley; Ray Conniff; Tony Hiller; Guess Who; Kenny Bernard.
Where the Action Is .... Design (M) DLP-210 10-20 65
Where the Action Is .... Design (S) SDLP-210 10-20 65
Jerry Lee Lewis; Neil Sedaka; Gene Pitney; Glen Campbell; Freddie Scott; Barry McGuire; Jan & Dean; Roy Orbison; Johnny Rivers; Floyd Cramer.
Where the Action Is .... International Award Series (S) AKS-277 8-12
Jerry Lee Lewis; Neil Sedaka; Gene Pitney; Glen Campbell; Freddie Scott; Barry McGuire; Jan & Dean; Roy Orbison; Johnny Rivers.
Where the Boys Are '84 .... RCA (S) ABL1-5039 8-10 84
(Soundtrack.) Judy Cole; Shandi; Rockats; Peter Beckett; Lisa Hartman; Toronto; Phil Seymour; Rick Derringer.
Where the Buffalo Roam .... Backstreet/MCA (S) 5126 10-15 80
(Soundtrack.) Jimi Hendrix; Wild Bill Band of Strings; Bob Dylan; Neil Young; Four Tops; Creedence Clearwater Revival; Temptations.
Where Were You When . . . . Dot (S) DLP-25979 10-15 70
Shields; Robin Ward; Dale Ward; Del-Vikings; Gale Storm; Jim Lowe; Tab Hunter; Gale Storm; Fontane Sisters; Rusty Bryant; Arthur Alexander; Hilltoppers; Sanford Clark; Dodie Stevens; Robin Luke; Carol Jarvis; Sonny Knight.
Wherehouse Singles of the Month .... Integrity (S) LP 6/13/79 20-30 79
(Promotional only issue.) Paul McCartney; others.
Whistle While You Work .... Somerset (M) P-3200 5-10
Ferko String Band; Plunketts; Joyce Romero; Sound Stage Orchestra; Ken Carson; Danube Strings.
White Mansions .... A&M (S) SP-6004 8-10 78
(Soundtrack.) Waylon Jennings; Jessi Colter; others.
White Nights .... Atlantic (S) 81273-1 10-15 85
(Soundtrack. Back cover has 10 photos of Hines and Baryshnikov.)
White Nights .... Atlantic (S) 81273-1E 8-10 85
(Soundtrack. Back cover has five photos, with clouds scene and two dancers on front cover.)
White Nights .... Atlantic (S) A1-81273 8-10 80s
(Soundtrack. Columbia House Record Club issue.) Phil Collins; Marilyn Martin; David Pack; Robert Plant; Roberta Flack; Sandy Stewart; Nile Rodgers; John Hiatt; Chaka Khan; Lou Reed; David Foster; Jenny Burton.White SpirtualsAtlantic (M) 134920-30 60
White Spirtuals .... Atlantic (S) SD-1349 25-35 60
Who Am I .... Wise Owl (S) 604 5-10 78
Chip Fields; Kim & Paula; others.
Who's News! .... Capitol (M) NP-1 15-30 62
(Promotional issue only. Issued in custom sleeve, not cardboard cover.) Vic Damone; Peggy Lee; Kingston Trio; Glen Gray; Stan Kenton; Four Preps; Jonah Jones; Lettermen; Nancy Wilson; Four Freshmen; Tennessee Ernie Ford; Brothers Castro.
Who's That Girl .... Sire (S) 1-25611-1 8-10 87
(Soundtrack.) Madonna; Duncan Faure; Club Nouveau; Michael Davidson; Scritti Politti; Coati Mundi.
Who's Who in the Swinging Sixties .... Columbia (M) CL-1765 15-25 62
Who's Who in the Swinging Sixties .... Columbia (S) CS-8565 15-25 62
Dave Brubeck Quartet; Sir Charles Thompson; Louis Armstrong; Gerry Mulligan Concert Jazz Band; Mose Allison; Chico Hamilton Quintet; Carmen McRae; Miles Davis Quintet; Jazz All-Stars; Lambert, Hendricks & Ross; Andre Previn; J.J. Johnson; Duke Ellington; Lionel Hampton.
Who's Who of Country and Western Music .... Capitol (M) T-2538 10-20 66
Who's Who of Country and Western Music .... Capitol (S) ST-2538 10-20 66
Buck Owens; Ferlin Husky; Jean Shepard; Sonny James; Wanda Jackson; Tennessee Ernie Ford; Bonnie Owens; Tex Ritter; Charlie Louvin; Ned Miller; Merle Haggard; Hank Thompson.
Whoppers .... Jubilee (M) JGM-1119 50-75 60
Dominoes; Orioles; Ravens; Four Tunes; Billy Ward; Sonny Til; Jimmy Ricks.
Why Study — Columbia LP Sampler .... Columbia (S) AS-1765 5-10
(Promotional issue only.) Translator; Elvis Costello; Wham; Paul Young; Midnight Oil.

Wild & Crazy Hits .... Era (S) BU 4910 8-12 78
Larry Verne; Rivingtons; Hollywood Argyles; Johnny Preston; Jewel Akens; Freddy Cannon; Fendermen; Coasters; Olympics; Johnny Cymbal; Lonnie Donegan; Trashmen; Paul Evans; Frankie Ford; John Fred; Jimmy Gilmer; Sam the Sham & Pharaohs.

Wild Angels: see ALLAN, Davie

Wild Hi-Fi/Stereo Drums .... Capitol (M) T-1553 10-20 61

Wild Hi-Fi/Stereo Drums .... Capitol (S) ST-1553 15-20 61

Wild Life .... MCA (S) 5523 8-10 84
(Soundtrack.) Edward Van Halen; Andy Summers; Three O'Clock; Louise Goffin; Charlotte Caffey; Peter Case; Bananarama; Charlie Sexton; Ron Wood; Van Stephenson; Hanover Fist.

Wild on the Beach .... RCA (M) LPM-3441 20-25 65

Wild on the Beach .... RCA (S) LSP-3441 25-35 65
(Soundtrack.) Astronauts; Frankie Randall; Sonny & Cher; Sandy Nelson; Jackie & Gayle; Cindy Malone.

Wild Thing (2 LP) .... Warner Special Products (SP) LSM-731 10-15 80
Troggs; Love; Knickerbockers; Guess Who; Castaways; Leaves; Paul Revere & Raiders; Kingsmen; Swingin' Medallions; Sir Douglas Quintet; Fireballs; Strangeloves; Music Explosion; Syndicate of Sound; Music Machine; Gentry; Swingin' Blue Jeans; Los Bravos; Bobby Fuller Four; Dino, Desi & Billy; Young Rascals; Human Beinz; ? & Mysterians; Five Americans; Seeds; Balloon Farm; Steppenwolf; Standells; Shadows of Knight; Count Five. (Special products. Made for Lakeside Productions.)

Wild Wheels .... RCA (S) LSO-1156 15-20 69
(Soundtrack.) Terry Stafford; Don Epperson; Thirteenth Committee; Billie & Blue; Saturday Revue; Three of August.

Wild, Wild Twist .... Chancellor (M) CHL-5017 20-25 61

Wild, Wild Twist .... Chancellor (S) CHLS-5017 25-35 61
Cousins; Playboys; Nite-rons; George Young; others. (Repackage of *Wild, Wild, Wildwood.*)

Wild, Wild, Wildwood .... Chancellor (M) CHL-5017 25-30 60

Wild, Wild, Wildwood .... Chancellor (S) CHLS-5017 30-40 60
Cousins; Playboys; Nite-rons; George Young; others.

Wild, Wild Winter .... Decca (M) DL-4699 12-15 66

Wild, Wild Winter .... Decca (S) DL-74699 25-30 66
(Soundtrack.) Astronauts; Jay & Americans; Beau Brummels; Dick & Deedee; Jackie & Gayle.

Wild, Wild Young Women .... Rounder (S) 1031 5-10 84
Janis Martin; Collins Kids; Nettles Singers with the Rodeo Tune Wranglers; Jean Chapel; Sparkle Moore; Joan King; Alvadean Coker & Cokers; Linda & Epics; Davis Sisters; Sparkle Moore with Dan Belloc; Rose Maddox.

Wildcats .... Warner Bros. (S) 1-25388 8-10 86
(Soundtrack.) Isley Brothers; Mavis Staples; Michael Jeffries; Randy Crawford; Sidney Justin; James Ingram; Tata Vega; James Newton Howard; Joe Cocker.

Will the Circle Be Unbroken (3 LP) .... United Artists (S) UAS-9801 10-20 72
Maybelle Carter; Earl Scruggs; Doc Watson; Roy Acuff; Merle Travis; Jimmy Martin; Vassar Clements; Junior Huskey; Norman Blake; Nitty Gritty Dirt Band; Pete Oswald Kirby.

Win a Trip with Me .... Prestige (S) 7539 15-20 60s
Lightning Hopkins; Holy Modal Rounders; others.

Windy City Harmonizers .... Chess (S) PLP 6082 5-10 80s
Moonglows; Quintones; Zeniths; Mellow Larks; Fair Lanes; Ravens.

Wings .... Capitol (S) SL-6621 8-10
Glen Campbell; Joe South; Corporation; Danny McCulloch; Stone Poneys; Bob Seeger System; Lothar & Hand People; Quicksilver Messenger Service; Linda Ronstadt. (Special products. Made for TG&Y.)

Wings of Sound .... K-Tel (S) TU-2730 8-12 80
Bob Dylan; Michael Jackson; Kool & Gang; Blondie; Nick Lowe; Journey; John Stewart; Little River Band; Kenny Loggins; Rupert Holmes; KC & Sunshine Band; Abba; France Joli; Sniff 'N' the Tears.

Winner Is .... Columbia (S) ???? 5-10
Andy Williams; Andre Kostelanetz; Jerry Vale; Johnny Mathis; Johnny Cash; June Carter; Terry Baxter; Columbia Pops Orchestra; Johnny Horton; Mantovani; Steve Lawrence.

Winners .... Buddah (S) 5624 8-12 75
Etta James; Glenn Yarbrough & Limeliters Reunion '74; Lettermen; James Cleveland; Al Wilson; Hagers; Molly Bee; Judy Kaye; Steven Geyer; Stampeders; Oak Ridge Boys; Sanford & Townsend.

Winners .... I&M (S) 017 5-10 80
Jacksons; Whispers; Shalamar; Rufus & Chaka Khan; Spinners; Carrie Lucas; Issac Hayes; Ray Goodman & Brown; Smokey Robinson; Commodores; Kool & Gang; G.Q.; Ray Parker & Raydio; Teddy Pendergrass; Dionne Warwick.

Winners .... Ronco (S) 2270 5-10 79
Barry Manilow; Al Steweart; Melissa Manchester; Toby Beau; Dave Mason; Dobie Gray; Alice Cooper; Eric Carmen; Taste of Honey; Boston; Hot Chocolate; Cheryl Ladd; Nick Gilder; Outlaws; Meatloaf; Johnny Mathis & Deniece Williams; Dr. Hook; Commodores.

Winners, Vol. 1 .... Harmony (S) HS-11310 8-12 69
Aretha Franklin; Everly Brothers; Dion; Cyrkle; Byrds; Chad & Jeremy; Bobby Vinton; Sonny & Cher; New Happiness.

Winners, Vol. 2 .... Harmony (SP) HS-11380 8-12 70
Aretha Franklin; Everly Brothers; Pozo Seco Singers; others.

Winners' Circle .... Columbia (M) GB-4 8-12
Duke Ellington; Les Brown; Woody Herman; Claude Thornhill; Pete Rugolo; Chubby Jackson; Les Elgart; Count Basie; Benny Goodman; Anita O'Day.

Winners Circle Number One Hits, Vol. 1 .... Motown (S) 935 5-10 80

Winners Circle Number One Hits, Vol. 2 .... Motown (S) 936 5-10 80
Four Tops; Supremes; Mary Wells; Temptations; Contours; Barrett Strong; Martha Reeves & Vandellas; Stevie Wonder; Smokey Robinson & Miracles; Brenda Holloway.

Winners of the 18 Band Surf Battle .... GNP/Crescendo (M) GNP-85

Winnin' Country .... 51 West/CBS (S) QR-16060 5-10 79
Johnny Cash; Johnny Duncan; Tammy Wynette; David Houston; Lynn Anderson.

Winter Gold (WCFL) .... WCFL (S) 142391 8-10
Tommy James & Shondells; Boyce & Hart; Ronnie Dove; Amboy Dukes; Barbara Mason; Five Americans; Toys; Turtles; Andy Kim; Deep Purple; J. Frank Wilson & Cavaliers; Peggy Scott & Jo Jo Benson; Bobby Darin; Mystics.

Winter Warnerland (2 LP) .... Warner Bros. (S) PRO-A-3328 15-25 88
(Promotional only issue. Colored vinyl.) Traveling Wilburys; others.

Winter Wonderland .... CBS (S) P-18403 5-10 85
Andy Williams; Tony Bennett; Percy Faith; Johnny Mathis; Ray Conniff; Englebert Humperdinck; Mel Torme; Barbra Streisand; Andre Kostelanetz; Steve Lawrence; Eydie Gorme.

Wired .... Varese Sarabande (S) VS-5237 12-15 88
(Soundtrack.) Michael Chicklis & Wired Band; Brian Francis Neary; Joe Strummer; Gary Groomes; Richie Havens; Ventures; Basil Poledouris.

Wishing You a Merry Christmas .... Columbia (S) 7322 5-8 69
Richard Tucker; Mormon Tabernacle Choir; Walter Carlos; Anna Moffo; others.

Wishing You a Merry Christmas .... RCA (S) LSP-4793 8-10 72
Wishing You a Merry Christmas .... RCA (S) ANLI-1952 5-8 76
Chet Atkins; Floyd Cramer: Willie Nelson; Jim Reeves; Dottie West; Hank Snow; Charley Pride; others.

Wisk 25th Anniversary Fabulous Fifties Favorites .... Columbia Special Products (S) P-16567 5-10 82
Elegants; Fiestas; Penguins; Crests; Connie Francis; Bobby Freeman; Frankie Ford; Diamonds; Danny & Juniors; Bobby Day. (Made for Wisk Detergent.)

With Love: A Pot of Flowers: see WILDFLOWER / Harbinger Complex / Euphoria / Other Side

With Strings Attached .... United Artists (S) SP-89 10-15 73
(Promotional issue only.) Shirley Bassey; Robert Thomas Velline; Bobby Goldsboro; John Barry; 50 Guitars of Tommy Garrett; Jim Bailey; Ferrente & Teicher; Francis Lai; Don McLean; Dory Previn; *Man of La Mancha* Soundtrack.

Withnail and I .... DRG (S) SBL-12590 8-10 87
(Soundtrack.) George Harrison; others.

Wiz (2 LP) .... MCA (S) 2-14000 10-12 78
(Soundtrack.) Diana Ross; Michael Jackson; Lena Horne; Richard Pryor; Nipsey Russell; Thelma Carpenter; Mabel King; Theresa Merritt; Ted Ross.

Wolfman Jack Presents 15 of the Best 45s, Vol. 1 .... Fairway (S) 1545 8-12 70s
(Mail order offer.) Wilbert Harrison; Bobby Lewis; Willows; Shepherd Sisters; Ritchie Valens; Jimmy Dorsey; Casinos; Little Richard; Fred Hughes Skyliners; Marvin & Johnny; Jerry Butler; Impressions.

Wolfman Jack Presents 15 of the Best 45s, Vol. 2 .... Fairway (S) 1545 8-12 70s
(Mail order offer.) Betty Everett; Dee Clark Gene Chandler; Teen Queens; Jesse Belvis; Maurice Williams & Zodiacs; Olympics; Chimes; Leaves; Bob & Earl; Terry Stafford; Spaniels; Isley Brothers; Dobie Gray; Crests.

Wolfman Jack Presents 15 of the Best 45s, Vol. 3 .... Fairway (S) 1545 8-12 70s
(Mail order offer.) Shirelles; Cannibal & Headhunters; Tee Set; Jody Reynolds; Huey "Piano" Smith; Rocky Fellers; Turtles; Lee Dorsey; Harptones; Gladys Knight & Pips; Dupress; Maxine Brown; Jimmy Clanton.

Wolfman Jack Presents 45 of the Best 45s (3 LP) .... Fairway (S) 4545 20-30 77
(Mail order offer.) Wilbert Harrison; Bobby Lewis; Willows; Shepherd Sisters; Ritchie Valens; Jimmy Dorsey; Casinos; Little Richard; Fred Hughes Skyliners; Marvin & Johnny; Jerry Butler; Impressions; Betty Everett; Dee Clark; Gene Chandler; Teen Queens; Jesse Belvin; Maurice Williams & Zodiacs; Olympics; Chimes; Leaves; Bob & Earl; Terry Stafford; Spaniels; Isley Brothers; Dobie Gray; Crests; Shirelles; Cannibal & Headhunters; Tee Set; Jody Reynolds; Huey "Piano" Smith; Rocky Fellers; Turtles; Lee Dorsey; Harptones; Gladys Knight & Pips; Dupress; Maxine Brown; Jimmy Clanton. (Repackage of the above three volumes.)

Women of the Blues .... RCA (M) LPV-534 10-15 66
Mamie Smith; Lizzie Miles; Sweet Peas; others.

Wonder Years .... Atlantic (S) 82032-1 8-15 89
(TV Soundtrack.) Joe Cocker; Was (Not Was); Judson Spence; Buffalo Springfield; Indigo Girls; Debbie Gibson; Escape Club; Julian Lennon; Van Morrison; Carole King; Crosby, Stills, Nash & Young.

Wonderful Waltzes of Country Music .... Starday (S) SLP-297 8-12
Cowboy Copas; Dean Manual; Blue Sky Boys; Red Sovine; Curly Fox; Johnny Bond; Pee Wee King; Red Stewart; Tommy Hill's String Band; Clyde Moody; Archie Campbell; Benny Martin; Lonesome Pine Fiddles; Shot Jackson; Buddy Emmons.

Wonderful World of Christmas .... Capitol (S) SL 800 5-10 75
Hollywood Pops Orchestra with Ralph Carmichael; Nat King Cole; Dinah Shore; Glen Campbell; Bing Crosby; New Christy Minstrels; Bobby Vinton; Anne Murray; Tennessee Ernie Ford; Tony Orlando.

Wonderful World of Christmas .... Capitol Special Markets (S) SL 8025 5-10
Merle Haggard; Pat Boone; Dinah Shore; Glen Campbell; Freddy Fender; Donna Fargo; Loretta Lynn; Ray Price; C.W. McCall; Jimmy Dean. (Made for Firestone.)

Wonderful World of Christmas, Vol. 2 .... Holiday (S) HDY-1933 5-10 81
Billy Vaughn; Bing Crosby; Frank Sinatra; Mantovani; Vienna Boys Choir; Roger Williams; 50 Guitars; Harry Simeone Chorale; Ronnie Aldrich; Vic Damone; Virtuoso Symphony of London.

Wonderful World of Country Music .... Camden (S) CAS-9032 5-10 72
Chet Atkins; Floyd Cramer; Skeeter Davis; Don Gibson; Dottie West; Dolly Parton; Jim Reeves; others.

Wonderful World of Country Music .... Starday (M) SLP 270 8-12
Wonderful World of Country Music .... Starday (S) SLP 270 8-12
Cowboy Copas; Jimmie Skinner; Willis Brothers; Red Sovine; Bobby Sykes; Leon Payne; Blue Sky Boys; Benny Martin; Lulu Belle & Scotty; George Jones; Curly Fox & Texas Ruby; Al Phipps Family; Lonzo & Oscar; Johnny Bond; Howard Vokes; Merle Kilgore.

Wonderful World of Gospel and Sacred Music .... Starday (S) SLP-255 15-20 63

Wonderful World of Word .... Word (M) W-3307 5-10
White Sisters; Frank Boggs; Don Hustad; Tedd Smith; Melody Four Quartet; Revivaltime Choir; Lew Charles; Cam Floria's Continentals; Ethel Waters; Fague Springman; Burl Ives; Salvation Army Band; Bill Pearce; Dick Anthony; Spurrlows; J.T. Adams; John Charles Thomas; Bill Mann; Kurt Kaiser.

Woodstock (3 LP) .... Cotillion (S) CT3-500 15-20 70
Woodstock (3 LP) .... Cotillion (S) SD3-500 15-20 Re
(Soundtrack.) Jimi Hendrix; Crosby, Stills, Nash & Young; Santana; Who; Ten Years After; Joe Cocker; Sha-Na-Na; John Sebastian; Canned Heat; Richie Havens; Country Joe McDonald; Joan Baez; Jeffrey Shurtleff; Jefferson Airplane; Sly & Family Stone; Butterfield Blues Band.

Woodstock II (2 LP) .... Cotillion (S) CT2-400 15-20 71
Woodstock II (2 LP) .... Cotillion (S) SD2-400 10-15 71
(Soundtrack.) Jimi Hendrix; Jefferson Airplane; Butterfield Blues Band; Joan Baez; Crosby, Stills, Nash & Young; Melanie; Mountain; Canned Heat.

Woodstock (5 LP) .... Mobile Fidelity (S) MFSL 5-200 80-100 87
(Soundtrack. Includes booklet.) Jimi Hendrix; Crosby, Stills, Nash & Young; Santana; Who; Ten Years After; Joe Cocker; Sha-Na-Na; John Sebastian; Canned Heat; Richie Havens; Country Joe McDonald; Joan Baez; Jeffrey Shurtleff; Jefferson Airplane; Sly & Family Stone; Butterfield Blues Band; Melanie; Mountain. (Repackaging of Cotillion releases.)

Woody Guthrie's "We Ain't Down Yet!" .... Cream (S) CR-1002 8-12 76
Arlo Guthrie; Seals & Crofts; Peter Yarrow; Hoyt Axton; Doug Dillard; John Hartford; Ramblin' Jack Elliot; John Beland; Jeff Gilkenson; others.

Working Class Hero .... Hollywood (S) ???? 10-12 95
(Promotional only issue, white vinyl.) Red Hot Chili Peppers; Toad the Wet Sprocket; Mary Chapin Carpenter; Candlebox; Blues Traveler; others.

Working Class Hero .... Hollywood PRCD 105322 8-12 95
(Promotional sampler.) Red Hot Chili Peppers; Toad *the* Wet Sprocket; Mary Chapin Carpenter; Candlebox; Blues Traveler.

World in Sound – 1977... Associated Press (M) AP-1977 80-100 77
Elvis Presley; others. (News highlights issue for radio stations.)

World of Blues... Imperial (M) 9210 20-30 63
T-Bone Walker; Charles Brown; others.

World of Country Giants... Columbia (S) G-30893 5-10 71
Marty Robbins; David Houston; Lynn Anderson; Carl Perkins; others.

World of Country Music (2 LP) .... Capitol (S) NPB-5 10-20 65
Buck Owens; Sonny James; Roy Clark; Jean Shepard; Hank Thompson; Ferlin Husky; Leon McAuliffe; Glen Campbell; Faron Young; Bobby Durham; Mary Taylor; Red Johnson; Tex Ritter; Wynn Stewart; Wanda Jackson; Charlie Louvin; Rose Maddox; Tommy Collins; Ira Louvin; Merle Travis; Neal Merritt; Ray Pillow; Mac Wiseman; Walter Hensley.

World of Country Music... Design (S) SDLP-640 8-12 60s
Hal Willis; Larry Steele; Stuart Hamblen; Maddox Brothers & Rose; Johnny & Jonie Mosby; T. Texas Tyler; Del Reeves; Glen Campbell; Wynn Stewart; Jimmy Newman.

World of Folk Music... FM (M) 319 8-12 60s
Big Three; Joe Mapes; Len Chandler; Allan & Grier; Fred Neil; Bob Carey.

World of Quadraphonic Sound, (An Introduction to) .... Columbia (Q) QX 31403 10-20 73
Paul Simon; Miles Davis; Santana; Peter Matz; Leonard Bernstein; Ray Conniff; Barbra Streisand; Andy Williams; Michael Tolan (narrator).

World of Swing (2 LP) .... Columbia (S) KG 32945 10-15 74
Baron Lee & Blue Rhythm Band; Don Redman; Claude Hopkins; Chick Webb; Teddy Hills; Stuff Smith & His Onyx Club Boys; Erskine Hawkins & Bama State Collegians; Mildred Bailey; Fletcher Henderson; Sedric & His Honey Bears; John Kirby; Jimmie Lunceford; Benny Carter; Coleman Hawkins; Cab Calloway; Benny Goodman; Harry James; Lionel Hampton; Duke Ellington; Count Basie; Woody Herman.

World of Surfin': see DALE, Dick / Surfaris / Fireballs

World Star Festival... Columbia (S) CSS-867 8-12
Frank Sinatra; Ray Conniff; Dionne Warwick; Ray Charles; Glen Campbell; Herb Alpert & Tijuana Brass; Julie Andrews; Mel Carter; Vikki Carr; Paul Mauriat; Andy Williams; Shirley Bassey; Tom Jones; Barbra Streisand; Sammy Davis Jr.; Dusty Sprngfield; Simon & Garfunkel; Bee Gees; Diana Ross & Supremes; Sonny & Cher.

World Wide Top 20 (2 LP)... Columbia Special Products (S) P-2-13749 8-12 76
Glen Campbell; Charlie Rich; Jessi Colter; Kenny Rogers & First Editon; Anne Murray; Linda Ronstadt; Mac Davis; Freddy Dender; Janis Joplin; B.J. Thomas; Emmylou Harris; Cal Smith; Merle Haggard; Ronnie Milsap; Crystal Gayle; Tanya Tucker; Freddie Hart; Willie Nelson; Tom T. Hall; Billy Crash Craddock.

World's Favorite Hymns .... Columbia (S) C-32246 5-10 73
Jim Nabors; Anita Bryant; Johnny Cash; Patti Page; others.

World's Greatest Bluegrass Bands .... CMH (S) 5900 5-10 77
Osborne Bros.; Joe Maphis; Carl Story; Mac Wiseman.

World's Greatest Bluegrass Bands (2 LP)... CMH (S) 5901 8-12 79
Osborne Brothers; Merle Travis; Joe Maphis; Pinnacle Boys; Lester Flatt; Nashville Grass; Benny Martin; Josh Graves; Grandpa Jones; Jim Silvers; Mac Wiseman; Paul Warren; Bluegrass Cardinals; Don Reno; Artuhur Smith; Bobby Smith; Boys from Shilott; Chubby Wise; Eddie Adcock & Martha; Carl Story; Tennessee Cut-ups.

World's Greatest Country Fiddlers (2 LP) .... CMH (S) 5904 8-12 82
Johnny Gimble; Buddy Spicher; Red Herron; Paul Warren; Ramona Jones; Benny Martin; Clarence Tate; Kenny Baker; Bobby Osborne; Chubby Wise; Cliff Bruner; Joe Maphis; Randall Collins; Jerry Moore; Ronnie Stewart; Paul Warren; Vassar Clements; Josh Graves; Chubby Anthony.

World's Greatest Rock Festival... Columbia (S) 1P-6145 5-10
(One LP. This LP was previously issued as *Reunion 74/2*.)

World's Greatest Rock Festival... Columbia (S) 2P-6144 10-12
(Two LPs. These two LPs were previously issued as *Reunion 74/1*.)

World's Greatest Rock Festival... Columbia (S) 6144 15-20
(All three LPs in two covers.)

World's Most Loved Christmas Classics .... Beautiful Music (S) BMR 3-0119 8-12
Dean Martin; others.

World's Worst Records .... Rhino (M) RNLP-809 5-10 83
Novas; Edith Massey; Jimmy Cross; Heathen Dan; Temple City Kazoo Orchestra; Gloria Balsam; Legendary Stardust Cowboy; Seven Stooges; Barnes & Barnes; Ogden Edsel; Turtles; Johnny Meeskite; Breakers; Wild Man Fischer.

World's Worst Records, Vol. 2 .... Rhino (M) RNLP-815 5-10 85
Mrs. Miller; Mickey Katz; Barnes & Barnes; Credibility Gap; Halos; Yogi Yorgesson; Shad O'Shea; Sticky Fingers; Debbie Dawn; Rockin' Richie Ray; Little Roger & Goosebumps; Napoleon XIV; Killer Pussy; Troggs.

Wraith .... Scotti Bros. (S) SZ-40429 8-10 86
(Soundtrack.) Tim Feehan; Honeymoon Suite; Stan Bush; LaMarca; Jil Michaels; Ozzy Osbourne; Lion; James House; Ian Hunter; Bonnie Tyler.

Wrinkles (Classic and Rare Chess Instrumentals)... Chess/MCA (M) CH-9293 5-10 89
Jody Williams; Big Three Trio; Little Walter; Chuck Berry; Paul Gayten; Otis Spann; Lloyd Glenn; Gene the Hat; J.C. Davis; Bo Diddley.

Wyatt Earp, Cheyenne and Other TV Favorites... RCA (M) LBY-1004 10-20
(Soundtrack.) Shorty Long & Happy Fellows; Prairie Chiefs; Sons of the Pioneers; Roy Rogers & Dale Evans.

Xanadu .... MCA (S) 6100 10-15 80
(Soundtrack.) Olivia Newton-John; Electric Light Orchestra; Cliff Richard; Gene Kelly; Tubes.

Y'all Come, Let's Have a Country Christmas... Starday (M) SLP-123 20-25 60

Year of the Ear, Vol. 1, the New Models, February 1977 .... Elektra (S) EA2-77 15-20 77
(Promotional issue only.) Cate Brothers; Corky Laing; Booker T. & MGs; Jelly; Television; Blondie Chaplin; Tom Waits; Andrew Gold.

Years to Remember .... Longine Symphonette (S) SYS 5384 8-10
Stan Kenton; Clyde McCoy; Paul Whiteman; Ray Anthony; Jerry Gray; Victor Lombardo; Johnny Long; Charlie Ventura; Charlie Spivak.

Years to Remember, the Big Bands .... Longine Symphonette/Capitol (S) SYS 5374 8-10
Les Brown; Glenn Miller; Artie Shaw; Billy May; Benny Goodman; Duke Ellington; Tommy Dorsey; Bob Crosby; Harry James; Claude Thornhill.

Yes L.A. .... Dangerous (S) 79 15-20 79
(Silk screened disc.) Germs; X; Bags; others.

Yesterday and Today .... York (M) YS-5001 8-10
Del-Vikings; Shirley & Lee; Willows; Harptones; Tokens; Shepherd Sisters; Gene & Eunice; Rocketones.

Yesterday's Apollo .... Harlem Hit Parade (S) HHP 5008 5-10 70s
Wilbert Harrison; Clovers; Platters; Moonglows; Lloyd Price; Huey Piano Smith; Jesters; Harptones; Paragons; Don Covay.

Yesterday's Gold (3 LP) .... Warner Special Products/Sessions (S) ARI 5002 10-15 76
(Mail order offer.) Byrds; Guy Mitchell; Marty Robbins; Percy Faith; Jimmy Dean; Johnny Horton; Bobby Vinton; Marvelettes; Blood, Sweat & Tears; O.C. Smith; Smokey Robinson & Miracles; Gary Puckett & Union Gap; Frankie Laine; Contours; Jr. Walker & All Stars; Johnny Horton; Buckinghams; Yardbirds; Marvin Gaye; Fantastic Johnny C.; Hollies; Ronnie Dyson; Shorty Long; Mark Lindsay; Spiral Staircase; Brenda Holloway; Roy Hamilton; Cyrkle; Marvelettes; Jimmy Ruffin; Robert John.

Yesterdays Goodies .... United Artists (M) UAL MX-22 20-25 61
Yesterdays Goodies .... United Artists (S) UAS SX-72 25-30 61
Marv Johnson; Clovers; Falcons; Tune Rockers; Lee Andrews & Hearts; Acorns; Jimmy Forest; Enzo Stuarti; Don Costa.

Yesterdays Goodies .... United Artists (M) UAL-3196 20-25 62
Yesterdays Goodies .... United Artists (S) UAS-6196 25-30 62
Marv Johnson; Clovers; Falcons; Tune Rockers; Lee Andrews & Hearts; Acorns; Jimmy Forest; Enzo Stuarti; Don Costa.

You Ain't Heard Nothing Yet .... Warner Bros. (M) PRO 113 20-30 59
George Greeley; Raoul Maynard; Don Ralke; Irving Taylor; Jim Timmens; David Terry; Marty Wilson; Billy Byrd; Marty Paich; Al Spider Gugan; Almanac Singers.

You Ain't Heard Nothing Yet .... Warner Bros. (S) XS-1307 20-30 59
Efrem Zimbalist Jr.; Roger Smith; James Garner; Edward Byrnes; William Holden; Matty Melneck; Mary Kaye Trio; John Scott Trotter; Trombones Inc.; Heindorf; Warren Barker; Garry Moore; Buddy Cole; Raoul Meynard; Ira Ironstrings; George Greeley.

You Are What You Eat .... Columbia (S) OS-3240 12-18 68
(Soundtrack.) Paul Butterfield; Electric Flag; Tiny Tim; Rosko; Peter Yarrow; John Herold; Hamsa El Din; John Simon; Eleanor Baruchian.

You Be a Disc Jockey (UBADJ) .... Cameo (M) C-1075 15-20 64
You; Don Bruce; Dee Dee Sharp; Bobby Rydell; Chubby Checker; Tymes; Orlons; Dovells; Rays; Tootie & Bouquets.

You Better Know It .... Impulse (M) A-78 10-20 65
You Better Know It .... Impulse (S) AS-78 10-20 65
Lionel Hampton; Clark Terry; Hank Jones; others.

You Can't Have Too Many Hits .... RCA (M) F7-MP-5774/5 10-20 55
(Promotional issue only. Issued in plain unmarked cover.) Eddie Fisher; Vaughn Monroe; Eartha Kitt; Lou Monte; Kay Starr; Nine LaFalce Brothers; Jaye P. Morgan; Perry Como; Henri Rene.

You Found the Vocal Group Sound, Vol. 1 .... Solid Smoke (M) SS 8031 5-10 84
Nutmegs; Edsels; Harptones; Del-Vikings; Mello-Kings; Fiestas; Dells; Danleers; Silhouettes; Capris; Hollywood Flames; Five Satins; Dion & Belmonts; Paradons.

You Found the Vocal Group Sound .... Solid Smoke (M) SS 8033 5-10 84
Little Caesar & Romans; Pentagons; Gallahads; Castaleers; Shadows; Valentino & Lovers; Pharaos.

You Must Have That Pure Religion .... Design (M) DLP-616 10-15 62
You Must Have That Pure Religion .... Design (S) SDLP-616 10-15 62
Wally Flowers; Texas Jim Robertson; T. Texas Tyler; Maddox Brothers & Rose.

You Must Remember These, Vol. 1 .... Bell (S) 6077 8-12 72
Five Satins; Silhouettes; Maurice Williams & Zodiacs; Tassels; Turbans; Nutmegs; Faye Adams; Don Gardner & Dee Dee Ford; Mello-Kings; Lee Allen; Bobby Marchan; Kodaks; Channels; Gladys Knight & Pips; Buster Brown.

You Must Remember These, Vol. 2 .... Bell (S) 6078 8-12 72
Box Tops; Syndicate of Sound; Crazy Elephant; Delfonics; Ronny & Daytonas; Edison Lighthouse; James & Bobby Purify; Joey Powers; Lee Dorsey; Merrilee Rush.

Young & Restless Album .... MCA (S) 6268 5-10 88
Patty Weaver; Beth Maitland; Michael Damian; Colleen Casey; Tracey E. Bregman.

Young America Rock 'N' Roll Songs (Milwaukee Sentinel Presents) .... Century (M) 3313 50-75 65
Coachmen; Shags; Seven Wonders; Fastbacks; Rogues; Yorks; Overtures; Woodsmen; Destinations; Ethics; Radicals; Patriots.

Young Love .... Era (S) BU 4810 8-12 78
Mamas & Papas; Ketty Lester; Kathy Young; Vogues; Jimmy Clanton; B.J. Thomas; Curtis Lee; Tab Hunter; Climax; Fleetwoods; Crystals; Gerry & Pacemakers; Austin Roberts; Dick & DeeDee; Brian Hyland; Pat Boone.

Young Love .... Dot (M) DLP-3183 25-35 59
Tab Hunter; Shields; Robin Luke; Del-Vikings; Sanford Clark; Jim Lowe; Bonnie Guitar; Carol Jarvis; Nick Todd; Rusty Bryant.

Young Lovers .... ABC (S) MD-11115 8-10 78
Sonny James; George Hamilton IV; Brian Hyland; Debbie Reynolds; Tommy Roe; Robin Luke; Hilltoppers; Andy Kim; Jimmie Rodgers; Fontane Sisters; Elegants; Robin Ward; Del-Vikings; Sanford Clark; Johnny Ace; Del Shannon. (Special products. Made for military sales as part of their "At Ease" series.)

Young Lovers (Design): see ROE, Tommy / Bobby Rydell / Ray Stevens

Young Sound '70 .... Somerset (S) 34400 5-10 70
Youngblood .... United Artists (S) UA-LA 904 10-12 78
Youngblood .... RCA (S) ABL1-7172 8-10 86
Youngblood .... Far Out (S) 904 5-8 Re
(Soundtrack.) Mickey Thomas; Starship; Mr. Mister; Autograph; Glenn Jones; Nick Gilder; Marc Johnson; John Hiatt; William Orbit.

Your Cheatin' Heart .... Columbia DS 683 5-10 76
(Columbia Record Club issue.) Stonewall Jackson; Billy Walker; Anita Bryant; Johnny Cash; Carl Smith; Marty Robbins; Charlie Walker; George Morgan; Johnny Horton; Frankie Laine.

Your Favorite Christmas Carols, Vol. 2 .... Firestone (SE) SLP 7011 5-10 63
Risë Stevens; Brian Sullivan; Columbus Choir; Firestone Orchestra & Choir.

Your Favorite Christmas Music, Vol. 4 .... Firestone (SE) SLP 7011 5-10 65
Julie Andrews; Vic Damone; Dorothy Kirsten; James McCracken; Young Americans; Milton Anderson; Firestone Orchestra.

Your Favorite Christmas Music, Vol. 6 .... Firestone (SE) SLP 7014 5-10 67
Jack Jones; Roberta Peters; Vienna Choir Boys; Firestone Orchestra & Choir; others.
Your Favorite Singing Groups .... Hull (M) 1002 300-400 63
Avons; Legends; Desires; Beltones; Pastels; Elegants; Monotones; Supremes; Carousels; Sparks.
Your Hit Parade (6 LP) .... Columbia Special Products (SE) P6 17180 20-30 83
(Boxed set.) Everly Brothers; Champs; Fred Astaire; Hal Kemp; Riley Farley Onyx Club Boys; Billie Holiday; Bing & Dixie Lee Crosby; Martha Raye with Dave Rose; Chick Webb; Mildred Bailey; Dorothy Lamour; Judy Garland; Kay Kyser; Kate Smith; Benny Goodman; Jimmy Dorsey with Bob Eberle & Helen O'Connell; Charlie Spivak; Cab Calloway; Harry James; Mills Brothers; Jo Stafford with Paul Weston; Les Brown with Doris Day; Pied Pipers; Dinah Shore; Modernaires; Kay Kyser; Al Jolson; Art Mooney; Ezio Pinza; Frankie Laine; Weavers with Gordon Jenkins; Patti Page; Tony Bennett; Guy Mitchell; Toni Arden; Percy Faith; Rosemary Clooney; Chordettes; Kitty Kallen; Mitch Miller; Roy Hamilton; Les Paul & Mary Ford; Vic Damone; Pat Boone; Johnny Mathis.
Your Hit Parade 1952 (2 LP) .... Time-Life (M) P2 20758 8-12 89
(Mail order offer.) Mills Brothers; Kay Starr; Perry Como; Eddie Fisher; Rosemary Clooney; Pee Wee King; Jo Stafford; Eddie Fisher; Percy Faith; Georgia Gibbs; Don Cornell; Johnnie Ray; Peggy Lee; Doris Day & Frankie Liane; Leroy Anderson; Patti Page; Tex Ritter; Les Paul & Mary Ford; Four Aces; Doris Day; Al Martino; Vera Lynn.
Your Musical Souvenir from QSP .... RCA Special Products (SP) QSP1-0042 50-70
Elvis Presley; others. (Special products. Made for QSP/Reader's Digest.)
Your Musical Souvenir from QSP .... RCA Special Products (SP) QSP1-0047 50-70
Elvis Presley; others. (Special products. Made for QSP/Reader's Digest.)
Your Old Favorites on the Old Town .... Old Town (M) OT LP-101 75-100 59
Fiestas; Robert & Johnny; Billy Bland; Royaltones; Keynotes; Solitaires; Valentines; Co-Eds; Harptones; Ruth McFadden.
Yulesville .... Warner Bros. (S) PRO-A-2896 10-15 87
(Promotional only issue.) George Harrison; others.
Zabriskie Point .... MGM (S) SE-4468 12-18 70
Zabriskie Point .... MCA (S) 25032 8-10 86
(Soundtrack.) Pink Floyd; Jerry Garcia & Grateful Dead; Youngbloods; Patti Page; John Fahey; Kaleidoscope; Roscoe Holcomb.
Zachariah .... ABC (S) ABC5-OC-13 15-25 70
(Soundtrack.) Country Joe & Fish; James Gang; Doug Kershaw; New York Rock Ensemble; White Lightnin'; Elvin Jones; Jimmie Haskell.
Zapped: see ZAPPA, Frank
Zapped .... Regency (S) 38-152 8-10 82
(Soundtrack.) David Pomeranz; Plain Jane; Rick Derringer; others.
Zenith Extended Range High Fidelity Demonstration Record .... Zenith (M) No Number Used 15-20 50s
(10-inch LP.) Doris Day; Tony DeSimone; Percy Faith; Brother Lee Roy & His Band; Jeff Morley; Eugene Ormandy & Philadelphia Orchestra; Jean Fournet Conding & Orchestra des Concerts Lamoureux; Paul Van Kempen with the Berlin Philharmonic; Corde Groot; Willem Van Otterloo & Hague Philharmonic.
Zenith High Fidelity Demonstration Record .... TV 20929 20-35 50
Eugene Ormandy & Philadelphia Orchestra; Jean Fournet Conding & Orchestra des Concerts Lamoureux; Paul Van Kempen & Berlin Philharmonic; Corde Groot & Willem Van Otterloo & Hague Philharmonic; Tony DeSimone; Percy Faith; Doris Day; Brother Lee Roy & His Band; Jeff Morley; Mike Wallace (narrator.).
Zenith Hootenanny Special .... Columbia Special Products (M) CS-216 15-25 63
Zenith Hootenanny Special .... Columbia Special Products (S) CSP-216 20-30 63
Bob Dylan; New Christy Minstrels; Brothers Four; Pete Seeger; Village Stompers; Clancy Brothers & Tommy Makem.
Zenith Jazz Set .... Columbia Special Products (S) CS-217 15-25 63
Zenith Jazz Set .... Columbia Special Products (S) CSP-217 20-30 63
Paul Winter; Andre Previn; Dave Brubeck; Duke Ellington; Village Stompers; Art Van Damme.
Zenith Presents a Christmas Gift of Music .... Columbia Special Products (S) CSS 834 8-12
Percy Faith; Ray Conniff; Mormon Tabernacle Choir; New York Philharmonic; Robert Goulet; Doris Day; Johnny Mathis; Patti Page; Bobby Vinton; Andre Kostelanetz; Charlie Byrd; Philadelphia Orchestra; Jerry Vale; Brothers Four; Norman Luboff Choir.
Zenith Presents Broadway & Hollywood .... Columbia Special Products (S) CSP-321 5-10 60s
Tony Bennett; Eydie Gorme; Steve Lawrence; Jane Morgan; Jerry Vale.
Zenith Presents Collectors Best (2 LP) .... Capitol Special Products (S) SL 6561/65 10-15 68
Hollywood Bowl Symphony Orchestra; Ella Fitzgerald; Gordon Jenkins; Nat King Cole; Guy Lombardo; Joao Gilberto & Antonio Carlos Jobim; David Rose; Seekers; Hollyridge Strings; Dinah Shore; Andre Previn; Jo Stafford; Whittemore & Lowe; Jackie Gleason; Kay Starr; Alfred Newman; Freddy Martin; Andy Russell; Miklos Rozsa; Glen Campbell; Frank Barber's Sound in the Round; Gordon MacRae; Rod McKuen; Franck Pourcel; Lettermen; George Shearing; Matt Monro; Nelson Riddle; Peggy Lee; Guitars Unlimited; Laurindo Almeida; Stu Phillips; Al Martino; Stan Kenton; Jimmie Haskell; Mexico's Golden Violins; Vic Damone; Glen Gray.
Zenith Presents Encore '72 (5 LP) .... Capitol Creative Products (S) SL 6734 15-25 72
Lettermen; Matt Monro; San Fernando Brass & Voices; Al Martino; Sounds of Our Times; Sandler & Young; Al DeLory; Peggy Lee; Tom Vaughn; Laurindo Almeida; Hollyridge Strings; Bobbie Gentry; Tennessee Ernie Ford; Glen Campbell; Nancy Wilson; Nat King Cole; Dean Martin; Joao Gilberto & Antonio Carlos Jobim; Xanadu Pleasure Dome; David Rose; John Williams; Ennio Morricone; Jackie Gleason; Tartaglia.
Zenith Presents Folk All Stars .... Columbia Special Products (S) CSP-324 10-15 60s
Back Porch Majority; Brothers Four; Clancy Brothers & Tommy Makem; New Christy Minstrels; Pete Seeger.
Zenith Presents From Broadway to Hollywood .... Columbia Special Products (S) CSP-213 15-20 60s
(Soundtrack.) Johnny Mathis; Andre Kostelanetz; Don Costa; Percy Faith; Julie Andrews; Ray Conniff.
Zenith Presents Jazz: Red Hot & Cool .... Columbia Special Products (S) CSS 326 5-10 60s
Dave Brubeck; Duke Ellington; Paul Winter; Thelonious Monk; Miles Davis.
Zenith Presents Romantic Moments .... Columbia Special Products (S) CSP-323 5-10 60s
Skitch Henderson; Percy Faith; Andre Kostelanetz; Ray Conniff; Andre Previn.
Zenith Presents Soft and Swinging .... Columbia Special Products (S) CSP-215 5-10 60s
Les & Larry Elgart; Glenn Miller Orchestra & Bobby Hackett; Lester Lanin; Ernie Heckscher; Ray Conniff; Andre Kostelanetz.
Zenith Presents the Best of the Easy Sounds .... Capitol Creative Products (S) SL-6564 5-10 70
(Issued in plain cover.) Laurindo Almeida; George Shearing; Nelson Riddle; Guitars Unlimited; Stu Phillips; Stan Kenton; Mexico's Golden Violins; Glen Gray; Gordon Jenkins; Joao Gilberto & Antonio Carlos Jobim; Hollyridge Strings.
Zenith Presents the Best of the Great Hits from Stage & Screen .... Capitol Creative Products (S) SL 6562 5-10 68
(Soundtrack.) Jackie Gleason; Matt Monro; Peggy Lee; Laurindo Almeida; Al Martino; Jimmie Haskell; Vic Damone; Lettermen.
Zenith Presents the Best of the Great Songs with a Folk Accent .... Capitol Creative Products (S) SL-6563 5-10 70
Ella Fitzgerald; Al Martino; Peggy Lee; Seekers; Jo Stafford; Glen Campbell; Kay Starr; Rod McKuen; Andy Russell; Guy Lombardo.

Zenith Presents the Hitmakers .... Columbia Special Products (M) CS-214 10-20 63

Zenith Presents the Hitmakers .... Columbia Special Products (S) CSP-214 15-25 63

Steve Lawrence; Eydie Gorme; Robert Goulet; Barbra Streisand; Patti Page; Tony Bennett.

Zenith Presents the Hitmakers, Vol. 2 .... Columbia Special Products (S) CSP-320 5-10 60s

Robert Goulet; Barbra Streisand; Andy Williams; Doris Day; Johnny Mathis.

Zenith Presents the Pop Stars .... Columbia Special Products (S) CSS-518 5-10 60s

Andy Williams; Eydie Gorme; John Davidson; Tony Bennett; Ray Conniff; Jerry Vale; Barbra Streisand.

Zenith Presents the Sounds of America .... Columbia Special Products (S) CSP-144 10-15 60s

Flatt & Scruggs; Halifax Three; Les & Larry Elgart; Village Stompers; New Christy Minstrels.

Zenith Presents the Thrilling World of Stereo .... Columbia (S) XTV-88654 8-12 60s

Les Elgart; Ray Conniff; Terry Snyder; Andy Williams; Andre Kostelanetz; Don Costa; Lionel Hampton; Art Van Damme; Skitch Henderson; New Christy Minstrels.

Zenith Presents Your Christmas Favorites, Vol. 3 .... FTP (M) MLP 7008 5-10

Zenith Presents Your Christmas Favorites, Vol. 3 .... FTP (S) SLP 7008 5-10

Gordon MacRae; Martha Wright; Franco Corelli; Roberta Peters; Columbus Boy Choir; Nat King Cole; Peggy Lee; Les Paul & Mary Ford; Les Baxter; Dean Martin; Tennessee Ernie Ford; Nelson Riddle; Sonny James; Kay Starr; Pee Wee Hunt.

Zenith Salutes the Broadway Musicals .... Columbia Special Products (S) CSS-520 8-12 60s

(Soundtrack.) Andy Williams; Robert Goulet; Julie Andrews; Henri Rene; Eydie Gorme; Ray Conniff; Andre Kostelanetz; Barbra Streisand; Steve Lawrence; Tony Bennett; Jerry Vale; Jane Morgan.

Zenith Salutes the Filmusic Scene .... Columbia Special Products (S) CSS 521 8-10 60s

Andy Williams; Andre Kostelanetz; Jerry Vale; Eydie Gorme; Tony Bennett; Jane Morgan; Robert Goulet; Barbra Streisand.

Zenith Salutes the Million Record Singers .... Columbia Special Products (S) CSS 519 5-10 60s

Barbra Streisand; Robert Goulet; Eydie Gorme; Johnny Mathis; Tony Bennett; Andy Williams.

Zenith Salutes the Mood Music Makers .... Columbia Special Products (S) CSS 522 5-10 60s

Andre Kostelanetz; Skitch Henderson; Percy Faith; Joe Harnell; Ray Conniff; Andre Previn.

Zenith Salutes . . . the Teen Sound .... Columbia Special Products (S) CSS-523 20-30 60s

Paul Revere & Raiders; Bob Dylan; Cyrkle; Byrds; Donovan; Chad & Jeremy; New Happiness; Dave Clark Five; Bobby Vinton.

Zig Zag Festival (2 LP) .... Mercury (SP) SRD-2-29 10-15 70

Blue Mink; Blue Cheer; Kenny Rankin; Screamin' Jay Hawkins; Linn County; Ekseption; Rod Stewart; David Bowie; Freedom Express; Mother Earth; Joe Cocker; Wayne Talbert; Lynn Hughes; Coven; Sir Douglas Quintet; Big Mama Thornton; Stephen Miller; Taos; Cuby & Blizzards; Tracy Nelson; Good, Bad & Ugly; Jesse Colin & Youngbloods; Fort Mudge Memorial Dump; Mickey Newbury; Jerry Lee Lewis.

MISCELLANEOUS PICTURE DISCS

ADVENTURES in AGAPELAND
Long Plays
MCA/SPARROW (2054 "Adventures in Agapeland")....10-15 83

AMERICA FREEDOM TRAIN
Long Plays
SEMAPHORE....50-60 76
(Boxed set includes picture disc, black vinyl EP, poster, book, and patch.)
SEMAPHORE....20-30 76
(Picture disc only.)

AMERICA LOOK & LISTEN
Long Plays
ADAMS (0001 "America Look & Listen")....40-50 76
(Promotional issue only.)

AMERICAN LEGION
Long Plays
SHINKYO (011 "American Legion")....75-100 68
(Made in Japan for distribution in Hawaii.)

AMERICAN REVOLUTION
Singles: 33rpm
AMERECARD ("1/2/3/4 "Bicentennial 1776-1976")....20-30 75
(Set of four postcards.)
AMERECARD....5-8 75
(Any individual postcard.)

ANCIENT AGE BOURBON
Singles: 45rpm
CBS ("Moments to Remember")....4-8 60s
(Square cardboard. No selection number used Promotional issue made for Ancient Age.)

ANNIE
Singles: 45rpm
CBS (169002 "Annie")....25-30 81
(Promotional issue only.)

AVE MARIA RADIO HOUR
Singles: 45rpm
COLUMBIA AURAVISION ("Sermon on the Mount")....15-25 59
(Square cardboard. No selection number used.)

BAKER, George: see RCA Victor Picture Discs

BALLANCE, Bill
Long Plays
MARK 56 (578 "Feminine Forum")....10-15 70s
(Radio feature hosted by Ballance.)

BAMBI
Long Plays
DISNEYLAND (3108 "Story and Songs of Bambi")....10-15 82
(Soundtrack.)

BARBI & HER FRIENDS
Long Plays
KID STUFF (6003 "Barbi & Her Friends")....10-15 81

BARRACAN, Arregio de J. Ruiz: see RCA Victor Picture Discs

BARRYMORE, Lionel
Singles: 78rpm
FAMOUS/RCA (3 "Hamlet")....30-45 41
(Laminated cardboard.)

BEAUTIFUL DREAMER
Singles: 33rpm
MUSICAL POSTCARD (1007 "Beautiful Dreamer")....5-10 50s
(Postcard disc.)

BENJI & HIS FRIENDS
Long Plays
KID STUFF (6004 "Benji & His Friends")....15-20 81

BERENSTEIN BEARS
Long Plays
KID STUFF (6014 "Meet the Berenstein Bears")....15-20 82

BERGEN, Edgar, & Charlie McCarthy
Long Plays
MARK 56 (615 "The Chase & Sandborn Show")....100-120 70s
(Original Radio Cast.)

BERRA, Larry "Yogi"
Singles: 78rpm
SPALDING ("How to Hit")....50-70 50s
(Square cardboard. No selection number used.)

BLONDIE
Long Plays
MARK 56 (624 "Blondie")....120-140 70s
(Original Radio Cast.)

BETTY BOOP
Long Plays
MARK 56 (658 "Scandals of 1974")....125-150 74
(Studio Cast.)

BOZO the CLOWN
Singles: 78rpm
CAPITOL/SIGHT 'N' SOUND (Bozo the Clown")....15-25 50s
(Square cardboard. Promotional issue made for Fedders Air Conditioners.)

BRENT, Bix, & 4 Cricketones: see Red Raven Movie Records

BROWN, Joe E.
Singles: 78rpm
FAMOUS/RCA (5 "The Cat and the Drunken Mouse")....40-60 41
(Laminated cardboard.)

BROWN'S, John, Raid
Singles: 45rpm
SCENIC SOUND ("John Brown's Raid at Harper's Ferry")....8-12 67
(Cardboard. Made for Kelo-Land TV. No selection number used.)

BUNNY PARADE
Singles: 78rpm
SOUND PACKAGING ("The Bunny Parade")....10-15 50s
(Cardboard.)

CAMPANELLA, Roy
Singles: 78rpm
SIGHT 'N' SOUND ("Brooklyn Dodgers")....150-200 50
(Square cardboard. No selection number used.)
SIGHT 'N' SOUND ("How to Catch")....125-175 52
(Cardboard. No selection number used.)

CAPE CANAVERAL MISSILE RANGE
Singles: 45rpm
MARX-ATOMIC ("Cape Canaveral Missile Range")....10-15 60s
(Square cardboard. No selection number used.)

CAPTAIN MIDNIGHT
Long Plays
MARK 56 (594 "Captain Midnight")....400-500 70s
(Original Radio Cast.)

CARE BEARS
Long Plays
KID STUFF (6016 "Introducing the Care Bears")....10-15 82

CARMICHAEL, Hoagy
Singles: 78rpm
CHARLES ECKART CO. ("Sing with the Road Show")....75-100 41
(Single-sided.)

CASA LOMA ORCHESTRA
Singles: 78rpm
CASA LOMA ("Glen Island Casino, New Rochelle, NY")....40-60 33
(Promotional only issue.)

CASPER THE FRIENDLY GHOST
Long Plays
PETER PAN (200 "Casper, the Friendly Ghost")....50-60 82

CAVANAUGH, Rose Stock: see Red Raven Movie Records

CELEBRATION '76
Long Plays
COLUMBIA/SCALES (1976 "Celebration '76")....20-25 76
(Musical score by Eugene Ormandy. Pictures Ben Franklin.)
COLUMBIA/SCALES (1976 "Celebration '76")....10-15 76
(Musical score by Eugene Ormandy. Pictures a shield.)

CHARLOTTE'S WEB
Long Plays
MCA (13302 "Charlotte's Web")....25-35 83

CHASE, Ilka
Singles: 78rpm
FAMOUS/RCA (4 "The Picnic")....30-50 41
(Laminated cardboard.)

CHATTERTON, Ruth, & Louella Parsons
Singles: 78rpm
FLEXO HOLLYWOOD ("Sunkist Radio Interview")....20-30 31
(One side is pink. No selection number used. Add $10 if with mailer-envelope.)
FLEXO HOLLYWOOD ("Sunkist Radio Interview")....20-30 31
(One side is pink. No selection number used. Add $10 if with mailer-envelope.)
Also see HARDING, Ann & Louella Parsons

CHICKEN DELIGHT
Singles: 45rpm
CHICKEN DELIGHT ("Chicken Delight Twist")....5-10
(Square cardboard. Promotional issue only, made for Chicken Delight fast-food chain. No selection number used.)

CHIQUITA BANANAS
Singles: 45rpm
EVA-TONE ("Hello, I'm Chiquita Banana")....5-10 75
(Square cardboard. No selection number used.)

CINDERELLA
Long Plays
DISNEYLAND (3107 "Cinderella")...20-30 81
(Soundtrack.)

CONFESSIONS OF A NYMPHOMANIAC
Singles: 45rpm
DIAMOND PUBLICATIONS....4-8

CONQUEST ALLIANCE RECORDS
Singles: 78rpm
CONQUEST ALLIANCE....60-80
(Set of both discs with mailer-envelope.)
CONQUEST ALLIANCE (170720 "En La Noche Que Te Vi")....25-35
CONQUEST ALLIANCE (170721 "Recuerdo Lejano")....25-35
(Shellac disc with cardboard base.)

COORS BICYCLE CLASSIC
Singles: 45rpm
CIBC (1109 "Theme from Coors Bicycle Classic")....8-12 85

COUNT CHOCULA
Singles: 45rpm
("Count Chocula Goes to Hollywood") . 4-8 80
(Cardboard cut-out from cereal box. No label or selection number used. Double price if still attached to box.)

DANCERINA
Singles: 45rpm
COLUMBIA/AURAVISION ("Nutcracker Suite")....8-12 68
(Cardboard. No selection number used.)

DANIS, Mel
Singles: 45rpm
AMERICAN AUDIOGRAPHICS ("Mad Look at Graduation Day")....8-12 81
(Square cardboard cutout from *Mad Magazine*. Pictures Alfred E. Neuman. No selection number used.)

DENVER UNIVERSITY
Long Plays
PACKER MURAL (0879 "Denver University")....20-25 81
(Promotional issue only.)

DIAMOND BAR HIGH SCHOOL
Singles: 45rpm
DIAMOND BAR ("Just You and I")....8-10 87
(Shaped disc. No selection number used.)

DISC JOCKEY JAMBOREE
Singles: 78rpm
PILLSBURY MILLS ("Disc Jockey Jamboree, Featuring Musical Guessing Game")....8-12
(Cardboard. Add $4 to $6 if with mailer-envelope.)

DORSEY, Tommy / Judy Garland: see Vogue (Sav-Way)

DRACULA
Long Plays
MARK 56 (720 "Dracula")....90-100 70s
(Original Radio Cast. Narrated by Orson Wells.)

DREW, Charlie
Singles: 78rpm
RECORD GUILD of AMERICA ("When the Old Village Clock Strikes Nine")....12-20 40s
(Cardboard. Promotional issue only made for Hotel Taft Bar & Tap Room.)
Picture Sleeves
RECORD GUILD of AMERICA....5-10 40s

DUNHAM, Sonny, & Orchestra: see Vogue (Sav-Way)

ECHO MAGAZINE
Singles: 45rpm
ECHO (Vol. 1 "A Magazine of Sight and Sound")....90-120 59
(Set of six cardboard discs with *Echo* magazine.)
ECHO....12-18 59
(Any individual disc.)

EDWARDS, Joan: see Vogue (Sav-Way)

EDWARDS, Webley
Singles: 78rpm
HISTORICAL BROADCASTING (1545 "Pearl Harbor Broadcast")....50-70 40s

ELECTRICAL WATER PAGEANT
Singles: 45rpm
DISNEY (WE-1 "Electrical Water Pageant")....30-40 73

EMPIRE STATE BUILDING
Singles: 78rpm
SIEMON ILLUSTRATED (170617 "Empire State Building")....60-80

ENFORCER
Long Plays
MARK 56 (707 "Enforcer")....90-100 79
(Soundtrack.)

EVERLAST PRODUCTS
Singles: 45rpm
EVERLAST....5-10 50s
(Postcard. No selection number or title used. Promotiona issue made for Everlast.)

FANTASY RECORDS
Singles: 45rpm
FANTASY....15-20 85
(Set of five adult-shaped discs.)
FANTASY....4-8 85
(Any individual disc.)

FEELING BA-A-AD
Singles: 45rpm
MUSICARDS (250 "Feeling Ba-a-ad, Get Well Soon")....3-6 80
(Square cardboard.)

FIELDS, Shep: see Vogue (Sav-Way)

FIELDS, W.C.
Long Plays
MARK 56 (571 "Nostalgia")....100-120 70s
(Original Radio Cast.)

FIRST NATIONAL CITY BANK OF N.Y.
Singles: 45rpm
1ST NATIONAL ("Christmas Greetings")....8-12
(Snowflake/star-shaped cardboard. No selection number used.)

FOR A CHRISTMAS RECORD
Singles: 78rpm
ANHEUSER-BUSCH ("For a Christmas Record: Jingle Bells")....10-15 50s
(Rectangular cardboard. No selection number used.)

FOX & THE HOUND
Long Plays
DISNEYLAND (3106 "The Fox & the Hound")....25-30 81
(Soundtrack.)

FROSTY THE SNOW MAN
Singles: 45rpm
PAMPERS ("Frosty The Snow Man & Santa Is Coming to Town")....8-12
(Square cardboard. Issued in box of diapers. Promotional issue made for Pampers. No selection number used.)

FRUIT LOOPS

Singles: 45rpm

FRUIT LOOPS....................................4-6
(Cutout from cereal box. Three different titles issued.)

GEM RAZORS

Singles: 78rpm

GEM ("Voices of Victory")................25-35 40s
(Cardboard. "Home Recordings" made by American Safety Razor Corp. with personal message from family to military member at war. Some have opening and/or closing comments by a Gem representative.)
Also see NELSON, Dick
Also see PEPSI
Also see SPECIAL SERVICES, U.S. MARINE CORPS
Also see USO/RAINBO

GET MORE from YOUR KENMORE

Singles: 33rpm

KENMORE (94404 "Get More from Your Kenmore")..8-12
(Promotional only issue. Square cardboard. Promotional issue made for Kenmore.)

GILLESPIE, Earl

Singles: 45rpm

VOCA-VISION (100 "Baseball Record Game: WEMP's Voice of the Brave")..........60-75 58
(Baseball-shaped disc. Includes picture sleeve mailer with instructions.)

GIRLS JUST WANT TO HAVE FUN

Singles: 45rpm

POLYGRAM (22062 "Girls Just Want to Have Fun")...50-60 85
(Soundtrack. Promotional issue only.)

GLEE HEART RECORDS

Singles: 78rpm

GLEE HEART (700 "Aries: Master of the Arcanes")....................................100-150 28
GLEE HEART (701 "Taurus: Crown of the Magic")..100-150 28
GLEE HEART (702 "Gemini: Chariot of Osirus")..100-150 28
GLEE HEART (703 "Cancer: The Balance & the Sword")..100-150 28
GLEE HEART (704 "Leo: The Tamed Lion")..100-150 28
GLEE HEART (705 "Virgo: The Wheel of Destiny")..100-150 28
GLEE HEART (706 "Libra: The Gate of the Sanctuary")..100-150 28
GLEE HEART (707 "Scorpio: TheTwo Lions")...100-150 28
GLEE HEART (708 "Sagitarius: The Two Ways")..100-150 28
GLEE HEART (709 "Capricorn: The Reading Skeleton")..100-150 28
GLEE HEART (710 "Aquarius: Iris, Urania")...100-150 28
GLEE HEART (711 "Pisces: The Dazzling Light")..100-150 28
(Artwork for this series provided by John Grippo.)

GLOBAL TV NETWORK

Singles: 45rpm

RHODES ("O Canada")......................15-20 74
(Canadian. Promotional only issue. No selection number used.)

GLYNN, Thomas

Singles: 78rpm

CHARLES ECKART CO. (Musical Gems from Mother Goose")..............................25-40 41
(Plastic coated cardboard flexi-disc. Several different titles exist. No selection numbers used.)

GOLDEN AGE OF R&B

Singles: 45rpm

ATLANTIC (1001 "Golden Age of R&B")..4-8 82
(Promotional issue only for Sounds Good Distributors.)

GRAHAM, Billy

Singles: 78rpm

BILLY GRAHAM EVANGELIST ASSOCIATION ("Billy Graham Family Gathered Around the Hearth")..20-30 52
(Square cardboard. No selection number used.)
BILLY GRAHAM EVANGELIST ASSOCIATION ("Responsibility of the American Home")..20-30 58
(Square cardboard. No selection number used.)
BILLY GRAHAM EVANGELIST ASSOCIATION ("Season's Greetings")...................20-30 52
(Square cardboard. No selection number used.)

Singles: 33prm

MANNA ("The Peace We Seek")......20-30 50s
(Square cardboard. Made for Billy Graham Evangelist Association. No selection number used.)

GRAHAM, Billy / Scottish Male Choir

Singles: 78rpm

BILLY GRAHAM EVANGELIST ASSOCIATION (5035 "24th Psalm"/All That Thrills My Soul")..20-30 55
(Square cardboard.)

GRAHAM, Billy / SHEA, George Beverly

Singles: 78rpm

MANNA (5067 "Meet the Billy Graham Team"/ "How Great Thou Art")....................20-30 55
(Square cardboard. Souvenir of a New York Crusade. Add $5 to $10 if with mailer-envelope.)
MANNA ("Ninety and Nine").............20-30 54
(Square cardboard. No selection number used.)

GRANT, Shauna

Singles: 45rpm

HUSTLER 4-8 87
(Shaped cardboard disc still intact with *Hustler* magazine.)
HUSTLER 3-5 87
(For disc itself.)

GREAT AMERICAN CAROUSEL CONVENTION

Singles: 45rpm

ERIKA ("Paul Link Medley").............10-15 84
(Shaped disc. No selection number used.)

GREAT MOMENTS IN ROCK & ROLL

Singles: 45rpm

QUAKER ("Guitar Heros")....................3-6 86
(Cardboard. Issued with box of Quaker Granola Dipp Bars. No selection number used. Has Jimmy Page, Jimi Hendrix, Jeff Beck, Eddie Van Halen.)
QUAKER ("Tribute to John Lennon")...10-15 86
(Cardboard. Issued with box of Quaker Granola Dipp Bars. No selection number used. Has excerpts from John Lennon songs.)
QUAKER ("Live Aid")..........................3-6 86
(Cardboard. Issued with box of Quaker Granola Dipp Bars. No selection number used. Has REO Speedwagon, Thompson Twin, Eric Clapton.)
QUAKER ("Motown Sound")..................3-6 86
(Cardboard. Issued with box of Quaker Granola Dipp Bars. No selection number used. Has Temptations, Jackson 5, De Barge, Commodores.)
QUAKER ("Rising Stars of Video Music")..3-6 86
(Cardboard. Issued with box of Quaker Granola Dipp Bars. No selection number used. Has Bangles, Alarm, Jon Bon Jovi, Psychedelic Furs, Romantics.)

GREETINGS and HERE'S GOOD WISHES FOR A 14 CARROT CHRISTMAS

Singles: 78rpm

CAPITOL ("Greetings and Here's Good Wishes for a 14 Carrot Christmas")..............50-75 47
(Pictures Bugs Bunny. Listed by title since no artist is credited. No selection number used.)

HANDLEY, Mary Louise

Singles: 78rpm

(1471 "Praise to the Lord")...........100-150
(No label name used.)

HAPPY BIRTHDAY

Singles: 78rpm

SEE HEAR (303 "Happy Birthday")...10-15 56
(Postcard.)

HARDING, Ann, & Louella Parsons

Singles: 78rpm

FLEXO HOLLYWOOD ("Sunkist Radio Interview").......................................20-30 31
(Single-sided, pink picture disc. No selection number used. Add $10 if with mailer-envelope.)
Also see CHATTERTON, Ruth & Louella Parsons

HAWAIIAN PICTURE RECORD

Singles: 45rpm

MUSICOLOR/PIPRECO (101 "Aloha Oe")...25-35 70s
(Made in Japan for distribution in Hawaii.)

HAWAII SINGS

Long Plays

MUSICOLOR (3005 "50th State Celebration")....................................15-20 75
(Made in Japan for distribution in Hawaii.)

HEIDI

Long Plays

K-TEL (5320 "Heidi's Song")............ 10-12 82

HELSTOSKI, Henry

Singles: 45rpm

ALLIED ("Listen")............................ 10-15 66
(Square-cardboard with picture of President Johnson and others. Made for New Jersey gubernatorial primary. No selection number used.)
ALLIED ("Listen")............................ 10-15 68
(Square cardboard with picture of Henry Helstoski for re-election to Congress. Track for above two includes L.B.J. and Kitty Kallen. No selection number used.)

HERM, David

Singles: 78rpm

BROWN & BIGELOW (123 "Merry Christmas")...................................... 10-15 51
(Square cardboard.)

HODGES, Gil

Singles: 78rpm

SIGHT 'N' SOUND ("Brooklyn Dodgers")................................ 100-125 50
(Square cardboard. No selection number used.)

HOUR of CHARM ALL GIRLS ORCHESTRA with Phil Spitalny: see Vogue (Sav-Way)

HOUR OF DECISION CHOIR / SMITH, Ted, & Paul Mickelson

Singles: 78rpm

BILLY GRAHAM EVANGELIST ASSOCIATION ("Wonderful Peace")....................... 20-30 55
(Square cardboard. No selection number used.)

IT'S A SMALL WORLD

Singles: 45rpm

DISNEY (WD-2 "It's a Small World").. 30-40 75
(Includes insert.)

JAMAL

Long Plays

TMS (1002 "Children's Musical for Christmas")...................................... 30-35 79
(Promotional only issue.)

JEWEL, James: see Vogue (Sav-Way)

JOE PALOOKA

Long Plays

MARK 56 (663 "Joe Palooka")..... 125-150 70s
(Original Radio Cast.)

JOHANNES PAULUS II

(Pope John Paul II)

Long Plays

SD (1984 "Message of Peace")........ 10-15 84

JOHNSON, Jimmy

Long Plays

WONDER (JJIDO "That's My L.A.") . 30-50 84
(Promotional issue made for L.A. Olympics.)

JUNGLE BOOK

Long Plays

DISNEYLAND (3105 "Jungle Book").. 10-15 81
(Soundtrack.)

KASSEL, Art: see Vogue (Sav-Way)

KIDDIE RECORDS

Singles: 78rpm

KIDDIE (1 "Song & Story Book #1")................................ 80-120 30s
(Has picture on non-playing side. Set with story book and six discs: 1001-1006.)
KIDDIE (2 "Song & Story Book #2")................................... 80-120 30s
(Has picture on non-playing side. Set with story book and six discs: 201-206.)
KIDDIE 15-20 30s
(For any individual disc.)

KING'S JESTERS & LOUISE: see Vogue (Sav-Way)

L&M QUARTET

Singles: 45rpm

CONSOLIDATED LITHO ("Christmas Carols").. 8-12 80
(Promotional only square cardboard. Made for Liggett & Meyers. No selection number used.)

LADY & THE TRAMP

Long Plays

DISNEYLAND (3103 "The Lady & the Tramp").. 15-18 80
(Soundtrack.)

LARGE, Don, Chorus: see Vogue (Sav-Way)

LASALLE, Dick: see Vogue (Sav-Way)

LAUREL & HARDY

Long Plays

MARK 56 (575 "Laurel & Hardy")... 80-100 78
(Soundtrack.)
MARK 56 (577 "Babes in Toyland")....................................... 90-120 78
(Soundtrack.)
MARK 56 (579 "Another Fine Mess").. 60-80 78
(Soundtrack.)

LEE, Nancy, & Hilltoppers: see Vogue (Sav-Way)

LEONARD, Gloria

Singles: 45rpm

HIGH SOCIETY (December 1979 "Opens Her Holiday Gift Box").............................. 5-8 80
(Square cardboard cutouts from *High Society* magazine.)
HIGH SOCIETY (May 1980 "Succulent Sounds of Double Trouble")............................ 5-8 80
(Square cardboard cutouts from *High Society* magazine.)
HIGH SOCIETY (October 1980 "Head of the Class").. 5-8 80
(Square cardboard cutouts from *High Society* magazine.)
HIGH SOCIETY 10-20 80
(For any magazine with picture disc intact.)

LIFE CEREAL: see Rock Music Mystery

LI'L WALLY & HIS FAMOUS POLKA BAND

Singles: 33rpm

MUSICAL POSTCARD (1009 "Seven Days & Seven Nights Without You") 5-10 50s
(Postcard.)

LIONEL TRAIN EFFECT SOUNDS

Singles: 78rpm

LIONEL.. 25-35 50s
(Laminated cardboard.) Issued in folder which adds $10 to value.)

LIPPMAN, Eva, & Gladys Gewirtz

Singles: 78rpm

MENORAH (P5/P6 "Candle Man")... 15-25 50s
(Children's series.)

LITTLE ORPHAN ANNIE

Long Plays

MARK 56 (593 "Little Orphan Annie")... 100-125 79
(Original Radio Cast.)

LOCKMAN, Whitey

Singles: 78rpm

SIGHT 'N' SOUND ("How to Play First Base").. 60-90 52
(Cardboard. No selection number used.)

LONGINES SYMPHONETTE

Singles: 45rpm

COLUMBIA SPECIAL PRODUCTS ("Choraliers Treasury")................................. 6-12 60s
(Narrated by Frank Knight. No selection number used.)

LOS ANGELES RAIDERS

Singles: 45rpm

RHINO (70260 "Silver")................... 10-15 86
(Raider's shield logo-shape.)

LULU BELLE & SCOTTY: see Vogue (Sav-Way)

LUTHER, Frank: see RCA Victor Picture Discs

MACK, Gilbert, & Peggy Allenby, & Walt Kelly

Singles: 78rpm

STORY BOOK.................................. 60-80
(Boxed four cardboard disc set.)
STORY BOOK.................................. 12-20
(For any individual disc.)

MAD MAN MATT

Singles: 45rpm

AZRA.. 8-12 86
(Hexagon shape.)

MacGREGOR, Scotty

Singles: 78rpm

PHONOGRAPH ("Record from Santa Claus")... 20-25 48
(Shaped disc. No selection number used.)

MADRIGUERA, Enric: see Vogue (Sav-Way)

MAGIC TALKING BOOKS

Singles: 78rpm

SIGHT-N-SOUND 25-35 55
(Cardboard disc is front cover of 28 page children's book. Nineteen different record books were issued: T-1 thru T-19.)
SIGHT-N-SOUND 10-20 55
(Cardboard disc without book.)

MAIN STREET ELECTRICAL PARADE
Singles: 45rpm
DISNEY (DE-1 "Main Street Electrical Parade")........................15-25 73
DISNEY (DE-4 "Main Street Electrical Parade")........................15-25 73
DISNEY (DE-5 "Main Street Electrical Parade")........................15-25 77
(With insert.)
DISNEY (WD-4 "Main Street Electrical Parade")........................15-25 74
DISNEY (WE-4 "Main Street Electrical Parade")........................15-25 73

MANN, Marion: see Vogue (Sav-Way)

MASTERS, Frankie: see Vogue (Sav-Way)

McCOY, Clyde: see Vogue (Sav-Way)

MARY POPPINS
Long Plays
DISNEYLAND (3104 "Mary Poppins")........................20-30 81
(Soundtrack.)

MASTERS OF THE UNIVERSE
Long Plays
KID STUFF (6018 "Masters of the Universe")........................50-60 84

McDONALD, Ronald
Singles: 45rpm
McDONALDS ("The Night Before Christmas")........................5-10 74
(Square cardboard. No selection number used.)

McDONALDLAND
Long Plays
KID STUFF (6017 "Welcome to McDonaldland")........................10-15 83

McHARGUE, Rosey
Singles: 45rpm
AMERIVENT ("Music to Install Gas Vents By")........................5-10
(Postcard. Promotional issue made for American Metal Products. No selection number used.)

McPHERSON, Aimee Semple
Singles: 78rpm
McPHERSON ("The Foursome Gospel")........................60-80
(Promotional issue made for National Voice Library Productions of Hollywood. No selection number used.)

MENORAH RECORDS
Singles: 78rpm
MENORAH........................15-25 50s
(Children's series.)
Also see LIPPMAN, Eva, & Gladys Gewirtz

MERCURY PICTURE DISC SERIES
Note: Discs in this series are found in the A-Z listings in the body of the book. Each is referenced here for easy access.
MERCURY (1027 "On the Sunny Side of the Street"): see LAINE, Frankie
MERCURY (1028 "West End Blues"): see LAINE, Frankie
MERCURY (3055/5026 "To Me"): see BABBIT, Harry / Tony Martin
MERCURY (3059/5041 "Ask Anyone Who Knows"): see ELLIS, Anita / Glen Gray & His Orchestra
MERCURY (3059/8040 "Ask Anyone Who Knows"): see ELLIS, Anita / Albert Ammons
MERCURY (3060/5049 "Here We Are"): see LORENZ, John / Starlighters
MERCURY (3066/5057 "Ragtime Cowboy"): see COOL, Harry / Frances Langford
MERCURY (5038 "Stardust"): see MELIS, Jose
MERCURY (5047 "Rhapsody in Blue"): see FINA, Jack
MERCURY (5053 "Ivy"): see DAMONE, Vic
MERCURY (5054 "Hawaiian War Chant"): see COURTNEY, Del
MERCURY (5056/5055 "You Do"): see DAMONE, Vic / Dick "Two Ton" Baker
MERCURY (5059 "Kiss Me Again"): see LAINE, Frankie
MERCURY (6045/6049 "Lemme Outa Here"): see CURTIS, Ken / Rex Allen & Arizona Wranglers

MERRY CHRISTMAS FROM CAPITOL RECORDS OF HOLLYWOOD
Singles: 78rpm
CAPITOL ("Merry Christmas from Capitol Records of Holly: a Happy '47 from the Entire Capitol Family")........................20-30 46
(Cardboard. No selection number used.)

MERRY CHRISTMAS! MERRY CHRISTMAS!
Singles: 78rpm
SEE HEAR (202 "Merry Christmas! Merry Christmas!")........................10-15 56
(Postcard. Has song in several languages.)

MERRY MELODY SINGERS
Singles: 78rpm
PLAYSONG (MM series)........................12-20 40s
(Cardboard. At least six different titles exist.)

MERRY SINGERS: see PicturTone Records

MESSAGE FROM SANTA CLAUS
Singles: 78rpm
PHONODISC (40/42 "Message from Santa Clause")........................25-35 48
(Shaped cardboard.)
Also see PHONODISC PICTURE RECORDS

MICKEY MOUSE
Singles: 78rpm
TALKIN' JECTOR........................50-75 33
(The "Talkie and Movie Jector" picture record. Made for a special projector/turntable.)
Long Plays
DISNEYLAND (3109 "Mickey's Christmas Carol")........................50-60 82
(Soundtrack.)
DISNEYLAND (3111 "Mickey Mouse Disco")........................15-20 82

MIGHTY AMERICA
Singles: 45rpm
L (5193 "Mighty America")........................15-25 81
(250 made.)

MITCHELL'S, Ollie, Sunday Band
Singles: 45rpm
CHEESE & OLIVE ("Apple Pie Seven Baseball")........................10-15
(Baseball-shaped disc. No selection number used.)

MITCHUM, Johnny
Long Plays
QUADDES (001 "Chicken Reel")......70-80 74
(Made for his band members upon winning National Fiddle Championship.)

MOJICA, Jose: see RCA Victor Picture Discs

MONSTER ADVENTURES in OUTER SPACE
Singles: 45rpm
("Monster Adventures in Outer Space")........................4-6
(Cardboard cutout from cereal box. No label name or selection number used. Double value if still attached to box.)

MONTANA, Patsy: see Vogue (Sav-Way)

MORE AMERICAN GRAFITTI
Long Plays
MCA........................30-40 79
(Soundtrack.)

MOTHER GOOSE PLAYERS
Singles: 78rpm
PLAYSONG (MG series)........................12-20 40s
(Cardboard. At least six different titles exist.)

MULLALY, Father Charles J., S.J.
Singles: 78rpm
NATIONAL FILM & DISC ("Words of the Holy Father")........................40-60 31
(English translation of *Voice & Words of His Holiness*, by Pope Pius XI. Has same picture. No selection number used.)
Also see POPE PIUS XI

MUSGRAVE, Jim
Singles: 45rpm
BLUE JAY VILLAGE ("It's Christmas in Blue Jay Village")........................15-20
(Promotional only issue. No selection number used.)

MUSIAL, Joe: see RCA VICTOR PICTURE DISCS

MUSICAL SOUVENIR
Long Plays
DISNEY (WD-3 "Musical Souvenir of America on Parade")........................75-100 75
DISNEY (WE-2 "Musical Sovenir of Walt Disney World's Magic Kingdom")........................80-120 73

NELSON, Dick
Singles: 78rpm
GEM RAZORS ("Gem Blade Reporter")........................40-50 40s
(War effort contribution disc "presented as a momento of your participation in a Salute to Our Commander-in-Chief." Has photo of President Roosevelt. Has two play holes.)
Also see GEM RAZORS
Also see ROOSEVELT, Franklin D.

NEW EBENEZER BAPTIST CHURCH
Long Plays
DELTRON ("Keep Your Head to the Sky")........................15-25 75
(Promotional only issue. No selection number used.)

NEW YORK JETS / NEW YORK GIANTS
Long Plays
("New York Jets/New York Giants") . 30-40 80s
(One side has sketch of Joe Namath, other side has one of Phil Sims. No label name or selection number used.)

NOCTURNE STRING QUARTET: see see Vogue (Sav-Way)

O COME ALL YE FAITHFUL
Singles: 78rpm
LOOK-N-LISTEN ("O Come All Ye Faithful")........................8-12 57
(Cardboard. "A Countess Fruit Cake Holiday Record." No selection number used.)

OPERETT SLAGEREK
Long Plays
GLOBE (568-89 "Operett Slagerek")........................6-12 81
(Original Cast. Hungarian opera.)
GLOBE (7301954 "Operett Slagerek")........................15-25 81
(Original Cast. Four disc set with one picture disc and three colored vinyl discs.)

ORTIZ, Alfonso: see RCA Victor Picture Discs

PADDINGTON
Long Plays
KID STUFF (6008 "Songs of Paddington")........................10-15 82

PARIS, Norman, Trio
Singles: 45rpm
("Sweatered Look for Knitted Outerware Foundation")........................5-10 60s
(Square cardboard. No label name or selection number used.)

PARK, Alvin
Singles: 78rpm
SPALDING ("How to Field")........................50-70 50s
(Square cardboard. No selection number used.)

PARNELL, Mel
Singles: 78rpm
SIGHT 'N' SOUND ("Red Sox")........ 50-70 47
(Square cardboard. No selection number used.)

PEPSI
Singles: 78rpm
RECORDISC ("Dear Friend from Pepsi")........................25-35 40s
(Cardboard. "Home Recordings" made by Pepsi Cola for those serving in the military to use as audio letters to family and friends.)
Also see Gem Razors

PETER PAN
Long Plays
DISNEYLAND (3110 "Peter Pan") ... 15-20 82
(Soundtrack.)

PHONODISC PICTURE RECORDS
Singles: 78rpm
PHONODISC (series)........................25-35 48
(Shaped cardboard.)
Also see MESSAGE FROM SANTA CLAUS
Also see VALENTINE GREETINGS SONGS

PHONOSCOPE POSTCARDS
Singles: 78pm
PHONOSCOPE........................15-20 57
(Postcard series. Made in Switzerland for USA distribution.)
Singles: 45rpm
PHONOSCOPE........................10-15 57
(Postcard series. Made in Switzerland for USA distribution.)

PICKWICK CAROL GROUP
Singles: 45rpm
HAWTHORNE HOUSE ("Silent Night")........................5-8
(Cardboard Christmas card. No selection number used.)

PICTORIAL RECORDS
Singles: 78rpm
PICTORIAL (10001 "Three Little Kittens")........................70-90
PICTORIAL (10002 "Little Bo Peep")........................70-90
PICTORIAL (10003 "Mary Had a Little Lamb")........................70-90
PICTORIAL (10005 "Little Boy Blue")........................70-90
PICTORIAL (20003 "Christ in the Temple")........................70-90
PICTORIAL........................70-90
(For any other individual discs not listed here.)
PICTORIAL........................250-300
(Set of three discs, with gatefold cover.)
Note: All of these discs were originally sold in sets of three. All were issued circa 1929.

PICTURTONE RECORDS
Singles: 78rpm
PICTURTONE (D series)........................12-20 48
(Cardboard. "Folk Dances" series.)
PICTURTONE (D series)........................45-65 48
(Three disc boxed set.)
PICTURTONE (G series)........................15-25 48
(Cardboard. "Greetings Songs" series.)
PICTURTONE (H series)........................12-20 48
(Cardboard. "Holiday Songs" series.)
PICTURTONE (H series)........................45-65 48
(Three disc boxed set.)
PICTURTONE (JCS series)........................15-25 48
(Cardboard.)
PICTURTONE (M series)........................12-20 48
(Cardboard. "Musical Tales" series. Many are credited to the Merry Singers.)
PICTURTONE (MAR series)........................12-20 48
(Cardboard. "Marching Songs" series.)
PICTURTONE (P series)........................15-25 48
(Cardboard. "Play-Party Songs" series. Many are credited to the Merry Singers.)
PICTURTONE (S series)........................12-20 48
(Cardboard. "Folk Songs" series.)
PICTURTONE (10000 series)........................20-25 48
(Cardboard. "Treasure Tales for Children" series.)

PINK PANTHER
Long Plays
KID STUFF (6010 "Country Album")........................15-20 82

PINOCCHIO
Long Plays
DISNEYLAND (3102 "Pinocchio") ... 15-18 80
(Soundtrack.)

PINOCCHIO" & "WIZARD of OZ
Long Plays
MCA (13301 "Pinocchio" & "Wizard of Oz")........................30-40 83
(Soundtrack.)

PIX RECORDS
Singles: 78rpm
PIX (101 "Mary Had a Little Lamb").. 30-40 41
PIX (102 "Humpty Dumpty")........................30-40 41
PIX (103 "Little Miss Muffet")........................30-40 41
PIX (104 "Little Jack Horner")........................30-40 41
PIX (105 "Hey Diddle Diddle")........................30-40 41
PIX (106 "Old Woman in the Shoe") 30-40 41
PIX (107 "Hickory Dickory Dock")........................30-40 41
PIX (108 "Jack and Jill")........................30-40 41
PIX (109 "Deedle Deedle Dumplings")........................30-40 41
Note: All of these are cardboard with clear sheet of lamination taped around outer edge. Manufactured by Dupli-Kut.)

PLAYOLA RECORDS
Singles: 78rpm
PLAYOLA (99 "A Little Story for You")........................75-125 48
(Cardboard. Comes with audio instructions and three songs. Also includes the Playola Player, a crank record player.)
PLAYOLA (99 "A Little Story for You")........................25-35 48
(Cardboard includes audio instructions and three songs. Sold with the Playola record player.)
PLAYOLA (101 "Goldilocks and the Three Bears")........................60-75 48
(Set of three in custom folder.)
PLAYOLA (102 "Cinderella")........................60-75 48
(Set of three in custom folder.)
PLAYOLA (103 "Gingerbread Boy"/Sleeping Beauty"/"Ugly Duckling")........................60-75 48
(Set of three in custom folder.)
PLAYOLA (104 "23 Children's Nursery Rhymes")........................60-75 48
(Set of three in custom folder.)
PLAYOLA (105 ""Wind and the Sun"/"Tortoise and the Hare"/"Wolf! Wolf!")........................60-75 48
(Set of three in custom folder. Titled *Famous Fables: Lion and the Mouse.*)
PLAYOLA........................15-20 48
(Each disc. All Playola discs are cardboard.)
PLAYOLA........................10-15 48
(Folder only.)

PLAYSONG RECORDS

Singles: 78rpm

PLAYSONG 10-20 40s
(Cardboard.)
Also see MOTHER GOOSE PLAYERS
Also see MERRY MELODY SINGERS
Also see WILD WEST SINGERS

PONY BOY

Singles: 78rpm

RAINBO RECARD ("Pony Boy")......... 8-15 50s
(Cardboard cutout from Wheaties cereal box. Quadruple value if still attached to box.)

POPE PIUS XI

Singles: 78rpm

("St. Peter's Prayer for the Holy Year") 35-50
(No label name or selection number used.)

Singles: 78rpm

AMERICAN PICTURE TALKING RECORD ("Voice & Words of His Holiness") ... 60-90 31
(Flexi-disc. No selection number used.)
Also see MULLALY, Father Charles J., S.J.

POPEYE

Long Plays

MARK 56 (715 "Popeye") 75-90 79
(Original Radio Cast.)
MARK 56 (715 "Popeye") 90-120 79
(Original Radio Cast. Has die-cut cover.)
PETER PAN (201 "Popeye the Sailor Man") 40-50 82

PROFESSOR BOP

Singles: 45rpm

ERIKA (007 "Santa's White Christmas") 10-15 84
(Square disc.)

PUFF THE MAGIC DRAGON

Long Plays

PETER PAN (202 "Puff the Magic Dragon") 10-15 82

RAGGEDY ANN & ANDY

Long Plays

KID STUFF (6001 "Happiness Album") 15-20 81

RAINBOW BRITE

Long Plays

HALLMARK (63156 "Paint a Rainbow in Your Heart") 10-15 85

RAINER, Luise

Singles: 78rpm

FAMOUS/RCA (2 "As Anna Held from the Great Ziegfeld") 30-45 41
(Laminated cardboard.)

RANDOLPH SINGERS

Singles: 78rpm

VISITONE (V-1/-2 "Abide with Me").. 40-50 50
VISITONE (V-3/-4 "Rock of Ages, Cleft for Me") 40-50 50
VISITONE (V-5/-6 "Nearer My God to Thee") 40-50 50

RCA VICTOR PICTURE DISCS (1931-1934)

Singles: 78rpm

RCA VICTOR (221 "Winnie the Pooh Stories") 150-200 30s
RCA VICTOR (222 "Winnie the Pooh Stories") 150-200 30s
RCA VICTOR (223 "Winnie the Pooh Stories") 150-200 30s
RCA VICTOR (221/222/223) 600-750 30s
(Three-disc set in an album cover. Not to be confused with less valuable set issued in non-picture disc format. Studio Cast. Above three by Frank Luther.)
RCA VICTOR (224 "Who's Afraid of the Big Bad Wolf") 150-200 30s
RCA VICTOR (225 "In a Silly Symphony"/ "Mickey Mouse & Minnie's in Town") 200-300 30s
RCA VICTOR (226 "Lullaby Land of Nowhere") 150-200 30s
RCA VICTOR (224/225/226) 600-750 30s
(Three disc set in album cover. Studio Cast. Above three by Frank Luther.)
RCA Victor (2000 "The Raven").... 300-400 30s
(Parts 1 & 2.)
RCA Victor (2000 "The Raven").... 300-400 30s
(Part 2. Same selection number.)
RCA Victor (2001 "The Raven").... 300-400 30s
(Parts 3 & 4.)
Note: Above three are by Leopold Stokowski & the Philadelphia Orchestra. Narration by Benjamin de Loache.

RCA VICTOR (17-4000 "Adorable") 250-350 30s
(From film Soundtrack. *Adorable.* By Leo Reisman & His Orchestra with Janet Gaynor & Henry Garat. One of only three cardboard picture discs in RCA series. All others are believed to be shellac.)
RCA VICTOR (17-4002 "Llora, Campana, Llora") 250-350 30s
(By Alfonso Ortiz. One of only three cardboard picture discs in RCA series. All others are believed to be shellac.)
RCA VICTOR (17-4003 "How Doth the Little Crocodile") 300-400 30s
(From film Soundtrack *Alice in Wonderland.* By George Baker.)
RCA VICTOR (17-4004 "Speak Roughly to Your Little Boy") 300-400 30s
(From film Soundtrack *Alice in Wonderland.* By George Baker.)
RCA VICTOR (17-5000 "Cancion de la Buenaventura") 300-400 30s
(From film Soundtrack *El Ray de los Gitanos.* By Jose Mojica.)
RCA VICTOR (17-5001 "A Granada") 400-550 30s
RCA VICTOR (17-5002 "Siempre") 300-400 30s
(From film Soundtrack *La Melodia Prohibida.* By Jose Mojica.)
RCA VICTOR (18-6000 "Cowhand's Last Ride"): see RODGERS, Jimmie
RCA VICTOR (18-6003 "Nabanera") 300-400 30s
(By Pablo Sarosote.)
RCA VICTOR (18-6003 "Nabanera") 400-600 30s
(Credits Pablo Sarosote, but due to a production error, plays Jimmie Rodgers songs.)
RCA Victor (18-6004 "La Sombra de Pancho Villa") 400-600 30s
(One of only three cardboard picture discs in RCA series. All others are believed to be shellac. Credits Arregio de J. Ruiz Barracan, but due to a production error, plays Jimmie Rodgers songs. We know of no copies with music by Barracan.)
RCA VICTOR (07864 "Matey Visits New York") 70-90 30s
(Cardboard. Identification number shown since no selection number is used. Issued in a picture book, which is valued at $25 to $50. By Joe Musial.)
RCA VICTOR (39000 "Night with Paul Whiteman at the Biltmore"): see WHITEMAN, Paul

Long Plays

RCA VICTOR (39001 "Music In the Air") 300-400 30s
(Original Cast. By Nat Shilkret.)
RCA VICTOR (39002 "RCA Presents Noel Coward"): see COWARD, Noel
RCA VICTOR (39003 "As Thousands Cheer"): see WHITEMAN, Paul
RCA VICTOR (67-2000 "Night with Paul Whiteman at the Biltmore"): see WHITEMAN, Paul

RECORD GUILD OF AMERICA

Singles: 78rpm

RECORD GUILD of AMERICA (1 Silent Night") 15-20
RECORD GUILD of AMERICA (2 "Come All Ye Faithful") 15-20
RECORD GUILD of AMERICA (3 "Noel Noel") 15-20
RECORD GUILD of AMERICA (4 "It Came Upon a Midnight Clear") 15-20
RECORD GUILD of AMERICA (5 "Jingle Bells") 15-20
RECORD GUILD of AMERICA (6 "Auld Lang Syne") 15-20
RECORD GUILD of AMERICA (1 thru 6) 100-120
(Complete set of all six, with greetings cards.)
RECORD GUILD of AMERICA (Album series) 60-80
(18 different boxed sets were issued, each containing three or four discs.)
RECORD GUILD of AMERICA (C1 thru C12) 15-25
RECORD GUILD of AMERICA (C3000, C5000, C7000 series) 12-20
RECORD GUILD of AMERICA (E series) 12-20
(E series are all cardboard.)
RECORD GUILD of AMERICA (F301 "Flash Gordon: City of Sea Caves") 40-50
(Cardboard.)
RECORD GUILD of AMERICA (F401 "Red Ryder: Hermit's Gold") 30-40
(Cardboard.)
RECORD GUILD of AMERICA (F501 "Terry & the Pirates: Million Dollar Ruby") 30-40
(Cardboard.)
RECORD GUILD of AMERICA (F601 "Popeye: Pirate Treasure") 50-60
(Cardboard.)
RECORD GUILD of AMERICA (G series) 12-15
(G series are all cardboard.)
RECORD GUILD of AMERICA (M series) 12-20
(Cardboard.)
RECORD GUILD of AMERICA (N series, except 101) 20-30
RECORD GUILD of AMERICA (N-101 "Santa's Surprise") 25-35
(Santa shaped cardboard.)
RECORD GUILD of AMERICA (P series, except P2001) 12-20
(Sold individually. These were also available in album box sets.)
RECORD GUILD of AMERICA (P-2001 "Blue Tail Fly") 15-25
RECORD GUILD of AMERICA (PR series) 35-45
(Also known as "Picture Play" series.)
RECORD GUILD of AMERICA (S series) 12-15
(Cardboard.)
RECORD GUILD of AMERICA (T series) 12-20
(Cardboard.)
Note: Our best guess is that all of the preceding Record Guild discs came out between 1948 and 1951.

RED RAVEN MOVIE RECORDS

Singles: 78rpm

RED RAVEN (MA-1 "Magic Mirror") 150-200 56
(Boxed set with Magic Mirror and two discs, M-1/2 and M-3/4. Has animated cartoon effect when used with 3 1/2–inch mirror attached to spindle)
RED RAVEN 70-90 56
(Magic Mirror 3 1/2–inch attachment.)
RED RAVEN (MA-2 "Magic Mirror") 75-100 56
(Boxed set with two discs, M-5/6 and M-7/8.)
RED RAVEN (MA-3 "Magic Mirror") 75-100 56
(Boxed set with two discs, M-9/10 and M-11/12.)
RED RAVEN (MA-4 "Magic Mirror") 75-100 56
(Boxed set with two discs, M-13/14 and M-15/16.)
RED RAVEN (MA-5 "Magic Mirror") 75-100 56
(Boxed set with two discs, M-17/18 and M-19/20.)
RED RAVEN (M-1/2 "Tootles the Tug") 30-45 56
(By Red Raven Orchestra.)
RED RAVEN (M-3/4 "Old MacDonald Had a Farm") 30-45 56
(A-side by Red Raven Orchestra, B-side by Betty Wells, Bill Marine & Playmates Orchestra.)
RED RAVEN (M-5/6 "Happy Birthday") 30-45 56
RED RAVEN (M-7/8 "Sidewalks of New York") 30-45 56
(By Red Raven Orchestra.)
RED RAVEN (M-9/10 "Me and My Teddy Bear") 30-45 56
(A-side by Red Raven Orchestra. B-side by Bix Brent & 4 Cricketones.)
RED RAVEN (M-11/12 "On the Merry-Go-Round") 30-45 56
(A-side by Rose Stock Cavanaugh, B-side by Red Raven Orchestra.)
RED RAVEN (M-13/14 "Mary Had a Little Lamb") 30-45 56
RED RAVEN (M-15/16 "Three Little Kittens") 30-45 56
RED RAVEN (M-17/18 "Rudolf the Red-Nosed Reindeer") 30-45 56
RED RAVEN (M-19/20 "Santa Claus Is Coming to Town") 30-45 56
Note: All of preceding Red Raven discs have a scratch resistent acetate surface on cardboard base with brass grommet protecting the play hole and cemented metal rim.)
RED RAVEN (Color vinyl series)...... 15-30 56
(Each have large picture label. At least 11 were issued.)

REISMAN, Leo, & His Orchestra with Janet Gaynor & Henry Garat: see RCA VICTOR PICTURE DISCS

RETURN of the JEDI

Long Plays

LUCAS FILM (63155 "Return of the Jedi") 25-35 83
(Soundtrack.)

RETURN OF THE LIVING DEAD

Long Plays

ENIGMA (72085 "Return of the Living Dead") 30-35 84
(Soundtrack.)

REYNOLDS, Allie

Singles: 78rpm

SIGHT 'N' SOUND ("How to Pitch").. 60-90 52
(Cardboard. No selection number used.)

ROBERTS, Oral

Singles: 45rpm

COLUMBIA/AURAVISION ("Oral Roberts University") 10-15 67
(Square cardboard. Issued in three page gatefold cover. No selection number used.)

ROCK MUSIC MYSTERY

Singles: 45rpm

QUAKER (Part 1"Rock Music Mystery") 3-6 86
(Cardboard. Issued with box of Life Cereal. Has Elton John; Katrina & the Waves; Aretha Franklin; and Spencer Davis Group.)
QUAKER (Part 2"Rock Music Mystery") 3-6 86
(Cardboard. Issued with box of Life Cereal. Has Kinks; others.)
QUAKER (Part 3"Rock Music Mystery") 3-6 86
(Cardboard. Issued with box of Life Cereal. Has Mamas & Papas; others.)

ROCKY HORROR PICTURE SHOW

Long Plays

ODE (91653 "Rocky Horror Picture Show") 20-30 78
(Soundtrack. Numbered edition.)
ODE (91653 "Rocky Horror Picture Show") 15-20 78
(Soundtrack. Reissue numbered edition has "Limited Edition II" sticker on cover.)

ROE, Preacher

Singles: 78rpm

SIGHT 'N' SOUND ("Brooklyn Dodgers") 100-125 50
(Square cardboard. No selection number used.)

RUDOLF THE RED-NOSED REINDEER

Singles: 45rpm

PHONOSCOPE (206 "Rudolf the Red-Nose Reindeer") 10-15 57
(Postcard.)
Also see PHONOSCOPE POSTCARDS

SANTA CLAUS IS COMING TO TOWN

Singles: 45rpm

PHONOSCOPE (208 "Santa Claus Is Coming to Town") 10-15 57
(Postcard.)
Also see PHONOSCOPE POSTCARDS

SAROSOTE, Pablo: see RCA Victor Picture Discs

SAWYER, Eddie

Singles: 78rpm

SIGHT 'N' SOUND ("Philadelphia Phillies") 50-60 51
(Square cardboard. No selection number used.)

SCOOBY DOO

Long Plays

PETER PAN (203 "Scooby Doo")..... 20-25 82

SCHRAFFT'S CHOCOLATE PLAY A TUNE

Singles: 78rpm

TALKING BOOK 25-35
(Square cardboard. Promotional issue for Schrafft's Candy Co. No selection number used.)

SHADOW, The

Long Plays

MARK 56 (608 "The Shadow, Vol. 2") 125-150 79
(Original Radio Cast.)
MARK 56 (771 "The Shadow, Vol. 4") 100-125 79
(Original Radio Cast.)

SHAHIN, Paul: see Vogue (Sav-Way)

SHARE YOUR FAITH THROUGH the FAMILY

Singles: 45rpm

SALVATION ARMY ("Share Your Faith Through the Family") 6-12
(Shaped cardboard. No selection number used.)

SHAVERS, Charlie, Quintet: see Vogue (Sav-Way)

SHIEK, The

Long Plays

MARK 56 (760 "The Shiek") 100-120 70s
(Original Radio Cast. Stars Rudolf Valentino.)

SILENT NIGHT
Singles: 45rpm
PHONOSCOPE (205 "Silent Night") 10-15 57
(Postcard.)
Also see PHONOSCOPE POSTCARDS

SLOWPOKES
Singles: 45rpm
EVATONE ("Happy Trails") 8-12 89
(Postcard made for Roy Rogers and Dale Evans Museum. From the book *Revenge of the Son of the World's Tackiest Postcards*. Has photo of Trigger after his visit with the taxidermist.)

SMURFS
Long Plays
POLY (1 "Smurfing Sing Along") 15-20 82
(Canadian.)
SESSIONS (1029 "Smurfing Sing Along") 15-20 82

SNIDER, Duke
Singles: 78rpm
SIGHT 'N' SOUND ("Tips on Batting") 125-175 52
(Cardboard. No selection number used.)
Singles: 78rpm
SIGHT 'N' SOUND ("Brooklyn Dodgers") 150-175 50
(Square cardboard. No selection number used.)

SNOW WHITE & SEVEN DWARFS
Long Plays
DISNEYLAND (3101 "Snow White & Seven Dwarfs") 15-18 80
(Soundtrack.)

SONG & STORY BOOK: see KIDDIE RECORDS

SONGS OF THE LETTER PEOPLE
Singles: 45rpm
NEW DIMENSION in EDUCATION ("Mr. A" through "Mr. Z.") 4-6 73
(Square cardboard. For andy of a series of 26 different titles—one for each alphabet letter. No selection number used.)

SOUNDS OF SELF-DEFENSE
Singles: 45rpm
COLUMBIA/AURAVISION ("Sounds of Self-Defense") 5-8 60s
(Square cardboard. Promotional issue made for Hai Karate After Shave & Cologne. Selection number not known.)

SPACE SHUTTLE
Long Plays
KID STUFF (6005 "A True Space Adventure") 15-25 82
(Reissue of Ronald Reagan's *Space Shuttle Columbia*.)

SPECIAL SERVICES, U.S. MARINE CORPS
Singles: 78rpm
U.S. MARINE CORP 25-35 43-45
(Cardboard. "Home Recordings" made for those serving in the military to use as audio letters to family and friends. Add $10 for custom mailer with two cardboard inserts.)
Also see Gem Razor

SPENCER, Eddie, & Kings of Hawaii
Long Plays
LEI WAS (1001 "Wahi Aloha") 10-20 75
(Promotional only issue. Made in Japan for Hawaii distribution.)

SPONSELLER, Gail, & Orchestra
Long Plays
MARK 56 (818 "Big Band Disco: the TA Disco") 20-25 79
(Promotional issue made for B.F. Goodrich. Same recording as *Dipsy Doodle Disco*.)
MARK 56 (818 "Dipsy Doodle Disco") 20-25 79
(Promotional issue made for B.F. Goodrich. Note title change.)

SPOOKY STORIES
Singles: 45rpm
PICKWICK (1 "Legend of Sleepy Hollow") 5-8 78
PICKWICK (2 "Miser's Gold") 5-8 78
PICKWICK (3 "The Hitch Hiker") 5-8 78
(Square cardboard. Two different graphics variations used. Though each disc lists all three songs, a number is stamped on each disc to identify the track.)

SPORTS CHALLENGE
Singles: 45rpm
SCARAB ("Henry Aaron: Hits First Met Homer") 15-20 70s
SCARAB ("Johnny Bench: Beats Pirates in '72 Playoff") 15-20 70s
SCARAB ("Jerry Koosman & Don Clendenon: 1969 Miracle Mets") 8-12 70s
SCARAB ("Don Larsen: '56 World Series Perfect Game") 8-12 70s
SCARAB ("Fred Lynn: Has Incredible Day in Detroit") 8-12 70s
SCARAB ("Willie Mays: Hits First Met Homer") 15-20 70s
SCARAB ("Bill Mazeroski: Wins 1960 World Series") 15-20 70s
SCARAB ("Frank Robinson: Homers First Time As an Indian") 15-20 70s
SCARAB ("Nolan Ryan: Fourth No-Hitter") 15-20 70s
SCARAB ("Tom Seaver: Cubs Ruin Perfect Game") 15-20 70s
SCARAB ("Bobby Thompson: Shot Heard 'Round the World") 8-12 70s
SCARAB ("Last Time at Bat in Boston") 15-20 70s
Note: The Scarab titles are all cardboard discs.

SPORTS CHAMPIONSHIPS
Singles: 45rpm
AURAVISION ("Bob Allison Story") 8-12 64
(Has 1963 statistics on back.)
AURAVISION ("Ernie Banks Story") 20-25 62
(Has 1961 statistics on back.)
AURAVISION ("Ernie Banks Story") 15-20 64
(Has 1963 statistics on back.)
AURAVISION ("Ken Boyer Story") 10-15 64
(Has 1963 statistics on back.)
AURAVISION ("Rocky Colavito Story") 25-30 62
(Has 1961 statistics on back; Detroit Tigers uniform on front.)
AURAVISION ("Rocky Colavito Story") 8-12 64
(Has 1963 statistics on back; Kansas City Athletics uniform on front.)
AURAVISION ("Don Drysdale Story") 10-15 64
(Has 1963 statistics on back.)
AURAVISION ("Whitey Ford Story") 20-30 62
(Has 1961 statistics on back.)
AURAVISION ("Whitey Ford Story") 15-20 64
(Has 1963 statistics on back.)
AURAVISION ("Jim Gentle Story") 30-35 62
(Has 1961 statistics on back; Baltimore Orioles uniform on front.)
AURAVISION ("Jim Gentle Story") 8-12 64
(Has 1963 statistics on back; Kansas City Athletics uniform on front.)
AURAVISION ("Al Kaline Story") 15-20 64
(Has 1963 statistics on back.)
AURAVISION ("Sandy Koufax Story") 25-35 64
(Has 1963 statistics on back.)
AURAVISION ("Mickey Mantle Story") 60-75 62
(Has 1961 statistics on back; full body batting pose on front.)
AURAVISION ("Mickey Mantle Story") 50-60 64
(Has 1963 statistics on back; upper body only batting pose on front.)
AURAVISION ("Roger Maris Story") 35-45 62
(Has 1961 statistics on back.)
AURAVISION ("Roger Maris Story") 25-35 64
(Has 1963 statistics on back.)
AURAVISION ("Willie Mays Story") .. 50-60 62
(Has 1961 statistics on back.)
AURAVISION ("Willie Mays Story") 35-45 64
(Has 1963 statistics on back.)
AURAVISION ("Bill Mazeroski Story") 8-12 64
(Has 1963 statistics on back.)
AURAVISION ("Frank Robinson Story") 15-20 64
(Has 1963 statistics on back.)
AURAVISION ("Warren Spahn Story") 15-20 62
(Has 1961 statistics on back.)
AURAVISION ("Warren Spahn Story") 8-12 64
(Has 1963 statistics on back.)
AURAVISION ("Pete Ward Story") 8-12 62
(Has 1961 statistics on back.)
Note: Auravision discs bove are all square cardboard. All, except where noted, have same picture on play side. No selection numbers used.)

ST. PAUL'S ABBEY
Singles: 45rpm
("Christmas Music") 8-12
(Square cardboard. No label name or selection number used.)

STANDARD PUBLISHING
Singles: 78rpm
STANDARD (701/2 "Noah's Ark") 10-15 40s
STANDARD (703/4 "Boy Who Listened") 10-15 40s
STANDARD (711/12 "Shepherds of Bethlehem") 10-15 40s
STANDARD (713/14 "Good Samaritan") 10-15 40s
STANDARD (715/16 "Jesus Loves Me") 10-15 40s
STANDARD (751/52 "When Jesus Was Born") 10-15 40s
STANDARD (753/54 "Jesus and the Children") 10-15 40s
STANDARD (755/56 "Good Morning") 10-15 40s
STANDARD (771/72 "Jacob's Dream") 10-15 40s
STANDARD (773/74 "Daniel and the Lion's Den") 10-15 40s
STANDARD (775/76 "Ruth") 10-15 40s
Note: The Standard discs above are cardboard, part of the "Bible Storytime" series.)

STAR WARS
Long Plays
20TH CENTURY (103 "The Story of Star Wars") 25-35 79
(Soundtrack.)

STOKOWSKI, Leopold, & Benjamin de Loache: see RCA Victor Picture Discs

STRAWBERRY SHORTCAKE
Long Plays
KID STUFF (6002 "And Her Friends") 15-20 81
KID STUFF (6011 "Over the Rainbow") 15-20 82
SCHOLASTIC (31088 "And the Winter That Would Not End") 8-12

STUNT ROCK
Long Plays
("Stunt Rock") 15-25 78
(Soundtrack. Includes map, bios, nine photos and poster. No label name or selection number used.)

SUGAR BEARS
Singles: 45rpm
POST 4-8 60s
(Cardboard cutouts from cereal box. Each disc lists five songs, a number is stamped on each disc to identify the track. Double value if still attached to box.)

SUPERMAN
Singles: 7–inch
MUSETTE (1 "The Flying Train"). 100-150 47
(Two records in folder with script and pictures.)
MUSETTE (2 "The Magic Ring") .. 100-150 47
(Two records in folder with script and pictures.)
Long Plays
MARK 56 (812 "Superman") 20-30 78
(Original Radio Cast. Has four episodes from 1940s.)
MARK 56 (812 "Superman") 40-50 78
(Original Radio Cast. Promotional issue made for Pepsi, with different picture on back side.)

SWARTHOUT, Gladys with Al Goodman & Deems Taylor
Singles: 78rpm
DUPLI-KUT ("Merry Christmas: The Family Hour") 70-90 42
(Cardboard. No selection number used.)

TAKE ME OUT TO THE BALLGAME
Singles: 78rpm
WHEATIES 15-20
(Cardboard cutout from cereal box. Triple value if still attached to box.)
Singles: 45rpm
MUSICAL POSTCARD 15-20 50s
(Postcard.)

TALKING BASEBALL CARDS
Singles: 45rpm
AMERICAN AUDIOGRAPHICS (1 "Mazeroski's 9th Inning Home Run Wins 1960 World Series") 8-10 89
AMERICAN AUDIOGRAPHICS (2 Bucky Dent's Playoff Game") 8-10 89
AMERICAN AUDIOGRAPHICS (3 "Hank Aaron Hits 715 Homers") 8-10 89
AMERICAN AUDIOGRAPHICS (4 "Pete Rose Sets N.L. Hitting Streak Record") 8-10 89
AMERICAN AUDIOGRAPHICS (5 Babe Ruth Day at Yankee Stadium") 8-10 89
AMERICAN AUDIOGRAPHICS (6 Carlton Fisk Hits World Series Game Winning Homer") 8-10 89
AMERICAN AUDIOGRAPHICS (7 "Don Larsen Pitches Only World Series Perfect Game") 8-10 89
AMERICAN AUDIOGRAPHICS (8 "Reggie Jackson Hits Three Home Runs in a World Series") 8-10 89
AMERICAN AUDIOGRAPHICS (9 "Willie Mays Game Winning Catch in 1954 World Series") 8-10 89
AMERICAN AUDIOGRAPHICS (10 "Roger Maris Breaks Babe Ruth's Season Home Run Record") 8-10 89
AMERICAN AUDIOGRAPHICS (11 "Miracle N.Y. Mets Win World Series") 8-10 89
AMERICAN AUDIOGRAPHICS (12 "Bobby Thompson's Shot Heard Around the World") 8-10 89
AMERICAN AUDIOGRAPHICS ("Jose Canesco") 8-10 89
(Selection number not known.)
AMERICAN AUDIOGRAPHICS ("Don Mattingly") 8-10 89
(Selection number not known.)
AMERICAN AUDIOGRAPHICS ("Mickey Mantle Talks About Switch Hitting") 8-10 89
(Selection number not known.)
Note: All of the above discs are square cardboard, from the "Great Moments in Baseball" series.")

TALKING BOOK CORP.
Singles: 78rpm
TALKING BOOK 50-100 18
(Pseudo-picture discs. Notable because 4 1/4–inch clear flexi-disc was adhered to oversized shape picture card, such as a lion or a parrot. Includes disc and backing card.)

TALK-O-PHOTO
Singles: 78rpm
TALK-O-PHOTO 50-75 23
(Pseudo-picture disc series with photo on non-playing B-side.)

TARZAN
Long Plays
MARK 56 (644 "Tarzan") 100-120 70s
(Original Radio Cast. Narrated by Edgar Ride Burroughs.)

3 BEARS
Singles: 78rpm
KIDISKS (KD-77 "3 Bears") 10-20 48

TIBBETTS, Birdie
Singles: 78rpm
SIGHT 'N' SOUND ("Red Sox") 50-70 47
(Square cardboard. No selection number used.)

TONE, Franchot
Singles: 78rpm
FAMOUS/RCA (1 "England, My England") 30-45 41
(Laminated cardboard. From the film *Lives of a Bengal Lancer*.)

TOUCAN SAM
Singles: 45rpm
KELLOGG (1 "Takes You on a Listening Safari") 8-12 83
(Cardboard.)
KELLOGG (2 "Toucan Sam at the Big Race") 8-12 83
(Cardboard.)
KELLOGG (3 "Toucan Sam Workout") 8-12 83
(Cardboard.)

TOY TOON RECORDS
Singles: 45rpm
TOY TOON ("A-PAK") 100-120 48-52
(Six disc cardboard set with custom cover. Other six packs have same value.)
TOY TOON 15-20 48-52
(Single-sided cardboard with lyrics on one side.)
TOY TOON 20-25 48-52
(Double-sided cardboard with picture on both sides.)

TRIUMPH MOTORCYCLE
Singles: 45rpm
COLUMBIA/AURAVISION ("Triple Scoop") 8-12 69
(Postcard. Promotional issue made for Triumph Motorcycles. No selection number used.)

TURNBILL, Bob
Long Plays
GOSPEL SOUNDS (80/81 "Chaplain of Waikiki Beach") 30-35 81

USO / RAINBO

Singles: 78rpm

USO/RAINBO 25-35 43-45
(Cardboard. "Home Recordings" made by National Catholic Community Service for those serving in the military to use as audio letters to family and friends. Has four play holes.)
Also see Gem Razor

U.S.S. ALABAMA

Long Plays

QUADDES (1 "Story of the U.S.S. Alabama BB-60")..60-80 76
(Promotional issue made for Crewmans Association.)

UNION PACIFIC

Long Plays

HAROLD DAGVE (6940 "Mainliner #1")..40-60 73
(Promotional issue only.)

UNTITLED

Long Plays

FIG (001) 10-15
(No artist or title is shown.)

VALENTINE GREETINGS SONGS

Singles: 78rpm

PHONODISC (41/42 "Valentine Greetings Songs")..25-35 48
(Heart-shaped cardboard. Add $10 for mailer envelope.)
Also see PHONODISC PICTURE RECORDS

VANDERBILT UNIVERSITY MARCHING BAND

Long Plays

LIT (7601 "Vanderbilt University Marching Band")..12-18 75

VELVET MAGAZINE

Singles: 45rpm

VELVET (7 "Velvet Talks #7")..............4-6 80
(Cardboard cutout from *Velvet* magazine.)
VELVET (7 "Velvet Talks #7")...........10-12 80
(Disc still attached in *Velvet* magazine.)

VI & VILMA

Singles: 78rpm

DUPLI-KUT ("I'm Tryin") 70-90 40s
(Cardboard. No selection number used.)

VISITONE

Singles: 78rpm

VISITONE (series)..............................40-50 50
Also see RANDOLF SINGERS

VOCO RECORDS

Singles: 78rpm

VOCO (200 series) 20-30 47
(Square cardboard.)
VOCO (500/600 thru 523/623)..........20-35 47
(All above are cardboard.)
VOCO (700/800 series) 25-35 48
(Cardboard with various animal shapes; rabbit, elephant, dog, kitten, etc.)
VOCO (35200 series)........................20-30 46
(Square cardboard.)
VOCO (EB1 "Bunny Easter") 25-40 48
(Rabbit-shaped cardboard. Includes picture sleeve.)
VOCO (SC1/1A "I Wish That I Were Santa")...20-30 48
(Santa-shaped cardboard.)

VOGUE (SAV-WAY)

Note: Some discs in this series are found in the A-Z listings in the body of the book. Those are referenced here for easy access. All of the Vogue discs listed here were issued circa 1946 or '47.

Singles: 78rpm

VOGUE ("Nursery Rhymes") 800-1200 40s
(Promotional only issue. No selection number used and no artist credited.)
VOGUE.......................................800-1200 40s
(Price for any of the five other 12–inch titles that reportedly exist.)
VOGUE ("Trolley Song"): see GARLAND, Judy / Tommy Dorsey
VOGUE (S100 "A Trip to Slumberland")............................800-1200 40s
(By the Vogue Players with the Vogue Recording Orchestra.)
VOGUE (V-100 "A Study in Blue")..150-300 40s
(R-725 & R726 in album folder.)
VOGUE (V-100 "A Study in Blue")..150-200 40s
(R-725 & R726 in boxed set with sleeves.)
VOGUE (V-101 "A Mooney Medley") 150-300 40s
(R730 & R713/R732 in boxed set with sleeves.)
VOGUE (V-102-1 "Learn to Dance the Rhumba: Beginners")....................................150-200 40s
(R737 & R738 in boxed set with sleeves. Add $20 to $30 for dance step inserts.)
VOGUE (V-102-2 "Learn to Dance the Rhumba: Intermediate") 150-250 40s
(R737 & R738 in boxed set with sleeves. Add $20 to $30 for dance step inserts.)
VOGUE (V-103 "Joan Edwards, Your Hit Parade Star")...250-350 40s
(R761 & R767 in boxed set with sleeves.)
VOGUE (V-104 "Society Rhumbas")...250-350 40s
(R747 & R748 in boxed set with sleeves.)
VOGUE (V-105 "Rural Rhythms"): see WOWO HOOSIER HOP GANG
VOGUE (V-106 "For the Children")..250-350 40s
(R745 & R746 in boxed set with sleeves.)
VOGUE (R707 "Sugar Blues")..........50-70 40s
(By Clyde McCoy.)
VOGUE (R708 "I Surrender, Dear")..60-80 40s
(By King's Jesters & Louise.)
VOGUE (R710 "The Bells of St. Marys") 60-80 40s
(By Don Large Chorus.)
VOGUE (R711 "Seems Like Old Time"/"Warsaw Concerto"): see MOONEY, Art
VOGUE (R711/R713 "Seems Like Old Time"/"I've Been Working on the Railroad"): see MOONEY, Art
VOGUE (R712 "Atlanta, GA") 60-80 40s
(By Shep Fields.)
VOGUE (R713 "I've Been Working on the Railroad"/You're Nobody 'Til Somebody Loves You"): see MOONEY, Art
VOGUE (R713/R732 "I've Been Working on the Railroad"/"I Don't Know Why"): see MOONEY, Art
VOGUE (R-713-2/R-732-13 "I've Been Working on the Railroad"/"I Don't Know Why"): see MOONEY, Art
VOGUE (R714 "Doodle Doo Doo")...60-80 40s
(By Art Kassel.)
VOGUE (R715 "Waitin' for the Train to Come")..400-600 40s
(By Shep Fields.)
VOGUE (R716 "Humphrey, the Sweet Singing Pig")....................................800-1200 40s
(By King's Jesters & Louise.)
VOGUE (R718 "Some Sunday Morning")..60-80 40s
(By Lulu Belle & Scotty.)
VOGUE (R719 "Have I Told You Lately That I Love You")...60-80 40s
(By Lulu Belle & Scotty.)
VOGUE (R720 "Grandpa's Gettin' Younger Every Day")..60-80 40s
(By Lulu Belle & Scotty.)
VOGUE (R721 "When I Get Where I'm Going") 90-120 40s
(By Patsy Montana.)
VOGUE (R722 "Tear It Down")..........60-80 40s
(By Clyde McCoy.)
VOGUE (R723 "Wave to Me My Lady")..80-100 40s
(By Art Kassel.)
VOGUE (R724 "Sweet I've Gotten on You")..80-100 40s
(By Frankie Masters.)
VOGUE (R725 "Rhapsody in Blue"/Alice Blue Gown")..60-80 40s
(By 'The Hour of Charm' All Girls Orchestra with Phil Spitalny.)
VOGUE (R725/726 "Rhapsody in Blue"/ "Part 2") 125-175 40s
(By 'The Hour of Charm' All Girls Orchestra with Phil Spitalny.)
VOGUE (R726 "Rhapsody in Blue"/"Blue Skies")..60-80 40s
(By 'The Hour of Charm' All Girls Orchestra with Phil Spitalny.)
VOGUE (R726/733 "Blue Skies"/ "Seville")..125-175 40s
(By 'The Hour of Charm' All Girls Orchestra with Phil Spitalny.)
VOGUE (R730 "Piper's Junction"): see MOONEY, Art
VOGUE (R731 "Between the Devil and the Deep Blue Sea").......................................70-80 40s
(By Marion Mann.)
VOGUE (R732 "In the Moonmist"): see MOONEY, Art
VOGUE (R732-13/R732 "In the Moonmist"): see MOONEY, Art
VOGUE (R733 "Blue Skies"/ "Seville")...60-80 40s
(By 'The Hour of Charm' All Girls Orchestra with Phil Spitalny.)
VOGUE (R734 "Sweetheart")........... 60-80 40s
(By Art Kassel.)
VOGUE (R735 "Anybody Home") 60-80 40s
(By Frankie Masters.)
VOGUE (R736 "Out Where the West Winds Blow"): see DOWNHOMERS
VOGUE (R737 "Rhumba Lesson #1 - the Hip Movement").. 60-80 40s
(By Paul Shahin.)
VOGUE (R738 "Rhumba Lesson #2 - the Forward & Backward Movement"/"Give Me All Your Heart") 60-80 40s
(A-side by Paul Shahin; B-side by Dick LaSalle.)
VOGUE (R738/747 "Rhumba Lesson #2 - The Forward & Backward Movement")....................................... 60-80 40s
(A-side by Paul Shahin; B-side by Dick LaSalle. Same as R738.)
VOGUE (R739 "Rhumba Lesson #1")...................................... 70-90 40s
(By Paul Shahin.)
VOGUE (R740 "Rhumba Lesson #2 "/"I Dreamed About You Last Night") 60-80 40s
(A-side by Paul Shahin, B-side by Dick LaSalle.)
VOGUE (R744 "Don't Tetch It")........ 70-90 40s
(A-side by Nancy Lee & Hilltoppers; B-side by Judy & Jen.)
VOGUE (R745 "Trial of Bumble the Bee, Part 1")...................................... 70-90 40s
(By James Jewel.)
VOGUE (R746 "Trial of Bumble the Bee, Part 2")...................................... 70-90 40s
(By James Jewel.)
VOGUE (R747 "Give Me All Your Heart").. 125-175 40s
(By Dick LaSalle.)
VOGUE (R748 "Let Me Take You in My Arms") 125-175 46-47
(By Dick LaSalle.)
VOGUE (R750 "Who's Got a Tent")... 100-140 40s
(By King's Jesters.)
VOGUE (R751 "Humphrey, the Sweet Singing Pig").. 80-100 40s
(By King's Jesters & Louise.)
VOGUE (R752 "Baby What You Do to Me") 60-80 40s
(By Clyde McCoy.)
VOGUE (R753 "At Sundown")........... 60-80 40s
(By Clyde McCoy.)
VOGUE (R754 "She's Funny That Way").. 80-90 40s
(By Charlie Shavers Quintet.)
VOGUE (R755 "Broadjump")............ 80-90 40s
(By Charlie Shavers Quintet.)
VOGUE (R756 "Musicomania")...... 90-100 40s
(By Charlie Shavers Quintet.)
VOGUE (R758 "You're Gonna Hate Yourself in the Morning") 80-90 40s
(By Marion Mann with Bob Haggart's Orchestra.)
VOGUE (R760 "So It Goes")............ 70-80 40s
(By Enric Madriguera.)
VOGUE (R761 "More Than You Know") 90-120 40s
(By Joan Edwards.)
VOGUE (R764 "I Guess I'll Get the Papers and Go Home")................................ 70-80 40s
(By Shep Fields.)
VOGUE (R765 "What Is Love").. 800-1200 40s
(By Shep Fields.)
VOGUE (R766 "G'wan Home, Your Mudder's Callin") 80-90 40s
(By King's Jesters.)
VOGUE (R767 "Love Means the Same Old Thing") 70-90 40s
(By Joan Edwards.)
VOGUE (R770 "Whiffenpoof Song").. 70-90 40s
(By Art Kassel.)
VOGUE (R771 "If I Could Be with You").. 80-90 40s
(By Art Kassel.)
VOGUE (R772 "All By Myself") 70-90 40s
(By Frankie Masters.)
VOGUE (R774 "Desert Fantasy") 70-90 40s
(By Sonny Dunham & Orchestra.)
VOGUE (R775 "I Love You in the Daytime Too") 80-100 40s
(By Sonny Dunham & Orchestra.)
VOGUE (R776 "Mujercita") 70-90 40s
(By Enric Madriguera.)
VOGUE (R777 "La Rhumbita")......... 60-80 40s
(By Enric Madriguera.)
VOGUE (R778 "Guilty of Love")...................................... 100-125 40s
(By Enric Madriguera.)
VOGUE (R779 "A Man, a Moon & a Maid")...................................... 60-80 40s
(By Enric Madriguera.)
VOGUE (R780 "Let's Get Married") . 60-80 40s
(By Art Kassel.)
VOGUE (R781 "I Love You for Sentimental Reasons") 60-80 40s
(By Art Kassel.)
VOGUE (R782 "What Am I Gonna Do About You") 70-90 40s
(By Joan Edwards.)
VOGUE (R784 "Queen for a Day").. 500-700 40s
(By Art Kassel.)
VOGUE (R785 "The Echo Said No").. 60-80 40s
(By Art Kassel.)
VOGUE (R786 "Boogie Woogie Yodel"): see DOWNHOMERS
VOGUE (GO 1007/1008 "That's for Me").. 600-900 40s
(Promotional only issue. A-side by Nocturne String Quartet; B-side was made for Butyl-Molded Transformers by G.E.)
VOGUE/PHILCO ("Rum and Coca-Cola"): see HELLER, Jackie / Glenn Miller

VOICE OF THE HOLY FATHER

Singles: 78rpm

ADALTO (199178 "Voice of the Holy Father") 15-20 49

WELLS, Betty, Bill Marine & Playmates Orchestra: see Red Raven Movie Records

WHEATIES MICKEY MOUSE CLUB

Singles: 78rpm

RAINBO RECARD ("Wheaties Mickey Mouse Club: Walt Disney's Mouseketeer Record" series) 10-20 50s
RAINBO RECARD ("Donald Duck: Donald Duck's Song")................................ 10-20 50s
RAINBO RECARD ("Goofy: It's Fun to Whistle") 10-20 50s
RAINBO RECARD ("Chip 'N' Dale: The Laughing Song").. 10-20 50s
RAINBO RECARD ("Mickey Mouse: Happy Mouse").. 10-20 50s
RAINBO RECARD ("Mickey Mouse: The Gadget Tree") 10-20 50s
RAINBO RECARD ("Mickey, Donald & Goofy: I'd Rather Be Me") 10-20 50s
Note: The above Rainbo Recards are cardboard cutouts from cereal box. No selection numbers are used. Quadruple value if still attached to box.

WHITE CHRISTMAS

Singles: 45rpm

PHONOSCOPE (207 "White Christmas") 10-15 57
(Postcard.)
Also see PHONOSCOPE POSTCARDS

WILD WEST SINGERS

Singles: 78rpm

PLAYSONG (WW series)................ 10-20 40s
(Cardboard. At least six titles were issued.)

WILLIAMS, Ted

Singles: 78rpm

SIGHT 'N' SOUND ("Red Sox").... 125-175 47
(Square cardboard. No selection number used.)

WKSS RADIO "KISS 96"

Singles: 45rpm

WKSS ("WKSS Radio KISS 96").......... 3-6 80
(Square cardboard. Promotional issue only.)

WOODY WOODPECKER

Long Plays

MCA (13300 "Family Album")........... 25-35 83

WORK, REST, PLAY

Long Plays

KINNEY SHOES (7770 "Work, Rest, Play").. 15-20
(Promotional issue only.)

WORLD'S FAIR

Long Plays

L (17478 "New Orleans, 1984")........ 70-90 84
(Four picture disc set.)
PARTNERSHIP (1001 "Knoxville, Tennessee 1982").. 20-25 82

YANKEE AIR PIRATES

Long Plays

MADOM (11338 "Dixieland Jazz Band") 10-15 83

YOLANDA the NYMPHO

Singles: 45rpm

VELVET ("Pounding Beat of Live Action Sex") 4-6
(Cardboard cutout from *Velvet* magazine.)
VELVET ("Pounding Beat of Live Action Sex") 10-12
(Disc still attached in *Velvet* magazine.)

YOUNGMAN, Henny

Singles: 78rpm

DUPLI-KUT ("A Command Performance in Which Kate Smith Presents Henny Youngman")....................................70-90 40s
(Cardboard. No selection number used.)

YOUR HOLSUM BAKER

Singles: 45rpm

BING CROSBY PHONOCARDS (2 "Gracious Living") 5-10 60s
(Square cardboard. Made for Holsum Bakery.)

YOUR OWN MICKEY MOUSE CLUB on RECORD

Singles: 78rpm

MATTEL/RAINBO ("Your Own Mickey Mouse Club on Record")..........................100-150 59
(Set of five 7-inch square cardboard cutouts. Packaged in over-sized accordian-like folder.)
MATTEL/RAINBO (11 "Mickey Mouse Club March & Mouseketters Song #11").......................................15-20 59
MATTEL/RAINBO (12 "Cartoon Time #12").......................................15-20 59
MATTEL/RAINBO (13 "Joe McDonald Musical on the Farm #13")................................15-20 59
MATTEL/RAINBO (14 "Mickey Mouse Club Circus Day #14") 15-20 59
MATTEL/RAINBO (15 "Toot-Toot Talent Roundup #15") 15-20 59

YOUR TRIP TO DISNEYLAND

MATTEL/RAINBO (D5140 "Your Trip to Disneyland")................................100-150 50s
(Set of five 7-inch square cardboard cutouts. Packaged in over-sized accordian-like folder.)
MATTEL/RAINBO (6 "Introduction to Disneyland #6")..15-20 50s
MATTEL/RAINBO (7 "Tomorrowland #7")...15-20 50s
MATTEL/RAINBO (8 "Fantasyland #8")...15-20 50s
MATTEL/RAINBO (9 "Frontierland #9) 15-20 50s
MATTEL/RAINBO (10 "Adventureland #10")...15-20 50s

THE KRAZY KATS

"BEAT OUT MY LOVE" b/w "WIGGLY LITTLE MAMA"
WILD unreleased rockers from 1959 by Missouri's finest!

PAUL WINCHELL and JERRY MAHONEY

HOORAY - HOORAH (It's Winchell-Mahoney Time)
FRIENDS, FRIENDS, FRIENDS (We Will Always Be)

FOX 311

MARILYN MONROE

SINGS

RIVER OF NO RETURN

and

ONE SILVER DOLLAR

From the 20th Fox Album—"MARILYN"—FXG 5000
"River of No Return" A 20th Century-Fox Film

MY FRAGILE HEART
The 5 Embers
FOR REVIEW NOT FOR SALE
X-BAT RECORDS
X-1006
Owensboro, Kentucky (1959) left to right:
Sonny Rates (2nd Tenor), Melvin Smith (Bass),
Richard Brown (Lead, 1st Tenor), Raymond Johnson (Baritone)
Charles Brown (Lead, 1st Tenor)
X-BAT GROUP VOCAL SERIES BY SPECIAL ARRANGEMENT
WITH BO-AN PUBLISHING CO.

HIGH PRIESTESS OF
ROCK 'N ROLL
LILLIAN
BRIGGS
EG 7163

BUYERS–SELLERS DIRECTORY

The pages in every *Rockin' Records* Buyers-Sellers Directory are packed with personal and business ads, certain to appeal to anyone with an interest in music collecting.

Most books in the Osborne series — including every edition of *Rockin' Records* — offer an outstanding opportunity to cost-effectively spread the word of your products and services to a targeted worldwide audience. An ad in the Buyers-Sellers Directory is also an excellent and inexpensive way to locate those elusive discs you've been seeking for your collection. For over 22 years, the results of advertising in the Osborne books have proven to be tremendous. We are especially proud of our high rate of repeat advertisers, one that far surpasses industry standards.

Look the ads over carefully. You might just find the dealer or contact you've been wanting to assist you in building your collection. When responding to any of our advertisers, be sure to say you saw their ad in Jerry Osborne's *Rockin' Records.*

You can advertise in the next *Rockin' Records,* or any of the other books in our series. Simply contact our office and ask for complete details. Let us do for you what we have done for many others!

Osborne Enterprises
Box 255
Port Townsend WA 98368
Phone: (360) 385-1200 — Fax: (360) 385-6572
e-mail: jpo@olympus.net web site: www.jerryosborne.com

Cool Cats
We're hep—
Specializing in the music of the 1950's, 33 1/3, 45, & 78 rpm.
Want lists filled; collections bought.
Over 100,000 records in stock at all times.
Victor Pearlin
VICTOR PEARLIN
PO Box 60299
Greendale Station
Worcester MA 01606 USA
e-mail: vpearlin@aol.com

Varèse Vintage

FINELY AGED MUSIC

Best Sellers

Steve Allen
On The Air-The Classic Comedy Of Steve Allen
VSD-5703

Bill Anderson
Bill Anderson's Greatest Hits
VSD-5643

Frankie Avalon
The Best Of Frankie Avalon
VSD-5594

Dick Bartley Presents Collectors Essentials
The '60s & The '70s
VSD-5705 & VSD-5706

Pat Boone
More Greatest Hits
VSD-5522

Bubblegum Classics Volume 1,2 & 3
(The Ultimate Collection Of Pure Pop Music)
VSD-5535, 5575, 5719

Gene Chandler
Nothing Can Stop Me-The Best Of Gene Chandler
VSD-5515

Roy Clark
Greatest Hits
VSD-5608

Dark Shadows
The 30th Anniversary Collection
VSD-5702

Dolenz, Jones, Boyce & Hart
Concert In Japan
VSD-5625

Donna Fargo
The Best Of Donna Fargo
VSD-5567

The Hi-Lo's
The Best Of The Hi-Lo's
VSD-5694

Jan & Dean
Teen Suite-The Best Of Jan & Dean, 1958-1962
VSD-5590

Enoch Light
Persuasive Percussion
VSD-5636

Leonard Nimoy
Mr. Spock's Music From Outer Space
VSD-5613

Neil Sedaka
Laughter In The Rain-The Best Of Neil Sedaka
VSD-5539

William Shatner
The Transformed Man
VSD-5614

The Surfaris
Wipe Out-The Best Of The Surfaris
VSD-5478

Johnny Tillotson
Poetry In Motion-The Best Of Johnny Tillotson
VSD-5570

Dick Hyman
***Moog-The Electric Eclectics of Dick Hyman*, VSD-5788**
Originally released in 1969 on Command Records, this album spent 30 weeks on the *Billboard* album chart and spawned the hit single *The Minotaur*, featured on this CD. Also included are three bonus tracks (12 Tracks)

Xavier Cugat
***Cugie A-Go-Go*, VSD-5790**
This collection compiles tracks from several of Xavier Cugat's albums recorded for Decca Records in the '60s, including *Bang Bang, Adios, Music To Watch Girls By*, and *Chim, Chim, Cher-ee* (16 Tracks)

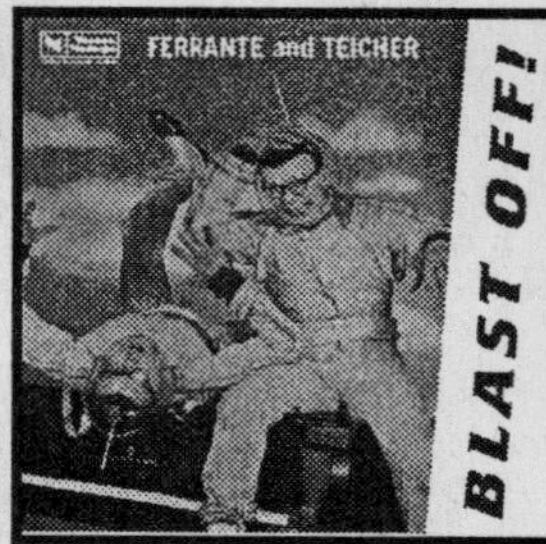

Ferrante & Teicher
***Blast Off*, VSD-5791**
Originally released in 1959 on ABC Records. These recordings represent the avant-garde experimental stereo sounds period of Ferrante & Teicher's career, and are quite different from the easy listening sound they were later known for (16 Tracks)

The Chad Mitchell Trio
***The Chad Mitchell Trio Collection*, VSD-5749**
"The Original Kapp Recordings" First time on CD, this compilation features some of their most sought after recordings including *The John Birch Society, Last Night I Had The Strangest Dream* and *Blowin' In The Wind* (17 Tracks)

Various Artists
***The '50s Remembered, Dick Haymes, Alan Dale, Johnny Desmond, Don Cherry*, VSD-5782**
Kicking off the first releases from our new series the "Pop Vocalist Era" are four popular male vocalists from the '50s who have little or no material available on CD. (16 Tracks)

Various Artists
***The '50s Remembered, Toni Arden, Kitty Kallen, Jane Morgan, Sylvia Syms*, VSD-5783**
Kicking off the first releases from our new series the "Pop Vocalist Era" are four popular female vocalists from the '50s who have little or no material available on CD. (16 Tracks)

Bill Deal & The Rhondells
***Vintage Rock*, VSD-5785**
This reissue from 1970 features two bonus tracks and includes all of the Bill Deal and The Rhondells chart hits, *What Kind of Fool Do You Think I Am, May I, I've Been Hurt, Nothing Succeeds Like Success* and both the album and single versions of *Swingin' Tight* (15 Tracks)

Michael Zager
***Let's All Chant-The Michael Zager Dance Collection*, VSD-5787**
An all-star dance music collection featuring vocal performances by **Whitney Houston, Peabo Bryson, Deniece Williams, Cissy Houston** and **Luther Vandross**. Also included are songs by **The Michael Zager Band** *Let's All Chant*, **The Andrea True Connection** *What's Your Name, What's Your Number* and **Johnny "Guitar" Watson** (11 Tracks)

The Casinos
***Then You Can Tell Me Goodbye*, VSD-5786**
The long awaited CD compilation by The Casinos, featuring the world-wide smash hit *Then You Can Tell Me Goodbye* as well as many songs that were top ten hits across the country. This package also contains many unreleased tracks (14 Tracks)

Available At Music Stores Everywhere!

If you wish to purchase any of our titles by mail please contact:
Collectors Choice Music
1(800) 923-1122

For a complete catalog, Please write to:
Varèse Sarabande Records/Varèse Vintage
11846 Ventura Blvd., Suite 130
Studio City, CA 91604

BUY YOUR RECORDS AT

The Record King
AKA J.J. Sales Co.
2113 Parkdale Ave.
Glenside, PA 19038
(215) 576-0102

Search Service: 11:00 a.m. - 11:00 p.m. EST (7 days a week)

LPs, cassettes, 8-tracks, CDs, 45s, EPs, videos, 12-inch singles, boxed sets, stereo & video equipment sold.
Karaoke distribution. Mail order anywhere.
U.S. funds only. Payable to J.J. Hollin only.
SASE or IRCs for reply. A-Z want lists welcome.
Free to 36 items. Buy & sell.
DISCoveries, Official Price Guides.
Other publications available.
8-Track catalog. . . video catalog. . . $10.00 each.
Soundtrack / Original Cast / Related LP catalog . . . $25.00.
All refundable with order plus lifetime updates.
Listings–Playboy Anniversary & Special Edition issues $1.00.
Miss America Pageant souvenir program (some with newspaper clipping): $2
Adult videos - $1.00. Beta videos - $1.00. Elvis $5.00 Beatles $5.00.
Spoken Word $1.00.
McNally's Picture Price Guide (Soundtrack): $29.95 + postage
Money order - shipped in 2 days. Checks - shipped in 1 week.
↳ Mail or Phone Orders Only

America's best disc, tape and component storage system

Stacking units hold all recording formats and audio/video components

Free mailorder brochure
(please mention Jerry Osborne)

Per Madsen Design (415) 822-4883
P.O. Box 882464, San Francisco, CA 94188

"The Truth About Me"

The original 20 MINUTE interview. Recorded in August 1956 – then lost for 40 years!

Our complete collector's set includes:

- Reprint of the original '56 *Elvis Answers Back* magazine, with gold, playable 2-minute record. 10-inch gold vinyl disc of 20-minute interview.
- Picture CD, also with 20-minute interview.

Shimandra Trading Co.
880 Mandalay Ave. #C603
Clearwater Beach FL 34630
Tel: (813) 446-9371 – Fax: (813) 447-1128
Wholesale inquiries welcome

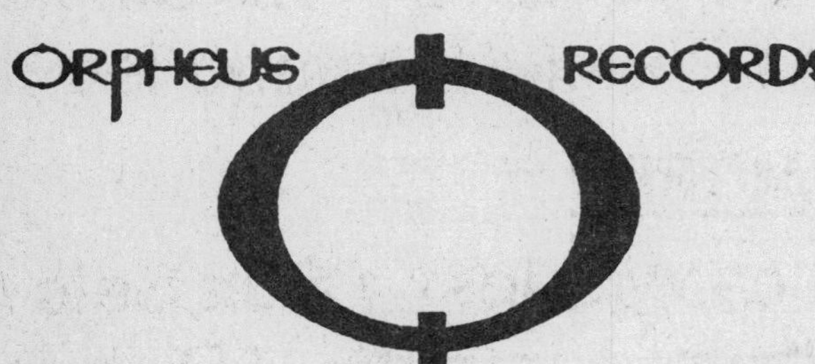

ORPHEUS
RECORDS

Vinylweb

DIRECTORY OF ADVERTISERS